# The Princeton Dictionary of Buddhism

PRINCETON
REFERENCE

# The Princeton Dictionary of Buddhism

Robert E. Buswell Jr. and Donald S. Lopez Jr.

WITH THE ASSISTANCE OF

Juhn Ahn
J. Wayne Bass
William Chu
Amanda Goodman
Hyoung Seok Ham
Seong-Uk Kim
Sumi Lee
Patrick Pranke
Andrew Quintman
Gareth Sparham
Maya Stiller
Harumi Ziegler

PRINCETON UNIVERSITY PRESS
PRINCETON AND OXFORD

Published by Princeton University Press, 41 William Street, Princeton, New Jersey 08540
In the United Kingdom: Princeton University Press, 6 Oxford Street, Woodstock, Oxfordshire OX20 1TW

press.princeton.edu

Jacket Photograph: Buddha portrait. © Anna Jurkovska. Courtesy of Shutterstock.



Library of Congress Cataloging-in-Publication Data

The Princeton dictionary of Buddhism / Robert E. Buswell, Jr. and Donald S. Lopez, Jr. ;
with the assistance of Juhn Ahn, J. Wayne Bass, William Chu, Amanda Goodman, Hyoung Seok Ham, Seong-Uk Kim,
Sumi Lee, Patrick Pranke, Andrew Quintman, Gareth Sparham, Maya Stiller, Harumi Ziegler.
pages cm
Includes bibliographical references.
ISBN-13: 978-0-691-15786-3 (cloth : alk. paper)
ISBN-10: 0-691-15786-3 (cloth : alk. paper) 1. Buddhism—Dictionaries. I. Buswell, Robert E., author, editor of compilation.
II. Lopez, Donald S., 1952- author, editor of compilation.
BQ130.P75 2013
294.303—dc23
2012047585

British Library Cataloging-in-Publication Data is available

This book has been composed in Adobe Garamond Pro with Myriad Display

Printed on acid-free paper. ∞

Printed in the United States of America

5 7 9 10 8 6

# Contents

# Preface

At more than one million words, this is the largest dictionary of Buddhism ever produced in the English language. Yet even at this length, it only begins to represent the full breadth and depth of the Buddhist tradition. Many great dictionaries and glossaries have been produced in Asia over the long history of Buddhism and Buddhist Studies. One thinks immediately of works like the *Mahāvyutpatti*, the ninth-century Tibetan-Sanskrit lexicon said to have been commissioned by the king of Tibet to serve as a guide for translators of the dharma. It contains 9,565 entries in 283 categories. One of the great achievements of twentieth-century Buddhology was the *Bukkyō Daijiten* ("Encyclopedia of Buddhism"), published in ten massive volumes between 1932 and 1964 by the distinguished Japanese scholar Mochizuki Shinkō. Among English-language works, there is William Soothill and Lewis Hodous's *A Dictionary of Chinese Buddhist Terms*, published in 1937, and, from the same year, G. P. Malalasekera's invaluable *Dictionary of Pāli Proper Names*. In preparing the present dictionary, we have sought to build upon these classic works in substantial ways.

Apart from the remarkable learning that these earlier works display, two things are noteworthy about them. The first is that they are principally based on a single source language or Buddhist tradition. The second is that they are all at least a half-century old. Many things have changed in the field of Buddhist Studies over the past fifty years, some for the worse, some very much for the better. One looks back in awe at figures like Louis de la Vallée Poussin and his student Msgr. Étienne Lamotte, who were able to use sources in Sanskrit, Pāli, Chinese, Japanese, and Tibetan with a high level of skill. Today, few scholars have the luxury of time to develop such expertise. Yet this change is not necessarily a sign of the decline of the dharma predicted by the Buddha; from several perspectives, we are now in the golden age of Buddhist Studies. A century ago, scholarship on Buddhism focused on the classical texts of India and, to a much lesser extent, China. Tibetan and Chinese sources were valued largely for the access they provided to Indian texts lost in the original Sanskrit. The Buddhism of Korea was seen as an appendage to the Buddhism of China or as a largely unacknowledged source of the Buddhism of Japan. Beyond the works of "the Pāli canon," relatively little was known of the practice of Buddhism in Sri Lanka and Southeast Asia. All of this has changed for the better over the past half century. There are now many more scholars of Buddhism, there is a much higher level of specialization, and there is a larger body of important scholarship on each of the many Buddhist cultures of Asia. In addition, the number of adherents of Buddhism in the West has grown significantly, with many developing an extensive knowledge of a particular Buddhist tradition, whether or not they hold the academic credentials of a professional Buddhologist. It has been our good fortune to be able to draw upon this expanding body of scholarship in preparing *The Princeton Dictionary of Buddhism*.

This new dictionary seeks to address the needs of this present age. For the great majority of scholars of Buddhism, who do not command all of the major Buddhist languages, this reference book provides a repository of many of the most important terms used across the traditions, and their rendering in several Buddhist languages. For the college professor who teaches "Introduction to Buddhism" every year, requiring one to venture beyond one's particular area of geographical and doctrinal expertise, it provides descriptions of many of the important figures and texts in the major traditions. For the student of Buddhism, whether inside or outside the classroom, it offers information on many fundamental doctrines and practices of the various traditions of the religion. This dictionary is based primarily on six Buddhist languages and their traditions: Sanskrit, Pāli, Tibetan, Chinese, Japanese, and Korean. Also included, although appearing much less frequently, are terms and proper names in vernacular Burmese, Lao, Mongolian, Sinhalese, Thai, and Vietnamese. The majority of entries fall into three categories: the terminology of Buddhist doctrine and practice, the texts in which those teachings are set forth, and the persons (both human and divine) who wrote those texts or appear in their pages. In addition, there are entries on important places—including monasteries and sacred mountains—as well as on the major schools and sects of the various Buddhist traditions. The vast majority of the main entries are in their original language, although cross-references are sometimes provided to a common English rendering. Unlike many terminological dictionaries, which merely provide a brief listing of meanings with perhaps some of the equivalencies in various Buddhist languages, this work seeks to function as an encyclopedic dictionary. The main entries offer a short essay on the extended meaning and significance of the terms covered, typically in the range of two hundred to six hundred words, but sometimes substantially longer. To offer further assistance in understanding a term or tracing related concepts, an extensive set of internal cross-references (marked in small capital letters) guides the reader to related entries throughout the dictionary. But even with over a million words and five thousand entries, we constantly had to make difficult choices about what to include and how much to say. Given the long history and vast geographical scope of the Buddhist traditions, it is difficult to imagine any dictionary ever being truly comprehensive. Authors also write about what they know (or would like to know); so inevitably the dictionary reflects our own areas of scholarly expertise, academic interests, and judgments about what readers need to learn about the various Buddhist traditions.

Despite the best efforts of the king of Tibet more than a thousand years ago, it has always been difficult for scholars of Buddhism to agree on translations. That difficulty persists in the present work for a variety of reasons, including the different ways that Buddhist scholiasts chose to translate technical terms into their various languages over the centuries, the preferences of the many modern scholars whose works we consulted, and the relative stubbornness of the authors. As a result, there will inevitably be some variation in the renderings of specific Buddhist terminology in the pages that follow. In our main entries, however, we have tried to guide users to the range of possible English translations that have been used to render a term. In addition, a significant effort has been made to provide the original language equivalencies in parentheses so that specialists in those languages can draw their own conclusions as to the appropriate rendering.

This book represents more than twelve years of effort. Donald Lopez initiated the project with the assistance of several of his graduate students at the University of Michigan, many of whom have now gone on to receive their degrees and be appointed to university positions. Around that time, Robert Buswell asked Lopez to serve as one of the editors of his two-volume *Encyclopedia of Buddhism* (New York: Macmillan Reference, 2004). When that project was completed, Lopez invited Buswell to join him as coauthor of the dictionary project, an offer he enthusiastically accepted, bringing with him his own team of graduate students from UCLA. In dividing up responsibilities for the dictionary, Buswell took principal charge of entries on mainstream Buddhist concepts, Indian abhidharma, and East Asian Buddhism; Lopez took principal charge of entries on Mahāyāna Buddhism in India, Buddhist tantra, and Tibetan Buddhism. Once drafts of the respective sections were complete, we exchanged files to review each other's sections. Over the last seven years, we were in touch almost daily on one or another aspect of the project as we expanded upon and edited each other's drafts, making this a collaborative project in the best sense of the term. Graduate students at both the University of Michigan and UCLA assisted in gathering materials for the dictionary, preparing initial drafts, and tracing the multiple cross-references to Asian language terms. This project would have been impossible without their unstinting assistance and extraordinary commitment; we are grateful to each of them. Those graduate students and colleagues who made particularly extensive contributions to the dictionary are listed on the title page.

In addition to its more than five thousand main entries, this volume also contains a number of reference tools. Because the various historical periods and dynasties of India, China, Korea, and Japan appear repeatedly in the entries, historical chronologies of the Buddhist periods of those four countries have been provided. In order to compare what events were occurring across the Buddhist world at any given time, we have provided a timeline of Buddhism. Eight maps are provided, showing regions of the Buddhist world and of the traditional Buddhist cosmology. We have also included a List of Lists. Anyone with the slightest familiarity with Buddhism has been struck by the Buddhist propensity for making lists of almost anything. The *Mahāvyutpatti* is in fact organized not alphabetically but by list, including such familiar lists as the four noble truths, the twelve links of dependent origination, and the thirty-two major marks of the Buddha, as well as less familiar lists, such as various kinds of grain (twenty items) and types of ornaments (sixty-four items). Here we have endeavored to include several of the most important lists, beginning with the one vehicle and ending with the one hundred dharmas of the Yogācāra school. After some discussion, we decided to forgo listing the 84,000 afflictions and their 84,000 antidotes.

# Acknowledgments

Our first debt of gratitude is to the several generations of scholars of Buddhism around the world whose research we have mined shamelessly in the course of preparing our entries. We are unable to mention them by name, but those who remain during the present lifetime will recognize the fruits of their research as they read the entries. In addition to our collaborators listed on the title page, we would like to thank the following graduate students and colleagues, each of whom assisted with some of the myriad details of such a massive project: Wesley Borton, Bonnie Brereton, Tyler Cann, Caleb Carter, Mui-fong Choi, Shayne Clarke, Jacob Dalton, Martino Dibeltulo, Alexander Gardner, Heng Yi fashi (Chi Chen Ho), Anna Johnson, Min Ku Kim, Youme Kim, Alison Melnick, Karen Muldoon-Hules, Cuong Tu Nguyen, Aaron Proffitt, Cedar Bough Saeji, and Sherin Wing. In addition, we would like to thank our long-suffering colleagues: William Bodiford, Gregory Schopen, Natasha Heller, Stephanie Jamison, and Jennifer Jung-Kim at UCLA, and Madhav Deshpande, Luis Gómez, Robert Sharf, and James Robson, now or formerly at the University of Michigan. The map of Tibet was designed by Tsering Wangyal Shawa; the map of Japan and Korea was designed by Maya Stiller; all other maps were designed by Trevor Weltman. Christina Lee Buswell also provided invaluable assistance with preparing the lists of language cross-references.

Financial support for the project was provided by the Numata Fund in Buddhist Studies and the 14th Dalai Lama Fund in Tibetan and Buddhist Studies at the UCLA Center for Buddhist Studies; the UCLA Academic Senate Faculty Research Grant Program; the UCLA International Institute; the University of Michigan Institute for the Study of Buddhist Traditions; and the University of Michigan College of Literature, Science, and the Arts. A generous supplemental grant to help complete the project was provided by Bukkyo Dendo Kyokai (America).

# Conventions

No single language crosses all of the linguistic and cultural boundaries of the Buddhist tradition. However, in order to present Buddhist terms that are used across this diverse expanse, it is convenient to employ a single linguistic vocabulary. For this reason European and North American scholars have, over the last century, come to use Sanskrit as the lingua franca of the academic discipline of Buddhist Studies. Following this scholarly convention we have used Sanskrit, and often Buddhist Hybrid Sanskrit forms, in our main entry headings for the majority of Indic-origin terms that appear across the Buddhist traditions. Pāli, Tibetan, or Chinese terms are occasionally used where that form is more commonly known in Western writings on Buddhism. We have attempted to avoid unattested Sanskrit equivalents for terms in Pāli and other Middle Indic languages, generally marking any hypothetical forms with an asterisk. These main entry headings are accompanied by cognate forms in Pāli, Tibetan, Chinese, Japanese, and Korean (abbreviated as P., T., C., J., and K., respectively), followed by the Sinographs (viz., Chinese characters) commonly used in the East Asian traditions. For those Indian terms that are known only or principally in the Pāli tradition, the main entry heading is listed in Pāli (e.g., bhavaṅga). Terms used across the East Asian traditions are typically listed by their Chinese pronunciation with Japanese and Korean cross-references, with occasional Japanese or Korean headings for terms that are especially important in those traditions. Tibetan terms are in Tibetan, with Sanskrit or Chinese cognates where relevant. In order that the reader may trace a standard term through any of the languages we cover in the dictionary, we also provide cross-references to each of the other languages at the end of the volume in a section called Cross-References by Language. In both the main entries and the Cross-References by Language, words have been alphabetized without consideration of diacritical marks and word breaks.

Book titles are generally given in the language of original provenance, e.g., *Saddharmapuṇḍarīkasūtra*, in Sanskrit, with cross-references to Tibetan, Chinese, Japanese, and Korean; *Dasheng qixin lun*, in Chinese, with cross-references to a putative Sanskrit reconstruction of the title, and Japanese and Korean. We also include some main entries to indigenous terms, book titles, personal names, or place names in other Asian languages, e.g.: Burmese, Thai, Lao, Nepalese, Sinhalese, Mongolian, and Vietnamese.

To reduce the amount of capitalization in the dictionary, as a general rule we capitalize only:

- proper names: e.g., of historical figures, specific buddhas, bodhisattvas, and divinities;
- historical schools: Madhyamaka, Mūlasarvāstivāda, Huayan zong, but not hīnayāna, ekayāna, tathāgatagarbha;
- titles of books: e.g., *Sukhāvatīvyūhasūtra*, *Saddharmapuṇḍarīkasūtra*;
- terrestrial place names: e.g., Jambudvīpa, Śrāvastī, Turfan, but not celestial realms (e.g., tuṣita), infernal realms (avīci), or ideal realms (sukhāvatī).

East Asian monks, especially those in the Chan, Sŏn, Zen, and Thiền schools, often use multiple names throughout their careers, e.g., ordination name, cognomen, toponym (e.g., the mountains, monasteries, hermitages, or regions where they dwelled), posthumous or funerary name, and honorary names and titles conferred by a monarch. Commonly, these monks are listed in their genealogical lineages by a four-Sinograph name, which gives this alternate name first, typically followed by their ordination name: e.g., Linji Yixuan (hermitage name + ordination name), Dongshan Liangjie (mountain name + ordination name), Pojo Chinul (posthumous name/official title + ordination name). The main entries for these monks are found under this common four-Sinograph lineage name, with a blind cross-reference in the main body of the dictionary for their two-Sinograph ordination name; e.g.: **Congshen.** (C) (從諗). See ZHAOZHOU CONGSHEN.

# Transcription Systems

The dictionary uses the standard Romanization systems for East Asian languages: viz., pinyin for Chinese (rather than the now-superseded Wade-Giles system that most pre-1990s scholarship on Chinese Buddhism used), Revised Hepburn for Japanese, and McCune-Reischauer for Korean, with the transcriptions in some cases modified slightly to conform more closely to the Chinese parsing of compounds. While this dictionary was being compiled, the Korean government unveiled its latest iteration of a Revised Romanization system, but that system is still rarely used in academic writing in the West and its acceptance is uncertain; we therefore chose to employ McCune-Reischauer for this edition of the dictionary.

For Tibetan, the dictionary uses the standard Wylie system of transliteration, with words alphabetized by the first letter, regardless of whether it is the root letter. Tibetan does not have a standard system for rendering words phonetically. For Tibetan terms that appear as main entries, a phonetic approximation has been placed in parentheses following the Wylie transliteration. In addition, a separate listing of Tibetan pronunciations has been provided in the Cross-References by Language, where readers may look up phonetic renderings in order to find the Wylie transliteration used in the main entries.

Unlike Tibetan, where there are generally standard translations for Indian terms, in the East Asian tradition there are a plethora of alternate Sinographic renderings, including both translations and transcriptions (i.e., using the Chinese characters purely for their phonetic value to render Sanskrit or Middle Indic terms). We obviously could not include all possible renderings and have typically chosen one or at most two of the most common, e.g., one translation and one transcription. In addition, in Tibet and China, translations of Indian terms and texts were often given in abbreviated forms. We have attempted to provide the full form in most cases, using the abbreviation when it is the better known version of the term or text.

As a general rule, we provide multiple language equivalencies only for terms that were traditionally known in the other languages. For this reason, many late tantric terms known only in India and Tibet will not have East Asian equivalents (even though equivalents were in some cases created in the twentieth century); Chinese texts not translated into Tibetan will give only Japanese and Korean equivalencies; Japanese and Korean figures and texts not generally known in China will have only Japanese and Korean transcriptions, and so forth.

# Asian Historical Periods

## Indian Historical Periods

| | |
|---|---|
| Vedic Period | c. 1500–600 BCE |
| Bimbisara Dynasty | c. 684–413 BCE |
| śramaṇa movements | c. 600–400 BCE |
| Śiśunāga Empire | c. 413–345 BCE |
| Nanda Empire | c. 424–321 BCE |
| Maurya Empire | c. 322–185 BCE |
| Mahāmeghavahana Dynasty | c. 250 BCE–400 CE |
| Śātavāhana Empire | c. 230 BCE–220 CE |
| Indo-Greek Kingdoms | c. 200 BCE–50 CE |
| Kulinda Kingdom | c. 200–100 BCE |
| Cōḷa Dynasty | c. 205 BCE–1279 CE |
| Śuṅga Empire | c. 187–71 BCE |
| Śaka Kingdom | c. 100–30 BCE |
| Kuṣāṇa Empire | c. 30–375 CE |
| Gupta Empire | c. 320–540 CE |
| Pāla Empire | 750–1174 CE |
| Rāṣṭrakūṭa Dynasty | 753–982 CE |
| Hoysala Empire | 1026–1343 CE |

## Chinese Historical Periods

| | |
|---|---|
| Shang 商 | c. 1600 BCE–1046 |
| Zhou 周 | c. 1046 BCE–256 |
| Qin 秦 | 221 BCE–206 |
| Western Han 西漢 | 206 BCE–9 CE |
| Eastern Han 東漢 | 25–220 CE |
| Three Kingdoms 三國 | 220–280 |
| Wei 魏 | 220–265 |
| Shu 蜀 | 221–263 |
| Wu 吳 | 229–280 |
| Western Jin 西晉 | 265–316 |
| Sixteen Kingdoms 十六國 | 304–439 |
| Former Zhao 前趙 | 304–329 |
| Later Zhao 後趙 | 319–351 |
| Cheng Han 成漢 | 304–347 |
| Former Liang前涼 | 320–376 |
| Later Liang 後涼 | 386–403 |
| Northern Liang 北涼 | 397–439 |
| Western Liang 西涼 | 400–421 |
| Southern Liang 南涼 | 397–414 |

| | | | |
|---|---|---|---|
| Former Yan 前燕 | | | 337–370 |
| Later Yan 後燕 | | | 384–409 |
| Northern Yan 北燕 | | | 407–436 |
| Southern Yan 南燕 | | | 398–410 |
| Former Qin 前秦 | | | 351–394 |
| Later Qin 後秦 | | | 384–417 |
| Western Qin 西秦 | | | 409–431 |
| Xia 夏 | | | 407–431 |
| Eastern Jin 東晉 | | | 317–420 |
| Southern and Northern Dynasties 南北朝 | | | 420–588 |
| Southern | | Northern | |
| Liu Song 劉宋 | 420–478 | Northern Wei 北魏 | 386–533 |
| Southern Qi 南齊 | 479–501 | Eastern Wei 東魏 | 534–549 |
| Liang 梁 | 502–556 | Western Wei 西魏 | 535–557 |
| Chen 陳 | 557–588 | Northern Qi 北齊 | 550–577 |
| | | Northern Zhou 北周 | 557–581 |
| Sui 隋 | | | 581–618 |
| Tang 唐 | | | 618–907 |
| Five Dynasties and Ten Kingdoms 五代十國 | | | 907–979 |
| Five Dynasties | | Ten Kingdoms | |
| Later Liang 後梁 | 907–923 | Wu 吳 | 907–937 |
| Later Tang 後唐 | 923–936 | Wuyue 吳越 | 907–978 |
| Later Jin 後晉 | 936–946 | Min 閩 | 909–945 |
| Later Han 後漢 | 947–950 | Chu 楚 | 907–951 |
| Later Zhou 後周 | 951–960 | Southern Han 南漢 | 917–971 |
| | | Former Shu 前蜀 | 907–925 |
| | | Later Shu 後蜀 | 934–965 |
| | | Jingnan 荊南 | 924–963 |
| | | Southern Tang 南唐 | 937–975 |
| | | Northern Han 北漢 | 951–979 |
| Liao 遼 | | | 907–1125 |
| Song 宋 | | | 960–1279 |
| Northern Song 北宋 | | | 960–1127 |
| Southern Song 南宋 | | | 1127–1279 |
| Western Xia 西夏 | | | 1038–1227 |
| Jin 金 | | | 1115–1234 |
| Yuan 元 | | | 1271–1368 |
| Ming 明 | | | 1368–1644 |
| Qing 清 | | | 1644–1911 |
| Republic of China 中華民國 (mainland) | | | 1912–1949 |
| Republic of China 中華民國 (Taiwan) | | | 1949–present |
| People's Republic of China 中華人民共和國 | | | 1949–present |
| Chinese Cultural Revolution | | | 1966–1976 |

## Korean Historical Periods

| | |
|---|---|
| Ko-Chosŏn 古朝鮮 | ?– 08 BCE |
| Proto–Three Kingdoms 原三國時代 | 3rd cent. BCE–4th cent. CE |
| Puyŏ 夫餘 | 2nd cent. BCE–494 CE |
| Okchŏ 沃沮 | 2nd cent. BCE–3rd cent. CE |
| Tongye 東濊 | 3rd cent. BCE–3rd cent. CE |
| Mahan 馬韓 | 1st cent. BCE–3rd cent. CE |
| Chinhan 辰韓 | 1st cent. BCE–4th cent. CE |
| Pyŏnhan 弁韓 | 1st cent.–4th cent. CE |

| | |
|---|---|
| Three Kingdoms 三國 | 1st cent. BCE–668 CE |
| Koguryŏ 高句麗 | 37 BCE–668 CE |
| Paekche 百濟 | 18 BCE–660 CE |
| Silla 新羅 | 57 BCE–668 CE (continues to 935) |
| Kaya 伽倻 | 42–562 |
| North-South States | 698–926 |
| Parhae 渤海 | 698–926 |
| Unified Silla 統一新羅 | 668–935 |
| Later Three Kingdoms 後三國 | 892–936 |
| Unified Silla 統一新羅 | (continues to 935) |
| Later Paekche 後百濟 | 892–936 |
| Later Koguryŏ 後高句麗 | 901–918 |
| Koryŏ 高麗 | 918–1392 |
| Chosŏn 朝鮮 | 1397–1897 |
| Korean Empire 大韓帝國 | 1897–1910 |
| Japanese Colonial Period | 1910–1945 |
| North and South Korea | 1948–present |

## Japanese Historical Periods

| | |
|---|---|
| Yayoi 弥生 | 300 BCE–300 CE |
| Kofun 古墳 | 300–538 |
| Asuka 飛鳥 | 538–710 |
| Nara 奈良 | 710–794 |
| Heian 平安 | 794–1185 |
| Kamakura 鎌倉 | 1185–1333 |
| Kenmu Restoration 建武の新政 | 1333–1336 |
| Muromachi 室町 | 1337–1573 |
| Azuchi–Mamoyama 安土桃山 | 1537–1603 |
| Edo 江戸 | 1603–1868 |
| Meiji 明治 | 1868–1912 |
| Taishō 大正 | 1912–1926 |
| Shōwa 昭和 | 1926–1986 |
| Heisei 平成 | 1986–present |

# Timeline of Buddhism

| Century | India | Sri Lanka | Southeast Asia | East Asia | Tibet and Central Asia | General world history |
|---|---|---|---|---|---|---|
| **600** BCE | 566: Birth of the Buddha according to the "long chronology" | | | c. 550: Life of Laozi<br>c. 551–479: Life of Confucius | | 550: Persian empire founded by Cyrus the Great |
| **500** BCE | 486: Death of the Buddha according to the "long chronology"<br>486 or 368: First Council at Rājagṛha<br>448: Birth of the Buddha according to the "short chronology" | | | | | 469–399: Life of Socrates<br>c. 427–347: Life of Plato |
| **400** BCE | 368: Death of the Buddha according to the "short chronology"<br>386 or 268: Second Council at Vaiśālī<br>Buddhism established in Kathmandu Valley | | | | | 384–322: Life of Aristotle<br>327: Alexander the Great (356–323) invades India |
| **300** BCE | 268–232: Reign of Aśoka<br>c. 250: Third Council at Pāṭaliputra under Aśoka | 247–207: Reign of Devānaṃpiyatissa in Sri Lanka<br>Buddhism established in Sri Lanka | | 221: Construction begins on Great Wall in China | | 287–212: Archimedes |
| **200** BCE | c. 150: King Menander (Milinda) | 161–137: Reign of King Duṭṭagāmaṇī Abhaya in Sri Lanka | | | | |
| **First century** BCE | Emergence of Mahāyāna<br>Bhārhut and Sāñcī stūpas established<br>Earliest phase of construction at Ajantā caves | c. 25: Recording of Pāli tipiṭaka under King Vaṭṭagāmaṇi of Sri Lanka | | | | 100–44: Life of Julius Caesar |

*(Continued)*

| Century | India | Sri Lanka | Southeast Asia | East Asia | Tibet and Central Asia | General world history |
|---|---|---|---|---|---|---|
| **First century** CE | Early first century: Kārli cave complex in Maharashtra established<br>First–second centuries: Earliest Buddha images in Mathurā and Gandhāra | | | 67: Indian monks Kāśyapa Mātaṅga and Zhu Falan said to arrive at the court of Emperor Ming of Han-dynasty China; emperor establishes first monastery, Baimasi | Buddhism spreads from Bactria throughout Central Asia | Jesus of Nazareth<br>47: Library of Alexandria destroyed by fire<br>70: Destruction of Second Temple in Jerusalem |
| **100** CE | c. 100 *Lotus Sūtra* composed<br>c. 127–151: Reign of Kaniṣka<br>c. Second century: Life of Nāgārjuna | | | 148: Parthian translator An Shigao arrives in Chinese capital of Luoyang | | c. 100–178: Life of Ptolemy |
| **200** CE | c. Second - third centuries: Development of Mathurā art | | Spread of Buddhism to regions of Burma, Cambodia, Laos, Thailand, Vietnam<br>Construction of pagodas at Luy-lau in Vietnam | | Third–fifth centuries: construction of caves and images at Bāmiyān in Afghanistan | |
| **300** CE | c. 320: Birth of Asaṅga and Vasubandhu | c. 362: Arrival of the Buddha's tooth relic | | 372: Monk-envoy Sundo arrives in Korean state of Koguryŏ; formal introduction of Buddhism into Korean peninsula | | 312: Emperor Constantine converts to Christianity |
| **400** CE | c. 450: Founding and flourishing of Nālandā<br>Aśoka's Mahābodhi temple rebuilt at Bodhgayā | c. 425: Buddhaghosa composes the *Visuddhimagga* and translates Sinhalese commentarial literature into Pāli<br>Fourth–fifth centuries: Height of Anurādhapura period | Fifth–eleventh centuries: Rāmaññadesa (Thaton), center of Mon and Buddhist culture in Burma<br>c. Fifth–sixth centuries: Buddha statues in South Indian style in Cambodia | 399–414: Faxian's visit to India<br>401: Kumārajīva arrives in China, establishes important translation bureau<br>Fifth–sixth centuries: Development of major cave temples at Yungang and Longmen | | 451: Attila the Hun crosses the Rhine into Gaul |
| **500** CE | Rock carvings at Ajaṇṭā, Ellorā | | c. 580: Thiền (Chan) monk Vinītaruci purported to arrive in Vietnam<br>Sixth–seventh centuries: Rise of Buddhism in Indonesia | c. 520: Bodhidharma said to arrive in China with Chan teachings<br>538–597: Life of Tiantai Zhiyi<br>552: Official date Buddhism is | c. 500–700: paintings at Qizil | 570–632: Life of Muhammed |

| Century | India | Sri Lanka | Southeast Asia | East Asia | Tibet and Central Asia | General world history |
|---|---|---|---|---|---|---|
| | | | c. Sixth century: Gupta influence in Buddhist statuary in Thailand<br>Buddhist establishments at Nakhon Panthom, Ku Bua, U Thong in Thailand | adopted in Japan from Korea state of Paekche<br>574–622: Prince Shōtoku patronizes Buddhism in Japan<br>Sixth–seventh centuries: Buddhist art flourishes in Korean states | | |
| **600 CE** | c. 600: First datable uses of the term "Mahāyāna" in Indian inscriptions | | Buddhist communities in Indonesia; beginnings of Śrīvijaya kingdom (Sumatra) and spread of Mahāyāna | 607: Hōryūji founded in Japan<br>617–686: Life of Korean monk Wŏnhyo<br>629–645: Xuanzang's sojourn in India<br>638–713: Life of Huineng in China<br>671–695: Yijing's travels to India<br>671: Ŭisang returns to Korea, founds Hwaŏm school<br>699: Fazang builds Huayan school | c. 640: Foundation laid for Jo khang temple in Lha sa<br>c. 605–650: Life of Srong bstan sgam po | 622: Muhammad departs from Mecca for Medina (the Hijra) |
| **700 CE** | c. 750: Pāla dynasty established<br>Spread of vajrayāna<br>Odantapurī founded<br>Śāntideva composes *Bodhicaryāvatāra* | 777–797: Buddhist establishments at Anurādhapura and Polonnarua | Śailendra dynasty established in Java; patronage of Mahāyāna<br>Borobudur constructed in Java<br>Late eighth century: Mahāyāna spreads in Vietnam | 720: Vajrabodhi and Amoghavajra arrive in China<br>724–727: Hyech'o's pilgrimage to India<br>745: Shenhui extols the teachings of Huineng<br>c. 751: *Mugujŏnggwang taedarani kyŏng*, world's oldest printed text, made in Silla Korea<br>767–822: Life of Saichō; Tendai school established<br>774–835: Life of Kūkai; Shingon tradition established | 754–c. 799: Reign of Khri srong lde bstan<br>c. 770: Padmasambhava invited to Tibet and construction of Bsam yas monastery begins<br>c. 797: Debate at Bsam yas monastery | 711–718: Muslim Arabs conquer much of Spain<br>*Beowulf* composed |

*(Continued)*

| Century | India | Sri Lanka | Southeast Asia | East Asia | Tibet and Central Asia | General world history |
|---|---|---|---|---|---|---|
| **800** CE | c. 800: Vikramaśīla founded<br>Mahābodhi temple at Bodhgayā restored | c. 840: Tamil Pāṇḍya invasion, sack of Anurādhapura | Śrīvijaya expands into Maenam Basin; surge of Mahāyāna Buddhism | 828: First mountain site of Nine Mountains School of Sŏn (Kusan Sŏnmun) founded in Korea<br>868: *Diamond Sūtra*, oldest extant printed book, printed in China<br>842–845: Huichang persecution of Buddhism | 838: Death of Ral pa can and end of earlier dissemination of Buddhism in Tibet<br>842: Assassination of Tibetan king Glang dar ma, ending his persecution of Buddhism and the Tibetan monarchy | 800: Charlemagne crowned<br>c. 850: Classic Mayan culture in central Yucatan collapses |
| **900** CE | 988–1069: Tantric siddha Tilopa in India | | Decline of Mahāyāna Buddhism in Maenam Basin<br>Second half of tenth century: Mahāyāna renaissance in Cambodia | 983: First printing of Chinese Buddhist canon (dazangjing) completed<br>985: Copy of Udāyana Buddha image made for Seiryōji, Japan | 958–1055: Life of translator Rin chen bzang po; beginning of the later dissemination of Buddhism in TIbet<br>996: Founding of Ta pho monastery in western Tibet | c. 900–950: Anasazi Indians move in to Chaco Canyon in northern New Mexico |
| **1000** CE | | | c. 1044–1077: Reign of King Anawrahta in Burma, construction of Shwezigon pagoda<br>1044–1287: Kingdom of Pagan | 1010: Koryŏ-dynasty Korean king orders carving of complete Buddhist canon; destroyed in 1232 by Mongols | 1028/40–1111/23: Life of Mi la ras pa<br>1042: Atiśa arrives in Tibet<br>1073: Founding of Sa skya (Sakya) monastery | 1096–1099: First crusades<br>c. 1000–1500: Inca civilization in South America |
| **1100** CE | c. 1100: Mahābodhi temple restored by Burmese<br>1192: Nālandā sacked by Muslim troops of Mohammed Al Ghauri | 1153–1186: Reign of Parākramabāhu I | 1113–c. 1145: Reign of Sūryavarman II, Angkor Wat founded as Vaiṣṇavite temple<br>1118–c. 1220: Khmer expansion into the Vientiane area of Laos<br>1181–c. 1218: Reign of Jayavarman VII in Cambodia; state support of Mahāyāna Buddhism, construction of Bayon and other Buddhist monuments | 1133–1212: Life of Honen in Japan; Jōdōshū established<br>1141–1215: Life of Myōan Eisai in Japan; Rinzaishū of Zen established<br>1158–1210: Life of Pojo Chinul in Korea, flourishing of Sŏn school<br>1173–1262: Life of Shinran in Japan | | c. 1150: Anasazi culture in Chaco Canyon, New Mexico collapses<br>1181–1226: Life of Francis of Assisi |

| Century | India | Sri Lanka | Southeast Asia | East Asia | Tibet and Central Asia | General world history |
|---|---|---|---|---|---|---|
| **1200** CE | 1203: Vikramaśīla sacked by Turkish troops; last abbot, Śākyaśrībhadra, declares Buddhism destroyed in India, flees to Tibet.<br>1295–1298: Second restoration of Mahābodhi Temple by Burmese | 1236–1270: Reign of Parākramabāhu II | c. 1220–1250: Thai kingdom of Sukhothai founded; promotion of Theravāda Buddhism<br>1279–1316: Sukhothai kingdom expands into Vientiane region of Laos<br>1279: Latest extant inscriptions of any Theravāda nunnery in Burma<br>1296: Visit of Chinese envoy Zhou Daguan to Cambodia | 1200–1253: Life of Dōgen Kigen in Japan; establishment of Sōtōshū of Zen<br>1222–1282: Life of Nichiren in Japan; Nichiren school established<br>1236: Korean court orders Sugi to edit and carve second Korean Buddhist canon, the *Koryŏ taejanggyŏng*; oldest extant complete xylographic canon | 1247: Meeting of Sa skya Paṇḍita of Tibet and Mongol Godan Khan | 1200: University of Paris founded<br>1225–1274: Life of Thomas Aquinas<br>1271–1292: Travels of Marco Polo<br>1288: Ottoman empire founded by Osman I |
| **1300** CE | | | 1327: King Jayavarman Parameśvara establishes Theravāda in Cambodia<br>1353–1373: Theravāda promoted as state religion in Laos by Fa Ngum<br>1350: Kingdom of Ayuthaya founded<br>1360: Theravāda adopted as state religion of Thailand | 1270: Mongol Yuan dynasty supports Tibetan Buddhist traditions in China<br>1392: Chosŏn dynasty established in Korea, leading to lengthy Confucian suppression of Buddhist institutions | 1357–1419: Life of Tsong kha pa<br>Editing of Tibetan canon by Bu ston | 1337–1453: Hundred Years' War<br>1347–1352: Black Death in Europe |
| **1400** CE | | 1412–1467: Reign of Parākramabāhu VI | c. 1475: Buddhist council at Chiangmai<br>Fifteenth–sixteenth centuries: Buddhist establishments at Pegu in Burma<br>Theravāda lineage restored in Thailand after reordination of Siamese monks in Sri Lanka | | | 1431: Joan of Arc burned at the stake<br>1452–1519: Life of Leonardo da Vinci<br>c. 1455: Gutenberg prints *Mazarin Bible* |

(Continued)

| Century | India | Sri Lanka | Southeast Asia | East Asia | Tibet and Central Asia | General world history |
|---|---|---|---|---|---|---|
| **1500 CE** | | | c. 1500: Angkor Wat in Cambodia reconceived as Buddhist site. | 1535–1615: Life of Yunqi Zhuhong, unification of Chan and pure land in China<br>1571: Japanese general Oda Nobunaga launches campaign against Buddhism<br>1592–1598: Korean monks Ch'ŏnghŏ Hyujŏng and Samyŏng Yujŏng help defeat Japanese Hideyoshi invasions | 1578: Altan Khan confers the title of Dalai Lama on Bsod nams rgya mtsho | 1483–1546: Life of Martin Luther<br>1564–1642: Life of Galileo |
| **1600 CE** | | 1687: Temple of the Tooth Relic established at Kandy | | | 1617–1682: Life of Fifth Dalai Lama<br>1634: Ngag dbang rnam rgyal unites Bhutan<br>1642: Beginning of political rule by Dalai Lamas | 1600: East India Company charter granted by Elizabeth I<br>English colonies at Jamestown (1607) and Plymouth (1620) |
| **1700 CE** | | 1753: King Kīrti Rājasiṃha reinstates Buddhism by inviting Thai monks to his court | 1784: "Emerald Buddha" installed at Wat Phra Kaew in Bangkok, Thailand | | 1749: Mongolian canon completed | Expansion of European empires and colonial occupation throughout Asia<br>French and American revolutions |
| **1800 CE** | 1891: Founding of the Mahābodhi Society | 1873: Pānadura Debate between Buddhist monk Guṇānanda and Methodist minister | 1830: Prince Mongkut (King Rāma IV) founds the Thammayut order<br>1871: Fifth Theravāda Council held at Mandalay | 1868: Meiji reforms of Buddhism begin in Japan, separating Shintō from Buddhism | "Non-sectarian" (ris med) movement in eastern Tibet | 1875 Founding of the Theosophical Society by Blavatsky and Olcott<br>1881: Founding of the Pali Text Society by T. W. Rhys-Davids |
| **1900 CE** | 1891–1956: Life of B. R. Ambedkar, leader in reestablishing Buddhism in India | | c. 1900: Forest monk traditions revived in Thailand<br>1902/1908: The Saṅgha Administration Act in Thailand standardizes monastic education and ordination procedures, grants the monarchy authority to appoint abbots | 1890–1947: Life of Chinese reformer Taixu<br>1924–1929: *Taisho Shinshū Daizōkyō* edition of Chinese Buddhist canon printed in Tokyo<br>1946: Founding of Sōka Gakkai in Japan<br>1955: Korean monks launch purification campaign to purge Japanese colonial influence | 1959: Fourteenth Dalai Lama goes into exile in India<br>1989: Fourteenth Dalai Lama awarded Nobel Peace Prize | 1910–1945: Japanese occupation of Korea<br>1952: Founding of World Fellowship of Buddhists |

# Maps

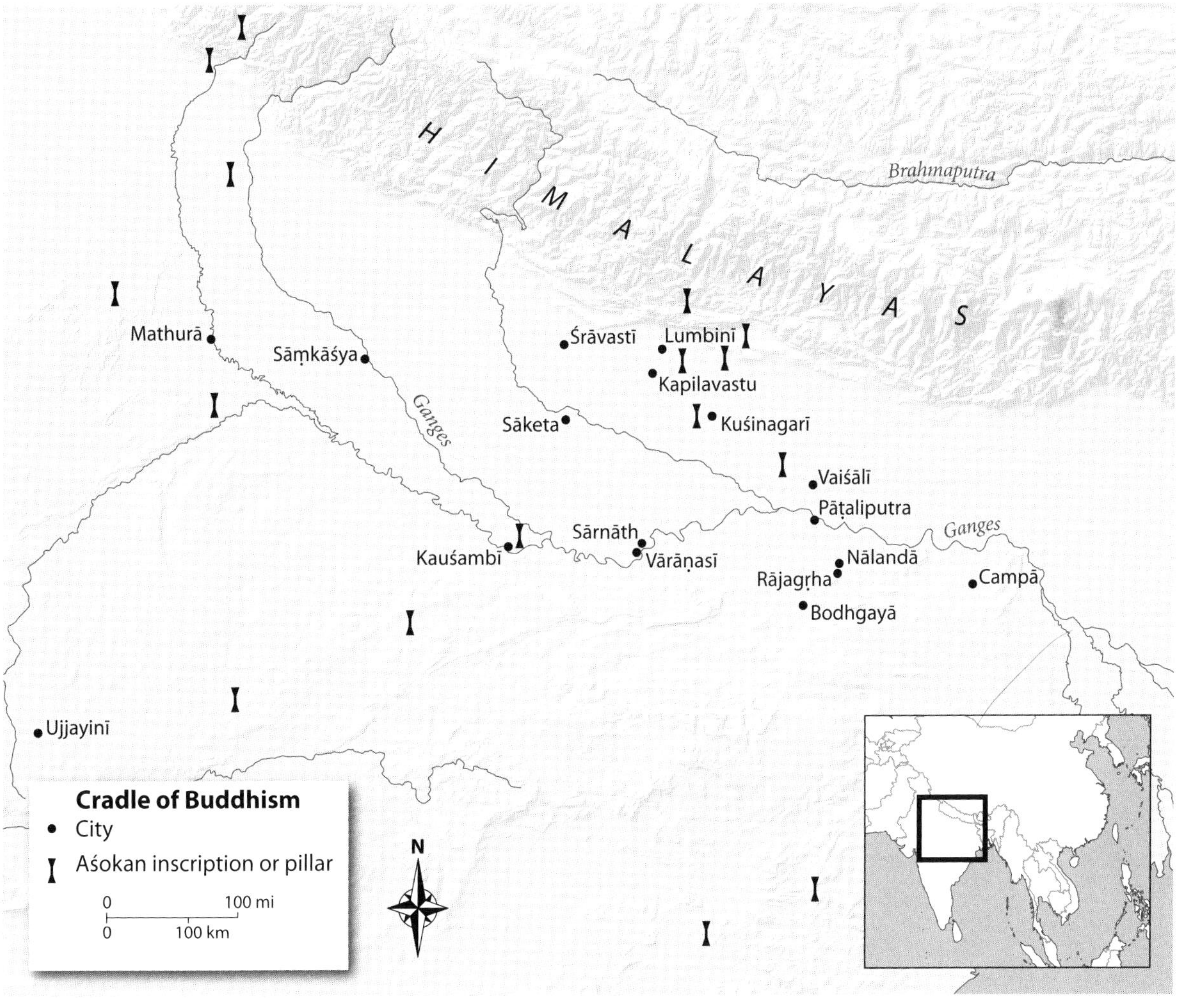

Brahmaputra
H I M A L A Y A S
Mathurā
Sāṃkāśya
Ganges
Śrāvastī
Lumbinī
Kapilavastu
Sāketa
Kuśinagarī
Vaiśālī
Pāṭaliputra
Ganges
Sārnāth
Kauśambī
Vārāṇasī
Nālandā
Rājagṛha
Campā
Bodhgayā
Ujjayinī
Cradle of Buddhism
City
Aśokan inscription or pillar
0
100 mi
0
100 km
N

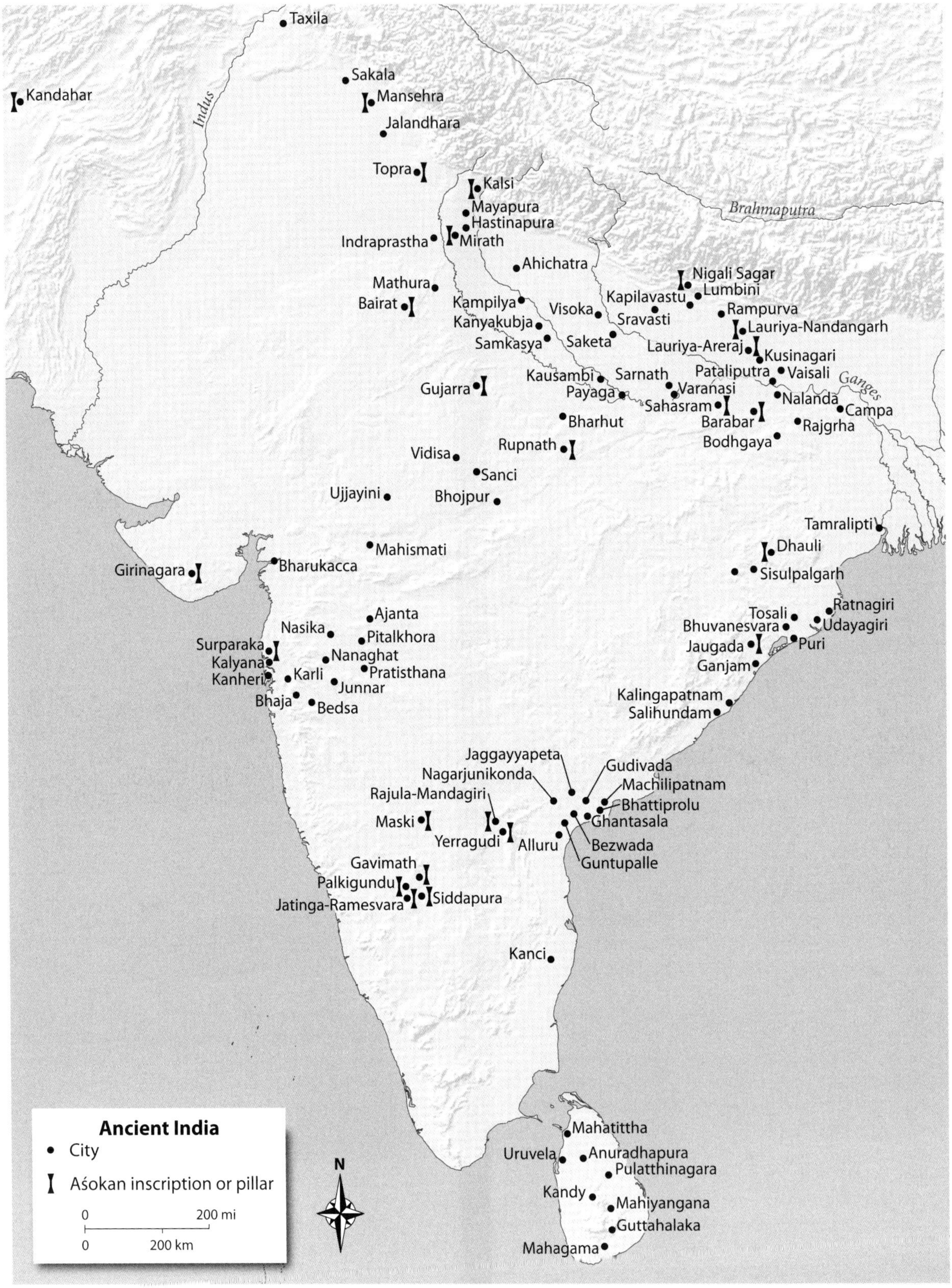
Taxila
Sakala
Kandahar
Mansehra
Indus
Jalandhara
Topra
Kalsi
Mayapura
Hastinapura
Brahmaputra
Indraprastha
Mirath
Ahichatra
Nigali Sagar
Lumbini
Mathura
Kapilavastu
Bairat
Kampilya
Visoka
Rampurva
Sravasti
Kanyakubja
Lauriya-Nandangarh
Samkasya
Saketa
Lauriya-Areraj
Kusinagari
Kausambi
Sarnath
Pataliputra
Vaisali
Gujarra
Payaga
Varanasi
Ganges
Sahasram
Nalanda
Campa
Bharhut
Barabar
Rajgrha
Rupnath
Bodhgaya
Vidisa
Sanci
Ujjayini
Bhojpur
Tamralipti
Mahismati
Dhauli
Girinagara
Bharukacca
Sisulpalgarh
Ratnagiri
Ajanta
Tosali
Nasika
Bhuvanesvara
Udayagiri
Pitalkhora
Surparaka
Jaugada
Puri
Kalyana
Nanaghat
Ganjam
Kanheri
Karli
Pratisthana
Junnar
Kalingapatnam
Bhaja
Bedsa
Salihundam
Jaggayyapeta
Gudivada
Nagarjunikonda
Machilipatnam
Rajula-Mandagiri
Bhattiprolu
Maski
Ghantasala
Yerragudi
Alluru
Bezwada
Guntupalle
Gavimath
Palkigundu
Siddapura
Jatinga-Ramesvara
Kanci
Ancient India
City
Aśokan inscription or pillar
0
200 mi
0
200 km
N
Mahatittha
Uruvela
Anuradhapura
Pulatthinagara
Kandy
Mahiyangana
Guttahalaka
Mahagama

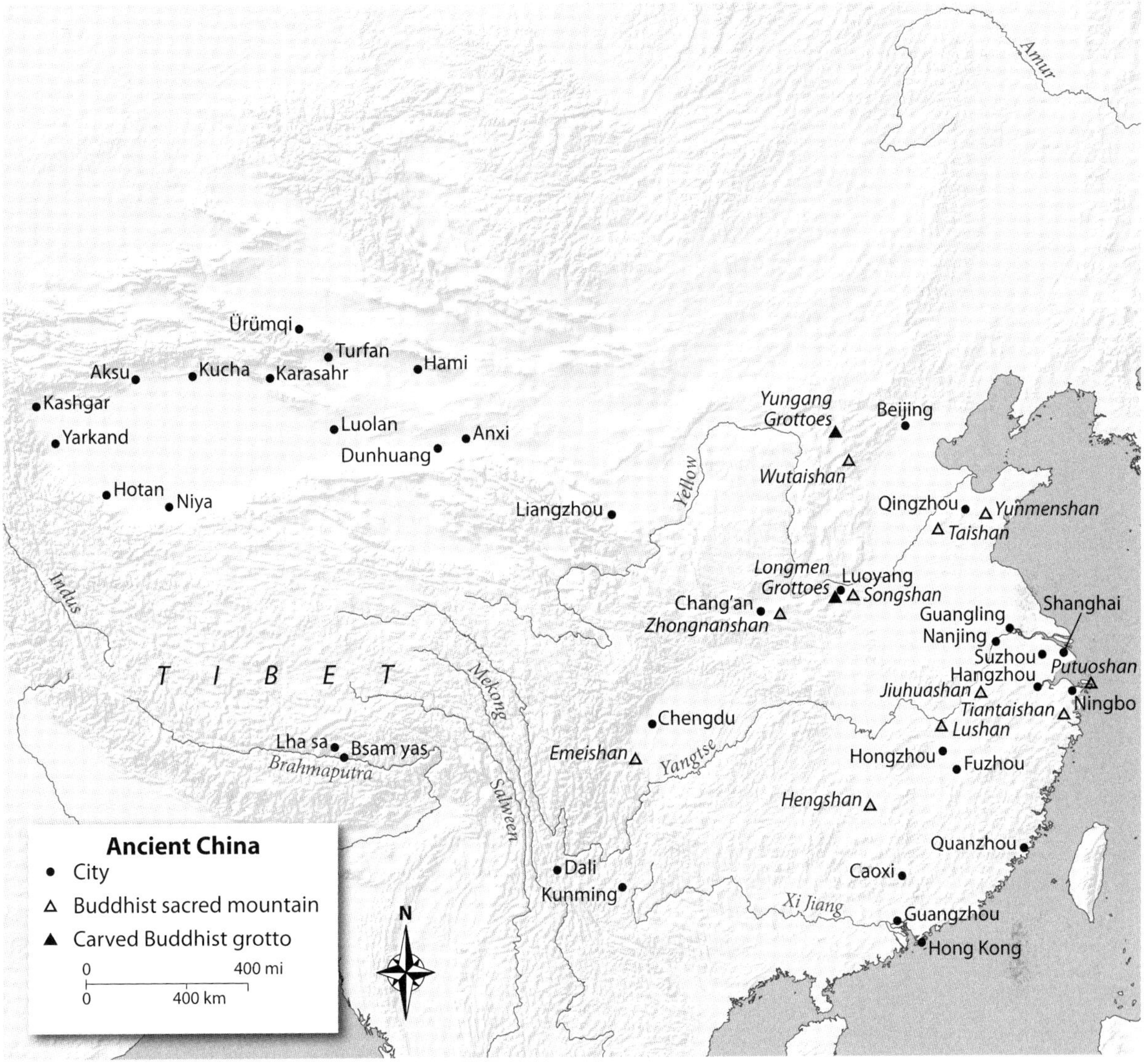
Ancient China
City
Buddhist sacred mountain
Carved Buddhist grotto
0 400 mi
0 400 km
N
Amur
Ürümqi
Turfan
Hami
Aksu
Kucha
Karasahr
Kashgar
Yarkand
Luolan
Anxi
Dunhuang
Hotan
Niya
Liangzhou
Yungang Grottoes
Beijing
Wutaishan
Yellow
Qingzhou
Yunmenshan
Taishan
Indus
Longmen Grottoes
Luoyang
Songshan
Chang'an
Zhongnanshan
Guangling
Shanghai
Nanjing
Suzhou
Hangzhou
Putuoshan
Jiuhuashan
Ningbo
Tiantaishan
Lushan
T I B E T
Mekong
Chengdu
Lha sa
Bsam yas
Brahmaputra
Emeishan
Yangtse
Hongzhou
Fuzhou
Salween
Hengshan
Quanzhou
Dali
Caoxi
Kunming
Xi Jiang
Guangzhou
Hong Kong

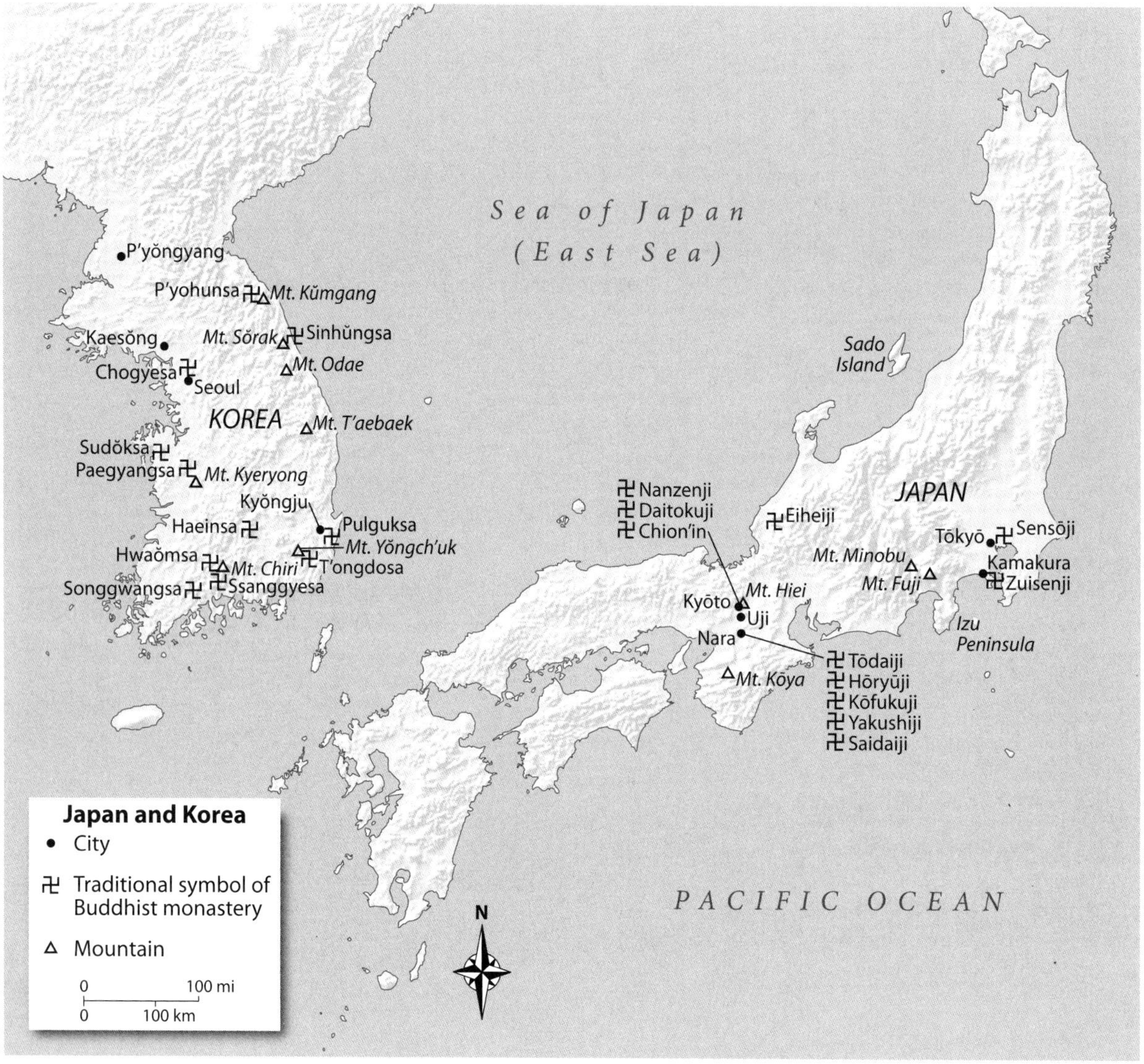
Sea of Japan
(East Sea)
P'yŏngyang
P'yohunsa
Mt. Kŭmgang
Kaesŏng
Mt. Sŏrak
Sinhŭngsa
Mt. Odae
Chogyesa
Seoul
KOREA
Mt. T'aebaek
Sudŏksa
Paegyangsa
Mt. Kyeryong
Kyŏngju
Haeinsa
Pulguksa
Mt. Yŏngch'uk
Hwaŏmsa
Mt. Chiri
T'ongdosa
Songgwangsa
Ssanggyesa
Sado Island
JAPAN
Nanzenji
Daitokuji
Chion'in
Eiheiji
Tōkyō
Sensōji
Mt. Minobu
Kamakura
Mt. Fuji
Zuisenji
Mt. Hiei
Kyōto
Uji
Nara
Izu Peninsula
Mt. Kōya
Tōdaiji
Hōryūji
Kōfukuji
Yakushiji
Saidaiji
PACIFIC OCEAN
N
Japan and Korea
City
Traditional symbol of Buddhist monastery
Mountain
0
100 mi
0
100 km

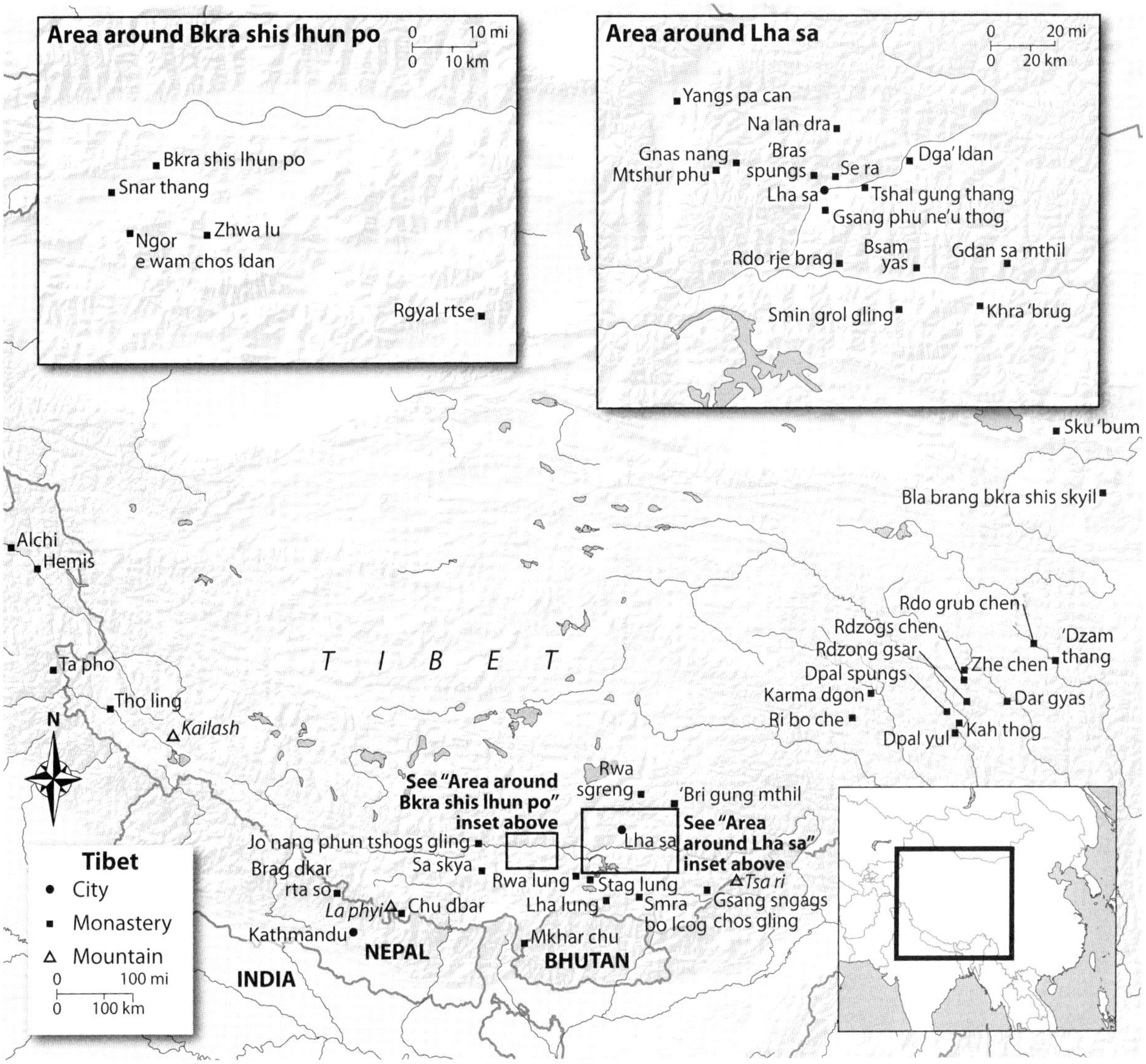
Area around Bkra shis lhun po
0 10 mi
0 10 km
Bkra shis lhun po
Snar thang
Ngor e wam chos ldan
Zhwa lu
Rgyal rtse
Area around Lha sa
0 20 mi
0 20 km
Yangs pa can
Na lan dra
Gnas nang
Mtshur phu
'Bras spungs
Se ra
Dga' ldan
Lha sa
Tshal gung thang
Gsang phu ne'u thog
Rdo rje brag
Bsam yas
Gdan sa mthil
Smin grol gling
Khra 'brug
Sku 'bum
Bla brang bkra shis skyil
Alchi
Hemis
Ta pho
Tho ling
Kailash
T I B E T
Rdo grub chen
Rdzogs chen
Rdzong gsar
Dpal spungs
Karma dgon
Ri bo che
'Dzam thang
Zhe chen
Dar gyas
Kah thog
Dpal yul
Rwa sgreng
'Bri gung mthil
See "Area around Bkra shis lhun po" inset above
See "Area around Lha sa" inset above
Lha sa
Jo nang phun tshogs gling
Sa skya
Brag dkar rta so
Rwa lung
Stag lung
Tsa ri
Gsang sngags chos gling
La phyi
Chu dbar
Lha lung
Smra bo lcog
Kathmandu
NEPAL
Mkhar chu
BHUTAN
INDIA
N
Tibet
City
Monastery
Mountain
0 100 mi
0 100 km

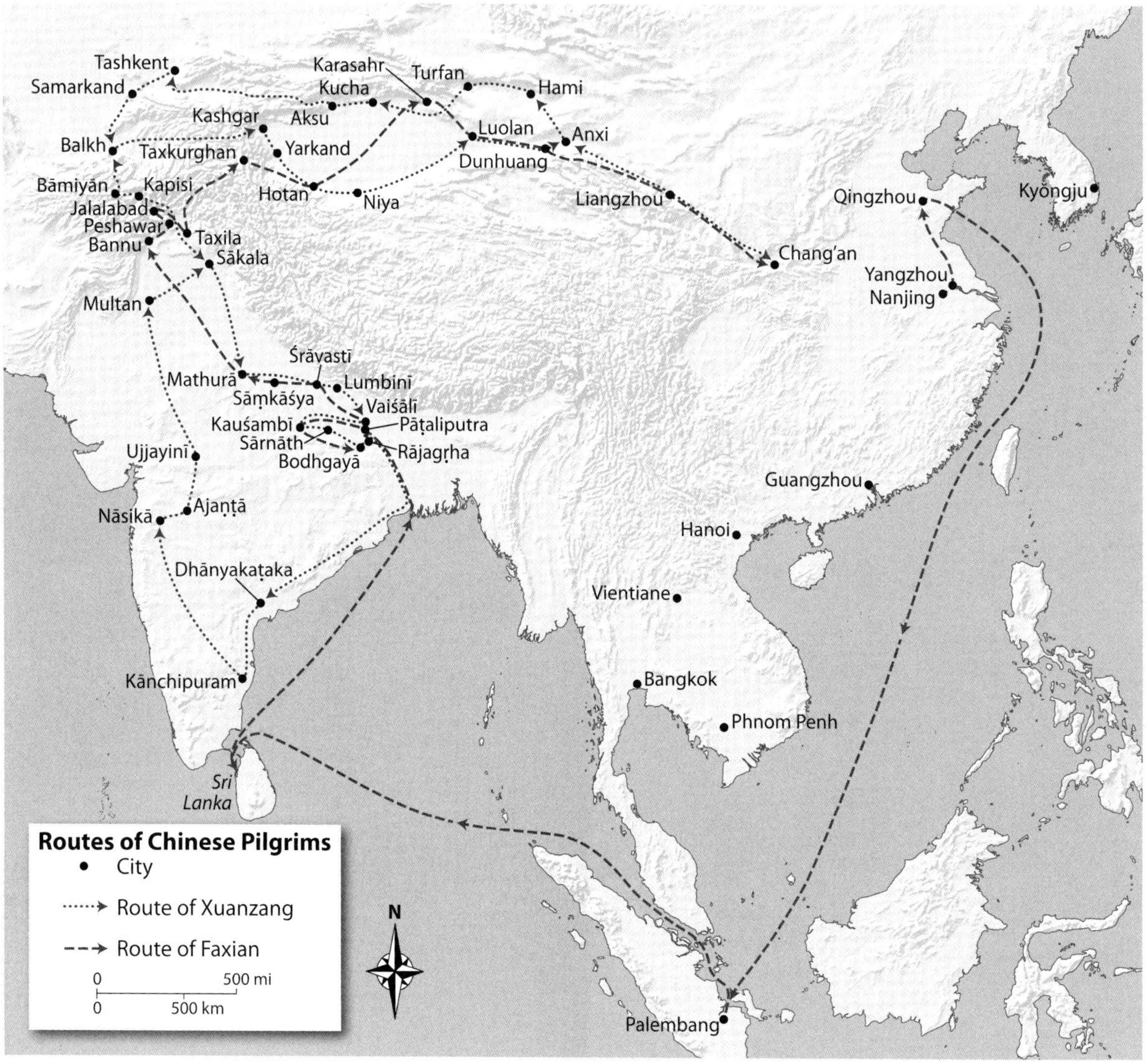
Routes of Chinese Pilgrims
City
Route of Xuanzang
Route of Faxian
0 500 mi
0 500 km
N
Tashkent
Samarkand
Balkh
Bāmiyān
Kapisi
Jalalabad
Peshawar
Bannu
Taxila
Sākala
Multan
Kashgar
Taxkurghan
Yarkand
Aksu
Kucha
Karasahr
Turfan
Hami
Luolan
Anxi
Dunhuang
Hotan
Niya
Liangzhou
Chang'an
Qingzhou
Kyongju
Yangzhou
Nanjing
Śrāvastī
Mathurā
Lumbinī
Sāṃkāśya
Vaiśālī
Kauśambī
Pāṭaliputra
Sārnāth
Rājagṛha
Bodhgayā
Ujjayinī
Ajaṇṭā
Nāsikā
Dhānyakaṭaka
Kānchipuram
Sri Lanka
Guangzhou
Hanoi
Vientiane
Bangkok
Phnom Penh
Palembang

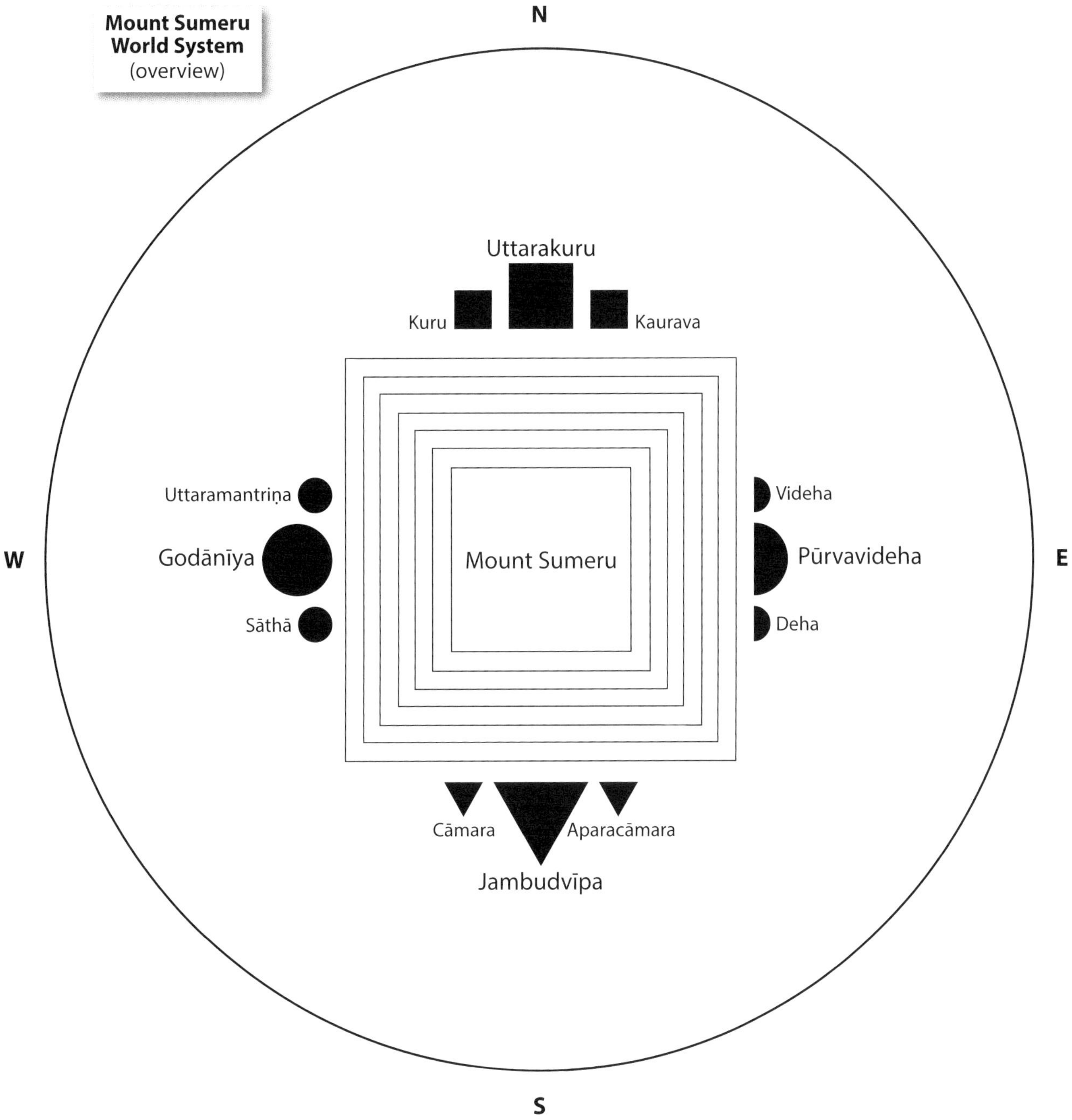
Mount Sumeru
World System
(overview)
N
Uttarakuru
Kuru
Kaurava
Uttaramantriṇa
Videha
W
Godānīya
Mount Sumeru
Pūrvavideha
E
Sāthā
Deha
Cāmara
Aparacāmara
Jambudvīpa
S

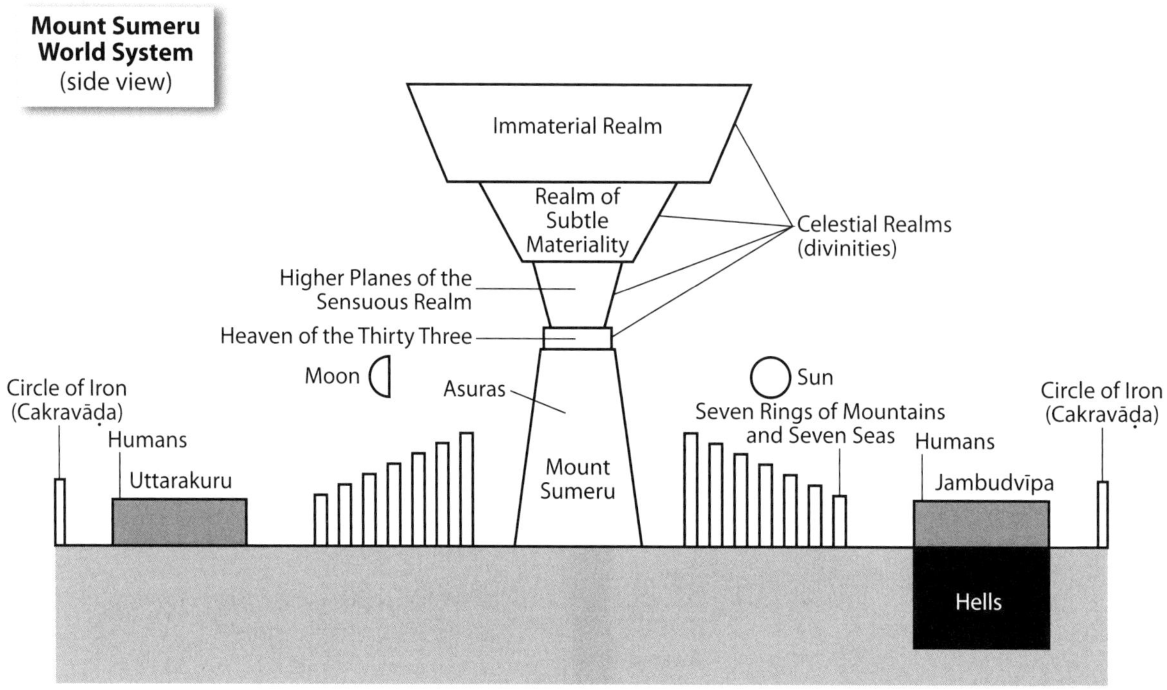
Mount Sumeru
World System
(side view)
Immaterial Realm
Realm of
Subtle
Materiality
Celestial Realms
(divinities)
Higher Planes of the
Sensuous Realm
Heaven of the Thirty Three
Moon
Asuras
Sun
Circle of Iron
(Cakravāḍa)
Humans
Uttarakuru
Mount
Sumeru
Seven Rings of Mountains
and Seven Seas
Humans
Jambudvīpa
Circle of Iron
(Cakravāḍa)
Hells

# The Princeton Dictionary of Buddhism

# A

**A**. The first vowel and letter in the Sanskrit alphabet. The phoneme "a" is thought to be the source of all other phonemes and its corresponding letter the origin of all other letters. As the basis of both the Sanskrit phonemic system and the written alphabet, the letter "a" thus comes to be invested with mystical significance as the source of truth, nondifferentiation, and emptiness (ŚŪNYATĀ), or even of the universe as a whole. The PRAJÑĀPĀRAMITĀSARVATATHĀGATAMĀTĀ-EKĀKṢARĀ, the shortest of the perfection of wisdom scriptures, also describes how the entirety of the perfection of wisdom is subsumed by this one letter. The letter in the Sanskrit SIDDHAM alphabet gained special significance within the esoteric Buddhist traditions in Japan (MIKKYŌ), such as Shingon (see SHINGONSHŪ), which considered it to be the "seed" (BĪJA) of MAHĀVAIROCANA, the central divinity of esoteric Buddhism, and used it in a distinctive type of meditation called AJIKAN ("contemplation of the letter 'a'"). The letter "a," which is said to be originally uncreated (AJI HONPUSHŌ), is interpreted to be the essence of all phenomena in the universe and the DHARMAKĀYA of the buddha Mahāvairocana. In the East Asian CHAN traditions, the letter "a" is also sometimes understood to represent the buddha-nature (FOXING, S. BUDDHADHĀTU) of all sentient beings.

**abhabbaṭṭhāna**. (S. *abhavyasthāna; T. *mi rung ba'i gnas; C. buwei; J. fui; K. purwi 不爲). In Pāli, "condition of being incapable" or "impossibility"; referring to nine immoral acts or inadequacies of character that an ARHAT is incapable of performing or possessing. Because he has destroyed the four ĀSRAVA, or contaminants—of sensuality (KĀMA), becoming (BHAVA), ignorance (AVIDYĀ), and wrong views (DṚṢṬI)—he is rendered forever "incapable" of engaging in the following acts: (1) deliberately killing any living being; (2) theft; (3) sexual intercourse; (4) deliberately lying; (5) accumulating personal possessions for sensual indulgence, as would a layperson; or performing wrong actions prompted by (6) attachment; (7) hatred; (8) stupidity; or (9) fear.

**ābhāsvaracitta**. In Sanskrit, "mind of clear light." See PRABHĀSVARACITTA.

**ābhāsvaraloka**. (P. ābhassaraloka; T. 'od gsal ba; C. jiguangjing tian/guangyintian; J. gokukōjōten/kōonten; K. kukkwangjŏng ch'ŏn/kwangŭmch'ŏn 極光淨天/光音天). In Sanskrit, the "heaven of radiant light" (in Chinese, the name is also parsed as the "heaven of radiant sound"), the highest of the three heavens associated with the second concentration (DHYĀNA) of the realm of subtle materiality (RŪPADHĀTU). As the BRAHMĀ divinities dwelling in this realm perpetually experience this profound state of meditation, they are described as subsisting on bliss (PRĪTI) and abiding in ease (SUKHA). Their bodies radiate light in all directions like lightning or like flames from a torch. While the bodies of the divinities of this realm are uniform, their perceptions are diverse, and there is no assurance that they will not be reborn in a lower realm of existence after their death. At the beginning of a world cycle, when the physical world (BHĀJANALOKA) of the sensuous realm (KĀMADHĀTU) has not yet been formed, and at the end of a world cycle when that physical world has been destroyed, many beings are reborn into the ābhāsvarāloka. A BODHISATTVA is never reborn in the immaterial realm (ĀRŪPYADHĀTU) even if he has achieved meditative states consistent with that realm, but he may be reborn in the ābhāsvarāloka. The Buddha once disabused a Brahmā god dwelling in that realm of the mistaken view that he was eternal. This god, whose name was Baka, had been the first living being born in the ābhāsvarāloka after a period of world dissolution, and presumed that no one had existed before him. When the divinities (DEVA) of the ābhāsvarāloka are first reborn in the realm of human beings (MANUṢYA), they may retain their divine attributes for a time, being spontaneously generated rather than born viviparously, and possessing bodies made from subtle materiality rather than gross matter. However, as time passes and they take on the physical and mental characteristics of ordinary human beings, they lose their luminosity, develop sexual characteristics, and come to subsist on solid foods.

**abhayadāna**. (T. mi 'jigs pa sbyin pa; C. wuwei [bu] shi/shi wuwei; J. mui[fu]se/semui; K. muoe[bo]si/si muoe 無畏[布]施/施無畏). In Sanskrit, the "gift of fearlessness"; said to be one of the expanded list of three (sometimes four) forms of giving/gifts (DĀNA), along with the "gift of dharma" (DHARMADĀNA) and the "gift of material goods" (ĀMIṢADĀNA). This particular type of gift is typically offered by BODHISATTVAs, whose encouragement, consolation, teaching of the dharma, and so forth relieve the fears, worries, and tribulations of the beneficiary. The common Buddhist practice of purchasing animals from butchers in order to save them from slaughter (see FANGSHENG) is considered to be a form of abhayadāna.

**Abhayadattaśrī**. (T. Mi 'jigs pa sbyin pa dpal). Indian author of the early twelfth century to whom the text of tantric hagiographies entitled *CATURAŚĪTISIDDHAPRAVṚTTI ("Lives of the Eighty-Four Siddhas") is ascribed. According to the colophon of this work, the author is known as "the great guru from Campara in India."

**Abhayagiri**. A Sri Lankan monastery built at the capital of ANURĀDHAPURA in first century BCE. The monastery was constructed for the elder Mahātissa by the Sinhala king VAṬṬAGĀMAṆI ABHAYA in gratitude for the monk's assistance during the king's political exile and his struggle for the throne. According to medieval Pāli historical chronicles, Mahātissa was said to have been unrestrained and base in his behavior, which eventually prompted the monks of the MAHĀVIHĀRA to pass an act of banishment (PRAVRĀJANĪYAKARMAN, P. pabbājanīyakamma) against him. Mahātissa thereafter conducted ecclesiastical ceremonies (SAṂGHAKARMAN, P. saṅghakamma) separately, and the Abhayagiri fraternity eventually seceded from the Mahāvihāra as a separate order of Sri Lankan Buddhism. The Abhayagiri flourished during the eleventh century, but, with the abandonment of Anurādhapura in the thirteenth century, ceased to exist as an active center. The site is today known for the massive Abhayagiri Thūpa (STŪPA), one of the largest in Sri Lanka, which was rediscovered deep in a forest at the end of the nineteenth century.

**Abhayākaragupta**. (T. 'Jigs med 'byung gnas sbas pa) (d. c. 1125). Indian tantric Buddhist master who was born into a brāhmaṇa family in either Orissa or northeast India near Bengal. Sources vary regarding his dates of birth and death, although most agree that he was a contemporary of the Pāla king Rāmapāla, who began his reign during the final quarter of the eleventh century. Abhayākaragupta became a Buddhist monk in response to a prophetic vision and trained extensively in the esoteric practices of TANTRA, while nevertheless maintaining his monastic discipline (VINAYA). Abhayākaragupta was active at the monastic university of VIKRAMAŚĪLA in Bihar and became renowned as both a scholar and a teacher. He was a prolific author, composing treatises in numerous fields of Buddhist doctrine, including monastic discipline and philosophy as well as tantric ritual practice and iconography. Many Sanskrit manuscripts of his works have been preserved in India, Nepal, and Tibet, and his writings were influential both in India and among Newari Buddhists in Nepal. Translations of his works into Tibetan were begun under his supervision, and more than two dozen are preserved in the Tibetan canon. To date, Abhayākaragupta's writings best known in the West are his treatises on tantric iconography, the *Vajrāvalī* and *Niṣpannayogāvalī*, and his syncretistic ABHIDHARMA treatise *Munimatālaṃkāra*.

**abhayamudrā**. (T. mi 'jigs pa'i phyag rgya; C. shiwuwei yin; J. semuiin; K. simuoe in 施無畏印). In Sanskrit, "the gesture of fearlessness" or "gesture of protection"; also sometimes called the gesture of granting refuge. This gesture (MUDRĀ) is typically formed with the palm of the right hand facing outward at shoulder height and the fingers pointing up, although both hands may simultaneously be raised in this posture in a double abhayamudrā. Occasionally, the index, second, or third finger touches the thumb, with the remaining fingers extended upward. This gesture is associated with ŚĀKYAMUNI Buddha immediately following his enlightenment, and standing buddha images will often be depicted with this mudrā, portraying a sense of the security, serenity, and compassion that derive from enlightenment. This gesture is also commonly associated with AMOGHASIDDHI.

**Abheda**. (T. Mi phyed pa). One of "the sixteen elders" or senior ARHATs in the Tibetan enumeration. See ṢOḌAŚASTHAVIRA.

**abhibhvāyatana**. (P. abhibhāyatana; T. zil gyis gnon pa'i skye mched; C. shengchu; J. shōsho; K. sŭngch'ŏ 勝處). In Sanskrit, "sphere of sovereignty" or "station of mastery"; eight stages of transcendence over the sense spheres (ĀYATANA), which are conducive to the development of meditative absorption (DHYĀNA). By recognizing from various standpoints that material forms are external, one trains oneself to let go of attachments to material objects and focus exclusively on the meditation subject. The standard list of eight is as follows. When one perceives forms internally (viz., on one's own person), one sees forms external to oneself that are (1) limited and beautiful or ugly (viz., pure and impure colors) or (2) unlimited, and beautiful or ugly, and masters them so that one is aware that one knows and sees them; when one does not perceive forms internally, one sees external forms that are (3) limited or (4) unlimited. When one does not perceive forms internally, one sees external forms that are (5) blue, (6) yellow, (7) red, or (8) white and masters them so that one is aware that one knows and sees them. In the Pāli meditative literature, the earth and the color devices (KASIṆA) are said to be especially conducive to developing these spheres of sovereignty. Progress through these spheres weans the mind from its attraction to the sensuous realm (KĀMADHĀTU) and thus encourages the advertence toward the four meditative absorptions (DHYĀNA; RŪPĀVACARADHYĀNA) associated with the realm of subtle materiality (RŪPADHĀTU), wherein the mind becomes temporarily immune to sensory input and wholly absorbed in its chosen object of meditation.

**abhicāra**. [alt. abhicara] (T. mngon spyod). In Sanskrit, "magic" or "wrathful action"; in ANUTTARAYOGATANTRA, the fourth of the four activities (CATURKARMAN) of the Buddhist tantric adept.

Abhicāra is broken down into māraṇa "killing," mohana "enchanting," stambhana "paralyzing," vidveṣaṇa "rendering harm through animosity," uccāṭana "removing or driving away," and vaśīkaraṇa "subduing." After initiation (ABHIṢEKA), adepts who keep their tantric commitments (SAMAYA) properly and reach the requisite yogic level are empowered to use four sorts of enlightened activity, as appropriate: these four types of activities are (1) those that are pacifying (S. ŚĀNTICĀRA); (2) those that increase prosperity, life span, etc. (PAUṢṬIKA), when necessary for the spread of the doctrine; (3) those that subjugate or tame (S. VAŚĪKARAṆA) the unruly; and finally (4) those that are violent or drastic measures (abhicāra) such as war, when the situation requires it. In the MAÑJUŚRĪNĀMASAṂGĪTI, Cānakya, Candragupta's minister, is said to have used abhicāra against his enemies, and because of this misuse of tantric power was condemned to suffer the consequences in hell. Throughout the history of Buddhist tantra, the justification of violence by invoking the category of abhicāra has been a contentious issue. PADMASAMBHAVA is said to have tamed the unruly spirits of Tibet, sometimes violently, with his magical powers, and the violent acts that RWA LO TSĀ BA in the eleventh century countenanced against those who criticized his practices are justified by categorizing them as abhicāra.

**Abhidhammatthasaṅgaha**. In Pāli, "Summary of the Meaning of Abhidharma"; a synoptic manual of Pāli ABHIDHARMA written by the Sri Lankan monk ANURUDDHA (d.u.), abbot of the Mūlasoma Vihāra in Polonnaruwa, sometime between the eighth and twelfth centuries CE, but most probably around the turn of the eleventh century. (Burmese tradition instead dates the text to the first century BCE.) The terse *Abhidhammatthasaṅgaha* has been used for centuries as an introductory primer for the study of abhidharma in the monasteries of Sri Lanka and the THERAVĀDA countries of Southeast Asia; indeed, no other abhidharma text has received more scholarly attention within the tradition, especially in Burma, where this primer has been the object of multiple commentaries and vernacular translations. The *Abhidhammatthasaṅgaha* includes nine major sections, which provide a systematic overview of Pāli Buddhist doctrine. Anuruddha summarizes the exegeses appearing in BUDDHAGHOSA's VISUDDHIMAGGA, though the two works could hardly be more different: where the *Visuddhimagga* offers an exhaustive exegesis of THERAVĀDA abhidharma accompanied by a plethora of historical and mythical detail, the *Abhidhammatthasaṅgaha* is little more than a list of topics, like a bare table of contents. Especially noteworthy in the *Abhidhammatthasaṅgaha* is its analysis of fifty-two mental concomitants (CETASIKA), in distinction to the forty-six listed in SARVĀSTIVĀDA ABHIDHARMA and the ABHIDHARMAKOŚABHĀṢYA. There is one major Pāli commentary to the *Abhidhammatthasaṅgaha* still extant, the *Porāṇaṭīkā*, which is attributed to Vimalabuddhi (d.u.). The *Abhidhammatthasaṅgaha* appears in the Pali Text Society's English translation series as *Compendium of Philosophy*.

**Abhidhammāvatāra**. In Pāli, "Introduction to Abhidhamma"; a primer of Pāli ABHIDHAMMA attributed to BUDDHADATTA (c. fifth century CE), who is said to have been contemporaneous with the premier Pāli scholiast BUDDHAGHOSA; some legends go so far as to suggest that the two ABHIDHAMMIKAS might even have met. The book was written in south India and is the oldest of the noncanonical Pāli works on abhidhamma. It offers a systematic scholastic outline of abhidhamma, divided into twenty-four chapters called niddesas (S. nirdeśa; "expositions"), and displays many affinities with Buddhaghosa's VISUDDHIMAGGA. These chapters include coverage of the mind (CITTA) and mental concomitants (CETASIKA), the various types of concentration (SAMĀDHI), the types of knowledge (JÑĀNA) associated with enlightenment, and the process of purification (visuddhi, S. VIŚUDDHI). The work is written in a mixture of prose and verse.

**abhidhammika**. [alt. ābhidhammika]. In Pāli, "specialist in the ABHIDHAMMA"; scholarly monks who specialized in study of the abhidhamma (S. ABHIDHARMA) section of the Buddhist canon. In the Pāli tradition, particular importance has long been attached to the study of abhidharma. The AṬṬHASĀLINĪ says that the first ABHIDHAMMIKA was the Buddha himself, and the abhidhammikas were presumed to be the most competent exponents of the teachings of the religion. Among the Buddha's immediate disciples, the premier abhidhammika was Sāriputta (S. ŚĀRIPUTRA), who was renowned for his systematic grasp of the dharma. Monastic "families" of abhidhamma specialists were known as abhidhammikagaṇa, and they passed down through the generations their own scholastic interpretations of Buddhist doctrine, interpretations that sometimes differed from those offered by specialists in the scriptures (P. sutta; S. SŪTRA) or disciplinary rules (VINAYA). In medieval Sri Lanka, the highest awards within the Buddhist order were granted to monks who specialized in this branch of study, rather than to experts in the scriptures or disciplinary rules. Special festivals were held in honor of the abhidhamma, which involved the recital of important texts and the granting of awards to participants. In contemporary Myanmar (Burma), where the study of abhidhamma continues to be highly esteemed, the seventh book of the Pāli ABHIDHARMAPIṬAKA, the PAṬṬHĀNA ("Conditions"), is regularly recited in festivals that the Burmese call pathan pwe. Pathan pwe are marathon recitations that go on for days, conducted by invited abhidhammikas who are particularly well versed in the *Paṭṭhāna*, the text that is the focus of the festival. The pathan pwe serves a function similar to that of PARITTA recitations, in that it is believed to ward off baleful influences, but its main designated purpose is to forestall the decline and disappearance of the Buddha's dispensation (P. sāsana; S. ŚĀSANA). The Theravāda tradition considers the *Paṭṭhāna* to be the Buddha's most profound exposition of ultimate truth (P. paramatthasacca; S. PARAMĀRTHASATYA), and according to the Pāli commentaries, the *Paṭṭhāna* is the first constituent of the Buddha's dispensation that will disappear from the world as the religion faces its inevitable decline. The abhidhammikas' marathon recitations of the *Paṭṭhāna*, therefore, help to ward off the eventual demise of the Buddhist religion. This practice speaks of a THERAVĀDA orientation in favor of scholarship that goes back well over a thousand years. Since at least the time of BUDDHAGHOSA (c. fifth century CE), the life of scholarship (P. PARIYATTI), rather than that of meditation or contemplation (P. PAṬIPATTI), has been the preferred vocational path within Pāli Buddhist monasticism. Monks who devoted themselves exclusively to meditation were often portrayed as persons who lacked the capacity to master the intricacies of Pāli scholarship. Even so, meditation was always recommended as the principal means by which one could bring scriptural knowledge to maturity, either through awakening or the realization (P. paṭivedha; S. PRATIVEDHA) of Buddhist truths. See also ĀBHIDHARMIKA.

**Abhidhānappadīpikā**. A Pāli dictionary of synonyms attributed to the twelfth-century Sinhalese scholar–monk Moggallāna, which, in style and method, is similar to the Sanskrit lexicon the *Amarakośa*. The text is arranged into three sections, dealing with celestial, terrestrial, and miscellaneous topics. The three sections are further subdivided into various chapters, each composed of groups of synonyms arranged in verse for ease of memorization. For example, the first section of the thesaurus includes 179 different entries, each of which offers multiple entries: e.-g., thirty-two different epithets for the Buddha and forty-six synonyms for nibbāna (S. NIRVĀṆA). The second section has six different chapters, which include twenty-four synonyms for a house, ten for man, fifteen for woman, etc. The third section has four chapters on miscellaneous topics. A Sinhalese paraphrase and commentary on this dictionary were produced in Sri Lanka by Caturaṅgabala (d.u.), while a Burmese commentary was composed by Ñāṇāvāsa (d.u.) in the fourteenth century during the reign of King Kittisīhasūra (c. 1351); a Burmese vernacular translation was subsequently made during the eighteenth century.

**Abhidhānottaratantra**. [alt. Avadānastotratantra] (T. Mngon par brjod pa'i rgyud bla ma). In Sanskrit, "Continuation of the Explanation [of the CAKRASAṂVARATANTRA]"; an Indian text describing the invocation of numerous tantric deities together with their seed syllables (BĪJA) and ritual meditations. The work was originally translated into Tibetan and edited by ATIŚA DĪPAṂKARAŚRĪJÑĀNA and RIN CHEN BZANG PO in the eleventh century.

**abhidharma**. (P. abhidhamma; T. chos mngon pa; C. apidamo/duifa; J. abidatsuma/taihō; K. abidalma/taebŏp 阿毘達磨/對法). In Sanskrit, abhidharma is a prepositional compound composed of abhi- + dharma. The compound is typically glossed with abhi being interpreted as equivalent to uttama and meaning "highest" or "advanced" DHARMA (viz., doctrines or teachings), or abhi meaning "pertaining to" the dharma. The SARVĀSTIVĀDA Sanskrit tradition typically follows the latter etymology, while the THERAVĀDA Pāli tradition prefers the former, as in BUDDHAGHOSA's gloss of the term meaning either "special dharma" or "supplementary dharma." These definitions suggest that abhidharma was conceived as a precise (P. nippariyāya), definitive (PARAMĀRTHA) assessment of the dharma that was presented in its discursive (P. sappariyāya), conventional (SAṂVṚTI) form in the SŪTRAs. Where the sūtras offered more subjective presentations of the dharma, drawing on worldly parlance, simile, metaphor, and personal anecdote in order to appeal to their specific audiences, the abhidharma provided an objective, impersonal, and highly technical description of the specific characteristics of reality and the causal processes governing production and cessation. There are two divergent theories for the emergence of the abhidharma as a separate genre of Buddhist literature. In one theory, accepted by most Western scholars, the abhidharma is thought to have evolved out of the "matrices" (S. MĀTṚKĀ; P. mātikā), or numerical lists of dharmas, that were used as mnemonic devices for organizing the teachings of the Buddha systematically. Such treatments of dharma are found even in the sūtra literature and are probably an inevitable by-product of the oral quality of early Buddhist textual transmission. A second theory, favored by Japanese scholars, is that abhidharma evolved from catechistic discussions (abhidharmakathā) in which a dialogic format was used to clarify problematic issues in doctrine. The dialogic style also appears prominently in the sūtras where, for example, the Buddha might give a brief statement of doctrine (uddeśa; P. uddesa) whose meaning had to be drawn out through exegesis (NIRDEŚA; P. niddesa); indeed, MAHĀKĀTYĀYANA, one of the ten major disciples of the Buddha, was noted for his skill in such explications. This same style was prominent enough in the sūtras even to be listed as one of the nine or twelve genres of Buddhist literature (specifically, VYĀKARAṆA; P. veyyākaraṇa). According to tradition, the Buddha first taught the abhidharma to his mother MAHĀMĀYĀ, who had died shortly after his birth and been reborn as a god in TUṢITA heaven. He met her in the heaven of the thirty-three (TRĀYASTRIṂŚA), where he expounded the abhidharma to her and the other divinities there, repeating those teachings to ŚĀRIPUTRA when he descended each day to go on his alms-round. Śāriputra was renowned as a master of the abhidharma. Abhidharma primarily sets forth the training in higher wisdom (ADHIPRAJÑĀŚIKṢĀ) and involves both analytical and synthetic modes of doctrinal exegesis. The body of scholastic literature that developed from this exegetical style was compiled into the ABHIDHARMAPIṬAKA, one of the three principal sections of the Buddhist canon, or TRIPIṬAKA, along with sūtra and VINAYA, and is concerned primarily with scholastic discussions on epistemology, cosmology, psychology, KARMAN, rebirth, and the constituents of the process of enlightenment and the path (MĀRGA) to salvation. (In the MAHĀYĀNA tradition, this abhidharmapiṭaka is sometimes redefined as a broader "treatise basket," or *ŚĀSTRAPIṬAKA.)

**Abhidharmadharmaskandha[pādaśāstra]**. (C. Apidamo fayun zu lun; J. Abidatsuma hōunsokuron; K. Abidalma pŏbon chok non 阿毘達磨法蘊足論). See DHARMASKANDHA [PĀDAŚĀSTRA].

**Abhidharmadhātukāya[pādaśāstra]**. (C. Apidamo jieshen zu lun; J. Abidatsuma kaishinsokuron; K. Abidalma kyesin chok non 阿毘達磨界身足論). See DHĀTUKĀYA[PĀDAŚĀSTRA].

**Abhidharmadīpa**. In Sanskrit, "Lamp of ABHIDHARMA"; an Indian scholastic treatise probably composed between 450 and 550 CE. Only fragments of the treatise (sixty-two of 150 folios) are extant; these were discovered in Tibet in 1937. The treatise is composed of two parts—the *Abhidharmadīpa*, written in verse (kārikā), and a prose autocommentary, the *Vibhāṣāprabhāvṛtti*—both of which were probably composed by the same anonymous author. The author, who refers to himself merely as the "Dīpakāra" ("author of the *Dīpa*") may be Vimalamitra (d.u.), an otherwise-unknown disciple of SAṂGHABHADRA. The structure of the text is modeled on that of the influential ABHIDHARMAKOŚABHĀṢYA, and almost half of the kārikā verses included in the *Abhidharmadīpa* are virtually identical to those found in the *Abhidharmakośa*. Although borrowing freely from the *Kośa*, the Dīpakāra launches a harsh critique of VASUBANDHU's (whom he calls the "Kośakāra," or "author of the *Kośa*") *Abhidharmakośabhāṣya*, from the standpoint of SARVĀSTIVĀDA abhidharma. Vasubandhu is criticized for the SAUTRĀNTIKA tendencies betrayed in his doctrinal analyses and also for being a Mahāyānist adherent of the teachings of the "three natures" (TRISVABHĀVA). As such, the *Abhidharmadīpa*'s author seems to have been a follower of SAṂGHABHADRA's *NYĀYĀNUSĀRA, and the text helps to clarify the positions of Saṃghabhadra and the orthodox VAIBHĀṢIKAS. The Dīpakāra shares the latter's concern with providing both a systematic exegesis of abhidharma theory and a vigorous polemical defense of Sarvāstivāda doctrinal positions. Since it presents theories of other thinkers not covered in the *Abhidharmakośabhāṣya*, the *Abhidharmadīpa* serves as an important source for studying the history of Indian abhidharma. For example, in his discussion of the eponymous Sarvāstivāda position that "everything exists" throughout all three time periods (TRIKĀLA) of past, present, and future, the Dīpakāra also critiques three rival positions: the VIBHAJYAVĀDA and Dārṣṭāntikas, who maintain that only "part" exists (viz., the present); the Vaitulika and Ayogaśūnyatāvāda, who say that nothing exists; and the PUDGALAVĀDA, who presume that existence is indeterminate (AVYĀKṚTA).

***Abhidharmahṛdaya**. (C. Apitan xin lun; J. Abidon shinron; K. Abidam sim non 阿毘曇心論). In Sanskrit, "Heart of ABHIDHARMA"; one of the first attempts at a systematic presentation of abhidharma according to the SARVĀSTIVĀDA school; the treatise is attributed to Dharmaśreṣṭhin (Fasheng, c. 130 BCE), who hailed from the GANDHĀRA region of Central Asia. The text is no longer extant in Sanskrit but survives only in a Chinese translation made sometime during the fourth century (alt. 376, 391) by Saṃghadeva and LUSHAN HUIYUAN. The treatise functions essentially as a handbook for meditative development, focusing on ways of overcoming the negative proclivities of mind (ANUŚAYA) and developing correct knowledge (JÑĀNA). The meditative training outlined in the treatise focuses on the four absorptions (DHYĀNA) and on two practical techniques for developing concentration: mindfulness of breathing (ĀNĀPĀNASMṚTI) and the contemplation of impurity (AŚUBHABHĀVANĀ). The text is also one of the first to distinguish the path of vision (DARŚANAMĀRGA), which involves the initial insight into the FOUR NOBLE TRUTHS, and the path of cultivation (BHĀVANĀMĀRGA), which eliminates all the remaining proclivities so that the adept may experience the stage of the worthy one (ARHAT).

**Abhidharmajñānaprasthāna**. (C. Apidamo fazhi lun; J. Abidatsuma hotchiron; K. Abidalma palchi non 阿毘達磨發智論). See JÑĀNAPRASTHĀNA.

**Abhidharmakośa**. See ABHIDHARMAKOŚABHĀṢYA.

**Abhidharmakośabhāṣya**. (T. Chos mngon pa'i mdzod kyi bshad pa; C. Apidamo jushe lun; J. Abidatsuma kusharon; K. Abidalma kusa non 阿毘達磨俱舍論). In Sanskrit, "A Treasury of ABHIDHARMA, with Commentary"; an influential scholastic treatise attributed to VASUBANDHU (c. fourth or fifth century CE). The *Abhidharmakośabhāṣya* consists of two texts: the root text of the *Abhidharmakośa*, composed in verse (kārikā), and its prose autocommentary (bhāṣya); this dual verse-prose structure comes to be emblematic of later SARVĀSTIVĀDA abhidharma literature. As the title suggests, the work is mainly concerned with abhidharma theory as it was explicated in the ABHIDHARMAMAHĀVIBHĀṢĀ, the principal scholastic treatise of the VAIBHĀṢIKA ĀBHIDHARMIKAS in the Sarvāstivāda school. In comparison to the *Mahāvibhāṣā*, however, the *Abhidharmakośabhāṣya* presents a more systematic overview of Sarvāstivāda positions. At various points in his expositions, Vasubandhu criticizes the Sarvāstivāda doctrine from the standpoint of the more progressive SAUTRĀNTIKA offshoot of the Sarvāstivāda school, which elicited a spirited response from later Sarvāstivāda–Vaibhāṣika scholars, such as SAṂGHABHADRA in his *NYĀYĀNUSĀRA. The *Abhidharmakośabhāṣya* has thus served as an invaluable tool in the study of the history of the later MAINSTREAM BUDDHIST SCHOOLS. The Sanskrit texts of both the kārikā and the bhāṣya were lost for centuries before being rediscovered in Tibet in 1934 and 1936, respectively. Two Chinese translations, by XUANZANG and PARAMĀRTHA, and one Tibetan translation of the work are extant. The *Kośa* is primarily concerned with a detailed elucidation of the polysemous term DHARMA, the causes (HETU) and conditions (PRATYAYA) that lead to continued rebirth in SAṂSĀRA, and the soteriological stages of the path (MĀRGA) leading to enlightenment. The treatise is divided into eight major chapters, called kośasthānas. (1) Dhātunirdeśa, "Exposition on the Elements," divides dharmas into various categories, such as tainted (SĀSRAVA) and untainted (ANĀSRAVA), or compounded (SAṂSKṚTA) and uncompounded (ASAṂSKṚTA), and discusses the standard Buddhist classifications of the five aggregates (SKANDHA), twelve sense fields (ĀYATANA), and eighteen elements (DHĀTU). This chapter also includes extensive discussion of the theory of the four great elements (MAHĀBHŪTA) that constitute materiality (RŪPA) and the Buddhist theory of atoms or particles (PARAMĀṆU). (2) Indriyanirdeśa, "Exposition on the Faculties," discusses a fivefold classification of dharmas into materiality (rūpa), thought (CITTA), mental concomitants (CAITTA), forces dissociated from thought (CITTAVIPRAYUKTASAṂSKĀRA), and the uncompounded (ASAṂSKṚTA). This chapter also has extensive discussions of the six causes (HETU), the four conditions (PRATYAYA), and the five effects or fruitions (PHALA). (3) Lokanirdeśa, "Exposition on the Cosmos," describes the formation and structure of a world system (LOKA), the different types of sentient beings, the various levels of existence, and the principle of dependent origination (PRATĪTYASAMUTPĀDA) that governs the process of rebirth, which is discussed here in connection with the three time periods (TRIKĀLA) of past, present, and future. (4) Karmanirdeśa, "Exposition on Action," discusses the different types of action (KARMAN), including the peculiar type of action associated with unmanifest materiality (AVIJÑAPTIRŪPA). The ten wholesome and unwholesome "paths of action" (KUŚALA-KARMAPATHA and AKUŚALA-KARMAPATHA) also receive a lengthy description. (5) Anuśayanirdeśa, "Exposition on the Proclivities," treats the ninety-eight types of ANUŚAYA in relation to their sources and qualities and the relationship between the anuśayas and other categories of unwholesome qualities, such as afflictions (KLEŚA), contaminants (ĀSRAVA), floods (OGHA), and yokes (yoga). (6) Mārgapudgalanirdeśa, "Exposition on the Path and the [Noble] Persons," outlines how either insight into the four noble truths and carefully following a series of soteriological steps can remove defilements and transform the ordinary person into one of the noble persons (ĀRYAPUDGALA). (7) Jñānanirdeśa, "Exposition on Knowledge," offers a detailed account of the ten types of knowledge and the distinctive attributes of noble persons and buddhas. (8) Samāpattinirdeśa, "Exposition on Attainment," discusses different categories of concentration (SAMĀDHI) and the attainments (SAMĀPATTI) that result from their perfection. (9) Appended to this main body is a ninth section, an independent treatise titled the *Pudgalanirdeśa*, "Exposition of the Notion of a Person." Here, Vasubandhu offers a detailed critique of the theory of the self, scrutinizing both the Buddhist PUDGALAVĀDA/VĀTSĪPUTRĪYA "heresy" of the inexpressible (avācya) "person" (PUDGALA) being conventionally real and Brahmanical theories of a perduring soul (ĀTMAN). Numerous commentaries to the *Kośa*, such as those composed by VASUMITRA, YAŚOMITRA, STHIRAMATI, and Pūrṇavardhana, attest to its continuing influence in Indian Buddhist thought. The *Kośa* was also the object of vigorous study in the scholastic traditions of East Asia and Tibet, which produced many indigenous commentaries on the text and its doctrinal positions.

**Abhidharmakośavyākhyā Sphuṭārthā**. See SPHUṬĀRTHĀ ABHIDHARMAKOŚAVYĀKHYĀ.

**Abhidharmamahāvibhāṣā**. (T. Chos mngon pa bye brag bshad pa chen po; C. Apidamo dapiposha lun; J. Abidatsuma daibibasharon; K. Abidalma taebibasa non 阿毘達磨大毘婆沙論). In Sanskrit, "Great Exegesis of ABHIDHARMA," also commonly known as *Mahāvibhāṣā*; a massive VAIBHĀṢIKA treatise on SARVĀSTIVĀDA abhidharma translated into Chinese by the scholar–pilgrim XUANZANG and his translation bureau between 656 and 659 at XIMINGSI in the Tang capital of Chang'an. Although no Sanskrit version of this text is extant, earlier Chinese translations by Buddhavarman and others survive, albeit only in (equally massive) fragments. The complete Sanskrit text of the recension that Xuanzang used was in 100,000 ślokas; his translation was in 200 rolls, making it one of the largest single works in the Buddhist canon. According to the account in Xuanzang's DA TANG XIYU JI, four hundred years after the Buddha's PARINIRVĀṆA, King KANIṢKA gathered five hundred ARHATs to recite the Buddhist canon (TRIPIṬAKA). The ABHIDHARMAPIṬAKA of this canon, which is associated with the Sarvāstivāda school, is said to have been redacted during this council (see COUNCIL, FOURTH). The central abhidharma treatise of the Sarvāstivāda school is KĀTYĀYANĪPUTRA's JÑĀNAPRASTHĀNA, and the *Abhidharmamahāvibhāṣā* purports to offer a comprehensive overview of varying views on the meaning of that seminal text by the five hundred arhats who were in attendance at the convocation. The comments of four major ĀBHIDHARMIKAS (Ghoṣa, DHARMATRĀTA, VASUMITRA, and Buddhadeva) are interwoven into the *Mahāvibhāṣā*'s contextual analysis of Kātyāyanīputra's material from the *Jñānaprasthāna*, making the text a veritable encyclopedia of contemporary Buddhist scholasticism. Since the *Mahāvibhāṣā* also purports to be a commentary on the central text of the Sarvāstivāda school, it therefore offers a comprehensive picture of the development of Sarvāstivāda thought after the compilation of the *Jñānaprasthāna*. The *Mahāvibhāṣā* is divided into eight sections (grantha) and several chapters (varga), which systematically follow the eight sections and forty-three chapters of the *Jñānaprasthāna* in presenting its explication. Coverage of each topic begins with an overview of varying interpretations found in different Buddhist and non-Buddhist schools, detailed coverage of the positions of the four major Sarvāstivāda ābhidharmikas, and finally the definitive judgment of the compilers, the Kāśmīri followers of Kātyāyanīputra, who call themselves the Vibhāṣāśāstrins. The *Mahāvibhāṣā* was the major influence on the systematic scholastic elaboration of Sarvāstivāda doctrine that appears (though with occasional intrusions from the positions of the Sarvāstivāda's more-progressive SAUTRĀNTIKA offshoot) in VASUBANDHU's influential ABHIDHARMAKOŚABHĀṢYA, which itself elicited a spirited response from later Sarvāstivāda–Vaibhāṣika scholars, such as SAṂGHABHADRA in his *NYĀYĀNUSĀRA. The *Mahāvibhāṣa* was not translated into Tibetan until the twentieth century, when a translation entitled *Bye brag bshad mdzod chen mo* was made at the Sino-Tibetan

Institute by the Chinese monk FAZUN between 1946 and 1949. He presented a copy of the manuscript to the young fourteenth DALAI LAMA on the Dalai Lama's visit to Beijing in 1954, but it is not known whether it is still extant.

***Abhidharmanyāyānusāra**. See *NYĀYĀNUSĀRA.

**abhidharmapiṭaka**. (P. abhidhammapiṭaka; T. chos mngon pa'i sde snod; C. lunzang; J. ronzō; K. nonjang 論藏). The third of the three "baskets" (PIṬAKA) of the Buddhist canon (TRIPIṬAKA). The abhidharmapiṭaka derives from attempts in the early Buddhist community to elucidate the definitive significance of the teachings of the Buddha, as compiled in the SŪTRAs. Since the Buddha was well known to have adapted his message to fit the predilections and needs of his audience (cf. UPĀYAKAUŚALYA), there inevitably appeared inconsistencies in his teachings that needed to be resolved. The attempts to ferret out the definitive meaning of the BUDDHADHARMA through scholastic interpretation and exegesis eventually led to a new body of texts that ultimately were granted canonical status in their own right. These are the texts of the abhidharmapiṭaka. The earliest of these texts, such as the Pāli VIBHAṄGA and PUGGALAPAÑÑATTI and the SARVĀSTIVĀDA SAṂGĪTIPARYĀYA and DHARMASKANDHA, are structured as commentaries to specific sūtras or portions of sūtras. These materials typically organized the teachings around elaborate doctrinal taxonomies, which were used as mnemonic devices or catechisms. Later texts move beyond individual sūtras to systematize a wide range of doctrinal material, offering ever more complex analytical categorizations and discursive elaborations of the DHARMA. Ultimately, abhidharma texts emerge as a new genre of Buddhist literature in their own right, employing sophisticated philosophical speculation and sometimes even involving polemical attacks on the positions of rival factions within the SAṂGHA. ¶ At least seven schools of Indian Buddhism transmitted their own recensions of abhidharma texts, but only two of these canons are extant in their entirety. The Pāli abhidhammapiṭaka of the THERAVĀDA school, the only recension that survives in an Indian language, includes seven texts (the order of which often differs): (1) DHAMMASAṄGAṆI ("Enumeration of Dharmas") examines factors of mentality and materiality (NĀMARŪPA), arranged according to ethical quality; (2) VIBHAṄGA ("Analysis") analyzes the aggregates (SKANDHA), conditioned origination (PRATĪTYASAMUTPĀDA), and meditative development, each treatment culminating in a catechistic series of inquiries; (3) DHĀTUKATHĀ ("Discourse on Elements") categorizes all dharmas in terms of the skandhas and sense-fields (ĀYATANA); (4) PUGGALAPAÑÑATTI ("Description of Human Types") analyzes different character types in terms of the three afflictions of greed (LOBHA), hatred (DVEṢA), and delusion (MOHA) and various related subcategories; (5) KATHĀVATTHU ("Points of Controversy") scrutinizes the views of rival schools of mainstream Buddhism and how they differ from the Theravāda; (6) YAMAKA ("Pairs") provides specific denotations of problematic terms through paired comparisons; (7) PAṬṬHĀNA ("Conditions") treats extensively the full implications of conditioned origination. ¶ The abhidharmapiṭaka of the SARVĀSTIVĀDA school is extant only in Chinese translation, the definitive versions of which were prepared by XUANZANG's translation team in the seventh century. It also includes seven texts: (1) SAṂGĪTIPARYĀYA[PĀDAŚĀSTRA] ("Discourse on Pronouncements") attributed to either MAHĀKAUṢṬHILA or ŚĀRIPUTRA, a commentary on the *Saṃgītisūtra* (see SAṄGĪTISUTTA), where Śāriputra sets out a series of dharma lists (MĀTṚKĀ), ordered from ones to elevens, to organize the Buddha's teachings systematically; (2) DHARMASKANDHA[PĀDAŚĀSTRA] ("Aggregation of Dharmas"), attributed to Śāriputra or MAHĀMAUDGALYĀYANA, discusses Buddhist soteriological practices, as well as the afflictions that hinder spiritual progress, drawn primarily from the ĀGAMAS; (3) PRAJÑAPTIBHĀṢYA[PĀDAŚĀSTRA] ("Treatise on Designations"), attributed to Maudgalyāyana, treats Buddhist cosmology (lokaprajñapti), causes (kāraṇa), and action (KARMAN); (4) DHĀTUKĀYA[PĀDAŚĀSTRA] ("Collection on the Elements"), attributed to either PŪRṆA or VASUMITRA, discusses the mental concomitants (the meaning of DHĀTU in this treatise) and sets out specific sets of mental factors that are present in all moments of consciousness (viz., the ten MAHĀBHŪMIKA) or all defiled states of mind (viz., the ten KLEŚAMAHĀBHŪMIKA); (5) VIJÑĀNAKĀYA[PĀDAŚĀSTRA] ("Collection on Consciousness"), attributed to Devaśarman, seeks to prove the veracity of the eponymous Sarvāstivāda position that dharmas exist in all three time periods (TRIKĀLA) of past, present, and future, and the falsity of notions of the person (PUDGALA); it also provides the first listing of the four types of conditions (PRATYAYA); (6) PRAKARAṆA[PĀDAŚĀSTRA] ("Exposition"), attributed to VASUMITRA, first introduces the categorization of dharmas according to the more developed Sarvāstivāda rubric of RŪPA, CITTA, CAITTA, CITTAVIPRAYUKTASAṂSKĀRA, and ASAṂSKṚTA dharmas; it also adds a new listing of KUŚALAMAHĀBHŪMIKA, or factors always associated with wholesome states of mind; (7) JÑĀNAPRASTHĀNA ("Foundations of Knowledge"), attributed to KĀTYĀYANĪPUTRA, an exhaustive survey of Sarvāstivāda dharma theory and the school's exposition of psychological states, which forms the basis of the massive encyclopedia of Sarvāstivāda-Vaibhāṣika abhidharma, the ABHIDHARMAMAHĀVIBHĀṢĀ. In the traditional organization of the seven canonical books of the Sarvāstivāda abhidharmapiṭaka, the JÑĀNAPRASTHĀNA is treated as the "body" (ŚARĪRA), or central treatise of the canon, with its six "feet" (pāda), or ancillary treatises (pādaśāstra), listed in the following order: (1) Prakaraṇapāda, (2) Vijñānakāya, (3) Dharmaskandha, (4) Prajñaptibhāṣya, (5) Dhātukāya, and (6) Saṃgītiparyāya. Abhidharma exegetes later turned their attention to these canonical abhidharma materials and subjected them to the kind of rigorous scholarly analysis previously directed to the sūtras. These led to the writing of innovative syntheses and synopses of abhidharma doctrine, in such texts as BUDDHAGHOSA's VISUDDHIMAGGA and ANURUDDHA's ABHIDHAMMATTHASAṄGAHA, VASUBANDHU's ABHIDHARMAKOŚABHĀṢYA, and SAṂGHABHADRA's *NYĀYĀNUSĀRA. In East Asia, this third "basket" was eventually expanded to include the burgeoning scholastic literature of the MAHĀYĀNA, transforming it from a strictly abhidharmapiṭaka into a broader "treatise basket" or *ŚĀSTRAPIṬAKA (C. lunzang).

**Abhidharmaprakaraṇapāda**. (S). See PRAKARAṆA[PĀDAŚĀSTRA].

**Abhidharmasamuccaya**. (T. Chos mngon pa kun las btus pa; C. Dasheng Apidamo ji lun; J. Daijō Abidatsuma jūron; K. Taesŭng Abidalma chip non 大乘阿毘達磨集論). In Sanskrit, "Compendium of Abhidharma"; an influential scholastic treatise attributed to ASAṄGA. The *Abhidharmasamuccaya* provides a systematic and comprehensive explanation of various categories of DHARMAS in ABHIDHARMA fashion, in five major sections. Overall, the treatise continues the work of earlier abhidharma theorists, but it also seems to uphold a MAHĀYĀNA and, more specifically, YOGĀCĀRA viewpoint. For example, unlike SARVĀSTIVĀDA abhidharma materials, which provide detailed listings of dharmas in order to demonstrate the range of factors that perdure throughout all three time periods (TRIKĀLA) of past, present, and future, Asaṅga's exposition tends to reject any notion that dharmas are absolute realities, thus exposing their inherent emptiness (ŚŪNYATĀ). The first section of the treatise, Lakṣaṇasamuccaya ("Compendium of Characteristics"), first explains the five SKANDHA, twelve ĀYATANA, and eighteen DHĀTU in terms of their attributes (MĀTṚKĀ) and then their includedness (saṃgraha), association (saṃprayoga), and accompaniment (samanvāgama). The second section of the treatise, Satyaviniścaya ("Ascertainment of the Truths"), is generally concerned with and classified according to the FOUR NOBLE TRUTHS (catvāry āryasatyāni). The third section, Dharmaviniścaya ("Ascertainment of the Dharma"), outlines the teachings of Buddhism in terms of the twelve divisions (DVĀDAŚĀṄGA [PRAVACANA]) of texts in the TRIPIṬAKA. The fourth section, Prāptiviniścaya ("Ascertainment of Attainments"), outlines the various types of Buddhist practitioners and their specific realizations (ABHISAMAYA). The fifth and last section, Sāṃkathyaviniścaya ("Ascertainment of Argumentation"), outlines specific modes of debate that will enable one to defeat one's opponents. Fragments of the Sanskrit text of the *Abhidharmasamuccaya* (discovered in Tibet in 1934) are extant, along with a Tibetan translation and a Chinese translation made by XUANZANG in 652 CE. A commentary on the treatise by STHIRAMATI, known as the *Abhidharmasamuccayavyākhyā(na)*, was also translated into Chinese by Xuanzang.

**Abhidharmavijñānakāyapādaśāstra**. See VIJÑĀNAKĀYA [PĀDAŚĀSTRA].

**ābhidharmika**. (P. ABHIDHAMMIKA; T. chos mngon pa ba; C. apidamo dalunshi/duifa zhushi; J. abidatsuma daironshi/taihō shashi; K. abidalma taeronsa/taebŏp chesa 阿毘達磨大論師/對法諸師). In Sanskrit, "specialist in ABHIDHARMA"; refers to exegetes and commentators specializing in the texts and teachings of the ABHIDHARMAPIṬAKA. In MAHĀYĀNA sources, ābhidharmika may also refer more generically to "scholars," not necessarily only to specialists in abhidharma. In Chinese Buddhism, for example, the eminent Indian scholiasts AŚVAGHOṢA, NĀGĀRJUNA, ĀRYADEVA, and Kumāralāta are said to be the four great ābhidharmikas of the Mahāyāna tradition. See also ABHIDHAMMIKA.

**abhidhyā**. (P. abhijjhā; T. brnab sems; C. tan; J. ton; K. t'am 貪). In Sanskrit, "covetousness"; a synonym for greed (LOBHA) and craving (TṚṢṆĀ), abhidhyā is listed as the eighth of ten unwholesome courses of action (AKUŚALA-KARMAPATHA). Abhidhyā is a more intense form of lobha in which one's inherent greed or lust for objects has evolved into an active pursuit of them in order to make them one's own ("Ah, would that they were mine," the commentaries say). The ten courses of action are divided into three groups according to whether they are performed by the body, speech, or mind. Covetousness is classified as an unwholesome mental course of action and forms a triad along with malice (VYĀPĀDA) and wrong views (MITHYĀDṚṢṬI). Only extreme forms of defiled thinking are deemed an unwholesome course of mental action (akuśalakarmapatha), such as the covetous wish to misappropriate someone else's property, the hateful wish to hurt someone, or adherence to pernicious doctrines. Lesser forms of defiled thinking are still unwholesome (AKUŚALA), but do not constitute a course of action. The unwholesome course of bodily action is of three types: killing, stealing, and unlawful sexual intercourse. The unwholesome course of verbal action includes four: false speech, slander, abusive speech, and prattle. The list of ten wholesome and ten unwholesome courses of action occurs frequently in mainstream Buddhist scriptures.

**abhijñā**. (P. abhiññā; T. mngon shes; C. shentong; J. jinzū; K. sint'ong 神通). In Sanskrit, "superknowledges"; specifically referring to a set of supranormal powers that are by-products of meditation. These are usually enumerated as six: (1) various psychical and magical powers (ṚDDHIVIDHĀBHIJÑĀ [alt. ṛddhividhi], P. iddhividhā), such as the ability to pass through walls, sometimes also known as "unimpeded bodily action" (ṛddhisākṣātkriyā); (2) clairvoyance, lit. "divine eye" (DIVYACAKṢUS, P. dibbacakkhu), the ability to see from afar and to see how beings fare in accordance with their deeds; (3) clairaudience, lit. "divine ear" (DIVYAŚROTRA, P. dibbasota), the ability to hear from afar; (4) the ability to remember one's own former lives (PŪRVANIVĀSĀNUSMṚTI, P. pubbenivāsānussati); (5) "knowledge of others' states of mind" (CETOPARYĀYĀBHIJÑĀNA/PARACITTAJÑĀNA, P. cetopariyañāṇa), e.g., telepathy; and (6) the knowledge of the extinction of the contaminants (ĀSRAVAKṢAYA, P. āsavakkhāya). The first five of these superknowledges are considered to be mundane (LAUKIKA) achievements, which are gained through still more profound refinement of the fourth stage of meditative absorption (DHYĀNA). The sixth power is said to be supramundane

(LOKOTTARA) and is attainable through the cultivation of insight (VIPAŚYANĀ) into the nature of reality. The first, second, and sixth superknowledges are also called the three kinds of knowledge (TRIVIDYĀ; P. tevijjā).

**abhilāṣa**. (P. abhilāsa; T. 'dod pa/mngon par 'dod pa; C. leqiu; J. gyōgu; K. nakku 樂求). In Sanskrit, "desire" or "longing"; in MAHĀYĀNA referring especially to the "longing" to remain at the level of a ŚRĀVAKA.

**abhimāna**. (T. mngon pa'i nga rgyal; C. man; J. man; K. man 慢). In Sanskrit and Pāli, "conceit," "haughtiness," or "arrogance"; an intensification of mere "pride" (MĀNA). In the YOGĀCĀRABHŪMIŚĀSTRA and Tibetan sources, abhimāna is listed as one of seven types of conceit. This conceit can refer either to views that one holds arrogantly, haughtiness regarding the status into which one is born, or arrogance regarding the extent of one's wealth and/or knowledge.

**abhimukhī**. (T. mngon du 'gyur ba/mngon du phyogs pa; C. xianqian [di]; J. genzen[chi]; K. hyŏnjŏn [chi] 現前[地]). In Sanskrit, "manifest" or "evident"; used with reference to a twofold classification of phenomena as manifest (abhimukhī)—viz., those things that are evident to sense perception—and hidden (S. PAROKṢA, T. lkog gyur)—viz., those things whose existence must be inferred through reasoning. ¶ Abhimukhī, as "immediacy" or "face-to-face," is the sixth of the ten stages (BHŪMI) of the BODHISATTVA path described in the DAŚABHŪMIKASŪTRA. The MAHĀYĀNASŪTRĀLAṂKĀRA interprets this bhūmi as "directly facing," or "face-to-face," implying that the bodhisattva at this stage of the path stands at the intersection between SAṂSĀRA and NIRVĀṆA. The bodhisattva here realizes the equality of all phenomena (dharmasamatā), e.g., that all dharmas are signless and free of characteristics, unproduced and unoriginated, and free from the duality of existence and nonexistence. Turning away from the compounded dharmas of saṃsāra, the bodhisattva turns to face the profound wisdom of the buddhas and is thus "face-to-face" with both the compounded (SAṂSKṚTA) and uncompounded (ASAṂSKṚTA) realms. This bhūmi is typically correlated with mastery of the sixth perfection (PĀRAMITĀ), the perfection of wisdom (PRAJÑĀPĀRAMITĀ).

**abhinirūpaṇāvikalpa**. (T. mngon par rtog pa/rnam par rtog pa; C. jidu fenbie; J. ketaku funbetsu; K. kyet'ak punbyŏl 計度分別). In Sanskrit, "conceptualizing discrimination" or "discursive thought"; the second of the three types of conceptual discrimination (VIKALPA). See TRIVIKALPA.

**Abhiniṣkramaṇasūtra**. (T. Mngon par 'byung ba'i mdo; C. Fo benxing ji jing; J. Butsuhongyōjukkyō; K. Pul ponhaeng chip kyŏng 佛本行集經). In Sanskrit, "Sūtra of the Great Renunciation"; this scripture relates the story of Prince SIDDHĀRTHA's "going forth" (abhiniṣkramaṇa; P. abhinikkhamaṇa) from his father's palace to pursue the life of a mendicant wanderer (ŚRAMAṆA) in search of enlightenment. There are no extant Sanskrit versions of the SŪTRA, but the work survives in Tibetan and in several distinct recensions available in Chinese translation, one dating to as early as the first century CE. The best-known Chinese translation is the *Fo benxing ji jing*, made by JÑĀNAGUPTA around 587 CE, during the Sui dynasty. The text claims to be a DHARMAGUPTAKA recension of the JĀTAKA, or past lives of the Buddha. (Franklin Edgerton has suggested that this text may instead be a translation of the MAHĀVASTU, "The Great Account," of the LOKOTTARAVĀDA offshoot of the MAHĀSĀṂGHIKA school.) Jñānagupta's recension has sixty chapters, in five major parts. The first part is an introduction to the work as a whole, which relates how rare it is for a buddha to appear in the world and why people should take advantage of this opportunity. Reference is made to the various meritorious roots (KUŚALAMŪLA) that ŚĀKYAMUNI acquired throughout his many lifetimes of training, in order to prepare for this final life when he would finally attain enlightenment. The second part enumerates the entire lineage of the buddhas of antiquity, a lineage that Śākyamuni would soon join, and the third part follows with a genealogy of the ŚĀKYA clan. The fourth part describes the decisive stages in Śākyamuni's life, from birth, through his awakening, to the first "turning of the wheel of the DHARMA" (DHARMACAKRAPRAVARTANA). The last part gives extended biographies (going even into their past lives) of his prominent disciples, of which the stories involving his longtime attendant, ĀNANDA, are particularly extensive. In 1876, SAMUEL BEAL translated this Chinese recension of the sūtra into English as *The Romantic Legend of Śākya Buddha*.

**abhiprāya**. (T. dgongs pa; C. yiqu; J. ishu; K. ŭich'wi 意趣). In Sanskrit, "hidden intention" or "purpose"; a term used in hermeneutics to refer to the concealed intent the Buddha had in mind when he made a statement that was not literally true (see also ABHISAṂDHI). In the MAHĀYĀNASŪTRĀLAṂKĀRA, there are four abhiprāyas. (1) The Buddha may say that two things are the same when in fact they are similar in only one, albeit important, feature. Thus, ŚĀKYAMUNI Buddha says that he is the past buddha VIPAŚYIN, thinking of the fact that there is not the slightest difference in their DHARMAKĀYAs. This is called the intention of sameness (samatābhiprāya). (2) The Buddha may say one thing while intending something else (arthāntarābhiprāya). This category is often invoked in YOGĀCĀRA exegesis to explain why the Buddha proclaimed the nonexistence of all phenomena in the PRAJÑĀPĀRAMITĀ sūtras when he in fact did not intend this statement to be taken literally, thinking instead of the three natures (TRILAKṢAṆA) of all phenomena propounded by the Yogācāra. (3) The buddha may make a statement intending another time (kālāntarābhiprāya) than that suggested by his words. For example, he may assure lazy persons who are incapable of any virtuous practice whatsoever that they will be reborn in SUKHĀVATĪ, the paradise of AMITĀBHA, if they will simply call on that buddha. He does this in order to encourage them to accumulate a modest amount of merit, although he knows that they will not be reborn there immediately or even in their next lifetime, but at some other time in the future. (4) The Buddha adjusts his teaching to the capacities of his students based on their dispositions (pudgalāntarābhiprāya). For example, the Buddha will extol the benefits of the practice of charity (DĀNA) to a person who is disposed toward the accumulation of merit (PUṆYA) but will underplay the importance of charity to a person who becomes complacently attached to that practice. See ABHISAṂDHI; SANDHYĀBHĀṢĀ.

**abhirati**. (T. mngon dga'; C. miaoxi/abiluoti; J. myōki/abiradai; K. myohŭi/abiraje 妙喜/阿比羅提). In Sanskrit, "delight," "repose," or "wondrous joy"; the world system (LOKADHĀTU) and buddha-field (BUDDHAKṢETRA) of the buddha AKṢOBHYA, which is said to be located in the east. Abhirati is one of the earliest of the buddha-fields to appear in Buddhist literature and is depicted as an idealized form of our ordinary SAHĀ world. As its name implies, abhirati is a land of delight, the antithesis of the suffering that plagues our world, and its pleasures are the by-products of Akṣobhya's immense merit and compassion. In his land, Akṣobhya sits on a platform sheltered by a huge BODHI TREE, which is surrounded by row after row of palm trees and jasmine bushes. The soil is golden in color and as soft as cotton. Although abhirati, like our world, has a sun and moon, both pale next to the radiance of Akṣobhya himself. In abhirati, there are gender distinctions, as in our world, but no physical sexuality. A man who entertains sexual thoughts toward a woman would instantly see this desire transformed into a DHYĀNA that derives from the meditation on impurity (AŚUBHABHĀVANĀ), while a woman can become pregnant by a man's glance (even though women do not experience menstruation). Food and drink appear spontaneously whenever a person is hungry or thirsty. Abhirati is designed to provide the optimal environment for Buddhist practice, and rebirth there is a direct result of an adept having planted meritorious roots (KUŚALAMŪLA), engaging in salutary actions, and then dedicating any merit deriving from those actions to his future rebirth in that land. Akṣobhya will eventually attain PARINIRVĀṆA in abhirati through a final act of self-immolation (see SHESHEN). Abhirati is described in the AKṢOBHYATATHĀGATASYAVYŪHA, an important precursor to the more famous SUKHĀVATĪVYŪHA that describes SUKHĀVATĪ, the buddha-field of AMITĀBHA.

**Abhirūpā Nandā**. In Pāli, "Nandā the Lovely"; one of three prominent nuns named Nandā mentioned in the Pāli canon (the others being JANAPADAKALYAṆĪ NANDĀ and SUNDARĪ NANDĀ), all of whom share similar stories. According to Pāli sources, Abhirūpā Nandā was said to be the daughter of the Sākiyan (S. ŚĀKYA) chieftain Khemaka and lived in Kapilavatthu (S. KAPILAVASTU). She was renowned for her extraordinary beauty, for which she was given the epithet Abhirūpā (Lovely). So popular was she that her parents became vexed by the many suitors who sought her hand in marriage. As was the Sākiyan custom, Nandā was entitled to choose her future husband, but on the day she was to wed, her fiancé died and her parents forced her into the monastic order against her will. Exceedingly proud of her beauty and having no real religious vocation, she avoided visiting the Buddha lest he rebuke her for her vanity. Learning of her reluctance, the Buddha instructed Mahāpajāpatī (S. MAHĀPRAJĀPATĪ), his stepmother and head of the nuns' order, to arrange for every nun in her charge to come to him for instruction. Nandā, in fear, sent a substitute in her place but the ruse was uncovered. When Nandā was finally compelled to appear before the Buddha, he created an apparition of lovely women standing and fanning him. Nandā was enthralled by the beauty of the conjured maidens, whom the Buddha then caused to age, grow decrepit, die, and rot, right before her eyes. The Buddha then preached to her about the fragility of physical beauty. Having been given a suitable subject of meditation (KAMMAṬṬHĀNA), Nandā eventually gained insight into the impermanence (ANITYA), suffering (DUḤKHA), and lack of self (ANĀTMAN) of all conditioned things and attained arahatship. The source for the stories related to Abhirūpā Nandā is the commentarial note to verses nineteen and twenty of the Pāli THERĪGĀTHĀ, a text only known to the Pāli tradition.

**abhisamācārikāsīla**. (C. biqiu weiyi; J. biku igi; K. pigu wiŭi 比丘威儀). In Pāli, "virtuous (or proper) conduct"; often abbreviated simply as abhisamācārikā. The term may be used generically to refer to the basic moral codes (ŚĪLA) that are followed by all Buddhists, whether lay or monastic. More specifically, in the context of the Buddhist monastic codes (VINAYA), abhisamācārikā refers to the broad standards of behavior and norms that are expected of a monk (BHIKṢU) or nun (BHIKṢUṆĪ) living in a monastery. In the monastic tradition, we find a distinction between two kinds of moral discipline. The first is abhisamācārikāsīla, which indicates a set of more mundane, external prescriptions including how a monk should treat his superior and how a monastery should be maintained from day to day. For example, the abhisamācārikā section of the MAHĀSĀṂGHIKA VINAYA includes detailed instructions on how and when to hold the recitation of the monastic rules (UPOṢADHA). The text lists the spaces that are appropriate for this ritual and gives detailed instructions on how the space is to be cleaned and prepared for the recitation. As with other monastic instructions, these rules are accompanied by a story that serves as an impetus for the making of the rule. The second type of moral discipline is ĀDIBRAHMACARIYAKASĪLA, which are rules of conduct that will lead one further toward the complete eradication of suffering (DUḤKHA). Abhisamācārikāsīla is understood to be the lesser discipline with mundane ends, while ādibrahmacariyakasīla is understood to be the higher transcendent discipline.

**abhisamaya**. (T. mngon rtogs; C. xianguan; J. genkan; K. hyŏn'gwan 現觀). In Sanskrit and Pāli, "comprehension," "realization," or "penetration"; a foundational term in Buddhist soteriological theory, broadly referring to training that results in the realization of truth (satyābhisamaya; P. saccābhisamaya). This realization most typically involves the direct insight into the FOUR NOBLE TRUTHS (catvary āryasatyāni) but may also be used with reference to realization of the twelvefold chain of dependent origination (PRATĪTYASAMUTPĀDA), the noble eightfold path (ĀRYĀṢṬĀṄGAMĀRGA), the thirty-seven wings of enlightenment (BODHIPĀKṢIKADHARMA), etc., thus making all these doctrines specific objects of meditation. The Pāli PAṬISAMBHIDĀMAGGA discusses forty-four specific kinds of abhisamaya, all related to basic doctrinal lists. In the SARVĀSTIVĀDA abhidharma, abhisamaya occurs on the path of vision (DARŚANAMĀRGA), through a "sequential realization" (anupūrvābhisamaya) of sixteen moments of insight into the four noble truths. This gradual unfolding of realization was rejected by the THERAVĀDA school and was strongly criticized in HARIVARMAN's *TATTVASIDDHI, both of which advocated the theory of instantaneous realization (ekakṣaṇābhisamaya). In the YOGĀCĀRA school of MAHĀYĀNA, abhisamaya is not limited to the path of vision, as in the Sarvāstivāda school, but also occurs on the path of preparation (PRAYOGAMĀRGA) that precedes the path of vision through the abhisamayas of thought, faith, and discipline, as well as on the path of cultivation (BHĀVANĀMĀRGA) through two abhisamayas associated with wisdom and an abhisamaya associated with the ultimate path (NIṢṬHĀMĀRGA). The term comes to be associated particularly with the ABHISAMAYĀLAṂKĀRA, attributed to MAITREYANĀTHA, which sets forth the various realizations achieved on the "HĪNAYĀNA" and MAHĀYĀNA paths. In the eight chapters of this text are delineated eight types of abhisamaya, which subsume the course of training followed by both ŚRĀVAKAS and BODHISATTVAS: (1) the wisdom of knowing all modes (SARVĀKĀRAJÑATĀ), (2) the wisdom of knowing the paths (MĀRGAJÑATĀ), (3) the wisdom of knowing all phenomena (SARVAJÑATĀ), (4) manifestly perfect realization of all (the three previous) aspects (sarvākārābhisambodha), (5) the summit of realization (mūrdhābhisamaya; see MŪRDHAN), (6) gradual realization (anupūrvābhisamaya), (7) instantaneous realization (ekakṣaṇābhisamaya), and (8) realization of the dharma body, or DHARMAKĀYA (dharmakāyābhisambodha).

**Abhisamayālaṃkāra**. (T. Mngon par rtogs pa'i rgyan). In Sanskrit, "Ornament of Realization"; a major scholastic treatise of the MAHĀYĀNA, attributed to MAITREYANĀTHA (c. 350 CE). Its full title is *Abhisamayālaṃkāranāmaprajñāpāramitopadeśaśāstra* (T. Shes rab kyi pha rol tu phyin pa'i man ngag gi bstan bcos mngon par rtogs pa'i rgyan) or "Treatise Setting Forth the Perfection of Wisdom called 'Ornament for Realization.'" In the Tibetan tradition, the *Abhisamayālaṃkāra* is counted among the five treatises of Maitreya (BYAMS CHOS SDE LNGA). The 273 verses of the *Abhisamayālaṃkāra* provide a schematic outline of the perfection of wisdom, or PRAJÑĀPĀRAMITĀ, approach to enlightenment, specifically as delineated in the PAÑCAVIṂŚATISĀHASRIKĀPRAJÑĀPĀRAMITĀ ("Perfection of Wisdom in Twenty-Five Thousand Lines"). This detailed delineation of the path is regarded as the "hidden teaching" of the prajñāpāramitā sūtras. Although hardly known in East Asian Buddhism (until the modern Chinese translation by FAZUN), the work was widely studied in Tibet, where it continues to hold a central place in the monastic curricula of all the major sects. It is especially important for the DGE LUGS sect, which takes it as the definitive description of the stages of realization achieved through the Buddhist path. The *Abhisamayālaṃkāra* treats the principal topics of the prajñāpāramitā sūtras by presenting them in terms of the stages of realizations achieved via the five paths (PAÑCAMĀRGA). The eight chapters of the text divide these realizations into eight types. The first three are types of knowledge that are essential to any type of practice and are generic to both the mainstream and Mahāyāna schools. (1) The wisdom of knowing all modes (SARVĀKĀRAJÑATĀ), for the bodhisattva-adepts who are the putative target audience of the commentary, explains all the characteristics of the myriad dharmas, so that they will have comprehensive knowledge of what the attainment of enlightenment will bring. (2) The wisdom of knowing the paths (MĀRGAJÑATĀ), viz., the paths perfected by the ŚRĀVAKAS, is a prerequisite to achieving the wisdom of knowing all modes. (3) The wisdom of knowing all phenomena (SARVAJÑATĀ) is, in turn, a prerequisite to achieving the wisdom of knowing the paths. With (4) the topic of the manifestly perfect realization of all aspects (sarvākārābhisambodha) starts the text's coverage of the path itself, here focused on gaining insight into all aspects, viz., characteristics of dharmas, paths, and types of beings. By reaching (5) the summit of realization (mūrdhābhisamaya; see MŪRDHAN), one arrives at the entrance to ultimate realization. All the realizations achieved up to this point are secured and commingled through (6) gradual realization (anupūrvābhisamaya). The perfection of this gradual realization and the consolidation of all previous realizations catalyze the (7) instantaneous realization (ekakṣaṇābhisamaya). The fruition of this instantaneous realization brings (8) realization of the dharma body, or DHARMAKĀYA (dharmakāyābhisambodha). The first three chapters thus describe the three wisdoms incumbent on the buddhas; the middle four chapters cover the four paths that take these wisdoms as their object; and the last chapter describes the resultant dharma body of the buddhas and their special attainments. The *Abhisamayālaṃkāra* provides a synopsis of the massive prajñāpāramitā scriptures and a systematic outline of the comprehensive path of Mahāyāna. The *Abhisamayālaṃkāra* spurred a long tradition of Indian commentaries and other exegetical works, twenty-one of which are preserved in the Tibetan canon. Notable among this literature are Ārya VIMUKTISEṆA's *Vṛtti* and the ABHISAMAYĀLAṂKĀRĀLOKĀ and *Vivṛti* (called *Don gsal* in Tibetan) by HARIBHADRA. Later Tibetan commentaries include BU STON RIN CHEN GRUB's *Lung gi snye ma* and TSONG KHA PA's LEGS BSHAD GSER PHRENG.

**Abhisamayālaṃkārakārikāprajñāpāramitopadeśa-śāstraṭīkā-Prasphuṭapadā**. (S). See PRASPHUṬAPADĀ.

**Abhisamayālaṃkārālokā-vyākhyā**. (T. Mngon rtogs rgyan gyi snang ba rgya cher bshad pa). In Sanskrit, "Illuminating the 'Ornament of Realization,'" by the Indian scholiast HARIBHADRA (c. 750 CE). This long commentary, summarized in his ABHISAMAYĀLAṂKĀRAVIVṚTI, correlates the 273 verses of MAITREYANĀTHA's ABHISAMAYĀLAṂKĀRA with the specific corresponding sections in the AṢṬASĀHASRIKĀPRAJÑĀPĀRAMITĀ ("Perfection of Wisdom in Eight Thousand Lines"). It was translated into Tibetan by RIN CHEN BZANG PO in the eleventh century and by RNGOG BLO LDAN SHES RAB and subsequently became a central text in the curricula of many Tibetan monasteries. See AṢṬASĀHASRIKĀPRAJÑĀPĀRAMITĀVYĀKHYĀBHISAMAYĀLAṂKĀRĀLOKĀ.

**Abhisamayālaṃkāravivṛti**. (T. [Shes rab phar phyin man ngag gi bstan bcos] mngon rtogs rgyan gyi 'grel pa). In Sanskrit, "Commentary on the Ornament of Realization" by HARIBHADRA. The work in four bundles (T. bam po) is a digest (called *'grel chung*, "short commentary") of his long detailed explanation of the AṢṬASĀHASRIKĀPRAJÑĀPĀRAMITĀ ("Perfection of Wisdom in Eight Thousand Lines"), the AṢṬASĀHASRIKĀPRAJÑĀPĀRAMITĀVYĀKHYĀBHISAMAYĀLAṂKĀRĀLOKĀ (called *'grel chen*, "long commentary"). The *Abhisamayālaṃkāravivṛti* gained considerable importance in Tibet after RNGOG BLO LDAN SHES RAB supplemented his translation of it with a summary (*bsdus don*) of its contents, beginning a tradition of PRAJÑĀPĀRAMITĀ commentary that spread from GSANG PHU NE'U THOG monastery into all four Tibetan sects. This tradition, which continues down to the present, uses the ABHISAMAYĀLAṂKĀRA and ABHISAMAYĀLAṂKĀRAVIVṚTI as twin root texts to structure wide-ranging discussions of abhidharma, right philosophical view and proper praxis. There are two subcommentaries to the work, Dharmamitra's PRASPHUṬAPADĀ and DHARMAKĪRTIŚRĪ's *Durbodhāloka*. PRAJÑĀKARAMATI, RATNAKĪRTI, and Buddhajñāna wrote summaries of the work, all extant in Tibetan translation. See also SPHUṬĀRTHĀ.

**abhisaṃdhi**. (T. ldem por dgongs pa; C. miyi; J. mitchi/mitsui; K. mirŭi 密意). In Sanskrit, "implied intention," a term used in hermeneutics to classify the types of statements made by the Buddha. In the MAHĀYĀNASŪTRĀLAṂKĀRA, there are four such abhisaṃdhi listed. (1) The first is implied intention pertaining to entrance (avatāraṇābhisaṃdhi). The Buddha recognizes that if he were to teach HĪNAYĀNA disciples that, in addition to the nonexistence of the self (ANĀTMAN), DHARMAS also did not exist (DHARMANAIRĀTMYA), they would be so terrified that they would never enter the MAHĀYĀNA. Therefore, in order to coax them toward the Mahāyāna, he teaches them that a personal self does not exist while explaining that phenomena other than the person do exist. (2) The second is implied intention pertaining to the [three] natures (lakṣaṇābhisaṃdhi). When the Buddha said that all phenomena are without own-nature, he had in mind the imaginary nature (PARIKALPITA) of phenomena. When he said that they were neither produced nor destroyed, he had in mind their dependent nature (PARATANTRA). When he said that they were inherently free from suffering, he had in mind their consummate nature (PARINIṢPANNA). (3) The third is implied intention pertaining to antidotes (pratipakṣābhisaṃdhi). In the hīnayāna, the Buddha teaches specific antidotes (PRATIPAKṢA) to various defilements. Thus, as an antidote to hatred, he teaches the cultivation of love; as an antidote to sensuality, he teaches meditation on the foul, such as a decomposing corpse; as an antidote to pride, he teaches meditation on dependent origination; and as an antidote to a wandering mind, he teaches meditation on the breath. He indicates that these faults can be completely destroyed with these antidotes, calling them a supreme vehicle (agrayāna). In fact, these faults are only completely destroyed with full insight into non-self. Thus, the Buddha intentionally overstated their potency. (4) The final type is implied intention pertaining to translation (pariṇāmanābhisaṃdhi). This category encompasses those statements that might be termed antiphrastic, i.e., appearing to say something quite contrary to the tenor of the doctrine, which cannot be construed as even provisionally true. A commonly cited example of such a statement is the declaration in the DHAMMAPADA (XXI.5–6) that one becomes pure through killing one's parents; the commentators explain that parents are to be understood here to mean negative mental states such as sensual desire. See also ABHIPRĀYA; SANDHYĀBHĀṢĀ.

**abhiṣeka**. (P. abhiseka; T. dbang bskur; C. guanding; J. kanjō; K. kwanjŏng 灌頂). In Sanskrit, "anointment," "consecration," "empowerment," or "initiation"; a term originally used to refer to the anointment of an Indian king or the investiture of a crown prince, which by extension came to be applied to the anointment of a BODHISATTVA as a buddha. Just as a wheel-turning monarch (CAKRAVARTIN) invests the crown prince by sprinkling the crown of his head with fragrant water from all the four seas, so too do the buddhas anoint the crown of a bodhisattva when he makes his vow to achieve buddhahood. The Chinese translation, lit. "sprinkling the crown of the head," conveys this sense of anointment. In the MAHĀVASTU, an early text associated with the LOKOTTARAVĀDA branch of the MAHĀSĀṂGHIKA school, the tenth and last stage (BHŪMI) of the bodhisattva path is named abhiṣeka, rather than the more commonly known DHARMAMEGHĀBHŪMI, indicating that the bodhisattva has then been initiated into the lineage of the buddhas. Abhiṣeka is used especially in tantric literature, such as the MAHĀVAIROCANĀBHISAṂBODHISŪTRA, to refer to an initiation ceremony that empowers disciples to "enter the MAṆḌALA," where they are then allowed to learn the esoteric formulae (MANTRA) and gestures (MUDRĀ) and receive the instructions associated with a specific tantric deity. In ANUTTARAYOGATANTRA, a series of four initiations or empowerments are described, the vase empowerment (KALAŚĀBHIṢEKA), the secret empowerment (GUHYĀBHIṢEKA), the knowledge of the wisdom empowerment (PRAJÑĀJÑĀNĀBHIṢEKA), and the word empowerment (śabdābhiṣeka), also known as the "fourth empowerment" (caturthābhiṣeka). The vase empowerment is the only one of the four that is used in the three other tantras of KRIYĀTANTRA, CARYĀTANTRA, and YOGATANTRA. A special type of consecration ceremony, called a BUDDHĀBHIṢEKA, is conducted at the time of the installation of a new buddha image, which vivifies the inert clay, metal, or wood of the image, invests the image with insight into the dharma (e.g., through reciting some version of the formula concerning causality, or PRATĪTYASAMUTPĀDA), and transforms the image into a living buddha.

**abhiṣekamudrā**. (T. dbang bskur phyag rgya; C. guanding yin; J. kanjōin; K. kwanjŏng in 灌頂印). In Sanskrit, "gesture of anointment." In this particular mudrā, the palms are held together with the forefingers extended against each other. See also MUDRĀ.

**abhūtaparikalpa**. (T. yang dag pa ma yin pa'i kun tu rtog pa/kun rtog; C. xuwang fenbie; J. komō funbetsu; K. hŏmang punbyŏl 虛妄分別). In Sanskrit, "false imagining" or "construction of what is unreal"; a pivotal Yogācāra term describing the tendency of the dependent (PARATANTRA) nature (SVABHĀVA) to project false constructions of a reality that is bifurcated between self and others. Sentient beings mistakenly assume that what has been constructed through consciousness has a static, unchanging reality. This process inserts into the perceptual process an imaginary bifurcation (VIKALPA) between perceiving subject (grāhaka) and perceived object (grāhya) (see GRĀHYAGRĀHAKAVIKALPA), which is the basis for a continued proliferation of such mental constructions. This subject–object dichotomy is then projected onto all sensory experience, resulting in the imagined (PARIKALPITA) nature (svabhāva). By relying on these false imaginings to construct our sense of what is real, we inevitably subject ourselves to continued suffering (DUḤKHA) within the cycle of birth-and-death (SAṂSĀRA). The term figures prominently in MAITREYNĀTHA's MADHYĀNTAVIBHĀGA ("Separating the Middle from the Extremes") and VASUBANDHU's commentary on the treatise, the *Madhyāntavibhāgabhāṣya*.

**abhyāyana**. (P. abbhāna; T. mngon par 'ongs; C. chuzui; J. shutsuzai; K. ch'ulchoe 出罪). In Sanskrit, the formal ecclesiastical act of "calling back" a monk into communion. In the Pāli VINAYA, for example, a monk who has committed a suspension (P. saṅghādisesa; S. SAṂGHĀVAŚEṢA) offense is required to undergo rehabilitation through either penance (P. manatta; S. MĀNATVA) or probation (PARIVĀSA) until his offense has been expiated. If he does not properly carry out his penalty, it will be reimposed until the community is satisfied with his performance. At that point, the community performs the abbhāna-kamma, the ecclesiastical act of "calling back," which restores the monk to functional membership in the SAṂGHA. A minimum of twenty monks must be present during the abhyāyana ritual for it to be valid. No member of the twenty may himself be observing either mānapya or parivāsa at the time, although such a monk may be present as long as the minimum number of blameless monks is participating.

**abhyudaya**. (T. mngon par mtho ba; C. shengsheng; J. shōsho; K. sŭngsaeng 勝生). In Sanskrit, lit. "rising"; viz., a "superior rebirth." In MAHĀYĀNA texts like NĀGĀRJUNA's RATNĀVALĪ, the term is typically used to refer to "rising" to a higher rebirth in the realms of the divinities (DEVA) or human beings (MANUṢYA); often paired with NIḤŚREYASA, a term for NIRVĀṆA that literally means "of which there is nothing finer."

**absorption**. See DHYĀNA; JHĀNA.

**acalā**. (T. mi g.yo ba; C. budong di; J. fudōji; K. pudong chi 不動地). In Sanskrit, "immovable" or "steadfast"; the name for the eighth of the ten BODHISATTVA grounds or stages (BHŪMI) according to the DAŚABHŪMIKASŪTRA. At this level of the path (MĀRGA), the bodhisattva realizes the acquiescence or receptivity to the nonproduction of dharmas (ANUTPATTIKADHARMAKṢĀNTI) and is no longer perturbed by either cause or absence of cause. The eighth-stage bodhisattva is able to project different transformation bodies (NIRMĀṆAKĀYA) anywhere in the universe. This bhūmi is sometimes correlated with mastery of the eighth perfection of resolve or aspiration (PRAṆIDHĀNAPĀRAMITĀ). According to some commentators, upon reaching this bhūmi, the bodhisattva has abandoned all of the afflictive obstructions (KLEŚĀVARAṆA) and is thus liberated from any further rebirth in a realm where he would be subject to defilement; for this reason, the eighth, ninth, and tenth bhūmis are sometimes called "pure bhūmis."

**Acalanātha-Vidyārāja**. (T. Mi g.yo mgon po rig pa'i rgyal po; C. Budong mingwang; J. Fudō myōō; K. Pudong myŏngwang 不動明王). In Sanskrit, a wrathful DHARMAPĀLA of the VAJRAYĀNA pantheon and the chief of the eight VIDYĀRĀJA. As described in the MAHĀVAIROCANĀBHISAṂBODHISŪTRA, he is the NIRMĀṆAKĀYA of VAIROCANA, a protector of boundaries and vanquisher of obstacles. A late Indian deity, Acalanātha-Vidyārāja possibly originated from the YAKṢA form of VAJRAPĀṆI, with whom he is associated in his form of Acalavajrapāṇi. Indian forms of the god from the eleventh century show him kneeling on his left leg, holding a sword (khaḍga). Vajrayāna images show him standing with one or three faces and varied numbers of pairs of hands, identified by his raised sword, snare, and ACALĀSANA. The cult of Acalanātha-Vidyārāja entered China during the first millennium CE, and was brought to Japan by KŪKAI in the ninth century, where the wrathful deity (known in Japanese as Fudō myōō) became important for the Shingon school (SHINGONSHŪ), even being listed by it as one of the thirteen buddhas. In East Asian iconography, Acalanātha-Vidyārāja holds the sword and a snare or lasso (pāśa), with which he binds evil spirits.

**acalāsana**. (T. mi g.yo ba'i 'dug stangs; C. budongzuo; J. fudōza; K. pudongjwa 不動坐). In Sanskrit, the "immovable posture"; a semi-kneeling position, where the left knee touches the ground, but the right knee is raised off the ground. This posture is commonly seen in figures bearing gifts, where the hands are clasped in front of the donor's chest in AÑJALI. This pose is also characteristic of the wrathful deity ACALANĀTHA-VIDYĀRĀJA, whose hands instead hold a snare (pāśa) in the left and a raised sword in the right. Bodhisattvas are also sometimes depicted in this posture.

**Acalavajrapāṇi**. See ACALANĀTHA-VIDYĀRĀJA.

**ācariya**. (S. ācārya, Thai, ăčhān; T. slob dpon; C. asheli; J. ajari; K. asari 阿闍梨). In Pāli, "teacher." A monk takes an ācariya if he has lost his preceptor (P. upajjhāya; S. UPĀDHYĀYA) and is still in need of guidance (nissaya, S. NIŚRAYA). A preceptor is said to be lost when he goes away, disrobes, dies, joins another religion, or has expelled the monk under his guidance for wrongdoing. To act as an ācariya, a monk must possess the same qualifications as required of an upajjhāya; namely, he must be competent in DHARMA and VINAYA and be of at least ten years standing in the order since his own ordination. The monk taken under the guidance of the ācariya is called his ANTEVĀSIKA, or pupil. The relationship between teacher and pupil is compared to that of father and son. The teacher is enjoined to teach dhamma and vinaya to his pupil and to supply him with all necessary requisites, such as robes (see TRICĪVARA) and alms bowl (PĀTRA). He should tend to him if he is ill and discipline him if he commits wrongdoing. If the pupil should begin to entertain doubts about the dispensation or his abilities to practice, the teacher must try to dispel them. If the pupil should commit a grave offense against the rules of the SAṂGHA, the teacher is to prevail upon him to go before the saṃgha to seek expiation. If the pupil misbehaves or is disobedient, the teacher is enjoined to expel him. But if the pupil shows remorse and asks forgiveness, the teacher is to take him again under guidance. A monk ceases to be an ācariya when he goes away, dies, disrobes, changes religion, or expels his pupil. See also ĀCĀRYA.

**ācārya**. (P. ācariya; Thai ăčhān; T. slob dpon; C. asheli; J. ajari; K. asari 阿闍梨). In Sanskrit, "teacher" or "master"; the term literally means "one who teaches the ācāra (proper conduct)," but it has come into general use as a title for religious teachers. In early Buddhism, it refers specifically to someone who teaches the supra dharma and is used in contrast to the UPĀDHYĀYA (P. upajjhāya) or "preceptor." (See ĀCARIYA entry supra.) The title ācārya becomes particularly important in VAJRAYĀNA Buddhism, where the officiant of a tantric ritual is often viewed as the vajra master (VAJRĀCĀRYA). The term has recently been adopted by Tibetan monastic universities in India as a degree (similar to a Master of Arts) conferred upon graduation. In Japan, the term refers to a wise teacher, saint, holy person, or a wonder-worker who is most often a Buddhist monk. The term is used by many Japanese Buddhist traditions, including ZEN, TENDAI, and SHINGON. Within the Japanese Zen context, an ajari is a formal title given to those who have been training for five years or more.

**ăčhān**. Thai pronunciation of the Sanskrit term ĀCĀRYA ("teacher"); also seen transcribed as AJAHN or acchan. See AJAHN.

**acintya**. (P. acinteyya; T. bsam gyis mi khyab pa; C. bukesiyi; J. fukashigi; K. pulgasaŭi 不可思議). In Sanskrit, "inconceivable"; a term used to describe the ultimate reality that is beyond all conceptualization. Pāli and mainstream Buddhist materials refer to four specific types of "inconceivables" or "unfathomables" (P. acinteyya): the range or sphere of a buddha, e.g., the extent of his knowledge and power; the range of meditative absorption (DHYĀNA); the potential range of moral cause and effect (KARMAN and VIPĀKA); and the range of the universe or world system (LOKA), i.e., issues of cosmogony, whether the universe is finite or infinite, eternal or transitory, etc. Such thoughts are not to be pursued, because they are not conducive to authentic religious progress or ultimately to NIRVĀṆA. See also AVYĀKṚTA.

**Acintyastava**. (T. Bsam gyis mi khyab par bstod pa). In Sanskrit, "In Praise of the Inconceivable One"; an Indian philosophical work by the MADHYAMAKA master NĀGĀRJUNA written in the form of a praise for the Buddha. In the Tibetan tradition, there are a large number of such praises (called STAVAKĀYA) in contrast to the set of philosophical texts (called YUKTIKĀYA) attributed to Nāgārjuna. Among these praise works, the *Acintyastava*, LOKĀTĪTASTAVA, NIRAUPAMYASTAVA, and PARAMĀRTHASTAVA are extant in Sanskrit and are generally accepted to be his work; these four works together are known as the CATUḤSTAVA. It is less certain that he is the author of the DHARMADHĀTUSTAVA or DHARMADHĀTUSTOTRA ("Hymn to the Dharma Realm") of which only fragments are extant in the original Sanskrit. The *Acintyastava* contains fifty-nine stanzas, many of which are addressed to the Buddha. The first section provides a detailed discussion of why dependently originated phenomena are empty of intrinsic nature (NIḤSVABHĀVA); this section has clear parallels to the MŪLAMADHYAMAKAKĀRIKĀ. The forty-fifth verse makes reference to the term PARATANTRA, leading some scholars to believe that Nāgārjuna was familiar with the LAṄKĀVATĀRASŪTRA. The second section describes wisdom (JÑĀNA); the third section sets forth the qualities of the true dharma (SADDHARMA); the fourth and final section extols the Buddha as the best of teachers (ŚĀSTṚ).

**ādānavijñāna**. (T. len pa'i rnam par shes pa; C. atuona shi/xiangxu shi; J. adanashiki/sōzokushiki; K. at'ana sik/sangsok sik 阿陀那識/相續識). In Sanskrit, "appropriating consciousness" or "retributory consciousness"; an alternate name for the ĀLAYAVIJÑĀNA, the eighth consciousness in the YOGĀCĀRA analysis of consciousness, which serves as a repository (ālaya) of the seeds (BĪJA) of past action (KARMAN) until they can come to fruition (VIPĀKA) in the future. Because that consciousness thus links the present with the future life, the ālayavijñāna also serves as the consciousness that "appropriates" a physical body at the moment of rebirth, hence, its name ādānavijñāna.

**ādarśajñāna**. [alt. mahādarśajñāna] (T. me long lta bu'i ye shes; C. dayuanjing zhi; J. daienkyōchi; K. taewŏn'gyŏng chi 大圓鏡智). In Sanskrit, "mirrorlike wisdom" or "great perfect mirror wisdom"; one of the five types of wisdom (PAÑCÁJÑĀNA) exclusive to a buddha according to the YOGĀCĀRA and tantric schools, along with the wisdom of equality (SAMATĀJÑĀNA), the wisdom of discriminating awareness (PRATYAVEKṢAṆAJÑĀNA), the wisdom that one has accomplished what was to be done (KṚTYĀNUṢṬHĀNAJÑĀNA), and the wisdom of the nature of the DHARMADHĀTU (DHARMADHĀTUSVABHĀVAJÑĀNA). This specific type of wisdom is a transformation of the eighth consciousness, the ĀLAYAVIJÑĀNA, in which the perfect interfusion between all things is seen as if reflected in a great mirror.

**adbhutadharma**. (P. abbhutadhamma; T. rmad du byung ba'i chos; C. xifa; J. kehō; K. hŭibŏp 希法). In Sanskrit, "marvelous events"; one of the nine (NAVAṄGA[PĀVACANA]) or twelve (DVĀDAŚĀṄGA[PRAVACANA]) categories (AṄGA) of scripture recognized in Pāli and Sanskrit sources, respectively, as classified according to their structure or literary style. This particular genre of SŪTRA is characterized by the presence of various miraculous or supernatural events that occur during the course of the narrative.

**Adbhutadharmaparyāyasūtra**. (T. Rmad du byung ba'i chos kyi rnam grangs; C. Shen xiyou jing/Weicengyou jing; J. Jinkeukyō/Mizōukyō; K. Sim hŭiyu kyŏng/Mijŭngyu kyŏng 甚希有經/未曾有經). In Sanskrit, "Discourse on the Wondrous Teachings"; a MAHĀYĀNA SŪTRA best known for advocating that the merit deriving from worshipping the Buddha, such as sponsoring the production of a buddha image or a STŪPA, surpasses that of all other activities. The sūtra states, for example, that erecting even a tiny stūpa containing the relics of a TATHĀGATA is more meritorious than building a large monastery. This text is extant only in three Chinese translations: the "Scripture on the Miraculous" (*Weicengyou jing*); "Scripture on the Rarest of Things" (*Shen xiyou jing*), translated by XUANZANG (600/602–664); and the "Chapter on Relative Merits" (*Xiaoliang gongde pin*), the first chapter of the "Scripture on the Unexcelled Basis" (*Fo shuo wushangyi jing*, S. *Anuttarāśrayasūtra), translated by PARAMĀRTHA (499–569).

**adhamapuruṣa**. (T. skyes bu chung ngu; C. xiashi; J. geshi; K. hasa 下士). In Sanskrit, "person of lesser capacity"; the lowest in a threefold classification of religious practitioners, together with madhyapuruṣa ("person of average capacity") and MAHĀPURUṢA ("person of great capacity"). The person of lesser capacity seeks only happiness in SAṂSĀRA, wishing to be reborn as a human (MANUṢYA) or a divinity (DEVA) in the next life. The three categories of persons are most famously set forth in ATIŚA's BODHIPATHAPRADĪPA and, deriving from that text, in the LAM RIM literature in Tibet. See also TRĪNDRIYA; MṚDVINDRIYA; TĪKṢṆENDRIYA.

**adhigama**. (T. rtogs pa; C. zheng; J. shō; K. chŭng 證). In Sanskrit, "realization," especially in the realization of truth, either conceptually or directly. In this context, adhigama is contrasted with ĀGAMA, the received scriptural tradition, as one of the two methods of realizing truth. See also ADHIGAMADHARMA.

**adhigamadharma**. (T. rtogs pa'i chos; C. zhengfa; J. shōhō; K. chŭngbŏp 證法). In Sanskrit, "realized dharma"; one of the two divisions of the dharma or teaching of the Buddha, together with the "scriptural dharma" (ĀGAMADHARMA). The adhigamadharma is the practice of the dharma, often identified in this context as the training in higher morality (ADHIŚĪLAŚIKṢĀ), the training in higher meditation (ADHISAMĀDHIŚIKṢĀ), and the training in higher wisdom (ADHIPRAJÑĀŚIKṢĀ), which leads to direct realization (ADHIGAMA), rather than mere conceptual understanding. It is also identified with the truths of cessation and path within the FOUR NOBLE TRUTHS. See also ĀGAMA; ĀGAMADHARMA.

**adhikaraṇa**. (T. rtsod pa; C. zhengshi/zhengsong; J. jōji/jōshō; K. chaengsa/chaengsong 諍事/諍訟). In Pāli and Sanskrit, "legal question" or "case," an important term in the VINAYA. Legal questions or cases are of four kinds: (1) those arising out of a dispute, (2) those arising out of censure, (3) those arising out of an offense, and (4) those arising out of an obligation. (1) Legal questions or cases arising out of a dispute are of eighteen kinds and deal primarily with what does and does not pertain to the monastic code, what is and is not sanctioned by the rules of vinaya, and what is an especially grievous offense, such as "defeat" (PĀRĀJIKA), vs. what is nongrievous. (2) Legal questions or cases arising out of censure are involved with whether or not a monk has fallen away from morality or good habits, fallen away from right view, or fallen away from right livelihood. (3) Legal questions or cases arising out of offenses deal with misdeeds classified under five headings: viz., pārājika, SAṂGHĀDIŚEṢA, PĀYATTIKA, PRATIDEŚANĪYA, or DUṢKṚTA, or under seven headings: viz., the above five plus miscellaneous grave, but unconsummated offenses (STHŪLĀTYAYA, P. thullaccaya), and mischievous talk (DURBHĀṢITA, P. dubbhāsita). (5) Legal questions or cases arising out of obligation concern the jurisdiction of resolutions and formal acts passed by the SAṂGHA. In the final section of the monastic codes of conduct (PRĀTIMOKṢA), seven specific methods of resolving disputes (ADHIKARAṆAŚAMATHA) are offered.

**adhikaraṇaśamatha**. (P. adhikaraṇasamatha; T. rtsod pa nye bar zhi ba; C. miezhengfa; J. metsujōhō; K. myŏlchaengpŏp

滅諍法). In Sanskrit, "settlement of a legal case," viz., rules for settling disputes, involving either confronting ordained monks and nuns who have transgressed the rules of the order (see PRĀTIMOKṢA) or dealing with differences that have arisen within the order. The settlement of a legal question or case (ADHIKARAṆA) within the SAṂGHA may be accomplished in seven ways (SAPTĀDHIKARAṆAŚAMATHA): (1) a verdict "in the presence of," viz., bringing disputants before a panel of competent monks or the saṃgha as a whole and rendering a verdict according to the appropriate legal procedure; (2) a verdict "of mindfulness": declaring the accused innocent by virtue of being pure and without offense—e.g., being an ARHAT—and thus incapable of wrongdoing; (3) declaring the accused not guilty by reason of insanity; (4) adding an additional punishment to a monk who confesses to a specific type of wrongdoing only after being interrogated; (5) rendering a verdict by majority vote of the whole saṃgha when a competent monk or a panel of competent monks is unable to reach a decision; (6) resolution through an admission of guilt; and (7) a verdict of "covering over as with grass": viz., settling a case between disputants through arbitration and compromise before bringing it before the saṃgha for a verdict. These seven methods of resolving disputes are typically placed at the end of the list of rules in the PRĀTIMOKṢA code and appear in the Pāli *Pāṭimokkha* in its CŪḶAVAGGA section. These seven types of verdicts are sometimes listed in different orders.

**adhimāna**. (T. lhag pa'i nga rgyal; C. zengshangman; J. zōjōman; K. chŭngsangman 增上慢). In Sanskrit and Pāli, "arrogance" or "haughtiness"; this term refers specifically to overestimation of oneself or boasting about one's spiritual accomplishments. When one is mistakenly convinced that one has attained one of the superknowledges (ABHIJÑĀ), meditative absorptions (DHYĀNA), or spiritual fruitions (PHALA), when in actuality one has not, one is said to possess adhimāna. When adhimāna is expressed verbally—that is, by bragging to others that one has mastered one of the aforementioned exceptional achievements for the purpose of winning reputation and material support—this braggadocio constitutes a grave offense, especially for ordained monks and nuns. According to the VINAYA, such overestimation of one's extraordinary spiritual achievements could constitute grounds for "defeat" (PĀRĀJIKA), the most serious transgression that can be committed by monks and nuns. In its more generic usage, adhimāna may also refer simply to particularly intense forms of "conceit" and "pride" (MĀNA).

**adhimokṣa**. (P. adhimokkha; T. mos pa; C. shengjie; J. shōge; K. sŭnghae 勝解). In Sanskrit, "determination," "resolution," or "zeal"; a general term denoting an inclination toward a virtuous object, sometimes used to indicate a preliminary stage prior to the conviction that results from direct experience; also seen written as adhimukti. The adhimukticaryābhūmi incorporates the stages of the path of accumulation (SAṂBHĀRAMĀRGA) and the path of preparation (PRAYOGAMĀRGA) prior to the path of vision (DARŚANAMĀRGA). In a more technical sense, adhimokṣa is a mental factor (CAITTA) that keeps consciousness intent on its object without straying to another object. It is listed among the ten major omnipresent mental concomitants (S. MAHĀBHŪMIKA) that are present in all in the dharma taxonomy of the SARVĀSTIVĀDA school, among the five determinative mental concomitants (S. VINIYATA) in the YOGĀCĀRA dharma system, and one of the six secondary (P. pakiṇṇaka) factors in the Pāli ABHIDHAMMA. Adhimokṣa is also used to describe the interests or dispositions of sentient beings, the knowledge of which contributes to a buddha's pedagogical skills.

**adhimukti**. In Sanskrit, "resolution" or "resolute faith." See ADHIMOKṢA.

**adhipatiphala**. (T. bdag po'i 'bras bu; C. zengshang guo; J. zōjōka; K. chŭngsang kwa 增上果). In Sanskrit, "predominant effects" or "sovereign effects"; this is one of the five effects (PHALA) enumerated in the SARVĀSTIVĀDA ABHIDHARMA and in YOGĀCĀRA. In the Sarvāstivāda–VAIBHĀṢIKA abhidharma system of six causes (HETU) and five effects (PHALA), the "predominant effect" is the result of the "efficient cause" (KĀRAṆAHETU), referring to causation in its broadest possible sense, in which every conditioned dharma serves as the generic, indirect cause for the creation of all things except itself. The kāraṇahetu provides the general background necessary for the operation of causality, and the results of the causal process it supports are the adhipatiphala.

**adhipatipratyaya**. (P. adhipatipaccaya; T. bdag po'i rkyen; C. zengshang yuan; J. zōjōen; K. chŭngsang yŏn 增上緣). In Sanskrit, "predominant" or "sovereign condition"; the fourth of the four types of conditions (PRATYAYA) recognized in the SARVĀSTIVĀDA–VAIBHĀṢIKA system of ABHIDHARMA and in YOGĀCĀRA; the term also appears as the ninth of the twenty-four conditions (P. paccaya) in the massive Pāli abhidhamma text, the PAṬṬHĀNA. In epistemology, the predominant condition is one of the three causal conditions necessary for perception to occur. It is the specific condition that provides the operative capability (kāraṇa) for the production of something else. In the case of sensory perception, the predominant condition for the arising of sensory consciousness (VIJÑĀNA) is the physical sense organ and the sensory object; but more generically even the seed could serve as the adhipatipratyaya for the generation of a sprout. The four primary physical elements (MAHĀBHŪTA) themselves serve as the predominant condition for the five physical sensory organs, in that they are the condition for the sensory organs' production and development.

**adhiprajñāśikṣā**. (T. lhag pa'i shes rab kyi bslab pa; C. zengshanghui xue; J. zōjōegaku; K. chŭngsanghye hak 增上慧學). In Sanskrit, "training in higher wisdom"; the third of the three trainings (TRIŚIKṢĀ) required to achieve enlightenment, said to be set forth primarily in the ABHIDHARMA basket of the TRIPIṬAKA. Adhiprajñāśikṣā is primarily associated with the first two constituents of the eightfold path (ĀRYĀṢṬĀṄGAMĀRGA), viz., right views (SAMYAGDṚṢṬI) and right intention (SAMYAKSAṂKALPA).

**adhisamādhiśikṣā**. (T. lhag pa'i ting nge 'dzin gyi bslab pa; C. zengshangding xue; J. zōjōjōgaku; K. chŭngsangjŏng hak 增上定學). In Sanskrit, "training in higher meditation"; the second of the three trainings (TRIŚIKṢĀ) required to achieve enlightenment, said to be set forth primarily in the SŪTRA basket of the TRIPIṬAKA. Adhisamādhiśikṣā is primarily associated with the last three constituents of the eightfold path (ĀRYĀṢṬĀṄGAMĀRGA), viz., right effort (SAMYAGVYĀYĀMA), right mindfulness (SAMYAKSMṚTI), and right concentration (SAMYAKSAMĀDHI).

**adhiśīlaśikṣā**. (T. lhag pa'i tshul khrims kyi bslab pa; C. zengshangjie xue; J. zōjōkaigaku; K. chŭngsanggye hak 增上戒學). In Sanskrit, "training in higher morality"; the first of the three trainings (TRIŚIKṢĀ) required to achieve enlightenment, said to be set forth primarily in the VINAYA basket of the TRIPIṬAKA. Adhiśīlaśikṣā is primarily associated with the middle three constituents of the eightfold path (ĀRYĀṢṬĀṄGAMĀRGA), viz., right speech (SAMYAGVĀC), right action (SAMYAKKARMĀNTA), and right livelihood (SAMYAGĀJĪVA).

**adhiṣṭhāna**. (P. adhiṭṭhāna; T. byin gyis brlabs pa; C. jiachi; J. kaji; K. kaji 加持). In Sanskrit, lit. "determination" or "decisive resolution" and commonly translated as "empowerment." Literally, the term has the connotation of "taking a stand," viz., the means by which the buddhas reveal enlightenment to the world, as well as the adept's reliance on the buddhas' empowerment through specific ritual practices. In the former sense, adhiṣṭhāna can refer to the magical power of the buddhas and bodhisattvas, in which contexts it is often translated as "blessing" or "empowerment." As the LAṄKĀVATĀRASŪTRA notes, it is thanks to the buddhas' empowerment issuing from their own original vows (PRAṆIDHĀNA) that BODHISATTVAS are able to undertake assiduous cultivation over three infinite eons (ASAṂKHYEYAKALPA) so that they may in turn become buddhas. The buddhas' empowerment sustains the bodhisattvas in their unremitting practice by both helping them to maintain tranquillity of mind throughout the infinity of time they are in training and, ultimately, once the bodhisattvas achieve the tenth and final stage (BHŪMI) of their training, the cloud of dharma (DHARMAMEGHĀ), the buddhas appear from all the ten directions to anoint the bodhisattvas as buddhas in their own right (see ABHIṢEKA). ¶ In mainstream Buddhist materials, adhiṣṭhāna refers to the first of a buddha's six or ten psychic powers (ṚDDHI), the ability to project mind-made bodies (MANOMAYAKĀYA) of himself, viz., to replicate himself ad infinitum. In Pāli materials, adhiṭṭhāna is also used to refer to the "determination" to extend the duration of meditative absorption (P. JHĀNA; S. DHYĀNA) and the derivative psychic powers (P. iddhi; S. ṚDDHI).

**Adhyardhaśatikāprajñāpāramitāsūtra/Prajñāpāramitānayaśatapañcaśatikā**. (T. Shes rab kyi pha rol tu phyin pa'i tshul brgya lnga bcu pa; C. Shixiang bore boluomi jing/Bore liqu fen; J. Jissō hannya haramitsukyō/Hannya rishubun; K. Silsang panya paramil kyŏng/Panya ich'wi pun 實相般若波羅蜜經/般若理趣分). In Sanskrit, "Perfection of Wisdom in One Hundred and Fifty Lines." The basic verses (in Sanskrit) and a commentary describing the ritual accompanying its recitation (originally in Khotanese), are found together as two YOGA class tantras, the *Śrīparmādhya* (T. Dpal mchog dang po) and *Śrīvajramaṇḍalālaṃkāra* (T. Dpal rdo rje snying po rgyan). In Japan, AMOGHAVAJRA's version of the text (called the *Rishukyō*) came to form an integral part of the philosophy and practice of the Japanese Shingon sect (SHINGONSHŪ).

**adhyāśaya**. (T. lhag bsam; C. zhengzhi xin; J. shōjiki no shin, K. chŏngjik sim 正直心). In Sanskrit, "determination" or "resolution"; a term used especially to describe the commitment of the BODHISATTVA to liberate all beings from suffering. In the Tibetan mind-training (BLO SBYONG) tradition, the bodhisattva's resolute commitment is the last in a series of six causes (preceded by recollecting that all beings have been one's mother, recollecting their kindness, wishing to repay them, love, and compassion), which culminate in BODHICITTA or BODHICITTOTPĀDA. See also XINXIN.

**adhyātmavidyā**. (T. nang rig pa; C. neiming; J. naimyō; K. naemyŏng 內明). In Sanskrit, "inner knowledge," viz. knowledge of the three trainings (TRIŚIKṢĀ) and the two stages (UTPATTIKRAMA and NIṢPANNAKRAMA) of TANTRA; the term is sometimes used to refer to knowledge of Buddhist (as opposed to non-Buddhist) subjects.

**ādibrahmacariyakasīla**. In Pāli, "higher rules of purity"; the more advanced of two types of moral discipline (P. sīla, S. ŚĪLA), referring to rules of conduct that will lead the practitioner further along toward the complete eradication of suffering. This type of discipline is contrasted with ABHISAMĀCĀRIKĀSĪLA, or lesser discipline, which indicates more mundane, external prescriptions, including how a monk should treat his superior and how a monastery should be maintained from day to day. While abhisamācārikāsīla is concerned with mundane ends, ādibrahmacariyakasīla is understood to be the higher, transcendent discipline.

**ādibuddha**. (T. dang po'i sangs rgyas/ye nas sangs rgyas; C. benchu fo; J. honshobutsu; K. ponch'o pul 本初佛). In Sanskrit, "original buddha" or "primordial buddha"; the personification of innate enlightenment. The term seems to appear for the first time in the MAHĀYĀNASŪTRĀLAṂKĀRA, where the existence of such a primordial buddha is refuted on the grounds that the achievement of buddhahood is impossible without the accumulation of merit (PUṆYA) and wisdom (JÑĀNA). However, the term reemerges in tantric literature, most prominently in the KĀLACAKRATANTRA. There, the term has two meanings, based on the reading of the term ādi. According to the first interpretation, ādi means "first" such that the ādibuddha was the first to attain buddhahood. According to the second interpretation, ādi means "primordial," which suggests an eternal and atemporal state of innate buddhahood. However, when the commentators on this tantra use the term in this second sense, they appear to be referring not to a person but to an innate wisdom that is present in the minds of all sentient beings and which is the fundamental basis of SAṂSĀRA and NIRVĀṆA. In Tibetan Buddhism, the term ādibuddha is often used to describe the buddha SAMANTABHADRA (according to the RNYING MA sect) or VAJRADHARA (for the GSAR MA sects); in East Asia, by contrast, the ādibuddha is typically considered to be VAIROCANA.

**ādikarmika**. (P. ādikammika; T. las dang po pa; C. shiye; J. shigō; K. siŏp 始業). In Sanskrit, "beginner" or "neophyte"; a term used to refer to someone who is a novice on the path (MĀRGA). More technically, it refers to a practitioner on the path of accumulation (SAṂBHĀRAMĀRGA), where the initial tools necessary for spiritual development are first beginning to be gathered.

**ādīnava**. (T. nyes dmigs; C. guohuan; J. kagen; K. kwahwan 過患). In Sanskrit and Pāli, "dangers." More generically, ādīnava refers to the evils that may befall a layperson who is made heedless (PRAMĀDA) by drinking, gambling, debauchery, and idleness. More specifically, however, the term comes to be used to designate a crucial stage in the process of meditative development (BHĀVANĀ), in which the adept becomes so terrified of the "dangers" inherent in impermanent, compounded things that he turns away from this transitory world and instead turns toward the radical nonattachment that is NIRVĀṆA. In the so-called graduated discourse (P. ANUPUBBIKATHĀ) that the Buddha used to mold the understanding of his new adherents, the Buddha would outline in his elementary discourse the benefits of giving (dānakathā), right conduct (śīlakathā), and the prospect of rebirth in the heavens (svargakathā). Once their minds were pliant and impressionable, the Buddha would then instruct his listeners in the dangers (ādīnava) inherent in sensuality (KĀMA), in order to turn them away from the world and toward the advantages of renunciation (P. nekkhamme ānisaṃsa; see NAIṢKRAMYA). This pervasive sense of danger thence sustains the renunciatory drive that ultimately will lead to nirvāṇa. See also ĀDĪNAVĀNUPASSANĀÑĀṆA.

**ādīnavānupassanāñāṇa**. In Pāli, "knowledge arising from the contemplation of danger (ĀDĪNAVA)"; this is the fourth of nine knowledges (ñāṇa) cultivated as part of the "purity of knowledge and vision of progress along the path" (PAṬIPADĀÑĀṆADASSANAVISUDDHI) according to the outline in the VISUDDHIMAGGA. This latter category, in turn, constitutes the sixth and penultimate purity (VISUDDHI) to be developed along the path to liberation. Knowledge arising from the contemplation of danger is developed by noting the frightfulness of conditioned formations (saṃkhāra; S. SAṂSKĀRA), that is to say, the mental and physical phenomena (NĀMARŪPA) comprising the individual and the universe. Having seen that all phenomena are fearful because they are impermanent (anicca; S. ANITYA) and destined for annihilation, the practitioner finds no refuge in any kind of existence in any of the realms of rebirth. He sees no conditioned formation or station on which he can rely or that is worth holding onto. The *Visuddhimagga* states that the practitioner sees the three realms of existence as burning charcoal pits, the elements of the physical world as venomous snakes, and the five aggregates (khandha; S. SKANDHA) comprising the person as murderers with drawn swords. Seeing danger in continued existence and in every kind of becoming (BHAVA), the practitioner realizes that the only safety and happiness are found in nibbāna (S. NIRVĀṆA).

**Ādittapariyāyasutta**. (S. *Ādityaparyāyasūtra; C. Ranshao; J. Nenshō; K. Yŏnso 燃燒). In Pāli, lit. "Discourse on the Manner of Being Aflame," usually known in English as the "Fire Sermon"; the third sermon spoken by the Buddha following his enlightenment. After his conversion of the three matted-hair ascetics Uruvela-Kassapa, Gayā-Kassapa, and Nadī-Kassapa, along with their one thousand disciples, the Buddha was traveling with them to Gayāsīsa, where he delivered this sermon. Because of his new disciples' previous devotions to the Brahmanical fire sacrifice, once they were ordained the Buddha preached to these new monks a targeted discourse that he called the "Fire Sermon." The Buddha explains that all of the six sense bases, six sensory objects, and six sensory consciousnesses, along with the sensory contacts (phassa; S. SPARŚA) and sensations (VEDANĀ) that accompany the senses, are burning with the fires of greed (LOBHA), hatred (P. dosa; S. DVEṢA), and delusion (MOHA) and with the fires of all the various types of suffering (dukkha; S. DUḤKHA). Only through dispassion toward the senses (see INDRIYASAṂVARA) will attachment diminish and liberation eventually be achieved. In the Pāli tradition, the sermon appears in the MAHĀVAGGA section of the Pāli VINAYAPIṬAKA, on the history of the dispensation, not in the SUTTAPIṬAKA; a parallel SARVĀSTIVĀDA recension appears in the Chinese translation of the SAṂYUKTĀGAMA.

**Ādityabandhu**. (P. Ādiccabandhu; T. Nyi ma'i gnyen; C. Rizhong; J. Nisshu; K. Ilchong 日種). In Sanskrit, "Kinsman of the Sun"; one of the common epithets for ŚĀKYAMUNI or GAUTAMA Buddha, from his lineage (GOTRA) name of Āditya. This epithet and gotra name led some early Western scholars, such as ÉMILE SENART, to presume (wrongly) that the Buddha was an Indian solar deity. Āditya is also the name of a past buddha.

**advaya**. (T. gnyis su med pa; C. bu'er; J. funi; K. puri 不二). In Sanskrit, "nonduality"; one of the common synonyms for the highest teachings of Buddhism and one of the foundational principles of the MAHĀYĀNA presentation of doctrine. Nonduality refers to the definitive awareness achieved through enlightenment, which transcends all of the conventional dichotomies into which compounded existence is divided (right and wrong, good and evil, etc.). Most specifically, nondual knowledge (ADVAYAJÑĀNA) transcends the subject–object bifurcation that governs all conventional states of consciousness and engenders a distinctive type of awareness that no longer requires an object of consciousness. See also WU'AIXING.

**advayajñāna**. (T. gnyis su med pa'i ye shes; C. bu'erzhi; J. funichi; K. puriji 不二智). In Sanskrit, "nondual knowledge"; referring to knowledge that has transcended the subject-object bifurcation that governs all conventional states of sensory consciousness, engendering a distinctive type of awareness that is able to remain conscious without any longer requiring an object of consciousness. See also WU'AIXING.

**Advayavajra**. (S). See MAITRĪPA/MAITRĪPĀDA.

**adveṣa**. (P. adosa; T. zhe sdang med pa; C. wuchen; J. mushin; K. mujin 無瞋). In Sanskrit, "absence of ill will" or "absence of hatred." One of the forty-six mental concomitants (CAITTA) according to the VAIBHĀṢIKA–SARVĀSTIVĀDA school of ABHIDHARMA, one of the fifty-one according to the YOGACĀRA school and one of the fifty-two in the Pāli ABHIDHAMMA, "absence of ill will" is the opposite of "ill will" or "aversion" (DVEṢA). The SARVĀSTIVĀDA exegetes posited that this mental quality accompanied all wholesome activities, and it is therefore classified as one of the ten omnipresent wholesome factors (KUŚALAMAHĀBHŪMIKA). "Absence of ill will" is listed as one of the three wholesome faculties (KUŚALAMŪLA), is one of the states of mind comprising right intention (SAMYAKSAṂKALPA) in the noble eightfold path (ĀRYĀṢṬAṄGIKAMĀRGA), and is traditionally presumed to be a precondition for the cultivation of loving-kindness (MAITRĪ).

**afflictions**. See KLEŚA.

**āgama**. (T. lung; C. ahan jing; J. agongyō; K. aham kyŏng 阿含經). In Sanskrit and Pāli, "text" or "scripture"; a general term for received scriptural tradition. The term āgama is commonly paired with two other contrasting terms: āgama and YUKTI (reasoning) are the means of arriving at the truth; āgama and ADHIGAMA (realization) are the two divisions of the BUDDHADHARMA—the verbal or scriptural tradition and that which is manifested through practice. In its Sanskrit usage, the term āgama is also used to refer more specifically to the four scriptural collections of the mainstream tradition (now lost in Sanskrit but preserved in Chinese translation), attributed to the Buddha and his close disciples, which correspond to the four Pāli NIKĀYAS: (1) DĪRGHĀGAMA or "Long Discourses," belonging to the DHARMAGUPTAKA school and corresponding to the Pāli DĪGHANIKĀYA; (2) MADHYAMĀGAMA or "Medium Discourses," associated with the SARVĀSTIVĀDA school and corresponding to the Pāli MAJJHIMANIKĀYA; (3) SAṂYUKTĀGAMA or "Connected Discourses," belonging to the Sarvāstivāda school (with a partial translation perhaps belonging to the KĀŚYAPĪYA school) and corresponding to the Pāli SAṂYUTTANIKĀYA; and (4) EKOTTARĀGAMA or "Numerically Arranged Discourses," variously ascribed to the Dharmaguptakas, or less plausibly to the MAHĀSĀṂGHIKA school or its PRAJÑAPTIVĀDA offshoot, and corresponding to the Pāli AṄGUTTARANIKĀYA. Despite the similarities in the titles of these collections, there are many differences between the contents of the Sanskrit āgamas and the Pāli nikāyas. The KHUDDAKANIKĀYA ("Miscellaneous Collection"), the fifth nikāya in the Pāli canon, has no equivalent in the extant Chinese translations of the āgamas; such miscellanies, or "mixed baskets" (S. kṣudrakapiṭaka), were however known to have existed in several of the MAINSTREAM BUDDHIST SCHOOLS, including the Dharmaguptaka, Mahāsāṃghika, and MAHĪŚĀSAKA.

**āgamadharma**. (T. lung gi chos; C. jiaofa, J. kyōhō, K. kyobŏp 教法). In Sanskrit, "scriptural dharma"; one of the two divisions of the dharma or teaching of the Buddha, together with the "realized dharma" (ADHIGAMADHARMA). This term refers to the scriptural dharma as the teaching of the Buddha in its verbal form and is often identified with the TRIPIṬAKA or with the twelve divisions (DVĀDAŚĀṄGA[PRAVACANA]) of the word of the Buddha (BUDDHAVACANA).

**āgantukakleśa**. (P. āgantukakilesa; T. glo bur gyi nyon mongs; C. kechen fannao; J. kyakujin bonnō; K. kaekchin pŏnnoe 客塵煩惱). In Sanskrit, "adventitious afflictions" or "adventitious defilements"; indicating that the KLEŚA are accidental and extrinsic qualities of the mind, rather than natural and intrinsic. This notion builds on an ancient strand in Buddhist thought, such as in the oft-quoted passage in the Pāli AṄGUTTARANIKĀYA: "The mind, O monks, is luminous but defiled by adventitious defilements" (pabhassaraṃ idaṃ bhikkave cittaṃ, tañ ca kho āgantukehi upakkilesehi upakkiliṭṭham). Since defilements are introduced into the thought processes from without, the intrinsic purity of the mind (CITTA) can be restored through counteracting the influence of the kleśa and overcoming the inveterate tendency toward attachment and its concomitant craving (LOBHA) and ill will (DVEṢA), which empower them.This concept of āgantukakleśa is critical to the MAHĀYĀNA doctrine of TATHĀGATAGARBHA (embryo of buddhahood), where the mind is presumed to be innately enlightened, but that enlightenment is temporarily obscured or concealed by defilements (KLEŚA) that are extrinsic to it.

**Aggaññasutta**. (C. Xiaoyuan jing; J. Shōengyō; K. Soyŏn kyŏng 小緣經). In Pāli, "Discourse on Origins" or "Sermon on Things Primeval"; the twenty-seventh sutta of the DĪGHANIKĀYA (a separate DHARMAGUPTAKA recension appears as the fifth SŪTRA in the Chinese translation of the DĪRGHĀGAMA); the sūtra provides a Buddhist account of the origins of the world and of human society. The Buddha preached the sermon at Sāvatthi (ŚRĀVASTĪ) to two ordinands, Vāsettha and Bhāradvāja, to disabuse them of the belief that the priestly brāhmaṇa caste was superior to the Buddha's khattiya (KṢATRIYA), or warrior, caste. The Buddha describes the fourfold caste system of traditional Indian society as a by-product of the devolution of sentient beings. In the beginning of the eon (KALPA), beings possess spiritual bodies that are luminous, able to travel through the air, and feed on joy. But out of greed for sensual gratification, they degenerate into physical beings with ever grosser propensities: e.g., the coarser the food they eat (first a cream on the surface of water, then creepers, then eventually rice), the coarser their bodies become, until the beings develop sex organs, begin to have intercourse, and in turn build dwellings in order to conceal their debauchery. As their bodies become ever more physical, their life spans in turn also decrease. Immorality, strife, and violence ensue until people finally realize they need a leader to save them from anarchy. They elect the first human king, named Mahāsammata, who was also the first kṣatriya. It was out of the kṣatriya lineage deriving from this first king that the other three classes—brāhmaṇa, vaiśya, and śūdra—also evolved. This account challenges the mainstream Indian belief that the brāhmaṇa caste is congenitally superior (descending, it claims, from the mouth of the god Brahmā himself) and posits that the effort of moral and spiritual perfection, not the accident of birth, is the true standard of human superiority. Although the Buddhist tradition presumes that this sermon offers a distinctively Buddhistic account of the origin and development of both the universe and society, many of the topoi adopted in the story derive from Brahmanical cosmogonies, perhaps employed here as a satire of Brahmanical pretensions in Indian society. The scripture has also been treated by modern interpreters as offering an incipient Buddhist "environmentalism," wherein human actions, motivated by greed and lust, cause deleterious effects on the physical world, turning, for example, naturally growing rice into a rice that must be cultivated.

**Aggavaṃsa**. A twelfth-century scholar monk of the Pāli tradition who wrote the *Saddanīti*, an important Pāli grammar, in 1154. Although some texts describe him as hailing from JAMBUDVĪPA (viz., India), he seems instead to have lived north of Pagan (Bagan), present-day Myanmar (Burma).

**aggregates**. See SKANDHA.

**Agni**. (T. Me lha; C. Huoshen; J. Kashin; K. Hwasin 火神). The Vedic fire deity adopted into the Buddhist pantheon as the guardian of the southeast. In the MAHĀVAIROCANĀBHISAMBODHISŪTRA, he is identified as an incarnation of VAIROCANA; in Tibet, he is associated with HEVAJRA. Agni is depicted riding a goat, with one face and two hands, the right holding a rosary, the left a vase full of the nectar of immortality (AMṚTA). The term also refers to a class of pre-Buddhist fire deities absorbed into the Tibetan Buddhist pantheon.

**Agonshū**. (阿含宗). In Japanese, "ĀGAMA School"; a Japanese "new religion" structured from elements drawn from esoteric Buddhism (MIKKYŌ) and indigenous Japanese religions; founded in 1970 by Kiriyama Seiyū (born Tsutsumi Masao in 1921). Kiriyama's teachings are presented first in his *Henshin no genri* ("Principles of Transformation"; 1975). Kiriyama believed he had been saved by the compassion of Kannon (AVALOKITEŚVARA) and was told by that BODHISATTVA to teach others using the HOMA (J. goma) fire rituals drawn from Buddhist esoteric (MIKKYŌ) traditions. Later, while Kiriyama was reading the āgama (J. agon) scriptures, he realized that Buddhism as it was currently constituted in Japan did not correspond to the original teachings of the Buddha. In 1978, Kiriyama changed the name of his religious movement to Agon, the Japanese pronunciation of the transcription of āgama, positing that his teachings derived from the earliest scriptures of Buddhism and thus legitimizing them. His practices are fundamentally concerned with removing practitioners' karmic hindrances (KARMĀVARAṆA). Since many of these hindrances, he claims, are the result of neglecting one's ancestors or are inherited from them, much attention is also paid in the school to transforming the spirits of the dead into buddhas themselves, which in turn will also free the current generation from their karmic obstructions. Spiritual power in the school derives from the shinsei busshari (true ŚARĪRA [relics] of the Buddha), a sacred reliquary holding a bone fragment of the Buddha himself, given to Kiriyama in 1986 by the president of Sri Lanka. Individual adherents keep a miniature replica of the śarīra in their own homes, and the relic is said to have the transformational power to turn ancestors into buddhas. A "Star Festival" (Hoshi Matsuri) is held in Kyōto on each National Foundation Day (February 11), at which time two massive homa fires are lit, one liberating the spirits of the ancestors (and thus freeing the current generation from inherited karmic obstructions), the other helping to make the deepest wishes of its adherents come true. Adherents write millions of prayers on wooden sticks, which are cast into the two fires.

**Agvaandandar**. (T. Ngag dbang bstan dar a.k.a. Bstan dar lha ram pa) (1759–1830). Mongolian scholar of the DGE LUGS sect of Tibetan Buddhism. He was born into a nomad family in the Eastern Qoshot banner of Alashan, entering the monastery at the age of seven. He was sent to 'BRAS SPUNGS monastery in LHA SA at the age of nineteen, where he completed the Dge lugs curriculum and received the highest rank of DGE BSHES, that of lha ram pa, around 1800. In Tibetan, he is often referred to as Bstan dar lha ram pa. He returned to his native Mongolia shortly thereafter where he was appointed to a high position at Eastern Monastery, before leaving again, this time for A mdo and the great Dge lugs monasteries of SKU 'BUM and BLA BRANG. He traveled extensively, visiting monasteries in both Inner and Outer Mongolia, and going also to China, where he visited Beijing and WUTAISHAN. He was regarded as one of the leading Dge lugs scholars of his generation. Agvaandandar returned to his native Alashan at the end of his life, where he died in 1830. His tomb at Sharil Chindar is still a place of worship. His collected works fill two volumes, comprising thirty-six titles, all written in Tibetan (two are bilingual Tibetan and Mongolian). He wrote on a wide range of topics in Buddhist philosophy, logic, poetics (based on Daṇḍin's *Kāvyādarśa*), and grammar (both Tibetan and Mongolian), including a Tibetan–Mongolian dictionary. His philosophical work included commentaries on the *Hetucakra* and the ĀLAMBANAPARIKṢĀ of DIGNĀGA, the *Saṃtānāntarasiddhi* of DHARMAKĪRTI, and on the PRAJÑĀPĀRAMITĀHṚDAYASŪTRA ("Heart Sūtra").

**agyo**. (C. xiayu; K. haŏ 下語). In Japanese, "appended words" or "granted words." Although the term is now used generally to refer to the instructions of a ZEN master, agyo can also more specifically refer to a set number of stereotyped sayings, often a verse or phrase, that were used in KŌAN (C. GONG'AN) training. Unlike the literate monks of the medieval GOZAN monasteries, monks of the RINKA, or forest, monasteries were usually unable to compose their own Chinese verses to express the insight that they had gained while struggling with a kōan. The rinka monks therefore began to study the "appended words" or "capping phrases" (JAKUGO) of a kōan text such as the BIYAN LU, which summarized or explained each segment of the text. The agyo are found in kōan manuals known as MONSAN, or Zen phrase manuals, such as the ZENRIN KUSHŪ, where they are used to explicate a kōan.

**Agyō**. (J) (阿形). See NIŌ.

**ahaṃkāra**. (T. ngar 'dzin; C. wozhi/woman; J. gashū/gaman; K. ajip/aman 我執/我慢). In Sanskrit and Pāli, "conception of I," "egotism," or "arrogance"; a synonym of ĀTMAGRĀHA (attachment to a conception of self). See ĀTMAGRĀHA.

**āhāra**. (T. zas; C. shi; J. jiki; K. sik 食) In Sanskrit and Pāli, lit. "food," i.e., "nutriment" in the broadest sense, which nourishes everything associated with the body and mind. Four types of nutriment are commonly listed in mainstream materials: (1) food (āhāra; P. kabaliṅkārāhāra) of both coarse and fine varieties, which nourishes the physical body; (2) sensory contact or impression (SPARŚA, P. phassa), which nourishes pleasant, unpleasant, and neutral sensations (VEDANĀ; see PRATĪTYASAMUTPĀDA); (3) intention (CETANĀ; P. manosañcetanā), which nourishes actions (KARMAN) performed via body, speech, and mind; and (4) consciousness (VIJÑĀNA; P. viññāṇa), which nourishes mentality and corporeality (NĀMARŪPA), specifically at the moment of conception in the next rebirth (see pratītyasamutpāda).

**ahiṃsā**. (T. 'tshe ba med pa; C. buhai; J. fugai; K. purhae 不害). In Sanskrit and Pāli, "absence of harmful intentions," "harmlessness," "noninjury," or "nonviolence." The religious ideal and ethical injunction of "harmlessness" toward all living beings was shared in some fashion by several of the Indian ŚRAMAṆA traditions, including the Buddhists as well as the JAINAS, who made it a central tenet of their religion. Some of the corollaries of this idea included the precept against killing, the injunction to refrain from physically and verbally abusing sentient beings, and vegetarianism. The Jainas were especially stringent in their interpretation of "harmlessness" toward all living creatures, demanding strict vegetarianism from their followers in order to avoid injuring sentient creatures, a requirement that the Buddha rejected when his rival in the order, DEVADATTA, proposed it in his list of austerities (see DHUTAṄGA). The Buddha's view was that monks were a "field of merit" (PUṆYAKṢETRA) for the laity and should accept all offerings made to them, including meat, unless the monk knew that the animal had been killed specifically to feed him, for example. The voluntary vegetarianism that is now prevalent in both Mahāyāna Buddhism and wider Indian Hindu culture is almost certainly a result of Jaina influence and constitutes that religion's most enduring contribution to Indian religion. Buddhism treated "absence of harmful intentions" as one of the forty-six mental factors (CAITTA) according to the SARVĀSTIVĀDA–VAIBHĀṢIKA school of ABHIDHARMA, one of the fifty-one according to the YOGACĀRA school, and one of the fifty-two CETASIKAS in the Pāli ABHIDHAMMA. It is the opposite of "harmful intention" or "injury" (VIHIṂSĀ, and is sometimes seen written as avihiṃsā) and one of the states of mind comprising right intention (S. samyaksaṃkalpa; P. sammāsaṅkappa) in the noble eightfold path (ĀRYĀṢṬĀṄGIKAMĀRGA). "Absence of harmful intentions" is also traditionally taken to be a precondition for the cultivation of "compassion" (KARUṆĀ). See VIHIṂSĀ.

**aiśvarya**. (T. dbang phyug; C. zizai; J. jizai; K. chajae 自在). In Sanskrit, lit. "sovereignty"; referring to the "self-mastery" or "autonomy" that is a product of religious training and/or related superknowledges (ABHIJÑĀ) that are gained thereby, such as clairvoyance, clairaudience, telepathy, the ability to manifest transformation bodies, and erudition.

**Aizen Myōō**. (愛染明王) (S. Rāgavidyārāja). In Japanese, lit. "Bright King of the Taint of Lust"; an esoteric deity considered to be the destroyer of vulgar passions. In stark contrast to the traditional Buddhist approach of suppressing the passions through various antidotes or counteractive techniques (PRATIPAKṢA), this VIDYĀRĀJA is believed to be able to transform attachment, desire, craving, and defilement directly into pure BODHICITTA. This deity became a principal deity of the heretical Tachikawa branch (TACHIKAWARYŪ) of the SHINGONSHŪ and was considered the deity of conception. As an emanation of the buddha MAHĀVAIROCANA or the bodhisattva VAJRASATTVA, Aizen Myōō was favored by many followers of Shingon Buddhism in Japan and by various esoteric branches of the TENDAISHŪ. Aizen Myōō was also sometimes held to be a secret buddha (HIBUTSU) by these traditions. The NICHIRENSHŪ was the last to adopt him as an important deity, but he played an important role in the dissemination of its cult. Aizen Myōō is well known for his fierce appearance, which belies the love and affection he is presumed to convey. Aizen Myōō usually has three eyes (to see the three realms of existence) and holds a lotus in his hand, which is symbolic of the calming of the senses, among other things. Other attributes of this deity are the bow and arrows, VAJRAS, and weapons that he holds in his hands.

**ajahn**. Thai pronunciation of the Sanskrit term ĀCĀRYA ("teacher"); also transcribed as āčhān.

**Ajahn Chah Bodhiñāṇa**. (1918–1992). A prominent Thai monk who was one of the most influential Thai forest-meditation masters (PHRA PA) of the twentieth century. Born in the village of Baan Gor in the northeastern Thai province of Ubon Ratchathani, he was ordained as a novice at his local temple, where he received his basic education and studied the Buddhist teachings. After several years of training, he returned to lay life to attend to the needs of his parents, but motivated by his religious calling, at the age of twenty, he took higher ordination (UPASAṂPADĀ) as a BHIKṢU and continued his studies of Pāli scripture. His father's death prompted him to travel to other monasteries in an effort to acquire a deeper understanding of Buddhist teaching and discipline under the guidance of different teachers. During his pilgrimage, he met AJAHN MUN BHŪRIDATTA, the premier meditation master of the Thai forest-dwelling (ARAÑÑAVĀSI) tradition. After that encounter, Ajahn Chah traveled extensively throughout the country, devoting his energies to meditation in forests and charnel grounds (ŚMAŚĀNA). As his reputation grew, he was invited to establish a monastery near his native village, which became known as Wat Pa Pong after the name of the forest (reputed to be inhabited by ghosts) in which it was located. Ajahn Chah's austere lifestyle, simple method of mindfulness meditation, and straightforward style of teaching attracted a large following of monks and lay supporters, including many foreigners. In 1966, he established Wat Pa Nanachat, a branch monastery specifically for Western and other non-Thai nationals, next to Wat Pa Pong. In 1976, he was invited to England, which led to the establishment of the first branch monastery of Wat Pa Pong there, followed by others in Switzerland, Australia, New Zealand, and Italy. He also visited the United States, where he spoke at retreats at the Insight Meditation Center in Barre, Massachusetts. Ajahn Chah died in 1992, after several years in a coma.

**Ajahn Mun Bhūridatta**. (1870–1949). Thai monk who revitalized the Thai forest-monk tradition (Thai PHRA PA), and the subject of a celebrated Thai hagiography by Ajahn Mahā Boowa Ñāṇasampaṇṇo (b. 1913). Born in 1870, in Ban Khambong village in the province of Ubon Ratchathani, Mun was ordained in 1893 at Wat Liab and began studying insight practice (VIPAŚYANĀ) under the guidance of Ajahn Sao Kantasīla (1861–1941). Through developing the meditation on foulness (AŚUBHABHĀVANĀ), he eventually had an experience of calmness (ŚAMATHA), and in order to enhance his practice, he embarked on the life of asceticism (P. DHUTAṄGA) as a forest dweller (P. ARAÑÑAVĀSI) in northeast Thailand and southern Laos. After every rains' retreat (VARṢĀ) was over, he would travel into the forests, staying just close enough to a few small villages in order to perform his alms round (PIṆḌAPĀTA) each morning. According to the hagiography, after first experiencing the fruition of the state of the nonreturner (ANĀGĀMIN), he eventually achieved the stage of a worthy one (ARHAT) in Chiang Mai, an experience that he said shook the entire universe and brought a roar of accolades from the heavenly hosts. Ajahn Mun became a widely known and respected meditator and teacher, who was invited to dwell in monasteries throughout much of Thailand. The hagiography compiled by Ajahn Mahā Boowa is filled with exuberantly told tales of his meditative visions, prophetic dreams, lectures and instructions, and encounters with other eminent monks, laypeople, and even with deceased arhats and divinities (DEVA) such as ŚAKRA with his 100,000 strong retinue. Ajahn Mun's many prominent disciples helped revive the Thai forest-monk tradition, especially in the northeast, and defined its austere practices (Thai, THUDONG; P. DHUTAṄGA) in their contemporary context.

**Ajaṇṭā**. A complex of some thirty caves and subsidiary structures in India, renowned for its exemplary Buddhist artwork. Named after a neighboring village, the caves are carved from the granite cliffs at a bend in the Wagurna River valley, northeast of AURANGĀBĀD, in the modern Indian state of Maharashtra. The grottoes were excavated in two phases, the first of which lasted from approximately 100 BCE to 100 CE, the second from c. 462 to 480, and consist primarily of monastic cave residences (VIHĀRA) and sanctuaries (CAITYA). The sanctuaries include four large, pillared STŪPA halls, each enshrining a central monumental buddha image, which renders the hall both a site for worship and a buddha's dwelling (GANDHAKUṬĪ), where he presides over the activities of the monks in residence. The murals and sculpture located at Ajaṇṭā include some of the best-preserved examples of ancient Buddhist art. Paintings throughout the complex are especially noted for their depiction of accounts from the Buddha's previous lives (JĀTAKA). Despite the presence of some AVALOKITEŚVARA images at the site, it is Sanskrit texts of mainstream Buddhism, and especially the MŪLASARVĀSTIVĀDA school, that are the source and inspiration for the paintings of Ajaṇṭā. Indeed, almost all of Ajaṇṭā's narrative paintings are based on accounts appearing in the MŪLASARVĀSTIVĀDA VINAYA, as well as the poems of Āryaśūra and AŚVAGHOṢA. On the other hand, the most common type of sculptural image at Ajaṇṭā (e.g., Cave 4) is a seated buddha making a variant of the gesture of turning the wheel of the dharma (DHARMACAKRAMUDRĀ), flanked by the two bodhisattvas AVALOKITEŚVARA and VAJRAPĀṆI. The deployment of this mudrā and the two flanking bodhisattvas indicates that these buddha images are of VAIROCANA and suggests that tantric elements that appear in the MAHĀVAIROCANĀBHISAṂBODHISŪTRA and the MAÑJUŚRĪMŪLAKALPA, both of which postdate the Ajaṇṭā images, developed over an extended period of time and had precursors that influenced the iconography at Ajaṇṭā. Inscriptions on the walls of the earliest part of the complex, primarily in Indian Prakrits, attest to an eclectic, even syncretic, pattern of religious observance and patronage. Later epigraphs found at the site associate various patrons with Hariṣeṇa (r. 460–477), the last known monarch of the Vākāṭaka royal family. Varāhadeva, for example, who patronized Cave 16, was one of Hariṣeṇa's courtiers, while Cave 1 was donated by Hariṣeṇa himself, and Cave 2 may have been patronized by a close relative, perhaps one of Hariṣeṇa's wives. Cave 16's central image, a buddha seated on a royal throne with legs pendant (BHADRĀSANA), is the first stone sculpture in this iconographic form found in western India. Introduced to India through the tradition of KUSHAN royal portraiture, the bhadrāsana has been interpreted as a position associated with royalty and worldly action. This sculpture may thus have functioned as a portrait sculpture; it may even allegorize Hariṣeṇa as the Buddha. In fact, it is possible that Varāhadeva may have originally intended to enshrine a buddha seated in the cross-legged lotus position (VAJRAPARYAṄKA) but changed his plan midway in the wake of a regional war that placed Hariṣeṇa's control over the Ajaṇṭā region in jeopardy. Around 480, the constructions at Ajaṇṭā came to a halt with the destruction of the Vākāṭaka family. The caves were subsequently abandoned and became overgrown, only to be discovered in 1819 by a British officer hunting a tiger. They quickly became the object of great archaeological and art historical interest, and were designated a UNESCO World Heritage Site in 1983.

**Ajātaśatru**. (P. Ajātasattu; T. Ma skyes dgra; C. Asheshi wang; J. Ajase ō; K. Asase wang 阿闍世王). In Sanskrit, "Enemy While Still Unborn," the son of King BIMBISĀRA of Magadha and his successor as king. According to the Pāli account, when Bimbisāra's queen VAIDEHĪ (P. Videhī) was pregnant, she developed an overwhelming urge to drink blood from the king's right knee, a craving that the king's astrologers interpreted to mean that the son would eventually commit patricide and seize the throne. Despite several attempts to abort the fetus, the child was born and was given the name Ajātaśatru. While a prince, Ajātaśatru became devoted to the monk DEVADATTA, the Buddha's cousin and rival, because of Devadatta's mastery of yogic powers (ṚDDHI). Devadatta plotted to take revenge on the Buddha through manipulating Ajātaśatru, whom he convinced to murder his father Bimbisāra, a close lay disciple and patron of the Buddha, and seize the throne. Ajātaśatru subsequently assisted Devadatta in several attempts on the Buddha's life. Ajātaśatru is said to have later grown remorseful over his evil deeds and, on the advice of the physician JĪVAKA, sought the Buddha's forgiveness. The Buddha preached to him on the benefits of renunciation from the SĀMAÑÑAPHALASUTTA, and Ajātaśatru became a lay disciple. Because he had committed patricide, one of the five most heinous of evil deeds that are said to bring immediate retribution (ĀNANTARYAKARMAN), Ajātaśatru was precluded from attaining any degree of enlightenment during this lifetime and was destined for rebirth in the lohakumbhiya hell. Nevertheless, Sakka (S. ŚAKRA), the king of the gods, described Ajātaśatru as the chief in piety among the Buddha's unenlightened disciples. When the Buddha passed away, Ajātaśatru was overcome with grief and, along with other kings, was given a portion of the Buddha's relics (ŚARĪRA) for veneration. According to the Pāli commentaries, Ajātaśatru provided the material support for convening the first Buddhist council (see COUNCIL, FIRST) following the Buddha's death. The same sources state that, despite his piety, he will remain in hell for sixty thousand years but later will attain liberation as a solitary buddha (P. paccekabuddha; S. PRATYEKABUDDHA) named Viditavisesa. ¶ Mahāyāna scriptures, such as the MAHĀPARINIRVĀṆASŪTRA and the GUAN WULIANGSHOU JING ("Contemplation Sūtra on the Buddha of Infinite Life"), give a slightly different account of Ajātaśatru's story. Bimbisāra was concerned that his queen, Vaidehī, had yet to bear him an heir. He consulted a soothsayer, who told him that an aging forest ascetic would eventually be reborn as Bimbisāra's son. The king then decided to speed the process along and had the ascetic killed so he would take rebirth in Vaidehī's womb. After the queen had already conceived, however, the soothsayer prophesized that the child she would bear would become the king's enemy. After his birth, the king dropped him from a tall tower, but the child survived the fall, suffering only a broken finger. (In other versions of the story, Vaidehī is so mortified to learn that her unborn son will murder her husband the king that she tried to abort the fetus, but to no avail.) Devadatta later told Ajātaśatru the story of his conception and the son then imprisoned his father, intending to starve him to death. But Vaidehī kept the king alive by smuggling food to him, smearing her body with flour-paste and hiding grape juice inside her jewelry. When Ajātaśatru learned of her treachery, he drew his sword to murder her, but his vassals dissuaded him. The prince's subsequent guilt about his intended matricide caused his skin break out in oozing abscesses that emitted such a foul odor that no one except his mother was able to approach him and care for him. Despite her loving care, Ajātaśatru did not improve and Vaidehī sought the Buddha's counsel. The Buddha was able to cure the prince by teaching him the "Nirvāṇa Sūtra," and the prince ultimately became one of the preeminent Buddhist monarchs of India. This version of the story of Ajātaśatru was used by Kosawa Heisaku (1897–1968), one of the founding figures of Japanese psychoanalysis, and his successors to posit an "Ajase (Ajātaśatru) Complex" that distinguished Eastern cultures from the "Oedipal Complex" described by Sigmund Freud in Western psychoanalysis. As Kosawa interpreted this story, Vaidehī's ambivalence or active antagonism toward her son and Ajātaśatru's rancor toward his mother were examples of the pathological relationship that pertains between mother and son in Eastern cultures, in distinction to the competition between father and son that Freud posited in his Oedipal Complex. This pathological relationship can be healed only through the mother's love and forgiveness, which redeem the child and thus reunite them.

**aji gatsurinkan**. (阿字月輪觀). In Japanese, "contemplation of the letter 'A' in the moon-wheel." See AJIKAN.

**aji honpushō**. (阿字本不生). In Japanese, "the letter 'A' that is originally uncreated." See AJIKAN.

**ajikan**. (阿字観). In Japanese, "contemplation of the letter 'A'"; a meditative exercise employed primarily within the the Japanese SHINGON school of esoteric Buddhism. The ajikan practice is also known as the "contemplation of the letter 'A' in the moon-wheel" (AJI GATSURINKAN). The letter "A" is the first letter in the Sanskrit SIDDHAM alphabet and is considered to be the "seed" (BĪJA) of MAHĀVAIROCANA, the central divinity of the esoteric traditions. The letter "A" is also understood to be the "unborn" buddha-nature (FOXING) of the practitioner; hence, the identification of oneself with this letter serves as a catalyst to enlightenment. In ajikan meditation, the adept draws a picture of the full moon with an eight-petaled lotus flower at its center. The Siddham letter "A" is then superimposed over the lotus flower as a focus of visualization. As the visualization continues, the moon increases in size until it becomes coextensive with the universe itself. Through this visualization, the adept realizes the letter "A" that is originally uncreated (AJI HONPUSHŌ), which is the essence of all phenomena in the universe and the DHARMAKĀYA of MAHĀVAIROCANA Buddha.

**Ajita**. (T. Ma pham pa; C. Ayiduo; J. Aitta; K. Ailta 阿逸多). In Sanskrit and Pāli, "Invincible"; proper name of several different figures in Buddhist literature. In the Pāli tradition, Ajita is said to have been one of the sixteen mendicant disciples of the brāhmaṇa ascetic Bāvarī who visited the Buddha at the request of their teacher. Upon meeting the Buddha, Ajita saw that he was endowed with the thirty-two marks of a great man (MAHĀPURUṢALAKṢAṆA) and gained assurance that the Buddha's renown was well deserved. Starting with Ajita, all sixteen of the mendicants asked the Buddha questions. Ajita's question is preserved as the *Ajitamānavapucchā* in the *Parāyanavagga* of the SUTTANIPĀTA. At the end of the Buddha's explanations, Ajita and sixteen thousand followers are said to have become worthy ones (ARHAT) and entered the SAṂGHA. Ajita returned to his old teacher Bāvarī and recounted to him what happened. Bāvarī himself converted and later became a nonreturner (ANĀGĀMIN). ¶ Another Ajita is Ajita-Keśakambala (Ajita of the Hair Blanket), a prominent leader of the LOKĀYATA (Naturalist) school of Indian wandering religious (ŚRAMAṆA) during the Buddha's time, who is mentioned occasionally in Buddhist scriptures. His doctrine is recounted in the Pāli SĀMAÑÑAPHALASUTTA, where he is claimed to have denied the efficacy of moral cause and effect because of his materialist rejection of any prospect of transmigration or rebirth. ¶ An Ajita also traditionally appears as the fifteenth on the list of the sixteen ARHAT elders (ṢOḌAŚASTHAVIRA), who were charged by the Buddha with protecting his dispensation until the advent of the next buddha, MAITREYA. Ajita is said to reside on Mt. GṚDHRAKŪṬA (Vulture Peak) with 1,500 disciples. He is known in Chinese as the "long-eyebrowed arhat" (changmei luohan) because he is said to have been born with long white eyebrows. In CHANYUE GUANXIU's standard Chinese depiction, Ajita is shown sitting on a rock, with both hands holding his right knee; his mouth is open, with his tongue and teeth exposed. East Asian images also sometimes show him leaning on a staff. In Tibetan iconography, he holds his two hands in his lap in DHYĀNAMUDRĀ. ¶ Ajita is finally a common epithet of the bodhisattva MAITREYA, used mostly when he is invoked in direct address.

**Ājīvaka**. [alt. Ājīvakā; Ājīvika]. (T. 'Tsho ba can; C. Xieming waidao; J. Jamyō gedō; K. Samyŏng oedo 邪命外道) In Sanskrit and Pāli, "Improper Livelihood"; one of the major early sects of Indian wandering religious (ŚRAMAṆA) during the fifth century BCE. Makkhali Gosāla (S. MASKARIN GOŚĀLĪPUTRA) (d. c. 488 BCE), the leader of the Ājīvakas, was a contemporary of the Buddha. No Ājīvaka works survive, so what little we know about the school derives from descriptions filtered through Buddhist materials. Buddhist explications of Ājīvaka views are convoluted and contradictory; what does seem clear, however, is that the Ājīvakas adhered to a doctrine of strict determinism or fatalism. The Ājīvakas are described as believing that there is no immediate or ultimate cause for the purity or depravity of beings; all beings, souls, and existent things are instead directed along their course by fate (niyati), by the conditions of the species to which they belong, and by their own intrinsic natures. Thus, attainments or accomplishments of any kind are not a result of an individual's own action or the acts of others; rather, according to those beings' positions within the various stations of existence, they experience ease or pain. Makkhali Gosāla is portrayed as advocating a theory of automatic purification through an essentially infinite number of transmigrations (saṃsāraśuddhi), by means of which all things would ultimately attain perfection. The Buddha is said to have regarded Makkhali Gosāla's views as the most dangerous of heresies, which was capable of leading even the divinities (DEVA) to loss, discomfort, and suffering. BUDDHAGHOSA explains the perniciousness of his error by comparing the defects of Makkhali's views to those of the views of two other heretical teachers, Pūraṇa Kassapa (S. Pūraṇa Kāśyapa) (d. c. 503 BCE), another Ājīvaka teacher, and AJITA-Kesakambala, a prominent teacher of the LOKĀYATA (Naturalist) school, which maintained a materialist perspective toward the world. Pūraṇa asserted the existence of an unchanging passive soul that was unaffected by either wholesome or unwholesome action and thereby denied the efficacy of KARMAN; Ajita advocated an annihilationist theory that there is no afterlife or rebirth, which thereby denied any possibility of karmic retribution. Makkhali's doctrine of fate or noncausation, in denying both action and its result, was said to have combined the defects in both those systems of thought.

**Ājñātakauṇḍinya**. (P. Aññātakoṇḍañña / Aññākoṇḍañña; T. Kun shes kauṇ ḍi nya; C. Aruojiaochenru; J. Anyakyōjinnyo; K. Ayakkyojinyŏ 阿若憍陳如). In Sanskrit, "Kauṇḍinya (P. Koṇḍañña) who Knows"; the first person to understand the insights of the Buddha, as delivered in the first sermon, the DHARMACAKRAPRAVARTANASŪTRA (P. DHAMMACAKKAPPAVATTANASUTTA), and the first disciple to take ordination as a monk (BHIKṢU), following the simple EHIBHIKṢUKĀ (P. ehi bhikkhu), or "come, monk," formula: "Come, monk, the DHARMA is well proclaimed; live the holy life for the complete ending of suffering." Kauṇḍinya was one of the group of five ascetics (BHADRAVARGĪYA) converted by the Buddha at the ṚSIPATANA (P. Isipatana) MṚGADĀVA (Deer Park), located just north-east of the city of Vārāṇasī. According to the Pāli account, he was a brāhmaṇa older than the Buddha, who was especially renowned in physiognomy. After the birth of the infant GAUTAMA, he was one of eight brāhmaṇas invited to predict the infant's future and the only one to prophesize that the child would definitely become a buddha rather than a wheel-turning monarch (CAKRAVARTIN). He left the world as an ascetic in anticipation of the bodhisattva's own renunciation and was joined by the sons of four of the other eight brāhmaṇas. Kauṇḍinya and the other four ascetics joined the bodhisattva in the practice of austerities, but when, after six years, the bodhisattva renounced extreme asceticism, they left him in disgust. After his enlightenment, the Buddha preached to the five ascetics at the Ṛsipatana deer park, and Kauṇḍinya was the first to realize the truth of the Buddha's words. The Pāli canon describes Kauṇḍinya's enlightenment as proceeding in two stages: first, when the Buddha preached the *Dhammacakkappavattanasutta*, he attained the opening of the dharma eye (DHARMACAKṢUS), the equivalent of stream-entry (SROTAĀPANNA), and five days later, when the Buddha preached his second sermon, the ANATTALAKKHAṆASUTTA, he attained the level of ARHAT. The Buddha praised him both times by exclaiming "Kauṇḍinya knows!," in recognition of which Ājñāta ("He Who Knows") was thereafter prefixed to his name. Later, at a large gathering of monks at JETAVANA grove in ŚRĀVASTĪ, the Buddha declared Ājñātakauṇḍinya to be preeminent among his disciples who first comprehended the dharma, and preeminent among his long-standing disciples. Ājñātakauṇḍinya received permission from the Buddha to live a solitary life in the Chaddantavana forest and only returned after twelve years to take leave of the Buddha before his own PARINIRVĀṆA. After his cremation, Ājñātakauṇḍinya's relics were given to the Buddha, who personally placed them in a silver reliquary (CAITYA) that spontaneously appeared from out of the earth.

**akalpikavastu**. (P. akappiyavatthu; T. rung ba ma yin pa'i dngos po; C. bujing wu; J. fujōmotsu; K. pujŏng mul 不淨物). In Sanskrit, "inappropriate possessions" or "improper matters"; eight kinds of possessions or activities that monks and nuns are expected to avoid, since they may compromise their status as renunciants: (1) gold, (2) silver, (3) servants or slaves, (4) cattle, (5) sheep, (6) safe deposits or warehouses, (7) engaging in trade, and (8) engaging in farming. (An alternative version of this list does not include "sheep," but instead distinguishes between male and female servants or slaves). Another list has the following: (1) possessing land or property, (2) engaging in animal husbandry, (3) maintaining storage of grains or food and silk or other cloth, (4) having servants or slaves, (5) keeping animals (as either pets or livestock), (6) keeping money, (7) keeping cushions and pans, and (8) keeping furniture gilded with gold, ivory, or precious jewels.

**akaniṣṭha**. (P. akaniṭṭha; T. 'og min; C. sejiujing tian; J. shikikukyōten; K. saekkugyŏng ch'ŏn 色究竟天). In Sanskrit, "highest"; akaniṣṭha is the eighth and highest level of the realm of subtle materiality (RŪPADHĀTU), which is accessible only through experiencing the fourth meditative absorption (DHYĀNA); akaniṣṭha is thus one of the BRAHMALOKAS (see DEVA). Akaniṣṭha is the fifth and highest class of the "pure abodes," or ŚUDDHĀVĀSA (corresponding to the five highest heavens in the realm of subtle materiality), wherein abide "nonreturners" (ANĀGĀMIN)—viz., adepts who need never again return to the KĀMADHĀTU—and some ARHATs. The pure abodes therefore serve as a way station for advanced spiritual beings (ĀRYA) in their last life before final liberation. According to some Mahāyāna texts, akaniṣṭha is also the name of the abode of the enjoyment body (SAMBHOGAKĀYA) of a buddha in general and of the buddha VAIROCANA in particular.

**Ākaṅkheyyasutta**. (C. Yuan jing; J. Gangyō; K. Wŏn kyŏng 願經). In Pāli, "Discourse on What One May Wish," the sixth sutta in the MAJJHIMANIKĀYA (a separate SARVĀSTIVĀDA recension appears as SŪTRA no. 105 in the Chinese translation of the MADHYAMĀGAMA, and a recension of uncertain affiliation in the Chinese translation of the EKOTTARĀGAMA); preached by the Buddha to a group of disciples in the JETAVANA grove in the town of ŚRĀVASTĪ. The Buddha describes how a monk who wishes for all good things to come to himself, his fellow monks, and his lay supporters should restrain his sense faculties by seeing danger (ĀDĪNAVA) in the slightest fault and by abiding by the dictates of the disciplinary codes (PRĀTIMOKṢA). This restraint will allow him to develop morality (ŚĪLA), meditative concentration (SAMĀDHI), and liberating wisdom (PRAJÑĀ), leading to the destruction of the contaminants (ĀSRAVAKṢAYA).

**ākāra**. (T. rnam pa; C. xingxiang; J. gyōsō; K. haengsang 行相). In Sanskrit, "aspect," "mode," "form," or "image"; a polysemous term that is notably employed in discussions of epistemology to describe an image cast by an object, which serves as the actual object of sense perception. At an early stage of its history (as ākṛti), the term refers to what a word articulates. Over time, it came to mean the content of a word (that may or may not be connected with an actual content in reality) and then the mediating mental image. Buddhist philosophical schools differ as to whether or not such an "aspect" is required in order for sense perception to occur. VAIBHĀṢIKAS are nonaspectarians (NIRĀKĀRAVĀDA) who say mind knows objects directly; SAUTRĀNTIKAS are aspectarians (SĀKĀRAVĀDA) who say mind knows through an image (ākāra) of the object that is taken into the mind. YOGĀCĀRAs are aspectarians insofar as they do not accept external objects; they are divided into satyākāravādin

(T. rnam bden pa), or true aspectarians, who assert that appearances as gross objects exist and are not polluted by ignorance; and alīkākāravādin (T. rnam rdzun pa), or false aspectarians, who assert that appearances as gross objects do not exist and are polluted by ignorance. In SARVĀKĀRAJÑATĀ ("knowledge of all modes"), the name in the perfection of wisdom (PRAJÑĀPĀRAMITĀ) literature for the omniscience of a buddha, ākāra is synonymous with DHARMAS. In the ABHISAMAYĀLAṂKĀRA, there are 173 aspects that define the practice (prayoga) of a bodhisattva. They are the forms of a bodhisattva's knowledge (of impermanence that counteracts the mistaken apprehension of permanence, for example) informed by BODHICITTA and the knowledge that the knowledge itself has no essential nature (SVABHĀVA).

**ākāśa**. (T. nam mkha'; C. xukong; J. kokū; K. hŏgong 虛空). In Sanskrit, "space" or "spatiality"; "sky," and "ether." In ABHIDHARMA analysis, ākāśa has two discrete denotations. First, as "spatiality," ākāśa is an absence that delimits forms; like the empty space inside a door frame, ākāśa is a hole that is itself empty but that defines, or is defined by, the material that surrounds it. Second, as the vast emptiness of "space," ākāśa comes also to be described as the absence of obstruction and is enumerated as one of the permanent phenomena (nityadharma) because it does not change from moment to moment. Space in this sense is also interpreted as being something akin to the Western conception of ether, a virtually immaterial, but glowing fluid that serves as the support for the four material elements (MAHĀBHŪTA). (Because this ethereal form of ākāśa is thought to be glowing, it is sometimes used as a metaphor for buddhahood, which is said to be radiant like the sun or space.) In addition to these two abhidharma definitions, the sphere of infinite space (ĀKĀŚĀNANTYĀYATANA) has a meditative context as well through its listing as the first of the four immaterial DHYĀNAS. Ākāśa is recognized as one of the uncompounded dharmas (ASAṂSKṚTADHARMA) in six of the mainstream Buddhist schools, including the SARVĀSTIVĀDA and the MAHĀSĀṂGHIKA, as well as the later YOGĀCĀRA; three others reject this interpretation, including the THERAVĀDA.

**Ākāśagarbha**. (T. Nam mkha'i snying po; C. Xukongzang pusa; J. Kokūzō bosatsu; K. Hŏgongjang posal 虛空藏菩薩). In Sanskrit, "Storehouse/Womb of Space"; a BODHISATTVA who is one of the MAHOPAPUTRA, whose position is the north; also known as Cakrapāṇi. He is usually considered to be a form of AKṢOBHYA, although sometimes he is instead said to be the emanation of VAIROCANA. He is depicted in bodhisattva form, with one face and two hands in various MUDRĀS; his most common attribute is a sun disc. His consort is Mālā, and he is the counterpart to KṢITIGARBHA, the "Womb of the Earth." The sūtra that describes his attributes, the *Ākāśagarbhasūtra*, was first translated into Chinese by BUDDHAYAŚAS at the beginning of the fifth century and again by Dharmamitra a few decades later.

**ākāśānantyāyatana**. (P. ākāsānañcāyatana; T. nam mkha' mtha' yas skye mched; C. kong wubian chu; J. kūmuhenjo; K. kong mubyŏn ch'ŏ 空無邊處). In Sanskrit, "sphere of infinite space"; the first and lowest (in ascending order) of the four levels of the immaterial realm (ĀRŪPYADHĀTU) and the first of the four immaterial absorptions (DHYĀNA). It is a realm of rebirth as well as a meditative state that is entirely immaterial (viz., there is no physical [RŪPA] component to existence) in which the mind comes to an awareness of unlimited pervasive space (ĀKĀŚA) without the existence of material objects. Beings reborn in this realm are thought to live as long as forty thousand eons (KALPAS). However, as a state of being that is still subject to rebirth, even the realm of infinite space remains part of SAṂSĀRA. Like the other levels of the realm of subtle materiality (RŪPADHĀTU) and the immaterial realm, one is reborn in this state by achieving the specific level of meditative absorption of that state in the previous lifetime. One of the most famous and influential expositions on the subject of these immaterial states comes from the VISUDDHIMAGGA of BUDDHAGHOSA, written in the fifth century. Although there are numerous accounts of Buddhist meditators achieving immaterial states of SAMĀDHI, they are also used polemically in Buddhist literature to describe the attainments of non-Buddhist yogins, who mistakenly identify these exalted states within saṃsāra as states of permanent liberation from rebirth. See also DHYĀNASAMĀPATTI; DHYĀNOPAPATTI.

**ākiñcanyāyatana**. (P. ākiñcaññāyatana; T. ci yang med pa'i skye mched; C. wu suoyou chu; J. mushousho; K. mu soyu ch'ŏ 無所有處). In Sanskrit, "sphere of nothing whatsoever," or "absolute nothingness," the third (in ascending order) of the four levels of the immaterial realm (ĀRŪPYADHĀTU) and the third of the four immaterial absorptions (SAMĀPATTI). It is "above" the first two levels of the immaterial realm, called infinite space (AKĀŚĀNANTYĀYATANA) and infinite consciousness (VIJÑĀNĀNANTYĀYATANA), but "below" the fourth level, called "neither perception nor nonperception" (NAIVASAṂJÑĀNĀSAṂJÑĀYATANA). It is a realm of rebirth as well as a meditative state that is entirely immaterial (viz., there is no physical [RŪPA] component to existence) in which all ordinary semblances of consciousness vanish entirely. Beings reborn in this realm are thought to live as long as sixty thousand eons (KALPAS). However, as states of being that are still subject to rebirth, all of these spheres remain part of SAṂSĀRA. See also DHYĀNASAMĀPATTI; DHYĀNOPAPATTI.

**akkhipūjā**. In Pāli lit. "ritual of [opening] the eyes," a consecration ceremony for a buddha image; the Pāli equivalent for the Sanskrit term NETRAPRATIṢṬHĀPANA. The Pāli term is attested at least as early as the sixth-century MAHĀVAṂSA and BUDDHAGHOSA's SAMANTAPĀSĀDIKĀ.

**akliṣṭājñāna**. (T. nyon mongs can ma yin pa'i mi shes pa; C. buran wuzhi; J. fuzen muchi; K. puryŏm muji 不染無知). In Sanskrit, "unafflicted ignorance," a form of ignorance that affects those who have destroyed the KLEŚĀVARAṆA (afflictive obstructions) but not the JÑEYĀVARAṆA (cognitive obstructions). The term is used specifically in the MAHĀYĀNA tradition to refer to ARHATs, who have been liberated from rebirth (SAṂSĀRA) but who are still presumed to possess this subtlest form of ignorance. These cognitive obstructions are considered to result from fundamental misapprehensions about the nature of reality and serve as the origin of the afflictive obstructions. The buddhas therefore encourage the arhats to overcome even this unafflicted ignorance and enter the BODHISATTVA path that leads to buddhahood.

**akopya**. (P. akuppa; T. mi 'khrugs pa; C. budong; J. fudō; K. pudong 不動). In Sanskrit, "imperturbable" or "unshakable"; used often in mainstream Buddhist materials in reference to the "imperturbable" liberation of mind (CETOVIMUKTI) that derives from mastering any of the four meditative absorptions (P. JHĀNA; S. DHYĀNA). The term is also deployed in treatments of mastery of the "adept path" (AŚAIKṢAMĀRGA) of the ARHAT: once the imminent arhat realizes the knowledge of the cessation (KṢAYAJÑĀNA) of the afflictions (KLEŚA), and becomes imperturbable in that experience, the "knowledge of nonproduction" (ANUTPĀDAJÑĀNA) arises—viz., the awareness that the kleśas, once eradicated, will never arise again.

**akṣaṇa**. (P. akkhaṇa; T. mi khom pa; C. nanchu; J. nansho; K. nanch'ŏ 難處). In Sanskrit, "inopportune birth" (lit. "not at the right moment"), referring specifically to a rebirth in which one will not be able to benefit from a buddha or his teachings. Eight such situations are typically listed: birth (1) as one of the hell denizens (NĀRAKA); (2) as an animal, (3) as a hungry ghost (PRETA), or (4) as a long-lived divinity (DEVA); (5) in a border land or barbarian region; (6) with perverted or heretical views; (7) as stupid and unable to understand the teachings; and (8) even if one could have understood the teachings, one is born at a time when or place where no buddhas have arisen. An opportune birth (KṢAṆA), by contrast, means to be born at a time and place where a buddha or his teachings are present and where one has the intellectual faculties sufficient to benefit from them.

**Akṣayamati**. (T. Blo gros mi zad pa; C. Wujinyi pusa; J. Mujin'i bosatsu; K. Mujinŭi posal 無盡意菩薩). In Sanskrit, "Inexhaustible Intention," a bodhisattva who expounds the AKṢAYAMATINIRDEŚA. Akṣayamati is also the foil for chapter twenty-five of the SADDHARMAPUṆḌARĪKASŪTRA ("Lotus Sūtra") where the Buddha explains the efficacy of calling AVALOKITEŚVARA's name; upon hearing the Buddha's discourse, Akṣayamati is said to have given Avalokiteśvara his crystal rosary.

**Akṣayamatinirdeśa**. (T. Blo gros mi zad pas bstan pa; C. Wujinyi pusa pin/Achamo pusa jing; J. Mujin'i bosatsubon/Asamatsu bosatsukyō; K. Mujinŭi posal p'um/Ach'amal posal kyŏng 無盡意菩薩品/阿差末菩薩經). In Sanskrit, "Exposition of Akṣayamati," a MAHĀYĀNA sūtra in which the BODHISATTVA AKṢAYAMATI expounds the "inexhaustible eightyfold doctrine," the method through which a BODHISATTVA should listen to and comprehend the dharma. Four Chinese translations are extant, including the *Wujinyi pusa pin* by Zhiyan and Baoyun and the *Achamo pusa jing* by DHARMARAKṢA (C. Zhu Fahu). The sūtra also exists in a Tibetan translation by Chos nyid tshul khrims. The sūtra is particularly important as the source of the doctrine that the only definitive (NĪTĀRTHA) statements are those in which a buddha teaches emptiness (ŚŪNYATĀ) with words like unceasing, unproduced (ANUTPĀDA), and so on; all other statements require interpretation (NEYĀRTHA). See also ALAKṢAṆADHARMACAKRA, ABHIPRĀYA.

**Akṣobhya**. (T. Mi bskyod pa; C. Achu fo; J. Ashuku butsu; K. Ach'ok pul 阿閦佛). In Sanskrit, "Immovable" or "Imperturbable"; the name given to the buddha of the East because he is imperturbable in following his vow to proceed to buddhahood, particularly through mastering the practice of morality (ŚĪLA). Akṣobhya is one of the PAÑCATATHĀGATA (five tathāgatas), the buddha of the vajra family (VAJRAKULA). There are references to Akṣobhya in the PRAJÑĀPĀRAMITĀ sūtras and the SADDHARMAPUṆḌARĪKASŪTRA ("Lotus Sūtra"), suggesting that his cult dates back to the first or second century of the Common Era, and that he was popular in India and Java as well as in the Himālayan regions. The cult of Akṣobhya may have been the first to emerge after the cult of ŚĀKYAMUNI, and before that of AMITĀBHA. In the *Saddharmapuṇḍarīkasūtra*, Akṣobhya is listed as the first son of the buddha Mahābhijñā Jñānābhibhu, and his bodhisattva name is given as Jñānākara. His cult entered China during the Han dynasty, and an early text on his worship, the AKṢOBHYATATHĀGATASYAVYŪHA, was translated into Chinese during the second half of the second century. Although his cult was subsequently introduced into Japan, he never became as popular in East Asia as the buddhas AMITĀBHA or VAIROCANA, and images of Akṣobhya are largely confined to MAṆḌALAs and other depictions of the pañcatathāgata. Furthermore, because Akṣobhya's buddha-field (BUDDHAKṢETRA) or PURE LAND of ABHIRATI is located in the East, he is sometimes replaced in maṇḍalas by BHAIṢAJYAGURU, who also resides in that same direction. Akṣobhya's most common MUDRĀ is the BHŪMISPARŚAMUDRĀ, and he often holds a VAJRA. His consort is either Māmakī or Locanā.

**Akṣobhyatathāgatasyavyūha**. (T. De bzhin gshegs pa mi 'khrugs pa'i bkod pa; C. Achu foguo jing; J. Ashuku bukkokukyō; K. Ach'ok pulguk kyŏng 阿閦佛國經). In Sanskrit, "The Array of the TATHĀGATA AKṢOBHYA"; a SŪTRA in which the Buddha, at ŚĀRIPUTRA's request, teaches his eminent disciple about the buddha AKṢOBHYA; also known as the *Akṣobhyavyūha*. It was first translated into Chinese in the mid-second century CE by LOKAKṢEMA, an Indo–Scythian monk from KUSHAN, and later retranslated by the Tang-period monk BODHIRUCI in the early eighth century as part of his rendering of the RATNAKŪṬASŪTRA. The scripture also exists in a

Tibetan translation by Jinamitra, Surendrabodhi, and Ye shes sde. The text explains that in the distant past, a monk made a vow to achieve buddhahood. He followed the arduous BODHISATTVA path, engaging in myriad virtues; the text especially emphasizes his practice of morality (ŚĪLA). He eventually achieves buddhahood as the buddha Akṣobhya in a buddha-field (BUDDHAKṢETRA) located in the east called ABHIRATI, which the sūtra describes in some detail as an ideal domain for the practice of the dharma. As its name implies, Abhirati is a land of delight, the antithesis of the suffering that plagues our world, and its pleasures are the by-products of Akṣobhya's immense merit and compassion. In his land, Akṣobhya sits on a platform sheltered by a huge BODHI TREE, which is surrounded by rows of palm trees and jasmine bushes. Its soil is golden in color and as soft as cotton, and the ground is flat with no gullies or gravel. Although Abhirati, like our world, has a sun and moon, both pale next to the radiance of Akṣobhya himself. In Abhirati, the three unfortunate realms (APĀYA) of hell denizens, ghosts, and animals do not exist. Among humans, there are gender distinctions but no physical sexuality. A man who entertains sexual thoughts toward a woman would instantly see that desire transformed into a DHYĀNA that derives from the meditation on impurity (AŚUBHABHĀVANĀ), while a woman can become pregnant by a man's glance (even though women do not experience menstruation). Food and drink appear spontaneously whenever a person is hungry or thirsty. There is no illness, no ugliness, and no crime. Described as a kind of idealized monastic community, Abhirati is designed to provide the optimal environment to engage in Buddhist practice, both for those who seek to become ARHATs and for those practicing the bodhisattva path. Rebirth there is a direct result of having planted virtuous roots (KUŚALAMŪLA), engaging in wholesome actions, and then dedicating any merit deriving from those actions to one's future rebirth in that land. One is also reborn there by accepting, memorizing, and spreading this sūtra. Akṣobhya will eventually attain PARINIRVĀṆA in Abhirati through a final act of self-immolation (see SHESHEN). After his demise, his teachings will slowly disappear from the world.

**akunin shōki**. (悪人正機). In Japanese, lit. "evil people have the right capacity"; the emblematic teaching of the JŌDO SHINSHŪ teacher SHINRAN (1173–1263), which suggests that AMITĀBHA's compassion is directed primarily to evildoers. When Amitābha was still the monk named DHARMĀKARA, he made a series of forty-eight vows (PRAṆIDHĀNA) that he promised to fulfill before he became a buddha. The most important of these vows to much of the PURE LAND tradition is the eighteenth, in which he vows that all beings who call his name will be reborn in his pure land of SUKHĀVATĪ. This prospect of salvation has nothing to do with whether one is a monk or layperson, man or woman, saint or sinner, learned or ignorant. In this doctrine, Shinran goes so far as to claim that if a good man can be reborn in the pure land, so much more so can an evil man. This is because the good man remains attached to the delusion that his virtuous deeds will somehow bring about his salvation, while the evil man has abandoned this conceit and accepts that only through Amitābha's grace will rebirth in the pure land be won.

**akuśala**. (P. akusala; T. mi dge ba; C. bushan; J. fuzen; K. pulsŏn 不善). In Sanskrit, "unsalutary," "unvirtuous," "inauspicious," "unwholesome," used to describe those physical, verbal, and mental activities (often enumerated as ten) that lead to unsalutary rebirths. An "unvirtuous" or "unwholesome" action generally refers to any volition (CETANĀ) or volitional action, along with the consciousness (VIJÑĀNA) and mental constructions (SAṂSKĀRA) associated with it, that are informed by the afflictions (KLEŚA) of greed (LOBHA), hatred (DVEṢA; P. dosa), or delusion (MOHA). Such volitional actions produce unfortunate results for the actor and ultimately are the cause of the unfavorable destinies (APĀYA; DURGATI) of hell denizens (NĀRAKA), hungry ghosts (PRETA), animals (TIRYAK), and (in some descriptions) titans or demigods (ASURA). A list of ten unwholesome courses of actions (see KARMAPATHA) are listed that lead to apāya and are equivalent to the ten wrong deeds (P. duccarita) as enumerated in the Nidānavagga of the SAṂYUTTANIKĀYA. The first three on the list are classified as bodily wrong deeds: killing (prāṇātipāta; P. pāṇātipāta), stealing (adattādāna; P. adinnādāna), and sexual misconduct (KĀMAMITHYĀCĀRA; P. kāmamicchācāra). The next four in the list are classified as verbal wrong deeds: lying (mṛṣāvāda; P. musāvāda), slander or malicious speech (PAIŚUNYA; P. pisuṇavācā), offensive or rough speech (pāraṣyavāda; P. pharusavācā), and frivolous prattle (saṃbhinnapralāpa; P. samphappalāpa). The final three on the list are classified as mental wrong deeds: covetousness (ABHIDHYĀ; P. abhijjhā), ill will (VYĀPĀDA), and wrong views (MITHYĀDṚṢṬI; P. micchādiṭṭhi).

**akuśaladṛṣṭi**. (C. ejian/xiejian; J. akuken/jaken; K. akkyŏn/sagyŏn 悪見/邪見). See MITHYĀDṚṢṬI.

**akuśalakarmapatha**. In Sanskrit, the ten "unwholesome courses of action." See KARMAPATHA.

**akuśalamahābhūmika**. (T. mi dge ba'i sa mang chen po; C. da bushandi fa; J. daifuzenjihō; K. tae pulsŏnji pŏp 大不善地法). In Sanskrit, "omnipresent unwholesome factors" or "unwholesome factors of wide extent"; the principal factors (DHARMA) that ground all unwholesome actions (AKUŚALA). In the SARVĀSTIVĀDA ABHIDHARMA system, two specific forces associated with mentality (CITTASAṂPRAYUKTASAṂSKĀRA) are identified as accompanying all unwholesome activities and are therefore described as "unwholesome factors of wide extent." The two dharmas are "lack of a sense of decency" (āhrīkya; cf. HRĪ, "sense of decency") and "lack of modesty" (anapatrāpya; cf. APATRĀPYA, "modesty").

**akuśalamūla**. (P. akusalamūla; T. mi dge ba'i rtsa ba; C. bushangen; J. fuzenkon; K. pulsŏn'gŭn 不善根). In Sanskrit, "unwholesome faculties," or "roots of evil"; these refer to the cumulative unwholesome actions performed by an individual throughout one's past lives, which lead that being toward the baleful destinies (DURGATI) of animals, hungry ghosts, and the denizens of hell. The Buddhist tradition offers various lists of these unwholesome faculties, the most common of which is threefold: craving or greed (LOBHA), aversion or hatred (DVEṢA), and delusion (MOHA). These same three are also known in the sūtra literature as the "three poisons" (TRIVIṢA). These three factors thus will fructify as unhappiness in the future and provide the foundation for unfavorable destinies or rebirths (APĀYA). These three unwholesome roots are the converse of the three wholesome faculties, or "roots of virtue" (KUŚALAMŪLA), viz., nongreed (alobha), nonhatred (adveṣa), and nondelusion (amoha), which lead instead to happiness or liberation (VIMOKṢA). See also SAMUCCHINNAKUŚALAMŪLA.

**Akutobhayā**. (T. Ga las 'jigs med). In Sanskrit, "Fearless," the abbreviated title of the *Mūlamadhyamakavṛtti-akutobhayā*, a commentary on NĀGĀRJUNA's MŪLAMADHYAMAKAKĀRIKĀ. In Tibet, the work has traditionally been attributed to Nāgārjuna himself, but scholars doubt that he is the author of this commentary on his own work, in part because the commentary cites the CATUḤŚATAKA of ĀRYADEVA, who was Nāgārjuna's disciple. In places, the work is identical to the commentary of BUDDHAPĀLITA. Regardless of the authorship, the work is an important commentary on Nāgārjuna's most famous work. In China, the commentary of Qingmu (*Piṅgala?), an influential work in the SAN LUN ZONG, is closely related to the *Akutobhayā*.

**Alagaddūpamasutta**. (C. Alizha jing; J. Aritakyō; K. Arit'a kyŏng 阿梨吒經). In Pāli, "Discourse on the Simile of the Snake," the twenty-second sutta of the MAJJHIMANIKĀYA (a separate Sarvāstivāda recension appears as the 200th sūtra in the Chinese translation of the MADHYAMĀGAMA, and the similes of the snake and of the raft are the subjects of independent sūtras in an unidentified recension in the EKOTTARĀGAMA). The discourse was preached by the Buddha at Sāvatthi (ŚRĀVASTĪ), in response to the wrong view (MITHYĀDṚṢṬI) of the monk Ariṭṭha. Ariṭṭha maintained that the Buddha taught that one could enjoy sensual pleasures without obstructing one's progress along the path to liberation, and remained recalcitrant even after the Buddha admonished him. The Buddha then spoke to the assembly of monks on the wrong way and the right way of learning the dharma. In his discourse, he uses several similes to enhance his audience's understanding, including the eponymous "simile of the snake": just as one could be bitten and die by grasping a poisonous snake by the tail instead of the head, so too will using the dharma merely for disputation or polemics lead to one's peril because of one's wrong grasp of the dharma. This sutta also contains the famous "simile of the raft," where the Buddha compares his dispensation or teaching (ŚĀSANA) to a makeshift raft that will help one get across a raging river to the opposite shore: after one has successfully crossed that river by paddling furiously and reached solid ground, it would be inappropriate to put the raft on one's head and carry it; similarly, once one has used the dharma to get across the "raging river" of birth and death (SAṂSĀRA) to the "other shore" of NIRVĀṆA, the teachings have served their purpose and should not be clung to.

**alakṣaṇadharmacakra**. (T. mtshan nyid med pa'i chos 'khor; C. wuxiang falun; J. musō hōrin; K. musang pŏmnyun 無相法輪). In Sanskrit, lit. "the dharma wheel of signlessness"; the second of the three turnings of the wheel of the dharma (DHARMACAKRAPRAVARTANA) described in the SAṂDHINIRMOCANASŪTRA. The sūtra, an important source for YOGĀCĀRA doctrine, explains that the Buddha turned the wheel of the dharma three times. According to the commentators on the sūtra, in the first turning of the wheel, called "the dharma wheel of the four noble truths" (CATUḤSATYADHARMACAKRA), the Buddha taught that dharmas exist in reality. This wheel is described as provisional (NEYĀRTHA). The second turning of the wheel, delivered on Vulture's Peak (GṚDHRAKŪṬAPARVATA) near RĀJAGṚHA, is called "the dharma wheel of signlessness" (alakṣaṇadharmacakra). Here, the Buddha taught that no dharmas exist. The sūtra also identifies this wheel as a provisional teaching (NEYĀRTHA). The third turning of the wheel is described as "well-differentiated" (suvibhakta), with the Buddha explaining that some dharmas exist and some do not. This wheel is described as definitive (NĪTĀRTHA). The description of the third wheel is an important scriptural source for the Yogācāra doctrine of the three natures (TRISVABHĀVA). Commentators identify this second turning of the wheel, the alakṣaṇadharmacakra, with the Mahāyāna doctrine set forth in the PRAJÑĀPĀRAMITĀSŪTRAS (perfection of wisdom sūtras) that all dharmas, even buddhahood and NIRVĀṆA, are without any intrinsic nature (NIḤSVABHĀVA). In Tibet, the schools of interpretation of the sūtra divided evenly into two camps: some (like TSONG KHA PA) assert that the *Saṃdhinirmocanasūtra*'s second turning of the wheel is the definitive teaching of the Buddha and that the third turning is an inferior YOGĀCĀRA teaching;, others (like DOL PO PA) assert that the third turning of the wheel is a definitive teaching and the second turning of the wheel is provisional. See also *SUVIBHAKTADHARMACAKRA.

**ālambana**. (P. ārammaṇa; T. dmigs pa; C. suoyuan; J. shoen; K. soyŏn 所緣). In Sanskrit, "objective support," "sense object," or "object of cognition"; in epistemology, the object of any one of the six sensory consciousnesses (VIJÑĀNA), i.e., visual, auditory, olfactory, gustatory, tactile, and mental objects. In the mainstream traditions, these objects were considered to be the external constituent in the cognitive relationship between subject and object, whereby the contact (SPARŚA) between, e.g., an olfactory sensory object (e.g., gandha) and the olfactory sense base (GHRAṆENDRIYA) produces a corresponding olfactory consciousness (GHRAṆAVIJÑĀNA). Sense objects thus correspond to the six external "sense-fields" or "spheres of perception" (ĀYATANA) and the six external "elements" (DHĀTU). The term ālambana is also used in instructions on meditation to describe the object upon which the meditator is to focus the mind. See also ĀLAMBANAPRATYAYA.

**Ālambanaparīkṣā**. (T. Dmigs pa brtag pa; C. Guan suoyuan yuan lun; J. Kanshoen nenron; K. Kwan soyŏn yŏn non 觀所緣緣論). In Sanskrit, "An Analysis of the Objects of Cognition," a text on YOGĀCĀRA epistemology by the early fifth-century Indian logician DIGNĀGA, which examines the objective support (ĀLAMBANA) of cognition. Dignāga argues that cognition cannot take for its object anything from the external world; instead, the object of cognition is actually the form of an object that appears within cognition itself. While the original Sanskrit is lost, the text is preserved in both Tibetan and Chinese translations. Dignāga also composed a commentary to this work, the *Ālambanaparīkṣāvṛtti*, as did Vinītadeva (c. eighth century), the *Ālambanaparīkṣāṭikā*.

**ālambanapratyaya**. (P. ārammaṇapaccaya; T. dmigs rkyen; C. suoyuan yuan; J. shoennen; K. soyŏn yŏn 所緣緣). In Sanskrit, "objective-support condition" or "observed-object condition," the third of the four types of conditions (PRATYAYA) recognized in both the VAIBHĀṢIKA ABHIDHARMA system of the SARVĀSTIVĀDA school and the YOGĀCĀRA school; the term also appears as the second of the twenty-four conditions (P. paccaya) in the massive Pāli abhidhamma text, the PAṬṬHĀNA. This condition refers to the role the corresponding sensory object (ĀLAMBANA) takes in the arising of any of the six sensory consciousnesses (VIJÑĀNA) and is one of the three causal conditions necessary for cognition to occur. Sensory consciousness thus cannot occur without the presence of a corresponding sensory object, whether that be visual, auditory, olfactory, gustatory, tactile, or mental.

**Alaungpaya**. Burmese king (r. 1752–1760) and founder of the Konbaung dynasty (1752–1885), the last Burmese royal house before the British conquest. He was born the son of the village headman of Mokesoebo in Upper Burma in 1711. Originally named Aungzeyya, he succeeded his father as headman and early on showed charismatic signs of leadership. By this time, the then Burmese empire of Taungoo, which had been founded in 1531, was on the verge of collapse. The Mon of Lower Burma, whose capital was Pegu, rebelled and soon swept northward, eventually capturing the Burmese capital, AVA, and executing its king. When emissaries from the Mon king, Binnya-dala, demanded the allegiance of Mokesoebo, Aungzeyya beheaded them and organized a rebellion to restore Burmese sovereignty. Gathering around him a loyal cohort of local chiefs and soldiers from Ava, he crowned himself king and established Mokesoebo as his first capital, which he renamed Shwebo. A brilliant tactician and masterful propagandist, he assumed the title Alaungpaya, meaning "Future Buddha," and waged war on the Mon as a BODHISATTVA intent on restoring the purity of the Buddha's religion and ushering in a golden age. In 1753, he recaptured Ava and subdued the Shan chieftains on his northern flank. In 1755, he captured the strategic port town of Dagon, which he renamed Yangon (Rangoon), meaning "End of Strife." In 1757, after a protracted siege, he destroyed Pegu, the last stronghold of Mon resistance, executing its king, Binnya-dala, and massacring its population. After consolidating Burmese control over the central provinces, Alaungpaya marched his armies against the Hindu kingdom of Manipur, which had taken advantage of the civil war to pillage Burma's western territories. Having vanquished Manipur, in 1760, he moved against the Thai kingdom of AYUTHAYA in the east in retaliation for fomenting anti-Burmese rebellions along the border. The Burmese seized Moulmein, Tavoy, and Tenasserim, but Alaungpaya was mortally wounded during the siege of Ayuthaya and died during the subsequent Burmese retreat. The empire created by Alaungpaya expanded under his sons and their descendants, eventually bringing it into conflict with the British East India Company.

**Ālavaka**. Name of a man-eating ogre (P. yakkha; S. YAKṢA) whose conversion by the Buddha is described in Pāli materials. Ālavaka dwelt in a tree near the town Ālavi and had been granted a boon by the king of the yakkhas that allowed him to eat anyone who came into the shadow of his tree. Even the sight of the ogre rendered the bodies of men as soft as butter. His tree was surrounded by a stout wall and covered with a metal net. Above it lay the sky passage to the Himālaya mountains traversed by those who possessed supernatural powers. Ascetics seeing the strange abode would descend out of curiosity, whereupon Ālavaka would ask them knotty questions about their beliefs. When they could not answer, he would penetrate their hearts with his mind and drive them mad. Ālavaka is most famous for the promise he extorted from the king of Ālavi, whom he captured while the monarch was on a hunting expedition. In order to save his life, the king promised to supply the ogre regularly with a human victim. The king first delivered convicted criminals for sacrifice, but when there were no more, he ordered each family to supply one child at the appointed time. Pregnant women fearing for their unborn infants fled the city, until after twelve years, only one child, the king's own son, remained. The child was duly made ready and sent to the ogre. The Buddha knew of the impending event and went to the ogre's abode to intervene. While Ālavaka was absent, the Buddha sat upon the ogre's throne and preached to his harem. Informed of the Buddha's brazenness, Ālavaka returned and attacked the Buddha with his superpowers to remove him from the throne, but to no avail. The Buddha only left when politely asked to do so. Still unwilling to admit defeat, the ogre invited the Buddha to answer questions put to him. So skillfully did the Buddha answer that Ālavaka shouted for joy and then and there became a stream-enterer (SROTAĀPANNA; P. sotāpanna). When the king's entourage delivered the young prince for sacrifice, Ālavaka, ashamed of his past deeds, surrendered the boy to the Buddha, who in turn handed him back to the king's men. Because he was handed from one to another, the boy was known as Hatthaka (Little Hand, or Handful) and in adulthood became one of the chief lay patrons of the Buddha. When the populace heard of the ogre's conversion, they were overjoyed and built a shrine for him, where they offered flowers and perfumes daily. Ālavaka is named in the *Aṭānāṭiyasutta* as one of several yakṣas who may be entreated for protection against dangers.

**ālayavijñāna**. (T. kun gzhi rnam par shes pa; C. alaiyeshi/zangshi; J. arayashiki/zōshiki; K. aroeyasik/changsik 阿賴耶識/藏識). In Sanskrit, "storehouse consciousness" or "foundational consciousness"; the eighth of the eight types of consciousness (VIJÑĀNA) posited in the YOGĀCĀRA school. All forms of Buddhist thought must be able to uphold (1) the principle of the cause and effect of actions (KARMAN), the structure of SAṂSĀRA, and the process of liberation (VIMOKṢA) from it, while also upholding (2) the fundamental doctrines of impermanence (ANITYA) and the lack of a perduring self (ANĀTMAN). The most famous and comprehensive solution to the range of problems created by these apparently contradictory elements is the ālayavijñāna, often translated as the "storehouse consciousness." This doctrinal concept derives in India from the YOGĀCĀRA school, especially from ASAṄGA and VASUBANDHU and their commentators. Whereas other schools of Buddhist thought posit six consciousnesses (vijñāna), in the Yogācāra system there are eight, adding the afflicted mind (KLIṢṬAMANAS) and the ālayavijñāna. It appears that once the Sarvāstivāda's school's eponymous doctrine of the existence of dharmas in the past, present, and future was rejected by most other schools of Buddhism, some doctrinal solution was required to provide continuity between past and future, including past and future lifetimes. The alāyavijñāna provides that solution as a foundational form of consciousness, itself ethically neutral, where all the seeds (BIJA) of all deeds done in the past reside, and from which they fructify in the form of experience. Thus, the ālayavijñāna is said to pervade the entire body during life, to withdraw from the body at the time of death (with the extremities becoming cold as it slowly exits), and to carry the complete karmic record to the next rebirth destiny. Among the many doctrinal problems that the presence of the ālayavijñāna is meant to solve, it appears that one of its earliest references is in the context not of rebirth but in that of the NIRODHASAMĀPATTI, or "trance of cessation," where all conscious activity, that is, all CITTA and CAITTA, cease. Although the meditator may appear as if dead during that trance, consciousness is able to be reactivated because the ālayavijñāna remains present throughout, with the seeds of future experience lying dormant in it, available to bear fruit when the person arises from meditation. The ālayavijñāna thus provides continuity from moment to moment within a given lifetime and from lifetime to lifetime, all providing the link between an action performed in the past and its effect experienced in the present, despite protracted periods of latency between seed and fruition. In Yogācāra, where the existence of an external world is denied, when a seed bears fruit, it bifurcates into an observing subject and an observed object, with that object falsely imagined to exist separately from the consciousness that perceives it. The response by the subject to that object produces more seeds, either positive, negative, or neutral, which are deposited in the ālayavijñāna, remaining there until they in turn bear their fruit. Although said to be neutral and a kind of silent observer of experience, the ālayavijñāna is thus also the recipient of karmic seeds as they are produced, receiving impressions (VĀSANĀ) from them. In the context of Buddhist soteriological discussions, the ālayavijñāna explains why contaminants (ĀSRAVA) remain even when unwholesome states of mind are not actively present, and it provides the basis for the mistaken belief in self (ātman). Indeed, it is said that the kliṣṭamanas perceives the ālayavijñāna as a perduring self. The ālayavijñāna also explains how progress on the path can continue over several lifetimes and why some follow the path of the ŚRĀVAKA and others the path of the BODHISATTVA; it is said that one's lineage (GOTRA) is in fact a seed that resides permanently in the ālayavijñāna. In India, the doctrine of the ālayavijñāna was controversial, with some members of the Yogācāra school rejecting its existence, arguing that the functions it is meant to serve can be accommodated within the standard six-consciousness system. The MADHYAMAKA, notably figures such as BHĀVAVIVEKA and CANDRAKĪRTI, attacked the Yogācāra proponents of the ālayavijñāna, describing it as a form of self, which all Buddhists must reject. ¶ In East Asia, the ālayavijñāna was conceived as one possible solution to persistent questions in Buddhism about karmic continuity and about the origin of ignorance (MOHA). For the latter, some explanation was required as to how sentient beings, whom many strands of MAHĀYĀNA claimed were inherently enlightened, began to presume themselves to be ignorant. Debates raged within different strands of the Chinese Yogācāra traditions as to whether the ālayavijñāna is intrinsically impure because of the presence of these seeds of past experience (the position of the Northern branch of the Chinese DI LUN ZONG and the Chinese FAXIANG tradition of XUANZANG and KUIJI), or whether the ālayavijñāna included both pure and impure elements because it involved also the functioning of thusness, or TATHATĀ (the Southern Di lun school's position). Since the sentient being has had a veritable interminable period of time in which to collect an infinity of seeds—which would essentially make it impossible to hope to counteract them one by one—the mainstream strands of Yogācāra viewed the mind as nevertheless tending inveterately toward impurity (dauṣṭhulya). This impurity could only be overcome through a "transformation of the basis" (ĀŚRAYAPARĀVṚTTI), which would completely eradicate the karmic seeds stored in the storehouse consciousness, liberating the bodhisattva from the effects of all past actions and freeing him to project compassion liberally throughout the world. In some later interpretations, this transformation would then convert the ālayavijñāna into a ninth "immaculate consciousness" (AMALAVIJÑĀNA). See also DASHENG QIXIN LUN.

**Alchi**. The name, possibly of early Dardic origin, of a monastic complex located approximately twenty miles northwest of Leh, in the Ladakh region of the northwestern Indian state of Kashmir. The complex is renowned for its exceptional collection of early Tibetan Buddhist painting and statuary. Local legend ascribes Alchi's foundation to the great eleventh-century translator RIN CHEN BZANG PO. While the monastery's early history is obscure, inscriptions within the complex attribute its foundation to Skal ldan shes rab (Kalden Sherap) and Tshul khrims 'od (Tsultrim Ö), active sometime between the eleventh and twelfth centuries. The complex of Alchi, called the chos 'khor ("dharma enclave"), comprises five main buildings: (1) the 'dus khang ("assembly hall"); (2) the lo tsā ba'i lha khang ("translator's temple"); (3) the 'Jam dpal lha khang ("Mañjuśrī temple"); (4) the gsum brtsegs ("three-storied [temple]"); and (5) the lha khang so ma ("new temple"). While the 'dus khang stands as the earliest and largest structure, the gsum brtsegs is perhaps most famous for its three-storied stucco statues of AVALOKITEŚVARA, MAITREYA, and MAÑJUŚRĪ, each painted in elaborate detail. The temple also contains extraordinary murals painted by western Tibetan and Kashmiri artisans.

**ālīḍha**. (T. g.yas brkyang ba). A Sanskrit term used to describe the Buddhist iconographic posture (ĀSANA) in which the figure holds one leg bent forward at the knee with the other leg stretched out in the opposite direction. While the term generally refers to standing postures, it may also apply to seated poses and is distinguished from PRATYĀLĪḌHA, where the leg positions are reversed. Sources vary in describing which leg is outstretched and which leg is bent. In Tibetan tantric art, the ālīḍha posture is often found in deities of the MOTHER TANTRA class. See also ĀSANA.

**ālikāli**. (T. ā li kā li). The letters of the Sanskrit alphabet (A being the first in the list of vowels and ka the first in the list of consonants), often recited or visualized in tantric practice. See also ARAPACANA; AJIKAN.

**alms bowl**. See PĀTRA.

**alms round**. See PIṆḌAPĀTA.

**alobha**. (T. ma chags pa; C. wutan; J. muton; K. mut'am 無貪). In Sanskrit and Pāli, "absence of craving" or "absence of greed"; one of the most ubiquitous of moral virtues (KUŚALA), which serves as an antidote to the KLEŚA of desire and as the foundation for progress on the path. Alobha is one of the forty-six mental factors (CAITTA) according to the SARVĀSTIVĀDA school and the ABHIDHARMAKOŚABHĀṢYA, one of the fifty-one according to the YOGĀCĀRA school, and one of the fifty-one of the Pāli abhidhamma. "Absence of craving" is the opposite of "craving" or "greed" (LOBHA). The Sarvāstivāda ABHIDHARMA system posited that this mental quality accompanied all wholesome activities, and therefore lists it as the seventh of the ten major omnipresent wholesome factors (KUŚALAMAHĀBHŪMIKA). Absence of craving is listed as one of the so-called three roots of virtue (KUŚALAMŪLA), one of the states of mind comprising right intention (SAMYAKSAṂKALPA) in the noble eightfold path (ĀRYĀṢṬĀṄGAMĀRGA), and is traditionally taken to be the precondition for the cultivation of equanimity (UPEKṢĀ).

**Āloka lena**. A cave near modern Matale in Sri Lanka where, during the last quarter of the first century BCE, during the reign of King VAṬṬAGĀMAṆI ABHAYA, the Pāli tipiṭaka (TRIPIṬAKA) and its commentaries (AṬṬHAKATHĀ) were said to have been written down for the first time. The DĪPAVAṂSA and MAHĀVAṂSA state that a gathering of ARHATs had decided to commit the texts to writing out of fear that they could no longer be reliably memorized and passed down from one generation to the next. They convened a gathering of five hundred monks for the purpose, the cost of which was borne by a local chieftain. The subcommentary by Vajirabuddhi and the *Sāratthadīpanī* (c. twelfth century CE) deem that the writing down of the tipiṭaka occurred at the fourth Buddhist council (see COUNCIL, FOURTH), and so it has been generally recognized ever since throughout the THERAVĀDA world. However, the fourteenth-century SADDHAMMASAṄGAHA, written at the Thai capital of AYUTHAYA, deems this to be the fifth Buddhist council (see COUNCIL, FIFTH), the fourth council being instead the recitation of VINAYA by Mahā Ariṭṭha carried out during the reign of King DEVĀNAṂPIYATISSA.

**ālokasyopalabdhiśa**. (T. nye bar thob pa'i snang ba). In Sanskrit "appearance of near-attainment," the penultimate stage in the final three stages of the dissolution of consciousness that culminates in the dawning of "clear light" (PRABHĀSVARA), the actual moment of death according to certain systems of ANUTTARAYOGATANTRA. After the gross elements and states of consciousness dissolve, a process that is accompanied by a series of signs, the subtler levels of consciousness appear: first an experience of radiant whiteness called appearance (āloka) like a night sky filled with moonlight, then an experience of redness, called increase (vṛddhi) like a clear sky filled with sunlight, and finally an experience called "near attainment" (upalabdha) like a black moonless sky, so called because it is the state nearest to the most subtle level of consciousness, the mind of clear light.

**Altan Khan**. (1507–1583). A ruler descending from the lineage of Genghis Khan who became the leader of the Tümed Mongols in 1543. In 1578, he hosted BSOD NAMS RGYA MTSHO, a renowned Tibetan lama of the DGE LUGS sect, bestowing on the prelate the appellation "DALAI LAMA" by translating part of his name, rgya mtsho ("ocean"), into the Mongolian word dalai. Bsod nams rgya mtsho was deemed the third Dalai Lama, with the title applied posthumously to his two predecessors. The Dge lugs gained influence under Tümed Mongol patronage, and, following the death of Bsod nams rgya mtsho, the grandson of Altan Khan's successor was recognized as the fourth Dalai Lama. See also DALAI LAMA.

**amalavijñāna**. (T. dri ma med pa'i rnam shes; C. amoluo shi/wugou shi; J. amarashiki/mukushiki; K. amara sik/mugu sik 阿摩羅識/無垢識). In Sanskrit, "immaculate consciousness"; a ninth level of consciousness posited in certain strands of the YOGĀCĀRA school, especially that taught by the Indian translator and exegete PARAMĀRTHA. The amalavijñāna represents the intrusion of TATHĀGATAGARBHA (womb or embryo of buddhahood) thought into the eight-consciousnesses theory of the YOGĀCĀRA school. The amalavijñāna may have antecedents in the notion of immaculate gnosis (amalajñāna) in the RATNAGOTRAVIBHĀGA and is claimed to be first mentioned in STHIRAMATI's school of Yogācāra, to which Paramārtha belonged. The term is not attested in Sanskrit materials, however, and may be of Chinese provenance. The most sustained treatment of the concept appears in the SHE LUN ZONG, an exegetical tradition of Chinese Buddhism built around Paramārtha's translation of ASAṄGA's MAHĀYĀNASAMGRAHA (*She Dasheng lun*). Paramārtha compares amalavijñāna to the perfected nature (PARINIṢPANNA) of consciousness, thus equating amalavijñāna with the absolute reality of thusness (TATHATĀ) and therefore rendering it the essence of all dharmas and the primary catalyst to enlightenment. As "immaculate," the amalavijñāna emulates the emphasis in tathāgatagarbha thought on the inherent purity of the mind; but as "consciousness," amalavijñāna could also be sited within the Yogācāra philosophy of mind as a separate ninth level of consciousness, now construed as the basis of all the other consciousnesses, including the eighth ĀLAYAVIJÑĀNA. See also BUDDHADHĀTU; FOXING.

**Amarapura**. The "Immortal City"; Burmese royal capital during the Konbaung period (1752–1885), built by King Bodawpaya (r. 1782–1819). Amarapura was one of five Burmese capitals established in Upper Burma (Myanmar) after the fall of Pagan between the fourteenth and nineteenth centuries, the others being Pinya, SAGAING, AVA (Inwa), and Mandalay. Located five miles north of the old capital of Ava (Inwa) and seven miles south of Mandalay on the southern bank of the Irrawaddy river, it served as the capital of the Burmese kingdom twice: from 1783 to 1823 and again from 1837 to 1857. The city was mapped out in the form of a perfect square, its perimeter surrounded by stout brick walls and further protected by a wide moat. The city walls were punctuated by twelve gates, three on each side, every gate crowned with a tiered wooden pavilion (B. pyatthat). Broad avenues laid out in a grid pattern led to the center of the city where stood the royal palace and ancillary buildings, all constructed of teak and raised above the ground on massive wooden pylons. Located to the north of the city was a shrine housing the colossal MAHĀMUNI image of the Buddha (see ARAKAN BUDDHA), which was acquired by the Burmese as war booty in 1784 when King Bodawpaya conquered the neighboring Buddhist kingdom of Arakan. Since its relocation at the shrine, the seated image has been covered with so many layers of gold leaf that its torso is now completely obscured, leaving only the head and face visible. In 1816, Bodawpaya erected the monumental Pahtodawgyi pagoda, modeled after the Shwezigon pagoda at Pagan. Its lower terraces are adorned with carved marble plaques depicting episodes from the JĀTAKAS. Another major shrine is the Kyauktawgyi pagoda, located to the southeast of the city on the opposite shore of Taungthaman lake. Kyauktawgyi pagoda is reached via the U Bein Bridge, a 3,000-foot- (1,200-meter) long bridge spanning the lake, which was constructed from teakwood salvaged from the royal palace at the vanquished capital of Ava. Amarapura was site of the THUDHAMMA (P. Sudhamma) reformation begun in 1782 under the patronage of Bodawpaya, which for a time unified the Burmese saṅgha under a single leadership and gave rise to the modern Thudhamma Nikāya, contemporary Burma's largest monastic fraternity. The Thudhamma council that Bodawpaya organized was directed to reform the Burmese saṅgha throughout the kingdom and bring it under Thudhamma administrative control. In 1800, the president of the council conferred higher ordination (UPASAṂPADĀ) on a delegation of five low-caste Sinhalese ordinands who returned to Sri Lanka in 1803 and established a branch of the reformed Burmese order on the island; that fraternity was known as the AMARAPURA NIKĀYA and was dedicated to opening higher ordination to all without caste distinction. In 1857, when the royal residence was shifted from Amarapura to nearby Mandalay, the city walls and palace compound of Amarapura were disassembled and used as building material for the new capital. Today, Amarapura is home to modern Burma's most famous monastic college, Mahagandayon Kyaung Taik, built during the British period and belonging to the Shwegyin Nikāya.

**Amarapura Nikāya**. One of three major monastic fraternities (NIKĀYA) within the modern Sinhalese THERAVĀDA saṅgha (S. SAṂGHA), the others being the majority SIYAM NIKĀYA and the RĀMAÑÑA NIKĀYA. The Amarapura Nikāya was founded in the early nineteenth century in opposition to the Siyam Nikāya's policy of restricting higher ordination (UPASAṂPADĀ) to the highest Goyigama caste. The Goyigama was concentrated in the interior highlands of Sri Lanka, which were governed by the Kandyan king. The lower castes—comprised of toddy tappers and cinnamon pickers, who formed the majority population in the British controlled coastal lowlands—were at most given lower ordination (PRAVRAJYĀ) as novices (ŚRĀMAṆERA). In protest, five low-caste Sinhalese novices journeyed to the Burmese capital of Amarapura in 1800 to receive higher ordination from the Burmese patriarch, Ñāṇabhivaṃsa. In 1803, they were ordained as monks (BHIKṢU) and, together with three Burmese elders (P. thera), returned to Sri Lanka to establish the reformist Amarapura Nikāya. The Amarapura Nikāya takes as its charter the KALYĀṆĪ INSCRIPTIONS of the Mon king Dhammazedi erected at Pegu in 1479, a recension of which it preserves in its monasteries as the *Kalyāṇipakaraṇa*. Following its establishment, the Amarapura Nikāya itself divided along caste lines into numerous subgroups, each group maintaining its own lineage of teachers that are traced back to the original founders of the Amarapura Nikāya. Continued sectarianism, along with doctrinal disagreements over the role of meditation, led to the formation of another reformist monastic order with Burmese roots, the Rāmañña Nikāya, in 1862.

**Amarāvatī**. (T. 'Chi med ldan). In Sanskrit, "Immortal"; is the modern name for Dhānyakaṭaka or Dharaṇikoṭa, the site of a monastic community associated with the MAHĀSĀṂGHIKA school, located in eastern Andhra Pradesh. The site is best known for its large main STŪPA, started at the time of AŚOKA (third century BCE), which, by the second century CE, was the largest monument in India. It is thought to have been some 140 feet in diameter and upwards of 100 feet tall, and decorated with bas-reliefs. The stūpa is mentioned in numerous accounts, including that by the Chinese pilgrim XUANZANG. Amarāvatī (as Dhānyakaṭaka) reached its historical zenith as the southern capital of the later Sātavāhana [alt. Śātavāhana] dynasty that ended in 227 CE. The last inscription found at the site is dated to the eleventh century, and when first excavated at the end of the eighteenth century by the British, the stūpa had long been reduced to a large mound of earth. Over the following centuries, it has been the focus of repeated archaeological excavations that yielded many important finds, making it one of the best researched Buddhist sites of ancient India. The site is important in Tibetan Buddhism because the Buddha is said to have taught the KĀLACAKRATANTRA at Dhānyakaṭaka. See also NĀGĀRJUNAKOṆḌĀ.

**Ambedkar, Bhimrao Ramji**. (1891–1956). Indian reformer and Buddhist convert, who advocated for reform of the caste system and improvements in the social treatment of "untouchables" or the Dalit community during the independence period. The fourteenth child of a Dalit caste family in the Indian state of Maharashtra, Ambedkar was one of the few members of his caste to receive a secondary-school education and went on to study in New York and London, eventually receiving a doctorate from Columbia University. Upon his return to India, he worked both for Indian independence from Britain and for the social and political rights of the untouchables. After independence, he served in Nehru's government, chairing the committee that drafted the constitution. Seeking a religious identity for Dalits that would free them from the caste prejudice of Hinduism, he settled on Buddhism after considering also Islam, Christianity, and Sikhism. Buddhism had been extinct in India for centuries, but Ambedkar's research led him to conclude that the Dalits were descendants of Buddhists who had been persecuted by Hindus for their beliefs. In 1956, six weeks before his death, Ambedkar publicly converted to Buddhism and then led an audience of 380,000 in taking refuge in the three jewels (RATNATRAYA) and in accepting the five precepts (PAÑCAŚĪLA) of lay Buddhists. Eventually, millions of other Indians, mostly from low-caste and outcaste groups, followed his example. In his writings, Ambedkar portrayed the Buddha as a social reformer, whose teachings could provide India with the foundation for a more egalitarian society.

**Amida**. Japanese pronunciation of the Sinographic transcripton of the name AMITĀBHA, the buddha who is the primary focus of worship in the PURE LAND traditions of Japan. See JŌDOSHŪ; JŌDO SHINSHŪ.

**āmiṣadāna**. (P. āmisadāna; T. zang zing gi sbyin pa; C. caishi; J. zaise; K. chaesi 財施). In Sanskrit, "the gift of material goods"; one of the two (or sometimes three) forms of giving (DĀNA) praised in the sūtras. The Sanskrit term āmiṣa connotes the venal world of the flesh—i.e., material goods, physical pleasures, and sensual enjoyment—as contrasted to the spiritual world of the dharma. Therefore, giving material goods, while certainly a salutary and meritorious act, is thought to be inferior to the "gift of dharma" (DHARMADĀNA), which is believed to bring greater merit (PUṆYA). Sometimes, a third form of giving, the "gift of fearlessness" (ABHAYADĀNA), viz., helping others to overcome their fear, is added to the list. The gift of material goods typically takes the form of laypeople providing material or monetary support to religious renunciants or institutions, or to the needy and indigent. See also WUJINZANG YUAN.

**Amitābha**. (T. 'Od dpag med/Snang ba mtha' yas; C. Amituo fo/Wuliangguang fo; J. Amida butsu/Muryōkō butsu; K. Amit'a pul/Muryanggwang pul 阿彌陀佛/無量光佛). In Sanskrit, "Limitless Light," the buddha of the western PURE LAND of SUKHĀVATĪ, one of the most widely worshipped buddhas in the MAHĀYĀNA traditions. As recounted in the longer SUKHĀVATĪVYŪHASŪTRA, numerous eons ago, a monk named DHARMĀKARA vowed before the buddha LOKEŚVARARĀJA to follow the BODHISATTVA path to buddhahood, asking him to set forth the qualities of buddha-fields (BUDDHAKṢETRA). Dharmākara then spent five KALPAS in meditation, concentrating all of the qualities of all buddha-fields into a single buddha field that he would create upon his enlightenment. He then reappeared before Lokeśvararāja and made forty-eight specific vows (PRAṆIDHĀNA). Among the most famous were his vow that those who, for as few as ten times over the course of their life, resolved to be reborn in his buddha-field would be reborn there; and his vow that he would appear at the deathbed of anyone who heard his name and remembered it with trust. Dharmakāra then completed the bodhisattva path, thus fulfilling all the vows he had made, and became the buddha Amitābha in the buddha-field called sukhāvatī. Based on the larger and shorter versions of the *Sukhāvatīvyūhasūtra* as well as the apocryphal GUAN WULIANGSHOU JING (**Amitāyurdhyānasūtra*), rebirth in Amitābha's buddha-field became the goal of widespread Buddhist practice in India, East Asia, and Tibet, with the phrase "Homage to Amitābha Buddha" (C. namo Amituo fo; J. NAMU AMIDABUTSU; K. namu Amit'a pul) being a central element of East Asian Buddhist practice. Amitābha's Indian origins are obscure, and it has been suggested that his antecedents lie in Persian Zoroastrianism, where symbolism of light and darkness abounds. His worship dates back at least as far as the early centuries of the Common Era, as attested by the fact that the initial Chinese translation of the *Sukhāvatīvyūhasūtra* is made in the mid-second century CE, and he is listed in the SADDHARMAPUṆḌARĪKASŪTRA ("Lotus Sūtra") as the ninth son of the buddha Mahābhijñā Jñānābhibhu. The Chinese pilgrims FAXIAN and XUANZANG make no mention of him by name in their accounts of their travels to India in the fifth and seventh centuries CE, respectively, though they do include descriptions of deities who seem certain to have been Amitābha. Scriptures relating to Amitābha reached Japan in the seventh century, but he did not become a popular religious figure until some three hundred years later, when his worship played a major role in finally transforming what had been previously seen as an elite and foreign tradition into a populist religion. In East Asia, the cult of Amitābha eventually became so widespread that it transcended sectarian distinction, and Amitābha became the most popular buddha in the region. In Tibet, Amitābha worship dates to the early propagation of Buddhism in that country in the eighth century, although it never became as prevalent as in East Asia. In the sixteenth century, the fifth DALAI LAMA gave the title PAṆ CHEN LAMA to his teacher, BLO BZANG CHOS KYI RGYAL MTSHAN, and declared him to be an incarnation of Amitābha (the Dalai Lama himself having been declared the incarnation of Avalokiteśvara, Amitābha's emanation). ¶ The names "Amitābha" and "Amitāyus" are often interchangeable, both deriving from the Sanskrit word "amita," meaning "limitless," "boundless," or "infinite"; there are some intimations that Amita may actually have been the original name of this buddha, as evidenced, for example, by the fact that the Chinese transcription Amituo [alt. Emituo] transcribes the root word amita, not the two longer forms of the name. The distinction between the two names is preserved in the Chinese translations "Wuliangguang" ("Infinite Light") for Amitābha and Wuliangshou ("Infinite Life") for Amitāyus, neither of which is used as often as the transcription Amituo. Both Amitābha and Amitāyus serve as epithets of the same buddha in the longer *Sukhāvatīvyūhasūtra* and the *Guan Wuliangshou jing*, two of the earliest and most important of the sūtras relating to his cult. In Tibet, his two alternate names were simply translated: 'Od dpag med ("Infinite Light") and Tshe dpag med ("Infinite Life"). Despite the fact that the two names originally refer to the same deity, they have developed distinctions in ritual function and iconography, and Amitāyus is now considered a separate form of Amitābha rather than just a synonym for him. ¶ Amitābha is almost universally shown in DHYĀNĀSANA, his hands at his lap in DHYĀNAMUDRĀ, though there are many variations, such as standing or displaying the VITARKAMUDRĀ or VARADAMUDRĀ. As one of the PAÑCATATHĀGATA, Amitābha is the buddha of the padma family and is situated in the west. In tantric depictions he is usually red in color and is shown in union with his consort Pāndarā, and in East Asia he is commonly accompanied by his attendants AVALOKITEŚVARA (Ch. GUANYIN) and MAHĀSTHĀMAPRĀPTA. See also JINGTU SANSHENG; WANGSHENG.

**Amitābhasūtra**. (C. Amituo jing; J. Amidakyō; K. Amit'a kyŏng 阿彌陀經). The popular title for the "shorter" or "smaller" version of the SUKHĀVATĪVYŪHASŪTRA, one of the three main texts of the PURE LAND tradition of East Asia. See SUKHĀVATĪVYŪHASŪTRA.

**Amitāyus**. (T. Tshe dpag med; C. Wuliangshou fo; J. Muryōju butsu; K. Muryangsu pul 無量壽佛). In Sanskrit, the buddha or bodhisattva of "Limitless Life" or "Infinite Lifespan." Although the name originally was synonymous with AMITĀBHA, in the tantric traditions, Amitāyus has developed distinguishing characteristics and is now sometimes considered to be an independent form of Amitābha. The Japanese SHINGON school, for example, uses Muryōju in representations of the TAIZŌKAI (garbhadhātumaṇḍala) and Amida (Amitābha) in the KONGŌKAI (vajradhātumaṇḍala). Amitāyus is often central in tantric ceremonies for prolonging life and so has numerous forms and appellations in various groupings, such as one of six and one of nine. He is shown in bodhisattva guise, with crown and jewels, sitting in DHYĀNĀSANA with both hands in DHYĀNAMUDRĀ and holding a water pot (kalaśa) full of AMṚTA (here the nectar of long life); like Amitābha, he is usually red.

**Amituo jingtu bian**. (阿彌陀淨土變). In Chinese, "transformation tableaux of the PURE LAND of AMITĀBHA Buddha," pictorial representations of Amitābha Buddha and his pure land of SUKHĀVATĪ. Typically in colors and occasionally hung on the western wall of some pure land monasteries, these elaborate illustrations were typically created as MAṆḌALA, visual supplements to public preaching, or as visualization aids for people on their deathbed intent on being reborn into the pure land. The illustrations themselves—viz., Amitābha Buddha with his two flanking bodhisattvas AVALOKITEŚVARA and MAHĀSTHĀMAPRĀPTA (see JINGTU SANSHENG), his celestial entourage, jeweled trees, singing birds, lotus pond, and palatial buildings—are usually rendered in East Asian artistic style and are based on the way sukhāvatī is described in pure land texts such as the GUAN WULIANGSHOU JING ("Sūtra on the Contemplation of the Buddha of Immeasurable Life"). See also JINGTU BIAN, BIANXIANG, and DIYU BIAN.

**Amituo jiupin yin**. (J. Amida kuhon'in; K. Amit'a kup'um in 阿彌陀九品印). In Chinese, lit. "the nine-levels gesture of AMITĀBHA"; in East Asian Buddhist iconography, the distinctive gesture (MUDRĀ) associated with images of Amitābha Buddha, whose western paradise of SUKHĀVATĪ is said to have nine levels through which devotees pass in the process of attaining enlightenment. The gesture is formed with the index finger and thumbs of both hands touching each other, with one hand typically raised in the air.

**Amoghapāśa (Lokeśvara)**. (T. Don yod zhags pa; C. Bukong Juansuo; J. Fukū Kenjaku; K. Pulgong Kyŏnsak 不空

羂索). A popular tantric form of AVALOKITEŚVARA, primarily distinguished by his holding of a snare (pāśa); his name is interpreted as "Lokeśvara with the unfailing snare." Like Avalokiteśvara, he is worshipped as a savior of beings, his snare understood to be the means by which he rescues devotees. His worship seems to have developed in India during the sixth century, as evidenced by the 587 Chinese translation of the *Amoghapāśahṛdayasūtra* (the first chapter of the much longer *Amoghapāśakalparājasūtra*) by Jñānagupta. Numerous translations of scriptures relating to Amoghapāśa by BODHIRUCI, XUANZANG, and AMOGHAVAJRA and others up into the tenth century attest to the continuing popularity of the deity. The earliest extant image of Amoghapāśa seems to be in Japan, in the monastery of TŌDAIJI in Nara, dating from the late seventh century. There are many extant images of the god in northwest India from the ninth and tenth centuries; some earlier images of Avalokiteśvara from the eighth century, which depict him holding a snare, have been identified as Amoghapāśa, although the identification remains uncertain. Tibetan translations of the *Amoghapāśahṛdayasūtra* and the *Amoghapāśakalparājasūtra* are listed in the eighth-century LDAN DKAR MA catalogue, though it is later translations that are included in the BKA' 'GYUR, where they are classified as kriyātantras. (The Tibetan canon includes some eight tantras concerning Amoghapāśa.) Numerous images of Amoghapāśa from Java dating to the early second millennium attest to his popularity in that region; in the Javanese custom of deifying kings, King Viṣṇuvardhana (d. 1268) was identified as an incarnation of Amoghapāśa. Amoghapāśa can appear in forms with any number of pairs of hands, although by far the most popular are the six-armed seated and eight-armed standing forms. Other than his defining snare, he often carries a three-pointed staff (tridaṇḍa) but, like other multiarmed deities, can be seen holding almost any of the tantric accoutrements. Amoghapāśa is depicted in bodhisattva guise and, like Avalokiteśvara, has an image of AMITĀBHA in his crown and is occasionally accompanied by TĀRĀ, BHṚKUṬĪ, Sudhanakumāra, and HAYAGRĪVA.

**Amoghasiddhi**. (T. Don yod grub pa; C. Bukong Chengjiu rulai fo; J. Fukū Jōju nyoraibutsu; K. Pulgong Sŏngch'wi yŏrae pul 不空成就如來佛). In Sanskrit, "He Whose Accomplishments Are Not in Vain," name of one of the PAÑCATATHĀGATA. He is the buddha of the KARMAN family (KARMAKULA) and his PURE LAND is located in the north. Amoghasiddhi is seldom worshipped individually and he appears to have been largely a creation to fill out the pañcatathāgata grouping. He is usually depicted in the guise of a buddha, green in color, and sitting in DHYĀNĀSANA with his right hand in DHYĀNAMUDRĀ or with a viśvavajra in his upturned palm; his left hand is held at his chest in ABHAYAMUDRĀ. In Nepal, he alone of the five buddhas is shown with a NĀGA above his face or coiled beside him. In East Asian representations of the pañcatathāgata, Amoghasiddhi is often replaced with ŚĀKYAMUNI Buddha.

**Amoghavajra**. (C. Bukong; J. Fukū; K. Pulgong 不空) (705–774). Buddhist émigré ĀCĀRYA who played a major role in the introduction and translation of seminal Buddhist texts belonging to the esoteric tradition or mijiao (see MIKKYŌ; TANTRA). His birthplace is uncertain, but many sources allude to his ties to Central Asia. Accompanying his teacher VAJRABODHI, Amoghavajra arrived in the Chinese capital of Chang'an in 720–1 and spent most of his career in that cosmopolitan city. In 741, following the death of his mentor, Amoghavajra made an excursion to India and Sri Lanka with the permission of the Tang-dynasty emperor and returned in 746 with new Buddhist texts, many of them esoteric scriptures. Amoghavajra's influence in the Tang court reached its peak when he was summoned by the emperor to construct an ABHIṢEKA, or consecration, altar on his behalf. Amoghavajra's activities in Chang'an were interrupted by the An Lushan rebellion (655–763), but after the rebellion was quelled, he returned to his work at the capital and established an inner chapel for HOMA rituals and abhiṣeka in the imperial palace. He was later honored by the emperor with the purple robe, the highest honor for a Buddhist monk and the rank of third degree. Along with XUANZANG, Amoghavajra was one of the most prolific translators and writers in the history of Chinese Buddhism. Among the many texts that he translated into Chinese, especially important are the SARVATATHĀGATATATTVASAṂGRAHA and the BHADRACARĪPRAṆIDHĀNA.

**amoha**. (T. gti mug med pa; C. wuchi; J. muchi; K. much'i 無癡). In Sanskrit and Pāli, "nondelusion"; one of the eleven wholesome (KUŚALA) mental concomitants (CAITTA) according to the YOGĀCĀRA school, "nondelusion" is the opposite of "delusion" (MOHA). This mental quality was presumed to be so central to all wholesome activities that it was listed as one of the three wholesome faculties, or roots of virtue (KUŚALAMŪLA). Nondelusion is interpreted variously as clarity in perception regarding the way things are (yathābhūta), the temporary suppression or permanent extirpation of ignorance (AVIDYĀ), the full comprehension of the FOUR NOBLE TRUTHS, or the clear seeing of the three marks of existence (TRILAKṢAṆA).

**Āmrapālī**. (P. Ambapālī [alt. Ambapālikā]; T. A mra skyong ma; C. Anpoluonü; J. Anbaranyo; K. Ambaranyŏ 菴婆羅女). A courtesan in the city of VAIŚĀLĪ (P. Vesāli) and famous patron of the Buddha, who donated her mango grove (the Āmrapālīvana) to the SAṂGHA. Pāli sources describe her as a woman of exceptional beauty, who is said to have been spontaneously born at the foot of a mango tree in the king's garden, whence her name. As a young maiden, many princes vied for her hand in marriage. To quell the unrest, she was appointed courtesan of the city. She is said to have charged her patrons the extraordinary amount of fifty kahāpaṇas for a night with her. So much revenue flowed into the coffers of Vaiśālī through her business that BIMBISĀRA, the king of RĀJAGṚHA, decided to install a courtesan at his capital as well. It was during the Buddha's last visit to Vaiśālī, shortly before his death, that Āmrapālī first encountered his teachings. Hearing that the famous sage was to preach in the nearby town of Kotigāma, she went there with a retinue of chariots to listen to him preach. Enthralled by his sermon, she invited him for his meal the next morning. Delighted at his acceptance and proud by nature, she refused to give way to the powerful Licchavi princes whom she met on the road, and who likewise had intended to invite the Buddha the next day. Knowing the effect such beauty could have on minds of men, the Buddha admonished his disciples to be mindful in her presence lest they become infatuated. At the conclusion of the meal, Āmrapālī offered to the Buddha and his order her park, Āmrapālīvana, which was the venue of several sermons on the foundations of mindfulness (S. SMṚTYUPASTHĀNA; P. SATIPAṬṬHĀNA). Āmrapālī's son Vimala Kauṇḍinya (P. Koṇḍañña) entered the order and became a renowned elder. Listening to him preach one day, Āmrapālī renounced the world and became a nun. Practicing insight (VIPAŚYANĀ) and contemplating the faded beauty of her own aging body, she became an ARHAT.

**amṛta**. (P. amata; T.'chi med/bdud rtsi; C. ganlu; J. kanro; K. kamno 甘露). In Sanskrit, lit. "deathless" or "immortal"; used in mainstream Buddhist materials to refer to the "end" (NIṢṬHĀ) of practice and thus liberation (VIMOKṢA). The term is also used to refer specifically to the "nectar" or "ambrosia" of the TRĀYASTRIṂŚA heaven, the drink of the divinities (DEVA) that confers immortality. It is also in this sense that amṛta is used as an epithet of NIRVĀṆA, since this elixir confers specific physical benefit, as seen in the descriptions of the serene countenance and clarity of the enlightened person. Moreover, there is a physical dimension to the experience of nirvāṇa, for the adept is said to "touch the 'deathless' element with his very body." Because amṛta is sweet, the term is also used as a simile for the teachings of the Buddha, as in the phrase the "sweet rain of dharma" (dharmavarṣaṃ amṛtaṃ). The term is also used in Buddhism to refer generically to medicaments, viz., the five types of nectar (PAÑCĀMṚTA) refer to the five divine foods that are used for medicinal purposes: milk, ghee, butter, honey, and sugar. Amṛtarāja (Nectar King) is the name of one of the five TATHĀGATAs in tantric Buddhism and is identified with AMITĀBHA. In ANUTTARAYOGATANTRA, there are five types of amṛta and five types of māṃsa ("flesh") that are transformed in a KAPĀLA ("skull cup") into a special offering substance called nang mchod, the "inner offering," in Tibetan. Giving it to the deities in the MAṆḌALA is a central feature in anuttarayogatantra practice (SĀDHANA) and ritual (VIDHI). The inner offering of important religious figures in Tibetan is often distilled into a pill (T. bdud rtsi ril bu) that is then given to followers to use. In tantric practices such as the visualization of VAJRASATTVA, the meditator imagines a stream of amṛta descending from the teacher or deity visualized on the top of the head; it descends into the body and purifies afflictions (KLEŚA) and the residual impressions (VĀSANĀ) left by earlier negative acts.

**A myes rma chen**. (Amnye Machen). A mountain that stands beside a bend in the Yellow River in the Chinese province of Qinghai (which Tibetans call the A mdo region), the seat of the Tibetan mountain god RMA CHEN SPOM RA. This mountain is an important pilgrimage site in northeastern Tibet.

**an**. (J. an; K. am 菴). In Chinese, "hermitage"; referring to residences where only a single hermit or a small number of monks are in residence; often used for smaller residences built in the mountains surrounding major monasteries. The term is also sometimes used for a nunnery or convent. See also ANJITSU.

**An**. (J. An; K. An 安). Sinograph used as an ethnikon for PARTHIA; the character is used to transcribe the surname of monks and missionaries who hailed from Aršak or Arsakes (C. ANXI GUO), the Arsacid kingdom (c. 250 BCE–224 CE) southeast of the Caspian Sea, in the region Roman geographers called Parthia. This Chinese character appears, for example, in the names of the prolific early translator AN SHIGAO (fl. c. 148–180 CE) and his compatriot An Xuan (fl. c. 168–189).

**anabhisaṃskāraparinirvāyin**. (T. mngon par 'du byed pa med par yongs su mya ngan las 'das pa; C. wuxing ban/wuxing banniepan; J. mugyōhatsu/mugyōhatsunehan; K. muhaeng pan/muhaeng panyŏlban 無行般/無行般涅槃). In Sanskrit, "one who achieves NIRVĀṆA without effort"; a particular sort of nonreturner (ANĀGĀMIN), one of the twenty members of the ĀRYASAṂGHA (see VIṂŚATIPRABHEDASAṂGHA). According to the ABHIDHARMAKOŚABHĀṢYA, the anabhisaṃskāraparinirvāyin are nonreturners who, having achieved any of the sixteen birth states of the realm of subtle materiality (RŪPADHĀTU), enter "nirvāṇa with remainder" (SOPADHIŚEṢANIRVĀṆA) in that state without having to apply any effort. They are distinguished from those who achieve nirvāṇa at birth (see UPAPADYAPARINIRVĀYIN) or those who need to apply themselves in order to achieve nirvāṇa (see SĀBHISAṂSKĀRAPARINIRVĀYIN).

**anabhraka**. (T. sprin med; C. wuyun tian; J. muunten; K. muun ch'ŏn 無雲天). In Sanskrit, "cloudless," the lowest of the eight heavens of the fourth concentration (DHYĀNA) of the realm of subtle materiality (RŪPADHĀTU). As with all the heavens of the realm of subtle materiality, one is reborn as a divinity (DEVA) there through achieving the same level of concentration (dhyāna) as the gods of that heaven during one's practice of meditation in the preceding lifetime. This heaven has no analogue in Pāli.

**anāgāmin**. (T. phyir mi 'ong ba; C. buhuan/bulai/anahan; J. fugen/furai/anagon; K. purhwan/pullae/anaham 不還/不來/阿那含). In Sanskrit and Pāli, "nonreturner"; the third of the four types of Buddhist saint or "noble person" (ĀRYAPUDGALA) in the mainstream traditions, along with the SROTAĀPANNA or "stream-enterer" (the first and lowest grade), the SAKṚDĀGĀMIN or "once-returner" (the second grade), and the ARHAT or "worthy-one" (the fourth and highest grade). The anāgāmin is one who has completely put aside the first five of ten fetters (SAṂYOJANA) that bind one to the cycle of rebirth: (1) belief in the existence of a perduring self (SATKĀYADṚṢṬI), (2) belief in the efficacy of rites and rituals (ŚĪLAVRATAPARĀMARŚA), (3) skeptical doubt about the efficacy of the path (VICIKITSĀ), (4) sensual craving (KĀMARĀGA), and (5) malice (VYĀPĀDA). The anāgāmin has also weakened considerably the last five of the ten fetters (including such affective fetters as pride, restlessness, and ignorance), thus enervating the power of SAṂSĀRA. Having completely eradicated the first five fetters, which are associated with the sensuous realm (KĀMADHĀTU), and weakened the latter five, the anāgāmin is a "nonreturner" in the sense that he will never be reborn in the kāmadhātu again; instead, he will either complete the path and become an arhat in the present lifetime or he will be reborn in the "pure abodes," or ŚUDDHĀVĀSA (corresponding to the five highest heavens in the subtle-materiality realm, or RŪPADHĀTU); and specifically, in the AKANIṢṬHA heaven, the fifth and highest of the pure abodes, which often serves as a way station for anāgāmins before they achieve arhatship. As one of the twenty members of the ĀRYASAṂGHA (see VIṂŚATIPRABHEDASAṂGHA), the anāgāmin is the name for a candidate (pratipannaka) for anāgāmin (the third fruit of the noble path). In addition, the ANĀGĀMIPHALASTHA is the basis for several subdivisions of the twenty members. The anāgamin may be either a follower through faith (ŚRADDHĀNUSĀRIN) or a follower through doctrine (DHARMĀNUSĀRIN) with either dull (MṚDVINDRIYA) or keen faculties (TĪKṢṆENDRIYA). The anāgāmins have eliminated all of the nine levels of afflictions that cause rebirth in the sensuous realm (kāmadhātu) that the ordinary (LAUKIKA) path of meditation (BHĀVANĀMĀRGA) removes. Depending on their earlier career, they may be VĪTARĀGAPŪRVIN (those who have already eliminated sensuous-realm faults prior to reaching the path of vision) and an ānupūrvin (those who reach the four fruits of the noble path in a series). Those with dull faculties are ānupūrvin who have earlier been SAKṚDĀGĀMIPHALASTHA. Those with keen faculties reach the third fruit when they attain the VIMUKTIMĀRGA (path of liberation from the afflictions, or KLEŚA) on the DARŚANAMĀRGA (path of vision). See also ANABHISAṂSKĀRAPARINIRVĀYIN; SĀBHISAṂSKĀRAPARINIRVĀYIN; UPAPADYAPARINIRVĀYIN.

**anāgāmiphalapratipannaka**. (P. anāgāmimagga; T. phyir mi 'ong zhugs pa; C. buhuan xiang; J. fugenkō; K. purhwan hyang 不還向). In Sanskrit, candidate for the fruit of nonreturner. If an anāgāmiphalapratipannaka is an ānupūrvin (one who reaches the four fruits of the noble path in a series), he is SAKṚDĀGĀMIPHALASTHA.

**anāgāmiphalastha**. (P. anāgāmiphala; T. phyir mi 'ong 'bras gnas; C. zheng buhuan guo; J. shōfugenka; K. chŭng purhwan kwa 證不還果). In Sanskrit, "one who has reached or is the recipient of the fruit of nonreturner"; the anāgāmiphalastha is the basis for the division into a number of the twenty members of the ĀRYASAṂGHA (see VIṂŚATIPRABHEDASAṂGHA). Among the anāgāmiphalastha are those who have aspired through faith (ŚRADDHĀDHIMUKTA), those who attain through seeing (DṚṢṬIPRĀPTA), and those who are ānupūrvin (those who reach the four fruits of the noble path in a series). See SAKṚDĀGĀMIPHALASTHA.

**anagārikā**. [alt. anāgārikā; anagāriyā] (P. anagāriya; T. khyim med pa; C. feijia; J. hike; K. piga 非家). In Sanskrit, "the homeless life," viz., to leave the home life behind and follow the ascetic existence of the wandering mendicant. The term was adopted in the twentieth century for unordained laymen who lived as monks. See DHARMAPĀLA, ANAGĀRIKA.

**Anāgatavaṃsa**. In Pāli, "Chronicle of Future Events"; a medieval Pāli work in verse detailing the advent of Metteya (MAITREYA) Buddha in the far distant future of this auspicious eon (bhaddakappa; S. BHADRAKALPA). The current eon is deemed auspicious because five buddhas—Maitreya being the fifth—appear during its duration, the maximum number possible. Attributed to Coḷa Kassapa, author of *Vimativinodanī*, the *Anāgatavaṃsa* claims to have been preached to ŚĀRIPUTRA by the Buddha. The text elaborates upon the prophecy of the coming of Maitreya found in the CAKKAVATTISĪHANĀDASUTTA of the DĪGHANIKĀYA. In eighteenth- and nineteenth-century Burma, the *Anāgatavaṃsa* became popular as a kind of charter for a host of millenarian movements and uprisings, including one that led in 1752 to the founding of Burma's last royal dynasty, the Konbaung. Its founder, Alaung hpaya (r. 1752–1760), and his sons utilized this text to justify claims that their wars of conquest were prophesied to usher in a Buddhist Golden Age. A synopsis in English of a nineteenth-century Burmese recension of the *Anāgatavaṃsa* appears in HENRY CLARK WARREN's *Buddhism in Translations* as "The Buddhist Apocalypse."

**Anakṣarakaraṇḍaka[Vairocanagarbha]sūtra**. (T. Yi ge med pa'i za ma tog rnam par snang mdzad kyi snying po'i mdo; C. Wuzi baoqie jing; J. Muji hōkyōgyō; K. Muja pohyŏp kyŏng 無字寶篋經). In Chinese translation from the Sanskrit, "The Letter-less Casket"; a Mahāyāna scripture best known for its statement that, in the enlightenment of the TATHĀGATAs, the nature of all factors (DHARMA) is discovered to be empty (ŚŪNYATĀ); it is neither produced nor extinguished; it neither increases nor decreases; it neither comes nor goes; it is neither obtained nor discarded; and it is free from all causes and conditions. There are three Chinese translations, the best known of which is the *Wuzi baoqie jing*, which was translated by BODHIRUCI (?–527) between 508 and 535. There are also two other Chinese recensions, both translated by Divākara (613–687), the first made in 683 and the second between 676 and 688.

**Ānanda**. (T. Kun dga' bo; C. Anan[tuo]; J. Anan[da]; K. Anan[da] 阿難[陀]). In Sanskrit and Pāli, literally "Bliss," the name of the Buddha's cousin, longtime attendant, and one of his chief disciples. According to tradition, in his previous life, he was a god in the TUṢITA heaven, who was born on the same day and into the same ŚĀKYA clan as the BODHISATTVA and future buddha who was born as prince SIDDHĀRTHA. Ānanda was born as the son of Amṛtodana, the brother of king ŚUDDHODANA. He was thus the Buddha's cousin and the brother of DEVADATTA. When the Buddha returned to his home town of KAPILĀVASTU in the second year after his enlightenment, many of the Śākyan men, such as Ānanda and Devadatta, wished to renounce the householder life and become the Buddha's disciples as monks. Not long after his ordination, Ānanda became a SROTAĀPANNA upon hearing a sermon by PŪRṆA. The Buddha did not have a personal attendant for the first twenty years after his enlightenment, with various monks occasionally offering various services to him. But after two decades of these ad hoc arrangements, the Buddha finally asked for someone to volunteer to be his personal attendant; all the monks volunteered except Ānanda, who said that he did not do so because the Buddha would choose the correct person regardless of who volunteered. The Buddha selected Ānanda, who accepted on the following conditions: the Buddha was never to give him any special food or robes that he had received as gifts; the Buddha was not to provide him with a special monk's cell; and the Buddha was not to include him in dining invitations he received from the laity. Ānanda made these conditions in order to prevent anyone from claiming that he received special treatment because of serving as the Buddha's attendant. In addition, he asked to be allowed to accept invitations on behalf of the Buddha; he asked to be allowed to bring to the Buddha those who came from great distances to see him; he asked to be able to bring any questions he had to the Buddha; and he asked that the Buddha repeat to him any doctrine that had been taught in his absence. Ānanda saw these latter conditions as the true advantages of serving the Buddha. For the next twenty-five years, Ānanda served the Buddha with great devotion, bringing him water, sweeping his cell, washing his feet, rubbing his body, sewing his robes, and accompanying him wherever he went. He guarded the Buddha's cell at night, carrying a staff and a torch, in order to make sure that his sleep was not disturbed and to be ready should the Buddha need him. As the Buddha grew older and more infirm, Ānanda provided devoted care, despite the fact that the two were exactly the same age. Because Ānanda was constantly in the Buddha's presence, he played a key role in many famous events of the early dispensation. For example, it was Ānanda who, on behalf of MAHĀPRAJĀPATI, requested that women be allowed to enter the SAṂGHA as nuns, persisting in his request despite the Buddha's initial refusal. He is therefore remembered especially fondly by the order of BHIKṢUṆĪs, and it is said that he often preached to nuns. In a famous tale reproduced in various sources, the daughter of a woman named Mātaṅgī attempted to seduce Ānanda with the help of her mother's magical powers, only to come to realize her wrongdoing with the intervention of the Buddha. Toward the end of his life, the Buddha mentioned to Ānanda that a buddha could live for a KALPA or until the end of the kalpa if he were asked to do so. (See CĀPĀLACAITYA.) Ānanda, distracted by MĀRA, failed to request the Buddha to do so, despite the Buddha mentioning this three times. Ānanda was chastised for this blunder at the first council (see infra). Ānanda figures prominently in the account of the Buddha's last days in the MAHĀPARINIBBĀNASUTTA, weeping at the knowledge that the Buddha was about to die and being consoled by him. Ānanda was known for his extraordinary powers of memory; he is said to have heard all 84,000 sermon topics (82,000 taught by the Buddha and 2,000 taught by other disciples) and was able to memorize 15,000 stanzas without omitting a syllable. He therefore played a key role in the recitation of the Buddha's teachings at the first council (SAṂGĪTI; see COUNCIL, FIRST) held at RĀJAGṚHA shortly after the Buddha's death. However, MAHĀKĀŚYAPA, who convened the council, specified that all five hundred monks in attendance must be ARHATs, and Ānanda was not. On the night before the opening of the council, Ānanda achieved the enlightenment of an arhat as he was lying down to sleep, as his head fell to the pillow and his feet rose from the ground. He is therefore famous for achieving enlightenment in none of the four traditional postures (ĪRYĀPATHA): walking, standing, sitting, or lying down. As an arhat, Ānanda was welcomed to the council, where he recounted all the words of the Buddha (except those concerning the VINAYA, or monastic rules, which were recited by UPĀLI). For this reason, most SŪTRAs open with the words, "Thus have I heard" (EVAṂ MAYĀ ŚRUTAM); the "I" is usually Ānanda. (For this reason, Ānanda is also known in China as Duowen Diyi, "First in Vast Hearing" or "He Who Heard the Most.") After the Buddha's death, the order of monks brought five charges against Ānanda: (1) the Buddha had said that after his passing, the monks could disregard the minor precepts, but Ānanda failed to ask him which those were; thus, all the precepts had to be followed; (2) Ānanda had once stepped on the Buddha's robe when sewing it; (3) Ānanda had allowed women to honor the Buddha's naked body after his death and their tears had fallen on his feet; (4) Ānanda failed to ask the Buddha to live on for the rest of the kalpa; and (5) Ānanda urged the Buddha to admit women to the order. Ānanda replied that he saw no fault in any of these deeds but agreed to confess them. According to FAXIAN, when Ānanda was 120 years old, he set out from MAGADHA to VAIŚĀLĪ in order to die. Seeking his relics (ŚARĪRA), AJĀTAŚATRU followed him to the Rohīni River, while a group from Vaiśālī awaited him on the other bank. Not wishing to disappoint either group, Ānanda levitated to the middle of the river in the meditative posture, preached the dharma, and then meditated on the TEJOKASIṆA, which prompted his body to burst into flames, with the relics dividing into two parts, one landing on each bank of the river. Ānanda has long been one of the most beloved figures in the history of Buddhism, in part because he was not the wisest of the Buddha's disciples but showed unstinting devotion to the Buddha, always seeking to understand him correctly and to bring his teachings to as many people as possible.

**Ananda Metteyya**. (1872–1923). Ordination name of the British Buddhist monk, born Charles Henry Allen Bennett. He was the son of an electrical engineer and studied science in his youth. In 1894, he joined the Hermetic Order of the Golden Dawn, a society devoted to esotericism, whence he gained a reputation as a magician and miracle worker, becoming the friend and teacher of Aleister Crowley. He became interested in Buddhism from reading EDWIN ARNOLD's *The Light of Asia*. In 1900, he traveled to Asia, both because of his interest in Buddhism and his hope of relieving his asthma. Bennett was ordained as a Buddhist novice (ŚRĀMAṆERA) in Akyab, Burma, in 1901 and received the higher ordination (UPASAMPADĀ) as a monk (BHIKṢU) in 1902. He was among the first Englishmen to be ordained as a bhikkhu, after Gordon Douglas (Bhikkhu Asoka), who was ordained in 1899 and the Irish monk U Dhammaloka, who was ordained some time prior to 1899. In 1903, he founded the International Buddhist Society (Buddhasasana Samagama) in Rangoon. Ananda Metteya led the first Buddhist mission to Britain with his patroness Hla Oung in 1908. In the previous year, in preparation for their visit, the Buddhist Society of Great Britain and Ireland was established, with THOMAS W. RHYS DAVIDS as president. He returned to Rangoon after six months. Plagued throughout his life with asthma, he disrobed in 1914 due to ill health and returned to England, where he continued his work to propagate Buddhism. Partly due to increasing drug dependency prompted by continuing medical treatments, he passed his final years in poverty. His published works include *An Outline of Buddhism* and *The Wisdom of the Aryas*.

**Ananda Temple**. A monumental THERAVĀDA Buddhist monastery located outside the Tharba Gate in the medieval Burmese capital of Pagan. The Ananda was built around 1105 by King Kyanzittha (r. 1084–1111), third monarch of the Pagan empire, and is dedicated to the four buddhas who have appeared during the present auspicious age: Krakucchanda (P. Kakusandha), Kanakamuni (P. Koṇāgamana), KĀŚYAPA, and GAUTAMA. In architectural style, the Ananda represents a fusion of Bengali, Burmese, and Pyu (precursors of the ethnic Burmans) elements. Legend states that eight ARHATs from Mount Gandhamadana in India visited King Kyanzittha, and he was so impressed that he constructed a monastery for them, and next to it founded the Ananda. Like all temples and pagodas of the city of Pagan, the Ananda is built of fired brick and faced with stucco. It is cruciform in plan following a Pyu prototype and crowned with a North Indian style tower, or śikhara. Its interior consists of two circumambulatory halls pierced by windows that allow a limited amount of light into the interior. The hallways are decorated with terracotta plaques depicting episodes from the Pāli JĀTAKAs, the *Mahānipāta*, and NIDĀNAKATHĀ. The inner hall contains niches housing numerous seated images of the Buddha that are rendered in a distinctive Pala style. The temple is entered from four entrances facing the four cardinal directions, which lead directly to four large inner chambers, each containing a colossal standing statue of a buddha. Two of the statues are original; a third was rebuilt in the eighteenth century; and the fourth has been repaired. Three of the statues are flanked by smaller images of their chief disciples. The exception is the statue of Gautama Buddha, located in the western chamber, which is flanked by what is believed to be portrait statues of King Kyanzitha and SHIN ARAHAN, the Mon monk said to have converted Pagan to Theravāda Buddhism, who was also Kyanzittha's preceptor.

**Anaṅgaṇasutta**. (C. Huipin jing; J. Ebongyō; K. Yep'um kyŏng 穢品經). In Pāli, "Discourse on Being Unblemished," the fifth sutta in the MAJJHIMANIKĀYA (a separate SARVĀSTIVĀDA recension appears as the eighty-seventh sūtra in the Chinese translation of the MADHYAMĀGAMA; there is also an unidentified recension in the Chinese translation of the EKOTTARĀGAMA); preached by ŚĀRIPUTRA to a group of monks in the JETAVANA grove in ŚRĀVASTĪ. Śāriputra describes how a monk will become blemished if he succumbs to evil wishes. In this regard, he explains that people are of four types: one who is impure who does not know his impurity, and one who is impure and knows his impurity; one who is pure and does not know his purity, and one who is pure who knows his purity. Of these four, the second of each pair is to be preferred: the one who knows his impurities can strive to remove them so that he dies with his mind undefiled; the one who knows that his mind is pure can continue to guard his senses so that he too keeps his mind without blemish until death.

**anantarapratyaya**. (P. anantarapaccaya; T. de ma thag pa'i rkyen; C. cidi yuan; J. shidaien; K. ch'aje yŏn 次第緣). In Sanskrit, "antecedent condition," one of the four kinds of conditions (PRATYAYA) recognized in the VAIBHĀṢIKA school of SARVĀSTIVĀDA ABHIDHARMA and the YOGĀCĀRA school; the term is also listed as one of the twenty-four conditions (P. paccaya) in the massive Pāli ABHIDHAMMA text, the PAṬṬHĀNA. This type of condition refers to the antecedent moment in the mental continuum (SAṂTĀNA), which through its cessation enables a subsequent moment of consciousness to arise. Any moment of consciousness in the conditioned (SAṂSKṚTA) realm serves as an antecedent condition. The only exception is the final thought-moment in the mental continuum of an ARHAT: because the next thought-moment involves the experience of the unconditioned (ASAṂSKṚTA), no further thoughts from the conditioned realm can ever recur. This type of condition is also called the "immediate-antecedent condition" (SAMANANTARAPRATYAYA); the VISUDDHIMAGGA explains that samanantarapratyaya and anantararapratyaya are essentially the same, except that the former emphasizes the immediacy of the connection between the two moments.

**ānantaryakarman**. (P. ānantariyakamma; T. mtshams med pa'i las; C. wujian ye; J. mukengō; K. mugan ŏp 無間業). In Sanskrit, "act that brings immediate retribution" or "inexpiable transgressions." This term refers to particularly heinous deeds that after death result in the "immediate retribution" of rebirth in the AVĪCI hell, without an intervening rebirth in another realm. They are often enumerated as five: patricide, matricide, killing an ARHAT, spilling the blood of a buddha, and causing schism in the monastic order (SAṂGHABHEDA). According to Pāli sources, this type of act also serves as a karmic obstruction (KARMĀVARAṆA) to concentration meditation (specifically of the KASIṆA visualization devices).

**ānantaryamārga**. (T. bar chad med lam; C. wujian dao; J. mukendō; K. mugan to 無間道). In Sanskrit, the "immediate path" or "uninterrupted path"; a term that refers to the two-stage process of abandoning the afflictions (KLEŚA). In the VAIBHĀṢIKA path (MĀRGA) schema, as one proceeds from the third level of the path, the path of vision (DARŚANAMĀRGA), to the fifth level, the adept path (AŚAIKṢAMĀRGA), the kleśa are abandoned in sequence through repeated occasions of yogic direct perception (YOGIPRATYAKṢA), which consists of two moments: the first is called the ānantaryamārga (uninterrupted path) in which the specific kleśa or set of kleśas is actively abandoned, followed immediately by a second moment, the path of liberation (VIMUKTIMĀRGA), which is the state of having been liberated from the kleśa. A similar description is found in YOGĀCĀRA and MADHYAMAKA presentations of the path.

**ānantaryasamādhi**. (T. bar chad med pa'i ting nge 'dzin; C. wujian ding; J. mukenjō; K. mugan chŏng 無間定). In Sanskrit, "unimpeded concentration"; the culmination of the path of preparation (PRAYOGAMĀRGA), the second segment of the five-path schema outlined in the VAIBHĀṢIKA school system of SARVĀSTIVĀDA ABHIDHARMA and treated similarly in YOGĀCĀRA soteriology. After mastering all four of the "aids to penetration" (NIRVEDHABHĀGĪYA) that catalyze knowledge of the reality of the FOUR NOBLE TRUTHS, the meditator acquires fully the highest worldly dharmas (LAUKIKĀGRADHARMA), the last of these aids, an experience that is marked by the ānantaryasamādhi. This distinctive type of SAMĀDHI receives its name from the fact that the adept then continues on without interruption to the path of vision (DARŚANAMĀRGA), the third stage of the path, which provides access to sanctity (ĀRYA) as a stream-enterer (SROTAĀPANNA).

**Ānāpānasatisutta**. (S. Ānāpānasmṛtisūtra; T. Dbugs rngub pa dang 'byung ba dran pa'i mdo; C. Annabannanian; J. Annahannanen; K. Annabannanyŏm 安那般那念). In Pāli, "The Mindfulness of Breathing Discourse," the 118th sutta (SŪTRA) in the MAJJHIMANIKĀYA (a separate SARVĀSTIVĀDA recension, as titled above, appears in the Chinese translation of the SAṂYUKTĀGAMA). In this discourse, the Buddha outlines a type of meditation where the meditator remains mindful of the process of breathing in and breathing out (P. ānāpānasati; S. ĀNĀPĀNASMṚTI). The meditator begins by developing an awareness of the physical processes involved in breathing, such as whether the breath is long or short; remaining cognizant of either the entire body during breathing or the entire process of breathing (as the commentaries typically interpret it), it culminates in breathing while consciously striving to calm the body. The meditator then follows the in- and out-breaths while developing salutary affective states, such as rapture (P. pīti, S. PRĪTI) and ease (SUKHA). The penultimate step is breathing while actively seeking to focus and liberate the mind. The meditation culminates in mindfulness of the breath while focusing on the awareness of the mental qualities of impermanence, cessation, and relinquishment. Through this progressive development, mindfulness of breathing thus leads from physical and mental calm, to direct insight into the value of nonattachment. The discourse ends with a treatment of the seven aspects of awakening (P. bojjhaṅga; S. BODHYAṄGA) with regard to the four foundations of mindfulness (P. satipaṭṭhāna; S. SMṚTYUPASTHĀNA) of the physical body, physical sensations, state of mind, and mental qualities. See also ANBAN SHOUYI JING.

**ānāpānasmṛti**. (P. ānāpānasati; T. dbugs rngub pa dang 'byung ba dran pa; C. shuxi guan/annabannanian; J. susokukan/annahannanen; K. susik kwan/annabannanyŏm 數息觀/安那般那念). In Sanskrit, lit. "mindfulness (SMṚTI) of inhalation (āna = prāṇa) and exhalation (apāna)," or simply, "mindfulness of breathing"; referring to one of the oldest and most basic meditative techniques found in Buddhism. The practice requires focusing on the breath as it moves into and out of the body during inhalation and exhalation, some say through attention to the sensation of the movement of breath at the tip of the nose, others say through attention to the rise and fall of the diaphragm. This passive following of the breath leads to physical and mental calm, which allows the meditator to focus on the generic aspect of breath: viz., the fact that the constant ebb and flow of the breath is emblematic of impermanence (ANITYA). This awareness may then lead to nonattachment and insight. The Pāli ĀNĀPĀNASATISUTTA provides a detailed description of the processes involved in developing this type of meditation. Unlike many of the other forty topics of meditation (KAMMAṬṬHĀNA) in Pāli Buddhism, which are said to suit specific types of personalities or as antidotes to specific negative tendencies, ānāpānasmṛti is claimed to be suitable for all, which may account for its continued popularity. Elsewhere, it is said to be a suitable object of meditation for those given to excessive thought. Some form of this practice is found in nearly every Buddhist tradition. There are various renderings of the term using Chinese Sinographs; although shuxi guan is one of the most common translations, there are others (e.g., chixi guan), as well as different ways of transcribing the Sanskrit into Chinese (e.g., anabona nian).

**anāsrava**. (P. anāsava; T. zag pa med pa; C. wulou; J. muro; K. muru 無漏). In Sanskrit, "uncontaminated" or "non-outflow"; referring to the absence of the "contaminants" (ĀSRAVA) of sensuality (KĀMA), the desire for continued existence (BHAVA), ignorance (AVIDYĀ), and sometimes wrong views (DṚṢṬI). The absence of these contaminants may be either the quality of a specific object, such as NIRVĀṆA, or a state achieved through meditative training. In the former sense, anāsrava refers both to freedom from the afflictions (KLEŚA) and to those factors that are uncontaminated in the sense that their observation does not serve to increase the afflictions (kleśa). Examples of the latter include true cessations (NIRODHASATYA) and true paths (MĀRGASATYA) among the FOUR NOBLE TRUTHS. The "uncontaminated actions" (anāsrava-KARMAN) performed after enlightenment by ARHATs and PRATYEKABUDDHAs, and by great BODHISATTVAs who have gained control (vaśitāprāptabodhisattva) may in some cases lead to rebirth, but they will not produce continued subjection to SAṂSĀRA as would be the case for ordinary beings. See also PARIṆĀMIKAJARĀMARAṆA ("transfigurational birth-and-death").

**anāsravadhātu**. (T. zag pa med pa'i dbyings; C. wulou jie; J. murokai; K. muru kye 無漏界). In Sanskrit, the "uncontaminated realm." According to those proponents of the MAHĀYĀNA who assert that all beings will eventually become buddhas, ARHATs do not enter the NIRVĀṆA without remainder (ANUPADHIŚEṢANIRVĀṆA) at the time of death but instead enter the anāsravadhātu. There, they abide in states of deep concentration until they are roused by the buddhas and exhorted to abandon their "unafflicted ignorance" (AKLIṢṬĀJÑĀNA) by following the BODHISATTVA path to buddhahood.

**Anāthapiṇḍada**. (P. Anāthapiṇḍika; T. Mgon med zas sbyin; C. Jigudu zhangzhe; J. Gikkodoku chōja; K. Kŭpkodok changja 給孤獨長者). In Sanskit, "Feeder of the Defenseless"; a wealthy merchant from the city of ŚRĀVASTĪ who became such a great patron of the SAṂGHA that the Buddha declared him to be chief among laymen (UPĀSAKA) in his munificence. His personal name was Sudatta; Anāthapiṇḍada was a sobriquet suggesting his philanthropic qualities. Anāthapiṇḍada's father-in-law introduced him to the Buddha, and he was quickly converted, becoming in the process a stream-enterer (SROTAĀPANNA). Anāthapiṇḍada built numerous dwellings, guest houses, and residential parks for the Buddha and his monastic order and was unstinting in his donation of requisites. The most famous of the residences he built was the JETAVANA park on the outskirts of Śrāvastī, which he purchased from the prince JETA (Jetakumāra) by covering the entire property with gold coins. Prince Jeta himself donated the entrance to the park, over which he built a splendid gate. Anāthapiṇḍada had numerous buildings constructed at the site—including the Buddha's own residence, the GANDHAKUṬĪ, or perfumed chamber—to serve the Buddha and the monastic community during the rains retreat (VARṢĀ). The very same spot had served as a monastery and rains retreat center for previous buddhas as well, although the extent of the establishments varied. Jeta's Grove was said to be the Buddha's favorite residence and, according to tradition, he passed nineteen rains retreats there. After the laywoman VIŚĀKHĀ built the grand monastery MṚGĀRAMĀTṚPRĀSĀDA in Śrāvastī, the Buddha would alternate between both residences, spending the day at one and the night at another. The Buddha preached numerous sermons to Anāthapiṇḍada who, in turn, was fond of debating with ascetics and teachers of other religions. Although skilled in business, Anāthapiṇḍada was in his later years reduced to penury. He is said to have died shortly after feeding the monks with gruel prepared from his own cooking pot. One of the more poignant exchanges in the Pāli canon involves Anāthapiṇḍada and is recorded in the *Anāthapiṇḍikovādasutta*, the 143rd sutta in the Pāli MAJJHIMANIKĀYA (a recension of unidentified affiliation appears in the Chinese translation of the EKOTTARĀGAMA). When Anāthapiṇḍada was on his deathbed, the Buddha sent ŚĀRIPUTRA, one of his two chief disciples, along with ĀNANDA as his attendant, to visit him. Learning that Anāthapiṇḍada was in great pain, Śāriputra taught him a fairly standard discourse on how to guard the senses (INDRIYASAṂVARA) so as to remain unattached toward sensory experience and thereby develop a state of consciousness that clings to nothing. At the conclusion of the discourse, Anāthapiṇḍada was brought to tears; seeing him weep, Śāriputra asked him whether he was deteriorating. Anāthapiṇḍada said that he was actually lamenting the fact that, throughout his years of attending the Buddha and his monks, he had not once heard this kind of instruction. Śāriputra responded that such teachings were intended for the monks, not the laity, but Anāthapiṇḍada begged him to make such teachings available to the laity as well, since some of them had "little dust in their eyes" and would be able to understand. Soon afterward that evening, Anāthapiṇḍada was reborn in TUṢITA heaven and, as a young divinity (DEVA), visited the Buddha and praised the virtues of the Jetavana and of Śāriputra, of whom Anāthapiṇḍada was especially fond.

**anātman**. (P. anattā; T. bdag med; C. wuwo; J. muga; K. mua 無我). In Sanskrit, "no self" or "nonself" or more broadly "insubstantiality"; the third of the "three marks" (TRILAKṢAṆA) of existence, along with impermanence (ANITYA) and suffering (DUḤKHA). The concept is one of the key insights of the Buddha, and it is foundational to the Buddhist analysis of the compounded quality (SAṂSKṚTA) of existence: since all compounded things are the fruition (PHALA) of a specific set of causes (HETU) and conditions (PRATYAYA), they are therefore absent of any perduring substratum of being. In the sūtra analysis of existence, the "person" (PUDGALA) is said to be a product of five aggregates (SKANDHA)—materiality (RŪPA), physical sensations (VEDANĀ), perception (SAṂJÑĀ), impulses (SAṂSKĀRA), and consciousness (VIJÑĀNA)—which together comprise the totality of the individual's physical, mental, and emotional existence. What in common parlance is called the person is a continuum (SAṂTĀNA) imputed to the construction of these aggregates, but when these aggregates are separated at the time of death, the person also simultaneously vanishes. This relationship between the person and the skandhas is clarified in the MILINDAPAÑHA's famous simile of the chariot: a chariot is composed of various constituent parts, but if that chariot is broken down into its parts, there is no sense of "chariot" remaining. So it is with the person and his constituent parts, the skandhas. The Buddha is rigorously against any analysis of phenomena that imputes the reality of a person: when a questioner asks him, "Who senses?," for example, the Buddha rejects the question as wrongly conceived and reframes it in terms of conditionality, i.e., "With what as condition does sensation occur?" ("Sensory contact" [SPARŚA] is the answer.) Buddhism thus rejects any notion of an eternal, perduring soul that survives death, or which transmigrates from lifetime to lifetime; rather, just as we can impute a conventional continuity to the person over one lifetime, so can this same continuity be imputed over several lifetimes. The continuum of karmic action and reaction ensures that the last moment of consciousness in the present life serves as the condition for the first moment of consciousness in the next. The next life is therefore neither the same as nor different from the preceding lifetime; instead, it is causally related to it. For this reason, any specific existence, or series of existences, is governed by the causes and conditions that create it, rendering life fundamentally beyond our attempts to control it (another connotation of "nonself") and thus unworthy as an object of attachment. Seeing this lack of selfhood in compounded things generates a sense of "danger" (ĀDĪNAVA) that catalyzes the aspiration to seek liberation (VIMOKṢA). Thus, understanding this mark of anātman is the crucial antidote (PRATIPAKṢA) to ignorance (AVIDYĀ) and the key to liberation from suffering (duḥkha) and the continuing cycle of rebirth (SAṂSĀRA). Although the notion of anātman is applied to the notion of a person in mainstream Buddhism, in the PRAJÑĀPĀRAMITĀ scriptures and the broader MAHĀYĀNA tradition the connotation of the term is extended to take in the "nonself of phenomena" (DHARMANAIRĀTMYA) as well. This extension may be a response to certain strands of the mainstream tradition, such as SARVĀSTIVĀDA (lit. the "Teaching That All [Dharmas] Exist"), which considered dharmas (i.e., the five skandhas and so on) to be factors that existed in reality throughout all three time periods (TRIKĀLA) of past, present, and future. In order to clarify that dharmas have only conventional validity, the Mahāyāna posited that they also were anātman, although the nature of this lack of self was differently understood by the YOGĀCĀRA and MADHYAMAKA schools.

**Anattalakkhaṇasutta**. (S. *Anātmalakṣaṇasūtra; C. Wuwo; J. Muga; K. Mua 無我). In Pāli, "Discourse on the Mark of Nonself," Gautama Buddha's second sermon, delivered five days after the DHAMMACAKKAPPAVATTANASUTTA (S. DHARMACAKRAPRAVARTANASŪTRA); the discourse appears in the MAHĀVAGGA section of the Pāli VINAYA, which recounts the founding of the dispensation (ŚĀSANA). (Separate SARVĀSTIVĀDA recensions, as titled above, appear in the Chinese translation of the SAṂYUKTĀGAMA.) In this second sermon delivered to the group of five new monks (BHADRAVARGĪYA, PAÑCAVARGIKA), the Buddha demonstrates that the five aggregates (SKANDHA) are not a perduring self, because they are impermanent (ANITYA), suffering (DUḤKHA), and therefore impossible to control, viz., "nonself" (ANĀTMAN). The Buddha concludes that any manifestation of the aggregates, whether past, present, or future, whether internal or external, etc., are not mine, are not what I am, and are not my self. This realization will lead, the Buddha says, to dispassion toward the aggregates and eventually liberation. After hearing the sermon, all five monks progressed from the stage of stream-enterer (SROTAĀPANNA) to worthy one (ARHAT).

**Anawrahta**. (S. Aniruddha; P. Anuruddha) (1015–1078). King of Pagan (r. c. 1044–1077 CE), who is celebrated in Burmese history and legend as the founder of the first Burmese empire and as having established THERAVĀDA Buddhism as the national religion of the Burmese people. Fifteenth-century Mon inscriptions record that Anawrahta conquered the Mon kingdom of Thaton in 1057 and carried off to his capital relics of the Buddha, Pāli texts, and orthodox Theravāda monks. With these acquisitions, he laid the foundation for Pāli Buddhism in his kingdom. Later Burmese chronicles recount that, prior to his invasion of the Mon kingdom, Anawrahta had been converted to Theravāda Buddhism by the Mon saint SHIN ARAHAN, who preached to the king the *Appamādasutta*. After his conversion, Anawrahta is alleged to have suppressed an already established sect of heretical Buddhist monks dwelling at Pagan known as the Ari, which seem to have been a MAHĀYĀNA strand that practiced some forms of tantra. Although supposedly reprehensible in their behavior, the Ari had enjoyed the patronage of Pagan's kings for generations. In revenge, the Ari monks attempted to harm Shin Arahan, whereupon Anawrahta defrocked them and conscripted them into his army. To firmly establish Theravāda Buddhism as the sole religion of Pagan, Shin Arahan advised Anawrahta to request Buddha relics and Pāli scriptures from the king of Thaton, the Mon Theravāda kingdom whence Shin Arahan hailed. When Manuha, the Thaton king in Rāmañña, refused Anawrahta's request, Anawrahta and his Burmese forces invaded and acquired these objects by force. Manuha was himself seized and transported to Pagan in golden chains where he and his family were dedicated to the Shwezigon Pagoda as temple slaves and allowed to worship the Buddha until the end of their days. Whatever the historical accuracy of the legend, epigraphic and archaeological evidence indicates that Anawrahta was more eclectic in his beliefs than traditional sources suggest. According to the CŪḶAVAṂSA, Anawrahta assisted the Sinhalese king Vijayabāhu I (r. 1055–1110) in reinstating a valid Theravāda ordination line in Sri Lanka, but Anawrahta also circulated in his own kingdom votive tablets adorned with Mahāyāna imagery, and seals bearing his name are inscribed in Sanskrit rather than in Pāli. In addition, Anawrahta supported a royal cult of spirits (Burmese NAT) propitiation at the Shwezigon pagoda in the capital, which was dedicated to the same deities said to have been worshipped by the heterodox Ari monks. All of this evidence suggests a religious environment at Pagan during Anawrahta's time that was far more diverse than the exclusivist Theravāda practices described in the chronicles; indeed, it is clear that more than one Buddhist tradition, along with brahmanism and the nat cult, received the patronage of the king and his court.

**Anban shouyi jing**. (J. Anpanshuikyō; K. Anban suŭi kyŏng 安般守意經). In Chinese, "The Ānāpāna Guarding the Mind Scripture" composed by the Parthian teacher and translator AN SHIGAO sometime during the second century. Although the text purports to be a translation of a Middle Indic analogue of the Pāli ĀNĀPĀNASATISUTTA, the text is interspersed with commentarial notes on the practice of mindfulness of the process of breathing in and breathing out (ĀNĀPĀNASMṚTI, P. ānāpānasati) and brief explanations of such numerical categories as the five SKANDHAs, twelve ĀYATANAs, and so on. The text is similar in content to certain sections of the ABHIDHARMAMAHĀVIBHĀṢĀ. The *Anban shouyi jing* relies heavily upon indigenous Chinese terminology and consequently serves as an important source for studying the process through which Buddhist meditative techniques were introduced into China. The Sogdian monk KANG SENGHUI wrote a preface and commentary to this text, but his commentary is no longer extant.

**anchin kokkahō**. (安鎮國家法). In Japanese, the "technique for pacifying the state." Japanese TENDAI priests often performed this ritual in the palace at the request of the emperor. Offerings were made to the deity Fudō myōō (S. ACALANĀTHA–VIDYĀRĀJA), who in return would quell the demons who were disturbing the peace of the state. A simplified version of this ritual known as kachin or chintaku is now commonly performed for laity at their homes.

**Andhakā**. In Pāli, "Those from Andhra," a collective designation used by BUDDHAGHOSA, in the introduction to his commentary to the KATHĀVATTHU, to refer to the Rājagirīya, Siddhārthika, PŪRVAŚAILA, and Aparaśaila MAINSTREAM BUDDHIST SCHOOLS, which seem to have been related to the CAITYA [alt. Caitiya] school, a collateral line of the MAHĀSĀṂGHIKA school.

**Āndhra**. In Sanskrit, "Those from Andhra," a Telegu-speaking region in central India now incorporated into the modern state of Andhra Pradesh. See ANDHAKĀ.

**aṅga**. (T. yan lag; C. zhi; J. shi; K. chi 支). In Sanskrit and Pāli, literally "branch" or "limb" but, in the context of Buddhist doctrine, usually connoting "section" or a constituent of a list. The term is used as an abbreviation for the Pāli NAVAṄGA and Sanskrit DVĀDAŚĀṄGA, the nine or twelve sections or categories of the Buddha's word (BUDDHAVACANA), divided according to structure, literary style, or content (see List of Lists). It is also widely used in Buddhist lists such as seven factors of enlightenment (BODHYAṄGA), eightfold noble path (ĀRYĀṢṬĀṄGAMĀRGA), and so on.

**Aṅgaja**. (T. Yan lag 'byung; C. Yinjietuo; J. Inkatsuda; K. In'get'a 因揭陀). The Sanskrit name of the thirteenth of the sixteen ARHAT elders (ṢOḌAŚASTHAVIRA), who were charged by the Buddha with protecting his dispensation until the advent of the next buddha, MAITREYA. He is said to reside on Guangxie Mountain with thirteen hundred disciples. According to the Chinese tradition, Aṅgaja had been a snake wrangler before he was ordained, so whenever he went into the mountains, he carried a cloth bag with him to catch snakes, which he would release after removing their fangs so they would not injure people. For this reason, he earned the nickname "Cloth-Bag Arhat" (BUDAI LUOHAN/heshang). In CHANYUE GUANXIU's standard Chinese depiction, Aṅgaja leans against a staff, with his head lowered, reading a SŪTRA that he holds in his left hand, his right hand counting recitation beads (JAPAMĀLĀ).

**Angkor Thom**. Twelfth-century Khmer (Cambodian) temple city constructed by Jayavarman VII (r. 1181–c. 1220) and dedicated to AVALOKITEŚVARA. Built shortly after the Khmer capital was sacked by invading Chams from the region of today's central Vietnam, Angkor Thom is surrounded by a hundred-meter-wide moat and an eight-meter-high wall. Arranged in the shape of a perfect rectangle oriented toward the cardinal directions, its walls are pierced at their center by gates that connect the city to the outside world via four broad avenues that bridge the moat. The avenues are flanked by massive railings in the form of a cosmic snake (NĀGA) held aloft on one side by divinities (DEVA) and on the other by ASURAs, a motif recalling the Hindu creation myth of the churning of the cosmic ocean. The avenues run at right angles toward the center of the city complex, where the famous funerary temple of BAYON is located. Constructed of sandstone and in the form of a terraced pyramid, the Bayon represents among other symbols Mt. SUMERU, the axis mundi of the Hindu–Buddhist universe. The temple is entered through four doorways, one on each side, that lead through galleries richly carved with bas-reliefs depicting scenes from contemporary life and Hindu mythology. The temple is crowned with fifty-two towers, the largest of which occupies the center and pinnacle of the structure. The four sides of every tower bear colossal guardian faces that are believed to be portraits of Jayavarman VII in the guise of the bodhisattva Avalokiteśvara. The Bayon is the first of Angkor's many temples dedicated to a MAHĀYĀNA Buddhist cult; those built earlier were exclusively Hindu in affiliation. Beneath the central tower is a chamber that once housed a buddha image protected by a hooded nāga. This image was situated above a receptacle intended to receive the king's ashes at death. The Bayon thus combines the function and architectural elements of a Hindu temple and a Buddhist STŪPA; and Jayavarman's identification with Avalokiteśvara was but an extension of

Angkor's long-standing Hindu devarāja (divine king) cult, which identified the reigning monarch as an incarnation of Śiva. Angkor Thom was the last of several temple cities that cover the large area known today as Angkor, each city having been built by a successive Khmer king and crowned with an elaborate funerary shrine at its center. The most famous of these is the nearby ANGKOR WAT, the largest religious structure in the world, built by Suryavarman II between 1131 and 1150.

**Angkor Wat**. Massive temple complex and religious monument located in northwest Cambodia; the name refers to both a specific temple and the larger archaeological site, which includes hundreds of temples, including ANGKOR THOM, an ancient capital city of the Khmer kingdom. The Angkor Wat temple was constructed under the auspices of King Suryavarman II (r. 1131–1150 CE) in honor of the Hindu god Viṣṇu. The temple is constructed in high Khmer (Cambodian) classical style and consists of five major towers, which are said to represent the five peaks surrounding Mt. SUMERU, the axis mundi of the universe in Indian cosmology; it also includes an extensive bas-relief, the longest continuous such carving in the world, that depicts famous episodes in Hindu mythology. As the fortunes of the Khmer empire declined along with the Hindu religion it had supported, Angkor Wat was later reconceived as a Buddhist monument, and a Hall of a Thousand Buddhas added to its main entrance. In 1992, UNECSCO designated the entire complex as a World Heritage Site.

**ango**. (S. vārṣika; P. vassa; C. anju; K. an'gŏ 安居). In Japanese, "peaceful dwelling"; also known as gegyō ("summer dwelling"), zage ("sitting in the summer"), zarō ("sitting age"), etc. The term is used in ZEN monasteries to refer either to the summer rainy season retreat, which usually lasts for three months, or to an intensive period of meditative training during the summer rain's retreat. The beginning of this period is known as kessei (C. JIEZHI), but this term is also occasionally used in place of ango to refer to the meditation retreat. In the Sōtō Zen tradition (SŌTŌSHŪ), ango is often used as a means of measuring the dharma age, or hōrō (C. FALA), of a monk. A monk who completes his first summer retreat is known as "one who has entered the community," five retreats or more a "saint," and ten retreats or more a "master." See also VARṢĀ.

**Aṅgulimāla**. (S. alt. Aṅgulimālīya; T. Sor mo phreng ba; C. Yangjuemoluo; J. Ōkutsumara; K. Anggulmara 央掘摩羅). In Sanskrit and Pāli, literally, "Garland of Fingers"; nickname given to Ahiṃsaka, a notorious murderer and highwayman who was converted by the Buddha and later became an ARHAT; the Sanskrit is also seen written as Aṅgulimālya and Aṅgulimālīya. Ahiṃsaka was born under the thieves' constellation as the son of a brāhmaṇa priest who served the king of KOŚALA. His given name means "Harmless," because even though his birth was attended by many marvels, no one was injured. The boy was intelligent and became a favorite of his teacher. His classmates, out of jealousy, poisoned his teacher's mind against him, who thenceforth sought Ahiṃsaka's destruction. His teacher instructed Ahiṃsaka that he must collect one thousand fingers as a gift. (In an alternate version of the story, the brāhmaṇa teacher's wife, driven by lust, attempted to seduce the handsome student, but when he rebuffed her, the resentful wife informed her husband that it was instead he who had attempted to seduce her. Knowing that he could not defeat his disciple by force, the vengeful brāhmaṇa teacher told his student that he must kill a thousand people and string together a finger from each victim into a garland as the final stage of his training.) Following his teacher's instructions, he began to murder travelers, cutting off a single finger from each victim. These he made into a garland that he wore around his neck, hence his nickname Aṅgulimāla, or "Garland of Fingers." With one finger left to complete his collection, Aṅgulimāla resolved to murder his own mother, who was then entering the forest where he dwelled. It was at this time that the Buddha decided to intervene. Recognizing that the thief was capable of attaining arhatship in this life but would lose that chance if he killed one more person, the Buddha taunted Aṅgulimāla and converted him through a miracle: although the Buddha continued to walk sedately in front of the brigand, Aṅgulimāla could not catch him no matter how fast he ran. Intrigued at this feat, Aṅgulimāla called out to the Buddha to stop, but the Buddha famously responded, "I have stopped, Aṅgulimāla; may you stop as well." Aṅgulimāla thereupon became a disciple of the Buddha and spent his time practicing the thirteen austere practices (see DHUTAṄGA), eventually becoming an ARHAT. Because of his former misdeeds, even after he was ordained as a monk and became an arhat, he still had to endure the hatred of the society he used to terrorize, sometimes suffering frightful beatings. The Buddha explained that the physical pain he suffered was a consequence of his violent past and that he should endure it with equanimity. His fate illustrates an important point in the theory of KARMAN: viz., even a noble one who has overcome all prospect of future rebirth and who is certain to enter NIRVĀṆA at death can still experience physical (but not mental) pain in his last lifetime as a result of past heinous deeds. Aṅgulimāla also became the "patron saint" of pregnant women in Buddhist cultures. Once, while out on his alms round, Aṅgulimāla was profoundly moved by the suffering of a mother and her newborn child. The Buddha recommended that Aṅgulimāla cure them by an "asseveration of truth" (SATYAVACANA). The Buddha first instructed him to say, "Sister, since I was born, I do not recall that I have ever intentionally deprived a living being of life. By this truth, may you be well and may your infant be well." When Aṅgulimāla politely pointed out that this was not entirely accurate, the Buddha amended the statement to begin, "since I was born with noble birth." The phrase "noble birth" can be interpreted in a number of ways, but here it seems to mean "since I became a monk." When Aṅgulimāla spoke these words to the mother and her child, they were cured. His statement has been repeated by monks to pregnant women over the centuries in the hope of assuring successful childbirth. See also AṄGULIMĀLĪYASŪTRA.

**Aṅgulimālīyasūtra**. (T. Sor mo'i phreng ba la phan pa'i mdo; C. Yangjuemoluo jing; J. Ōkutsumarakyō; K. Anggulmara kyŏng 央掘摩羅經). In Sanskrit, "The Discourse on AṄGULIMĀLA"; a TATHĀGATAGARBHA sūtra that tells the story of Aṅgulimāla. Aṅgulimāla's story (see previous entry) also serves here as a frame for several sermons concerning the EKAYĀNA and tathāgatagarbha doctrine. When asked by the Buddha about the meaning of "one learning," for example, Aṅgulimāla replies that the path to awakening consists of a single vehicle (ekayāna), a single act of taking refuge, and a single truth. In reply to the BODHISATTVA MAÑJUŚRĪ's questions about the meaning of tathāgatagarbha, the Buddha teaches that every sentient being possesses the tathāgatagarbha, which remains concealed (S. saṃdhi/abhisaṃdhi, C. yinfu) and covered by afflictions (KLEŚA); this is one of the two major interpretations of the concept. The Buddha proclaims the tathāgatagarbha to be the only true foundation of the bodhisattva path.

**Aṅgulimālya**. (S). See AṄGULIMĀLA.

**Aṅguttaranikāya**. (S. Ekottarāgama; T. Gcig las 'phros pa'i lung; C. Zengyi ahan jing; J. Zōichiagongyō; K. Chŭngil aham kyŏng 增壹阿含經). In Pāli, "Collection of Numerically Arranged Discourses"; the fourth division of the Pāli SUTTAPIṬAKA (S. SŪTRAPIṬAKA). This collection, which may date from as early as the first century BCE, is composed of 2,198 suttas organized into nine nipātas, or sections. It corresponds in general structure to the EKOTTARĀGAMA, extant only in Chinese translation (and of unidentified affiliation), which is much smaller at only 471 sūtras. The suttas in the Pāli collection are arranged sequentially in numbered lists according to their subject matter, beginning with discussions of singularities, such as nibbāna (NIRVĀṆA), and progressing up to sets of eleven. Its Pāli commentary, the MANORATHAPŪRAṆĪ, was probably composed during the fifth century CE. The *Aṅguttaranikāya* appears in the Pali Text Society's English translation series as *The Book of Gradual Sayings*.

**Anham**. (安含) (c. 579–640). Korean pilgrim-monk of the Silla dynasty. According to the HAEDONG KOSŬNG CHŎN, in 600, Anham attempted with a fellow monk by the name of Hyesuk to travel to China in search of the teachings of the Buddha but had to turn back due to a heavy rainstorm. The following year, a royal decree permitted him to accompany a Silla envoy to China. At the behest of the Chinese emperor, he studied various scriptures at the monastery of Xingshengsi in the imperial capital of Chang'an for five years. Anham returned to Silla in 605 with foreign monks from Khotan, Serindia, India, and China. While residing at the monastery of HWANGNYONGSA, these monks are claimed to have translated together a scripture known as the *Zhantanxianghuo xingguang miaonü jing*, which emphasizes the efficacy of a DHĀRAṆĪ called zhantanxiang shen. Anham might also be identical to another Korean monk by the name of Anhong who is said to have brought the LAṄKĀVATĀRASŪTRA, ŚRĪMĀLĀDEVĪSIṂHANĀDASŪTRA, and relics of the Buddha to Korea in 576. Anham was renowned for his superknowledges (ABHIJÑĀ) and was worshipped as one of the "ten worthies of Silla" (Silla sipsŏng) at Hwangnyongsa. A text known as the *Tongdo sŏngnip ki* ("Record of the Establishment of the Eastern Capital") is attributed to Anham.

**ānimitta**. (P. animitta; T. mtshan ma med pa; C. wuxiang; J. musō; K. musang 無相). In Sanskrit, "signless"; one of three "gates to deliverance" (VIMOKṢAMUKHA), along with emptiness (ŚŪNYATĀ) and wishlessness (APRAṆIHITA). A sign or characteristic (NIMITTA) refers to the generic appearance of an object, in distinction to its secondary characteristics or ANUVYAÑJANA. Advertence toward the generic sign and secondary characteristics of an object produces a recognition or perception (SAṂJÑĀ) of that object, which may in turn lead to clinging or rejection and ultimately suffering. Hence, signlessness is crucial in the process of sensory restraint (INDRIYASAṂVARA), a process in which one does not actively react to the generic signs of an object (i.e., treating it in terms of the effect it has on oneself), but instead seeks to halt the perceptual process at the level of simple recognition. By not seizing on these signs, perception is maintained at a pure level prior to an object's conceptualization and the resulting proliferation of concepts (PRAPAÑCA) throughout the full range of sensory experience. As the frequent refrain in the SŪTRAs states, "In the seen, there is only the seen," and not the superimpositions (cf. SAMĀROPA) created by the intrusion of ego (ĀTMAN) into the perceptual process. Mastery of this technique of sensory restraint provides access to the signless gate to deliverance. Signlessness is produced through insight into impermanence (ANITYA) and serves as the counteragent (PRATIPAKṢA) to attachments to anything experienced through the senses; once the meditator has abandoned all such attachments to the senses, he is then able to advert toward NIRVĀṆA, which ipso facto has no sensory signs of its own by which it can be recognized. In the PRAJÑĀPĀRAMITĀ literature, signlessness, emptiness, and wishlessness are equally the absence of the marks or signs of intrinsic existence (SVABHĀVA). The YOGĀCĀRABHŪMIŚĀSTRA says when signlessness, emptiness, and wishlessness are spoken of without differentiation, the knowledge of them is that which arises from hearing or learning (ŚRUTAMAYĪPRAJÑĀ), thinking (CINTĀMAYĪPRAJÑĀ), and meditation (BHĀVANĀMAYĪPRAJÑĀ), respectively.

**animittayoga**. (T. mtshan med kyi rnal 'byor). Literally, "yoga without signs," a term that occurs in Buddhist tantric literature and is especially associated with YOGATANTRA among the four classes of tantric texts. It refers to those meditation practices in which one meditates on emptiness (ŚŪNYATĀ) in such a way that there are no dualistic appearances or "signs." It is contrasted with SANIMITTAYOGA or "yoga with signs," practices that entail dualistic appearances or signs in the sense that the meditator visualizes seed syllables (BĪJA) and deities.

**aniñjyakarman**. [alt. aniñjanakarman] (P. aniñjitakamma; T. mi g.yo ba'i las; C. budong ye; J. fudōgō; K. pudong ŏp 不動業). In Sanskrit, "invariable" or "unwavering action"; usually appearing in conjunction with the dichotomies of wholesome (KUŚALA) and unwholesome (AKUŚALA) or meritorious (PUṆYA) and demeritorious (APUṆYA) in referring to types of action (KARMAN) or the states of existence resulting therefrom. Wholesome and unwholesome actions lead to rebirth, but other actions may intervene and produce their results first. In particular, according to the ABHIDHARMAKOŚABHĀṢYA, when a meditator attains the fundamental state (maula) of a DHYĀNA (concentration) in the realm of subtle materiality (RŪPADHĀTU) or the immaterial realm (ĀRŪPYADHĀTU), the force of the action is aniñjya and will definitely lead to rebirth as a deity in the corresponding heaven in the next life. It is said, however, that BODHISATTVAs are able to circumvent birth as a long-lived divinity in one of the heavens of the realm of subtle materiality or immaterial realm so that they can better offer assistance to sentient beings. Thus, aniñjyakarman indicates the "invariable" connection or continuity between the achievement of those states in this lifetime and the subsequent rebirth: for example, a person who achieves the fourth immaterial absorption in this lifetime will "invariably" be reborn as a BHAVĀGRA deity in the fourth immaterial heaven in the next lifetime.

**aniruddha**. (T. ma 'gags pa; C. bumie; J. fumetsu; K. pulmyŏl 不滅). In Sanskrit, "unextinguished"; a term used to describe uncompounded (ASAṂSKṚTA) phenomena, especially NIRVĀṆA, which are not subject either to production or extinction. In some MAHĀYĀNA SŪTRAs, all phenomena, including compounded (SAṂSKṚTA) phenomena, are described as being aniruddha, which is interpreted to mean that from the standpoint of absolute truth (PARAMĀRTHASATYA), they are not produced and therefore are not extinguished or do not cease. See NIRODHA.

**Aniruddha**. (P. Anuruddha; T. Ma 'gags pa; C. Analü; J. Anaritsu; K. Anayul 阿那律). One of the ten great disciples of the Buddha, who was GAUTAMA's first cousin and brother of MAHĀNĀMAN. Along with many others of the Buddha's relatives in the ŚĀKYA clan, such as ĀNANDA and DEVADATTA, Aniruddha renounced the life of a householder to become a disciple of the Buddha when the Buddha returned to his home town of KAPILAVASTU after his enlightenment. According to legend, Aniruddha was once scolded by the Buddha for sleeping too much. Aniruddha subsequently devoted himself to vigorous practice without sleep (see DHUTAṄGA), as a consequence of which he became blind. The Pāli THERAGĀTHĀ notes that he did not sleep at all for twenty-five years, and that for the last thirty years of his life, he slept only during the last watch of the night. Despite his physical blindness, he attained through his meditative practice the divine eye (DIVYACAKṢUS) and came to be ranked as foremost among the Buddha's disciples in that attainment. For this reason, in East Asia, he is given the epithet Tianyan Diyi or "First of Those Who Have the Divine Eye." According to Pāli tradition, after the recitation of the Buddha's teachings at the first Buddhist council (COUNCIL, FIRST), Aniruddha and his disciples were entrusted with preserving the AṄGUTTARANIKĀYA. Aniruddha and the Buddha held one another in particularly high regard, and many of the Buddha's discourses were addressed personally to him. In assemblies, Aniruddha always sat near the Buddha, and he was present at the Buddha's death. He consoled his fellow monks at their master's passing (PARINIRVĀṆA) and advised the MALLĀ on how properly to carry out the funerary rites.

**anisong**. In Thai, "blessings" (from the Pāli ānisaṃsa [S. ANUŚAṂSA], "blessing" or "merit"), referring to a type of text in the northern Thai tradition that explains the benefits of certain merit-making rituals. The anisong may have been written specifically to encourage participation in Buddhist rituals and festivals.

**anitya**. [alt. anityatā] (P. anicca; T. mi rtag pa; C. wuchang; J. mujō; K. musang 無常). In Sanskrit, "impermanence"; the first of the "three marks" (TRILAKṢAṆA) of existence, along with suffering (DUḤKHA), and nonself (ANĀTMAN). "Impermanence" refers to the fact that compounded objects (SAṂSKṚTA) created by causes (HETU) and conditions (PRATYAYA) are inevitably subject to change, decline, and finally destruction. Because conditioned objects are subject to such impermanence, they are seen to be unsuitable objects for either desire (LOBHA) or hatred (DVEṢA), thus prompting the meditator to turn away from conditioned objects and toward the unconditioned (ASAṂSKṚTA). Mistaking what is in fact impermanent for something permanent is one of the four fundamental "inverted views" (VIPARYĀSA) and a primary cause of suffering. Two kinds of impermanence (see ER WUCHANG) are sometimes delineated: "impermanence marked by a successive period" (S. prabandhānitya, C. xiangxu wuchang), i.e., when an event or length of time has elapsed, such as the ending of a human life or the waning daylight at dusk; and "impermanence that occurs at every thought-instant" (S. kṣaṇikānitya, C. niannian wuchang), i.e., the inexorable change that is taking place anytime and anywhere, even before an event has come to an end (e.g., even before a person's biological death, the person "dies" every instant in the continuum of flux that defines his existence). ¶ In the SARVĀSTIVĀDA ABHIDHARMA system, anityatā (more technically "desinence," viz., death) is treated as a "conditioned force dissociated from thought" (CITTAVIPRAYUKTASAṂSKĀRA), which functions as one of the four conditioned characteristics (CATURLAKṢAṆA, SAṂSKṚTALAKṢAṆA) that are associated with all conditioned objects. Because the ontology of the Sarvāstivāda school, as its name implies, postulated that "everything exists" in all three time periods (TRIKĀLA) of past, present, and future, the school had to posit some mechanism through which to account for the apparent change that conditioned objects underwent through time. Therefore, along with the other three characteristics of birth (JĀTI), continuance (STHITI), and senescence (JARĀ), desinence was posited as a "conditioned force dissociated from thought" that serves as the predominant condition of an object's death. The very definition of conditioned objects is that they are subject to these conditioned characteristics, including this inevitability of death, and this is what ultimately distinguishes them from the unconditioned (asaṃskṛta), viz., NIRVĀṆA.

**aniyata**. (T. gzhan 'gyur; C. buding; J. fujō; K. pujŏng 不定). In Sanskrit and Pāli, "undetermined" or "indeterminate"; the term has separate usages in both ABHIDHARMA and VINAYA materials. In the abhidharma analysis of mind, among the mental constituents (CAITTA, P. CETASIKA), "indeterminate" refers to mental factors that, depending on the intention of the agent, may be virtuous, nonvirtuous, or neutral. They are variously listed as four (in the YOGĀCĀRA hundred-dharmas list) or eight (in the seventy-five dharmas list of the SARVĀSTIVĀDA school) and include sleep (MIDDHA), contrition (KAUKṚTYA, which can be nonvirtuous when one regrets having done a good deed), applied thought or investigation (VITARKA), and sustained thought or analysis (VICĀRA). ¶ In the vinaya (rules of discipline), "undetermined" refers to a category of ecclesiastical offenses of "uncertain" gravity, which therefore must be evaluated by the SAṂGHA in order to make a determination. Aniyata offenses are of two types and always concern the conduct of a monk toward a woman in either (1) private or (2) semiprivate situations. For the monk, even to place himself in such a potentially compromising situation is an offense, since it can arouse suspicion among the laity about the monk's intentions. After learning of such an offense, the saṃgha must then determine the seriousness of the monk's offense by evaluating his conduct while in that situation. After due evaluation, his "undermined" offense will then be judged accordingly as one of three types: (1) PĀRĀJIKA, or most grave, entailing "defeat"; (2) SAṂGHĀVAŚEṢA (P. saṅghādisesa), the second most serious category, entailing confession before the assembly and expiation; and (3) PĀYATTIKA (P. pācittiya), the least serious offense, requiring only confession.

**aniyatagotra**. (T. rigs ma nges pa; C. buding zhongxing; J. fujōshushō; K. pujŏng chongsŏng 不定種姓). In Sanskrit, "indeterminate lineage"; referring to those beings who are not predestined to a particular path and who, depending on circumstances, may follow one path and then change to another. According to some YOGĀCĀRA schools, at birth some beings are endowed with an inherent lineage (PRAKṚTISTHAGOTRA) directing them toward one of three vehicles: the ŚRĀVAKAYĀNA, PRATYEKABUDDHAYĀNA, or BODHISATTVAYĀNA. The difficulty or ease with which they proceed on the path results from a developed lineage (SAMUDĀNĪTAGOTRA) obtained from cultivating earlier wholesome roots (KUŚALAMŪLA). For such persons, the lineages of the śrāvaka, pratyekabuddha, and bodhisattva remain definite even when facing great hindrances. There are also persons of indeterminate or indefinite lineage. For such persons, whether they follow the śrāvaka, pratyekabuddha, or bodhisattva path depends on circumstances, such as which teacher they encounter. Persons of this lineage can therefore change their path. For example, beginner (ĀDIKARMIKA) bodhisattvas may revert to a śrāvaka path and seek personal NIRVĀṆA when faced with either the prospect of the difficult deeds (duṣkaracaryā) that bodhisattvas must perform for the sake of others or the seemingly interminable length of time (see ASAṂKHYEYAKALPA) required to achieve full enlightenment (ANUTTARASAMYAKSAṂBODHI). In addition, a śrāvaka may be inspired to seek buddhahood for the sake of all beings and thus switch to the bodhisattva path.

**añjali[mudrā]**. (T. thal mo sbyar ba; C. hezhang; J. gasshō; K. hapchang 合掌). In Sanskrit and Pāli, "gesture of supplication" or "gesture of greeting." The añjali is a traditional Indian gesture of salutation and respect wherein the palms of the hands are pressed together with fingers pointing up, usually at the level of the heart or the forehead. As a specific type of gesture (MUDRĀ), añjali is used to symbolize thusness (TATHATĀ). In Buddhist iconography, this is one of the principal mudrās of AVALOKITEŚVARA, who in several forms holds a wish-fulfilling gem (CINTĀMAṆI) between cupped palms at his heart. This gesture is also commonly seen in images of religious donors and patrons.

**anjitsu**. (C. anshi; K. amsil 庵室). In Japanese "hut" or "hermitage"; the term is used for a small residence often used by monks to further their training away from the company of others. According to various sources, such as the SHASEKISHŪ, an anshitsu was preferably built deep in the mountains, far away from the hustle and bustle of cities and towns, which might distract monks from their practice. See also AN.

**ankokuji**. (安國寺). In Japanese, "temples for the pacification of the country." After the Ashikaga shogunate took over control of the capital of Kyōto from the rapidly declining forces of Emperor Godaigo (1288–1339) between the years 1336 and 1337, they sought to heal the scars of civil war by following the suggestions of the ZEN master MUSŌ SOSEKI and building pagodas and temples in every province of Japan. By constructing these temples, the shogunate also sought to subsume local military centers under the control of the centralized government, just as the monarch Shōmu (r. 724–749) had once done with the KOKUBUNJI system. These pagodas were later called rishōtō, and the temples were given the name ankokuji in 1344. Many of these temples belonged to the lineages of the GOZAN system, especially that of Musō and ENNI BEN'EN.

**anleguo**. (J. anrakukoku; K. allakkuk 安樂國). In Chinese, the "land of peace and happiness." One of the many names in Chinese for the buddha-field (BUDDHAKṢETRA) of AMITĀBHA known as SUKHĀVATĪ or the "realm of bliss." Other terms such as JILE or JINGTU, however, are more commonly used to translate the Sanskrit term sukhāvatī.

**Anle ji**. (安樂集). In Chinese, "Collected Writings on the Land of Peace and Happiness"; an influential Chinese Buddhist treatise compiled by the monk DAOCHUO sometime during the early seventh century. The text is divided into twelve sections that largely consist of scriptural quotations and exhortations to seek rebirth in AMITĀBHA's PURE LAND, otherwise known as the land of peace and happiness (ANLEGUO). The *Anle ji* classifies the Buddha's teachings into two "gates" known as the "sagely way" (shengdao men) and the "pure land" (jingtu men). The latter refers to the teachings of the Buddha that emphasize the chanting of his name and especially that of the buddha Amitābha, and the former refers to those teachings that expound the means of attaining NIRVĀṆA or enlightenment. This classification became the standard defense for the practice of NIANFO, or "chanting the name of the Buddha." Many of Daochuo's contemporaries, such as Jiacai (d.u.), also noted inconsistencies in certain parts of the text that have even led some to argue that the text was not compiled by Daochuo.

**Anlu**. (C) (安錄). See ZONGLI ZHONGJING MULU.

**Annen**. (安然) (841–889?). Japanese TENDAI (C. TIANTAI) monk considered to be the founder of Japanese Tendai esoterism and thus also known as Himitsu daishi. Annen studied under ENNIN and initiated a reform of the Japanese Tendai tradition by incorporating new teachings from China called MIKKYŌ, or esoteric Buddhism. He received the bodhisattva precepts at ENRYAKUJI on Mt. Hiei (HIEIZAN) in 859 and by 884 had become the main dharma lecturer at Gangyoji. He subsequently was the founder of a monastery called Godaiin and is therefore often known to the tradition as "master Godaiin" (Godaiin daitoku or Godaiin ajari). Over one hundred works are attributed to Annen on both the exoteric and esoteric teachings of Tendai as well as on Sanskrit SIDDHAM orthography; dozens are extant, including texts that are considered primary textbooks of the Japanese Tendai tradition, such as his *Hakke hiroku*, *Kyōjijō*, and *Shittanzō*. Annen is especially important for having examined comprehensively the relationship between precepts associated with the esoteric tradition and the Buddhist monastic precepts, including the bodhisattva precepts (BODHISATTVAŚĪLA); his ultimate conclusion is that all precepts ultimately derive from specific sets of esoteric precepts.

**An Shigao**. (J. An Seikō; K. An Sego 安世高) (fl. c. 148–180 CE). An early Buddhist missionary in China and first major translator of Indian Buddhist materials into Chinese; he hailed from Arsakes (C. ANXI GUO), the Arsacid kingdom (c. 250 BCE–224 CE) of PARTHIA. (His ethnikon AN is the Chinese transcription of the first syllable of Arsakes.) Legend says that he was a crown prince of Parthia who abandoned his right to the throne in favor of a religious life, though it is not clear whether he was a monk or a layperson, or a follower of MAHĀYĀNA or SARVĀSTIVĀDA, though all of the translations authentically ascribed to him are of mainstream Buddhist materials. An moved eastward and arrived in 148 at the Chinese capital of Luoyang, where he spent the next twenty years of his life. Many of the earliest translations of Buddhist texts into Chinese are attributed to An Shigao, but few can be determined with certainty to be his work. His most famous translations are the *Ren benyu sheng jing* (MAHĀNIDĀNASUTTANTA), ANBAN SHOUYI JING (ĀNĀPĀNASATISUTTA), *Yinchiru jing*, and *Daodi jing*. Although his *Anban shouyi jing* is called a SŪTRA, it is in fact made up of both short translations and his own exegesis on these translations, making it all but impossible to separate the original text from his exegesis. An Shigao seems to have been primarily concerned with meditative techniques such as ĀNĀPĀNASMṚTI and the study of numerical categories such as the five SKANDHAS and twelve ĀYATANAS. Much of An's pioneering translation terminology was eventually superseded as the Chinese translation effort matured, but his use of transcription, rather than translation, in rendering seminal Buddhist concepts survived, as in the standard Chinese transcriptions he helped popularize for buddha (C. FO) and BODHISATTVA (C. pusa). Because of his renown as an early translator, later Buddhist scriptural catalogues (JINGLU) in China ascribed to An Shigao many works that did not carry translator attributions; hence, there are many indigenous Chinese Buddhist scriptures (see APOCRYPHA) that are falsely attributed to him.

**antagrāhadṛṣṭi**. (T. mthar 'dzin gyi lta ba; C. bianjian; J. henken; K. pyŏn'gyŏn 邊見). In Sanskrit, "extreme views"; one of the five major types of (wrong) views (DṚṢṬI), along with the view that there is a perduring self, or soul (SATKĀYADṚṢṬI); fallacious views (MITHYĀDṚṢṬI); the attachment to views (DṚṢṬIPARĀMARŚA); and attachment to rites and rituals (ŚĪLAVRATAPARĀMARŚA). "Extreme views" refers specifically to the mistaken notion that there is a perduring soul that continues to be reborn unchanged from one lifetime to the next, or to the self as being annihilated at death and thus not subject to rebirth. The former view is called the extreme of eternalism (ŚĀŚVATADṚṢṬI; P. sassatadiṭṭhi); the latter, the extreme of annihilationism (UCCHEDADṚṢṬI; P. ucchedadiṭṭhi). The Buddhist middle way (MADHYAMAPRATIPAD) between these two extremes posits that there is no permanent, perduring soul (countering eternalism), and yet there is karmic continuity from one lifetime to the next (countering annihilationism).

**antarābhava**. (T. bar do'i srid pa/bar do; C. zhongyin/zhongyou; J. chūin/chūu; K. chungŭm/chungyu 中陰/中有). In Sanskrit, "intermediate state" or "transitional existence," a transitional state between death (maraṇabhava) and rebirth (upapattibhava), distinct from the five or six destinies of SAṂSĀRA (see GATI), during which time the transitional being (GANDHARVA) prepares for rebirth. The antarābhava is considered one of sentient beings' "four modes of existence" (catvāro bhavāḥ), along with birth/rebirth (upapattibhava), life (pūrvakālabhava), and death (maraṇabhava). The notion of an intermediate state was controversial. Schools that accepted it, including the SARVĀSTIVĀDA and most MAHĀYĀNA traditions, resorted to scriptural authority to justify its existence, citing, for example, SŪTRAs that refer to seven states of existence (bhava), including an antarābhava. A type of nonreturner (ANĀGĀMIN), the third stage of sanctity in the mainstream Buddhist schools, was also called "one who achieved NIRVĀṆA while in the intermediate state" (ANTARĀPARINIRVĀYIN), again suggesting the scriptural legitimacy of the antarābhava. There were several views concerning the maximum duration of the ANTARĀBHAVA. The ABHIDHARMAMAHĀVIBHĀṢĀ, for example, lists such variations as instantaneous rebirth, rebirth after a week, indeterminate duration, and forty-nine days. Of these different durations, forty-nine days became dominant, and this duration is found in the ABHIDHARMAKOŚABHĀṢYA and the YOGĀCĀRABHŪMIŚĀSTRA. Ceremonies to help guide the transitional being toward a more salutary rebirth, if not toward enlightenment itself, take place once weekly (see QIQI JI); these observances culminate in a "forty-ninth day ceremony" (SISHIJIU [RI] ZHAI), which is thought to mark the end of the process of transition, when rebirth actually occurs. The transitional being in the intermediate state is termed either a gandharva (lit. "fragrance eater"), because it does not take solid food but is said to subsist only on scent (gandha), or sometimes a "mind-made body" (MANOMAYAKĀYA). During the transitional period, the gandharva is searching for the appropriate place and parents for its next existence and takes the form of the beings in the realm where it is destined to be reborn. In the Tibetan tradition, the antarābhava is termed the BAR DO, and the guidance given to the transitional being through the process of rebirth is systematized in such works as the BAR DO THOS GROL CHEN MO, commonly known in the West as *The Tibetan Book of the Dead*. Like several of the MAINSTREAM BUDDHIST SCHOOLS, the THERAVĀDA scholastic tradition rejects the notion of an intermediate state, positing instead that an instantaneous "connecting" or "linking" consciousness (P. paṭisandhiviññāna; S. *pratisaṃdhivijñāna) directly links the final moment of consciousness in the present life to the first moment of consciousness in the next.

**antaradhāna**. In Pāli, "disappearance [of the Buddha's teachings]." According to the Pāli commentaries, the true dharma (saddhamma) or teaching (sāsana) of the Buddha is destined to survive in the world for at most five thousand years, during which time it will suffer a steady decline in five stages, called the pañcantaradhānāni. There are several alternate theories found in the commentaries as to the specifics of the decline. One version of the five disappearances, which appears in the MANORATHAPŪRAṆĪ, the commentary to the AṄGUTTARANIKĀYA, describes the sequential disappearance of (1) the four noble (āriya) attainments, (2) observance of the precepts, (3) knowledge of the texts, (4) outward signs of monasticism, and (5) the Buddha's relics. In the PRAJÑĀPĀRAMITĀ (perfection of wisdom) literature, there are similarly a number of explanations of the disappearance or extinction of the teaching (saddharmakṣaya). The *Śatasāhasrikāprajñāpāramitābṛhaṭṭīkā*, an early commentary extant only in Tibetan, subdivides the five thousand years that the teaching lasts into ten periods of five hundred years each. The first three (the period of understanding) are when people realize the doctrine and attain results of ARHAT, ANĀGĀMIN (nonreturner), and SROTAĀPANNA (stream-enterer), respectively; the second three (the period of practice) are when people cultivate insight (VIPAŚYANĀ), serenity (ŚAMATHA), and morality (ŚĪLA), respectively; the third three are when the majority have a scripture-centered religious life based on the ABHIDHARMA, SŪTRA, and VINAYA sections of the TRIPIṬAKA; and the final five hundred years are when there is just the mere show of the dharma. See also MOFA; SADDHARMAVIPRALOPA.

**antarāparinirvāyin**. (T. bar ma dor yongs su mya ngan las 'das pa; C. zhong ban/zhong banniepan; J. chūhatsu/chūhatsunehan; K. chung pan/chung panyŏlban 中般/中般涅槃). In Sanskrit, "one who achieves NIRVĀṆA in the ANTARĀBHAVA (intermediate state)"; a specific type of nonreturner (ANĀGĀMIN), one of the twenty members of the āryasaṃgha (see VIṂŚATIPRABHEDASAṂGHA). According to the ABHIDHARMAKOŚABHĀṢYA, the antarāparinirvāyin are nonreturners who, having been reborn in any of the seventeen intermediate states that would have led to rebirth in the realm of subtle materiality (RŪPADHĀTU) (with the exception of the great Brahmā heaven), enter "nirvāṇa without remainder" (NIRUPADHIŚEṢANIRVĀṆA) on the basis of that support. There are three types: those who enter into nirvāṇa without remainder immediately after the intermediate state comes into being; those who enter after it has come into being and just before the sequence of events leading to the conception state begins; and those who enter when thoughts begin to turn toward the conception state.

**antarvāsas**. (P. antaravāsaka; T. smad g.yogs; C. neiyi; J. naie; K. naeŭi 内衣). In Sanskrit, the "lower robe" or "waist cloth"; one of the "three robes" (TRICĪVARA) worn by a monk or nun, along with the larger outer robe (S. SAṂGHĀṬĪ; P. saṅghāṭi) and the upper robe (S. UTTARĀSAṂGA; P. uttarāsaṅga). See also CĪVARA; KĀṢĀYA.

**antevāsika**. [alt. antevāsī] (T. nye gnas; C. jinzhu dizi; J. gonjū deshi; K. kŭnju cheja 近住弟子). In Pāli and Sanskrit, a "pupil" who dwells with a teacher. A monk who loses his preceptor (P. upajjhāya; S. UPĀDHYĀYA) while still in need of "guidance" (P. NISSAYA; S. NIŚRAYA) must seek instruction and training under another qualified master. This new master is called the ĀCARIYA (S. ĀCĀRYA), or "teacher," and the monk is then designated an antevāsika, or "pupil." The same relationship pertains between the antevāsika and the ācariya as between a *SĀRDHAVIHĀRIN (P. saddhivihārika) and an upajjhāya, and it is described as being like that of a son and father. Accordingly, the pupil is required to serve the daily needs of his teacher, by, for example, providing him with water, washing and preparing his robes and alms bowl, cleaning his residence, accompanying him on journeys, attending him when he is sick, and so forth. As part of his responsibilities toward the teacher, if the teacher should begin to entertain doubts about the doctrine or his ability to practice, the pupil is to try to dispel them. If the teacher should commit a grave offense against the rules of the saṃgha, the pupil is supposed to try to prevail upon his teacher to go before the saṃgha to receive its judgment. An antevāsika requires the permission of his ācariya to attend to others, to accompany others on alms round (PIṆḌAPĀTA), to seek instruction from others, etc. The antevāsika is required to seek pardon from his ācariya for any wrongdoing, and may be expelled for bad behavior. A fully ordained monk (P. bhikkhu; S. BHIKṢU) must remain under the guidance (nissaya) of either his upajjhāya or an ācariya or for a minimum of five years from the time of his ordination. A monk may be required to live under nissaya for a longer period, or for his whole life, if he is unable to become competent in DHARMA and VINAYA.

**antidote**. See PRATIPAKṢA.

**anubhāva**. (T. mthu; C. weishen; J. ijin; K. wisin 威神). In Sanskrit and Pāli, "majesty" or "splendor"; referring to the inconceivable power and glory of the buddhas, the spiritual equivalent to the majesty of royalty. The term is often found in compound to express different aspects of Buddhistic splendor. For example, the buddhas are said to have the ability to display various psychic powers (ṚDDHI), including telekinesis, and the ability to walk through walls and to project themselves infinitely (see ADHIṢṬHĀNA); the majestic power displayed through these thaumaturgic abilities is termed ṛddhyanubhāva (P. iddhānubhāva).

**anujñā**. (T. rjes gnang). In Sanskrit, "authorization"; referring to a ritual less elaborate than the ABHIṢEKA (consecration) rite, which imparts the authorization to perform certain practices within a particular cycle of tantric instructions, including deity yoga (DEVATĀYOGA) and MANTRA recitation, but excluding the activities of teaching and bestowing consecrations authorized by the final part of the abhiṣeka, the ĀCĀRYA (teacher) consecration.

**anulomañāṇa**. In Pāli, "conformity knowledge"; according to the VISUDDHIMAGGA, this is the ninth and last of nine knowledges (P. ñāṇa, S. JÑĀNA) cultivated as part of the purity of knowledge and vision of progress along the path (P. paṭipadāñāṇadassanavisuddhi). This latter category, in turn, constitutes the sixth of the seven purities (VIŚUDDHI) to be developed along the path to liberation. "Conformity knowledge" refers to the last three so-called impulsion moments (javana) of consciousness that arise in the mind of the practitioner preceding his perception of the nibbāna element (NIRVĀṆADHĀTU). This knowledge is so named because it conforms itself to the preceding eight stages of knowledge, as well as to the immediately following supramundane path (P. āriyamāgga, S. ĀRYAMĀRGA) and the thirty-seven constituents of enlightenment (P. bodhipakkhiyadhamma, S. BODHIPĀKṢIKADHARMA). When the three moments are treated separately, they receive different names. The first impulsion moment is called "preparation" (P. parikamma), when adaptation knowledge takes as its object the compounded formations (SAṂSKĀRA) as being something impermanent (ANITYA), suffering (DUḤKHA), and nonself (ANĀTMAN). Immediately thereafter, the second impulsion moment arises, which takes the same formations as its object and is called "access" (upacāra). Immediately following that the third impulsion moment arises taking the same object, which is called "conformity" (anuloma). At this point, the practitioner is at the threshold of liberation (P. vimokkha, S. VIMOKṢA), and, therefore, conformity knowledge is described as the final stage in what is called "insight leading to emergence" (P. vuṭṭhānagāminivipassanā). This category includes the sixth, seventh, and eighth knowledges (ñāṇa) in the ninefold schema: namely, "knowledge arising from the desire for deliverance" (P. MUCCITUKAMYATĀÑĀṆA), "knowledge arising from the contemplation on reflection" (P. PAṬISAṄKHĀNUPASSANĀÑĀṆA), and "knowledge arising from equanimity regarding all formations of existence" (P. SAṄKHĀRUPEKKHĀÑĀṆA).

**anulomapratiloma**. (P. anulomapaṭiloma; T. lugs 'byung lugs ldog; C. shunni; J. jungyaku; K. sunyŏk 順逆). In Sanskrit, "forward and reverse"; a term most commonly used in discussions of the twelvefold chain of dependent origination (PRATĪTYASAMUTPĀDA). The "forward" order of the twelve constituents provides an account of the origin of SAṂSĀRA, i.e., an ontology, whereby ignorance produces predispositions, (linking) consciousness, and name-and-form, ultimately leading to birth, aging, and death. The "reverse" order refers to the soteriological sequence, whereby birth, aging, and death are ended by bringing an end ultimately to ignorance; thus, from the cessation of ignorance, volitional action ceases; from the cessation of volitional action, consciousness ceases; and so on.

**anumāna**. (T. rjes su dpag pa; C. biliang; J. hiryō; K. piryang 比量). In Sanskrit and Pāli, "inference." In Buddhist logic and epistemology, inference is considered to be one of the two forms of valid knowledge (PRAMĀṆA), along with direct perception (PRATYAKṢA). Inference allows us to glean knowledge concerning objects that are not directly evident to the senses. In the Buddhist logical traditions, inferences may be drawn from logical signs (HETU, LIṄGA): e.g., there is a fire on the mountain (SĀDHYA), because there is smoke (SĀDHANA), like a stove (SAPAKṢA), unlike a lake (VIPAKṢA).

**Anumānasutta**. (C. Biqiu qing jing; J. Bikushōkyō; K. Pigu ch'ong kyŏng 比丘請經). In Pāli, "Discourse on Inference," the fifteenth sutta of the MAJJHIMANIKĀYA (a separate SARVĀSTIVĀDA recension appears as the eighty-ninth SŪTRA in the Chinese translation of the MADHYAMĀGAMA). The sūtra was preached by MAHĀMAUDGALYĀYANA (P. Mahāmoggallāna) to a large group of monks at Suṃsumāragiri in the Bhagga country. Mahāmaudgalyāyana enumerates sixteen faults that make it difficult for a monk to be admonished by his teachers or fellow monks, such as evil wishes, conceit, deceit, anger, resentment, stubbornness, defensiveness, and prevarication. Should a monk discover any of these negative traits within himself, he should strive to remove them.

**anumodana**. (T. rjes su yi rang; C. suixi; J. zuiki; K. suhŭi 隨喜). In Sanskrit and Pāli, "admiration" or "gratification," also written anumodanā; the act of taking delight in the virtuous acts of others, which, in contrast to the unwholesome emotion of envy (ĪRṢYĀ), enables one also to accumulate virtue for oneself. It is considered an effective means of gaining merit (PUṆYA) and figures as a standard component in MAHĀYĀNA liturgies, including the three-part Mahāyāna liturgy (TRISKANDHAKA) and the sevenfold PŪJĀ (SAPTĀṄGAVIDHI). Anumodanā is also used in mainstream Buddhism to refer to the "benedictions" (C. zhouyuan) that monks recite after receiving a meal or a gift, which express thanks or "gratification" to the donors for their offerings.

**Anūnatvāpūrṇatvanirdeśa**. (C. Buzeng bujian jing; J. Fuzōfugengyō; K. Pujŭng pulgam kyŏng 不增不減經). In Sanskrit, the "Neither Increase nor Decrease Sūtra," one of the earliest TATHĀGATAGARBHA (embryo of the tathāgatas) scriptures, along with the TATHĀGATAGARBHASŪTRA and the ŚRĪMĀLĀDEVĪSIṂHANĀDASŪTRA. The text, only a single roll in length, was far more influential in the development of tathāgatagarbha thought in East Asia than its length might suggest. The complete text survives only in a Chinese translation made in 525 by BODHIRUCI (d. 527). Neither Sanskrit nor Tibetan recensions of the text are extant, although the RATNAGOTRAVIBHĀGA includes many quotations from the scripture. The *Anūnatvāpūrṇatvanirdeśa* explains the absolute identity between sentient beings and the DHARMAKĀYA of the buddhas through the concept of tathāgatagarbha. According to the scripture, although sentient beings endure endless rebirths among the six destinies (GATI) because of afflictions (KLEŚA), they in fact neither arise nor perish because they are all actually manifestations of the unchanging dharmakāya. Since sentient beings are therefore nothing other than the dharmakāya—and since the dharmakāya is unchanging, ever-present, and subject neither to increase nor to decrease—the sentient beings who possess the dharmakāya as their nature also "neither increase nor decrease." The scripture also explains that such wrong views as the notion that sentient beings are subject to increase or decrease are caused by not realizing that the realms of sentient beings and tathāgatas are in fact one and the same. When the dharmakāya is obscured by afflictions and resides in the suffering of SAṂSĀRA, it is called a sentient being; when it is cultivating the perfections (PĀRAMITĀ) and developing a repugnance for the suffering of saṃsāra, it is called a BODHISATTVA; when it is pure and free from all afflictions, it is called a tathāgata. Sentient beings, tathāgatagarbha, and dharmakāya are therefore merely different names for the one realm of reality (DHARMADHĀTU). The *Anūnatvāpūrṇatvanirdeśa* thus emphasizes the immanent aspect of tathāgatagarbha, whereas the *Śrīmālāsūtra* emphasizes its transcendent aspect.

**anupadhiśeṣanirvāṇa**. [alt. nirupadhiśeṣanirvāṇa] (P. anupādisesanibbāna; T. phung po'i lhag ma med par mya ngan las 'das ba / lhag med myang 'das; C. wuyu niepan; J. muyonehan; K. muyŏ yŏlban 無餘涅槃). In Sanskrit, "the nirvāṇa without remainder"; one of the two kinds of NIRVĀṆA, along with "the nirvāṇa with remainder" (SOPADHIŚEṢANIRVĀṆA). After a buddha or, in some interpretations, an ARHAT has achieved awakening (BODHI), some Buddhist schools distinguish between the experience of nirvāṇa while it is still accompanied by a substratum of existence (upadhi = SKANDHA) and the nirvāṇa that is completely freed from that substratum. According to this view, at the time of his enlightenment under the BODHI TREE, the Buddha achieved the nirvāṇa with remainder, because he had destroyed all causes for future rebirth, but the "remainder" of his mind and body persisted. The anupadhiśeṣanirvāṇa subsequently occurred at the time of the Buddha's death. It was achieved through having brought an absolute end to any propensity toward defilement (KLEŚA) and of the causes that would lead to any prospect of future rebirth; it is therefore the total extinction of all conventional physical and mental existence. The nirvāṇa that is experienced at death is thus "without remainder" because there are no physical or mental constituents remaining that were the products of previous KARMAN; anupadhiśeṣanirvāṇa is therefore synonymous with PARINIRVĀṆA. Since this type of nirvāṇa results from the complete eradication of the afflictive destructions (KLEŚĀVARAṆA), MAINSTREAM BUDDHIST SCHOOLS typically claim that it is accessible by ŚRĀVAKAS and PRATYEKABUDDHAS. However, according to those proponents of the MAHĀYĀNA who assert that all beings will eventually become buddhas, arhats do not enter anupādiśeṣanirvāṇa upon death but instead enter the uncontaminated realm (ANĀSRAVADHĀTU), where they remain in states of deep concentration until they are roused by the buddhas and exhorted to abandon their "unafflicted ignorance" (AKLIṢṬĀJÑĀNA). In the YOGĀCĀRA school, anupādiśeṣanirvāṇa is one of the four kinds of nirvāṇa, which entails the cessation of any tendency toward delusion through the transformation of the eighth consciousness, the storehouse consciousness (ĀLAYAVIJÑĀNA), into the mirrorlike knowledge (ĀDARŚAJÑĀNA).

**anupalabdhi**. [alt. anupalambha] (T. mi dmigs pa / dmigs med; C. bukede; J. fukatoku; K. pulgadŭk 不可得). In Sanskrit, "unascertainable," "noncognition," or "non-observation," describing the peculiar type of cognition inherent in enlightenment, in which perception occurs without any bifurcation between subject and object in the case of YOGĀCĀRA or without any perception or "observation" of intrinsic existence (SVABHĀVA) in the case of MADHYAMAKA and is thus freed from any kind of false dichotomization. This type of perception is therefore "unascertainable," viz., freed from conventional types of cognition and thus "noncognition."

**anupassanā**. (S. ANUPAŚYANĀ). In Pāli, "contemplation." A term applied to several sets of meditation practices, most notably as enumerated under the category of the four "foundations of mindfulness" (P. satipaṭṭhāna; S. SMṚTYUPASTHĀNA). The first foundation is called "contemplation of the body" (kāyānupassanā, S. KĀYĀNUPAŚYANĀ) and comprises fourteen practices, which include mindfulness of breathing (P. ānāpānasati, S. ĀNĀPĀNASMṚTI), mindfulness of postures or deportments (P., iriyāpatha, S. ĪRYĀPATHA), full awareness of bodily actions, contemplation of bodily impurities, contemplation of the four physical elements (DHĀTU, MAHĀBHŪTA), and nine cemetery meditations (P. asubhabhāvanā, S. AŚUBHABHĀVANĀ). The second foundation is called "contemplation of sensations" (P. vedanānupassanā, S. vedanānupasyanā) and consists of one practice: mindfulness of physical sensations (VEDANĀ) as pleasant, unpleasant, or neutral. The third foundation is called "contemplation of mind" (P. cittānupassanā, S. cittānupasyanā) and consists of one practice: mindfulness of one's general state of mind (CITTA), e.g. as calm or distracted, elated or depressed, etc. The fourth foundation is "contemplation of mind-objects" (P. dhammānupassanā, S. dharmānupasyanā) and includes five meditations on specific categories of factors (P. dhamma, S. DHARMA), namely: the five hindrances (NĪVARAṆA), the five aggregates (SKANDHA), the six sense bases and six sense objects (ĀYATANA), the seven enlightenment factors (BODHYAṄGA), and the FOUR NOBLE TRUTHS. In the Pāli SATIPAṬṬHĀNASUTTA, the four anupassanās are extolled as the one path leading to the realization of nibbāna (NIRVĀṆA). Another common set of anupassanās found in the Pāli tradition includes three members: (1) contemplation of impermanence (aniccānupassanā), (2) contemplation of suffering (dukkhānupassanā), and (3) contemplation of nonself (anattānupassanā). In the PAṬISAMBHIDĀMAGGA, this list is expanded to ten with the addition of (4) contemplation of nirvāṇa (nibbānānupassanā), (5) contemplation of dispassion (virāgānupassanā), (6) contemplation of cessation (nirodhānupassanā), (7) contemplation of renunciation (paṭinissaggānupassanā), (8) contemplation of signlessness (animittānupassanā), (9) contemplation of desirelessness (appaṇihitānupassanā), and (10) contemplation of emptiness (suññatānupassanā).

**anupaśyanā**. (T. rjes su lta ba; C. xunguan; J. junkan; K. sun'gwan 循觀). In Sanskrit, "contemplation" or "consideration." See ANUPASSANĀ (P).

**anupubbikathā**. (S. anupūrvikathā; T. mthar gyis pa; C. cidi shuofa/jianwei shuofa; J. shidai seppō/zen'i seppō; K. ch'aje sŏlbŏp/chŏmwi sŏlbŏp 次第說法/漸爲說法). In Pāli, "graduated discourse" or "step-by-step instruction"; the systematic outline of religious benefits that the Buddha used to mold the understanding of new lay adherents and to guide them toward the first stage of enlightenment. In this elementary discourse, the Buddha would outline the benefits of generosity (dānakathā) and morality (sīlakathā) before finally holding out for the laity the prospect of rebirth in the heavens (svargakathā). Once their minds were pliant and impressionable, the Buddha then would instruct his listeners in the dangers (ĀDĪNAVA) inherent in sensuality (KĀMA) in order to turn them away from the world and toward the advantages of renunciation (P. nekkhamme ānisaṃa; S. NAIṢKRAMYA). Only after his listeners' minds were made fully receptive would the Buddha then go on to teach them the doctrine that was unique to the buddhas: the FOUR NOBLE TRUTHS of suffering, origination, cessation, and path. Understanding the pervasive reality of the fact that "all that is subject to production is subject to cessation" (yaṃ kiñci samudayadhammaṃ taṃ nirodhadhammaṃ), the laity would then gain a profound personal understanding of the dharma, which often prompted the experience of "stream-entry" (SROTAĀPANNA). The "graduated discourse" was such a stock formula in the standard sermon to the laity that it appears only in summary form in the NIKĀYAs and ĀGAMAs. The only detailed treatment of the graduated discourse appears in the *Tuṇḍilovādasutta* (Advice to Layman Tuṇḍila), a late Pāli apocryphon (see APOCRYPHA) probably composed in Sri Lanka in the eighteenth century. This late text provides a systematic outline of the specifics of the practice of generosity (DĀNA), morality (ŚĪLA), the heavens (SVARGA), the dangers in sensual desires, and the benefits of renunciation, leading up to the "perfect peace" of nibbāna (S. NIRVĀṆA).

**anupūrvikathā**. In Sanskrit, "graduated discourse." See ANUPUBBIKATHĀ.

**Anurādhapura**. Ancient capital of Sri Lanka nearly continuously from the fourth century BCE to the ninth century CE, with interludes of foreign occupation by Cōḷa forces from South India. To the south of the city was the MAHĀMEGHAVANA park, which was gifted to the elder MAHINDA by King DEVĀNAṂPIYATISSA when the latter converted to Buddhism in the third century BCE. Soon, the MAHĀVIHĀRA and the shrine of the southern branch of the BODHI TREE were built there. In the second century BCE, King DUṬṬHAGĀMAṆĪ built the seven-storied LOHAPĀSĀDA and the MAHĀTHŪPA. The site also housed the ABHAYAGIRI monastery, built in the first century BCE by King VAṬṬAGĀMAṆI, and the JETAVANA monastery built in the fourth century CE by King Mahāsena. The latter two monasteries were headquarters of the two eponymous secessionist fraternities of Sri Lankan Buddhism. Although Anurādhapura was abandoned in favor of Pulatthipura as the capital in the ninth century, it remained a center of pilgrimage and religious activity.

**Anuruddha**. (P) The Pāli name for one of the ten chief disciples of the Buddha; see ANIRUDDHA. ¶ Anuruddha is also the name of the author of the THERAVĀDA abhidhamma manual ABHIDHAMMATTHASAṄGAHA, as well as the *Paramatthavinicchaya* and the *Nāmarūpapariccheda*. Anuruddha flourished during the eleventh or twelfth century and was the abbot of Mūlasoma Vihāra. His *Abhidhammatthasaṅgaha* has for centuries been the most widely used introductory text for the study of ABHIDHAMMA (S. ABHIDHARMA) in monastic colleges throughout the Pāli Buddhist world.

**anuśaṃsa**. [alt. ānuśaṃsa; ānuśaṃsā, etc.] (P. ānisaṃsa; T. phan yon; C. gongde/liyi; J. kudoku/riyaku; K. kongdŏk/iik 功德/利益). In Buddhist Hybrid Sanskrit, "blessing," "benefit," "reward," or "advantage" that accrues from leading a virtuous life or performing various types of virtuous actions. In the Pāli MAHĀPARINIBBĀNASUTTANTA, for example, while preaching on the benefits of moral rectitude to a gathering of lay disciples in the city of Pāṭaligāma (see PĀṬALIPUTRA), the Buddha enumerates five such blessings that a morally upright person can expect to acquire in this lifetime: first, great wealth (bhogakkhandha); second, a good reputation (kittisadda); third, self-confidence (visārada); fourth, a peaceful death (asammūḷho kālaṃ karoti); and fifth, after he dies, a happy rebirth (saggaṃ lokaṃ upapajjati). In contrast, a morally dissolute person can expect in this lifetime: first, poverty due to sloth; second, a bad reputation; third, shame in the presence of others; fourth, an anxious death; and fifth, after he dies, an unhappy rebirth. In the so-called graduated discourse (P. ANUPUBBIKATHĀ), the Buddha also teaches the blessings of renunciation (nekkhamme ānisaṃsa) as a prerequisite to understanding the FOUR NOBLE TRUTHS. Different lists of five, ten, or eighteen such blessings appear in Sanskrit sources. The PRAJÑĀPĀRAMITĀ literature has long passages praising the merit gained from writing out in book form, reading, memorizing, and generally worshipping the prajñāpāramitā as compared, in particular, to worshiping a STŪPA containing the relics of a TATHĀGATA, and the commentarial literature lists the benefits (anuśaṃsa) of the BODHISATTVA's path of vision (DARŚANAMĀRGA) when compared with the earlier understanding of the FOUR NOBLE TRUTHS.

**anuśaya**. (P. anusaya; T. bag la nyal ba; C. suimian; J. zuimen; K. sumyŏn 隨眠). In Sanskrit, "proclivity" or "predisposition"; various unwholesome mental states that lead eventually to suffering. There are several lists, most common of which is a list of six or seven principal proclivities: sensual passion (KĀMARĀGA; see also RĀGA), hostility (PRATIGHA), pride (MĀNA), ignorance (AVIDYĀ), views (DṚṢṬI), and skeptical doubt (VICIKITSĀ); sometimes, passion for existence (bhavarāga) is added as a seventh. The SARVĀSTIVĀDA school of ABHIDHARMA offers an extensive list of ninety-eight proclivities, in which dṛṣṭi is subdivided into five subtypes, giving ten, which are then further subdivided into ninety-eight in relation to the three realms of existence (sensual, subtle materiality, and immaterial) and the five classes of discipline.

**anusmaraṇavikalpa**. (T. rjes su dran pa'i rnam rtog; C. suinian fenbie; J. zuinen funbetsu; K. sunyŏm punbyŏl 隨念分別). In Sanskrit, "discrimination involving reflection on past events"; the third of the three types of conceptual discrimination (VIKALPA). See TRIVIKALPA.

**anusmṛti**. (P. anussati; T. rjes su dran pa; C. nian; J. nen; K. yŏm 念). In Sanskrit, "recollection." The Pāli form anussati is applied to a number of mental exercises enumerated in the Pāli tradition under the category of KAMMAṬṬHĀNA, or topics of meditation. The fifth-century VISUDDHIMAGGA lists ten such recollections conducive to the cultivation of concentration (SAMĀDHI): namely, recollection of (1) the BUDDHA, (2) the DHARMA, (3) the SAMGHA, (4) morality, (5) generosity, (6) the gods, (7) death, (8) the body, (9) the in-breath and out-breath, and (10) peace. Of these, recollection or mindfulness (P. sati; S. SMṚTI) of the in-breath and out-breath can produce all four meditative absorptions (DHYĀNA; P. JHĀNA), while recollection of the body can produce the first absorption. The remaining recollections can produce only "access concentration" (UPACĀRASAMĀDHI), which immediately precedes but does not quite reach the first absorption. In East Asia, the practice of recollection of the Buddha (BUDDHĀNUSMṚTI) evolved into the recitation of name of the buddha AMITĀBHA in the form of the Chinese phrase namo Amituo fo (Homage to the buddha Amitābha; see NAMU AMIDABUTSU). See also BUDDHĀNUSMṚTI.

**anuśrava**. (P. anussava; T. gsan pa; C. suiwen; J. zuimon; K. sumun 隨聞). In Sanskrit, "tradition," "hearsay," or "report" (in Chinese, it is, literally, "according to what has been heard"), referring to knowledge learned from received tradition, which is said to be unreliable as a standard for judging truth and falsity. In the Pāli KĀLĀMASUTTA, the Buddha rejects the validity of testimony based on anussava (tradition) in favor of what practitioners learn through their own personal training to be blameworthy or praiseworthy, harmful or beneficial.

**anutpāda**. [alt. anutpanna] (T. skye med; C. wusheng; J. mushō; K. musaeng 無生). In Sanskrit, "unproduced" or "nonproduction"; a term used to describe unconditioned phenomena, especially NIRVĀṆA, which are not subject to either production or cessation. In some MAHĀYĀNA sūtras, all phenomena, including impermanent phenomena, are described as anutpāda; this is interpreted to mean that they ultimately are neither produced nor extinguished.

**anutpādajñāna**. (T. mi skye ba shes pa; C. wusheng zhi; J. mushōchi; K. musaeng chi 無生智). In Sanskrit, "knowledge of nonproduction"; one of the two knowledges (along with KṢAYAJÑĀNA) that accompanies liberation from rebirth (SAṂSĀRA). Anutpādajñāna refers specifically to the knowledge that the afflictions (KLEŚA), once destroyed, will never be produced again. See also ANUTPATTIKADHARMAKṢĀNTI.

**anutpanna**. (S; T. skye med). See ANUTPĀDA.

**anutpattikadharmakṣānti**. (T. mi skye ba'i chos la bzod pa; C. wushengfaren; J. mushōbōnin; K. musaeng pŏbin 無生法忍). In Sanskrit, the "acquiescence" or "receptivity" "to the nonproduction of dharmas." In the MAHĀYĀNA, a BODHISATTVA is said to have attained the stage of "nonretrogression" (AVAIVARTIKA) when he develops an unswerving conviction that all dharmas are "unproduced" (ANUTPĀDA) and "empty" (ŚŪNYATĀ) in the sense that they lack any intrinsic nature (NIḤSVABHĀVA). This stage of understanding has been variously described as occurring on either the first or eighth BHŪMIs of the bodhisattva path. This conviction concerning emptiness is characterized as a kind of "acquiescence," "receptivity," or "forbearance" (KṢĀNTI), because it sustains the bodhisattva on the long and arduous path of benefiting others, instilling an indefatigable equipoise, and preventing him from falling back into the selfish preoccupation with personal liberation. The bodhisattva "bears" or "acquiesces to" the difficulty of actively entering the world to save others by residing in the realization that ultimately there is no one saving others and no others being saved. In other words, all dharmas—including sentient beings and the rounds of rebirth—are originally and eternally "unproduced" or "tranquil." This realization of nonduality—of the self and others, and of SAṂSĀRA and NIRVĀṆA—inoculates the bodhisattva from being tempted into a premature attainment of "cessation," wherein one would escape from personal suffering through the extinction of continual existence, but at the cost of being deprived of the chance to attain the even greater goal of buddhahood through sustained practice along the bodhisattva path. Anutpattikadharmakṣānti is sometimes used in a nonpolemical context, where it refers both to the Mahāyāna realization of the truth of "emptiness" and to the non-Mahāyāna realization of no-self (ANĀTMAN) and the FOUR NOBLE TRUTHS. In a non-Mahāyāna context, the term corresponds to the path of vision (DARŚANAMĀRGA).

**anuttarasamyaksaṃbodhi**. (T. bla na med pa yang dag par rdzogs pa'i byang chub; C. wushang zhengdeng jue/anouduoluo sanmiao sanputi; J. mujōshōtōgaku/anokutarasanmyaku-sanbodai; K. musang chŏngdŭng kak/anyoktara sammyak sambori 無上正等覺/阿耨多羅三藐三菩提). In Sanskrit, "unsurpassed (anuttara), complete (samyak), and perfect enlightenment (SAṂBODHI)"; the enlightenment (BODHI) of a buddha, superior to all other forms of enlightenment. The term is often used to distinguish the enlightenment of a buddha from that of an ARHAT, with the former deemed superior because it is the result of the sustained practice of the BODHISATTVA path over the course of many eons (KALPA) of lifetimes. According to Mahāyāna schools, in anuttarasamyaksaṃbodhi, both of the two kinds of obstructions, the afflictive obstructions (KLEŚĀVARAṆA) and the obstructions to omniscience (JÑEYĀVARAṆA), have been completely overcome. Although ARHATS also achieve enlightenment (BODHI), they have overcome only the first of the obstructions, not the second, and thus have still not realized anuttarasamyaksaṃbodhi. This enlightenment, which is unique to the buddhas, surpasses all other types of realization and is thus unsurpassed, complete, and perfect. See also MAHĀBODHI; SAṂBODHI.

**anuttarayogatantra**. (T. bla na med pa'i rnal 'byor rgyud). In Sanskrit, "unsurpassed yoga tantra." According to an Indian classification system, later adopted in Tibet, anuttarayogatantra is the highest category in the fourfold division of tantric texts, above YOGATANTRA, CARYĀTANTRA, and KRIYĀTANTRA. Texts classified as unsurpassed yoga tantras include such works as the GUHYASAMĀJATANTRA, the HEVAJRATANTRA, and the CAKRASAṂVARATANTRA. These tantras were further divided into mother tantras (MĀTṚTANTRA) and father tantras (PITṚTANTRA). The mother tantras, also known as ḌĀKINĪ tantras, are traditionally said to emphasize wisdom (PRAJÑĀ) over method (UPĀYA), especially wisdom in the form of the mind of clear light (PRABHĀSVARACITTA). The father tantras are those that, between method (upāya) and wisdom (prajñā), place a particular emphasis on method, especially as it pertains to the achievement of the illusory body (MĀYĀDEHA) on the stage of generation (UTPATTIKRAMA). According to Tibetan exegetes, buddhahood can only be achieved through the practice of anuttarayogatantra; it cannot be achieved by the three "lower tantras" or by the practice of the PĀRAMITĀYĀNA. The many practices set forth in the anuttarayogatantras are often divided into two larger categories, those of the stage of generation (utpattikrama) and those of the stage of completion (NIṢPANNAKRAMA). The latter typically includes the practice of sexual yoga. The status of the KĀLACAKRATANTRA, historically the latest of the unsurpassed yoga tantras (the text includes apparent references to Muslim invaders in the Indian subcontinent), was accorded special status by DOL PO PA SHES RAB RGYAL MTSHAN; TSONG KHA PA in his SNGAGS RIM CHEN MO ("Great Exposition of the Stages of Tantra") gave it a separate place within a general anuttarayogatantra category, while others such as Red mda' ba Gzhon nu blo gros said it was not a Buddhist tantra at all.

**anuvyañjana**. (T. dpe byad; C. hao; J. kō; K. ho 好). In Sanskrit and Pāli, "minor mark" or "secondary characteristic"; the secondary characteristics of an object, in distinction to its generic appearance, or "sign" (NIMITTA). Advertence toward the generic sign and secondary characteristics of an object produces a recognition or perception (SAṂJÑĀ) of that object, which may then lead to clinging or rejection and ultimately suffering. ¶ The term anuvyañjana [alt. vyañjana] also refers specifically to the eighty minor marks of a "great man" (MAHĀPURUṢA) and specifically of a buddha; these are typically mentioned in conjunction with the thirty-two major marks of a great man (MAHĀPURUṢALAKṢAṆA). These are set forth at length in, for example, the PAÑCAVIṂŚATISĀHASRIKĀPRAJÑĀPĀRAMITĀ (see PRAJÑĀPĀRAMITĀ) and chapter eight of the ABHISAMAYĀLAṂKĀRA and are known as well in mainstream Buddhist sources.

**anuyoga**. (T. a nu yo ga). In Sanskrit, "subsequent yoga" or "further yoga," the eighth of the nine vehicles (THEG PA DGU) of Buddhism according to the RNYING MA sect of Tibetan Buddhism. Here, the system of practice described elsewhere as ANUTTARAYOGATANTRA is divided into three: MAHĀYOGA, anuyoga, and ATIYOGA, with anuyoga corresponding to the practices of the "stage of completion" (NIṢPANNAKRAMA), mahāyoga to the stage of generation (UTPATTIKRAMA) and atiyoga to the great completion (RDZOGS CHEN) and the spontaneous achievement of buddhahood. Thus, such stage of completion practices as causing the winds (PRĀṆA) to move through the channels (NĀḌĪ) to the CAKRAs are set forth in anuyoga. In Rnying ma, anuyoga is also a category of texts in the RNYING MA'I RGYUD 'BUM, divided under the following headings: the four root sūtras (rtsa ba'i mdo bzhi), the six tantras clarifying the six limits (mtha' drug gsal bar byed pa'i rgyud drug), the twelve rare tantras (dkon rgyud bcu gnyis), and the seventy written scriptures (lung gi yi ge bdun bcu).

**anvayajñāna**. (S). See DHARMAKṢĀNTI.

**Anxi guo**. (J. Ansoku koku; K. Ansik kuk 安息國). Chinese transcription of the Parthian proper name Aršak, referring to the Arsacid kingdom (c. 250 BCE–224 CE) in the region Roman geographers called PARTHIA. Aršak was the name adopted by all Parthian rulers, and the Chinese employed it to refer to the lands that those rulers controlled to the southeast of the Caspian Sea. In the Marv oasis, where the old Parthian city of Margiana was located, Soviet archeologists discovered the vestiges of a Buddhist monastic complex that has been dated to the third quarter of the fourth century CE, as well as birch-bark manuscripts written in the BRĀHMĪ script that are associated with the SARVĀSTIVĀDA school of mainstream Buddhism. There is therefore archaeological evidence of at least a semblance of Buddhist presence in the area during the fourth through sixth centuries. Parthian Buddhists who were active in China enable us to push this dating back at least two more centuries, for two of the important early figures in the transmission of Buddhist texts into China also hailed from Parthia: AN SHIGAO (fl. c. 148–180 CE), a prolific translator of mainstream Buddhist works, and An Xuan (fl. c. 168–189), who translated the UGRAPARIPṚCCHĀ with the assistance of the Chinese Yan Fotiao. (The AN in their names is an ethnikon referring to Parthia.) There is, however, no extant Buddhist literature written in the Parthian language and indeed little evidence that written Parthian was ever used in other than government documents and financial records until the third century CE, when Manichaean texts written in Parthian begin to appear.

**anxin**. (J. anjin; K. ansim 安心). In Chinese, "pacification of mind" or "peace of mind." Used generally to refer to an enlightened state of mind, anxin is used specifically in the Chan school (CHAN ZONG) in the more active sense of focusing one's attention in "wall contemplation" (BIGUAN) and thereby calming or "pacifying" the mind. According to the ERRU SIXING LUN attributed to the founder of Chan, BODHIDHARMA, the result of such cultivation is said to be an immovable state of mind. In the PURE LAND traditions, the "pacification of mind" refers to the firm establishment of a sense of faith in the teachings of the buddhas and the patriarchs (ZUSHI).

**Anyang jie**. (J. Annyōkai; K. Anyang kye 安養界). In Chinese, the "realm of peace and nurturance"; also known as the Anyang jingtu, or "pure land of peace and nurturance." One of the many names in Chinese for SUKHĀVATĪ ("land of bliss"), the purified buddha-field (BUDDHAKṢETRA) of AMITĀBHA Buddha. Sukhāvatī is, however, more commonly translated as JILE ("ultimate bliss").

**Anzhai shenzhou jing**. (J. Antaku jinshukyō; K. Ant'aek sinju kyŏng 安宅神呪經). In Chinese, the "Spirit-Spell Scripture for Pacifying Homes"; together with the *Anzhai tuolunizhou jing* ("DHĀRAṆĪ-Spell Scripture for Pacifying Homes"), both SŪTRAs detail the ritual known as anzhai zhai ("feast for pacifying homes"). According to this scripture, a merchant's sons were anguished by the unending travails that befell their household and asked the Buddha for help. The Buddha went to the merchant's house, reprimanded the spirits who were supposed to be protecting the home (anzhai jingshen), and expounded the means of preparing the feast for pacifying homes. This ritual, which had to be supervised by a BHIKṢU, entailed burning incense, lighting lamps, and chanting the *Anzhai shenzhou jing*. The scripture is claimed to have been translated during the Eastern Han dynasty (25–220 CE) by an unidentified translator, but no Indian or Tibetan recension is known, and it is suspected to be an indigenous Chinese composition (see APOCRYPHA).

**Apabhraṃśa**. In Sanskrit, literally "corrupt," or "ungrammatical"; a term used in ancient Sanskrit works to refer to the dialects of northern India. The term is used with reference to a number of north Indian languages, including Bengali, between the sixth and thirteenth centuries CE. A number of important tantric texts, such as the CARYĀGĪTIKOṢA, were composed in Apabhraṃśa.

**Apadāna**. In Pāli, "Heroic Tales" or "Narratives" (cf. S. AVADĀNA); the thirteenth book of the KHUDDAKANIKĀYA of the Pāli SUTTAPIṬAKA, this collection includes hagiographies of 547 monks and forty nuns, all arahant (S. ARHAT) disciples who lived during the lifetime of the Buddha. The text also contains two introductory chapters in verse. The first, the "Buddhāpadāna," is a series of encomiums praising the merits and perfections (P. pāramī; S. PĀRAMITĀ) of the Buddha and an account of the past lives during which he mastered these qualities. The second chapter, the "Paccekabuddhāpadāna," deals with solitary buddhas who do not teach (paccekabuddha; S. PRATYEKABUDDHA). Quite distinctively, the *Apadāna* names thirty-five buddhas of antiquity, in contrast to the twenty-four listed in the BUDDHAVAṂSA; this is one of the reasons that the *Apadāna* is presumed to be one of the latest books in the Pāli canon. The third and fourth chapters offer accounts of the noble deeds of the senior disciples, including many of the most famous names in Buddhist history. Each story focuses on a specific meritorious action performed by one of these elders while they trained under a buddha in a previous lifetime, followed by an account of what wholesome result that action produced in subsequent lifetimes, and how this ultimately led them to achieve arahantship in the present life. The collection thus highlights the merit that results from perfecting specific types of moral actions.

**aparagodānīya**. (S). See GODĀNĪYA.

**Aparamitāyurnāmamahāyānasūtra**. (S). See AMITĀBHASŪTRA.

**Aparānta**. [alt. Aparāntaka]. A territory in western India traversing modern Rajasthan and Gujarat along the Narmada River; according to the Pāli tradition, it was one of the nine regions to which Buddhist missions were dispatched during the reign of King AŚOKA. After the completion of the third Buddhist council (see COUNCIL, THIRD) in the third century BCE, the elder MOGGALIPUTTATISSA dispatched the elder Yonaka Dhammarakkhita from Pāṭaliputta (S. PĀṬALIPUTRA) to Aparānta to promote Buddhism. Burmese and Thai chroniclers, by contrast, variously identify Aparānta with Chiangmai, AYUTHAYA, and the Irrawaddy river basin in Middle Burma. The third Buddhist council at Pāṭaliputta and the nine Buddhist missions are known only in Pāli sources and are first recorded in the fifth-century DĪPAVAṂSA.

**āpas**. (P. āpo; T. chu; C. shuida; J. suidai; K. sudae 水大). In Sanskrit, lit. "water," viz., the property of "cohesion"; also seen written as āpodhātu. One of the four "great elements" (MAHĀBHŪTA) or "major elementary qualities" of which the physical world of materiality (RŪPA) is composed, along with earth (viz., solidity; PṚTHIVĪ, P. paṭhavī), wind (viz., motion, movement, or oscillation; VĀYU, P. vāyu/vāyo), and fire (viz., temperature, warmth; TEJAS, P. tejo). "Water" is defined as that which is moist and fluid and refers to the principle of liquidity; it also is the agent that binds the other elements together. Since water can convey things, such as ships (viz., earth), has relative temperature (viz., fire), and is capable of motion (viz., wind), the existence of all the other three elements may also be inferred even in that single element. In the physical body, this water element is associated with blood, tears, urine, sweat, phlegm, and so on.

**apatrāpya**. (P. ottappa; T. khrel yod pa; C. kui; J. gi, K. koe 愧). In Sanskrit, "modesty" or "blame"; one of the fundamental mental concomitants thought to accompany all wholesome actions (KUŚALA) and therefore listed as the sixth of the ten "wholesome factors of wide extent" (KUŚALAMAHĀBHŪMIKA) in the SARVĀSTIVĀDA ABHIDHARMA and one of the twenty-five wholesome (P. kusala) mental concomitants (CETASIKA) in the Pāli ABHIDHAMMA. It refers to a fear of blame or condemnation that prevents one from engaging in nonvirtuous deeds. "Modesty" is often seen in compound with the term "shame" or "decency" (HRĪ), where hrī refers to the sense of shame or the pangs of moral conscience that one feels oneself at the prospect of engaging in an immoral act, whereas apatrāpya refers to the fear of being blamed or embarrassed by others for engaging in such acts. This dual sense of "shame and blame" was thought to be foundational to progress in morality (ŚĪLA).

**apavāda**. (T. skur 'debs; C. sunjian; J. songen; K. son'gam 損減). In Sanskrit, "denigration" or "slander"; denying the presence of positive qualities and falsely ascribing negative qualities. Philosophically, the term is used to describe the underestimation or denigration of the status of phenomena, by claiming, for example, that phenomena do not exist conventionally. Wrong views (MITHYĀDṚṢṬI) themselves are considered to be the "denigration" of that which really exists, such as the truth of suffering (DUḤKHA); other specific sorts of wrong views may also be the "erroneous affirmation" or "superimposition" (SAMĀROPA) of things that actually do not exist in reality. Four types of apavāda are mentioned in the ABHIDHARMAMAHĀVIBHĀṢĀ: denigration of (1) cause, which is countered by understanding the noble truth of origination; (2) effect, which is countered by the noble truth of suffering; (3) the path, which is countered by the noble truth of the path; and (4) cessation, which is countered by the noble truth of cessation.

**apāya**. (T. ngan song; C. equ; J. akushu; K. akch'wi 惡趣). In Sanskrit and Pāli, lit. "falling away," or "misfortune," viz., "baleful destinies," and synonymous with the unfortunate destinies (DURGATI); refers to an unsalutary rebirth that occurs as a consequence of performing unwholesome actions (S. AKUŚALA; P. akusala). Three such unfortunate rebirth destinies (GATI) are typically enumerated in the literature: rebirth as (1) a denizen of the hells (S. NĀRAKA; P. nirāya); (2) an animal (S. TIRYAK, P. tiracchāna); or (3) a ghost (S. PRETA; P. peta); birth as a demigod or titan (ASURA) is sometimes added as a fourth. Unwholesome actions that lead to unfortunate rebirth are classified into ten types of wrong deeds (S. duṣcarita; P. duccarita), which include (1) intentionally killing living beings (S. prāṇātipāta; P. pāṇātipāta); (2) stealing (S. adattādāna; P. adinnādāna); and (3) sexual misconduct (S. KĀMAMITHYĀCĀRA; P. kāmamicchācāra). The next four in the list are classified as verbal wrong deeds and include (4) lying (S. mṛṣāvāda; P. musāvāda); (5) malicious speech (S. PAIŚUNYA; P. pisuṇavācā); (6) harsh speech (S. PĀRAṢYAVĀDA; P. pharusavācā); and (7) frivolous prattle (S. sampralāpa; P. samphappalāpa). The final three of the list are classified as mental wrong deeds and include (8) covetousness (S. ABHIDHYĀ; P. abhijjhā); (9) malice (S. VYĀPĀDA; P. vyāpāda); and (10) wrong views (S. MITHYĀDṚṢṬI; P. micchādiṭṭhi). Other sūtra literature, such as the SĀMAÑÑAPHALASUTTA, attribute rebirth in this state to reviling the noble ones (ĀRYA), keeping wrong views, and performing unwholesome acts as a result of those wrong views. See also BHAVACAKRA.

**apocrypha**. (C. yijing/weijing; J. gikyō/gikyō; K. ŭigyŏng/wigyŏng 疑經/僞經). Buddhist scholars have appropriated (though not without some controversy) the Judeo-Christian religious term "apocrypha" to refer to indigenous sūtras composed outside the Indian cultural sphere, but on the model of translated Indian or Serindian scriptures. Such scriptures were sometimes composed in conjunction with a revelatory experience, but many were intentionally forged using their false ascription to the Buddha or other enlightened figures as a literary device to enhance both their authority and their prospects of being accepted as authentic scriptures. Many of the literary genres that characterize Judeo-Christian apocrypha are found also in Buddhist apocrypha, including the historical, didactic, devotional, and apocalyptic. Both were also often composed in milieus of social upheaval or messianic revivalism. As Buddhism moved outside of its Indian homeland, its scriptures had to be translated into various foreign languages, creating openings for indigenous scriptures to be composed in imitation of these translated texts. Ferreting out such inauthentic indigenous scripture from authentic imported scripture occupied Buddhist bibliographical cataloguers (see JINGLU), who were charged with confirming the authenticity of the Buddhist textual transmission. For the Chinese, the main criterion governing scriptural authenticity was clear evidence that the text had been brought from the "Outer Regions" (C. waiyu), meaning India or Central Asia; this concern with authenticating a text partially accounts for why Chinese translations of Buddhist scriptures typically included a colophon immediately following the title, giving the name of the translator (who was also sometimes the importer of the scripture), along with the place where, and often the imperial reign era during which the translation was made. Scriptures for which there was no such proof were in danger of being labeled as texts of "suspect" or "suspicious" authenticity (yijing) or condemned as blatantly "spurious" or "counterfeit" scriptures (weijing). The presence of indigenous cultural elements, such as yin-yang cosmology, local spirits, or rituals and liturgies associated with folk religion could also be enough to condemn a scripture as "spurious." In Tibet, "treasure texts" (GTER MA) were scriptures or esoteric teachings attributed to enlightened beings or lineage holders that purported to have been buried or hidden away until they could be rediscovered by qualified individuals. Because of their association with a revelatory experience, such "treasure texts" carried authority similar to that of translated scripture. Different classifications of apocryphal scriptures have been proposed, based on genre and style, social history, and doctrinal filiations. In one of the ironies of the Buddhist textual transmission, however, many of the scriptures most influential in East Asian Buddhism have been discovered to be indigenous "apocrypha," not translated scriptures. Such indigenous scriptures were able to appeal to a native audience in ways that translated Indian materials could not, and the sustained popularity of many such "suspect" texts eventually led cataloguers to include them in the canon, despite continuing qualms about their authenticity. Such "canonical apocrypha" include such seminal scriptures as the FANWANG JING ("Brahmā's Net Sūtra"), RENWANG JING ("Humane Kings Sūtra"), and the YUANJUE JING ("Perfect Enlightenment Sūtra"), as well as treatises like the DASHENG QIXIN LUN ("Awakening of Faith"). Similar questions of authenticity can be raised regarding scriptures of Indian provenance, since it is virtually impossible to trace with certainty which of the teachings ascribed to the Buddha in mainstream canonical collections (TRIPIṬAKA) such as the Pāli canon can be historically attributed to him. Similarly, the MAHĀYĀNA sūtras, which are also attributed to the Buddha even though they were composed centuries after his death, are considered apocryphal by many of the MAINSTREAM BUDDHIST SCHOOLS, including the modern THERAVĀDA tradition; however, modern scholars do not use the term "Buddhist apocrypha" to describe Mahāyāna texts.

**apoha**. (T. gzhan sel; C. chu; J. jo; K. che 除). In Sanskrit, "exclusion"; a technical term in later Indian Buddhist philosophy of language and epistemology, which describes comprehension through the negative process of exclusion: i.e., only by excluding everything that is other than the target concept will the significance of that concept be comprehended. Buddhist apoha theory therefore posits that concepts convey meaning only to the extent that they "exclude" other meanings: e.g., the concept "chair" is understood only by the mental consciousness excluding everything else that is "not chair." Concepts thus do not denote the actual objects that they purport to reference but instead denote the mere "exclusion" of everything else that is not relevant. See also VYATIREKA.

**appanāsamādhi**. In Pāli, "absorptive concentration"; the more advanced of the two broad types of concentration (SAMĀDHI) discussed in Pāli commentarial literature. Both of these two types of samādhi are used with reference to meditators who are specializing in calmness (samatha; S. ŚAMATHA) techniques. The preliminary "threshold concentration" (UPACĀRASAMĀDHI) helps to calm and focus the mind but is too discursive to lead to full meditative absorption (JHĀNA; S. DHYĀNA). In order to develop jhāna, meditators must proceed to cultivate less discursive topics of meditation (KAMMAṬṬHĀNA) that will lead to "absorptive concentration" and thence jhāna: e.g., mindfulness of breathing (ānāpānasati, S. ĀNĀPĀNASMṚTI); the four "divine abidings" (BRAHMAVIHĀRA; [alt. P. appamañña], S. APRAMĀṆA), namely, loving-kindness (P. mettā; S. MAITRĪ), compassion (KARUṆĀ), altruistic or empathetic joy (MUDITĀ), and equanimity or impartiality (P. upekkhā; S. UPEKṢĀ); and the ten "visual devices" (KASIṆA)—devices that are constructed from the elements earth, water, fire, and air; the colors blue, yellow, red, and white; and light and space. See also KHANIKASAMĀDHI.

**apramāda**. (P. appamāda; T. bag yod pa; C. bufangyi; J. fuhōitsu; K. pulbangil 不放逸). In Sanskrit, "heedfulness" or "vigilance"; one of the forty-six mental concomitants (CAITTA) according to the SARVĀSTIVĀDA-VAIBHĀṢIKA school of ABHIDHARMA and one of the fifty-one according to the YOGACĀRA school. Heedfulness is the opposite of "heedlessness" (PRAMĀDA) and is the vigilant attitude that strives toward virtuous activities and remains ever watchful of moral missteps. Heedfulness fosters steadfastness regarding spiritual and ethical matters; it was presumed to be so foundational to any kind of ethical or wholesome behavior that the Sarvāstivāda abhidharma system included it among the predominant wholesome factors of wide extent (KUŚALAMAHĀBHŪMIKA). Heedfulness is also an integral part of the path of cultivation (BHĀVANĀMĀRGA), where certain types of proclivities (ANUŚAYA)—such as passion for sensual pleasure (RĀGA)—can only be removed by consistent and vigilant training, rather than simply through correct insight, as on the path of vision (DARŚANAMĀRGA). Heedfulness was so crucial to spiritual progress that the Buddha recommended it in his last words delivered on his deathbed, as related in the Pāli MAHĀPARINIBBĀNASUTTANTA: "Indeed, monks, I declare to you: decay is inherent in all compounded things; strive on with vigilance." (Handa 'dāni bhikkhave āmantayāmi vo: vayadhammā saṅkhārā; appamādena sampādetha.)

**apramāṇa**. (P. appammaññā; T. tshad med pa; C. wuliangxin; J. muryōshin; K. muryangsim 無量心). In Sanskrit, "the boundless states," "unlimiteds," or "limitless qualities." This list is identical to the four "divine abidings" (BRAHMAVIHĀRA) of loving-kindness (MAITRĪ), compassion (KARUṆĀ), empathetic joy (MUDITĀ), and equanimity or impartiality (UPEKṢĀ). When taken as objects of concentration and extended in meditation to all beings without limit, the divine abidings then become "boundless states" (apramāṇa). The meditator is taught to take up each of the boundless states in the same way: starting with the first apramāṇa, for example, filling his mind with loving-kindness, he pervades the world with it, first in one direction, then in a second direction, then a third and a fourth, then above, below, and all around, identifying himself with all beings and remaining free from hatred and ill will. In the same way, he takes up compassion, empathetic joy, and equanimity. These four factors are taken up as objects of meditation to counter the influence of specific unwholesome states of mind: viz., loving-kindness counteracts hostility (VYĀPĀDA); compassion counters harmfulness (VIHIṂSĀ); empathetic joy counters dissatisfaction or envy regarding others' achievements (arati); and equanimity counters both the desire and hostility arising from sensuality (KĀMARĀGA-VYĀPĀDA) and the desire to win the approval of others (anunaya). Of these boundless states, the first three are capable of producing the first three of the four DHYĀNAs, or meditative absorptions; the fourth divine abiding is the only one capable of producing the fourth meditative absorption.

**apramāṇābha**. (P. appamāṇābha; T. tshad med 'od; C. wuliangguang tian; J. muryōkōten; K. muryanggwang ch'ŏn 無量光天). In Sanskrit, "immeasurable radiance"; the second of the three heavens of the second meditative absorption (DHYĀNA) of the realm of subtle materiality (RŪPADHĀTU). The divinities of this heaven are so-called because their bodies emanate limitless light. As with all the heavens of the realm of subtle materiality, one is reborn as a divinity in this realm through achieving the same level of concentration (dhyāna) as the gods of that heaven during one's practice of meditation in a previous lifetime.

**apramāṇaśubha**. (P. appamāṇasubha; T. tshad med dge; C. wuliangjing tian; J. muryōjōten; K. muryangjŏng ch'ŏn 無量淨天). In Sanskrit, "immeasurable purity"; the second of the three heavens of the third meditative absorption (DHYĀNA) of the realm of subtle materiality (RŪPADHĀTU).

**apraṇihita**. (P. appaṇihita; T. smon pa med pa; C. wuyuan; J. mugan; K. muwŏn 無願). In Sanskrit, "wishless"; apraṇihita is one of the three "gates to deliverance" (VIMOKṢAMUKHA), along with emptiness (ŚŪNYATĀ) and signlessness (ĀNIMITTA). Once signlessness has exposed the dangers (ĀDĪNAVA) inherent in sensory perception, the meditator loses all desire for the compounded (SAṂSKṚTA) things of this world and adverts instead toward the uncompounded (ASAṂSKṚTA), which is NIRVĀṆA. The wishless is produced through insight into suffering (DUḤKHA) and serves as the counteragent (PRATIPAKṢA) to all the intentions (āśaya) and aspirations (PRAṆIDHĀNA) one has toward any compounded dharma. Once the meditator has abandoned all such aspirations, he or she is then able to advert toward nirvāṇa, which has no relation to anything that can be desired (VAIRĀGYA). This leads to the seeming conundrum of Buddhist soteriology, viz., that nirvāṇa can only be attained once the meditator no longer has any desire for anything, including nirvāṇa itself. The SARVĀSTIVĀDA and YOGĀCĀRA schools sought to resolve this conundrum about nirvāṇa being uncaused by positing that nirvāṇa was a specific type of effect, the VISAṂYOGAPHALA, or "disconnection fruition," which was disconnected from the afflictions (KLEŚA).

**aprāpti**. (T. 'thob pa med pa; C. feide; J. hitoku; K. pidŭk 非得). In Sanskrit, "dispossession" or "nonacquisition"; the second of the fourteen "conditioned forces dissociated from thought" (CITTAVIPRAYUKTASAṂSKĀRA) listed in the SARVĀSTIVĀDA–VAIBHĀṢIKA ABHIDHARMA and in the YOGĀCĀRA system. It is the opposite of the dissociated force of "possession" (PRĀPTI), which serves as a kind of glue that causes the various independent constituents of reality (DHARMA) to stick together into apparently permanent constructs. Aprāpti is the absence of such possession: when, for example, the afflictions (KLEŚA) are eliminated through the experience of sanctity, there is a "dispossession" between the afflictions and the mental continuum (SAṂTĀNA) of that sage to whom they were previously attached.

Similarly, the state of an ordinary person (PṚTHAGJANA) involves the "dispossession" of the noble (ĀRYA) dharmas.

**apratisaṃkhyānirodha**. (T. so sor brtags min gyi 'gog pa; C. feizemie; J. hichakumetsu; K. pit'aekmyŏl 非擇滅). In Sanskrit, "nonanalytical suppression" or "nonanalytical cessation," one of the uncompounded factors (ASAṂSKṚTADHARMA) listed by both the VAIBHĀṢIKA-SARVĀSTIVĀDA and the YOGĀCĀRA schools. In the Vaibhāṣika dharma theory, where all factors were presumed to exist in all three time periods (TRIKĀLA) of past, present, and future, this dharma was posited to suppress the production of all other dharmas, ensuring that they remain ever positioned in future mode and never again able to arise in the present. Whenever any specific factor is unproduced, this is due to its position in the present mode being occupied by the nonanalytical suppression; thus the number of apratisaṃkhyānirodha is coextensive with the number of factors. Because this dharma is not produced, not an object of knowledge, and not a result of insight, it is considered to be "nonanalytical." Other schools, such as the SAUTRĀNTIKA, presume that this factor has only nominal validity and refers to dharmas when they are in their unproduced state. The term also refers to states of temporary absence or cessation that do not occur as the result of meditative practice, such as the cessation of hunger after eating a meal. See also PRATISAṂKHYĀNIRODHA.

**apratiṣṭhitanirvāṇa**. (T. mi gnas pa'i mya ngan las 'das pa; C. wuzhu niepan; J. mujūnehan; K. muju yŏlban 無住涅槃). In Sanskrit, "unlocated nirvāṇa" or "nirvāṇa that is not permanently fixed"; the MAHĀYĀNA description of the NIRVĀṆA of the buddhas, which is "not permanently fixed" at either the extreme of the SAṂSĀRA of ordinary beings (PṚTHAGJANA) or what is presented as the overly quietistic nirvāṇa of the ARHAT. Since the buddhas' nirvāṇa is "unlocated," the buddhas are free to return to this world in order to save all sentient beings from suffering, without becoming in any way entangled by the prospect of rebirth, and without having passed completely away into the nirvāṇa of the arhat. Nirvāṇa as it is experienced by the buddhas, who have eradicated both the afflictive obstructions (KLEŚĀVARAṆA) and obstructions to omniscience (JÑEYĀVARAṆA), is therefore qualitatively different from that of the arhats, who have eradicated only the former.

**apsaras**. (P. accharā; T. chu skyes mo; C. tiannü; J. tennyo; K. ch'ŏnnyŏ 天女). In Sanskrit, "celestial nymph" (lit. "between the vapors [of the clouds]"); female divinities who dwell in the sky but have the capacity to visit the earth at will and thus occupy a liminal state between the celestial and the terrestrial worlds; they are eventually incorporated into Buddhist cosmology as one of several different types of nonhuman beings who dwell in the sensuous realm (KĀMADHĀTU). According to Indian mythology, they are married to the "celestial musicians" (GANDHARVA). The apsaras occupy an ambivalent position in Buddhist cosmology, since they are sometimes depicted as the debauched seductresses of Buddhist ascetics, at other times as the heavenly reward of leading a spiritual life. In Buddhist art, the apsaras are typically depicted as aerial beings fluttering above Buddhist deities or saints.

**Ārāḍa Kālāma**. (P. Āḷāra Kālāma; T. Sgyu rtsal shes kyi bu ring du 'phur; C. Aluoluojialan; J. Ararakaran; K. Araragaran 阿羅邏迦蘭). The Sanskrit name of one of the Buddha's two teachers of meditation (the other being UDRAKA RĀMAPUTRA) prior to his enlightenment. He was known as a meditation master who once sat in deep concentration without noticing that five hundred carts had passed by. He explained to GAUTAMA that the goal of his system was the attainment of the "state of nothing whatsoever" (ĀKIÑCANYĀYATANA), which the BODHISATTVA quickly attained. Ārāḍa Kālāma then regarded the bodhisattva as his equal. However, Gautama eventually recognized that this state was not NIRVĀṆA and left to begin the practice of austerities. Upon his eventual achievement of buddhahood, Gautama surveyed the world to identify the most worthy recipient of his first sermon. He thought first of Ārāḍa Kālāma but determined that he had unfortunately died just seven days earlier.

**arahant**. (S. arhat). In Pāli, "worthy one"; the highest of the four grades of Buddhist saint or "noble person" (ariyapuggala) recognized in the mainstream Buddhist schools. For a full description see ARHAT; LUOHAN.

**Arakan Buddha**. A colossal buddha image that is one of the most sacred images in Arakan, a coastal kingdom along the west coast of what eventually became the country of Burma after the Burmese conquest of the region in the eighteenth century; also known as the MAHĀMUNI Buddha or the Candasāra Buddha. This twelve-foot, seven-inch, tall bronze image of the Buddha as Mahāmuni ("Great Sage") is claimed by tradition to have been cast in 197 CE, during the reign of the Arakan king Candrasurya, and is assumed to be an exact replica of the Buddha himself, which was made at the time of his putative visit to the Arakan kingdom. The image is cast in the "earth-touching gesture" (BHŪMISPARŚAMUDRĀ) and is now enshrined in the Arakan pagoda (Mahāmuni Paya), located near the old capital of AMARAPURA on the outskirts of the city of Mandalay, which was constructed to house it. The image was coveted by several of Arakan's neighboring kingdoms, including Prome, Pagan, Pegu, and the Shan, but was eventually carried off to Mandalay by the Burmese as war booty in 1784 when King Bodawpaya finally conquered the kingdom. Since its relocation to the shrine, the seated image has been covered by worshippers with so many layers of gold leaf that its torso is now totally obscured, leaving only the head and face fully visible. The image is embellished with a pointed crown and earrings made in 1884 in the JAMBUPATI style, with a royal insignia across its chest; the Buddha is also draped in shawls by the temple vergers every night to ward off the evening chill.

**ārāma**. (T. kun dga' ra ba; C. yuan; J. on; K. wŏn 園). In Sanskrit and Pāli, "park" or "pleasure grove"; a term that originally referred to a garden, a favorite site for the teaching or practice of the dharma. The term came to mean an enclosed area, often in or near a city, which contained permanent dwellings for the use of monks during the annual rains retreat (VARṢĀ). The dwellings were built and maintained by a donor (DĀNAPATI), who offered them to the SAṂGHA for its use. An ārāma donated as property to the saṃgha was called a saṃghārāma and is considered to be the forerunner of the monastery, or VIHĀRA. These residences were often named after their donors, e.g., the JETAVANA-ārāma in ŚRĀVASTĪ, named after Prince JETA.

**araññavāsi**. In Pāli, "forest-dweller"; in the Pāli Buddhist tradition, a monk who is principally dedicated to meditative training (VIPASSANĀDHURA); contrasted with "town-dweller" (GĀMAVĀSI), who lives in a village or town monastery and whose monastic vocation focuses on doctrinal study and teaching, or "book work" (GANTHADHURA). In Sri Lankan Buddhism, the emphases within the Buddhist order on both meditation and study led to the evolution over time of these two major practice vocations. The araññavāsi remained in solitude in the forest to focus principally on their meditative practice. The gāmavāsi, by contrast, were involved in studying and teaching the dhamma, especially within the lay community of the village, and thus helped to disseminate Buddhism among the people. The araññavāsi were not necessarily hermits, but they did live a more secluded life than the gāmavāsi, devoting most of their time to meditation (either individually or in smaller groups) and keeping their contact with the laity to a minimum. According to the VINAYA, a monk cannot remain constantly alone in the forest by himself; at a minimum, he must join together with the saṅgha at least once a fortnight to participate in the uposatha (S. UPOṢADHA) rite, when the monks gather to confess any transgressions of the precepts and to listen to a recitation of the rules of discipline (P. pāṭimokkha; S. PRĀTIMOKṢA). These two vocations have a long history and have continued within the saṅgha into modern times. In a sense, the Buddha himself was an araññavāsi for six years before he attained enlightenment; subsequently, he then passed much of his time as a gāmavāsi, teaching people the dharma and encouraging them to practice to bring an end to their suffering. See also PHRA PA; THUDONG.

**araṇya**. (P. arañña; T. dgon pa; C. [a]lanruo; J. [a]rannya; K. [a]ranya [阿]蘭若). In Sanskrit, "forest" or "wilderness"; the ideal atmosphere for practice, and one of the various terms used to designate the residences of monks. The solitude and contentment fostered by forest dwelling was thought to provide a better environment for meditation (BHĀVANĀ) than the bustle and material comforts of city monasteries, and there is some evidence in mainstream Buddhist materials of discord between monks who followed the two different ways of life. Forest dwelling was frequently championed by the Buddha, and living at the root of a tree was one of the thirteen specific ascetic practices (S. DHŪTAGUṆA, P. DHUTAṄGA) authorized by the Buddha. Forest dwelling is also used as a metaphor for the renunciation and nonattachment that monks were taught to emulate. Forest dwellers are called araṇyaka (P. araññaka or āraññaka). See also ARAÑÑAVĀSI; PHRA PA.

**arapacana**. (T. a ra pa dza na). The arapacana is a syllabary of Indic or Central Asian origin typically consisting of forty-two or forty-three letters, named after its five initial constituents a, ra, pa, ca, and na. The syllabary appears in many works of the MAHĀYĀNA tradition, including the PRAJÑĀPĀRAMITĀ, GAṆḌAVYŪHA, LALITAVISTARA, and AVATAṂSAKA SŪTRAs, as well as in texts of the DHARMAGUPTAKA VINAYA (SIFEN LÜ) and MŪLASARVĀSTIVĀDA VINAYA. It occurs in both original Sanskrit works and Chinese and Tibetan translations. In most cases, each syllable in the list is presumed to correspond to a key doctrinal term beginning with, or containing, that syllable. A, for example, is associated with the concept of ANUTPĀDA (nonarising), ra with rajo'pagata (free from impurity), and so forth. Recitation of the syllabary, therefore, functioned as a mystical representation of, or mnemonic device (DHĀRAṆĪ) for recalling, important Mahāyāna doctrinal concepts, somewhat akin to the MĀTṚKĀ lists of the ABHIDHARMA. Other interpretations posit that the syllables themselves are the primal sources whence the corresponding terms later developed. The syllabary includes: a, ra, pa, ca, na, la, da, ba, ḍa, ṣa, va, ta, ya, ṣṭa, ka, sa, ma, ga, stha, tha, ja, śva, dha, śa, kha, kṣa, sta, jña, rta, ha, bha, cha, sma, hva, tsa, gha, ṭha, ṇa, pha, ska, ysa, śca, ṭa, ḍha. The arapacana also constitutes the central part of the root MANTRA of the BODHISATTVA MAÑJUŚRĪ; its short form is oṃ a ra pa ca na dhi. It is therefore also considered to be an alternate name for Mañjuśrī.

**Arbuda**. (S). One of the twenty-four sacred sites associated with the CAKRASAṂVARATANTRA. See PĪṬHA.

**arciṣmatī**. (T. 'od 'phro ba; C. yanhui di; J. enneji; K. yŏmhye chi 焰慧地). In Sanskrit, "radiance" or "effulgence"; the fourth of the ten BODHISATTVA grounds or stages (BHŪMI) according to the DAŚABHŪMIKASŪTRA. At this stage, the bodhisattva masters the thirty-seven wings of enlightenment (BODHIPĀKṢIKADHARMA), whose radiance becomes so intense that it incinerates all the obstructions and afflictions. The bodhisattva thus develops inexhaustible energy for his quest for enlightenment; this bhūmi is therefore often correlated with mastery of the fourth perfection (PĀRAMITĀ), the perfection of vigor or energy (VĪRYAPĀRAMITĀ). The fourth-stage bodhisattva also shows special devotion to the fourth means of conversion (SAṂGRAHAVASTU), that of the common good, or consistency between words and deeds (SAMĀNĀRTHATĀ).

**ardhapadmāsana**. (T. pad ma'i skyil krung phyed pa; C. ban lianhuazuo; J. hanrengeza; K. pan yŏnhwajwa 半蓮華坐). In Sanskrit, "half-lotus posture" a position in which only one leg is crossed completely over the top of the opposite thigh, the other leg being simply folded underneath. (In full-lotus posture, both legs would be crossed completely over the opposite thigh.) See also PADMĀSANA; ARDHAPARYAṄKA.

**ardhaparyaṅka**. (T. skyil krung phyed pa; C. ban jiafuzuo; J. hankafuza; K. pan kabujwa 半跏趺坐). In Sanskrit, the "half cross-legged" posture (ĀSANA). This particular posture may be formed in a number of ways. As a seated pose, either foot rests on the opposite thigh with the remaining leg bent forward. Alternatively, both shins may be loosely crossed at the ankles while resting or crouching on the seat. As a standing pose, it may form a dancing posture sometimes described as NṚTYĀSANA. Some standing Japanese images described as being in ardhaparyaṅka may show a raised foot lifted straight up off the ground, as if about to stomp down. See also VAJRAPARYAṄKA; ARDHAPADMĀSANA.

**arhat**. (P. arahant; T. dgra bcom pa; C. aluohan/yinggong; J. arakan/ōgu; K. arahan/ŭnggong 阿羅漢/應供). In Sanskrit, "worthy one"; one who has destroyed the afflictions (KLEŚA) and all causes for future REBIRTH and who thus will enter NIRVĀṆA at death; the standard Tibetan translation dgra bcom pa (drachompa) ("foe-destroyer") is based on the paronomastic gloss ari ("enemy") and han ("to destroy"). The arhat is the highest of the four grades of Buddhist saint or "noble person" (ĀRYAPUDGALA) recognized in the mainstream Buddhist schools; the others are, in ascending order, the SROTAĀPANNA or "stream-enterer" (the first and lowest grade), the SAKṚDĀGĀMIN or "once-returner" (the second grade), and the ANĀGĀMIN or "nonreturner" (the third and penultimate grade). The arhat is one who has completely put aside all ten fetters (SAṂYOJANA) that bind one to the cycle of rebirth: namely, (1) belief in the existence of a perduring self (SATKĀYADṚṢṬI); (2) skeptical doubt (about the efficacy of the path) (VICIKITSĀ); (3) belief in the efficacy of rites and rituals (ŚĪLAVRATAPARĀMARŚA); (4) sensual craving (KĀMARĀGA); (5) malice (VYĀPĀDA); (6) craving for existence as a divinity (DEVA) in the realm of subtle materiality (RŪPARĀGA); (7) craving for existence as a divinity in the immaterial realm (ĀRŪPYARĀGA); (8) pride (MĀNA); (9) restlessness (AUDDHATYA); and (10) ignorance (AVIDYĀ). Also described as one who has achieved the extinction of the contaminants (ĀSRAVAKṢAYA), the arhat is one who has attained nirvāṇa in this life, and at death attains final liberation (PARINIRVĀṆA) and will never again be subject to rebirth. Although the arhat is regarded as the ideal spiritual type in the mainstream Buddhist traditions, where the Buddha is also described as an arhat, in the MAHĀYĀNA the attainment of an arhat pales before the far-superior achievements of a buddha. Although arhats also achieve enlightenment (BODHI), the Mahāyāna tradition presumes that they have overcome only the first of the two kinds of obstructions, the afflictive obstructions (KLEŚĀVARAṆA), but are still subject to the noetic obstructions (JÑEYĀVARAṆA); only the buddhas have completely overcome both and thus realize complete, perfect enlightenment (ANUTTARASAMYAKSAṂBODHI). Certain arhats were selected by the Buddha to remain in the world until the coming of MAITREYA. These arhats (called LUOHAN in Chinese, a transcription of arhat), who typically numbered sixteen (see ṢOḌAŚASTHAVIRA), were objects of specific devotion in East Asian Buddhism, and East Asian monasteries will often contain a separate shrine to these luohans. Although in the Mahāyāna sūtras, the bodhisattva is extolled over the arhats, arhats figure prominently in these texts, very often as members of the assembly for the Buddha's discourse and sometimes as key figures. For example, in the SADDHARMAPUṆḌARĪKASŪTRA ("Lotus Sūtra"), ŚĀRIPUTRA is one of the Buddha's chief interlocutors and, with other arhats, receives a prophecy of his future buddhahood; in the VAJRACCHEDIKĀPRAJÑĀPĀRAMITĀSŪTRA, SUBHŪTI is the Buddha's chief interlocutor; and in the VIMALAKĪRTINIRDEŚA, Śāriputra is made to play the fool in a conversation with a goddess.

**arhatpratipannaka**. (P. arahattamagga; T. dgra bcom zhugs pa; C. aluohan xiang; J. arakankō; K. arahan hyang 阿羅漢向). In Sanskrit, "candidate for worthy one"; one of the VIṂŚATIPRABHEDASAṂGHA ("twenty varieties of the ārya saṃgha") based on the list given in the ABHISAMAYĀLAṂKĀRA. The arhatpratipannaka is usually an ANĀGĀMIPHALASTHA (one who has reached, or is the recipient of the fruit of nonreturner) who is making an effort to eliminate any fault that could cause rebirth in SAṂSĀRA, including the very last, ninth fetter to the BHAVĀGRA (summit of existence) that only the supramundane (LOKOTTARA) path of meditation (BHĀVANĀMĀRGA) can eliminate. See ARHAT.

**Ariyapariyesanāsutta**. (C. Luomo jing; J. Ramakyō; K. Rama kyŏng 羅摩經). In Pāli, "Discourse on the Noble Quest"; the twenty-sixth sutta (SŪTRA) in the MAJJHIMANIKĀYA, also known as the *Pāsarāsisutta* (a separate SARVĀSTIVĀDA recension appears as the 204th SŪTRA in the Chinese translation of the MADHYAMĀGAMA); preached by the Buddha to an assembly of monks at the hemitage of the brāhmaṇa Rammaka in the town of ŚRĀVASTĪ. The Buddha explains the difference between noble and ignoble quests and recounts his own life as an example of striving to distinguish between the two. Beginning with his renunciation of the householder's life, he tells of his training under two meditation masters, his rejection of this training in favor of austerities, and ultimately his rejection of austerities in order to discover for himself his own path to enlightenment. The Buddha also relates how he was initially hesitant to teach what he had discovered, but was convinced to do so by the god BRAHMĀ SAHĀṂPATI, and how he then converted the "group of five" ascetics (PAÑCAVARGIKA) who had been his companions while he practiced austerities. There is an understated tone of the narrative, devoid of the detail so familiar from the biographies. There is no mention of the opulence of his youth, no mention of his wife, no mention of the chariot rides, no description of the departure from the palace in the dead of night, no mention of MĀRA. Instead, the Buddha states, "Later, while still young, a black-haired young man endowed with the blessing of youth, in the prime of life, though my mother and father wished otherwise and wept with tearful faces, I shaved off my hair and beard, put on the yellow robe, and went forth from the home life into homelessness." Although the accounts of his study with other meditation masters assume a sophisticated system of states of concentration, the description of the enlightenment itself is both simple and sober, portrayed as the outcome of long reflection rather than as an ecstatic moment of revelation.

**Ariyaratne, A. T.** See SARVODAYA.

**Arnold, Edwin.** (1832–1904). Sir Edwin Arnold was educated at Oxford and served as principal of a government college in Pune, India, from 1856 to 1861, during which time he studied Indian languages and published translations from the Sanskrit. He eventually returned to England, due primarily to the death of a child and his wife's illness. Upon his return, he became a writer for *The Daily Telegraph* newspaper, where he was appointed chief editor in 1873. He wrote his most famous work, *The Light of Asia*, during this period. After leaving his editorial position, he traveled widely in Asia, especially in Japan, and published popular accounts of his travels. Although largely forgotten today, *The Light of Asia* was in its own time a foundational text for anyone in the English-speaking world interested in Buddhism. First published in 1879, *The Light of Asia* was a poetic rendering of the life of the Buddha. Arnold used as his chief source a French translation of the LALITAVISTARA, one of the more ornate and belletristic Indian biographies of the Buddha. Arnold, however, added his own embellishments and deployed important scenes from the life of the Buddha differently than had previous authors in order to intensify the narrative. Despite the animosity it aroused in many Christian pulpits, the book was a favorite of Queen Victoria, who subsequently knighted Arnold. Although it has long been rendered obsolete, *The Light of Asia* played a seminal role in introducing the history and belief systems of Buddhism to the West. Arnold also played an important role in rallying support worldwide for the restoration of the important Buddhist pilgrimage site of BODHGAYĀ, the place where the Buddha achieved enlightenment. He and Reverend SUMAṄGALA sent a petition to the Queen of England requesting permission to buy the land and the temple from the Hindus and restore the neglected site. Although unsuccessful, his efforts eventually came to fruition after Indian independence in 1949, when the Indian government returned control of Bodhgayā to the Buddhists.

**āropa.** (S). See SAMĀROPA.

**artha.** (P. attha/aṭṭha; T. don; C. yi; J. gi; K. ŭi 義). In Sanskrit, "meaning" or "object"; a polysemous term of wide import in Buddhist materials. In perhaps its most common usage, artha refers to the meaning or denotation of a term (and is always spelled aṭṭha in Pāli in this meaning), and, as the first of the four reliances (PRATISARAṆA), suggests that adepts should rely on the real meaning (artha) of words rather than their mere "letter" (vyañjana). In other contexts, however, artha may also be contrasted with DHARMA to refer to the principal denotation of a word rather than its interpreted connotations, implying the "literal meaning" of a term rather than its imputed "true spirit." Artha, as extensive understanding of meaning, is also listed as one of the four discriminating insights (PRATISAṂVID), along with knowledge of reasons or causal interconnections (DHARMA), explanation (NIRUKTI), and eloquence (PRATIBHĀNA). In other contexts, artha also can mean a sensory object; an event, matter, or aim; and welfare, benefit, profit, or even wealth. Thus, the bodhisattva seeks the welfare (artha) of others.

**arthacaryā.** (S). See SAṂGRAHAVASTU.

**arthakriyā.** (T. don byed nus pa; C. liyi; J. riyaku; K. iik 利益). In Sanskrit, "efficiency" or "capable of functioning"; a term used to describe the capacity of impermanent phenomena to produce effects. Arthakriyā as "actions that bring spiritual benefit to others," is also sometimes listed as one of the four means of conversion (SAṂGRAHAVASTU), in place of the more typical arthacaryā (actions that benefit others, i.e., helpfulness). The term is also important in YOGĀCĀRA and MADHYAMAKA philosophy in describing conventional truths (SAṂVṚTISATYA), which, although empty of intrinsic nature (NIḤSVABHĀVA), are nonetheless able to perform a function. Thus, for example, although the water in a mirage and the water in a glass are both empty of intrinsic nature, the water in a glass is nonetheless conventionally existent because it can perform the function of slaking thirst.

**arūpadhātu.** (S, P). See ĀRŪPYADHĀTU.

**arūpaloka.** In Sanskrit and Pāli, "immaterial world." See AVACARA.

**ārūpyadhātu.** [alt. in S. and P. arūpadhātu] (T. gzugs med pa'i khams; C. wuse jie; J. mushikikai; K. musaek kye 無色界). In Sanskrit, "immaterial" or "formless" "realm"; the highest of the three realms of existence (TRAIDHĀTUKA) within SAṂSĀRA, along with the sensuous realm (KĀMADHĀTU) and the realm of subtle materiality (RŪPADHĀTU). The heavens of the immaterial realm are comprised of four classes of divinities (DEVA) whose existence is entirely mental, no longer requiring even a subtle material foundation for their ethereal states of mind: (1) the sphere of infinite space (ĀKĀŚĀNANTYĀYATANA); (2) the sphere of infinite consciousness (VIJÑĀNĀNANTYĀYATANA); (3) the sphere of nothing whatsoever or absolute nothingness (ĀKIÑCANYĀYATANA); (4) the sphere of neither perception nor nonperception (NAIVASAṂJÑĀNĀSAṂJÑĀYATANA, see also BHAVĀGRA). Rebirth in these different spheres is based on mastery of the corresponding four immaterial meditative absorptions (ĀRŪPYĀVACARADHYĀNA) in previous lives. Because they have transcended all materiality, the beings here retain only the subtlest form of the last four aggregates (SKANDHA). For a detailed description, see DEVA.

**ārūpyarāga**. (P. arūparāga; T. gzugs med pa'i 'dod chags; C. wuse tan; J. mushikiton; K. musaek t'am 無色貪). In Sanskrit, "craving for immaterial existence"; the seventh of ten "fetters" (SAṂYOJANA) that keep beings bound to the cycle of rebirth (SAṂSĀRA). Ārūpyarāga is the desire to be reborn as a divinity (DEVA) in the immaterial realm (ĀRŪPYADHĀTU), where beings are composed entirely of mentality and are perpetually absorbed in the meditative bliss of the immaterial absorptions or attainments (ĀRŪPYĀVACARADHYĀNA). Craving for immaterial existence is permanently eliminated upon attaining the stage of a worthy one (ARHAT), the fourth and highest degree of Buddhist sanctity (ĀRYAPUDGALA) in the mainstream schools.

**ārūpyāvacaradhyāna**. (P. arūpāvacarajhāna; T. gzugs med na spyod pa'i bsam gtan; C. wusejie ding; J. mushikikaijō; K. musaekkye chŏng 無色界定). In Sanskrit, "meditative absorption associated with the immaterial realm"; equivalent to S. ārūpyadhyāna (q.v. DHYĀNA) and synonymous with "immaterial attainment" (arūpasamāpatti). One of two broad varieties of DHYĀNA or meditative absorption; the other being RŪPĀVACARADHYĀNA (P. rūpāvacarajhāna) or meditative absorption belonging to the realm of subtle materiality. In both cases, dhyāna refers to the attainment of single-pointed concentration of the mind on an ideational object of meditation. Ārūpyāvacaradhyāna is described as accessible only to those who have already mastered the fourth absorption of the realm of subtle materiality, and is itself merely a refinement of that state. In the immaterial absorptions, the "object" of meditation is gradually attenuated until the meditator abides in the sphere of infinite space (S. ĀKĀŚĀNANTYĀYATANA; P. ākāsānañcāyatana). In the second immaterial absorption, the meditator sets aside infinite space and abides in the sphere of infinite consciousness (S. VIJÑĀNĀNANTYĀYATANA; P. viññāṇānañcāyatanta). In the third immaterial absorption, one sets aside the perception of infinite consciousness and abides in the sphere of nothingness (S. ĀKIÑCANYĀYATANA; P. ākiñcaññāyatana). In the fourth immaterial absorption, one sets aside the perception of nothingness and abides in the sphere of neither perception nor nonperception (S. NAIVASAṂJÑĀNĀSAṂJÑĀYATANA; P. nevasaññānāsaññāyatana). Mastery of any of the absorptions of the immaterial realm can result in rebirth as a divinity (DEVA) within the corresponding plane in the immaterial realm (ārūpyāvacara or ĀRŪPYADHĀTU); see ANIÑJYAKARMAN. See also KAMMAṬṬHĀNA.

**ārya**. (P. ariya; T. 'phags pa; C. sheng; J. shō; K. sŏng 聖). In Sanskrit, "noble" or "superior." A term appropriated by the Buddhists from earlier Indian culture to refer to its saints and used technically to denote a person who has directly perceived reality and has become a "noble one." In the fourfold path structure of the mainstream schools, an ārya is a person who has achieved at least the first level of sanctity, that of stream-enterer (SROTAĀPANNA), or above. In the fivefold path system, an ārya is one who has achieved at least the path of vision (DARŚANAMĀRGA), or above. The SARVĀSTIVĀDA (e.g., ABHIDHARMAKOŚABHĀṢYA) and THERAVĀDA (e.g., VISUDDHIMAGGA) schools of mainstream Buddhism both recognize seven types of noble ones (ārya, P. ariya). In e.g., the VISUDDHIMAGGA, these are listed in order of their intellectual superiority as (1) follower of faith (P. saddhānusāri; S. ŚRADDHĀNUSĀRIN); (2) follower of the dharma (P. dhammānusāri; S. DHARMĀNUSĀRIN); (3) one who is freed by faith (P. saddhāvimutta; S. ŚRADDHĀVIMUKTA); (4) one who has formed right view (P. diṭṭhippatta; S. DṚṢṬIPRĀPTA), by developing both faith and knowledge; (5) one who has bodily testimony (P. kāyasakkhi; S. KĀYASĀKṢIN), viz., through the temporary suspension of mentality in the equipoise of cessation (NIRODHASAMĀPATTI); (6) one who is freed by wisdom (P. paññāvimutta; S. PRAJÑĀVIMUKTA), by freeing oneself through analysis; and (7) one who is freed both ways (P. ubhatobhāgavimutta; S. UBHAYATOBHĀGAVIMUKTA), by freeing oneself through both meditative absorption (P. jhāna; S. DHYĀNA) and wisdom (P. paññā; S. PRAJÑĀ). In the *Abhidharmakośabhāṣya*, the seven types of ārya beings are presented in a slightly different manner, together with the list of eight noble persons (ĀRYAPUDGALA) based on candidates for (pratipannika) and those who have reached the result of (phalastha) stream-enterer (srotaāpanna), once-returner (SAKṚDĀGĀMIN), nonreturner (ANĀGĀMIN), and ARHAT; these are again further expanded into a list of twenty members of the ārya VIṂŚATIPRABHEDASAṂGHA and in Mahāyāna explanations into forty-eight or more ĀRYABODHISATTVAs. The Chinese character sheng, used to render this term in East Asia, has a long indigenous history and several local meanings; see, for example, the Japanese vernacular equivalent HIJIRI. It is also the name of one of two Indian esoteric GUHYASAMĀJATANTRA traditions, receiving its name from Ārya Nāgārjuna, the author of the PAÑCAKRAMA.

**āryabodhisattva**. (T. byang chub sems dpa' 'phags pa). In Sanskrit, superior bodhisattva, a bodhisattva who has achieved either the path of vision (DARŚANAMĀRGA) or the path of cultivation (BHĀVANĀMĀRGA).

**Āryadeva**. (T. 'Phags pa lha; C. Tipo; J. Daiba; K. Cheba 提婆). While traditional sources are often ambiguous, scholars have identified two Āryadevas. The first Āryadeva (c. 170–270 CE) was an important Indian philosopher, proponent of MADHYAMAKA philosophy, and a direct disciple of the Madhyamaka master NĀGĀRJUNA. According to traditional accounts, he was born to a royal family in Sri Lanka. Renouncing the throne at the time of his maturity, he instead sought monastic ordination and met Nāgārjuna at PĀṬALIPUTRA. After his teacher's death, Āryadeva became active at the monastic university of NĀLANDĀ, where he is said to have debated and defeated numerous brahmanic adherents, eventually converting them to Buddhism. He is the author of the influential work CATUḤŚATAKA ("The Four Hundred"). He is also said to be the author of the *ŚATAŚĀSTRA (C. BAI LUN), or "The Hundred Treatise," counted as one of the "three treatises" of the SAN LUN ZONG of Chinese Buddhism, together with the *Zhong lun* ("Middle Treatise," i.e., MŪLAMADHYAMAKAKĀRIKĀ) and SHI'ERMEN LUN ("Twelve [Chapter] Treatise"), both attributed to Nāgārjuna. The **Śataśāstra* is not extant in Sanskrit or Tibetan, but is preserved only in Chinese. ¶ The second Āryadeva [alt. Āryadevapāda; d.u.] trained in yogic practices under the tantric master Nāgārjuna at Nālandā. In the Tibetan tradition, this Āryadeva is remembered for his great tantric accomplishments, and is counted among the eighty-four MAHĀSIDDHAS under the name Karṇari or Kaṇheri. His important tantric works include the *Caryāmelapakapradīpa* ("Lamp that Integrates the Practices") and *Cittaviśuddhiprakaraṇa* [alt. *Cittāvaraṇaviśuddhiprakaraṇa*] ("Explanation of Mental Purity").

**āryamārga**. (P. ariyamagga; T. 'phags lam; C. shengdao; J. shōdō; K. sŏngdo 聖道). In Sanskrit, "noble path"; the path of vision (DARŚANAMĀRGA), of cultivation (BHĀVANĀMĀRGA), and of the adept who has nothing more to learn (AŚAIKṢAMĀRGA), in either the mainstream or MAHĀYĀNA traditions. On these three paths, the practitioner becomes a noble person (ĀRYA) as a result of a direct perception of the truth. The paths of the stream-enterer (SROTAĀPANNA), once-returner (SAKṚDĀGĀMIN), and nonreturner (ANĀGĀMIN) would all be classified as noble paths. See also ĀRYĀṢṬĀṄGAMĀRGA.

**āryamārgaphala**. (P. ariyamaggaphala; T. 'phags lam gyi 'bras bu; C. shengdaoguo; J. shōdōka; K. sŏngdo kwa 聖道果). In Sanskrit, "noble path and fruit"; the four supramundane (LOKOTTARA) paths (MĀRGA) and the four supramundane fruitions (PHALA) that mark the attainment of sanctity (ĀRYA). Attainment of the path refers to the first moment of entering into or becoming a candidate (pratipannaka) for any of the four stages of sanctity; viz., stream-enterer (SROTAĀPANNA), once-returner (SAKṚDĀGĀMIN), nonreturner (ANĀGĀMIN), and worthy one (ARHAT). During this initial moment of path attainment, the mind takes the nirvāṇa element (NIRVĀṆADHĀTU) as its object. Path attainment is brought about by insight (VIPAŚYANĀ) into the three universal marks (TRILAKṢAṆA) of existence that characterize all phenomena: impermanence (ANITYA), suffering (DUḤKHA), and nonself (ANĀTMAN). Attainment of the fruit refers to the moments of consciousness that immediately follow attainment of the path. Attainment of any of the four paths occurs only once, while attainment of the fruit can be repeated indefinitely during a lifetime, depending on the circumstances. It is said that, by virtue of attaining the path, one "becomes" free in stages of the ten fetters (SAṂYOJANA) that bind one to the cycle of rebirth, and, by virtue of attaining the fruit, one "is" free from the fetters. The ten fetters that are put aside in stages are (1) belief in the existence of a self (ĀTMAN) in relation to the body (SATKĀYADṚṢṬI; P. sakkāyadiṭṭhi); (2) belief in the efficacy of rites and rituals (ŚĪLAVRATAPARĀMARŚA; P. sīlabbataparāmāsa) as a means of salvation; (3) doubt about the efficacy of the path (VICIKITSĀ; P. vicikicchā); (4) sensual craving (KĀMACCHANDA); (5) malice (VYĀPĀDA); (6) craving for existence as a divinity in the realm of subtle materiality (RŪPARĀGA); (7) craving for existence as a divinity in the immaterial realm (ĀRŪPYARĀGA; P. arūparāga); (8) pride (MĀNA); (9) restlessness (AUDDHATYA; P. uddhacca); and (10) ignorance (AVIDYĀ; P. avijjā). See also ŚRĀMAṆYAPHALA.

**āryapudgala**. (P. ariyapuggala; T. 'phags pa'i gang zag; C. xiansheng; J. kenjō; K. hyŏnsŏng 賢聖). In Sanskrit, "noble person"; an epithet given to enlightened beings, i.e., those who have reached at least the path of vision (DARŚANAMĀRGA). There is a well-known list of four types of noble persons, from stream-enterer (SROTAĀPANNA) to once-returner (SAKṚDĀGĀMIN), nonreturner (ANĀGĀMIN), and worthy one (ARHAT). This list is then subdivided into eight types or grades of noble persons according to their respective attainment of the paths and fruits of the noble path (ĀRYAMĀRGAPHALA). These are (1) the person who has entered the path of stream-enterer (SROTAĀPANNAPHALAPRATIPANNAKA); (2) the person who abides in the fruit of stream-enterer (SROTAĀPANNAPHALASTHA); (3) the person who has entered the path of once-returner (SAKṚDĀGĀMIPHALAPRATIPANNAKA); (4) the person who abides in the fruit of once-returner (SAKṚDĀGĀMIPHALASTHA); (5) the person who has entered the path of nonreturner (ANĀGĀMIPHALAPRATIPANNAKA); (6) the person who abides in the fruit of nonreturner (ANĀGĀMIPHALASTHA); (7) the person who has entered the path of a worthy one (ARHATPRATIPANNAKA); and (8) the person who has attained that fruition and become a worthy one (arhat). In some treatments, this list is presented together with a list of seven types of noble ones (ĀRYA) in order of intellectual superiority. By attaining the path and fruit of stream-entry, that is, by becoming a srotaāpanna, a person becomes free of the first three of the ten fetters (SAṂYOJANA) that bind one to the cycle of rebirth: namely, (1) belief in the existence of a perduring self in relation to the body (SATKĀYADṚṢṬI, P. sakkāyadiṭṭhi); (2) belief in the efficacy of rites and rituals (ŚĪLAVRATAPARĀMARŚA, P. sīlabbataparāmāsa) as a means of salvation; and (3) skeptical doubt (VICIKITSĀ, P. vicikicchā) about the efficacy of the path. By attaining the path and fruit of once-returning, i.e., becoming a sakṛdāgāmin, a person in addition severely weakens the effects of the fourth and fifth fetters, namely, (4) sensual craving (KĀMACCHANDA) and (5) malice (VYĀPĀDA). By attaining the path and fruit of nonreturning, i.e., becoming an anāgāmin, a person is completely freed of the first five fetters. Finally, by attaining the path and fruit of a worthy one and becoming an arhat, a person is additionally freed of the last five of the ten fetters: (6) craving for existence as a divinity (DEVA) in the realm of subtle materiality (RŪPARĀGA); (7) craving for existence as a divinity in the immaterial realm (ĀRŪPYARĀGA; P. arūparāga); (8) pride (MĀNA); (9) restlessness (AUDDHATYA, P. uddhacca); and (10) ignorance (AVIDYĀ, P. avijjā).

**āryasaṃgha**. (P. ariyasaṅgha; T. 'phags pa'i dge 'dun; C. shengseng; J. shōsō; K. sŏngsŭng 聖僧). "Noble community" or "community of noble ones"; the community of followers of the Buddha who are noble persons (ĀRYAPUDGALA). There are eight types or grades of noble persons according to their respective attainment of the paths and fruits of the noble path (ĀRYAMĀRGAPHALA). These are (1) the person who has entered the path of stream-enterer (SROTAĀPANNAPHALAPRATIPANNAKA); (2) the person who abides in the fruit of stream-enterer (SROTAĀPANNAPHALASTHA); (3) the person who has entered the path of once-returner (SAKṚDĀGĀMIPHALAPRATIPANNAKA); (4) the person who abides in the fruit of once-returner (SAKṚDĀGĀMIPHALASTHA); (5) the person who has entered the path of nonreturner (ANĀGĀMIPHALAPRATIPANNAKA); (6) the person who abides in the fruit of nonreturner (ANĀGĀMIPHALASTHA); (7) the person who has entered the path of a worthy one (ARHATPRATIPANNAKA); and (8) the person who has attained the fruit of a worthy one (ARHAT) (see also VIṂŚATIPRABHEDASAṂGHA). These eight persons are said to constitute the "SAṂGHA jewel" among the three jewels (RATNATRAYA) to which Buddhists go for refuge (ŚARAṆA).

**āryāṣṭāṅgamārga**. (P. ariyāṭṭhaṅgikamagga; T. 'phags lam yan lag brgyad; C. bazhengdao; J. hasshōdō; K. p'alchŏngdo 八正道). In Sanskrit, "noble eightfold path"; the path (MĀRGA) that brings an end to the causes of suffering (DUḤKHA); the fourth of the FOUR NOBLE TRUTHS (catvāry āryasatyāni). This formulation of the Buddhist path to enlightenment appears in what is regarded as the Buddha's first sermon after his enlightenment, the "Setting Forth the Wheel of Dharma" (DHARMACAKRAPRAVARTANASŪTRA), in which he sets forth a middle way (MADHYAMAPRATIPAD) between the extremes of asceticism and sensual indulgence. That middle way, he says, is the eightfold path, which, like the four truths, he calls "noble" (ĀRYA); the term is therefore commonly rendered as "noble eightfold path." However, as in the case of the four noble truths, what is noble is not the path but those who follow it, so the compound might be more accurately translated as "eightfold path of the [spiritually] noble." Later in the same sermon, the Buddha sets forth the four noble truths and identifies the fourth truth, the truth of the path, with the eightfold path. The noble eightfold path is comprised of (1) right views (SAMYAGDṚṢṬI; P. sammādiṭṭhi), which involve an accurate understanding of the true nature of things, specifically the four noble truths; (2) right intention (SAMYAKSAṂKALPA; P. sammāsaṅkappa), which means avoiding thoughts of attachment, hatred, and harmful intent and promoting loving-kindness and nonviolence; (3) right speech (SAMYAGVĀC; P. sammāvācā), which means refraining from verbal misdeeds, such as lying, backbiting and slander, harsh speech and abusive language, and frivolous speech and gossip; (4) right action or right conduct (SAMYAKKARMĀNTA; P. sammākammanta), which is refraining from physical misdeeds, such as killing, stealing, and sexual misconduct; (5) right livelihood (SAMYAGĀJĪVA; P. sammājīva), which entails avoiding trades that directly or indirectly harm others, such as selling slaves, selling weapons, selling animals for slaughter, dealing in intoxicants or poisons, or engaging in fortune-telling and divination; (6) right effort (SAMYAGVYĀYĀMA; P. sammāvāyāma), which is defined as abandoning unwholesome states of mind that have already arisen, preventing unwholesome states that have yet to arise, sustaining wholesome states that have already arisen, and developing wholesome states that have yet to arise; (7) right mindfulness (SAMYAKSMṚTI; P. sammāsati), which means to maintain awareness of the four foundations of mindfulness (SMṚTYUPASTHĀNA), viz., body, physical sensations, the mind, and phenomena; and (8) right concentration (SAMYAKSAMĀDHI; P. sammāsamādhi), which is one pointedness of mind. ¶ The noble eightfold path receives less discussion in Buddhist literature than do the four noble truths (of which they are, after all, a constituent). Indeed, in later formulations, the eight factors are presented not so much as a prescription for behavior but as eight qualities that are present in the mind of a person who has understood NIRVĀṆA. The eightfold path may be reduced to a simpler, and more widely used, threefold schema of the path that comprises the "three trainings" (TRIŚIKṢĀ) or "higher trainings" (adhiśikṣā) in morality (ŚĪLA; P. sīla; see ADHIŚĪLAŚIKṢĀ), concentration (SAMĀDHI, see ADHISAMĀDHIŚIKṢĀ), and wisdom (PRAJÑĀ; P. paññā; see ADHIPRAJÑĀŚIKṢĀ). In this schema, (1) right views and (2) right intention are subsumed under the training in higher wisdom (adhiprajñāśikṣā); (3) right speech, (4) right conduct, and (5) right livelihood are subsumed under higher morality (adhiśīlaśikṣā); and (6) right effort, (7) right mindfulness, and (8) right concentration are subsumed under higher concentration (adhisamādhiśikṣā). According to the MADHYĀNTAVIBHĀGA, a MAHĀYĀNA work attributed to MAITREYANĀTHA, the eightfold noble path comprises the last set of eight of the thirty-seven constituents of enlightenment (BODHIPĀKṢIKADHARMA), where enlightenment (BODHI) is the complete, nonconceptual awakening achieved during the path of vision (DARŚANAMĀRGA). After that vision, following the same pattern as the Buddha, right view is the perfect understanding of the vision, and right intention is the articulation of the vision that motivates the teaching of it. Right mindfulness, right effort, and right concentration correspond respectively to the four types of mindfulness (SMṚTYUPASTHĀNA), four efforts (PRAHĀṆA), and four ṚDDHIPĀDA ("legs of miraculous attainments," i.e., samādhi) when they are perfect or right (samyak), after the vision of the four noble truths.

**āryavaṃśa**. (P. ariyavaṃsa; T. 'phags pa'i rigs; C. shengzhong; J. shōshu; K. sŏngjong 聖種). In Sanskrit, "[attitudes of] the noble lineage." A list of four such attitudes commonly appears in the literature: contentment with robes, food, and beds, and devotion to the way of liberation. In

MAHĀYĀNA literature, the meaning of lineage changes, and the word GOTRA or DHĀTU is used in place of vaṃśa.

**aśaikṣa**. (P. asekha; T. mi slob pa; C. wuxue; J. mugaku; K. muhak 無學). In Sanskrit, lit. "one for whom no further training is necessary," an "adept"; a term for one who has completed the path (see AŚAIKṢAMĀRGA), used especially as an epithet of the ARHAT. The aśaikṣa has completed the three "higher trainings" (adhiśikṣā; P. adhisikkhā) in morality (ADHIŚĪLAŚIKṢĀ), concentration (ADHISAMĀDHIŚIKṢĀ), and wisdom (ADHIPRAJÑĀŚIKṢĀ).

**aśaikṣamārga**. (T. mi slob lam; C. wuxuedao; J. mugakudō; K. muhakto 無學道). In Sanskrit, "the path of the adept" (lit. "the path where there is nothing more to learn" or "the path where no further training is necessary"); the fifth of the five-path schema (PAÑCAMĀRGA) used in both SARVĀSTIVĀDA ABHIDHARMA and the YOGĀCĀRA and MADHYAMAKA schools of MAHĀYĀNA. It is the equivalent of the path of completion (NIṢṬHĀMĀRGA) and is synonymous with aśaikṣapatha. With the consummation of the "path of cultivation" (BHĀVANĀMĀRGA), the adept (whether following the ŚRĀVAKA, PRATYEKABUDDHA, or BODHISATTVA path) achieves the "adamantine-like concentration" (VAJROPAMASAMĀDHI), which leads to the permanent destruction of even the subtlest and most persistent of the ten fetters (SAṂYOJANA), resulting in the "knowledge of cessation" (KṢAYAJÑĀNA) and in some presentations an accompanying "knowledge of nonproduction" (ANUTPĀDAJÑĀNA), viz., the knowledge that the fetters are destroyed and can never again recur. Because the adept now has full knowledge of the eightfold path (ĀRYĀṢṬĀṄGAMĀRGA) and has achieved full liberation (VIMOKṢA) as either an ARHAT or a buddha, he no longer needs any further instruction—thus he has completed the "path where there is nothing more to learn."

**asamayavimukta**. (T. dus dang mi sbyor bar rnam par grol ba; C. bushi jietuo; J. fujigedatsu; K. pulsi haet'al 不時解脫). In Sanskrit, "one who is liberated regardless of occasion," in the sense that there is no occasion in which the meditative concentration of such an ARHAT will degenerate; one of the twenty members of the ĀRYASAṂGHA (see VIṂŚATIPRABHEDASAṂGHA).

**asaṃjñāsamāpatti**. [alt. asaṁjñisamāpatti] (P. asaññasamāpatti; T. 'du shes med pa'i snyoms par 'jug pa; C. wuxiang ding; J. musōjō; K. musang chŏng 無想定). In Sanskrit, "equipoise of nonperception" or "unconscious state of attainment"; viz., a "meditative state wherein no perceptual activity remains." It is a form of meditation with varying, even contradictory, interpretations. In some accounts, it is positively appraised: for example, the Buddha was known for entering into this type of meditation in order to "rest himself" and, on another occasion, to recover from illness. In this interpretation, asaṃjñāsamāpatti is a temporary suppression of mental activities that brings respite from tension, which in some accounts, means that the perception (SAṂJÑĀ) aggregate (SKANDHA) is no longer functioning, while in other accounts, it implies the cessation of all conscious thought. In such cases, asaṁjñasamāpatti is similar to ānimittasamāpatti in functions and contents, the latter being a meditative stage wherein one does not dwell in or cling to the "characteristics" (NIMITTA) of phenomena, and which is said to be conducive to the "liberation of the mind through signlessness (ĀNIMITTA)" (P. ānimittacetovimutti)—one of the so-called three gates to deliverance (VIMOKṢAMUKHA). Elsewhere, however, asaṁjñāsamāpatti is characterized negatively as a nihilistic state of mental dormancy, which some have mistakenly believed to be final liberation. Non-Buddhist meditators were reported to mistake this vegetative state for the ultimate, permanent quiescence of the mind and become attached to this state as if it were liberation. In traditional Buddhist classificatory systems (such as those of the YOGĀCĀRA school and the ABHIDHARMAKOŚABHĀṢYA), asaṃjñāsamāpatti is sometimes also conflated with the fourth DHYĀNA, and the karmic fruition of dwelling in this meditation is the rebirth in the asaṃjñā heaven (ASAṂJÑIKA) located in the "realm of subtle materiality," where the heavens corresponding to the fourth dhyāna are located (see RŪPADHĀTU). Together with the "trance of cessation" (NIRODHASAMĀPATTI), these two forms of meditation are classified under the CITTAVIPRAYUKTASAṂSKĀRA ("forces dissociated from thought") category in SARVĀSTIVĀDA ABHIDHARMA texts, as well as in the one hundred dharmas of the Yogācāra school, and are also called in the East Asian tradition "the two kinds of meditation that are free of mental activity" (er wuxin ding).

**asaṃjñika**. (P. asañña; T. 'du shes med pa; C. wuxiang tian; J. musōten; K. musang ch'ŏn 無想天). In Sanskrit, "free from discrimination," or "nonperception"; according to some systems, one of the heavens of the fourth meditative absorption (DHYĀNA) associated with the realm of subtle materiality (RŪPADHĀTU; see RŪPĀVACARADHYĀNA). In the Pāli tradition, it is one of the seven heavens of the fourth dhyāna; in Sanskrit sources, in some cases, it is considered a ninth heaven of the fourth dhyāna, and in other cases, it is considered to be a region of the BṚHATPHALA heaven. It is a place of rebirth for those who, during their lifetimes as humans, have cultivated the trance of nonperception (ASAṂJÑĀSAMĀPATTI), a state of meditative trance in which there is no mental activity; it is compared to dreamless sleep. During their long lifetime in this heaven, these divinities have a slight perception of having been born there and then have no other thoughts, sensations, or perceptions until the end of their period of rebirth in that heaven. Such beings are called asaññasatta ("unconscious beings") in Pāli. This particular state is often described as the attainment of non-Buddhist ascetics, who mistake it for the state of liberation (VIMOKṢA).

**asaṃkhya**. (P. asaṅkhya; T. grangs med pa; C. asengqi; J. asōgi; K. asŭnggi 阿僧祇). In Sanskrit, literally, "incalculable" or "infinite"; often used with reference to "infinite" eons of time (ASAṂKHYEYAKALPA).

**asaṃkhyeyakalpa**. (P. asaṅkheyyakappa; T. bskal pa grangs med pa; C. asengqi jie; J. asōgikō; K. asŭnggi kŏp 阿僧祇劫). In Sanskrit, "incalculable eon" or "infinite eon." The longest of all KALPAs is named "incalculable" (ASAṂKHYA); despite its name, it has been calculated by dedicated Buddhist scholiasts as being the length of a mahākalpa (itself, eight intermediate kalpas in duration) to the sixtieth power. The BODHISATTVA path leading to buddhahood is presumed to take not one but three "incalculable eons" to complete, because the store of merit (PUṆYA), knowledge (JÑĀNA), and wholesome actions (KUŚALA-KARMAPATHA) that must be accumulated by a bodhisattva in the course of his training is infinitely massive. Especially in the East Asian traditions, this extraordinary period of time has been taken to mean that practice is essentially interminable, thus shifting attention from the goal to the process of practice. For example, the AVATAṂSAKASŪTRA's statement that "at the time of the initial arousal of the aspiration for enlightenment (BODHICITTOTPĀDA), complete, perfect enlightenment (ANUTTARASAMYAKSAṂBODHI) is already achieved" has been interpreted in the East Asian HUAYAN ZONG to imply that enlightenment is in fact achieved at the very inception of religious training—a realization that renders possible a bodhisattva's commitment to continue practicing for three infinite eons. In YOGĀCĀRA and MADHYAMAKA presentations of the path associated with the ABHISAMAYĀLAMKĀRA, the three incalcuable eons are not considered infinite, with the bodhisattva's course divided accordingly into three parts. The first incalcuable eon is devoted to the paths of accumulation (SAMBHĀRAMĀRGA) and preparation (PRAYOGAMĀRGA); the second incalculable eon devoted to the path of vision (DARŚANAMĀRGA) and the first seven bodhisattva stages (BHŪMI); and the third incalculable eon devoted to the eighth, ninth, and tenth stages.

**asaṃprajanya**. (P. asampajañña; T. shes bzhin med pa; C. buzhengzhi; J. fushōchi; K. pujŏngji 不正知). In Sanskrit, "without circumspection" or "without clear comprehension." In Buddhist psychological analysis, when contact with sensory objects is made "without circumspection" (asaṃprajanya), then "attachment" (RĀGA), "greed" (LOBHA), "aversion" (DVEṢA), or "delusion" (MOHA) may result. The YOGĀCĀRA school lists asaṃprajanya in its hundred dharmas (C. BAIFA) list as the last of twenty secondary afflictions (UPAKLEŚA). Asaṃprajanya is the opposite of SAṂPRAJANYA (P. sampajañña), a term closely related to "mindfulness" (S. SMṚTI; P. sati), with which is it often used in compound as "mindfulness and clear comprehension."

**asaṃskṛta**. (P. asaṅkhata; T. 'dus ma byas; C. wuwei; J. mui; K. muwi 無爲). In Sanskrit, "uncompounded" or "unconditioned"; a term used to describe the few factors (DHARMA), especially NIRVĀṆA and in some schools space (ĀKĀŚA), that are not conditioned (SAṂSKṚTA) and are thus not subject to the inevitable impermanence (ANITYA) that plagues all conditioned dharmas. See ASAṂSKṚTADHARMA.

**asaṃskṛtadharma**. (P. asaṅkhatadhamma; T. 'dus ma byas kyi chos; C. wuweifa; J. muihō; K. muwibŏp 無爲法). In Sanskrit, "uncompounded" or "unconditioned" "factors"; a term used to describe the few DHARMAs that are not conditioned (SAṂSKṚTA) and are therefore perduring phenomena (NITYADHARMA) that are not subject to impermanence (ANITYA). The lists differ in the various schools. The Pāli tradition's list of eighty-two dharmas (P. dhamma) recognizes only one uncompounded dharma: NIRVĀṆA (P. nibbāna). The SARVĀSTIVĀDA school recognizes three out of seventy-five: space (ĀKĀŚA), and two varieties of nirvāṇa: "analytical" "suppression" or "cessation" (PRATISAṂKHYĀNIRODHA) and "nonanalytical suppression" (APRATISAṂKHYĀNIRODHA). YOGĀCĀRA recognizes six of its one hundred dharmas as uncompounded: the preceding three, plus "motionlessness" (āniñjya, [alt. aniñjya]), the "cessation of perception and sensation" (SAṂJÑĀVEDAYITANIRODHA), and "suchness" (TATHATĀ). Nirvāṇa is the one factor that all Buddhist schools accept as being uncompounded. It is the one dharma that exists without being the result of a cause (ahetuja), though it may be accessed through the three "gates to deliverance" (VIMOKṢAMUKHA). Because nirvāṇa neither produces nor is produced by anything else, it is utterly distinct from the conditioned realm that is subject to production and cessation; its achievement, therefore, means the end to the repeated cycle of rebirth (SAṂSĀRA). In several schools of Buddhism, including the Sarvāstivāda, nirvāṇa is subdivided into two complementary aspects: an "analytical cessation" (pratisaṃkhyānirodha) that corresponds to earlier notions of nirvāṇa and "nonanalytical suppression" (apratisaṃkhyānirodha), which ensures that the enlightened person will never again be subject to the vagaries of the conditioned world. "Analytical cessation" (pratisaṃkhyānirodha) occurs through the direct meditative insight into the FOUR NOBLE TRUTHS (catvāry āryasatyāni) and the cognition of nonproduction (ANUTPĀDAJÑĀNA), which brings about the disjunction (visaṃyoga) from all unwholesome factors (AKUŚALADHARMA). "Nonanalytical suppression" (apratisaṃkhyānirodha) prevents the dharmas of the conditioned realm from ever appearing again for the enlightened person. In the VAIBHĀṢIKA interpretation, this dharma suppresses the conditions that would lead to the production of dharmas, thus ensuring that they remain forever positioned in future mode and unable ever again to arise in the present. Because this dharma is not a result of insight, it is called "nonanalytical." Space (ākāśa) has two discrete denotations. First, space is an absence that delimits forms; like the empty space inside a door frame, ākāśa is a hole that is itself empty but that defines, or is defined by, the material that surrounds it. Second, as the vast emptiness of space, space comes also to be described as the absence of obstruction; in this sense, space also comes to be interpreted as something akin to the Western conception of ether, a virtually immaterial, but glowing fluid that serves as the support for the four material elements (MAHĀBHŪTA). Space is accepted as an uncompounded dharma in six of the mainstream Buddhist schools, including the SARVĀSTIVĀDA and the MAHĀSĀṂGHIKA, as well as the later YOGĀCĀRA; three others reject this interpretation, including the THERAVĀDA. The Yogācāra additions to this list essentially subsume the upper reaches of the immaterial realm (ārūpyāvacara) into the listing of uncompounded dharmas. Aniñjya, or motionlessness, is used even in the early Buddhist tradition to refer to actions that are neither wholesome nor unwholesome (see ANIÑJYAKARMAN), which lead to rebirth in the realm of subtle materiality or the immaterial realm and, by extension, to those realms themselves. The "cessation of perception and sensation" (saṃjñāvedayitanirodha) is the last of the eight liberations (VIMOKṢA; P. vimokkha) and the ninth and highest of the immaterial attainments (SAMĀPATTI). "Suchness" (TATHATĀ) is the ultimate reality (i.e., ŚŪNYATĀ) shared in common by a TATHĀGATA and all other afflicted (SAṂKLIṢṬA) and pure (VIŚUDDHI) dharmas; the "cessation of perception and sensation" (saṃjñāvedayitanirodha) is not only "a meditative trance wherein no perceptual activity remains," but one where no feeling, whether pleasant, unpleasant, or neutral, is experienced.

**asaṃvāsa**. (T. gnas par mi bya; C. bugongzhu; J. fugūjū; K. pulgongju 不共住). In Sanskrit and Pāli, "not in communion"; the lifelong punishment enjoined in the VINAYA on monks (and nuns) who have transgressed one of the major offenses that bring "defeat" (PĀRĀJIKA), such as the prohibition against engaging in sexual intercourse. The monk who is asaṃvāsa is not permitted to participate in any of the official monastic proceedings or ecclesiastical acts (KARMAN); thus he is effectively ostracized from the formal activities of the monastery. Although this term has sometimes been interpreted as "expulsion," asaṃvāsa does not necessarily mean that the monk is banished from the monastery but simply that he is "no longer in communion" with the work, rules, and training of the monastic community as a whole. Indeed, there is evidence from virtually all recensions of the vinaya (except the Pāli recension of the THERAVĀDA school), that pārājika monks continued to live in the monastery even after their transgressions, in the special status of pārājika penitents (ŚIKṢĀDATTAKA).

**āsana**. (T. 'dug stangs; C. zuofa/zuo; J. zahō/za; K. chwabŏp/chwa 坐法/座). In Sanskrit, "posture"; commonly referring to the position of the legs and feet in representations of Buddhist images. Āsanas may be seated or standing, passive or active, and, in the context of esoteric imagery, they are usually prescribed in literary sources such as TANTRAs and SĀDHANAs. The term may also be used to refer to the physical support or seat for a Buddhist deity. See also ACALĀSANA; ĀLĪḌHA; ARDHAPARYAṄKA; BHADRĀSANA; LALITĀSANA; MAITREYĀSANA; NṚTYĀSANA; PADMĀSANA; PRALAMBAPĀDĀSANA; PRATYĀLĪḌHA; RĀJALĪLĀSANA; SATTVAPARYAṄKA; SATTVĀRDHAPARYAṄKA; VAJRAPARYAṄKA; VAJRĀSANA.

**Asaṅga**. (T. Thogs med; C. Wuzhao; J. Mujaku; K. Much'ak 無著) (c. 320–c. 390 CE). a.k.a. Ārya Asaṅga, Indian scholar who is considered to be a founder of the YOGĀCĀRA school of MAHĀYĀNA Buddhism. In the Tibetan tradition, he is counted as one of the "six ornaments of JAMBUDVĪPA" ('dzam gling rgyan drug), together with VASUBANDHU, NĀGĀRJUNA and ĀRYADEVA, and DIGNĀGA and DHARMAKĪRTI. Born into a brāhmaṇa family in Puruṣapura (modern-day Peshawar, Pakistan), Asaṅga originally studied under SARVĀSTIVĀDA (possibly MAHĪŚĀSAKA) teachers but converted to the Mahāyāna later in life. His younger brother was the important exegete Vasubandhu; it is said that he was converted to the Mahāyāna by Asaṅga. According to traditional accounts, Asaṅga spent twelve years in meditation retreat, after which he received a vision of the future buddha MAITREYA. He visited Maitreya's abode in TUṢITA heaven, where the bodhisattva instructed him in Mahāyāna and especially Yogācāra doctrine. Some of these teachings were collected under the name Maitreyanātha, and the Buddhist tradition generally regards them as revealed by Asaṅga through the power of the future buddha. Some modern scholars, however, have posited the existence of a historical figure named MAITREYANĀTHA or simply Maitreya. Asaṅga is therefore associated with what are known as the "five treatises of Maitreyanātha" (the ABHISAMAYĀLAṂKĀRA, the DHARMADHARMATĀVIBHĀGA, the MADHYĀNTAVIBHĀGA, the MAHĀYĀNASŪTRĀLAṂKĀRA, and the RATNAGOTRAVIBHĀGA). Asaṅga was a prolific author, composing commentaries on the SAṂDHINIRMOCANASŪTRA and the VAJRACCHEDIKĀPRAJÑĀPĀRAMITĀSŪTRA. Among his independent treatises, three are particularly important. The ABHIDHARMASAMUCCAYA sets forth the categories of the ABHIDHARMA from a Yogācāra perspective. The MAHĀYĀNASAṂGRAHA is a detailed exposition of Yogācāra doctrine, setting forth such topics as the ĀLAYAVIJÑĀNA and the TRISVABHĀVA as well as the constituents of the path. His largest work is the compendium entitled YOGĀCĀRABHŪMIŚĀSTRA. Two of its sections, the ŚRĀVAKABHŪMI and the BODHISATTVABHŪMI, circulated as independent works, with the former important for its exposition of the practice of DHYĀNA and the latter for its exposition of the bodhisattva's practice of the six PĀRAMITĀ; the chapter on ŚĪLA is particularly influential. These texts have had a lasting and profound impact on the development of Buddhism, especially in India, Tibet, and East Asia. Among the great figures in the history of Indian Buddhism, Asaṅga is rare for the breadth of his interests and influence, making significant contributions to philosophy (as the founder of Yogācāra), playing a key role in TATHĀGATAGARBHA thought (through the *Ratnagotravibhāga*), and providing significant expositions of Buddhist practice (in the *Yogācārabhūmi*).

**āsava**. (S. āsrava). In Pāli, "contaminants" or "outflows"; mental contaminants that are eradicated upon attaining arahantship. They are: (1) the contaminant of sensuality (P. kāmāsava); (2) the contaminant of continuing existence (P. bhavāsava); and (3) the contaminant of ignorance (P. avijjāsava); to this list is sometimes added (4) the contaminant of views (P. diṭṭhāsava). See also ĀSAVAKKHAYA; and the more extensive discussion in ĀSRAVA s.v.

**āsavakkhaya**. (S. āsravakṣaya). In Pāli, "extinction of the contaminants" or "destruction of the outflows"; a supramundane (lokuttara) supernormal power (abhiññā) produced through the perfection of insight (VIPASSANĀ). It is equivalent to the attainment of "worthiness" (arahatta) or perfect sainthood. One who achieves this is a "worthy one" (arahant), attains in this life deliverance of mind (cetovimutti) and deliverance through wisdom (paññāvimutti), and at death passes into nibbāna never to be reborn. See ĀSRAVAKṢAYA.

**asceticism**. (S. duṣkaracaryā; P. dukkarakārikā; T. dka' ba spyod pa; C. kuxing; J. kugyō; K. kohaeng 苦行). Derived from the Greek term askesis, "to exercise"; the performance of austerities, both mental and physical, for the purpose of attaining enlightenment (BODHI) and, in certain cases, special powers or knowledges (ABHIJÑĀ). The basic Buddhist attitude toward asceticism, as found in the narrative surrounding the life of the Buddha, has been a negative one, particularly with regard to those practices associated with physical torment, such as fasting. The Buddha himself is said to have once practiced asceticism with five fellow ascetics in the forest of URUVILVĀ, only to eventually abandon it for the middle way (MADHYAMAPRATIPAD) between sensual indulgence and mortification of the flesh. Ascetic practices nevertheless continued to be important in the various Buddhist traditions, as attested to by the life stories of the teachers MI LA RAS PA (Milarepa), BODHIDHARMA, and HAKUIN EKAKU to name but a few. See also DUṢKARACARYĀ; DHUTAṄGA; TAPAS.

**asipattravana**. (P. asipattavana; T. ral gri'i lo ma'i nags; C. jianye lin; J. ken'yōrin; K. kŏmyŏp rim 劍葉林). In Sanskrit, "forest with leaves of swords," one of the neighboring hells (PRATYEKANARAKA) surrounding the eight hot hells, through which the denizens of the hells (NĀRAKA) must pass as they depart from those baleful realms. It is classified as part of the third of the four neighboring hells, called "razor road" (KṢURAMĀRGA). From a distance, the forest appears to be a forest of mango trees, and the denizens of hell approach in the hope of eating the mangoes. Upon arrival, they find that the leaves on the trees are swords and, as the denizens of hell pass through the forest, the leaves fall from the trees, lacerating their bodies.

**Asita**. (T. Mdog nag po; C. Asituo; J. Ashida; K. Asat'a 阿私陀). Sanskrit and Pāli name for an Indian brāhmaṇa who, according to Pāli sources, was chaplain to the BODHISATTVA's grandfather Sīhahanu (S. Siṃhahanu) and teacher of the bodhisattva's father Suddhodana (S. ŚUDDHODANA). After his retirement from the world, Asita developed various supranormal powers through his mastery of meditation and used them to sojourn in the realm of the divinities (DEVA). Once while staying in TRĀYASTRIṂŚA heaven, he learned that the future buddha SIDDHĀRTHA GAUTAMA had been born as the son of King Śuddhodana. Asita went to the palace to examine the infant and saw that the child was endowed with the thirty-two marks of a MAHĀPURUṢA, or great man. From these signs, he realized that Siddhārtha was destined to become a fully enlightened buddha. Despite his great joy, Asita was also dismayed to realize that, at his current age of ninety, he would not live long enough to witness this event. Instead, he would die and be reborn in the immaterial realm (ĀRŪPYADHĀTU), where he would not be able to hear the Buddha preach and could not be liberated by his salvific message. Asita urged his nephew Nālaka to renounce the world in anticipation of the future buddha's enlightenment. The boy complied and later attained arhatship after reflecting on the sermon the Buddha delivered to him in the *Nālakasutta*.

**Aśoka**. (P. Asoka; T. Mya ngan med; C. Ayu wang; J. Aiku ō; K. Ayuk wang 阿育王) (c. 300–232 BCE; r. c. 268–232 BCE). Indian Mauryan emperor and celebrated patron of Buddhism; also known as Dharmāśoka. Son of Bindusāra and grandson of Candragupta, Aśoka was the third king of the Mauryan dynasty. Aśoka left numerous inscriptions recording his edicts and proclamations to the subjects of his realm. In these inscriptions, Aśoka is referred to as DEVĀNĀṂ PRIYAḤ, "beloved of the gods." These inscriptions comprise one of the earliest bodies of writing as yet deciphered from the Indian subcontinent. His edicts have been found inscribed on boulders, on stone pillars, and in caves and are widely distributed from northern Pakistan in the west, across the Gangetic plain to Bengal in the east, to near Chennai in South India. The inscriptions are ethical and religious in content, with some describing how Aśoka turned to the DHARMA after subjugating the territory of Kaliṅga (in the coastal region of modern Andhra Pradesh) in a bloody war. In his own words, Aśoka states that the bloodshed of that campaign caused him remorse and taught him that rule by dharma, or righteousness, is superior to rule by mere force of arms. While the Buddha, dharma, and SAṂGHA are extolled and Buddhist texts are mentioned in the edicts, the dharma that Aśoka promulgated was neither sectarian nor even specifically Buddhist, but a general code of administrative, public, and private ethics suitable for a multireligious and multiethnic polity. It is clear that Aśoka saw this code of ethics as a diplomatic tool as well, in that he dispatched embassies to neighboring states in an effort to establish dharma as the basis for international relations. The edicts were not translated until the nineteenth century, however, and therefore played little role in the Buddhist view of Aśoka, which derives instead from a variety of legends told about the emperor. The legend of Aśoka is recounted in the Sanskrit DIVYĀVADĀNA, in the Pāli chronicles of Sri Lanka, DĪPAVAṂSA and MAHĀVAṂSA, and in the Pāli commentaries, particularly the SAMANTAPĀSĀDIKĀ. Particularly in Pāli materials, Aśoka is portrayed as a staunch sectarian and exclusive patron of the Pāli tradition. The inscriptional evidence, as noted above, does not support that claim. In the *Mahāvaṃsa*, for example, Aśoka is said to have been converted to THERAVĀDA Buddhism by the novice NIGRODHA, after which he purifies the Buddhist SAṂGHA by purging it of non-Theravāda heretics. He then sponsors the convention of the third Buddhist council (SAṂGĪTĪ; see COUNCIL, THIRD) under the presidency of MOGGALIPUTTATISSA, an entirely Theravāda affair. Recalling perhaps the historical Aśoka's diplomatic missions, the legend recounts how, after the council, Moggaliputtatissa dispatched Theravāda missions, comprised of monks, to nine adjacent lands for the purpose of propagating the religion, including Aśoka's son (MAHINDA) and daughter (SAṄGHAMITTĀ) to Sri Lanka. In Sri Lanka, where the legend appears to have originated, and in the Theravāda countries of Southeast Asia, the Pāli account of King Aśoka was adopted as one of the main paradigms of Buddhist kingship and models of ideal governance and proper saṃgha-state relations. A different set of legends, which do not recount the conversion of Sri Lanka, appears in Sanskrit sources, most notably, the AŚOKĀVADĀNA.

**Aśokan pillars**. Stone pillars erected or embellished during the reign of King AŚOKA, many of which bear royal edicts attesting to the king's support of the "dharma" and putatively of Buddhism. Although later Buddhist records mention more than forty such pillars, less than half of these have been identified. At least some pillars predate Aśoka's ascendance, but most were erected by the king to commemorate his pilgrimage to sacred Buddhist sites or as Buddhist memorials. One representative example, located at Lauriyā Nandangaṛh, stands nearly forty feet tall and extends over ten feet below the ground. The heaviest may weigh up to 75,000 pounds. The pillar edicts form some of the earliest extant written records in the Indian subcontinent and typically avoid mentioning Buddhist philosophy, offering instead general support of dharma, or righteousness, and in some cases of the Buddhist SAṂGHA. At one time, the pillars supported stone capitals in the form of animals such as the bull. One Aśokan innovation was the use of lion capitals, the most famous being a lotus vase supporting a drum of four wheels and other animals, topped with four lions and a wheel (now missing). The use of lion symbolism may have been a direct reference to the ŚĀKYA clan of the Buddha, which took the lion (siṃha) as its emblem.

**Aśokāvadāna**. (T. Ku ṇā la'i rtogs pa brjod pa; C. Ayu wang zhuan; J. Aiku ō den; K. Ayuk wang chŏn 阿育王傳). In Sanskrit, "The Story of Aśoka," a text belonging to the category of "edifying tales" (AVADĀNA), which narrates the major events in the life of King AŚOKA of the Indian Mauryan dynasty. The work focuses primarily on Aśoka's conversion to Buddhism, his subsequent support of the DHARMA and monastic community (SAṂGHA), his visits to the major sites of the Buddha's life (MAHĀSTHĀNA), and his construction of STŪPAs. It also records the transmission of the Buddhist teachings by five early teachers: MAHĀKĀŚYAPA, ĀNANDA, MADHYĀNTIKA, ŚĀṆAKAVĀSIN, and UPAGUPTA. The *Aśokāvadāna* relates that, in a previous life, Aśoka (then a small boy named Jaya) placed a handful of dirt in the Buddha's begging bowl (PĀTRA). The Buddha predicted that one hundred years after his passage into nirvāṇa, the child would become a DHARMARĀJA and CAKRAVARTIN named Aśoka. As emperor, Aśoka becomes a devout Buddhist and righteous king, renowned for collecting the relics (ŚARĪRA) of the Buddha from eight (or in one version, seven of eight) stūpas and redistributing them in 84,000 stūpas across his realm. Parts of the Sanskrit text have been preserved in the DIVYĀVADĀNA, and the entire work is extant in Chinese. Only the Kunāla chapter of the *Aśokāvadāna* was rendered into Tibetan, in the eleventh century, by Padmākaravarman and RIN CHEN BZANG PO.

**āśraddhya**. [alt. aśrāddhya] (P. asaddhā/asaddhiya; T. ma dad pa; C. buxin; J. fushin; K. pulsin 不信). In Sanskrit, "lack of faith," "disbelief." In the roster of seventy-five factors (DHARMA) in the SARVĀSTIVĀDA school of ABHIDHARMA, āśraddhya is listed as the fourth of the six major afflicted factors of wide extent (KLEŚAMAHĀBHŪMIKA) that are associated with all defiled thoughts and afflictions (KLEŚA), together with delusion (MOHA), heedlessness (PRAMĀDA), indolence (KAUSĪDYA), sloth (STYĀNA), and restlessness (AUDDHATYA). The YOGĀCĀRA school lists it in its roster of a hundred dharmas (C. BAIFA) as the thirteenth of the twenty secondary afflictions (UPAKLEŚA). Āśraddhya refers to the inability of a person to generate the tacit belief or confidence in a teacher and the doctrines that is necessary to undertake practice in earnest; it has a stronger affective dimension than the intellectual skepticism of the related term doubt (VICIKITSĀ).

**āsrava**. (P. ĀSAVA; T. zag pa; C. lou; J. ro; K. nu 漏). In Sanskrit, "contaminants," "outflows," or "fluxes"; mental contaminants that are eradicated upon attaining the status of a "worthy one" (ARHAT); also written as āśrava. They are (1) the contaminant of sensuality (kāmāsrava; KĀMA); (2) the contaminant of continuing existence (bhavāsrava; BHAVA); and (3) the contaminant of ignorance (avidyāsrava; AVIDYĀ); to this list is often added (4) the contaminant of views (dṛṣṭyāsrava; DṚṢṬI). Since the āsravas bind or immerse one in the cycle of existence, they are also sometimes called the "floods" (OGHA) and the "yokes" (yoga). The term āsrava is used in both Buddhism and Jainism, suggesting that it is one of the earliest such terms for the mental contaminants used within the tradition. (In the Buddhist interpretation, an āsrava is more of an "outflow," because the contaminants flow out from the mind and affect the ways in which one interacts with the external world; indeed, the Chinese translation of the term means literally to "leak." In the JAINA tradition, an āsrava is more of an "inflow," because the contaminants flow into the body, where they adhere to the ĀTMAN, thus defiling it.) The term is a synonym of the KLEŚAs (afflictions, defilements), since objects (such as the five SKANDHAs) that can serve as objects of defilement are "contaminated" (sāsrava). The contaminants are permanently overcome through insight into such fundamental Buddhist truths as the FOUR NOBLE TRUTHS, conditioned origination (PRATĪTYASAMUTPĀDA), or the three marks of existence (TRILAKṢAṆA). Because the ARHAT has permanently uprooted the contaminants from the mind, he or she receives the epithet KṢĪṆĀSRAVA ("one whose contaminants are extinguished"). See also ĀSAVA, ANĀSRAVA, ĀSRAVAKṢAYA.

**āsravakṣaya**. (P. āsavakkhaya; T. zag pa zad pa; C. loujin [zhi]; J. rojin[chi]; K. nujin[ji] 漏盡[智]). In Sanskrit, "extinction of the contaminants"; a supranormal power (ABHIJÑĀ) produced through the perfection of insight (VIPAŚYANĀ), and one of the three knowledges (TRIVIDYĀ) that are the products of enlightenment (BODHI). One who achieves this state is a "worthy one" (ARHAT) and at death passes into NIRVĀṆA, never to be reborn. See also ANĀSRAVA; ĀSRAVA.

**āśraya**. (T. gnas; C. suoyi; J. sho'e; K. soŭi 所依). In Sanskrit, lit. "basis." In the SAUTRĀNTIKA school, the term is used idiosyncratically to refer to the "substratum" of existence. This substratum is the psychophysical entity that was presumed to exist independently from the momentary flow of the conscious continuum (SAṂTĀNA) and thus to provide the physical support for thought (CITTA) and the mental concomitants (CAITTA). This Sautrāntika teaching was critiqued by other Buddhist schools as skirting dangerously close to the proscribed notion of a perduring self (ĀTMAN). The term is also adopted subsequently in the YOGĀCĀRA school to refer to the "transformation of the basis" (ĀŚRAYAPARĀVṚTTI) of the mind, the path, and the proclivities, which transforms an ordinary person (PṚTHAGJANA) into a noble one (ĀRYA).

**āśrayaparāvṛtti**. [alt. āśrayaparivṛtti] (T. gnas yongs su 'gyur pa; C. zhuanyi; J. ten'e; K. chŏnŭi 轉依). In Sanskrit, "transformation of the basis" or "fundamental transmutation"; the transmutation of the defiled state in which one has not abandoned the afflictions (KLEŚA) into a purified state in which the kleśas have been abandoned. This transmutation thus transforms an ordinary person (PṚTHAGJANA) into a noble one (ĀRYA). In the YOGĀCĀRA school's interpretation, by understanding (1) the emptiness (ŚŪNYATĀ) of the imagined reality (PARIKALPITA) that ordinary people mistakenly ascribe to the sensory images they experience (viz., "unreal imaginings," or ABHŪTAPARIKALPA) and (2) the conditioned origination of things through the interdependent aspect of cognition (PARATANTRA), the basis will be transformed into the perfected (PARNIṢPANNA) nature, and enlightenment realized. STHIRAMATI posits three aspects to this transformation: transformation of the basis of the mind (cittāśrayaparāvṛtti), transformation of the basis of the path (mārgāśrayaparāvṛtti), and transformation of the basis of the proclivities (dauṣṭhulyāśrayaparāvṛtti). "Transformation of the basis of mind" transmutes the imaginary into the perfected through the awareness of emptiness. Insight into the perfected in turn empties the path of any sense of sequential progression, thus transmuting the mundane path (LAUKIKAMĀRGA) with its multiple steps into a supramundane path (lokottaramārga, cf. LOKUTTARAMAGGA) that has no fixed locus; this is the "transformation of the basis of the path." Finally, "transformation of the basis of the proclivities" eradicates the seeds (BĪJA) of action (KARMAN) that are stored in the storehouse consciousness (ĀLAYAVIJÑĀNA), liberating the bodhisattva from the effects of any past unwholesome actions and freeing him to project compassion liberally throughout the world.

**Aṣṭabhayatrāṇa-Tārā**. (S). See TĀRĀ.

**aṣṭaduḥkha**. (T. sdug bsngal brgyad; C. baku; J. hakku; K. p'algo 八苦). In Sanskrit, "eight types of suffering" (DUḤKHA), sometimes specificed as the eight sufferings of humans. The eight are the suffering associated with (1) birth (jātiduḥkha), (2) aging (jarāduḥkha), (3) sickness (vyādhiduḥkha), and (4) death (maraṇaduḥkha); (5) "the suffering of being separated from persons and things one likes" (priyaviprayogaduḥkha); (6) "the suffering of being associated with persons and things one dislikes" (apriyasaṃprayogaduḥkha); (7) "the suffering of not getting what one wants" (yad api icchayā paryeṣamāṇo na labhate tad api duḥkham); and (8) "the suffering inherent in the five aggregates" (saṃkṣepeṇa pañcopādānaskandhaduḥkham); the eighth appears in some lists as "the suffering of getting what one does not want." See discussion in DUḤKHA entry.

**aṣṭakṣaṇa**. (T. dal ba brgyad). In Sanskrit, lit. "eight moments," i.e., eight qualities of an opportune [human] rebirth (these are defined in Tibetan as "eight freedoms"). The eight are freedom from (1) birth as one of the hell denizens (NĀRAKA); (2) birth as an animal (TIRYAK), (3) birth as a ghost (PRETA), or (4) birth as a long-lived divinity (DEVA); (5) birth in a border land or barbarian region; (6) birth in a place with perverted or heretical views; (7) birth as a stupid person who is unable to understand the teachings; and (8) birth at a time when or a place where no buddhas have arisen. In Tibetan LAM RIM literature, one is instructed to contemplate the rarity of such an opportune birth in order to take full advantage of it by practicing the path. See KṢAṆA.

**aṣṭalokadharma**. (T. 'jig rten gyi chos brgyad). In Sanskrit, "eight mundane dharmas" or "eight worldly concerns"; the preoccupation with gain (lābha) and loss (alābha), pleasure (SUKHA) and pain (DUḤKHA), praise (praśaṃsā) and blame (nindā), and fame (yaśas) and disgrace (ayaśas). This list encapsulates the concerns of foolish (BĀLA) ordinary persons (PṚTHAGJANA) who in each case desire to attain the first and avoid the second, unlike those who practice asceticism (DHUTAṄGA), understand impermanence (ANITYA), and are motivated to attain both a better rebirth and the state of NIRVĀṆA and BODHI.

**aṣṭamahābodhisattva**. In Sanskrit, "eight great BODHISATTVAs." See AṢṬAMAHOPAPUTRA.

**aṣṭamahāśmaśāna**. (T. dur khrod chen po brgyad). In Sanskrit, "eight great charnel grounds." See ŚMAŚANA.

**aṣṭamahopaputra**. (T. nye ba'i sras chen brgyad; C. ba da pusa; J. hachidai bosatsu; K. p'al tae posal 八大菩薩). In Sanskrit, the "eight great associated sons"; a group of eight bodhisattvas also known as the AṢṬAMAHĀBODHISATTVA or "eight great bodhisattvas"; they are KṢITIGARBHA, ĀKĀŚAGARBHA, AVALOKITEŚVARA, VAJRAPĀṆI, MAITREYA, SARVANĪVARAṆAVIṢKAMBHIN, SAMANTABHADRA, and MAÑJUŚRĪ. Textual evidence for the grouping is found as early as the third century, the date of ZHI QIAN's Chinese translation of the *Aṣṭabuddhakasūtra* (*Fo shuo ba jixiangshen zhoujing*). In earlier representations, they flank either ŚĀKYAMUNI or AMITĀBHA. Their roles are laid out in the *Aṣṭamaṇḍalakasūtra*, where the aims of their worship are essentially mundane—absolution from transgressions, fulfillment of desires, and protection from ills. The grouping is known throughout Asia, from northern India, where they first appeared in ELLORĀ, Ratnagiri, and NĀLANDĀ, and from there as far east as Japan and Indonesia—indeed, virtually anywhere MAHĀYĀNA and tantric Buddhism flourished. They figure as a group in TANTRAs of various classes, where their number of arms corresponds to the main deity of the MAṆḌALA and their colors correspond to the direction in which they are placed. In the maṇḍala of the GUHYASAMĀJATANTRA, they flank the central figure AKṢOBHYA, who appears in the form of Vajradhṛk and his consort Sparśavajrā. When each has a consort, the females are called the aṣṭapūjādevī ("eight offering goddesses"). There are four in the *Guhyasamājatantra* maṇḍala: Rūpavajrā, Śabdavajrā, Gandhavajrā, and Rasavajrā. In the vajradhātu mahāmaṇḍala, the group of bodhisattvas is expanded to sixteen.

**aṣṭamaṅgala**. (T. bkra shis rtags brgyad; C. ba jixiang; J. hachikichijō; K. p'al kilsang 八吉祥). In Sanskrit, "eight auspicious symbols"; eight Indian emblems of good fortune, which became especially popular in Nepal and Tibet but are also known in China. The eight include the lotus (PADMA), the endless knot (śrīvatsa, T. dpal be'u), the pair of golden fish (suvarṇamatsya, T. gser nya), the parasol (chattra, T. gdugs), the victory banner (ketu, T. rgyal mtshan), the treasure vase (dhanakumbha, T. gter gyi bum pa), the white conch shell (śaṅkha, T. dung dkar), and the wheel (CAKRA, T. 'khor lo). VAJRAYĀNA Buddhism deified the symbols as eight goddesses, the aṣṭamaṅgaladevī, who each carry one of these emblems as their attribute. Chinese Buddhism regards the symbols as representing eight organs of the Buddha's body, and in one Tibetan tradition the eight are collectively identified as forming the body of the Buddha. Designs of these symbols are found throughout both sacred and secular artwork and commonly adorn furniture, murals, carpets, and brocade hangings. In Tibetan communities, the eight symbols are traditionally drawn on the ground out of sprinkled flour or powder as a greeting to visiting religious teachers.

**aṣṭamāyopamā**. (T. sgyu ma'i dpe brgyad; C. ruhuan yu; J. nyogen no yu; K. yŏhwan yu 如幻喩). In Sanskrit, "eight similes of illusion"; teaching that all dharmas lack an inherent nature (NIḤSVABHĀVA). In the PAÑCAVIṂŚATSĀHASRIKĀPRAJÑĀPĀRAMITĀSŪTRA, these are listed as a dream (svapna); an illusion (MĀYĀ); a mirage (marīci); an echo (pratiśabda); an optical illusion (pratibhāsa); a reflection (pratibimba), such as of the moon reflected in water (udakacandra); a city of the GANDHARVAS (GANDHARVANAGARA); and a tathāgata's magical creation (tathāgatanirmita). Other famous metaphors or similes for the insubstantiality of the five aggregates (SKANDHA) include the five in the *Pheṇapiṇḍūpamasutta* of the SAṂYUTTANIKĀYA, which compare form to a lump of foam (P. pheṇapiṇḍa), feeling to a water bubble (P. bubbuḷaka), perception to a mirage (P. marīcikā), conditioned formations to the trunk of a plantain tree (P. kadalikkhandha), and consciousness to a conjurer (māyākāra). See also LIUYU ("six similes").

**aṣṭāṅgasamanvāgataṃ upavāsaṃ**. (P. aṭṭhaṅgasamannāgataṃ uposathaṃ; T. yan lag brgyad pa'i gso sbyong; C. bazhaijie; J. hassaikai; K. p'alchaegye 八齋戒). In Sanskrit, the "fortnightly assembly with its eight constituents," more popularly known as the eight rules of conduct (ŚIKṢĀPADA; P. sikkhāpada). On the fortnightly UPOṢADHA days, Buddhist laity would take three additional precepts beyond their standard list of five precepts (PAÑCAŚĪLA) to help foster a sense of renunciation. The full list of eight includes prohibitions against (1) killing, (2) stealing, (3) engaging in sexual misconduct, (4) lying, and (5) consuming intoxicants; these are supplemented by these three extra precepts prohibiting (6) resting on a high or luxurious bed, (7) using makeup and perfumes and enjoying music and dance, and (8) eating at improper times (viz., after midday). See also BAGUAN ZHAI; ŚĪLA.

**aṣṭāṅgikamārga**. In Sanskrit, "eightfold path." See ĀRYĀṢṬĀṄGAMĀRGA.

**aṣṭānta**. (T. mtha' brgyad; C. babu; J. happu; K. p'albul 八不). In Sanskrit, "eight extremes," an important term in the MADHYAMAKA school, referring to eight qualities of which all phenomena are said to be empty (see ŚŪNYATĀ). The eight (in four pairs) are cessation and production, annihilation and permanence, coming and going, and difference and sameness. The locus classicus for the list is the opening passage of NĀGĀRJUNA's MŪLAMADHYAMAKAKĀRIKĀ, which reads, "Homage to the perfect Buddha, best of teachers, who taught that what is dependently arisen has no cessation and no production, no annihilation and no permanence, no coming and no going, no difference and no sameness, is free of elaborations and is at peace." See also BABU.

**aṣṭāryapudgala**. (P. aṭṭhāriyapuggala; T. 'phags pa'i gang zag brgyad/gang zag ya brgyad; C. badaren; J. hachidainin; K. p'altaein 八大人). In Sanskrit, "eight noble persons"; referring to those who have achieved the four right paths and four fruitions of sanctity. See ĀRYAPUDGALA.

**Aṣṭasāhasrikāprajñāpāramitāvyākhyābhisamayālaṃkārālokā**. (T. Brgyad stong 'grel chen/Rgyan snang). In Sanskrit, "Light for the Ornament of Clear Realizations, a Commentary on the Perfection of Wisdom in Eight Thousand Lines," by the Indian scholiast HARIBHADRA. See ABHISAMAYĀLAṂKĀRĀLOKĀVYĀKHYĀ.

**Aṣṭasāhasrikāprajñāpāramitā**. (T. Sher phyin brgyad stong pa; C. Xiaopin bore jing; J. Shōbon hannyakyō; K. Sop'um panya kyŏng 小品般若經). In Sanskrit, "Perfection of Wisdom in Eight Thousand Lines." This scripture is now generally accepted to be the earliest of the many PRAJÑĀPĀRAMITĀ sūtras and thus probably one of the very earliest of the MAHĀYĀNA scriptures. The *Aṣṭa*, as it is often referred to in the literature, seems to have gradually developed over a period of about two hundred years, from the first century BCE to the first century CE. Some of its earliest recensions translated into Chinese during the Han dynasty do not yet display the full panoply of self-referentially Mahāyāna terminology that characterize the more elaborate recensions translated later, suggesting that Mahāyāna doctrine was still under development during the early centuries of the Common Era. The provenance of the text is obscure, but the consensus view is that it was probably written in central or southern India. The *Aṣṭa*, together with its verse summary, the RATNAGUṆASAṂCAYAGĀTHĀ, probably represents the earliest stratum of the prajñāpāramitā literature; scholars believe that this core scripture was subsequently expanded between the second and fourth centuries CE into other massive Prajñāpāramitā scriptures in as many as 100,000 lines (the ŚATASĀHASRIKĀPRAJÑĀPĀRAMITĀ). By about 500 CE, the *Aṣṭa*'s basic ideas had been abbreviated into shorter condensed statements, such as the widely read, 300-verse VAJRACCHEDIKĀPRAJÑĀPĀRAMITĀ ("Diamond Sūtra"). (Some scholars have suggested instead that the "Diamond Sūtra" may in fact represent one of the earliest strata of the prajñāpāramitā literature.) The Mahāyāna tradition's view of its own history, however, is that the longest of the prajñāpāramitā scriptures, the 100,000-line *Śatasāhasrikāprajñāpāramitā*, is the core text from which all the other perfection of wisdom sūtras were subsequently excerpted. The main interlocutor of the *Aṣṭa*, as in most of the prajñāpāramitā scriptures, is SUBHŪTI, an ARHAT foremost among the Buddha's disciples in dwelling at peace in remote places, rather than ŚĀRIPUTRA, who much more commonly appears in this role in the mainstream Buddhist scriptures (see ĀGAMA; NIKĀYA). The prominent role accorded to Subhūti suggests that the prajñāpāramitā literature may derive from forest-dwelling (āraṇyaka) ascetic traditions distinct from the dominant, urban-based monastic elite. The main goal of the *Aṣṭa* and other prajñāpāramitā scriptures is rigorously to apply the foundational Buddhist notion of nonself (ANĀTMAN) to the investigation of all phenomena—from the usual compounded things (SAṂSKĀRA) and conditioned factors (SAṂSKṚTADHARMA), but even to such quintessentially Buddhist summa bona as the fruits of sanctity (ĀRYAMĀRGAPHALA) and NIRVĀṆA. The constant refrain of the *Aṣṭa* is that there is nothing that can be grasped or to which one should cling, not PRAJÑĀ, not PĀRAMITĀ, not BODHISATTVA, and not BODHI. Even the six perfections (ṢAḌPĀRAMITĀ) of the bodhisattva are subjected to this same refutation: for example, only when the bodhisattva realizes that there is no giver, no recipient, and no gift will he have mastered the perfection of giving (DĀNAPĀRAMITĀ). Such radical nonattachment even to the central concepts of Buddhism itself helps to foster a thoroughgoing awareness of the emptiness (ŚŪNYATĀ) of all things and thus the perfection of wisdom (prajñāpāramitā). Even if the *Aṣṭa*'s area of origin was in the south of India, the prajñāpāramitā scriptures seem initially to have found their best reception in the northwest of India during the KUSHAN dynasty (c. first century CE), whence they would have had relatively easy entrée into Central Asia and then East Asia. This geographic proximity perhaps accounts for the early acceptance the *Aṣṭa* and the rest of the prajñāpāramitā literature received on the Chinese mainland, helping to make China the first predominantly Mahāyāna tradition.

***aṣṭasenā**. (T. lha srin sde brgyad; C. tianlong babu; J. tenryū hachibu; K. ch'ŏnnyong p'albu 天龍八部). Sanskrit term for a grouping of eight nonhuman beings associated with the sensuous realm (KĀMADHĀTU); they are often listed as being in attendance when the Buddha speaks the MAHĀYĀNA sūtras. There are various lists, but a standard grouping includes divinities (DEVA), dragons (NĀGA), demons (YAKṢA), demigods or titans (ASURA), demigod musicians (GANDHARVA), mythical birds (GARUḌA), half-horse/half-men (KIṂNARA), and great snakes (MAHORĀGA).

**aṣṭavimokṣa**. (P. aṭṭhavimokkha; T. rnam par thar pa brgyad; C. ba jietuo; J. hachigedatsu; K. p'al haet'al 八解脱). In Sanskrit, "eight liberations"; referring to a systematic meditation practice for cultivating detachment and ultimately liberation (VIMOKṢA). There are eight stages in the attenuation of consciousness that accompany the cultivation of increasingly deeper states of meditative absorption (DHYĀNA). In the first four dhyānas of the realm of subtle materiality (RŪPĀVACARADHYĀNA), the first three stages entail (1) the perception of materiality (RŪPA) in that plane of subtle materiality (S. rūpasaṃjñin, P. rūpasaññī), (2) the perception of external forms while not perceiving one's own form (S. arūpasaṃjñin, P. arūpasaññī), and (3) the developing of confidence through contemplating the beautiful (S. śubha, P. subha). The next five stages transcend the realm of subtle materiality to take in the four immaterial dhyānas (ĀRŪPYĀVACARADHYĀNA) and beyond: (4) passing beyond the material plane with the idea of "limitless space," one attains the plane of limitless space (ĀKĀŚĀNANTYĀYATANA); (5) passing beyond the plane of limitless space with the idea of "limitless consciousness," one attains the plane of limitless consciousness (VIJÑĀNĀNANTYĀYATANA); (6) passing beyond the plane of limitless consciousness with the idea that "there is nothing," one attains the plane of nothingness (ĀKIÑCANYĀYATANA), (7) passing beyond the plane of nothingness, one attains the plane of neither perception nor nonperception (NAIVASAMJÑĀNĀSAMJÑĀYATANA); and (8) passing beyond the plane of neither perception nor nonperception, one attains the cessation of all perception and sensation (SAṂJÑĀVEDAYITANIRODHA). ¶ The ABHIDHARMASAMUCCAYA and YOGĀCĀRABHŪMIŚĀSTRA give an explanation of the first three of the eight vimokṣas within the larger context of bodhisattvas who compassionately manifest shapes, smells, and so on for the purpose of training others. Bodhisattvas who have reached any of the nine levels (the RŪPADHĀTU, the four subtle-materiality DHYĀNAs, and four immaterial attainments) engage in this type of practice. In the first vimokṣa, they destroy "form outside," i.e., those in the rūpadhātu who have not destroyed attachment to forms (to their own color, shape, smell, and so on) cultivate detachment to the forms they see outside. (Other bodhisattvas who have reached the first dhyāna and so on do this by relaxing their detachment for the duration of the meditation.) In the second vimokṣa, they destroy the "form inside," i.e., they cultivate detachment to their own color and shape. (Again, others who have reached the immaterial attainments and have no attachment to their own form relax that detachment for the duration of the meditation.) In the third, they gain control over what they want to believe about forms by meditating on the relative nature of beauty, ugliness, and size. They destroy grasping at anything as having an absolute pleasant or unpleasant identity, and perceive them all as having the same taste as pleasant, or however else they want them to be. These texts finally give an explanation of the remaining five vimokṣas, "to loosen the rope of craving for the taste of the immaterial levels."

**aśubhabhāvanā**. (P. asubhabhāvanā; T. mi sdug pa bsgom pa; C. bujing guan; J. fujōkan; K. pujŏng kwan 不淨觀). In Sanskrit, the "contemplation on the impure" or "foul"; a set of traditional topics of meditation (see KAMMAṬṬHĀNA) that were intended to counter the affliction of lust (RĀGA), develop mindfulness (SMṚTI; P. SATI) regarding the body, and lead to full mental absorption (DHYĀNA). In this form of meditation, "impure" or "foul" is most often used to refer either to a standardized list of thirty-one or thirty-two foul parts of the body or to the various stages in the decay of a corpse. In the case of the latter, for example, the meditator is to observe nine or ten specific types of putrefaction, described in gruesome detail in the Buddhist commentarial literature: mottled discoloration of the corpse (vinīlakasaṃjñā), discharges of pus (vipūyakasaṃjñā), decaying of rotten flesh (vipaḍumakasaṃjñā), bloating and tumefaction (vyādhmātakasaṃjñā), the exuding of blood and the overflow of body fluids (vilohitakasaṃjñā), infestation of worms and maggots (vikhāditakasaṃjñā), the dissolution of flesh and exposure of bones and sinews (vikṣiptakasaṃjñā), the cremated remains (vidagdhakasaṃjñā), and the dispersed skeletal parts (asthisaṃjñā). The *Kāyagatāsatisutta* of the MAJJHIMANIKĀYA includes the contemplation of the impure within a larger explanation of the contemplation of one's body with mindfulness (KĀYĀNUPAŚYANĀ; see also SMṚTYUPASTHĀNA); before the stages in the decay of the corpse, it gives the standardized list of thirty-one (sometimes thirty-two) foul parts of the body: the head hairs, body hairs, nails, teeth, skin, flesh, tendons, bones, bone marrow, kidneys, heart, liver, diaphragm, spleen, lungs, large intestines, small intestines, gorge, feces, bile, phlegm, pus, blood, sweat, fat, tears, skin-oil, saliva, mucus, fluid in the joints, and urine. These parts are chosen specifically because they will be easily visualized, and may have been intended to be the foul opposites of the thirty-two salutary marks of the great man (MAHĀPURUṢALAKṢAṆA). The Chinese tradition also uses a contemplation of seven kinds of foulness regarding the human body in order to counter lust and to facilitate detachment. (1) "Foulness in their seeds" (C. zhongzi bujing): human bodies derive from seminal ejaculate and, according to ancient medicine, mother's blood. (2) "Foulness in their conception" (C. shousheng bujing): human bodies are conceived through sexual intercourse. (3) "Foulness in their [gestational] residence" (C. zhuchu bujing): human bodies are conceived and nurtured inside the mother's womb. (4) "Foulness in their nutriments" (C. shidan bujing): human bodies in the prenatal stage live off and "feed on" the mother's blood. (5) "Foulness in their delivery" (C. chusheng bujing): it is amid the mess of delivery, with the discharge of placenta and placental water, that human bodies are born. (6) "Foulness in their entirety" (C. jüti bujing): human bodies are innately impure, comprising of innards, excrement, and other foul things underneath a flimsy skin. (7) "Foulness in their destiny" (C. jiujing bujing): human bodies are destined to die, followed by putrid infestation, decomposition, and utter dissolution. There is also a contemplation on the nine bodily orifices (C. QIAO), which are vividly described as constantly oozing pus, blood, secretions, etc. ¶ As contemplation on foulness deepens, first an eidetic image (S. udgrahanimitta, P. UGGAHANIMITTA), a perfect mental reproduction of the visualized corpse, is maintained steadily in mind; this is ultimately followed by the appearance of the representational image (S. pratibhāganimitta, P. PAṬIBHĀGANIMITTA), which the VISUDDHIMAGGA (VI.66) describes as a perfectly idealized image of, for example, a bloated corpse as "a man with big limbs lying down after eating his fill." Continued concentration on this representational image will enable the meditator to access up to the fourth stage of the subtle-materiality dhyānas (ĀRŪPYĀVACARADHYĀNA). After perfecting dhyāna, this meditation may also be used to develop wisdom (PRAJÑĀ) through developing increased awareness of the reality of impermanence (ANITYA). Foulness meditation is ritually included as part of the THERAVĀDA ordination procedure, during which monks are taught the list of the first five of the thirty-two foul parts of the body (viz., head hair, body hair, nails, teeth, and skin) in order to help them ward off lust.

**Asuka**. (飛鳥). Japan's first historical epoch, named after a region in the plains south of modern NARA. Until the eighth century (710) when the capital was moved to Nara, a new palace, and virtually a new capital, was built every time a new ruler succeeded to the throne. One of the earliest capitals was located in the region of Asuka. The Asuka period is characterized by the rise of powerful aristocratic clans such as the Soga and Mononobe and attempts such as the Taika reform (646) to counteract the rise of these clans and to strengthen the authority of the emperor. According to the NIHON SHOKI ("Historical Records of Japan"), the inception of Buddhism occurred in the Japanese isles during this period, when Emperor Kimmei (r. 532–571) received an image of the Buddha from the King Sŏngmyŏng of the Korean kingdom of Paekche in 552 (var. 538). Buddhism became the central religion of the Asuka court with the support of such famous figures as Prince SHŌTOKU, Empress Suiko (r. 593–628), and Empress Jitō (r. 686–697). After the establishment of the grand monastery ASUKADERA by the descendants of a Korean clan, other temples modeled after early Chinese monastery campuses, such as HŌRYŪJI, were also constructed during this period. These temples enshrined the magnificent sculptures executed by Tori Busshi.

**Asukadera**. (飛鳥寺) In Japanese, "Asuka Temple"; also known as Hōkōji ("Monastery of the Flourishing Dharma"), the Asukadera was built during the ASUKA period on a site known as the Amakashi no Oka by the Asuka River near Nara, Japan. Shortly after the death of Emperor Yōmei in 587, the powerful vassals Mononobe no Moriya (d. 587), who represented the indigenous ritual specialists, and Soga no Umako (551?–626), a supporter of Buddhism who came from the Korean peninsula, found themselves caught in battle over imperial succession. In celebration of the Soga clan's victory over the Mononobe and the death of Moriya, the Soga commenced the construction of the first complete monastic compound in Japan, which they named Hōkōji in 588. Hōkōji was completed nine years later in 596 and for more than a century served as the central monastic complex of the Yamato court. The large monastic compound contained a central hall or KONDŌ and a central pagoda flanked by two other halls. A large lecture hall flanked by a belfry and SŪTRA repository was located behind the main monastic complex. According to the NIHON SHOKI ("Historical Records of Japan"), Empress Suiko commissioned two sixteen-feet gilt-bronze icons of the Buddha to be made by Tori Busshi for installment in Hōkōji. When the capital was moved from Fujiwarakyō to Heijōkyō (modern-day Nara) in 710, the major monasteries including Hōkōji were moved as well. Hōkōji, otherwise known as Asukadera, was subsequently renamed Gangōji.

**asura**. (T. lha ma yin; C. axiuluo; J. ashura; K. asura 阿修羅). In Sanskrit and Pāli, lit., "nongods," also translated rather arcanely as "demigod" and "titan," referring to both a class of divinities and the destiny where those beings reside in the sensuous realm (KĀMADHĀTU); in the list of six destinies (GATI), the asuras are ranked between the realms of the divinities (DEVA) and human beings (MANUṢYA) and are usually considered to be a baleful destiny (see APĀYA, DURGATI). The asuras live in the oceans surrounding the central continent of the world and in the lower reaches of Mount SUMERU. The asuras are said to be constantly jealous of the good fortunes of the divinities (deva), which prompted the king of the gods INDRA [alt. ŚAKRA] to expel them from their original home in the heaven of the thirty-three (TRĀYASTRIṂŚA); the asuras continue to engage in futile warfare against the devas above them to regain access to their lost realm. Many indigenous non-Buddhist deities, such as the Tibetan srung ma (sungma), were placed in this realm as they were assimilated into the Buddhist pantheon.

**Asura Cave**. A cave south of the Kathmandu Valley in Nepal where PADMASAMBHAVA is said to have meditated and conquered the twelve bstan ma (tenma) goddesses. It is an important pilgrimage place, considered sacred by Tibetan and Newar Buddhists as well as Hindus, and the site of several Tibetan monasteries. According to the writings of one Tibetan lama, the fourth KHAMS SPRUL (Khamtrul) Rin po che, the cave may take its name from a small passage at its rear that is purported to lead to the realm of the ASURAS.

**Asvabhāva**. (T. Ngo bo nyid med pa). Name of the author of the *Mahāyānasamgrahopanibandhana*, a commentary on Asaṅga's *Mahāyānasaṃgraha*. See also NIḤSVABHĀVA ("without self-nature").

**Aśvaghoṣa**. (T. Rta dbyangs; C. Maming; J. Memyō; K. Mamyŏng 馬鳴) (c. second century CE). An Indian Buddhist poet from ŚRĀVASTĪ, renowned for his epic kāvya poem, the BUDDHACARITA, the first complete biography of the Buddha. According to traditional accounts, Aśvaghoṣa was born into a brāhmaṇa family in Ayodhyā during the reign of the KUSHAN king KANIṢKA and was converted to Buddhism by the VAIBHĀṢIKA teacher PĀRŚVA. His poetic works are esteemed for their distinguished artistic merit, considered representative of the high Sanskritic literary tradition. While the *Buddhacarita* is Aśvaghoṣa's most famous work, he authored numerous other epic poems including the *Saundarananda* ("The Handsome Nanda," an account of NANDA's conversion) and the *Śāriputraprakaraṇa* ("Story of ŚĀRIPUTRA"). East Asian tradition also attributes to Aśvaghoṣa the DASHENG QIXIN LUN (*Awakening of Faith*), a treatise on TATHĀGATAGARBHA thought that is now widely presumed to be an indigenous Chinese treatise (see APOCRYPHA). ¶ A second tantric Aśvaghoṣa, author of the GURUPAÑCĀŚIKĀ (a brief text detailing the proper worship of a tantric guru), lived in about the tenth century.

**Aśvajit**. (P. Assaji; T. Rta thul; C. Ashuoshi; J. Asetsuji; K. Asŏlsi 阿說示). The fifth of the five ascetics (PAÑCAVARGIKA), along with ĀJÑĀTAKAUṆḌINYA (P. Aññātakoṇḍañña), BHADRIKA (P. Bhaddiya), VĀṢPA (P. Vappa), and MAHĀNĀMAN (P. Mahānāma), who practiced austerities with GAUTAMA prior to his enlightenment. Subsequently, when Gautama abandoned the severe asceticism they had been practicing in favor of the middle way (MADHYAMAPRATIPAD), Aśvajit and his companions became disgusted with Gautama's backsliding and left him, going to the ṚṢIPATANA (P. Isipatana) deer park, located in the northeast of Vārāṇasī. After the Buddha's enlightenment, however, the Buddha sought them out to teach them the first sermon, the DHARMACAKRAPRAVARTANASŪTRA (P. DHAMMACAKKAPAVATTANASUTTA); while listening to this sermon, Aśvajit achieved the first stage of awakening or "opening of the dharma eye" (DHARMACAKṢUS), becoming a stream-enterer (SROTAĀPANNA), and was immediately ordained as a monk using the informal EHIBHIKṢUKĀ, or "come, monk," formula. Five days later, the Buddha then preached to the group of five new monks the second sermon, the **Anātmalakṣaṇasūtra* (P. ANATTALAKKHAṆASUTTA), which led to Aśvajit's becoming a worthy one (ARHAT). It was through an encounter with Aśvajit that ŚĀRIPUTRA and MAHĀMAUDGALYĀYANA, the Buddha's two chief disciples, were initially converted. Śāriputra witnessed Aśvajit's calm demeanor while gathering alms in the city of RĀJAGṚHA. Impressed, he approached Aśvajit and asked who his teacher was and what were his teachings. In response, Aśvajit said that he was new to the teachings and could offer only the following summary: "Of those phenomena produced through causes, the Tathāgata has proclaimed their causes and also their cessation. Thus has spoken the great renunciant." His description, which came to known as the YE DHARMĀ (based on its first two words of the summary), would become perhaps the most commonly repeated statement in all of Buddhist literature. Upon hearing these words, Śāriputra attained the stage of stream-entry (see SROTAĀPANNA), and when he repeated what he heard to his friend Maudgalyāyana, he also did so. The two then agreed to become the Buddha's disciples. According to Pāli sources, Aśvajit once was approached by the ascetic Nigaṇṭha Saccaka, who inquired of the Buddha's teachings. Aśvajit explained the doctrine of nonself (ANĀTMAN) with a summary of the *Anattalakkhaṇasutta*, which the Buddha had taught him. Convinced that he could refute that doctrine, Nigaṇṭha Saccaka challenged the Buddha to a debate and was vanquished. The Pāli commentaries say that Aśvajit intentionally offered only the briefest of explanations of the nonself doctrine as a means of coaxing the ascetic into a direct encounter with the Buddha.

**Ātānātiyasutta**. In Pāli, "Discourse on the Ātānātiya Protective Spell," the thirty-second sutta of the DĪGHANIKĀYA (there is no equivalent recension in the Chinese translations of the ĀGAMAS). The discourse was preached by the Buddha to an assembly of deities on Vulture Peak (GṚDHRAKŪṬAPARVATA) in RĀJAGṚHA. The divinities of the four directions, together with a retinue of lesser deities, told the Buddha that there are many unbelievers among gods and men who might bring harm to the faithful. They requested that the Buddha allow them to teach his monks the ātānātiya PARITTA, a protective spell to ward off danger; the lengthy spell lists the names of the seven buddhas of antiquity (SAPTATATHĀGATA) and the virtues of the current buddha GAUTAMA, to whom even the ogres (P. yakkha; S. YAKṢA) pay homage. The Buddha consented and advised that monks, nuns, laymen, and laywomen memorize the spell so that they might dwell in comfort and safety.

**atapa**. (P. atappa; T. mi gdung ba; C. wure; J. munetsu; K. muyŏl 無熱). In Sanskrit, "not burning" (viz., "cool"), or "without torment" (also seen spelled as atapas, anavatapta); the second of the five pure abodes (ŚUDDHĀVĀSA), where those who have attained the rank of ANĀGĀMIN become ARHATs, and the highest level of the fourth meditative realm of subtle materiality (RŪPADHĀTU); it is also the name of the divinities (DEVA) who reside there. As with all the heavens of the realm of subtle materiality, one is reborn as a god there through achieving the same level of concentration (DHYĀNA) during one's practice of meditation as the gods of that heaven. According to BUDDHAGHOSA, the heaven is called "without torment" because the gods born there torment no one.

**Atigupta**. (S). See ATIKŪṬA.

**Atikūṭa**. (C. Adiquduo; J. Ajikuta; K. Ajiguda 阿地瞿多) (c. seventh century). An Indian translator who traveled to the Chinese capital of Chang'an in 652, during the Tang dynasty. (His Chinese name may also be transcribed as Atigupta.) His major translation was the *Dhāraṇīsamuccaya* (*Tuoluoni ji jing*), which was completed in a total of twelve rolls in 653–654.

**Atiśa Dīpaṃkaraśrījñāna**. (T. A ti sha Mar me mdzad dpal ye shes) (982–1054). Indian Buddhist monk and scholar revered by Tibetan Buddhists as a leading teacher in the later dissemination (PHYI DAR) of Buddhism in Tibet. His name, also written as Atisha, is an Apabhraṃśa form of the Sanskrit term atiśaya, meaning "surpassing kindness." Born into a royal family in what is today Bangladesh, Atiśa studied MAHĀYĀNA Buddhist philosophy and TANTRA as a married layman prior to being ordained at the age of twenty-nine, receiving the ordination name of Dīpaṃkaraśrījñāna. After studying at the great monasteries of northern India, including NĀLANDĀ, ODANTAPURĪ, VIKRAMAŚĪLA, and SOMAPURA, he is said to have journeyed to the island of Sumatra, where he studied under the CITTAMĀTRA teacher Dharmakīrtiśrī (also known as guru Sauvarṇadvīpa) for twelve years; he would later praise Dharmakīrtiśrī as a great teacher of BODHICITTA. Returning to India, he taught at the Indian monastic university of VIKRAMAŚĪLA. Atiśa was invited to Tibet by the king of western Tibet YE SHES 'OD and his grandnephew BYANG CHUB 'OD, who were seeking to remove perceived corruption in the practice of Buddhism in Tibet. Atiśa reached Tibet in 1042, where he initially worked together with the renowned translator RIN CHEN BZANG PO at THO LING monastery in the translation of PRAJÑĀPĀRAMITĀ texts. There, he composed his famous work, the BODHIPATHAPRADĪPA, or "Lamp for the Path to Enlightenment," an overview of the Mahāyāna Buddhist path that served as a basis for the genre of literature known as LAM RIM ("stages of the path"). He spent the remaining twelve years of his life in the central regions of Tibet, where he formed his principal seat in Snye thang (Nyetang) outside of LHA SA where he translated a number of MADHYAMAKA works into Tibetan. He died there and his relics were interred in the SGROL MA LHA KHANG. Atiśa and his chief disciples 'BROM STON RGYAL BA'I 'BYUNG GNAS and RNGOG LEGS PA'I SHES RAB are considered the forefathers of the BKA' GDAMS PA sect of Tibetan Buddhism. In Tibet, he is commonly known by the honorific title Jo bo rje (Jowoje), "the Superior Lord."

**atiyoga**. (T. a ti yo ga/shin tu rnal 'byor). In Sanskrit, "surpassing yoga"; the ninth and most advanced of the nine vehicles according to the RNYING MA sect of Tibetan Buddhism. Here, the system of practice described elsewhere as ANUTTARAYOGATANTRA is divided into three: MAHĀYOGA, ANUYOGA, and atiyoga, with atiyoga referring to the practice of the great completion (RDZOGS CHEN) in which all the phenomena of SAṂSĀRA and NIRVĀṆA appear as the sport of self-arisen wisdom.

**ātmabhāvaparityāga**. (S). See SHESHEN.

**ātmagraha**. (P. attagaha; T. bdag 'dzin; C. wozhi; J. gashū; K. ajip 我執). In Sanskrit, "clinging to self" or "conception of self"; the fundamental ignorance that is the ultimate cause of suffering (DUḤKHA) and rebirth (SAṂSĀRA). Although the self does not exist in reality, the mistaken conception that a self exists (SATKĀYADṚṢṬI) constitutes the most fundamental form of clinging, which must be eliminated through wisdom (PRAJÑĀ). Two types of attachment to self are mentioned in MAHĀYĀNA literature: the type that is constructed or artificial (S. parakalpita; T. kun btags; C. fenbie wozhi) and that type that is innate (S. sahaja; T. lhan skyes; C. jusheng wozhi). The former is primarily an epistemic error resulting from unsystematic attention (AYONIŚOMANASKĀRA) and exposure to erroneous philosophies and mistaken views (VIPARYĀSA); it is eradicated at the stage of stream-entry (see SROTAĀPANNA) for the ŚRĀVAKA and PRATYEKABUDDHA and at the DARŚANAMĀRGA for the BODHISATTVA. The latter is primarily an affective, habitual, and instinctive clinging, conditioned over many lifetimes in the past, which may continue to be present even after one has abandoned the mistaken conception of a perduring self after achieving stream-entry. This innate form of clinging to self is only gradually attenuated through the successive stages of spiritual fruition, until it is completely extinguished at the stage of arhatship (see ARHAT) or buddhahood. In the Mahāyāna philosophical schools, the conception of self is said to be twofold: the conception of the self of persons (pudgalātmagraha) and the conception of the self of phenomena or factors (dharmātmagraha). The second is said to be more subtle than the first. The first is said to be abandoned by followers of the HĪNAYĀNA paths in order to attain the rank of arhat, while both forms must be abandoned by the BODHISATTVA in order to achieve buddhahood. See also ĀTMAN; PUDGALANAIRĀTMYA.

**ātman**. (P. attan; T. bdag; C. wo; J. ga; K. a 我). In Sanskrit, "self" or "I," with a similar range of meanings as the terms possess in English, but used especially to refer to a perduring substratum of being that is the agent of actions, the possessor of mind and body (NĀMARŪPA), and that passes from lifetime to lifetime. The misconception that there is an "I" (ātman), a perduring soul that exists in reality (SATKĀYADṚṢṬI), and a "mine" (ātmīya), viz., things that belong to me, injects a "point of view" into all of one's perception (SAṂJÑĀ), which inevitably leads to clinging (toward things we like, viz., LOBHA) and hatred (toward things we dislike, viz., DVEṢA). This mistaken belief that there is such a permanent self is regarded as fundamental ignorance (AVIDYĀ) and the root cause of all suffering (DUḤKHA). The Buddha therefore taught "nonself" (ANĀTMAN) as a palliative to this misconception of permanence. The precise meaning of ātman, the ways in which the misconception arises, and how that misconception is then extended beyond the person are considered in great detail in the various Buddhist philosophical schools. See also PUDGALA.

**ātmavāda**. (P. attavāda; T. bdag tu smra ba; C. woyu; J. gago; K. aŏ 我語). In Sanskrit, the mistaken "notion of a self"; viz., the misconception that there is a perduring soul that exists in reality (SATKĀYADṚṢṬI), which constitutes the most fundamental form of clinging. The false notion of a self is commonly listed as the fourth of the four kinds of attachments (UPĀDĀNA), along with the attachments to sensuality (KĀMA), views (DṚṢṬI), and the soteriological efficacy of rites and rituals (ŚĪLAVRATA).

**attachment**. See UPĀDĀNA; NONATTACHMENT.

**Aṭṭhakanāgarasutta**. (C. Bacheng jing; J. Hachijōkyō; K. P'alsŏng kyŏng 八城經). In Pāli, "Discourse to the Man from Aṭṭhaka"; the fifty-second sutta in the MAJJHIMANIKĀYA (a separate SARVĀSTIVĀDA recension appears as SŪTRA no. 217 in the Chinese translation of the MADHYAMĀGAMA); preached by the Buddha's attendant ĀNANDA to the householder Dasaka of Aṭṭhaka at Beluvagāmaka near Vesālī (VAIŚĀLĪ). According to the Pāli recension, a merchant from the town (nāgara) of Aṭṭhaka named Dasaka approaches Ānanda and asks him if there was any one thing that could lead to liberation from bondage. Ānanda teaches him the eleven doors of the deathless, by means of which it is possible to attain liberation from bondage. These doors are made up of the four meditative absorptions (JHĀNA; S. DHYĀNA), the four BRAHMAVIHĀRA meditations, and the three immaterial meditations of infinite space (ĀKĀŚĀNANTYĀYATANA), infinite consciousness (VIJÑĀNĀNANTYĀYATANA), and nothing-whatsoever (ĀKIÑCANYĀYATANA). Ānanda states that by contemplating the conditioned and impermanent nature of these eleven doors to liberation, one can attain arhatship (see ARHAT) in this life or short of that will attain the stage of a nonreturner (ANĀGĀMIN), who is destined to be reborn in the pure abodes (ŚUDDHĀVĀSA), whence he will attain arhatship and final liberation.

**aṭṭhakathā**. In Pāli, lit. "recital of meaning" or "exegesis"; referring specifically to the "commentaries" to the first four NIKĀYAS, or scriptural collections, that comprise the Pāli Buddhist canon (tipiṭaka; S. TRIPIṬAKA). According to THERAVĀDA tradition, MAHINDA brought the Pāli tipiṭaka and aṭṭhakathās to Sri Lanka from the Indian mainland during the third century CE, during the time of King AŚOKA. The language of those Indian commentaries is unknown, but they were initially written down in Sri Lanka in some sort of Sinhalese PRAKRIT. That first Sinhalese recension of the four aṭṭhakathās was superseded when, two centuries later, the renowned Theravāda scholiast, BUDDHAGHOSA, rewrote them in Pāli and wrote a lengthy prolegomenon to this massive body of commentarial literature, which he titled the VISUDDHIMAGGA ("Path of Purification"). In conjunction with the systematic overview provided in the *Visuddhimagga*, the aṭṭhakathās thus claim to offer a comprehensive account of the full panoply of Buddhist doctrine. The aṭṭhakathā to the last, and latest, of the nikāyas, the KHUDDAKANIKĀYA ("Miscellaneous Discourses"), was composed separately, probably sometime between 450 and 600 CE, by the prolific Pāli commentator DHAMMAPĀLA, and seems to draw on a separate textual recension from that used by Buddhaghosa.

**Aṭṭhakavagga**. (S. Arthavargīya; C. Yizu jing; J. Gisokukyō; K. Ŭijok kyŏng 義足經). In Pāli, "The Octet Chapter" [alt. "The Chapter on Meaning," as the Chinese translation suggests], an important chapter of the SUTTANIPĀTA. Based on analysis of the peculiar meters and grammatical formations used in this text, philologists have reached a broad consensus that the Aṭṭhakavagga and its companion chapter, the Pārāyanavagga, are among the very earliest strata of extant Pāli literature and may have existed even during the Buddha's own lifetime. The Pāli suttas include citations and exegeses of some of the verses from the Aṭṭhakavagga, and the MAHĀNIDESA, a commentary that covers the text, is accepted as canonical in the Pāli canon (tipiṭaka, S. TRIPIṬAKA). All this evidence suggests its relative antiquity within the canon. The teachings contained in the chapter seem to suggest an early stratum of Buddhist teachings, prior to their formalization around fixed numerical lists of doctrines. The technical terminology that becomes emblematic of the standardized Buddhist presentation of doctrine is also relatively absent in its verses (GĀTHĀ). The Aṭṭhakavagga offers a rigorous indictment of the dangers inherent in "views" (P. diṭṭhi; S. DṚṢṬI) and displays a skepticism about religious dogmas in general, seeing them as virulent sources of attachment that lead ultimately to conceit, quarrels, and divisiveness. Some scholars have suggested that the kind of thoroughgoing critique of views presented in the Aṭṭhakavagga might have been the prototype of the later MADHYAMAKA logical approach, which sought to demonstrate the fallacies inherent in any philosophical statement. The verses also seem to represent an earlier stage in the evolution of Buddhist institutions, when monks still lived alone in the forest or with small groups of fellow ascetics, rather than in larger urban monasteries. Monks are still referred to as hermits or "seers" (P. isi, S. ṛṣi), a generic Indian term for religious recluses, rather than the formal Buddhist term bhikkhu (BHIKṢU) as is seen in the prose passages. A two-roll Chinese translation of a Sanskrit or Middle Indic recension of the text was made by ZHI QIAN during the Wu dynasty (c. 223–253 CE).

**Aṭṭhasālinī**. In Pāli, "Exposition of Meaning," commentary by BUDDHAGHOSA on the DHAMMASAṄGAṆI, the first book of the Pāli ABHIDHAMMAPIṬAKA (S. ABHIDHARMAPIṬAKA). The MAHĀVAṂSA and SĀSANAVAṂSA state that the *Aṭṭhasālinī* was originally written in India; the commentary also mentions by name the SAMANTAPĀSĀDIKĀ (the commentary to the Pāli VINAYA) and the VISUDDHIMAGGA, suggesting that it comes from a relatively late stratum of Pāli commentarial writings. The *Aṭṭhasālinī* provides a spirited defense of the claim that the seven books of the Pāli abhidhammapiṭaka were actually spoken by the Buddha himself, rather than being later scholastic elaborations; they are the Buddha's own enunciations of his enlightenment experience, which were handed down to ŚĀRIPUTRA and an unbroken succession of ABHIDHAMMIKAS until they were brought to Sri Lanka. The *Aṭṭhasālinī*'s extended defense suggests that this claim was a matter of much controversy, even within the tradition. The third chapter of the *Aṭṭhasālinī* presents some of the most comprehensive and detailed explanations of the workings of KARMAN theory found in Pāli literature. The *Aṭṭhasālinī* appears in the Pali Text Society's English translation series as *The Expositor*.

**auddhatya**. (P. uddhacca; T. rgod pa; C. diao; J. jō; K. to 掉). In Sanskrit, "restlessness," "agitation," or "distraction"; along with its related "worry" or "regret" (KAUKṚTYA), with which it is often seen in compound, auddhatya constitutes the fourth of the five hindrances (NĪVARAṆA) to the attainment of meditative absorption (DHYĀNA). Auddhatya-kaukṛtya is the specific hindrance to joy (SUKHA), the fourth of the five factors of dhyāna (DHYĀNĀṄGA). Restlessness and worry are fostered by unwise attention (AYONIŚOMANASKĀRA) to mental unrest and are overcome through learning and reflecting on the SŪTRAS and VINAYA and by associating with elders of calm demeanor. Restlessness and worry are countered by SAMĀDHI, the fourth of the five spiritual faculties (INDRIYA) and the sixth of the factors of enlightenment (BODHYAṄGA), together with development of the factors of tranquillity (PRAŚRABDHI), and equanimity (UPEKṢĀ).

**Aurangābād**. A complex of twelve rock-cut Buddhist caves located at the outskirts of the city of Aurangābād in the modern Indian state of Maharashtra. The oldest structure at the site is the severely damaged Cave 4, which dates to the beginning of the Common Era. The complex functioned as a center of popular devotion and secular patronage in the region. This strong linkage of the site with popular religiosity is particularly evident in Cave 2, with its central sanctum and pradakṣiṇapatha for

absorbed in immaterial trance states, and rebirth there is the result of mastery of one or all of the immaterial dhyānas (ĀRŪPYĀVACARADHYĀNA).

**avadāna**. (P. apadāna; T. rtogs par brjod pa; C. apotuona/piyu; J. ahadana or apadana/hiyu; K. ap'adana/piyu 阿波陀那/譬喻). In Sanskrit, "tales" or "narrative"; a term used to denote a type of story found in both Buddhist and non-Buddhist literature. The precise meaning of the word has been the subject of much discussion. In the Indian Brāhmaṇas and śrauta literature, the term denotes either something that is sacrificed or a portion of a sacrifice. The term avadāna was originally thought to mean "something cut off; something selected" and was presumed to derive from the prefix ava- + the Sanskrit root √dā. Feer, who published a French translation of the AVADĀNAŚATAKA in 1891, tentatively translated it as "légende, action héroïque," while noting that the Tibetans, the Chinese, and the Mongols all employed differing translations of the word as well. (The Chinese use a transcription, apotuona, as well as a translation, piyu, meaning "simile." The Tibetan rtogs brjod has been rendered as "judgment" or "moral legend"; literally, it means the presentation or expression of the realizations [of an adept]. The Mongolian equivalent is domok.) Feer's rendering of avadāna is closer to its meaning of "heroic action" in classical Indian works such as the *Raghuvaṃśa* and the *Kumārasambhava*. Avadānas are listed as the tenth of the twelvefold (DVĀDAŚĀṄGA) division of the traditional genres of Buddhist literature, as classified by compositional style and content. The total corpus of the genre is quite extensive, ranging from individual avadānas embedded in VINAYA texts, or separate sūtras in the SŪTRAPIṬAKA, to avadānas that circulated either individually or in avadāna collections. These stories typically illustrate the results of both good and bad KARMAN, i.e., past events that led to present circumstances; in certain cases, however, they also depict present events that lead to a prediction (VYĀKARAṆA) of high spiritual attainment in the future. Avadānas are closely related to JĀTAKAS, or birth stories of the Buddha; indeed, some scholars have considered jātakas to be a subset of the avadāna genre, and some jātaka tales are also included in the AVADĀNAŚATAKA, an early avadāna collection. Avadānas typically exhibit a three-part narrative structure, with a story of the present, followed by a story of past action (karman), which is then connected by identifying the past actor as a prior incarnation of the main character in the narrative present. In contrast to the jātakas, however, the main character in an avadāna is generally not the Buddha (an exception is Kṣemendra's eleventh-century *Bodhisattvāvadānakalpalatā*) but rather someone who is or becomes his follower. Moreover, some avadānas are related by narrators other than the Buddha, such as those of the AŚOKĀVADĀNA, which are narrated by UPAGUPTA. Although the avadāna genre was once dismissed as "edifying stories" for the masses, the frequent references to monks as listeners and the directives to monks on how to practice that are embedded in these tales make it clear that the primary audience was monastics. Some of the notations appended to the stories in Śūra's [alt. Āryaśūra; c. second century CE] JĀTAKAMĀLĀ suggest that such stories were also used secondarily for lay audiences. On the Indian mainland, both mainstream and MAHĀYĀNA monks compiled avadāna collections. Some of the avadānas from northwestern India have been traced from kernel stories in the MŪLASARVĀSTIVĀDA VINAYA via other mainstream Buddhist versions. In his French translation of the *Avadānaśataka*, Feer documented a number of tales from earlier mainstream collections, such as the *Avadānaśataka*, which were reworked and expanded in later Mahāyāna collections, such as the *Ratnāvadānamālā* and the *Kalpadrumāvadānamālā*, which attests to the durability and popularity of the genre. Generally speaking, the earlier mainstream avadānas were prose works, while the later Mahāyāna collections were composed largely in verse.

**Avadānaśataka**. (T. Rtogs pa brjod pa brgya pa; C. Zhuanji baiyuan jing; J. Senjū hyakuengyō; K. Ch'anjip paegyŏn kyŏng 撰集百緣經). In Sanskrit, "A Hundred Tales" (AVADĀNA). The collection was originally ascribed to the SARVĀSTIVĀDA school but is now thought to belong to the MŪLASARVĀSTIVĀDA, because of the large number of stereotyped passages that the *Avadānaśataka* shares with the DIVYĀVADĀNA and the Mūlasarvāstivāda VINAYA and its close correlation with certain other elements of the Mūlasarvāstivāda vinaya. Hence, the *Avadānaśataka* most likely originated in the northwest of the Indian subcontinent, a provenance confirmed with the recent discovery of fragments of the text in the Schøyen Collection that most likely come from BĀMIYĀN. The *Avadānaśataka* is one of the earliest avadāna collections and was translated into Chinese (*Zhuanji baiyuan jing*), a translation traditionally attributed to ZHI QIAN. The Tibetan translation (*Gang po la sogs pa rtogs pa brjod pa brgya pa*) was carried out in the early ninth century by the monk Jinamitra and Devacandra. The composition date of the *Avadānaśataka* is uncertain. A date c. 100 CE has been proposed, based on Zhi Qian's putative Chinese translation, whose traditional date of c. 223–253 CE provided a terminus ante quem for the compilation of the anthology. Recent scholarship, however, has questioned this attribution to Zhi Qian and indicates that the translation probably dates instead to the late fifth or early sixth century CE. The significant degree of divergence between the known Sanskrit texts and the Chinese recension may indicate that two or more Sanskrit versions were in circulation. The Chinese text also includes interpolations of story elements that derive from another Chinese collection, the *Xian yu jing*. In terms of structure, the stories in the *Avadānaśataka* are arranged symmetrically in ten chapters of ten stories apiece, each with a central theme: (1) prophecies (VYĀKARAṆA) of buddhahood, (2) JĀTAKA tales, (3) prophecies of pratyeka ("solitary") buddhahood (see PRATYEKABUDDHA), (4) more jātakas, (5) tales of PRETA or "hungry ghosts," (6) heavenly rebirths as DEVA ("divinities"), (7)–(9) male and female disciples who become ARHATS, and (10) stories of suffering resulting from misdeeds in past lives. The structure of a typical avadāna story includes (1) a frame story told in the narrative present; (2) a story of past deeds (which is the cause of the present achievement or suffering); and (3) a bridge between the two, linking the past actor with the person presently experiencing its consequence. Major motifs include devotion to the Buddha, the benefits of donation (DĀNA), and the workings of moral cause and effect (see KARMAN), as indicated in the stock passage with which more than half of the tales end: "Thus, O monks, knowing that black actions bear black fruits, white actions white fruits, and mixed ones mixed fruits, you should shun the black and the mixed and pursue only the white." Although avadānas have often been assumed to target the laity, the reference to monks in this stock passage clearly indicates the monastic audience to which these tales were directed.

**avadhūtī**. (T. rtsa dbu ma; C. afudi; J. abatei; K. abujŏ 阿嚩底). In Sanskrit, "channel," "vein," or "canal." According to various systems of tantric physiognomy, the avadhūtī refers to the central channel that runs from either the tip of the genitals or the base of the spine to either the crown of the head or the point between the eyebrows, with a number of "wheels" (CAKRA) along its course. To its left and right are two channels, both smaller in diameter, the RASANĀ (the left channel in males and the right channel in females) and the LALANĀ (the right channel in males and the left channel in females). Much tantric practice is devoted to techniques for causing the winds or energies that course through the other channels to enter into this central channel.

**Avadhūtipāda**. (S). See MAITRĪPA/MAITRĪPĀDA.

**avaivartika**. (T. phyir mi ldog; C. butuizhuan; J. futaiten; K. pult'oejŏn 不退轉). In Sanskrit, "nonretrogression" or "irreversible"; a term used to describe a stage on the path (MĀRGA) at which further progress is assured, with no further possibility of retrogressing to a previous stage. For the BODHISATTVA, different texts posit this crucial transition as occurring at various points along the path, such as on the path of preparation (PRAYOGAMĀRGA), where there is then no danger of the bodhisattva turning back to seek instead to become an ARHAT; the first BHŪMI; or the eighth bhūmi, when the bodhisattva is then certain to continue forward to complete, perfect enlightenment (ANUTTARASAMYAKSAMBODHI). There are many variant forms in Sanskrit (e.g., avaivarya, avinivartya, avinivartanīya, and anivartiya), of which avaivartika is among the most common. The state of nonretrogression is also termed the avaivartyabhūmi. Nonretrogression is also listed in the MAHĀVASTU as the highest of four stages of practice (CARYĀ). In the PURE LAND schools, taking rebirth (WANGSHENG) in AMITĀBHA's PURE LAND of SUKHĀVATĪ is said to constitute the stage of nonretrogression.

**āvajjana**. In Pāli, "advertence," that is, adverting the mind toward a sensory object, which is the first of seven functions in the cognitive process that ultimately lead to sensory consciousness (P. viññāṇa, S. VIJÑĀNA). When the unconscious mind (P. BHAVAṄGASOTA) is interrupted by the presence of a sensory object, the mind first performs the function of "adverting" toward the object. Thereafter, the mind performs in sequence the functions of "seeing" (P. dassana), "receiving" (P. sampaṭicchana), "investigating" (P. santīrana), and "determining" (P. votthapana). Immediately after this, the mind generates six or seven "impulse moments" (P. javanacitta) associated with either wholesome, unwholesome, or neutral classes of consciousness, after which it reverts to the bhavaṅga.

**Avalokitavrata**. (T. Spyan ras gzigs brtul zhugs). Indian scholiast of the eighth century CE and successor to BHĀVAVIVEKA [alt. Bhavya] in the SVĀTANTRIKA school of MADHYAMAKA. Avalokitavrata wrote the *Prajñāpradīpaṭīkā*, an extensive subcommentary to Bhāvaviveka's PRAJÑĀPRADĪPA, his commentary on NĀGĀRJUNA's MŪLAMADHYAMAKAKĀRIKĀ, in which he defends Bhāvaviveka from CANDRAKĪRTI's critiques. That subcommentary is extant only in Tibetan translation.

**Avalokiteśvara**. (T. Spyan ras gzigs; C. Guanshiyin/Guanyin; J. Kanzeon/Kannon; K. Kwanseŭm/Kwanŭm 觀世音/觀音). In Sanskrit, "Lord who Looks Down [in Empathy]"; the BODHISATTVA of compassion, the most widely worshipped of the MAHĀYĀNA bodhisattvas and one of the earliest to appear in Buddhist literature. According to legend, Avalokiteśvara was produced from a beam of light that radiated from the forehead of AMITĀBHA while that buddha was deep in meditation. For this reason, Buddhist iconography often depicts Amitābha as embedded in Avalokiteśvara's crown. His name dates back to the beginning of the Common Era, when he replaced the Vedic god BRAHMĀ as the attendant to ŚĀKYAMUNI Buddha, inheriting in turn Brahmā's attribute of the lotus (PADMA). Images of Avalokiteśvara as PADMAPĀṆI LOKEŚVARA ("Lord with a Lotus in his Hand"), an early name, are numerous. Avalokiteśvara is the interlocutor or main figure in numerous important Mahāyāna sūtras, including the PRAJÑĀPĀRAMITĀHṚDAYASŪTRA ("Heart Sūtra"). His cult was introduced to China in the first century CE, where his name was translated as Guanshiyin ("Perceiver of the Sounds of the World") or GUANYIN ("Perceiver of Sounds"); his cult entered Korea and Japan with the advent of Buddhism in those countries. Avalokiteśvara was once worshipped widely in Southeast Asia as well, beginning at the end of the first millennium CE. Although the Mahāyāna tradition eventually faded from the region, images of Avalokiteśvara remain. Avalokiteśvara is also the patron deity of Tibet, where he is said to have taken the form of a monkey and mated with TĀRĀ in the form of a local demoness to produce the Tibetan race. Tibetan political and religious leaders have been identified as incarnations of him, such as the seventh-century king SRONG BTSAN SGAM PO (although that attribution was most likely a later addition to the king's legacy) and, notably, the DALAI LAMAS. The

PO TA LA Palace, the residence of the Dalai Lamas, in the Tibetan capital of LHA SA is named for Avalokiteśvara's abode on Mount POTALAKA in India. In China, Avalokiteśvara as Guanyin underwent a transformation in gender into a popular female bodhisattva, although the male iconographic form also persists throughout East Asia. PUTUOSHAN, located off the east coast of China south of Shanghai, is said to be Potalaka. Avalokiteśvara is generally depicted in the full raiments of a bodhisattva, often with an image of Amitābha in his crown. He appears in numerous forms, among them the two-armed Padmapāṇi who stands and holds a lotus flower; the four-armed seated Avalokiteśvara, known either as Caturbhuja Avalokiteśvara [Caturbhujāvalokiteśvara] or Cintāmaṇi Avalokiteśvara [Cintāmaṇyavalokiteśvara], who holds the wish-fulfilling jewel (CINTĀMAṆI) with his central hands in AÑJALIMUDRĀ, and a lotus and crystal rosary in his left and right hands, respectively; the eleven-armed, eleven-faced EKĀDAŚAMUKHA; and the thousand-armed and thousand-headed SĀHASRABHUJASĀHASRANETRĀVALOKITEŚVARA (q.v. MAHĀKARUṆIKA). Tradition holds that his head split into multiple skulls when he beheld the suffering of the world. Numerous other forms also exist in which the god has three or more heads, and any number of arms. In his wrathful form as Aṣṭabhayatrāṇāvalokiteśvara (T. Spyan ras gzigs 'jigs pa brgyad skyob), "Avalokiteśvara who Protects against the Eight Fears," the bodhisattva stands in ARDHAPARYAṄKA ("half cross-legged posture") and has one face and eight hands, each of which holds a symbol of one of the eight fears. This name is also given to eight separate forms of Avalokiteśvara that are each dedicated to protecting from one of the eight fears, namely: Agnibhayatrāṇāvalokiteśvara ("Avalokiteśvara Who Protects from Fear of Fire") and so on, replacing fire with Jala (water), Siṃha (lion), Hasti (elephant), Daṇḍa (cudgel), Nāga (snake), Ḍākinī (witch) [alt. Piśācī]; and Cora (thief). In addition to his common iconographic characteristic, the lotus flower, Avalokiteśvara also frequently holds, among other accoutrements, a jeweled rosary (JAPAMĀLĀ) given to him by Akṣamati (as related in chapter twenty-five of the SADDHARMAPUṆḌARĪKASŪTRA), or a vase. In East Asia, Avalokiteśvara often appears in a triad: the buddha Amitābha in the center, flanked to his left and right by his two bodhisattva attendants, Avalokiteśvara and MAHĀSTHĀMAPRĀPTA, respectively. In Tibet, Avalokiteśvara is part of a popular triad with VAJRAPĀṆI and MAÑJUŚRĪ. As one of the AṢṬAMAHOPAPUTRA, Avalokiteśvara also appears with the other bodhisattvas in group representation. The tantric deity AMOGHAPĀŚA is also a form of Avalokiteśvara. The famous mantra of Avalokiteśvara, OṂ MAṆI PADME HŪṂ, is widely recited in the Mahāyāna traditions and nearly universally in Tibetan Buddhism. In addition to the twenty-fifth chapter of the *Saddharmapuṇḍarīkasūtra*, the KĀRAṆḌAVYŪHA is also devoted to him. See also BAIYI GUANYIN; GUANYIN; MIAOSHAN; MAṆI BKA' 'BUM.

**Avalokiteśvaraguṇa-Kāraṇḍavyūha**. (S). See KĀRAṆḌAVYŪHA.

**Avalokiteśvarasahasrabhujanetra**. In Sanskrit, "Thousand-Armed and Thousand-Eyed AVALOKITEŚVARA"; one of the manifestations of the bodhisattva of compassion, Avalokiteśvara. See SĀHASRABHUJASĀHASRANETRĀVALOKITEŚVARA.

**Avanti**. (T. Srung byed; C. Abanti [guo]; J. Ahandai[koku]; K. Abanje [kuk] 阿般提[國]). In Sanskrit and Pāli, an Indian kingdom in the southwest subcontinent, north of present-day Mumbai; its capital was Ujjayinī (P. Ujjenī); the dialect spoken there was related to, and perhaps the ancestor of, the language used in the Pāli canon. Avanti was located along the major southern Indian trade route (the Dakṣiṇāpatha) that passed through ŚRĀVASTĪ in central India, one of the main centers of early Buddhism. Buddhist missionaries following this trade route began to proselytize in the southwest even during the Buddha's lifetime. Kātyāyana, also known as "Kātyāyana the Great" (MAHĀKĀTYĀYANA; P. Mahākaccāna), one of the Buddha's ten major disciples, hailed from the Avanti region and later returned to his native land to disseminate Buddhism. He is said to have requested that the Buddha allow for special dispensation to ordain new monks in outlying regions without the requisite number of ten monastic witnesses. PŪRṆA (P. Puṇṇa) was another important disciple from the coastal area of this region (Sūrpāraka), who returned there to proselytize as well. He is the subject of the *Puṇṇovādasutta* (no. 145 in the Pāli MAJJHIMANIKĀYA) and the *Pūrṇāvadāna*, which describe his resolve to spread the teachings of Buddhism. Buddhism became firmly established in the Avanti region at least by the time of King AŚOKA; Aśoka's son, MAHINDA, who later transmitted Buddhism to the island kingdom of Sri Lanka (Ceylon), is said to have been a native of its capital, Ujjayinī. Avanti was a stronghold of the STHAVIRANIKĀYA, and its monks led the opposition to ten disputed items in the monastic discipline that resulted in the schism with the MAHĀSĀṂGHIKA order.

**āvaraṇa**. (T. sgrib pa; C. zhang; J. shō; K. chang 障). In Sanskrit and Pāli, "obstruction," "obstacle," or "hindrance." In MAHĀYĀNA literature, two types of āvaraṇa are commonly described: "obstructions that are the afflictions," or "afflictive obstructions" (KLEŚĀVARAṆA), and cognitive or noetic obstructions, viz., "obstructions to omniscience" (JÑEYĀVARAṆA). ŚRĀVAKAS and PRATYEKABUDDHAS can be freed from the afflictive obstructions, but only BODHISATTVAS are able to free themselves from the cognitive obstructions. In the YOGĀCĀRA system, the cognitive obstructions result from fundamental misapprehensions about the nature of reality. Because of the attachment that derives from the reification of what are actually imaginary external phenomena, conceptualization and discrimination arise in the mind, which in turn lead to pride, ignorance, and wrong views. Based on the mistakes in understanding generated by these cognitive obstructions, the individual engages in defiled actions motivated by anger, envy, etc., which constitute the afflictive obstructions. The afflictive obstructions may be removed by followers of the śrāvaka, pratyekabuddha, and beginning bodhisattva paths by applying various antidotes or counteragents (PRATIPAKṢA) to the afflictions or defilements (KLEŚA); overcoming these types of obstructions will lead to freedom from further rebirth. The cognitive obstructions, however, can only be overcome by advanced bodhisattvas who seek instead to achieve buddhahood, by perfecting their understanding of emptiness (ŚŪNYATĀ) and compassion (KARUṆĀ) and amassing a great store of merit (PUṆYA) by engaging in the bodhisattva deeds (CARYĀ). Buddhas, therefore, are the only class of beings who have overcome both types of obstructions and thus are able simultaneously to cognize all objects of knowledge in the universe. The jñeyāvaraṇa are therefore sometimes translated as "obstructions to omniscience." In the elaboration of the obstructions in the Yogācāra text CHENG WEISHI LUN (**Vijñaptimātratāsiddhi*), there are ten types of āvaraṇa that are specifically said to obstruct the ten types of suchness (TATHATĀ) correlated with the ten stages of the bodhisattva path (DAŚABHŪMI): (1) the obstruction of the common illusions of the unenlightened (pṛthagjanatvāvaraṇa; C. yishengxing zhang); (2) the obstruction of deluded conduct (mithyāpratipattyāvaraṇa; C. xiexing zhang); (3) the obstruction of dullness (dhaṇḍhatvāvaraṇa; C. andun zhang); (4) the obstruction of the manifestation of subtle afflictions (sūkṣmakleśasamudācārāvaraṇa; C. xihuo xianxing zhang); (5) the obstruction of the lesser HĪNAYĀNA ideal of PARINIRVĀṆA (hīnayānaparinirvāṇāvaraṇa; C. xiasheng niepan zhang); (6) the obstruction of the manifestation of coarse characteristics (sthūlanimittasamudācārāvaraṇa; C. cuxiang xianxing zhang); (7) the obstruction of the manifestation of subtle characteristics (sūkṣmanimittasamudācārāvaraṇa; C. xixiang xianxing zhang); (8) the obstruction of the continuance of activity even in the immaterial realm that is free from characteristics (nirnimittābhisaṃskārāvaraṇa; C. wuxiang jiaxing zhang); (9) the obstruction of not desiring to act to bring salvation to others (parahitacaryākāmanāvaraṇa; C. buyuxing zhang); and (10) the obstruction of not yet acquiring mastery over all things (dharmeṣuvaśitāpratilambhāvaraṇa; fa weizizai zhang). These ten obstructions are overcome by practicing, respectively: (1) the perfection of giving (DĀNAPĀRAMITĀ); (2) the perfection of morality (ŚĪLAPĀRAMITĀ); (3) the perfection of forbearance (KṢĀNTIPĀRAMITĀ); (4) the perfection of energetic effort (VĪRYAPĀRAMITĀ); (5) the perfection of meditative absorption (DHYĀNAPĀRAMITĀ); (6) the perfection of wisdom (PRAJÑĀPĀRAMITĀ); (7) the perfection of expedient means (UPĀYAPĀRAMITĀ); (8) the perfection of the vow (to attain enlightenment) (PRAṆIDHĀNAPĀRAMITĀ); (9) the perfection of powers (BALAPĀRAMITĀ); and (10) the perfection of omniscience (jñānapāramitā). See also KARMĀVARAṆA; NĪVARAṆA.

**Avataṃsakasūtra**. (T. Mdo phal po che; C. Huayan jing; J. Kegongyō; K. Hwaŏm kyŏng 華嚴經). In Sanskrit, "Garland Scripture"; also known as the BUDDHĀVATAṂSAKASŪTRA ("Scripture of the Garland of Buddhas"), or **Buddhāvataṃsakanāmamahāvaipulyasūtra*, the Sanskrit reconstruction of the title of the Chinese translation *Dafangguang fo huayan jing*, which is usually abbreviated in Chinese simply as the HUAYAN JING ("Flower Garland Scripture"). The sūtra is one of the most influential Buddhist scriptures in East Asia and the foundational text of the indigenous East Asian HUAYAN ZONG. The first major edition of the *Avataṃsakasūtra* was said to have been brought from KHOTAN and was translated into Chinese by BUDDHABHADRA in 421; this recension consisted of sixty rolls and thirty-four chapters. A second, longer recension, in eighty rolls and thirty-nine chapters, was translated into Chinese by ŚIKṢĀNANDA in 699; this is sometimes referred to within the Huayan tradition as the "New [translation of the] *Avataṃsakasūtra*" (*Xin Huayan jing*). A Tibetan translation similar to the eighty-roll recension also exists. The *Avataṃsakasūtra* is traditionally classified as a VAIPULYASŪTRA; it is an encyclopedic work that brings together a number of heterogeneous texts, such as the GAṆḌAVYŪHA and DAŚABHŪMIKASŪTRA, which circulated independently before being compiled together in this scripture. No Sanskrit recension of the *Avataṃsakasūtra* has been discovered; even the title is not known from Sanskrit sources, but is a reconstruction of the Chinese. (Recent research in fact suggests that the correct Sanskrit title might actually be *Buddhāvataṃsakasūtra*, or "Scripture of the Garland of Buddhas," rather than *Avataṃsakasūtra.*) There are, however, extant Sanskrit recensions of two of its major constituents, the *Daśabhūmikasūtra* and *Gaṇḍavyūha.* Given the dearth of evidence of a Sanskrit recension of the complete *Avataṃsakasūtra*, and since the scripture was first introduced to China from Khotan, some scholars have argued that the scripture may actually be of Central Asian provenance (or at very least was heavily revised in Central Asia). There also exists in Chinese translation a forty-roll recension of the *Avataṃsakasūtra*, translated by PRAJÑA in 798, which roughly corresponds to the *Gaṇḍavyūha*, otherwise known in Chinese as the Ru fajie pin or "Chapter on the Entry into the DHARMADHĀTU." Little attempt is made to synthesize these disparate materials into an overarching narrative, but there is a tenuous organizational schema involving a series of different "assemblies" to which the different discourses are addressed. The Chinese tradition presumed that the *Avataṃsakasūtra* was the first sermon of the Buddha (see HUAYAN ZHAO), and the sūtra's first assembly takes place at the BODHI TREE two weeks after he had attained enlightenment while he was still immersed in the samādhi of oceanic reflection (SĀGARAMUDRĀSAMĀDHI). The *Avataṃsaka* is therefore believed to provide a comprehensive and definitive description of the Buddha's enlightenment experience from within this profound state of samādhi. The older sixty-roll recension includes a total of eight assemblies held at seven different locations: three in the human realm and the rest in the heavens. The later eighty-roll recension, however, includes a total of nine assemblies at seven locations, a discrepancy that led to much ink in Huayan exegesis. In terms of its content, the sūtra offers exuberant descriptions of myriads of world systems populated by buddhas and bodhisattvas, along with elaborate imagery focusing especially on radiant light and boundless space. The scripture is also the inspiration for the famous metaphor of INDRAJĀLA (Indra's Net), a canopy made of transparent jewels in which each jewel is reflected in all the others, suggesting the multivalent levels of interaction between all phenomena in the universe. The text focuses on the unitary and all-pervasive nature of enlightenment, which belongs to the realm of the Buddha of Pervasive Light, VAIROCANA, the central buddha in the *Avataṃsaka*, who embodies the DHARMAKĀYA. The sūtra emphasizes the knowledge and enlightenment of the buddhas as being something that is present in all sentient beings (see TATHĀGATAGARBHA and BUDDHADHĀTU), just as the entire universe, or trichiliocosm (S. TRISĀHASRAMAHĀSĀHASRALOKADHĀTU) is contained in a minute mote of dust. This notion of interpenetration or interfusion (YUANRONG) is stressed in the thirty-second chapter of Buddhabhadra's translation, whose title bears the influential term "nature origination" (XINGQI). The sūtra, especially in FAZANG's authoritative exegesis, is presumed to set forth a distinctive presentation of dependent origination (PRATĪTYASAMUTPĀDA) in terms of the dependence of the whole on its parts, stressing the unity of the universe and its emptiness (ŚŪNYATĀ) of inherent nature; dependent origination here emerges as a profound ecological vision in which the existence of any one thing is completely dependent on the existence of all other things and all things on any one thing. Various chapters of the sūtra were also interpreted as providing the locus classicus for the exhaustive fifty-two stage Mahāyāna path (MĀRGA) to buddhahood, which included the ten faiths (only implied in the scripture), the ten abodes, ten practices, ten dedications, and ten stages (DAŚABHŪMI), plus the two stages of awakening itself: virtual enlightenment (dengjue) and sublime enlightenment (miaojue). This soteriological process was then illustrated through the peregrinations of the lad SUDHANA to visit his religious mentors, each of whom is identified with one of these specific stages; Sudhana's lengthy pilgrimage is described in great detail in the massive final chapter (a third of the entire scripture), the *Gaṇḍavyūha*, titled in the *Avataṃsakasūtra* the "Entry into the Dharmadhātu" chapter (Ru fajie pin). The evocative and widely quoted statement in the "Brahmacarya" chapter that "at the time of the initial arousal of the aspiration for enlightenment (BODHICITTOTPĀDA), complete, perfect enlightenment (ANUTTARASAMYAKSAṂBODHI) is already achieved" was also influential in the development of the East Asian notion of sudden enlightenment (DUNWU), since it implied that awakening could be achieved in an instant of sincere aspiration, without requiring three infinite eons (ASAṂKHYEYAKALPA) of religious training. Chinese exegetes who promoted this sūtra reserved the highest place for it in their scriptural taxonomies (see JIAOXIANG PANSHI) and designated it the "perfect" or "consummate" teaching (YUANJIAO) of Buddhism. Many commentaries on and exegeses of the sūtra are extant, among which the most influential are those written by FAZANG, ZHIYAN, CHENGGUAN, LI TONGXUAN, GUIFENG ZONGMI, WŎNHYO, ŬISANG, and MYŌE KŌBEN.

**avavāda**. (P. ovāda; T. gdams ngag; C. jiaodaolun; J. kyōdōron; K. kyodoron 教導論). In Sanskrit, "admonitions" or "instructions"; oral instructions that provide practical advice to a student. These may include instructions given to a monk or nun, or instructions on how to put into practice a particular doctrine or teaching. The term carries the connotation of advice drawn from experience in contrast to learning derived from books, although a true practitioner is said to be someone who can see all of the SŪTRAs and ŚĀSTRAs as avavāda. The term often appears in compound with its near-synonym anuśāsanī as "admonition and instruction" (avavādānuśāsanī). The compound OVĀDAPĀṬIMOKKHA (S. *avavādaprātimokṣa) is also used to refer to a foundational disciplinary code (PRĀTIMOKṢA) handed down by the past buddha VIPAŚYIN (P. Vipassī), which is believed to summarize the teachings fundamental to all the buddhas; it is found in the MAHĀPADĀNASUTTANTA [DĪGHANIKĀYA no. 14] and DHAMMAPADA v. 183: "Not doing anything evil,/Undertaking what is wholesome,/Purifying one's mind:/This is the teaching of the buddhas" (P. sabbapāpassa akaraṇaṃ/kusalassūpasampadā/sacittapariyodapanaṃ/etaṃ buddhāna sāsanaṃ). This verse has been widely incorporated into THERAVĀDA Buddhist rituals and ceremonies. According to the ABHISAMAYĀLAṂKĀRA, in the PRAJÑĀPĀRAMITĀ sūtras, there are distinct avavāda for each stage of the bodhisattva path (MĀRGA) corresponding to the twenty-two stages of BODHICITTA.

**āveṇika[buddha]dharma**. (T. chos ma 'dres pa/ma 'dres pa'i chos; C. bugong[fo]fa; J. fugūhō/fugūbuppō; K. pulgong [bul]bŏp 不共[佛]法). In Sanskrit and Pāli, "unshared factors"; special qualities that are unique to the buddhas. They usually appear in a list of eighteen (aṣṭādaśa āveṇikā buddhadharmāḥ): (1)–(2) the buddhas never make a physical or verbal mistake; (3) their mindfulness never diminishes; (4) they have no perception of difference; (5) they are free from discursiveness; (6) their equanimity is not due to a lack of discernment; (7)–(12) they do not regress in their devotion, perseverance, recollection, concentration, wisdom, or liberation; (13)–(15) all their physical, verbal, and mental actions are preceded and followed by gnosis; and (16)–(18) they enter into the perception of the gnosis that is unobstructed and unimpeded with respect to the past, future, and present. An expanded listing of 140 such unshared factors is given in the YOGĀCĀRABHŪMIŚĀSTRA.

**āveśa**. (T. 'bebs pa; C. aweishe; J. abisha; K. amisa 阿尾捨). In Sanskrit, "possession"; the possession of shamans and mediums by a spirit or divinity so they could serve as oracles. Specific rites are outlined in esoteric Buddhist materials to incite possession in young children of usually seven or eight years of age; once the children began to shake from their inhabitation by the possessing deity, they would be asked a series of questions regarding portents for the future. In China, the tantric master VAJRABODHI was said to have used two seven-year-old girls as oracles in the palace, who were claimed to have been possessed by two deceased princesses. In Tibet, some of the bodies (rten, sku rten) through which an oracle (lha) speaks attained considerable importance in the religious and even political affairs of the state; among them the GNAS CHUNG (Nechung) oracle, said to be the pre-Buddhist spirit PE HAR, who was tamed by PADMASAMBHAVA and tasked with protecting the Buddha's teaching, has the status of state oracle.

**avīci**. (T. mnar med; C. abi diyu/wujian diyu; J. abijigoku/mukenjigoku; K. abi chiok/mugan chiok 阿鼻地獄/無間地獄). In Sanskrit and Pāli, "interminable," "relentless," "incessant"; referring to the deepest, largest, and most tortuous of the eight great, or eight hot, hells (see NĀRAKA). (The Chinese use either a transcription corresponding to the first two syllables of the Sanskrit avīci or else the translation "interminable," combined with their own cultural translation of "hell" as a "subterranean prison.") This hell is said to be located twenty thousand YOJANAs below the continent of JAMBUDVĪPA and is the destination of beings whose "wholesome faculties are eradicated" (SAMUCCHINNAKUŚALAMŪLA) or who have committed the most heinous of acts, which, after death, result in immediate rebirth in the avīcı hell: patricide, matricide, killing an ARHAT, wounding a buddha, and causing schism in the SAṂGHA (see ĀNANTARYAKARMAN). Because beings reborn in this hell are being constantly burned alive in hot flames, with no respite in their torture, the agony they experience is said to be "Interminable." (*Editors' note*: According to one esoteric lineage, there is a special level of the avīci hell reserved especially for compilers of dictionaries, where, no matter how many terms the authors have defined, an interminable list remains.) Another seven levels of the hot hells are either situated above, or in other interpretations, at the same level as avīci. The ABHIDHARMAKOŚABHĀṢYA lists a corresponding series of bitterly cold hells beginning with the arbuda hell. Avīci and its seven companion hells each have sixteen (four in each direction) neighboring hells (PRATYEKANARAKA) or subhells (utsada), where supplementary tortures are meted out to the unfortunate inhabitants, such as plains of ash that burn their feet; swamps of excrement and corpses in which maggots eat their flesh; roads and forests of razor blades that slice off their flesh; and rivers of boiling water in which they are plunged. Like all levels of hell, however, avīci is ultimately impermanent and, once the previous unwholesome actions of the inhabitant are expiated after many eons, that being will be reborn elsewhere according to his KARMAN.

**avidyā**. (P. avijjā; T. ma rig pa; C. wuming; J. mumyō; K. mumyŏng 無明). In Sanskrit, "ignorance"; the root cause of suffering (DUḤKHA) and one of the key terms in Buddhism. Ignorance occurs in many contexts in Buddhist doctrine. For example, ignorance is the first link in the twelvefold chain of dependent origination (PRATĪTYASAMUTPĀDA) that sustains the cycle of birth and death (SAṂSĀRA); it is the condition that creates the predispositions (SAṂSKĀRA) that lead to rebirth and thus inevitably to old age and death. Ignorance is also listed as one of the root afflictions (S. MŪLAKLEŚA) and the ten "fetters" (SAṂYOJANA) that keep beings bound to saṃsāra. Avidyā is closely synonymous with "delusion" (MOHA), one of the three unwholesome roots (AKUŚALAMŪLA). When they are distinguished, moha may be more of a generic foolishness and benightedness, whereas avidyā is instead an obstinate misunderstanding about the nature of the person and the world. According to ASAṄGA's ABHIDHARMASAMUCCAYA, for example, moha is the factor of nescience, while avidyā is the active misconstruction of the nature of reality; he uses the analogy of twilight (= moha) falling on a coiled rope (= reality), which someone in the darkness wrongly conceives to be a snake (= avidyā). Due to the pervasive influence of ignorance, the deluded sentient being (PṚTHAGJANA) sees what is not self as self, what is impermanent as permanent, what is impure as pure, and what is painful as pleasurable (see VIPARYĀSA); and due to this confusion, one is subject to persistent suffering (duḥkha) and continued rebirth. The inveterate propensity toward ignorance is first arrested in the experience of stream-entry (see SROTAĀPANNA), which eliminates the three cognitive fetters of belief in a perduring self (SATKĀYADṚṢṬI), attachment to rules and rituals (S. ŚĪLAVRATAPARĀMARŚA), and skeptical doubt (S. VICIKITSĀ). Avidyā is gradually alleviated at the stages of once-returners (SAKṚDĀGĀMIN) and nonreturners (ANĀGĀMIN), and permanently eliminated at the stage of arhatship (see ARHAT), the fourth and highest degree of sanctity in mainstream Buddhism (see ĀRYAPUDGALA).

**avijñaptirūpa**. (T. rnam par rig byed ma yin pa'i gzugs; C. wubiaose; J. muhyōjiki; K. mup'yosaek 無表色). In Sanskrit, "unmanifest material force," or "hidden imprints"; a special type of materiality (RŪPA) recognized in the SARVĀSTIVĀDA school of ABHIDHARMA, especially. The Sarvāstivāda school notably makes recourse to this unique type of materiality as one way of reconciling the apparent contradiction in Buddhism between advocating the efficacy of moral cause and effect and rejecting any notion of an underlying substratum of being (ANĀTMAN), as well as issues raised by the teaching of momentariness (KṢAṆIKAVĀDA). When a person forms the intention (CETANĀ) to perform an action (KARMAN), whether wholesome (KUŚALA) or unwholesome (AKUŚALA), that intention creates an "unmanifest" type of materiality that imprints itself on the person as either bodily or verbal information, until such time as the action is actually performed via body or speech. Unmanifest materiality is thus the "glue" that connects the intention that initiates action with the physical act itself. Unmanifest material force can be a product of both wholesome and unwholesome intentions, but it is most commonly associated in Sarvāstivāda literature with three types of restraint (SAṂVARA) against the unwholesome specifically: (1) the restraint proffered to a monk or nun when he or she accepts the disciplinary rules of the order (PRĀTIMOKṢASAṂVARA); (2) the restraint that is produced through mental absorption (dhyānajasaṃvara); and (3) the restraint that derives from being free from the contaminants (anāsravasaṃvara). In all three cases, the unmanifest material force creates an invisible and impalpable force field that helps to protect the monk or nun from unwholesome action. Prātimokṣasaṃvara, for example, creates a special kind of force that dissuades people from unwholesome activity, even when they are not consciously aware they are following the precepts or when they are asleep. This specific type of restraint is what makes a man a monk, since just wearing robes or following an ascetic way of life would not itself be enough to instill in him the protective power offered by the PRĀTIMOKṢA. Meditation was also thought to confer on the monk protective power against physical harm while he was absorbed in DHYĀNA: the literature abounds with stories of monks who saw tiger tracks all around them after withdrawing from dhyāna, thus suggesting that dhyāna itself provided a protective shield against accident or injury. Finally, anāsravasaṃvara is the restraint that precludes someone who has achieved the extinction of the outflows (ĀSRAVA)—that is, enlightenment—from committing any action (KARMAN) that would produce a karmic result (VIPĀKA), thus ensuring that their remaining actions in this life do not lead to any additional rebirths. Because avijñaptirūpa sounds as much like a force as a type of matter, later authors, such as HARIVARMAN in his TATTVASIDDHI, instead listed it among the "conditioned forces dissociated from thought" (CITTAVIPRAYUKTASAṂSKĀRA).

**Avikalpapraveśadhāraṇī**. (T. Rnam par mi rtog pa la 'jug pa'i gzungs). In Sanskrit, "DHĀRAṆĪ for Entrance into the Nonconceptual"; also called the Drumavikalpapraveśadhāraṇī, or "Dhāraṇī for Entrance to the [Wish Fulfilling] Tree of Paradise." The text is cited in the DHARMADHARMATĀVIBHĀGA and appears to be the source of a number of its doctrines. There is a commentary on the text by KAMALAŚĪLA.

**avṛha**. (P. aviha; T. mi che ba; C. wufan tian; J. mubonten; K. mubŏn ch'ŏn 無煩天). In Sanskrit, "free from afflictions"; the name of the fifth highest of the eight heavens of the fourth concentration (DHYĀNA) of the realm of subtle materiality (RŪPADHĀTU), and one of the five heavens within the fourth dhyāna that constitute the ŚUDDHĀVĀSA, the "pure abodes," where those who have attained the rank of ANĀGĀMIN become ARHATs. As with all the heavens of the realm of subtle materiality, one is reborn as a divinity there through achieving the same level of concentration (dhyāna) as the gods of that heaven during one's previous practice of meditation.

**avyākṛta**. (P. avyākata; T. lung du ma bstan pa/lung ma bstan; C. wuji; J. muki; K. mugi 無記). In Sanskrit, "indeterminate" or "unascertainable"; used to refer to the fourteen "indeterminate" or "unanswered" questions (avyākṛtavastu) to which the Buddha refuses to respond. The American translator of Pāli texts HENRY CLARKE WARREN rendered the term as "questions which tend not to edification." These questions involve various metaphysical assertions that were used in traditional India to evaluate a thinker's philosophical lineage. There are a number of versions of these "unanswerables," but one common list includes fourteen such questions, three sets of which are framed as "four alternatives" (CATUṢKOṬI): (1) Is the world eternal?, (2) Is the world not eternal?, (3) Is the world both eternal and not eternal?, (4) Is the world neither eternal nor not eternal?; (5) Is the world endless?, (6) Is the world not endless?, (7) Is the world both endless and not endless?, (8) Is the world neither endless nor not endless?; (9) Does the tathāgata exist after death?, (10) Does the tathāgata not exist after death?, (11) Does the tathāgata both exist and not exist after death?, (12) Does the tathāgata neither exist nor not exist after death?; (13) Are the soul (jīva) and the body identical?, and (14) Are the soul and the body not identical? It was in response to such questions that the Buddha famously asked whether a man shot by a poisoned arrow would spend time wondering about the height of the archer and the kind of wood used for the arrow, or whether he should seek to remove the arrow before it killed him. Likening these fourteen questions to such pointless speculation, he called them "a jungle, a wilderness, a puppet-show, a writhing, and a fetter, and is coupled with misery, ruin, despair, and agony, and does not tend to aversion, absence of passion, cessation, quiescence, knowledge, supreme wisdom, and nirvāṇa." The Buddha thus asserted that all these questions had to be set aside as unanswerable for being either unexplainable conceptually or "wrongly framed" (P. ṭhapanīya). Questions that were "wrongly framed" inevitably derive from mistaken assumptions and are thus the products of wrong reflection (AYONIŚOMANASKĀRA); therefore, any answer given to them would necessarily be either misleading or irrelevant. The Buddha's famous silence on these questions has been variously interpreted, with some seeing his refusal to answer these questions as deriving from the inherent limitations involved in using concepts to talk about such rarified existential questions. Because it is impossible to expect that concepts can do justice, for example, to an enlightened person's state of being after death, the Buddha simply remains silent when asked this and other "unanswerable" questions. The implication, therefore, is that it is not necessarily the case that the Buddha does not "know" the answer to these questions, but merely that he realizes the conceptual limitations inherent in trying to answer them definitively and thus refuses to respond. Yet other commentators explained that the Buddha declined to answer the question of whether the world (that is, SAṂSĀRA) will ever end because the answer ("no") would prove too discouraging to his audience.

**avyākṛtadharma**. (P. avyākatadhamma; T. lung du ma bstan pa'i chos; C. wujifa; J. mukihō; K. mugibŏp 無記法). In Sanskrit, "indeterminate," "neutral," or "indifferent" dharmas. This term is used in contrast to dharmas that are wholesome (KUŚALA) or unwholesome (AKUŚALA); avyākṛtadharmas are neither wholesome nor unwholesome, and therefore "neutral." Such "interdeterminate dharmas" include the KLIṢṬAMANAS, ĀLAYAVIJÑĀNA, and the results of KARMAN. The term is also used more generally for deeds that in themselves are neither virtuous nor nonvirtuous but may become so depending on the intention with which they are performed.

**Awakening of Faith (in Mahāyāna)**. See DASHENG QIXIN LUN.

**ayaḥśālmalīvana**. (P. simbalivana; T. lcags kyi shing shal ma li'i nags; C. tieci lin; J. tesshirin; K. ch'ŏlcha rim 鐵刺林). In Sanskrit "forest of iron thorns"; one of the neighboring hells (PRATYEKANARAKA) surrounding the eight hot hells, through which the denizens of hell must pass as they depart from hell. It is classified as part of the third of the four neighboring hells, called "razor road" (KṢURAMĀRGA). The denizens of this hell arrive at a tree, where a loved one sits at the top of the tree beckoning. As the denizen climbs the tree, its body is lacerated by iron thorns in the bark of the tree. When it reaches the top, the loved one is gone and is now beckoning from the bottom of the tree. Climbing down, the body is again lacerated. The process is repeated until the unwholesome action has been expiated.

**āyatana**. (T. skye mched; C. chu; J. sho; K. ch'ŏ 處). In Sanskirt and Pāli, "sense-fields" or "bases of cognition." In epistemology, these twelve sense-fields, which serve as the bases for the production of consciousness, are the six internal sense bases, or sense organs (the "faculties" or INDRIYA, i.e., eye, ear, nose, tongue, body, and mind) and the six external sense objects (the "objective supports" or ĀLAMBANA, i.e., forms, sounds, odors, tastes, tangible objects, and mental phenomena). The contact (SPARŚA) between a sense base and its corresponding sense object would lead to specific sensory consciousnesses (VIJÑĀNA); hence, the āyatanas are considered to be the "access" (āya) of the mind and mental states. In the context of the twelvefold chain of dependent origination (PRATĪTYASAMUTPĀDA), the āyatanas are usually described as comprising only the six sense bases. The twelve āyatana are subsumed as the first twelve of the eighteen elements (DHĀTU). The āyatanas are one of the three major taxonomies of factors (along with SKANDHA and dhātu) found in the SŪTRAs, and represent a more primitive stage of DHARMA classification than the elaborate analyses found in the later ABHIDHARMA literature. In compound words like ĀKĀŚĀNANTYĀYATANA, ABHIBHAVĀYATANA, and so on, āyatana means simply "stage" or "level."

**ayoniśomanaskāra**. [alt. ayoniśomanasikāra] (P. ayonisomanasikāra; T. tshul bzhin ma yin pa'i yid la byed pa/tshul min yid byed; C. feili zuoyi/buzheng siwei; J. hiri no sai/fushōshiyui; K. piri chagŭi/pujŏng sayu 非理作意/不正思惟). In Sanskrit, "unsystematic attention" or "wrong reflection"; attention directed to an object in a superficial manner, without thoroughgoing attention. This term refers especially to the entrancement with the compounded forms of things as revealed through their external marks (LAKṢAṆA) and secondary characteristics (ANUVYAÑJANA), so that one does not perceive that they are impermanent (ANITYA). It also entails wrongly ascribing a notion of permanent selfhood (SATKĀYADṚṢṬI) to things that are compounded and thus lacking a perduring substratum of being. Because of unsystematic attention to sensory experience, the sentient being becomes subject to an inexorable process of conceptual proliferation (PRAPAÑCA), in which everything that can be experienced in this world is tied together into a labyrinthine network of concepts, all connected to oneself and projected outward as craving (TṚṢṆĀ), conceit (MĀNA), and wrong views (DṚṢṬI), thus creating bondage to SAṂSĀRA.

**āyuṣman**. (P. āvuso; T. tshe dang ldan pa; C. jushou; J. guju; K. kusu 具壽). In Sanskrit, "friend" or "brother" (lit. "endowed with life," which is the meaning of the Chinese translation "full of life"); a polite form of monastic address, usually used between equals or when a teacher or senior monk addresses a student or junior monk.

**Ayuthaya**. [alt. Ayutthaya]. There are two important places called Ayuthaya in the Buddhist tradition. ¶ Ayuthaya was a city in north-central India, prominent in early Buddhist texts, that is identified as the ancient city of SĀKETA; it was said to be the birthplace of the Indian divine-king Rāma. ¶ Ayuthaya is the name of a major Thai kingdom and its capital that flourished between 1350 and 1767 CE. The city of Ayuthaya was built on an island at the confluence of the Chao Phraya, Pasak, and Lopburi rivers and grew in importance as the power of its neighbor, the Thai kingdom of SUKHOTHAI, waned. Strategically located and easy to defend, Ayuthaya was accessible to seagoing vessels and commanded the northward trade of the entire Menam basin, whence it grew rapidly into a major Asian entrepôt. Merchant ships from China, Java, Malaya, Japan, India, Sri Lanka, Persia, Portugal, Holland, France, and England regularly docked at its port. One of the world's wealthiest capitals, Ayuthaya contained hundreds of gilded monasteries, temples, and pagodas within its walls and was traversed by grand canals and waterways that served as avenues. Strong Khmer influence is evident in the architecture of Ayuthaya, which developed a distinctive stepped-pyramidal pagoda form called prang. The city's magnificence was extolled in the travelogues of European and Asian visitors alike. Soon after the city's founding, Ayuthaya's kings became enthusiastic patrons of reformed Sinhalese-style THERAVĀDA Buddhism, inviting missionaries from their stronghold in Martaban to reform the local saṅgha. The same form of Buddhism was adopted by neighboring Thai states in the north, the Mon kingdom of Pegu, and later the Burmese, making it the dominant form of Buddhism in Southeast Asia. In 1548, the Burmese king, Tabin Shwehti, invaded the kingdom of Ayuthaya and laid siege to its capital, initiating more than two centuries of internecine warfare between the Burmese and the Thai kingdoms, which culminated in the destruction of Ayuthaya in 1767 and the building of a new Thai capital, Bangkok, in 1782.

circumambulation (PRADAKṢIṆA) left undecorated to display a number of individually commissioned votive panels. The arrangement combines the ritual need for circumambulation with the preference for placing the main buddha against the rear wall by creating a corridor around the entire shrine. The entrance to the shrine is flanked by the BODHISATTVAs MAITREYA and AVALOKITEŚVARA, both attended by serpent kings (NĀGA); the shrine itself contains a seated buddha making the gesture of turning the wheel of the DHARMA (DHARMACAKRAMUDRĀ) flanked by two bodhisattvas. The creation of the Aurangābād cave site appears to have been connected with the collapse of the Vākāṭakas, who had patronized the cave temples at AJAṆṬĀ. Aurangābād rose in response, testimony to the triumph of the regional powers and local Buddhist forces at the end of the fifth century. The small number of cells for the SAṂGHA, the presence of the life-size kneeling devotees with a portrait-like appearance and royal attire sculpted in Cave 3, and the individually commissioned votive panels in Cave 2 indicate the growing importance of the "secular" at Aurangābād. The strong affinities in design, imagery, and sculptural detail between Aurangābād Cave 3 and Caves 2 and 26 at Ajaṇṭā indicate that the same artisans might have worked at both sites. The sculptural panels in Cave 7, which date to the mid-sixth century, may demonstrate the growing importance of tantric sects, with their use of the imagery of voluptuous females with elaborate coiffures serving as attendants to bodhisattvas or buddhas.

**aureole**. See KĀYAPRABHĀ.

**auspicious symbols, eight**. See AṢṬAMAṄGALA.

**Ava**. [alt. Inwa]. Name of the chief Burmese (Myanmar) kingdom and its capital that flourished in Upper Burma between the fourteenth and sixteenth centuries CE. Founded in 1364 at the confluence of the Irrawaddy and Myitnge rivers, the city of Ava, whose official Pāli name is Ratanapura, was the successor state of the PAGAN empire (1044–c. 1287), whose cultural, religious, and political traditions Ava's kings consciously sought to preserve. While occupying a much reduced realm compared to imperial Pagan and hemmed in by the hostile Mon kingdom of Rāmañña (Pegu) in the south, and Shan warlords in the north and east, Ava remained the preeminent military power in the region through its strategic control of the irrigated district of Kyaukse. Ava's kings were lavish in their support of Buddhist institutions as testified by the numerous pagodas and temples constructed within the environs of the city. Especially important were the Sagaing hills on the opposite shore of the Irrawaddy river, where successive kings built scores of monasteries and colleges, making it one of Southeast Asia's major Theravāda scholastic centers. In contrast to the neighboring Mon and Thai kingdoms, which by the fifteenth century had largely adopted the reformed THERAVĀDA Buddhism of Sri Lankan tradition, Ava continued to patronize its own native "unreformed" saṅgha, which was descended from Pagan and which Ava regarded as possessing a purer and more ancient pedigree than that of the Sinhalese. The political and religious traditions preserved at Ava came to an abrupt end, however, when in 1527, Shan armies overran the capital and three years later massacred its monks. Ava's glory was resurrected in 1635 when King Thalun (r. 1629–1648) rebuilt the city and made it the capital of the restored Burmese empire of Taungoo. From the throne of Ava, Thalun orchestrated a major Buddhist revival in which he rebuilt the kingdom's ancient national shrine of Shwesettaw near Minbu and erected the gigantic Kaungmudaw pagoda in Sagaing. In addition to the construction of monuments, Thalun held an inquest into monastic lands and instituted the office of ecclesiastical censor (B. mahadan-wun) to oversee religious affairs throughout the country, an office that survived into the British period. Ava was again sacked and its king executed by Mon rebels in 1752, an event that marked the end of the Taungoo dynasty. It was rebuilt and served twice as the capital of the third Burmese empire of Konbaung in 1765–1783 and 1823–1837.

**avacara**. (T. spyod pa; C. jieji; J. kaike; K. kyegye 界繫). In Sanskrit and Pāli, when used at the end of compound words, means "sphere," "domain," or "realm of existence." In Buddhist cosmology, the term refers to the things that "belong to the sphere" of the three realms of existence (traidhātukāvacara, see TRAIDHĀTUKA), which comprise the entire phenomenal universe: the sensuous realm (kāmāvacara or KĀMADHĀTU), the realm of subtle materiality or form (rūpāvacara or RŪPADHĀTU), and the immaterial or formless realm (ārūpyāvacara or ĀRŪPYADHĀTU). The three realms of existence taken together comprise all of SAṂSĀRA, the cycle of rebirth, and are the spheres within which beings take rebirth: there are no realms of existence that are unoccupied, and no beings are born anywhere other than in these three spheres. The sensuous realm is the lowest stratum of the universe and contains the following destinies (GATI), in ascending order: denizens of hell, hungry ghosts, animals, humans, demigods (ASURA), and divinities (DEVA). Rebirth in the sensuous realm is the result of past performance of either predominantly unwholesome deeds (in the case of hell denizens, hungry ghosts, animals, and asuras), a mix of unwholesome and wholesome deeds (as with human beings), or predominantly wholesome deeds (the divinities). The beings in the sensuous realm all have a coarser physical constituent. The realm of subtle materiality is occupied by the BRAHMĀ and other gods, whose minds are perpetually absorbed in one of the four subtle-materiality meditative absorptions (RŪPĀVACARADHYĀNA). Rebirth in the realm of subtle materiality is the result of mastery of one or all of these four dhyānas, and the beings residing there are refined enough that they require only the subtlest of material foundations for their consciousnesses. The immaterial realm is occupied by divinities who are entirely mental, no longer requiring even a subtle-material foundation for their ethereal states of mind. The divinities in the immaterial realm are perpetually

# B

**babu**. (J. happu; K. p'albul 八不). In Chinese, "eight extremes" (the Chinese is a free rendering of the Sanskrit AṢṬĀNTA): the antinomies of production and cessation, eternality and annihilation, sameness and difference, and coming and going, which constitute eight misconceptions of sentient beings. The negation of these eight extremes is a central philosophical and soteriological tenet of the SAN LUN ZONG (the East Asian equivalent of the MADHYAMAKA school) and is adapted from the opening verse of NĀGĀRJUNA's MŪLAMADHYAMAKAKĀRIKĀ. See also CATUṢKOṬI.

**ba bushan jue**. (C) (八不善覺). See BA JUE.

**Bactria**. The name of a region of Central Asia, located between the Hindu Kush range and the Amu Darya River (now lying in Afghanistan, Uzbekistan, and Tajikistan), which was an active center of Buddhism in the centuries immediately preceding and following the onset of the Common Era. A Greco-Bactrian kingdom was established by Diodotus I around 250 BCE. The Greek rulers received Buddhist emissaries from AŚOKA and the MAHĀVAṂSA describes the monk Mahādharmarakṣita as ordaining Greeks as monks. Buddhism would flourish under later Greek kings, most notably Menander, the putative interlocutor of the MILINDAPAÑHA. Buddhist texts written in cursive Greek have been discovered in Afghanistan. Clement of Alexandria seems to mention Buddhists among the Bactrians during the second century CE, when, in describing the gymnosophists, he writes, "Some of the Indians obey the precepts of Boutta; whom, on account of his extraordinary sanctity, they have raised to divine honors." The SARVĀSTIVĀDA school of mainstream Buddhism, especially its VAIBHĀṢIKA strand, seems to have been active in the region.

**ba da zizai wo**. (J. hachidai jizaiga; K. p'al tae chaje a 八大自在我). In Chinese, the "eight great types of autonomy of the self." In distinction to mainstream Buddhist teachings about the absence of a perduring self (ANĀTMAN), the Chinese recension of the MAHĀYĀNA MAHĀPARINIRVĀṆASŪTRA teaches a doctrine of a "great self" (dawo, S. mahātman) that is realized through enlightenment. According to the Chinese renderings, a buddha, having realized this great self, is capable of eight kinds of miraculous transformations (ba shenbian; ba zizai): (1) self-manifesting (he has the power to make his body appear as multiple emanations; nengshi yishen wei duoshen); (2) infinite enlargement (his physical body appears to fill the myriad world systems; shi yichenshen man daqian jie); (3) levitation and translocation (viz., to transport himself to remote places through space; dashen qingju yuandao); (4) incarnating into myriad species or categories of sentient beings (xian wulianglei changju); (5) intentional synesthesia (e.g., to see with his ears, to smell with his eyes, etc.; zhugen huyong); (6) attaining any ability imaginable, but without giving rise to the (conceited) thought of attainment (de yiqie fa wude xiang); (7) elaborating on the meaning of a single scriptural stanza for innumerable eons (before exhausting his knowledge and eloquence; shuo yiji yi jing wuliang jie); (8) pervading all of infinite space (shenbian zhuchu youru xukong). Other Mahāyāna scriptures outline similarly fantastic and dramatic depictions of greatly apotheosized buddhas and advanced bodhisattvas.

**baguan zhai**. (S. aṣṭāṅgasamanvāgataṃ upavāsaṃ; P. aṭṭhaṅgasamanāgataṃ uposathaṃ; T. yan lag brgyad dang ldan pa'i bsnyen gnas; J. hakkansai; K. p'algwan chae 八關齋). In Chinese, "eight-restrictions fast"; also known as bajie ("eight precepts"), bajie zhai ("eight-precepts fast"), bafenzhaijie ("eightfold fasting precepts"), etc. This fast was held on specific days when the laity was expected to observe a temporary set of more restrictive moral precepts. For one day and night, the laity would leave their homes and keep eight precepts (AṢṬĀṄGASAMANVĀGATAṂ UPAVĀSAṂ; see ŚĪLA), as if they had entered the SAṂGHA, effectively becoming monks or nuns for a day. According to the Chinese Buddhist calendar, the UPOṢADHA days reserved for the eight-precepts fast were the eighth, fourteenth, fifteenth, twenty-third, twenty-ninth, and thirtieth of each month. The eight precepts prohibit (1) killing, (2) stealing, (3) engaging in sexual misconduct, (4) lying, (5) consuming intoxicants, (6) resting on a high or luxurious bed, (7) using makeup and perfumes and enjoying music and dance, and (8) eating at improper times. Monasteries sometimes handed out certificates to those laypeople who participated in the precepts ceremony. In Korea, the p'algwan chae (which in Korean is usually called the P'ALGWANHOE, or "eight-restrictions festival") became an important winter festival of thanksgiving held over two full-moon days of the eleventh lunar month; the festival combined indigenous religious practices propitiating the spirits of mountains and rivers with tributes to the memory of fallen warriors. In Tibet, important religious dignitaries customarily give the precepts to both ordained and lay followers before sunrise on days marking important festivals. See also UPAVĀSA; JINGDU SANMEI JING.

**Bāhiranidāna**. In Pāli, lit., the "Outer Origin," a work by BUDDHAGHOSA, conceived as a preface to his SAMANTAPĀSĀDIKĀ, his commentary on the VINAYA, considered by some to be his most important work. The *Bāhiranidāna* recounts the early history of the dispensation (ŚĀSANA), from the Buddha's death through the convocation of the first three Buddhist councils and on to the recitation of the vinaya in Sri Lanka by MAHĀRIṬṬHA during the reign of the Sinhalese king DEVĀNAṂPIYATISSA. Although not technically a VAṂSA, or "chronicle," the work is based on the same sources as the DĪPAVAṂSA, seeking to establish the authenticity of the vinaya by tracing it back to its origins, before beginning the formal commentary upon it. A translation of the *Bahīranidāna* appears in the Pali Text Society's English translation series as *The Inception of Discipline*.

**bahirdhā**. (P. bahiddhā; T. phyi; C. wai; J. ge; K. oe 外). In Sanskrit, "outer" (also written bāhya); usually paired with "inner" (adhyātma) and sometimes with a third "both" (ubhaya), particularly in lists of the types of emptiness (ŚŪNYATĀ) in the PRAJÑĀPĀRAMITĀ SŪTRAs. Outer refers to the first six external sense-fields (ĀYATANA, the objects of eye, ear, nose, and so on); inner to the six internal sense-fields (from the eye- to mind-faculties); and both to the inner and outer sense-fields of other persons. The emptiness of these three categories completes the presentation of the emptiness of a person (PUDGALA); it is followed by the demonstration of the emptiness of emptiness itself. See also BĀHYĀRTHA.

**Bāhiya-Dārucīriya**. (C. Poxijia; J. Bakika; K. Pasaga 婆呬迦). A lay ARHAT (P. arahant), who is declared by the Buddha to be foremost among those of swift intuition (khippābhiññānaṃ). According to Pāli accounts, Bāhiya was a merchant from the town of Bāhiya (whence his toponym), who was engaged in maritime trade. He sailed seven times across the seas in search of profit and seven times returned home safely. On an eighth journey, however, he was shipwrecked and floated on a plank until he came ashore near the seaport town of Suppāraka. Having lost his clothes, he dressed himself in tree bark and went regularly to the town to beg for alms with a bowl. Impressed with his demeanor, the people of Suppāraka were exceedingly generous, offering him luxurious gifts and fine clothes, which he consistently refused. Over time, he came to be regarded by the populace as an arhat, and, infatuated with his growing fame, Bāhiya also came to believe that he had attained that state of holiness. A BRAHMĀ god, who had been Bāhiya's friend in a previous existence, convinced him out of kindness that he was mistaken and recommended that he seek out the Buddha in ŚRĀVASTĪ (P. Sāvatthi). The Brahmā god transported Bāhiya to the city of RĀJAGṚHA (P. Rājagaha) where the Buddha was then staying and told him to meet the Buddha during his morning alms round. Bāhiya approached the Buddha and requested to be taught what was necessary for liberation, but the Buddha refused, saying that alms round was not the time for teaching. Bāhiya persisted three times in his request, whereupon the Buddha consented. The Buddha gave him a short lesson in sensory restraint (INDRIYASAṂVARA): i.e., "in the seen, there is only the seen; in the heard, only the heard; in what is thought, only the thought," etc. As he listened to the Buddha's terse instruction, Bāhiya attained arhatship. As was typical for laypersons who had attained arhatship, Bāhiya then requested to be ordained as a monk, but the Buddha refused until Bāhiya could be supplied with a bowl and robe. Bāhiya immediately went in search of these requisites but along the path encountered an ox, which gored him to death. Disciples who witnessed the event informed the Buddha, who from the beginning had been aware of Bāhiya's impending demise. He instructed his disciples to cremate the body and build a reliquary mound (P. thūpa, S. STŪPA) over the remains; he then explained that Bāhiya's destiny was such that he could not be ordained in his final life.

**Bahuśrutīya**. (P. Bahussutaka/Bahulika; T. Mang du thos pa; C. Duowenbu; J. Tamonbu; K. Tamunbu 多聞部). In Sanskrit, lit. "Great Learning"; one of the traditional eighteen schools of mainstream Indian Buddhism. The Bahuśrutīya was one of the two subschools of the KAUKKUṬIKA branch of the MAHĀSĀṂGHIKA school, along with the PRAJÑAPTIVĀDA, which may have split off as a separate school around the middle of the third century CE. The school was based in NĀGĀRJUNAKOṆḌĀ in the Andhra region of India, although there is also evidence it was active in the Indian Northwest. One of the few extant texts of the Bahuśrutīya is HARIVARMAN's c. third-century CE *TATTVASIDDHI ([alt. *Satyasiddhi]; C. CHENGSHI LUN, "Treatise on Establishing Reality"), a summary of the school's lost ABHIDHARMA; this text is extant only in its Chinese translation. The positions the Bahuśrutīya advocates are closest to those of the STHAVIRANIKĀYA and SAUTRĀNTIKA schools, though, unlike the Sthaviranikāya, it accepts the reality of "unmanifest materiality" (AVIJÑAPTIRŪPA) and, unlike the Sautrāntika, rejects the notion of an "intermediate state" (ANTARĀBHAVA) between existences. The Bahuśrutīya also opposed the SARVĀSTIVĀDA position that dharmas exist in both past and future, the Mahāsāṃghika view that thought is inherently pure, and the VĀTSĪPUTRĪYA premise that the "person" (PUDGALA) exists. The Bahuśrutīya thus seems to have adopted a middle way between the extremes of "everything exists" and "everything does not exist," both of which it views as expediencies that do not represent ultimate reality. The Bahuśrutīya also claimed that the Buddha offered teachings that were characterized by both supramundane (LOKOTTARA) and mundane (LAUKIKA) realities, a position distinct from the LOKOTTARAVĀDA, one of the other main branches of the Mahāsāṃghika, which claimed that the Buddha articulates all of his teachings in a single utterance that is altogether transcendent (lokottara). The Bahuśrutīya appears to be one of the later subschools of mainstream Buddhism; its views are not discussed in the Pāli KATHĀVATTHU. They are also claimed to have attempted a synthesis of mainstream and MAHĀYĀNA doctrine.

**bāhya**. (S). See BAHIRDHĀ.

**bāhyārtha**. (T. phyi don; C. waijing; J. gekyō; K. oegyŏng 外境). In Sanskrit, "external object"; referring specifically to sensory objects (ĀYATANA) that exist externally to the sensory consciousnesses (VIJÑĀNA) that perceive them; the term is sometimes also seen in Sanskrit as bahirdhārtha. Such objects are knowable because there is some feature or quality (ĀKĀRA) that is specific to that particular sense datum. In the MADHYAMAKA school, the conventional existence of external objects is sometimes upheld, although they are said to lack intrinsic nature (SVABHĀVA). External objects are built up out of atoms (PARAMĀṆU), the smallest particles, sometimes compared to a mote of dust. These indivisible atoms serve as building blocks that coalesce to create an external object large enough to have an impact on a sensory faculty (INDRIYA). In his critique of individual atoms in his MADHYAMAKĀLAṂKĀRA, ŚĀNTARAKṢITA describes three basic assertions about how this process happens: (1) different atoms are connected with one another; (2) the atoms are surrounded by external atoms of the same class, with interstices in between, each grounding the others' potential; they cohere and do not drift apart because of a reciprocal energy but do not touch each other; (3) there are no interstices at all between the atoms. In the YOGĀCĀRA school, external objects are presumed not to exist prior to and separate from the sensory consciousnesses that perceive them, and thus lack any intrinsic reality of their own. VASUBANDHU's VIṂŚATIKĀ presents the Yogācāra view that indivisible atoms of any type cannot form gross objects. The Yogācāra refutation is part of a larger project to demonstrate that Buddhist notions of causality are tenable only in the absence of external objects. According to this view, the conscious experience of apparent external objects is in fact the result of residual impressions (VĀSANĀ) left by earlier, similar experiences on an eighth consciousness, the storehouse-like subconscious (ĀLAYAVIJÑĀNA).

**Bai lun**. [alt. Bo lun]. (J. Hyakuron; K. Paek non 百論). In Chinese, "The Hundred Treatise," a philosophical work attributed to the MADHYAMAKA master ĀRYADEVA, and counted as one of the "three treatises" of the SANLUN ZONG of Chinese Buddhism. See *ŚATAŚĀSTRA.

**Baiḍūrya dkar po**. (Vaidurya Karpo). In Tibetan, "White Beryl." The monumental astronomical and astrological treatise written in 1685 by the regent of the fifth DALAI LAMA, SDE SRID SANGS RGYAS RGYA MTSHO; the full title is *Phug lugs rtsis kyi legs bshad mkhas pa'i mgul rgyan baiḍūrya dkar po'i do shal dpyod ldan snying nor*. It deals with the principles of astrology, astronomy, geomancy, and calendrical calculations based on the five elements of wood, fire, earth, metal, and water. Like the larger BAIḌŪRYA SNGON PO, it is supplemented by detailed illustrations. The author's *Baiḍūrya dkar po las 'phros pa'i snyan sgron dang dri lan g.ya' sel* (known as *Baiḍūrya g.ya' sel*) clarifies and further elucidates controversial points in the text.

**Baiḍūrya gser po**. (Vaidurya Serpo). In Tibetan, "Golden Beryl." The text is a history of the DGE LUGS sect of Tibetan Buddhism, its principal teachers, and its institutions, written in 1698 by the regent of the fifth DALAI LAMA, SDE SRID SANGS RGYAS RGYA MTSHO; also known as the *Dga' ldan chos 'byung* ("History of the Dga' ldan pa [= Dge lugs pa]"); the full title is *Dpal mnyam med ri bo dga' ldan pa'i bstan pa zhwa ser cod pan 'chang ba'i ring lugs chos thams cad kyi rtsa ba gsal bar byed pa baiḍūrya ser po'i me long*. Vostrikov's *Tibetan Historical Literature* gives a summary of the contents of the work.

**Baiḍūrya sngon po**. (Vaidurya Ngonpo). In Tibetan, "Blue Beryl"; a commentary composed by the regent of the fifth DALAI LAMA, SDE SRID SANGS RGYAS RGYA MTSHO on the "four tantras" (rgyud bzhi), the basic texts of the Tibetan medical system. Completed in 1688, the work's full title is *Gso ba rig pa'i bstan bcos sman bla'i dgongs rgyan rgyud bzhi'i gsal byed baiḍūrya sngon po*; it is an important treatise on the practice of Tibetan medicine (gso rig). Its two volumes explain the Tibetan medical treatise *Bdud rtsi snying po yan lag brgyad pa gsang ba man ngag gi rgyud*, a text probably by G.yu thog yon tan mgon po (Yutok Yonten Gonpo) the younger, but accepted by Sangs rgyas rgya mtsho to be an authentic work of the "Medicine Buddha" BHAIṢAJYAGURU. The *Baiḍūrya sngon po* covers a wide range of medical topics approximating physiology, pathology, diagnosis, and cure; although based on the four tantras, the text is a synthesis of earlier medical traditions, particularly those of the Byang (Jang) and Zur schools. Its prestige was such that it became the major reference work of a science that it brought to classical maturity. Sangs rgyas rgya mtsho's original commentary on the four tantras was supplemented by a set of seventy-nine (originally perhaps eighty-five) THANG KA (paintings on cloth) that he commissioned to elucidate his commentary. Each painting represented in detail the contents of a chapter, making up in total 8,000 vignettes, each individually captioned. These famous paintings, a crowning achievement in medical iconography, adorned the walls of the Lcags po ri (Chakpori) medical center that Sangs rgyas rgya mtsho founded in LHA SA in 1696; they were destroyed in 1959. It is the commentary most widely studied in the Sman rtsis khang (Mentsikang), a college founded by the thirteenth DALAI LAMA for the study of traditional Tibetan medicine.

**baifa**. (S. śatadharma; J. hyappō; K. paekpŏp 百法). In Chinese, the "hundred DHARMAS"; the standard YOGĀCĀRA classification of factors, classified in five major categories: (1) Eight dharmas concerning the mind (CITTA)—the five affective consciousnesses associated with the five senses, plus the mental consciousness (MANOVIJÑĀNA), mentality (MANAS), and the "storehouse consciousness" (ĀLAYAVIJÑĀNA). (2) Fifty-one forces associated with thought (CITTASAṂPRAYUKTASAṂSKĀRA), such as "applied thought" (VITARKA), "sustained attention" (VICĀRA), and "envy" (ĪRṢYĀ); these are the mental concomitants (CAITTA). (3) Eleven "material" (RŪPA) dharmas, including the eye organ and visual objects, and formal thought objects (dharmāyatanikarūpa). (4) Twenty-four forces dissociated from thought (CITTAVIPRAYUKTASAṂSKĀRA); these are either subconscious or involuntary phenomena, such as "life force" (jīvitendriya) and the "meditative trance wherein no perceptual activities remain" (ASAṂJÑĀSAMĀPATTI), or abstract notions, such as "possession" (PRĀPTI), which are nonetheless classified as real existents. (5) Six "uncompounded" (ASAṂSKṚTA) dharmas, such as "space" (ĀKĀŚA) and "suchness" (TATHATĀ), which are taken to be neither contingent on nor susceptible to causal forces, since they are unproduced by conditions and eternally unchanging. For the full roster of the hundred dharmas, see the List of Lists (s.v.).

**Bai Juyi**. (C) (白居易). See BO JUYI.

**Bailian jiao**. (白蓮教). In Chinese, "White Lotus teachings." As with the BAILIAN SHE, this name was used frequently during the Ming dynasty to refer pejoratively to various religious teachings and magical techniques deemed heretical or traitorous by local officials and Buddhist leaders. No specific religious group, however, seems to coincide precisely with this appellation. The White Lotus teachings are nonetheless often associated with millenarian movements that began to appear during the Mongol Yuan dynasty. Religious groups associated with these movements compiled their own scriptures, known as "precious scrolls" (BAOJUAN), which spoke of the future buddha MAITREYA and the worship of Wusheng Laomu ("Eternal Venerable Mother").

**Bailian she**. (J. Byakurensha; K. Paengnyŏnsa 白蓮社). In Chinese, "White Lotus Society." In the late fourth and early fifth centuries, the Chinese monk LUSHAN HUIYUAN assembled a group of 123 monks and laymen on LUSHAN and contemplated the image of the buddha AMITĀBHA; this group came to be known as the White Lotus Society. This name was also used by putatively heterodox lay Buddhist organizations that flourished during the Tang, Song, and early Yuan dynasties, as well as by monks mainly associated with the TIANTAI school. Inspired by Huiyuan's White Lotus Society and the repentance rituals of the Tiantai school, Mao Ziyuan (c. 1086–1166) constructed halls for repentance called White Lotus repentance halls and promoted the practice of NIANFO (see BUDDHĀNUSMṚTI) as a means of maintaining the five moral precepts (PAÑCAŚĪLA). Mao Ziyuan's White Lotus Society was further popularized by the monk Pudu (1255–1330), who compiled an influential treatise known as the *Lushan lianzong baojian* ("Precious Mirror of the Lotus Tradition at Mt. Lu"). Despite ongoing governmental suppression, he and many other lay followers established cloisters and worship halls all over the country. There seems to be little if any connection between these later organizations and that of Lushan Huiyuan. These lay organizations primarily focused on the recitation of the name of Amitābha in hopes of ensuring rebirth in his PURE LAND. During the early Ming, the name White Lotus Society was frequently associated with rebellious millenarian movements that worshipped the future buddha MAITREYA, which prompted the Ming government to ban any use of the name. Another more common name for these millenarian movements was BAILIAN JIAO. White Lotus societies also flourished in Korea during the Koryŏ dynasty, where they were called Paengnyŏn kyŏlsa (White Lotus retreat societies). Especially well known was the White Lotus Society (Paengnyŏnsa) established at Mandŏksa in 1211 by WŎNMYO YOSE (1163–1240), the mid-Koryŏ revitalizer of the Korean CH'ŎNT'AE (TIANTAI) tradition and a colleague of POJO CHINUL. See also JIESHE.

**Baimasi**. (J. Hakubaji; K. Paengmasa 白馬寺). In Chinese, "White Horse Monastery"; according to tradition, the oldest Buddhist monastery in China; putatively founded in 75 CE in the Chinese capital of Luoyang by MINGDI (r. 58–75), emperor of the Latter Han dynasty. According to a well-known legend found in the preface to the SISHI'ER ZHANG JING ("Sūtra in Forty-Two Sections"), in 67 CE, Emperor Ming had a dream of a radiant golden figure flying through the air, whom his vassals later told him was the Buddha. He subsequently sent envoys to the Western Regions (Xiyu, viz., Central Asia), where this divine being was presumed to reside. The envoys were said to have returned three years later with a copy of the *Sishi'er zhang jing* and two foreign missionaries, KĀŚYAPA MĀTAṄGA and Zhu Falan (Dharmaratna). The emperor ordered that a monastery be built on their behalf in the capital of Luoyang; this monastery was named Baimasi because the two Indian monks were said to have arrived in China with scriptures carried on white horses. This legend probably originated in the third century as a means of legitimizing the apocryphal *Sishi'er zhang jing*. A second founding narrative, which occurs in the GAOSENG ZHUAN ("Biographies of Eminent Monks"), begins with a monastery in India of the same name. According to this legend, a king ordered the destruction of all Buddhist monasteries, but spared one monastery because in his dream he saw a white horse circumambulating the monastery and took this to be an auspicious omen. This king then renamed the monastery White Horse monastery, and, in a reversal of his previous order, began establishing new monasteries throughout India. Emperor Ming thus imitated him in building his own White Horse Monastery in Luoyang. Baimasi quickly became a center for Buddhist study and practice, housing both foreign and Chinese monks. During the Wei dynasty (220–265 CE), SAMGHAVARMAN stayed there; during the Six Dynasties period (420–589 CE), DHARMARAKṢA, Dharmaruci, and Buddhaśānta (d.u.); and during the Tang dynasty, BUDDHATRĀTA. During the Five Dynasties period (the transition from the Tang to the Song dynasties), Baimasi flourished as a residence for CHAN masters, and during the later Jin dynasty (936–947 CE), it also served as a center for the HUAYAN ZONG. The monastery burned down during the early twelfth century but was rebuilt in 1175 CE by the Jin-dynasty prince Sengyan and was extensively renovated during both the Ming and Qing dynasties.

**Baiyi Guanyin**. (S. Pāṇḍaravāsinī; T. Gos dkar mo; J. Byakue kannon; K. Paegŭi Kwanŭm 白衣觀音). In Chinese, "White-Robed GUANYIN (Perceiver of Sounds)." An esoteric form of the BODHISATTVA AVALOKITEŚVARA (known as Guanyin in Chinese), who became a popular focus of cultic worship in East Asia. The cult of Baiyi Guanyin began around the tenth century in China, whence it spread to Korea and Japan. Several indigenous Chinese scriptures praise the compassion and miraculous powers of White-Robed Guanyin. According to the various Baiyi Guanyin APOCRYPHA, she was also a grantor of children, as was Songzi Guanyin. Many testimonials from literati are appended to these scriptures, which attest to Baiyi Guanyin's ability to ensure the birth of sons, although it is also said that she granted children of both genders. Like many other Guanyin-related texts, the White-Robed Guanyin texts frequently invoke esoteric Buddhist terminology such as DHĀRAṆĪ, MUDRĀ, and MANTRA. Beginning in the tenth century, Baiyi Guanyin's cult was associated with the founding of temples, as well as the production of countless images commissioned by both religious and laity. Many worshippers, especially monastics and royalty, had visions of White-Robed Guanyin. These dreams range from being promised children in return for a residence (such as the Upper Tianzhu monastery outside of Hangzhou, later also associated with Princess MIAOSHAN), to enlarging existing structures or even restoring them once a vision or dream of White-Robed Guanyin occurred. In such visions and dreams, White-Robed Guanyin appeared as a female, thus differentiating this form of the bodhisattva from SHUIYUE GUANYIN (Moon-in-the-Water Avalokiteśvara), who was similarly dressed in a white robe, but appeared as a male. Some miracle tales highlighting the donors' names were also produced in honor of Baiyi Guanyin, lending further credence to the accounts of the bodhisattva's miraculous powers.

**Baiyun Shouduan**. (J. Hakuun Shutan; K. Paegun Sudan 白雲守端) (1025–1072). Chinese CHAN master of the LINJI ZONG. Baiyun was a native of Hengyang in present-day Hunan province. After studying with various teachers, Baiyun eventually became a disciple of the Chan master YANGQI FANGHUI (992–1049) and inherited his YANGQI PAI collateral lineage of the Linji school. Baiyun's illustrious career took him to such monasteries as Shengtian Chanyuan in Jiangzhou, Shongsheng Chanyuan in Yuantong, Zhengdao Chanyuan on Mt. Fahua, Ganming Chanyuan on Mt. Longmen, and Haihui Chanyuan on Mt. Baiyun, whence he acquired his toponym. The Yangqi lineage came to dominate the Chan tradition of the Song dynasty largely through the efforts of Baiyun and his disciples. Among Baiyun's disciples, WUZU FAYAN (1024?–1104) is most famous. His teachings can be found in the *Baiyun Shouduan yulu, Baiyun Duan heshang guanglu*, and *Baiyun Duan heshang yuyao*.

**Baizhang Huaihai**. (J. Hyakujō Ekai; K. Paekchang Hoehae 百丈懷海) (749–814). Chinese CHAN monk of the Tang dynasty, who was a dharma successor (FASI) of MAZU DAOYI. Mazu's disciples dedicated a monastery known as Dazhi Shengshou Chansi (Chan Monastery of Great Wisdom and Sagacious Longevity) on Mt. Baizhang (whence Huaihai derived his toponym) and appointed Baizhang Huaihai to be its founding patriarch (kaizu). According to later Song-dynasty accounts, Baizhang compiled for this first independent Chan monastery a novel code of monastic regulations known as the BAIZHANG QINGGUI. This text was said to have been compiled so that Chan monks would no longer need to reside in VINAYA monasteries, where they were regulated by the imported monastic rules of the Indian vinaya tradition, but could now follow a code unique to their own tradition. Because of this supposedly momentous development in Chan history, Baizhang is often heralded as a revolutionary figure within the Chan tradition. However, thus far, no conclusive evidence exists from the time of Baizhang to support this claim. The famous Chan maxim "a day without work is a day without food" is also attributed to Baizhang. He left many famous disciples, among whom GUISHAN LINGYOU and HUANGBO XIYUN are best known.

**Baizhang qinggui**. (J. Hyakujō shingi; K. Paekchang ch'ŏnggyu 百丈清規). In Chinese, "Baizhang's Rules of Purity"; a monastic code distinctive to the CHAN school, attributed to the eminent Tang dynasty monk BAIZHANG HUAIHAI; the text is no longer extant, but it is abridged in the CHANMEN GUISHI. According to later Song-dynasty accounts, Baizhang wrote this QINGGUI ("pure rules") for the new monastery that he had helped establish on Mt. Baizhang. This monastery is considered by the Chan tradition to be the first independent Chan institution, and its unique monastic code is thus a symbol of the school's emancipation from the regulations of the Indian VINAYA tradition. The *Baizhang qinggui* is said to have emphasized the role of the abbot within monastic administration, the precedence of ordination age over monastic rank, and the importance of communal labor. The code also divides the Chan monastic institution into ten administrative offices and provides a general outline of the daily ritual activities in the monastery. This story of the promulgation of the code can be found in the biography of Baizhang in the SONG GAOSENG ZHUAN and JINGDE CHUANDENG LU, as well as in the preface attributed to Yang Yi (968–1024) in the 1335 edition of the *Baizhang guishi*. Whether Baizhang's monastic codes were ever compiled in written form, and if so, whether they bore this title, remain matters of scholarly controversy.

**ba jue**. (J. hachikaku/hakkaku; K. p'algak 八覺). In Chinese, "eight kinds of [misplaced] attention": (1) that directed at desire (yu; S. CHANDA), (2) that directed at aversion (chen; S. DVEṢA),

(3) harmful intent (hai; S. VIHIṂSĀ), (4) partiality and nostalgia for one's loved ones and relatives (QINLI JUE), (5) chauvinistic identification with one's land or country (guotu jue), (6) the delusion that one is safe from death (busi jue), (7) identification with or pride in one's clan or family or lineage (zuxing jue), and (8) belittlement of or contempt toward others (qingwu jue).

**Ba Khin, U**. (1899–1971). Influential lay Burmese teacher of insight meditation (S. VIPAŚYANĀ; P. VIPASSANĀ). Born to a working-class family in Rangoon, U Ba Khin was educated in Christian middle and high schools. Married with six children, he began his career as a government clerk during the British colonial period, later becoming accountant general of independent Burma. He began practicing vipassanā in 1937 under the guidance of Saya Thet Gyi, a lay meditation teacher and disciple of the Burmese monk LEDI SAYADAW. He explored several styles of tranquility (P. samatha, S. ŚAMATHA) and insight meditation and eventually developed his own technique of vipassanā by drawing on his own experiences. The method he devised focuses on physical sensations (VEDANĀ), beginning at the crown of the head and continuing throughout the body; his approach is considered to be especially effective in producing states of deep concentration (SAMĀDHI). In 1941, U Ba Khin met the famous meditation teacher Webu Sayadaw, who encouraged him to teach his meditation technique to others. He began teaching small groups informally and eventually, while accountant general, taught vipassanā to his staff. Under his influence, the government of Burma instituted a policy of encouraging civil servants to practice meditation as part of their daily routine. In 1952, U Ba Khin established the International Meditation Centre in Rangoon, where he taught meditation and began holding intensive ten-day vipassanā retreats on a regular basis. After his retirement from government service in 1953, he devoted all of his time to promoting vipassanā practice. He also played an active role in the sixth Buddhist council (see COUNCIL, SIXTH), held in Rangoon from 1954–1956. His style of vipassanā is one of the most widely disseminated techniques internationally, and his disciples include such well-known meditation teachers as S. N. Goenka.

**Bakkula**. [alt. Nakula; Vakula; etc.] (P. Bakkula; T. Ba ku la; C. Bojuluo; J. Hakukura; K. Pakkura 薄拘羅). Sanskrit and Pāi name of an ARHAT disciple of the Buddha, who became an arhat only eight days after ordaining at the age of eighty. The Buddha declared him to be foremost among those who enjoyed good health, and also one of the four monks most proficient in superknowledges (ABHIJÑĀ), supernatural powers that are the by-products of meditation. ¶ Bakkula is also traditionally listed as fifth (or, in Tibetan, ninth) of the sixteen arhat elders (ṢOḌAŚASTHAVIRA), who are charged by the Buddha with protecting his dispensation until the advent of the next buddha, MAITREYA. He is said to reside in JAMBUDVĪPA with eight hundred disciples. According to the East Asian tradition, Bakkula was a fierce warrior. After he ordained, the Buddha calmed him by making him sit in meditation, whence he became known as the "Quietly Sitting Arhat" (Jingzuo Luohan). Bakkula may be the arhat known by the epithet of Kundovahan (Holder of the Mongoose; C. Juntoupohan) referred to in the *Śāriputraparipṛcchā* ("Sūtra of Śāriputra's Questions"). In Tibetan iconography he holds a mongoose (nakula) spitting out jewels; East Asian images have him seated in a chair holding a mongoose, sometimes accompanied by a beggar child. In CHANYUE GUANXIU's standard Chinese depiction, Bakkula is shown sitting cross-legged on a rock, with both hands holding a backscratcher over his left shoulder. In Tibetan Buddhism, Bakkula (or Bakula) is the first figure in an important incarnation (SPRUL SKU) lineage of the DGE LUGS sect. The nineteenth Bakula Rinpoche (1917–2003) served in the Indian parliament and as the Indian ambassador to Mongolia. Bakkula is alternatively known in Sanskrit as Bakula, Vakkula, Vakula, Vatkula (cf. P. Bākula; Vakkula).

**bala**. (T. stobs; C. li; J. riki; K. yŏk 力). In Sanskrit and Pāli, "power" or "strength"; used in a variety of lists, including the five powers (the eighteenth to twenty-second of the BODHIPĀKṢIKADHARMAS, or "thirty-seven factors pertaining to awakening"), the ten powers of a TATHĀGATA, the ten powers of a BODHISATTVA, and the ninth of the ten perfections (PĀRAMITĀ). The five powers are the same as the five spiritual faculties (INDRIYA)—faith (ŚRADDHĀ), perseverance (VĪRYA), mindfulness (SMṚTI), concentration (SAMĀDHI), and wisdom (PRAJÑĀ)—but now fully developed at the LAUKIKĀGRADHARMA stage of the path of preparation (PRAYOGAMĀRGA), just prior to the path of vision (DARŚANAMĀRGA). A tathāgata's ten powers are given in both Pāli and Sanskrit sources as the power of the knowledge (jñānabala) of: (1) what can be and cannot be (sthānāsthāna), (2) karmic results (karmavipāka), (3) the various dispositions of different beings (nānādhimukti), (4) how the world has many and different elements (nānādhātu), (5) the higher (or different) faculties people possess (indriyaparāpara), (6) the ways that lead to all destinations (sarvatragāminīpratipad), (7) the defilement and purification of all meditative absorptions (DHYĀNA), liberations (VIMOKṢA), samādhis, and trances (SAMĀPATTI) (sarvadhyānavimokṣasamādhisamāpatti-saṃkleśavyavadānavyavasthāna), (8) recollecting previous births (PŪRVANIVĀSĀNUSMṚTI), (9) decease and birth (cyutyupapatti), and (10) the extinction of the contaminants (ĀSRAVAKṢAYA). Another list gives the Buddha's ten powers as the power of aspiration (āśaya), resolution (ADHYĀŚAYA), habit (abhyāsa), practice (PRATIPATTI), wisdom (prajñā), vow (PRAṆIDHĀNA), vehicle (YĀNA), way of life (caryā), thaumaturgy (vikurvaṇa), the power derived from his bodhisattva career, and the power to turn the wheel of dharma (DHARMACAKRAPRAVARTANA). When the Mahāyāna six perfections (PĀRAMITĀ) are expanded and linked to the ten bodhisattva stages (DAŚABHŪMI), four perfections are added: the perfections of skillful means (UPĀYA), vow, power, and knowledge (JÑĀNA). Thus the perfection of power (BALAPĀRAMITĀ) is linked with the ninth bodhisattva stage (BHŪMI). When the ten powers are listed as a bodhisattva's perfection of power, they are sometimes explained to be the powers of a tathāgata before they have reached full strength.

**bāla**. (T. byis pa; C. yutong; J. gudō; K. udong 愚童). In Sanskrit and Pāli, "foolish," "childish"; a pejorative term used to describe a worldling (PṚTHAGJANA), especially one who is ignorant or heedless of the DHARMA. The two terms often appear in a compound as bālapṛthagjana (foolish worldling).

**balapāramitā**. (T. stobs kyi pha rol tu phyin pa; C. li boluomi; J. rikiharamitsu; K. yŏk paramil 力波羅蜜). In Sanskrit, "perfection of power" or "strength"; the ninth of the ten perfections (PĀRAMITĀ), which is mastered at the ninth stage (BHŪMI) of the BODHISATTVA path, viz., SĀDHUMATĪ. The bodhisattva's strength of intellect achieved through this perfection allows him to master the four analytical knowledges (PRATISAṂVID), which gives him the subtlety of thought necessary to craft his understanding of dharma so that it is relevant to each and every sentient being. See DAŚABHŪMI.

**Bāmiyān**. (C. Fanyanna; J. Bon'enna; K. Pŏmyŏnna 梵衍那) (The Chinese is probably a transcription of the Indian equivalency Bayana). A complex of several hundred Buddhist caves situated in the heart of the Hindu Kush mountains, some seventy miles northwest of the modern city of Kabul, Afghanistan; renowned for two massive standing buddhas carved into the cliff face, which were the largest in the world. The Bāmiyān Valley was a thriving Buddhist center of the LOKOTTARAVĀDA school from the second through roughly the ninth century CE, until Islam entered the region. Scholars tend to divide the valley into three sections: the western section contained a giant standing buddha (some 177 feet, or fifty-five meters high) and numerous painted caves; the eastern section contained a second large-scale buddha statue (some 124 feet, or thirty-eight meters high); and the central section is marked by a smaller buddha image. The seventh-century Chinese pilgrim XUANZANG described a giant reclining buddha at Bāmiyān, although no archaeological evidence of such a statue has been found. The series of caves excavated between the massive statues vary in size and layout and include both monastic residences (VIHĀRA) as well as cave basilicas perhaps used for worship by passing monks and traveling merchants. The diversity of artistic styles found at Bāmiyān, like those in the caves at DUNHUANG, is a reminder of its crucial position along the ancient SILK ROAD. In 1222 CE, the Mongol ruler Genghis Khan defaced some of the statues, and the Taliban of Afghanistan shelled the two large buddha statues and destroyed them in March 2001. In 2003, the archaeological remains of the Bāmiyān Valley were listed as a UNESCO World Heritage site.

**Bandhudatta**. (C. Pantoudaduo; J. Banzudatta; K. Pandudalta 槃頭達多). A teacher of KUMĀRAJĪVA, the scholar-monk who eventually became the preeminent translator of Indian Buddhist materials into Chinese. Kumārajīva's mother became a Buddhist nun when her son was seven years old. She also had her son ordained at that time and two years later took him to Kashmir to further his studies. There, over the course of the next three years, he was instructed in the ĀGAMAS and SARVĀSTIVĀDA doctrine by Bandhudatta. Kumārajīva later invited his teacher to KUCHA, where he sought to convert him to the MAHĀYĀNA. Bandhudatta initially resisted, comparing the doctrine of ŚŪNYATĀ to an invisible garment worn by a madman, but Kumārajīva was eventually able to win him over.

**banghe**. (J. bōkatsu; K. ponghal 棒喝). In Chinese, literally "the stick and the shout." Also known as fojuanbanghe ("fly whisk, fist, stick, and shout"). A method of pedagogical engagement associated with the "question-and-answer" (WENDA) technique and employed primarily by teachers of the CHAN, SŎN, and ZEN traditions. In response to questions about the nature of the mind or the teachings of BODHIDHARMA, Chan masters of the Tang dynasty began to respond by hitting, kicking, and shouting at their students. This illocutionary method of instruction is said to have been pioneered by such eminent masters of the Chinese Chan school as HUANGPO XIYUN, DESHAN XUANJIAN, and LINJI YIXUAN. According to his recorded sayings (YULU), Linji Yixuan would often strike or shout at his students before they could even begin to respond. The BIYAN LU ("Blue Cliff Record") specifically refers to "Deshan's stick and Linji's shout" (Deshan bang Linji he) in describing this pedagogical style.

**Bankei Yōtaku**. (盤珪永琢) (1622–1693). Japanese ZEN master of the Tokugawa period; also known as Eitaku. Bankei was born in the district of Hamada in present-day Hyōgō prefecture. According to his sermons, Bankei was dissatisfied with the standard explanations of the concept of "bright virtue" (mingde) found in the CONFUCIAN classic *Daxue* ("Great Learning"), and sought explanations elsewhere. His search eventually brought him to the temple of Zuiōji, the residence of Zen master Unpo Zenshō (1568–1653). After he received ordination and the dharma name Yōtaku from Unpo, Bankei left his teacher to perform a long pilgrimage (angya) to various temples and hermitages. After what he describes in sermons as an awakening at the age of twenty-six, Bankei continued his post-awakening training under Unpo's senior disciple, Bokuō Sogyū (d. 1694), and perfected the teaching of FUSHŌ ZEN ("unborn Zen"). Upon hearing of the arrival of the Chinese monk DAOZHE CHAOYUAN in Nagasaki (1651), Bankei traveled to Sōfukuji where Daozhe was residing and furthered his studies under the Chinese master. Bankei spent the rest of his life teaching his "unborn Zen" to both lay and clergy in various locations. He also built and restored a great number of temples and hermitages, such as Ryūmonji in his native Hamada. In 1672 he was appointed the abbot of the RINZAI monastery of MYŌSHINJI in Kyōto.

**banruo**. (C) (般若). Alternative Sinographic transcription for the Sanskrit PRAJÑĀ (wisdom). The preferred transcription is BORE. See BORE (for related Chinese terms); PRAJÑĀ (for Sanskrit).

**Bao'en**. (J. Hōon; K. Poŭn 報恩). See DAHONG BAO'EN.

**Bao'en fengben jing**. (J. Hōonbubongyō; K. Poŭn pongbun kyŏng 報恩奉盆經). In Chinese, "Scripture for Offering Bowls to Requite Kindness." Along with the YULANBEN JING, the *Bao'en fengben jing* details the practice of the ghost festival (YULANBEN) and its mythology. These scriptures describe the pious efforts of Mulian (the Chinese transcription of the Sanskrit name MAUDGALYĀYANA), one of the two main disciples of the Buddha, to save his mother from the tortures of her rebirth as a hungry ghost (PRETA). In this scripture, the Buddha explains to Mulian that if someone should make offerings to the SAṂGHA in a bowl, the power of the order's meditative practices will be sufficient to save one's ancestors and loved ones from unfortunate rebirths (see APĀYA, DURGATI).

**Bao'ensi**. (報恩寺). In Chinese, "Requiting Kindness Monastery"; located in Jiangsu province. Sometime during the first half of the third century, the Sogdian monk KANG SENGHUI brought to the Wu dynasty (222–264) of the Chinese Three Kingdoms period (c. 220–280 CE) a relic (ŚARĪRA) of the Buddha. The Wu emperor ordered the construction of a monastery called JIANCHUSI (First Built Monastery), where he installed a legendary AŚOKA STŪPA to enshrine that relic. The monastery went through several renovations and relocations during the successive dynasties that had suzerainty over the region. The establishment of the Ming dynasty's capital in the nearby city of Nanjing helped the monastery regain imperial patronage. In 1412, the Yongle emperor of the Ming dynasty began repairs on the monastery in commemoration of his wife's death and renamed it Bao'ensi. He also ordered the construction of a new nine-story stūpa there, now known as the "Porcelain Pagoda," which was decorated with white bricks, glazed tiles, and murals executed by leading artists of the day.

**baohua ershen**. (J. hōke nishin; K. pohwa isin 報化二身). In Chinese, "the enjoyment body and the transformation body [of a buddha]," Two of the three bodies (TRIKĀYA) of a buddha described in the MAHĀYĀNA. The "enjoyment body" (SAṂBHOGAKĀYA) is described as the product of eons of bodhisattva activities, which resides forever in that buddha's PURE LAND. The "transformation body" or "emanation body" (NIRMĀṆAKĀYA) is, by contast, a magical emanation of a buddha in ordinary realms of rebirth, which appears to be subject to old age and death. By inference, the "true essence" of a buddha's PURE LAND, which is beyond the dualities of purity and impurity, is eternally abiding, and is called the "pure land of the enjoyment body" (baotu). The magically transformed buddha lands (huatu), in contrast, may manifest as either pure or impure in varying degrees according to the mental condition and collective karma (see BUDDHAKṢETRA and GONG BUGONG YE) of their inhabitants, and are subject to the laws of formation and dissolution. See TRIKĀYA.

**Baojing sanmei**. (J. Hōkyō sanmai/zanmai; K. Pogyŏng sammae 寶鏡三昧). In Chinese, "Jeweled-Mirror SAMĀDHI"; a definitive poem on enlightenment and practice from the standpoint of the Chinese CAODONG ZONG; otherwise known as the *Baojing sanmei ge*, or "GĀTHĀ of the Jeweled-Mirror Samādhi." This lengthy Chinese song is attributed to the Chan master DONGSHAN LIANGJIE and, along with the CANTONG QI, is revered in the Chinese Caodong and Japanese SŌTŌ schools of CHAN and ZEN as the foundational scripture of their tradition. Although the song is traditionally attributed to Dongshan, a number of sources note that Dongshan secretly received this song from his teacher Yunyan Tansheng (780–841), and Dongshan in turn transmitted it to his head disciple CAOSHAN BENJI. The earliest version of this song appears in the entry on Caoshan in the CHANLIN SENGBAO ZHUAN, written in 1123. The *Baojing sanmei* emphasizes the "inherent enlightenment" (BENJUE; cf. HONGAKU) of sentient beings and the futility of seeking that enlightenment through conscious reflection. Instead, the song urges its audience to allow one's inherently pure enlightened nature to "silently illuminate" itself through meditation (MOZHAO CHAN), as the Buddha did under the BODHI TREE. Numerous commentaries on this song are extant.

**baojuan**. (寶卷). In Chinese, "precious scrolls" or "treasure scrolls"; a genre of scripture produced mainly by popular religious sects with Buddhist orientations during the Ming and Qing dynasties. The baojuan are believed to have been divinely revealed to select beings who often became the leaders of these new religious movements (see also T. GTER MA). The earliest extant baojuan, which focuses on the worship of MAITREYA, the future buddha, is dated 1430, shortly after the fall of the Yuan dynasty. Lo Qing (1442–1527), a lay Buddhist, founded the Wuwei jiao ("Teachings of Noninterference"), for instance, for which he produced "five books and six volumes" of baojuan. Precious scrolls seem to share certain mythological elements, such as a new cosmogony of both the creation and demise of the world. Many of them also expound a new soteriology based on CHAN meditation and Daoist alchemy. The baojuan genre seems to be an evolutionary development from the earlier Buddhist vernacular narrative known as "transformation texts" (BIANWEN). Like bianwen, the baojuan were also employed for both popular entertainment and religious propagation.

**Baolin zhuan**. (J. Hōrinden; K. Porim chŏn 寶林傳). In Chinese, "Chronicle of the Bejeweled Forest (Monastery)"; an important early lineage record of the early Chinese CHAN tradition, in ten rolls; also known as *Da Tang Shaozhou Shuangfeng shan Caoxi Baolin zhuan* or *Caoxi Baolin zhuan*. The title refers to Baolinsi, the monastery in which HUINENG, the legendary "sixth patriarch" (LIUZU) of Chan, resided. The *Baolin zhuan* was compiled by the obscure monk Zhiju (or Huiju) in

801, and only an incomplete version of this text remains (rolls 7, 9, 10 are no longer extant). As one of the earliest extant records of the crucial CHAN legend of patriarchal succession (cf. FASI, ZUSHI), the *Baolin zhuan* offers a rare glimpse into how the early Chan tradition conceived of the school's unique place in Buddhist history. Texts like the *Baolin zhuan* helped pave the way for the rise of a new genre of writing, called the "transmission of the lamplight records" (CHUANDENG LU), which provides much more elaborate details on the principal and collateral lineages of the various Chan traditions. The *Baolin zhuan*'s list of patriarchs includes the buddha ŚĀKYAMUNI, twenty-eight Indian patriarchs beginning with MAHĀKĀŚYAPA down to BODHIDHARMA (the *Baolin Zhuan* is the earliest extant text to provide this account), and the six Chinese patriarchs: Bodhidharma, HUIKE, SENGCAN, DAOXIN, HONGREN, and HUINENG (the *Baolin zhuan*'s entries on the last three figures are no longer extant). For each patriarch, the text gives a short biography and transmission verse (GĀTHĀ).

**Baomingsi**. (保明寺). In Chinese, "Protecting the Ming [Dynasty] Monastery"; located in West Huang Village in the Western Hills near Beijing and closely associated with the Ming imperial family. According to legend, the monastery was established by the Ming dynasty emperor Yingzong (r. 1457–1464 CE) in 1457 CE, in honor of a nun known only by her surname, Lü. While the Ming emperor was being held captive by the Mongols, Nun Lü, who by that time had died, is said to have provided him with food and drink to keep him alive. After he returned to power in 1457 CE, the Yingzong Emperor gave the nun the posthumous imperial rank of "imperial younger sister" (yumei) and built a convent in her honor. Due to her rank, Nun Lü subsequently came to be called an "imperial aunt" (huanggu), and the monastery was renamed Huanggusi. Later in the Ming, its original name Baomingsi was restored. Baomingsi benefited from its close relationship to Ming royalty. During the Chenghua reign era of the Ming (1465–1487 CE), a petition was made for it to receive an imperially bestowed plaque, which was eventually granted during the reign of the Xiaozong emperor (r. 1488–1505 CE). This bestowal brought the monastery imperial protection and exemption from taxes and corvée labor. During the reign of the Jiajing emperor (r. 1507–1567 CE), a period during which Buddhist monasteries and convents were severely persecuted, the emperor spared Baomingsi because of its patronage by two empress dowagers: his own and his predecessor's mothers. A bell was cast for the Guanyin Hall of Baomingsi during the reign of the Longqing emperor (r. 1537–1572 CE) commemorating Nun Lü. The inscriptions on the bell include one commemorating the date of its casting. The other inscription is a list of more than a hundred donors, headed by Empress Dowager Cisheng, further legitimizing the relationship of Baomingsi with the Ming imperial family.

**Baotang Wuzhu**. (J. Hotō Mujū; K. Podang Muju 保唐無住) (714–774). Chinese monk in the early CHAN school, who is considered the founder of the BAOTANG ZONG during the Tang dynasty. Baotang is the name of the monastery where Wuzhu resided (located in present-day Sichuan province). Wuzhu is said to have attained awakening through the influence of Chen Chuzhang (d.u.), a lay disciple of the monk Hui'an (582–799; a.k.a. Lao'an); Chen was thought to be an incarnation of the prototypical Buddhist layman VIMALAKĪRTI. According to the LIDAI FABAO JI, Wuzhu attended a mass ordination performed by the Korean monk CHŎNGJONG MUSANG at Jingzhong monastery in the city of Chengdu. Upon hearing Musang's instructions to practice in the mountains, Wuzhu left for Baiyaishan, where he remained for the next seven years (759–766). He subsequently went to the monastery Konghuisi, until he finally moved to Baotangsi, where he passed away in the summer of 774. Wuzhu was famous for his antinomian teachings that rejected all devotional practices, and is remembered as the founder of the eponymous BAOTANG ZONG. Wuzhu's successor was a lay disciple by the name of Tu Hongjian, deputy commander-in-chief and vice president of the Imperial Chancellery.

**Baotang zong**. (J. Hotōshū; K. Podang chong 保唐宗). An important school of the early Chinese CHAN tradition, known for its radically antinomian doctrines. The school takes its name from the monastery (Baotangsi) where the school's putative founder, BAOTANG WUZHU, resided. The monastery was located in Jiannan (in modern-day Sichuan province), in the vicinity of the city of Chengdu. Until the recent discovery of the LIDAI FABAO JI at DUNHUANG, information on this school was limited to the pejorative comments found in the writings of the ninth-century CHAN historian GUIFENG ZONGMI. Owing perhaps to the antinomian teachings espoused by its members, the school was short-lived. The school rejected all soteriological practices and devotional activities. No images of the Buddha were enshrined in their monasteries, and they questioned the value of chanting scriptures and performing repentance rituals. Instead, they insisted on "simply sitting in emptiness and quietude" (zhikong xianzuo) and transmitting "no thought" (WUNIAN) in lieu of formal precepts. The Baotang lineage is often traced back to Hui'an (582–709; also known as Lao'an, "Old An," because of his long life), a disciple of the fifth patriarch HONGREN, and to Hui'an's lay disciple Chen Chuzhang (d.u.), through whose influence Baotang Wuzhu is said to have attained awakening. Although the author of the *Lidai fabao ji*, a disciple of Wuzhu, attempts to associate the Baotang lineage with that of CHŎNGJONG MUSANG, the founder of the JINGZHONG ZONG, these schools are now considered to have been two distinct traditions. Like the Jingzhong school, the Baotang zong also seems to have exerted considerable influence on the development of Tibetan Buddhism, especially on the early teachings of RDZOGS CHEN (dzogchen).

**Baozang lun**. (J. Hōzōron; K. Pojang non 寶藏論). In Chinese, "Treasure Store Treatise," in one roll, attributed to SENGZHAO. The treatise comprises three chapters. (1) the broad illumination of emptiness and being, (2) the essential purity of transcendence and subtlety, and (3) the empty mystery of the point of genesis. Doctrinally, the *Baozang lun* resembles works associated with the NIUTOU ZONG of the CHAN school, such as the JUEGUAN LUN, XINXIN MING, and WUXIN LUN. In both terminology and rhetorical style, the treatise is also similar to the *Daode jing* and to texts that belong to the Daoist exegetical tradition known as Chongxuan. The author(s) of the *Baozang lun* thus sought to synthesize the metaphysical teachings of the Buddhist and Daoist traditions.

**Baozhi**. (J. Hōshi; K. Poji 保誌/寶誌) (418–514). Chinese monk and well-known thaumaturge who comes to be especially revered by the CHAN school. The earliest sources referring to Baozhi are his epitaph written by Lu Chui (470–526) and his hagiography in the GAOSENG ZHUAN. According to these two texts, Baozhi's secular surname was Zhu, and he was a native of Jinling (in present-day Jiansu); he is therefore sometimes known as Jinling Baozhi, using this toponym. Baozhi became a monk at a young age and around 466 suddenly turned eccentric: he would go for days without food, showing no sign of hunger, let his hair grow several inches long, and wander around the streets barefoot with a pair of scissors, a mirror, and a few strips of silk dangling from a long staff that he carried over his shoulder. Portraits of Baozhi often picture him carrying his staff with its various accoutrements, all symbols of his prescience. He also would work miracles, giving predictions and appearing in many places simultaneously. By the middle of the Tang dynasty, he was believed to be an incarnation of AVALOKITEŚVARA and was widely worshipped. Baozhi was especially venerated by Emperor Wu of the Liang dynasty (r. 502–549) and appears in the famous GONG'AN that relates Emperor Wu's encounter with the Chan founder BODHIDHARMA; there, Baozhi played the role of a clairvoyant witness who revealed to the emperor Bodhidharma's true identity as an incarnation of Avalokiteśvara; YUANWU KEQIN's (1063–1135) commentary to this gong'an in the BIYAN LU ("Blue Cliff Record") refers briefly to the notion that Bodhidharma and Baozhi were both incarnations of Avalokiteśvara. A few verses attributed to Baozhi are included in such Chan writings as HUANGBO XIYUN's CHUANXIN FAYAO, GUIFENG ZONGMI's commentary to the YUANJUE JING (*Yuanjue xiuduoluo liaoyi jing lüeshu*), and YONGMING YANSHOU's ZONGJING LU; these refer, for example, to the metaphor of wheat flour and flour products, and the nonduality between ordinary activities and the functioning of the buddha-nature (BUDDHADHĀTU; FOXING). These verses, however, are retrospective attributions, since they contain Chan ideas that postdate Baozhi and include terminology and ideology similar to later HONGZHOU ZONG texts, which could not have derived from Baozhi.

**Barabuḍur**. See BOROBUDUR.

**'bar ba spun bdun**. (barwa pündün). A group of seven Tibetan dharma protectors (DHARMAPĀLA), who are the commanders of the BTSAN (tsen) class of native Tibetan deities. They are chief among the native spirits who attempted to prevent the propagation of Buddhism in Tibet and were subdued by PADMASAMBHAVA, who accomplished this feat through meditating on HAYAGRĪVA, a wrathful tantric deity. Their chief is the dharmapāla TSI'U DMAR PO. An important place of worship of the 'bar ba spun bdun is in Dpal ti (Palti) near Yar 'brog mtsho (Lake Yardrok) and Rgyal rtse (Gyantse) in the Gtsang (Tsang) region of central Tibet. Seven temples, or btsan khang, were erected to house them, and travelers would stop and present offerings, from simple red flowers to elaborate red GTOR MA or a bla rdo (life stone). They are also known as dam can mched bdun, drag btsan mched bdun, btsan rgod 'bar ba, and btsan rgod zangs ri spun bdun.

**bar bskor**. (barkor) In Tibetan, "middle circuit"; the middle of three main ritual circuits in the Tibetan capital of LHA SA, skirting the outer walls of the JO KHANG temple and its surrounding structures. The other two circuits are the "inner circuit" (nang bskor) going around the central statue in the Jo khang, and the "sanctuary circuit" (gling bskor) around what used to be the limits of the city of Lha sa. The bar bskor is a major center for religious activity in the city, drawing devotees from all parts of the Tibetan Buddhist world to walk, prostrate, pray, and perform offerings around the ambulatory. It is also an important social venue and marketplace, where individuals meander through street vendors' stalls and modern Chinese department stores. Since the late 1980s, the bar bskor has become the stage for political protest, merging civil expression with religious and social ritual space.

**bar do**. In Tibetan, literally "between two"; often translated as "intermediate state"; the Tibetan translation of the Sanskrit ANTARĀBHAVA, the intermediate state between death and rebirth, posited by some, but not all, Buddhist schools (the STHAVIRANIKĀYA, for example, rejects the notion). In Tibet, the term received considerable elaboration, especially in the RNYING MA sect, most famously in a cycle of treasure texts (GTER MA) discovered in the fourteenth century by KARMA GLING PA entitled "The Profound Doctrine of Self-Liberation of the Mind [through Encountering] the Peaceful and Wrathful Deities" (*Zab chos zhi khro dgongs pa rang grol*) also known as the "Peaceful and Wrathful Deities According to Karmalingpa" (*Kar gling zhi khro*). A group of texts from this cycle is entitled BAR DO THOS GROL CHEN MO ("Great Liberation in the Intermediate State through Hearing"). Selections from this group were translated by KAZI DAWA-SAMDUP and published by WALTER Y. EVANS-WENTZ in 1927 as *The Tibetan Book of the Dead*. In Karma gling pa's texts, the universe through which the dead wander is composed of three bar dos. The first, and briefest, is the bar do of the moment of death ('chi kha'i bar do), which occurs with the dawning of the profound state of consciousness called the clear light (PRABHĀSVARACITTA). If one is able to recognize the clear light as reality, one is immediately liberated from rebirth. If not, the second bar do begins, called the bar do of reality (chos nyid bar do). The disintegration of the personality brought on by death reveals reality, but in this case, not in the form of clear light, but in the form of a MAṆḌALA of fifty-eight wrathful deities and a maṇḍala of forty-two peaceful deities from the GUHYAGARBHATANTRA. These deities appear in sequence to the consciousness of the deceased in the days immediately following death. If reality is not recognized in this second bar do, then the third bar do, the bar do of existence (srid pa'i bar do), dawns, during which one must again take rebirth in one of the six realms (ṢAḌGATI) of divinities, demigods, humans, animals, ghosts, or hell denizens. The entire sequence may last as long as seven days and then be repeated seven times, such that the maximum length of the intermediate state between death and rebirth is forty-nine days. This is just one of many uses of the term bar do in Tibetan Buddhism; it was used to describe not only the period between death and rebirth but also that between rebirth and death, and between each moment of existence, which always occurs between two other moments. Cf. also SISHIJIU [RI] ZHAI.

**Bar do thos grol chen mo**. (Bardo Tödröl Chenmo). In Tibetan, "Great Liberation through Hearing in the Intermediate State." It is a section of large cycle of mortuary texts entitled "The Profound Doctrine of Self-Liberation of the Mind [through Encountering] the Peaceful and Wrathful Deities" (*Zab chos zhi khro dgongs pa rang grol*) also known as the "Peaceful and Wrathful Deities according to Karmalingpa" (*Kar gling zhi khro*). The *Bar do thos grol chen mo* is a treasure text (GTER MA) of the RNYING MA sect of Tibetan Buddhism, discovered in the fourteenth century by KARMA GLING PA. Selections from it were translated by KAZI DAWA SAMDUP and published by WALTER Y. EVANS-WENTZ in 1927 as *The Tibetan Book of the Dead*. See also ANTARĀBHAVA, BAR DO.

**Bareau, André**. (1921–1993). A distinguished French scholar of Sanskrit and Pāli who made important contributions to scholarly understanding of the early history of Buddhism in India. While studying philosophy at the Sorbonne, Bareau first became interested in Sanskrit and Pāli. Studying with Jean Filliozat and PAUL DEMIÉVILLE, in 1951 he completed his doctoral thesis, which dealt with the evolution of the notion of the unconditioned (ASAṂSKṚTA) in Buddhism. Bareau would go on to publish thirteen books and more than one hundred articles. Among these books, his most important monographs include *Les Sectes bouddhiques du petit véhicule* (1955) and *Recherches sur la biographie du Buddha dans les Sūtrapiṭaka et les Vinayapiṭaka anciens* (1963). Among his greatest contributions was his work on the earliest sources for the life of the Buddha, which he traced to the third century BCE, more than a century after the Buddha's death. He held the chair in Buddhist Studies at the Collège de France from 1971 to 1991.

**Barlaam and Josaphat**. A Christian saint's tale that contains substantial elements drawn from the life of the Buddha. The story tells the tale of the Christian monk Barlaam's conversion of an Indian prince, Josaphat. (Josaphat is a corrupted transcription of the Sanskrit term BODHISATTVA, referring to GAUTAMA Buddha prior to his enlightenment.) The prince then undertakes the second Christian conversion of India, which, following the initial mission of the apostle Thomas, had reverted to paganism. For their efforts, both Barlaam and Josaphat were eventually listed by the Roman Catholic Church among the roster of saints (their festival day is November 27). There are obvious borrowings from Buddhist materials in the story of Josaphat's life. After the infant Josaphat's birth, for example, astrologers predict he either will become a powerful king or will embrace the Christian religion. To keep his son on the path to royalty, his pagan father has him ensconced in a fabulous palace so that he will not be exposed to Christianity. Josaphat grows dissatisfied with his virtual imprisonment, however, and the king eventually accedes to his son's request to leave the palace, where he comes across a sick man, a blind man, and an old man. He eventually meets the monk Barlaam, who instructs him using parables. Doctrines that exhibit possible parallels between Buddhism and Christianity, such as the emphasis on impermanence and the need to avoid worldly temptations, are a particular focus of Barlaam's teachings, and the account of the way of life followed by Barlaam and his colleagues has certain affinities with that of wandering Indian mendicants (ŚRAMAṆA). By the late nineteenth century, the story of Barlaam and Josaphat was recognized to be a Christianized version of the life of the Buddha. The Greek version of the tale is attributed to "John the Monk," whom the Christian scholastic tradition assumed to be St. John of Damascus (c. 676–749). The tale was, however, first rendered into Greek from Georgian in the eleventh century, perhaps by Euthymius (d. 1028). The Georgian version, called the *Balavariani*, appears to be based on an Arabic version, *Kitāb Bilawhar wa Būdhāsaf*. The source of the Arabic version has not been identified, nor has the precise Buddhist text from which the Buddhist elements were drawn. After the Greek text was translated into Latin, the story was translated into many of the vernaculars of Europe, becoming one of the most popular saint's tales of the Middle Ages.

**'Ba' rom bka' brgyud**. (Barom Kagyü). One of the eight Tibetan subsects of the BKA' BRGYUD sect of Tibetan Buddhism, originating with 'Ba' rom Dar ma dbang phyug (Barom Darma Wangchuk, 1127–1199), a disciple of SGAM PO PA BSOD NAMS RIN CHEN.

**Ba shenbian**. (C) (八神變). See BA DA ZIZAI WO.

**Bashō**. (J) (芭蕉). See MATSUO BASHŌ.

**Bassui Tokushō**. (拔隊得勝) (1327–1387). Japanese monk of the Hottō branch of the RINZAISHŪ of ZEN; also known as Bassui Zenji. Ordained at the age of twenty-nine, Bassui subsequently began a pilgrimage around the Kantō area of Japan in search of enlightened teachers. He eventually met Kohō Kakumyō (1271–1361) of Unjuji in Izumo, and received from him the name Bassui, which means "well above average," lit., "to rise above the rank-and-file." Their relationship, however, remains unclear. After taking leave from Kohō, Bassui continued traveling on pilgrimage until he settled down in Kai, where his local patrons established for him the monastery of Kōgakuji ("Facing Lofty Peaks Monastery"). Bassui's teachings stress the importance of KŌAN (C. GONG'AN) training and especially the notion of doubt (see YIJING; YITUAN). Bassui was also extremely critical of SŌTŌ teachers of his day, despite the fact that his own teacher Kohō was once a Sōtō monk, and he was strongly critical of their use of kōan manuals called MONSAN in their training. Although his teacher Kohō employed Sōtō-style "lineage charts" (see KECHIMYAKU SŌJŌ) as a means of attracting lay support, Bassui rejected their use and instead stressed the importance of practice.

**ba wei**. (J. hachimi; K. p'al mi 八味). In Chinese, lit. "eight tastes"; a numerical list derived from Chinese translations of the MAHĀPARINIRVĀṆASŪTRA, where the Buddha's experience of NIRVĀṆA is said to be characterized by eight "tastes," or experiences: (1) it is perpetually abiding (changzhu), (2) calm and extinguished (viz., of suffering and afflictions) (jimie), (3) not subject to old age (bulao), (4) deathless (busi), (5) immaculate (qingjing), (6) unobstructed like space (xutong), (7) imperturbable (budong), and (8) blissful (kuaile).

**ba wu san er**. (八五三二). In Chinese, "[teaching involving] eight, five, three, and two [dharmas]"; a numerical schema used in the Chinese FAXIANG ZONG (YOGĀCĀRA) to summarize key tenets of its analysis of factors (DHARMA). In this schema, "eight" refers to "eight consciousnesses" (the six sensory consciousnesses; the seventh consciousness, or KLIṢṬAMANAS; and the eighth consciousness, or ĀLAYAVIJÑĀNA); "five" refers to the "five [aspects of] dharmas" (WUFA); the "three" refers to "three natures" (TRISVABHĀVA); and the "two" to "two kinds of nonself" (see PUDGALANAIRĀTMYA and DHARMANAIRĀTMYA).

**baxiang**. (J. hassō; K. p'alssang 八相). In Chinese, "eight episodes"; eight archetypal events in the life of any buddha: (1) descending from TUṢITA heaven to undertake his final life as a BODHISATTVA; (2) entering the womb of his mother for his final life; (3) birth; (4) renunciation (i.e., leaving home to become a monk); (5) subjugating MĀRA; (6) attaining enlightenment; (7) turning the wheel of the dharma (DHARMACAKRAPRAVARTANA) at the first sermon; (8) passing into PARINIRVĀṆA. Another common list is (1) descent from tuṣita heaven; (2) birth in LUMBINĪ; (3) seeing the four portents (CATURNIMITTA); (4) going forth into homelessness (PRAVRAJITA); (5) ascetic practice in the Himālayas; (6) subjugating Māra beneath the BODHI TREE and attaining enlightenment; (7) turning the wheel of the dharma in the Deer Park (MṚGADĀVA); (8) passing into parinirvāṇa beneath twin ŚĀLA trees. The lists may differ slightly, e.g., replacing subjugating Māra with gestation in the womb. These eight episodes are common themes in Buddhist art. See also TWELVE DEEDS OF A BUDDHA.

**ba xunsi**. (C) (八尋思). See BA JUE.

**Bayinnaung**. (r. 1551–1581). Burmese king and third monarch of the Taungoo dynasty. Bayinnaung was the brilliant general and brother-in-law of King Tabinshwehti (r. 1531–1550), who first expanded the territory of the city-state Taungoo to create the Taungoo empire (1531–1752). Tabinshwehti sought to reunify the various kingdoms and petty states that had once been vassals to the first Burmese empire of Pagan (1044–1287). To this end, he followed a policy of conciliation toward vanquished peoples, especially the Mon, whose brand of reformed Sinhalese THERAVĀDA Buddhism he favored. Bayinnaung continued this ecumenical religious policy even while he aggressively extended the borders of his empire eastward through military campaigns launched in the name of the Buddha. In a series of campaigns, he subdued the Shan tribes, the Lao kingdom of Vientiane, and the Thai kingdoms of AYUTHAYA and Chiangmai, creating briefly Southeast Asia's largest polity. Throughout these territories, he built pagodas and distributed copies of PĀLI scriptures. In the Shan hills, he compelled the local warlords to abandon human sacrifice and convert to Buddhism, requiring them to provide material support to missionary monks dispatched from his capital. While officially promoting the reformed Buddhism of the Mon, Bayinnaung remained tolerant of local Buddhist custom and allowed independent monastic lineages to continue. He maintained close diplomatic relations with the Buddhist kingdom of Sri Lanka and offered munificent gifts to its palladium, the TOOTH RELIC at Kandy. In 1560, when the Portuguese captured the relic, Bayinnaung sought to ransom it for 300,000 ducats, only to have his emissaries witness its destruction in a public ceremony ordered by the archbishop of Goa. Legend says that the tooth miraculously escaped and divided itself into two, one of which was returned to Kandy, while the other was gifted to Bayinnaung, who enshrined it in the Mahazedi pagoda at his capital Pegu. The religious policies of Bayinnaung and his successors greatly influenced the character of Burmese Buddhism and society. Royal patronage of Buddhist scholarship coupled with the proliferation of village monastery schools fostered a common Buddhist identity among the populace that crossed ethnic boundaries and facilitated a degree of peasant literacy that was unusual in premodern societies.

**Bayon**. One of the most important Buddhist temples sites at ANGKOR THOM, the temple-city of the ancient Khmer kingdom; built by the Khmer king Jayavarman VII (r. 1181–c. 1220). The Bayon is a funerary temple located at the center of the Angkor Thom city complex. Constructed of sandstone and in the form of a terraced pyramid, the Bayon represents among other symbols Mt. SUMERU, the axis mundi of the Hindu-

Buddhist universe. The temple is entered through four doorways, one on each side, that lead through galleries richly carved with bas-reliefs depicting scenes from contemporary life and Hindu mythology. The temple is crowned with fifty-two towers, the largest of which occupies the center and pinnacle of the structure. The four sides of every tower bear colossal guardian faces that are believed to be portraits of Jayavarman VII in the guise of the bodhisattva AVALOKITEŚVARA. The Bayon is the first of Angkor's many temples specifically dedicated to a MAHĀYĀNA Buddhist cult; those built earlier were exclusively Hindu in affiliation. Beneath the central tower is a chamber that once housed a buddha image protected by a hooded cobra. This image was situated above a receptacle intended to receive the king's ashes at death. The Bayon thus combines the function and architectural elements of a Hindu temple and a Buddhist STŪPA, while Jayavarman's identification with Avalokiteśvara was but an extension of Angkor's long-standing Hindu devarājan (divine king) cult.

**Ba zizai**. (C) (八自在). See BA DA ZIZAI WO.

**bca' yig**. (chayik). In Tibetan, "constitution" or "charter"; the monastic codes promulgated at individual monasteries, which govern life at those centers. These individual codes supplement the much larger MŪLASARVĀSTIVĀDA VINAYA, the primary source for the monastic code, and its summary in GUṆAPRABHA's VINAYASŪTRA, a medieval Indian summary of the monastic code. Each monastery has its own bca' yig, which sometimes is an oral code of best practices, sometimes a written document drawn up by a respected party. The bca' yig condenses customs, oral lore, and traditional documentation into a single constitution for the community, addressing specific questions to do with the governance of the monastery, the duties, responsibilities, and dress of monastic officers, the order of priority among members, and the procedures for arriving at binding decisions. It also codifies the observance of ritual activities. See also QINGGUI.

**Bdag med ma**. (Dakmema) (fl. c. eleventh century). Chief of the nine wives of the renowned Tibetan translator MAR PA CHOS KYI BLO GROS. Bdag med ma plays a leading role in the life story of Marpa's chief disciple MI LA RAS PA, as his benefactor, confidant, and teacher. Her name, literally "selfless woman," is the Tibetan translation for the Sanskrit goddess NAIRĀTMYĀ, consort of the deity HEVAJRA. Marpa's principal chosen deity (YI DAM) was Hevajra, and it is believed that Marpa's family represented the nine deity Hevajra MAṆḌALA (Kye'i rdo rje lha dgu) consisting of Hevajra and Nairātmyā in the center surrounded by eight goddesses.

**Bde lam lam rim**. (Delam Lamrim). In Tibetan, "The Stages of the Easy Path," an important "stages of the path" (LAM RIM) treatise composed by the first PAṆ CHEN LAMA BLO BZANG CHOS KYI RGYAL MTSHAN. The work's complete title is *Byang chub lam gyi rim pa'i khrid yig thams cad mkhyen par bgrod pa'i bde lam*.

**bdud**. (dü). In Tibetan, "demon"; a class of pre-Buddhist harmful spirits, who are said to cause fits of unconsciousness and other illnesses, and are counteracted through a glud (lü) ceremony known as the brgya bzhi (gyashi). The bdud are depicted as black wrathful gods, carrying a snare (S. pāśa, T. zhags pa) or notched staff (T. khram shing) and riding black horses. There are also female bdud, known as bdud mo. The bdud are classified according to numerous schemata that include a different deity as the king. In BON texts, they are commonly grouped in classes of four or five: the sa (earth) bdud in the east, rlung (wind) bdud in the north, me (fire) bdud in the west and chu (water) bdud in the south; sometimes a fifth class, the lha (god) bdud, is added at the zenith. Bdud is also used as the Tibetan translation of MĀRA, evil personified.

**Bdud 'joms Rin po che**. (Düdjom Rinpoche) (1904–1987). An influential twentieth-century Tibetan master who served for a time as the head of the RNYING MA sect of Tibetan Buddhism. Born in the southern Tibetan region of PADMA BKOD, Bdud 'joms Rin po che was recognized at the age of three as the reincarnation of the treasure revealer (GTER STON) Bdud 'joms gling pa (Düdjom Lingpa). He trained primarily at SMIN GROL GLING monastery in central Tibet, establishing himself as a leading exponent of Rnying ma doctrine, especially the instructions of RDZOGS CHEN or "great completion." Following his flight into exile in 1959, Bdud 'joms Rin po che became the religious leader of the Rnying ma sect, while actively supporting the educational activities of the Tibetan diasporic community in India. He spent much of his later life in the West, establishing centers and garnering a wide following in the United States and France. He died in 1987 at his religious institution in Dordogne, France. Renowned as a treasure revealer, scholar, and poet, Bdud 'joms Rin po che is especially known for his extensive historical writings, including the comprehensive *The Nyingma School of Tibetan Buddhism: Its Fundamentals and History*. His full name is 'Jigs bral ye shes rdo rje (Jikdral Yeshe Dorje).

**Beal, Samuel**. (1825–1889). British translator of Chinese Buddhist works. A graduate of Trinity College, Cambridge, he worked as a chaplain in the British navy and rector of various Anglican parishes, including Wark and Northumberland. In 1877, Beal was appointed as lecturer, and later professor, of Chinese at University College, London, where he specialized in Chinese Buddhist materials. Beal is perhaps best known for his translations of the travelogues of Chinese Buddhist pilgrims to India, including FAXIAN (c. 399/337–422), Song Yun (c. 516–523), and XUANZANG (600/602–664). Especially influential was his translation of Xuanzang's travelogue DA TANG XIYU JI, which he rendered as *Si-Yu-Ki: Buddhist Records of the Western World* (two volumes, 1884). Beal's anthology of

Chinese Buddhist texts, *A Catena of Buddhist Scriptures from the Chinese* (1872), includes translations of a wide range of important Buddhist texts. Beal also compiled one of the first Western-language catalogues of the Chinese Buddhist canon. Other books of his include *The Romantic Legend of Śākya Buddha* (1876) and *Texts from the Buddhist Canon, commonly known as Dhammapada* (1878).

**begging bowl**. See PĀTRA; PIṆḌAPĀTA.

**Beg tse**. In Tibetan, "Hidden Coat of Mail"; an important wrathful deity in Tibetan Buddhism, one of the eight DHARMAPĀLA (chos skyong) or protectors of the dharma. He is also known as Lcam sring ("Brother and Sister") and as Srog bdag or Srog bdag dmar po ("Lord of the Life Force" or "Red Lord of the Life Force"). According to legend, he was a war god of the Mongols prior to their conversion to Buddhism. In 1575, he tried to prevent the third DALAI LAMA BSOD NAMS RGYA MTSHO from visiting the Mongol khan but was defeated by the Buddhist cleric and converted to Buddhism as a protector of the dharma. According to some descriptions, he is a worldly protector ('jig rten pa'i srung ma); according to others, he is a transcendent protector ('jig rten las 'das pa'i srung ma). In texts devoted to HAYAGRĪVA, Beg tse is sometimes represented as the principal protector deity.

**beidou qixing**. (J. hokuto shichishō; K. puktu ch'ilsŏng 北斗七星). In Chinese, "seven stars of the Northern Dipper" (viz., the Big Dipper, or Ursa Major); Daoist divinities that are also prominent in Korean Buddhism, where they are typically known as the ch'ilsŏng. The cult of the seven stars of the Big Dipper developed within Chinese Buddhist circles through influence from indigenous Daoist schools, who worshipped these seven deities to guard against plague and other misfortunes. The apocryphal *Beidou qixing yanming jing* ("Book of the Prolongation of Life through Worshipping the Seven Stars of the Northern Dipper"), suggests a correlation between the healing buddha BHAIṢAJYAGURU and the Big Dipper cult by addressing the seven-star TATHĀGATAS (qixing rulai) with names that are very similar to Bhaiṣajyaguru's seven emanations. This indigenous Chinese scripture (see APOCRYPHA), which derives from an early Daoist text on Big Dipper worship, is certainly dated no later than the late thirteenth or early fourteenth centuries but may have been composed as early as the middle of the eighth century; it later was translated into Uighur, Mongolian, and Tibetan, as part of the Mongol Yuan dynasty's extension of power throughout the Central Asian region. Thanks to this scripture, the seven-star cult became associated in Buddhism with the prolongation of life. We know that seven-star worship had already been introduced into esoteric Buddhist ritual by at least the eighth century because of two contemporary manuals that discuss HOMA fire offerings to the seven stars: VAJRABODHI's (671–741) *Beidou qixing niansong yigui* ("Ritual Procedures for Invoking the Seven Stars of the Northern Dipper") and his disciple AMOGHAVAJRA's (705–774) *Beidou qixing humo miyao yigui* ("Esoteric Ritual Procedure for the Homa Offering to the Seven Stars of the Northern Dipper"). Renderings of DHĀRAṆĪ sūtras dedicated to the tathāgata TEJAPRABHA (Qixingguang Rulai), who is said to be master of the planets and the twenty-eight asterisms, are also attributed to Amoghavajra's translation bureau. Worship of the seven stars within esoteric Buddhist circles was therefore certainly well established in China by the eighth century during the Tang dynasty and probably soon afterward in Korean Buddhism. ¶ The worship of the Big Dipper in Korea may date as far back as the Megalithic period, as evidenced by the engraving of the Big Dipper and other asterisms on dolmens or menhirs. In the fourth-century Ji'an tombs of the Koguryŏ kingdom (37 BCE–668 CE), one of the traditional Three Kingdoms of early Korea, a mural of the Big Dipper is found on the north wall of tomb no. 1, along with an accompanying asterism of the six stars of Sagittarius (sometimes called the Southern Dipper) on the south wall; this juxtaposition is presumed to reflect the influence of the Shangqing school of contemporary Chinese Daoism. Court rituals to the seven stars and the tathāgata Tejaprabha date from the twelfth century during the Koryŏ dynasty. By at least the thirteen century, the full range of texts and ritual practices associated with the seven-star deities were circulating in Korea. At the popular level in Korea, the divinities of the Big Dipper were thought to control longevity, especially for children, and the ch'ilsŏng cult gained widespread popularity during the Chosŏn dynasty (1392–1910). This popularization is in turn reflected in the ubiquity in Korean monasteries of "seven-stars shrines" (ch'ilsŏnggak), which were typically located in less-conspicuous locations along the outer perimeter of the monasteries and were worshipped primarily by the nonelite. Inside these shrines were hung seven-star paintings (T'AENGHWA), which typically depict the tathāgatas of the seven stars, with the tathāgata Tejaprabha presiding at the center. There are also several comprehensive ritual and liturgical manuals compiled during the Chosŏn dynasty and Japanese colonial period in Korea that include rituals and invocations to the seven stars and Tejaprabha, most dedicated to the prolongation of life. Along with the mountain god (sansin), who also often has his own shrine in the monasteries of Korea, the role of the ch'ilsŏng in Korean Buddhism is often raised in the scholarship as an example of Buddhism's penchant to adapt beliefs and practices from rival religions. Although ch'ilsŏng worship has declined markedly in contemporary Korea, the ch'ilsŏkche, a worship ceremony dedicated to the tathāgata Tejaprabha, is occasionally held at some Buddhist monasteries on the seventh day of the seventh lunar month, with lay believers praying for good fortune and the prevention of calamity.

**Beishan lu**. (北山録). In Chinese, lit. "North Mountain Record"; a lengthy treatise in ten rolls, compiled by the Chinese monk Shenqing (d. 1361). This comprehensive treatise provides a detailed account of the formation of the world, the appearance of sages and sacred texts, and the history of Chinese thought. Among its many claims, the harmony of Buddhist, Daoist, and Confucian thought and its harsh critique of the CHAN school's "transmission of the lamplight" (chuandeng; see CHUANDENG LU) theory were the most controversial and came under attack later by FORI QISONG.

**Bei zong**. (J. Hokushū; K. Puk chong 北宗). In Chinese, "Northern school"; a designation for an early tradition of the CHAN school that flourished in the seventh and eighth centuries, and referring specifically to the lineage of SHENXIU and his disciples. The doctrines of the "Northern school" are known to have focused on the transcendence of thoughts (linian) and the five expedient means (fangbian; S. UPĀYA); these teachings appear in "Northern school" treatises discovered at Dunhuang, such as the DASHENG WUSHENG FANGBIAN MEN, YUANMING LUN, and *Guanxin lun*. The appellations "Northern school" and "Southern school" (NAN ZONG) began to be used widely throughout the Tang dynasty, largely due to the efforts of HEZE SHENHUI and his followers. As a result of Shenhui's polemical attacks on Shenxiu and his followers, later Chan historians such as GUIFENG ZONGMI came to speak of a "Northern school" whose teachings promoted a "gradual awakening" (JIANWU) approach to enlightenment (see SUDDEN-GRADUAL ISSUE); this school was distinguished from a superior "Southern school," which was founded on the prospect of "sudden awakening" (DUNWU). While such a characterization is now known to be misleading, subsequent genealogical histories of the Chan tradition (see CHUANDENG LU) more or less adopted Shenhui's vision of early Chan wherein the legendary sixth patriarch (LIUZU) HUINENG, rather than Shenxiu, became the bearer of the orthodox transmission from the fifth patriarch HONGREN. The LIUZU TAN JING played an important role in making this characterization of a gradualist Northern school and a subitist Southern school part of the mainstream tradition. Despite Shenhui's virulent attacks, Shenxiu and his disciples YIFU (661–736), PUJI (651–739), and XIANGMO ZANG played a much more important role in the early growth of Chan than the later tradition generally acknowledges. There is strong evidence, in fact, that Shenxiu was considered by his contemporaries to be the legitimate successor to the fifth patriarch Hongren and he and his followers were part of the metropolitan elite and wielded deep influence at the Chinese imperial court. The Northern school also seems to have been a force in Tibetan Buddhism during the eighth century and the Northern-school monk Heshang MOHEYAN was the Chinese protagonist in the famous BSAM YAS DEBATE.

**Bendōhō**. (辨道法). In Japanese, "Techniques for Pursuing the Way"; a work devoted to the rules of the SAṂGHA hall (see C. SENGTANG), written by DŌGEN KIGEN. Primarily during his stays at the monasteries Daibutsuji and EIHEIJI, Dōgen wrote a number of related manuals on monastic rules (C. QINGGUI), of which the *Bendōhō* is perhaps most important. These manuals, including the *Bendōhō*, were later collected and published together as a single text known as the EIHEI SHINGI. Dōgen modeled his regulations after those found in an earlier code of monastic rules produced in China, the CHANYUAN QINGGUI. The *Bendōhō* was therefore heavily influenced by the Chinese Chan master CHANGLU ZONGZE's manual of meditation, ZUOCHAN YI, which was embedded in the *Chanyuan qinggui*. The text includes guidelines for all of the activities of the saṃgha hall, from sitting, walking, sleeping, and cleaning to the practice of seated meditation (J. zazen; C. ZUOCHAN). The *Bendōhō* also contains a version of Dōgen's FUKAN ZAZENGI.

**Bendōwa**. (辦道話). In Japanese, "A Talk on Pursuing the Way"; a short essay written in vernacular Japanese by the SŌTŌ ZEN monk DŌGEN KIGEN in 1231. Dōgen's earliest extant work, the *Bendōwa* contains a brief description of the orthodox transmission to the East of the "true dharma" (shōbō; S. SADDHARMA) of the Buddha and also a succinct explanation of Zen in a series of eighteen questions and answers. The *Bendōwa* was later incorporated into Dōgen's magnum opus, the SHŌBŌGENZŌ. The teachings on Zen meditation found in the *Bendōwa* are similar to those of Dōgen's FUKAN ZAZENGI.

**Ben'en**. (J) (辯圓). See ENNI BEN'EN.

**Benevolent Kings Sūtra**. See RENWANG JING.

**Benji**. (J. Honjaku; K. Ponji 本寂). See CAOSHAN BENJI.

**benji**. (J. honzai; K. ponje 本際). In Chinese, "point of genesis"; the term frequently appears in Buddhist and Chongxuan Daoist texts. Buddhist writers used the term to translate the Sanskrit terms BHŪTAKOṬI ("ultimate state"), pūrvakoṭi ("absolute beginning"), and KOṬI ("end"), which all denote a sense of limit, end, or origin. The term benji was also sometimes used as a synonym for NIRVĀṆA and for "absolute truth" (PARAMĀRTHASATYA); in certain texts, it could also refer to the origin of SAṂSĀRA. Other terms, such as zhenji ("apex of truth") or shiji ("apex of reality"), are also used in place of benji as expressions for ultimate truth.

**benjue**. (J. hongaku; K. pon'gak 本覺). In Chinese, lit. "original enlightenment"; also sometimes translated as "inherent" or "intrinsic" enlightenment. The term was apparently coined in China and explicated in many Buddhist APOCRYPHA, such as the DASHENG QIXIN LUN and the KŬMGANG SAMMAE KYŎNG. The *Dasheng qixin lun* synthesized the earlier Indian theories of TATHĀGATAGARBHA and ĀLAYAVIJÑĀNA, which came to stand for two different aspects of the one mind (YIXIN). The *Dasheng qixin lun* also posited a difference between attaining awakening through a process of cultivation known as "actualizing enlightenment" (SHIJUE) and the inherent purity of the mind represented by the term "original enlightenment" (benjue). From the standpoint of the buddhas and sages, the mind of the ordinary sentient being is seen as being inherently endowed with the tathāgatagarbha, the embryo of buddhahood and thus intrinsically in a state of "original enlightenment" (benjue). From the standpoint of sentient beings, however, the foundation of that same mind is the ālayavijñāna, which, as a storehouse of a seemingly infinite number of seeds or potencies (BĪJA) of past unwholesome deeds, is defiled and thus in need of purification through a process of "actualizing enlightenment" (shijue). Once that actualization process is completed, however, one realizes that the enlightenment achieved through cultivation is in fact identical to the enlightenment that is innate, viz., "original enlightenment" (benjue). Hence, the difference between these two types of enlightenment is ultimately a matter of perspective: the buddhas and sages see the mind as the innately pure tathāgatagarbha and thus originally enlightened, while ordinary persons (PṚTHAGJANA) see the mind as defiled and thus needing purification through the process of actualizing enlightenment. See also HONGAKU.

**Benkenmitsu nikyōron**. (辯顯密二教論). In Japanese, literally "Distinguishing the Two Teachings of the Exoteric and Esoteric"; a relatively short treatise composed by the Japanese SHINGON monk KŪKAI in the early ninth century. The text is commonly known more simply as the *Nikyōron*. As the title suggests, the central theme of the *Benkenmitsu nikyōron* is the elaboration of the difference between the exoteric and esoteric teachings of Buddhism and the demonstration of the latter's superiority. The text begins with a brief introduction, followed by a series of questions and answers, and a short conclusion. The *Benkenmitsu nikyōron* describes the relation between the exoteric teachings preached by the NIRMĀṆAKĀYA of the Buddha and the esoteric teachings preached by his DHARMAKĀYA as that between provisional words spoken according to the different capacities of sentient beings and ultimate truth. By meticulously citing scriptural references, such as the LAṄKĀVATĀRASŪTRA, the *Benkenmitsu nikyōron* shows that the dharmakāya, like the nirmāṇakāya and SAṂBHOGAKĀYA, can indeed preach and that it does so in a special language best articulated in such esoteric scriptures as the MAHĀVAIROCANĀBHISAṂBODHISŪTRA. Whereas the nirmāṇakāya speaks the DHARMA with reference to the six perfections (PĀRAMITĀ), the dharmakāya employs the language of the three mysteries: the body, speech, and mind of MAHĀVAIROCANA expressed in MUDRĀ, MANTRA, and MAṆḌALA. Like many of Kūkai's other writings, the arguments presented in his *Benkenmitsu nikyōron* helped him legitimize the introduction and installment of the new teachings, now known as MIKKYŌ or esoteric Buddhism, which he had brought back from China. There are several commentaries on the text, including those composed by Seisen (1025–1115), Raiyu (1226–1304), Yūkai (1345–1416), and Kaijō (1750–1805).

**benlai mianmu**. (J. honrai no menmoku; K. pollae myŏnmok 本來面目). In Chinese, "original face"; an expression used in the CHAN school to describe the inherent state of enlightenment and often synonymous with buddha-nature (BUDDHADHĀTU; C. FOXING). The term is best known in the GONG'AN attributed by the tradition to the sixth patriarch (LIUZU) HUINENG (638–713), "Not thinking of good, not thinking of evil, at this very moment, what is your original face before your parents conceived you?" (The last line is often found translated as "what is your original face before your parents were born," but the previous rendering is preferred.) This gong'an is often one of the first given to RINZAI ZEN neophytes in Japan as part of their meditation training; the term, however, does not appear in the earlier DUNHUANG version of the LIUZU TAN JING ("Platform Sūtra of the Sixth Patriarch"), but only in later Song-dynasty recensions, suggesting it is actually a Song-period locution.

**Benye jing**. (C) (本業經). See PUSA BENYE JING.

**benyou zhongzi**. (C) (本有種子). In Chinese, "primordial seeds." See BĪJA.

**betsuji nenbutsu**. (別時念佛). In Japanese, lit. "special-time recitation of the Buddha's name," also known as nyohō nenbutsu; a term for an intensive nenbutsu (C. NIANFO) practice, usually the chanting of the name of the buddha AMITĀBHA, as mentioned in the ŌJŌ YŌSHŪ and SHASEKISHŪ. This type of recitation is mainly practiced among the followers of the JŌDOSHŪ for a special period of one, seven, ten, or ninety days as a means of overcoming torpor and sluggishness.

**Bezeklik**. In Uighur, "Place of Paintings"; an archeological site in Central Asia with more than seventy cave temples unique for their Uighur Buddhist wall paintings and inscriptions. Situated near the ruins of the ancient Uighur capital of Gaochang (Kharakhoja) and east of the modern city of TURFAN (in China's Xinjiang province), the Bezeklik caves were in use from roughly the fourth to the twelfth centuries CE. In addition to the extensive Buddhist presence in the caves, scholars have also found evidence of Manichaean Christian influence at the site. Nearby cave complexes include Toyuk and Sangim. In 1905, the German explorer Albert von Le Coq visited the site and removed many of its painted wall murals so that they could be sent back to Europe for study and safekeeping. Ironically, many of the murals von Le Coq removed were destroyed during the Allied bombing of Berlin during World War II. What remains of his collection is now housed in museums in Berlin.

**Bhaddā-Kuṇḍalakesā**. (S. *Bhadrā-Kuṇḍalakeśā; C. Batuo Juntuoluojuyiguo; J. Batsuda Gundarakuikoku; K. Palt'a Kundaraguiguk 拔陀軍陀羅拘夷國). A female ARHAT whom the Buddha declared foremost among his nun disciples in swift intuition (khippābhiññā). According to Pāli sources, Bhaddā was the daughter of the treasurer of Rājagaha (S. RĀJAGṚHA). She witnessed once from her window a handsome thief named Sattuka being led off to execution and instantly fell in love with him. Pleading that she could not live without the young man, she persuaded her father to bribe the guard to release the thief into his custody. Sattuka was bathed and brought to the treasurer's home, where Bhaddā bedecked in her finest jewelry waited upon him. Sattuka feigned love for her, all the while plotting to murder her for her jewelry. One day he informed her that he had once promised the deity of Robbers' Cliff that, if he were ever to escape punishment, he would make an offering to the god, and that now the time was at hand to fulfill his promise. Bhaddā trusted him and, after preparing an offering for the deity, she accompanied Sattuka to the cliff adorned in her finest jewelry. Once they reached the edge of the cliff, he informed her of his real intentions, and without hesitation, she begged him to let her embrace him one last time. He agreed and, while feigning an embrace, Bhaddā pushed him over the cliff to his death. The local deity commended her for her cleverness and presence of mind. Bhaddā refused to return to her father's house after what had happened and joined the JAINA nuns' order. As part of her ascetic regime, she pulled out her hair with a palmyra comb, but it grew back in curls, hence her epithet Kuṇḍalakesā, "Curly Hair." Bhaddā was exceptionally intelligent and soon grew dissatisfied with Jain teachings. She wandered as a solitary mendicant, challenging all she encountered to debate and quickly proved her proficiency. Once she debated Sāriputta (S. ŚĀRIPUTRA), one of the Buddha's two chief disciples, who answered all her questions. He then asked her, "One: What is that?," which left her speechless. She asked Sāriputta to be her teacher, but he instead brought her before the Buddha, who preached her a sermon about it being better to know one verse bringing tranquillity than a thousand profitless verses. Hearing the Buddha's words, she immediately became an ARHAT and the Buddha personally ordained her as a nun in his order.

**Bhaddekarattasutta**. In Pāli, "The Ideal Lover of Solitude," the 131st sūtra in the MAJJHIMANIKĀYA (there is no corresponding version in the Chinese translations of the ĀGAMAs); spoken at Jeta's Grove in Sāvatthi (ŚRĀVASTĪ); several related DHARMAGUPTAKA recensions appear in the Chinese translation of the MADHYAMĀGAMA, although none with a corresponding title. The Buddha recites an enigmatic verse, in which he defines ideal solitude as letting go of everything involving the past or the future and dwelling solely in the present moment, discerning phenomena with wisdom as they appear. In his own exposition of the meaning of his verses, the Buddha explains that tracing back the past means not so much remembering the past but rather binding oneself to one's past aggregates (SKANDHA) through delighting in them; similarly, yearning for the future means the desire to have one's aggregates appear a certain way in the future. Instead, the religious should not identify with any of the five skandhas as being oneself; such a one is called an "ideal lover of solitude." The *Majjhimanikāya* collects subsequent expositions of these same verses by the Buddha's attendant ĀNANDA, Mahākaccāna (MAHĀKĀTYĀYANA), and Lomasakaṅgiya. The term bhaddekaratta has given traditional Pāli commentators difficulties and has sometimes been interpreted to mean "one who is happy [viz., auspicious?] for one night" (bhaddakassa ekarattassa) because he possesses insight, an interpretation that has its analogues in the Chinese translation of the Sanskrit title BHADRAKĀRĀTRĪ as shanye (a good night).

**Bhaddiya-Kāḷigodhāputta**. (S. *Bhadrika-Kāligodhāputrika; C. Bati; J. Batsudai; K. Palche 跋提). An ARHAT whom the Buddha declared foremost among his disciples of aristocratic birth (P. uccakulika). According to Pāli sources, Bhaddiya was the son of lady Kāḷigodhā and belonged to the royal Sākiyan (S. ŚĀKYA) clan of Kapilavatthu (S. KAPILAVASTU) and entered the order together with Anuruddha (S. ANIRUDDHA) and other nobles in the Anupiya mango grove. Bhaddiya and Anuruddha were childhood friends. When Anuruddha decided to renounce the world, his mother agreed, but only on the condition that Bhaddiya accompany him. Her hope was that Bhaddiya would dissuade him, but in the end Anuruddha instead convinced Bhaddiya to join him as a renunciant. Soon after his ordination, Bhaddiya attained arhatship and subsequently dwelled in solitude beneath a tree, exclaiming, "Oh happiness, Oh happiness!," as he reveled in the bliss of NIRVĀṆA. When the Buddha queried him about his exclamation, he explained that as a prince in his realm he was well guarded but nevertheless always felt anxious of enemies; now, however, having renounced all worldly things, he was finally free from all fear. Bhaddiya was regal in bearing, a consequence of having been born a king five hundred times in previous lives. During the time of Padumuttara Buddha, he was the son of a wealthy family and performed numerous meritorious deeds, which earned him this distinction under the current buddha GAUTAMA.

**Bhadra**. (P. Bhadda; T. Bzang po; C. Batuoluo zunzhe; J. Batsudara sonja; K. Palt'ara chonja 跋陀羅尊者). The Sanskrit name of the sixth of the sixteen ARHAT elders (ṢOḌAŚASTHAVIRA), who are charged by the Buddha with protecting his dispensation until the advent of the next buddha, MAITREYA. He is said to reside in Sri Lanka with nine hundred disciples. His mother gave birth to him under the bhadra (auspicious) tree, hence his name. A cousin of the Buddha, he served as his attendant and was famed for his clear exposition of the teachings. In the Chinese tradition, he is charged with matters related to bathing and his image is therefore enshrined in bath houses in some mountain monasteries. In CHANYUE GUANXIU's standard Chinese depiction, Bhadra typically sits on a rock in meditation. His forehead is high, his cheeks plump, and his gaze is turned slightly upward. His right hand is hidden under his robes and his left hand rests on his knee, holding prayer beads (JAPAMĀLĀ). Some East Asian images also show him accompanied by a tiger. In Tibetan iconography, he holds his left hand at his chest in VITARKAMUDRĀ, his right at his lap in DHYĀNAMUDRĀ.

**Bhadracarīpraṇidhāna**. (T. Bzang po spyod pa'i smon lam; C. Puxian pusa xingyuan zan; J. Fugen bosatsu gyōgansan; K. Pohyŏn posal haengwŏn ch'an 普賢菩薩行願讚). In Sanskrit, "Vows of Good Conduct," the last section of the GAṆḌAVYŪHA in the AVATAṂSAKASŪTRA and one of the most beloved texts in all of Mahāyāna Buddhism; also known as the *Samantabhadracarīpraṇidhānarāja*. The *Bhadracarīpraṇidhāna* focuses on the ten great vows (PRAṆIDHĀNA) taken by SAMANTABHADRA to realize and gain access to the DHARMADHĀTU, which thereby enable him to benefit sentient beings. The ten vows are: (1) to pay homage to all the buddhas, (2) to praise the tathāgatas, (3) to make unlimited offerings, (4) to repent from one's transgressions in order to remove karmic hindrances (cf. KARMĀVARAṆA), (5) to take delight in others' merit, (6) to request the buddhas to turn the wheel of dharma (DHARMACAKRAPRAVARTANA), (7) to request the buddhas to continue living in the world, (8) always to follow the teachings of the Buddha, (9) always to comply with the needs of sentient beings, and (10) to transfer all merit to sentient beings for their spiritual edification. The text ends with a stanza wishing that sentient beings still immersed in evil be reborn in the PURE LAND of AMITĀBHA. The text was translated into Chinese in 754 by AMOGHAVAJRA (705–774). Other Chinese recensions appear in the *Wenshushili fayuan jing* ("Scripture on the Vows made by MAÑJUŚRĪ"), translated in 420 by BUDDHABHADRA (359–429), which corresponds to the verse section from *Ru busiyi jietuo jingjie Puxian xingyuan pin*, the last roll of the forty-roll recension of the *Huayan jing* translated by PRAJÑA in 798. (There is no corresponding version in either the sixty- or the eighty-roll translations of the *Huajan jing*.) The verses are also called the "Précis of the *Huayan jing*" (*Lüe Huayan jing*), because they are believed to constitute the core teachings of the *Avataṃsakasūtra*. In the main Chinese recension by Amoghavajra, the text consists of sixty-two stanzas, each consisting of quatrains with lines seven Sinographs in length, thus giving a total number of 1,736 Sinographs. In addition to the sixty-two core stanzas, Amoghavajra's version adds ten more stanzas of the *Bada pusa zan* ("Eulogy to the Eight Great Bodhisattvas") from the *Badapusa mantuluo jing* ("Scripture of the MAṆḌALAs of the Eight Great Bodhisattvas") (see AṢṬAMAHĀBODHISATTVA; AṢṬAMAHOPAPUTRA). Buddhabhadra's version consists of forty-four stanzas with 880 Sinographs, each stanza consisting of a quatrain with lines five Sinographs in length. Prajña's version contains fifty-two stanzas with each quatrain consisting of lines seven sinographs in length. There are five commentaries on the text attributed to eminent Indian exegetes, including NĀGĀRJUNA, DIGNĀGA, and VASUBANDHU, which are extant only in Tibetan translation. In the Tibetan tradition, the prayer is called the "king of prayers" (smon lam gyi rgyal po). It is incorporated into many liturgies; the opening verses of the prayer are commonly incorporated into a Tibetan's daily recitation.

**bhadrakalpa**. (P. bhaddakappa; T. bskal pa bzang po; C. xianjie; J. kengō/gengō; K. hyŏn'gŏp 賢劫). In Sanskrit, "auspicious eon"; the current of the numerous "great eons" (MAHĀKALPA), or cyclic periods in the existence of a universe, that are recognized in Buddhist cosmology. The "auspicious eon" along with the last and the next "great eons"—that is, the "glorious eon" (vyūhakalpa) and "the eon of the constellations" (nakṣatrakalpa)—are together termed the "three great eons." Each great eon is presumed to consist of four "intermediate eons" (antarakalpa), viz., an "eon of formation" (VIVARTAKALPA); "stability" or "abiding" (VIVARTASTHĀYIKALPA); "decay" (SAṂVARTAKALPA); and "dissolution" (SAṂVARTASTHĀYIKALPA). A bhadrakalpa refers specifically to an eon in which buddhas appear, the present eon being such an era. The bhadrakalpa occurs during an eon (KALPA) of stability, following a period when the lifespan of human beings has been gradually reduced from innumerable years to eighty thousand. The number of buddhas who take rebirth during a bhadrakalpa varies widely in the texts, some stating that five buddhas will appear during this era, others that upward of a thousand buddhas will appear. In many texts, ŚĀKYAMUNI is presumed to have been preceded by six previous buddhas, bridging two different eons, who together are called the "seven buddhas of antiquity" (SAPTATATHĀGATA). Elsewhere, it is presumed that a thousand buddhas appear during the "eon of stability" in each of the three preceding great eons. The full list of the thousand buddhas of the present bhadrakalpa is extolled in the BHADRAKALPIKASŪTRA, a MAHĀYĀNA scripture that lists the names of the buddhas, their entourages, and their places of residence and enjoins the practice of various concentrations (SAMĀDHI) and perfections (PĀRAMITĀ). In this sūtra, the current buddha Śākyamuni is said to be the fourth buddha of the present kalpa, MAITREYA is to follow him, and another 995 buddhas will follow in succession, in order to continually renew Buddhism throughout the eon. A bhadrakalpa is presumed to last some 236 million years, of which over 151 million years have already elapsed in our current eon.

**Bhadrakalpikasūtra**. (T. Bskal pa bzang po'i mdo/Mdo sde bskal bzang; C. Xianjie jing; J. Gengōgyō; K. Hyŏn'gŏp kyŏng 賢劫經). In Sanskrit, "Auspicious Eon Scripture"; a MAHĀYĀNA text in twenty-four chapters, written c. 200–250 CE and translated into Chinese by DHARMARAKṢA in either 291 or 300 CE. In this scripture, the Buddha teaches a special concentration (SAMĀDHI) through the mastery of which bodhisattvas come to be equipped with 2,100 perfections (PĀRAMITĀ), 84,000 samādhis and 84,000 codes (DHĀRAṆĪ). He then lists the names of a thousand buddhas who will appear during the "auspicious eon" (BHADRAKALPA) due to the merit they obtained from practicing this samādhi, as well as their residences, parents, disciples, spiritual powers, teachings, and so on. In the Tibetan BKA' 'GYUR the *Bhadrakalpikasūtra* takes pride of place as the first in the sūtra section (mdo sde); it is recited often, and it is not uncommon for the elaborate hagiographies (RNAM THAR) of important Tibetan religious figures or incarnations (SPRUL SKU) to identify their subject as an earlier rebirth of one of the thousand buddhas.

**Bhadra-Kapilānī**. (P. Bhaddā-Kapilānī; C. Batuoluo Jiabeiliye; J. Batsudara Kahiriya; K. Palt'ara Kabiriya 跋陀羅迦卑梨耶). A female ARHAT whom the Buddha declared to be foremost among his nun disciples in her ability to recall former lives (PŪRVANIVĀSĀNUSMṚTI). According to Pāli sources, she was the daughter of a wealthy man named Kapila and was married to Pipphali, a landlord's son who later was to become the great arhat Mahākassapa (S. MAHĀKĀŚYAPA). It is said that Pipphali was inclined toward renunciation and only agreed to his parents' request that he marry on the condition that it be a woman as lovely as a beautiful statue he had crafted. Bhaddā was found to be the equal of the statue in beauty and arrangements were made for their wedding. But Bhaddā too was similarly inclined toward renunciation and, although she and Pipphali finally consented to marry for the sake of their parents, they chose not to consummate their marriage. Pipphali was master of a grand estate and one day, while observing a plowman plow one of his fields, saw birds eating worms turned up by the plow. At the same time, Bhaddā witnessed crows eating insects as they scurried among sesame seeds drying in the sun. Filled with pity and remorse for indirectly causing the death of those creatures, the couple resolved to renounce the world and take up the life of mendicancy. After shaving their heads and donning the yellow robes of mendicants, Pipphali and Bhaddā abandoned their estate and wandered forth into homelessness, parting company at a fork in the road. Pipphali met the Buddha and was ordained as Mahākāssapa and soon attained arhatship. Bhaddā took up residence in a hermitage near the JETAVANA Grove named Titthiyārāma. There she dwelled for five years, unable to take ordination because the nuns' (BHIKṢUṆĪ) order had not yet been established. When MAHĀPRAJĀPATĪ GAUTAMĪ was finally granted permission to begin a nuns' order, Bhaddā took ordination from her and quickly attained arhatship. Bhaddā Kapilānī became a famous preacher, though several of her disciples are recorded as having been unruly and ill disciplined.

**Bhadrakārātrī**. (T. Mtshan mo bzang po; C. Shanye jing; J. Zen'yakyō; K. Sŏnya kyŏng 善夜經). In Sanskrit, "Scripture of One Fine Night," an apotropaic and soteriological text, in one roll, with close parallels to the Pāli BHADDEKARATTASUTTA; translated into Chinese in 701 by YIJING (635–713), and into Tibetan by YE SHES SDE (fl. c. 800). The Sanskrit title, which is found in the colophon of the Tibetan translation of the sūtra (three folios in length) is otherwise unattested in the literature. The title is interpreted in Chinese as meaning "a fine night" and is used as an analogy for the mind of a person who is freed from all kinds of suffering (DUḤKHA) and afflictions (KLEŚA). The text seems to have its origins in an incantation that the Buddha had spoken previously. One day, a divinity (DEVA) visited a monk who was then staying with the Buddha in the Bamboo Grove (S. VEṆUVANAVIHĀRA) in RĀJAGṚHA, to ask about this verse. The monk, who did not know the verse, went to the Buddha, informed him of the divinity's request, and asked him to teach it. The Buddha then explained this scripture, which he said had the power to protect human beings from baleful spirits. One who follows the teachings of the scripture would also be relieved from all miseries and transgressions and could soon attain awakening. If one recites the scripture or one of its verses, or explains it to others, one would experience no misfortunes and would acquire knowledge of one's past and future lives. A recension of the text is also included in the Chinese translation of the MADHYAMĀGAMA (no. 165), which partially corresponds to the Pāli *Bhaddekarattasutta* spoken by Mahākaccāna (MAHĀKĀTYĀYANA), the 133rd sutta in the MAJJHIMANIKĀYA.

***Bhadra-Kuṇḍalakeśā** (S). See BHADDĀ-KUṆḌALAKESĀ.

**Bhadrapāla**. (T. Bzang skyong; C. Xianhu/Batuoboluo; J. Kengo/Batsudahara; K. Hyŏnho/Palt'abara 賢護/跋陀波羅) In Sanskrit, "Auspicious Protector"; a lay (GṚHAPATI) BODHISATTVA who is listed as one of the eight great bodhisattvas (S. AṢṬAMAHOPAPUTRA), who have vowed to protect and propagate the true dharma (S. SADDHARMA) in the age of decline (S. SADDHARMAVIPRALOPA; C. MOFA) after ŚĀKYAMUNI Buddha's death and to guard sentient beings. He is also listed in the DAZHIDU LUN (**Mahāprajñāpāramitāśāstra*) as one of the sixteen great bodhisattvas who have remained a householder. In the RATNAKŪṬASŪTRA, Bhadrapāla is described as the son of a wealthy merchant (gṛhapati) whose enjoyments surpassed even those of INDRA, the king of the gods, himself. In the *Banzhou sanmei jing* (PRATYUTPANNABUDDHASAṂMUKHĀVASTHITASAMĀDHISŪTRA), Bhadrapāla appears together with his five hundred attendant bodhisattvas to ask the Buddha how bodhisattvas can obtain wisdom that is as deep and broad as the ocean. In the twentieth chapter of the SADDHARMAPUṆḌARĪKASŪTRA ("Lotus Sutra"), Bhadrapāla is identified as someone who slighted the Buddha in a previous lifetime and as a result fell into AVĪCI hell. After suffering there for a thousand eons (KALPA) and requiting his offenses, Bhadrapāla was again able to encounter the Buddha and finally accept his teaching. He is also mentioned as one of the eighty thousand bodhisattvas who attended the assembly on Vulture Peak (GṚDHRAKŪṬAPARVATA) where Śākyamuni preached in the opening chapter of the *Saddharmapuṇḍarīkasūtra*. Bhadrapāla eventually became a buddha who attained enlightenment through the contemplation of water. Drawing on this experience, the Chinese apocryphal *ŚŪRAṂGAMASŪTRA (*Shoulengyan jing*) says that Bhadrapāla became enlightened as he entered the bathhouse; hence, the Chinese CHAN tradition enshrined an image of Bhadrapāla in the monastic bathhouse and some Japanese Buddhist schools similarly considered him to be the patron of the temple bathhouse.

**bhadrāsana**. (T. bzang po'i 'dug stangs) In Sanskrit, "auspicious posture" or "posture of good fortune." See PRALAMBAPADĀSANA.

**bhadravargīya**. (S). See PAÑCAVARGIKA.

**Bhadrayānīya**. See VĀTSĪPUTRĪYA.

**Bhadrika**. (P. Bhaddiya; T. Bzang ldan; C. Poti/Renxian; J. Badai/Ninken; K. Paje/Inhyŏn 婆提/仁賢). In Sanskrit, "Felicitous," one of the five ascetics (S. PAÑCAVARGIKA; P. pañcavaggiyā), along with ĀJÑĀTAKAUṆḌINYA (P. Aññakoṇḍañña), AŚVAJIT (P. Assaji), VĀṢPA (P. Vappa), and MAHĀNĀMAN (P. Mahānāma), who practiced austerities with GAUTAMA before his enlightenment; he later became one of the Buddha's first disciples upon hearing the first "turning of the wheel of the DHARMA" (DHARMACAKRAPRAVARTANA; P. dhammacakkappavatana) at the ṚṢIPATANA (P. Isipatana) deer park. When Gautama first renounced the world to practice austerities, Bhadrika and his four companions accompanied him (some texts say that the Buddha's father, King ŚUDDHODANA, dispatched them to ensure his son's safety). Later, when Gautama abandoned the severe asceticism they had been practicing in favor of the middle way (MADHYAMAPRATIPAD), Bhadrika and his companions became disgusted with Gautama's backsliding and left him, going to practice in the Ṛṣipatana deer park, located in the northeast of Benares. After the Buddha's enlightenment, however, the Buddha sought them out to teach them the first sermon, the DHARMACAKRAPRAVARTANASŪTRA (P. DHAMMACAKKAPPAVATTANASUTTA); Bhadrika became a stream-enterer (SROTAĀPANNA) while listening to this sermon and was immediately ordained as a monk using the informal EHIBHIKṢUKĀ (P. ehi bhikkhu), or "come, monk," formula. Five days later, the Buddha then preached to the group of five monks the second sermon, the **Anātmalakṣaṇasūtra* (P. ANATTALAKKHAṆASUTTA), which led to Bhadrika becoming an arhat. Bhadrika is presumed to have been related to the Buddha on his father King Śuddhodana's side and was the son of one of the eight brāhmaṇas who attended Gautama's naming ceremony, when it was predicted he would become either a wheel-turning monarch (CAKRAVARTIN; P. cakkavattin) or a buddha. There are several variant transcriptions of Bhadrika's name in Chinese and a number of different translations, including Xiaoxian (J. Shōken; K. Sohyŏn), Shanxian (J. Zenken; K. Sŏnhyŏn), Renxian (J. Ninken; K. Inhyŏn), and Youxian (J. Yūken; K. Yuhyŏn). ¶ For another Bhadrika (P. Bhaddiya) known in the mainstream Buddhist literature as chief among monks of aristocratic birth, see BHADDIYA-KĀḶIGODHĀPUTTA.

***Bhadrika-Kāligodhāputrika**. (S). See BHADDIYA-KĀḶIGODHĀPUTTA.

**bhāga**. (T. cha; C. fen; J. bun; K. pun 分). In Sanskrit, "part" or "portion"; a term used in the YOGĀCĀRA school to describe the functioning of consciousness. As a seed (BĪJA) from the eighth storehouse consciousness (ĀLAYAVIJÑĀNA) fructifies, it simultaneously produces both a moment of consciousness (VIJÑĀNA) and a corresponding sensory object (ĀLAMBANA). The object, which is in fact not external to the mind, is called the "image portion" (nimittabhāga) or the "grasped" (grāhya). The perception of that object is called the "perceiving portion" (darśanabhāga) or the "grasper " (grāhaka). The awareness that perception has occurred is called the "self-witnessing portion" (svasaṃvittibhāga).

**bhagavat**. [alt. bhagavant] (T. bcom ldan 'das; C. shizun; J. seson; K. sejon 世尊). In Sanskrit and Pāli, lit. "endowed with fortune"; one of the standard epithets of a buddha, commonly rendered in English as "Blessed One," "Exalted One," or simply "Lord." The term means "possessing fortune," "prosperous," and, by extension, "glorious," "venerable," "divine." In Sanskrit literature, bhagavat is reserved either for the most honored of human individuals, or for the gods. In Buddhist literature, however, the term is used almost entirely with reference to the Buddha, and points to the perfection of his virtue, wisdom, and contentment. There are several transcriptional and declensional variants of the term commonly found in English-language sources, including bhagavān (nominative singular), bhagavat (weak stem), bhagavad (a saṃdhi pronunciation change), bhagawan, and bhagwan. The Chinese translation of bhagavat, shizun, means "World-Honored One." The Tibetan translation may be rendered as "Transcendent and Accomplished Conqueror," as it indicates a conqueror (bcom) who is endowed with all good qualities (ldan) and has gone beyond SAṂSĀRA ('das).

**bhāgyacāra**. (S). See VAŚĪKARAṆA.

**Bhairava**. (T. 'Jigs byed; C. Buwei; J. Fui; K. P'ooe 怖畏). In Sanskrit, "Fierce," "Frightening," "Horrible"; the name of a Śaivite Hindu and Buddhist deity. Bhairava first appears as one of the emanations of the Hindu god Śiva. Many stories appear in the Hindu tradition explaining how and why Śiva first took this wrathful form. In Buddhism, Bhairava, or commonly VAJRABHAIRAVA, is closely related to YAMĀNTAKA, "He who Brings an End (antaka) to Death (yama)." Vajrabhairava and Yamāntaka are understood to be emanations of the BODHISATTVA MAÑJUŚRĪ. Bhairava is particularly popular in Nepal and Tibet. In Tibetan Buddhism, Bhairava is both a meditative deity (YI DAM), where his wrathful appearance is said to frighten away the mistaken belief in a self (ĀTMAN), as well as a protector of the dharma (DHARMAPĀLA) who frightens away baleful spirits with his terrifying appearance. In Buddhist art, Bhairava is typically depicted with black or dark-blue skin, a single head (often that of a buffalo), and multiple arms brandishing a variety of weapons. He may also have a necklace made of skulls, a mouth stained with blood, and have his feet holding down a prone figure he has vanquished.

**Bhaiṣajyaguru**. (T. Sman bla; C. Yaoshi rulai; J. Yakushi nyorai; K. Yaksa yŏrae 藥師如來). In Sanskrit, "Medicine Teacher"; the "Healing Buddha" or "Medicine Buddha," who was the focus of an important salvific cult in the early MAHĀYĀNA tradition. According to his eponymous scripture, the BHAIṢAJYAGURUSŪTRA, he has a body more brilliant than the sun, which was the color of lapis lazuli (vaiḍūryamaṇi) and possessed the power to heal illness and physical deformities; his pure land of Vaiḍūryanirbhāsa is located in the east. The origin of Bhaiṣajyaguru and his healing cult is unclear, although his worship seems to have arisen contemporaneously with the rise of the Mahāyāna. BHAIṢAJYARĀJA and Bhaiṣajyasamudgata, two bodhisattvas mentioned in the SADDHARMAPUṆḌARĪKASŪTRA ("Lotus Sūtra"), are likely antecedents, and similarities with other "celestial" buddhas like AMITĀBHA and AKṢOBHYA also suggest possible influence from those rival cults. The *Bhaiṣajyagurusūtra* was translated into Chinese in the seventh century, during the Tang dynasty, when his worship finally achieved the wide recognition that it continues to enjoy within the Chinese tradition. The *Bhaiṣajyagurusūtra* is also cited in the eighth-century tantric text, MAÑJUŚRĪMŪLAKALPA, indicating that his cult had by then achieved widespread acclaim throughout Asia. Bhaiṣajyaguru was one of the earliest buddhas to gain popularity in Japan, although initially he was familiar only within the imperial court, which constructed monasteries in his honor beginning in the sixth century. By the eighth century, his cult had spread throughout the country, with Bhaiṣajyaguru being invoked both to cure illness and to ward off dangers. The worship of Bhaiṣajyaguru seems to have entered Tibet during the eighth century, two versions of the *Bhaiṣajyagurusūtra* having been translated into Tibetan by the prolific YE SHES SDE and others. Early in the development of his cult, Bhaiṣajyaguru was divided into a group of eight medicine buddhas (aṣṭa-bhaiṣajyaguru), made up of seven of his emanations plus the principal buddha. Their names vary according to source, and none save Bhaiṣajyaguru are worshipped individually. Two of these emanations—Sūryaprabha and Candraprabha—are often depicted in a triad with Bhaiṣajyaguru. Further, Bhaiṣajyaguru is also said to command twelve warriors (YAKṢA) related to various astrological categories and to wage war on illness in the name of their leader. Indic images of Bhaiṣajyaguru are rare, but his depictions are common across both the East Asian and Tibetan cultural spheres. East Asian images are almost uniform in depicting him seated, with his right hand in the gesture of fearlessness (ABHAYAMUDRĀ) or the gesture of generosity (VARADAMUDRĀ), his left in his lap, occasionally holding a medicine bowl. In Tibet, he is also shown holding the fruit of the medicinal myrobalan plant.

**Bhaiṣajyagurusūtra**. [alt. Bhaiṣajyaguruvaiḍūryaprabhārājasūtra] (T. Sman gyi bla bai ḍūrya'i 'od kyi rgyal po'i sngon gyi smon lam gyi khyad par rgyas pa'i mdo; C. Yaoshi benyuan jing; J. Yakushi hongangyō; K. Yaksa ponwŏn kyŏng 藥師本願經). An eponymous MAHĀYĀNA SŪTRA that recounts the qualities, vows, and PURE LAND (BUDDHAKṢETRA) of the buddha BHAIṢAJYAGURU—the Master of Healing, also known as the Medicine Buddha, or the Tathāgata of Lapis-Lazuli Light. The scripture was most likely written in northern India during the early centuries of the Common Era. In this sūtra, at the request of MAÑJUŚRĪ-kumāra, ŚĀKYAMUNI describes this buddha and his pure land. Bhaiṣajyaguru's pure land lies in the east, separated from our world system by innumerable buddhakṣetras. Like other pure lands, Bhaiṣajyaguru's realm is free from the miseries that invariably plague existence and is ideal for the acquisition of the dharma as taught by Bhaiṣajyaguru himself and his retinue of BODHISATTVAS. The ground in this realm is made of lapis lazuli. Its roads, also made of precious stones, are marked with ropes of gold. Its houses are made of jewels. Śākyamuni also describes the bodhisattva vows taken by Bhaiṣajyaguru in his quest for awakening. Bhaiṣajyaguru vowed that his name, if merely uttered, would cure diseases, free prisoners, secure food and clothing for the impoverished, and produce other similar benefits. He also vowed that his body would be as resplendent as lapis lazuli itself so that it might illuminate the world. This sūtra describes methods by which one may gain Bhaiṣajyaguru's favor; these methods include making an image of Bhaiṣajyaguru, reciting the text of the *Bhaiṣajyagurusūtra*, or merely thinking of his name. Chinese translations of this sūtra were made by Dharmagupta in 616 and by XUANZANG in 650 at DACI'ENSI in the Tang capital of Chang'an.

**Bhaiṣajyaguruvaiḍūryaprabhārājasūtra**. (S). See BHAIṢAJYAGURUSŪTRA.

**Bhaiṣajyarāja**. (T. Sman gyi rgyal po; C. Yaowang pusa; J. Yakuō bosatsu; K. Yagwang posal 藥王菩薩). In Sanskrit, "Medicine King"; a BODHISATTVA brother and probable antecedent of the buddha BHAIṢAJYAGURU. Like his younger brother Bhaiṣajyasamudgata (C. Yaoshang), Bhaiṣajyarāja is mentioned in both the SADDHARMAPUṆḌARĪKASŪTRA ("Lotus Sūtra") as well as in the *Foshuo Guan Yaowang Yaoshang er pusa jing* ("Sūtra Spoken by the Buddha on Visualizing the Two Bodhisattvas Bhaiṣajyarāja and Bhaiṣajyasamudgata") translated into Chinese by KĀLAYAŚAS between 424–442 CE. The appearance of the brothers in the *Saddharmapuṇḍarīkasūtra* suggests that a cult of a medicine bodhisattva or buddha had developed in India by at least the third century CE. The *Saddharmapuṇḍarīkasūtra* tells of the elder brother Bhaiṣajyarāja offering his own body to a buddha by burning himself on a pyre, a fire that is said to have burned for twelve hundred years. As their own sūtra (the *Guan Yaowang Yaoshang er pusa jing*) relates, the two brothers did not make their initial bodhisattva aspirations before a buddha, as would typically be the case, but in front of an as-yet unenlightened monk named Sūryagarbha, though both have the buddhas of the ten directions in their headdresses. That sūtra further describes the myriad benefits attained through visualization of the two, an indication that the bodhisattvas were evolving from models of behavior to emulate, as they are depicted in the *Saddharmapuṇḍarīkasūtra* into objects of worship. With the rise of the cult of the buddha Bhaiṣajyaguru, however, the two bodhisattvas assumed subservient positions, becoming the two main figures in that buddha's group of seven acolytes. See also SHESHEN.

**Bhaiṣajyasamudgata**. (S). See BHAIṢAJYARĀJA.

**Bhājā**. One of the earliest and best-preserved Buddhist cave temples in western India, located around 150 miles south of Mumbai (Bombay). According to the paleography of the inscriptions on site and the stylistic features of the monuments, the site seems to have been excavated around 100–70 BCE. Early Buddhist rock-cut cave temples like Bhājā, AJAṆṬĀ, and KĀRLI were located along ancient trade routes, especially those connecting ports with inland towns. The architecture of these temples generally included one worship hall (CAITYA) containing a STŪPA with an ambulatory that enabled circumambulation (PRADAKṢIṆA), as well as numerous other cells that comprised the living quarters for the monks (VIHĀRA). At Bhājā, a large caitya hall dominates the site, featuring stylistic characteristics typical of this early phase of Buddhist architecture: a simple apsidal plan, divided into a nave and side aisles, crowned by a tunnel vault; the imitation of wooden prototypes in the detailing of the surface and the almost complete absence of sculptural decoration in the interior (though paintings may have once adorned the walls). The caitya hall is accompanied by seventeen further caves, which supposedly once housed a community of Buddhist nuns.

**bhājanaloka**. (T. snod kyi 'jig rten; C. qishijian; J. kiseken; K. kisegan 器世間) In Sanskrit, lit. "container world," referring to the wider environment, or the physical or inanimate world, whose function is to serve merely as a "container" for the lives of ordinary sentient beings (SATTVA). Bhājanaloka is used in contrast to and in conjunction with SATTVALOKA, the world of sentient beings, who are the inhabitants of that "container." Its ancillary production and cessation as well as its overall physical qualities were considered to be byproducts of the actions (KARMAN) of sentient beings. In the YOGĀCĀRA school, the physical world is viewed as a product of the storehouse consciousness (ĀLAYAVIJÑĀNA).

**Bhallika**. (T. Bzang pa; C. Boli; J. Hari; K. P'ari 波利). In Sanskrit and Pāli, one of the two merchants (together with his brother TRAPUṢA, P. Tapussa) who became the first lay Buddhists (UPĀSAKA). Following his enlightenment, the Buddha remained in the vicinity of the BODHI TREE. In the seventh week, he went to the Rājāyatana tree to continue his meditation. Two merchants, Bhallika and his older brother Trapuṣa, who were leading a large trading caravan with five hundred carts, saw him there and, realizing that he had not eaten for weeks (as many as eight weeks, in some accounts), offered the Buddha sweet rice cakes with butter and honey. In response to their act of charity (DĀNA), the Buddha spoke with them informally and gave them the Buddha and dharma refuges (ŚARAṆA) (the SAṂGHA had not yet been created), making them the first lay Buddhists. The Buddha is said to have given the two brothers eight strands of hair from his head, which they took back to their homeland and interred for worship as relics (ŚARĪRA) in a STŪPA. According to Mon-Burmese legend, Tapussa and Bhallika were Mon natives, and their homeland of Ukkala was a place also called Dagon in the Mon homeland of Rāmañña in lower Burma. The stūpa they constructed at Ukkala/Dagon, which was the first shrine in the world to be erected over relics of the present buddha, was to be enlarged and embellished over the centuries to become, eventually, the golden SHWEDAGON PAGODA of Rangoon. Because of the preeminence of this shrine, some Burmese chroniclers date the first introduction of Buddhism among the Mon in Rāmañña to Tapussa and Bhallika's time. Bhallika eventually ordained and became an ARHAT; Trapuṣa achieved the stage of stream-enterer (SROTAĀPANNA). The merchants were also the subject of a Chinese apocryphal text, the TIWEI [BOLI] JING, written c. 460–464, which praises the value of the lay practices of giving and of keeping the five precepts (PAÑCAŚĪLA).

**bhāṇaka**. In Sanskrit and Pāli, "reciter," especially referring to monks in a monastic community whose vocation was to memorize, recite, and transmit to the next generation one of the various collections (NIKĀYA, ĀGAMA) of the scriptural canon (SŪTRAPIṬAKA). See DHARMABHĀṆAKA.

**bhaṅgānupassanāñāṇa**. In Pāli, "knowledge arising from the contemplation of dissolution"; according to BUDDHAGHOSA's VISUDDHIMAGGA, the second of nine types of knowledge (P. ÑĀṆA) cultivated as part of the "purity of knowledge and vision of progress along the path" (PAṬIPADĀÑĀṆADASSANAVISUDDHI). This latter category, in turn, constitutes the sixth and penultimate purity (VIŚUDDHI) that is to be developed along the path to liberation. "Knowledge arising from the contemplation of dissolution" is developed by observing the dissolution of material and mental phenomena (NĀMARŪPA). Having keenly observed the arising, subsistence, and decay of phenomena, the meditator turns his attention solely to their dissolution or destruction (bhaṅga). He then observes, for example, that consciousness arises because of causes and conditions: namely, it takes as its objects the five aggregates (P. khandha, S. SKANDHA) of matter (RŪPA), sensation (VEDANĀ), perception (P. saññā, S. SAṂJÑĀ) conditioned formations (P. saṅkhāra, S. SAMSKĀRA) and consciousness (P. viññāṇa, S. VIJÑĀNA), after which it is inevitably dissolved. Seeing this, the meditator understands that all consciousness is characterized by the three marks of existence (tilakkhaṇa; S. TRILAKṢAṆA); namely, impermanence (anicca; S. ANITYA), suffering (dukkha; S. DUḤKHA) and nonself (anattā; S. ANĀTMAN). By understanding these three marks, he feels aversion for consciousness and overcomes his attachment to it. Eight benefits accrue to one who develops knowledge arising from the contemplation of dissolution; (1) he overcomes the view of eternal existence, (2) he abandons attachment to life, (3) he develops right effort, (4) he engages in a pure livelihood, (5 & 6) he enjoys an absence of anxiety and of fear, (7) he becomes patient and gentle, and (8) he overcomes boredom and sensual delight.

**Bharadvāja**. [alt. Bhāradvāja] (T. Bha ra dhwa dza / Bha ra dhwa dza'i bu / Rgyal mtshan 'dzin). In Sanskrit, "One Who Carries a Banner," or "Son of the One Who Carries a Banner"; found in the names PIṆḌOLA BHARADVĀJA and KANAKA BHĀRADVĀJA (the Tibetan transcriptions do not always clearly differentiate between the two forms of the names), both counted among the sixteen ARHATS (ṢOḌAŚASTHAVIRA); also the name of one of the sixteen sons of the past buddha Mahābhijñā Jñānābhibhu.

**Bhārhut**. An important Buddhist archeological site in India; located in central India, in northeastern Madhya Pradesh. In 1873, the British general Alexander Cunningham discovered at the site an ancient Buddhist STŪPA, or reliquary mound, dating as far back as the third century BCE. Surrounding this stūpa are a series of sculptures that date to the second and first centuries BCE. The antiquity of these works, and the quality of their preservation, render them invaluable to the study of Indian Buddhist iconography. The structure follows the general Indian stūpa design, with a central mound surrounded by a fence-like enclosure with four gates. The stūpa is illustrated with several aniconic representations of the Buddha. These images include an empty throne (VAJRĀSANA), a BODHI TREE, a set of the Buddha's footprints (BUDDHAPĀDA), the triple gem (RATNATRAYA) and a dharma wheel (DHARMACAKRA). This stūpa also includes a number of reliefs depicting various episodes in the life of the Buddha (see BAXIANG; TWELVE DEEDS OF A BUDDHA), including the dream of queen MĀYĀ when he was conceived, the battle with MĀRA, and his enlightenment. Also depicted are a number of the Buddha's birth stories (JĀTAKA). The stūpa's sculptural remains are now housed in the Indian Museum in Kolkata (Calcutta) and in the Municipal Museum of Allahabad. See also SĀÑCĪ.

**Bhartṛhari**. (fl. c. 475). Sanskrit proper name of an important Indian grammarian and author of the *Vākyapadīya*, the central text of the Śabdabrahman school of Indian philosophy; thought by some to be a teacher of DIGNĀGA, who cites lines from Bhartṛhari in his seminal work the PRAMĀṆASAMUCCAYA. Dignāga's theory of APOHA (exclusion), a central tenet in his system, is central to SAUTRĀNTIKA and some YOGĀCĀRA interpretations of the two truths (SAṂVṚTISATYA and PARAMĀRTHASATYA). The apoha theory holds that objects of conceptual thought have only a shared (sāmānya) essence and appear only as the exclusion of other categories. Some suggest this theory can be traced back through Bhartṛhari to the grammarian Vyāḍi. Bhartṛhari himself was not a follower of any Buddhist school, and his views are briefly refuted by ŚĀNTARAKṢITA in his TATTVASAṂGRAHA.

**bhāṣya**. (T. bshad pa; C. lun; J. ron; K. non 論). In Sanskrit, "commentary," or "exposition"; especially an exegesis on a set of aphoristic statements (SŪTRAS) or kārikās (the same in verse form): e.g., ABHIDHARMAKOŚABHĀṢYA. In East Asia, the term lun was reserved for the commentaries of the eminent bodhisattva-exegetes of Indian MAHĀYĀNA Buddhism, such as VASUBANDHU, ASAṄGA, and MAITREYA/MAITREYANĀTHA; commentaries by indigenous East Asian exegetes are usually termed shu. One of the very few exceptions is the "Exposition of the **Vajrasamādhisūtra* (KŬMGANG SAMMAE KYŎNG)" (KŬMGANG SAMMAEGYŎNG NON), by the Korean exegete WŎNHYO, which was so highly regarded that it was given this special designation.

**bhautika**. (T. 'byung 'gyur; C. youda; J. udai; K. yudae 有大). In Sanskrit, a secondary formation from BHŪTA ("element"), and therefore often rendered in English as "secondary element" or "sensible phenomenon." According to the VAIBHĀṢIKA and SAUTRĀNTIKA schools, any material object (ĀLAMBANA) except sound (viz., an object of sight, smell, taste, and touch) is made up of eight components: the four elements (MAHĀBHŪTA) of earth, water, fire, and wind; and the four secondary elements (bhautika) of form, smell, taste, and touch. These eight components are inseparable from each other.

**bhava**. (T. srid pa; C. you; J. u; K. yu 有). In Sanskrit and Pāli, "becoming" or "existence," conceived of as a process; the tenth link in the twelve-linked chain of dependent origination (PRATĪTYASAMUTPĀDA; P. paṭiccasamuppāda). In Pāli sources, bhava is of three types depending on the strata of the universe in which it occurs: namely, sensuous becoming (kāmabhava) in the sensuous realm (KĀMADHĀTU), subtle-material becoming (rūpabhava) in the subtle-materiality realm (RŪPADHĀTU), and immaterial becoming (arūpabhava) in the immaterial realm (ĀRŪPYADHĀTU). Wherever it occurs, bhava can be divided into an active process (P. kammabhava) or a passive process (P. uppattibhava). The active process is ethically charged, that is to say it is comprised of virtuous and unvirtuous volitional action (KARMAN) which leads to fortunate and unfortunate rebirth according to the deeds performed. The passive process refers to rebirth and all other events that befall an individual as a consequence of previous action. As such events or phenomena are automatic effects and are not volitional, they are ethically neutral. According to the ABHIDHARMAKOŚABHĀṢYA and MAHĀYĀNA sources, the word bhava as the tenth link in the chain of dependent origination is a case of ascribing the name of the result ("becoming" reborn) to its cause (the most intense moment of upādāna attraction that fully ripens the volitional action in the instant prior to rebirth). The term is also used in a more general sense as "existence" and hence in some cases as a synonym of SAṂSĀRA. See BHAVACAKRA. In Tibetan, the translation of the term, srid, also denotes the secular realm, as opposed to the religious realm (chos).

**bhavacakra**. (P. bhavacakka; T. srid pa'i khor lo; C. youlun; J. urin; K. yuryun 有輪). In Sanskrit, "wheel of existence"; a visual depiction of SAṂSĀRA in the form of a wheel, best known in its Tibetan forms but widely used in other Buddhist traditions as well. The BHAVACAKRA is a seminal example of Buddhist didactic art. The chart is comprised of a series of concentric circles, each containing pictorial representations of some of the major features of Buddhist cosmology and didactics. Standard versions consist of an outer ring of images depicting the twelve-linked chain of dependent origination (PRATĪTYASAMUTPĀDA). Within this ring is another circle broken into six equal sectors—one for each of the six realms of existence in saṃsāra. The salutary realms of divinities (DEVA), demigods (ASURA), and humans (MANUṢYA) are found in the top half of the circle, while the unfortunate realms (DURGATI; APĀYA) of animals (TIRYAK), hungry ghosts (PRETA), and hell denizens (NĀRAKA) are found in the bottom half. Inside this circle is a ring that is divided evenly into dark and light halves. The most popular interpretation of these two halves is that the light half depicts the path of bliss, or the path that leads to better rebirth and to liberation, while the dark half represents the path of darkness, which leads to misfortune and rebirth in the hells. Finally, in the center of the picture is a small circle in which can be seen a bird, a snake, and a pig. These three animals represent the "three poisons" (TRIVIṢA)—the principal afflictions (KLEŚA) of greed or sensuality (LOBHA or RĀGA), hatred or aversion (DVEṢA), and delusion (MOHA)—that bind beings to the round of rebirth. The entire wheel is held in the jaws and claws of a demon whose identity varies from version to version. Often this demon is presumed to be MĀRA, the great tempter who was defeated in his attempt to sway GAUTAMA from enlightenment. Another common figure who grips the wheel is YAMA, the king of death, based on the idea that Yama was the original being, the first to die, and hence the ruler over all caught in the cycle of birth and death. Often outside the circle appear one or more buddhas, who may be pointing to a SŪTRA, or to some other religious object. The buddhas' location outside the circle indicates their escape from the cycle of birth and death. The same figure of a buddha may be also found among the denizens of hell, indicating that a buddha's compassion extends to beings in even the most inauspicious destinies. According to several Indian texts, the Buddha instructed that the bhavacakra should be painted at the entrance of a monastery for the instruction of the laity; remnants of a bhavacakra painting were discovered at AJAṆṬĀ.

**bhavāgra**. (P. bhavagga; T. srid rtse; C. youding tian; J. uchōten; K. yujŏng ch'ŏn 有頂天). In Sanskrit, the "summit of existence" or "apex of the universe"; one of the names for the fourth and highest level of heavens of the immaterial realm of existence (ĀRŪPYADHĀTU), which is also known as the sphere of neither perception nor nonperception (NAIVASAṂJÑĀNĀSAṂJÑĀYATANA). As the highest level of existence, bhavāgra is also sometimes used in contrast to the lowest level of the hells, the AVĪCI.

**bhāvanā**. (T. sgom pa; C. xiuxi; J. shujū; K. susŭp 修習). In Sanskrit and Pāli, "cultivation" (lit. "bringing into being"); a Sanskrit term commonly translated into English as "meditation." It is derived from the root √bhū, "to be" or "to become," and has a wide range of meanings including cultivating, producing, manifesting, imagining, suffusing, and reflecting. It is in the first sense, that of cultivation, that the term is used to mean the sustained development of particular states of mind. However, bhāvanā in Buddhism can include studying doctrine, memorizing sūtras, and chanting verses to ward off evil spirits. The term thus refers broadly to the full range of Buddhist spiritual culture, embracing the "bringing into being" (viz., cultivating) of such generic aspects of training as the path (MĀRGA), specific spiritual exercises (e.g., loving-kindness, or MAITRĪ), or even a general mental attitude, such as virtuous (KUŚALA) states of mind. The term is also used in the specific sense of a "path of cultivation" (BHĀVANĀMĀRGA), which "brings into being" the insights of the preceding path of vision (DARŚANAMĀRGA). Hence, bhāvanā entails all the various sorts of cultivation that an adept must undertake in order to enhance meditation, improve its efficacy, and "bring it into being." More specifically as "meditation," two general types of meditation are sometimes distinguished in the commentarial literature: stabilizing meditation (ŚAMATHA) in which the mind focuses with one-pointedness on an object in an effort to expand the powers of concentration; and analytical meditation (VIPAŚYANĀ), in which the meditator conceptually investigates a topic in order to develop insight into it.

**Bhāvanākrama**. (T. Sgom rim). In Sanskrit, "Stages of Meditation," the title of three separate but related works by the late-eighth century Indian master KAMALAŚĪLA. During the reign of the Tibetan king KHRI SRONG LDE BTSAN at the end of the eighth century, there were two Buddhist factions at court, a Chinese faction led by the Northern Chan (BEI ZONG) monk Heshang Moheyan (Mahāyāna) and an Indian faction of the recently deceased ŚĀNTARAKṢITA, who with the king and PADMASAMBHAVA had founded the first Tibetan monastery at BSAM YAS (Samye). According to traditional accounts, Śāntarakṣita foretold of dangers and left instructions in his will that his student Kamalaśīla should be summoned from India. A conflict seems to have developed between the Indian and Chinese partisans (and their allies in the Tibetan court) over the question of the nature of enlightenment, with the Indians holding that enlightenment takes place as the culmination of a gradual process of purification, the result of perfecting morality (ŚĪLA), concentration (SAMĀDHI), and wisdom (PRAJÑĀ). The Chinese spoke against this view, holding that enlightenment was the intrinsic nature of the mind rather than the goal of a protracted path, such that one need simply to recognize the presence of this innate nature of enlightenment by entering a state of awareness beyond distinctions; all other practices were superfluous. According to both Chinese and Tibetan records, a debate was held between Kamalaśīla and Moheyan at Bsam yas, circa 797, with the king himself serving as judge (see BSAM YAS DEBATE). According to Tibetan reports (contradicted by the Chinese accounts), Kamalaśīla was declared the winner and Moheyan and his party banished from Tibet, with the king proclaiming that thereafter the MADHYAMAKA school of Indian Buddhist philosophy (to which Śāntarakṣita and Kamalaśīla belonged) would have pride of place in Tibet. ¶ According to Tibetan accounts, after the conclusion of the debate, the king requested that Kamalaśīla compose works that presented his view, and in response, Kamalaśīla composed the three *Bhāvanākrama*. There is considerable overlap among the three works. All three are germane to the issues raised in the debate, although whether all three were composed in Tibet is not established with certainty; only the third, and briefest of the three, directly considers, and refutes, the view of "no mental activity" (amanasikāra, cf. WUNIAN), which is associated with Moheyan. The three texts set forth the process for the potential BODHISATTVA to cultivate BODHICITTA and then develop ŚAMATHA and VIPAŚYANĀ and progress through the bodhisattva stages (BHŪMI) to buddhahood. The cultivation of vipaśyanā requires the use of both scripture (ĀGAMA) and reasoning (YUKTI) to understand emptiness (ŚŪNYATĀ); in the first *Bhāvanākrama*, Kamalaśīla sets forth the three forms of wisdom (prajñā): the wisdom derived from learning (ŚRUTAMAYĪPRAJÑĀ), the wisdom derived from reflection (CINTĀMAYĪPRAJÑĀ), and the wisdom derived from cultivation (BHĀVANĀMAYĪPRAJÑĀ), explaining that the last of these gradually destroys the afflictive obstructions (KLEŚĀVARAṆA) and the obstructions to omniscience (JÑEYĀVARAṆA). The second *Bhāvanākrama* considers many of these same topics, stressing that the achievement of the fruition of buddhahood requires the necessary causes, in the form of the collection of merit (PUṆYASAṂBHĀRA) and the collection of wisdom (JÑĀNASAṂBHĀRA). Both the first and second works espouse the doctrine of mind-only (CITTAMĀTRA); it is on the basis of these and other statements that Tibetan doxographers classified Kamalaśīla as a YOGĀCĀRA-SVĀTANTRIKA-MADHYAMAKA. The third and briefest of the *Bhāvanākrama* is devoted especially to the topics of śamatha and vipaśyanā, how each is cultivated, and how they are ultimately unified. Kamalaśīla argues that analysis (VICĀRA) into the lack of self (ĀTMAN) in both persons (PUDGALA) and phenomena (DHARMA) is required to arrive at a nonconceptual state of awareness. The three texts are widely cited in later Tibetan Buddhist literature, especially on the process for developing śamatha and vipaśyanā.

**bhāvanāmārga**. (T. sgom lam; C. xiudao; J. shudō; K. sudo 修道). In Sanskrit, "the path of cultivation" or "path of meditation"; the fourth of the five stages of the path (MĀRGA) in the SARVĀSTIVĀDA soteriological system (also adopted in the MAHĀYĀNA), which follows the path of vision or insight (DARŚANAMĀRGA) and precedes the adept path where no further training is necessary (AŚAIKṢAMĀRGA). In the Sarvāstivāda path schema, the path of vision consists of fifteen thought-moments, with a subsequent sixteenth moment marking the beginning of the path of cultivation (BHĀVANĀMĀRGA). This sixteenth moment, that of subsequent knowledge (ANVAYAJÑĀNA) of the truth of the path (mārga), is, in effect, the knowledge that all of the afflictions (KLEŚA) of both the subtle-materiality realm (RŪPADHĀTU) and the immaterial realm (ĀRŪPYADHĀTU) that are associated with the FOUR NOBLE TRUTHS have been abandoned. As a result, the meditator destroys all causes for future rebirth as an animal, ghost, or hell denizen, but is not liberated from rebirth altogether and may still be reborn as a human or divinity. The more deeply rooted afflictions are destroyed over the course of the path of cultivation. For each of the nine levels of the three realms of rebirth—the sensuous realm (with one level), the realm of subtle materiality (with four levels), and the immaterial realm (with four levels)—there are nine levels of afflictions (KLEŚA), from the most coarse to the most insidious, making eighty-one levels of affliction to be destroyed. As was the case with the path of vision, these defilements must be destroyed in a two-step process: the actual destruction of the particular affliction and the knowledge that it has been destroyed. There are therefore 162 "moments" of the abandoning of afflictions. This process, which takes place over the course of the path of cultivation, may occur over several lifetimes. However, when the 162nd stage is reached, and the subtlest of the subtle afflictions associated with the ninth level—that is, the fourth absorption of the immaterial realm—has been abandoned, the adept is then liberated from rebirth. The bhāvanāmārga is one of the "paths of the nobles" (ĀRYAMĀRGA) and one on this stage is immune to any possibility of retrogression and is assured of eventually achieving NIRVĀṆA. Reference is also sometimes made to the mundane path of cultivation (LAUKIKA-bhāvanāmārga), which refers to the three trainings (TRIŚIKṢĀ) in morality (ŚĪLA), concentration (SAMĀDHI), and wisdom (PRAJÑĀ) as they are developed before the first of the three fetters (SAṂYOJANA) is eradicated and insight achieved. In the Mahāyāna path system, with variations between YOGĀCĀRA and MADHYAMAKA, the bhāvanāmārga is the period in which the BODHISATTVA proceeds through the ten BHŪMIs and destroys the afflictive obstructions (KLEŚĀVARAṆA) and the obstructions to omniscience (JÑEYĀVARAṆA).

**bhāvanāmayīprajñā**. (P. bhāvanāmayapañña; T. bsgoms pa las byung ba'i shes rab; C. xiuhui; J. shue; K. suhye 修慧). In Sanskrit, lit. "wisdom generated by cultivation"; often translated as "wisdom derived from meditation"; the third of the three types of wisdom, together with ŚRUTAMAYĪPRAJÑĀ (wisdom derived from what is heard, viz., learning) and CINTĀMAYĪPRAJÑĀ (wisdom derived from reflection or analysis). Although the general understanding is that this third and final manifestation of wisdom comes after, and is largely dependent on, the previous two types, bhāvanāmayīprajñā is considered to be the highest of these three because it is the culmination of one's efforts to cultivate the path (MĀRGA) and the product of direct spiritual experience. This third type of wisdom is a form of VIPAŚYANĀ, an understanding of reality at the level of ŚAMATHA—profound concentration coupled with tranquility.

**bhavaṅgasota**. In Pāli, "subconscious continuum"; a concept peculiar to later Pāli epistemological and psychological theory, which the ABHIDHAMMA commentaries define as the foundation of experience. The bhavaṅgasota is comprised of unconscious moments of mind that flow, as it were, in a continuous stream (sota) or continuum and carry with them the impressions or potentialities of past experience. Under the proper conditions, these potentialities ripen as moments of consciousness, which, in turn, interrupt the flow of the bhavaṅga briefly before the mind lapses back into the subconscious continuum. Moments of consciousness and unconsciousness are discreet and never overlap in time, with unconsciousness being the more typical of the two states. This continuum is, therefore, what makes possible the faculty of memory. The bhavaṅgasota is the Pāli counterpart of idealist strands of Mahāyāna Buddhist thought, such as the "storehouse consciousness" (ĀLAYAVIJÑĀNA) of the YOGĀCĀRA school. See also CITTASAṂTĀNA; SAṂTĀNA.

**Bhavasaṃkrānti**. (T. Srid pa 'pho ba). In Sanskrit, "Transference of Existence," a brief work ascribed to NĀGĀRJUNA; also known as *Madhyamakabhavasaṃkrānti*. The title seems to suggest that it deals with the practice of transferring one's consciousness from one body to another, but this topic is actually not covered in the text. It discusses instead standard MADHYAMAKA topics such as the function of VIKALPA as the source of the world, the ultimate nonexistence of all phenomena, the six perfections (PĀRAMITĀ), UPĀYA and PRAJÑĀ, and the two truths (SATYADVAYA). Nāgārjuna's major commentators (BHĀVAVIVEKA, CANDRAKĪRTI et al.) do not cite the work, which raises questions about its authorship.

**Bhāvaviveka**. (T. Legs ldan 'byed; C. Qingbian; J. Shōben; K. Ch'ŏngbyŏn 淸辯) (c. 500–570). Also known as Bhāviveka and Bhavya, an important Indian master of the MADHYAMAKA school, identified in Tibet as a proponent of SVĀTANTRIKA MADHYAMAKA and, within that, of SAUTRĀNTIKA-SVĀTANTRIKA-MADHYAMAKA. He is best known for two works. The first is the PRAJÑĀPRADĪPA, his commentary on NĀGĀRJUNA's MŪLAMADHYAMAKAKĀRIKĀ; this work has an extensive subcommentary by AVALOKITAVRATA. Although important in its own right as one of the major commentaries on the central text of the Madhyamaka school, the work is most often mentioned for its criticism of the commentary of BUDDHAPĀLITA on the first chapter of Nāgārjuna's text, where Bhāvaviveka argues that it is insufficient for the Madhyamaka only to state the absurd consequences (PRASAṄGA) that follow from the position of the opponent. According to Bhāvaviveka, the Madhyamaka must eventually state his own position in the form of what is called an autonomous inference (svatantrānumāna) or an autonomous syllogism (SVATANTRAPRAYOGA). In his own commentary on the first chapter of Nāgārjuna's text, CANDRAKĪRTI came to the defense of Buddhapālita and criticized Bhāvaviveka, stating that it is inappropriate for the Madhyamaka to use autonomous syllogisms. It is on the basis of this exchange that Tibetan exegetes identified two schools within Madhyamaka: the Svātantrika, which includes Bhāvaviveka, and the Prāsaṅgika, which includes Buddhapālita and Candrakīrti. ¶ The other major work of Bhāvaviveka is his MADHYAMAKAHṚDAYA, written in verse, and its prose autocommentary, the TARKAJVĀLĀ. The *Madhyamakahṛdaya* is preserved in both Sanskrit and Tibetan, the *Tarkajvālā* only in Tibetan. It is a work of eleven chapters, the first three and the last two of which set forth the main points in Bhāvaviveka's view of the nature of reality and the Buddhist path, dealing with such topics as BODHICITTA, the knowledge of reality (tattvajñāna), and omniscience (SARVAJÑĀTĀ). The intervening chapters set forth the positions (and Bhāvaviveka's refutations) of various Buddhist and non-Buddhist schools, including the ŚRĀVAKA, YOGĀCĀRA, Sāṃkhya, Vaiśeṣika, Vedānta, and Mīmāṃsā. These chapters (along with ŚĀNTARAKṢITA's TATTVASAṂGRAHA) are an invaluable source of insight into the relations between Madhyamaka and other contemporary Indian philosophical schools, both Buddhist and non-Buddhist. The chapter on the śrāvakas, for example, provides a detailed account of the reasons put forth by the ŚRĀVAKAYĀNA schools of mainstream Buddhism as to why the Mahāyāna sūtras are not the word of the Buddha (BUDDHAVACANA). Bhāvaviveka's response to these charges, as well as his refutation of YOGĀCĀRA in the subsequent chapter, are particularly spirited, arguing that reality (TATHATĀ) cannot be substantially existent (dravyasat), as those rival schools claim. However, Bhāvaviveka made extensive use of both the logic and epistemology of DIGNĀGA, at least at the level of conventional analysis. Bhāvaviveka appears to have been the first Madhyamaka author to declare that the negations set forth by the Madhyamaka school are nonaffirming (or simple) negations (PRASAJYAPRATIṢEDHA) rather than affirming (or implicative) negations (PARYUDĀSAPRATIṢEDHA). Also attributed to Bhāvaviveka is the *Karatalaratna* ("Jewel in Hand Treatise"; *Zhangzhen lun*), a work preserved only in the Chinese translation of XUANZANG. Bhāvaviveka's MADHYAMAKĀRTHASAṂGRAHA is a brief text in verse. As the title suggests, it provides an outline of the basic topics of MADHYAMAKA philosophy, such as the middle way (S. MADHYAMAPRATIPAD) between the extremes of existence and nonexistence, Madhyamaka reasoning, and the two truths (SATYADVAYA). The MADHYAMAKARATNAPRADĪPA is likely the work of another author of the same name, since it makes reference to such later figures as Candrakīrti and DHARMAKĪRTI.

**Bhāviveka**. (S). See BHĀVAVIVEKA.

**Bhavya**. (S). See BHĀVAVIVEKA.

**Bhayabheravasutta**. In Pāli, "Discourse on Fear and Dread," the fourth sutta in the MAJJHIMANIKĀYA (an untitled recension of uncertain affiliation appears in the Chinese translation of the EKOTTARĀGAMA); preached by the Buddha to a brāhmaṇa named Jāṇussoṇi in the JETAVANA Grove in ŚRĀVASTĪ. The Buddha explains how a monk living alone in a fearful jungle must guard his thoughts, words, and deeds from evil.

He then explains how he had to guard his own thoughts, words, and deeds while he strove to attain enlightenment as he sat beneath the BODHI TREE.

**bhayatupaṭṭhānañāṇa**. In Pāli, "knowledge arising from the awareness of terror"; according to the VISUDDHIMAGGA, the third of nine knowledges (ñāṇa; JÑĀNA) cultivated as part of "purity of knowledge and vision of progress along the path" (PAṬIPADĀÑĀṆADASSANAVISUDDHI). This latter category, in turn, constitutes the sixth and penultimate purity (VISUDDHI) to be developed along the path to liberation. Knowledge arising from the contemplation of terror is developed by noting how all conditioned formations (saṅkhāra; SAṂSKĀRA) or mental and physical phenomena (NĀMARŪPA) of the past, present and future have either gone, are going, or are destined to go to destruction. A simile given in the *Visuddhimagga* is that of a woman whose three sons have offended the king. The woman, who has already witnessed the beheading of her eldest son, witnesses the beheading of her middle son. And having witnessed the beheadings of her two older sons, the woman is filled with terror at the knowledge that her youngest son will likewise be executed. In the same way, the practitioner observes how phenomena of the past have ceased, how phenomena of the present are ceasing, and how those of the future are likewise destined to cease. Seeing conditioned formations as destined to destruction in this way, that is, as impermanent (anicca; ANITYA), the practitioner is filled with terror. Similarly, the practitioner sees conditioned formations as suffering (dukkha; DUḤKHA), and as impersonal and nonself (anattā; ANĀTMAN) and is filled with terror. In this way, the practitioner comes to realize that all mental and physical phenomena, being characterized by the three universal marks of existence (tilakkhaṇa; TRILAKṢAṆA), are frightful.

**bhikkhu**. In Pāli, "mendicant"; a fully ordained Buddhist monk, who is enjoined to observe 227 rules of discipline according to the Pāli VINAYA. Upon receiving higher ordination (UPASAṂPADĀ), the new monk is required to remain under the guidance (nissaya; NIŚRAYA) of his preceptor (upajjhāya; UPĀDHYĀYA) for at least five years, until he becomes sufficiently skilled in dhamma and vinaya. After ten years, the monk becomes an elder (thera) in the saṅgha and is allowed to serve as an upajjhāya and ordain others. See also BHIKṢU.

**bhikkhunī**. (P). See BHIKṢUṆĪ.

**bhikṣu**. (P. bhikkhu; T. dge slong; C. biqiu; J. biku; K. pigu 比丘). In Sanskrit, lit. "beggar"; a male "religious mendicant" or, as commonly translated, "monk." The female counterparts of bhikṣu are BHIKṢUṆĪ (nuns). The term is derived from the Sanskrit root √bhikṣ meaning, among other things, "to beg for alms." The Tibetan translation of the term literally means "virtuous beggar"; the Chinese instead uses a transcription. Buddhism was one of the principal early groups of wandering religious (ŚRAMAṆA), which constituted a new religious movement in the fifth century BCE, and coined the term bhikṣu to distinguish its wanderers from those of other śramaṇa sects, such as the JAINA and ĀJĪVAKA. A bhikṣu holds the higher ordination (UPASAṂPADĀ) of his VINAYA lineage and is thus distinguished from a novice, or ŚRĀMAṆERA. Novitiate status is attained by undergoing the "going forth" (pravrajyā; see PRAVRAJITA) ceremony and accepting a set of ten (and, in some traditions, expanded to thirty-six) precepts (ŚĪLA). After a period of service in the order, one may undergo the upasaṃpadā ceremony, by which one attains full ordination. At that point, the bhikṣu is expected to adhere to all the rules found in the litany of monastic discipline, or PRĀTIMOKṢA, e.g., 227 in the Pāli vinaya used in Southeast Asia, 250 in the DHARMAGUPTAKA vinaya used in much of East Asia, 253 in the MŪLASARVĀSTIVĀDA vinaya followed in Tibet, etc. By rule, although not necessarily in practice, a bhikṣu is allowed to possess only a set of four or eight "requisites" (PARIṢKĀRA, P. parikkhāra), which provide him with the minimal necessities of food, clothing, and shelter. The duties of a bhikṣu vary widely across the Buddhist tradition. These duties include, but are not limited to, preserving the teaching by memorizing, copying and/or reciting the scriptures; instructing younger monks, novices, and lay adherents; conducting a variety of different kinds of ceremonies; maintaining the monastery grounds, etc. Bhikṣus were customarily presumed to be dependent on lay followers for their material requirements and, in return, served as a field of merit (PUṆYAKṢETRA) for them by accepting their donations (DĀNA). Within any given monastery, bhikṣus maintain hierarchical relationships. Depending on the monk's tradition, seniority may be determined by the number of years since full ordination (see VARṢĀ; C. JIELA), one's performance in examinations, or other factors. Literary evidence suggests that the first Buddhist monks were itinerant ascetics who resided in communities only during the monsoon season. Later, as the tradition grew, these temporary residences evolved into permanent monasteries. In the Hindu tradition, the term bhikṣu may sometimes also be used to signify the fourth stage (āśrama) of life, in which one renounces worldly attachments for the sake of study and reflection (although this stage is more commonly referred to as saṃnyāsin); in this context, however, no formal renunciation through ordination is necessarily required. Throughout much of the history of Buddhism, there have been regions and historical periods in which Buddhist monks married but continued to maintain the appearance of a fully-ordained bhikṣu, including wearing monastic robes and shaving their heads. In English, such religious might better be called "priests" rather than "monks." See also BHIKKHU.

**bhikṣuṇī**. (P. bhikkhunī; T. dge slong ma; C. biqiuni; J. bikuni; K. piguni 比丘尼) In Sanskrit, "beggar (female)," commonly translated as "nun." A bhikṣuṇī holds full ordination in her VINAYA lineage and is distinguished from a novice nun (ŚRĀMAṆERIKĀ) or a probationary postulant (ŚIKṢAMĀṆĀ) who both accept only the preliminary training rules. The bhikṣuṇī is enjoined to observe the full set of rules of monastic discipline, or PRĀTIMOKṢA, governing fully ordained nuns, which vary from 311 in the Pāli vinaya to 364 in the MŪLASARVĀSTIVĀDA vinaya followed in Tibet (although the order of bhikṣuṇī was never established there). These rules mirror closely those also incumbent on monks (BHIKṢU) (although there are substantially greater numbers of rules in all categories of the bhikṣuṇī prātimokṣa); an important exception, however, is that nuns are also required to adhere to the eight "weighty" or "deferential" "rules" (GURUDHARMA), a set of special rules that nuns alone are enjoined to follow, which explicitly subordinate the bhikṣuṇī to the bhikṣu SAṂGHA. Upon receiving higher ordination (UPASAMPADĀ), the new nun is required to remain under the guidance (NIŚRAYA; P. nissaya) of her preceptor (UPĀDHYĀYĀ; P. upajjhāyā) for at least two years until she becomes skilled in dharma and vinaya. After ten years, the nun becomes an elder (sthavirī; P. therī) in the bhikṣuṇī saṃgha and, after another two years, may act as a preceptor and ordain new nuns into the order. In South Asia, the formal upasaṃpadā ordination of nuns is thought to have died out sometime during the medieval period, and there is little evidence that a formal bhikṣuṇī saṃgha was ever established in Southeast Asia. The only surviving bhikṣuṇī ordination lineages are in China, Korea, and Taiwan. Apart from East Asia, most Buddhist women known as "nuns" are actually only ordained with the eight, nine, or ten extended lay precepts (as in Southeast Asia), as śrāmaṇerikā (as in Tibet), or else take the East Asian bodhisattva precepts of the FANWANG JING (as in Japan). In recent years there has been a concerted effort to reintroduce the bhikṣuṇī ordination to countries where it had died out or was never established.

**bhrāntijñāna**. (T. 'khrul shes; C. luanshi; J. ranjiki; K. nansik 亂識). In Sanskrit, "mistaken consciousness"; an epistemological term that is used to describe a consciousness that is mistaken with regard to its external sensory object, or "appearing object" (T. snang yul). Hence, according to the SAUTRĀNTIKA school, all conceptual consciousnesses, even those that are veridical, are mistaken in the sense that they mistake a generic image (arthasāmānya) of an object for the actual object. YOGĀCĀRA schools say all consciousness of external appearance is mistaken, and some MADHYAMAKA schools say basic ignorance makes even nonconceptual sensory perceptions mistaken. In addition to mistaken consciousnesses that arise from such forms of ignorance (AVIDYĀ), there are also mistaken consciousnesses produced by superficial causes—inner and outer causes and conditions that distort the five physical senses and sixth mental sense. For example, jaundice may cause something that is white to appear yellow and summer sunlight and sand may cause a mirage, in which the mistaken consciousness sees water where there is none.

**Bhṛkutī**. (T. Khro gnyer can; C. Pijuzhi; J. Bikutei; K. Piguji 毘俱胝). In Sanskrit, lit. "She who Frowns"; a wrathful deity understood to be a form of TĀRĀ, who is reputed to have been born from a frown of the BODHISATTVA AVALOKITEŚVARA. An alternate account is that she arose from a ray of light emanating out of Avalokiteśvara's left eye at the same time Tārā was born from the right eye. Bhṛkutī is sometimes said to be an emanation of the buddha AMITĀBHA as well, particularly in Japan, and often appears with an image of Amitābha in her crown. Although she can appear in peaceful form, she is generally depicted as a wrathful deity, most commonly with one face with three eyes, and four arms holding a trident, vase, and rosary and displaying the VARADAMUDRĀ, and either standing in ĀLĪḌHA posture or sitting in LALITĀSANA. ¶ Bhṛkutī is also the name of the Nepali princess who married SRONG BTSAN SGAM PO. According to the MAṆI BKA' 'BUM, she was the daughter of the Nepalese king Aṃśuvarman and was brought to Tibet by the famed minister Mgar stong btsan after Srong btsan sgam po saw her in a prophetic dream. The Nepalese king initially refused to send her, deriding Tibet as a land of savagery, lacking not only the teachings of the Buddha but basic civil laws as well. Mgar convinced the king that Srong btsan sgam po was sincere in desiring the DHARMA, and was able to return with her, after which he set out to China to bring back the Tang princess WENCHENG. Bhṛkūti is said to have brought with her to Tibet the statue of ŚĀKYAMUNI called JO BO MI BSKYOD RDO RJE, which was eventually housed in RA MO CHE. The historicity of both Bhṛkūti and her father has been called into question by recent scholarship. The Nepalese princess is said to have also brought a sandalwood statue of Bhṛkuṭī to Tibet, but (if it ever existed) it had disappeared by the seventeenth century, when the fifth DALAI LAMA, in his guidebook to the temples of LHA SA, reported it missing.

**bhūmi**. (T. sa; C. di; J. ji; K. chi 地). In Sanskrit, lit. "ground"; deriving from an ABHIDHARMA denotation of bhūmi as a way or path (MĀRGA), the term is used metaphorically to denote a "stage" of training, especially in the career of the BODHISATTVA or, in some contexts, a ŚRĀVAKA. A list of ten stages (DAŚABHŪMI) is most commonly enumerated, deriving from the DAŚABHŪMIKASŪTRA ("Discourse on the Ten Bhūmis"), a sūtra that is later subsumed into the massive scriptural compilation, the AVATAṂSAKASŪTRA. The bodhisattva does not enter the ten bhūmis immediately after generating the aspiration for enlightenment (BODHICITTOTPĀDA); rather, the first bhūmi coincides with the attainment of the path of vision (DARŚANAMĀRGA) and the remaining nine to the path of cultivation (BHĀVANĀMĀRGA). The ultimate experience of buddhahood is sometimes referred to (as in the LAṄKĀVATĀRASŪTRA) as an eleventh TATHĀGATABHŪMI, which the MAHĀVYUTPATTI designates as the samantaprabhābuddhabhūmi. The stage of the path prior to entering the path of vision is sometimes referred to as the adhimukticaryābhūmi ("stage of the practice of resolute faith"), a term from the BODHISATTVABHŪMI. An alternative list of "ten shared stages" of spiritual progress common to all three vehicles of ŚRĀVAKA, PRATYEKABUDDHA, and bodhisattva is described in the *MAHĀPRAJÑĀPĀRAMITĀSŪTRA and the DAZHIDU LUN (*Mahāprajñāpāramitāśāstra*). An alternative list of seven bhūmis of the bodhisattva path, as found in MAITREYANĀTHA and ASAṄGA's *Bodhisattvabhūmi*, is also widely known in Mahāyāna literature. For full treatment of each the bhūmi system, see BODHISATTVABHŪMI, DAŚABHŪMI; ŚRĀVAKABHŪMI; see also individual entries for each BHŪMI.

**bhūmisparśamudrā**. (T. sa gnon gyi phyag rgya; C. chudi yin; J. sokujiin; K. ch'okchi in 觸地印). In Sanskrit, "gesture of touching the earth"; this MUDRĀ is formed by the right hand touching the ground with extended fingers, usually across the right knee, while the left hand remains resting in the lap. It is the most common mudrā depicted in seated images of ŚĀKYAMUNI Buddha. The bhūmisparśamudrā recalls a specific moment in Śākyamuni's biography. After MĀRA had sought to dislodge the future buddha from his seat under the BODHI TREE by attacking him with his minions and seducing him with his daughters, he ultimately tried to cause the Buddha to move by claiming that he had no right to occupy that spot. The bodhisattva then touched the earth, thereby calling on the goddess of the earth Pṛthivī or STHĀVARĀ to bear witness to his practice of virtue over his many lifetimes on the bodhisattva path. The goddess responded affirmatively by causing the earth to quake. With that, Māra withdrew for good and the bodhisattva went on to achieve buddhahood that evening. In Southeast Asia, this scene is elaborated to include the goddess, called THORANI, emerging from the earth to wring from her hair all of the water that the Buddha had offered during his lifetimes as a BODHISATTVA. The water creates a flood that sweeps away Māra and his horde. The mudrā is also considered a gesture of immovability (acala) and is thus the mudrā associated with the buddha AKṢOBHYA.

**Bhūridatta**. See AJAHN MUN BHŪRIDATTA.

**bhūta**. (T. 'byung po; C. zhen/gui; J. shin/ki; K. chin/kwi 眞/鬼). The past passive particle of the Sanskrit root √bhū (cognate with English "be"); in compound words in Buddhist texts, it means "element," "true," or "real"; the word alone also means a class of harm-inflicting and formless obstructing spirits (i.e., "elemental spirits"). The MAHĀBHŪTA (literally "great elements") are the well-known elements of earth, water, fire, and wind; the BHŪTAKOṬI ("ultimate state") is a technical term used in the MAHĀYĀNA to distinguish between different levels of spiritual achievement; BHŪTATATHATĀ ("true suchness") is the eternal nature of reality that is "truly thus" and free of all conceptual elaborations. The bhūta ("elemental") spirits, who are sometimes equivalent to PRETA ("hungry ghost"), are said to inhabit the northeast quarter of the universe, or in some descriptions, all of the ten directions (DAŚADIŚ). Because they obstruct rainfall, the bhūta are propitiated by rituals to cause precipitation, as are the NĀGA ("serpent spirits, spirits of the watery subsoil") who inhabit rivers and lakes. Tibetan medical texts also identify eighteen elemental spirits ('byung po'i gdon) that invade the psyche and cause mental problems.

**bhūtaḍāmaramudrā**. (T. 'byung po 'dul byed kyi phyag rgya; C. xiang sanshi yin; J. gōzanzein; K. hang samse in 降三世印). In Sanskrit, "spirit-subduing gesture," a gesture (MUDRĀ) formed by crossing the left wrist in front of the right with palms facing forward and linking the little fingers; the thumbs hold down the two middle fingers and the forefingers of both hands stick out in the threatening gesture (TARJANĪMUDRĀ). In Tibet, the mudrā is specific to Bhūtaḍāmara, a name for a four-armed wrathful form of VAJRAPĀṆI; the Chinese translation of the term means "gesture that subjugates the three time periods" of past, present, and future.

**bhūtakoṭi**. (T. yang dag pa'i mtha'; C. shiji; J. jissai; K. silche 實際). In Sanskrit, lit. "end," "limit," or perhaps "edge" or "apex" (KOṬI) of "reality" (BHŪTA); the "peak experience" or "ultimate state" that is realized in the experience of the absolute (PARAMĀRTHA). Both buddhas and ARHATs are said to reside in the bhūtakoṭi, which in this context is synonymous with absolute truth (PARAMĀRTHASATYA). The DAZHIDU LUN (*Mahāprajñāpāramitāśāstra*) glosses the term as follows: "In the term bhūtakoṭi, "real" (bhūta) refers to the DHARMATĀ; because it is realized, it is called the "end" (koṭi)." While dharmatā as the "nature of reality" is used interchangeably with "things as they are" (TATHATĀ, yathābhūta) to refer to the nature of reality itself, bhūtakoṭi appears along with NIRVĀṆA to imply the "peak experience" or "ultimate state" that is reached in the realization of that nature of reality. The ABHISAMAYĀLAṂKĀRA commentarial tradition also describes the bhūtakoṭi as a limit that bodhisattvas must cross over. In those contexts bhūtakoṭi is equivalent to the partial nirvāṇa of the arhat that bodhisattvas must avoid falling into, and hence is the extreme of tranquility. Bodhisattvas finally cross over that "reality limit" when they reach the state of full enlightenment.

**bhūtatathatā**. (C. zhenru; J. shinnyo; K. chinyŏ 眞如). In Sanskrit, "true suchness." See TATHATĀ.

**biandi**. (J. henji; K. pyŏnji 邊地). In Chinese, "peripheral," or "outlying" "regions"; referring to the regions beyond the civilizing influences of Buddhism and higher spiritual culture. The corresponding Sanskrit term YAVANA was used to designate Greeks (Ionians) and later even Arab Muslims. In Buddhist cosmology, the term refers to regions north and west of India proper, which are inhabited by illiterate, barbaric peoples hostile to Buddhism. The birth into a "peripheral region" is considered to be one of the states that constitute an "inopportune moment or birth" (AKṢAṆA), i.e., a state that precludes attainment of enlightenment in the present lifetime. In other contexts, as in the SUKHĀVATĪVYŪHASŪTRA, a PURE LAND devotee who practices with doubt, hesitancy, and intermittent faith, or who eventually regrets and regresses from his or her devotion, will not be able to be reborn directly into AMITĀBHA Buddha's pure land (see SUKHĀVATĪ). Instead, he or she would be reborn first in the biandi ("outlying region") of the pure land for five hundred years before being granted access to sukhāvatī proper. The outlaying region of the pure land is depicted as a bejeweled place landscaped with lotus ponds and teeming with palatial buildings; it is almost as blissful and trouble-free as the pure land itself, except that its denizens lack the freedom to roam anywhere beyond its confines.

**bianwen**. (變文). In Chinese, "transformation texts"; the earliest examples of Chinese vernacular writings, many drawing on prominent Buddhist themes. Produced during the Tang dynasty (c. seventh through tenth centuries), they were lost to history until they were rediscovered among the manuscript cache at DUNHUANG early in the twentieth century. The vernacular narratives of bianwen are probably descended from BIANXIANG, pictorial representations of Buddhist and religious themes. The Sinograph bian in both compounds refers to the "transformations" or "manifestations" of spiritual adepts, and seems most closely related to such Sanskrit terms as nirmāṇa ("magical creation" or "magical transformation," as in NIRMĀṆAKĀYA) or ṚDDHI ("magical powers"). Bianwen were once thought to have been prompt books that were used during public performances, but this theory is no longer current. Even so, bianwen have a clear pedigree in oral literature and are the first genre of Chinese literature to vary verse recitation with spoken prose (so-called "prosimetric" narratives). As such, the bianwen genre was extremely influential in the evolution of Chinese performing arts, opera, and vernacular storytelling. Bianwen are primarily religious in orientation, and the Buddhist bianwen are culled from various sources, such as the JĀTAKAMĀLĀ, SADDHARMAPUṆḌARĪKASŪTRA, and VIMALAKĪRTINIRDEŚA. The genre does, however, include a few examples drawn from secular subjects. Bianwen may also have led to the development of later vernacular genres of literature with a religious orientation, such as the "treasure scrolls," or BAOJUAN.

**bianxiang**. (變相) In Chinese, "transformation tableaux"; pictorial representations of Buddhist narratives, which seem to have been the antecedent for later vernacular narratives of the same themes known as BIANWEN. As is the case with the compound bianwen, the logograph bian here refers to the "transformations" or "manifestations" of spiritual adepts. Bianxiang deal almost entirely with religious topics and involve especially pictorial representations of AMITĀBHA's PURE LAND (JINGTU) of SUKHĀVATĪ, famous episodes in the lives and activities of the Buddha and BODHISATTVAS (especially AVALOKITEŚVARA), and synopses of important sūtras (such as the SADDHARMAPUṆḌARĪKASŪTRA). A great number of bianxiang were discovered at DUNHUANG and provide a window on the popular practices in medieval Chinese Buddhism. See also AMITUO JINGTU BIAN; DIYU BIAN [XIANG]; JINGTU BIAN.

**bianyi shengsi**. (J. hen'i shōji; K. pyŏni saengsa 變異生死). In Chinese, "birth and death as alternation and change"; one of the two types of rebirth (see SAṂSĀRA) described in the Chinese FAXIANG (YOGĀCĀRA) and TIANTAI schools, along with "birth and death in punctuated succession" (FENDUAN SHENGSI). This type refers either to the process of positive psychological transformation, wherein a person could be "reborn" symbolically while still in the same physical body, or to the subtle mental instabilities a novice BODHISATTVA experiences due to the presence of minor, but as yet unresolved, afflictions (KLEŚA).

**Bianzheng lun**. (J. Benshōron; K. Pyŏnjŏng non 辯正論). In Chinese, "Treatise on Determining Orthodoxy"; a polemical treatise composed in 626 by the Tang dynasty monk Falin (d.u.) in response to such treatises as the *Shiyi jiumi lun* ("Treatise on the Ten Differences and Nine Obscurities") and *Xuanzheng lun* ("Treatise on Manifesting Orthodoxy") presented to the court by Daoist priests in defense of their own religion. The *Bianzheng lun* compares the teachings of Buddhists, Confucians, and Daoists in order to demonstrate the superiority of Buddhism. The Buddhist response to such theories as Laozi's conversion of the barbarians (see LAOZI HUAHU JING) and early Chinese notions of qi (pneuma or energy) and DAO (way or path) can be found in the *Bianzheng lun*. The treatise is therefore a valuable resource for studying Buddhist perspectives on Chinese thought.

**biexiang sanguan**. (C) (J. bessō no sangan; K. pyŏlsang samgwan 別相三觀). See SANGUAN.

**biexu**. (C) (別序). See ER XU.

**biguan**. (J. hekikan; K. pyŏkkwan 壁觀). In Chinese, "wall contemplation" or "wall gazing"; a type of meditative practice reputedly practiced by the putative founder of the CHAN school, the Indian monk BODHIDHARMA, whom legend says spent nine years in wall contemplation in a small cave near the monastery SHAOLINSI on SONGSHAN. This practice is explained as a meditation that entails "pacifying the mind" (ANXIN) and is the putative origin of contemplative practice in the CHAN school. Despite the prestige the term carries within the Chan tradition because of its association with Bodhidharma, precisely what "wall contemplation" means has remained fraught with controversy since early in the school's history. Two of the more commonly accepted explanations are that the practitioner renders his or her mind and body silent and still like a wall, or that the mind is "walled in" and kept isolated from sensory disturbance. Some scholars have suggested that the term might actually be a combination of a transcription bi and a translation kuan, both referring to VIPAŚYANĀ (insight) practice, but this theory is difficult to reconcile with the historical phonology of the Sinograph bi. Tibetan translations subsequently interpret biguan as "abiding in luminosity" (lham mer gnas), a gloss that may have tantric implications. Whatever its actual practice, the image of Bodhidharma sitting in a cross-legged meditative posture while facing a wall becomes one of the most frequent subjects of Chan painting.

**bīja**. (T. sa bon; C. zhongzi; J. shuji; K. chongja 種子). In Sanskrit, "seed," a term used metaphorically in two important contexts: (1) in the theory of KARMAN, an action is said to plant a "seed" or "potentiality" in the mind, where it will reside until it fructifies as a future experience or is destroyed by wisdom; (2) in tantric literature, many deities are said to have a "seed syllable" or seed MANTRA that is visualized and recited in liturgy and meditation in order to invoke the deity. In the Chinese FAXIANG (YOGĀCĀRA) school, based on similar lists found in Indian Buddhist texts like the MAHĀYĀNASAṂGRAHA, a supplement to the YOGĀCĀRABHŪMI, various lists of two different types of seeds are mentioned. (1) The primordial seeds (BENYOU ZHONGZI) and the continuously (lit. newly) acquired seeds (XINXUN ZHONGZI). The former are present in the eighth "storehouse consciousness" (ĀLAYAVIJÑĀNA) since time immemorial, and are responsible for giving rise to a sentient being's basic faculties, such as the sensory organs (INDRIYA) and the aggregates (SKANDHA). The latter are acquired through the activities and sense impressions of the other seven consciousnesses (VIJÑĀNA), and are stored within the eighth storehouse consciousness as pure, impure, or indeterminate seeds that may become activated again once the right conditions are in place for it to fructify. (2) Tainted seeds (youlou zhongzi) and untainted seeds (wulou zhongzi). The former are sowed whenever unenlightened activities of body, speech, and mind and the contaminants (ĀSRAVA) of mental defilements take place. The latter are associated with enlightened activities that do not generate such contaminants. In all cases, "full emergence" (SAMUDĀCĀRA, C. xiangxing) refers to the sprouting of those seeds as fully realized action. ¶ In tantric Buddhism the buddha field (BUDDHAKṢETRA) is represented as a MAṆḌALA with its inhabitant deities (DEVATĀ). The sonic source of the maṇḍala and the deities that inhabit it is a "seed syllable" (bīja). In tantric practices (VIDHI; SĀDHANA) the meditator imagines the seed syllable emerging from the expanse of reality, usually on a lotus flower. The seed syllable is then visualized as transforming into the maṇḍala and its divine inhabitants, each of which often has its own seed syllable. At the end of the ritual, the process is reversed and collapsed back into the seed syllable that then dissolves back into the nondual original expanse. Seed syllables in tantric Buddhism are connected with DHĀRAṆĪ, mnemonic codes widespread in Mahāyāna sūtras that consist of strings of letters, often the first letter of profound terms or topics. These strings of letters in the dhāraṇī anticipate the MANTRAs found in tantric ritual practices. The tantric "seed syllable" is thought to contain the essence of the mantra, the letters of which are visualized as standing upright in a circle around the seed syllable from which the letters emerge and to which they return.

**Bi ma snying thig**. (Bime Nyingtik) In Tibetan, "Heart Essence of VIMALAMITRA"; associated with KLONG CHEN RAB 'BYAMS whose collection of RDZOGS CHEN teaching of the "instruction class" (MAN NGAG SDE) are loosely referred to by this name. The *Bi ma snying thig* itself is a collection of five texts attributed to Vimalamitra, rediscovered as treasure texts (GTER MA) by Lce btsun Seng ge dbang phyug in CHIMS PHU near BSAM YAS, and passed down through Zhang ston Bkra shis rdo rje (1097–1167) to Klong chen pa who established the SNYING THIG ("heart essence") as the central element in the rdzogs chen tradition. He gave an exegesis on the theory and practice of rdzogs chen in his MDZOD BDUN ("seven great treasuries") and NGAL GSO SKOR GSUM ("Trilogy on Rest"), and in his *Bla ma yang thig*, revealed the contents of the Bi ma snying thig itself.

**Bimbisāra**. (T. Gzugs can snying po; C. Pinposuoluo; J. Binbashara; K. Pinbasara 頻婆娑羅) (r. c. 465–413 BCE). King of MAGADHA, and chief royal patron of the Buddha during his lifetime, who reigned from his capital city of RĀJAGṚHA (P. Rājagaha). There are several accounts of how the two first met. According to the Pāli JĀTAKA, the two first met at Rājagṛha just after GAUTAMA had renounced the world when the BODHISATTVA passed beneath the king's window. Impressed with the mendicant's demeanor, Bimbisāra invited him to join his court. When the bodhisattva refused, Bimbisāra wished him success in his quest for enlightenment and requested that he visit his palace as soon as he achieved his goal. The Buddha honored his request and, soon after attaining enlightenment, returned to Rājagṛha to preach to Bimbisāra and his courtiers. Immediately upon listening to the sermon, the king and his attendants became stream-enterers (SROTAĀPANNA). The Pāli MAHAVAṂSA, however, states instead that they were childhood friends. Bimbisāra was munificent in his support for the Buddha and his SAṂGHA. The most famous of his donations was the VEṆUVANA (P. Veḷuvana) bamboo grove, where it is said he constructed a multistoried residence for the monks. He repaired the road from Rājagṛha to the Ganges River, a distance of five leagues, just so the Buddha would have an easier walk on his way to VAIŚĀLĪ. With such gifts, Bimbisāra declared that the five ambitions of his life had been fulfilled: that he would become king, that the Buddha would visit his kingdom, that he would render service to the Buddha, that the Buddha would preach to him, and that he would understand the meaning of the Buddha's teachings. Bimbisāra met a tragic death at the hands of his son AJĀTAŚATRU (P. Ajātasattu). Even as his son was conceived, according to some accounts, astrologers had predicted that the unborn child would kill his father and recommended to the king that the fetus be aborted. The king would not hear of it and instead showered affection on his son throughout his childhood. Ajātaśatru was persuaded to murder his father by DEVADATTA, the Buddha's evil cousin, who saw Bimbisāra's continued patronage of the Buddha as the chief obstacle to his ambition to become leader of the saṃgha himself. According to some reports, it was only upon the birth of his own son that he realized the paternal love that his father had had for him. According to the Pāli account, Bimbisāra was reborn as a yakkha (YAKṢA) named Janavasabha and is said to have visited the Buddha in that form. See also VAIDEHĪ.

**bindu**. (T. thig le). In Sanskrit, "drop," as in the title of Buddhist texts like DHARMAKĪRTI's NYĀYABINDU ("Drop of Reasoning"). In Buddhist tantra, bindu is BODHICITTA, seminal fluids in the ordinary sense, and in an extraordinary sense the seed of the illusory world and enlightenment; in this tantric sense, bindu is either red (from the female) or white (from the male). A second meaning of bindu found widely in tantric literature in Tibet, and in the RNYING MA sect in particular, is in words like thig le chen po (great circle) and thig le nyag chig (single circle, single sphere), words for the primordial basis: the natural state of the mind as empty, creative, and a state of great bliss both in ordinary beings, and as the DHARMAKĀYA at the time of enlightenment. This bindu is understood as including all phenomena, in a causal sense, and as their essence. According to tantric physiology, the bindu resides in the channels (NĀḌĪ) and is the source of bliss when manipulated in meditation practice through the control of the energies (PRĀṆA). Iconographically, it is represented as a curved line on the top of the circular symbol placed on the top of letters to represent the nasalization of vowels (anusvāra).

**bingfu**. (J. hinpotsu; K. pyŏngbul 秉拂). In Chinese, lit. "to take hold of the whisk"; dharma discourses delivered by a CHAN master from the high seat while holding the fly whisk or "chowrie" (see VĀLAVYAJANA; C. FUZI). The chowrie, a yak-tail fan that Buddhist monks used to keep flies and mosquitoes away, is presumed to have originally been used among followers of the JAINA tradition to shoo away flies without injuring them and came to be used widely throughout India. In the Chinese CHAN tradition, the fly whisk (which in East Asia is usually made from a horse tail) became a symbol of the office or privilege of a Chan master and the first thing the Chan master would do after ascending to his seat for his formal dharma discourse (see SHANGTANG) was to "take up the whisk"; by metonymy, the term came to be used to refer to a formal Chan sermon. The head monks in a Chan monastery who are privileged to "take hold of the whisk" in the Chan master's stead are called the "chief officers" (C. TOUSHOU): i.e., the chief seat (C. SHOUZUO), scribe (C. SHUJI), library prefect (C. ZANGZHU), guest prefect (C. ZHIKE), bath prefect (C. ZHIYU), and hall prefect (C. ZHIDIAN).

**Binglingsi**. (J. Heireiji; K. Pyŏngnyŏngsa 炳靈寺). In Chinese, "Bright and Numinous Monastery"; site of a Buddhist cave complex, located fifty miles outside Lanzhou, the capital of the present-day Chinese province of Gansu, and accessible only by boat. The complex contains 183 caves with 694 stone and eighty-two clay statues. Binglingsi, along with MAIJISHAN, developed under the patronage of the Qifu rulers of the Western Qin dynasty (385–43). The carving of Buddhist caves at Binglingsi may have started as early as the late fourth century; however, the earliest inscription was found in cave 169 and is dated 420. Two novel features can be found in cave 169. One is the stylistic link of some of its sculptures with the Buddhist art of KHOTAN on the southern SILK ROAD. For example, five seated buddhas in niche 23 inside the cave are attired in their monastic robes and perform the meditation gesture (DHYĀNAMUDRĀ), backed by a large aureole. Second, numerous inscriptions identify the sculptures and painted images in this cave, which include AMITĀBHA Buddha, accompanied by AVALOKITEŚVARA (GUANYIN) and MAHĀSTHĀMAPRĀPTA (Dashizi). This triad in niche 6 closely resembles the style of Liangzhou, and thus KUCHA. Among the painted images are the buddhas of the ten directions (see DAŚADIŚ), members of the Qin dynastic house, and the state preceptor (GUOSHI) Tanmobi (Dharmapriya), cotranslator with ZHU FONIAN of the AṢṬASĀHASRIKĀPRAJÑĀPĀRAMITĀ. The representations in cave 169 depict the content of then-newly translated scriptures such as the VIMALAKĪRTINIRDEŚA, SADDHARMAPUṆḌARĪKASŪTRA, and the shorter SUKHĀVATĪVYŪHASŪTRA (see also AMITĀBHASŪTRA), which had been translated by KUMĀRAJĪVA in Chang'an around 400–410. The sculptures and paintings at Binglingsi serve as precedents for the subsequent Northern Wei sculpture found at YUNGANG and LONGMEN.

**Biographies of Eminent Monks**. See GAOSENG ZHUAN.

**Biqiuni zhuan**. (J. Bikuniden; K. Piguni chŏn 比丘尼傳). In Chinese, "Lives of the Nuns," the major Chinese collection of biographies of eminent BHIKṢUṆĪ, compiled c. 516 CE by Shi Baochang, a Buddhist monk whose own biography can be found in the XU GAOSENG ZHUAN ("Continued Lives of Eminent Monks"). The anthology consists of sixty-five nuns' biographies, arranged chronologically beginning in the Eastern Jin (317–420 CE) and continuing through the period of the Northern and Southern dynasties (420–588 CE). The introduction lists several characteristics that Shi Baochang deems worthy of emulation and special mention. These include steadfast asceticism, skill in meditation and study, chastity, and teaching abilities. The hagiographies themselves emphasize the following activities: over half of the nuns included in the anthology excelled in either scriptural study or meditation and religious practice. Almost half taught scripture and established convents. One-third of the nuns are said to have practiced strict vegetarianism. The same number is also said to have excelled in chanting scriptures: the most frequently named scriptures as the object of this devotion include the SADDHARMAPUṆḌARĪKASŪTRA, the MAHĀPARINIRVĀṆASŪTRA, and the MAHĀPRAJÑĀPĀRAMITĀSŪTRA. The majority of nuns are also said to have inspired numerous monastic and secular followers. Many of the lay followers came from the highest reaches of society: governors and lords are regularly mentioned as patrons who often were instrumental in the founding of a new convent by donating land, funding construction, or both. In addition, almost half of the nuns were praised for their pure faith in the Buddha. In the instances where age was mentioned, almost half of the nuns were said to have adopted their vocation when they were still quite young (preadolescent); in contrast, only one-third were said to have left secular life once they were adults. The legitimacy of the Chinese nuns' order was specifically addressed in at least three hagiographies, where it is asserted that the subjects' ordinations were performed by foreign monks and nuns and was therefore valid.

**Birushana nyorai**. (J) (毗盧遮那如來). See NARA DAIBUTSU.

**Biyan lu**. (J. Hekiganroku; K. Pyŏgam nok 碧巖錄). In Chinese, "Emerald Grotto Record" or, as it is popularly known in the West, the "Blue Cliff Record"; compiled by CHAN master YUANWU KEQIN; also known by its full title of *Foguo Yuanwu chanshi biyan lu* ("Emerald Grotto Record of Chan Master Foguo Yuanwu"). The *Biyan lu* is one of the two most famous and widely used collection of Chan cases (GONG'AN), along with the WUMEN GUAN ("The Gateless Checkpoint"). The anthology is built around XUEDOU CHONGXIAN's *Xuedou heshang baice songgu*, an earlier independent collection of one hundred old Chan cases (GUCE) with verse commentary; Xuedou's text is embedded within the *Biyan lu* and Yuanwu's comments are interspersed throughout. Each of the one hundred cases, with a few exceptions, is introduced by a pointer (CHUISHI), a short introductory paragraph composed by Yuanwu. Following the pointer, the term "raised" (ju) is used to formally mark the actual case. Each case is followed by interlinear notes known as annotations or capping phrases (ZHUOYU; J. JAKUGO) and prose commentary (PINGCHANG), both composed by Yuanwu. The phrase "the verse says" (song yue) subsequently introduces Xuedou's verse, which is also accompanied by its own capping phrases and prose commentary, both added by Yuanwu. The cases, comments, and capping phrases found in the *Biyan lu* were widely used and read among both the clergy and laity in China, Korea, Japan, and Vietnam as an contemplative tool in Chan meditation practice and, in some contexts, as a token of social or institutional status. A famous (or perhaps infamous) story tells of the Chan master DAHUI ZONGGAO, the major disciple of Yuanwu, burning his teacher's *Biyan lu* for fear that his students would become attached to the words of Xuedou and Yuanwu. The *Biyan lu* shares many cases with the *Wumen guan*, and the two texts continue to function as the foundation of training in the Japanese RINZAI Zen school.

**Bka' babs bdun ldan gyi brgyud pa'i rnam thar**. (Kabap Dünden gyi Gyüpe Namtar). In Tibetan, "Biographies of the Seven Instruction Lineages"; a collection of brief biographies composed by the Tibetan historian TĀRANĀTHA (1575–1634). It documents the lives of fifty-nine Indian SIDDHAs involved in the early transmission of tantric instructions that came to be important and widely practiced later in Tibet. Although it serves to legitimize the author's own lineage, the text is considered to be an important source of historical information, because Tāranātha had direct contact with several of these masters. According to the text's colophon, Tāranātha composed the work when he was twenty-six, in about the year 1601. Its complete title is: *Bka' babs bdun ldan gyi brgyud pa'i rnam thar ngo mtshar rmad du byung ba rin po che'i lta bu'i rgyan*.

**bka' babs bzhi**. (kabap shi). In Tibetan, "four instructional lineages" (bka' means words—of a buddha or enlightened master—and babs means to descend in a stream); a series of tantric instructions that the Indian SIDDHA TILOPA received from various masters, codified, and then passed on to his disciple NĀROPA. These later became foundational teachings for the BKA' BRGYUD sect of Tibetan Buddhism and were incorporated into the six doctrines of Nāropa (NĀ RO CHOS DRUG). Tibetan sources vary widely regarding the lineage and content of these four transmissions. According to a biography of Tilopa composed by MAR PA CHOS KYI BLO GROS, they are (1) the transmission of illusory body (T. sgyu lus kyi bka' babs) received from the siddha NĀGĀRJUNA; (2) the transmission of dreams (T. rmi lam gyi bka' babs) received from the siddha Caryāpa; (3) the transmission of clear light (T. 'od gsal gyi bka' babs) received from the siddha Lavapa; and (4) the transmission of inner heat (T. gtum mo'i bka' babs) received from Jñānaḍākinī. According to other sources, these four may alternatively include the transmissions of MAHĀMUDRĀ, the intermediate state (BAR DO), mother tantra (MĀTṚTANTRA), father tantra (PITṚTANTRA), and individual tantras such as the tantra of CAKRASAṂVARA, HEVAJRA, and GUHYASAMĀJA.

**Bka' brgyud**. (Kagyü). In Tibetan, "Oral Lineage" or "Lineage of the Buddha's Word"; one of the four main sects of Tibetan Buddhism. The term bka' brgyud is used by all sects of Tibetan Buddhism in the sense of an oral transmission of teachings from one generation to the next, a transmission that is traced back to India. Serving as the name of a specific sect, the name Bka' brgyud refers to a specific lineage, the MAR PA BKA' BRGYUD, the "Oral Lineage of Mar pa," a lineage of tantric initiations, instructions, and practices brought to Tibet from India by the translator MAR PA CHOS KYI BLO GROS in the eleventh century. Numerous sects and subsects evolved from this lineage, some of which developed a great deal of autonomy and institutional power. In this sense, it is somewhat misleading to describe Bka' brgyud as a single sect; there is, for example, no single head of the sect as in the case of SA SKYA or DGE LUGS. The various sects and subsects, however, do share a common retrospection to the teachings that Mar pa retrieved from India. Thus, rather than refer to Bka' brgyud as one of four sects (chos lugs), in Tibetan the Mar pa Bka' brgyud is counted as one of the eight streams of tantric instruction, the so-called eight great chariot-like lineages of achievement (SGRUB BRGYUD SHING RTA CHEN PO BRGYAD), a group which also includes the RNYING MA, the BKA' GDAMS of ATIŚA, and the instructions on "severance" (GCOD) of MA GCIG LAB SGRON. In some Tibetan histories, Mar pa's lineage is called the Dkar brgyud ("White Lineage"), named after the white cotton shawls worn by its yogins in their practice of solitary meditation. The reading

Dka' brgyud ("Austerities Lineage") is also found. The lineage from which all the sects and subsects derive look back not only to Mar pa, but to his teacher, and their teachers, traced back to the tantric buddha VAJRADHARA. Vajradhara imparted his instructions to the Indian MAHĀSIDDHA TILOPA, who in turn transmitted them to the Bengali scholar and yogin NĀROPA. It was Nāropa (in fact, his disciples) whom Mar pa encountered during his time in India, receiving the famous NĀ RO CHOS DRUG, or the six doctrines of Nāropa. Mar pa returned to Tibet, translated the texts and transmitted these and other teachings (including MAHĀMUDRĀ, the hallmark practice of Bka' brgyud) to a number of disciples, including his most famous student, MI LA RAS PA. These five figures—the buddha Vajradhara, the Indian tantric masters Tilopa and Nāropa, and their Tibetan successors Mar pa and Mi la ras pa (both of whom were laymen rather than monks)—form a lineage that is recognized and revered by all forms of Bka' brgyud. One of Mi la ras pa's chief disciples, the physician and monk SGAM PO PA BSOD NAMS RIN CHEN united the tantric instructions he received from Mi la ras pa and presented them in the monastic and exegetical setting that he knew from his studies in the Bka' gdams sect. Sgam po pa, therefore, appears to have been instrumental in transforming an itinerant movement of lay yogins into a sect with a strong monastic element. He established an important monastery in the southern Tibetan region of Dwags po; in acknowledgment of his importance, the subsequent branches of the Bka' brgyud are sometimes collectively known as the DWAGS PO BKA' BRGYUD. The Bka' brgyud later divided into what is known in Tibetan as the "four major and eight minor Bka' brgyud" (BKA' BRGYUD CHE BZHI CHUNG BRGYAD). A number of these subsects no longer survive as independent institutions, although the works of their major figures continue to be studied. Among those that survive, the KARMA BKA' BRGYUD, 'BRI GUNG BKA' BRGYUD, and 'BRUG PA BKA' BRGYUD continue to play an important role in Tibet, the Himalayan region, and in exile.

**Bka' brgyud che bzhi chung brgyad**. (Kagyü che shi chung gye). In Tibetan, the "Four Major and Eight Minor Bka' brgyud." A division of the BKA' BRGYUD sect of Tibetan Buddhism into various sects and subsects stemming from the disciples of SGAM PO PA BSOD RNAM RIN CHEN. The terms "major" and "minor" indicate a relative proximity to the master Sgam po pa and carry no quantitative or qualitative overtones. The four major subsects follow from the direct disciples of Sgam po pa and his nephew Dwags po Sgom tshul (Dakpo Gomtshul, 1116–1169):

1. KARMA BKA' BRGYUD, also called the Karma kam tshang, originating with the first KARMA PA DUS GSUM MKHYEN PA—a disciple of Sgam po pa
2. TSHAL PA BKA' BRGYUD originating with Zhang tshal pa Brtson 'grus grags pa (Shangtsalpa Tsöndru Drakpa, 1123–1193)—a disciple of Dwags po Sgom tshul
3. 'BA' ROM BKA' BRGYUD originating with 'Ba' rom Dar ma dbang phyug (Barom Darma Wangchuk, 1127–1199)—a disciple of Sgam po pa
4. Phag gru bka' brgyud (Pakdru Kagyü) originating with PHAG MO GRU PA RDO RJE RGYAL PO—a disciple of Sgam po pa.

The eight minor subsects stem from disciples of Phag mo gru pa:

1. 'BRI GUNG BKA' BRGYUD originating with 'JIG RTEN GSUM MGON
2. STAG LUNG BKA' BRGYUD originating with STAG LUNG THANG PA BKRA SHIS DPAL
3. Gling ras bka' brgyud (Lingre Kagyü) originating with Gling rje ras pa Padma rdo rje (Lingje Repa Pema Dorje, 1128–1288), this later became the 'BRUG PA BKA' BRGYUD under his disciple GTSANG PA RGYA RAS YE SHES RDO RJE
4. G.ya' bzang bka' brgyud (Yasang Kagyü) originating with Zwa ra ba Skal ldan ye shes seng ge (Sarawa Kalden Yeshe Senge, d. 1207)
5. KHRO PHU BKA' BRGYUD originating with Rgya tsha (Gyatsa, 1118–1195), Kun ldan ras pa (Kunden Repa, 1148–1217), and their nephew Khro phu lo tsā ba Byams pa dpal (Trophu Lotsāwa Jampapal, 1173–1228)
6. SHUG GSEB BKA' BRGYUD originating with GYER SGOM TSHUL KHRIMS SENG GE
7. YEL PA BKA' BRGYUD originating with Ye shes brtsegs pa (Yeshe Tsekpa, d.u.)
8. SMAR TSHANG BKA' BRGYUD originating with Smar pa grub thob Shes rab seng ge (Marpa Druptob Sherap Senge, d.u.)

**Bka' brgyud mgur mtsho**. (Kagyü Gurtso). In Tibetan, "An Ocean of Songs of the Bka' brgyud"; a collection of spiritual songs and poetry composed by eminent masters of the BKA' BRGYUD sect of Tibetan Buddhism. It was compiled by the eighth KARMA PA MI BSKYOD RDO RJE in about 1542, originally intended as a liturgical text to be recited as an invocation of the entire Bka' brgyud lineage. The text is also part biographical recollection and doctrinal catalogue and is still much loved and widely read by adherents of the tradition. Its complete title is: *Mchog gi dngos grub mngon du byed pa'i myur lam bka' brgyud bla ma rnams kyi rdo rje'i mgur dbyangs ye shes char 'bebs rang grol lhun grub bde chen rab 'bar nges don rgya mtsho'i snying po.*

**Bka' brgyud pa**. (Kagyüpa). A person affiliated with the BKA' BRGYUD sect of Tibetan Buddhism.

**Bka' brgyud sngags mdzod**. (Kagyü Ngagdzö). In Tibetan, "Treasury of Bka' brgyud Mantra"; a compilation of tantric teachings belonging to the BKA' BRGYUD sect of Tibetan Buddhism, compiled and edited in six volumes by the nineteenth-century Tibetan master 'Jam mgon kong sprul Blo gros mtha' yas. The collection forms one of the five treasuries of Kong sprul (Kong sprul mdzod lnga), and largely preserves the esoteric instructions transmitted by Bka' brgyud founder Mar pa Chos kyi blo gros to his disciple Rngog Chos sku rdo rje (Ngok Chöku Dorje).

**Bka' chems ka khol ma**. (Kachem Kakölma). In Tibetan, "The Pillar Testament"; an early historiographic text, purportedly the testament of the seventh-century Tibetan religious king Srong bstan sgam po. It is said to have been discovered in the hollow of a pillar in the Jo khang Temple of Lha sa by the Indian master Atiśa Dīpaṃkaraśrījñāna in about 1049. The circumstances of both the author and revealer, however, have recently been called into question. The text details the reign of Srong bstan sgam po and likely served as a primary source for later accounts of the early royal dynastic period in Tibet.

**Bka' gdams**. (Kadam). An early sect of Tibetan Buddhism. In Tibetan, bka' (ka) is the word of the Buddha or an enlightened master, and gdams (dam) means "to instruct"; traditionally the compound is parsed as "those who take all of the Buddha's words as instruction." Another etymology associates the word bka' with the words of Atiśa Dīpaṃkaraśrījñāna, whose followers began the early sect of Tibetan Buddhism, and in place of gdams "to advise" understands dam "to bind," hence, "those who hold his sacred words as binding." The origins of the sect are traced back to the founding of Rwa sgreng monastery in 1056 by Atiśa's foremost disciple and interpreter 'Brom ston Rgyal ba'i 'byung gnas. The three main students of 'Brom ston pa are Po to ba Rin chen gsal (Potowa), Spyan mnga' ba Tshul khrims 'bar (Chen Ngawa), and Bu chung ba Gzhon nu rgyal mtshan (Bu chungwa), from whom originate the three principal Bka' gdams lineages (bka' babs): (1) the authoritative treatises (gzhung) lineage, (2) the essential instruction (gdams ngag) lineage, and (3) the oral instruction (man ngag) lineage, respectively. Po to ba's authoritative treatise lineage emphasized the close study of six paired fundamental Buddhist treatises: the Bodhisattvabhūmi and Mahāyānasūtrālaṃkāra, the Bodhicaryāvatāra and Śikṣāsamuccaya, and the Jātakamālā and Udānavarga. The teachings of the lineage of oral instructions are collected in the Bka' gdams glegs bam pha chos bu chos. The sect is probably best known for its strict discipline and austerity of practice, but the Gsang phu ne'u thog Bka' gdams lineage that is traced back to the founding of the monastery of Gsang phu ne'u thog in about 1073 by Rngog legs pa'i shes rab, an immediate disciple of Atiśa, and his nephew, the translator Rngog blo ldan shes rab, gave the Bka' gdams a well-deserved reputation as a sect of great learning. Monks from Gsang phu ne'u thog like Phywa pa Chos kyi seng ge wrote important works on pramāṇa (logic and epistemology) and formalized debate (rtsod rigs). The Bka' gdams was responsible for the distinctive Tibetan bstan rim (tenrim) ("stages of teaching") genre, based on Atiśa's seminal work, the Bodhipathapradīpa. This genre was later adapted and popularized by Tsong kha pa in his influential Lam rim chen mo. Tsong kha pa idealized Atiśa as the perfect teacher and his early Dge lugs pa followers, first called Dga' ldan pa (Gandenpa) after the Dga' ldan monastery he founded, were also known as the new Bka' gdams pa. After the rise of the Dge lugs sect, the Bka' gdams disappeared from Tibetan history, for reasons still not fully understood, with only the monasteries of Rwa sgreng and Snar thang retaining their original affiliation.

**Bka' gdams glegs bam pha chos bu chos**. (Kadam Lekbam Pachö Buchö). In Tibetan, "The Book of Bka' gdams, Dharma of the Father and Sons" originating with the Indian master Atiśa Dīpaṃkaraśrījñāna a seminal work of the Bka' gdams sect of Tibetan Buddhism, being the primary text of the oral-instruction (man ngag) lineage organized into its present version by Mkhan chen Nyi ma rgyal mtshan (Kenchen Nyima Gyaltsen) in 1302. "Dharma of the Father" refers to Atiśa's responses to questions posed by his foremost Tibetan student 'Brom ston Rgyal ba'i 'byung gnas (the two "fathers" of Bka' gdams); "Dharma of the Sons" refers to Atiśa's responses to questions posed by Rngog Legs pa'i shes rab and Khu ston Brtson 'grus g.yung drung (Kutön Tsondrü Yungdrung), the spiritual sons of Atiśa and 'Brom ston pa.

**bka' 'gyur**. (kangyur). In Tibetan, "translation of the word [of the Buddha]," one of the two traditional divisions of the Tibetan Buddhist canon, along with the bstan 'gyur, the translation of the treatises (śāstra). The bka' 'gyur comprises those sūtras and tantras that were accepted by the tradition as spoken or directly inspired by the Buddha. The collection was redacted, primarily by the fourteenth-century polymath Bu ston Rin chen grub, based upon earlier catalogues, lists, and collections of texts, particularly a major collection at Snar thang monastery. The four major editions of the bka' 'gyur presently in circulation (called the Co ne, Snar thang, Sde dge, and Beijing editions after the places they were printed) go back to two earlier branches of the textual tradition, called Them spangs ma and 'Tshal pa in modern scholarship. The first xylographic print of the bka' 'gyur was produced in China in 1410; the Sde dge bka' 'gyur, edited by Si tu Gstug lag chos kyi 'byung gnas (1700–1774) was printed in the Tibetan kingdom of Sde dge (in present-day Sichuan province) in 1733. While the collection is traditionally said to include 108 volumes (an auspicious number), most versions contain somewhat fewer. The Snar thang edition holds ninety-two volumes, divided as follows: thirteen volumes of vinaya, twenty-one volumes of prajñāpāramitā, six volumes of the

Avataṃsakasūtra, six volumes of the Ratnakūṭasūtra, thirty volumes of other sūtras, and twenty-two volumes of tantras. The Bon tradition formulated its own bka' 'gyur, based on the Buddhist model, in the late fourteenth or early fifteenth century.

**bka' ma**. (kama). In Tibetan "words"; in the Tibetan Rnying ma sect, referring particularly to the mahāyoga, anuyoga, and atiyoga tantras. The term is contrasted with gter ma ("treasure text"), which is also accepted as authentic scripture, but hidden and rediscovered at a later time, or directly transmitted through the medium of the mind. Two collections of the teachings of the Rnying ma sect in fifty-eight and 120 volumes are called Bka' ma; they include the entire range of texts, from vinaya to modern commentaries on the tantras and gter ma.

**Bka' thang gser 'phreng**. (Katang Sertreng). In Tibetan, "The Golden Rosary Chronicle"; a treasure text (gter ma) containing a well-known biography of Padmasambhava, discovered by the treasure revealer (gter ston) Sangs rgyas gling pa. Its complete title is: *O rgyan gu ru padma 'byung gnas kyi rnam par thar pa gser gyi phreng ba thar lam gsal byed.*

**bka' thang sde lnga**. (katang denga). In Tibetan, "the five chronicles"; treasure texts (gter ma) describing the times and events surrounding the life of Padmasambhava, and discovered in stages by the treasure revealer (gter ston) O rgyan gling pa during the late fourteenth century. The collection contains five books: the kings (rgyal po), queens (btsun mo), ministers (blon po), translators and paṇḍitas (lo paṇ), and gods and ghosts (lha 'dre). These accounts contain many early legends and myths but also sections of historical value and interest, including descriptions of Chinese Chan Buddhist doctrine.

**Bka' thang zangs gling ma**. (Katang Sanglingma). In Tibetan, "The Copper Island Chronicle"; the earliest of the many treasure texts (gter ma) containing biographies of Padmasambhava, discovered by the twelfth-century treasure revealer (gter ston) Nyang ral Nyi ma 'od zer.

**Bka' tshal**. (Katsel). In Tibetan, one of the four "edge-taming temples" or "edge-pinning temples" (mtha' 'dul gtsug lag khang) said to have been constructed during the time of the Tibetan king Srong btsan sgam po to pin down the limbs of the demoness (T. srin mo) who was impeding the introduction of Buddhism into Tibet. The temple is located on the head flank (T. dbu ru) and pins down her right hip.

**Bkra shis lhun po**. (Tashi Lhunpo). A Tibetan monastery that served as the seat of the Paṇ chen Lamas, located in the Tibetan city of Gzhi ka rtse (Shigatse), and considered one of the six great institutions of the Dge lugs sect of Tibetan Buddhism. The others include Se ra, 'Bras spungs, and Dga' ldan, all located near Lha sa, together with Bla brang bkra shis 'khyil and Sku 'bum, in the northeast region of A mdo. Bkra shis lhun po was founded in 1447 by Dge 'dun grub, a disciple of the Dge lugs luminary Tsong kha pa. In 1618, the Karma Bka' brgyud monastery Bkra shis zil gnon (Tashi Silnön, "Tashi Lhunpo Suppressor") was established on a nearby hill and, for a short while, superceded Bkra shis lhun po, but it was eventually destroyed amid sectarian strife between the rival institutions. The cleric Blo bzang chos kyi rgyal mtshan enlarged Bkra shis lhun po's original structure, and the fifth Dalai Lama Ngag dbang blo bzang rgya mtsho conferred upon him the title of Paṇ chen Lama, "Great Scholar." Blo bzang chos kyi rgyal mtshan was affirmed as the fourth such master, with the first three prelates recognized posthumously, beginning with Tsong kha pa's disciple Mkhas grub Dge legs dpal bzang. The Paṇ chen Lama was elevated to a position of great religious and political authority, officially ranking second after the Dalai Lama but often acting as his tutor and occasionally rivaling him in political power. His monastery thus became a key institution in the religious and political history of central and western Tibet from the seventeenth century onward. The large monastic complex of assembly halls, temples, and residences, including its famous golden roof, was spared major destruction during the Chinese Cultural Revolution (1966–1976).

**bkra shis tshe ring mched lnga**. (tashi tsering chenga). In Tibetan, "the five long-life sisters," a group of pre-Buddhist Tibetan deities who were subdued and converted to Buddhism by Padmasambhava; the sisters also make an appearance in the songs of Mi la ras pa (Mi la'i mgur 'bum) collected by Gtsang smyon Heruka, where they give the yogin access to the highest states of bliss. According to the Dge lugs tradition, they are dharma protectors (dharmapāla) who have not transcended existence in saṃsāra (although both the Rnying ma and Bka' brgyud sects assert that they have done so). They reside at either Mount Everest or La phyi, on the border between Tibet and Nepal. Their leader is Bkra shis tshe ring ma/Rdo rje kun grags ma or Tshe yi dbang phyug ma. The other members are Mthing gi zhal bzang ma, Mi g.yo glang bzang ma, Cod pan mgrin bzang ma, and Gtal dkar 'gro bzang ma. They are also known as the bkra shis tshe yi lha mo lnga.

**Bla brang bkra shis 'khyil**. (Labrang Tashikyil). One of the six great monasteries of Tibet belonging to the Dge lugs sect of Tibetan Buddhism; located in the northeast region of A mdo near the traditional border with China. The other five include Se ra, 'Bras spungs, Dga' ldan, and Bkra shis lhun po, all located in central Tibet, together with Sku 'bum in A mdo. The monastery was established in 1709 by the first 'Jam dbyangs bzhad pa incarnation, Ngag dbang brtson grus, and became the principal seat of his subsequent incarnations. At its peak, Bla brang bkra shis 'khyil housed four thousand monks and several colleges, making it the largest and most powerful in A mdo.

**Black Hats**. (C. heimao 黑帽). A popular designation in both European languages and Chinese for the KARMA PA lineage of incarnate lamas in the KARMA BKA' BRGYUD subsect of the BKA' BRGYUD sect of Tibetan Buddhism. Because of his black crown, the Karma pa is sometimes called the "black hat" (zhwa nag) lama. In the nineteenth century, a Western misunderstanding of this term led to the presumption that there was a "Black Hat" sect of Tibetan Buddhism, a mistake that persists in some accounts of Tibetan Buddhism. The Western and Chinese division of major Tibetan sects into YELLOW HATS, RED HATS, and Black Hats has no corollary in Tibetan Buddhism and should be avoided.

**bla ma**. (lama). A Tibetan term of uncertain derivation, used to translate the Sanskrit word GURU, or "teacher." According to traditional paranomastic glosses, it means "none higher" and "high mother." Outside of Tibet, it is sometimes assumed that any Tibetan monk is a lama, but this is not the case. This misconception is reflected in the Chinese term lama jiao, or "teachings of the lama," the source of the European misnomer for Tibetan Buddhism, "Lamaism." Within Tibetan Buddhism, the term may be applied to any religious teacher, especially one's own teacher, regardless of whether the teacher is a monk or a layperson. In common Tibetan parlance, bla ma usually denotes an incarnate lama (SPRUL SKU).

**Bla ma g.yung drung dgon pa**. (Lama Yuru). The oldest Buddhist monastery in Ladakh and Zangskar; located 125 kilometers west of Leh, the capital of Ladakh. Bla ma g.yung drung is thought to have been founded between the tenth and eleventh centuries; the site is also believed to be a sacred BON site. According to traditional accounts, when NĀROPA came to the area to meditate in the eleventh century, he decided where the monastery would be built. He then magically drained a lake in the valley in order to make way for its construction. It is a 'BRUG PA BKA' BRGYUD monastery, and currently one of the most active monasteries in the region. Bla ma g.yung drung's library is also thought to be one of the oldest in Ladakh. The translator RIN CHEN BZANG PO built many temples at Bla ma g.yung drung.

**Bla ma Zhang**. [full name, Zhang tshal pa Brtson 'grus grags pa] (Shangtsalpa Tsöndrü Drakpa) (1123–1193). The founder of the TSHAL PA BKA' BRGYUD, one of the four major and eight minor subsects of the BKA' BRGYUD sect of Tibetan Buddhism (BKA' BRGYUD CHE BZHI CHUNG BRGYAD). He was an important figure in twelfth-century Tibet in both the religious and political realms. Born into an aristocratic family near LHA SA, he is said to have studied black magic in his youth. When both of his parents soon died, he attributed their deaths to his negative deeds and decided to become a Buddhist monk, receiving BHIKṢU ordination in 1148. In 1152, he met the nephew of SGAM PO PA, from whom he received instructions in MAHĀMUDRĀ, the subject of his best known work, *Phyag chen lam mchog mthar thug* ("Supreme Path of Mahāmudrā"). In 1175 he established his own community, Tshal gung thang, north of Lha sa, controlling the region with a law code of his own composition and his own militia, dismissing criticisms of his use of force with the claim that such acts were the skillful methods of the tantric master. However, he eventually agreed to renounce violence when he was requested to do so by the first KARMA PA, DUS GSUM MKHYEN PA.

**Blavatsky, Helena Petrovna**. (1831–1891). A founding member of the Theosophical Society, Blavatsky was born in Ukraine to an aristocratic family, the daughter of a military officer and a well-known novelist. She was largely self-educated, and traveled throughout the world for more than twenty years. Arriving in New York from Paris in 1873, two years later she and HENRY STEEL OLCOTT founded the Theosophical Society, an organization that played a prominent role in the introduction of Asian religions to Europe and America. The society's purpose focused on promoting the understanding and awareness of the nature of reality through various disciplines. Madame Blavatsky claimed to have spent seven years in Tibet studying with masters whom she called "mahatmas," preservers of an ancient wisdom that provided the foundation for all mystical traditions. She also claimed to have remained in telepathic communication with these masters throughout her life and to have translated their teachings from the Senzar language into English. After attempts at alliances with various Asian teachers in India, Madame Blavatsky concluded that the modern manifestations of Hinduism and Buddhism had drifted far from their original essence, so she devoted much of her writing to expounding the true teachings, which she sometimes referred to as "Esoteric Buddhism." Two of her most important works are *The Secret Doctrine* (1888) and *The Voice of the Silence* (1889); these provide an account of, and commentary on, the theory of spiritual evolution that she is said to have discovered in the ancient *Book of Dzyan*, written in the secret language of Senzar. Although this text has not been found, nor the Senzar language identified, *The Voice of the Silence* has been considered to be a Buddhist text by some prominent figures within the modern Buddhist tradition.

**Blo bzang chos kyi rgyal mtshan**. (Losang Chökyi Gyaltsen) (1570–1662). A Tibetan Buddhist scholar and incarnate lama (SPRUL SKU), revered as the first or the fourth PAṆ CHEN LAMA; he was the first to receive the title. He entered BKRA SHIS LHUN PO monastery at age seventeen and in 1601 ascended the throne as the monastery's abbot. He also later served as abbot of 'BRAS SPUNGS and SE RA. He lived during a formative period in Tibetan history that saw the rise to power of the DALAI

LAMA institution and the DGA' LDAN PHO BRANG government, and the demise of the political power of the KARMA BKA' BRGYUD sect and their Gtsang patrons. Blo bzang chos kyi rgyal mtshan was instrumental in forging alliances between the emerging DGE LUGS sect and powerful families associated with the RNYING MA sect. He discovered and served as tutor to the fifth Dalai Lama, NGAG DBANG BLO BZANG RGYA MTSHO, who recognized Blo bzang chos kyi rgyal mtshan's achievements and conferred on him the title paṇḍita chen po, or "great scholar," from which the name Paṇ chen Lama is derived. Blo bzang chos kyi rgyal mtsan is traditionally viewed as the fourth such master, with the first three prelates recognized posthumously as the previous incarnations, beginning with the Dge lugs founder TSONG KHA PA's disciple MKHAS GRUB DGE LEGS DPAL BZANG. For this reason, Blo bzang chos kyi rgyal mtshan is also sometimes considered the fourth Paṇ chen Lama.

**blo rigs**. [alt. blo rig] (lorik). In Tibetan, "mind and reasoning," "categories of mind" or "mind and awareness" (when spelled blo rig); a genre of Tibetan monastic textbook literature (yig cha) that sets forth the categories of mind so that beginners can learn the basic concepts of Buddhist epistemology and logic. This genre supplements, or is a subset of, the "collected topics" (BSDUS GRWA) genre of textbook that forms the basis of the curriculum during the first years of study in many Tibetan monasteries. The categories of mind are not fixed, but usually include subdivisions into seven, three, and pairs. The seven minds range on a scale from wrong consciousness (log shes), through doubt, assumption, and inference (ANUMĀNA), to direct perception (PRATYAKṢA); among the contrasting pairs of minds are "sense consciousness" (dbang shes) via the sense faculties (INDRIYA) and "mental consciousness" (yid shes) based on MANAS; minds that are tshad ma ("valid") and tshad min ("invalid"); conceptual (rtog bcas) and nonconceptual minds (rtog med); and minds that have a specifically characterized (SVALAKṢAṆA) appearing object (snang yul) and a generally characterized (SĀMĀNYALAKṢAṆA) appearing object. The last of the contrasting pairs is primary and secondary minds, or minds (CITTA) and mental factors (CAITTA). Longer discussion of this topic includes a discussion of the fifty-one mental factors in several subcategories. The explanation of mind in blo rigs draws mainly on terminology found in DHARMAKĪRTI's PRAMĀṆAVĀRTTIKA and its commentarial tradition, as well as the ABHIDHARMAKOŚABHĀṢYA.

**blo sbyong**. (lojong). In Tibetan, "mind training"; a tradition of Tibetan Buddhist practice associated especially with the BKA' GDAMS sect and providing pithy instructions on the cultivation of compassion (KARUṆĀ) and BODHICITTA. The trainings are based primarily on the technique for the equalizing and exchange of self and other, as set forth in the eighth chapter of ŚĀNTIDEVA's BODHICARYĀVATĀRA, a poem in ten chapters on the BODHISATTVA path. The practice is to transform the conception of self (ĀTMAGRAHA), characterized as a self-cherishing attitude (T. rang gces 'dzin) into cherishing others (gzhan gces 'dzin), by contemplating the illusory nature of the self, the faults in self-cherishing, and the benefits that flow from cherishing others. The training seeks to transform difficulties into reasons to reaffirm a commitment to bodhicitta. Dharmarakṣita's *Blo sbyong mtshon cha'i 'khor lo* (sometimes rendered as "Wheel of Sharp Weapons"), translated into Tibetan by ATIŚA DĪPAṂKARAŚRĪJÑĀNA and 'BROM STON, founders of the Bka' gdam sect, in the eleventh century; Glang ri thang pa's (Langri Thangpa) (1054–1123) BLO SBYONG TSHIG BRGYAD MA ("Eight Verses on Mind Training"); 'CHAD KA BA YE SHES RDO RJE's BLO SBYONG DON BDUN MA (Lojong döndünma) ("Seven Points of Mind Training"), and Hor ston Nam mkha'i dpal bzang's (1373–1447) *Blo sbyong nyi ma'i 'od zer* ("Mind Training like the Rays of the Sun") are four among a large number of widely studied and practiced blo sbyong texts. The *Blo sbyong mtshon cha'i 'khor lo*, for example, compares the bodhisattva to a hero who can withstand spears and arrows, and to a peacock that eats poison and becomes even more beautiful; it says difficulties faced in day-to-day life are reasons to strengthen resolve because they are like the spears and arrow of karmic results launched by earlier unsalutary actions. From this perspective, circumstances that are ordinarily upsetting or depressing are transformed into reasons for happiness, by thinking that negative KARMAN has been extinguished. The influence of tantric Buddhism is discernable in the training in blo sbyong texts like the *Mtshon cha'i 'khor lo* that exhorts practitioners to imagine themselves as the deity YAMĀNTAKA and mentally launch an attack on the conception of self, imagining it as a battle. The conception of self is taken as the primary reason for the earlier unsalutary actions that caused negative results, and for engaging in present unsalutary deeds that harm others and do nothing to advance the practitioner's own welfare.

**Blo sbyong don bdun ma**. (Lojong Döndünma). In Tibetan, "Seven Points of Mind Training"; an influential Tibetan work in the BLO SBYONG ("mind training") genre. The work was composed by the BKA' GDAMS scholar 'CHAD KA BA YE SHES RDO RJE, often known as Dge bshes Mchad kha ba, based on the tradition of generating BODHICITTA known as "mind training" transmitted by the Bengali master ATIŚA DĪPAṂKARAŚRĪJÑĀNA. It also follows the system laid out previously by Glang ri thang pa (Langri Tangpa) in his BLO SBYONG TSHIG BRGYAD MA ("Eight Verses on Mind Training"). Comprised of a series of pithy instructions and meditative techniques, the *Blo sbyong don bdun ma* became influential in Tibet, with scholars from numerous traditions writing commentaries to it. According to the commentary of the nineteenth-century Tibetan polymath 'JAM MGON KONG SPRUL, the seven points covered in the treatise are: (1) the preliminaries to mind training, which include the contemplations on the preciousness of human rebirth, the reality of death and impermanence, the shortcomings of SAṂSĀRA, and the effects of KARMAN; (2) the actual practice of training in bodhicitta; (3) transforming adverse conditions into the path of awakening; (4) utilizing the practice in one's entire life; (5) the evaluation of mind training; (6) the commitments of mind training; and (7) guidelines for mind training.

**Blo sbyong tshig brgyad ma**. (Lojong Tsikgyema). In Tibetan, "Eight Verses on Mind Training"; a text composed by the BKA' GDAMS scholar Glang ri thang pa (Langri Thangpa, 1054–1123), based upon the instructions for generating BODHICITTA transmitted to Tibet by the Bengali master ATIŚA DĪPAṂKARAŚRĪJÑĀNA. The work became famous in Tibet for its penetrating advice for the practice of compassion (KARUṆĀ). It formed the basis for future influential works, including the often-quoted BLO SBYONG DON BDUN MA ("Seven Points of Mind Training"), by the Bka' gdams scholar 'CHAD KA BA YE SHES RDO RJE, written several decades later. The first seven verses teach the practice of conventional (SAṂVṚTI) bodhicitta, and the last verse ultimate (PARAMĀRTHA) bodhicitta. The first training is to view sentient beings as wish-granting gems because it is only by feeling compassion for beings that bodhisattvas reach enlightenment; the second is to cultivate an attitude similar to a person of low status whose natural place is serving others; and the third is to immediately confront and counteract afflictions (KLEŚA) (here understood specifically as selfishness, attachment to one's own interests, and hatred for those who oppose them). The fourth training is to treat people who are actually cruel as extremely rare and precious because they present an opportunity to practice patience and compassion, without which enlightenment is impossible; the fifth is the famous advice to "give all victory to others; take all defeat for yourself;" the sixth is to treat ungrateful persons as special gurus, and the seventh is to practice GTONG LEN (giving and taking), a practice of breathing out love and compassion and breathing in the sufferings of others. The eighth training is in a mind free from all conceptions.

**Blue Cliff Record**. See BIYAN LU.

**Blyth, Reginald H**. (1898–1964). An early English translator of Japanese poetry, with a particular interest in ZEN Buddhism. Blyth was born in Essex; his father was railway clerk. He was imprisoned for three years during the First World War as a conscientious objector. In 1925, he traveled to Korea, then a Japanese colony, where he taught English at Keijō University in Seoul. It was there that he developed his first interest in Zen through the priest Hanayama Taigi. After a brief trip to England, he returned to Seoul and then went to Japan, where he taught English in Kanazawa. With the outbreak of the Pacific War, Blyth was interned as an enemy alien, despite having expressed sympathy for the Japanese cause. Although he remained interned throughout the war, he was allowed to continue his studies, and in 1942 published his most famous work, *Zen in English Literature and Oriental Classics*, which sought to identify Zen elements in a wide range of literature. After the war, Blyth served as a liaison between the Japanese imperial household and the Allies, later becoming a professor of English at Gakushuin University, where one of his students was the future emperor Akihito (b. 1933). After the war, he published a four-volume collection of his translations of Japanese haiku poetry, which was largely responsible for European and American interest in haiku during the 1950s, among the Beat Poets and others, and the writing of haiku in languages other than Japanese. Subsequent scholarship has questioned the strong connection that Blyth saw between Zen and haiku. Blyth died in Japan and is buried in Kamakura next to his friend D. T. SUZUKI.

**Bo**. (J. Haku; K. Paek 帛). Ethnikon used in China for monks who hailed from KUCHA, an Indo-European oasis kingdom along the SILK ROAD, at the northern edge of the Takla Makhan desert in Central Asia. The Chinese is the transcription of the surname of the royal family of Kucha, and thus applied to everyone who came from the region. See FOTUDENG; SHI.

**bodaiji**. (菩提寺). In Japanese, literally "BODHI temple"; also known as bodaiin, bodaisho, or DANNADERA. Bodaiji are temples that flourished mainly during the Edo period under the parish system (DANKA SEIDO) established by the Tokugawa shogunate. Parishioners, known as danka or DAN'OTSU, were required to register at these local temples. By establishing the danka and terauke ("temple support") system, the early Tokugawa shogunate hoped to eradicate the threat of Christianity as they had witnessed it in the Christian-led Shimabara Uprising of 1637. During the Edo period, the bodaiji primarily offered funerary and memorial services for the ancestors of its parishioners and in many cases came to function as cemeteries. Festivals for the dead such as bon (see YULANBEN) and higan were also held annually at these temples. Although the danka system was abolished during the Meiji period, the bodaiji continue to function as memorial temples in modern Japan.

**Bodawpaya**. (r. 1782–1819). Burmese king and sixth monarch of the Konbaung dynasty (1752–1885). Originally known as Badon Min, he was the fourth son of Alaungpaya (r. 1752–1760), founder of the dynasty, and ascended to the throne through usurpation. His official regnal title was Hsinpyumyashin, "Lord of Many White Elephants"; the name by which he is most commonly known, Bodawpaya, "Lord Grandfather," is a posthumous sobriquet. Immediately upon becoming king in 1782, he began construction of a new capital, AMARAPURA, and convened a conclave of abbots, known as the THUDHAMMA (P. Sudhamm) council, to oversee a reform of the Burmese SAṂGHA. In 1784, he conquered the kingdom of Arakan and transported its colossal palladium, the MAHĀMUNI image of the Buddha (see ARAKAN BUDDHA), to Amarapura and enshrined it in a temple to the north of the city. Later, in 1787 he dispatched a Buddhist mission to Arakan to bring the Arakanese THERAVĀDA saṃgha into conformity with Thudhamma standards. In 1791 Buddhist missions were sent from the capital to forty-two cities around the realm, each equipped with Thudhamma handbooks and newly edited copies of the Buddhist canon (tipiṭaka; S. TRIPIṬAKA). The missions were charged with the threefold task of defrocking unworthy monks, disestablishing local monastic fraternities, and reordaining worthy monks from these local groups into a single empire-wide monastic order under Thudhamma control. In conjunction with this policy of saṃgha unification, a standardized syllabus for monastic education was promulgated and monks and novices throughout the realm were thenceforth required to pass state-administered Pāli examinations or to leave the order. That same year (1791), Bodawpaya retired from the palace, placing the daily affairs of the kingdom in the hands of his son, the crown prince. While retaining ultimate royal authority, he donned the robes of a mendicant and took up residence at Mingun, some fifteen miles north of Amarapura on the opposite bank of the Irrawaddy River. There, he oversaw for several years the construction of the great Mingun pagoda, which, if it had been completed, would have been the largest pagoda in the world. The labor force for this project, numbering some twenty thousand people, was conscripted from the vanquished kingdom of Arakan. Strict and austere in temperament, Bodawpaya was quick to suppress heresy and banned the use of intoxicants and the slaughter of cattle, on penalty of death. He was enamored of Hindu science and sent several missions to India to acquire Brahmanical treatises on medicine, alchemy, astrology, calendrics, and what he hoped would be original Indian recensions of Buddhist scriptures. His missions reached BODHGAYĀ and returned with models of the main shrine and maps of its environs, which were used to create a miniature replica of the site at Mingun. He appointed Indian brāhmaṇas to refine court punctilio and attempted to reform the Burmese calendar along Indian lines. The calendar reforms were rejected by monastic leaders and this rebuff appears to have caused the king to become increasingly critical of the monkhood. Toward the end of his reign, Bodawpaya defrocked the Thudhamma patriarch, declaring the dispensation (P. sāsana; S. ŚĀSANA) of Gotama (GAUTAMA) Buddha to be extinct and its saṃgha therefore defunct. This attempt to disestablish the Burmese saṃgha met with little success outside the capital and was later abandoned. Bodawpaya's military campaigns against Arakan and Assam extended the borders of the Burmese empire to the frontiers of the British East India Company. The cruelty of Bodawpaya's rule in Arakan created an influx of refugees into British territory, who were regularly pursued by Burmese troops. Although British diplomacy kept tensions with the Burmese kingdom under control throughout Bodawpaya's reign, the stage was set for eventual military conflict between the two powers and the subsequent British conquest of Burma in three wars during the nineteenth century.

**Bodhgayā**. (S. Buddhagayā). Modern Indian place name for the most significant site in the Buddhist world, renowned as the place where ŚĀKYAMUNI Buddha (then, still the BODHISATTVA prince SIDDHĀRTHA) became a buddha while meditating under the BODHI TREE at the "seat of enlightenment" (BODHIMAṆḌA) or the "diamond seat" (VAJRĀSANA). The site is especially sacred because, according to tradition, not only did Śākyamuni Buddha attain enlightenment there, but all buddhas of this world system have or will do so, albeit under different species of trees. Bodhgayā is situated along the banks of the NAIRAÑJANĀ river, near RĀJAGṚHA, the ancient capital city of the MAGADHA kingdom. Seven sacred places are said to be located in Bodhgayā, each being a site where the Buddha stayed during each of the seven weeks following his enlightenment. These include, in addition to the bodhimaṇḍa under the Bodhi tree: the place where the Buddha sat facing the Bodhi tree during the second week, with an unblinking gaze (and hence the site of the animeṣalocana caitya); the place where the Buddha walked back and forth in meditation (CAṄKRAMA) during the third week; the place called the ratnagṛha, where the Buddha meditated during the fourth week, emanating rays of light from his body; the place under the ajapāla tree where the god BRAHMĀ requested that the Buddha turn the wheel of the dharma (DHARMACAKRAPRAVARTANA) during the fifth week; the lake where the NĀGA MUCILINDA used his hood to shelter the Buddha from a storm during the sixth week; and the place under the rājāyatana tree where the merchants TRAPUṢA and BHALLIKA met the Buddha after the seventh week, becoming his first lay disciples. ¶ Located in the territory of MAGADHA (in modern Bihar), the ancient Indian kingdom where the Buddha spent much of his teaching career, Bodhgayā is one of the four major pilgrimage sites (MAHĀSTHĀNA) sanctioned by the Buddha himself, along with LUMBINĪ in modern-day Nepal, where the Buddha was born; the Deer Park (MṚGADĀVA) at SĀRNĀTH, where he first taught by "turning the wheel of the dharma" (DHARMACAKRAPRAVARTANA); and KUŚINAGARĪ in Uttar Pradesh, where he passed into PARINIRVĀṆA. According to the AŚOKĀVADĀNA, the emperor AŚOKA visited Bodhgayā with the monk UPAGUPTA and established a STŪPA at the site. There is evidence that Aśoka erected a pillar and shrine at the site during the third century BCE. A more elaborate structure, called the vajrāsana GANDHAKUṬĪ ("perfumed chamber of the diamond seat"), is depicted in a relief at Bodhgayā, dating from c. 100 BCE. It shows a two-storied structure supported by pillars, enclosing the Bodhi tree and the vajrāsana, the "diamond seat," where the Buddha sat on the night of his enlightenment. The forerunner of the present temple is described by the Chinese pilgrim XUANZANG. This has led scholars to speculate that the structure was built sometime between the third and sixth centuries CE, with subsequent renovations. Despite various persecutions by non-Buddhist Indian kings, the site continued to receive patronage, especially during the Pāla period, from which many of the surrounding monuments date. A monastery, called the Bodhimaṇḍavihāra, was established there and flourished for several centuries. FAXIAN mentions three monasteries at Bodhgayā; Xuanzang found only one, called the Mahābodhisaṃghārāma (see MAHĀBODHI TEMPLE). The temple and its environs fell into neglect after the Muslim invasions that began in the thirteenth century. British photographs from the nineteenth century show the temple in ruins. Restoration of the site was ordered by the British governor-general of Bengal in 1880, with a small eleventh-century replica of the temple serving as a model. There is a tall central tower some 165 feet (fifty meters) in height, with a high arch over the entrance with smaller towers at the four corners. The central tower houses a small temple with an image of the Buddha. The temple is surrounded by stone railings, some dating from 150 BCE, others from the Gupta period (300–600 CE) that preserve important carvings. In 1886, EDWIN ARNOLD visited Bodhgayā. He published an account of his visit, which was read by ANAGĀRIKA DHARMAPĀLA and others. Arnold described a temple surrounded by hundreds of broken statues scattered in the jungle. The Mahābodhi Temple itself had stood in ruins prior to renovations undertaken by the British in 1880. Also of great concern was the fact that the site had been under Śaiva control since the eighteenth century, with reports of animal sacrifice taking place in the environs of the temple. Dharmapāla visited Bodhgayā himself in 1891, and returned to Sri Lanka, where he worked with a group of leading Sinhalese Buddhists to found the MAHĀBODHI SOCIETY with the aim of restoring Bodhgayā as place of Buddhist worship and pilgrimage. The society undertook a series of unsuccessful lawsuits to that end. In 1949, after Indian independence, the Bodhgayā Temple Act was passed, which established a committee of four Buddhists and four Hindus to supervise the temple and its grounds. The Government of India asked Anagārika Munindra, a Bengali monk and active member of the Mahābodhi Society, to oversee the restoration of Bodhgayā. Since then, numerous Buddhist countries —including Bhutan, China, Japan, Myanmar, Nepal, Sikkim, Sri Lanka, Thailand, Tibet, and Vietnam—have constructed (or restored) their own temples and monasteries in Bodhgayā, each reflecting its national architectural style. In 2002, the Mahābodhi Temple was named a UNESCO World Heritage Site.

**bodhi**. (T. byang chub; C. puti/jue; J. bodai/kaku; K. pori/kak 菩提/覺). In Sanskrit and Pāli, "awakening," "enlightenment"; the consummate knowledge that catalyzes the experience of liberation (VIMOKṢA) from the cycle rebirth. Bodhi is of three discrete kinds: that of perfect buddhas (SAMYAKSAṂBODHI); that of PRATYEKABUDDHAs or "solitary enlightened ones" (pratyekabodhi); and that of ŚRĀVAKAs or disciples (śrāvakabodhi). The content of the enlightenment experience is in essence the understanding of the FOUR NOBLE TRUTHS (catvāry āryasatyāni): namely, the truth of suffering (DUḤKHA), the truth of the cause of suffering (SAMUDAYA), the truth of the cessation of suffering (NIRODHA), and the truth of the path leading to the cessation of suffering (MĀRGA). Bodhi is also elaborated in terms of its thirty-seven constituent factors (BODHIPĀKṢIKADHARMA) that are mastered in the course of perfecting one's understanding, or the seven limbs of awakening (BODHYAṄGA) that lead to the attainment of the "threefold knowledge" (TRIVIDYĀ; P. tevijjā): "recollection of former lives" (S. PŪRVANIVĀSĀNUSMṚTI; P. pubbenivāsānussati), the "divine eye" (DIVYACAKṢUS; P. dibbacakkhu), which perceives that the death and rebirth of beings occurs according to their actions (KARMAN), and the "knowledge of the extinction of the contaminants" (ĀSRAVAKṢAYA; P. āsavakkayañāṇa). Perfect buddhas and solitary buddhas (pratyekabuddha) become enlightened through their own independent efforts, for they discover the four noble truths on their own, without the aid of a teacher in their final lifetime (although pratyekabuddhas may rely on the teachings of a buddha in previous lifetimes). Of these two types of buddhas, perfect buddhas are then capable of teaching these truths to others, while solitary buddhas are not. Śrāvakas, by contrast, do not become enlightened on their own but are exposed to the teachings of perfect buddhas and through the guidance of those teachings gain the understanding they need to attain awakening. Bodhi also occupies a central place in MAHĀYĀNA religious conceptions. The Mahāyāna ideal of the BODHISATTVA means literally a "being" (SATTVA) intent on awakening (bodhi) who has aroused the aspiration to achieve buddhahood or the "thought of enlightenment" (BODHICITTA; BODHICITTOTPĀDA). The Mahāyāna, especially in its East Asian manifestations, also explores in great detail the prospect that enlightenment is something that is innate to the mind (see BENJUE; HONGAKU) rather than inculcated, and therefore need not be developed gradually but can instead be realized suddenly (see DUNWU). The Mahāyāna also differentiates between the enlightenment (bodhi) of śrāvakas and pratyekabuddhas and the full enlightenment (samyaksaṃbodhi) of a buddha. According to Indian and Tibetan commentaries on the PRAJÑĀPĀRAMITĀ sūtras, buddhas achieve full enlightenment not beneath the BODHI TREE in BODHGAYĀ, but in the AKANIṢṬHA heaven in the form of a SAṂBHOGAKĀYA, or enjoyment body remaining for eternity to work for the welfare of sentient beings. The bodhisattva who strives for enlightenment and achieves buddhahood beneath the Bodhi tree is a NIRMĀṆAKĀYA, a conjured body meant to inspire the world. See also WU; JIANWU.

**Bodhicaryāvatāra**. (T. Byang chub sems dpa'i spyod pa la 'jug pa; C. Putixing jing; J. Bodaigyōkyō; K. Porihaeng kyŏng 菩提行經). In Sanskrit, lit. "Introduction to the Practice of Enlightenment," a.k.a. *Bodhisattvacaryāvatāra*, "Introduction to the Bodhisattva Practice"; a poem about the BODHISATTVA path, in ten chapters, written by the Indian poet ŚĀNTIDEVA (fl. c. 685–763). The verse is regarded as one of the masterpieces of late Indian MAHĀYĀNA Buddhism, eliciting substantial commentary in both India and Tibet. The most influential of the Indian commentaries is the *Bodhicaryāvatārapañjikā* by PRAJÑĀKARAMATI. The text is especially important in Tibetan Buddhism, where it has long been memorized by monks and where stanzas from the text are often cited in both written and oral religious discourse. The poem is an extended reverie on the implications of the "aspiration for enlightenment" (BODHICITTA) that renders a person a bodhisattva, and on the deeds of the bodhisattva, the six perfections (PĀRAMITĀ). In the first chapter, Śāntideva distinguishes between two forms of bodhicitta, the intentional (PRAṆIDHICITTOTPĀDA) and the practical (PRASTHĀNACITTOTPĀDA), comparing them to the decision to undertake a journey and then actually setting out on that journey. In the fifth chapter he provides a famous argument for patience (KṢĀNTI), stating that in order to walk uninjured across a surface of sharp stones, one can either cover the entire world with leather or one can cover the sole of one's foot with leather; in the same way, in order to survive the anger of enemies, one can either kill them all or practice patience. In the eighth chapter, he sets forth the technique for the equalizing and exhange of self and other, regarded in Tibet as one of the two chief means of cultivating bodhicitta. The lengthiest chapter is the ninth, devoted to wisdom (PRAJÑĀ). Here Śāntideva refutes a range of both non-Buddhist and Buddhist positions. On the basis of this chapter, Śāntideva is counted as a PRĀSAṄGIKA in the Tibetan doxographical system. According to legend, when Śāntideva recited this chapter to the monks of NĀLANDĀ monastery, he began to rise into the air, leaving some questions as to precisely how the chapter ends. The final chapter is a prayer, often recited independently.

**bodhicitta**. (T. byang chub kyi sems; C. putixin; J. bodaishin; K. porisim 菩提心). In Sanskrit, "thought of enlightenment" or "aspiration to enlightenment"; the intention to reach the complete, perfect enlightenment (ANUTTARASAMYAKSAṂBODHI) of the buddhas, in order to liberate all sentient beings in the universe from suffering. As the generative cause that leads to the eventual achievement of buddhahood and all that it represents, bodhicitta is one of the most crucial terms in MAHĀYĀNA Buddhism. The achievement of bodhicitta marks the beginning of the BODHISATTVA path: bodhicitta refers to the aspiration that inspires the bodhisattva, the being who seeks buddhahood. In some schools of Mahāyāna Buddhism, bodhicitta is conceived as being latent in all sentient beings as the "innately pure mind" (prakṛtipariśuddhacitta), as, for example, in the MAHĀVAIROCANĀBHISAṂBODHISŪTRA: "Knowing one's own mind according to reality is BODHI, and bodhicitta is the innately pure mind that is originally existent." In this sense, bodhicitta was conceived as a universal principle, related to such terms as DHARMAKĀYA, TATHĀGATA, or TATHATĀ. However, not all schools of the Mahāyāna (e.g., some strands of YOGĀCĀRA) hold that all beings are destined for buddhahood and, thus, not all beings are endowed with bodhicitta. Regardless of whether or not bodhicitta is regarded as somehow innate, however, bodhicitta is also a quality of mind that must be developed, hence the important term BODHICITTOTPĀDA, "generation of the aspiration to enlightenment." Both the BODHISATTVABHŪMI and the MAHĀYĀNASŪTRĀLAṂKĀRA provide a detailed explanation of bodhicitta. In late Indian Mahāyāna treatises by such important authors as ŚĀNTIDEVA, KAMALAŚĪLA, and ATIŚA DĪPAṂKARAŚRĪJÑĀNA, techniques are set forth for cultivating bodhicitta. The development of bodhicitta also figures heavily in Mahāyāna liturgies, especially in those where one receives the bodhisattva precepts (BODHISATTVASAṂVARA). In this literature, two types of bodhicitta are enumerated. First, the "conventional bodhicitta" (SAṂVṚTIBODHICITTA) refers to a bodhisattva's mental aspiration to achieve enlightenment, as described above. Second, the "ultimate bodhicitta" (PARAMĀRTHABODHICITTA) refers to the mind that directly realizes either emptiness (ŚŪNYATĀ) or the enlightenment inherent in the mind. This "conventional bodhicitta" is further subdivided between PRAṆIDHICITTOTPĀDA, literally, "aspirational creation of the attitude" (where "attitude," CITTA, refers to bodhicitta), where one makes public one's vow (PRAṆIDHĀNA) to attain buddhahood; and PRASTHĀNACITTOTPĀDA, literally "creation of the attitude of setting out," where one actually sets out to practice the path to buddhahood. In discussing this latter pair, Śāntideva in his BODHICARYĀVATĀRA compares the first type to the decision to undertake a journey and the second type to actually setting out on the journey; in the case of the bodhisattva path, then, the first therefore refers to the process of developing the aspiration to buddhahood for the sake of others, while the second refers to undertaking the various practices of the bodhisattva path, such as the six perfections (PĀRAMITĀ). The AVATAṂSAKASŪTRA describes three types of bodhicitta, those like a herder, a ferryman, and a king. In the first case the bodhisattva first delivers all others into enlightenment before entering enlightenment himself, just as a herder takes his flock into the pen before entering the pen himself; in the second case, they all enter enlightenment together, just as a ferryman and his passengers arrive together at the further shore; and in the third, the bodhisattva first reaches enlightenment and then helps others to reach the goal, just as a king first ascends to the throne and then benefits his subjects. A standard definition of bodhicitta is found at the beginning of the ABHISAMAYĀLAṂKĀRA, where it is defined as an intention or wish that has two aims: buddhahood, and the welfare of those beings whom that buddhahood will benefit; the text also gives a list of twenty-two types of bodhicitta, with examples for each. Later writers like Ārya VIMUKTISENA and HARIBHADRA locate the *Abhisamayālaṃkāra*'s twenty-two types of bodhicitta at different stages of the bodhisattva path and at enlightenment. At the beginning of his MADHYAMAKĀVATĀRA, CANDRAKĪRTI compares compassion (KARUṆĀ) to a seed, water, and crops and says it is important at the start (where compassion begins the bodhisattva's path), in the middle (where it sustains the bodhisattva and prevents a fall into the limited NIRVĀṆA of the ARHAT), and at the end when buddhahood is attained (where it explains the unending, spontaneous actions for the sake of others that derive from enlightenment). Karuṇā is taken to be a cause of bodhicitta because bodhicitta initially arises and ultimately will persist, only if MAHĀKARUṆĀ ("great empathy for others' suffering") is strong. In part because of its connotation as a generative force, in ANUTTARAYOGATANTRA, bodhicitta comes also to refer to semen, especially in the practice of sexual yoga, where the physical seed (BĪJA) of awakening (representing UPĀYA) is placed in the lotus of wisdom (PRAJÑĀ).

**Bodhicittavivaraṇa**. (T. Byang chub sems 'grel). In Sanskrit, "Exposition of the Mind of Enlightenment"; a work traditionally ascribed to NĀGĀRJUNA, although the text is not cited by Nāgārjuna's commentators BUDDHAPĀLITA, CANDRAKĪRTI, or BHĀVAVIVEKA. This absence, together with apparently tantric elements in the text and the fact that it contains a sustained critique of VIJÑĀNAVĀDA, have led some scholars to conclude that it is not the work of the same Nāgārjuna who authored the MŪLAMADHYAMAKAKĀRIKĀ. Nonetheless, the work is widely cited in later Indian Mahāyāna literature and is important in Tibet. The text consists of 112 stanzas, preceded by a brief section in prose. It is essentially a compendium of MAHĀYĀNA theory and practice, intended for bodhisattvas, both monastic and lay, organized around the theme of BODHICITTA, both in its conventional aspect (SAṂVṚTIBODHICITTA) as the aspiration to buddhahood out of compassion for all sentient beings, and in its ultimate aspect (PARAMĀRTHABODHICITTA) as the insight into emptiness (ŚŪNYATĀ). In addition to the refutation of Vijñānavāda, the text refutes the self as understood by the TĪRTHIKAS and the SKANDHAS as understood by the ŚRĀVAKAS.

**bodhicittotpāda**. (T. byang chub kyi sems bskyed pa; C. fa puti xin; J. hotsubodaishin; K. pal pori sim 發菩提心). In Sanskrit, "generating the aspiration for enlightenment," "creating (utpāda) the thought (CITTA) of enlightenment (BODHI)"; a term used to describe both the process of developing BODHICITTA, the aspiration to achieve buddhahood, as well as the state achieved through such development. The MAHĀYĀNA tradition treats this aspiration as having great significance in one's spiritual career, since it marks the entry into the Mahāyāna and the beginning of the BODHISATTVA path. The process by which this "thought of enlightenment" (bodhicitta) is developed and sustained is bodhicittotpāda. Various types of techniques or conditional environments conducive to bodhicittotpāda are described in numerous Mahāyāna texts and treatises. The BODHISATTVABHŪMI says that there are four predominant conditions (ADHIPATIPRATYAYA) for generating bodhicitta: (1) witnessing an inconceivable miracle (ṛddhiprātihārya) performed by a buddha or a bodhisattva, (2) listening to a teaching regarding enlightenment (BODHI) or to the doctrine directed at bodhisattvas (BODHISATTVAPIṬAKA), (3) recognizing the dharma's potential to be extinguished and seeking therefore to protect the true dharma (SADDHARMA), (4) seeing that sentient beings are troubled by afflictions (KLEŚA) and empathizing with them. The *Fa putixinjing lun* introduces another set of four conditions for generating bodhicitta: (1) reflecting on the buddhas; (2) contemplating the dangers (ĀDĪNAVA) inherent in the body; (3) developing compassion (KARUṆĀ) toward sentient beings; (4) seeking the supreme result (PHALA). The Chinese apocryphal treatise DASHENG QIXIN LUN ("Awakening of Faith According to the Mahāyāna") refers to three types of bodhicittotpāda: that which derives from the accomplishment of faith, from understanding and practice, and from realization. JINGYING HUIYUAN (523–592) in his DASHENG YIZHANG ("Compendium on the Purport of Mahāyāna") classifies bodhicittotpāda into three groups: (1) the generation of the mind based on characteristics, in which the bodhisattva, perceiving the characteristics of SAṂSĀRA and NIRVĀṆA, abhors saṃsāra and aspires to seek nirvāṇa; (2) the generation of the mind separate from characteristics, in which the bodhisattva, recognizing that the nature of saṃsāra is not different from nirvāṇa, leaves behind any perception of their distinctive characteristics and generates an awareness of their equivalency; (3) the generation of the mind based on truth, in which the bodhisattva, recognizing that the original nature of bodhi is identical to his own mind, returns to his own original state of mind. The Korean scholiast WŎNHYO (617–686), in his *Muryangsugyŏng chongyo* ("Doctrinal Essentials of the 'Sūtra of Immeasurable Life'"), considers the four great vows of the bodhisattva (see C. SI HONGSHIYUAN) to be bodhicitta and divides its generation into two categories: viz., the aspiration that accords with phenomena (susa palsim) and the aspiration that conforms with principle (suri palsim). The topic of bodhicittotpāda is the subject of extensive discussion and exegesis in Tibetan Buddhism. For example, in his LAM RIM CHEN MO, TSONG KHA PA sets forth two techniques for developing this aspiration. The first, called the "seven cause and effect precepts" (rgyu 'bras man ngag bdun) is said to derive from ATIŚA DIPAṂKARAŚRĪJÑĀNA. The seven are (1) recognition of all sentient beings as having been one's mother in a past life, (2) recognition of their kindness, (3) the wish to repay their kindness, (4) love, (5) compassion, (6) the wish to liberate them from suffering, and (7) bodhicitta. The second, called the equalizing and exchange of self and other (bdag gzhan mnyam brje) is derived from the eighth chapter of ŚĀNTIDEVA's BODHICARYĀVATĀRA. It begins with the recognition that oneself and others equally want happiness and do not want suffering. It goes on to recognize that by cherishing others more than oneself, one ensures the welfare of both oneself (by becoming a buddha) and others (by teaching them the dharma). Mahāyāna sūtra literature typically assumes that, after generating the bodhicitta, the bodhisattva will require not one, but three "incalculable eons" (ASAṂKHYEYAKALPA) of time in order to complete all the stages (BHŪMI) of the bodhisattva path (MĀRGA) and achieve buddhahood. The Chinese HUAYAN ZONG noted, however, that the bodhisattva had no compunction about practicing for such an infinity of time, because he realized at the very inception of the path that he was already a fully enlightened buddha. They cite in support of this claim the statement in the "Brahmacaryā" chapter of the AVATAṂSAKASŪTRA that "at the time of the initial generation of the aspiration for enlightenment (bodhicittotpāda), complete, perfect enlightenment (ANUTTARASAMYAKSAṂBODHI) is already achieved."

**Bodhidharma**. (C. Putidamo; J. Bodaidaruma; K. Poridalma 菩提達磨) (c. late-fourth to early-fifth centuries). Indian monk who is the putative "founder" of the school of CHAN (K. SŎN, J. ZEN, V. THIỀN). The story of a little-known Indian (or perhaps Central Asian) emigré monk grew over the centuries into an elaborate legend of Bodhidharma, the first Chinese patriarch of the Chan school. The earliest accounts of a person known as Bodhidharma appear in the *Luoyang qielan ji* and XU GAOSENG ZHUAN, but the more familiar and developed image of this figure can be found in such later sources as the BAOLIN ZHUAN, LENGQIE SHIZI JI, LIDAI FABAO JI, ZUTANG JI, JINGDE CHUANDENG LU, and other "transmission of the lamplight" (CHUANDENG LU) histories. According to these sources, Bodhidharma was born as the third prince of a South Indian kingdom. Little is known about his youth, but he is believed to have arrived in China sometime during the late fourth or early fifth century, taking the southern maritime route according to some sources, the northern overland route according to others. In an episode appearing in the *Lidai fabao ji* and BIYAN LU, after arriving in southern China, Bodhidharma is said to have engaged in an enigmatic exchange with the devout Buddhist emperor Wu (464–549, r. 502–549) of the Liang dynasty (502–557) on the subject of the Buddha's teachings and merit-making. To the emperor's questions about what dharma Bodhidharma was transmitting and how much merit (PUṆYA) he, Wudi, had made by his munificent donations to construct monasteries and ordain monks, Bodhidharma replied that the Buddha's teachings were empty (hence there was nothing to transmit) and that the emperor's generous donations had brought him no merit at all. The emperor seems not to have been impressed with these answers, and Bodhidharma, perhaps disgruntled by the emperor's failure to understand the profundity of his teachings, left for northern China, taking the Yangtze river crossing (riding a reed across the river, in a scene frequently depicted in East Asian painting). Bodhidharma's journey north eventually brought him to a cave at the monastery of SHAOLINSI on SONGSHAN, where he sat in meditation for nine years while facing a wall (MIANBI), in so-called "wall contemplation" (BIGUAN). During his stay on Songshan, the Chinese monk HUIKE is said to have become Bodhidharma's disciple, allegedly after cutting off his left arm to show his dedication. This legend of Bodhidharma's arrival in China is eventually condensed into the famous Chan case (GONG'AN), "Why did Bodhidharma come from the West?" (see XILAI YI). Bodhidharma's place within the lineage of Indian patriarchs vary according to text and tradition (some list him as the twenty-eighth patriarch), but he is considered the first patriarch of Chan in China. Bodhidharma's name therefore soon became synonymous with Chan and subsequently with Sŏn, Zen, and Thiền. Bodhidharma, however, has often been confused with other figures such as BODHIRUCI, the translator of the LAṄKĀVATĀRASŪTRA, and the Kashmiri monk DHARMATRĀTA, to whom the DHYĀNA manual DAMODUOLUO CHAN JING is attributed. The *Lidai fabao ji*, for instance, simply fused the names of Bodhidharma and Dharmatrāta and spoke of a Bodhidharmatrāta whose legend traveled with the *Lidai fabao ji* to Tibet. Bodhidharma was even identified as the apostle Saint Thomas by Jesuit missionaries to China, such as Matteo Ricci. Several texts, a number of which were uncovered in the DUNHUANG manuscript cache in Central Asia, have been attributed to Bodhidharma, but their authorship remains uncertain. The ERRU SIXING LUN seems to be the only of these texts that can be traced with some certainty back to Bodhidharma or his immediate disciples. The legend of Bodhidharma in the *Lengqie shizi ji* also associates him with the transmission of the *Laṅkāvatārasūtra* in China. In Japan, Bodhidharma is often depicted in the form of a round-shaped, slightly grotesque-looking doll, known as the "Daruma doll." Like much of the rest of the legends surrounding Bodhidharma, there is finally no credible evidence connecting Bodhidharma to the Chinese martial arts traditions (see SHAOLINSI).

**bodhimaṇḍa**. (T. byang chub snying po; C. daochang; J. dōjō; K. toryang 道場). In Sanskrit (and very late Pāli), "seat of enlightenment" or "platform of enlightenment," the place in BODHGAYĀ under the BODHI TREE where the Buddha sat when he achieved liberation from the cycle of birth and death (SAṂSĀRA). (The word maṇḍa in this compound refers to the scum that forms on the top of boiling rice or the heavy cream that rises to the top of milk, thus suggesting the observable and most essential signs of the supreme act of BODHI, or enlightenment. Note that Western literature sometimes wrongly transcribes the term as *bodhimaṇḍala rather than bodhimaṇḍa.) All buddhas are associated with such a place, and it is presumed that all BODHISATTVAs of this world system as well will sit on such a seat before attaining buddhahood. The term is also used to refer to the region surrounding the seat itself, which, in the case of ŚĀKYAMUNI, is Bodhgayā. The bodhimaṇḍa is also known as the VAJRĀSANA ("diamond seat"), since it is the only site on earth strong enough to bear the pressures unleashed by the battle for enlightenment. Buddhist iconography often depicts the Buddha just prior to his enlightenment sitting on the bodhimaṇḍa in the "earth-touching gesture" (BHŪMISPARŚAMUDRĀ), i.e., with his right hand touching the ground, calling the earth to bear witness to his achievement. The bodhimaṇḍa is often said to be the center or navel of the world and thus can be understood as what early scholars of religion called an axis mundi—the liminal site between divine and profane realms; according to the ABHIDHARMAKOŚABHĀṢYA, the various hot and cold hells (see NĀRAKA) are located not below Mount SUMERU but below the bodhimaṇḍa. In medieval East Asia, the Chinese term for bodhimaṇḍa began to be used to designate a "ritual precinct," viz., a site where such critical Buddhist rituals as ordinations were held, and by the seventh century came to be commonly used as the equivalent of "monastery" (si). In Korea, toryang (= bodhimaṇḍa) is also used to designate the central courtyard around which are arrayed the most important shrine halls in a monastery.

**Bodhiñāṇa**. (1917–1992). See AJAHN CHAH BODHIÑĀṆA.

**bodhipakṣa**. (S). See BODHIPĀKṢIKADHARMA.

**bodhipākṣikadharma**. [alt. -pakṣa-; -pakṣika-] (P. bodhipakkhiyadhamma; T. byang chub kyi phyogs kyi chos; C. puti fen/sanshiqi daopin; J. bodaibun/sanjūshichidōbon; K. pori pun/samsipch'il top'um 菩提分/三十七道品). In Sanskrit, "factors pertaining to awakening" or "wings of awakening." There are thirty-seven factors pertaining to enlightenment (saptatriṃśad bodhipākṣikā dharmāḥ), a conflation of seven distinct lists of practices: (1–4) the four foundations of mindfulness (SMṚTYUPASTHĀNA, P. SATIPAṬṬHĀNA), (5–8) the four right efforts or abandonments (SAMYAKPRADHĀNA, P. sammāpadhāna), (9–12) the four requisites of supranormal power (ṚDDHIPĀDA, P. iddhipāda), (13–17) the five spiritual faculties (INDRIYA), (18–22) the five mental powers (BALA), (23–29) the seven factors of enlightenment (BODHYAṄGA, P. bojjhaṅga), and (30–37) the noble eightfold path (ĀRYĀṢṬĀṄGAMĀRGA). This comprehensive list is said to encompass the entire teachings of the Buddha and may constitute one of, if not the, earliest examples in Buddhist literature of "matrices" (MĀTṚKĀ; P. mātikā), the dharma lists that were the foundation of the ABHIDHARMA. As additional psychic characteristics associated with meditative states were added to this original list of bodhipākṣikadharmas, the various factors listed in these mātṛkā came to be considered an exhaustive accounting of the "elements of reality" (DHARMA).

**Bodhipathapradīpa**. (T. Byang chub lam gyi sgron ma). In Sanskrit, "Lamp for the Path to Enlightenment"; a work composed by the Indian scholar ATIŚA DĪPAṂKARAŚRĪJÑĀNA at THO LING GTSUG LAG KHANG shortly after he arrived in Tibet in 1042. Tibetan histories often note that Atiśa wrote this text in order to clarify problematic points of Buddhist practice, especially TANTRA, which were thought to have degenerated and become distorted, and to show that tantra did not render basic Buddhist practice irrelevant. The *Bodhipathapradīpa* emphasizes a gradual training in the practices of the MAHĀYĀNA and VAJRAYĀNA and became a prototype and textual basis first for the bstan rim, or "stages of the teaching" genre, and then for the genre of Tibetan religious literature known as LAM RIM, or "stages of the path." It is also an early source for the instructions and practice of BLO SBYONG, or "mind training." Atiśa wrote his own commentary (pañjikā) (*Commentary on the Difficult Points of the Lamp for the Path to Enlightenment*) to the text. The text says bodhisattvas must first follow one of the sets of PRĀTIMOKṢA disciplinary rules; based on those precepts, they practice the six perfections (PĀRAMITĀ); with those perfections as a solid foundation, they finally practice Buddhist tantra.

**Bodhirak, Phra**. (P. Bodhirakkha) (b. 1934). Thai Buddhist leader who is the founder of the SANTI ASOKE movement. Born in 1934 in northeastern Thailand as Mongkhon Rakphong, he became a well-known TV entertainer, songwriter, and movie producer before abruptly walking away from his career at the age of thirty-six to seek the dhamma. He was ordained in 1970 into first the THAMMAYUT and later the MAHĀNIKAI orders, but eventually left both orders to establish the independent Santi Asoke ("People of Asoke") movement, which grew rapidly. Bodhirak was finally excommunicated from the Thai saṅgha in 1989 for defying national ecclesiastical law (including publicly proclaiming himself to be a "once-returner," or sakadāgāmi [S. SAKṚDĀGĀMIN]) and for his controversial views on Buddhism, which mainstream traditions found to be iconoclastic and doctrinaire. He continues to live as a monk and is an influential figure in contemporary Thai Buddhism; he and his movement have also come to play a role in Thai politics through the Phalang Dhamma Party, which has ties to Santi Asoke.

**Bodhiruci**. (C. Putiliuzhi; J. Bodairushi; K. Poriryuji 菩提流支) (fl. sixth century). A renowned Indian translator and monk (to be distinguished from a subsequent Bodhiruci [s.v.] who was active in China two centuries later during the Tang dynasty). Bodhiruci left north India for Luoyang, the Northern Wei capital, in 508. He is said to have been well versed in the TRIPIṬAKA and talented at incantations. Bodhiruci stayed at the monastery of YONGNINGSI in Luoyang from 508 to 512 and with the help of Buddhaśānta (d.u.) and others translated over thirty MAHĀYĀNA sūtras and treatises, most of which reflect the latest developments in Indian Mahāyāna, and especially YOGĀCĀRA. His translations include the DHARMASAṂGĪTI, SHIDIJING LUN, LAṄKĀVATĀRASŪTRA, VAJRACCHEDIKĀPRAJÑĀPĀRAMITĀSŪTRA, and the WULIANGSHOU JING YOUPOTISHE YUANSHENG JI, attributed to VASUBANDHU. Bodhiruci's translation of the *Shidijing lun*, otherwise known more simply as the *Di lun*, fostered the formation of a group of YOGĀCĀRA specialists in China that later historians retroactively call the DI LUN ZONG. According to a story in the LIDAI FABAO JI, a jealous Bodhiruci, assisted by a monk from SHAOLINSI on SONGSHAN named Guangtong (also known as Huiguang, 468–537), is said to have attempted on numerous occasions to poison the founder of the CHAN school, BODHIDHARMA, and eventually succeeded. Bodhiruci is also said to have played an instrumental role in converting the Chinese monk TANLUAN from Daoist longevity practices to the PURE LAND teachings of the GUAN WULIANGSHOU JING.

**Bodhiruci**. (C. Putiliuzhi; J. Bodairushi; K. Poriryuji 菩提流支) (d. 727). A renowned Indian translator and monk (to be distinguished from an earlier Bodhiruci [s.v.], who was active two centuries earlier during the Northern Wei dynasty). Bodhiruci is said to have been a south Indian who was invited to China by Emperor Gaozong (r. 649–683) of the Tang dynasty in 663, but did not arrive until thirty years later, in 693, during the reign of Empress WU ZETIAN (r. 684–704). He is said to have changed his name from Dharmaruci to Bodhiruci at the request of Empress Wu. He resided in the monastery of Foshoujisi, where he dedicated himself to the translation of several scriptures, including the RATNAMEGHASŪTRA

(*Baoyun jing*), ADHYARDHAŚATIKĀPRAJÑĀPĀRAMITĀSŪTRA (*Shixiang bore bolomi jing*), and *Gayāśīrṣasūtra*. Bodhiruci also assisted ŚIKṢĀNANDA in his translation of the AVATAṂSAKASŪTRA. In 706, he resided in the monastery Chongfusi and commenced the translation of the lengthy RATNAKŪṬASŪTRA, which the famed Chinese pilgrim and translator XUANZANG had failed to complete earlier. Bodhiruci's translation, edited into 120 rolls, was completed in 713.

**bodhisaṃbhāra**. (T. byang chub kyi tshogs; C. puti ju/puti ziliang; J. bodaigu/bodaishiryō; K. pori ku/pori charyang 菩提具/菩提資糧). In Sanskrit, "collection" of, or "equipment" (SAṂBHĀRA) for, "enlightenment" (BODHI); the term refers to specific sets of spiritual requisites (also called "accumulations") necessary for the attainment of awakening. The BODHISATTVA becomes equipped with these factors during his progress along the path (MĀRGA) leading to the attainment of buddhahood. In a buddha, the amount of this "enlightenment-collection" is understood to be infinite. These factors are often divided into two major groups: the collection of merit (PUṆYASAṂBHĀRA) and the collection of knowledge (JÑĀNASAṂBHĀRA). The collection of merit (PUṆYA) entails the strengthening of four perfections (PĀRAMITĀ): generosity (DĀNA), morality (ŚĪLA), patience (KṢĀNTI), and energy (VĪRYA). The collection of knowledge entails the cultivation of meditative states leading to the realization that emptiness (ŚŪNYATĀ) is the ultimate nature of all things. The bodhisaṃbhāra were expounded in the **Bodhisaṃbhāraka*, attributed to the MADHYAMAKA exegete NĀGĀRJUNA, which is now extant only in Dharmagupta's 609 CE Chinese translation, titled the *Puti ziliang lun*. In this treatise, Nāgārjuna explains that the acquisition, development, and fruition of these factors is an essentially interminable process: enlightenment will be achieved when these factors have been developed for as many eons as there are grains of sand in the Ganges River (see GAṄGĀNADĪVĀLUKĀ). The text also emphasizes the importance of compassion (KARUṆĀ), calling it the mother of perfect wisdom (PRAJÑĀPĀRAMITĀ). The perfection of wisdom sūtras stress that PARIṆĀMANĀ (turning over [merit]) and ANUMODANA (rejoicing [in the good deeds of others]) are necessary to amass the collection necessary to reach the final goal.

**bodhisattva**. (P. bodhisatta; T. byang chub sems dpa'; C. pusa; J. bosatsu; K. posal 菩薩). In Sanskrit, lit. "enlightenment being." The etymology is uncertain, but the term is typically glossed to mean a "being (SATTVA) intent on achieving enlightenment (BODHI)," viz., a being who has resolved to become a buddha. In the MAINSTREAM BUDDHIST SCHOOLS, the Buddha refers to himself in his many past lifetimes prior to his enlightenment as a bodhisattva; the word is thus generally reserved for the historical Buddha prior to his own enlightenment. In the MAHĀYĀNA traditions, by contrast, a bodhisattva can designate any being who resolves to generate BODHICITTA and follow the vehicle of the bodhisattvas (BODHISATTVAYĀNA) toward the achievement of buddhahood. The Mahāyāna denotation of the term first appears in the AṢṬASĀHASRIKĀPRAJÑĀPĀRAMITĀ, considered one of the earliest Mahāyāna sūtras, suggesting that it was already in use in this sense by at least the first century BCE. Schools differ on the precise length and constituent stages of the bodhisattva path (MĀRGA), but generally agree that it encompasses a huge number of lifetimes—according to many presentations, three incalculable eons of time (ASAṂKHYEYAKALPA)—during which the bodhisattva develops specific virtues known as perfections (PĀRAMITĀ) and proceeds through a series of stages (BHŪMI). Although all traditions agree that the bodhisattva is motivated by "great compassion" (MAHĀKARUṆĀ) to achieve buddhahood as quickly as possible, Western literature often describes the bodhisattva as someone who postpones his enlightenment in order to save all beings from suffering. This description is primarily relevant to the mainstream schools, where an adherent is said to recognize his ability to achieve the enlightenment of an ARHAT more quickly by following the teachings of a buddha, but chooses instead to become a bodhisattva; by choosing this longer course, he perfects himself over many lifetimes in order to achieve the superior enlightenment of a buddha at a point in the far-distant future when the teachings of the preceding buddha have completely disappeared. In the Mahāyāna, the nirvāṇa of the arhat is disparaged and is regarded as far inferior to buddhahood. Thus, the bodhisattva postpones nothing, instead striving to achieve buddhahood as quickly as possible. In both the mainstream and Mahāyana traditions, the bodhisattva, spending his penultimate lifetime in the TUṢITA heaven, takes his final rebirth in order to become a buddha and restore the dharma to the world. MAITREYA is the bodhisattva who will succeed the dispensation (ŚĀSANA) of the current buddha, GAUTAMA or ŚĀKYAMUNI; he is said to be waiting in the tuṣita heaven, until the conditions are right for him to take his final rebirth and become the next buddha in the lineage. In the Mahāyāna tradition, many bodhisattvas are described as having powers that rival or even surpass those of the buddhas themselves, and come to symbolize specific spiritual qualities, such as AVALOKITEŚVARA (the bodhisattva of compassion), MAÑJUŚRĪ (the bodhisattva of wisdom), VAJRAPĀṆI (the bodhisattva of power), and SAMANTABHADRA (the bodhisattva of extensive practice). In Western literature, these figures are sometimes referred to as "celestial bodhisattvas." ¶ In Korea, the term posal also designates laywomen residents of monasteries, who assist with the menial chores of cooking, preserving food, doing laundry, etc. These posal are often widows or divorcées, who work for the monastery in exchange for room and board for themselves and their children. The posal will often serve the monastery permanently and end up retiring there as well.

**bodhisattvabhūmi**. (T. byang chub sems dpa'i sa; C. pusa di; J. bosatsuji; K. posal chi 菩薩地). In Sanskrit, lit. "ground" or "stage" (BHŪMI) of a BODHISATTVA, referring to the systematic stages along the path (MĀRGA) of a bodhisattva's maturation into a buddha. A normative list of ten bhūmis, which becomes standard in many MAHĀYĀNA accounts of the bodhisattva path, appears in the DAŚABHŪMIKASŪTRA, a sūtra that was later incorporated into the AVATAṂSAKASŪTRA compilation. These ten stages (DAŚABHŪMI) of the *Daśabhūmikasūtra* correspond to the forty-first to fiftieth stages among the fifty-two bodhisattva stages, the comprehensive outline of the entire bodhisattva path taught in such scriptures as the Avataṃsakasūtra, the PUSA YINGLUO BENYE JING, and the RENWANG JING. The first bhūmi begins on the path of vision (DARŚANAMĀRGA), and the other nine bhūmis occur on the path of cultivation (BHĀVANĀMĀRGA). (For detailed explication of each stage, see DAŚABHŪMI s.v.) The PRAJÑĀPĀRAMITĀ SŪTRAS, and the MAHĀYĀNASŪTRĀLAṂKĀRA and ABHISAMAYĀLAṂKĀRA in their exegesis of these stages, explain that bodhisattvas reach each higher level along the path after completing the preparations (parikarman) for it; they set forth the same ten levels as the *Daśabhūmikasūtra* with the same names. Ārya VIMUKTISENA, in his exegesis of the *Abhisamayālaṃkāra*, says bodhisattvas on the tenth bhūmi are like TATHĀGATAS who have passed beyond all stages, and lists eight other stages corresponding roughly to the stages of the eight noble persons (ĀRYAPUDGALA), with the first through ninth bodhisattva bhūmis described as a transcendent ninth level. In contrast to the normative ten bhūmis described in the *Daśabhūmikasūtra*, MAITREYANĀTHA/ASAṄGA in the BODHISATTVABHŪMI instead outlines a system of seven stages (bhūmi), which are then correlated with the thirteen abodes (VIHĀRA). (See the following entry on the treatise for further explication.) The seven-bhūmi schema of the *Bodhisattvabhūmi* and the ten-bhūmi schema of the *Daśabhūmikasūtra* are independent systematizations.

**Bodhisattvabhūmi**. (T. Byang chub sems dpa'i sa; C. Pusa dichi jing; J. Bosatsujijikyō; K. Posal chiji kyŏng 菩薩地持經). In Sanskrit, "The Bodhisattva Stages"; a treatise on the entire vocation and training of a BODHISATTVA, attributed to MAITREYA/MAITREYANĀTHA or ASAṄGA (c. fourth century CE), the effective founder of the YOGĀCĀRA school. Sanskrit and Tibetan recensions are extant, as well as three different renderings in Chinese: (1) *Pusa dichi jing*, translated by DHARMAKṢEMA between 414–421 CE, which is also abbreviated as the "Treatise on the Bodhisattva Stages" (C. Dichi lun; J. Jijiron; K. Chiji non); (2) *Pusa shanjie jing*, translated by GUṆAVARMAN in 431 CE; and (3) a version incorporated as the fifteenth section of XUANZANG's Chinese translation of Asaṅga's YOGĀCĀRABHŪMIŚĀSTRA. In the Tibetan BSTAN 'GYUR, the *Bodhisattvabhūmi* appears as the sixteenth and penultimate part of the fundamental section (sa'i dngos gzhi) of the *Yogācārabhūmi* (which has a total of seventeen sections), but it is set apart as a separate work in 6,000 lines. The *Bodhisattvabhūmi* explains in three major sections the career and practices of a bodhisattva. The chapters on the abodes (vihārapaṭala) in the second major division and the chapter on stages (bhūmipaṭala) in the third section are considered especially important, because they provide a systematic outline of the soteriological process by which a bodhisattva attains enlightenment. ¶ In contrast to the ten stages (DAŚABHŪMI) of the bodhisattva path that are described in the DAŚABHŪMIKASŪTRA, the *Bodhisattvabhūmi* instead outlines a system of seven stages (BHŪMI), which are then correlated with the thirteen abodes (VIHĀRA): (1) The stage of innate potentiality (gotrabhūmi), which corresponds to the abode of innate potentiality (gotravihāra); (2) the stage of the practice of resolute faith (adhimukticaryābhūmi), corresponding to the abode of resolute faith (adhimukticaryāvihāra); (3) the stage of superior aspiration (śuddhādhyāśayabhūmi), which corresponds to the abode of extreme bliss (pramuditavihāra); (4) the stage of carrying out correct practices (caryāpratipattibhūmi), which includes the abode of superior morality (adhiśīlavihāra), the abode of superior concentration (adhicittavihāra), and the abode of the superior wisdom (adhiprajñavihāra), i.e., the abode of superior insight associated with the factors of enlightenment (bodhipakṣyapratisaṃyukto 'dhiprajñavihāra), the abode of superior insight associated with the truths (satyapratisaṃyukto 'dhiprajñavihāra), the abode of superior insight associated with the cessation of dependently arisen transmigration (pratītyasamutpādapravṛttinivṛttipratisaṃyukto 'dhiprajñavihāra), and the signless abode of applied practices and exertion (sābhisaṃskārasābhoganirnimittavihāra); (5) the stage of certainty (niyatabhūmi), which is equivalent to the signless abode that is free from application and exertion (anābhoganirnimittavihāra); (6) the stage of determined practice (niyatacaryābhūmi), which corresponds to the abode of analytical knowledge (pratisaṃvidvihāra); (7) the stage of arriving at the ultimate (niṣṭhāgamanabhūmi), which correlates with the abode of ultimate consummation [viz., of bodhisattvahood] (paramavihāra) and the abode of the tathāgata (tathāgatavihāra). In this schema, the first two stages are conceived as preliminary stages of the bodhisattva path: the first stage, the stage of innate potentiality (gotrabhūmi), is presumed to be a state in which the aspiration for enlightenment (BODHICITTA) has yet to be generated; the second stage, the stage of the practice of resolute faith (adhimukticaryābhūmi), is referred to as the stage of preparation (saṃbhārāvasthā) and applied practice (prayogāvasthā) in the case of the fivefold YOGĀCĀRA mārga schema, or alternatively to the ten faiths, ten abodes, ten practices, and ten dedications in the case of the comprehensive fifty-two stage bodhisattva path presented in the AVATAṂSAKASŪTRA, PUSA YINGLUO BENYE JING, and RENWANG JING. The third stage, the stage of superior aspiration, is regarded as corresponding to the first of the ten bhūmis in the *Daśabhūmikasūtra*; the fourth stage of carrying out correct practices corresponds to the second through seventh bhūmis in that rival schema; the fifth stage of certainty pertains to the eighth bhūmi; the stage of determined practice to the ninth bhūmi; and the stage of arriving at the ultimate to the tenth bhūmi. In fact, however, the seven-bhūmi schema of the *Bodhisattvabhūmi* and the ten-bhūmi schema of the *Daśabhūmikasūtra* developed independently of each other and it requires consider exegetical aplomb to correlate them. ¶ The *Bodhisattvabhūmi* also serves as an important source of information on another crucial feature of bodhisattva practice: the Mahāyāna interpretation of a set of moral codes specific to bodhisattvas (BODHISATTVAŚĪLA). The chapter on precepts (śīlapaṭala) in the first major section of the text provides an elaborate description of Mahāyāna precepts, which constitute the bodhisattva's perfection of morality (ŚĪLAPĀRAMITĀ). These precepts are classified into the "three sets of pure precepts" (trividhāni śīlāni; C. sanju jingjie, see ŚĪLATRAYA; TRISAṂVARA): (1) the saṃvaraśīla, or "restraining precepts," (cf. SAṂVARA), which refers to the "HĪNAYĀNA" rules of discipline (PRĀTIMOKṢA) that help adepts restrain themselves from all types of unsalutary conduct; (2) practicing all virtuous deeds (kuśaladharmasaṃgrāhakaśīla), which accumulates all types of salutary conduct; and (3) sattvārthakriyāśīla, which involve giving aid and comfort to sentient beings. Here, the first group corresponds to the generic hīnayāna precepts, while the second and third groups are regarded as reflecting a specifically Mahāyāna position on morality. Thus, the three sets of pure precepts are conceived as a comprehensive description of Buddhist views on precepts, which incorporates both hīnayāna and Mahāyāna perspectives into an overarching system. A similar treatment of the three sets of pure precepts is also found in the Chinese apocryphal sūtra FANWANG JING (see APOCRYPHA), thus providing a scriptural foundation in East Asia for an innovation originally appearing in an Indian treatise. ¶ In Tibet, the *Bodhisattvabhūmi* was a core text of the BKA' GDAMS sect, and its chapter on śīla was the basis for a large body of literature elaborating a VINAYA-type ritual for taking bodhisattva precepts in a Mahāyāna ordination ceremony. The SA SKYA PA master Grags pa rgyal mtshan's explanation of CANDRAGOMIN's synopsis of the morality chapter, and TSONG KHA PA's *Byang chub gzhung lam* are perhaps the best known works in this genre. In Tibet, the SDOM GSUM genre incorporates the *Bodhisattvabhūmi*'s three sets of pure precepts into a new scheme that reconciles hīnayāna and Mahāyāna with TANTRA.

**Bodhisattvacaryāvatāra**. (T. Byang chub sems dpa'i spyod pa la 'jug pa). An alternate title of the BODHICARYĀVATĀRA by ŚĀNTIDEVA. See BODHICARYĀVATĀRA.

**bodhisattva path**. See BODHISATTVAYĀNA; MĀRGA.

**Bodhisattvapiṭaka**. (T. Byang chub sems dpa'i sde snod; C. Pusazang jing; J. Bosatsuzōkyō; K. Posalchang kyŏng 菩薩藏經). In Sanskrit, "The Bodhisattva Basket," one of the earliest MAHĀYĀNA scriptures, written by at least the first century CE and perhaps even as early as the first century BCE. The text is no longer extant, but its antiquity is attested by its quotation in some of the earliest Mahāyāna sūtras translated into Chinese, including *LOKAKṢEMA's translation of the KĀŚYAPAPARIVARTA made in 179 CE and in DHARMARAKṢA's 289 CE rendering of the *Vimaladattāparipṛcchā*. The content of the anthology is unknown, but based on much later compilations bearing the same title (and which therefore might have been derived from the original *Bodhisattvapiṭaka*), the text must have been substantial in size (one later Chinese translation is twenty rolls in length) and have offered coverage of at least the six perfections (PĀRAMITĀ). Sections of the *Bodhisattvapiṭaka* may also have been subsumed in later collections of Mahāyāna materials, such as the RATNAKŪṬASŪTRA.

**bodhisattvapraṇidhāna**. (T. byang chub sems pa'i smon lam; C. pusa yuan; J. bosatsugan; K. posal wŏn 菩薩願). In Sanskrit, "bodhisattva vow"; the vow to achieve buddhahood in order to liberate all beings from suffering. Following the BODHICARYĀVATĀRA, the MAHĀYĀNA commentarial tradition considers this vow to be the point at which one makes a public pronouncement of one's aspiration to achieve buddhahood (PRAṆIDHICITTOTPĀDA), which is distinguished from the subsequent practice of this aspiration (PRASTHĀNACITTOTPĀDA), i.e., cultivating specific bodhisattva precepts (see BODHISATTVASAṂVARA) and mastering the six perfections (PĀRAMITĀ). In Mahāyāna sūtras, which tend to be less systematized, this vow is typically made before a buddha, who then offers a prediction (VYĀKARAṆA) that the aspirant will succeed in his quest; the person is then called one who will not turn back, or "irreversible" (AVAIVARTIKA). The recitation of the bodhisattva vow is a central component in many Mahāyāna liturgies. See also BODHICITTOTPĀDA.

**bodhisattva precepts**. See BODHISATTVASAṂVARA; BODHISATTVAŚĪLA; PUSA JIE; SDOM GSUM.

**bodhisattvasaṃvara**. (T. byang chub sems dpa'i sdom pa; C. pusa jie; J. bosatsukai; K. posal kye 菩薩戒). In Sanskrit, lit. "restraints for the BODHISATTVA"; the "restraints," "precepts," or code of conduct (SAṂVARA) for someone who has made the bodhisattva vow (BODHISATTVAPRAṆIDHĀNA; PRAṆIDHĀNA) to achieve buddhahood in order to liberate all beings from suffering. The mainstream moral codes for monastics that are recognized across all forms of Buddhism are listed in the PRĀTIMOKṢA, which refers to rules of discipline that help adepts restrain themselves from all types of unwholesome conduct. With the rise of various groups that came to call themselves the MAHĀYĀNA, different sets of moral codes developed. These are formulated, for example, in the BODHISATTVABHŪMI and Candragomin's *Bodhisattvasaṃvaraviṃśaka*, and in later Chinese apocrypha, such as the FANWANG JING. The mainstream prātimokṣa codes are set forth in the *Bodhisattvabhūmi* as saṃvaraśīla, or "restraining precepts." These are the first of three types of bodhisattva morality, called the "three sets of restraints" (TRISAṂVARA), which are systematized fully in Tibet in works like TSONG KHA PA's *Byang chub gzhung lam*. It seems that in the early Mahāyāna, people publicly took the famous bodhisattva vow, promising to achieve buddhahood in order to liberate all beings. A more formal code of conduct developed later, derived from a number of sources, with categories of root infractions and secondary infractions. The bodhisattva precepts, however, could be taken equally by laypeople and monastics, men and women, and formal ceremonies for conferring the precepts are set forth in a number of Mahāyāna treatises. In addition, there appear to have been ceremonies for the confession of infractions, modeled on the UPOṢADHA rituals. Some of the precepts have to do with interpersonal relations, prescribing the kind of altruistic behavior that one might expect from a bodhisattva. Others are grander, such as the precept not to destroy cities, and appear to presuppose a code of conduct for kings or other important figures in society. There is also the suggestion that the bodhisattva precepts supersede the prātimokṣa precepts: one of the secondary infractions of the bodhisattva code is not to engage in killing, stealing, sexual misconduct, lying, divisive speech, harsh speech, or senseless speech when in fact it would be beneficial to do so. The great weight given to the precept not to reject the Mahāyāna as being the word of the Buddha (BUDDHAVACANA) suggests that, throughout the history of the Mahāyāna in India, there were concerns raised about the questionable origin of the Mahāyāna sūtras. With the rise of TANTRA, the "three restraints" (trisaṃvara) of bodhisattva morality were refigured as the second of a new set of precepts, preceded by the prātimokṣa precepts and followed by the tantric vows. There was much discussion, especially in Tibetan SDOM GSUM (dom sum) literature, of the relationships among the three sets of restraints and of their compatibility with each other. ¶ Although there is much variation in the listings of bodhisattva precepts, according to one common list, the eighteen root infractions are: (1) to praise oneself and slander others out of attachment to profit or fame; (2) not to give one's wealth or the doctrine, out of miserliness, to those who suffer without protection; (3) to become enraged and condemn another, without listening to his or her apology; (4) to abandon the Mahāyāna and teach a poor facsimile of its excellent doctrine; (5) to steal the wealth of the three jewels (RATNATRAYA); (6) to abandon the excellent doctrine; (7) to steal the saffron robes of a monk and beat, imprison, and or expel him from his life of renunciation, even if he has broken the moral code; (8) to commit the five deeds of immediate retribution (ĀNANTARYAKARMAN) i.e., patricide, matricide, killing an arhat, wounding a buddha, or causing dissent in the saṃgha; (9) to hold wrong views; (10) to destroy cities and so forth; (11) to discuss emptiness (ŚŪNYATĀ) with sentient beings whose minds have not been trained; (12) to turn someone away from buddhahood and full enlightenment; (13) to cause someone to abandon completely the prātimokṣa precepts in order to practice the Mahāyāna; (14) to believe that desire and so forth cannot be abandoned by the vehicle of the ŚRĀVAKAS and to cause others to believe that view; (15) to claim falsely, "I have withstood the profound emptiness (śūnyatā)"; (16) to impose fines on renunciates; to take donors and gifts away from the three jewels; (17) to cause meditators to give up the practice of ŚAMATHA; to take the resources of those on retreat and give them to reciters of texts; (18) to abandon the two types of BODHICITTA (the conventional and the ultimate). See also BODHISATTVAŚĪLA.

**bodhisattvaśīla**. (T. byang chub sems dpa'i tshul khrims; C. pusa jie; J. bosatsukai; K. posal kye 菩薩戒). In Sanskrit, "BODHISATTVA morality" or "bodhisattva precepts"; the rules of conduct prescribed by MAHĀYĀNA literature for bodhisattvas, or beings intent on achieving buddhahood. These precepts appear in a variety of texts, including the chapter on morality (śīlapaṭala) in the BODHISATTVABHŪMI and the Chinese FANWANG JING (**Brahmajālasūtra*). Although there is not a single universally recognized series of precepts for bodhisattvas across all traditions of Buddhism, all lists include items such as refraining from taking life, refraining from boasting, refraining from slandering the three jewels (RATNATRAYA), etc. In the *Bodhisattvabhūmi*, for example, the Mahāyāna precepts are classified into the "three sets of pure precepts" (trividhāni śīlāni; C. sanju jingjie): (1) the saṃvaraśīla, or "restraining precepts," which refers to the so-called HĪNAYĀNA rules of discipline (PRĀTIMOKṢA) that help adepts restrain themselves from all types of unsalutary conduct; (2) practicing all virtuous deeds (kuśaladharmasaṃgrāhakaśīla), which accumulates all types of salutary conduct; and (3) sattvārthakriyāśīla, which involve giving aid and comfort to sentient beings. Here, the first group corresponds to the preliminary hīnayāna precepts, while the second and third groups reflect a uniquely Mahāyāna position on morality. Thus, the three sets of pure precepts are conceived as a comprehensive description of Buddhist views on precepts (sarvaśīla), which incorporates both hīnayāna and Mahāyāna perspectives into an overarching system. A similar treatment of the three sets of pure precepts is also found in such Chinese indigenous sūtras as *Fanwang jing* ("Sūtra of Brahmā's Net") and PUSA YINGLUO BENYE JING (see APOCRYPHA), thus providing a scriptural foundation in East Asia for an innovation originally appearing in an Indian treatise. The *Fanwang jing* provides a detailed list of a list of ten major and forty-eight minor Mahāyāna precepts that came to be known as the "Fanwang Precepts"; its listing is the definitive roster of bodhisattva precepts in the East Asian traditions. As in other VINAYA ordination ceremonies, the bodhisattva precepts are often taken in a formal ritual along with the bodhisattva vows (BODHISATTVAPRAṆIDHĀNA; PRAṆIDHĀNA). However, unlike the majority of rules found in the mainstream vinaya codes (prātimokṣa), the bodhisattva precepts are directed not only at ordained monks and nuns, but also may be taken by laypeople. Also, in contrast to the mainstream vinaya, there is some dispensation for violating the bodhisattvaśīla, provided that such violations are done for the welfare and weal of other beings. See also BODHISATTVASAṂVARA.

**bodhisattva vow**. See BODHISATTVAPRAṆIDHĀNA; BODHISATTVASAṂVARA; BODHISATTVAŚĪLA.

**bodhisattvayāna**. (T. byang chub sems dpa'i theg pa; C. pusa sheng; J. bosatsujō; K. posal sŭng 菩薩乘). In Sanskrit, lit. "BODHISATTVA vehicle," the path (MĀRGA) that begins with the initial activation of the aspiration for enlightenment

(BODHICITTOTPĀDA) and culminates in the achievement of buddhahood; one of the early terms used for what eventually comes to be called the "Great Vehicle" (MAHĀYĀNA). The bodhisattvayāna focuses on the development of the six perfections (PĀRAMITĀ) over a period as long as three incalculable eons of time (ASAṂKHYEYAKALPA). At the culmination of this essentially interminable process, the bodhisattva becomes a buddha, with the full range of unique qualities (ĀVEṆIKA[BUDDHA] DHARMA) that are developed only as a result of mastering the perfections. The bodhisattvayāna is distinguished from the ŚRĀVAKAYĀNA, in which teachings were learned from a buddha or an enlightened disciple (ŚRĀVAKA) of the Buddha and which culminates in becoming a "worthy one" (ARHAT); and the PRATYEKABUDDHAYĀNA, the vehicle of those who reach their goal in solitude. The bodhisattvayāna, by contrast, is modeled on the accounts of the current buddha ŚĀKYAMUNI's extensive series of past lives, during which he was motivated by the altruistic aspiration to save all beings from suffering by becoming a buddha himself, not simply settling for arhatship. The śrāvakayāna, pratyekabuddhayāna, and bodhisattvayāna together constitute the TRIYĀNA, or "three vehicles," mentioned in many Mahāyāna sūtras, most famously in the SADDHARMAPUṆḌARĪKASŪTRA.

**Bodhisena**. (C. Putixianna; J. Bodaisenna; K. Porisŏnna 菩提僊那) (704–760). Indian monk who traveled first to Southeast Asia and China starting in 723 and subsequently continued on to Japan in 736 at the invitation of the Japanese emperor Shōmu (r. 724–749), where he resided at DAIANJI in Nara. Bodhisena was instrumental in helping to introduce the teachings of the HUAYAN (Kegon) school of Buddhism to Japan. Shōmu also asked Bodhisena to perform the "opening the eyes" (KAIYAN; NETRAPRATIṢṬHĀPANA) ceremony for the 752 dedication of the great buddha image of VAIROCANA (see NARA DAIBUTSU; Birushana Nyorai) at TŌDAIJI. At forty-eight feet high, this image remains the largest extant gilt-bronze image in the world and the Daibutsuden (Great Buddha Hall) where the image is enshrined is the world's largest surviving wooden building.

**Bodhi tree**. (S. bodhidruma [alt. bodhivṛkṣa; bodhiyaṣṭi; bodhivaṭa]; P. bodhirukkha; T. byang chub shing; C. puti shu; J. bodaiju; K. pori su 菩提樹). The name for the sacred tree under which each buddha achieves enlightenment (BODHI), according to the standard hagiographies; sometimes abbreviated as the "bo tree" in English. The Bodhi tree is one of the elements in all stories of a buddha's enlightenment and each buddha has a specific type of tree associated with him. In the case of the current buddha, GAUTAMA or ŚĀKYAMUNI, the tree under which he sat when he attained enlightenment is a pipal, or fig, tree (*Ficus religiosa*). The original Bodhi tree was located at the "seat of enlightenment" (BODHIMAṆḌA, VAJRĀSANA) in BODHGAYĀ, in northern India, but cuttings from it have throughout history been replanted at Buddhist sites around Asia, and now the world. It is said that the Buddha authorized a seed from the tree to be planted in JETAVANA. Its veneration and protection are a common theme in Buddhist literature, figuring prominently, for example, in the story of AŚOKA. The tree was cut, burned, and uprooted by various Hindu kings, including Saśāṅka of Bengal in the seventh century. It was subsequently replaced by a seedling derived from a cutting that had been taken to Sri Lanka in the third century BCE. The Pāli MAHĀBODHIVAṂSA (c. tenth–eleventh century CE) tells the history of the Bodhi tree, the arrival of a cutting from it in Sri Lanka, and the beginnings of the Sinhalese worship of the tree as a Buddhist relic. The large seeds of the Bodhi tree are commonly used to make Buddhist rosaries (JAPAMĀLĀ).

**Bodhnāth Stūpa**. (T. Bya rung kha shor). The popular Nepali name for a large STŪPA situated on the northeast edge of the Kathmandu Valley in Nepal. Venerated by both Newar and Tibetan Buddhists, it has become one of Nepal's most important and active Buddhist pilgrimage sites. The base, arranged on three terraces in a multiangled shape called viṃśatikoṇa (lit. "twenty angles"), is more than 260 feet on each side with the upper dome standing some 130 feet high. At the structure's south entrance stands a shrine to the Newar goddess known as Ajima or HĀRĪTĪ. Together with SVAYAMBHŪ and NAMO BUDDHA, Bodhnāth forms a triad of great stūpas often depicted together in Tibetan literature. The stūpa's origins are unclear and a variety of competing traditions account for its founding and subsequent development. Most Nepali sources agree that the mahācaitya was founded through the activities of King Mānadeva I (reigned 464–505), who unwittingly murdered his father but later atoned for his patricide through a great act of contrition. Among Newars, the stūpa is commonly known as the Khāsticaitya, literally "the dew-drop CAITYA." This name is said to refer to the period in which King Mānadeva founded the stūpa, a time of great drought when cloth would be spread out at night from which the morning dew could be squeezed in order to supply water necessary for the construction. The site is also called Khāsacaitya, after one legend which states that Mānadeva was the reincarnation of a Tibetan teacher called Khāsā; another well-known tradition explains the name as stemming from the buddha KĀŚYAPA, whose relics are said to be enclosed therein. The major Tibetan account of the stūpa's origin is found in a treasure text (GTER MA) said to have been hidden by the Indian sage PADMASAMBHAVA and his Tibetan consort YE SHES MTSHO RGYAL. According to this narrative, the monument was constructed by a widowed poultry keeper. The local nobility grew jealous that such a grand project was being undertaken by a woman of such low status. They petitioned the king, requesting that he bring the construction to a halt. The king, however, refused to intervene and instead granted permission for the work to be completed, from which its Tibetan name *Bya rung kha shor* (Jarung Kashor, literally "permission to do what is proper") is derived. The stūpa was renovated under the guidance of Tibetan lamas on numerous occasions and it eventually came under the custodial care of a familial lineage known as the Chini Lamas. Once surrounded by a small village, since 1959 Bodhnāth has become a thriving center for Tibetan refugee culture and the location for dozens of relocated Tibetan monasteries.

**bodhyaṅga**. (P. bojjhaṅga; T. byang chub kyi yan lag; C. juezhi/qijuezhi; J. kakushi/shichikakushi; K. kakchi/ch'ilgakchi 覺支/七覺支). In Sanskrit, "branches of enlightenment," or "limbs of awakening"; seven qualities attained at the point of realizing the path of vision (DARŚANAMĀRGA): mindfulness (SMṚTI; P. sati), investigation of factors (dharmapravicaya; P. dhammavicaya), energy (VĪRYA; P. viriya), rapture (PRĪTI; pīti), tranquility (PRAŚRABDHI; passaddhi), concentration (SAMĀDHI), and equanimity (UPEKṢĀ; upekkhā). In their roles as "branches of enlightenment," mindfulness, first, refers to the "four foundations of mindfulness" (SMṚTYUPASTHĀNA; P. SATIPAṬṬHĀNA), where the practitioner dwells contemplating four types of objects: namely, the body (KĀYA), sensations (VEDANĀ), the mind (CITTA), and mental objects (DHARMA). Investigation of factors refers to investigating, examining, and reflecting on the teachings and numerical lists of factors taught by the Buddha. Energy refers to firm and unshaken energy that arises in the mind of the practitioner while investigating factors, etc. Rapture refers to the supersensuous bliss that arises as a consequence of contemplating with energy. Tranquility refers to the tranquility that arises as a consequence of the mind experiencing rapture. Concentration refers to the mental absorption that arises as a consequence of tranquility. Finally, equanimity refers to the sense of complete composure that arises as a consequence of the mind being well concentrated on an object. These are called factors of "enlightenment," because they lead to awakening (BODHI) or more specifically to the attainment of the "threefold knowledge" (TRIVIDYĀ; P. tevijjā): "recollection of former lives" (S. PŪRVANIVĀSĀNUSMṚTI; P. pubbenivāsānussati), the "divine eye" (DIVYACAKṢUS; P. dibbacakkhu), which sees the death and rebirth of beings occurring according to their actions, and the "knowledge of the extinction of the contaminants" (ĀSRAVAKṢAYA JÑĀNA; P. āsavakhayañāṇa).

**bodhyaṅgīmudrā**. (T. byang chub mchog gi phyag rgya; C. zhiquan yin; J. chiken'in; K. chigwŏn in 智拳印). In Sanskrit, "gesture of the branches of enlightenment"; a gesture (MUDRĀ) found primarily with images of VAIROCANA, the DHARMAKĀYA buddha, the central figure of the esoteric traditions of Buddhism and the chief buddha of the TATHĀGATA family (see PAÑCAKULA). The gesture is typically formed with the right fist clasping the raised left index finger at the level of the heart, although the hand positions may be reversed. (This gesture is known in Chinese as the zhiquan yin, or "wisdom-fist gesture" a rendering often found in English accounts.) Alternatively, the raised thumb of the left fist may be clasped by the four fingers of the right fist, symbolizing the MAṆḌALA of the five buddhas (PAÑCATATHĀGATA). The gesture is interpreted to indicate the unity in the DHARMAKĀYA of the divergent experience of ordinary beings (PṚTHAGJANA) and buddhas, SAṂSĀRA and NIRVĀṆA, ignorance (AVIDYĀ) and wisdom (PRAJÑĀ), and delusion (MOHA) and enlightenment (BODHI). See also JÑĀNAMUṢṬI.

**Bo dong**. Name of a place in central Tibet and of a small, institutionally independent Tibetan Buddhist sect with its major seat at Bo dong E monastery. The sect was founded in about 1049 in the Shigatse region of Tibet by the BKA' GDAMS geshe (DGE BSHES) Mu dra pa chen po, who invited Sthirapāla ('Bum phrag gsum pa), a contemporary of ATIŚA DĪPAMKARAŚRĪJÑĀNA, to stay in the monastery on his arrival from India. The monastery's earlier history is not well known, though it is compared by some to the more famous Bka' gdams monastery GSANG PHU NE'U THOG, founded by RNGOG LEGS PA'I SHES RAB. KO BRAG PA BSOD NAMS RGYAL MTSHAN, an abbot of Bo dong, is known for his teaching of the KĀLACAKRA ṣaḍaṅgayoga practice, and for propagating a lineage of the LAM 'BRAS "path and result" teaching that was later subsumed into the SA SKYA tradition. The Bo dong sect, as it is now known, begins properly with BO DONG PHYOGS LAS RNAM RGYAL, who wrote a huge encyclopedic work *De nyid 'dus pa* ("Compendium of the Principles") in 137 volumes (in the incomplete published edition). The monastary of Bsam lding (Samding) overlooking Yam 'brog mtsho retains an affiliation with the Bo dong sect; it was founded for a student of Phyogs las rnam rgyal, the Gung thang princess Chos kyi sgron me (1422–1455). It is the only Tibetan monastery whose abbot is traditionally a woman; her incarnations are said to be those of the goddess VAJRAVĀRĀHĪ (T. Rdo rje phag mo), "Sow-Headed Goddess."

**Bo dong Phyogs las rnam rgyal**. (Chokle Namgyal) (1376–1451). The twenty-third abbot of Bo dong E monastery, founded in about 1049 by the BKA' GDAMS geshe (DGE BSHES) Mu dra pa chen po, and the founder of the BO DONG tradition. His collected works, said to number thirty-six titles, include his huge encyclopedic work *De nyid 'dus pa* ("Compendium of the Principles"); it alone runs to 137 volumes in the incomplete edition published by Tibet House in Delhi. Phyogs las rnam rgyal (who is sometimes confused with Jo nang pa Phyogs las rnam rgyal who lived some fifty years earlier) was a teacher of DGE 'DUN GRUB (retroactively named the first DALAI LAMA) and MKHAS GRUB DGE LEGS DPAL BZANG, both students of TSONG KHA PA. Among his leading disciples was the king of Gung thang, Lha dbang rgyal mtshan (1404–1463), whose daughter Chos kyi sgron me (1422–1455) became a nun after the death of her daughter and then the head of Bsam lding (Samding) monastery, which her father founded for her. The monastery is the only Tibetan monastery whose abbot is traditionally a woman; incarnations are said to be those of the goddess VAJRAVĀRĀHĪ (T. Rdo rje phag mo), "Sow-Headed Goddess."

**Bo Juyi**. [alt. Bai Juyi] (J. Haku Kyoi; K. Paek Kŏi 白居易) (772–846). A celebrated Chinese poet of the Tang dynasty; also known as Yaotian (Enjoying Heaven) and Layman Xiangshan. Bo Juyi was born in Henan to a destitute family with a scholarly background. He passed the civil examinations at the age of twenty-seven and held various government positions throughout his political career. Bo Juyi was exiled in 815 from the capital of Chang'an for his criticisms of governmental policies, after which he turned to Buddhism for solace. Bo Juyi befriended numerous CHAN masters of his time and studied under Foguang Ruman (d.u.), a disciple of the renowned Chan master MAZU DAOYI. He acquired his Buddhist toponym Xiangshan during his residence at the monastery of XIANGSHANSI. In addition to his famous collections of poems, such as the *Changhen ge*, Bo Juyi also left numerous funerary inscriptions that he composed for deceased monks. His writings were compiled together in his *Baishi wenji*, in seventy-five rolls.

**bokuseki**. (墨蹟). In Japanese, "ink traces"; generally referring to any sort of calligraphy executed by an ink brush on paper or silk. The Japanese monk Murata Jukō (1422–1502) is said to have hung in his tea room the calligraphy of the Song-dynasty CHAN master YUANWU KEQIN, which he had received from his teacher IKKYŪ SŌJUN, a practice that seems to have had no precedent in Japan. Following his lead, monks largely from the GOZAN lineage began to collect the calligraphy of eminent Song-dynasty Chan masters such as DAHUI ZONGGAO and XUTANG ZHIYU to display in their private quarters and tea rooms. From the time of the Zen and tea master Sen no Rikyū (Sōeki Rikyū; 1521–1591), the calligraphy of Japanese Zen monks such as MYŌAN EISAI, DŌGEN KIGEN, and MUSŌ SŌSEKI began to be seen as valuable commodities. The calligraphy of Zen masters belonging to the DAITOKUJI lineage such as SŌHŌ MYŌCHŌ, Ikkyū Sōjun, and TAKUAN SŌHŌ also came to be highly prized. Beginning with Sen no Rikyū, the practice of collecting relatively simple calligraphy, comprised largely of a single, horizontally executed line, came to be favored over those containing longer poems or sermons written in vertical lines.

**Bon**. In Tibetan, "reciter"; originally a term for a category of priest in the royal cult of pre-Buddhist Tibet. Traditional Tibetan histories present these priests as opponents of the introduction of Buddhism in Tibet during the seventh and eighth centuries. In the eleventh century, Bon emerged as fully elaborated sect of Tibetan religion, with its own buddha, its own pantheon, and its own path to liberation from rebirth. Bon should not be regarded as the pre-Buddhist religion of Tibet, but rather as the leading non-Buddhist religion of Tibet, which has had a long history of mutual influence and interaction with the Buddhist sects.

**Bon Festival**. [alt. Obon] (J. 盆/お盆). See *ULLAMBANA.

**bonze**. (J. bonsō/bossō 凡僧). An early English term for a Buddhist monk, especially in East Asia, deriving from the Portuguese pronunciation of the Japanese bonsō ("ordinary cleric"). Although occasionally still used in reference to Japanese Buddhist priests, this sixteenth-century term is long outmoded and should be discarded.

**bore**. (C) (般若). The preferred Sinographic transcription for "PRAJÑĀ"; the term is also sometimes seen transcribed as BANRUO or BORUO.

**Bore wuzhi lun**. (J. Hannya muchiron; K. Panya muji non 般若無知論). In Chinese, the "Nescience of Prajñā Treatise"; a subtreatise in a larger work entitled the ZHAO LUN, attributed to the Chinese monk SENGZHAO. In this treatise, the author claims that because wisdom (PRAJÑĀ) is quiescent, empty, and lacking any perduring essence, any conscious awareness of it is impossible. Although prajñā is itself formless, it interacts with the realm of perceived objects through a process known as GANYING, or "sympathetic resonance." This treatise is said to have been based on KUMĀRAJĪVA's translation of the PAÑCAVIṂŚATISĀHASRIKĀPRAJÑĀPĀRAMITĀSŪTRA.

**Borobudur**. [alt. Barabuḍur]. A massive Indonesian Buddhist monument located in a volcanic area west of Yogyakarta, in the south-central region of the island of Java. Although there are no written records concerning the monument's dating, archaeological and art-historical evidence suggests that construction started around 790 CE during the Śailendra dynasty and continued for at least another three-quarters of a century. The derivation of its name remains controversial. The anglicized name Borobudur was given to the site by the colonial governor Sir Thomas Raffles, when Java was under British colonial rule. The name "budur" occurs in an old Javanese text referring to a Buddhist site and Raffles may have added the "boro" to refer to the nearby village of Bore. Borobudur is a pyramid-shaped MAṆḌALA with a large central STŪPA, which is surrounded by three concentric circular tiers that include a total of seventy-two individual stūpas, and four square terraces, giving the monument the appearance of a towering mountain. The maṇḍala may have been associated with the pilgrimage of the lad SUDHANA described in the GAṆḌAVYŪHA (and its embedded version in the "Entering the Dharmadhātu" chapter of the AVATAṂSAKASŪTRA). This structure is without analogue anywhere else in the Buddhist world, but seems to have influenced Khmer (Cambodian) architectural traditions. The central stūpa houses a buddha image, and originally may have also enshrined a relic (ŚARĪRA). Each of the seventy-two smaller stūpas also enshrines an image of a BODHISATTVA, of whom MAÑJUŚRĪ and SAMANTABHADRA are most popular. The walls of Borobudur are carved with some 1,350 bas-reliefs that illustrate tales of the Buddha's past and present lives from the JĀTAKA and AVADĀNA literature, as well as events from such texts as the LALITAVISTARA, Gaṇḍavyūha, and the BHADRACARĪPRAṆIDHĀNA. There are also niches at the upper parts of the walls that are enshrined with buddha images employing different hand gestures (MUDRĀ). The three circular tiers of Borobudur are presumed to correspond to the three realms of Buddhist cosmology (TRAIDHĀTUKA); thus, when pilgrims circumambulated the central stūpa, they may have also been traveling symbolically through the sensuous realm (KĀMADHĀTU), the subtle-materiality realm (RŪPADHĀTU) and the immaterial realm (ĀRŪPYADHĀTU). There are also ten series of bas-reliefs, which suggest that pilgrims making their way through the monument were also ritually reenacting a bodhisattva's progression through the ten stages (DAŚABHŪMI) of the bodhisattva path (MĀRGA). The monument is constructed on hilly terrain rather than flat land, and there is also some geological evidence that it may have originally been built on a lakeshore, as if it were a lotus flower floating in a lake. Borobudur is aligned with two other Buddhist temples in the area, Pawon and Mendu, an orientation that may well have had intentional ritual significance. By at least the fifteenth century, Borobudur was abandoned. There are two main theories regarding its fate. Since Borobudur was buried under several layers of volcanic ash at the time of its rediscovery, one theory is that a famine resulting from a volcanic eruption prompted the depopulation of the region and the monument's abandonment. A second explanation is that the rise of Islam hastened the downfall of Buddhism in Java and the neglect of the monument.

**Borommaracha I**. (P. Paramarājā) (r. 1370–1388). Thai king of AYUTHAYA. During his reign, the Thai monk Dhammakitti Mahāsāmī returned to Ayuthaya from Sri Lanka and wrote the SADDHAMMASAṄGAHA, the earliest-known Buddhist chronicle written in Southeast Asia. The *Saddhammasaṅgaha* borrows its account of PARĀKRAMABĀHU's reforms of the Buddhist order from the historical introduction of the MAHĀPARĀKRAMABĀHU-KATIKĀVATA.

**Borommaracha II**. (P. Paramarājā) (r. 1424–1448). Thai king of AYUTHAYA, who expanded the city-state's boundaries, turning it into a regional power. He destroyed the Khmer empire of Ankhor to the east and absorbed the kingdom of SUKHOTHAI. In 1442 he attacked the Thai kingdom of Lānnā, beginning a century of warfare between Ayuthaya and Chiangmai. Toward the end of his life he received a delegation of reordained monks from Sri Lanka headed by MEDHAṄKARA AND ÑĀṆAGAMBHĪRA and at their prompting made their reformed Sinhalese NIKĀYA the only orthodox fraternity in the kingdom. The PADAENG CHRONICLE states that the senior monk of Ayuthaya, Mahā Dhammasārada, ordered all younger monks laicized and reordained at the residence of Ñāṇagambhīra. The delegation resided at Ayuthaya for four years, during which time they reordained many local monks. Afterward, they traveled to Chiangmai and other northern city-states to propagate their reforms.

**boruo**. (C) (般若). Alternate Chinese transcription for Sanskrit PRAJÑĀ (wisdom); the preferred transcription is BORE. See BORE for related Chinese terms and PRAJÑĀ for Sanskrit equivalents.

**Bo tree**. See BODHI TREE.

**Brag dkar rta so**. (Drakar Taso). In Tibetan, lit. "White Rock Horse Tooth"; a complex of meditation caves and small temples located close to the Nepalese border in the SKYID GRONG valley of southwestern Tibet. It was one of the primary meditation retreats of the eleventh-century yogin MI LA RAS PA, who was born nearby and later spent many years in the area in strict meditation retreat, especially at the site called Dbu ma rdzong (Uma dzong), "Fortress of the Central [Channel]." In the sixteenth century, a small monastery was founded at Brag dkar rta so by the 'BRUG PA BKA' BRGYUD master LHA BTSUN RIN CHEN RNAM RGYAL, and the location became an important xylographic printing house specializing in the biographies of BKA' BRGYUD masters. The center also became the seat of an important incarnation lineage, the Brag dkar rta so incarnations.

**Brag yer pa**. [alt. Yer pa; G.yer pa] (Drak Yerpa). A complex of meditation caves and temples northeast of LHA SA, regarded as one of the premier retreat locations of central Tibet. The ancient hermitage complex was founded by queen Mong bza' khri lcam (Mongsa Tricham) and her children and was inhabited during the imperial period by Tibet's religious kings SRONG BTSAN SGAM PO, KHRI SRONG LDE BTSAN, and RAL PA CAN. The Indian sage PADMASAMBHAVA is said to have spent some seven months in retreat there and hid numerous treasure texts (GTER MA) in the area. Brag yer pa is considered one of his three primary places of attainment (grub gnas), together with CHIMS PHU and Shel brag (Sheldrak). Lha lung Dpal gyi rdo rje (Lhalung Palgyi Dorje), assassin of King GLANG DAR MA, is said to have spent more than twenty-two years in retreat there. Brag yer pa later gained prominence under the influence of the BKA' GDAMS sect after the Bengali scholar ATIŚA passed some three years at the site.

**Brahmā**. [alt. Mahābrahmā] (T. Tshangs pa; C. Fantian; J. Bonten; K. Pŏmch'ŏn 梵天). An Indian divinity who was adopted into the Buddhist pantheon as a protector of the teachings (DHARMAPĀLA) and king of the BRAHMALOKA (in the narrow sense of that term). A particular form of the god Brahmā, called SAHĀṂPATI, plays a crucial role in the inception of the Buddhist dispensation or teaching (ŚĀSANA). During the seven weeks following his enlightenment, the newly awakened buddha GAUTAMA was unsure as to whether he should teach, wondering whether there would be anyone in this world who would be able to duplicate his experience. Brahmā descended to earth and convinced him that there were persons "with little dust in their eyes" who would be able to understand his teachings. The Buddha then surveyed the world to determine the most suitable persons to hear the DHARMA. Seeing that his former meditation teachers had died, he chose the "group of five" (PAÑCAVARGIKA) and proceeded to ṚṢIPATANA, where he taught his first sermon, the "Turning of the Wheel of the Dharma" (DHARMACAKRAPRAVARTANASŪTRA; P. DHAMMACAKKAPPAVATTANASUTTA). Because of this intervention, Brahmā is considered one of the main dharmapālas. BUDDHAGHOSA explains, however, that the compassionate Buddha never had any hesitation about teaching the dharma but felt that if he were implored by the god Brahmā, who was revered in the world, it would lend credence to his mission. Brahmā is depicted with four faces and four arms, and his primary attributes are the lotus and the CAKRA. The figure of Brahmā also fused with early Indian BODHISATTVAS such as PADMAPĀṆI (AVALOKITEŚVARA). In Tibet the dharmapāla TSHANGS PA DKAR PO is a fusion of Brahmā and PE HAR RGYAL PO.

**brahmacarya**. (P. brahmacariya; T. tshangs spyod; C. fanxing; J. bongyō; K. pŏmhaeng 梵行). In Sanskrit, lit. "holy lifeway" or "religious life"; a term used most typically to mean "celibacy," viz., a religious way of life based on renunciation and chastity, and by extension to the monks and ascetics who follow that way of life. Within the Brahmanical tradition, brahmacarya refers to unmarried students of the Vedas, but the term was adopted by the Buddhists to refer more broadly to a religious mendicant's celibate way of life. Cf. PĀRĀJIKA.

**Brahmajālasuttanta**. (C. Fandong jing; J. Bondōkyō; K. Pŏmdong kyŏng 梵動經) In Pāli, "Discourse on BRAHMĀ's Net"; the first sutta of the DĪGHANIKĀYA (a separate DHARMAGUPTAKA recension appears as the twenty-first SŪTRA in the Chinese translation of the DĪRGHĀGAMA). While dwelling in the Ambalaṭṭhikā grove, the Buddha preaches this sermon to the ascetic Supiyya and his disciple Brahmadatta, in order to allay their disagreement over the merits and demerits of the Buddha. The Buddha first explains that there are some who praise him for his observation of moral precepts (sīla; S. ŚĪLA), which, he notes, are merely abstentions from wrongdoing. These he elaborates in increasing detail in three sections and concludes by saying that those who judge him by these abstentions have only a trivial understanding of his virtues. The Buddha then describes sixty-two theories regarding the existence of the self (attan; S. ĀTMAN) advocated by other recluses (samaṇa, S. ŚRAMAṆA) and brāhmaṇas, all of which he rejects. These he classifies as the doctrines of eternalism (sassatavāda, see S. ŚĀŚVATADṚṢṬI), semieternalism (ekaccasassatavāda), extensionism (antānantavāda), equivocation or eel-wriggling (amarāvikkhepavāda), causeless originationism (adhiccasamuppannavāda), the belief in conscious existence after death (saññīvāda), unconscious existence after death (asaññīvāda), existence after death that is neither conscious or unconscious (nevasaññīnāsaññīvāda), annihilationism (UCCHEDAVĀDA), and hedonism (diṭṭhadhammanibbānavāda). All of these theories the Buddha rejects as examples of wrong views (diṭṭhi, S. DṚṢṬI), which are advocated by other recluses and brāhmaṇas through their contact with, and experience of, sensory objects. Because of their wrong views, these theories produce craving (taṇhā, S. TṚṢṆĀ) and grasping (UPĀDĀNA), which in turn fuel the process of becoming (BHAVA) and leads to continued rebirth (JĀTI), old age and death (JARĀMARAṆA), sorrow (śoka), lamentation (parideva), pain (DUḤKHA), grief (daurmanasya), and despair (upāyāsa) (see PRATĪTYASAMUTPĀDA). The *Brahmajālasuttanta* is valued by scholars as a source for understanding the range of philosophical views present in India at the time of the early Buddhist community.

**brahmakāyika**. (P. brahmapārisajjā; T. tshangs ris; C. fanzhong tian; J. bonshuten; K. pŏmjung ch'ŏn 梵衆天). In Sanskrit, "brahmā's retainers"; the lowest of the three heavens that constitute the first concentration (DHYĀNA) of the realm of subtle materiality (RŪPADHĀTU) in the Buddhist cosmological system. In Pāli, the term brahmakāyika seems to be used at times for a general term for all the inhabitants of the BRAHMALOKA; the inhabitants of the lowest of the three heavens are instead called brahmāpārisajjā (the "assembly of BRAHMĀ"). However, brahmakāyika more commonly refers to the lowest of the three heavens, whose inhabitants are divinities (DEVA) who are subordinates of the god Brahmā. As with the other inhabitants of the realm of subtle materiality, the divinities there have only three sense organs: of sight, hearing, and touch. Also as with all the heavens of the subtle-materiality realm, one is reborn as a divinity there through mastering during one's meditative practice in a preceding lifetime the same level of dhyāna as those divinities.

**brahmaloka**. (T. tshangs pa'i 'jig rten; C. fanjie; J. bonkai; K. pŏmgye 梵界). In Sanskrit and Pāli, the "BRAHMĀ worlds." In its narrowest sense, brahmaloka refers to the first three heavens of the realm of subtle materiality (RŪPADHĀTU), whose denizens live perpetually immersed in the bliss of the first meditative absorption (DHYĀNA; P. jhāna): BRAHMAKĀYIKA (heaven of Brahmā's followers), BRAHMAPUROHITA (heaven of Brahmā's vassals), and MAHĀBRAHMĀ (heaven of Brahmā himself). The ruler of these three heavens is named either Brahmā or Mahābrahmā, and he mistakenly believes that he is the creator of the universe. In a more general sense, the brahmaloka can also refer collectively to all the heavens of both the realm of subtle materiality and the immaterial realm (ĀRŪPYADHĀTU). The two realms are divided into twenty heavens, the top four of which comprise the immaterial realm. Denizens of the immaterial realm have no physical dimension but are entirely mental and are perpetually immersed in one of the four immaterial absorptions (ĀRŪPYĀVACARADHYĀNA). The realm of subtle materiality is divided into sixteen heavens, the top five of which are called the "pure abodes" (ŚUDDHĀVĀSA), where nonreturners (ANĀGĀMIN) are reborn. When the time is right, inhabitants of the pure abodes descend to earth in the guise of brāhmaṇas to leave portents of the advent of future buddhas so that they can be recognized when they appear in the human realm. One heaven in the realm of subtle materiality is reserved for unconscious beings (S. asaṃjñisattva; P. asaññasatta) who pass their entire lives (which can last eons) in dreamless sleep, only to die the moment they awaken. As with the immaterial realm, the realm of subtle materiality is also divided into four broad strata that correspond to the four form-based meditative absorptions (RŪPĀVACARADHYĀNA) and the denizens of these strata perpetually experience the bliss of the corresponding dhyāna. Regardless of the particular heaven they occupy, all inhabitants of the brahmaloka are all classified as brahmā gods and live in splendor that far exceeds that of the divinities in the lower sensuous realm of existence (KĀMADHĀTU).

**Brahmanimantanikasutta**. (C. Fantian qing fo jing; J. Bonten shōbutsukyō; K. Pŏmch'ŏn ch'ŏngbul kyŏng 梵天請佛經). In Pāli, "Discourse on the Invitation of a BRAHMĀ"; the forty-ninth sutta of the MAJJHIMANIKĀYA, preached by the Buddha to a gathering of monks at the JETAVANA Grove in the town of Sāvatthi (S. ŚRĀVASTĪ). (A separate SARVĀSTIVĀDA version appears as the seventy-eighth SŪTRA in the Chinese translation of the MADHYAMĀGAMA.) The Buddha recounts to his disciples how he once visited the divine abode of the brahmā god Baka to dissuade him of the wrong view of eternalism (S. ŚĀŚVATADṚṢṬI). Because Baka had lived a very long time as lord of his realm—so long that his memory had failed him—the wrong view occurred to him that everything in his heaven was permanent, everlasting, and eternal; that nothing was beyond it; that nothing in his heaven was born, grew old, or died; that nothing passed away or reappeared; and that beyond his heavenly realm there was no escape. The Buddha tells Baka he knows more than Baka knows, that there are in fact other heavens more resplendent than his, and that because of their awakening, the Buddha and his disciples are quite beyond and free from all realms of existence.

**brahmapurohita**. (T. tshangs pa'i mdun na 'don; C. fanfu tian; J. bonhoten; K. pŏmbo ch'ŏn 梵輔天). In Sanskrit and Pāli "brahmā's ministers"; the second of the three heavens that constitute the first concentration (DHYĀNA) of the realm of subtle materiality (RŪPADHĀTU) in the Buddhist cosmological system. The inhabitants of this heaven are divinities (DEVA) who serve as the attendants, ministers, and officials of the god BRAHMĀ. As with the other inhabitants of the realm of subtle materiality, the divinities there have only three physical sense organs: of sight, hearing, and touch. As with all the heavens of the subtle-materiality realm, one is reborn as a god there through mastering during one's meditative practice in a preceding lifetime the same level of dhyāna as those divinities.

**Brahmā's Net Sūtra**. See FANWANG JING; cf. BRAHMAJĀLASUTTANTA.

**brahmavihāra**. (T. tshangs pa'i gnas; C. fanzhu; J. bonjū; K. pŏmju 梵住). In Sanskrit and Pāli, "divine abidings," or "highest religious state." This is a classification of four meditative topics used for the cultivation of tranquility meditation (ŚAMATHĀ): loving-kindness (MAITRĪ; P. mettā), compassion (KARUṆĀ), empathetic joy (MUDITĀ), and equanimity or impartiality (UPEKṢĀ; P. upekkhā). The meditator is taught to take up each of the divine abidings in the same way: starting with the first brahmavihāra, for example, filling his mind with loving-kindness, he pervades the world with it, first in one direction; then in a second direction; then a third and a fourth; then above, below, and all around; always identifying himself with all beings and keeping himself free from hatred and ill will. In the same way, he develops compassion, empathetic joy, and equanimity. These four factors are taken up as objects of meditation to counter the influence of specific unwholesome (AKUŚALA) states of mind: viz., loving-kindness counteracts hostility (VYĀPĀDA), compassion counters harmfulness (VIHIṂSĀ), empathetic joy counters dissatisfaction or envy regarding others achievements (arati), and equanimity counters both the desire and hostility arising from sensuality (kāmarāgavyāpāda) as well as the desire to win the approval of others (anunaya). Of these divine abidings, the first three are capable of producing the first three of the four meditative absorptions (DHYĀNA); the fourth divine abiding is the only one capable of producing the fourth meditative absorption. The four divine abidings are listed in the VISUDDHIMAGGA as four of the forty meditative topics (KAMMAṬṬHĀNA) that may be pursued by the meditator. The *Visuddhimagga* notes they are useful only for the cultivation of tranquility (P. samatha; S. śamatha), and not for the cultivation of insight (P. VIPASSANĀ; S. VIPAŚYANĀ). Taken as objects of concentration and extended in meditation to all beings without limit, the divine abidings also come to be known as the "boundless states" (APRAMĀṆA).

**Brāhmī**. In Sanskrit, "Holy Script"; name for one of the two predominant scripts (along with KHAROṢṬHĪ) used in the GANDHĀRA region of northwest India; Buddhist texts using this script are found in Sanskritized Gāndhārī and other Prakrit vernaculars (known as BUDDHIST HYBRID SANSKRIT). Buddhist documents were written in the Kharoṣṭhī script at least as early as the first half of the first century CE; these are now generally conceded to be the oldest extant Indian and Buddhist documents, although stone and coin inscriptions and edicts in Aśokan Brāhmī date from considerably earlier. Documents using the Brāhmī script date from about one or two centuries later, during the second or third centuries CE; the latest Brāhmī documents date from the eighth century CE, around the time that Buddhism begins to vanish from the Gandhāra region. The Brāhmī manuscripts are often written on palm leaves, while many of the Kharoṣṭhī manuscripts instead use birch bark. The greatest cache of Brāhmī manuscripts discovered so far are extensive fragments of a Sanskrit recension of the DĪRGHĀGAMA ("Long Discourses"; see also DĪGHANIKĀYA) attributed to the SARVĀSTIVĀDA school or its MŪLASARVĀSTIVĀDA offshoot. Aśokan-period Brāhmī has ten vowels and thirty-eight consonants and is written like all Indian alphabets from left to right; Kharoṣṭhī is written from right to left and appears to be based on an Aramāic script. In the modern period, the Brāhmī script was deciphered by James Prinsep (1799–1840) of the Asiatic Society of Bengal. Brāhmī is also related to the SIDDHAM script used in East Asian for transcribing Sanskit DHĀRAṆĪs and MANTRAs.

**'Bras spungs**. (Drepung). In Tibetan, literally "Rice Heap"; one of the three monastic seats (GDAN SA GSUM) of the DGE LUGS sect of Tibetan Buddhism; located eight kilometers west of the Tibetan capital of LHA SA. The monastery is named after the Dhanyakaṭaka stūpa in AMARĀVATĪ in southern India, where the Buddha is said to have first taught the KĀLACAKRATANTRA. It was founded in 1416 by 'JAM DBYANGS CHOS RJE BKRA SHIS DPAL LDAN, one of TSONG KHA PA's leading disciples, and after only a few years in operation already housed over 2,000 monks. In the early sixteenth century, the second DALAI LAMA Dge 'dun rgya mtsho (Gendün Gyatso, 1475–1542) became the monastery's abbot; in 1530, he established a residence and political institution there called the DGA' LDAN PHO BRANG or "Palace of TUṢITA." Following him, Bsod nams grags pa (Sönam Drakpa, 1478–1554) became the abbot. Thereafter, until the ascendancy of the Dalai Lamas, the most powerful religious dignitaries in the monastery were the Dalai Lamas and the reincarnations of Bsod nams grags pa. In the seventeenth century, under the direction of the fifth Dalai Lama NGAG DBANG BLO BZANG RGYA MTSHO, the Dga' ldan pho brang (also known as the gzims khang 'og ma or "lower chambers" to distinguish it from the "upper chambers," gzims khang gong ma, where the incarnations of Bsod nams grags pa resided), was moved to the PO TA LA palace. There it functioned as the seat of the Tibetan government until the Chinese occupation of Tibet in 1959. The monastery is an enormous complex of assembly halls, temples, chapels, living quarters and mountain hermitages. At the time of the fifth Dalai Lama, 'Bras spungs housed over 10,000 monks divided into seven (and later four) colleges (grwa tshang), more than fifty regional dormitories (khams tshan), and occupied an area of some 180,000 square feet, easily forming the largest monastery in Tibet. At the height of its florescence, 'Bras spungs drew applicants from all quarters of the Tibetan cultural world including the far east and northeast in A mdo, as well as Mongolia, Kalmykia, and Buryatia. The monastery was large enough to accommodate individuals of a wide range of capacities and interests. A large percentage of its monks engaged in little formal intellectual study, instead choosing to work for the institution as laborers, cooks, and ritual assistants. Even so, 'Bras spungs's numerous monastic colleges also attracted some of Tibet's most talented and gifted scholars, producing a line of elite academicians and authors. The complex was sacked a number of times, first by the King of Gtsang (Tsang) during a civil war in 1618, then by the Mongol army in 1635, and again by Lha bzang Khan in 1706. It was most recently plundered by the People's Liberation Army during the Chinese Cultural Revolution but opened again in 1980 with five hundred monks.

**bṛhatphala**. (P. vehapphala; T. 'bras bu che; C. guangguo tian; J. kōkaten; K. kwanggwa ch'ŏn 廣果天). In Sanskrit, "great fruition," the third and lowest of the eight heavens of the fourth concentration (DHYĀNA) of the realm of subtle materiality (RŪPADHĀTU); in Pāli sources, this is the lowest of the seven heavens of the fourth DHYĀNA of the realm of subtle materiality (RŪPADHĀTU).The heaven is so called because it is the greatest fruition among all places of rebirth in SAṂSĀRA for ordinary persons (PṚTHAGJANA) who have not achieved the state of ĀRYAPUDGALA or noble person. As with all the heavens of the subtle-materiality realm, one is reborn as a god there through mastering during one's meditative practice in a preceding lifetime the same level of dhyāna as those divinities.

**'Bri gung bka' brgyud**. (Drigung Kagyü). A subsect of the BKA' BRGYUD sect of Tibetan Buddhism, counted among the "four major and eight minor Bka' brgyud subsects" (BKA' BRGYUD CHE BZHI CHUNG BRGYAD). The lineage stems from the twelfth-century meditation master 'JIG RTEN GSUM MGON, who founded the sects seat at 'BRI GUNG MTHIL monastery in 1179, from which the lineage derives its name. Although the 'Bri gung bka' brgyud wielded political power at times during the thirteenth century, members of the tradition are primarily renowned as great meditators. The sect established prominent retreat centers around Mount KAILĀSA in western Tibet and LA PHYI in the south. It has remained an active Bka' brgyud subsect under the guidance of its principal reincarnate teachers, the Che tshang and Chung tshang lamas. The former has established an exile seat in Dehra Dun, Uttar Pradesh in northern India, with numerous affiliated centers in India, Nepal, and the West, while the latter remains in Tibet.

**'Bri gung mthil**. (Drigung Til). An important monastery affiliated with the 'BRI GUNG BKA' BRGYUD sect of Tibetan Buddhism, located northeast of the Tibetan capital of LHA SA. A hermitage was initially established at the site in 1167 by Mi nyag sgom ring (Minyak Gomring), a disciple of the influential Bka' brgyud hierarch PHAG MO GRU PA RDO RJE RGYAL PO. In 1179 Phag mo gru pa's disciple 'JIG RTEN GSUM MGON, founder of the 'Bri gung bka' brgyud sect, constructed a monastery there, deriving its name (literally "back of a female yak") from the contour of the surrounding ridge. The institution was renowned for its excellence in meditative training and gained great political power during the thirteenth century when it rivaled even the SA SKYA establishment. 'Bri gung mthil was sacked by the Mongol-backed Sa skyas in 1290 but was rebuilt and later flourished as an active, though politically insignificant, religious center for the 'Bri gung bka' brgyud teachings. One of central Tibet's most famous sky-burial sites is affiliated with the monastery.

**Brin**. (Drin) A village and its surrounding region of the Rongshar Valley in southern Tibet, close to the Nepalese border, chiefly associated with the eleventh-century Tibetan YOGIN MI LA RAS PA. According to the yogin's biographies, the region was home to numerous patrons, and many of his favored retreat caves are located here. Also spelled Ding ma brin, or Brin thang.

**'Brog mi Shākya Ye shes**. (Drogmi Shākya Yeshe) (c. 992–1072?). Tibetan scholar and founder of the SA SKYA sect of Tibetan Buddhism; one of the foremost translators of the new traditions (GSAR MA) in Tibet. Also known as 'Brog mi Lo tsā ba

("Drokmi the Translator"), 'Brog mi traveled to Nepal and India and studied for thirteen years under numerous masters and at the monastic university of VIKRAMAŚĪLA. After returning to Tibet, he translated a variety of Sanskrit works, including important tantric treatises and commentaries. Chief among these were the HEVAJRATANTRA and the RDO RJE TSHIG RKANG ("Vajra Verses") of the adept VIRŪPA. He received the latter in Tibet from the Indian master Gyadhara (d. 1103) and it formed a scriptural basis for the seminal Sa skya tradition known as LAM 'BRAS, or "path and result." His chief disciple, DKON MCHOG RGYAL PO, is credited with founding SA SKYA monastery.

**'Brom ston Rgyal ba'i 'byung gnas**. (Dromton Gyalwe Jungne) (1004–1064). The foremost Tibetan disciple of the Bengali scholar ATIŚA, and central figure in the founding of the BKA' GDAMS sect of Tibetan Buddhism during the period known as the later dissemination (PHYI DAR) of Buddhism in Tibet. Born in central Tibet, he began his education at an early age. Toward the middle years of his life, news of Atiśa's arrival in western Tibet reached him, and he set out on the arduous journey to meet the master. 'Brom ston pa became an early and close student of Atiśa and made arrangements for his Indian guru's tour of central Tibet in 1045. After Atiśa's death, 'Brom ston pa established RWA SGRENG monastery in 1056, consolidating his career as translator and teacher at this important religious institution. He is remembered especially for the firm austerity of his religious practice. 'Brom ston pa's instructions, as recorded in Bka' gdams pa works such as the *Bka' gdams gtor bu* ("Bka' gdams Miscellania"), perhaps wary of the potential abuses of tantric practice, instead emphasize meditation on impermanence and compassion coupled with adherence to strict ethical principles and monastic discipline.

**brtan** [alt. bstan] **ma bcu gnyis**. (denma chunyi). A group of twelve pre-Buddhist Tibetan deities converted to Buddhism by PADMASAMBHAVA. The site of their subjugation is said to have been either Kha la brag (Kaladrak) or 'U yug, although individual members have variant legends. They are considered to be subordinate to the BKRA SHIS TSHE RING MCHED LNGA, "five long-life sisters," and, like that group of deities, frequently appear in the retinue of DPAL LDAN LHA MO. Their status in the world is ambiguous, considered by some to be enlightened, by others to be mundane. Rdo rje g.yu sgron ma (Dorje Yudronma) is generally considered to be their leader, though sometimes Rdo rje grags mo rgyal (Dorje Drakmo Gyel) is given that honor. All members are said to take possession of female mediums, some of whom were sponsored by the powerful DGE LUGS monasteries of SE RA and 'BRAS SPUNGS. The brtan ma are divided into three groups of four members each: the bdud mo (dumo) (female BDUD), gnod sbyin (nöjin) (female YAKṢA), and sman mo (menmo). Their names, without the epithet "Rdo rje" (i.e., "Vajra") are Kun grags ma, G.ya' ma skyong, Kun bzang mo, and Bgegs kyi gtso in the group of bdud mo; Spyan gcig ma, Dpal gyi yum, Drag mo rgyal, and Klu mo dkar in the group of gnod sbyin chen mo; and Bod khams skyong, Sman gcig ma, G.yar mo sil, and G.yu sgron ma in the group of sman mo. There are numerous variations in the names.

**'Brug chen incarnations**. (Drukchen). An important "incarnate lama" (SPRUL SKU) lineage of Tibetan masters, esteemed as prominent teachers of the 'BRUG PA BKA' BRGYUD sect of Tibetan Buddhism. The recognized line began in the fifteenth century, although the first embodiment is held to be GTSANG PA RGYA RAS YE SHES RDO RJE who lived several centuries earlier. Perhaps most famous among the 'Brug chen incarnations was the fourth, PADMA DKAR PO, an exceptional scholar and prolific author and historian. The current 'Brug chen incarnation established a residence in India following the Chinese occupation of Tibet. The lineage includes:

1. Gtsang pa rgya ras Ye shes rdo rje (1161–1211)
2. Chos rje Kun dga' dpal 'byor (Chöje Kunga Paljor, 1426–1476)
3. 'Jam dbyangs chos grags (Jamyang Chödrak, 1477–1523),
4. Padma dkar po (1527–1592)
5. 'Phags bsam dbang po (Paksam Wangpo, 1593–1641)
6. Mi pham dbang po (Mipam Wangpo, 1641–1717)
7. Phrin las shing rta (Trinle Shingta, 1718–1766)
8. Kun gzigs chos kyi snang ba (Kunsik Chökyi Nangwa, 1767–1822)
9. 'Jigs med mi 'gyur dbang rgyal (Jikme Migyur Wangyal, 1823–1883)
10. Mi pham chos kyi dbang po (Mipam Chökyi Wangpo, 1884–1930)
11. Bstan 'dzin mkhyen rab dge legs dbang po (Tendzin Khyenrap Gelek Wangpo, 1931–1960)
12. 'Jigs med padma dbang chen (Jikme Pema Wangchen, b. 1963).

**'Brug pa bka' brgyud**. (Drukpa Kagyü). A lineage counted among the four major and eight minor BKA' BRGYUD subsects (BKA' BRGYUD CHE BZHI CHUNG BRGYAD) of Tibetan Buddhism, which maintained an active presence throughout central and western Tibet and became a predominant tradition in neighboring Bhutan. Its practitioners were widespread and renowned for their simple lifestyle and intensive meditative practices. For this reason, a Tibetan proverb arose that said, "Half of the people are 'Brug pas. Half of the 'Brug pas are beggars. Half of the beggars are saints." The lineage originated with GLING RAS PA PADMA RDO RJE (1128–1188), student of renowned Bka' brgyud master PHAG MO GRU PA RDO RJE RGYAL PO, and his disciple GTSANG PA RGYA RAS YE SHES RDO RJE. The sect eventually divided into three branches, known as (1) Upper 'Brug (stod 'brug), established by Gtsang pa rgya ras's disciple RGOD TSHANG PA MGON PO RDO RJE; (2) Middle 'Brug (bar 'brug), established by Gtsang pa rgya ras's disciple Lo ras pa Dar ma [alt. Grags pa] dbang phyug (Lorepa Darma Wangchuk)

(1187–1250); and (3) Lower 'Brug (smad 'brug) established by Gtsang pa rgya ras himself. It was the Middle 'Brug tradition that was transmitted to Bhutan by ZHAB DRUNG NGAG DBANG RNAM RGYAL.

**'Brug pa kun legs**. (Drukpa Kunlek) (1455–1529). Also known as 'Brug smyon pa, "the Drukpa madman"; stories about his exploits, similar to the exploits of A khu ston pa (Aku Tönpa), are much beloved in Tibetan society; they draw on Tibetan folk narratives, the Indian SIDDHA tradition, and the Tibetan holy madman (smyon pa) tradition, poking fun at powerful interests and figures of religious authority, particularly monks, and often referring obliquely to esoteric tantric practices; the stories often suggest he engages in profane sexual and scatological activities in order to awaken people from ignorance to an understanding of Buddhist truths. The historical 'Brug pa kun leg (his given name was Kun dga' legs pa; 'Brug pa is short for 'BRUG PA BKA' BRGYUD, a BKA' BRYUD subsect) was born into the noble Rgya (Gya) lineage of RWA LUNG; he was a student of Lha btsun Kun dga' chos kyi rgya mtsho and possibly the Bhutanese saint and RNYING MA treasure revealer (GTER STON) PADMA GLING PA. His lineage was carried on after his death by his son. In his autobiography he describes himself as a difficult and contrary person from an early age; he was an adept at the practice of MAHĀMUDRĀ. Later biographies of Kun dga' legs pa give anachronistic accounts of him making fun of SA SKYA PAṆḌITA and TSONG KHA PA, iconic figures in Tibetan Buddhism, describe his appetite for barley beer and his fantastic love life; some accounts say he was the paramour of over five thousand women whom he enlightened by his teaching and practice. There is a small monastery of 'Brug pa kun legs with a phallic symbol in Bhutan where he is especially revered.

**Bsam gtan mig sgron**. (Samten Mikdrön). In Tibetan, literally "Lamp of the Eye of Concentration"; the title of a ninth-century treatise by GNUBS CHEN SANGS RGYAS YE SHES that discusses four main philosophical approaches prevalent during the early spread (SNGA DAR) of Buddhism in Tibet. These include (1) the gradual path (rim gyis pa); (2) the sudden path (cig car ba); (3) the tradition of MAHĀYOGA; and (4) the RDZOGS CHEN teachings. The text is an important source for understanding the range of meditative practice and theory in Tibet in the period after the BSAM YAS DEBATE and before the persecution of Buddhism under King GLANG DAR MA. The work makes clear reference to the teachings of the Chinese CHAN school in its discussion of the sudden teachings (see DUNJIAO).

**Bsam yas**. (Samye). Tibet's first Buddhist monastery, constructed on the north bank of the Gtsang po (Tsangpo) River in central Tibet, probably circa 779. The Tibetan king KHRI SRONG LDE BTSAN invited the renowned Indian Buddhist preceptor ŚĀNTARAKṢITA to found the institution and ordain Tibet's first monks. According to traditional accounts, local spirits hostile to Buddhism blocked the completion of the project. Unable to continue his work, Śāntarakṣita convinced the Tibetan ruler to invite the powerful Indian tantric master PADMASAMBHAVA to his kingdom in order to subdue these autochthonous spirits. Padmasambhava reached the site and, from atop the nearby hill called He po ri, he subjugated the demons, binding them by oath to become protectors of the dharma (DHARMAPĀLA). The Bsam yas complex was subsequently constructed in the form of a MAṆḌALA arranged in the shape of the universe according to Buddhist cosmological accounts, based on the model of ODANTAPURĪ, a Pāla-dynasty monastery located in the present-day Indian state of Bihar. At the center stands the main basilica, serving as Mount SUMERU, surrounded by chapels representing the four continents and eight subcontinents in the four cardinal directions, all of which is ringed by a massive wall capped with a thousand STŪPAs. According to Tibetan and Chinese sources, in about 797 the monastery served as the venue for a great dispute between proponents of Indian and Chinese Buddhist perspectives on enlightenment and meditation. The outcome of this famous BSAM YAS DEBATE, in which the Indian view is said to have prevailed, greatly influenced the development of Buddhism in Tibet, which subsequently became a tradition that looked more to India than China for inspiration. Bsam yas was a religiously and politically vibrant institution from its inception up to the tenth century, after which its influence waned under BKA' GDAMS, SA SKYA, and eventually DGE LUGS control. Bsam yas's central basilica is renowned for its art and its architectural design, said to be a fusion of styles from India, China, Tibet, and Central Asia. The complex suffered on numerous occasions due to fires and, most recently, at the hands of the Chinese military during the Cultural Revolution. Extensive reconstruction and renovations were begun in the 1980s and Bsam yas remains an important pilgrimage destination and a potent symbol of Tibet's Buddhist heritage.

**Bsam yas debate**. An important event in the early dissemination (SNGA DAR) of Buddhism in Tibet. During the reign of the king KHRI SRONG LDE BRTSAN at the end of the eighth century, there were two Buddhist factions at court, a Chinese faction led by the Northern Chan (BEI ZONG) monk Heshang MOHEYAN (the Chinese transcription of "Mahāyāna") and an Indian faction associated with the recently deceased ŚĀNTARAKṢITA who, with the king and PADMASAMBHAVA, had founded the first Tibetan monastery at BSAM YAS. According to traditional accounts, Śāntarakṣita foretold of dangers and left instructions in his will that his student KAMALAŚĪLA be called from India. A conflict seems to have developed between the Indian and Chinese partisans (and their allies in the Tibetan court) over the question of the nature of enlightenment, with the Indians holding that enlightenment takes place as the culmination of a gradual process of purification, the result of combining ethical practice (ŚĪLA), meditation (SAMĀDHI), and wisdom (PRAJÑĀ). The Chinese spoke against this view, holding that enlightenment was the intrinsic nature of the mind itself rather than the goal of a protracted path of practice. Therefore, to recognize the presence of this innate nature of enlightenment, one need only enter a state of awareness beyond distinctions; all other practices were superfluous. According to both Chinese and Tibetan records, a debate was held between Kamalaśīla and Moheyan at Bsam yas, circa 797, with the king himself serving as judge. According to Tibetan records (contradicted by Chinese accounts), Kamalaśīla was declared the winner and Moheyan and his party were banished from Tibet, with the king proclaiming that the MADHYAMAKA school of Indian Buddhist philosophy (to which Śāntarakṣita and Kamalaśīla belonged) would thereafter be followed in Tibet. Kamalaśīla died shortly after the debate, supposedly assassinated by members of the Chinese faction. Scholars have suggested that although a controversy between the Indian and Chinese Buddhists (and their Tibetan partisans) occurred, it is unlikely that a face-to-face debate took place or that the outcome of the controversy was so unequivocal. The "debate" may instead have been an exchange of statements; indeed, Kāmalaśīla's third BHĀVANĀKRAMA seems to derive from this exchange. It is also important to note that, regardless of the merits of the Indian and Chinese philosophical positions, China was Tibet's chief military rival at the time, whereas India posed no such threat. The debate's principal significance derives from the fact that from this point on, Tibet largely sought its Buddhism from India; no school of Chinese Buddhism subsequently exerted any major influence in Tibet. It is said that when he departed, Moheyan left behind one shoe, indicating that traces of his view would remain in Tibet; some scholars have suggested possible connections between Chan positions and the RDZOGS CHEN teachings that developed in the ninth century. In Tibetan polemics of later centuries, it was considered particularly harsh to link one's opponent's views to the antinomian views of Moheyan. Moheyan himself was transformed into something of a trickster figure, popular in Tibetan art and drama. This event is variously referred to in English as the Council of Samye, the Council of Lha sa, and the Samye Debate. See also DUNWU.

**bsdus grwa**. (dudra). A distinctively Tibetan genre of monastic textbook (used widely in DGE LUGS monasteries) that introduces beginners to the main topics in PRAMĀṆA (T. tshad ma) and ABHIDHARMA. The genre probably originated with the summaries (bsdus pa) of important pramāṇa texts composed by the translator RNGOG BLO LDAN SHES RAB of GSANG PHU NE'U THOG monastery. PHYWA PA CHOS KYI SENG GE is credited with originating the distinctively Tibetan dialectical form that strings together a chain of consequences linked by a chain of reasons that distinguishes bsdus grwa. Beginners are introduced to the main topics in abhidharma and pramāṇa using this formal language, a language that has been heard in Tibetan debate institutions (RTSOD GRWA) down to the present day.

**bshad grwa**. (shedra). In Tibetan, lit. "commentarial institution" or simply "teaching institute"; a part of a monastic complex devoted to the study of scripture, sometimes contrasted with a meditation center (sgrub khang, literally "practice house"). The institution possibly originates with SA SKYA PAṆḌITA who in his *Mkhas pa la 'jug pa'i sgo* proposed a model of intellectual inquiry based on exposition, composition, and debate. In a traditional bshad grwa, the teacher explains line by line an authoritative Indian text, often referring to a Tibetan commentary; this may be followed by a formal period of debate; the teacher then calls on the monks during the next class to give an explanation of the part of the Indian text they have learned. The bshad grwa is contrasted with the RTSOD GRWA (tsödra) "debating institution," the origins of which may go back to the model of study followed in BKA' GDAMS monasteries like GSANG PHU NE'U THOG. The best known rtsod grwa are the six great DGE LUGS monasteries of pre-1959 Tibet, which rarely emphasized the ability to give an explanation of the Indian text, but rather followed strict debating periods where particular points of doctrine were investigated in great detail. In the rtsod grwa, debate was raised to a high level, forming a central part of the curriculum, and the examination system that provided access to important and remunerative ecclesiastical postings in the Dge lugs establishment was based almost entirely on debating, as distinct from the ability to give a full commentary on an Indian text. The bshad grwa appears to have gained particular importance in areas of Khams, in Eastern Tibet, after the rise of the so-called RIS MED (rime) movement in the nineteenth century; of particular note there is the Khams bye bshad grwa in the RDZONG GSAR region of SDE DGE, and the considerable number of new bshad grwa opened by learned monks from the Khams region as annexes of older monasteries that earlier were devoted entirely to ritual. See RDZONG GSAR.

**Bsod nams rgya mtsho**. (Sönam Gyatso) (1543–1588). A Tibetan Buddhist prelate officially identified as the third DALAI LAMA, although he was the first to actually hold the title. Recognized as an accomplished scholar and Buddhist master, he served as the abbot of 'BRAS SPUNGS Monastery. In 1578 he traveled to Mongolia at the invitation of the Tümed ruler Altan Khan, and served as religious instructor to the court. He convinced the Mongols to ban blood sacrifice and other indigenous rites in favor of Buddhist practice. In return, the Mongol Khan bestowed upon his guru the title "Dalai Lama," literally translating the Tibetan's name rgya mtsho ("ocean") into the Mongolian equivalent dalai. The name Dalai Lama was posthumously applied to Bsod nams rgya mtsho's two previous incarnations, DGE 'DUN GRUB and Dge 'dun rgya mtsho (Gendün Gyatso), who became respectively the first and second members of the lineage. Bsod nams rgya mtsho traveled widely throughout eastern Tibet and China, teaching and establishing monastic centers.

**Bsod nams rtse mo**. (Sönam Tsemo) (1142–1182). A renowned scholar of the SA SKYA sect of Tibetan Buddhism, considered one of the five Sa skya forefathers (SA SKYA GONG MA RNAM LNGA). He was born the second son of the great Sa skya founder SA CHEN KUN DGA' SNYING PO. His brother was another of the Sa skya forefathers, Grags pa rgyal mtshan (Drakpa Gyaltsen). He was the uncle of SA SKYA PAṆḌITA. Bsod nams rtse mo was a devoted student of PHYWA PA CHOS KYI SENG GE, studying MADHYAMAKA and PRAMĀṆA with him over the course of eleven years. Bsod nams rtse mo was famous for his commentarial work on Indian tantra, which he categorized in works such as his *Rgyu sde spyi rnam par bzhag pa* ("A General Presentation on the Divisions of Tantra").

**bstan 'gyur**. (tengyur). In Tibetan, "the translated treatises," or ŚĀSTRA collection; referring to the second of the two major divisions of the Tibetan Buddhist canon, along with the BKA' 'GYUR, or "translated word [of the Buddha]." The bstan 'gyur collection contains approximately 225 volumes of commentarial literature and independent works, comprising more than 3,500 texts, most of which were written by Indian Buddhist exegetes. It exists in numerous editions, but was less frequently printed than its companion collection, the bka' 'gyur. Subjects covered include hymns of praise (stotra), SŪTRA commentaries, works on PRAJÑĀPĀRAMITĀ, MADHYAMAKA and YOGĀCĀRA philosophies, ABHIDHARMA, and VINAYA, TANTRA commentaries, and technical treatises on logic, grammar, poetics, medicine, and alchemy.

**bstan rim**. (tenrim). In Tibetan, "stages of the doctrine"; a genre of Tibetan Buddhist literature similar to the "stages of the path" (LAM RIM), of which it is a precursor. Bstan rim texts present a systematic and comprehensive outline of Tibetan Buddhist thought, although they generally differ from "stages of the path" works by referring strictly to MAHĀYĀNA doctrine and avoiding the typology of three spiritual levels of individuals (skyes bu gsum): these are, following the explanation of TSONG KHA PA in his LAM RIM CHEN MO, the individual whose practice leads to a good rebirth, a middling type of individual whose practice leads to NIRVĀṆA, and the great person whose Mahāyāna practice as a BODHISATTVA leads to buddhahood for the sake of all beings. However, the differences between bstan rim and lam rim texts are often blurred; the THAR PA RIN PO CHE'I RGYAN ("Jewel Ornament of Liberation") by SGAM PO PA BSOD NAMS RIN CHEN, for example, is often designated as a "stages of the path" work, although it might more precisely be classified as "stages of the doctrine." Early examples of bstan rim treatises were written at GSANG PHU NE'U THOG monastery by RNGOG BLO LDAN SHES RAB and his followers.

**btsan**. (tsen). A class of Tibetan harmful deities that antedate the introduction of Buddhism. The btsan are said to be subservient to the converted 'BAR BA SPUN BDUN, although they continue to be seen as malicious disease-causing demons. As such, they are sometimes the object of the wrath of the dharma-protectors (DHARMAPĀLA), who carry snares designed to catch them. There are numerous subcategories of btsan, including combinations with other spirits, such as klu btsan and lha btsan; as well as listings according to their abodes: e.g., sa btsan, who live in the soil, brag btsan, who live in rock faces, and so forth.

**Bu chu**. In Tibetan, one of the four "extra taming temples" or "extra pinning temples" (YANG 'DUL GTSUG LAG KHANG) said to have been constructed during the time of the Tibetan king SRONG BTSAN SGAM PO to pin down the limbs of the demoness (T. srin mo) who was impeding the introduction of Buddhism into Tibet. The temple is located in Kong po and pins down her right elbow.

**bucidi sanguan**. (J. fushidai no sangan; K. pulch'aje samgwan 不次第三觀). See SANGUAN.

**Budai**. (J. Hotei; K. P'odae 布袋) (d. 916). A legendary Chinese monk, whose name literally means "Hemp Sack"; also occasionally referred to as Fenghua Budai, Changtingzi, and Budai heshang. He is said to have hailed from Fenghua county in Ningbo prefecture of Zhejiang province. Budai is often depicted as a short figure with an enormous belly and a staff or walking stick on which he has hung a hemp bag or sack (budai), whence derives his name. Budai wandered from one town to the next begging for food, some of which he saved in his sack. This jolly figure is remembered as a thaumaturge who was particularly famous for accurately predicting the weather. On his deathbed, Budai left the following death verse, which implied he was in fact a manifestation of the BODHISATTVA MAITREYA: "Maitreya, true Maitreya, / His thousands, hundreds, and tens of millions of manifestations, / From time to time appear among his fellow men, / But remain unrecognized by his fellow men." Budai is also associated in China with AṄGAJA, the thirteenth of the sixteen ARHATs (see ṢOḌAŚASTHAVIRA) who serve as protector figures. Aṅgaja had been a snake wrangler before he ordained, so whenever he went into the mountains, he carried a cloth bag with him to catch snakes, which he would release after removing their fangs so they would not injure people. For this reason, he earned the nickname "Cloth-Bag Arhat" (Budai luohan/heshang). In Zhejiang province, many images of Budai were made for worship, and an image of Budai installed in the monastery of MANPUKUJI on Mt. Ōbaku in Japan is still referred to as that of the bodhisattva Maitreya. The local cult hero and thaumaturge Budai was quickly appropriated by the CHAN community as a trickster-like figure, leading to Budai often being as called the "Laughing Buddha." In Japan, Budai is also revered as one of the seven gods of virtue (see SHICHIFUKUJIN). It is Budai who is commonly depicted in all manner of kitschy knickknacks and called the "Fat Buddha." He has never been identified with, and is not to be mistaken for, ŚĀKYAMUNI Buddha.

**buddha**. (T. sangs rgyas; C. fo; J. butsu/hotoke; K. pul 佛). In Sanskrit and Pāli, "awakened one" or "enlightened one"; an epithet derived from the Sanskrit root √budh, meaning "to awaken" or "to open up" (as does a flower) and thus traditionally etymologized as one who has awakened from the deep sleep of ignorance and opened his consciousness to encompass all objects of knowledge. The term was used in ancient India by a number of different religious groups, but came to be most strongly associated with followers of the teacher GAUTAMA, the "Sage of the ŚĀKYA Clan" (ŚĀKYAMUNI), who claimed to be only the most recent of a succession of buddhas who had appeared in the world over many eons of time (KALPA). In addition to Śākyamuni, there are many other buddhas named in Buddhist literature, from various lists of buddhas of the past, present, and future, to "buddhas of the ten directions" (daśadigbuddha), viz., everywhere. Although the precise nature of buddhahood is debated by the various schools, a buddha is a person who, in the far distant past, made a previous vow (PŪRVAPRAṆIDHĀNA) to become a buddha in order to reestablish the dispensation or teaching (ŚĀSANA) at a time when it was lost to the world. The path to buddhahood is much longer than that of the ARHAT—as many as three incalculable eons of time (ASAṂKHYEYAKALPA) in some computations—because of the long process of training over the BODHISATTVA path (MĀRGA), involving mastery of the six or ten "perfections" (PĀRAMITĀ). Buddhas can remember both their past lives and the past lives of all sentient beings, and relate events from those past lives in the JĀTAKA and AVADĀNA literature. Although there is great interest in the West in the "biography" of Gautama or Śākyamuni Buddha, the early tradition seemed intent on demonstrating his similarity to the buddhas of the past rather than his uniqueness. Such a concern was motivated in part by the need to demonstrate that what the Buddha taught was not the innovation of an individual, but rather the rediscovery of a timeless truth (what the Buddha himself called "an ancient path" [S. purāṇamārga, P. purāṇamagga]) that had been discovered in precisely the same way, since time immemorial, by a person who undertook the same type of extended preparation. In this sense, the doctrine of the existence of past buddhas allowed the early Buddhist community to claim an authority similar to that of the Vedas of their Hindu rivals and of the JAINA tradition of previous tīrthaṅkaras. Thus, in their biographies, all of the buddhas of the past and future are portrayed as doing many of the same things. They all sit cross-legged in their mother's womb; they are all born in the "middle country" (madhyadeśa) of the continent of JAMBUDVĪPA; immediately after their birth they all take seven steps to the north; they all renounce the world after seeing the four sights (CATURNIMITTA; an old man, a sick man, a dead man, and a mendicant) and after the birth of a son; they all achieve enlightenment seated on a bed of grass; they stride first with their right foot when they walk; they never stoop to pass through a door; they all establish a SAṂGHA; they all can live for an eon if requested to do so; they never die before their teaching is complete; they all die after eating meat. Four sites on the earth are identical for all buddhas: the place of enlightenment, the place of the first sermon that "turns the wheel of the dharma" (DHARMACAKRAPRAVARTANA), the place of descending from TRĀYASTRIṂŚA (heaven of the thirty-three), and the place of their bed in JETAVANA monastery. Buddhas can differ from each other in only eight ways: life span, height, caste (either brāhmaṇa or KṢATRIYA), the conveyance by which they go forth from the world, the period of time spent in the practice of asceticism prior to their enlightenment, the kind of tree they sit under on the night of their enlightenment, the size of their seat there, and the extent of their aura. In addition, there are twelve deeds that all buddhas (dvādaśabuddhakārya) perform. (1) They descend from TUṢITA heaven for their final birth; (2) they enter their mother's womb; (3) they take birth in LUMBINĪ Garden; (4) they are proficient in the worldly arts; (5) they enjoy the company of consorts; (6) they renounce the world; (7) they practice asceticism on the banks of the NAIRAÑJANĀ River; (8) they go to the BODHIMAṆḌA; (9) they subjugate MĀRA; (10) they attain enlightenment; (11) they turn the wheel of the dharma; and (12) they pass into PARINIRVĀṆA. They all have a body adorned with the thirty-two major marks (LAKṢANA; MAHĀPURUṢALAKṢAṆA) and the eighty secondary marks (ANUVYAÑJANA) of a great man (MAHĀPURUṢA). They all have two bodies: a physical body (RŪPAKĀYA) and a body of qualities (DHARMAKĀYA; see BUDDHAKĀYA). These qualities of a buddha are accepted by the major schools of Buddhism. It is not the case, as is sometimes suggested, that the buddha of the mainstream traditions is somehow more "human" and the buddha in the MAHĀYĀNA somehow more "superhuman"; all Buddhist traditions relate stories of buddhas performing miraculous feats, such as the ŚRĀVASTĪ MIRACLES described in mainstream materials. Among the many extraordinary powers of the buddhas are a list of "unshared factors" (ĀVEṆIKA[BUDDHA]DHARMA) that are unique to them, including their perfect mindfulness and their inability ever to make a mistake. The buddhas have ten powers specific to them that derive from their unique range of knowledge (for the list, see BALA). The buddhas also are claimed to have an uncanny ability to apply "skill in means" (UPĀYAKAUŚALYA), that is, to adapt their teachings to the specific needs of their audience. This teaching role is what distinguishes a "complete and perfect buddha" (SAMYAKSAṂBUDDHA) from a "solitary buddha" (PRATYEKABUDDHA) who does not teach: a solitary buddha may be enlightened but he neglects to develop the great compassion (MAHĀKARUṆĀ) that ultimately prompts a samyaksaṃbuddha to seek to lead others to liberation. The Mahāyāna develops an innovative perspective on the person of a buddha, which it conceived as having three bodies (TRIKĀYA): the DHARMAKĀYA, a transcendent principle that is sometimes translated as "truth body"; an enjoyment body (SAṂBHOGAKĀYA) that is visible only to advanced bodhisattvas in exalted realms; and an emanation body (NIRMĀṆAKĀYA) that displays the deeds of a buddha to the world. Also in the Mahāyāna is the notion of a universe filled with innumerable buddha-fields (BUDDHAKṢETRA), the most famous of these being SUKHĀVATĪ of Amitābha. Whereas the mainstream traditions claim that the profundity of a buddha is so great that a single universe can only sustain one buddha at any one time, Mahāyāna SŪTRAs often include scenes of multiple buddhas appearing together. See also names of specific buddhas, including AKṢOBHYA, AMITĀBHA, AMOGHASIDDHI, RATNASAMBHAVA, VAIROCANA. For indigenous language terms for buddha, see FO (C); HOTOKE (J); PHRA PHUTTHA JAO (Thai); PUCH'Ŏ(NIM) (K); SANGS RGYAS (T).

**Buddhabhadra**. (C. Fotuobatuoluo; J. Butsudabatsudara; K. Pult'abaltara 佛陀跋陀羅) (359–429). Important early translator of Indian Buddhist texts into Chinese, also known by the Chinese translation of his name, Juexian, or "Enlightened Sage" (the Chinese above is the more common transcription of his Sanskrit name). According to the "Biographies of Eminent Monks" (GAOSENG ZHUAN), Buddhabhadra was born in north India and joined the SAṂGHA after losing both his parents at an early age. Buddhabhadra studied various scriptures and was adept in both meditation and observing the precepts; he was also renowned for his thaumaturgic talents. At the behest of a Chinese monk named ZHIYAN, Buddhabhadra traveled to China along the southern maritime route. Upon learning of the eminent Kuchean monk KUMĀRAJĪVA's arrival in Chang'an, Buddhabhadra went to the capital in 406 to meet him. Due to a difference of opinion with Kumārajīva, however, Buddhabhadra left for LUSHAN, where he was welcomed by LUSHAN HUIYUAN and installed as the meditation instructor in Huiyuan's community; Buddhabhadra came to be known as one of the eighteen worthies of Lushan. He devoted the rest of his career to translating such scriptures as the DAMODUOLUO CHAN JING, *Guanfo sanmei hai jing*, and AVATAṂSAKASŪTRA, to name just a few. Buddhabhadra also translated the MAHĀSĀṂGHIKA VINAYA with the assistance of FAXIAN and contributed significantly to the growth of Buddhist monasticism in China.

**buddhābhiṣeka**. In Sanskrit, "buddha [image] consecration." See ABHIṢEKA; DIANYAN; NETRAPRATIṢṬHĀPANA.

**Buddhabhūmiśāstra**. (C. Fodijing lun; J. Butsujikyōron; K. Pulchigyŏng non 佛地經論). In Sanskrit, "Exposition of the Stage of Buddhahood"; an influential commentary on the BUDDHABHŪMISŪTRA, attributed to Bandhuprabha (Qinguang; d.u.), a disciple of DHARMAPĀLA (530–561), and collaborators. The commentary is extant only in a seven-roll Chinese translation made by XUANZANG and his translation team in 649–650.

**Buddhabhūmisūtra**. (T. Sangs rgyas kyi sa'i mdo; C. Fodi jing; J. Butsujikyō; K. Pulchi kyŏng 佛地經). In Sanskrit, "Scripture on the Stage of Buddhahood," an important MAHĀYĀNA scripture on the experience of enlightenment. The sūtra begins with a description of the PURE LAND in which the scripture is taught and its audience of BODHISATTVAS, mahāśrāvakas, and MAHĀSATTVAS. The text goes on to describe the five factors that exemplify the stage of buddhahood (buddhabhūmi). The first of these is (1) the wisdom of the DHARMADHĀTU, which is likened to space (ĀKĀŚA) itself, in that it is all-pervasive and uncontained. The next two factors are (2) mirror-like wisdom, or great perfect mirror wisdom (ĀDARŚAJÑĀNA), in which the perfect interfusion between all things is seen as if reflected in a great mirror, and (3) the wisdom of equality, or impartial wisdom (SAMATĀJÑĀNA), which transcends all dichotomies to see everything impartially without coloring by the ego. The scripture then describes (4) the wisdom of specific knowledge (PRATYAVEKṢAṆĀJÑĀNA) and (5) the wisdom of having accomplished what was to be done (KṚTYĀNUṢṬHĀNAJÑĀNA), both of which are attained as a result of the subsequently attained wisdom (TATPṚṢṬHALABDHAJÑĀNA); these two types of knowledge clarify that the dharmadhātu is a realm characterized by both emptiness (ŚŪNYATĀ) and compassion (KARUṆĀ). Finally, similes are offered to elucidate the nature of these wisdoms. The Chinese translation, in one roll, was made by XUANZANG and his translation team in 645 CE. In tantric Buddhism, these five wisdoms or knowledges (JÑĀNA) are linked with the five "buddha families" (see PAÑCATATHĀGATA).

**buddha bodies**. See BUDDHAKĀYA.

**buddhacakṣus**. (P. buddhacakkhu; T. sangs rgyas kyi spyan; C. foyan; J. butsugen; K. puran 佛眼). In Sanskrit, "buddha eye"; one of the five eyes or five sorts of vision (PAÑCACAKṢUS) similar to the five (or six) "clairvoyances" or "superknowledges" (ABHIJÑĀ). In mainstream Buddhist materials, the buddha eye is one of the five sorts of extraordinary vision of a buddha and includes the other four sorts of vision: fleshly eye (MĀṂSACAKṢUS, P. maṅsacakkhu), divine eye (DIVYACAKṢUS, P. dibbacakkhu), wisdom eye (PRAJÑĀCAKṢUS, P. paññācakkhu), and all-seeing eye (samantacakṣus, P. samantacakkhu). In Mahāyāna texts, the buddha eye is described as the eye that knows all dharmas in the full awakening of final enlightenment (ANUTTARASAMYAKSAṂBODHI).

**Buddhacarita**. (T. Sangs rgyas kyi spyod pa; C. Fosuoxing zan; J. Butsushogyōsan; K. Pulsohaeng ch'an 佛所行讚). In Sanskrit, "Acts [viz., Life] of the Buddha"; the title of two verse compositions written in the first and second centuries CE that were intended to serve as a complete biography of the historical Buddha. The first was by the monk Saṅgharakṣa (c. first century CE), whose work survives today only in its Chinese translation. The second version, which became hugely popular across Asia, was composed by the well-known Indian philosopher–poet AŚVAGHOṢA (c. second century), who was supposedly an opponent of Buddhism until he converted after losing a debate with the VAIBHĀṢIKA teacher PĀRŚVA. Because of the early date of Aśvaghoṣa's epic poem, it is of great importance for both the history of Indian Buddhism, as well as the study of classical Indian linguistics and thought. Aśvaghoṣa's version of the Buddha's life begins with a description of his parents—King ŚUDDHODANA and Queen MĀYĀ—and ends with the events that immediately follow his death, or PARINIRVĀṆA. His text is written in the style of high court poetry, or kāvya. In keeping with this style, the *Buddhacarita* is characterized by lengthy digressions and elaborate descriptions. For example, one entire canto is devoted to a detailed description of the sight of the women sleeping in the palace that precedes GAUTAMA's renunciation (pravrajya; see PRAVRAJITA). Canto XII provides an invaluable outline of the ancient Indian Sāṃkhya philosophical system. The *Buddhacarita* has served an important role within the Buddhist tradition itself, as the canonical works do not offer a systematic, chronological account of the Buddha's life from his birth through his death. Only the first half of the *Buddhacarita* is extant in its original Sanskrit; the remainder survives in Tibetan and Chinese translations.

**Buddhadāsa**. (1906–1993). Prominent Thai monk, Buddhist reformer, teacher of meditation, and ecumenical figure. Born the son of a merchant in the village of Pum Riang in southern Thailand, he was educated at Buddhist temple schools. It was customary for males in Thailand to be ordained as Buddhist monks for three months at the age of twenty and then return to lay life. Buddhadāsa decided, however, to remain a monk and quickly gained a reputation as a brilliant thinker, meditator, and teacher. He dwelled for several years in the Thai capital of Bangkok to further his studies but grew disillusioned with the prevailing practices of the SAṂGHA in the city, which he perceived to be lax and corrupt. In 1932, he returned home to an abandoned monastery near his native village to live a simple life, practice meditation, and teach the dharma. He named his monastery Wat Suan Mokkhabalārāma (Garden of the Power of Liberation), which is usually abbreviated to Suan Mokkh, the Garden of Liberation. The monastery became one of the first VIPASSANĀ (S. VIPAŚYANĀ) (insight meditation) centers in southern Thailand. Buddhadāsa spent most of his life at this forest monastery overlooking the sea. Although his formal scholastic training was limited, Buddhadāsa studied Pāli scriptures extensively, in particular the SUTTAPIṬAKA, to uncover their true meaning, which he felt had become obscured by centuries of commentarial overlays, ritual practices, and monastic politics. A gifted orator, his numerous sermons and talks were transcribed and fill an entire room of the National Library in Bangkok. In his writings, many of which are his transcribed sermons, he eschewed the formal style of traditional scholastic commentary in favor of a more informal, and in many ways controversial, approach in which he questioned many of the more popular practices of Thai Buddhism. For example, he spoke out strongly against the practice of merit-making in which lay people offer gifts to monks in the belief that they will receive material reward in their next life. Buddhadāsa argued that this traditionally dominant form of lay practice only keeps the participants in the cycle of rebirth because it is based on attachment, whereas the true form of giving is the giving up of the self. Instead, Buddhadāsa believed that, because of conditioned origination (PRATĪTYASAMUTPĀDA), people are naturally connected through a shared environment and are in fact capable of living harmoniously together. The hindrance to such a harmony comes from attachments to "I" and "mine," which must therefore be severed. Modern and ecumenical in perspective, Buddhadāsa sought to strip traditional Buddhism of what he regarded as obscurantism and superstition, and present the Buddha's teachings in a rational scientific idiom that acknowledged kindred teachings in other religions. Buddhadāsa's interpretations of the dharma have had a great impact on contemporary Buddhist thought in Thailand and are especially influential among the urban intelligentsia, social reformers, and environmentalists. His teachings are often cited as foundational by advocates of engaged Buddhism. The monastery he founded has become a venue for the training of foreign monks and nuns and for interfaith dialogue between Buddhists of different traditions, as well as between Buddhists and adherents of other religions.

**Buddhadatta**. (fl. c. fifth century CE). A prominent Pāli scholar-monk from South India who is presumed by the tradition to have been a personal acquaintance of the preeminent Pāli commentator BUDDHAGHOSA. Buddhadatta lived and wrote his several works at Bhūtamangalagāma monastery in the Cōḷa country (Tamil Nadu) of South India, although it is also said he trained at the MAHĀVIHĀRA in ANURĀDHAPURA in Sri Lanka. Buddhadatta is best known as the author of the ABHIDHAMMĀVATĀRA, the oldest of the noncanonical Pāli works on ABHIDHAMMA (S. ABHIDHARMA). The text is a primer of Pāli abhidhamma, divided into twenty-four chapters called niddesa (S. nirdeśa; "exposition"), which displays many affinities with Buddhaghosa's VISUDDHIMAGGA. Other works attributed to Buddhadatta include the *Vinayavinicchaya*, the *Uttaravinicchaya*, and the *Rūpārūpavibhāga*. Some authorities also attribute to him the *Madhuratthavilāsinī* and the *Jinālaṅkāra*.

**buddhadharma**. (P. buddhadhamma; T. sangs rgyas pa'i chos; C. fofa; J. buppō; K. pulpŏp 佛法). In Sanskrit, "the teachings of the Buddha"; one of the closest Indian equivalents to what in English is called "Buddhism," along with DHARMAVINAYA (teaching and discipline), BUDDHĀNUŚĀSANA (teaching, dispensation, or religion of the Buddha), and ŚĀSANA (teaching or dispensation). ¶ This term is also used with reference to the "unshared factors" (ĀVEṆIKA[BUDDHA]DHARMA), a list of eighteen (or sometimes as many as 140) special qualities (dharma) that are unique to the buddhas, such as their perfect mindfulness and their inability to make a physical or verbal mistake, or for all the qualities that together make up a buddha.

**buddhadhātu**. (T. sangs rgyas kyi khams; C. foxing; J. busshō; K. pulsŏng 佛性). In Sanskrit, "buddha-element," or "buddha-nature"; the inherent potential of all sentient beings to achieve buddhahood. The term is also widely used in Buddhist Sanskrit with the sense of "buddha relic," and the term DHĀTU alone is used to mean "buddha-element" (see also GOTRA, KULA). The term first appears in the MAHĀYĀNA recension of the MAHĀPARINIRVĀṆASŪTRA, now available only in Chinese translation, which states that all sentient beings have the "buddha-element" (FOXING). (The Chinese translation foxing literally means "buddha-nature" and the Chinese has often been mistakenly back-translated as the Sanskrit buddhatā; buddhadhātu is the accepted Sanskrit form.) The origin of the term may, however, be traced back as far as the

AṢṬASĀHASRIKĀPRAJÑĀPĀRAMITĀ, one of the earliest Mahāyāna SŪTRAS, where the fundamental substance of the mind is said to be luminous (prakṛtiś cittasya prabhāsvarā), drawing on a strand of Buddhism that has its antecedents in such statements as the Pāli AṄGUTTARANIKĀYA: "The mind, O monks, is luminous but defiled by adventitious defilements" (pabhassaraṃ idaṃ bhikkhave cittaṃ, tañ ca kho āgantukehi upakkilesehi upakkiliṭṭhaṃ). Because the BODHISATTVA realizes that the buddha-element is inherent in him at the moment that he arouses the aspiration for enlightenment (BODHICITTOTPĀDA) and enters the BODHISATTVAYĀNA, he achieves the profound endurance (KṢĀNTI) that enables him to undertake the arduous training, over not one, but three, incalculable eons of time (ASAṂKHYEYAKALPA), that will lead to buddhahood. The buddhadhātu is a seminal concept of the Mahāyāna and leads to the development of such related doctrines as the "matrix of the tathāgatas" (TATHĀGATAGARBHA) and the "immaculate consciousness" (AMALAVIJÑĀNA). The term is also crucial in the development of the teachings of such indigenous East Asian schools of Buddhism as CHAN, which telescope the arduous path of the bodhisattva into a single moment of sudden awakening (DUNWU) to the inherency of the "buddha-nature" (foxing), as in the Chan teaching that merely "seeing the nature" is sufficient to "attain buddhahood" (JIANXING CHENGFO).

**buddha field**. See BUDDHAKṢETRA.

**Buddhaghosa**. (S. Buddhaghoṣa) (fl. c. 370–450 CE). The preeminent Pāli commentator, who translated into Pāli the Sinhalese commentaries to the Pāli canon and wrote the VISUDDHIMAGGA ("Path of Purification"), the definitive outline of THERAVĀDA doctrine.There are several conflicting accounts of Buddhaghosa's origins, none of which can be dated earlier than the thirteenth century. The Mon of Lower Burma claim him as a native son, although the best-known story, which is found in the CŪḶAVAṂSA (chapter 37), describes Buddhaghosa as an Indian brāhmaṇa who grew up in the environs of the MAHĀBODHI temple in northern India. According to this account, his father served as a purohita (brāhmaṇa priest) for King Saṅgāma, while he himself became proficient in the Vedas and related Brahmanical sciences at an early age. One day, he was defeated in a debate by a Buddhist monk named Revata, whereupon he entered the Buddhist SAṂGHA to learn more about the Buddha's teachings. He received his monk's name Buddhaghosa, which means "Voice of the Buddha," because of his sonorous voice and impressive rhetorical skills. Buddhaghosa took Revata as his teacher and began writing commentaries even while a student. Works written at this time included the *Ñāṇodaya* and AṬṬHASĀLINĪ. To deepen his understanding (or according to some versions of his story, as punishment for his intellectual pride), Buddhaghosa was sent to Sri Lanka to study the Sinhalese commentaries on the Pāli Buddhist canon (P. tipiṭaka; S. TRIPIṬAKA). These commentaries were said to have been brought to Sri Lanka in the third century BCE, where they were translated from Pāli into Sinhalese and subsequently preserved at the MAHĀVIHĀRA monastery in the Sri Lankan capital of ANURĀDHAPURA. At the Mahāvihāra, Buddhghosa studied under the guidance of the scholar-monk Saṅghapāla. Upon completing his studies, he wrote the great compendium of Theravāda teachings, *Visuddhimagga*, which summarizes the contents of the Pāli tipiṭaka under the threefold heading of morality (sīla; S. ŚĪLA), meditative absorption (SAMĀDHI), and wisdom (paññā; S. PRAJÑĀ). Impressed with his expertise, the elders of the Mahāvihāra allowed Buddhaghosa to translate the Sinhalese commentaries back into Pāli, the canonical language of the Theravāda tipiṭaka. Attributed to Buddhaghosa are the VINAYA commentaries, SAMANTAPĀSĀDIKĀ and *Kaṅkhāvitaraṇī*; the commentaries to the SUTTAPIṬAKA, SUMAṄGALAVILĀSINĪ, PAPAÑCASŪDANĪ, SĀRATTHAPPAKĀSINĪ, and MANORATHAPŪRAṆĪ; also attributed to him is the PARAMATTHAJOTIKĀ (the commentary to the KHUDDAKAPĀṬHA and SUTTANIPĀTA). Buddhaghosa's commentaries on the ABHIDHAMMAPIṬAKA (see ABHIDHARMA) include the SAMMOHAVINODANĪ and PAÑCAPPAKARAṆAṬṬHAKATHĀ, along with the *Aṭṭhasālinī*. Of these many works, Buddhaghosa is almost certainly author of the *Visuddhimagga* and translator of the commentaries to the four nikāyas, but the remainder are probably later attributions. Regardless of attribution, the body of work associated with Buddhaghosa was profoundly influential on the entire subsequent history of Buddhist scholasticism in the Theravāda traditions of Sri Lanka and Southeast Asia.

**Buddhaguhya**. (fl. c. 760) (T. Sangs rgyas gsang ba). Sanskrit proper name of the author of a detailed commentary on the MAHĀVAIROCANĀBHISAṂBODHISŪTRA ("Great Vairocana's Enlightenment Discourse"); his commentary (*Mahāvairocanābhisaṃbodhi-vikurvitādhiṣṭhāna-vaipulyasūtrendrarāja-nāma-dharmaparyāyabhāṣya*), and his *Tantrārthā-vatāra* ("Introduction to the Meaning of the Tantras") are said to have been the primary resource for Tibetan translators of tantra during the earlier spread of the doctrine (SNGA DAR). He is claimed to have been the teacher of VIMALAMITRA. His views on KRIYĀTANTRA and CARYĀTANTRA are considered authoritative by later Tibetan writers.

**buddhahood**. See BUDDHAYĀNA; BODHISATTVAYĀNA.

**buddhakāya**. (T. sangs rgyas sku; C. foshen; J. busshin; K. pulsin 佛身). In Sanskrit, literally "body of the buddha." Throughout the history of the Buddhist tradition, there has been a great deal of debate, and a good many theories, over the exact nature of a buddha's body. In the Pāli NIKĀYAS and the Sanskrit ĀGAMAS, we find a distinction made between various possible bodies of ŚĀKYAMUNI Buddha. There are references, for example, to a pūtikāya, or corruptible body, which was born from the womb of his mother; a MANOMAYAKĀYA, or mind-made body, which he uses to visit the heavens; and a DHARMAKĀYA, the buddhas' corpus of unique qualities (ĀVEṆIKA[BUDDHA]DHARMA), which is worthy of greater honor than the other two bodies and is the body of the buddha in which one seeks refuge (ŚARAṆA). Perhaps the most popular of these theories on the nature of the buddhakāya is the MAHĀYĀNA notion of the "three bodies," or TRIKĀYA. According to this doctrine, a buddha is indistinguishable from absolute truth, but will still appear in various guises in the relative, conditioned world in order to guide sentient beings toward enlightenment. To distinguish these differing roles, Mahāyāna thus distinguishes between three bodies of a buddha. First, a buddha has a dharmakāya, which is identical to absolute reality. Second, a buddha has a SAṂBHOGAKĀYA, or "enjoyment body," which resides in a buddha land (BUDDHAKṢETRA); this is the body that is visible only to the BODHISATTVAS. Finally, a buddha possesses a NIRMĀṆAKĀYA, a "transformation" or "emanation body," which are the various earthly bodies that a buddha makes manifest in order to fulfill his resolution to help all different types of sentient beings; this type of body includes the Buddha who achieved enlightenment beneath the BODHI TREE. These are many other theories of the buddhakāya that have developed within the tradition.

**buddhakṣetra**. (T. sangs rgyas zhing; C. focha; J. bussetsu; K. pulch'al 佛刹). In Sanskrit, "buddha field," the realm that constitutes the domain of a specific buddha. A buddhakṣetra is said to have two aspects, which parallel the division of a world system into a BHĀJANALOKA (lit. "container world," "world of inanimate objects") and a SATTVALOKA ("world of sentient beings"). As a result of his accumulation of merit (PUṆYASAṂBHĀRA), his collection of knowledge (JÑĀNASAṂBHĀRA), and his specific vow (PRAṆIDHĀNA), when a buddha achieves enlightenment, a "container" or "inanimate" world is produced in the form of a field where the buddha leads beings to enlightenment. The inhabitant of that world is the buddha endowed with all the BUDDHADHARMAS. Buddha-fields occur in various levels of purification, broadly divided between pure (VIŚUDDHABUDDHAKṢETRA) and impure. Impure buddha-fields are synonymous with a world system (CAKRAVĀḌA), the infinite number of "world discs" in Buddhist cosmology that constitutes the universe; here, ordinary sentient beings (including animals, ghosts, and hell beings) dwell, subject to the afflictions (KLEŚA) of greed (LOBHA), hatred (DVEṢA), and delusion (MOHA). Each cakravāḍa is the domain of a specific buddha, who achieves enlightenment in that world system and works there toward the liberation of all sentient beings. A pure buddha-field, by contrast, may be created by a buddha upon his enlightenment and is sometimes called a PURE LAND (JINGTU, more literally, "purified soil" in Chinese), a term with no direct equivalent in Sanskrit. In such purified buddha-fields, the unfortunate realms (APĀYA, DURGATI) of animals, ghosts, and hell denizens are typically absent. Thus, the birds that sing beautiful songs there are said to be emanations of the buddha rather than sentient beings who have been reborn as birds. These pure lands include such notable buddhakṣetras as ABHIRATI, the buddha-field of the buddha AKṢOBHYA, and SUKHĀVATĪ, the land of the buddha AMITĀBHA and the object of a major strand of East Asian Buddhism, the so-called pure land school (see JŌDOSHŪ, JŌDO SHINSHŪ). In the VIMALAKĪRTINIRDEŚA, after the buddha reveals a pure buddha land, ŚĀRIPUTRA asks him why ŚĀKYAMUNI's buddha-field has so many faults. The buddha then touches the earth with his toe, at which point the world is transformed into a pure buddha-field; he explains that he makes the world appear impure in order to inspire his disciples to seek liberation.

**buddhakula**. (T. sangs rgyas rigs; C. rulai jia; J. nyoraike; K. yŏrae ka 如來家). In Sanskrit, "buddha family"; synonymous with GOTRA ("lineage"); buddhakula and gotra, like BUDDHADHĀTU and TATHĀGATAGARBHA refer to the potential inherent in all sentient beings to achieve buddhahood. The RATNAGOTRAVIBHĀGA describes a confluence of three necessary factors: the altruistic effort that buddhas make out of their great compassion (MAHĀKARUṆĀ) to disseminate their doctrines; the ultimate nature of beings that is purified of any essential defilement; and, last, buddhakula or gotra, i.e., belonging to a lineage that does not lead to endless rebirth or to a final end in the limited NIRVĀṆA of HĪNAYĀNA adepts, but rather to the royal state of a buddha. The defining mark of the buddhakula is the seed of great compassion (mahākaruṇā). Because of the confluence of these three factors, all beings are said to have the TATHĀGATAGARBHA, which in this interpretation of the compound means the womb or embryo of a tathāgata. In tantric Buddhism, there are typically five (but sometimes more and sometimes less, depending on the tantra) buddha families (see PAÑCAJINA, PAÑCATATHĀGATA), the families of VAIROCANA, AKṢOBHYA, RATNASAMBHAVA, AMITĀBHA, and AMOGHASIDDHI. These buddhas (regarded as the final purification and transformation of the five SKANDHAS) are the forms in which adepts with differing personality types, those in whom the five KLEŚAS of delusion (MOHA), hatred (DVEṢA), pride (MĀNA), desire (RĀGA), and jealousy (ĪRṢYĀ), respectively, predominate, reach the goal. The five buddha families are also connected with the five YOGĀCĀRA knowledges or wisdoms (JÑĀNA) (see BUDDHABHŪMISŪTRA; PAÑCAJÑĀNA).

**Buddhamitra**. (C. Fotuomiduoluo; J. Butsudamitsutara; K. Pult'amiltara 佛陀蜜多羅). In Sanskrit, literally "Friend of the Buddha"; one of the Indian patriarchs listed in Chinese lineage records. He is variously listed in Chinese sources as the ninth (e.g., in the LIDAI FABAO JI and BAOLIN ZHUAN), the eighth (e.g., FU FAZANG YINYUAN ZHUAN), or the fifteenth (e.g., LIUZU TAN JING) patriarch of the Indian tradition. He is said to have been born into the vaiśya caste of agriculturalists, in the kingdom of Daigya. His master was the patriarch BUDDHANANDI. According to tradition, when Buddhamitra was fifty years old, Buddhanandi was passing by the house in which Buddhamitra lived; seeing a white light floating above the house, Buddhanandi immediately recognized that his successor was waiting inside. Buddhamitra is also said to be one of the teachers of the Indian Buddhist philosopher VASUBANDHU and is considered the author of a work known as the *Pañcadvāradhyānasūtramahārthadharma*.

**Buddhanandi**. (C. Fotuonanti; J. Butsudanandai; K. Pult'ananje 佛陀難提). In Sanskrit, literally "Joy of the Buddha"; one of the Indian patriarchs listed in Chinese lineage records. He is variously listed in Chinese sources as the eighth (e.g., in the LIDAI FABAO JI and BAOLIN ZHUAN), the seventh (e.g., FU FAZANG YINYUAN ZHUAN), or the fourteenth (e.g., LIUZU TAN JING) patriarch of the Indian tradition. He is said to hail from the Indian country of Kamala, and is a member of the Gautama family. According to some records (e.g., BAOLIN ZHUAN), his master was the patriarch VASUMITRA.

**buddha-nature**. See BUDDHADHĀTU; FOXING.

**buddhānuśāsana**. In Sanskrit, "the dispensation of the Buddha." See ŚĀSANA; BUDDHAVACANA.

**buddhānusmṛti**. (P. buddhānussati; T. sangs rgyas rjes su dran pa; C. nianfo; J. nenbutsu; K. yŏmbul 念佛). In Sanskrit, "recollection of the Buddha"; one of the common practices designed to develop concentration, in which the meditator reflects on the meritorious qualities of the Buddha, often through contemplating a series of his epithets. The oldest list of epithets of the Buddha used in such recollection, which is found across all traditions, is worthy one (ARHAT), fully enlightened (SAMYAKSAṂBUDDHA), perfect in both knowledge and conduct (vidyācaraṇasampanna), well gone (SUGATA), knower of all worlds (lokavid), teacher of divinities (or kings) and human beings (śāstṛ devamanuṣyānaṃ), buddha, and BHAGAVAT. Buddhānusmṛti is listed among the forty meditative exercises (KAMMAṬṬHĀNA) discussed in the VISUDDHIMAGGA and is said to be conducive to gaining access concentration (UPACĀRASAMĀDHI). In East Asia, this recollection practice evolved into the recitation of the name of the buddha AMITĀBHA (see NIANFO) in the form of the phrase namo Amituo fo ("homage to Amitābha Buddha"; J. NAMU AMIDABUTSU). This recitation was often performed in a ritual setting accompanied by the performance of prostrations, the burning of incense, and the recitation of scriptures, all directed toward gaining a vision of Amitābha's PURE LAND (SUKHĀVATĪ), which was considered proof that one would be reborn there. Nianfo practice was widely practiced across schools and social strata in China. In Japan, repetition of the phrase in its Japanese pronunciation of namu Amidabutsu (homage to Amitābha Buddha) became a central practice of the Japanese Pure Land schools of Buddhism (see JŌDOSHŪ, JŌDO SHINSHŪ).

**buddhapāda**. (T. sangs rgyas kyi zhabs; C. fozu; J. bussoku; K. pulchok 佛足). In Sanskrit and Pāli, lit. "the feet of the Buddha"; typically referring to "the Buddha's footprints," which became objects of religious veneration in early Buddhism. There are typically three kinds of footprints of the Buddha, all of which are treated as a type of relic (ŚARĪRA, DHĀTU). At the incipiency of the tradition, the Buddha's footprints were a popular aniconic representation of the Buddha; the oldest of these, from the BHĀRHUT reliquary mound (STŪPA), dates to the second century BCE. The second are natural indentations in rock that are said to have been made by the Buddha's feet; an example is the Sri Lankan mountain known as Śrī Pāda, or "Holy Foot," which is named after an impression in the rock of the mountain's summit that the Sinhalese people believe to be a footprint of GAUTAMA Buddha. Both these first and second types are concave images and are presumed to be a sign of the Buddha's former presence in a specific place. Such footprints are also often important as traditional evidence of a visit by the Buddha to a distant land. The third form of footprint are convex images carved in stone, metal, or wood (or in some cases painted), which represent the soles of the Buddha's feet in elaborate detail and are often covered with all manner of auspicious symbols. They may bear the specific physical marks (LAKṢAṆA) said to be present on the feet of a fully awakened being, such as having toes that are all the same length, or having dharma-wheels (DHARMACAKRA) inscribed on the soles (see MAHĀPURUṢALAKṢAṆA). In the Pāli tradition, there is a practice of making buddhapāda in which the central wheel is surrounded by a retinue (parivāra) of 108 auspicious signs, called MAṄGALA. Symbolically, the footprints point to the reality of the Buddha's erstwhile physical presence in our world. At the same time, the footprints also indicate his current absence and thus may encourage the observer to reflect on nonattachment. Veneration of the Buddha's footprints occurs throughout the Buddhist world but is particularly popular in Sri Lanka, Burma, and Thailand. Of his footprints, tradition reports that the Buddha said, "In the future, intelligent beings will see the scriptures and understand. Those of less intelligence will wonder whether the Buddha appeared in the world. In order to remove their doubts, I have set my footprints in stone."

**Buddhapālita**. (T. Sangs rgyas bskyang) (c. 470–540). An Indian Buddhist scholar of the MADHYAMAKA school, who is regarded in Tibet as a key figure of what was dubbed the *PRĀSAṄGIKA school of Madhyamaka. Little is known about the life of Buddhapālita. He is best known for his commentary on NĀGĀRJUNA's MŪLAMADHYAMAKAKĀRIKĀ, a commentary that was thought to survive only in Tibetan translation, until the recent rediscovery of a Sanskrit manuscript. Buddhapālita's commentary bears a close relation in some chapters to the AKUTOBHAYĀ, another commentary on Nāgārjuna's *Mūlamadhyamakakārikā* of uncertain authorship, which is sometimes attributed to Nāgārjuna himself. In his commentary, Buddhapālita does not adopt some of the assumptions of the Buddhist logical tradition of the day, including the need to state one's position in the form of an autonomous inference (SVATANTRĀNUMĀNA). Instead, Buddhapālita merely states an absurd consequence (PRASAṄGA) that follows from the opponent's position. In his own commentary on the first chapter of Nāgārjuna's text, BHĀVAVIVEKA criticizes Buddhapālita's method, arguing for the need for the Madhyamaka adept to state his own position after refuting the position of the opponent. In his commentary on the same chapter, CANDRAKĪRTI in turn defended the approach of Buddhapālita and criticized Bhāvaviveka. It was on the basis of these three commentaries that later Tibetan exegetes identified two schools within Madhyamaka, the SVĀTANTRIKA, in which they included Bhāvaviveka, and the Prāsaṅgika, in which they included Buddhapālita and Candrakīrti.

**buddhapātramudrā**. (T. sangs rgyas kyi lhung bzed phyag rgya; C. foboyin; J. buppatsuin; K. pulbarin 佛鉢印). In Sanskrit, "the gesture of the Buddha's begging bowl." In this symbolic posture or gesture (MUDRĀ), the Buddha holds a begging bowl (PĀTRA) that sits in his lap. In some variations, the hands hold a jewel, or ornate treasure box, instead. In esoteric rituals, variations of this mudrā may be used for a number of different outcomes. For example, one Chinese indigenous SŪTRA (see APOCRYPHA) suggests that forming and holding this gesture will cure stomach ailments. In another Japanese ritual, this mudrā is used to invite autochthonous deities to join the audience in attendance. The buddhapātramudrā is typically associated with images of the Buddha AMITĀBHA, whose begging bowl is filled with the nectar of immortality (AMṚTA).

**buddhatā**. (S). See BUDDHADHĀTU.

**Buddhatrāta**. (C. Fotuoduoluo; J. Butsudatara; K. Pult'adara 佛陀多羅). Proper name of the putative translator of the YUANJUE JING (*Dafangguang yuanjue xiuduoluo liaoyi jing*; "Book of Perfect Enlightenment"). According to the KAIYUAN SHIJIAO LU, Zhisheng's catalogue of Chinese Buddhist scriptural translations, Buddhatrāta hailed from Kashmir (see KASHMIR-GANDHĀRA) and translated this text, in 693, at BAIMASI outside the Chinese capital of Luoyang. Although Zhisheng's attribution is followed by all subsequent cataloguers, this scripture is now generally recognized to be an indigenous Chinese Buddhist scripture (see APOCRYPHA) from the eighth century CE, so his ascription is dubious. There are a few other works attributed to a Buddhatrāta in the Chinese catalogues, including a vinaya text and a commentary to the YULANBEN JING, but it is unclear whether these are the same Buddhatrāta; nothing else is known about his life or activities in China.

**buddhavacana**. (T. sangs rgyas kyi bka'; C. foyu; J. butsugo; K. purŏ 佛語). In Sanskrit and Pāli, "word of the Buddha"; those teachings accepted as having been either spoken by the Buddha or spoken with his sanction. Much traditional scholastic literature is devoted to the question of what does and does not qualify as the word of the Buddha. The SŪTRAPIṬAKA and the VINAYAPIṬAKA of the Buddhist canon (TRIPIṬAKA), which are claimed to have been initially redacted at the first Buddhist council (see COUNCIL, FIRST), held in RĀJAGṚHA soon after the Buddha's death, is considered by the tradition—along with the ABHIDHARMAPIṬAKA, which was added later—to be the authentic word of the Buddha; this judgment is made despite the fact that the canon included texts that were spoken, or elaborated upon, by his direct disciples (e.g., separate versions of the BHADDEKARATTASUTTA, which offer exegeses by various disciples of an enigmatic verse the Buddha had taught) or that included material that clearly postdated the Buddha's death (such as the MAHĀPARINIRVĀṆASŪTRA, which tells of the events leading up to, and immediately following, the Buddha's demise, or the *Nāradasutta*, which refers to kings who lived long after the Buddha's time). Such material could still be considered buddhavacana, however, by resort to the four references to authority (MAHĀPADEŚA; CATURMAHĀPADEŚA). These four types of authority are found listed in various SŪTRAS, including the eponymous Pāli *Mahāpadesasutta*, and provide an explicit set of criteria through which to evaluate whether a teaching is the authentic buddhavacana. Teachings could be accepted as authentic if they were heard from four authorities: (1) the mouth of the Buddha himself; (2) a SAMGHA of wise elders; (3) a group of monks who were specialists in either the dharma (dharmadhara), vinaya (vinayadhara), or the proto-abhidharma (mātṛkādhara); or (4) a single monk who was widely learned in such specializations. The teaching should then be compared side by side with the authentic SŪTRA and VINAYA; if found to be compatible with these two strata of the canon and not in contradiction with reality (DHARMATĀ), it would then be accepted as the buddhavacana and thus marked by the characteristics of the Buddha's words (buddhavacanalakṣaṇa). Because of this dispensation, the canons of all schools of Buddhism were never really closed, but could continue to be reinvigorated with new expressions of the Buddha's insights. In addition, completely new texts that purported to be from the mouths of the buddha(s) and/or BODHISATTVAS, such as found in the MAHĀYĀNA or VAJRAYĀNA traditions, could also begin to circulate and be accepted as the authentic buddhavacana since they too conformed with the reality (dharmatā) that is great enlightenment (MAHĀBODHI). For example, a Mahāyāna sūtra, the *Adhyāśayasañcodanasūtra*, declares, "All which is well-spoken, Maitreya, is spoken by the Buddha." The sūtra qualifies the meaning of "well spoken" (subhāṣita), explaining that all inspired speech should be known to be the word of the Buddha if it is meaningful and not meaningless, if it is principled and not unprincipled, if it brings about the extinction and not the increase of the afflictions (KLEŚA), and if it sets forth the qualities and benefits of NIRVĀṆA and not the qualities and benefits of SAṂSĀRA. However, the authenticity of the Mahāyāna sūtras (and later the tantras) was a topic of great contention between the proponents of the Mahāyāna and mainstream schools throughout the history of Indian Buddhism and beyond. Defenses of the Mahāyāna as buddhavacana appear in the Mahāyāna sūtras themselves, with predictions of the terrible fates that will befall those who deny their authenticity; and arguments for the authenticity of the Mahāyāna sūtras were a stock element in writings by Mahāyāna authors as early as NĀGĀRJUNA and extending over the next millennium. Related, and probably earlier, terms for buddhavacana are the "teaching of the master" (S. śāstuḥ śāsanam) and the "dispensation of the Buddha" (buddhānuśāsanam). See also APOCRYPHA, DAZANGJING, GTER MA.

**Buddhavaṃsa**. In Pāli, "The Chronicle of the Buddhas"; the fourteenth book of the KHUDDAKANIKĀYA of the Pāli SUTTAPIṬAKA. A work in verse, it contains the life histories of twenty-five buddhas, concluding with that of the historical Buddha, Gotama (S. GAUTAMA). Details of each buddha are given, such as the species of the BODHI TREE under which he sat at the time of attaining enlightenment, as well as the name that the future buddha Gotama assumed under each previous buddha. The final chapter concerns the distribution of the relics (sarīra; S. ŚARĪRA) of Gotama Buddha. According to Theravāda tradition, the *Buddhavaṃsa* was preached at the request of the Buddha's disciple Sāriputta (S. ŚĀRIPUTRA), following the Buddha's display of the "jeweled-walk" (ratanacaṅkama) miracle, which is the name of the chronicle's first chapter. The *Madhuratthavilāsinī* is the Pāli commentary to the *Buddhavaṃsa*.

**buddhavarṣa**. (P. buddhavassa; T. sangs rgyas kyi lo; C. foji; J. butsuki; K. pulgi 佛紀). In Sanskrit, "Buddhist Era." The term used for the Buddhist calendar calculated from the date of the final demise (S. PARINIRVĀṆA; P. parinibbāna) of the Buddha. There is general agreement among Buddhist traditions that the Buddha died in his eightieth year, but no consensus as to the date of his death and hence no agreement regarding the commencement of the Buddhist era. Dates for the parinirvāṇa given in texts and inscriptions from across Buddhist Asia range from 2420 BCE to 290 BCE. One of the more commonly used dates is 544/543 BCE, which is the year asserted for the Buddha's death by the THERAVĀDA tradition of Sri Lanka and Southeast Asia. Use of the Theravāda calendar most likely originated in Sri Lanka, where it is attested in inscriptions dating from as early as the first century BCE. The same calendar appears in Burmese inscriptions beginning in the eleventh century, which coincides with that country's adoption of Theravāda Buddhism as its dominant faith. The earliest known record of its use in India is likewise relatively late, and dates from the thirteenth century in an inscription erected at BODHGAYĀ. Since at least the fifth century, the Theravāda traditions have asserted that the religion of the Buddha (P. buddhasāsana; see ŚĀSANA) would endure for five thousand years. Accordingly, in 1956 the halfway point in the life span of the religion was presumed to have been reached, an event that was celebrated with considerable millenarian overtones throughout the Theravāda world in the Buddha Jayantī ("Celebration of Buddhism"). A historically significant feature of the Theravāda calendar is that it places the coronation of the Mauryan emperor AŚOKA 218 years after the parinirvāṇa of the Buddha. This contrasts with another ancient Buddhist calendar tradition, preserved primarily in Sanskrit sources, which instead places Aśoka's coronation one hundred years after the parinirvāṇa. The two calendars have come to be designated in modern scholarship as the "long chronology" and "short chronology," respectively. According to the long chronology, the Buddha's dates would be 566–486 BCE. According to the short chronology, they would be 448–368 BCE. The precise dating of the Buddha's parinirvāṇa has been a contested issue among scholars for well over a century, and both the long and the short chronologies, as well as permutations thereof, have had their supporters. At present, there is widespread consensus, based primarily on Greek accounts and Aśoka's own inscriptions, that Aśoka ascended to the Mauryan throne in c. 265 BCE, or approximately sixty years later than what is reported in the long chronology. Scholars who accept this dating, but who still adhere to the Theravāda claim that the Buddha died 218 years before this event, therefore place the parinirvāṇa at c. 480 BCE. This is known as the "corrected long chronology" and is the theory upheld by many contemporary scholars of Indian Buddhism. Recently however, a number of historians have argued, based primarily on a reevaluation of evidence found in the DĪPAVAṂSA, that the short chronology is the earlier and more accurate calendar, and that the parinirvāṇa should be moved forward accordingly to between c. 400 and 350 BCE. Many contemporary traditions of East Asian Buddhism now also follow the modern Theravāda system in which the Buddha's parinirvāṇa is calculated as 544/543 BCE.

**Buddhāvataṃsakasūtra**. In Sanskrit, "Scripture of the Garland of Buddhas." See AVATAṂSAKASŪTRA.

**buddhayāna**. (T. sangs rgyas kyi theg pa; C. fo sheng; J. butsujō; K. pul sŭng 佛乘). In Sanskrit, "buddha vehicle," the conveyance leading to the state of buddhahood. In general, the buddhayāna is synonymous with both the BODHISATTVAYĀNA and the MAHĀYĀNA, although in some contexts it is considered superior to them, being equivalent to a supreme EKAYĀNA. When this path is perfected, the adept achieves the full range of special qualities unique to the buddhas (ĀVEṆIKA[BUDDHA]DHARMA), which result from mastery of the perfections (PĀRAMITĀ). This understanding of the term buddhayāna and its significance is explained in chapter two of the SADDHARMAPUṆḌARĪKASŪTRA ("Lotus Sūtra"). There, the Buddha compares three means of salvation to three carts promised to children in an effort to convince them to come out from a burning house. The three carts are said to correspond to the three vehicles (TRIYĀNA). The first is the ŚRĀVAKAYĀNA, the vehicle for ŚRĀVAKAS ("disciples"), in which teachings were learned from a buddha and which culminates in becoming a "worthy one" (ARHAT). Next is the PRATYEKABUDDHAYĀNA, the vehicle of the PRATYEKABUDDHA or "solitary buddha," those who strive for enlightenment but do not rely on a buddha in their last life. The third is the bodhisattvayāna, the path followed by the BODHISATTVA to buddhahood. In the parable in the "Lotus Sūtra," the Buddha uses the prospect of these three vehicles to entice the children to leave the burning house; once they are safely outside, they find not three carts waiting for them but instead a single magnificent cart. The Buddha then declares the three vehicles to be a form of skillful means (UPĀYAKAUŚALYA), for there is in fact only one vehicle (ekayāna), also referred to as the buddha vehicle (buddhayāna). Later exegetes, especially in East Asia, engaged in extensive scholastic investigation of the relationships between the terms bodhisattvayāna, buddhayāna, and ekayāna.

**Buddhayaśas**. (C. Fotuoyeshe; J. Butsudayasha; K. Pult'ayasa 佛陀耶舍) (d.u.; fl. c. early fifth century). A monk from Kashmir (see KASHMIR-GANDHĀRA) who became an important early translator of Indic Buddhist texts into Chinese. Buddhayaśas is said to have memorized several million words worth of both mainstream and Mahāyāna materials and became a renowned teacher in his homeland. He later taught the SARVĀSTIVĀDA VINAYA to the preeminent translator KUMĀRAJĪVA and later joined his star pupil in China, traveling to the capital of Chang'an at Kumārajīva's invitation in 408. While in China, he collaborated with the Chinese monk ZHU FONIAN (d.u.) in the translation of two massive texts of the mainstream Buddhist tradition: the SIFEN LÜ ("Four-Part Vinaya," in sixty rolls), the vinaya collection of the DHARMAGUPTAKA school, which would become the definitive vinaya used within the Chinese tradition; and the DĪRGHĀGAMA, also generally presumed to be associated with the Dharmaguptakas. Even after returning to Kashmir four years later, Buddhayaśas is said to have continued with his translation work, eventually sending back to China his rendering of the *Ākāśagarbhasūtra*.

**buddhi**. (T. blo; C. siwei; J. shiyui; K. sayu 思惟). In Sanskrit and Pāli, "intelligence," "comprehension," or "discernment"; referring specifically to the ability to fashion and retain concepts and ideas (related etymologically to the words buddha and BODHI, from the root √budh "to wake up"). In Buddhist usage, buddhi sometimes denotes a more elevated faculty of mind that surpasses the rational and discursive in its ability to discern truth. Buddhi is thus a kind of intuitive intelligence, comprehension, or insight, which can serve to catalyze wisdom (PRAJÑĀ) and virtuous (KUŚALA) actions. According to some strands of MAHĀYĀNA philosophy, this discernment is an inherent and fundamental characteristic of the mind, which is essentially free of all mistaken discriminations and devoid of distinction or change. In such contexts, buddhi is often associated with the original nature of the mind. See RIG PA.

**Buddhism**. See BUDDHADHARMA; BUDDHAVACANA; DHARMA-VINAYA; ŚĀSANA.

**Buddhist Councils**. See SAṂGĪTI and listings under COUNCIL, FIRST, etc.

**Buddhist Hybrid Sanskrit**. A term coined by the Sanskritist FRANKLIN EDGERTON, who compiled the definitive grammar and dictionary of the language, to refer to the peculiar Buddhist argot of Sanskrit that is used both in many Indic MAHĀYĀNA scriptures, as well as in the MAHĀVASTU, a biography of the Buddha composed within the LOKOTTARAVĀDA subgroup of the MAHĀSĀṂGHIKA school. Edgerton portrays Buddhist Hybrid Sanskrit texts as the products of a gradual Sanskritization of texts that had originally been composed in various Middle Indic dialects (PRAKRIT). Buddhist Hybrid Sanskrit (BHS) texts were not wholesale renderings of vernacular materials intended to better display Sanskrit vocabulary, grammar, and syntax, but rather were ongoing, and often incomplete, reworkings of Buddhist materials, which reflected the continued prestige of Sanskrit within the Indic scholarly community. This argot of Sanskrit is sometimes called the "GĀTHĀ dialect," because its peculiarities are especially noticeable in Mahāyāna verse forms. Edgerton describes three layers of Buddhist Hybrid Sanskrit based on the extent of their hybridization (and only loosely chronological). The first, and certainly earliest, class consists solely of the *Mahāvastu*, the earliest extant BHS text, in which both the prose and verse portions of the scripture contain many hybridized forms. In the second class, verses remain hybridized, but the prose sections are predominantly standard Sanskrit and are recognizable as BHS only in their vocabulary. This second class includes many of the most important Mahāyāna scriptures, including the GAṆḌAVYŪHA, LALITAVISTARA, SADDHARMAPUṆḌARĪKASŪTRA, and SUKHĀVATĪVYŪHASŪTRA. In the third class, both the verse and prose sections are predominantly standard Sanskrit, and only in their vocabulary would they be recognized as BHS. Texts in this category include the AṢṬASĀHASRIKĀPRAJÑĀPĀRAMITĀ, BODHISATTVABHŪMI, LAṄKĀVATĀRASŪTRA, MŪLASARVĀSTIVĀDA VINAYA, and VAJRACCHEDIKĀPRAJÑĀPĀRAMITĀSŪTRA.

**bugongye**. (C) (不共業). See GONG BUGONG YE.

**Bukai nanshin**. (J) (霧海南針). See MUKAI NANSHIN.

**Bukkoku Kokushi**. (J) (佛國國師). See KŌHŌ KENNICHI.

**buli wenzi**. (J. furyūmonji; K. pullip muncha 不立文字). In Chinese, lit. "not establishing words and letters"; a line summarizing the CHAN school's unique sense of its own pedigree, as a school of Buddhism that does not rely on the scriptural teachings of Buddhism but has a direct connection through the "buddhas and patriarchs" (FOZU) to the mind of the Buddha himself. The saying is later attributed to the school's traditional founder, BODHIDHARMA. According to GUIFENG ZONGMI's CHANYUAN ZHUQUANJI DUXU, the Indian monk Bodhidharma taught that the mind was the DHARMA and he transmitted this teaching from mind to mind (YIXIN CHUANXIN) without establishing words or letters. This phrase also often appears together with three other phrases: JIAOWAI BIECHUAN ("a special transmission outside the teachings"), ZHIZHI RENXIN ("directly pointing to the human mind"), and JIANXING CHENGFO ("seeing one's own nature and becoming a buddha"). They appear together for the first time in the ZUTING SHIYUAN compiled in

1108 and soon became a normative teaching in the subsequent CHAN, SŎN, THIỀN, and ZEN traditions. As a radical interpretation of the notion of UPĀYA, the phrase buli wenzi remains to this day a controversial and frequently debated topic. Song-dynasty exponents of "lettered Chan" (WENZI CHAN), such as JUEFAN HUIHONG (1071–1128), decried the bibliophobic tendencies epitomized in this line and advocated instead that Chan insights were made manifest in both Buddhist SŪTRAs as well as in the uniquely Chan genres of discourse records (YULU), lineage histories (see CHUANDENG LU), and public-case anthologies (GONG'AN).

**Bum thang**. A district of central Bhutan. Considered one of the country's most sacred regions, it was the birthplace of PADMA GLING PA and is home to numerous important monasteries including GTAM ZHING, Sku rje (Kuje), and Byams pa lha khang (Jampa Lhakang).

**Bunkyō hifuron**. (文鏡秘府論). In Japanese, "A Mirror on Literature and a Treasury of Marvels Treatise"; a work on classical Chinese poetics and prosody, composed by the Japanese SHINGONSHŪ monk KŪKAI, probably in the early ninth century. The work was intended to serve as a vade mecum on classical Chinese writing style and literary allusions for Japanese ranging from novice monks who needed to know how to parse Buddhist MANTRAS and DHĀRAṆĪs to diplomats or scribes who had to compose elegant Chinese prose and verse. The treatise is titled a "mirror on literature" because it describes correct Chinese style and a "treasury of marvels" because it serves as a literary compendium and thesaurus. The text is significant not only because of its impact on the development of Japanese classical-Chinese writing, but also because its extensive extracts of original Chinese sources (most now lost) stand as a valuable resource for the study of Tang literature.

**Burnouf, Eugène**. (1801–1852). French orientalist and seminal figure in the development of Buddhist Studies as an academic discipline. He was born in Paris on April 8, 1801, the son of the distinguished classicist Jean-Louis Burnouf (1775–1844). He received instruction in Greek and Latin from his father and studied at the Lycée Louis-le-Grand. He entered the École des Chartes in 1822, receiving degrees in both letters and law in 1824. He then turned to the study of Sanskrit, both with his father and with Antoine Léonard de Chézy (1773–1832). In 1826, Burnouf published, in collaboration with the young Norwegian-German scholar Christian Lassen (1800–1876), *Essai sur le pâli* ("Essay on PĀLI"). After the death of Chézy, Burnouf was appointed to succeed his teacher in the chair of Sanskrit at the Collège de France. His students included some of the greatest scholars of day; those who would contribute to Buddhist studies included Philippe Edouard Foucaux (1811–1894) and FRIEDRICH MAX MÜLLER. Shortly after his appointment to the chair of Sanskrit, the Société Asiatique, of which Burnouf was secretary, received a communication from BRIAN HOUGHTON HODGSON, British resident at the court of Nepal, offering to send Sanskrit manuscripts of Buddhist texts to Paris. The receipt of these texts changed the direction of Burnouf's scholarship for the remainder his life. After perusing the AṢṬASĀHASRIKĀPRAJÑĀPĀRAMITĀ and the LALITAVISTARA, he decided to translate the SADDHARMAPUṆḌARĪKASŪTRA. Having completed the translation, he decided to precede its publication with a series of studies. He completed only the first of these, published in 1844 as *Introduction à l'histoire du Buddhisme indien*. This massive work is regarded as the foundational text for the academic study of Buddhism in the West. It contains Burnouf's highly influential analyses of various aspects of Sanskrit Buddhism as he understood them from the works received from Hodgson. It also contains hundreds of pages of translations of previously unknown works, drawn especially from the DIVYĀVADĀNA and the AVADĀNAŚATAKA. Burnouf died, apparently of kidney failure, on May 28, 1852. His translation of the *Saddharmapuṇḍarīka*, *Le Lotus de la bonne loi*, appeared that same year.

**Bu ston chos 'byung**. (Butön Chöjung). A history of Buddhism in India and Tibet composed in 1322 by the Tibetan polymath BU STON RIN CHEN GRUB. The full name of the work is *Bde bar gshegs pa'i bstan pa'i gsal byed chos kyi 'byung gnas gsung rab rin po che'i mdzod*; it is available in English in the 1931–1932 translation of major parts by EUGÈNE OBERMILLER, done in collaboration with Mongolian monks educated in Tibetan monasteries. The text is in two parts: a history and an important general catalogue of Tibetan Buddhist canonical literature, one of the first of its kind. The first chapter of the *Chos 'byung* draws on the VYĀKHYĀYUKTI and is a general discussion of the exposition and study of Buddhist doctrine. The second chapter is a traditional history dealing with the spread of the doctrine in the human world, the three turnings of the wheel of DHARMA (DHARMACAKRAPRAVARTANA), the councils (SAṂGĪTI), the collection of the Buddhist doctrine into authoritative scriptures, the date of the Buddha, the followers who came after him, and the decline of the doctrine in India. The history of Buddhism in Tibet is divided into a section on the earlier (SNGA DAR) and later spread (PHYI DAR) of the doctrine. The third section is the general catalogue of Buddhist canonical literature in Tibetan translation. It is divided into SŪTRAs and TANTRAs, then again into the words of the Buddha (bka') and authoritative treatises (bstan bcos). The words of the Buddha are subdivided based on the three turnings of the wheel of the dharma with a separate section on MAHĀYĀNA sūtras; treatises are divided into treatises explaining specific works of the Buddha (again subdivided based on the three turnings of the wheel of the dharma), general expositions, and miscellaneous treatises. Bu ston similarly divides the tantras into words of the Buddha and authoritative treatises and deals with both under the division into four "sets" (sde) of KRIYĀ, CARYĀ, and YOGA, and MAHĀYOGA tantras. This latter division is again subdivided into method (UPĀYA), wisdom (PRAJÑĀ), and both (ubhaya) tantras.

In Mkhas grub Dge legs dpal bzang's explanation (*Rgyud sde spyi'i rnam bzhag*), a work based on Bu ston's model, but incorporating the influential scheme of Tsong kha pa, the divisions of mahāyoga are subsumed under the general category of anuttarayogatantra (highest yoga tantra). The tantric commentaries are organized following the same schema.

**Bu ston rin chen grub**. (Butön Rinchen Drup) (1290–1364). A Tibetan scholar, translator, and encyclopedist, renowned for systematizing the Tibetan Buddhist canon into its present form. According to Tibetan hagiographies, Bu ston was born into a lineage of tantric practitioners and considered a reincarnation of the Kashmiri master Śākyaśrībhadra. Having mastered tantric ritual at an early age, he then received ordination at the age of eighteen. He trained under numerous teachers, studying all branches of Buddhist learning and eventually earned a reputation especially for his knowledge of the Kālacakratantra. At age thirty, Bu ston accepted the abbacy of Zhwa lu monastery in central Tibet, where he authored and taught his most influential works; his entire corpus fills twenty-eight volumes in one edition. Bu ston's tenure at Zhwa lu was so influential that it provided the name for a new lineage, the so-called Zhwa lu pa (those of Zhwa lu) or the Bu lugs tshul (the tradition of Bu ston). In about 1332 Bu ston completed his famous history of Buddhism (Bu ston chos 'byung) and it was during this time that, based on previous canonical lists, he began to reformulate a classification system for organizing the Tibetan canon. Bu ston was not the only editor (among them were Dbu pa blo gsal and Bcom ldan rig pa'i ral gri), but he was the most important figure in the final redaction of the bka' 'gyur and bstan 'gyur; he compared manuscripts from the two major manuscript collections at Snar thang and 'Tshal, added other works not found there, eliminated indigenous Tibetan works, decided on criteria for inclusion in the canon, standardized terminology, and decided on categories under which to include the many volumes. It is customary in modern works to include Bu ston in the Sa skya sect and indeed his explanations of the Abhisamayālaṃkāra and the Abhidharmasamuccaya, among others, are considered authoritative by that sect. But his influence is not limited to that sect; for example, Tsong kha pa's commentary on the perfection of wisdom (Legs bshad gser 'phreng), and his explanation of the different types of tantra (Sngags rim chen mo) (both authoritative texts in the Dge lugs sect) borrow heavily from Bu ston's work. Bu ston is one of several key figures in the history of Tibetan Buddhism to be referred to as kun mkhyen, or "all knowing."

**butsudan**. (佛壇). In Japanese, literally "buddha platform"; a platform on which an image of a buddha and/or bodhisattva is placed and worshipped; also known as shūmidan ("Sumeru platform"). A butsudan can be made of stone, clay, or wood and can take the shape of a lotus platform, niche, or portable shrine. According to the Baizhang qinggui, a butsudan houses the image of the saṃbhogakāya of the Buddha. The *Nihon shoki* also notes that the practice of making butsudan had spread widely among Japanese commoners as early as the Nara and Heian periods. Nowadays, butsudan are owned by most households and take the form of a portable shrine that houses icons, sacred objects of a particular school or sect, and mortuary tablets, known as ihai, for deceased family members. They are thus used primarily for private worship and mortuary practice.

**Buttō Kokushi**. (J) (佛燈國師). See Rankei Dōryū.

**Byams chos sde lnga**. In Tibetan, "the five books of Maitreya" said to have been presented to Asaṅga by the bodhisattva Maitreya in the tuṣita heaven; they are the Mahāyānasūtrālaṃkāra, Abhisamayālaṃkāra, Madhyāntavibhāga, Dharmadharmatāvibhāga, and the Ratnagotravibhāga (*Uttaratantra*). See Maitreyanātha.

**Byang chub 'od**. (Jangchup Ö) (late tenth century). Grandnephew of King Ye shes 'od who successfully invited the Indian Buddhist monk and scholar Atiśa Dīpaṃkaraśrījñāna to Tibet. During the second half of the tenth century, Ye shes 'od (also known as Song nge) became the king of Mnga' ris (Ngari), now the far western region of Tibet. He sent a number of Tibetans to Kashmir (see Kashmir-Gandhāra) to study Buddhism, among them the translator Rin chen bzang po whose return to Tibet in 978 marks the beginning of the later spread of Buddhism (phyi dar). (Others date the beginning to the start of the second Mūlasarvāstivāda ordination line, which began at about the same period.) According to a well-known story, Ye shes 'od wanted to invite the foremost Indian Buddhist scholar of the day, Atiśa, to Tibet and traveled to the Qarluq (T. gar log) kingdom (probably to Khotan in present-day Chinese Xianjiang province), to raise funds. He was captured by the chieftain and held for ransom. Ye shes 'od sent a letter to his nephew Byang chub 'od, saying that rather than use money for a ransom to free him, he should use any money collected for his release to invite Atiśa. Ye shes 'od died in captivity, but Byang chub 'od succeeded in convincing Atiśa to come to Tibet where he had a great influence, particularly on the earlier followers of the Bka' gdams sect. The history of this period becomes more important in later Tibetan history when Tsong kha pa, the founder of the Dge lugs sect, described Atiśa as the perfect teacher in his seminal work the Lam rim chen mo. In the seventeenth century, when the Dge lugs rose to political power under the fifth Dalai Lama and his supporters, Byang chub 'od and Atiśa were incorporated into a complex founding myth legitimating Dge lugs ascendancy and the Dga' ldan pho brang government.

**Byōdōin**. (平等院). A famous Japanese temple located in Uji, south of Kyōto, now associated with the Tendaishū and Jōdoshū sects. Byōdōin is especially famous for its Phoenix Hall (Hōōdō), which houses a magnificent image of Amitābha made by the artist Jōchō (d. 1057). The hall, the statue, and fifty-two other small sculptures of bodhisattvas making offerings of music to the central Amitābha statue have been designated as national treasures. The Byōdōin Amitābha image is highly regarded as a representative piece of the refined art of the Fujiwara period (894–1185). Byōdōin was originally a villa that belonged to the powerful regent Fujiwara no Michinaga (966–1027). The private villa was later transformed by Michinaga's son Yorimichi (992–1074) into a temple in 1052, and the Phoenix Hall was constructed the following year. Many halls dedicated to the buddha Amitābha were built in this period by powerful aristocrats who were influenced by the growing belief in the notion of mappō (see MOFA), or "the demise of the dharma," wherein the only means of salvation was the practice of nenbutsu, the recitation of Amitābha's name (see also NIANFO; BUDDHĀNUSMṚTI). The monk Myōson (d. 1063), originally the abbot of another temple called ONJŌJI, was installed as the first abbot of Byōdōin.

# C

**Caitika**. (S). See CAITYA.

**caitta**. [alt. caitasika] (P. cetasika; T. sems byung; C. xinsuo; J. shinjo; K. simso 心所). In Sanskrit, "mental concomitants" or "mental factors." In the ABHIDHARMA, the term encompasses those mental factors that accompany, in various combinations, the mind (CITTA) and its six sensory consciousnesses (VIJÑĀNA), viz., visual (lit. eye), auditory (ear), olfactory (nose), gustatory (tongue), tactile (body), and mental. The VAIBHĀṢIKA school of SARVĀSTIVĀDA abhidharma lists forty-six caittas, the Pāli ABHIDHAMMA lists fifty-two (called CETASIKA), while the mature YOGĀCĀRA system of MAHĀYĀNA abhidharma gives a total of fifty-one specific mental concomitants, listed in six categories. The first, mental concomitants of universal application (SARVATRAGA), includes the five factors of sensory contact (SPARŚA), sensations (VEDANĀ), intention or volition (CETANĀ), perception (SAṂJÑĀ), and attention (MANASKĀRA). The second category, five concomitants that are of specific application (VINIYATA) in spiritual progress, includes mindfulness (SMṚTI), concentration (SAMĀDHI), and wisdom (PRAJÑĀ). The third category, salutary (KUŚALA) factors, includes nine positive mental states such as faith (ŚRADDHĀ), lack of greed (ALOBHA), lack of hatred (ADVEṢA), and vigor (VĪRYA). The fourth category, the primary afflictions (KLEŚA), includes six negative mental states such as sensuality (RĀGA), aversion (PRATIGHA), pride (MĀNA), and doubt (VICIKITSĀ). The fifth category, secondary afflictions (UPAKLEŚA), includes twenty lesser forms of negative mental states, such as envy (ĪRṢYĀ), harmfulness (VIHIṂSĀ), and carelessness (PRAMĀDA). The sixth and final category, mental concomitants of indeterminate (ANIYATA) quality, includes the four factors of remorse (KAUKṚTYA), torpor (MIDDHA), thought (VITARKA), and analysis (VICĀRA). See also CETASIKA.

**caitya**. (P. cetiya; T. mchod rten; C. zhiti; J. shidai; K. chije 支提). In Sanskrit, "cairn," "tumulus," "sanctuary," or "shrine." The term is used sometimes to refer to a Buddhist reliquary, or STŪPA, sometimes to a cave or sanctuary that enshrines a stūpa, and sometimes to local or non-Buddhist shrines. Where a distinction is made between caitya and stūpa, a stūpa contains a relic (ŚARĪRA) of the Buddha or an eminent saint, while a caitya does not and is erected solely as a commemorative shrine. Many early Indian cave monasteries, such as ELLORĀ, included a rectangular caitya hall as a central assembly room, with three naves and a stūpa in the apse as the object of worship. Early on, these caitya halls were superseded by rooms that instead enshrined a buddha image, the standard form subsequently found in Buddhist monasteries. The VAJRACCHEDIKĀPRAJÑĀPĀRAMITĀSŪTRA famously declares that any place where even a four-lined stanza from the sūtra is taught will become a caitya for divinities and humans.

**Caitya**. [alt. Caitika; Caityaśaila] (P. Cetiyavāda; T. Mchod rten pa; C. Zhiduoshanbu; J. Seitasanbu/Seitasenbu; K. Chedasanbu 制多山部). In Sanskrit, "The Caitya Worshippers"; one of the three main subgroups of the MAHĀSĀṂGHIKA school of mainstream Buddhism, along with the KAUKKUṬIKA and LOKOTTARAVĀDA [alt. Ekavyavahārika]. Inscriptional evidence places the school in the Andhra region of India in the early second century CE, suggesting their possible association with the groups that Pāli materials refer to collectively as the ANDHAKĀ. The Caitya school seems to have been named after its distinctive practice of worshipping shrines and sanctuaries (CAITYA). The founder of the school is presumed to have been a second MAHĀDEVA, who led a reconsideration of the five propositions about the qualities of an ARHAT offered by an earlier MAHĀDEVA, whom Buddhist sources from northern India consider to have fomented the initial schism of the mainstream Buddhist schools between the Mahāsāṃghika and the STHAVIRANIKĀYA.

**Cakkavattisīhanādasutta**. (C. Zhuanlun shengwang xiuxing jing; J. Tenrinjōō shugyōkyō; K. Chŏllyun sŏngwang suhaeng kyŏng 轉輪聖王修行經). In Pāli, "Discourse on the Lion's Roar of the Wheel-Turning Emperor"; the twenty-sixth sutta of the DĪGHANIKĀYA (a separate DHARMAGUPTAKA recension appears as the sixth SŪTRA in the Chinese translation of the DĪRGHĀGAMA and a separate Sarvāstivāda recension as the seventieth sūtra in the Chinese translation of the MADHYAMĀGAMA); the scripture is known especially for being the only sutta in the Pāli canon that mentions the name of the Buddha's successor, Metteya (MAITREYA). Before a gathering of monks at the town of Mātulā in MAGADHA, the Buddha tells the story of a universal or wheel-turning monarch (cakkavattin; S. CAKRAVARTIN) named Daḷhanemi, wherein he explains that righteousness and order are maintained in the world so long as kings observe their royal duties. Daḷhanemi's successors, unfortunately, gradually abandoned their responsibilities, leading to immorality, strife, and the shortening of life spans from eighty thousand years to a mere ten; the sutta thus attributes the origins of evil in the world to the neglect of royal duty. Upon reaching this nadir, people finally recognize the error of their ways and begin anew to practice morality. The observance of morality leads to improved conditions, until eventually a universal monarch named Saṅkha appears, who will prepare the way for the advent of the future-Buddha Metteya (Maitreya).

**cakra**. (P. cakka; T. 'khor lo; C. lun; J. rin; K. yun 輪). In Sanskrit, "wheel," "disc," or "circle"; a frequent symbol used to represent various aspects of Buddhism, from the Buddha, to the DHARMA, to Buddhist notions of kingship. When the Buddha first taught his new religion, it is said that he "turned the wheel of dharma" (DHARMACAKRAPRAVARTANA) and the eight-spoked "wheel of dharma" (DHARMACAKRA) is subsequently used as a symbol for both the teachings as well as the person who rediscovered and enunciated those teachings. The ABHIDHARMAKOŚABHĀṢYA explains that the noble eightfold path (ĀRYĀṢṬĀṄGAMĀRGA) is like a wheel because it is similar in terms of the hub that is the support of the wheel, the spokes, and the containment rim. Right speech, action, and livelihood are like the hub, because they are the training in morality that provides support for concentration (DHYĀNA) and wisdom (PRAJÑĀ). Right view, thought, and effort are like spokes, because they are the training in wisdom. Right mindfulness and concentration are like the rim because the spokes of right view and so forth provide the objective support (ĀLAMBANA) in a one-pointed manner in dependence on them. The dharmacakra appears in some of the earliest Buddhist art, often as an iconographic symbol standing in for the Buddha himself. The sign of a thousand-spoked wheel on the palms of the hands and the soles of the feet is one of the thirty-two major marks of a great man (MAHĀPURUṢALAKṢAṆA), which is said to adorn the body of both a Buddha and a "wheel-turning emperor" (CAKRAVARTIN), his secular counterpart. A cakravartin's power is said to derive from his wheel of divine attributes, which rolls across different realms of the earth, bringing them under his dominion. The realm of SAṂSĀRA is sometimes depicted iconographically in the form of a wheel, known as the "wheel of existence" (BHAVACAKRA), with a large circle divided into the six realms of existence (ṢAḌGATI), surrounded by an outer ring representing the twelve links of dependent origination (PRATĪTYASAMUTPĀDA). ¶ The term cakra is also important in Buddhist TANTRA, especially in ANUTTARAYOGATANTRA. According to various systems of tantric physiognomy, a central channel (AVADHŪTĪ) runs from either the tip of the genitals or the base of the spine to either the crown of the head or the point between the eyebrows, with a number of "wheels" (cakra) along its course. In one of the systems, these wheels are located at the point between the eyebrows, the crown of the head, the throat, the heart, the navel, the base of the spine, and the opening of the sexual organ. Running parallel to the central channel to the right and left are two channels, both smaller in diameter, the LALANĀ and the RASANĀ. It is said that the right and left channels wrap around the central channel, forming knots at the cakras. Much tantric practice is devoted to techniques for loosening these knots in order to allow the winds (PRĀṆA) or energies that course through the other channels to flow freely and enter into the central channel. The cakras themselves are essential elements in this practice and other tantric meditative practices, with seed syllables (BĪJA), spells (MANTRA), deities, and diagrams (MAṆḌALA) visualized at their center. The cakras themselves are often described as open lotus blossoms, with varying numbers of petals in different colors.

**Cakrasaṃvara**. (T. 'Khor lo bde mchog). See CAKRASAṂVARATANTRA

**Cakrasaṃvaratantra**. (T. 'Khor lo bde mchog gi rgyud). In Sanskrit, the "Binding of the Wheel Tantra" an important Buddhist tantra, often known simply as the Cakrasaṃvara (T. 'Khor lo bde mchog). The text is extant in Sanskrit and in a Tibetan translation in seven hundred stanzas, which is subdivided into fifty-one sections; it is also known by the name *Śrīherukābhidhāna* (a name appearing at the end of each section), and commonly known in Tibet as the *Cakrasaṃvara Laghutantra* ("short tantra" or "light tantra") or *Mūlatantra* ("root tantra") because, according to legend, there was once a longer text of one hundred thousand stanzas. The main deity of the tantra is HERUKA (also known as Cakrasaṃvara) and his consort is VAJRAVĀRĀHĪ. Historically, the tantra originated as part of a literature that focused on a class of female divinities called YOGINĪ or ḌĀKINĪ. It and its sister tantra, the HEVAJRATANTRA, probably appeared toward the end of the eighth century, and both show the influence of the *Sarvabuddhasamayoga-ḍākinījālasaṃvaratantra* (referred to by Amoghavajra after his return from India to China in 746 CE). All are classed as yoginītantras. The use of skulls, the presence of the KHATVĀṄGA staff, and the references to sites holy to Śaivite Kāpālikas (those who use skulls) point to a very close relationship between the Śaiva Kāpālika literature and the early yoginītantras, such that some scholars have suggested an actual appropriation of the Śaiva literature by Buddhists outside mainstream Buddhist practice. Other scholars suggest this class of tantric literature originates from a SIDDHA tradition, i.e., from individual charismatic yogins and yoginīs with magical powers unaffiliated with particular religions or sects. Among the four classes of tantras—KRIYĀTANTRA, CARYĀTANTRA, YOGATANTRA, and ANUTTARAYOGATANTRA—the *Cakrasaṃvaratantra* is included in the last category; between the father tantras (PITṚTANTRA) and mother tantra (MĀTṚTANTRA) categories of anuttarayogatantras, it is classified in the latter category. The siddhas Luipa and SARAHA are prominent in accounts of its origin and transmission, and the siddha NĀROPA is of particular importance in the text's transmission in India and from there to Tibet. Like many root tantras, the text contains very little that might be termed doctrine or theology, focusing instead on ritual matters, especially the use of MANTRA for the achievement of various powers (SIDDHI), especially the mundane (LAUKIKA) powers, such as the ability to fly, become invisible, etc. The instructions are generally not presented in a systematic way, although it is unclear whether this is the result of the development of the text over time or the intention of the authors to keep practices secret from the uninitiated. Later commentators found references in the text to elements of both the stage of generation (UTPATTIKRAMA) and stage of completion (NIṢPANNAKRAMA). The *Ḍākārṇavatantra* is included within the larger category of tantras related to the Cakrasaṃvara cycle, as is the *Abhidhanottara* and the *Saṃvarodayatantra*. The tantra describes, in greater and less detail, a MAṆḌALA with goddesses in sacred places in India (see PĪṬHA) and the process of ABHIṢEKA. The practice of the MĀYĀDEHA (T. sgyu lus, "illusory body") and CAṆḌĀLĪ (T. gtum mo, often translated as "psychic heat") are closely associated with this tantra. It was translated twice into Tibetan and is important in all three new-translation (GSAR MA) Tibetan sects, i.e., the SA SKYA, BKA' BRGYUD, and DGE LUGS. Iconographically, the Cakrasaṃvara maṇḍala, starting from the outside, has first eight cremation grounds (ŚMAŚĀNA), then a ring of fire, then VAJRAS, then lotus petals. Inside that is the palace with five concentric placement rings going in toward the center. In the center is the main deity Heruka with his consort Vajravārāhī trampling on BHAIRAVA and his consort Kālarātri (deities associated with Śaivism). There are a number of different representations. One has Heruka (or Cakrasaṃvara) dark blue in color with four faces and twelve arms, and Vārāhī with a single face and two hands, red and naked except for bone ornaments. In the next circles are twenty-four vīras (heroes) with their consorts (related with the twenty-four pīṭha), with the remaining deities in the maṇḍala placed in different directions in the outer circles.

**cakravāḍa**. [alt. cakravāla] (P. cakkavāḷa; T. 'khor yug ri; C. tiewei shan; J. tetchisen; K. ch'ŏrwi san 鐵圍山). In Sanskrit, "ring of mountains"; the proper name of the eight ranges of metallic mountains that are presumed in Buddhist cosmology to surround the world system of the sensuous realm (KĀMALOKA) and thus sometimes used by metonymy to designate the entire universe or "world system." Eight concentric mountain ranges are said to surround the central axis of the world system, Mount SUMERU or Mount Meru. The seven innermost ranges are made of gold, and seven seas fill the valleys between these concentric ranges. In some representations, the mountain ranges are in the form a circle; in others, they are in the form of a square, consistent with the shape of Mount Sumeru. Located in a vast ocean that exists beyond these seven innermost concentric rings are laid out the four continents, including JAMBUDVĪPA (the Rose-Apple Continent) to the south, where human beings dwell; VIDEHA to the east; GODĀNĪYA to the west; and UTTARAKURU to the north. At the outer perimeter of the world system is a final range of iron mountains, which surrounds and contains the outermost sea. The universe was presumed to be occupied by an essentially infinite number of these cakravāḍa world systems, each similarly structured, and each world system was the domain of a specific buddha, where he achieved enlightenment and worked toward the liberation of all sentient beings. See also BUDDHAKṢETRA.

**cakravāla**. (S). See CAKRAVĀḌA.

**cakravartin**. (P. cakkavattin; T. 'khor lo sgyur ba'i rgyal po; C. zhuanlun wang; J. tenrin'ō; K. chŏllyun wang 轉輪王). In Sanskrit, lit. "wheel-turning emperor" or "universal monarch"; a monarch who rules over the entire universe (CAKRAVĀḌA), commonly considered in Buddhism to be an ideal monarch who rules his subjects in accordance with the DHARMA. Just as with a buddha, only one cakravartin king can appear in a world system at any one time. Also like a buddha, a cakravartin is endowed with all the thirty-two major marks of a great man (MAHĀPURUṢALAKṢAṆA). Hence, when the future buddha GAUTAMA was born with these marks, seers predicted that he had two possible destinies: to become a cakravartin if he remained in the world, or a buddha if he renounced it. A cakravartin's power derives from a wheel or disc of divine attributes (CAKRA) that rolls across different realms of the earth, bringing them under his dominion. The ABHIDHARMAKOŚABHĀṢYA lists four classes of cakravartin, depending on the basic element from which his disc is forged: (1) a suvarṇacakravartin (referred to in some texts as a caturdvīpakacakravartin, or "cakravartin of four continents"), whose wheel is gold, who reigns over all the four continents of a world system (see CAKRAVĀḌA), and who conquers the world through the spontaneous surrender of all rival kings whose lands his wheel enters; (2) a rūpyacakravartin, whose wheel is silver, who reigns over three continents (all except UTTARAKURU), and who conquers territory by merely threatening to move against his rivals; (3) a tāmracakravartin, whose wheel is copper, who reigns over two continents (JAMBUDVĪPA and VIDEHA), and who conquers territory after initiating battle with his rivals; (4) an ayaścakravartin, whose wheel is iron, who reigns over one continent (Jambudvīpa only), and who conquers territory only after extended warfare with his rivals. Some texts refer to a balacakravartin or "armed cakravartin," who corresponds to the fourth category. The cakravartins discussed in the sūtras typically refers to a suvarṇacakravartin, who conquers the world through the sheer power of his righteousness and charisma. He possesses the ten royal qualities (rājadharma) of charity, good conduct, nonattachment, straightforwardness, gentleness, austerity, nonanger, noninjury, patience, and tolerance. A cakravartin is also said to possess seven precious things (RATNA): a wheel (cakra), an elephant (HASTINĀGA), a horse (aśva), a wish-granting gem (MAṆI), a woman (strī), a financial steward or treasurer (GṚHAPATI), and a counselor (pariṇāyaka). Various kings over the course of Asian history have been declared, or have declared themselves to be, cakravartins. The most famous is the Mauryan emperor AŚOKA, whose extensive territorial conquests, coupled with his presumed support for the dharma and the SAṂGHA, rendered him the ideal paradigm of Buddhist kingship.

**cakṣurāyatana**. (P. cakkhāyatana; T. mig gi skye mched; C. yanchu; J. gensho; K. anch'ŏ 眼處). In Sanskrit, "visual sense base" or "base of cognition"; the visual sense base or eye sense organ (CAKṢURINDRIYA) as it occurs in the list of the twelve sense fields (ĀYATANA). These āyatanas are also called "bases of cognition," because each pair of sense base and sense object produces its respective sensory consciousness. In this case, the contact (SPARŚA) between a visual sensory object (RŪPA) and the visual sense base (cakṣurindriya) produces a visual consciousness (CAKṢURVIJÑĀNA).

**cakṣurindriya**. (P. cakkhundriya; T. mig gi dbang po; C. yangen; J. genkon; K. an'gŭn 眼根). In Sanskrit, "visual sense base" or "eye sense organ"; the physical organ located in the eye that makes it possible to see forms (RŪPA). This sense base is not the eyeball itself, but a subtle type of materiality that is located within the eye and invisible to the naked eye. It is said to be shaped like the bud of a flax flower. If this sense organ is absent or damaged, vision is not possible. The visual sense base serves as the dominant condition (ADHIPATIPRATYAYA) for the production of visual consciousness (CAKṢURVIJÑĀNA). The visual sense base is counted among the six sense bases or sense organs (INDRIYA), the twelve bases of cognition (ĀYATANA), and eighteen sensory elements (DHĀTU).

**cakṣurvijñāna**. (P. cakkhuviññāṇa; T. mig gi rnam par shes pa; C. yanshi; J. genshiki; K. ansik 眼識). In Sanskrit, "visual consciousness" or "eye consciousness"; one of the five types of consciousness of physical objects (along with those of the ear, nose, tongue, and body) and one of the six sensory consciousnesses (adding the mental consciousness, or MANOVIJÑĀNA). The visual consciousness perceives forms (RŪPA), i.e., colors and shapes. Like the other consciousness of physical objects, visual consciousness is produced through the contact (SPARŚA) between a visual sensory object (RŪPA) and the visual sense base or eye sense organ (CAKṢURINDRIYA), and in dependence on three conditions (PRATYAYA): the object condition (ĀLAMBANAPRATYAYA), in this case, a form; a dominant condition (ADHIPATIPRATYAYA), here, the visual sense base (cakṣurindriya); and the immediately preceding condition (SAMANANTARAPRATYAYA), a prior moment of consciousness. The visual consciousness is counted as one of the six sensory consciousnesses (VIJÑĀNA) and eighteen sensory elements (DHĀTU).

**cakṣus**. (P. cakkhu; T. mig; C. yan; J. gen; K. an 眼). In Sanskrit, lit. "eye"; the base associated with the full range of types of vision (DARŚANA), from sensory perception that occurs via the visual base (ĀYATANA), through extrasensory perception that was a product of meditative development (YOGIPRATYAKṢA). Buddhist literature often refers to five types of "eyes" (pañcacakṣus), viz., the physical eye (māṃsacakṣus), which is the sense base (āyatana) associated with visual consciousness; the divine eye (DIVYACAKṢUS), the vision associated with the divinities (DEVA) in the heavens or the spiritual power (ABHIJÑĀ) of clairvoyance; the wisdom eye (prajñācakṣus), which is the insight (PRAJÑĀ) that derives from mainstream Buddhist practices; the dharma eye (dharmacakṣus) that is exclusive to the BODHISATTVAS; and the buddha eye (buddhacakṣus), which subsumes all other four. The cakṣus is said to be impossible to perceive with the naked eye and differs from the gross physical eyeball that is called the basis of the faculty.

**Cāmadevīvaṃsa**. In Pāli, "History of Queen Cāma"; a chronicle in mixed prose and verse written by Mahāthera Bodhiraṃsi at Lamphun (Haripuñjaya) in northern Thailand, sometime between 1460 and 1530 CE. The text recounts the accession of Queen Cāma to the throne of Haripuñjaya in the seventh century CE and the introduction of THERAVĀDA Buddhism as the state religion under her patronage. The work begins with an account of the legendary visit by the Buddha to the site of Lamphun, where he prophesied the city's future greatness, and goes on to describe its founding under the direction of various sages. The narrative concludes with accounts of the reigns of kings after Queen Cāma, culminating with Ādityarājā who flourished in the eleventh century.

**cāmara**. (S). See VĀLAVYAJANA.

**caṇḍālī**. (T. gtum mo; C. zhantuoli; J. sendari; K. chŏndari 旃陀利). In Sanskrit, "fierce woman." In ordinary usage, this is a term for an outcaste or low-caste woman. However, in ANUTTARAYOGATANTRA, it refers to a meditation practice sometimes described in English as "inner heat" or "psychic heat." It is one of the "six yogas of Nāropa" (NA RO CHOS DRUG) but it figures in many practices of the completion stage (NIṢPANNAKRAMA). In this practice, the meditator imagines a seed syllable (BĪJA) in the middle of the central channel (AVADHŪTĪ) at the navel CAKRA. As the meditator concentrates on the letter, it begins to glow with bright light and emits intense heat. That heat rises slowly up the central channel, first to the cakra at the heart, then to the cakra at the throat, and finally to the cakra at the crown of the head. When it reaches the crown of the head, the heat of the inner fire begins to melt the white drop (BINDU) located there, causing it to begin to melt. As it melts, it descends through the central channel, first to the cakra at the throat, then to the cakra at the heart, the cakra at the navel, and finally to the cakra at the end of the central channel. As the drop moves slowly down through each cakra, a different type of bliss is experienced. This practice is said to produce physical heat in the body; according to tradition, yogins in Tibet, most notably MI LA RAS PA, were able to survive the cold in mountain caves through this practice.

**Candasāra Buddha**. One of the most sacred of Burmese Buddha images. See ARAKAN BUDDHA.

**Candragarbhaparipṛcchā**. (T. Zla ba'i snying pos zhus pa'i mdo; C. Yuezang fen; J. Gatsuzōbun; K. Wŏlchang pun 月藏分). In Sanskrit, "Dialogue with Candragarbha"; a MAHĀYĀNA sūtra that is important, especially in East Asia and Tibet, for its prediction of the demise of the dharma (MOFA; SADDHARMAVIPRALOPA); also known as the *Candragarbhasūtra*. There are three versions of the text, in Chinese, Khotanese, and Tibetan. In the Tibetan version, the BODHISATTVA Candragarbha asks the Buddha how and when his dharma will disappear. The Buddha replies that it will last for two thousand years, in four periods of five hundred years each. During the first period, his dharma will be taught and people will put it into practice and achieve liberation. In the second period, very few will be able to achieve liberation. In the third, the dharma will be taught but no one will put it into practice. In the fourth the guardian deities will stop protecting Buddhists from disease, famine, and warfare, and monks will begin to engage in commerce. In the Chinese version, the Buddha explains that his teaching will last for one thousand five hundred years, with five hundred years of "true dharma" and one thousand years of "semblance dharma" (XIANGFA).

**Candragomin**. (T. Btsun pa zla ba). Fifth-century CE Indian lay poet and grammarian, who made substantial contributions to Sanskrit grammar, founding what was known as the Cāndra school. A junior contemporary of the great Kālidāsa, Candragomin was one of the most accomplished poets in the history of Indian Buddhism. His play *Lokānanda*, which tells the story of the BODHISATTVA king Maṇicūḍa, is the oldest extant Buddhist play and was widely performed in the centuries after its composition. He was a devotee of TĀRĀ and composed several works in her praise. Tibetan works describe him as a proponent of VIJÑĀNAVĀDA who engaged in debate with CANDRAKĪRTI, but there is little philosophical content in his works that can be confidently ascribed to him. Among those works are the "Letter to a Disciple" (*Śiṣyalekha*), the "Confessional Praise" (*Deśanāstava*), and perhaps the "Twenty Verses on the Bodhisattva Precepts" (*Bodhisattvasaṃvaraviṃśaka*).

**Candrakīrti**. (T. Zla ba grags pa) (c. 600–650). An important MADHYAMAKA master and commentator on the works of NĀGĀRJUNA and ĀRYADEVA, associated especially with what would later be known as the PRĀSAṄGIKA branch of Madhyamaka. Very little is known about his life; according to Tibetan sources, he was from south India and a student of Kamalabuddhi. He may have been a monk of NĀLANDĀ. He wrote commentaries on Nāgārjuna's YUKTIṢAṢṬIKĀ and ŚŪNYATĀSAPTATI as well as Āryadeva's CATUḤŚATAKA. His two most famous and influential works, however, are his PRASANNAPADĀ ("Clear Words"), which is a commentary on Nāgārjuna's MŪLAMADHYAMAKAKĀRIKĀ, and his MADHYAMAKĀVATĀRA ("Entrance to the Middle Way"). In the first chapter of the *Prasannapadā*, he defends the approach of BUDDHAPĀLITA against the criticism of BHĀVAVIVEKA in their own commentaries on the *Mūlamadhyamakakārikā*. Candrakīrti argues that it is inappropriate for the Madhyamaka to use what is called an autonomous syllogism (SVATANTRAPRAYOGA) in debating with an opponent and that the Madhyamaka should instead use a consequence (PRASAṄGA). It is largely based on Candrakīrti's discussion that Tibetan scholars retrospectively identified two subschools of Madhyamaka, the SVĀTANTRIKA (in which they placed Bhāvaviveka) and the Prāsaṅgika (in which they placed Buddhapālita and Candrakīrti). Candrakīrti's other important work is the *Madhyamakāvatāra*, written in verse with an autocommentary. It is intended as a general introduction to the *Mūlamadhyamakakārikā*, and provides what Candrakīrti regards as the soteriological context for Nāgārjuna's work. It sets forth the BODHISATTVA path, under the rubric of the ten bodhisattva stages (BHŪMI; DAŚABHŪMI) and the ten perfections (PĀRAMITĀ). By far the longest and most influential chapter of the text is the sixth, dealing with the perfection of wisdom (PRAJÑĀPĀRAMITĀ), where Candrakīrti discusses the two truths (SATYADVAYA), offers a critique of CITTAMĀTRA, and sets forth the reasoning for proving the selflessness of phenomena (DHARMANAIRĀTMYA) and the selflessness of the person (PUDGALANAIRĀTMYA), using his famous sevenfold analysis of a chariot as an example. Candrakīrti seems to have had little influence in the first centuries after his death, perhaps accounting for the fact that his works were not translated into Chinese (until the 1940s). There appears to have been a revival of interest in his works in India, especially in Kashmir, in the eleventh and twelfth centuries, at the time of the later dissemination (PHYI DAR) of Buddhism to Tibet. Over the next few centuries, Candrakīrti's works became increasingly important in Tibet, such that eventually the *Madhyamakāvatāra* became the locus classicus for the study of Madhyamaka in Tibet, studied and commented upon by scholars of all sects and serving as one of the "five texts" (GZHUNG LNGA) of the DGE LUGS curriculum. ¶ There appear to be later Indian authors who were called, or called themselves, Candrakīrti. These include the authors of the *Triśaraṇasaptati* and the *Madhyamakāvatāraprajñā*, neither of which appears to have been written by the author described above. Of particular importance is yet another Candrakīrti, or Candrakīrtipāda, the author of the *Pradīpoddyotana*, an influential commentary on the GUHYASAMĀJATANTRA. Scholars often refer to this author as Candrakīrti II or "the tantric Candrakīrti."

**caṅkrama**. (P. caṅkama; T. 'chag pa; C. jingxing; J. kyōgyō/kinhin; K. kyŏnghaeng 經行). In Sanskrit, lit. "walking"; referring to both the physical act of walking itself and, by extension, composed, meditative walking, as well as the mendicant life of wandering as a vocation. Caṅkrama is the most active of the four postures (ĪRYĀPATHA), and is one of the specific objects of mindfulness of the body (see SMṚTYUPASTHĀNA). Caṅkrama also refers to walking in a calm, collected manner, while maintaining one's object of meditation. Finally, caṅkrama refers to the wandering, "homeless" life (see PRAVRAJITA) of the Indian recluse, which was the model for the Buddhist SAṂGHA. In East Asia, in addition to walking meditation per se, the term is also used to describe short periods of walking that break up extended periods of seated meditation (ZUOCHAN). In Korean meditation halls, for example, a three-hour block of meditation practice will be divided into three fifty-minute blocks of seated meditation, punctuated by ten-minutes of walking meditation. The Japanese ZEN tradition reads these Sinographs as kinhin.

**canon**. A term used generically to designate Buddhist scriptural collections in a whole range of canonical Asian languages, including the Indic "three baskets" (TRIPIṬAKA), the East Asian "scriptures of the great repository" (DAZANGJING), and the Tibetan BKA' 'GYUR and BSTAN 'GYUR. Beyond these canons, Buddhists in these various traditions also typically used their own local collections of texts, collections that often were quite distinct from those of the officially sanctioned canons. See also KORYŎ TAEJANGGYŎNG; TAISHŌ SHINSHŪ DAIZŌKYŌ; SŪTRA; ŚĀSTRA; BODHISATTVAPIṬAKA; APOCRYPHA.

**Cantong qi**. (J. Sandōkai; K. Ch'amdong kye 参同契). A famous verse attributed to the Chinese CHAN master SHITOU XIQIAN. Along with the BAOJING SANMEI, the *Cantong qi* is revered in the Chinese CAODONG ZONG and Japanese SŌTŌSHŪ traditions as the foundational scripture of the tradition. The *Cantong qi* is relatively short (forty-four five-character stanzas, for a total of 220 Sinographs), but Shitou's verse is praised for its succinct and unequivocal expression of the teaching of nonduality. The Sinograph "can" in the title means to "consider," "compare," or "differentiate"; it thus carries the connotation of "difference" and is said to refer to the myriad phenomena. The Sinograph "tong" means "sameness" and is said to refer to the oneness of all phenomena. The Sinograph "qi" means "tally" and is said to refer to the tallying of oneself and all phenomena. The title might be alluding to an earlier verse bearing the same title, which is attributed to the renowned Daoist master Wei Boyang. The *Cantong qi* also seems to be the root source from which were derived core concepts in the "five ranks" (WUWEI) doctrine, an emblematic teaching of the mature Caodong school.

**Caodong zong**. (J. Sōtōshū; K. Chodong chong 曹洞宗). One of the so-called "five houses and seven schools" (WU JIA QI ZONG) of the mature Chinese CHAN tradition. The school traces its own pedigree back to the sixth patriarch (LIUZU) HUINENG via a lineage that derives from QINGYUAN XINGSI and SHITOU XIQIAN, but its history begins with the two Tang-dynasty Chan masters who lend their names to the school: DONGSHAN LIANGJIE and his disciple CAOSHAN BENJI. The name of this tradition, Caodong, is derived from the first characters of the two patriarchs' names, viz., Caoshan's "Cao" and Dongshan's "Dong." (The disciple's name is said to appear first in the school's name purely for euphonic reasons.) One of the emblematic teachings of the Caodong tradition is that of the "five ranks" (WUWEI), taught by Dongshan and further developed by Caoshan, which was a form of dialectical analysis that sought to present the full panoply of MAHĀYĀNA Buddhist insights in a compressed rubric. During the Song dynasty, the Caodong school also came to be associated with the contemplative practice of "silent illumination" (MOZHAO CHAN), a form of meditation that built upon the normative East Asian notion of the inherency of buddhahood (see TATHĀGATAGARBHA) to suggest that, since enlightenment was the mind's natural state, nothing needed to be done in order to attain enlightenment other than letting go of all striving for that state. Authentic Chan practice therefore entailed only maintaining this original purity of the mind by simply sitting silently in meditation. The practice of silent illumination is traditionally attributed to HONGZHI ZHENGJUE (see MOZHAO MING) and ZHENGXIE QINGLIAO, who helped revive the moribund Caodong lineage during the late eleventh and early twelfth centuries and turned it into one of the two major forces in mature Song-dynasty Chan. The silent-illumination technique that they championed was harshly criticized by teachers in the rival LINJI ZONG, most notably Hongzhi's contemporary DAHUI ZONGGAO. In Japan, the ZEN master DŌGEN KIGEN is credited with transmitting the Caodong lineage to the Japanese isles in the thirteenth century, where it is known as the SŌTŌSHŪ (the Japanese pronunciation of Caodong zong); it became one of the three major branches of the Japanese Zen school, along with RINZAISHŪ and ŌBAKUSHŪ. In Korea, just one of the early Nine Mountains schools of SŎN (see KUSAN SŎNMUN), the Sumisan school, is presumed to trace back to a teacher, Yunju Daoying (d. 902), who was also a disciple of Dongshan Liangjie; the Caodong school had no impact in the subsequent development of Korean Sŏn, where Imje (C. Linji zong) lineages and practices dominated from the thirteenth century onwards.

**Caoqishan**. (C) (曹溪山). See CAOXISHAN.

**Caoshan Benji**. (J. Sōzan Honjaku; K. Chosan Ponjŏk 曹山本寂) (840–901). Chinese CHAN master and reputed cofounder of the CAODONG line of Chan; also known as Danzhang. Caoshan was a native of Quanzhou in present-day Fujian province. After leaving home at age eighteen and fully ordaining at twenty-five, Caoshan visited the Chan master DONGSHAN LIANGJIE and became his disciple. Caoshan was later invited to Mt. Heyu in Fuzhou (present-day Jiangxi province), and there he established his unique style of Chan. He later renamed the mountain Mt. Cao (or Caoshan) after the sixth patriarch HUINENG's own residence of CAOXISHAN. Caoshan's line of Chan came to be known as Caodong, which is derived eponymously from the first Sinograph in both Caoshan and Dongshan's names. One of the most emblematic teachings of the Caodong tradition is that of the "five ranks" (WUWEI), taught by Dongshan and further developed by Caoshan, a form of dialectical analysis that JUEFAN HUIHONG (1071–1128) considered to be the origin of "lettered Chan" (WENZI CHAN). Caoshan was later given the posthumous title Great Master Yunzheng. Although Caoshan had many disciples, his own lineage did not survive into the

Song dynasty and the Caodong line was carried on by the lineage of Yunju Daoying (d. 902), a fellow student of Dongshan.

**Caoxi baolin zhuan**. (C) (曹溪寶林傳). See BAOLIN ZHUAN.

**Caoxishan**. [alt. Caoqishan] (J. Sōkeizan; K. Chogyesan 曹溪山). A sacred mountain in the south of China, located in Shaozhou, present-day Guangdong province, and closely associated with the CHAN ZONG. According to legend, an Indian brāhmaṇa who arrived at the mountain in 502 was so moved by the taste of its spring water that he suggested that a monastery be constructed there. The monastery was built and named Baolinsi, or Bejeweled Forest Monastery. The brāhmaṇa also predicted that a great teacher would one day preach the DHARMA at the monastery and awaken beings as numerous as the trees in the forest. This tale may be attributed to followers of the legendary sixth patriarch (LIUZU) of the Chan school, HUINENG, who purportedly arrived at Baolinsi in 677. Upon his arrival, Huineng is also said to have established separate quarters for meditative practice within the monastery's compounds, which later came to be known as Huoguoyuan or NANHUASI. The mountain's name of Caoxi is sometimes also used as a toponym of Huineng, its most famous inhabitant. Caoxishan (in its Korean pronunciation of Chogyesan) is also an important Buddhist mountain in Korea and is the site of the famous practice monastery of SONGGWANGSA. See also CHOGYE CHONG.

**Caoyuan Daosheng**. (J. Sōgen Dōshō; K. Chowŏn Tosaeng 曹源道生) (d. 1192). A Chinese CHAN master of the LINJI ZONG. Caoyuan was a native of Nanjian in present-day Fujian province. He later became a student of the eminent Chan master MI'AN XIANJIE and made a name for himself at the monastery of Ruguosi in Jiangxi province. Caoyuan subsequently resided at such monasteries as Guifengsi and Qianfusi, also in Jiangxi province. Those in his lineage are sometimes specifically referred to as the Caoyuan branch of the Linji lineage. Caoyuan's teachings are found in his *Caoyuan heshang yulu* and *Caoyuan Sheng chanshi yuyao*.

**Cao Zhi**. (曹植) (192–232). Reputed founder of the distinctive Chinese style of Buddhist chanting. See FANBAI.

**Cāpālacaitya**. (P. Cāpālacetiya; T. Tsa pa la mchod rten; C. Zhepoluo ta; J. Shabara no tō; K. Ch'abara t'ap 遮婆羅塔) In Sanskrit, "Cāpāla shrine"; the site near the city of VAIŚĀLĪ where the Buddha GAUTAMA announced his intention to die and enter PARINIRVĀṆA. According to the Pāli MAHĀPARINIBBĀNASUTTANTA, on an excursion to the shrine with his attendant, ĀNANDA, the Buddha mentioned that, because he had fully mastered the four bases of psychic power (P. iddhipāda, S. ṚDDHIPĀDA), he had the ability to extend his life "for an eon or until the end of the eon" (P. kappa; S. KALPA). (The Pāli commentaries take "eon" here to mean "his full allotted lifespan," not a cosmological period.) Although he raised this prospect a second and third time, Ānanda did not take the hint, and the Buddha finally "consciously and deliberately" renounced his remaining lifespan and proclaimed he would pass away in three months' time. When the earth quaked at his decision, Ānanda finally realized what had happened and earnestly entreated the Buddha to extend his lifespan. However, the Buddha refused, enumerating the many occasions in the past when the Buddha had made the same statement and Ānanda had failed to make the request. Ānanda would later explain that he had been distracted by MĀRA. For his error, Ānanda was publicly censured by his colleagues at the time of the first Buddhist council following the Buddha's death (see COUNCIL, FIRST). The Cāpāla shrine was probably some sort of pre-Buddhist tree shrine; it was almost certainly not a Buddhist reliquary or commemorative tumulus (CAITYA).

**carita**. (T. spyod pa; C. xing; J. gyō; K. haeng 行). In Sanskrit and Pāli, "conduct," "behavior," or "temperament"; an alternative form is Sanskrit caryā (P. cariyā). As "behavior," carita is typically bifurcated into either good (sucarita) or bad (S. duścarita; P. duccarita) conduct. As "temperament," carita is used to indicate six general character types, which are predominantly biased toward the negative temperaments of greedy (RĀGA), hateful (S. DVEṢA; P. dosa), and deluded (MOHA), or the more positive temperaments of faithful (S. ŚRADDHĀ; P. saddhā), intelligent (BUDDHI), and discursive (S. VITARKA; P. vitakka), a taxonomy found in the VISUDDHIMAGGA. The first three types of temperaments are negative and thus need to be corrected. (1) A greedy temperament is constantly searching out new sensory experiences and clings to things that are not beneficial. (2) A hateful temperament is disaffected, always finding imaginary faults in others; along with the intelligent temperament, he is less prone to clinging than the other character types. (3) A deluded temperament is agitated and restless, because he is unable to make up his mind about anything and follows along with others' decisions. The latter three types of temperaments are positive and thus need to be enhanced. (4) A faithful temperament is like a greedy type who instead cultivates wholesome actions and clings to what is beneficial. (5) An intelligent temperament is like a hateful type who performs salutary actions and points out real faults; along with the hateful temperament, he is less prone to clinging than the other character types. (6) A discursive temperament is characterized by a restlessness of mind that constantly flits from topic to topic and vacillates due to his constant conjecturing; if these discursive energies can be harnessed, however, that knowledge may lead to wisdom. The *Visuddhimagga* also provides detailed guidelines for determining a person's temperament by observing their posture, their preferences in food, and the sort of mental concomitants with which they are typically associated. This knowledge of temperaments is important as a tool of practice (BHĀVANĀ), because in the *Visuddhimagga*'s account of visualization (P. KASIṆA) exercises, the practitioner is taught to use an appropriate kasiṇa device or meditation topic (P. KAMMAṬṬHĀNA) either to mitigate the influence of the negative temperaments or enhance the influence of the positive ones. Thus, a practitioner with a greedy temperament is advised to emphasize the cemetery contemplations on foulness (S. AŚUBHABHĀVANĀ; P. asubhabhāvanā) and mindfulness of the body (S. KĀYĀNUPAŚYANĀ; P. kāyānupassanā; see also SMṚTYUPASTHĀNA); the hateful temperament, the four divine abidings (BRAHMAVIHĀRA) and the four color kasiṇas (of blue, yellow, red, white); the deluded temperament, mindfulness of breathing (S. ĀNĀPĀNASMṚTI; P. ānāpānasati); the discursive temperament, also mindfulness of breathing; the faithful temperament, the first six recollections (S. ANUSMṚTI; P. anussati), viz., of the Buddha, the DHARMA, the SAṂGHA, morality, generosity, and the divinities; and the intelligent temperament, the recollections of death and peace, the analysis of the four elements, and the loathsomeness of food. Suitable to all six temperaments are the other six kasiṇas (viz., of earth, water, fire, air, light, and empty space) and the immaterial absorptions (S. ĀRŪPYĀVACARADHYĀNA; P. arūpāvacarajhāna). ¶ In the MAHĀYĀNA, caryā, carita, and related terms (e.g., Sanskrit compounds such as duścara) refer specifically to the difficult course of action that a BODHISATTVA pursues in order to reach the goal of enlightenment. These actions include the unending search or pilgrimage for a teacher, the sacrifices required to meet with an authentic teacher who can teach Mahāyāna doctrines (see SADĀPRARUDITA, SUDHANA), and the difficult practices of charity, such as giving away all possessions, including family members and even one's body (see DEHADĀNA; SHESHEN). The JĀTAKAMĀLĀ of Śura, the BODHICARYĀVATĀRA of ŚĀNTIDEVA, and to a certain extent the BUDDHACARITA of AŚVAGHOṢA set forth a model of the authentic bodhisattva's behavior for aspirants to emulate. In Buddhist TANTRA, caryā refers to a code of ritual purity, and to an esoteric practice called "yoga with signs" (SANIMITTAYOGA) followed by CARYĀTANTRA practitioners.

**Cariyāpiṭaka**. In Pāli, "The Basket of Conduct"; fifteenth book of the KHUDDAKANIKĀYA of the Pāli SUTTAPIṬAKA. According to traditional accounts, the text was preached by Gotama (S. GAUTAMA) Buddha immediately after the BUDDHAVAṂSA at the request of Sāriputta (S. ŚĀRIPUTRA). Centuries later, the missionary MAHINDA is said to have converted thousands of Sri Lankans to Buddhism when he recited it in ANURĀDHAPURA. Divided into three chapters (vagga), the book contains thirty-five stories in verse of previous lives of the Buddha. These stories recount and extol the ten perfections (P. pāramī, S. PĀRAMITĀ) that Gotama developed while striving for enlightenment through many lives as a bodhisatta (S. BODHISATTVA). The stories in this collection are called cariyā ("conduct," or "act"), whence the name of the text, and in content they parallel corresponding prose narratives found in the JĀTAKA. The Pāli tradition recognizes ten perfections as requisite for attaining buddhahood: generosity (DĀNA), morality (sīla, S. ŚĪLA), renunciation (nekkhamma, S. NAIṢKRAMYA), wisdom (paññā, S. PRAJÑĀ), energy (viriya, S. VĪRYA), patience (khanti, S. KṢĀNTI), truthfulness (sacca, S. SATYA), resolution (adhiṭṭhāna, S. ADHIṢṬHĀNA), loving-kindness (mettā, S. MAITRĪ) and equanimity (upekkhā, S. UPEKṢĀ). Of these ten, only seven are enumerated in this text. The first vagga is comprised of ten stories concerning the perfection of generosity. The second vagga has ten stories concerning morality. The third vagga contains fifteen stories, five of which are devoted to renunciation, six to truthfulness, two to loving-kindness, and one each to the perfections of resolution and equanimity. A commentary to the text, attributed to DHARMAPĀLA, is included in the PARAMATTHADĪPANĪ.

**Carus, Paul**. (1852–1919). An early supporter of Buddhism in America and the proponent of the "religion of science": a faith that claimed to be purified of all superstition and irrationality and that, in harmony with science, would bring about solutions to the world's problems. Carus was born in Ilsenberg in Harz, Germany. He immigrated to America in 1884, settling in LaSalle, Illinois, where he assumed the editorship of the Open Court Publishing Company. He attended the World Parliament of Religions in Chicago in 1893 and became friends with several of the Buddhist delegates, including DHARMAPĀLA and SHAKU SŌEN, who were among the first to promote his writing. Later, Shaku Sōen's student, DAISETZ TEITARO SUZUKI, would spend eleven years working with and for Carus in LaSalle. In 1894, Carus published *The Gospel of Buddha according to Old Records*, an anthology of passages from Buddhist texts drawn from contemporary translations in English, French, and German, making particular use of translations from the Pāli by THOMAS W. RHYS DAVIDS, as well as translations of the life of the Buddha from Chinese and Tibetan sources. Second only to Edwin Arnold's *Light of Asia* in intellectual influence at the time, *The Gospel* was arranged like the Bible, with numbered chapters and verses and a table at the end that listed parallel passages from the New Testament. *The Gospel* was intended to highlight the many agreements between Buddhism and Christianity, thereby bringing out "that nobler Christianity which aspires to the cosmic religion of universal truth." Carus was free in his manipulation of his sources, writing in the preface that he had rearranged, retranslated, and added emendations and elaborations in order to make them more accessible to a Western audience; for this reason, the translated sources are not always easy to trace back to the original literature. He also makes it clear in the preface that his ultimate goal is to lead his readers to the Religion of Science. He believed that both Buddhism and Christianity, when understood correctly, would point the way to the Religion of Science. Although remembered today for his *Gospel*, Carus wrote some seventy books and more than a thousand articles. His books include studies of Goethe, Schiller, Kant, and Chinese thought.

**caryā**. (S). See CARITA.

**Caryāgītikoṣa**. (T. Spyod pa'i glu'i mdzod). In Sanskrit, "Anthology of Songs on Practice"; a collection of fifty songs, dating from the eighth through the twelfth centuries, that represent some of the oldest examples of specifically tantric literature written in an Indian vernacular language (see APABHRAṂŚA). The manuscript was discovered in Nepal in 1907 and published in 1916, and contained four sections. The first section in the collection, *Caryācaryābhiniścaya*, was written in the Bengali vernacular, while the three other sections were written in Eastern Apabhraṃśa, a late Middle Indic dialect from the Bengal region. The original manuscript of the *Caryāgītikoṣa* contained sixty-nine folios, which included the fifty songs, with exegeses in Sanskrit. By the time of the text's rediscovery, however, five folios were lost, leaving sixty-four folios containing the text of forty-six full songs and the first six lines of another ten-lined song. The names of twenty-three different authors are ascribed to the songs themselves; the authorship of the Sanskrit commentary to the Bengali songs is attributed to Munidatta. The songs were handed down orally before they were committed to writing, and even today they are sung in the Buddhist communities of Nepal, Tibet, and other neighboring areas of the Himālayas. Most of the songs deal with gaining release from the bondage of the illusory world and enjoying the great bliss of enlightenment, by employing worldly similes drawn from marriage and such daily activities as fermenting wine and rowing a boat.

**caryātantra**. (T. spyod rgyud). In Sanskrit, "performance tantra"; in a traditional fourfold division of tantric practices and texts, it is the second of the four, ranked above KRIYĀTANTRA and below YOGATANTRA and ANUTTARAYOGATANTRA. According to the Indian commentator BUDDHAGUHYA, this class of tantras derives its name from the fact that it set forth an equal "performance" of both external rituals and internal yoga. This also explains the placement of this class of tantras between krīya and yoga. The most important tantra in the performance class is the MAHĀVAIROCANĀBHISAṂBODHI. There are three buddha families (BUDDHAKULA) in caryātantra: TATHĀGATAKULA, PADMAKULA, and VAJRAKULA. According to Tibetan exegetes, caryātantra for the most part does not set forth practices for meditating upon oneself as a buddha but rather prescribes methods for gaining feats (SIDDHI).

**catuḥpratisaraṇa**. See PRATISARAṆA.

**catuḥsaṃgrahavastu**. See SAṂGRAHAVASTU.

**catuḥsamudācāra**. See CATURKARMAN.

**Catuḥśataka**. (T. Bzhi brgya pa; C. Guang Bai lun ben; J. Kōhyakuronpon; K. Kwang Paengnon pon 廣百論本). In Sanskrit, "Four Hundred [Stanzas]"; the magnum opus of ĀRYADEVA, a third century CE Indian monk of the MADHYAMAKA school of MAHĀYĀNA philosophy and the chief disciple of NĀGĀRJUNA, the founder of that tradition. The four-hundred verses are divided into sixteen chapters of twenty-five stanzas each, which cover many of the seminal teachings of Madhyamaka philosophy. The first four of the sixteen chapters are dedicated to arguments against erroneous conceptions of permanence, satisfaction, purity, and a substantial self. In chapter 5, Āryadeva discusses the career of a BODHISATTVA, emphasizing the necessity for compassion (KARUṆĀ) in all of the bodhisattva's actions. Chapter 6 is a treatment of the three afflictions (KLEŚA) of greed or sensuality (LOBHA or RĀGA), hatred or aversion (DVEṢA), and delusion (MOHA). Chapter 7 explains the need to reject sensual pleasures. In chapter 8, Āryadeva discusses the proper conduct and attitude of a student of the TATHĀGATA's teaching. Chapters 9 through 15 contain a series of arguments refuting the erroneous views of other Buddhist and non-Buddhist schools. These refutations center on Āryadeva's understanding of emptiness (ŚŪNYATĀ) as the fundamental characteristic of reality. For example, in chapter 9, Āryadeva argues against the conception that anything, including liberation, is permanent and independent of causes. In chapter 11, Āryadeva argues against the SARVĀSTIVĀDA claim that dharmas exist in reality in the past, present, and future. Chapter 16, the final chapter, is a discussion of emptiness and its centrality to the Madhyamaka school and its doctrine. There is a lengthy and influential commentary on the text by CANDRAKĪRTI, entitled *Catuḥśatakaṭīkā*; its full title is *Bodhisattvayogacaryācatuḥśatakaṭīkā*. The *Catuḥśataka* was translated into Chinese by XUANZANG and his translation team at DACI'ENSI, in either 647 or 650–651 CE. The work is counted as one of the "three treatises" of the Chinese SAN LUN ZONG, where it is treated as Āryadeva's own expansion of his *ŚATAŚĀSTRA (C. BAI LUN; "One Hundred Treatise"); hence, the Chinese instead translates the title as "Expanded Text on the One Hundred [Verse] Treatise." Some have speculated, to the contrary, that the *Śataśāstra* is an abbreviated version of the *Catuḥśataka*. The two works consider many of the same topics, including the nature of NIRVĀṆA and the meaning of emptiness in a similar fashion and both refute Sāṃkhya and Vaiśeṣika positions, but the order of their treatment of these topics and their specific contents differ; the *Śataśāstra* also contains material not found in the *Catuḥśataka*. It is, therefore, safer to presume that these are two independent texts, not that one is a summary or expansion of the other. It is possible that the *Śataśāstra* represents Kumārajīva's interpretation of the *Catuḥśataka*, but this is difficult to determine without further clarity on the Indian text that Kumārajīva translated.

**catuḥsatyadharmacakra**. (T. bden bzhi'i chos 'khor; C. sidi falun; J. shitai hōrin; K. saje pŏmnyun 四諦法輪). In Sanskrit, lit. "the dharma wheel of the four truths"; the wheel of the dharma (DHARMACAKRA) delivered in ṚSIPATANA. In this first turning of the wheel of dharma, the Buddha set in motion a wheel with twelve aspects, by setting forth the four noble truths three separate times. He addressed the original group of five disciples (PAÑCAVARGIKA), telling them that they should not fall into extremes of asceticism or indulgence, and laid out for them the eightfold noble path (AṢṬĀṄGIKAMĀRGA). He set forth the four truths the first time by saying that the five aggregates

(SKANDHA) qualified by birth, aging, sickness, and death are the noble truth of suffering, craving is the noble truth of their origination, the elimination of that craving is the noble truth of their cessation, and that the eightfold noble path is the noble truth of the path leading to their cessation. He set forth the four truths a second time when, in the same extended discourse, he said, "I knew well that the truth of suffering was what I had to comprehend; I knew well that the truth of the origin was what I had to eliminate; I knew well that the truth of cessation was what I had to realize; and I knew well that the truth of the path was what I had to cultivate." He then set forth the four truths a third and final time when he said, "I comprehended the truth of suffering, I eliminated the true origin of suffering, I realized the true cessation of suffering, and I cultivated the true path." There are twelve aspects to this triple wheel because for each of the three stages there is (1) a vision that sees reality directly with the wisdom eye that is free from contaminants, (2) a knowledge that is free from doubt, (3) an understanding of the way things are, and (4) an intellectual comprehension of an idea never heard of before. ¶ The SAṂDHINIRMOCANASŪTRA calls the triple turning of the catuḥsatyadharmacakra with its twelve aspects the "first turning of the wheel." According to its commentaries, it is a demonstration that all dharmas, the skandhas, sense-fields (ĀYATANA), elements (DHĀTU), and so forth, exist. This teaching is provisional (NEYĀRTHA) because it must be interpreted in order to understand what the Buddha really means. A second "middle" dispensation, called "the dharma wheel of signlessness" (ALAKṢAṆADHARMACAKRA), is the teaching of the Mahāyāna doctrine, as set forth in the PRAJÑĀPĀRAMITĀ SŪTRAs, that all dharmas, even buddhahood and NIRVĀṆA, are without any intrinsic nature (NIḤSVABHĀVA). The first turning of the wheel is directed toward the ŚRĀVAKAs and PRATYEKABUDDHAs, who tremble at this doctrine of emptiness (ŚŪNYATĀ). The second turning is also not a final, definitive (NĪTĀRTHA) teaching. The ultimate teaching is the final turning of the wheel of dharma, called "the dharma wheel that makes a fine delineation" (*SUVIBHAKTADHARMACAKRA), i.e., the *Saṃdhinirmocanasūtra* itself. Here the Buddha, through his amanuensis Paramārthasamudgata, sets forth in clear and plain language what he means: that dharmas are endowed with three natures (TRISVABHĀVA) and each of those is, in a distinctive way, free from intrinsic nature (niḥsvabhāva). The doctrine of the first, middle, and final wheels of dharma is not intended to be a historical presentation of the development of Buddhist doctrine, but the first turning does loosely equate to the early teachings of the Buddha, the second to early Mahāyāna, and the third to the emergence of the later YOGĀCĀRA school of Mahāyāna philosophy. In Tibet, there is no argument over this first turning of the wheel of dharma: it is always understood to refer to the basic teachings of the Buddha for those of a HĪNAYĀNA persuasion. There is, however, substantial argument over the status of the second and third turnings of the wheel.

***catuḥśrāvakanikāya**. (T. nyan thos rtsa ba'i sde pa bzhi). In Sanskrit, "four main ŚRĀVAKA schools"; according to BHĀVAVIVEKA's PRAJÑĀPRADĪPA, the SARVĀSTIVĀDA, STHAVIRANIKĀYA, MAHĀSĀṂGHIKA, and SAṂMITĪYA schools. The *Prajñāpradīpa* identifies a total of eighteen śrāvaka schools by again dividing these main schools into seven, five, three, and three, respectively. See also MAINSTREAM BUDDHIST SCHOOLS; SAMAYABHEDOPARACANACAKRA.

**Catuḥstava**. (T. Bstod pa bzhi). In Sanskrit, "Four Songs of Praise"; a set of four devotional hymns attributed to the Indian monk NĀGĀRJUNA, the founder of the MADHYAMAKA school of MAHĀYĀNA philosophy. More than four such hymns have survived, so it is uncertain which were the original four. The four hymns now included in this set are entitled LOKĀTĪTASTAVA ("Hymn to He Who Transcends the World"), NIRAUPAMYASTAVA ("Hymn to He Who Is Unequaled"), ACINTYASTAVA ("Hymn to the Inconceivable"), and PARAMĀRTHASTAVA ("Hymn to the Ultimate"). These verses are addressed to the Buddha himself, in honor of his virtues and various aspects of his enlightenment. The author praises the Buddha for his supreme insight, his compassion, and his efforts to awaken all beings. The hymns also contain many important aspects of the philosophy of the Madhyamaka school. For example, verses five through ten of the *Lokātītastava* are used to explain the interdependence, and therefore inessential nature, of each of the five aggregates (SKANDHA).

***caturāpattidvāra**. (T. ltung ba'i sgo bzhi / sdom pa nyams pa'i rgyu bzhi; C. si fanzui men; J. shibonzaimon; K. sa pŏmjoe mun 四犯罪門). In Sanskrit, "the four doors through which transgression comes." According to the BODHISATTVABHŪMI, the best way to guard against transgression (āpatti) is to block these four doors. The first door is not knowing boundaries relative to which transgression does, or does not, occur; to counteract it, one should know the moral code (S. PRĀTIMOKṢA) well. The second is knowing the code, but not respecting virtuous persons; to counteract it, one should conquer pride and have respect. The third is having respect but being heedless (PRAMĀDA); to counteract it, one must be guided by one's conscience (APRAMĀDA). The fourth door is when one has knowledge, respect, and a conscience but where KLEŚA (affliction) predominates; to counteract it, one must apply an antidote (S. PRATIPAKṢA) and focus on reducing the powers of the kleśas.

**caturapramāṇa**. In Sanskrit, "four boundless states." See APRAMĀṆA; BRAHMAVIHĀRA.

***Caturaśītisiddhapravṛtti**. (T. Grub thob brgyad bcu rtsa bzhi'i lo rgyus). In Sanskrit, "The Lives of the Eighty-four Siddhas"; a tantric doxography ascribed to the early twelfth-century Indian author ABHAYADATTAŚRĪ. The original Sanskrit version has been lost, but the text is preserved in Tibetan translation. The work records brief vitae for the great SIDDHAS (or mahāsiddhas) of Indian tantric Buddhism, who are commonly enumerated in a list of eighty-four. While the list varies, according to Abhayadattaśrī's work, the eighty-four siddhas include Lūyipa, Līlapa, VIRŪPA, Ḍombipa, Śavaripa, SARAHA, Kankaripa, Mīnapa, Goraksa, Caurāṅgi, Vīnapa, Śāntipa, Tantipa, Camaripa, Khaḍgapa, NĀGĀRJUNA, Kāṇḥapa, Karṇaripa, Thaganapa, NĀROPA, Śalipa, TILOPA, Catrapa, Bhadrapa, Dhukhandi, Ajokipa, Kalapa, Dhombipa, Kaṅkana, Kambala, Ṭeṅgipa, Bhandhepa, Tandhepa, Kukkuripa, Kucipa, Dharmapa, Mahipa, Acinta, Babhahi, Nalina, Bhusuku, INDRABHŪTI, Mekopa, Koṭali, Kamparipa, Jālandhari, RĀHULA, Dharmapa, Dhokaripa, Medhina, Paṅkaja, Ghaṇḍhapa, Yogipa, Caluki, Gorura, Lucika, Niguṇa, Jayānanda, Pacari, Campaka, Bhikṣana, Telopa, Kumaripa, Caparipa, Maṇibhadrā, Mekhalā, Kanakhalā, Kalakala, Kantali, Dhahuli, Udheli, Kapalapa, Kirava, Sakara, Sarvabhakṣa, Nāgabodhi, Dārika, Putali, Panaha, Kokali, Anaṅga, Lakṣmīnkarā, Samudra, and Vyali. See MAHĀSIDDHA.

**caturkarman**. (T. las bzhi). In Sanskrit, "four activities"; the four types of activities set forth in the Buddhist tantras. It is a general rubric for the classification of rituals, based on the means or the goal of the ritual. The four types are activities of pacification (ŚĀNTICĀRA), activities of increase (PAUṢṬIKA), activities of control (VAŚĪKARAṆA), and wrathful activities (ABHICĀRA).

**caturlakṣaṇa**. (T. mtshan nyid bzhi; C. sixiang; J. shisō; K. sasang 四相). In Sanskrit, "four marks of existence"; also known as the four "conditioned marks" (SAṂSKṚTALAKṢAṆA. These four characteristics governing all conditioned objects are "origination" or birth (JĀTI), "maturation" or continuance (STHITI), "senescence" or decay (JARĀ), and "desinence" or extinction, viz., death (ANITYA). In the SARVĀSTIVĀDA school, these four were treated as "forces dissociated from thought" (CITTAVIPRAYUKTASAṂSKĀRA), which exerted real power over compounded objects, escorting an object along from one force to another, until the force "desinence" extinguishes it; this explanation was necessary in order to explain how factors that the school presumed continued to exist in all three time periods of past, present, and future nevertheless still appeared to undergo change. Some Sarvāstivāda ABHIDHARMA texts, however, accept only three characteristics, omitting continuance. See also DHARMAMUDRĀ; LAKṢAṆA.

**caturmahāpadeśa**. In Sanskrit, "four resorts to authority." See MAHĀPADEŚA.

**caturmahārāja**. (S). See LOKAPĀLA.

**cāturmahārājakāyika**. (P. cātummahārājikā; T. rgyal chen rigs bzhi; C. sitianwang tian; J. shitennōten; K. sach'ŏnwang ch'ŏn 四天王天). In Sanskrit, "heaven of the assemblage of the four great kings"; the lowest of all the heavens in Buddhist cosmology and the lowest of the six heavens located in the sensuous realm (KĀMADHĀTU). The heaven is located on the upper slopes of MOUNT SUMERU and is presided over by four kings, one in each of the cardinal directions. The four kings are DHṚTARĀṢṬRA in the east; VIRŪḌHAKA in the south; VIRŪPĀKṢA in the west; and VAIŚRAVAṆA in the north. These four are known collectively as the LOKAPĀLAS, or protectors of the world. There are many divinities (DEVA) inhabiting this heaven: GANDHARVAS in the east, KUMBHĀṆḌAS in the south, NĀGAS in the west, and YAKṢAS in the north. As vassals of ŚAKRO DEVĀNĀM INDRAḤ (lit. "Śakra, the lord of the gods"; see INDRA; ŚAKRA), the four heavenly kings serve as protectors of the dharma (DHARMAPĀLA) and of sentient beings who are devoted to the dharma. They are said to have protected the Buddha from the time that he entered his mother's womb and also to have presented him with his alms bowl after his enlightenment. They survey their respective quadrants of the world and report on the deeds of humans to the divinities of the TRĀYASTRIṂŚA heaven.

**caturmudrā**. (T. phyag rgya bzhi; C. siyin; J. shiin; K. sain 四印). In Sanskrit, lit. "four seals" or "four assertions"; the Tibetan translation lta ba bkar btags kyi phyag rgya bzhi literally means "the four seals that mark a view as the word [of the Buddha]," i.e., that mark a philosophical system or certify a doctrine as being Buddhist. The four seals are: all compounded factors (SAṂSKṚTADHARMA) are impermanent (ANITYATĀ), all contaminated things are suffering (DUḤKHA), all things are devoid of any perduring self (ANĀTMAN), and NIRVĀṆA is peace (śānta). In the MAHĀYĀNASŪTRĀLAṂKĀRA, the four seals are connected with the three "gates to deliverance" (VIMOKṢAMUKHA), which mark the transition from the compounded (SAṂSKṚTA) realm of SAṂSĀRA to the uncompounded (ASAṂSKṚTA) realm of NIRVĀṆA. "All compounded factors are impermanent" and "all contaminated things are suffering" are the cause of the SAMĀDHI of wishlessness (APRAṆIHITA). "All phenomena are selfless" is the cause of the samādhi of emptiness (ŚŪNYATĀ). "Nirvāṇa is peace" is the cause of the samādhi of signlessness (ĀNIMITTA).

**caturnimitta**. (P. catunimitta; T. mtshan ma bzhi; C. sixiang; J. shisō; K. sasang 四相). In Sanskrit, the "four signs," "sights," or "portents," which were the catalysts that led the future buddha SIDDHĀRTHA GAUTAMA to renounce the world (see PRAVRAJITA) and pursue liberation from the cycle of birth and death (SAṂSĀRA): specifically, an old man, a diseased man, a dead man, and a religious mendicant (ŚRAMAṆA). According to the many traditional biographies of the Buddha, eight brāhmaṇa seers predicted at the time of his birth that, were Gautama to see all four of these portents, he would be led inexorably toward renunciation of his royal heritage. His father, ŚUDDHODANA, who wanted Siddhārtha to succeed him, sought to shield the prince from these sights. While distracting his son with all the sensual pleasures available in his palaces, the prince, at the age of twenty-nine, eventually became curious about the world beyond the palace and convinced his father to allow him to go out in his chariot, accompanied by the charioteer CHANDAKA. On four successive chariot rides, the prince saw an old man, a sick man, a corpse being taken to the charnel ground, and a mendicant. Gautama eventually determined to go forth (pravrajita) into homelessness after witnessing the four portents. The first three sights demonstrated to Gautama the vanity of life and the reality of suffering (DUḤKHA), and the sight of a religious mendicant provided him with the prospect of freedom of mind and a model to follow in finding a way leading to liberation. Some versions of the Buddha's biography refer only to the first three of these signs. In some versions, it is said that the four sights were not actually an old man, sick man, corpse, and mendicant, but apparitions of these created by the gods in order to spur the bodhisattva to renounce the world. In the LALITAVISTARA, it is the prince himself who creates the old man, the sick man, the corpse, and the mendicant, and then asks his charioteer who they are, pretending not to know the answer. Biographies of previous buddhas, such as VIPAŚYIN, typically mention the role similar encounters played in their own renunciations.

**caturthābhiṣeka**. (T. dbang bzhi pa; C. disi guanding; J. daishi kanjō; K. chesa kwanjŏng 第四灌頂). In Sanskrit, "fourth empowerment"; the fourth of the four empowerments or initiations employed in ANUTTARAYOGATANTRA, the other three being the vase empowerment (KALAŚĀBHIṢEKA), the secret empowerment (GUHYĀBHIṢEKA), and the knowledge of the consort empowerment (PRAJÑĀJÑĀNĀBHIṢEKA). After having engaged in sexual union with a consort in the third empowerment, in this fourth and final empowerment, the practitioner seeks to attain the state of innate bliss (sahajānanda) with the mind of clear light (PRABHĀSVARACITTA), in a vision like the natural color of the autumn sky at dawn, free from moonlight, sunlight, and darkness. The initiation is also called the "word empowerment" (śabdābhiṣeka) because the teacher will identify this state for the disciple.

**caturyoni**. (S). See YONI.

**caturyuga**. In Sanskrit, "four eons." See YUGA.

**catuṣkoṭi**. (T. mu bzhi; C. siju fenbie; J. shiku funbetsu; K. sagu punbyŏl 四句分別). In Sanskrit, "four antinomies" or "four alternatives"; a dialectical form of argumentation used in Buddhist philosophy to categorize sets of specific propositions, i.e., (1) A, (2) B, (3) both A and B, (4) neither A nor B; or (1) A, (2) not A, (3) both A and not A, 4) neither A nor not A. For instance, something may be said to (1) exist, (2) not exist, (3) both exist and not exist, and (4) neither exist nor not exist. Or, 1) everything is one, (2) everything is many, (3) everything is both one and many, 4) everything is neither one nor many. In the sūtra literature, the catuṣkoṭi is employed to categorize the speculative philosophical propositions of non-Buddhists (TĪRTHIKA) in a list of fourteen "indeterminate" or "unanswered" (AVYĀKṚTA) questions to which the Buddha refused to respond. These questions involve various metaphysical assertions that were used in traditional India to evaluate a thinker's philosophical pedigree. In the case of ontology, for example: (1) Is the world eternal? (2) Is the world not eternal? (3) Is the world both eternal and not eternal? (4) Is the world neither eternal nor not eternal? Or, in the case of soteriology, for a TATHĀGATA, or an enlightened person: (1) Does the tathāgata exist after death? (2) Does the tathāgata not exist after death? (3) Does the tathāgata both exist and not exist after death? (4) Does the tathāgata neither exist nor not exist after death? Because of the conceptual flaws inherent in any prospective answer to these sets of questions, the Buddha refused to answer them and his silence is sometimes interpreted to mean that his teachings transcend conceptual thought (PRAPAÑCA). This transcendent quality of Buddhist philosophy is displayed in the MADHYAMAKA school, which seeks to ascertain the conceptual flaws inherent in any definitive philosophical proposition and show instead that all propositions—even those made by Buddhists—are "empty" (śūnya). NĀGĀRJUNA, the founder of the Madhyamaka school, analyzes many philosophical positions in terms of a catuṣkoṭi to demonstrate their emptiness. In analyzing causality, for example, Nāgārjuna in the opening lines of his MŪLAMADHYAMAKAKĀRIKĀ analyzes the possible philosophical positions on the connection between cause (HETU) and effect (PHALA) as a catuṣkoṭi: (1) cause and effect are identical, as the Sāṃkhya school claims; (2) cause and effect are different, as the Buddhists propose; (3) cause and effect are both identical and different, and thus the effect is both continuous with as well as emergent from the cause, as the JAINA school claims; (4) cause and effect are neither identical nor different, and thus things occur by chance, as the materialists and skeptics advocate. Nāgārjuna instead reveals the absurd consequences inherent in all of these positions to show that the only defensible position is that cause and effect are "empty"; thus, all compounded things are ultimately unproduced (ANUTPĀDA) and empty of intrinsic existence (NIḤSVABHĀVA). Classifications of teachings using the catuṣkoṭi are widely found in Buddhist literature of all traditions.

**catuṣkuśalamūla**. (T. dge rtsa bzhi; C. si shangen; J. shizenkon; K. sa sŏn'gŭn 四善根). In Sanskrit, "four spiritual faculties"; an alternate name for the four "aids to penetrations" (NIRVEDHABHĀGĪYA), the full name of which is the nirvedhabhāgīya-kuśalamūla.

**catvāro yonayaḥ**. See YONI.

**catvāry āryasatyāni**. (P. cattāri ariyasaccāni; T. 'phags pa'i bden pa bzhi; C. si shengdi; J. shishōdai; K. sa sŏngje 四聖諦). In Sanskrit, "four noble truths." See FOUR NOBLE TRUTHS.

**causality**. See PRATĪTYASAMUTPĀDA; HETUPRATYAYA.

**cause**. See HETU.

**causes and conditions**. See HETUPRATYAYA.

**celestial bodhisattva**. An English term coined to describe BODHISATTVAS appearing in the MAHĀYĀNA pantheons, who are objects of specific types of devotions or cultic practices. These include AVALOKITEŚVARA, MAÑJUŚRĪ, VAJRAPĀṆI, KṢITIGARBHA, and SAMANTABHADRA, among many others. See also AṢṬAMAHOPAPUTRA.

**celibacy**. See BRAHMACARYA; PĀRĀJIKA.

**central channel**. See AVADHŪTĪ.

**cessation**. See NIRODHA.

**cetanā**. (T. sems pa; C. si; J. shi; K. sa 思). In Sanskrit and Pāli, "intention," "volition," or "stimulus"; one of the omnipresent mental factors (MAHĀBHŪMIKA; SARVATRAGA) that accompanies each moment of consciousness; intention directs the mind toward either salutary (KUŚALA), unsalutary (AKUŚALA), or neutral (AVYĀKṚTA) objects. Intention is of crucial importance in the theory of action (KARMAN), where the intent defines the eventual quality of the action: "Action is volition, for after having intended something, one accomplishes action through body, speech, and mind." Hence, cetanā functions as both the stimulus and driving force behind all action, framing the ways in which beings choose to interact with the world at large and coordinating the functioning of the various mental concomitants (CAITTA) that are necessary in order to respond accordingly. In this sense, in a simile drawn from the AṬṬHASĀLINĪ, cetanā functions like a general, who commands and coordinates the activities of all the soldiers on the battlefield. The emphasis on cetanā in the larger sense of intention is sometimes identified as a Buddhist innovation in KARMAN theory, where the intention motivating a deed plays a significant role in the positive or negative karmic weight of the deed itself.

**cetasika**. In Pāli, "mental concomitant" or "mental factor"; the Pāli equivalent of the Sanskrit term caitasika (see CAITTA). Mental concomitants are factors associated with the arising of consciousness (CITTA or viññāṇa; S. VIJÑĀNA). According to the Pāli ABHIDHAMMA, there are fifty-two mental concomitants, of which twenty-five are either karmically salutary or neutral, fourteen are karmically unsalutary, and thirteen are simply neutral. Out of the fifty-two types of cetasikas, seven are invariably associated with all moments of consciousness—viz., consciousness cannot arise without these seven all being present: (1) sensory contact or sense impression (phassa; S. SPARŚA), (2) sensation or feeling (VEDANĀ), (3) perception or conception (saññā; S. SAṂJÑĀ), (4) volition (CETANĀ), (5) concentration (SAMĀDHI), (6) vitality (JĪVITA), and (7) attention, viz., the advertence of the mind toward an object (manasikāra; S. MANASKĀRA). See also CAITTA; List of Lists.

**Cetiyagiri**. In Pāli, "Shrine Mountain"; name given to the mountain of MISSAKAPABBATA (see MIHINTALE) in Sri Lanka, because of the many shrines and reliquaries (P. cetiya; S. CAITYA) located there; also called Cetiyapabbata. The Sinhalese king DEVĀNAṂPIYATISSA built a monastery for the elder MAHINDA atop the mountain. Relics acquired from AŚOKA and from Sakka (S. ŚAKRA), king of the gods, were temporarily kept at that site; a sapling from the southern branch of the BODHI TREE brought to Sri Lanka from India by the elder nun, SAṄGHAMITTĀ, was also planted there. Mahinda dwelt for several years at Cetiyagiri and passed away there; his remains were cremated at the site and a reliquary (P. thūpa; S. STŪPA) erected over them. In the first century BCE, King Kaṇirajānutissa once had sixty monks from Cetiyagiri executed for treason. Over time, Cetiyagiri became an important monastic center, and the Chinese pilgrim FAXIAN records that when he visited the site in the early fifth century, there were more than two thousand monks in residence.

**Cetokhilasutta**. (C. Xinhui jing; J. Shinnekyō; K. Simye kyŏng 心穢經). In Pāli, "Discourse on Mental Obstructions"; the sixteenth sutta of the MAJJHIMANIKĀYA (a separate Sarvāstivāda recension appears as the 206th sūtra in the Chinese translation of the MADHYAMĀGAMA; a recension of unidentified affiliation also occurs in the Chinese translation of the EKOTTARĀGAMA), preached by the Buddha to a gathering of monks in the JETAVANA grove in the town of Sāvatthi (ŚRĀVASTĪ). The Buddha describes five mental obstructions and five fetters that constitute impediments to overcoming suffering. The five obstructions include (1) doubt about the teacher, the Buddha; (2) doubt about the dhamma (DHARMA); (3) doubt about the SAṂGHA; (4) doubt about the value of morality (sīla; S. ŚĪLA), meditative concentration (SAMĀDHI), and wisdom (paññā; S. PRAJÑĀ); 5) ill will and animosity toward one's fellow monks. The five fetters include (1) attachment to sensual desires, (2) attachment to a sense of self, (3) attachment to material possessions, (4) excessive sleeping and eating, and (5) adopting the life of renunciation merely for the limited goal of a blissful existence in the heavens.

**cetoparyāyābhijñāna**. (S). See PARACITTAJÑĀNA.

**cetovimukti**. (P. cetovimutti; T. sems rnam par grol ba; C. xin jietuo; J. shingedatsu; K. sim haet'al 心解脫). In Sanskrit, "liberation of mind"; a meditative concept associated with the mastery of any of the four meditative absorptions (P. JHĀNA; S. DHYĀNA). Cetovimukti results in the temporary suppression of the contaminants (P. āsava; S. ĀSRAVA) through the force of concentration (SAMĀDHI). It is also associated with the acquisition of the "superknowledges" (P. abhiññā; S. ABHIJÑĀ). Cetovimukti alone is insufficient to bring about the attainment of enlightenment (BODHI) or the cessation of rebirth and must therefore be complemented by the "liberation through wisdom" (P. paññāvimutti; S. prajñāvimukti; see PRAJÑĀVIMUKTA).

**Chach'o**. (K) (自超). See MUHAK CHACH'O.

**'Chad ka ba Ye shes rdo rje**. (Chekawa Yeshe Dorje) (1102–1176). A scholar of the BKA' GDAMS sect of Tibetan

Buddhism, most famous for his influential work on the practice of "mind training" (BLO SBYONG) called BLO SBYONG DON BDUN MA ("The Seven Points of Mind Training"). He is also known as Dge bshes Mchad kha ba (Geshe Chekawa).

**Chaiya**. One of the oldest cities in Thailand, located south of Bangkok, and famous for its Buddhist archaeological remains. The city was a center of the kingdom of ŚRĪVIJAYA, a MAHĀYĀNA Buddhist empire that dominated the island of Sumatra, the Malay peninsula, and parts of Thailand and Java from the seventh through the thirteenth centuries. Mahāyāna monasteries still exist at the city, which were constructed during this period, such as Wat Hua Wieng and Wat Keu. Chaiya monasteries display a unique architectural style: the tops of the structures have five towers, with a large tower on the center and four smaller towers on the corners. Strong Indian Gupta influences are seen in a sculpture of the Buddha under the hooded protection of the NĀGA king and in depictions of Mahāyāna deities, in particular, AVALOKITEŚVARA. The city thrived until the thirteenth century, when Śrīvijaya fell to invasion from neighboring kingdoms.

**Chajang**. (慈藏) (d.u.; fl. c. 590–658/alt. 608–686). Korean VINAYA master (yulsa) of the Silla dynasty. Born into the royal "true bone" (chin'gol) class of the Silla aristocracy, Chajang lost his parents at an early age and was ordained at the monastery of Wŏnnyŏngsa. Chajang traveled to China in 636 and during his sojourn on the mainland made a pilgrimage to WUTAISHAN, where he had a vision of the BODHISATTVA MAÑJUŚRĪ. Returning to Silla Korea in 643, he is said to have brought back a set of the Buddhist canon and packed the boat on which he returned with Buddhist banners, streamers, and other ritual items. He is also claimed to have returned with treasures he had received directly from Mañjuśrī, including ŚĀKYAMUNI Buddha's own gold-studded monk's robe (K. kasa; KAṢĀYA) wrapped in purple silk gauze, as well as the Buddha's skull bone and finger joint. Back in Silla, Chajang began looking for the place where Mañjuśrī had told him the relics should be enshrined. After a long search, he finally found the spot in 646, where he constructed a "Diamond Precept Platform" (Kŭmgang kyedan) and enshrined one portion of the Buddha's relics. This platform was the origin of the important Korean monastery of T'ONGDOSA, which became the center of vinaya practice in Korea. Chajang is also said to have established SINHŬNGSA, WŎLCHŎNGSA, and HWANGNYONGSA and supervised the construction of the famous nine-story wooden pagoda at Hwangnyongsa, which was completed in 645. He was also appointed the state overseer of the SAṂGHA (taegukt'ong), the top ecclesiastical office in the Silla Buddhist institution. Chajang was in charge of regulations concerning the conduct of monks and nuns all over the country, as well as overseeing at a state level the repair and maintenance of temples, the correct attention to the details of Buddhist ceremonial ritual, and the proper display of Buddhist religious images. His concern to improve the discipline and decorum of Korean monks led to his emphasis on vinaya study and practice, and he did much to encourage the study and dissemination of the vinaya in Korea, including writing commentaries to the SARVĀSTIVĀDA and DHARMAGUPTAKA vinayas. Chajang also instituted the UPOṢADHA rite of having monks recite the PRĀTIMOKṢA once every fortnight on full- and new-moon days. For his efforts, Chajang was revered by later generations as a teacher of the Dharmaguptaka vinaya (known in East Asia as the "Four-Part Vinaya"; see SIFEN LÜ) and the founder of the Korean analogue to the Chinese NANSHAN LÜ ZONG of DAOXUAN. In 650, at Chajang's suggestion, the Silla court adopted the Tang Chinese calendrical system, an important step in the Sinicization of the Korean monarchy. Various works attributed to Chajang include the *Amit'a kyŏng ŭigi* ("Notes on the AMITĀBHASŪTRA"), *Sabun yul kalma sagi* ("Personal Notes on the Karman Section of the Four-Part Vinaya"), and *Kwanhaeng pŏp* ("Contemplative Practice Techniques"); none of his writings are extant.

**chakpŏp**. (作法). In Korean, lit. "to create DHARMA"; a generic term for Korean Buddhist rituals, and especially ritual dances, such as the butterfly dance (NABICH'UM), cymbal dance (PARACH'UM), and the dharma drum dance (PŎPKOCH'UM). Outdoor performances, called toryanggye chakbŏp, might include the butterfly dance (nabich'um) performed together with an accompaniment of ritual chanting (PŎMP'AE) and a traditional band.

**'cham**. A Tibetan term for precisely choreographed ritual dances usually performed by a group of monks in a monastery courtyard and generally coinciding with a major monastic festival or important religious event. In many cases, the dancers are dressed in elaborate costumes, including painted masks, with the performance involving varied routines during the course of several days. Some dances, such as the zhwa nag (black hat) dance, symbolize the subjugation of forces inimical to Buddhism. Others may represent episodes from the life of Buddhist personalities, including PADMASAMBHAVA and MI LA RAS PA, or aspects of their spiritual attainment. Monks generally begin to train while quite young, although the most experienced performers practice 'cham as a form of active meditation. The dances are most often public events, performed before crowds of lay Buddhists from surrounding villages. Most performances are therefore a combination of religious ritual and social gathering and nearly every large dance festival will include several jester figures to keep the public entertained during slow periods in the program. See also LHA MO.

**Chan**. (J. Zen; K. Sŏn; V. Thiền 禪). In Chinese, the "Meditation," or Chan school (CHAN ZONG); one of the major indigenous schools of East Asian Buddhism. The Sinograph "chan" is the first syllable in the transcription channa, the Chinese transcription of the Sanskrit term DHYĀNA (P. JHĀNA); thus chan, like the cognate term chanding (chan is a transcription and ding a translation, of dhyāna), is often translated in English simply as "meditation." For centuries, the title CHANSHI (meditation master) was used in such sources as the "Biography of Eminent

Monks" (GAOSENG ZHUAN) to refer to a small group of elite monks who specialized in the art of meditation. Some of these specialists adopted the term chan as the formal name of their community (Chan zong), perhaps sometime during the sixth or seventh centuries. These early "Chan" communities gathered around a number of charismatic teachers who were later considered to be "patriarchs" (ZUSHI) of their tradition. The legendary Indian monk BODHIDHARMA was honored as the first patriarch; it was retrospectively claimed that he first brought the Chan teachings to China. Later Chan lineage histories (see CHUANDENG LU) reconstructed elaborate genealogies of such patriarchs that extended back to MAHĀKĀŚYAPA, the first Indian patriarch, and ultimately to the Buddha himself; often, these genealogies would even go back to all of the seven buddhas of antiquity (SAPTABUDDHA). Six indigenous patriarchs (Bodhidharma, HUIKE, SENGCAN, DAOXIN, HONGREN, and HUINENG) are credited by the established tradition with the development and growth of Chan in China, but early records of the Chan school, such as the LENGQIE SHIZI JI and LIDAI FABAO JI, reveal the polemical battles fought between the disparate communities to establish their own teachers as the orthodox patriarchs of the tradition. A particularly controversial dispute over the sixth patriarchy broke out between the Chan master SHENXIU, the leading disciple of the fifth patriarch Hongren, and HEZE SHENHUI, the purported disciple of the legendary Chinese monk Huineng. This dispute is often referred to as the "sudden and gradual debate," and the differing factions came to be retrospectively designated as the gradualist Northern school (BEI ZONG; the followers of Shenxiu) and the subitist Southern school (NAN ZONG; the followers of Huineng). The famous LIUZU TANJING ("Platform Sūtra of the Sixth Patriarch"), composed by the followers of this putative Southern school, is an important source for the history of this debate. Following the sixth patriarch, the Chan lineage split into a number of collateral lines, which eventually evolved into the so-called "five houses and seven schools" (WU JIA QI ZONG) of the mature Chan tradition: the five "houses" of GUIYANG (alt. Weiyang), LINJI, CAODONG, YUNMEN, and FAYAN, and the subsequent bifurcation of Linji into the two lineages of HUANGLONG and YANGQI, giving a total of seven schools. ¶ The teachings of the Chan school were introduced to Korea perhaps as early as the end of the seventh century CE and the tradition, there known as SŎN, flourished with the rise of the Nine Mountains school of Sŏn (KUSAN SŎNMUN) in the ninth century. By the twelfth century, the teachings and practices of Korean Buddhism were dominated by Sŏn; and today, the largest Buddhist denomination in Korea, the CHOGYE CHONG, remains firmly rooted in the Sŏn tradition. The Chan teachings were introduced to Japan in the late twelfth century by MYŌAN EISAI (1141–1215); the Japanese tradition, known as ZEN, eventually developed three major sects, RINZAISHŪ, SŌTŌSHŪ, and ŌBAKUSHŪ. The Chan teachings are traditionally assumed to have been transmitted to Vietnam by VINĪTARUCI (d. 594), a South Indian brāhmaṇa who is claimed (rather dubiously) to have studied in China with the third Chan patriarch SENGCAN before heading south to Guangzhou and Vietnam. In 580, he is said to have arrived in Vietnam and settled at Pháp Vân monastery, where he subsequently transmitted his teachings to Pháp Hiền (d. 626), who carried on the Chan tradition, which in Vietnamese is known as THIỀN. In addition to the Vinītaruci lineage, there are two other putative lineages of Vietnamese Thiền, both named after their supposed founders: VÔ NGÔN THÔNG (reputedly a student of BAIZHANG HUAIHAI), and THẢO ĐƯỜNG (reputedly connected to the YUNMEN ZONG lineage in China). Chan had a presence in Tibet during the early dissemination (SNGA DAR) of Buddhism, and the Chan monk MOHEYAN was an influential figure at the Tibetan court in the late eighth century, leading to the famous BSAM YAS DEBATE.

**chanda**. (T. 'dun pa; C. yu; J. yoku; K. yok 欲). In Sanskrit and Pāli, "zeal" or "desire to act"; one of the ten mental factors or mental concomitants (CAITTA) of wide extent (MAHĀBHŪMIKA) that the VAIBHĀṢIKA school of SARVĀSTIVĀDA ABHIDHARMA says accompany all consciousness activity; alternatively, it is listed as one of the five VINIYATA or pratiniyama mental factors of specific application according to the YOGĀCĀRA school, and one of the six pakiṇṇaka (miscellaneous) CETASIKAs of the Pāli abhidhamma. Chanda plays an important role in motivating all wholesome (and unwholesome) activity, and is particularly important in the cultivation of ŚAMATHA (serenity or calm abiding). According to the MADHYĀNTAVIBHĀGA, there are eight forces that counteract five hindrances (NĪVARAṆA) to reaching śamatha. Chanda is called the ground of all eight forces because, based on ŚRADDHĀ (faith or confidence), it leads to a resolute effort (vyāyāma) to apply SMṚTI (mindfulness), SAṂPRAJANYA (circumspection), and UPEKṢĀ (equanimity) to reach the final goal.

**Chandaka**. (P. Channa; T. 'Dun pa; C. Cheni; J. Shanoku; K. Ch'anik 車匿). The charioteer and groom of SIDDHĀRTHA GAUTAMA, who accompanied the BODHISATTVA prince on two momentous occasions. First, Chandaka drove the prince's chariot when he ventured outside the palace, where he was confronted with the four portents (CATURNIMITTA), encountering on separate occasions an old man, a sick man, a corpse, and a mendicant. Having been confronted with these realities, the prince resolved to go forth in search of liberation from birth and death. According to the story, during his youth, the prince had never seen an old person, a sick person, or a corpse before and so asked Chandaka what each was. Chandaka's explanation that old age, sickness, and death were the ultimate fate of all humans led the prince to decide to renounce his royal inheritance and go out in search of a state beyond aging, sickness, and death. Second, Chandaka accompanied the prince on his ride into renunciation as a mendicant (see PRAVRAJITA). When Gautama left his father's palace in KAPILAVASTU to lead the homeless life, Chandaka departed with him, together with Gautama's noble steed, KAṆṬHAKA. Once outside the city, after cutting off his topknot, the prince removed his jewelry and handed it over to Chandaka, exchanged clothes with him, and then ordered his groom to return to the palace with his horse and inform his father that he would not return to the city until his quest for enlightenment was fulfilled. Kaṇṭhaka was so grief-stricken at his master's departure that he died on the spot, and Chandaka, crushed at both losses, asked for permission to join the prince in mendicancy but was refused. (Some accounts state instead that Chandaka feared for his life if he returned alone with all the prince's possessions, and so left the worldly life that very night.) Chandaka was eventually ordained by the Buddha. Because he was so swollen with pride at his close relationship with his former charge Gautama, it is said that he was arrogant in accepting discipline from his colleagues and was ostracized from the order more than once, in one case for siding with nuns in a dispute with monks, in another for repeatedly reviling ŚĀRIPUTRA and MAHĀMAUDGALYĀYANA. In the account of the Buddha's final days in the MAHĀPARINIBBĀNASUTTANTA, the Buddha's last disciplinary act before he died was to pass the penalty of brahmadaṇḍa (lit. the "holy rod") on Chandaka, which required that he be ostracized by his fellow monks. When the Buddha's attendant ĀNANDA went to Chandaka to announce the penalty, it is said that Chandaka finally was contrite and became an ARHAT on the spot.

**Changansa**. (長安寺). In Korean, "Monastery of Extended Peace"; was one of the major monasteries on the Korean sacred mountain of KŬMGANGSAN (Diamond Mountains), now in North Korea. There are two different accounts of the monastery's foundation: it was built either by an unidentified figure during the rule of the Silla king Pŏphŭng (r. 514–540) or by the Koguryŏ monk Hyeryang (d.u) in 551, which he was proselytizing in the Silla dynasty. The monastery was frequently rebuilt with state support. Especially elaborate was the reconstruction project sponsored in 1323 by the empress Ki (d.u.), a Koryŏ native and consort of Emperor Shundi (r. 1333–1368) of the Mongol Yuan dynasty, on behalf of the emperor and her son, the prince. The Chosŏn-dynasty Sŏn monk SŎSAN HYUJŎNG (1520–1604) and his disciple SAMYONG YUCHŎNG (1544–1610) are both said to have practiced at Changansa. During the Korean War (1950–1953), most of the monastery burned to the ground and the campus has yet to be restored.

**changjwa purwa**. (S. naiṣyadika; P. nesajjika; T. cog bu pa; C. changzuo buwo; J. jōza/chōza fuga 長坐不臥). In Korean, "constantly sitting without lying down." This practice is the last of a list of twelve or thirteen voluntarily ascetic practices (see DHUTAṄGA) sanctioned by the Buddha, and is used as a countermeasure (PRATIPAKṢA) against sloth and torpor (P. thīnamiddha; S. STYĀNA-MIDDHA). In Korean Sŏn (C. CHAN) monasteries, this is typically the only one of the list of the ascetic practices that is still in general practice. Although the practice of never lying down is recommended during intensive periods of practice during the summer and winter meditative retreats (kyŏlche; see JIEZHI), in some cases, the practice is carried out for months or years at a time. Unlike ascetics in the Chinese and Tibetan traditions, however, Korean monks never use physical supports to prop up the body. During periods of "ferocious effort" (YONGMAENG CHŎNGJIN), typically the one-week period during the winter meditation retreat preceding the enlightenment day of the Buddha (the eighth day of the twelfth lunar month), the monks and nuns in the meditation hall often undertake changjwa purwa for the entire seven days.

**Changlu Zongze**. (J. Chōro Sōsaku; K. Changno Chongsaek 長蘆宗賾) (d.u.; fl. c. late eleventh to early twelfth centuries). Chinese CHAN monk of the YUNMEN ZONG. Little is known about his life, but Changlu is said to have been a native of Yongnian in Luozhou, in present-day Henan province. Changlu also seems to have had a close relation to the disciples of Tianyi Yihuai (993–1064), himself a disciple of the Yunmen Chan master XUEDOU CHONGXUAN. Changlu eventually became a student of Tianyi's disciples Fayun Faxiu (1027–1090) and Changlu Yingfu (d.u.), and later inherited the latter's lineage. Changlu Zongze is most famous for his compilation of the influential text on Chan monastic regulations or "rules of purity" (QINGGUI), the CHANYUAN QINGGUI, during his tenure at the Chan monastery Hongji chanyuan in 1103. When a revised edition of the *Chanyuan qinggui* was published in 1202, the meditation manual ZUOCHAN YI, probably composed by Changlu or his colleagues, was included. Changlu is also remembered as a PURE LAND adept renowned for his rigorous practice of NIANFO, the recitation of the name of the buddha AMITĀBHA. He later moved to Changlu in present-day Jiangxi province, whence he acquired his toponym. Changlu was later given the title Chan master Cijue (Compassionate Enlightenment).

**Changuan cejin**. (J. Zenkan sakushin; K. Sŏn'gwan ch'aekchin 禪關策進). In Chinese, "Spurring Advancement through the Chan Barrier"; composed by the CHAN master YUNQI ZHUHONG in 1600. The text has long been used in Chan monasteries as a primer in meditation. From various Chan lineage histories (CHUANDENG LU) and recorded sayings (YULU), Yunqi compiled over a hundred anecdotes and legends about Chan masters that cogently demonstrated the value of diligence and intense practice. The *Changuan cejin* consists of two general collections. The first collection itself is further divided into two sections, entitled "Zhuzu fayu jieyao" ("Essential Selections of Dharma Talks by Various Masters") and "Zhuzu kugong jielüe" ("Brief Selections of the Painful Effort of Various Masters"). The first section consists largely of public lectures delivered by famous Chan masters, with Yunqi's own evaluation and notes appended at the end of each lecture. Similarly, the second section consists largely of stories of courageous efforts in practice made by various monks of the past, again with Yunqi's evaluations appended at the end of each story. The second collection, entitled "Zhujing yinzheng jielüe" ("Brief Selections of Verified Passages from Various Scriptures"), also consists of short passages quoted from various scriptures, with Yunqi's evaluation appended at the end of each passage.

**changzhu**. (J. jōjū; K. sangju 常住). In Chinese, lit. "constantly abiding"; this term refers, first, to the doctrine of the eternality of the Buddha's "three bodies" (TRIKĀYA), especially as elaborated in the ŚRĪMĀLĀDEVĪSIṂHANĀDASŪTRA and the MAHĀPARINIRVĀṆASŪTRA. According to this doctrine, it is not just the "dharma body" (DHARMAKĀYA) of the Buddha that is eternal; rather, these sūtras explain that even his "enjoyment body" (SAṂBHOGAKĀYA) and "emanation body" (NIRMĀṆAKĀYA) also perdure and are imperishable. Second, in the East Asian traditions, changzhu refers to the communal, shared property and equipment within the monastic compound. Such communal property was not permitted to be appropriated for private, personal use, but was intended to be the common possession of the entire monastic community and was therefore subjected to the collective oversight of the SAṂGHA. The monastic office in charge of overseeing, allocating, maintaining the common monastic property was, by extension, also called the changzhu.

**Chanlin baoxun**. (J. Zenrin hōkun; K. Sŏllim pohun 禪林寶訓). In Chinese, "Treasured Instructions of the Chan Grove"; edited by the CHAN monk Jingshan (d.u.) and published in 1378. Jingshan expanded upon an earlier collection of one hundred or so anecdotes that the eminent Chan master DAHUI ZONGGAO and Longxiang Shigui (d. 1149) had culled from the recorded sayings (YULU) and biographies of various Chan masters. Jingshan's edition contains more than three hundred anecdotes, which he divided into two rolls. The *Chanlin baoxun* was a popular text and numerous commentaries and annotations, such as Dajian Jiaoding's (d.u.) *Chanlin baoxun yinyi*, Xingsheng's (d.u.) *Chanlin baoxun niansong*, and Pinji Zhixiang's (d.u.) *Chanlin baoxun bishuo*, were appended to the end of some editions of the text.

**Chanlin sengbao zhuan**. (J. Zenrin sōbōden; K. Sŏllim sŭngbo chŏn 禪林僧寶傳). In Chinese, "Chronicles of the SAṂGHA Jewel in the Forests of CHAN"; compiled in the twelfth century by the "lettered Chan" (WENZI CHAN) monk JUEFAN HUIHONG (1071–1128). Huihong intended for this chronicle to serve as a supplement to his own "Biographies of Eminent Monks" (GAOSENG ZHUAN), which is no longer extant. Huihong collected the biographies of over a hundred eminent Chan masters who were active in the lettered Chan movement between the late Tang and early Song dynasties, appending his own comments to each biography. Huihong's collection is said to have been pared down to eighty-one biographies by the Chan master DAHUI ZONGGAO. Later, Dahui's disciple Jinglao (d.u.) of Tanfeng added a biography of WUZU FAYAN, the teacher of Dahui's own master YUANWU KEQIN, and two other masters to the conclusion of Huihong's text, giving a total of eighty-four biographies in the extant collection. A postscript by XUTANG ZHIYU appears at the end of the compilation. Unlike Chan "lamplight histories" (CHUANDENG LU), which are typically arranged according to principal and collateral lineages, the monks treated in this compilation are listed according to their significance in the origin and development of the "lettered Chan" movement; Huihong's treatment undermines the neat charts of master–disciple connections deriving from the lamplight histories, which have become so well known in the literature. In Japan, a copy of the *Chanlin sengbao zhuan* was published as early as 1295 and again in 1644.

**Chanmen guishi**. (J. Zenmon kishiki; K. Sŏnmun kyusik 禪門規式). In Chinese, "Pure Regulations of the Gate of Chan"; a synopsis of the eminent CHAN master BAIZHANG HUAIHAI's legendary text on monastic regulations (BAIZHANG QINGGUI). This text appears in the official Chan lineage history JINGDE CHUANDENG LU, written in 1004, as an appendix to its biography of Baizhang. The *Chanmen guishi* speaks of such unique Chan practices as establishing the dharma hall in lieu of the Buddha Hall, the emphasis on the abbot's quarters (FANGZHANG) and the SAṂGHA hall (SENGTANG), and the ritual of entering the abbot's room (rushi). As Baizhang's original text is now lost (if, in fact, it ever existed), the *Chanmen guishi* serves as an important source for the study of Baizhang's putative innovations in monastic regulations.

**Chanmen miyao jue**. (C) (禪門秘要訣/決). See ZHENGDAO GE.

**Chan miyaofa jing**. (J. Zenpiyōhōkyō; K. Sŏn piyobŏp kyŏng 禪秘要法經). In Chinese, "Scripture on the Essential Techniques of Meditation"; translated by KUMĀRAJĪVA. The scripture details the practice of meditation, visualization, and controlling the breath. Among the different meditative practices discussed in the text, the meditations on foulness (AŚUBHABHĀVANĀ) serves as the foundational practice.

**Chan Preface**. See CHANYUAN ZHUQUANJI DUXU.

**chanshi**. (J. zenji; K. sŏnsa 禪師). In Chinese, lit. "DHYĀNA master," "meditation master," and, later, "CHAN master." Various "biographies of eminent monks" (GAOSENG ZHUAN) collections mention specialists of meditation known as chanshi, many of whom appear in a section typically entitled "practitioners of meditation" (xichan). Teachers of the TIANTAI, PURE LAND, and SANJIE JIAO are often referred to as chanshi. After the rise of the CHAN school in China, the term typically referred more specifically to the eminent teachers of this specific tradition. Often the formal title of chanshi (Chan master) was bestowed upon exceptional teachers by the monarchs of China, Korea, and Japan.

**Chanxian**. (C) (禪賢). See ZHIKONG CHANXIAN.

**Chanyao**. (J. Zen'yō; K. Sŏnyo 禪要). In Chinese, "Essentials of Chan." See GAOFENG HESHANG CHANYAO.

**Chanyuan qinggui**. (J. Zen'on shingi; K. Sŏnwŏn ch'ŏnggyu 禪苑清規). In Chinese, "Pure Rules of the Chan

Garden"; compiled by the CHAN master CHANGLU ZONGZE, in ten rolls. According to its preface, which is dated 1103, the *Chanyuan qinggui* was modeled on BAIZHANG HUAIHAI's legendary "rules of purity" (QINGGUI) and sought to provide a standardized set of monastic rules and an outline of institutional administration that could be used across all Chan monasteries. As the oldest extant example of the qinggui genre, the *Chanyuan qinggui* is an invaluable source for the study of early Chan monasticism. It was the first truly Chinese set of monastic regulations that came to rival in importance and influence the imported VINAYA materials of Indian Buddhism and it eventually came to be used not only in Chan monasteries but also in "public monasteries" (SHIFANG CHA) across the Chinese mainland. The *Chanyuan qinggui* provides meticulous descriptions of monastic precepts, life in the SAṂGHA hall (SENGTANG), rites and rituals, manners of giving and receiving instruction, and the various institutional offices at a Chan monastery. A great deal of information is also provided on the abbot and his duties, such as the tea ceremony. Semi-independent texts such the ZUOCHAN YI, a primer of meditation, the *Guijing wen*, a summary of the duties of the monastic elite, and the *Baizhang guisheng song*, Zongze's commentary on Baizhang's purported monastic code, are also appended at the end of the *Chanyuan qinggui*. The Japanese pilgrims MYŌAN EISAI, DŌGEN KIGEN, and ENNI BEN'EN came across the *Chanyuan qinggui* during their visits to various monastic centers in China and, upon their return to Japan, they used the text as the basis for the establishment of the Zen monastic institution. Copies of a Chinese edition by a certain Yu Xiang, dated 1202, are now housed at the Tōyō and Kanazawa Bunkō libraries. The *Chanyuan qinggui* was also imported into Korea, which printed its own edition of the text in 1254; the text was used to reorganize Korean monastic institutions as well.

**Chanyuan zhuquanji duxu**. (J. Zengen shosenshū tojo; K. Sŏnwŏn chejŏnjip tosŏ 禪源諸詮集都序). In Chinese, lit., "Prolegomenon to the 'Collected Writings on the Source of Chan'"; composed by the CHAN and HUAYAN exegete GUIFENG ZONGMI sometime between 828 and 835; typically known by its abbreviated title of "Chan Prolegomenon" (C. Duxu; J. Tojo; K. Tosŏ) and often referred to in English as the "Chan Preface." The text is a comprehensive overview of the Chan collection (*Chanyuan zhuquanji*), which is said to have been one hundred rolls (juan) in length, but is now entirely lost. Pei Xiu's (787?–860) own preface to Zongmi's "Prolegomenon" describes this collection as a massive anthology of essential prose and verse selections drawn from all the various Chan schools, which was so extensive that Pei says it deserves to be designated as a separate "Chan basket" (Chanzang; see PIṬAKA), complementing the other "three baskets" (TRIPIṬAKA) of the traditional Buddhist canon. In order to provide a comprehensive overview of this massive collection of Chan material, Zongmi seeks to assess in his "Prolegomenon" the teachings of eight representative schools of Tang-dynasty Chan: JINGZHONG ZONG, Northern school (BEI ZONG), BAOTANG ZONG, Nanshan Nianfo men Chan zong, the Shitou school of SHITOU XIQIAN (which would eventually evolve into the CAODONG and YUNMEN schools), NIUTOU ZONG, the Heze school of HEZE SHENHUI, and the HONGZHOU ZONG (or "Jiangxi" as it is called in the text) of MAZU DAOYI. In an effort to bridge both the ever-growing gap between the contending Chan lineages and also their estranged relations with the doctrinal schools (C. jiao, see K. KYO) that derive from the written scriptures of Buddhism, Zongmi provides in his "Prolegomenon" an overarching hermeneutical framework (see JIAOXIANG PANSHI) through which to evaluate the teachings of both the Chan and doctrinal schools. This framework is built around a series of polarities, such as the three core teachings of the scriptures and the three axiomatic perspectives of Chan, the words of the Chan masters and the mind of the Buddha, sudden awakening and gradual practice, and original enlightenment (BENJUE) and nonenlightenment. In order to demonstrate the continuities between Chan and jiao, Zongmi proceeds to demonstrate how various doctrinal traditions align with the three core teachings of the scriptures and how the eight representative Chan schools correlate with the three axiomatic perspectives of Chan. He then correlates the three doctrinal teachings with the three Chan perspectives, thus demonstrating the fundamental correspondence between the Chan and the scriptures. The last polarity he examines, that between original enlightenment and nonenlightenment, also enables Zongmi to outline an etiology of both delusion and awakening, which provides the justification for a soteriological schema that requires an initial sudden awakening followed by continued gradual cultivation (DUNWU JIANXIU). Zongmi's luster faded in China during the Song dynasty, but his vision of the Chan tradition as outlined in his "Prolegomenon" was extremely influential in YONGMING YANSHOU's ZONGJING LU; indeed, it is now believed that the Zongjing lu subsumes a substantial part of Zongmi's lost "Chan Canon" (viz., his *Chanyuan zhuquanji*). Zongmi and his "Prolegomenon" found a particularly enthusiastic proponent in Korean Sŏn in the person of POJO CHINUL, who placed Zongmi's preferred soteriological schema of sudden awakening followed by gradual cultivation at the core of Korean Sŏn practice. Zongmi's works continued to be widely read in Korea after Chinul's time and, since the seventeenth century, Korean Buddhist seminaries (kangwŏn) included the "Prolegomenon" (K. Tosŏ) in the SAJIP ("Fourfold Collection"), the four key texts of the Korean monastic curriculum.

**Chanyue Guanxiu**. (J. Zengetsu Kankyū; K. Sŏnwŏl Kwanhyu 禪月貫休) (832–912). A Chinese CHAN monk famous as a poet and painter. His CHANYUE JI ("Collection of the Moon of Meditation") is one of the two most important collections of Chan poetry, along with the HANSHAN SHI. His rendering of the sixteen ARHAT protectors of Buddhism (ṢOḌAŚASTHAVIRA) became the standard Chinese presentation. His vivid portrayal of the arhats offers an extreme, stylized rendition of how the Chinese envisioned "Indians" (fan) or "Westerners" (hu), and gives each of his subjects a distinctive bearing and deportment and unique phrenological features and physical characteristics; these features are subsequently repeated routinely in the Chinese artistic tradition.

**Chanyue ji**. (J. Zengetsu shū; K. Sŏnwŏl chip 禪月集). In Chinese, "Collection of the Moon of Meditation"; a popular anthology of poetry by the poet and painter monk CHANYUE GUANXIU (832–912), otherwise known by his sobriquet of Chanyue dashi (Great Master Meditation Moon), whence the collection acquired its name. The *Chanyue ji* is said to have originally consisted of twenty-five or twenty-six rolls, of which only eleven are extant. A copy was made in 923 and again in 1240. Along with the HANSHAN SHI, the *Chanyue ji* is often considered one of the most lucid collections of CHAN poetry and is thus favored by many monks within the Chan tradition.

**Chan zong**. (J. Zenshū; K. Sŏn chong 禪宗). The Chan, or Meditation, school. See CHAN.

**Chan zong Yongjia ji**. (J. Zenshū Yōkashū; K. Sŏnjong Yŏngga chip 禪宗永嘉集). In Chinese, "Collection of Yonjia of the Chan School," attributed to the CHAN master YONGJIA XUANJUE; also known as the *Yongjia ji*, *Yongjia chanzong ji*, and *Yongjia chanji*. This text was an influential collection of poems that delineated the fundamental principles of meditation and the proper means of practice. The collection consists of ten major sections: (1) "intent and formalities in appreciating the way," (2) "haughtiness in keeping moral precepts (ŚĪLA)," (3) "the pure cultivation of the three modes of action," (4) "song of ŚAMATHA," (5) "song of VIPAŚYANĀ," (6) "song of UPEKṢĀ," (7) "gradual cultivation of the three vehicles," (8) "principle and phenomena are nondual," (9) "letters of encouragement to a friend," and (10) "vows." There is a famous commentary on this text by the Song-dynasty monk Xingding (d.u.) entitled the (*Chan zong*) *Yongjia ji zhu*. In 1464, a vernacular Korean translation of Xingding's text, with translation and commentary attributed to King Sejo (1455–1468) of the Chosŏn dynasty, was published in Korea by the official Bureau of Scriptural Publication; this was one of the earliest texts composed in the new vernacular writing system of Han'gŭl.

**Chaoyuan**. (J. Chōgen; K. Ch'owŏn 超元). See DAOZHE CHAOYUAN.

**Chapada**. A Mon disciple of Uttarajīva Thera who introduced reformed Sinhalese Buddhism into the Pagan empire of Burma during the reign of King Narapatisithu (r. 1173–1210 CE). According to the KALYĀṆĪ INSCRIPTIONS (1479), where his story is first told, Chapada traveled to Sri Lanka as a twenty-year-old novice in the company of his preceptor, Uttarajīva, shortly after the THERAVĀDA tradition of the island kingdom had been reformed by Parākramabāhu I in accordance with the orthodox standards of the MAHĀVIHĀRA. Chapada was given the UPASAṂPADĀ higher ordination by both Uttarajīva and other patriarchs of the Sinhalese saṅgha (S. SAṂGHA), thus becoming the first monk from Burma to be ordained into the Mahāvihāra tradition. The joint ceremony is described as having symbolized the essential unity of the Burmese-Mon and Sinhalese monastic lineages. Despite this initial ecumenism, when Chapada returned to Burma after ten years of study on the island, he and his cohorts refused to join with the existing saṅgha of Pagan, and instead organized themselves into a separate monastic fraternity at the capital. The fraternity thus established became known as the Sīhaḷa saṅgha, while the older "unreformed" congregation of monks of Pagan came to be known as the Ariya Arahanta saṅgha. The Sīhaḷa saṅgha founded by Chapada continued to fragment so that by the end of the Pagan empire (late thirteenth century), there were at least ten separate monastic fraternities in Burma. The "Kalyāṇī Inscriptions" decry this disunity as a factor that ultimately weakened the vitality of the religion.

**Chengguan**. (J. Chōkan; K. Chinggwan 澄觀) (738–839). Putative fourth patriarch of the Chinese HUAYAN tradition; also known as Daxiu, Huayan pusa, Huayan shuzhu, and Qingliang GUOSHI. Chengguan is said to have entered the monastery in 746 under the guidance of a monk named Tizhen (d.u.). Although little is known of Chengguan's early training, he is supposed to have studied a broad range of scriptures and commentaries including the PRAJÑĀPĀRAMITĀ SŪTRAS, MAHĀPARINIRVĀṆASŪTRA, DASHENG QIXIN LUN, YOGĀCĀRABHŪMIŚĀSTRA, and others. In 757, he received the full monastic precepts from a certain Tanyi (d.u.) of the NANSHAN LÜ ZONG and studied for several years under Tanyi's prominent disciple JINGXI ZHANRAN. Chengguan is also said to have studied CHAN during this period under various masters. After his training under Fashen (718–778), second-generation disciple of the Huayan master FAZANG, Chengguan left for WUTAISHAN, the earthly abode of the BODHISATTVA MAÑJUŚRĪ, in 776. Chengguan was a prolific exegete, whose writings amount to over four hundred rolls in total. Chengguan is best known for his massive commentary on ŚIKṢĀNANDA's new translation of the AVATAṂSAKASŪTRA, entitled the [*Dafangguang fo*] HUAYAN JING SHU, in sixty rolls. This work rivaled and may even have surpassed in influence the most popular commentary on the *Avataṃsakasūtra* of his day, viz., Fazang's HUAYAN JING TANXUAN JI. Chengguan also wrote a comprehensive autocommentary to his commentary, entitled the HUAYAN JING SUISHU YANYI CHAO, in a total of ninety rolls. In these works, Chengguan expands upon the Huayan master DUSHUN's work on the notion of the realm of reality (DHARMADHĀTU), the HUAYAN FAJIE GUANMEN. Chengguan approached the dharmadhātu from four interrelated perspectives, viz., the dharmadhātu of phenomena (SHI FAJIE), dharmadhātu of principle (LI FAJIE), the dharmadhātu of the mutual nonobstruction between principle and phenomena (LISHI WU'AI FAJIE), and the dharmadhātu of the mutual nonobstruction between phenomenon and phenomena (SHISHI WU'AI FAJIE). As the premier Huayan exegete of his generation, Chengguan also was summoned to the Tang capital of Chang'an in 796 to collaborate with the northwest Indian monk PRAJÑA in preparing a new translation of the GAṆḌAVYŪHA, the forty-roll final chapter of the *Avataṃsakasūtra*. Among Chengguan's many disciples, the CHAN and Huayan exegete GUIFENG ZONGMI is most famous.

**Chengshi lun**. (S. *Tattvasiddhi; J. Jōjitsuron; K. Sŏngsil non 成實論). In Chinese, "Treatise on Establishing Reality"; a summary written c. 253 CE by the third century CE author HARIVARMAN of the lost ABHIDHARMA of the BAHUŚRUTĪYA school, a branch of the MAHĀSĀṂGHIKA. (The Sanskrit reconstruction **Tattvasiddhi* is now generally preferred over the outmoded **Satyasiddhiśāstra*). The *Tattvasiddhi* is extant only in KUMĀRAJĪVA's Chinese translation, made in 411–412, in sixteen rolls (juan) and 202 chapters (pin). The treatise is especially valuable for its detailed refutations of the positions held by other early MAINSTREAM BUDDHIST SCHOOLS; the introduction, for example, surveys ten different grounds of controversy separating the different early schools. The treatise is structured in the form of an exposition of the traditional theory of the FOUR NOBLE TRUTHS, but does not include listings for different factors (DHARMA) that typify many works in the abhidharma genre. The positions advocated in the text are closest to those of the STHAVIRANIKĀYA and SAUTRĀNTIKA schools, although, unlike the Sthaviranikāya, the treatise accepts the reality of "unmanifest materiality" (AVIJÑAPTIRŪPA) and, unlike Sautrāntika, rejects the notion of an "intermediate state" (ANTARĀBHAVA) between existences. Harivarman opposes the SARVĀSTIVĀDA position that dharmas exist in past, present, and future, the Mahāsāṃghika view that thought is inherently pure, and the VĀTSĪPUTRĪYA premise that the "person" (PUDGALA) exists. The *Chengshi lun* thus hones to a "middle way" between the extremes of "everything exists" and "everything does not exist," both of which it views as expediencies that do not represent ultimate reality. The text advocates, instead, the "voidness of everything" (sarvaśūnya) and is therefore sometimes viewed within the East Asian traditions as representing a transitional stage between the mainstream Buddhist schools and Mahāyāna philosophical doctrine. The text was so widely studied in East Asia, especially during the fifth and sixth centuries, that reference is made to a *Tattvasiddhi school of exegesis (C. Chengshi zong; J. Jōjitsushū; K. Sŏngsilchong); indeed, the Jōjitsu school is considered one of the six major schools of Japanese Buddhist scholasticism during the Nara period.

**Chengshi zong**. (J. Jōjitsushū; K. Sŏngsil chong 成實宗). In Chinese, "*Tattvasiddhi school" of scholastic exegesis. See CHENGSHI LUN.

**Cheng weishi lun**. (S. *Vijñaptimātratāsiddhi; J. Jōyuishikiron; K. Sŏng yusik non 成唯識論). In Chinese, "Demonstration of Consciousness-Only"; a magnum opus of Sino-Indian YOGĀCĀRA Buddhism and the foundational text of the Chinese WEISHI, or FAXIANG, school. The text is often cited by its reconstructed Sanskrit title *VIJÑAPTIMĀTRATĀSIDDHI, and its authorship attributed to DHARMAPĀLA (530–561), but the text as we have it in Chinese translation has no precise analogue in Sanskrit and was never used within the Indian or Tibetan traditions. Its Chinese translator XUANZANG (600/602–664), one of the most important figures in the history of Chinese Buddhist scholasticism, traveled to India in the seventh century, where he specialized in Yogācāra doctrine at NĀLANDĀ monastic university under one of Dharmapāla's disciples, ŚĪLABHADRA (529–645). At Nālandā, Xuanzang studied VASUBANDHU's TRIṂŚIKĀ (*Triṃśikāvijñaptimātratā[siddhi]kārikā*), the famous "Thirty Verses on Consciousness-Only," along with ten prose commentaries on the verses by the prominent Yogācāra scholiasts Dharmapāla, STHIRAMATI, Nanda, Citrabhānu, Guṇamati, Jinamitra, Jñānamitra, Jñānacandra, Bandhuśrī, Śuddhacandra, and Jinaputra. After his return to China in 645, Xuanzang set to work translating this massive amount of new material into Chinese. Rather than translate in their entirety all ten commentaries, however, on the advice of his translation team Xuanzang chose to focus on Dharmapāla's exegesis, which he considered orthodox, rather than muddy the waters in China with the divergent interpretations of the other teachers. As a foil for Dharmapāla's interpretation, Xuanzang uses the commentaries by Sthiramati, Nanda, and occasionally Citrabhānu, but he typically concludes any discussion with Dharmapāla's definitive view. This decision to rely heavily on Dharmapāla's interpretation probably comes from the fact that Xuanzang's own Indian teacher, Śīlabhadra, was himself a pupil of Dharmapāla. ¶ The *Cheng weishi lun* is principally concerned with the origination and removal of ignorance (AVIDYĀ), by clarifying the processes by which erroneous perception arises and enlightened understanding is produced. Unlike the writings of STHIRAMATI, which understood the bifurcation of consciousness into subject and object to be wholly imaginary, the *Cheng weishi lun* proposed instead that consciousness in fact always appears in both subjective and objective aspects, viz., a "seeing part" (darśanabhāga) and a "seen part" (nimittabhāga). The apparent dichotomy between inner self and external images is a supposition of mentality (MANAS), which in turn leads to the various afflictions (KLEŚA), as the mind clings to those images it likes and rejects those it dislikes; thus, suffering (DUḤKHA) is created and the cycle of rebirth (SAṂSĀRA) sustained. Both the perceiving self and the perceived images are therefore both simply projections of the mind and thus mere-representation (VIJÑAPTIMĀTRA) or, as Xuanzang translated the term, consciousness-only (WEISHI). This clarification of the perceptual process produces an enlightened understanding that catalyzes a transmutation of the basis (ĀŚRAYAPARĀVṚTTI), so that the root consciousness (MŪLAVIJÑĀNA), or ĀLAYAVIJÑĀNA, no longer serves as the storehouse of either wholesome or unwholesome seeds (BĪJA), thus bringing an end to the subject–object bifurcation. In the course of its discussion, the *Cheng weishi lun* offers an extensive treatment of the Yogācāra theory of the eight consciousnesses

(VIJÑĀNA) and especially the storehouse consciousness (ālayavijñāna) that stores the seeds, or potentialities, of these representational images. The text also offers an overview of the three-nature (TRISVABHĀVA) theory of vijñaptimātra as imaginary (PARIKALPITA), dependent (PARATANTRA), and perfected (PARINIṢPANNA). Finally, the *Cheng weishi lun* provides such exhaustive detail on the hundred dharmas (BAIFA) taxonomical system of the Yogācāra that it has been used within the tradition as a primer of Yogācāra dharma theory.

**Cheng weishi lun shu ji**. (J. Jōyuishikiron jukki; K. Sŏng yusik non sulgi 成唯識論述記). In Chinese, "Explanatory Notes on the CHENG WEISHI LUN" (**Vijñaptimātratāsiddhi*); by the Chinese YOGĀCĀRA monk KUIJI and probably compiled sometime between 659 and 682. In his preface, Kuiji praises VASUBANDHU and his TRIṂŚIKĀ, DHARMAPĀLA's **Vijñaptimātratāsiddhi* (C. *Cheng weishi lun*) and XUANZANG for translating DHARMAPĀLA's text. Then, as do most commentaries of that period, Kuiji expounds upon the title of Dharmapāla's text. In his subsequent introduction, Kuiji largely divides his commentary into five sections. In the first section, he ascertains the period in the Buddha's life to which the teachings belong (see JIAOXIANG PANSHI; PANJIAO) and discusses its audience, the BODHISATTVAS. In the second section, Kuiji discusses the tenets of the *Cheng weishi lun*, which he subsumes under the notion of "mind-only" (CITTAMĀTRA). In third section, Kuiji demonstrates that the *Cheng weishi lun* belongs to the "one vehicle" (EKAYĀNA) and the BODHISATTVAPIṬAKA. In the fourth section, short biographies and dates of the ten masters of the YOGĀCĀRA are provided. Kuiji then provides a detailed analysis of the *Cheng weishi lun* itself in the last section. Several commentaries on Kuiji's text have been written throughout the ages in East Asia. The *Cheng weishi lun shu ji* also exerted a considerable amount of influence on Silla-period Korean Buddhism and among the Nara schools of early Japanese Buddhism (see NARA BUDDHISM, SIX SCHOOLS OF).

**Chian**. (K) (志安). See HWANSŎNG CHIAN.

**Chijang**. (C. Dizang 地藏) (628–726). A Korean monk of the Silla dynasty, also known as KIM KYOGAK, who was closely associated with the cult of KṢITIGARBHA (K. Chijang) on the Chinese sacred mountain of JIUHUASHAN. According to his biography in the SONG GAOSENG ZHUAN ("Biographies of Eminent Monks Compiled During the Song Dynasty"); Kim was a scion of the Silla royal family, who ordained as a Buddhist monk at around the age of twenty-three and then traveled to Tang China on pilgrimage. Eventually arriving at Jiuhuashan in southeastern China, Chijang ended up residing there for some seventy-five years. Chijang is said to have spent his time in meditation, surviving by eating only rice that he cooked together with "white soil" (perhaps lime or gypsum). Deeply moved by his asceticism, the laity decided to build a large monastery for him. Around 780 CE, Zhang Gongyan brought the new name plaque for Chijang's monastery, designating it Huachengsi, and many laypeople made the arduous journey from Silla Korea to visit. In the summer of 803 CE, at the age of ninety-nine, Chijang bid farewell to his congregation, sat down in full lotus position, and passed away. His corpse was placed in seated position inside a coffin but even after three years it had not decayed and his face still looked as if he were alive. People eventually came to believe that he was the manifestation of his namesake, the BODHISATTVA KṢITIGARBHA (K. Chijang). A shrine hall, named Dizang dian (K. Chijang chŏn), was built on the site where he died, which could only be reached by pulling oneself by rope up eighty-one precarious stone steps.

**Chikchisa**. (直指寺). In Korean, "Direct Pointing Monastery"; the eighth district monastery (PONSA) of the contemporary CHOGYE CHONG of Korean Buddhism, located on Mount Hwangak in North Kyŏngsang province. The monastery purports to have been founded in 418 CE by the Koguryŏ monk Ado (fl. c. 418). There are three different stories about how the monastery got its name. The first version states that the name originated when Ado pointed directly at Mount Hwangak and said, "At that place, a large monastery will be established." The second story says that a monk called Nŭngyŏ (fl. c. 936) laid out the monastery campus using only his hands and without using any other measuring devices; hence, the monastery was given the name "Direct Measuring" (chikchi). A third story connects the name to the famous line concerning the soteriological approach of the SŎN or CHAN school: "direct pointing to the human mind" (K. chikchi insim; C. ZHIZHI RENXIN). With the support of the Koryŏ king Taejo (r. 918–943), Nŭngyo restored the monastery in 936; major renovations followed in the tenth century and again during the Chosŏn dynasty. In 1595, during the Japanese Hideyoshi invasions, all its buildings except the Ch'ŏnbul Chŏn (Thousand Buddhas Hall), Ch'ŏnwang Mun (Heavenly Kings Gate), and Chaha Mun (Purple-Glow Gate) were burned to the ground. The monastery was rebuilt in a massive construction project that began in 1602 and lasted for seventy years. The monastery enshrines many treasures, including a seated figure of the healing buddha BHAIṢAJYAGURU and a hanging picture of a Buddha triad (Samjonbul T'AENGHWA). Two three-story stone pagodas are located in front of the main shrine hall (TAEUNG CHŎN) and other three-story pagodas are located in front of the Piro chŏn (VAIROCANA Hall).

**Chikchi simch'e yojŏl**. (K) (直指心體要節). See PULCHO CHIKCHI SIMCH'E YOJŎL.

**'Chi med lha khang**. (Chime Lhakang). A small temple founded in 1499 near Punakha in central Bhutan, dedicated to the mad YOGIN 'BRUG PA KUN LEGS, who is believed to have stayed there.

**Chims** [alt. Mchims] **'Jam pa'i dbyangs**. (d. 1267). A Tibetan scholar who is renowned as the author of the *Chos mngon pa mdzod kyi tshig le'ur byas pa'i 'grel pa mngon pa'i rgyan,* better known by its abbreviation *Chims mdzod*, an extensive commentary on Vasubandhu's ABHIDHARMAKOŚABHĀṢYA. His commentary was widely used for detailed study of ABHIDHARMA in large DGE LUGS monasteries in Tibet.

**Chims phu**. [alt. Mchims phu]. A conglomeration of meditation caves and hermitages on the side of a low ridge near BSAM YAS monastery south of LHA SA; also known as Mchims phu. It forms one of central Tibet's most important and active pilgrimage sites. The location's principal cave, Brag dmar ke'u tshang (Drakmar Ke'utsang), is one of eight major centers connected with PADMASAMBHAVA, and is considered the representation of the Indian master's speech. It is identified as the place where Padmasambhava first gave the instructions known as the "eight transmitted precepts of attainment" (SGRUB PA BKA' BGYAD) to his eight main disciples, including the Tibetan king KHRI SRONG LDE BTSAN. It is also the location where Padmasambhava resurrected Khri srong lde btsan's young daughter PADMA GSAL, and gave her the teachings of the MKHA' 'GRO SNYING THIG for the first time. The Chims phu complex also contains a natural representation of Padmasambhava's pure land, ZANGS MDOG DPAL RI, the glorious copper-colored mountain, as well as meditation caves of YE SHES MTSHO RGYAL, VAIROCANA, and KLONG CHEN RAB 'BYAMS, who died there. Many of the caves and hermitages at Chims phu are still used for meditation retreat by Tibetan men and women.

**Chin'gak Hyesim**. (眞覺慧諶) (1178–1234). Korean SŎN master during the Koryŏ dynasty, also known as Yŏngŭl and Muŭija. Although he sought to ordain as a monk at an early age, his mother adamantly opposed his wish and he instead studied to become a Confucian literatus. It was not until 1202, after his mother's death, that he finally was able to join the SUSŎNSA community established by POJO CHINUL and become his principal disciple. Hyesim was known for his intense style of practice: he is said, for example, to have been so absorbed in his meditation while he was at CHIRISAN that snow had piled up to his head. Although Chinul had decided to pass the leadership of his community on to Hyesim in 1208, Hyesim declined and went into hiding on Chirisan. In 1210, when Chinul passed away, some of his disciples notified the king of their master's death and he issued a royal decree, ordering Hyesim to return to Susŏnsa and succeed Chinul. Hyesim thus became the second teacher of the Susŏnsa community. He spent the rest of his life building the community and teaching the kanhwa Sŏn (see KANHUA CHAN), or "questioning meditation," technique that Chinul had first championed in Korea. Hyesim compiled the first indigenous kongan (C. GONG'AN) collection, the SŎNMUN YŎMSONG CHIP, and the emphasis on kanhwa Sŏn in subsequent Korean Buddhist practice owes much to his fervent advocacy of the technique. Hyesim passed away at the age of fifty-seven and received the posthumous title Chin'gak kuksa (State Preceptor Authentic Enlightenment). His other works include the CHOGYE CHIN'GAK KUKSA ŎROK and the *Sŏnmun gangyo*.

**Chin'gam Hyeso**. (眞鑑慧昭) (774–850). A Korean SŎN master and pilgrim during the Silla dynasty, also known as Chin'gam Sŏnsa. Hyeso is famous for introducing a traditional Indian Buddhist chanting style (K. pŏmp'ae; C. FANBAI) to Korea. In 804, Hyeso accompanied the official embassy to China, where he studied under a disciple of the eminent CHAN master MAZU DAOYI in the HONGZHOU school of early Chan. In China, Hyeso is said to have been often referred to as the Sage of the East (Dongfang shengren) and the Black-Headed Ascetic (Heidoutuo) because of his dark skin. In 810, Hyeso received full monastic precepts at the monastery of SHAOLINSI on SONGSHAN, where he met a fellow Korean monk TOŬI. Hyeso later traveled to Zhongnanshan, where he practiced ŚAMATHA and VIPAŚYANĀ meditation for three years. In 830, he returned to Korea and became the king's personal teacher. He later established the monasteries of Changbaeksa on Sŏraksan and Okch'ŏnsa on CHIRISAN, where he constructed an image hall for the sixth patriarch (LIUZU) HUINENG. King Chŏnggang (r. 886–887) gave him the posthumous title Chin'gam (True Mirror) and changed the name of his monastery from Okch'ŏnsa to SSANGGYESA (Paired Brooks Monastery). Hyeso is also renowned for introducing tea and tea culture to the Korean peninsula and green tea from the mountains surrounding SSANGGYESA is still renowned in Korea for its quality. Chin'gam Hyeso is also reputed to have introduced the distinctive "Indian style" of chanting to Korea around 830, and current pŏmp'ae specialists trace their lineage back to him.

**Chinhŭng wang**. (眞興王) (534/540–576). Twenty-fourth king of the Korean Silla dynasty; his secular name was Kim Kongnŭngjong and his dharma name, Pŏbun (Dharma Cloud). He succeeded King Pŏphŭng at the age of seven and reigned for thirty-six years (r. 540–576). Later in his life he became a Buddhist monk and promoted the propagation of Buddhism in Silla. Following his footsteps, his queen, Lady Sado, also entered the SAṂGHA and received the dharma name Myoju (Sublime Dwelling); she resided at a monastery called Yŏnghŭngsa. King Chinhŭng's reign is considered to be a turning point in the development of Buddhism in Silla. King Chinhŭng ordered the construction of the royal monastery Hŭngnyunsa, and after its completion allowed commoners for the first time to enter the saṃgha. At his request, the hundred high-seat ceremony (paekkojwa pŏphoe) for the recitation of the RENWANG JING as well as the eight restrictions festival (P'ALGWANHOE; cf. C. BAGUAN ZHAI) were held for the first time in Silla. HWANGNYONGSA, the grandest monastery in Korea, was also built during his reign.

**Chinjong**. (K) (震鐘). See YONGSŎNG CHINJONG.

**Chinmyŏng Honwŏn**. (眞明混元) (1191–1271). A Korean SŎN master during the Koryŏ dynasty. Honwŏn was ordained in 1203 and studied under various teachers before visiting the Sŏn master CHIN'GAK HYESIM. He began his training in Sŏn

(CHAN) meditation under Hyesim's disciple Mongyŏ (d. 1252), who became the third state preceptor (kuksa, C. GUOSHI) to lead the SUSŎNSA community established by POJO CHINUL. Honwŏn eventually became Mongyŏ's disciple. In 1245, Honwŏn was invited by the powerful military commander Ch'oe U (d. 1249) to the newly founded monastery of Sŏnwŏnsa that he had established in the Koryŏ capital of Kaesŏng. There, Honwŏn attracted many talented disciples including CH'UNGGYŎNG CH'ŎNYŎNG. When Mongyŏ passed away in 1252, Honwŏn became the fourth state preceptor of Susŏnsa, but he quickly abdicated this position to his disciple Ch'ŏnyŏng in 1259 to become the personal teacher of the king (wangsa). He was later given the posthumous title Chinmyŏng (True Illumination).

**Chinp'yo**. (眞表) (fl. c. eighth century). Korean VINAYA master (yulsa) during the Silla dynasty. Chinp'yo was a native of Mangyŏng county in Wansan province (present-day Chŏnju). According to legend, Chinp'yo is said to have been a student of a certain dharma master named Sungje (d.u.) of the monastery of KŬMSANSA, and was himself responsible for a major expansion of the monastery that took place between 762 and 766. Sungje, who purportedly studied under the eminent Chinese monk SHANDAO, informed Chinp'yo of his vision of MAÑJUŚRĪ on WUTAISHAN, after which Chinp'yo decided to devote himself to the practice of body-discarding repentance (mangsinch'am) at Pusaŭiam (Inconceivable Hermitage). In 740, after seven nights of ascetic repentance, Chinp'yo had a vision of the BODHISATTVA KṢITIGARBHA. Chinp'yo continued his training at the monastery Yŏngsansa, where he had a vision of the bodhisattva MAITREYA. From Maitreya, Chinp'yo received the divination scripture, ZHANCHA SHANE YEBAO JING, and 189 divination sticks made of sandalwood, two of which were said to have been made of Maitreya's fingers. In 766, he began teaching at Kŭmsansa, where he installed six gilded images of Maitreya in the main shrine hall (TAEUNG CHŎN). King Kyŏngdŏk (r. 742–764) later invited Chinp'yo to the palace and received the bodhisattva precepts (K. posal kye, C. PUSA JIE). Chinp'yo had many disciples, among whom Yŏngsim (d.u.) is most famous.

**Chinul**. (K) (知訥). See POJO CHINUL.

**chinyŏng**. (C. zhenying; J. shin'ei 眞影). In Korean, lit. "true image"; viz., a "monk's portrait." Although the term is known throughout the East Asian Buddhist traditions, it is especially associated with Korea; the related term DINGXIANG (J. chinzō, lit. "head's appearance") is more typically used within the Chinese and Japanese traditions. The employment of the term chinyŏng in Korea is a late Chosŏn dynasty development; different terms were used in Korea before that era to refer to monk's portraits, including chinhyŏng ("true form"), sinyŏng ("divine image"), chinyong ("true appearance") and yŏngja ("small portrait image"). "Chin" ("true") in the compound refers to the inherent qualities of the subject, while "yŏng" ("image") alludes to his physical appearance; thus, a chinyŏng is a portrait that seeks to convey the true inner spirituality of the subject. Images of eminent masters who had been renowned patriarchs of schools, courageous monk soldiers, or successful fund-raisers were enshrined in a monastery's portrait hall. These portraits were painted posthumously—and, unlike Chinese dingxiang portraits, typically without the consent of the subjects—as one means of legitimizing the dharma-transmission lineage of their religious descendants; this usage of portraits is seen in both meditation (SŎN) and doctrinal (KYO) monasteries. Korean monk portraits were not given out to individual disciples or lay adherents, as occurred in Chinese and Japanese Buddhism, where dozens and even hundreds of portraits were produced by and for a variety of persons. In the context of the Korean Sŏn school, the pictures additionally enhanced the Sŏn Buddhist emphasis on the direct spiritual transmission (see YINKE) between master and disciple. The development of monk portraiture was closely tied to annual commemorative practices in Buddhist monasteries, which sought to maintain the religious bonds between the dharma ancestors and their descendants.

**Chion'in**. (知恩院). In Japanese, "Knowing Beneficence Cloister"; the headquarters of the JŌDOSHŪ, or PURE LAND school of Japanese Buddhism, which was founded by HŌNEN (1133–1212); located in the Higashiyama district of Kyōto. Chion'in was the site where Hōnen taught and where he died after a long period of fasting. His disciple Genchi (1183–1238) built the complex in his honor in 1234 and, still today, a statue of Hōnen is enshrined in the founder's hall. Most of the monastery was destroyed by fire in 1633, but the third Tokugawa shōgun rebuilt the monastery in the middle of the seventeenth century with the structures present today. These include the main gate, or sanmon, built in 1619 and the largest gate of this type in Japan at seventy-nine feet tall. The oldest building on the monastery campus is the hondō, or main Buddha hall, built in 1633, which can hold three thousand people. Guesthouses from 1641 are roofed in the Irimoya style, and the roof beams on many of the buildings are capped with the Tokugawa three-hollyhock leaf crest. Various hallways in the monastery have also been built with "nightingale floors" (J. uguisubari)—floorboards with metal ends that rub on metal joints when someone walks across them, making them extremely squeaky. This flooring was specifically designed to sound an alarm in case any assassin might try to sneak into the sleeping quarters when the Tokugawa family stayed over at the monastery. The monastery's bell was cast in 1633 and weighs seventy-four tons; it is so massive that it takes seventeen monks to ring it when it is rung annually on New Year's Day.

**Chirisan**. (智異山). In Korean, "Mountain of the Wise and Extraordinary [Bodhisattva]" (though the term more probably means "round mountain"; see below); a Buddhist sacred mountain and the second highest mountain in Korea (its highest peak is Ch'onwangbong at 5,745 ft./1,915 m.) after Hallasan.

Chirisan is located on the southern end of the Paektu taegan, the marchmount that is regarded geographically and spiritually as the geomantic "spine" of the Korean peninsula, and is the widest and highest section of the Sobaeksan subrange. Chiri Mountain stretches across the three southernmost provinces of the Korean peninsula: North Chŏlla, South Chŏlla, and South Kyŏngsang and has been considered a place where the BODHISATTVA MAÑJUŚRĪ is constantly preaching. Because of this association, Buddhists have traditionally interpreted the Chinese characters used to transcribe the mountain's name Chiri as deriving from the -ri in the Sino-Korean transcription of Mañjuśrī's name (K. Munsusari) combined with the character chi(-ji) in his epithet "He of Great Wisdom" (Taeji); the near-homophone i ("extraordinary") was ultimately substituted for the character -ri to indicate that Mañjuśrī represents himself in various "extraordinary" guises in order to save sentient beings. Recent research by historical linguists has, however, called this Buddhist parsing of the name into question. One of the earliest names found in Korean sources for the mountain is Turyu (lit. "Head Flowing"), which seems to be a transcription using Sinographs of the indigenous Korean word turu (now the adverb "widely" but previously used as an adjective meaning "round"), which in the local dialect changed from turuto turi, tŭri, tiri, to finally chiri. Hence, Chirisan is actually the transcription of an indigenous Korean word meaning "round mountain," referring to the many rounded peaks, punctuated by winding valleys, that dominate the massif. Chirisan's steepest summit is Ch'onwangbong Peak (5,745 ft/ 1,915 m) in the north, but its principal peaks include Songnisan (3,171 ft./1,057 m) in the south, Nogodan (4,521 ft/1,507 m) in the west, and Panyabong (5,271 ft/1,751 m) in the north central region of the massif. Chirisan has long been considered one of the "three spiritual mountains" (samsinsan) of Korea, along with KŬMGANGSAN and Hallasan, and has been a major center of Buddhist practice on the peninsula. There are currently 350 to 400 monasteries and hermitages on Chirisan, the three largest of which are HWAŎMSA, SSANGGYESA, and CHŎNŬNSA. Chiri Mountain is now protected as a national park, the first such designation made in Korea.

**chiroutuan**. (J. shakunikudan; K. chŏgyuktan 赤肉團). In Chinese, "lump of red (viz., raw) flesh"; a CHAN expression attributed to LINJI YIXUAN (d. 867) to refer to the physical body that is constantly buffeted by the senses. Linji contrasts this lump of flesh with the "true man of no rank" (C. WUWEI ZHENREN), which is equivalent to the sentience, or numinous awareness (LINGZHI), that enables sensory experience.

**Ch'obalsim chagyŏng mun**. (初發心自警文). In Korean, "Personal Admonitions to Neophytes Who Have First Aroused the Mind," a primer of three short texts used to train Korean postulants and novices in the basics of Buddhist morality and daily practice, compiled during the middle of the Chosŏn dynasty (1392–1910). The title of the primer is constructed by combining elements from its three constituent texts: (1) POJO CHINUL'S (1158–1210) *Kye ch'osim hagin mun* ("Admonitions to Neophytes"), a vade mecum for monastic conduct directed to novices, monks, and SŎN monks residing in the meditation hall; (2) WŎNHYO'S (617–686) PALSIM SUHAENG CHANG ("Arouse Your Mind and Practice") (-balsim is the first two Sinographs in the title of *Palsim suhaeng chang*); and (3) Yaun Kagu's (fl. c. 1376) *Chagyŏng* or *Chagyŏng mun* ("Self-Admonitions"), a set of ten behavioral codes to follow in religious development. The *Ch'obalsim Chagyŏng mun* continues today to be among the very first works read by male and female postulants in the monastic community.

**Chodang chip**. (C. Zutang ji; J. Sodōshū 祖堂集). In Korean, "Patriarchs' Hall Collection"; one of the earliest "lamplight histories" (CHUANDENG LU), viz., lineage records, of the CHAN tradition, compiled in 952 by the monks Jing (K. Chŏng) (d.u.) and Yun/Jun (K. Un/Kyun) (d.u.) of the monastery of Chaojingsi in Quanzhou (in present-day Fujian provine). The *Chodang chip* builds on an earlier Chan history, the BAOLIN ZHUAN, on which it seems largely to have been based. According to one current theory, the original text by Jing and Yun was a short work in a single roll, which was expanded into ten rolls early in the Song dynasty and subsequently reissued in twenty rolls in the definitive 1245 Korean edition. The anthology includes a preface by the compilers' teacher and collaborator Zhaoqing Shendeng/Wendeng (884–972), also known as the Chan master Jingxiu, who also appends verse panegyrics after several of the biographies in the collection. The *Chodang chip* provides biographies of 253 figures, including the seven buddhas of the past (SAPTATATHĀGATA), the first Indian patriarch (ZUSHI) MAHĀKĀŚYAPA up to and including the sixth patriarch (LIUZU) of Chan in China, HUINENG, and monks belonging to the lineages of Huineng's putative disciples QINGYUAN XINGSI and NANYUE HUAIRANG. In contrast to the later JINGDE CHUANDENG LU, the *Chodang chip* mentions the lineage of Qingyuan before that of Nanyue. In addition to the biographical narrative, the entries also include short excerpts from the celebrated sayings and dialogues of the persons it covers. These are notable for including many features that derive from the local vernacular (what has sometimes been labeled "Medieval Vernacular Sinitic"); for this reason, the text has been the frequent object of study by Chinese historical linguists. The *Chodang chip* is also significant for containing the biographies of several Silla-dynasty monks who were founders of, or associated with, the Korean "Nine Mountains School of Sŏn" (KUSAN SŎNMUN), eight of whom had lineage ties to the Chinese HONGZHOU ZONG of Chan that derived from MAZU DAOYI; the anthology in fact offers the most extensive body of early material on the developing Korean Sŏn tradition. This emphasis suggests that the two compilers may themselves have been expatriate Koreans training in China and/or that the extant anthology was substantially reedited in Korea. The *Chodang chip* was lost in China after the Northern Song dynasty and remained completely unknown subsequently to the Chinese Chan and

Japanese Zen traditions. However, the 1245 Korean edition was included as a supplement to the Koryŏ Buddhist canon (KORYŎ TAEJANGGYŎNG), which was completed in 1251 during the reign of the Koryŏ king Kojong (r. 1214–1259), and fortunately survived; this is the edition that was rediscovered in the 1930s at the Korean monastery of HAEINSA. Because the collection is extant only in a Koryŏ edition and because of the many Korean monks included in the collection, the *Chodang chip* is often cited in the scholarly literature by its Korean pronunciation.

**Ch'oesangsŭng non**. (K) (最上乘論). Original Korean title of the *Xiuxin yao lun*. See XIUXIN YAO LUN.

**Chogye Chin'gak kuksa ŏrok**. (曹溪眞覺國師語録). In Korean, "Recorded Sayings of the National Master Chin'gak of Mt. Chogye"; a collection of the sayings of the Korean SŎN master CHIN'GAK HYESIM. As the first and oldest recorded saying (YULU) collection in Korea, the *Chogye Chin'gak kuksa ŏrok* has served as an important source for studying the early history of kongan studies in that region (see GONG'AN). The oldest extant edition of the text dates to 1526. The collection consists largely of Hyesim's various public lectures (e.g., SHANGTANG, shizhong, and FAYU), private lessons (DUIJI, xiaocan, and AGYO), and letters to his students. Many of his lectures are concerned with the famous kongan attributed to ZHAOZHOU CONGSHEN, wherein Zhaozhou offers the reply "wu" ("no") to the question, "Does a dog have buddha nature, or not?" (see GOUZI WU FOXING).

**Chogye chong**. (曹溪宗). In Korean, the "Chogye order"; short for Taehan Pulgyo Chogye chong (Chogye Order of Korean Buddhism); the largest Buddhist order in Korea, with and some fifteen thousand monks and nuns and over two thousand monasteries and temples organized around twenty-five district monasteries (PONSA). "Chogye" is the Korean pronunciation of the Chinese Caoxi, the name of the mountain (CAOXISHAN) where the sixth patriarch (LIUZU) of CHAN, HUINENG, resided; the name is therefore meant to evoke the order's pedigree as a predominantly Chan (K. SŎN) tradition, though it seeks also to incorporate all other major strands of Korean Buddhist thought and practice. The term Chogye chong was first used by the Koryŏ monk ŬICHŎN to refer to the "Nine Mountains school of Sŏn" (KUSAN SŎNMUN), and the name was used at various points during the Koryŏ and Chosŏn dynasties to designate the indigenous Korean Sŏn tradition. The Chogye order as it is known today is, however, a modern institution. It was formed in 1938 during the Japanese colonial administration of Korea, a year after the monastery of T'aegosa was established in central Seoul and made the new headquarters of Chosŏn Buddhism (Chosŏn Pulgyo ch'ongbonsan). This monastery, later renamed CHOGYESA, still serves today as the headquarters of the order. The constitution of the order traces its origins to Toŭi (d. 825), founder of the Kajisan school in the Nine Mountains school of Sŏn; this tradition is said to have been revived during the Koryŏ dynasty by POJO CHINUL, who provided its soteriological grounding; finally, the order's lineage derives from T'AEGO POU, who returned to Korea at the very end of the Koryŏ dynasty with dharma transmission in the contemporary Chinese LINJI ZONG. In 1955, following the end of the Korean War, Korean Buddhism entered into a decade-long "purification movement" (chŏnghwa undong), through which the celibate monks (pigu sŭng) sought to remove all vestiges of Japanese influence in Korean Buddhism, and especially the institution of married monks (taech'ŏ sŭng). This confrontation ultimately led to the creation of two separate orders: the Chogye chong of the celibate monks, officially reconstituted in 1962, and the much smaller T'AEGO CHONG of married monks.

**Chogye order**. See CHOGYE CHONG.

**Chogyesa**. (曹溪寺). In Korean, "Chogye Monastery"; the administrative headquarters of the CHOGYE CHONG, the largest Buddhist order in contemporary Korea, and its first district monastery (PONSA). In an attempt to unify Korean Buddhist institutions during the Japanese colonial period, Korean Buddhist leaders prepared a joint constitution of the SŎN and KYO orders and established the Central Bureau of Religious Affairs (Chungang Kyomuwŏn) in 1929. Eight years later, in 1937, the Japanese government-general decided to help bring the Buddhist tradition under centralized control by establishing a new headquarters for Chosŏn Buddhism (Chosŏn Pulgyo Ch'ongbonsan) in the capital of Seoul. With financial and logistical assistance from the Japanese colonial administration, the former headquarters building of a proscribed Korean new religion, the Poch'ŏn'gyo, was purchased, disassembled, and relocated from the southwest of Korea to the site of Kakhwangsa in the Chongno district of central Seoul. That new monastery was given the name T'aegosa, after its namesake T'AEGO POU, the late-Koryŏ Sŏn teacher who received dharma transmission in the Chinese LINJI ZONG. After the split in 1962 between the celibate monks of the Chogye chong and the married monks (taech'ŏ sŭng), who organized themselves into the T'AEGO CHONG, T'aegosa was renamed Chogyesa, from the name of the mountain where the sixth patriarch (LIUZU) of Chan, HUINENG, resided (see CAOXISHAN). This monastery continues to serve today as the headquarters of the Chogye chong. In addition to the role it plays as the largest traditional monastery in the city center of Seoul, Chogyesa also houses all of the administrative offices of the order.

**chŏl**. Vernacular Korean term for a Buddhist "monastery" and the indigenous Korean equivalent of the Sino-Korean term sach'al (see, e.g., SAMBO SACH'AL). The derivation of the term is uncertain: some historical linguists derive it by metonymy as a place where "bows" (chŏl) are performed; others scholars, from the Pāli/Prakrit term THERA (elder). Cf. TERA.

**Ch'ŏnch'aek**. (天頙) (1206–?). The fourth patriarch of the Korean White Lotus Society (PAENGNYŎN KYŎLSA) during the middle of the Koryŏ dynasty; also known as State Preceptor Chinjŏng ("True Calmness" or "True Purity," using homophonous Sinographs). Ch'ŏnch'aek was a descendent of a Koryŏ merit official, who devoted himself to Confucian studies from a young age and passed the civil-service examinations at the age of twenty. At twenty-three, he became a monk under the tutelage of State Preceptor WŎNMYO YOSE (1163–1245), the founder of the White Lotus Society (cf. BAILIAN SHE) at Mount Mandŏk in T'amjin county (present-day Kangjin in South Chŏlla province), and subsequently assisted his teacher Yose in the Society's campaign. In 1244, Ch'ŏnch'aek traveled to Mimyŏnsa on Mount Kongdŏk in Sangju county (present-day Mun'gyŏng in North Kyŏngsang province) to open and lead the society there at the request of the renowned magistrate of Sangju, Ch'oe Cha (1188–1260). The Kongdŏksan branch of the society was called the East White Lotus; the Mandŏksan branch was by contrast called the South White Lotus. In the late 1250s or early 1260s, Ch'ŏnch'aek returned to Mandŏksan to become the fourth patriarch of the White Lotus Society. He later retired to Yonghyŏram (Dragon Cavity Hermitage) on Mount Tŏngnyong, south of Mandŏksan, where he continued an active correspondence with literati. Indeed, Ch'ŏnch'aek maintained close associations with several of the famous literati of his time and invited them to participate in the activities of the White Lotus Society. Ch'ŏnch'aek's thought reflects the historical realities of Korea during the Mongol invasion. In his letters to civil and military officials, Ch'ŏnch'aek opined that killing the invading Mongol army would be an appropriate act for a BODHISATTVA, because it would stop the invaders from performing evil actions that would lead them to endless suffering in the hells. His *Haedongjŏn hongnok* ("Extended Record of the Transmission [of Buddhism] in Korea"), a four-roll collection of miracle tales related to worship of the SADDHARMAPUṆḌARĪKASŪTRA ("Lotus Sūtra") , sought to popularize that scripture also in order to help bring peace to the Korean peninsula. Ch'ŏnch'aek's literary talent was so renowned that the famous Chosŏn literatus Chŏng Yagyong (1762–1836) counted him among the three greatest writers of the Silla and Koryŏ dynasties. Ch'ŏnch'aek's works, none of which are extant in full, include the *Haedongjŏn hongnok* and his literary collection, the *Hosan nok* ("Record of Lakes and Mountains"). Authorship of the SŎNMUN POJANGNOK is attributed to Ch'ŏnch'aek, although this attribution is still in question.

**Chongfasi**. (崇法寺). In Chinese, "Esteeming the Dharma Monastery"; Song dynasty name for WUZHENSI.

**Chŏngho**. (K) (鼎鎬). See HANYŎNG.

**Ch'ŏnghŏ Hyujŏng**. (清虛休靜) (1520–1604). Korean SŎN master of the Chosŏn dynasty; best known to Koreans by his sobriquet Sŏsan taesa (lit. the Great Master "West Mountain," referring to Mt. Myohyang near present-day P'yŏngyang in North Korea). Hyujŏng was a native of Anju in present-day South P'yŏngan province. After losing his parents at an early age, Hyujŏng was adopted by the local magistrate of Anju, Yi Sajŭng (d.u.), and educated at the Sŏnggyun'gwan Confucian academy. In 1534, Hyujŏng failed to attain the chinsa degree and decided instead to become a monk. He was ordained by a certain Sungin (d.u.) on CHIRISAN in 1540, and he later received the full monastic precepts from Hyuong Ilsŏn (1488–1568). Hyujŏng later became the disciple of the Sŏn master Puyong Yŏnggwan (1485–1571). In 1552, Hyujŏng passed the clerical exams (SŬNGKWA) revived by HŎŬNG POU, who later appointed Hyujŏng the prelate (p'ansa) of both the SŎN and KYO traditions. Hyujŏng also succeeded Pou as the abbot of the monastery Pongŭnsa in the capital, but he left his post as prelate and spent the next few years teaching and traveling throughout the country. When the Japanese troops of Hideyoshi Toyotomi (1536/7–1598) invaded Korea in 1592, Hyujŏng's disciple Kihŏ Yŏnggyu (d. 1592) succeeded in retaking the city of Ch'ŏngju, but died shortly afterward in battle. Hyujŏng himself was then asked by King Sŏnjo (r. 1567–1608) to lead an army against the invading forces. His monk militias (ŭisŭnggun) eventually played an important role in fending off the Japanese troops. When the king subsequently gave Hyujŏng permission to retire, the master left his command in the hands of his disciple SAMYŎNG YUJŎNG; he died shortly thereafter. Hyujŏng is said to have had more than one thousand students, among whom Yujŏng, P'yŏnyang Ŭn'gi (1581–1644), Soyo T'aenŭng (1562–1649), and Chŏnggwan Ilsŏn (1533–1608) are best known. Hyujŏng left a number of writings, including the SŎN'GA KWIGAM, which is one of the most widely read works of the Korean Buddhist tradition. Other important works include the *Samga kwigam*, *Sŏn'gyo sŏk*, *Sŏn'gyo kyŏl*, and *Sŏlsŏn ŭi*. In these works, Hyujŏng attempted to reconcile the teachings of the Sŏn and Kyo traditions of Buddhism, as well as the doctrines of Buddhism and Confucianism.

**Chonghŏn**. (K) (宗憲). See MANAM CHONGHŎN.

**Chŏnghye Kyŏlsa**. (定慧結社). In Korean, the "SAMĀDHI and PRAJÑĀ Society"; an important Korean "retreat society" (kyŏlsa; C. JIESHI) during the Koryŏ dynasty. The first Samādhi and Prajñā Society was established by the Korean SŎN master POJO CHINUL at the monastery of Kŏjosa on Mt. Kong in 1188. At the invitation of a monk by the name of Tŭkchae (d.u.), Chinul and a handful of monks gathered at Kŏjosa in 1188 and formally began their retreat two years later in 1190. Throughout the retreat, Chinul continued to invite willing participants, both clergy and laity, to join the community. Among the most renowned of these recruits was the Korean CHŎNT'AE CHONG (TIANTAI ZONG) adept WŎNMYO YOSE (1163–1240). Seven years later, in 1197, the community had grown to such a size that Chinul began looking for a larger, more suitable site to relocate the community. A small, dilapidated monastery known as Kilsangsa on Mt. Songgwang was chosen as the new site, and reconstruction of the temple began immediately. King Hŭijong (r. 1204–1211) later renamed Kilsangsa SUSŎNSA, or Sŏn Cultivation Community; it is now the major monastery of SONGGWANGSA, the so-called Saṃgha-Jewel monastery (Sŭngbo sach'al) of Korean Buddhism. Chinul's first composition, the *Kwŏn su Chŏnghye kyŏlsa mun* ("Encouragement to Practice: The Compact of the Samādhi and Prajñā Society"), written in 1290, provides the rationale behind the establishment of the community and critiques PURE LAND adepts who claim that buddhahood cannot be achieved in the present lifetime.

**chongjŏng**. (宗正). In Korean, "supreme patriarch" (lit. "primate of the order"); the spiritual head of the CHOGYE CHONG (Chogye order) of Korean Buddhism. The term chongjŏng first began to be used in Korean Buddhism during Japanese colonial rule (1910–1945) and has continued to be employed since 1954 when the celibate monks (pigu sŭng) established an independent Chogye order, which eventually excluded the married monks (taech'ŏ sŭng) who had dominated monastic positions during the colonial period. A Korean Supreme Court ruling in 1962 ultimately gave the celibate monks title to virtually all the major monasteries across the nation and led to the Chogye order's official re-establishment as the principal ecclesiastical institution of Korean Buddhism, with the chongjŏng serving as its primate. The married monks subsequently split off from the Chogye order to form the independent T'AEGO CHONG. ¶ To be selected as chongjŏng, a candidate must be a minimum of sixty-five years of age and have been a monk for at least forty-five years; his rank in the Chogye order must be that of Taejongsa (great master of the order), the highest of the Chogye order's six ecclesiastical ranks. To select the chongjŏng, a committee of seventeen to twenty-five monks is appointed, which includes the Chogye order's top executive (ch'ongmuwŏnjang), council representative (chonghoe ŭijang), and head vinaya master (hogye wiwŏnjang); the selection is finalized through a majority vote of the committee members. The chongjŏng is initially appointed for a five-year term and is eligible for reappointment for one additional term. The contemporary Chogye order counts Wŏnmyŏng Hyobong (1888–1966), appointed in 1962, as its first chongjŏng.

**Chŏngjung Musang**. (C. Jingzhong Wuxiang; J. Jōshu Musō 淨衆無相) (680–756, alt. 684–762). Korean-Chinese CHAN master of the Tang dynasty; because he was of Korean heritage, he is usually called Musang in the literature, following the Korean pronunciation of his dharma name, or Master Kim (K. Kim hwasang; C. Jin heshang), using his Korean surname. Musang is said to have been the third son of a Silla king and was ordained in Korea at the monastery of Kunnamsa. In 728, he arrived in the Chinese capital of Chang'an (present-day Xi'an) and had an audience with the Tang emperor Xuanzong (r. 712–756), who appointed him to the monastery of Chandingsi. Musang subsequently traveled to Chu (in present-day Sichuan province) and became a disciple of the monk Chuji (alt. 648–734, 650–732, 669–736), who gave him dharma transmission at the monastery of Dechunsi in Zizhou (present-day Sichuan province). He later resided at the monastery of Jingzhongsi in Chengdu (present-day Sichuan province; later known as WANFOSI), which gave him his toponym Chŏngjung (C. Jingzhong). Musang became famous for his ascetic practices and meditative prowess. Musang also began conferring a unique set of precepts known as the three propositions (SANJU): "no recollection" (wuji), which was equated with morality (ŚĪLA); "no thought" (WUNIAN) with concentration (SAMĀDHI); and "no forgetting" (mowang) with wisdom (PRAJÑĀ). He also taught a practice known as YINSHENG NIANFO, a method of reciting the name of the Buddha by extending the length of the intonation. Musang's prosperous lineage in Sichuan came to be known as the JINGZHONG ZONG line of Chan. Musang seems to have taught or influenced several renowned Chan monks, including HEZE SHENHUI (668–760), BAOTANG WUZHU (714–774), and MAZU DAOYI (707–786); he also played an important role in transmitting Chan to Tibet in the 750s and 760s.

**ch'ongnim**. (叢林). In Korean, lit., "dense grove"; a large, ecumenical monastery. In Korea, the term ch'ongnim is used in the contemporary CHOGYE CHONG to refer to a handful of major monasteries that are able to provide training in the full range of practices that exemplify the major strands of the Korean Buddhist tradition, including SŎN meditation, KYO (and especially Hwaŏm, C. HUAYAN) doctrine, PURE LAND recitation of the buddha AMITĀBHA'S name (K. yŏmbul; see NIANFO), and VINAYA (monastic discipline) observance. While most monasteries are primarily devoted to one or another of these types of training, a ch'ongnim serves as a center where all can be practiced. These monasteries thus typically are larger comprehensive training centers, with a meditation hall (sŏnbang) and a monks' seminary or lecture hall (kangwŏn) on the campus; additionally, their spiritual head is called a pangjang (C. FANGJANG) rather than the usual chosil ("occupant of the patriarchs' room"). A monastery designated as a ch'ongnim receives a second name, most of which designate the mountain at which they are located. The five current Korean ch'ongnims are HAEINSA (also known as the Haein Ch'ongnim), SONGGWANGSA (Chogye Ch'ongnim), T'ONGDOSA (Yŏngch'uk Ch'ongnim), SUDŎKSA (Tŏksung Ch'ongnim), and PAEGYANGSA (Kobul Ch'ongnim). See also CONGLIN.

**Ch'ŏnt'ae chong**. (C. Tiantai zong; J. Tendaishū 天台宗). In Korean, "Altar of Heaven order"; a new order of Korean Buddhism, founded in 1966 by Wŏn'gak Sangwŏl (1911–1974). Despite the order's name, which evokes that of the Chinese TIANTAI ZONG, the Ch'ŏnt'ae chong is not heavily beholden to traditional Tiantai (K. Ch'ŏnt'ae) doctrine and practice but is a thoroughly modern order, which seeks to respond to contemporary religious and social concerns. The school professes "aeguk Pulgyo" (patriotic Buddhism), which purports to contribute to the development of the nation through personal cultivation and social-welfare activities. Its primary method of spiritual cultivation involves the repetitive recitation of the name of Kwanseŭm posal (AVALOKITEŚVARA bodhisattva), based in part on the constant-action SAMĀDHI (K. sanghaeng sammae; C. changxing sanmei), one of the four kinds of samādhi attributed to the Chinese TIANTAI monk TIANTAI ZHIYI (538–597). The Ch'ŏnt'ae order introduced a few distinctive elements that distinguish it from other Korean Buddhist orders, e.g., (1) all its followers, whether monks, nuns, or lay people, participate together in a one-month retreat each summer and winter, although monks and nuns have an additional fifty-five day retreat period that immediately follows the winter retreat; (2) monks observe the tradition of shaving their heads, while nuns keep their hair in a small chignon in order to distinguish themselves from laywomen. Since its inception, the order has emphasized lay activities: it encourages lay people to involve themselves in administrative affairs, such as temple finance; it founded the Kŭmgang Buddhist seminary, which offers a two-year program to educate lay people on Tiantai and general Buddhist doctrines and a one-year program to train lay propagators of Buddhism (p'ogyosa); finally, the order has also established Kŭmgang University (Geumgang Daehakkyo), which offers a full range of majors in both Buddhism and secular topics. The order is also active in social activities, such as the promotion of social welfare and environmental preservation. Its major temples are the Kuinsa headquarters founded by Sangwŏl in 1945 in North Ch'ungch'ŏng province; and Samgwangsa, founded in 1969 in Pusan. The school also has overseas branches in Canada, the United States, Denmark, and Mongolia.

**Ch'ŏntae marhak Unmuk hwasang kyŏngch'aek**. (天台末學雲默和尚警策). In Korean, "Admonitions of the Preceptor Unmuk, a Latter-day Scholar of Ch'ŏnt'ae/Tiantai," in one roll, by the late-Koryŏ monk Unmuk (d.u.; fl. late fourteenth century?). See UNMUK.

**Ch'ŏnt'ae sagyo ŭi**. (C. Tiantai sijiao yi; J. Tendai shikyōgi 天台四教儀). In Korean, the "Principle of the Fourfold Teachings of the Tiantai [School]," composed by the Korean monk Ch'egwan (d. 970); an influential primer of TIANTAI ZONG (K. Chŏnt'ae chong) doctrine. The loss of the texts of the Tiantai tradition in China after the chaos that accompanied the fall of the Tang dynasty prompted the king of the Wuyue kingdom to seek copies of them elsewhere in East Asia. King Kwangjong (r. 950–975) of the Koryŏ dynasty responded to the Wuyue king's search by sending the monk Ch'egwan to China in 961. In order to summarize the major teachings of the Tiantai school, Ch'egwan wrote this one-roll abstract of TIANTAI ZHIYI's *Sijiao yi,* which also draws on other of Zhiyi's writings, including his FAHUA XUANYI. Ch'egwan's text is especially known for its summary of Zhiyi's doctrinal classification schema (see JIAOXIANG PANSHI) on the different (chronological) stages of the Buddha's teaching career and the varying methods he used in preaching to his audiences; these are called the "five periods and eight teachings" (WUSHI BAJIAO). The five periods correspond to what the Tiantai school considered to be the five major chronological stages in the Buddha's teaching career, each of which is exemplified by a specific scripture or type of scripture: (1) HUAYAN (AVATAṂSAKASŪTRA), (2) ĀGAMA, (3) VAIPULYA, (4) PRAJÑĀPĀRAMITĀ, and (5) SADDHARMAPUṆḌARĪKASŪTRA and MAHĀPARINIRVĀṆASŪTRA. The different target audiences of the Buddha's message lead to four differing varieties of content in these teachings (huafa): (1) the PIṬAKA teachings, which were targeted at the two-vehicle adherents (ER SHENG) of disciples (ŚRĀVAKA) and solitary buddhas (PRATYEKABUDDHA); (2) the common teachings, which were intended for both two-vehicle adherents and neophyte bodhisattvas of the MAHĀYĀNA; (3) the distinct teachings, which targeted only bodhisattvas; (4) the perfect or consummate teachings (YUANJIAO), which offered advanced bodhisattvas an unvarnished assessment of Buddhist truths. In speaking to these audiences, which differed dramatically in their capacity to understand his message, the Buddha is said also to have employed four principal techniques of conversion (huayi), or means of conveying his message: sudden, gradual, secret, and indeterminate. Ch'egwan's text played a crucial role in the revitalization of the Tiantai tradition in China and has remained widely studied since. The *Ch'ŏnt'ae sagyo ŭi* was also influential in Japan, where it was repeatedly republished. Numerous commentaries on this text have also been written in China, Korea, and Japan.

**Ch'ŏnŭng**. (K) (處能). See PAEKKOK CH'ŎNŬNG.

**Chŏnŭnsa**. (泉隱寺). In Korean, "Monastery of the Hidden Fount"; one of the three major monasteries located on the Buddhist sacred mountain of CHIRISAN. The monastery is said to have been founded in 828 by an Indian monk named Tŏgun (d.u.) and was originally named Kamnosa (either "Sweet Dew Monastery" or "Responsive Dew Monastery"), after a spring there that would clear the minds of people who drank its ambrosial waters. During the Koryŏ dynasty, Chŏnŭnsa was elevated to the status of first Sŏn monastery of the South, during the rule of Ch'ŭngnyŏl wang (r. 1275–1308). Most of the monastery was destroyed during the Japanese Hideyoshi invasion (1592–1598). In 1679, a Sŏn monk named Tanyu (d.u.) rebuilt the monastery, but changed the name to Chŏnŭn (Hidden Fount), because the spring had disappeared after a monk killed a snake that kept showing up around it. Subsequently, fires of unknown origin repeatedly occurred in the monastery, which stopped only after hanging up a board with the name of the monastery written in the "water" calligraphic style by Wŏn'gyo Yi Kwangsa (1705–1777), one of the four preeminent calligraphers of the Chosŏn dynasty.

**Ch'ŏnyŏng**. (K) (天英). See CH'UNGGYŎNG CH'ŎNYŎNG.

**Chŏryo**. (K) (節要). See PŎPCHIP PYŎRHAENG NOK CHŎRYO PYŎNGIP SAGI.

**chōsan**. (朝参). In Japanese, lit. "morning meditation"; the morning-period ZAZEN that begins the day at a Japanese ZEN monastery.

**Chos 'byung mkhas pa'i dga' ston**. (Chöjung Kepe Gatön). In Tibetan, "A Scholar's Feast of Doctrinal History"; the title of a seminal historical study of Indian and Tibetan Buddhism, composed between 1545 and 1564 by the renowned scholar DPA' BO GTSUG LAG PHRENG BA. Due to the author's lineage affiliation as an incarnation (SPRUL SKU) of the BKA' BRGYUD sect, the text emphasizes the history and doctrine of the KARMA BKA' BRGYUD, tracing lines of transmission and doctrinal development, although it also addresses other Tibetan traditions more cursorily. There is an extensive section on Tibet's early imperial period, likely written on the basis of first-hand access to many original documents, ledgers, royal receipts, and historical notes, all long since lost. This religious history is therefore held by both Tibetan and Western scholars to be an authoritative and historically reliable source. It is also known as the *Lho brag chos 'byung* ("The Lho brag History of the Doctrine") in reference to the author's principal seat in the region of Lho brag in southern Tibet. Its complete title is *Dam pa'i chos kyi 'khor los bsgyur ba rnams kyi byung ba gsal bar byed pa mkhas pa'i dga' ston*.

**Chos grub**. (Chö drup) (C. Facheng 法成) (c. 755–849). Tibetan translator of Chinese Buddhist texts into Tibetan during the early ninth century; he worked at the Chinese outpost of DUNHUANG along the SILK ROAD. At the command of King RAL PA CAN, Chos grub translated what the Tibetans know as the "Great Chinese Commentary" on the SAṂDHINIRMOCANASŪTRA, a massive exegesis to this important YOGĀCĀRA text that was composed by the Korean commentator WŎNCH'ŬK; Chos grub's rendering was an important source for TSONG KHA PA's *Drang nges* LEGS BSHAD SNYING PO ("Essence of Eloquence on the Definitive and Provisional"). Chos grub was also the translator of the Chinese apocryphon YULANBEN JING ("Book of the Yulan Vessel"), an influential text on the "Ghost Festival" (YULANBEN).

**Chos kyi 'byung gnas**. (Chökyi Jungne) (1700–1774). Tibetan Buddhist scholar recognized as the eighth TAI SI TU incarnation, remembered for his wide learning and his editorial work on the Tibetan Buddhist canon. He traveled extensively throughout his life, maintaining strong relationships with the ruling elite of eastern Tibet and the Newar Buddhists of the Kathmandu Valley. Born in the eastern Tibetan region of SDE DGE, Chos kyi 'byung gnas was recognized as a reincarnate lama (SPRUL SKU) by the eighth ZHWA DMAR, from whom he received his first vows. He would go on to study with KAḤ THOG Rigs 'dzin Tshe dbang nor bu (1698–1755), from whom he learned about GZHAN STONG ("other emptiness"). At the age of twenty-one, he accompanied several important Bka' brgyud hierarchs, the Zhwa dmar and the twelfth KARMA PA, to Kathmandu, a journey that was to have a profound impact on the young Si tu's life. He returned to eastern Tibet in 1724, where he was received favorably by the king of Sde dge, Bstan pa tshe ring (Tenpa Tsering, 1678–1738). Under the latter's patronage, Chos kyi 'byung gnas founded DPAL SPUNGS monastery in 1727, which became the new seat for the Si tu lineage (they are sometimes called the Dpal spungs si tu). Between the years 1731 and 1733, he undertook the monumental task of editing and correcting a new redaction of the BKA' 'GYUR section of the Tibetan Buddhist canon, to be published at the printing house of Sde dge. Although in his day Tibetan knowledge of Indian linguistic traditions had waned, Chos kyi 'byung gnas devoted much of his later life to the study of Sanskrit grammar and literature, which he had first studied with Newar paṇḍitas during his time in Kathmandu. He sought out new Sanskrit manuscripts in order to establish more precise translations of Sanskrit works already translated in the Tibetan canon; he is esteemed in Tibet for his knowledge of Sanskrit grammar. In addition to his prolific scholarly work, Chos kyi 'byung gnas was an accomplished painter as well as a gifted physician, much sought after by the aristocracy of eastern Tibet. In 1748, he visited Nepal once again, where he translated the *Svayambhūpurāṇa*, the legends concerning the SVAYAMBHŪ STŪPA, into Tibetan. He was received amicably by the rulers Jayaprakāśamalla (1736–1768) of Kathmandu, Raṇajitamalla (1722–1769) of what is now Bhaktapur, and Pṛthvīnārāyaṇa Śāha, who would unify the Kathmandu Valley under Gorkhali rule several decades later. Chos kyi 'byung gnas' collected writings cover a vast range of subjects including lengthy and detailed diaries and an important history of the KARMA BKA' BRGYUD sect coauthored by his disciple Be lo Tshe dbang kun khyab (Belo Tsewang Kunkyap, b. 1718). He is retrospectively identified as an originator of what would become known as Khams RIS MED movement, which gained momentum in early nineteenth century Sde dge.

**Chosŏn Pulgyo t'ongsa**. (朝鮮佛教通史). In Korean, "A Comprehensive History of Chosŏn Buddhism"; compiled by the Buddhist historian Yi Nŭnghwa (1868–1943). Yi's *Chosŏn Pulgyo t'ongsa* is the first modern attempt to write a comprehensive history of Korean (or Chosŏn as it was then known) Buddhism. The text was first published by Sinmun'gwan in 1918. The first volume narrates the history of Korean Buddhism from its inception during the Three Kingdoms period up until the time of the Japanese occupation. Information on the temples and monasteries established by Koreans and a report on the current number of monks and nuns are also appended to end of this volume. The second volume narrates the history of Buddhism in India after the Buddha's death. The compilation of the canon (TRIPIṬAKA; DAZANGJING) and the formation of the various schools and traditions are provided in this volume. The third and final volume provides a commentary on some of the more important events described in volume one. Yi relied heavily on biographies of eminent monks and stele inscriptions. Yi's text is still considered an important source for studying the history of Korean Buddhism.

**Chosŏn Pulgyo yusin non**. (朝鮮佛教唯新論). In Korean, "Treatise on the Reformation of Korean Buddhism"; composed by the Korean monk-reformer HAN YONGUN in 1910. While sojourning in Japan, Han personally witnessed what to him seemed quite innovative ways in which Japanese Buddhists were seeking to adapt their religious practices to modern society and hoped to implement similar ideas in Korea. This clarion call for Buddhist reform was one of the first attempts by a Korean author to apply Western liberalism in the context of Korean society. Han attributed many of the contemporary problems Korean Buddhism was facing to its isolation from society at large, a result of the centuries-long persecution Buddhism had suffered in Korea at the hands of Confucian ideologues during the previous Chosŏn dynasty (1392–1910). To help restore Buddhism to a central place in Korean society and culture, Han called for what were at the time quite radical reforms, including social and national egalitarianism, the secularization of the SAṂGHA, a married clergy, expanded educational opportunities for monks, the transfer of monasteries from the mountains to the cities, and economic self-reliance within the monastic community. Both the Japanese government-general and the leaders of the Korean Buddhist community rebuffed most of Han's proposals (although several of his suggestions, including a married clergy, were subsequently co-opted by the Japanese colonial administration), but the issues that he raised about how to make Buddhism relevant in an increasingly secularized and capitalist society remain pertinent even to this day.

**Chos rgyam Drung pa**. See TRUNGPA, CHÖGYAM.

**Ch'oŭi Ŭisun**. (草衣意恂) (1786–1866). Korean SŎN master of the Chosŏn period; also known as Ilchiam ("One-Finger Hermitage"). He received the full monastic precepts and the name Ch'oŭi from the monk Wanho Yunu (1758–1826). Ch'oŭi became Yunu's disciple, and made a name for himself as an influential Sŏn master. Ch'oŭi is perhaps most renowned for his efforts to revitalize the art of tea in Korea. He developed the tea ceremony as a form of religious practice and is known for synthesizing the tea ceremony and Sŏn practice, as exemplified in his slogan ta sŏn ilmi ("tea and Sŏn are a single taste"). Ch'oŭi also wrote several guides to growing, preparing, and drinking tea, such as the *Tongdasong* and the *Tasin chŏn*, which is based on the Chinese classic *Wanbao quanshu*. Ch'oŭi's other writings include a collection of his poetry, the *Ch'oŭi shigo*, and a biography of the eminent Korean monk Chinmuk Irok (1562–1633), the *Chinmuk chosa yujŏkko*. Among his writings, the *Sŏnmun sabyŏn manŏ* ("Prolix Discourse on Four Distinctive Types in the Sŏn School") in particular played a major role in determining the future of Sŏn discourse in Korea. The text was written as a critique of PAEKP'A KŬNGSŎN'S equally influential text, the *Sŏnmun sugyŏng* ("Hand Mirror on the Sŏn School").

**chuandeng lu**. (J. dentōroku; K. chŏndŭng nok 傳燈録). In Chinese, "transmission of the lamplight record"; a generic term for a genre of historical writing associated with the CHAN school, or more specifically to the most representative text of that genre, the JINGDE CHUANDENG LU. These so-called "lamp" or "lamplight histories" (denglu) include the CHODANG CHIP (C. *Zutang ji*), CHUANFA ZHENGZONG JI, *Tiansheng guangdeng lu*, *Wudeng huiyuan* ("Collected Essentials of the Five Lamplight Histories"), and others. These texts were composed primarily to establish a genealogical map of Chan orthodoxy and to reinforce the legitimacy for the lineages, teachings, and practices of the various Chan lines. These mature Chan histories were strongly influenced by earlier genealogical histories compiled during the Tang dynasty, such as the CHUAN FABAO JI, LENGQIE SHIZI JI, LIDAI FABAO JI, and BAOLIN ZHUAN. In these earlier texts, contending groups of masters and their disciples wove together intricate lineages that they traced back to the legendary Indian founder of Chan, BODHIDHARMA, and his immediate successors. These texts began using the metaphor of a "lamplight" (deng) being transmitted from lamp to lamp to suggest the wordless, mind-to-mind transmission (YIXIN CHUANXIN) of the Buddha's insight from master to disciple and down through the generations. These chuandeng lu also came to serve another important purpose as the primary source of the stories about the interactions between masters and students, from which important precedents or cases (GONG'AN) were collected for contemplation or testing of meditative experience.

**chuanfa**. (J. denbō/denpō; K. chŏnpŏp 傳法). In Chinese, lit., "transmit the dharma"; the transmission from master to disciple that constitutes the genealogy or lineage of different schools of Buddhism. See CHUANDENG LU; CHUANFA ZHENGZONG JI; FASI; YINKE.

**Chuan fabao ji**. (J. Denbōhōki; K. Chŏn pŏppo ki 傳法寶紀). In Chinese, "Annals of the Transmission of the Dharma Jewel"; compiled c. 713 by the layman Du Fei (d.u.) for followers of the so-called Northern School (BEI ZONG) of CHAN. Along with the LENGQIE SHIZI JI, the *Chuan fabao ji* is probably one of the earliest Chan chronicles that delineate the theory of the "transmission of the lamplight" (see CHUANDENG LU). The narrative of transmission that appears in the *Chuan fabao ji* seems to be based on an epitaph for the monk Faru (638–689), which is the oldest extant document outlining the transmission of the lamplight theory (written in 689). According to Faru's epitaph and the *Chuan fabao ji*, the wordless teaching of Chan that ŚĀKYAMUNI transmitted to his disciple ĀNANDA was inherited by BODHIDHARMA, HUIKE, SENGCAN, DAOXIN, HONGREN, Faru, and finally by SHENXIU. The *Chuan fabao ji* is largely comprised of the biography of these figures.

**chuanfa ji**. (J. denbōge/denpōge; K. chŏnpŏp ke 傳法偈). In Chinese, "dharma-transmission GĀTHĀ." See YIJI.

**Chuanfa zhengzong ji**. (J. Denbōshōshūki; K. Chŏnpŏp chŏngjong ki 傳法正宗記). In Chinese, "Record of the Orthodox Tradition's Transmission of the Dharma"; edited by FORI QISONG (1007–1072) and published in 1591; an influential history of the CHAN tradition, the *Chuanfa zhengzong ji* largely follows the genealogies delineated in the JINGDE CHUANDENG LU, with the crucial difference of accepting a roster of only twenty-four, not twenty-eight, patriarchs (ZUSHI) in the Chan tradition. In its first roll, the *Chuanfa zhengzong ji* begins with the biography of the Buddha, and follows in the next few rolls with the biographies of his successors, starting with MAHĀKĀŚYAPA and the twenty-four Indian patriarchs of Chan, continuing through to the sixth Chinese patriarch HUINENG. In rolls seven and eight, approximately thirteen hundred short biographies of monks who trace their lineages back to Huineng are provided. The last roll offers more than two hundred biographies of important meditators, ascetics, and Chan masters who predate Huineng, as well as brief notes on monks who thus do not belong to the "orthodox" Chan lineage outlined above. One of the primary purposes of this text was to argue against the dominant "twenty-eight Indian patriarchs" model borrowed from the apocryphal FUFAZANG YINYUAN ZHUAN (the model used, for instance, in the *Jingde chuandeng lu*) and substantiate instead the alternative paradigm of twenty-four Indian patriarchs.

**Chuanxin fayao**. (J. Denshinhōyō; K. Chŏnsim pŏbyo 傳心法要). In Chinese, "Essential Teachings on the Transmission of the Mind"; by the CHAN master HUANGBO XIYUN, also known as the *Huangboshan Duanji chanshi chuanxin fayao*. Huangbo's prominent lay disciple Pei Xiu's (787?–860) preface to the text was prepared in 857. Pei Xiu, the powerful Tang-dynasty minister of state, is said to have recorded the lectures delivered by Huangbo at the monasteries of Longxingsi and Kaiyuansi, and edited his notes together as the *Chuanxin fayao* and WANLING LU. The two texts seem to have circulated together until the eleventh century. The central tenet of the *Chuanxin fayao* is the teaching of the "one mind" (YIXIN). Since everything, including buddhas and sentient beings, are all considered to be aspects of the one mind, Huangbo's use of this term underscores the fundamental unity of all things. Huangbo also likens this mind to space, a common metaphor for emptiness (ŚŪNYATĀ). Chan practice entails bringing an end to the discriminative process of thought, so that this one mind will be made manifest. Since all beings are inherently endowed with this one mind, which is complete in and of itself, there is no need to develop a series of practices, such as the six PĀRAMITĀs, or to amass stores of merit (PUṆYA), in order to perfect that one mind. Simply awakening to that one mind will itself be sufficient to transform an ignorant sentient being into an enlightened buddha.

**Chu dbar**. (Chubar). A Tibetan name for the region of the Rongshar Valley in southern Tibet close to the Nepalese border, chiefly associated with the eleventh-century Tibetan YOGIN MI LA RAS PA; also spelled Chu 'bar. According to Mi la ras pa's biographies, many of the yogin's favored retreat sites were located in the Chu dbar area, a short distance from the famed enclave of LA PHYI. Foremost among these was 'Bri lce phug (Driche puk), or "Dri's Tongue Cave," which served as the site for his cremation. Many of Mi la ras pa's patrons hailed from Chu dbar and the neighboring village BRIN, both of which later came under the administrative control of 'BRI GUNG BKA' BRGYUD hierarchs. The region is also home to Chu dbar monastery, which was eventually directed by the tenth KARMA PA Chos dbying rdo rje (Chöying Dorje, 1604–1674), but was destroyed during the Cultural Revolution. Nearby is Mt. Tseringma (Nepalese: Gaurishanker) which, together with four surrounding peaks, is believed to be the divine residence of the five long-life sister goddesses (TSHE RING MCHED LNGA) who were converted to Buddhism and became disciples of Mi la ras pa.

**chuin'gong**. (主人公). In Korean, lit. "master" or "owner"; a term used within the SŎN and CHAN tradition to refer to "buddha-nature" (C. FOXING) or "true mind" (C. zhenxin). See ZHURENGONG.

**chuishi**. (J. suiji; K. susi 垂示). In Chinese, lit "giving instructions," viz., a "pointer"; also known as shizhong (instructing the assembly), chuiyu (giving words), and suoyu (searching for words). In order to measure the depth of a student's understanding, CHAN masters often challenged him with a question, word, or phrase. This process of interrogation was referred to as chuishi. In various case (GONG'AN) collections, such as the BIYAN LU, the term chuishi also began to refer to the introductory words, or "pointers," placed before the actual case (bence). These introductory words often included questions and anecdotes. Similarly, the CONGRONG LU used the term shizhong to refer to these introductory words.

**chūkai**. (抽解). In Japanese, "to take off"; referring to the rest period between meditation periods for monks practicing in the sōdō, or SAṂGHA hall. In between meditation sessions, monks are allowed to leave the SAṂGHA hall and take off their robes to lie down and rest.

**chukpi**. (竹篦). In Korean, "bamboo clacker"; an instrument used in Korea to mark the beginning and end of Buddhist ceremonies and meditation sessions. The instrument is a hollow stick of bamboo split down the middle, which, when struck, produces a clacking noise. The chukpi is typically clacked three times to signal the beginning and end of a ceremony or meditation session. Cf. MOKT'AK.

**Chulalongkorn**. (Thai). See RĀMA V.

**Ch'unggyŏng Ch'ŏnyŏng**. (冲鏡天英) (1215–1286). Korean monk of the Koryŏ dynasty and fifth patriarch of the SUSŎNSA community established by POJO CHINUL. Ch'unggyŏng was ordained by CHIN'GAK HYESIM in 1229 and passed the national clerical examinations (SŬNGKWA) in 1236. He subsequently began his studies under Hyesim's disciple Mongyŏ (d. 1252), and he later became the student of Mongyŏ's disciple CHINMYŎNG HONWŎN. Ch'unggyŏng continued studying with his teacher while they were living at the monastery of Sŏnwŏnsa and in the Susŏnsa community. When Chinmyŏng stepped down as patriarch of Susŏnsa in 1256, the king gave Ch'unggyŏng the title of Great Sŏn Master (taesŏnsa) and appointed him as Chinmyŏng's successor. The community flourished under Ch'unggyŏng's supervision. He passed away at the monastery of Pulgaesa in 1286 and was succeeded as patriarch of the Susŏnsa community by his chief disciple MIRAM CH'UNGJI.

**Chunghyangsŏng**. (K) (衆香城). "City of Multitudinous Fragrances"; city where the AṢṬASĀHASRIKĀPRAJÑĀPĀRAMITĀ says the BODHISATTVA DHARMODGATA lived and taught the perfection of wisdom (PRAJÑĀPĀRAMITĀ); an alternate name for the Korean "Diamond Mountains." See GANDHAVATĪ, KŬMGANGSAN; DHARMODGATA.

**Ch'ungji**. (K) (沖止). See MIRAM CH'UNGJI.

**Chungwŏn**. (K) (重遠). See HANAM CHUNGWŎN.

**Chu sanzang jiji**. (J. Shutsusanzōki shū; K. Ch'ul samjang kijip 出三藏記集). In Chinese, "Compilation of Notices on the Translation of the TRIPIṬAKA"; edited by the monk SENGYOU (445–518) and published around 515. The *Chu sanzang jiji* is the first extant scriptural catalogue (JINGLU) and incorporates in its listings an even earlier catalogue by DAO'AN (312–385), the ZONGLI ZHONGJING MULU, which is now lost. The *Chu sanzang jiji* consists of five principal sections: (1) a discussion on the provenance of translated scriptures, (2) a record of (new) titles and their listings in earlier catalogues, (3) prefaces to scriptures, (4) miscellaneous treatises on specific doctrines, and (5) biographies of translators. Sengyou's catalogue established the principal categories into which all subsequent cataloguers would classify scriptures, including new or old translations, anonymous or variant translations, APOCRYPHA, anonymous translations, MAHĀYĀNA and HĪNAYĀNA literature divided according to the three divisions of the TRIPIṬAKA, and so forth. The roster of texts includes translations of scriptures and commentaries from the Han to the Liang dynasties and compares the listings of these various translations in official scriptural catalogues in order to determine their authenticity. Short biographies of the various translators are also provided. Sengyou also discusses indigenous Buddhist literature, such as biographical and historiographical collections, scriptural prefaces, and the catalogues themselves, in order to provide subsequent generations with guidance on how properly to transmit Buddhist literature. Sengyou's text is as an important source for studying the early history of translation work and indigenous scriptural creation (see APOCRYPHA) in Chinese Buddhism.

**cibu/cibu tong**. (祠部/祠部筒). In Chinese, "tonsure certificate" and "tonsure-certificate canister." Monks and nuns in China were subject to governmental supervision through tonsure certificates (cibu) and either annual and/or triennial registration. Starting as early as 729 during the Tang dynasty, the Chinese state required monks to register their ordinations, with one copy of the registration kept at the central Bureau of Sacrifices and the other at the local government office. By the Song dynasty, monks could no longer be ordained by a monastery without having first received official government permission, and anyone not formally registered would be laicized. Tonsure certificates were issued by the Bureau of Sacrifices (Cibu), the name thus referring to the government office that issued them. Tonsure certificates are traditionally presumed to have first been issued in 747 during the Tang dynasty, and were required in order to hold any kind of monastic position. Certificates imprinted with a postulant's name were typically issued only after a candidate had passed a required set of monastic examinations; blank certificates were sometimes simply sold on the open market, with the number varying according to the revenue needs of the state. The price of blank certificates in particular varied widely, sometimes becoming so expensive that monasteries had to take up donations in order to fund their postulants' registrations. Such tonsure certificates became an important revenue source for the Chinese state, rivaling the taxes placed on salt and commercial activity, and were a valuable commodity because they came with a substantial tax exemption. Tonsure certificates were kept in a special canister known as the cibu tong, which the CHANYUAN QINGGUI ("Pure Rules from the Chan Grove") lists as one of the standard requisites that a Chinese monk should carry with him as he traveled from monastery to monastery. By requiring that all monks receive and carry such tonsure certificates, the government ensured that the Buddhist ecclesia remained under strict government regulation.

**cidi sandi**. (J. shidai no santai; K. ch'aje samje 次第三諦). In Chinese, "sequential three truths"; also known as the "differentiated three truths" (GELI SANDI). See SANDI, YUANRONG.

**cidi sanguan**. (J. shidai sangan; K. ch'aje samgwan 次第三觀). In Chinese, the "sequential threefold contemplation." *See* SANGUAN.

**cidi xingbu men**. (次第行布門). In Chinese, the "approach of sequential practices." See YUANRONG.

**Ci'en (dashi) Kuiji**. (慈恩[大師]窺基). See KUIJI.

**Ci'en xuepai**. (C) (慈恩學派). In Chinese, "The Ci'en Scholastic Lineage" of the Chinese YOGĀCĀRA school, which is associated with KUIJI. See FAXIANG ZONG.

**Cihang**. (慈航) (1895–1954). Chinese monk during the Republican Era and prominent disciple of the influential Buddhist reformer TAIXU; his mummified remains continue to be a major focus of relic worship in Taiwan. Cihang was first educated in the traditional Chinese Buddhist exegetical traditions of the CHAN, TIANTAI, and PURE LAND schools before beginning his studies in 1927 at Taixu's modern Buddhist academy in Minnan. It was there that Cihang was exposed to, and inspired by, Taixu's reformist ideals, and began his own active missionary career. Cihang's achievements as a missionary included establishing various Chinese Buddhist organizations and lecturing on Buddhism throughout Southeast Asia, including the Philippines, Singapore, Burma, and Malaysia, where he was credited with promoting a type of "socially engaged Buddhism." Cihang was also the founder and editor of the Buddhist monthly *Renjian* ("Human Realm"), and served as abbot of various monasteries. Most notably, Cihang founded the renowned Mile Neiyuan (MAITREYA Buddhist Academy) in Taiwan for training young clergy who had recently relocated from the Chinese mainland, so that they would be able to minister to new Taiwanese converts to Buddhism. Cihang's classes on YOGĀCĀRA and other MAHĀYĀNA traditions in and outside of the academy were influential on the way Chinese Buddhism spread, developed, and took root in Taiwan after the retreat of the Kuomintang (Guomindang) from the Chinese mainland in 1949. Cihang's mummified remains—in the form of his largely intact body—continue to be a source of great fascination and controversy in Taiwan. In addition to the many debates within both the secular and religious communities concerning his "whole-body relic" (QUANSHEN SHELI), a new cult of relic worship began in earnest as soon as the existence of his mummified body became publicized. Cihang's pious followers undertook extra measures to ensure the lasting preservation of his body. Cihang's mummy, still sitting in a meditative posture, remains on display inside the memorial building (Cihang guan) dedicated to him.

**Cimin Huiri**. (J. Jimin Enichi; K. Chamin Hyeil 慈愍慧日) (680–748). Founder of the Cimin lineage of Chinese PURE LAND Buddhism. Inspired by his meeting with the pilgrim and translator YIJING (635–713), Huiri also traveled to India between 702 and 719, where he is said to have studied with Indian teachers about SUKHĀVATĪ, the pure land of AMITĀBHA and had a vision in which the BODHISATTVA AVALOKITEŚVARA personally instructed him in pure land teachings. After Huiri returned to China, he taught an ecumenical approach to pure land practice, which combined the practices of meditation, recitation, and discipline. Because Huiri's approach differs markedly from that offered by LUSHAN HUIYUAN (334–416) and TANLUAN (476–542), his teachings are sometimes considered to constitute a separate Cimin line of the Chinese pure land tradition. Huiri also made a concerted effort to respond to critiques of pure land practice made by adepts within the CHAN ZONG, who disparaged the pure land approach as an expedient intended for spiritually inferior practitioners. The Tang emperor Xuanzong (r. 712–756) bestowed on Huiri the posthumous title of Cimin Sanzang (TREPITAKA Compassionate Sympathy) for his service in transmitting the pure land teaching. Cimin's combination of recitation of the Buddha's name (NIANFO) with meditation subsequently influenced the nianfo Chan of YONGMING YANSHOU (904–975).

**cintāmaṇi**. (T. yid bzhin nor bu; C. ruyi baozhu; J. nyoihōju; K. yŏŭi poju 如意寶珠). In Sanskrit, "wish-fulfilling gem"; in Indian mythology a magical jewel possessed by DEVAS and NĀGAS that has the power to grant wishes. The term is often as a metaphor for various stages of the path, including the initial aspiration to achieve buddhahood (BODHICITTOTPĀDA), the rarity of rebirth as a human being with access to the dharma, and the merit arising from the teachings of the Buddha. According to the *Ruyi baozhu zhuanlun mimi xianshen chengfo jinlunzhouwang jing* (also known simply as the *Jinlunzhouwang jing*), which describes in great detail the inexhaustible merit of this gem, the cintāmaṇi is rough in shape and is comprised of eleven precious materials, including gold and silver, and has thirty-two pieces of the Buddha's relics (ŚARĪRA) at its core, which give it its special power. In the DAZHIDU LUN, the gem is said to derive from the brain of the dragon king (nāgarāja), the undersea protector of Buddhism, or, alternatively, to be the main jewel ornamenting the top of his head. The text claims that it has the power to protect its carrier from poison and fire; other texts say that the cintāmaṇi has the capacity to drive away evil, clarify muddy water, etc. This gem is also variously said to come from the head of a great makara fish (as in the RATNAKŪṬASŪTRA) or the heart of a GARUḌA bird (as in the GUAN WULIANGSHOU JING). Other texts suggest that while the king of the gods, INDRA, was fighting with the demigods (ASURA), part of his weapon dropped to the world and became this gem. The bodhisattvas AVALOKITEŚVARA and KṢITIGARBHA are also depicted holding a cintāmaṇi so that they may grant the wishes of all sentient beings.

**cintāmayīprajñā**. (P. cintāmayapaññā; T. bsam pa las byung ba'i shes rab; C. sihui; J. shie; K. sahye 思慧). In Sanskrit, "wisdom derived from reflection [or analysis]"; the second of the three types of wisdom, together with ŚRUTAMAYĪPRAJÑĀ (wisdom derived from what is heard, viz., study) and BHĀVANĀMAYĪPRAJÑĀ (wisdom generated by cultivation or meditation). Building upon what one has learned through śrutamayīprajñā, the practitioner deepens that knowledge by reflecting upon its significance and its application in understanding the nature of this world and beyond. This reflection may involve a certain level of mental attention and concentration, but not yet full meditative calmness (ŚAMATHA). This level of understanding is therefore not as profound as the third and final stage of wisdom, bhāvanāmayīprajñā, where the knowledge first learned and subsequently developed over the preceding two stages of wisdom is now authenticated at the level of VIPAŚYANĀ.

**cishi song**. (J. jiseiju; K. sase song 辭世頌). In Chinese, lit., "taking leave of the world hymn"; alternate name for a "bequeathed verse." See YIJI.

**Citipati**. (T. Dur khrod bdag po). In Sanskrit, "Lord of the Funeral Pile"; a pair of male and female dancing skeletons associated with the CAKRASAṂVARATANTRA and who are often depicted as protectors of VAJRAYOGINĪ. They are also called śrīśmaśānādhipati or "lords of the charnel ground" and are regarded as enlightened beings and emanations of CAKRASAṂVARA. They are also propitiated for wealth and for protection from thieves. According to legend, they are the spirits of two Indian ascetics who were murdered by thieves while practicing austerities in a charnel ground (ŚMAŚĀNA). They each hold a daṇḍa or staff made of bone and a KAPĀLA and dance on corpses in ARDHAPARYAṄKA pose, either in YAB YUM posture or side by side. They are not to be confused with the skeleton dancers in Tibetan 'CHAM performances, who represent servants of YAMA, the deity of death.

**citta**. (T. sems; C. xin; J. shin; K. sim 心). In Sanskrit and Pāli, "mind," "mentality," or "thought"; used broadly to refer to general mentality, citta is the factor (DHARMA) that is present during any type of conscious activity. Citta is contrasted with the physical body or materiality (RŪPA), and is synonymous in this context with "name" (NĀMA), as in the term NĀMARŪPA. In this sense, citta corresponds to the last four of the five aggregates (SKANDHA), excluding only the first aggregate, of materiality (RŪPA), i.e., sensation (VEDANĀ), perception (SAṂJÑĀ), conditioning factors (SAṂSKĀRA), and consciousness (VIJÑĀNA). (Where the correspondences on this list are further refined, the first three of these mentality aggregates correspond to the mental concomitants, viz., CAITTA, while citta is restricted to the last aggregate, that of consciousness, or vijñāna.) Citta in this broad sense is synonymous with both mentality (MANAS) and consciousness (vijñāna): mind is designated as citta because it "builds up" (cinoti) virtuous and nonvirtuous states; as manas, because it calculates and examines; and as vijñāna, because it discriminates among sensory stimuli. Mind as "consciousness" refers to the six consciousnesses (ṣaḍvijñāna): the five sensory consciousnesses of the visual (CAKṢURVIJÑĀNA), auditory (ŚROTRAVIJÑĀNA), olfactory (GHRĀṆAVIJÑĀNA), gustatory (JIHVĀVIJÑĀNA), and tactile (KĀYAVIJÑĀNA), along with the mental consciousness (MANOVIJÑĀNA). In some strands of MAHĀYĀNA thought, such as YOGĀCĀRA, mind is instead considered to encompass not only mentality but all dharmas, and the distinction between mentality and materiality is presumed to be merely nominal; Yogācāra is thus sometimes called the school of CITTAMĀTRA, or "mind-only." Citta as mentality serves as one of the four foundations of mindfulness (SMṚTYUPASTHĀNA) in Buddhist meditative training, and refers to various general states of mind, e.g., a mind (citta) that is depressed, distracted, developed, concentrated, or freed. Citta is also used to signify mind itself in distinction to various sets of mental concomitants (caitta) that accompany the basic sensory consciousnesses. The DHAMMASAṄGAṆI, the first of the seven books of the Pāli ABHIDHAMMAPIṬAKA, classifies citta as the first of a fourfold division of factors into mind (citta), mental concomitants (P. CETASIKA), materiality or form (rūpa), and NIRVĀṆA (P. nibbāna). In this text's treatment, a moment of consciousness (citta) will always arise in association with a variety of associated mental factors (P. cetasika), seven of which are always present during every moment of consciousness: (1) sensory contact or sense impression (P. phassa; S. SPARŚA), (2) feeling or sensation (VEDANĀ), (3) perception or conception (P. saññā; S. SAṂJÑĀ), (4) volition (CETANĀ), (5) concentration (SAMĀDHI), (6) vitality (JĪVITA), and (7) attention, viz., the advertence of the mind toward an object (P. manasikāra; S. MANASKĀRA). The SARVĀSTIVĀDA ABHIDHARMA instead divides all dharmas into five groups: mind (citta), mental concomitants (caitta), materiality (rūpa), forces dissociated from thought (CITTAVIPRAYUKTASAṂSKĀRA), and the unconditioned (ASAṂSKṚTA). In this system, ten specific factors are said universally to accompany all conscious activity and are therefore called "factors of wide extent" or "omnipresent mental factors" (MAHĀBHŪMIKA): (1) sensation (vedanā); (2) volition (cetanā); (3) perception (saṃjñā); (4) zeal or "desire-to-act" (CHANDA) (5) sensory contact (sparśa); (6) discernment (mati); (7) mindfulness (SMṚTI); (8) attention (manaskāra); (9) determination (ADHIMOKṢA); (10) concentration (samādhi). According to the system set forth by ASAṄGA in his ABHIDHARMASAMUCCAYA, this list is divided into two sets of five: the five omnipresent (SARVATRAGA) mental factors (vedanā, saṃjñā, cetanā, sparśa, and manaskāra) and the five determining (pratiniyama) mental factors (chanda, adhimokṣa, smṛti, samādhi, and prajñā). ¶ In the experience of enlightenment (BODHI), the citta is said to be "freed" from the "point of view" that is the self (ĀTMAN). The citta is then no longer subject to the limitations perpetuated by ignorance (AVIDYĀ) and craving (TṚṢṆĀ) and thus becomes nonmanifesting (because there is no longer any projection of ego into the perceptual process), infinite (because the mind is no longer subject to the limitations of conceptualization), and lustrous (because the ignorance that dulls the mind has been vanquished forever). Scriptural statements attest to this inherent luminosity of the citta, which may be revealed through practice and manifested in enlightenment. For example, in the Pāli AṄGUTTARANIKĀYA, the Buddha says, "the mind, O monks, is luminous" (P. pabhassaraṃ idaṃ bhikkhave cittaṃ). Such statements are the strands from which the Mahāyāna subsequently derives such concepts as the inherent quality of buddhahood (BUDDHADHĀTU; C. FOXING) or the embryo of the TATHĀGATAS (TATHĀGATAGARBHA) that is said to be innate in the mind.

**Citta**. A lay follower of the Buddha, mentioned in Pāli sources as being foremost among laymen who preached the DHARMA; also known as Cittagahapati. Citta was treasurer for the township of Macchikāsaṇḍa in the kingdom of Kāsī. When he was born, the sky rained flowers of many hues, hence his name which means variegated color. Citta was converted to Buddhism when he encountered the elder Mahānāma (S. MAHĀNĀMAN) while the latter was sojourning in Macchikāsaṇḍa. Citta was greatly impressed by the monk's demeanor and built a monastery for him in his park named Ambāṭakārāma. There, listening to Mahānāma preach on the subject of the six senses, he attained to state of a nonreturner (ANĀGĀMIN). On one occasion, Citta visited the Buddha in the company of two thousand laypeople, bringing with him five hundred cartloads of offerings. When he bowed at the Buddha's feet, flowers in a variety of colors rained down from the heavens. Like Mahānāma, the Buddha preached a sermon on the six senses to him. Citta distributed offerings for a fortnight, the gods continuously refilling the carts. Citta was endowed with a great intellect and was a gifted speaker. His conversations with members of the order are recorded in the "Citta Saṃyutta" of the Pāli SAṂYUTTANIKĀYA, and he is also described as having refuted the views of non-Buddhist teachers, such as Nigaṇṭha Nātaputta (S. NIRGRANTHA-JÑĀTĪPUTRA, viz., Mahāvīra), the eminent JAINA teacher, and Acela Kassapa. Although he was not an ARHAT, he possessed the analytical knowledge (P. paṭisambhidā; S. PRATISAṂVID) of a learner (P. sekha). It was for these aptitudes that he earned preeminence. On his deathbed, divinities visited him and encouraged him to seek rebirth as a heavenly king, but he refused, stating that such an impermanent reward was not his goal. He then preached to them, and to all the kinfolk who had gathered around him, before passing away. Together with HATTHAKA ĀḶAVAKA, Citta is upheld as an ideal layman worthy of emulation.

**cittaikāgratā**. (P. cittekaggatā; T. sems rtse gcig pa; C. xin yijing xing; J. shin ikkyō shō; K. sim ilgyŏng sŏng 心一境性). In Sanskrit, "one-pointedness of mind"; a deep state of meditative equipoise in which the mind is thoroughly concentrated on the object of meditation. In the progression of the four meditative absorptions associated with the subtle-materiality realm (RŪPĀVACARADHYĀNA), the first absorption (DHYĀNA) still involves the first two of the five constituents of dhyāna (DHYĀNĀṄGA): i.e., the application of thought to the meditative object (VITARKA) and sustained attention to that object (VICĀRA). As concentration deepens from the second dhyāna onward, applied and sustained thought vanish and the meditator moves from the mental "isolation" or "solitude" (VIVEKA) that characterizes the first dhyāna, to the true one-pointedness of mind (cittaikāgratā) that characterizes all higher stages of dhyāna; in this state of one-pointedness, the mind is so completely absorbed in the meditative object that even these most subtle varieties of thinking have disappeared.

**cittamahābhūmika**. In Sanskrit, "omnipresent mental factors." See MAHĀBHŪMIKA, SARVATRAGA.

**cittamātra**. (T. sems tsam; C. weixin; J. yuishin; K. yusim 唯心). In Sanskrit, lit. "mind-only"; a term used in the LAṄKĀVATĀRASŪTRA to describe the notion that the external world of the senses does not exist independently of the mind and that all phenomena are mere projections of consciousness. Because this doctrine is espoused by the YOGĀCĀRA, that school is sometimes referred to as cittamātra. The doctrine is closely associated with the eight consciousness (VIJÑĀNA) theory set forth in the "Viniścayasaṃgrahaṇī" of the YOGĀCĀRABHŪMIŚĀSTRA and in the MAHĀYĀNASAṂGRAHA and ABHIDHARMASAMUCCAYA that are supplemental to that work. In East Asia, these texts are associated with the name of the Mahāyāna writer ASAṄGA and his quasi-mythological teacher MAITREYA or MAITREYANĀTHA. According to this theory, there are not only six consciousnesses (vijñāna), viz., the visual, auditory, olfactory, gustatory, and tactile consciousnesses, and the mental consciousness (manovijñāna) well known to canonical Buddhism; there are two further consciousnesses, called the afflicted mind (KLIṢṬAMANAS) and the storehouse consciousness (ĀLAYAVIJÑĀNA). The ālayavijñāna is also known as the sarvabīja, or the consciousness that carries all the seeds or potentialities (BĪJA). The Cittamātra school holds that mental states leave a residual impression that is carried by the ālayavijñāna. These impressions (VĀSANĀ) literally "perfume" or "suffuse" this underlying consciousness, where they lie dormant as seeds. Among the many categories of seeds, two are principal: the residual impressions giving rise to a new form of life (VIPĀKA) in the six realms of existence, and the residual impression that is basic ignorance causing all ordinary mental states to appear in a distorted way, i.e., bifurcated into subject and object. Vasubandhu, who is said to have been converted to the Cittamātra doctrine by his brother Asaṅga, argues in his TRIṂŚIKĀ (*Triṃśikāvijñaptimātratā[siddhi]kārikā*), the famous "Thirty Verses on Consciousness-Only," that there could not possibly be an atomic basis for objects known by mind. In the absence of an atomic basis, only the ripening of the residual impressions left on the ālayavijñāna can account for the variety of mental states and experience, and only this doctrine of mind-only can properly account for the purification of mind and the final attainment of BODHI. The object and subject share the same mental nature because they both arise from the residual impressions left on the ālayavijñāna, hence the doctrine of cittamātra, mind-only.

**cittasaṃprayuktasaṃskāra**. (T. sems dang mtshungs ldan gyi 'du byed; C. xin xiangying fa; J. shinsōōbō; K. sim sangŭng pŏp 心相應法). In Sanskrit, "conditioned forces associated with thought"; an ABHIDHARMA term synonymous with the mental concomitants (CAITTA), the dharmas that in various combinations accompany mind or thought (CITTA). The ABHIDHARMAKOŚABHĀṢYA, for example, explains that mind and its concomitants always appear in conjunction with one another and cannot be independently generated. These factors are "associated" because of five equalities that they share with mind, i.e., equality as to (1) support (ĀŚRAYA), in this context, meaning the six sensory bases; (2) object (ĀLAMBANA), viz., the six sensory objects; (3) aspect (ĀKĀRA), the aspects of sensory cognition; (4) time (kāla), because they occur simultaneously; and (5) the number of their substance (DRAVYA), because mind and its concomitants are in a one-to-one association. The different schools of ABHIDHARMA enumerate various lists of such forces. The VAIBHĀṢIKA school of SARVĀSTIVĀDA abhidharma lists forty-six cittasamprayuktasaṃskāras, while the mature YOGĀCĀRA system of MAHĀYĀNA scholasticism gives a total of fifty-one, listed in six categories. The Vaibhāṣika and Yogācāra schools also posited a contrasting category of "conditioned forces dissociated from thought" (CITTAVIPRAYUKTASAṂSKĀRA), which served to account for specific types of complex moral and mental processes (such as where both physicality and mentality were temporarily suspended in higher meditative absorptions), and anomalous doctrinal problems. (The Pāli equivalent cittasaṃpayuttasaṅkhāra is attested, but only rarely, in Pāli commentarial literature; it does not appear in canonical ABHIDHAMMA texts. This doctrinal category therefore has no significance in the THERAVĀDA abhidhamma.) For more detailed discussion, see CAITTA; and for the complete lists, see SEVENTY-FIVE DHARMAS OF THE SARVĀSTIVĀDA SCHOOL and ONE-HUNDRED DHARMAS OF THE YOGĀCĀRA SCHOOL in the List of Lists.

**cittasaṃtāna**. [alt. cittasaṃtati] (P. cittasantāna; T. sems rgyud/sems rgyun; C. xin xiangxu; J. shinsōzoku; K. sim sangsok 心相續). In Sanskrit, "mental continuum." The notion of a continuum is employed in the ABHIDHARMA traditions to clarify that there is continuity between an action (KARMAN) that an individual undertakes and its eventual effect (VIPĀKA) as well as continuity between one lifetime and the next, without going so far as to posit a perduring self (ĀTMAN). In the theory of karman, the fruition of action is experienced by the mental continuum (cittasaṃtāna) of the being who initially performed the action, not by another; thus in mainstream Buddhism one can neither receive the fruition of another's karman, nor redeem another's actions. This notion of a mental continuum also serves to counter annihilationist interpretations (see UCCHEDAVĀDA; UCCHEDĀNTA) of the quintessential Buddhist doctrine of nonself (ANĀTMAN): there may be no permanent, underlying substratum of being that we can designate a self or soul, but this does not negate the continuity that pertains in the flow of moral cause and effect or the possibility of rebirth. Hence, there can be rebirth, moral efficacy, and spiritual progress despite the lack of a permanent self. See also BHAVAṄGASOTA; SAṂTĀNA.

**cittaviprayuktasaṃskāra**. (T. sems dang ldan pa ma yin pa'i 'du byed; C. xin buxiangying fa; J. shinfusōōbō; K. sim pulsangŭng pŏp 心不相應法). In Sanskrit, "conditioned forces dissociated from thought"; forces that are associated with neither materiality (RŪPA) nor mentality (CITTA) and thus are listed in a separate category of factors (DHARMA) in ABHIDHARMA materials associated with the SARVĀSTIVĀDA school and in the hundred-dharmas (BAIFA) list of the YOGĀCĀRA school. These conditioned forces were posited to account for complex moral and mental processes (such as the states of mind associated with the higher spheres of meditation, where both physicality and mentality were temporarily suspended), and anomalous doctrinal problems (such as how speech was able to convey meaning or how group identity was established). A standard listing found in the DHARMASKANDHA and PRAKARAṆAPĀDA, two texts of the Sarvāstivāda abhidharma canon, includes sixteen dissociated forces: (1) possession (PRĀPTI); (2) equipoise of nonperception (ASAṂJÑĀSAMĀPATTI); (3) equipoise of cessation (NIRODHASAMĀPATTI); (4) nonperception (āsaṃjñika); (5) vitality (JĪVITA); (6) homogeneity (sabhāgatā); (7) acquisition the corporeal basis (*āśrayapratilābha); (8) acquisition of the given entity (*vastuprāpti); (9) acquisition of the sense spheres (*āyatanaprāpti); the four conditioned characteristics (SAṂSKṚTALAKṢAṆA), viz., (10) origination, or birth (JĀTI); (11) continuance, or maturation (STHITI); (12) senescence, or decay (JARĀ); and (13) desinence, or death (anityatā); (14) name set (nāmakāya); (15) phrase set (padakāya); 16) syllable set (vyañjanakāya). The later treatise ABHIDHARMAKOŚABHĀṢYA includes only fourteen, dropping numbers 7, 8, 9 and adding nonpossession (APRĀPTI). These listings, however, constituted only the most generic and comprehensive types employed by the VAIBHĀṢIKA school of Sarvāstivāda abhidharma; the cittaviprayuktasaṃskāras thus constituted an open category, and new forces could be posited as the need arose in order to resolve thorny doctrinal issues. The four conditioned characteristics (saṃskṛtalakṣaṇa) are a good example of why the cittaviprayuktasaṃskāra category was so useful in abhidharma-type analysis. In the Sarvāstivāda treatment of causality, these four characteristics were forces that exerted real power over compounded objects, escorting an object along from origination, to continuance, to senescence or decay, until the force "desinence," or death finally extinguishes it; this rather tortured explanation was necessary in order to explain how factors that the school presumed continued to exist in all three time periods (TRIKĀLA) of past, present, and future nevertheless still appeared to undergo change. The YOGĀCĀRA school subsequently includes twenty-four cittaviprayuktasaṃskāras in its list of one hundred dharmas (see BAIFA), including such elements as the state of an ordinary being (pṛthagjanatva), time (KĀLA), place (deśa), and number (saṃkhyā).

**cittavisuddhi**. (S. cittaviśuddhi). In Pāli, "purity of mind"; according to the VISUDDHIMAGGA, the second of seven "purities" (VISUDDHI) to be developed along the path to liberation. Purity of mind refers to the eight meditative absorptions (P. JHĀNA; S. DHYĀNA) or attainments (SAMĀPATTI) belonging to the subtle-materiality realm (rūpāvacara) and the immaterial realm (ārūpyāvacara). Meditative absorption belonging to the subtle-materiality realm (P. rūpāvacarajhāna; S. RŪPĀVACARADHYĀNA) is subdivided into four stages, each of which is characterized by an increasing attenuation of consciousness as the meditator progresses from one stage to the next. Meditative absorption belonging to the immaterial realm (P. arūpāvacarajhāna; S. ĀRŪPYĀVACARADHYĀNA) is likewise subdivided into four stages, but in this case it is the object of meditation that becomes attenuated from one stage to the next. In the first immaterial absorption, the meditator sets aside the perception of materiality and abides in the sphere of infinite space (P. ākāsānañcāyatana; S. ĀKĀŚĀNANTYĀYATANA). In the second immaterial absorption, the meditator sets aside the perception of infinite space and abides in the sphere of infinite consciousness (P. viññaṇañcāyatana; S. VIJÑĀNĀNANTYĀYATANA). In the third immaterial absorption, the meditator sets aside the perception of infinite consciousness and abides in the sphere of nothingness (P. ākiñcaññāyatana; S. ĀKIÑCANYĀYATANA). In the fourth immaterial absorption, the meditator sets aside the perception of nothingness and abides in the sphere of neither perception nor nonperception (P. nevasaññānāsaññāyatana; S. NAIVASAṂJÑĀNĀSAṂJÑĀYATANA). To this list of eight absorptions is added "access" or "neighborhood" "concentration" (P. UPACĀRASAMĀDHI), which is the degree of concentration present in the mind of the meditator just prior to entering any of the four jhānas.

**cīvara**. (T. chos gos; C. yi; J. e/koromo; K. ŭi 衣). In Pāli and Sanskrit, "monastic robe"; the generic term for the robes worn by Buddhist monks, nuns, female probationers, and male and female novices. The cīvara may be made of cotton, wool, linen, or silk. Initially, the robe was to be made of rags discarded in the rubbish heap (S. pāṃsukūla; P. paṃsukūla) or from funeral shrouds. The rule was amended by the Buddha to allow monks also to accept cloth offered by the laity. A full set of monastic robes is comprised of three robes (S. TRICĪVARA; P. ticīvara): the larger outer robe (S. SAṂGHĀṬĪ; P. saṅghāṭi), the upper robe (S. UTTARĀSAṂGA; P. uttarāsaṅga), and the lower robe or waistcloth (S. ANTARVĀSAS; P. antaravāsaka). The antarvāsas is the smallest of the three robes: normally made of one layer of cloth, it is worn about the waist and is intended to cover the body from the navel to the middle of the calf. The uttarāsaṃga is worn over one or both shoulders, depending on whether one is inside or outside the monastery grounds, and is large enough to cover the body from the neck to the middle of the calf; it too is normally made of one layer of cloth. The saṃghāṭī or outer robe is the same size as the uttarāsaṃga but is normally made of two layers of cloth rather than one; it is worn over one or both shoulders, depending on whether one is inside or outside the monastery grounds. The saṃghāṭī was required to be tailored of patches, ranging in number from nine up to twenty-five, depending on the VINAYA recension; this use of patches of cloth is said to have been modeled after plots of farmland in MAGADHA that the Buddha once surveyed. All three robes must be dyed a sullied color, interpreted as anything from a reddish- or brownish-yellow saffron color to an ochre tone (see KĀṢĀYA). Robes were one of the four major requisites (S. NIŚRAYA; P. nissaya) of the monks and nuns, along with such basics as a begging bowl and lodging, and were the object of the KAṬHINA ceremony in which the monastics were offered cloth for making new sets of robes at the end of each rains' retreats (VARṢĀ).

**clear light**. See PRABHĀSVARACITTA; 'OD GSAL.

**compassion**. See KARUṆĀ.

**conditioned origination**. See PRATĪTYASAMUTPĀDA.

**confession**. See PĀPADEŚANĀ.

**conglin**. (J. sōrin; K. ch'ongnim 叢林). In Chinese, a "dense grove"; also known as chanlin, or "CHAN grove"; the term translates the Sanskrit vana (trees) or vindhyavana (grove). The term conglin is a metaphorical reference to the monastic grounds: like trees densely gathered in a grove, monks quietly gather together in a monastery to train together. More specifically, the term refers to the monastic training grounds of Chan, SŎN, and ZEN monks. In Korea, the term CH'ONGNIM is used in the contemporary CHOGYE CHONG to refer to a handful of larger monasteries that are able to provide training in the full range of practices that exemplify the major strands of the Korean Buddhist tradition. While most Korean monasteries are primarily devoted to one or another of these types of training, the ch'ongnims offer a center where all can be practiced together.

**Conglin dashi**. (C) (叢林大士). See FU DASHI.

**Congrong lu**. (J. Shōyōroku; K. Chongyong nok 從容錄). In Chinese, "Encouragement (Hermitage) Record"; edited by Chan master Wansong Xingxiu (1165–1246). Also known as the *Congrong an lu* and *Wansong laoren pingzhang Tiantong Jue heshang songgu Congrong an lu* ("Encouragement Hermitage Record of the Prose Commentaries by Old Man Wansong on the Case and Verse [Collection] by Master Jue of Tiantong"). In 1223, while residing at the hermitage Congrong'an at the monastery of Bao'ensi near Yanjing, Wansong was asked by the famous layman and statesman Yelü Chucai (1190–1244) to expound upon an earlier collection of one hundred cases (GONG'AN) and their verse commentaries (SONGGU) prepared by the Chan master HONGZHI ZHENGJUE. In the *Congrong lu*, Wansong added some introductory words (shizhong; see CHUISHI), prose commentaries (pingchang), and capping phrases (ZHUYU) to Hongzhi's collection. The *Congrong lu* is considered one the most important scriptures of the CAODONG ZONG lineage of Chan and demonstrates definitively that the Caodong school (J. SŌTŌSHŪ) employed gong'ans (J. koan) as part of its training.

**Congshen**. (C) (從諗). See ZHAOZHOU CONGSHEN.

**consciousness**. See VIJÑĀNA.

**contaminants**. See ĀSRAVA.

**Conze, Edward**. [Eberhard (Edward) Julius Dietrich Conze] (1904–1979). An influential Anglo-German Buddhist scholar and practitioner, Edward Conze was born in London, the son of the then German vice consul, but was raised in Germany. He attended the universities of Cologne, Bonn, and Hamburg, where he studied both Western and Indian philosophy and Buddhist languages, including Sanskrit, Pāli, and Tibetan. Conze was raised as a Protestant, but he also explored Communism and had a strong interest in Theosophy. Because of his deep opposition to the Nazi ideology, he became persona non grata in Germany and in 1933 moved to England. Although initially active with English socialists, he eventually became disillusioned with politics and began to study the works of DAISETZ TEITARO SUZUKI, whom he came to consider his informal spiritual mentor. Conze taught at various universities in the UK between 1933 and 1960, expanding the range of his visiting professorships to the USA and Canada in the 1960s. However, the Communist affiliations of his youth and his outspoken condemnation of the Vietnam War put him at odds with American authorities, prompting him to return to England. Conze was especially enamored of the perfection of wisdom (PRAJÑĀPĀRAMITĀ) texts and the related MADHYAMAKA strand of Buddhist philosophy and became one of foremost scholarly exponents of this literature of his day. He saw Buddhism and especially Madhyamaka philosophy as presenting an "intelligible, plausible, and valid system" that rivaled anything produced in the West and was therefore worthy of the close attention of Western philosophers. He translated several of the major texts of the prajñāpāramitā, including *The Perfection of Wisdom in Eight Thousands Lines and Its Verse Summary* (1973), and *The Large Sutra on Perfect Wisdom with the Divisions of the Abhisamayālaṃkāra* (1975), as well as the VAJRACCHEDIKĀPRAJÑĀPĀRAMITĀSŪTRA ("Diamond Sūtra") and the PRAJÑĀPĀRAMITĀHṚDAYASŪTRA ("Heart Sūtra"). His compilation of terminology derived from this translation work, *Materials for a Dictionary of the Prajñāpāramitā Literature* (1967), did much to help establish many of the standard English equivalencies of Sanskrit Buddhist terms. Conze also wrote more general surveys of Buddhist philosophy and history, including *Buddhism: Its Essence and Development* (1951) and *Buddhist Thought in India* (1962).

**correct action**. See SAMYAKKARMĀNTA.

**correct concentration**. See SAMYAKSAMĀDHI.

**correct effort**. See SAMYAGVYĀYĀMA.

**correct intention**. See SAMYAKSAṂKALPA.

**correct livelihood**. See SAMYAGĀJĪVA.

**correct mindfulness**. See SAMYAKSMṚTI.

**correct speech**. See SAMYAGVĀK.

**correct view**. See SAMYAGDṚṢṬI.

**Council, 1st**. The term translated as "council" is SAṂGĪTI, literally "recitation," the word used to describe the communal chanting of the Buddha's teaching. The term suggests that the purpose of the meeting was to recite the TRIPIṬAKA in order to codify the canon and remove any discrepancies concerning what was and was not to be included. The first Buddhist council is said to have been held in a cave at RĀJAGṚHA shortly after the Buddha's passage into PARINIRVĀṆA, although its historicity has been questioned by modern scholars. There are numerous accounts of the first council and much scholarship has been devoted to their analysis. What follows draws on a number of sources to provide a general description. The accounts agree that, in the SAṂGHA, there was an elderly monk named SUBHADRA, a former barber who had entered the order late in life. He always carried a certain animus against the Buddha because when Subhadra was a layman, the Buddha supposedly refused to accept a meal that he had prepared for him. After the Buddha's death, Subhadra told the distraught monks that they should instead rejoice because they could now do as they pleased, without the Buddha telling them what they could and could not do. MAHĀKĀŚYAPA overheard this remark and was so alarmed by it that he thought it prudent to convene a meeting of five hundred ARHATs to codify and recite the rules of discipline (VINAYA) and the discourses (SŪTRA) of the Buddha before they became corrupted. With the patronage of King AJĀTAŚATRU, a meeting was called. At least one arhat, GAVĀMPATI, declined to participate, deciding instead to pass into nirvāṇa before the council began. This led to an agreement that no one else would pass into nirvāṇa until after the conclusion of the council. At the time that the council was announced, ĀNANDA, the Buddha's personal attendant and therefore the person who had heard the most discourses of the Buddha, was not yet an arhat and would have been prevented from participating. However, on the night before the council, he fortuitously finished his practice and attained the status of arhat. At the council, Mahākāśyapa presided. He interrogated UPĀLI about the rules of discipline (PRĀTIMOKṢA) of both BHIKṢUs and BHIKṢUṆĪs. He then questioned Ānanda about each of the discourses the Buddha had delivered over the course of his life, asking in each case where and on whose account the discourse had been given. In this way, the VINAYAPIṬAKA and the SŪTRAPIṬAKA were established. (In many accounts, the ABHIDHARMAPIṬAKA is not mentioned, but in others it is said the abhidharmapiṭaka was recited by Mahākāśyapa or by Ānanda.) Because of his extraordinary powers of memory, Ānanda was said to be able to repeat sixty thousand words of the Buddha without omitting a syllable and recite fifteen thousand of his stanzas. It was at the time of his recitation that Ānanda informed the council that prior to his passing the Buddha told him that after his death, the saṃgha could disregard the minor rules of conduct. Since he had neglected to ask the Buddha what the minor rules were, however, it was decided that all the rules would be maintained. Ānanda was then chastised for (1) not asking what the minor rules were, (2) stepping on the Buddha's robe while he was sewing it, (3) allowing the tears of women to fall on the Buddha's corpse, (4) not asking the Buddha to live for an eon

(KALPA) or until the end of the eon although the Buddha strongly hinted that he could do so (see CĀPĀLACAITYA), and (5) urging the Buddha to allow women to enter the order. (There are several versions of this list, with some including among the infractions that Ānanda allowed women to see the Buddha's naked body.) The entire vinayapiṭaka and sūtrapiṭaka was then recited, which is said to have required seven months. According to several accounts, after the recitation had concluded, a group of five hundred monks returned from the south, led by a monk named Purāṇa. When he was asked to approve of the dharma and vinaya that had been codified by the council, he declined, saying that he preferred to remember and retain what he had heard directly from the mouth of the Buddha rather than what had been chanted by the elders. Purāṇa also disputed eight points of the vinaya concerning the proper storage and consumption of food. This incident, whether or not it has any historical basis, suggests that disagreements about the contents of the Buddha's teaching began to arise shortly after his death.

**Council, 2nd**. The second council was held at VAIŚĀLĪ, some one hundred years after the Buddha's death. It is said that the monk YAŚAS was traveling in Vaiśālī when he observed the monks from the city, identified as VṚJIPUTRAKAS, receiving alms in the form of gold and silver directly from the laity, in violation of the disciplinary prohibition against monks' handling gold and silver. He also found that the monks had identified ten points in the VINAYA that they considered were sufficiently minor to be ignored, despite the decision at the first council (see COUNCIL, FIRST) not to disregard any of the minor precepts. The ten violations in question were: (1) carrying salt in an animal horn; (2) eating when the shadow of the sundial is two fingerbreadths past noon; (3) after eating, traveling to another village on the same day to eat another meal; (4) holding several assemblies within the same boundary (SĪMĀ) during the same fortnight observance; (5) making a monastic decision with an incomplete assembly and subsequently receiving the approval of the absent monks; (6) citing precedent as a justification for violating monastic procedures; (7) drinking milk whey after mealtime; (8) drinking unfermented wine; (9) using mats with fringe; and (10) accepting gold and silver. Yaśas informed the monks that these were indeed violations of the disciplinary code, at which point the monks are said to have offered him a share of the gold and silver they had collected; when he refused, they expelled him from the order. Yaśas sought support of several respected monks in the west, including ŚĀṆAKAVĀSIN and REVATA, and together with other monks, they travelled together to Vaiśālī. Once there, Revata went to Sarvagāmin, the senior-most monk in the order, who was said to have been a disciple of ĀNANDA. However, when Revata questioned him about the ten points, the elder monk refused to discuss them in private. At Revata's suggestion, a jury of eight monks was appointed, with four representatives from each party. Revata was selected as one of four from the party declaring the ten practices to be violations, and it was Revata who publicly put the questions to Sarvagāmin. In each case, he said that the practice in question was a violation of the vinaya. Seven hundred monks then gathered to recite the vinaya. Those who did not accept the decision of the council held their own convocation, which they called the MAHĀSĀMGHIKA, or "Great Assembly." This event is sometimes referred to as "the great schism." The second council is generally accepted as a historical event. ¶ Some accounts make MAHĀDEVA a participant at the second council, which is said to have resulted in the schism of the SAMGHA into the conservative STHAVIRANIKĀYA and the more liberal Mahāsāṃghika. However, the chief points of controversy that led to the convening of the council seem not to have been Mahādeva's five theses, but rather these ten relatively minor rules of monastic discipline. If Mahādeva was a historical figure, it is more likely that he was involved in a later schism that occurred within the Mahāsāṃghika, as a result of which the followers of Mahādeva formed the CAITYA sect. See also SAṂGĪTI.

**Council, 3rd**. The third council is said to have been held at PĀṬALIPUTRA under the patronage of the Mauryan Emperor AŚOKA. According to Pāli sources, Aśoka's lavish support of the Buddhist SAṂGHA had prompted many non-Buddhist mendicants and brāhmaṇas to don the robes of Buddhist monks in order to receive alms. With the legitimate saṃgha unable to forcibly remove the false monks from their midst, the UPOṢADHA ceremony was suspended. The emperor sent a minister to order the monks to continue to perform the ceremony. When they refused, he beheaded a number of monks, only stopping when he was about to behead the emperor's ordained brother. The emperor eventually summoned the distinguished monk MOGGALIPUTTATISSA, who taught him the correct DHARMA and VINAYA in order that Aśoka might intervene on behalf of the legitimate party. Aśoka interrogated the saṃgha and, using the authority of the state, defrocked those found to be false monks. With the saṃgha thus purified of corruption, Moggaliputtatissa selected a group of one thousand monks from a total of sixty thousand and convened a council to rehearse the Buddha's teachings as preserved in the Pāli tipiṭaka (S. TRIPIṬAKA) and its commentaries (AṬṬHAKATHĀ). At that same time, Moggaliputtatissa composed the KATHĀVATTHU, the seventh and last book of the Pāli abhidhammapiṭaka, in order to refute various heretical Buddhist views; he also declared the dharma as it was understood by the VIBHAJYAVĀDA to be orthodox. At the conclusion of the council, Moggaliputtatissa dispatched missionaries to nine neighboring lands to propagate the newly purified teaching. Since accounts of this council only appear in Pāli sources, the historicity of this council has been questioned by modern scholars. It is possible that such a council occurred only within the STHAVIRANIKĀYA tradition, but perhaps a century later, in the last half of the second century BCE, at which time the *Kathāvatthu* was compiled. See also SAṂGĪTI.

**Council, 4th**. Two different events are referred to as the fourth council. According to the account of the Chinese pilgrim XUANZANG, four hundred years after the Buddha's death, King

Kaniṣka called an assembly of five hundred arhats, either in Gandhāra or Kashmir, to compile the canon once again. Under the direction of the monk Vasumitra, the Sarvāstivāda monks compiled the vinaya and composed the Abhidharmamahāvibhāṣā. This council is not now considered to have been a historical event and the *Mahāvibhāṣā* was likely composed long after the reign of Kaniṣka. The second event that is known as the fourth council took place in Sri Lanka under King Vaṭṭagāmaṇi Abhaya in 25 bce. Up until this time the canon (P. tipiṭaka, S. tripiṭaka) had been maintained entirely orally, with different monastic families of monks responsible for its recitation (see dharmabhāṇaka). Fearing that famine and social discord might lead to the death of those monks and hence the loss of the canon, the king convened a council at the Mahāvihāra in the capital of Anurādhapura, where the canon was recited by five hundred monks and then inscribed onto palm leaves. According to tradition this was the first time that the canon was committed to writing. See also saṃgīti.

**Council, 5th**. What Burmese Buddhism regards as the fifth council was convened in 1868, when King Mindon Min summoned 2,400 learned monks from throughout the kingdom to Mandalay to revise and recite the Pāli tipiṭaka. The recitation of the canon lasted over a period of seven months. In 1871, the revised Burmese canon was inscribed in Burmese script on 729 stone slabs that were erected, each in its own shrine, in concentric rings around the massive Kuthodaw Pagoda (Pagoda of Great Merit). The entire complex occupies fourteen acres and is situated to the northeast of the fortified city at the base of Mandalay Hill. Nearby is the Sandamuni Pagoda, constructed along a similar plan; it enshrines 1,171 slabs on which are inscribed the Pāli commentaries.

**Council, 6th**. What the Theravāda school calls the sixth council was held in Rangoon from 1954 to 1956, commemorating the 2,500th anniversary of the Buddha's passage into parinirvāṇa. The convocation was sponsored by the Burmese government under Prime Minister U Nu. A special cave was constructed for the purpose, since the first council was also said to have been held in a cave. At this event, attended by some two thousand five hundred monks from eight Theravāda countries, the Pāli canon was edited and recited, with discrepancies among versions in the various Southeast Asian scripts noted and corrected. Mahasi Sayadaw was appointed to the dual position of pucchaka (questioner) and osana (editor). See also saṃgīti.

**Council of Bsam yas**. See Bsam yas Debate.

**Council of Lha sa**. See Bsam yas Debate.

**craving**. See tṛṣṇā; taṇhā; cf. lobha.

**Csoma de Kőrös, Alexander**. (1784–1842). Early European scholar of Tibet and its Buddhist culture. Csoma de Kőrös was born in Transylvania, to a family descended from Magyar nobility. He developed an early interest in the origins of his Hungarian ancestry, which led him to dedicate himself to learning more about the history of the Hungarian language. Through his studies in Arabic, he eventually came to the conclusion that Hungarian had developed in the Tarim Basin of modern Xinjiang province in China, and so in 1819 he set out on foot for Yarkand in Turkestan. He crossed the mountains into Ladakh and reached Kashmir in 1822. There, he spent a year travelling between Srinagar and Leh (the capital of Ladakh) in the hopes of finding a caravan to join in order to make his way to Yarkand. On one of these journeys, Csoma de Kőrös met William Moorcroft, a veterinarian working for the British government. Moorcroft suggested that Csoma de Kőrös' research might benefit more from traveling to Lha sa to learn about Tibetan language and literature. Although he never reached Lha sa, Csoma de Kőrös spent nine years in monasteries in Ladakh and Zanskar learning Tibetan and studying Tibetan Buddhist texts. He devoted much of his research time to mastering Buddhist terminology. In 1830, he left for Calcutta, where he would live for eleven years. In Calcutta, Csoma de Kőrös worked for the British East Indian Company through the Asiatic Society cataloguing Tibetan texts that were sent by Brian Houghton Hodgson (1800–1894). He also published the first Tibetan grammar and dictionary in English, a translation of a ninth-century catalogue of Buddhist terminology, the Mahāvyutpatti, and a number of scholarly articles on the Tibetan canon. He died of malaria in Darjeeling (1842) as he continued his search for the ancestral homeland of the Hungarian people. Although Csoma de Kőrös was not a Buddhist, he was declared a bodhisattva by Taishō University in Tokyo in 1933 and is often described as the "Father of Tibetology."

**Cūḍapanthaka**. (P. Cūḷapanthaka/Cullapantha; T. Lam phran bstan; C. Zhutubantuojia; J. Chūdahantaka; K. Chudobant'akka 注荼半托迦). An eminent arhat declared in Pāli sources as foremost among the Buddha's disciples in his ability to create mind-made bodies (manomayakāya) and to manipulate mind (cittavivaṭṭa). Cūḍapanthaka was the younger of two brothers born to a merchant's daughter from Rājagṛha who had eloped with a slave. Each time she became pregnant, she wanted to return home to give birth to her children, but both were born during her journey home. For this reason, the brothers were named "Greater" Roadside (Mahāpanthaka; see Panthaka) and "Lesser" Roadside. The boys were eventually taken to Rājagṛha and raised by their grandparents, who were devoted to the Buddha. The elder brother Panthaka often accompanied his grandfather to listen to the Buddha's sermons and was inspired to be ordained. He proved to be an able monk, skilled in doctrine, and eventually attained arhatship. He later ordained his younger brother Cūḍapanthaka but was gravely disappointed in his brother's inability to memorize even a single verse of the dharma. Panthaka was so disappointed that he advised his brother to leave the order, much to the latter's distress. Once, the Buddha's physician Jīvaka invited the

Buddha and his monks to a morning meal. Panthaka gathered the monks together on the appointed day to attend the meal but intentionally omitted Cūḍapanthaka. So hurt was Cūḍapanthaka by his brother's contempt that he decided to return to lay life. The Buddha, knowing his mental state, comforted the young monk and taught him a simple exercise: he instructed him to sit facing east and, while repeating the phrase "rajoharaṇaṃ" ("cleaning off the dirt"), continue to wipe his face with a clean cloth. As Cūḍapanthaka noticed the cloth getting dirty from wiping off his sweat, he gained insight into the reality of impermanence (ANITYA) and immediately attained arhatship and was equipped with the four analytical knowledges (PRATISAṂVID), including knowledge of the entire canon (TRIPIṬAKA). (According to other versions of the story, he came to a similar realization through sweeping.) Thereafter Cūḍapanthaka became renowned for his vast learning, as well as for his supranormal powers. He was a master of meditative concentration (SAMĀDHI) and of the subtle-materiality absorptions (RŪPĀVACARADHYĀNA). He could simultaneously create a thousand unique mind-made bodies (MANOMAYAKĀYA), while other meditative specialists in the order could at best produce only two or three. ¶ Cūḍapanthaka is also traditionally listed as the last of the sixteen arhat elders (ṢOḌAŚASTHAVIRA), who were charged by the Buddha with protecting his dispensation until the advent of the next buddha, MAITREYA. In CHANYUE GUANXIU's standard Chinese depiction, Cūḍapanthaka sits among withered trees, his left hand raised with fingers slightly bent, and his right hand resting on his right thigh, holding a fan.

**Cūḷadhammasamādānasutta**. (C. Shoufa jing; J. Juhōkyō; K. Subŏp kyŏng 受法經). In Pāli, "Shorter Discourse on Undertaking the Dharma"; the forty-fifth sutta of the MAJJHIMANIKĀYA (a separate SARVĀSTIVĀDA recension appears as the 174th sūtra in the Chinese translation of the MADHYAMĀGAMA); preached by the Buddha to a gathering of monks in the JETAVANA Grove at Sāvatthi (S. ŚRĀVASTĪ). The Buddha describes four ways of undertaking things in this life and the good and bad consequences that accrue to one who follows these ways. The first way is to live happily in the present, but suffer a painful consequence in the future, e.g., when a person wantonly indulges in sensual pleasures in the present life and, as a result, is reborn into a woeful state later. The second way is to live a painful existence in the present, and suffer a painful consequence in the future; this is the case with ascetics who mortify their flesh only to be reborn in a woeful state. The third way is to live a painful existence in the present, but enjoy a happy consequence in the future; this is the case with a person who suffers in this life due to greed, hatred, and delusion but nevertheless strives to lead a blameless life and is consequently reborn in a happy existence as a human or lesser divinity (DEVA). The fourth way is to live happily in the present, and enjoy a happy consequence, as is the case with a person who cultivates the meditative absorptions (JHĀNA; S. DHYĀNA); he is happy in the present life and is rewarded with a happy rebirth as a BRAHMĀ divinity. An expanded version of this sermon is found in the MAHĀDHAMMASAMĀDĀNASUTTA, or "Longer Discourse on Undertaking the Dharma," also contained in the *Majjhimanikāya*.

**Cūḷadukkhakkhandhasutta**. (C. Kuyin jing; J. Kuongyō; K. Koŭm kyŏng 苦陰經). In Pāli, "Shorter Discourse on the Mass of Suffering"; the fourteenth sutta in the MAJJHIMANIKĀYA (a separate SARVĀSTIVĀDA recension appears as the one hundredth sūtra in the Chinese translation of the MADHYAMĀGAMA); preached by the Buddha to the Sakiyan prince Mahānāma at Kapilavatthu (S. KAPILAVASTU). The Buddha explains the full implications of sensual pleasures, the advantages of renouncing them, and the path needed to escape from their influence. In a discussion with JAINA ascetics, he describes how greed, ill-will, and ignorance cause moral defilement and misery.

**Cūḷagopālakasutta**. In Pāli, "Shorter Discourse on the Cowherd"; the thirty-fourth sutta in the MAJJHIMANIKĀYA (separate recensions appear, but without title, in the Chinese translations of the EKOTTARĀGAMA and SAṂYUKTĀGAMA); preached by the Buddha to an assembly of monks at Ukkācelā in the land of the Vajji (S. Vṛji). The Buddha explains that if monks are not equipped with the requisite skills in understanding this world and the next, the realm of death and the deathless, etc., the teachings cannot be expected to prosper. He uses the example of an unskillful cowherd under whose guidance a herd is led across a river, only to meet with destruction before they reach the other shore.

**Cūḷagosiṅgasutta**. (C. Niujiaosuoluolin jing; J. Gokakusararingyō; K. Ugaksararim kyŏng 牛角娑羅林經). In Pāli, "Shorter Discourse in Gosiṅga Park"; the thirty-first sutta in the MAJJHIMANIKĀYA (a separate SARVĀSTIVĀDA recension appears as the 185th sūtra in the Chinese translation of the MADHYAMĀGAMA; there is also a recension of uncertain affiliation that appears without title in the Chinese translation of the EKOTTARĀGAMA). The Buddha visits the eminent monks, Anuruddha (S. ANIRUDDHA), Nandiya, and Kimila while the three are residing in the Gosiṅga grove. The monks describe to him how they carry out their daily activities in cooperation with one another and the Buddha praises them for their harmonious lifestyle, declaring it to be an adornment to the grove.

**Cūḷahatthipadopamasutta**. (C. Xiangjiyu jing; J. Zōshakuyugyō; K. Sangjŏgyu kyŏng 象跡喻經). In Pāli, "Shorter Discourse on the Simile of the Elephant's Footprint"; the twenty-seventh sutta in the MAJJHIMANIKĀYA (a separate SARVĀSTIVĀDA recension appears as the 146th sūtra in the Chinese translation of the MADHYAMĀGAMA), preached by the Buddha to the brāhmaṇa Jāṇussoṇi at the JETAVANA grove in the city of Sāvatthi (ŚRĀVASTĪ). Jāṇussoṇi asks the Buddha whether a person could infer something of the virtues of the Buddha and his teachings in the same way that a hunter can infer the size of an elephant from its footprint. The Buddha responds that the virtues of the Buddha and his teachings could only be fully comprehended by following the teachings oneself until one has attained the final goal of NIRVĀṆA; this is just as with a hunter, who can only truly know the size of an elephant by following its tracks and seeing it directly at its watering hole. The Buddha then provides a systematic outline of his path of training, from morality (sīla, S. ŚĪLA), through the four meditative absorptions (jhāna; S. DHYĀNA), to the three higher knowledges (tevijjā; S. TRIVIDYĀ).

**Cūḷaniddesa**. In Pāli, "Shorter Exposition," second part of the *Niddesa* ("Exposition"), an early commentarial work on the SUTTANIPĀTA included in the Pāli SUTTAPIṬAKA as the eleventh book of the KHUDDAKANIKĀYA; also written as *Cullaniddesa*. Attributed by tradition to the Buddha's chief disciple, Sāriputta (S. ŚĀRIPUTRA), the *Niddesa* is divided into two sections: the MAHĀNIDDESA ("Longer Exposition"), and *Cūḷaniddesa*. The *Mahāniddesa* comments on the sixteen suttas (S. SŪTRA) of the AṬṬHAKAVAGGA chapter of the *Suttanipāta*, while the *Cūḷaniddesa* comments on the sixteen suttas of the Parāyaṇavagga chapter and on the *Khaggavisānasutta* (see KHAḌGAVIṢĀṆA). The *Mahāniddesa* and *Cūḷaniddesa* do not comment on any of the remaining contents of the *Suttanipāta*, a feature that has suggested to historians that at the time of their composition the Aṭṭhakavagga and Parāyaṇavagga were autonomous anthologies not yet incorporated into the *Suttanipāta*, and that the *Khaggavisānasutta* likewise circulated independently. The exegesis given to the *Suttanipāta* by the *Mahā-* and *Cūḷaniddesa* displays the influence of the Pāli ABHIDHAMMA (S. ABHIDHARMA) and passages from it are frequently quoted in the VISUDDHIMAGGA. Both parts of the *Niddesa* are formulaic in structure, a feature that appears to have been designed as a pedagogical aid to facilitate memorization. In Western scholarship, there has long been a debate regarding the dates of these two compositions, with some scholars dating them as early as the third century BCE, others to as late as the second century CE. The *Mahā-* and *Cūḷaniddesa* are the only commentarial texts besides the SUTTAVIBHAṄGA of the VINAYAPIṬAKA to be included in the Sri Lankan and Thai recensions of the Pāli canon. In contrast, the Burmese canon includes two additional early commentaries, the NETTIPAKARAṆA and PEṬAKOPADESA, as books sixteen and seventeen in its version of the *Khuddakanikāya*.

**Cūḷasaccakasutta**. In Pāli, "Shorter Discourse to Saccaka"; thirty-fifth sutta contained in the MAJJHIMANIKĀYA (two separate recensions appear, but without title, in the Chinese translations of the EKOTTARĀGAMA and SAṂYUKTĀGAMA); preached by the Buddha to the wandering ascetic Saccaka in the Mahāvana forest outside the city of Vesālī (S. VAIŚĀLĪ). Saccaka maintained that that the five aggregates (P. khandha; S. SKANDHA) of materiality (RŪPA), sensations (VEDANĀ), perception (P. saññā; S. saṃjñā), conditioning factors (P. saṅkhāra; S. SAṂSKĀRA), and consciousness (P. viññāṇa; S. VIJÑĀNA) are one's self (P. attan; S. ĀTMAN), and that it was this self that experienced the results of good and bad deeds (P. kamma; S. KARMAN). The Buddha refutes this view by pointing out that all of the aggregates are impermanent (P. anicca; S. ANITYA), unsatisfactory or suffering (P. dukkha; S. DUḤKHA), nonself (P. anatta; S. ANĀTMAN) and beyond one's control.

**Cūḷasāropamasutta**. In Pāli, "Shorter Discourse on the Simile of the Heartwood"; thirtieth sutta in the MAJJHIMANIKĀYA (a separate unidentified recension appears, without title, in the Chinese translation of the EKOTTARĀGAMA), preached by the Buddha to the brāhmaṇa Piṅgalakoccha at the JETAVANA Grove in the town of Sāvatthi (S. ŚRĀVASTĪ). Piṅgalakoccha asks whether the six mendicant teachers (P. samaṇa ; ŚRAMAṆA) who were the Buddha's rivals were, as they claimed, all buddhas themselves. The Buddha responds by explaining that, whereas the religious practices set forth by his rivals could lead to fame and profit and to the attainment of supranormal powers (P. abhiññā; S. ABHIJÑĀ), these were but like the leaves and twigs of a tree. Only the holy life (P. brahmacariya; S. BRAHMACARYA) set forth by the Buddha leads to the status of arahant (S ARHAT), which is like the heartwood of a tree.

**Cūḷasīhanādasutta**. (C. Shizihou jing; J. Shishikukyō; K. Sajahu kyŏng 師子吼經). In Pāli, "Shorter Discourse on the Lion's Roar"; eleventh sutta in the MAJJHIMANIKĀYA (a SARVĀSTIVĀDA recension appears as the 103rd sūtra in the Chinese translation of the MADHYAMĀGAMA; a separate recension of unidentified affiliation appears, without title, in the Chinese translation of the EKOTTARĀGAMA), preached by the Buddha to a group of monks in the JETAVANA grove in the city of Sāvatthi (S. ŚRĀVASTĪ). The Buddha explains how only in his teachings can one attain any of the four degrees of sanctity (see ĀRYAPUDGALA): stream-enterer, once-returner, nonreturner, and perfected ARHAT; all other teachings lack these. Also, only in his teachings are found a rejection of all notions of a perduring self (P. atta; S. ĀTMAN).

**Cūḷāssapurasutta**. (C. Mayi jing; J. Meyūkyō; K. Maŭp kyŏng 馬邑經). In Pāli, "Shorter Discourse at Assapura"; the fortieth sutta in the MAJJHIMANIKĀYA (a separate SARVĀSTIVĀDA recension appears as the 183rd sūtra in the Chinese translation of the MADHYAMĀGAMA); preached by the Buddha to a group of monks dwelling in the market town of Assapura in the country of the Aṅgans. The people of Assapura were greatly devoted to the Buddha, the DHARMA, and the SAṂGHA and were especially generous in their support of the community of monks. In recognition of their generosity, the Buddha advised his monks that the true path of the recluse is not concerned with mere outward purification through austerities but rather with inward purification through freedom from passion and mental defilements. The dedicated monk should therefore devote himself to the path laid down by the Buddha until he has abandoned twelve unwholesome states of mind: (1)

covetousness, (2) ill will, (3) anger, (4) resentment, (5) contempt, (6) insolence, (7) envy, (8) greed, (9) fraud, (10) deceit, (11) evil wishes, and (12) wrong view. Having abandoned these twelve, the monk should then strive to cultivate the divine abidings (BRAHMAVIHĀRA) of loving-kindness, compassion, sympathetic joy, and equanimity; through those virtues, the monk attains inner peace and thereby practices the true path of the recluse.

**Cūḷataṇhāsaṅkhayasutta**. In Pāli, "Shorter Discourse on the Destruction of Craving"; the thirty-seventh sutta in the MAJJHIMANIKĀYA (two separate recensions appear, but without title, in the Chinese translations of the EKOTTARĀGAMA and SAṂYUKTĀGAMA), preached by the Buddha to Sakka (S. ŚAKRA), king of the gods, in the city of Sāvatthi (S. ŚRĀVASTĪ). Sakka inquires how the Buddha trained himself so that he achieved the destruction of craving and reached the ultimate goal of liberation, whereby he became foremost among humans and gods. In response, the Buddha describes how a householder, after renouncing the world, trains himself to purify his mind of mental defilements and reaches the final goal. Mahāmoggallāna (MAHĀMAUDGALYĀYANA) overhears the sermon and travels to the heaven of the thirty-three (P. tāvatiṃsa; S. TRĀYASTRIṂŚA) to find out whether Sakka had correctly understood the meaning of the Buddha's words. While there, Sakka gives Mahāmoggallāna a tour of his magnificent palace, which the king explains was constructed following the defeat of the demigods (ASURA).

**Cūḷavagga**. [alt. Cullavagga]. In Pāli, "Lesser Chapter"; one of the sections of the Pāli "basket of discipline" (VINAYAPIṬAKA). The second major division of the Pāli VINAYA, the KHANDHAKA (Collections), is subdivided between the MAHĀVAGGA ("Great Chapter") and the *Cūḷavagga*. The *Cūḷavagga* includes twelve sections, in two parts that differ markedly in length and scope. The first part (chaps. 1–10) covers a variety of disciplinary regulations and relatively minor rules of monastic etiquette, ranging from transactions (P. saṅghakamma; S. SAṂGHAKARMAN) for imposing penance and probation on monks to methods of settling disputes within the order, apportioning lodging, handling schism within the order, and proper procedures for the ordination of nuns (P. bhikkhunī; S. BHIKṢUṆĪ). The second part (chaps. 11–12) continues the *Mahāvagga*'s narrative on the history of the SAṂGHA, relating events that followed the Buddha's PARINIRVĀṆA, including the first council at RĀJAGṚHA shortly after his death and the second council at VAIŚĀLĪ a century or so later (see COUNCIL, FIRST; COUNCIL, SECOND).

**Cūḷavaṃsa**. In Pāli, "The Shorter Chronicle"; a historical chronicle of Sri Lanka and a continuation of the MAHĀVAṂSA. Written in segments by several authors beginning in the thirteenth century and continuing through the eighteenth century, the text offers a synopsis of the history of the island and its religion from the reign of Sirimeghavaṇṇa (362–390 CE) to that of Sirivikkamarājasīha (1798–1815 CE).

**Cūḷavedallasutta**. (C. Fale biqiuni jing; J. Hōraku bikunikyō; K. Pŏmnak piguni kyŏng 法樂比丘尼經). In Pāli, "Shorter Discourse on Points of Doctrine"; the forty-fourth sutta in the MAJJHIMANIKĀYA (a separate SARVĀSTIVĀDA recension appears as the 210th sūtra in the Chinese translation of the MADHYAMĀGAMA; the entire discourse is also subsumed in the Tibetan translation of Śamathadeva's commentary to the ABHIDHARMAKOŚABHĀṢYA), expounded by the nun Dhammadinnā (S. DHARMADINNĀ) to her former husband, the householder Visākha, at the Veḷuvana (S. VEṆUVANAVIHĀRA) bamboo grove in Rājagaha (S. RĀJAGṚHA). Visākha approached Dhammadinnā and questioned her concerning a number of points of doctrine preached by the Buddha. These questions included: what is the nature of this existing body (P. sakkāya; S. satkāya); what is its origin (SAMUDAYA), its cessation (NIRODHA), and the path (P. magga; S. MĀRGA) leading to its cessation; how does wrong view concerning this body (P. sakkāyadiṭṭhi; S. SATKĀYADṚṢṬI) arise and how is it removed; what is the noble eightfold path; what is concentration (SAMĀDHI); what are bodily, verbal, and mental formations; what is the attainment of cessation (nirodha); what is sensation (VEDANĀ); what are the underlying tendencies with regard to pleasant, painful, and neutral sensations and how should these be overcome; and what are the counterparts of pleasant, painful, and neutral sensations. Dhammadinnā answered all of the questions put to her to the satisfaction of the householder Visākha—proving why the Buddha considered her foremost among his nun disciples in the gift of preaching.

**Cullavagga**. (P). See CŪḶAVAGGA.

**Cunda**. (T. Skul byed; C. Zhuntuo; J. Junda; K. Chunda 準陀). In Sanskrit and Pāli, the proper name of a metalworker famous, or perhaps infamous, for having offered the Buddha his final meal before his demise. According to the Pāli account, the Buddha was traveling to Kusinārā (S. KUŚINAGARĪ) and interrupted his journey to rest at Cunda's mango grove in Pāvā. Cunda paid his respects to the Buddha and invited him and his followers for the morning meal the next day. Cunda prepared for them sweet rice, cakes, and SŪKARAMADDAVA, literally "tender boar" or "soft boar's [food]." There has been much debate, both in the tradition and among modern scholars, as to the meaning of this term. It is unclear whether it means something soft that is consumed by boars (such as a type of mushroom, truffle, or bamboo shoots that had been trampled by boars) or some kind of pork dish. The Indian and Sinhalese commentators prefer, although not unanimously, the latter interpretation. Some East Asian recensions of Cunda's story state that he offered the Buddha mushrooms rather than pork for his last meal, thus preserving the idea that the Buddha was vegetarian. At the meal, the Buddha announced that he alone should be served the dish, and what was left over should be buried, for none but a buddha could survive eating it. This has led some modern interpreters to suggest that the meal had been poisoned, but no such implication appears in traditional commentaries. Shortly thereafter, the Buddha became afflicted with the dysentery from which he would eventually die. Shortly before his death, the Buddha instructed his disciple ĀNANDA to visit Cunda and reassure the layman that he was blameless; in fact, he should rejoice at the great merit he earned for having given the Buddha his last meal. In an earlier meeting, Cunda remarked to the Buddha that he approved of Brahmanical rites of purification, to which the Buddha responded with a sermon on the threefold defilement and purification of the body, the fourfold defilement and purification of speech, and the threefold defilement and purification of the mind. Although Cunda is not recorded as having ever reached any degree of spiritual attainment, he did have his doubts removed by the Buddha, whom he regarded as his teacher. There are a variety of different transcriptions of the name in Chinese, of which the above is among the most common.

**Cundī**. (T. Skul byed ma; C. Zhunti; J. Juntei; K. Chunje 准提). In Sanskrit, the name Cundī (with many orthographic variations) probably connotes a prostitute or other woman of low caste but specifically denotes a prominent local ogress (YAKṢIṆĪ), whose divinized form becomes the subject of an important Buddhist cult starting in the eighth century. Her worship began in the Bengal and Orissa regions of the Indian subcontinent, where she became the patron goddess of the Pāla dynasty, and soon spread throughout India, and into Sri Lanka, Southeast Asia, and Tibet, eventually making its way to East Asia. Cundī was originally an independent focus of cultic worship, who only later (as in the Japanese SHINGONSHŪ) was incorporated into such broader cultic practices as those focused on the "womb MAṆḌALA" (see TAIZŌKAI). Several scriptures related to her cult were translated into Chinese starting in the early eighth century, and she lends her name to both a MUDRĀ as well as an influential DHĀRAṆĪ: namaḥ saptānāṃ samyaksaṃbuddhakoṭīṇāṃ tadyathā: oṃ cale cule cunde svāhā. The dhāraṇī attributed to Cundī is said to convey infinite power because it is in continuous recitation by myriads of buddhas; hence, an adept who participates in this ongoing recitation will accrue manifold benefits and purify himself from unwholesome actions. The efficacy of the dhāraṇī is said to be particularly pronounced when it is recited before an image of Cundī while the accompanying Cundī mudrā is also being performed. This dhāraṇī also gives Cundī her common epithet of "Goddess of the Seventy Million [Buddhas]," which is sometimes mistakenly interpreted (based on a misreading of the Chinese) as the "Mother of the Seventy Million Buddhas." The texts also provide elaborate directions on how to portray her and paint her image. In Cundī's most common depiction, she has eighteen arms (each holding specific implements) and is sitting atop a lotus flower (PADMA) while being worshipped by two ophidian deities.

**cyutyupapādānusmṛti**. (S). See CYUTYUPAPATTIJÑĀNA.

**cyutyupapattijñāna**. [alt. cyutyupapādānusmṛti] (P. cutūpapātañāṇa; T. 'chi 'pho ba dang skye ba rjes su dran pa; C. shengsizhi; J. shōjichi; K. saengsaji 生死智). In Sanskrit, lit., "recollection of the disappearance [in one life] and rebirth [in another]," viz., "insight into the future rebirth destinies" of all other beings, a by-product of the "divine eye" (DIVYACAKṢUS), or clairvoyance, and the second of the "three knowledges" (TRIVIDYĀ). This recollection comes as a by-product of the enlightenment experience of a "worthy one" (ARHAT), and is an insight achieved by the Buddha during the second watch of the night of his own enlightenment. Through his enlightenment, the adept realizes not only that himself and all beings have been governed by the association between past actions (KARMAN) and their fruitions (VIPĀKA) throughout all their past lives; but through this insight, he also realizes that all other beings continue to be governed by their actions, and he is able to observe where beings will be reborn in the future as well. Specifically, one who possesses this insight sees the disappearance and arising of beings as low or noble, beautiful or ugly, etc., according to their good and evil deeds (KARMAN) performed through body, speech, and mind. Those who revile the noble ones (ĀRYAPUDGALA), hold perverse views (MITHYĀDṚṢṬI), and act in accordance with perverse views are observed to be reborn in lower realms of existence, e.g., in baleful destinies (APĀYA; DURGATI) such as the hells. Those who honor the noble ones, hold right views, and act in accordance with right views are observed to be reborn in higher realms of existence, e.g., in pleasant destinies such as the heavens. This ability is also listed as one of the superknowledges (ABHIJÑĀ).

# D

**Da banniepan jing jijie**. (J. Daihatsunehangyō juge; K. Tae panyŏlban kyŏng chiphae 大般涅槃經集解). In Chinese, "Compilation and Explanation of the MAHĀPARINIRVĀṆASŪTRA"; compiled by the monk Baoliang (444–509); the oldest and most comprehensive collection of commentaries on the *Mahāparinirvāṇasūtra*, in a total of seventy-one rolls. The *Da banniepanjing jijie* explicates the title and content of each chapter of the sūtra by quoting the words and sayings of different commentators, of whom Baoliang is but one. The influential Chinese commentaries on the *Mahāparinirvāṇasūtra* by JIZANG and GUANDING rely heavily upon this work.

**Dabei zhou**. (J. Daihiju; K. Taebi chu 大悲咒). In Chinese, "Great Compassion Spell," also known as the Qianshou zhou; an esoteric code (DHĀRAṆĪ) associated with the BODHISATTVA AVALOKITEŚVARA in his guise as MAHĀKARUṆIKA, which is widely used liturgically in East Asian Buddhism, especially in funeral ceremonies. See the extensive treatment of this dhāraṇī in QIANSHOU JING, s.v.

**Daci'ensi**. (J. Daijionji; K. Taejaŭnsa 大慈恩寺). In Chinese, the "Beneficence of Great Compassion Monastery" or "Great Maternal Grace Monastery"; a major scholastic center during the Sui and Tang dynasties, located in the imperial capital of Chang'an (present-day Xi'an). Originally founded in 589 CE during the Sui dynasty as Wulousi (Free of Contaminants Monastery), it was later rebuilt in 648 CE during the Tang by the prince who would later become the Gaozong emperor (r. 649–683). The monastery was rebuilt to honor the prince's deceased mother, Empress Wende (601–636 CE), in whose memory it was given its new name. The monastery became best known as the base for the translation bureau established by the pilgrim and scholar XUANZANG (600/602–664 CE) and his collaborators, including WŎNCH'ŬK (C. Yuance) and KUIJI. At the monastery, Xuanzang and his team translated much of the scholastic literature of Indian Buddhism, including the ABHIDHARMAMAHĀVIBHĀṢĀ, *ABHIDHARMANYĀYĀNUSĀRA, NYĀYAMUKHA, and CHENG WEISHI LUN. In 652 CE, Xuanzang commissioned a pagoda, named the DAYAN TA (Great Wild Goose Pagoda), in order to house the numerous Sanskrit manuscripts and Buddhist images he had brought back with him from his sojourn in India; the originally five-story stone pagoda is still a major tourist attraction in Xi'an.

**dade**. (J. daitoku; K. taedŏk 大德). In Chinese, "great virtue"; a reference to spiritual virtuosi, such as buddhas, BODHISATTVAs, and eminent monks. During the Tang dynasty, the special title dade was given periodically to ten worthy monks. The term dade also was used as a second-person pronoun in certain periods. Elderly monks were also sometimes referred to as dade, especially in the CHAN tradition. In Korea, the term continues to be used to designate an official monastic office that is occupied by the most senior monks of the CHOGYE CHONG, whose only primary duty is to advise the order through their "great virtue" and help in the selection of the most senior members of the ecclesiastical hierarchy. See also SŬNGKWA.

**Dafangguang yuanjue xiuduoluo liaoyi jing**. (大方廣圓覺修多羅了義經). In Chinese, "The Expanded Sūtra of Perfect Enlightenment, a Book of Definitive Meaning (NĪTĀRTHA)"; the extended Chinese title of the YUANJUE JING ("Book of Perfect Enlightenment"). See YUANJUE JING.

**dāgoba**. Also dāgaba; the Sinhalese word for STŪPA. See STŪPA.

**Dag pa shel ri**. (T). See TSA RI.

**Daguan Zhenke**. (J. Takkan Shinka; K. Talgwan Chin'ga 達觀眞可) (1543–1603). Chinese CHAN master of the Ming dynasty, also known as ZIBO. Daguan was a native of Jugu prefecture in Jiangsu province. He was ordained at age sixteen and is said to have attained awakening after reading the following verse by the layman Zhang Zhuo (d.u.), a disciple of the Chan master SHISHUANG QINGZHU: "Cutting off deluded thoughts increases maladies ever more,/ Heading out toward true suchness is also heresy" (duanji wangxiang zhongzeng bing,/ quxiang zhenru yishi xie). Like his influential contemporaries HANSHAN DEQING and YUNQI ZHUHONG, he was renowned for his advocacy of NIANFO Chan, in which Chan meditative practice was combined with the invocation or recitation of the name of the buddha AMITĀBHA. Daguan was known as one of the four great monks of the Ming dynasty along with Hanshan Deqing (1546–1623), Yunqi Zhuhong (1535–1615), and OUYI ZHIXU (1599–1655). Daguan's teachings are recorded in the *Zibo zunzhe quanji* and *Zibo laoren shiji*.

**Dahong Bao'en**. (J. Daikō Hōon; K. Taehong Poŭn 大洪報恩) (1058–1111). Chinese CHAN master of the CAODONG lineage. Dahong was a native of Liyang in present-day Henan province. Raised in a traditional family, he became an official at an early age, but later abandoned the position, with the court's permission, in order to ordain as a monk. He studied under the Chan master TOUZI YIQING and became his disciple. Dahong was later invited by the prime minister to lecture at the famed monastery of SHAOLINSI. In response to still another request, he moved to Mt. Dahong in Suizhou prefecture (present-day Hubei province), whence he acquired his toponym, and became the first Chan monk to convert a VINAYA monastery into a Chan center, which he named Chongning Baoshou Chanyuan. Dahong also became close friends with the powerful and outspoken statesman ZHANG SHANGYING (1043–1122). Dahong is known to have composed several texts including a history of the Caodong tradition, *Caodong zongpai lu*, and manuals for conferring the precepts, such as the *Shou puti xinjie wen* and *Luofa shoujie yiwen*; none of these texts are extant.

**Dahong Shousui**. (J. Daikō Shusui; K. Taehong Susu 大洪守遂) (1072–1147). Chinese CHAN master in the CAODONG lineage. Dahong was a native of Suining in present-day Sichuan province. He was ordained at the age of twenty-seven and became the student of DAHONG BAO'EN of Mt. Dahong and acquired the same toponym. In 1118, the title Great Master Jingyan (Pure and Strict) was bestowed upon him. After the invasion of Jin dynasty troops, Dahong moved south and became the abbot of the monastery Shuinan Chanyuan. Later he moved back to Mt. Dahong where he and his seven hundred disciples devoted themselves to its restoration.

**Dahui Pujue chanshi shu**. (J. Daie Fukaku zenji sho; K. Taehye Pogak sŏnsa sŏ 大慧普覺禪師書). In Chinese, "CHAN Master Dahui Pujue's Letters"; also known as the *Dahui shumen*, DAHUI SHUZHUANG, SHUZHUANG, and *Dahui shu*. Its colophon is dated to 1166. In reply to the letters he received from his many students, both ordained and lay, the Chan master DAHUI ZONGGAO wrote back with detailed instructions on meditation practice, especially his signature training in "observing the meditative topic," or more freely "questioning meditation" (KANHUA CHAN); after his death, his letters were compiled and edited in two rolls by his disciples Huiran and Huang Wenchang. Numerous editions of this collection were subsequently printed in China, Korea, and Japan. Many practitioners of Chan, SŎN, and ZEN favored the *Dahui Pujue chanshi shu* for its clarity, intelligibility, and uniquely personal tone. The text was especially influential in the writings of the Korean Sŏn master POJO CHINUL (1158–1210), who first learned about the Chan meditative technique of kanhua Chan from its pages and who attributed one of his three awakenings to his readings of Dahui. Dahui's letters were formally incorporated into the Korean Sŏn monastic curriculum by at least the seventeenth century, as one of books in the "Fourfold Collection" (SAJIP), where it is typically known by its abbreviated title of "Dahui's Letters" (K. TAEHYE SŎJANG) or just "Letters" (K. SŎJANG; C. Shuzhuang). The Japanese monk and historian MUJAKU DŌCHŪ (1653–1744) also wrote an important commentary to the text, known as the *Daiesho kōrōju*.

**Dahui Pujue chanshi zongmen wuku**. (J. Daie Fukaku zenji shūmon muko; K. Taehye Pogak sŏnsa chongmun mugo 大慧普覺禪師宗門武庫). In Chinese, "CHAN Master Dahui Pujue's Arsenal of the Tradition," edited in one roll by the monk Daoqian (d.u.); also known by the abbreviated titles *Dahui wuku* and *Zongmen wuku*. The preface to the text is dated 1186. Daoqian edited together over a hundred of his teacher DAHUI ZONGGAO's stories, anecdotes, inscriptions, and poems. The wide range of material that appears in the *Dahui Pujue chanshi zongmen wuku* serves as an important source for the study of the lives and thoughts of eminent monks and laymen, some of whom would otherwise no longer be known to us. Most of the stories, however, concern the deeds and words of Dahui's teachers YUANWU KEQIN and Dantang Wenzhun (1061–1115), Yuanwu's teacher WUZU FAYAN, and Dantang's teacher ZHENJING KEWEN.

**Dahui shuzhuang**. (J. Daie shojō; K. Taehye sŏjang 大慧書狀). See DAHUI PUJUE CHANSHI SHU.

**Dahui's Letters**. See DAHUI PUJUE CHANSHI SHU.

**Dahui Zonggao**. (J. Daie Sōkō; K. Taehye Chonggo 大慧宗杲) (1089–1163). Influential Song-dynasty Chinese CHAN master in the LINJI ZONG; also known as Miaoxi, Yunmen, Tanhui, or more typically just Dahui (J. Daie; K. Taehye). Dahui was a native of Ningguo in Xuanzhou (present-day Anhui province). After studying at LUSHAN and Mt. Dong, Dahui became the student of the Chan master DANTANG WENZHUN; in 1115, aware of his impending death, Dantang encouraged Dahui to continue his studies under YUANWU KEQIN. Before approaching Yuanwu, Dahui visited the Chan master JUEFAN HUIHONG, at which time he also met the powerful statesman and layman ZHANG SHANGYING. In 1124, while Yuanwu was serving under imperial orders as abbot of the monastery of Tianningsi in Dongjing, Dahui became his disciple and later inherited his Linji lineage. At the recommendation of the current grand councilor, Dahui was given the title Fori Dashi (Great Master Buddha Sun). After Yuanwu returned to his home province of Sichuan, Dahui moved to the hermitage of Yunmen'an in Haihun (present-day Jiangxi province) to avoid the invading forces of the Jin dynasty. In 1134, Dahui moved again to the hermitage of Yangyuan in Fujian province, where he launched a harsh critique against the practice of "silent-illumination Chan" (MOZHAO CHAN), championing instead the "investigation of the meditative topic" (KANHUA CHAN) method of meditation. Dahui later served as abbot of the powerful monastery Nengren Chanyuan on Mt. Jing (see WANSHOUSI) and revitalized the teachings of the Chan master LINJI YIXUAN. While a truce with the rival Jin dynasty was being negotiated, Dahui was accused of collaborating with Jin forces, for which he was exiled to Hengzhou in present-day Hunan province. During this period, Dahui composed his magnum opus, ZHENGFAYANZANG. After he was absolved of his alleged crime of treason, Dahui began his residence on Mt. Ayuwang and befriended the CAODONG ZONG Chan master HONGZHI ZHENGJUE, who was the preeminent advocate of the "silent-illumination" technique that Dahui so harshly criticized, suggesting that this professional disagreement did not affect their personal ties. Dahui later returned to his post at Nengren Chanyuan and became the teacher of Emperor Xiaozong (r. 1162–1189), who gave him the title Chan Master Dahui (Great Wisdom). He was also given the posthumous title Chan Master Pujue (Universal Enlightenment), the name typically used in his publications. Dahui's teachings are recorded in his *Dahui chanshi yulu*, DAHUI PUJUE CHANSHI SHU, and DAHUI PUJUE CHANSHI ZONGMEN WUKU.

**Daianji**. (大安寺). In Japanese, "Great Peace Monastery"; one of the seven great monasteries of the ancient Japanese capital of Nara (NANTO SHICHIDAIJI). Daianji was founded in the Asuka area and, according to internal monastery records, was originally the Kudara no Ōdera (Great Paekche Monastery) that was founded by Emperor Jomei in 639. When this monastery burned down in 642, Empress Kōgyoku had it rebuilt and renamed it Daianji. If this identification with Kudara no Ōdera is correct, Daianji has the distinction of being the first monastery in Japan founded by the court. The monastery moved to Nara in 716, following the relocation of the capital there in 710. The Koguryŏ monk Tohyŏn (J. Tōgen, fl. c. seventh century) lived at Daianji during the seventh century, where he wrote the *Nihon segi*, an early historical chronicle, which is no longer extant. Daianji was also the residence of the Indian monk BODHISENA (704–760), who lived and taught there until the end of his life. Bodhisena performed the "opening the eyes" (C. KAIYAN; J. KAIGEN; NETRAPRATIṢṬHĀPANA) ceremony for the 752 dedication of the great buddha image of Vairocana (NARA DAIBUTSU; Birushana Nyorai) at TŌDAIJI, another of the great Nara monasteries. Daianji was also home to the Korean monk SIMSANG (J. Shinjō, d. 742) from the Silla kingdom, who was instrumental in introducing the teachings of the Kegon (C. HUAYAN; K. Hwaŏm) school of Buddhism to Japan. Since the time of another famous resident, KŪKAI (774–835), Daianji has been associated with the SHINGONSHŪ of Japanese Buddhism. Daianji was at times quite grand, with two seven-story pagodas and many other buildings on its campus. After a fire destroyed much of the monastery in the 1200s, rebuilding was slow and the renovated structures were damaged once again by an earthquake in 1449. Daianji's fireproof treasury holds nine wooden images from the eighth century, including three different representations of the BODHISATTVA AVALOKITEŚVARA, including both his representations as AMOGHAPĀŚA (J. Fukū Kenjaku) and his thousand-armed manifestation (SĀHASRABHUJASĀHASRANETRĀVALOKITEŚVARA), as well as two of the four heavenly kings (S. CĀTURMAHĀRĀJAKĀYIKA; J. shitennō). The monastery also retains two famous images that are brought out for display for one month each year: in March, HAYAGRĪVA, and in October, the eleven-headed Avalokiteśvara (Jūichimen Kannon).

**daibutsu**. (大佛). In Japanese, "great buddha"; referring to colossal wooden or cast-bronze buddha images, such as the forty-eight-foot-high image of VAIROCANA enshrined at TŌDAIJI and the image of AMITĀBHA in Kāmakura. As a specific example, see NARA DAIBUTSU.

**dai-gohonzon**. (大御本尊). In Japanese, lit. "great object of devotion"; the most important object of worship in the NICHIREN SHŌSHŪ school of Japanese Buddhism. The dai-gohonzon is a plank of camphor wood that has at its center an inscription of homage to the title of the SADDHARMAPUṆḌARĪKASŪTRA ("Lotus Sūtra")—NAMU MYŌHŌ RENGEKYŌ, as well as the name of NICHIREN (1222–1282), surrounded by a cosmological chart (MAṆḌALA) of the Buddhist universe, written in Nichiren's own hand in 1279. By placing namu Myōhōrengekyō and his name on the same line, the school understands that Nichiren meant that the teachings of the *Saddharmapuṇḍarīkasūtra* and the person who proclaimed those teachings (Nichiren) are one and the same (ninpō ikka). The dai-gohonzon has been enshrined at TAISEKIJI, the administrative head temple of Nichiren Shōshū, since the temple's foundation in 1290; for this reason, the temple remains the major pilgrimage center for the school's adherents. The dai-gohonzon itself, the sanctuary (kaidan) where it is enshrined at Taisekiji, and the teaching of namu Myōhōrengekyō, are together called the "three great esoteric laws" (SANDAI HIHŌ), because they were hidden between the lines of the *Saddharmapuṇḍarīkasūtra* until Nichiren discovered them and revealed them to the world. Transcriptions of the maṇḍala, called simply GOHONZON, are inscribed on wooden tablets in temples or on paper scrolls when they are enshrined in home altars. See also DAIMOKU.

**Daigu Sōchiku**. (大愚宗築) (1584–1669). Japanese ZEN master of the RINZAISHŪ lineage. Daigu was born in Mino, present-day Gifu prefecture. In his twenties, Daigu went on a pilgrimage around the country with several other young monks, including GUDŌ TŌSHOKU and Ungo Kiyō (1582–1659), in search of a teacher. In his thirties, Daigu built the monastery of Nansenji in the capital Edo, which he named after his home temple in Mino. He also founded the monasteries of Enkyōji in Kinkō (present-day Shiga prefecture) and Enichiji in Tanba (present-day Hyōgo prefecture). Daigu was active in restoring dilapidated temples. In 1656, he was invited as the founding abbot of the temple Daianji in Echizen (present-day Fukui prefecture). During the Tokugawa period, temples were mandated by the bakufu to affiliate themselves with a main monastery (honzan), thus becoming a branch temple (matsuji). The temples that Daigu built or restored became branch temples of MYŌSHINJI. Daigu's efforts thus allowed the influence of Myōshinji, where he once served as abbot, to grow. Along with

Gudō, Daigu also led a faction within Myōshinji that rejected the invitation of the Chinese Chan master YINYUAN LONGQI to serve as abbot of the main temple.

**daijue ermiao**. (待絶二妙). In Chinese, "marvelous in comparison and marvelous in its own right." In the TIANTAI school's system of doctrinal classification (see JIAOXIANG PANSHI), Buddhist teachings and scriptures were classified into four modes of instruction (according to their different doctrinal themes; see TIANTAI BAJIAO) and five periods (according to the presumed chronological order by which the Buddha propounded them; see WUSHI). The most sophisticated pedagogical mode and the culminating chronological period are called, respectively, "the perfect teaching" (YUANJIAO) and the "Fahua-Niepan period." The teachings and scriptures associated with the highest mode and the culminating period—the paradigmatic example being the SADDHARMAPUṆḌARĪKASŪTRA ("Lotus Sūtra") and the teachings it embodied for the Tiantai school—are called truly "marvelous" for two reasons. First, they are "marvelous in comparison to the teachings and scriptures of all other 'modes' and 'periods'" (xiangdai miao) because they are the definitive expressions of the Buddha's teachings; second, they are also "marvelous in their own right" (juedai miao), i.e., they are wonderful and profound in an absolute sense, and not just comparatively.

**daimoku**. (題目). In Japanese, lit. "title" of a scripture; the term comes to be used most commonly in the NICHIRENSHŪ and associated schools of Japanese Buddhism to refer specifically to the title of the SADDHARMAPUṆḌARĪKASŪTRA ("Lotus Sūtra"). The title is presumed to summarize the gist of the entire scripture, and the recitation of its title in its Japanese pronunciation (see NAMU MYŌHŌRENGEKYŌ) is a principal religious practice of the Nichiren and SŌKKA GAKKAI schools. Recitation of the title of the *Saddharmapuṇḍarīkasūtra* is called specifically the "diamoku of the essential teaching" (honmon no daimoku) in the Nichiren school. The Japanese reformer NICHIREN (1222–1282) advocated recitation of this daimoku as one of the "three great esoteric laws" (SANDAI HIHŌ), and he claimed it exemplified mastery of wisdom (PRAJÑĀ) in the three trainings (TRIŚIKṢĀ).

**Dainichi(bō) Nōnin**. (大日[房]能忍) (d.u.). Japanese monk of the late Heian and early Kamakura eras; his surname was Taira. Nōnin is the reputed founder of the short-lived ZEN sect known as the DARUMASHŪ, one of the earliest Zen traditions to develop in Japan. Nōnin was something of an autodidact and is thought to have achieved awakening through his own study of scriptures and commentaries, rather than through any training with an established teacher. He taught at the temple of Sanbōji in Suita (present-day Ōsaka prefecture) and established himself as a Zen master. Well aware that he did not have formal authorization (YINKE) from a Chan master in a recognized lineage, Nōnin sent two of his disciples to China in 1189. They returned with a portrait of BODHIDHARMA inscribed by the Chan master FOZHAO DEGUANG (1121–1203) and the robe of Fozhao's influential teacher DAHUI ZONGGAO. Fozhao also presented Nōnin with a portrait of himself (see DINGXIANG), on which he wrote a verse at the request of Nōnin's two disciples. Such bestowals suggested that Nōnin was a recognized successor in the LINJI lineage. In 1194, the monks of HIEIZAN, threatened by Nōnin's burgeoning popularity, urged the court to suppress Nōnin and his teachings as an antinomian heresy. His school did not survive his death, and many of his leading disciples subsequently became students of other prominent teachers, such as DŌGEN KIGEN; this influx of Nōnin's adherents introduced a significant Darumashū component into the early SŌTŌSHŪ tradition. Nōnin was later given the posthumous title Zen Master Shinpō [alt. Jinhō] (Profound Dharma).

**Daiō Kokushi**. (J) (大應國師). See NANPO JŌMYŌ.

**Daitō Kokushi**. (J) (大燈國師). See SŌHŌ MYŌCHŌ.

**Daitokuji**. (大德寺). A famous Japanese ZEN monastery in Kyōto; also known as Murasakino Daitokuji. After his secluded training at the hermitage of Ungoan in eastern Kyōto in 1319, the Japanese RINZAI Zen master SŌHŌ MYŌCHŌ, or Daitō Kokushi, was invited by his uncle Akamatsu Norimura to Murasakino located in the northeastern part of Kyōto. There a dharma hall was built and inaugurated by Daitō in 1326. Daitō was formally honored as the founding abbot (kaizan; C. KAISHAN) and he continued to serve as abbot of Daitokuji until his death in 1337. In an attempt to control the influential monasteries in Kyōto, Emperor Godaigo (1288–1339), who was a powerful patron of Daitō and Daitokuji, decreed in 1313 that only those belonging to Daitō's lineage could become abbot of Daitokuji and added Daitokuji to the official GOZAN system. Two years later, Daitokuji was raised to top rank of the gozan system, which it shared with the monastery NANZENJI. These policies were later supported by retired Emperor Hanazono (1297–1348), another powerful patron of Daitō and his monastery. Daitokuji was devastated by a great fire in 1453 and suffered further destruction during the Ōnin War (1467–1477). The monastery was restored to its former glory in 1474, largely through the efforts of its prominent abbot IKKYŪ SŌJUN. A famous sanmon gate was built by the influential tea master Sen no Rikyū. During its heyday, Daitokuji had some twenty-four inner cloisters (tatchū), such as Ikkyū's Shinjuan and Rikyū's Jukōin and over 173 subtemples (matsuji).

**daiyu**. (J. daigo; K. taeŏ 代語). In Chinese, "substitute reply." When a CHAN master asks a question to the assembly and answers his own question before anyone else responds, his or her response is known as the "substitute reply."

**ḍāka**. (T. mkha' 'gro). In Sanskrit, a donor or sacrifice; in tantric Buddhism, another name for a VĪRA "hero"; the male counterpart of a ḌĀKINĪ, particularly in the GANACAKRA, a ritual tantric feast that may have originated as an actual assembly of tāntrikas engaged in antinomian behavior, including ingesting ritually impure foods and engaging in sexual relations. In Tibetan, the term dpa' bo (vīra) or "hero" is typically used instead of mkha' 'gro (ḍāka), although the latter term appears in traditional lists of the beings invited to the gaṇacakra (T. tshogs). In the title of such tantras as the ḌĀKĀRṆAVAMAHĀYOGINĪTANTRA and the VAJRAḌĀKATANTRA, ḍāka seems to be used as an abbreviation of ḌĀKINĪ.

**Ḍākārṇavamahāyoginītantra**. [alt. Dākārṇavatantra] (T. Mkha' 'gro rgya mtsho rnal 'byor ma'i rgyud). In APABHRAṂŚA, an early medieval Indian vernacular based on Sanskrit, literally, "Ḍāk[inī] Ocean Yoginī Tantra"; the yoginī, or "mother," tantras are a subdivision of ANUTTARAYOGATANTRA. A manuscript of the tantra is extant in the Nepalese National Archives; the Tibetan translation is by Jayasena and Dharma yon tan. It is one of the four CAKRASAṂVARATANTRA explanatory (vākhyā) tantras.

**ḍākinī**. (T. mkha' 'gro ma; C. tuzhini; J. dakini; K. tojini 荼枳尼). In Sanskrit, a cannibalistic female demon, a witch; in ŚĀNTIDEVA's BODHICARYĀVATĀRA, a female hell guardian (narakapālā); in tantric Buddhism, ḍākinīs, particularly the vajraḍākinī, are guardians from whom tāntrikas obtain secret doctrines. For example, the VAJRABHAIRAVA adept Lālitavajra is said to have received the YAMĀNTAKA tantras from vajraḍākinīs, who allowed him to bring back to the human world only as many of the texts as he could memorize in one night. The ḍākinī first appears in Indian sources during the fourth century CE, and it has been suggested that they evolved from local female shamans. The term is of uncertain derivation, perhaps having something to do with "drumming" (a common feature of shamanic ritual). The Chinese, Japanese, and Korean give simply a phonetic transcription of the Sanskrit. In Tibetan, ḍākinī is translated as "sky goer" (mkha' 'gro ma), probably related to the Sanskrit khecara, a term associated with the CAKRASAṂVARATANTRA. Here, the ḍākinī is a goddess, often depicted naked, in semi-wrathful pose (see VAJRAYOGINĪ); they retain their fearsome element but are synonymous with the highest female beauty and attractiveness and are enlightened beings. They form the third of what are known as the "inner" three jewels (RATNATRAYA): the guru, the YI DAM, and the ḍākinīs and protectors (DHARMAPĀLA; T. chos skyong). The archetypical Tibetan wisdom or knowledge ḍākinī (ye shes mkha' 'gro) is YE SHES MTSHO RGYAL, the consort of PADMASAMBHAVA. Ḍākinīs are classified in a variety of ways, the most common being mkha' 'gro sde lnga, the female buddhas equivalent to the PAÑCATATHĀGATA or five buddha families (PAÑCAKULA): Buddhaḍākinī [alt. Ākāśadhātvīśvarī; Sparśavajrā] in the center of the maṇḍala, with Locanā, Māmakī, Pāṇḍaravāsinī, and TĀRĀ in the cardinal directions. Another division is into three: outer, inner, and secret ḍākinīs. The first is a YOGINĪ or a YOGIN's wife or a regional goddess, the second is a female buddha that practitioners visualize themselves to be in the course of tantric meditation, and the last is nondual wisdom (ADVAYAJÑĀNA). This division is also connected with the three bodies (TRIKĀYA) of Mahāyāna Buddhism: the NIRMĀṆAKĀYA (here referring to the outer ḍākinīs), SAṂBHOGAKĀYA (meditative deity), and the DHARMAKĀYA (the knowledge ḍākinī). The word ḍākinī is found in the title of the explanation (vākhyā) tantras of the yoginī class or mother tantras included in the *Cakrasaṃvaratantra* group.

**Dalada Maligawa**. (Sinhalese). See TOOTH RELIC.

**Dalai Lama**. (T. Dā la'i bla ma). An honorific title given to members of a prominent Tibetan incarnation (SPRUL SKU) lineage belonging to the DGE LUGS sect of Tibetan Buddhism. The Dalai Lamas are traditionally revered as earthly manifestations of AVALOKITEŚVARA, the BODHISATTVA of compassion and protector of Tibet. Although the term has become widely known outside the region, Tibetans most frequently refer to the Dalai Lama as Rgyal ba rin po che (Gyalwa Rinpoche) "Precious Conqueror," Sku mdun (Kundun) "The Presence," or Yid bzhin nor bu (Yishin Norbu) "Wish-fulfilling Gem." The name originated during the sixteenth century when ALTAN KHAN, ruler of the Tümed Mongols, bestowed the title on the Dge lugs teacher BSOD NAMS RGYA MTSHO by translating the prelate's name rgya mtsho ("ocean") into Mongolian as dalai. The name thus approximately means "ocean teacher." It is not the case, as is often reported, that the Dalai Lamas are so named because their wisdom is as vast as the ocean. After Bsod nams rgya mtsho, all subsequent incarnations have rgya mtsho as the second component of their name. At the time of his meeting with the Altan Khan, Bsod nams rgya mtsho was already a recognized incarnate lama of the Dge lugs. Bsod nams rgya mtsho became the third Dalai Lama and two of his previous incarnations were posthumously recognized as the first and second holders of the lineage. From that time onward, successive incarnations have all been known as the Dalai Lama. Although writings outside Tibet often describe the Dalai Lama as the head of the Dge lugs sect, that position is held by a figure called the DGA' LDAN KHRI PA, the "Throneholder of Ganden Monastery." The fourteen Dalai Lamas are:

1. Dge 'dun grub (Gendün Drup, 1391–1475)
2. Dge 'dun rgya mtsho (Gendün Gyatso, 1475–1542)
3. Bsod nams rgya mtsho (Sönam Gyatso, 1543–1588)
4. Yon tan rgya mtsho (Yönten Gyatso, 1589–1617)
5. Ngag dbang blo bzang rgya mtsho (Ngawang Losang Gyatso, 1617–1682)
6. Tshangs dbyangs rgya mtsho (Tsangyang Gyatso, 1683–1706?)
7. Skal bzang rgya mtsho (Kalsang Gyatso, 1708–1757)
8. 'Jam dpal rgya mtsho (Jampal Gyatso, 1758–1804)
9. Lung rtogs rgya mtsho (Lungtok Gyatso, 1805–1815)
10. Tshul khrims rgya mtsho (Tsultrim Gyatso, 1816–1837)
11. Mkhas grub rgya mtsho (Kedrup Gyatso, 1838–1855)
12. 'Phrin las rgya mtsho (Trinle Gyatso, 1856–1875)

13. Thub bstan rgya mtsho (Tupten Gyatso, 1876–1933)
14. Bstan 'dzin rgya mtsho (Tenzin Gyatso, b. 1935)

The first Dalai Lama, DGE 'DUN GRUB, was known as a great scholar and religious practitioner. A direct disciple of TSONG KHA PA, he is remembered for founding BKRA SHIS LHUN PO monastery near the central Tibetan town of Shigatse. The second Dalai Lama, Dge 'dun rgya mtsho, was born the son of a RNYING MA YOGIN and became a renowned tantric master in his own right. ¶ It is with the third Dalai Lama, BSOD NAMS RGYA MTSHO, that the Dalai Lama lineage actually begins. Recognized at a young age as the reincarnation of Dge 'dun rgya mtsho, he was appointed abbot of 'BRAS SPUNGS monastery near LHA SA and soon rose to fame throughout central Asia as a Buddhist teacher. He served as a religious master for the Mongol ruler Altan Khan, who bestowed the title "Dalai Lama," and is credited with converting the Tümed Mongols to Buddhism. Later in life, he traveled extensively across eastern Tibet and western China, teaching and carrying out monastic construction projects. ¶ The fourth Dalai Lama, Yon tan rgya mtsho, was recognized in the person of the grandson of Altan Khan's successor, solidifying Mongol-Tibetan ties. ¶ While the first four Dalai Lamas served primarily as religious scholars and teachers, the fifth Dalai Lama, NGAG DBANG BLO BZANG RGYA MTSHO, combined religious and secular activities to become one of Tibet's preeminent statesmen. He was a dynamic political leader who, with the support of Gushi Khan, defeated his opponents and in 1642 was invested with temporal powers over the Tibetan state, in addition to his religious role, a position that succeeding Dalai Lamas held until 1959. A learned and prolific author, he and his regent, SDE SRID SANGS RGYAS RGYA MTSHO, were largely responsible for the identification of the Dalai Lamas with the bodhisattva Avalokiteśvara. The construction of the PO TA LA palace began during his reign (and was completed after this death). He is popularly known as the "Great Fifth." ¶ The sixth Dalai Lama, TSHANGS DBYANGS RGYA MTSHO, was a controversial figure who chose to abandon the strict monasticism of his predecessors in favor of a life of society and culture, refusing to take the vows of a fully ordained monk (BHIKṢU). He is said to have frequented the drinking halls below the Po ta la palace. He constructed pleasure gardens and the temple of the NĀGAS, called the KLU KHANG, on the palace grounds. He is remembered especially for his poetry, which addresses themes such as love and the difficulty of spiritual practice. Tibetans generally interpret his behavior as exhibiting an underlying tantric wisdom, a skillful means for teaching the dharma. His death is shrouded in mystery. Official accounts state that he died while under arrest by Mongol troops. According to a prominent secret biography (GSANG BA'I RNAM THAR), however, he lived many more years, traveling across Tibet in disguise. ¶ The seventh Dalai Lama, SKAL BZANG RGYA MTSHO, was officially recognized only at the age of twelve, and due to political complications, did not participate actively in affairs of state. He was renowned for his writings on tantra and his poetry. ¶ The eighth Dalai Lama, 'Jam dpal rgya mtsho (Jampal Gyatso, 1758–1804), built the famous NOR BU GLING KHA summer palace. ¶ The ninth through twelfth Dalai Lamas each lived relatively short lives, due, according to some accounts, to political intrigue and the machinations of power-hungry regents. According to tradition, from the death of one Dalai Lama to the investiture of the next Dalai Lama as head of state (generally a period of some twenty years), the nation was ruled by a regent, who was responsible for discovering the new Dalai Lama and overseeing his education. If the Dalai Lama died before reaching his majority, the reign of the regent was extended. ¶ The thirteenth Dalai Lama, THUB BSTAN RGYA MTSHO, was an astute and forward-looking political leader who guided Tibet through a period of relative independence during a time of foreign entanglements with Britain, China, and Russia. In his last testament, he is said to have predicted Tibet's fall to Communist China. ¶ The fourteenth and present Dalai Lama, Bstan 'dzin rgya mtsho, assumed his position several years prior to reaching the age of majority as his country faced the Chinese invasion of Tibet in 1950. In 1959, he escaped into exile, establishing a government-in-exile in the Himalayan town of Dharamsala (DHARMAŚĀLĀ) in northwestern India. Since then, he has traveled and taught widely around the world, while also advocating a nonviolent solution to Tibet's occupation. He was born in the A mdo region of what is now Qinghai province in China to a farming family, although his older brother had already been recognized as an incarnation at a nearby important Dge lugs monastery (SKU 'BUM). On his becoming formally accepted as Dalai Lama, his family became aristocrats and moved to Lha sa. He was educated traditionally by private tutors (yongs 'dzin), under the direction first of the regent Stag brag rin po che (in office 1941–1950), and later Gling rin po che Thub bstan lung rtogs rnam rgyal (1903–1983) and Khri byang rin po che Blo bzang ye shes (1901–1981). His modern education was informal, gained from conversations with travelers, such as the Austrian mountaineer Heinrich Harrer. When the Chinese army entered the Khams region of eastern Tibet in 1951, he formally took over from the regent and was enthroned as the head of the DGA' LDAN PHO BRANG government. In the face of Tibetan unrest as the Chinese government brought Tibet firmly under central control, the Dalai Lama fled to India in 1959; the Indian government accorded the Dalai Lama respect as a religious figure but did not accept his claim to be the head of a separate state. In 1989, the Dalai Lama was awarded the Nobel Peace Prize, an event that increased his prominence around the world. He is the author of many books in English, most of them the written record of lectures and traditional teachings translated from Tibetan.

**ḍamaru**. (T. ḍa ma ru). In Sanskrit, the name of an hourglass-shaped, two-sided hand drum, used in tantric liturgy. Two small strikers are attached to strings at the drum's waist, making a rattling sound as they strike the alternate faces when the drum is rotated back and forth in the upraised right hand. This type of drum appears in pictograms from as early as the Indus Valley civilization and is commonly used by street performers in India. The Śaivite ḍamaru, slightly extended in the middle, is called cang te'u in Tibetan. The Buddhist ḍamaru comes in a number of sizes, from the small drum about four inches in diameter, up to the large drum used in GCOD (severance) practice, which is up to sixteen inches in diameter. The true KAPĀLA (skull) ḍamaru used by tāntrikas is fashioned from two human craniums facing outward and joined together by human bone; an ornate tail made of brocade with the five colors signifying the PAÑCATATHĀGATA is attached to the waist of the drum and hangs down when the drum is played. The large gcod rnga used in gcod practice is made of wood; it is shaken slowly and rhythmically while chanting, accompanied by intermittent blasts through a rkang gling (kangling), a trumpet-like instrument ideally fashioned from a human leg bone. See also DRUM.

**dam can**. (damchen). In Tibetan, "bound by oath"; a term for the pre-Buddhist Tibetan deities, also called ordinary or mundane (LAUKIKA) deities, who have been subjugated and made to take a solemn oath (SAMAYA) to protect Buddhism. According to traditional accounts, the Tibetan king KHRI SRONG SDE BTSAN encountered many hindrances during the construction of the first Buddhist monastery in Tibet at BSAM YAS. The Indian teacher ŚĀNTARAKṢITA advised the king to invite PADMASAMBHAVA to subdue the malevolent spirits; these spirits, referred to generally as the "eight classes of gods and demons" (lha srin sde brgyad; see AṢṬASENĀ), include the BRTAN MA BCU GNYIS, various local deities (yul lha) inhabiting mountain passes, plains, and peaks, and the spirits of powerful deceased persons (rgyal po). Illustrative is the account of the subjugation of the powerful rgyal po spirit RDO RJE GRAGS LDAN (in some accounts the emissary of a powerful spirit called PE HAR RGYAL PO), who becomes an important protector, particularly of the RNYING MA sect, and through the GNAS CHUNG oracle a protector of the Tibetan state.

**Dam can chos rgyal**. (Damchen Chögyal). A popular Tibetan form of YĀMA, the first person to die, hence the ruler of the kingdom of the dead. He is the chief DHARMAPĀLA in the retinue of VAJRABHAIRAVA, a YAMĀNTAKA deity popular in the DGE LUGS sect because of its association with TSONG KHA PA. He serves as the DHARMAPĀLA of DGA' LDAN PHUN TSHOGS GLING (formerly JO NANG PHUN TSHOGS GLING, the JO NANG seat of TĀRANĀTHA) in central Tibet. He has one face of an angry bull, two hands holding a staff and a pāśa (noose), an erect phallus, and stands on a water buffalo, which itself is lying atop a human figure.

**Đàm Lựu**. (曇榴) (1933–1999). A prominent Vietnamese nun, born on April 8, 1933, in Hà Đông province (in northern Vietnam). At the age of two, she visited Cự Đà Temple with her parents but refused to leave and so spent her childhood there. In 1948, she took novice precepts and was sent to study Buddhism at various temples in North Vietnam. In 1951, she received full ordination as a nun and, in 1952, followed her teacher to South Vietnam when he was appointed abbot of Dược Sư Temple in Gò Vấp. After completing her baccalaureate degree, she moved to Phước Hòa Temple in Saigon. In 1964, she earned a scholarship to study social work in West Germany. While in Freiburg, she divided her time between her studies and assisting Vietnamese orphans in Germany. After returning to South Vietnam in 1969, she was appointed director of Lumbini Orphanage in Saigon. In 1977, she escaped from Vietnam and, in 1979, settled in San José, California. In 1991, she founded Đức Viên Temple, which has subsequently served as a site for Buddhist practice and a center for many Vietnamese cultural activities. Until her death in 1999, Đàm Lựu oversaw the training of many young nuns and encouraged them to enroll in colleges and universities in North America, as well as in India and Taiwan. She also gave financial assistance to various Buddhist colleges in Vietnam.

**Damoduoluo chan jing**. (J. Darumatara zenkyō; K. Talmadara sŏn kyŏng 達摩多羅禪經). In Chinese, the "Dhyāna Sūtra of Dharmatrāta"; a scripture on meditation (DHYĀNA) attributed to the SARVĀSTIVĀDA teacher DHARMATRĀTA (c. fourth century CE) and translated into Chinese by BUDDHABHADRA in the early fifth century. Buddhabhadra arrived in the Chinese capital of Chang'an in 406 and briefly stayed at LUSHAN HUIYUAN's (334–416) monastery on LUSHAN, where he translated the text at the latter's request. The *Damoduoluo chan jing* describes the transmission of the oral teachings of the Buddha from master to disciple and details the various practices of meditation (GUAN) such as mindfulness of breathing (S. ĀNĀPĀNASMṚTI; P. ānāpānasati) and meditation on the foul (AŚUBHABHĀVANĀ), as well as the categories of, SKANDHA, ĀYATANA, and DHĀTU. The text includes a listing of patriarchs of the tradition before and after Dharmatrāta, which begins with MAHĀKĀŚYAPA and ĀNANDA, continues through MADHYĀNTIKA, ŚĀṆAKAVĀSIN, UPAGUPTA, VASUMITRA, and Saṃgharakṣa, leading up to Dharmatrāta, who is then followed in turn by Puṇyamitra. This lineage seems to derive from the SARVĀSTIVĀDA school in the KASHMIR-GANDHĀRA region and suggests that the notion of a teaching geneaology as a central part of Buddhist religious identity has its start in the Indian tradition. Prefaces to the *Damoduoluo chan jing* by Lushan Huiyuan and Huiguan subsequently connect versions of this lineage to BODHIDHARMA, the putative founder of the CHAN school in East Asia, suggesting this text exerted some influence in the rise of transmission lineages within the early Chan tradition.

**dāna**. (T. sbyin pa; C. bushi; J. fuse; K. posi 布施). In Sanskrit and Pāli, "giving," "generosity," or "charity"; one of the most highly praised of virtues in Buddhism and the foundational practice of the Buddhist laity, presumably because of its value in weaning the layperson from attachment to material possessions while providing essential material support to the

SAṂGHA. It is the chief cause of prosperity in future lives and rebirth as a divinity (DEVA) in one of the heavens of the sensuous realm (KĀMADHĀTU). There are numerous stories in the AVADĀNA and JĀTAKA literatures that illustrate the virtues of giving, the most famous being that of Prince Viśvaṃtara (P. VESSANTARA), whose generosity was so profound that he gave away not only all his worldly possessions but even his wife and children. In other stories, BODHISATTVAs often give away their body or parts of their body (see DEHADĀNA; SHESHEN). The immediate karmic result of the practice of giving is said to be wealth in the future, especially as a divinity in one of the heavens. Giving, especially to the SAṂGHA, is presumed to generate merit (PUṆYA) that will accrue to the benefit of the donor in both this and future lifetimes; indeed, giving is the first in a standard list of meritorious acts, along with morality (ŚĪLA) and religious development (BHĀVANĀ). In the "graduated discourse" (S. ANUPŪRVIKATHĀ; P. ANUPUBBIKATHĀ) that the Buddha commonly used in instructing the laity, the discourse on giving (dānakathā) was even more fundamental than the succeeding discourses on right conduct (śīlakathā) and the joys of rebirth in the heavens (svargakathā). Eight items are typically presumed to make appropriate offerings: food, water, clothing, vehicles, garlands, perfume, beds and dwellings, and lights. In yet another enumeration, there are three kinds of dāna: the "gift of material goods" (ĀMIṢADĀNA); the gift of fearlessness (ABHAYADĀNA), and the "gift of the dharma" (DHARMADĀNA). Of all gifts, however, the greatest was said to be the "gift of the dharma" (dharmadāna), viz., spiritual instruction that will lead not just to better rebirths but to liberation from SAṂSĀRA; it is this gift that the saṃgha offers reciprocally to the laity. In MAHĀYĀNA soteriology, giving is listed as the first of the six perfections (PĀRAMITĀ) cultivated on the bodhisattva path (see DĀNAPĀRAMITĀ). According to the Pāli tradition, dāna is the first of ten perfections (P. pāramī). In some schools, a being who is incapable of even the modicum of detachment that is required to donate one's possessions through charity is thought to have eradicated his wholesome spiritual faculties (SAMUCCHINNAKUŚALAMŪLA; see also ICCHANTIKA) and to have lost for an indeterminate period any prospect of enlightenment.

**Dānapāla**. (C. Shihu; J. Sego; K. Siho 施護) (d.u.; fl. c. 980 CE). In Sanskrit, lit. "Protector of Giving"; one of the last great Indian translators of Buddhist texts into Chinese. A native of Oḍḍiyāna in the GANDHĀRA region of India, he was active in China during the Northern Song dynasty. At the order of the Song Emperor Taizhong (r. 960–997), he was installed in a translation bureau to the west of the imperial monastery of Taiping Xingguosi (in Yuanzhou, present-day Jiangxi province), where he and his team are said to have produced some 111 translations in over 230 rolls. His translations include texts from the PRAJÑĀPĀRAMITĀ, MADHYAMAKA, and tantric traditions, including the AṢṬASĀHASRIKĀPRAJÑĀPĀRAMITĀ, SUVARṆAPRABHĀSOTTAMASŪTRA, SARVATATHĀGATATATTVASAṂGRAHA, HEVAJRATANTRA, NĀGĀRJUNA's YUKTIṢAṢṬIKĀ and DHARMADHĀTUSTAVA, and KAMALAŚĪLA's BHĀVANĀKRAMA, as well as several DHĀRAṆĪ texts.

**dānapāramitā**. (P. dānapāramī; T. sbyin pa'i pha rol tu phyin pa; C. bushi boluomi; J. fuseharamitsu; K. posi paramil 布施波羅蜜). In Sanskrit, the "perfection of giving"; the first of the six [or ten] perfections (PĀRAMITĀ) cultivated on the BODHISATTVA path. According to the Pāli tradition, dāna is the first of ten perfections (P. PĀRAMĪ). Three kinds of DĀNA are often enumerated in this context: the "gift of material goods" (ĀMIṢADĀNA); the "gift of fearlessness" (ABHAYADĀNA) and the "gift of the dharma" (DHARMADĀNA). Giving (DĀNA) is perfected on the first of the ten stages (DAŚABHŪMI) of the bodhisattva path, PRAMUDITĀ (joyful), where the bodhisattva's vision into the emptiness (ŚŪNYATĀ) of all things motivates him to perfect the practice of giving, learning to give away those things most precious to him, including his wealth, his wife, and family, and even his very body (see DEHADĀNA; SHESHEN). Thanks to his understanding of emptiness (ŚŪNYATĀ), the bodhisattva masters the perfection of giving by realizing there is no donor, no recipient, and no gift. It is with this insight that ordinary giving becomes perfected giving. The perfection of giving brings an end to the obstruction of the common illusions of the unenlightened (pṛthagjanatvāvaraṇa; C. yishengxing zhang), leading in turn to the awareness of universal suchness (sarvatragatathatā; C. bianxing zhenru). See DAŚABHŪMI, VESSANTARA.

**dānapati**. (T. sbyin pa'i bdag po/sbyin bdag; C. tanyue/shizhu; J. dan'otsu/seshu; K. tanwŏl/siju 檀越/施主). In Sanskrit and Pāli, lit. "master of giving," viz., a "generous donor"; a "patron" of individual monks and nuns, or of the SAṂGHA as a whole. Being a willing dānapati is also one of the expectations of a wise ruler. Among the disciples of the Buddha, the most famous dānapati was ANĀTHAPIṆḌADA. In Tibet, the denotation of the term is extended to include those who commission prayers, rituals, and particularly public discourses by well-known teachers. For large public discourses there is a primary sbyin bdag (jindak), who at the start ritually offers to the teacher a small statue of the Buddha, a religious book, and a STŪPA (together called the maṇḍal rten gsum) representing the body, speech, and mind of the Buddha, while holding a white scarf (kha btags), along with a small gift. The primary sbyin bdag is the person who originally asked the teacher to give the discourse, and whose request was accepted; it is not necessarily the person who actually sponsored the event. At the end of the teaching, the primary sbyin bdag heads a line of all those who have contributed (also called sbyin bdag) who give gifts to the teacher. The Chinese use both the translation shizhu (lit. "master of giving") and the transcription tanyue, which transcribes a Prakrit form of the Indic term.

**danka seido**. (檀家制度). In Japanese, "parish-household system"; danka (parish household) is synonymous with DANNA, and the more common form after the mid-Tokugawa period. See DANNA.

**danna**. (檀那). This Japanese term is originally a transcription of the Sanskrit term DĀNA, or "giving." When referring to a patron of a monk, nun, or monastery, the term danna is used with reference to a "donor" (J. dan'otsu, dan'ochi, dannotsu; S. DĀNAPATI) or "parish temple" (DANKA). During the Tokugawa period (1603–1868), the Japanese shogunate required every family to register at and support a local temple, called the DANNADERA, which in turned entitled that family to receive funerary services from the local priest. The dannadera, also called the BODAIJI and dankadera, thus served as a means of monitoring the populace and preventing the spread in Japan of subversive religions, such as Christianity and the banned Nichiren–Fuju–Fuse sect of the NICHIREN school. By requiring each Japanese family to be registered at a specific local temple and obligating them to provide for that temple's economic support and to participate in its religious rituals, all Japanese thus became Buddhist in affiliation for the first time in Japanese history.

**dannadera**. (J) (檀那寺). In Japanese, "parish temple"; a Japanese Buddhist institutional system that reached its apex in the sixteenth and seventeenth centuries. See DANNA.

**dantadhātu**. (S/P). See TOOTH RELIC.

**dao**. (J. dō; K. to 道). In Chinese, lit. "way" or "path"; a polysemous term in Chinese, which in Buddhist texts is used variously as the translation for terms related to "path" (MĀRGA) and "awakening" (BODHI); thus, "cultivating the way" (xiudao) means "practicing Buddhism" and "entering the way" (rudao) comes to be used as the equivalency in Chinese Buddhist texts for the idea of attaining enlightenment. But dao also has numerous other usages, including as a translation for the DHARMA as teachings (dao or daofa), the dharmas as factors (e.g., daopin for the BODHIPĀKṢIKADHARMA), and the realms of rebirth (e.g., edao as one of the translations of unfortunate destinies, viz., DURGATI or APĀYA). In the premodern period, dao is also one of the closer Chinese equivalents for what in the West would simply be called "religion," so that the compound DAOREN ("person of the way") refers more generally to an accomplished adherent of a religion; in DAOSU, the term refers generically to a "religious" (dao) or renunciant, especially in distinction to a layperson (su), etc. The term is still often seen transcribed in English as tao or Tao, using the older Wade–Giles transcription. In East Asian Buddhist texts, dao only rarely refers to the religious tradition of Daoism/Taoism.

**Dao'an**. (J. Dōan; K. Toan 道安) (312–385). In Chinese, "Peace of the Way"; monk-exegete and pioneer of Buddhism during the Eastern Jin dynasty. A native of Fuliu in present-day Hebei province, at the age of eleven he became a student of the famous Kuchean monk and thaumaturge FOTUDENG. Fleeing from the invasions of the so-called northern barbarians, Dao'an and his teacher relocated frequently, with Dao'an finally settling down in the prosperous city of Xiangyang in Hubei province, where he taught for fifteen years. Learning of Dao'an's great reputation, the Former Qin ruler Fu Jian (338–385) amassed an army and captured Xiangyang. After the fall of Xiangyang, Fu Jian invited Dao'an to the capital of Chang'an and honored him as his personal teacher. Dao'an later urged Fu Jian to invite the eminent Central Asian monk KUMĀRAJĪVA to China. In order to determine the authenticity and provenance of the various scriptural translations then being made in China, Dao'an compiled an influential catalogue of scriptures known as the ZONGLI ZHONGJING MULU, which was partially preserved in the CHU SANZANG JIJI. He also composed various prefaces and commentaries, and his exegetical technique of dividing a scripture into three sections (SANFEN KEJING)—"preface" (xufen), "text proper" *(*zhengzongfen), and "dissemination section" (liutongfen)—is still widely used even today in East Asian scriptural exegesis. In Dao'an's day, the Indian VINAYA recensions had not yet been translated into Chinese, so Dao'an took it upon himself to codify an early set of indigenous monastic regulations known as the *Sengni guifan fofa xianzhang* (no longer extant) as a guide for Chinese monastic practice. Also traced to Dao'an is the custom of monks and nuns abandoning their secular surnames for the surname SHI (a transcription of the Buddha's clan name ŚĀKYA; J. Shaku; K. Sŏk; V. Thích), as a mark of their religious ties to the Buddha's lineage. Among his many disciples, LUSHAN HUIYUAN is most famous.

**daochang**. (J. dōjō; K. toryang 道場). In Chinese, literally "place of the way"; daochang is the Chinese translation for the Sanskrit technical term BODHIMAṆḌA, the "seat of enlightenment" or "platform of enlightenment," viz., the place under the BODHI TREE where the Buddha sat when he achieved enlightenment. The term is now used more generally by various religious and secular groups to refer to a place of worship, practice, and training. In Korean monasteries, the toryang typically refers to the large open courtyard in front of the main shrine hall (TAEUNG CHŎN).

**Daochuo**. (J. Dōshaku; K. Tojak 道綽) (562–645). Chinese monk and putative second patriarch of the JINGTU (pure land) tradition; also known as Chan Master Xihe (West River). Daochuo was a native of Bingzhou in present-day Shanxi province. He left home at an early age and studied the MAHĀPARINIRVĀṆASŪTRA. According to legend, in 609, Daochuo is said to have been inspired by TANLUAN's epitaph to continue the latter's efforts to further PURE LAND thought and practice. Daochuo is then said to have devoted himself to the practice of NIANFO, the invocation of the name of the buddha AMITĀBHA, and the daily recitation of the SUKHĀVATĪVYŪHASŪTRA. Daochuo is perhaps more famous than even Tanluan for advocating the practice of recitation of the Buddha's name (NIANFO) over all other practices. He is also known for using small beans (xiaodou) to keep count of the number of recitations; some believe his habit of using counting beans is the origin of rosaries (JAPAMĀLĀ) in China. The influential pure land treatise ANLE JI is attributed to Daochuo.

**daofeng**. (J. tōfū; K. top'ung 刀風). In Chinese, lit. "knife wind"; an allegory for the disintegrating forces that cause the dissolution of the world at the end of an eon according to Buddhist cosmology (see KALPA), or the end of a person's physical life (when the "primary elements," the MAHĀBHŪTA, from which the body is believed to be composed, disintegrate).

**Đạo Hạnh**. (道行) (died 1117). Vietnamese monk, popularly known as Từ Đạo Hạnh; CHAN master and thaumaturge, whose miraculous exploits have captured the imagination of Vietnamese Buddhists for centuries. His personal name was Từ Lộ. The Thiền Uyển Tập Anh relates that as a young man he was a free spirit who harbored great aspirations. He befriended people of various social backgrounds and was a serious student, passing the royal examination for tăng quan (monk officers). After his father was killed by a sorcerer, Đạo Hạnh went to Mount Từ Sơn to live in seclusion and devoted himself to chanting the "Great Compassion" DHĀRAṆĪ (see DABEI ZHOU) daily. After chanting it 108,000 times, he gained magical powers and avenged his father's death. He later began to wander to various Buddhist monasteries in search of enlightenment; eventually, under the guidance of Sùng Phạm (1004–1087), he gained realization. He is said to have tamed mountain snakes and wild beasts, burned his finger to pray for rain, and blessed water with mantras to cure disease. It is believed that Đạo Hạnh used his magical powers to reincarnate himself as the son of King Lý Nhân Tông (r. 1072–1127) and was eventually enthroned as King Lý Thần Tông (r. 1128–1138). In northern Vietnam, the story of Đạo Hạnh is still reenacted during festivals.

**Daojiao yishu**. (J. Dōkyō gisū; K. Togyo ŭich'u 道教義樞). In Chinese, "The Pivotal Meaning of the Teachings of the DAO"; a text attributed to the Daoist priest Meng Anpai (d.u.); an encyclopedic work that provides a detailed explanation of thirty-seven matters of Daoist doctrine, five of which are now lost. Among the thirty-seven concepts explained in the text, there are concepts borrowed directly from Buddhism, such as the dharma body (DHARMAKĀYA), three jewels (RATNATRAYA), three vehicles (TRIYĀNA), three realms of existence (TRILOKA [DHĀTU]), knowledge of external objects, and the PURE LAND of SUKHĀVATĪ. The text also employs Buddhist terms, concepts, and classificatory systems throughout. The greatest Buddhist influence on this text came from the SAN LUN ZONG and especially from the teachings of the Sanlun master JIZANG. The *Daojiao yishu* was, in fact, written to demonstrate the sophistication of Daoist thought in response to Buddhist criticisms during the Tang dynasty. This text influenced the compilation of many later Daoist works, such as the *Yunji qiqian*.

**Daokai**. (C) (道楷). See FURONG DAOKAI.

**Daolong**. (C) (道隆). See LANXI DAOLONG.

**daoren**. (J. dōnin; K. toin 道人). In Chinese, lit. "person of the way"; a "religious adherent" or "a religious." The term is used by many different religious and secular groups in China to refer generally to any person who has perfected a path of cultivation and training or attained a special skill or knowledge. Among Buddhists, the term has also come to refer more generally to anyone who has made some progress in following the Buddha's path (dao; S. MĀRGA) to enlightenment. In East Asian Buddhist texts, the term daoren only rarely refers to a "Daoist adherent"; most commonly it refers to a Buddhist adherent or generically to any "religious."

**Daosheng**. (C) (道生). See CAOYUAN DAOSHENG.

**Daosheng**. (J. Dōshō; K. Tosaeng 道生) (355–434). Influential Chinese monk during the Eastern Jin dynasty and renowned scholar of the MAHĀPARINIRVĀṆASŪTRA; also known as ZHU DAOSHENG. Daosheng was a native of Julu in present-day Hebei province. He became a student of the monk Zhu Fatai (320–387), changing his surname to Zhu in his honor. Daosheng received the full monastic precepts in his nineteenth year and took up residence at the monastery of Longguangsi in Jianye. Later, he moved to LUSHAN, where he studied under the eminent monk LUSHAN HUIYUAN. Daosheng also continued his studies under the famed translator and MADHYAMAKA scholar KUMĀRAJĪVA, and was later praised as one of Kumārajīva's four great disciples. In 409, Daosheng returned to Jianye and made the controversial claim that even incorrigibles (ICCHANTIKA) may eventually attain enlightenment and that buddhahood is attained in an instant of awakening (DUNWU). For these claims, Daosheng was harshly criticized by the community of scholars in Jianye, which prompted Daosheng to return to Lushan once more. His interpretations were eventually corroborated in subsequent Chinese translations of the MAHĀPARINIRVĀṆASŪTRA and become emblematic of many important strands of indigenous Chinese Buddhism. Daosheng's teachings are quoted in many of his contemporaries' works and Daosheng himself is known to have composed numerous treatises and commentaries, including the *Foxing dangyou lun* ("Buddha Nature Perforce Exists"), *Fashen wuse lun* ("DHARMAKĀYA Lacks Form"), *Fo wu jingtu lun* ("The Buddha has no Pure Land"), and *Fahua jing yishu* (a commentary on the SADDHARMAPUṆḌARĪKASŪTRA).

**daosu**. (道俗). In Chinese, "the religious and the laity." See DAO; DAOREN.

**daotong**. (J. dōtsū; K. tot'ong 道通). In Chinese, lit. "penetrate the way"; a term used by many different Chinese religious and secular groups to refer generally to the act of "penetrating," attaining, accomplishing, or completing a path of cultivation and training. Daotong can also refer to the state of perfection achieved through such practice.

**daotu**. (J. tōzu; K. todo 刀塗). In Chinese, lit. "destiny of knives," viz., "butchery"; a descriptive term to refer to the realm of animals (TIRYAK). This rebirth destiny (GATI) is typically depicted in Buddhist cosmology as highly undesirable, one of the reasons being that many animals inevitably suffer the fate of being butchered to feed others. The Sanskrit tiryaggati literally means the destiny of those who go horizontally, i.e., on all four legs, rather than standing up straight.

**Daoxin**. (J. Dōshin; K. Tosin 道信) (580–651). Chan monk and reputed fourth patriarch of the CHAN tradition. Although Daoxin's birthplace is not certain, some sources say he was a native of Qizhou in present-day Hubei province, while others mention Henei in Henan province. Little is known of his early training, but early Chan sources such as the LENGQIE SHIZI JI and CHUAN FABAO JI claim that Daoxin studied under SENGCAN, the putative third patriarch of Chan and supposed successor to BODHIDHARMA and HUIKE, his connection to this dubious figure is tenuous at best, however, and is probably a retrospective creation. The earliest biography of Daoxin, recorded in the XU GAOSENG ZHUAN ("Supplementary Biographies of Eminent Monks"), not only does not posit any connection of Daoxin to the preceding three patriarchs but does not even mention their names. The *Chuan fabao ji* states that Daoxin was fully ordained in 607, after his purported period of study under Sengcan. Daoxin is subsequently known to have resided at the monastery of Dalinsi on LUSHAN in Jiangxi province for ten years. At the invitation of the inhabitants of his native Qizhou, Daoxin moved again to Mt. Shuangfeng in Huangmei (perhaps in 624), where he remained in seclusion for about thirty years. He is therefore sometimes known as Shuangfeng Daoxin. During his residence at Mt. Shuangfeng, Daoxin is claimed to have attracted more than five hundred students, among whom HONGREN, the fifth patriarch of Chan, is most famous. The lineage and teachings attributed to Daoxin and Hongren are typically called the East Mountain Teachings (DONGSHAN FAMEN) after the easterly peak of Mt. Shuangfeng, where Hongren dwelled. Daoxin was given the posthumous title Chan Master Dayi (Great Physician) by Emperor Daizong (r. 762–779) of the Tang dynasty. According to the *Lengqie shizi ji*, Daoxin composed the *Pusajie zuofa* ("Method of Conferring the BODHISATTVA Precepts"), which is no longer extant, and the *Rudao anxin yaofangbian famen* ("Essentials of the Teachings of the Expedient Means of Entering the Path and Pacifying the Mind"), which is embedded in the *Lengqie shizi ji*. This latter text employs the analogy of a mirror from the *Banzhou sanmei jing* (S. PRATYUTPANNABUDDHASAṂMUKHĀVASTHITASAMĀDHISŪTRA) to illustrate the insubstantiality of all phenomena, viz., one's sensory experiences are no more substantial than the reflections in a mirror. The text then presents the "single-practice SAMĀDHI" (YIXING SANMEI) as a practical means of accessing the path leading to NIRVĀṆA, based on the *Wenshushuo bore jing* ("Perfection of Wisdom Sūtra Spoken by Manjuśrī"). Single-practice samādhi here refers to sitting in meditation, the supreme practice that subsumes all other practices. In single-practice samādhi, the meditator contemplates every single aspect of one's mental and physical existence until one realizes they are all empty, and "guards that one without deviation" (shouyi buyi).

**Daoxuan**. (J. Dōsen; K. Tosŏn 道宣) (596–667). Chinese VINAYA master and reputed patriarch of the Nanshan vinaya school (NANSHAN LÜZONG); also known as Fabian. Daoxuan was a native of Wuxing in present-day Zhejiang province (or, according to another report, Runzhou in Jiangsu province). Daoxuan became a monk at age fifteen and studied monastic discipline under the vinaya master Zhishou. He later moved to ZHONGNANSHAN and established the monastery of Nanquansi. Daoxuan was also a prolific writer. In 626, he composed the *Sifen lü shanfan buque xingshi chao*, one of the most influential commentaries on the SIFEN LÜ ("Four-Part Vinaya") of the DHARMAGUPTAKA school. The next year, he composed the *Sifen lü shi pini yichao* and the XU GAOSENG ZHUAN, *Shijia fangzhi*, JI GUJIN FODAO LUNHENG, and other texts in the following years. When the monastery XIMINGSI was established in 658 by Emperor Gaozong (r. 649–683) in the Tang capital of Chang'an, Daoxuan was invited to serve as its abbot. In 664, while at Ximingsi, Daoxuan compiled a comprehensive catalogue of scriptures known as the DA TANG NEIDIAN LU and, in continuation of his earlier *Ji gujin fodao lunheng*, wrote a collection of essays in defense of Buddhism entitled the GUANG HONGMING JI.

**Daoyi**. (C). See MAZU DAOYI.

**Daozhe Chaoyuan**. (J. Dōsha Chōgen; K. Toja Ch'owŏn 道者超元) (1630–1698). Chinese CHAN and ZEN master in the LINJI lineage. Daozhe was a native of Xinghua prefecture in present-day Fujian province. He became a student of Gengxin Xingmi (1603–1659), a direct disciple of the Chan master FEIYIN TONGRONG and, after inheriting Gengxin's lineage, became a dharma cousin of the renowned Chan master YINYUAN LONGQI. In 1651, Daozhe traveled to Nagasaki, Japan, where he served as abbot of the monastery Sōfukuji for the next five years. During his stay in Japan, a number of important Buddhist figures visited him for instruction, including the monks Dokuan Genkō (1630–1698), Kengan Zen'etsu (1618–1690), EGOKU DŌMYŌ, Chōon Dōkai (1628–1695), and BANKEI YŌTAKU. Unlike his compatriot Yinyuan, who continued to reside in Japan, Daozhe returned to China in 1658 and died shortly thereafter. Daozhe played an important role in preparing the ground for Yinyuan's later establishment of the ŌBAKUSHŪ in Japan.

**Dari jing shu**. (J. Dainichikyōsho; K. Taeil kyŏng so 大日經疏). In Chinese, "Commentary on the MAHĀVAIROCANASŪTRA"; dictated by ŚUBHAKARASIṂHA and committed to writing with additional notes by his disciple YIXING. After Yixing's death, the *Dari jing shu* was further edited and expanded by the monks Zhiyan (d.u.) and Wengu (d.u.), and this new edition is known as the DARI JING YISHI. Both editions were transmitted to Japan (the *Dari jing shu* by KŪKAI, *Dari jing yishi* by ENNIN) and they seem to have circulated without a determinate number of volumes or fixed title. SAICHŌ, for example, cites a fourteen-roll edition of the *Dari jing shu*, and Kūkai cites a twenty-roll edition; Ennin cites a fourteen-roll edition of the *Dari jing yishi*, and ENCHIN cites a ten-roll edition. Those belonging to the Tōmitsu line of Kūkai's SHINGON tradition thus began to exclusively paraphrase the twenty-roll edition of the *Dari jing shu*, while those of the Taimitsu line of the TENDAI tradition relied solely on the version Ennin had brought back from China. The exact relation between the two editions remains a matter for further study. The first two rolls of the *Dari jing shu*, known more popularly in Japan as the "Kuchi no sho," provide notes and comments on the first chapter of the MAHĀVAIROCANĀBHISAṂBODHISŪTRA and serve as an important source for the study of the *Mahāvairocanasūtra's* central doctrines. Numerous studies and commentaries on the Kuchi no sho exist. The rest of Yixing's commentary, known as the "Oku no sho," is largely concerned with matters of ritual and art (see MAṆḌALA). Further explanations of the Oku no sho were primarily transmitted from master to disciple as an oral tradition in Japan; twelve such oral traditions are known to exist. The *Dari jing shu* played an important role in the rise of esoteric Buddhism (see TANTRA) in East Asia, and particularly in Japan.

**Dari jing yishi**. (J. Dainichikyō gishaku; K. Taeil kyŏng ŭisŏk 大日經義釋). In Chinese, "Interpretation of the Meaning of the MAHĀVAIROCANĀBHISAṂBODHISŪTRA." The monks Zhiyan (d.u.) and Wengu (d.u.) further edited and expanded upon the famous commentary on the *Mahāvairocanābhisaṃbodhisūtra*, the DARI JING SHU. The *Dari jing shu* was dictated by ŚUBHAKARASIṂHA and written down by his disciple YIXING, with further notes. Both texts were transmitted to Japan (the *Dari jing shu* by KŪKAI and *Dari jing yishi* by ENNIN); monks connected with the Taimitsu strand of the TENDAI tradition exclusively relied on the *Dari jing yishi* that Ennin had brought back from China. The eminent Japanese monk ENCHIN paid much attention to the *Dari jing yishi* and composed a catalogue for the text known as *Dainichigyō gishaku mokuroku*, wherein he details the provenance of the text and the circumstances of its arrival in Japan. Enchin also discusses three different points on which the *Dari jing yishi* was superior to the *Dari jing shu*. These points were further elaborated in his other commentaries on the *Dari jing yishi*. Few others besides Enchin have written commentaries on this text. In China, the Liao dynasty monk Jueyuan (d.u.) composed a commentary entitled the *Dari jing yishi yanmi chao*.

**Dar ma mdo sde**. (Darma Dode, eleventh century). Chief son of the renowned Tibetan translator MAR PA CHOS KYI BLO GROS. According to Mar pa's traditional biographies, he originally intended to make Dar ma mdo sde the principal heir to his most important teachings, especially the practice of transferring consciousness into—and thereby reanimating—a corpse (GRONG 'JUG). The son, however, died as a youth in an equestrian accident. As he was about to die, Mar pa gave him the instructions, and Dar ma mdo sde transferred his consciousness into the corpse of a nearby pigeon, who then flew to India, where he again transferred his consciousness into the corpse of a young brāhmaṇa child. The revived brāhmaṇa grew up to become a tantric adept named TI PHU PA ("Pigeon Man") and became an important link in the transmission of the nine aural lineage cycles of the formless ḍākinīs (LUS MED MKHA' 'GRO SNYAN RGYUD CHOS SKOR DGU) for the BKA' BRGYUD sect of Tibetan Buddhism. According to some traditions, the translator RWA LO TSĀ BA RDO RJE GRAGS PA used black magic to cause Dar ma mdo sde's fatal accident.

**darśana**. (P. dassana; T. mthong ba; C. jian; J. ken; K. kyŏn 見). In Sanskrit, lit. "seeing," viz., "vision," "insight," or "understanding." In a purely physical sense, darśana refers most basically to visual perception that occurs through the ocular sense organ. However, Buddhism also accepts a full range of sensory and extrasensory perceptions, such as those associated with meditative development (see YOGIPRATYAKṢA), that also involve "vision," in the sense of directly perceiving a reality hidden from ordinary sight. Darśana may thus refer to the seeing that occurs through any of the five types of "eyes" (CAKṢUS) mentioned in Buddhist literature, viz., (1) the physical eye (MĀṂSACAKṢUS), the sense base (ĀYATANA) associated with visual consciousness; (2) the divine eye (DIVYACAKṢUS), the vision associated with the spiritual power (ABHIJÑĀ) of clairvoyance; (3) the wisdom eye (PRAJÑĀCAKṢUS), which is the insight that derives from cultivating mainstream Buddhist practices; (4) the dharma eye (DHARMACAKṢUS), which is exclusive to the BODHISATTVAS; and (5) the buddha eye (BUDDHACAKṢUS), which subsumes all the other four. When used in its denotation of "insight," darśana often appears in the compound "knowledge and vision" (JÑĀNADARŚANA), viz., the direct insight that accords with reality (YATHĀBHŪTA) of the three marks of existence (TRILAKṢAṆA)—impermanence (ANITYA), suffering (DUḤKHA), and nonself/insubstantiality (ANĀTMAN)—and one of the qualities perfected on the path leading to the state of "worthy one" (ARHAT). Darśana is usually considered to involve awakening (BODHI) to the truth, liberation (VIMUKTI) from bondage, and purification (VIŚUDDHI) of all afflictions (KLEŚA). The perfection of knowledge and vision (jñānadarśanapāramitā) is also said to be an alternate name for the perfection of wisdom (PRAJÑĀPĀRAMITĀ), one of the six perfections (PĀRAMITĀ) of the bodhisattva path. In the fivefold structure of the Buddhist path, the DARŚANAMĀRGA constitutes the third path. The related term "view" (DṚṢṬI), which derives from the same Sanskrit root √dṛś ("to see"), is sometimes employed similarly to darśana, although it also commonly conveys the more pejorative meanings of dogma, heresy, or extreme or wrong views regarding the self and the world, often as propounded by non-Buddhist philosophical schools. Darśana is also sometimes used within the Indian tradition to indicate a philosophical or religious system, a usage still current today.

**darśanamārga**. (T. mthong lam; C. jiandao; J. kendō; K. kyŏndo 見道). In Sanskrit, "path of vision"; the third of the five paths (PAÑCAMĀRGA) to liberation and enlightenment, whether as an ARHAT or as a buddha. It follows the second path, the path of preparation (PRAYOGAMĀRGA) and precedes the fourth path, the path of meditation or cultivation (BHĀVANĀMĀRGA). This path marks the adept's first direct perception of reality, without the intercession of concepts, and brings an end to the first three of the ten fetters (SAṂYOJANA) that bind one to the cycle of rebirth: (1) belief in the existence of a self in relation to the body (SATKĀYADṚṢṬI), (2) belief in the efficacy of rites and rituals (ŚĪLAVRATAPARĀMARŚA) as a means of salvation, and (3) doubt about the efficacy of the path (VICIKITSĀ). Because this vision renders one a noble person (ĀRYA), the path of vision marks the inception of the "noble path" (āryamārga). According to the Sarvāstivāda soteriological system, the darśanamārga occurs over the course of fifteen moments of realization of the FOUR NOBLE TRUTHS, with the sixteenth moment marking the beginning of the BHĀVANĀMĀRGA. There are four moments of realization for each of the four truths. The first moment is that of doctrinal acquiescence (DHARMAKṢĀNTI) with regard to the sensuous realm (KĀMADHĀTU). In that moment, the afflictions (KLEŚA) of the sensuous realm associated with the truth of suffering are abandoned. This is followed by a moment of doctrinal knowledge (DHARMAJÑĀNA) of the truth of suffering with regard to the sensuous realm, which is the state of understanding that the afflictions of that level have been abandoned. Next comes a moment of realization called subsequent acquiescence (anvayakṣānti), in which the afflictions associated with the truth of suffering in the two upper realms, the realm of subtle materiality (RŪPADHĀTU) and the immaterial realm (ĀRŪPYADHĀTU) are abandoned; there is finally a moment of subsequent knowledge (anvayajñāna) of the truth of suffering with regard to the two upper realms. This sequence of four moments—doctrinal acquiescence and doctrinal knowledge (which are concerned with the sensuous realm) and subsequent acquiescence and subsequent knowledge (which are concerned with the two upper realms)—is repeated for the remaining truths of origin, cessation, and path. In each case, the moments of realization called acquiescence are the time when the afflictions are actually abandoned; they are called uninterrupted paths (ANANTARYAMĀRGA) because they cannot be interrupted or impeded in severing the hold of the afflictions. The eight moments of knowledge are the state of having realized that the afflictions of the particular level have been abandoned. They are called paths of liberation (VIMUKTIMĀRGA). An uninterrupted path, followed by a path of liberation, are likened to throwing out a thief and locking the door behind him. The sixteenth moment in the sequence—the subsequent knowledge of the truth of the path with regard to the upper realms—constitutes the first moment of the next path, the bhāvanāmārga. For a BODHISATTVA, the attainment of the path of vision coincides with the inception of the first BODHISATTVABHŪMI (see also DAŚABHŪMI). The ABHIDHARMASAMUCCAYA explains that the bodhisattva's path of vision is also a direct perception of reality and is focused on the four noble truths; unlike the mainstream account, however, all three realms are considered simultaneously, and the sixteenth moment is not the first instant of the path of cultivation (bhāvanāmārga). The YOGĀCĀRA system is based on their doctrine of the falsehood of the subject/object bifurcation. The first eight instants describe the elimination of fetters based on false conceptualization (VIKALPA) of objects, and the last eight the elimination of fetters based on the false conceptualization of a subject; thus the actual path of vision is a direct realization of the emptiness (ŚŪNYATĀ) of all dharmas (sarvadharmaśūnyatā). This view of the darśanamārga as the first direct perception (PRATYAKṢA) of emptiness is also found in the MADHYAMAKA school, according to which the bodhisattva begins to abandon the afflictive obstructions (KLEŚĀVARAṆA) upon attaining the darśanamārga. See also DHARMAKṢĀNTI; JIEWU; DUNWU JIANXIU.

**Darumashū**. (達摩宗). In Japanese, the "BODHIDHARMA sect"; one of the earliest Japanese Buddhist ZEN sects, established in the tenth century by DAINICHI NŌNIN; the sect takes its name from the putative founder of the CHAN tradition, Bodhidharma. Little was known about the teachings of the Darumashū until the late-twentieth century apart from criticisms found in the writings of its contemporary rivals, who considered the school to be heretical. Criticisms focused on issues of the authenticity of Nōnin's lineage and antinomian tendencies in Nōnin's teachings. A recently discovered Darumashū treatise, the *Jōto shōgakuron* ("Treatise on the Attainment of Complete, Perfect Enlightenment"), discusses the prototypical Chan statement "mind is the buddha," demonstrating that a whole range of benefits, both worldly and religious, would accrue to an adept who simply awakens to that truth. As a critique of the Darumashū by Nōnin's rival MYŌAN EISAI states, however, since the school posits that the mind is already enlightened and the afflictions (KLEŚA) do not exist in reality, its adherents claimed that there therefore no precepts that had to be kept or practices to be followed, for religious cultivation would only serve to hinder the experience of awakening. The Darumashū also emphasized the importance of the transmission of the patriarchs' relics (J. shari; S. ŚARĪRA) as a mark of legitimacy. Although the Darumashū was influential enough while Nōnin was alive to prompt other sects to call for its suppression, it did not survive its founder's death, and most of Nōnin's leading disciples affiliated themselves with other prominent teachers, such as DŌGEN KIGEN. These Darumashū adherents had a significant influence on early SŌTŌSHŪ doctrine and self-identity and seem to have constituted the majority of the Sōtōshū tradition into its third generation of successors. ¶ Darumashū, as the Japanese pronunciation of the Chinese term Damo zong (Bodhidharma lineage), can also refer more generally to the CHAN/SŎN/ZEN school, which traces its heritage back to the founder and first Chinese patriarch, Bodhidharma.

**daśabhūmi**. (T. sa bcu; C. shidi; J. jūji; K. sipchi 十地). In Sanskrit, lit., "ten grounds," "ten stages"; the ten highest reaches of the bodhisattva path (MĀRGA) leading to buddhahood. The most systematic and methodical presentation of the ten BHŪMIs appears in the DAŚABHŪMIKASŪTRA ("Ten Bhūmis Sūtra"), where each of the ten stages is correlated with seminal doctrines of mainstream Buddhism—such as the four means of conversion (SAṂGRAHAVASTU) on the first four bhūmis, the FOUR NOBLE TRUTHS (CATVĀRY ĀRYASATYĀNI) on the fifth bhūmi, and the chain of dependent origination (PRATĪTYASAMUTPĀDA) on the sixth bhūmi, etc.—as well as with mastery of one of a list of ten perfections (PĀRAMITĀ) completed in the course of training as a bodhisattva. The list of the ten bhūmis of the *Daśabhūmikasūtra*, which becomes standard in most Mahāyāna traditions, is as follows: (1) PRAMUDITĀ (joyful) corresponds to the path of vision (DARŚANAMĀRGA) and the bodhisattva's first direct realization of emptiness (ŚŪNYATĀ). The bodhisattva masters on this bhūmi the perfection of giving (DĀNAPĀRAMITĀ), learning to give away those things most precious to him, including his wealth, his wife and family, and even his body (see DEHADĀNA); (2) VIMALĀ (immaculate, stainless) marks the inception of the path of cultivation (BHĀVANĀMĀRGA), where the bodhisattva develops all the superlative traits of character incumbent on a buddha through mastering the perfection of morality (ŚĪLAPĀRAMITĀ); (3) PRABHĀKARĪ (luminous, splendrous), where the bodhisattva masters all the various types of meditative experiences, such as DHYĀNA, SAMĀPATTI, and the BRAHMAVIHĀRA; despite the emphasis on meditation in this bhūmi, it comes to be identified instead with the perfection of patience (KṢĀNTIPĀRAMITĀ), ostensibly because the bodhisattva is willing to endure any and all suffering in order to master his practices; (4) ARCIṢMATĪ (radiance, effulgence), where the flaming radiance of the thirty-seven factors pertaining to enlightenment (BODHIPĀKṢIKADHARMA) becomes so intense that it incinerates obstructions (ĀVARAṆA) and afflictions (KLEŚA), giving the bodhisattva inexhaustible energy in his quest for enlightenment and thus mastering the perfection of vigor or energy (VĪRYAPĀRAMITĀ); (5) SUDURJAYĀ (invincibility, hard-to-conquer), where the bodhisattva comprehends the various permutations of truth (SATYA), including the four noble truths, the two truths (SATYADVAYA) of provisional (NEYĀRTHA) and absolute (NĪTĀRTHA), and masters the perfection of meditative absorption (DHYĀNAPĀRAMITĀ); (6) ABHIMUKHĪ (immediacy, face-to-face), where, as the name implies, the bodhisattva stands at the intersection between SAṂSĀRA and NIRVĀṆA, turning away from the compounded dharmas of saṃsāra and turning to face the profound wisdom of the buddhas, thus placing him "face-to-face" with both the compounded (SAṂSKṚTA) and uncompounded (ASAṂSKṚTA) realms; this bhūmi is correlated with mastery of the perfection of wisdom (PRAJÑĀPĀRAMITĀ); (7) DŪRAṄGAMĀ (far-reaching, transcendent), which marks the bodhisattva's freedom from the four perverted views (VIPARYĀSA) and his mastery of the perfection of expedients (UPĀYAPĀRAMITĀ), which he uses to help infinite numbers of sentient beings; (8) ACALĀ (immovable, steadfast), which is marked by the bodhisattva's acquiescence or receptivity to the nonproduction of dharmas (ANUTPATTIKADHARMAKṢĀNTI); because he is now able to project transformation bodies (NIRMĀṆAKĀYA) anywhere in the universe to help sentient beings, this bhūmi is correlated with mastery of the perfection of aspiration or resolve (PRAṆIDHĀNAPĀRAMITĀ); (9) SĀDHUMATĪ (eminence, auspicious intellect), where the bodhisattva acquires the four analytical knowledges (PRATISAṂVID), removing any remaining delusions regarding the use of the supernatural knowledges or powers (ABHIJÑĀ), and giving the bodhisattva complete autonomy in manipulating all dharmas through the perfection of power (BALAPĀRAMITĀ); and (10) DHARMAMEGHĀ (cloud of dharma), the final bhūmi, where the bodhisattva becomes autonomous in interacting with all material and mental factors, and gains all-pervasive knowledge that is like a cloud producing a rain of dharma that nurtures the entire world; this stage is also described as being pervaded by meditative absorption (DHYĀNA) and mastery of the use of codes (DHĀRAṆĪ), just as the sky is filled by clouds; here the bodhisattva achieves the perfection of knowledge (JÑĀNAPĀRAMITĀ). As the bodhisattva ascends through the ten bhūmis, he acquires extraordinary powers, which CANDRAKĪRTI describes in the eleventh chapter of his MADHYAMAKĀVATĀRA. On the first bhūmi, the bodhisattva can, in a single instant (1) see one hundred buddhas, (2) be blessed by one hundred buddhas and understand their blessings, (3) live for one hundred eons, (4) see the past and future in those one hundred eons, (5) enter into and rise from one hundred SAMĀDHIs, (6) vibrate one hundred worlds, (7) illuminate one hundred worlds, (8) bring one hundred beings to spiritual maturity using emanations, (9) go to one hundred BUDDHAKṢETRA, (10), open one hundred doors of the doctrine (DHARMAPARYĀYA), (11) display one hundred versions of his body, and (12) surround each of those bodies with one hundred bodhisattvas. The number one hundred increases exponentially as the bodhisattva proceeds; on the second bhūmi it becomes one thousand, on the third one hundred thousand, and so on; on the tenth, it is a number equal to the particles of an inexpressible number of buddhakṣetra. As the bodhisattva moves from stage to stage, he is reborn as the king of greater and greater realms, ascending through the Buddhist cosmos. Thus, on the first bhūmi he is born as king of JAMBUDVĪPA, on the second of the four continents, on the third as the king of TRĀYATRIṂŚA, and so on, such that on the tenth he is born as the lord of AKANIṢṬHA. ¶ According to the rather more elaborate account in chapter eleven of the CHENG WEISHI LUN (**Vijñaptimātratāsiddhi*), each of the ten bhūmis is correlated with the attainment of one of the ten types of suchness (TATHATĀ); these are accomplished by discarding one of the ten kinds of obstructions (āvaraṇa) by mastering one of the ten perfections (pāramitā). The suchnesses achieved on each of the ten bhūmis are, respectively: (1) universal suchness (sarvatragatathatā; C. bianxing zhenru), (2) supreme suchness (paramatathatā; C. zuisheng zhenru), (3) ubiquitous, or "supreme outflow" suchness (paramaniṣyandatathatā; C. shengliu zhenru), (4) unappropriated suchness (aparigrahatathatā; C. wusheshou zhenru), (5) undifferentiated suchness (abhinnajātīyatathatā; C. wubie zhenru), (6) the suchness that is devoid of maculations and contaminants (asaṃkliṣṭāvyavadātatathatā; C. wuranjing zhenru), (7) the suchness of the undifferentiated dharma (abhinnatathatā; C. fawubie zhenru), (8) the suchness that neither increases nor decreases (anupacayāpacayatathatā; C. buzengjian), (9) the suchness that serves as the support of the mastery of wisdom (jñānavaśitāsaṃniśrayatathatā; C. zhizizai suoyi zhenru), and (10) the suchness that serves as the support for mastery over actions (kriyādivaśitāsaṃniśrayatathatā; C. yezizai dengsuoyi). These ten suchnessses are obtained by discarding, respectively: (1) the obstruction of the common illusions of the unenlightened (pṛthagjanatvāvaraṇa; C. yishengxing zhang), (2) the obstruction of the deluded (mithyāpratipattyāvaraṇa; C. xiexing zhang), (3) the obstruction of dullness (dhandhatvāvaraṇa; C. andun zhang), (4) the obstruction of the manifestation of subtle afflictions (sūkṣmakleśasamudācārāvaraṇa; C. xihuo xianxing zhang), (5) the obstruction of the lesser HĪNAYĀNA ideal of parinirvāṇa (hīnayānaparinirvāṇāvaraṇa; C. xiasheng niepan zhang), (6) the obstruction of the manifestation of coarse characteristics (sthūlanimittasamudācārāvaraṇa; C. cuxiang xianxing zhang), (7) the obstruction of the manifestation of subtle characteristics (sūkṣmanimittasamudācārāvaraṇa; C. xixiang xianxing zhang), (8) the obstruction of the continuance of activity even in the immaterial realm that is free from characteristics (nirnimittābhisaṃskārāvaraṇa; C. wuxiang jiaxing zhang), (9) the obstruction of not desiring to act on behalf of others' salvation (parahitacaryākāmanāvaraṇa; C. buyuxing zhang), and (10) the obstruction of not yet acquiring mastery over all things (fa weizizai zhang). These ten obstructions are overcome by practicing, respectively: (1) the perfection of giving (dānapāramitā), (2) the perfection of morality (śīlapāramitā), (3) the perfection of forbearance (kṣāntipāramitā), (4) the perfection of energetic effort (vīryapāramitā), (5) the perfection of meditation (dhyānapāramitā), (6) the perfection of wisdom (prajñāpāramitā), (7) the perfection of expedient means (upāyapāramitā), (8) the perfection of the vow (to attain enlightenment) (praṇidhānapāramitā), (9) the perfection of power (balapāramitā), and (10) the perfection of knowledge (jñānapāramitā). ¶ The eighth, ninth, and tenth bhūmis are sometimes called "pure bhūmis," because, according to some commentators, upon reaching the eighth bhūmi, the bodhisattva has abandoned all of the afflictive obstructions (KLEŚĀVARAṆA) and is thus liberated from any further rebirth. It appears that there were originally only seven bhūmis, as is found in the BODHISATTVABHŪMI, where the seven bhūmis overlap with an elaborate system of thirteen abidings or stations (vihāra), some of the names of which (such as pramuditā) appear also in the standard bhūmi schema of the *Daśabhūmikasūtra*. Similarly, though a listing of ten bhūmis appears in the MAHĀVASTU, a text associated with the LOKOTTARAVĀDA subsect of the MAHĀSĀṂGHIKA school, only seven are actually discussed there, and the names given to the stages are completely different from those found in the later *Daśabhūmikasūtra*; the stages there are also a retrospective account of how past buddhas have achieved enlightenment, rather than a prescription for future practice. ¶ The daśabhūmi schema is sometimes correlated with other systems of classifying the bodhisattva path. In the five levels of the Yogācāra school's outline of the bodhisattva path (PAÑCAMĀRGA; C. wuwei), the first bhūmi (pramuditā) is presumed to be equivalent to the level of proficiency (*prativedhāvasthā; C. tongdawei), the third of the five levels; while the second bhūmi onward corresponds to the level of cultivation (C. xiuxiwei), the fourth of the five levels. The first bhūmi is also correlated with the path of vision (DARŚANAMĀRGA), while the second and higher bhūmis correlate with the path of cultivation (BHĀVANĀMĀRGA). In terms of the doctrine of the five acquiescences (C. ren; S. kṣānti) listed in the RENWANG JING, the first through the third bhūmis are equivalent to the second acquiescence, the acquiescence of belief (C. xinren; J. shinnin; K. sinin); the fourth through the sixth stages to the third, the acquiescence of obedience (C. shunren; J. junnin; K. sunin); the seventh through the ninth stages to the fourth, the acquiescence to the nonproduction of dharmas (anutpattikadharmakṣānti; C. wushengren; J. mushōnin; K. musaengin); the tenth stage to the fifth and final acquiescence, to extinction (jimieren; J. jakumetsunin; K. chŏngmyŏrin). FAZANG's HUAYANJING TANXUAN JI ("Notes Plumbing the Profundities of the AVATAṂSAKASŪTRA") classifies the ten bhūmis in terms of practice by correlating the first bhūmi to the practice of faith (ŚRADDHĀ), the second bhūmi to the practice of morality (ŚĪLA), the third bhūmi to the practice of concentration (SAMĀDHI), and the fourth bhūmi and higher to the practice of wisdom (PRAJÑĀ). In the same text, Fazang also classifies the bhūmis in terms of vehicle (YĀNA) by correlating the first through third bhūmis with the vehicle of humans and gods (rentiansheng), the fourth through the seventh stage to the three vehicles (TRIYĀNA), and the eighth through tenth bhūmis to the one vehicle (EKAYĀNA). ¶ Besides the list of the daśabhūmi outlined in the *Daśabhūmikasūtra*, the MAHĀPRAJÑĀPĀRAMITĀSŪTRA and the DAZHIDU LUN (**Mahāprajñāpāramitāśāstra*) list a set of ten bhūmis, called the "bhūmis in common" (gongdi), which are shared between all the three vehicles of ŚRĀVAKAS, PRATYEKABUDDHAS, and bodhisattvas. These are the bhūmis of: (1) dry wisdom (śuklavidarśanābhūmi; C. ganhuidi), which corresponds to the level of three worthies (sanxianwei, viz., ten abidings, ten practices, ten transferences) in the śrāvaka vehicle and the initial arousal of the thought of enlightenment (prathamacittotpāda) in the bodhisattva vehicle; (2) lineage (gotrabhūmi; C. xingdi, zhongxingdi), which corresponds to the stage of the "aids to penetration" (NIRVEDHABHĀGĪYA) in the śrāvaka vehicle, and the final stage of the ten transferences in the fifty-two bodhisattva stages; (3) eight acquiescences (aṣṭamakabhūmi; C. barendi), the causal incipiency of stream-enterer (SROTAĀPANNA) in the case of the śrāvaka vehicle and the acquiescence to the nonproduction of dharmas (anutpattikadharmakṣānti) in the bodhisattva path (usually corresponding to the first or the seventh through ninth bhūmis of the bodhisattva path); (4) vision (darśanabhūmi; C. jiandi), corresponding to the fruition or fulfillment (PHALA) level of the stream-enterer in the śrāvaka vehicle and the stage of nonretrogression (AVAIVARTIKA), in the bodhisattva path (usually corresponding to the completion of the first or the eighth bhūmi); (5) diminishment (tanūbhūmi; C. baodi), corresponding to the fulfillment level (phala) of stream-enterer or the causal incipiency of the once-returner (sakṛdāgāmin) in the śrāvaka vehicle, or to the stage following nonretrogression before the attainment of buddhahood in the bodhisattva path; (6) freedom from desire (vītarāgabhūmi; C. liyudi), equivalent to the fulfillment level of the nonreturner in the śrāvaka vehicle, or to the stage where a bodhisattva attains the five supernatural powers (ABHIJÑĀ); (7) complete discrimination (kṛtāvibhūmi), equivalent to the fulfillment level of the ARHAT in the śrāvaka vehicle, or to the stage of buddhahood (buddhabhūmi) in the bodhisattva path (buddhabhūmi) here refers not to the fruition of buddhahood but merely to the state in which a bodhisattva has the ability to exhibit the eighteen qualities distinctive to the buddhas (ĀVEṆIKA[BUDDHA]DHARMA); (8) pratyekabuddha (pratyekabuddhabhūmi); (9) bodhisattva (bodhisattvabhūmi), the whole bodhisattva career prior to the fruition of buddhahood; (10) buddhahood (buddhabhūmi), the stage of the fruition of buddhahood, when the buddha is completely equipped with all the buddhadharmas, such as omniscience (SARVĀKĀRAJÑATĀ). As is obvious in this schema, despite being called the bhūmis "common" to all three vehicles, the shared stages continue only up to the seventh stage; the eighth through tenth stages are exclusive to the bodhisattva vehicle. This anomaly suggests that the last three bhūmis of the bodhisattvayāna were added to an earlier śrāvakayāna seven-bhūmi scheme. ¶ The presentation of the bhūmis in the PRAJÑĀPĀRAMITĀ commentarial tradition following the ABHISAMAYĀLAṂKĀRA uses the names found in the *Daśabhūmikasūtra* for the bhūmis and understands them all as bodhisattva levels; it introduces the names of the ten bhūmis found in the *Dazhidu lun* as levels that bodhisattvas have to pass beyond (S. atikrama) on the tenth bodhisattva level, which it calls the buddhabhūmi. This tenth bodhisattva level is not the level of an actual buddha, but the level on which a bodhisattva has to transcend attachment (abhiniveśa) to not only the levels reached by the four sets of noble persons (ĀRYAPUDGALA) but to the bodhisattvabhūmis as well. See also BHŪMI.

**Daśabhūmikasūtra**. (T. Sa bcu pa'i mdo; C. Shidi jing/Shizhu jing; J. Jūjikyō/Jūjūkyō; K. Sipchi kyŏng/Sipchu kyŏng 十地經/十住經). In Sanskrit, "Scripture of the Ten Stages"; the definitive scriptural account of the ten "grounds" or "stages" (DAŚABHŪMI) at the upper reaches of the BODHISATTVA path (MĀRGA). In the sūtra, each of the ten stages is correlated with seminal doctrines of mainstream Buddhism, as well as with mastery of one of a list of ten perfections (PĀRAMITĀ) completed in the course of training as a bodhisattva. The sūtra appears as one of the chapters of the AVATAṂSAKASŪTRA and also circulated as an independent text. For a full treatment, see DAŚABHŪMI; BHŪMI.

**Daśabhūmivyākhyāna**. (T. Sa bcu pa'i rnam par bshad pa; C. Shidijing lun; J. Jūjikyōron; K. Sipchigyŏng non 十地經論). In Sanskrit, "Explanation of the DAŚABHŪMIKASŪTRA"; a commentary on the *Daśabhūmikasūtra* attributed to the Indian exegete VASUBANDHU. The work served as the basis for the Chinese DI LUN ZONG, "School of *Di lun* Exegetes," a lineage of Buddhist scholiasts who studied this text. (*Di lun* is an abbreviation of the *Shidijing lun*, the Chinese translation of the *Daśabhūmivyākhyāna*.) The school is considered to be one of the earliest of the indigenous scholastic traditions of East Asian MAHĀYĀNA Buddhism, and its thought draws on strands of Indic thought that derive from both the YOGĀCĀRA and TATHĀGATAGARBHA traditions.

**daśadhātu**. (T. [gzugs can gyi] khams bcu; C. shijie; J. jikkai; K. sipkye 十界). In Sanskrit, "ten elements"; an ABHIDHARMA classification referring to the five physical sense organs (eyes, ears, nose, tongue, and body) plus the five sense objects (visual, auditory, olfactory, gustatory, and tactile objects). ¶ In MAHĀYĀNA Buddhism, and especially in the East Asian TIANTAI schools, the term was appropriated to refer to ten "realms" or "destinies" of being; in East Asian Buddhism, this denotation is by far the most common. These destinies are, from the bottom up, the six rebirth destinies (GATI) in SAṂSĀRA, viz., (1) hells (naraka; see NĀRAKA), (2) hungry ghosts (PRETA), (3) animals (TIRYAK), (4) demigods (ASURA), (5) human beings (MANUṢYA), and (6) divinities (DEVA), plus the four destinies of enlightened beings, viz., (7) disciples of the Buddha (ŚRĀVAKA), (8) solitary buddhas (PRATYEKABUDDHA), (9) BODHISATTVAs, and (10) buddhas. According to Tiantai doctrine, since these ten destinies are mutually pervasive (C. shijie huju), each of these realms pervades, and is pervaded by, all the nine other realms; hence, the potential for buddhahood is inherent even in the most dire destiny in the hells.

**daśadiś**. [alt. diśā] (P. dasadisā; T. phyogs bcu; C. shifang; J. jippō; K. sibang 十方). In Sanskrit, "ten directions"; the four cardinal directions (north, east, south, west), the four intermediate directions (northeast, southeast, southwest, northwest), plus the zenith and the nadir. By covering every possible direction, the "ten directions" therefore comes to be used by extension to mean "everywhere," in the sense of an all-pervasive completeness or comprehensiveness, whether of activities, states, or occurrences. The MAHĀYĀNA tradition presumes that there are innumerable world systems in all the ten directions (S. daśadiglokadhātu; C. shifang shijie), as well as innumerable "buddhas of the ten directions" (daśadigbuddha). See also SHIFANG CHA; PĀPADEŚANĀ.

**daśaśīla**. (P. dasasīla; T. tshul khrims bcu; C. shijie; J. jikkai; K. sipkye 十戒). In Sanskrit, "ten precepts"; an expansion and enhancement of the five lay precepts (PAÑCAŚĪLA), which all male novices (ŚRĀMAṆERA) and female novices (ŚRĀMAṆERIKĀ) were required to follow as part of their training; also known as the "restraints for novices" (ŚRĀMAṆERASAṂVARA). The ten are framed in terms of training rules (ŚIKṢĀPADA), viz., "I undertake the training rule to abstain from": (1) killing; (2) stealing; (3) sexual activity; (4) false speech; (5) intoxicants; (6) eating after midday; (7) dancing, singing, music, and other unseemly forms of entertainment; (8) using garlands, perfumes, and unguents to adorn the body; (9) using high and luxurious beds and couches; and (10) handling money. On full- and new-moon days (UPOṢADHA), the laity have the option of taking all these precepts except the tenth; numbers 7 and 8 were then combined to give a set of eight precepts to be specially followed on these retreat days (S. upoṣadhaśīla; P. uposathasīla) as a sort of temporary renunciation. In the MŪLASARVĀSTIVĀDA VINAYA followed in Tibet, these ten precepts are expanded to thirty-six.

**Dasheng dayi zhang**. (J. Daijō daigishō; K. Taesŭng taeŭi chang 大乘大義章). In Chinese "Compendium of the Great Purport of the Mahāyāna," in three rolls; also known as the *Jiumoluoshi fashi dayi*, or "The Great Purport of the Great Master KUMĀRAJĪVA." The *Dasheng dayi zhang* is a compendium of letters that Kumārajīva wrote in reply to LUSHAN HUIYUAN's inquiries about MAHĀYĀNA doctrine. There are a total of eighteen categories of questions that are concerned largely with the nature of the dharma body (DHARMAKĀYA), emptiness (ŚŪNYATĀ), and the mind (CITTA). The *Dasheng dayi zhang* is a valuable source for studying the development of Mahāyāna thought in China.

**Dasheng faxiang jiao**. (C) (大乘法相教). See HUAYAN WUJIAO.

**Dasheng fayuan yilin zhang**. (J. Daijō hōon girinjō; K. Taesŭng pŏbwŏn ŭirim chang 大乘法苑義林章). In Chinese, "(Edited) Chapters on the Forest of Meaning of the Dharma-Garden of MAHĀYĀNA"; composed by the eminent Chinese monk KUIJI. This treatise consists of twenty-nine chapters in seven rolls, but a thirty-three chapter edition is known to have been transmitted to Japan in the second half of the twelfth century. Each chapter is concerned with an important doctrinal matter related to the YOGĀCĀRABHŪMIŚĀSTRA. Some chapters, for instance, discuss the various canons (PIṬAKA), two truths (SATYADVAYA), five faculties (INDRIYA), the sixty-two views (DṚṢṬI), eight liberations (AṢṬAVIMOKṢA), and buddha-lands (BUDDHAKṢETRA), to name but a few. Because of its comprehensive doctrinal coverage, the *Dasheng fayuan yilin zhang* has served as an invaluable source of information on early YOGĀCĀRA thought in China.

**Dasheng poxiang jiao**. (C) (大乘破相教). See HUAYAN WUJIAO.

**Dasheng qixin lun**. (S. *Mahāyānaśraddhotpādaśāstra; J. Daijō kishinron; K. Taesŭng kisin non 大乘起信論). In Chinese, "Treatise on the Awakening of Faith According to the MAHĀYĀNA"; attributed to the Indian author AŚVAGHOṢA, but now widely assumed to be an indigenous Chinese text (see APOCRYPHA) composed in the sixth century; typically known in English as simply the "Awakening of Faith." Since its composition, the text has remained one of the most influential treatises in all of East Asian Buddhism. The earliest and most widely used "translation" (c. 550) is attributed to the famous YOGĀCĀRA scholar PARAMĀRTHA, although some scholars have speculated that Paramārtha may in fact have composed the treatise after his arrival in China, perhaps even in Sanskrit, and then translated it into Chinese. The author of the *Dasheng qixin lun* sought to reconcile two of the dominant, if seemingly incompatible, strands in Mahāyāna Buddhism: TATHĀGATAGARBHA (embryo or womb of the buddhas) thought and the ĀLAYAVIJÑĀNA (storehouse consciousness) theory of consciousness. Tathāgatagarbha thought taught that all sentient beings have the potential to achieve enlightenment because that enlightenment is in fact inherent in the minds of sentient beings. What that doctrine did not seem to explain well to the East Asians, however, was why sentient beings who were inherently enlightened would have become deluded in the first place. Ālayavijñāna theory, by contrast, posited that the foundational recesses of the mind serve as a storehouse of the essentially infinite numbers of potentialities or seeds (BĪJA) of all past actions, including unsalutary deeds; this interpretation suggested to the East Asians that mental purity was not innate and that enlightenment therefore had to be catalyzed by some external source, such as "hearing the dharma," which would then prompt a "transformation of the basis" (ĀŚRAYAPARĀVṚTTI) that could lead to purity of mind. The ālayavijñāna thus explained the intractability of ignorance and delusion, but did not seem to offer ready accessibility to enlightenment. In its search for common ground between these two doctrines, the *Dasheng qixin lun* instead describes the mind as being comprised of two distinct, but complementary, aspects: true thusness (ZHENRU; S. TATHATĀ) and production-and-cessation (shengmie), which correspond respectively to ultimate truth (PARAMĀRTHASATYA) and conventional truth (SAṂVṚTISATYA) or the unconditioned (ASAṂSKṚTA) and conditioned (SAṂSKṚTA) realms. Since the mind that is subject to production and cessation (which the treatise identifies with ālayavijñāna) remains always grounded on the mind of true thusness (which the treatise identifies with tathāgatagarbha), the mind is therefore simultaneously deluded and enlightened. This distinction between this enlightened essence of the mind as "true thusness" and its various temporal manifestations as "production and cessation" is also described in terms of "essence" (TI) and "function" (YONG). From the standpoint of the buddhas and sages, the mind of the sentient being is therefore seen as being perpetually in a state of "original enlightenment" or "intrinsic enlightenment" (BENJUE; see also HONGAKU), while from the standpoint of sentient beings that same mind is seen as being deluded and thus in need of purification through a process of "actualizing enlightenment" (SHIJUE). Actualizing enlightenment involves the cultivation of calmness (ji; S. ŚAMATHA) and insight (guan; S. VIPAŚYANĀ), as well as the development of no-thought (WUNIAN), aspects of training that receive extensive discussion in the treatise. Once the process of actualizing enlightenment is completed, however, the student realizes that the enlightenment achieved through cultivation is in fact identical to the enlightenment that is innate. Hence, the difference between these two types of enlightenment is ultimately a matter of perspective: the buddhas and sages see the innate purity of the tathāgatagarbha as something intrinsic; ordinary persons (PṚTHAGJANA) see it as something that must be actualized through practice. Some East Asian Buddhists, such as WŎNHYO (617–686), seem to have presumed that the KŬMGANG SAMMAE KYŎNG (S. *Vajrasamādhisūtra*) was the scriptural source of the *Dasheng qixin lun*'s emblematic teaching of the one mind and its two aspects, even though we now know that that scripture was a Korean apocryphon that was not composed until over a century later. The most important commentaries to the Dasheng qixin lun are Wŏnhyo's TAESŬNG KISIN NON SO and TAESŬNG KISIN NON PYŎLGI, FAZANG's DASHENG QIXIN LUN YI JI, and JINGYING HUIYUAN's *Dasheng qixin lun yishu*.

**Dasheng qixin lun yi ji**. (J. Daijō kisihinron giki; K. Taesŭng kisin non ŭi ki 大乘起信論義記). In Chinese, "Notes on the Meaning of the 'Awakening of Faith According to the Mahāyāna'"; composed by the Chinese HUAYAN monk FAZANG. In addition to exegeses by WŎNHYO (see TAESŬNG KISIN NON SO) and JINGYING HUIYUAN, this commentary has been traditionally regarded as one of the three great commentaries on the DASHENG QIXIN LUN. Fazang's commentary relies heavily upon that by Wŏnhyo. Throughout the centuries, numerous other commentaries on the *Dasheng qixin lun* appeared in China, and most of them are based on Fazang's work. According to this commentary, the *Dasheng qixin lun* speaks of one mind, two gates, three greats, four faiths, and five practices. Fazang also categorizes the entire history of Buddhism into four traditions: (1) the tradition of grasping at the characteristics of dharmas (i.e., the HĪNAYĀNA), (2) the tradition of no characteristics and only true emptiness (i.e., the PRAJÑĀPĀRAMITĀ SŪTRAS and the MADHYAMAKA), (3) the tradition of YOGĀCĀRA and consciousness-only (i.e., the SAṂDHINIRMOCANASŪTRA and YOGĀCĀRABHŪMIŚĀSTRA), and (4) the tradition of conditioned origination from the TATHĀGATAGARBHA (i.e., the LAṄKĀVATĀRASŪTRA and *Dasheng qixin lun*). The notion of "conditioned origination from the tathāgatagarbha" (rulaizang yuanqi) reflects the author's Huayan training deriving from the AVATAMSAKASŪTRA and its notion of "nature origination" (XINGQI).

**Dasheng wusheng fangbian men**. (J. Daijō mushō hōbenmon; K. Taesŭng musaeng pangp'yŏn mun 大乘無生方便門). In Chinese, "Expedient Means of [Attaining] Nonproduction according to the MAHĀYĀNA"; a summary of the teachings of the Northern School (BEI ZONG) of CHAN. Several different recensions of this treatise were discovered at DUNHUANG; the text is also known as the *Dasheng wufangbian Beizong* ("Five Expedient Means of the Mahāyāna: the Northern School"). These different editions speak of five expedient means (UPĀYA): (1) a comprehensive explanation of the essence of buddhahood (corresponding to the DASHENG QIXIN LUN), (2) opening the gates of wisdom and sagacity (viz., the SADDHARMAPUṆḌARĪKASŪTRA), (3) manifesting the inconceivable dharma (the VIMALAKĪRTINIRDEŚA), (4) elucidating the true nature of dharmas (*Sūtra of [the god] Siyi*), and (5) the naturally unobstructed path to liberation (the AVATAṂSAKASŪTRA). Although this arrangement of scriptures bears a superficial resemblance to a taxonomy of texts (see JIAOXIANG PANSHI), a common feature of Chinese Buddhist polemics and exegesis, this listing was not intended to be hierarchical. The explanation of the five expedient means occurs largely in dialogic format. Unlike the *Dasheng wufangbian Beizong*, the *Dasheng wusheng fangbian men* also provides a description of the method of conferring the BODHISATTVA precepts (PUSA JIE). In its discussions of both the five expedient means and the bodhisattva precepts, great emphasis is placed on the need for purity of mind.

**Dasheng xuanlun**. (J. Daijō genron; K. Taesŭng hyŏn non 大乘玄論). In Chinese, "Profound Treatise on the MAHĀYĀNA"; one of most influential treatises of the SAN LUN ZONG, the Chinese branch of the MADHYAMAKA school of Indian philosophy; composed by JIZANG, in five rolls. The treatise is primarily concerned with eight general topics: the two truths (SATYADVAYA), eight negations, buddha-nature (FOXING), EKAYĀNA, NIRVĀṆA, two wisdoms, teachings, and treatises. The section on teachings explains the notions of sympathetic resonance (GANYING) and the PURE LAND. Explanations of Madhyamaka epistemology, the "four antinomies" (CATUṢKOṬI), and the MŪLAMADHYAMAKAKĀRIKĀ appear in the last section on treatises.

**Dasheng yi zhang**. (J. Daijō gishō; K. Taesŭng ŭi chang 大乘義章). In Chinese, "Compendium of the Purport of Mahāyāna"; compiled by JINGYING HUIYUAN; a comprehensive dictionary of Buddhist numerical lists that functions as a virtual encyclopedia of MAHĀYĀNA doctrine. Huiyuan organized 249 matters of doctrine into five sections: teachings, meanings, afflictions, purity, and miscellaneous matters (this last section is no longer extant). Each section is organized numerically, much as are some ABHIDHARMA treatises. The section on afflictions begins, for instance, with the meaning of the two hindrances and ends with the 84,000 hindrances. These various listings are then explained from a Mahāyāna perspective, with corroboration drawn from quotations from scriptures, treatises, and the sayings of other teachers. The *Dasheng yi zhang* serves as an important source for the study of Chinese Mahāyāna thought as it had developed during the Sui dynasty (589–618).

**dashi**. (J. daiji; K. taesa 大事). In Chinese, the "great enterprise" or "great matter"; often seen also as the "one great matter" (C. yidashi). The Chinese term dashi appears in KUMĀRAJĪVA's translation of the SADDHARMAPUṆḌARĪKASŪTRA ("Lotus Sūtra") regarding the reason why the buddhas appear in the world, but has no precise relation there to a specific Sanskrit term; possible equivalencies might be mahākṛtya, "the great action," or mahānuśaṃsa, "the great blessing." According to the MAHĀYĀNA tradition, the Buddha taught most of his teachings as provisional, transitional, and adaptive instructions that catered to the special contingencies of the spiritually less advanced. However, the Buddha's ultimate concern is the revelation of an ultimate and overriding message, the "great enterprise." Different Mahāyāna scriptures and schools interpret this ultimate message differently and often purport uniquely to convey that message. For example, according to the *Saddharmapuṇḍarīkasūtra* and the TIANTAI ZONG, the "great enterprise" is the revelation of the one vehicle (EKAYĀNA), through which all individuals without exception are able to enter the Mahāyāna path and realize the knowledge and vision of perfect buddhahood. According to the MAHĀPARINIRVĀṆASŪTRA, it is the eternal, absolute characteristics of the buddha-nature (FOXING; BUDDHADHĀTU). According to the SUKHĀVATĪVYŪHASŪTRA and the PURE LAND schools, it is the revelation of the paradisiacal pure land of SUKHĀVATĪ and the "original vows" of AMITĀBHA Buddha. And, finally, in the CHAN ZONG, the "great enterprise" refers to the general process of awakening to one's own original nature and becoming a buddha (JIANXING CHENGFO).

**'das log**. (delok). In Tibetan, literally "returned from beyond"; referring to an individual who dies but then returns to life, describing the horrors and suffering of the lower realms of rebirth (DURGATI). In Tibetan culture, such individuals are generally women and their testimony to the reality of karmic retribution often becomes a strong exhortation to practice virtue and to adopt such religious activities as reciting the famous six-syllable MANTRA (OṂ MAṆI PADME HŪṂ) of AVALOKITEŚVARA.

**Da Song seng shi lüe**. (J. Dai Sō sōshiryaku; K. Tae Song sŭng sa nyak 大宋僧史略). In Chinese, "Abbreviated History of the SAṂGHA, [compiled during] the Great Song [Dynasty]"; compiled by the monk ZANNING, in three rolls. Zanning began to write this institutional history of Buddhism in 978 and finished it in 999. In the first roll, Zanning describes the life of ŚĀKYAMUNI Buddha and the transmission of Buddhism to China. He also provides a brief history of monasteries, translation projects, and scriptural exegeses, as well as an explanation of the ordination procedure and the practice of repentance. The first roll ends with a history of the CHAN school. The second roll delineates the organization of the Buddhist monkhood and its recognition by the court in China. The last roll offers a history of Buddhist retreat societies, precept platforms (SĪMĀ), and émigré monks; in addition, it provides an explanation of the significance of bestowing the purple robe (of a royal master) and receiving the appellation of "great master" (dashi). As one of the earliest attempts to provide a comprehensive account of the history of Buddhism across Asia, the *Da Song seng shi lüe* serves as an invaluable source for the study of premodern Buddhist historiography.

**Dasuttarasutta**. (S. Daśottarasūtra; C. Shishang jing; J. Jūjōkyō; K. Sipsang kyŏng 十上經). In Pāli, "Discourse on Expanding Decades," or "Tenfold Series"; the thirty-fourth, and last, sutta of the DĪGHANIKĀYA. Several fragments of the Sanskrit recension of the text, the *Daśottarasūtra*, were discovered in TURFAN and these appear to represent the same SARVĀSTIVĀDA recension that was translated in Chinese by AN SHIGAO (*Chang ahan shibaofa jing*) sometime between 148 and 170 CE; this was one of the earliest Chinese renderings of a Buddhist scripture. A DHARMAGUPTAKA recension also appears as the tenth sūtra in the Chinese translation of the DĪRGHĀGAMA. According to this Pāli version, this scripture was preached by Sāriputta (ŚĀRIPUTRA) in Campā to a congregation of five hundred monks. For the edification of his listeners, and so that they might more easily be liberated and attain nibbāna (NIRVĀṆA), Sāriputta presents a systematic outline of the dhamma (DHARMA), using a schema of numerical classification that organizes the doctrine into groups ranging from a single factor (e.g., "the one thing to be developed," viz., mindfulness of the body) up to groups of ten (e.g., the ten wholesome ways of action). This sūtta thus provides one of the first canonical recensions of the "matrices" (P. mātikā; S. MĀTṚKĀ) that are thought to mark the incipiency of abhidhamma (S. ABHIDHARMA) exegesis, and its exegetical style is closely connected to that used in the SAṄGĪTISUTTA (S. *Saṃgītisūtra*); several of its exegetical categories are also reproduced in the SAṂGĪTIPARYĀYA of the Sarvāstivāda abhidharma.

**Da Tang neidian lu**. (J. Dai Tō naitenroku; K. Tae Tang naejŏn nok 大唐内典録). In Chinese, "The Great Tang Record of Inner [viz., Buddhist] Classics"; a catalogue of the Buddhist canon compiled by the Chinese monk DAOXUAN (596–667). While preparing an inventory of scriptures for the newly established library at the monastery of XIMINGSI, Daoxuan was unsatisfied with the quality of existing scriptural catalogues (JINGLU) and decided to compile his own. Daoxuan's catalogue draws heavily on earlier catalogues, such as the LIDAI SANBAO JI, CHU SANZANG JIJI, *Fajing lu*, and *Renshou lu*. The *Da Tang neidian lu* consists of ten major sections. The first section is the comprehensive catalogue of scriptures, which more or less corresponds to the list found in the *Lidai sanbao ji*. The second section, a taxonomy of scriptures, also largely corresponds to the *Renshou lu*. The third section lists the actual contents of Ximingsi's library and thus serves as an important source for studying the history of this monastery and its scriptural collection. The fourth section provides a list of texts appropriate for recitation. The fifth section deals with texts that contain mistakes and discusses their significance. The sixth section lists texts composed in China. The seventh and eighth sections cover miscellaneous texts and APOCRYPHA (162 in total). The ninth section lists previous scriptural catalogues of the past, and the tenth section discusses the virtues of reciting scriptures.

**Da Tang Xiyu ji**. (J. Dai Tō Saiiki ki; K. Tae Tang Sŏyŏk ki 大唐西域記). In Chinese, "The Great Tang Record of [Travels to] the Western Regions"; a travelogue of a pilgrimage to India by the Chinese translator and exegete XUANZANG (600/602–664) written in 646 at the request of the Tang emperor Taizong and edited by the monk Bianji (d. 652). Xuanzang was already a noted Buddhist scholiast in China when he decided to make the dangerous trek from China, through the Central Asian oases, to the Buddhist homeland of India. Xuanzang was especially interested in gaining access to the full range of texts associated with the YOGĀCĀRA school, only a few of which were then currently available in Chinese translation. He left on his journey in 627 and eventually spent fourteen years in India (629–643), where he traveled among many of the Buddhist sacred sites, collected manuscripts of Buddhist materials as yet untranslated into Chinese, and studied Sanskrit texts with various eminent teachers, most notably DHARMAPĀLA'S disciple ŚĪLABHADRA, who taught at the Buddhist university of NĀLANDĀ. The *Da Tang xiyu ji* provides a comprehensive overview of the different countries that Xuanzang visited during his travels in India and Central Asia, offering detailed descriptions of the geography, climate, customs, languages, and religious practices of these various countries. Xuanzang paid special attention to the different ways in which the teachings of Buddhism were cultivated in different areas of the Western Regions. The *Da Tang xiyou ji* thus serves as an indispensible tool in the study of the geography and Buddhist history of these regions. Xuanzang's travelogue was later fictionalized in the narrative *Xiyou ji* ("Journey to the West"), written c. 1592 during the Ming dynasty and attributed to Wu Cheng'en. The *Xiyou ji* is one of the greatest of Chinese vernacular novels and is deservedly famous for its fanciful accounts of the exploits of the monk-pilgrim, here called Sanzang (TREPIṬAKA), and especially of his protector, Monkey. See also CHENG WEISHI LUN.

**Da Tang Xiyu qiufa gaoseng zhuan**. (J. Dai Tō Saiiki guhō kōsōden; K. Tae Tang Sŏyŏk kubŏp kosŭng chŏn 大唐西域求法高僧傳). In Chinese, "The Great Tang Biographies of Eminent Monks who Sought the Dharma in the Western Regions"; compiled by the Chinese pilgrim and translator YIJING (635–713). Yijing's record, modeled after other texts in the "eminent monks" (GAOSENG ZHUAN) genre, provides biographies of fifty-six contemporary and near-contemporary East Asian monks who made the arduous journey from China to the Buddhist homeland of India. Forty-nine of the pilgrims discussed are Chinese and seven are identified as Korean. Yijing's account of his own pilgrimage to Sumatra and India appears independently in his NANHAI JIGUI NEIFA ZHUAN.

**Dāṭhāvaṃsa**. In Pāli, "History of the Tooth Relic"; a Pāli chronicle in verse, attributed to Dhammakitti, that records the history of the Buddha's TOOTH RELIC before its c. fourth century CE arrival in Sri Lanka; also known as the *Dantadhātuvaṃsa*. The work begins with an account of the previous buddha Dīpaṅkara (S. DĪPAṂKARA), followed by the story of Gotama (S. GAUTAMA) Buddha, his visit to Sri Lanka, his decease (P. parinibbāna; S. PARINIRVĀṆA), and the distribution of his relics (P. sarīra; S. ŚARĪRA). The history of the Tooth Relic at the city of Dantapura in the Indian kingdom of Kaliṅga follows. Finally, there is a detailed accounting of the circumstances that culminated in the relic's arrival at Sri Lanka during the reign of Sirimeghavaṇṇa in the fourth century CE and the building of a shrine to house it.

**Datong heshang**. (大通和尚). See SHENXIU.

**David-Néel, Alexandra**. (1868–1969). A famous traveler to Tibet. Born Alexandra David to a bourgeois family in Paris, she was educated in a Calvinist convent before studying Indian and Chinese philosophy at the Sorbonne and the Collège de France. In 1888, she traveled to London, where she became interested in Theosophy. In 1891, she journeyed to Ceylon and India (where she studied Vedānta) and traveled as far as Sikkim over eighteen months. Upon returning to France, she began a career as a singer and eventually was offered the position of female lead in the Hanoi Opera. Some years later, in Tunis, she met and married a railroad engineer, Philippe Néel, who insisted that she retire from the stage. She agreed to do so if he would finance a one-year trip to India for her. He ended up not seeing his wife again for another fourteen years. David-Néel became friends with THOMAS and CAROLINE RHYS DAVIDS in London, leading scholars of THERAVĀDA Buddhism, and corresponded with the ZEN scholar DAISETZ TEITARO SUZUKI, before publishing her first book on Buddhism in 1911, entitled, *Le modernisme bouddhiste et le bouddhisme du Bouddha*. She continued to Sikkim, where she met the thirteenth DALAI LAMA in Darjeeling in 1912, while he was briefly in residence there after fleeing a Chinese invasion of Tibet. David-Néel spent two years in retreat receiving instructions from a RNYING MA hermit-lama. In 1916, the British expelled her from Sikkim, so she traveled to Japan, where she was the guest of D. T. Suzuki. From there she went to China, traveling west in the company of a young Sikkimese monk named Yongden. Disguised as a pilgrim, she arrived in LHA SA in 1924, presumably the first European woman to reach the Tibetan capital. She returned to France as a celebrity the following year. She published the best-selling book *My Journey to Lhasa*, followed by a succession of books based on her travels in Tibet and her study and practice of Tibetan Buddhism. She built a home in Digne, which she named Samten Dzong, "Fortress of Concentration." David-Néel made one final trip to Asia as World War II began, but spent the rest of her life writing in Digne, where she died at the age of one hundred.

**Daxiu Zhengnian**. (J. Daikyū Shōnen; K. Taehyu Chŏngnyŏm 大休正念) (1215–1289). Chinese CHAN master in the LINJI ZONG. A native of Wenzhou in present-day Zhejiang province, Daxiu began his training under the CAODONG master Donggu Miaoguang (d. 1253) of Linyinsi, and later became the disciple of Shiqi Xinyue (d. 1254). In 1269, Daxiu left for Japan, where he received the patronage of the powerful regent Hōjō Tokimune (1251–1284). In Kamakura, Daxiu established the monastery Jōchiji, which came to be ranked fourth in the Kamakura GOZAN system. Daxiu also served as abbot of the monasteries ZENKŌJI, Juhukuji, and KENCHŌJI. In 1288, Daxiu became the abbot of ENGAKUJI, but passed away the next year in 1289. He was given the posthumous title Zen Master Butsugen ("Source of the Buddhas"). His teachings can be found in the *Daikyū oshō goroku*.

**Dayang Jingxuan**. (J. Taiyō Kyōgen; K. Taeyang Kyŏnghyŏn 大陽警玄) (942–1027). Chinese CHAN master in the CAODONG ZONG. A native of Jiangxia in present-day Hubei province, Dayang was ordained at the monastery of Chongxiaosi in Jinleng by his uncle, who had also become a monk. After traveling throughout China, Dayang visited the Chan master Liangshan Yuanguan (d.u.) in Dingzhou prefecture (present-day Sichuan province) and became his disciple. Later, he became a student of the Caodong monk Huijian (d.u.) and took over his lecture seat on Mt. Dayang, which became his toponym. Before his death, Dayang entrusted his portrait (DINGXIANG), leather shoes, and patched robe to his friend Fushan Fayuan (991–1067) of the LINJI ZONG in hopes of continuing his Caodong lineage and the incumbent annual memorial services to the patriarchs in his line. Fushan in turn transferred these items to his student TOZI YIQING, who embraced Dayang's line and became a Caodong lineage holder. Dayang was bestowed the posthumous title Great Master Ming'an ("Illuminating Peace"). His teachings are recorded in the *Dayang Ming'an dashi shibaban miaoyu*.

**Dayan ta**. (大雁塔). In Chinese, "Big Wild Goose Pagoda." See DACI'ENSI.

**dazangjing**. (J. daizōkyō; K. taejanggyŏng 大藏經). In Chinese, "scriptures of the great repository"; the term the Chinese settled upon to describe their Buddhist canon, supplanting the Indian term TRIPIṬAKA ("three baskets"). The myriad texts of different Indian and Central Asian Buddhist schools were transmitted to China over a millennium, from about the second through the twelfth centuries CE, where they were translated with alacrity into Chinese. Chinese Buddhists texts therefore came to include not only the tripiṭakas of several independent schools of Indian Buddhism, but also different recensions of various MAHĀYĀNA scriptures and Buddhist TANTRAs, sometimes in multiple translations. As the East Asian tradition developed its own scholarly traditions, indigenous writings by native East Asian authors, composed in literary Chinese, also came to be included in the canon. These materials included scriptural commentaries, doctrinal treatises, biographical and hagiographical collections, edited transcriptions of oral lectures, Chinese–Sanskrit dictionaries, scriptural catalogues (JINGLU), and so on. Because the scope of the Buddhist canon in China was therefore substantially broader than the traditional tripartite structure of an Indian tripiṭaka, the Chinese coined alternative terms to refer to their collection of Buddhist materials, including "all the books" (yiqie jing), until eventually settling on the term dazangjing. The term dazangjing seems to derive from a Northern Song-dynasty term for an officially commissioned "great library" (dazang) that was intended to serve as a repository for "books" (jing) sanctioned by the court. Buddhist monasteries were the first places outside the imperial palaces that such officially sanctioned libraries were established. These collections of the official canonical books of Chinese Buddhism were arranged not by the VINAYA, SŪTRA, ABHIDHARMA, and ŚĀSTRA categories of India, but in shelf lists that were more beholden to the categorizations used in court libraries. The earliest complete Buddhist canons in China date from the fifth century; by the eighth century, these manuscript collections included over one thousand individual texts in more than five thousand rolls. By the tenth century, woodblock printing techniques had become sophisticated enough that complete printed Buddhist canons began to be published, first during the Song dynasty, and thence throughout East Asia. The second xylographic canon of the Korean Koryŏ dynasty, the KORYŎ TAEJANGGYŎNG, was especially renowned for its scholarly accuracy; it included some 1,514 texts, in 6,815 rolls, carved on 81,258 individual woodblocks, which are still housed today in the scriptural repository at the monastery of HAEINSA. The second Koryŏ canon is arranged with pride of place given to texts from the Mahāyāna tradition:

1. Major Mahāyāna scriptures (K 1–548), beginning with the PRAJÑĀPĀRAMITĀ, followed by the MAHĀRATNAKŪṬASŪTRA, and continuing through all the major Mahāyāna sūtras and sūtra collections, from the AVATAṂSAKASŪTRA, to the MAHĀPARINIRVĀṆASŪTRA, SAṂDHINIRMOCANASŪTRA, and LAṄKĀVATĀRASŪTRA
2. Mahāyāna śāstras and scriptural commentaries, beginning with the DAZHIDU LUN (**Mahāprajñāpāramitāśāstra*) (K 549–646)
3. ĀGAMA collections and HĪNAYĀNA sūtras (K 647–888)
4. Vinaya materials (K 889–937)
5. Abhidharma texts (K 938–977)
6. AVADĀNA and JĀTAKA tales and miscellaneous materials (K 978–1034)
7. Biographies of individual monks, starting with AŚVAGHOṢA, NĀGĀRJUNA, etc. (K 1035–1049)
8. Rosters of numerical lists and scriptural catalogues (K 1050–1064)
9. Travelogues and "Biographies of Eminent Monks" anthologies (K 1065–1086)

10. Miscellaneous sūtras, DHĀRAṆĪ scriptures and dhāraṇī anthologies (K 1087–1242)
11. Other miscellaneous sūtras (K 1243–1496)
12. References, Chan anthologies, indigenous Korean works (K 1497–1514)

The second Koryŏ canon was used as the basis of the modern Japanese TAISHŌ SHINSHŪ DAIZŌKYŌ ("New Edition of the Buddhist Canon Compiled during the Taishō Reign Era"), edited by TAKAKUSU JUNJIRŌ and Watanabe Kaikyoku and published using movable-type printing between 1924 and 1935, which has become the standard reference source for East Asian Buddhist materials. The *Taishō* canon includes 2,920 texts in eighty-five volumes (each volume is about one thousand pages in length), along with twelve volumes devoted to iconography, and three volumes of bibliography and scriptural catalogues. The *Taishō's* arrangement is constructed following modern scholarly views regarding the historical development of the Buddhist scriptural tradition, with mainstream Buddhist scriptures opening the canon, followed by Indian Mahāyāna materials, indigenous Chinese writings, and Japanese writings:

1. ĀGAMA (vols. 1–2, nos. 1–151)
2. AVADĀNA (vols. 3–4, nos. 152–219)
3. PRAJÑĀPĀRAMITĀ (vols. 5–8, nos. 220–261)
4. SADDHARMAPUṆḌARĪKA (vol. 9, nos. 262–277)
5. AVATAṂSAKA/GAṆḌAVYŪHA (vols. 9–10, nos. 278–309)
6. RATNAKŪṬASŪTRA (vols. 11–12, nos. 310–373)
7. MAHĀPARINIRVĀṆA (vols. 12, nos. 374–396)
8. MAHĀSAṂNIPĀTA (vol. 13, nos. 397–424)
9. Miscellaneous sūtras (vols. 14–17, nos. 425–847), e.g.,
   YOGĀCĀRABHŪMIŚĀSTRA (nos. 602–620)
   RATNAMEGHASŪTRA (nos. 658–660)
   SUVARṆAPRABHĀSOTTAMASŪTRA (nos. 663–665)
   TATHĀGATAGARBHASŪTRA (nos. 666–667)
   LAṄKĀVATĀRASŪTRA (nos. 670–672)
   SAṂDHINIRMOCANASŪTRA (nos. 675–679)
   BUDDHABHŪMISŪTRA (no. 680)
   GHANAVYŪHA (nos. 681–682)
10. Esoteric Buddhism (vols. 18–21, nos. 848–1420), e.g.,
    SARVATATHĀGATATATTVASAṂGRAHA (vol. 18, no. 866)
    MAHĀMĀYŪRĪ (vol. 19, no. 982–988)
11. VINAYA (vols. 22–24, nos. 1421–1506), e.g.:
    MAHĪŚĀSAKA (nos. 1421–1424)
    MAHĀSĀṂGHIKA (nos. 1425–1427)
    DHARMAGUPTAKA (nos. 1428–1434)
    SARVĀSTIVĀDA (nos. 1435–1441)
    MŪLASARVĀSTIVĀDA (nos. 1442–1459)
    Mahāyāna-Bodhisattva (nos. 1487–1504)
12. Commentaries to Sūtras (vols. 24–26, nos. 1505–1535), e.g.,
    Āgamas (nos. 1505–1508)
    Mahāyāna sūtras (nos. 1509–1535)
13. ABHIDHARMA (vols. 26–29, nos. 1536–1563), e.g.:
    JÑĀNAPRASTHĀNA (nos. 1543–1544)
    MAHĀVIBHĀṢĀ (nos. 1545)
    Vibhāṣā (nos. 1546–1547)
    ABHIDHARMAKOŚABHĀṢYA (nos. 1558–1559)
14. MADHYAMAKA (vol. 30, nos. 1564–1578), e.g.,
    MŪLAMADHYAMAKAKĀRIKĀ (no. 1564)
    ŚATAŚĀSTRA (no. 1569)
15. YOGĀCĀRA (vols. 30–31, nos. 1579–1627), e.g.,
    YOGĀCĀRABHŪMIŚĀSTRA (no. 1579)
    *Vijñaptimātratāsiddhiśāstra (CHENG WEISHI LUN; no. 1585)
    MAHĀYĀNASAṂGRAHA (nos. 1592–1598)
16. Treatises (vol. 32, nos. 1628–1692), e.g.,
    SŪTRASAMUCCAYA (no. 1635)
    ŚIKṢĀSAMUCCAYA (no. 1636)
    DASHENG QIXIN LUN (nos. 1667–1668)
17. Chinese sūtra commentaries (vols. 33–39)
18. Chinese vinaya commentaries (vols. 40)
19. Chinese śāstra commentaries (vols. 40–44)
20. Chinese sectarian writings (vols. 44–48), e.g.,
    HUAYAN school (vol. 45, nos. 1866–1890)
    TIANTAI school (vol. 46, nos. 1911–1950)
    PURE LAND school (vol. 47, nos. 1957–1984)
    CHAN school (vols. 47–48, nos. 1985–2025)
21. Histories (vols. 49–52, nos. 2026–2120), e.g.,
    FOZU TONGJI (vol. 49, no. 2035)
    GAOSENG ZHUAN collections (vols. 50–51, nos. 2059–2066)
    GUANG HONGMINGJI (vol. 52, no. 2103)
22. Encyclopedias and references (vols. 53–54, nos. 2121–2136), e.g.,
    FAYUAN ZHULIN (vol. 53, no. 2122)
    YIQIEJING YINYI (vol. 54, no. 2128)
23. Non-Buddhist schools (vol. 54, nos. 2137–2144), e.g.,
    Saṃkhyakārikā (vol. 54, no. 2137)
24. Scriptural Catalogues (vol. 55, nos. 2145–2184), e.g.,
    KAIYUAN SHIJIAO LU (vol. 55, no. 2152)
25. Japanese Buddhist writings (vols. 56–84)
26. Buddhist apocrypha and fragments (vol. 85)
27. Iconography (vols. 86–92)
28. Bibliography and catalogues (vols. 93–100)

Even though the *Taishō* is often considered to be the definitive East Asian canon, it does not offer truly critical editions of its texts. The second Koryŏ canon's reputation for accuracy was so strong that the Japanese editors adopted it wholesale as the textus receptus for the modern *Taishō* edition of the canon, i.e., where there was a Koryŏ edition available for a text, the *Taishō* editors simply copied it verbatim, listing in footnotes alternate readings found in other canons, but not attempting to evaluate the accuracy of those readings or to establish a critical edition. Hence, to a large extent, the *Taishō* edition of the dazangjing is a modern typeset edition of the xylographical Koryŏ canon, with an updated arrangement of its contents based on modern historiographical criteria.

**Dazhidu lun**. (J. Daichidoron; K. Taejido non 大智度論). In Chinese, "Treatise on the Great Perfection of Wisdom"; an important Chinese text that is regarded as the translation of a Sanskrit work whose title has been reconstructed as **Māhāprājñāpāramitāśāstra* or **Mahāprajñāpāramitopedeśa*. The work is attributed to the MADHYAMAKA exegete NĀGĀRJUNA, but no Sanskrit manuscripts or Tibetan translations are known and no references to the text in Indian or Tibetan sources have been identified. The work was translated into Chinese by the KUCHA monk KUMĀRAJĪVA (344–413) between 402 and 406; it was not translated into Chinese again. Some scholars speculate that the work was composed by an unknown Central Asian monk of the SARVĀSTIVĀDA school who had "converted" to MADHYAMAKA, perhaps even Kumārajīva himself. The complete text was claimed to have been one hundred thousand ślokas or one thousand rolls (zhuan) in length, but the extant text is a mere one hundred rolls. It is divided into two major sections: the first is Kumārajīva's full translation of the first fifty-two chapters of the text; the second is his selective translations from the next eighty-nine chapters of the text. The work is a commentary on the PAÑCAVIMŚATISĀHASRIKĀPRAJÑĀPĀRAMITĀSŪTRA, and is veritable compendium of Buddhist doctrine, replete with quotations from a wide range of Indian texts. Throughout the translation, there appear frequent and often substantial interlinear glosses and interpolations, apparently provided by Kumārajīva himself and targeting his Chinese readership; it is the presence of such interpolations that has raised questions about the text's Indian provenance. In the first thirty-four rolls, the *Dazhidu lun* provides a detailed explanation of the basic concepts, phrases, places, and figures that appear in the *Pañcaviṃśatisāhasrikāprajñāpāramitā* (e.g., BHAGAVAT, EVAM MAYĀ ŚRUTAM, RĀJAGṚHA, buddha, BODHISATTVA, ŚRĀVAKA, ŚĀRIPUTRA, ŚŪNYATĀ, NIRVĀṆA, the six PĀRAMITĀ, and ten BALA). The scope of the commentary is extremely broad, covering everything from doctrine, legends, and rituals to history and geography. The overall concern of the *Dazhidu lun* seems to have been the elucidation of the concept of buddhahood, the bodhisattva career, the MAHĀYĀNA path (as opposed to that of the HĪNAYĀNA), PRAJÑĀ, and meditation. The *Dazhidu lun* thus served as an authoritative source for the study of Mahāyāna in China and was favored by many influential writers such as SENGZHAO, TIANTAI ZHIYI, FAZANG, TANLUAN, and SHANDAO. Since the time of the Chinese scriptural catalogue KAIYUAN SHIJIAO LU (730), the *Dazhidu lun*, has headed the roster of ŚĀSTRA materials collected in the Chinese Buddhist canon (DAZANGJING; see also KORYŎ TAEJANGGYŎNG); this placement is made because it is a principal commentary to the PRAJÑĀPĀRAMITĀ sūtras that open the SŪTRA section of the canon. Between 1944 and 1980, the Belgian scholar ÉTIENNE LAMOTTE published an annotated French translation of the entire first section and chapter 20 of the second section as *Le Traité de la Grande Vertu de Sagesse*, in five volumes.

**Dazhu Huihai**. (J. Daiju Ekai; K. Taeju Hyehae 大珠慧海) (d.u.). Chinese CHAN master of the Tang dynasty. Dazhu was a native of Jianzhou in present-day Fujian province, who was tonsured by a certain Daozhi at the monastery Dayunsi in Yuezhou (present-day Zhejiang province). He later studied under the eminent Chan master MAZU DAOYI for six years and inherited his HONGZHOU lineage. Dazhu then returned to Yuezhou where he devoted himself to teaching. Dazhu is most famous for his work the DUNWU RUDAO YAOMEN LUN, one of the definitive accounts in the CHAN ZONG of the notion of "sudden awakening" (DUNWU).

**Dazu shike**. (大足石刻). In Chinese, "Dazu rock carvings"; a series of Chinese religious sculptures and carvings located on the steep hillsides of Dazu County, in Sichuan province near the city of Chongqing. The Dazu grottoes are considered one of the four greatest troves of rock sculptures in China, along with the LONGMEN grottoes in LUOYANG, the MOGAO Caves in DUNHUANG, and the YUNGANG grottoes in Shanxi province. Listed by UNESCO as a World Heritage Site in 1999, the Dazu rock carvings consist of seventy-five sites, all under state protection, which contain some fifty thousand statues, along with epigraphs and inscriptions numbering over one hundred thousand inscribed Sinographs. There are five sites that are particularly large and well preserved: Baodingshan (Treasure Peak Mountain), Beishan (North Mountain), Nanshan (South Mountain), Shizhuanshan (Rock-Carving Mountain), and Shimenshan (Stone-Gate Mountain). Among the five major sites, the grottoes on Baodingshan and Nanshan are the largest in scale, the richest in content, and the most refined in artistic skill, although other sites are also noteworthy for their many statues integrating Buddhism, Confucianism, and Daoism. The earliest carvings of the Dazu grottoes were begun in the early seventh century during the Tang dynasty, but the main creative period began in the late ninth century, when Wei Junjing, the prefect of Changzhou, initiated the carvings on Beishan. Even after the collapse of the Tang dynasty, his example continued to be emulated by local gentry, government officials, Buddhist monks and nuns, and ordinary people. From the late Tang dynasty through the reign of the Song Emperor Gaozong (r. 1127–1131), some ten thousand sculptures of Buddhist figures were carved at the site in varied styles. The most famous carving on Beishan is a Song-dynasty statue of GUANYIN (AVALOKITEŚVARA). In the twelfth century, during the Song dynasty, a Buddhist monk named Zhao Zhifeng began to work on the sculptures and carvings on Baodingshan, dedicating seventy years of his life to the project. He produced some ten thousand Buddhist statues, as well as many carvings depicting scenes from daily life that bear inscriptions giving religious rules of behavior, teaching people how to engage in correct moral action. Along with EMEISHAN, Baodingshan became one of the most sacred Buddhist sites in Sichuan. Although the Dazu grottoes primarily contain Buddhist statues, they also include Daoist, Confucian, and historical figures, as well as many valuable inscriptions describing people's daily lives, which make the Dazu grottoes unique. The Yungang grottoes, created during the fourth and fifth centuries, represent an early stage of Chinese cave art and were greatly influenced by Indian culture. The Longmen grottoes, begun in the fifth century, represent the middle period of cave art, blending Indian and Chinese characteristics. The Dazu grottoes represent the highest level of grotto art in China and demonstrate breakthroughs in both carving technique and subject matter. They not only provide outstanding evidence of the harmonious synthesis of Buddhism, Daoism, and Confucianism in Chinese local religious practice but also mark the completion of the localization process of China's grotto art, reflecting great changes and developments in China's folk religion and rock carvings. The Dazu grottoes are thus remarkable for their high aesthetic quality, their rich diversity of style and subject matter (including both secular and religious topics), and the light that they shed on everyday life in China.

**Dbang phyug rdo rje**. (Wangchuk Dorje) (1556–1603). A revered Tibetan Buddhist master, recognized as the ninth KARMA PA. A prolific author, Dbang phyug rdo rje wrote three important treatises on MAHĀMUDRĀ that remain central BKA' BRGYUD texts: PHYAG CHEN NGAS DON RGYA MTSHO ("Mahāmudrā: Ocean of Definitive Meaning"), PHYAG CHEN MA RIG MUN GSAL ("Mahāmudrā: Eliminating the Darkness of Ignorance"), and PHYAG CHEN CHOS SKU MDZUB TSHUGS ("Mahāmudrā: Pointing Out the DHARMAKĀYA"). He traveled throughout Mongolia and Bhutan and established several monasteries in Sikkim. One of these, Rum theg monastery located near Gangtok, became the Karma pa's main seat when the sixteenth Karma pa RANG 'BYUNG RIG PA'I RDO RJE (Rangjung Rikpe Dorje) fled into exile in 1959.

**dbu ma chen po**. (uma chenpo) [alt. dbu ma pa chen po]. In Tibetan, "great MADHYAMAKA"; a term central to the "self empty, other empty" (RANG STONG GZHAN STONG) debate in Tibetan Buddhism, on the question of which Indian masters are the true representatives of the Madhyamaka. According to the DGE LUGS view, among the three turnings of the wheel of the dharma as described in the SAṂDHINIRMOCANASŪTRA, the second wheel, generally identified with the view of emptiness as set forth in the PRAJÑĀPĀRAMITĀ sūtras and propounded by the Madhyamaka, is definitive (NĪTĀRTHA), while the third wheel, generally identified with YOGĀCĀRA and TATHĀGATHAGARBHA teachings, is provisional (NEYĀRTHA). Other sects, most notably the JO NANG PA, as well as certain BKA' BRGYUD and RNYING MA thinkers, especially of the so-called RIS MED movement, disagreed, asserting that the third wheel is the definitive teaching while the second wheel is provisional. (Both agree that the first wheel, setting forth the FOUR NOBLE TRUTHS to ŚRĀVAKAS, is provisional.) For the Dge lugs pas, the highest of all Buddhist doctrines is that all phenomena in the universe are empty of an intrinsic nature (SVABHĀVA); emptiness is the lack of any substantial existence. The Dge lugs pas are therefore proponents of "self-emptiness" (rang stong), arguing that that each object of experience is devoid of intrinsic nature; the unenlightened wrongly believe that such a nature is intrinsic to the object itself. In reality, everything, from physical forms to the omniscient mind of a buddha, is equally empty, and this emptiness is a nonaffirming negation (PRASAJYAPRATIṢEDHA), an absence with nothing else implied in its place. Furthermore, this emptiness of intrinsic nature is the ultimate truth (PARAMĀRTHASATYA). The Jo nang pa's look to the third wheel, especially to those statements that describe the nonduality of subject and object to be the consummate nature (PARINIṢPANNA) and the understanding of that nonduality as the highest wisdom, described as eternal, self-arisen, and truly established. This wisdom exists autonomously and is thus not empty in the way that emptiness is understood by the Dge lugs. Instead, this wisdom consciousness is empty in the sense that it is devoid of all defilements and conventional factors, which are extraneous to its true nature. Hence, the Jo nang pas speak of "other emptiness" (gzhan stong) the absence of extrinsic and extraneous qualities. For the Dge lugs pas, the supreme interpreter of the doctrine of emptiness (as they understand it) is CANDRAKĪRTI. The Jo nang pas do not dispute the Dge lugs reading of Candrakīrti but they deny Candrakīrti the rank of premier expositor of NĀGĀRJUNA's thought. For them, Candrakīrti teaches an emptiness that is a mere negation of intrinsic existence, which they equate with nihilism. They also do not deny that such an exposition is found in Nāgārjuna's philosophical treatises (YUKTIKĀYA). However, they claim that those works do not represent Nāgārjuna's final view, which is expressed instead in his devotional corpus (STAVAKĀYA), notably the DHARMADHĀTUSTAVA, and, according to some, in the works of VASUBANDHU, the author of two defenses of the prajñāpāramitā sūtras. Those who would deny the ultimate existence of wisdom, such as Candrakīrti, are classed as "one-sided Madhyamakas" (phyogs gcig pa'i dbu ma pa) as opposed to the great Madhyamakas among whom they would include the Nāgārjuna of the hymns and ĀRYADEVA as well as thinkers whom the Dge lugs classify as Yogācāra or SVĀTANTRIKA MADHYAMAKA: ASAṄGA, Vasubandhu, MAITREYANĀTHA, and ŚĀNTARAKṢITA.

**Deb ther dmar po**. (Depter Marpo). In Tibetan, lit. "The Red Annals"; an influential Tibetan religious and political history written by 'Tshal pa Kun dga' rdo rje (1309–1364). The work shows evidence of Mongolian influence, likely due to the strong Tibeto-Mongolian ties at the time. The title word deb ther is likely a Mongolian loan word and, although it became a subgenre in Tibetan literature, this appears to be the first instance of its usage. The text is also known as the *Hu lan deb ther*, where hu lan derives from the Mongolian word for "red."

**Deb ther dmar po gsar ma**. (Depter Marpo Sarma). In Tibetan, lit. "The New Red Annals"; a Tibetan historical work written by the famed DGE LUGS scholar Paṇ chen Bsod nams grags pa (1478–1554). The text was intended as a supplement to the DEB THER DMAR PO ("Red Annals") written almost a century previously, and covers the political and religious history of Tibet, with information about India, China, Mongolia, and the fabled land of ŚAMBHALA.

**Deb ther sngon po**. (Depter Ngonpo). In Tibetan, lit. "The Blue Annals"; a Tibetan historical work written by 'Gos lo tsā ba Gzhon nu dpal (1392–1481) between 1476 and 1478. It provides a broad history of Buddhism in Tibet, divided into sections covering various periods and transmission lineages. It is especially valued for its detailed history of the transmission of specific texts and practices from India to Tibet. It was one of the first comprehensive Tibetan works to be translated into English, by the Russian scholar GEORGE ROERICH and the Tibetan savant DGE 'DUN CHOS 'PHEL.

**decline of the dharma**. See SADDHARMAVIPRALOPA; MOFA.

**Deer Park**. See MṚGADĀVA.

**defilement**. See KLEŚA.

**Deguang**. (C). See FOZHAO DEGUANG.

**dehadāna**. (T. lus kyi sbyin pa; C. sheshen; J. shashin; K. sasin 捨身). In Sanskrit, "gift of the body," a form of charity (DĀNA) in which one gives away one's body or a part of one's body. Stories of such gifts abound in both the JĀTAKA and AVADĀNA literature, where a bodhisattva will give away a body part (including the head) or sacrifice his life as a way of easing others' suffering. Among the more famous stories are that of King ŚIBI, who cuts off some of his own flesh to ransom the life of a dove from a hawk, Prince Mahāsattva who commits suicide by jumping off a cliff in order that his corpse can feed a starving tigress and her cubs, and King Candraprabha who gives his head to an evil brāhmaṇa. Such gifts are often counted among the bodhisattva's fulfillment of the perfection of giving (DĀNAPĀRAMITĀ), but it is sometimes said that a bodhisattva who has not yet understood emptiness (ŚŪNYATĀ) should not make such a gift. The person who asks for the body part is often the god ŚAKRA in disguise, and the body part that was offered is then often restored upon making an "asseveration of truth" (SATYAVACANA). See also SHESHEN.

**deity yoga**. See DEVATĀYOGA.

**delusion**. See MOHA.

**Demiéville, Paul**. (1894–1979). Distinguished French Buddhologist and Sinologist. He was born in Lausanne, Switzerland, and educated in Bern, Munich, and London. He began his study of Chinese at King's College, London, in 1915, continuing in Paris, studying Chinese with Edouard Chavannes and Sanskrit with SYLVAIN LÉVI. In 1919, he became a member of the École française d'Extrême-Orient, spending 1920–24 in Hanoi, 1924–26 teaching Sanskrit and philosophy at Amoy University in Xiamen, China, and 1926–30 in Tokyo, where he served as editor-in-chief of the Buddhist dictionary HŌBŌGIRIN, which had been founded by Lévi and TAKAKUSU JUNJIRŌ. Returning to Paris, Demiéville held positions at the École des languages orientales vivantes and the École pratique des hautes études, before being appointed to succeed Henri Maspero in the chair of Chinese language and literature at the Collège de France, where he spent the remainder of his academic career. The majority of his publications, on a remarkable range of Buddhological and Sinological topics, were published as articles (many quite substantial) in journals such as *Bulletin de l'École française d'Extrême-Orient*, *T'oung Pao* (where he served as editor), and in *Hōbōgirin*. Many of these later writings were gathered into two collections, *Choix d'études sinologiques* and *Choix d'études bouddhiques*. Demiéville published a detailed study of the Chinese version of the MILINDAPAÑHA and worked extensively on the DUNHUANG manuscripts. Two of his monographs are particularly well known, *Entretiens de Lin-tsi* (1972) on the Chan master LINJI and *Le Concile de Lhasa* (1952), still regarded as the definitive study on the BSAM YAS DEBATE.

**Dengyō Daishi**. (J) (傳教大師). See SAICHŌ.

**Denkōroku**. (傳光録). In Japanese, "Record of the Transmission of the Light"; a text also known by its full title, *Keizan oshō denkōroku* ("A Record of the Transmission of the Light by Master Keizan"). The anthology is attributed by Sōtō tradition to KEIZAN JŌKIN, but was most probably composed posthumously by his disciples. The *Denkōroku* is a collection of pithy stories and anecdotes concerning fifty-two teachers recognized by the Japanese SŌTŌSHŪ as the patriarchs of the school, accompanied by the author's own explanatory commentaries and concluding verses. Each chapter includes a short opening case (honsoku), which describes the enlightenment experience of the teacher; a longer section (called a kien) offering a short biography and history of the teacher, including some of his representative teachings and exchanges with students and other teachers; a prose commentary (teishō; C. TICHANG) by the author; and a concluding appreciatory verse (juko). The teachers discussed in the text include twenty-seven Indian patriarchs from MAHĀKĀŚYAPA to Prajñātāra; six Chinese patriarchs from BODHIDHARMA through HUINENG; seventeen Chinese successors of Huineng in the CAODONG ZONG, from QINGYUAN XINGSI to TIANTONG RUJING; and finally the two Japanese patriarchs DŌGEN KIGEN and Koun Ejō (1198–1280). The *Denkōroku* belongs to a larger genre of texts known as the CHUANDENG LU ("transmission of the lamplight records"), although it is a rigidly sectarian lineage history, discussing only the single successor to each patriarch with no treatment of any collateral lines.

**Denson**. (J) (傳尊). See TENKEI DENSON.

**dependent origination**. See PRATĪTYASAMUTPĀDA.

**Deqing**. (德清). See HANSHAN DEQING.

**Deshan Xuanjian**. (J. Tokusan Senkan; K. Tŏksan Sŏn'gam 德山宣鑑) (780/2–865). Chinese CHAN master of the Tang dynasty; famous for the fearsome "blows" (bang) through which he expressed his understanding of enlightenment, similar to the terrifying shouts (he) of Chan master LINJI YIXUAN (see BANGHE). A native of Jiannan in present-day Sichuan province, Deshan first studied the scriptures and the VINAYA, and became famous as a teacher of the VAJRACCHEDIKĀPRAJÑĀPĀRAMITĀSŪTRA ("Diamond Sūtra"). According to his hagiography, he was determined to defeat the Chan masters of the south with his knowledge of the sūtra, but on his way in Lizhou (present-day Hunan province), Deshan was rendered speechless by the following question from an old woman: "The 'Diamond Sūtra' says that neither the past mind, present mind, nor future mind can be grasped; so which mind does the elder desire to refresh?" He later became a student of the Chan master Longtan Chongxin (d.u.) and inherited his lineage. After his thirty-year residence at Lizhou, Deshan was forced by Emperor Wuzong's (840–846) persecution of Buddhism (see HUICHANG FANAN) to hide on Mt. Dufu. He was later invited by the governor of Wuleng (present-day Hunan province) to reside on Deshan ("Mount Virtue"), whence he acquired his toponym. Deshan's most famous disciple was XUEFENG YICUN, and their joint lineage leads ultimately to the mature Chan schools of the YUNMEN ZONG and FAYAN ZONG.

**Desideri, Ippolito**. (1684–1733). Jesuit missionary to Tibet. He was born in the town of Pistoia in Tuscany in 1684 and entered the Jesuit order in 1700, studying at the Collegio Romano. Following two years of instruction in theology, he requested permission to become a missionary, departing for India in 1712 and reaching Goa the following year. Assigned to the Tibet mission, Desideri and another priest, the Portuguese Manoel Freyre, traveled by ship, horseback, and on foot to Leh, the capital of Ladakh, the westernmost Tibetan domain. Setting out for LHA SA, they were able to survive the difficult seven-month journey thanks to the protection of a Mongolian princess who allowed the two priests to join her caravan. They reached the Tibetan capital on March 18, 1716. After just a month in Lha sa, Desideri's companion decided to return to India. Desideri received permission from the ruler of Tibet, the Mongol warlord Lha bzang Khan, to remain in Tibet. He arranged for Desideri to live at RA MO CHE, and then at SE RA monastery. His notes from his studies indicate that he worked through textbooks on elementary logic through to the masterworks of the DGE LUGS sect, including the LAM RIM CHEN MO of TSONG KHA PA, which Desideri would eventually translate into Italian (the translation is lost). He would go on also to write a number of works in Tibetan, both expositions of Christianity and refutations of Buddhism. The most substantial of these was his unfinished "Inquiry into the Doctrines of Previous Lives and of Emptiness, Offered to the Scholars of Tibet by the White Lama called Ippolito" (*Mgo skar [sic] gyi bla ma i po li do zhes bya ba yis phul ba'i bod kyi mkhas pa rnams la skye ba snga ma dang stong pa nyid kyi lta ba'i sgo nas zhu ba*). Desideri remained in Tibet until 1721, when Tibet became a mission field of the Capuchins, requiring that the Jesuit abandon his work. After several years in India, he returned to Italy in 1727. Desideri arrived in Rome in the midst of the Rites Controversy, the question of whether non-Christian rituals (such as Chinese ancestor worship) had a place in the methods of the missionaries. As a Jesuit, Desideri was on the losing side of this debate. The last years of his life were consumed with composing long defenses of his work, as well as the remarkable account of his time in Tibet, the *Relazione de' viaggi all' Indie e al Thibet*. He died in Rome on April 13, 1733. Because of the suppression of the Jesuit order, Desideri's works remained largely unknown, both in Italian and Tibetan, until the twentieth century.

**desire**. See LOBHA; RĀGA; TṚṢṆĀ.

**detachment**. See VIVEKA.

**deva**. (T. lha; C. tian; J. ten; K. ch'ŏn 天). In Sanskrit and Pāli, lit., "radiant one" or "shining one"; a "divinity," "heavenly being," or "god," as one of the five [alt. six] rebirth destinies (GATI) of SAṂSĀRA. When it is said that Buddhism has "gods" but no "God," the devas are being referred to. The term deva derives from the Sanskrit root √div and is related etymologically to the English word "divinity." Rebirth as a deva is considered to be the beneficial result of virtuous actions (KARMAN) performed in a previous lifetime, and all of the many heavenly realms in Buddhist cosmology are therefore salutary levels of existence. However, they are temporary abodes within saṃsāra, rather than eternal heavens. ¶ There are a total of twenty-seven [alt. twenty-six or twenty-eight] different categories of devas, which are subdivided according to where their abode (DEVALOKA) is located within the three realms of existence (TRAIDHĀTUKA, trailokya), viz., the sensuous or desire realm (KĀMADHĀTU), the materiality or form realm (RŪPADHĀTU) and the immaterial or formless realm (ĀRŪPYADHĀTU). ¶ There are six heavens of the sensuous realm (KĀMADHĀTU). The first two are located on Mount SUMERU; the other four are located in the sky above its summit. One is reborn into these heavens as a result of virtuous deeds done in the past, especially deeds of charity (DĀNA). They include six deva abodes:

1. The heaven of the four heavenly kings (CĀTURMAHĀRĀJAKĀYIKA) located on the slopes of Mount Sumeru
2. The heaven of the thirty-three [gods] (TRĀYASTRIṂŚA), located on the summit of Mount Sumeru
3. The heaven of YĀMA, also known as SUYĀMA ("where the seasons are always good")

4. The heaven of the contented (TUṢITA), where the BODHISATTVA ŚVETAKETU resided before descending to earth to be reborn as prince SIDDHĀRTHA and where the future buddha MAITREYA currently resides
5. The heaven of the enjoyment of creation (NIRMĀṆARATI), where the gods are able to convert their mental and emotional desires into palpable physical pleasures
6. The heaven of the gods who have power over the creations of others, or the gods who partake of the pleasures created in other heavens (PARANIRMITAVAŚAVARTIN)

The four heavenly kings of the first and lowest of the six heavens are DHṚTARĀṢṬRA in the east, VIRŪḌHAKA in the south, VIRŪPĀKṢA in the west, and VAIŚRAVAṆA in the north. There are many devas inhabiting this heaven: GANDHARVAs in the east, KUMBHĀṆḌAs in the south, NĀGAs in the west, and YAKṢAs in the north. As vassals of ŚAKRO DEVĀNĀM INDRAḤ (lit. "Śakra, the lord of the gods"; see INDRA; ŚAKRA; DEVARĀJAN), the four heavenly kings serve as protectors of the dharma (DHARMAPĀLA) and of sentient beings who are devoted to the dharma. They dwell at the four gates in each direction at the midslope of the world's central axis, Mt. Sumeru. The thirty-three gods of the second heaven are the eight vāsava, two aśvina, eleven rudra, and twelve āditya. They live on the summit of Mt. Sumeru and are arrayed around the city of Sudarśana, the capital of their lord Śakra. Śakra is also known as Indra, the war god of the Āryans, who became a devotee of the Buddha as well as a protector of the dharma. The remaining four heavens are located in the sky above Mt. Sumeru. At the highest level of the sensuous realm, the paranirmitavaśavartin heaven, dwells MĀRA, the Evil One. The four heavenly kings and the thirty-three gods are called the "divinities residing on the ground" (bhūmyavacaradeva) because they dwell on Mt. Sumeru, while the gods from the Yāma heaven up to the gods of the realm of subtle materiality are known as "divinities residing in the air" (antarikṣavāsin, antarīkṣadeva), because they reside in the sky above the mountain. The higher one ascends into the heavens of both the sensuous realm and the subsequent realm of subtle materiality, the larger and more splendid the bodies of those gods become and the longer their life spans. Related to the devas of the sensuous realm are the demigods or titans (S. ASURA), jealous gods whom Indra drove out of the heaven of the thirty-three; they now live in exile in the shadows of Mt. Sumeru. ¶ The heavens of the realm of subtle materiality (rūpadhātu) consist of sixteen (according to the SARVĀSTIVĀDA school), seventeen (the SAUTRĀNTIKA school), or eighteen (the THERAVĀDA/STHAVIRANIKĀYA school) levels of devas. These levels, which are collectively called the BRAHMALOKA (world of the Brahmā gods), are subdivided into the four classes of the dhyāna or "concentration" heavens, and rebirth there is dependent on specific meditative attainments in previous lives. One of the most extensive accounts on these heavens appears in the ABHIDHARMAKOŚABHĀṢYA, which presents seventeen levels of the subtle-materiality devas. Whereas rebirth in the heavens of the sensuous realm are the result of a variety of virtuous deeds done in a previous life, rebirth in the heavens of the realm of subtle materiality or in the immaterial realm is the result of what is called a "nonfluctuating" or "unwavering" action (ANIÑJYAKARMAN). Here, the only cause that will produce rebirth in one of these heavens is the achievement of the level of meditative concentration or absorption of that particular heaven in the immediately preceding lifetime. Such meditation is called a "nonfluctuating deed" because it always produces the effect of that particular type of rebirth. The first set of dhyāna heavens, where those who practiced the first meditative absorption in the previous lifetime are born, is comprised of three levels:

1. The heaven of Brahmā's retainers (BRAHMAKĀYIKA)
2. The heaven of Brahmā's ministers (BRAHMAPUROHITA)
3. The heaven of the great Brahmā himself (MAHĀBRAHMĀ)

The inhabitants of these heavens lack olfactory and gustatory sense organs, and thus do not need to consume food, but do possess the other sense organs of sight, hearing, and touch, as well as mentality (MANENDRIYA). According to Buddhist accounts, Mahābrahmā, the inhabitant of the highest of the first dhyāna heavens, presumed himself to be the creator of the world and father of all beings, but after being taught by the Buddha he subsequently realized how arrogant had been his misapprehension; he became the Buddha's follower and protector of his teachings (dharmapāla), along with the four heavenly kings and Śakra. The second set of dhyāna heavens, where those who practiced the second meditative absorption in their previous lifetime are reborn, is also comprised of three levels:

1. The heaven of lesser radiance (PARĪTTĀBHA)
2. The heaven of immeasurable radiance (APRAMĀṆĀBHA)
3. The heaven of ultimate radiance (ĀBHĀSVARALOKA)

These heavens are said to be equal in size to a small chiliocosm. The third set of dhyāna heavens, where those who practiced the third meditative concentration in the previous lifetime are reborn, is also comprised of three levels:

1. The heaven of lesser purity (PARĪTTAŚUBHA)
2. The heaven of immeasurable purity (APRAMĀṆĀŚUBHA)
3. The heaven of pervasive purity (ŚUBHAKṚTSNA)

These heavens are said to be equal in size to a medium chiliocosm; its inhabitants also possess only the mind organ and experience great joy. The fourth set of dhyāna heavens, where those who practiced the fourth meditative concentration in the previous lifetime are reborn, is comprised of eight levels:

1. The cloudless heaven (ANABHRAKA)
2. The heaven of blessed birth (PUṆYAPRASAVA)
3. The heaven of extensive fruition (BṚHATPHALA)
4. The heaven that is free from afflictions (AVṚHA)

5. The heaven that is not burning, or without torment (ATAPA)
6. The heaven of perfect form (SUDṚŚA)
7. The heaven of perfect vision (SUDARŚANA)
8. The highest heaven (AKANIṢṬHA)

In schemata where there are nine levels of the Brahmā heavens, a ninth nonperceptual heaven [asaṃjñika] is added to the list as an eighteenth heaven of the rūpadhātu. The last five heavens of the fourth dhyāna level (levels thirteen through seventeen) are collectively designated as the five pure abodes (ŚUDDHĀVĀSAKĀYIKA), and the divinities residing there are called the śuddhāvāsakāyika devas. In some interpretations, the śuddhāvāsa are said to be the abode of nonreturners (ANĀGĀMIN), the third of the four types of advanced adepts who are in their final rebirth before achieving arhatship (see ARHAT) and thus need never again be reborn in the sensuous realm. Since nonreturners have removed the first five fetters (SAṂYOJANA) associated with the sensuous realm and weakened the latter five, they are "nonreturners" to the sensuous realm and are instead reborn into the pure abodes, whence they will complete their practice and attain enlightenment, entering NIRVĀṆA from that abode. The pure abodes therefore serve as a kind of way station for advanced spiritual beings (ĀRYA) in their last lives before final liberation. In the *Abhidharmakośabhāṣya*, the explanation of nonreturners differs: before they reach nirvāṇa they never take rebirth in the sensuous realm, but they may pass through each of the heavens, or skip one or more heavens, and enter into nirvāṇa, depending on their aptitude, in any heaven. Furthermore, certain persons with sharp faculties (TĪKṢṆENDRIYA) even enter nirvāṇa in the sensuous realm itself. In certain Mahāyāna interpretations, such as in the ABHISAMAYĀLAṂKĀRA commentarial tradition, especially in Tibet, the pure abodes are adjacent to the fourth dhyāna, and the akaniṣṭha heaven pure abode is considered to be the abode of the enjoyment body (SAṂBHOGAKĀYA) of a buddha. According to some accounts, the pure abodes remain empty for several eons (KALPA) when there are no buddhas. ¶ The heavens of the immaterial realm (ārūpyadhātu) are comprised of four classes of devas whose existence is entirely mental, no longer requiring a body or even a subtle material foundation for their ethereal states of mind. These heavens are:

1. The sphere of infinite space (ĀKĀŚĀNANTYĀYATANA)
2. The sphere of infinite consciousness (VIJÑĀNĀNANTYĀYATANA)
3. The sphere of nothing whatsoever, or absolute nothingness (ĀKIÑCANYĀYATANA)
4. The sphere of neither perception nor nonperception (NAIVASAṂJÑĀNĀSAṂJÑĀYATANA [alt. BHAVĀGRA])

In each case, the name of the realm indicates the object of meditation of the beings reborn there. Hence, in the first, for example, the beings perceive only infinite space. Rebirth in these different spheres is based on mastery of the corresponding four immaterial meditative absorptions (ĀRŪPYĀVACARADHYĀNA; ārūpyasamāpatti) in the previous life. While the devas of the sensuous realm and the realm of subtle materiality come to have larger and ever more splendid bodies at the more advanced levels of their heavens, the devas of the immaterial realm do not have even the subtlest foundation in materiality; their existence is so refined that it is not even possible to posit exactly where they dwell spatially. In some schools, such as the Sarvāstivāda, the immaterial realm does not even exist as a discrete place: rather, when a being who has mastered the immaterial absorptions dies, he is reborn at the very same location where he passed away, except now he is "immaterial" or "formless" and thus invisible to coarser beings. According to the Theravāda, even a mind-made body (MANOMAYAKĀYA) is excluded from this realm, for the devas here possess only the mind base (MANĀYATANA), mental objects (P. dhammāyatana), the elements of mental consciousness (P. manoviññāṇadhātu), and the element of mental objects (P. dhammadhātu), needing only three nutriments (ĀHĀRA) to survive—contact (P. phassa), mental cognition (P. manosañcetana), and consciousness (P. viññāṇa). The Buddha claims to have lived among the devas of the immaterial realm in certain of his previous lives, but without offering any detailed description of those existences. ¶ In all realms, devas are born apparitionally. In the sensuous realm, devas are born in their mother's lap, appearing as if they are already five to ten years old at birth; by contrast, devas of the subtle-materiality and immaterial realms appear not to need the aid of parents; those in the subtle-materiality realm appear fully grown, while those in the immaterial realm do not appear at all, because they have no form. It is also said that, when devas are reborn, they are aware of their prior existence and of the specific KARMAN that led to their rebirth in the heavenly realms. The different deva realms are also distinguished by differences in nutriment, sexuality, requisites, and life span. The devas of the lower heavens of the sensuous realm consume ordinary food; those in the upper spheres of the sensuous realm and the lower levels of the realm of subtle materiality feed only on sensory contact; the devas of the upper levels of the realm of subtle materiality feed only on contemplation; those in the immaterial realm feed on cognition alone. Sexual differentiation remains only in the sensuous realm: in the heaven of the four heavenly kings and the heaven of the thirty-three, the devas engage in physical copulation, the devas of the yāma heaven engage in sexual union by embracing one another, the devas of the tuṣita heaven by holding hands, those of the nirmāṇarati heaven by smiling at one another, and those of the paranirmitavaśavartin heaven by exchanging a single glance. Clothes are said to be used in all deva worlds except in the immaterial realm. The life spans of devas in the sensuous realm range from five hundred years for the gods of the heaven of the four heavenly kings to one thousand years for the trāyastriṃśa gods, two thousand years for the yāma gods, four thousand years for the tuṣita gods, eight thousand years for the nirmāṇarati gods, and sixteen thousand years for the paranirmitavaśavartin gods. However, there is a range of opinion of what constitutes a year in these heavens. For example, it is said that in the tuṣita heaven, four hundred human years equal one day in the life of a god of that heaven. The life spans of devas in the realm of subtle materiality are measured in eons (KALPA). The life spans of devas in the immaterial realm may appear as essentially infinite, but even those divinities, like all devas, are subject to impermanence (ANITYA) and will eventually die and be subject to further rebirths once the salutary meditative deed that caused them to be reborn there has been exhausted. The sūtras say that for a deva of the sensuous realm, there are five portents of his impending death: the garlands of flowers he wears begin to fade, his clothes become soiled and his palace dusty, he begins to perspire, his body becomes opaque and loses its luster, and his throne becomes uncomfortable. At that point, the deva experiences a vision of his next place of rebirth. This vision is said to be one of the most horrible sufferings in saṃsāra, because of its marked contrast to the magnificence of his current life. There are also said to be four direct reasons why devas die: exhaustion of their life spans, their previous merit, their food, and the arising of anger. ¶ Rebirth as a deva is presumed to be the reward of virtuous karman performed in previous lives and is thus considered a salutary, if provisional, religious goal. In the "graduated discourse" (P. ANUPUBBIKATHĀ; S. ANUPŪRVIKATHĀ) taught by the Buddha, for example, the Buddha uses the prospect of heavenly rebirth (svargakathā), and the pleasures accruing thereto, as a means of attracting laypersons to the religious life. Despite the many appealing attributes of these heavenly beings, such as their physical beauty, comfortable lives, and long life span, even heavenly existence is ultimately unsatisfactory because it does not offer a definitive escape from the continued cycle of birth and death (saṃsāra). Since devas are merely enjoying the rewards of their previous good deeds rather than performing new wholesome karman, they are considered to be stagnating spiritually. This spiritual passivity explains why they must be reborn in lower levels of existence, and especially as human beings, in order to further their cultivation. For these reasons, Buddhist soteriological literature sometimes condemns religious practice performed solely for the goal of achieving rebirth as a deva. It is only certain higher level of devas, such as the devas belonging to the five pure abodes (śuddhāvāsa), that are not subject to further rebirth, because they have already eliminated all the fetters (saṃyojana) associated with that realm and are destined to achieve arhatship. Nevertheless, over the history of Buddhism, rebirth in heaven as a deva has been a more common goal for religious practice, especially among the laity, than the achievement of nirvāṇa. ¶ The sūtras include frequent reference to "gods and men" (S. devamanuṣya; C. tianren) as the objects of the Buddha's teachings. Despite the fact that this is how most Buddhist traditions have chosen to translate the Sanskrit compound, "gods" here is probably meant to refer to the terrestrial divinities of "princes" or "kings," rather than heavenly beings; thus, the compound should be more properly (if, perhaps, pedantically) rendered "princes and peoples." Similarly, as the "divinities" of this world, buddhas, bodhisattvas, and arhats are also sometimes referred to as devas. See also DEVALOKA; DEVATĀ.

**Devadatta**. (T. Lhas sbyin; C. Tipodaduo; J. Daibadatta; K. Chebadalta 提婆達多). Sanskrit and Pāli proper name for a cousin and rival of the Buddha; he comes to be viewed within the tradition as the embodiment of evil for trying to kill the Buddha and split the SAṂGHA (SAṂGHABHEDA). Devadatta is said to have been the brother of ĀNANDA, who would later become the Buddha's attendant. According to Pāli sources, when Gotama (GAUTAMA) Buddha returned to Kapalivatthu (KAPILAVASTU) after his enlightenment to preach to his native clan, the Sākiyans (ŚĀKYA), Devadatta along with ĀNANDA, Bhagu, Kimbila, BHADDIYA-KĀḶIGODHĀPUTTA, Anuruddha (ANIRUDDHA), and UPĀLI were converted and took ordination as monks. Devadatta quickly attained mundane supranormal powers (iddhi; S. ṚDDHI) through his practice of meditation, although he never attained any degree of enlightenment. For a period of time, Devadatta was revered in the order. Sāriputta (ŚĀRIPUTRA) is depicted as praising him, and the Buddha lists him among eleven chief elders. Devadatta, however, always seems to have been of evil disposition and jealous of Gotama; in the final years of the Buddha's ministry, he sought to increase his influence and even usurp leadership of the saṃgha. He used his supranormal powers to win over the patronage of Prince Ajātasattu (AJĀTAŚATRU), who built for him a monastery at Gayāsīsa (Gayāśīrṣa). Emboldened by this success, he approached the Buddha with the suggestion that the Buddha retire and pass the leadership of the saṃgha to him, whereupon the Buddha severely rebuked him. It was then that Devadatta conceived a plan to kill the Buddha even while he incited Ajātasattu to murder his father BIMBISĀRA, king of MAGADHA, who was the Buddha's chief patron. At Devadatta's behest, Ajātasattu dispatched sixteen archers to shoot the Buddha along a road, but the Buddha, using his supranormal powers, instead converted the archers. Later, Devadatta hurled a boulder down the slope of Mt. Gijjhakūṭa (GṚDHRAKŪṬAPARVATA) at the Buddha, which grazed his toe and caused it to bleed. Finally, Devadatta caused the bull elephant NĀLĀGIRI, crazed with toddy, to charge at the Buddha, but the Buddha tamed the elephant with the power of his loving-kindness (P. mettā; S. MAITRĪ). Unsuccessful in his attempts to kill the Buddha, Devadatta then decided to establish a separate order. He approached the Buddha and recommended that five austere practices (DHUTAṄGA) be made mandatory for all members of the saṃgha: forest dwelling, subsistence only on alms food collected by begging, use of rag robes only, dwelling at the foot of a tree, and vegetarianism. When the Buddha rejected his recommendation, Devadatta gathered around him five hundred newly ordained monks from Vesāli (VAIŚĀLĪ) and, performing the fortnightly uposatha (UPOṢADHA) ceremony separately at Gayāsīsa, formally seceded from the Buddha's saṃgha. When the five hundred Vesāli monks were won back to the fold by

Sāriputta (ŚĀRIPUTRA) and Moggallāna (MAHĀMAUDGALYĀYANA), Devadatta grew sick with rage, coughing up blood, and never recovered. It is said that toward the end of his life, Devadatta felt remorse and decided to journey to see the Buddha to ask him for his forgiveness. However, spilling the blood of a Buddha and causing schism in the saṃgha are two of the five "acts that brings immediate retribution" (P. ānantariyakamma; S. ĀNANTARYAKARMAN), viz., rebirth in hell. In addition, Devadatta is said to have beaten to death the nun UTPALAVARṆĀ when she rebuked him for attempting to assassinate the Buddha. She was an arhat, and killing an arhat is another of the "acts that bring immediate retribution." When Devadatta was on his way to visit the Buddha (according to some accounts, to repent; according to other accounts, to attempt to kill him one last time by scratching him with poisoned fingernails), the earth opened up and Devadatta fell into AVĪCI hell, where he will remain for one hundred thousand eons. His last utterance was that he had no other refuge than the Buddha, an act that, at the end of his torment in hell, will cause him to be reborn as the paccekabuddha (PRATYEKABUDDHA) Atthissara. In many JĀTAKA stories, the villain or chief antagonist of the BODHISATTVA is often identified as a previous rebirth of Devadatta. In the "Devadatta Chapter" of the SADDHARMAPUṆḌARĪKASŪTRA ("Lotus Sūtra"), the Buddha remarks that in a previous life, he had studied with the sage Asita, who was in fact Devadatta, and that Devadatta would eventually become a buddha himself. This statement was used in the Japanese NICHIREN school as proof that even the most evil of persons (see ICCHANTIKA; SAMUCCHINAKUŚALAMŪLA) still have the capacity to achieve enlightenment. In their accounts of India, both FAXIAN and XUANZANG note the presence of followers of Devadatta who adhered to the austere practices he had recommended to the Buddha.

**devaloka**. (T. lha'i 'jig rten; C. tianshijie/tianjie/tianshang; J. tensekai/tengai/tenjō; K. ch'ŏnsegye/ch'ŏn'gye/ch'ŏnsang 天世界/天界/天上). In Sanskrit and Pāli, the "heavenly world," the abodes of the divinities (DEVA); the highest and most salutary of the five or six rebirth destinies (GATI) of SAṂSĀRA. Rebirth as a deva is considered to be the beneficial result of virtuous actions (KARMAN) performed in a previous lifetime, and all the devalokas are thus regarded as salutary levels of existence. There are a total of twenty-seven [alt. twenty-six or twenty-eight] different heavenly worlds (see DEVA), subdivided according to where their abode is located within the three realms of existence (TRAIDHĀTUKA; trailokya), viz., the sensuous or desire realm (KĀMADHĀTU), the realm of subtle materiality or form (RŪPADHĀTU), and the immaterial or formless realm (ĀRŪPYADHĀTU). The devalokas in Buddhist cosmology seem to be an adaptation and enhancement of pre-Buddhistic Indian notions of the cosmos. For instance, the six heavens of the sensuous realm in the Buddhist schema seem to be developed from the "six spaces" (rajāṃsi), the six subdivisions of the two upper strata of the Vedic cosmos. One of the earliest formulations of the Buddhist devalokas appears in the Buddha's first sermon, the "Setting in Motion the Wheel of the Dharma" (P. DHAMMACAKKAPPAVATTANASUTTA; S. DHARMACAKRAPRAVARTANASŪTRA), included in the Pāli MAHĀVAGGA, where the seven heavens are said to be comprised of the six heavens of the sensuous realm and the heaven of the BRAHMĀ gods in the realm of subtle materiality. Even so, it appears that the early Buddhists were aware of the presence of even more devalokas, since the AṄGUTTARANIKĀYA notes that there are still more divinities even beyond those of the Brahmā heavens. A more or less complete roster of all the devalokas appears in the Pāli SĀḶEYYAKASUTTA, which enumerates twenty-five heavens extending throughout all three realms of existence. For an extended discussion of specific heavenly realms, see DEVA.

**devamāna**. (T. lha'i nga rgyal). In Sanskrit, lit. "divine pride"; a term that appears in tantric literature in connection with the practice of deity yoga (DEVATĀYOGA). In general, pride (MĀNA) is regarded as a negative mental state, one of the root afflictions (MŪLAKLEŚA), and therefore an affliction to be abandoned. However, in one of the inversions typical of the tantric context, although one should abandon ordinary pride, one should cultivate pride in oneself as being a deity, that is, in this case, as being a buddha. It is by imagining oneself to have the mind, body, abode, and resources of a buddha now that one is said to proceed quickly to the state of true buddhahood via the tantric path. Therefore, one should imagine oneself as having already achieved the goal that one is in fact seeking.

**Devānaṃpiyatissa**. (r. 247–207 BCE). Sinhalese king who, according to the Sri Lankan tradition, was the ruler under whom the island kingdom of Sri Lanka first accepted Buddhism. According to these accounts, Devānaṃpiyatissa was a contemporary of the Indian emperor Asoka (S. AŚOKA), who is said to have encouraged Devānaṃpiyatissa to convert to Buddhism. Asoka dispatched his son, the Buddhist monk MAHINDA (S. Mahendra), as head of a delegation to Sri Lanka (Ceylon) in the third century BCE to minister to Devānaṃpiyatissa and the Sinhalese court. Mahinda preached for the king the CŪḶAHATTHIPADOPAMASUTTA ("Shorter Discourse on the Simile of the Elephant's Footprint"), the twenty-seventh sutta of the MAJJHIMANIKĀYA, where the Buddha uses the simile of a woodsman tracking an elephant's footprints to explain to his audience how to reach complete certainty regarding the truth of the path, which he calls the footprints of the Tathāgata. After hearing the discourse, Devānaṃpiyatissa converted and was accepted as a Buddhist layman (UPĀSAKA). The king offered Mahinda the Mahāmeghavana, a royal pleasure garden on the outskirts of the Sinhalese capital of ANURĀDHAPURA, where he built the MAHĀVIHĀRA, which thenceforth served as the headquarters of the major Theravāda fraternity on the island. It was also at Devānaṃpiyatissa's behest that Asoka sent his daughter, the Buddhist nun SAṄGHAMITTĀ (S. Saṃghamitrā), to Sri Lanka to establish the order of nuns (P. bhikkhunī; S. BHIKṢUṆĪ) there. Saṅghamittā also brought with her a branch of the BODHI TREE, which Devānaṃpiyatissa planted at Mahāmeghavana, initiating an important site of cultic worship that continued for centuries afterward. The evidence of the Aśokan edicts and Sanskrit AVADĀNA literature suggest that the Pāli MAHĀVAṂSA account of the spread of Buddhism to Sri Lanka through the work of Devānaṃpiyatissa, whom Aśoka's son Mahinda converted to Buddhism, is probably not meant to be a historical account, but was instead intended to lend prestige to the THERAVĀDA tradition.

**Devānāṃ Priyaḥ**. [alt. Devapriya] (P. Devānaṃpiya; T. Lha rnams kyi dga' bo; C. Tian'ai; J. Ten'ai; K. Ch'ŏnae 天愛). In Sanskrit, "Beloved of the Gods"; Emperor AŚOKA's name for himself in a number of his rock edicts (see AŚOKA PILLARS).

**devarājan**. (T. lha'i rgyal po; C. tianwang; J. tennō; K. ch'ŏnwang 天王). In Sanskrit and Pāli, "king of the divinities (DEVA)"; an epithet of ŚAKRO DEVĀNĀM INDRAḤ, viz., "ŚAKRA, the king of the gods," who is also known as INDRA (Lord). Śakra resides in his capital city of Sudarśana, which is centered in the heaven of the thirty-three [gods] (TRĀYASTRIṂŚA), the second of the six heavens of the realm of sensuality (KĀMALOKA). Southeast Asian Buddhism also drew on the Hindu cult of the devarājan (divine king), which identified the reigning monarch as an incarnation of the god Śiva. See also BAYON.

**devatā**. (T. lha; C. tianshen; J. tenjin; K. ch'ŏnsin 天神). In Sanskrit and Pāli, "state of being a divinity," referring to all classifications of heavenly beings or divinities (DEVA) in the abstract. Deriving from the principle that any being who is worshipped or to whom offerings are made may be called a devatā, the connotation of divinities was broadly expanded to include not only the higher gods of the heavenly realms (DEVALOKA) proper but also religious mendicants; domesticated animals; powerful earthly forces such as fire and wind; lesser gods such as NĀGAS, GANDHARVAS, and YAKṢAS; and local ghosts and spirits, including devatās of homes, trees, and bodies of water. As Buddhism moved into new regions, various indigenous local deities thus came to be assimilated into the Buddhist pantheon by designating them as devatās.

**devatāyoga**. (T. lha'i rnal 'byor). In Sanskrit, "deity yoga"; tantric practice in which a deity (often a buddha or bodhisattva) is visualized in the presence of the practitioner, the deity is propitiated through offerings, prayers, and the recitation of MANTRA, and is then requested to bestow SIDDHIS. Two types are sometimes enumerated: one in which the deity is visualized in front of the practitioner and another in which the practitioner imagines himself or herself to be the deity. According to TSONG KHA PA, the practice of this latter type of deity yoga is the distinguishing characteristic of the VAJRAYĀNA, differentiating it from the PĀRAMITĀYĀNA. He argues that both forms of deity yoga are to be found in all classes of tantra: KRIYĀ, CARYĀ, YOGA, and ANUTTARAYOGA. Devatāyoga is a central feature of the two stages of anuttarayoga tantra (UTPATTIKRAMA and NIṢPANNAKRAMA); in the former "generation" stage, guided by a SĀDHANA, the tāntrika visualizes a MAṆḌALA, with its central and surrounding deities. Through meditation on ANĀTMAN (nonself) or ŚŪNYATĀ (emptiness), the practitioner imagines himself or herself to be the central deity of the maṇḍala. In certain forms of practice, the practitioner will also imagine the entire maṇḍala and its deities as residing within the practitioner's body. When the practitioner has developed the ability to visualize the maṇḍala and its deities in minute detail, one moves to the second "completion" stage (niṣpannakrama), in which the complex of NĀḌIS (channels) and CAKRAS (wheels) of the human body are utilized to achieve buddhahood.

**devātideva**. (T. lha'i yang lha; C. tian zhong tian; J. tenchūten; K. ch'ŏn chung ch'ŏn 天中天). In Sanskrit and Pāli, "god of gods"; an epithet of the Buddha, as someone whose divinity surpasses that of all other divinities and whose superiority is acknowledged by them, as, for example, when the infant prince SIDDHĀRTHA was taken to the temple by his father, King ŚUDDHODANA, and the statues of the deities bowed down to the child; and later when, after his enlightenment, the god BRAHMĀ implored the Buddha to teach the dharma. Thus, although the Buddha was reborn as a human, he is superior to the gods because he discovered and taught the path to NIRVĀṆA, something that gods, despite their great powers, are unable to do.

**devāvatāra**. (T. lha yul nas babs pa; C. tianxialai/Tianxiachu; J. tengerai/Tengesho; K. ch'ŏnharae/Ch'ŏnhach'ŏ 天下來/天下處). In Sanskrit, "descent from the realm of the divinities (DEVA)"; a term that describes the Buddha's return to earth after he spent the rain's-retreat season (VARṢĀ) teaching the ABHIDHARMA to his mother in the heaven of the thirty-three (TRĀYASTRIṂŚA). Because the Buddha's mother, MAHĀMĀYĀ, had died seven days after his birth, she was not able to benefit from her son's teaching; she was reborn in the TUṢITA heaven. Therefore, in the seventh year after his enlightenment, the Buddha magically ascended to the trāyastriṃśa, to which his mother descended, where he taught the abhidharma to his mother and the assembled divinities. He would descend briefly each day to collect alms and at that time would repeat to ŚĀRIPTURA what he had taught to the gods. Pining for the Buddha during his long absence from the world, King PRASENAJIT had a sandalwood statue of the Buddha carved; this statue was claimed to have been the first buddha image. The Buddha is said to have descended from the summit of Mount SUMERU to the continent of JAMBUDVĪPA on a stairway of gems that was flanked by stairways of gold and silver. Devāvatāra (Tianxiachu) is also the name of the city or country of SĀṄKĀŚYA (P. Saṅkassa), where this descent from the trayastriṃśa heaven occurred. This scene is commonly depicted in Buddhist iconography and is the subject of an eponymous SŪTRA.

**Devīkoṭa**. (S). One of the twenty-four sacred sites associated with the CAKRASAṂVARATANTRA. See PĪṬHA.

**dewachen**. A phonetic rendering of the Tibetan bde ba can, the Tibetan translation of SUKHĀVATĪ, the pure land of the buddha AMITĀBHA. The term in this form was popularized by HELENA PETROVNA BLAVATSKY and appears in a variety of European and American books on Buddhism from the nineteenth century.

**Dewa sanzan**. (出羽三山). In Japanese, the "three mountains of Dewa"; referring to Mount Haguro, Mount Gassan, and Mount Yudono in what was once known as Dewa province (in modern-day Yamagata prefecture). The region is particularly important in SHUGENDŌ and has long been a place of pilgrimage; it was visited by BASHŌ.

**Dga' ldan**. (Ganden). The Tibetan translation of the Sanskrit TUṢITA, the joyous, or contented, heaven (see DEVA), which is the abode of the future buddha MAITREYA. ¶ The short name for Dga' ldan rnam rgyal gling (Ganden Namgyal Ling), one of the three chief monasteries (known as the GDAN SA GSUM or "three seats") of the DGE LUGS sect of Tibetan Buddhism and one of the sect's principal monasteries, located twenty-eight miles (forty-five kilometers) east of LHA SA. Named after the tuṣita heaven, the monastery was established by the Dge lugs founder TSONG KHA PA in 1409 near a hill originally associated with the consecration rituals performed after the birth of the king SRONG BTSAN SGAM PO. A nearby ridge was the favored picnic ground of the king's royal wives. According to legend, the JO BO statue of Lha sa's JO KHANG temple miraculously confirmed the location's significance to Tsong kha pa. The great assembly hall was added in 1417, followed by the two colleges, Byang rtse (Jangtse) and Shar rtse (Shartse). Tsong kha pa died at Dga' ldan in 1419 and was entombed there in a STŪPA. Following Tsong kha pa's death, the abbacy passed to two of his foremost disciples, first, RGYAL TSHAB DAR MA RIN CHEN, then twelve years later to MKHAS GRUB DGE LEGS DPAL BZANG. Thus, the tradition of the DGA' LDAN KHRI PA or Throne Holder of Dga' ldan was established. Because Dga' ldan was the seat of Tsong kha pa and his two chief disciples, his followers were initially called Dga' ldan pa'i lugs, "the system of Dga' ldan." This was shortened to Dga' lugs and eventually to Dge lugs. Dga' ldan monastery was traditionally said to have 3,300 monks, although over the course of its history it often housed twice that number, forming a vast monastic complex. It was completely destroyed by the Chinese in the 1960s but has since been partially rebuilt. It has also been reestablished in exile in southern India.

**Dga' ldan khri pa**. (Ganden Tripa). In Tibetan, lit. "Holder of the Dga' ldan Throne"; title of the head of the DGE LUGS sect of Tibetan Buddhism, who is regarded as the successor of TSONG KHA PA. The first two Dga' ldan khri pas were Tsong kha pa's disciples; the first was RGYAL TSHAB DAR MA RIN CHEN and the second was MKAS GRUB DGE LEGS DPAL BZANG. Together with Tsong kha pa, they are traditionally considered to be the founders of the Dge lugs sect. The fifteenth Dga' ldan khri pa Pan chen Bsod nams grags pa (Panchen Sönam Drakpa) (1478–1554) is known for his role during the terms of the third and fourth DALAI LAMAS. At present, the Dga' ldan khri pa is selected by the Dalai Lama from a group of candidates who have already served in a number of specific positions in the major Dge lugs monasteries and tantric colleges; the term of office is generally seven years. It is not the case, as is often imagined, that the Dalai Lama is the head of the Dge lugs sect, or that the Dga' ldan khri pa is necessarily an incarnate lama (SPRUL SKU). According to the traditional system of selection, the monk who became the Dga' ldan khri pa had to rise through several ranks of the Dge lugs sect. First, he completed the prescribed course of study in one of the three GDAN SA (the major Dge lug monasteries in the LHA SA area) and achieved the highest degree in the Dge lugs academy, that of DGE BSHES lha ram pa. He then entered one of the two Dge lugs tantric colleges in Lha sa (see RGYUD STOD and RGYUD SMAD) and became a dge bshes sngags ram pa (ngakrampa). Only a dge bshes sngags ram pa could become a dge skos (gekö) (disciplinarian) of a tantric college. Rgyud stod and Rgyud smad chose three disciplinarians each year, and the bla ma dbu mdzad (lama umdze), literally "leader of the chant," i.e., vice abbot, was chosen from among the former dge skos and served for three years. Following that period, he became the abbot (mkhan po) of his tantric college for three years. The seniormost former abbot (mkhan zur) received the title Byang rtse chos rje, if he attended Rgyud smad, and Shar rtse chos rje if he attended Rgyud stod. (Byang rtse and Shar rtse are two colleges of Dga' ldan monastery.) Since the time of the eighth Dga' ldan khri pa these two alternated in the position of Dga' ldan khri pa. To date there have been 102 Dga' ldan khri pas.

**Dga' ldan pho brang**. (Ganden Podrang). In Tibetan, lit. "Palace of TUṢITA," the name by which the central government of Tibet was known from the time of fifth DALAI LAMA's ascension to power in the seventeenth century until 1959. The Dga' ldan pho brang was originally the residence or estate of Dge 'dun rgya mtsho (retrospectively named the second Dalai Lama) in 'BRAS SPUNGS monastery. He was a learned and diplomatic figure who protected the interests of the fledgling DGE LUGS sect during a difficult period when its original patron, the Sne'u dong royal family, was in decline. The residence, originally called the Rdo khang sngon mo, was given to him by the Sne'u dong princes in 1518, when he was the unquestioned leader of the major emerging Dge lugs monasteries. From this point, the Dga' ldan pho brang became the seat of the Dalai Lamas. NGAG DBANG BLO BZANG RGYA MTSHO, the fifth Dalai Lama, enlisted the help of the Qoshot Mongols and their leader, Gushri Khan, to decisively crush the KARMA PA and his patron, the King of Gtsang. From this point, the Dga' ldan pho brang came to designate not the residence of the Dalai Lama but the seat of the Dalai Lama's rulership of substantial regions of Tibet, from which he collected taxes. By extension, the term Dga' ldan pho brang has come to mean the government of Tibet during the reign of the Dalai Lamas. To consolidate Dge lugs power and prevent the the large Dge lugs monasteries (GDAN SA GSUM) from usurping his power, the fifth Dalai Lama moved the Dga' ldan pho brang into the PO TA LA palace, which then became the seat of the government he established.

**Dga' ldan phun tshogs gling**. (Ganden Puntsok Ling). A Tibetan monastery located in Gtsang province, founded by TĀRANĀTHA in 1615, who named it Rtag brtan phun tshogs gling. It was also known as JO NANG PHUN TSHOGS GLING. He hired artists from Nepal to decorate it, eventually making it the most lavishly appointed monastery in central Tibet. Under Tāranātha, it became the primary seat of the JO NANG sect. After his death, the monastery was forcibly converted to a DGE LUGS establishment by order of the fifth DALAI LAMA, who opposed the Jo nang and is said to have had a personal animosity against Tāranātha. The monastery was thus renamed Dga' ldan phun tshogs gling and the printing of the Jo nang texts held there was banned; permission to print them was not granted until the late nineteenth century.

**Dga' rab rdo rje**. (Garap Dorje). In Tibetan, the name of a semimythological figure in the early lineage of the RNYING MA sect's RDZOGS CHEN "great completion" teachings. The transmission of the teaching is said to have passed from the primordial buddha SAMANTABHADRA (T. Kun tu bzang po) to VAJRASATTVA, who transmitted it to the first human lineage holder, Dga' rab rdo rje; from him, rdzogs chen passed to MAÑJUŚRĪMITRA and ŚRĪSIṂHA, and to the Tibetan translator Ba gor VAIROCANA (fl. c. 800 CE). See RDZOGS CHEN.

**dge bshes**. (geshe). A Tibetan abbreviation for dge ba'i bshes gnyen, or "spiritual friend" (S. KALYĀṆAMITRA). In early Tibetan Buddhism, the term was used in this sense, especially in the BKA' GDAMS tradition, where saintly figures like GLANG RI THANG PA are often called "geshe"; sometimes, however, it can have a slightly pejorative meaning, as in the biography of MI LA RAS PA, where it suggests a learned monk without real spiritual attainment. In the SA SKYA sect, the term came to take on a more formal meaning to refer to a monk who had completed a specific academic curriculum. The term is most famous in this regard among the DGE LUGS, where it refers to a degree and title received after successfully completing a long course of Buddhist study in the tradition of the three great Dge lugs monasteries in LHA SA: 'BRAS SPUNGS, DGA' LDAN, and SE RA. According to the traditional curriculum, after completing studies in elementary logic and epistemology (BSDUS GRWA), a monk would begin the study of "five texts" (GZHUNG LNGA), five Indian ŚĀSTRAs, in the following order: the ABHISAMAYĀLAMKĀRA of MAITREYANĀTHA, the MADHYAMAKĀVATĀRA of CANDRAKĪRTI, the ABHIDHARMAKOŚABHĀṢYA of VASUBANDHU, and the VINAYASŪTRA of GUṆAPRABHA. Each year, there would also be a period set aside for the study of the PRAMĀṆAVĀRTTIKA of DHARMAKĪRTI. The curriculum involved the memorization of these and other texts, the study of them based on monastic textbooks (yig cha), and formal debate on their content. Each year, monks in the scholastic curriculum (a small minority of the monastic population) were required to pass two examinations, one in memorization and the other in debate. Based upon the applicant's final examination, one of four grades of the dge bshes degree was awarded, which, in descending rank, are: (1) lha rams pa, (2) tshogs rams pa, (3) rdo rams pa; (4) gling bsre [alt. gling bseb], a degree awarded by a combination of monasteries; sometimes, the more scholarly or the religiously inclined would choose that degree to remove themselves from consideration for ecclesiastical posts so they could devote themselves to their studies and to meditation practice. The number of years needed to complete the entire curriculum depended on the degree, the status of the person, and the number of candidates for the exam. The coveted lha rams pa degree, the path to important offices within the Dge lugs religious hierarchy, was restricted to sixteen candidates each year. The important incarnations (SPRUL SKU) were first in line, and their studies would be completed within about twelve years; ordinary monks could take up to twenty years to complete their studies and take the examination. Those who went on to complete the course of study at the tantric colleges of RGYUD STOD and RYUD SMAD would be granted the degree of dge bshes sngags ram pa.

**Dge 'dun chos 'phel**. (Gendun Chopel) (1903–1951). A distinguished essayist, poet, painter, translator, historian, and philosopher; one of the most important Tibetan intellectuals of the first half of the twentieth century. He was born in the Reb kong region of A mdo, the son of a respected SNGAGS PA. At the age of five, he was recognized as the incarnation (SPRUL SKU) of an abbot of the famous RNYING MA monastery, RDO RJE BRAG. Following his father's untimely death, he entered a local DGE LUGS monastery, eventually moving to BLA BRANG BKRA' SHIS 'KHYIL. He gained particular notoriety as a debater but apparently criticized the monastery's textbooks (yig cha). In 1927, he traveled to LHA SA, where he entered Sgo mang College of 'BRAS SPUNGS monastery. In 1934, the Indian scholar and nationalist Rahul Sankrityayan (1893–1963) arrived in Lha sa in search of Sanskrit manuscripts, especially those dealing with Buddhist logic. He enlisted Dge 'dun chos 'phel as his guide, just as he was completing the final examinations at the end of the long curriculum of the DGE BSHES. After visiting many of the monasteries of southern Tibet, Sankrityayan invited Dge 'dun chos 'phel to return with him to India. Over the next decade, he would travel extensively, and often alone, across India and Sri Lanka, learning Sanskrit, Pāli, several Indian vernaculars, and English. He assisted the Russian Tibetologist, GEORGE

ROERICH, in the translation of the important fifteenth-century history of Tibetan Buddhism by 'Gos lo tsā ba, DEB THER SNGON PO ("The Blue Annals"). He visited and made studies of many of the important Buddhist archaeological sites in India, writing a guide (lam yig) that is still used by Tibetan pilgrims. He studied Sanskrit erotica and frequented Calcutta brothels, producing his famous sex manual, the *'Dod pa'i bstan bcos* ("Treatise on Passion"). During his time abroad, he also spent more than a year in Sri Lanka. In January 1946, after twelve years abroad, Dge 'dun chos 'phel returned to Lha sa. He taught poetry and also gave teachings on MADHYAMAKA philosophy, which would be published posthumously as the controversial *Klu sgrub dgongs rgyan* ("Adornment for NĀGĀRJUNA's Thought"). Within a few months of his arrival in Lha sa, Dge 'dun chos 'phel was arrested by the government of the regent of the young fourteenth Dalai Lama on the fabricated charge of counterfeiting foreign currency. Sentenced to three years, he served at least two, working on his unfinished history of early Tibet, *Deb ther dkar po* ("The White Annals"), and composing poetry. He emerged from prison a broken man and died in October 1951 at the age of forty-eight.

**Dge 'dun grub**. (Gendün Drup) (1391–1475). A revered scholar of the DGE LUGS sect of Tibetan Buddhism, posthumously recognized as the first DALAI LAMA. He was from the clan of Ngar tso in the region of Ru lug and received his early training at SNAR THANG monastery, where he earned fame for his erudition. In 1415, he traveled to central Tibet, where he became a close disciple of the Dge lugs polymath TSONG KHA PA in the years before the master's death in 1419. He went on to serve as the abbot of DGA' LDAN monastery. In 1447, Dge 'dun grub founded BKRA SHIS LHUN PO monastery, later the seat of the PAṆ CHEN LAMAS in the central Tibetan city of Gzhis ka rtse (Shigatse). After the Mongolian ruler Altan Khan bestowed the title Dalai Lama on BSOD NAMS RGYA MTSHO in 1578, Dge 'dun grub was posthumously identified as the lineage's first incarnation. He was a renowned scholar, writing influential works on both VINAYA and ABHIDHARMA.

**Dge lugs**. (Geluk). In Tibetan, lit. "System of Virtue"; one of the four major sects of Tibetan Buddhism (see also BKA' BRYUD, SA SKYA, RNYING MA). Originating among the disciples of TSONG KHA PA, it was originally referred to as the Dga' ldan pa'i lugs (abbreviated as Dga' lugs) "the system of those from Dga' ldan Mountain," where Tsong kha pa, with the patronage of the powerful Phag mo gru family, founded Ri bo DGA' LDAN monastery in 1409. (The name Dge lugs may have originally been an abbreviation of Dga' ldan pa'i lugs.) Within a few years of the founding of Dga' ldan, two followers of Tsong kha pa, 'JAM DBYANGS CHOS RJE BKRA SHIS DPAL LDAN and Byams chen chos rje Shākya ye shes (1354–1435), founded 'BRAS SPUNGS (1416) and SE RA (1419) monasteries, respectively, apparently at Tsong kha pa's urging. These three monasteries developed into the institutional center of Dge lugs power and influence; Tsong kha pa with his two most prominent followers, RGYAL TSHAB DARMA RIN CHEN (called Rgyal tshab rje) and MKHAS GRUB DGE LEGS DPAL BZANG PO (called Mkhas grub rje)—both important scholars in their own right—became the cultic center, called rje yab sras gsum ("the lord and his two spiritual sons"). BKRA SHIS LHUN PO monastery, the fourth great Dge lugs monastery, was founded in Gzhis ka rtse (Shigatse) in 1447 by another of Tsong kha pa's followers, the scholarly and politically astute DGE 'DUN GRUB, providing a basis for Dge lugs power in the west. Dge 'dun grub was posthumously recognized as the first DALAI LAMA. The fifth Dalai Lama NGAG DBANG BLO BZANG RGYA MTSHO and BLO BZANG CHOS KYI RGYAL MTSHAN, with the help of the Mongols, established the Dge lugs as the largest and most powerful Buddhist sect in Tibet. After the founding of the DGA' LDAN PHO BRANG government in 1642, the Dalai Lama was invested with temporal power, making the Dge lugs the de facto ruling party and bringing an end to the political instability that accompanied the rise of the sect during the sixteenth and seventeenth centuries. Blo bzang chos kyi rgyal mtshan became abbot of Bkra shis lhun po and began the lineage of powerful PAṆ CHEN BLA MAS, after the Dalai Lamas, the second most powerful lineage of Dge lugs incarnate lamas (see SPRUL SKU). The influence of the Dge lugs sect over Tibet was based on an elaborate system of regional monasteries with ties to the four central Dge lugs monasteries; the two largest of the regional monasteries, BLA BRANG BKRA SHIS DKYIL and SKU 'BUM in A mdo, rivaled the central monasteries in size and stature. The sect is known for its scholastic curriculum, and for a rigorous examination system that culminates in the rank of DGE BSHES, providing a steady stream of abbots and incarnate lamas to administer the system in collaboration with the aristocratic elite under the oversight of the Dga' ldan pho brang government. In its rise to power, the Dge lugs incorporated doctrines and monasteries that were earlier separate and distinct traditions.

**Dge lugs pa**. (Gelukpa). A person affiliated with the DGE LUGS sect of Tibetan Buddhism.

**Dge rgyas**. (Gegye). In Tibetan, one of the four "extra taming temples" or "extra pinning temples" (YANG 'DUL GTSUG LAG KHANG) said to have been constructed during the time of the Tibetan king SRONG BTSAN SGAM PO to pin down the limbs of the demoness (T. srin mo) who was impeding the introduction of Buddhism into Tibet. The temple is located in Byams sprin (Jamtrin) and pins down her right knee.

**dgon pa**. (gompa). In Tibetan, literally, "remote place"; the most common term for "monastery." See ARAṆYA.

**dgra lha**. (dralha). In Tibetan, literally "enemy god"; a class of Tibetan deities that fights against the enemy of those who propitiate and worship them. Tibetans speak of both a personal dgra lha, which abides on one's right shoulder to protect one from enemies and promote one's social status, as well as various groupings of dgra lha invoked in both Buddhist and BON ritual. Dgra lha is also a common epithet of wrathful DHARMAPĀLAS who protect the dharma against its enemies, both internal and external.

**dhamma**. In Pāli, "factor," "element," "doctrine." See DHARMA.

**Dhammacakkappavattanasutta**. (S. Dharmacakrapravartanasūtra; T. Chos 'khor bskor ba'i mdo; C. Zhuan falun jing; J. Tenbōringyō; K. Chŏn pŏmnyun kyŏng 轉法輪經). In Pāli, "Discourse on Turning the Wheel of the DHARMA"; often referred to as GAUTAMA Buddha's "first sermon," delivered after his enlightenment to the "group of five" (PAÑCAVARGIKA; bhadravargīya), at the Deer Park (P. Migadāya; S. MṚGADĀVA) in ṚSIPATANA near SĀRNĀTH. In its Pāli version, the discourse appears in the MAHĀVAGGA section of the VINAYA, which recounts the founding of the dispensation, rather than in the suttapiṭaka (S. SŪTRAPIṬAKA). (A separate SARVĀSTIVĀDA recension appears in the Chinese translation of the SAṂYUKTĀGAMA; there is also an early Chinese translation by AN SHIGAO that circulated independently.) Following his enlightenment, the Buddha considered who might be able to comprehend what he had experienced and remembered the "group of five" ascetics, with whom he had previously engaged in self-mortification practices (TAPAS). Although initially reticent to receive Gautama because he had abandoned his asceticism and had become "self-indulgent," they soon relented and heard Gautama relate his realization of the deathless state. Their minds now pliant, the Buddha then "set rolling the wheel of the dharma" (DHARMACAKRAPRAVARTANA), which is the first enunciation of his liberation. In the sermon, the Buddha advocates a middle way (P. majjhimapaṭipadā; S. MADHYAMAPRATIPAD) between sensual indulgence and self-mortification, and equates the middle way to the noble eightfold path (P. ariyāṭṭhaṅgikamagga; S. ĀRYĀṢṬĀṄGAMĀRGA). He follows with a detailed account of the FOUR NOBLE TRUTHS, the full knowledge and vision (P. ñāṇadassana; S. JÑĀNADARŚANA) of which leads to liberation. While listening to the discourse, ĀJÑĀTAKAUṆḌINYA (P. Aññātakoṇḍañña) understood the principle of causation—that all things produced will also come to an end—and achieved the first level of sanctity, that of stream-enterer (P. sotāpanna; S. SROTAĀPANNA). He was the first disciple to take ordination (UPASAMPADĀ) as a monk (P. BHIKKHU; S. BHIKṢU), following the simple "come, monk" formula (P. ehi bhikkhu; S. EHIBHIKṢUKĀ): "Come, monk, the dharma is well proclaimed; live the holy life for the complete ending of suffering." Soon afterward, he was followed into the order by the rest of the "group of five" monks. The site where the first sermon was delivered—the Deer Park (Mṛgadāva) in Ṛṣipatana (P. Isipatana), the modern Sārnāth, near Vārāṇasī—subsequently became one of the four major Buddhist pilgrimage sites (MAHĀSTHĀNA) in India.

**Dhammacetī**. (r. 1472–1492). Mon king of Rāmaññadesa (Lower Burma) whose capital was Pegu (Hanthawaddi). His regnal title, by which he is known in inscriptions, is Rāmādhipatimahārājā. Dhammacetī conducted a purification of the Mon Sāsana of Rāmaññadesa between 1476 and 1479, during which time the entire Mon saṅgha (SAṂGHA) was reordained according to Sihala procedures. The purification is recorded in the KALYĀṆĪ INSCRIPTIONS, erected in 1479 at the site of the Kalyāṇī Sīmā Hall in Pegu. The SĪMĀ hall was named after the Kalyāṇī River in Sri Lanka where, in 1476, a delegation of twenty-two Mon monks dispatched by Dhammacetī took reordination to form the nucleus of the reformed Mon saṅgha.

**Dhammadāyādasutta**. (C. Qiufa jing; J. Guhōgyō; K. Kupŏp kyŏng 求法經). In Pāli, "Discourse on Heirs of the Dharma"; third sutta in the MAJJHIMANIKĀYA (a separate SARVĀSTIVĀDA recension appears as the eighty-eighth sūtra in the Chinese translation of the MADHYAMĀGAMA; another recension of uncertain affiliation also appears in the Chinese translation of the EKOTTARĀGAMA.) This sutta contains two discourses preached at the JETAVANA Grove in Sāvatthi (ŚRĀVASTĪ), the first by the Buddha and the second by Sāriputta (ŚĀRIPUTRA). The Buddha urges his monks to give priority to the dharma, not to material possessions, and to receive as their true legacy from him the constituents of enlightenment (bodhipakkhiyadhamma; S. BODHIPAKṢIKADHARMA), rather than the four requisites (nissaya; S. NIŚRAYA) of mendicancy. Sāriputta advises the monks to live in solitude for the attainment of meditative absorption (jhāna; S. DHYĀNA) and to abandon greed (LOBHA), hatred (P. dosa; S. DVEṢA), and delusion (MOHA) in order to attain nibbāna (NIRVĀṆA).

**Dhammakāya**. (Thai, Thammakai). A Buddhist reform movement in Thailand that originated in 1916, when a monk named Luang Phor Sodh is said to have rediscovered a technique of meditation that had been lost since the time of the Buddha. The movement began to gain impetus in 1970, when one of the abbot's disciples, a nun known as Khun Yay Upāsika, founded Wat Phra Dhammakāya. Dhammakāya meditation practice consists of visualizing a small crystal sphere entering one's body through the nasal passage; the sphere settles in the solar plexus and eventually becomes transformed into a crystal image of the Buddha. While engaging in this visualization, the meditator is supposed to focus on the MANTRA "samma arahang." The practice is supposed to culminate in the ability to see a buddha image (the dhammakāya, or "truth body" of the Buddha; see DHARMAKĀYA) inside oneself, an experience compared to tasting NIRVĀṆA in the present life. Meditation is the principal Dhammakāya practice, and the organization encourages its followers to meditate twice a day as a way of improving self-confidence and as a tool for success, well being, and fostering family life. Dhammakāya also offers group training courses for adults in the private and public sectors. Devotees dress in white, and temple buildings are simple in design. Dhammakāya is also known for organizing massive ceremonies involving several thousand monks and tens of thousands of laypeople on Buddhist holy days. Rather than following the traditional lunar calendar and practicing on the days of the waning and waxing moon, Dhammakāya practice is held every Sunday, with meditation in the morning, followed by a sermon on topics relevant to the problems and concerns of everyday life. Its adherents are also encouraged to take part in such activities as retreats, youth camps, and massive ordinations for college students during the summer break. The Dhammakāya movement also differs from mainstream Thai Buddhism in that it requires monks to be ordained for life rather than the temporary ordination that is common among Thai laymen. In addition to its massive WAT outside of Bangkok, it has established branches throughout Thailand and overseas. Many Thais, especially intellectuals who support the forest meditation tradition, criticize Dhammakāya for its "direct marketing" type of organization and its quick-fix solutions to complex problems.

**Dhammapada**. (S. Dharmapada; T. Chos kyi tshigs su bcad pa; C. Faju jing; J. Hokkugyō; K. Pŏpku kyŏng 法句經). In Pāli, "Verses of Dharma"; the second book of the KHUDDAKANIKĀYA of the Pāli SUTTAPIṬAKA. The *Dhammapada* is an anthology of verses, arranged topically, many of which are also found in other books of the Pāli canon, although it is unclear whether the *Dhammapada* was compiled from them. Some of the same verses are also found in JAINA and Hindu sources. The current Pāli text contains 423 verses divided into twenty-six chapters; the verses are broadly associated with the topic of each particular chapter, which have predominantly ethical themes. The verses and chapters are sometimes arranged in pairs, e.g., "The Fool" and "The Sage," "The World" and "The Buddha," etc. As possible evidence of the popularity of the collection, there are several extant recensions of *Dharmapadas* in languages other than Pāli, including a GĀNDHĀRĪ version and several in Chinese translation that derive from Sanskrit or Middle Indic versions of the collection. The chapters and verses of these other recensions often bear little resemblance to the Pāli version, some having alternate arrangements of the chapters and verses, others having many more total verses in their collections. These differences suggest that such anthologies of gnomic verses were being made independently in disparate Buddhist communities throughout India and Central Asia, often borrowing liberally, and haphazardly, from earlier recensions. A version of the UDĀNAVARGA compiled by Dharmatrāta, a larger work containing all the verses from the *Dhammapada*, became a basic text of the BKA' GDAMS sect in Tibet; the Pāli version of the *Dhammapada* was translated into Tibetan by the twentieth-century scholar DGE 'DUN CHOS 'PHEL. The *Dhammapada* has long been one of the most beloved of Buddhist texts in the West. Since its first translation into a Western language (Latin) in 1855 by the Danish scholar Victor Fausbøll (1821–1908), it has been rendered numerous times into English (well over fifty translations have been made) and other languages.

**Dhammapadaṭṭhakathā**. In Pāli, "Commentary to the DHAMMAPADA"; attributed to BUDDHAGHOSA. The text is comprised of stories similar to the JĀTAKAS, recounting the occasions on which the verses of the *Dhammapada* were uttered. Many of the stories are also found in the SUTTA and VINAYA PIṬAKAS, as well as in the jātaka commentary, *Jātakatthavaṇṇanā*. The *Dhammapadaṭṭhakathā* appears in the Pali Text Society's English translation series as *Buddhist Legends*.

**Dhammapāla**. (d.u.). A celebrated Pāli commentator and author, Dhammapāla is known to have flourished sometime after the time of BUDDHAGHOSA (fl. fifth century CE), though his precise dates are uncertain. Numerous works are attributed to him, although the accuracy of these attributions is sometimes suspect because of the many Pāli authors who have the same name. The SĀSANAVAṂSA states that Dhammapāla lived at Badaratittha in southern India. In several of his works, Dhammapāla records that he is a native of Kañcipuram and that he studied at the MAHĀVIHĀRA in the Sinhalese capital of ANURĀDHAPURA. THERAVĀDA congregations affiliated with the Mahāvihāra existed among the Tamils in South India, and it appears that he was familiar with their commentarial traditions. According to one legend, Dhammapāla was so renowned for his intelligence that the local king of Kañcipuram offered him his daughter in marriage. Being interested instead in a life of renunciation and scholarship, Dhammapāla prayed for his release before an image of the Buddha, whereupon the gods carried him away to a place where he could be ordained as a Buddhist monk. Seven of Dhammapāla's commentaries (AṬṬHAKATHĀ) are devoted to the KHUDDAKANIKĀYA division of the SUTTAPIṬAKA; these include the PARAMATTHADĪPANĪ (a commentary on the UDĀNA, ITIVUTTAKA, VIMĀNAVATTHU, PETAVATTHU, THERAGĀTHĀ, and THERĪGĀTHĀ), as well as exegeses of the *Vimānavatthu, Petavatthu, Itivuttaka*, and CARIYĀPIṬAKA. He also wrote commentaries to the NETTIPPAKARAṆA and the VISUDDHIMAGGA, the latter of which is titled the PARAMATTHAMAÑJŪSĀ. Dhammapāla also wrote several subcommentaries (ṭīkā) on Buddhaghosa's exegeses of the Pāli canon, including the *Līnatthavannanā* on the suttapiṭaka, and subcommentaries on the JĀTAKA, the BUDDHAVAṂSA, and the ABHIDHAMMAPIṬAKA.

**Dhammaruci Nikāya**. The name of a Sri Lankan THERAVĀDA monastic order, which, according to Sinhalese chronicles, is named after a Vajjiputaka (S. VṚJIPUTRAKA) monk named Dhammaruci. Dhammarui is said to have brought his disciples from India to Sri Lanka, where they were welcomed by a group of monks at ABHAYAGIRI who had seceded from the MAHĀVIHĀRA when a monk named Mahātissa was expelled from the Mahāvihāra for inappropriate interaction with the laity.

This secession is said to have occurred not long after the founding of Abhayagiri in the late first century BCE. The Dhammaruci Nikāya is considered a heterodox sect of Sri Lankan Theravāda because of disagreements over minor points in the VINAYA. They nonetheless received royal patronage during several periods of Sri Lankan history. The Abhayagiri Nikāya, which maintained close ties with India and adopted some MAHĀYĀNA teachings, is sometimes referred to as the Dhammaruci Nikāya.

**Dhammasaṅgaṇi**. [alt. Dhammasaṅgaṇī]. In Pāli, lit. "Enumeration (saṅgaṇī) of Factors (dhamma)"; the first of the seven books of the THERAVĀDA ABHIDHAMMAPIṬAKA. The text undertakes a systematic analysis of all the elements of reality, or factors (dhamma; S. DHARMA), discussed in the suttapiṭaka, organizing them into definitive rosters. The elaborate analysis of each and every element of existence provided by the *Dhammasaṅgaṇi* is considered to be foundational to the full account of the conditional relations pertaining between all those dharmas found in the PAṬṬHĀNA, the last book of the Pāli abhidhamma. ¶ The *Dhammasaṅgaṇi* consists of an initial "matrix" (mātikā; S. MĀTṚKĀ), followed by four main divisions: (1) mind (CITTA) and mental concomitants (CETASIKA), (2) materiality (RŪPA), (3) analytical summaries (nikkhepa; S. NIKṢEPA), and (4) exegesis (AṬṬHAKATHĀ). In the opening matrix, the complete list of subjects to be treated in both the *Dhammasaṅgaṇi*, as well as the entire abhidhammapiṭaka, is divided into three groups. (1) The triad matrix (tikamātikā) consists of twenty-two categories of factors (dhamma; S. DHARMA), each of which is treated as triads. For example, in the case of the matrix on wholesomeness (kusala; S. KUŚALA), the relevant factors are divided into wholesome factors (kusaladhamma; S. kuśaladharma), unwholesome factors (akusaladhamma; S. akuśaladharma), and neither wholesome nor unwholesome factors (avyākatadhamma; S. AVYĀKṚTA-DHARMA). (2) The dyad matrix (dukamātikā) consists of one hundred categories of factors, treated as dyads. For example, in the matrix on cause (HETU), factors are divided between factors that are root causes (hetudhamma) and factors that are not root causes (na hetudhamma). (3) The dyad matrix from the sūtras (suttantikadukamātikā) consists of forty-six categories of factors found in the suttapiṭaka that are treated as dyads. According to the AṬṬHASĀLINĪ, the commentary to the *Dhammasaṅgaṇi*, this section was added by Sāriputta (S. ŚĀRIPUTRA), one of the two main disciples of the Buddha, to facilitate understanding of the suttapiṭaka. Of the four main divisions of the *Dhammasaṅgaṇi* that follow this initial matrix, the first two, the division on mind and mental concomitants (cittuppādakaṇḍa) and the division on materiality (rūpakaṇḍa), expound upon the first category in the triad matrix, the matrix on wholesomeness, so as to provide a basis for the analysis of other categories of dharmas. The division on mind and mental concomitants contains the analysis of wholesome factors, unwholesome factors, and the first two of the four categories of factors that are neither wholesome nor unwholesome (avyākata; S. AVYĀKṚTA), namely, resultant (VIPĀKA) and noncausative action (kiriya); the division on materiality (rūpakaṇḍa) treats the remaining two categories of abyākatadhammas, namely, materiality (rūpa) and nibbāna (S. NIRVĀṆA), although nibbāna does not receive a detailed explanation. In the first division on wholesomeness in the triad category, each aspect is analyzed in relation to the various realms of existence: wholesome states of mind and mental concomitants: (1) pertaining to the sensuous realm (KĀMĀVACARA) (P. kāmāvacara-aṭṭhamahācitta), (2) pertaining to the realm of subtle materiality (rūpāvacara) (P. rūpāvacarakusala), (3) pertaining to the immaterial realm (arūpāvacara) (P. arūpāvacarakusala), (4) leading to different levels of existence within the three realms, and (5) leading to liberation from the three realms (lokuttaracitta). The third division, the division on analytical summaries (nikkhepakaṇḍa), provides a synopsis of the classifications found in all the triads and dyads, organized in eight categories: roots (mūla), aggregates (khandha; S. SKANDHA), doors (dvāra), field of occurrence (BHŪMI), meaning (attha; S. ARTHA), doctrinal interpretation (dhamma), nomenclature (nāma), and grammatical gender (liṅga). The final division on exegesis (aṭṭhakathākaṇḍa) offers additional detailed enumeration of other triads and dyads.

**Dhanapāla**. [alt. Nālāgiri] (T. Nor skyong; C. Hucai/Shoucai; J. Gozai/Shuzai; K. Hojae/Sujae 護財/守財). In Sanskrit and Pāli, "Wealth Protector"; alternate name of a ferocious elephant whom the Buddha tamed with his loving-kindness (MAITRĪ) on the streets of RĀJAGṚHA. See NĀLĀGIRI.

**Dharamsala**. See DHARMAŚĀLĀ.

**dhāraṇī**. (T. gzungs; C. tuoluoni/zongchi; J. darani/sōji; K. tarani/ch'ongji 陀羅尼/總持). In Sanskrit, "mnemonic device," "code." The term is derived etymologically from the Sanskrit root √dhṛ ( "to hold" or "to maintain"), thus suggesting something that supports, holds, or retains; hence, a verbal formula believed to "retain" or "encapsulate" the meaning of lengthier texts and prolix doctrines, thus functioning as a mnemonic device. It is said that those who memorize these formulae (which may or may not have semantic meaning) gain the power to retain the fuller teachings that the dhāraṇī "retain." Commenting on the BODHISATTVABHŪMISŪTRA, Buddhist exegetes, such as the sixth-century Chinese scholiast JINGYING HUIYUAN, describe dhāraṇī as part of the equipment or accumulation (SAṂBHĀRA) that BODHISATTVAs need to reach full enlightenment, and classify dhāraṇī into four categories, i.e., those associated with (1) teachings (DHARMA), (2) meaning (ARTHA), (3) spells (MANTRA), and (4) acquiescence (KṢĀNTI). The first two types are involved with learning and remembering the teachings and intent of Buddhist doctrine and thus function as "codes." In the PRAJÑĀPĀRAMITĀ literature, for example, a dhāraṇī can be a letter of the alphabet associated with a meaningful term: e.g., the letter "a" serves as code for remembering the term "ādy-anutpannatva" ("unproduced from the very beginning").

The third type (mantradhāraṇī) helps the bodhisattva to overcome adversity, counter baleful influences, and bestow protection (see PARĪTTA). The fourth type assists the bodhisattva in acquiescing to the true nature of dharmas as unproduced (ANUTPATTIKADHARMAKṢĀNTI), giving him the courage to remain in the world for the sake of all sentient beings. Dhāraṇī sometimes occur at the conclusion of a Mahāyāna sūtra as a terse synopsis of the fuller teaching of the sūtra, again drawing on their denotation as codes. The DHARMAGUPTAKA school of mainstream Buddhism, which may date to as early as the third or second century BCE, included a dhāraṇī collection (dhāraṇīpiṭaka) as an addition to the usual tripartite division of the Buddhist canon (TRIPIṬAKA), an indication of how widespread the use of dhāraṇī was across the Buddhist tradition. Dhāraṇī also appear often in Buddhist tantras and one prevailing theory in the scholarship had been that they were the root source from which tantric literature developed. The connection between dhāraṇī and the TANTRAs is tenuous, however, and seems not to be found before eighth-century materials. More likely, then, dhāraṇī should be treated as a pan-Buddhistic, rather than a proto-tantric, phenomenon. Indeed, the DAZHIDU LUN (*Mahāprajñāpāramitāśāstra*), attributed to NĀGĀRJUNA, includes facility in dhāraṇī among the skills that all ordained monks should develop and mastery of ten different types of dhāraṇī as a central part of the training of bodhisattvas. See also MANTRA.

**dharma**. (P. dhamma; T. chos; C. fa; J. hō; K. pŏp 法). In Sanskrit, "factor," or "element"; a polysemous term of wide import in Buddhism and therefore notoriously difficult to translate, a problem acknowledged in traditional sources; as many as ten meanings of the term are found in the literature. The term dharma derives from the Sanskrit root √dhṛ, which means "to hold" or "to maintain." In Vedic literature, dharma is often used to refer to the sacrifice that maintains the order of the cosmos. Indian kings used the term to refer to the policies of their realms. In Hinduism, there is an important genre of literature called the dharmaśāstra, treatises on dharma, which set forth the social order and the respective duties of its members, in relation to caste, gender, and stage of life. Based on this denotation of the term, many early European translators rendered dharma into English as "law," the same sense conveyed in the Chinese translation of dharma as fa (also "law"). ¶ In Buddhism, dharma has a number of distinct denotations. One of its most significant and common usages is to refer to "teachings" or "doctrines," whether they be Buddhist or non-Buddhist. Hence, in recounting his search for truth prior to his enlightenment, the Buddha speaks of the dharma he received from his teachers. After his enlightenment, the Buddha's first sermon was called "turning the wheel of the dharma" (DHARMACAKRAPRAVARTANA). When the Buddha described what he himself taught to his disciples, he called it the DHARMAVINAYA, with the vinaya referring to the rules of monastic discipline and the dharma referring presumably to everything else. This sense of dharma as teaching, and its centrality to the tradition, is evident from the inclusion of the dharma as the second of the three jewels (RATNATRAYA, along with the Buddha and the SAṂGHA, or community) in which all Buddhists seek refuge. Commentators specified that dharma in the refuge formula refers to the third and fourth of the FOUR NOBLE TRUTHS: the truth of the cessation (NIRODHASATYA) of the causes that lead to suffering and the truth of the path (MĀRGA) to that cessation. Here, the verbal root of dharma as "holding" is evoked etymologically to gloss dharma as meaning something that "holds one back" from falling into states of suffering. A distinction was also drawn between the dharma or teachings as something that is heard or studied, called the scriptural dharma (ĀGAMA-dharma), and the dharma or teachings as something that is made manifest in the consciousness of the practitioner, called the realized dharma (ADHIGAMA-dharma). ¶ A second (and very different) principal denotation of dharma is a physical or mental "factor" or fundamental "constituent element," or simply "phenomenon." In this sense, the individual building blocks of our compounded (SAṂSKṚTA) existence are dharmas, dharma here glossed as something that "holds" its own nature. Thus, when Buddhist texts refer to the constituent elements of existence, they will often speak of "all dharmas," as in "all dharmas are without self." The term ABHIDHARMA, which is interpreted to mean either "higher dharma" or "pertaining to dharma," refers to the analysis of these physical and mental factors, especially in the areas of causation and epistemology. The texts that contain such analyses are considered to be one of the three general categories of the Buddhist canon (along with SŪTRA and vinaya), known as the TRIPIṬAKA or "three baskets." ¶ A third denotation of the term dharma is that of "quality" or "characteristic." Thus, reference is often made to dharmas of the Buddha, referring in this sense not to his teachings but to his various auspicious qualities, whether they be physical, verbal, or mental. This is the primary meaning of dharma in the term DHARMAKĀYA. Although this term is sometimes rendered into English as "truth body," dharmakāya seems to have originally been meant to refer to the entire corpus (KĀYA) of the Buddha's transcendent qualities (dharma). ¶ The term dharma also occurs in a large number of important compound words. SADDHARMA, or "true dharma," appears early in the tradition as a means of differentiating the teachings of the Buddha from those of other, non-Buddhist, teachers. In the MAHĀYĀNA sūtras, saddharma was used to refer, perhaps defensively, to the Mahāyāna teachings; one of the most famous Mahāyāna sūtras is the SADDHARMAPUṆḌARĪKASŪTRA, known in English as the "Lotus Sūtra," but whose full title is "White Lotus of the True Dharma Sūtra." In Buddhist theories of history, the period after the death of the Buddha (often said to last five hundred years) is called the time of the true dharma. This period of saddharma is followed, according to some theories, by a period of a "semblance" of the true dharma (SADDHARMAPRATIRŪPAKA) and a period of "decline" (SADDHARMAVIPRALOPA). The term DHARMADHĀTU refers to the ultimate nature of reality, as does DHARMATĀ, "dharma-ness." It should also be noted that dharma commonly appears in the designations of persons. Hence, a DHARMABHĀṆAKA is a preacher of the dharma, a DHARMAPĀLA is a deity who protects the dharma; in both terms, dharma refers to the Buddhist doctrine. A DHARMARĀJAN is a righteous king (see CAKRAVARTIN), especially one who upholds the teachings of the Buddha. For various rosters of dharmas, see the List of Lists appendix.

**dharmabhāṇaka**. (P. dhammabhāṇaka; T. chos smra ba; C. shuofashi; J. seppōshi; K. sŏlbŏpsa 說法師). In Sanskrit, "reciter of the dharma"; a term used to describe a monastic vocation. Before the Buddhist canon was committed to writing, perhaps four hundred years after the Buddha's death, the canon was transmitted orally within monastic families of reciters. In the Pāli tradition, "reciters" were typically assigned to memorize one specific subcategory of the canon, i.e., Mahjjhimabhāṇaka ("reciters of the MAJJHIMANIKĀYA"), Jātakabhāṇaka ("reciters of the JĀTAKA"), etc. The term also occurs in the MAHĀYĀNA sūtras to describe a teacher of the Mahāyāna; indeed, such teachers may have played an important role in the dissemination of the Mahāyāna sūtras.

**dharmacakra**. (P. dhammacakka; T. chos kyi 'khor lo; C. falun; J. hōrin; K. pŏmnyun 法輪). In Sanskrit, "wheel of the DHARMA"; the eight-spoked wheel that symbolizes the teaching of the Buddha (eight representing the eightfold noble path, or ĀRYĀṢṬĀṄGAMĀRGA). Before human images of the Buddha began to be made in India due to Greek or JAINA influence, the Buddha was often represented visually by the dharmacakra, as a symbol of the "turning the wheel of the dharma" (DHARMACAKRAPRAVARTANA), viz., the dispensation that he set in motion at his first sermon in SĀRNĀTH. In Indian mythology, one of the possessions of a "universal emperor," or CAKRAVARTIN (literally, "wheel turner"), was a magical wheel that rolled around the world, bringing the lands it entered under the king's domain. At his birth, it was prophesied that Prince SIDDHĀRTHA would become either a cakravartin or a buddha. His dharmacakra is seen as the counterpart of the more worldly wheel of the cakravartin, and the Buddha's teaching is thus described as his setting that wheel of the dharma in motion.

**dharmacakramudrā**. (T. chos kyi 'khor lo'i phyag rgya; C. zhuan falun yin; J. tenbōrin'in; K. chŏn bŏmnyun in 轉法輪印). In Sanskrit, "wheel of dharma gesture," sometimes referred to as the "teaching MUDRĀ," is commonly found in images of the buddha ŚĀKYAMUNI where it represents his teaching the dharma. Representations of other buddhas, such as AMITĀBHA, VAIROCANA, and MAITREYA, may also exhibit this gesture. The dharmacakramudrā is formed with the left palm turned inward toward the body, in front of the chest, and the right palm turned outward. The index finger and thumb of each hand form circles that lightly touch each other. In an alternate position, the thumb and index fingers of the right hand may touch one of the left fingers. Occasionally, the right hand forms this gesture alone, with the left hand situated in the DHYĀNAMUDRĀ.

**dharmacakrapravartana**. (P. dhammacakkappavattana; T. chos 'khor bskor ba; C. zhuan falun; J. tenbōrin; K. chŏn pŏmnyun 轉法輪). In Sanskrit, "turning the wheel of the DHARMA"; a term used generally to describe the Buddha's teaching; specifically, it refers the Buddha's first sermon, delivered at the Deer Park (S. MṚGADĀVA) in ṚṢIPATANA, the modern SĀRNĀTH, as described in the Pāli DHAMMACAKKAPPAVATTANASUTTA (S. Dharmacakrapravartanasūtra), when he first declared the FOUR NOBLE TRUTHS (catvāry āryasatyāni) and the noble eightfold path (ĀRYĀṢṬĀṄGAMĀRGA). As Buddhist doctrine expanded exponentially in size and complexity, Buddhists were hard put to explain the apparent divergences in the teachings found in various recensions of the sūtras. In order to account for the critical differences in these sūtra explications of the Buddhist teachings, different traditions began to suggest that the Buddha had actually "turned the wheel of the dharma" more than one time. Certain perfection of wisdom (PRAJÑĀPĀRAMITĀ) sūtras refer to the Buddha's teaching of the perfection of wisdom as the second turning of the wheel of dharma. The SAṂDHINIRMOCANASŪTRA posits that the Buddha actually turned the wheel of the dharma three separate times, a description that came to figure prominently in MAHĀYĀNA scholastic literature: the first, called CATUḤSATYADHARMACAKRA, when he taught the four noble truths of the HĪNAYĀNA traditions; the second, called the ALAKṢAṆADHARMACAKRA ("dharma-wheel of signlessness"), when he taught the emptiness (ŚŪNYATĀ) doctrine as understood by the MADHYAMAKA school; and a third, the *SUVIBHAKTADHARMACAKRA ("dharma-wheel possessed of good differentiation"), when he taught the Yogācāra TRISVABHĀVA doctrine. The *Saṃdhinirmocanasūtra* claims that the teachings of the first two dharma-wheels were provisional (NEYĀRTHA), while the third was definitive (NĪTĀRTHA). This threefold taxonomy of the Buddhist teachings was one of the most influential hermeneutical schema (see JIAOXIANG PANSHI) created in the Mahāyāna and elicited extensive commentary in India, Tibet, and East Asia. Proponents of the Madhyamaka, who identified the second wheel with the PRAJÑĀPĀRAMITĀSŪTRAS, claimed to the contrary that the second wheel was definitive and the first and third were provisional.

**Dharmacakrapravartanasūtra**. In Sanskrit, "Setting in Motion the Wheel of the Dharma." See DHAMMACAKKAPPAVATTANASUTTA.

**dharmacakṣus**. (P. dhammacakkhu; T. chos kyi mig; C. fayan; J. hōgen; K. pŏban 法眼). In Sanskrit, "eye of dharma"; the enlightened capacity to cognize the inherent truth of impermanence (ANITYA). The term also frequently appears in the sūtras in the stock formula of comprehension, where an interlocutor's "eye of dharma" opens as he or she understands the meaning of the Buddha's instruction. As one of the

PAÑCACAKṢUS ("five eyes"), it sees all that the noble persons (ĀRYAPUDGALA) see. See also ABHIJÑĀ.

**dharmadāna**. (P. dhammadāna; T. chos kyi sbyin pa; C. fashi; J. hōse; K. pŏpsi 法施). In Sanskrit, "gift of dharma"; one of the two (or sometimes three) forms of giving (DĀNA) praised in the sūtras, along with the "gift of material goods" (ĀMIṢADĀNA). Occasionally, a third form of giving, the "gift of fearlessness" (ABHAYADĀNA), viz., helping others to become courageous, is added to the list. "The gift of dharma" means to share the Buddhist teachings with others through such means as delivering sermons, copying sūtras, encouraging others to cultivate the path (MĀRGA), and writing dictionaries.

**Dharmadharmatāvibhāga**. (T. Chos dang chos nyid rnam par 'byed pa). In Sanskrit, "Distinguishing Dharma and Dharmatā"; a short YOGĀCĀRA work attributed to MAITREYA or MAITREYANĀTHA; it survives only in Tibetan translation (in the SDE DGE BSTAN 'GYUR, there are two translations); it is one of the five works of Maitreya (BYAMS CHOS SDE LNGA). The text explains SAṂSĀRA (= DHARMA) and the NIRVĀṆA (= DHARMATĀ) attained by the ŚRĀVAKA, PRATYEKABUDDHA, and BODHISATTVA; like the MADHYĀNTAVIBHĀGA, it uses the three-nature (TRISVABHĀVA) terminology to explain that, because there is no object or subject, the transcendent is beyond conceptualization. It presents the paths leading to transformation of the basis (ĀŚRAYAPARĀVṚTTI), and enumerates ten types of TATHATĀ (suchness). There is a commentary by VASUBANDHU, the *Dharmadharmatāvibhāgavṛtti*.

**dharmadhātu**. (P. dhammadhātu; T. chos kyi dbyings; C. fajie; J. hokkai; K. pŏpkye 法界). In Sanskrit, "dharma realm," viz., "realm of reality," or "dharma element"; a term that has two primary denotations. In the ABHIDHARMA tradition, dharmadhātu means an "element of the dharma" or the "reality of dharma." As one of the twelve ĀYATANA and eighteen DHĀTU, the dharmadhātu encompasses every thing that is or could potentially be an object of cognition and refers to the "substance" or "quality" of a dharma that is perceived by the mind. Dhātu in this context is sometimes read as "the boundary" or "delineation" that separates one distinct dharma from the other. The ABHIDHARMAKOŚABHĀṢYA lists the sensation aggregate (VEDANĀ-SKANDHA), the perception aggregate (SAṂJÑĀ-skandha), the conditioning forces aggregate (SAṂSKĀRA-skandha), unmanifest materiality (AVIJÑAPTIRŪPA), and unconditioned dharmas (viz., NIRVĀṆA) to be the constituents of this category. ¶ In the MAHĀYĀNA, dharmadhātu is used primarily to mean "sphere of dharma," which denotes the infinite domain in which the activity of all dharmas takes place—i.e., the universe. It also serves as one of several terms for ultimate reality, such as TATHATĀ. In works such as the DHARMADHĀTUSTAVA, the purpose of Buddhist practice is to recognize and partake in this realm of reality. ¶ In East Asian Mahāyāna, there is a list of "ten dharmadhātus," which are the six traditional levels of nonenlightened existence—hell denizens (NĀRAKA), hungry ghosts (PRETA), animals (TIRYAK), demigods (ASURA), humans (MANUṢYA), and divinities (DEVA)—together with the four categories of enlightened beings, viz., ŚRĀVAKAS, PRATYEKABUDDHAS, BODHISATTVAS, and buddhas. ¶ The Chinese HUAYAN school recognizes a set of four dharmadhātus (SI FAJIE), that is, four successively more profound levels of reality: (1) the dharmadhātu of phenomena (SHI FAJIE); (2) the dharmadhātu of principle (LI FAJIE); (3) the dharmadhātu of the unimpeded interpenetration between phenomena and principle (LISHI WU'AI FAJIE); and (4) the dharmadhātu of unimpeded interpenetration of phenomenon and phenomena (SHISHI WU'AI FAJIE). ¶ In YOGATANTRA, the dharmadhātu consists of the realms of vajradhātu (see KONGŌKAI) and garbhadhātu (see TAIZŌKAI), categories that simultaneously denote the bivalence in cosmological structure, in modes of spiritual practice, and in the powers and qualities of enlightened beings. Dharmadhātu is believed to be the full revelation of the body of the cosmic buddha VAIROCANA.

**dharmadhātuprakṛtijñāna**. See DHARMADHĀTUSVABHĀVAJÑĀNA.

**Dharmadhātustava**. [alt. Dharmadhātustotra] (T. Chos dbyings bstod pa; C. Zan fajie song; J. San hokkaiju; K. Ch'an pŏpkye song 讚法界頌). In Sanskrit, "Praise of the DHARMADHĀTU," a hymn in 101 stanzas attributed to NĀGĀRJUNA. It is cited by BHĀVAVIVEKA as a work by Nāgārjuna, but its authorship has been questioned by scholars because its substantialist elements seem at odds with the doctrine of emptiness (ŚŪNYATĀ), as espoused by Nāgārjuna in works such as the MŪLAMADHYAMAKAKĀRIKĀ. The text is also not counted among the "four hymns" (CATUḤSTAVA), which can be more confidently ascribed to Nāgārjuna. However, in the Tibetan tradition, it is regarded as his work and is counted among his "devotional corpus" (STAVAKĀYA). Apart from a few stanzas quoted in extant Sanskrit works, the text is lost in the original Sanskrit and is preserved in Tibetan and Chinese (translated by DĀNAPĀLA). The *Dharmadhātustava* describes the nature of the realm of reality (dharmadhātu) as being pure in its essence but is hidden by the afflictions (KLEŚA); when those taints are removed, the nature of reality is made manifest. Many of the metaphors in the text are similar to those found in the TATHĀGATAGARBHA literature. However, the dharmadhātu is also described in ontological terms as the cause of SAṂSĀRA, uncreated, immovable, certain, pure, the seed, etc., descriptions that seem at odds with Nāgārjuna's more famous views. In Tibet, this apparent contradiction figured prominently in the so-called RANG STONG GZHAN STONG debates, where the proponents of the rang stong position, especially the DGE LUGS, saw Nāgārjuna's exposition of emptiness to be his definitive position and explained the dharmadhātu as emptiness. The proponents of the gzhan stong position, most famously the JO NANG, argued for a more substantialist reality that is not empty of its own nature

(SVABHĀVA) but is devoid of adventitious defilements. They found support for this position in the *Dharmadhātustava*.

**dharmadhātusvabhāvajñāna**. [alt. dharmadhātuprakṛtijñāna] (T. chos dbyings ye shes; C. fajie tixingzhi; J. hokkai taishōchi; K. pŏpkye ch'esŏngji 法界體性智). In Sanskrit, "the wisdom of the essential nature of the reality-realm"; one of five wisdoms of a buddha. The five are the wisdom of the essential nature of the DHARMADHĀTU (dharmadhātuprakṛtijñāna or dharmadhātusvabhāvajñāna), the mirror-like wisdom (ADARŚAJÑĀNA), the wisdom of equality (SAMATĀJÑĀNA), the wisdom of specific knowledge (PRATYAVEKṢAṆAJÑĀNA), and the wisdom of having accomplished what was to be done (KṚTYĀNUṢṬHĀNAJÑĀNA). The five wisdoms are considered to derive from specific transformations of the nine types of consciousness (VIJÑĀNA), which occur when a cultivator consummates one's practice: dharmadhātuprakṛtijñāna is derived from the transformation of the ninth consciousness, the "immaculate consciousness" (AMALAVIJÑĀNA); adarśajñāna from the eighth, the "storehouse consciousness" (ĀLAYAVIJÑĀNA); samatājñāna from the seventh, "defiled mental consciousness" (KLIṢṬAMANAS); the pratyavekṣaṇajñāna from the sixth, "mental consciousness" (MANOVIJÑĀNA); and kṛtyānuṣṭhānajñāna from the five sensory consciousnesses. The YOGĀCĀRA school initially discussed only the latter four types of wisdom, without the dharmadhātuprakṛtijñāna that derived from amalavijñāna. The full list of five wisdoms appears to derive from the "Sūtra of the Buddha Stage" (S. BUDDHABHŪMISŪTRA; C. Fodi jing), which refers to five kinds of dharmas that are incorporated in the stage of great enlightenment, viz., the four earlier types of wisdom listed in Yogācāra materials, plus the pure dharmadhātu, corresponding to dharmadhātuprakṛtijñāna. In esoteric Buddhism, these wisdoms are personified as the five buddhas depicted in the diamond-realm MAṆḌALA (vajradhātumaṇḍala). The five wisdoms of the diamond-realm (S. vajradhātu; see KONGŌKAI) represent the aspect of wisdom of the DHARMAKĀYA buddha, Mahāvairocana (see VAIROCANA). In contrast, the womb-realm (garbhadhātu; see TAIZŌKAI) is interpreted as the store or womb of Mahāvairocana Buddha, that is, the fundamental principle underlying those five types of wisdom. These are represented by Mahāvairocana in the center, AKṢOBHYA in the east, RATNASAMBHĀVA in the south, AMITĀBHA in the west and AMOGHASIDDHI or ŚĀKYAMUNI in the north.

**Dharmadinnā**. (P. Dhammadinnā; T. Chos kyis sbyin; C. Tanmotina biqiuni/Fale biqiuni; J. Donmadaina bikuni/Hōraku bikuni; K. Tammajena piguni/Pŏmnak piguni 曇摩提那比丘尼/法樂比丘尼). An eminent ARHAT nun, declared by the Buddha to be foremost among his nun disciples in the gift of preaching. According to Pāli sources, she was married to a rich merchant of Rājagaha (S. RĀJAGṚHA) named VISĀKHA. Visākha was a lay disciple of the Buddha, but his behavior toward his wife changed after he became a nonreturner (ANĀGĀMIN). When he explained why, Dhammadinnā requested permission to renounce the world and become a Buddhist nun. So highly did Visākha regard his wife's piety that he informed Bimbisāra, the king of MAGADHA, who arranged for her to be carried to the nuns' convent on a golden palanquin. Dhammadinnā dwelled in solitude and soon became an arhat of the highest degree, equipped with the four analytical knowledges (paṭisambhidā; S. PRATISAṂVID), which included knowledge of the entire Buddhist canon. When she returned to Rājagaha to venerate the Buddha, her former husband Visākha approached her with questions on doctrine, which she easily answered. Visākha reported this to the Buddha, who praised Dhammadinnā's proficiency in preaching. Dhammadinnā's preeminence in preaching was a result of a vow she made during the time of the past buddha Padumuttara, when she witnessed a nun who was praised for her eloquence and vowed to achieve the same.

**Dharmagupta**. (C. Damojiduo; J. Darumagyūta; K. Talmagŭpta 達摩笈多) (d. 619). A South Indian monk-translator who traveled to China during the Sui dynasty; sometimes known by his abbreviated name Jiduo. Arriving in the Chinese capital of Chang'an in 590, he set to translating several scriptures into Chinese, including sūtras on the buddha BHAIṢAJYAGURU, one of the later recensions of the SADDHARMAPUṆḌARĪKASŪTRA, which he cotranslated with JÑĀNAGUPTA, and Vasubandhu's commentary on the VAJRACCHEDIKĀPRAJÑĀPĀRAMITĀSŪTRA. Some ten different translations are attributed to him. He should be distinguished from the Dharmagupta (c. third century BCE) who was the eponymous founder of the DHARMAGUPTAKA school.

**Dharmaguptaka**. (T. Chos sbas pa; C. Fazangbu/Tanwudebu; J. Hōzōbu/Donmutokubu; K. Pŏpchangbu/Tammudŏkpu 法蔵部/曇無德部). In Sanskrit, "Adherents of Dharmagupta"; one of the eighteen traditional "mainstream" (that is, non-MAHĀYĀNA) schools of early Indian Buddhism. There are various theories on the origin of the school in Buddhist literature. The SARVĀSTIVĀDA treatise SAMAYABHEDOPARACANACAKRA states that the Dharmaguptaka separated from the MAHĪŚĀSAKA school, one of the collateral branches of the Sarvāstivāda school (probably sometime around the late second or early first centuries BCE), while inscriptional evidence and Tibetan sources instead suggest it was one strand of the VIBHAJYAVĀDA (P. Vibhajjavāda) school, a collateral line of the STHAVIRANIKĀYA that was most active in KASHMIR-GANDHĀRA, and Sri Lanka. There is inscriptional evidence from the northwest of the Indian subcontinent for the continued existence of the school into the seventh century. The school is named after the eponymous teacher Dharmagupta (c. third century BCE), even though the school itself traces its lineage back to MAHĀMAUDGALYĀYANA (P. Mahāmoggallāna), one of the two main disciples of the Buddha. Unlike the typical tripartite division of the canon (TRIPIṬAKA), viz., SŪTRAPIṬAKA, VINAYAPIṬAKA, and ABHIDHARMAPIṬAKA, the Dharmaguptaka canon is said to have consisted of five divisions, adding to the usual three a collection on BODHISATTVA doctrines and practices (BODHISATTVAPIṬAKA) and a DHĀRAṆĪ collection (dhāraṇīpiṭaka). Some of the distinctive tenets of the school are (1) the Buddha is not included among the members of the SAṂGHA and thus a gift given to him is superior to offerings made to the community as a whole; (2) there are four characteristics (CATURLAKṢAṆA) of compounded things—origination, maturation, decay, and extinction—of which the first three were conditioned (SAṂSKṚTA) and the last unconditioned (ASAṂSKṚTA); (3) the path of the buddhas and bodhisattvas is distinct from that of the ŚRĀVAKAS; (4) non-buddhists (TĪRTHIKA) cannot attain the five kinds of superknowledge (ABHIJÑĀ); (5) the body of an ARHAT is free from the contaminants (ANĀSRAVA). Because of their views about the Buddha's superiority to the broader saṃgha, the school also emphasized the extraordinary merit accruing from offerings made to a STŪPA, which was considered to be the contemporary representation of the Buddha because of the relics (ŚARĪRA) it enshrined. Due to the convergence of some of the school's doctrines with those of the MAHĀSĀṂGHIKA, it has been suggested that the school may have had its origins within the Sthaviranikāya but was subsequently influenced by Mahāsāṃghika ideas. One of the enduring influences of the Dharmaguptaka school in Buddhist history comes from its vinaya, which came to be adopted widely throughout East Asia; this so-called "Four-Part Vinaya" (SIFEN LÜ, *Dharmaguptaka vinaya) was translated into Chinese in 405 by BUDDHAYAŚAS (c. fifth century CE) and is still used today in the East Asian Buddhist traditions. The recension of the DĪRGHĀGAMA (C. *Chang Ahan jing*) that was translated into Chinese in 413 CE by Buddhayaśas and ZHU FONIAN is also attributed to the Dharmaguptaka school.

**dharma heir**. See FASI.

**dharmajñāna**. (S). See DHARMAKṢĀNTI.

**Dharmākara**. (T. Chos kyi 'byung gnas; C. Fazang biqiu; J. Hōzō biku; K. Pŏpchang pigu 法藏比丘). The bodhisattva-monk (BHIKṢU) who became the buddha AMITĀBHA. According to the longer SUKHĀVATĪVYŪHASŪTRA (C. *Wuliangshou jing*), in the distant past, Dharmākara was a monk under the tutelage of the buddha LOKEŚVARARĀJA. At Dharmākara's request, Lokeśvararāja described and displayed millions of buddha-fields (BUDDHAKṢETRA) to the monk. Dharmākara then selected the best qualities of each and concentrated them in his conception of a single buddha-field, which he described to Lokeśvararāja in terms of forty-eight vows. The most important of these vows for the PURE LAND tradition is the eighteenth, in which he vows that all beings who call upon him (with the possible exception of those who have committed the five ĀNANTARYAKARMAN, the heinous crimes that bring immediate retribution, or who have slandered the DHARMA) will be reborn in his pure land of SUKHĀVATĪ. Since Dharmākara was eventually successful in his quest and became the buddha Amitābha, his vows have been fulfilled and all sentient beings therefore have access to his buddha land.

**dharmakāya**. (T. chos sku; C. fashen; J. hosshin; K. pŏpsin 法身). In Sanskrit, often translated as "truth body," one of the two (along with the RŪPAKĀYA) or three (along with the SAṂBHOGAKĀYA and NIRMĀṆAKĀYA) bodies of a buddha. In early discussions of the true nature of the Buddha, especially regarding the person of the Buddha to whom one goes for refuge (ŚARAṆA), the term dharmakāya seems to have been coined to refer to the corpus or collection (KĀYA) of the auspicious qualities (DHARMA) of the Buddha, including his wisdom, his compassion, his various powers, etc.; it also referred to the entire corpus (kāya) of the Buddha's teachings (dharma). In the MAHĀYĀNA, the term evolved into a kind of cosmic principle that was regarded as the true nature of the Buddha and the source from which his various other forms derived. In the perfection of wisdom (PRAJÑĀPĀRAMITĀ) commentarial tradition, a dispute arose over the interpretation of the eighth chapter of the ABHISAMAYĀLAṂKĀRA, with VIMUKTISENA arguing that the SVĀBHĀVAKĀYA is the ultimate nature of a buddha and HARIBHADRA arguing that there are two aspects of the dharmakāya: a JÑĀNADHARMAKĀYA (knowledge truth body), i.e., the nondual omniscient knowledge of a buddha, and a svābhāvakāya. Later commentators in India and Tibet explored the ramifications of this distinction at length. See also TRIKĀYA.

**Dharmakīrti**. (T. Chos kyi grags pa; C. Facheng; J. Hōshō; K. Pŏpch'ing 法稱) (c. 600–670 CE). Indian Buddhist logician, who was one of the most important and influential figures in the history of Buddhist philosophy. Dharmakīrti was the author of a series of seminal works building on his predecessor DIGNĀGA's PRAMĀṆASAMUCCAYA ("Compendium on Valid Knowledge"), defending it against criticism by Brahmanical writers and explaining how accurate knowledge could be gleaned (see PRAMĀṆA). His "seven treatises on pramāṇa" (T. TSHAD MA SDE 'DUN) are the PRAMĀṆAVĀRTTIKA ("Commentary on Valid Knowledge") and PRAMĀṆAVINIŚCAYA ("Determination of Valid Knowledge"), as well as the NYĀYABINDU ("Drop of Reasoning"), the *Hetubindu* ("Drop of Reasons"), the *Sambandhaparīkṣā* ("Analysis of Relations"), the *Saṃtānāntarasiddhi* ("Proof of Other Mental Continuums"), and the *Vādanyāya* ("Reasoning for Debate"). Dharmakīrti proposed a causal efficacy connecting the sense object and sensory perception as the basis of reliable perception (PRATYAKṢA), thereby attempting to remove the potential fallacy in Dignāga's acceptance of the infallibility of sense data themselves. Dharmakīrti wrote explanations of many of his own works, and DHARMOTTARA, Śākyamati, PRAJÑĀKARAGUPTA, and Manorathanandin, among others, wrote detailed commentaries on his works. He had a profound influence on the exchange between subsequent Indian Buddhist writers, such as ŚĀNTARAKṢITA, KAMALAŚĪLA, and HARIBHADRA, and contemporary Brahmanical

Naiyāyika and Mīmāṃsaka thinkers. His work subsequently became the focus of intense study in Tibet, first in GSANG PHU NE'U THOG monastery where RNGOG BLO LDAN SHES RAB and later PHYWA PA CHOS KYI SENG GE established through their commentaries on the PRAMĀṆAVINIŚCAYA an influential tradition of interpretation; it was questioned by SA SKYA PAṆḌITA in his TSHAD MA RIGS GTER, giving rise to a second line of interpretation more in line with Dharmakīrti's original works. There is a question of Dharmakīrti's philosophical affiliation, with elements in his works that reflect both SAUTRĀNTIKA and YOGĀCĀRA doctrinal positions.

**Dharmakīrtiśrī**. (T. Chos kyi grags pa dpal). Buddhist paṇḍita better known by his Tibetan name Gser gling pa (Serlingpa), "The Man from Suvarṇadvīpa"; also known as Kulānta (T. Rigs sbyin). He was a GURU of ATIŚA, who traveled by sea to Suvarṇadvīpa (generally regarded as referring to the region of lower Burma, the Malay Peninsula, and Sumatra) in order to study with him. Atiśa is said to have praised him as his supreme teacher of BODHICITTA. His doctrinal affiliation was said to be YOGĀCĀRA. He is the author of the *Durbodhāloka*, a widely cited subcommentary on HARIBHADRA's ABHISAMAYĀLAṂKĀRAVIVṚTI. The *Durbodhāloka* is only extant in Tibetan translation and was written later than the PRASPHUṬAPADĀ of Dharmamitra. It is the only extant Buddhist scholastic text from that period by a writer from that region.

**dharmakṣānti**. (T. chos bzod; C. faren; J. hōnin; K. pŏbin 法忍). In Sanskrit, "acquiescence," "receptivity," or "forbearance" (KṢĀNTI) to the "truth" or the "doctrine" (DHARMA); a term that occurs in SARVĀSTIVĀDA descriptions of the path of vision (DARŚANAMĀRGA). In this path schema, the path of vision consists of fifteen thought moments, with a subsequent sixteenth moment marking the beginning of the path of cultivation (BHĀVANĀMĀRGA). There are four moments of "acquiescence" to, or realization of, the "dharmas" of each of the FOUR NOBLE TRUTHS (catvāry āryasatyāni). The first moment is that of acquiescence to the truth of suffering with regard to the sensuous realm (KĀMADHĀTU); in this moment, the afflictions (KLEŚA) of the sensuous realm associated with the truth of suffering are abandoned. This is followed by a moment of doctrinal knowledge (dharmajñāna) of the truth of suffering with regard to the sensuous realm, which is the understanding that the kleśas of that realm associated with the truth of suffering have been abandoned. This is then followed by a moment of subsequent acquiescence (anvayakṣānti) to the truth of suffering in which the kleśas of the upper realms of existence (the RŪPADHĀTU and ĀRŪPYADHĀTU) associated with the truth of suffering are abandoned. This is followed finally by a fourth moment, called subsequent knowledge (anvayajñāna) of the truth of suffering, which is the understanding that the kleśas of the two upper realms associated with the truth of suffering have been abandoned. This same fourfold sequence is repeated for the truth of origin, the truth of cessation, and the truth of the path. The sixteenth moment, that is, the moment of subsequent knowledge (anvayajñāna) of the truth of the path (MĀRGASATYA) is, in effect, the knowledge that all of the kleśas of both the subtle-materiality realm and the upper immaterial realm that are associated with the four truths have been abandoned. This moment marks the beginning of the path of cultivation (bhāvanāmārga). The term is also sometimes an abbreviation for the receptivity to the nonproduction of dharmas (ANUTPATTIKADHARMAKṢĀNTI). For an explanation of dharmakṣānti and the other instants from a Mahāyāna perspective, based on the ABHIDHARMASAMUCCAYA, see DARŚANAMĀRGA.

**Dharmakṣema**. (C. Tanwuchen; J. Donmusen; K. Tammuch'am 曇無讖) (385–433 CE). Indian Buddhist monk who was an early translator of Buddhist materials into Chinese. A scion of a brāhmaṇa family from India, Dharmakṣema became at the age of six a disciple of Dharmayaśas (C. Damoyeshe; J. Donmayasha) (d.u.), an ABHIDHARMA specialist who later traveled to China c. 397–401 and translated the *Śāriputrābhidharmaśāstra*. Possessed of both eloquence and intelligence, Dharmakṣema was broadly learned in both monastic and secular affairs and was well versed in mainstream Buddhist texts. After he met a meditation monk named "White Head" and had a fiery debate with him, Dharmakṣema recognized his superior expertise and ended up studying with him. The monk transmitted to him a text of the MAHĀPARINIRVĀṆASŪTRA written on bark, which prompted Dharmakṣema to embrace the MAHĀYĀNA. Once he reached the age of twenty, Dharmakṣema was able to recite over two million words of Buddhist texts. He was also so skilled in casting spells that he earned the sobriquet "Great Divine Spell Master" (C. Dashenzhou shi). Carrying with him the first part of the *Mahāparinirvāṇasūtra* that he received from "White Head," he left India and arrived in the KUCHA kingdom in Central Asia. As the people of Kucha mostly studied HĪNAYĀNA and did not accept the Mahāyāna teachings, Dharmakṣema then moved to China and lived in the western outpost of DUNHUANG for several years. Juqu Mengxun, the non-Chinese ruler of the Northern Liang dynasty (397–439 CE), eventually brought Dharmakṣema to his capital. After studying the Chinese language for three years and learning how to translate Sanskrit texts orally into Chinese, Dharmakṣema engaged there in a series of translation projects under Juqu Mengxun's patronage. With the assistance of Chinese monks, such as Daolang and Huigao, Dharmakṣema produced a number of influential Chinese translations, including the *Dabanniepan jing* (S. *Mahāparinirvāṇasūtra*; in forty rolls), the longest recension of the sūtra extant in any language; the *Jinguangming jing* ("Sūtra of Golden Light"; S. SUVARṆAPRABHĀSOTTAMASŪTRA; in four rolls); and the *Pusa dichi jing* (S. BODHISATTVABHŪMISŪTRA; in ten rolls). He is also said to have made the first Chinese translation of the LAṄKĀVATĀRASŪTRA (C. *Ru Lengqie jing*), but his rendering had dropped out of circulation at least by 730 CE, when the Tang Buddhist cataloguer ZHISHENG (700–786 CE) compiled the KAIYUAN SHIJIAO LU. The Northern Wei ruler Tuoba Tao, a rival of Juqu Mengxun's, admired Dharmakṣema's esoteric expertise and requested that the Northern Liang ruler send the Indian monk to his country. Fearing that his rival might seek to employ Dharmakṣema's esoteric expertise against him, Juqu Mengxun had the monk assassinated at the age of forty-nine. Dharmakṣema's translation of Indian Buddhist texts into Chinese had a significant impact on Chinese Buddhism; in particular, the doctrine that all beings have the buddha-nature (FOXING), a teaching appearing in Dharmakṣema's translation of the *Mahāparinirvāṇasūtra*, exerted tremendous influence on the development of Chinese Buddhist thought.

**dharmameghā**. (T. chos kyi sprin; C. fayun di; J. hōunji; K. pŏbun chi 法雲地). In Sanskrit, "cloud of dharma," the tenth and final "ground" or stage (BHŪMI) of the BODHISATTVA path, just prior to the attainment of buddhahood. On the dharmameghā bhūmi, the bodhisattva is at the point of attaining the dharma-body (DHARMAKĀYA) that is as vast as the sky, becomes autonomous in interacting with all material and mental factors, and gains all-pervasive knowledge, which causes the excellent dharma to fall like rain from a cloud, nurturing the entire world and increasing the harvest of virtue for sentient beings. This stage is also described as being pervaded by meditative absorption (DHYĀNA) and mastery of the use of DHĀRAṆĪ, just as the sky is filled with clouds. According to the CHENG WEISHI LUN (**Vijñaptimātratāsiddhiśāstra*; chap. 11), each of the ten stages of the bodhisattva path leads to the attainment of one of the ten types of suchness (TATHATĀ); these are accomplished by discarding one of the ten kinds of obstructions (ĀVARAṆA) through practicing one of the ten perfections (PĀRAMITĀ). In the case of the dharmameghā bhūmi, the obstruction of not yet acquiring mastery over all dharmas (fa wei zizai zhang) is removed through the perfection of knowledge (JÑĀNAPĀRAMITĀ), leading to the suchness that serves as the support for mastery over action (ye zizai deng suoyi zhenru; *kriyādivaśitāsaṃniśrayatathatā) and the ability of the bodhisattva to ripen the minds of sentient beings. The tenth stage thus removes any remaining delusions regarding the use of the supernatural knowledges or powers (ABHIJÑĀ) or the subtle mysteries, giving the bodhisattva complete autonomy in manipulating all dharmas. As the culminating stage of the "path of cultivation" (BHĀVANĀMĀRGA), the dharmameghā bhūmi still contains the last and most subtle remnants of the cognitive obstructions (JÑEYĀVARAṆA). These obstructions will be completely eradicated through the adamantine-like concentration (VAJROPAMASAMĀDHI), which marks the transition to the "ultimate path" (NIṢṬHĀMĀRGA), or "path where no further training is necessary" (AŚAIKṢAMĀRGA), i.e., an eleventh stage of the buddhas (TATHĀGATABHŪMI) that is sometimes also known as the "universally luminous" (samantaprabhā).

**dharmamudrā**. (P. dhammamuddā; T. chos [rtags] kyi phyag rgya; C. fayin; J. hōin; K. pŏbin 法印). In Sanskrit, "the seal" or "distinguishing mark" (MUDRĀ) "of the dharma." This mark may refer either to the objective qualities of all phenomena or to the doctrinal insights that distinguish either the definitive teachings (NĪTĀRTHA) of Buddhism from the provisional teachings (NEYĀRTHA), or the Buddhist teachings from non-Buddhist (TĪRTHIKA) ones. In the mainstream traditions, there are generally presumed to be three distinguishing marks of all phenomena or three doctrinal features that constitute the genuine Buddhist teachings. In one typology, the "three marks" refer to "all compounded things are characterized by impermanence" (ANITYA) "all existing things are characterized by the lack of a self" (ANĀTMAN) and "nirvāṇa is characterized by uncompounded quiescence"; in an alternate typology, the third mark is replaced by the typical "all experiences are characterized by unsatisfactoriness" (DUḤKHA). In the MAHĀYĀNA, one or four marks are typically listed. In the first case, the "true distinguishing mark corresponding to the true nature of all things" (yi shixiang yin) is taken to be the only true dharmamudrā. In the second case, the dharmamudrā of "all dharmas are empty in their self-nature" (NIḤSVABHĀVA; ŚŪNYATĀ) is added to either group of the three marks of the mainstream tradition listed earlier to make four dharmamudrās. In Tibet, the usual locution is "four seals that mark a doctrine as the word [of the Buddha]" (lta ba bka' btags kyi phyag rgya bzhi). See CATURMUDRĀ.

**dharmanairātmya**. (T. chos kyi bdag med; C. fawuwo; J. hōmuga; K. pŏmmua 法無我). In Sanskrit, "insubstantiality of dharmas," viz., the lack of self in all the phenomena in the universe, a second, and more advanced, level of emptiness (ŚŪNYATĀ) than the insubstantiality of the person (PUDGALANAIRĀTMYA). The doctrine of nonself (ANĀTMAN) is a fundamental tenet of Buddhism and is directed primarily at the denial of any notion of a perduring soul. Sentient beings (SATTVA) are viewed as merely a collection of aggregates (SKANDHA) or elements of reality (DHARMA), which are temporarily concatenated through an impersonal, causal process; thus, the person (PUDGALA) is lacking any eternal self (pudgalanairātmya). The mainstream Buddhist ABHIDHARMA schools began to compile extensive lists of the elements of reality (dharma) from which the compounded things of this world were comprised, and the SARVĀSTIVĀDA school was especially known for propounding the view that all these dharmas were real and existed throughout all the three time periods (TRIKĀLA) of the past, present, and future (the school's name literally means "those who say that all exists," S. sarvam asti). This view that dharmas were permanent, while compounded things were not, was strongly critiqued by the MAHĀYĀNA tradition as the unwarranted intrusion into Buddhism of a notion of permanence (NITYA). The MADHYAMAKA school in particular was well known for its thoroughgoing denial of the substantiality not only of the compounded person, but of the constituents of reality as well (dharmanairātmya). The selflessness of dharmas is synonymous with the emptiness (śūnyatā) of dharmas, and the fact that all things in existence are devoid of intrinsic nature

(S. NIḤSVABHĀVA). It was furthermore said in the Mahāyāna that in order to achieve buddhahood, the BODHISATTVA had to gain direct realization of both pudgalanairātmya as well as the more subtle dharmanairātmya; there was disagreement over whether the ARHAT had to gain understanding of dharmanairātmya in order to achieve NIRVĀṆA.

**dharmānusārin**. (P. dhammānusāri; T. chos kyi rjes su 'brang ba; C. suifaxing; J. zuihōgyō; K. subŏphaeng 隨法行). In Sanskrit, "follower of the dharma," one who arrives at a realization of the dharma or truth through his or her own analysis of the teachings; contrasted with "follower of faith" (ŚRADDHĀNUSĀRIN) whose religious experience is grounded in the faith or confidence in what others tell him about the dharma. The SARVĀSTIVĀDA (e.g., as described in the ABHIDHARMAKOŚABHĀṢYA) and THERAVĀDA (e.g., VISUDDHIMAGGA) schools of mainstream Buddhism both recognize seven types of noble ones (ĀRYA, P. ariya), listed in order of their intellectual superiority: (1) follower of faith (S. śraddhānusārin; P. saddhānusāri); (2) follower of the dharma (S. dharmānusārin; P. dhammānusāri); (3) one who is freed by faith (S. ŚRADDHĀVIMUKTA; P. saddhāvimutta); (4) one who has formed right view (S. DṚṢṬIPRĀPTA; P. diṭṭhippatta), by developing both faith and wisdom; (5) one who has bodily testimony (S. KĀYASĀKṢIN; P. kāyasakkhi), viz., through the temporary suspension of mentality in the absorption of cessation (NIRODHASAMĀPATTI); (6) one who is freed by wisdom (S. PRAJÑĀVIMUKTA; P. paññāvimutta), by freeing oneself through analysis; and (7) one who is freed both ways (S. UBHAYATOBHĀGAVIMUKTA; P. ubhatobhāgavimutta), by freeing oneself through both meditative absorption and wisdom. According to the Sarvāstivāda VAIBHĀṢIKA school of ABHIDHARMA, an ARHAT whose liberation is grounded in faith may be subject to backsliding from that state, whereas those who are dharmānusārin are unshakable (AKOPYA), because they have experienced the knowledge of nonproduction (ANUTPĀDAJÑĀNA), viz., that the afflictions (kleśa) can never occur again, the complement of the knowledge of extinction (KṢAYAJÑĀNA). ¶ The Theravāda school, which does not accept this dynamic interpretation of an arhat's spiritual experience, develops a rather different interpretation of these types of individuals. BUDDHAGHOSA explains in his VISUDDHIMAGGA that one who develops faith by contemplating the impermanent nature of things is a follower of faith at the moment of becoming a stream-enterer (sotāpanna; S. SROTAĀPANNA) and is one who is freed by faith at the subsequent moments of the fruition of the path; one who is tranquil and develops concentration by contemplating the impermanent nature of things is one who has bodily testimony at all moments; one who develops the immaterial meditative absorptions (arūpajhāna; S. ARŪPĀVACARADHYĀNA) is one freed both ways; one who develops wisdom is one who follows the dharma (dhammānusāri) at the moment of entry into the rank of stream-enterer and is one who has formed right view at the subsequent moments of path entry. When one achieves highest spiritual attainment, one is called freed by wisdom. In another classification of six individuals found in the Pāli CŪḶAGOPĀLAKASUTTA, dhammānusāri is given as the fifth type, the other five being the worthy one (arahant; S. ARHAT), nonreturner (anāgāmi; S. ANĀGĀMIN), once-returner (sakadāgāmi; S. SAKṚDĀGĀMIN), stream-enterer (sotāpanna; S. srotaāpanna), and follower of faith (saddhānusāri). The Indriyasaṃyutta in the SAṂYUTTANIKĀYA also mentions these same six individuals and explains their differences in terms of their development of the five spiritual faculties (INDRIYA): faith, energy, mindfulness, concentration, and wisdom. An arahant has matured the five faculties; a nonreturner has all five faculties, but they are slightly less developed than in the arahant; a once-returner is slightly less developed than a nonreturner; a stream-enterer slightly less than a once-returner; a dhammānusāri slightly less than a stream-enterer; and a saddhānusāri slightly less than a dhammānusāri. The saddhāvimutta and dhammānusāri are also distinguished depending on when they reach higher spiritual attainment: one who is following faith at the moment of accessing the path (maggakkhana) is called saddhāvimutta, one liberated through faith; the other, who is following wisdom, is called dhammānusāri, one who is liberated by wisdom at the moment of attainment (phalakkhana). ¶ The dharmānusārin is also found in the list of the members of the saṃgha when it is subdivided into twenty (VIṂŚATIPRABHEDASAṂGHA). Among the dharmānusārin there are candidates for the fruit of stream-enterer (SROTAĀPANNAPRATIPANNAKA), once-returner (SAKṚDĀGĀMIPRATIPANNAKA), and nonreturner (ANĀGĀMIPRATIPANNAKA). The Mahāyāna carries over the division of dharmānusārin and śraddhānusārin into its discussion of the path to enlightenment. The PAÑCAVIṂŚATISĀHASRIKĀPRAJÑĀPĀRAMITĀ takes the seven types of noble ones (ārya) listed in order of intellectual superiority, and the eight noble beings (stream-enterer and so on) as examples for bodhisattvas at different stages of the path; the dharmānusārin more quickly reaches the AVAIVARTIKA (irreversible) stage, the śraddhānusārin more slowly, based on the development of wisdom (PRAJÑĀ) that has forbearance for the absence of any ultimately existing goal to be reached, and skillful means (UPĀYA) that places pride of place on the welfare of others (PARĀRTHA).

**Dharmapada**. (S). See DHAMMAPADA.

**dharmapāla**. (P. dhammapāla; T. chos skyong; C. fahu; J. hōgo; K. pŏpho 法護). In Sanskrit, "protector of the DHARMA"; in Mahāyāna and tantric texts, dharmapālas are divinities, often depicted in wrathful forms, who defend Buddhism from its enemies and who guard Buddhist practitioners from various forms of external and internal dangers. The histories of many Buddhist nations often involve the conversion of local deities into dharma protectors. In Tibet, for example, the worship of dharmapālas is said to have begun in the early eighth century CE at the instigation of PADMASAMBHAVA (c. eighth century), when he was invited to the country by the Tibetan king KHRI SRONG LDE BTSAN. On his arrival, Padmasaṃbhava is said to have used his powers to subdue baleful local deities he encountered along the way and spared only those who promised to become dharmapālas. In Tibetan Buddhism, dharmapālas are divided into two groups, the mundane ('jig rten pa), who are worldly deities who protect the dharma, and the supramundane ('jig rten las 'das pa), enlightened beings who appear in wrathful form to defend the dharma. The eight types of nonhuman beings (AṢṬASENĀ) are also sometimes listed as dharma-protectors, viz., GARUḌA, DEVA, NĀGA, YAKṢA, GANDHARVA, ASURA, KIṂNARA, and MAHORĀGA.

**Dharmapāla**. (T. Chos skyong; C. Hufa; J. Gohō; K. Hobŏp 護法) (530–561). One of the ten great YOGĀCĀRA philosophers of Indian Buddhism. He was born in southern India in the middle of the sixth century CE, to the family of a high government minister. At around the age of twenty, on the evening that he was to be married, he ran away to a mountain monastery to become a monk. After mastering the teachings of both mainstream and MAHĀYĀNA Buddhism, Dharmapāla traveled extensively, becoming renowned for his debating skills. Later, he studied under the YOGĀCĀRA specialist and logician DIGNĀGA (d.u.) at NĀLANDĀ, where he became chief instructor despite his youth. His teaching focused especially on Yogācāra doctrine, and he produced many excellent disciples. XUANZANG (600/602–664), one of the most important figures in the history of Chinese Buddhist scholasticism, traveled to India in the seventh century, where he studied Dharmapāla's doctrines at Nālandā under one of his principal disciples, ŚĪLABHADRA (529–645), and brought Dharmapāla's scholastic lineage back to China. Xuanzang edited and translated some of the materials he had collected in India into the CHENG WEISHI LUN (**Vijñaptimātratāsiddhiśāstra*; "Demonstration of Consciousness-Only"), a synopsis of ten separate commentaries on VASUBANDHU's TRIṂŚIKĀ ("Thirty Verses") but heavily focused on the insights of Dharmapāla, which Xuanzang considered orthodox. Unlike STHIRAMATI, who understood the bifurcation of consciousness into subject and object to be wholly imaginary, Dharmapāla proposed instead that consciousness always appears in both subjective and objective aspects, viz., a "seeing part" (darśanabhāga) and a seen part (nimittabhāga). His interpretations regarding the nature of consciousness became predominant in the Chinese FAXIANG (alt. Weishi) school of Yogācāra, which was developed by Xuanzang and his two main disciples, WŎNCH'ŬK and KUIJI. Dharmapāla retired to Asaṃbodhi monastery at the age of twenty-nine and passed away at the age of thirty-one.

**Dharmapāla, Anagārika**. (1864–1933). An important figure in the revival of Buddhism in Sri Lanka and the dissemination of Buddhism in the West. Born Don David Hēvāvirtarne in Sri Lanka, at that time the British colony of Ceylon, he was raised in the English-speaking middle class of Colombo and educated in Christian schools run by Anglican missionaries, where he is said to have memorized large portions of the Bible. His family was Buddhist, however, and in 1880, at the age of sixteen, he met HENRY STEEL OLCOTT and MADAME BLAVATSKY, founders of the Theosophical Society, during their visit to Sri Lanka in support of Buddhism. In 1881, he took the Buddhist name Dharmapāla, "Protector of the Dharma," and in 1884 was initiated into the Theosophical Society by Colonel Olcott, later accompanying Madame Blavatsky to the headquarters of the Society in Adyar, India. Under the initial patronage of Theosophists, he studied Pāli, choosing to adopt the lifestyle of a celibate lay religious. Prior to that time in Sri Lanka, the leadership in Buddhism had been provided exclusively by monks and kings. Dharmapāla established a new role for Buddhist laypeople, creating the category of the anagārika (meaning "homeless wanderer"), a layperson who studied texts and meditated, as did monks, but who remained socially active in the world, as did laypeople. Free from the restrictions incumbent on the Sinhalese monkhood, yet distinct from ordinary laity, he regarded this new lifestyle of the anagārika as the most suitable status for him to work for the restoration and propagation of Buddhism. A social reformer, rationalist, and religious nationalist, he promoted rural education and a reformist style of Buddhism, stripped of what he considered extraneous superstitions, as a means of uplifting Sinhalese society and gaining independence for his country as a Buddhist nation. While he was in India in 1891, he was shocked to see the state of decay of the great pilgrimage sites of India, all then under Hindu control, and most especially of BODHGAYĀ, the site of the Buddha's enlightenment. In that same year, he joined a group of leading Sri Lankan Buddhists to found the MAHĀBODHI SOCIETY, which called on Buddhists from around the world to work for the return of important Indian Buddhist sites to Buddhist control, and one of whose aims was the restoration of the MAHĀBODHI TEMPLE at Bodhgayā. This goal only came to fruition in 1949, well after his death, when the newly independent Indian government granted Buddhists a role in administering the site. His influential Buddhist journal, *The Mahā-Bodhi*, also established in 1891, continues to be published today. A gifted orator, in 1893 Anagārika Dharmapāla addressed the World's Parliament of Religions, held in conjunction with the Columbian Exhibition in Chicago, drawing much acclaim. Although he was one of several Buddhist speakers, his excellent English and Anglican education made him an effective spokesperson for the dharma, demonstrating both its affinities with, and superiority to, Christianity. In 1925, he founded the British Mahā Bodhi Society in London and a year later established the first THERAVĀDA monastery in the West, the London Buddhist Vihāra. In 1931, he was ordained as a monk (bhikkhu; BHIKṢU), taking the name Devamitta. He died in 1933 at SĀRNĀTH, site of the Buddha's first sermon.

**dharmaparyāya**. (P. dhammapariyāya; T. chos kyi rnam grangs; C. famen; J. hōmon; K. pŏmmun 法門). In Sanskrit, lit. "method" or "sequence of the doctrine," denoting both "ways of teaching the dharma" as well as the "dharma discourse" itself. As implied in the Pāli interpretation of the term as "an explanation of one thing that stands for many," these dharmaparyāya may entail types of discourse (P. kathā) that are both indirect (P. sapariyāya), and thus not meant to be taken literally, as when the Buddha refers to a person (P. puggala; S. PUDGALA) or a self (P. atta; S. ĀTMAN); and direct (P. nippariyāya), and thus able to be construed literally and without interpretation. Since the term involves ways of framing the instruction to fit the needs of the target audience, dharmaparyāya has close connections to UPĀYAKAUŚALYA, "skill in means," or "stratagems." The Chinese translation famen means literally "dharma gate," implying an "approach to dharma," a "way of accessing the dharma," or sometimes simply a "teaching."

**dharmaprīti**. (P. dhammapīti; T. chos la dga' ba; C. faxi; J. hōki; K. pŏphŭi 法喜). In Sanskrit, "joy of the dharma"; the uplifting feelings of joy or enthusiasm that derive from properly observing the precepts (i.e., to be morally "blameless" and thus harboring no regrets or shame) and from hearing, understanding, or practicing the dharma. Depending on its intensity, this joy may manifest itself in several different ways, ranging from a radiant complexion, horripilation (the body hair standing on end), and goose bumps, to ecstatic physical levitation. In the context of meditative training, such joy is said to be conducive to the development of concentration (SAMĀDHI) and serenity (PRAŚRABDHI).

**dharmarājan**. (P. dhammarājā; T. chos kyi rgyal po; C. fawang; J. hōō; K. pŏbwang 法王). In Sanskrit, "king of dharma"; one of the epithets of the Buddha used generally across traditions. The term dharmarājan is also used to designate a monarch with faith in the BUDDHADHARMA, who rules in accordance with Buddhist, or simply broader religious, principles. Some monarchs have claimed the appellation for themselves, and many have been so designated posthumously, most notably AŚOKA. In certain Mahāyāna contexts, dharmarājan is also a title for King YAMA, so named because he administers punishments to moral transgressors in the netherworld according to the law of karmic retribution. In Tibet, the term is used to refer to the three kings credited with the introduction of Buddhism into Tibet: SRONG BRTSAN SGAM PO, KHRI SRONG LDE BRTSAN, and RAL PA CAN. The term was also used as a reverential title that the Chinese imperial court bestowed on eminent Tibetan lamas (BLA MA), beginning in the Mongol period. In Sikkim, during the Rnam rgyal dynasty (1642–1975), the king was referred to as the chos rgyal, the Tibetan translation of dharmarājan.

**Dharmarakṣa**. (C. Zhu Fahu; J. Jiku Hōgo; K. Ch'uk Pŏpho 竺法護) (c. 233–310). One of the most prolific translators in early Chinese Buddhism, who played an important role in transmitting the Indian scriptural tradition to China. Presumed to be of Yuezhi heritage, Dharmarakṣa was born in the Chinese outpost of DUNHUANG and grew up speaking multiple languages. He became a monk at the age of eight and in his thirties traveled extensively throughout the oasis kingdoms of Central Asia, collecting manuscripts of MAHĀYĀNA scriptures in a multitude of Indic and Middle Indic languages, which he eventually brought back with him to China. Because of his multilingual ability, Dharmarakṣa was able to supervise a large team in rendering these texts into Chinese; the team included scholars of Indian and Central Asian origin, as well as such Chinese laymen as the father-and-son team Nie Chengyuan and Nie Daozhen. Some 150 translations in over three hundred rolls are attributed to Dharmarakṣa, including the first extant translation of the SADDHARMAPUṆḌARĪKASŪTRA, the VIMALAKĪRTINIRDEŚA, the LALITAVISTARA, the BHADRAKALPIKASŪTRA, and some of the PRAJÑĀPĀRAMITĀ literature. Although many of Dharmarakṣa's pioneering renderings were later superseded by the fourth-century retranslations of KUMĀRAJĪVA, Dharmarakṣa is generally considered the most important translator of the early Chinese Buddhist saṃgha.

**Dharmaśālā**. [alt. Dharmshala, Dharmsala, Dharamsala]. A former British hill station in the foothills of the Himalayas that has become the seat of the Tibetan government in exile; located in the northern Indian state of Himachal Pradesh, in the upper reaches of the Kangra Valley, with the Dhauladhar Mountains as its backdrop. The Kangra Valley is rich in Buddhist archaeological sites. In the seventh century, the Chinese monk-pilgrim XUANZANG recorded that there were fifty monasteries in the region with some two thousand monks in residence. Most evidence of Buddhism vanished a century later, however, amid an upsurge of Brahmanical revivalism. Today, Dharmaśālā is renowned as the "LHA SA of India," because it is the headquarters of the Tibetan government in exile and the seat of the fourteenth DALAI LAMA. The town is populated by Tibetan refugees and several institutes have been established to preserve the artistic, cultural, and religious traditions of Tibet, including the Library of Tibetan Works and Archives. Rnam rgyal (Namgyel) monastery, located in upper Dharmaśālā, is the personal monastery of the Dalai Lama.

**Dharmasaṃgīti**. (T. Chos yang dag par sdud pa; C. Faji jing; J. Hōjūkyō; K. Pŏpchip kyŏng 法集經). In Sanskrit, "Recitation of Dharma," a SŪTRA that contains references to doctrines that become emblematic of MAHĀYĀNA and especially YOGĀCĀRA thought, such as the notion of the nominal reality of all dharmas and the eight levels of consciousness (VIJÑĀNA). The sūtra does not survive in Sanskrit, and is extant only in Tibetan and Chinese. The Chinese translation was made by the Indian monk BODHIRUCI (fl. sixth century) in 515 CE, during the Northern Wei dynasty, at its capital Luoyang. The *Dharmasaṃgīti*, translated in six rolls, is one of over thirty Mahāyāna sūtras and treatises that Bodhiruci translated during his sojourn in China, most of which reflect the latest developments in Indian Mahāyāna. Besides the *Dharmasaṃgīti*, Bodhiruci's translations that were related to the developing

Yogācāra tradition include the LAṄKĀVATĀRASŪTRA, the SAṂDHINIRMOCANASŪTRA, and the SHIDIJING LUN; his translation of the latter treatise led to the development of the Yogācāra-influenced DI LUN ZONG in China.

**dharmaśarīra**. (T. chos sku'i ring bsrel; C. fa[shen] sheli; J. hosshinshari/hōshari; K. pŏp[sin] sari 法[身]舍利). In Sanskrit, "relics of the dharma [body]"; the Buddha's incorporeal relics, viz., his scriptures, verses, and doctrines, or the immutable truth "embodied" therein. "Relics" (ŚARĪRA) literally means "body," but in Buddhist usage comes to refer most often to the sacred physical relics found in the cremated remains of the Buddha or of an eminent monk. In contrast to these physical relics remaining after cremation, "the relics of the dharma [body]" refers to the corpus of Buddhist literature and/or the DHARMAVINAYA embodied therein that were left behind by the Buddha as his incorporeal legacy; therefore they can be worshiped as śarīra. As the SADDHARMAPUṆḌARĪKASŪTRA ("Lotus Sūtra"), for example, notes, "Wherever this sūtra is spoken, read, recited, written out, or stored, one should build a STŪPA of the seven jewels (RATNA), making it high, broad, and adorned. It is not necessary to place śarīra in it. Why is this? Within it already is the complete body of the TATHĀGATA. To this stūpa one should make offerings of all kinds of flowers, incenses, beads, silk canopies, banners, vocal and instrumental music, honoring and praising it."

**Dharmaskandha[pādaśāstra]**. (T. Chos kyi phung po; C. Fayun zu lun; J. Hōunsokuron; K. Pŏbon chok non 法蘊足論). In Sanskrit, "Aggregation of Factors," or "Collection of Factors"; one of the two oldest works in the SARVĀSTIVĀDA ABHIDHARMA, along with the SAṂGĪTIPARYĀYA, and traditionally placed as the third of the six "feet" (pāda) of the JÑĀNAPRASTHĀNA, the central treatise in the Sarvāstivāda ABHIDHARMAPIṬAKA. The text is attributed to ŚĀRIPUTRA or MAHĀMAUDGALYĀYANA. It is considered an early work, with some scholars dating it as early as c. 300 BCE. It draws principally from the ĀGAMA scriptures to provide an account of Buddhist soteriological practices, as well as the afflictions that hinder spiritual progress. In coverage, the closest analogues to the *Dharmaskandha* are the VIBHAṄGA of the Pāli *abhidhammapiṭaka* and the first half of the *Śāriputrābhidharmaśāstra* (probably associated with the DHARMAGUPTAKA school), but it appears to be the most primitive of the three in the way it organizes DHARMA classifications, listing them as sense-fields or bases (ĀYATANA), aggregates (SKANDHA), and elements (DHĀTU), rather than the standard Sarvāstivāda listing of aggregates, bases, and elements (as is also found in the Pāli abhidhamma). The exposition of dharmas in the first half of the text follows the primitive arrangement of the thirty-seven factors pertaining to enlightenment (BODHIPĀKṢIKADHARMA), probably the earliest of the MĀTṚKĀ (matrices) listings that were the origin of the abhidharma style of dharma analysis. The *Dharmaskandha* provides one of the earliest attempts in Sarvāstivāda literature to organize the constituents of the path (MĀRGA) and introduce the crucial innovation of distinguishing between a path of vision (DARŚANAMĀRGA) and a path of cultivation (BHĀVANĀMĀRGA). This distinction would be of crucial importance in the mature systematizations of the path made by the VAIBHĀṢIKAS and would profoundly influence later MAHĀYĀNA presentations of the path. The second half of the text covers various other classification schema, including the āyatanas and dhātus. The sixteenth chapter synthesizes these two divisions, and focuses especially on the afflictions (KLEŚA) and their removal. Despite being one of the earliest of the Sarvāstivāda abhidharma texts, the mature tradition considers the *Dharmaskandha* to be one of the "feet" (pāda) of the JÑĀNAPRASTHĀNA, the central treatise in the Sarvāstivāda abhidharmapiṭaka. The *Dharmaskandha* does not survive in an Indic language and is only extant in a Chinese translation made by XUANZANG's translation team in 659 CE.

**Dharmāśoka**. (S). See AŚOKA.

**dharmatā**. (T. chos nyid; C. faxing; J. hosshō; K. pŏpsŏng 法性). In Sanskrit, "the nature of reality," or "the nature of things," interpreted in Chinese as the "dharma-nature"; the intrinsic nature (SVABHĀVA) of dharmas, which is constant (NITYA) and transcends all discriminative phenomena. Dharmatā is also sometimes used to mean "the way things are," and is used interchangeably with other terms that have the connotation of "the real nature of things," such as "suchness," or "things as they are" (TATHATĀ), dharma realm (DHARMADHĀTU), emptiness (ŚŪNYATĀ), the "real end" (BHŪTAKOṬI), ultimate truth (PARAMĀRTHASATYA), etc., and is sometimes used in compound with those terms. Dharmatā is said to be that which constantly exists in the world (nityasthita), whether or not the TATHĀGATAs appear to rediscover it. The DAZHIDU LUN explains that dharmatā is that unitary characteristic that combines both the generic characteristics (zongxiang) and the distinctive characteristics (biexiang) of objects (see LIUXIANG). In the East Asian Buddhist traditions, the dharma-nature, which is described as constant, equipoised, absolute, and essential reality, is contrasted with phenomenal characteristics, which are changing, discriminative, relative, and mere conventional reality. According to the East Asian YOGĀCĀRA tradition of the FAXIANG ZONG, the dharma-nature refers to reality itself, while phenomenal characteristics refer to the three natures (TRISVABHĀVA) of imaginary (PARIKALPITA), dependent (PARATANTRA), and consummate (PARINIṢPANNA); alternatively, dharma nature means the true suchness (BHŪTATATHATĀ; zhenru) of pariniṣpannasvabhāva, and phenomenal characteristics refer to the dependent nature (paratantrasvabhāva) of all dharmas. Certain strands of Mahāyāna Buddhism also view dharmatā as one aspect of the dharma body (DHARMAKĀYA), bifurcating the dharmakāya between the dharma body as the true nature of things (*dharmatā–dharmakāya; C. faxing fashen) and dharma body as skill in means (*upāya–dharmakāya; C. fangbian fashen). The former refers to the dharma body that is free from appearances, viz., the constant dharma that is neither created nor destroyed; the latter refers to both the enjoyment body (SAṂBHOGAKĀYA) and transformation body (NIRMĀṆAKĀYA), which take on phenomenal appearances in order to guide sentient beings. Because dharmatā was considered to be the ultimate nature of reality, it also came to be viewed as the foundational nature of even deluded sentient beings. This notion that dharmatā was thus in some sense the original nature of sentient beings eventually evolved into the related notions of the embryo or womb of the buddhas (TATHĀGATAGARBHA) or the buddha-nature (BUDDHADHĀTU; FOXING), which posit that enlightenment is somehow innate in the minds of sentient beings. The HUAYAN school eventually comes to distinguish buddha-nature (foxing), which is the innate prospect sentient beings have of achieving buddhahood, from dharmatā, which is considered the principle of true suchness (bhūtatathatā) that underlies even inanimate objects. When dharmatā means "the nature of things," it is referring to dependent origination (PRATĪTYASAMUTPĀDA).

**dharmātmagraha**. (T. chos kyi bdag 'dzin; C. fawozhi; J. hōgashū; K. pŏbajip 法我執). In Sanskrit, the "conception of a self with regard to phenomena"; a term that is used in combination with PUDGALĀTMAGRAHA, the "conception of a self with regard to persons." In the MAHĀYĀNA philosophical schools, the false notion of self (ĀTMAN) is expanded beyond that of a permanent soul inherent in each person, to that of a broader sense of an independent existence or intrinsic existence (SVABHĀVA) that is falsely imagined to exist in all objects of experience. Sentient beings are thus said to falsely imagine the presence of such a self in two broad categories: persons (PUDGALA) and all other phenomena (DHARMA). Wisdom (PRAJÑĀ) entails understanding the lack of self in both of these categories, referred to as the lack of self of persons (PUDGALANAIRĀTMYA) and the lack of self of phenomena (DHARMANAIRĀTMYA). Among the soteriological theories of YOGĀCĀRA and MADHYAMAKA there are differences of opinion as to whether the false conception of the selfhood of persons is more easily uprooted than the conception of the selfhood of phenomena. In addition, although all Mahāyāna philosophical schools agree that both forms of the conception of self must be uprooted by the BODHISATTVA in order to become a buddha, there are differences of opinion as to whether both must be uprooted by the ŚRĀVAKA and PRATYEKABUDDHA in order to become an ARHAT.

**dharma transmission**. See CHUANFA; FASI; YINKE.

**Dharmatrāta**. (T. Chos skyob; C. Damoduoluo; J. Darumatara; K. Talmadara 達摩多羅). The proper name of two well-known masters of the ABHIDHARMA. ¶ The first Dharmatrāta (fl. c. 100–150 CE), sometimes known to the tradition as the Bhadanta Dharmatrāta and commonly designated Dharmatrāta I in the scholarship, was a Dārṣṭāntika from northwest India. This Dharmatrāta, along with VASUMITRA, Ghoṣa[ka], and Buddhadeva, was one of the four great ĀBHIDHARMIKAS whom Xuanzang says participated in the Buddhist council (SAṂGĪTI) conveyed by the KUSHAN king KANIṢKA (r. c. 144–178 CE), which was headed by PĀRŚVA (see COUNCIL, FOURTH). The views of these four masters are represented in the ABHIDHARMAMAHĀVIBHĀṢĀ, a massive commentary on KĀTYĀYANĪPUTRA's JÑĀNAPRASTHĀNA, which functions as a virtual encyclopedia of SARVĀSTIVĀDA abhidharma. ¶ A second Dharmatrāta (fl. c. fourth century CE), known as Dharmatrāta II, is also the putative author of the SAṂYUKTĀBHIDHARMAHṚDAYA (C. *Za apitan xinlun*; "The Heart of Scholasticism with Miscellaneous Additions"), the last of a series of expository treatises that summarized Sarvāstivāda abhidharma philosophy as it was then prevailing in BACTRIA and GANDHĀRA; the text was based on Dharmaśresthin's ABHIDHARMAHṚDAYA. Dharmatrāta II also composed the *Pañcavastuvibhāṣā* (C. *Wushi piposha lun*; "Exposition of the Five-Fold Classification"), a commentary on the first chapter of Vasumitra's PRAKARAṆAPĀDA, one of the seven major texts of the Sarvāstivāda ABHIDHARMAPIṬAKA, which was also translated by Xuanzang in 663; it involves a discussion of the mature Sarvāstivāda fivefold classification system for dharmas: materiality (RŪPA), mentality (CITTA), mental constituents (CAITTA), forces dissociated from thought (CITTAVIPRAYUKTASAṂSKĀRA), and the unconditioned (ASAṂSKṚTA). The DAMODUOLUO CHAN JING, a meditation manual that proved influential in early Chinese Buddhism, is also attributed to him.

**dharmavinaya**. (P. dhammavinaya; T. chos 'dul ba; C. falü; J. hōritsu; K. pŏmnyul 法律). In Sanskrit, the "teaching" (DHARMA) and "discipline" (VINAYA) expounded by the Buddha and recommended to his followers as the highest refuge and spiritual guide after his demise. The compound dharmavinaya, with dharma referring to the Buddha's discourses (SŪTRA) and vinaya referring to monastic discipline, appears to be an early term used prior to the development of the ABHIDHARMA as a separate category of teachings and the tripartite division of the Buddhst canon (TRIPIṬAKA). Dharmavinaya is one of the terms (along with BUDDHADHARMA) within the tradition that is closest to what in the West is called "Buddhism." Generally, the sūtras and the vinaya were collectively called dharmavinaya; the Chinese term falü may also less precisely refer only to the monastic precepts (see PRĀTIMOKṢA) and does not always denote two separate categories.

**dharmāyatana**. (P. dhammāyatana; T. chos kyi skye mched; C. fachu; J. hōsho/hossho; K. pŏpch'ŏ 法處). In Sanskrit, "the sense-field of mental objects," that is, objects of the mind or mental phenomena (DHARMA) as they occur in the list of twelve sense faculties or "bases of cognition" (ĀYATANA), which serve as the bases for the production of consciousness, viz., the six internal sense bases, or sense organs (eye, ear, nose, tongue, body, and mind) and the six external sense objects (forms, sounds, odors, tastes, tangible objects, and mental phenomena). The contact (SPARŚA) between the mental sense base

(MANENDRIYA) and its corresponding mental object (dharma) leads to mental consciousness (MANOVIJÑĀNA). Although the other organs (INDRIYA) are limited to their respective objects (the eye to forms, the ear to sounds, etc.), any phenomenon may be a dharmāyatana because it can be an object of thought.

**Dharmodgata**. (T. Chos 'phags; C. Faqi pusa; J. Hōki bosatsu; K. Pŏpki posal 法起菩薩). In Sanskrit, "Elevated Dharma," or "Dharma Arising," the name of a BODHISATTVA whom the AVATAṂSAKASŪTRA describes as residing in the Diamond (S. VAJRA) Mountains. According to the Chinese translations of the *Avataṃsakasūtra*, Dharmodgata lives in the middle of the sea in the Diamond Mountains (C. Jingangshan; J. KONGŌSAN; K. KŬMGANGSAN), where he preaches the dharma to his large congregation of fellow bodhisattvas. The AṢṬASĀHASRIKĀPRAJÑĀPĀRAMITĀ also says that Dharmodgata (his name there is transcribed as C. Tanwujian, J. Donmukatsu, and K. Tammugal) preaches the PRAJÑĀPĀRAMITĀ three times daily at the City of Fragrances (S. Gandhavatī; C. Zhongxiangcheng; J. Shukōjō; K. Chunghyangsŏng), now used as the name of one of the individual peaks at the Korean KŬMGANGSAN. Since the Chinese Tang dynasty and the Korean Silla dynasty, East Asian Buddhists have presumed that Dharmodgata resided at the Diamond Mountains, just as the bodhisattva MAÑJUŚRĪ lived at WUTAISHAN. In his HUAYAN JING SHU, CHENGGUAN's massive commentary to the *Avataṃsakasūtra*, Chengguan explicitly connects the sūtra's mention of the Diamond Mountains to the Kŭmgangsan of Korea. At Kŭmgangsan, there are many place names associated with Dharmodgata and several legends and stories concerning him have been transmitted. Records explain that P'YOHUNSA, an important monastery at Kŭmgangsan, at one time had an image of Dharmodgata enshrined in its main basilica (although the image is now lost). According to the Japanese ascetic tradition of SHUGENDŌ, the semilegendary founder of the school, EN NO OZUNU (b. 634), is considered to be a manifestation of Dharmodgata, and his principal residence, Katsuragi Mountain in Nara prefecture, is therefore also sometimes known as the Diamond Mountains (KONGŌSAN).

**Dharmottara**. (T. Chos mchog) (fl. eighth century). Indian author of a number of works on PRAMĀṆA, the most important of which are his detailed commentary on DHARMAKĪRTI's PRAMĀṆAVINIŚCAYA and a shorter commentary on his NYĀYABINDU. A contemporary or student of PRAJÑĀKARAGUPTA, Dharmottara was influential in the transmission of PRAMĀṆA (T. tshad ma) studies in Tibet. RNGOG BLO LDAN SHES RAB's translation of Dharmakīrti's *Pramāṇaviniścaya* and *Nyāyabindu* into Tibetan together with Dharmottara's commentaries and his own explanations laid the foundations for the study of pramāṇa in GSANG PHU NE'U THOG monastery. This importance continued unchallenged until SA SKYA PAṆḌITA's detailed explanation of Dharmakīrti's ideas based on all his seven major works, particularly his PRAMĀṆAVĀRTTIKA, opened up a competing tradition of explanation.

**dhātu**. (T. khams; C. jie; J. kai; K. kye 界). In Sanskrit and Pāli, "element"; a polysemous term with wide application in Buddhist contexts. ¶ In epistemology, the dhātus refer to the eighteen elements through which sensory experience is produced: the six sense bases, or sense organs (INDRIYA; viz., eye, ear, nose, tongue, body, and mind); the six corresponding sense objects (ĀLAMBANA; viz., forms, sounds, odors, tastes, tangible objects, and mental phenomena); and the six sensory consciousnesses that result from contact (SPARŚA) between the corresponding base and object (VIJÑĀNA; viz., visual, auditory, olfactory, gustatory, tactile, and mental consciousnesses). As this list makes clear, the eighteen dhātus also subsume the twelve ĀYATANA (sense-fields). The dhātus represent one of the three major taxonomies of dharmas found in the sūtras (along with SKANDHA and āyatana), and represent a more primitive stage of dharma classification than the elaborate analyses found in much of the mature ABHIDHARMA literature (but cf. DHARMASKANDHA). ¶ In cosmology, dhātu is used in reference to the three realms of existence (TRILOKADHĀTU), which comprise all of the phenomenal universe: the sensuous realm (KĀMADHĀTU), the subtle-materiality realm (RŪPADHĀTU), and the immaterial realm (ĀRŪPYADHĀTU). The three realms of existence taken together comprise all of SAMSĀRA, and are the realms within which beings take rebirth. In this cosmological sense, dhātu is synonymous to AVACARA (sphere, domain); see AVACARA for further details. ¶ In a physical sense, dhātu is used to refer to the constituent elements of the physical world (see MAHĀBHŪTA), of which four are usually recognized in Buddhist materials: earth, water, fire, and wind. Sometimes two additional constituents are added to the list: space (ĀKĀŚA) and consciousness (VIJÑĀNA). ¶ The term dhātu may also refer to an "elemental physical substance," that is, the physical remains of the body, and this context is synonymous with ŚARĪRA (relic), with which it is often seen in compound as śarīradhātu (bodily relic). Sometimes three types of relics are differentiated: specific corporeal relics (śarīradhātu), relics of use (pāribhogikadhātu), and relics of commemoration (uddeśikadhātu). In a further development of this usage, in the RATNAGOTRAVIBHĀGA, dhātu is synonymous with GOTRA, the final element that enables all beings to become buddhas; see BUDDHADHĀTU.

**Dhātukathā**. In Pāli, "Discourse on Elements"; traditionally listed as the third of the seven canonical books of the THERAVĀDA abhidhammapiṭaka, and probably deriving from the middle stratum of Pāli abhidhamma literature, after the earlier VIBHAṄGA and PUGGALAPAÑÑATTI, but before the later KATHĀVATTHU; the proposed dating varies widely, but the first century BCE is its terminus ad quem. The *Dhātukathā* presents a psychological analysis of noble states of mind, supplementing the subject matter of the DHAMMASAṄGAṆI. Its fourteen chapters are presented in catechetic style, describing the relationship that pertains between specific factors (dhamma; S. DHARMA) and the three broader categories of the aggregates (khandha; S. SKANDHA), elements (DHĀTU), and sense-fields (ĀYATANA). In its analysis of the relationships that pertain between these various factors and categories, rigorous definitions of each factor are provided. The analytical approach taken in the text—e.g., whether a specific factor is both included and not included in a particular category, etc.—anticipates the sophisticated logical analysis found later in the four antinomies (CATUṢKOṬI). The *Dhātukathā* is reminiscent in style and exegetical approach to the SARVĀSTIVĀDA DHĀTUKĀYA, and may derive from a common urtext, although there are few similarities in their respective contents.

**Dhātukāya[pādaśāstra]**. (T. Khams kyi tshogs; C. Jieshen lun; J. Kaishinron; K. Kyesin non 界身論). In Sanskrit, "Collection of Elements"; traditionally placed as the fifth of the six "feet" (pāda) of the JÑĀNAPRASTHĀNA, the central treatise in the SARVĀSTIVĀDA ABHIDHARMAPIṬAKA. The text, which is attributed to either VASUMITRA or PŪRṆA, probably dates from the middle stratum of Sarvāstivāda abhidharma materials, together with the VIJÑĀNAKĀYA, and probably the PRAJÑAPTIBHĀṢYA and PRAKARAṆAPĀDA as well; the first century BCE is the terminus ad quem for its composition. As its title suggests, the *Dhātukāya* is a collection of various schemata for organizing the diverse mental concominants (CAITTA) that had been listed in previous ABHIDHARMA materials. The text is in two major sections, the first of which, the *mūlavastuvarga, provides a roster of ninety-one different types of mentality (CITTA) and mental concomintants (caitta) in fourteen different lists of factors (DHARMA). The second major section, the *vibhajyavarga, provides a series of analyses that details the intricate interrelationships among the various factors included in these dharma lists. The text concludes with an analysis of each individual factor in terms of its association with, or dissociation from, the eighteen elements (DHĀTU), twelve sense-fields (ĀYATANA), and five aggregates (SKANDHA). The idiosyncratic lists of dharmas found in the *Dhātukāya* are ultimately standardized in the later *Prakaraṇapāda*. Because the *Dhātukāya*'s preliminary rosters are ultimately superseded by the more developed and comprehensive treatment of dharmas found in the *Prakaraṇapāda*, the *Dhātukāya* is less commonly read and consulted within the later Sarvāstivāda tradition and is, in fact, never cited in the ABHIDHARMAMAHĀVIBHĀṢĀ, the Sarvāstivāda's encyclopedic treatment of doctrine. The fact that the Chinese tradition ascribes authorship of both of these texts to Vasumitra suggests that the *Prakaraṇapāda* may have been intended to be the definitive and complete systematization of dharmas that are outlined only tentatively, and incompletely, in the *Dhātukāya*. The *Dhātukāya* is reminiscent in style and exegetical approach to the Pāli PAṬṬHĀNA and especially the DHĀTUKATHĀ (both of which may derive from a common urtext), although there are few similarities in their respective contents. The *Dhātukāya* does not survive in an Indic language and is only extant in a Chinese translation made by XUANZANG's translation team in 663 CE. The text is said to have been composed originally in six thousand ślokas, although the recension Xuanzang translated apparently derived from an abbreviated edition in 830 ślokas.

**Dhītika**. (S). See DHṚṬAKA.

**Dhṛṭaka**. [alt. Dhītika] (C. Tiduojia; J. Daitaka; K. Chedaga 提多迦). The fifth of the twenty-eight Indian patriarchs of Buddhism listed in the LIDAI FABAO JI, the important lineage history of the CHAN school. Dhṛṭaka is said to have been a disciple of UPAGUPTA and is best known for having converted to Buddhism the religious teacher Micchaka [alt. Mikkaka], who became his successor and the sixth patriarch, along with his eight thousand followers.

**Dhṛtarāṣṭra**. (P. Dhataraṭṭha; T. Yul 'khor srung; C. Chiguo Tian; J. Jikokuten; K. Chiguk Ch'ŏn 持國天). In Sanskrit, "He whose Empire is Unyielding," or "He who Preserves the Empire"; one of the four "great kings" of heaven (CATURMAHĀRĀJA), who are also known as "world guardians" (LOKAPĀLA); he is said to be a guardian of the DHARMA and of sentient beings who are devoted to the dharma. Dhṛtarāṣṭra guards the gate that leads to the east at the midslope of the world's central axis of Mount SUMERU; this gate leads to pūrvavideha (see VIDEHA), one of the four continents (dvīpa), which is located in the east. Dhṛtarāṣṭra and his fellow great kings reside in the first and lowest of the six heavens of the sensuous realm of existence (KĀMADHĀTU), the heaven of the four great kings (CATURMAHĀRĀJAKĀYIKA). Dhṛtarāṣṭra is a vassal of ŚAKRO DEVĀNĀM INDRAḤ (see INDRA; ŚAKRA), the king of the gods, who is lord of the heaven of the thirty-three divinities (TRĀYASTRIṂŚA), the second of the six sensuous-realm heavens, which is located at the peak of Mount SUMERU. Among the eight classes of demigods, Dhṛtarāṣṭra rules over the "heavenly musicians" (GANDHARVA) and the "stinking hungry demons" (pūtana). Dhṛtarāṣṭra and the four heavenly kings were originally indigenous Indian or Central Asian deities, who were eventually "conquered" by the Buddha and incorporated into Buddhism; they seem to have been originally associated with royal (KṢATRIYA) lineages, and their connections with royal warfare are evidenced in the suits of armor they come to wear as their cult is transmitted from Central Asia to China, Korea, and Japan. According to the *Dhāraṇīsamuccaya*, Dhṛtarāṣṭra is to be depicted iconographically with his sword in his left hand and his right fist akimbo on his waist.

**dhūtaguṇa**. [alt. dhūta/dhuta]. In Buddhist Hybrid Sanskrit, "austerities." See DHUTAṄGA.

**dhutaṅga**. [alt. dhūtaṅga] (S. dhūtaguṇa/dhūta/dhuta; T. sbyang pa'i yan lag; C. toutuo[xing]; J. zuda[gyō]; K. tut'a[haeng] 頭陀[行]). In Pāli, lit. "limbs of scrupulousness," viz., "austerities," or "ascetic practices." The term is alternately known as simply dhuta/dhūta in both Pāli and Sanskrit; the BUDDHIST HYBRID SANSKRIT term dhūtaguṇa means the "qualities" (GUṆA) of the "purified" (dhuta) person, viz., an "ascetic." Dhūtaṅga refers to a specific set of thirteen ascetic practices that the Buddha authorized monks to adopt voluntarily for the purposes of cultivating contentedness with little, detachment, energy, and moderation. These austerities are not enjoined on monks and nuns by the VINAYA, but are rather optional practices that monastics were sanctioned to adopt for limited periods of time in order to foster sensory restraint (INDRIYASAMVARA), an important constituent of morality (ŚĪLA). Based on the Buddha's own failed experiments with extreme mortification of the flesh (see TAPAS) as a practice conducive to enlightenment while he was a BODHISATTVA, this specific set of practices was considered to provide a middle way (MADHYAMAPRATIPAD) between self-mortification and sensual indulgence. The thirteen authorized practices are (1) wearing patched robes made from discarded cloth rather than from cloth donated by laypeople; (2) wearing only three robes; (3) going for alms; (4) not omitting any house while on the alms round, rather than begging only at those houses known to provide good food; (5) eating only what can be eaten in one sitting; (6) eating only food received in the alms bowl (PĀTRA), rather than more elaborate meals presented to the SAṂGHA; (7) refusing more food after indicating one has eaten enough; (8) dwelling in the forest; (9) dwelling at the root of a tree; (10) dwelling in the open air, using only a tent made from one's robes as shelter; (11) dwelling in a charnel ground (ŚMAŚĀNA); (12) satisfaction with whatever dwelling one has; and (13) sleeping in a sitting position without ever lying down (see CHANGJWA PURWA). The comparable Mahāyāna list of twelve dhūtaguṇas is essentially the same, dropping the two practices involving eating (5, 6) and adding an additional rule on wearing only garments made of coarse hemp and wool. The VISUDDHIMAGGA recommends these ascetic practices especially to those of either greedy (RĀGA) or deluded (MOHA) temperaments (CARITA), because greed and delusion both wane through, respectively, the continued practice of asceticism and the clarification of what is important in life; sometimes a person of hateful temperament is also said to benefit, because conflict abates as one becomes content with little. The Buddha offered this authorized list of voluntary practices after explicitly rejecting a more severe set of austerities proposed by his cousin and rival DEVADATTA that would have been mandatory for all members of the saṃgha: forest dwelling (see ARAÑÑAVĀSI), subsistence on gathered alms food only, use of rag robes only, dwelling at the foot of a tree, and strict vegetarianism. With the growth of settled monasticism, the practice of the austerities waned, although asceticism continues to be a major prestige factor within the Buddhist lay and monastic communities. In their accounts of India, both FAXIAN and XUANZANG note the presence of followers of Devadatta who adhered to the austere practices he had recommended to the Buddha. The dhutaṅgas should be distinguished from TAPAS, "severe austerities," or DUṢKARACARYĀ, "difficult feats" of religious virtuosity, practices that do not necessarily involve the authorized types of ascetic practices. See also THUDONG.

**dhyāna**. (P. jhāna; T. bsam gtan; C. chan/chanding; J. zen/zenjō; K. sŏn/sŏnjŏng 禪/禪定). In Sanskrit, "meditative absorption," specific meditative practices during which the mind temporarily withdraws from external sensory awareness and remains completely absorbed in an ideational object of meditation. The term can refer both to the practice that leads to full absorption and to the state of full absorption itself. Dhyāna involves the power to control the mind and does not, in itself, entail any enduring insight into the nature of reality; however, a certain level of absorption is generally said to be necessary in order to prepare the mind for direct realization of truth, the destruction of the afflictions (KLEŚA), and the attainment of liberation (VIMUKTI). Dhyāna is classified into two broad types: (1) meditative absorption associated with the realm of subtle materiality (RŪPĀVACARADHYĀNA) and (2) meditative absorption of the immaterial realm (ĀRŪPYĀVACARADHYĀNA). Each of these two types is subdivided into four stages or degrees of absorption, giving a total of eight stages of dhyāna. The four absorptions of the realm of subtle materiality are characterized by an increasing attenuation of consciousness as one progresses from one stage to the next. The deepening of concentration leads the meditator temporarily to allay the five hindrances (NĪVARAṆA) and to put in place the five constituents of absorption (DHYĀNĀṄGA). The five hindrances are: (1) sensuous desire (KĀMACCHANDA), which hinders the constituent of one-pointedness of mind (EKĀGRATĀ); (2) malice (VYĀPĀDA), hindering physical rapture (PRĪTI); (3) sloth and torpor (STYĀNA-MIDDHA), hindering applied thought (VITARKA); (4) restlessness and worry (AUDDHATYA-KAUKṚTYA), hindering mental ease (SUKHA); and (5) skeptical doubt (VICIKITSĀ), hindering sustained thought (VICĀRA). These hindrances thus specifically obstruct one of the specific factors of absorption and, once they are allayed, the first level of the subtle-materiality dhyānas will be achieved. In the first dhyāna, all five constituents of dhyāna are present; as concentration deepens, these gradually fall away, so that in the second dhyāna, both types of thought vanish and only prīti, sukha, and ekāgratā remain; in the third dhyāna, only sukha and ekāgratā remain; and in the fourth dhyāna, concentration is now so rarified that only ekāgratā is left. Detailed correlations appear in meditation manuals describing specifically which of the five spiritual faculties (INDRIYA) and seven constituents of enlightenment (BODHYAṄGA) serves as the antidote to which hindrance. Mastery of the fourth absorption of the realm of subtle materiality is required for the cultivation of the supranormal powers (ABHIJÑĀ) and for the cultivation of the four ārūpyāvacaradhyānas, or meditative absorptions of the immaterial realm. The immaterial absorptions themselves represent refinements of the fourth rūpāvacaradhyāna, in which the "object" of meditation is gradually attenuated. The four immaterial absorptions instead are named after their respective objects: (1) the sphere of infinite space (ĀKĀŚĀNANTYĀYATANA), (2) the sphere of infinite consciousness (VIJÑĀNĀNANTYĀYATANA), (3) the sphere of nothingness (ĀKIÑCANYĀYATANA), and (4) the sphere of neither perception nor nonperception (NAIVASAṂJÑĀNĀSAṂJYYATANA). Mastery of the subtle-materiality realm absorptions can also result in rebirth as a divinity (DEVA) in the subtle-materiality realm, and mastery of the immaterial absorptions can lead to rebirth as a divinity in the immaterial realm (see ANIÑJYAKARMAN). Dhyāna occurs in numerous lists of the constituents of the path, appearing, for example, as the fifth of the six perfections (PĀRAMITĀ). The term CHAN (J. zen), the name adopted by an important school of indigenous East Asian Buddhism, is the Chinese phonetic transcription of the Sanskrit term dhyāna. See also JHĀNA; SAMĀDHI; SAMĀPATTI.

**dhyānamudrā**. (T. mnyam bzhag gi phyag rgya; C. dingyin; J. jōin; K. chŏngin 定印). In Sanskrit, "gesture of meditation"; also sometimes written as dhyānimudrā. This MUDRĀ is formed with both hands resting in the lap, the back of the right hand resting on the palm of the left and both thumbs lightly touching. In this version, the right hand represents the world of enlightenment, which subdues the world of appearance symbolized by the left hand, or, alternatively, the absolute realm of reality in which NIRVĀṆA and SAṂSĀRA are nondual. This gesture may also be made with the left hand only, while the right hand is positioned in another mudrā. This gesture is commonly found in images of ŚĀKYAMUNI and AMITĀBHA buddhas and is also a basic hand position used in the practice of meditation.

**dhyānāṅga**. (P. jhānaṅga; T. bsam gtan gyi yan lag; C. chanzhi; J. zenshi; K. sŏnji 禪支). In Sanskrit, the "constituents of meditative absorption" (DHYĀNA); according to mainstream Buddhist materials, five factors that must be present in order to enter into the first meditative absorption of the subtle-materiality realm (RŪPĀVACARADHYĀNA): (1) applied thought (VITARKA), (2) sustained thought (VICĀRA), (3) physical rapture (PRĪTI), (4) mental ease (SUKHA), and (5) one-pointedness (EKĀGRATĀ; cf. CITTAIKĀGRATĀ) or equanimity (UPEKṢĀ). Each constituent results from the temporary allayment of a specific mental hindrance (NĪVARAṆA): vitarka allays sloth and torpor (STYĀNA-MIDDHA); vicāra allays skeptical doubt (VICIKITSĀ); prīti allays malice (VYĀPĀDA); sukha allays restlessness and worry (AUDDHATYA–KAUKṚTYA); and ekāgratā allays sensuous desire (KĀMACCHANDA). Each higher dhyāna has a decreasing number of factors, with both types of thought dropping away in the second dhyāna, physical rapture dropping away in the third, and mental ease vanishing in the fourth, when only one-pointedness remains. The ABHIDHARMAKOŚABHĀṢYA and related MAHĀYĀNA accounts say the first dhyāna has five branches: applied and sustained thought, rapture, bliss, and SAMĀDHI (meditative stabilization); the second, four branches: rapture, bliss, samādhi, and PRASĀDA (calm clarity); the third, five branches: equanimity, SMṚTI (recollection), SAṂPRAJANYA (introspection), happiness, and one-pointedness; and the fourth, four branches: equanimity, recollection, an equanimous feeling that is neither painful nor pleasant, and samādhi. See also DHYĀNA; NĪVARAṆA.

**dhyānapāramitā**. (P. jhānapāramī; T. bsam gtan gyi pha rol tu phyin pa; C. jinglü boluomiduo; J. jōryoharamita; K. chŏngnyŏ paramilta 靜慮波羅蜜多). In Sanskrit, the "perfection of meditative absorption" or "concentration"; the fifth of the six [alt. ten] perfections (PĀRAMITĀ) cultivated on the BODHISATTVA path. It is perfected on the fifth of the ten stages (DAŚABHŪMI) of the bodhisattva path, SUDURJAYĀ (invincibility), where the bodhisattva comprehends the various permutations of truth (SATYA), including the FOUR NOBLE TRUTHS, the provisional (NEYĀRTHA) and definitive (NĪTĀRTHA), etc., and masters infinite numbers of samādhis.

**dhyānasamāpatti**. [alt. samāpattidhyāna] (P. jhānasamāpatti; T. bsam gtan snyoms 'jug; C. xiude ding; J. shutokujō; K. sudŭk chŏng 修得定). In Sanskrit, "meditative absorption attained through cultivation"; one of the two types of meditative absorption, along with "innate meditative absorption" (DHYĀNOPAPATTI). Whereas "innate meditative absorption" is attained once one is reborn into the "field of meditative concentration" (dhyānabhūmi), i.e., the subtle-materiality realm (RŪPADHĀTU) or the immaterial realm (ĀRŪPYADHĀTU), this "meditative absorption attained by cultivation" is the meditative state attained in the "field of distraction" (asamāhitatva) of the sensuous realm (KĀMADHĀTU) through meditative practice. Rebirth into the subtle-materiality or immaterial realms is presumed to occur as the reward for having performed in the preceding lifetime cultivation of the subtle-material absorptions (RŪPĀVACARADHYĀNA) or immaterial absorptions (ĀRŪPYĀVACARADHYĀNA). The ABHIDHARMAKOŚABHĀṢYA and related MAHĀYĀNA accounts parse the compound dhyāna-samāpatti as a dual compound (dvandva) and construe dhyāna as referring to the four levels of the dhyānas of the subtle-materiality realm and samāpatti to the four levels of dhyāna of the immaterial realm.

**dhyānibuddha**. In Sanskrit, "meditation buddhas"; a term used to refer to the five central buddhas of VAJRAYĀNA Buddhism: AKṢOBHYA, AMITĀBHA, AMOGHASIDDHI, RATNASAMBHAVA, and VAIROCANA (see PAÑCATATHĀGATA). Although these five buddhas commonly appear as a group, the collective designation of them as dhyānibuddhas does not seem to be attested in a Buddhist textual source. The term first appears in the essays of BRIAN HOUGHTON HODGSON, British Resident at the Court of Nepal in the early nineteenth century, who may have learned the term from his Newari informant, the pundit Amṛtānanda. Hodgson distinguished these more celestial buddhas from the mānuṣibuddhas, or human buddhas, buddhas such as ŚĀKYAMUNI who appear on earth as the human manifestations of the dhyānibuddhas. Through Hodgson, the term was widely used in Europe in the nineteenth century, and was appropriated by HELENA PETROVNA BLAVATSKY, who explained in *The Secret Doctrine* that there are not five but seven dhyānibuddhas.

**dhyānopapatti**. (C. shengde ding; J. shōtokujō; K. saengdŭk chŏng 生得定). In Sanskrit, "innate meditative absorption";

one of the two types of meditative absorption (DHYĀNA), along with "meditative absorption attained through cultivation" (DHYĀNASAMĀPATTI). The innate type of meditative absorption refers to the state of deep concentration that is possessed congenitally by a being who is born into either the subtle-materiality realm (RŪPADHĀTU) or the immaterial realm (ĀRŪPYADHĀTU). For this reason, the subtle-materiality and the immaterial realms are termed "fields of meditative concentration" (dhyānabhūmi), while the sensuous realm (KĀMADHĀTU) is the "field of distraction" (asamāhitatva).

**Dhyānottarapaṭala**. (T. Bsam gtan phyi ma rim par phye ba). In Sanskrit, the "Chapter on the Subsequent Stages of Concentration"; a brief work in seventy-four verses regarded as a chapter of the lost *Vajroṣṇīṣatantra*. It also is related to the fifth chapter of the MAHĀVAIROCANĀBHISAṂBODHISŪTRA. The work, preserved only in Tibetan, is classified as a KRIYĀTANTRA, and provides instruction on MANTRA recitation and yogic breath practice (PRĀṆĀYĀMA), which are to be undertaken subsequent to the practice of DHYĀNA. There is a detailed commentary on the text by BUDDHAGUHYA.

**diamond maṇḍala**. See KONGŌKAI.

**Diamond Mountains**. See KŬMGANGSAN.

**Diamond Sūtra**. See VAJRACCHEDIKĀPRAJÑĀPĀRAMITĀSŪTRA.

**dianyan**. (J. tengen; K. chŏman 點眼). In Chinese, lit. "dotting the eyes," also known as "opening the eyes" (KAIYAN; T. spyan phye); a consecration ceremony for a buddha image (BUDDHĀBHIṢEKA) that serves to make the icon come alive. The term refers to a ceremony, or series of ceremonies, that accompanies the installation of a buddha image or painting, which specifically involves dotting the pupils onto the inert eyes of the icon in order to animate it. Until this ceremony is performed, the icon remains nothing more than an inert block of wood or lump of clay; once its eyes are dotted, however, the image is thought to become invested with the power and charisma of a living buddha. The related term kaiyan has the same denotation, but may in some contexts it refer more broadly to "opening up the eyes" of an image by ritually dropping eye drops into its eyes. Both dianyan or kaiyan occurred in conjunction with esoteric Buddhist rituals. The *Yiqie rulai anxiang sanmei yigui jing* provides an elaborate set of instructions on how to consecrate buddha images, in which "dotting the eyes" accompanies the performance of other esoteric practices, such as MANTRA and MUDRĀ. When a bodhisattva wonders why buddha images are installed if the DHARMAKĀYA of a buddha has no physical form, the Buddha replies that images are used as an expedient for guiding neophytes who have first aroused the thought of enlightenment (BODHICITTOTPĀDA). In Korea, where this term chŏman is typically used for this ceremony rather than kaean (C. kaiyan), there were different "dotting the eyes" consecrations for different types of Buddhist images and requisites, including images of a buddha, ARHAT, the ten kings of hell (shiwang), and the kings of heaven, as well as in conjunction with ceremonies for erecting a STŪPA or offering robes (KAṢĀYA). Through these chŏman ceremonies, Buddhist artifacts are transformed from mere physical objects into spiritually sanctioned religious items imbued with spiritual efficacy. The Korean *Chinŏn chip* ("Mantra Anthology"), extant in several editions of which the oldest is dated 1476, includes a "mantra for dotting the eyes" (chŏman mun) along with its Sanskrit and Chinese transliterations. In Japan, this ceremony is usually called kaigen (C. kaiyan) rather than tengen. In Chinese CHAN texts, "dotting the eyes" of a buddha image is also sometimes used as a metaphor for a Chan adept's final achievement of awakening. See also NETRAPRATIṢṬHĀPANA.

**dianzuo**. (J. tenzo; K. chŏnjwa 典座). In Chinese, lit. "in charge of seating"; the term that comes to be used for a cook at a Buddhist monastery, who supervises the preparation and distribution of meals. In Indian VINAYA texts, the term was used to designate a "manager," the service monk (S. VAIYĀPṚTYA[KARA]; P. veyyāvaccakara) who assigned seating at assemblies and ceremonies and arranged for the distribution of material objects or donations in addition to food. In the pilgrimage records of YIJING in India and ENNIN in China, the term always referred to a "manager," not someone who worked in the monastic kitchen. But sometime after the tenth century, during the Northern Song dynasty, the term came to be used in Chinese monasteries to refer to the cook. In East Asian CHAN monasteries, the cook and five other officers, collectively known as the ZHISHI (J. chiji), oversaw the administration of the monastic community. Typically, the dianzuo position was considered a prestigious position and offered only to monks of senior rank. The Japanese Zen monk DŌGEN KIGEN wrote a famous essay on the responsibilities of the cook entitled *Tenzo kyōkun* ("Instructions to the Cook"). Cf. DRAVYA MALLAPUTRA.

**Diệu Nhân**. (妙仁) (1042–1113). The only nun whose biography is recorded in the Vietnamese lineage history THIỀN UYỂN TẬP ANH. Diệu Nhân's personal name was Lý Ngọc Kiều. She came from Phù Đổng village, Tiên Du prefecture in northern Vietnam, the eldest daughter of Lord Phụng Yết. She was raised in the imperial palace by King Lý Thánh Tông (r. 1054–72) and married a man named Lê, a provincial governor. Upon his death, she vowed not to remarry and, moved by the Buddhist teaching on impermanence, decided to give away all her belongings and enter the Buddhist order. She studied under the monk Chân Không of Phù Đổng District who gave her the sobriquet Diệu Nhân. Diệu Nhân devoted herself to keeping the precepts and practicing meditation and was highly revered among nuns. Later, Chân Không appointed her head of the Hương Hải Convent.

**Dīghanikāya**. In Pāli, "Collection of Long Discourses"; the first division of the Pāli SUTTAPIṬAKA. It is comprised of thirty-four lengthy suttas (SŪTRA) arranged rather arbitrarily into three major sections: "morality" (sīlakkhanda), comprising suttas 1–14; "great division" (mahāvagga), comprising suttas 14–23; and the "charlatan" (pāṭikavagga), comprising suttas 24–34. Among the suttas contained in the *Dīghanikāya* are such renowned and influential scriptures as the AGGAÑÑASUTTA, MAHĀPARINIBBĀNASUTTA, SĀMAÑÑAPHALASUTTA, and the SATIPAṬṬHĀNASUTTA. The Pāli tradition asserts that the texts of the *Dīghanikāya* were first recited orally during the first Buddhist council (SAṂGĪTI; see COUNCIL, FIRST) following the Buddha's death and were officially transcribed into written form in Sri Lanka during the reign of King VAṬṬAGĀMAṆI ABHAYA in the first century BCE. An analogous recension of the "Long Discourses" appears in the Sanskrit DĪRGHĀGAMA (all but three of its thirty sūtras have their equivalents in Pāli). Fragments of the Sanskrit recension, which is associated with the SARVĀSTIVĀDA school or its MŪLASARVĀSTIVĀDA offshoot, were rediscovered in Afghanistan in the 1990s. Before that rediscovery, only a Chinese translation of the *Dīrghāgama* survived, which was attributed to the DHARMAGUPTAKA school; the translation was finished in 413 CE. Although all three recensions of this collection have a tripartite structure, only the first section of the Pāli, the sīlakkhanda, has a counterpart in the Sarvāstivāda and Dharmaguptaka recensions. The *Dīghanikāya* appears in the Pali Text Society's English translation series as *Dialogues of the Buddha*.

**Dignāga**. [alt. Diṅnāga] (T. Phyogs glang; C. Chenna; J. Jinna; K. Chinna 陳那) (c. 480–c. 540). Indian monk regarded as the formalizer of Buddhist logic (NYĀYA; HETUVIDYĀ). Dignāga was an influential innovator in Buddhist inferential reasoning or logical syllogisms (PRAYOGA; SĀDHANA), an important feature of Indian philosophy more broadly, which occupies a crucial place in later Indian and Tibetan philosophical analysis. The Indian Nyāya (Logic) school advocated that there were five necessary stages in syllogistic reasoning: (1) probandum or proposition (PRATIJÑĀ), "The mountain is on fire"; (2) reason (HETU), "because there is smoke," (3) analogy (udāharaṇa), "Whatever is smoky is on fire, like a stove, but unlike a lake"; (4) application (upanāya), "Since this mountain is smoky, it is on fire"; (5) conclusion (nigamana), "The mountain is on fire." Using the same example, Dignāga by contrast reduced the syllogism down to only three essential steps: (1) probandum or proposition (PAKṢA), "the mountain is on fire"; (2) reason (hetu), "because there is smoke"; (3) exemplification (dṛṣṭānta), "whatever is smoky is on fire, like a stove," and "whatever is not on fire is not smoky, like a lake," or, more simply, "like a stove, unlike a lake." Dignāga is also the first scholiast to incorporate into Buddhism the Vaiśeṣika position that there are only two valid means of knowledge (PRAMĀṆA): direct perception (PRATYAKṢA, which also includes for Buddhists the subcategory of YOGIPRATYAKṢA) and inference (ANUMĀNA). Dignāga's major works include his PRAMĀṆASAMUCCAYA ("Compendium on Valid Means of Knowledge"), ĀLAMBANAPARĪKṢĀ ("Investigation of the Object"), and *Nyāyamukha* ("Primer on Logic"), which is available only in Chinese translation. See also DHARMAKĪRTI.

**Dil mgo mkhyen brtse**. [alt. Ldil go] (Dilgo Kyentse) (1910–1991). One of the most highly revered twentieth-century teachers of the RNYING MA sect of Tibetan Buddhism, renowned both for his scholarship and meditative mastery of RDZOGS CHEN practices. His full name was Rab gsal zla ba gzhan dga'. Born in eastern Tibet, he was recognized at the age of twelve as the mind incarnation of the illustrious nineteenth-century savant 'JAM DBYANGS MKHYEN BRTSE DBANG PO and enthroned at ZHE CHEN monastery. He studied under a number of masters, including the fourth Zhe chen Rgyal tshabs and 'JAM DBYANGS MKHYEN BRTSE CHOS KYI BLO GROS, and then spent close to thirteen years in solitary meditation retreat. At the suggestion of his teachers, he married while in his mid-twenties and fathered several children. Escaping the Communist invasion of Tibet in 1959, he fled to Bhutan where he was invited to live as the spiritual master of the royal family. A prolific author, Dil mgo mkhyen brtse was recognized as a modern-day treasure revealer (GTER STON) and eventually served a period of time as the spiritual head of the Rnying ma. In the early 1980s he founded a new Zhe chen monastery in Kathmandu where his grandson, recognized as the monastery's throne holder, the seventh Rab 'byams incarnation, resides. On December 29, 1995, a young boy named O rgyan bstan 'dzin 'jigs med lhun grub (Orgyan Tendzin Jikme Lhundrup, b. 1993) was enthroned as Dil mgo mkhyen brtse's reincarnation in a ceremony at MĀRATIKA cave in eastern Nepal.

**Di lun zong**. (J. Jironshū; K. Chi non chong 地論宗). In Chinese, "School of *Di lun* Exegetes"; a lineage of Buddhist scholastics who studied the *Di lun*, an abbreviation of the *Shidijing lun*, or DAŚABHŪMIVYĀKHYĀNA, a commentary on the DAŚABHŪMIKASŪTRA attributed to the Indian exegete VASUBANDHU. The school is considered one of the earliest of the indigenous scholastic traditions of Chinese MAHĀYĀNA Buddhism, and its thought draws on strands of Indic thought that derive from both the YOGĀCĀRA and TATHĀGATAGARBHA traditions. At the Northern Wei capital of Luoyang, BODHIRUCI, Ratnamati (d.u.), and Buddhaśānta (d.u.) began the translation of the *Daśabhūmivyākhyāna* into Chinese in 508. However, disagreements between the collaborators over the nature of ĀLAYAVIJÑĀNA (viz., whether it was pure, impure, or both) led them to produce different translations. This controversy about the real nature of this eighth storehouse consciousness derived from VASUBANDHU's ambiguous position in his commentary. In some passages, Vasubandhu implied that the ālayavijñāna was the tainted source from which SAṂSĀRA arises and thus impure; in others, he implied instead that the ālayavijñāna was coextensive with suchness (TATHATĀ) and thus fundamentally pure. Those who studied Bodhiruci's rendering came to be known as the Northern Di lun school, while the followers of Ratnamati's version were known as the Southern Di lun school. The Northern Di lun school advocated that the ālayavijñāna was only provisionally real (SAṂVṚTISATYA) and was impure; it was a tainted source that produced only defiled dharmas. By contrast, the southern branch advocated that the ālayavijñāna was fundamentally pure but came to be associated with impure elements: it was the functioning of suchness and thus pure, but it also was subject to the same laws of conditioned origination (PRATĪTYASAMUTPĀDA) as the sensory consciousnesses and thus impure. The two contrasting renderings of the treatise were later edited together by the Southern Di lun monk Huiguang (468–537), also known as VINAYA master Guangtong, and it is this edition in twelve rolls that we have today. Studies of the *Shidijing lun* continued with Fashang (495–580), Huishun (d.u.), JINGYING HUIYUAN, and others. Interest in the theories of the *Shidijing lun* largely waned, as new YOGĀCĀRA texts from India were introduced to China by the pilgrim and translator XUANZANG and the work of HUAYAN scholars such as FAZANG on the AVATAṂSAKASŪTRA (within which the *Daśabhūmikasūtra* is incorporated) began to gain prominence. Despite being superseded by these later schools, however, the positions of the Southern Di lun school lived on in the Huayan school of the mature Chinese tradition, while the Northern Di Lun school positions were taken up by the Chinese Yogācāra tradition of the FAXIANG ZONG. See also SHE LUN ZONG.

**dingxiang**. (J. chinzō; K. chŏngsang 頂相). In Chinese, lit. "mark on the forehead" or "head's appearance." The term dingxiang was originally coined as the Chinese translation of the Sanskrit term UṢṆĪṢA, but the term also came to be used to refer to a portrait or image of a monk or nun. Written sources from as early as the sixth century, such as the GAOSENG ZHUAN ("Biographies of Eminent Monks"), recount the natural mummification of eminent Buddhist monks, and subsequently, the making of lifelike sculptures of monks made from ashes (often from cremation) mixed with clay. The earliest extant monk portraits date from the ninth century and depict the five patriarchs of the esoteric school (C. Zhenyan; J. SHINGONSHŪ); these portraits are now enshrined in the collection of TŌJI in Kyoto, Japan. Another early example is the sculpture of the abbot Hongbian in cave 17 at DUNHUANG. Dingxiang portraits were largely, but not exclusively, used within the CHAN, SŎN, and ZEN traditions, to be installed in special halls prepared for memorial and mortuary worship. After the rise of the SHIFANGCHA (monasteries of the ten directions) system in the Song dynasty, which guaranteed the abbacy to monks belonging to a Chan lineage, portraits of abbots were hung in these image halls to establish their presence in a shared spiritual genealogy. The portraits of the legendary Indian monk BODHIDHARMA and the Chan master BAIZHANG HUAIHAI were often placed at the center of these arrangements, symbolizing the spiritual and institutional foundations of Chan. The practice of inscribing one's own dingxiang portrait before death also flourished in China; inscribed portraits were presented to disciples and wealthy supporters as gifts and these portraits thus functioned as highly valued commodities within the Buddhist religious community. The practice of preparing dingxiang portraits was transmitted to Japan. Specifically noteworthy are the Japanese monk portrait sculptures dating from the Kamakura period, known for their lifelike appearance. The making of dingxiang portraits continues to flourish even to this day. In Korea, the related term CHINYŎNG ("true image") is more commonly used to refer to monks' portraits.

**Diṅnāga**. See DIGNĀGA.

**Dīpaṃkara**. (P. Dīpaṅkara; T. Mar me mdzad; C. Dingguang rulai; J. Jōkō nyorai; K. Chŏnggwang yŏrae 定光如來). In Sanskrit, "Maker of Light"; a buddha of the past, who preceded the current buddha ŚĀKYAMUNI in the succession lineage of buddhas. It was in the presence of this buddha that the hermit SUMEDHA, who would eventually become ŚĀKYAMUNI Buddha, made his initial vow (PŪRVAPRAṆIDHĀNA) to attain buddhahood and received the prophecy (VYĀKARAṆA) of his enlightenment. Dīpaṃkara is sometimes presumed to be the fourth in a line of twenty-seven buddhas preceding Śākyamuni, but the first to have met the BODHISATTVA who would become the current Buddha. He is therefore sometimes referred to as the first of twenty-four previous buddhas, or the fourth of twenty-eight, the last being Śākyamuni. Later enumerations found in Sanskrit and Chinese Mahāyāna texts count as many as eighty-one predecessor buddhas. Dīpaṃkara is said to have lived on earth for one hundred thousand years, three thousand of which he passed before he met a worthy recipient of his dharma. His name is explained by the legend of his birth. According to the MAHĀVASTU, he was born on an island that miraculously appeared in a bathing tank as his mother neared childbirth, at which point a great many lamps appeared. An alternate name of this buddha, Dvīpaṃkara, means "Island Maker." He is frequently depicted to the left of Śākyamuni Buddha and MAITREYA in a triad of the three buddhas of the past, present, and future. His right hand is commonly in the "gesture of fearlessness" (ABHAYAMUDRĀ), and he either stands or sits.

**Dīpaṃkaraśrījñāna**. See ATIŚA DĪPAṂKARAŚRĪJÑĀNA.

**Dīpavaṃsa**. In Pāli, the "Island Chronicle"; the earliest surviving Pāli chronicle of Sri Lanka. Written in verse, the *Dīpavaṃsa* is based on a collation of earlier Sinhalese commentaries passed down in the MAHĀVIHĀRA tradition. In its present form, it probably dates from the fourth-century CE. The bulk of the work concerns the history of THERAVĀDA Buddhism in Sri Lanka from the conversion of the Sinhalese king DEVĀNAṂPIYATISSA by the elder MAHINDA in the third-century BCE to the reign of king Mahāsena in the fourth-century CE. Immensely important to the development of Theravāda historiography, the *Dīpavaṃsa* contains the earliest Pāli accounts of the Indian emperor AŚOKA and his patronage of the third

Buddhist council (see COUNCIL, THIRD) at Pāṭaliputta (S. PĀṬALIPUTRA). It also reports on the dispatch of missionaries to nine foreign lands at the command of MOGGALIPUTTATISSA, the leader of the third council. These lands included Sīhaḷadīpa (Sri Lanka) and Suvaṇṇabhūmi, the latter variously identified by Buddhist geographers as Lower Burma, the Malay Peninsula, and/or Thailand. The *Dīpavaṃsa* provided the basic outline and contents for the later MAHĀVAṂSA, and it is quoted in the *Bāhiranidāna*, the historical introduction to the VINAYA commentary (SAMANTAPĀSĀDIKĀ). A critical edition and English translation of the Dīpavaṃsa was produced by Hermann Oldenberg in 1879, entitled *The Dipavaṃsa: An Ancient Buddhist Historical Record.*

**Dīrghāgama**. (T. Lung ring po; C. Chang Ahan jing; J. Jōagongyō; K. Chang Aham kyŏng 長阿含經). In Sanskrit, "The Collection of Long Scriptures"; the Sanskrit scriptural collection (ĀGAMA) that is analogous to the Pāli DĪGHANIKĀYA. (All but three of the *Dīrghāgama*'s thirty SŪTRAS have equivalents in the Pāli *Dīghanikāya.*) The Sanskrit recension was long lost and survived only in a Chinese translation made in 413 CE by BUDDHAYAŚAS and ZHU FONIAN; that Chinese recension is attributed to the DHARMAGUPTAKA school. In the 1990s, however, extensive fragments of a Sanskrit recension of the *Dīrghāgama* in BRĀHMĪ script were discovered in Afghanistan, a recension that is instead associated with the SARVĀSTIVĀDA school or its MŪLASARVĀSTIVĀDA offshoot. These fragments, which constitute about fifty-five percent of the complete manuscript, are the object of intensive scholarly investigation. Small fragments of this same Sarvāstivāda or Mūlasarvāstivāda recension have also been discovered in Central Asia. All three major recensions of the *Dīrghāgama* (including the Pāli *Dīghanikāya*) have a tripartite structure, but two of the three sections in the Sarvāstivāda manuscript are radically different from the other two recensions, suggesting that it comes from an independent textual lineage. In the Sarvāstivāda Sanskrit recension, part one, the "six sūtra section" (ṣaṭsūtrakanipāta), and part two, the "section on pairs" (yuganipāta), have no counterpart in the Pāli or Dharmaguptaka recensions. Part three, the "section on morality" (śīlaskandhanipāta), has an analogue in the other two recensions, but the titles and sequence of the incorporated sūtras differs. The first section of the Sarvāstivāda *Dīrghāgama* with its six major sūtras—the *Daśottarasūtra* (P. DASUTTARASUTTA), *Arthavistarasūtra, Saṃgītisūtra* (P. SAṄGĪTISUTTA), *Catuspariṣatsūtra, Mahāvadānasūtra* (P. MAHĀPADĀNASUTTANTA), and MAHĀPARNIRVĀṆASŪTRA (P. MAHĀPARINIBBĀNASUTTANTA)—was not preserved in the Afghan manuscripts and is extant only in fragments from Central Asia, where it was popular in its own right and often circulated independently.

**disciple**. See ŚRĀVAKA.

**diṭṭhivisuddhi**. In Pāli, "purity of understanding"; the third of seven purities (P. visuddhi; S. VIŚUDDHI) that are to be developed along the path to liberation according to THERAVĀDA Buddhist soteriological theory. In the VISUDDHIMAGGA, purity of understanding refers to correct knowledge according to reality (YATHĀBHŪTA) of the nature of mentality and materiality (NĀMARŪPA) through reliance on discriminative wisdom, having overcome all mistaken belief in the existence of a perduring soul (attan; S. ĀTMAN). The ordinary person (puggala; S. PUDGALA) and, indeed, all of the phenomenal universe or realm of rebirth (SAṂSĀRA) are comprised merely of mentality and materiality. Mind and matter, whether taken singly or together, do not constitute a self; but there is also no self existing apart from mind and matter that possesses them as their controller. Rather, the self is to be correctly regarded as merely a conventional expression (vohāradesanā) that does not designate a real, existing thing. The purity of understanding thus reveals that everything that exists is selfless (anattā; S. ANĀTMAN). Such an understanding of the selflessness of mind and matter penetrates the veil of conventional truth (sammutisacca; S. SAṂVṚTISATYA) and apprehends ultimate truth (paramatthasacca; S. PARAMĀRTHASATYA).

**divine ear**. See DIVYAŚROTRA.

**divine eye**. See DIVYACAKṢUS.

**divyacakṣus**. (P. dibbacakkhu; T. lha'i mig; C. tianyan; J. tengen; K. ch'ŏnan 天眼). In Sanskrit, lit. "divine eye," viz., "clairvoyance"; one of the five (or six) superknowledges (ABHIJÑĀ) and one of the three "knowledges" (TRIVIDYĀ). The divine eye refers to the ability to observe things from afar, as well as to see the "mind-made bodies" (MANOMAYAKĀYA) that are the products of meditation or enlightenment. It also provides the ability to observe where beings will be reborn after they die (S. CYUTYUPAPĀDĀNUSMṚTI), the second of the TRIVIDYĀ. One who possesses this power sees the disappearance and arising of beings as low or noble, beautiful or ugly, etc., according to their wholesome and unwholesome deeds (KARMAN) in body, speech, and mind. Those who revile the noble ones (ĀRYAPUDGALA), hold perverse views (MITHYĀDṚṢṬI), and act in accordance with perverse views are observed to be reborn in lower realms of existence, or in painful realms such as the hells. Those who honor the noble ones, hold right views, and act in accordance with right views are observed to be reborn in higher realms of existence, and in pleasant realms such as the heavens. On the night of his enlightenment, the Buddha gained the divine eye during the second watch of the night. This superknowledge is considered to be a mundane (LAUKIKA) achievement and is gained through refinement of the fourth stage of meditative absorption (DHYĀNA; RŪPĀVACARADHYĀNA).

**divyaśrotra**. (P. dibbasota; T. lha'i rna ba; C. tian'er; J. tenni; K. ch'ŏni 天耳). In Sanskrit, lit. "divine ear," viz., "clairaudience"; one of the five (or six) superknowledges (ABHIJÑĀ). With the divine ear, one can hear heavenly and earthly sounds both far and near just as if one were a divinity. This superknowledge is considered to be a mundane (LAUKIKA) achievement and is gained through refinement of the fourth stage of meditative absorption (DHYĀNA; RŪPĀVACARADHYĀNA).

**Divyāvadāna**. In Sanskrit, "Divine Exploits"; a collection of thirty-eight "heroic tales" or "narratives" (AVADĀNA). Avadānas are the tenth of the twelvefold (DVĀDAŚĀṄGA[PRAVACANA]) categorization of the traditional genres of Buddhist literature and relate the past and present deeds of a person, either lay or ordained, who in some specific fashion exemplifies Buddhist ethics and practice. The present characters in the stories in the *Divyāvadāna* are often identified as persons whom the Buddha encountered in a former life. Thus, its tales have a narrative structure similar to JĀTAKA stories, in which an event in the present offers an opportunity to recount a story from the past, which in turn illuminates details regarding present circumstances. Themes that run throughout the *Divyāvadāna* include the realization of positive or negative consequences of action (KARMAN), the importance of moral discipline, and the great merit (PUṆYA) that can be accrued through service or reverence offered to the buddhas or to sites related to the buddhas, such as a STŪPA. The *Divyāvadāna* includes thirty-six avadānas and two SŪTRAs. Famous stories found in the *Divyāvadāna* collection include the *Pūrṇāvadāna*, the story of the monk PŪRṆA, and the AŚOKĀVADĀNA, which recounts the birth, life, and reign of King AŚOKA, the monarch whom the Buddhist tradition considers the great protector of the religion. Although the style and language of the works vary tremendously, more than half of the tales also appear in the MŪLASARVĀSTIVĀDA VINAYA. Given their debt to vinaya literature, it is not surprising that many of the tales in the *Divyāvadāna* often make reference to points of monastic discipline (VINAYA). This association with the Mūlasarvāstivāda vinaya suggests that these stories could date as far back as the beginning of the Common Era. However, the oldest extant manuscript of the *Divyāvadāna* dates only to the seventeenth century, and there is no reference to a text by that title in a Buddhist source prior to that date. There also is no Tibetan or Chinese translation of the text, although many of its stories are found in the Tibetan and Chinese canons. (For example, twenty-one of the thirty-eight stories of the collection are found in the vinaya section of the Tibetan canon.) This has led some scholars to conclude that, although the stories themselves are quite old, the particular compilation as the *Divyāvadāna* may be rather late. A number of stories from the *Divyāvadāna* were translated by EUGÈNE BURNOUF in his 1844 *Introduction à l'histoire du Buddhisme indien*. The first Sanskrit edition of the entire text was undertaken in 1866 by Edward B. Cowell and Robert A. Neil. The *Divyāvadāna* legends had a significant influence on Buddhist art and were often the subject of Buddhist sculptures and paintings. For instance, in the "Sahasodgata" chapter of this collection, the Buddha describes the "wheel of existence" (BHAVACAKRA), which became a popular subject of painting in many of the Buddhist traditions.

**Diyu bian[xiang]**. (J. Jigoku hen[sō]; K. Chiok pyŏn[sang] 地獄變[相]). In Chinese, "transformation tableaux of the hells"; pictorial representations of scenes from various hells, which were used as dramatic visual aids in storytelling and preaching. Often graphic and gory, these paintings depict the denizens of hells (NĀRAKA) as being variously devoured by beasts, boiled in cauldrons, inundated in rivers of blood, having their limbs amputated, etc. In East Asia, one of the earliest reported examples of this type of transformation tableaux (BIANXIANG) was in the form of paintings made on the walls of the Jingong monastery in 736 by the famous Tang-dynasty artist Wu Daozi. Legend has it that the sensationalized depictions of the hells in this transformation tableaux so shocked the butchers of the Tang capital that they all switched professions. See also AMITUO JINGTU BIAN; JINGTU BIAN.

**dkar po chig thub**. (karpo chiktup). In Tibetan, "self-sufficient white [remedy]" or "white panacea"; in Tibetan pharmacology, a single remedy that has the ability to effect a cure by itself alone. In Tibetan Buddhism, the term was used as a metaphor to describe certain doctrines or methods said to be self-sufficient for bringing about awakening. Although found in various contexts, the term is best known from its use by members of the DWAGS PO BKA' BRGYUD, including SGAM PO PA BSOD NAMS RIN CHEN and his nephew's disciple BLA MA ZHANG. This method is often equated with the introduction to the nature of mind (sems kyi ngo sprod) or the direct realization of the mind's true nature, and is deeply rooted in the tradition of MAHĀMUDRĀ transmitted by Sgam po pa. In Sgam po pa's own words, "I value the realization of the nature of mind as better than excellent meditation." Some Tibetan scholars, most notably SA SKYA PAṆḌITA KUN DGA' RGYAL MTSHAN, rejected the notion that any single method or factor (even insight into ŚŪNYATĀ, or emptiness) could be soteriologically sufficient. He also argued that the fruit of mahāmudrā practice could never be gained through wholly nonconceptual means. Nor, he argued, could it be gained outside of strictly tantric practice, in contrast to Sgam po pa's tradition, which advocated both SŪTRA and TANTRA forms of mahāmudrā. Such arguments often disparagingly associate dkar po chig thub with the subitism of MOHEYAN, the Chinese CHAN protagonist in the BSAM YAS DEBATE, who is known to have also used the metaphor.

**Dkon mchog rgyal po**. (Könchok Gyalpo) (1034–1102). A Tibetan master renowned as the founder of the SA SKYA sect of Tibetan Buddhism. He was a member of the 'Khon clan and a descendent of one of the first seven Tibetans to be ordained as a Buddhist monk (SAD MI BDUN). He studied primarily under the translator 'BROG MI SHĀKYA YE SHES, receiving teachings and initiations of the new translations (GSAR MA), particularly the HEVAJRATANTRA. He was also instructed in the doctrine of "path and result" (LAM 'BRAS), which had originally been transmitted by the great Indian adept VIRŪPA.

In 1073, Dkon mchog rgyal po founded SA SKYA monastery, one of the sect's principal institutions, and the seat of Tibetan political power for nearly a century; he also served as its first abbot. His son, SA CHEN KUN DGA' SNYING PO, became another important Sa skya hierarch and served as the monastery's third abbot.

**Dōchū**. (J) (道忠). See MUJAKU DŌCHŪ.

**Dōgen Kigen**. (道元希玄) (1200–1253). Japanese ZEN monk who is regarded as the founder of the SŌTŌSHŪ. After losing both his parents at an early age, Dōgen became the student of a relative, the monk Ryōkan (d.u.), who lived at the base of HIEIZAN, the headquarters of the TENDAI school (C. TIANTAI) in 1212; Ryōkan subsequently recommended that Dōgen study at the famed training center of Senkōbō. The next year, Dōgen was ordained by Kōen (d.u.), the abbot of the powerful Tendai monastery of ENRYAKUJI. Dōgen was later visited by the monk Kōin (1145–1216) of Onjōji, who suggested the eminent Japanese monk MYŌAN EISAI as a more suitable teacher. Dōgen visited Eisai at his monastery of KENNINJI and became a student of Eisai's disciple Myōzen (1184–1225). In 1223, Dōgen accompanied Myōzen to China as his attendant and made a pilgrimage to various important monastic centers on Mts. Tiantong, Jing, and Yuwang. Before returning to Japan in 1227, Dōgen made another trip in 1225 to Mt. Tiantong to study with the CAODONG ZONG Chan master TIANTONG RUJING (1162–1227), from whom he is said to have received dharma transmission. During his time there, Dōgen overheard Rujing scolding a monk who was sleeping, saying, "The practice of zazen (C. ZUOCHAN) is the sloughing off of body and mind. What does sleeping accomplish?" Dōgen reports that he experienced awakening upon hearing Rujing's words "sloughing off body and mind" (SHINJIN DATSURAKU), a phrase that would figure prominently in his later writings. The phrase, however, is not common in the Chan tradition, and scholars have questioned whether Dōgen's spoken Chinese was up to the task of understanding Rujing's oral instructions. Dōgen also attributes to Rujing's influence the practice of SHIKAN TAZA, or "just sitting," and the notion of the identity of practice and attainment: that to sit correctly in meditative posture is to enact one's own buddhahood. After Rujing's death, Dōgen returned to Japan, famously reporting that he had learned only that noses are vertical and eyes are horizontal. He returned to Kenninji, but relocated two years later in 1229 to the monastery of Anyōin in Fukakusa. In 1233, Dōgen moved to Kōshōji, on the outskirts of Kyōto, where he established one of the first monasteries in Japan modeled on Song-dynasty Chan monastic practice. Dōgen resided there for the next ten years and attracted a large following, including several adherents of the DARUMASHŪ, who became influential in his burgeoning community. When the powerful monastery of Tōfukuji was established by his RINZAISHŪ rival ENNI BEN'EN, Dōgen moved again to remote area of Echizen (present-day Fukui prefecture), where he was invited to reside at the newly established monastery of Daibutsuji; Dōgen renamed the monastery EIHEIJI in 1246. There, he composed several chapters of his magnum opus, SHŌBŌGENZŌ ("Treasury of the True Dharma Eye"). In 1253, as his health declined, Dōgen entrusted Eiheiji to his successor Koun Ejō (1198–1280), a former disciple of the Darumashū founder DAINICHIBŌ NŌNIN, and left for Kyōto to seek medical treatment. He died that same year. Dōgen was a prolific writer whose work includes the FUKAN ZAZENGI, EIHEI SHINGI, *Eihei kōroku*, BENDŌWA, HŌKYŌKI, GAKUDŌ YŌJINSHU, *Tenzo kyōkun*, and others. Dōgen's voluminous oeuvre has been extremely influential in the modern construction of the Japanese Zen tradition and its portrayal in Western literature. See also GENJŌ KŌAN; SHIKAN TAZA.

**dohā**. (T. nyams mgur). In Sanskrit, the name of a meter in poetry; hence, a name for a poetic form of religious expression most commonly employing this meter, which began to appear as early as the seventh century CE. These verses are of varying lengths, usually in rhymed couplets, and are composed in APABHRAṂŚA, an early medieval protovernacular from northeastern India. These songs offer an expression of the beauty and simplicity of tantric experience (the Tibetan translation means "song of experience"). There are collections of dohā by the SIDDHAS TILOPA, Kṛṣṇācārya (Kāṇha), and SARAHA (see MAHĀSIDDHA); Saraha's DOHĀKOŚA ("Treasury of Dohā Verses") was especially influential in Tibet. In the early BKA' BRGYUD tradition, the songs (mgur) of MI LA RAS PA (see MI LA'I MGUR 'BUM) show the influence of dohā.

**Dohākośa**. [alt. Dohākośagīti] (T. Do ha mdzod). In Sanskrit, "Treasury of Dohā Verses"; a collection of DOHĀ verses sung by SARAHA (perhaps fl. in the tenth century, one of the eighty-four MAHĀSIDDHAS); the verses express the immediacy of the ultimate spiritual experience and the inadequacy of language to convey it, often using sarcasm to mock social conventions. At the same time, the work is based on the traditional tantric premise that meditative practice, motivated by BODHICITTA, and undertaken with devotion to one's GURU, can bring about the bliss of enlightenment within the present lifetime. The order and number of the verses vary significantly among the different versions of the text, reflecting the interests and views of the Nepalese or Tibetan compilers and exegetes. The verses were transmitted sixteen times to Tibet and gave rise to a large and varied commentarial literature; Advayavajra's (1007–1085) *Dohākośapañjikā* is extant in Sanskrit. See also DO HA SKOR GSUM.

**Dōhaku**. (J) (道白). See MANZAN DŌHAKU.

**Dōhan**. (道範) (1179–1252). A Kamakura-period SHINGON scholar-monk from KŌYASAN, who wrote extensively on the works of KŪKAI and KAKUBAN. He is well known for his esoteric writings on the PURE LAND, especially the *Himitsu nenbutsushō* ("Compendium on the Secret Contemplation of Buddha").

Dōhan was ordained at the age of fourteen under Myōnin (1148–1229) at Shōchiin, and he later studied under KAKUKAI at Keōin. In 1237, Dōhan was appointed head administrator of Shōchiin. In 1243, a violent dispute erupted between Kongōbuji and Daidenbōin, which resulted in the exile of Dōhan and around thirty other Kōyasan elders. Dōhan's travel diary, *Nankai rurōki* ("Record of Wandering by the Southern Sea"), records his time in exile on the island of Shikoku, traveling to many sites associated with Kūkai. One of his dharma lectures from his time in exile survives as *Dōhan goshōsoku* ("Dōhan's Letter"), a short discussion of AJIKAN, or contemplation of the letter "a." In 1249, Dōhan was pardoned by imperial decree and permitted to return to Kōyasan, where he passed away in 1252.

**Do ha skor gsum**. (Doha korsum). In Tibetan, "Three Cycles of Spiritual Songs"; a collection of spiritual songs (DOHĀ) composed by the Indian sage SARAHA. Originally recorded in an eastern APABHRAṂŚA dialect, they were later compiled and translated into Tibetan. The title refers to the work's three chapters: "king dohās," "queen dohās," and "people dohās," although there is some debate as to whether the divisions were Saraha's own or a later Tibetan innovation. See also DOHĀKOŚA.

**Dokuan Genkō**. (独庵玄光) (1630–1698). Japanese ZEN monk in the SŌTŌSHŪ. Dokuan was ordained by the monk Tenkoku (d.u.) at the temple of Kōdenji in his hometown of Saga. After traveling around the country on pilgrimage, Dokuan visited the émigré Chinese CHAN monk DAOZHE CHAOYUAN in Nagasaki and studied under him for eight years. When Daozhe returned to China in 1658, Dokuan continued his training under the Zen master Gesshū Sōrin (1614–1687) at Kōtaiji in Nagasaki and remained at Kōtaiji after Gesshū's death. Dokuan was a prolific writer whose work includes the *Gohōshū*, *Shūi sanbō kannō den*, and the *Zenaku genken hōō hen*.

**dokusan**. (C. ducan; K. tokch'am 獨參). In Japanese, lit. a "private consultation" between a ZEN student and master, which is conducted in the privacy of the master's room. This consultation is an important element of training in the Japanese RINZAISHŪ, and allows the master to check the progress of the student in his meditation, and the student to ask questions regarding his practice. Dokusan is also the formal occasion where the student is expected to express his understanding of a specific Zen kōan (GONG'AN) so that the master can gauge his development (see J. JAKUGO; C. ZHUOYU).

**Dol po pa Shes rab rgyal mtshan**. (Dolpopa Sherap Gyaltsen) (1292–1361). An innovative and controversial Tibetan Buddhist scholar, who is regarded as an early master of the JO NANG lineage. He is best known for promulgating the view of extrinsic emptiness (GZHAN STONG), for his writings on the KĀLACAKRATANTRA, and for constructing a massive multiroom STŪPA temple (SKU 'BUM) above JO NANG PHUN TSHOGS GLING monastery. He was born in the region of Dol po in present-day northwestern Nepal, from which his toponym (literally "the man from Dol po") is derived. Although his family was affiliated with the RNYING MA sect of Tibetan Buddhism, he formed an early connection with the SA SKYA teacher Skyi ston 'Jam dbyangs grags pa rgyal mtshan (Gyidön Jamyang Drakpa Gyaltsen, d.u.). As a seventeen-year-old novice monk, Dol po pa fled his home, against the wishes of his parents and without their knowledge, in order to study with this master. He arrived first in the nearby region of Mustang and in 1312 continued on to the Tibetan monastery of SA SKYA itself. He was a gifted student, mastering a broad range of MAHĀYĀNA subjects in a short period of time. His erudition was so great that while still in his early twenties he earned the title "omniscient" (kun mkhyen), an epithet by which he was known for the rest of his life. He was ordained as a BHIKṢU in 1314, going on to study with leadings masters from various sects, including the third KARMA PA. He spent several years in strict meditation retreat, during which time he began to formulate his understanding of extrinsic emptiness. In 1326 he formally ascended the abbatial throne at Jo nang, dividing his time between meditative retreats and teaching the monastic community. In 1333, Dol po pa completed construction of the sku 'bum chen po stūpa, one of the largest in Tibet. Dol po pa developed a rich new vocabulary for discussing his controversial notion of extrinsic emptiness. Public reaction was mixed, and many Sa skya scholars in particular appear to have felt betrayed by this new doctrine, which seemed to contradict their own. Among his major works written at this time was the *Ri chos nges don rgya mtsho* ("The Ocean of Definitive Meaning: A Mountain Dharma"). Another of Dol po pa's major projects was a revised translation and reinterpretation of the *Kālacakratantra* and VIMALAPRABHĀ, both important sources for his major doctrinal theories. In 1338, Dol po pa retired from his position at Jo nang, after which he remained in isolated retreat, in part to discreetly avoid an invitation to the court of the Mongol ruler Toghon Temür (r. 1333–1370). By the end of his life, Dol po pa ranked as one of the leading masters of his time. During a 1358 trip to LHA SA toward the end of his life, the halls in which he taught literally collapsed from the enormous size of the crowds in attendance. On his return to Jo nang, he visited the monastery of ZHWA LU, home of another leading scholar and Kālacakra expert of the day, BU STON RIN CHEN GRUB. According to several accounts, Bu ston declined the opportunity to debate, but Dol po pa uttered the opening exclamation for debate as he departed, which cracked the walls of Bu ston's residence. While Dol po pa's views were considered unorthodox, even heterodox, particularly in the DGE LUGS sect, his works made a lasting impression on the landscape of Buddhism in Tibet.

**Ḍombī Heruka**. A tantric adept counted among the eighty-four MAHĀSIDDHAS, often depicted riding a tiger with his consort. As recorded in his hagiographies, he was originally king of the Indian region of MAGADHA and received teachings on the HEVAJRATANTRA from the SIDDHA VIRŪPA. These he practiced for twelve years in secret while continuing to skillfully administer his kingdom. He then secretly took a low-caste musician, a ḍombī, as his consort and continued his practice of TANTRA with her. (The word heruka is rendered khrag thung, "blood drinker," in Tibetan.) When his subjects discovered their king's transgression of customary social and caste restrictions, Ḍombī Heruka abdicated the throne and disappeared with his consort into the jungle, where they continued to practice tantric yoga for twelve years. Later, the kingdom was wrought with famine and the subjects searched for their former king to request his assistance. Ḍombī Heruka then emerged from the jungle astride a tigress, brandishing a snake in one hand. Displaying miraculous signs of his mastery, he denied the subjects' request and departed for the celestial realms. Ḍombī Heruka is an important member of the lineage of the *Hevajratantra* and, according to some accounts, was a disciple of NĀROPA as well as a teacher of ATIŚA DĪPAṂKARAŚRĪJÑĀNA. Seventeen texts attributed to him are preserved in the BSTAN 'GYUR section of the Tibetan Buddhist canon. He is also known as Ḍombīpa.

**Donglinsi**. (J. Tōrinji; K. Tongnimsa 東林寺). In Chinese, "Eastern Grove Monastery"; located in the forest on the eastern side of LUSHAN, a Buddhist sacred mountain in Jiangxi province. The monastery was founded between 380 CE and 386 CE by the early advocate of PURE LAND visualization LUSHAN HUIYUAN (334–416 CE) and became an important early center of Buddhism in China, especially of the White Lotus retreat society (BAILIAN SHE). The monastery also hosted such monks as Saṃghadeva, who translated important works of ABHIDHARMA and SARVĀSTIVĀDA scholasticism, and BUDDHABHADRA (359–429). Donglinsi continued to be a center of Buddhist activity during subsequent dynasties and its influence reached its zenith during the Tang dynasty, when it attracted both monks and leading literati, such as the renowned Tang poet BO JUYI (772–846 CE).

**Dongshan famen**. (J. Tōzan hōmon; K. Tongsan pŏmmun 東山法門). In Chinese, lit. "East Mountain Dharma Gate" or "East Mountain Teachings"; one of the principal early CHAN schools, which is associated with the putative fourth and fifth patriarchs of the tradition, DAOXIN (580–651) and HONGREN (602–675). The name of the school is a toponym for the location of Hongren's monastery, at Huangmei in Qizhou (present-day Hubei province). "East Mountain" refers to the easterly of the "twin peaks" of Mount Shuangfeng, where Hongren taught after the death of his master Daoxin, who had taught on the westerly peak; the term "East Mountain Teachings," however, is typically used to refer to the tradition associated with both masters. The designations Dongshan famen and Dongshan jingmen (East Mountain Pure Gate) first appear in the LENGQIE SHIZI JI ("Records of the Masters and Disciples of the Laṅkā[vatāra]") and were used in the Northern school of Chan (BEI ZONG) by SHENXIU (606?–706) and his successors to refer to the lineage and teachings that they had inherited from Daoxin and Hongren. ¶ Although later Chan lineage texts list Daoxin and Hongren as respectively the fourth and the fifth Chan patriarchs, succeeding BODHIDHARMA, HUIKE, and SENGCAN, the connection of the East Mountain lineage to these predecessors is tenuous at best and probably nonexistent. The earliest biography of Daoxin, recorded in the XU GAOSENG ZHUAN ("Supplementary Biographies of Eminent Monks"), not only does not posit any connection between Daoxin and the preceding three patriarchs, but does not even mention their names. This connection is first made explicit in the c. 713 CHUAN FABAO JI ("Annals of the Transmission of the Dharma-Jewel"), one of the earliest Chan "transmission of the lamplight" (CHUANDENG LU) lineage texts. Unlike many of the Chan "schools" that were associated with a single charismatic teacher, the "East Mountain Teachings" was unusual in that it had a single, enduring center in Huangmei, which attracted increasing numbers of students. Some five or six names of students who studied with Daoxin survive in the literature, with another twenty-five associated with Hongren. Although Hongren's biography in the *Chuan fabao ji* certainly exaggerates when it says that eight to nine out of every ten Buddhist practitioners in China studied under Hongren, there is no question that the number of students of the East Mountain Teachings grew significantly over two generations. ¶ The fundamental doctrines and practices of the East Mountain Teachings can be reconstructed on the basis of the two texts: the RUDAO ANXIN YAO FANGBIAN FAMEN ("Essentials of the Teachings of the Expedient Means of Entering the Path and Pacifying the Mind") and the XIUXIN YAO LUN ("Treatise on the Essentials of Cultivating the Mind"), ascribed respectively to Daoxin and Hongren. The *Rudao anxin yao fangbian famen*, which is included in the *Lengqie shizi ji,* employs the analogy of a mirror from the *Banzhou sanmei jing* (S. PRATYUTPANNABUDDHASAṂMUKHĀVASTHITASAMĀDHISŪTRA) to illustrate the insubstantiality of all phenomena, viz., one's sensory experiences are no more substantial than the reflections in a mirror. The text then presents the "single-practice SAMĀDHI" (YIXING SANMEI) as a practical means of accessing the path leading to NIRVĀṆA, based on the *Wenshushuo bore jing* ("Perfection of Wisdom Sūtra Spoken by MAÑJUŚRĪ"). Single-practice samādhi here refers to sitting in meditation, the supreme practice that subsumes all other practices; it is not one samādhi among others, as it is portrayed in the MOHE ZHIGUAN ("Great Calming and Contemplation"). Single-practice samādhi means to contemplate every single aspect of one's mental and physical existence until one realizes they are all empty, just like the reflections in the mirror, and "to guard that one without deviation" (shouyi buyi). The *Xiuxin yao lun*, which is attributed to Hongren, stresses the importance of "guarding the mind" (SHOUXIN). Here, the relationship between the pure mind and the afflictions (KLEŚA) is likened to that between the sun and clouds: the pure mind is obscured by afflictions, just as the sun is covered by layers of clouds, but if one can guard the mind so that it is kept free from false thoughts and delusions, the sun of NIRVĀṆA will then appear. The text suggests two specific meditation techniques for realizing this goal: one is continuously to visualize the original, pure mind (viz., the sun) so that it shines without obscuration; the other is to concentrate on one's own deluded thoughts (the clouds) until they disappear. These two techniques purport to "guard the mind" so that delusion can never recur. The East Mountain Teachings laid a firm foundation for the doctrines and practices of later Chan traditions like the Northern school.

**Dongshan Liangjie**. (J. Tōzan Ryōkai; K. Tongsan Yanggae 洞山良价) (807–869). Chinese CHAN master of the Tang dynasty and reputed founder of the CAODONG lineage of Chan; also known as Xinfeng. Dongshan was a native of Yuezhou in present-day Zhejiang province. He left home at an early age and became the student of the Chan master Lingmo (747–818). Having received full monastic precepts from a certain VINAYA master Rui on SONGSHAN, Dongshan visited the Chan masters NANQUAN PUYUAN and GUISHAN LINGYOU and later continued his studies under Yunyan Tancheng (782–841). Dongshan is said to have attained awakening under Yunyan's guidance and eventually inherited his lineage. During the HUICHANG FANAN, Dongshan remained in hiding until the persecution ran its course, eventually reemerging at Xinfeng tong in Jiangxi province. With the support of his followers, Dongshan later established the monastery Guangfusi (later renamed Puli yuan) on Mt. Dong (Dongshan), whence he acquired his toponym. Among his many disciples, Yunju Daoying (d. 902) and CAOSHAN BENJI are most famous. Dongshan was renowned for his poetry and verse compositions and his teaching of the "five ranks" (WUWEI). His teachings are recorded in the *Dongshan yulu* ("The Record of Dongshan"), but the most famous of his works is the BAOJING SANMEI ("Jeweled-Mirror Samādhi"), a definitive verse on enlightenment and practice from the standpoint of the CAODONG ZONG. The *Baojing sanmei* emphasizes the "original enlightenment" (BENJUE; cf. HONGAKU) of sentient beings and the futility of seeking that enlightenment through conscious thought. Instead, the song urges its audience to allow one's inherently pure, enlightened nature to "silently illuminate" itself through meditation (see MOZHAO CHAN), as the Buddha did under the BODHI TREE.

**Dongshan Shouchu**. (J. Tōsan Shusho; K. Tongsan Such'o 洞山守初) (910–990). Successor in the Chinese YUNMEN lineage of the CHAN school. See MA SANJIN.

**Dongta lü zong**. (J. Tōtō Risshū; K. Tongt'ap yul chong 東塔律宗). In Chinese, the "East Pagoda VINAYA School"; one of the three major exegetical traditions of the DHARMAGUPTAKA school's SIFEN LÜ ("Four-Part Vinaya"); the other traditions are DAOXUAN's NANSHAN LÜ ZONG (South Mountain) and Fali's XIANGBU LÜ ZONG (Xiang Region) vinaya schools. The reputed patriarch of the Dongta tradition is the vinaya master HUAISU. This exegetical tradition derived its name from Huaisu's residence near the east pagoda of the monastery of Xidayuansi in the Chinese capital of Chang'an. Huaisu's disciple Fashen (d.u.) firmly established his teacher's *Sifen lü kaizong ji* (composed in 682), also known as the "new commentary" (xinshu), as the authoritative commentary on the "Four-Part Vinaya." The tradition thrived under Emperor Daizong (r. 762–779), thanks to the grand councilor's support of Huaisu, but was subsequently eclipsed by the Nanshan school.

**Dongyang dashi**. (C) (東陽大士). See FU DASHI.

**doors of liberation**. See VIMOKṢAMUKHA.

**Dorzhiev, Agvan**. (T. Ngag dbang rdo rje) (1854–1938). Influential Mongol-Russian monk in the Tibetan Buddhist tradition; born in the Siberian region of Buryatia to a seminomadic Buddhist family. As a child, Dorzhiev was introduced to Buddhism at the monastery at Atsagat, receiving his first tantric empowerment (ABHIṢEKA) at the age of thirteen. He continued his education in Urga after his father died in 1868, at which time there were thirteen thousand monks in the city. For a time he was married to a woman named Kholintsog and worked in the local government. In 1873, he began his first journey to LHA SA and spent a few months in eastern China. Because of his linguistic and academic prowess, he was sent to 'BRAS SPUNGS monastery, where he became a scholar at Sgo mang (Gomang) College. In 1880, he settled in Lha sa, and rapidly completed his DGE BSHES degree. By 1888, he was teaching logic, debate, and language at 'Bras spungs. At this time, the thirteenth DALAI LAMA was twelve or thirteen years old, and Dorzhiev became one of his religious teachers and political advisors. Dorzhiev displayed great ability in political diplomacy and served as the only emissary between Russia and Tibet for many years. He feared that British influence in Tibet could be detrimental to the future of the country, and advised the Dalai Lama to initiate relations between Lha sa and St. Petersburg as a counter. In 1898, Prince Ukhtomsky summoned him to St. Petersburg, where he met with Tsar Nicholas II. From there, he traveled to Paris, where he lectured on Buddhism at the Musée Guimet. He then went to Kalmykia and Buryatia before returning to Lha sa. Dorzhiev sought to improve the quality of Buddhist practice in Russia, specifically in Buryatia and Kalmykia, where he opened monasteries, initiated monks, and opened a school for Tibetan Buddhist doctors. In 1915 he opened a temple and monastery in St. Petersburg, the first in the West. Dorzhiev was arrested at the onset of the "Red Terror" of 1918, but was soon released. Buddhism remained comparatively inviolable over the next decade, although other Russian religions suffered. Dorzhiev wrote his memoirs in Tibetan around 1924. In 1922, an "All-Buryat Buddhist Congress" was held, followed by a 1927 "Congress of Soviet Buddhists" in Moscow. Russian Buddhism entered a bleak period after the death of Lenin in 1924; in 1930, an antireligion campaign began in Buryatia, during which the aged Dorzhiev was placed under house arrest. He wrote his will in 1937, at which time he left house arrest in Leningrad and traveled to

Ulan Udé, Buryatia. In Ulan Udé, he was arrested and interrogated before being sent to the prison hospital, where he died in January of 1938.

**doṣa**. (P. dosa; T. skyon/zhe sdang; C. guo; J. ka; K. kwa 過). In Sanskrit, "fault"; a general term for a mental or physical defect, used also as a synonym for affliction (KLEŚA). In addition, the classical Sanskrit term DVEṢA (P. dosa), "anger," is frequently written as doṣa in BUDDHIST HYBRID SANSKRIT.

**Dōshō**. (道昭) (629–700). Japanese monk and reputed founder of the Japanese Hossō (YOGĀCĀRA) school in the seventh century. A native of Kawachi province, Dōshō became renowned for his strict adherence to the precepts while he was residing at the monastery of Gangōji. In 653, Dōshō made a pilgrimage to China, where he studied under the Chinese monk–translator and Yogācāra scholar XUANZANG. In 660, Dōshō returned to Gangōji and devoted the rest of his life to the dissemination of the Yogācāra teachings that he had brought back with him from China.

**doubt**. See VICIKITSĀ; YIQING.

**Dpa' bo Gtsug lag phreng ba**. (Pawo Tsuklak Trengwa) (1504–1566). A renowned master and historian of the KARMA BKA' BRGYUD sect of Tibetan Buddhism, second in the line of DPA' BO INCARNATIONS. Born in the region of Snye thang (Nyethang), south of LHA SA in central Tibet, Gtsug lag phreng ba was recognized at the age of five as the embodiment of his predecessor, Dpa' bo Chos dbang lhun grub (Pawo Chöwang Lhundrup). At nine, he received monastic ordination from the fourth ZHWA DMAR, Chos grags ye shes (Chödrak Yeshe, 1453–1524), and he later studied with masters such as Dwags po paṇḍita Chos rgyal Bstan pa'i rgyal mtshan (Chögyal Tenpe Gyaltsen, b. fifteenth century), the mad yogin of central Tibet Dbus smyon Kun dga' bzang po (Ü Nyön Kunga Sangpo, 1458–1532) Heruka. At the age of twenty-nine he received the name Gtsug lag phreng ba from the eighth KARMA PA MI BSKYOD RDO RJE. He was active throughout his life in the southern Tibetan region of LHO BRAG; he became the abbot of LHA LUNG monastery and later renovated SRAS MKHAR DGU THOG, the famed site of MI LA RAS PA's tower, commissioning many religious paintings, adding a large a golden roof and constructing a large monastic complex. Among Gtsug lag 'phreng ba's major literary works is the famous history of Indian and Tibetan Buddhism CHOS 'BYUNG MKHAS PA'I DGA' STON, composed between 1544 and 1564.

**Dpa' bo incarnations**. (Pawo). A lineage of incarnate lamas (SPRUL SKU), members of the KARMA BKA' BRGYUD sect of Tibetan Buddhism and traditionally responsible for the propitiation of the sect's protector deities. The second incarnation, DPA' BO GTSUG LAG 'PHRENG BA, was a renowned scholar and historian. The incarnation line includes:

1. Chos dbang lhun grub (Chöwang Lhundrup, 1440–1503)
2. Gtsug lag phreng ba (Tsuklak Trengwa, 1504–1566)
3. Gtsug lag rgya mtsho (Tsuklak Gyatso, 1568–1630)
4. Gtsug lag kun bzang (Tsuklak Kunsang, b.1633)
5. Gtsug lag 'phrin las rgya mtsho (Tsuklak Trinle Gyatso, 1650–1699)
6. Gtsug lag chos kyi don grub (Tsuklak Chökyi Döndrup, 1701–1718?)
7. Gtsug lag dga' ba (Tsuklak Gawa, 1718–1781)
8. Gtsug lag chos kyi rgyal po (Tsuklak Chökyi Gyalpo, d.u.)
9. Gtsug lag nyin byed (Tsuklak Nyinje, d. 1911)
10. Gtsug lag smra ba'i dbang phyug (Tsuklak Mawe Wangchuk, 1912–1991)
11. Gtsug lag smra ba'i rta dbyang (Tsuklak Mawe Tayang, b. 1993)

**Dpal brtsegs**. (Paltsek) (fl. late eighth-early ninth centuries). A translator (LO TSĀ BA) during the early spread of Buddhism in Tibet; a native of 'Phan yul of the Ska ba (Kawa) clan; translator of a large number of VINAYA, PRAJÑĀPĀRAMITĀ, and tantric texts, and the author of the *Lta ba'i rim pa'i man ngag* (also known as *Snang ba bcu bdun*) and *Chos kyi rnam grangs kyi brjed byang*, a work that mainly consists of a list of standard Buddhist terms. See also YE SHES SDE; KLU'I RGYAL MTSHAN.

**Dpal ldan lha mo**. (S. Śrīdevī). In Tibetan, "Glorious Goddess"; a literal translation of the Sanskrit name for a form of a female divinity ubiquitous in the northeast and mountainous regions of the Indian subcontinent. In her usual form, she has one face, is wrathful, holds a kaḍga (sword) and KAPĀLA (skull cup), and rides a barren mule above a churning ocean of blood. The mule has an eye in his rump, caused by an arrow shot by her husband after she killed their son and used his skin as a saddle. She is found in the retinue (parivāra) of the Sarvavighnavināyaka (Obstacle-Removing) MAHĀKĀLA, but as a central figure she is surrounded by a large retinue that includes the goddesses Ākāśāmbarā, Svayambhu-rājñī, and Nīleśvarī. She is always a supramundane (LOKOTTARA) being and is considered to be a protector of all Tibet; in this role she is seen as a wrathful form of TĀRĀ. In the DGE LUGS sect, she is an important protector, particularly as the main protectress of the DALAI LAMAS; she is propitiated daily in rituals and a THANG KA of her is always kept in the presence of the Dalai Lama. Each Dalai Lama would try to visit her sacred lake, LHA MO BLA MTSHO, at least once during his life to receive visions on the water's surface regarding his future activities and death, a tradition said to date back to the first Dalai Lama, DGE 'DUN GRUB. The lake is also believed to display signs concerning the future rebirth of the Dalai Lama and PAṆ CHEN LAMA. Most recently, in 1933 the regent of Tibet, Rwa sgreng Rin po che, saw visions in the lake that indicated the birthplace and circumstances of the fourteenth Dalai Lama. At Tibetan Buddhist temples, long lines of ordinary people are often seen at the chapel of Dpal ldan lha mo carrying small bottles of chang (barley beer) or black tea as offerings for her.

**Dpal sprul Rin po che**. (Patrul Rinpoche) (1808–1887). One of the most important teachers of the RNYING MA sect of Tibetan Buddhism during the nineteenth century, famous for his great humility and simple lifestyle. Recognized as an incarnate lama (SPRUL SKU) while a child, Dpal sprul Rin po che trained under the great ascetic 'Jigs med rgyal ba'i myu gu (Jigme Gyalwe Nyugu), himself a disciple of the renowned treasure revealer (GTER STON) 'JIGS MED GLING PA, from whom he received instructions on the KLONG CHEN SNYING THIG, "Heart Essence of the Great Expanse." He later studied with many other great masters, including MDO MKHYEN RTSE YE SHES RDO RJE, mind emanation (thugs sprul) of 'Jigs med gling pa. Although he established himself as one of the foremost scholars of his time, Dpal sprul Rin po che emulated the renunciate lifestyle of his masters, wandering from place to place with few possessions, often in the guise of an ordinary beggar. He was known for his exceptional kindness, treating both king and pauper with equal compassion. The author of numerous commentaries and treatises on Buddhist philosophy and doctrine, he is perhaps best known for his KUN BZANG BLA MA'I ZHAL LUNG ("Words of My Perfect Teacher"), an explanation of the preliminary practices of the klong chen snying thig. Together with other great lamas of eastern Tibet, Dpal sprul Rin po che was also an active participant in the so-called RIS MED (nonsectarian) movement, which sought to cut through the rampant sectarian controversies of the time. According to one account, when asked what religious affiliation he maintained, Dpal sprul Rinpoche famously remarked that he was only a follower of the Buddha. He is also known as Rdza Dpal sprul (Dza Patrul) and O rgyan 'jigs med chos kyi dbang po.

**Dpal spungs**. (Palpung). A large fortress-like monastic compound located near SDE DGE in the eastern Tibetan region of Khams belonging to the BKA' BRGYUD sect of Tibetan Buddhism and serving as the seat of the TAI SI TU INCARNATION lineage; its full name is Dpal spungs thub brtan chos 'khor gling (Palpung Tupten Chökorling). The center was established in 1727 by the eighth Si tu CHOS KYI 'BYUNG GNAS, a great Bka' brgyud scholar, historian, and linguist, with support from Derge's ruler Bstan pa tshe ring (Tenpa Tsering, 1678–1738). Prior to this, the Si tu line mainly resided at the nearby Karma dgon monastery. Dpal spungs was also home to the nineteenth-century luminary 'JAM MGON KONG SPRUL BLO GROS MTHA' YAS and became one of the largest and most powerful Bka' brgyud institutions in eastern Tibet. An important monastic college (BSHAD GRWA) and several centers for practicing the traditional three-year meditation retreat are located nearby. Not far from Dpal spungs is one of the region's premier retreat locations, Tsa 'dra Rin chen brag—a locale reckoned to be equivalent in spiritual power to the famed region of TSĀ RI in southern Tibet. The founding of Dpal spungs coincides with the start of the so-called RIS MED (nonsectarian) movement in Khams.

**Dpal yul**. (Payul). The Tibetan short name of a monastery in Khams (now part of the Chinese province of Sichuan). The name is an abbreviation of Dpal yul rnam rgyal byang chub chos gling, one of the four main RNYING MA monasteries in eastern Tibet, the others being KAḤ THOG, RDZOGS CHEN, and ZHE CHEN; founded in 1665 by Kun bzang shes rab (1636–1699). The monastery specializes in the GTER MA (treasure text) teachings of KARMA CHAGS MED; members of the monastery follow a set course of preliminary practices and engage in a three-year retreat. The monastery, destroyed during the Chinese Cultural Revolution (1966–76), has been rebuilt and currently houses about three hundred monks. The eleventh khri 'dzin (throne-holder) Thub bstan legs bshad chos kyi sgra dbyangs, Penor Rin po che (1932–2009), established a new monastery called Rnam grol gling with great success near Bylakuppe in South India; at present it is the largest Rnying ma institution outside Tibet, with perhaps as many as five thousand monks and nuns. The present throne-holder is the fifth Karma sku chen (b. 1970).

**Drang nges legs bshad snying po**. See LEGS BSHAD SNYING PO.

**dravya**. (T. rdzas; C. shishi; J. jitsuji; K. silsa 實事). In Sanskrit "substance," "constituent," or "real entity"; a term with wide-ranging use in Buddhism, from the "ingredients" of a medicine or magic potion to "substance" in an ontological sense. The various schools of Indian Buddhism made use of the term in different ways. Although the term is virtually unknown in Pāli materials (where the equivalent is dabba), including its abhidhamma literature, in the VAIBHĀṢIKA school of the SARVĀSTIVĀDA ABHIDHARMA, dravya became virtually synonymous with DHARMA. The Vaibhāṣikas conceived that all things that were "real entities" (DRAVYA) had unique characteristics of their own (SVALAKṢAṆA), were not subject to any further division, and had specific modes of being (what the Vaibhāṣikas termed their "own being," or SVABHĀVA). All material objects were said to be composed of eight dravya: earth, water, fire, air, form, smell, taste, and touch. In MAHĀYĀNA, the YOGĀCĀRA school argued that because there is no external world, there were no physical constituents; only consciousness (VIJÑĀNA) possessed dravya. By contrast, the MADHYAMAKA school, in keeping with its doctrine of emptiness (ŚŪNYATĀ), saw dravya as almost a synonym of inherent existence (SVABHĀVA) and said that all things were ultimately devoid of dravya. See also DRAVYASAT.

**Dravya Mallaputra**. (P. Dabba Mallaputta; C. Tapomoluo; J. Tōbamara; K. Tappamara 沓婆摩羅). An important ARHAT, whom the Buddha declared to be foremost among his monk disciples in service (S. VAIYĀPṚTYA[KARA]; P. veyyāvaccakara) to the community of monks, specifically in assigning residence quarters and arranging meals. According to Pāli sources, Dravya (P. Dabba) belonged to the Malla clan and had a most unusual birth: he was born to his mother while her corpse was burning on the funeral pyre and was discovered lying amid the ashes after the flames were extinguished. He was seven when he first saw the Buddha and immediately asked his grandmother to allow him to join the order. She gave her consent and he became an arhat while he was being ordained as a novice. Because he was already enlightened, he was given the higher ordination as a BHIKṢU while he was still only seven years old. Wishing to be useful, Dravya assumed the task of assigning night lodgings to visiting monks. So diligent and efficient was the young boy that he quickly became famous. Monks used to arrive late in the evening intentionally so they could witness his special thaumaturgic skill: he would burst into flames and use his body as a lamp to show his guests to their quarters. Dravya appears to have had several encounters with the infamous "group of six" (S. ṢAḌVĀRGIKA), a notorious band of recalcitrant malefactors in the order. Twice these monks falsely accused him of seducing women, and once for neglecting his duties, but Dravya was vindicated of all charges. Dravya was fated to die young and had a premonition of his own demise. With his death imminent, he bid farewell to the Buddha and passed away in his presence amid a marvelous display of ṚDDHI power. Cf. DIANZUO.

**dravyasat**. (T. rdzas yod; C. shi you; J. jitsuu; K. sil yu 實有). In Sanskrit, "substantially existent," or "existent in substance"; a term used in Buddhist philosophical literature to describe phenomena whose inherent nature is more real than those designated as PRAJÑAPTISAT, "existent by imputation." The contrast drawn in doctrinal discussions between the way things appear to be and the way they exist in reality appears to have developed out of the early contrast drawn between the false view (MITHYĀDṚṢṬI) of a perduring self (ĀTMAN) and five real aggregates (SKANDHA). The five aggregates as the real constituents of compounded things were further elaborated into the theory of factors (DHARMA), which were generally conceived as dravyasat, although the ABHIDHARMA schools differed regarding how they defined the term and which phenomena fell into which category. In the SARVĀSTIVĀDA abhidharma, for example, dharmas are categorized as dravyasat because they have "inherent existence" (SVABHĀVA), while all compounded things, by contrast, are prajñaptisat, or merely conventional constructs that derive from dravyasat. In the MADHYAMAKA school of MAHĀYĀNA scholasticism, however, all things are considered to lack any inherent existence (NIḤSVABHĀVA). Therefore, Madhyamaka asserts that even dharmas are marked by emptiness (ŚŪNYATĀ) and thus nothing is "substantially existent" (dravyasat). In contrast to the Madhyamaka's exclusive rejection of anything being dravyasat, the YOGĀCĀRA school maintained that at least one thing, the flow of consciousness or the process of subjective imputation (VIJÑAPTI), was substantially existent (dravyasat). For Yogācāra followers, however, the reason that the flow of consciousness is dravyasat is not because it is free from causal conditioning and thereby involves inherent existence (svabhāva), but because the Yogācāra denies the ontological claim that causal conditioning involves the absence of svabhāva, or vice versa. Thus the flow of consciousness, even though it is causally conditioned, may still be conceived as "substantially existent" (dravyasat) because its inherent existence is "dependent" (PARATANTRA), one of the three natures (TRISVABHĀVA) recognized in the school. Another strand of Mahāyāna thought that asserts there is something that is substantially existent is the doctrine of the buddha-nature (BUDDHADHĀTU) or TATHĀGATAGARBHA. As the potentiality inherent in each sentient being to become a buddha, the tathāgatagarbha is sometimes said to be both empty (of all afflictions) and nonempty (of all the attributes and qualities inherent in enlightenment). In this context, there has been some dispute as to whether the buddhadhātu or tathāgatagarbha should be conceived as only dravyasat, or as both dravyasat and prajñaptisat.

**'dre**. Tibetan term for a class of baleful spirits that includes what might be termed demons, ghosts, and goblins in English.

**Droṇa**. (P. Doṇa; T. Bre bo; C. Xiangxing poluomen; J. Kōshō baramon; K. Hyangsŏng paramun 香姓婆羅門). A renowned brāhmaṇa who is remembered for resolving the dispute that arose over control of the Buddha's relics following his cremation. Droṇa was a brāhmaṇa with many disciples who came upon the Buddha once while traveling. After hearing the Buddha's discourse, he became a once-returner (ANĀGĀMIN) and wrote an extended verse eulogizing the Buddha. Droṇa was revered by the secular rulers of his day, so while he was sojourning in the city of KUŚINAGARĪ (P. Kusinārā), he was able to mediate among the various competing groups concerning who would take charge of the Buddha's relics (ŚARĪRA) following the teacher's cremation. His solution was to divide the relics into eight parts, which he distributed among the factions to take back to their regions for enshrinement. After the division of the relics into eight shares, there remained the ashes from the cremation fire and the bucket (droṇa) that Droṇa had used to divide the relics. Droṇa received permission to keep the bucket himself and erected a reliquary STŪPA in Kuśinagarī to house the vessel that had temporarily held the relics. A young brāhmaṇa who arrived late for the division of the relics received the ashes and built a tenth stūpa to house them.

**dṛṣṭi**. (P. diṭṭhi; T. lta ba; C. jian; J. ken; K. kyŏn 見). In Sanskrit, "view" or "opinion"; nearly always used pejoratively in Buddhism to refer to a "wrong view." In the AṬṬHAKAVAGGA chapter of the SUTTANIPĀTA, which seems to belong to the earliest stratum of Pāli Buddhist literature, the Buddha offers a rigorous indictment of the dangers inherent in "views" and displays a skepticism about religious dogmas in general, seeing them as virulent sources of attachment that lead ultimately to conceit, quarrels, and divisiveness. Some scholars have suggested that the thoroughgoing critique of views may have been the core teaching of Buddhism and might have served as the prototype of the later MADHYAMAKA logical approach of reductio ad absurdum, which sought to demonstrate the fallacies inherent in any philosophical statement. A standardized list of five types of wrong views (pañcadṛṣṭi) is commonly found in the literature: (1) the view that there is a perduring self, or soul, that exists in reality (SATKĀYADṚṢṬI); (2) extreme views (ANTAGRĀHADṚṢṬI), viz., in permanence or annihilation (dhruvoccheda); (3) fallacious views (MITHYĀDṚṢṬI), the denial of or disbelief in the efficacy of KARMAN, rebirth, and causality; (4) the rigid attachment to views (DṚṢṬIPARĀMARŚA), viz., mistakenly and stubbornly clinging to one's own speculative views as being superior to all others; and (5) the rigid attachment to the soteriological efficacy of rites and rituals (ŚĪLAVRATAPARĀMARŚA). There are numerous other kinds of wrong views listed in the literature. Views are also commonly listed as the second of the four attachments (UPĀDĀNA), along with the attachments to sensuality (KĀMA), the soteriological efficacy of rites and rituals (śīlavrata), and mistaken notions of a perduring soul (ĀTMAVĀDA). Views are also the third of the four contaminants (ĀSRAVA), along with sensuality (KĀMA), the desire for continued existence (BHAVA), and ignorance (AVIDYĀ).

**dṛṣṭiparāmarśa**. (P. diṭṭhiparāmāsa; T. lta ba mchog tu 'dzin pa; C. jianqu; J. kenju; K. kyŏnch'wi 見取). In Sanskrit, "attachment to (wrong) views"; the fourth of the five types of wrong views (DṚṢṬI), along with the view that there exists in reality a perduring self, or soul (SATKĀYADṚṢṬI); extreme views (ANTAGRĀHADṚṢṬI), viz., in permanence or annihilation; fallacious views (MITHYĀDṚṢṬI); and the rigid attachment to the soteriological efficacy of rites and rituals (ŚĪLAVRATAPARĀMARŚA). Dṛṣṭiparāmarśa suggests that a person mistakenly and stubbornly clings to one's own speculative views as being correct and superior to all others. In practice, the term refers specifically to the stubborn attachment to self-view (satkāyadṛṣṭi), extreme views (antagrāhadṛṣṭi), and false views (mithyādṛṣṭi).

**dṛṣṭiprāpta**. (P. diṭṭhippatta; T. mthong bas thob pa; C. jianzhi/jiande; J. kenji/kentoku; K. kyŏnji/kyŏndŭk 見至/見得). In Sanskrit, "one who has attained understanding" or "one who attains through seeing"; one of the seven noble persons (ĀRYAPUDGALA; P. ariyapuggala) listed in the MAJJHIMANIKĀYA; parallel to the DHARMĀNUSĀRIN (P. dhammānusāri), or "follower of the dharma." The dṛṣṭiprāpta is one in the list of the members of the SAṂGHA when it is subdivided into twenty (VIṂŚATIPRABHEDASAṂGHA). Among the dṛṣṭiprāpta, there are recipients of the fruit of stream-enterer (SROTAĀPANNAPHALASTHA), once-returner (SAKṚDĀGĀMIPHALASTHA), and nonreturner (ANĀGĀMIPHALASTHA). The dharmānusārin and dṛṣṭiprāpta are characterized as having keen faculties (TĪKṢNENDRIYA), unlike the ŚRADDHĀNUSĀRIN and ŚRADDHĀVIMUKTA who have dull faculties (MṚDVINDRIYA).

**drum**. (S. dundubhi, mṛdaṅga; P. dundubhi, mutiṅga; T. rnga bo che; C. gu; J. ku; K. ko 鼓). Drums and other percussion instruments are used in many Buddhist cultures to signal the events of the daily monastic schedule, to call the monks and nuns to assembly, and in Buddhist liturgical activities. Drums also appear frequently in Buddhist literature as a symbol of the power of the dharma to encourage good and frighten away evil. In Chinese monasteries, a drum is beaten at dawn and dusk to gather the monastic residents for services; a "cloud drum," viz., a drum ornamented with clouds, calls the monks to the midday meal; and a bathing drum is used to announce bath time in CHAN monasteries. The Chinese typically use four instruments to mark the schedule of events in a monastery: the dharma drum, temple bell, cloud-shaped gong, and wooden fish (C. muyu = K. MOKTAK). Especially interesting is the wooden fish, a wooden percussion instrument carved in the shape of a fish that is used for calling the monks to meals and to mark time during chanting. Because a fish's eyes are always open day and night, the wooden fish is a subtle admonition to monks and nuns to remain ever vigilant about their practice. Drums are often used together with other instruments during Buddhist liturgical activities. Small drums, bells, and gongs, for example, are used to mark time during Buddhist rituals and while chanting the Buddha's name (C. NIANFO). ¶ Drums often appear in conjunction with heavenly divinities (DEVA) in Buddhist literature. Dundubhisvara-rāja is the lord of the sound of celestial drums, viz., the thunder. Meghasvara-rāja, a son of Mahābhijñābhibhu, is the ruler of the cloud drums in the SADDHARMAPUṆḌARĪKASŪTRA. The heavenly drum in the TRĀYASTRIṂŚA heaven spontaneously emits a sublime sound without being struck; it warns the divine inhabitants that even their lives are impermanent and subject to the law of causality. Drums are a common metaphor for the Buddha or dharma in Buddhist literature. "Great Drum of the Dharma" is one of the epithets of a Buddha, since he exhorts sentient beings to perform wholesome actions and frightens away baleful influences and demons. The YOGĀCĀRABHŪMIŚĀSTRA describes one of the characteristics of the divine voice of a Buddha as being like the thunderous sound of a heavenly drum. The drum of dharma is also likened to both a noxious drum that helps to repress unwholesome action and evil, as well as a heavenly drum that offers kind and gentle encouragement to sentient beings to perform wholesome deeds. The noxious drum is likened also to the buddha-nature (C. FOXING), which can help overcome all evil. There are many variant Sanskrit names for drums and percussion instruments, including bherī, ghaṭṭita, GHAṆṬA, dundubha, and paṇava. See also MOKT'AK; ḌAMARU.

**Drumavikalpapraveśadhāraṇī**. (S). See AVIKALPAPRAVEŚADHĀRAṆĪ.

**duanzhu**. (C) (短珠). In Chinese, "short rosary." See JAPAMĀLĀ.

**Du Fei**. (C) (杜朏). See CHUAN FABAO JI.

**duḥkha**. (P. dukkha; T. sdug bsngal; C. ku; J. ku; K. ko 苦). In Sanskrit, "suffering" or "unsatisfactoriness"; the first of the

FOUR NOBLE TRUTHS (CATVĀRY ĀRYASATYĀNI) of Buddhism and a concept foundational to Buddhism's worldview and religious practice. The emblematic description of duḥkha, as found in the first noble truth, is, "Birth is suffering, aging is suffering, sickness is suffering, death is suffering. To be conjoined with what one dislikes is suffering and to be separated from what one likes is suffering. Not to get what one wants is suffering. In short, grasping at the five aggregates (SKANDHA) is suffering." Suffering thus not only includes the suffering that will invariably be associated with ordinary life, such as birth, aging, disease, and death, but also subsumes a full range of mental, emotional, and spiritual dissatisfactions, and ultimately is seen to be inherent to life itself. The teaching of suffering therefore seeks to change one's ordinary perspectives on the things of this world as objects worthy of pursuit, so that instead one realizes their nature of impermanence (ANITYA), suffering, and nonself (ANĀTMAN), viz., the three marks of existence (TRILAKṢAṆA). Through this sort of systematic attention (YONIŚOMANASKĀRA), even the pleasures of life are ultimately realized to be "unsatisfactory," because, like all compounded things, they are impermanent and thus inevitably destined to pass away. This awareness of suffering produces a sense of the "dangers" (ĀDĪNAVA) inherent in this world and prompts the practitioner to turn away from this world and toward the radical nonattachment that is NIRVĀṆA. ¶ Many types of duḥkha are enumerated in the literature, including forms specific to each of the six realms of rebirth (GATI). Most common are lists of three, four, and eight types of suffering. The three major categories of suffering are: (1) "misery caused by (physical and mental) suffering" (DUḤKHADUḤKHATĀ), viz., the full range of unpleasant or painful sensations (VEDANĀ) that are associated with either the physical body or the mind; (2) "misery caused by change" (VIPARIṆĀMADUḤKHATĀ), i.e., pleasant sensations may be a cause of suffering because they do not perdure and eventually turn into pain; (3) "misery caused by conditioning" (SAṂSKĀRADUḤKHATĀ), i.e., sensations that are neither painful nor pleasant may still be a cause of suffering because they are impermanent and thus undependable; because of past KARMAN, suffering may always occur unexpectedly in the next moment. The four types of suffering are the suffering associated with birth (jātiduḥkha), senescence or aging (jarāduḥkha), sickness (vyādhiduḥkha), and death (maraṇāduḥkha); various sūtras describe the Buddha's quest for enlightenment as motivated by the impulse to overcome these four types of sufferings. The eight types of suffering comprise the above four types plus an additional four: "the suffering of being separated from persons and things one likes" (priyaviprayogaduḥkha), "the suffering of being associated with persons and things one dislikes" (apriyasaṃprayogaduḥkha), "the suffering of not getting what one wants" (yad api icchayā paryeṣamāṇo na labhate tad api duḥkhaṃ), and "the suffering inherent in the five aggregates that are objects of clinging" (saṃkṣepeṇa pañcopādānaskandhaduḥkha). In addition to these three typical categories of suffering, there are other lists, from the eighteen types of suffering listed in the *Śāriputrābhidharmaśāstra* (*Shelifu apitan lun*) to the one hundred and ten types enumerated in the YOGĀCĀRABHŪMIŚĀSTRA. NĀGĀRJUNA's SUHṚLLEKHA gives a list of six sufferings: uncertainty, insatiability, casting off bodies repeatedly, repeated rebirth, repeatedly descending from high to low, and having no companions when dying and being reborn. Tibetan sources stress the role that meditation on suffering plays in producing a feeling of disgust (NIRVEDA; T. nges 'byung), that is, the preliminary turning away from the things of this world and turning toward nirvāṇa.

**duḥkhaduḥkhatā**. (P. dukkhadukkhatā; T. sdug bsngal gyi sdug bsngal; C. kuku; J. kuku; K. kogo 苦苦). In Sanskrit, "misery caused by (physical and mental) suffering"; one of the three principal categories of suffering (DUḤKHA), along with "suffering caused by conditioning" (SAṂSKĀRADUḤKHATĀ), and "suffering caused by change" (VIPARIṆĀMADUḤKHATĀ). Misery caused by suffering is defined as the full range of unpleasant and painful sensations (VEDANĀ) that rack the body and mind. The specific constituents of misery caused by suffering vary in different texts but typically include, among the physical components, birth (JĀTI), aging (JARĀ), disease (vyādhi), death (maraṇā), and physical pain (duḥkha) and, among the mental and emotion components, sorrow (śoka), lamentation (parideva), despair (daurmanasya), irritation (upāyāsa), being associated with persons and things that one dislikes, being dissociated from persons and things that one likes, and being unable to get what one wants. Many texts explain in great detail how these ordinary experiences involve or generate duḥkha. For example, according to the VISUDDHIMAGGA, the suffering associated with birth indicates all kinds of discomfort and pain to which a fetus is subject during gestation: the unpleasant conditions of stench, darkness, and physical constraint in the mother's womb, the nauseating feelings produced when the mother moves, and the excruciating pain that the newborn suffers during the birth process. By contrast, the "misery caused by conditioning" (saṃskāraduḥkhatā) means that sensations that are neither painful nor pleasant may still be a cause of suffering because they are impermanent and thus undependable. The "misery caused by change" (vipariṇāmaduḥkhatā) means that even pleasant sensations may be a cause of suffering because they do not perdure.

**duḥkhasatya**. (P. dukkhasacca; T. sdug bsngal gyi bden pa; C. kudi; J. kutai; K. koje 苦諦). In Sanskrit, "truth of suffering," or "true suffering," the first of the FOUR NOBLE TRUTHS (CATVĀRY ĀRYASATYĀNI), set forth in the Buddha's first sermon (DHAMMACAKKAPPAVATTANASUTTA), where he enumerated eight types of suffering (see DUḤKHA) and identified as suffering the five aggregates (SKANDHA) that are produced by contaminated (ĀSRAVA) actions (KARMAN) and afflictions (KLEŚA). Thus, the minds and bodies of ordinary sentient beings, as well as the environments they inhabit, which are also the byproducts of the actions of these beings, are forms of suffering. The term satya in

Sanskrit can mean "truth" in the abstract sense, but it can also have the more concrete meaning of a fact, a reality, or a constituent of experience. In this sense, the constituents of SAṂSĀRA, both sentient beings and their environments, can be called "true sufferings." More generally, the truth of suffering encompasses the three forms of suffering: (1) "misery caused by (physical and mental) suffering" (DUḤKHADUḤKHATĀ), (2) "misery caused by change" (VIPARIṆĀMADUḤKHATĀ), and (3) "misery caused by conditioning" (SAṂSKĀRADUḤKHATĀ), as well as the specific sufferings of the six realms (GATI) of rebirth. Each of the four truths has four aspects (ĀKĀRA), which are specific objects of SAMĀDHI on the mainstream Buddhist path. The four aspects of the truth of suffering are impermanence (ANITYA), misery (duḥkha), emptiness (śūnya; see ŚŪNYATĀ), and nonself (anātmaka; see ANĀTMAN). The five aggregates are forms of suffering because they are impermanent in the sense that they are constantly disintegrating; by meditating on the impermanence of mind and body, one overcomes the wrong view that they are permanent. The five aggregates are miserable in the sense that they are produced by contaminated actions and afflictions and thus are subject to the three types of suffering; by meditating on their misery one overcomes the wrong view that they are pure and pleasurable. The five aggregates are empty and nonself in the sense that they lack a permanent self and are not the possessions of such a self. By meditating on their emptiness and lack of selfhood, one overcomes the wrong view that a self is present among the five aggregates.

**duiji**. (J. taiki; K. taegi 對機). In Chinese, lit. teaching "in accord with capacity"; an abbreviation of the phrase duiji shuofa, or "speaking the DHARMA in accord with [the student's] capacity," referring to the Buddha's propensity to tailor his message through stratagems (UPĀYA) in order to respond to the specific needs of his audience and his listeners' ability to understand him. The term comes to be used in the CHAN school to refer to a formal exchange between a Chan master and disciple that takes place in the master's room (see FANGZHANG). This exchange between master and disciple is typically a "private" affair, for the master's answers are designed to respond to the spiritual capacity of that specific student. These exchanges constitute much of the content of the discourse records (YULU) of Chan, SŎN, and ZEN masters.

**duiji shuofa**. (J. taiki seppō; K. taegi sŏlbop 對機說法). In Chinese, "speaking the dharma in accord with [the student's] capacity." See DUIJI.

**dukkha**. In Pāli, "suffering." See DUḤKHA.

**Dung dkar**. (Dungkar). A valley in western Tibet (Mnga' ris) about thirty kilometers from THO LING with 1,150 caves, most of which were used as dwellings but twenty of which are cave temples with mural paintings. The area appears to have become the capital of the Pu rang GU GE kingdom at the beginning of the twelfth century, and the cave temples with mural paintings and mud sculptures were probably founded by the descendents of the Gu ge royal family during that period. Of the three main caves, the most important has statues of the seven buddhas of the past (SAPTATATHĀGATA) and the future buddha MAITREYA, a ceiling mural of the VAJRADHĀTU MAṆḌALA, and walls covered with bodhisattvas. Another has a GUHYASAMĀJA MAṆḌALA, suggesting development at a later period. The caves have been documented a number of times, first by GIUSEPPE TUCCI in the 1930s.

**Dunhuang**. (J. Tonkō; K. Tonhwang 敦煌). A northwest Chinese garrison town on the edge of the Taklamakan desert in Central Asia, first established in the Han dynasty and an important stop along the ancient SILK ROAD; still seen written also as Tun-huang, followed the older Wade–Giles transcription. Today an oasis town in China's Gansu province, Dunhuang is often used to refer to the nearby complex of approximately five hunded Buddhist caves, including the MOGAO KU (Peerless Caves) to the southeast of town and the QIANFO DONG (Caves of the Thousand Buddhas) about twenty miles to the west. Excavations to build the caves at the Mogao site began in the late-fourth century CE and continued into the mid-fourteenth century CE. Of the more than one thousand caves that were hewn from the cliff face, roughly half were decorated. Along with the cave sites of LONGMEN and YUNGANG further east and BEZEKLIK and KIZIL to the west, the Mogao grottoes contain some of the most spectacular examples of ancient Buddhist sculpture and wall painting to be found anywhere in the world. Legend has it that in 366 CE a wandering monk named Yuezun had a vision of a thousand golden buddhas at a site along some cliffs bordering a creek and excavated the first cave in the cliffs for his meditation practice. Soon afterward, additional caves were excavated and the first monasteries established to serve the needs of the monks and merchants traveling to and from China along the Silk Road. The caves were largely abandoned in the fourteenth century. In the early twentieth century, Wang Yuanlu (1849–1931), self-appointed guardian of the Dunhuang caves, discovered a large cache of ancient manuscripts and paintings in Cave 17, a side chamber of the larger Cave 16. As rumors of these manuscripts reached Europe, explorer-scholars such as SIR MARC AUREL STEIN and PAUL PELLIOT set out across Central Asia to obtain samples of ancient texts and artwork buried in the ruins of the Taklamakan desert. Inside were hundreds of paintings on silk and tens of thousands of manuscripts dating from the fifth to roughly the eleventh centuries CE, forming what has been described as the world's earliest and largest paper archive. The texts were written in more than a dozen languages, including Chinese, Tibetan, Sanskrit, Sogdian, Uighur, Khotanese, Tangut, and TOCHARIAN and consisted of paper scrolls, wooden tablets, and one of the world's earliest printed books (868 CE), a copy of the VAJRACCHEDIKĀPRAJÑĀPĀRAMITĀSŪTRA ("Diamond Sūtra").

In the seventh-century, a Tibetan garrison was based at Dunhuang, and materials discovered in the library cave also include some of the earliest documents in the Tibetan language. This hidden library cave was apparently sealed in the eleventh century. As a result of the competition between European, American, and Japanese institutions to acquire documents from Dunhuang, the material was dispersed among collections worldwide, making access to all the manuscripts difficult. Many items have still not been properly catalogued or conserved and there are scholarly disputes over what quantity of the materials are modern forgeries. In 1944 the Dunhuang Academy was established to document and study the site and in 1980 the site was opened to the public. In 1987 the Dunhuang caves were listed as a UNESCO World Heritage site and today are being preserved through the efforts of both Chinese and international groups.

**dunjiao**. (J. tongyō; K. ton'gyo 頓教). In Chinese, "sudden teachings," or "subitism"; a polemical term used by HOZE SHENHUI in the so-called "Southern school" (NAN ZONG) of Chan to disparage his rival "Northern school" (BEI ZONG) as a gradualist, and therefore inferior, presentation of Chan teachings and practice. Unlike the Northern school's more traditional soteriological approach, which was claimed to involve gradual purification of the mind so that defilements would be removed and the mind's innate purity revealed, the Southern school instead claimed to offer immediate access to enlightenment itself (viz., "sudden awakening"; see DUNWU) without the necessity of preparatory practices or conceptual mediation. See also LIUZU TAN JING. ¶ The "sudden teaching" (dunjiao) was also the fourth of the five classifications of the teachings in the Huayan school (see HUAYAN WUJIAO), as outlined by DUSHUN and FAZANG (643–712). In a Huayan context, the sudden teachings were ranked as a unique category of subitist teachings befitting sharp people of keen spiritual faculties (S. TĪKṢNENDRIYA), which therefore bypassed systematic approaches to enlightenment. Huayan thus treats the Chan school's touted methods involving sudden enlightenment (dunwu) and its rejection of reliance on written texts (BULI WENZI) as inferior to the fifth and final category of the "perfect" or "consummate teaching" (YUANJIAO), which was reserved for the HUAYAN ZONG.

**dunwu**. (J. tongo; K. tono 頓悟). In Chinese, "sudden awakening," or "sudden enlightenment"; the experience described in the CHAN school that "seeing the nature" (JIANXING) itself is sufficient to enable the adept to realize one's innate buddhahood (JIANXING CHENGFO). The idea of a subitist approach (DUNJIAO) to awakening was also used polemically by HOZE SHENHUI in the so-called "Southern school" (NAN ZONG) of Chan to disparage his rival "Northern school" (BEIZONG) as a gradualist, and therefore inferior, presentation of Chan soteriological teachings. Although debates over gradual vs. sudden enlightenment are most commonly associated with the East Asian Chan schools, there are also precedents in Indian Buddhism. The so-called BSAM YAS DEBATE, or "Council of LHA SA," that took place in Tibet at the end of the eighth century is said to have pitted the Indian monk KAMALAŚĪLA against the Northern Chan monk HESHANG MOHEYAN in a debate over gradual enlightenment vs. sudden enlightenment. ¶ In two-tiered path (MĀRGA) schemata, such as "sudden awakening [followed by] gradual cultivation" (DUNWU JIANXIU), this initial experience of sudden awakening constitutes an "understanding–awakening" (JIEWU), in which the adept comes to know that he is not a deluded sentient being but is in fact a buddha. (In this context, the understanding–awakening is functionally equivalent to the path of vision [DARŚANAMĀRGA] in ABHIDHARMA path systems.) But this sudden awakening is not sufficient in itself to generate the complete, perfect enlightenment of buddhahood (ANUTTARASAMYAKSAMBODHI), where one is able to manifest all the potential inherent in that exalted state. That realization comes only through continued gradual cultivation (jianxiu) following this initial sudden awakening, so that one will learn not only to be a buddha but to act as one as well. That point where knowledge and action fully correspond marks the final "realization–awakening" (ZHENGWU) and is the point at which buddhahood is truly achieved. See also WU; JIANWU.

**dunwu jianxiu**. (J. tongo zenshu; K. tono chŏmsu 頓悟漸修). In Chinese, "sudden awakening [followed by] gradual cultivation"; a path (MĀRGA) schema emblematic of such CHAN masters as GUIFENG ZONGMI (780–841) in the Chinese Heze school of Chan, and POJO CHINUL (1158–1210) of the Korean CHOGYE school of Sŏn. In this outline of the Chan mārga, true spiritual practice begins with an initial insight into one's true nature (viz., "seeing the nature"; JIANXING), through which the Chan adept comes to know that he is not a deluded sentient being but is in fact a buddha. This experience is called the "understanding–awakening" (JIEWU) and is functionally equivalent to the path of vision (DARŚANAMĀRGA) in ABHIDHARMA path systems. Simply knowing that one is a buddha through this sudden awakening of understanding, however, is not sufficient in itself to generate the complete, perfect enlightenment of buddhahood (ANUTTARASAMYAKSAMBODHI) and thus to ensure that one will always be able to act on that potential. Only after continued gradual cultivation (jianxiu) following this initial understanding–awakening will one remove the habituations (VĀSANĀ) that have been engrained in the mind for an essentially infinite amount of time, so that one will not only be a buddha, but will be able to act as one as well. That point where knowledge and action fully correspond marks the final "realization-awakening" (ZHENGWU) and is the point at which buddhahood is truly achieved. This soteriological process is compared by Zongmi and Chinul to that of an infant who is born with all the faculties of a human being (the sudden understanding–awakening) but who still needs to go a long process of maturation (gradual cultivation) before he will be able to live up to his full potential as an adult human being (realization–awakening). See also WU.

**Dunwu rudao yaomen lun**. (J. Tongo nyūdō yōmonron; K. Tono ipto yomun non 頓悟入道要門論). In Chinese, "Treatise on the Essential Gate of Entering the Way through Sudden Awakening," composed by the Tang dynasty CHAN master DAZHU HUIHAI (d.u.); also known as the *Dunwu yaomen*. The monk Miaoxie (d.u.) discovered this text in a box and published it in 1369 together with Dazhu's recorded sayings that he selectively culled from the JINGDE CHUANDENG LU. Miaoxie's edition is comprised of two rolls. The first roll contains Dazhu's text the *Dunwu rudao yaomen lun*, and the second contains his sayings, which Miaoxie entitled the *Zhufang menren canwen yulu*. A preface to this edition was prepared by the monk Chongyu (1304–1378). The *Dunwu rudao yaomen lun* focuses on the notion of "sudden awakening" (DUNWU) and attempts to explicate various doctrinal concepts, such as ŚĪLA, DHYĀNA, PRAJÑĀ, TATHATĀ, BUDDHA-NATURE (FOXING), and "no-thought" (WUNIAN), from the perspective of sudden awakening. The text explains sudden awakening as the "sudden" (dun) eradication of deluded thoughts and "awakening" (WU) to nonattainment or the fundamental absence of anything that needs to be achieved. Citing such scriptures as the LAṄKĀVATĀRASŪTRA and VIMALAKĪRTINIRDEŚA, the text also contends that the mind itself is the foundation of cultivation and practice. The primary method of cultivation discussed in the text is seated meditation (ZUOCHAN), which it describes as the nonarising of deluded thoughts and seeing one's own nature (JIANXING). The *Dunwu rudao yaomen lun* also contends that sudden awakening begins with the perfection of giving (DĀNAPĀRAMITĀ).

**dūraṅgamā**. (T. ring du song ba; C. yuanxing di; J. ongyōji; K. wŏnhaeng chi 遠行地). In Sanskrit, "gone afar," or "transcendent"; the seventh of the ten "stages" or "grounds" (BHŪMI) of the bodhisattva path (MĀRGA). The name of this stage is interpreted to mean that the bodhisattva has here reached the culmination of moral discipline (ŚĪLA) and hereafter proceeds to focus more on meditation (SAMĀDHI) and wisdom (PRAJÑĀ). This stage marks the bodhisattva's freedom from the four perverted views (VIPARYĀSA) and his mastery of the perfection of expedients (UPĀYAKAUŚALYA), which he uses to help infinite numbers of sentient beings. Although at this stage the bodhisattva abides in signlessness (ĀNIMITTA), he does not negate the conventions that create signs, thereby upholding the conventional nature of phenomena. He remains at this stage until he is able to abide spontaneously and effortlessly in the signless state. According to CANDRAKĪRTI in his MADHYAMAKĀVATĀRA, at this stage the bodhisattva, in each and every moment, is able to enter into and withdraw from the equipoise of cessation (NIRODHASAMĀPATTI) in which all elaborations (PRAPAÑCA) cease. For Candrakīrti, at the conclusion of the seventh stage, the bodhisattva is liberated from rebirth, having destroyed all of the afflictive obstructions (KLEŚĀVARAṆA). The seventh stage is thus the last of the impure bhūmis. The bodhisattva then proceeds to the three pure stages (the eighth, ninth, and tenth bhūmis), over the course of which he abandons the obstructions to omniscience (JÑEYĀVARAṆA).

**durbhāṣita**. (P. dubbhāsita; T. nyes par smra ba; C. eshuo; J. akusetsu; K. aksŏl 惡說). In Sanskrit, "mischievous talk"; a supplementary category of ecclesiastical offenses. See DUṢKṚTA; PRĀTIMOKṢA; VINAYA.

**durgati**. (P. duggati; T. ngan 'gro; C. equ; J. akushu; K. akch'wi 惡趣). In Sanskrit, "unfortunate destinies." These destinies refer to the unfortunate or unfavorable rebirths (APĀYA) that occur as a consequence of performing demeritorious actions (AKUŚALAKARMAN). Typically a list of three (or sometimes four) such destinies is found in the literature: (1) a denizen of hell (S. NĀRAKA; P. nerayika), (2) an animal (S. TIRYAK; P. tiracchāna), (3) a hungry ghost (S. PRETA; P. peta), and (4) a demigod or titan (ASURA). According to the ABHIDHARMAKOŚABHĀṢYA, the eight hot and eight cold hells are the lowest place beneath JAMBUDVĪPA; the pretas are ruled by YAMA and primarily live in a region five hundred yojanas (a YOJANA is the distance a pair of bulls can pull a cart in a day) below; animals primarily live on the land, in the water, and in the air. The life spans of beings in the unfortunate destinies are longest in the hells and shortest for animals. The life span of the least-painful, topmost hell is five hundred years calculated as follows: fifty human days makes a day in the life of the lowest level sensuous realm (KĀMADHĀTU) divinity who lives five hundred years; one day in the topmost hell is equal to the life span of that god. The length of life span becomes even more dire for the lower hells. A day for a preta who lives for five hundred years is one month for a human being. Animal life spans range widely, some seeming almost evascent by human standards, others, such as the NĀGA, supposedly able to live for an eon (KALPA). See also APĀYA; BHAVACAKRA.

**Dus gsum mkhyen pa**. (Dusum Kyenpa) (1110–1193). A renowned Tibetan master recognized as the first in the lineage of KARMA PA incarnations and early founder of the KARMA BKA' BRGYUD sect of Tibetan Buddhism. He was born in the Tre shod region of eastern Tibet and at the age of sixteen was ordained by a monk of the BKA' GDAMS sect and received tantric instruction from a disciple of ATIŚA DĪPAṂKARAŚRĪJÑĀNA. He went on to study MADHYAMAKA and the KĀLACAKRATANTRA with some of the leading scholars of the day. At the age of thirty, Dus gsum mkhyen pa met his principal GURU, SGAM PO PA BSOD NAMS RIN CHEN, from whom he received many teachings, including so-called "heat yoga" (gtum mo; see CAṆḌĀLĪ). He also studied with MI LA RAS PA's renowned disciple RAS CHUNG PA. He devoted himself to the teachings that would become the hallmark of the Bka' brgyud, such as the six yogas of NĀROPA and MAHĀMUDRA, but he also received teachings from a number of Bka' gdams and SA SKYA masters. He went on to found three important Bka' brgyud monasteries: Kam po gnas nang in 1164, KARMA DGON in 1184, both in eastern Tibet, and MTSHUR PHU northwest of LHA SA in 1187. The latter became a powerful central-Tibetan institution as the primary seat of the Karma pas up to 1959. It is said that at the age of sixteen Dus gsum mkhyen pa received a hat woven from the hair of one hundred thousand ḌĀKINĪs. This hat has been passed down to subsequent Karma pas, and seen in the so-called "black hat ceremony" (zhwa nag).

**Dushun**. (J. Tojun; K. Tusun 杜順) (557–640). Chinese monk thaumaturge, meditator, and exegete who is recognized by tradition as the founder and putative first patriarch of the HUAYAN ZONG of East Asian Buddhism; also known as Fashun. Dushun was a native of Wengzhou in present-day Shaanxi province. He became a monk at the age of seventeen and is said to have studied meditation under a certain Weichen (d.u.) at the monastery of Yinshengsi. Later, he retired to the monastery of Zhixiangsi on ZHONGNANSHAN, where he devoted himself to study of the AVATAṂSAKASŪTRA. The monk ZHIYAN (602–668) is presumed to have studied under Dushun at Zhixiangsi and subsequently came to be recognized as Dushun's formal successor. Some fourteen different works have been ascribed to Dushun at various points in history, but it is now presumed that only two of these can definitively be associated with him: the *Huayan yisheng shixuan men* ("The Ten Arcane Gates of the One Vehicle of the *Avataṃsaka*"), which was composed by Dushun's successor, Zhiyan, supposedly from his teacher's oral teachings; and the HUAYAN FAJIE GUANMEN, one of the foundational texts of the nascent Huayan school. (Some scholars have proposed that this text may have been excerpted from FAZANG's *Fa putixin zhang*, and only later attributed to Dushun, but this hypothesis is not widely accepted.) Dushun is also portrayed as an advocate of various Sui- and Tang-dynasty cults associated with MAÑJUŚRĪ and AMITĀBHA that were popular among the laity. Because of the sweeping scope of his religious career, Dushun is sometimes considered to be emblematic of the emerging "new Buddhism" of sixth- and seventh-century China, which sought to remake Buddhism into forms that would be more accessible to an indigenous audience.

**dusi**. (J. tsūsu; K. tosa 都寺/司). In Chinese, "prior's assistant," or later "prior"; a principal administrative post in a CHAN monastery, the officer in charge of supplies and finances and the main staff person of the prior (JIANYUAN). Along with the rector (WEINUO), cook (DIANZUO), superintendent (ZHISUI), comptroller (JIANSI), and assistant comptroller (FUSI), the prior is one of the six stewards (ZHISHI) at an East Asian Chan monastery. The comptroller and assistant comptroller are usually under the prior's direct supervision, and the prior himself is second only to the abbot (ZHUCHI) in administrative rank.

**duṣkaracaryā**. (P. dukkarakārikā; T. dka' ba spyod pa; C. kuxing; J. kugyō; K. kohaeng 苦行). In Sanskrit, "difficult feats" of religious practice, referring especially to the extreme asceticism in which Śākyamuni Buddha engaged as the BODHISATTVA, prior to finding the middle way (MADHYAMAPRATIPAD) between mortification of the flesh and sensual indulgence. For the authorized list of ascetic practices, see DHUTAṄGA.

**duṣkṛta**. (P. dukkaṭa; T. nyes byas; C. ezuo/tujiluo; J. akusa/tokira; K. akchak/tolgilla 惡作/突吉羅). In Sanskrit, "wrongdoing"; a general category for the least serious of ecclesiastical offenses; for this reason, the term is also rendered in Chinese as "minor misdeed" (xiaoguo) or "light fault" (qingguo). In some recensions of the VINAYA, such as the Pāli, wrongdoings are treated as a category supplementary to the eight general classifications of rules and regulations appearing in the monastic code of conduct (PRĀTIMOKṢA). The eight are: (1) PĀRĀJIKA ("defeat," entailing expulsion from the order in some vinaya recensions); (2) SAṂGHĀVAŚEṢA (requiring a formal meeting and temporary suspension from the order); (3) ANIYATA (undetermined or indefinite offenses); (4) NAIḤSARGIKAPĀYATTIKA (offenses entailing expiation and forfeiture); (5) PĀYATTIKA (offenses entailing confession and forfeiture); (6) PRATIDEŚANĪYA (offenses that are to be publicly acknowledged); (7) ŚAIKṢADHARMA (minor rules of training); and (8) ADHIKARAṆA (rules for settling disputes). Other such supplementary categories include STHŪLĀTYAYA (various grave, but unconsummated offenses), and DURBHĀṢITA (mischievous talk). In such treatments, the duṣkṛta category typically is said to entail deliberate disobeying of any of the śaikṣadharma rules, which involve a whole range of possible transgressions of monastic decorum and public conduct, such as improperly wearing one's robes, misconduct during alms round (PIṆḌAPĀTA), or incorrect toilet habits. In addition, failed attempts to break any of rules in the relatively minor categories of the pāyattika, or pratideśanīya are a duṣkṛta, while failed attempts to break the much more serious pārājika and saṃghāvaśeṣa rules are both a duṣkṛta and a sthūlātyaya. Finally, various offenses that are not specifically treated in a formal rule in the prātimokṣa may also be treated as a duṣkṛta, e.g., striking a layperson, which is not specifically enjoined in the prātimokṣa, although striking a monk is. Other vinayas, however, such as the DHARMAGUPTAKA VINAYA (C. *Sifen lü*), list the duṣkṛta offenses as one of the five categories of precepts, along with pārājika, saṃghāvaśeṣa, pāyattika, and pratideśanīya; alternatively, the Dharmaguptaka vinaya also lists seven categories of precepts, which include the preceding five categories, plus stūlātyaya and durbhāṣita. In such categorizations, the duṣkṛta essentially replace the śaikṣadharma rules of other vinayas. These duṣkṛta offenses are typically said to be expiated through confession; more specifically, the Dharmaguptaka vinaya stipulates that a deliberate wrongdoing should be confessed to a single monk or nun, while an accidental case of wrongdoing may simply be repented in the mind of the offender. Similarly, the MŪLASARVĀSTIVĀDA VINAYA includes the 112 duṣkṛta in the 253 PRĀTIMOKṢA rules recited during the UPOṢADHA confession. In MAHĀYĀNA discussions of bodhisattva precepts (according to ASAṄGA and others, these are a second set of precepts that supplement the prātimokṣa rules but do not contradict them), all offenses except the eighteen involving defeat (pārājika) [alt. mūlāpatti, T. rtsa ltung] are classified as "minor offenses" (C. qing gouzui; T. nyas byas), i.e., duṣkṛta. There are, for instance, forty-two types of duṣkṛta discussed in the BODHISATTVABHŪMI (*Pusa dichi jing*), forty-eight in the FANWANG JING, and fifty in the *Pusa shanjie jing*. In tantric Buddhism, gross infractions (sthūla) are any form of behavior that does not constitute defeat (mūlāpatti), but are a weaker form of the infraction.

**Dus ldan**. (T). See KĀLIKA.

**Duṭṭhagāmaṇī**. [alt. Sinhalese: Dutugümunu] (r. 101–77 BCE). Sinhalese king best known for restoring Sinhalese suzerainty over the entire island of Sri Lanka after his first century BCE defeat of King Eḷāra of the predominantly Hindu Damiḷas (Tamil). According to the MAHĀVAṂSA, Duṭṭhagāmaṇī had been a monk in his previous life, when he vowed to be reborn as a CAKRAVARTIN. As king, he went to war against the enemies of the dharma, carrying a spear with a relic of the Buddha attached to it. The battle ended when he killed the enemy king, the pious but non-Buddhist Eḷāra. After his victory, he planted his spear in the earth. When he attempted to extract it, he failed, and so decided to have a STŪPA built around it, making the instrument of his victory a site for merit-making. Like AŚOKA, Duṭṭhagāmaṇī was troubled by the carnage he had caused, specifically the death of sixty thousand of his enemies. But a delegation of ARHATs assured him that, because his victims were not Buddhists, he had only accrued the negative KARMAN of having killed just one and a half persons. As a result of meritorious deeds, Duṭṭhagāmaṇī is said to have been reborn in the TUṢITA heaven, awaiting rebirth as a disciple of MAITREYA. The story of Duṭṭhagāmaṇī continues to be told in Sri Lanka, and was deployed during the late-twentieth century to defend the violence of Sinhalese Buddhists against non-Buddhist Tamils. After his victory over Eḷāra at his capital of ANURĀDHAPURA, the king began a series of construction projects in support of Buddhism, culminating in the MAHĀTHŪPA, the great stūpa [alt. Ruwanwelisaya], at the site where the Buddha is thought to have made his third visit to the island of Sri Lanka. Duṭṭhagāmaṇī fell ill before this massive project was completed, but according to legend his brother Saddhātissa draped the site in white cloth so that the king could visualize it in all its glory prior to his death.

**Dutugümunu**. (Sinhalese). See DUṬṬHAGĀMAṆĪ.

**Duxu**. (C) (都序). See CHANYUAN ZHUQUANJI DUXU.

***Dvādaśamukhaśāstra**. (S). See SHI'ERMEN LUN.

**dvādaśāṅga[pravacana]**. (T. gsung rab yan lag bcu gnyis; C. shi'erbu jing; J. jūnibukyō; K. sibibu kyŏng 十二部經). In Sanskrit, "twelve categories"; the twelve traditional divisions of the Buddha's teachings based on content and literary style, according to Sanskrit Buddhist sources. The Sanskrit list adds three more genres—framing stories or episodes (NIDĀNA), heroic tales or narratives (AVADĀNA), and instructions (UPADEŚA)—to the nine divisions (P. NAVAṄGA[PĀVACANA]) listed in mainstream Buddhist sources: discourses (SŪTRA), aphorisms in mixed prose and verse (GEYA), prophetic teachings or expositions (VYĀKARAṆA), verses (GĀTHĀ), utterance or meaningful expressions (UDĀNA), fables (ITIVṚTTAKA), tales of previous lives (JĀTAKA), marvelous events (ADBHUTADHARMA), and catechisms or works of great extent (VAIPULYA). In Sanskrit sources, these twelve are called vacana or pravacana (P. pāvacana), viz., the words of the Buddha. See also AṄGA.

**Dvāranikāya**. See DWAYA.

**dvārapāla**. (T. sgo bsrungs pa; C. shoumenren; J. shumonnin; K. sumunin 守門人). In Sanskrit, "gatekeepers"; Indian Buddhist wrathful deities (see YAKṢA), who protect the entrances to monasteries, marking the passage from mundane to sacred space. Four names generally appear in the literature: Vajrāṅkuśa, Vajrapāśa, Vajrasphoṭa, and Vajrāveśa/Vajraghaṇṭa. Statues of dvārapāla are often placed on either side of a monastery's main gate and the entrances to holy sanctuaries. They are typically depicted as male warriors, carrying weapons or emblems, and wrathful in appearance, sometimes with two fangs at each corner of mouth, and displaying imposing strength that can frighten away evil spirits and baleful influences before they can disturb the quietude of the monastery. Dvārapāla are connected with dragon or snake spirits (NĀGA) and are often depicted in South Asia with sacred threads (upavīta) in the guise of snakes encircling their waists or knees. They are mighty in battle and can uproot trees or hurl mountaintops to thwart their enemies. They are also skilled in magic and can transform themselves into all sorts of shapes, whether human or nonhuman, in order better to protect their monastery. ¶ Dvārapāla also guard the four gates of the MAṆḌALA. MAÑJUŚRĪ in the GARBHADHĀTU maṇḍala is portrayed with two guardians of the dharma, called the Durdharṣadvārapāla, to his sides. They are typically portrayed standing with one hand raised, eyes bulging, and naked to the waist. Sometimes they are portrayed with the right hand raised, holding a long club. See also DHARMAPĀLA.

**Dvāravatī**. Name given to the Mon civilization that flourished in the region of present-day Thailand from roughly the sixth through the eleventh centuries, occupying chiefly the Menam valley and extending northward to Lamphun. Little is known of the political organization of Dvāravatī, that is, whether it was an empire that had one or more capitals, or whether it was instead a collection of autonomous city-states. The geographic distribution of urban sites suggests an economy based on control of trade routes, particularly across the Three Pagodas Pass into Burma, northward up the Chaophraya River toward Chiangmai, and eastward into Cambodia. The chief Dvāravatī centers of the Menam valley were U Thong, Lopburi, Khu Bua, and Nakhon Pathom. In the north near Lamphun was the kingdom of Haripuñjaya, which, according to the Thai chronicles, was founded in the seventh century by sages and governed by a heroic Mon queen named Cāma (cf. CĀMADEVĪVAṂSA). Common at all of the sites are inscriptions written in Mon, with a smaller number in Sanskrit and Pāli. The sites are typically fortified with moats and earthen walls and display extensive Buddhist remains, which include ruins of monasteries, temples, and pagodas and stone and bronze sculpture and statuary. Much of Dvāravatī art shows strong Indian influence reminiscent of the Amaravatī and Gupta styles, while in later centuries a distinctive Khmer influence becomes evident. The overall religious culture of the Dvāravatī civilization appears to have been mixed, with evidence of multiple forms of Buddhism, Brahmanism, and indigenous cults receiving patronage. By the mid-eleventh century, the cities occupying the eastern portion of the Dvāravatī cultural zone were absorbed by the expanding Khmer empire of Angkor, while in the west they fell to the newly emergent Burmese empire of Pagan. Haripuñjaya alone retained a degree of autonomy until the thirteenth century, when it was conquered by the northern Thai kingdom of Lānnā (Lan Na).

**dvātriṃśadvaralakṣaṇa**. (T. mtshan gsum bcu so gnyis; C. sanshi'er xiang; J. sanjūnisō; K. samsibi sang 三十二相). In Sanskrit, the "thirty-two marks" unique to a buddha or CAKRAVARTIN king. See MAHĀPURUṢALAKṢAṆA.

**Dvedhāvitakkasutta**. (C. Nian jing; J. Nengyō; K. Yŏm kyŏng 念經). In Pāli, "Discourse on Two Kinds of Thoughts"; the nineteenth sutta contained in the MAJJHIMANIKĀYA (a separate SARVĀSTIVĀDA recension appears as the 102nd sūtra in the Chinese translation of the MADHYAMĀGAMA); preached by the Buddha to his disciples gathered at the JETAVANA Grove in the town of Sāvatthi (ŚRĀVASTĪ). The Buddha explains that thoughts can be divided into two categories: unsalutary (P. akusala; S. AKUŚALA) thoughts associated with sensual desire, ill will, and harmfulness; and salutary (P. kusala; S. KUŚALA) thoughts associated with renunciation, non-ill will, and harmlessness. He describes his own practice prior to his enlightenment as discerning between these two types of thoughts and recognizing the advantages that come from developing the salutary and the disadvantages of the unsalutary. He advises his monks to examine their minds in the same way so that they too would develop salutary thoughts and overcome unsalutary thoughts.

**dveṣa**. (P. dosa; T. zhe sdang; C. chen; J. shin; K. chin 瞋). In Sanskrit, "aversion," "ill will," or "hatred"; it is frequently written DOṢA in BUDDHIST HYBRID SANSKRIT; closely synonymous also to "hostility" (PRATIGHA). "Aversion" is one of the most ubiquitous of defilements and is listed, for example, among the six fundamental "afflictions" (KLEŚA), ten "fetters" (SAṂYOJANA), ten "proclivities" (ANUŚAYA), five "hindrances" (NĪVARAṆA), and "three poisons" (TRIVIṢA). It is also one of the forty-six mental factors (CAITTA) according to the VAIBHĀṢIKA school of SARVĀSTIVĀDA ABHIDHARMA, one of the fifty-one according to the YOGĀCĀRA school, and one of fifty-two in the Pāli abhidhamma. In Buddhist psychology, when contact with sensory objects is made "without introspection" (ASAMPRAJANYA), "passion" (RĀGA) or "greed" (LOBHA), "aversion," and/or "delusion" (MOHA) arise as a result. In the case of "aversion"—which is a psychological reaction that is associated with repulsion, resistance, and active dislike of a displeasing stimulus—one of the possible derivative emotions typically ensue. These derivative emotions—which include "anger" (KRODHA), "enmity" (UPANĀHA), "agitation" (PRADĀSA), "envy" (ĪRṢYĀ), "harmfulness" (VIHIṂSĀ)—all have "aversion" as their common foundation.

**Dwags lha sgam po**. (Daklha Gampo). The site of an important BKA' BRGYUD monastic complex in the Dwags po (Dakpo) region of south-central Tibet, founded in 1121 by SGAM PO PA BSOD RNAM RIN CHEN. Flanked by an unusual range of mountains, the location was originally developed by the Tibetan king SRONG BTSAN SGAM PO, who constructed one of his many "taming temples" (mtha' 'dul) there in order to pin down the head of the supine demoness (srin mo) believed to be hindering the spread of Buddhism in Tibet. It is said that PADMASAMBHAVA later hid several treasure texts (GTER MA) in the surrounding peaks, foremost among which was the BAR DO THOS GROL CHEN MO, or "Liberation Through Hearing in the Intermediate State," usually known in English as *The Tibetan Book of the Dead*, which was unearthed by the treasure revealer (GTER STON) KARMA GLING PA. Dwags lha sgam po is best known, however, as the seat of the important Bka' brgyud hierarch Sgam po pa and under his direction it became an active center for meditative retreats. His numerous disciples, from whom stem the four major and eight minor Bka' brgyud subsects, include the first KARMA PA DUS GSUM MKHYEN PA and PHAG MO GRU PA RDO RJE RGYAL PO. Following Sgam po pa's death, the complex was directed by masters in his familial lineage, and later, Sgam po pa's incarnation lineage, including lamas such as DWAGS PO BKRA SHIS RNAM RGYAL. It was destroyed by the invading Dzungar Mongol army in 1718 and rebuilt, only to be completely destroyed once again during the Chinese Cultural Revolution (1966–1976). Several small chapels have since been renovated.

**Dwags po Bka' brgyud**. (Dakpo Kagyü). The main branch of the BKA' BRGYUD sect of Tibetan Buddhism stemming from MAR PA CHOS KYI BLO GROS, MI LA RAS PA, and SGAM PO PA BSOD NAMS RIN CHEN. It refers to the various Bka' brgyud branches, known as the four major and eight minor Bka' brgyud subsects (BKA' BRGYUD CHE BZHI CHUNG BRGYAD) that formed and flourished due to the activities of Sgam po pa and his immediate disciples. The name Dwags po Bka' brgyud is derived from Sgam po pa's main seat, DWAGS LHA SGAM PO, located in the Dwags po region of southern Tibet.

**Dwags po Bkra shis rnam rgyal**. (Dakpo Tashi Namgyal) (1512/13–1587). An abbot of the Tibetan monastery of DWAGS LHA SGAM PO, founded by SGAM PO PA BSOD NAMS RIN CHEN, from which he receives his toponym. In his early years he studied with SA SKYA teachers and was abbot of NA LAN DRA monastery. He is known in particular for his writing on the HEVAJRATANTRA and MAHĀMUDRĀ; his *Nges don phyag rgya chen po'i sgom rim gsal bar byed pa'i legs bshad zla ba'i 'od zer* is a definitive text of mahāmudrā, giving a presentation of the graduated stages of HĪNAYĀNA and MAHĀYĀNA practices and a scholarly explanation of mahāmudrā. Among his students was the scholar PADMA DKAR PO, the fourth head of the BRUG PA BKA' BRYUD sect and the systematizer of its teachings.

**Dwags po thar rgyan**. (T). See THAR PA RIN PO CHE'I RGYAN.

**Dwaya**. (P. Dvāra). The third largest monastic fraternity (B. GAING; P. gaṇa, cf. NIKĀYA) of modern Myanmar (Burmese) Buddhism, following the THUDHAMMA (P. Sudhammā) and the SHWEGYIN fraternities. The Dwaya fraternity was founded as a dissident group within the Burmese saṅgha (S. SAṂGHA) in the mid-nineteenth century by the Okpo Sayadaw, U Okkamwuntha (P. Okkaṃvaṃsa), who hailed from the Okpo region between Yangon (Rangoon) and Bago (Pegu) in Lower Burma. During his lifetime, Lower Burma was conquered by the British with the result that many Buddhist monks fled north to seek the protection of the Burmese crown. The Okpo Sayadaw recommended against this move, claiming that if the saṅgha strictly observed the VINAYA, it did not need royal protection but could resist the political and religious encroachments of the British and their Christian missionaries on its own. This led him to challenge the authority of the Burmese king to direct saṅgha affairs in the British-controlled south. In 1857, he seceded from the royally backed Thudhamma fraternity and established an independent ordination line that came to be known as the Dwaya Gaing. The fraternity derives its name from the Okpo Sayadaw's interpretation of the correct way to take refuge in the three jewels (P. ratanattaya; S. RATNATRAYA), viz., not through one's literal acts (P. kamma; S. KARMAN) of body, speech, and mind, but rather through the "doors" (B. dwaya; P. dvāra) or "intentions" that inform one's acts of body, speech, and mind. True worship thus derives from correct mental volition (CETANĀ), not from ritual acts themselves. The Dwaya fraternity is well-known for its strict interpretation of the vinaya, and sectarian aloofness. Dwaya monks are not allowed to handle money or even to use umbrellas, preferring instead large fans made of palmyra leaf; they also are prohibited from living, eating, or otherwise associating with members of other monastic fraternities. Following the Okpo Sayadaw's death, the fraternity split into rival factions. As of 1980, the Burmese Ministry of Religious Affairs officially recognizes three independent Dwaya gaing.

**'Dzam gling rgyas bshad**. (Dzamling gyeshe). In Tibetan, "An Extensive Exposition on the World"; one of the first works in Tibetan to present a systematic geographical and cultural description of the world, although that world is substantially limited to the sacred Buddhist geography of India, Nepal, and Tibet. The text was composed in 1820 (1830 according to one source) by the fourth Bstan po No mon han (Tsenpo Nomonhan) incarnation of SMIN GROL GLING 'Jam dpal chos kyi bstan 'dzin 'phrin las (Jampal Chökyi Tendzin Trinle, 1789–1838). The complete title is *'Dzam gling chen po'i rgyas bshad snod bcud kun gsal me long*.

**'Dzam thang**. A monastic complex in eastern Tibet founded in 1658 in the 'Dzam thang region of A mdo; the major monastric seat of the JO NANG tradition following the suppression of the Jo nang sect in central Tibet by the fifth DALAI LAMA. Following the death of TĀRANĀTHA, the fifth Dalai Lama forcibly converted the main seat of the Jo nang sect at Phun tshogs gling in central Tibet into a DGE LUGS monastery (see DGA' LDAN PHUN TSHOGS GLING) in 1658 and sealed the works of DOL PO PA and TĀRANĀTHA as heretical. Long unknown to modern scholarship, the tradition flourished in the far east of Tibet since that time. Important masters from the monastery are Thub bstan dge legs rgya mtsho (Tupten Gelek Gyatso) (1844–1904) from 'Bam mda', who studied with the luminaries of the Khams RIS MED movement; and Ngag dbang blo gros grags pa (1920–1975) and his disciple Ngag dbang yon tan rgya mtsho, who died in 2002. In the early twenty-first century, there were about fifteen hundred residents of the monastic complex.

# E

**e**. (C) (阿). Sinograph adopted in Chinese Buddhist texts to transcribe the Sanskrit and Middle Indic phoneme "a." Following common practice in Buddhist studies, Chinese transcriptions using this character are listed under "A," e.g., Emituo is listed as Amituo, emaluo as amaluo, etc.

**Ebisu**. (J) (恵比須). See SHICHIFUKUJIN.

**Edgerton, Franklin**. (1885–1963). American scholar of Sanskrit; born in Le Mars, Iowa, he received his undergraduate education at Cornell. He then studied at Munich and Jena before returning to the United States, where he studied Sanskrit and comparative philology at Johns Hopkins. Edgerton taught at the University of Pennsylvania, before moving to Yale in 1926 as Salisbury Professor of Sanskrit. He remained there for the remainder of his academic career, retiring in 1953. Edgerton's great contribution to Buddhist studies was the 1953 publication of his *Buddhist Hybrid Sanskrit Grammar and Dictionary* and his *Buddhist Hybrid Sanskrit Reader*, the result of some three decades of work. Edgerton coined the term BUDDHIST HYBRID SANSKRIT to describe the language of PRAKRIT, mixed Sanskrit, and Sanskrit that occurs in many Buddhist Sanskrit texts, especially the MAHĀYĀNA SŪTRA literature. Prior to Edgerton, this language was sometimes called the Gāthā dialect because it occurred frequently in the verses, or GĀTHĀ, in the Mahāyāna sūtras. Edgerton divided Buddhist Hybrid Sanskrit into three classes based on the degree of hybridization within a given text. Since its publication, Edgerton's work, and the entire category of Buddhist Hybrid Sanskrit itself, has been the subject of much scholarly debate, but Edgerton's dictionary remains widely used.

**ehibhikṣukā**. (P. ehi bhikkhu; T. dge slong tshur shog; C. shanlai bichu; J. zenrai bisshu; K. sŏllae p'ilch'u 善來苾芻). In Sanskrit, the "come, monk" formula; the oldest of the four types of ordination (UPASAṂPADĀ), the ehibhikṣukā was primarily performed at the inception of the Buddhist dispensation before the establishment of a formal procedure for admission into the order; for this reason, many of the Buddha's most famous early disciples were called the ehibhikṣu UPĀLI, etc. Early in his teaching career, when a disciple sought to enter formally the Buddha's incipient order, the Buddha would ordain them via this simple formula, the full form of which is "Come, monk, the DHARMA is well proclaimed; live the holy life for the complete ending of suffering." Some women were also ordained as nuns following a parallel exhortation. In the AVADĀNA literature, when the Buddha ordains monks with this famous phrase, the following description of the new monks often appears, "No sooner had the BHAGAVAT pronounced these words than they found themselves shaved, covered with the robe and provided with the alms-bowl and the pitcher that ends in the beak of a bird; having beard and hair of seven days, they appeared with the proper aspect of monks who had received ordination a hundred years ago."

**eight auspicious symbols**. See AṢṬAMAṄGALA.

**eight bodhisattvas**. See AṢṬAMAHOPAPUTRA.

**eight classes of nonhuman beings**. In Sanskrit, AṢṬASENĀ; a listing of eight types of mythical and semi-mythical beings associated with the sensuous realm (KĀMADHĀTU); they are often listed as being in attendance when the Buddha speaks the MAHĀYĀNA SŪTRAS. There are various lists, but a standard grouping includes divinities (DEVA), serpent deities (NĀGA), demons (YAKṢA), titans (ASURA), demigod musicians (GANDHARVA), mythical birds (GARUḌA), half-horse/half-men (KIṂNARA), and great snakes (MAHORĀGA). For fuller treatments, see AṢṬASENĀ and entries for the individual beings.

**eighteen arhats**. Cf. ṢOḌAŚASTHAVIRA.

**eight episodes in the life of a buddha**. See BAXIANG.

**eight extremes**. (S. aṣṭānta; T. mtha' brgyad; C. babu; J. happu; K. p'albul 八不). The antinomies of production and cessation, eternality and annihilation, sameness and difference, and coming and going, which constitute the eight deluded views of sentient beings. See AṢṬĀNTA; BABU.

**eightfold path**. (S. aṣṭāṅgamārga; P. aṭṭhaṅgikamagga; T. lam yan lag brgyad; C. bazhengdao; J. hasshōdō; K. p'alchŏngdo 八正道). One of the basic formulations of the Buddhist path (MĀRGA) to enlightenment, comprised of the following: (1) right views (SAMYAGDṚṢṬI; P. sammādiṭṭhi), (2) right intention (SAMYAKSAṂKALPA; P. sammāsaṅkappa), (3) right speech (SAMYAGVĀC; P. sammāvācā), (4) right conduct (SAMYAKKARMĀNTA; P. sammākammanta), (5) right livelihood (SAMYAGĀJĪVA; P. sammājīva), (6) right effort (SAMYAGVYĀYĀMA; P. sammāvāyāma), (7) right mindfulness (SAMYAKSMṚTI; P. sammāsati), and (8) right concentration (SAMYAKSAMĀDHI; P. sammāsamādhi). For a full treatment of this formulation, see ĀRYĀṢṬĀṄGAMĀRGA s.v..

**eighth consciousness**. See ĀLAYAVIJÑĀNA.

**eight liberations**. See AṢṬAVIMOKṢA.

**eight minor Bka' brgyud subsects**. See BKA' BRGYUD CHE BZHI CHUNG BRGYAD.

**eight precepts**. See AṢṬĀṄGASAMANVĀGATAṂ UPAVĀSAṂ; ŚĪLA.

**Eight Verses on Mind Training**. See BLO SBYONG TSHIG BRGYAD MA.

**Eiheiji**. (永平寺). In Japanese, "Eternal Peace Monastery." Eiheiji is currently the headquarters (honzan) of the SŌTŌSHŪ. Eiheiji was founded by the Zen master DŌGEN KIGEN. A lay follower named Hatano Yoshishige offered his property in Echizen as a site for the new monastery and invited Dōgen to lead the community. In 1243, Dōgen moved to Echizen and resided in a dilapidated temple named Kippōji. In the meantime, Hatano and others began constructing a new DHARMA hall and SAṂGHA hall (see C. SENGTANG), which they quickly finished by 1244. The new monastery was named Daibutsuji and renamed Eiheiji by Dōgen in 1246. The name Eihei is said to derive from the Han-dynasty reign period, Yongping (58–75 CE; J. Eihei), when Buddhism first arrived in China. In 1248, the mountain on which Eiheiji is located was renamed Mt. Kichijō. In 1372, Eiheiji was declared a shusse dōjō, an official monastery whose abbot is appointed by the state. In 1473, Eiheiji was devastated by war and fire, and reconstruction efforts began in 1487. Since its foundation, Eiheiji has continued to serve as one of the most important Zen institutions in Japan.

**Eihei shingi**. (永平清規). In Japanese, "Pure Rules for EIHEI(JI)"; a collection of essays on the ZEN monastic codes or "pure rules" (QINGGUI), composed by DŌGEN KIGEN. The work is composed in two rolls, in six major sections. The Tenzo Kyōkun section, composed while Dōgen was still residing at Koshōji in 1237, discusses the duties of the cook. The BENDŌHŌ details the daily duties at the monastery of Daibutsuji and the practices, such as meditation, carried out in the SAṂGHA hall (see C. SENGTANG). The Fu shukuhanpō explains the proper method of preparing and consuming rice gruel. The Shuryō shingi of 1249 describes the proper deportment of monks in training at Eiheiji's shuryō. The Tai taiko goge jarihō, composed in 1244, deals with the proper ritual decorum or means of respecting a master (ĀCĀRYA). The final section, the Chiji shingi, from 1246, details the duties of the officers of the monastery. In 1667, these essays were edited together and published by Kōshō Chidō (d. 1670), the thirtieth abbot of Eiheiji. The fiftieth abbot, Gentō Sokuchū (1729–1807), republished Kōshō's edited volume with minor corrections in 1794.

**Eikan**. (J) (永觀). See YŌKAN.

**Eisai**. (榮西). See MYŌAN EISAI.

**Eison**. [alt. Eizon] (叡尊) (1201–1290). In Japanese, "Lord of Sagacity"; founder of Shingon Risshū, a Kamakura-period school that combined the esoteric teachings of the SHINGONSHŪ with VINAYA disciplinary observance. After beginning his career as a monk at the age of eleven, he initially studied Shingon teachings at DAIGOJI in Kyōto and in 1224 moved to KŌYASAN, the mountain center of esoteric teachings and practices. In 1235, while studying vinaya at SAIDAIJI, Eison came to realize the centrality of the PRĀTIMOKṢA precepts to a monastic vocation; however, since the custom of full monastic ordination (J. gusokukai) had died out in Japan long before, he was unable to be properly ordained. Eison decided that his only recourse was to take the precepts in a self-administrated ceremony (J. jisei jukai) before an image of the Buddha. Eison and three other monks conducted such a self-ordination at TŌDAIJI in 1236, after which he traveled around the country, ordaining monks and lecturing on the Buddhist precepts, before eventually returning to Saidaiji to stay. That monastery is now regarded as the center of the Shingon Risshū school. Eison is also known for his extensive charitable activities and his attempts to disseminate the recitation of the MANTRA of light (J. kōmyō shingon) among the laity. When the Mongols invaded Japan in 1274 and 1281, Eison performed esoteric rituals on behalf of the court to ward off the invasions. Among Eison's works are the *Bonmōkyō koshakuki bugyō monjū*, a sub-commentary to the *Pŏmmanggyŏng kojŏkki*, the Korean YOGĀCĀRA monk T'AEHYŎN's (d.u.) commentary on the FANWANG JING; and the *Kanjingaku shōki*, his autobiography, compiled at the age of eighty-six. Eison was given the posthumous name Kōshō Bosatsu (Promoting Orthodoxy BODHISATTVA).

**Ekādaśamukhāvalokiteśvara**. (T. Spyan ras gzigs bcu gcig zhal; C. Shiyimian Guanyin; J. Jūichimen Kannon; K. Sibilmyŏn Kwanŭm 十一面觀音). In Sanskrit, "Eleven-Headed AVALOKITEŚVARA," one of the most common iconographic forms of the BODHISATTVA of compassion. While theories abound about why he has eleven heads, it is likely that the ten small bodhisattva heads topped by a buddha head represent the ten stages (DAŚABHŪMI) of the bodhisattva path, along with the final attainment of buddhahood. The facial expressions of these heads range from kind to ferocious and were meant to symbolize the bodhisattva's various abilities to destroy illusions and help all sentient beings attain liberation. According to legend, Avalokiteśvara was so exhausted and desperate after trying to save innumerable beings that his skull shattered. AMITĀBHA came to help him and formed new heads from the pieces, which he then arranged on AVALOKITEŚVARA's head like a crown, finally putting an image of his own head at the very top. While this eleven-headed form is frequently found in later Buddhist art in Tibet, Nepal, and East Asia, an image from the Indian cave site of KĀNHERI is the only extant artistic evidence that this iconographic form is originally of Indian provenance.

**ekāgratā**. In Sanskrit, "one-pointedness." See CITTAIKĀGRATĀ.

**Ekajaṭā**. [alt. Ekajaṭī] (T. Ral gcig ma; C. Dujimu; J. Dokukeimo; K. Tokkyemo 獨髻母). In Sanskrit, "Having One Lock of Hair," an emanation of AKṢOBHYA; she is often depicted in that Buddha's crown, with a single lock or knot of hair on her head. The wrathful goddess Mahācīnakrama-TĀRĀ or Ugra-Tārā (who is dark and short, with a protruding belly, fanged, with three eyes, a lolling tongue, and a single tawny-colored knot of hair) is iconographically identical to several forms of the Ekajaṭā worshiped in later Hinduism. According to one tradition, this form of Tārā was originally a pre-Buddhist Tibetan goddess who entered into Buddhist TANTRA with the tantric NĀGĀRJUNA in the seventh century. In the RNYING MA sect, in particular, she is said to be a form of DPAL LDAN LHA MO and is called Sngags srung (protectress of the MANTRAS). In this form, she is the protector of the RDZOGS CHEN tantras; she has a single eye, one sharp tooth, a single breast, and a single lock of hair above her head, and she wields a triśūla (trident) and KAPĀLA (skull cup). She also serves as the consort of several forms of MAHĀKĀLA and YAMA and is also found as a member of the PARIVĀRA (retinue) of Dpal ldan lha mo. In other forms, she has one face and two or four hands and twelve faces and twenty-four hands.

**Ekaku**. (J) (慧鶴). See HAKUIN EKAKU.

**ekavīcika**. (T. bar chad gcig pa; C. yijian; J. ikken; K. ilgan 一間). In Sanskrit, "one who has a single obstacle," a particular sort of SAKṚDĀGĀMIPHALASTHA who is one of the twenty members of the ĀRYASAṂGHA (see VIṂŚATIPRABHEDASAṂGHA). According to the ABHIDHARMAKOŚABHĀṢYA, these sorts of once-returners are those who have eliminated the seventh and eighth sets of afflictions (KLEŚA) that cause rebirth in the sensuous realm (KĀMADHĀTU). These are impediments to the first DHYĀNA, which the mundane (LAUKIKA) path of meditation (BHĀVANĀMĀRGA) removes. They receive the name ekavīcika because they will take only one more rebirth in the sensuous realm before they become ARHATs. They are also ānupūrvin (those who reach the four fruits of the noble path in a series), and ANĀGĀMIPHALAPRATIPANNAKA, because they will reach the third fruit of nonreturner before they reach the final fruit of arhat.

**Ekavyavahārika**. (P. Ekabbohārika; T. Tha snyad gcig pa'i sde; C. Yishuobu; J. Issetsubu; K. Ilsŏlbu 一說部). In Sanskrit, "Those who Make a Single Utterance," an alternate name for the LOKOTTARAVĀDA collateral line of the MAHĀSĀṂGHIKA school of mainstream Buddhism. See LOKOTTARAVĀDA.

**ekavyūhasamādhi**. (S). See YIXING SANMEI.

**ekayāna**. (T. theg pa gcig pa; C. yisheng; J. ichijō; K. ilsŭng 一乘). In Sanskrit, lit. "one vehicle" or "single vehicle." "Vehicle" literally means "conveyance" or "transportation," viz., the conveyance that carries sentient beings from SAṂSĀRA to NIRVĀṆA; the term may also refer to the actual person who reaches the destination of the path. The doctrine of a single vehicle is set forth in certain MAHĀYĀNA SŪTRAs, most famously, the SADDHARMAPUṆḌARĪKASŪTRA ("Lotus Sūtra"), which declares that the three vehicles of the ŚRĀVAKA (disciple), PRATYEKABUDDHA (solitary buddha), and BODHISATTVA are actually just three expedient devices (UPĀYAKAUŚALYA) for attracting beings to the one buddha vehicle, via which they all become buddhas. It is important to note that, although it is often claimed that a central tenet of the MAHĀYĀNA is that all sentient beings will eventually achieve buddhahood, this view is not universally set forth in the Mahāyāna sūtras and philosophical schools. A number of important sūtras, notably the SAṂDHINIRMOCANASŪTRA, maintained that there are three final vehicles and that those who successfully followed the path of the śrāvaka and pratyekabuddha would eventually become ARHATs and would not then go on to achieve buddhahood (cf. GOTRA; BUDDHADHĀTU). This position was also held by such major YOGĀCĀRA figures as ASAṄGA. In the *Saddharmapuṇḍarīkasūtra*, however, the Buddha reveals that his earlier teachings of the three vehicles were in fact three expedient forms suited to specific beings' capacities; the sūtra's exposition of the one buddha vehicle is said to be the unifying, complete, and final exposition of his teachings. Since this one-vehicle teaching is the teaching that leads to buddhahood, it is synonymous with the "buddha vehicle" (BUDDHAYĀNA), the "great vehicle" (MAHĀYĀNA), and sometimes the "bodhisattva vehicle" (BODHISATTVAYĀNA). In East Asia, there was substantial consideration given to the precise relations among these terms. Thus, the FAXIANG school of Chinese YOGĀCĀRA interprets the "one vehicle" of the three-vehicle system as being equivalent to the bodhisattva vehicle, while the HUAYAN and TIANTAI schools distinguish between the one buddha vehicle and the bodhisattva vehicle that is included within the three vehicles. The Faxiang school also distinguishes between two levels of the ekayāna, the "inclusive" Mahāyāna (sheru dasheng) and the "derivative" Mahāyāna (chusheng dasheng). According to the explanation of KUIJI (632–682), the first is an expedient like that used in the *Saddharmapuṇḍarīkasūtra* to attract people of indeterminate nature to the one buddha vehicle. Because this type of sentient being is incapable of immediately attaining buddhahood, this teaching does not fully correspond to the meaning of the ekayāna. However, because all members of the *Saddharmapuṇḍarīkasūtra*'s audience have the potential to become buddhas through hearing this teaching, it is still considered to be true and effective. The second type means that all teachings of the Buddha are "born from" or "derive from" a single Mahāyāna teaching; Kuiji says that this type corresponds to the teaching of the ŚRĪMĀLĀDEVĪSIṂHANĀDASŪTRA and the MAHĀPARINIRVĀṆASŪTRA.

**Ekottarāgama**. [alt. Ekottarikāgama] (P. Aṅguttaranikāya; T. Gcig las 'phros pa'i lung; C. Zengyi ahan jing; J. Zōichiagongyō; K. Chŭngil aham kyŏng 增壹阿含經). In Sanskrit, "Numerically Arranged Discourses," the Sanskrit analogue of the Pāli AṄGUTTARANIKĀYA, in which the collected sūtras are putatively arranged sequentially in numbered lists of "ones," "twos," etc.; the extant version of this collection, however, has a pronounced topical arrangement like the SAṂYUTTANIKĀYA. The collection probably dates from sometime between the second century and the first part of the fourth century CE. The *Ekottarāgama*'s sectarian affiliation remains in dispute. Some scholars have attributed it to the MAHĀSĀṂGHIKA school of the mainstream Buddhist tradition, but this attribution has been called into question because certain passages of the text contradict established Mahāsāṃghika doctrine (such as the standard Mahāsāṃghika assertion that ARHATs are subject to backsliding) and show serious inconsistencies with the Mahāsāṃghika VINAYA. Because of these issues, other scholars have instead ascribed the text to the PRAJÑAPTIVĀDA, an offshoot of the Mahāsāṃghika. Because of some seeming consistencies between the *Ekottarāgama* and DHARMAGUPTAKA doctrine and because the text refers to 250 PRĀTIMOKṢA rules for monks, a number that corresponds to the Dharmaguptaka recension of that code, it is possible that the collection may belong to the Dharmaguptaka school. The text is only extant in a Chinese recension, *Zengyi Ahan jing*, translated by Gautama Saṃghadeva in 397 during the Eastern Jin dynasty, in fifty-one rolls. It contains translations of only 471 sūtras, far fewer than the 2,198 suttas in the Pāli *Aṅguttaranikāya*.

**element**. See MAHĀBHŪTA; DHĀTU.

**Ellorā**. [alt. Elūrā]. Among the many cave complexes scattered throughout Asia, perhaps the most famous are Ellorā and AJAṆṬĀ in India; YUNGANG, DUNHUANG, and DAZU in China; and SŎKKURAM in Korea. The site of Ellorā is located near Ajaṇṭā, eighteen miles north of the present-day city of Aurangabad, in the state of Maharashtra. From the sixth through the tenth centuries, there were thirty-four caves carved out of the solid rock of its cliffs. Twelve of these caves date from c. 600 to 730 CE and are Buddhist in orientation. They are rather modest in comparison to the site's Hindu and JAINA caves, which were built at a later date. As monks and nuns built retreats at the site, cave complexes were dug into the base of the cliffs. Some of these excavations were plain cells; others were more elaborate sanctuaries, adorned with paintings, statues, and bas-reliefs. Constructed in the late-seventh or early-eighth centuries, the three-storied Cave 12 was probably one of the last Buddhist caves created at Ellorā. While the central shrine on each floor shows a buddha flanked by the two BODHISATTVAS AVALOKITEŚVARA and VAJRAPĀṆI, it is especially noteworthy that Cave 12's interior artistic scheme also illustrates the early development of diagrams (MAṆḌALA), both in two-dimensional relief and three-dimensional sculpture. The so-called eight-bodhisattva maṇḍala (aṣṭabodhisattvamaṇḍala) is depicted on each floor. In addition, in some sections of the cave, the eight bodhisattvas (AṢṬAMAHOPAPUTRA) surround a central buddha in a nine-square diagram. The maṇḍalas shown in this cave attest to the highly developed ritual environments at Ellorā and also demonstrate that over the course of time artistic imagery was used in the service of specific Buddhist beliefs. The developments documented in exceptional caves like this one were nurtured by lay patronage and royal support. Stylistically, the Ellorā caves are similar to those of neighboring Ajaṇṭā, and may have been crafted by sculptors who worked at that earlier cave site.

**Elūrā**. See ELLORĀ.

**Emeishan**. (C. 峨嵋山/峨眉山). In Chinese, lit. "Delicate Eyebrows Mountain," a mountain located in Sichuan province that is traditionally listed as one of the four sacred Buddhist mountains of China, along with JIUHUASHAN in Anhui province, PUTUOSHAN in Zhejiang, and WUTAISHAN in Shanxi. The name Emeishan is derived from its two peaks, which face each other and are said to look like the delicate eyebrows of a classic Chinese beauty. The mountain covers more than 58 square miles (150 square kilometers), and its tallest peak, Wanfo Ding (Myriad Buddhas Summit), is 10,167 feet (3,099 meters) high, over 3280 feet (1,000 meters) higher than the other three sacred Buddhist mountains of China. The charming scenery of Emeishan has won it since ancient times the name "the greatest beauty under heaven." The patron BODHISATTVA of Emeishan is SAMANTABHADRA (C. Puxian pusa), who was said to have resided in Emeishan. Because of this connection, most monasteries on Emeishan house a statue of Samantabhadra. Emeishan is of exceptional cultural significance because Chinese tradition assumes it was the place where Buddhism first became established on Chinese territory and whence it spread widely. The first Buddhist monastery in China is said to have been built on Emeishan in the first century CE during the Eastern Han dynasty (25–220). There were once more than a hundred monasteries and temples located on the mountain, but only about twenty remain today. These active monasteries include Baoguosi, Wanniansi, Fuhusi, Leiyinsi, Xianfengsi, Qianfosi, Huazangsi on the Golden Summit, and the Xixiangshi (Elephant Washing Pool) hermitage. At the foot of Emeishan, Baoguosi, built between 1573 and 1619 during the Ming dynasty, is the largest surviving monastery, and is the center of Buddhist activity on the mountain. Wanniansi, originally named Puxiansi, is one of the major monasteries and houses an exquisite copper statue of Samantabhadra riding a white elephant; made in 980 CE during the Song dynasty, the image is 24.11 feet (7.35 meters) high. The Jinding (Golden Summit), one of the mountain's main peaks, is 10,095 feet (3,077 meters) high and is the ideal place to view the sunrise, the sea of clouds, and strange atmospheric phenomena called Buddhist lights and sacred lamps. Emeishan is also a well-known nature preserve and is home to more than three thousand species of plants and two thousand species of animals, including groups of monkeys that often appear on the mountain roads. Near Emeishan is the remarkable Great Buddha of Leshan (C. LESHAN DAFO); the world's largest stone statue of MAITREYA, this image is 233 feet (71 meters) high and was carved out of a hillside in the eighth century during the Tang dynasty. In 1996, UNESCO listed Emeishan and the Great Buddha of Leshan as a World Heritage Site.

**Emerald Buddha**. See PHRA KAEW MORAKOT.

**empowerment**. See ADHIṢṬHĀNA.

**emptiness**. See ŚŪNYATĀ.

**Enchin**. (圓珍) (814–891). Japanese monk affiliated with the TENDAISHŪ (C. TIANTAI ZONG) and reputed founder of the Jimon branch of the school. Enchin was a native of Sanuki in present-day Kagawa and a cousin of the SHINGON master KŪKAI. At age fourteen, Enchin became the student of GISHIN, the abbot of ENRYAKUJI, and four years later received the full monastic precepts from him. For the next twelve years, Enchin remained in retreat on HIEIZAN. In 853, Enchin traveled to Fuzhou, China, and stayed at the nearby monastery of Kaiyuansi. There he studied the Sanskrit SIDDHAM script under the Indian TREPIṬAKA Boredaluo (Prajñātāra?). Enchin later visited Yuezhou and Taizhou (present-day Zhejiang province), where he studied Tiantai doctrine and practice. In 855, Enchin entered the Chinese capital of Chang'an with his fellow Japanese monk Ensai (d. 877), where they are believed to have received the "dharma-transmission ABHIṢEKA" (denbō kanjō) from Faquan (d.u.) at the monastery of Qinglongsi, as well as the secret of teachings of the "two realms" (RYŌBU) from Prajñācakra (d.u.). Enchin then returned to Mt. Tiantai in Taizhou with the new translations of esoteric scriptures that he acquired in Chang'an. Enchin returned to Japan in 858 and resided at the monastery of Onjōji (see MIIDERA). In 866, Enchin became the fifth head (zasu) of Enryakuji and was given imperial permission to transform Onjōji into the official grounds of "dharma-transmission abhiṣeka." A schism between the lineages of Enchin and ENNIN over the issue of succession in 993 led to the split between Ennin's Sanmon branch of Hieizan and Enchin's Jimon branch of Onjōji. Enchin was later given the posthumous title Great Master Chishō (Realization of Wisdom).

**Engakuji**. (圓覺寺). A large monastery in Kamakura, Japan, that is currently the headquarters (honzan) of the Engakuji branch of the RINZAISHŪ of the ZEN tradition. Engakuji was once listed as a second-rank monastery in the influential GOZAN system. The monastery was established by the powerful regent Hōjō Tokimune (1251–1284) in 1282. When LANXI DAOLONG, the prominent Chinese abbot of the influential monastery of KENCHŌJI, died in 1274, Hōjō Tokimune immediately sought a replacement, and his envoys returned from China escorting the CHAN master WUXUE ZUYUAN. Wuxue, who was serving as abbot of Kenchōji, was installed as the founding abbot (J. kaisan; C. KAISHAN) of the new monastery of Engakuji. In 1400, Engakuji was devastated by a great fire, but restoration efforts in 1625 refurbished the monastery to its current size and form. Since its foundation, Engakuji has remained a center of Zen culture and training in Japan.

**enlightenment**. See ANUTTARASAMYAKSAṂBODHI; BODHI; DUNWU; NIRVĀṆA; WU.

**Enni Ben'en**. (C. Yuan'er Bianyuan 圓爾辨圓) (1202–1280). Japanese ZEN master in the Chinese LINJI ZONG and Japanese RINZAISHŪ. Enni was tonsured at the TENDAI monastery of Onjōji (see MIIDERA) at the age of seventeen, and received the full monastic precepts at the precepts platform (kaidan) in the monastery of TŌDAIJI. In 1235, Enni left for China and visited the CHAN masters Chijue Daochong (1169–1250), Xiaoweng Miaokan (1177–1248), and Shitian Faxun (1171–1245). Enni eventually visited the Chan master WUZHUN SHIFAN at the monastery of WANSHOUSI on Mt. Jing and inherited his Linji lineage. In 1241, Enni returned to Japan and began to teach at the capital Kyōto at the invitation of the powerful Fujiwara minister Kujō Michiie (1191–1252). In 1243, Enni was given the title Shōichi (Sacred Unity). Enni also won the support of the powerful regent Hōjō Tokiyori (1227–1263). Michiie later installed Enni as the founding abbot (J. kaisan; C. KAISHAN) of his powerful monastery of Tōfukuji. Enni also served as abbot of the Zen monastery of KENNINJI in Kyōto. In 1311, Enni was named State Preceptor Shōichi. His teachings are recorded in the *Shōichi Kokushi goroku* and *Shōichi kokushi kana hōgo*.

**Ennin**. (C. Yuanren 圓仁) (794–864). Japanese monk of the TENDAISHŪ (C. TIANTAI ZONG), who wrote a classic account of his ninth-century pilgrimage to China. A native of Tochigi prefecture, Ennin lost his father when young, and became a student of the eminent Japanese monk SAICHŌ at the monastery of ENRYAKUJI on HIEIZAN. Ennin was ordained on Mt. Hiei in 814 and received the full monastic precepts three years later at the precepts platform (kaidan) on the grounds of the monastery of TŌDAIJI. In 838, Ennin traveled to China with his companions Engyō (799–852) and Jōkyō (d. 866), arriving in Yangzhou (present-day Jiangsu province) at the mouth of the Yangzi River. The next year, he visited the monastery of Kaiyuansi, where he received the teachings and rituals of the various KONGŌKAI (vajradhātu) deities from the monk Quanya (d.u.). Ennin also studied the Sanskrit SIDDHAM script while in China. When adverse winds kept him from returning to Japan, he remained behind at the monastery of Fahuayuan on Mt. Chi in Dengzhou (present-day Shandong province). From there, Ennin made a pilgrimage to WUTAISHAN and studied Tiantai doctrine and practice. In 840, Ennin arrived in the capital of Chang'an, where he studied the kongōkai MAṆḌALA under Yuanzheng (d.u.) of the monastery of Daxingshansi. The next year, Ennin also studied the teachings of the TAIZŌKAI (garbhadhātu) and *SUSIDDHIKARASŪTRA under Yizhen (d.u.) of the monastery of Qinglongsi. In 842, Ennin furthered his studies of the taizōkai under Faquan (d.u.) at the monastery of Xuanfasi, siddham under Yuanjian (d.u.) of Da'anguosi, and siddham pronunciation under the Indian ĀCĀRYA Baoyue (d.u.). In 845, Ennin fled from the Huichang persecution of Buddhism (see HUICHANG FANAN) that then raged in Chang'an, and arrived back in Japan in 847. Ennin kept a detailed record of his sojourn in China in his famed diary, the NITTŌ GUHŌ JUNREI GYŌKI (translated into English as *A Pilgrimage to China in Search of the Law*). In 854, Ennin was appointed the head (zasu) of Enryakuji and three years later was allowed to perform the RYŌBU ABHIṢEKA for Emperor Buntoku (r. 850–858) in the palace. Ennin promoted the Tendai/Tiantai teachings of the four kinds of SAMĀDHI (sizhong sanmei), which he had brought back to Japan from China. He also made an effort to continue his teacher Saichō's attempt to implement the use of the bodhisattva precepts (see FANWANG JING) in Japan.

**En no Gyōja**. (J) (役行者). See EN NO OZUNU.

**En no Ozunu**. (役小角) (b. 634). Also known as En no Gyōja (lit. "En the Ascetic"), a semi-legendary figure associated with SHUGENDŌ (lit. the "Way of Cultivating Supernatural Power") who is known for his shamanic abilities and mountain austerities. Practitioners of Shugendō, Japan's tradition of mountain asceticism, regard him as their founder and view him as the archetypal ascetic. The earliest accounts of En no Ozunu appear in the *Shoku Nihongi* (797) and the *Nihon Ryōiki* (810–824). He subsequently became the subject of numerous medieval texts, although many of the details of his life are sketchy. Allegedly born in Chihara in present-day Nara prefecture, he spent three decades of practice in KATSURAGISAN, where legend holds that he worked to convert malicious spirits. In 699, he was exiled to Izu (in present-day Shizuoka prefecture) by Emperor Monmu because of accusations made by his disciple, Karakuni no Muraji Hirotari that he was practicing sorcery. Shugendō considers En no Ozunu to be a manifestation of Hōki Bosatsu (DHARMODGATA), whose sphere of practice in the Katsuragi mountains includes KONGŌSAN (see also KŬMGANGSAN), the traditional residence of this BODHISATTVA. In 1799, in conjunction with the alleged eleven hundredth anniversary of En no Ozunu's death, Emperor Kōkaku bestowed on him the title Jinben Daibosatsu (Great Bodhisattva Mysterious Change).

**Enpō dentōroku**. (延寶傳燈錄). In Japanese, "The Enpō Reign-Era Transmission of the Lamplight Record"; a late Japanese genealogical history of the ZEN school, written by the RINZAISHŪ monk Mangen Shiban (1626–1710) and completed in 1678 and published in 1706, in a total of 41 rolls. Like the earlier Chinese lamplight record JINGDE CHUANDENG LU, which was named after the Chinese reign-era during which the text was compiled, Mangen used the Japanese reign-era Enpō to designate his collection. The text includes the biographies of over one thousand Zen clerics and lay practitioners in the major Zen lineages of the Japanese Rinzaishū and SŌTŌSHŪ, with excerpts from their sermons and verses. Because of its vast scope, the collection offers a comprehensive overview of the history of the Japanese Zen tradition up to Mangen's time. In his preface, Shiban states that his source materials were these masters' discourse records (J. goroku; C. YULU), biographies, and stele and pagoda inscriptions, which he had collected for over thirty years since his youth. Mangen subsequently collected the biographies of 1,662 Buddhist monks from a range of Japanese sects and compiled them into the HONCHŌ KŌSŌDEN, completed in 1702 in a total of 75 rolls.

**Enryakuji**. (延暦寺). An important monastery located on HIEIZAN (Mt. Hiei), near Kyōto, Japan, which has served as the headquarters (honzan) of the TENDAISHŪ (C. TIANTAI ZONG) since its foundation. Enryakuji, or Hieizanji, started from humble beginnings in 785, when the Japanese monk SAICHŌ built a straw hut on Mt. Hiei. Three years later he built Ichijō shikan'in, the famous main hall that later was named Konpon chūdō and is currently designated a national treasure (kokuhō). In 806, with Emperor Kanmu's (r. 781–806) support, Saichō's residence was firmly established as a powerful monastery, whose function was to protect the new capital Heijōkyō (present-day Kyōto) from the demons that threatened the capital from the northeast. In 822, the year of Saichō's death, the emperor granted permission to construct a MAHĀYĀNA precepts platform (daijō kaidan) at the site, and a year later the monastery was renamed Enryakuji. In 824, the monk GISHIN was appointed the first head (zasu) of Enryakuji and the Tendai school. In 828, the Mahāyāna precepts platform was constructed on Mt. Hiei, which gave the Tendai monks freedom from the monopoly over ordination that the powerful monasteries in Nara had wielded up to that time. In 834, the Shakadō was constructed in the Saitō (West Hall) subcomplex. In 848, ENNIN established the Shūryōgon'in complex at YOKAWA and in 858 the monk ENCHIN established the subtemple Onjōji (see MIIDERA) as his separate residence. A schism between the lineages of Enchin and Ennin over the issue of succession in 993 led to the split between Ennin's Sanmon branch of Mt. Hiei and Enchin's Jimon branch of Onjōji. This schism grew into a violent battle that involved the recruiting of so-called warrior monks (SŌHEI). In 1571, Oda Nobunaga (1534–1582) burned a large number of monasteries on Mt. Hiei to the ground, including Enryakuji. Enryakuji now largely consists of three independent subcomplexes known as the Tōdō (East Pagoda), Saitō (West Pagoda), and Yokawa.

**er bao**. (J. nihō; K. i po 二報). In Chinese, "two kinds of karmic retribution." One's actions, or KARMAN, are said to lead to "retribution proper" (C. zheng bao; J. shōhō; K. chŏngbo) and "adjunct retribution" (C. yi bao; J. ehō; K. ŭibo). The former directly affects the individual, in that it creates and conditions one's physical body and psychological makeup (see VIPĀKAPHALA). The latter affects the individual in a less direct way, in that it creates and conditions the quality of one's possessions and property (e.g., homes, land, and personal acquaintances) and determines such external factors as the household and country into which one is reborn (see ADHIPATIPHALA). This expression is also sometimes used to refer to the buddhas of MAHĀYĀNA; in that context, "retribution proper" determines the longevity and other personal attributes of a given buddha, whereas "adjunct retribution" influences the relative desirability and objective features of his PURE LAND (cf. GONG BUGONG YE and ER SHIJIAN). See BUDDHAKṢETRA.

**er chao**. (二超). In Chinese, "two modes of deliverance" or "escape." See HENGCHAO and SHUCHAO.

**er chi**. (J. niji; K. i chi 二持). In Chinese, "two modes of observing the precepts": the observance of prohibitive precepts (zhi chi) and the observance of exhortative precepts (zuo chi). The former refers to the "passive" restraint that comes from simply following the monastic regulations specified in the VINAYA proper. The latter refers to the "active" cultivation of virtue and "constructive" undertaking of those wholesome activities that are elaborated in the SKANDHAKA (P. Khandhaka) section of the vinaya (cf. ER FAN).

**er chu san hui**. (J. nisho san'e; K. i ch'ŏ sam hoe 二處三會). In Chinese, "the two locations and three assemblies," the sites where the Buddha is presumed to have preached the SADDHARMAPUṆḌARĪKASŪTRA; a TIANTAI term. The two locations are Vulture Peak (GṚDHRAKŪṬAPARVATA) and the sky. According to the account in the *Saddharmapuṇḍarīkasūtra*, the Buddha preached, first, chapters one through the middle of the eleventh chapter on Vulture Peak; continuing on to, second, the end of the twenty-second chapter in the sky; and, finally, third, the twenty-third chapter to the end of the sūtra back at Vulture Peak.

**er de**. (J. nitoku; K. i tŏk 二德). In Chinese, "dual virtues" or "two meritorious qualities." There are at least three different sets of "dual virtues": (1) the virtue of wisdom (zhi de) and the virtue of cessation (duan de) (e.g., of ignorance, suffering, and the fetters), (2) the virtue of wisdom (zhi de) and the virtue of compassion (bei de), (3) virtues that are inherent (xing de, i.e., those inherent in one's buddha-nature, or FOXING) and virtues that are cultivated (xiu de).

**er fan**. (J. nibon; K. i pŏm 二犯). In Chinese, "two kinds of transgressions [against precepts]": the transgression of precepts through a failure to act (zhi fan), and the transgression of precepts through action (zuo fan). Through neglect, laziness, or a lack of motivation, one commits the former transgression when one is delinquent in cultivating the "exhortative precepts"—the undertaking of wholesome activities. In contrast to the former's "guilt due to passivity," one's active and willful breach of "prohibitive precepts" constitutes the latter transgression. Cf. ER CHI.

**er he**. (J. niwa; K. i hwa 二和). In Chinese, "two kinds of harmony." The monastic community is exhorted to achieve both harmony in "principle" (li, viz., doctrinal or ideological consensus [lihe]) and harmony in "practice" (shi, viz., freedom from verbal, physical, economic, and institutional conflicts [shihe]). These two kinds of harmony are sometimes expanded to a list of six (liu he): harmony in observation of the precepts (jiehe), harmony in understanding (jianhe), harmony in sharing a residence (shenhe), harmony in sharing the requisites (lihe), harmony in verbal activity (kouhe), and harmony in mutual goodwill (yihe).

**er jia**. (J. nika; K. i ka 二加). In Chinese, "two kinds of empowerment (ADHIṢṬHĀNA) [of the Buddha]": "manifest empowerment" (xian jia) and "covert empowerment" (min jia). Manifest empowerment is the direct, physical assistance provided by the Buddha through such acts as aiding and protecting the empowered with his psychic powers (S. ṚDDHI); verbally communicating with and speaking the dharma to them; displaying physical gestures, such as rubbing the disciple's head, in order to increase the latter's faith; verbal exhortation in order to enhance the eloquence (S. PRATISAṂVID) of the empowered, etc. Because this type of empowerment is visible to all, it is manifest empowerment. Covert empowerment has been variously interpreted to be the Buddha's telepathic assistance to his disciples, or his disciples' ability to partake mystically in the Buddha's powers by recollecting him or invoking his name. Because such empowerment is typically hidden from view, it is covert.

**er liu**. (J. niru; K. i nyu 二流). In Chinese, "two currents": going against the current (ni liu) and following the current (shun liu). The former means to turn against the powerful currents that drive the cycle of rebirth (see SAṂSĀRA), by practicing the path (MĀRGA) and stopping the contaminants (see ĀSRAVA). The latter means to be unrestrained in one's worldly pursuits, not undertake religious training, and thus following the currents of saṃsāra.

**er mi**. (J. nimitsu; K. i mil 二密). In Chinese, "two aspects of esoteric Buddhism." "Esoteric as to principle" (li mi) refers to the doctrines and conceptual understanding of esoteric Buddhism. "Esoteric as to practices" (shi mi) refers to the physical enactment of the "esoteric principle," either in tantric rituals and practices or in the Buddha's unfathomable activities. The Japanese TAIMITSU sect of esoteric Buddhism (as advocated by Japanese TENDAISHŪ) regards the SADDHARMAPUṆḌARĪKASŪTRA and MAHĀPARINIRVĀṆASŪTRA as representative of esoteric as to principle, whereas the sūtras promoted by SHINGONSHŪ are esoteric with regard to both principle and practices.

**er quan**. (J. nisen; K. i chŏn 二詮). In Chinese, "two modes of explication": apophatic (negative) and kataphatic (positive) discourse. The former describes something by pointing to what the thing is not. For example, the Buddhist description of NIRVĀṆA often employs "negative statement"—i.e., nirvāṇa is neither a kind of existence nor is it nonexistence; it can neither be characterized by any of the primary factors nor can it be localized. A "positive statement," by contrast, delineates and defines something by pointing to what the thing is. For example, the Buddhist idea of right understanding may be described by a positive statement—i.e., it is the intellectual and intuitive acceptance of the law of conditionality, the reality of KARMAN and rebirth, and the FOUR NOBLE TRUTHS.

**er ren**. (J. ninin; K. i in 二忍). In Chinese, "the two kinds of forbearances (KṢĀNTI)": The first is the endurance, patience, and forbearance a BODHISATTVA has toward sentient beings, referring to the ability to withstand insults and obstacles posed by them and to undertake altruistic deeds (sheng ren). The second is ANUTPATTIKADHARMAKṢĀNTI, the receptivity to the fact that dharmas are unproduced (fa ren).

**er ru**. (J. ninyū; K. i ip 二入). In Chinese, "the two accesses," or "two entrances." The putative Indian founder of the CHAN ZONG, BODHIDHARMA, taught in his ERRU SIXING LUN ("Treatise on the Two Accesses and Four Practices") that enlightenment could be gained by two complementary methods. The "access of principle" (li ru) was a more static approach to practice, which sought an intuitive insight into the DHARMA and a recognition of the fact that each and every person was innately endowed with the capacity for enlightenment. The "access of practice" (xing ru) was a set of four dynamic practices that teach the student how to act with correct understanding of SAṂSĀRA and that ultimately culminates in the same understanding achieved through the access of principle. The four practices are: retribution of enmity, acquiescing to conditions, seeking nothing, and practicing in accord with the dharma. Later Chan adepts sometimes sought to ascribe to these two accesses the original inspiration for the Chan notion of sudden enlightenment (see DUNWU), or the soteriological approach of sudden awakening followed by gradual cultivation (see DUNWU JIANXIU).

**Erru sixing lun**. (J. Ninyū shigyōron; K. Iip sahaeng non 二入四行論). In Chinese, "Treatise on the Two Accesses and Four Practices," attributed to the legendary Indian monk BODHIDHARMA, putative founder of the CHAN ZONG; regardless of the authenticity of this ascription, the text is legitimately regarded as the earliest text of the Chan school. The treatise provides an outline of "two accesses" (ER RU): the access of principle (liru) a more static approach to practice, which sought an intuitive insight into the DHARMA and a recognition of the fact that each and every person was innately endowed with the capacity for enlightenment. This was complemented by the access of practice (xingru), which was subdivided into four progressive practices: retribution of enmity, acquiescing to conditions, seeking nothing, and practicing in accord with the dharma. The treatise underscores the inherent purity of the practitioner, which it glosses as the dharma or principle, and betrays little evidence of features that come to characterize the later Chan tradition, such as the debate over sudden or gradual enlightenment, the rejection of traditional meditative techniques, etc. Numerous copies of this treatise were found in DUNHUANG, and citations of this text are found in the XU GAOSENG ZHUAN, LENGQIE SHIZI JI, and JINGDE CHUANDENG LU. The text was published in Korea as part of the SŎNMUN CH'WARYO and in Japan as the SHŌSHITSU ROKUMONSHŪ. A preface to this relatively short treatise was prepared by the monk Tanlin (fl. 506–574) and some editions of the treatise also contain two letters attributed to Bodhidharma's disciple HUIKE.

**er sheng**. (S. yānadvaya; J. nijō; K. i sŭng 二乘). In Chinese, "two vehicles," referring to adherents of the "two vehicles" of disciples (ŚRĀVAKA) and solitary buddhas (PRATYEKABUDDHA), and thus often functionally equivalent to the "lesser vehicle" (HĪNAYĀNA). The Chinese translates literally the Sanskrit yānadvaya (two vehicles), but the Chinese term is often used as an abbreviated translation for the Sanskrit compound śrāvaka-pratyekabuddha (disciples and solitary buddhas). In many contexts, therefore, the term means "two-vehicle adherents," in distinction to the BODHISATTVAs and buddhas of the MAHĀYĀNA.

**er shijian**. (J. niseken; K. i segan 二世間). In Chinese, lit. "the two kinds of worlds." Following the ABHIDHARMAKOŚABHĀṢYA, the Chinese distinguish between the reality associated with the sentient and inanimate realms. The sentient aspect of reality refers to the living beings who are endowed with consciousness (SATTVALOKA); the inanimate aspect is the physical environment in which sentient beings exist (BHĀJANALOKA). According to this cosmology, both the sentient and inanimate aspects of reality are created and conditioned by living beings' KARMAN—the former by the so-called individual karman and the latter by "collective karman." (cf. ER BAO and GONG BUGONG YE).

**ershiwu yuantong**. (J. nijūgoenzū; K. isibo wŏnt'ong 二十五圓通). In Chinese, "twenty-five kinds of consummate interpenetration." According to the *ŚŪRAṂGAMASŪTRA (*Shoulengyan jing*), twenty-five of the Buddha's disciples and bodhisattvas have each mastered a concentration (SAMĀDHI) pertaining to one of the twenty-five objects of meditation. The latter include the six sensory objects (liu chen; S. ĀLAMBANA), the six sensory faculties (liu gen; S. INDRIYA), the six sensory consciousnesses (liu shi; S. VIJÑĀNA), and the seven primary elements (qi da). It is said that enlightenment is possible by accessing any of the twenty-five masteries even though the bodhisattva AVALOKITEŚVARA's mastery over the "ear faculty," or auditory sense-base, has been singled out as a particularly efficacious method for practice.

**er wozhi**. (J. nigashū; K. i ajip 二我執). In Chinese, "two kinds of attachment to self" (ĀTMAGRĀHA): "self-attachment that arises from discriminatory cognition" (fenbie wozhi) and "innate self-attachment" (jusheng wozhi). The former is primarily an epistemic error resulting from improper thinking and exposure to fallacious doctrines (MITHYĀDṚṢṬI); it is eradicated at the stage of stream-enterer (SROTAĀPANNA). The latter is primarily an affective, habitual, and instinctive clinging (conditioned for many lifetimes in the past) that may be present whether or not one subscribes to fenbie wozhi, the "view of self." "Innate self-attachment" is only gradually attenuated through the successive stages of spiritual fruition until it is completely extinguished at the stage of the ARHAT. See FAZHI and PUDGALANAIRĀTMYA.

**er wuchang**. (J. nimujō; K. i musang 二無常). In Chinese, "two kinds of impermanence" (ANITYA): "impermanence marked by a successive period" (xiangxu wuchang; T. bya rdzogs kyi skad cig ma) and "impermanence that occurs at every instant" (niannian wuchang; T. dus mtha'i skad cig pa). The former is visible when an episodic event or arbitrary length of time has elapsed, such as the ending of a human life, the waning daylight at dawn, the extinguishing light at candle's end, etc. The latter, by contrast, refers to the inexorable change that is taking place anytime and anywhere, even before an arbitrary episodic event has come to an end (e.g., even before a person's biological death, the person "dies" every instant in the continuum of flux that defines his existence). Cf. FENDUAN SHENGSI and BIANYI SHENGSI, respectively.

**er xiashi**. (C) (二挾侍). See ER XIESHI.

**er xieshi**. (J. nikyōji; K. i hyŏpsa 二脇士). In Chinese, "the two flanking attendants." In Buddhist art and literature, ŚĀKYAMUNI and other buddhas are often depicted flanked by two companions, usually either BODHISATTVAS or disciples (ŚRĀVAKA). In the case of Śākyamuni, typically ŚĀRIPUTRA and MAHĀMAUDGALYĀYANA, the bodhisattvas MAÑJUŚRĪ and SAMANTABHADRA, or the disciples ĀNANDA and MAHĀKĀŚYAPA are at his sides. In the case of the buddha AMITĀBHA, the bodhisattvas AVALOKITEŚVARA and MAHĀSTHĀMAPRĀPTA are his "two flanking attendants." In the case of BHAIṢAJYAGURU, the bodhisattvas Sunlight (C. Riguang; S. Sūryaprabha) and Moonlight (C. Yueguang; S. Candraprabha) are his ancillary companions. See MCHOG ZUNG.

**er xu**. (J. nijo; K. i sŏ 二序). In Chinese, the "two kinds of prefaces" appearing in most SŪTRAs according to Chinese Buddhist exegetical traditions. The first kind is the so-called generic preface (tongxu)—the phrase "thus have I heard" (C. rushi wowen; S. EVAṂ MAYĀ ŚRUTAM). The second kind is called the "specific preface" (biexu), which stipulates the particular location and audience of a sermon and is different between sūtras. See also NIDĀNA.

**er yingshen**. (J. niōjin; K. i ŭngsin 二應身). In Chinese, "the two kinds of emanation bodies" (NIRMĀṆAKĀYA): superior transformation body (sheng yingshen) and inferior transformation body (lie yingshen). In the MAHĀYĀNA, the Buddha's magical "emanation body" (nirmāṇakāya) is said to correspond to the audience's karmic predispositions and spiritual attainments. The "superior transformation body"—with its celestial features and immeasurable longevity—is said to be only visible to highly advanced bodhisattvas (those who have attained the tenth BHŪMI or higher). All other beings have only access to the Buddha's "inferior transformation body." See SPRUL SKU.

**erzhong gongyang**. (J. nishu no kuyō; K. ijong kongyang 二種供養). In Chinese, "two kinds of offerings" (S. PŪJĀ/pūjanā). There are several lists. (1) The offering that is in accord with principle (LI gongyang), and the offering that is in accord with phenomena (SHI gongyang). The former is the "glorifying" of the three jewels (RATNATRAYA) by means of attaining spiritual realization and undertaking spiritual practice; the latter are offerings of material support. (2) The offering made to those who are freed from the fetters, or SAṂYOJANA (chuchan gongyang), and the offering made to those who are still subject to the fetters (zaichan gongyang). (3) Material offerings (cai gongyang) and offerings of the DHARMA (fa gongyang): the former involves material goods; the latter involves the explication, promotion, implementation, and promulgation of the Buddhist teachings.

**erzhong sanguan**. (J. nishu no sangan; K. ijong samgwan 二種三觀). See SANGUAN.

**erzhong yuanli**. (J. nishuonri; K. ijong wŏlli 二種遠離). In Chinese, "two kinds of seclusion" (S. VIRATI; VIVEKA): physical seclusion (shen yuanli) and seclusion of the mind (xin yuanli). Removing oneself from a distracting, unwholesome, and disquieting environment by leaving it behind constitutes "physical seclusion." Seclusion of the mind usually refers to "guarding one's senses" (see INDRIYASAṂVARA) with mindfulness so that the mind will neither cling to nor be repulsed by, sensory stimuli; it also refers to the "withdrawal" from sensory stimulations and the collectedness of attention during meditative states (see DHYĀNA).

**er zong**. (J. nishū; K. i chong 二宗). In Chinese, "the two [primary] scholastic traditions," or "two [rival] tenets," of which there are three different schemata. (1) kong zong vs. you zong: In this model, Buddhism is divided into the school that posits the insubstantiality of things (C. kong; S. ŚŪNYATĀ) and that which posits the substantiality of things (C. you; S. BHAVA), respectively. One such dichotomy involves the BAHUŚRUTĪYA, the school associated with the CHENGSHI LUN (**Tattvasiddhi*), which teaches the "emptiness of everything" (sarva-ŚŪNYATĀ), including factors (DHARMANAIRĀTMYA), and the SARVĀSTIVĀDA school, which assumes that things could be reduced to fundamentally real, indivisible factors (DHARMA) that exist independently and are endowed with unique, irreducible properties. (2) XING ZONG vs. XIANG ZONG: In this model, Buddhist teaching is said to consist of the doctrine that deals with the "nature of things" (C. xing; this doctrine has been variously interpreted as being associated with the MADHYAMAKA and TATHĀGATAGARBHA schools), and the doctrine that deals with the "characteristics/phenomenal aspects of things" (C. xiang; this doctrine has been variously interpreted to be associated with the YOGĀCĀRA and Sarvāstivāda schools), respectively. (3) kong zong vs. xing zong: In the third model, Buddhism is said to contain two antithetical strands of thought (that may or may not be ultimately complementary). One strand upholds the reality of "emptiness" (C. kong) and denies any "self" or substantiality in all dharmas. The other strand affirms a discoverable and real "essence" (C. xing) of dharmas. Traditionally, Madhyamaka has been identified to be the paradigmatic "school of emptiness," and tathāgatagarbha to be the paragon of the "school of [real] nature."

**Eshin Sōzu**. (J) (惠心僧都). See GENSHIN.

**evaṃ mayā śrutam**. (P. evaṃ me sutaṃ; T. 'di skad bdag gis thos pa; C. rushi wowen; J. nyozegamon; K. yŏsi amun 如是我聞). In Sanskrit, "thus have I heard," the stock phrase that begins most SŪTRAS, certifying that the teachings about to be recounted were heard from the mouth of the Buddha (or, in some cases, were spoken with his sanction by insightful disciples). The "I" in the phrase is generally assumed to refer to the Buddha's attendant ĀNANDA, who recited the SŪTRAPIṬAKA at the first Buddhist council (see COUNCIL, FIRST) following the Buddha's PARINIRVĀṆA. In MAHĀYĀNA scholastic literature, however, where the argument is made that the Buddha taught many sūtras that were not heard by Ānanda, it is sometimes advocated that the "I" instead refers to a particular BODHISATTVA who serves as the interlocutor for the scripture, such as MAÑJUŚRĪ. There is also some debate within scholarly circles, following the commentarial interpretations of certain Buddhist traditions, whether this stock opening should also include the phrase "at one time" (ekasmin samaye) that usually follows, viz., "thus I have heard at one time" or "thus I once heard" (evaṃ mayā śrutaṃ ekasmin samaye). See also ER XU; cf. GUHYASAMĀJATANTRA.

**Evans-Wentz, Walter Y**. (1878–1965). American Theosophist, best known as the editor of THE TIBETAN BOOK OF THE DEAD. Walter Wentz was born in Trenton, New Jersey, the son of a German immigrant and an American Quaker. As a boy he took an early interest in books on spiritualism he found in his father's library, reading as a teen both *Isis Unveiled* and *The Secret Doctrine* by Madame HELENA PETROVNA BLAVATSKY of the Theosophical Society. He moved to California at the turn of the century, where in 1901, he joined the American section of the Theosophical Society. After graduating from Stanford University, Wentz went to Jesus College at Oxford in 1907 to study Celtic folklore. He later traveled to Sri Lanka (Ceylon) and then on to India. In 1919, he arrived in the British hill station of Darjeeling, where he acquired a Tibetan manuscript. The manuscript was a portion of a cycle of treasure texts (GTER MA) discovered by RATNA GLING PA, entitled "The Profound Doctrine of Self-Liberation of the Mind [through Encountering] the Peaceful and Wrathful Deities" (*Zab chos zhi khro dgongs pa rang grol*), said to have been discovered in the fourteenth century. Since he could not read Tibetan, Evans-Wentz took the text to KAZI DAWA SAMDUP, the English teacher at a local school. Kazi Dawa Samdup provided Evans-Wentz with a translation of a portion of the text, which Evans-Wentz augmented with his own introduction and notes, publishing it in 1927 as *The Tibetan Book of the Dead*. Since its publication, various editions of the book have sold over 500,000 copies in English, making it the most famous Tibetan Buddhist text in the world. The text describes the process of death and rebirth, focusing on the intervening transition period called the BAR DO, or "intermediate state" (ANTARĀBHAVA). The text provides instructions on how to recognize reality in the intermediate state and thus gain liberation from rebirth. Through listening to the instructions in the text being read aloud, the departed consciousness is able to gain liberation; the Tibetan title of the text, BAR DO THOS GROL CHEN MO, means "Great Liberation in the Intermediate State through Hearing." Evans-Wentz's approach to the text reflects his lifelong commitment to Theosophy. Other translations that Kazi Dawa Samdup made for Evans-Wentz were included in *Tibetan Yoga and Secret Doctrines* (1935). In 1924, after Kazi Dawa Samdup's death, Evans-Wentz visited his family in Kalimpong, from whom he received a manuscript translation of the MI LA RAS PA'I RNAM THAR, a biography of MI LA RAS PA, which Evans-Wentz subsequently edited and published as *Tibet's Great Yogi Milarepa* (1928). He returned to Darjeeling in 1935 and employed two Sikkimese monks to translate another work from the same cycle of texts as the *Bar do thos grol*, entitled "Self-Liberation through Naked Vision Recognizing Awareness" (*Rig pa ngo sprod gcer mthong rang grol*). During the same visit, he received a summary of a famous biography of PADMASAMBHAVA. These works formed the last work in his series, *The Tibetan Book of the Great Liberation*, eventually published in 1954.

**exchange of self and other**. See PARĀTMAPARIVARTANA.

**expedient**. See UPĀYA.

**eye-opening ceremony**. See DIANYAN; KAIYAN; NETRAPRATIṢṬHĀPANA.

F

**Fachang**. (C) (法常) (d.u.). In Chinese, "Constancy of the Dharma"; proper name of the first "state preceptor" appointed in China, during the reign of Emperor Wenxian (r. 550–559) of the Northern Qi dynasty. See GUOSHI.

**fachuang**. (J. hōdō; K. pŏptang 法幢). In Chinese, "banner of dharma"; in its literal usage, this term refers to the banners that would be raised whenever dharma sermons, rituals, or festivals were held. By extension, the opening or founding of a monastery or lecture hall came to be called the "establishment of the dharma banner" (ji'an fachuang). Metaphorically, the proclamation or exposition of the Buddhist truths was also said to be like raising the dharma banner, which would terrify MĀRA's legions, thus symbolizing the vanquishing of Buddhism's ideological opponents.

**Fafang**. (法舫) (1904–1951). In Chinese, "Skiff of Dharma"; distinguished Chinese Buddhist scholar and activist who initiated some of the earliest ecumenical dialogues between Chinese MAHĀYĀNA and Sri Lankan THERAVĀDA Buddhists. Ordained at the age of eighteen, Fafang was one of the first students to study in the Chinese Buddhist Academy that TAIXU founded in Wuchang (Wuchang Foxue Yuan). He eventually taught at the academy, as well as at other leading Chinese Buddhist institutions of his time, contributing significantly to Taixu's attempts to found international Buddhist research centers and libraries. He also was longtime chief editor of the influential and long-running Buddhist periodical *Haichao yin* ("Sound of the Tide"). In 1946, Fafang traveled to Sri Lanka after becoming proficient in Sanskrit, Pāli, Japanese, and English and studied Theravāda Buddhism with Kirwatatuduwe Prasekene. Among his later accomplishments, Fafang taught at the University of Sri Lanka, served as one of the chief editors for the compilation of Taixu's collected works, founded one of the first Pāli learning centers in China, and created a student exchange program for Chinese and Sri Lankan monks.

**Fahai**. (J. Hōkai; K. Pŏphae 法海) (d.u.). In Chinese, "Sea of Dharma": a disciple of HUINENG, the sixth patriarch (LIUZU) of the CHAN ZONG. Fahai is said to have been the head monk of the monastery of Tafansi in Shaozhou Prefecture, where Huineng is presumed to have delivered a sermon on the "sudden" teachings (DUNJIAO) of the Southern school (NAN ZONG) of Chan. Fahai is dubiously credited with compiling the written record of this sermon, the LIUZU TAN JING ("Platform Sūtra of the Sixth Patriarch"). A rather late "brief preface" (luexu) to the *Liuzu tan jing* is also retrospectively attributed to Fahai. The story of this figure may have been based on a monk by the same name who was affiliated with the NIUTOU ZONG of Chan.

**Fahua anle xingyi**. (J. Hokke anrakugyōgi; K. Pŏphwa allak haengŭi 法華安樂行義). In Chinese, "Exegesis on the 'Blissful Practice' Section of the 'Lotus Sūtra,'" treatise composed by NANYUE HUISI and one of the earliest texts of the nascent TIANTAI ZONG. The text situated the SADDHARMAPUṆḌARĪKASŪTRA at the locus of Tiantai teachings and outlined the archetypal contemplative techniques that were subsequently developed by TIANTAI ZHIYI. It contained both the incipient Tiantai understanding of the notion of "emptiness according to the PRAJÑĀPĀRAMITĀ" (bore kongxing) and the ritualistic elements of visualization and chanting that became central in subsequent iterations of Tiantai practice.

**Fahua chanfa**. (J. Hokke senbō; K. Pŏphwa ch'ambŏp 法華懺法). In Chinese, "penance ritual according to the 'Lotus Sūtra.'" Despite its name, this intensive twenty-one-day ritual was based as much on the *Guan Puxian pusa xingfa jing* ("The Sūtra on the Procedures for Visualizing the Bodhisattva SAMANTABHADRA") as it was on the SADDHARMAPUṆḌARĪKASŪTRA. As explained in TIANTAI ZHIYI's *Fahua sanmei chanfa* ("Penance Ritual according to the Lotus Samādhi"), the goal of the ritual is to ensure visions of celestial buddhas and/or BODHISATTVAs, which were taken to be signs that the one's unwholesome actions (AKUŚALA-KARMAN) had been expiated. The penitent was required to refrain from lying down for the full duration of the ritual, by constantly alternating between walking and sitting postures. Demanding intense mental and physical devotion, the ritual involves extensive contemplation of the TIANTAI teachings, making vows and supplications, uttering prescribed words of repentance, chanting the *Saddharmapuṇḍarīkasūtra* and performing intermittent circumambulation.

**fahua ermiao**. (C) (法華二妙). See DAIJUE ERMIAO.

**Fahua jing lüeshu**. (J. Hokekyō ryakusho; K. Pŏphwa kyŏng yakso 法華經略疏). In Chinese, "A Brief Commentary on the 'Lotus Sūtra,'" the earliest extant Chinese commentary on the SADDHARMAPUṆḌARĪKASŪTRA, though there is considerable controversy regarding its authenticity. The text is attributed to DAOSHENG from the Liu-Song period (420–479), who was one of the direct disciples of the Kuchean translator KUMĀRAJĪVA. Daosheng claimed that the treatise combined the famous translator's lectures notes on the *Saddharmapuṇḍarīkasūtra* with Daosheng's own insights. If authentic, this commentary would be Daosheng's only surviving work, offering a rare perspective into the way the *Saddharmapuṇḍarīkasūtra* was understood and interpreted by Kumārajīva and his circle of adherents. Employing expressions found in the Chinese "Book of Changes" (*Yijing*), this commentary discusses the notions of "consummate perfection" (yuan) and a peculiar MAHĀYĀNA definition of the "middle way" (C. zhongdao, MADHYAMAPRATIPAD), notions that were further elaborated by subsequent TIANTAI and HUAYAN exegetes.

**Fahua jing shu**. (C) (法華經疏). See FAHUA JING LÜESHU.

**Fahua jing yi ji**. (J. Hokekyō giki; K. Pŏphwa kyŏng ŭi ki 法華經義記). In Chinese, "Notes on the Meaning of the 'Lotus Sūtra,'" also known as "Commentary on the Meaning of the 'Lotus Sūtra'" (*Fahua yi shu*), eight-roll text composed by Fayun (467–529). This commentary is the second-oldest extant treatise in Chinese on the SADDHARMAPUṆḌARĪKASŪTRA, after the FAHUA JING LÜESHU. These two commentaries played an important role in shaping early HUAYAN and TIANTAI thought.

**Fahua sanbu [jing]**. (J. Hokke sanbu[kyō]; K. Pŏphwa sambu [kyŏng] 法華三部[經]). In Chinese, "The Three [Sister] Sūtras of the 'Lotus,'" and often referred to in English as the "Threefold 'Lotus Sūtra.'" The three scriptures are: the WULIANG YI JING ("Sūtra of Immeasurable Meanings"); the SADDHARMAPUṆḌARĪKASŪTRA ("Lotus Sūtra") itself; and the GUAN PUXIAN PUSA XINGFA JING ("Sūtra on the Procedures for Visualizing the Bodhisattva SAMANTABHADRA"). They are called "sister sūtras" in East Asia because they seem to contain internal references to one other, which implied that they were propounded in this order during the final period of the Buddha's ministry (according to the TIANTAI school's temporal taxonomy of the scriptures; see WUSHI). The first of the three scriptures, the *Wuliang yi jing*, was presumed to be the prequel to the influential *Saddharmapuṇḍarīkasūtra* (although the text is now generally believed to be an indigenous Chinese composition, see APOCRYPHA); the last, the *Guan Puxian pusa xingfa jing*, was considered its sequel. The three texts are also called "sister sūtras" because they all figured prominently in Tiantai teachings, although the *Saddharmapuṇḍarīkasūtra* far eclipsed the other two sūtras in importance in the school's exegetic tradition.

**Fahua wenju**. (J. Hokke mongu; K. Pŏphwa mun'gu 法華文句). In Chinese, "Words and Phrases of the 'Lotus Sūtra'"; a major commentary on the SADDHARMAPUṆḌARĪKASŪTRA, taught by TIANTAI ZHIYI and put into writing by his disciple Guanding (561–632), in alt. ten or twenty rolls. Along with the MOHE ZHIGUAN and the FAHUA XUANYI, the *Fahua wenju* is considered one of Zhiyi's three great commentaries. The lectures that formed the basis of the *Fahua wenju* were delivered by Zhiyi in 587 at the monastery of Jinzhaisi in Jinling (present-day Jiangsu province), and they offered a thorough exegetical analysis of the *Saddharmapuṇḍarīkasūtra*. The *Fahua wenju* was incorporated in the Song-dynasty Buddhist canon at the recommendation of the Tiantai monk Ciyun Zunshi (964–1032) in 1024. The treatise employs a fourfold exegetical technique (sishi) unique to Zhiyi and his TIANTAI ZONG, viz., exegesis via: (1) causes and conditions, (2) classification of the teachings (see JIAOXIANG PANSHI), (3) fundamentals and traces, and (4) contemplation on the mind. Throughout the *Fahua wenju*, the interpretations of other teachers, such as DAOSHENG, are critiqued. An influential commentary on the *Fahua wenju* known as the *Fahua wenju ji* was prepared by JINGXI ZHANRAN.

**Fahua wubai wen lun**. (J. Hokke gohyakumonron; K. Pŏphwa obaek mun non 法華五百問論). In Chinese, "Treatise on Five Hundred Questions Regarding the 'Lotus Sūtra,'" in three rolls; text composed by JINGXI ZHANRAN (711–782) to refute the Chinese YOGĀCĀRA school's (see FAXIANG ZONG) interpretation of the SADDHARMAPUṆḌARĪKASŪTRA. It is so named because it contains roughly five hundred entries offering rejoinders (mainly from a TIANTAI position) against hypothetical Faxiang argumentations. Questions such as whether one's spiritual potential is determined and fixed (see GOTRA), whether consciousness is fundamentally defiled or innately immaculate, and the relation between the different Buddhist "vehicles" (YĀNA) have been addressed in this polemical work.

**Fahua wuchong xuanyi**. (J. Hokke gojūgengi; K. Pŏphwa ojung hyŏnŭi 法華五重玄義). In Chinese, "The Five Layers of Profound Meaning according to the Fahua (TIANTAI) [school]," a standardized set of interpretive tools devised by TIANTAI ZHIYI to be used in composing Buddhist scriptural commentaries. The five topics of exegesis that Zhiyi states should be covered in any comprehensive sūtra commentary are: (1) "explanation of the title [of the sūtra]" (shiming); (2) "discernment of its main theme" (bianti); (3) "elucidation of its cardinal doctrine or main tenet" (mingzong); (4) "discussion of the sūtra's intent or purpose" (lunyong); (5) "adjudication of its position in a hermeneutical taxonomy of the scriptures" (panjiao; see JIAOXIANG PANSHI). These five topics are covered in most East Asian sūtra commentaries written after Zhiyi's time.

**Fahua xuanyi**. (J. Hokke gengi; K. Pŏphwa hyŏnŭi 法華玄義). In Chinese, "Profound Meaning of the 'Lotus Sūtra,'" taught by the eminent Chinese monk TIANTAI ZHIYI and put into writing by his disciple Guanding (561–632). Along with the MOHE ZHIGUAN and FAHUA WENJU, the *Fahua xuanyi* is considered one of Zhiyi's three great commentaries. The lectures that form the basis of the *Fahua xuanyi* were delivered by Zhiyi in 593, perhaps at the monastery of Yuquansi in Jingzhou (present-day Hubei province), and they are concerned with the thorough analysis of the SADDHARMAPUṆḌARĪKASŪTRA. The treatise is divided into two broader methods of interpretation: general (tongshi) and specific (bieshi). The general interpretation further consists of seven subtypes, such as a listing of the chapters, citations, provenance, and so forth. The specific interpretation consists of five subtypes (see FAHUA WUCHONG XUANYI): the interpretation of the title, determination of its main theme, clarification of its main tenet, discussion of its purpose, and classification of its teachings (panjiao; see JIAOXIANG PANSHI). Nearly two-thirds of the treatise is dedicated to the first two characters in the title of the Chinese translation of the *Saddharmapuṇḍarīka*, "subtle" (miao) and "dharma" (fa).

**Fahua xuanzan**. (T. Dam pa'i chos puṇḍa rī ka'i 'grel pa [rgya las bsgyur pa]; J. Hokke genzan; K. Pŏphwa hyŏnch'an 法華玄贊). In Chinese, "Profound Panegyric to the 'Lotus Sūtra,'" a commentary to the SADDHARMAPUṆḌARĪKASŪTRA composed by KUIJI, whose unique YOGĀCĀRA perspective on the text set him at odds with the more influential commentaries written by earlier and contemporaneous TIANTAI and HUAYAN exegetes. This commentary is still extant in both Chinese and, notably, a Tibetan translation.

**Fahua zhuan[ji]**. (J. Hokke den[ki]; K. Pŏphwa chŏn['gi] 法華傳[記]). In Chinese, "Compendium of the 'Lotus Sūtra,'" also known as the *Hongzan fahua zhuan*[*ji*], was composed by Huixiang during the Tang dynasty. This work included much information regarding the translation, circulation, commentaries, epigraphy, illustrations, magical lore, and other aspects of the SADDHARMAPUṆḌARĪKASŪTRA. Several other comparable compendia devoted exclusively to the *Saddharmapuṇḍarīkasūtra* are still extant (by authors from China, Korea, and Japan), testifying to the scripture's popularity throughout East Asia.

**faith**. See ŚRADDHĀ; XINXIN.

**Fajie guanmen**. (C) (法界觀門). See HUAYAN FAJIE GUANMEN.

**fajie jiachi**. (J. hokkai kaji; K. pŏpkye kaji 法界加持). In Chinese "the empowerment of the DHARMADHĀTU." According to the MAHĀVAIROCANĀBHISAṂBODHISŪTRA, the buddhas, the TANTRAS, and sentient beings (SATTVA) mutually pervade and "empower" (ADHIṢṬHĀNA) each other. This mutual interfusion is what makes the dharmadhātu unfathomably profound and interconnected.

**fajie yuanqi**. (J. hokkai engi; K. pŏpkye yŏn'gi 法界緣起). In Chinese, "conditioned origination (PRATĪTYASAMUTPĀDA) of the dharma-element (DHARMADHĀTU)," an East Asian theory of causality elaborated within the HUAYAN school. Unlike the Indian systematization of the twelvefold chain of pratītyasamutpāda, which views existence as an endless cycle of painful rebirths that begins with ignorance (AVIDYĀ) and ends with old age and death (jarāmaraṇa; see JARĀ), this Huayan vision of causality instead regards the infinitely interdependent universe as the manifestation of the truth to which the Buddha awakens. The term "fajie yuanqi" does not appear in the *Huayan jing* (AVATAṂSAKASŪTRA) itself and seems to have been first coined by ZHIYAN (602–668), the "second patriarch" of the Huayan lineage. Zhiyan used fajie yuanqi to refer to the concurrency between cause (C. yin; S. HETU) and fruition (C. guo; S. PHALA), here meaning the "causal" practices (hsing) that are conducive to enlightenment and their "fruition" in the realization (zheng) of the quiescence that is NIRVĀṆA. As this Huayan theory of pratītyasamutpāda is elaborated within the tradition, it is broadened to focus on the way in which every single phenomenal instantiation of existence both contains, and is contained by, all other instantiations, so that one existence is subsumed by all existences (yi ji yiqie) and all existences by one existence (yiqie ji yi); in this vision, all things in the universe are thus mutually creative and mutually defining, precisely because they all lack any independent self-identity (SVABHĀVA). Each phenomenon constitutes a part of an organic whole that is defined by the harmonious relationship between each and every member: just as the whole is defined by all of its independent constituents, each independent constituent is defined by the whole with which it is integrated. This relationship is called endless multiplication (chongchong wujin), because the process of mutual penetration and mutual determination (xiangru xiangji) is infinite. Due to this unlimited interdependence among all phenomena, this type of pratītyasamutpāda may also be termed "inexhaustible conditioned origination" (wujin yuanqi). This interdependence between one phenomenon and all other phenomena developed through fajie yuanqi is indicative also of the Huayan "dharmadhātu of the unimpeded interpenetration of phenomenon with phenomena" (SHISHI WU'AI FAJIE). The Huayan doctrines of the "ten profound mysteries" (SHI XUANMEN) and the "consummate interfusion of the six aspects" (LIUXIANG YUANRONG) also offer systematic elaborations of the doctrine of fajie yuanqi.

**fala**. (J. hōrō; K. pŏmnap 法臘). In Chinese, "dharma age," the number of years since one has been ordained as a novice or monk or nun. See JIELA.

**Famensi**. (法門寺). In Chinese, "Dharma-Gate Monastery," located approximately seventy miles outside the city of Chang'an (present-day Xi'an) in Shaanxi province, China. Though the exact dates of its construction are unknown, the monastery claims to have been built during the Eastern Han dynasty but more likely dates from the Northern Wei period (386–534). One of only four monasteries in China to house a relic (ŚARĪRA) of the Buddha, Famensi was particularly renowned for its four finger-bone relics, which were displayed in the Tang-dynasty capital several times during the seventh and eighth centuries. Famensi's renowned thirteen-story, octagonal brick pagoda (STŪPA) collapsed in 1981 after a torrential rainfall, and excavations in 1987 revealed three secret stone chambers under the foundations, which had remained unopened since the ninth century. The chambers housed a large number of precious objects, including incense burners (see GANDHAGHAṬIKĀ), jewelry, and textile items, as well as 122 gold and silver objects that are exhaustively inventoried in two stone tablets written in 874 and left with the cache. An exquisite, gilded reliquary casket containing a nested series of smaller reliquaries was also discovered in the chamber. One of the purported finger-bone relics of the Buddha was found intact within the innermost reliquary; the other three were located elsewhere in the chambers.

**faming**. (T. chos ming; J. hōmyō; K. pŏmmyŏng 法名). In Chinese, "dharma name." In East Asian Buddhism, the given name in one's dharma lineage is typically a new religious name —often consisting of two Sinographs for monks, nuns, and laymen, or sometimes three Sinographs for laywomen—that is conferred by the preceptor to a person who has undergone either the three refuges (RATNATRAYA) ceremony or monastic ordination. After ordination, monks and nuns no longer use their secular names but will subsequently be known only by their dharma names. In many East Asian traditions, following long-established Chinese practice going back to the time of DAO'AN (312–385), monks and nuns also often abandon their secular surname and take in its place the surname SHI (J. Shaku; K. Sŏk; V. Thích), a transliteration of the first syllable of ŚĀKYA, the Buddha's own clan name, as a mark of their spiritual ties to the clan of the Buddha. In the case of monks and nuns and people of notable accomplishment, this dharma name is traditionally preceded by another cognomen or cognomina that alludes to one's lineage group, place of residence (such as one's home monastery or mountain), an imperially bestowed title, and/or other known virtues. ¶ In Tibet, two names are given and the first name is typically the first name of the preceptor; thus, those ordained by Bstan 'dzin rgya mtsho (Tenzin Gyatso) (the fourteenth Dalai Lama) will have Bstan 'dzin (Tenzin) as the first of their two dharma names.

**fanan**. (J. hōnan; K. pŏmnan 法難). In Chinese, "calamities that befall the dharma," referring to political persecutions of Buddhism, or other forms of systematic harassment of the religion and its adherents. Examples of such persecutions abound throughout Buddhist history. In India, e.g., there were Indian rulers who were hostile to Buddhism, such as King Puśyamitra (c. end of the second century BCE) and those of the Sena dynasty (c. eleventh to twelfth centuries), as well as Muslim generals and rulers who sacked Buddhist centers and forced the conversion of the local populace. In East Asia, China saw the systematic persecution by four emperors with Daoist affinities, as well as the infamous Huichang persecution (HUICHANG FANAN). More recent periods saw Japan's suppression of Buddhism during the Meiji period (beginning in 1868; cf. SHINBUTSU BUNRI) and the Korean Chosŏn dynasty's five centuries of persecution of Buddhism, which extended into the late nineteenth century. Related Chinese terms are feifo ("abolition of Buddhism"), miefo ("annihilation of Buddhism"), pofo ("destruction of Buddhism"), huifa ("damage to Buddhism"), and mie-Shi ("annihilation of [the teachings of] ŚĀKYAMUNI").

**fanbai**. (J. bonbai; K. pŏmp'ae 梵唄). In Chinese, lit., "the speech of BRAHMĀ," Buddhist ritual chanting performed in a distinctively clear, melodious, and resonate voice; "fan," lit. Brahmā, is generically used in China to refer to all things Indian, and "bai" is a transcription of the Sanskrit word bhāṣā, or "speech," so fanbai means something like "Indian-style chanting." Although the historical origins of fanbai are uncertain, according to legend, it derives from the singing of the heavenly musicians (GANDHARVA) or from the chants of Gadgadasvara (Miaoyin), a bodhisattva appearing in the SADDHARMAPUṆḌARĪKASŪTRA who eulogized the virtues of ŚĀKYAMUNI Buddha. An account in the NANHAI JIGUI NEIFA CHUAN, a pilgrimage record written by the Chinese monk YIJING (635–713), who sojourned in India for twenty-five years, confirms that fanbai chanting was still popular on the Indian subcontinent during the seventh century. Fanbai was transmitted to China almost simultaneously with the introduction of Buddhism. The Chinese developed their own style of fanbai by at least the third century CE: Cao Zhi (192–232) of the Wei dynasty is said to have created it inspired by a fish's movement, leading to the use of the term yushan (lit. "fish mountain") as an alternate name for fanbai. According to the Korean SAMGUK YUSA, the transmission of fanbai (K. pŏmp'ae) from China to Korea occurred perhaps as early as the first half of the seventh century; subsequently, the monk CHIN'GAM HYESO (774–850) is said to have introduced the Tang-Chinese style of fanbai to the Silla kingdom around 830. The NITTŌ KYŪHŌ JUNREIGYŌKI by ENNIN (794–864), a Japanese pilgrim monk who visited both Silla Korea and Tang China, reports that both Silla and Tang styles of pŏmp'ae were used in Korean Buddhist ceremonies. The Chosŏn monk Taehwi (fl. c. 1748), in his *Pŏmŭmjong po* ("The Lineage of the Brahmā's Voice School"), traces his Korean lineage of pŏmp'ae monks back to the person of Chin'gam Hyeso. Fanbai was preserved orally in China and Korea, but was recorded in Japan using the Hakase neume style of notation. The fanbai chanting style involves special vocalization techniques with complex ornamentation that are thought to have been introduced from India, but uses lyrics that derive from Chinese verse; these lyrics are usually in non-rhyming patterns of five- or seven-character lines, making up four-line verses that praise the virtues of the Buddha. Vocables are sometimes employed in fanbai, unlike in sūtra chanting. The different fanbai chants are traditionally performed solo or by a chorus, often in a call and response format. Only in Korea has fanbai branched into two distinct types: hossori pŏmp'ae and chissori pŏmp'ae. Some pŏmp'ae texts can be performed only in one style, but others, such as porye and toryanggye, leave the choice to the performer. Hossori pŏmp'ae is performed in a melismatic style that is elegantly simple, in a vocal style somewhat similar to Western music. By contrast, chissori pŏmp'ae is solemn, highly sophisticated, and utilizes a tensed throat and falsetto for high notes. Although chissori pŏmp'ae is considered to be a more important vocal musical form, there are only twelve extant compositions in this style. Owing to how texts and melodic phrases are organized, even though it uses a shorter text, chissori pŏmp'ae takes two or three times longer to complete than hossori. Of the two, only hossori can be accompanied by musicians or sung to accompany dance. Korean pŏmp'ae is also performed during Buddhist ceremonies such as YŎNGSANJAE.

**Fangshan shijing**. (房山石經). In Chinese, "Lithic Scriptures of Fangshan," the world's largest collection of scriptures written on stone, located in the Fangshan district about forty miles southwest Beijing. The blocks are now stored on Shijingshan (Stone Scriptures Hill) in nine separate caves, among them the Leiyindong (Sound of Thunder Cave), near the monastery of YUNJUSI (Cloud Dwelling Monastery). The carving of the lithic scriptures was initiated during the Daye era (604–617) by the monk Jingwan (d. 639) with the support of Empress Xiao (?-630) and her brother Xiao Yu (574–647). Among the scriptures carved during Jingwan's lifetime were the SADDHARMAPUṆḌARĪKASŪTRA ("Lotus Sūtra"), the MAHĀPARINIRVĀṆASŪTRA ("Nirvāna Sūtra"), and the AVATAṂSAKASŪTRA ("Flower Garland Sūtra"). The project continued up through the Tianqi era (1621–1627) of the Ming dynasty. The collection now includes 1,122 Buddhist scriptures carved on 14,278 lithographs, or stone slabs. The Fangshan canon is a product of the Chinese belief that Buddhism had entered the "dharma-ending age" (MOFA; see SADDHARMAVIPRALOPA): by carving the Buddhist canon on stone, this project was thus one way of helping to ensure that the Buddhist scriptures would survive the inevitable demise of the religion. Most of the scriptures in the Fangshan canon represent textual lineages that derive from recensions that circulated during the Tang and Khitan Liao dynasties. The monk Xuanfa (fl. c. 726–755) initiated a project to carve the entire canon after being presented with a copy of the handwritten Kaiyuan manuscript canon (see KAIYUAN SHIJIAO LU) by the Tang princess Jinxian (689–732). During the rule of the Khitan Liao emperors Shengzong (r. 983–1031), Xingzong (r. 1032–1054), and Daozong (r. 1055–1100), the new Qidan canon was carved on xylographs (viz., woodblocks), with the lithic carving of the same texts carried out in tandem at Yunjusi for several decades. By the late eleventh century, all nine caves had been filled to capacity. Consequently, in 1117, a pit was excavated in the southwestern section of Yunjusi to bury a new set of carvings initiated by the monk Tongli (1049–1098); these texts were mostly commentarial and exegetical writings, rather than sūtra translations. By the time of the Jin dynasty (1115–1234), most of the mainstream Mahāyāna canonical scriptures had been carved. In the twelfth century, during the Song dynasty, the growing popularity of tantric materials and the ĀGAMAS prompted a supplementary carving project to add them to the Fangshan canon. However, the Fangshan Shijing does not exclusively contain Buddhist texts. In the third year of the Xuande era (1428) of the Ming dynasty, many Daoist scriptures were carved with an intent similar to that of the Buddhists: to ensure that these texts were transmitted to posterity. The Buddhist Association of China made rubbings of a substantial part of the extant lithographs in 1956. For modern historians, these rubbings offer a rich tapestry of information for studying the textual history of the Buddhist canon and the social history and culture of Buddhism in northern China. See also DAZANGJING.

**fangsheng**. (T. srog blu/tshe thar; J. hōjō; K. pangsaeng 放生). In Chinese, "releasing living creatures," referring to the practice of buying captured animals, such as fish, turtles, or birds, and then setting them free; the focus of a ritual popular in East Asian Buddhism, the "ceremony of releasing living creatures" (FANGSHENG HUI). The Buddhist tradition asserts that merit (PUṆYA) is produced by both actively pursuing wholesome actions (KUŚALA-KARMAPATHA) as well as refraining from unwholesome actions (AKUŚALA-KARMAPATHA); fangsheng is regarded as an enhancement of both types of action, by furthering the first lay precept (ŚĪLA) that forbids the unsalutary action of killing, as well as the MAHĀYĀNA precept that encourages the salutary act of vegetarianism. ¶ The two representative scriptures on fangsheng are the FANWANG JING ("Book of Brahmā's Net") and the SUVARṆAPRABHĀSOTTAMASŪTRA (C. *Jinguangming jing*; "Sūtra of Golden Light"), the former providing the doctrinal basis for the practice of fangsheng, the latter a protypical example of a fangsheng hui. The *Fanwang jing* says that because all sentient beings in the six destinies (ṢAḌGATI; see also GATI) have at some time or other during the vastness of SAṂSĀRA been one's parents, a person should always strive to rescue creatures from people who would kill them in order to save them from their torment. The *Suvarṇaprabhāsottamasūtra* tells a story about Jalavāhana (ŚĀKYAMUNI Buddha in an earlier life), who saved ten thousand fish who were dying in a dried up pond by bringing water to refill it. He then recited for them the ten epithets of the buddha Ratnaśikhin/Ratnabhava, since he had been told that any creatures who heard that Buddha's name at the time of their deaths would be reborn in the heavens. The fish were reborn as divinities in the TRĀYASTRIṂŚA heaven, who then rained jewels down on the earth.¶ In China, the Buddhist custom of vegetarianism had started to pervade the culture by the Qi (479–501) and Liang (502–556) dynasties, a custom that encouraged the freeing of animals. In 619, an imperial decree prohibited fishing, hunting, and the slaughter of animals during the first, fifth, and ninth months of the year. A decree of 759 established eighty-one ponds for the release and protection of fish. Fangsheng appears to have been practiced not only by individual laypeople and monks. There is a record of the Liang dynasty monk Huiji (456–515) who practiced mendicancy so he could buy and release captured animals. TIANTAI ZHIYI (538–597), the founder of the TIANTAI ZONG, is known to have performed a formal ceremony for releasing animals in 575. Zhiyi lamented the fact that local folk made their living by catching fish, so he built a "pond where creatures could be released" (fangsheng chi) and preached to the freed fish the SADDHARMAPUṆḌARĪKASŪTRA and the *Suvarṇaprabhāsottamasūtra*. Zhiyi thus established the *Suvarṇaprabhāsottamasūtra* as the scriptural authority for fangsheng. Following Zhiyi, the fangsheng ceremony subsequently became one of the important rituals used within the Tiantai school. Ciyun Zunshi (964–1032) and SIMING ZHILI (960–1028), both Tiantai monks during the Song dynasty, were ardent advocates of fangsheng, who established ponds for releasing creatures and performed the ceremony of releasing creatures, especially in conjunction with celebrations of the Buddha's birthday. In the CHAN school, YONGMING YANSHOU (904–975) and YUNQI ZHUHONG (1535–1615) were among the most enthusiastic proponents of fangsheng. Zhuhong wrote works regarding the practice of vegetarianism, including the *Shirou* ("On Meat-Eating") and the *Shasheng feirensuowei* ("Killing Is Not What Humans Are Supposed To Do"), and also composed tracts on the ritual practice of fangsheng, such as the *Fangsheng yi* ("Rite for Releasing Living Creatures") and the *Jiesha fangsheng wen* ("Text on Prohibiting Killing and Releasing Living Creatures"). His *Fangsheng yi* is still considered today one of the standard sources for the Fangsheng ritual. Eventually, almost every large monastery in China had a pool for releasing fish and pens for the care of livestock that had been rescued from the butcher. Because these animals had been given Buddhist precepts, they were encouraged to observe them, with males and females segregated and carnivorous fish kept separately. Birds, turtles, and fish were more popular for release than domesticated animals because they required no further assistance. The pious who delivered cows and pigs to the monastery, however, were required to contribute toward their sustenance. ¶ The practice was popular in other Buddhist countries. In medieval Japan the imperial government would order the capture of three times the number of fish needed to be released at a ceremony in order that the requisite number—often from one to three thousand—would still be alive by the time the ceremony took place. In such cases, the practice of releasing animals resulted in the unfortunate death of many before they could be liberated. Among Tibetan Buddhists, the killing of animals is normatively deplored, and protecting the life of even the tiniest insect (srog skyob) is a common practice; in the LHA SA region, a small Muslim community traditionally performed the task of killing and butchering animals; farmers and nomads butcher some of their animals each year. Vegetarianism (sha med) is admired, but not widespread in Tibet, except during the first two weeks of the fourth Tibetan month SA GA ZLA BA when, it is believed, the results of wholesome actions increase one hundred thousand times. Buying an animal destined for slaughter to protect one's own life, or more commonly to protect the life of an important religious figure, is also common; that practice is known as *tshe thar*, lit., "liberating life" in Tibetan.

**fangsheng hui**. (J. hōjōe; K. pangsaeng hoe 放生會). In Chinese, "ceremony for releasing living creatures," a Buddhist ceremony held throughout East Asian Buddhism, usually on the fifteenth day of the eighth month of the lunar calendar or the third day of the third month. The practice of releasing animals is claimed to have been initially established as a formal ceremony by TIANTAI ZHIYI (538–597), who followed the account presented in the SUVARṆAPRABHĀSOTTAMASŪTRA (C. *Jinguangming jing*; "Sūtra of Golden Light"), which describes the practice of releasing captured animals (FANGSHENG), especially fish. The *Suvarṇaprabhāsottamasūtra* tells a story about Jalavāhana (Śākyamuni Buddha in an earlier incarnation), who saved ten thousand fish by bringing water to a dried-up pond. He then recited for them the ten epithets of the buddha Ratnaśikhin/Ratnabhava, since he had been told that any creatures who heard that buddha's name at the time their deaths would be reborn in the heavens; he continued on to teach them the doctrine of conditioned origination (PRATĪTYASAMUTPĀDA). In 575, Zhiyi is said to have lamented the fact that local folk made their living by catching fish, so he built a "pond where creatures could be released" (fangsheng chi) and preached to the freed fish the SADDHARMAPUṆḌARĪKASŪTRA and the *Suvarṇaprabhāsottamasūtra*. The fangsheng ceremony subsequently became one of the important rituals within the TIANTAI ZONG, even though there is no extant record of its performance until it was revived by Luoxi Yiji (919–987), the fifteenth head of the Tiantai school. Public ceremonies of releasing animals were also held at court, particularly on the Buddha's Birthday, and lay groups were organized at the local level to release animals. The Ming-dynasty monk YUNQI ZHUHONG's (1535–1615) *Fangsheng yi* ("Rite for Releasing Living Creatures") is considered one of the standard sources for the fangsheng ritual. This ritual entails bestowing the three refuges (TRIŚARAṆA) on the creatures to be released, reciting the ten epithets of the buddha Ratnaśikhin/Ratnabhava, teaching the creatures the twelvefold chain of dependent origination (a difficult doctrine even for bipeds), and concluding with a repentance rite for the animals' transgressions.

**fang yankou**. (S. pretamukhāgnivālāyaśarakāra; J. hōenkō; K. pang yŏmgu 放焰口). In Chinese, "releasing the burning mouths," Chinese esoteric Buddhist ritual for those dead who have been reborn as hungry ghosts (PRETA). The "burning mouths" refers specifically to hungry ghosts, whose tiny mouths and narrow gullets leave them congenitally incapable of filling their distended bellies; even worse, as they try to feed themselves such tiny morsels, the tidbits turn into fire, ash, and burning iron in their mouths. The ritual is performed by monks during the ULLAMBANA festival for the dead or at the request of laypeople on behalf of their ancestors. The ritual typically takes five hours to complete and is always held in the evening when hungry ghosts can more easily travel from their realm of existence to attend. During the performance, the monks wear red or golden hats in the shape of a five-pointed crown, which symbolizes the five buddhas (S. PAÑCATATHĀGATA). At first, the five buddhas and other divinities are invited and offered "sweet dew" (C. ganlu; S. AMṚTA), viz., water consecrated through the recitation of a MANTRA. After summoning all the inhabitants of the six realms of existence (ṢAḌGATI), the hungry ghosts are then released and feted; purged of their afflictions (KLEŚA), they then pay homage to the three jewels (RATNATRAYA) and make a vow to become BODHISATTVAs. Finally, after being taught the Buddhist teachings, they are sent on their way to the PURE LAND. The ritual is accompanied by such features as ringing hand bells, chanting mantras, and performing MUDRĀ in order symbolically to open both the gates of the hells and the throats of the hungry ghosts and to remove their karmic obstructions (KARMĀVARAṆA). The ritual is supposed to have been created in response to a nightmare of the Buddha's attendant ĀNANDA: after dreaming one night about the horrible plight of the hungry ghosts, Ānanda asked the Buddha to help beings avoid such a baleful rebirth and to rescue all the current residents of that bourne. The Buddha then recited DHĀRAṆĪ on all their behalves. The *Jiuba yankou egui tuoluoni jing* (S. *Pretamukhāgnivālāyaśarakāradhāraṇī*; T. *Yi dwags kha la me 'bar ma la skyabs mdzad pa'i gzungs*, "Dhāraṇī-Sūtra for Liberating the Burning Mouth Hungry Ghosts"), translated by AMOGHAVAJRA during the eighth century, includes the earliest version of the ritual. The fangyan kou is still performed today within the Chinese Buddhist community, especially in Taiwan and Hong Kong.

**fangzhang**. (J. hōjō; K. pangjang 方丈). In Chinese, lit. "a square zhang," the "abbot's quarters" at a CHAN monastery. This term comes from the Chinese translation of the VIMALAKĪRTINIRDEŚA, where it is said that the layman VIMALAKĪRTI was able to accomplish the miraculous feat of seating thirty-two thousand beings in his small room measuring only one square (fang) zhang (a Chinese measurement of length equivalent to a little more than three meters or ten feet) in size. The notion of a fangzhang was appropriated by the Chan tradition as the technical term for the abbot's quarters at a Chan monastery. The abbot, a Chan master, would often have private interviews there with students and greet private visitors to the monastery. In some contexts, the "abbot's quarters" comes by metonymy to refer to the abbot himself. Korean monasteries distinguish between a chosil (lit. occupant of the patriarch's room), the Sŏn master at a regular monastery, and a pangjang, the Sŏn master at a CH'ONGNIM, one of the large ecumenical monastic centers where the full panoply of Buddhist training is maintained, such as HAEINSA or SONGGWANGSA. At the ch'ongnim, the pangjang is then considered the Sŏn master who heads the practice centers in the monastery, while the chuji (C. ZHUCHI; abbot) is the head of monastic administration.

**Fanwang jing**. (J. Bonmōkyō; K. Pŏmmang kyŏng 梵網經). In Chinese, "Brahmā's Net Sūtra," the scripture is often cited by its reconstructed, but unattested, Sanskrit title, the **Brahmajālasūtra*. This scripture is reputed to have been translated by KUMĀRAJĪVA in 406, but it is most likely an indigenous Chinese scripture (see APOCRYPHA) composed during the middle of the fifth century. The *Fanwang jing*, in its current recension in two rolls, purports to be the tenth chapter of a much longer, 120-roll scripture titled the *Bodhisattvaśīlasūtra*, which is otherwise unknown. The first roll provides a description of the buddha VAIROCANA and the ten different stages of the BODHISATTVA path. Because subsequent Chinese indigenous scriptures that were closely related to the *Fanwang jing*, such as the PUSA YINLUO PENYE JING, provided more systematic presentations of these soteriological models, this first roll was not widely studied and was typically omitted in commentaries on the scripture. Far more important to the tradition is the second roll, which is primarily concerned with the "bodhisattva precepts" (BODHISATTVAŚĪLA); this roll has often circulated independently as PUSAJIE JING (**Bodhisattvaśīlasūtra*; "The Book of the Bodhisattva Precepts"). This roll provides a list of ten major and forty-eight minor MAHĀYĀNA precepts that come to be known as the "Fanwang Precepts," which became a popular alternative to the 250 monastic precepts of the DHARMAGUPTAKA VINAYA (also known as the SIFEN LÜ). Unlike the majority of rules found in other non-Mahāyāna vinaya codes, the bodhisattva precepts are directed not only at ordained monks and nuns, but also may be taken by laymen and laywomen. The *Fanwang jing* correlates the precepts with Confucian virtues such as filial piety and obedience, as well as with one's buddha-nature (FOXING). Numerous commentaries on this text were composed, and those written by FAZANG, Mingkuang (fl. 800 CE), and the Korean monk T'AEHYŎN (d.u.) were most influential. As the primary scriptural source in East Asia for the bodhisattva precepts, the *Fanwang jing* was tremendously influential in subsequent developments in Buddhist morality and institutions throughout the region. In Japan, for example, the TENDAISHŪ monk SAICHŌ (767–822) disparaged the PRĀTIMOKṢA precepts of the traditional vinaya as being the precepts of HĪNAYĀNA adherents, and rejected them in favor of having all monastics take instead the MAHĀYĀNA precepts of the *Fanwang jing*. In Korea, all monastics and laypeople accept the bodhisattva precepts deriving from the *Fanwang jing*, but for monks and nuns these are still seen as complementary to their main monastic vows.

**fanzhao**. (J. henshō; K. panjo 返照). In Chinese, "tracing back the radiance," or "counter-illumination," a description used in the CHAN school for the underlying process governing a variety of different types of meditation, referring specifically to the process of introspection or "counter-illumination" that moves the mind away from its attachment to sensory objects and back toward its fundamental source, called variously the "numinous awareness" (LINGZHI), buddha-nature (BUDDHADHĀTU; C. FOXING), TATHĀGATAGARBHA, or the DHARMADHĀTU. "Tracing back the radiance" receives one of its most detailed treatments in the writings of the Korean Sŏn adept POJO CHINUL (1158–1210). Chinul's Korean commentator Yŏndam Yuil (1720–1799), e.g., defines the term as follows: "To trace back the radiance means to trace the radiance back to the numinous awareness of one's own mind.... It is like seeing the radiance of the sun's rays and following it back until you see the orb of the sun itself." The original enlightenment (BENJUE) of the mind is naturally luminous, shining ever outward and allowing beings to experience their external world. This natural quality of luminosity is what is meant by "sentience," and the very fact that "sentient" beings are conscious is proof that they are inherently enlightened. If this meditator can turn this radiance emanating from his mind back to its source, he would rediscover that luminous core of the mind and be instantly enlightened. This inherent radiance of the mind does not merely shine over the sense realms; in addition, as the mind's natural brightness is restored through meditative introspection, it comes virtually to shine through objects, exposing their inherent emptiness (ŚŪNYATĀ). Hence, numinous awareness is the quality that constitutes sentient beings' ultimate capacity to attain enlightenment. It serves as both the inherent faculty that allows meditation to develop and the quality of mind perfected through that meditation. By starting at the sensory level of what is seen, heard, etc., the meditator then trains to trace these sensory experiences back to their perceptual source in the quality of sentience itself, just as if he were following the rays emanating from the sun back to the sun itself; the perception of that sentience then constitutes "seeing the buddha-nature" (JIANXING), or the "understanding awakening" (JIEWU). The term is also known by its expanded form "follow back the light and trace back the radiance" (HUIGUANG FANZHAO), and various other permutations.

**faqi**. (S. *dharmabhājana; T. chos kyi snod; J. hōki; K. pŏpki 法器). In Chinese, "dharma vessel" or "implement of dharma." When referring to objects, faqi is the collective name for all the implements used either for ritual and liturgical purposes (e.g., bells, drums, and wooden fish) or for decorative purposes (e.g., canopies, banners, flower vases, censers, and lamps). The term is also used to refer to the few possessions allowable to a monk or nun, such as the begging bowl (PĀTRA), recitation beads (JAPAMĀLĀ), and the staff; see also PARIṢKĀRA. One of the six forms of AVALOKITEŚVARA, the Thousand-Hands and Thousand-Eyes emanation (S. SĀHASRABHUJASĀHASRANETRĀVALOKITEŚVARA; C. Qianshou Qianyan Guanshiyin Pusa), is commonly depicted in abbreviated form with forty hands, each of which holds a different faqi (cf. T. phyag mtshan, lag cha). According to the *Nīlakantha[ka] sūtra*, these forty faqi include weapons, precious jewels, liturgical instruments, the sun and moon, and plants. The bodhisattva uses these various faqi to protect and save the sentient beings of the continent of JAMBUDVĪPA. When used metaphorically to refer to a person, faqi is a term of praise, meaning "one who has been, or has the potential to be, molded into a vessel of the dharma," or "someone who is suitably prepared to believe in and understand the teachings of Buddhism." In the CHAN tradition, one who is capable of being entrusted with the store of the proper dharma eye (ZHENFAYANZANG), the sublime mind of NIRVĀṆA, is called a "dharma vessel."

**Faqin**. (J. Hōkin; K. Pŏphŭm 法欽) (714–792). In Chinese, "Dharma Reverence"; CHAN master in the NIUTOU ZONG, also known as Daoqin. A chance encounter with the monk HELIN XUANSU when Faqin was twenty-eight is said to have resulted in his decision to become a monk. In 741, Faqin went to Mt. Jing, where he established a small hut to study. Faqin was later summoned in 768 by Emperor Daizong (r. 762–779) to give a lecture in the imperial palace. In honor of his achievements, the emperor bestowed upon him the title Great Master Guoyi (Foremost of the Country) and a plaque for Faqin's monastery that bore the name Jingshansi, or Mt. Jing monastery, which later came to be known as WANSHOUSI. Faqin had many famous disciples; in addition, masters in other Chan lineages, such as XITANG ZHIZANG, TIANHUANG DAOWU, and DANXIA TIANRAN, also sought instruction from Faqin. In 790, Faqin moved to the hermitage Jingtuyuan at the monastery Rongxingsi, where he passed away two years later at the age of seventy-nine. Emperor Dezong (r. 779–805) later gave Faqin the posthumous title Chan master Dajue (Great Awakening).

**Farong**. (C) (法融). See NIUTOU FARONG.

**fashen sheli**. (J. hosshinshari; K. pŏpsin sari 法身舍利). In Chinese, "relics of the dharma body," Buddhist scriptures that were enshrined in STŪPAs and worshipped as if they were physical remains. See DHARMAŚARĪRA; ŚARĪRA.

**fashu**. (J. hossū; K. pŏpsu 法數). In Chinese, "enumerations of dharmas," the numerical schemes involving successive integers used to organize and memorize Buddhist teachings, such as the one path, two truths, three refuges, FOUR NOBLE TRUTHS, etc. This classificatory and mnemonic device is frequently employed in both SŪTRAs (such as the "Numerically-Arranged Discourses," or AṄGUTTARANIKĀYA/EKOTTARĀGAMA) and ŚĀSTRAs. East Asian exegeses, compendia, and concordances were also often arranged by, or composed exclusively of, such sequential set of numerical headings. See also GEYI.

**Fashun**. (C) (法順). See DUSHUN.

**fasi**. (J. hōshi/hassu; K. pŏpsa 法嗣). In Chinese, lit., "DHARMA heir"; a disciple who has received transmission (see YINKE) in his or her master's lineage. Generally, a fasi refers to a disciple whose understanding has been certified by his teacher, thereby becoming his inheritor. Histories of the CHAN tradition, such as the JINGDE CHUANDENG LU can largely be characterized as the history of the dharma heirs of such thriving Chan lineages as the LINJI ZONG, CAODONG ZONG, etc. See also CHUANFA; PARAMPARĀ.

**Faxian**. (J. Hōken/Hokken; K. Pŏphyŏn 法顯) (c. 337–422). In Chinese, "Display of Dharma"; a Chinese monk pilgrim of the Eastern Jin dynasty, who is best known for his pilgrimage record of his travels to India, titled the FAXIAN ZHUAN. The text, also known as the FOGUO JI, ("Record of Buddhist Kingdoms") is an invaluable source for understanding South Asian Buddhism in the early fifth century. Motivated by a desire to procure a complete recension of an Indian VINAYA, in 399 Faxian left the Chinese capital of Chang'an for India, together with his fellow monks Hujing, Daozheng, and others. He left a detailed record of his journey through numerous kingdoms in Central Asia, his arduous path through the Himalayas, and various pilgrimage sites (see MAHĀSTHĀNA) in central India. He ended up staying for several years in India, studying Sanskrit and copying various SŪTRAs and vinayas such as the MAHĀSĀṂGHIKA vinaya, SAMYUKTĀGAMA, and MAHĀPARINIRVĀṆASŪTRA, before leaving for Sri Lanka. Taking the southern sea route home from Sri Lanka, Faxian's ship was damaged in a typhoon and he was forced to stay on the island of Java for five months, finally returning to China in 413. Faxian brought back with him the new texts that he had collected overseas, and spent the rest of his life translating them into Chinese, several in collaboration with the Indian monk BUDDHABHADRA.

**Faxiang zong**. (J. Hossōshū; K. Pŏpsang chong 法相宗). In Chinese, "Dharma Characteristics School," the third and most important of three strands of YOGĀCĀRA-oriented MAHĀYĀNA Buddhism to emerge in China, along with the DI LUN ZONG and SHE LUN ZONG. The name Faxiang (originally coined by its opponents and having pejorative connotations) comes from its detailed analysis of factors (DHARMA) on the basis of the Yogācāra doctrine that all phenomena are transformations of consciousness, or "mere-representation" (VIJÑAPTIMĀTRATĀ). The school's own preferred name for itself was the WEISHI ZONG (Consciousness/Representation-Only School). Interest in the theories of the SHIDIJING LUN (viz., *Di lun*) and the MAHĀYĀNASAṂGRAHA (viz., *She lun*) largely waned as new YOGĀCĀRA texts from India were introduced to China by the pilgrim and translator XUANZANG (600/602–664) and the work of HUAYAN scholars such as FAZANG (643–712) on the AVATAṂSAKASŪTRA (within which the *Daśabhūmikasūtra* is incorporated) began to gain prominence. One of the reasons motivating Xuanzang's pilgrimage to India, in fact, was to procure definitive Indian materials that would help to resolve the discrepancies in interpretation of Yogācāra found in these different traditions. Because of the imperial patronage he received upon his return, Xuanzang became one of the most prominent monks in Chinese Buddhist history and attracted students from all over East Asia. The Faxiang school was established mainly on the basis of the CHENG WEISHI LUN (**Vijñaptimātratāsiddhi*; "The Treatise on the Establishment of Consciousness-Only"), a text edited and translated into Chinese by Xuanzang, based on material that he brought back with him from India. Xuanzang studied under ŚĪLABHADRA (529–645), a principal disciple of DHARMAPĀLA (530–561), during his stay in India, and brought Dharmapāla's scholastic lineage back with him to China. Xuanzang translated portions of Dharmapāla's **Vijñaptimātratāsiddhi*, an extended commentary on VASUBANDHU's TRIṂŚIKĀ ("Thirty Verses on Consciousness-Only"). Dharmapāla's original exegesis cited the different interpretations of Vasubandhu's treatise offered by himself and nine other major scholiasts within the Yogācāra tradition; Xuanzang, however, created a précis of the text and translated only the "orthodox" interpretation of Dharmapāla. Xuanzang's disciple KUIJI (632–682) further systematized Xuanzang's materials by compiling the CHENG WEISHI LUN SHUJI ("Commentarial Notes on the **Vijñaptimātratāsiddhi*") and the *Cheng weishi lun shuyao* ("Essentials of the **Vijñaptimātratāsiddhi*"); for his efforts to build the school, Kuiji is traditionally regarded as the first Faxiang patriarch. The Faxiang school further developed under Huizhao (650–714), its second patriarch, and Zhizhou (668–723), its third patriarch, but thereafter declined in China. ¶ The teachings of the Faxiang school were transmitted to Korea (where it is called the Pŏpsang chong) and were classified as one of the five major doctrinal traditions (see KYO) of the Unified Silla (668–935) and Koryŏ (935–1392) dynasties. The Korean expatriate monk WŎNCH'ŬK (613–696) was one of the two major disciples of Xuanzang, along with Kuiji, and there are reports of intense controversies between Kuiji's Ci'en scholastic line (CI'EN XUEPAI) and Wŏnch'uk's Ximing scholastic line (XIMING XUEPAI) due to their differing interpretations of Yogācāra doctrine. Wŏnch'ŭk's commentary to the SAṂDHINIRMOCANASŪTRA, the *Jieshenmi jing shu* (K. *Haesimmil kyŏng so*), was transmitted to the DUNHUANG region and translated into Tibetan by CHOS GRUB (C. Facheng, c. 755–849) at the behest of the Tibetan king RAL PA CAN (806–838), probably sometime between 815 and 824. Wŏnch'ŭk's exegesis of the scripture proved to be extremely influential in the writings of TSONG KHA PA (1357–1419), and especially on his LEGS BSHAD SNYING PO, where Wŏnch'ŭk's work is called the "Great Chinese Commentary." ¶ The Japanese Hossōshū developed during the Nara period (710–784) after being transmitted from China and Korea, but declined during the Heian (794–1185) due to persistent attacks from the larger TENDAI (C. TIANTAI) and SHINGON (C. Zhenyan) schools. Although the Hossōshū survived, it did not have the wide influence over the Japanese tradition as did its major rivals. ¶ Faxiang is known for its comprehensive list of one hundred DHARMAS, or "factors" (BAIFA), in which all dharmas—whether "compounded" or "uncompounded," mundane or supramundane—are subsumed; this list accounts in large measure for its designation as the "dharma characteristics" school. These factors are classified into five major categories:

1. Eight dharmas concerning the mind (CITTA)—the five sensory consciousnesses associated with the five senses, plus the mental consciousness (MANOVIJÑĀNA), ego-mentality (MANAS), and the "storehouse consciousness" (ĀLAYAVIJÑĀNA).

2. Fifty-one forces associated with thought (CITTASAṂPRAYUKTASAṂSKĀRA), such as "applied thought" (VITARKA), "sustained attention" (VICĀRA), and "envy" (ĪRṢYĀ). These are mental concomitants (CAITTA).
3. Eleven "form" or "material" (RŪPA) dharmas, the eye organ, visual object, etc., and formal thought objects (dharmāyatanika-rūpa).
4. Twenty-four forces dissociated from thought (CITTAVIPRAYUKTASAṂSKĀRA). These are either subconscious or involuntary phenomena such as "life force" (jīvitendriya) and the "meditative trance wherein no perceptual activities remain" (ASAṂJÑĀSAMĀPATTI), or abstract notions such as "possession" (PRĀPTI), which are nonetheless classified as real existents.
5. Six "uncompounded" (ASAṂSKṚTA) dharmas, such as "space" (ĀKĀŚA) and "suchness" (TATHATĀ), which are taken to be neither contingent on nor susceptible to causal forces, since they are unproduced by conditions and eternally unchanging.

All of these factors were seen by the Faxiang school as being simply projections of consciousness (VIJÑAPTIMĀTRATĀ). As noted earlier, consciousness (VIJÑĀNA) was itself subdivided into an eightfold schema: the six sensory consciousnesses (visual, auditory, gustatory, olfactory, tactile, and mental), plus the seventh ego consciousness (manas, or KLIṢṬAMANAS), which invests these sensory experiences with selfhood, and an eighth "storehouse consciousness" (ālayavijñāna), which stores the seeds or potentialities (BĪJA) of these experiences until they sprout as new cognition. One of the most controversial doctrines of the Faxiang school was its rejection of a theory of inherent enlightenment or buddhahood (i.e., TATHĀGATAGARBHA) and its advocacy of five distinct spiritual lineages or destinies (PAÑCAGOTRA): (1) the TATHĀGATA lineage (GOTRA), for those destined to become buddhas; (2) the PRATYEKABUDDHA lineage, for those destined to become ARHATS via the pratyekabuddha vehicle; (3) the ŚRĀVAKAYĀNA lineage, for those who will become arhats via the ŚRĀVAKA vehicle; (4) those of indefinite (ANIYATA) lineage, who may follow any of three vehicles; and (5) those without lineage (agotra), who are ineligible for liberation or who have lost the potential to become enlightened by becoming "incorrigibles" (ICCHANTIKA). The Faxiang school's claim that beings belonged to these various lineages because of the seeds (BĪJA) already present in the mind seemed too fatalistic to its East Asian rivals. In addition, Faxiang's acceptance of the notion that some beings could completely lose all yearning for enlightenment and fall permanently into the state of icchantikas so profoundly conflicted with the pervasive East Asian acceptance of innate enlightenment that it thwarted the school's aspirations to become a dominant tradition in China, Korea, or Japan. Even so, much in the Faxiang analysis of consciousness, as well as its exegetical techniques, were incorporated into mainstream scholasticism in East Asia and continued to influence the subsequent development of Buddhism in the region.

**Faxian zhuan**. (J. Hokken den; K. Pŏphyŏn chŏn 法顯傳). In Chinese, "The Record of Faxian," commonly known as the FOGUO JI (translated into English as *A Record of Buddhistic Kingdoms*), the record of the Chinese monk FAXIAN's pilgrimage to India. Faxian left the Chinese capital of Chang'an in 399 and visited numerous cities and kingdoms in Central Asia, India, Sri Lanka, and the island of Java. He traveled to many sacred sites in India and Sri Lanka until his return to China in 413. Faxian left a fairly detailed record of the various ways in which Buddhism was practiced in these kingdoms. His record is replete with myths and legends associated with the pilgrimage sites he visited. Faxian's record also served as an authoritative guidebook for many pilgrims who later followed in his footsteps. As one of the earliest records of its kind, the *Faxian zhuan* serves as an indispensable tool for studying Buddhist pilgrimage, the state of Buddhism across the continent during the early fifth century, and the history of various kingdoms that once flourished in Asia. It was among the first Buddhist texts to be translated in Europe, published in Paris in 1836 as *Foĕ Kouĕ Ki ou Relation des royaumes bouddhiques: Voyage dans la Tartarie, dans l'Afghanistan et dans l'Inde, exécuté à la fin du IV^e siècle, par Chỹ Fă Hian*. The translation of the text was undertaken by Jean-Pierre Abel-Rémusat (1788–1832). The Chinese text is relatively short, but Abel-Rémusat provided detailed notes, in which he sought to identify and explain the many Buddhist persons, places, and doctrines that occur in Faxian's work. Abel-Rémusat died in the cholera epidemic of 1832, when the book was only half-finished. Heinrich Julius von Klaproth (1783–1835) took over the project until his own death. It was completed by Ernest-Augustin Xavier Clerc de Landresse (1800–1862) and published in 1836. Until the publication of EUGÈNE BURNOUF's *Introduction à l'histoire du Buddhisme indien* in 1844, this was the most detailed study of Buddhism to be produced in Europe. Faxian's text was translated into English by SAMUEL BEAL in 1869 and by James Legge in 1886.

**Faxing zong**. (J. Hosshōshū; K. Pŏpsŏng chong 法性宗). In Chinese, "Dharma Nature school," the intellectual tradition in East Asian Buddhism that was concerned with the underlying essence or "nature" (xing) of reality; contrasted with the "Dharma Characteristics School" (FAXIANG ZONG), the tradition that analyzed the different functions of various phenomena. The term "Faxing zong" was employed to refer to more advanced forms of the MAHĀYĀNA, such as to the MADHYAMAKA teachings of the SAN LUN ZONG, the TATHĀGATAGARBHA teachings, or to the last three of the five teachings in the Huayan school's hermeneutical taxonomy (see JIAOXIANG PANSHI): viz., the advanced teaching of Mahāyāna (Dasheng zhongjiao), the sudden teaching (DUNJIAO), and the perfect teaching (YUANJIAO). By contrast, "Faxiang zong" was a pejorative term referring to the Chinese YOGĀCĀRA school that was established on the basis of the new Yogācāra texts introduced from India by XUANZANG (600/602–664) and elaborated upon in his lineage. The

Huayan exegete CHENGGUAN (738–839) first used the term Faxing zong to differentiate it from the Faxiang zong. In his *Dafangguang fo huayanjing shu* ("Commentary on the AVATAṂSAKASŪTRA"), Chengguan presents ten differences between the two schools of Faxing and Faxiang, and in his own hermeneutic taxonomy, Chengguan polemically equates the elementary teaching of the Mahāyāna (Dasheng shijiao) with Faxiang, and the advanced (Dasheng zhongjiao) and perfect teachings (yuanjiao) of the Mahāyāna with the Faxing school. The contrast between "nature" (xing) and "characteristics" (xiang) was used in FAZANG's (643–712) HUAYAN WUJIAO ZHANG as a means of reconciling the differences in the approaches taken by the Madhyamaka and Yogācāra schools. Although Fazang did not use the term Faxing zong himself, he did coin the term "Faxiang zong" to refer pejoratively to Xuanzang's lineage of Yogācāra teachings. It appears, then, that Chengguan projected the concept of Faxing and Faxiang schools onto Fazang's doctrinal notions as well, for Chengguan sometimes interprets Fazang's notions of the "provisional" and "definitive" teachings (see QUAN SHI) as the Faxiang and the Faxing schools, respectively, or sometimes replaces a concept such as "true nature" (zhenxing) with the term faxing.

**Fayan Wenyi**. (J. Hōgen Mon'eki; K. Pŏban Munik 法眼文益) (885–958). Chinese CHAN master and reputed founder of the FAYAN ZONG of Chan. Fayan was a native of Yuhang in present-day Zhejiang province. At the age of six, he was ordained by the monk Quanwei (d.u.) of the monastery Xinding Zhitongyuan and later received the full monastic precepts at the monastery of KAIYUANSI in Yuezhou. Fayan first visited the Chan master Changqing Huiling (854–932); later, while staying at the monastery Dizangyuan on Mt. Shi (present-day Fujian province), he met Luohan Guichen (867–928) and eventually became his disciple. Later, Fayan arrived in Linchuan (present-day Jiangxi province) where he was invited by the steward to serve as abbot of the monastery of Chongshouyuan. Admired by the local ruler, Fayan was again invited as the abbot of the monastery of BAO'ENSI in Jinling (present-day Jiangsu province) and was given the title Chan master Jinghui (Pure Wisdom). Fayan later moved to the monastery of Qingliangyuan in Shengzhou (present-day Jiangsu province), which flourished under his guidance and the support of the ruler of the state of Wuye. He was also given the posthumous title Chan master Dafayan (Great Dharma Eye). Fayan composed the ZONGMEN SHIGUI LUN ("Treatise on the Ten Rules of the Tradition"), which outlines ten defects of Chan practice; the text is also important for being the first to name the so-called five houses (wu jia), viz., schools or lineages, of the mature Chan tradition (see WU JIA QI ZONG).

**Fayan zong**. (J. Hōgenshū; K. Pŏban chong 法眼宗). In Chinese, the "Dharma Eye School," one of the "five houses" (wu jia; see WU JIA QI ZONG), or distinct schools, that had developed with the mature Chinese CHAN lineage during the late Tang dynasty, c. ninth to tenth centuries CE. Chan genealogical histories (see CHUANDENG LU) speak of a lineage of monks that can be traced back to the eminent Chan master FAYAN WENYI (885–958), who himself inherited the lineage(s) of XUEFENG YICUN (822–908), XUANSHA SHIBEI (835–908), and their student Luohan Guichen (867–928). With the support of the ruler of the state of Wuyue, Fayan and his monastery of Qingliangyuan in Shengzhou (present-day Jiangsu province) flourished. Fayan's prominent students TIANTAI DESHAO (891–972), Baizhang Daoheng (d. 991), Guizong Yirou (d.u.), and Bao'en Fa'an (d.u.) firmly established Fayan's line in the area of Zhejiang and Fujian provinces. Chengtian Daoyuan (d.u.), the compiler of the influential genealogical history of Chan known as the JINGDE CHUANDENG LU, also belongs to the Fayan line of Chan through his teacher Tiantai Deshao.The Fayan line's interest in harmonizing the iconoclastic aspects of Chan with the exegetical tradition of HUAYAN and the recitative practices of PURE LAND (see NIANFO) is best exemplified in the Fanyan Chan master YONGMING YANSHOU's magnum opus ZONGJING LU. The works of Fayan masters also exerted much influence in Korean Sŏn Buddhism. Although the Fayan zong did not survive into the Song dynasty as an active lineage, it remained an integral part of the retrospective imagining of the Chan tradition that took place during the Song.

**fayou wowu zong**. (J. hōugamushū; K. pŏbyu amu chong 法有我無宗). In Chinese, "the school that posits that 'DHARMAS are real but the self is nonexistent.'" The HUAYAN ZONG in particular uses this label polemically to denigrate the majority of the ŚRĀVAKAYĀNA or HĪNAYĀNA traditions. The latter group was presumed to have inferior doctrinal understanding, because it acknowledged that compounded things have no existent self, while positing (mistakenly) that the constituent dharmas that make up those illusory, compounded things are in fact real. So, e.g., while the hīnayāna may posit that there is no "self" to be found in a person because he/she is contingent on and comprised of a whole range of constituent factors (dharma), the physical and psychological aggregates (S. SKANDHA) that make up that person would be considered objectively real and not lacking a real substance. By contrast, Huayan exegetes would suggest that a distinguishing doctrinal theme in the MAHĀYĀNA tradition is the acknowledgment of the "emptiness" (S. ŚŪNYATĀ) or "selflessness" (S. ANĀTMAN) of not just the individual person but also the constituent factors (dharma) from which that person is constructed. This supposedly superior doctrinal stance is advocated by "the school that posits that both self and dharmas are nonexistent" (wofa juwu zong). See also PUDGALANAIRĀTMYA; DHARMANAIRĀTMYA.

**fayu**. (J. hōgo; K. pŏbŏ 法語). In Chinese, "dharma talk" or "religious discourse," referring broadly to sermons by the Buddha or eminent teachers, teachings that accord with reality (yathābhūta), or talks on topics related to the dharma; rhyming verses or terse essays containing spiritual exhortations are also sometimes called fayu. In the CHAN zong, fayu refer to anecdotal conversations or formal lectures of the patriarchs and masters of the tradition. Chan fayu are typically in colloquial prose, and often offer transcripts of Chan masters' spontaneous utterances on, or specific responses to, real-life contingencies. There are many such anthologies of Chan fayu in the literature, including both collections of the sayings of an individual master and anthologies of the sayings of multiple teachers. See also YULU.

**Fayuan zhulin**. (J. Hōon jurin; K. Pŏbwŏn churim 法苑珠林). In Chinese, "A Grove of Pearls in the Garden of the Dharma," compiled in 668 by the Tang-dynasty monk Daoshi (d. 683) of XIMINGXI; a comprehensive encyclopedia of Buddhism, in one hundred rolls and one hundred chapters, based on the DA TANG NEIDIAN LU and XU GAOSENG ZHUAN, which were compiled by Daoshi's elder brother, the monk DAOXUAN (596–667). The encyclopedia provides definitions and explanations for hundreds of specific Buddhist concepts, terms, and numerical lists. Each chapter deals with a single category such as the three realms of existence (TRILOKA[DHĀTU]), revering the Buddha, the DHARMA, and the SAṂGHA, the monastery, relics (ŚARĪRA), repentance, receiving the precepts, breaking the precepts, and self-immolation (SHESHEN), covering these topics with numerous individual entries. The *Fayuan zhulin* is characterized by its use of numerous passages quoted from Buddhist scriptures in support of its explanations and interpretations. Since many of the texts that Daoshi cites in the *Fayuan zhulin* are now lost, the encyclopedia serves as an invaluable source for the study of medieval Chinese Buddhism.

**Fazang**. (J. Hōzō; K. Pŏpchang 法藏) (643–712). Tang-dynasty Chinese monk and putative third patriarch of the HUAYAN ZONG, also known as Xianshou, Dharma Master Guoyi (Nation's Best), Great Master Xiangxiang (Fragrant Elephant), and state preceptor (GUOSHI) Kang Zang. Fazang was the third-generation descendent of immigrants to China from the kingdom of SOGDIANA in Central Asia (the Greek Transoxiana) and thus used as his secular surname the ethnicon KANG. At a young age, Fazang became a student of the Chinese monk ZHIYAN, and studied the AVATAṂSAKASŪTRA. Fazang was also fluent in several Central Asian languages, and assisted the monks ŚIKṢĀNANDA and YIJING in translating new recensions of the *Avataṃsakasūtra* (699) and the LAṄKĀVATĀRASŪTRA (704). Empress WU ZETIAN often requested Fazang to lecture on the *Avataṃsakasūtra* and its teachings on PRATĪTYASAMUTPĀDA. Fazang devoted the rest of his career to the study of the *Avataṃsakasūtra* and composing commentaries on the *Laṅkāvatārasūtra*, FANWANG JING, DASHENG QIXIN LUN, and other texts. Many of Fazang's compositions sought to systematize his teacher Zhiyan's vision of the *Avataṃsakasūtra* in terms drawn from indigenous Chinese Buddhist materials, such as the *Dasheng qixin lun*. In so doing, Fazang developed much of the specific doctrinal terminology and worldview that comes to be emblematic of the Huayan zong, making him the de facto founder of this indigenous school of Chinese Buddhist philosophy. Among Fazang's many works, his HUAYAN JING TANXUAN JI, HUAYAN WUJIAO ZHANG, and his commentary to the *Dasheng qixin lun shu* ("Awakening of Faith According to the Mahāyāna") are most famous. Fazang passed away while residing at the monastery of Da Qianfusi. Fazang remained close throughout his life to his Korean colleague ŬISANG, the founder of the Korean Hwaŏm school, with whom he studied together under Zhiyan, and some of his correspondence with Ŭisang survives. SIMSANG (J. Shinjō) (d. c. 744), another Korean who is claimed to have been a direct disciple of Fazang, was the first transmitter of the Huayan teachings in Japan, and Simsang's own disciple RYŌBEN [alt. Rōben] (689–773) is considered the founder of the Japanese Kegon school. For discussion of Fazang's philosophical views, see also HUAYAN ZONG; INDRA'S NET; SI FAJIE.

**fazhan**. (法戰). In Chinese, "dharma combat." See JIFENG.

**Fazhao**. (J. Hōshō; K. Pŏpcho 法照) (d.u.). Tang-dynasty Chinese monk, now revered by followers of the Japanese JŌDOSHŪ and JŌDO SHINSHŪ as the fifth patriarch of the PURE LAND (JINGTU ZONG) tradition in China. Fazhao resided at LUSHAN early in his career, where he devoted himself to recitation of the name of the buddha AMITĀBHA (see NIANFO); there, Fazhao had a vision of AMITĀBHA, who personally taught him about the pure land. Fazhao subsequently traveled to the Chinese capital of Chang'an, where he developed the method of WUHUI NIANFO, or "five-tempo intonation of [the name of] the Buddha." When he demonstrated this practice in 767 at the monastery of Yunfengsi, the practice is said to have resulted in a series of miracles, such as the appearance of Amitābha amid the clouds, which in turn purportedly led Emperor Daizong (762–779) to invite Fazhao to the imperial palace. In addition to demonstrating the value of buddha-recitation practice, Fazhao also sought to explain pure land teachings in terms drawn from TIANTAI doctrine, bringing pure land beliefs into the mainstream of contemporary Buddhist intellectual discourse. Because of his success in propagating pure land teachings, his peers called Fazhao the "latter-day SHANDAO." Fazhao later moved to the monastery of Zhulinsi on WUTAISHAN and acquired the cognomen Wuhui fashi (Dharma Master Five-Tempo).

**fazhi**. (J. hōshū/hosshū; K. pŏpchip 法執). In Chinese, "attachment to factors"; in contrast to ĀTMAGRĀHA, the attachment to a self, attachment to factors (DHARMA) refers to either a clinging to the constituent aggregates that make up a person as ultimately real, or an attachment to the Buddhist teachings themselves. In the former scenario, the SARVĀSTIVĀDA, for example, rejects the reality of a self among the constituent factors (DHARMA) that constitute the person, but maintained that constituent parts themselves do have a perduring, ultimate reality. Rival Buddhist schools, most notably the MADHYAMAKA tradition, criticize such a view as being emblematic of an attachment to the dharmas. In the latter scenario, dharma-attachment is the clinging to Buddhist teachings and other heuristic devices as being ultimately real (cf. PARAMĀRTHASATYA). Various Buddhist scriptures tout the Buddhist teachings as skillful strategems (UPĀYA) that serve a provisional purpose. Buddhist teachings are likened to a raft that could be used to cross a river, but once having reached the other shore, the traveler should leave the raft behind lest it become a burden. Doctrinaire interpretations of, or an undue fascination with, the Buddhist teachings, especially when they are ill-suited for the present situation, is said to be a kind of dharma-attachment. Traditionally, two kinds of dharma-attachment are delineated: "dharma-attachment that arises from discriminatory cognition" (fenbie fazhi) and "inborn dharma-attachment" (jusheng fazhi). The former is primarily an epistemic error resulting from improper thinking and exposure to fallacious doctrines—it is eradicated at the path of vision (DARŚANAMĀRGA). The latter is primarily an affective, habitual, and instinctive clinging (conditioned by similar tendencies accrued from previous lives) that may be present whether or not one subscribes to fenbie fazhi—the view of independent, irreducibly real dharmas. "Inborn dharma-attachment" is only gradually attenuated through the successive stages of the path of cultivation (BHĀVANĀMĀRGA). In Mahāyāna polemics, the so-called HĪNAYĀNA can only lead to the eradication of the attachment to self but never to the attachment to dharmas. Cf. DHARMANAIRĀTMYA.

**fazhu**. (J. hōshu/hosshu; K. pŏpchu 法主). In Chinese, "Lord of the DHARMA," a reverential epithet for the Buddha, e.g., "The World Honored One is the source of the dharma; the World Honored One is the lord of the dharma." In addition, the term fazhu is used to refer to the chief officiant of a religious ritual or ceremony, and with reference to a teacher who give dharma lectures. In China during the Southern and Northern Dynasties (Nanbei chao) period (c. 420–589), fazhu was the title of a minor SAṂGHA official who oversaw a monastery's internal affairs. In modern Japan, the term is also used as a title for leaders of different Buddhist sects (when it is then pronounced as hosshu or hossu).

**fazi**. (J. hōshu/hosshu; K. pŏpcha 法子). In Chinese, "progenies of the dharma," an expression referring to Buddhist renunciants, viz., those who have entered homelessness and received ordination. They are said to have been reborn through "the mouth of the Buddha" and belong to the same "clan lineage" of the Buddha. Sometimes this term refers to all Buddhists, both clergy and laity. In another context and in East Asian monasteries, designated successors of the abbot are called fazi, "successors to the dharma [of the lineage]."

**Fazun**. (法尊) (T. Blo bzang chos 'phags) (1902–1980). Twentieth-century Chinese translator of Buddhist scriptures and scholar of Tibetan religious and political history. In 1920, Fazun was ordained as a novice on WUTAISHAN. He became acquainted with Dayong (1893–1929), a student of TAIXU's who introduced him to the techniques of Buddhist TANTRA, at the time a popular strand of Buddhism in China in its Japanese (MIKKYŌ) and Tibetan forms. Fully ordained in Beijing in 1922, Fazun trained under Taixu's patronage in the tenets of the PURE LAND and TIANTAI schools at the Wuchang Institute for Buddhist Studies. During the same years, Taixu urged Dayong to train in Japanese mikkyō on KŌYASAN. Taixu's aim was to verify and rectify the opinions about Buddhist tantra that circulated in China, where this form of Indian Buddhism had flourished at the Tang court. Upon his return, Dayong conferred on Fazun several ABHIṢEKAS of the lower tantric cycles that he had brought from Japan. He also instructed Fazun in the *Mizong gangyao* ("Essentials of Tantra"), a primer for students of Buddhist tantra by the Japanese SHINGONSHŪ scholar Gonda Raifu (1846–1934) that Wang Hongyuan (1876–1937), a Chinese student of Gonda's, had translated in 1918. After an introduction to the Tibetan tantric traditions by Bai Puren (1870–1927), a Mongolian lama stationed at Beijing's Yonghe Gong, Dayong became gradually dissatisfied with Japanese mikkyō. With Taixu's endorsement, he resolved to study Buddhist tantra in its Tibetan form. In 1924, Fazun joined Dayong's Group for Learning the Dharma in Tibet (Liu Zang Xuefa Tuan), a team of some thirty Chinese monks who were studying the basics of the Tibetan language in Beijing. From 1925 to 1929, Fazun carried on his language learning in eastern Tibet and began his training in the classics of the DGE LUGS monastic curriculum, which in the ensuing years would become his main focus of translation. After Dayong's passing in 1929, Fazun followed his Tibetan teacher, DGE BSHES A mdo, to central Tibet. He stayed at 'BRAS SPUNGS monastery from 1930 to 1933. In 1934, Taixu asked Fazun to take on the position of director at the newly established Sino-Tibetan Institute (Hanzang Jiaoli Yuan) near Chongqing. The thirteenth DALAI LAMA also encouraged Fazun to spread TSONG KHA PA's synthesis of the Buddhist teachings in China. Hence from 1935, under the Japanese occupation and during the Chinese civil war, Fazun served as an educator of young monks in Tibetan Buddhism and as a translator of Tibetan scriptures at the Sino-Tibetan Institute. These years of prolific translation work established Fazun as the foremost translator of Buddhism from Tibetan sources in the history of Chinese Buddhism. Among his translations are Tsong kha pa's LAM RIM CHEN MO (*Putidao cidi guanglun*), LEGS BSHAD SNYING PO (*Bian liaoyi buliaoyi lun*), SNGAGS RIM CHEN MO (*Mizong daocidi lun*); MAITREYA's ABHISAMAYĀLAMKĀRA (*Xianguan zhuangyan lun*); CANDRAKĪRTI's MADHYAMAKĀVATĀRA (*Ru zhonglun*); and ĀRYADEVA's CATUḤŚATAKA (*Sibailun song*). Fazun also translated into Tibetan the ABHIDHARMAMAHĀVIBHĀṢA, extant in the two hundred rolls of XUANZANG's Chinese rendering (*Da piposha lun*), by the title *Bye brag bshad mdzod chen mo*. In 1950, after the Communist authorities discontinued the activities of the Institute, Fazun moved to Beijing. The Committee for Minority Affairs appointed him as a translator of communist propaganda materials, including Chairman Mao's *Xin minzhu zhuyi*

("New Democracy") and *Lun renmin minzhu zhuanzheng* ("On the People's Democratic Dictatorship"), for the education of the new generation of cadres in occupied Tibet. In 1966, as the Cultural Revolution set in, he was charged with expressing anti-Communist sentiments during the 1930s. He was confined in a labor camp until his release in 1972. During the 1970s Fazun resumed his translation activity from Tibetan with DHARMAKĪRTI's PRAMĀṆAVĀRTTIKA (*Shiliang lun*), DIGNĀGA's PRAMĀṆASAMUCCAYA (*Jiliang lun*), and ATIŚA DĪPAṂKARAŚRĪJÑĀNA's BODHIPATHAPRADĪPA (*Putidao deng lun*). Fazun suffered a fatal heart attack in 1980. Because of his unsurpassed knowledge of Tibetan language, religion, and history, and his writing style inspired by KUMĀRAJĪVA's and Xuanzang's Buddhist Chinese, Fazun is often referred to as "the Xuanzang of modern times."

**Feilaifeng**. (J. Hiraihō; K. Piraebong 飛来峰). In Chinese, "Flying-In Peak," site of Buddhist rock carvings and grottoes, located in front of LINGYINSI in Hangzhou, Zhejiang province. Feilaifeng houses the most important sculptural works of Tibetan Buddhism found in Han Chinese territory. The name of the peak was inspired by a legend, according to which Vulture Peak (GṚDHRAKŪṬAPARVATA) flew to this location from India. There are more than three hundred carved images still in existence at the site, with eleven from the Five Dynasties period, more than two hundred from the Song dynasty, and around one hundred from the Yuan. The Song-dynasty images were mostly carved during the Xianping era (998–1003) under Emperor Zhenzong. Many of these figures are ARHATS (C. LUOHAN), but some works illustrate special themes, such as XUANZANG's pilgrimage to India or MAITREYA's "Hemp Sack" (BUDAI) form. The gilded, colorfully painted Yuan images are delicately carved and constitute a significant development in the history of Chinese sculpture. Nearly half of these images depict esoteric themes, with buddhas, bodhisattvas, female deities, and dharma protectors (DHARMAPĀLA). The image enshrined in Niche 25 is VAJRADHARA. Also found here are images of MAÑJUŚRĪ, AVALOKITEŚVARA, and VAJRASATTVA. The female deity SITĀTAPATRĀ is depicted in Niche 22; she was highly venerated by the Yuan rulers because she was believed to be able to destroy armies and overcome disasters.

**Feiyin Tongrong**. (J. Hiin Tsūyō; K. Piŭn T'ongyong 費隱通容) (1593–1661). Chinese CHAN master in the LINJI ZONG, who lived at the end of the Ming dynasty. Feiyin was a native of Min Prefecture in present-day Fujian province. After losing his father at age six and his mother at eleven, Feiyin entered the monastery two years later and became the student of a certain Huishan (d.u.) of Sanbaosi. Feiyin subsequently studied under the renowned Chan masters ZHANRAN YUANDENG, Wuming Huijing, and Wuyi Yuanlai. In 1622, he departed Jiangxi province for Mt. Tiantai, where he continued his studies under MIYUN YUANWU. Feiyin eventually became Miyun's disciple and inherited his lineage. In 1633, Feiyin served as abbot of Wanfusi on Mt. Huangbo. He subsequently resided at such monasteries as Tianningsi and WANSHOUSI in Zhejiang province. His disciple YINYUAN LONGQI edited Feiyin's teachings together in the *Feiyin chanshi yulu*. Feiyin himself composed several texts including the Chan primer ZUTING QIANCHUI LU and the Chan history *Wudeng yantong*.

**fenbie fazhi**. (C) (分別法執). See ER FAZHI.

**fenbie wozhi**. (C) (分別我執). See ER WOZHI.

**fenduan shengsi**. (J. bundanshōji; K. pundan saengsa 分段生死). In Chinese, "birth and death in punctuated succession," one of the two types of rebirth (SAṂSĀRA) described in the Chinese FAXIANG (YOGĀCĀRA) and TIANTAI schools; the other is "birth and death as alteration and change" (BIANYI SHENGSI). This type refers to the actual physical process of death and rebirth into new bodies, bodies that are the products of our previous actions (KARMAN) and whose duration is therefore measured by the life span of the individual physical body.

**Fengfa yao**. (J. Hōhōyō; K. Pongpŏp yo 奉法要). In Chinese, "Essentials of Upholding the DHARMA," a short Buddhist catechism, composed by Xichao (336–377), a lay follower of the monk ZHI DUN, which is preserved in the HONGMING JI. The *Fengfa yao* provides a brief overview of a number of important doctrinal concepts and categories, such as the three refuges (TRIŚARAṆA), five precepts (PAÑCAŚĪLA), fasting, six recollections (ANUSMṚTI), five rebirth destinies (GATI), five aggregates (SKANDHA), five hindrances (NĪVARAṆA), six sense bases (INDRIYA), mind (CITTA), KARMAN, patient endurance (KṢĀNTI), NIRVĀṆA, six perfections (PĀRAMITĀ), FOUR NOBLE TRUTHS, confession, doing good works, etc. These notions are sometimes explained with reference to Daoist thought and historical and mythical events in China. As such, the *Fengfa yao* is an important source for studying the manner in which Buddhist doctrine was understood in early China.

**Fenggan**. (C) (風干). See SHIDE.

**Fenollosa, Ernest Francisco (Kano Yeitan)**. (1853–1908). An American proponent of Japanese Buddhism and Japanese art. Born in Salem, Massachusetts, to a mother from Salem and a Spanish father, he was part of Boston's East Asian renaissance during the 1890s and one of the first students of the incipient discipline of art history. He studied philosophy at Harvard and attended the School of the Museum of Fine Arts, Boston. At the age of twenty-five, Fenollosa went to teach at the Imperial University in Japan, where his students introduced him to Buddhism. His interest in the religion grew through his visits to temples near Nara and Kyōto. Fenollosa also became interested in traditional Japanese art and met the aristocratic families who had been court painters during the Tokugawa shogunate. By 1882, Fenollosa was considered enough of an expert to lecture at the Ryuchikai Club and, in 1884, he was named an imperial commissioner of fine arts. Sakurai Keitaku

Ajari, the head of the Hoyugin Temple at MIIDERA, became Fenollosa's teacher of Buddhism. Fenollosa received the precepts of TENDAI Buddhism in 1885, making him one of the first Americans to practice MAHĀYĀNA Buddhism. During his time in Japan, he was adopted into the Kano family and received the name Kano Yeitan. He was also presented with the "Order of the Sacred Mirror" by the Meiji emperor. After returning to the United States in 1890, Fenollosa lectured and wrote about Buddhism, became the curator of Far Eastern Art at the Boston Museum of Fine Arts, and in 1893 published a poem called *East and West*. In 1895, he married his second wife, Mary McNeil Scott, and they returned together to Japan, where Fenollosa taught English at Tōkyō Higher Normal School. He and Mary remained in Japan until 1900. *Epochs of Chinese and Japanese Art*, his magnum opus, was published posthumously, with help from Ezra Pound.

**Fire Sermon**. See ĀDITTAPARIYĀYASUTTA.

**first sermon**. See DHAMMACAKKAPPAVATTANASUTTA; DHARMACAKRAPRAVARTANASŪTRA; PAÑCAVARGIKA.

**five buddha families**. See PAÑCATATHĀGATA; PAÑCAKULA.

**five houses (of the Chan school)**. See WU JIA QI ZONG.

**five mountains**. See GOZAN.

**five nikāyas**. See DĪGHANIKĀYA; MAJJHIMANIKĀYA; SAṂYUTTANIKĀYA; AṄGUTTARANIKĀYA; KHUDDAKANIKĀYA.

**five periods and eight teachings**. See WUSHI BAJIAO.

**five precepts**. See PAÑCAŚĪLA.

**Flower Garland Sūtra**. See AVATAṂSAKASŪTRA.

**Flower Sermon**. See NIANHUA WEIXIAO.

**fo**. [alt. fotuo/futu] (J. butsu/budda/fuda; K. pul/pult'a/fudu/pudo 佛/佛陀/浮屠). In Chinese, the transcription of "buddha" and the term most often used to render the Sanskrit. Fo, the first syllable of the transcription, is ubiquitous in premodern Buddhist Chinese. (In premodern Chinese, the full transcription fotuo is more often found in the names of Indian figures, such as BUDDHABHADRA, BUDDHAYAŚAS, etc.) In modern Chinese, both colloquial and written, the compound fotuo is generally employed to refer to the Buddha. The pronunciations of the Sinographs fotuo have been tentatively reconstructed as *but-da in Early Middle Chinese (c. seventh century), demonstrating that, when the transcription was created, it was a close approximation of the original Sanskrit or Middle Indic phonology. The Sinograph is composed of the phonetic element fo and the semantic component "man"; thus, in a Buddhist context, the character can be construed to mean "the man whose name is fo." Buddhist exegetes typically glossed fo with the Sinographs juezhe ("the awakened one"). Buddhist translators into Chinese often preferred to transcribe, rather than translate, especially sacred or polysemous Buddhist terms like NIRVĀṆA, PĀRAMITĀ, or SAṂGHA; thus it was with the term buddha, where a semantic translation seems never to have been used in China. In the early centuries of the dissemination of Buddhism in China, several competing transcriptions of buddha were in use, such as the archaic form futu (reconstructed as *buw-dɔ) in the entry heading for fo above, which represented different stages in the phonology of premodern Chinese, or local dialectical variations. These were eventually superseded by fo when Buddhist translators and exegetes active in the region of the Chinese capital of Luoyang adopted it in their court-sponsored translations.

**Foguo ji**. (C) (佛國記). In Chinese, "A Record of Buddhist Kingdoms." See FAXIAN ZHUAN.

**Foguo Yuanwu chanshi biyan lu**. (C) (佛果圜悟禪師碧巖録). See BIYAN LU.

**footprints of the Buddha**. See BUDDHAPĀDA.

**forest monks**. See ARAÑÑAVĀSI.

**Fori Qisong**. (J. Butsunichi Kaisū; K. Puril Kyesung 佛日契嵩) (1007–1072). In Chinese, "Buddha Sun, Accords with Loftiness"; renowned scholar-monk during the Song dynasty and fifth-generation successor in the YUNMEN ZONG of the Chan school. After entering the monastery in his seventh year and being ordained in his thirteenth year, he traveled widely throughout China to meet with the famous Chan masters of his age. He eventually received formal dharma transmission from Dongshan Xiaocong (d.u.) in the Yunmen school. Qisong served as abbot of Jinghuisi, a monastery located nearby the city of Hangzhou on Mt. Fori, hence his toponym. He was known as a severe abbot, and his presence led many of the less serious monks who had been residing there to leave the monastery. Around 1061, Qisong completed an early history of the Chan school titled *Chuanfa zhengzong ji* ("Essay on the Authentic Lineage of Dharma Transmission"), which contains the first reference to the five houses schema of the mature Chan school (see WU JIA QI ZONG): the GUIYANG ZONG (which Qisong says was virtually extinct in his day), CAODONG ZONG (which he says is barely extant), and the LINJI ZONG, Yunmen zong, and FAYAN ZONG (all three of which he says were flourishing). Qisong also wrote a widely read and cited introduction to the Yuan-dynasty edition of the "Platform Sūtra of the Sixth Patriarch" (LIUZU TAN JING), the edition of that text most commonly used in the Chan school from that point forward. Qisong died in 1072 in his sixty-sixth year. Many relics (ŚARĪRA) remained after his cremation and near-contemporary records say that his eyes, tongue, and penis survived the flames. These relics were enshrined in a reliquary (STŪPA) at Lingyinsi in Hangzhou. We know of only one named disciple of Qisong's, and the Yunmen school with which he was affiliated faded soon after his demise.

**form is emptiness, emptiness is form**. See RŪPAṂ ŚŪNYATĀ ŚŪNYATAIVA RŪPAM.

**forty-ninth day ceremony**. See SISHIJIU [RI] ZHAI; ANTARĀBHAVA.

**Fotudeng**. [alt. Fotucheng] (J. Butsutochō/Buttochō; K. Pultojing 佛圖澄) (232–348). A monk and thaumaturge, perhaps from the Central Asian kingdom of KUCHA, who was a pioneer in the transmission of Buddhism to China. According to his hagiography in the GAOSENG ZHUAN, Fotudeng was a foreign monk, whose surname was BO, the ethnikon used for Kuchean monks; in some sources, his name is transcribed as Buddhasiṃha. He was talented at memorizing and expounding scriptures, as well as in debate. Fotudeng is said to have received training in Kashmir (see KASHMIR-GANDHĀRA) and to have arrived in China in 310 intending to spread the DHARMA. Fotudeng is described as a skilled magician who could command spirits and predict the future. Despite his initial failure to establish a monastery in the Chinese capital of Luoyang, Fotudeng was able to convert the tyrannical ruler of the state of Later Zhao, Shi Le (r. 319–333), with a demonstration of his thaumaturgic skills. Fotudeng's continued assistance of Shi Le won him the title Daheshang (Great Monk). After Shi Le's general Shi Hu (r. 334–339) usurped the throne, Fotudeng was elevated to the highest status at the palace, and he continued to play the important role of political and spiritual advisor to the ruler. During his illustrious career as royal advisor, Fotudeng also taught many Buddhist disciples and is said to have established hundreds of monasteries. Among his disciples Zhu Faya (d.u.), DAO'AN, and Chu Fatai (320–387) are most famous.

**four extremes**. See CATUṢKOṬI.

**four great vows**. See SI HONGSHIYUAN.

**four immeasurables**. See APRAMĀṆA; BRAHMAVIHĀRA.

**four noble truths**. (S. catvāry āryasatyāni; P. cattāri ariyasaccāni; T. 'phags pa'i bden pa bzhi; C. si shengdi; J. shishōdai; K. sa sŏngje 四聖諦). Although the term "four noble truths" is well established in English-language works on Buddhism, it is a misleading translation of the original Sanskrit and Pāli terms. The term translated as "noble" (ĀRYA) refers not to the truths themselves, but to those who understand them; thus, the compound may more accurately, if less euphoniously, be rendered as "four truths [known by the spiritually] noble"; they are four facts known to be true by those "noble ones" with insight into the nature of reality, but not known by ordinary beings (PṚTHAGJANA). The four truths are: suffering (DUḤKHA), origination (SAMUDAYA), cessation (NIRODHA), and path (MĀRGA). The four noble truths are the subject of extensive exegesis in the tradition, but the four terms and the relationships among them may be summarized as follows. Existence in the realms that are subject to rebirth, called SAMSĀRA, is qualified by suffering (duḥkha), the first truth (the Sanskrit term may also be rendered as "sorrow," "pain," or more generally "unsatisfactoriness"). The types of sufferings that beings undergo in the various destinations of rebirth are enumerated at great length in Buddhist texts. In his first sermon delivered after his enlightenment (see DHARMACAKRAPRAVARTANASŪTRA), the Buddha identifies the following as forms of suffering: birth, aging, sickness, death, encountering what is unpleasant, separation from what is pleasant, not gaining what one desires, and the five SKANDHAS. The second truth is the origination (samudaya), or cause, of suffering. In his first sermon, the Buddha identifies the cause of suffering as craving (TṚṢṆĀ) or attachment; in his second sermon, the ANATTALAKKHAṆASUTTA, said to have been delivered five days later, he suggests that the belief is self (ĀTMAN) is the cause of suffering. In other works, he lists two causes of suffering: unwholesome or unsalutary (AKUŚALA) actions (KARMAN) such as killing, stealing, and lying, and the unwholesome mental states (see CAITTA) that motivate unwholesome actions. These unwholesome mental states include greed (LOBHA), hatred (DVEṢA), and ignorance (MOHA), with ignorance referring here to an active misperception of the nature of the person and the world or, more technically, to an unsystematic attention (AYONIŚOMANASKĀRA) to the true nature of things, leading to the following "inverted views" (VIPARYĀSA): seeing pleasure where there is actually pain, purity where there is impurity, permanence where there is impermanence, and self where there is no self. The third truth is the cessation (nirodha) of suffering, which refers to NIRVĀṆA, the "deathless" (AMṚTA) state that transcends all suffering. The fourth and final truth is that of the path (mārga) to the cessation of suffering. The path is delineated in exhaustive detail in Buddhist texts; in his first sermon, the Buddha describes an eightfold path (ĀRYĀṢṬĀṄGAMĀRGA). The four truths therefore posit the unsatisfactory nature of existence, identify its causes, hold out the prospect of a state in which suffering and its causes are absent, and set forth a path to that state. Suffering is to be identified, its origin destroyed, its cessation realized, and the path to its cessation followed. The four truths demonstrate the importance of causality (see HETUPRATYAYA) in Buddhist thought and practice. Suffering is the effect of the cause, or origin, viz., "craving." Cessation is the absence of suffering, which results from the destruction of suffering's origin, craving. The path is the means by which one attains that cessation. The Buddha states in his first sermon that when he gained absolute and intuitive knowledge of the four truths, he achieved complete enlightenment and freedom from future rebirth. The four truths are also often described in terms of their sixteen aspects (ṣoḍaśākāra), which counteract four inverted views (viparyāsa) for each truth. For the truth of suffering, the four aspects are knowledge that the aggregates (SKANDHA) are impermanent, suffering, empty, and selfless; these counteract seeing permanence, pleasure, mine (MAMAKĀRA), and I (AHAṂKĀRA), respectively. For the truth of origination, the four aspects are knowledge that KLEŚA (affliction) and action (karman) are cause (HETU), origination (samudaya), producer (saṃbhava), and condition (PRATYAYA); they counteract the view that there is no cause, that there is a single cause, that the cause is transformation of a fundamental nature, and that the cause is a prior act of divine will, respectively. For the truth of cessation, the four aspects are knowledge that nirvāṇa is cessation (NIRODHA), peace (śānta), sublime (praṇīta), and a definite escape (niryāṇa); these counteract the view that there is no liberation, that liberation is suffering, that the pleasure of meditative absorption (DHYĀNA) is unmitigated, and that NIRVĀṆA is not firmly irreversible. And for the truth of the path, the four aspects are knowledge that the eightfold noble path is a path (mārga), correct method (UPĀYA), practice (PRATIPATTI), and brings a definite escape (nairyāṇika); these counteract the view that there is no path, that this eightfold noble path is vile, that something else is also a path, and that this path is reversible. Some Mahāyāna sūtras say that those who are attached to (ABHINIVEŚA) the four noble truths as being essentially true do not understand the purport of the Buddha's doctrine; only the teaching of the third noble truth, NIRVĀṆA, is definitive (NĪTĀRTHA), the statements about the other truths require interpretation (NEYĀRTHA). See also DARŚANAMĀRGA.

**Four-Part Vinaya**. See SIFEN LÜ, DHARMAGUPTAKA.

**four seals**. Four assertions that mark a philosophical system as Buddhist. See CATURMUDRĀ.

**four signs/sights**. See CATURNIMITTA.

**four truths, sixteen aspects of**. See FOUR NOBLE TRUTHS.

**foxing**. (J. busshō; K. pulsŏng 佛性). In Chinese, "buddha-nature," a translation of the Sanskrit term BUDDHADHĀTU (buddha-element). According to the East Asian YOGĀCĀRA tradition (see FAXIANG ZONG), there are "two kinds of buddha-nature" (er foxing), referring to the "buddha-nature of principle" (li foxing) and the "functional buddha-nature" (xing foxing), or literally, "buddha-nature of the nature." The former type is said to be the true nature of factors (DHARMA), which is beyond production and cessation, birth and death, conceptualization and designation—a "principle" (li) discoverable by all through wisdom. The latter type is a latent seed or potentiality (BĪJA) within the eighth storehouse consciousness (ĀLAYAVIJÑĀNA) that may, if it is activated and matured, eventually result in the achievement of buddhahood. According to the Faxiang school, the "buddha-nature of principle" is "universal" in the sense that all sentient beings partake in it. Only some sentient beings, however, are endowed with the "functional buddha-nature"; others are said to be devoid of the potential to achieve buddhahood for all eternity (see ICCHANTIKA). The FOXING LUN, an important treatise on the buddha-nature and TATHĀGATAGARBHA thought, discusses three types of foxing: (1) "the buddha-nature that dwells in itself," viz., that is inherent in the minds of deluded ordinary beings (PṚTHAGJANA); (2) "the emergent buddha-nature," which emerges as a result of practice, and which is initiated when the adept first generates the aspiration for enlightenment (BODHICITTOTPĀDA); and (3) "the attained buddha-nature," which is achieved once the BODHISATTVA path (MĀRGA) is completed and the fruition of buddhahood attained. See also the extended coverage in BUDDHADHĀTU.

**Foxing lun**. (J. Busshōron; K. Pulsŏng non 佛性論). In Chinese, "Treatise on the Buddha-Nature," an important exposition of the MAHĀYĀNA theories of buddha-nature (FOXING) and storehouse, womb, or matrix of the tathāgatas (TATHĀGATAGARBHA). Authorship of the treatise is traditionally attributed to the Indian scholiast VASUBANDHU (fl. c. mid-fourth to mid-fifth centuries CE), with the Chinese translation made by the Indian YOGĀCĀRA exegete PARAMĀRTHA (499–569). Scholars now generally accept, however, that the text at the very least displays the heavy editorial hand of Paramārtha and may in fact have been written by him. The text offers a tripartite account of the buddha-nature as "dwelling in itself," "emergent," and "attained" (see discussion in FOXING, s.v.). It is also well known for its outline of three aspects of the tathāgatagarbha, as (1) the contained, (2) the concealed or hidden, and (3) the container. The "contained" means the "embryo" of enlightenment that is contained within the womb of the tathāgatas. "Concealment" denotes both the tathāgata as (a) an active agent of liberation, secreting himself inside the minds of ordinary sentient beings in order to motivate them toward enlightenment, and (b) a passive factor that is covered over and hidden by the afflictions (KLEŚA). As the "container," the tathāgatagarbha is the fulfillment of the infinite numbers of meritorious qualities perfected by the buddhas. See also RATNAGOTRAVIBHĀGA.

**Foxin zong**. (J. Busshinshū; K. Pulsim chong 佛心宗). In Chinese, "Buddha-Mind School"; a term used largely as a synonym for the CHAN ZONG. According to the BIYAN LU, for instance, NĀGĀRJUNA, the fourteenth patriarch in the Chan patriarchal lineage, is said to have transmitted the Buddha-Mind School to the fifteenth patriarch Kānadeva. The term "buddha-mind" also functions in certain cases as a synonym for BUDDHADHĀTU (FOXING) or TATHĀGATAGARBHA.

**Fo yijiao jing**. (佛遺教經). In Chinese, "Scripture on the Teachings Bequeathed by the Buddha." See YIJIAO JING.

**Fozhao Deguang**. (J. Busshō Tokkō; K. Pulcho Tŏkkwang 佛照德光) (1121–1203). Chinese CHAN master in the LINJI ZONG. Fozhao studied under DAHUI ZONGGAO at Mt. Ayuwang and took the name of the mountain, Yuwang, as his toponym. He later served as preceptor of Emperor Xiaozong (r. 1162–1189), from whom he received the title Chan master Fozhao. His conversations with the emperor were recorded in the *Fozhao chanshi qindui lu* and his teachings in the *Fozhao Guang heshang yuyao*.

**fozu**. (J. busso; K. pulcho 佛祖). In Chinese, "buddhas and patriarchs," referring to the ancestors of the Buddhist tradition. Many traditions of Buddhism, especially those in East Asia, trace their pedigree back through an unbroken lineage of patriarchs (cf. ZUSHI) to the Buddha or buddhas. Positing such a succession of teachers directly connects the contemporary tradition both temporally and geographically to the founder of the religion himself and thus authenticates the school's presentation of the Buddhist tradition. The buddhas in these rosters typically refer to the seven buddhas of antiquity (SAPTATATHĀGATA), the last of whom in the succession is ŚĀKYAMUNI, the founder of the current dispensation (ŚĀSANA) of Buddhism. Śākyamuni in turn is followed by a succession of Indian patriarchs (ZUSHI), whose numbers vary: in East Asia, the CHAN ZONG ultimately accepts a list of twenty-eight Indian patriarchs, beginning with MAHĀKĀŚYAPA and ending with BODHIDHARMA; the TIANTAI ZONG accepts twenty-four Indian patriarchs, beginning with Mahākāśyapa and ending with Siṃha bhikṣu. These Indian predecessors would then be followed in turn by a list of Chinese patriarchs, of whom six are best known in the Chan school (ending with the sixth patriarch, LIUZU, HUINENG) and nine in the Tiantai school. Especially for a school like Chan, which claims not to base its presentation of Buddhism on the scriptures of the religion (see BULI WENZI) but instead on its direct connection to the mind of the Buddha (foxin), the existence of such an unbroken lineage of "buddhas and patriarchs" is a principal means of legitimating the school. See also FOZU TONGJI; JINGDE CHUANDENG LU.

**Fozu sanjing**. (J. Busso sangyō; K. Pulcho samgyŏng 佛祖三經). In Chinese, "The Three Scriptures of the Buddhas and Patriarchs," referring to a collection of three texts, YIJIAO JING, SISHI'ER ZHANG JING, and GUISHAN JINGCE. The *Fozu sanjing* texts were compiled together sometime during the late Tang and early Song dynasties as an accessible primer of Buddhist doctrine and practice, recommended to all beginners in the CHAN ZONG for its simple and clear exposition of the Buddhist teachings. The earliest extant commentary on this compilation was composed by the CAODONG ZONG monk DAHONG SHOUSUI (1072–1147). Interestingly, the first two texts in the anthology are now presumed to be Chinese APOCRYPHA, indigenous scriptures composed on the model of Indian scriptures, suggesting that they appealed to their Chinese audience in a way that translated Indian scriptures did not.

**Fozu tongji**. (J. Busso tōki; K. Pulcho t'onggi 佛祖統紀). In Chinese, "Chronicle of the Buddhas and Patriarchs," a massive history of Buddhism and TIANTAI orthodoxy written in the manner of an official chronicle, composed by ZHIPAN (1220–1275) in fifty-four rolls. The chronicle begins with the life of the Buddha, the division of his relics (ŚARĪRA), and the compilation of the Buddhist canon (see TRIPIṬAKA; DAZANGJING). The fifth roll details the lives of the twenty-four Indian patriarchs, beginning with MAHĀKĀŚYAPA and ending with Siṃha bhikṣu. This theory of the twenty-four patriarchs is also found in TIANTAI ZHIYI's magnum opus MOHE ZHIGUAN, wherein it is stated that the transmission ends after Siṃha bhikṣu was killed by the tyrant Mihirakula, the king of Damiḷa. Rolls six and seven discuss the nine patriarchs in China, starting with Huiwen (d.u.), NANYUE HUISI, Zhiyi, Guanding (561–632), Zhiwei (d. 680), Huiwei (634–713), and JINGXI ZHANRAN; roll eight covers the rest in the series of patriarchs leading up to SIMING ZHILI. The rest of the chronicle details the lives of worthy monks of other traditions. Other important charts and histories are provided in the last few rolls. The *Fozu tongji* thus serves as an important source for studying the history of the Tiantai tradition and the ways in which the school envisioned Buddhist orthodoxy during the Song dynasty.

**Frauwallner, Erich**. (1898–1974). Austrian scholar of Sanskrit philology; professor at the University of Vienna and a member of the Austrian Academy of Sciences. Frauwallner wrote some twenty monographs on various strands of Indian Buddhist literature, especially concerning the VINAYA and ABHIDHARMA, and broader surveys of Indian philosophy. His works include his *The Earliest Vinaya and the Beginnings of Buddhist Literature* (1956) and *Abhidharmastudien* (translated into English as *Studies in Abhidharma Literature and the Origins of Buddhist Philosophical Systems*), which treats the analytical structure of early Buddhist abhidharma as the inception of systematic philosophical thought in Buddhism. Frauwallner was also one of the first Western scholars to explore the writings of DHARMAKĪRTI on Buddhist logic and epistemology and especially the APOHA theory, laying the foundation for PRAMĀṆA studies in Austria. Frauwallner, with other Indologists like Ludwig Alsdorf, were tainted by their association with Nazism and anti-Semitism; Frauwallner, however, later acknowledged the great contributions that the Alsatian Jewish scholar SYLVAIN LÉVI had made to Buddhist studies.

**Fu dashi**. (J. Fu daishi; K. Pu taesa 傅大士) (497–569). In Chinese, "Great Layman Fu," his secular name was Xi and he is also known as Shanhui, Conglin, and Dongyang dashi. Fu dashi was a native of Wuzhou in present-day Zhejiang province. At fifteen, he married and had two sons, Pujian and Pucheng. Originally a fisherman, he abandoned his fishing basket after hearing a foreign mendicant teach the dharma and moved to SONGSHAN (Pine Mountain). After attaining awakening beneath a pair of trees, he referred to himself as layman Shanhui (Good Wisdom) of Shuanglin (Paired Trees). While continuing with his severe ascetic practices, Fu and his wife hired out their services as laborers during the day and he taught at night, ultimately claiming that he had come from TUṢITA heaven, where the future buddha MAITREYA was currently residing. He is said to have been summoned to teach at court during the reign of the Liang-dynasty emperor Wudi (r. 502–549). In 539, Fu dashi is said to have established the monastery Shuanglinsi at the base of Songshan. His collected discourses, verses, and poetry are preserved in the *Shanhui dashi yulu*, in four rolls, which also includes his own biography as well as those of four other monks who may have been his associates. Fu is also credited with inventing the revolving bookcase for scriptures, which, like a prayer wheel (cf. MA ṆI 'KHOR LO), could yield merit (PUṆYA) simply by turning it. This invention led to the common practice of installing an image of Fu and his family in monastic libraries. In painting and sculpture, Fu dashi is typically depicted as a tall bearded man wearing a Confucian hat, Buddhist raiments, and Daoist shoes and accompanied by his wife and two sons.

**Fudōchi shinmyōroku**. (不動智神妙録). In Japanese, "Record of the Mental Sublimity of Immovable Wisdom," a treatise on ZEN and sword fighting composed by the Japanese RINZAISHŪ monk TAKUAN SŌHŌ (1573–1645). In the first half of the seventeenth century, Takuan found himself in the middle of a political battle known as the "purple robe incident" (shi'e jiken), which, in 1629, ultimately led to his exile to Kaminoyama in Uzen (present-day Yamagata Prefecture). There, he composed this treatise on the proper use of the mind in Zen and sword fighting for the samurai sword master Yagyū Muneori (1571–1646), the personal instructor to the shōgun. Takuan first describes the afflictions that rise from ignorance (AVIDYĀ) as hindrances to proper sword fighting. Then he explains the "immovable wisdom" as the unclinging, unstopping mind. Takuan likens this unmoving state to the concept of "no-mind" (J. mushin; C. WUXIN) in the "Platform Sūtra" (LIUZU TANJING), wherein one's movements are not calculated, but instinctual; thus, there should be no gap between mind and sword. The rest of the treatise expounds upon the proper means of attaining this state of no-mind.

**Fu fazang yinyuan zhuan**. (J. Fuhōzō innenden; K. Pu pŏpchang inyŏn chŏn 付法藏因緣傳). In Chinese, "History of the Transmission of the Dharma-Storehouse," a lineage history of the Indian Buddhist patriarchs, purportedly translated in 472 by Kiṅkara (d.u.) and Tanyao (fl. 450–490) of the Northern Wei dynasty, but now known to be an indigenous Chinese composition, in six rolls. The *Fu fazang yinyuan zhuan* outlines the history of the transmission of the dharma-storehouse (fazang), viz., the lineage of teachers, following the BUDDHA's PARINIRVĀṆA, beginning with the first patriarch of the tradition, the elder MAHĀKĀŚYAPA, and ending with the beheading of the putative twenty-fourth patriarch, Siṃha bhikṣu, at the hand of the tyrant Mihirakula, the king of Damiḷa. This account of the Buddhist transmission lineage was adopted in TIANTAI ZHIYI's magnum opus MOHE ZHIGUAN and exerted much influence over the development of the transmission histories of the the TIANTAI ZONG and the CHAN ZONG (see CHUANDENG LU). Both the Tiantai and Chan schools thus hold this text in high esteem, as offering documentary evidence for their sectarian accounts of the Buddhist transmission lineage. Despite the wide influence of the *Fu fazang yinyuan zhuan* within Chinese Buddhism, however, the text seems not to be a translation of an Indian original but is instead a Chinese composition (see APOCRYPHA). As the discussions of the text in the DA TANG NIEDIAN LU and LIDAI SANBAO JI both suggest, the *Fu fazang yinyuan zhuan* may have been compiled in response to the persecution of Buddhism that occurred during the reign of the Northern Wei emperor Taiwu (r. 441–451). Later, after his successor, Emperor Wencheng (r. 452–465), had ascended to the throne and revived Buddhism, Tanyao and his collaborator Kiṅkara were inspired to compose this book at the cave site of Beitai in order to clarify definitively the orthodox lineage of ŚĀKYAMUNI Buddha. The book also largely resembles Chinese recensions of the biography of King AŚOKA and thus probably could not have been a translation of an Indian text. Finally, many of the sources cited in the book are otherwise unknown and their authenticity is dubious. For all these reasons, it is now generally accepted that the text is of Chinese provenance.

**Fukan zazengi**. (普勸坐禪儀). In Japanese, "General Advice on the Principles of Seated Meditation," an important meditation manual composed by the eminent Japanese ZEN master DŌGEN KIGEN. Although this treatise is traditionally dated to 1227, recent discoveries of a hitherto unknown copy of the *Fukan zazengi* suggest the date of 1233. The *Fukan zazengi* is a relatively short treatise on seated meditation (ZAZEN), which is also embedded in Dōgen's magnum opus, the SHŌBŌGENZŌ. The treatise underscores the need to practice seated meditation as a corrective against excessive indulgence in "words and letters," viz., scholastic interpretations of Buddhist doctrine (cf. BULI WENZI). The explanation of how to perform seated meditation starts with preparing a quiet spot for practice and following a proper diet. The correct posture for meditation is then described. The actual practice of seated meditation begins with the regulation of breathing, which is followed by an injunction to stay aware of all thoughts that arise in the mind. The treatise then briefly explains the psychosomatic effects of meditation and the proper way to rise from seated meditation. The importance of seated meditation is reiterated at the end. Dōgen's manual is in large part a revision of the Chinese Chan master CHANGLU ZONGZE's influential primer of meditation, the ZUOCHAN YI.

**Fukeshū**. (普化宗). In Japanese, "Puhua Sect"; a secondary sect of the Japanese ZEN school, founded by SHINCHI KAKUSHIN (1207–1298). While Kakushin was in China studying under WUMEN HUIKAI (1183–1260), he is said to have met a layman, the otherwise-unknown Zhang Can (J. Chō San; d.u.), who claimed to be a sixteenth-generation successor of the little-known Tang-dynasty monk Puhua (J. Fuke; d.u.), supposedly an eccentric friend of LINJI YIXUAN and a successor of MAZU DAOYI. Four lay disciples of Zhang's accompanied Kakushin when he returned to Japan, helping Kakushin to establish the sect. There is no evidence of the existence of a Puhua school in China apart from Kakushin's account, however, and the school seems to be a purely Japanese creation. During the Tokugawa era (1603–1867), in particular, the school attracted itinerant lay Zen practitioners, known as "clerics of emptiness" (kamusō), who played the bamboo flute (shakuhachi) as a form of meditation and wore a distinctive bamboo hat that covered their entire face as they traveled on pilgrimage around the country. Because masterless samurai (rōnin) and bandits began adopting Fuke garb as a convenient disguise during the commission of their crimes, the Meiji government proscribed the school in 1871 and it vanished from the scene.

**Fukurokuju**. (J) (福祿壽). See SHICHIFUKUJIN.

**full-lotus posture**. See VAJRAPARYAṄKA; PADMĀSANA.

**Fumon**. (J) (普門). See MUKAN FUMON.

**Fumu enzhong jing**. (J. Bumo onjūgyō; K. Pumo ŭnjung kyŏng 父母恩重經). In Chinese, "The Scripture on the Profundity of Parental Kindness," an indigenous Buddhist scripture, composed in the seventh century that extols the virtues of filial piety (C. xiao). There are several different recensions of this sūtra, including one discovered in the caves of DUNHUANG. The scripture denounces unfilial sons who, after their marriages, neglect and abuse their parents, and instead urges that they requite the kindness of their parents by making offerings at the ghost festival (C. YULANBEN; S. *ULLAMBANA) and by copying this scripture and reciting it out loud. This text seems to be related to other earlier Chinese APOCRYPHA, such as the *Fumu enzhong nanbao jing* ("The Scripture on the Difficulty of Requiting Parental Kindness") and the YULANPEN JING ("Ullambana Scripture"), and displays the possible influence of the indigenous Confucian tradition. The *Fumu enzhong jing* continues to be one of the most popular scriptures in East Asian Buddhism and is frequently cited in the Buddhist literature of China, Korea, and Japan.

**Furong Daokai**. (J. Fuyō Dōkai; K. Puyong Tohae 芙蓉道楷) (1043–1118). Chinese CHAN master in the CAODONG ZONG, a native of Yizhou in present-day Shandong province. When he was young, Daokai is said to have trained to become a Daoist transcendent (shenxian). He later became a monk at the monastery Shushengyuan (or Shutaisi) in Jingshi, where he studied under a monk named Dexian (d.u.); and, in 1074, he received the full monastic precepts. Daokai later became a disciple of the Chan master TOUZI YIQING at the Chan monastery of Haihui Chansi on Mt. Baiyun in Shuzhou prefecture (present-day Anhui province). In 1082, he established himself on Mt. Xiantong in Yizhou and in 1103 became the second abbot of the influential Chan monastery of Baoshou Chanyuan on Mt. Dahong (present-day Hubei province). A year later he relocated to the Chan monastery of Shifang Jingyin Chanyuan in Dongjing (present-day Henan province) and again to the nearby Tianningsi in 1107. The emperor offered him a purple robe and the title Chan Master Dingzhao (DHYĀNA Illumination), but Daokai declined. Later, a prominent lay follower built a hermitage for him on Furong island (present-day Shandong province), whence he acquired his toponym. The community at Furong quickly grew into a prominent monastery. In 1117, Daokai's hermitage was given the official plaque Huayan Chansi, thereby elevating it to an official "monastery of the ten directions" (SHIFANGCHA). Inheriting his lineage were twenty-nine disciples, of whom the most famous was Danxia Zichun (1064–1117). Furong's teachings are recorded in the *Furong Kai chanshi yuyao*.

**fushō Zen**. (不生禪). In Japanese, "unborn Zen"; a form of ZEN meditation popularized by the RINZAISHŪ master BANKEI YŌTAKU. The teaching of the "unborn" (fushō) functioned as the central theme of Bankei's vernacular sermons (kana hōgo). According to Bankei, the unborn is none other than buddhanature (FOXING), or buddha mind, itself. As such, he emphatically notes that there is little need actually to seek buddhahood, since everyone is already born with the innate, unborn buddha mind. Bankei's teaching of unborn Zen was harshly criticized by the fellow Rinzai Zen master HAKUIN EKAKU.

**fusi**. (J. fūsu; K. pusa 副司). In Chinese, "assistant comptroller," the third assistant to the prior (JIANYUAN) in an East Asian Buddhist monastery. Along with the rector (WEINUO), cook (DIANZUO), superintendent (ZHISUI), prior's assistant (DUSI), and comptroller (JIANSI), the assistant comptroller is one of the six stewards (ZHISHI) at an East Asian CHAN monastery.

**fuzangwu**. (J. fukuzōmotsu; K. pokchangmul 腹藏物). In Chinese, "interred objects," referring to items enshrined within the cavities of buddha images, a practice widespread in the Buddhist traditions of East Asia (if not throughout all of Buddhism). Typically the "lost-wax" casting process for creating iron or bronze images would leave a substantial cavity inside the image, in which could be interred such sacred objects as written or printed scriptures, DHĀRAṆĪ, and MANTRA; smaller images of buddhas and bodhisattvas; information on the creation of the image, lists of sponsoring donors, and various dedications and vows; replicas of internal organs carved from wood or sown from cloth; or paddy rice, hulled rice, and soy beans as a form of permanent offering to the Buddha. The sealing of such things inside an image often took place as part of the consecration ritual for the image. Wooden images were also often carved in imitation of cast images in order to leave such an interment cavity. By serving as a repository of sacred objects, the image could thus serve not only as an object of worship but also play a role similar to that of a STŪPA or CAITYA.

**fuzi**. (S. vālavyajana; P. vālavījanī; T. rnga yab; J. hossu; K. pulcha 拂子). In Chinese, "fly whisk" or "chowrie," a yak-tail fan that Buddhist monks used to keep flies and mosquitoes away, which comes to be a symbol of the office of CHAN master. The chowrie is presumed to have originally been used among followers of the JAINA tradition to shoo away flies without injuring them and came to be used widely throughout India. In the Chinese Chan tradition, the fly whisk (which in East Asia is usually made from a horse tail) became a symbol of the office or privilege of a Chan master and is one of the accoutrements he traditionally is depicted as holding in formal portraits. "Taking up the fly whisk" (BINGFU) is, by metonymy, a term used to refer to a formal Chan sermon delivered by a master. See also VĀLAVYAJANA.

# G

**gaing**. (P. gaṇa). In Burmese, lit. "group" or "association"; the Myanmar (Burmese) term for a monastic fraternity or denomination within the Burmese saṅgha (S. SAṂGHA). Used in this sense, gaing is sometimes replaced with its Pāli equivalent NIKĀYA. As of 1980, there are nine officially recognized monastic gaing registered with the Burmese government's Ministry of Religious Affairs. The two largest are (1) THUDHAMMA (P. Sudhammā) and (2) SHWEGYIN. Next is a smaller but stricter DWAYA fraternity, which is subdivided into: (3) Dhammanudhamma Maha Dwaya (P. Dhammānudhamma Mahā Dvāra), (4) Dhamma Vinayanuloma Mula Dwaya (P. Dhamma Vinayānuloma Mūla Dvāra), and (5) Anauk Kyaung Dwaya. The remaining gaing are: (6) Satubhummika Maha Thatipatan Hngetwin (P. Catubhummika Mahā Satipaṭṭhāna), (7) Weluwun, (P. Veḷuvana), (8) Ganawimotti Kuto (P. Gaṇavimutti), and (9) Dhammayutti Mahayin. Of these nine monastic gaing, the oldest is the Thudhamma, which traces its origins to an ecclesiastical council named the Thudhamma Thabin (P. Sudhammā Sabhā) that was established in 1782 by the Burmese king, BODAWPAYA (r. 1782–1819). The Thudhamma Council was organized to reform the Burmese saṅgha and unite its various factions under centralized control, a task at which it seems to have been relatively successful. The influence of the royally backed Thudhamma Council greatly diminished by the mid-nineteenth century as a consequence of the British conquest of Lower Burma during the first and second Anglo-Burmese Wars (1824–6 and 1852). It is following this territorial loss, during the reign of King MINDON (r. 1853–1878), that the Shwegyin, Dwaya, and Hngetwin gaing begin to coalesce into separate fraternities. All three were founded by ultra-orthodox scholar-monks who broke with the Thudhamma Council over issues of monastic discipline. The Dwaya Gaing, which had its center in British-controlled Lower Burma, later divided into the three separate fraternities recognized today. The Weluwun, another southern gaing, had similar beginnings except that it was established following the British conquest of Upper Burma and termination of the Burmese monarchy in 1885. The Shwegyin, Dwaya, Hngetwin, and Weluwun gaing thus all can be seen as ultimately descending from the Thudhamma. The Ganawimotti Kuto Gaing (lit., "Gaṇa-free") regards itself as autonomous of gaing affiliation, as its name suggests. The Dhammayutti Mahayin Gaing, a late nineteenth-century Mon reform tradition, traces its lineage to the Thai THAMMAYUT order. ¶ Outside of the monastic context, the term gaing is most frequently used to refer to Burmese occult associations that follow a popular tradition known as the weikza-lam, lit. "path of esoteric knowledge." Such an association is called a WEIKZA gaing and typically will be devoted to the cultivation of supranormal powers and virtual immortality through the application of various "sciences" (B. weikza, P. vijjā), such as alchemy and the casting of runes, that weikza-lam practitioners will have learned from their spiritual masters.

**gāmavāsi**. In Pāli, "town dweller"; in the THERAVĀDA tradition, a monk who lives in a village or town monastery and whose monastic vocation focuses on doctrinal study and teaching, or lit."book work" (P. GANTHADHURA); such a monk is often contrasted with a "forest dweller" (P. ARAÑÑAVĀSI), who is principally dedicated to meditative training (P. VIPASSANĀDHURA). In Sri Lankan Buddhism, the emphases within the Buddhist order on study and meditation led to the evolution over time of these two major practice vocations. The gāmavāsi were involved in studying and teaching the dhamma, especially within the lay community of the village, and thus helped to disseminate Buddhism among the people and maintain the institutions and history of the order. Because of their active engagement in society, the gāmavāsi have thus historically enjoyed closer relations with the social elite. The araññavāsi, by contrast, remained in solitude in the forest to focus principally on their meditative practice. The araññavāsi were not necessarily hermits, but they lived a more secluded life than the gāmavāsi, devoting most of their time to meditation, either individually or in smaller groups, and keeping their contact with the laity to a minimum. These two vocations have a long history and have continued within the saṅgha (S. SAṂGHA) into modern times. In a sense, the Buddha himself was an araññavāsi for six years before he attained enlightenment; subsequently, he then passed much of his time as a gāmavāsi, teaching people the dharma and encouraging them to practice to bring an end to their suffering. See also PARIYATTI; PAṬIPATTI.

**gaṇacakra**. (T. tshogs kyi 'khor lo/tshogs). In Sanskrit, lit. "circle of assembly" or "feast"; originally, the term may have referred to an actual gathering of male and female tāntrikas engaging in antinomian behavior, including ingesting substances ordinarily deemed unclean, and sexual activities ordinarily deemed taboo. In Tibet, the gaṇacakra is typically a ritualized tantric liturgy, often performed by celibate monks, that involves visualizing impure substances and transforming them into a nectar (AMṚTA; PAÑCĀMṚTA), imagining the bliss of high tantric attainment, and mentally offering this to buddhas, bodhisattvas, and various deities (see T. TSHOGS ZHING) and to oneself visualized as a tantric deity. The ritual is regarded as a rapid means of accumulating the equipment (SAṂBHĀRA) required for full enlightenment. In Tibet the word is inextricably linked with rituals for worshipping one's teacher (GURUYOGA) and in that context means an extended ritual performed on special days based on practices of highest yoga tantra (ANUTTARAYOGATANTRA). ¶ To start the gaṇacakra ritual, a large accumulation of food, including GTOR MA, bread, sweets, and fruit is placed near the altar, often supplemented by offerings from participants; a small plate with tiny portions of meat, a small container of an alcoholic beverage, and yogurt mixed with red jam is placed in a small container nearby. After visualizing one's teacher in the form of the entire pantheon of buddhas, bodhisattvas, and so on, the gaṇacakra consists of worship on the model of the BHADRACARĪPRAṆIDHĀNA, i.e., the seven-branch worship (SAPTĀṄGAVIDHI) of going for refuge, confessing transgressions, giving gifts, rejoicing, asking the teacher to turn the wheel of dharma, asking the buddhas not to pass into NIRVĀṆA, and, finally, dedicating the merit to full enlightenment (see PARIṆĀMANĀ). Following this, the participants visualize the nectar (AMṚTA) and the bliss of high tantric attainment. Three participants then line up in front of the officiating master (VAJRĀCĀRYA) and ritually offer a plate with a gtor ma and other parts of the collected offerings, along with a tiny bit of meat, a slight taste of alcohol, and a drop of the mixed yogurt and jam. While singing tantric songs extolling the bliss of tantric attainment, the rest of the offerings are divided up equally among the other participants, who are also given a tiny bit of meat, a slight taste of alcohol, and a drop of the mixed yogurt and jam. The gaṇacakra forms the central part of the worship of the teacher (T. bla ma mchod pa) ritual and is a marker of religious identity in Tibetan Buddhism, because participants visualize their teacher in the form of the head of the particular sect, tradition, or monastery to which they are attached, with the historical buddha, and the tantric buddha telescoped into smaller and smaller figures in his heart; the entire pantheon of buddhas, bodhisattvas and so on are then arrayed around that form. A gaṇacakra is customarily performed at the end of a large ABHIṢEKA (consecration) or teaching on TANTRA, where participants can number in the thousands.

**Gaṇḍavyūha**. (T. Sdong po bkod pa; C. Dafangguang fo huayan jing; J. Daihōkō butsu kegongyō; K. Taebanggwang pul hwaŏm kyŏng 大方廣佛華嚴經). In Sanskrit, loosely translatable as "Multivalent Array Scripture," an important Sanskrit SŪTRA that served as a virtual "pilgrim's progress" of MAHĀYĀNA Buddhism; later incorporated into the large scriptural omnibus, the AVATAṂSAKASŪTRA or BUDDHĀVATAṂSAKASŪTRA, where the text becomes known as the "Entering the DHARMADHĀTU" chapter (C. Ru fajie pin; S. *Dharmadhātupraveśanaparivarta). The *Gaṇḍavyūha* describes the youth SUDHANA's spiritual journey in search of enlightenment through a series of fifty-three spiritual mentors (KALYĀṆAMITRA), who serve as the personification of the fifty-two stages of the bodhisattva path, or MĀRGA (Sudhana's first and last teacher, the bodhisattva MAÑJUŚRĪ, are the same, giving a total of fifty-three). At the conclusion of his journey, Sudhana has a vision of SAMANTABHADRA and fully merges with him. The text is especially influential for its description of the accomplishment of the conducts and vows (see BHADRACARĪPRAṆIDHĀNA) of Samantabhadra, who comes to be considered the patron bodhisattva of the HUAYAN ZONG of Chinese Buddhism. The first Chinese translation of the *Avataṃsakasūtra*, in sixty rolls and thirty-four chapters, was translated by the North Indian monk BUDDHABHADRA (359–429) between 418 and 421, but it included only a severely truncated version of the *Gaṇḍavyūha* chapter. The second translation, in eighty rolls and thirty-nine chapters, completed between 695 and 704 by the Khotanese monk ŚIKṢĀNANDA (652–710), included the full chapter. Since the earlier version was still incomplete, however, a third translation, specifically of the *Gaṇḍavyūha* section, was translated in forty rolls as the *Dafangguang fo huayan jing* (*Avataṃsakasūtra*) by PRAJÑA, between 795 and 798. The *Gaṇḍavyūha* is also included among the nine sacred books (NAVAGRANTHA) of the Newar tradition of Nepal.

**gandha**. (T. dri; C. xiang; J. kō; K. hyang 香). In Sanskrit and Pāli, "smell," "odor," or "fragrance," the olfactory objects of the olfactory or nose consciousness (GHRĀṆAVIJÑĀNA). The Sanskrit term has a more neutral sense than the pleasing "fragrance" or the unpleasant "smell" or "odor" in English. There are said to be two basic types of olfactory objects, the pleasant and the unpleasant, with each category further subdivided into two based on whether the fragrance of the pleasant or the odor of the unpleasant infuses other objects, like the fragrance of garlic, or does not, like the fragrance of sesame. A particular class of demigod, the GANDHARVA, is said to consume fragrances.

**gandhaghaṭikā**. (T. spos snod; C. xianglu; J. kōro; K. hyangno 香爐). In Sanskrit, "censer," "incense burner"; a small stove with a perforated lid, both typically made of bronze or pottery, in which incense is burned as an offering during the performance of a ritual. In certain VINAYA traditions, such as the DHARMAGUPTAKA (see SIFEN LÜ), the censer is included in a list of eighteen requisites (S. aṣṭādaśadravya; see PARIṢKĀRA; NIŚRAYA) that monks were allowed to keep, along with tooth cleaners, soap, the three robes, water bottle, begging bowl, sitting mat, walking staff, water filter, handkerchief, knife, fire starter, tweezers, sleeping hammock, sūtras, vinaya texts, buddha images, and bodhisattva images.

**gandhakuṭī**. (T. dri gtsang khang; C. xiangshi; J. kōshitsu; K. hyangsil 香室). In Sanskrit and Pāli, "perfumed chamber," the name given to the Buddha's personal dwelling place in JETAVANA monastery. Later in India, a room called the perfumed chamber, where an image of the Buddha was installed, became a standard component in many traditional Indian monasteries, symbolizing that the Buddha himself was in residence and presiding over the administration of the monastic institution. When ĀNANDA was asked by the Buddha to be his personal attendant, one of Ānanda's conditions for acceptance was that he not be given his own "perfumed chamber," to avoid any suspicion that he would receive special treatment as the Buddha's attendant. See also AJAṆṬĀ.

**Gandhāra**. (T. Sa 'dzin; C. Jiantuoluo; J. Kendara; K. Kŏndara 健馱羅). An ancient center of Indic Buddhism, located in the northwest of the subcontinent in the region of present-day northern Pakistan and southeastern Afghanistan. The Gandhāra region included the entire Peshawar valley up to its border along the Indus River to the east and also extended to include the Swat valley and the region around Gandhāra's central city of TAKṢAŚILA (Taxila), located near what is today Peshawar, Pakistan. For the five centuries bracketing the beginning of the Common Era, Gandhāra was a cosmopolitan cultural center and a crossroads of the major trade routes between Europe, the Middle East, Central Asia, China, and the Indian subcontinent (see SILK ROAD). As traders from these various areas moved through Gandhāra, the region became a place of cultural exchange. Four major empires were centered in Gandhāra: the Indo-Greek, Indo-Scythian, Indo-Parthian, and KUSHAN. Tradition claims that AŚOKA supported Buddhism in the Gandhāra region during the third century BCE, although the first physical evidence of Buddhism in the region dates from the second and first centuries CE. Gandhāra was conquered by Demetrius I of Bactria around 185 BCE and, although Greek rule in the region was brief, Greek art and culture had an enduring effect on the Gandhāran community. Some of the oldest known Buddhist art comes from this region, more specifically the "Greco-Buddhist" style of sculpture that was a product of this period. The earliest iconographic representations of the Buddha, in fact, are thought by some art historians to come from second century BCE Gandhāra. During the first and second centuries CE, Gandhāra became the principal gateway through which Buddhism traveled to Persia, China, and the rest of Asia. Between the years 50 and 320 CE, the KUSHANs were pushed south out of Central Asia and occupied Gandhāra. Gandhāra, along with KASHMIR, supported and housed a large SARVĀSTIVĀDA community, and Gandhāra was long recognized as a principal bastion of this important MAINSTREAM BUDDHIST SCHOOL. Around the first or second century CE, when the Sarvāstivāda school was at its peak, the fourth Buddhist council (see COUNCIL, FOURTH) is said to have taken place in Gandhāra, sponsored by KANIṢKA I, the third king of the Kushan dynasty. According to traditional accounts, there were 499 monks in attendance, although that large number is probably intended to represent the importance of the convention rather than a literal count of the number of people present. VASUMITRA presided over the fourth council, with the noted poet and scholarly exegete AŚVAGHOṢA assisting him. In addition to recording a new VINAYA, the council also resulted in the compilation of a massive collection of Sarvāstivāda ABHIDHARMA philosophy, known as the ABHIDHARMAMAHĀVIBHĀṢĀ, or "Great Exegesis of Abhidharma," which functions as a virtual encyclopedia of different scholastic perspectives on Buddhism of the time. The VAIBHĀṢIKA school of Sarvāstivāda abhidharma exegesis, which based itself on this compilation, was centered in the regions of Gandhāra and Kashmir. The KĀŚYAPĪYA and BAHUŚRUTĪYA schools added to the significant presence of Buddhism in the region.

**Gāndhārī**. A PRAKRIT language of the GANDHĀRA region of northwest India, which was one of the principal languages used in the early transmission of Buddhism into China. The transcriptions of Buddhist technical terminology found in many of the earliest Buddhist texts translated into Chinese indicate that these texts were written in the Gāndhārī language, not classical Sanskrit. These Chinese transcriptional data from Gāndhārī and other Prakrits have also been used by historical linguists to reconstruct early Chinese phonology and Han-dynasty spoken dialects. Gāndhārī exhibits some tendency toward metathesis (transposition) of syllables—e.g., G. jambodaṇa for S. jāmbūnada or P. jambonada ("golden")—a tendency that is noted in Chinese transcriptions. Gāndhārī also tends to show vocalic weakening, e.g., S. ajita > G. ayuda. The extant Gāndhārī corpus consists entirely of mainstream Buddhist materials with little evidence of the MAHĀYĀNA.

**gandharva**. (P. gandhabba; T. dri za; C. gantapo/zhongyun youqing; J. kendatsuba/chūun'ujō; K. kŏndalba/chungon yujŏng 乾闥婆/中蘊有情). A Sanskrit term whose folk etymology is "fragrance eaters"; in Buddhist cosmology it is most often translated as "celestial musicians"; in the context of the cycle of rebirth, gandharva refers to a "transitional being" that bridges the current and future existence. (The CJK uses a transcription for the former denotation, and the translation "intermediary being" for the latter.) In the Buddhist cosmological schema, gandharvas are a sort of demigod and one of the eight classes of beings (AṢṬASENĀ); they fly through space and serve as musicians in the heavenly court of INDRA or ŚAKRA, the king of the gods, who presides over the heaven of the thirty-three (TRĀYASTRIṂŚA) in the sensuous realm of existence (KĀMADHĀTU). According to Indian mythology, they are married to the celestial nymphs (APSARAS). The gandharvas get their name from the presumption that they subsist on fragrance (GANDHA). The term gandharva is also the designation given to the transitional being in the intermediate state (ANTARĀBHAVA; see also BAR DO), the forty-nine-day period between rebirths in the five or six destinies (GATI) of SAṂSĀRA. Since the transitional being does not take solid food but subsists only on scent, it is also referred to as a gandharva. During this transitional period, the gandharva is searching for the appropriate place and parents for its next existence and takes the form of the beings in the realm where it is destined to be reborn.

**gandharvanagara**. (T. dri za'i grong khyer; C. gantapo cheng; J, kendatsubajō/gendatsubajō; K. kŏndalba sŏng 乾闥婆城). In Sanskrit, "city of the GANDHARVA," a simile frequently employed in Buddhist literature for something that appears to be real but is not. The gandharvanagara is one of the standard similes used to illustrate the premise that all DHARMAS are illusory and unreal. Other similes include a dream, an illusion, a mirage, an echo, a hallucination, a reflection, an apparition, a flower in the sky (KHAPUṢPA), and the core of a plantain tree. In NĀGĀRJUNA's treatment of moral cause and effect, he concludes that the whole apparatus of the Buddhist teaching on KARMAN—the afflictions (KLEŚA; of greed, hatred, and delusion), specific actions, the different bodies beings take depending on their actions, as well as the actors and receivers of the fruition of action—is all like a gandharvanagara, a ray of light or a spark, or a dream. There are several alternative transcriptions of the Sanskrit term in Chinese Buddhist literature. See also AṢṬAMĀYOPAMĀ.

**Gandhavaṃsa**. In Pāli, "History of Books," a traditional history of Pāli literature, written in Burma by a forest-dwelling monk named Nandapaññā. The text, which is in mixed prose and verse, is dated to the seventeenth century by some scholars and to the nineteenth century by others. The text discusses the arrangement of the tipiṭaka (S. TRIPIṬAKA) and the authorship of the commentaries, subcommentaries, and numerous extracanonical treatises on various topics, ranging from grammar to doctrine. While exceedingly short (the original manuscript consisted of only twelve palm leaves), the *Gandhavaṃsa* has proven invaluable for the historical understanding of the development of Pāli literature.

**Gandhavatī**. (T. Spos ldan ma; C. Zhongxiangcheng; J. Shukōjō; K. Chunghyangsŏng 衆香城). In Sanskrit, "City of [Multitudinous] Fragrances," the city where the AṢṬASĀHASRIKĀPRAJÑĀPĀRAMITĀ says that the BODHISATTVA DHARMODGATA lived and taught the perfection of wisdom (PRAJÑĀPĀRAMITĀ); an alternate name for the Korean "Diamond Mountains" (KŬMGANGSAN).

**gandhāyatana**. (T. dri'i skye mched; C. xiangchu; J. kōsho; K. hyangch'ŏ 香處). In Sanskrit and Pāli, "olfactory sense field," i.e., odor (GANDHA) as it occurs in the list of twelve sense faculties or "bases of cognition" (ĀYATANA), which serve as the bases for the production of consciousness, viz., the six internal sense bases, or sense organs (eye, ear, nose, tongue, body, and mind) and the six external sense objects (forms, sounds, odors, tastes, tangible objects, and mental phenomena). In the case of odor, the contact (SPARŚA) between the olfactory sense base (GHRĀṆENDRIYA) and its corresponding olfactory sensory object (gandha) leads to olfactory consciousness (GHRĀṆAVIJÑĀNA).

**Gaṅgānadī**. (T. Gang gā'i klung; C. Henghe; J. Gōga; K. Hangha 恒河). In Sanskrit and Pāli, the "Ganges River," the major river in the north of India and, according to Buddhist cosmology, one of the four sacred rivers that flow through the southernmost continent of JAMBUDVĪPA, along with the Sindhu, Vakṣu, and Sītā. Several of the important Indian kingdoms that supported the growth of Buddhism were based in the Ganges River valley, including KOŚALA in the middle and MAGADHA in the lower Ganges valley. The Mauryan dynasty, including its most renowned ruler, AŚOKA, had its capital at the city of PĀṬALIPUTRA on the banks of the river, as did the Gupta dynasty that followed. The sand in the Ganges River (GAṄGĀNADĪVĀLUKĀ) was reputed to be extremely fine in texture, and so is often used in similes in Buddhist texts to refer to an infinity, viz., "as numerous as the sands of the Ganges."

**Gaṅgānadīvālukā**. [alt. -vālikā] (T. Gang gā'i klung gi bye ma; C. Henghesha; J. Gōgasha; K. Hanghasa 恒河沙). In Sanskrit and Pāli, "sands of the Ganges," viz., an "incalculable number." The sands of the Ganges River were universally reputed to be extremely fine in texture, so the term is often used in similes in Buddhist texts to refer to an "infinity," e.g., "for world systems as numerous as the sands of the Ganges" (Gaṅgānadīvālukāsamā lokadhātavaḥ), "eons as numerous as the sands of the Ganges" (Gaṅgānadīvālukāsamān kalpān).

**Gangōji**. (J) (元興寺). See ASUKADERA.

**Gangs ri thod dkar**. (Gangri Tokar). In Tibetan, lit. "White Skull Snow Mountain," a mountain and retreat hermitage above SHUG GSEB nunnery in central Tibet, near LHA SA. The central meditation cave, O rgyan rdzongs, was a primary residence of the RNYING MA master KLONG CHEN RAB 'BYAMS and is the location where he composed, edited, and redacted many of his works on the Rnying ma teachings of RDZOGS CHEN.

**Ganjin**. (C. Jianzhen 鑑眞) (688–763). Chinese VINAYA master and reputed founder of the RISSHŪ and the monastery of TŌSHŌDAIJI in Japan; also known as Tōdai Wajō. Ganjin was a native of Guangling, Yangzhou, in present-day Jiangsu province. He studied TIANTAI thought and practice and the vinaya under the vinaya master Dao'an (654–717). Having returned to Yangzhou from his studies in Chang'an and Luoyang, he led an illustrious career at the monastery of Damingsi as a famous lecturer on the vinaya of the NANSHAN LÜ ZONG, and is credited with the establishment of many monasteries. In 733, two monks from Nara, Eiei (d. 748) and Fushō (d.u.), arrived in China. While studying in Chang'an, they learned of Ganjin and headed for Damingsi in 742 to meet him. The next year, Ganjin made his first attempt to go to Japan. After four more failed attempts, Ganjin was finally able to arrive in Japan in 754. During his earlier attempts, Ganjin had lost his eyesight and Eiei had lost his life. Upon his arrival, he was warmly welcomed by retired Emperor Shōmu (r. 724–749) and the Buddhist community in Japan. In the summer of 754, an ordination platform was prepared at the great Nara monastery of TŌDAIJI, where Ganjin conferred the precepts on Emperor Shōmu and others. A precepts hall was constructed the next year in 755. In 756, Ganjin and RYŌBEN (689–773), the abbot of Tōdaiji, were appointed to senior ecclesiastical positions at court. A year after Empress Kōken (r. 749–758) abdicated the throne in 758, a new monastery, named Tōritsu Shōdaiji (alt. Tōshōdaiji), was built and granted to Ganjin. In 763, as death neared, Ganjin had a statue of himself made and installed in his quarters at Tōshōdaiji, which remains to this day.

**ganshijue**. (J. kanshiketsu; K. kŏnsigwŏl 乾屎橛). In Chinese, "dried shit stick," a CHAN expression attributed to LINJI YIXUAN (d. 867), who dismissed the buddha-nature, or FOXING (what he calls the "true man of no rank"; C. WUWEI ZHENREN), as being nothing more than a "dried shit stick," i.e., "useless." This expression becomes a famous meditative topic (HUATOU) used in Chan questioning meditation (see KANHUA CHAN). It also appears in a GONG'AN exchange attributed to the Tang-dynasty monk YUNMEN WENYAN (864–949): Once when Yunmen was asked, "What is the Buddha?," he replied, "A dried shit stick." This gong'an appears as case no. 21 in the WUMEN GUAN ("Gateless Checkpoint"). This phrase has sometimes been translated as "dried turd," but the term refers to the toilet utensil, not the excrement.

**ganthadhura**. In Pāli, lit. the "burden of book learning," often rendered as the "duty of study," a term used to describe the monastic vocation of scriptural study. The term is often paired with VIPASSANĀDHURA, the "burden of insight," referring to the vocation of meditation. Although each of these vocations may be pursued by a monk, in the THERAVĀDA tradition it has historically typically been the case that a monk chooses one over the other. In Sri Lanka, for example, the more scholarly pursuit of scriptural study is sometimes perceived as the more prestigious course to be undertaken by younger monks, while those who ordain late in life undertake the vocation of meditation. See also PARIYATTI.

**ganying**. (J. kannō; K. kamŭng 感應). In Chinese, "sympathetic resonance," or "stimulus and response," a seminal concept in traditional Chinese philosophy, which is appropriated in early Chinese Buddhism to explain the Buddhist concepts of action (KARMAN) and grace (i.e., the "response" of a buddha or BODHISATTVA to a supplicant's invocation, or "stimulus"). Ganying is a mode of seemingly spontaneous (although not "uncaused") response that occurs naturally in a universe conceived holistically in terms of pattern or "principle" (LI) and interdependent order. The notion itself is deceptively simple: objects belonging to the same category or class are conceived as resonating spontaneously with each other, just as would two identically tuned strings on a pair of zithers. The notion of resonance was used in traditional Chinese philosophy to explain or rationalize the mechanism behind the elaborate system of correlated categories generally known as five-phase (wuxing) thought—viz., the primary elements of metal, wood, water, fire, and soil. According to early Chinese cosmology, the underlying principles and patterns of the universe seemingly give rise to, or resonate spontaneously with, correlative manifestations in the physical world. The Chinese conception of the universe as an interconnected harmonious whole finds expression in theories concerning the cyclic progression of the five phases and yin (dark) and yang (light), as well as in elaborate prescriptions pertaining to the ritual life of the court. The universe, according to this view, is in a state of continual motion and flux. The patterns of change are the result of the cyclic interactions between the five phases and the forces (or vital energies, C. qi) of yin and yang, which tend naturally in the direction of rhythmic balance and harmony. Humans do not stand apart from the natural universe but rather constitute a fundamental and integral part of this whole. Early Buddhist thinkers in China adapted the mechanism of sympathetic resonance to explain in Chinese terms how an action (karman) performed in one time period could evoke a corresponding response, or fruition (VIPĀKA), in another. In addition, sympathetic resonance was used by early Chinese Buddhist thinkers to make sense of the notion of grace. In this later sense, sentient beings' faith (ŚRADDHĀ) and/or roots of virtue (KUŚALAMŪLA) would invoke a "sympathetic response" in the minds of the buddhas and bodhisattvas, which prompts them to respond accordingly with salvific grace. In the PURE LAND traditions, sentient beings' recitation of the name of AMITĀBHA (see NIANFO) creates a sympathetic response in the mind of that buddha, which prompts him in turn to bring them to his pure land, where they may become enlightened. The rubric of ganying is just as prevalent in popular religious tracts in China, where it refers to the principle of moral retribution—the belief that one's good and evil deeds will result in corresponding rewards and punishments. While the Chinese notion of moral retribution (bao) meted out in this life or the next was indebted to Buddhist notions of karman and rebirth, in the premodern period, such retribution emerged as a fundamental principle of Chinese popular religious belief and practice, irrespective of one's specific religious affiliation. This doctrine was propagated through innumerable tales of miraculous retribution—such as "numinous attestation" (lingyan), "responsive attestation" (yingyan), or "numinous response" (lingying), and so on—that "attested" (yan) to the reality of the "numinous" or "supernatural" (ling) and the inevitability of divine justice.

**Gaofeng heshang Chanyao**. (J. Kōhō oshō Zen'yō/Kōbō oshō Zen'yō; K. Kobong hwasang Sŏnyo 高峰和尚禪要). In Chinese, "Master Gaofeng's Essentials of CHAN," often known by its abbreviated title *Chanyao* (J. Zenyō; K. Sŏnyo), "Essentials of Chan." The text is best known for its exposition of the "three essentials" (SANYAO) of Chan questioning meditation (KANHUA CHAN): the great faculty of faith, great fury, and great doubt (YIQING). The text was republished in Korea in 1399, where it became widely read as a primer on the practice of GONG'AN meditation. Since the seventeenth century, Korean Buddhist seminaries (kangwŏn) have included the *Chanyao/Sŏnyo* as one of the four books in the SAJIP (Fourfold Collection), the core of the Korean monastic curriculum.

**Gaofeng Yuanmiao**. (J. Kōhō Genmyō; K. Kobong Wŏnmyo 高峰原妙) (1238–1295). Yuan-dynasty Chinese CHAN monk in the YANGQI PAI of the LINJI ZONG. Gaofeng was a native of Suzhou in present-day Jiangsu province. He was ordained at the age of fourteen and two years later began his studies of TIANTAI thought and practice under Fazhu (d.u.) at the monastery of Miyinsi. He later continued his studies under Chan master WUZHUN SHIFAN's disciples Duanqiao Miaolun (1201–1261) and Xueyan Zuqin (1215–1287). Gaofeng trained in Chan questioning meditation (KANHUA CHAN), and Xueyan Zuqin taught him the necessity of contemplating his meditative topic (HUATOU) not just while awake, but also during dreams, and even in dreamless sleep. (In his own instructions on GONG'AN practice, Gaofeng eventually used the same question Zuqin had asked him: "Do you have mastery of yourself even in dreamless sleep?") In 1266, Gaofeng went into retreat at Longxu in the Tianmu mountains of Linan (in present-day Zhejiang province) for five years, after which he is said to have had a great awakening when the sound of a falling pillow shattered his doubt (YIQING). In 1274, he began his residence at a hermitage on Shuangji peak in Wukang (present-day Zhejiang province), and in 1279 he began teaching at Shiziyan on the west peak of the Tianmu mountains. He subsequently established the monasteries of Shizisi and Dajuesi, where he attracted hundreds of disciples, including the prominent ZHONGFENG MINGBEN (1263–1323). He was given the posthumous title Chan Master Puming Guangji (Universal Radiance and Far-reaching Salvation). Gaofeng is most renowned for his instruction on the "three essentials" (SANYAO) of kanhua Chan practice: the great faculty of faith, great fury, and great doubt. Gaofeng's teachings are recorded in his discourse record, the *Gaofeng dashi yulu*, and his GAOFENG HESHANG CHANYAO, better known as simply the *Chanyao* ("Essentials of Chan"; K. Sŏnyo), which has been a principal text in Korean monastic seminaries since at least the seventeenth century. Gaofeng is also known for his famous gong'an: "Harnessing the moon, the muddy ox enters the sea."

**Gaoseng zhuan**. (J. Kōsōden; K. Kosŭng chŏn 高僧傳). In Chinese "Biographies of Eminent Monks," also known as the *Liang gaoseng zhuan*, a collection of biographies of famous and/or archetypal monks compiled by the monk Huijiao (497–554) of the Liang dynasty. The *Gaoseng zhuan* contains the biographies of nearly five hundred monks (253 full biographies and 243 miscellaneous figures) who were active in China from 67 to 519 CE. In compiling his collection, Huijiao drew upon various sources, including epigraphy, oral interviews, and extant literary works. He categorized the biographies into ten sections: translators, exegetes, thaumaturges (shenyi), meditators, VINAYA masters, self-immolators (wangshen), chanters of scriptures, benefactors, hymnodists (jingshi), and propagators (changdao). Huijiao's collection became the standard followed in subsequent biographical collections, such as DAOXUAN's XU GAOSENG ZHUAN and ZANNING's SONG GAOSENG ZHUAN.

**garanbō**. (伽藍法). In Japanese, lit. "temple dharma," viz., "temple lineage." Garanbō refers to the practice of inheriting the lineage of a temple (i.e., the lineage of the temple's founder) regardless of the monastic lineage one might have inherited earlier from one's teacher. By the Edo period, most temples and monasteries belonging to the ZENSHŪ in Japan required monks to follow the garanbō system. Through the garanbō system, monasteries built by the founder of a lineage were able to secure financial and spiritual support from a network of temples belonging to that lineage.

**garbhadhātu**. (S). See TAIZŌKAI.

**Garland Sutra**. See AVATAṂSAKASŪTRA.

**garuḍa**. (P. garuḍa/garuḷa; T. khyung/mkha' lding; C. jialouluo; J. karura; K. karura 迦樓羅). In Sanskrit and Pāli, mythical "golden-winged bird," one of the eight classes of nonhuman beings (AṢṬASENĀ) who are often in attendance during ŚĀKYAMUNI's sermons. In traditional Indian mythology, the garuḍa was a golden-winged bird who was the deification of the sun's brilliance; thus, like the phoenix in Western mythology, it served as a symbol of fire or flame. Garuḍas served as the mount of Viṣṇu and were the mortal enemies of NĀGAs and snakes. The garuḍa was said to be fantastic in size, with a massive wingspan (some texts say as wide as 330 YOJANAs), and carried either a wish-fulfilling gem (CINTĀMAṆI) or a talisman around its neck. Its wings were said to be adorned with marvelous gems, and it had a huge gullet that would allow it slowly to digest enormous amounts of food. Garuḍas are sometimes portrayed in Buddhist art as having the head and wings of an eagle and the body of a man. JĀTAKA stories describe garuḍas as giant birds, massive in both size and strength, which are capable of splitting the ocean by flapping their wings, creating an enormous breeze known as the garuḍa wind. The SAṂYUTTANIKĀYA mentions that garuḍas roost in the forest of silk-cotton trees, and their nests are in danger of being crushed by Sakka's (S. ŚAKRA; INDRA) chariot as it speeds through the forest. Garuḍas eat only flesh and are the enemies of nāgas, which are their main food. In the jātakas, garuḍas are said to live on the nāga island of Seruma (also called, simply, NĀGADĪPA). With their garuḍa wind, they can lift into the air nāgas that are a thousand fathoms long, uprooting the banyan trees around which the snakes wrap themselves. Besides possessing impressive strength, garuḍas are also described in the jātakas as having supernatural powers, such as in the *Sussondī Jātaka*, where garuḍas use their special powers to plunge the whole city into darkness in order to carry off Queen Sussondī. Garuḍas were formerly considered to be wrathful creatures but, after having been converted by the Buddha, they now protect his teachings. In both mainstream and MAHĀYĀNA materials, garuḍas are said to pay homage to the Buddha as one of a group of eight mythical classes of nonhuman beings (aṣṭasenā): divinities (DEVA), nāgas, demons (YAKṢA), celestial musicians (GANDHARVA), demigods (ASURA), half-human half-horse (or half-bird) celestial musicians (KIṂNARA), and snake spirits (MAHORĀGA). In Buddhist tantra garuḍas are a DHARMAPĀLA and appear in the PARIVĀRA (retinue) of various tantric deities, as both companion and mount. In tantric Buddhism there exists a group known as the pañcagaruḍa (khyung rigs lnga): the garuḍas of the Buddha, karma, ratna, vajra, and padma families.

**gate gate pāragate pārasaṃgate bodhi svāhā**. (T. ga te ga te pā ra ga te pā ra saṃ ga te bo dhi svā hā; C. jiedi jiedi boluojiedi boluosengjiedi puti sapohe; J. gyatei gyatei haragyatei harasōgyatei boji sowaka; K. aje aje paraaje parasŭngaje moji sabaha 揭帝揭帝波羅揭帝波羅僧揭帝菩提薩婆訶). A Sanskrit MANTRA contained in the PRAJÑĀPĀRAMITĀHṚDAYASŪTRA ("Heart Sūtra"). At the conclusion of the SŪTRA, the BODHISATTVA AVALOKITEŚVARA says to ŚĀRIPUTRA, "Therefore, the mantra of the perfection of wisdom is the mantra of great wisdom, the unsurpassed mantra, the unequalled mantra, the mantra that completely pacifies all suffering. Because it is not false, it should be known to be true. The mantra of the perfection of wisdom is stated thus: gate gate pāragate pārasaṃgate bodhi svāhā." Although most mantras are not translatable, this one can be roughly rendered into English as "gone, gone, gone beyond, gone completely beyond, enlightenment, svāhā" (svāhā is an interjection, meaning "hail," commonly placed at the end of a mantra). "Gate" in the mantra is most probably a vocative of gatā addressed to the goddess PRAJÑĀPĀRAMITĀ (the iconographic representation of perfect wisdom); hence, the mantra may be addressed to Prajñāpāramitā and mean, "You who have gone, gone, gone beyond," etc. Given the ubiquity of the *Prajñāpāramitāhṛdayasūtra* in MAHĀYĀNA Buddhism and its frequent ritual chanting by monks in both East Asia and Tibet, the mantra has been the subject of extensive commentary. Thus, some commentators correlate the first five words with the five paths (PAÑCAMĀRGA) to buddhahood: the first "gate" indicates the path of accumulation (SAṂBHĀRAMĀRGA); the second "gate," the path of preparation (PRAYOGAMĀRGA); "pāragate," the path of vision (DARŚANAMĀRGA); "pārasaṃgate," the path of cultivation (BHĀVANĀMĀRGA); and BODHI, the adept path (AŚAIKṢAMĀRGA). Such an interpretation is in keeping with the Indian scholastic view of the PRAJÑĀPĀRAMITĀ sūtras, where it is said that the sūtras have two teachings, one explicit and one implicit. The explicit teaching is emptiness (ŚŪNYATĀ) and the implicit teaching is the various realizations (ABHISAMAYA) of the bodhisattva along the path to buddhahood. From this perspective, everything in the sūtra up to the mantra provides the explicit teaching and the mantra provides the implicit teaching. Other commentators state that the first part of the sūtra (up to the mantra) is intended for bodhisattvas of dull faculties and that the mantra is intended for bodhisattvas of sharp faculties (TĪKṢṆENDRIYA). Some of the commentators include "it is thus" (tadyathā) in the mantra and add oṃ at the beginning. Although the presence of DHĀRAṆĪ is relatively common in Mahāyāna sūtras, something that is explicitly called a mantra is not, leading some commentators to consider whether the *Prajñāpāramitāhṛdayasūtra* should be classified as a sūtra or a TANTRA.

**gāthā**. (T. tshigs su bcad pa; C. ji; J. ge; K. ke 偈). In Sanskrit and Pāli, "odes" or "religious verse," typically listed as the fourth of the Pāli ninefold (NAVAṄGA[PĀVACANA]) and Sanskrit twelvefold (DVĀDAŚĀṄGA[PRAVACANA]) divisions of the traditional genres of Buddhist literature as classified by composition style and content. Gāthās are often written in quatrains of four lines of eight syllables apiece. The gāthā genre is closely related to GEYA, "verse narratives" or "verse interspersed with prose"; however, gāthā does not include the geya's interspersed prose narration and is not necessarily the verse reiteration of a preceding prose narrative.

**gati**. (T. 'gro ba; C. qu; J. shu; K. ch'wi 趣). In Sanskrit and Pāli, "destiny," "destination," or "bourne," one of the five or six places in SAṂSĀRA where rebirth occurs. In ascending order, these bournes are occupied by hell denizens (NĀRAKA), hungry ghosts (PRETA), animals (TIRYAK), humans (MANUṢYA), and divinities (DEVA); sometimes, demigods (ASURA) are added between humans and divinities as a sixth bourne. These destinies are all located within the three realms of existence (TRILOKA[DHĀTU]), which comprises the entirety of our universe. At the bottom of the sensuous realm (KĀMADHĀTU) are located the denizens of the eight hot and cold hells (nāraka), of which the lowest is the interminable hell (see AVĪCI). These are said to be located beneath the continent of JAMBUDVĪPA. This most ill-fated of existences is followed by hungry ghosts, animals, humans, demigods, and the six sensuous-realm divinities, who live on MOUNT SUMERU or in the heavens directly above it. Higher levels of the divinities occupy the upper two realms of existence. The divinities of the BRAHMALOKA, whose minds are perpetually absorbed in one of the four meditative absorptions (DHYĀNA), occupy seventeen levels in the realm of subtle materiality (RŪPADHĀTU). Divinities who are so ethereal that they do not require even a subtle material foundation occupy four heavens in the immaterial realm (ĀRŪPYADHĀTU). The divinities in the immaterial realm are perpetually absorbed in formless trance states, and rebirth there is the result of mastery of one or all of the immaterial dhyānas (ĀRŪPYĀVACARADHYĀNA). The bottom three destinies, of hell denizens, hungry ghosts, and animals, are referred to as the three evil bournes (DURGATI); these are destinies where suffering predominates because of the past performance of primarily unvirtuous actions. In the various levels of the divinities, happiness predominates because of the past performance of primarily virtuous deeds. By contrast, the human destiny is thought to be ideally suited for religious training because it is the only bourne where both suffering and happiness can be readily experienced in the proper balance (not intoxicated by pleasure or racked by pain), allowing one to recognize more easily the true character of life as impermanent (ANITYA), suffering (DUḤKHA), and nonself (ANĀTMAN). Some schools posit a transitional "intermediate state" (ANTARĀBHAVA) of being between past and future lives within these destinies. See also DAŚADHĀTU.

**Gautama**. (P. Gotama; T. Go ta ma; C. Jutan; J. Kudon; K. Kudam 瞿曇). The family name of the historical Buddha, also known as ŚĀKYAMUNI Buddha. He was a member of the ŚĀKYA tribe of what is today southern Nepal (hence his epithet Śākyamuni, "Sage of the Śākyas"). Within that group, his family or clan (GOTRA) was Gautama. His name means "descendants of Gotama" in Sanskrit, with Gotama (lit. "Excellent Cow") being the name of several brāhmaṇas of ancient India, including a poet of the *Ṛg Veda*. Thus, the name of the Buddha's tribe or ethnic group was Śākya, the name of his family or clan was Gautama, and his given name was SIDDHĀRTHA. In Pāli literature, he is more commonly referred to as Gotama Buddha; in Mahāyāna texts, Śākyamuni Buddha is more common.

**Gautamī, Mahāprajāpatī**. See MAHĀPRAJĀPATĪ.

**Gavāṃpati**. (P. Gavampati; T. Ba glang bdag; C. Jiaofanboti/Niuzhu; J. Kyōbonhadai/Goshu; K. Kyobŏmbaje/Uju 憍梵波提/牛主). In Sanskrit and Pāli sources, the name of an ARHAT disciple of the Buddha. His name literally means "Lord of Cattle," after a previous lifetime in which he owned many head of cattle. (The Chinese both transcribe, and translate, his name.) Gavāṃpati was a companion of the Buddha's sixth disciple, YAŚAS; he followed his friend into the order and like him also became an arhat. Gavāṃpati was known for his special ability in supernatural powers (ṚDDHI), which he used in one instance to stem advancing floodwaters that were endangering the lives of the monks. Gavāṃpati is said to have been summoned to attend the first Buddhist council (see COUNCIL, FIRST) of arhats following the Buddha's PARINIRVĀṆA, but decided to pass into NIRVĀṆA rather than attend; as a result of his death, a rule was made that none of the arhats invited to the council were allowed to die until the conclusion of the council. In the eponymous *Gavampatisutta* (in the Pāli SAṂYUTTANIKĀYA), the elder explains that the understanding of suffering (P. dukkha; S. DUḤKHA) subsumes all four of its aspects: its implications, its production, its cessation, and the path leading to its cessation. The Sanskrit text *Mahākarmavibhaṅga* also speaks of an Ārya Gavāṃpati who converted the inhabitants of Suvarṇabhūmi (P. SUVAṆṆABHŪMI) for a distance of one hundred YOJANAS. ¶ In Burma, Mon legend has it that the novice Gavāṃpati invited the Buddha to preach the dhamma (S. DHARMA) to the people of Suvaṇṇabhūmi in Lower Burma. The Buddha complied with his request, converting many inhabitants of that border region. The Buddha promised Sirimāsoka, the king of Suvaṇṇabhūmi, that after his parinibbāna (S. parinirvāṇa), Gavāṃpati would carry thirty-two tooth relics to the kingdom so that the king might enshrine them in pagodas for the faithful to worship. The Mons identify their homeland in Lower Burma with Suvaṇṇabhūmi, and date the initial foundation of Buddhism in their region to the Buddha's visit and the arrival of the tooth relics. This Gavāṃpati legend finds no parallel in Pāli sources and most likely derives from Sanskrit sources.

**Gayā-Kāśyapa**. (P. Gayā-Kassapa; T. Ga ya 'od srung; C. Qieye Jiashe; J. Gaya Kashō; K. Kāya Kasŏp 伽耶迦葉). A matted-hair ascetic who was ordained with his two brothers and became an early enlightened disciple of the Buddha. According to the Pāli account, the three brothers were fire worshippers, who practiced austerities on the banks of the Nerañjarā (S. NAIRAÑJANĀ) river. Gayā-Kāśyapa dwelt at Gayāsīsa with two hundred disciples, while his older brother URUVILVĀ-KĀŚYAPA (P. Uruvela-Kassapa), dwelled upriver at Uruvelā with five hundred disciples, and the middle brother NADĪ-KĀŚYAPA (P. Nadī-Kassapa) with three hundred disciples. All three brothers were devoted to the observance of brahmanical fire rituals. Gayā-Kāśyapa also observed the practice of bathing three times in the river in order to wash away sins during the festival of Gayāphaggu. Not long after his enlightenment, the Buddha visited the hermitage of Uruvilvā-Kāśyapa with the intention of converting him and his disciples. Uruvilvā-Kāśyapa mistakenly believed that he was already an arahant (S. ARHAT) himself and was liberated from the bonds of rebirth. Knowing that Uruvilvā-Kāśyapa could be dissuaded from his false views by a display of yogic power, the Buddha performed numerous magical feats to demonstrate his mastery of iddhi (S. ṚDDHI), including subduing a fire serpent (NĀGA) without being burned, a scene depicted in Indian rock carvings. Using his ability to read Uruvilvā-Kāśyapa's mind, the Buddha was able to dispel his view that he was an arahant and converted him and his disciples. As part of their conversion, they shaved off their long locks and threw them in the river. When Uruvilvā-Kāśyapa's younger brothers Gayā-Kāśyapa and Nadī-Kāśyapa saw all the hair floating downstream, they came to investigate. They in turn accepted the Buddha as their teacher and entered the order of monks (SAṂGHA), bringing all their disciples along with them. As a result, the Buddha's community gained a thousand monks. Because of their previous devotions to fire rituals, after their ordination, the Buddha preached to all these new monks the renowned "Fire Sermon" (ĀDITTAPARIYĀYASUTTA), whereupon the three brothers and their disciples attained arahantship. Gayā-Kāśyapa earned the merit to encounter the Buddha and attain arahantship in a previous life during the time of the buddha Sikhī (S. Sikhin), when, as a hermit, he encountered that previous buddha walking in the woods and offered him fruit.

**gcod**. (chö). A Tibetan term, from the verb "to cut" or "to sever;" a Tibetan tantric practice for severing attachment. The full name of the practice is bdud kyi gcod yul, or "the demon to be severed," and is a Tibetan tantric practice in which the meditator, through visualization, offers his or her body to an assembly of benevolent and malevolent deities as a means of accumulating merit and eliminating attachment to the body. The tradition of gcod, together with that of ZHI BYED or "pacification," is commonly classified among eight important tantric traditions and transmission lineages that spread throughout Tibet, the so-called "eight great conveyances that are lineages of achievement" (SGRUB BRGYUD SHING RTA CHEN PO BRGYAD). The practice was originally promulgated by the twelfth-century female adept MA GCIG LAB SGRON, who described it as a practice that severs (gcod) attachment to one's body, dualistic thinking, and conceptions of hope and fear. Although usually practiced by solitary meditators in isolated and frightening locations, gcod liturgies are also performed by monastic assemblies—both accompanied by the ritual music of the hand drum (see ḌAMARU) and the human leg-bone trumpet. The meditation, rooted in PRĀJÑĀPĀRAMITĀ and MAHĀMUDRĀ, involves the visualized offering of the adept's body, flesh, blood, bones, and organs, as food for a vast assembly of beings, including local spirits and demons. It is also commonly used as a ritual for healing or protection.

**Gcung ri bo che**. (Chung Riwoche). A residence of the renowned Tibetan adept THANG STONG RGYAL PO, founded by the master between the years 1449 and 1456. Situated west of Ding ri on the banks of the Gtsang po (Tsangpo) river, it is one of several large multichapel STŪPAS located in central Tibet. Others include the Rgyal rtse sku 'bum, Jo nang sku 'bum, Byams pa gling sku 'bum, and Rgyang bum mo che. The seven-story structure contains murals inspired by the cross-cultural fusion of styles at ZHWA LU monastery, marking an important period in the history of Tibetan painting.

**Gdams ngag mdzod**. (Dam Ngak Dzö). In Tibetan, lit. "Treasury of Practical Instructions," an encyclopedic and systematic presentation of the practical instructions (S. UPADEŚA; T. gdams ngag) of tantra according to numerous traditions of Tibetan Buddhist teaching, compiled and edited by the nineteenth-century master 'JAM MGON KONG SPRUL BLO GROS MTHA' YAS. The collection, encompassing ten volumes, forms one of Kong sprul's five treasuries (KONG SPRUL MDZOD LNGA) and illustrates his nonsectarian (RIS MED) perspective by including instructions from all traditions counted among the so-called "eight great conveyances that are lineages of attainment" (SGRUB BRGYUD SHING RTA CHEN PO BRGYAD).

**gdan sa gsum**. (den sa sum). In Tibetan, lit. "three seats" or "three foundations," a term that refers to the three principal monasteries of the DGE LUGS sect of Tibetan Buddhism in the LHA SA area: DGA' LDAN, 'BRAS SPUNGS, and SE RA. TSONG KHA PA, with the patronage of the powerful Phag mo gru family, founded Dga' ldan monastery in 1409; two followers of Tsong kha pa, 'JAM DBYANGS CHOS RJE BKRA SHIS DPAL LDAN and Byams chen chos rje Shākya ye shes (1354–1435), founded 'Bras spungs (1416) and Se ra (1419) monasteries, respectively, apparently at Tsong kha pa's urging. These three monasteries developed into the institutional center of Dge lugs power and influence.

**Gdan sa mthil**. (Den sa til). A monastery in southern Tibet, north of Rtsed thang (Tsetang), founded in 1158 by the influential BKA' BRGYUD hierarch PHAG MO GRU PA RDO RJE RGYAL PO. It became a powerful political center during the late fourteenth and fifteenth centuries under the patronage of the Phag mo gru family.

**geli**. (J. kyakuryaku; K. kyŏngnyŏk 隔歷). In Chinese, "separation," a term used in the HUAYAN and TIANTAI traditions to refer to the understanding of reality in terms of the discriminative phenomena of the conventional realm. "Separation" is distinguished from "consummate interfusion" (C. YUANRONG), which refers to the ultimate state of reality wherein all individual phenomena are perceived to be perfectly interfused and completely harmonized with one another. See YUANRONG.

**geli sandi**. (J. kyakuryaku no santai; K. kyŏngnyŏk samje 隔歷三諦). In Chinese, "differentiated three truths," also known as the "sequential three truths" (cidi sandi 次第三諦). See SANDI, YUANRONG.

**Gengo**. (J) (玄悟). See MUKAN FUMON.

**genjō kōan**. (C. xiancheng gong'an; K. hyŏnsŏng kongan 現[見]成公案). In Japanese, lit. "presently manifest case," or "actualized case," deriving from a term in Chinese law for an "open and shut case," or someone "caught dead to rights." The term is sometimes used in the CHAN school to refer to the universality of buddhahood in all aspects of the mundane world and, for this reason, is occasionally interpreted (rather too freely) as the "kōan of everyday life." Genjō kōan is one of the seminal terms in the writings of DŌGEN KIGEN (1200–1253), the putative founder of the SŌTŌSHŪ of Japanese ZEN, and is the title of a treatise written in 1233 that was later anthologized as the first roll of the sixty- and the seventy-five-roll recensions of his magnum opus, the SHŌBŌGENZŌ ("Treasury of the True Dharma Eye"). The term seems to have first been used by the Tang Chan master Muzhou Daoming (780–877), and more often later by such Song Chan masters as HONGZHI ZHENGJUE (1091–1157) and YUANWU KEQIN (1063–1135). Dōgen deploys the term to criticize the RINZAI (LINJI) usage of kōan (C. GONG'AN) as a means of catalyzing a breakthrough into awakening, thus making genjō kōan a polemical device for distinguishing his presentation of Zen thought and practice from rival schools. Although Dōgen never directly defines it, in his usage, genjō kōan indicates the way in which all things are constantly manifesting their inherent buddhahood in the here and now; thus, Buddhist cultivation entails simply performing a single practice, such as seated meditation (J. ZAZEN), so completely that the enlightenment inherent in that practice becomes "an open and shut case."

**Genshin**. (源信) (942–1017). Japanese TENDAISHŪ monk, scholar, and artist, popularly known as ESHIN SŌZU (Head Monk of Eshin) because he spent much of his life at the monastery of Eshin at YOKAWA on HIEIZAN. Genshin was born in Yamato province (present-day Nara prefecture), but after losing his father at a young age, he was put in the care of the Tendai center on Mt. Hiei. It is believed that during his teens he formally joined the institution and became a student of the Tendai reformer RYŌGEN (912–985). Genshin first gained a name for himself in 974 due to his sterling performance in an important debate at Mt. Hiei. Eventually, Genshin retired to the secluded monastery of Shuryōgon'in in Yokawa, where he devoted the rest of his life primarily to scholarship. Genshin wrote on a wide array of Buddhist topics related to both Tendai and PURE LAND practices and is also regarded as the founder of the Eshin school of Tendai, which espoused the notion that everyone is inherently awakened (J. HONGAKU). While it is uncertain if any of his art is extant, Genshin was both a sculptor and painter, and his paintings of the buddha Amida (S. AMITĀBHA) welcoming believers into the PURE LAND, referred to as raigōzu, helped to popularize this subject in Japan. The most influential of Genshin's works was the ŌJŌ YŌSHŪ ("Collection of Essentials on Going to Rebirth" [in the pure land]), written in 985, one of the first Japanese treatises on the practice of nenbutsu (C. NIANFO) and the soteriological goal of rebirth in the pure land, playing an important role in laying the groundwork for an independent pure land tradition in Japan a century later. The *Ōjō yōshū* offers a systematic overview of pure land thought and practice, using extensive passages culled from various scriptures and treatises, especially the writings of the Chinese pure land monks DAOCHUO and SHANDAO. Genshin contends that the practice of nenbutsu is relatively easy for everyone and is appropriate for people during the dharma-ending age (mappō; see MOFA), especially as a deathbed practice. The *Ōjō yōshū* was also one of the few texts written in Japan that made its way to China, where it influenced the development of pure land Buddhism on the mainland. Japanese Buddhists have long debated whether Genshin should be primarily viewed as affiliated with either the Tendai or pure land schools. In fact, however, this distinction was not relevant during Genshin's own lifetime, since an independent pure land tradition did not yet exist at that point. Given the Tendai notion that all beings can attain buddhahood through a variety of means, an argument he supports in his *Ichijō yōketsu* ("Essentials of the One Vehicle"), Genshin asserts that nenbutsu (C. nianfo) practice is the best method for reaching this goal. Pure land practice for Genshin therefore fits under the larger umbrella of Tendai thought. Nonetheless, Genshin's presentation of pure land beliefs and practice offered a foundation for the development of pure land Buddhism in Japan, notably in its influence on HŌNEN (1133–1212) and SHINRAN (1173–1263); for this reason, the JŌDO SHINSHŪ school considers Genshin to be the sixth patriarch in its lineage.

**Ge sar**. A legendary king who is the hero of the most famous Tibetan cycle of epic poetry, traditionally sung by bards; it is said to be the longest work of literature in the world. The songs recount the birth and adventures of Ge sar, the king of the land of Gling. The name Ge sar apparently derives from Zoroastrian sources and stories of Ge sar appear in a number of Central Asian languages. It is unclear whether Ge sar was a historical figure; elements of the songs seem to derive from the period of the later dissemination (PHYI DAR) of Buddhism to Tibet, although the earliest version of the songs in the form they are known today dates to the fifteenth century. In the songs, the world has fallen into chaos and various gods such as Brahmā and ŚAKRA, and various Buddhist figures, such as PADMASAMBHAVA and the buddha AMITĀBHA, decide that a hero should descend into the world to restore order. That hero is Ge sar, who defeats many foes, including the evil king of Hor.

**Geshe Rabten**. See RABTEN, GESHE.

**Geshe Wangyal**. See WANGYAL, GESHE.

**geteng Chan**. (J. kattōzen; K. kaltŭng Sŏn 葛藤禪). In Chinese, "kudzu Chan", a term for convoluted conceptual descriptions of CHAN doctrine or elaborate belletristic accounts of Chan, which are compared to the creeping vines of the kudzu plant. Just as the kudzu plant completely entangles everything in its vicinity, creating an impenetrable mass of vines, so too do the creeping tendrils of conceptualization (cf. PRAPAÑCA) entangle the mind, eventually overwhelming it. The term is often used as a synonym for the "lettered chan" (WENZI CHAN) approach championed by JUEFAN HUIHONG (1071–1128) of the Northern Song dynasty.

**gewai Chan**. (J. kakugai no Zen/kakuge no Zen; K. kyŏgoe Sŏn 格外禪). In Chinese, lit. "unconventional Chan" (lit. "the Chan that goes beyond all conventions"), referring to one of the styles of practice and pedagogy associated with the CHAN ZONG; often considered to be equivalent to the supreme vehicle Chan (ZUISHANGSHENG CHAN; K. ch'oesangsŭng Sŏn) that is transmitted by the patriarchs (ZUSHI). This form of Chan is said to transcend all conventional standards and styles because its approach transcends all explanations that rely upon language. Based on its fundamental distrust of the ability of language to convey truth, this form of Chan is said to use "unconventional words" (gewai ju; K. kyŏgoe ku) in its teachings, i.e., absurdities, contradictions, negations, double negations, etc., so that its listeners will come to realize the limits of language itself and thereby seek instead true knowledge that transcends verbal explanations. In addition to this unconventional usage of language, gewai Chan also uses nonverbal expressions, such as shouting and beatings, and many other illocutionary means of teaching. The ideas implicit in this form of Chan are formulated in the well-known phrases retrospectively attributed to BODHIDHARMA by the Chan masters of the Song dynasty: "a separate transmission outside the teaching" (JIAOWAI BIEZHUAN), "mind-to-mind transmission" (YIXIN CHUAN XIN), "no establishment of words and letters" (BULI WENZI), and "directly pointing to the human mind" (ZHIZHI RENXIN). The idea of unconventional Chan also was at times used polemically, i.e., to refer to a form of Chan superior to the more expository style of its opponents, which was denigrated as "theoretical Chan" (yili Chan) or "lettered Chan" (WENZI CHAN).

**geya**. (P. geyya; T. dbyangs bsnyad; C. qiye; J. giya; K. kiya 祇夜). In Sanskrit, "verse narrations," or "songs"; the verse summaries, sometimes with preceding prose material, included in the Buddhist scriptures. The geya are typically listed as the second of the Pāli ninefold (NAVAṄGA) and Sanskrit twelvefold (DVĀDAŚĀṄGA) divisions of the traditional genres of Buddhist literature as classified by composition style and content. These verses are sometimes written in the traditional Sanskrit ŚLOKA form, with four lines of eight syllables apiece. The geya genre is closely related to GĀTHĀ, religious verse, but may in some cases be distinguished by being the verse reiteration of a preceding prose narrative or by sometimes having verse interspersed with prose narration.

**geyi**. (J. kakugi; K. kyŏgŭi 格義). In Chinese, "matching concepts," or "categorized concepts"; geyi has typically been explained as a method of translation and exegesis that was supposedly popular during the incipiency of Buddhism in China. It has been presumed that Buddhist translators of the Wei and Jin dynasties borrowed terms and concepts drawn from indigenous Chinese philosophy (viz., "Daoism") to "match" (ge) the "meaning" (yi) of complicated and poorly understood Sanskrit Buddhist terminology. For instance, translators borrowed the term wuwei, used in both Chinese Daoist and Confucian writings to refer to "nonaction" or "nondeliberative activity," to render the seminal Buddhist concept of NIRVĀṆA. Misunderstandings were rife, however, since the matches would as often distort the Buddhist denotations of terms as clarify them. The technique of geyi has often been assumed by scholars to demonstrate that early Buddhism in China drew from the indigenous Daoist tradition in its initial attempts to make its message intelligible to its new Chinese audience. This view would correspondingly suggest that Daoism provided the inspiration for much of early Buddhist writing in China. This practice of drawing parallels to native Chinese concepts was criticized as early as the fourth century by the translator and cataloguer DAO'AN (312–385), who lobbied for the creation of a distinctive Chinese Buddhist vocabulary. Eventually Chinese Buddhists created their own neologisms for Buddhist technical terms, or resorted to transcription (viz., using Sinographs phonetically to transcribe the sound of the Sanskrit words) in order to render particularly significant, or polysemous, terms: e.g., using the transcription niepan, rather than the translation wuwei, as the standard rendering for nirvāṇa. In fact, however, the term geyi is quite rare in Chinese Buddhist literature from this incipient period. In the few instances where the term is attested, geyi seems instead to refer to Chinese attempts to cope with the use of lengthy numerical lists of seminal factors found in Indian Buddhist doctrinal formulations. This Indian proclivity for categorization is seldom evident in traditional Chinese philosophy and it would have been an extraordinary challenge for Chinese Buddhists to learn how to employ such lists skillfully. Against the received understanding of geyi as "matching concepts," then, the term may instead mean something more akin to "categorized concepts," referring to this Buddhist proclivity for producing extensive numerical lists of dharmas. See also FASHU.

**Ghanavyūha**. (T. Rgyan stug po bkod pa/Stug po bkod pa; C. Dasheng miyan jing; J. Daijō mitsugongyō; K. Taesŭng mirŏm kyŏng 大乘密嚴經). In Sanskrit, the "Dense Array" scripture, now extant only in Chinese and Tibetan translations. This sūtra discusses rebirth in the "dense-array PURE LAND" of the buddha VAIROCANA, which is known also in the AVATAṂSAKASŪTRA (C. *Huayan jing*) as the lotus-womb (C. huazang; S. kusumatalagarbhavyūhālaṃkāra) world. Like the LAṄKĀVATĀRASŪTRA, the *Ghanavyūha* expounds upon the doctrines of the matrix of buddhahood (TATHĀGATAGARBHA) and the storehouse consciousness (ĀLAYAVIJÑĀNA) and teaches that all phenomena emerge from the storehouse consciousness. The Chinese recension of the sūtra is divided into eight chapters, which describe ŚĀKYAMUNI Buddha's visit to Vairocana's pure land, where he ascends Vairocana's throne to speak the dharma to the BODHISATTVA Vajragarbha. Vajragarbha asks for an explanation of absolute truth (PARAMĀRTHASATYA), which Śākyamuni describes in terms of the nonproduction (ANUTPĀDA) and nonextinction (anuccheda) of the tathāgatagarbha. Vajragarbha then explains to other bodhisattvas the characteristics of the tathāgatagarbha and ālayavijñāna. Two Chinese translations, both in three rolls, were made: the first time c. 676–688 by Divākara, which was most influential within the tradition; the second by AMOGHAVAJRA (705–774). There is also a Tibetan translation, which is composed of nine chapters and differs slightly from the Chinese.

**ghaṇṭā**. (T. dril bu; C. jianzhi; J. kenchi; K. kŏnch'i 犍稚). In Sanskrit, "gong"; a resonant instrument used in Buddhist monasteries to announce the time of events, or to assemble the congregation. According to such texts as the MAHĪŚĀSAKA VINAYA, ghaṇṭās are to be sounded when it is time to recite

SŪTRAS and to assemble SAṂGHA members for meals and other activities, or to announce the time of the UPOṢADHA observance. Ghaṇṭhās are also ritual bells used in tantric liturgy. When used in conjunction with the VAJRA, the ghaṇṭā is said to represent wisdom (PRAJÑĀ), while the vajra represents method (UPĀYA).

**Ghost Festival**. See YULANPEN.

**ghrāṇavijñāna**. (P. ghānaviññāṇa; T. sna'i rnam par shes pa; C. bishi; J. bishiki; K. pisik 鼻識). In Sanskrit, "olfactory consciousness" or "nose consciousness"; one of the five consciousnesses of physical objects (along with those of the eye, ear, tongue, and body) and one of the six sensory consciousnesses (adding the mental consciousness, or MANOVIJÑĀNA). The olfactory consciousness perceives olfactory objects or fragrances (GANDHA). Like the other consciousnesses of physical objects, an olfactory consciousness is produced through the contact (SPARŚA) between an olfactory sensory object (gandha) and the olfactory sense base or nose sense organ (GHRĀṆENDRIYA) and in dependence on three conditions (PRATYAYA): the object condition (ĀLAMBANAPRATYAYA), in this case, a fragrance; a dominant condition (ADHIPATIPRATYAYA), here, the olfactory sense base (ghrāṇendriya); and the immediately preceding condition (SAMANANTARAPRATYAYA), a prior moment of consciousness. The olfactory consciousness is counted as one of the six sensory consciousnesses (VIJÑĀNA) and eighteen elements (DHĀTU).

**ghrāṇāyatana**. (P. ghānāyatana; T. sna'i skye mched; C. bichu; J. bisho; K. pich'ŏ 鼻處). In Sanskrit, "olfactory sense base," or "base of cognition"; the olfactory sense base or nose sense organ (GHRĀṆENDRIYA) as it occurs in the list of the twelve sense fields (ĀYATANA), which are called "bases of cognition" because each pair of sense base and sense object produces its respective sensory consciousness. In this case, the contact (SPARŚA) between an olfactory sensory object (GANDHA) and the olfactory sense base (ghrāṇendriya) produces an olfactory consciousness (GHRĀṆAVIJÑĀNA).

**ghrāṇendriya**. (P. ghānindriya; T. sna'i dbang po; C. bigen; J. bikon; K. pigŭn 鼻根). In Sanskrit, "olfactory sense base" or "nose sense organ," the physical organ located in the nose that makes it possible to perceive fragrances (GANDHA). This sense base is not the nose itself, but a form of subtle materiality (RŪPA) located within the nose and invisible to the naked eye; it is said to be shaped like two hollow needles at the root of the nostrils. If this sense organ is absent or damaged, the sense of smell does not function. The olfactory sense base serves as the dominant condition (ADHIPATIPRATYAYA) for the production of olfactory consciousness (GHRĀṆAVIJÑĀNA). The olfactory sense base is counted among the six sense bases or sense organs (INDRIYA), the twelve sense fields (ĀYATANA), and eighteen elements (DHĀTU).

**Gilgit**. A region on the northwestern frontier of KASHMIR in northern Pakistan, also the name of the township where the river Gilgit meets the Indus; a trade route passed through the region, giving it strategic importance. Some associate Gilgit with a region the Tibetans call Bru sha. Its rulers (especially the Turuṣka) supported Buddhism at a number of times during its history, particularly between the sixth and eighth centuries; it fell under the control of the Tibetan kingdom for a time in the late eighth century. A STŪPA discovered in Gilgit in 1931 yielded one of the largest troves ever discovered of Indian Buddhist manuscripts, associated especially with the MŪLASARVĀSTIVĀDA offshoot of the SARVĀSTIVĀDA school and with the MAHĀYĀNA. The discoveries included manuscripts of significant portions of the MŪLASARVĀSTIVĀDA VINAYA, and numerous Mahāyāna texts, including the SADDHARMAPUṆḌARĪKASŪTRA and various PRAJÑĀPĀRAMITĀ sūtras.

**Ginsberg, Allen**. (1926–1997). American Beat poet and Buddhist born in Newark, New Jersey. Ginsberg attended Columbia University with the intent of becoming a labor lawyer, but soon fell in with a group that included students such as JACK KEROUAC, and nonstudents, such as William Burroughs, with whom he shared common interests, both literary and otherwise. In 1948, he had a transformative vision while reading William Blake in his Harlem apartment. He moved to San Francisco where he joined the burgeoning poetry movement. In October 1955, he read his most famous work, *Howl*, at the Six Gallery. By his own account, Ginsberg was first introduced to Buddhism in letters he received from Kerouac, in which his friend wrote of suffering as the fundamental fact of existence. He began to read the works of DAISETZ TEITARO SUZUKI, whom he later met in New York in the company of Kerouac. Ginsberg was intimately involved in the various cultural movements of the 1960s, collaborating with Timothy Leary, Bob Dylan, and Ken Kesey, and protesting actively against the Vietnam War. In 1962, he traveled to India with GARY SNYDER, visiting BODHGAYĀ and SĀRNĀTH; he also had an audience with the fourteenth DALAI LAMA, who had arrived from Tibet just three years earlier. After experimenting with various forms of Hindu practice, Ginsberg met the Tibetan lama CHÖGYAM TRUNGPA in 1970, and remained his disciple until Trungpa's death, helping to found the Jack Kerouac School of Disembodied Poetics at Trungpa's Naropa Institute in Boulder, Colorado; in his last years, Ginsberg became a disciple of another Tibetan lama, Gelek Rinpoche. Buddhist themes figure prominently in much of Ginsberg's poetry.

**Gishin**. (義眞) (781–833). Japanese monk who was the first head (zasu) of the TENDAISHŪ. At a young age, Gishin became the student of the Japanese monk SAICHŌ, who dwelled on HIEIZAN. He later went to the monastery of DAIANJI and studied the VINAYA under the Chinese vinaya master GANJIN. Gishin also studied Chinese under Jiken (d.u.) of TŌDAIJI. In 804, the novice Gishin followed his teacher Saichō to China where he primarily served as an interpreter for his teacher. That same year, Saichō and Gishin arrived at the monastery of Guoqingsi on Mt. Tiantai (in present-day Zhejiang province). There, Gishin was ordained, receiving the full monastic precepts. The next year, both Saichō and Gishin received the "perfect teaching" (C. YUANJIAO) BODHISATTVA precepts (engyō bosatsukai) of the FANWANG JING from the reputed seventh patriarch of the TIANTAI tradition Daosui (d.u.) at the monastery of Longxingsi. Before their return to Japan that year, both Saichō and Gishin purportedly received initiation into the "two realms" (RYŌBU) of the KONGŌKAI (vajradhātu) and TAIZŌKAI (garbadhātu) MAṆḌALAS from a certain Shunxiao (d.u.) during their sojourn in Yuezhou (present-day Zhejiang province). After Saichō's death in 823, Gishin was given permission to construct a MAHĀYĀNA precepts platform (daijō kaidan) at his monastery of ENRYAKUJI. In 832, he was appointed the first head (zasu) of the Tendai school on Mt. Hiei.

**Glang dar ma**. (Langdarma) (r. c. 838–842). The forty-second king of the imperial Tibetan dynasty and, according to traditional sources, an infamous persecutor of Buddhism. Tibetan Buddhist histories portray Glang dar ma as a villainous figure who assassinated his brother, King RAL PA CAN, in 838 in order to seize the throne. For the next four years, he is said to have engaged in the suppression of Buddhist institutions in favor of the indigenous BON priests. While his rule did interrupt the process of translating and disseminating Indian Buddhist literature that had commenced during the previous century, recent scholarship maintains that Glang dar ma's persecution amounted to withdrawing state patronage from the increasingly powerful monastic institutions. According to Buddhist chronicles, his reign came to an abrupt end with his assassination in 842 at the hands of the cleric Lha lung Dpal gyi rdo rje. This marked the termination of the royal lineage and the demise of the Tibetan empire, traditionally understood as the end of the early dissemination of Buddhism (SNGA DAR) and portrayed as the beginning of a dark period that lasted for more than a century.

**Glang 'khor**. (Langkor). A site in central Tibet associated principally with the eleventh-century Indian adept PHA DAM PA SANGS RGYAS. The small temple of Glang 'khor, located in a village of the same name near the town of Ding ri, marks the location where Pha dam pa sangs rgyas disseminated his teachings on pacification (ZHI BYED) and severance (GCOD), primarily to his foremost Tibetan disciple MA GCIG LAB SGRON.

**Glass Palace Chronicle**. See HMANNAN MAHAYAZAWIN-DAW-GYI.

**Gling ras pa Padma rdo rje**. (Lingrepa Pema Dorje) (1128–1188). A Tibetan YOGIN venerated as a founder of the 'BRUG PA BKA' BRGYUD sect of Tibetan Buddhism; also known as Gling chen ras pa (Lingchen Repa) and Gling rje ras pa (Lingje Repa). He trained under the renowned BKA' BRGYUD master PHAG MO GRU PA RDO RJE RGYAL PO at GDAN SA MTHIL monastery and later spent numerous years in solitary meditation retreat. He consecrated the site upon which his principal disciple, GTSANG PA RGYA RAS YE SHES RDO RJE, founded the important 'BRUG PA monastery of RWA LUNG.

**Gnam lcags bar ba**. (Namchak Barwa). In Tibetan, "Blazing Meteor"; a mountain located in southern Tibet considered to demarcate the western border of the famed hidden land (SBAS YUL) of PADMA BKOD and venerated as the repository of numerous hidden treasure texts (GTER MA). Treasure revealers (GTER STON) who were active in the area include Sangs rgyas gling pa (Sangye Lingpa, 1340–1396) and Bdud 'dul rdo rje (Dudul Dorje, 1615–1672). According to one explanation of the region's sacred geography, the mountain forms the left breast of the deity VAJRAVĀRĀHĪ.

**Gnas chung**. (Nechung). In Tibetan, lit. "Small Place," a monastery serving as the seat of the GNAS CHUNG ORACLE, Tibet's state oracle, located near 'BRAS SPUNGS monastery outside LHA SA. According to tradition, on the advice of ŚĀNTARAKṢITA, KHRI SRONG SDE BTSAN invited the tantric thaumaturge PADMASAMBHAVA to Tibet to subdue spirits hostile to the introduction of Buddhism. Padmasambhava appointed a powerful spirit PE HAR as the protector of Buddhism of Tibet in general and of BSAM YAS monastery in particular. The main place (T. gnas chen) of Pe har is in Bsam yas, and a smaller shrine dedicated to his worship (and to the worship of RDO RJE GRAGS LDAN, the chief form in which Pe har carries out his work in Tibet) was located on the site of the present Gnas chung monastery. The monastery became important during the time of the fifth DALAI LAMA (1617–1682) and his regent SDE SRID SANGS RGYAS RGYA MTSHO, who completed an extensive expansion of the monastery in 1683 as part of a strategy to legitimatize the new government of Tibet (the DGA' LDAN PHO BRANG). They expanded the role of Pe har and made Nechung monastery the seat of Tibet's state oracle, introducing new invocations and rituals as an integral part of the monastery's practices. In the late nineteenth century, O rgyan Phrin las chos 'phel, a lama from SMIN GROL GLING monastery, introduced a number of RNYING MA tantric practices to the monastery; his incarnations are called the Gnas chung sprul skus.

**Gnas chung oracle**. (Nechung). The state oracle of Tibet, known as the Gnas chung chos rje, traditionally based at GNAS CHUNG monastery outside of LHA SA. During the time of the fifth DALAI LAMA, PE HAR rgyal po shifted residence from BSAM YAS to Gnas chung monastery. It is said that, at that time, the medium of Pe har, in a form known as Rdo rje grags ldan, saved the Tibetan people by uncovering a Nepalese plot to poison Tibetan wells. The oracle played an important role in contentious successions of the sixth and seventh Dalai Lamas, acting as a voice of the Tibetans against Chinese interests and predicting the birth of the seventh Dalai Lama in Li thang in Khams, and again assisting in the nineteenth century in the discovery of the thirteenth Dalai Lama. The oracle briefly lost favor due to erroneous predictions regarding the 1904 British invasion of Tibet, but regained his status by exposing a plot against the thirteenth Dalai Lama's life and then predicting his death in 1933. The oracle was consulted in the search for the current fourteenth Dalai Lama, and in matters relating to the 1950 Chinese Communist invasion of Tibet and subsequent events of the Chinese occupation, leading up to the Dalai Lama's escape into exile in 1959. In exile the Gnas chung chos rje has continued to play his traditional role of advising the Tibetan government.

**gnas skor ba**. (nekorwa). In Tibetan, lit. "going around a [sacred] place," generally translated as "pilgrimage," a pervasive practice of Tibetan Buddhism. Tibetan pilgrimage is most often a communal practice, involving a group of persons of the same family, the same village, or the same monastery, in some cases led by one or more monks or lamas who provide information and religious instruction along the route. Pilgrimage is undertaken to accrue merit and to expiate transgressions, but it also plays an important social and economic role in Tibetan society. Once the pilgrimage begins, pilgrims will do everything possible not to turn back; failure to complete the journey is thought to be like breaking a vow. Pilgrims generally traverse the pilgrimage route on foot; it is said that more merit is accrued if one walks rather than travels on horseback. The length of the pilgrimage varies according to the distance traveled, the season, the number of mountain passes to be crossed, and the number of sites to be visited. The trip can sometimes take several years, especially if the pilgrims perform prostrations along the entire route. Pilgrims make offerings at the monasteries and temples they visit, both on behalf of themselves but also for relatives who have not made the journey. Monasteries offer pilgrims ceremonial scarves (kha btags), blessed pills, and sometimes also food and lodging. Among the most important destinations for pilgrims is the city of LHA SA. There are eight famous mountains and mountain ranges, including Mount KAILĀSA in western Tibet and Dag pa shel ri (the Crystal Mountain) in TSA RI, a site sacred to CAKRASAṂVARA on the border with eastern Nepal, and further afield the sacred sites in India (BODHGAYĀ, SĀRNĀTH, etc.) and in China (WUTAISHAN, etc.). See also MAHĀSTHĀNA.

**gnosis**. See JÑĀNA.

**Gnubs chen Sangs rgyas ye shes**. (Nupchen Sangye Yeshe) (c. 832–962). A Tibetan Buddhist master revered as one of the twenty-five original disciples of the Indian tantric adept PADMASAMBHAVA. He is the author of the BSAM GTAN MIG SGRON, an early text explaining, among other systems, RDZOGS CHEN. According to traditional biographies, he was born in to the Gnubs (Nup) clan, an important clan that provided ministers to the kings in central Tibet. In his youth, he studied with Padmasambhava and numerous other masters in India, Nepal, and northwest India. He later made seven trips to Nepal and India, collecting and translating tantric texts. He is considered to be the chief recipient of the ANUYOGA teachings. Other sources state that he frightened away king GLANG DAR MA with his magical powers when the king threatened his community of practitioners. ZHI BA 'OD and others criticized the RNYING MA PA for claiming an Indian origin for texts that they alleged had in fact been composed by Gnubs chen Sangs rgyas ye shes.

**Gnyan chen thang lha**. (Nyenchen Tangla). An important Tibetan mountain god, sometimes said to be an emanation of VAJRAPĀṆI, despite being a worldly DHARMAPĀLA. He was subdued by PADMASAMBHAVA; some accounts say that his domestication occurred in four settings, with Padmasambhava in four different guises: first in the heavens, with Padmasambhava assuming the guise of Vajrapāṇi; the second at He po ri near BSAM YAS, with Padmasambhava in the form of Padma HERUKA; the third time on the very peak of Bsam yas monastery, with Padmasambhava in the form of VAJRAHŪṂKĀRA; and finally as Padmasambhava himself. His connection with Bsam yas is furthered by his identification with a NĀGA king named Zur phud lnga pa; this serpent king was asked by Padmasambhava to be the protector of the monastery, but he refused, recommending instead that Padmasambhava travel to Hor and bring back PE HAR RGYAL PO for the job. Gnyan chen thang lha is said to be the chief of all SA BDAG (earth spirits) in central Tibet and the protector of Dmar po ri, the hill in LHA SA on which the PO TA LA stands, although his principal seat is in northern Tibet, at the mountain range that bears his name. Gnyan chen thang lha appears as a member of numerous groupings of Tibetan deities, often as their leader. He is the leader of the 360 mountain gods, the chief of the ser bdag bco brgyad (the eighteen masters of hail), and one of the mgur lha bcu gsum of the BON pantheon. He is also called Thang lha yar shur, Thang lha yab shur, Yar shur gnyan gyi lha, and Gter bdag gnyan chen thang lha.

**Go bo rab 'byams pa Bsod nams seng ge**. [alt. Go rams pa Bsod nams seng ge] (1429–1489). A renowned philosopher and logician of the SA SKYA sect of Tibetan Buddhism, he studied at NA LAN DRA (founded in 1435 by RONG STON SMRA BA'I SENG GE) then NGOR (founded in 1429 by Ngor chen KUN DGA' BZANG PO), where he later became the sixth abbot. His complete works in five volumes, included in the set of works of the great masters of the Sa skya sect, present the authoritative interpretation of statements by the five Sa skya hierarchs (SA SKYA GONG MA RNAM LNGA) on important topics in ABHIDHARMA and epistemology (PRAMĀṆA). Particularly highly regarded are his works on MADHYAMAKA and the thought of DHARMAKĪRTI, as well as his explanation of Sa skya Paṇḍita's SDOM GSUM RAB DBYE, a core text of the Sa skya curriculum explaining the three ŚRĀVAKA, BODHISATTVA, and tantric moral codes, written as a corrective to the work of his contemporary SHĀKYA MCHOG LDAN.

**godānīya**. (P. goyāniya; T. ba lang spyod; C. qutuoni; J. kudani; K. kudani 瞿陀尼). One of the four continents of our world system, located to the west of Mount SUMERU, also known as aparagodānīya or "western godānīya." According to the ABHIDHARMAKOŚABHĀṢYA, this continent is circular in shape and is twenty-five thousand leagues (YOJANA) in diameter. It is flanked by two smaller islands, sāthā and uttaramantriṇa. The inhabitants of the continent are said to be sixteen cubits tall and have a life span of five hundred years. The continent is home to a wish-granting cow, which provides the inhabitants with whatever they wish; this feature may account for the name of the continent, which means, "using cattle."

**Godāvarī**. (S). One of the twenty-four sacred sites associated with the CAKRASAṂVARATANTRA. See PĪṬHA.

**Goddard, Dwight**. (1861–1939). American popularizer of Buddhism and author of the widely read *A Buddhist Bible*. He was born in Massachusetts and educated in both theology and mechanical engineering. Following the death of his first wife, he enrolled at Hartford Theological Seminary and was ordained as a minister in the Congregational Church. He went to China as a missionary and it was there that he visited his first Buddhist monastery. After holding pastoral positions in Massachusetts and Chicago, he left the ministry to become a mechanical engineer. An invention that he sold to the government made him independently wealthy and allowed him to retire in 1913. He traveled to China several times in the 1920s, where he met a Lutheran minister who was seeking to promote understanding between Buddhists and Christians. Goddard first learned of Zen Buddhism from a Japanese friend in New York in 1928 and later traveled to Japan where he met DAISETZ TEITARO SUZUKI and practiced ZAZEN for eight months in Kyōto. Upon his return to America, Goddard attempted in 1934 to form an American Buddhist community, called the Followers of the Buddha. With property in Vermont and California, the organization was to include a celibate monkhood, called the Homeless Brothers, supported by lay members. Goddard also published a Buddhist magazine, *Zen, A Magazine of Self-Realization*, before bringing out, with his own funds, what would become his most famous work, *A Buddhist Bible*, in 1932. The purpose of the anthology was to "show the unreality of all conceptions of the personal ego" and inspire readers to follow the path to buddhahood. It was Goddard's conviction that Buddhism was the religion most capable of meeting the problems of European civilization. Commercially published in 1938, the contents of *A Buddhist Bible* were organized by the language of a text's origins and contained works that had not been translated into English before. The works came mostly from Chinese, translated by the Chinese monk Wai-tao, in collaboration with Goddard. Tibetan selections were drawn from W. Y. EVANS-WENTZ. *A Buddhist Bible* is not without its eccentricities. For example, Goddard rearranged the VAJRACCHEDIKĀPRAJÑĀPĀRAMITĀSŪTRA ("Diamond Sūtra") into a more "sensible" order, and he included in his anthology a classic of Chinese philosophy, the *Daode jing* (*Tao te ching*). Goddard also composed his own treatise to provide practical guidance in meditation, which he felt was difficult for Europeans and Americans. As one of the first anthologies of Buddhist texts widely available in the West, and especially because it was one of the few that included MAHĀYĀNA works, *A Buddhist Bible* remained widely read for decades after its publication.

**Goddess of Mercy**. See GUANYIN.

**Godenshō**. (御伝鈔). In Japanese, "Biographical Notes," an important early biography of SHINRAN (1163–1273), in two rolls; written in 1295 by his great-grandson KAKUNYO (1270–1351), the third abbot of HONGANJI. Godenshō is the abbreviated title of this work favored in JŌDO SHINSHŪ communities; its full title is *Honganji Shōnin Shinran den e* ("Biography with Illustrations of the Honganji Sage Shinran"). This text is often paired with illustrations in a version that is presumed to have been composed by Kakunyo's son Zonkaku (1290–1373) and painted by Jōga Hogen. As few documents survive from Shinran's time, this biography is especially important in detailing the events in Shinran's life, and all later biographies draw upon it. One of the most important features of the Godenshō is its identification of Shinran as being an earthly manifestation of AMITĀBHA.

**gohonzon**. (御本尊). In Japanese, "object of devotion." See DAI-GOHONZON.

**Gokulika**. (S). See KAUKKUṬIKA.

**Golden Light Sūtra**. See SUVARṆAPRABHĀSOTTAMASŪTRA.

**Gombojab**. (T. Mgon po skyabs). (fl. eighteenth century). An important Mongolian scholar and translator, renowned for his knowledge of the four languages of the Qing dynasty: Chinese, Tibetan, Manchu, and Mongol. He was appointed by Emperor Yongzheng as director of the School of the Tibetan Language (Xi fan xue zong guan) and provided translations from Tibetan into Chinese for the Chinese canon (including a work by the fifth DALAI LAMA on the seven medicine buddhas) as well as a work on the correct proportions of Buddha images. He translated from Chinese into Tibetan XUANZANG's account of his journey to the West, the DA TANG XIYU JI. His most influential work was the "History of Buddhism in China" (*Rgya nag chos 'byung*), which remained a major Tibetan source on Chinese history and Buddhism. It had three parts: a general geographical and historical description of China, a history of Buddhism in China based on "Lives of Eminent Monks" (GAO SENG ZHUAN), and a Tibetan translation of the catalogue (C. JINGLU) of the Chinese Buddhist canon (C. DAZANGJING). The work also contained historical information on Buddhism in Mongolia. Other works include a book on WUTAISHAN in Tibetan; the story of the sandalwood Buddha, also in Tibetan; a Tibetan–Mongolian dictionary; and a work in Mongolian on the proper pronunciation of Sanskrit. Lesser works include a Tibetan–Chinese glossary of medicines for Mongolian visitors to Chinese pharmacies.

**gong'an**. (J. kōan; K. kongan 公案). In Chinese, "public case," or "precedent"; better known in the West by its Japanese pronunciation kōan, a word that has now entered common English parlance as "koan." Gong'an was originally a legal term, referring to the magistrate's (gong) table (an), which by metonymy comes to refer to a legal precedent or an authoritative judgment; the term also comes to mean simply a "story" (gong'an in vernacular Chinese refers to the genre of detective stories). The term is widely used in the CHAN school in a way that conveys both denotations of a legal precedent and a story. The study of gong'an seems to have had its beginnings in the practice, probably dating from the late-Tang dynasty, of commenting on the exchanges or "ancient precedents" (guce) culled from Chan genealogical histories (e.g., JINGDE CHUANDENG LU) and the recorded sayings or discourse records (YULU) of the Chan masters of the past. Commenting on old cases (niangu), often using verses (SONGGU), seems to have become a well-established practice by the early Song dynasty, as more recorded sayings began to include separate sections known as nianggu and songgu. Perhaps one of the most famous collections of verse commentaries on old cases is the Chan master XUEDOU CHONGXIAN's *Xuedou heshang baice songgu*, which now exists only as part of a larger influential collection of gong'ans known as the BIYAN LU. Other famous gong'an collections, such as the CONGRONG LU and WUMEN GUAN, were compiled during the Song dynasty and thereafter. These collections often shared a similar format. Each case (bence), with some exceptions, begins with a pointer (CHUISHI), a short introductory paragraph. The actual case, often a short anecdote, is interspersed with interlinear notes known as "annotations" or "capping phrases" (C. zhuoyu/zhuyu; see J. JAKUGO). After the case, a prose commentary (pingchang), verse commentary (songgu), and subcommentary on the verse commentary follow. Traditionally, 1,700 specific gong'an are said to have been in circulation in the Chan school. Although this number does have antecedents within the tradition, there are no fixed numbers of cases included in Chan gong'an anthologies; for example, a late Qing-dynasty collection, the 1712 *Zongjian falin,* includes 2,720 gong'an, which were claimed to be all the gong'an then in active use within the tradition. Whatever the number, there seems not to have been any kind of systematic curriculum within the Chinese Chan or Korean Sŏn traditions using this full panoply of gong'an. The creation of a pedagogical system of training involving mastery of a series of many different kōans is commonly attributed to HAKUIN EKAKU (1685–1769) in the Japanese RINZAISHŪ of ZEN. The widespread reference to 1,700 gong'an in Western-language materials may derive from accounts of Japanese government attempts in 1627 to routinize the Rinzai monastic curriculum, by promulgating a regulation requiring all Zen abbots to master 1,700 cases as part of their training. ¶ The literary endeavor of studying old cases also gave rise to new forms of meditation. The Chan master DAHUI ZONGGAO in the YANGQI PAI of the LINJI ZONG systematized a practice in which one focuses on what he termed the "meditative topic" (HUATOU), which in some contexts refers to the "keyword," or "critical phrase" of a gong'an story. For instance, the famous huatou "WU" (no) that Dahui used as a meditative topic was derived from a popular gong'an attributed to ZHAOZHOU CONGSHEN: A student asked Zhaozhou, "Does a dog have buddha nature, or not?," to which Zhaozhou replied "wu" (no; lit., "it does not have it") (see WU GONG'AN; GOUZI WU FOXING). This new practice was called the "Chan of observing the meditative topic" or, more freely, "questioning meditation" (KANHUA CHAN). During the Song dynasty, students also began to seek private instruction on gong'an from Chan masters. These instructions often occurred in the abbot's quarters (FANGZHANG). ¶ The active study of gong'an in Korean SŎN begins with POJO CHINUL and his disciple CHIN'GAK HYESIM, who learned of Dahui's kanhua Chan largely through the writings of their Chinese counterpart. Hyesim was also the first Korean Sŏn monk to compile his own massive collection of cases, titled the SŎNMUN YŎMSONG CHIP. The use of cases was later transmitted to Japan by pilgrims and émigré monks, where kōan study became emblematic of the Rinzaishū. Because rote memorization of capping phrases came to take precedence over skilled literary composition in classical Chinese, the Japanese compiled large collections of capping phrases, such as the ZENRIN KUSHŪ, to use in their training.

**gong bugong ye**. (S. *sādhāraṇāsādhāraṇakarman; T. thun mong dang thun mong ma yin pa'i las; J. gūfugūgō; K. kong pulgong ŏp 共不共業). In Chinese, "collective KARMAN and individual karman." In both the MAHĀYĀNA and ABHIDHARMA literature, a distinction is made between collective (or communal, shared) action (sādhāraṇakarman) and individual (or unshared) action (asādhāraṇakarman). The former is the combined and mixed force of multiple individual's karman, which creates and conditions the shared physical habitat in which those sentient beings live (cf. BHĀJANALOKA). The latter is individual-specific and produces karmic effects that could only be reaped by the primary agent of that karman. However, there is an overlap between collective and individual karman, as the two interact with and, to an extent, influence one another. According to the YOGĀCĀRABHŪMIŚĀSTRA, for example, such geographical features as rivers and mountains are products of "absolute collective karman" (gong zhong gong); but other physical objects like homes and private lands are of "individuated instances of collective karman" (gong zhong bugong), since they are personal property enjoyed by the primary agent. Other possible combinations of collective and individual karman are also outlined in the same text (cf. ER BAO and ER SHIJIAN).

**gongde yuan**. (J. kudokuin; K. kongdŏk wŏn 功德院). In Chinese, "merit cloister," a semiprivate Buddhist institution common during the Tang and Song dynasties. These merit cloisters were sometimes private monasteries established on the burial grounds of elite Chinese families; in many cases, however, they were not new temples at all but instead appendages to officially sanctioned monasteries. Once the merit cloister was established on the monastery's grounds, the family could then claim the entire monastery as its own, transfer title of its landed estate to the monastery—and, like a premodern tax shelter, avoid paying property taxes to the government—but still retain control over the entire property. Unlike public monasteries, where offerings made by private donors became the permanent property of the monastery, the merit cloister was a hybrid institution: donated lands were considered to be the monastery's property in the eyes of the government, but the families in reality retained effective control over the disposition of those lands, even using the tax-free income they generated to acquire still more property for the family. The family that established the merit cloister also retained control over the administration of the monastery, including the right to hire, and fire, the abbot. As one transnational example, Huiyinsi (Ocean Seal Monastery) in the Southern Song capital of Hangzhou effectively became a merit cloister for the ruling family of the Korean Koryŏ dynasty (918–1392). ŬICH'ŎN (1055–1101), the prominent monk and fourth son of the Koryŏ king Munjong (r. 1047–1083), studied at Huiyinsi with the Huayan teacher Jingyuan (1011–1088). After Ŭich'ŏn's death, the Koryŏ dynasty continued to provide an annual stipend to Huiyinsi to maintain a virtual merit cloister for the deceased prince, and retained the authority at certain points in the monastery's history to appoint its abbot. Koryŏ support was so substantial and continuous that the monastery came to be better known by its nickname Gaolisi (Korea Monastery).

**gongye**. (C) (共業). See GONG BUGONG YE.

**Gopaka**. (T. Sbed byed). One of the ṢOḌAŚASTHAVIRA ("the sixteen elders") in the Tibetan enumeration. See ṢOḌAŚASTHAVIRA.

**gotra**. (P. gotta; T. rigs; C. zhongxing; J. shushō; K. chongsŏng 種姓/種性). In Sanskrit, "family" or "lineage," used in a figurative sense. The VINAYA explains that those in a noble family or line are those monks who are content with their robes, with whatever they receive in their begging bowls, and with low-quality bedding, and who take pleasure in forsaking the unwholesome (AKUŚALA) and cultivating the wholesome (KUŚALA). In the Pāli ABHIDHAMMA, the moment when one's concentration or insight moves from one "family" to another is called "change of lineage" (GOTRABHŪ). In Mahāyāna literature (especially that associated with the YOGĀCĀRA), gotra refers to a destiny, almost in the sense of a spiritual disposition, that prompts one to follow a particular path to enlightenment. There is typically a list of five such spiritual destinies (pañcagotra) found in Yogācāra literature: (1) the TATHĀGATA lineage, for those destined to become buddhas; (2) the PRATYEKABUDDHA lineage, for those destined to become ARHATs via the PRATYEKABUDDHAYĀNA; (3) the ŚRĀVAKA lineage, for those who will become arhats via the ŚRĀVAKAYĀNA; (4) those of indefinite (ANIYATA) lineage, who may change from any of three vehicles to another; and (5) those without lineage (agotra), who are ineligible for liberation or who have lost the prospect of becoming enlightened by being "incorrigibles" (ICCHANTIKA). Another division of lineage is into PRAKṚTISTHAGOTRA (naturally present) and SAMUDĀNĪTAGOTRA (developed). According to the YOGĀCĀRABHŪMIŚĀSTRA, the former refers to one's innate potential for spiritual achievement; the latter refers to the specific individual habits one can develop that will help speed the mastery of that potential. See also FAXIANG ZONG; ŚRĀVAKABHŪMI.

**gotrabhū**. In Pāli, "entering the lineage (of the noble ones)," or "maturity moment," the momentary, transitional state of consciousness that takes the NIRVĀṆA element (P. nibbānadhātu) as its object for the first time. At that moment, the adept is no longer an ordinary unenlightened "worldling" (P. puthujjana; S. PṚTHAGJANA) and will transition in the following moment onto the path of the enlightened "noble ones" (P. ariya; ĀRYA) as a "stream-enterer" (P. sotāpanna; S. SROTAĀPANNA). Gotrabhū belongs to the class of mental processes called javana, or "impulsion moments."

**gotrabhūñāṇa**. In Pāli, "change-of-lineage knowledge," a specific type of knowledge (P. ñāṇa; S. JÑĀNA) included in the category "purity of knowledge and vision" (ÑĀṆADASSANAVISUDDHI), which is the seventh and final purity (P. VISUDDHI) to be developed along the path to liberation. Change-of-lineage knowledge takes as its object the unconditioned NIRVĀṆA element (P. nibbānadhātu), by virtue of which the practitioner leaves the lineage of ordinary worldlings (P. puthujjanagotta; cf. S. PṚTHAGJANA; GOTRA) and enters the lineage of the noble ones (P. ariyagotta; S. āryagotra). Change-of-lineage knowledge itself is reckoned as a transitional moment of consciousness in that it has not yet entered onto any one of the four supramundane or noble paths (P. ariyamagga; S. ĀRYAMĀRGA), viz., that of the stream-enterer (P. sotāpanna; S. SROTAĀPANNA), once-returner (P. sakadāgāmi; S. SAKṚDĀGĀMIN), nonreturner (ANĀGĀMI) or worthy one (P. arahant; S. ARHAT). Immediately following the occurrence of change-of-lineage knowledge there arises a moment of consciousness called MAGGACITTA, or "path consciousness," that signals the practitioner's actual entry into the noble path. It is this path consciousness that, technically speaking, constitutes the aforementioned "purity of knowledge and vision." At this point, if the practitioner has entered the path of the stream-enterer, he has permanently uprooted the first three of ten fetters (SAṂYOJANA) that bind beings to the cycle of existence, viz., (1) belief in the existence of a self in relation to the body (P. sakkāyadiṭṭhi; S. SATKĀYADṚṢṬI), (2) doubt about the efficacy of the path (P. vicikicchā; S. VICIKITSĀ), and (3) belief in the efficacy of rites and rituals (P. sīlabbataparāmāsa; S. ŚĪLAVRATAPARĀMARŚA). Having become a stream-enterer, the practitioner is destined never again to be reborn in any of the three unfortunate realms (DURGATI) of the hells, hungry ghosts, or animals, and is guaranteed to attain nirvāṇa in at most seven more lifetimes.

**gouzi wu foxing**. (J. kushi mubusshō; K. kuja mu pulsŏng 狗子無佛性). In Chinese, "a dog has no buddha-nature"; a CHAN expression that becomes a famous meditative topic (HUATOU) and is used as the subject of a Chan "questioning meditation" (see KANHUA CHAN). This phrase refers to a GONG'AN exchange attributed to the Tang-dynasty monk ZHAOZHOU CONGSHEN (778–897): Once when Zhaochou was asked, "Does a dog have buddha-nature (FOXING), or not?" Zhaochou answered, "No" (lit. "It does not have it."). This gong'an exchange is the famous "no" (WU) huatou, the first case of the WUMEN GUAN ("Gateless Checkpoint"), which is often the initial meditation topic given to neophyte Chan monks in the LINJI ZONG and Linji-oriented traditions in China, Korea, and Japan.

**Govinda, Lama Anagarika**. (1898–1985). Born Ernst Lothar Hoffmann in Kassel, Germany, he served in the German army during World War I, after which he continued his studies at Freiburg University in Switzerland. He became interested in Buddhism while living with expatriate European and American artists on the Italian island of Capri, during which time he published his first book, *The Basic Ideas of Buddhism and Its Relationship to Ideas of God* (1920). In 1928, he sailed for Ceylon, where he studied meditation and Buddhist philosophy briefly with the German-born THERAVĀDA monk ÑĀṆATILOKA MAHĀTHERA (who gave him the name Govinda), before leaving to travel in Burma and India. While visiting Darjeeling in the Himalayas in 1931, he was driven by a spring snowstorm to a Tibetan monastery at Ghoom, where he met Tomo (Gro mo) Geshe Rimpoche, a DGE LUGS PA lama. Govinda later held brief teaching positions at the University of Patna and at Shantiniketan, publishing essays in *The Mahā Bodhi*, the journal of the MAHĀBODHI SOCIETY, as well as various Theosophical journals. His lectures at Patna resulted in his book *The Psychological Attitude of Early Buddhist Philosophy* (1961) and his lectures at Shantiniketan led to *Psycho-Cosmic Symbolism of the Buddhist Stūpa*. While at Shantiniketan he met a Parsi woman, Rati Petit (who assumed the name Li Gotami), whom he would marry in 1947. In 1942, he was interned by the British at Dehra Dun along with other German nationals, including Heinrich Harrer. During 1947–1948, Lama Govinda and Li Gotami traveled to some of the temples of western Tibet. During their travels, they met a lama named Ajorepa Rimpoche, who, according to Govinda, initiated them into the BKA' BRGYUD order. Returning from Tibet, Lama Govinda and Li Gotami set up permanent residence in India, publishing *Foundations of Tibetan Mysticism* in 1960. He spent the last two decades before his death in 1985 lecturing in Europe and the United States. His last years were spent in a home in Mill Valley, California, provided by the San Francisco Zen Center.

**gozan**. (五山). In Japanese, "five mountains"; a medieval Japanese ranking system for officially sponsored ZEN monasteries, which may derive from Chinese institutional precedents. Large and powerful public monasteries in China known as "monasteries of the ten directions" (SHIFANGCHA) came under the control of the Chinese state during the Song dynasty and were designated either as VINAYA or CHAN monasteries. Government administration of these monasteries eventually ceased, but it is widely believed that five major Chan monasteries in Zhejiang province (ranked in the order of WANSHOUSI, Lingyinsi, Jingdesi, Jingci Bao'en Guangxiaosi, and Guanglisi) were selected to be protected and governed by the state, largely through the efforts of the Chan master DAHUI ZONGGAO and his disciples. Whether this is indeed the beginning of a "five-mountain ranking system" is unclear, but by the Yuan dynasty the term was clearly in use in China. The implementation of this system in Japan began under the rule of the Kamakura shōgun Hōjō Sadatoki (1271–1311). Five illustrious RINZAISHŪ monasteries in Kamakura, including KENCHŌJI and ENGAKUJI, were granted gozan status and given a specific rank. A reordering of the gozan ranks occurred when Emperor Godaigo (1288–1339) came to power in 1333. The powerful Zen monasteries in Kyōto, NANZENJI and DAITOKUJI, replaced Kenchōji and Engakuji as the top-ranking monasteries, and the monastery of TŌFUKUJI was added to the gozan system. The gozan ranks were changed again several times by the Ashikaga shogunate. By the Muromachi period, some three hundred official monasteries (kanji) were ranked either gozan, jissatsu (ten temples), or shozan (many mountains). The term gozan also came to denote the prosperous lineages of MUSŌ SOSEKI and ENNI BEN'EN, who populated the gozan monasteries; monks in these lineages were particularly renowned for their artistic and literary talents in classical Chinese and brushstroke art. There seems also to have been a five-mountain convent system (amadera gozan or niji gozan) for Japanese nuns, which paralleled the five-mountain monastery system of the monks, but little is known about it.

**gradual enlightenment**. See JIANWU.

**graduated discourse**. See ANUPUBBIKATHĀ.

**grāhyagrāhakavikalpa**. (T. gzung ba dang 'dzin pa'i rnam par rtog pa; C. suoqu nengqu fenbie; J. shoshunōshu funbetsu; K. soch'wi nŭngch'wi punbyŏl 所取能取分別). In Sanskrit, "discrimination between the grasped and the grasper," or "false conception of apprehended and apprehender," a specific kind of discrimination (VIKALPA) used in the YOGĀCĀRA school to refer to the misconception that there is an inherent bifurcation between a perceiving subject (grāhaka) and its perceived objects (grāhya). This bifurcation occurs because of false imagining (ABHŪTAPARIKALPA), the tendency of the relative (PARATANTRA) nature (SVABHĀVA) to project both a false sense of a perceiving self and of perceived objects that are external to it. By relying on these false imaginings to construct our sense of what is real, we inevitably subject ourselves to continued suffering (DUḤKHA) within the cycle of rebirth SAṂSĀRA. Overcoming this bifurcation leads to the nondiscriminative wisdom (NIRVIKALPAJÑĀNA), which marks the inception of the path of vision (DARŚANAMĀRGA).

**'Gram**. (Dram). In Tibetan, one of the four "edge-taming temples" or "edge-pinning temples" (MTHA' 'DUL GTSUG LAG KHANG) said to have been constructed during the time of the Tibetan king SRONG BTSAN SGAM PO to pin down the limbs of the demoness (T. srin mo) who was impeding the introduction of Buddhism into Tibet. The temple is located on the right ru or flank in Gtsang to the west of LHA SA, and pins down her left shoulder.

**Gṛdhrakūṭaparvata**. (P. Gijjhakūṭapabbata; T. Bya rgod phung po'i ri; C. Lingjiushan; J. Ryōjusen; K. Yŏngch'uksan [alt. Yŏngch'wisan/Yŏngch'usan] 靈鷲山). In Sanskrit, "Vulture Peak," one of the five hills surrounding the city of RĀJAGṚHA, a favored site of GAUTAMA Buddha and several of his most important disciples in mainstream Buddhist materials and the site where the Buddha is said to have delivered many renowned sūtras in the NIKĀYAS and ĀGAMAS; in the MAHĀYĀNA, Gṛdhrakūṭa is also the location where ŚĀKYAMUNI Buddha is purported to have preached such important Mahāyāna scriptures as the SADDHARMAPUṆḌARĪKASŪTRA ("Lotus Sūtra") and the perfection of wisdom sūtras (PRAJÑĀPĀRAMITĀ). The hill was so named either because it was shaped like a vulture's beak or a flock of vultures, or because vultures roosted there. In another legend, the peak is said to have received its name when, in an attempt to distract ĀNANDA from his meditation, the demon MĀRA turned himself into a frightening vulture; Ānanda, however, was unswayed by the provocation and eventually became enlightened. In one of the most famous episodes in the life of the Buddha, his evil cousin DEVADATTA, in attempting to kill the Buddha, instead wounded him when he hurled a boulder down on him from the hill, cutting his toe; for this and other "acts that bring immediate retribution" (ĀNANTARYAKARMAN), Devadatta fell into AVĪCI hell. Because many important Mahāyāna sermons are said to have been spoken on the peak, some schools—specifically the Japanese NICHIRENSHŪ—believe that the mountain itself is a PURE LAND. Other sources state that because of the sūtras set forth there, the peak has become a STŪPA, and like the Buddha's seat (VAJRĀSANA) in BODHGAYĀ, it will not be destroyed by fire at the end of the KALPA. Although beings in the intermediate state (ANTARĀBHAVA) are said to be able to pass through mountains, they are not able to pass through Vulture Peak. The first Buddhist council (see COUNCIL, FIRST), in which a group of five hundred ARHATS met to recite the Buddha's teaching after his death, is said to have been held in a cave on Vulture Peak.

**great completion**. See RDZOGS CHEN.

**great doubt**. See YIQING.

**great perfection**. See RDZOGS CHEN.

**Great Vehicle**. See MAHĀYĀNA.

**greed**. See LOBHA.

**Gṛhadevatā**. (S). One of the twenty-four sacred sites associated with the CAKRASAṂVARATANTRA. See PĪṬHA.

**gṛhapati**. (P. gahapati; T. khyim bdag; C. zhangzhe/jushi; J. chōja/koji; K. changja/kŏsa 長者/居士). In Sanskrit, "householder" or "pater familias," typically used to refer to an affluent lay supporter of Buddhism. The gṛhapati were wealthy gentry or businessmen, who were often classed together with priests (brāhmaṇa) and warriors (kṣatriya) to refer to respectable society in traditional India. The Buddha often uses gṛhapati in address to mean something close to "gentlemen" or "sirs." The term is also often seen in compound with śreṣṭhin ("distinguished") to indicate wealthy merchants or guild leaders (S. śreṣṭhigṛhapati; P. seṭṭhigahapati). Finally, gṛhapati appears in lists of the seven "jewels" (RATNA) associated with a wheel-turning monarch (CAKRAVARTIN): his role is to locate unclaimed possessions or wealth through his "divine eye" (DIVYACAKṢUS), which the king can then appropriate for the crown. In this capacity, gṛhapati has sometimes been translated as a "financial steward," or "treasurer," although his role is really more that of a thaumaturgic treasure hunter than a quotidian accountant. Although GṚHASTHA or "householder" is sometimes used interchangeably with gṛhapati, gṛhapati seems to connote an especially wealthy and influential householder who is a patron of Buddhism.

**gṛhastha**. (P. gahaṭṭha; T. khyim na gnas pa; C. zaijia; J. zaike; K. chaega 在家). In Sanskrit, lit. "householder," a married male who has a family and supports his household through his labor. The householder is often contrasted with the ŚRAMAṆA or BHIKṢU, who has renounced the life of the householder and the social entanglements it entails (see PRAVRAJITA). The term is often translated simply as "layman" to indicate this distinction from the Buddhist clergy. It is important to note, however, that a householder is not necessarily an UPĀSAKA, a term also often translated as "layman," but perhaps better rendered as "lay [male] disciple." An upāsaka is a householder who has at minimum taken refuge in the three jewels (RATNATRAYA), and who may also hold any of the five upāsaka precepts (see PAÑCAŚĪLA). Householders play important roles in Buddhism, primarily by providing alms to the SAṂGHA.

The Buddha offered specific teachings for them, generally consisting of advice on how to live an ethical life and accumulate merit so that they will be reborn in heaven (see P. ANUPUBBIKATHĀ, the "graduated discourse"). A number of householders figure prominently in the canon, including the Buddha's wealthy patron ANĀTHAPIṆḌADA. Although among the Buddha's disciples, householders generally do not practice or excel at meditation, there are some exceptions, most notably CITTA. It is said that householders who excel at the practice of meditation achieve the state of the ANĀGĀMIN. Pāli texts state that a layperson who becomes an ARHAT must be ordained as a monk or nun within seven days or die; the body of a layperson, unpurified by monastic vows, is considered incapable of supporting such a state of enlightenment. Although gṛhastha is sometimes used interchangeably with GṚHAPATI, the latter term seems to connote an especially wealthy and influential householder who is a patron of Buddhism.

**Gro bo lung**. (Drowolung). Residence of the Tibetan translator MAR PA CHOS KYI BLO GROS and the surrounding area, located in the southern Tibetan region of LHO BRAG close to the Bhutanese border.

**Grum pa rgyang**. (Drumpa gyang). In Tibetan, one of the four "edge-taming temples" or "edge-pinning temples" (MTHA' 'DUL GTSUG LAG KHANG) said to have been constructed during the time of the Tibetan king SRONG BTSAN SGAM PO to pin down the limbs of the demoness (T. srin mo) who was impeding the introduction of Buddhism into Tibet. The temple is located at Lha rtse on the auxiliary flank (ru lag) and pins down her left hip.

**gsang ba'i rnam thar**. (sang we nam tar). In Tibetan, "secret autobiography," one of the three types of RNAM THAR (sacred biography or autobiography), focusing on a subject's religious experiences, visions, and past-life experiences, with the author often writing from the perspective of an omniscient subject. They are called secret not because they are hidden away from general readership, but because of the esoteric tantric practices that form part of the subject matter. A well-known example of secret autobiography is 'JIGS MED GLING PA's *Gsang ba chen po nyams snang gi rtogs brjod chu zla'i gar mkhan* (translated as "Dancing Moon"), at least one purpose of which was demonstrating the authenticity of the KLONG CHEN SNYING THIG, a GTER MA (treasure text) that he revealed.

**Gsang phu ne'u thog**. (Sangphu Ne'utok). A monastery associated with the BKA' GDAMS sect established south of LHA SA in 1073 by RNGOG LEGS PA'I SHES RAB; for many centuries one of the premier institutions of learning in central Tibet. The abbacy passed to the scholar and translator RNGOG BLO LDAN SHES RAB, Legs pa'i shes rab's nephew, on his thirty-fifth birthday. Blo ldan shes rab's translations and summaries (bsdus don) of all the major works of DHARMAKĪRTI, together with the commentaries of DHARMOTTARA, as well as his two major commentaries (rnam bshad) established Gsang phu as the unchallenged center for the study of epistemology (T. tshad ma; S. PRAMĀṆA) until SA SKYA PAṆḌITA's masterly presentation of Dharmakīrti's thought in about 1219 in his TSHAD MA RIGS GTER; it criticized some aspects of the Gtsang phu tradition. Most illustrious of the line of pramāṇa scholars after Rngog at GSANG PHU was PHYWA PA CHOS KYI SENG GE who is credited with originating the distinctively Tibetan BSDUS GRWA genre of textbook (used widely in DGE LUGS monasteries) that introduces beginners to the main topics in ABHIDHARMA in a particular dialectical form that strings together a chain of consequences linked by a chain of reasons. Gtsang phu was also the center of PRAJÑĀPĀRAMITĀ studies based on the ABHISAMAYĀLAṂKĀRA, originating again with Blo ldan shes rab's translation, summary, and a major commentary. It attracted great masters of various sectarian affiliations including DUS GSUM MKHYEN PA, the first KARMA PA. The monastery divided into two colleges in the twelfth century; Gnyal [alt. Mnyal] zhig 'Jam pa'i rdo rje (fl. c. 1200) was abbot during Sa skya Paṇḍita's early years. Gnyal zhig's students passed on the traditions down to ZHWA LU monastery and to BU STON RIN CHEN GRUB and his followers. Like many former Bka' gdams institutions, it faded into obscurity with the rise of the DGE LUGS sect.

**gsar ma**. (sarma). In Tibetan, "new," and taken to mean, "followers of the new translations," in contradistinction to the RNYING MA, the "old" or "followers of the old translations." Tibetan historians describe the dissemination of Buddhism to Tibet as occurring in two waves, the first, called the earlier dissemination (SNGA DAR), beginning in the seventh century and ending with the persecutions of Buddhism under King GLANG DAR MA in the ninth century. The second wave, called the latter dissemination (PHYI DAR), is generally marked by the return of the Tibetan translator RIN CHEN BZANG PO from India and the new translations undertaken by him and others of TANTRAs that had been translated in the earlier period and the translations of a range of texts not previously translated. These are called the "new translations." By extension, the sects that developed subsequently based on the translations of these texts are called collectively the "new sects" (gsar ma), identified as the three sects of BKA' BRGYUD, SA SKYA, and BKA' GDAMS (later DGE LUGS). Those who continued to rely on the earlier translations (which included works that some members of the new sects would claim to be apocryphal) came to be known as the "old sect" (RNYING MA).

**Gtam zhing**. (Tamshing). A monastery founded in 1501–1505 by the Bhutanese treasure revealer (GTER STON) PADMA GLING PA, located in the Chos skor valley of Bum thang, central Bhutan; its full name is Gtam zhing lhun grub chos gling. The monastery contains some of the oldest extant mural painting in Bhutan, executed based upon the iconographic canons laid down by Padma gling pa himself.

**Gter bdag gling pa**. (Terdak Lingpa) (1646–1714). Also known as Smin gling Gter dag gling pa 'Gyur med rdo rje, an important monk and lama of the RNYING MA sect of Tibetan Buddhism and brother of the prominent teacher Lo chen Dharma shrī. He studied widely with masters of the major traditions of Tibetan Buddhism and was a close associate of the fifth DALAI LAMA, both receiving teachings from him and giving teachings to him. As his name Gter bdag ("Lord of Treasure") suggests, he was an important GTER STON, or discoverer of treasure texts (GTER MA). In addition to discovering important treasure texts, he complied and commented upon the BKA' MA. In 1676, he founded the monastery of SMIN GROL GLING, which would become one of the six major monasteries of the Rnying ma sect.

**gter ma**. (terma). In Tibetan, "hidden treasures" or "treasure text," a source of Tibetan Buddhist and BON sacred objects, including a wide range of manuscripts, relics, statuary, and ritual implements from earlier periods. Such treasure texts have been found in caves, mountains, lakes, valleys, or sequestered away in monasteries, sometimes within a pillar. Whether gter ma are BUDDHAVACANA, i.e., authentic words of the Buddha (or a buddha) or whether they are APOCRYPHA, is contested. In the RNYING MA canon, a division is made between gter ma and BKA' MA, the latter made up of commonly authenticated canonical works. Some gter ma are authentic (although proper criteria for authenticity is a subject of debate in both traditional and modern sources), and some are clearly forgeries and fabricated antiquities. Gter ma are of three types: sa gter ("earth treasure"), dgongs gter ("mind treasure"), and dag snang ("pure vision"). Those physically discovered in caves and so on are sa gter; they may be revealed in a public gathering (khrom gter) or found privately (gsang gter) and then shown to others; they may be accompanied by a prophecy (lung bstan; gter lung; see VYĀKARAṆA) of the discovery, made at the time of concealment; the gter ma may have a guardian (gter srung), and the revealer (GTER STON) is often assisted by a ḌĀKINĪ. Dgongs gter are discovered in the mindstream of the revealer, placed there as seeds to be found, coming from an earlier lifetime, often as a direct disciple of PADMASAMBHAVA. Dag snang are discovered by the revealer through the power of the innate purity of the mind. Gter ma are associated most closely with the RNYING MA sect, although not exclusively so. The basic account of gter ma, in which myth and historical fact are interwoven, relates that prior to the persecution of Buddhism by GLANG DAR MA (reigned c. 838–842), PADMASAMBHAVA hid many teachings, often dictated to YE SHES MTSHO RGYAL, as treasures to be discovered in later times in order to ensure the continuation of the doctrine and to provide appropriate teachings for future generations. The first Tibetan gter ma appear sometime after the start of the second dispensation (PHYI DAR), c. 1000, with the rise of the new (GSAR MA) sects of BKA' GDAMS, SA SKYA, AND BKA' BRGYUD, who in many cases call into question the authenticity of earlier Tibetan practices and translations. Gter ma became more common in the thirteenth and early fourteenth centuries. Prominent among the revealers is PADMA LAS 'BREL RTSAL, a shadowy figure who revealed the RDZOGS CHEN SNYING THIG that KLONG CHEN RAB 'BYAMS PA then systematized into the definitive RDZOGS CHEN teachings. Klong chen pa's scholarly presentation was again made more accessible through a series of gter ma (called the KLONG CHEN SNYING THIG) discovered by 'JIGS MED GLING PA. These are the basis of the rdzogs chen teachings as they are commonly found today in most branches of the Rnying ma sect. According to traditional accounts, Padmasambhava taught a system of meditation called the MKHA' 'GRO SNYING THIG ("Heart Essence of the Ḍākinī") to PADMA GSAL, the daughter of king KHRI SRONG SDE BTSAN, in whose heart he had inscribed a sacred syllable after bringing her back from the dead. They were discovered there by Padma las 'brel rtsal and Klong chen pa, who are her reincarnations. Besides this widely acknowledged tradition, there are numerous other gter ma that form the basis of practices and rituals in specific Rnying ma monasteries. For example, the main line of teachings and consecrations (ABHIṢEKA) in the DPAL YUL monastery in the Khams region of eastern Tibet, and in its reestablished Indian branch near Mysore in South India, is based on gter ma teachings combining Rnying ma and Bka' brgyud practices, revealed by Mi 'gyur rdo rje and redacted by KARMA CHAGS MED; the gter ma discovered by PADMA GLING PA are held in great reverence by the 'BRUG PA BKA' BRGYUD sect in Bhutan; and the secret teachings of the fifth DALAI LAMA (1617–1682) that later locate and legitimate the role of the Dalai Lamas in the Dge lugs pa sect originated in gter ma that he revealed. The different gter ma were brought together in a quasi-canonical form by 'JAM MGON KONG SPRUL BLO GROS MTHA' YAS in his RIN CHEN GTER MDZOD ("Treasury of Precious Treasure Teachings"). It is believed that the sacred and even political space of Tibet is empowered through the discovery of gter ma and, by extension, that the religious practice of a region is empowered through the discovery of treasures within it.

**gter ston**. (tertön). In Tibetan, lit., "treasure revealer," a person who discovers GTER MA or "treasure," Tibetan Buddhist and BON sacred objects, including a wide range of manuscripts, relics, statuary, and ritual implements, which are presumed to have been buried in earlier periods for discovery later. See GTER MA.

**gter ston rgyal po lnga**. (tertön gyalpo nga). A Tibetan term, lit. "the five kingly treasure revealers," referring to a list of five renowned treasure revealers (GTER STON) believed to be reincarnations of the king KHRI SRONG LDE BTSAN. The list is found most often in writings of the RNYING MA sect of Tibetan Buddhism. The five include:

1. NYANG RAL NYI MA 'OD ZER
2. GURU CHOS KYI DBANG PHYUG

3. RDO RJE GLING PA
4. PADME GLING PA
5. 'JAM DBYANGS MKHYEN BRTSE DBANG PO

**gtong len**. (tonglen). In Tibetan, lit. "giving and taking"; a well-known BLO SBYONG (mind training) practice. In this practice, as the meditator inhales, he or she imagines all the suffering of all beings, in the form of smoke, darkness, and various frightening creatures, being lifted from the bodies of all beings and entering the meditator's body. Then, as he or she exhales, the meditator imagines all of his or her own happiness and merit (PUṆYA) going out to all beings in the form of light and descending upon them. The practice is considered to be one of the techniques for developing BODHICITTA and is often set forth in connection with the practice of exchanging self and other (PARĀTMAPARIVARTANA) described in the eighth chapter of the BODHICARYĀVATĀRA of ŚĀNTIDEVA. See BLO SBYONG TSHIG BRGYAD MA.

**gtor ma**. (torma). The Tibetan translation of the Sanskrit term bali (offering, tribute), an offering of food to propitiate a deity. There are ritual texts (S. balividhi) for constructing and offering gtor ma, differing based on the purpose of the offering and the status of the recipient. In Tibet the gtor ma is always a distinctive conical shape, and became a canvas for extremely ornate butter sculpture. The spectacular gtor ma ritual culminated in the gtor bzlog (tordok) or gtor rgyag (torgyak) on the last day of the Tibetan year, during which the monastic assembly would march out with the gtor ma. All negativities and bad spirits of the departing year are drawn to the offering, which is then hurled into a blazing pyre accompanied by a cacophony of instruments and the loud bangs of firecrackers. On the last of the fifteen days of festivities celebrating lo gsar (new year) in LHA SA, the bco lnga mchod pa competition to judge the best gtor ma was held; it is reported that some gtor ma were so high that ladders had to be used to reach the top; they were decorated with extremely ornate butter sculptures, including figures manipulated like puppets with hidden strings. There are a variety of gtor mas in Tibet, usually made of barley flour with butter if they are expected to last and be eaten, or with water if they are to be thrown out; they may be painted red if the recipient protector or deity is wrathful, and clear or whitish in color if in a peaceful form.

**Gtsang pa rgya ras Ye shes rdo rje**. (Tsangpa Gyare Yeshe Dorje) (1161–1211). The founder of the 'BRUG PA BKA' BRGYUD sect of Tibetan Buddhism, and considered to be the first in the line of 'BRUG CHEN INCARNATIONS that begins historically with Chos rje Kun dga' dpal' 'byor (Chöje Kunga Paljor, 1426/8–1476). His works include the *Rten 'brel rab bdun* ("Seven Auspicious Dharmas") and the *Ro snyom skor drug* ("Six Spheres of Equal Taste"), said to be teachings concealed as GTER MA (treasure) by RAS CHUNG PA, the disciple of MI LA RAS PA and discovered by Gtsang pa rgya ras. These works were systematized by PADMA DKAR PO, a prolific author and scholar, and fourth in the line of reincarnations. The students of Gtsang pa rgya ras founded three 'Brug pa bka' brgyud subsects; of the three, the so-called Bar 'Brug (middle Drukpa) was passed down through Gtsang pa rgya ras's family to the fourth incarnation, Padma dkar po. Of the two candidates to the lineage throne on his death, ZHABS DRUNG NGAG DBANG RNAM RGYAL fell afoul of strong political forces in Dbus (central Tibet) and was forced to flee to Bhutan where he founded the southern sect (Lho 'brug bka' brgyud) and became both the spiritual and temporal head of the country. The name of Bhutan, 'Brug yul (Drukpa Lands), stems from that time.

**Gtsang smyon Heruka**. (Tsangnyön Heruka) (1452–1507). Tibetan iconoclast, best known as Gtsang smyon, the "madman of Gtsang"; revered especially for his literary works, including the biography of eleventh-century master MI LA RAS PA. Gtsang smyon Heruka began his career as a monk, receiving Buddhist ordination at the age of seven. He studied various systems of tantra and meditation under his chief guru, the Bka' brgyud master Shes rab 'byams pa, and later under several Sa skya teachers. Discouraged by the limitations of life as a monk and scholar, he adopted the life of a wandering YOGIN, engaging in the unusual behavior for which he earned the appellation smyon pa, "madman." His actions have been interpreted as part of a fifteenth-century reaction and reform movement against the growing wealth and power of elite incarnation lineages and religious institutions of his day. He and other "mad yogins" affiliated with the Bka' brgyud sect, such as 'BRUG BA KUN LEGS, and the lesser known Dbu smyon Kun dga' bzang po (1458–1532), sought to reemphasize the importance of meditation and retreat over strict adherence to monastic discipline or intellectual study—a tradition reaching back to the renowned Bka' brgyud founder, Mi la ras pa. Gtsang smyon Heruka himself spent many years visiting the meditation caves and retreat sites associated with Mi la ras pa. He also attempted to preserve important Bka' brgyud instruction lineages that were in danger of being lost, and toward the end of his life compiled an enormous thirteen-volume synthesis of the aural instructions (snyan brgyud) stemming from three of Mi la ras pa's principal disciples, RAS CHUNG PA RDO RJE GRAGS, SGAM PO PA BSOD NAMS RIN CHEN, and Ngan rdzongs rdo rje rgyal po (late eleventh century). He visited Nepal on several occasions, directing the renovation of SVAYAṂBHŪ STŪPA, one of the Kathmandu Valley's principal Buddhist pilgrimage centers. He is perhaps best remembered as the author of the widely read MI LA RAS PA'I RNAM THAR ("Life of Milarepa") and MI LA RAS PA'I MGUR 'BUM ("Hundred Thousand Songs of Milarepa"), as well as a biography of Milarepa's guru MARPA CHOS KYI BLO GROS.

**Guanding jing**. (J. Kanjōgyō; K. Kwanjŏng kyŏng 灌頂經). In Chinese, "Consecration Scripture." Although the *Guanding jing* claims to be a translation by Śrīmitra (d. 343), the scripture is almost certainly a indigenous Chinese scripture (see

APOCRYPHA) composed in the mid-fifth century. The *Guanding jing* is largely a collection of twelve semi-independent scriptures on magical spells (DHĀRAṆĪ). They are the (1) spells of the 72,000 spirit kings that protect BHIKṢUs; (2) spells of the 120,000 spirit kings that protect BHIKṢUṆĪs; (3) protective spells of the three refuges and five precepts to be carried on one's person; (4) protective spells of the hundred-knotted spirit kings; (5) incantations of spirit kings who guard one's surroundings; (6) the circumstances of tombs and the spells of the four quarters; (7) devil-subduing seals and great spells; (8) great spells of Maṇiratna; (9) summoning the dragon kings of the five directions and treating pestilent infections; (10) the oracle of Brahmā; (11) rebirth in the ten pure lands of one's desire; and (12) eliminating faults and transcending life and death. The twelfth scripture is currently the oldest extant Chinese version of the BHAIṢAJYAGURUSŪTRA. The *Guanding jing* also contains one of the earliest extant Chinese descriptions of a full Buddhist consecration (ABHIṢEKA) ritual, and serves as an important source for studying the influence of Daoism on early Buddhism.

**Guang hongming ji**. (J. Kōgumyōshū; K. Kwang hongmyŏng chip 廣弘明集). In Chinese, "Expanded Collection on the Propagation and Clarification [of Buddhism]," a collection of materials pertaining to the propagation and protection of Buddhism in China, compiled by DAOXUAN in 644 CE. As the title indicates, the *Guang hongming ji* is an updated version of the HONGMING JI compiled by SENGYOU. Daoxuan's text, however, differs from Sengyou's in several respects. Unlike the *Hongming ji*, which focused on treatises written by the SAṂGHA, Daoxuan's text also cites non-Buddhist texts written by Daoists, monks' petitions to the court, court documents, imperial decrees, poetry, and songs. While the *Hongming ji* was primarily concerned with the Buddhists' attempts to protect their tradition from the attack of the Confucian elite who dominated the courts of the Five Dynasties, the *Guang hongming ji* had less to do with the Confucians than the Daoist priests of the Tang dynasty. Among the various sources cited in the *Guang hongming ji* are the Daoist renegade Zhen Luan's *Xiaodao lun* ("Laughing at the Dao Treatise") and DAO'AN's *Erjiao lun* ("Two Teachings Treatise"). The *Guang hongming ji* serves as an important source not only for understanding the different ways in which Chinese Buddhists sought to defend their "foreign" religion, but also for information on the relationship between Buddhism and Daoism in medieval China.

**Guangshengsi**. (廣勝寺). In Chinese, "Monastery of Vast Triumph"; located in the Zhaocheng county seat in southern Shanxi province, the monastery's foundation legend traces its history back to 147 CE. The monastery is comprised of two monastic compounds, called the lower (xiasi) and upper (shangsi) Guangsheng monasteries. The upper monastery was rebuilt in 769 CE during the Tang, when the Taizong emperor (r. 762–779 CE) bestowed upon it the current name of Guangsheng or "Vast Triumph." Upper Guangsheng monastery was known for housing both Buddhist relics and two editions of the Buddhist canon (DAZANGJING), one dating from the Jin dynasty (1115–1234 CE), the other from the Yuan (1271–1368 CE). Lower Guangsheng monastery was originally an independent monastery. It is unique in that its main shrine hall, which dates from 1319 CE during the Yuan dynasty, was not specifically Buddhist or Daoist but was instead dedicated to a local god—Mingying Wang, the King of Righteous Response. The monastery was later subsumed by its neighbor, Upper Guangsheng monastery, and since the Ming dynasty (1368–1644 CE) has been known as Lower Guangsheng monastery.

**Guangxiaosi**. (光孝寺). In Chinese, "Radiant Filiality Monastery"; located in Guangzhou, it was formerly the residence of Prince Zhao Jiande of the Western Han dynasty. In 401 CE, during the Eastern Jin dynasty (317–420), the GANDHĀRA monk, Dharmayaśas (Tanmoyeshe), is said to have converted the residence into a monastery. When BODHIDHARMA (c. early fifth century), the legendary founder of the CHAN school, traveled to China, he is said to have arrived in Guangzhou and visited the monastery before proceeding north. But the monk most closely associated with Guangxiaosi was a native of the region, HUINENG (638–713 CE), the putative sixth patriarch (LIUZU) of Chan Buddhism. Chan doxographies state that Huineng initially arrived at the monastery, which was then called Faxingsi, as a novice during the 660s. Huineng's arrival coincided with an ongoing debate among some resident monks: when the breeze blew a banner located nearby, was it the breeze or the banner that moved? Huineng famously replied that it was actually the minds of the two monks that moved. The story is commemorated in a hall constructed at the monastery named Banner Hall. Huineng is said to have accepted his monastic vows under a BODHI TREE located at the monastery, thus fulfilling a prophecy made over a century earlier, and later became its abbot. Huineng's monastery was renamed Guangxiaosi during the Song dynasty; by the Yuan dynasty, it had achieved fame for being the former residence of Zhao Jiande, as well as for housing the aforementioned bodhi tree and Banner Hall. During the Ming dynasty, the monastery was favored by poets seeking refuge from the summer heat. Three of the Pearl River delta's most celebrated poets, Ou Daren, Li Minbiao, and Liang Youyu, founded a poetry society while residing at the monastery. Guangxiaosi was rebuilt during the Qing dynasty (1644–1911 CE) in its present form. The monastery is also famous for housing the first iron STŪPAs in China, which still exist. The west courtyard houses the square West Iron Pagoda, which was cast in 963 CE, during the Five Dynasties period. Only three of the original seven stories still exist. The East Iron Pagoda, cast in 967 CE, was also seven stories high and is preserved on the monastery grounds.

**Guan Puxian pusa xingfa jing**. (J. Kan Fugen bosatsu gyōbōkyō; K. Kwan Pohyŏn posal haengbŏp kyŏng 觀普賢菩薩行法經). In Chinese, "Sūtra on the Procedures for Visualizing the Bodhisattva SAMANTABHADRA"; one of the "Three [Sister] Sūtras of the 'Lotus'" (FAHUA SANBU [JING]), along with the WULIANG YI JING ("Sūtra of Immeasurable Meanings") and the SADDHARMAPUṆḌARĪKASŪTRA ("Lotus Sūtra") itself. The extant text, in one roll, was translated into Chinese by Dharmamitra (356–442) sometime between 424 and 442; two earlier translations, neither of which is extant, are mentioned in the scriptural catalogues (JINGLU): the *Puxian guan jing* by *Gītamitra (c. fourth century) and the *Guan Puxian pusa jing*, attributed to KUMĀRAJĪVA. There is no extant Sanskrit recension of the scripture. While the *Wuliang yi jing* is presumed to be the prequel to the *Saddharmapuṇḍarīkasūtra*, the *Guan Puxian pusa xingfa jing* is usually considered its sequel, being similar in content to the twenty-eighth and final chapter of the *Saddharmapuṇḍarīkasūtra*. In this scripture, the Buddha provides a detailed account of a meditation that will generate a vision of the bodhisattva Samantabhadra in all his glory, including the majesty of the snowy-white elephant on which he rides. Once Samantabhadra is visible, he will then reveal to the meditator all the buddhas of the ten directions, as well as various other pure lands and bodhisattvas. The scripture concludes with Samantabhadra's explanation of how to conduct a repentance ritual that will purify the six sense organs, thus ensuring that the meditator will never again engage in unwholesome acts (AKUŚALA-KARMAN) and will no longer be subject to rebirth in the three realms of existence (TRILOKA[DHĀTU]).

**Guanshiyin**. (J. Kanzeon; Kwanseŭm 觀世音). In Chinese, "Perceiver of the World's Sounds"; one of the popular Chinese translations of the name of the bodhisattva AVALOKITEŚVARA. See GUANYIN.

**Guan Wuliangshou jing**. (S. *Amitāyurdhyānasūtra; J. Kan Muryōjukyō; K. Kwan Muryangsu kyŏng 觀無量壽經). In Chinese, "Sūtra on the Visualization of [the Buddha of] Immeasurable Life"; often called simply the *Guan jing*, or "Visualization Scripture." Along with the AMITĀBHASŪTRA and SUKHĀVATĪVYŪHASŪTRA, the *Guan Wuliangshou jing* has been considered one of the three central scriptures of the PURE LAND tradition(s) (JINGTU SANBU JING). The *Guan jing* was extremely influential in East Asian Buddhism for advocating specific types of visualizations or contemplations (guan) on the person of the buddha AMITĀBHA (C. Wuliangshou; S. Amitāyu), and for encouraging oral recitation of Amitābha's name (chengming; see NIANFO). Early commentaries on the scripture were written by SHANDAO (613–681), an important Chinese exponent of pure land practice, as well as by TIANTAI ZHIYI (538–597), and JINGYING HUIYUAN (523–592), all attesting to the text's centrality to the East Asian Buddhist tradition. Although the *Guan Wuliangshou jing* purports to be a translation by the monk KĀLAYAŚAS (fl. c. 383–442), no Sanskrit or Tibetan recension is known to have ever existed; Uighur versions of the *Guan Wuliangshou jing* are extant, but they are translations of the Chinese version. The scripture also contains specific Chinese influences, such as references to earlier Chinese translations of pure land materials and other contemplation sūtras (guan jing), which has suggested to some scholars that the text might be a Chinese indigenous composition (see APOCRYPHA). It is now generally accepted that the scripture outlines a visualization exercise that was practiced in Central Asia, perhaps specifically in the TURFAN region, but includes substantial Chinese admixtures. ¶ The *Guan Wuliangshou jing* tells the story of prince AJĀTAŚATRU who, at the urging of DEVADATTA, imprisons his father, king BIMBISĀRA, and usurps the throne. After Ajātaśatru learns that his mother, queen VAIDEHĪ, has been surreptitiously keeping her husband alive by sneaking food in to him, he puts her under house arrest as well. The distraught queen prays to the Buddha for release from her suffering and he immediately appears in her chambers. Vaidehī asks him to show her a land free from sorrow and he displays to her the numerous buddha fields (BUDDHAKṢETRA) throughout the ten directions (DAŚADIŚ) of the universe. Queen Vaidehī, however, chooses to be reborn in the buddha AMITĀBHA's pure land of SUKHĀVATĪ, so the Buddha instructs her in sixteen visualizations that ensure the meditator will take rebirth there, including visualizations on the setting sun, the lotus throne of Amitābha, Amitābha himself, as well as the bodhisattvas AVALOKITEŚVARA and MAHĀSTHĀMAPRĀPTA. The visualizations largely focus on the details of sukhāvatī's beauty, such as its beryl ground, jeweled trees, and pure water. In the last three visualizations, the Buddha expounds the nine grades of rebirth (JIUPIN) in that land, which became a favorite topic among exegetes in China, Korea, and Japan. The *Guan Wuliangshou jing* has also exerted much influence in the realm of art. A number of exquisite mural representations of sukhāvatī and the sixteen contemplations adorn the walls of the DUNHUANG cave complex, for example.

**Guanxiu**. (J. Kankyū; K. Kwanhyu 貫休). See CHANYUE GUANXIU.

**Guanyin**. (J. Kannon; K. Kwanŭm 觀音). In Chinese, "Perceiver of Sounds," an abbreviation of the longer name Guanshiyin (J. Kanzeon; K. Kwanseŭm; Perceiver of the World's Sounds); the most famous and influential BODHISATTVA in all of East Asia, who is commonly known in Western popular literature as "The Goddess of Mercy." Guanyin (alt. Guanshiyin) is the Chinese translation of AVALOKITEŚVARA, the bodhisattva of compassion; this rendering, popularized by the renowned Kuchean translator KUMĀRAJĪVA in his 405–406 CE translation of the SADDHARMAPUṆḌARĪKASŪTRA ("Lotus Sūtra"), derives from an earlier form of this bodhisattva's name, Avalokitasvara, which is attested in some Sanskrit manuscripts of this scripture; Kumārajīva interprets this name as "gazing" (avalokita; C. guan) on the "sounds" (svara; C. yin) [of this wailing "world" (C. shi) of suffering]. Avalokitasvara was supplanted during the seventh century CE by the standard Sanskrit form Avalokiteśvara, the "gazing" (avalokita) "lord" (īśvara); this later form is followed in XUANZANG's Chinese rendering Guanzizai (J. Kanjizai; K. Kwanjajae), as found in his 649 CE translation of the PRAJÑĀPĀRAMITĀHṚDAYASŪTRA ("Heart Sūtra"). The primary textual source for Guanyin worship is the twenty-fifth chapter of the *Saddharmapuṇḍarīkasūtra*; that chapter is devoted to the bodhisattva and circulated widely as an independent text in East Asia. The chapter guarantees that if anyone in danger calls out Guanshiyin's name with completely sincerity, the bodhisattva will "perceive the sound" of his call and rescue him from harm. Unlike in India and Tibet, Avalokiteśvara took on female form in East Asia around the tenth century. In traditional China, indigenous forms of Guanyin, such as BAIYI GUANYIN (White-Robed Guanyin), Yulan Guanyin (Guanyin with Fish Basket), SHUIYUE GUANYIN (Moon in Water Guanyin), Songzi Guanyin (Child-Granting Guanyin), MALANG FU, as well as Princess MIAOSHAN, became popular subjects of worship. Guanyin was worshipped in China by both monastics and laity, but her functions differed according to her manifestation. Guanyin thus served as a protectress against personal misfortune, a symbol of Buddhist ideals and restraint, or a granter of children. Various religious groups and lay communities also took one of her various forms as their patroness, and in this role, Guanyin was seen as a symbol of personal salvation. Beginning in the tenth century, these different manifestations of Guanyin proliferated throughout China through indigenous sūtras (see APOCRYPHA), secular narratives, miracle tales, monastic foundation legends, and images. In later dynasties, and up through the twentieth century, Guanyin worship inspired both male and female religious groups. For example, White Lotus groups (see BAILIAN SHE; BAILIAN JIAO) during the Song dynasty included members from both genders, who were active in erecting STŪPAs and founding cloisters that promoted Guanyin worship. In the twentieth century, certain women's groups were formed that took Princess Miaoshan's refusal to marry as inspiration to reject the institution of marriage themselves and, under the auspices of a Buddhist patron, pursue other secular activities as single women. ¶ In Japan, Kannon was originally introduced during the eighth century and took on additional significance as a female deity. For example, Kannon was often invoked by both pilgrims and merchants embarking on long sea voyages or overland travel. Invoking Kannon's name was thought to protect travelers from seven different calamities, such as fire, flood, storms, demons, attackers, lust and material desires, and weapons. Moreover, Kannon worship in Japan transcended sectarian loyalties, and there were numerous miracle tales concerning Kannon that circulated throughout the Japanese isles. ¶ In Korea, Kwanŭm is by far the most popular bodhisattva and is also known there as a deity who offers succor and assistance in difficult situations. The cult of Kwanŭm flourished initially under the patronage of the aristocracy in both the Paekche and Silla kingdoms, and historical records tell of supplications made to Kwanŭm for the birth of children or to protect relatives who were prisoners of war or who had been lost at sea. Hence, while the cult of AMITĀBHA was principally focused on spiritual liberation in the next life, Kwanŭm instead was worshipped for protection in this life. Still today, Kwanŭm is an object of popular worship and a focus of ritual chanting in Korean Buddhist monasteries by both monks and, especially, laywomen (and usually chanted in the form Kwanseŭm).

**Guanzizai**. (J. Kanjizai; K. Kwanjajae 觀自在). In Chinese, "Gazing Lord"; later Chinese translation of the name of the bodhisattva AVALOKITEŚVARA. See GUANYIN.

**Gudō Tōshoku**. (愚堂東寔) (1579–1661). Japanese ZEN master in the RINZAISHŪ. Gudō Tōshoku was born in Mino, present-day Gifu prefecture. In his twenties, he went on a pilgrimage around the country with several other young monks, such as DAIGU SŌCHIKU and Ungo Kiyō (1582–1659), in search of a teacher. Gudō later travelled to Shōtakuin, a memorial chapel (tatchū) at the Rinzai monastery of MYŌSHINJI, where he found a teacher by the name of Yōzan Keiyō (1559–1626). Gudō later became Yōzan's DHARMA heir (see FASI). In 1614, Gudō became the abbot of a dilapidated monastery named Zuiganji in his native Mino. He was also invited as the abbot of the nearby monastery of Shōdenji. In 1621, he was once again invited to restore Daisenji, another dilapidated monastery in Mino. With the support of powerful local patrons, Gudō was able to restore all these monasteries. In 1628, he became the abbot of Myōshinji and served as abbot a total of three times. During his stay at Myōshinji, Gudō led a faction within the monastery that opposed tendering an invitation to the Chinese Chan master YINYUAN LONGQI to serve as abbot of the monastery. Yinyuan instead was invited to Uji in 1661 to establish a new monastery, MANPUKUJI, which led to the foundation of the ŌBAKUSHŪ of Japanese Zen. Gudō later returned to his efforts to restore monasteries throughout the country. During the Tokugawa period, monasteries were mandated by the military government (bakufu) to affiliate themselves with a main monastery (honzan), thus becoming branch temples (matsuji). The monasteries that Gudō restored became branch temples of Myōshinji. Through Gudō's efforts, the influence of Myōshinji thus grew extensively. The influential Zen master HAKUIN EKAKU traced his lineage back to Gudō through the latter's disciple Shidō Bunan (1603–1676) and Shidō's disciple Dōkyō Etan (1642–1721). Gudō later received the honorary title Daien Hōkan kokushi (State Preceptor Great and Perfect Jeweled Mirror). His teachings can be found in the *Hōkanroku*.

**Gu ge**. The name of a kingdom in Mnga' ris (western Tibet) founded by descendants of the royal line that fled after the breakup of the central Tibetan kingdom following the rule and assassination of GLANG DAR MA. The kingdom lasted until the sixteenth century, with its capitals at Rtsa rang, THO LING, and DUNG DKAR; it reached its zenith during the tenth to thirteenth centuries. During the second half of the tenth century, the king of the Gu ge kingdom Lha bla ma YE SHES 'OD, a strong supporter of Buddhism, sent the translator RIN CHEN BZANG PO and a number of other Tibetans to India to study Buddhism. Rin chen bzang po's return in 978 marks the beginning of the later spread of Buddhism (PHYI DAR). Ye shes 'od's nephew BYANG CHUB 'OD successfully invited the famous Indian teacher ATIŚA DĪPAṂKARAŚRĪJÑĀNA to Tibet; under him and his successors, temple building and scholarship flourished. The sculpture and wall paintings executed by artists from Kashmir and other areas, whom they invited to decorate the temples in their capitals as well as at ALCHI, TA PHO, and numerous smaller shrines, are still extant. Because of their remoteness, and because some of the areas formerly part of the Gu ge kingdom are now under the political jurisdiction of India, many of the temples from that period have escaped destruction and contain some of the most important examples of Buddhist art from that period.

**guhyābhiṣeka**. (T. gsang dbang; C. mimi guanding; J. himitsukanjō; K. pimil kwanjŏng 秘密灌頂). In Sanskrit, "secret empowerment," the second of the four empowerments or initiations employed in the ANUTTARAYOGA tantras, the other three being the vase empowerment (KALAŚĀBHIṢEKA), which precedes the secret empowerment (guhyābhiṣeka), and the knowledge of the consort empowerment (PRAJÑĀJÑĀNĀBHIṢEKA) and the fourth empowerment (CATURTHĀBHIṢEKA), which both follow it. The secret empowerment is intended for initiates who have already received the full vase empowerment. In the secret empowerment, the disciple presents his master with a fully qualified consort. The consort, representing wisdom (PRAJÑĀ), and the master, representing method (UPĀYA), then unite sexually. A drop of the fluid that results from their union, called BODHICITTA, is then placed on the tongue of the disciple, who swallows it. In the next empowerment, "the knowledge of the consort," the disciple then engages in sexual union with the same consort, inducing increasing levels of bliss. Although later monastic exegetes would interpret these empowerments symbolically, it appears that they were actually practiced as the tantric systems developed in India, and they continued to be practiced among certain groups of adepts in Tibet.

**Guhyagarbhatantra**. (T. Gsang ba'i snying po'i rgyud). In Sanskrit, the "Secret Essence Tantra," a central text of the RNYING MA sect of Tibetan Buddhism and the RDZOGS CHEN tradition. The tantra is regarded as an expression of the enlightened intention of the primordial DHARMAKĀYA, the buddha SAMANTABHADRA. It is a work of Indic origin, appearing around mid-eighth century, probably after the GUHYASAMĀJATANTRA. It is unclear whether the text was called *Guhyagarbha* at the time of its composition or whether that title was added later. In DUNHUANG documents, it is usually referred to as the *Māyājālatantra*. By the time of a late tenth-century manuscript, it is called the *Guhyagarbhatantra*. The later Tibetan tradition identifies the *Guhyagarbha* as the root tantra of the MAHĀYOGA class, as well as the main tantra of the MĀYĀJĀLA cycle of tantras, a group of eighteen mahāyoga tantras. The *Guhyagarbha* was particularly influential in late eighth- and early ninth-century Tibet, when it was a principal inspiration for the early rdzogs chen movement. Its Māyājāla MAṆḌALA of one hundred deities (forty-two peaceful and fifty-eight wrathful) was widely employed. In the PHYI DAR period, the tantra was condemned by a number of GSAR MA figures (especially the eleventh-century translator 'Gos khug pa lhas btsas) as an apocryphal Tibetan creation, probably because of its importance in the Rnying ma sect and in the still-developing rdzogs chen tradition. However, a Sanskrit copy of the tantra was discovered at BSAM YAS and verified by ŚĀKYAŚRĪBHADRA. In the thirteenth century, Lcom ldan rig ral ordered a new translation on the basis of the manuscript. Major commentators include Rong zom chos bzang (eleventh century) and KLONG CHEN RAB 'BYAMS, and eventually, two schools of interpretations formed, the Rong klong lugs and the Zur lugs. The tantra exists in three distinct versions: in twenty-two, forty-six, and eighty-two chapters. The shorter version is considered the root tantra and is the subject of most commentary.

**guhyamantrayāna**. (T. gsang sngags kyi theg pa). In Sanskrit, "secret MANTRA vehicle," a synonym for the VAJRAYĀNA, used especially in Tibet. According to the contextual etymology, tantric practice is secret both in the sense that it is not taught openly and because it remains secret, i.e., not understood, by those who are not suitable vessels for it. In this context, mantra is glossed to mean "mind protection," in the sense that it protects the mind from ordinary appearances. The *guhyamantrayāna* is regarded as one of the two branches of the MAHĀYĀNA, together with the PĀRAMITĀYĀNA.

**Guhyasamājatantra**. (T. Gsang ba 'dus pa'i rgyud; C. Yiqie rulai jingang sanye zuishang mimi dajiaowang jing; J. Issainyorai kongōsangōsaijōhimitsu daikyōōgyō; K. Ilch'e yŏrae kŭmgang samŏp ch'oesang pimil taegyowang kyŏng 一切如來金剛三業最上秘密大教王經). In Sanskrit, "Secret Assembly Tantra"; referred to in Tibet as the "king of tantras" (rgyud kyi rgyal po), it is among the most important of what later come to be called ANUTTARAYOGATANTRAs, or highest yoga tantras. It is also classified as a "father tantra" (PITṚTANTRA). The text was likely composed sometime between about 750 and 850 CE. It consists of eighteen chapters, the last of which is a supplement, referred to as the uttaratantra. The *Guhyasamāja* is one of the earliest tantras to present overtly antinomian practices, notably of a sexual nature, as well as the practices of ingesting impure substances. The text begins with a surprising rendition of the opening line of a Buddhist sūtra (see EVAṂ MAYĀ ŚRUTAM), when it states, "Thus have I heard. At one time the Bhagavān was residing in the vaginas of the women who are the vajra essence of the body, speech, and mind of all the tathāgatas." Such passages led to the development of sophisticated hermeneutical systems for interpreting the tantras to discover their hidden meaning. Important Indian commentaries on this tantra include the PAÑCAKRAMA attributed to NĀGĀRJUNA, the *Caryāmelāpakapradīpa* attributed to ĀRYADEVA, and the *Pradīpoddyotana* attributed to CANDRAKĪRTI. In the MAṆḌALA associated with the Ārya tradition of commentary (deriving from Nāgārjuna) there are thirty-two deities. The central deity of the maṇḍala is Guhyasamāja, a manifestation of AKṢOBHYA, surrounded by VAIROCANA in the east, RATNASAMBHAVA (or Ratnaketu) in the south, AMITĀBHA in the west, and AMOGHASIDDHI in the north, each in sexual union with a consort. The central deity is blue in color, with three faces and six arms. Seated in the posture of sexual union, he embraces his consort Sparśavajra. In addition, there are the ten "fierce kings" (krodharāja), eight bodhisattvas, and four goddesses. Like other tantras of its class, the SĀDHANAS of the Guhyasamāja set forth the practice of the stage of generation (UTPATTIKRAMA) and the stage of completion (NIṢPANNAKRAMA), with its attendant sexual yogas, toward the achievement of an illusory body (MĀYĀKĀYA). The text was translated into Chinese by Dānapāla around 1002, but was not particularly influential in East Asian Buddhism, where its explicit sexual language offended more prudish Confucian sensibilities. It was translated into Tibetan in the eleventh century by RIN CHEN BZANG PO and Śraddhākaravarman. In Tibet, the tantra was highly influential, ranking in importance with the HEVAJRATANTRA, CAKRASAṂVARATANTRA, and KĀLACAKRATANTRA.

**Guhyasiddhi**. (T. Gsang ba grub pa). A tantric work by Padmavajra or Devacandra, probably written in the ninth century; it praises the GUHYASAMĀJATANTRA and posits the bliss of sexual union as a prerequisite for attaining the highest, essenceless state that is beyond the contemplation even of the Buddha.

**Guifeng Zongmi**. (J. Keihō Shūmitsu; K. Kyubong Chongmil 圭峰宗密) (780–841). Chinese CHAN master and historian; putative fifth patriarch of the HUAYAN tradition and successor in the Heze school of CHAN; best known for positing the fundamental harmony between the scriptural teachings of Buddhism and Chan practice. Zongmi was a native of Xichong in present-day Sichuan province. Although little is known of his early life, Zongmi is said to have received a classical Confucian education. In 804, Zongmi encountered the monk Daoyuan (d.u.), purportedly a fourth-generation lineage holder of the Heze line of Chan (see HEZE SHENHUI), and became his student. During this period, Zongmi also carried on his studies of the YUANJUE JING. In 808, Zongmi received the full monastic precepts from Daoyuan, who then recommended the monk Nanyin Weizhong (d. 821) as a suitable teacher. In 810, Zongmi met the monk Lingfeng (d.u.), a disciple of the Huayan monk CHENGGUAN, at the monastery of Huijuesi. Two years later Zongmi began his studies of the AVATAṂSAKASŪTRA under CHENGGUAN in Chang'an. In 816, Zongmi began his residence at the monastery of Zhijusi on ZHONGNANSHAN and in 821 he retired to the temple Caotangsi on Gui peak (Guifeng), whence he acquired his toponym. There, Zongmi devoted himself to such works as his influential commentary on the *Yuanjue jing*, the *Yuanjue jing dashu*. In 828, Zongmi was invited to the palace and given a purple robe and the title Dade (Great Virtue). During his stay at the capital he met many important statesmen including Pei Xiu (787–860). Zongmi was a prolific writer whose works include commentaries on the *Avataṃsakasūtra*, VAJRACCHEDIKĀPRAJÑĀPĀRAMITĀSŪTRA, DASHENG QIXIN LUN, MAHĀPARINIRVĀṆASŪTRA, SIFEN LÜ ("Four-Part Vinaya"), and others. He also composed a massive, 100-roll history of the Chan school, the *Chanyuan zhuquanji* ("Collected Writings on the Source of Chan"), only the prolegomenon to which is extant (see CHANYUAN ZHUQUANJI DUXU). Zongmi's writings were extremely influential in the mature Korean SŎN school and, especially, in the thought and practice of POJO CHINUL (1158–1210), who drew on Zongmi to advocate an accord between the traditions of Sŏn (C. Chan; meditation) and Kyo (C. JIAO; doctrine). See also LINGZHI; FANZHAO.

**guiku**. (J. kikutsu; K. kwigul 鬼窟). In Chinese, "ghost cave," a CHAN Buddhist expression referring to a fallacious kind of meditative state or spiritual understanding, wherein the practitioner mistakes the nihilistic void he experiences for the realization of emptiness (ŚŪNYATĀ), stagnant inactivity for tranquility, or gratuitous sensory deprivation for freedom from mental afflictions. Those misled or mired in this trap often profess denial of, or apathy toward, conditioned reality as well as its causal and karmic laws and the apparent suffering that sentient beings experience. For these reasons, this is also called "the pit of spurious liberation" (jia jietuo keng) and is one of the dangers about which Chan teachers vehemently caution their students. By extension, the fallacious view that there is no fruition of action and that ultimate reality consists of utter vacuity is called guijian—"the view of a ghost," who dwells in the aforementioned cave.

**Guishan jingce**. [alt. Weishan jingce] (J. Isan kyōsaku [alt. keisaku]; K. Wisan kyŏngch'aek 潙山警策). In Chinese, "Guishan's Admonitions," also known as the *Guishan Dayuan chanshi jingce*. This treatise by the CHAN master GUISHAN LINGYOU (771–853) warns novices against laziness and lays out in straightforward fashion the proper manner of cultivating oneself. Along with the YIJIAO JING and the SISHI'ER ZHANG JING, the *Guishan jingce* has been cherished by the CHAN tradition for its simple and accessible style of writing. Sometime during the late Tang and early Song dynasties, the three texts were edited together as the FOZU SANJING ("The Three Scriptures of the Buddhas and Patriarchs") and were recommended to neophytes in Chan practice. (Note in this and following entries that both pronunciations for the Sinograph Gui/Wei are attested in Chinese dictionaries of historical phonology, but in modern times the character is more commonly pronounced Wei.)

**Guishan Lingyou**. [alt. Weishan Lingyou] (J. Isan Reiyū; K. Wisan Yŏngu 潙山靈祐) (771–853). Chinese CHAN master and cofounder of the GUIYANG ZONG of the mature Chan tradition. Guishan was a native of Fuzhou prefecture in present-day Fujian province. He was ordained at the age of fifteen and studied SŪTRA and VINAYA at Longxingsi in Hangzhou prefecture (present-day Zhejiang province). Later, Guishan became the disciple of the eminent Chan master BAIZHANG HUAIHAI (720–814) of Hongzhou prefecture (present-day Jiangxi province). Along with HUANGBO XIYUN (d. 850?), Guishan became one of Baizhang's most prominent disciples and an emblematic teacher of Tang-dynasty Chan. He later moved to Guishan, whence he acquired his toponym, and taught more than forty close disciples. Among his disciples, the most important is YANGSHAN HUIJI (807–883). The names of the mountains on which Guishan and his student Yangshan resided were used collectively to refer to their prosperous Chan lineage, the Guiyang. He was later bestowed the title Chan master Dayuan (Great and Perfect). His teachings are recorded in the *Tanzhou Guishan Lingyou chanshi yulu* and GUISHAN JINGCE.

**Guiyang zong**. [alt. Weiyang zong] (J. Igyōshū; K. Wiang chong 潙仰宗). In Chinese, the "Guiyang school," one of the "five houses" (wu jia; see WU JIA QI ZONG), or distinct schools, that developed within the mature Chinese CHAN lineage during the late-Tang dynasty, or c. ninth century CE. The Guiyang school is named after its cofounders, GUISHAN LINGYOU (771–853) and YANGSHAN HUIJI (807–883), whose lineage derives from the HONGZHOU school of MAZU DAOYI (709–788) and BAIZHANG HUAIHAI (720–814). The Guiyang school is recognized for its distinctive pedagogical style, which privileged nonverbal expressions of enlightenment over verbal descriptions. For example, once Lingyou's teacher, Huaihai, placed a water jug before the assembly of monks and asked them, "If you don't call this a water jug, what can you call it?" Lingyou's response was to kick over the jug and walk away. This combination of action and silence was said to be the way in which the Guiyang school would express the relationship between essence (TI) and function (YONG). The Guiyang school is also known for its use of circular figures, including an intricate set of ninety-seven circular symbols that Yangshan Huiji used to express different aspects of Buddhist ontology and soteriology. Although the Guiyang zong did not survive into the Song dynasty as an active lineage, it remained an integral part of the retrospective imagining of the Chan tradition that took place during the Song.

**guṇa**. (T. yon tan; C. gongde; J. kudoku; K. kongdŏk 功德). In Sanskrit and Pāli, lit. "string," or "strand," by extension a "quality" or "spiritual virtue." In the sense of a "quality," or "constituent part," the term appears in lists such as the five "strands" or "aspects" of "sensuality" (kāmaguṇa), viz., the sensual pleasures associated with the five physical senses. Guṇa as "spiritual virtue" or "meritorious quality" (S. guṇa; C. gongde) is sometimes contrasted with "merit" (S. PUṆYA; C. fude), i.e., practices that lead to worldly rewards and/or better rebirths but not necessarily to enlightenment. In general, such religious deeds as building monasteries, erecting STŪPAS, making images of the Buddha, transcribing sūtras, and chanting all help to generate merit that can lead to better quality of life in this and other existences but will not in themselves produce the spiritual virtue (guṇa) that will be sufficient to bring about liberation from the cycle of rebirth (SAṂSĀRA). See also GUṆAPĀRAMITĀ.

**Guṇabhadra**. (C. Qiunabatuoluo; J. Gunabaddara; K. Kunabaltara 求那跋陀羅) (394–468). Indian scholiast and major translator of Buddhist scriptures into Chinese during the Liu Song period (420–479). Born in central India into a brāhmaṇa family, he is said to have studied in his youth the five traditional Indian sciences, as well as astronomy, calligraphy, mathematics, medicine, and magic. He was converted to Buddhism and began systematically to study Buddhist texts, starting with the ABHIDHARMA and proceeding through the most influential MAHĀYĀNA texts, such as the MAHĀPRAJÑĀPĀRAMITĀSŪTRA and AVATAṂSAKASŪTRA. Around 435, he departed from Sri Lanka for China, arriving in Guangzhou by sea. In China, he devoted himself to teaching and translating Buddhist scriptures, carrying out most of his translations of Mahāyāna and mainstream Buddhist texts while residing at Qiyuansi in Jiankang and Xinsi in Jingzhou. He translated a total of fifty-two scriptures in 134 rolls, including the SAṂYUKTĀGAMA and the PRAKARAṆAPĀDA [ŚĀSTRA], both associated with the SARVĀSTIVĀDA school, such seminal Mahāyāna texts as the ŚRĪMĀLĀDEVĪSIṂHANĀDASŪTRA and the LAṄKĀVATĀRASŪTRA. In the LENGQIE SHIZI JI, a CHAN genealogical history associated with the Northern school (BEI ZONG) of the early Chan tradition, Guṇabhadra is placed before BODHIDHARMA in the Chan patriarchal lineage, perhaps because of his role in translating the *Laṅkāvatārasūtra*, an important scriptural influence in the early Chan school.

**Guṇānanda**. (1823–1890). Also known as Migettuwatte Guṇānanda Thera; prominent figure in the Buddhist revival in Ceylon (now Sri Lanka) during the 1860s. Born into a wealthy Buddhist family in Mohottiwatta (Migettuwatta), near Balapitiya in southern Sri Lanka, as a child he studied the Bible and Christianity with a Roman Catholic priest at a local church. He was ordained as a novice Buddhist monk in 1835 and received full ordination in 1844. Guṇānanda is best known for his involvement in five debates between Christian missionaries and Buddhist monks. (He was a contemporary of SUMAṄGALA, who helped him prepare for the debates.) An impressive orator, Guṇānanda's extensive knowledge of both Christian and Buddhist doctrine allowed him to present a nuanced critique of Christianity and the superiority of Buddhism. The last of the debates, between Guṇānanda and Reverend David de Silva, took place at Panadura over two days in 1873, with an audience of some five to seven thousand spectators. The audience included the ten-year-old David Hevavitarne, who would later become ANAGĀRIKA DHARMAPĀLA. An edited transcript of the debate, known as the *Pānaduravādaya*, was published in English in the book *Buddhism and Christianity Face to Face* in 1878. This book inspired Colonel HENRY STEEL OLCOTT and Madame HELENA PETROVNA BLAVATSKY, founders of the Theosophical Society, to travel to Ceylon, where they played active roles in the revival of Buddhism. Guṇānanda wrote many articles and edited three texts on Buddhism. He also sought to revive Sinhala language and literature.

**guṇapāramitā**. (T. yon tan pha rol tu phyin pa; C. gongde boluomi; J. kudokuharamitsu; K. kongdŏk paramil 功德波羅蜜). In Sanskrit, "the perfection of qualities," referring to the four salutary qualities of the TATHĀGATAGARBHA: permanence, purity, bliss, and self, as described in the ŚRĪMĀLĀDEVĪSIṂHANĀDASŪTRA. These qualities are in distinction to the four perverted views (VIPARYĀSA), where ignorant sentient beings regard the conditioned realm of SAṂSĀRA as being permanent, pure, blissful, and self when in fact it is impermanent (ANITYA), impure (aśubha), suffering (DUḤKHA), and not-self (ANĀTMAN). More specifically, according to the *Ratnagotravibhāgavyākyā*, sentient beings assume that all the conditioned phenomena they experience are permanent and real: they consider their own bodies to be pure, regard their five aggregates (SKANDHA) as having a perduring self (ĀTMAN), falsely imagine permanence in the transitory, and mistakenly regard saṃsāra as a source of real happiness. In order to counter these attachments, the Buddha therefore taught that saṃsāra is impermanent, impure, suffering, and not-self. However, the *Ratnagotravibhāgavyākyā* says it would be wrong to assume that these four qualities also apply to the tathāgatagarbha or the DHARMAKĀYA; the Buddha teaches that it is endowed with the four guṇapāramitā, or perfect qualities, of permanence, purity, bliss, and self. The FOXING LUN ("Buddha-Nature Treatise") additionally presents the guṇapāramitā as resulting from the perfection of four soteriological practices, e.g., bliss refers to the condition of being free from suffering, which is experienced through cultivating a SAMĀDHI that overcomes wrong conceptions of emptiness (ŚŪNYATĀ); permanence indicates the endless variety of acts that bodhisattvas cultivate on the path of great compassion (MAHĀKARUṆĀ), etc. This positive valorization of the qualities of the tathāgatagarbha serves to counteract any mistaken tendency toward nihilism that might be prompted by the apophatic language used within the PRAJÑĀPĀRAMITĀ literature or the MADHYAMAKA school.

**Guṇaprabha**. (T. Yon tan 'od; C. Deguang/Junabolapo; J. Tokkō/Kunaharaba; K. Tŏkkwang/Kunaballaba 德光/瞿拏鉢剌婆) (d.u.; c. seventh century). Indian YOGĀCĀRA scholar and VINAYA specialist. In the Tibetan tradition, he is considered one of the most important of the Indian scholars because of his exposition of the vinaya. In the list of the "six ornaments and two supreme ones of JAMBUDVĪPA," the six ornaments are NĀGĀRJUNA and ĀRYADEVA, ASAṄGA and VASUBANDHU, and DIGNĀGA and DHARMAKĪRTI; the two supreme ones are Guṇaprabha and ŚĀKYAPRABHA. Guṇaprabha is said to have been an adviser to King Harṣa, who unified most of northern India following the demise of the Gupta empire. Born into a brāhmaṇa family in MATHURĀ during the seventh century, Guṇaprabha is said to have first studied the MAHĀYĀNA teachings and wrote several treatises on YOGĀCĀRA. He is known as the author of the *Bodhisattvabhūmivṛtti*, a commentary on the BODHISATTVABHŪMI, the *Bodhisattvaśīlaparivartabhāṣya*, an expansion of that commentary, and the *Pañcaskandhavivaraṇa*, an exegesis of VASUBANDHU's work. Subsequently, this same Guṇaprabha seems to have abandoned Yogācāra for ŚRĀVAKAYĀNA teachings and thereafter devoted several of his works to critiquing various aspects of the Mahāyāna. (There is some controversy as to whether Guṇaprabha the Yogācāra teacher is the same as Guṇaprabha the vinaya specialist, but prevailing scholarly opinion now accepts that they are identical.) Taking up residence at a monastery in Mathurā, he became a master of the vinaya, with a specialty in the monastic code of the MŪLASARVĀSTIVĀDA school (see MŪLASARVĀSTIVĀDA VINAYA). His most influential work is the VINAYASŪTRA. Despite its title, the work is not a sūtra (in the sense of a work ascribed to the Buddha) but is instead an authored work composed of individual aphoristic statements (sūtra). The text offers a summary or condensation of the massive Mūlasarvāstivāda vinaya. At approximately one quarter the length of this larger vinaya, Guṇaprabha's abridgment seems to have functioned as a kind of primer on the monastic code, omitting lengthy passages of scripture and providing the code of conduct that monks were expected to follow. In this sense, the text is an important work for determining what lived monastic practice may actually have been like in medieval India. The *Vinayasūtra* became the most important vinaya text for Tibetan Buddhism, being studied in all of the major sects; in the DGE LUGS, it is one of the five books (GZHUNG LNGA) that served as the basis of the monastic curriculum. According to legend, Guṇaprabha traveled to the TUṢITA heaven in order to discuss with MAITREYA his remaining doubts regarding ten points of doctrine. The accounts of this trip say that Guṇaprabha did not learn anything, either because Maitreya was not an ordained monk and hence was unable to teach him anything or because Maitreya saw that Guṇaprabha did not require any additional teaching. XUANZANG writes about Guṇaprabha in his DA TANG XIYU JI ("Great Tang Dynasty Record of [Travels to] the Western Regions").

**Guṇavarman**. (C. Qiunabamo; J. Gunabatsuma; K. Kunabalma 求那跋摩) (367–431 CE). A Kashmiri monk who was an important early translator of Buddhist VINAYA and BODHISATTVA preceptive materials into Chinese. He was a prince of Kubhā, who was ordained at the age of twenty and eventually became known as a specialist in the Buddhist canon (TREPIṬAKA). Upon his father's death, he was offered the throne, but refused, and instead embarked on travels throughout Asia to preach the dharma, including to Java, where he helped to establish the Buddhist tradition. Various miracles are associated with the places he visited, such as fragrance wafting in the air when he meditated and a dragon-like creature who was seen ascending to heaven in his presence. In 424 CE, Guṇavarman traveled to China and was invited by Emperor Wen of the Liu Song dynasty to come to the capital in Nanjing. Upon his arrival, a monastery was built in his honor and Guṇavarman lectured there on various sūtras. During his sojourn in China, he translated some eighteen rolls of seminal Buddhist texts into Chinese, including the BODHISATTVABHŪMI, and several other works associated with the BODHISATTVAŚĪLA, the DHARMAGUPTAKA VINAYA (SIFEN LÜ), and monastic and lay precepts. Guṇavarman was a central figure in founding the order of nuns (BHIKṢUṆĪ) in China and he helped arrange the ordination of several Chinese nuns whose hagiographies are recorded in the BIQIUNI ZHUAN.

**Guoqing bailu**. (J. Kokusei hyakuroku; K. Kukch'ŏng paengnok 國清百録). In Chinese, "One Hundred Records from Guoqing [Monastery]," compiled by the TIANTAI ZONG monk GUANDING. Although the title refers to one hundred records, the *Guoqing bailu* in fact contains 104 documents that Guanding compiled in memory of his teacher TIANTAI ZHIYI. These documents include Zhiyi's letters, memorial tablets, imperial decrees, ritual manuals, and monastic rules. The *Guoqing bailu* provides a wealth of information on Zhiyi's thought and career.

**guoshi**. (J. kokushi; K. kuksa 國師). In Chinese, "state preceptor," a high ecclesiastical office in East Asian Buddhist religious institutions. The first record of a "state preceptor" in China occurs during the reign of Emperor Wenxian (r. 550–559) of the Northern Qi dynasty, who is said to have appointed the monk Fachang (d.u.) as a guoshi after listening to his disquisition at court on the MAHĀPARINIRVĀṆASŪTRA. During the Tang dynasty, many renowned monks were appointed as guoshi, including FAZANG (643–712) as the Kangzang guoshi, CHENGGUAN (738–839) as the Qingliang guoshi, and NANYANG HUIZHONG (d. 775) as the Nanyang guoshi. In Japan, the term kokushi was used during the Nara period to refer to the highest ecclesiastical office accredited to each province (koku) by the central government. In Korea, kuksa were appointed from the Silla through early Chosŏn dynasties and the term referred to a senior monk who served as a symbolic religious teacher and adviser to the state. The kuksa system appears to have become firmly established in Korea during the Koryŏ dynasty, which treated Buddhism as a virtual state religion. The first king of the Koryŏ dynasty, Wang Kŏn (T'aejo, r. 918–943), established a system of "royal preceptors" (wangsa) for his own religious edification, in distinction to the "state preceptors" who ministered to the government more broadly. The institution of ecclesiastical examinations (SŬNGKWA) during the reign of the king Kwangjong (r. 949–975) further systematized the appointments of both kuksa and wangsa. The kuksa and wangsa were compared to the parents of sentient beings and were thus placed at a status higher than even the king himself in state ceremonies. A monk could be posthumously appointed as a kuksa, and it was common during the Koryŏ dynasty for the king to reverentially appoint his wangsa as a kuksa following his spiritual adviser's death. Because Confucian ideologues during the late Koryŏ criticized the political roles played by kuksa and wangsa as examples of the corruption of Buddhism, the offices were eventually abolished during the reign of the third king of the Confucian-oriented Chosŏn dynasty, T'aejong (r. 1400–1418).

**guru**. (T. bla ma; C. shi; J. shi; K. sa 師). In Sanskrit, lit. "heavy," hence "venerable" and thus "religious guide or teacher." In mainstream Buddhism, the UPĀDHYĀYA (novice monk's preceptor) takes the role of the guru; the preceptor and disciple are said to be like father and son; the preceptor teaches the disciple and gives him his robes and alms bowl. In MAHĀYĀNA SŪTRA literature, the increased importance of the guru is evident in the story of SADĀPRARUDITA and his teacher DHARMODGATA, from whom he seeks to learn the PRAJÑĀPĀRAMITĀ, and in the GAṆḌAVYŪHA section of the AVATAṂSAKASŪTRA, which recounts SUDHANA's spiritual journey in search of enlightenment through a series of fifty-three spiritual mentors (KALYĀṆAMITRA, a word often synonymous with guru). In tantric Buddhism, the guru is of greatest importance: the first of the SAMAYAS (tantric vows) is not to despise one's guru, who is considered to be the equal of all the TATHĀGATAS. The GURUPAÑCĀŚIKĀ ("Fifty Verses on the Guru") explains the proper conduct students should observe in the presence of a tantric guru. In Tibetan Buddhism, the ritual worship of a guru is crucially important, supported by the doctrine that it is only through one's guru that one hears the Buddha's teaching; for only when the buddhas take the form of a personal guru can they convey the salvific doctrine to students. The ritual worship of the guru (see GAṆACAKRA) in the form of the entire Buddhist pantheon (TSHOGS ZHING) is common to all Tibetan sects.

**Gu ru chos kyi dbang phyug**. (Guru Chökyi Wangchuk) (1212–1270). Also known as Gu ru chos dbang (Guru Chöwang); a Tibetan Buddhist master who was considered to be the second of the "five kingly treasure revealers" (GTER STON RGYAL PO LNGA) and the reincarnation of NYANG RAL NYI MA 'OD ZER. According to traditional accounts, at the time of his birth, his father was reading the MAÑJUŚRĪNĀMASAṂGĪTI ("Litany of the Names of Mañjuśrī") and had just reached the words "lord of doctrine"; hence, the infant was given the name Chos kyi dbang phyug (lit. "lord of doctrine"). A gifted youth, he studied both the ancient (RNYING MA) and new (GSAR MA) traditions of SŪTRA and TANTRA, including the doctrinal systems of pacification (ZHID BYED), severance (GCOD), MAHĀMUDRĀ, and RDZOGS CHEN. At twenty-two, he discovered a set of treasure texts (GTER MA), the first of thirteen great collections of treasures attributed to him. He established a seat in the southern Tibetan region of LHO

BRAG, and was later renowned by masters of other religious sects such as BU STON RIN CHEN GRUB. His teachings also spread to Nepal through his Newar disciple Bharo Gtsug 'dzin.

**gurudharma**. (P. gurudhamma/garudhamma; T. lci ba'i chos; C. jingfa; J. kyōhō; K. kyŏngbŏp 敬法). In Sanskrit, "weighty" or "deferential" "rules," a list of eight special precepts the Buddha issued as a condition of admitting women to the Buddhist order, which explicitly subordinates the BHIKṢUṆĪ to the BHIKṢU SAṂGHA. According to traditional accounts, the Buddha was initially reluctant to admit women into the order, for fear that their presence would exacerbate the decline of the dharma (see SADDHARMAVIPRALOPA; MOFA). It was only after the earnest pleas of his aunt and stepmother, MAHĀPRAJĀPATĪ GAUTAMĪ, and the continued requests of his attendant, ĀNANDA, that the Buddha is said to have relented and ordained his aunt as the first BHIKṢUṆĪ. (Ānanda's support for the ordination of women would be one of the charges brought against him at at the first Buddhist council (see COUNCIL, FIRST), following the Buddha's PARINIRVĀṆA.) As a condition of ordination, however, the Buddha required that women would have to accept the following list of eight "deferential rules" (the lists vary slightly by VINAYA tradition): (1) Although seniority within the order of monks was based on the length of time since ordination (see JIELA), a nun who had been ordained for even a hundred years must rise and pay respects to a monk ordained for a day; (2) a nun must not spend the annual rains retreat (VARṢĀ) in a place where there are no monks; (3) nuns must ask the order of monks for instruction in the dharma and for the appropriate time to hold the fortnightly confession assembly (UPOṢADHA) (an alternative rendering of this rule says, "Every half month the nuns must request a monk to give them the exhortation to keep the eight rules, and they should ask him when the confession rite should be performed"); (4) after the rains retreat, a nun should perform the rite of confessing any infractions (PRAVĀRAṆĀ) that they have seen, heard, or suspected to both the order of monks and the order of nuns; (5) a nun who has committed an important infraction, or who fails to comply with any of the gurudharmas, must submit to the MĀNATVA discipline of probationary penance from both orders before she is reinstated before a quorum of twenty monks and twenty nuns; (6) women are required to receive ordination in both orders, in contrast to men, who need only be ordained in the bhikṣusaṃgha (other lists add that a woman must train for a period of two years as a probationary postulant, or ŚIKṢAMĀṆĀ, before seeking her dual ordination); (7) a nun should never abuse or revile a monk in any way; and (8) although a monk may point out a nun's transgressions, it is forbidden for a nun ever to admonish a monk. Some modern Buddhist reform movements have advocated the repeal of the eight deferential precepts for exemplifying an outmoded and sexist model of monasticism.

**Gurupañcāśikā**. (T. Bla ma lnga bcu pa). In Sanskrit, "Fifty Verses on the GURU," a short work attributed to one AŚVAGHOṢA (a tenth-century figure not to be confused with the earlier poet) that details the proper conduct students observe in the presence of a tantric guru. Respect for one's tantric guru was the first point in the code of tantric morality (T. rig 'dzin gyi sdom pa) (see SDOM GSUM). The *Gurupañcāśikā* sets forth the proper physical behavior and deferential language that should be employed in the presence of one's guru in order to avoid incurring serious infractions.

**Guru Rin po che**. A devotional title for PADMASAMBHAVA. The name, mixing Sanskrit and Tibetan, literally means "precious teacher" and is the appellation of Padmasambhava most commonly used by Tibetans.

**guruyoga**. (T. bla ma'i rnal 'byor). The practice of GURU devotion, considered especially important in tantric practice, in which one's teacher is regarded as a buddha. In Tibetan Buddhism, guruyoga is included in a series of preliminary practices (SNGON 'GRO) to be undertaken before receiving a consecration. According to such works as DPAL SPRUL's KUN BZANG BLA MA'I ZHAL LUNG ("Words of My Perfect Teacher"), guruyoga includes reciting one hundred thousand repetitions of the name MANTRA of one's guru, visualized in the form of an enlightened being (in the case of that text, PADMASAMBHAVA). Guruyoga also includes the proper attitude toward a guru, as set forth in the GURUPAÑCĀŚIKĀ and expanded on at length at the beginning of works of the LAM RIM-type genre. See also GAṆACAKRA.

**G.ya' bzang bka' brgyud**. (Yasang Kagyü). One of the four major and eight minor subsects of the Bka' brgyud sect of Tibetan Buddhism (BKA' BRGYUD CHEN BZHI CHUNG BRGYAD), originating with Zwa ra ba Skal ldan ye shes seng ge (Sarawa Kalden Yeshe Senge, d. 1207), a disciple of the BKA' BRGYUD hierarch PHAG MO GRU PA RDO RJE RGYAL PO.

**Gyer sgom Tshul khrims seng ge**. (Gyergom Tsultrim Senge) (1144–1204). A Tibetan student of the BKA' BRGYUD hierarch PHAG MO GRU PA RDO RJE RGYAL PO, considered the founder of the SHUG GSEB BKA' BRGYUD—one of the four major and eight minor subsects of the Bka' brgyud sect of Tibetan Buddhism (BKA' BRGYUD CHEN BZHI CHUNG BRGYA). He founded the retreat center located at SHUG GSEB nunnery, south of LHA SA.

**Gyi jo lo tsā ba Zla ba'i 'od zer**. (Gyijo lotsāwa Dawe Öser) (c. eleventh century). A Tibetan translator renowned as the first scholar to render the KĀLACAKRATANTRA into Tibetan. The year in which this project was completed, 1027, marks the beginning of the modern Tibetan calendar. Gyi jo lo tsā ba composed translations of many other tantric works still preserved in both the BKA' 'GYUR and BSTAN 'GYUR sections of the Tibetan Buddhist canon.

**Gyōgi**. (行基) (668–749). Japanese monk of the Hossō (FAXIANG ZONG) tradition; his name is sometimes also seen transcribed as Gyōki, although Gyōgi is to be preferred. Gyōgi was a native of Ōtori in Izumi no kuni (present Sakai-shi, Ōsaka prefecture). He was ordained in 682, perhaps at the monastery of YAKUSHIJI, by the eminent monk DŌSHŌ. Almost two decades later, Gyōgi is said to have taken the rather unconventional route of directly preaching to the public in the capital and the countryside. He also became famous for building monasteries, bridges, roads, and irrigation systems. As a large number of the taxable population sought ordination from Gyōgi, in 717 the court issued an edict banning private ordination, leaving temple grounds, and performing rites for the sick without official sanction. The court then increased its control of the Buddhist SAṂGHA by requiring government certification (kokuchō) of all ordinations. The court's hostile attitude toward Gyōgi later changed and in 743 he was asked to assist in the construction of the great VAIROCANA statue at TŌDAIJI. Shortly thereafter, Gyōgi was appointed by Emperor Shōmu (r. 724–749) as the supreme priest (daisōjō) of the office of priestly affairs (sōgō) in 745.

**Gyōnen**. (凝然) (1240–1321). Japanese monk associated with the Kegonshū doctrinal school (HUAYAN ZONG). Gyōnen was a scion of the Fujiwara clan, one of the most influential aristocratic families in Japan, who ordained at sixteen and subsequently moved to TŌDAIJI, where he eventually became abbot. At Tōdaiji, he lectured frequently on the AVATAṂSAKASŪTRA, the central text of the Kegonshū, and was also invited to lecture on FAZANG's WUJIAO CHANG at the imperial court, which awarded him the honorary title of state preceptor (J. kokushi; C. GUOSHI). Gyōnen wrote over 125 works, all in literary Chinese, which ran the gamut from SŪTRA exegesis, to biography, to ritual music. Gyōnen's interest in Buddhist doctrine was not limited to the Kegon school. His most famous work is his HASSHŪ KŌYŌ ("Essentials of the Eight Traditions"), which provides a systematic overview of the history and doctrines of the eight major schools that were dominant in Japanese Buddhism during the Nara and Heian periods. Gyōnen's portrayal of Japanese Buddhism as a collection of independent schools identified by discrete doctrines and independent lines of transmission had a profound impact on Japanese Buddhist studies into the modern period.

**gzhan stong**. (shentong). In Tibetan, "other-emptiness" or "extrinsic emptiness"; as contrasted with RANG STONG "self-emptiness" or "intrinsic emptiness." DOL PO PA SHES RAB RGYAL MTSHAN, the third KARMA PA RANG 'BYUNG RDO RJE, and TĀRANĀTHA are the best-known proponents of this position. For a detailed discussion see RANG STONG GZHAN STONG.

# H

**Hachiman**. (八幡). In Japanese, "God of Eight Banners," a popular SHINTŌ deity (KAMI), who is also considered a "great BODHISATTVA"; also known as Hachiman jin. Although his origins are unclear, Hachiman can at least be traced back to his role as the tutelary deity of the Usa clan in Kyūshū during the eighth century. Hachiman responded to an oracle in 749, vouchsafing the successful construction of the Great Buddha (DAIBUTSU) image at TŌDAIJI and quickly rose in popularity in both Kyūshū and the Nara capital. In 859, the Buddhist monk Gyōkyō established the Iwashimizu Hachiman Shrine near the capital of Kyōto that was dedicated to the deity. Hachiman's oracles continued to play decisive roles in Nara politics, leading to a worship cult devoted to him. The Hachiman cult expanded throughout the Heian period (794–1185), and in 809, he was designated a "great bodhisattva" (daibosatsu) by drawing on the concept of HONJI SUIJAKU (buddhas or bodhisattvas appearing in the world as gods). Hachiman also came to be considered a manifestation of the semi-legendary ancient sovereign Ōjin and was likewise seen as guardian of the monarch. From the eleventh century, the Minamoto warrior clan also linked itself with Hachiman. Through this patronage, Hachiman became increasingly associated with warfare. During the Meiji persecution of Buddhism in 1868, which separated the gods from the buddhas and bodhisattvas (SHINBUTSU BUNRI), Hachiman was divorced from his Buddhist identity and recast as a purely Shintō deity. Currently, there are approximately 25,000 Hachiman shrines across Japan.

**Haedong kosŭng chŏn**. (海東高僧傳). In Korean, "Lives of Eminent Korean Monks," putatively compiled in 1215 by the monk Kakhun (d.u.), abbot of the monastery of Yŏngt'ongsa, and the only such indigenous biographical collection of its kind (see GAOSENG ZHUAN) extant in Korea. A copy of the *Haedong kosŭng chŏn* was ostensibly discovered by the monk Hoegwang Sasŏn (1862–1933; also known as Yi Hoegwang) amid a pile of old documents housed at a "certain" monastery in North Kyŏngsang province. A critical edition of this copy was published by Ch'oe Namsŏn (1809–1957) in the magazine *Pulgyo* ("Buddhism") in 1927; the original document has never been seen again. The published recension of the *Haedong kosŭng chŏn* contains only the first two chapters, on yut'ong, or propagators of the religion. The first chapter is largely concerned with the history of the transmission of Buddhism from India to China and Korea. This roll contains the biographies of eight Korean monks and briefly mentions three others. The second roll contains the biographies of ten eminent Silla monks who made pilgrimages to India and China (e.g., WŎN'GWANG and ANHAM) and also mentions the activities of eleven other figures; large portions of this roll are derived from the Chinese hagiographical anthology XU GAOSENG ZHUAN. There is also considerable overlap between the *Haedong kosŭng chŏn* and Iryŏn's (1206–1289) supposedly contemporaneous Buddhist history SAMGUK YUSA ("Memorabilia of the Three Kingdoms"). These several overlaps in material, as well as issues involving the provenance of the manuscript discovered by Yi Hoegwang, raise concerns about the authenticity of the *Haedong kosŭng chŏn* that have yet to be resolved.

**Haeinsa**. (海印寺). In Korean, "Ocean-Seal Monastery," or "Oceanic-Reflection Monastery"; the twelfth district monastery (PONSA) of the contemporary CHOGYE CHONG of Korean Buddhism, located on Kaya Mountain, in Hapch'ŏn, South Kyŏngsang province. Along with SONGGWANGSA and T'ONGDOSA, Haeinsa is considered to be one of the "three-jewel monasteries" (SAMBO SACH'AL) which represent one of the three jewels of Buddhism (RATNATRAYA); Haeinsa is traditionally designated the "Dharma-Jewel Monastery" (Pŏppo sach'al) because of its pair of scriptural repositories, which house the woodblocks of the second Koryŏ-dynasty carving of the Buddhist canon (KORYŎ TAEJANGGYŎNG; see also DAZANGJING). These paired halls are placed on top of a hill overlooking the main buddha hall in order to accentuate Haeinsa's role as a surrogate for the DHARMA. Haeinsa was established in 802 to celebrate the successful healing of King Aejang's (r. 800–808) queen by the two monks Sunŭng (d.u.) and Yijŏng (d.u.). The woodblock canon carved in the first half of the thirteenth century was moved to Haeinsa during the reign of King T'aejo (r. 1392–1398). In 1392, King T'aejo also repaired Haeinsa's old pagoda, and King Sejo (r. 1455–1468) later repaired the library halls housing the canon (Changgyŏnggak). The monastery went through extensive repairs again for three years from 1488 to 1490, but most of its treasures of old (with the fortunate exception of the woodblocks) were lost in a series of fires that broke out in the compounds between the years 1862 and 1874. Most of the buildings that stand today were rebuilt after those conflagrations.

**Haein to**. (K) (海印圖). See HWAŎM ILSŬNG PŎPKYE TO.

**haibutsu kishaku.** (排佛毀釋). In Japanese, "abolishing Buddhism and destroying [the teachings of] ŚĀKYAMUNI"; a slogan coined to describe the extensive persecution of Buddhism that occurred during the Meiji period (1868–1912). The rise of Western-derived notions of nationalism, kokugaku (national learning), and SHINTŌ as a new national ideology raised serious questions about the role of Buddhism in modern Japan. Buddhism was characterized as a foreign influence and the institution suffered the disestablishment of thousands of temples, the desecration of its ritual objects, and the defrocking of monks and nuns. When an edict was issued separating Shintō from Buddhism in 1868 (see SHINBUTSU BUNRI), Buddhist monasteries and temples where local deities (KAMI) were worshipped as manifestations of a buddha or BODHISATTVA (see HONJI SUIJAKU) sustained the most damage. The forced separation of Shintō and Buddhism eventually led to the harsh criticism of Buddhism as a corrupt and superstitious institution. Buddhists sought to counter the effects of these attacks through a rapid transformation of the SAṂGHA in order to make their religion more relevant to the needs of modern, secular society.

**haihui.** (J. kaie; K. haehoe 海會). In Chinese, lit. "oceanic congregation," referring, e.g., to congregations of sages, divinities, bodhisattvas, etc., that are said to be as vast as the ocean. "A congregation that is [as vast as] the ocean" is a common motif in MAHĀYĀNA sutras, whose expositions are typically attended by astronomical numbers of beings. Such "oceanic congregations" also sometimes refer to the extraordinary entourages of celestial buddhas. For example, "the oceanic congregation of SUKHĀVATĪ" (jile haihui) usually involves a religious vision of the buddha AMITĀBHA and the infinite numbers of inhabitants resident in his PURE LAND. Congregations in Chan monasteries (see CONGLIN) are also called a "congregation that is [as vast as the confluence of rivers in] the ocean" to symbolize the coming together of many sincere practitioners.

**Haimavata.** (P. Hemavataka; T. Gangs ri'i sde; C. Xueshanbu; J. Sessenbu; K. Sŏlsanbu 雪山部). In Sanskrit, "Inhabitants of the Himālayas," one of the traditional eighteen schools of the mainstream Indian Buddhist tradition, alternatively associated with either the MAHĀSĀṂGHIKA, SARVĀSTIVĀDA, or STHAVIRANIKĀYA traditions. The name of the school is generally regarded as deriving from school's location in the Himalayan region. There are various theories on the origin of this school. The Pāli DĪPAVAṂSA states that the Haimavata arose during the second century after the Buddha's death, and lists it separately along with the schools of Rājagirīya, Siddhārthika, PŪRVAŚAILA, Aparaśaila (the four of which were collectively designated as the ANDHAKĀ schools by BUDDHAGHOSA in the introduction to his commentary on the KATHĀVATTHU) and Apararājagirika, but without identifying their respective origins. According to northwest Indian tradition, a view represented in the Sarvāstivāda treatise SAMAYABHEDOPARACANACAKRA (C. *Yibuzong lun lun*) by VASUMITRA (c. first to second centuries, CE), the Haimavata is considered the first independent school to split off from the Sthaviranikāya line. KUIJI's commentary to the *Samayabhedoparacanacakra* explains the name pejoratively to refer to the desolation of the freezing breeze coming down from the Himālayas, in contrast to the prosperity that accompanies the Sarvāstivāda teachings. However, given that the Haimavata school does not seem to have been particularly influential (even if had been part of the original Sthaviranikāya line) and that, moreover, all the other Sthavira lineages are posited to derive from the Sarvāstivāda by this tradition, the account of the *Samayabhedoparacanacakra* is usually dismissed as reflecting Sarvāstivāda polemics more than historical fact. The *Samayabhedoparacanacakra* also attributes to the Haimavata school MAHĀDEVA's five propositions about the status of the ARHAT, the propositions that prompted, at the time of the second Buddhist council (see COUNCIL, SECOND), the schism in the SAṂGHA between the STHAVIRA and the nascent Mahāsāṃghika order. These five propositions were: the arhats (1) are still subject to sexual desire (RĀGA); (2) may have a residue of ignorance (ajñāna); (3) retain certain types of doubt (kāṅkṣā); (4) gain knowledge through others' help; and finally, (5) have spiritual experience accompanied by an exclamation, such as "aho." It is probably because of this identification with Mahādeva's propositions that BHĀVAVIVEKA (c. 490–570) classified the Haimavata among the Mahāsāṃghika. Other doctrines that Vasumitra claimed were distinctive to the Haimavata were (1) a BODHISATTVA is an ordinary person (PṚTHAGJANA); (2) a bodhisattva does not experience any desire (KĀMA) when he enters the mother's womb; (3) non-Buddhists (TĪRTHIKA) cannot develop the five kinds of supernatural powers (ABHIJÑĀ); and (4) the divinities (DEVA) cannot practice a religious life (BRAHMACARYA). Vasumitra asserts that these and other of its views were similar to those of the Sarvāstivāda, thus positing a close connection between the doctrines of the two schools.

**Hakuin Ekaku.** (白隱慧鶴) (1685–1769). Japanese ZEN master renowned for revitalizing the RINZAISHŪ. Hakuin was a native of Hara in Shizuoka Prefecture. In 1699, Hakuin was ordained and received the name Ekaku (Wise Crane) from the monk Tanrei Soden (d. 1701) at the nearby temple of Shōinji. Shortly thereafter, Hakuin was sent by Tanrei to the temple of Daishōji in Numazu to serve the abbot Sokudō Fueki (d. 1712). Hakuin is then said to have lost faith in his Buddhist training and devoted much of his time instead to art. In 1704, Hakuin visited the monk Baō Sōchiku (1629–1711) at the temple Zuiunji in Mino province. While studying under Baō, Hakuin is said to have read the CHANGUAN CEJIN by YUNQI ZHUHONG, which inspired him to further meditative training. In 1708, Hakuin is said to have had his first awakening experience upon hearing the ringing of a distant bell. That same year, Hakuin met Dōju Sōkaku (1679–1730), who urged him to visit the Zen master Dōkyō Etan (1642–1721), or Shōju Rōnin, at the hermitage of Shōjuan in Iiyama. During one of his begging rounds, Hakuin is said to have had another important awakening after an old woman struck him with a broom. Shortly after his departure from Shōjuan, Hakuin suffered from an illness, which he cured with the help of a legendary hermit named Hakuyū. Hakuin's famous story of his encounter with Hakuyū was recounted in his YASENKANNA, *Orategama*, and *Itsumadegusa*. In 1716, Hakuin returned to Shōinji and devoted much of his time to restoring the monastery, teaching students, and lecturing. Hakuin delivered famous lectures on such texts as the VIMALAKĪRTINIRDEŚA, SADDHARMAPUṆḌARĪKASŪTRA, VAJRACCHEDIKĀPRAJÑĀPĀRAMITĀSŪTRA, BIYAN LU, BAOJING SANMEI, DAHUI PUJUE CHANSHI SHU, and YUANREN LUN, and the recorded sayings (YULU) of LINJI YIXUAN, WUZU FAYAN, and XUTANG ZHIYU. He also composed a number of important texts during this period, such as the *Kanzan shi sendai kimon*, *Kaian kokugo*, and SOKKŌROKU KAIEN FUSETSU. Prior to his death, Hakuin established the monastery of Ryūtakuji in Mishima (present-day Shizuoka prefecture). Hakuin was a strong advocate of "questioning meditation" (J. kanna Zen; C. KANHUA CHAN), which focused on the role of doubt in contemplating the kōan (GONG'AN). Hakuin proposed that the sense of doubt was the catalyst for an initial SATORI (awakening; C. WU), which had then to be enhanced through further kōan study in order to mature the experience. The contemporary Rinzai training system involving systematic study of many different kōans is attributed to Hakuin, as is the famous kōan, "What is the sound of one hand clapping?" (see SEKISHU KŌAN). Hakuin was a prolific writer who left many other works as well, including the *Dokugo shingyō*, *Oniazami*, *Yabukōji*, *Hebiichigo*, *Keisō dokuzui*, *Yaemugura*, and *Zazen wasan*. Hakuin also produced many prominent disciples, including TŌREI ENJI, Suiō Genro (1716–1789), and GASAN JITŌ. The contemporary Japanese Rinzai school of Zen traces its lineage and teachings back to Hakuin and his disciples.

**Hamhŏ Tŭkt'ong**. (K) (涵虛得通). See KIHWA.

**Hanam Chungwŏn**. (漢岩重遠) (1876–1951). First supreme patriarch (CHONGJŎNG) of the Korean Buddhist CHOGYE CHONG (between 1941 and 1945), before the split between the Chogye order and T'AEGO CHONG; he is also known as Pang Hanam, using his secular surname. In 1899, Hanam went to the hermitage Sudoam in Ch'ŏngamsa to study with KYŎNGHŎ SŎNGU, the preeminent SŎN master of his generation. In 1905, after three years of lecturing throughout the country, Hanam became the Sŏn master of Naewŏn Meditation Center at the monastery of T'ONGDOSA. In 1926, he moved to Sangwŏnsa on Odae Mountain, which remained his primary residence for the rest of his life. Hanam's best-known work is the biography he wrote of his teacher Kyŏnghŏ; some twenty-three correspondences between him and his teacher are also still extant. More recently, in 1995, a collection of Hanam's own dharma talks was published as the *Hanam ilbal nok* ("Hanam's One-Bowl Record"). Hanam's "five regulations for the SAṂGHA," which he promulgated when he first arrived at Sangwŏnsa, outlined what he considered to be the main constituents of Korean Buddhist practice: (1) Sŏn meditation, (2) "recollection" of the Buddha's name (K. yŏmbul; C. NIANFO), (3) doctrinal study, (4) ritual and worship, and (5) maintaining the monastery. Hanam was a strong advocate for the revitalization of "questioning meditation" (K. kanhwa Sŏn; C. KANHUA CHAN) in Korean Buddhism, although he was more flexible than many Korean masters—who typically used ZHAOZHOU CONGSHEN'S "No" (K. mu; C. wu) gong'an (see WU GONG'AN; GOUZI WU FOXING) exclusively—in recommending also a variety of other Chan cases. Hanam also led a move to reconceive "recitation of the Buddha's name," a popular practice in contemporary Korean Buddhism, as "recollection of the Buddha's name," in order better to bring out the contemplative dimensions of yŏmbul practice and its synergies with gong'an meditation. During the four years he was supreme patriarch of the Chogye order, Hanam was especially adept at avoiding entanglement with the Japanese colonial authorities, refusing, for example, to visit the governor-general in the capital of Seoul but accepting visits from Japanese authorities who came to Sangwŏnsa to "pay respects" to him. Hanam's emphasis on the monastic context of Sŏn practice was an important influence in post-liberation Korean Buddhism after the end of World War II.

**Hannya shingyō hiken**. (般若心經秘鍵). In Japanese, "Secret Key to the PRAJÑĀPĀRAMITĀHṚDAYASŪTRA"; attributed to the Japanese SHINGONSHŪ monk KŪKAI. According to its colophon, Kūkai composed the *Hannya shingyō hiken* upon imperial request during a great epidemic in 818, but an alternative theory rejects the colophon's claim and dates the text to 834. The *Hannya shingyō hiken* claims that the *Prajñāpāramitāhṛdaya*, the famous "Heart Sūtra," is actually an esoteric scripture (see TANTRA) that explicates the "great mind-MANTRA SAMĀDHI" of the BODHISATTVA Prajñā. The treatise first provides a synopsis of the scripture and an explanation of its title, followed by a detailed interpretation of its teachings, in a total of five sections (each corresponding to a certain part of the scripture). In its first section, entitled "the complete interpenetration between persons and DHARMAS," the treatise describes the practice of the bodhisattva AVALOKITEŚVARA in terms of five factors (cause, practice, attainment, entrance, and time). The next section, entitled "division of the various vehicles," divides the different vehicles (YĀNA) of Buddhism into the vehicles of construction, destruction, form, two, and one, and also mentions the vehicles of SAMANTABHADRA (see HUAYAN ZONG), MAÑJUŚRĪ (see SANLUN ZONG), MAITREYA (see YOGĀCĀRA), ŚRĀVAKAS, PRATYEKABUDDHAS, and Avalokiteśvara (see TIANTAI ZONG). In the third section, entitled "benefits attained by the practitioner," the treatise discusses seven types of practitioners (Huayan, Sanlun, Yogācāra, śrāvaka, pratyekabuddha, Tiantai, and Shingon) and four varieties of dharmas (cause, practice, attainment, and entrance). The fourth section, entitled "clarification of the DHĀRAṆĪ," explains the MANTRA "GATE GATE PĀRAGATE PĀRASAṂGATE BODHI SVĀHĀ" in terms of its name, essence, and function, and also divides it into four types, which are associated with the śrāvaka, pratyekabuddha, MAHĀYĀNA, and esoteric (himitsu) vehicles. The fifth section, entitled "secret mantra," further divides the spell into five different types and explains the attainment of BODHI within the various vehicles. Commentaries on this treatise were written by DŌHAN (1178–1252), Saisen (1025–1115), KAKUBAN (1095–1143), Innyū (1435–1519), Donjaku (1674–1742), and others.

**Hanshan**. (J. Kanzan; K. Hansan 寒山) (d.u.; fl. mid-eighth century). In Chinese, "Cold Mountain"; sobriquet of a legendary Tang dynasty poet and iconoclast of near-mythic status within Chinese Buddhism. The HANSHAN SHI, one of the best-loved collection of poems in the Chinese Buddhist tradition, is attributed to this obscure figure. Hanshan (Cold Mountain) is primarily known as a hermit who dwelled on Mt. Tiantai, in present-day Zhejiang province. References to Hanshan are scattered throughout the discourse records (YULU) of various Chan masters and biographies of eminent monks (GAOSENG ZHUAN). Hanshan also became a favored object in brushstroke art (BOKUSEKI), in which he is often depicted together with SHIDE and FENGGAN. Together, these three iconoclasts are known as the "three recluses of Guoqing [monastery]."

**Hanshan Deqing**. (J. Kanzan Tokusei; K. Kamsan Tŏkch'ŏng 憨山德清) (1546–1623). In Chinese, "Crazy Mountain, Virtuous Clarity"; Ming-dynasty Chinese CHAN master of the LINJI ZONG; also known as Chengyin. Hanshan was a native of Quanjiao in Jinling (present-day Nanjing in Jiangsu province). He entered the monastery at age eleven and was ordained at the age of eighteen. Hanshan then studied under the monks Yungu Fahui (d.u.) and Fangguang (d.u.) of Mt. Funiu and later retired to WUTAISHAN. In 1581, Hanshan organized an "unrestricted assembly" (WUZHE DAHUI) led by five hundred worthies (DADE) on Mt. Wutai. In 1587, Hanshan received the patronage of the empress dowager, who constructed on his behalf the monastery Haiyinsi in Qingzhou (present-day Shandong province) and granted the monastery a copy of the Buddhist canon. Hanshan, however, lost favor with Emperor Shenzong (r. 1572–1620) and was sent to prison in Leizhou (present-day Guangdong province). In 1597, Hanshan reestablished himself on CAOXISHAN, where he devoted most of his time to restoring the meditation hall, conferring precepts, lecturing on scriptures, and restructuring the monastic regulations. In 1616, he established the Chan monastery of Fayunsi on LUSHAN's Wuru Peak. In 1622, Hanshan returned to Mt. Caoxi and passed away the next year. Hanshan was particularly famous for his cultivation of Chan questioning meditation (KANHUA CHAN) and recollection of the Buddha's name (NIANFO). Along with YUNQI ZHUHONG (1535–1615), DAGUAN ZHENKE (a.k.a. Zibo) (1542–1603), and OUYI ZHIXU (1599–1655), Hanshan was known as one of the four great monks of the Ming dynasty. Hanshan was later given the posthumous title Chan master Hongjue (Universal Enlightenment). His teachings are recorded in the *Hanshan dashi mengyou quanji*.

**Hanshan shi**. (J. Kanzan shi; K. Hansan si 寒山詩). In Chinese, "Cold Mountain's Poems," attributed to the legendary Chinese iconoclast HANSHAN (Cold Mountain); also known as *Hanshan shiji*. Sometime between 766 and 779, Hanshan is presumed to have retired to Mt. Tiantai (in present-day Zhejiang province), where he composed his famous poetry. The poems of the legendary monks FENGGAN and SHIDE are also included at the end of Hanshan's poetry collection. During the Song dynasty, the *Hanshan shi* was also known as the *Sanyin ji* ("Collection of the Three Recluses"). The *Hanshan shi* was widely read for its sharp satire of his times and its otherworldliness. The earliest edition was published in 1189 at the monastery of Guoqingsi on Mt. Tiantai.

**Hanthawaddi**. (Burmese). See PEGU.

**Hanyŏng Chŏngho**. (漢永鼎鎬) (1870–1948). Korean monk renowned for his efforts to revitalize Buddhist education during the Japanese colonial period. Hanyŏng Chŏngho studied the Confucian classics when young and entered the SAṂGHA at seventeen. He became a disciple of Sŏryu Ch'ŏmyŏng (1858–1903), from whom he received the dharma name Hanyŏng. In 1909, he traveled to Seoul and helped lead the Buddhist revitalization movement, along with fellow Buddhist monks HAN YONGUN and Kŭmp'a Kyŏngho (1868–1915). In 1910, shortly after Japan's formal annexation of Korea, Hoegwang Sasŏn (1862–1933) and others signed a seven-item treaty with the Japanese SŌTŌSHŪ, which sought to assimilate Korean Buddhism into the Sōtō order. In response to this threat to Korean Buddhist autonomy, Hanyŏng Chŏngho helped Han Yongun and other Korean Buddhist leaders establish the IMJE CHONG order in Korea. In 1913, he published the journal *Haedong Pulgyo* ("Korean Buddhism") in order to inform the Buddhist community of the need for revitalization and self-awareness. Beginning with his teaching career at Kodŭng Pulgyo Kangsuk in 1914, he devoted himself to the cause of education and went on to teach at various other Buddhist seminaries (kangwŏn) throughout the country. His many writings include the *Sŏngnim sup'il* ("Jottings from Stone Forest"), *Chŏngsŏn Ch'imunjiphwa* ("Selections from *Stories of Admonitions*"), and *Chŏngsŏn Yŏmsong sŏrhwa* ("Selections from the YŎMSONG SŎRHWA"), a digest of the most-famous Korean kongan (C. GONG'AN) collection.

**Han Yongun**. (韓龍雲) (1879–1944). Korean monk, poet, and writer, also known by his sobriquet Manhae or his ordination name Pongwan. In 1896, when Han was sixteen, both his parents and his brother were executed by the state for their connections to the Tonghak ("Eastern Learning") Rebellion. He subsequently joined the remaining forces of the Tonghak Rebellion and fought against the Chosŏn-dynasty government but was forced to flee to Oseam hermitage on Mt. Sŏrak. He was ordained at the monastery of Paektamsa in 1905. Three years later, as one of the fifty-two monastic representatives, he participated in the establishment of the Wŏn chong (Consummate Order) and the foundation of its headquarters at Wŏnhŭngsa. After returning from a sojourn in Japan, where he witnessed Japanese Buddhism's attempts to modernize in the face of the Meiji-era persecutions, Han Yongun wrote an influential tract in 1909 calling for radical changes in the Korean Buddhist tradition; this tract, entitled CHOSŎN PULGYO YUSIN NON ("Treatise on the Reformation of Korean Buddhism"), set much of the agenda for Korean Buddhist modernization into the contemporary period. After Korea was formally annexed by Japan in 1910, Han devoted the rest of his life to the fight for independence. In opposition to the Korean monk Hoegwang Sasŏn's (1862–1933) attempt to merge the Korean Wŏn chong with the Japanese SŌTŌSHŪ, Han Yongun helped to establish the IMJE CHONG (Linji order) with its headquarters at PŎMŎSA in Pusan. In 1919, he actively participated in the March First independence movement and signed the Korean Declaration of Independence as a representative of the Buddhist community. As a consequence, he was sentenced to three years in prison by Japanese colonial authorities. In prison, he composed the *Chosŏn Tongnip ŭi sŏ* ("Declaration of Korea's Independence"). In 1925, three years after he was released from prison, he published a book of poetry entitled *Nim ŭi ch'immuk* ("Silence of the Beloved"), a veiled call for the freedom of Korea (the "beloved" of the poem) and became a leader in resistance literature; this poem is widely regarded as a classic of Korean vernacular writing. In 1930, Han became publisher of the monthly journal *Pulgyo* ("Buddhism"), through which he attempted to popularize Buddhism and to raise the issue of Korean political sovereignty. Han Yongun continued to lobby for independence until his death in 1944 at the age of sixty-six, unable to witness the long-awaited independence of Korea that occurred a year later on August 15th, 1945, with Japan's surrender in World War II.

**Haribhadra**. (T. Seng ge bzang po) (c. 800). Indian Buddhist exegete during the Pāla dynasty, whom later Tibetan doxographers associate with the YOGĀCĀRA-*SVĀTANTRIKA syncretistic strand of Indian philosophy. He may have been a student of ŚĀNTARAKṢITA and was a contemporary of KAMALAŚĪLA; he himself lists Vairocanabhadra as his teacher. Haribhadra is known for his two commentaries on the AṢṬASĀHASRIKĀPRAJÑĀPĀRAMITĀSŪTRA ("PRAJÑĀPĀRAMITĀ in Eight Thousand Lines"): the longer ABHISAMAYĀLAṂKĀRĀLOKĀ-*Prajñāpāramitāvyākhyā*, and its summary, the ABHISAMAYĀLAṂKĀRAVIVṚTI. He is also known for his recasting of the twenty-five-thousand-line version of the prajñāpāramitā (PAÑCAVIṂŚATISĀHASRIKĀPRAJÑĀPĀRAMITĀSŪTRA) in a work entitled the *Le'u brgyad ma* in Tibetan. Each of these works is based on the interpretative scheme set forth in the ABHISAMAYĀLAṂKĀRA ("Ornament for Clear Realizations"), a guide to the *Pañcaviṃśati* that Haribhadra explicitly attributes to MAITREYA. His *Abhisamayālaṃkārālokā* builds upon PRAMĀṆA, MADHYAMAKA, and ABHIDHARMA literature and was extremely influential in Tibet; its summary (known as "'grel pa don gsal" in Tibetan) is the root text (rtsa ba) for commentaries in the GSANG PHU NE'U THOG monastery tradition originating with RNGOG BLO LDAN SHES RAB. It is the most widely studied prajñāpāramitā commentary in Tibetan Buddhism to the present day. Haribhadra is known for his explanation of a JÑĀNADHARMAKĀYA (knowledge truth-body) in addition to a SVĀBHĀVAKĀYA, viz., the eternally pure DHARMADHĀTU that is free from duality. He is characterized as an alīkākāravādin ("false-aspectarian") to differentiate him from Kamalaśīla, a satyākāravādin ("true-aspectarian") who holds that the objects appearing in the diverse forms of knowledge in a buddha's all-knowing mind are truly what they seem to be. He cites DHARMAKĪRTI frequently but appears to accept that scripture (ĀGAMA) is also a valid authority (PRAMĀṆA). There are two principal commentaries on his work, by Dharmamitra and Dharmakīrtiśrī. Buddhaśrījñāna (or simply Buddhajñāna) was his disciple. The *Subodhinī*, a commentary on the RATNAGUṆASAMCAYAGĀTHĀ, is also attributed to him.

**Hārītī**. (T. 'Phrog ma; C. Guizimushen; J. Kishimojin; K. Kwijamosin 鬼子母神). In Sanskrit, Hārītī, "the mother of demons," is a ravenous demoness (alternatively called either a yakṣiṇī or a rākṣasī), who is said to eat children. At the pleading of her victims' distraught mothers, ŚĀKYAMUNI Buddha kidnapped one of Hārītī's own five hundred children and hid the child in his begging bowl (PĀTRA) so she would experience the same kind of suffering she had caused other parents; realizing the pain she had brought others prompted her to convert to Buddhism. Subsequently, Hārītī came to be recognized specifically as a protector of both pregnant women and children, and laywomen made pilgrimages to sites associated with her and her manifestations. More generally, Hārītī is also thought to protect the SAṂGHA and, indeed, all sentient beings (SATTVA), from depredations by evil spirits. Monasteries may have a small shrine to Hārītī near the entrance gate or kitchen, where monks and nuns will leave a small offering of food to her before meals. She is often paired with her consort Pāñcika (KUBERA), one of the twenty-eight YAKṢA generals in VAIŚRAVAṆA's army, who fathered her five hundred children; indeed, all demons (yakṣa) are said to be the "sons of Hārītī" (Hārītīputra). The couple is commonly depicted surrounded by young children, offering the laity a positive portrayal of marital fidelity and reproductive fecundity, which contrasts with the world-renouncing stereotypes of Buddhism.

**Harivarman**. (T. Seng ge go cha; C. Helibamo; J. Karibatsuma; K. Haribalma 訶梨跋摩). Indian Buddhist exegete who probably lived between the third and fourth centuries CE (c. 250–350 CE). Harivarman was a disciple of Kumāralabdha and is the author of the CHENGSHI LUN (**Tattvasiddhi*; "Treatise on Establishing Reality"), a summary of the lost ABHIDHARMA of the BAHUŚRUTĪYA school, a branch of the MAHĀSĀṂGHIKA school of the mainstream Buddhist tradition. The **Tattvasiddhi*, extant only in Chinese translation as the *Chengshi lun*, is especially valuable for its detailed refutations of the positions held by other early ŚRĀVAKAYĀNA schools; the introduction, e.g., surveys ten different bases of controversy that separate the different early schools. The treatise is structured in the form of an exposition of the traditional theory of the FOUR NOBLE TRUTHS, but does not include the listings for different factors (DHARMA) that typify many works in the abhidharma genre. The positions that Harivarman advocates are closest to those of the STHAVIRANIKĀYA and SAUTRĀNTIKA schools, although, unlike the Pāli texts, he accepts the reality of "unmanifest materiality" (AVIJÑAPTIRŪPA) and, unlike Sautrāntika, rejects the notion of an "intermediate state" (ANTARĀBHAVA) between existences. Harivarman opposes the SARVĀSTIVĀDA position that dharmas exist in both past and future, the MAHĀSĀṂGHIKA view that thought is inherently pure, and the VĀTSĪPUTRĪYA premise that the "person" (PUDGALA) exists in reality. Harivarman seems to hone to a middle way between the extremes of "everything exists" and "everything does not exist," both of which he views as expediencies that do not represent ultimate reality. Harivarman advocates, instead, the "emptiness of everything" (sarva-ŚŪNYATĀ) and is therefore sometimes viewed within the East Asian traditions as representing a transitional stage between the mainstream Buddhist schools and MAHĀYĀNA philosophical doctrine.

**Hasshū kōyō**. (八宗綱要). In Japanese, "Essentials of the Eight Traditions"; an influential history of Buddhism in Japan composed by the Japanese KEGONSHŪ (C. HUAYAN ZONG) monk GYŌNEN (1240–1321). Gyōnen first divides the teachings of the Buddha into the two vehicles of MAHĀYĀNA and HĪNAYĀNA, the two paths of the ŚRĀVAKA and BODHISATTVA, and the three baskets (PIṬAKA) of SŪTRA, VINAYA, and ABHIDHARMA. He then proceeds to provide a brief history of the transmission of Buddhism from India to Japan. Gyōnen subsequently details the division of the Buddha's teachings into the eight different traditions that dominated Japanese Buddhism during the Nara (710–794) and Heian (794–1185) periods. This outline provides a valuable summary of the teachings of each tradition, each of their histories, and the development of their distinctive doctrines in India, China, and Japan. The first roll describes the Kusha (see ABHIDHARMAKOŚABHĀṢYA), Jōjitsu (*Tattvasiddhi; see CHENGSHI LUN), and RITSU (see VINAYA) traditions. The second roll describes the Hossō (see FAXIANG ZONG; YOGĀCĀRA), Sanron (see SAN LUN), TENDAI (see TIANTAI), Kegon (see HUAYAN), and SHINGON traditions. Brief introductions to the ZENSHŪ and JŌDOSHŪ, which were more recent additions to Japanese Buddhism, appear at the end of the text. The *Hasshū kōyō* has been widely used in Japan since the thirteenth century as a textbook of Buddhist history and thought. Indeed, Gyōnen's portrayal of Japanese Buddhism as a collection of independent schools identified by discrete doctrines and independent lineages of transmission had a profound impact on Japanese Buddhist studies into the modern period.

**hastināga**. (P. hatthināga; C. longxiang; J. ryūzō; K. yongsang 龍象). In Sanskrit, "elephant," often referring to an especially magnificent or noble elephant, but sometimes parsed, especially in translation, as the dual compound "elephants and NĀGAS"; a metaphor for a highly advanced Buddhist practitioner. (The Chinese characters translate the compound as "dragons and elephants.") Hastināgas were said to be synonymous with religious virtuosi or worthies (DADE), because dragons and elephants were respectively the most powerful animals in water (and in the water vapor of clouds) and on land. In the East Asia CHAN (J. Zen; K. Sŏn) tradition, "dragons and elephants" as advanced adepts are contrasted with YUNSHUI (J. unsui; K. unsu), lit. "clouds and water," referring to itinerant practitioners and especially novice monks, who were expected to travel to various monasteries to learn from different teachers as part of their training. In Korean monasteries, the "dragons and elephants" (yongsang; C. longxiang) roster is a list of monastic duties, along with the assigned incumbents of the offices, that is posted during the retreat periods (K. kyŏlche; C. JIEZHI) of winter and summer.

**Hatthaka Āḷavaka**. An eminent lay disciple of the Buddha, declared by him to be foremost among laymen who attract followers by means of the four means of conversion (S. SAṂGRAHAVASTU). According to the Pāli account, he was the son of the king of Āḷavī, and received his name Hatthaka (which in Pāli means "handed over" as a child), because he had once been given to the Buddha by an ogre (S. YAKṢA), who, in turn, handed him back to the king. The ogre, the yakkha Āḷavaka, was going to eat the boy but was converted by the Buddha and persuaded to release him, instead. When he grew up, Hatthaka heard the Buddha preach and became a nonreturner (S. ANĀGĀMIN). A gifted preacher, Hatthaka had a following of five hundred disciples who always accompanied him. The suttapiṭaka records several conversations he had with the Buddha. On one occasion, after the Buddha asked him how he was able to gather such a large following around him, Hatthaka responded that it was through four means of conversion: giving gifts, kind words, kind deeds, and equality in treatment. It was for this capacity that Hatthaka won eminence. The Buddha declared him to be endowed with eight qualities: faith, virtue, conscientiousness, shame, the ability to listen, generosity, wisdom, and modesty. When he died, Hatthaka was reborn as a divinity in avihā heaven in the subtle materiality realm (RŪPALOKA), where he was destined to attain final nibbāna (S. NIRVĀṆA). Once, he visited the Buddha from his celestial world but collapsed in his presence, unable to support his subtle material body on earth; the Buddha instructed him to create a gross material body, by means of which he was then able to stand. He told the Buddha that he had three regrets upon his death: that he had not seen the Buddha enough, that he had not heard the DHARMA enough, and that he had not served the SAṂGHA enough. Together with the householder CITTA (Cittagahapati), Hatthaka Āḷavaka is upheld as an ideal layman, who is worthy of emulation.

**Hayagrīva**. (T. Rta mgrin; C. Matou Guanyin; J. Batō Kannon; K. Madu Kwanŭm 馬頭觀音). In Sanskrit, "Horse-Necked One"; an early Buddhist deity who developed from a YAKṢA attendant of AVALOKITEŚVARA into a tantric wrathful deity important in the second diffusion of Buddhism in Tibet. The name "Hayagrīva" belonged to two different Vedic deities, one an enemy of VIṢṆU, another a horse-headed avatāra, or manifestation, of that deity. Eventually the two merged, whence he was absorbed into the Buddhist pantheon. In early Buddhist art, Hayagrīva frequently appears as a smallish yakṣa figure attending Avalokiteśvara, Khasarpaṇa, AMOGHAPĀŚA, and TĀRĀ; by the mid-seventh century, however, Hayagrīva had merged with Avalokiteśvara to become a wrathful form of that bodhisattva. He appears in this new form, Hayagrīva–Avalokiteśvara, in the Avalokiteśvara sections of the *Dhāraṇīsaṃgraha* (where his DHĀRAṆĪs are said to be effective in destroying mundane obstacles) and later Chinese translations of the *Amoghapāśahṛdaya*, as well as in the MAHĀVAIROCANASŪTRA. While he does appear with a horse's head in Japan (where he is considered a protective deity of horses), Hayagrīva is customarily shown with a horse head emerging from his flaming hair. In the tantric pantheon, Hayagrīva initially occupied outer rings of the MAṆḌALA, but eventually came to be considered a YI DAM in his own right, a transformation that would grant him the status of a fully enlightened being. In Mongolia he is worshipped as the god of horses. In Tibet he is primarily worshipped as a LOKOTTARA (supramundane) DHARMAPĀLA (dharma protector).

**Heart Sūtra**. See PRAJÑĀPĀRAMITĀHṚDAYASŪTRA.

**heaven**. See DEVA; SVARGA.

**Helin Xuansu**. (J. Kakurin Genso; K. Hangnim Hyŏnso 鶴林玄素) (668–752). Chinese CHAN master in the NIUTOU ZONG, also known as Daoqing or Masu (from his secular surname Ma). Helin was ordained at the monastery of Changshousi in present-day Jiangsu province, but later in his life moved to Youqisi, where he became a disciple of the fifth-generation Niutou successor Zhiwei (646–722). At another monk's request, Helin moved once again to the monastery of Helinsi on Mt. Huanghe in Yunzhou prefecture, whence he acquired his toponym. He died without any symptoms of illness in 752 at the age of eighty-four. He was subsequently given the posthumous title Chan master Dalü (Great Discipline). He claims among his disciples Jingshan Daoqin (714–792) and FAHAI, whom the Dunhuang edition of the LIUZU TAN JING ("Platform Sūtra of the Sixth Patriarch") states is the compiler of the text.

**hells**. See NĀRAKA (hell denizens).

**Hemis Monastery**. A monastery located about twenty-five miles (forty km.) southeast of Leh, the capital of Ladakh. Hemis Monastery is sited just south of the Indus River, within present-day Hemis National Park. The largest monastery in the kingdom of Ladakh, Hemis Monastery was founded in the mid-seventeenth century by Stag tsang ras pa (Taktsang Repa), who was supported by King Seng ge rnam rgyal (Senge Namgyal, 1570–1642), one of the most important kings in the history of Ladakhi Buddhism. Hemis is central to the 'BRUG PA BKA' BRGYUD community in the region, and the two-day 'CHAM (sacred dance) festival that is held each summer in honor of PADMASAMBHAVA is widely known throughout the area.

**hengchao**. (J. ōchō; K. hoengch'o 橫超). In Chinese, "the expeditious (lit. horizontal) deliverance/escape." In the PURE LAND traditions, it is said that deliverance through the aid of "other power" (TARIKI)—i.e., by relying on the vows and saving grace of the buddha AMITĀBHA—is a faster and easier approach to enlightenment than is that found in traditional Buddhist soteriological systems. Since the mainstream conception of transcendence from the round of rebirth (SAṂSĀRA) involves a tortuous (lit. vertical) ascent (SHUCHAO) through successive levels of ever-deeper meditative absorptions (DHYĀNA) and ever-more-daunting spiritual fruitions (PHALA), pure land followers argue that their method "cuts horizontally across the three realms of existence" (hengchao sanjie) and bypasses the difficult sequential stages of mainstream approaches. The pure land "shortcut" is conceptualized as a "horizontal" approach partly because, by traveling "westward" instead of "upward"—i.e., being reborn into the western pure land (see SUKHĀVATĪ)—one is more easily liberated from the round of rebirth.

**Heruka**. (T. Khrag 'thung; C. Xilujia; J. Kiruoka; K. Hŭiroga 呬嚕迦). Sanskrit proper name of a spirit that perhaps originally was associated with cremation grounds (ŚMAŚĀNA) and was a form of Śiva (Maheśvara). The name appears commonly in tantric Buddhism as a generic name for a buddha appearing in a wrathful (KRODHA) aspect, especially in the form of CAKRASAṂVARA, and either with or without a consort. The name is translated into Chinese and Tibetan as "blood drinker," an interpretation not reflected in the Sanskrit. Heruka also appears in the HEVAJRATANTRA as the name of a deity who is essentially the same as Hevajra. See also CAKRASAṂVARATANTRA.

**heshang**. (J. oshō; K. hwasang 和尚). In Chinese, "monk," one of the most common Chinese designations for a senior Buddhist monk. The term is actually an early Chinese transcription of the Khotanese translation of the Sanskrit UPĀDHYĀYA, meaning "preceptor." The transcription heshang originally was used in Chinese to refer specifically to the upādhyāya, the monk who administered the precepts at the ordination of either a novice (ŚRĀMAṆERA) or fully ordained monk (BHIKṢU), but over time the term entered the vernacular Chinese lexicon to refer more generically to any senior monk. The term heshang has several variant readings in Japanese, depending on the sectarian affiliation: it is read OSHŌ in the JŌDO and ZEN schools; WAJŌ in the HOSSŌ (C. FAXIANG ZONG), SHINGON, and RITSU schools; and kashō in the TENDAI school.

**hetu**. (T. rgyu; C. yin; J. in; K. in 因). In Sanskrit and Pāli, "cause." In one of the first accounts of the Buddha's teachings, he was said to have "set forth the causes of things that have causes and also set forth their cessation." The process of causality is provisionally divided between hetu and PRATYAYA, "causes and conditions": hetu designates the main or primary cause of production, which operates in conjunction with pratyaya, the concomitant conditions or secondary, supporting causes; these two together produce a specific "fruition" or result (PHALA): thus, the fruition of a tree is the result of a primary cause (hetu), its seed; supported by such subsidiary conditions as soil, sunlight, and water; and only when all the relevant causes and conditions in their totality are functioning cooperatively will the prospective fruition or effect occur. ¶ The JÑĀNAPRASTHĀNA, the central text of the SARVĀSTIVĀDA ABHIDHARMA, designates six specific types of hetu: (1) the "cause as a reason for being" (KĀRAṆAHETU), the efficient cause or generic cause, referring to causation in its broadest possible sense, in which every conditioned dharma serves as the generic, indirect cause for the creation of all things except itself; (2) the coexistent cause (SAHABHŪHETU), where dharmas simultaneously condition one another, as with a material element (MAHĀBHŪTA) and its derivatives, or a dharma and its four conditioned characteristics (SAṂSKṚTALAKṢAṆA); (3) associative cause (SAṂPRAYUKTAHETU), wherein mental events cannot exist in isolation but instead mutually condition one another; (4) homogenous cause (SABHĀGAHETU), wherein cause is always antecedent to its incumbent effect, ensuring that apple seeds always produce apples, wholesome causes lead to wholesome effects, etc.; (5) all-pervasive, or universally active, cause (SARVATRAGAHETU), wherein afflictions (KLEŚA) produce not only identical types of subsequent afflictions but also serve as the root cause of all other afflictions, obstructing a person's capacity to intuit empirical reality; (6) retributive cause (VIPĀKAHETU), i.e., the unwholesome dharmas and wholesome dharmas associated with the contaminants (ĀSRAVA) that produce subsequent "retribution," viz., pleasant, unpleasant, or neutral effects, or ultimately rebirth. ¶ In Indian Buddhist logic, the hetu also refers to the second step, or "reason," in a syllogism (SĀDHANA): e.g., "The mountain is on fire,/because there is smoke,/like a stove (and unlike a lake)"; see also LIṄGA.

**hetupratyaya**. (P. hetupaccaya; T. rgyu rkyen; C. yin yuan; J. innen; K. in yŏn 因緣). In Sanskrit, "causes and conditions," or "causality"; one of the cardinal teachings of Buddhism, which applies to all aspects of the physical, emotional, and spiritual realms. In the Buddhist account of this causal process, HETU designates the main or primary cause of production and PRATYAYA are the subsidiary factors that contribute to the production of an effect, or "fruit" (PHALA), from that cause. In the production of a sprout from a seed, e.g., the seed would be the cause (hetu), such factors as light and moisture would be conditions (pratyaya), and the sprout itself would be the result or "fruit" (phala). Given the centrality of the doctrine of causality of Buddhist thought, detailed lists and descriptions of causes and conditions appear in all strata of Buddhist literature (see separate entries on HETU and PRATYAYA). ¶ The VIJÑĀNAKĀYA, the fifth book of the SARVĀSTIVĀDA school of ABHIDHARMA, lists hetupratyaya, the "condition qua cause" or "causal condition," as the first in a list of four specific types of pratyaya. In this type, a condition serves as the direct cause of an effect; thus, a seed would be the hetupratyaya of a sprout. In the Sarvāstivāda list of the six types of causes (hetu), all except the "efficient cause" or "generic cause" (KĀRAṆAHETU) are subsumed under the hetupratyaya. ¶ The PAṬṬHĀNA, the seventh book of the PĀLI ABHIDHAMMA, also recognizes hetupaccaya, or "root condition," as the first in a list of twenty-four conditions. The "root condition" is described as the condition upon which all mental states depend, just as a tree depends on its root. These root conditions are greed (LOBHA), hatred (P. dosa, S. DVEṢA), and delusion (MOHA) in the case of unwholesome (AKUŚALA) mental states, or greedlessness (alobha), hatelessness (adosa), and nondelusion (amoha) in the case of wholesome (KUŚALA) mental states. Without the presence of these roots, the respective mental states cannot exist.

**hetuvidyā**. (T. gtan tshigs kyi rig pa; C. yinming; J. inmyō; K. inmyŏng 因明). In Sanskrit, the "science of reasoning," hence "logic and dialectics"; in Indian Buddhism, the term refers generally to a scholarly tradition that begins with DIGNĀGA and DHARMAKĪRTI, a tradition known for an epistemological theory based on two means of knowledge (PRAMĀṆA)—direct perception (PRATYAKṢA) and inference (ANUMĀNA)—and rejecting ĀGAMA, i.e., the authority of the scriptures, specifically the Vedas. Much of hetuvidyā focuses on the correct form of the syllogism (PRAYOGA) that underpins correct inference.

**Hevajra**. (T. Kye rdo rje; C. Jingangwang; J. Kongōō; K. Kŭmgangwang 金剛王). An important Indian tantric deity in the ANUTTARAYOGA class of tantras, who is the central figure in the HEVAJRATANTRA MAṆḌALA. The cult of Hevajra developed in India at least by the eighth century, the date generally given for that TANTRA. A number of Indian images from the eleventh century have been identified as HERUKA Hevajra, although the identification is uncertain. The tantric deity Hevajra is most commonly depicted as dark blue in color and naked. One of his most common forms is the Kapāladhārin ("Skull Bearing") Hevajra, with four legs, eight faces with three eyes each, and sixteen hands, each of which holds a skull cup. Each face has three bloodshot eyes, four fangs, and a protruding tongue. The skulls in his right hands hold various animals and the skulls in his left hand hold various deities. He is often depicted in sexual union with his consort is Nairātmyā ("Selflessness"), who holds a curved knife and skull cup, the couple surrounded by a retinue of eight yoginīs. There are eight famous forms of Hevajra: four called the body (KĀYA), speech (vāc), mind (CITTA), and heart (hṛdaya) Hevajras, as described in the *Hevajratantra* (the Kapāladhārin Hevajra corresponds to the heart Hevajra);

and the body, speech, mind, and heart Hevajras, as described in the *Saṃpuṭatantra*. His name literally means "Hey, Vajra."

**Hevajratantra/Hevajraḍākinījālasaṃvaratantra**. (T. Kye rdo rje'i rgyud; C. Dabei kongzhi jingang dajiao wang yigui jing; J. Daihi kūchi kongō daikyōō gikikyō; K. Taebi kongji kŭmgang taegyo wang ŭigwe kyŏng 大悲空智金剛大教王儀軌經). An important Indian Buddhist TANTRA, classified as an ANUTTARAYOGATANTRA, and within that group, a YOGINĪTANTRA and a mother tantra (MĀTṚTANTRA). Likely composed in the eighth century, the work consists of seven hundred fifty stanzas written in a mixture of Sanskrit and APABHRAṂŚA; it is traditionally said to be a summary of a larger work in five hundred thousand stanzas, now lost. The tantra is presumed to derive from the SIDDHA movement of north India, and the central deity, HEVAJRA, is depicted as a naked siddha. Like most tantras, the text is particularly concerned with ritual, especially those that result in the attainment of worldly (LAUKIKA) powers. It famously recommends the use of "intentional language" or "coded language" (SANDHYĀBHĀṢĀ) for tantric practitioners. The widespread ANUTTARAYOGA system of the channels (NĀḌĪ), winds (PRĀṆA), and drops (BINDU), and the various levels of bliss achieved through the practice of sexual yoga is particularly associated with the *Hevajratantra*. It sets forth the so-called four joys, the greatest of which is the "innate" or "natural" (SAHAJA) joy. A Chinese translation of the *Hevajratantra* was made in 1055 by Dharmapāla, but neither the text nor its central deity gained particular popularity in East Asian Buddhism. The text was much more important in Tibet. The tantra was rendered into Tibetan by the Sa skya translator 'BROG MI SHĀKYA YE SHES in the early eleventh century and popularized by MAR PA, whose Indian master NĀROPA wrote a well-known commentary to the text. The scriptures associated with the *Hevajratantra* were the basis for the Indian adept VIRŪPA's LAM 'BRAS ("path and result") systematization of tantric doctrine. This practice is central in the SA SKYA tradition of Tibetan Buddhism. The *Saṃpuṭatantra* is regarded as an explanatory tantra of the Hevajra. There are a number of important commentaries to this tantra written in the Indian tradition and dozens composed in Tibet.

**Heze Shenhui**. (J. Kataku Jinne; K. Hat'aek Sinhoe 荷澤神會) (684–758). Chinese CHAN master and reputed main disciple of the sixth patriarch HUINENG; his collateral branch of Huineng's lineage is sometimes referred to as the Heze school. Shenhui was a native of Xiangyang in present-day Hubei province. He became a monk under the master Haoyuan (d.u.) of the monastery of Kuochangsi in his hometown of Xiangyang. In 704, Shenhui received the full monastic precepts in Chang'an, and extant sources provide differing stories of Shenhui's whereabouts thereafter. He is said to have become a student of SHENXIU and later visited MT. CAOXI where he studied under Huineng until the master's death in 713. After several years of traveling, Shenhui settled down in 720 at the monastery of Longxingsi in Nanyang (present-day Henan province). In 732, during an "unrestricted assembly" (WUZHE DAHUI) held at the monastery Dayunsi in Huatai, Shenhui engaged a monk by the name of Chongyuan (d.u.) and publicly criticized the so-called Bei zong (Northern school) of Shenxiu's disciples PUJI and XIANGMO ZANG as being a mere collateral branch of BODHIDHARMA's lineage that upheld a gradualist soteriological teaching. Shenhui also argued that his teacher Huineng had received the orthodox transmission of Bodhidharma's lineage and his "sudden teaching" (DUNJIAO). In 745, Shenhui is said to have moved to the monastery of Hezesi in Luoyang, whence he acquired his toponym. He was cast out of Luoyang by a powerful Northern school follower in 753. Obeying an imperial edict, Shenhui relocated to the monastery of Kaiyuansi in Jingzhou (present-day Hubei province) and assisted the government financially by performing mass ordinations after the economic havoc wrought by the An Lushan rebellion in 755. He was later given the posthumous title Great Master Zhenzong (Authentic Tradition). Shenhui also plays a minor, yet important, role in the LIUZU TAN JING ("Platform Sūtra of the Sixth Patriarch"). A treatise entitled the XIANZONGJI, preserved as part of the JINGDE CHUANDENG LU, is attributed to Shenhui. Several other treatises attributed to Shenhui were also discovered at DUNHUANG. Shenhui's approach to Chan practice was extremely influential in GUIFENG ZONGMI's attempts to reconcile different strands of Chan, and even doctrine, later in the Tang dynasty; through Zongmi, Shenhui's teachings also became a critical component of the Korean Sŏn master POJO CHINUL's accounts of Chan soteriology and meditation.

**hibutsu**. (秘仏). In Japanese, "secret buddha." A hibutsu refers to a Buddhist icon in a Japanese monastery that is more or less kept out of public view. In some cases, the hibutsu icon is periodically brought out for public showing, but even then only once in perhaps several decades. The Amida (see AMITĀBHA) triad purportedly housed at the monastery of ZENKŌJI is one famous example of a hibutsu.

**Hieizan**. (比叡山). In Japanese "Mt. Hiei," a sacred mountain best known as the headquarters of the TENDAISHŪ (see TIANTAI ZONG). Mt. Hiei is located northeast of Kyōto on the border of present-day Kyōto and Shiga prefectures, and rises to 2,600 feet (848 meters). In 785, SAICHŌ, founder of the Tendai school, left Nara for Hieizan after receiving ordination. Dissatisfied with the Nara Buddhist schools, he resided in a hut on the mountain and gradually attracted a small group of followers. In 788, Saichō built the hall Ichijō shikan'in (later renamed Konpon chūdō), which became incorporated into the larger monastery of ENRYAKUJI, headquarters for the Tendai school. As Tendai Buddhism rose to dominance in medieval Japan, Hieizan became extremely influential not only in religious matters, but also in politics, the economy, and military affairs. In addition to Enryakuji and numerous other Tendai monasteries, the mountain also housed three aristocratic temples (monzeki), which further extended its ties to the court in Kyōto. Hieizan's power was not maintained without its share of violence. Conflict erupted in the late tenth century with the nearby Tendai temple Onjōji, when succession over the position of head priest at Enryakuji broke down in armed disputes between ENNIN and ENCHIN and their respective followers and warrior monks (SŌHEI). In order to wrest control of Hieizan's military and economic strength, Oda Nobunaga (1534–1582) led an attack on the mountain in 1571, burning many of its monasteries to the ground. The mountain's influence was further supplanted during the Tokugawa period when Tenkai (1536?–1643), a Tendai priest and advisor to Shōgun Tokugawa Ieyasu (1543–1616), presided over the construction of Kan'eiji in 1625, which the Shogunate ranked above Hieizan. Hieizan also served as home to many KAMI, notably Ōbie and Kobie (Great and Small Hie), who developed close ties with Tendai monasteries as early as the Heian period (794–1185) through a process known as SHINBUTSU SHŪGŌ ("unity of spirits and buddhas"). SHUGENDŌ practices eventually took root on Hieizan as well. The practice of "circumambulating the mountain" (KAIHŌGYŌ), which reputedly dates back to the ninth century, consists of ascetics running a course around the mountain for as many as one thousand days.

**Higashi Honganjiha**. (東本願寺派). In Japanese, "Eastern Honganji sect," the second largest of the two major subsects of JŌDO SHINSHŪ; also known as the ŌTANIHA. See HONGANJI; ŌTANIHA.

**hihan Bukkyō**. (C. pipan Fojiao; K. pip'an Pulgyo 批判佛教). In Japanese, "critical Buddhism." A contemporary intellectual controversy fostered largely by the Japanese Buddhist scholars and SŌTŌSHŪ ZEN priests Hakamaya Noriaki and Matsumoto Shirō and their followers. In a series of provocative essays and books, Hakamaya and Matsumoto have argued for a more engaged form of Buddhist scholarship that sought a critical pursuit of truth at the expense of the more traditional, accommodative approaches to Buddhist thought and history. "Critical" here refers to the critical analysis of Buddhist doctrines using modern historiographical and philological methodologies in order to ascertain the authentic teachings of Buddhism. "Critical" can also connote an authentic Buddhist perspective, which should be critical of intellectual misconstructions and/or societal faults. Critical Buddhists polemically dismiss many of the foundational doctrines long associated with East Asian Buddhism, and especially Japanese Zen, as corruptions of what they presume to have been the pristine, "original" teachings of the Buddha. In their interpretation, true Buddhist teachings derive from a critical perspective on the nature of reality, based on the doctrines of "dependent origination" (PRATĪTYASAMUTPĀDA) and "nonself" (ANĀTMAN); for this reason, the style of critical philosophical analysis used in the MADHYAMAKA school represents an authentic approach to Buddhism. By contrast, more accommodative strands of Buddhism that are derived from such teachings as the "embryo of buddhahood" (TATHĀGATAGARBHA), buddha-nature (FOXING), and original enlightenment (HONGAKU) were considered heretical, because they represented the corruption of the pristine Buddhist message by Brahmanical notions of a perduring self (ĀTMAN). The Mahāyāna notion of the nonduality between such dichotomies as SAṂSĀRA and NIRVĀṆA, the Critical Buddhists also claim, fostered a tendency toward antinomianism or moral ambiguity that had corrupted such Buddhist schools as CHAN or Zen and encouraged those schools to accept social inequities and class-based persecution (as in Sōtō Zen's acquiescence to the persecution of Japanese "untouchables," or burakumin). Opponents of "Critical Buddhism" suggest that efforts to locate what is "original" in the teachings of Buddhism are inevitably doomed to failure and ignore the many local forms Buddhism has taken throughout its long history; the "Critical Buddhism" movement is therefore sometimes viewed as social criticism rather than academic scholarship.

**hijiri**. (聖). In Japanese, "holy man" or "saint." The term hijiri is polysemous and may refer generally to an eminent monk or more specifically to those monks who have acquired great merit through rigorous cultivation. A hijiri may also refer to an ascetic monk who rejects monastic life in favor of a more reclusive, independent lifestyle and practice. Historically, the term hijiri was also often used to refer to itinerant preachers, who converted the masses by means of healing, divination, and thaumaturgy, as well as by building basic infrastructure, such as bridges, roads, and irrigation systems. The holy men of KŌYASAN, the Kōya hijiri, and the saints of the JISHŪ tradition, the Yugyō hijiri, are best known in Japan. See also ĀRYA.

**Himālaya**. (S). One of the twenty-four sacred sites associated with the CAKRASAṂVARATANTRA. See PĪṬHA.

**Himavanta**. In Pāli, "The Snowy Region," one of nine adjacent lands (paccantadesa) converted to Buddhism by missionaries dispatched in the third century BCE by the elder MOGGALIPUTTATISSA at the end of the third Buddhist council (see COUNCIL, THIRD). Himavanta is identified with the Himalaya mountain range and is also known as Himavā or Himācala. This land was converted by the elder Majjhima, who preached the DHAMMACAKKAPPAVATTANASUTTA during his mission there. The third Buddhist council (SAṂGĪTI; see COUNCIL, THIRD), which was held in Pāṭaliputta (S. PĀṬALIPUTRA) during the reign of King Asoka (S. AŚOKA), and the nine Buddhist missions it fostered, are known only in STHAVIRANIKĀYA sources and are first recorded in Pāli in the fifth-century DĪPAVAṂSA. Himavanta was renowned as a refuge for ascetics and hermits and as an abode of solitary buddhas (P. paccekabuddha; S. PRATYEKABUDDHA).

**Himitsu mandara jūjūshinron**. (秘密曼荼羅十住心論). In Japanese, "Ten Abiding States of Mind According to the Sacred MAṆḌALA"; a treatise composed by the Japanese SHINGONSHŪ monk KŪKAI; often referred to more briefly as the *Jūjūshinron*. In 830, Kūkai submitted this treatise in reply to Emperor Junna's (r. 823–833) request to each Buddhist tradition in Japan to provide an explanation of its teachings. In his treatise, Kūkai systematically classified the various Buddhist teachings (see JIAOXIANG PANSHI) and placed them onto a spiritual map consisting of the ten stages of the mind (jūjūshin). The first and lowest stage of the mind ("the deluded, ram-like mind") is that of ignorant beings who, like animals, are driven by their uncontrolled desires for food and sex. The beings of the second stage ("the ignorant, childlike, but tempered mind") display ethical behavior consistent with the teachings of Confucius and the lay precepts of Buddhism. The third stage of mind ("the infant-like, fearless mind") is the state in which one worships the various gods and seeks rebirth in the various heavens, as would be the case in the non-Buddhist traditions of India and in Daoism. The fourth stage ("recognizing only SKANDHAs and no-self") corresponds to the ŚRĀVAKAYĀNA and the fifth stage ("mind free of karmic seeds") to that of the PRATYEKABUDDHAYĀNA. The sixth stage ("the mind of MAHĀYĀNA, which is concerned with others") corresponds to the YOGĀCĀRA teachings, the seventh ("mind awakened to its unborn nature") to MADHYAMAKA, the eighth ("mind of one path devoid of construction") to TIANTAI (J. TENDAI), and the ninth ("mind completely devoid of self-nature") to HUAYAN (J. Kegon). Kūkai placed his own tradition of Shingon at the last and highest stage of mind ("the esoteric and adorned mind"). Kūkai also likened each stage of mind to a palace and contended that these outer palaces surround an inner palace ruled by the buddha MAHĀVAIROCANA. To abide in the inner palace one must be initiated into the teachings of Shingon by receiving consecration (ABHIṢEKA). Kūkai thus provided a Buddhist (or Shingon) alternative to ideal rulership. To demonstrate his schema of the mind, Kūkai frequently cites numerous scriptures and commentaries, which made his treatise extremely prolix; Kūkai later provided an abbreviated version of his argument, without the numerous supporting references, in his HIZŌ HŌYAKU.

**hīnayāna**. (T. theg pa dman pa; C. xiaosheng; J. shōjō; K. sosŭng 小乘). In Sanskrit, "lesser vehicle," a pejorative term coined by the MAHĀYĀNA ("Great Vehicle") tradition of Buddhism to refer to the (in their minds' discredited) doctrines and practices of its rival ŚRĀVAKAYĀNA schools of the mainstream Buddhist tradition. Hīna has the negative connotations of "lesser," "defective," and "vile," and thus the term hīnayāna is inevitably deprecatory. It should be understood that the term hīnayāna is never used self-referentially by the śrāvakayāna schools of mainstream Buddhism and thus should never be taken as synonymous with the THERAVĀDA school of contemporary Sri Lankan and Southeast Asian Buddhism. Hīnayāna does, however, have a number of usages in Buddhist literature. (1) Hīnayāna is used by proponents of the Mahāyāna to refer specifically to those who do not accept the Mahāyāna sūtras as being the authentic word of the Buddha (BUDDHAVACANA). (2) Hīnayāna is used in Mahāyāna literature to refer collectively to the paths of the ŚRĀVAKAs and the PRATYEKABUDDHAs (see also ER SHENG), i.e., those who, out of a desire to attain enlightenment for themselves alone, lack sufficient compassion to undertake the BODHISATTVA path leading ultimately to buddhahood. (3) Hīnayāna has been used both by traditional Buddhist exegetes and by modern scholars of Buddhism to refer to the non-Mahāyāna schools of Indian Buddhism, traditionally numbered as eighteen, which themselves each set forth the three paths of the śrāvaka, pratyekabuddha, and bodhisattva. See MAINSTREAM BUDDHIST SCHOOLS.

**hindrance**. See ĀVARAṆA; NĪVARAṆA.

**Hiuen Tsiang**. (C). Obsolete transcription of the Chinese pilgrim and translator Xuanzang. See XUANZANG.

**Hizō hōyaku**. (秘藏寶鑰). In Japanese, "Jeweled Key to the Secret Treasury," a text composed by the Japanese SHINGONSHŪ monk KŪKAI. The *Hizō hōyaku* is a summary (one-fifth the length) of Kūkai's dense magnum opus HIMITSU MANDARA JŪJŪSHINRON. The title refers metaphorically to the "jeweled key" of the special teachings that will unlock the "secret treasury" that is the buddha-nature (C. FOXING) of all sentient beings. In contrast to the *Himitsu mandara jūjūshinron*, the *Hizō hōyaku* provides far fewer supporting references and introduces a fictional debate between a Confucian official and a Buddhist priest and a set of questions and answers from the *Sŏk Mahayŏn non*.

**Hmannan Mahayazawin-daw-gyi**. In Burmese, "The Great Glass Palace Chronicle"; the best-known Burmese YAZAWIN, or royal chronicle, of the Konbaung dynasty (1752–1885). It was written by a committee of scholars headed by the royal minister and former saṅgharājā, Mahadhamma thin gyan, at Amarapura in 1831. It copies verbatim U Kala's MAHAYAZAWIN GYI, making occasional alterations to the narrative and adding criticisms and learned observations. An interesting feature of this text is its criticism of the legend of SHIN UPAGOT (UPAGUPTA), a key element in the story of King Asoka (S. AŚOKA) found in the *Mahayazawin gyi*, as being inauthentic, because it is not attested in Pāli sources. The portion of the *Hmannan Mahayazawin-daw-gyi* that relates the ancient history of Burma from the founding of Tagaung to the fall of PAGAN to Chinese forces in 1284 CE has been translated by Pe Maung Tin and Gordon Luce as *The Glass Palace Chronicle of the Kings of Burma*.

**Hodgson, Brian Houghton**. (1801–1894). An early British scholar of Sanskrit Buddhism. He was born in Derbyshire. At age fifteen, he gained admission to Haileybury, the college that had been established by the East India Company in 1806 to train its future employees. He excelled at Bengali, Persian, Hindi, political economy, and classics. Following the standard curriculum of the company, after two years at Haileybury, he went to the College of Fort William in Calcutta to continue his studies. Once in India, he immediately began to suffer liver problems and was eventually assigned to Kathmandu as Assistant Resident and later Resident to the Court of Nepal. He began his studies of Buddhism at this time (Buddhism, although long dead in India, still flourished in the Newar community of the Kathmandu Valley). Working with the assistance of the distinguished Newar scholar Amṛtānanda, Hodgson published a number of essays on Buddhism in leading journals of the day. However, he is largely remembered for his collection and distribution of Sanskrit manuscripts. In 1824, he began accumulating Buddhist works in Sanskrit (and Tibetan) and dispatching them around the world, beginning with the gift of sixty-six manuscripts to the library of the College of Fort William in 1827 and continuing until 1845: ninety-four to the Library of the Asiatic Society of Bengal, seventy-nine to the Royal Asiatic Society, thirty-six to the India Office Library, seven to the Bodleian, eighty-eight to the Société Asiatique, and later fifty-nine more to Paris. A total of 423 works were provided. The manuscripts sent to Paris drew the immediate attention of EUGÈNE BURNOUF, who used them as the basis for his monumental 1844 *Introduction à l'histoire du Buddhisme indien*. Hodgson's contributions to the study of Buddhism occurred in the early decades of his career; he later turned his attention to Himalayan natural history and linguistics, where he made important contributions as well.

**Hokke gisho**. (法華義疏). In Japanese, "Commentary on the SADDHARMAPUṆḌARĪKASŪTRA," attributed to the Japanese prince SHŌTOKU TAISHI (574–622). Along with his commentaries on the ŚRĪMĀLĀDEVĪSIṂHANĀDASŪTRA and VIMALAKĪRTINIRDEŚA, the *Hokke gisho* is known as one of the "three SŪTRA commentaries" (sangyō gisho) of Shōtoku Taishi. According to Shōtoku Taishi's biography, the *Hokke gisho* was composed in 615, but the exact dates of its compilation remain uncertain. The *Hokke gisho* relies on the Chinese monk Fayun's (467–529) earlier commentary, the *Fahua yiji*, to KUMĀRAJĪVA's Chinese translation of the *Saddharmapuṇḍarīkasūtra*. Because of its attribution to Shōtoku Taishi, the *Hokke gisho* is considered an important source for studying the thought of this legendary figure in the evolution of Japanese Buddhism, but the extent of its influence on the early Japanese tradition remains a matter of debate.

**Hōkōji**. (J) (法興寺). See ASUKADERA.

**Hōkyōki**. (寶慶記). In Japanese, "Record from the Baoqing era," a treatise attributed to Japanese SŌTŌSHŪ ZEN master DŌGEN KIGEN. The *Hōkyōki* was discovered after Dōgen's death by his disciple Koun Ejō (1198–1280) and a preface was prepared in 1750. The *Hōkyōki* is purportedly a record of Dōgen's tutelage under the Chinese CAODONG ZONG master TIANTONG RUJING during his sojourn in China during the Baoqing reign era (1225–1227) of the Southern Song dynasty. The *Hōkyōki* records specific instructions attributed to Rujing, including such topics as the "sloughing off body and mind" (J. SHINJIN DATSURAKU), seated meditation (J. zazen; C. ZUOCHAN), and his doctrinal teachings.

**homa**. (T. sbyin sreg; C. humo; J. goma; K. homa 護摩). In Sanskrit, "burnt offering," an esoteric Buddhist ritual in which various offerings are consigned to flames. In the older Brahmanical traditions of the Indian subcontinent, burnt offerings were made through the medium of the deity AGNI (the god of fire) to the Vedic gods, in exchange for the boon of cattle and other forms of wealth. These rituals were systematized first in the Brāhmaṇas, and subsequently in the Āraṇyaka literature, where the exoteric homa rituals were questioned and reconceptualized as inner worship. Buddhist TANTRA includes both an outer offering of grain and other materials into a fire, and an inner offering into the fire of transcendental wisdom. In the latter, the inner offering is done by visualizing a skull cup (KAPĀLA) atop a triangular fire in a hearth made of three skulls. Impure objects are visualized as melting into a bliss-producing nectar (AMṚTA) that is then offered to one's GURU and to oneself visualized as the meditation deity. In Tibetan Buddhism, a homa ritual is often performed at the end of a meditation retreat as a means of purification.

**Honchō kōsōden**. (本朝高僧伝). In Japanese, "Biographies of Eminent Clerics of Japan"; a late Japanese biographic collection, written by the RINZAISHŪ ZEN monk Mangen Shiban (1626–1710) in 1702, in a total of seventy-five rolls. The *Honchō kōsōden* includes the biographies of 1,662 Japanese priests affiliated with a variety of Buddhist sects (except, prominently, the JŌDO SHINSHŪ and NICHIRENSHŪ) from the sixth century onward. Unlike Shiban's 1678 ENPŌ DENTŌROKU, which contains over one thousand biographies of only Zen clerics and lay practitioners, the *Honchō kōsōden* also discusses clerics from other schools of Japanese Buddhism. The biographies are divided into ten general categories: founders, exegetes, meditators, thaumaturges, VINAYA specialists, propagators, ascetics, pilgrims, scriptural reciters, and others. As the most comprehensive and voluminous Japanese collection of biographies of eminent clerics, the text is an indispensable work for research into the lineage histories of many of the most important schools of Japanese Buddhism. In 1867, the SHINGONSHŪ monk Hosokawa Dōkai (1816–1876) compiled a supplement to this collection, titled the *Zoku Nippon kōsōden* ("Supplement to the Eminent Clerics of Japan"), which including biographies of over two hundred clerics of the premodern period, in a total of eleven rolls.

**Hōnen**. (法然) (1133–1212). Japanese monk regarded as the founder of the JŌDOSHŪ, or PURE LAND school. Hōnen was a native of Mimasaka province. After his father's violent death, Hōnen was entrusted to his uncle, a monk at the nearby monastery of Bodaiji. Hōnen later headed for HIEIZAN in 1147 to received ordination. He began his studies under the TENDAISHŪ (C. TIANTAI ZONG) monks Genkō (d.u.) and Kōen (d. 1169), but the corruption he perceived within the Tendai community at ENRYAKUJI led Hōnen to seek teachings elsewhere. In 1150, he visited the master Eikū (d. 1179), a disciple of the monk RYŌNIN, in Kurodani on Mt. Hiei, where he remained for the next twenty years. Under Eikū's guidance, Hōnen studied GENSHIN's influential treatise, the ŌJŌ YŌSHŪ and became a specialist in the practice of nenbutsu ("recollecting the Buddha's name"; see C. NIANFO). Hōnen is also said to have devoted himself exclusively to the practice of invoking the name of the buddha AMITĀBHA (a type of nenbutsu) after perusing the Chinese monk SHANDAO's influential commentary on the GUAN WULIANGSHOU JING, the *Guan Wuliangshou jing shu*. In 1175, Hōnen left Mt. Hiei and established himself in the district of Higashiyama Yoshimizu in the capital Kyōto. His fame grew after his participation in the Ōhara discussion of 1186, which explored how pure land beliefs and practices could help overcome human suffering. Hōnen soon attracted many followers, including such prominent figures as the regent Kujō Kanezane (1149–1207). In 1198, Hōnen compiled his influential treatise, SENCHAKUSHŪ. Due perhaps to his growing influence and his purported rejection of the Tendai teachings of original enlightenment (HONGAKU), the monks of Enryakuji began attacking Hōnen, banning his practice of nenbutsu in 1204. The monks of the Nara monastery of KŌFUKUJI also petitioned the retired emperor Gotoba (r. 1183–1198) to ban the practice in 1205. A scandal involving two of Hōnen's disciples led to his exile to Shikoku in 1207 and the execution of four of his disciples. He was later pardoned and returned to Kyōto in 1211. Due to illness, he died the next year in what is now known as the Seishidō in the monastery of Chion'in. Hōnen preached that, in the current degeneration age of the dharma (J. mappō; C. MOFA), the exclusive practice of nenbutsu was the only way through which salvation could be achieved. Due in part to Hōnen's advocacy, nenbutsu eventually became one of the predominant practices of Japanese Buddhism. Hōnen's preeminent disciple was SHINRAN (1173–1262), who further radicalized pure land practice by insisting that salvation was only possible through the grace of Amitābha, rather than through continuous nenbutsu practice.

**hongaku**. (本覺). In Japanese, "original enlightenment." The notion that enlightenment was a quality inherent in the minds of all sentient beings (SATTVA) initially developed in East Asia largely due to the influence of such presumptive APOCRYPHA as the DASHENG QIXIN LUN. The *Dasheng qixin lun* posited a distinction between the potentiality to become a buddha that was inherent in the minds of every sentient being, as expressed by the term "original enlightenment" (C. BENJUE; pronounced hongaku in Japanese); and the soteriological process through which that potential for enlightenment had to be put into practice, which it called "actualized enlightenment" (C. SHIJUE; J. shikaku). This distinction is akin to the notion that a person may in reality *be* enlightened (original enlightenment), but still needs to learn through a course of religious training how to *act* on that enlightenment (actualized enlightenment). This scheme was further developed in numerous treatises and commentaries written by Chinese exegetes in the DI LUN ZONG, HUAYAN ZONG, and TIANTAI ZONG. ¶ In medieval Japan, this imported soteriological interpretation of "original enlightenment" was reinterpreted into an ontological affirmation of things just as they are. Enlightenment was thence viewed not as a soteriological experience, but instead as something made manifest in the lived reality of everyday life. Hongaku thought also had wider cultural influences, and was used, for example, to justify conceptually incipient doctrines of the identity between the buddhas and bodhisattvas of Buddhism and the indigenous deities (KAMI) of Japan (see HONJI SUIGAKU; SHINBUTSU SHŪGŌ). Distinctively Japanese treatments of original enlightenment thought begin in the mid-eleventh century, especially through oral transmissions (kuden) within the medieval TENDAISHŪ tradition. These interpretations were subsequently written down on short slips of paper (KIRIGAMI) that were gradually assembled into more extensive treatments. These interpretations ultimately came to be attributed by tradition to the great Tendai masters of old, such as SAICHŌ (767–822), but connections to these earlier teachers are dubious at best and the exact dates and attributions of these materials are unclear. During the late Heian and Kamakura periods, hongaku thought bifurcated into two major lineages, the Eshin and Danna (both of which subsequently divided into numerous subbranches). This bifurcation was largely a split between followers of the two major disciples of the Tendai monk RYŌGEN: GENSHIN (942–1017) of Eshin'in in YOKAWA (the famous author of the ŌJŌ YŌSHŪ); and Kakuun (953–1007) of Danna'in in the Eastern pagoda complex at ENRYAKUJI on HIEIZAN. The Tendai tradition claims that these two strands of interpretation derive from Saichō, who learned these different approaches while studying Tiantai thought in China under Daosui (J. Dōsui/Dōzui; d.u.) and Xingman (J. Gyōman; d.u.), and subsequently transmitted them to his successors in Japan; the distinctions between these two positions are, however, far from certain. Other indigenous Japanese schools of Buddhism that developed later during the Kamakura period, such as the JŌDOSHŪ and JŌDO SHINSHŪ, seem to have harbored more of a critical attitude toward the notion of original enlightenment. One of the common charges leveled against hongaku thought was that it fostered a radical antinomianism, which denied the need for either religious practice or ethical restraint. In the contemporary period, the notion of original enlightenment has been strongly criticized by advocates of "Critical Buddhism" (HIHAN BUKKYŌ) as an infiltration into Buddhism of Brahmanical notions of a perduring self (ĀTMAN); in addition, by valorizing the reality of the mundane world just as it is, hongaku thought was said to be an exploitative doctrine that had been used in Japan to justify societal inequality and political despotism. For broader East Asian perspectives on "original enlightenment," see BENJUE.

**Honganji**. (本願寺). In Japanese, "Original Vow Monastery." Honganji is the headquarters (honzan) of the JŌDO SHINSHŪ sect in Japan; it is located in the Shimogyō district of Kyōto. In 1277, Kakushinni (1224–1283), the daughter of the Japanese PURE LAND monk SHINRAN, designated her father's grave in the Ōtani district near Kyōto to be the primary memorial site for his worship. The site was later transformed into a temple, where an image of the buddha AMITĀBHA was installed. After a long period of factional disputes, the various groups of Shinran's followers were reunited by the eighth head priest of Honganji, RENNYO. In 1465, warrior monks from HIEIZAN razed Honganji and turned the site into one of their own branch temples (matsuji). In 1478, having gained enough support to counter any threat from Mt. Hiei, Rennyo moved Honganji to the Yamashina area of Kyōto. The move was completed in 1483 with the completion of the Amida hall. Under Rennyo's leadership, Honganji became the central monastery of the Jōdo Shinshū tradition. Rennyo built a broad network of temples that was consolidated under the sole administration of Honganji. After a brief move to Ōsaka, Honganji was relocated to its current site in Kyōto on the order of Toyotomi Hideyoshi (1536–1598). A split occurred between two factions shortly thereafter, and ever since the early seventeenth century the Nishi (West) and Higashi (East) Honganji complexes have served as the religious centers of these two major branches of Jōdo Shinshū, the NISHI HONGANJIHA and the HIGASHI HONGANJIHA (also known as the ŌTANIHA).

**Honggi**. (K) (洪基). See UDAM HONGGI.

**Hongming ji**. (J. Gumyōshū; K. Hongmyŏng chip 弘明集). In Chinese, "Collection on the Propagation and Clarification [of Buddhism]," compiled by the monk SENGYOU (445–518) of the Liang dynasty sometime between 515 and 518. The *Hongming ji* is a fourteen-roll collection of Buddhist apologetics, prepared in response to growing criticisms of the religion by rival Confucians and Daoists, and to interference in Buddhism's religious affairs by the government. Against these challenges, the *Hongming ji* attempted to defend the authenticity of the translated scriptures of Buddhism and its seminal doctrines. In its explanation and defense of such concepts as buddha or KARMAN, the *Hongming ji* drew not just on Buddhist sources, but also on the common terminology of its opponents. For this reason, the *Hongming ji* serves as an important source for studying the interactions between the different Chinese religious traditions and the process through which Buddhism was appropriated in early China. Sengyou's *Hongming ji* was expanded to thirty rolls by DAOXUAN in his *Guang hongming ji*.

**Hongren**. (J. Kōnin/Gunin; K. Hongin 弘忍) (601–674). Chinese Chan master and the reputed fifth patriarch of the Chan zong. Hongren was a native of Huangmei in Qizhou (present-day Hubei province). Little is known of his early life, but he eventually became the disciple of the fourth patriarch DAOXIN. After Daoxin's death in 651, Hongren succeeded his teacher and moved to Mt. Fengmao (also known as Dongshan or East Mountain), the east peak of Mt. Shuangfeng (Twin Peaks) in Huangmei. Hongren's teachings thus came to be known as the "East Mountain teachings" (DONGSHAN FAMEN), although that term is later applied also to the lineage and teachings of both Daoxin and Hongren. After his move to Mt. Fengmao, disciples began to flock to study under Hongren. Although Hongren's biography in the CHUAN FABAO JI certainly exaggerates when it says that eight to nine out of every ten Buddhist practitioners in China studied under him, there is no question that the number of students of the East Mountain teachings grew significantly over two generations. The twenty-five named disciples of Hongren include such prominent figures as SHENXIU, Zhishen (609–702), Lao'an (d. 708), Faru (638–689), Xuanze (d.u.), and HUINENG, the man who would eventually be recognized by the mature Chan tradition as the sixth, and last, patriarch. The legendary account of Hongren's mind-to-mind transmission (YIXIN CHUANXIN) of the DHARMA to Huineng can be found in the LIUZU TAN JING. Later, Emperor Daizong (r. 762–779) bestowed upon Hongren the title Chan master Daman (Great Abundance). The influential treatise XIUXIN YAO LUN ("Treatise on the Essentials of Cultivating the Mind") is attributed to Hongren; it stresses the importance of "guarding the mind" (SHOUXIN). In that text, the relationship between the pure mind and the afflictions (KLEŚA) is likened to that between the sun and the clouds: the pure mind is obscured by afflictions just as the sun is covered by layers of clouds; but if one can guard the mind so that it is kept free from false thoughts and delusions, the sun of NIRVĀṆA will then appear. The text suggests two specific meditation techniques for realizing this goal: one is continuously to visualize the original, pure mind (viz., the sun) so that it shines without obscuration; the other is to concentrate on one's own deluded thoughts (the clouds) until they disappear. These two techniques purport to "guard the mind" so that delusion can never recur.

**Hongzan fahua zhuan**. (C) (弘贊法華傳). See FAHUA ZHUAN.

**Hongzhi Zhengjue**. (J. Wanshi Shōgaku; K. Koengji Chŏnggak 宏智正覺) (1091–1157). Chinese CHAN master in the CAODONG ZONG. Hongzhi was a native of Xizhou in present-day Shanxi province, and later came to be known as the "Old Buddha of Xizhou." At age ten, he entered the monastery of Jingmingsi under the monk Benzong (d.u.) and four years later received the full monastic precepts from Zhiqiong (d.u.) at Ciyunsi. Hongzhi then set out to visit various teachers throughout the country and first studied under the Chan master Kumu Facheng (1071–1128). Hongzhi eventually became a student of the Chan master Danxia Zichun (1064–1117) and inherited his Caodong lineage. In 1124, Hongzhi became the abbot of Puzhaosi in Sizhou (present-day Anhui province). After holding posts at various other monasteries, Hongzhi was finally invited to Mt. Tiantong (in present-day Zhejiang province) in 1129 and spent the next three decades restoring his monastery at that mountain site. The great SAMGHA hall (SENGTANG) that he constructed there is said to have housed more than twelve hundred monks. Hongzhi is thus often referred to as the reviver of Mt. Tiantong. Hongzhi is best known within the Chan tradition for teaching a style of meditation he called "silent-illumination chan" (MOZHAO CHAN). Hongzhi also maintained a lengthy and close relationship with his friend and rival, the eminent LINJI ZONG master DAHUI ZONGGAO, who was a virulent critic of mozhao Chan. Hongzhi composed the MOZHAO MING and his teachings can be found in the *Hongzhi Jue chanshi yuyao*, *Hongzhi Jue chanshi yulu*, and *Hongzhi guanglu*. Hongzhi's famous verse commentaries on a hundred "old cases" (see GONG'AN) can be found in the CONGRONG LU. Emperor Gaozong subsequently bestowed upon him the title Chan master Hongzhi (Expansive Wisdom).

**Hongzhou zong**. (J. Kōshūshū; K. Hongju chong 洪州宗). The Hongzhou school of Chinese CHAN derives its name from the Hongzhou region in Jiangxi province, where the Chan master MAZU DAOYI developed his unique style of Chan pedagogy. The name was first used by the Chan historian GUIFENG ZONGMI to refer primarily to those who traced their lineage back to Mazu and his immediate disciples. According to traditional accounts of their teachings, Chan masters in the Hongzhou line regarded all activities of everyday life as the very functioning of the buddha-nature (FOXING) itself. Since everything in the conditioned realm, therefore, was presumed to be a manifestation of the buddha-nature, Hongzhou adepts were said to claim that all actions, whether right or wrong, good or evil, and so forth, were equally the functioning of the enlightened mind. Zongmi criticized this view as promoting a dangerous antinomianism in Chan, which fostered unrestrained conduct (see WU'AI XING). Normative portrayals in Chan literature of iconoclastic masters striking their students, shouting, and pinching their students' noses derive from stereotypes fostered within the Hongzhou school. Largely through the efforts of Mazu's prominent disciples BAIZHANG HUAIHAI and NANQUAN PUYUAN, the Hongzhou line came to be the dominant Chan lineage in medieval China and eventually evolved into the GUIYANG ZONG and LINJI ZONG of the mature Chan tradition. The Hongzhou lineage was also extremely influential in Silla and Koryŏ-period Korea as well, where eight of the nine sites associated with the Korean Nine Mountains Sŏn school (KUSAN SŎNMUN) were founded during the ninth century by teachers who studied in China with Hongzhou masters.

**honji suijaku**. (本地垂迹). In Japanese, "manifestation from the original state"; an indigenous Japanese explanation of the way in which the imported religion of Buddhism interacted with local religious cults. In this interpretation, an originally Indian buddha, BODHISATTVA, or divinity (the "original ground," or "state"; J. honji) could manifest or incarnate in the form of a local Japanese deity (KAMI) or its icon, which was then designated the "trace it dropped" (J. suijaku). The notion of honji suijaku was derived from the earlier Buddhist doctrine of multiple buddha bodies (BUDDHAKĀYA), especially the so-called transformation body (NIRMĀṆAKĀYA). The honji suijaku doctrine thus facilitated the systematic incorporation of local deities within Buddhism, speeding the localization of Buddhism within the religious culture of Japan. A movement forcefully to separate from Buddhism the local deities, now known collectively as SHINTŌ, occurred during the Meiji period (see HAIBUTSU KISHAKU). See also SHINBUTSU SHŪGŌ.

**honmon**. (C. benmen; K. ponmun 本門). In Japanese, lit. "fundamental teaching" or "origin teaching"; the essential core of the SADDHARMAPUṆḌARĪKASŪTRA ("Lotus Sūtra"), which is detailed in the latter fourteen of the scripture's twenty-eight chapters; in distinction to the SHAKUMON (lit. "trace teaching"), the provisional first half of the sūtra. The term is especially important in both the TIANTAI (J. TENDAI) and NICHIREN-oriented schools of East Asian Buddhism. The honmon is regarded as the teaching preached by the true Buddha, who attained buddhahood an infinite number of KALPAS ago. Traditionally, the sixteenth chapter of the *Saddharmapuṇḍarīkasūtra*, "The Longevity of the TATHĀGATA," is believed to constitute the central chapter of the honmon. In this chapter, the Buddha reveals his true identity: he became enlightened in the remote past, yet he appears to have a limited lifespan and to pass into NIRVĀṆA in order to inspire sentient beings' spiritual practice, since if they were to know about the Buddha's eternal presence, they might not exert themselves. Honmon is also called the "effect" or "fruition" section of the scripture, since it preaches the omnipresence of the Buddha, which is a consequence of the long process of training that he undertook in the course of achieving enlightenment. The Tiantai master TIANTAI ZHIYI (538–597) first applied the two terms honmon and shakumon to distinguish these two parts of the *Saddharmapuṇḍarīkasūtra*; he compared the two teachings to the moon in the sky and its reflection on the surface of a pond, respectively. Zhiyi considered the honmon to be different from the shakumon and other scriptural teachings in that it alone revealed the fundamental enlightenment of the Buddha in the distant past. He thus argued that, even though the honmon and shakumon are inconceivably one, the timeless principle of enlightenment itself is revealed in the honmon and all other teachings are merely the "traces" of this principle. The Japanese Tendai tradition offered a slightly different understanding of honmon: despite the fact that ŚĀKYAMUNI Buddha attained buddhahood numerous eons ago, his manifestation in this world served as a metaphor for the enlightenment inherent in all living things. Tendai thus understood honmon to mean "original enlightenment" (HONGAKU; see also C. BENJUE) and the dynamic phase of suchness (TATHATĀ) that accorded with phenomenal conditions, while "shakumon" was the "acquired enlightenment" (see C. SHIJUE) and the immutable phase of suchness as the unchanging truth. Most crucially, the Tendai tradition emphasized the superiority of honmon over shakumon. The two terms are also important in the various Nichiren-related schools of Japanese Buddhism. NICHIREN (1222–1282) maintained that *myōhōrengekyō*, the Japanese title (DAIMOKU) of the *Saddharmapuṇḍarīkasūtra*, was in fact the true honmon of the sutra.

**honmon no daimoku**. (本門の題目). In Japanese, lit. "DAIMOKU of the essential teaching"; term used specifically in the NICHIREN and associated schools of Japanese Buddhism to refer to the essential teaching epitomized in the title of the SADDHARMAPUṆḌARĪKASŪTRA ("Lotus Sūtra"). The title of the sūtra is presumed to summarize the gist of the entire scripture and it is recited in its Japanese pronunciation (see NAM MYŌHŌRENGEKYŌ) as a principal religious practice of the Nichiren and SŌKA GAKKAI schools. Recitation of the title of the *Saddharmapuṇḍarīkasūtra* was advocated as one of the "three great esoteric laws" (SANDAIHIHŌ) by the Japanese reformer NICHIREN (1222–1282) and was said to exemplify mastery of wisdom (PRAJÑĀ) in the three trainings (TRIŚIKṢĀ).

**Honwŏn**. (K) (混元). See CHINMYŎNG HONWŎN.

**Hōōdō**. (J) (鳳凰堂). See BYŌDŌIN.

**Horner, Isaline Blew**. (1896–1981). British translator of Pāli texts, who published as I. B. Horner. She was born in Walthamstow, England, in 1896 and attended Newnham College at Cambridge in 1914. When she was twelve years of age, her grandmother had introduced her to the pioneering Pāli scholars THOMAS RHYS DAVIDS and CAROLINE RHYS DAVIDS. Thomas Rhys Davids had founded the PĀLI TEXT SOCIETY in 1881; Horner would eventually become its fourth president in 1959. Horner traveled extensively in Sri Lanka (then Ceylon), India, and Burma. Over a four-decade-long career, Horner was a prolific editor and translator of Pāli texts. Her most significant contribution to the field of Pāli studies was a six-volume translation of the VINAYAPIṬAKA, which she worked on from 1938–1966. Her most important original piece of scholarship was her book *Women under Primitive Buddhism: Laywomen and Almswomen*, which was published in 1930. Her account of Buddhist women and their roles in sixth century BCE India was the first of its kind to be published in the West and has served as an important source for the study of gender in Buddhism. Horner also published a study of the arahant/ARHAT in her book *The Early Buddhist Theory of Man Perfected* (1934).

**Hōryūji**. (法隆寺). In Japanese, "Dharma Flourishing Monastery." Hōryūji is considered one of the seven great monasteries in former capital of Nara. The monastery is currently affiliated with the Shōtoku tradition and serves as the headquarters (honzan) of the Hossō school (C. FAXIANG ZONG). According to extant inscriptions, Empress Suiko (r. 592–628) and SHŌTOKU TAISHI (574–622) built Hōryūji in 607 to honor the deathbed wishes of retired Emperor Yōmei (r. 585–587). Prince Shōtoku's estate in Ikaruga was chosen as the site for the construction project. A famous Shaka (ŚĀKYAMUNI) triad produced perhaps in the early seventh century is installed in its Golden Hall (Kondō). Hōryūji is also famous for its numerous ancient icons and ritual artifacts and also for its five-story pagoda and Golden Hall, which is one of the oldest standing wooden structures in Japan. The monastery is currently divided into eastern and western cloisters.

**hotoke**. (佛). A vernacular Japanese term for "buddha." Colloquially, hotoke is also used to refer to a deceased person or the soul of a deceased person.

**Hottō Kokushi**. (J) (法燈國師). See SHINCHI KAKUSHIN.

**Hŏŭng Pou**. (虚應普雨) (1515–1565). Korean SŎN monk of the mid-Chosŏn dynasty, also known as Naam. In 1530, Pou entered the hermitage of Mahayŏnam on KŬMGANGSAN. In 1548, with the help of queen dowager Munjŏng (1501–1565), Pou became the abbot of the monastery of Pongŭnsa and, again with her help, he resuscitated the two traditions of SŎN (Meditation) and KYO (Doctrine) in Korea. In 1551, he was appointed the deputy chief of the Sŏn school (Sŏnjong p'ansa). With the help of some loyal officials, Pou also registered more than three hundred monasteries as officially sanctioned "pure monasteries" (chŏngch'al). Following the guidelines of the clerical certification system (toch'ŏpche), Pou reinstituted the clerical exams (SŬNGKWA) and oversaw the selection of four thousand monks. He was later given the title Sŏn master Todae (Capital's Greatest). In 1565, after the death of queen dowager Munjŏng, anti-Buddhist memorials to the throne led to Pou losing his clerical certification and he was exiled to, and eventually executed on, Cheju Island. His teachings are recorded in the *Hŏŭngdang chip* and *Naam chapchŏ*. He also composed the influential treatises *Suwŏltoryang konghwabulsa yŏhwanbinju mongjung mundap* (usually abbreviated as *Mongjung mundap*) and *Kwŏnnyŏm yorok*.

**hrī**. (P. hiri; T. ngo tsha shes pa; C. can; J. zan; K. ch'am 慚). In Sanskrit, "decency," "shame," or "conscience," one of the fundamental mental concomitants (CAITTA) presumed to accompany all wholesome actions (KUŚALA) and therefore listed as the fifth of the ten "omnipresent wholesome factors" (kuśala-MAHĀBHŪMIKA) in the SARVĀSTIVĀDA ABHIDHARMA and the second of eleven wholesome mental concomitants in the hundred-dharma list (see BAIFA) of the YOGĀCĀRA school. It is also one of the twenty-five wholesome mental factors in the Pāli abhidhamma. "Decency" is often seen in compound with the term "modesty" or "fear" of wrongdoing (APATRĀPYA), where hrī refers to the pangs of moral conscience that one feels at the prospect of engaging in an immoral act, whereas apatrāpya refers to the fear of being blamed by others for engaging in such acts. This dual sense of "shame and blame" was thought to be foundational to progress in morality (ŚĪLA).

**Hsüan-tsang**. (C). Outmoded Wade-Giles transcription of the Chinese pilgrim and translator Xuanzang. See XUANZANG.

**huafa sijiao**. (C) (化法四教). See TIANTAI BAJIAO.

**Huahu jing**. (C) (化胡經). See LAOZI HUAHU JING.

**Huaihai**. (C) (懷海). See BAIZHANG HUAIHAI.

**Huairang**. (C) (懷讓). See NANYUE HUAIRANG.

**Huaisu**. (J. Kaiso; K. Hoeso 懷素) (634–707). Chinese VINAYA master of the Tang dynasty. Huaisu was ordained at the age of eleven by XUANZANG, under whom he studied various SŪTRAS and ŚĀSTRAS. After receiving his precepts, Huaisu studied the *Sifen lü xingshi chao* with its author, the renowned vinaya master DAOXUAN. Huaisu also studied Fali's *Sifen lü shu* under one of his major disciples. After studying the SIFEN LÜ ("Four-Part Vinaya") of the DHARMAGUPTAKA school with these teachers, Huaisu decided to rectify what he considered flaws in earlier studies of the vinaya and composed the *Sifen lü kaizong ji*, in twenty rolls. Huaisu's text soon came to known as the "new commentary" (xinshu), and he and his followers came to be called the East Pagoda vinaya school (DONGTA LÜ ZONG) in distinction to Daoxuan's NANSHAN LÜ ZONG (Mt. Nan vinaya school) and Fali's XIANGBU LÜ ZONG (Xiang Region vinaya school). Huaisu also authored commentaries on the ABHIDHARMAKOŚABHĀṢYA, the Dharmaguptaka BHIKṢU precepts and their ecclesiastical procedures (karmavācanā), and various other texts.

**Huangbo Xiyun**. (J. Ōbaku Kiun; K. Hwangbyŏk Hŭiun 黃檗希運) (d. 850). Chinese CHAN master of the Tang dynasty. Huangbo was a native of Min in present-day Fujian province. Little is known of his early life, but he eventually became a monk on Mt. Huangbo in Fuzhou (present-day Fuzhou province). Huangbo later became the disciple of the eminent Chan master BAIZHANG HUAIHAI, a first-generation successor to MAZU DAOYI. After he left Baizhang's side, Huangbo became the abbot of the monastery of Da'ansi where he trained many students. At the invitation of the powerful minister of state Pei Xiu (787–860), Huangbo left for Zhongling (present-day Jiangxi province) and began to reside on a local mountain that he renamed Mt. Huangbo, whence he acquired his toponym. During this period, Huangbo acquired many more disciples and established himself as a major Chan master. In 842, Huangbo relocated to the monastery of Longxingsi and again to Kaiyuansi in Wanling (present-day Anhui province) in 848. His most famous disciple is LINJI YIXUAN (d. 867) whose lineage became the dominant Chan school in China, the eponymous LINJI ZONG. Huangbo's teachings focus on the notion of the "one mind" (YIXIN) that vivifies all things, including enlightened buddhas and unenlightened sentient beings. Chan practice therefore involves simply bringing an end to all discriminative thought so that the one mind will be made manifest. Pei Xiu compiled his notes of Huangbo's lectures, which he titled the CHUANXIN FAYAO. Huangbo received the posthumous title Chan master Duanji (Eradicating Limits).

**Huanglong Huinan**. (J. Ōryō/Ōryū Enan; K. Hwangnyong Hyenam 黃龍慧南) (1002–1069). Song-dynasty Chan monk who is regarded as the founder of the HUANGLONG PAI collateral lineage of the LINJI ZONG. He ordained as a monk at the age of eleven, eventually becoming a disciple of Shishuang Chuyuan (986–1039), a sixth-generation successor in the Linji school. He spent much of his life teaching at Mt. Huanglong in Xiushui county of Jiangxi province, whence he acquired his toponym. Huanglong was famous for employing three crucial questions to challenge his students and encourage their cultivation; these are known as "Huanglong's Three Checkpoints" (Huanglong sanguan): What conditioned your birth (viz., why were you born)? Why are my hands like the Buddha's? Why are my feet like a donkey's? His Huanglong lineage lasted for about one hundred fifty years, before being reabsorbed into the rival YANGQI PAI.

**Huanglong pai**. (J. Ōryōha/Ōryūha; K. Hwangnyong p'a 黃龍派). In Chinese, "Huanglong school"; collateral lineage of the CHAN school's LINJI ZONG, one of the five houses and seven schools (WU JIA QI ZONG) of the Chan during the Northern Song dynasty (960–1126). The school's name comes from the toponym of its founder, HUANGLONG HUINAN (1002–1069), who taught at Mt. Huanglong in present-day Jiangxi province; Huinan was a disciple of Shishuang Chuyuan (986–1039), himself a sixth-generation successor in the Linji school. The Huanglong school was especially known for "lettered Chan" (WENZI CHAN), a style of Chan that valorized belle lettres, and especially poetry, in Chan practice. Many of the most influential monks in the Huanglong school exemplified a period when Chan entered the mainstream of Chinese intellectual life: their practice of Chan was framed and conceptualized in terms that drew from their wide learning and profound erudition, tendencies that helped make Chan writings particularly appealing to wider Chinese literati culture. JUEFAN HUIHONG (1071–1128), for example, decried the bibliophobic tendencies in Chan that were epitomized in the aphorism that Chan "does not establish words and letters" (BULI WENZI) and advocated that Chan insights were in fact made manifest in both Buddhist sūtras and the uniquely Chan genres of discourse records (YULU), lineage histories (see CHUANDENG LU), and public-case anthologies (GONG'AN). Huanglong and YUNMEN ZONG masters made important contributions to the development of the Song Chan literary styles of songgu ([attaching] verses to ancient [cases]) and niangu (raising [and analyzing] ancient [cases]). Because of their pronounced literary tendencies, many Huanglong monks became close associates of such Song literati-officials as Su Shi (1036–1101), Huang Tingjian (1045–1105), and ZHANG SHANGYING (1043–1122). After the founder's death, discord appeared within the Huanglong lineage: the second-generation master Baofeng Kewen (1025–1102) and his disciple Juefan Huihong criticized the practices of another second-generation master Donglin Changzong (1025–1091) and his disciples as clinging to silence and simply waiting for enlightenment; this view may have influenced the subsequent criticism of the CAODONG ZONG by DAHUI ZONGGAO (1089–1163), who trained for a time with the Huanglong master Zhantang Wenjun (1061–1115). The Huanglong pai was the first school of Chan to be introduced to Japan: by MYŌAN EISAI (1141–1215), who studied with the eighth-generation Huanglong teacher Xu'an Huaichang (d.u.). The Huanglong pai did not survive as a separate lineage in either country long after the twelfth century, as its rival YANGQI PAI came to prominence; it was eventually reabsorbed into the Yangqi lineage.

**huatou**. (J. watō; K. hwadu 話頭). In Chinese, "topic of inquiry"; in some contexts, "critical phrase" or "keyword." The Song-dynasty CHAN master DAHUI ZONGGAO, in the LINJI ZONG, popularized a meditative technique in which he urged his students (many of whom were educated literati) to use a Chan case (GONG'AN) as a "topic of meditative inquiry" (huatou) rather than interpret it from purely intellectual or literary perspectives. Perhaps the most famous and most widely used huatou is the topic "no" (WU) attributed to the Chan master ZHAOZHOU CONGSHEN: A monk asked Zhaozhou, "Does a dog have buddha-nature (FOXING), or not?," to which Zhaozhou replied "WU" ("no"; lit. "it does not have it"; see GOUZI WU FOXING; WU GONG'AN). Because of the widespread popularity of this particular one-word topic in China, Korea, and Japan, this huatou is often interpreted as a "critical phrase'" or "keyword," in which the word "wu" is presumed to be the principal topic and thus the "keyword," or "critical phrase," of the longer gong'an exchange. Because Zhaozhou's answer in this exchange goes against the grain of East Asian Mahāyāna Buddhism—which presumes that all sentient beings, including dogs, are inherently enlightened—the huatou helps to foster questioning, or technically "doubt" (YIQING), the focus of a new type of Chan meditation called KANHUA CHAN, "the Chan of investigating the huatou." Huatou (which literally means "head of speech," and thus "topic") might best be taken metaphorically as the "apex of speech," or the "point at which (or beyond which) speech exhausts itself." Speech is of course initiated by thought, so "speech" in this context refers to all the discriminative tendencies of the mind, viz., conceptualization. By leading to the very limits of speech—or more accurately thought—the huatou acts as a purification device that frees the mind of its conceptualizing tendencies, leaving it clear, attentive, and calm. Even though the huatou is typically a word or phrase taken from the teachings of previous Chan masters, it is a word that is claimed to bring an end to conceptualization, leaving the mind receptive to the influence of the unconditioned. As Dahui notes, huatou produces a "cleansing knowledge and vision" (see JÑĀNADARŚANA) that "removes the defects of conceptual understanding so that one may find the road leading to liberation." Huatou is thus sometimes interpreted in Chinese Buddhism as a type of meditative "homeopathy," in which one uses a small dosage of the poison of concepts to cure the disease of conceptualization. Dahui's use of the huatou technique was first taught in Korea by POJO CHINUL, where it is known by its Korean pronunciation as hwadu, and popularized by Chinul's successor, CHIN'GAK HYESIM. Investigation of the hwadu remains the most widespread type of meditation taught and practiced in Korean Buddhism. In Japanese Zen, the use of the watō became widespread within the RINZAISHŪ, due in large part to the efforts of HAKUIN EKAKU and his disciples.

**Huayan bu**. (J. Kegonbu; K. Hwaŏm pu 華嚴部). In Chinese, the "Huayan Division," one of the four major divisions into which the MAHĀYĀNA section of the Chinese Buddhist canon (see DAZANGJING) is divided. This division contains primarily the different Chinese translations of the AVATAṂSAKASŪTRA and its independent chapters. According to the scriptural catalogue (JINGLU) KAIYUAN SHIJIAO LU, this division comprises twenty-six texts (in 187 rolls) that were catalogued along with the different recensions of the *Avataṃsakasūtra*.

**Huayan dashu**. (C) (華嚴大疏). In Chinese, "Great Commentary to the *Huayan [Jing]*." See HUAYAN JING SHU.

**Huayan fajie guanmen**. (J. Kegon hokkai kanmon; K. Hwaŏm pŏpkye kwanmun 華嚴法界觀門). In Chinese, "Gate to the Discernments of the DHARMADHĀTU in the AVATAṂSAKASŪTRA," a seminal text of the HUAYAN ZONG, attributed to DUSHUN, the putative first patriarch of the school. The *Fajie guanmen* no longer exists as an independent text but is extant only in citations found in other works, such as FAZANG's *Fa putixin zhang* ("Treatise on Generating the Thought of Enlightenment"), the commentaries of CHENGGUAN and ZONGMI, and YONGMING YANSHOU's ZONGJING LU. The *Fajie guanmen* largely consists of three "discernments" (guan), of true emptiness, the mutual nonobstruction between principle and phenomena, and total pervasion and accommodation. The text outlines some of the fundamental principles that will govern future doctrinal development within the Huayan school, including the causal relationship that pertains between principle (LI) and phenomena (SHI). The text is characterized by its validation of the reality of the phenomenal world, which is commonly considered to be one of the fundamental characteristics of indigenous Chinese Buddhism.

**Huayan jing**. (C) (華嚴經). See AVATAṂSAKASŪTRA.

**Huayan jing ganying zhuan**. (J. Kegongyō kannōden; K. Hwaŏm kyŏng kamŭng chŏn 華嚴經感應傳). In Chinese, "Record of Miraculous Responses to the AVATAṂSAKASŪTRA," originally compiled by Huiying (a disciple of the HUAYAN patriarch FAZANG) and redacted by Hu Youzhen during the Tang dynasty (618–907). The "Record of Miraculous Responses" is a collection of miracle tales reportedly recounted by devotees of the *Avataṃsakasūtra*. Meant as a compilation of testimonial accounts of the magical efficacy of reciting, circulating, and revering the *Avataṃsakasūtra*, this work was the forerunner of analogous works created in subsequent dynasties in honor of the same scripture.

**Huayan jing helun**. (J. Kegongyō gōron; K. Hwaŏm kyŏng hap non 華嚴經合論). In Chinese, "A Comprehensive Exposition of the AVATAMSAKASŪTRA," a commentary written by LI TONGXUAN in the Tang dynasty (618–907), a reclusive lay Huayan adept and contemporary of the HUAYAN patriarch FAZANG. The commentary is also known as the "Commentary to the New [Translation] of the *Avataṃsakasūtra*" (*Xin Huayan jing lun*), because it comments on ŚIKṢĀNANDA's "new" eighty-roll translation of the *Avataṃsakasūtra*, rather than Buddhabhadra's "old" sixty-roll rendering, which had been the focus of all earlier Huayan commentarial writing. Li Tongxuan's "Exposition of the *Avataṃsakasūtra*" contained ideas that were quite distinct from standard Huayan interpretations, such as the emphasis on the centrality of the preliminary soteriological stage of the "ten faiths" (shixin), rather than the "ten abodes" (shizhu) that had been stressed in previous Huayan accounts. Li's work subsequently played a key role in the revitalization of the Chinese Huayan exegetical tradition, especially in the thought of the Huayan patriarch CHENGGUAN. Li's worked dropped out of circulation soon after its composition, but after centuries in obscurity, the exposition was rediscovered by Chinese CHAN adepts during the Song dynasty, such as DAHUI ZONGGAO, and by Korean SŎN adepts during the Koryŏ dynasty for the provocative parallels they perceived between Li Tongxuan's treatment of Huayan soteriology and the Chan approach of sudden awakening (DUNWU). The Korean Sŏn exegete POJO CHINUL (1158–1210) was so inspired by the text that he wrote a three-roll abridgment of it entitled "Excerpts from the *Exposition of the Avataṃsakasūtra*" (*Hwaŏm non chŏryo*), which he used to demonstrate the parallels between the Huayan soteriological schema and his preferred meditative approach of "sudden awakening followed by gradual cultivation" (K. tono chŏmsu; C. TUNWU JIANXIU). In Japan, Li Tongxuan's advocacy of meditating on the light emanating from the Buddha's body was also a major influence on MYŌE KŌBEN.

**Huayan jingnei zhangmendeng za kongmu zhang**. (C) (華嚴經內章門等雜孔目章). See KONGMU ZHANG.

**Huayan jing shu**. (J. Kegongyōsho; K. Hwaŏm kyŏng so 華嚴經疏). In Chinese, "Commentary to the AVATAṂSAKASŪTRA"; the sixty-roll work of the HUAYAN patriarch CHENGGUAN, who is widely considered the principal force behind the revitalization of the Huayan exegetical tradition. Praised within the tradition as one of the two greatest commentaries on the *Avataṃsakasūtra*, along with FAZANG's HUAYAN TANXUAN JI, this work epitomizes Chengguan's attempt to salvage what he perceived to be the orthodox teachings of the patriarch FAZANG, whose intellectual legacy was presumed to have been misunderstood and misrepresented by some of his direct disciples. A comparable text aimed at resuscitating Huayan orthodoxy was Chengguan's *Huayan xuantan*. *Huayan jing shu* is also sometimes used as an alternate title for Fazang's *Huayan tanxuan ji*.

**Huayan jing souxuan ji**. (J. Kegongyō sōgenki; K. Hwaŏm kyŏng suhyŏn ki 華嚴經搜玄記). In Chinese, "Notes on Fathoming the Profundities of the AVATAṂSAKASŪTRA," a ten-roll exegesis of the *Avataṃsakasūtra*, written by the HUAYAN patriarch ZHIYAN. Using the Huayan school's idiosyncratic "Ten Profound Categories [of Dependent Origination]" (see SHI XUANMEN) to explain the intent of the sūtra, this work became the blueprint that FAZANG would later follow in writing his influential HUAYAN JING TANXUAN JI.

**Huayan jing suishu yanyi chao**. (J. Kegongyō zuisho engishō; K. Hwaŏm kyŏng suso yŏnŭi ch'o 華嚴經隨疏演義鈔). In Chinese, "Autocommentary to the Exegesis of the AVATAṂSAKASŪTRA," a ninety-roll autocommentary by the Huayan patriarch CHENGGUAN to his own sixty-roll exegesis of the *Avataṃsakasūtra*, the HUAYAN JING SHU; this massive work provides the most exhaustive presentation of Chengguan's thought in his oeuvre. In the autocommentary, Chengguan provides a general overview of the history and thought of the HUAYAN tradition, along with a painstaking line-by-line commentary to the text of the *Avataṃsakasūtra*. Chengguan explains the rise of the Huayan teachings and offers a classification of teachings (see JIAOXIANG PANSHI). These sections are followed by an explanation of such seminal Huayan doctrines as the dependent origination of the DHARMADHĀTU (FAJIE YUANQI). Chengguan also outlines the different capacities of sentient beings and provides a summary of the teachings of the different exegetical traditions in China. A comparative study of the various Chinese translations of the *Avataṃsakasūtra* follows, culminating in an analysis of the title of the sūtra. The autocommentary then follows with a detailed treatment of specific passages in the sūtra. Chengguan's attempt to define clearly the boundaries between the different traditions of Buddhism, as well as his emphasis on a distinctively Huayan style of meditation, are noteworthy aspects of his commentary.

**Huayan jing tanxuan ji**. (J. Kegongyō tangenki; K. Hwaŏm kyŏng t'amhyŏn ki 華嚴經探玄記). In Chinese, "Notes Plumbing the Profundities of the AVATAṂSAKASŪTRA," FAZANG's twenty-roll commentary to BUDDHABHADRA's sixty-roll translation of the *Huayan jing* and one of the key texts that shaped the mature teachings of the HUAYAN ZONG. Fazang's commentary was especially beholden to ZHIYAN's HUAYAN JING SOUXUAN JI, which uses the idiosyncratic "Ten Profound

Categories [of Dependent Origination]" (see SHI XUANMEN) of the Huayan school to explain the meanings of the sūtra. Fazang's work was praised within the Huayan tradition as one of the two greatest commentaries to the *Avataṃsakasūtra*, along with CHENGGUAN's HUAYAN JING SHU and its accompanying autocommentary HUAYAN JING SUISHU YANYI CHAO.

**Huayan jing zhigui**. (J. Kegongyō shiki; K. Hwaŏm kyŏng chigwi 華嚴經旨歸). In Chinese, "A Guide to the AVATAṂSAKASŪTRA," one of FAZANG's several commentaries to the *Avataṃsakasūtra*; its format is unique in that it explains ten aspects of the sūtra, each argued with ten theses or examples. The symbolic ten sections and one hundred theses/examples (ten sections times ten theses/examples) that make up the commentary are consistent with the HUAYAN school's fascination with those two numbers, which were taken to represent notions such as "consummate interfusion" (YUANRONG) and "unimpeded interpenetration between all phenomena" (see SHISHI WU'AI FAJIE).

**Huayan jing zhuan[ji]**. (J. Kegongyō den[ki]; K. Hwaŏm kyŏng chŏn['gi] 華嚴經傳[記]). In Chinese, "Notes on the Transmission of the AVATAṂSAKASŪTRA," composed by the HUAYAN patriarch FAZANG; Fazang did not finish the text before he passed away, so his disciples Huiyuan and Huiying completed it posthumously. The work offers a treatment of the pre-eighth century history of the *Avataṃsakasūtra* in Chinese Buddhism, including discussions of the translators and translations of the sūtra, its circulation and instances of its recitation and explanation, commentaries, and other related texts relevant to the study of the scripture.

**Huayan Qingliang shu**. (C) (華嚴清涼疏). In Chinese, "Qingliang's [viz., Chengguan] Commentary to the *Huayan* [*Jing*]. See HUAYAN JING SHU.

**Huayan sansheng**. (J. Kegon no sanshō; K. Hwaŏm samsŏng 華嚴三聖). In Chinese, "the Three Sages of HUAYAN," refer to the three primary deities of the lotus-womb world (lianhuazang shijie; cf. TAIZŌKAI), the universe as described in the AVATAṂSAKASŪTRA, which contains infinitely layered cosmoses and interpenetrating realms. (1) VAIROCANA Buddha is considered to be the dharma body (DHARMAKĀYA) itself, who pervades the entire universe and from whom all other buddhas arose; he symbolizes the utmost fruition of bodhisattva practice. (2) SAMANTABHADRA, an advanced BODHISATTVA depicted as standing to Vairocana's right, symbolizes the profound aspiration and all-embracing practices undertaken by the bodhisattvas. (3) MAÑJUŚRĪ, another advanced bodhisattva depicted as standing to Vairocana's left, symbolizes the wisdom gleaned through mastering the bodhisattva path. The primary virtues represented by these two bodhisattvas are said to culminate in the perfection of the cosmic Vairocana. In the Huayan tradition, in particular, various other attributes and symbolisms are also attributed to the three deities.

**Huayanshe**. (J. Kegonsha; K. Hwaŏmsa 華嚴社). In Chinese, the "Huayan Society," founded by Nanchao of Hengzhou Longxing monastery in 822; it held regular congregations for the communal chanting of, and public lecturing on, the AVATAṂSAKASŪTRA. The famous poet BO JUYI (722–847) was a member of this prominent organization when it was at the height of its influence.

**Huayan shiyi**. (J. Kegon no jūi; K. Hwaŏm sibi 華嚴十異). In Chinese, "Ten Distinctions of the AVATAṂSAKASŪTRA," ten reasons why HUAYAN exegetes consider the *Avataṃsakasūtra* to be superior to all other scriptures and thus the supreme teaching of the Buddha. (1) The "time of its exposition" was unique (shiyi): the sūtra was supposedly the first scripture preached after the Buddha's enlightenment and thus offers the most unadulterated enunciation of his experience. (2) The "location of its exposition" was unique (chuyi): it is said that the BODHI TREE under which the sūtra was preached was the center of the "oceans of world systems of the lotus womb world" (S. padmagarbhalokadhātu; C. lianhuazang shijie; cf. TAIZŌKAI). (3) The "preacher" was unique (zhuyi): The sūtra was supposedly preached by VAIROCANA Buddha, as opposed to other "emanation buddhas." (4) The "audience" was unique (zhongyi): only advanced BODHISATTVAS—along with divinities and demigods who were in actuality emanations of the Buddha—were present for its preaching; thus, there was no division between MAHĀYĀNA and HĪNAYĀNA. (5) The "basis" of the sūtra was unique (suoyiyi): its teaching was based on the one vehicle (EKAYĀNA), not the other provisional vehicles created later within the tradition. (6) The "exposition" of the sūtra was unique (shuoyi): the *Avataṃsakasūtra* preached in this world system is consistent with the sūtra as preached in all other world systems; this is unlike other sūtras, which were provisional adaptations to the particular needs of this world system only. (7) The "status" of the vehicles in the sūtra were unique (weiyi): no provisional categorization of the three vehicles of Buddhism (TRIYĀNA) was made in this sūtra. This is because, according to the sūtra's fundamental theme of "unimpeded interpenetration," any one vehicle subsumes all other vehicles and teachings. (8) Its "practice" was unique (xingyi): the stages (BHŪMI) of the BODHISATTVA path are simultaneously perfected in this sūtra's teachings, as opposed to having to be gradually perfected step-by-step. (9) The enumeration of "dharma gates," or list of dharmas, was unique (famenyi): whereas other sūtras systematize doctrinal formulas using different numerical schemes (e.g., FOUR NOBLE TRUTHS, eightfold path, etc.), this sūtra exclusively employs in all its lists the number "ten"—a mystical number that symbolizes the sūtra's infinite scope and depth. (10) Its "instantiation" was unique (shiyi): even the most mundane phenomena described in the *Avataṃsakasūtra* (such as trees, water, mountains, etc.) are expressions of the deepest truth; this is unlike other sūtras that resort primarily to abstract, philosophical concepts like "emptiness" (ŚŪNYATĀ) or "suchness" (TATHATĀ) in order to express their profoundest truths.

**Huayan shiyi**. (J. Kegon no jūgi; K. Hwaŏm sibŭi 華嚴十義). In Chinese, "Ten Meanings [propounded by] the Huayan [School]." A central thesis of HUAYAN philosophy is the "unimpeded interpenetration of all phenomena" (shishi wu'ai; see SHISHI WU'AI FAJIE). In order to provide some sense of what this "unimpeded interpenetration" entails, Huayan exegetes employed ten examples to explain how each constituent of a pair of concepts mutually validates and subsumes the other constituent: (1) the "teaching" and the "meaning" it designates (jiaoyi); (2) "phenomena" and their underlying "principle" (lishi); (3) "understanding" and its "implementation" (jiexing); (4) "causes" and their "results" (yinguo); (5) the "expounders" of the dharma and the "dharma" they expound (renfa); (6) the "distinction" and "unity" between distinct things (fenqi jingwei); (7) the "teacher," his "disciple," the "dharma" that is imparted from the former to the latter, and the "wisdom" that the disciple receives from that dharma (shidi fazhi); (8) the "dominant" and the "subordinate," the "primary" and the "secondary," and relations that pertain between things (zhuban yizheng); (9) the enlightened sages who "respond" to the spiritual maturity of their audiences and the audiences whose spiritual maturity "solicited" the appearance of the enlightened sages in the world (suishenggen yushixian); and (10) the spiritual "obstacles" and their corresponding "antidotes," the "essence" of phenomena and their "functions" or "efficacy" (nishun tiyong zizai). Each constituent of the above ten dichotomies derives its contextualized meaning and provisional existence from its opposite, thereby illustrating the Huayan teaching of the interconnectedness and mutual interpenetration between all things.

**Huayan wujiao**. (J. Kegon no gokyō; K. Hwaŏm ogyo 華嚴五教). In Chinese, "Huayan's five classifications of the teachings." The HUAYAN ZONG recognizes two different versions of this doctrinal-classification schema, which ranks different strands of Buddhist teachings. The best-known version was outlined by DUSHUN and FAZANG: (1) The HĪNAYĀNA teachings (xiaojiao; cf. XIAOSHENG JIAO), also known as the śrāvakayāna teaching (shengwenjiao), was pejoratively referred to as "teachings befitting the [spiritually] obtuse" (yufa). The ĀGAMAS and the ABHIDHARMAS were relegated to this class, which supposedly dealt primarily with theories of elements (DHĀTU) and more basic concepts such as dependent origination (PRATĪTYASAMUTPĀDA). (2) The "elementary teaching [of Mahāyāna]" ([Dasheng] SHIJIAO). Within this category, two additional subgroups were differentiated. The first was the "initial teaching pertaining to emptiness" (kong shijiao), which encompassed the PRAJÑĀPĀRAMITĀ literature and exegetical traditions such as MADHYAMAKA. This class of teachings was characterized by an emphasis (or, in Huayan's polemical assessment, an overemphasis) on the doctrine of emptiness (ŚŪNYATĀ). The second subgroup, the "initial teaching pertaining to phenomena" (xiang shijiao), broaches the dynamic and phenomenal aspects of reality and did not confine itself to the theme of emptiness. YOGĀCĀRA and its traditional affiliate sūtras and commentaries were classified under this subgroup. Together, these two subgroups were deemed the provisional teachings (quanjiao) within the MAHĀYĀNA tradition. (3) The "advanced [Mahāyāna] teachings" ([Dasheng] ZHONGJIAO) focused on the way true suchness (ZHENRU; S. TATHATĀ) was innately immaculate but could be activated in response to myriad conditions. The DASHENG QIXIN LUN ("Awakening of Faith"), ŚRĪMĀLĀDEVĪSIṂHANĀDASŪTRA, and LAṄKĀVATĀRASŪTRA are examples of texts belonging to this doctrinal category. The treatment in these texts of the one mind (YIXIN) and TATHĀGATAGARBHA thought was considered a more definitive rendition of the MAHĀYĀNA teachings than were the elementary teachings (shijiao). (4) The "sudden teachings" (DUNJIAO), which includes texts like the VIMALAKĪRTINIRDEŚA, was ranked as a unique category of subitist teachings befitting people of keen spiritual faculties (TĪKṢṆENDRIYA), and therefore bypasses traditional, systematic approaches to enlightenment. The CHAN ZONG's touted soteriological methods involving sudden enlightenment (DUNWU) and its rejection of reliance on written texts led some Huayan teachers to relegate that school to this advanced, but still inferior, category of the teachings. Chan was thus superseded by, (5) the "perfect teachings" or "consummate teachings" (YUANJIAO). This supposedly most comprehensive and definitive strand of Buddhist teaching was reserved for the Huayan school and especially its definitive scripture, the AVATAṂSAKASŪTRA. ¶ The second version of five classifications was made by GUIFENG ZONGMI (780–841) in his YUANREN LUN: (1) The "teachings pertaining to the human and heavenly realms" (RENTIAN JIAO) encompassed "mundane" (LAUKIKA) practices, such as the observation of the five precepts (PAÑCAŚĪLA) and the ten wholesome ways of action (KUŚALA-KARMAPATHA); this classification was named because of its believed efficacy to lead practitioners to higher realms of rebirth. (2) The "HĪNAYĀNA teachings" (XIAOSHENG JIAO), which were similar to the previous "xiaojiao." (3) The "dharma-characteristics teachings of MAHĀYĀNA" (Dasheng faxiang jiao), which was analogous to the aforementioned "elementary teaching pertaining to phenomena" (xiang shijiao) in the preceding classification scheme. (4) The "characteristics-negating teachings of MAHĀYĀNA" (Dasheng poxiang jiao) was analogous to the preceding "elementary teaching pertaining to emptiness." (5) The "nature-revealing teaching of the one vehicle" (yisheng xiangxing jiao) was equivalent to the last three categories Fazang's system combined together. See also HUAYAN WUJIAO ZHANG.

**Huayan wujiao zhang**. (J. Kegon gokyōshō; K. Hwaŏm ogyo chang 華嚴五教章). In Chinese, "Essay on the Five [Categories of] Teachings According to Huayan" is one of the foundational treatises on the HUAYAN ZONG; composed by DUSHUN. The essay offers a systematic analysis and classification of all major Buddhist teachings according to their thematic differences, which were discussed in reference to such basic Huayan tenets as the ten profound meanings (see HUAYAN SHIYI) and the six aspects of phenomena (LIUXIANG). Dushun's influential work is the foundation of the Huayan doctrinal taxonomy, which divided the Buddhist scriptures into five levels based on the profundity of their respective teachings: HĪNAYĀNA (viz., the ĀGAMAS), elementary MAHĀYĀNA (viz., YOGĀCĀRA and MADHYAMAKA), advanced Mahāyāna (SADDHARMAPUṆḌARĪKASŪTRA), sudden teachings (typically CHAN), and perfect teachings (AVATAṂSAKASŪTRA). See also HUAYAN WUJIAO.

**Huayan youyi**. (J. Kegon yūi; K. Hwaŏm yuŭi 華嚴遊意). In Chinese, "An Excursion through the Meaning of the AVATAṂSAKASŪTRA," a brief one-roll commentary on the *Avataṃsakasūtra*, composed by JIZANG, between 597 and 599; it is reported to be a record of his oral lectures on the scripture delivered in Yangzhou. The work contains a rare SAN LUN ZONG perspective on the *Avataṃsakasūtra*, before the HUAYAN ZONG's own influential commentaries came to monopolize the interpretation of the scripture. This work is of particular interest because it also critiqued contemporaneous exegetical traditions in both north and south China.

**Huayan zhao**. (J. Kegon wa asa; K. Hwaŏm cho 華嚴朝). In Chinese, "the morning [when] the *Huayan* [*Jing* was preached]"; the first half of a popular expression describing the two major stages in the teaching career of the Buddha. According to Chinese Huayan legend, immediately following his enlightenment, the Buddha initially preached the AVATAṂSAKASŪTRA, or *Huayan jing*. "Morning" in this expression thus refers to the early stage of the Buddha's preaching career, which was likened to the sun rising at dawn. This statement is typically followed by NIEPAN XI, "dusk [when] the MAHĀPARINIRVĀṆASŪTRA [was preached]," since, according to the same legend, the Buddha preached that scripture just before he passed away (PARINIRVĀṆA)—a time that was likened to the sun setting at dusk.

**Huayan zong**. (J. Kegonshū; K. Hwaŏm chong 華嚴宗). In Chinese, "Flower Garland School," an important exegetical tradition in East Asian Buddhism. Huayan takes its name from the Chinese translation of the title of its central scripture, the AVATAṂSAKASŪTRA (or perhaps BUDDHĀVATAṂSAKASŪTRA). The Huayan tradition is also sometimes referred to the Xianshou zong, after the sobriquet, Xianshou, of one of its greatest exegetes, FAZANG. A lineage of patriarchs, largely consisting of the tradition's great scholiasts, was retrospectively created by later followers. The putative first patriarch of the Huayan school is DUSHUN, who is followed by ZHIYAN, Fazang, CHENGGUAN, and GUIFENG ZONGMI. The work of these exegetes exerted much influence in Korea largely through the writings of ŬISANG (whose exegetical tradition is sometimes known as the Pusŏk chong) and WŎNHYO. Hwaŏm teachings remained the foundation of Korean doctrinal exegesis from the Silla period onward, and continued to be influential in the synthesis that POJO CHINUL in the Koryŏ dynasty created between SŎN (CHAN) and KYO (the teachings, viz., Hwaŏm). The Korean monk SIMSANG (J. Shinjō; d. 742), a disciple of Fazang, who transmitted the Huayan teachings to Japan in 740 at the instigation of RYŌBEN (689–773), was instrumental in establishing the Kegon school in Japan. Subsequently, such teachers as MYŌE KŌBEN (1173–1232) and GYŌNEN (1240–1321) continued Kegon exegesis into the Kamakura period. In China, other exegetical traditions such as the DI LUN ZONG, which focused on only one part of the *Avataṃsakasūtra*, were eventually absorbed into the Huayan tradition. The Huayan tradition was severely weakened in China after the depredations of the HUICHANG FANAN, and because of shifting interests within Chinese Buddhism away from sūtra exegesis and toward Chan meditative practice and literature, and invoking the name of the buddha AMITĀBHA (see NIANFO). ¶ The Huayan school's worldview is derived from the central tenets of the imported Indian Buddhist tradition, but reworked in a distinctively East Asian fashion. Huayan is a systematization of the teachings of the *Avataṃsakasūtra*, which offered a vision of an infinite number of interconnected world systems, interfused in an all-encompassing realm of reality (DHARMADHĀTU). This profound interdependent and ecological vision of the universe led Huayan exegetes to engage in a creative reconsideration of the central Buddhist doctrine of dependent origination (PRATĪTYASAMUTPĀDA), which in their interpretation meant that all phenomena in the universe are mutually creating, and in turn are being mutually created by, all other phenomena. Precisely because in the traditional Buddhist view any individual phenomenon was devoid of a perduring self-nature of its own (ANĀTMAN), existence in the Huayan interpretation therefore meant to be in a constant state of multivalent interaction with all other things in the universe. The boundless interconnectedness that pertains between all things was termed "dependent origination of the dharmadhātu" (FAJIE YUANQI). Huayan also carefully examines the causal relationships between individual phenomena or events (SHI) and the fundamental principle or patterns (LI) that govern reality. These various relationships are systematized in Chengguan's teaching of the four realms of reality (dharmadhātu): the realm of principle (LI FAJIE), the realm of individual phenomena (SHI FAJIE), the realm of the unimpeded interpenetration between principle and phenomena (LISHI WU'AI FAJIE), and the realm of the unimpeded interpenetration between phenomenon and phenomena (SHISHI WU'AI FAJIE). Even after Huayan's decline as an independent school, it continued to exert profound influence on both traditional East Asian philosophy and modern social movements, including engaged Buddhism and Buddhist environmentalism.

**huayi sijiao**. (C) (化儀四教). See TIANTAI BAJIAO.

**huazhu**. (J. keshu; K. hwaju 化主). In Chinese, lit. "chief of propagation," originally referring to the Buddha himself, but later in East Asia a term for a "fund-raiser" at a Buddhist monastery. The fund-raiser was the equivalent of a director of development in a modern nonprofit organization, who would journey outside the monastery walls to cultivate potential new donors and maintain relations with current donors. The huazhu would also secure letters to the donors from the relevant authorities such as the abbot and convey the needs and wishes of the monastery to the donors. He also was in charge of inventorying the gifts that donors offered, arranging their transport back to the monastery, and paying taxes on items received, where warranted.

**Huệ Trung**. [alt. Tuệ Trung] (慧忠[上士]) (1230–1291). Vietnamese Buddhist teacher, more popularly known as Huệ Trung Thượng Sĩ (the Eminent Huệ Trung); he was also one of the major literary figures of medieval Vietnam. His personal name was Trần Tung. He belonged to the Trần royal clan and was the older brother of Queen Nguyên Thánh Thiên Cảm, the mother of Trần Nhân Tông (1258–1308). He himself was Lord Hưng Ninh, a general in the two battles against the Mongols in 1285 and 1288. Huệ Trung was a lay disciple of Tiêu Diêu, a THIỀN (C. CHAN) master of the Yên Tử lineage. Although he never took ordination as a monk, he was a well-respected Chan master. Many Buddhists of his time were inspired by his unconventional behavior and approach to Chan philosophy and practice. He instructed Trần Nhân Tông on Chan Buddhism when the latter was crown prince. Huệ Trung's extant writings are collected in the *Huệ Trung Thượng Sĩ Ngữ Lục* ("Recorded Sayings of the Eminent Huệ Trung").

**hugui**. (J. koki; K. hogwe 胡跪). In Chinese, "genuflect in foreign fashion," a half-kneeling posture of respect, with one knee touching the ground, the opposite calf and knee raised off the ground, and the palms clasped in front of one's chest in AÑJALI. The posture is characteristic of figures bearing gifts or making entreaties, as in the opening lines of Chinese translations of Indian scriptures, where the interlocutors are often said to "genuflect in foreign fashion" before asking a question of the Buddha.

**huguo Fojiao**. (J. gokoku Bukkyō; K. hoguk Pulgyo 護國佛教). In Chinese, "state-protection Buddhism," referring to the sociopolitical role Buddhism played in East Asia to protect the state against war, insurrection, and natural disasters. The doctrinal justification for such a protective role for Buddhism derives from the "Guanshiyin pusa pumen pin" ("Chapter on the Unlimited Gate of the BODHISATTVA AVALOKITEŚVARA") and the "Tuoluoni pin" (DHĀRAṆĪ chapter) of the SADDHARMAPUṆḌARĪKASŪTRA ("Lotus Sūtra"), the "Huguo pin" ("Chapter on Protecting the State") of the RENWANG JING ("Scripture for Humane Kings"), and the "Zhenglun pin" ("Chapter on Right View") of the SUVARṆAPRABHĀSOTTAMASŪTRA ("Golden Light Sūtra"). For example, the *Suvarṇaprabhāsottamasūtra* states that a ruler who accepts that sūtra and has faith in the dharma will be protected by the four heavenly kings (CĀTURMAHĀRĀJAKĀYIKA); but if he neglects the dharma, the divinities will abandon his state and calamity will result. The "Huguo pin" of the *Renwang jing* notes that "when the state is thrown into chaos, facing all sorts of disasters and being destroyed by invading enemies," kings should set up in a grand hall one hundred buddha and bodhisattva images and one hundred seats, and then invite one hundred eminent monks to come there and teach the *Renwang jing*. This ritual, called the "*Renwang* Assembly of One-Hundred Seats" (C. Renwang baigaozuo hui; J. Ninnō hyakukōzae; K. Inwang paekkojwa hoe) would ward off any calamity facing the state and was held in China, Japan, and Korea from the late sixth century onward. In Japan, these three scriptures were used to justify the role Buddhism could play in protecting the state; and the Japanese reformist NICHIREN (1222–1282) cites the *Suvarṇaprabhāsottamasūtra* in his attempts to demonstrate that the calamities then facing Japan were a result of the divinities abandoning the state because of the government's neglect of the true teachings of Buddhism. The notion of state protection also figured in the introduction of ZEN to Japan. In 1198, the TENDAI and ZEN monk MYŌAN EISAI (1141–1215) wrote his KŌZEN GOKOKURON ("Treatise on the Promulgation of Zen as a Defense of the State"), which explained why the new teachings of Zen would both protect the state and allow the "perfect teachings" (see JIAOXIANG PANSHI) of Tendai to flourish. ¶ "State-protection Buddhism" has also been posited as one of the defining characteristics of Korean Buddhism. There are typically four types of evidence presented in support of this view. (1) Such rituals as the Inwang paekkojwa hoe (*Renwang jing* recitation) were held at court at least ten times during the Silla dynasty and increased dramatically to as many as one hundred twenty times during the succeeding Koryŏ dynasty. (2) Monasteries and STŪPAS were constructed for their apotropaic value in warding off calamity. During the Silla dynasty, e.g., HWANGNYONGSA and its nine-story pagoda, as well as Sach'ŏnwangsa (Four Heavenly Kings Monastery), were constructed for the protection of the royal family and the state during the peninsular unification wars. During the succeeding Koryŏ dynasty, the KORYŎ TAEJANGGYŎNG (Korean Buddhism canon) was carved (twice) in the hopes that state support for this massive project would prompt the various buddhas and divinities (DEVA) to ward off foreign invaders and bring peace to the kingdom. (3) Eminent monks served as political advisors to the king and the government. For example, Kwangjong (r. 949–975), the fourth monarch of the Koryŏ dynasty, established the positions of wangsa (royal preceptor) and kuksa (state preceptor, C. GUOSHI), and these offices continued into the early Chosŏn dynasty. (4) Monks were sometimes at the vanguard in repelling foreign invaders, such as the Hangmagun (Defeating Māra Troops) in twelfth-century Koryŏ, who fought against the Jurchen, and the Chosŏn monks CH'ŎNGHŎ HYUJŎNG (1520–1604) and SAMYŎNG YUJŎNG (1544–1610), who raised monks' militias to fight against the Japanese during the Hideyoshi invasions of the late sixteenth century. In the late twentieth century, revisionist historians argued that the notion of "state-protection Buddhism" in Korea may reflect as much the political situation of the modern and contemporary periods as any historical reality, and may derive from the concept of "chingo kokka" (protecting the state) advocated by Japanese apologists during the Buddhist persecution of the Meiji period (1868–1912).

**Huichang fanan**. (J. Kaishō no hōnan; K. Hoech'ang pŏmnan 會昌法難). In Chinese, "Huichang persecution of the dharma"; one of the worst persecutions in the history of Chinese Buddhism, which took place during the Huichang reign era (843–844) of the Tang-dynasty emperor Wuzong (r. 840–846). Factional disputes at court, growing economic strains, and opposition from Confucian officials and Daoist priests seem to have helped precipitate the Huichang persecution. The illicit buying and selling of ordination certificates (CIBU TONG) in order to avoid taxation may also have been a contributing factor in the restrictions the government imposed on Buddhism. Emperor Wuzong conducted a census of the monastic community and the number of temples in order to begin systematically to attack the Buddhist institution and to reassess the size of the population that was exempt from taxation and corvée labor. Over 260,000 monks and nuns were defrocked and returned to lay life, ostensibly for practicing alchemy or violating the precepts; this move, however, also returned them to the tax roles. Subsequently, the state placed heavy restrictions on the numbers of ordinands and their age (no one under the age of forty was allowed to ordain). Hundreds of monasteries were destroyed and much of the wealth confiscated from those temples that escaped destruction. Thousands of Buddhist images were melted down to be made into coinage. As with most persecutions, the effects were most deeply felt in the capital and major cities, effects that weakened considerably the farther away one moved from centralized power. Buddhist schools that were based on the capital, such as the HUAYAN ZONG and the Northern school (BEI ZONG) of the CHAN ZONG, were dealt such a severe blow that they were never able to fully recover. By contrast, schools located in isolated mountain sites in the countryside, such as other strands of the Chan school (e.g., HONGZHOU ZONG), were able to survive the persecution and subsequently flourish. Although the Huichang persecution indelibly scarred the Chinese Buddhist community, Buddhism continued to flourish, and even prosper, after the death of Wuzong. See also FANAN.

**Huiguang**. (C) (慧光). See DI LUN ZONG.

**huiguang fanzhao**. (J. ekō henjō; K. hoegwang panjo 迴/回光返照). In Chinese, "follow back the light and trace back the radiance," the quality of introspection that is operative during all types of meditation, according to some strands of the CHAN ZONG. See FANZHAO.

**Huiguo**. (J. Keika; K. Hyegwa 惠果) (746–805). Tang-dynasty Chinese monk, reputed seventh patriarch of esoteric Buddhism (J. MIKKYŌ), and a master especially of the KONGŌKAI and TAIZŌKAI transmissions. Huiguo was a native of Shaanxi province. He became a monk at an early age and went to the monastery of Qinglongsi in the Chinese capital of Chang'an, where he became a student of the master (ĀCĀRYA) AMOGHAVAJRA's disciple Tanchen (d.u.). In 765, Huiguo received the full monastic precepts, after which he is said to have received the teachings on the VAJRAŚEKHARASŪTRA from Amoghavajra himself. Two years later, Huiguo is also said to have received instructions on the taizōkai and the SUSIDDHIKARASŪTRA from the obscure Korean monk Hyŏnch'o (d.u.), a purported disciple of ācārya ŚUBHAKARASIṂHA. In 789, Huiguo won the support of Emperor Dezong (r. 779–805) by successfully praying for rain. Huiguo's renown was such that he received disciples from Korea, Japan, and even Java. In 805, Huiguo purportedly gave instructions on the kongōkai and taizōkai to the eminent Japanese pilgrim KŪKAI during the three months prior to the master's death, and eventually performed the consecration ritual (ABHIṢEKA) for his student. Kūkai thus claimed that Huiguo was the Chinese progenitor of the Japanese SHINGONSHŪ. That same year, Huiguo passed away at his residence in the Eastern Pagoda cloister at Qinglongsi.

**Huihai**. (C) (慧海). See DAZHU HUIHAI.

**Huihong**. (C) (慧洪). See JUEFAN HUIHONG.

**Huiji**. (C) (慧寂). See YANGSHAN HUIJI.

**Huikai**. (C) (慧開). See WUMEN HUIKAI.

**Huike**. (J. Eka; K. Hyega 慧可) (c. 487–593). "Wise Prospect"; putative second patriarch of the CHAN ZONG. Huike (a.k.a. Sengke) was a native of Hulao (alt. Wulao) near Luoyang in present-day Henan province. When he was young, Huike is said to have mastered the Confucian classics and Daoist scriptures in addition to the Buddhist SŪTRAS. He was later ordained by a certain Baojing (d.u.) on Mt. Xiang near Longmen, and received the full monastic precepts at Yongmusi. In 520, he is said to have made his famous visit to the monastery of SHAOLINSI on SONGSHAN, where he became the disciple of the Indian monk and founder of Chan, BODHIDHARMA. According to legend, Huike is said to have convinced the Indian master to accept him as a disciple by cutting off his left arm as a sign of his sincerity. (His biography in the GAOSENG ZHUAN tells us instead that he lost his arm to robbers.) Once Bodhidharma finally relented, Huike asked him to pacify his mind. Bodhidharma told him in response to bring him his mind, but Huike replied that he has searched everywhere for his mind but has not been able to find it anywhere. "Well, then," said Bodhidharma, in a widely quoted response, "I've pacified it for you." This brief encounter prompted Huike's awakening experience. Later, Huike taught at the capital Ye (present-day Henan province), where he is said to have amassed a large following. In 550, Huike ostensibly transmitted Bodhidharma's DHARMA to the obscure monk SENGCAN (the putative third patriarch of Chan) and later went into hiding during Emperor Wu's (r. 560–578) persecution of Buddhism (574–578).

**Huinan**. (C) (慧南). See HUANGLONG HUINAN.

**Huineng**. (J. Enō; K. Hyenŭng 慧能) (638–713). Chinese Chan master and reputed sixth patriarch (LIUZU) of the CHAN ZONG. While little is known of the historical figure, the legendary Huineng of the LIUZU TAN JING ("Platform Sūtra of the Sixth Patriarch") is an ubiquitous figure in Chan literature. According to his hagiography, Huineng was born in Xinzhou (present-day Guangdong province). As a youth, he cared for his poor mother by gathering and selling firewood. One day at the market he heard someone reciting the famous VAJRACCHEDIKĀPRAJÑĀPĀRAMITĀSŪTRA ("Diamond Sūtra") and immediately decided to enter the monastery. Huineng subsequently visited HONGREN, the fifth Chan patriarch, on East Mountain in Qizhou (present-day Hubei province). After spending eight years in the threshing room, the illiterate Huineng heard a monk reciting a verse that had just been posted on a wall of the monastery, a verse written secretly by Hongren's senior disciple, SHENXIU: "The body is the BODHI TREE, / The mind is like a bright mirror's stand. / Be always diligent in polishing it, / Do not let any dust alight." Immediately recognizing that the writer's understanding was deficient, Huineng in response composed a verse reply, which he asked a colleague to write down for him: "BODHI fundamentally has no tree, / The bright mirror also has no stand. / Fundamentally there is not a single thing, / Where could any dust alight?" After reading the verse the next day, Hongren secretly called Huineng to his room in the middle of the night and recited a line from the "Diamond Sūtra," which prompted in Huineng a great awakening. Hongren then secretly transmitted the robe and bowl of Chan's founder and first patriarch, BODHIDHARMA, to Huineng, making him the sixth (and ultimately last) patriarch of the Chan school; but he ordered his successor to go into hiding, lest he be harmed by followers of Shenxiu. Huineng then fled south. In 677, he received the full monastic precepts from the dharma master Yinzong (d.u.) at the monastery of Faxingsi in Nanhai (present-day Guangdong province). The next year, Huineng relocated to the monastery of Baolinsi on CAOXISHAN, the mountain that remains forever associated with him, where he attracted many students and followers. In 815, Emperor Xianzong (r. 805–820) bestowed upon him the posthumous title Chan master Dajian (Great Speculum). The monks QINGYUAN XINGSI, NANYUE HUAIRANG, HEZE SHENHUI, and YONGJIA XUANJUE are said to have been Huineng's preeminent disciples. Huineng is claimed to have been the founder of the so-called "Southern school" (NAN ZONG) of Chan, and to have instructed his students in the "sudden teachings" (DUNJIAO), the explication of which prompted much of the Chan school's subsequent soteriological developments and intrasectarian polemics. Although we have little historical evidence about either Huineng the person or his immediate disciples, all the various strands of the mature Chan tradition retrospectively trace their pedigrees back to him, making the legend of the sixth patriarch one of the most influential in the development of the Chan school.

**Huiri**. (C) (慧日). See CIMIN HUIRI.

**Huisi**. (C) (慧思). See NANYUE HUISI.

**Huiyuan**. (C) (惠/慧遠). See JINGYING HUIYUAN or LUSHAN HUIYUAN.

**Huizhong**. (C) (慧忠). See NANYANG HUIZHONG.

**hūṃkāramudrā**. (T. hūm mdzad kyi phyag rgya). In Sanskrit, "the gesture of the syllable hūṃ"; this MUDRĀ is formed by crossing the left wrist in front of the right wrist at the level of the heart. This gesture is commonly found in depictions of semiwrathful tantric deities such as SAṂVARA, HERUKA, GUHYASAMĀJA, and KĀLACAKRA as well as VAJRADHARA. In many instances, the right hand holds a VAJRA, symbolizing method (UPĀYA), and the left a bell, symbolizing wisdom (PRAJÑĀ).

**Humphreys, Christmas**. (1901–1983). Early British popularizer of Buddhism and founder of the Buddhist Society, the oldest lay Buddhist organization in Europe. Born in London in 1901, Humphreys was the son of Sir Travers Humphreys (1867–1956), a barrister perhaps best known as the junior counsel in the prosecution of the Irish writer Oscar Wilde (1854–1900). Following in his father's footsteps, Humphreys studied law at Cambridge University and eventually became a senior prosecutor at the Old Bailey, London, the central criminal court, and later a circuit judge; he was also involved in the Tokyo war crimes trials as a prosecutor, a post he accepted so he could also further in Japan his studies of Buddhism. (Humphreys's later attempts to inject some Buddhist compassion into his courtroom led to him being called the "gentle judge," who gained a reputation for being lenient with felons. After handing down a six-month suspended sentence to an eighteen-year-old who had raped two women at knifepoint, the public outcry that ensued eventually led to his resignation from the bench in 1976.) Humphreys was interested in Buddhism from his youth and declared himself a Buddhist at age seventeen. In 1924, at the age of twenty-three, he founded the Buddhist Society, London, and served as its president until his death; he was also the first publisher of its journal, *The Middle Way*. Humphreys strongly advocated a nonsectarian approach to Buddhism, which embraced the individual schools of Buddhism as specific manifestations of the religion's central tenets. His interest in an overarching vision of the whole of the Buddhist tradition led him in 1945 to publish his famous *Twelve Principles of Buddhism*, which has been translated into fourteen languages. These principles focus on the need to recognize the conditioned nature of reality, the truth of impermanence and suffering, and the path that Buddhism provides to save oneself through "the intuition of the individual." A close associate of DAISETZ TEITARO SUZUKI and a contemporary of EDWARD CONZE, Humphreys himself wrote over thirty semischolarly and popular books and tracts on Buddhism, including *Buddhism: An Introduction and Guide*, published in 1951.

**hundred dharmas**. See BAIFA.

**hundred-syllable mantra**. See VAJRASATTVA.

**Hundred Thousand Songs of Milarepa**. See MI LA'I MGUR 'BUM.

**Hŭngch'ŏnsa**. (興天寺). In Korean, "Flourishing Heaven Monastery"; the head monastery of the school of Doctrine (KYO) during the Chosŏn dynasty, located in Sŏngbuk-ku in the capital of Seoul. When Queen Sindŏk (d. 1395) died, King Taejo (r. 1392–1398) ordered in 1396 that this monastery be constructed to the east of the queen's royal tomb. At the king's command, a Sarigak (a three-story reliquary pavilion) and a Sarit'ap (a reliquary STŪPA) were erected at the north side of the monastery. Ceremonies to guide the spirit of the deceased queen, including the Uranbun ritual (see ULLAMBANA), were held during the seventh and eighth months. In 1408, Hŭngch'ŏnsa was officially affiliated with the Hwaŏm school (C. HUAYAN ZONG), but was designated a generic Kyo monastery in 1424, when the seven schools of Chosŏn-dynasty Buddhism were amalgamated into the two schools of Kyo (Doctrine) and SŎN (Meditation). The Buddhist canon (taejanggyŏng; C. DAZANGJING; see KORYŎ TAEJANGGYŎNG) was enshrined at the monastery in the ninth month of 1440. The monastery burned to the ground in 1510, and its large bronze monastery bell was moved to Tŏksu Palace. At King Sŏnjo's (r. 1567–1608) command, the monastery was reconstructed in 1569 at the old location of the Hamch'wi kiosk. The monastery's name was changed to Sinhŭngsa in 1794, but then changed back to Hŭngch'ŏnsa in 1865. The monastery is known for its Kŭngnak pojŏn (SUKHĀVATĪ Hall) and MYŎNGBU CHŎN (Hall of Judgment), both of which are Seoul municipal cultural properties.

**Hŭngdŏksa**. (興德寺). In Korean, "Flourishing Virtue Monastery"; the head monastery of the school of SŎN (Meditation) during the Chosŏn dynasty, located in Sŏdaemun-ku in the capital of Seoul. The monastery was constructed in 1401 at the command of the abdicated first king of Chosŏn, Taejo (r. 1392–1398), to the east of the king's old residence; it was intended to serve as a source of blessings for his kingdom, his ancestors, his people, and his royal lineage. This monastery became the chief head monastery (tohoeso) in 1424, when the seven schools of Chosŏn-dynasty Buddhism were amalgamated into the two schools of KYO (doctrine) and SŎN (meditation). To the sides of the main shrine hall were two halls, one for Sŏn meditation, the other for doctrinal lectures. The monastery was destroyed during the reign of King Yŏnsan (r. 1494–1506) and never reconstructed.

**hungry ghost**. See PRETA.

**hutuktu**. (T. ho thug thu). The Mongolian translation of "noble" (ĀRYA), used in Mongolia as a title for high lamas, especially incarnate lamas (SPRUL SKU).

**Huyền Quang**. (玄光) (1254–1334). Third patriarch of the TRÚC LÂM school of the Vietnamese THIỀN (C. Chan) tradition; his personal name was Lý Đạo Tái and he was a native of Giang Hạ (present-day Hà Bắc province). After passing the civil-service examination and serving as a scholar-official, he left home to become a monk in 1305, when he was already fifty-one years old. He first studied under Chan master Bão Phác of Lễ Vĩnh monastery and then became a follower of Trần Nhân Tông and, after the latter's death, of Pháp Loa, who was thirty years his junior. After a short stint as abbot of Vân Yên monastery on Mount Yên Tử, he moved to Côn Sơn monastery. Huyền Quang was already seventy-seven years old when he succeeded Pháp Loa as the third patriarch of the Trúc Lâm school in 1331 but seems never to have had the ambition to lead the Buddhist order. He died at Côn Sơn in 1334. Huyền Quang was a talented poet, who left behind more than twenty poems, most of which deal with the beauty of the natural world.

**Huyin Daoji**. (J. Koin Dōsai; K. Hoŭn Toje 湖隱道濟) (1150–1209). Chinese monk and thaumaturge who is associated with the YANGQI PAI of the LINJI ZONG of CHAN school; he is most commonly known in Chinese as JIGONG (Sire Ji) and sometimes as Jidian (Crazy Ji). A popular subject in vernacular Chinese fiction and plays, it has become difficult to separate the historical Jigong from the legend. Jigong is said to have been a native of Linhai in present-day Zhejiang province. He later visited the Chan master Xiatang Huiyuan (1103–1176), received the full monastic precepts at his monastery of Lingyinsi (present-day Jiangsu province), and became his disciple. After he left Xiatang's side, Jigong is said to have led the life of an itinerant holy man. During this period, Jigong's antinomian behavior, most notably his drinking and meat eating, along with his accomplishments as a trickster and wonderworker, became the subject of popular folklore. His unconventional behavior seems to have led to his ostracism from the SAṂGHA. Jigong later moved to the monastery of Jingcisi, where he died in 1209. His teachings are recorded in the *Jidian chanshi yulu* (first printed in 1569).

**hwajaeng**. (C. hezheng; J. wajō 和諍). In Korean, lit. "resolving disputes," "reconciling doctrinal controversies"; a hermeneutical technique associated with the Silla scholiast WŎNHYO (617–686), which seeks to demonstrate that various

Buddhist doctrines, despite their apparent differences and inconsistencies, can be integrated into a single coherent whole. This "ecumenical" approach is pervasive throughout Wŏnhyo's works, though its basic principle is explained chiefly in his *Simmun hwajaeng non* ("Ten Approaches to the Reconciliation of Doctrinal Controversy"; only fragments are extant), TAESŬNG KISILLON SO ("Commentary to the 'Awakening of Faith according to the Mahāyāna'"), and KŬMGANG SAMMAEGYŎNG NON ("Exposition of the *VAJRASAMĀDHISŪTRA"). Wŏnhyo was versed in the full range of Buddhist philosophical doctrines then accessible to him in Korea, including MADHYAMAKA, YOGĀCĀRA, HWAŎM, and TATHĀGATAGARBHA thought, and hwajaeng was his attempt to demonstrate how all of these various teachings of the Buddha were part of a coherent heuristic plan within the religion. All the Buddha's teachings were in fact representations of the one mind (K. ilsim; C. YIXIN); whatever doctrinal differences seem to exist between them result merely from the limitations inherent in conventional language to express the truth, not from substantive differences in the teachings themselves. One of the means through which Wŏnhyo seeks to demonstrate the truth of hwajaeng is to deploy the dichotomy of "analysis and synthesis" (kaehap)—lit. to "open up" all the various teachings for analysis and to "fold them together" into an overarching synthesis. This process of exegesis was then applied to the hermeneutical schema of "doctrines and essential" (chongyo)—i.e., the various doctrines of Buddhism and their essential truth. Buddhism's essential truth (yo) is "opened up" (kae) for analysis into all its various doctrines, and those doctrines (chong) are then returned to the one mind when they are "folded together" (hap) into a synthesis. Many of Wŏnhyo's scriptural commentaries use this hermeneutical technique in their exegeses, especially his seventeen exegetical commentaries (five of which are extant) that are titled chongyo, e.g., his *Yŏlban kyŏng chongyo* ("Doctrines and Essentials of the MAHĀPARINIRVĀṆASŪTRA"). As one specific example, Wŏnhyo's analysis of the DASHENG QIXIN LUN ("Awakening of Faith according to the Mahāyāna") attempts to demonstrate how the emptiness (ŚŪNYATĀ) doctrine of the Madhyamaka—which Wŏnhyo characterizes as apophasis or lit. "destruction" (K. p'a, C. po)—may been reconciled with the representation-only (VIJÑAPTIMĀTRATĀ) teachings of the Yogācāra—which he characterizes as a kataphasis, or lit. "establishment" (K. ip, C. li)—by reducing them both to the single principle of the "one mind." The Koryŏ monk ŬICH'ŎN (1055–1101) first posited that the notion of hwajaeng was emblematic of Wŏnhyo's philosophical approach and petitioned his brother, King Sukchong (r. 1095–1105), to grant Wŏnhyo the posthumous title of Hwajaeng KUKSA (the state preceptor Resolving Controversy) in 1101. Since that time, Wŏnhyo has been viewed as the embodiment of hwajaeng thought in Korea and hwajaeng has often been portrayed as characteristic of a distinctively Korean approach to Buddhist thought.

**Hwangnyongsa**. (皇/黃龍寺). In Korean, "royal," or "Yellow Dragon Monastery" ("royal" and "yellow" are homophonous in Korean); an important Korean monastery located in the Silla-dynasty capital of Kyŏngju. The monastery was constructed between 553 and 569, during the reign of the Silla king Chinhŭng (r. 540–576) and was especially renowned for its sixteen-foot high image of ŚĀKYAMUNI Buddha (completed in 574) and its massive, nine-story pagoda (STŪPA), which was built in 645 during the reign of Queen Sŏndŏk (r. 632–647). In the winter of 1238, during the succeeding Koryŏ dynasty (918–1392), the entire monastery, including the buddha image and the pagoda, was totally destroyed by invading Mongol troops, and only the foundation stones currently remain. The site of the monastery was excavated by the Kyŏngju National Research Institute of Cultural Heritage between 1976 and 1983. Royal Dragon monastery flourished due to the support of the Silla royal family, which sought to use Buddhism as an unifying political ideology; The stories told concerning the foundation of the monastery, the image, and the pagoda all reflect this fact. The construction of the monastery is thus often cited as an example of "state-protection Buddhism" hoguk Pulgyo; C. HUGUO FOJIAO) in Korea. According to the SAMGUK YUSA ("Memorabilia of the Three Kingdoms"), in the second month of 553, King Chinhŭng was building a new palace to the south of his Dragon Palace and east of Wŏlsŏng palace, when a yellow dragon (hwangnyong) appeared at the site. Yellow dragons were popular autochthonous deities in Silla; hence, given the auspicious nature of this apparition, the king changed plans and instead built a Buddhist monastery on the site, which is called both Yellow Dragon and Royal Dragon monastery in the literature. When the Silla monk CHAJANG (d.u.; fl. c. 590–658) was training at WUTAISHAN in China, an emanation of the bodhisattva MAÑJUŚRĪ told him that Hwangnyongsa was constructed on the site of the dispensation of the previous buddha KĀŚYAPA. Not long after the monastery's completion, a ship with 57,000 pounds of iron and 30,000 ounces of gold aboard appeared at Sap'o Harbor in Hagok County (currently Kokp'o near Ulsan, on the southeast coast of the peninsula). The ship also carried an inscription, which said that the Indian king AŚOKA, having tried and failed three times to forge a Śākyamuni triad from these metals, had finally decided to load the materials aboard ship, along with models of the images, and send them off in search of a land with the requisite metallurgical skill to craft such a statue. King Chinŭng ordered his metallurgists to forge this sixteen-foot statue of the Buddha, and they succeeded on the first attempt in the third month of 574. Chajang also was told by MAÑJUSRĪ that the queen belonged to the Indian KṢATRIYA caste. He was later told by a divine being that if a nine-story pagoda were constructed within the precincts of Royal Dragon monastery, the kingdoms bordering Silla would surrender and submit to Silla hegemony. Hearing Chajang's prediction, in 645, the queen built the pagoda, which was 224 feet tall and made entirely of wood. Chajang placed within its columns some of the relics (ŚARĪRA) of the Buddha that he had received at Wutaishan. (Another portion was enshrined at T'ONGDOSA, where they remain still today.) It was said that the nine stories of the pagoda symbolized the nine kingdoms and tribal leagues surrounding Silla. During the time when Hwangnyongsa was constructed, the unification wars between the three Korean kingdoms of Silla, Koguryŏ, and Paekche were raging. The Silla monarchs at this time tried to justify their royal authority by relying on Buddhism, particularly by comparing the Silla rulers to the imported Buddhist notion of the ideal Buddhist ruler, or CAKRAVARTIN (wheel-turning emperor) and by positing that the royal family was genealogically related to the kṣatriya clan of the Buddha. These associations are also obvious in the personal names of Silla kings, queens, and other royal family members. For example, the names of the King Chinhŭng's two princes were Tongnyun (Copper Wheel) and Kŭmnyun (Gold Wheel), both specific types of cakravartins; additionally, King Chinp'yŏng's personal name was Paekchŏng and his queen's was Maya, the Sino-Korean translation and transcription, respectively, of the names of Śākyamuni Buddha's father and mother, ŚUDDHODANA and MĀYĀ. The foundation of Hwangnyongsa was intimately associated with these attempts by the royal family to employ Buddhism as a tool for justifying and reinforcing its authority. The monastery sponsored the Inwang Paekkojwa hoe (Humane Kings Assembly of One-Hundred Seats), a state-protection (hoguk) rite based on the RENWANGJING ("Scripture for Humane Kings"), in the hopes that the power of the buddhadharma would protect and promote the royal family and the kingdom. According to both the *Samguk yusa* and the *Samguk Sagi* ("Historical Records of the Three Kingdoms"), such a ceremony was held at Hwangnyongsa in 613 and 636, before the unification of the three kingdoms, as well as several times subsequently. Monks who resided at Hwangnyongsa also played important roles in Silla politics and religion. WŎN'GWANG (532–630), who composed the five codes of conduct for the "flower boys" (hwarang), an elite group of male aristocratic youths, may have written there a letter to ask Emperor Yangdi (r. 604–618) of the Sui dynasty to attack Koguryŏ on Silla's behalf. Another resident, Chajang, encouraged the royal family to adopt Chinese official attire and the Chinese chronological era at the Silla court and was appointed kukt'ong (state superintendent), to supervise the entire Silla Buddhist ecclesia. Several other Hwangnyongsa monks, including Hyehun (fl. c. 640), Kangmyŏng (fl. 655), and Hunp'il (fl. 879), were appointed to kukt'ong and other important Silla ecclesiastical positions. Finally, several important Silla scholar-monks resided at Hwangnyongsa, including WŎNHYO (617–686), who delivered his first public teaching of the KŬMGANG SAMMAEGYŎNG NON ("Exposition of the *Vajrasamādhisūtra*") at the monastery.

**Hwansŏng Chian**. (喚醒志安) (1664–1729). Korean monk from the mid-Chosŏn dynasty. Hwansŏng Chian was a disciple of Wŏltam Sŏlche (1632–1704) and of Moun Chinŏn (1622–1703), at the time the most respected Hwaŏm (HUAYAN) scholar in the kingdom. At Chinŏn's request, Hwansŏng Chian began to lecture on the AVATAṂSAKASŪTRA in Chinŏn's place. Chinŏn eventually entrusted his disciples to Chian, and Chian thus acquired a name for himself as a Hwaŏm master. In 1725, he held a grand Hwaŏm lecture and attracted more than fourteen hundred listeners. Given the suspicion Buddhist activities engendered during this time of the religion's persecution, the government was deeply concerned about the potentially seditious impact of his lectures and consequently had him arrested and imprisoned. Chian was released after it was eventually revealed that he was falsely accused. Subsequently, a high Confucian official from Chŏlla province petitioned for his arrest, and he was sent into exile on Cheju island, where he died seven days later on July 7, 1729. His writings include the *Sŏnmun ojong kangyo* and the *Hwansŏng chip*.

**Hwaŏm ilsŭng pŏpkye to**. (C. Huayan yisheng fajie tu; J. Kegon ichijō hokkaizu 華嚴一乘法界圖). In Korean, "Diagram of the DHARMADHĀTU according to the One Vehicle of Hwaŏm (C. HUAYAN)," composed by ŬISANG in 670 and presented to his Chinese teacher, ZHIYAN. Ŭisang first provides a wavelike diagram of the dharmadhātu (also sometimes referred to as the Haein to, or "Oceanic-Reflection Diagram"), which contains a verse in two hundred and ten Chinese characters summarizing the gist of the Huayan school's interpretation of the AVATAṂSAKASŪTRA. The diagram and its subsumed verse are then followed by Ŭisang's own (auto)commentary, itself divided into two major sections: the fundamental purport of the diagram and the detailed interpretation of the verse. In the diagram itself, the path meanders along a single line in order to show that all phenomena are interconnected through the single principle of the dharma nature. The diagram begins and ends at the same place in the center of the maze, to suggest that the inception of practice in the generation of the thought of enlightenment (BODHICITTOTPĀDA) and its consummation through enlightenment are identical. The diagram is broadly divided into four equal sections to demonstrate that the dharma nature is perfected through the four means of conversion (SAṂGRAHAVASTU: viz., giving, kind words, helpfulness, and cooperation). The single path that meanders through the diagram includes fifty-four curves to indicate the teachers that the pilgrim SUDHANA in the GAṆḌAVYŪHA section of the *Avataṃsakasūtra* consulted in the course of his training—and thus by extension the stages of the BODHISATTVA path. The "Hwaŏm ilsŭng pŏpkye to" served as the foundation of Hwaŏm thought in Korea. There is some controversy over whether the verse itself may have in fact been composed by Zhiyan, with Ŭisang's contribution being to create the diagram for the verse and write the commentary, but there is not currently a scholarly consensus concerning this issue.

**Hwaŏmsa**. (華嚴寺). In Korean, "Flower Garland Monastery"; the nineteenth of the major district monasteries (PONSA) in the contemporary CHOGYE order and the largest monastery on the Buddhist sacred mountain of CHIRISAN. According to the Hwaŏmsa monastery history, the monastery was founded in 544 by the obscure monk Yŏn'gi (d.u.), an Indian monk who is claimed to have been the first figure to spread the teaching of the AVATAMSAKASŪTRA in Korea. (Five works related to the *Avataṃsakasūtra* and the DASHENG QIXIN LUN are attributed to Yŏn'gi in Buddhist catalogues, but none are extant.) In 645, during the Silla dynasty, the VINAYA master CHAJANG constructed at the monastery a three-story stone STŪPA with four lions at the base, in which to preserve the relics (ŚARĪRA) of the Buddha. The eminent scholiast WŎNHYO (617–686) is said to have taught at the monastery the "flower boys" (hwarang) group of Silla elite young men. In 677, the important vaunt courier in the Korean Hwaŏm school, ŬISANG (625–702), constructed a main shrine hall, the Changyukchŏn, where a gold buddha image six-chang (sixty feet) high was installed, and had inscribed the eighty-roll recension of the *Avataṃsakasūtra* on the four stone walls of the hall; since his time, the monastery was known as one of the centers of the Hwaŏm school (HUAYAN ZONG) in Korea. In 1462, during the Chosŏn dynasty, Hwaŏmsa was raised to the status of a main monastery in the Sŏn school (CHAN ZONG) of Buddhism. The monastery burned down during the Japanese Hideyoshi invasion of (1592–1598) and was rebuilt several times afterward. In 1702, the Sŏn monk Kyeba (d.u.) built a new main shrine hall, Kakhwangjŏn, to replace the ruined Changyukchŏn, and the monastery was elevated to a main monastery of both the Sŏn and Kyo (Doctrine) schools. The monastery is the nineteenth of the major parish monasteries (PONSA) in the contemporary CHOGYE order.

**Hyech'o**. (C. Huichao 慧[惠]超) (d.u.; c. 704–780). Korean monk from the Silla kingdom, best known as the writer of the WANG O CH'ŎNCH'UKKUK CHŎN, translated into English as *Memoir of the Pilgrimage to the Five Regions of India*. After ordaining in Korea, Hyech'o left for China sometime around 721 and spent perhaps three years on the mainland before departing via the southern sea route for India (the Ch'ŏnch'ukkuk of his travel diary) in 724. After landing on the eastern coast of the subcontinent, Hyech'o subsequently spent about three years on pilgrimage to many of the Buddhist sacred sites, including BODHGAYĀ, KUŚINAGARĪ, and SĀRNĀTH, and visits to some of the major cities in north central India. He then traveled in both southern and western India before making his way toward the Northwest, whence he journeyed on into Kashmir, GANDHĀRA, and Central Asia. Making his way overland across the Central Asian SILK ROADS, Hyech'o arrived back in Chinese territory in December of 727. For the rest of his life, Hyech'o remained in China, collaborating with AMOGHAVAJRA (705–774) and perhaps VAJRABODHI (671–741) in translating esoteric Buddhist scriptures into Chinese (see VAJRAYĀNA, TANTRA, and MIKKYŌ). Hyech'o is mentioned prominently in Amoghavajra's will as one of his six greatest living disciples. In May 780, Hyech'o left the Chinese capital of Chang'an for the Buddhist pilgrimage site of WUTAISHAN, where he seems to have spent the last months or years of his life.

**Hyegŭn**. (K) (慧勤). See NAONG HYEGŬN.

**Hyemyŏng chŏn**. (K) (惠明殿). See WANGNYUNSA.

**Hyesim**. (K) (慧諶). See CHIN'GAK HYESIM.

**Hyeso**. (K) (慧昭). See CHIN'GAM HYESO.

**Hyeyŏng**. (惠永) (1228–1294). Korean monk of the Koryŏ dynasty. In 1238, Hyeyŏng was ordained by Ch'ungyŏn (d.u.) at the monastery of Nambaegwŏlsa. Hyeyŏng passed the Sŏn (CHAN) examinations held at WANGNYUNSA in 1244 and was subsequently given a position at Hŭngdŏksa. In 1259, he was given the title Samjung taesa, and four years later, he was elevated to the status of head seat (sujwa). In 1267, Hyeyŏng moved to the temple Songnisa. Hyeyŏng's reputation grew, and he was eventually elevated to the highest status of SAṂGHA overseer (sŭngt'ong) in 1269. He also resided at such monasteries as PULGUKSA, T'ONGDOSA, and Chunghŭngsa. In 1290, he led a mission of one hundred monks who specialized in copying Buddhist scriptures to Yuan China and delivered a lecture in the capital. He also copied the Buddhist canon in gold. In 1292, he was given the title Poja Kukchon (National Worthy whose Compassion is Universal) and was also given the title of saṃgha overseer of the five teachings (Ogyodo Sŭngtong). He resided at the monastery of Tonghwasa and remained there until his death in 1294. Hyeyŏng composed a treatise entitled the *Paegŭihae*.

**Hyŏnjŏng non**. (顯正論). In Korean, "Treatise on the Exposition of Orthodoxy," composed by the Chosŏn-dynasty monk KIHWA (1376–1433). In this one-roll treatise, composed probably sometime after 1398, Kihwa attempted to counter the anti-Buddhist polemic of Confucian scholars of his time (e.g., Buddhism as a foreign religion that is financially corrupt, socially parasitic, and philosophically nihilistic) by clarifying the truths of Buddhism. First, Kihwa explains that the nature of the mind is inherently pure and free from discrimination and thus implicitly transcending all religious differences. Kihwa then demonstrates that, despite their differences, Confucianism, Daoism, and Buddhism each exhibits in its own way the practice of "humaneness," or "altruism," toward others, which ensures that all beings have shared responsibility for each others' quality of life. In the course of his examination, Kihwa clarifies the various attitudes of Buddhists and Confucians toward religious teachings, societal obligations, harming life, drinking liquor, wealth accumulation, and so forth. Kihwa also defends the Buddhist practice of cremation and the notion of KARMAN. Kihwa ultimately contends that a harmonious relation between Confucian and Buddhist teachings is required to regulate the family and govern the state.

**Hyujŏng**. (K) (休靜). See CH'ŎNGHŎ HYUJŎNG.

# I

**Icchānaṅgala**. [alt. Icchānaṅkala]. Pāli name of a brāhmaṇa village in the Indian kingdom of KOŚALA, on the outskirts of which was a grove where the Buddha preached the Pāli *Ambaṭṭhasutta* to the brāhmaṇa youth, Ambaṭṭhamānava. The Pāli SUTTANIPĀTA states that the town was the residence of several eminent brāhmaṇas. Elsewhere it is said that brāhmaṇas were in the habit of visiting the grove to discuss their interpretations of the Vedas. The Pāli *Vāseṭṭhasutta* states that two brāhmaṇa youths well versed in the Vedas, Vāseṭṭha and Bhāradvāja, once sought out the Buddha's counsel to resolve a debate while the Buddha was sojourning at the town. In the SAṂYUTTANIKĀYA, the Buddha is described as having once spent a rains retreat (S. VARṢĀ) in solitude at the Icchānaṅgala grove while attended by a single disciple, the monk Nāgita. After a while, the local villagers discovered his presence and disturbed his solitude with constant visits and noise. At the end of the three months' rains retreat, the Buddha preached the *Icchānaṅgalasutta* to a gathering of monks at the village, in which he described how he had spent his time while in solitary retreat practicing mindfulness on breathing (ĀNĀPĀNASMṚTI). He declares dedication to this practice to be a life lived according to the noble (ĀRYA) way and one that leads to the destruction of the contaminants (ĀSRAVA) and the attainment of ARHATship.

**icchantika**. (T. 'dod chen; C. yichanti; J. issendai; K. ilch'ŏnje 一闡提). In Sanskrit, "incorrigibles"; a term used in the MAHĀYĀNA tradition to refer to a class of beings who have lost all potential to achieve enlightenment or buddhahood. The term seems to derive from the present participle icchant (desiring), and may be rendered loosely into English as something like "hedonist" or "dissipated" (denotations suggested in the Tibetan rendering 'dod chen (po), "subject to great desire"). (The Sinographs are simply a transcription of the Sanskrit.) The Mahāyāna MAHĀPARINIRVĀṆASŪTRA states that persons become icchantika when they refuse to accept such basic principles as the law of causality, have lost their moral compass, are no longer concerned about either present actions or their future consequences, do not associate with spiritual mentors, and generally do not follow the teachings of the Buddha. In the LAṄKĀVATĀRASŪTRA, an icchantika is defined as a being who is explicitly antagonistic to the "bodhisattva collection" (BODHISATTVAPIṬAKA) of the canon, viz., to Mahāyāna scriptures, and who falsely claims that those scriptures do not conform to the SŪTRA and the VINAYA. As a consequence of their disdain for the dharma, icchantikas were commonly assumed to be condemned to an indefinite period (and, according to some texts, an eternity) in the hells (see NĀRAKA). Certain bodhisattvas, such as KṢITIGARBHA, could, however, voluntarily choose to become icchantikas by renouncing all of their own wholesome faculties (KUŚALAMŪLA) in order to save even the denizens of the hells. In East Asia, there was a major debate about whether icchantikas were subject to eternal damnation or whether even they retained the innate capacity to attain enlightenment. The Chinese monk DAOSHENG (355–434) rejected the implication that Buddhism would condemn any class of being to hell forever. He went so far as to reject the accuracy of passages suggesting such a fate that appeared in the first Chinese rendering of the *Mahāparinirvāṇasūtra* made by FAXIAN and BUDDHABHADRA in 418. DHARMAKṢEMA's subsequent translation of the sūtra in 421, however, affirmed Daosheng's view that the buddha-nature (C. FOXING; S. BUDDHADHĀTU) was inherent in all beings, even icchantikas. The FAXIANG school of YOGĀCĀRA Buddhism was the only school of East Asian Buddhism that posited the existence of icchantikas, which it viewed as beings who had destroyed the pure seeds (BĪJA) innate in the mind through their heinous actions and thus had lost all hope of becoming buddhas. Virtually all other schools of East Asian Buddhism, however, asserted the doctrine of the universality of the buddha-nature in all sentient beings (and, in some cases, even in inanimate objects), and thus rejected any implication that icchantikas were bereft of all prospect of achieving buddhahood. See also SAMUCCHINNAKUŚALAMŪLA; QINI[ZUI].

**ichinengi**. (一念義). In Japanese, "the doctrine of a single recitation," in the Japanese PURE LAND traditions, the practice of a single verbal recitation of the buddha AMITĀBHA's name (J. nenbutsu; C. NIANFO). This doctrine refers to a position held by some of HŌNEN's (1133–1212) major disciples in the early JŌDOSHŪ, especially Jōkakubō Kōsai (1163–1247), and to a lesser extent SHINRAN (1163–1273). After Hōnen passed away, a debate emerged among his followers over whether salvation in Amitābha's pure land of SUKHĀVATĪ was attained through a "single recitation" of the Buddha's name, or "multiple recitations" (see TANENGI). The single-recitation position advocates that a single moment of faith would be sufficient to ensure rebirth in that pure land, because the person would then be receptive to Amitābha's grace. Due to this near-exclusive emphasis on the role of grace in effecting salvation, some of the proponents of single-recitation practice apparently engaged in antinomian behavior, such that the doctrine of ichinengi came to be associated with subversive political activities. The degree to which this single moment of faith arises from the "self-power" (JIRIKI) of the aspirant or the "other-power" (TARIKI) of Amitābha was also debated. Although Shinran seems to have favored the single-recitation position, he also argued that neither the single- nor multiple-recitation position provided a comprehensive perspective on the prospect of salvation. (For the JISHU practice of ippen nenbutsu, the one-time invocation of the Buddha's name as if it were the time of one's death, see IPPEN.)

**ignorance**. See AVIDYĀ.

**Ikeda Daisaku**. (池田大作) (b. 1928). Third president of SŌKA GAKKAI, Japan's largest lay Buddhism organization, which is considered one of Japan's "new religions." Ikeda also helped found Sōka Gakkai International (SGI), which in 2008 claimed twelve million members in 192 countries and territories. He is a prolific author, who also founded a number of institutions, including Sōka University, the Kōmeitō political party, the Institute of Oriental Philosophy, and the Tōkyō Fuji Art Museum. Ikeda was born on January 2, 1928, in the Ota Ward of Tōkyō, to parents who cultivated and sold seaweed. After graduating from Fuji Junior College, he took employment under Toda Josei (1900–1958), the second president of Sōka Gakkai. Ikeda received intensive mentoring from Toda and accompanied him on most of his travels. Ikeda also helped carry out Toda's propagation (shakubuku) campaigns. Ikeda served as the third president of Sōka Gakkai from 1960 to 1979 until disagreements with the NICHIREN SHŌSHŪ priesthood, notably its head priest, Nikken (b. 1922), led to his resignation from the organization. In 1991, poor relations with the priesthood culminated in his excommunication. While remaining as Sōka Gakkai's spiritual leader, Ikeda has additionally served as the president of SGI since its founding in 1975. Throughout his career with Sōka Gakkai and SGI, Ikeda has met with both criticism and praise. At times, the organization's aggressive proselytizing efforts have made Ikeda and Sōka Gakkai objects of suspicion, and its political activities have led to several scandals: the 1956 "Ōsaka incident" in which he was charged with election fraud after engineering the election of a Kōmeitō party member; and a 1979 controversy over the suppression of several publications that criticized Ikeda and Sōka Gakkai. At the same time, Ikeda is respected as a leader on human rights and peace issues. He has been a strong supporter of the United Nations and has engaged in discussions with political leaders around the world. The expansive growth of both Sōka Gakkai and SGI can in large measure be attributed to his leadership.

**Ikkyū Sōjun**. (一休宗純) (1394–1481). Japanese ZEN master in the RINZAISHŪ, also known by his sobriquet Kyōun shi (Master Crazy Cloud). Materials on Ikkyū's life are an often indistinguishable mixture of history and legend. Little is known of Ikkyū's early years, but he is said to have been the illegitimate son of Emperor Gokomatsu (r. 1382–1392, 1392–1412). In 1399, Ikkyū was sent to the monastery of ANKOKUJI in Kyōto. In 1410, he left Ankokuji to study under Ken'ō Sōi (d. 1414), who belonged to the MYŌSHINJI branch of Rinzai Zen. After Ken'ō's death in 1414, Ikkyū continued his studies under the monk Kasō Sōdon (1352–1428) in Katada (present-day Shiga prefecture) near Lake Biwa. Kasō gave him the name Ikkyū, which he continued to use. While studying under Kasō, Ikkyū had his first awakening experience and also acquired some notoriety for his antinomian behavior. Perhaps because of his rivalry with a fellow student named Yōsō Sōi (1378–1458), Ikkyū left Kasō shortly before his death and headed for the city of Sakai. During this transition period, Ikkyū is said to have briefly returned to lay life, marrying a blind singer and fathering a son. Ikkyū's life in Sakai is shrouded in legend (most of which date to the Tokugawa period). There, he is said to have led the life of a mad monk, preaching in taverns and brothels. In 1437, Ikkyū is also said to have torn up the certificate of enlightenment that his teacher Kasō had prepared for him before his death. In 1440, Ikkyū was called to serve as the abbot of the monastery of DAITOKUJI, but he resigned his post the next year. Ikkyū devoted much of his later life to his famous poetry and brush-stroke art. Later, Ikkyū had a falling out with Yōsō, who as abbot secured Daitokuji's prominent place in Kyōto. In 1455, Ikkyū published a collection of his poems, the *Jikaishū* ("Self-Admonishment Collection"), and publicly attacked Yōsō. In 1456, Ikkyū restored the dilapidated temple Myōshōji in Takigi (located halfway between Sakai and Kyōto). There, he installed a portrait of the Zen master Daitō (see SŌHŌ MYŌCHŌ). Ikkyū also began identifying himself with the Chinese Chan master XUTANG ZHIYU, the spiritual progenitor of the Daitokuji lineage(s), by transforming portraits of Xutang into those of himself. In 1474, Ikkyū was appointed abbot of Daitokuji, which had suffered from a devastating fire during the Ōnin war, and he committed himself to its reconstruction, until his death in 1481. Among his writings, his poetry collection *Kyōunshū* ("Crazy Cloud Anthology") is most famous. Also well known is his *Gaikotsu* ("Skeletons"), a work, illustrated by Ikkyū himself, about his conversations with skeletons. See also WU'AI XING.

**illusory body**. See MĀYĀDEHA.

**Imje chong**. (臨濟宗). The Korean pronunciation of the Chinese LINJI ZONG; the name of a short-lived school of Korean Buddhism during the Japanese colonial period (1910–1945). In 1910, shortly after Japan's formal annexation of Korea, Hoegwang Sasŏn (1862–1933, a.k.a. Yi Hoegwang) and other Korean monks signed a seven-item treaty with the

Japanese SŌTŌSHŪ, which would have assimilated their newly formed Wŏn chong (Consummate Order) of Korean Buddhism into the Sōtō order. In response to this threat to Korean Buddhist autonomy, such renowned monks as HANYŎNG CHŎNGHO (1870–1948), HAN YONGUN (1879–1944), and other Korean Buddhist leaders established the Imje chong, with its headquarters at the monastery of PŎMŌSA in Pusan. These monks adopted this name to demonstrate that they considered the practices of the Sōtō school to be anathema to the fundamentally Linji orientation of Korean Sŏn practice. Both the Wŏn chong and the Imje chong were ultimately disestablished in 1912 by the Japanese colonial administration after the promulgation of the 1911 Monastery Ordinance, in which all aspects of Korean Buddhist institutional life were brought under the administrative control of the Japanese government-general.

**impermanence**. See ANITYA.

**imwŏtko**. (C. shi shenme; J. kore ikan; K. 이뭣고/si simma 是甚麽). In vernacular Korean (and specifically the dialect of Kyŏngsang province), "What is this?"; the foundational contemplative question (K. hwadu; C. HUATOU) used within the Korean SŎN (C. CHAN) tradition. This hwadu was taught by both KYŎNGHŎ SŎNGU (1849–1912) and YONGSŎNG CHINJONG (1864–1940) as part of their attempts to revive Korean kanhwa Sŏn (C. KANHUA CHAN) practice at the turn of the twentieth century. Imwŏtko is a dialectical contraction of the standard vernacular Korean phrase "Igŏsi muŏsin ko" ("What is this?"), which is the translation of the classical Chinese question "What is this?" (C. SHI SHENME; K. si simma) that was frequently raised by teachers in the Chinese Chan tradition. For example, the sixth patriarch HUINENG (638–713) is said to have asked, "There is this one thing that supports the heavens above and opens the earth below. It is as bright as the sun and moon and as dark as a lacquer barrel. It is constantly inside all my activities. What is that thing?" And MAZU DAOYI (709–788) asked, "It is not mind, not buddha, not a thing. So, what is it?" Imwŏtko differs from the enigmatic expressions of the enlightenment experience that appear in many of the Sŏn exchanges between master and disciple; it is instead presumed to ask the fundamental question about what existence itself means, such as what is my original face (K. pollae myŏnmok; C. BENLAI MIANMU). By asking this most basic of existential questions, imwŏtko is thought to generate the sensation of doubt (K. ŭijŏng; C. YIJING) more readily than might the standard Sŏn GONG'AN and is often thus the first hwadu given to beginning meditators, and especially laypersons, in Korean Sŏn training. But because the doubt generated by imwŏtko may not be as intense and sustained as that generated by the standard kongan, monks and nuns will typically shift from imwŏtko to one of those cases as their meditation progresses.

**indeterminate questions**. See AVYĀKṚTA.

**Indra**. (P. Inda; T. Dbang po; C. Yintuoluo/Di-Shi; J. Indara/Taishaku; K. Indara/Che-Sŏk 因陀羅/帝釋). In Sanskrit, Indra is an abbreviation for ŚAKRO DEVĀNĀM INDRAḤ ("ŚAKRA, the king of the gods"). Indra is the Vedic king of the gods of the atmosphere or sky, who eventually becomes the chief of all divinities in Indian popular religion. Indra is incorporated into the Buddhist pantheon as a guardian of the DHARMA and the king of the DEVA realm. Indra is always depicted in Indian Buddhist iconography as subservient to the Buddha: he worships the Buddha, holds an umbrella over him to shield him from the sun, or carries his alms bowl for him. Indra presides over the heaven of the thirty-three divinities (TRĀYASTRIṂŚA), the second of the six heavenly realms that exist within the sensuous realm (KĀMADHĀTU), located on the summit of MOUNT SUMERU. In the middle of this heaven is found Indra's royal city, Sudarśana, at the center of which is his royal palace, Vaijayanta. See also INDRAJĀLA; ŚAKRA.

**Indrabhūti**. (T. In dra bo dhi). There are at least three figures by this name known to the Indian and Tibetan traditions. Perhaps the most important is a semimythical king of OḌḌIYĀNA ([alt. Uḍḍiyāna], probably the Swat region of northwest India but also identified as Orissa) at the time of the miraculous birth of PADMASAMBHAVA; according to tradition, he had no male heir, and so he installed Padmasambhava as crown prince. A second Indrabhūti is listed among the eighty-four MAHĀSIDDHA as a teacher of TILOPA; he may be the Indrabhūti, closely associated with mahāsiddha Lawapa, who is first in the lineage list (T. gsan yig) of the VAJRAYOGINĪ practices of the Tibetan SA SKYA sect and a brother of Lakṣmīṅkarā. There is also a ninth-century Indian king and tantric master, a student of Ācārya Kukurāja, who authored the *Cittaratnaviśodhana*, called Indrabhūti.

**Indrajāla**. (T. Dbang po'i dra ba; C. Yintuoluo wang/Di-Shi wang; J. Indaramō/Taishakumō; K. Indara mang/Che-Sŏk mang 因陀羅網/帝釋網). In Sanskrit, "Indra's net"; a metaphor used widely in the HUAYAN ZONG of East Asian Buddhism to describe the multivalent web of interconnections in which all beings are enmeshed. As depicted in the AVATAṂSAKASŪTRA, the central scripture of the Huayan school, above the palace of INDRA, the king of the gods, is spread an infinitely vast, bejeweled net. At each of the infinite numbers of knots in the net is tied a jewel that itself has an infinite number of facets. A person looking at any single one of the jewels on this net would thus see reflected in its infinite facets not only everything in the cosmos but also an infinite number of other jewels, themselves also reflecting everything in the cosmos; thus, every jewel in this vast net is simultaneously reflecting, and being reflected by, an infinite number of other jewels. This metaphor of infinite, mutually reflecting jewels is employed to help convey how all things in existence are defined by their interconnection with all other things, but without losing their own independent identity in the process. The metaphor of Indra's net thus offers a profound vision of the universe, in which all things are mutually interrelated to all other things, in simultaneous mutual identity and mutual intercausality. The meditation on Indra's net (C. Diwang guan; J. Taimō kan; K. Chemang kwan) is the last of the six contemplations outlined by Fazang in his *Xiu Huayan aozhi wangjin huanyuan guan* ("Cultivation of the Inner Meaning of Huayan: The Contemplations That End Delusion and Return to the Source"), which helps the student to visualize the DHARMADHĀTU of the unimpeded interpretation between phenomenon and phenomena (SHISHI WU'AI FAJIE).

**Indra's net**. See INDRAJĀLA.

**indriya**. (T. dbang po; C. gen; J. kon; K. kŭn 根). In Sanskrit and Pāli, "faculty," "dominant," or "predominant factor"; a polysemous term of wide import in Buddhist soteriological and epistemological literature. In the SŪTRA literature, indriya typically refers to the five or six sense bases: e.g., the visual, auditory, olfactory, gustatory, and tactile faculties associated with the physical sense organs and the mental base associated with the mind; in the case of the physical senses, the indriya are forms of subtle matter located within the organs of the eye, ear, nose, tongue, and body that enable the functioning of the senses. The mind (MANAS) is typically listed as a sixth, internal sensory faculty. The six sense faculties (ṣaḍindriya) are subsumed as well within the list of the twelve ĀYATANA (sense-fields) and eighteen DHĀTU (elements). ¶ Indriya is also used soteriologically to describe the five "dominants" or "spiritual faculties" that are crucial to development along the path: faith (ŚRADDHĀ), effort (VĪRYA), mindfulness (SMṚTI), concentration (SAMĀDHI), and wisdom (PRAJÑĀ). These two denotations for indriya are subsumed by the VAIBHĀṢIKA school of SARVĀSTIVĀDA abhidharma into a more extensive list of twenty-two faculties: (1–5) the five physical sense faculties, which are the predominant factors in the rise of the sensory consciousnesses, etc.; (6–7) the "female" (strīndriya) and "male" (puruṣendriya) faculties, which are the predominant factors in distinguishing sex organs and marking physical gender; (8) the "life force" (jīvitendriya; see JĪVITA), the predominant factor in birth and prolonging the physical continuum up through the "intermediate state" (ANTARĀBHAVA); (9) the mental faculty (MANENDRIYA), the predominant factor that governs both rebirth and the associations between an individual and the world at large; (10–14) the five faculties of sensation or feeling—viz., pleasure (SUKHA), suffering (DUḤKHA), satisfaction (saumanasya), dissatisfaction (daurmanasya), and indifference (UPEKṢĀ)—the predominant factors with regard to contamination (SAṂKLEŚA), for passions such as attachment, hatred, conceit, delusion, etc., attach themselves to these five sensations, creating bondage to worldly objects; (15–22) the eight faculties—viz., the five moral faculties of faith (śraddhā), energy (vīrya), mindfulness (smṛti), concentration (samādhi), and wisdom (prajñā), and the three immaculate faculties of (1) anājñātam ājñāsyāmī 'ndriyam ("the faculty of resolving to understand that which is yet to be understood"), (2) ājñātendriya ("the faculty of having understood"), and (3) ājñātāvīndriya ("the faculty of perfecting one's understanding")—which are the predominant factors regarding purification (VIŚUDDHI); this is because the five moral faculties are the predominant factors that purify beings of their bondage to worldly objects and offer access to NIRVĀṆA, and the three immaculate faculties are the predominant factors in the origin, duration, and enjoyment of nirvāṇa. ¶ Indriya is also used to refer to "three capacities" (see TRĪNDRIYA) of the disciples of the Buddha or of a particular teaching, based on their level of aptitude or capacity for understanding: viz., those of dull faculties (MṚDVINDRIYA), those of intermediate faculties (MADHYENDRIYA), and those of sharp faculties (TĪKṢṆENDRIYA).

**indriyasaṃvara**. (T. dbang po sdom pa; C. genlüyi; J. konritsugi; K. kŭnyurŭi 根律儀). In Sanskrit and Pāli, "sensory restraint," or "guarding the sense organs"; an important factor in the development of mindfulness (SMṚTI, P. SATI) and eventually concentration (SAMĀDHI), in which the meditator trains to see things as they actually are, rather than only in terms of oneself—i.e., as things we like, dislike, or are indifferent toward. In addition to its role in formal meditative training, indriyasaṃvara should also be maintained throughout the ordinary activities of everyday life, in order to control the inveterate tendency toward craving. Maintaining sensory restraint helps the meditator to control one's reaction to the generic signs (NIMITTA) or secondary characteristics (ANUVYAÑJANA) of an object; instead, one halts the perceptual process at the level of simple recognition, simply noting what is seen, heard, etc. By not seizing on these signs and characteristics, perception is maintained at a level prior to an object's conceptualization and the resulting proliferation of concepts (PRAPAÑCA) throughout the full range of one's sensory experience. As the frequent refrain in the sūtras states, "In the seen, there is only the seen," and not the superimpositions created by the intrusion of ego (ĀTMAN) into the perceptual process. Mastery of this technique of sensory restraint provides access to the signless (ĀNIMITTA) gate to deliverance (VIMOKṢAMUKHA).

**Inhŭi chŏn**. (K) (仁熙殿). See WANGNYUNSA.

**in'in ekishi**. (因院易師). In Japanese, "changing teachers in accordance with the temple." Since the fifteenth century, members of the SŌTŌSHŪ of the ZEN tradition have participated in the practice of taking the lineage of the monastery where one was appointed abbot, even if that lineage was different from one's own. The practice of inheriting the temple's lineage was known as the "temple dharma lineage" (GARANBŌ), and the practice of switching lineages was called in'in ekishi. Basing his claims on the teachings found in the SHŌBŌGENZŌ, the Sōtō Zen master MANZAN DŌHAKU attempted to reform this practice by asserting the importance of the direct, face-to-face transmission (menju shihō) from one master to his disciple (isshi inshō). In 1700, he made a request to the Agency of Temples and Shrine (jisha bugyō) to intervene in the garanbō system. Despite fierce opposition from such figures as TENKEI DENSON (1646–1735), the Tokugawa government banned the practice in 1703.

**initiation**. See ABHIṢEKA.

**inka**. (印可). In Japanese, "certification." See YINKE.

**insight meditation**. See VIPASSANĀ; VIPAŚYANĀ.

**Inwa**. (Burmese). See AVA.

**ip'ansŭng**. (理判僧). In Korean, "practice monk," monks who engaged in meditation, scriptural study, and chanting; one of the two general types of Korean monastic vocations, along with SAP'ANSŬNG, administrative monks, who were responsible for the administrative and financial affairs of the monastery. Ip'ansŭng traditionally enjoyed higher standing within the monastery than the administrative monks, and the meditation monks had generally more status than doctrinal specialists. During the post-1945 "Purification Movement" (Chŏnghwa undong) within the Korean SAṂGHA, the celibate monks called themselves ip'ansung, while pejoratively referring to married monks as sap'ansung.

**Ippen**. (一遍) (1239–1289). Japanese itinerant holy man (HIJIRI) and reputed founder of the JISHU school of the Japanese PURE LAND tradition. Due perhaps to his own antinomian proclivities, Ippen's life remains a mixture of history and legend. Ippen was a native of Iyo in Shikoku. In 1249, after his mother's death, Ippen became a monk at the urging of his father, a Buddhist monk, and was given the name Zuien. In 1251, Ippen traveled to Dazaifu in northern Kyūshū, where he studied under the monk Shōdatsu (d.u.). In 1263, having learned of his father's death, Ippen returned to Iyo and briefly married. In 1271, Ippen visited Shōdatsu once more and made a pilgrimage to the monastery of ZENKŌJI in Shinano to see its famous Amida (AMITĀBHA) triad. His visit to Zenkōji is said to have inspired Ippen to go on retreat, spending half a year in a hut that he built in his hometown of Iyo. The site of his retreat, Sugō, was widely known as a sacred place of practice for mountain ascetics (YAMABUSHI). In 1272, Ippen set out for the monastery of SHITENNŌJI in Ōsaka, where he is said to have received the ten precepts. At this time, Ippen also developed the eponymous practice known as ippen nenbutsu (one-time invocation of the name [see NIANFO] of the buddha Amitābha), which largely consists of the uttering the phrase NAMU AMIDABUTSU as if this one moment were the time of one's death. Ippen widely propagated this teaching wherever he went, and, to those who complied, he offered an amulet (fusan), which he said would assure rebirth in Amitābha's pure land. From Shitennōji, Ippen made a pilgrimage to KŌYASAN and a shrine at KUMANO, where he is said to have had a revelation from a local manifestation of Amitābha. Ippen then began the life of an itinerant preacher, in the process acquiring a large following now known as the Jishū. In 1279, Ippen began performing nenbutsu while dancing with drums and bells, a practice known as odori nenbutsu and developed first by the monk KŪYA. Ippen continued to wander through the country, spreading his teaching until his death. A famous set of twelve narrative hand scrolls known as the *Ippen hijiri e* ("The Illustrated Biography of the Holy Man Ippen") is an important source for the study of Ippen's life. Currently designated a Japanese national treasure (kokuhō), the *Ippen hijiri e* was completed in 1299 on the tenth anniversary of Ippen's death. See also ICHINENGI.

**īrṣyā**. (P. issā; T. phrag dog; C. ji; J. shitsu; K. chil 嫉). In Sanskrit, "envy" or "jealousy," one of the forty-six mental concomitants (CAITTA) according to the SARVĀSTIVĀDA school of ABHIDHARMA, one of the fifty-one according to the YOGĀCĀRA school and one of fifty-two according to the Pāli abhidhamma. Envy is the unwholesome displeasure one experiences when witnessing others' virtues, gains, and rewards, or simply general well-being, and is the opposite of the salutary mental state of sympathetic joy (MUDITĀ), which is one of the four BRAHMAVIHĀRAS. "Envy" is also taken to be one of the possible derivative emotions of "aversion" (DVEṢA) and cannot exist independent of that latter mental state.

**irwŏnsang**. (一圓相). In Korean, "one-circle symbol"; the central doctrinal concept and object of religious devotion in the modern Korean religion of WŎNBULGYO, considered to be functionally equivalent to the notion of the DHARMAKĀYA buddha (pŏpsinbul) in mainstream MAHĀYĀNA Buddhism. The founder of Wŏnbulgyo, PAK CHUNGBIN (later known by his sobriquet SOT'AESAN), believed that worshipping buddha images, as symbols of the physical body of the buddha, no longer inspired faith in Buddhist adherents and was thus a hindrance to religious propagation in the modern age; he instead instructed Wŏnbulgyo dharma halls to enshrine on their altars just the simple circle that is the irwŏnsang. This irwŏnsang was the "symbol" (sang) of the ineffable reality of the "unitary circle" (irwŏn). In Sot'aesan's view, different religions may have various designations for ultimate truth, but all of their designations ultimately refer to the perfect unity that is the irwŏn. Sot'aesan described the irwŏn as the mind-seal of all the buddhas and sages, the original nature of all sentient beings, and the ineffable realm of SAMĀDHI that transcends birth and death; but it simultaneously also served as the monistic source from which the phenomenal world in all its diversity arises. By understanding this irwŏn through tracing the radiance of the mind back to its fundamental source (K. hoegwang panjo; see HUIGUANG FANZHAO), Wŏnbulgyo adherents seek to recognize the fundamental nonduality of, and unity between, all things in existence and thus master the ability to act with utter impartiality and selflessness in all their interactions with the world and society.

**īryāpatha**. (P. iriyāpatha; T. spyod lam; C. weiyi; J. igi; K. wiŭi 威儀). In Sanskrit, lit. "movement," referring specifically to a set of four "postures," "deportments," or modes of physical activity, in progressive order of ease: walking (CAṄKRAMA [alt. gamana]; P. caraṃ), standing (sthāna; P. ṭhāna, tiṭṭhaṃ), sitting (niṣaṇṇa; P. nisinna), and lying down (śaya/śayana; P. sayaṃ/sayāna). Because the body was presumed typically to be always in one or another of these postures, they constituted specific objects of mindfulness of the body (KĀYĀNUPAŚYANĀ; P. kāyānupassanā; see also SMṚTYUPASTHĀNA) and there are accounts of monks attaining the rank of ARHAT in each of the four postures. The īryāpatha figure prominently in ĀNANDA's enlightenment experience. After striving in vain all night to perfect his practice before the start of the first Buddhist council (see COUNCIL, FIRST), where the canon was to be redacted, Ānanda had given up, only to become enlightened as he was in the process of lying down to rest—and thus technically *between* postures. ¶ The term īryāpatha can refer in other contexts to general behavior or "deportment" (but typically to religiously salutary deportment) or to a specific "course" of religious and/or ascetic practice.

**Iryŏn**. (一然) (1206–1289). Korean monk-literatus during the Koryŏ dynasty, known as the author of the SAMGUK YUSA ("Memorabilia of the Three Kingdoms"), the source for much of the lore concerning the incipiency and early development of Buddhism in Korea. Iryŏn was born in KYŎNGJU, the ancient capital of the Silla dynasty, became a monk while still a child, and passed the monk's examination (SŬNGKWA) in the SŎN school at the age of twenty-two. Iryŏn became a well-known literatus of both Buddhist and Confucian literature and was close to the royal family of the Koryŏ dynasty, including King Ch'ungnyŏl (r. 1236–1308), who visited Iryŏn at KWANGMYŎNGSA in 1282. The *Samguk yusa* was written ca. 1282–1289, during the period of Mongol suzerainty over Korea, which began in 1259. In his miscellany, Iryŏn includes a variety of hagiographies of eminent monks in the early Korean Buddhist tradition, often drawing from local accounts of conduct (haengjang), rather than official biographies, and reams of material on early Korean Buddhist miracles and anomalies drawn from regional lore. In its emphasis on local narrative, where Buddhism dominated, over official discourse, Iryŏn's *Samguk yusa* contrasts with Kim Pusik's (1075–1151) earlier *Samguk sagi* ("Historical Records of the Three Kingdoms"), which included little information on Buddhism. Iryŏn's funerary inscription refers to seven other works written by him, in over one hundred rolls; interestingly, however, the *Samguk yusa* is not included in that list, suggesting that it may have been published posthumously, perhaps sometime around 1310. The only other extant work of Iryŏn's besides the *Samguk yusa* is his *Chungp'yŏn Ch'odong owi* ("Five Ranks of the Caodong School, Revised"), in two (alt. three) rolls. No longer extant are his *Ŏrok* ("Discourse Record"; two rolls), *Kesong chapchŏ* ("Miscellany of Gāthās and Verses"; three rolls), and his massive *Sŏnmun yŏmsong sawŏn* ("Chrestomathy of Selected Verses of the Sŏn school"), in thirty rolls.

**Ishin Sūden**. (以心崇傳) (1569–1633). Japanese ZEN master in the RINZAISHŪ. Sūden was born in Kii (present-day Wakayama prefecture) and, while still a youth, left home to become a monk at the Zen monastery of NANZENJI. In 1608, he was appointed the scribe of the new shōgun Tokugawa Ieyasu (1543–1616). Sūden was put in charge of foreign correspondence and was also given the important title of sōroku, or registrar general of monks. As sōroku, Sūden established the hatto ("laws") for temples and monasteries and put them under the direct control of the bakufu government. Sūden thus came to be known as the kokui no saishō, or "black-robed minister." With the assistance of the bakufu, Sūden also restored Nanzenji to its former glory. Konchi'in, the name of Sūden's residences at both Nanzenji and Edo, came to be synonymous with Sūden and his policies. After Ieyasu's death, Sūden continued to assist the second shōgun Tokugawa Hidetada (1579–1632) in political and religious affairs. In 1626, Sūden was given the honorary title Enshō Honkō kokushi (State Preceptor Perfectly Illuminating, Original Radiance) from Emperor Gomizunoo (r. 1611–1629). His diary, the *Honkō kokushi nikki*, is a valuable source for studying the sociopolitical history of the early Tokugawa bakufu. Sūden also left a collection of poems known as the *Kanrin gohōshū*.

**itivṛttaka**. (P. itivuttaka; T. de lta bu byung ba). In Sanskrit, "fables"; one of the nine (NAVAṄGA) (Pāli) or twelve (DVĀDAŚĀṄGA[PRAVACANA]) (Sanskrit) categories (AṄGA) of Buddhist scripture according to their structure or literary style. See also ITIVUTTAKA.

**Itivuttaka**. In Pāli, lit., "This Was Said"; fourth of the fifteen books contained in the KHUDDAKANIKĀYA of the Pāli SUTTAPIṬAKA. The collection is comprised of 110 suttas, each prefaced with the words vuttaṃ hetaṃ Bhagavatā ("This was said by the Blessed One"), rather than the more typical evaṃ me sutaṃ ("thus have I heard"; see EVAṂ MAYĀ ŚRUTAM). The suttas were preached to the slave woman Khujjutarā, who, to indicate that these were the Buddha's words and not her own, introduced the suttas in this way when repeating them to her mistress.

# J

**Jagaddala**. An important Buddhist monastery located in Naogaon district in modern Bangladesh. It was founded on the banks of the GAṄGĀNADĪ and Karatoya River in northern Bengal by King Rāmapāla (1077–1120). Reports from the early thirteenth century indicate that the monastery continued to flourish after the destruction of ODANTAPURĪ and VIKRAMAŚĪLA, serving as a refuge for such renowned Vikramaśīla scholars as ABHAYĀKARAGUPTA and Śubhākaragupta. Vidyākara, the author of the *Subhāṣitaratnakośa*, a famous anthology of aphorisms, served as abbot of Jagaddala.

**Jaina**. In Sanskrit, lit., "followers of The Victor [JINA]"; one of the major early sects of Indian wandering religious (ŚRAMAṆA), a movement in the fifth-century BCE that included Buddhism among its groups. One of the founders of Jainism, NIRGRANTHA-JÑĀTĪPUTRA (P. Nigaṇṭha Nātaputta), who is also known by his title of MAHĀVĪRA (Great Victor) (d. c. 488 BCE), was a contemporary of the Buddha and figures prominently in Buddhist literature. The Buddhists classified the Jainas among the TĪRTHIKA groups, the adherents of non-Buddhist religions who are sometimes mistranslated as "heretics." The Jainas were the śramaṇa group closest to Buddhism in its beliefs and practices, and the Buddha often used their teachings as a foil in order to present his own interpretations of important religious principles. Mahāvīra claimed to have achieved enlightenment and become one in a long line of jinas ("victors," e.g., over ignorance) or tīrthaṃkaras ("ford-makers") going back through twenty-four generations to Pārśva; this notion of an enlightened lineage of spiritual leaders is found also in Buddhism's doctrine that the Buddha was the latest in a series of previous buddhas (see SAPTATATHĀGATA). The Jainas believed in a theory of KARMAN, as did the Buddhists, but treated karman as a physical substance created through previous unwholesome actions, which constrained the soul and hindered its ability to rise above the physical world to the highest sphere of being; although the Buddhists accepted the notion of moral causality, as did the Jainas, they redefined karman instead as mental intention (CETANĀ). In order to free the soul from the bonds created through past actions, the Jainas held that the body had therefore to be rigorously cleansed of this karmic substance. The foundation of this cleansing process was the five great vows, the basic Jaina code of moral discipline, which parallel the Buddhist five precepts (PAÑCAŚĪLA). The Jainas also practiced more severe austerities than did the Buddhists, including a stricture requiring "non-harming" (AHIṂSĀ) of living creatures, rather than Buddhism's somewhat more lenient prohibition against "killing" living creatures. The Jainas also demanded strict vegetarianism from their followers in order to avoid injuring sentient creatures, a requirement that the Buddha rejected when his rival in the order, DEVADATTA, proposed it in his list of austerities (see DHUTAṄGA). The Buddha's view was that monks were a "field of merit" (PUṆYAKṢETRA) for the laity and it was be inappropriate to refuse offerings of meat made to them, except in a very limited number of specific situations (such as if the monk, for example, knew that the animal had been killed specifically to feed him). The vegetarianism that is now prevalent in both MAHĀYĀNA Buddhism and wider Indian Hindu culture is almost certainly a result of Jaina influence and constitutes that religion's most enduring contribution to Indian religion. One branch of the Jainas, the Digambara (lit. "Sky Clad"), took the prohibition against material possessions so strictly that their male adherents were forbidden from even wearing clothing; hence, the Jainas are often referred to in translations of Pāli materials as "naked ascetics." The Jainas were the only one of the six major śramaṇa traditions to survive into the present day on the Indian subcontinent, until Buddhism was reintroduced in the twentieth century by B. R. AMBEDKAR (1891–1956). In Buddhist texts, the Jainas are most commonly referred to as NIRGRANTHA, literally "freed from all ties."

**jakugo**. (C. zhuoyu/zhuyu; K. ch'agŏ 著語). In Japanese, "annotation," "attached word," or "capping phrase." Such "annotations" abound in several early Chinese collections of CHAN "cases," or GONG'AN (J. kōan), but they are most emblematic of the approach to kōan training taught in the Japanese RINZAISHŪ of ZEN. The use of capping phrases in Japan is largely due to the influence of SŌHŌ MYŌCHŌ (1282–1337), who introduced them in his interpretations of kōans. "Capping phrases" are brief phrases that are intended to offer a comment upon a specific Zen case, or kōan, to express one's own enlightened understanding, or to catalyze insight in another. These phrases were originally composed in literary Chinese and are taken as often from secular Chinese literature as they are from the Zen tradition's own stories. These phrases range from as few as one word (e.g., Right!, Finished!) to parallel eight-character phrases ("But for the rule and the compass, the square and the round could not be determined,/ But for the plumb-line, the straight and the crooked could not be rectified"), but they are rarely more than twenty-five Sinographs in total. In the Japanese Rinzai system of kōan meditative training, a student would demonstrate his understanding of the significance of a kōan by submitting to the teacher an (or even the) appropriate jakugo, often taken from such traditional anthologies of these phrases as the seventeenth-century ZENRIN KUSHŪ ("An Anthology of Phrases from the Zen Grove"). Once the student's understanding of a specific kōan was "passed" by the Zen master, the student would then continue on through a whole sequence of other kōans, each answered in turn by another jakugo. See also KIRIKAMI.

**Jakushitsu Genkō**. (C. Jishi Yuanguang 寂室元光) (1290–1367). Japanese ZEN monk in the RINZAISHŪ and founder of the Eigenji branch of the school. After entering the monastery at the age of thirteen, Jakushitsu studied under several Zen masters, including Yakuō Tokken (1244–1320) of ZENKŌJI in Kamakura, who administered to him the complete monastic precepts (gusokukai) of a BHIKṢU, and Yishan Yining (J. Issan Ichinei; 1247–1317) of NANZENJI in Kyōto, a Chinese LINJI ZONG monk who was active in Japan. Jakushitsu traveled to Yuan China in 1320 together with another Rinzai monk named Kaō Sōnen (d.1345). There, he studied with such eminent Linji Chan masters as ZHONGFENG MINGBEN (1263–1323), who gave him the cognomen Jishi (J. Jakushitsu), and Yuansou Xingduan (1255–1341). After returning to Japan in 1326, Jakushitsu spent the next twenty-five years traveling around the country as an itinerant monk, until 1362, when he assumed the abbacy of Eigenji, a monastery built for him by Sasaki Ujiyori (1326–1370) in Ōmi no kuni (present-day Shiga prefecture). The emperor subsequently invited him to stay at Tenryūji in Kyōto and KENCHŌJI in Kamakura, but he refused, choosing to remain at Eigenji for the remainder of his life. Jakushitsu is well known for his flute playing and his refined Zen poetry, which is considered some of the finest examples of the genre. He was given the posthumous title Ennō Zenji (Zen Master Consummate Response).

**Jālandhara**. (S). One of the twenty-four sacred sites associated with the CAKRASAṂVARATANTRA. See PĪṬHA.

**Jāliyasutta**. In Pāli, "Jāliya's Sermon"; the seventh sutta of the DĪGHANIKĀYA (there is no equivalent recension in the Chinese translation of the ĀGAMAS); preached by the Buddha to the mendicant (paribbājaka) Jāliya and his companion Maṇḍissa at the Ghositārāma monastery in Kosambī. The sermon is a disquisition on the virtues of leading the life of a mendicant and was given in response to a metaphysical question posed by Jāliya as to whether the soul and the body are one or different. The whole of this sermon is also subsumed within the *Mahālisutta* (the sixth sutta of the *Dīghanikāya*). The Buddha explains the benefits of Buddhist practice and the attainments beginning with taking refuge in the three jewels (P. ratanattaya; S. RATNATRAYA) of the Buddha, the DHARMA, and the SAMGHA, observing the precepts, renouncing the world to become a Buddhist monk, and controlling the senses with mindfulness (P. sati; S. SMṚTI), to cultivating the four meditative absorptions (P. JHĀNA; S. DHYĀNA), and developing the six higher knowledges or supranormal powers (P. abhiññā; S. ABHIJÑĀ). These include the following: (1) various magical powers (P. iddhividhābhiññāna; S. ṚDDHIVIDHĀBHIJÑĀ) such as the ability to pass through walls, (2) the divine ear (P. dibbasota; S. DIVYAŚROTRA), (3) the ability to know the minds of others (P. cetopariyañāṇa/paracittavijānanā; S. cetoparyāyābhijñāna/PARACITTAJÑĀNA), (4) the divine eye (P. dibbacakkhu; S. DIVYACAKṢUS), (5) the recollection of former existences (P. pubbenivāsānussati; S. PŪRVANIVĀSĀNUSMṚTI), and finally (6) the extinction of the contaminants (P. āsavakkhaya; S. ĀSRAVAKṢAYA), which is equivalent to arahantship (see S. ARHAT) and liberation from the cycle of rebirth.

**'ja' lus**. (jalu). In Tibetan, "rainbow body." In both Tibetan Buddhism and Bon, particularly in explanations of RDZOGS CHEN, the physical body dissolves into light when the adept reaches the final goal (often attained through a practice called THOD RGAL). This dissolution may be in the form of a miraculous disappearance while meditating, but is more usually associated with the time of the adept's death. The elements of the material body that remain at death depend upon the spiritual level of the deceased adept; the very highest leave no physical remnant at all, or in some explanations just hair and nails, and disappear with just a rainbow left behind. The colors in the rainbow body are sometimes associated with the transformation of the five aggregates (SKANDHA) into the colors of the five buddhas (PAÑCATATHĀGATA).

**Jambhala**. [alt. Jambhāla; Jambhīra] (T. Dzambala, Rmug 'dzin). In Sanskrit, a YAKṢA god of wealth; the Buddhist parallel to KUBERA, often equivalent to VAIŚRAVAṆA. In his various forms, he always holds in his left hand a mongoose with a jewel in its mouth. His śakti is Vasudharā. Statues of Jambhala have been found in Sri Lanka; he was also a popular figure in the Javanese Buddhist pantheon and is common in Tibet.

**Jambudvīpa**. (P. Jambudīpa; T. 'Dzam bu gling; C. Yanfuti; J. Enbudai; K. Yŏmbuje 閻浮提). In Sanskrit, "The Rose-Apple Continent"; corresponding to India. Jambudvīpa is the southernmost of the four continents where human beings reside in this world, along with VIDEHA (to the east of the world's axis mundi, MT. SUMERU), GODĀNĪYA (to the west), and UTTARAKURU (to the north). (Alternatively, Jambudvīpa is also said to be the central of seven continents that surround Mt. Sumeru.) At the center of Jambudvīpa is found the VAJRĀSANA ("diamond seat"), the spot where the buddhas realize their enlightenment; hence, Jambudvīpa is always the continent where buddhas spend their final lifetimes establishing their dispensations and is therefore the most auspicious site for beings to take rebirth. Also unique in this world, Jambudvīpa is ruled by a wheel-turning monarch (CAKRAVARTIN), the only continent that is so governed. Jambudvīpa is so named either because of the large number of rose-apple trees that grow there, or because of a large rose-apple tree at the top of Mt. Sumeru that is visible from there. It is shaped like a triangular cart, and has two subcontinents, cāmara and aparacāmara. On its eastern side are ten mountain ranges, the last and highest of which is the Himavanta (the Himālayas). From its deep lake Anavatapta flow its four major rivers: the GAṄGĀNADĪ (the Ganges), Sindhu, Vakṣu, and Sītā. The life span of human beings in Jambudvīpa drops as low as ten years at the end of a KALPA, increasing to incalculable years at the beginning of the eon (prāthamakalpika). The system of hells (see NĀRAKA) is located beneath Jambudvīpa.

**Jambupati**. In Pāli, lit. "Lord of the Rose Apple"; a type of buddha image found most commonly in the art of Burma (Myanmar) and its Shan state, in which the Buddha is adorned in the royal attire of a "wheel-turning monarch" (CAKRAVARTIN), wearing a magnificent crown and jewels, and seated on a throne. This image derives from a Southeast Asian Buddhist legend (which is apparently unknown in India) about an arrogant king named Jambupati, who terrorized his people. In order to convince him to repent of his unwholesome actions and practice compassion toward his subjects, the Buddha had himself adorned with full royal regalia and seated in a magnificent palace; when Jambupati was brought before the crowned Buddha, he was so humbled by the Buddha's majesty that he repented of his arrogance and took the five precepts (PAÑCAŚĪLA) of a Buddhist layman (UPĀSAKA). In this royal form, the Buddha's UṢṆĪṢA is often extended into a pronounced spire, perhaps suggesting the form of a STŪPA. Jambupati Buddha images are most commonly seated in the "earth-touching gesture" (BHŪMISPARŚAMUDRĀ), although sometimes standing images are also found. The famous ARAKAN BUDDHA, viz., the Mahāmuni image in Arakan (present-day Mandalay), is now crowned in the Jambupati style.

**'Jam dbyangs bzhad pa**. (Jamyang Shepa). The name of a line of SPRUL SKU (incarnations) that are the head lamas of BLA BRANG BKRA SHIS DKYIL monastery in A mdo in northeastern Tibet, now part of the Chinese province of Gansu. The first, 'JAM DBYANGS BZHAD PA'I RDO RJE NGAG DBANG BRTSON 'GRUS, founded Bla brang; the second, Dkon mchog 'jig med dbang po (Könchok Jigme Wangpo, 1728–1791), was a prolific scholar and writer. There have been a total of six incarnations.

**'Jam dbyangs bzhad pa'i rdo rje Ngag dbang brtson 'grus**. (Jamyang Shepe Dorje Ngawang Tsondrü) (1648–1722). The originator, and first in the line of 'JAM DBYANGS BZHAD PA SPRUL SKU (incarnations) that are the head lamas of BLA BRANG BKRA SHIS DKYIL monastery in A mdo, northeastern Tibet, now part of Gansu province in northwest China. He arrived in LHA SA in 1668 and entered Sgo mang grwa tshang (monastic college) of 'BRAS SPUNGS monastery. He received both his ŚRĀMAṆERA and BHIKṢU ordinations from the fifth DALAI LAMA. In 1676, he entered the tantric college of RGYUD SMAD. A prolific writer, his collected works (gsung 'bum) in fifteen volumes include commentaries on the GUHYASAMĀJATANTRA and VAJRABHAIRAVATANTRA, and long and detailed commentaries on ABHIDHARMA, PRAJÑĀPĀRAMITĀ, VINAYA, and a range of issues in MADHYAMAKA and YOGĀCĀRA philosophy; these works replaced those of Gung ru Chos kyi 'byung gnas as the authoritative standard works (yig cha) studied in the Sgo mang college of 'Bras spungs monastery, and in the network of provincial monasteries associated with it. Among his most famous works is his doxography of the Indian philosophical schools, both Buddhist and non-Buddhist, known as *Grub mtha' chen mo*. In the political turmoil that followed the death of the fifth DALAI LAMA in 1682 and the rule of SDE SRID SANGS RGYAS RGYA MTSHO in his name, 'Jam dbyangs bzhad pa was appointed abbot of Sgo mang in 1700. However, he came into conflict with the Sde srid over the latter's attempt to force a change in the monastic curriculum at 'Bras spungs, stepping down from the abbacy. He developed a friendship with Lha bzang Khan, the military ruler of central Tibet, accepting from him the hermitage of Pha bong kha located above SE RA monastery. He apparently sought to pacify the strained relations between the Sde srid and the Lha bzang Khan, but after the execution of the Sde srid by Mongolian forces in 1705, he left central Tibet for A mdo in 1709 where he founded Bla brang bkra shis dkyil. It grew into a huge monastery and a center of scholarship in its own right. The monastery attracted many Mongolian students and its influence was instrumental in consolidating the power of the DGE LUGS sect and the new DGA' LDAN PHO BRANG government over the A mdo regions.

**'Jam dbyangs chos rje Bkra shis dpal ldan**. (Jamyang Chöje Tashi Palden) (1379–1449). An important figure in the early history of the DGE LUGS sect. After studying at GSANG PHU and BSAM YAS monasteries, he became a follower of TSONG KHA PA and in 1414 founded 'BRAS SPUNGS, eventually the largest monastery in Tibet. Little is known about him, but his views came to be considered controversial and his writings were eventually lost to posterity. After the death of RGYAL TSHAB DAR MA RIN CHEN he was passed over as DGA' LDAN KHRI PA in favor of MKHAS GRUB DGE LEGS DPAL BZANG.

**'Jam dbyangs mkhyen brtse Chos kyi blo gros**. (Jamyang Khyentse Chökyi Lodrö) (1893–1959). A Tibetan visionary closely associated with what is known as the RIS MED or nonsectarian movement, in eastern Tibet. He is sometimes known as Rdzong gsar mkhyen brtse (Dzongsar Khyentse) due to his affiliation with RDZONG GSAR monastery in Khams, eastern Tibet. He was recognized by 'JAM MGON KONG SPRUL as one of five reincarnations of 'JAM DBYANGS MKHYEN BRTSE DBANG PO. At KAḤ THOG monastery, he studied both the treasure texts

(GTER MA) discovered by his previous incarnation as well as the curriculum of Indian texts. At the age of fifteen, he was appointed abbot of Rdzongs gsar. This remained his base for much of his life, but he traveled widely, receiving instruction from BKA' RGYUD, SA SKYA, and RNYING MA teachers. At the age of fifty-six, he married and went into retreat in a hermitage above Rdzongs gsar but also continued to give teachings. In 1955, he made a final pilgrimage to the sacred sites of Tibet and then went to Sikkim, where he died in 1959. Over the course of his life, he served as a teacher to many of the twentieth century's greatest Tibetan Buddhist masters.

**'Jam dbyangs mkhyen brtse dbang po**. (Jamyang Khyentse Wangpo) (1820–1892). A celebrated Tibetan Buddhist luminary, considered to be the last of the "five kingly treasure revealers" (GTER STON RGYAL PO LNGA). Together with 'JAM MGON KONG SPRUL BLO GROS MTHA' YAS and MCHOG 'GYUR GLING PA, he was a leading figure in the RIS MED or nonsectarian movement in eastern Tibet. He was identified at age twelve as the incarnation (SPRUL SKU) of a prominent SA SKYA lama. Later in life, he would be recognized as the mind incarnation (thugs sprul) of the acclaimed eighteenth-century treasure revealer (GTER STON) 'JIGS MED GLING PA. He was a prolific author, collecting numerous "path and result" (LAM 'BRAS) teachings and discovering many important treasure texts. In addition to his editions of other works, his own collected works encompass twenty-four volumes. Among his best known works is a pilgrimage guide to central Tibet. 'Jam dbyangs mkhyen brtse dbang po taught extensively, primarily from his seat at RDZONG GSAR monastery in Khams, attracting numerous students and gaining patronage from the region's most influential families; he served as chaplain at the Sde sge court. After his death, five "mkhyen brtse" (Khyentse) incarnations were recognized, including 'JAM DBYANGS MKHYEN BRTSE CHOS KYI BLO GROS and DIL MGO MKHYEN BRTSE.

**'Jam mgon kong sprul Blo gros mtha' yas**. (Jamgon Kongtrül Lodrö Thaye) (1813–1899). A renowned Tibetan Buddhist master, prolific scholar, and proponent of the RIS MED or nonsectarian movement, of eastern Tibet. He is often known as 'Jam mgon kong sprul (Jamgon Kongrtul) or simply Kong sprul. Born to a BON family in the eastern Tibetan region of Rong rgyab (Rongyap), 'Jam mgon kong sprul studied Bon doctrine as a youth, eventually receiving Buddhist ordination first in the RNYING MA and then the BKA' BRGYUD sects of Tibetan Buddhism. He was a gifted pupil, studying under at least sixty different masters representing all the various sects and lineages of Tibet. Early experiences with the sectarianism and religious intolerance rampant in many Buddhist institutions of his time left him somewhat disaffected and were to have a profound impact on his later career. He resided at DPAL SPUNGS monastery near Derge, where his reputation as a brilliant scholar spread widely. When Kong sprul was in danger of being drafted into the provincial administrative offices, the ninth TAI SI TU, Padma nyin byed (Pema Nyinje, 1774–1853), abbot of Dpal spungs, recognized him as the reincarnation of the former Si tu's servant, thereby exempting him from government service. In his autobiography, Kong sprul himself appears to have looked upon this event with some dismay. Together with other luminaries of the period such as 'JAM DBYANG MKHYEN RTSE DBANG PO, MCHOG 'GYUR GLING PA, and MI PHAM RGYA MTSHO, Kong sprul strove to collect, compile, and transmit a multitude of teachings and instruction lineages that were in danger of being lost. The impartial (ris med) approach with which he undertook this project has led him to be credited with spearheading a "nonsectarian" or "eclectic" movement in eastern Tibet. He was a proponent of the "other emptiness" (GZHAN STONG) view, which gained new impetus when his associate Blo gsal bstan skyong was able to arrange for the printing of the woodblocks preserved at TĀRANĀTHA's former seat at DGA' LDAN PHUN TSHOGS GLING, works that had been banned since the time of the fifth DALAI LAMA. 'Jam mgon kong sprul was a prolific author whose writings fill more than ninety volumes. These works are divided into the so-called KONG SPRUL MDZOD LNGA (Five Treasuries of Kongtrul), which cover the breadth of Tibetan Buddhist culture. Since the death of Blo gros mtha' yas, a line of Kong sprul incarnations has been recognized and continues to play an important role within the KARMA BKA' BRGYUD sect. The lineage is:

1. Kong sprul Blo gros mtha' yas (Kongtrül Lodrö Thaye, 1813–1899)
2. Kong sprul Mkhyen brtse 'od zer (Kongtrül Khyentse Öser, 1904–1953)
3. Kong sprul Blo gros chos kyi seng ge (Kongtrül Lodrö Chökyi Senge, 1954–1992)
4. Kong sprul Blo gros chos kyi nyi ma (Kongtrül Lodrö Chökyi Nyima, b. 1995)

**Janapadakalyāṇī Nandā**. (S. Janapandakalyāṇī Rūpanandā; T. Yul gyi bzang mo dga' mo). In Pāli, "Nandā, the Prettiest in the Land"; one of three prominent nuns named Nandā mentioned in the Pāli canon (the others being ABHIRŪPĀ NANDĀ and SUNDARĪ NANDĀ), all of whom share similar stories. According to Pāli sources, Janapadakalyāṇī Nandā was a Sākiyan (S. ŚĀKYA) woman of great beauty, who was betrothed to the Buddha's half-brother NANDA. On their wedding day, the Buddha visited her fiancé Nanda's palace in Kapilavatthu (S. KAPILAVASTU) and extended his felicitations. He caused Nanda to accompany him on his return to the monastery where he was staying and there asked Nanda to enter the order; Nanda reluctantly assented, but only after the Buddha used his supernatural powers to show him his prospects for enjoying heavenly maidens far more beautiful than his betrothed if he practiced well. Later, Nanda became an arahant (S. ARHAT). Janapadakalyāṇī was overcome with grief at Nanda's ordination. Since she felt she had nothing else to live for, as soon as women were allowed to enter the order, she decided to become a nun under the leadership of Mahāpajāpatī (S. MAHĀPRAJĀPATĪ). Still attached to her own loveliness, for a long time Janapadakalyāṇī refused to visit the Buddha for fear that he would speak disparagingly of physical beauty. When finally one day she went together with her companions to hear the Buddha preach, the Buddha, knowing her state of mind, created an apparition of an extraordinarily beautiful woman fanning him. Janapadakalyāṇī was transfixed by the beauty of the maiden, whom the Buddha then caused to age, die, and decompose right before her very eyes. As the Buddha described the impermanence of physical beauty, Janapadakalyāṇī attained stream-entry (P. sotāpatti; see SROTAĀPANNA) and, shortly thereafter, arahanthip (see S. ARHAT). The source for the stories related to JANAPADAKALYĀṆĪ NANDĀ are the DHAMMAPADAṬṬHAKATHĀ and the *Udāya*, both texts known only to the Pāli tradition.

**Janapandakalyāṇi Rūpanandā**. (S). See JANAPADAKALYĀṆĪ NANDĀ.

**Janavasabhasuttanta**. (C. Shenisha jing; J. Janishakyō; K. Sanisa kyŏng 闍尼沙經). In Pāli, the "Discourse on Janavasabha"; the eighteenth sutta of the DĪGHANIKĀYA (a Dharmaguptaka recension appears as the fourth sūtra in the Chinese translation of the DĪRGHĀGAMA). During the last year of his life, the Buddha addressed this discourse to his attendant ĀNANDA, who wished to know the destinies of deceased lay disciples from the country of MAGADHA. The Buddha replied that numerous lay disciples from Magadha had been reborn in the realms of the divinities (DEVA) as non-returners (S. ANĀGĀMIN), once-returners (S. SAKṚDĀGĀMIN), and stream-enterers (S. SROTAĀPANNA) through their faith in the three jewels (S. RATNATRAYA) of the Buddha, the DHARMA, and the SAṂGHA. The Buddha received this information from a divinity named Janavasabha, after whom the discourse is named, who in his preceding life had been King BIMBISĀRA of Magadha.

**janmanirmāṇakāya**. (T. skye ba'i sprul sku). In Sanskrit, "created emanation body"; a form of the NIRMĀṆAKĀYA in which a buddha, in order subdue the afflictions (KLEŚA) of sentient beings, takes an animate form (such as that of a god, a deer, or a bird) or an inanimate form (such as a bridge or a tree). See also UTTAMANIRMĀṆAKĀYA; SPRUL SKU; TRIKĀYA.

**japa**. (T. bzlas brjod; C. niansong; J. nenju; K. yŏmsong 念誦). In Sanskrit and Pāli, "recitation"; usually oral recitations of invocations or MANTRAS, often counted by fingering a rosary (JAPAMĀLĀ). The various merits forthcoming from specific numbers of such recitations are related in different scriptures. The number of such recitations to be performed in a single sitting is often related to specific numerical lists, such as varying rosters of stages on the BODHISATTVA path. The recitation would then constitute a reenactment of the path, or a process of purification. Perhaps the most common number across traditions is 108, but these numbers range from as few as seven, to fourteen, twenty-one, twenty-seven, thirty-six, forty-two, or fifty-four, up to as many as 1,080. The common figure of 108 is typically said to correspond to a list of 108 proclivities or afflictions (see KLEŚA), although other texts say it refers instead to lists of 108 enlightened ones or 108 SAMĀDHIS; 1,080 would then constitute these 108 across all the ten directions (DAŚADIŚ). (See also other explanations in JAPAMĀLĀ, s.v.)

**japamālā**. (T. bzlas brjod kyi 'phreng ba; C. shuzhu/nianzhu; J. juzu/nenju; K. suju/yŏmju 數珠/念珠). In Sanskrit and Pāli, lit. "garland for recitation," thus "prayer beads" or "rosary"; a string of beads held usually in the right hand and fingered by adherents to keep count of the number of recitations made in the course of a worship service, MANTRA recitation, or meditation session. The beads are often made from sandalwood or seeds of the BODHI TREE (*Ficus religiosa*), the tree under which the Buddha gained enlightenment, although rosaries made from a range of other materials are also common; in some tantric practices, a rosary with beads made from human bone is used. The number of beads on a rosary varies widely. The most common number is 108, the significance of which receives widely varying explanations. One common interpretation is that this number refers to a list of 108 afflictions (KLEŚA); fingering all 108 beads in the course of a recitation would then be either a reminder to remain mindful of these afflictions or would constitute their symbolic purification. Alternatively, this 108 can refer to all of phenomenal existence, i.e., the eighteen elements (DHĀTU), viz., the six sense bases, six sense objects, and six sensory consciousnesses, in all of the six states of existence (GATI) (18 × 6 = 108). In Tibetan Buddhism, the number 111 is sometimes used, based on the assumption that for each ten mantras recited, one will be mistaken and need to be repeated, thus adding an additional ten beads for 110. An additional bead is then added to account for the mistaken recitation among the additional ten. Thus, although a mantra might be recited 111 times, only 100 are counted. The Chinese PURE LAND advocate DAOCHUO (562–645) is famous for having used small beans (xiaodou) to keep track of the number of times he had recited the buddha AMITĀBHA's name (see NIANFO); some believe his habit of using such counting beans is the origin of the East Asian japamālā. In many Buddhist traditions, carrying a rosary serves almost as a symbol of the faith. In East Asia, Buddhist monks and nuns, and even many lay adherents, will commonly wear the full-length rosary around their necks. Rosaries of abbreviated lengths, which are more typically worn around the wrist, are sometimes designated duanzhu (J. tanju; K. tanju), or "short rosary." These rosaries will be a maximum of fifty-four beads in length (half the usual length), which would require two repetitions to complete a full round of recitation, and a minimum of nine beads, which would take twelve repetitions. In Tibetan Buddhism, a short rosary is sometimes worn around the right hand while doing prostrations. The CHAN school often uses a short rosary with eighteen beads, requiring six repetitions. See also JAPA.

**jarā**. (T. rga ba; C. lao; J. rō; K. no 老). In Sanskrit and Pāli, "senescence," "aging," or "decay." Aging and death (JARĀMARAṆA) are one of the varieties of the suffering (DUḤKHA) that is said to be inherent in the conditioned realm of existence and together constitute the last of the twelve links of dependent origination (PRATĪTYASAMUTPĀDA). The future buddha is said to have left the life of the householder in search of a state beyond birth, aging, sickness, and death. In the SARVĀSTIVĀDA ABHIDHARMA system, senescence is treated as a "conditioned force dissociated from thought" (CITTAVIPRAYUKTASAṂSKĀRA), which functions as one of the four conditioned characteristics (SAṂSKṚTALAKṢAṆA) that is associated with all conditioned objects. Because the ontology of the Sarvāstivāda school, as its name implies, postulated that "everything exists" in all three time periods (TRIKĀLA) of past, present, and future, there had to be some mechanism to account for the apparent change that conditioned objects underwent through time. Therefore, along with the other three characteristics of origination (JĀTI), continuance (STHITI), and desinence (ANITYATĀ; viz., death), aging was posited as a "conditioned force dissociated from thought," which causes the active functioning (kāritra) of a conditioned object to degenerate, initiating the process that leads to its inevitable death. The very definition of conditioned objects is that they are subject to these conditioned characteristics, including this process of decay and change; this is what ultimately distinguishes them from the unconditioned (ASAṂSKṚTA), viz., NIRVĀṆA.

**jarāmaraṇa**. (T. rga shi; C. laosi; J. rōshi; K. nosa 老死). In Sanskrit and Pāli, "aging and death"; the twelfth and final link in the chain of conditioned origination (PRATĪTYASAMUTPĀDA), preceded by JĀTI, the eleventh link. In some formulations of the twelve links of the chain, old age and death are presumed to occur in the last of a sequence of three lifetimes, with the first two links in the chain, ignorance and predispositions, assigned to the previous lifetime; consciousness, name and form, sense fields, contact, sensation, thirst, grasping, and existence to the current lifetime, leading to future birth, old age, and death in the immediately following lifetime. ¶ In some compounds, jarāmaraṇa does not mean only "old age and death," but is used as an abbreviation for the whole panoply of human existence, viz., "birth, old age, sickness, and death"; this accounts for its alternate translation as "birth and death" (shengsi) in Chinese. This usage of the term is found in two different types of jarāmaraṇa that are distinguished in the literature: (1) determinative birth-and-death (PARICCHEDAJARĀMARAṆA), referring to the physical existence of ordinary sentient beings, whose bodies are restricted in their longevity, appearance, and size; and (2) transfigurational birth-and-death (PARIṆĀMIKAJARĀMARAṆA), referring to the mind-made bodies (MANOMAYAKĀYA) of ARHATs, PRATYEKABUDDHAs, and great BODHISATTVAs, who are able to change their appearance and life span at will.

**jātaka**. (T. skyes rabs; C. bensheng jing; J. honshōkyō; K. ponsaeng kyŏng 本生經). In Sanskrit and Pāli, literally, "birth," or "nativity"; a term used in Buddhism to refer by extension to narrative accounts of previous births or lives, especially of a buddha. The jātaka constitute one of the nine (NAVAṄGA[PĀVACANA]) (Pāli) or twelve (DVĀDAŚĀṄGA [PRAVACANA]) (Sanskrit) categories (AṄGA) of Buddhist scripture that are delineated according to their structure or literary style. There are hundreds of such stories (547 in the Pāli collection alone) and together they form one of the most popular genres of Buddhist literature. In a typical tale, GAUTAMA Buddha will recount a story from one of his past lives as a human or an animal, demonstrating a particular virtue, or perfection (PĀRAMITĀ), after which he will identify the other characters in the story as the past incarnations of members of his present audience. A jātaka story usually has five components: (1) an introduction, in which the Buddha recounts the circumstances leading up to the story to be recounted; (2) a prose narrative, in which the story from one of the Buddha's past lives is related; (3) stanzas of poetry, which often contain the moral of the story; (4) a prose commentary on the stanzas; and (5) a conclusion that connects the past with the present, in which the Buddha identifies members of his current audience as incarnations in the present of the characters in the story from the past. ¶ The Pāli *Jātaka* is the tenth book of the KHUDDAKANIKĀYA of the SUTTAPIṬAKA. The collection is comprised of 547 stories of former lives of Gotama Buddha while he was a bodhisatta (S. BODHISATTVA). The *Jātaka* itself is made up entirely of short verses, but these are accompanied by prose commentary called the JĀTAKAṬṬHAKATHĀ, which recounts the relevant stories. Some of the *Jātakas* have been included in another collection contained in the KHUDDAKANIKĀYA, the CARIYĀPIṬAKA. In Sanskrit, the most famous jātaka collection is the JĀTAKAMĀLĀ by Śūra. Over the course of the history of Buddhism and throughout the Buddhist world, jātakas have been one of the most popular forms of Buddhist literature, especially among the laity, due both to their entertaining plots and their edifying moral lessons. Scenes from various jātaka stories are widely depicted in Buddhist art and occur among some of the earliest Buddhist stone carvings in India. Scholarship has demonstrated that the plots of many of the jātakas derive from Indian folklore, with the same story occurring in Hindu, JAINA, and Buddhist works. In the Buddhist versions, the plot has been adapted by adding a prologue and epilogue that identifies the protagonist as the bodhisattva and the other characters as members of the Buddha's circle in a former life; the hero's antagonist in the story is often identified as DEVADATTA in a former life. In addition to their general popularity, individual jātakas have had great influence, such as the VESSANTARA JĀTAKA in Southeast Asia.

**Jātakamālā**. (T. Skyes pa'i rabs kyi rgyud; C. Pusa benshengman lun; J. Bosatsu honjōmanron; K. Posal ponsaengman non 菩薩本生鬘論). In Sanskrit, "Garland of Birth Stories," by the poet Śūra [alt. Āryaśūra; c. second-century CE], a collection of thirty-four JĀTAKA tales related in an elegant and elliptical literary style. Each story includes Śūra's introduction relating the specific point of morality illustrated in the story. This narrative is in mixed prose and verse (a style that comes to be termed campū), with a variety of different meters employed. The beauty of Śūra's literary renderings was so renowned that the *Jātakamālā* often came to be even more widely read than the *Jātaka* collections themselves. In Tibet it is a custom for a senior monk to give an explanation of one of the tales from the *Jātakamālā* on the opening day of the SMON LAM CHEN MO (Great Prayer Festival). ¶ The story surrounding the Chinese "translation" of the *Jātakamālā*, the *Pusa benshengman lun* ("Treatise on the Bodhisattva's Garland of Birth Stories"), may be one of the strangest tales in the annals of the translation of Buddhist texts. As modern scholarship has shown, the Chinese "translators" had so much difficulty in construing Śūra's elaborate style that they managed to produce an "apocryphal" scripture while having the Sanskrit text right in front of them. Working without dictionary or grammar, or the luxury of an Indian paṇḍita to help them construe the text, and apparently faced with an impossible deadline, the translators simply resorted to forgery: where they found a few random words of Śūra's that they could construe, they lifted wholesale from other texts stories that happened to contain the same words. Except for the titles of some of the stories, there is almost nothing in the Chinese translation that corresponds to Śūra's Sanskrit.

**Jātakaṭṭhakathā**. [alt. Jātakatthavaṇṇanā]. In Pāli, "Commentary on the JĀTAKA," is a prose exegesis of the verses included in the *Jātaka* collection. Authorship is traditionally attributed to BUDDHAGHOSA, although the prose is a Pāli translation of a commentary written originally in Sinhalese. The commentary on each jātaka tale includes an introduction relating how the story came to be told and an epilogue correlating the major characters in the tale with the Buddha's current contemporaries. The commentary is preceded by a lengthy introduction, the NIDĀNAKATHĀ, which recounts the buddha's previous birth as SUMEDHA and his last life as Siddhattha (S. SIDDHĀRTHA) from the time of his birth, through his enlightenment and early teaching, ending with the donation of JETAVANA by Anāthapiṇḍika (S. ANĀTHAPIṆḌADA). The *Jātakaṭṭhakathā* appears in the Pali Text Society's English translation series as *Stories of the Buddha's Former Births*; the *Nidānakathā* appears separately as *The Story of Gotama Buddha*.

**jāti**. (T. skye ba; C. sheng; J. shō; K. saeng 生). In Sanskrit and Pāli, "birth," "origination." Birth is one of the varieties of the suffering (DUḤKHA) that is inherent in the conditioned realm of existence and the eleventh of the twelve links in the chain of dependent origination (PRATĪTYASAMUTPĀDA). The future buddha is said to have left the life of the householder in search of a state beyond birth, aging, sickness, and death. In the SARVĀSTIVĀDA ABHIDHARMA system, origination is treated as a "conditioned force dissociated from thought" (CITTAVIPRAYUKTASAṂSKĀRA), which functions as one of the four conditioned characteristics (SAṂSKṚTALAKṢAṆA) that is associated with all conditioned objects. Because the ontology of the Sarvāstivāda school, as its name implies, postulated that "everything exists" in all three time periods (TRIKĀLA) of past, present, and future, there had to be some mechanism to account for the apparent change that conditioned objects underwent through time. Therefore, along with the other three characteristics of continuance (STHITI), senescence (JARĀ), and desinence (ANITYATĀ; viz., death), origination was posited as a "conditioned force dissociated from thought," which prepares an object to be produced and thus pulls that object out of the future and into the present. The very definition of conditioned objects is that they are subject to these conditioned characteristics, including this process of production, and this is what ultimately distinguishes them from the unconditioned (ASAṂSKṚTA), viz., NIRVĀṆA. In less technical contexts, beginning with the Buddha's first sermon (see DHAMMACAKKAPPAVATTANASUTTA), jāti appears in various lists of the sufferings of SAṂSĀRA, with a variety of texts describing at length the pain experienced in the womb and during birth.

**jātismara**. (P. jātissara; T. tshe rabs dran pa; C. suming; J. shukumyō; K. sungmyŏng 宿命). In Sanskrit, "memory of previous births," is synonymous with "recollection of past lives" (PŪRVANIVĀSĀNUSMṚTI); a supernatural power often mentioned in the early Buddhist scriptures as accessible to religious virtuosi. This talent is listed as the first of three knowledges (TRIVIDYĀ), the fourth of five or six supranormal powers (ABHIJÑĀ), and the eight of the ten powers (BALA) of a TATHĀGATA. In the context of the supranormal powers, this ability to remember one's past lives is considered to be a mundane (LAUKIKA) achievement that is gained through still more profound refinement of the fourth stage of meditative absorption (DHYĀNA). In other contexts, however, this power is accessible only to those who are ARHATs, buddhas, or otherwise in no further need of training (AŚAIKṢA). In later MAHĀYĀNA materials, however, bodhisattvas sometimes give even unenlightened ordinary beings (PṚTHAGJANA) this insight into their past lives as a way of inspiring them in their religious practice. In other Mahāyāna texts, such as the SUVARṆAPRABHĀSOTTAMASŪTRA ("Golden Light Sūtra"), this talent is a by-product not of meditation but of specific types of ritual activity, a "blessing" (ANUŚAṂSA) that accrues, for example, from formulaic exaltations of the qualities of the buddhas, recitation of lists of their names, repetitions of mnemonic codes (DHĀRAṆĪ), or copying of scriptures. The ability to remember one's past lives is said to extend back to hundreds, thousands, or even millions of one's previous births. On the night of his enlightenment, the Buddha remembered all of his previous births.

**jedi**. [alt. zedi]. The Burmese pronunciation of Pāli cetī/cetiya, Sanskrit CAITYA or STŪPA; an architectural structure at a monastery, usually in the shape of a cone, with a bell-shaped base, but sometimes obelisque in form, containing relics (S. ŚARĪRA) of revered monks or in some cases, of the buddha.

**Jeta**. [alt. Jetakumāra]. (S. Jetṛ; T. Rgyal byed; C. Zhituo taizi; J. Gida taishi; K. Kit'a t'aeja 祇陀太子). In BUDDHIST HYBRID SANSKRIT and Pāli, "Victorious"; a prince of the Indian kingdom of ŚRĀVASTĪ (P. Sāvatthi), commonly referred to as Jetakumāra (Prince Jeta), and original owner of the JETAVANA park. Prince Jeta was approached by the banker ANĀTHAPIṆḌADA (P. Anāthapiṇḍika) who wished to purchase his park and donate it to the Buddha. Demanding that the banker cover the entire grounds with gold coins as the purchase price, Jeta finally consented once Anāthapiṇḍada had covered all but the entrance with eighteen crores (one hundred million) worth of coins. Jeta donated the entrance himself and then used the entire purchase price to erect a grand gateway over the entrance. Different explanations are given as to how the prince came to be so named: because he vanquished his enemies, because he was born during the reign of a victorious king, or because the name itself was thought to be auspicious for him. Sanskrit sources claim that Jeta was the son of King PRASENAJIT and was murdered by his half-brother Viḍuḍabha for refusing to participate in the extermination of the ŚĀKYA clan to which the Buddha belonged.

**Jetāri**. (S). See JITĀRI.

**Jetavana**. (T. Rgyal byed kyi tshal; C. Zhishu Jigudu yuan; J. Giju Gikkodokuon; K. Kisu Kŭpkodok wŏn 祇樹給孤獨園). In Pāli and Sanskrit, "Prince Jeta's Grove" (C. Zhishu), located in "Anāthapiṇḍika's Park" (S. Anāthapiṇḍadārāma; P. Anāthapiṇḍikārāma; C. Jigudu yuan); a park located to the south of the city of ŚRĀVASTĪ (P. Sāvatthi), which was donated to the Buddha and his disciples by the banker ANĀTHAPIṆḌADA (P. Anāthapiṇḍika). The park, which is also called Jetavanārama, is named after its original owner, Prince Jeta (Jetakumāra), from whom Anāthapiṇḍada purchased it for an extraordinary price. Anāthapiṇḍada had invited the Buddha to Śrāvastī and resolved to provide him with a suitable residence during his sojourn in the city. Knowing that Jetakumāra's park on the city's outskirts was the loveliest place in town, he offered to buy the park from the prince. But Jeta was unwilling to sell the property and rebuffed Anāthapiṇḍada, stating that the banker would have to cover the entire site in coins if he wanted to buy it. Undeterred, Anāthapiṇḍada brought the case before the city fathers, who agreed that if he could gather Jeta's stated purchase price, he would be entitled to Jetakumāra's park. Anāthapiṇḍada had his servants bring cartloads of gold coins from his treasury, some eighteen crores in total, with which he was able to cover the entire grounds of the park, except for the entrance. Impressed by the banker's generosity, Jetakumāra donated that spot himself, and with the vast purchase price he received, erected a grand entrance over it. Anāthapiṇḍada built numerous buildings at the park to serve the Buddha and the monastic community during the rains retreat (VARṢĀ). Among these was the Buddha's own residence, the so-called perfumed chamber, or GANDHAKUṬĪ. The same spot had served as a monastery and rains-retreat residence for previous buddhas also, although the extent of the grounds varied. According to Pāli sources, during the time of the buddha Vipassī (S. VIPAŚYIN), the merchant Punabbasumitta built a monastery that extended a league, while during the time of the buddha Vessabhū, the merchant Sotthika built another that extended half a league. Anāthapiṇḍada's monastery covered eighteen karīsa (a square measure of land). Traditional sources often state that Jetavanārāma was GAUTAMA Buddha's favorite residence and he is said to have is passed nineteen rains retreats there. After the laywoman VIŚĀKHĀ built another grand monastery named Migāramātupāsāda in Śrāvastī, the Buddha would alternate between both residences, spending the day at one and the night at another. ¶ Jetavana also refers to a monastery built at ANURĀDHAPURA in the fourth-century CE by the Sinhala king MAHĀSENA for the elder Saṅghamitta. Saṅghamitta felt great animosity toward the monks of the MAHĀVIHĀRA sect, which prompted him to lobby the king to confiscate its property and pass it on to the Jetavana.

**Jewel Ornament of Liberation**. See THAR PA RIN PO CHE'I RGYAN.

**jhāna**. In Pāli, "meditative absorption," corresponding to the Sanskrit DHYĀNA (s.v.). Jhāna refers to the attainment of single-pointed concentration, whereby the mind is withdrawn from external sensory input and completely absorbed in an ideational object of meditation (see KAMMAṬṬHĀNA). Jhāna involves the power to control the mind and does not, in itself, entail any enduring insight into the nature of reality; however, a certain level of concentration is generally said to be necessary in order to prepare the mind for direct realization of truth, the destruction of the afflictions, and the attainment of liberation. Jhāna is classified into two broad types: (1) meditative absorption of the subtle-materiality realm (P. rūpāvacarajhāna; S. RŪPĀVACARADHYĀNA) and (2) meditative absorption of the immaterial realm (P. arūpāvacarajhāna; S. ĀRŪPYĀVACARADHYĀNA). Each of these two types is subdivided into four stages or degrees of absorption, giving a total of eight stages of jhāna. These stages are sometimes called the eight "attainments" (SAMĀPATTI). The four absorptions of the subtle-materiality realm are characterized by an increasing attenuation of consciousness as one progresses from one stage to the next. By entering into any one of the jhānas, the meditator temporarily overcomes the five hindrances (NĪVARAṆA) through the force of concentration. This is called "overcoming by repression" (P. vikkhambhanappahāna). The five hindrances are (1) "sensuous desire" (KĀMACCHANDA), which hinders one-pointedness of mind (P. cittekaggatā; S. CITTAIKĀGRATĀ); (2) "malice" (P. byāpāda; S. VYĀPĀDA), hindering rapture (P. pīti; S. PRĪTI); (3) "sloth and torpor" (P. thīnamiddha; S. STHYĀNA-MIDDHA), hindering applied thought (P. vitakka; S. VITARKA); (4) "restlessness and worry" (P. uddhaccakukkucca; S. AUDDHATYA-KAUKṚTYA), hindering joy (SUKHA); and (5) "skeptical doubt" (P. vicikicchā;

S. VICIKITSĀ), which hinders sustained thought (VICĀRA). These hindrances thus specifically obstruct one of the factors of absorption (P. jhānaṅga; S. DHYĀNĀṄGA), and once they are allayed the first level of the subtle-materiality jhānas will be achieved. In the first jhāna, all five constituents of jhāna are present; as concentration deepens, these gradually fall away, so that in the second jhāna, both types of thought vanish and only pīti, sukha, and ekaggatā remain; in the third jhāna, only sukha and ekaggatā remain; and in the fourth jhāna, concentration is now so rarified that only ekaggatā is left. Detailed correlations appear in meditation manuals describing specifically which of the five spiritual faculties (INDRIYA) and seven constituents of enlightenment (P. bojjhaṅga; S. BODHYAṄGA) serve as the antidote to which hindrance. Mastery of the fourth absorption of the subtle-materiality realm is required for the cultivation of supranormal powers (P. abhiññā; S. ABHIJÑĀ) and for the cultivation of the four arūpāvacarajhānas, or meditative absorptions of the immaterial realm. The immaterial absorptions themselves represent refinements of the fourth rūpāvacarajhāna, in which the "object" of meditation is gradually attenuated. The four immaterial absorptions instead take as their objects: (1) the sphere of infinite space (P. ākāsānañcāyatana; S. ĀKĀŚĀNANTYĀYATANA), (2) the sphere of infinite consciousness (P. viññāṇañcāyatana; S. VIJÑĀNĀNANTYĀYATANA), (3) the sphere of nothingness (P. ākiñcaññāyatana; S. ĀKIÑCANYĀYATANA), and (4) the sphere of neither perception nor nonperception (P. nevasaññānāsaññāyatana; S. NAIVASAMJÑĀNĀSAMJÑĀYATANA). Mastery of the absorptions of either the subtle-materiality or immaterial realms results in rebirth in the corresponding heaven of each respective absorption.

**jia**. (J. ke; K. ka 家). In Chinese, lit. "house" referring especially to the "five houses" (wu jia), viz., the five principal lineages of the mature CHAN school of the Song dynasty. See WU JIA QI ZONG.

**Jianchusi**. (建初寺). In Chinese, lit. "First-Built Monastery"; a monastery constructed during the Wu dynasty (222–264) of the Chinese Three Kingdoms Period (c. 220–280 CE); the monastery's name Jianchu ostensibly derives from the fact that it was the first monastery to be built in southern China. The monastery was constructed by the Wu emperor to enshrine the relic (ŚARĪRA) of the Buddha that the Sogdian monk KANG SENGHUI brought to the kingdom of Wu during the first half of the third century. The relic was enshrined in one of the legendary AŚOKA STŪPAs that the emperor installed in Jianchusi. The monastery was abandoned and rebuilt on several occasions and is now known as BAO'ENSI.

**Jianfusi**. (建福寺). In Chinese, "Establishing Blessings Monastery"; located in Luoyang, the capital of the Eastern Jin dynasty (217–420 CE) and reputed to be the first Buddhist convent in China. Originally a residence of the Jin dynasty's minister of public works, he is said to have donated his residence out of respect toward Kang Minggan and Huizhan, two of the earliest Buddhist nuns appearing in Chinese records. According to the BIQIUNI ZHUAN ("Lives of the Nuns"), Kang Minggan was also responsible for naming the convent. "Blessings" in the convent's name refers first to the fact that she considered the establishment of the convent to be a blessing for all Buddhist practitioners in China, both monastic and lay; secondly, the convent itself was a physical symbol of the act of bestowing blessings. Several nuns whose biographies are contained in the "Lives of the Nuns" resided there, including Fasheng (368–439 CE) of the Liu-Song dynasty (420–479 CE) who became a nun at age seventy. Another Liu-Song resident, Dao Qiong, was said to have displayed such exemplary skill in practice that an empress personally solicited her advice in religious matters. Dao Qiong later commissioned an image of a reclining buddha to be enshrined in the convent. Zhisheng (427–492 CE) of the Southern Qi dynasty (479–502 CE) also is said to have inspired royalty, the Qi heir-apparent Wenhui (458–493 CE), who often summoned her to the imperial palace to seek her guidance on religious matters.

**jianhuo**. (J. kenwaku; K. kyŏnhok 見惑). In Chinese, "misapprehensions associated with views"; false impressions acquired and developed as a result of wrong views (MITHYĀDṚṢṬI). These are the kinds of attachments, confused ways of thinking, and unwholesome mental states that are induced and facilitated by fallacious views and conceptions, and a failure to grasp properly the FOUR NOBLE TRUTHS (catvāry āryasatyāni). These misapprehensions are therefore also called misapprehensions that "arise from discriminative cognition" (fengbie qi). And because it is said that at the moment when one attains the path of vision (DARŚANAMĀRGA), one is no longer under the sway of wrong views (mithyādṛṣṭi)—e.g., personality view (SATKĀYADṚṢṬI), the extreme views of eternalism or annihilationism, belief in the spiritual efficacy of rituals and superstitions (ŚĪLAVRATAPARĀMARŚA)—these misapprehensions are also called "the misapprehensions [eradicated at the stage of the path] of vision" (darśanaheya, one of the Sanskrit terms that jianhuo translates). Compared with "the misapprehensions [eradicated at the stage of the path] of cultivation" (see SIHUO), the jianhuo are crude and can be cut off at the relatively early stage of stream-entry (SROTAĀPANNA).

**jiansi**. (J. kansu 監司). In Chinese, "comptroller"; one of the six stewards (C. ZHISHI) at a CHAN monastery. Along with the prior (C. DUSI) and the assistant comptroller (C. FUSI), the comptroller is largely in charge of the monastery's finances. He prepares the annual budget, monastic purchases, and ensures the availability of funds for the various feasts held at the monastery.

**jianwu**. (J. zengo; K. chŏmo 漸悟). In Chinese, "gradual awakening" or "gradual enlightenment." In contrast to "sudden awakening" (DUNWU), gradual awakening refers to the view that enlightenment is the result of a process of the purification of the mind over the course of a number of stages, which may occur over many lifetimes. Sudden enlightenment, in contrast, refers to the view that the mind is naturally pure (viz., "buddha-nature," or FOXING) and that enlightenment entails an instantaneous re-cognition of this purity. Although debates over gradual vs. sudden enlightenment are most commonly associated in East Asia with the CHAN ZONG, there are precedents in Indian Buddhism. In addition, the so-called BSAM YAS DEBATE or Council of LHA SA that took place in Tibet at the end of the eighth century is said to have pitted the Indian monk KAMALAŚĪLA against the Northern school (BEI ZONG) Chan monk HESHANG MOHEYAN in a debate over gradual enlightenment vs. sudden enlightenment. See also WU; DUNWU JIANXIU.

**jianxing**. (J. kenshō; K. kyŏnsŏng 見性). In Chinese, "see one's nature"; an expression used in the CHAN school to refer to the recognition of one's innate buddha-nature (FOXING), often through sudden awakening (DUNWU). This recognition of the fact that one is inherently a buddha constitutes enlightenment (BODHI) in some Chan systems. In two-tiered models of the MĀRGA followed in some Chan schools (see DUNWU JIANXIU), this initial insight into one's true nature is called the "understanding–awakening" (JIEWU) and is functionally equivalent to the path of vision (DARŚANAMĀRGA) in ABHIDHARMA path systems; it is not, however, sufficient in itself to generate the complete, perfect enlightenment of buddhahood (ANUTTARASAMYAKSAMBODHI). See also KANHUA CHAN.

**jianxing chengfo**. (J. kenshō jōbutsu; K. kyŏnsŏng sŏngbul 見性成佛). In Chinese, lit. "see one's nature and become a buddha"; a line summarizing the CHAN school's unique approach to Buddhist meditative practice and attributed retrospectively to the school's putative founder, BODHIDHARMA. This phrase seems to have first appeared in Baoliang's (444–509) *Niepan jing ji jie* but appears in conjunction with the meaning of Bodhidharma's "coming from the West" (XILAI YI) for the first time in HUANGBO XIYUN's CHUANXIN FAYAO. The phrase jianxing chengfo appears together with another phrase, ZHIZHI RENXIN ("directly point to the human mind"), in the *Chuanxin fayao*; these two phrases would eventually appear together later with two other phrases, BULI WENZI ("without establishing words or letters") and JIAOWAI BIECHUAN ("a special transmission outside the teachings"), in the ZUTING SHIYUAN, compiled in 1108. These four phrases subsequently became a normative teaching within the Chan school and also the foundation on which the Chan traditions constructed their self-identities in China, Korea, and Japan.

**jianxiu**. (J. zenshu/zenshū; K. chŏmsu 漸修). In Chinese, "gradual cultivation." See DUNWU JIANXIU.

**jianyuan**. (J. kannin; K. kamwŏn 監院). In Chinese, lit. "overseer of the campus"; the "prior" in a Buddhist monastery. According to the Chan monastic code CHANYUAN QINGGUI, the prior is in charge of supplies, finances, and interaction with both local government officials and lay donors. He purchases staples and supervises oil and flour production in the monastery. Other duties include the management of various ceremonies and festivals, such as the New Year's and winter solstice festivities, and retreat-ending and retreat-commencing feasts (see JIEZHI). The prior had at least one principal assistant (see DUSI), and, during the Yuan dynasty, typically had in addition both a second assistant, called the comptroller (JIANSI), and a third, called the assistant comptroller (FUSI). Later, in certain contexts, the term for the prior's assistant (dusi) came to refer instead to the prior.

**Jianzhen**. (C) (鑑眞) (688–763). Chinese VINAYA master and reputed founder of the Japanese RITSU school (cf. NANSHAN LÜ ZONG) and the monastery of TŌSHŌDAIJI in Japan. See GANJIN.

**jiaowai biechuan**. (J. kyōge betsuden; K. kyooe pyŏlchŏn 教外別傳). In Chinese, "a special transmission outside the teachings," a line stating the CHAN school's own sense of its unique pedigree within Buddhism, and later attributed to the school's traditional founder, BODHIDHARMA. The phrase first appears in the ZUTANG JI (K. CHODANG CHIP), compiled in 952. Later, in the ZUTING SHIYUAN compiled in 1108, the phrase appeared together with three other phrases: BULI WENZI ("not establishing words and letters"), ZHIZHI RENXIN ("directly pointing to the human mind"), and JIANXING CHENGFO ("seeing one's nature and achieving buddhahood"). These four phrases subsequently became a normative teaching within the school and the foundation on which the East Asian Chan traditions constructed their self-identity.

**jiaoxiang panshi**. (J. kyōsō hanjaku; K. kyosang p'ansŏk 教相判釋). In Chinese, lit., "classification and interpretation of the characteristics of the doctrine"; also known as jiaopan or PANJIAO (tenet classification). Tenet classification was a fundamental exegetical practice in East Asian Buddhism, in which scriptures or Buddhist teachings were ranked in order of their supposed relative profundity. The practice flourished in East Asia, especially during the fifth, sixth, and seventh centuries. As more translations of Buddhist texts became available in East Asia, indigenous exegetes struggled with the question of why this plethora of scriptural material, all of which purported to have been spoken by the Buddha himself, offered such differing presentations of Buddhist thought and practice. Drawing on the notion of UPĀYA, or skill in means, exegetes began to reflect on the context and intent of the different Buddhist scriptures that were now available to them. The origin of scriptures and their teachings were analyzed and evaluated comparatively; after which the texts were organized in a hierarchical or, in some cases, chronological, order. Different exegetical traditions adopted different classification criteria.

The TIANTAI ZONG, for example, based its classification schema on the different (chronological) stages of the Buddha's teaching career, the content of those teachings, and the varying methods he used in preaching to his audience (see WUSHI BAJIAO). The HUAYAN ZONG, following the lead of FAZANG and CHENGGUAN, divided scriptures into five levels based on the profundity of their respective teachings: HĪNAYĀNA (viz., the ĀGAMAS), elementary MAHĀYĀNA (viz., YOGĀCĀRA and MADHYAMAKA), advanced Mahāyāna (SADDHARMAPUṆḌARĪKASŪTRA), sudden teachings (typically CHAN), and perfect teachings (AVATAṂSAKASŪTRA). Most exegetes placed the central scripture of their schools at the apex of their classificatory hierarchy, thereby using the tenet-classification system as a polemical tool to demonstrate the superiority of their own traditions. See also SIDDHĀNTA.

**Jie Daishi**. (J) (慈恵大師). See RYŌGEN.

**jiela**. (J. kairō; K. kyerap 戒臘). In Chinese, "ordination age." According to the VINAYA, a monk's or nun's seniority is determined by the number of years he or she has been ordained as a monk or nun and not by the biological age or apparent spiritual accomplishments of the individual. Ordination seniority determines seating order within the congregation and walking order during alms-round. Seniority within the ranks of novice and fully ordained monks and nuns (BHIKṢU; BHIKṢUṆĪ) is counted separately, so that even a novice of many years standing will again be the youngest after receiving full ordination. Monastic "years" are in turn calculated by counting the number of completed summer "rains retreats" (VARṢĀ)—held once annually during that period that corresponds to the traditional summer monsoon season in South Asia—one has completed. The alternate terms fala ("dharma age") and xiala ("summer-retreat age") are also employed.

**jienei jiao**. (J. kainai no kyō; K. kyenae kyo 界內教). In Chinese, "[mundane] teachings relating to [affairs found within] the three realms of existence." In the Chinese TIANTAI system of doctrinal classification (see JIAOXIANG PANSHI), those Buddhist teachings that have the aim of facilitating worldly happiness and rebirth into more desirable realms of existence are described as jienei jiao. Cf. JIAOWAI JIAO.

**ji er changzhao**. (J. jakunijōshō; K. chŏk i sangjo 寂而常照). In Chinese, "quiescent, yet constantly illumining"; a CHAN Buddhist expression that can be interpreted both ontologically and soteriologically. Ontologically, ji er changzhao describes the nature of the mind as imperturbable in its essence but as always dynamically responsive to external objects in its functioning. Soteriologically, ji er changzhao refers to the meditative technique wherein one trains the mind to be focused and tranquil with regard to all things that arise in the mind, while nevertheless remaining simultaneously vigilant and observant of them. This expression typically appears in a parallel couplet along with "illumining, yet always quiescent" (C. zhao er changji; J. shōnijōjaku; K. cho i sangjŏk).

**jieshe**. (J. kessha; K. kyŏlsa 結社). In Chinese, "retreat society"; a generic designation for various religious reform movements that were especially popular during Song-dynasty China and Koryŏ-dynasty Korea. These fraternal societies had their antecedents in the AMITĀBHA society of LUSHAN HUIYUAN (334–416) during the Eastern Jin dynasty and were widespread by the ninth century. By the Song dynasty, such communities were pervasive throughout China, especially in the south. These societies were typically involved in TIANTAI, HUAYAN, and PURE LAND practice, though some were dedicated to the worship of a specific BODHISATTVA, such as SAMANTABHADRA. These societies were typically founded outside the ecclesiastical establishment and, by encouraging both lay and ordained adepts to train together, they fostered some measure of religious egalitarianism within East Asian Buddhism. The jieshe movement was especially influential in Koryŏ-dynasty Korea, where some fourteen separate kyŏlsa sites are mentioned in the *Koryŏsa* ("History of Koryŏ"), from Kangwŏn province in the north to South Chŏlla province in the south. The best known is the CHŎNGHYE KYŎLSA (Samādhi and Prajñā Society) initiated in 1180 by POJO CHINUL (1158–1210) and formally established in 1188, which was dedicated to SŎN (Chan) cultivation. In 1197, the community had grown so large that it was relocated to Kilsangsa on Mt. Songgwang, the site of the major present-day monastery of SONGGWANGSA. The residents of the society are said to have gathered together to recite sūtras, train in meditation, and engage in group work activity. Chinul's first composition, the *Kwŏn su Chŏnghye kyŏlsa mun* ("Encouragement to Practice: The Compact of the Samādhi and Prajñā Society"), written in 1290, provided the rationale behind the establishment of the community and critiqued pure land adepts who claim that buddhahood cannot be achieved in the present lifetime. Chinul was joined at his community by the Ch'ŏnt'ae (TIANTAI) adept WŎNMYO YOSE (1163–1240), who subsequently founded the Paengnyŏn kyŏlsa (White Lotus Society) in 1211 at Mandŏksan in the far southwest of the peninsula, which was engaged in Ch'ŏnt'ae practice.

**jiewai jiao**. (J. kaige no kyō; K. kyeoe kyo 界外教). In Chinese, "[supramundane] teachings relating to [affairs beyond] the three realms of existence." In the Chinese TIANTAI system of doctrinal classification (see JIAOXIANG PANSHI), those Buddhist teachings that seek to do more than simply facilitate worldly happiness and rebirth into more desirable realms of existence—teachings that conduce to liberation from rebirth altogether—are described as jiewai jiao. Cf. JIAONEI JIAO.

**jiewu**. (J. gego; K. haeo 解悟). In Chinese, "understanding–awakening"; the most elementary of the two types of awakening (C. WU; S. BODHI) discussed in some CHAN schools, equivalent to "seeing the nature" (JIANXING). This type of awakening is achieved through a sudden awakening (DUNWU) that marks the inception of the path (MĀRGA), variously described as being the equivalent of the beginning of either the ten faiths (ŚRADDHĀ) or the ten abidings (VIHĀRA) (see BHŪMI), and is functionally equivalent to the path of vision (DARŚANAMĀRGA) in ABHIDHARMA path systems. Through this initial comprehension one's true nature, the Chan adept comes to know that he is not a deluded sentient being but is in fact a buddha. Simply knowing that one is a buddha through this sudden awakening of understanding, however, is not sufficient in itself to generate the complete, perfect enlightenment of buddhahood (ANUTTARASAMYAKSAṂBODHI) that ensures that one will always be able to act as a buddha. Only after continued gradual cultivation (JIANXIU) following this initial understanding–awakening will one remove the habituations (VĀSANĀ) that have been engrained in the mind for an essentially infinite amount of time, so that one will not only be a buddha, but will be able to act as one as well. That point where knowledge and action fully correspond marks the final "realization–awakening" (ZHENGWU). This two-tiered approach to awakening is the hallmark of the sudden awakening/gradual cultivation (DUNWU JIANXIU) path schema of certain Chan masters, such as GUIFENG ZONGMI (780–841) in the Chinese Heze school of Chan and POJO CHINUL (1158–1210) of the Korean CHOGYE CHONG.

**jiezhi**. (J. kessei; K. kyŏlche 結制). In Chinese, lit. "binding rule"; the initiation of an intensive period of meditative retreat during the summer season (anju; see ANGO), sometimes applied to the winter retreat season as well. The term is most commonly used within the CHAN (ZEN and SŎN) tradition with reference to its meditative retreats. The two terms jiezhi and anju are often used interchangeably or even in compound to generally refer to this three-month-long summer retreat. The term contrasts with the homophonous JIEZHI, "relaxed rule," the conclusion of a retreat.

**jiezhi**. (J. kaisei; K. haeje 解制). In Chinese, lit. "relaxed rule"; the end of an intensive period of meditation during the summer season (anju; see ANGO), sometimes applied to the end of the winter retreat season as well. The term is most commonly used within the CHAN (ZEN and SŎN) tradition with reference to its meditative retreats. The term contrasts with the homophonous JIEZHI, "binding rule," the initiation of a retreat.

**jifeng**. (J. kihō; K. kibong 機鋒). In Chinese, the "sharpness of one's responsiveness." In CHAN Buddhism, especially after the middle of the Tang dynasty (c. eighth to ninth centuries), a practitioner's level of spiritual comprehension or profundity of his or her enlightenment was often determined by jifeng. The tester or challenger would raise an illogical, perplexing puzzle, an anecdotal account of Chan patriarch's conversations (see GONG'AN), or a mundane occurrence; the monk being tested was expected to offer a spontaneous, impromptu reply to the challenge. In Chan monasteries, abbots or other senior monks randomly cited events described in a gong'an and challenged the tested students or colleagues on their abilities to respond to or explain the apparently enigmatic phrases contained therein. On other occasions, they would have monks debate in groups about the meanings of these accounts; these occasions were called "dharma combat" or "dharma confrontations" (fazhan) and usually took place as a series of mutually and alternately directed questions and answers.

**Jigong**. (J. Sai kō; K. Chegong 濟公) (1150–1209). In Chinese, "Sire Ji"; the name by which Huyin Daoji, a Chinese monk and thaumaturge who is associated with the CHAN school, is commonly known. See HUYIN DAOJI.

**'Jig rten gsum mgon**. [alt. 'Jig gsum mgon po] (Jikten Sumgön) (1143–1217). A disciple of PHAG MO GRU PA RDO RJE RGYAL PO, himself a disciple of SGAM PO PA from whom the four major and eight minor Bka' brgyud subsects (BKA' BRGYUD CHE BZHI CHUNG BRGYAD) originate. 'JIG RTEN GSUM MGON is the founder of the 'BRI GUNG BKA' BRGYUD sect, named after the hermitage he founded in 1179. His collected works are in fifty sections (chos tshan).

**'Jig rten mgon po**. [alt. 'Jig gsum mgon po] (Jikten Gönpo). A Tibetan rendering of [Tri]lokanātha, "Lord of the Three Worlds"; an epithet of AVALOKITEŚVARA.

**'Jigs med gling pa**. (Jikme Lingpa) (1729–1798). A Tibetan exegete and visionary, renowned as one of the premier treasure revealers (GTER STON) in the RNYING MA sect of Tibetan Buddhism. 'Jigs med gling pa was born in the central Tibetan region of 'Phyong rgyas (Chongye), and from an early age recalled many of his previous incarnations, including those of the Tibetan king KHRI SRONG LDE BTSAN, the scholars SGAM PO PA and KLONG CHEN PA and, in his immediately preceding birth, Chos rje gling pa. After a period of monastic education, in his late twenties, he undertook an intense series of meditation retreats, first at Dpal ri monastery and then at the CHIMS PHU cave complex near BSAM YAS. In one of the numerous visions he experienced during this period, he received the KLONG CHEN SNYING THIG, or "Heart Sphere of the Great Expanse," from a ḌĀKINĪ at the BODHNĀTH STŪPA in Kathmandu. The revelation of this text is considered a "mind treasure" (dgongs gter), composed by Padmasambhava and revealed to the mind of a later disciple. 'Jigs med gling pa kept this revelation secret for seven years before transcribing it. The klong chen snying thig corpus systematized by 'Jigs med gling pa, including numerous explanatory texts, tantric initiations, and ritual cycles, became a seminal component of the RDZOGS CHEN teachings in the Rnying ma sect. While based in central Tibet, 'Jigs med gling pa was also influential in Tibet's eastern regions, serving as spiritual teacher to the royal family of SDE DGE and supervising the printing of the collected Rnying ma tantras in twenty-eight volumes. His patrons and disciples included some of the most powerful and prestigious individuals from Khams in eastern

Tibet, and his active participation in reviving Rnying ma traditions during a time of persecution earned him a place at the forefront of the burgeoning eclectic or nonsectarian (RIS MED) movement. Numerous subsequent visionaries involved in promulgating the movement identified themselves as 'Jigs med gling pa's reincarnation, including 'JAM DBYANG MKHYEN BRTSE DBANG PO, MDO MKHYEN BRTSE YE SHES RDO RJE, DPAL SPRUL RIN PO CHE, and DIL MGO MKHYEN BRTSE. See also GTER MA.

**Ji gujin fodao lunheng**. (J. Shū kokonbutsudō ronkō; K. Chip kogŭm pulto nonhyŏng 集古今佛道論衡). In Chinese, "A Collection of Past and Present Treatises of the Buddhist and Daoists"; compiled in 661 by the Chinese VINAYA master DAOXUAN. The *Ji gujin fodao lunheng* is a collection of works pertaining to the history of the Buddho–Daoist conflict in China from the Han to the Tang dynasties. Daoxuan records, for instance, that the famous pilgrim-translator XUANZANG was once ordered to translate the *Daode jing* into Sanskrit. Because Daoxuan makes frequent reference to works that are now lost, the *Ji gujin fodao lunheng* serves as an important source for studying the history of the interactions between Buddhism and Daoism in China. Doaxuan's efforts were continued in Zhisheng's (d.u.) *Xu ji gujin fodao lunheng*.

**jihvāvijñāna**. (P. jivhāviññāṇa; T. lce'i rnam par shes pa; C. sheshi; J. zesshiki; K. sŏlsik 舌識). In Sanskrit, "gustatory consciousness"; one of the five consciousnesses of physical objects (along with those of the eye, ear, nose, and body) and one of the six sensory consciousnesses (adding the mental consciousness, or MANOVIJÑĀNA). The gustatory consciousness perceives flavors (RASA). Like the other consciousness of physical objects, gustatory consciousness is produced through the contact (SPARŚA) between a gustatory sensory object (ĀLAMBANA) and the gustatory sense base or tongue sense organ (JIHVENDRIYA) and in dependence on three conditions (PRATYAYA): the object condition (ĀLAMBANAPRATYAYA), in this case, a flavor; a dominant condition (ADHIPATIPRATYAYA), here, the gustatory sense base (jihvendriya); and the immediately preceding condition (SAMANANTARAPRATYAYA), a prior moment of consciousness. The gustatory consciousness is counted as one of the six sensory consciousnesses (VIJÑĀNA), and eighteen elements (DHĀTU).

**jihvāyatana**. (P. jivhāyatana; T. lce'i skye mched; C. shechu; J. zessho; K. sŏlch'ŏ 舌處). In Sanskrit, "gustatory base of cognition"; the gustatory sense organ (JIHVENDRIYA) as it occurs in the list of the twelve sense fields (ĀYATANA), which are called "bases of cognition" because each pair of sense base and sense object produces its respective sensory consciousness. In this case, the contact (SPARŚA) between a gustatory sensory object (ĀLAMBANA) and the gustatory sense base (INDRIYA) produces a gustatory consciousness (JIHVĀVIJÑĀNA).

**jihvendriya**. (P. jivhindriya; T. lce'i dbang po; C. shegen; J. zekkon; K. sŏlgŭn 舌根). In Sanskrit, "gustatory sense base" or "tongue sense organ"; the physical organ located in the tongue that makes it possible to perceive flavors (RASA). This sense base is not the tongue itself, but a form of subtle materiality located in the tongue and invisible to the naked eye. It is said to be shaped like many tiny half moons on the surface of the tongue. If this sense organ is absent or damaged, taste is not possible. The gustatory sense base serves as the dominant condition (ADHIPATIPRATYAYA) for the production of gustatory consciousness (JIHVĀVIJÑĀNA). The gustatory sense base is counted among the six sense bases or sense organs (INDRIYA), the twelve sources (ĀYATANA), and eighteen elements (DHĀTU).

**Jikaku Daishi**. (J) (慈覺大師). See ENNIN.

**jile**. (J. Gokuraku; K. Kŭngnak 極樂). In Chinese, "extreme happiness" or "ultimate bliss." The term is most often used as a Chinese translation of SUKHĀVATĪ and frequently, but not necessarily, appears in this context in conjunction with the term JINGTU ("PURE LAND"). In the wider context of East Asian Buddhism, the term is also sometimes used to refer generally to a better afterlife or to heaven, and not specifically to the buddha-land of sukhāvatī.

**jina**. (T. rgyal ba; C. zuisheng; J. saishō; K. ch'oesŭng 最勝). In Sanskrit and Pāli, "conqueror," or "victor," one of the epithets of a buddha. In this sense, a buddha is said to be one who has either conquered MĀRA or vanquished the unwholesome (AKUŚALA) dharmas. The term is also used also to refer to founders, or even the current leaders, of other religious sects, including the Buddha's contemporaries ĀRĀḌA KĀLĀMA and UDRAKA RĀMAPUTRA. Jina is also used as the title for the twenty-four teachers in the JAINA lineage.

**Jinakālamālī**. [alt. Jinakālamālīpakaraṇam]. In Pāli, "Garland of the Epochs of the Conqueror"; a Pāli historical chronicle written by Ratanapañña Thera at Chiangmai during the first half of the sixteenth-century CE. The text recounts the history of the THERAVĀDA from its inception in India to its propagation in the Lānnā (La Na) kingdom of northern Thailand. The narrative begins with a synopsis of the former lives of the Buddha, and continues through his enlightenment and parinibbāna (S. PARINIRVĀṆA) and the distribution of his relics. An account of the three Buddhist councils in India follows, as a prelude to a history of the religion in Sri Lanka. Attention is then given to the religious and political history of the kingdom of Haripuñjaya (Lamphun) in northern Thailand from the reign of Cāmadevī (see CĀMADEVĪVAṂSA) in the seventh century to its annexation by the Lānnā king Mengrai in the thirteenth century. The text continues with a history of the Lānnā kingdom, including an account of the missionary activity of Medaṅkara Thera who, under the patronage of the Lānnā king Tiloka, established reformed Sinhalese Buddhism as the dominant religion throughout the realm. The text concludes with an account of the activities of Tiloka's grandson, Phra Muang Keo. The

Jinakālamālī has been edited for the Pāli Text Society and translated by N. A. Jayawickrama as *The Sheaf of Garlands of the Epochs of the Conqueror.*

**jinaputra**. (T. rgyal sras; C. zuishengzi; J. saishōshi; K. ch'oesŭngja 最勝子). In Sanskrit, "progeny of the conqueror"; one of the epithets of BODHISATTVAS, who are like the offspring of the JINA, the Buddha.

**Jingang pi**. (J. Kongōbei; K. Kŭmgang pi 金剛錍). In Chinese, "Adamantine Scalpel"; a treatise composed by the TIANTAI exegete JINGXI ZHANRAN. The adamantine (S. VAJRA) scalpel was an ancient Indian tool used in cataract surgery; the title of the text thus alludes to its function as a tool for removing the ignorance that obscures the vision of sentient beings. The *Jingang pi* is a narrative conveyed in the form of a dream, which is structured around a dialogue with an unidentified stranger. The *Jingang pi* is largely concerned with the issue of buddha-nature (FOXING), and particularly with the controversy over whether insentient beings possess the buddha-nature. Zhanran seems to be the first Tiantai exegete to advance the argument that the buddha-nature was inherent in even insentient things, such as grass, trees, tiles, and rocks, thus corroborating a statement that appears in the MAHĀPARINIRVĀṆASŪTRA. This argument was later adopted by Tiantai scholars of the Song dynasty and by TENDAI and ZEN exegetes in Japan.

**Jingde chuandeng lu**. (J. Keitoku dentōroku; K. Kyŏngdŏk chŏndŭng nok 景德傳燈録). In Chinese, "Record of the Transmission of the Lamplight [Compiled during the] Jingde [Era]." A comprehensive, thirty-roll genealogical collection of short hagiographical notes and anecdotes of the ancient "patriarchs" and teachers (see ZUSHI) of the CHAN school, compiled by Daoyuan (d.u.) in 1004. Beginning with the seven buddhas of the past (SAPTATATHĀGATA) and up to the dharma heirs (see FASI) of the Tang-dynasty Chan monk FAYAN WENYI, the *Jingde chuandeng lu* provides a record of 1,701 Indian and Chinese successors in different main and collateral lineages of the Chan school. The first twenty-six rolls of the *Jingde chuandeng lu* is a series of hagiographies of Chan masters, focusing on their enlightenment experiences, and arranged genealogically; roll twenty-seven discusses eminent monks who do not belong to the Chan tradition; and the last three rolls contain YULU, viz., discourse records (roll twenty-eight), poetry and verses (roll twenty-nine), and other miscellaneous materials, such as the XINXIN MING (roll thirty). As the earliest and most influential of the many lamplight histories (denglu) compiled during the Song dynasty, the *Jingde chuandeng lu* is an invaluable resource for understanding the origins and development of the Chan school in China.

**Jingdu sanmei jing**. (J. Jōdo sanmaikyō; K. Chŏngdo sammae kyŏng 淨度三昧經). In Chinese, "SAMĀDHI-SŪTRA on Liberation through Purification," sometimes also known as the *Jingtu sanmei jing* ("Samādhi-Sūtra on the PURE LAND") and other variations; allegedly translated by Tanyao during the Northern Wei period (386–557) but suspected of being an indigenous Chinese scripture (see APOCRYPHA), perhaps composed in order to assist in the revival of Buddhism following the persecution (FANAN) that occurred from 446 to 452. This sanmei jing offers a detailed account of the thirty separate levels of the hells and the incumbent punishments meted out there. In order to avoid the torments of the hells and to secure the protection of guardian deities, promote long life, and ensure rebirth in the heavens, the scripture describes the merits that accrue to laypeople who observe the five precepts (PAÑCAŚĪLA) and perform the "eight-restrictions feast" (BAGUAN ZHAI) on specific Chinese seasonal days, thus betraying its Chinese provenance. The scripture was discovered in both the DUNHUANG manuscript cache and in Japan manuscript collections.

**Jingjue**. (J. Jōkaku; K. Chŏnggak 淨覺) (683–c. 760). Chinese author of the LENGQIE SHIZI JI ("Records of the Masters and Disciples of the LAṄKĀVATĀRASŪTRA"); an early lineage record of the CHAN ZONG, presented from the standpoint of the so-called Northern school (BEI ZONG). See LENGQIE SHIZI JI.

**jinglu**. (J. kyōroku; K. kyŏngnok 經錄). In Chinese, "scriptural catalogues"; a genre of Buddhist literature unique to East Asian Buddhism. Because the Chinese state presumed the authority to authorize which texts (including Buddhist scriptures) were allowed to circulate, the Chinese Buddhist institution from early in its history began to compile catalogues of scriptures that were deemed authentic, and thus suitable for inclusion in the Buddhist canon (DAZANGJING), and texts that were deemed suspect and thus potentially to be excluded from the canon (see APOCRYPHA). Scriptural catalogues began to be compiled within a century of the beginnings of the translation of Buddhist texts into Chinese, or sometime around the middle of the third century, and some eighty catalogues were compiled over the next one thousand five hundred years, with the majority dating from the Tang dynasty (618–907) or before. As Buddhist canons came to be compiled in Korea and Japan as well, those countries also began to create their own catalogues. For the Chinese cataloguers, the main standard of scriptural authority was whether there was clear evidence that a scripture had been imported from outside China and then translated into Chinese; any evidence that indigenous material had intruded into texts, whether that evidence involved vocabulary, thought, or practice, could lead to those texts being judged as apocrypha. Important catalogues include DAO'AN'S ZONGLI ZHONGJING MULU, the earliest catalogue, composed c. 374; Sengyou's CHU SANZANG JIJI from 515, which established the principal categories into which all subsequent cataloguers would classify texts; Fei Changfang's LIDAI SANBAO JI from 597, which fabricated many translator attributions to texts that had previously been listed as anonymous, so as to quash potential questions about the reliability of the Buddhist textual transmission; DAOXUAN'S DA TANG NEIDIAN LU from 664; and Zhisheng's

Kaiyuan Shijiao lu from 730, the catalogue par excellence, whose scriptural listings would provide the definitive content and organization of the East Asian Buddhist canon from that point onward.

**Jinglü yixiang**. (J. Kyōritsu isō; K. Kyŏngnyul isang 經律異相). In Chinese, lit., "Peculiarities of the Sūtras and Vinayas"; an encyclopedia of exotics found in both SŪTRA and VINAYA literature compiled in 516 CE by the monk Baochang, at the request of the martial emperor of the Liang dynasty (Liang Wudi). The encyclopedia is composed of fourteen chapters: heaven, earth, BUDDHAS, BODHISATTVAS, ŚRĀVAKAS, kings, crown princes, elders, laymen (UPĀSAKA) and laywomen (UPĀSIKĀ), non-Buddhist sages, other laymen and commoners, ghosts, animals, and hells. The *Jinglü yixiang* serves as an important resource for studying the ways in which Buddhism as a foreign religion was understood and adopted by medieval Chinese Buddhists.

**Jingshan**. (C) (徑山). See WANSHOUSI.

**jingtu**. (J. jōdo; K. chŏngt'o 浄土). In Chinese, "pure land." See PURE LAND; PARIŚUDDHABUDDHAKṢETRA; SUKHĀVATĪ.

**jingtu bian**. (J. jōdohen; K. chŏngt'o pyŏn 浄土變). In Chinese, "transformation tableaux of the PURE LAND"; pictorial representations of scenes of the various pure lands. Found throughout East Asia, and discovered also at DUNHUANG and other Central Asian locations, these paintings are the counterparts of what are known as "transformation paintings" (BIANXIANG). Often used as diagrams (MAṆḌALA) and dramatic visual aids for disseminating pure land ideas, these paintings are termed "transformations" (bian) possibly because they were meant to portray "animated" scenes to supplement storytelling and preaching. The transformation pictures of AMITĀBHA's pure land SUKHĀVATĪ were by far the most popular theme, although examples of the pure lands and abodes of VAIROCANA, BHAIṢAJYAGURU, AVALOKITEŚVARA, and MAITREYA were also known. See also AMITUO JINGTU BIAN and DIYU BIAN.

**Jingtu lun**. (J. Jōdoron; K. Chŏngt'o non 浄土論). In Chinese, "Treatise on the PURE LAND," composed by the Chinese monk Jiacai (fl. c. 627). In the nine chapters of this treatise, Jiacai attempts to reorganize systematically the arguments of DAOZHUO's ANLE JI. Jiacai's own interests in the MAHĀYĀNASAṂGRAHA and the teachings of VIJÑAPTIMĀTRATĀ and TATHĀGATAGARBHA are also reflected in his treatise. The treatise is largely concerned with the issues of the multiple buddha bodies (BUDDHAKĀYA), types of rebirth in the pure land, and the means of taking rebirth there. In the first chapter, Jiacai contends that there are three types of lands that correspond to the three buddha bodies: DHARMAKĀYA, SAṂBHOGAKĀYA, and NIRMĀṆAKĀYA. The second chapter is concerned with the rebirth of ordinary beings (PṚTHAGJANA). The third chapter discusses the different methods of attaining rebirth in the pure land: the general cause (e.g., arousing the BODHICITTA) vs. the special cause (e.g., NIANFO). The fourth chapter details the practice of mindfully invoking the buddha AMITĀBHA's name ten times (shinian) before death and the practice of invoking his name for seven days. In chapter 5, Jiacai provides scriptural evidence that it is ordinary beings who are reborn in the pure land, not solely advanced bodhisattvas. Chapter 6 contains the biographies of twenty people who attained rebirth in the pure land; this chapter is the oldest extant collection of rebirth testimonials in East Asia (see JINGTU RUIYING ZHUAN). In chapter 7, Jiacai compares rebirth in a pure land with rebirth in TUṢITA heaven. Chapter 8 discusses the benefits of repentance and chapter 9 underscores the importance of practicing the ten repetitions of Amitābha's name (shinian). Jiacai's text should be distinguished from the **Aparimitāyussūtropadeśa* ("Exegesis of the *Wuliangshou jing*"), commonly known to the pure land tradition as the *Jingtu lun* (J. *Jōdoron*) and attributed to VASUBANDHU (see WULIANGSHOU JING YOUPOTISHE YUANSHENG JI).

**Jingtu lun zhu**. (C) (浄土論註). See WULIANGSHOU JING YOUPOTISHE YUANSHENG JIE.

**Jingtu qunyi lun**. (J. Jōdo gungiron; K. Chŏngt'o kunŭi non 浄土群疑論). In Chinese, "Treatise on Myriad Doubts concerning the PURE LAND," composed by the monk Huaigan (fl. c. seventh century CE). In this treatise, written largely in dialogic format, Huaigan attempts to address systematically various questions concerning the notion of rebirth in AMITĀBHA Buddha's pure land. The seven-roll treatise is divided into twelve sections in a total of 116 chapters, which cover a wide range of subjects concerning pure land doctrine. These include, as but a few representative examples, the location of the pure land within the three realms of existence (TRILOKA[DHĀTU]), the destiny (GATI) to which beings reborn there belong, where pure land rebirth belongs on MĀRGA schemata, and Huaigan's attempts to reconcile inconsistencies in different scriptures' accounts of the pure land. The *Jingtu qunyi lun* has therefore functioned almost as an encyclopedia for adherents of pure land teachings. The questions raised anticipate the criticisms of Huaigan's contemporaries, who specialized in the exegesis of the MAHĀYĀNASAṂGRAHA and the new YOGĀCĀRA translations of XUANZANG; Huaigan's answers also reflect his own training in Yogācāra doctrine and his extensive command of Buddhist scriptural and commentarial literature.

**Jingtu ruiying zhuan**. (J. Jōdo zuiōden; K. Chŏngt'o sŏŭng chŏn 浄土瑞應傳). In Chinese, "Legends of Auspicious Resonance in the PURE LAND"; attributed to the monks Wenshen (fl. c. nine CE) and Shaokang (d. 805), although their authorship remains a matter of debate. The *Jingtu ruiying zhuan* is a collection of forty-eight testimonials of rebirth in the pure land of SUKHĀVATĪ, offering proof that the prospect of rebirth there is a viable reason for faith in the salvific grace of AMITĀBHA Buddha. This text is one of the earliest examples of a genre of Buddhist literature called rebirth testimonials (wangsheng zhuan), which is unique to East Asia. The *Jingtu ruiying zhuan* also served as a prototype for later collections, such as the *Jingtu wangsheng zhuan*, attributed to Jiezhu (985–1077).

**jingtu sanbu jing**. (J. jōdo sanbukyō; K. chŏngt'o sambu kyŏng 淨土三部經). In Chinese, "the three scriptures on the pure land," a designation for three main sūtras that focus on AMITĀBHA Buddha and his PURE LAND of SUKHĀVATĪ; these are generally considered to be the central canonical sūtras of the pure land schools, and especially of the Japanese JŌDOSHŪ and JŌDO SHINSHŪ. The three scriptures are (1) SUKHĀVATĪVYŪHASŪTRA, the "[Larger] Sūtra on the Buddha of Immeasurable Life" (*Wuliangshou jing*); (2) "Sūtra on the Contemplation of the Buddha of Immeasurable Life" (GUAN WULIANGSHOU JING); and (3) AMITĀBHASŪTRA, the "[Smaller] Sūtra on the Buddha Amitābha" *(Amituo jing)*. The writings of the pure land school are to a large extent commentaries on or exegeses of these three scriptures.

**Jingtu sanmei jing**. (淨土三昧經). In Chinese, "Samādhi-Sūtra on the Pure Land." See JINGDU SANMEI JING.

**jingtu sansheng**. (J. jōdo no sanshō; K. chŏngt'o samsŏng 淨土三聖). In Chinese, "the pure land trinity," or "the three saints of the pure land"; referring to the buddha AMITĀBHA (Amituo fo, usually depicted as standing in the middle), the BODHISATTVA AVALOKITEŚVARA (Guanshiyin pusa, usually depicted as flanking left), and bodhisattva MAHĀSTHĀMAPRĀPTA (Dashizhi pusa, usually depicted as flanking right). These are the three deities featured most prominently in sūtras on the PURE LAND of SUKHĀVATĪ and its pictorial representations (see JINGTU BIAN).

**Jingtu shiyi [lun]**. (J. Jōdo jūgi[ron]; K. Chŏngt'o sibŭi [non] 淨土十疑[論]). In Chinese, "Ten Doubts regarding the PURE LAND"; a popular text on pure land beliefs and practices composed by TIANTAI ZHIYI. As the title suggests, the treatise is an apologia for the practice and verity of the pure land, even though it is exclusively directed at AMITĀBHA's pure land of SUKHĀVATĪ. The "doubts" that Zhiyi addresses in his treatise include: "Doesn't it show a lack of compassion to seek rebirth in the pure land (and thus leave behind those who are suffering in this world)?" "Isn't seeking rebirth in the pure land contradictory to the teaching of non-production (which nullifies the prospect of further rebirths)?" "Why focus on Amitābha and his pure land (as one's sole choice of devotion)?" "How is it that unenlightened beings who are entangled in the fetters (SAṂYOJANA) are capable of being reborn in the pure land (and thereby transcend the rounds of rebirth)?" "How could it be that the pure land of sukhāvatī (being entirely male) has no women and no one with HĪNAYĀNA inclinations?"

**jingtu wuzu**. (J. jōdo no goso; K. chŏngt'o ojo 淨土五祖). In Chinese, the "five patriarchs of pure land"; according to the most common retrospective lineage, these are TANLUAN (476–?), DAOCHUO (562–645), SHANDAO (613–681), Huaigan (d.u.), and Shaokang (?–805). Of the five, Daochuo, Shandao, and Huaigan might actually have had at least a tenuous master–disciple relation, although this would not be sufficient in itself to constitute an authentic "pure land school" in China. It is among the Japanese pure land schools (e.g., JŌDOSHŪ and JŌDO SHINSHŪ) that these retrospective Chinese lineages carry real authority, since they authenticate the teachings and practices associated with those Japanese traditions.

**Jingtu zhuan**. (J. Jōdoden; K. Chŏngt'o chŏn 淨土傳). In Chinese, "biographies of PURE LAND [practitioners]," also called "biographies of those who have gone to rebirth in the pure land" (*wangsheng Jingtu zhuan*); several such compilations are extant. Most of these anthologies were made by selecting examples from the various biographies of eminent monks (GAOSENG ZHUAN) of persons who were reported, first, to have shown "auspicious signs" (ruixiang) at the time of their deaths and, second, were noted for their exceptional devotion to pure land practice. Visions of AMITĀBHA and his entourage, an inexplicable radiance filling the site, heavenly fragrances, and prescience and/or predictions of one's imminent death and rebirth into the pure land were taken to be such "auspicious signs" and are common themes in the hagiographical accounts recorded in these anthologies. One of the earliest extant examples of the genre is the *Jingtu zhuan* compiled in the eleventh century by Jiezhu (985–1077), but many other anthologies were compiled in later centuries and were widely circulated. The stories they contain became popular testimonials to the efficacy and verity of pure land practice. These pure land anthologies are notable for their inclusive nature, and they collect biographies not only of eminent monks, but also of nuns, laypeople, and even persons of ill repute and low social status.

**jingtu zong**. (jōdoshū; K. chŏngt'o chong 淨土宗). In Chinese "pure land school." See JINGTU WUZU; JISHŪ; JŌDOSHŪ; JŌDO SHINSHŪ; ŌJŌ YŌSHŪ; YŪZŪ NENBUTSUSHŪ.

**Jingxi Zhanran**. (J. Keikei Tannen; K. Hyŏnggye Tamyŏn 荊溪湛然) (711–782). Chinese monk who is the putative ninth patriarch of the TIANTAI ZONG; also known as Great Master Miaole (Sublime Bliss) and Dharma Master Jizhu (Lord of Exegesis). Zhanran was a native of Jingqi in present-day Jiangsu province. At age nineteen, Zhanran became a student of the monk Xuanlang (673–754), who had revitalized the community on Mt. Tiantai. After Xuanlang's death, Zhanran continued his efforts to unify the disparate regional centers of Tiantai learning under the school's banner; for his efforts, Zhanran is remembered as one of the great revitalizers of the Tiantai tradition. A gifted exegete who composed numerous commentaries on the treatises of TIANTAI ZHIYI, Zhanran established Zhiyi's MOHE ZHIGUAN, FAHUA XUANYI, and FAHUA WENJU as the three central texts of the Tiantai exegetical tradition. His commentary on the *Mohe zhiguan*, the MOHE ZHIGUAN FUXING ZHUANHONG JUE, is the first work to correlate ZHIGUAN (calmness and insight) practice as outlined by Zhiyi with the teachings of the SADDHARMAPUṆḌARĪKASŪTRA ("Lotus Sūtra"), the central scripture of the Tiantai tradition. In his JINGANG PI ("Adamantine Scalpel"), Zhanran argued in favor of the controversial proposition that insentient beings also possess the buddha-nature (FOXING). Zhanran's interpretation of Tiantai doctrine and the distinction he drew between his own tradition and the rival schools of the HUAYAN ZONG and CHAN ZONG set the stage for the internal Tiantai debates during the Song dynasty between its on-mountain (shanjia) and off-mountain (shanwai) branches (see SHANJIA SHANWAI). Zhanran lectured at various monasteries throughout the country and was later invited by emperors Xuanzong (r. 712–756), Suzong (r. 756–762), and Daizong (r. 762–779) to lecture at court, before retiring to the monastery Guoqingsi on Mt. Tiantai.

**Jingxuan**. (C) (警玄). See DAYANG JINGXUAN.

**Jingying Huiyuan**. (J. Jōyō Eon; K. Chŏngyŏng Hyewŏn 浄影慧遠) (523–592). Chinese monk and putative DI LUN exegete during the Sui dynasty. Huiyuan was a native of DUNHUANG. At an early age, he entered the monastery of Guxiangusi in Zezhou (present-day Shanxi province) where he was ordained by the monk Sengsi (d.u.). Huiyuan later studied various scriptures under the VINAYA master Lizhan (d.u.) in Ye, the capital of the Eastern Wei dynasty. In his nineteenth year, Huiyuan received the full monastic precepts from Fashang (495–580), ecclesiastical head of the SAṂGHA at the time, and became his disciple. Huiyuan also began his training in the DHARMAGUPTAKA "Four-Part Vinaya" (SIFEN LÜ) under the vinaya master Dayin (d.u.). After he completed his studies, Huiyuan moved back to Zezhou and began his residence at the monastery Qinghuasi. In 577, Emperor Wu (r. 560–578) of Northern Zhou began a systematic persecution of Buddhism, and in response, Huiyuan is said to have engaged the emperor in debate; a transcript of the debate, in which Huiyuan defends Buddhism against criticisms of its foreign origins and its neglect of filial piety, is still extant. As the persecution continued, Huiyuan retreated to Mt. Xi in Jijun (present-day Henan province). Shortly after the rise of the Sui dynasty, Huiyuan was summoned by Emperor Wen (r. 581–604) to serve as overseer of the saṃgha (shamendu) in Luozhou (present-day Henan). He subsequently spent his time undoing the damage of the earlier persecution. Huiyuan was later asked by Emperor Wen to reside at the monastery of Daxingshansi in the capital. The emperor also built Huiyuan a new monastery named Jingyingsi, which is often used as his toponym to distinguish him from LUSHAN HUIYUAN. Jingying Huiyuan was a prolific writer who composed numerous commentaries on such texts as the AVATAṂSAKASŪTRA, MAHĀPARINIRVĀṆASŪTRA, VIMALAKĪRTINIRDEŚA, SUKHĀVATĪVYŪHASŪTRA, ŚRĪMĀLĀDEVĪSIṂHANĀDASŪTRA, SHIDI JING LUN (VASUBANDHU's commentary on the DAŚABHŪMIKASŪTRA), DASHENG QIXIN LUN, and others. Among his works, the DASHENG YI ZHANG ("Compendium of the Purport of Mahāyāna"), a comprehensive encyclopedia of Mahāyāna doctrine, is perhaps the most influential and is extensively cited by traditional exegetes throughout East Asia. Jingying Huiyuan also plays a crucial role in the development of early PURE LAND doctrine in East Asia. His commentary on the GUAN WULIANGSHOU JING, the earliest extant treatise on this major pure land scripture, is critical in raising the profile of the *Guan jing* in East Asian Buddhism. His commentary to this text profoundly influenced Korean commentaries on the pure land scriptures during the Silla dynasty, which in turn were crucial in the evolution of Japanese pure land thought during the Nara and Heian periods. Jingying Huiyuan's concept of the "dependent origination of the TATHĀGATAGARBHA" (rulaizang yuanqi)—in which tathāgatagarbha is viewed as the "essence" (TI) of both NIRVĀṆA and SAṂSĀRA, which are its "functioning" (YONG)—is later adapted and popularized by the third HUAYAN patriarch, FAZANG, and is an important precursor of later Huayan reconceptualizations of dependent origination (PRATĪTYASAMUTPĀDA; see FAJIE YUANQI).

**Jingzhongsi**. (C) (淨衆寺). See WANFOSI.

**Jingzhong zong**. (J. Jōshūshū; K. Chŏngjung chong 淨衆宗). A branch of the early CHAN ZONG that flourished at the monastery Jingzhongsi in Chengdu (present-day Sichuan province). The history of the Jingzhong line is documented in the LIDAI FABAO JI. According to this text, the Jingzhong line is derived from the Chan master Zhishen (609–702), a disciple of the fifth patriarch HONGREN. Zhishen is also said to have received the purple robe of the Chan founder BODHIDHARMA from Empress Dowager WU ZETIAN, which was ostensibly transmitted to Zhishen's disciple Chuji (648–734/650–732/669–736) and then to CHŎNGJUNG MUSANG (C. Jingzhong Wuxiang) and BAOTANG WUZHU. The *Lidai fabao ji*, authored by a disciple of Wuzhu, claims that the Jingzhong lineage is eventually absorbed into the BAOTANG ZONG, though the two seem in fact to have been distinct lineages. The eminent Chan masters MAZU DAOYI and GUIFENG ZONGMI are also known to have once studied under teachers of the Jingzhong line of Chan. The school is most closely associated with the so-called three propositions (sanju), a unique set of Chan precepts that were equated with the traditional roster of the three trainings (TRIŚIKṢĀ): "no recollection" (wuyi), which was equated with morality (ŚĪLA); "no thought" (WUNIAN) with concentration (SAMĀDHI); and "no forgetting" (mowang) with wisdom (PRAJÑĀ). These three propositions are associated most closely with Musang, but other texts attribute them instead to Musang's putative successor, Wuzhu. The portrayal in the literature of the teachings of the Jingzhong school divides along the fault line of these two great teachers, with Musang's Chan adaptation of mainstream Buddhist teachings contrasting markedly with Wuzhu's more radical, even antinomian approach, deriving from HEZE SHENHUI. The

Jingzhong masters are also said to have had some influence in Tibet (see BSAM YAS DEBATE), including on the development of MAHĀYOGA and RDZOGS CHEN.

**Jinling Baozhi**. (C) (金陵寶誌). See BAOZHI.

**jiriki**. (C. zili; K. charyŏk 自力). In Japanese, "self power." The term jiriki came to be used frequently in the pure land schools by the followers of HŌNEN and SHINRAN and their JŌDOSHŪ and JŌDO SHINSHŪ traditions. Jiriki, or "self power," is often contrasted with the term TARIKI, or "other power." While tariki refers to the practitioner's reliance on the power or grace of the buddha AMITĀBHA, jiriki is often used pejoratively to refer to practices requiring personal effort, such as keeping the precepts (ŚĪLA) and cultivating the six perfections (PĀRAMITĀ). Reliance on jiriki was often condemned as a difficult path to enlightenment, especially as compared to practices based on tariki, such as reciting Amitābha's name (J. nenbutsu; see C. NIANFO). Exegetes also attempted to underscore the futility of jiriki practices by suggesting that the world was currently in the mappō (C. MOFA), or dharma-ending age, when personal power alone was no longer sufficient to bring one to enlightenment, requiring instead the intervention of an external force. The jiriki–tariki dichotomy was often used polemically by Jōdoshū and Jōdo Shinshū exegetes to condemn the practices of rival Japanese traditions, such as the TENDAISHŪ and ZENSHŪ, which they claimed were ineffective in the current degenerate age of the dharma.

**Jishu**. [alt. Jishū] (時衆/時宗). In Japanese, "Time Assembly" or "Time school"; referring to followers of the Japanese itinerant holy man (HIJIRI) IPPEN (1239–1289). The name comes from this community's practice of rotating leadership in invoking the name of the buddha AMITĀBHA (J. nenbutsu; see NIANFO) at different time intervals. Ippen developed a practice known as ippen nenbutsu (single-time invocation of the name [see NIANFO] of the Amitābha), which largely consists of the uttering the phrase NAMU AMIDABUTSU as if that one time were the moment of one's death. Ippen widely propagated this teaching wherever he went, and to those who complied, he offered an amulet (fusan), which he claimed assured them rebirth in Amitābha's pure land of SUKHĀVATĪ. In 1279, Ippen also began performing nenbutsu while dancing with drums and bells, a practice known as odori nenbutsu (dancing recitation) and first developed by the monk KŪYA. During the course of his life as an itinerant preacher, Ippen acquired a large following that eventually became known as the Jishū. The number of Jishū followers grew greatly during the Kamakura period. The Jishū community was guided by a set of eighteen vows devised by Ippen and was distinguished from monks of other traditions by their unique robes. An intense rivalry seems to have existed between the leaders of the Jishū and the JŌDO SHINSHŪ tradition of Japanese pure land Buddhism. A large portion of the Jishū community was later absorbed into the Jōdo Shinshū community, largely through the efforts of RENNYO. The current head temple of Jishū is Shōjōkōji in Fujisawa, Kanagawa Prefecture.

**Jitāri**. [alt. Jetāri] (T. Dgra las rnam rgyal) (fl. c. 940–980). Sanskrit proper name of the author of the *Hetutattopadeśa* and a number of short works on PRAMĀṆA in the tradition that follows DHARMAKĪRTI; later Tibetan doxographers (see SIDDHĀNTA) characterize him as interpreting Dharmakīrti's works from a MADHYAMAKA perspective, leading them to include him in a YOGĀCĀRA–SVĀTANTRIKA–MADHYAMAKA school following the false aspect (alīkākara) position. A Jitāri also appears in the list of the eighty-four MAHĀSIDDHAs as a tantric adept; he is also listed as a teacher of ATIŚA DĪPAṂKARAŚRĪJÑĀNA.

**Jiuhuashan**. (九華山). In Chinese, "Nine Florate Mountain"; located in southeastern China, in Qingyang county, Anhui province. Jiuhuashan is one of the four Buddhist sacred mountains of China, along with PUTUOSHAN in Zhejiang, EMEISHAN in Sichuan, and WUTAISHAN in Shanxi. Each mountain is said to be the residence of a specific BODHISATTVA, with Jiuhuashan considered the holy mountain of KṢITIGARBHA (DIZANG pusa), a revered bodhisattva in China, who is regarded as the redeemer of the denizens of the hells (NĀRAKA). Jiuhuashan, the major mountain center in southeastern China, covers more than sixty square miles (one hundred square kilometers) and is famous for its spectacular peaks, perilous cliffs, huge boulders, ancient caves, and myriads of springs, streams, waterfalls, ancient pines, and bamboo forests. Jiuhuashan was originally known as Jiuzifeng (lit. Nine Children Mountain) because its nine major peaks had the shape of children; it was renamed Jiuhuashan after a description of the mountain in a poem by Li Bo (701–762 CE), the renowned Tang-dynasty poet. Jiuhuashan is said to have been the residence of a Korean monk named CHIJANG (C. Dizang; S. Kṣitigarbha), also known as KIM KYOGAK (628–726). Chijang was a scion of the royal family of the Silla dynasty, who ended up spending some seventy-five years meditating at Jiuhuashan. He is said to have survived by eating only rice that had been cooked together with white soil (perhaps lime or gypsum) dug from between the rocks. The laity were so moved by his asceticism that they built the monastery of Huachengsi for him. When Chijang passed away, his body did not decay and people came to believe that he was the manifestation of his namesake, Kṣitigarbha. A shrine hall named Dizang dian was built on the site where he died, which could only be reached by pulling oneself by rope up eighty-one precarious stone steps. Because of this connection to Chijang, by at least the Ming dynasty, Jiuhuashan was considered the sacred site of Kṣitigarbha. Jiuhuashan at one time housed more than three hundred monasteries and four thousand monks. The grand scale of its monastic architecture and the large numbers of pilgrims it attracted throughout the year led to its recognition as a Buddhist sacred mountain.

**Jiun Onkō**. (慈雲飲光) (1718–1804). In Japanese, "Cloud of Compassion, Drinker of Light"; a monk of the Shingon Risshū school, which combined the esoteric teachings of the SHINGONSHŪ with disciplinary observance of the VINAYA; also known as Jiun Sonja. Up to the age of twelve, he received a traditional Confucian education, but after his father's death the following year, he was entrusted to Hōrakuji, a Shingon Risshū monastery in Kawachi (present-day Ōsaka prefecture), where he studied esoteric teachings and the SIDDHAM Sanskrit syllabary. During his early studies of Buddhism, Jiun came to realize the centrality of the PRĀTIMOKṢA precepts to a monastic vocation, and in 1738 decided to take the full set of monk's precepts (J. gusokukai) at the monastery of Yachūji. In the following year, Jiun was appointed abbot of his old monastery of Hōrakuji, but he resigned two years later to dedicate himself to ZEN practice in the SŌTŌSHŪ. In his late twenties, he founded a movement called the "vinaya of the true dharma" (shōbōritsu), which encouraged Buddhist clerics to commit themselves to the prātimokṣa precepts, regardless of their sectarian affiliations. In 1758, Jiun wrote a massive textbook on Sanskrit, the thousand-roll *Bongaku shinryō* ("The Ford and Bridge to Sanskrit Studies"), the first such study aid published in Japan. In 1775, he compiled his *Juzen hōgo* ("Dharma Discourses on the Ten Wholesome Ways of Action"), a collection of lectures on the KUŚALA-KARMAPATHA that he had delivered the two previous years at Amidadera in Kyōto. Late in his life, he moved to KATSURAGISAN, where he pioneered an eclectic religious movement that came to be called Unden SHINTŌ ("Shintō transmitted by Jiun") or Katsuragi Shintō, which integrated Shingon, Zen, and Confucianism with Japanese indigenous religion.

**jiupin**. (J. kuhon; K. kup'um 九品). In Chinese, "nine grades." According to the PURE LAND school, beings who succeed in being reborn into a pure land are divided into "nine grades," e.g., "the uppermost in the top grade (shangshang)," "the intermediate in the top grade (shangzhong)," "the lowest in the top grade (shangxia)," "the uppermost in the intermediate grade (zhongshang),"…"the lowest in the bottom grade (xiaxia)." One's rebirth "grade" is determined by one's previous practice, the amount of meritorious actions one has performed, and the greatness of one's aspiration for enlightenment, among other factors. For example, according to the GUAN WULIANGSHOU JING ("Sūtra on the Visualization of the Buddha of Immeasurable Life"), the "uppermost in the top grade" is won by possessing the utmost sincerity (zhicheng xin), profound aspiration (shenxin), and a desire to direct one's highest aspiration to the purpose of being reborn in the pure land (huixiang fayuan xin) during a lifetime of practice. By contrast, the "lowest in the bottom grade" is secured by a penitent reprobate who is able to chant the name of AMITĀBHA up to ten times (shinian) right before his or her death. One's reborn "grade" will affect things such as the time one will take to reach buddhahood in the pure land (the higher the grade, the quicker one will the attainment). See also AMITUO JIUPIN YIN.

**jiushi**. (J. kuse; K. kuse 九世). In Chinese, the "nine time periods," or "nine temporal modes." In each of the so-called three time periods (viz., past, present, future) there are three time periods posited, viz., a past, present, and future of the past, present, and future, giving a total of nine time periods.

**jiuyi**. (J. kugi; K. kuŭi 九儀). In Chinese, "nine modes [of showing respect]." According to the Chinese pilgrim XUANZANG's observations as recounted in his DA TANG XIYU JI, Indian Buddhists expressed their veneration through these nine modes: verbal greetings/asking about each other's welfare, bowing, holding high their clasped hands, bowing with clasped hands, bending one knee so it touches the ground, kneeling, prostration with the forehead, two hands and two knees touching the ground, and whole-body prostration with the front of the body touching the ground.

**Jīvaka**. (T. 'Tsho byed; C. Qipo/Shubojia; J. Giba/Jubaka/Jubakuka; K. Kiba/Subakka 耆婆/戍博迦). A famous physician and lay disciple of the Buddha, declared foremost among laymen beloved by the people. The son of a courtesan, he was abandoned at birth on a dust heap. He was rescued by a prince who, when he was told the infant was still alive, gave him the name Jīvaka, meaning "Living" in Sanskrit and Pāli. As the adopted son of the prince, he was also known in Pāli as Jīvaka Komārabhacca, meaning Jīvaka who was "raised by the prince." (Alternatively, Komārabhacca may mean "master of pediatrics," as in the science of kaumārabhṛtya, the treatment of infants.) As a young man, Jīvaka studied medicine and soon became a renowned and wealthy doctor. It is said that his first patient gave him sixteen thousand coins, a pair of servants, and a coach with horses. King BIMBISĀRA of MAGADHA hired him as his royal physician and also assigned him to look after the health of the Buddha and his monks. Jīvaka continued to serve Bimbisāra's son AJĀTAŚATRU, who murdered his father to usurp the throne, and it was Jīvaka who escorted the patricide before the Buddha, so he could repent from his crime. Jīvaka attended the Buddha on many occasions. He bandaged the Buddha's foot when it was injured by the rock hurled by DEVADATTA on GṚDHRAKŪṬAPARVATA. Once, Jīvaka noted how the monks were pale and unhealthy in appearance and recommended that the Buddha require them to exercise regularly. He treated rich and poor alike and those who could not pay he treated without charge. So popular was Jīvaka that he could not treat all who came to him, yet he never neglected to serve the SAṂGHA. For this reason, the poor and indigent began to enter the order simply to receive medical attention. When Jīvaka became aware of this trend, he recommended to the Buddha that persons suffering from certain diseases not be allowed to ordain. Jīvaka became a stream-enterer (SROTAĀPANNA) and is included in a list of good men assured of realization of the deathless. ¶ Jīvaka is also traditionally listed as ninth of the sixteen ARHAT elders (ṢOḌAŚASTHAVIRA), who were charged by the Buddha with protecting his dispensation until the advent of the next buddha,

MAITREYA. Jīvaka is said to reside in Gandhamādana with nine hundred disciples. The Chinese tradition says that this Jīvaka was originally a prince in a central Indian kingdom, whose younger brother wanted to fight him for the throne. But Jīvaka told his brother that he thought only of the Buddha and had never wanted to be king. He then exposed his chest, and his younger brother saw a buddha image engraved over his heart. Realizing his brother's sincerity, he then dismissed his troops. Jīvaka thus earned the nickname "Heart-Exposing ARHAT" (Kaixin Luohan). In CHANYUE GUANXIU's standard Chinese depiction, Jīvaka sits slightly leaning on a rock. He has an aquiline nose and deep-set eyes, a high forehead, and bright eyes staring forward. He holds a fan in his left hand, and his right fingers are bent.

**Jīvakasutta**. In Pāli, "Discourse to Jīvaka," fifty-fifth sutta in the MAJJHIMANIKĀYA (there is no equivalent recension in the Chinese translations of the ĀGAMAS). The Buddha addressed this discourse to his physician, JĪVAKA Komārabhacca, while he dwelled in the physician's mango grove in Rājagaha (S. RĀJAGṚHA). Jīvaka inquires whether it is true that the Buddha eats meat prepared for him from animals killed for his sake, or whether this is a misrepresentation of his practice. The Buddha explains that there are three instances when a monk should not eat meat that has been offered to him: when it is heard, seen, or suspected that a living creature has been intentionally slaughtered to feed him. Apart from these three exceptions, a monk is permitted to accept and eat meat. He further explains that a monk should not show preference for one kind of food over another, nor be greedy in eating. Rather he should eat what he receives dispassionately, noting that food is eaten only to sustain the health of the body in order vigorously to pursue the path to liberation. Pleased by the discourse, Jīvaka Komārabhacca dedicates himself as a lay disciple of the buddha.

**jīvita**. (T. srog; C. shouming/minggen; J. jumyō/myōkon; K. sumyŏng/myŏnggŭn 壽命/命根). In Sanskrit and Pāli, "vitality" or "life force." Jīvita appears in the Buddhist scriptures as a predominant factor (INDRIYA), the jīvitendriya, governing birth and prolonging the physical continuum up through the "intermediate state" (ANTARĀBHAVA), which leads to the next rebirth. Early ABHIDHARMA texts equate jīvita with "life" (ĀYUS) itself, viz., the life force that sustains and animates all sentient beings. In the SARVĀSTIVĀDA abhidharma, jīvita is listed as the seventh of fourteen conditioned forces dissociated from thought (CITTAVIPRAYUKTASAṂSKĀRA), which is characterized by bodily warmth and serves as the basis for perceptual consciousness. In the Pāli abhidharma, life-force appears twice as the support of both the physical body (as derived materiality, or upādārūpa) and the mind (as a morally indeterminate mental concomitant). When jīvita, which is the support of warmth and consciousness, is no longer associated with the physical body, death occurs.

**Jizang**. (J. Kichizō; K. Kilchang 吉藏) (549–623). In Chinese, "Storehouse of Auspiciousness"; Chinese Buddhist monk of originally Parthian descent and exegete within the SAN LUN ZONG, the Chinese counterpart of the MADHYAMAKA school of Indian thought. At a young age, he is said to have met the Indian translator PARAMĀRTHA, who gave him his dharma name. Jizang is also known to have frequented the lectures of the monk Falang (507–581) with his father, who was also ordained monk. Jizang eventually was ordained by Falang, under whom he studied the so-called Three Treatises (SAN LUN), the foundational texts of the Chinese counterpart of the Madhyamaka school: namely, the *Zhong lun* (MŪLAMADHYAMAKĀRIKĀ), BAI LUN (*ŚATAŚĀSTRA), and SHI'ERMEN LUN (**Dvādaśamukhaśāstra*). At the age of twenty-one, Jizang received the full monastic precepts. After Falang's death in 581, Jizang moved to the monastery of Jiaxiangsi in Huiji (present-day Zhejiang province). There, he devoted himself to lecturing and writing and is said to have attracted more than a thousand students. In 598, Jizang wrote a letter to TIANTAI ZHIYI, inviting him to lecture on the SADDHARMAPUṆḌARĪKASŪTRA. In 606, Emperor Yang (r. 604–617) constructed four major centers of Buddhism around the country and assigned Jizang to one in Yangzhou (present-day Jiangsu province). During this period, Jizang composed his influential overview of the doctrines of the Three Treatises school, entitled the SAN LUN XUANYI. Jizang's efforts to promote the study of the three treatises earned him the name "reviver of the San lun tradition." Jizang was a prolific writer who composed numerous commentaries on the three treatises, the *Saddharmapuṇḍarīkasūtra*, MAHĀPARINIRVĀṆASŪTRA, VIMALAKĪRTINIRDEŚA, SUKHĀVATĪVYŪHASŪTRA, etc., as well as an overview of Mahāyāna doctrine, entitled the *Dasheng xuan lun*.

**jñāna**. (P. ñāṇa; T. ye shes; C. zhi; J. chi; K. chi 智). In Sanskrit, "gnosis," "knowledge," "awareness," or "understanding," numerous specific types of which are described in Buddhist literature. Jñāna in the process of cognition implies specific understanding of the nature of an object and is necessarily preceded by SAMJÑĀ ("perception"). Jñāna is also related to PRAJÑĀ ("wisdom"); where prajñā implies perfected spiritual understanding, jñāna refers to more general experiences common to a specific class of being, such as the knowledge of a ŚRĀVAKA, PRATYEKABUDDHA, or buddha. The YOGĀCĀRA school discusses four or five specific types of knowledge exclusive to the buddhas. The four knowledges are transformations of the eighth consciousnesses (VIJÑĀNA): (1) Mirror-like knowledge, or great perfect mirror wisdom (ĀDARŚAJÑĀNA; mahādarśajñāna), a transformation of the eighth consciousness, the ĀLAYAVIJÑĀNA, in which the perfect interfusion between all things is seen as if reflected in a great mirror. (2) The knowledge of equality, or impartial wisdom (SAMATĀJÑĀNA), a transformation of the seventh KLIṢṬAMANOVIJÑĀNA, which transcends all dichotomies to see everything impartially without coloring by the ego. (3) The knowledge of specific knowledge or sublime contemplation (PRATYAVEKṢANĀJÑĀNA), a transformation of the sixth MANOVIJÑĀNA, which recognizes the unique and common characteristics of all DHARMAS, thus giving profound intellectual understanding. (4) The knowledge that one has accomplished what was to be done (KṚTYĀNUṢṬHĀNAJÑĀNA), a transformation of the five sensory consciousnesses, wherein one perfects actions that benefit both oneself and others. The fifth of the five knowledges is the "knowledge of the nature of the DHARMADHĀTU" (DHARMADHĀTUSVABHĀVAJÑĀNA). Each of these knowledges is then personified by one of the PAÑCATATHĀGATAS, sometimes given the names VAIROCANA, AKṢOBHYA, RATNASAMBHAVA, AMITĀBHA, and AMOGHASIDDHI.

**jñānadarśana**. (P. ñāṇadassana; T. ye shes mthong ba; C. zhijian; J. chiken; K. chigyŏn 知見). In Sanskrit, "knowledge and vision"; the direct insight into the reality of the three marks of existence (TRILAKṢAṆA)—impermanence (ANITYA), suffering (DUḤKHA), and nonself/insubstantiality (ANĀTMAN)—and one of the qualities perfected on the path leading to the stage of a worthy one (ARHAT). The term often appears in a stock description of the transition from the meditative absorption that is experienced during the four levels of DHYĀNA to the insight generated through wisdom (PRAJÑĀ): after suffusing one's mind with concentration, purity, malleability, and imperturbability, the meditator directs his or her attention to "knowledge and vision." In this vision of truth, the meditator then recognizes that the self (ĀTMAN) is but the conjunction of a physical body constructed from the four great elements (MAHĀBHŪTA) and a mentality (VIJÑĀNA, CITTA) that is bound to and dependent upon that physical body (see NĀMARŪPA). Letting go of attachment to body and mind, the meditator finally gains the knowledge that he is no longer subject to rebirth and becomes an arhat. The Pāli abhidhamma includes "knowledge and vision" within the last three types of purifications of practice (P. visuddhi; S. VIŚUDDHI): the fifth "purification of the knowledge and vision of what constitutes the path" (P. MAGGĀMAGGAÑĀṆADASSANAVISUDDHI), the sixth "purification of the knowledge and vision of the method of salvation" (P. PAṬIPADĀÑĀṆADASSANAVISUDDHI), and finally the seventh "purification of knowledge and vision" itself (P. ÑĀṆADASSANAVISUDDHI), which constitutes the pure wisdom that derives from the experience of enlightenment. In the MAHĀYĀNA, the perfection of knowledge and vision (jñānadarśanapāramitā) is also said to be an alternate name for the perfection of wisdom (PRAJÑĀPĀRAMITĀ), one of the six or ten perfections (PĀRAMITĀ) of the BODHISATTVA path.

**jñānadharmakāya**. (T. ye shes chos sku). In Sanskrit, "knowledge truth body," one of the two divisions (along with the SVABHĀVAKĀYA) of the DHARMAKĀYA of a buddha. With the development of MAHĀYĀNA thought, the dharmakāya became a kind of transcendent principle in which all buddhas partake, and it is in this sense that the term is translated as "truth body." In the later Mahāyāna scholastic tradition, the dharmakāya was said to have two aspects. The first is the svabhāvakāya (alt. svābhāvikakāya), or "nature body," which is the ultimate nature of a buddha's mind; the second is the jñānakāya or "knowledge body," a buddha's omniscient gnosis. The final chapter of the ABHISAMAYĀLAṂKĀRA sets forth an elliptic presentation of the svabhāvakāya that led to a number of different later interpretations. According to Ārya VIMUKTISENA's interpretation, the svabhāvakāya is not a separate buddha body, but rather the ultimate nature underpinning the other three bodies (the dharmakāya, SAṂBHOGAKĀYA, and NIRMĀṆAKĀYA). HARIBHADRA, influenced by YOGĀCĀRA scholastic positions, privileges the dharmakāya and says it has two parts: a knowledge body (jñānadharmakāya) and a svabhāvakāya, its ultimate nature. This controversy was widely debated in Tibet in the commentarial tradition. See also TRIKĀYA.

**Jñānagarbha**. (T. Ye shes snying po) (c. 700–760). Indian scholar of the syncretic Yogācāra–Madhyamaka school of philosophy, identified by the Tibetan tradition as a proponent of YOGĀCĀRA–SVĀTANTRIKA–MADHYAMAKA. He is counted in Tibet, together with ŚĀNTARAKṢITA and KAMALAŚĪLA, as one of the "three Eastern Svātantrikas," suggesting that he was from Bengal. He is said to have been the disciple of Śrīgupta and the teacher of Śāntarakṣita. His most famous work is the SATYADVAYAVIBHAṄGA ("Analysis of the Two Truths").

**Jñānagupta**. (C. Shenajueduo; J. Janakutta; K. Sanagulta 闍那崛多) (523–600). Indian monk from GANDHĀRA, who arrived in China around 559 and became a prolific translator of Indian materials into Chinese; some thirty-five of his translations are still extant and preserved in the Chinese canon (DAZANGJING). He is perhaps best known for his retranslation of the SADDHARMAPUṆḌARĪKASŪTRA ("Lotus Sūtra"), which included portions of the scripture that did not appear in KUMĀRAJĪVA's pioneering translation made two centuries before, especially the important "Chapter on Devadatta." He also translated the *Adhyāśayasañcodana*, the VIMALAKĪRTINIRDEŚA, the *Abhiniṣkramaṇasūtra* (a possible translation of the MAHĀVASTU), and several DHĀRAṆĪ sūtras.

**jñānamudrā**. (T. ye shes phyag rgya). In Sanskrit, "knowledge seal"; a term used to refer to an imagined or visualized female consort in the practice of sexual yoga in ANUTTARAYOGATANTRA. In the context of sexual yoga, three types of female consorts or VIDYĀ ("knowledge women") are sometimes enumerated. The first is the jñānamudrā or "knowledge seal," who is an imagined or visualized partner, not an actual consort. The second and third types of consorts are both actual consorts. The SAMAYAMUDRĀ, or "pledge seal," is a consort who is fully qualified for the practice of sexual yoga, in the sense that she is of the appropriate age and caste, has practiced the common path, and maintains the tantric pledges (SAMAYA). The third and final type is the KARMAMUDRĀ, "action seal," who is also an actual consort but who may not possess the qualifications of a samayamudrā. In some expositions of tantric practice, these three types of "seals" are discussed with reference to MAHĀMUDRĀ, or "great seal," a multivalent term sometimes defined as the union of method (UPĀYA) and wisdom (PRAJÑĀ), which does not require a consort.

**jñānamuṣṭi**. (T. ye shes khu tshur; C. zhiquan yin; J. chiken'in; K. chigwŏn in 智拳印). In Sanskrit, "wisdom/knowledge fist [gesture]"; in esoteric Buddhist iconography, the distinctive gesture (MUDRĀ) associated with images of the buddha VAIROCANA, the central figure of the esoteric traditions of Buddhism and the chief buddha of the tathāgata family (see PAÑCAKULA). The gesture is formed with the index finger of the left hand grasped by the fist of the right hand, and both hands raised in front of the image's chest. The gesture is interpreted to indicate the unity in the DHARMAKĀYA of the divergent experience of ordinary beings and buddhas, SAṂSĀRA and NIRVĀṆA, ignorance and wisdom, and delusion and enlightenment. See also BODHYAṄGĪMUDRĀ.

**Jñānaprasthāna**. (T. Ye shes la 'jug pa; C. Fazhi lun; J. Hotchiron; K. Palchi non 發智論). In Sanskrit, "Foundations of Knowledge," the central text, or "body" (śarīra), of the ABHIDHARMAPIṬAKA of the SARVĀSTIVĀDA school; attributed to KĀTYĀYANĪPUTRA and probably composed around the last half of the first-century BCE. The other six treatises of the Sarvāstivāda ABHIDHARMA are considered to be the ancillary texts, or "feet" (pādaśāstra), of the *Jñānaprasthāna*. The text is extant only in two Chinese translations, the earliest made in 383 by the Kashmiri monk Saṃghadeva and ZHU FONIAN (titled the *Bajiandu lun*, or *Aṣṭagrantha*, after the eight major sections into which the text is divided), the second, definitive translation by XUANZANG and his translation team between 657 and 660. Both recensions divide the treatise into eight sections, with forty-four chapters in total, but there are enough differences in the structure of the discussion to suggest that they may represent Gandhārin and Kashmiri recensions, respectively. The organization of material is as follows:

Section One: Miscellaneous Topics, including discussions of the highest worldly factors (LAUKIKĀGRADHARMA) and the NIRVEDHABHĀGĪYA
Section Two: Afflictions (KLEŚA)
Section Three: Knowledge (JÑĀNA)
Section Four: Action (KARMAN)
Section Five: Elements (BHŪTA)
Section Six: Dominant Factors (INDRIYA)
Section Seven: Meditative Absorption (DHYĀNA)
Section Eight: Vision (DARŚANA)

A few centuries after the composition of the *Jñānaprasthāna*, or c. first half of the second-century CE, Sarvāstivāda exegetes compiled a massive commentary to the text, entitled the ABHIDHARMAMAHĀVIBHĀṢĀ, which followed the root text's chapters and section divisions but exponentially expanded the coverage of the school's teachings. Because of their adherence to the exegetical approaches outlined in that commentary, later masters of the Sarvāstivāda school in KASHMIR–GANDHĀRA termed themselves "VAIBHĀṢIKA." ¶ The *Jñānaprasthāna* is probably the last of the canonical Sarvāstivāda abhidharma texts to have been composed and contains a systematic overview of the emblematic doctrines of the mature school. Distinctive Sarvāstivāda doctrines treated in the text include the full roster of the four conditions (PRATYAYA) and six causes (HETU); the Sarvāstivāda's eponymous teaching that factors (dharma) exist in all three time periods (TRIKĀLA) of the past, present, and future; the definitive classification schema for the mental concomitants (CAITTA); and the listing of the four conditioned characteristics (SAṂSKṚTALAKṢAṆA) of dharmas, viz., origination (JĀTI), continuance (STHITI), senescence (JARĀ), and desinence (anityatā, ANITYA; viz., death). The *Jñānaprasthāna*'s outline of Sarvāstivāda abhidharma is based on a soteriological schema, ultimately deriving from the FOUR NOBLE TRUTHS. The opening chapter on miscellaneous factors begins with a discussion of the highest worldly factors (laukikāgradharma), perhaps the major conceptual innovation of the text, that is, dharmas at the moment of the transition from ordinary person (PṚTHAGJANA) to noble one (ĀRYA), when they catalyze access to the path of vision (DARŚANAMĀRGA). The *Jñānaprasthāna* thus uses its treatment of the highest worldly dharmas as an interpretative tool to integrate its discussion of the major stages in the path, from the mundane path of practice (LAUKIKA-BHĀVANĀMĀRGA), to the path of vision, the supramundane path of cultivation (LOKOTTARA-BHĀVANĀMĀRGA), and the path of the realized adept (AŚAIKṢAMĀRGA; see also PAÑCAMĀRGA). This focus also highlights the major difference between Sarvāstivāda and Pāli abhidharma materials: whereas Pāli texts include substantial coverage of such preliminary practices as morality and choosing a meditation subject, the *Jñānaprasthāna* is principally concerned with the more advanced stages of the path. The second critical contribution of the *Jñānaprasthāna* is its systematization of the six causes (HETU). These six are not found in the ĀGAMAs, and only four are listed in earlier Sarvāstivāda abhidharma texts, such as the VIJÑĀNAKĀYA[PĀDAŚĀSTRA]. Kātyāyanīputra's systematization of this list seems to have been intended to demonstrate the causal connections that pertained between the stages of the path. Overall, the *Jñānaprasthāna* is best known not for its doctrinal innovations but instead for its grand systematization of Sarvāstivāda abhidharma.

**jñānasaṃbhāra**. (T. ye shes kyi tshogs; C. zhiju; J. chiju; K. chich'wi 智聚). In Sanskrit, the "collection," or "equipment," "of knowledge"; along with the "collection of merit" (PUṆYASAṂBHĀRA), one of the two types of qualities with which BODHISATTVAs must equip themselves in the course of achieving buddhahood. Between the two poles of method (UPĀYA) and wisdom (PRAJÑĀ), the collection of knowledge is associated with wisdom. Among the six perfections (PĀRAMITĀ), the last two, meditative absorption (DHYĀNA) and wisdom (PRAJÑĀ), are traditionally associated with the collection of knowledge (the perfection of effort, VĪRYAPĀRAMITĀ, contributes to both collections). The DHARMAKĀYA is said to be the result of the buddhas having equipped themselves with knowledge, while the RŪPAKĀYA is said to be the result of the collection of merit.

**Jñānasārasamuccaya**. (T. Ye shes snying po kun las btus pa). A treatise of MADHYAMAKA scholasticism, traditionally attributed to ĀRYADEVA, but probably composed by a Madhyamaka exegete following the development of Madhyamaka and YOGĀCĀRA; the author sets forth Madhyamaka positions and denies the reality of consciousness (VIJÑĀNA). It describes the doctrines of the later Indian philosophical schools, both Hindu and Buddhist. Although the work does not contain overtly tantric elements, it may be the work of the so-called tantric Āryadeva or Āryadevapāda. There is a commentary on the text by Bodhibhadra (c. 1000), the *Jñānasārasamuccayanibandhana*.

**jñānasattva**. (T. ye shes sems dpa'). In Sanskrit, "knowledge being;" in later tantric visualization practice, one is first instructed to create a visualized image, called the "pledge being" (SAMAYASATTVA), of the deity (DEVATĀ) being propitiated. Once that image is perfectly visualized, the true form of the deity, called the "knowledge being," is invited to come from his or her abode and fuse with the visualized form created by the meditator during the SĀDHANA ritual.

**Jñānaśrīmitra**. (T. Ye shes dpal bshes gnyen) Late Indian YOGĀCĀRA philosopher and logician of the school of DHARMAKĪRTI at VIKRAMAŚILA monastery, born between 975 and 1000. Within the Yogācāra, he held the so-called "aspectarian" (SĀKĀRA) position regarding the nature of cognition, taking a position opposed to that of RATNĀKARAŚĀNTI. He is credited as the author of twelve treatises, including an important work on APOHA, the *Apohaprakaraṇa*. In his works on logic, he upholds the interpretation of DHARMAKĪRTI by PRAJÑĀKARAGUPTA against the interpretation by DHARMOTTARA.

**jñapti**. (P. ñatti; T. gsol ba; C. bai; J. byaku; K. paek 白). In Sanskrit, lit. "understanding": in the context of the monastic code (VINAYA), a formal "motion" or "resolution" put before an assembly of the SAṂGHA for the purpose of carrying out a SAṂGHAKARMAN, an ecclesiastical act. Depending upon the requirements of the particular ecclesiastical act, the jñapti may or may not be followed by a KARMAVĀCANĀ, or "proceeding," which is a formalized recitation of a prescribed ritual text. There are three kinds, based on the number of times the motion must be stated in order to give all the monks present the opportunity to raise objections prior to the motion being carried. Some saṃghakarman do not require the recitation of a karmavācanā. Others require that the jñapti and the karmavācanā be recited once (JÑAPTIDVITĪYĀ KARMAVĀCANĀ). Yet others require that the jñapti and the karmavācanā be recited three times. There is no saṃghakarman that require the recitation of a karmavācanā two times.

**jñaptidvitīyā karmavācanā**. (P. ñattidutiyakammavācā; T. gsol ba dang gnyis kyi las brjod pa; C. boyi jiemo; J. byakuichikonma; K. paegil kalma 白一羯磨). In Sanskrit, "statement of a matter or 'proceeding' (KARMAVĀCANĀ) involving a 'motion' (JÑAPTI) accompanied by a single 'repetition' (dvitīya) of the formal question," that is, a motion made before the congregation of monks that may be approved by silent assent, rather than being followed by a request for a voicing of approval. According to the VINAYA, jñaptidvitīyā karmavācanā is the procedure that is to be followed during certain specific formal occasions within the SAṂGHA, such as the ordination ceremony, the adjudication of rules, the administration of punishments to transgressors of the precepts, and the settlement of disputes among the clergy. A motion or proposal is made formally one time to the attendees, and repeated once to solicit any additional responses. If the proposal is read in this manner with no audible objections from the group (silence indicating approval), it is passed and considered binding on the participants. For matters of greater importance or formality, there are also procedures involving three formal questions, which require an audible response before they are considered to be decided. See also SAṂGHAKARMAN; KARMAN.

**jñeyāvaraṇa**. (T. shes bya'i sgrib pa; C. suozhizhang; J. shochishō; K. sojijang 所知障). In Sanskrit, "cognitive obstructions," or "noetic obscurations"; the second of the two categories of obstructions (ĀVARAṆA), together with the afflictive obstructions (KLEŚĀVARAṆA), that must be overcome in order to perfect the BODHISATTVA path and achieve buddhahood. In the YOGĀCĀRA and MADHYAMAKA systems, the cognitive obstructions are treated as subtler hindrances that serve as the origin of the afflictive obstructions, and result from fundamental misapprehensions about the nature of reality. According to Yogācāra, because of the attachment deriving ultimately from the reification of what are actually imaginary external phenomena, conceptualization and discrimination arise in the mind, which lead in turn to pride, ignorance, and wrong views. Based on these mistakes in cognition, then, the individual engages in defiled actions, such as anger, envy, etc., which constitute the afflictive obstructions. The afflictive obstructions may be removed by followers of the ŚRĀVAKA, PRATYEKABUDDHA, and beginning BODHISATTVA paths, by applying various antidotes or counteragents (PRATIPAKṢA) to the afflictions (KLEŚA); overcoming these types of obstructions will lead to freedom from further rebirth. The cognitive obstructions, however, are more deeply ingrained and can only be overcome by advanced bodhisattvas who seek instead to achieve buddhahood, by perfecting their understanding of emptiness (ŚŪNYATĀ). Buddhas, therefore, are the only class of beings who have overcome both types of obstructions and thus are able simultaneously to cognize all objects of knowledge in the universe; this is one of the sources for their unparalleled skills as teachers of sentient beings. The jñeyāvaraṇa are therefore sometimes translated as "obstructions to omniscience."

**Jo bo mi bskyod rdo rje**. (Jowo Mikyur Dorje). A statue of ŚĀKYAMUNI Buddha as an eight-year-old BODHISATTVA, which was brought to Tibet by the Nepali Princess BHṚKUṬĪ during the reign of the Tibetan King SRONG BTSAN SGAM PO. Originally placed in the JO KHANG in LHA SA, it was later moved to the Lha sa RA MO CHE Temple. The statue disappeared sometime during the Chinese Cultural Revolution (1966–1976) but was later recovered by the tenth PAṆ CHEN LAMA and returned to Ra mo che.

**Jo bo Shākyamuni**. Chief image of the JO KHANG and of Tibet's most sacred Buddhist images. Called the Jo bo (Jowo, "Lord") or Jo bo rin po che ("Precious Lord"), this statue of ŚĀKYAMUNI as a young man is claimed to have been crafted in India during the Buddha's lifetime and brought to Tibet by the Chinese princess WENCHENG during the reign of the Tibetan King SRONG BTSAN SGAM PO. It lends its name to the monastery where it is enshrined, the Jo khang.

**Jōdo**. (J) (浄土). See PURE LAND.

**Jōdo Shinshū**. (浄土眞宗). In Japanese, the "True Pure Land school"; referring to the followers of the Japanese PURE LAND monk SHINRAN (1173–1262) and often called simply the Shinshū ("True School"). The central scriptures of the Jōdo Shinshū are the so-called three pure land SŪTRAS (J. jōdo sanbukyō, see JINGTU SANBUJING): the longer SUKHĀVATĪVYŪHASŪTRA, the shorter *Sukhāvatīvyūhasūtra* (also known as the AMITĀBHASŪTRA) and the GUAN WULIANGSHOU JING, as well as the writings of Shinran, such as his magnum opus, KYŌGYŌ SHINSHŌ. Following the example of Shinran's own vocation, the school is distinguished from the earlier JŌDOSHŪ by its more liberal attitude toward the Buddhist VINAYA rules of conduct, permitting its clergy to marry, have families, and eat meat, and its faith-oriented approach to practice, which placed relatively less emphasis on the efficacy of nenbutsu (C. NIANFO), the invocation of the name of the buddha AMITĀBHA, and greater stress on the power and grace of Amitābha. Because Shinran believed that people in this degenerate age of the dharma (J. mappō; C. MOFA) had little hope of gaining salvation through through own power (JIRIKI), he taught instead the complete reliance on Amitābha's salvific power (TARIKI). And because there was no possibility of effecting salvation on one's own, Shinran advocated that just a single sincere recitation of his name (ICHINENGI) would be sufficient to earn Amitābha's grace, in distinction to other of Hōnen's successors, who advocated multiple or even continuous recitations of Amitābha's name (TANENGI). Shinran's teachings spread from the capital of Kyōto to the countryside, largely through the proselytizing efforts of his disciples. The followers of Shinran eventually formed regional centers known as dōjō (cultivation sites), which later came under control of the monastery HONGANJI, thus developing a unified sectarian identity. This process largely began with the development of a memorial cult surrounding Shinran. KAKUNYO (1270–1351), Shinran's great-grandson, formalized the memorial services (hōonkō) for Shinran and transformed his mausoleum in Ōtani into a temple, which he later named Honganji. The regional centers also developed into contending factions (e.g., the Bukkōji, Senjuji, and Kinshokuji branches), but they were eventually unified under the strong leadership of RENNYO (1415–1499), the eighth abbot of Honganji. In 1465, warrior monks from HIEIZAN razed Honganji and turned the site into one of their own branch temples (matsuji). In 1478, having gained enough support to counter any threat from Mt. Hiei, Rennyo moved Honganji to the Yamashina area of Kyōto. The move was completed in 1483 with the completion of the Amida hall. Under Rennyo's leadership, Honganji became the central monastery of the Jōdo Shinshū tradition. Rennyo built a broad network of temples that was consolidated under the sole administration of Honganji. After a brief move to Ōsaka, Honganji was relocated to its current site in Kyōto on the order of Toyotomi Hideyoshi (1536–1598). A split occurred between two factions shortly thereafter, and ever since the early seventeenth century the Nishi (West) and Higashi (East) Honganji complexes have served as the religious centers of these two major branches of Jōdo Shinshū, the NISHI HONGANJIHA and the HIGASHI HONGANJIHA (also known as the ŌTANIHA). See also JŌDOSHŪ.

**Jōdoshū**. (浄土宗). In Japanese, the "PURE LAND school"; referring to the followers of HŌNEN (1133–1212), who formed the first indigenous school of Japanese Buddhism outside the aegis of the imperial court. The central scriptures of the school are the so-called three pure land SŪTRAS (jōdo sanbukyō; see JINGTU SANBUJING): the longer SUKHĀVATĪVYŪHASŪTRA, the shorter *Sukhāvatīvyūhasūtra* (also known as the AMITĀBHASŪTRA), and the GUAN WULIANGSHOU JING; as well as the **Aparimitāyussūtropadeśa* ("Exegesis of the *Wuliangshou jing*"), commonly known as the *Jingtu lun* (J. *Jōdoron*) ("Treatise on the Pure Land") and attributed by tradition to VASUBANDHU (see WULIANGSHOU JING YOUPOTISHE YUANSHENG JI). Hōnen's teachings focused on the "easy path" to NIRVĀṆA and the prospect of achieving enlightenment exclusively through recitation of the nenbutsu (C. NIANFO), which would lead to rebirth in the buddha AMITĀBHA's pure land. Hōnen's teachings quickly spread throughout Japan largely through the efforts of his disciples SHINRAN (1173–1262), Ryūkan (1148–1228), Shōkōbō Benchō (1162–1238), Zen'ebō Shōkū (1177–1247), Jōkakubō Kōsai (1163–1247), and Kakumyōbō Chōsai (1184–1366). While his disciples all agreed on the efficacy of the recitation of the nenbutsu as advocated by Hōnen, they developed different interpretations of this practice. These divisions eventually led to the formation of disparate factions within the school. Those who followed Benchō came to be known as the Chinzei branch; their spirit of tolerance for other practices allowed the Chinzei branch to thrive. Shōkū's followers, now known as the Seizan branch, held the position that rebirth in the pure land is possible only through continuous repetition of the nenbutsu (TANENGI); indeed, Shōkū himself was said to recite the nenbutsu as many as sixty thousand times a day. Kōsai, and to a lesser extent Shinran, held the more radical position that a single invocation of the name of Amitābha (ICHINENGI) would suffice. In 1207, in an effort to suppress the spread of Hōnen's teaching of exclusive nenbutsu, Hōnen, Kōsai, and Shinran, were exiled to different regions of the country. In 1227, the Jōdo movement was further suppressed when Hōnen's grave was desecrated by HIEIZAN monks and Kōsai was again sent into exile. In 1450, the Chinzei branch came to dominate the other branches when the Chinzei adherent Keijiku (1403–1459) assumed the position of abbot of the monastery CHION'IN (built at Hōnen's grave site) in Kyōto. The Chinzei branch firmly established itself as the leading branch with the support of the Tokugawa bakufu. The teachings of Benchō's disciple Ryōchū (1199–1287), who advocated the active use of the nenbutsu for purifying bad KARMAN in order to attain rebirth in pure land, came to be the official position of the Chinzei branch and thus of the wider Jōdoshū tradition. See also JŌDO SHINSHŪ.

**Jogye Order**. (K) (曹溪宗). See CHOGYE CHONG.

**Jo khang**. In Tibetan, "House of the Lord"; the earliest Tibetan temple and monastery, located in the capital of LHA SA. The central image is a statue of ŚĀKYAMUNI Buddha as a youth, said to have been sculpted in India during the Buddha's lifetime. This statue, the most sacred in Tibet, is known simply as the JO BO ("Lord") SHĀKYAMUNI or Jo bo Rin po che ("Precious Lord"). The temple takes its name from this image housed within it. Indeed, the name Lha sa ("Place of the Gods") may have referred originally to the Jo khang, only later becoming by extension to be the name of the city that surrounds it. The Jo khang stands at the heart of the old city, and is the central point for three circumambulation routes. The most famous of these is the BAR BSKOR, or middle circuit, which passes around the outer walls and surrounding structures of the Jo khang. The Jo khang and bar bskor together have long been Lha sa's primary religious space, with pilgrims circling it in a clockwise direction each day. The central market of Lha sa is also located along the bar bskor. Despite its well-known name, Tibetans tend to refer to the Jo khang simply as the Gtsug lag khang (Tsuklakang), the Tibetan term for VIHĀRA, meaning "monastery"; the original structure was likely laid out by Newari artisans following the plan of an Indian Buddhist vihāra. Western sources have rather misleadingly dubbed the Jo khang the "Cathedral of Lhasa." According to traditional Tibetan sources (most importantly, the MAṆI BKA' 'BUM) the original structure was established by the Tibetan king SRONG BTSAN SGAM PO and his two queens (one Chinese and one Nepalese), around 640 CE. The statue of Śākyamuni, said to have been crafted during the Buddha's lifetime, eventually made its way to China. It is said to have been brought to Tibet from China by the king's Chinese bride, Princess WENCHENG. The many difficulties she encountered en route from China convinced her that the landscape of Tibet was in fact a supine demoness (SRIN MO), who was inimical to the introduction of Buddhism. On her advice, the king (who had recently converted to Buddhism), the Chinese princess, and the king's other wife, the Nepalese princess BHṚKUTĪ, built the Jo khang directly over the heart of the demoness; according to Tibetan legends, the king himself built much of the first-floor structure. Other temples were subsequently built across Tibet, corresponding to other parts of the demoness's vast body, in order essentially to nail her to the earth and prevent her further obstruction of the dharma (see MTHA' 'DUL GTSUG LAG KHANG). When the Jo khang was completed, a different statue than the more famous Jo bo Shākyamuni or Jo bo rin bo che, was the central image; it was a statue of the buddha called JO BO MI BSKYOD RDO RJE brought to Tibet by Bhṛkutī. The statue brought by Wencheng (known as Jo bo rin bo che) was housed in the nearby RA MO CHE temple, founded by Wencheng. After the king's death, the two statues were switched, moving the Jo bo Shākyamuni statue to the Jo khang and the Jo bo mi bskyod rdo rje statue to Ra mo che, where they would remain over the subsequent centuries. Modern scholarship has raised questions about many details of this tale, including the degree of Srong btsan sgam po's devotion to Buddhism and the existence of his Nepalese queen. However, the story of the Jo khang's founding, depicted on murals inside the temple itself, is widely known, and the Jo khang remains central to the sacred geography of the Tibetan Buddhist world. The Jo khang has been the site of many important moments of Tibetan history, including the establishment of the SMON LAM CHEN MO festival in 1409, when TSONG KHA PA offered a crown to the Jo bo statue, giving it the aspect of a SAṂBHOGAKĀYA. Over the course of its long history, the Jo khang has been enlarged and renovated many times (although elements of the original structure, such as juniper beams, are still visible) to become a complex of chapels, courtyards, residential quarters (including those for the DALAI LAMA and PAṆ CHEN LAMA), monastic dormitories, government offices, and storerooms. The temple suffered during the Chinese Cultural Revolution (1966–1976), when parts of the complex and much of its original statuary and murals were damaged or destroyed, including the central image. During this period, the complex was occupied by Red Guards and People's Liberation Army troops, and the temple was used as a pigsty. The temple has since been restored, beginning in 1972 and again during the early 1990s. In 2000, it was listed by UNESCO as a World Heritage Site.

**Jōmyō**. (J) (紹明). See NANPO JŌMYŌ.

**Jo nang**. A sect of Tibetan Buddhism that flourished between the thirteenth and seventeenth centuries, seated primarily at the monastery of JO NANG PHUN TSHOGS GLING, northwest of Shigatse. The lineage of masters affiliated with the Jo nang, traditionally said to begin with the eleventh-century yogin-scholar Yu mo Mi bskyod rdo rje (Yumo Mikyö Dorje), includes such highly acclaimed luminaries as DOL PO PA SHES

RAB RGYAL MTSHAN and TĀRANĀTHA. Jo nang scholars are often noted for their interest in the KĀLACAKRATANTRA and the controversial doctrine of GZHAN STONG, or "extrinsic emptiness," developed and promulgated by Dol po pa. This theory, and its attendant interpretation of TATHĀGATAGARBHA, was later adopted, reformulated, and actively transmitted by numerous other masters, especially those of the BKA' BRGYUD and RNYING MA sects. Others, especially SA SKYA and later DGE LUGS adherents, presumed that these doctrines were incorrect and even heretical. In 1650, under the aegis of the fifth DALAI LAMA, the monastery of Jo nang was forcibly converted to the Dge lugs sect, its books locked under state seal. The Jo nang tradition survived, however, secretly in small pockets throughout central and western Tibet, and at 'DZAM THANG monastery in A mdo in eastern Tibet, where it has been practiced openly up to the present day. The name is also used to designate the principal central Tibetan monastery affiliated with the Jo nang tradition, Phun tshogs gling; see JO NANG PHUN TSHOGS GLING.

**Jo nang phun tshogs gling**. (Jonang Puntsokling). A monastery in west-central Tibet, northwest of Shigatse, which served as the principal seat of the JO NANG tradition of Tibetan Buddhism. Its foundation was laid by Kun spangs pa Thugs rje brtson 'grus (Kunpangpa Tukje Tsöndrü, 1243–1313), and was later expanded by the Jo nang luminary DOL PO PA SHES RAB RGYAL MTSHAN, who became the monastery's principal teacher in 1326. Dol po pa also established his own hermitage in a valley above the monastery, the site where he later constructed his famed STŪPA, based upon descriptions in the KĀLACAKRATANTRA. The massive structure, standing nearly seventy feet tall, was consecrated in 1333. The monastic structure was again expanded by the sixteenth-century Jo nang scholar TĀRANĀTHA, who gave it the name Phun tshogs gling. The full name of the monastery is Rtag brtan dam chos phun tshogs gling (or Rtag brtan dam chos gling); it is referred to as Jo nang phun tshogs gling because it was the seat of the Jo nang sect. The monastery is particularly famous for its extensive murals depicting the events in the life of ŚĀKYAMUNI Buddha, based on the biography of the Buddha by Tāranātha. The monastery was converted to a DGE LUGS establishment under the fifth DALAI LAMA and renamed DGA' LDAN PHUN TSHOGS GLING.

**Josaphat**. See BARLAAM AND JOSAPHAT.

**juedai miao**. (絶待妙). See DAIJUE ERMIAO.

**Juefan Huihong**. (J. Kakuhan Ekō; K. Kakpŏm Hyehong 覺範慧洪) (1071–1128). Chinese CHAN monk in the HUANGLONG PAI collateral line of the LINJI ZONG during the Northern Song dynasty (960–1127) and major proponent of "lettered Chan" (WENZI CHAN), which valorized belle lettres, and especially poetry, in the practice of Chan. Huihong entered the monastery after he was orphaned at fourteen, eventually passing the monastic examinations at age nineteen and receiving ordination at Tianwangsi in the eastern capital of Kaifeng. After studying the CHENG WEISHI LUN (**Vijñaptimātratāsiddhi*) for four years, he eventually began to study at LUSHAN with the Chan master Zhenjing Kewen (1025–1102), under whom he achieved enlightenment. Because of Huihong's close ties to the famous literati officials of his day, and especially with the statesman and Buddhist patron ZHANG SHANGYING (1043–1122), his own career was subject to many of the same political repercussions as his associates; indeed, Huihong himself was imprisoned, defrocked, and exiled multiple times in his life when his literati colleagues were purged. Compounding his problems, Huihong also suffered along with many other monks during the severe Buddhist persecution (see FANAN) that occurred during the reign of Emperor Huizong (r. 1100–1125). Even amid these trying political times, however, Huihong managed to maintain both his monastic vocation and his productive literary career. Huihong is in fact emblematic of many Chan monks during the Song dynasty, when Chan enters the mainstream of Chinese intellectual life: his practice of Chan was framed and conceptualized in terms that drew from his wide learning and profound erudition, tendencies that helped make Chan writings particularly appealing to wider Chinese literati culture. Huihong decried the bibliophobic tendencies in Chan that were epitomized in the aphorism that Chan "does not establish words and letters" (BULI WENZI) and advocated that Chan insights were made manifest in both Buddhist sūtras as well as in the uniquely Chan genres of discourse records (YULU), genealogical histories (see CHUANDENG LU), and public-case anthologies (GONG'AN). Given his literary penchant, it is no surprise that Huihong was a prolific author. His works associated with Chan lineages include the CHANLIN SENGBAO ZHUAN ("Chronicles of the SAṂGHA Jewel in the Chan Grove"), a collection of biographies of about a hundred eminent Chan masters important in the development of lettered Chan; and the *Linjian lu* ("Anecdotes from the Groves [of Chan]"), completed in 1107 and offering a record of Huihong's own encounters with fellow monks and literati and his reflections on Buddhist practice. Huihong also wrote two studies of poetics and poetic criticism, the *Lengzhai yehua* ("Evening Discourses from Cold Studio") and *Tianchu jinluan* ("Forbidden Cutlets from the Imperial Kitchen"), and numerous commentaries to Buddhist scriptures, including the SADDHARMAPUṆḌARĪKASŪTRA ("Lotus Sūtra"), SHOULENGYAN JING, and YUANJUE JING.

**Jueguan lun**. (J. Zetsukanron; K. Chŏlgwan non 絶觀論). In Chinese, "Extinguishing Cognition Treatise," (translated into English as *A Dialogue on the Contemplation-Extinguished*), attributed to the legendary Indian founder of the CHAN school, BODHIDHARMA. The treatise largely consists of an imaginary dialogue between a certain learned man named Master Entrance-into-Principle (Ruli xiansheng) and his student Conditionality (Yuanmen), which unfolds as a series of questions and answers. In this dialogue, Entrance-into-Principle continuously negates the premises that underlie the questions his student Conditionality raises about the mind and its pacification, the nature of enlightenment, as well as other matters related to practice, meditation, and attainment. For example, in the opening dialogue, Conditionality asks, "What is the mind? How do we pacify it?" Master Entrance-into-Principle replies, "Neither positing 'mind' nor trying to 'pacify' it—this is pacifying it." By rejecting the dualistic perspectives inherent in Conditionality's questions, the Master finally opens his student to an experience of the pure wisdom that transcends all dualities. This style of negative argumentation, derived from MADHYAMAKA antecedents, is believed to be characteristic of the NIUTOU ZONG of the Chan school; the treatise is therefore often assumed to have been written by an adherent of that school, perhaps even by its seventh-century founder NIUTOU FARONG himself, or else during the zenith of the Niutou school in the third quarter of the eighth century. The treatise also makes use of Daoist terminology and thus serves as a valuable source for studying Chinese reinterpretations of sophisticated Buddhist doctrines. A controversial argument claiming that insentient beings also possess the buddha-nature (FOXING) also appears in the *Jueguan lun*. The treatise seems to have gone through several editions, some of which were preserved in the DUNHUANG caves in Chinese Xinjiang.

**jushenguang**. (J. koshinkō; K. kŏsin'gwang 擧身光). In Chinese, lit. "whole-body light"; a "mandorla" surrounding the body of holy figures in Buddhist painting and sculpture. See KĀYAPRABHĀ.

**Jushi zhuan**. (居士傳). In Chinese, "Record of [Eminent] Laymen," by the Qing-dynasty author PENG SHAOSHENG (1740–1796), a Confucian literatus turned Buddhist layman; in fifty-six rolls. Written between 1770 and 1775, the record collects 312 biographies of Chinese Buddhist laymen (C. jushi; S. UPĀSAKA) from the inception of Buddhism in China through the reign of the Qing-dynasty Kangxi emperor (r. 1662–1722). The compilation was intended to give appropriate recognition to the contributions laymen made to the development of the Buddhist tradition in China. Its entries are adapted from the occasional biographies of laymen that are widely scattered throughout such collections as the HONGMING JI, *Fofa jintang*, *Faxi zhi*, FOZU TONG JI, JINGDE CHUANDENG LU, *Wudeng hui yuan*, *Donglin zhuan*, and WANGSHENG JINGTU ZHUAN. Although there had been some biographical collections of laymen affiliated with the Chan school, such as the *Jushi fendeng lu*, *Xianjue zongsheng*, and *Jushi Chandeng lu*, the records of laymen involved with other schools were much more widely dispersed. To prepare a more comprehensive and accurate portrayal of Chinese laymen, Peng Shaosheng reexamined the aforementioned works and excerpted certain portions from them, discarding many spurious records and adding corroborating information taken from additional historical, biographical, and genealogical works. His biographies thus describe in detail the individual backgrounds and religious experiences of the laymen profiled, and provide much broader and rich coverage of lay activities throughout the full panoply of Chinese Buddhism. Although Peng Shaosheng himself was a PURE LAND adherent, his *Jushi zhuan* includes figures associated with Chan, pure land, and various Buddhist doctrinal schools. This book provides valuable information for understanding the motivations underlying lay Buddhist practice and the changes that practice took over time. Peng Shaosheng followed his record of male householders with a parallel collection of the biographies of Buddhist laywomen, the SHANNÜREN ZHUAN.

# K

**Kaḥ thog**. An important monastery affiliated with the Rnying ma sect of Tibetan Buddhism, founded in 1159 by Kaḥ thog Dam pa bde gshegs (Katok Dampa Deshek, 1122–1192) in the eastern Tibetan region of Khams, also called Kaḥ thog rdo rje gdan (Katok Dorjeden). It is situated on the ridge of a mountain said to be shaped like the Tibetan letter "ka," from which the institution takes its name. One of the oldest surviving Rnying ma monasteries in Tibet, along with Bsam yas, Kaḥ thog has had a long and active history and maintained numerous rare instruction lineages that were lost in central Tibet. Widely famed for its philosophical studies, the monastery's college traditionally drew students from all parts of eastern Tibet. Kaḥ thog's monks were also renowned for their meditative training. The institution was home to the great scholar and historian Kaḥ thog rig 'dzin Tshe dbang nor bu (Katok Rikdzin Tsewang Norbu, 1698–1755). More contemporary figures associated with the monastery include the third Kaḥ thog Si tu, Chos kyi rgya mtsho (Chökyi Gyatso, 1880–1925); the scholar Mkhan po Sngags ga (Khenpo Ngakga, 1879–1941); and the meditation master Bya bral Sangs rgyas rdo rje (Jadral Sangye Dorje, 1913–). It is one of the four major Rnying ma monasteries in eastern Tibet, the others being Zhe chen, Rdzogs chen, and Dpal yul.

**Kaḥ thog Si tu**. A line of Tibetan sprul sku (incarnate lamas) at Kaḥ thog monastery, an important Rnying ma monastery in Khams, eastern Tibet; they are accepted to be the reincarnations of the erudite and accomplished eighth Si tu, Chos kyi 'byung gnas, the great scholar of Dpal spungs, himself the eighth Tai Si tu incarnation. The third Kaḥ thog Si tu was a nephew of 'Jam dbyangs mkhyen brtse dbang po, one of the leading figures in the so-called nonsectarian (ris med) movement of the nineteenth century and the main teacher of 'Jam dbyangs mkhyen brtse Chos kyi blo gros, the teacher of many of the twentieth-century's greatest Tibetan Buddhist masters.

**Kaian kokugo**. (槐安國語). In Japanese, "Words on the Peaceful Land of the Locust-Trees," composed by the Japanese Rinzai Zen master Hakuin Ekaku. The peaceful land of the locust-trees (Sophora japonica) is an allusion to the tale of a retired official who dreams of a peaceful paradise, but upon waking realizes that it was nothing but a mound of ants living underneath a locust-tree in the yard. This tale is found in the *Nanke taishou zhuan* ("Biography of the Governor of Nanke"), written by Li Gongzuo (c. 778–848), and retold in the *Nanke ji* ("Record of the Southern Bough") by the Ming-dynasty playwright Tang Xianzu (1550–1617). Hakuin composed this treatise in 1749 and published it the next year in 1750. The treatise, which was written at the request of his students, consists largely of Hakuin's prose commentary and notes on the recorded sayings (yulu) of the Zen master Daitō (see Sōhō Myōchō). The entire treatise was written in literary Chinese.

**kaihōgyō**. (回峰行). In Japanese, lit. "the practice of circumambulating the mountain," a Shugendō-related ascetic practice of running a course around the mountain of Hieizan, which is undertaken by Japanese Tendai monks and nuns within the Sanmon branch of the school. The central deity of veneration for kaihōgyō is Fudō Myōō (S. Acalanātha-Vidyārāja). While engaged in running the course, one chants, meditates, and stops to pray at temples, shrines, and natural elements along the route. Kaihōgyō can be practiced for as little as one day or for a 100-day period as part of a monk or nun's training. Best known, however, is its 1,000-day practice (sennichi kaihōgyō), which is carried out over a seven-year period. This route consists of twenty-five to fifty miles of running a day, depending on the stage of practice, which is broken up into 100-day terms. The first 700 days of practice benefits the practitioner (gyōja) himself (jiriki), while the last 300 days benefits others (tariki) and is thus known as the bodhisattva practice (bosatsugyō). Between these two stages, the *gyōja* undergoes a severe nine-day rite referred to as a dōiri (lit. "entering the hall"), during which he completely forgoes food, water, rest, or sleep. One who successfully completes the 1,000-day practice receives the title Daigyōman Ajari (Ācārya whose Great Practice is Fulfilled). Kaihōgyō dates back to at least the fourteenth century, and an earlier form of it may have been practiced as early as the ninth century. The origin of kaihōgyō is attributed to the Tendai monk Sōō (b. 831).

**Kailāsa**. The Sanskrit name for one of the most important sacred mountains in Asia, generally referred to in English as Kailash or Mount Kailash. It is 21,778 ft. high and is located in southwestern Tibet, not far from the current borders of India and Nepal. Lake Manasarovar is located eighteen miles to the southeast; these two sites have long been places of pilgrimage for Buddhists, Hindus, Jains, and followers of Tibetan BON, some of whom have regarded the striking dome-shaped peak as Mount SUMERU. The mountain is particularly important in Tibetan Buddhism, where it is called Gangs dkar Ti se ("White Snow Mountain Ti se") or simply Gangs rin po che ("Precious Snow Mountain"). Pilgrims from across the Tibetan Buddhist world visit Mount Kailāsa, especially in the Year of the Horse, which occurs once every twelve years in the Tibetan calendrical cycle. Within that year, it is considered auspicious to visit the mountain at the time that marks the Buddha's birth, enlightenment, and passage into PARINIRVĀṆA (generally falling in May or June, depending on the lunar calendar). The primary form of practice is the thirty-two mile clockwise circumambulation of the mountain, often completed in a single day, with specific rituals and practices performed along the route. It is said that one circumambulation purifies the negative KARMAN of one lifetime, ten circumambulations purify the negative KARMAN accumulated over the course of a KALPA, and one hundred circumambulations ensure enlightenment. The mountain came to take on numerous tantric associations beginning in the eleventh century. According to a popular story, the yogin MI LA RAS PA won control of the mountain for the Buddhists by defeating a rival Bon priest, Na ro bon chung, in a contest of miracles. The mountain later became an important meditation site for the followers of Mi la ras pa, principally members of the 'BRUG PA BKA' BRGYUD and 'BRI GUNG BKA' BRGYUD sects. Both ŚĀKYAMUNI Buddha and PADMASAMBHAVA are said to have visited Kailāsa. One of the most important associations of Mount Kailāsa is with the CAKRASAṂVARATANTRA, which names twenty-four sacred lands (PĪṬHA) as potent locations for tantric practice. The Cakrasaṃvara literature recounts how long ago these twenty-four lands came under the control of Maheśvara (Śiva) in the form of Rudra Bhairava. The buddha VAJRADHARA, in the wrathful form of a HERUKA deity, subdued BHAIRAVA, transforming each of the twenty-four sites into a MAṆḌALA of the deity Cakrasaṃvara and his retinue. In Tibetan literature, Mount Kailāsa came to be identified with one of the twenty-four sites, the one called Himavat or Himālaya ("The Snowy," or "The Snow Mountain"); this was one of several important transpositions of sacred locations in India onto Tibetan sites. The BKA' BRGYUD sect grouped the peak together with two other important mountain pilgrimage sites in southern Tibet, LA PHYI and TSA RI, identified respectively as Cakrasaṃvara's body, speech, and mind. These claims drew criticism from some Tibetan quarters, such as the renowned scholar SA SKYA PAṆḌITA, who argued that the sites associated with Cakrasaṃvara were located not in Tibet but in India. Such criticism has not prevented Mount Kailāsa from remaining one of the most important pilgrimage places in the Tibetan cultural domain.

**Kaimokushō**. (開目鈔). In Japanese, "Opening the Eyes"; one of the major writings of NICHIREN. Nichiren composed this treatise in 1273 while he was living in exile in a graveyard on Sado Island. Nichiren's motivation for writing this treatise is said to have come from the doubts that he came to harbor about the efficacy of the teachings of the SADDHARMAPUṆḌARĪKASŪTRA due to the government's repeated persecution of him and his followers. The *Kaimokushō* details the reasons behind the persecutions: bad KARMAN from the past, the abandonment of the country by the gods (KAMI), life in the impure realm of SAHĀLOKA, and the trials and tribulations of the BODHISATTVA path. In the *Kaimokushō*, Nichiren professes to have overcome his doubts and welcomes the bodhisattva path of martyrdom. The treatise explains the path that leads to "opening the eyes" as a journey from the teachings of the heretics to those of the HĪNAYĀNA, the MAHĀYĀNA, and finally culminating in the teachings of the *Saddharmapuṇḍarīkasūtra* (see JIAOXIANG PANSHI). According to Nichiren tradition, because Nichiren claims at the conclusion of the text to be the "sovereign, teacher, and mother and father to all the people of Japan," he has thus revealed himself to be the Buddha of the degenerate age of the dharma (MAPPŌ).

**kaishan**. (J. kaisan; K. kaesan 開山). In Chinese, lit. "opener of the mountain," a term used in East Asian Buddhism to refer to the founder of a monastery or sectarian tradition.

**kaiyan**. (J. kaigen; K. kaean 開眼). In Chinese, "opening the eyes," also known as "dotting the eyes" (DIANYAN); the ritual of consecrating a newly carved or cast buddha image (see BUDDHĀBHIṢEKA). "Opening the eyes" refers to a ceremony, or series of ceremonies, that accompanies the installation of a buddha image or painting, which specifically involves either dotting the pupils of an image or ritually dropping eyedrops into its eyes, in order to animate it. After the image has been "enspirited" (rushen) by placing on the image embroidered five-colored thread, coins (to represent dragon's eyes), and a mirror, the formal ritual begins by making offerings of incense, flowers, and lamps or candles before the newly installed image; at the conclusion of the ceremony, while reciting various MANTRA, the pupils of the eyes of the image are dotted with ink, thus literally "opening" them. (For this reason, in Korea, the ritual is most commonly known as "dotting the eyes," or chŏman; see DIANYAN.) By thus opening the buddha-eye (foyan) through the performance of this ritual, the image is vested with numinous power, thus making it "come alive." In Japan, the term kaigen is generally used for this buddha-consecration ceremony rather than tengen. Kaigen is then divided into the kaigen of phenomena (*ji*; see SHI) and the kaigen of principle (*ri*; see LI), which refer respectively to ceremonies consecrating a buddha image or the scriptures that might be enshrined inside the image and ceremonies that imbue the image with spiritual charisma. The ritual is also known as "opening the light [of the eyes]" (kaiguang; kaiguangming), and other variations. See also NETRAPRATIṢṬHĀPANA.

**Kaiyuan Shijiao lu**. (J. Kaigen Shakkyōroku; K. Kaewŏn Sŏkkyo nok 開元釋教録). In Chinese, "Record of ŚĀKYAMUNI's

Teachings, Compiled during the Kaiyuan Era"; a comprehensive catalogue (JINGLU) of Buddhist texts compiled by the monk Zhisheng (658–740) in 730. The catalogue began as Zhisheng's own private record of Buddhist scriptures but was adopted soon afterward by the Tang imperial court as an official catalogue of the Chinese Buddhist canon (DAZANGJING) and entered into the canon as well. Zhisheng divided his catalogue into two major sections, a chronological register (rolls one through ten) and a topical register (rolls eleven through twenty). The chronological register contains a list of translated scriptures, organized according to translator's name and the period during which the text was translated. Because this register provides alternative titles of texts, numbers of volumes and rolls, names of translators, and a list of alternate translations, it is an invaluable tool for studying the production and circulation of Buddhist texts in medieval China. The topical register contains "lists of canonical texts" (ruzang lu), which subsequently became the standard rosters from which East Asian Buddhism constructed its canon. This roster also includes 406 titles of texts classified as APOCRYPHA, that is, scriptures listed as either of "doubtful authenticity" (YIJING) or explicitly "spurious" (weijing), which Zhisheng determined were probably of indigenous Chinese origin and therefore not authentic translations of the Buddha's words (BUDDHAVACANA). The renown of the catalogue is due to the great strides Zhisheng made toward eliminating discrepancies between the chronological and topical rosters, inconsistencies that had marred previous catalogues. The content and structure of all later catalogues is derived from Zhisheng's work, making the *Kaiyuan Shijiao lu* the most important of all the Buddhist scriptural catalogues compiled in East Asia.

**Kakacūpamasutta**. (C. Moulipoqunna jing; J. Murihagunnakyō; K. Morip'agunna kyŏng 牟犁破群那經). In Pāli, "Simile of the Saw Discourse"; the twenty-first sutta of the MAJJHIMANIKĀYA (a separate SARVĀSTIVĀDA recension appears as the 193rd SŪTRA in the Chinese translation of the MADHYAMĀGAMA). According to the Pāli recension, the Buddha preached this sutta at Sāvatthi (ŚRĀVASTĪ), in conjunction with the admonishment of the monk Moliya Phagguna, who was overly friendly with nuns and angry at others' criticism of his behavior. Moliya Phagguna remained recalcitrant even after being admonished; in response, the Buddha spoke to his disciples of the harmfulness of anger and of the need for patience even in the most heinous of circumstances, such as if someone were sawing off one's limbs. Instead of giving in to hatred, such an event would offer an opportunity to develop loving-kindness by radiating loving thoughts even to one's attackers.

**Kaksŏng**. (K) (覺性). See PYŎGAM KAKSŎNG.

**Kakuban**. (覺鑁) (1095–1143). Japanese monk and putative founder of the Shingi branch of the SHINGONSHŪ, also known as Mitsugon Sonja (Venerable Secret Adornment). Kakuban was a native of Fujitsu no shō in Hizen (present-day Saga). In 1107, Kakuban became a monk at the monastery NINNAJI in Kyōto and studied the fundamentals of esoteric teachings (MIKKYŌ) under the eminent master Kanjo (1052–1125). Kakuban spent the next year in Nara, where he is said to have immersed himself in doctrinal studies at the monasteries of KŌFUKUJI and TŌDAIJI. In 1110, he returned to Ninnaji and was tonsured by Kanjo. In 1112, Kakuban began studying the eighteen ritual procedures according to KŪKAI's *Jūhachi geiin*, and the next year he received the KONGŌKAI and TAIZŌKAI MAṆḌALAS. In 1114, Kakuban received the full monastic precepts at Tōdaiji, and later that year he climbed KŌYASAN where he met the monk Shoren (d.u.). The next year, Kakuban studied a ritual known as the kumonjihō dedicated to ĀKĀŚAGARBHA under the monk Myōjaku (d.u.), and, during his stay on Mt. Kōya, Kakuban is said to have also received the consecration (ABHIṢEKA) of DHARMA transmission (J. denbō kanjō) eight times. In 1121, Kakuban received the three SAMAYA precepts and consecration of the two maṇḍalas from Kanjo at the sanctuary (dōjō) located in Ninnaji. In 1130, Kakuban established the temple Denbōin on Mt. Kōya with the support of retired Emperor Toba (1107–1123). There he attempted to reinstate a ritual of esoteric transmission known as the denbōe. When the temple proved to be too small to hold a great assembly, Kakuban again established the larger temples Daidenbōin and Mitsugon'in on Kōyasan in 1132. Kakuban subsequently devoted himself to developing a new esoteric ritual tradition that could incorporate the disparate ritual traditions that had developed in Kyōto, Nara, HIEIZAN, and other monastic centers. This new ritual tradition came to be known as the Denbōinryū. In 1134, Kakuban was appointed the head (zasu) of the monasteries of Daidenbōin and Kongōbuji on Mt. Kōya, but Kakuban's rise to power was soon contested by the conservative factions of Kongōbuji monks with ties to the monasteries of TŌJI and Daigoji. As a result, Kakuban retired to his monastery of Mitsugon'in. In 1140, the monks of Kongōbuji launched a violent attack on Daidenbōin and Mitsugon'in, which forced Kakuban to flee to Mt. Negoro in Wakayama. In 1288, the split between Kakuban's new ritual tradition (later known as Shingi or "new meaning") and the old traditions of Tōji and Kongōbuji was formalized by the monk Raiyu's (1226–1304) move of Daidenbōin and Mitsugon'in to Mt. Negoro. Kakuban is particularly well known for his efforts towards reestablishing the study of Kūkai's writings as the central organizing principle for the study of mikkyō ritual traditions. Kakuban is commonly regarded as having developed a new approach to nenbutsu (see NIANFO), or invocation of the name of the buddha AMITĀBHA, known as the "esoteric recitation," or himitsu nenbutsu. However, by Kakuban's time nenbutsu practice in esoteric Buddhist contexts had already become a nearly ubiquitous feature of monastic and lay practice in Japan, and it would therefore be more accurate to regard Kakuban's writings on this topic as an attempt to propose a unified nenbutsu perspective for the diverse factions of monks and ascetics (HIJIRI) who had come to Mt. Kōya in search of rebirth in the pure lands and abodes of

MAITREYA, Amitābha, MAÑJUŚRĪ, AVALOKITEŚVARA, etc. Long after his death, Emperor Higashiyama (r. 1687–1709) in 1690 gave Kakuban the title Kōgyō Daishi.

**Kakuda Kātyāyana**. (P. Pakudha Kaccāyana; T. Ka tya'i bu nog can; C. Jialuojiutuo jiazhanyan; J. Karakuda Kasen'en; K. Karagut'a Kajŏnyŏn 迦羅鳩馱迦旃延). One of the so-called six heretical teachers mentioned in the Buddhist scriptures as rivals or opponents of the Buddha; he is associated with MASKARIN GOŚĀLĪPUTRA (d. c. 488 BCE) and the ĀJĪVAKA group. Kakuda's doctrine is described as that of nonaction (P. akiriyavāda), viz., a type of antinomianism: because there are seven eternal and unchangeable elements—earth, water, fire, air, pleasure, pain, and the soul—there is therefore no KARMAN and no such thing as knowledge and ignorance, good and bad, etc. He also argued that there is no such thing as murder, because when a sword splits a head in half, the sword has simply passed between the spaces in the seven elements. As a teacher, Kakuda was apparently annoyed by questions. He considered it a sin to touch cold water, refusing to bathe when hot water was not available and constructing a mound of earth in expiation whenever it was necessary for him to ford a stream. In some sources, he is described as having a large and devoted following; in others, as not commanding the respect of his disciples.

**Kakukai**. [alt. Kakkai] (覺海) (1142–1223). An early Kamakura-period Japanese scholar-monk from Keōin temple on Mt. Kōya (see KŌYASAN), and the thirty-seventh temple administrator (J. kengyō) of Kongōbuji; his sobriquet was Nanshōbō. Kakukai is especially known for his "immanentalist" SHINGON pure land thought, emphasizing the position that this very world is itself the PURE LAND, and that seeking rebirth in the pure land as a post-mortem destination should not be the main goal of Buddhist practice. His views on the pure land are similar to those of KAKUBAN. However, Kakuban, like Kakukai's student DŌHAN, viewed the post-mortem attainment of rebirth in a pure land as a worthwhile goal. Many of Kakukai's students, such as Dōhan, Hosshō, Shinben, and others, came to be regarded as paragons of the Shingon academic tradition on Mt. Kōya. Kakukai is also the author of an important medieval dharma lecture (J. hōgo) written in vernacular Japanese entitled *Kakukai hokkyō hōgo*.

**Kakunyo**. (覺如) (1270–1351). A Japanese priest of the JŌDO SHINSHŪ tradition, also known by his posthumous name Shūshō. Kakunyo was the great-grandson of the Jōdo Shinshū patriarch SHINRAN. As a young man, Kakunyo first studied on HIEIZAN and in Nara, and later studied Jōdo Shinshū teachings under Nyoshin (1239–1300), the second main priest of HONGANJI. In 1310, Kakunyo became the third main priest of Honganji. Thereafter, he spent much of his time traveling to spread Shinran's teachings, before passing away in 1351. He authored a number of texts, including the *Hōonkō shiki*, the *Shinran shōnin den e*, the *Shūi kotokuden*, the *Kudenshō*, the *Kaijashō*, the *Shūjishō*, the *Honganshō*, the *Ganganshō*, the *Shusse gan'i*, and the *Saiyōshō*.

**kāla**. In Sanskrit, "time." See TRIKĀLA.

**Kālacakratantra**. (T. Dus kyi 'khor lo rgyud). A late ANUTTARAYOGATANTRA that was highly influential in Tibet. Although the title of the tantra is often translated as "Wheel of Time," this translation is not attested in the text itself. Kālacakra is the name of the central buddha of the tantra, and the tantra deals extensively with time (kāla) as well as various macrocosmic and microcosmic cycles or wheels (CAKRA). According to legend, King SUCANDRA came to India from his kingdom of ŚAMBHALA and asked that the Buddha set forth a teaching that would allow him to practice the dharma without renouncing the world. In response, the Buddha, while remaining at Vulture Peak (GṚDHRAKŪṬAPARVATA) in RĀJAGṚHA in the guise of a monk, set forth the *Kālacakratantra* at Dhānyakaṭaka in southern India (near present-day Amarāvatī) in the guise of the buddha Kālacakra. The king returned to śambhala, where he transcribed the tantra in twelve thousand verses. This text is referred to as the root tantra (mūlatantra) and is no longer extant. He also wrote a commentary in sixty thousand verses, also lost. He built a three-dimensional Kālacakra MAṆḌALA at the center of the country, which was transformed into an ideal realm for Buddhist practice, with 960 million villages. The eighth king of śambhala, Mañjuśrīkīrti, condensed the original version of the tantra into the abridged version (the *Laghukālacakra*). A later king of śambhala, Puṇḍarīka, composed the VIMALAPRABHĀ commentary, considered crucial for understanding the tantra. These two texts were eventually transported from śambhala to India. Internal evidence in the text makes it possible to date the composition of the tantra rather precisely to between the dates 1025 and 1040 CE. This was the period of Muslim invasions of northern India under Mahmud of Ghazni, during which great destruction of Buddhist institutions occurred. The tantra, drawing on Hindu mythology, describes a coming apocalyptic war in which Buddhist armies will sweep out of śambhala, defeat the barbarians (mleccha), described as being followers of Madhumati (i.e., Muhammad), and restore the dharma in India. After its composition in northern India, the tantra was promulgated by such figures as Piṇḍo and his disciple ATIŚA, as well as NĀROPA. From India, it spread to Nepal and Tibet. The millennial quality of the tantra has manifested itself at particular moments in Tibetan history. Prior to World War II, the PAṆ CHEN LAMA bestowed the Kālacakra initiation in China in an effort to repel the Japanese invaders. The fourteenth DALAI LAMA has given the initiation many times around the world to promote world peace. ¶ The tantra is an anuttarayogatantra dedicated to the buddha Kālacakra and his consort Viśvamātā. However, it differs from other tantras of this class in several ways, including its emphasis on the attainment of a body of "empty form" (śūnyatābimba) and on its six-branched yoga (ṣaḍaṅgayoga). The tantra itself, that is, the *Laghukālacakra* or

"Abridged Kālacakra," has five chapters, which in the Tibetan commentarial tradition is divided into three sections: outer, inner, and other or alternative. The outer, corresponding to the first chapter, deals with the cosmos and treats such topics as cosmology, astrology, chronology, and eschatology (the story of the apocalyptic war against the barbarians is told there). For example, this section describes the days of the year; each of the days is represented in the full Kālacakra maṇḍala as 360 golden (day/male) and dark (night/female) deities in union, with a single central Kālacakra and consort (YAB YUM) in the center. The universe is described as a four-tiered maṇḍala, whose various parts are homologous to the cosmic body of a buddha. This section was highly influential in Tibetan astrology and calendrics. The new calendar of the Tibetans, used to this day, starts in the year 1027 and is based on the Kālacakra system. The inner Kālacakra, corresponding to the second chapter, deals with human embryology, tantric physiology, medicine, yoga, and alchemy. The human body is described as a microcosm of the universe. The other or alternative Kālacakra, corresponding to the third, fourth, and fifth chapters, sets forth the practice of Kālacakra, including initiation (ABHIṢEKA), SĀDHANA, and knowledge (JÑĀNA). Here, in the stage of generation (UTPATTIKRAMA), the initiate imagines oneself experiencing conception, gestation, and birth as the child of Kālacakra and Viśmamātā. In the stage of completion (NIṢPANNAKRAMA), one practices the six-branched yoga, which consists of retraction (pratyāhāra), concentration (DHYĀNA), breath control (PRĀṆĀYĀMA), retention (dhāraṇā), recollection (ANUSMṚTI), and SAMĀDHI. In the last of these six branches, 21,600 moments of immutable bliss are created, which course through the system of channels and CAKRAS to eliminate the material aspects of the body, resulting in a body of "empty form" and the achievement of buddhahood as Kālacakra. The *Sekoddeśaṭīkā* of Naḍapāda (or Nāropa) sets forth this distinctive six-branched yoga, unique to the Kālacakra system. ¶ BU STON, the principal redactor of the canon in Tibetan translation, was a strong proponent of the tantra and wrote extensively about it. DOL PO PA SHES RAB RGYAL MTSHAN, a fourteenth-century JO NANG PA writer, championed the *Kālacakra* over all other Buddhist writings, assigning its composition to a golden age (kṛtayuga). Red mda' ba gzhon nu blo gros, an important scholar associated with SA SKYA sect, regarded the tantra as spurious. TSONG KHA PA, who was influenced by all of these writers, accepted the *Kālacakratantra* as an authentic ANUTTARAYOGATANTRA but put it in a category by itself.

**Kālāmasutta**. (C. Qielan jing; J. Garankyō; K. Karam kyŏng 伽藍經). In Pāli, "Instruction to the Kālāmas"; popular Western designation for a Pāli sutta (SŪTRA) in the AṄGUTTARANIKĀYA; delivered to the Kālāma people of Kesaputta, which is more commonly titled in modern Southeast Asian editions of the Pāli canon as the *Kesamuttisutta* or *Kesaputtisutta*. (A separate SARVĀSTIVĀDA recension appears as the sixteenth SŪTRA in the Chinese translation of the MADHYAMĀGAMA; the Sinographs Qielan are a transcription of Kālāma, so this seems to have been the title used for the scripture in the northwest Indian tradition). The sermon is prominently cited in Western writings on Buddhism for its advocacy of free inquiry and a putatively rational approach to religion, which is exempt from intolerance and dogmatism. In classical commentarial materials, however, the text is not interpreted in this way and is rarely mentioned. According to the Pāli recension, the Kālāmas had been visited by many religious teachers and had received conflicting testimony from them on what constituted the religious life; they also were put off by these teachers' tendency to praise only their own dogmas and to revile those of their rivals. Confused, the Kālāmas asked the Buddha to arbitrate. In his response, the Buddha rejects the validity of testimony simply because it is widely known, grounded in "tradition" (anussava; S. ANUŚRAVA), appearing in scripture, or taught by a respected teacher. All these standards are said to be unreliable for understanding truth and falsity. Instead, the Buddha encourages them to follow what they themselves learn through their own training to be blamable or praiseworthy, harmful or beneficial. The Buddha then helps the Kālāmas to understand for themselves that the three afflictions of greed or craving (RĀGA; LOBHA), hatred (DVEṢA; P. dosa), and delusion (MOHA) are harmful and should therefore be abandoned, while their absence is beneficial and should therefore be developed. The discourse concludes with the Buddha's instruction on how to project in all directions the four divine abidings (BRAHMAVIHĀRA) of loving-kindness (MAITRĪ), compassion (KARUṆĀ), empathetic joy (MUDITĀ), and impartiality (UPEKṢĀ) and a brief account of the solace that comes to those whose minds are free from hatred and defilement.

**kalaśābhiṣeka**. (T. bum dbang; C. baoping guanding; J. hōbyōkanjō; K. pobyŏng kwanjŏng 寶瓶灌頂). In Sanskrit, "vase empowerment," "jar empowerment," or "pot empowerment"; one of the four empowerments or initiations (ABHIṢEKA) of ANUTTARAYOGATANTRA, the other three being the secret empowerment (GUHYĀBHIṢEKA), the knowledge of the consort empowerment (PRAJÑĀJÑĀNĀBHIṢEKA), and the fourth empowerment (CATURTHĀBHIṢEKA). The vase empowerment is the only one of the four that is used in the three other tantras of KRIYĀTANTRA, CARYĀTANTRA, and YOGATANTRA. The term itself generally is meant to designate a series of empowerments or initiations, variously enumerated, but commonly counted as five: the water, crown, vajra, bell, and name empowerments, with a sixth, called the vajra master (VAJRĀCĀRYA) added in yogatantra and *anuttarayogatantra*. The vase empowerment may be publicly performed, often in large gatherings, and is considered a prerequisite for the three other empowerments.

**kālasūtra**. (T. thig nag; C. heisheng diyu; J. kokujō jigoku; K. hŭksŭng chiok 黑繩地獄). In Sanskrit, "black string"; the second of the eight hot hells (see NĀRAKA) of the Buddhist cosmos. In this hell, the henchmen of YAMA tie the unfortunate denizens to the ground with hot iron chains; then, marking lines on their victims' bodies with black string, they use those lines as guides to cut the body into pieces with burning saws. After the bodies of the denizens of this hell have been cut into pieces, they are made whole again and the process is repeated.

**kalaviṅka**. (T. ka la ping ka; C. jialupinqie niao; J. karyōbinga chō; K. karyukpin'ga cho 迦陸頻伽鳥). In Sanskrit, "kalaviṅka (cuckoo) bird"; a mythical bird from the HIMĀLAYA mountains with a call said to be far more beautiful than that of all other birds and so compelling that it could be heard even before the bird had hatched. The bird and its call are used as a simile for the BODHISATTVAs and their aspiration for enlightenment (BODHICITTA), which are so compelling and persuasive that, even before they have achieved complete, perfect enlightenment (ANUTTARASAMYAKSAṂBODHI), they are still far superior to all other spiritual adepts. As the AVATAṂSAKASŪTRA says, "It is like the kalaviṅka bird, which, even before it has hatched, has such great dynamism that other birds cannot challenge it. BODHISATTVA-MAHĀSATTVAS are just the same: even before they have hatched from inside the egg of birth-and-death, the dynamism deriving from the merit associated with generating the aspiration for enlightenment is so compelling that ŚRĀVAKAS and PRATYEKABUDDHAs cannot challenge them." The DAZHIDU LUN explains, "It is like the kalaviṅka bird, which even before it has hatched, has a call that is far more subtle and sublime than that of other birds. Bodhisattva-mahāsattvas are also just the same: although they may not have yet hatched from the egg of ignorance, the sound of their preaching and discoursing is far superior to that of the śrāvakas, pratyekabuddhas, and non-Buddhists."

**Kālayaśas**. (C. Jiangliangyeshe; J. Kyōryōyasha; K. Kangnyangyasa 畺良耶舍) (383–442). A Central Asian monk who was one of the early translators of Buddhist texts into Chinese. Kālayaśas arrived at Jiankang, the capital of the Liu-Song dynasty, in 424, where he became an adviser to Emperor Wen. Two works of translation are attributed to him in the Buddhist catalogues. Perhaps the most influential work with which he is associated is the GUAN WULIANGSHOU JING, the "meditation-sūtra" on AMITĀBHA Buddha, which is one of the three foundational texts of the East Asian PURE LAND traditions. Because no Sanskrit recension of this sūtra is attested, this scripture is now considered to be either a Central Asian or a Chinese indigenous scripture (see APOCRYPHA), and its ascription to Kālayaśas is problematic. The second text that he translated is the *Guan Yaowang Yaoshang er pusa jing* ("Sūtra on Visualizing the Two Bodhisattvas Bhaiṣajyarāja and Bhaiṣajyasamudgata"), an early sūtra on the Medicine Buddha/Bodhisattva cult associated with the bodhisattva BHAIṢAJYARĀJA and the buddha BHAIṢAJYAGURU.

**Kālika**. [alt. Karīka] (T. Dus ldan; C. Jialijia zunzhe; J. Karika sonja; K. Kariga chonja 迦里迦尊者). The Sanskrit name of one of the sixteen ARHAT elders (ṢOḌAŚASTHAVIRA), who were charged by the Buddha with protecting his dispensation until the advent of the next Buddha, MAITREYA. Kālika is said to reside in the Lion's Island (Siṃhatā; viz., Sri Lanka) with one thousand disciples. According to Chinese tradition, Kālika used to be an elephant tamer. (Because elephants have both great strength and endurance, they are a common symbol of the BUDDHADHARMA.) Because of this talent, he earned the nickname "Elephant-Riding Arhat" (Jixiang Luohan). In Tibetan iconography, he holds two earrings; East Asian images often portray him as an old man reading a scroll. In Chanyue Guanxiu's standard Chinese depiction, Kālika is encircled by long eyebrows, sitting in easy comfort on a rock, with his right arm wrapped around his right knee, and his long eyebrows twisted around his fingers. His right hand is placed naturally on an adjacent rock.

**Kālī Kururagharikā**. (C. Jialijia; J. Karika; K. Kariga 迦梨迦). Lay disciple of the Buddha, whom he declared to be foremost among laywomen who are able to generate faith even from hearsay; she was also well known as the mother of the arahant (ARHAT) SOṆA-KOṬIKAṆṆA (S. Śroṇa-Koṭikarṇa). According to the Pāli account, Kālī was born in Rājagaha (RĀJAGṚHA) but lived with her husband in the city of Kururaghara in the kingdom of AVANTI. When she was pregnant with her son Soṇa, she returned to her parent's house, and there one evening, while relaxing on a balcony of the house, she overheard two disciples of the Buddha discuss the marvelous qualities of their teacher and his teachings. As she listened, faith (saddhā; S. ŚRADDHĀ) grew in her and she became a stream-enterer (sotāpanna; S. SROTAĀPANNA). That same night she gave birth to Soṇa. When Kālī returned to Kururaghara, she devoted herself to serving the arhat MAHĀKĀTYĀYANA, who was a family friend and who frequently visited their town. Her son became a merchant, but on a caravan journey he encountered a series of frightful visions that inspired him to take ordination under Mahākātyāyana, who served as his preceptor (upajjhāya; S. UPĀDHYĀYA). When Soṇa later visited the Buddha, Kālī prepared a costly rug and asked that he spread it out in the Buddha's chamber. Soṇa had won praise from the Buddha for his eloquence (PRATIBHĀNA), and, on his return to Kururaghara, Kālī requested that he preach to her in the same manner as he had before the Buddha. Kālī Kururagharikā was considered the most senior of female disciples to have attained stream-entry. She was the devoted friend and companion of KĀTIYĀNĪ, another eminent laywoman praised by the Buddha.

**Kaliṅga**. (T. Ka ling ga; Jielingqie; J. Karyōga; K. Kallŭngga 羯陵伽). An Indian kingdom on the eastern coast of the subcontinent; identified with the modern state of Orissa. In the eighth year of his reign, the Mauryan emperor AŚOKA (third century BCE) conquered Kaliṅga. In his inscriptions, Aśoka states that the resulting carnage caused him to turn away from violence and toward the dharma. Kaliṅga is mentioned in the Pāli canon as one of seven states that flourished at the time of the mythical king, Renu, but it is not included in the classical list of sixteen nations (janapada). During his previous life as VESSANTARA, the BODHISATTVA gave the kingdom of Kaliṅga his white elephant, Pacaya, in order to alleviate that country's drought. A TOOTH RELIC of the Buddha is said to have been enshrined at the Kaliṅga capital, Dantapura, and, later during the reign of the Sinhalese king, Sirimeghavanna, it was carried to Sri Lanka, where it was installed as the palladium of the Sinhalese royal house. From ancient times, there were close relations between the kings of Kaliṅga and Sri Lanka. During the reign of Aggabodhi II, the king and queen of Kaliṅga came to the island, renounced their thrones, and entered the order. The royal houses of both kingdoms frequently exchanged brides, and many descendants of the Kaliṅga dynasty are mentioned as having been crowned king of Sri Lanka. Māgha, the twelfth-century invader and scourge of Buddhism on the island, is also said to have hailed from Kaliṅga. During the early centuries of the Common Era, Kaliṅga was an important source for Buddhist and Brahmanical cultural influence among the Pyu and Mon peoples of Burma, contributing to the emergence of Buddhist civilization in Southeast Asia. Kaliṅga is also one of the twenty-four sacred sites associated with the CAKRASAṂVARATANTRA. See also PĪṬHA.

**Kālodāyin**. (P. Kāḷudāyin; T. 'Char byed nag po; C. Jialiutuoyi; J. Karudai; K. Karyut'ai 迦留陀夷). An ARHAT elder, whom the Buddha declared to be foremost among his ordained disciples in gladdening clans. According to the Pāli tradition, he was the son of one of King ŚUDDHODANA's ministers (purohita) at KAPILAVASTU and a playmate of the young BODHISATTVA SIDDHĀRTHA. After his son renounced the world, Śuddhodana made Kālodāyin his most trusted councilor. When the king heard that his son had won enlightenment, he repeatedly sent delegations from his court to invite the Buddha to the palace; but on each occasion the delegates became arhats after hearing the Buddha preach and forgot their mission. Finally, the king sent Kālodāyin to invite the Buddha at a suitable time. Like his predecessors, Kālodāyin also was ordained and soon became an arhat, but he did not neglect his commitment to the king. Conveying the invitation when the countryside was in full bloom, he accompanied the Buddha on a sixty-day journey from RĀJAGṚHA to Kapilavastu, each day flying with his ṚDDHI powers to Śuddhodana's palace to keep the king and his people appraised of the Buddha's progress. By the time the Buddha reached his hometown, the entire city of Kapilavastu was anticipating the Buddha's arrival. It was for this accomplishment that Kālodāyin was honored by the Buddha as the foremost in gladdening clans or reconciling families. Different traditions describe Kālodāyin's ghastly end. According to the SARVĀSTIVĀDA VINAYA, Kālodāyin was beheaded by the jealous husband of one of his lay supporters, and the severed head was buried in horse manure. Another account states that Kālodāyin by chance learned of a brāhmaṇa wife's affair; in order to keep the affair secret, she had her servant behead the monk.

**kalpa**. (P. kappa; T. bskal pa; C. jie; J. kō; K. kŏp 劫). In Sanskrit, "eon" or "age"; the unit of measurement for cosmological time. There are a number of types of kalpas. An "intermediate kalpa" (antarakalpa), often a synonym of the generic kalpa, is said to mark the aeon during which the lifetime gradually decreases from being essentially eternal down to ten years. A "great kalpa" (mahākalpa) is composed of eighty intermediate kalpas and is the longest of the kalpas governing creation. (In the Pāli tradition, a mahākappa is instead said to be four "incalculable eons.") In the cycle of creation and dissolution of the universe, a great kalpa is divided into four periods of twenty intermediate kalpas. These are (1) the "kalpa of creation" (VIVARTAKALPA), the period from the arising of the primordial wind that produces the receptacle world and the arising of the hell denizens; this is followed by (2) the "kalpa of abiding" (VIVARTASTHĀYIKALPA); (3) the "kalpa of dissolution" (SAṂVARTAKALPA), the period between the time when the hell denizens vanish through the dissolution of the receptacle world (BHĀJANALOKA), viz., the physical environment; and finally (4) the "kalpa of nothingness" (SAṂVARTASTHĀYIKALPA). The longest of all kalpas is called the "incalculable kalpa" (ASAṂKHYEYAKALPA), which, despite its name, has been calculated as a mahākalpa to the sixtieth power. The BODHISATTVA path leading to buddhahood is presumed to take not one, but three, "incalculable eons" to complete. A kalpa during which a buddha appears in the world is known as an "auspicious" or "fortunate" kalpa (BHADRAKALPA).

**kalpanā**. [alt. kalpana] (T. rtog pa; C. fenbie; J. funbetsu; K. punbyŏl 分別). In Sanskrit, "thought," "imagination," or "conceptual construction"; generally carrying the negative connotation of a delusive fantasy and misconception, in which the object of thought is either nonexistent or falsely imagined. (The Chinese translates instead the connotation of conceptual "discrimination.") Kalpanā is often contrasted negatively with direct perception (PRATYAKṢA), especially yogic direct perception (YOGIPRATYAKṢA), in which reality is perceived directly without the medium of mental images. See also VIKALPA; WANGXIANG.

**kalpavṛksa**. (T. dpag bsam shing; C. yuanshengshu; J. enshōju; K. wŏnsaengsu 圓生樹). In Sanskrit, "wish-granting tree"; a magical tree whose fruit takes the form of whatever one wishes for. Numerous such trees appear in Buddhist legends. Perhaps the most famous of them is said to grow on the slopes of Mount SUMERU, with its roots located in the realm of the demigods (ASURA) but its leaves, branches, and fruit located above in the realm of the divinities (DEVA). Because the demigods were thus unable to enjoy the fruit of the tree that grows in their land, they became jealous of the divinities and fought against them. There are several varieties of wish-granting trees, including the pārijāta.

**kalpikāraka**. (P. kappiyakāraka; T. rung ba byed pa; C. jingren; J. jōnin; K. chŏngin 淨人). In Sanskrit, lit. "one who makes it appropriate," viz., "legalizer," referring to a lay "steward" or "surrogate"; one who receives donations on behalf of monks and converts them into appropriate requisites. Monks are forbidden to physically touch certain kinds of donated goods. The VINAYA rules entailing forfeiture and confession (NAIḤSARGIKAPĀYATTIKA; P. nissaggiyapācittiya), for example, prohibit monks from handling gold and silver, so a monk out on his daily alms round (PIṆḌAPĀTA) would not be allowed to receive a monetary donation offered by a layperson. The kalpikāraka attending the monk would instead serve as his stand-in, receiving the money in the monk's stead and keeping it until such time as the monk required some necessity or requisite. The kalpikāraka would then use the money to purchase the required item on the monk's behalf. This is the only major ecclesiastical office that is held by a layman, not a monk. See also VAIYĀPṚTYA (KARA).

**Kalu Rinpoche**. (1905–1989). An important modern meditation master and teacher of Tibetan Buddhism. Recognized as an incarnation (SPRUL SKU) of the KARMA BKA' BRGYUD master 'JAM MGON KONG SPRUL, Kalu Rinpoche was ordained at the age of thirteen by the eleventh SI TU RINPOCHE. Kalu Rinpoche began serious meditation study at an early age, undertaking his first three-year retreat at the age of sixteen. He also received the transmission of the teachings of the SHANGS PA sect of Bka' brgyud. He later served as the meditation teacher at DPAL SPUNGS monastery. Following the Chinese invasion, Kalu Rinpoche left Tibet in 1962 and first stayed at a small monastery outside of Darjeeling, India. He later settled in Sonada, West Bengal, where he built a three-year retreat center, teaching there before traveling internationally for ten years (1971–1981). In 1971, he traveled to France and the United States, at the request of the DALAI LAMA and the KARMA PA, in order to educate Westerners in Buddhism. During those ten years, Kalu Rinpoche founded many meditation and dharma centers in Canada, the United States, and Europe, with his main meditation school in Vancouver, Canada. Kalu Rinpoche led his first three-year retreat for Western students of Tibetan Buddhism in France in 1976. His full name is Kar ma rang 'byung kun khyab phrin las.

**kalyāṇamitra**. (P. kalyāṇamitta; T. dge ba'i bshes gnyen; C. shanzhishi; J. zenchishiki; K. sŏnjisik 善知識). In Sanskrit, lit. "good friend"; viz., "spiritual guide," or "religious mentor"; a spiritual companion or mentor (sometimes, though rarely, referring even to the Buddha himself) who encourages one in salutary directions and helps one to remain focused on matters of real religious import. Association with a kalyāṇamitra is said to be one of the foundations of religious progress: it is one of the seven things conducive to the welfare and weal of monks and one of the indicators that a monk will perfect the seven constituents of awakening (BODHYAṄGA). In the absence of "good friends," it was thought preferable for monks to lead the solitary life of the rhinoceros (see KHAḌGAVIṢĀṆA; KHAḌGAVIṢĀṆAKALPA). Three kinds of kalyāṇamitra are described in the literature: an instructor, a fellow practitioner, and a lay supporter (DĀNAPATI). The Tibetan title "geshe" (DGE BSHES), referring to a monk who has successfully completed the scholastic curriculum of the DGE LUGS sect, is a contraction of the Tibetan translation of kalyāṇamitra.

**Kalyāṇī inscriptions**. The Pāli term for a set of stele inscriptions erected at PEGU, the capital of the Mon kingdom of Rāmañña, by King DHAMMACETĪ in 1479. The inscriptions are written in Pāli and Mon and celebrate the successful purification of the Mon SAṂGHA through the introduction of the Sri Lankan MAHĀVIHĀRA ordination lineage. As a document, the Kalyāṇī inscriptions follow the conventions of a Sinhalese sāsana katikāvata: that is, they are composed of a list of monastic regulations imposed by the court on the entire saṃgha throughout the realm, prefaced by a long historical introduction. The purpose of the introduction, in part, is to legitimate the new regulations by appealing to historical precedent, such as the legend of Dhammāsoka (AŚOKA).

**Kalyāṇīsīmā**. An ordination site established at the Mon capital of Pegu in 1476 by King DHAMMACETĪ (r. 1472–1492). The construction of the Kalyāṇīsīmā marked the beginning of the reformation of the Mon SAṂGHA in accordance with orthodox Sinhalese standards. The reformation is recorded by Dhammacetī in the KALYĀṆĪ INSCRIPTIONS that were erected at the site. Dhammacetī selected a delegation of twenty-two Mon monks to travel to Sri Lanka, where, at a site of the Kalyāṇīvihāra near modern Colombo, the monks were laicized and reordained into the MAHĀVIHĀRA tradition. Upon their return, the newly reordained monks consecrated the Kalyāṇīsīmā at Pegu. Under the leadership of an elder monk ordained in Sri Lanka some twenty-six years earlier, the king ordered all new monks in his realm to be ordained into the MAHĀVIHĀRA tradition at the Kalyāṇīsīmā. Simultaneously, the existing saṃgha was purged of malefactors, and monks found to be worthy of continuing in the order were encouraged to return to lay status and be reordained at the Kalyāṇīsīmā. In this way, the Mon saṃgha, which had been long divided into rival monastic lineages, was reunited into a single fraternity descended from the Mahāvihāra tradition in Sri Lanka. The procedures employed by Dhammacetī to effect his reforms of the Mon saṃgha were taken as a blueprint for the later THUDHAMMA reformation of the Burmese saṃgha carried out by King BODAWPAYA beginning in 1782.

**kāma**. (T. 'dod pa; C. yu; J. yoku; K. yok 欲). In Sanskrit and Pāli, "sensuality," especially in the sense of sexual desire. Kāma often appears compounded with various intensifiers to emphasize its affective dimensions. KĀMARĀGA means "sensual craving" and is listed as the fourth of ten fetters (SAṂYOJANA) that keep beings bound to the cycle of rebirth (SAṂSĀRA). Kāmarāga is the desire for physical pleasure and sensuality; it belongs to the more general psychological category of craving (S. TṚṢṆĀ;

P. taṇhā, lit. "thirst"), which ceaselessly seeks pleasure here and there and is the chief root of suffering. The five "strands of sensuality" (kāmaguṇa) refer to the sensual pleasures of the five physical senses (see GUṆA). KĀMACCHANDA means "sensual pleasure" or "sensual gratification" and is also classified as one of five hindrances (NĪVARAṆA) that prevent the mind from achieving meditative absorption (DHYĀNA). Kāmacchanda is temporarily overcome with the attainment of the first meditative absorption and is eradicated in its grosser forms by attaining the stage of once-returner (SAKṚDĀGĀMIN), the second degree of Buddhist sanctity or holiness (ĀRYAPUDGALA); it is completely eliminated upon attaining the stage of nonreturner (ANĀGĀMIN), the third and penultimate degree of Buddhist holiness. Finally, KĀMADHĀTU, or the sensuous realm, is the lowest of the three realms of existence (TRAIDHĀTUKA) (excluding the realms of subtle materiality and immateriality) and receives this name because of the predominance of sensuous desire among the beings reborn there.

**kāmacchanda**. (T. 'dod pa la 'dun pa; C. haoyu; J. kōyoku; K. hoyok 好欲). In Sanskrit and Pāli, "sensual pleasure" or "sensual gratification"; an intensification of mere "sensuality" (KĀMA), which is classified as one of five hindrances (NĪVARAṆA) that prevent the mind from achieving meditative absorption (DHYĀNA). Kāmacchanda is temporarily overcome with the attainment of the first meditative absorption and is eradicated in its grosser forms by attaining the stage of once-returner (SAKṚDĀGĀMIN), the second degree of Buddhist sanctity (ĀRYAPUDGALA); it is completely eliminated upon attaining the stage of nonreturner (ANĀGĀMIN), the third and penultimate degree of Buddhist sanctity.

**kāmadhātu**. (T. 'dod khams; C. yujie; J. yokukai; K. yokkye 欲界). In Sanskrit and Pāli, "sensuous realm" or "desire realm"; the lowest of the three realms of existence, so named because the beings there are attached to pleasures derived from the five sense organs (INDRIYA). The dominant force among beings born into this realm is therefore sensuality (KĀMA), and especially the sex drive. The sensuous realm includes the following six rebirth destinies (GATI), in ascending order: denizens of hell (NĀRAKA), hungry ghosts (PRETA), animals (TIRYAK), humans (MANUṢYA), demigods (ASURA), and six levels of sensuous-realm divinities (DEVA). Rebirth in the sensuous realm is the result of past performance of either predominantly unwholesome deeds (in the case of hell denizens, hungry ghosts, animals, and demigods), a mix of unwholesome and wholesome deeds (as with human beings), or predominantly wholesome deeds (the divinities). The beings in the sensuous realm all have a coarser physical constituent. Above the kāmadhātu are the realm of subtle materiality (RŪPADHĀTU) and the realm of immateriality (ĀRŪPYADHĀTU), where sensuality exerts only minimal sway over its beings. The kāmadhātu may also be designated as a world (LOKA), worldly realm (LOKADHĀTU), or "sphere"/"domain" (AVACARA).

**Kamakura daibutsu**. (鎌倉大佛). In Japanese, "Great Buddha of Kamakura"; a colossal bronze buddha image located at KŌTOKUIN, a JŌDOSHŪ temple in Kamakura City, Kanagawa Prefecture, Japan. The Kamakura daibutsu is a huge bronze statue of Amida (S. AMITĀBHA) and is one of Japan's most renowned buddha images. It is forty-four feet high and weighs about ninety-three tons. The first Kamakura shōgun, Minamoto no Yoritomo (1147–1199), saw the colossal buddha image at TŌDAIJI (see NARA DAIBUTSU) that had been restored in 1185 and, inspired, proposed erecting a similar image in his capital of Kamakura. After his premature death, the building campaign was carried out by his court lady Ineda no Tsubone (d.u.) and the monk Jōkō (d.u.) and the image cast by Ōno Gorōemon and Tanji Hisatomo from eight separate bronze plates that were ingeniously pieced together. Casting and gilding of the bronze image began in 1252 and took some twelve years to complete; the new image replaced an earlier wooden statue from 1243 that had been badly damaged in a storm. It was originally located inside a huge wooden shrine hall; the building was destroyed by a tsunami that demolished the entire temple in 1495 but that was not strong enough to budge the massive statue. Without funds for repairs, the image was neglected for years until the Jōdo monk Yūten Ken'yo (1637–1718) arranged for needed restorations in 1712; just behind the image are four bronze plates in the shape of lotus petals, on which are engraved the names of the donors who contributed to the restoration project. The image's head is covered with 656 stylized curls and is disproportionately large so that it will not look small to people viewing it from the ground; the hands are in the meditation gesture (DHYĀNAMUDRĀ) typical of Amitābha images, with both hands displaying encircled thumb and index fingers. The image was repaired in 1923 after the Great Kantō earthquake and once again in 1960–1961. The image is one of the most famous sites in Japan and draws well over a million visitors a year.

**Kamalaśīla**. (T. Ka ma la shī la) (c. 740–795). One of the most important Madhyamaka authors of late Indian Buddhism, a major representative of the Yogācāra-Madhyamaka synthesis, and a participant in the famous BSAM YAS DEBATE. According to Tibetan doxographies, he was a proponent of the YOGĀCĀRA-SVĀTANTRIKA-MADHYAMAKA. Although little is known about his life, according to Tibetan sources he was a monk and teacher at NĀLANDĀ. Tibetan sources also count him as one of three (together with ŚĀNTARAKṢITA and JÑĀNAGARBHA) "Eastern Svātantrikas" (RANG RGYUD SHAR GSUM), suggesting that he was from Bengal. He was clearly a direct disciple of Śāntarakṣita, composing important commentaries on his teacher's two major works, the MADHYAMAKĀLAṂKĀRA and the TATTVASAṂGRAHA. The latter commentary, which is extant in Sanskrit, is an important source for both Hindu and Buddhist philosophical positions in the eighth century. Śāntarakṣita had gone to Tibet at the invitation of the Tibetan king KHRI SRONG LDE BTSAN, where, with the assistance of PADMASAMBHAVA, he founded BSAM

YAS, the first Buddhist monastery in Tibet. According to tradition, at the time of his death Śāntarakṣita warned that a mistaken philosophical view would become established in Tibet and advised the king to invite Kamalaśīla to come to Tibet in order to dispel it. This mistaken view was apparently that of Heshang MOHEYAN, a Northern CHAN (BEI ZONG) monk who had developed a following at the Tibetan court. Kamalaśīla was invited, and a debate was held between the Indian monk and his Chinese counterpart, with the king serving as judge. It is unclear whether a face-to-face debate took place or rather an exchange of documents. According to Tibetan sources, the king declared Kamalaśīla the winner, named MADHYAMAKA as the official philosophical school of his realm, and banished the Chinese contingent. (Chinese records describe a different outcome.) This event, variously known as the BSAM YAS DEBATE, the Council of Bsam yas, and the Council of Lhasa, is regarded as one of the key moments in the history of Tibetan Buddhism. Three of Kamalaśīla's most important works appear to have been composed in response to the issues raised in the debate, although whether all three were composed in Tibet is not established with certainty. These texts, each entitled BHĀVANĀKRAMA or "Stages of Meditation," set forth the process for the potential BODHISATTVA to cultivate BODHICITTA and then develop ŚAMATHA and VIPAŚYANĀ and progress through the bodhisattva stages (BHŪMI) to buddhahood. The cultivation of vipaśyanā requires the use of both scripture (ĀGAMA) and reasoning (YUKTI) to understand emptiness (ŚŪNYATĀ); in the first *Bhāvanākrama*, he sets forth the three forms of wisdom (PRAJÑĀ): the wisdom derived from hearing or learning (ŚRUTAMAYĪPRAJÑĀ), the wisdom derived from thinking and reflection (CINTĀMAYĪPRAJÑĀ), and the wisdom derived from meditation (BHĀVANĀMAYĪPRAJÑĀ). This "gradual" approach, very different from what was advocated in the Chinese CHAN ZONG, is set forth in all three of the *Bhāvanākrama*, which, according to Tibetan tradition, were composed in Tibet after the Bsam yas debate, at the request of the king. However, only the third, and the briefest, directly considers, and refutes, the view of "no mental activity" (amanasikāra), which is associated with Moheyan. It was also during his time in Tibet that Kamalaśīla composed his most important independent (i.e., noncommentarial) philosophical work, the MADHYAMAKĀLOKA, or "Illumination of the Middle Way," a wide-ranging exposition of the Yogācāra-Madhyamaka synthesis. It deals with a number of central epistemological and logical issues to articulate what is regarded as the defining tenet of the Yogācāra-Svātantrika-Madhyamaka school: that major YOGĀCĀRA doctrines, such as "mind-only" (CITTAMĀTRA), and the three natures (TRISVABHĀVA) are important in initially overcoming misconceptions, but they are in fact only provisional (NEYĀRTHA) teachings for those who have not yet understood the Madhyamaka view. The *Madhyamakāloka* is also important for its exploration of such central MAHĀYĀNA doctrines as the TATHĀGATAGARBHA and the question of the EKAYĀNA. On this latter point, Kamalaśīla argues against the Yogācāra position that there are three final vehicles (for the ŚRĀVAKA, PRATYEKABUDDHA, and BODHISATTVA, with some beings excluded from any path to liberation) in favor of the position that there is a single vehicle to buddhahood (BUDDHAYĀNA) for all beings. Kamalaśīla is said to have been murdered in Tibet by partisans of the Chinese position, who caused his death by squeezing his kidneys.

**kāmaloka**. (S). See KĀMADHĀTU.

**kāmamithyācāra**. (P. kāmamicchācāra; T. 'dod pas log par g.yem pa; C. xieyin; J. jain; K. saŭm 邪淫). In Sanskrit, lit. "wrong conduct due to sensuality," the term is generally translated into English as "sexual misconduct"; synonymous with abrahmacarya, lit. "impure conduct." Sexual misconduct constitutes the third of the ten unwholesome courses of action or nonvirtuous deeds (AKUŚALA-KARMAPATHA) and figures prominently in the precepts of both Buddhist clergy and laity. In its most straightforward formulation, sensual misconduct is defined (from the male perspective) as sexual intercourse with an inappropriate partner, often defined as a woman who is under the protection of another male. This would include females who are still under the protection of their father or mother, brother, sister, or relatives; married women; female convicts; and betrothed women. It would also include women who are members of a religious community, such as Buddhist nuns. Such a formulation would seem to permit sexual intercourse between consenting adults, whether married or not. However, further forms of sexual misconduct are often mentioned, including having sexual intercourse at an improper place, such as near a temple, monastery, or STŪPA, in the presence of a religious statue or painting, a relic, or one's teacher; sexual intercourse at an improper time, such as a religious holiday, the night of the full moon or new moon retreats, during the daytime, or when a woman is menstruating or breast-feeding; and sexual intercourse in an improper orifice, defined as any orifice other than the vagina. From this perspective, many sexual practices may be classed as sexual misconduct. In the VINAYA literature, a wide range of what is considered deviant sexual behavior is proscribed, ranging from masturbation to necrophilia. Among the many forms of sexual misconduct, sexual acts that entail "defeat" (PĀRĀJIKA) for a BHIKṢU are those that involve the penetration by the penis of any orifice "to the depth of a sesame seed." For a BHIKṢUṆĪ, acts that entail expulsion include sexual intercourse, lustfully allowing a man to touch her anywhere between the collarbone and the knees, or to lustfully stand with a man, converse with a man, or go to a rendezvous with a man.

**kāmarāga**. (T. 'dod pa la 'dod chags; C. yutan; J. yokuton; K. yokt'am 欲貪). In Sanskrit and Pāli, "sensual craving,"; an intensification of mere "sensuality" (KĀMA), which is listed as the fourth of the ten fetters (SAṂYOJANA) that keep beings bound to the cycle of rebirth (SAṂSĀRA). Kāmarāga is the desire for physical pleasure and sensuality; it belongs to the more general psychological category of craving (S. TṚṢṆĀ; P. taṇhā, lit. "thirst"), which ceaselessly seeks pleasure here and there and is the chief root of suffering.

**Kāmarūpa**. (S). One of the twenty-four sacred sites associated with the CAKRASAṂVARATANTRA. See PĪṬHA.

**kāmāvacara**. (S). See KĀMADHĀTU.

**kami**. (神). In Japanese, "spirits," "gods," or "deities" (the term is not gender-specific and can be used as either singular or plural). Kami worship preceded the arrival of Buddhism in Japan and much later came to be regarded as the putative indigenous religion of SHINTŌ. Kami is a complicated concept in Japanese religion, because the term applies to several different entities. Kami were perhaps most commonly considered to be spirits associated with physical objects; in the natural world, this meant that kami inhabited everything from rocks and trees to rivers and mountains. Kami could also designate ancestors or ancient heroes. The early historical record *Kojiki* (712), for example, recorded the names of various gods (kami) who created Japan and the Japanese people. In this text, all recognized clans (J. uji) had ancestries that linked themselves back to these local spirits. The tutelary deity of the ruling family, for example, was an anthropomorphized solar spirit named Amateru/Amaterasu ōmikami (lit. "Great Honorable Spirit Heavenly Radiance"), who was claimed to reside at the Ise shrine. From the Heian (794–1185) through the Tokugawa (1600–1868) periods, in conjunction with the ongoing Buddhist appropriation of native cults, kami were largely regarded as the local physical manifestations of buddhas and BODHISATTVAS, a theory of correlation known as HONJI SUIJAKU. In addition, local kami were also presumed to have converted to Buddhism and become protectors of specific shrines (both portable and fixed) and monasteries. The nativist (J. kokugaku) movement during the Tokugawa period, which developed as a reaction against such so-called foreign elements in Japanese culture as Buddhism and Confucianism, began to explore ways of distinguishing Buddhism from indigenous cults and held up the kami as something uniquely Japanese. From the inception of the Meiji period (1868–1912) up until 1945, the notion of kami became heavily politicized due to the government-mandated separation of buddhas and kami (J. SHINBUTSU BUNRI) and the proposition that the emperor (J. tennō) was a kami whose lineage could be traced back to the gods of the *Kojiki*. During this period, Japanese soldiers who died for the empire were interred at the Yasukuni shrine where they were venerated as kami; with the Japanese defeat in World War II, the Japanese government was compelled publicly to renounce this position. See also SHINBUTSU SHŪGŌ, HAIBUTSU KISHAKU.

**kammaṭṭhāna**. In Pāli, lit. "working ground," viz., "meditative topic"; a topic or object of meditation (BHĀVANĀ) used for training the mind and cultivating mental concentration (SAMĀDHI). The term originally referred to an occupation or vocation, such as farmer, merchant, or mendicant, but was adopted as a technical term to refer generically to various types of meditative exercises. The VISUDDHIMAGGA lists forty topics used for this purpose. First are ten "visualization devices" (KASIṆA)—devices that are constructed from the elements earth, water, fire, and air; the colors blue, yellow, red, and white, and light and space—to develop concentration. Kasiṇa exercises can produce all four of the "meditative absorptions" (JHĀNA; DHYĀNA) associated with the realm of subtle materiality. Next are ten "loathsome topics" (asubha; see S. AŚUBHABHĀVANĀ), such as the decaying of a corpse, which can lead only to the first meditative absorption (dhyāna). These are followed by ten "recollections" (P. anussati; S. ANUSMṚTI): viz., of (1) the Buddha, (2) the dhamma (DHARMA), (3) the saṅgha (SAṂGHA), (4) morality, (5) generosity, (6) the divinities, (7) death, (8) the body, (9) the inbreath and outbreath (P. ānāpānasati, S. ĀNĀPĀNASMṚTI), and (10) peace. Of these, recollection or mindfulness (P. sati; S. SMṚTI) of the inbreath and outbreath can produce all four meditative absorptions, while recollection of the body can produce the first absorption; the remaining recollections only lead to "access concentration" (UPACĀRASAMĀDHI), which immediately precedes but does not reach the level of the first absorption. Next are four "immaterial spheres" (arūpāyatana), viz., the "sphere of infinite space" (ākāsānañcāyatana, S. ĀKĀŚĀNANTYĀYATANA); of "infinite consciousness" (viññāṇañcāyatana, S. VIJÑĀNĀNANTYĀYATANA); of "nothingness" (ākiñcaññāyatana, S. ĀKIÑCANYĀYATANA); and of "neither perception nor nonperception" (nevasaññānāsaññāyatana, S. NAIVASAṂJÑĀNĀSAṂJÑĀYATANA). Meditation on these objects involves the increasing refinement of the fourth absorption and leads to the acquisition of the "immaterial attainments" (ARŪPASAMĀPATTI), also called "immaterial absorptions" (P. arūpāvacarajhāna; S. ĀRŪPYĀVACARADHYĀNA, see DHYĀNA, SAMĀPATTI). Four positive affective states or "divine abidings" (BRAHMAVIHĀRA; [alt. P. appamaññā]; S. APRAMĀṆA), are loving-kindness (mettā; MAITRĪ), compassion (KARUṆĀ), altruistic or empathetic joy (MUDITĀ), and equanimity or impartiality (upekkhā; UPEKṢĀ). Of these, loving-kindness, compassion, and altruistic joy can produce only the first three meditative absorptions, but equanimity can produce all four. There is one perception of the loathsomeness of food (āhāre paṭikkūlasaññā) and one analysis of the four elements (catudhātu vavatthāna), both of which can produce access concentration. Certain of these topics were said to be better suited to specific character types, such as the loathsome topics to persons with strong tendencies toward lust or the perception of the loathsomeness of food for gluttons; others, such as the meditation on the in- and outbreaths, were universally suitable to all character types. The Buddha was said to have had the ability to assess his disciples' character types and determine which topics of meditation would best suit them; as later generations lost this assessment ability, the number of kammaṭṭhānas in regular use dropped dramatically, with mindfulness of breathing being by far the most popular topic.

**Kanaka Bharadvāja**. (T. Bha ra dhwa dza bsod snyoms len; C. Jianuojiabaliduoshe; J. Kanyakabaridaja; K. Kanakkaballit'asa 迦諾迦跋釐墮闍). The Sanskrit name of the third of the sixteen ARHAT elders (ṢOḌAŚASTHAVIRA), who are charged by the Buddha with protecting his dispensation until the advent of the next buddha, MAITREYA. He holds a PĀTRA and lives in the eastern continent of VIDEHA with 3,600 disciples. Because he would lift his bowl up every time he received food on alms round, he was known in Chinese as the "Raising his Bowl Arhat" (Jubo Luohan). In CHANYUE GUANXIU's standard Chinese depiction, Kanaka Bharadvāja is depicted as skinny and emaciated as a stick, his eyes staring in anger, his mouth closed, and his eyebrows sticking out horizontally like a sword. Holding a chowrie in his right hand and resting his left hand on his knee, he sits leaning against a rock.

**Kanakavatsa**. (T. Gser be'u; C. Jianuojiafacuo; J. Kanyakabassa; K. Kanakkabŏlch'a 迦諾迦伐蹉). The Sanskrit name of the second of the sixteen ARHAT elders (ṢOḌAŚASTHAVIRA), who are charged by the Buddha with protecting his dispensation until the advent of the next buddha, MAITREYA; he is said to reside in Kashmir with five hundred disciples. In the East Asian tradition, he is known as the "ŚRĀVAKA who knows all the wholesome and unwholesome dharmas." Because he was renowned as a dynamic debater, one day a person approached him and asked, "What is happiness?" He answered, "It is the contentment that is gained through sensuality in hearing, viewing, smelling, tasting, and touching." The person continued, "Then what is joy?" He replied, "It is the contentment that is gained not through sensuality, but instead through the sincerity and joy one feels in the Buddha's existence." For this reason, Kanakavatsa is also known as the "Happiness and Joy Arhat." In CHANYUE GUANXIU's standard Chinese depiction, Kanakavatsa is portrayed in a gray robe, sitting in meditation on a rock, with his hands forming a MUDRĀ, and carrying a staff on his shoulder. His face is full of wrinkles, with eyebrows hanging downward and his gaze turned slightly upward.

**kanbian**. (J. kanben; K. kambyŏn 勘辨). In Chinese, "critical examinations"; a technical term used within the CHAN school to refer to the encounters between Chan monks and masters in which each questions and challenges the understanding of the other. These examinations are often in the form of an extended exchange or dialogue, which will often involve successive series of verbal and gesticulative joustings between the parties. Paradigmatic examples of kanbian are found in the second section of the LINJI LU ("The Record of Linji"), the discourse record (YULU) attributed to LINJI YIXUAN (d. 867).

**Kāñci**. (S). One of the twenty-four sacred sites associated with the CAKRASAṂVARATANTRA. See PĪṬHA.

**Kandarakasutta**. In Pāli, "Discourse to Kandaraka," the fifty-first sutta of the MAJJHIMANIKĀYA (there is no equivalent recension in the Chinese translations of the ĀGAMAS), preached by the Buddha to a gathering of monks on the banks of Gaggarā lake at Campā. Kandaraka, a wandering ascetic, visits the Buddha in the company of Pessa, the son of an elephant driver, and marvels at the silence maintained by the Buddha's congregation of disciples. The Buddha tells him that his disciples are self-controlled through their practice of the four foundations of mindfulness (P. satipaṭṭhāna; S. SMṚTYUPASTHĀNA). He then tells Pessa about four types of persons in the world: those who torment themselves, those who torment others, those who torment both themselves and others, and those who torment neither themselves nor others. After their departure, the Buddha addresses his disciples and elaborates on what he means by the four types of persons. Those who torment themselves are ascetics who undertake various mortification practices (see TAPAS). Those who torment others are butchers, hunters, fishermen, thieves, executioners, and prison wardens. Those who torment themselves and others are kings and their consorts who sponsor sacrifices wherein they undergo severe penances themselves and order the slaughter of sacrificial animals. Finally, those who torment neither themselves nor others are persons who have renounced the household life and gone forth as disciples of the Buddha. They abstain from extreme asceticism and harming others; they abstain from acquisitiveness and abide by the monastic rules; they practice meditation and quiet the mind; and they attain the four degrees of meditative absorption (JHĀNA; S. DHYĀNA) and the three knowledges (tevijjā; S. TRIVIDYĀ). The Buddha enumerates the three knowledges as (1) recollection of one's own previous lives (pubbenivāsānussati; S. PŪRVANIVĀSĀNUSMṚTI); (2) the divine eye (dibbacakkhu; S. DIVYACAKṢUS), or the ability to see the demise and rebirth of beings according to their good and evil deeds; and (3) knowledge of the extinction of the contaminants (āsavakkhāya; S. ĀSRAVAKṢAYA), which encompasses knowledge of the FOUR NOBLE TRUTHS (ariyasacca; S. āryasatya) and is equivalent to arhatship.

**Kang**. (J. Kō; K. Kang 康). A Sinograph used as an ethnikon for monks, missionaries, and translators who hailed from the kingdom of SOGDIANA in Central Asia (the Greek Transoxiana), as in the name of the translator KANG SENGHUI. Chinese descendants of Sogdian ancestry, such as FAZANG, also carried this ethnikon as their secular surname.

**Kang Senghui**. (J. Kō Sōe; K. Kang Sŭnghoe 康僧會) (d. 280). Sogdian monk and early translator of numerous mainstream Buddhist texts into Chinese. Kang Senghui emigrated in 247 to Jianye, the capital of the Wu dynasty (222–264). According to his hagiography, Kang Senghui was brought to the court of Wu as part of the court's investigation into Buddhism. As evidence of the truth of his religion, Kang Senghui miraculously manifested a relic (ŚARĪRA) of the Buddha, for which the marquis of Wu, Sun Quan, built a monastery near the capital named JIANCHUSI. When Sun Quan's grandson, Sun

Hao (r. 264–280), attempted to destroy all Buddhist structures in his kingdom, Kang Senghui is said to have successfully dissuaded him from doing so by making recourse to the notion of "sympathetic resonance" (GANYING). Kang Senghui translated several texts, including a collection of AVADĀNAS called the *Liudu ji jing*, and he wrote an important preface and commentary on the ANBAN SHOUYI JING, a Chinese recension of the **Smṛtyupasthānasūtra* (P. SATIPAṬṬHĀNASUTTA). As a learned scholar of Buddhism who was also well versed in the Confucian classics, astronomy, and divination, Kang Senghui played a crucial role in the development of a gentry Buddhist culture in the south, which was heavily influenced by indigenous Chinese philosophy.

**Kangzang guoshi**. (C) (康藏國師). See FAZANG.

**Kāṇha**. (S). See KṚṢṆĀCĀRYA.

**Kānheri**. The most extensive Buddhist monastic cave site in India, located six miles southeast of Borivili, a suburb of present-day Mumbai (Bombay), in the modern Indian state of Maharashtra. The name derives from the Sanskrit Kṛṣṇagiri, or "Black Mountain," probably because of the dark basalt from which many of the caves were excavated. Over 304 caves were excavated in the hills of the site between the first and tenth centuries CE. During the fifth and sixth centuries, older caves were modified and refurbished, while new caves were added, presumably initiated under the patronage of the Traikuṭakas (388–456 CE). While many of the new caves are architecturally rather plain, a number of important images were produced. The most extraordinary images are found in caves 90 and 41. The walls of cave 90 are abundantly, but haphazardly, carved with a myriad of images, suggesting that this hall was not intended for congregational purposes but rather as a place where believers could fund carvings as a way of making merit (PUṆYA). On the left side wall of cave 90 is an especially complex iconographic arrangement. It shows VAIROCANA Buddha in the center, making the gesture of turning the wheel of the dharma (DHARMACAKRAMUDRĀ) and seated in the so-called European pose (PRALAMBAPĀDĀSANA); accompanying Vairocana are four smaller images at the four corners of the composition. Together, these comprise the five buddhas (PAÑCATATHĀGATA or PAÑCAJINA). At each side of the composition is a vertical row of four buddhas, who together represent the eight buddhas of the past. By the sixth century, female images had emerged as a common part of Buddhist iconographic conceptions in South Asia, and Kānheri is no exception. Flanking the central Buddha in this same arrangement is a pair of BODHISATTVAS, each accompanied by a female consort. Depicted next to the stalk upon which rests the central Buddha's lotus pedestal are several subordinate figures: INDRA and BRAHMĀ, with female consorts, as well as male and female NĀGA. Kānheri was also a crucial site for both transoceanic and overland trade and pilgrimage networks, which probably accounts for the presence of images of AVALOKITEŚVARA, a bodhisattva who could be called upon by seafarers and merchants who were in distress. Avalokiteśvara's image in cave 90 shows him in the center, flanked by his attendants, and surrounded by scenes of the eight dangers, including shipwreck. In the bottom right-hand corner, seafarers are depicted praying to him. In cave 41, the unusual form of an Eleven-Headed Avalokiteśvara (EKĀDAŚAMUKHĀVALOKITEŚVARA), which is dated to the late fifth or early sixth century, indicates advanced and esoteric Buddhist practices at Kānheri. While frequently found in later Buddhist art in Tibet, Nepal, and East Asia, this image is the only extant artistic evidence that this iconographic type is of Indian provenance. A sixteenth-century Portuguese traveler reported that the Kānheri caves were the palace built by Prince Josaphat's father to shield him from knowledge of the sufferings of the world. (cf. BARLAAM AND JOSAPHAT). See also AJAṆṬĀ.

**kanhua Chan**. (J. kannazen/kanwazen; K. kanhwa Sŏn 看話禪). In Chinese, "Chan of investigating the topic of inquiry," or, more freely, "questioning meditation." The systematization of this meditative practice is commonly traced back to the writings of the Song-dynasty CHAN master DAHUI ZONGGAO. The kanhua Chan technique grew out of the growing interest in the study of "public cases" (GONG'AN), viz., old stories and anecdotes of Chan masters, which flourished during the Song dynasty. Dahui's teacher YUANWU KEQIN is also known to have lectured on numerous public cases, and his anthology of gong'an, along with his analysis of them, was recorded in the famous collection the BIYAN LU ("Blue Cliff Records"). Dahui further elaborated upon Yuanwu's investigation of public cases and applied this process to the practice of Chan meditation. In his lectures and letters (DAHUI PUJUE CHANSHI SHU), Dahui urged his students (many of whom were educated literati) to use the gong'an as a "topic of meditative inquiry" (HUATOU, K. hwadu), rather than interpret it from purely intellectual or conceptual perspectives. Perhaps the most famous huatou is the topic "no" (WU) attributed to the Chan master ZHAOZHOU CONGSHEN: A monk asked Zhaozhou, "Does a dog have buddha-nature (FOXING), or not?" to which Zhaozhou replied "WU" ("no"; lit. "it does not have it"). (See WU GONG'AN; GOUZI WU FOXING.) (Because of the popularity of this one-word meditative topic, kanhua Chan is often interpreted to mean the investigation of the "critical phrase" or "keyword," in which the "keyword" "wu" is presumed to have been extracted from the longer gong'an exchange.) The investigation of this huatou starts by "investigating the meaning" (C. canyi; K. ch'amŭi) of the huatou: what could Zhaozhou have meant by answering "no" to this question, when the right answer should be "yes"? The mainstream of East Asian Buddhist doctrine insists that all sentient beings, including dogs, are inherently enlightened and thus do in fact possess the buddha-nature, so this question promotes inquiry. Examining what Zhaozhou might have meant by saying "no" has what Dahui termed "taste" (C. wei, K. mi), meaning intellectual interest. As one's intellectual inquiry into this question continues, however, the student is ultimately left with "doubt" (YIQING), viz., the inability of the (unenlightened) mind to understand Zhaozhou's motive in giving this response to the student's question. Doubt, Dahui says, renders the mind "puzzled, frustrated, and tasteless" (viz., lacking intellectual interest), just as if you were gnawing on an iron rod." Once doubt arises, there is no longer any conceptual support for the meditation, and the student moves on to "investigating the word" (C. canju; K. ch'amgu), viz., just sitting with the huatou wu and no longer trying to understand Zhaozhou's motive in offering this response. At this point, the huatou becomes a "live word" (C. huoju; K. hwalgu) that helps to free the mind from conceptualization and to lead the meditator forward toward liberation. As the sense of doubt becomes more and more intense, it finally "explodes" (C. po; K. p'a), bringing an end to the deluded processes of thought and removing the limiting point of view that is the self. Once the distinctions between self and other disintegrate, the meditator experiences the interconnection between himself or herself and all the phenomena in the universe (SHISHI WU'AI). Kanhua Chan, therefore, employs the inevitable doubt that a benighted person would have about the sayings of the enlightened Chan masters of old to create a powerful sense of inquiry that leads the meditator toward the experience of nonconceptualization and finally enlightenment. ¶ Dahui's system of kanhua Chan was first taught in Korea by POJO CHINUL, where it is known as kanhwa Sŏn, and popularized by Chinul's successor, CHIN'GAK HYESIM. Kanhwa Sŏn continues to be the most common contemplative technique practiced in Korean Sŏn halls. Korean Sŏn monks typically work on one hwadu—often Zhaozhou's "no"—for much of their career, continually deepening their experience of that topic. In China, after the Ming dynasty, kanhua Chan merged with the recitation of the buddha AMITĀBHA's name (NIANFO), so that Chan meditators would turn the recitation into a huatou by reflecting on the topic "Who is reciting the Buddha's name?" In Japanese Zen, due in large part to the efforts of HAKUIN EKAKU and his disciples, kannazen became widespread within the RINZAI ZEN tradition, where it was incorporated into an elaborate system of kōan training, involving the systematic investigation of many different kōans.

**Kanhwa kyŏrŭi non**. (看話決疑論). In Korean, "Resolving Doubts about Observing the Keyword"; attributed to the Korean SŎN master POJO CHINUL. Shortly after Chinul's death in 1210, his disciple CHIN'GAK HYESIM is said to have discovered the *Kanhwa kyŏrŭi non* among Chinul's effects and arranged for the text to be published in 1215. The treatise displays the rapid crystallization of Chinul's thought around kanhwa Sŏn (see KANHUA CHAN), but its occasionally polemical tone suggests Hyesim's editorial hand. In the *Kanhwa kyŏrŭi non*, Chinul carefully expounds on the practice of observing the hwadu (HUATOU), the "meditative topic" or "keyword" deriving from a Chan public case (kongan; C. GONG'AN). He underscores the efficacy of the hwadu technique in counteracting the defects of conceptual understanding. In a series of questions and answers, Chinul also attempts to clarify the relation between the hwadu technique, the consummate interfusion of the DHARMADHĀTU, and the so-called sudden teachings (DUNJIAO) of Buddhism, as defined in the HUAYAN tenet-classification system (see JIAOXIANG PANSHI; HUAYAN WUJIAO). Chinul demonstrates that the goal of kanhwa Sŏn is not simply to abandon words and thought, as in the "sudden teachings," but to realize the unimpeded interpenetration of all phenomena (SHISHI WU'AI), the consummate description of enlightened experience according to the Huayan school. Unlike the prolix, scholastic explanations of Huayan, however, kanhwa Sŏn relies much less on conceptual descriptions in its soteriology and thus provides a more direct "shortcut" (kyŏngjŏl) to enlightenment than is offered in Huayan. Kanhwa Sŏn therefore offers the only truly perfect and sudden (wŏndon; C. yuandun) approach to enlightenment.

**kanhwa Sŏn**. (看話禪). In Korean, the Sŏn of investigating the topic of meditative inquiry (hwadu; C. HUATOU), or more freely, "questioning meditation." See KANHUA CHAN.

**Kaniṣka**. (T. Ka ni ska; C. Jianisejia wang; J. Kanishika ō; K. Kanisaekka wang 迦膩色迦王) (c. 127–151 CE). Third king of the KUSHAN kingdom in the northwest of India and legendary patron of Buddhism, rivaled, according to the tradition, only by AŚOKA, some four centuries later. The story of his conversion to Buddhism is widely found in the literature, but it seems to belong to the realm of legend, not history. Kaniṣka is said to have convened the fourth Buddhist council (see COUNCIL, FOURTH), which led to the compilation of the ABHIDHARMAMAHĀVIBHĀṢĀ ("Great Exegesis of Abhidharma").Thanks to Kaniṣka's putative support, the Kushan kingdom has traditionally been assumed to have been an important conduit for the introduction of Buddhist materials into China via the SILK ROAD of Central Asia. Recent evidence of the decline in western Central Asian trade during the Kushan period, however, may suggest instead that the Kushans were more of an obstacle than a help to this dissemination. Hence, it may not have been the Kushans who facilitated the transmission of Buddhism but their Indo-Scythian predecessors in the region, the Saka (S. Śaka) tribe. The emerging scholarly consensus is that Kaniṣka's reign began in 127 CE; if accepted, this date will allow much more precise dating of the cultural products of the KASHMIR–GANDHĀRA region.

**kaṅkhāvitaraṇavisuddhi**. In Pāli, "the purity of overcoming doubt"; the fourth of seven "purities" (VISUDDHI) to be developed along the path to liberation, according to the VISUDDHIMAGGA. The purity of overcoming doubt refers to the understanding of the conditions that give rise to name and form (NĀMARŪPA), viz., mentality and materiality, with reference to the three time periods (S. TRIKĀLA) of past, present, and future. The practitioner notes that no instance of name and form arisen in the present came into being through the will of a creator, nor did it arise spontaneously by itself without a cause.

Rather, the practitioner understands that everything that has arisen has occurred because of a specific cause or condition. Thus, the practitioner understands, for example, that, due to the contact of the eye sense base with a visible object, a moment of visual consciousness arises. In the same way, the practitioner understands that what has arisen in the present because of causes and conditions (HETUPRATYAYA) becomes the cause and condition for something arising in the future. This knowledge encompasses knowledge of the relationship between volitional action (KARMAN) and its result (VIPĀKA) and that future existence within the cycle of rebirth occurs as a result of volitional action. In addition, the practitioner clearly understands the distinction between volitional action and its result, that is, that there is neither volitional action in the result nor result in the volitional action. In this way, the practitioner overcomes doubt regarding causality underlying the appearance of name and form in relation to the three times.

**Kaṅkhāvitaraṇī**. [alt. Mātikaṭṭhakathā]. A Pāli commentary written by BUDDHAGHOSA on the pāṭimokkha (S. PRĀTIMOKṢA) of the VINAYAPIṬAKA.

**Kāṅkṣā-Revata**. (P. Kaṅkhā-Revata; T. Nam gru; C. Lipoduo; J. Ribata; K. Rip'ada 離婆多). An important ARHAT who was foremost among the Buddha's monk disciples in mastery of meditative absorption (JHĀNA; DHYĀNA). He is typically known as Kāṅkṣā-Revata (Doubting Revata), to distinguish him from several other REVATAs who appear in the literature, because, prior to his enlightenment, Revata was troubled by doubt concerning what was permissible and what was not. According to Pāli sources, he was born into a wealthy family in the city of Sāvitthi (S. ŚRĀVASTĪ). One day, he heard the Buddha preach in Kapilavatthu (S. KAPILAVASTU) and resolved to renounce the world and enter the order. He attained arahantship by relying on jhāna and his exceptional skill in these meditative states won him distinction. Revata had resolved to attain this distinction in a previous life as a brāhmaṇa, when, during the time of Padumuttara Buddha, he heard the Buddha describe one of his disciples as preeminent in his attainment of jhāna. In another famous story, the mother of Uttara had been reborn as a hungry ghost (P. peta; S. PRETA) and after fifty-five years of wandering encountered Revata and begged him for relief. He relieved her suffering by making various offerings to the SAṂGHA in her name.

**Kaṇṭhaka**. [alt. Kanthaka] (T. Bsngags ldan; C. Jianzhi; J. Kenjoku; K. Kŏnch'ŏk 犍陟). In Sanskrit and Pāli, the name of the horse that GAUTAMA rode when he departed from his father's palace in KAPILAVASTU and renounced the world (PRAVRAJITA). Kaṇṭhaka was born on the same day as Gautama, as was his groom CHANDAKA. Kaṇṭhaka was destined from birth to carry the future buddha from the household life into homelessness and was suitably magnificent in stature for that honor. Eighteen cubits in length, he was white, the color of a conch shell, and the sound of his neighing and gallop resounded throughout the kingdom of Kapilavastu. When he was saddled to carry his master into the wilderness, Kaṇṭhaka realized the significance of the event and neighed in exultation. Lest Gautama's father be forewarned and attempt to prevent his departure, the divinities muffled his neighing and the sound of his hoofs. The prince rode on Kaṇṭhaka's back, while Chandaka held onto his tail. Outside the city gates, Gautama turned to take a final look at his capital; a shrine (CAITYA) was later erected on the spot in commemoration. Between midnight and dawn, they traveled thirty leagues to the river Anomā. Kaṇṭhaka crossed the river in one jump and Gautama and Chandaka dismounted on the other side. There, the BODHISATTVA gave Chandaka his ornaments and directed him to take Kaṇṭhaka back to the palace; a shrine commemorating the event was later erected on the spot as well. Kaṇṭhaka continued to look at his master as he departed, and when he disappeared from view, Kaṇṭhaka died of a broken heart. He was immediately reborn in TRAYASTRIṂŚA heaven as a deity named Kaṇṭhakadevaputra and dwelled in a magnificent palace made of gems, where the ARHAT MAHĀMAUDGALYĀYANA later visited him.

**Kanzan Egen**. (關山慧玄) (1277–1360). Japanese ZEN master of the RINZAI Zen tradition and founder of the influential monastery of MYŌSHINJI in Kyōto. Kanzan was a native of Shinano in present-day Nagano prefecture and at a young age was ordained at the monastery KENCHŌJI in Kamakura. In 1307, he met the eminent Zen master NANPO JŌMYŌ when the latter was appointed the abbot of Kenchōji. In 1327, Kanzan visited Nanpo's leading disciple SŌHŌ MYŌCHŌ, also known as Daitō, to continue his studies with him at the monastery DAITOKUJI in Kyōto. In 1303, Kanzan is said to have attained awakening while struggling with the kōan (C. GONG'AN) of YUNMEN WENYAN's "barrier" (case 8 of the BIYAN LU). Daitō himself had penetrated this kōan earlier at Kenchōji under Nanpo's guidance. In recognition of his disciple's achievement, Daitō gave him the name Kanzan (Barrier Mountain). In place of his teacher Daitō, Kanzan later became the personal instructor to Emperor Godaigo (r. 1318–1339) and Hanazono (r. 1308–1318). After Daitō's death in 1337, Emperor Hanazono converted his country villa into a monastery and invited Kanzan to serve as its founding abbot (kaisan, C. KAISHAN); this monastery was subsequently given the name Myōshinji.

**kapāla**. (T. thod pa; C. dulou qi/jiebobei; J. dokuroki/kōhahai; K. ch'ongnu ki/kŏpp'abae 髑髏器/劫波杯). In Sanskrit, "skull"; used in Buddhist TANTRA to refer to the skull cup that is often one of the accoutrements of MAHĀSIDDHAs and wrathful deities. The vessel, made from the cranium of a human skull, is often elaborately carved and inlaid with precious metals. The symbolism of the skull cup is variously explained; most generally, it is yet another antinomian aspect of Buddhist tantra, in which things that would be regarded as polluting in Indian culture (in this case the skull of a corpse) are put to use to overcome dualities. It is also said that the skull cup is a constant reminder of death. In tantric SĀDHANAs, the skull cup is often said to contain the elixir of immortality (AMṚTA). The skull cup figures prominently in tantric iconography (being held, for example, by PADMASAMBHAVA) and in tantric practice. For example, in GCOD practice, one visualizes the top of one's own head being cut off and transformed into a huge vessel, where one's own body is cooked and offered to VAJRAYOGINĪ.

**Kapilavastu**. (P. Kapilavatthu; T. Ser skya'i gzhi; C. Jiapiluowei; J. Kabirae; K. Kabirawi 迦毘羅衛). In Sanskrit, the capital city of the ŚĀKYA tribe and the hometown of the buddha GAUTAMA. The city was located north of the larger region of KOŚALA, in the foothills of modern-day Nepal. Kapilavastu is the town where SIDDHĀRTHA Gautama was raised and lived as a prince until he renounced worldly life. Later, after his enlightenment, he stayed often at Nigrodha's Park in the precincts of the city, together with his growing band of disciples. In Kapilavastu, his cousins ĀNANDA and DEVADATTA, his half-brother NANDA, and his barber UPĀLI were converted and became monks (BHIKṢU). When the Buddha ordained his then seven-year-old son RĀHULA as a novice (ŚRĀMAṆERA) without the knowledge of the boy's mother, YAŚODHARĀ, the Buddha's father, ŚUDDHODANA, protested, and a rule was created stating that ordinations would not take place without prior parental consent. After the death of his father, the Buddha's foster mother MAHĀPRAJĀPATĪ begged the Buddha to be allowed to join the SAṂGHA, thus initiating the order of nuns (BHIKṢUṆĪ).

**Kapimala**. (C. Jiapimoluo; J. Kabimara; K. Kabimara 迦毘摩羅). Sanskrit name of an Indian monk who lived during the second century CE, who is listed as one of the successors in the Indian Buddhist lineage that traces itself back to the person of the Buddha himself. An Indian brāhmaṇa who was a native of PĀṬALIPUTRA (modern Patna), the capital of the kingdom of MAGADHA, he is said to have challenged the exegete AŚVAGHOṢA with his superpowers (ABHIJÑĀ) but was defeated by Aśvaghoṣa's profound learning and became his disciple, along with his three thousand adherents. He is typically listed as twelfth of twenty-three or thirteenth of twenty-four primary successors to ŚĀKYAMUNI Buddha.

**Kapleau, Philip**. (1912–2004). Influential twentieth-century American teacher of Zen Buddhism. Kapleau worked as a court reporter at the war crimes trials following World War II, first in Nuremberg and then in Tokyo. He met D. T. SUZUKI in Japan in 1948 and later attended his lectures at Columbia University in 1950. He returned to Japan in 1953, where he spent the next thirteen years practicing Zen, the last ten under YASUTANI HAKUUN (1885–1973), a Zen priest who had severed his ties to the SŌTŌ sect in order to form his own organization, called Sanbōkyōdan, the "Three Treasures Association," which taught Zen meditation to laypeople. Kapleau returned to the United States in 1965 and in the following year founded the Zen Center of Rochester, New York. While in Japan, Kapleau drew on his training as a court reporter to transcribe and translate Yasutani's instructions on Zen meditation, along with his formal interviews (DOKUSAN) with his students, and testimonials of their enlightenment experiences. These were compiled into *The Three Pillars in Zen*, first published in Japan in 1965, a work that influenced many Westerners to undertake Zen practice; it is widely recognized as a classic of the nascent American tradition of Zen Buddhism. As one of the first non-Japanese Zen teachers in America, Kapleau set out in this book to adapt some of the forms of Zen practice that he thought would be better suited to an American audience. Kapleau's modifications included an English translation of the PRAJÑĀPĀRAMITĀHṚDAYASŪTRA ("Heart Sūtra"). Yasutani was strongly opposed to the use of the translation, arguing that the sound of the words was more important than their meaning. Teacher and student broke over this question in 1967 and never spoke again. Kapleau, however, remained dedicated to Yasutani, and the Rochester Zen Center flourished under Kapleau's direction.

**kāraṇahetu**. (T. byed pa'i rgyu; C. nengzuo yin; J. nōsain; K. nŭngjak in 能作因). In Sanskrit, the "efficient," "generic," or "enabling" "cause," the first of the six causes (HETU) recognized in the SARVĀSTIVĀDA-VAIBHĀṢIKA ABHIDHARMA system. This category of cause subsumes all five other causes within it, and it corresponds with the predominant effect (ADHIPATAPHALA) as its specific effect. Each conditioned DHARMA serves as the enabling cause for all other dharmas besides itself by the mere fact that it does not obstruct the others' arising. The kāraṇahetu provides the broad context necessary for the operation of causality, so that the process of production and cessation will continue unabated.

**Kāraṇḍavyūha**. [alt. Karaṇḍavyūha; Avalokiteśvaraguṇa-kāraṇḍavyūha] (T. Za ma tog bkod pa'i mdo; C. Dasheng zhuangyan baowang jing; J. Daijō shōgon hōōgyō; K. Taesŭng changŏm powang kyŏng 大乘莊嚴寶王經). In Sanskrit, "Description of the Casket [of AVALOKITEŚVARA's Qualities]"; the earliest textual source for the BODHISATTVA Avalokiteśvara's MANTRA "OṂ MAṆI PADME HŪṂ" (oṃ, O Jewel-Lotus); the extended version of the title is *Avalokiteśvaraguṇa-kāraṇḍavyūha*. The earliest version of the *Kāraṇḍavyūha* is presumed to have been composed in Kashmir sometime around the end of the fourth or beginning of the fifth centuries CE. There are Tibetan and Chinese translations, including a late Chinese rendering made by the Kashmiri translator TIAN XIZAI (d. 1000) in 983. The *Kāraṇḍavyūha* displays characteristics of both sūtra and TANTRA literature in its emphasis on the doctrine of rebirth in AMITĀBHA Buddha's pure land (SUKHĀVATĪ), as well as such tantric elements as the mantra "oṃ maṇi padme hūṃ" and the use of MAṆḌALAs; it is thought to represent a transitional stage between the two categories of texts. The sūtra is composed as a dialogue between ŚĀKYAMUNI Buddha and the bodhisattva SARVANĪVARAṆAVIṢKAMBHIN. While describing Avalokiteśvara's supernal qualities and his vocation of saving sentient beings,

Śākyamuni Buddha tells his audience about the mantra "oṃ maṇi padme hūṃ" and the merits that it enables its reciters to accrue. Avalokiteśvara is said to be the embodiment of the SAṂBHOGAKĀYA (enjoyment body), the body of the buddha that remains constantly present in the world for the edification of all beings, and the dharma that he makes manifest is expressed in this six-syllable mantra (ṢAḌAKṢARĪ), the recitation of which invokes the power of that bodhisattva's great compassion (MAHĀKARUṆĀ). The sūtra claims that the benefit of copying this mantra but once is equivalent to that of copying all the 84,000 teachings of the DHARMA; in addition, there are an infinite number of benefits that derive from a single recitation of it.

**Karīka**. (S). See KĀLIKA.

**Kārli**. [alt. Kārle]. Buddhist cave temple site in western India, situated halfway between Mumbai (Bombay) and Pune in Maharashtra. Based on inscriptional evidence, the excavation of the site began around 124 CE, toward the end of the reign of Nahapāna, who ruled over much of western India during the early second century. The veranda and doorways to the site are decorated with outstanding sculptural features: flanking the doorways are carvings of couples in sexual union (MAITHUNA); these images are stylistically similar to contemporary carvings in the city of MATHURĀ. The end wall of the veranda features carvings of almost life-size elephants, which appear to support the architectural structure. The images of buddhas and BODHISATTVAS also found on the veranda were carved in the late fifth century, when the iconographic profile of the cave was modified. The interior of the cave's CAITYA hall, which is South Asia's largest, is characterized by an impressive, harmonious balance of architectural and sculptural elements. A STŪPA appears at the end of the long nave, with an ambulatory that allows its circumambulation (PRADAKṢIṆA). A row of pillars carved directly out of the rock parallels the shape of the cave itself. These pillars are adorned with capitals that depict sculpted images of figures riding animals, which are stylistically close to those of the contemporary or slightly earlier images at the great stūpa at SĀÑCĪ.

**Karma Bka' brgyud**. (Karma Kagyü). One of four major subsects of the BKA' BRGYUD sect of Tibetan Buddhism. Also known as the Karma kaṃ tshang, it dates to the first KARMA PA, DUS GSUM MKHYEN PA. Headed by a lineage of incarnate lamas (SPRUL SKU), who each hold the title of Karma pa, the sect held great political power from the late fourteenth through the early seventeenth century, until the ascendancy of the DGE LUGS at the time of the fifth DALAI LAMA. It continues to be strong in exile. The Karma bka' brgyud is known for its equal emphasis on study and practice, and in the realm of practice, on MAHĀMUDRĀ. Because of the black crown worn by the Karma pa, the sect is sometimes mistakenly referred to in the West as the "BLACK HATS." For a detailed history, see KARMA PA.

**Karma chags med**. (a.k.a. Rā ga a sya) (1613–1678). A KARMA BKA' BRGYUD teacher born near the RI BO CHE monastery in eastern Tibet, an unsuccessful candidate for the position of ninth KARMA PA and founder of the Gnas mdo branch of the Karma kaṃ tshang tradition, named after the monastery Gnas mdo that he established; at the same time, a founding figure in the lineage of the RNYING MA monastery DPAL YUL, one of the four great Rnying ma monasteries of Khams. A prolific author, he is known for his devotion to AMITĀBHA; his *Rnam dag bde chen zhing gi smon lam* ("Prayer to Be Reborn in SUKHĀVATĪ") is recited in all sects. As redactor of the GTER MA (treasure texts) revealed by his student and teacher Mi 'gyur rdo rje, he originated a fusion of BKA' BRGYUD and RNYING MA teachings that spread widely in Khams.

**karmadāna**. (S). See WEINUO.

**Karma gling pa**. (Karma Lingpa) (1326–1386). A treasure revealer (GTER STON) of the RNYING MA sect of Tibetan Buddhism. He is best known for unearthing the treasure cycle entitled the *Zhi khro dgongs pa rang grol* ("Peaceful and Wrathful Deities, the Natural Liberation of Intention") from a mountain peak in his native region of Dwags po (Dakpo). Part of this doctrinal cycle, called the BAR DO THOS GROL CHEN MO ("Great Liberation through Hearing in the Intermediate State"), became widely known in the West as the so-called *Tibetan Book of the Dead*. See also BAR DO; ANTARĀBHAVA.

**Karma kaṃ tshang**. See KARMA PA; KARMA BKA' BRGYUD.

**karmakula**. (T. las kyi rigs; C. jiemo bu; J. katsumabu; K. kalma pu 羯磨部). In Sanskrit, "action family"; one of the "five lineages" or "five families" (PAÑCAKULA) of tantric Buddhism. The five are usually given as the TATHĀGATAKULA, VAJRAKULA, PADMAKULA, RATNAKULA, and KARMAN families (different tantras have different lists). Those in the karmakula become enlightened in the form of the buddha AMOGHASIDDHI. Each of the five families is associated with one of the five aggregates (SKANDHA), five wisdoms (JÑĀNA), five afflictions (KLEŚA), five elements (MAHĀBHUTA), and five colors. For the karman family, these are the conditioning factors (SAṂSKĀRA) skandha, the wisdom of having accomplished what was to be done (KṚTYĀNUṢṬHĀNAJÑĀNA), the affliction of envy, the element air, and the color green. See also PAÑCATATHĀGATA.

**karmamudrā**. (T. las kyi phyag rgya). In Sanskrit, "action seal"; a term used to refer to the female consort in the practice of sexual yoga in ANUTTARAYOGATANTRA. In the context of sexual yoga, three types of female consorts or VIDYĀ ("knowledge women") are sometimes enumerated. The first is the JÑĀNAMUDRĀ, or "wisdom seal," who is an imagined or visualized partner and is not an actual consort. The second and third types of consorts are both actual consorts. The SAMAYAMUDRĀ, or "pledge seal," is a consort who is fully qualified for the practice of sexual yoga, in the sense that she is of the appropriate age and caste, has practiced the common path, and maintains the tantric pledges (SAMAYA). The third and final type is the karmamudrā, who is also an actual consort but who may not possess the qualifications of a samayamudrā. In some expositions of tantric practice, these three types of "seals" are discussed with reference to MAHĀMUDRĀ, or "great seal," a multivalent term sometimes defined as the union of method (UPĀYA) and wisdom (PRAJÑĀ), which does not require a consort.

**karman**. (P. kamma; T. las; C. ye; J. gō; K. ŏp 業). In Sanskrit, "action"; in its inflected form "karma," it is now accepted as an English word; a term used to refer to the doctrine of action and its corresponding "ripening" or "fruition" (VIPĀKA), according to which virtuous deeds of body, speech, and mind produce happiness in the future (in this life or subsequent lives), while nonvirtuous deeds lead instead to suffering. In Vedic religion, karman referred especially to ritual actions. The term came to take on wider meanings among the ŚRAMAṆA movements of wandering ascetics, to which Buddhism belonged. The JAINAS, for example, have a theory of karman as a physical substance created through unwholesome actions, which hinder the soul's ability to achieve liberation; in order to free the soul from the bonds created through past actions, the body had to be rigorously cleansed of this karmic substance through moral discipline and asceticism. Although the Buddhists accepted the notion of moral causality, as did the Jainas, they redefined karman instead as mental intention (CETANĀ) or intentional (cetayitvā) acts: the Buddha specifically says, "Action is volition, for after having intended something, one accomplishes action through body, speech, and mind." These actions are of four types: (1) wholesome (KUŚALA), which lead to wholesome results (vipāka); (2) unwholesome (AKUŚALA), which lead to unwholesome results; (3) mixed, with mixed results that may be partially harmful and partially beneficial; and (4) indeterminate (AVYĀKṚTA), which are actions done after enlightenment, which yield no result in the conditioned realm. The term karman describes both the potential and kinetic energy necessary to sustain a process; and, just as energy is not lost in a physical process, neither is it lost in the process of moral cause and effect. The Buddhists assert that there is a necessary relationship that exists between the action and its fruition, but this need not manifest itself in the present life; rather, when the complex of conditions and the appropriate time for their fruition come together, actions will bear their retributive fruit, even after an interval of hundreds of millions of eons (KALPA). The fruition of action is also received by the mental continuum (CITTASAṂTĀNA) of the being who initially performed the action, not by another; thus, in mainstream Buddhism, one can neither receive the fruition of another's karman nor redeem another's actions. The physical universe (BHĀJANALOKA) and all experience within it are also said to be the products of karman, although in a passive, ethically neutral sense (viz., upapattibhava; see BHAVA). The goal of the Buddhist path is to be liberated from the effects of karman and the cycle of rebirth (SAṂSĀRA) by destroying attachment to the sense of self (ĀTMAN). The doctrine of karman is meant to counter the errors of antinomianism (that morality is unnecessary to salvation), annihilationism, and materialism. Actions do, in fact, matter, even if there is ultimately no self that is the agent of action. Hence, karman as representing the continuity between action and result must be understood in conjunction with the teaching of discontinuity that is ANĀTMAN: there is indeed a causal chain connecting the initiator of action and the recipient of its result, but it is not the case that the person who performs the action is the same as the person who experiences the result (the wrong view of eternality) or that the agent is different from the experiencer (the wrong view of annihilationism). This connection is likened to milk changing to its different forms of curds, butter, and ghee: the milk and the ghee are neither identical nor different, but they are causally connected. The process that connects karmic cause and effect, as well as the process by which that connection is severed, is detailed in the twelvefold chain of dependent origination (PRATĪTYASAMUTPĀDA). Enlightened beings, such as a buddha or an ARHAT, have destroyed this chain and thus have eradicated all attachment to their past karmic continuums; consequently, after their enlightenment, they can still perform actions, but those will not lead to results that would lead to additional lifetimes in saṃsāra. Although the Buddha acknowledges that the connections between karman and its effect may seem so complex as to appear unfathomable (why, for example, does the evil person who harms others live in wealth, while the good Samaritan who helps others lives in poverty?), he is adamant that those connections can be known, and known with perfect precision, through the experience of awakening (BODHI). Indeed, two of the three kinds of knowledge (TRIVIDYĀ; P. tevijja) and one of the superknowledges (ABHIJÑĀ) that are by-products of enlightenment involve insight into the validity of the connection between karmic cause and effect for both oneself and for all beings: viz., the ability to remember one's own former lives (PŪRVANIVĀSĀNUSMṚTI: P. pubbenivāsānunssati) in all their detail; and the insight into the karmic destinies of all other beings as well (CYUTYUPAPATTIJÑĀNA; P. cutūpapātānuñāṇa). Distinguish KARMAN, "ecclesiastical proceeding," s.v.; see also ĀNANTARYAKARMAN; ANIÑJYAKARMAN; ER BAO; KARMĀVARAṆA.

**karman**. (P. kamma; T. las; C. jiemo; J. katsuma/konma; K. kalma 羯磨). In Sanskrit, "ecclesiastical proceeding"; from the literal meaning of karman as an "act." (To distinguish karman as "action" from "ecclesiastical proceeding," the Chinese uses a translation for the former and a transcription for the latter.) Such proceedings include admission into the order as novices (pravrajyā, see PRAVRAJITA), full ordination of monks and nuns (UPASAMPADĀ), the fortnightly confession ceremony (UPOṢADHA) for recitation of the PRĀTIMOKṢA precepts, the invitation ceremony (PRAVĀRAṆĀ) closing the rain's retreat (VARṢĀ), giving cloth for robes (KAṬHINA), the adjudication of rules, the administration of punishments to transgressors of the precepts, and the settlement of disputes among the clergy. At such formal proceedings, a motion is made before the congregation of monks that may be approved by silent assent (see JÑAPTIDVITĪYĀ KARMAVĀCANĀ [P. ñattidutiyakammavācā]; KARMAVĀCANĀ). In responding to monks who have transgressed the precepts, for example, the VINAYA provides for seven different ecclesiastical proceedings, depending on the kind and severity of the infraction. They are reprimands; expulsion from the clergy; the appointment of an overseeing mentor (see ĀCĀRYA; ANTEVĀSIKA); temporary proscription against contact with the laity; confronting with incriminating evidence a suspect who refuses to confess; confronting an unrepentant transgressor with incriminating evidence; and correcting someone who intransigently holds on to the pernicious view that certain precepts are expendable. Distinguish KARMAN, "action," s.v.; see also SAṂGHAKARMAN.

**Karma pa**. In Tibetan, a title given to the incarnate lama (SPRUL SKU) identified at birth in each generation as the head of the KARMA BKA' BRGYUD subsect of the BKA' RGYUD sect of Tibetan Buddhism. The term is commonly etymologized as "man of [enlightened] action." In the history of Tibetan Buddhism, the lineage of the Karma pas is considered to be the first to institutionalize its succession of incarnate lamas, a practice later adopted by the other sects. According to tradition, at the time of his death, each Karma pa composes a letter that specifies the date and location of his next incarnation. This letter is given to a close disciple, who then reveals its contents upon the death of the Karma pa, with the information in the letter used to locate the child who has been born as the next Karma pa. Among the most famous and sacred possessions of the Karma pa is a black crown, said to be made from the hair of one hundred thousand ḌĀKINĪS. The actual crown is said to be invisible to persons lacking sufficient merit. However, during the Ming dynasty, the Yongle emperor (r. 1402–1424) presented the fifth Karma pa with a visible physical replica of the crown. The replica itself is said to have great power; the "black hat ceremony," in which the Karma pa dons the crown, is among the most important in the sect. In the ceremony, the Karma pa holds the hat upon his head; otherwise, it is said, it will fly off into space. It is also said that those who see the crown will be liberated from rebirth. Due to the importance of the crown, the Karma pas are sometimes called the "black crowned" (zhwa nag). In the nineteenth century, a Western misunderstanding of this term led to the identification of a sect of Tibetan Buddhism called the "BLACK HATS," a mistake that persists in some accounts of Tibetan Buddhism. Like the DALAI LAMAS, the Karma pas are considered to be emanations of the BODHISATTVA AVALOKITEŚVARA. Also like the Dalai Lamas, the Karma pas have been among the most important and revered religious figures in the history of Tibet; they include many great scholars and yogins. Some have also had political power, at times leading to conflicts, sometimes polemical, and sometimes military, with the DGE LUGS PA. Although the main seat of the Karma pas was MTSHUR PHU Monastery in central Tibet, the Karma pas tended to travel widely. Their importance and influence extended throughout the Tibetan cultural domain, including China. The lineage includes:

1. Karma pa DUS GSUM MKHYEN PA (1110–1193)
2. Karma pa KARMA PAKSHI (1203–1283)
3. Karma pa RANG 'BYUNG RDO RJE (1284–1339)
4. Karma pa Rol pa'i rdo rje (Rolpe Dorje, 1340–1383)
5. Karma pa Bde bzhin gshegs pa (Deshin Shekpa, 1384–1415)
6. Karma pa Mthong ba don ldan (Tongwa Dönden, 1416–1453)
7. Karma pa Chos grags rgya mtsho (Chödrak Gyatso, 1454–1506)
8. Karma pa MI BSKYOD RDO RJE (1507–1554)
9. Karma pa DBANG PHYUG RDO RJE (1556–1603)
10. Karma pa Chos dbying rdo rje (Chöying Dorje, 1604–1674)
11. Karma pa Ye shes rdo rje (Yeshe Dorje, 1676–1702)
12. Karma pa Byang chub rdo rje (Jangchub Dorje, 1703–1732)
13. Karma pa Bdud 'dul rdo rje (Dudül Dorje, 1733–1797)
14. Karma pa Theg mchog rdo rje (Tekchok Dorje, 1798–1868)
15. Karma pa Mkha' khyab rdo rje (Kakyap Dorje, 1871–1922)
16. Karma pa RANG 'BYUNG RIG PA'I RDO RJE (1924–1982)
17. Karma pa O rgyan 'phrin las rdo rje (Orgyan Trinle Dorje, b. 1985).

The line of Karma pas originated during the twelfth century with DUS GSUM MKHYEN PA, a close disciple of SGAM PO PA BSOD NAMS RIN CHEN, who had himself studied under the famous YOGIN MI LA RAS PA. Dus gsum mkhyen pa established several important monasteries, including Mtshur phu, which served as the main seat of the Karma pas and the Karma bka' brgyud in central Tibet. Dus gsum mkhyen pa's successor, the second Karma pa KARMA PAKSHI, is remembered especially for his prowess in meditation and thaumaturgy. He was patronized by the Mongols, first by Möngke (1209–1259) and later by his brother, the Yuan emperor Qubilai Khan (r. 1260–1294) before losing the emperor's support. The third Karma pa RANG 'BYUNG RDO RJE continued this affiliation with the Mongol court, playing a role in emperor Toghun Temür's (r. 1333–1368) ascension to the throne. The fourth Karma pa Rol pa'i rdo rje and fifth Karma pa Bde bzhin gshegs pa maintained ties with the Chinese court—the former with Toghun Temür and the latter serving as the preceptor of the Yongle emperor (reigned 1402–1424) of the Ming dynasty, a position of great influence. The sixth Karma pa Mthong ba don ldan did not maintain the same political connections of his predecessors; he is remembered especially for his contributions to the religious life of the Karma bka' brgyud, producing meditation and ritual manuals. The seventh Karma pa Chos grags rgya mtsho is known primarily for his philosophical works on logic and epistemology (PRAMĀṆA); his voluminous text on the topic is still used today as a principal textbook in many Bka' brgyud monasteries. The eighth Karma pa MI BSKYOD RDO RJE is among the most renowned scholars of his generation, a prolific author whose writings encompassed Sanskrit, poetry, and art, as well as MADHYAMAKA philosophy and tantra. The ninth Karma pa DBANG PHYUG RDO RJE is revered for his influential works on the theory and practice of MAHĀMUDRĀ. It was during his lifetime that the DGE LUGS hierarchs ascended to power, with an attendant decline in the political fortunes of his sect in central Tibet. His successor, the tenth Karma pa Chos kyi dbang phyug, was thus forced into a life of virtual exile near the Sino-Tibetan border in the east as his patron, the king of Gtsang, was defeated by the Gushri Khan, patron of the Dge lugs. As the war came to an end, the tenth Karma pa returned to LHA SA where he established ties with the fifth Dalai Lama NGAG DBANG BLO BZANG RGYA MTSHO. The eleventh Karma pa Ye shes rdo rje and twelfth Karma pa Byang chub rdo rje lived relatively short lives, although the latter made an important journey through Nepal together with his disciple, the brilliant scholar and Sanskritist Si tu CHOS KYI 'BYUNG GNAS. The life of the thirteenth Karma pa Bdud 'dul rdo rje was, for the most part, lived outside the sphere of politics. He is remembered for his love of animals, to which he taught the dharma. Beginning during his lifetime and continuing into that of the fourteenth Karma pa Theg mchog rdo rje, there was a revival of Bka' brgyud doctrine in the eastern Tibetan province of Khams, as part of what has come to be called the RIS MED or non-sectarian movement. The fourteenth Karma pa's disciple, 'JAM MGON KONGS SPRUL BLO GROS MTHA' YAS, played a leading role. The fifteenth Karma pa Mkha' khyab rdo rje, a principal disciple of 'Jam mgon kongs sprul, was a prolific scholar. The sixteenth Karma pa RANG 'BYUNG RIG PA'I RDO RJE, like other lamas of his generation, saw the Communist Chinese occupation of Tibet, fleeing to India in 1959 and establishing an exile seat at Rumtek Monastery in Sikkim. He was the first Karma pa to visit the West. The seventeenth Karma pa O rgyan 'phrin las rdo rje was enthroned at Mtshur phu monastery on September 27, 1992. In late December 2000, he escaped into exile, establishing a residence in Dharamsala, India. Although his identification as the Karma pa has been disputed by a small number of followers of a rival candidate, O rgyan 'phrin las rdo rje is regarded as the seventeenth Karma pa by the majority of the Tibetan community, including the Dalai Lama.

**Karma Pakshi**. (1203–1283). A Tibetan Buddhist master recognized as the second KARMA PA, renowned for his virtuosity in meditation, thaumaturgy, and his activities at the Mongol court. The name "Pakshi" is derived from the Mongolian word for "teacher" or "master," and the second Karma pa is also frequently known by the epithet grub chen, or MAHĀSIDDHA. In his youth, Karma Pakshi was recognized as a child of great intellectual ability and skill in meditation. He conducted his early training under the BKA' BRGYUD teacher Spom brag pa Bsod rnams rdo rje (Pomdrakpa Sönam Dorje, 1170–1249) and spent a great period of his time in meditation retreat near the monastery of MTSHUR PHU in central Tibet. Traveling to eastern Tibet, he founded a monastery at Spungs ri (Pungri) and renovated the Bka' brgyud institution of KARMA DGON established by his predecessor DUS GSUM MKHYEN PA. Karma Pakshi's fame spread throughout the Tibetan border regions to the north and east. In about 1251, the Mongol prince Qubilai (later Khan, r. 1260–1294) sent an invitation to Karma Pakshi, who was residing at Mtshur phu. He arrived at the Mongol court several years later. Karma Pakshi was one of numerous religious figures present at court, including the SA SKYA hierarch 'PHAGS PA BLO GROS RGYAL MTSHAN. Karma Pakshi quickly impressed Qubilai with a display of magical powers, and the Mongol prince requested him to remain permanently at court. The relationship soured, however, when Karma Pakshi refused the offer. On his return to Tibet, he formed a relationship with Qubilai's elder brother and political rival Möngke (1209–1259) and consented to visit Möngke's palace in Liangzhou. He taught the Mongol ruler and his court Buddhist doctrine, especially TANTRA based on the CAKRASAṂVARATANTRA. For ten years, Karma Pakshi traveled across China, Mongolia, and Tibet and is also said to have debated with numerous Daoist practitioners. Qubilai assumed the role of high Khan after Möngke's death in 1259. Angered at Karma Pakshi's support of his rival brother, and still smarting from his refusal to remain at court, Qubilai ordered Karma Pakshi's capture and exile. Qubilai eventually relented and allowed the Karma pa to return to Tibet. Upon his return to Mtshur phu, he constructed a massive statue of ŚĀKYAMUNI called the "ornament of the world" ('dzam gling rgyan). The completed statue, however, was slightly tilted. In a famous account, Karma Pakshi is said to have straightened the statue by first assuming the same tilted posture and then righting himself, simultaneously moving the statue. Among his principal disciples was O rgyan pa Rin chen dpal (Orgyenpa Rinchenpal), who would become the guru of the third Karma pa, RANG 'BYUNG RDO RJE.

**karmapatha**. (P. kammapatha; T. las kyi lam; C. yedao; J. gōdō; K. ŏpto 業道). In Sanskrit, "course of action"; the name given to a standardized list of ten types of wholesome (KUŚALA) and unwholesome (AKUŚALA) actions (KARMAN), which lead respectively to salutary rebirths (viz., in the realms of humans and divinities) or unsalutary rebirths (APĀYA; DURGATI, viz., in the realms of hungry ghosts, animals, or hell denizens). The respective ten types are further subdivided into three subsets according to whether they pertain to physical actions, speech acts, or mental actions. The ten unwholesome courses of action (akuśalakarmapatha) include, under the category of the body: (1) killing (prāṇātipāta; P. pāṇātipāta), (2) stealing (adattādāna; P. adinnādāna), and (3) sexual misconduct (KĀMAMITHYĀCĀRA; P. kāmamicchācāra); under the category of speech: (4) lying (mṛṣāvāda; P. musāvāda), (5) slander or malicious speech (paiśunyavāda; P. pisuṇavācā), (6) offensive or harsh speech (pāraṣyavāda; P. pharusavācā), and (7) frivolous prattle (saṃbhinnapralāpa; P. samphappalāpa); and under the category of mind: (8) covetousness (ABHIDHYĀ; P. abhijjhā), (9) ill will (VYĀPĀDA), and (10) wrong views (MITHYĀDṚṢṬI; P. micchādiṭṭhi). The root causes of the ten unwholesome courses of action are greed (LOBHA), hatred (DVEṢA), or delusion (MOHA): for example, killing, ill will, and offensive speech are generally motivated by hatred; sexual misconduct, covetousness, and stealing are generally motivated by desire and greed; wrong views are generally motivated by delusion; and lying, slander, and frivolous prattle are motivated by a combination of all three. For a thought to be classified as an unwholesome mental course of action, it must be particularly extreme—for example, the wish to misappropriate someone else's property, the malicious intention to harm someone, or the adherence to pernicious doctrines. The ten wholesome courses of action (kuśalakarmapatha) are the opposite of those given in the preceding list: under the category of body, the avoidance of killing, the avoidance of stealing, and the avoidance of sexual misconduct; under the category of speech, the avoidance of lying, the avoidance of slander, the avoidance of offensive speech, and the avoidance of prattle; under the category of mind, unselfishness, good will, and right views (SAMYAGDṚṢṬI). The list of ten wholesome and ten unwholesome courses of action is frequently found in all strata of Buddhist literature.

**Karmasiddhiprakaraṇa**. (T. Las grub pa'i rab tu byed pa; C. Dasheng chengye lun; J. Daijō jōgōron; K. Taesŭng sŏngŏp non 大乘成業論). In Sanskrit, "Investigation Establishing [the Correct Understanding] of Karman"; an important treatise written c. 360 CE by the Indian scholiast VASUBANDHU, which seeks to explain karmic continuity by resorting to the quintessential YOGĀCĀRA doctrine of the storehouse consciousness (ĀLAYAVIJÑĀNA). The Sanskrit recension has not survived, so the text is known only through its translations into Chinese (by Vimokṣaprajña and XUANZANG) and Tibetan. Vasubandhu critiques different theories propounded concerning the interconnections between KARMAN (action) and VIPĀKA (fruition) discussed in rival Buddhist schools, including the VAIBHĀṢIKA, SAṂMITĪYA, and SAUTRĀNTIKA. Through this exhaustive analysis, Vasubandhu concludes that, while everything may be momentary (KṢAṆIKA), karman and vipāka are connected through the requital of causal associations that are embedded in the storehouse consciousness. This storehouse consciousness is the repository of the seeds (BĪJA) of past actions and serves as a retributory or appropriating consciousness (ĀDĀNAVIJÑĀNA), which manifests karmic fruitions based on the wholesome and unwholesome influences arising in the other consciousnesses (VIJÑĀNA) to which it is related. The storehouse consciousness is thus the repository for the seeds of all past experiences, as well as the consciousness that "appropriates" a physical body at the moment of rebirth. Vasubandhu's analysis reconciles momentariness (KṢAṆIKAVĀDA), one of the most radical framings of nonself doctrine (ANĀTMAN), with the imperishability of karman.

**karmavācanā**. (P. kammavācā; T. las su bsko ba; C. baijiemo; J. byakukonma; K. paekkalma 白羯磨). In Sanskrit, a "proceeding" or "stating of the matter"; carried out as part of the performance of an ecclesiastical act or saṅghakamma (S. SAṂGHAKARMAN; see also KARMAN) that involves the recitation of a prescribed ritual text. In the Pāli tradition, not all ecclesiastical acts require the performance of a kammavācanā; those that do not are called P. ñattikamma. Ecclesiastical acts that do require a formal "statement of the matter" may be one of two types. The first is the P. ñattidutiyakammavācā (S. JÑAPTIDVITĪYA KARMAVĀCANĀ), an ecclesiastical act that requires the performance of a kammavācanā once. This is the dictated procedure that is to be followed during certain formal occasions within the SAṂGHA, such as the ordination ceremony, the adjudication of rules, the administration of punishments to transgressors of the precepts, and the settlement of disputes among the clergy. A motion or proposal is made formally one time to the attendees and repeated once to solicit additional comment. If the proposal is read in this manner with no audible objections from the group (silence thus indicates approval), it is passed and considered binding on the participants. The second is the P. ñatticatutthakammavācā (S. jñapticaturtha karmavācanā), an ecclesiastical act that requires the performance of a kammavācanā three times. This type involves matters of greater importance or formality and requires three formal questions and an audible response before they are considered decided. There are no saṅghakamma in the Pāli tradition that require the recitation of a kammavācā two times.

**karmāvaraṇa**. (P. kammāvaraṇa; T. las kyi sgrib pa; C. yezhang; J. gōshō/gosshō; K. ŏpchang 業障). In Sanskrit, "karmic obstruction," or "hindered by KARMAN." The term is used in the VISUDDHIMAGGA with reference to meditators who are incapable of making any progress in concentration (SAMĀDHI) exercises, specifically involving the KASIṆA visualization devices. The text notes that a practitioner who has engaged in any of the five types of unwholesome "acts that are of immediate effect" (P. ānantariyakamma; S. ĀNANTARYAKARMAN), such as patricide or causing schism in the community of monks (SAṂGHBHEDA), is "obstructed by his acts" and will therefore never be able to develop a viable meditation practice. ¶ The relation of karmāvaraṇa to meditation practice continues in Korean Buddhism, where the term ŏpchang is colloquially used to refer to any kind of persistent physical, mental, or emotional obstacle to meditation practice, whether that be, for example, constant pain in one's legs that makes it difficult to sit in meditation for long periods, an inability to concentrate, or emotional distress caused by being apart from one's family. Anything that continually inhibits one's ability to practice effectively may be termed an ŏpchang (karmāvaraṇa). In the

ABHIDHARMAKOŚABHĀṢYA, obstacles to meditation practice are referred to as vimokṣāvaraṇa, obstruction to the production of the eight VIMOKṢAS, that is, physical and mental inflexibility (akarmaṇyatā). The ARHAT who is free in both ways (ubhayatobhāgavimukta) is free from this as well as from the KLEŚĀVARAṆA.

**karuṇā**. (T. snying rje; C. bei; J. hi; K. pi 悲). In Sanskrit and Pāli, "compassion," or "empathy"; the wish that others be free from suffering, as distinguished from loving-kindness (MAITRĪ; P. mettā), the wish that others be happy. Compassion is listed as the second of the four divine abidings (BRAHMAVIHĀRA) along with loving-kindness, empathetic joy (MUDITĀ), and equanimity (UPEKṢĀ). As one of the forty topics of meditation (P. KAMMAṬṬHĀNA), compassion is used only for the cultivation of tranquillity (ŚAMATHA), not insight (VIPAŚYANĀ). Compassion is to be developed in the following manner: filling one's mind with compassion, one pervades the world with it, first in one direction, then in a second direction, then a third, a fourth, then above, below, and all around. Of the four divine abidings, compassion, along with loving-kindness and empathetic joy, is capable of producing the first three of the four stages of meditative absorption (DHYĀNA). This mainstream Buddhist notion of compassion is to be distinguished from the "great compassion" (MAHĀKARUṆĀ) of the BODHISATTVA, whose compassion inspires them to develop BODHICITTA, the aspiration to achieve buddhahood in order to liberate all beings from suffering. This great compassion is distinguished both by its scope (all sentient beings) and its agency (one personally seeks to remove the suffering of others). Great compassion thus becomes the primary motivating force that enables the BODHISATTVA to endure the three infinite eons (ASAṂKHYEYAKALPA) necessary to consummate the path to buddhahood. In Mahāyāna literature, numerous techniques are set forth to develop compassion, including acknowledging the kindness one has received from other beings in past lifetimes.

**Karuṇāpuṇḍarīka**. (T. Snying rje pad ma dkar po; C. Beihua jing; J. Hikekyō; K. Pihwa kyŏng 悲華經). In Sanskrit, "Lotus of Compassion"; a MAHĀYĀNA SŪTRA important in the developing cult surrounding worship of the buddha AMITĀBHA. The sūtra was translated into Chinese in ten rolls by DHARMAKṢEMA and seems to have been compiled from various shorter texts. The sūtra tells the story of how a king and his thousand sons aroused the aspiration for enlightenment (BODHICITTOTPĀDA) and received a prediction that they would each be reborn in the PURE LAND. The sūtra is important in the pure land schools for its listing of fifty-one vows of the buddha AMITĀBHA, indicating that it was closely aligned with the teachings of the SUKHĀVATĪVYŪHASŪTRA.

**kaṣāya**. (P. kasāya; T. snyigs ma; C. zhuo; J. joku; K. t'ak 濁). In Sanskrit, lit. "turbidity," "degeneration," or "degradation," etc., referring especially to a list of five degradations that are said to mark the period of degeneracy in the cosmic cycle, when the human life span has declined to between one hundred years and ten years. (Humans are thought to have longer, even much longer, life spans in more salutary periods of the eon.) The five are (1) degeneration of the life span (āyuḥkaṣāya), because the life span has diminished; (2) degeneration of views (dṛṣṭikaṣāya), because wrong views (MITHYĀDṚṢṬI) are so prevalent; (3) degeneration of afflictions (kleśakaṣāya), because the afflictions (KLEŚA) have become so much worse; (4) degeneration of sentient beings (sattvakaṣāya), because living creatures are mentally and physically inferior; and (5) degeneration of the age (kalpakaṣāya), because the world and the environment have worsened. A buddha does not appear in the world during a period marked by the five degenerations, but only during the salutary eon (see BHADRAKALPA).

**kāṣāya**. (P. kāsāya; T. ngur smrig; C. jiasha; J. kesa; K. kasa 袈裟). In Sanskrit, "dyed" (lit. "turbid-colored") robes (CĪVARA), referring to the robes of an ordained monk or nun, which were traditionally required to be sewn from pieces of soiled cloth and "dyed" to a reddish- or brownish-yellow saffron color or ochre tone; also spelled kaṣāya. Although the color that eventually came to be used in different Buddhist traditions varied, the important feature was that it be a mixed or muddied hue—and thus impure—and not a pure primary color. This impurity would help monastics develop a sense of nonattachment even toward their own clothing. According to the VINAYA, the kāṣāya robe is also supposed to be sewn from sullied cloth that ordinary laypeople would be loath to use for clothing, such as rag cloth or funerary shrouds. Even new cloth offered to the SAṂGHA will typically be ritually defiled so that it fulfills this requirement. The final requirement for the kāṣāya robe is that it be sewn from pieces of cloth, not single sheets of new cloth, which were thought to be too luxurious. Robes were sewn from an odd-numbered series of vertical panels, typically five, seven, or nine in number, with each panel also in segments and the whole construction surrounded by a cloth edging. The Buddha is said to have received his inspiration for this patchwork design of the kāṣāya while he was looking over a field of rice paddies with their surrounding embankments. Robes were one of the four major requisites (S. NIŚRAYA; P. nissaya) of the monks and nuns, along with such basics as a begging bowl (PĀTRA), and were the object of the KAṬHINA ceremony, in which the monastics were offered cloth for making new sets of robes at the end of each rain's retreat (VARṢĀ). Robes eventually became symbolic of sectarian affiliation and institutional status within the various Buddhist traditions and are made in an array of bright colors and luxurious fabrics; but even the fanciest of robes will still typically be sewn in the patchwork fashion of the original kāṣāya. See also CĪVARA; TRICĪVARA.

**Kashmir-Gandhāra**. [alt. Kāśmīra-Gandhāra]. A district in northwest India corresponding to modern Kashmir. According to Pāli tradition, this area was the destination of one of the nine Buddhist missions dispatched from Pāṭaliputta (S. PĀṬALIPUTRA) to adjacent lands (paccantadesa) by the elder MOGGALIPUTTATISSA; this mission is said to have occurred during the reign of the Mauryan king AŚOKA, following the third Buddhist council (see COUNCIL, THIRD) in the third century BCE. The elder Majjhantika (S. MADHYĀNTIKA) was said to have been in charge of the mission to this region. The third council at Pāṭaliputta and the nine Buddhist missions are known only in Pāli sources and are first recorded in the fifth century CE DĪPAVAMSA. Burmese chroniclers instead identify Kashmir–Gandhāra with the kingdom of Nanchao in what is the modern Chinese province of Yunnan. See also GANDHĀRA.

**kasiṇa**. (S. *kṛtsna/*kṛtsnāyatana; T. zad par gyi skye mched; C. bianchu; J. hensho; K. p'yŏnch'ŏ 遍處). In Pāli, lit. "totality" or "universal" [alt. kasiṇāyatana], a "visualization device" that serves as the meditative foundation for the "totality" of the mind's attention to an object of concentration. Ten kasiṇa are generally enumerated: visualization devices that are constructed from the physical elements (MAHĀBHŪTA) of earth, water, fire, and air; the colors blue, yellow, red, and white; and light and empty space. The earth device, for example, might be constructed from a circle of clay of even texture, the water device from a tub of water, and the red device from a piece of red cloth or a painted red disc. The meditation begins by looking at the physical object; the perception of the device is called the "beginning sign" or "preparatory sign" (P. PARIKAMMANIMITTA). Once the object is clearly perceived, the meditator then memorizes the object so that it is seen as clearly in his mind as with his eyes. This perfect mental image of the device is called the "eidetic sign," or "learning sign" (P. UGGAHANIMITTA) and serves subsequently as the object of concentration. As the internal visualization of this eidetic sign deepens and the five hindrances (NĪVARAṆA) to mental absorption (P. JHĀNA; S. DHYĀNA) are temporarily allayed, a "representational sign" or "counterpart sign" (P. PAṬIBHĀGANIMITTA) will emerge from out of the eidetic image, as if, the texts say, a sword is being drawn from its scabbard or the moon is emerging from behind clouds. The representational sign is a mental representation of the visualized image, which does not duplicate what was seen with the eyes but represents its abstracted, essentialized quality. The earth disc may now appear like the moon, the water device like a mirror suspended in the sky, or the red device like a bright jewel. Whereas the eidetic sign was an exact mental copy of the visualized beginning sign, the representational sign has no fixed form but may be manipulated at will by the meditator. Continued attention to the representational sign will lead to all four of the meditative absorptions associated with the realm of subtle materiality. Perhaps because of the complexity of preparing the kasiṇa devices, this type of meditation was superseded by techniques such as mindfulness of breathing (P. ānāpānasati; S. ĀNĀPĀNASMṚTI) and is rarely practiced in the THERAVĀDA world today. But its notion of a purely mental object being somehow a purer "representation" of the external sense object viewed by the eyes has compelling connections to later YOGĀCĀRA notions of the world being a projection of mind.

**Kassapasīhanādasutta**. (S. Kāśyapasiṃhanādasūtra; C. Luoxing fanzhi jing; J. Ragyōbonjikyō; K. Nahyŏng pŏmji kyŏng 倮形梵志經). In Pāli, "Discourse on the Lion's Roar of Kassapa"; the eighth sutta of the DĪGHANIKĀYA (a separate DHARMAGUPTAKA recension appears as the twenty-fifth SŪTRA in the Chinese translation of the DĪRGHĀGAMA), preached by the Buddha to the naked ascetic Acela Kassapa at Ujuñña in the Kaṇṇakattha deer park. Acela Kassapa approaches the Buddha and inquires whether it is true that he reviles all ascetic practices (see TAPAS) or whether this is a misrepresentation of his teachings. The Buddha states that he does not revile ascetic practices but that the proper course of action for mendicants is to follow the noble eightfold path (P. ariyāṭṭhaṅgikamagga; S. ĀRYĀṢṬĀṄGAMĀRGA). Acela Kassapa inquires about the efficacy of numerous ascetic practices engaged in by mendicants of the time. The Buddha responds that, even should one follow all of these practices scrupulously but still not be perfect in morality (sīlasampadā), in mentality (cittasampadā), and in wisdom (paññāsampadā), he will not be a true ascetic (samaṇa; ŚRAMAṆA) or a true brāhmaṇa; only when one has attained the destruction of the contaminants (āsavakkhāya; ĀSRAVAKṢAYA), or arahantship (see ARHAT), will one be so recognized. The Buddha then explains in detail Buddhist practice and the attainments, beginning with taking refuge in the three jewels (S. RATNATRAYA) of the Buddha, the dhamma, and the saṅgha, observing the precepts, renouncing the world to become a Buddhist monk, and controlling the senses with mindfulness (sati; SMṚTI), to cultivating the four meditative absorptions (JHĀNA; S. DHYĀNA) and developing the six higher knowledges or superpowers (abhiññā; ABHIJÑĀ) that culminate in the destruction of the contaminants. The sutta concludes by noting that, upon hearing the discourse, Acela Kassapa entered the Buddhist order and in due course attained arahantship.

**Kāśyapa**. (P. Kassapa; T. 'Od srung; C. Jiashe; J. Kashō; K. Kasŏp 迦葉). Sanskrit proper name of one of the seven buddhas of antiquity (SAPTATATHĀGATA) who preceded the current buddha ŚĀKYAMUNI and, by some accounts, the buddha who predicted Śākyamuni's own eventual enlightenment. He is also sometimes mentioned in a list of three past buddhas, along with Krakucchanda and Kanakamuni. ¶ Kāśyapa is also the name of one of the Buddha's ten main disciples, who is usually known to the tradition as "Kāśyapa the Great"; see MAHĀKĀŚYAPA.

**Kāśyapa Mātaṅga**. (C. Jiashe Moteng; J. Kashō Matō; K. Kasŏp Madŭng 迦葉摩騰) (d.u.). Indian monk whom Chinese tradition credits with first introducing Buddhism to East Asia. Emperor Ming (r. 57–75) of the Later Han dynasty is said to have had a dream about a golden man and sent out emissaries to find out who he was. His emissaries traveled to the Western Regions, where they invited Kāśyapa Mātaṅga and his colleague Zhu Falan (Dharmaratna) to China to teach about the golden man, the Buddha. The two monks arrived in the Chinese capital of Louyang in 67 CE with scriptures carried on white horses. Emperor Ming had a monastery built for them in Luoyang, which was accordingly named the White Horse Monastery (BAIMASI). The two missionaries were said to have translated the SISHI'ER ZHANG JING ("Sūtra in Forty-Two Sections"), the first translation of a Buddhist text into Chinese. The *Sishi'er zhang jing* is now known to be a Chinese indigenous composition (see APOCRYPHA), and its translators, Kāśyapa Mātaṅga and Zhu Falan, are considered to be legendary figures.

**Kāśyapaparivarta**. (T. 'Od srung gi le'u; C. Yiri monibao jing; J. Yuinichi manihōkyō; K. Yuil manibo kyŏng 遺日摩尼寶經). In Sanskrit, "The KĀŚYAPA Chapter"; a SŪTRA from one of the earliest strata of Indian MAHĀYĀNA Buddhism, probably dating from sometime in the first century CE. The sūtra offers an overview of practices emblematic of BODHISATTVAs, which are arranged in several groups of four practices apiece. The text cites a "bodhisattva canon" (BODHISATTVAPIṬAKA) as the source for the teaching on the six perfections (PĀRAMITĀ) and offers one of the earliest mentions of the "thought of enlightenment" (BODHICITTA) in its Mahāyāna interpretation as the aspiration to achieve buddhahood. A bodhisattva who generates this thought even for the first time is said to be superior to the solitary buddhas (PRATYEKABUDDHA) and disciples (ŚRĀVAKA). Disciples are also censured as not being true sons of the Buddha, an early expression of the later Mahāyāna school's more explicit denunciations of the so-called HĪNAYĀNA. The sūtra also refers to bodhisattva precepts (see BODHISATTVAŚĪLA), which will subsequently be elaborated upon in such texts as MAITREYA/ASAṄGA's BODHISATTVABHŪMI and in such Chinese APOCRYPHA as the FANWANG JING. The *Kāśyapaparivarta* was one of the first sūtras translated into Chinese, by the Indo-Scythian monk *LOKAKṢEMA (c. 178–198 CE) in 179 CE; a later recension is also included in the massive RATNAKŪṬA collection of sūtras. The *Kāśyapaparivarta* is one of a substantial number of scriptures in the *Ratnakūṭa* collection for which Sanskrit recensions have been rediscovered and edited. Its Sanskrit manuscript was first discovered in KHOTAN in the 1890s and was more than one thousand years old; other Sanskrit fragments have subsequently been recovered.

**Kāśyapīya**. (P. Kassapīya/Kassapika; T. 'Od srung ba'i sde; C. Jiasheyibu/Yinguangbu; J. Kashōyuibu/Onkshō; K. Kasŏbyubu/Ŭmgwangbu 迦葉遺部/飲光部). In Sanskrit, "Followers of Kāśyapa"; one of the eighteen traditional schools of the mainstream Indian Buddhist tradition. There have been several accounts of the identity of the founder Kāśyapa. PARAMĀRTHA and KUIJI presume he was the Indian sage Kāśyapa (MAHĀKĀŚYAPA), while others opine that he was a Kāśyapa who was born some three centuries after the Buddha's death. DAOXUAN (596–667) in his *Sifen lü kaizong ji* says that Jiashe (Kāśyapa) was the personal name of the founder of the Kāśyapīya school and Shansui (SUVARŚAKA) his surname. According to the tradition he is relating, Kāśyapa was one of the five disciples of UPAGUPTA, the fifth successor in the Buddha's lineage about one hundred years following his death. These five disciples established their own schools based on their differing views regarding doctrine and redacted the VINAYA into five distinct recensions (C. Wubu lü). The so-called **Prātimokṣavinaya* of the Kāśyapīya school is not extant, but it is known through the *Prātimokṣasūtra* (*Jietuojie jing*), a primer of the school's monastic discipline. There are several competing theories regarding the lineage of the Kāśyapīya school. The SAMAYABHEDOPARACANACAKRA posits that the Kāśyapīya split off from the SARVĀSTIVĀDA school about three hundred years after the Buddha's death and identifies it with the Suvarśaka school (C. Shansuibu). But other texts, such as the *Śariputraparipṛcchāsūtra,* state that the Kāśyapīya and Suvarśaka schools are distinct, with the former having descended from the STHAVIRANIKĀYA and the latter from the Sarvāstivāda school. (The name of the Suvarśaka school is, however, not attested in Pāli sources.) The *Mañjuśrīparipṛcchā* instead claims that the school derived from the DHARMAGUPTAKA school, while the Tibetan tradition considers it as a collateral lineage of the VIBHAJYAVĀDA school. The most plausible scenario is that the Kāśyapīya, MAHĪŚĀSAKA, and Dharmaguptaka were each subsections of the Vibhajyavāda, which was a loose umbrella term for all those schools (except the Sarvāstivāda) that split off from the Sthaviranikāya. Inscriptional evidence for all three schools survives in northwestern India. The doctrines of the Kāśyapīya tend to be closest to those ascribed to the Sarvāstivāda and Dharmaguptaka schools. The arrangement of its TRIPIṬAKA also seems to have paralleled that of the Dharmaguptaka school, and its ABHIDHARMAPIṬAKA in particular seems to have been similar in structure to the *Śāriputrābhidharmaśāstra* of the Dharmaguptakas. Some of the doctrines that are peculiar to the Kāśyapīyas are as follows: (1) Past KARMAN that has not yet borne fruit exists (but the rest of the past does not), the present exists, and some of the future exists. By limiting the existence of past objects, the Kāśyapīyas reject the Sarvāstivāda position that dharmas perdure in all three time periods. (2) All compounded things (SAṂSKĀRA) are instantly destroyed. (3) Whatever is compounded (SAṂSKṚTA) has its cause in the past, while the uncompounded (ASAṂSKṚTA) has its cause in the future. This view also contrasts with that of the Sarvāstivāda, which holds that future actions can serve as either the retributive cause (VIPĀKAHETU) or the efficient or generic cause (KĀRAṆAHETU) of compounded objects, such that every conditioned dharma serves as the generic, indirect cause for the creation of all other compounded things, except itself. (4) The worthy ones (ARHAT) perfect both the knowledge of cessation (KṢAYAJÑĀNA) and the knowledge of nonproduction (ANUTPĀDAJÑĀNA), the two types of knowledge that accompany liberation from rebirth (SAṂSĀRA); thus, they are no longer subject to the afflictions (KLEŚA).

**Kathāvatthu**. In Pāli, "Points of Controversy"; the fifth of the seven books of the Pāli abhidhammapiṭaka (SEE ABHIDHARMAPIṬAKA). The Pāli tradition ascribes this text to MOGGALIPUTTATISSA, who is credited with having composed the work at the conclusion of the third Buddhist council (COUNCIL, THIRD) held at Pāṭaliputta (S. PĀṬALIPUTRA) in the third century BCE. In its twenty-three chapters, the treatise analyzes a wide range of doctrines held by contemporary Buddhist schools and demonstrates the orthodoxy of STHAVIRANIKĀYA positions. The work presumes the existence of the DHAMMASAṄGAṆI, the VIBHAṄGA, and the PAṬṬHĀNA as definitive abhidhamma sources for resolving doctrinal controversies.

**kaṭhina**. (T. sra brkyang; C. jiachinayi/jianguyi; J. kachinae/kengoe; K. kach'inaŭi/kyŏn'goŭi 迦絺那衣/堅固衣). In Sanskrit and Pāli, "robe-cloth ceremony," referring to the ceremony held in the fourth month of the rainy season, at which time the SAṂGHA as a whole receives gifts of robes or plain cloth from the laity; the cloth or robes are then distributed to individual monastics who have properly observed the rains retreat (VARṢĀ; P. VASSA). If cloth is given, the recipient must stitch it into one of three types of proper robe (TRICĪVARA; see also KAṢĀYA) on the same day. A monk selected to receive a kaṭhina robe or cloth is entitled to five privileges that remain in force for five months: (1) he may accept a meal invitation without telling anyone, (2) he may dwell without one of his three robes, (3) he may eat in a group with other monks, (4) he may keep any number of robes, and (5) he is entitled to a share of the robes donated to the saṃgha. A monk loses his right to receive kaṭhina robes or cloth if he is absent for more than a week from the monastery where he is observing the rains retreat.

**Kātiyānī**. (T. Kā ti bu mo). Sanskrit and Pāli proper name of a lay disciple of the Buddha, who is declared in Pāli sources to be foremost among laywomen in unswerving trust. According to Pāli sources, she was a resident of the city of Kururaghara and a devoted friend of the laywoman KĀLĪ KURURAGHARIKĀ. Kālī was a stream-enterer (SROTAĀPANNA) whose son, SOṆA-KOṬIKAṆṆA, was an arahant (S. ARHAT) renowned for his eloquence. One day, Kātiyānī accompanied Kālī to hear Soṇa preach to his mother. While the two women listened to the sermon, thieves broke into Kātiyānī's house, and when a servant girl, who had been sent back to fetch oil for lamps, returned and reported the theft, Kātiyānī refused to leave until the sermon was finished. At the end of the sermon, she became a stream-enterer. She became renowned for her resoluteness in listening to the dhamma (DHARMA), an honor she had resolved to attain in a previous life during the time of Padumuttara Buddha. The chief of the thieves witnessed all that had transpired and was so moved at Kātiyānī's faith that he ordered that all of her property be returned. The thieves then begged Kātiyānī to forgive them for their wrongdoing. She forgave them and brought them to Soṇa-Koṭikaṇṇa who, seeing their underlying virtue, ordained them. All of the former thieves in turn became arahants as well.

**Katsuragisan**. (J) (葛城山). Mountain practice site on the border between the present-day Japanese prefectures of Nara and Ōsaka, which was an important center of SHUGENDŌ practice. The semilegendary founder of Shugendō, EN NO OZUNU (b. 634), is said to have lived for some thirty years in a cave on this mountain. Since En no Ozunu was considered to be a manifestation of Hōki Bosatsu (DHARMODGATA) who, according to the AVATAMSAKASŪTRA, lived in the Diamond Mountains, the Katsuragi range includes the appositely named KONGŌSAN (Mt. Kongō; see also KŬMGANGSAN). Like many sacred mountains around Japan, there are encased sūtras known to be interred in Katsuragisan region. Twenty-eight buried scrolls (J. kyōzuka) of the SADDHARMAPUṆḌARĪKASŪTRA ("Lotus Sūtra")—corresponding to its twenty-eight chapters—were presumed to have been buried at Mt. Katsuragi, according to the late twelfth-century *Shozan engi* text. Also purportedly interred on the mountain are twenty-nine scrolls of the *Nyohōkyō* (C. **Rufa jing*) and eight hannyakyō (PRAJÑĀPĀRAMITĀ) scrolls. During the Heian period, burying Buddhist scriptures at mountains in Japan served the dual role of physically sacralizing the mountain and also preserving the dharma in the face of the religion's predicted demise (J. mappō; C. MOFA).

**kaṭvāṅga**. (S). See KHAṬVĀṄGA.

**Kātyāyana**. (P. Kaccāna; T. Ka tya'i bu; C. Jiazhanyan; J. Kasen'en; K. Kajŏnyŏn 迦旃延). One of the ten main disciples of the Buddha, who is usually known to the tradition as "Kātyāyana the Great." See MAHĀKĀTYĀYANA.

**Kātyāyanīputra**. (T. Kā ta'i bu mo'i bu; C. Jiaduoyannizi; J. Kataennishi; K. Kadayŏnnija 迦多衍尼子) (c. second to first century BCE). Important scholiast in the SARVĀSTIVĀDA school to whom the tradition attributes authorship of the JÑĀNAPRASTHĀNA, the central text of the Sarvāstivāda ABHIDHARMA.

**Kaukkuṭika**. [alt. Gokulika] (T. Bya gag 'tshong ba; C. Jiyin bu; J. Keiinbu; K. Kyeyunpu 鷄胤部). In Sanskrit, "those from KUKKUṬĀRĀMA"; a major monastery in PĀṬALIPUTRA; one of the three main subgroups of the MAHĀSĀṂGHIKA school of mainstream (NIKĀYA) Buddhism, along with the LOKOTTARAVĀDA [alt. Ekavyavahārika] and the CAITYA. The school is said to have placed pride of place on the ABHIDHARMAPIṬAKA, treating the VINAYA and SŪTRA as preparatory training, and emphasized the logical analysis of the abhidharma to the more expository and provisional expressions of truth found in the other two sections of the canon. This early collateral line of the Mahāsāṃghika school seems to have been most prominent around the end of the second century BCE, before it eventually split into the BAHUŚRUTĪYA and PRAJÑAPTIVĀDA subbranches.

**kaukṛtya**. (P. kukkucca; T. 'gyod pa; C. hui; J. ke; K. hoe 悔). In Sanskrit, "worry," "remorse," or perhaps "crisis of conscience"; along with the related "restlessness" or "distraction" (AUDDHATYA), with which it is often seen in compound (as auddhatya-kaukṛtya); it constitutes the fourth of the five hindrances (NĪVARAṆA) to the attainment of meditative absorption (DHYĀNA). Auddhatya-kaukṛtya is the specific hindrance to joy (SUKHA), the fourth of the five factors of dhyāna (DHYĀNĀṄGA), and is fostered by unwise attention (AYONIŚOMANASKĀRA) to mental unrest and is overcome through learning and reflecting on the SŪTRA and VINAYA, and associating with elders of calm demeanor. Restlessness and worry are countered by SAMĀDHI, the fourth of the five spiritual faculties (INDRIYA) and the sixth of the factors of enlightenment (BODHYAṄGA), together with development of the tranquillity (PRAŚRABDHI), and equanimity (UPEKṢĀ) enlightenment factors.

**Kauṇḍinya**. (S). See ĀJÑĀTAKAUṆḌINYA.

**Kaung-hmu-daw Pagoda**. A massive PAGODA (Burmese, JEDI) located five miles north of SAGAING City in Upper Burma (Myanmar). The Kaung-hmu-daw pagoda was built by King Thalun of AVA (r. 1629–1648) between 1636 and 1648 and houses the Buddha's alms bowl (PĀTRA) and an assortment of gems presented by the king of Sri Lanka. In recognition of its contents, the pagoda also receives the epithet Raza-mani-sula ("Lesser Royal Jewel"). The Kaung-hmu-daw was constructed on a massive scale (214 ft high and 243 ft in diameter) in order to protect the relics it enshrines from the ravages of earthquakes and pillagers. It is similar in shape to the MAHĀTHŪPA of Sri Lanka. Both pagodas are hemispherical and take as their prototype the reliquary STŪPA used in ancient India and Sri Lanka.

**kausīdya**. (P. kusīta; T. le lo; C. jietai; J. kedai; K. haet'ae 懈怠). In Sanskrit, "indolence," "laziness," or "lassitude." According to the SARVĀSTIVĀDA school of ABHIDHARMA, indolence is one of the six "fundamental afflictions" or "defiled factors of wide extent" (KLEŚA-MAHĀBHŪMIKA) that are associated with all defiled thoughts, together with delusion (MOHA), heedlessness (PRAMĀDA), lack of faith (ĀŚRADDHYA), sloth (STYĀNA), and restlessness (AUDDHATYA); the YOGĀCĀRA school also lists indolence among the twenty secondary afflictions (UPAKLEŚA). In addition to the general sense of laziness suggested by the English translations, the term also encompasses a sense of inferiority that discourages one from undertaking the practice of virtue. Indolence encourages attachment to unwholesome activities and the investment of energy in worldly deeds. In each of these senses, kausīdya serves as an obstacle to wholesome deeds, including the practice of meditation. Its antidote is effort (VĪRYA). Eight occasions of indolence are listed in the mainstream NIKĀYAS and ĀGAMAS (ranging from "I may get busy and become tired, so let me lie down now," to "I've been very ill and am not fully recovered, so let me lie down now"), each of which prompts laziness and discourages the adept from arousing the energy necessary to attain, achieve, or realize what is not yet attained, and so forth.

**Kauśika**. (P. Kosiya; T. Ka'u shi ka; C. Jiaoshijia; J. Kyōshika; K. Kyosiga 憍尸迦). The name for the king of the heaven of the thirty-three (TRĀYASTRIṂŚA), ŚAKRO DEVĀNĀM INDRAḤ (known more simply as ŚAKRA or INDRA), during a previous human lifetime as a brāhmaṇa priest. Śakra is often addressed more intimately as Kauśika in Buddhist texts.

**Kauṣṭhila**. (P. Koṭṭhita; T. Gsus po che; C. Juchiluo; J. Kuchira; K. Kuch'ira 拘絺羅). One of the principal arhat disciples of the Buddha deemed foremost among his monk disciples in analytical knowledge (S. PRATISAṂVID; P. paṭisambhidā), viz., of (1) true meaning, (2) the dharma, (3) language, and (4) ready wit. During the time of a previous buddha, Kauṣṭhila was said to have been a wealthy householder, who happened to overhear the Buddha praise one of his disciples as being foremost in analytical knowledge. It was then that he resolved to achieve the same preeminence during the dispensation of a future buddha. According to the Pāli account, Kauṣṭhila/Koṭṭhita was the son of a wealthy brāhmaṇa family from ŚRĀVASTĪ, who was learned in the Vedas and who converted while listening to the Buddha preach to his father. He entered the SAṂGHA and, taking up a topic of meditation (KAMMAṬṬHĀNA), soon attained arhatship. Kauṣṭhila is a frequent interlocutor in the NIKĀYAS and ĀGAMAS and often engages in doctrinal exchanges with ŚĀRIPUTRA, such as regarding what exists after NIRVĀṆA or the relative quality of various types of liberation (VIMUKTI; P. vimutti). Other topics on which Kauṣṭhila discourses in the SŪTRAS include discussions on action (KARMAN); the arising of phenomena, ignorance, and knowledge; the nature of the senses and sense objects; the fate of ARHATS after their deaths; things not revealed by the Buddha; and so on. On one occasion, during a discussion among the elders, a dispute erupted between Kauṣṭhila and a monk named Citta. Citta continually interrupted the discussion by insisting on his views, to the point that Kauṣṭhila had to remind him to let others speak. Citta's supporters objected that their favorite's views were eminently sound; but Kaṣṭhila replied that not only were Citta's views mistaken but he would soon reject the Buddha's teachings and leave the order. Kauṣṭhila's reputation was burnished when events unfolded exactly as he had foretold. Śāriputra held Kauṣṭhila in such high regard that he praises him in three verses preserved in the Pāli THERAGĀTHĀ. His fame was such that he is often known within the tradition as Kauṣṭhila the Great (Mahākauṣṭhila; P. Mahākoṭṭhita).

**kāya**. (T. lus/sku/tshogs; C. shen; J. shin; K. sin 身). In Sanskrit and Pāli, "body"; a term used to refer to the ordinary human body as well as the exalted body, or bodies, of a buddha (for which see TRIKĀYA, or "three bodies"). The body can serve as an object of meditation, as in "mindfulness of the body" (KĀYĀNUPAŚYANĀ; P. kāyānupassanā; see SMṚTYUPASTHĀNA), which involves practices associated with mindfulness of breathing (S. ĀNĀPĀNASMṚTI; P. ānāpānasati), mindfulness of the physical postures (ĪRYĀPATHA), full awareness of bodily actions, contemplation of bodily impurities, contemplation of elements, and nine cemetery meditations (AŚUBHABHĀVANĀ). ¶ The term is also used to refer to a group, collection, or mass, typically as the final member of a compound, for example, a mass or crowd of people (janakāya), or the "collection of names," viz., "letters" (nāmakāya; see CITTAVIPRAYUKTASAṂSKĀRA). ¶ From this sense of kāya as a group evolves the notion of the DHARMAKĀYA, originally meaning the "whole mass" (viz., "all") of the dharmas, and more specifically the "corpus" of a buddha's auspicious qualities (DHARMA). From this latter sense it would come to mean the foundational "dharma-body" of the buddhas.

**kāyānupaśyanā**. (P. kāyānupassanā; T. lus dran pa nye bar bzhag pa; C. shenguan; J. shinkan; K. sin'gwan 身觀). In Sanskrit, "mindfulness of the body." See SMṚTYUPASTHĀNA.

**kāyaprabhā**. (T. lus kyi snang ba/lus 'od; C. guangbei; J. kōhai; K. kwangbae 光背). In Sanskrit, lit. "body light"; a "nimbus," "mandorla," or "aureole" of light that encircles either the head or the body of holy figures in Buddhist painting and sculpture. The radiance surrounding the body of a buddha, bodhisattva, or other sacred being helps to highlight the sacred character of the iconography. This use of light in Buddhist art may derive from depictions of the supernatural-fire motif in Zoroastrian iconography. The Chinese offers several related terms in addition to guangbei (lit. "lighted back") that more precisely delineate what kind of light is being described. "Head light" (C. touguang; J. tōkō; K. tugwang) originally referred to light emanating from between the eyebrows (see ŪRṆĀKEŚA), but it also is used to refer to a halo of light encircling the head, thus a "nimbus." "Body light" (C. shenguang; J. sinkō; K. sin'gwang) or "light [surrounding] the whole body" (C. jushenguang; J. kyosinkō; K. kŏsin'gwang) refers to a halo of light encircling the entire body, or what is usually referred to in the West as a "mandorla" (lit. the "almond" of light surrounding an image). The outdated art-historical term "aureole" may refer to the radiance enveloping either the head or the body in Buddhist iconography.

**kāyasākṣin**. (P. kāyasakkhi; T. lus kyi mngon sum du byed pa; C. shenzheng; J. shinshō; K. sinjŭng 身證). In Sanskrit, "bodily witness" or "one who has bodily testimony"; the fifth of the seven noble disciples (ĀRYA) listed in the MAJJHIMANIKĀYA; a particular sort of nonreturner (ANĀGĀMIN), one of the twenty members of the ĀRYASAṂGHA (see VIṂŚATIPRABHEDASAṂGHA). According to commentaries on the ABHIDHARMAKOŚABHĀṢYA, there are two types of kāyasākṣin. The kāyasākṣin who is a dṛṣṭadharmaśama (one for whom there is peace in this life) is a nonreturner who does not journey to the realms of subtle materiality or immateriality and is not reborn in the sensuous realm either, but enters into NIRODHASAMĀPATTI (equipoise of cessation) during a final life in the sensuous realm, and, without that cessation weakening, enters nirvāṇa. Other kāyasākṣins are nonreturners who are born as subtle materiality realm deities, enter into nirodhasamāpatti on that basis, and enter NIRVĀṆA in that life, or nonreturners who are born as subtle materiality realm deities, enter into nirodhasamāpatti on that basis, die, and enter nirvāṇa as a divinity in the immaterial realm.

**kāyavijñāna**. (P. kāyaviññāṇa; T. lus kyi rnam par shes pa; C. shenshi; J. shinshiki; K. sinsik 身識). In Sanskrit, "tactile consciousness" or "body consciousness"; one of the five consciousnesses of physical objects (along with those of the eye, ear, nose, and tongue) and one of the six sensory consciousnesses (adding the mental consciousness, or MANOVIJÑĀNA). The tactile consciousness perceives tangible objects (SPRAṢṬAVYA). Like the other consciousnesses of physical objects, tactile consciousness is produced through the contact (SPARŚA) between a tactile sensory object (spraṣṭavya) and the tactile sense base or body sense organ (KĀYENDRIYA) and in dependence on three conditions (PRATYAYA): the object condition (ĀLAMBANAPRATYAYA), in this case, a tangible object; a dominant condition (ADHIPATIPRATYAYA), here, the tangible sense base or body sense organ (KĀYENDRIYA); and the immediately preceding condition (SAMANANTARAPRATYAYA), a prior moment of consciousness. The tactile consciousness is counted as one of the six sensory consciousnesses (VIJÑĀNA) and eighteen elements (DHĀTU).

**kāyaviññāṇa**. (P). See KĀYAVIJÑĀNA.

**kāyāyatana**. (T. lus kyi skye mched; C. shenchu; J. shinsho; K. sinch'ŏ 身處). In Sanskrit and Pāli, "tactile sense base" or "base of tactile cognition"; the tactile or body sense organ (KĀYENDRIYA), as it occurs in the list of the twelve sense-fields (ĀYATANA), which are called "bases of cognition" because each pair of sense base and sense object produces its respective sensory consciousness. In this case, the contact (SPARŚA) between a tactile sensory object (SPRAṢṬAVYA) and the tactile sense base (kāyendriya) produces a tactile consciousness (KĀYAVIJÑĀNA).

**kāyendriya**. (P. kāyindriya; T. lus kyi dbang po; C. shengen; J. shinkon; K. sin'gŭn 身根). In Sanskrit and Pāli, "tactile sense base" or "body sense organ"; the physical organ located in the body that makes it possible to perceive tangible objects (SPRAṢṬAVYA). This sense base is not the body itself, but a form of subtle materiality located on the body and invisible to the naked eye. It is said to be like a thin layer of skin covering the entire body. If this sense organ is absent or damaged, physical sensation is not possible. The tactile sense organ serves as the dominant condition (ADHIPATIPRATYAYA) for the production of tactile consciousness (KĀYAVIJÑĀNA). The tactile sense base is counted among the six sense bases or sense organs (INDRIYA), the twelve sources (ĀYATANA), and eighteen elements (DHĀTU).

**Kazi Dawa Samdup**. (Ka dzi Zla ba bsam 'grub) (1868–1922). An early translator from Tibetan to English, best known for his work with WALTER EVANS-WENTZ as translator of *The Tibetan Book of the Dead*. He apparently had wished to pursue the religious life but, as the eldest son in his family, was unable to do so. He was a disciple of a Bhutanese lama, one Guru Norbu, who was affiliated with the 'BRUG PA BKA' BRGYUD sect. Kazi Dawa Samdup served as a translator for such figures as ALEXANDRA DAVID-NÉEL, Charles Bell, and John Woodroffe (Arthur Avalon) and also was a member of the political staff of the thirteenth DALAI LAMA during his sojourn in Sikkim and India. In 1919, he published a 20,000-word English–Tibetan dictionary. Also in 1919, he was serving as the English teacher at the Maharaja's Boys' School in Gangtok, when the local police chief introduced him to Evans-Wentz. He agreed to provide a translation of a Tibetan text that Evans-Wentz had acquired, the BAR DO THOS GROL CHEN MO. The translations that Kazi Dawa Samdup made for Evans-Wentz eventually appeared in three books: *The Tibetan Book of the Dead* (1927), *Tibetan Yoga and Secret Doctrines* (1935), and *The Tibetan Book of the Great Liberation* (1954). He was subsequently appointed to the post of lecturer in Tibetan at the University of Calcutta. In 1924, after his death, Evans-Wentz visited Kazi Dawa Samdup's family in Kalimpong, from whom he received a manuscript translation of the MI LA RAS PA'I RNAM THAR, a famous biography of MI LA RAS PA, which Evans-Wentz subsequently edited and published as *Tibet's Great Yogi Milarepa* (1928). Although Evans-Wentz's notes and prefaces to these works contain many fanciful elements, Kazi Dawa Samdup's translations are generally well regarded.

**kechimyaku sōjō**. (血脈相承). In Japanese, "transmission of the bloodline"; a term used to refer to the unbroken transmission of the dharma from master to disciple down through the generations, which is like the bloodline in a family being passed from parents to child. The term is especially used in the ZEN (CHAN) and esoteric Buddhist sects in Japan, but later is adopted by the JŌDOSHŪ and NICHIRENSHŪ as well. Cf. XUEMO LUN.

**Keizan Jōkin**. (瑩山紹瑾) (1268–1325). Japanese ZEN master and putative second patriarch of the SŌTŌ Zen tradition. Keizan was a native of Echizen in present-day Fukui prefecture. Little is known of his early years, but Keizan is said to have been influenced by his mother, who was a pious devotee of the BODHISATTVA AVALOKITEŚVARA. Keizan went to the nearby monastery of EIHEIJI and studied under the Zen master Gikai (1219–1309), a disciple of DŌGEN KIGEN (1200–1253). He was later ordained by the monk Ejō (1198–1280). After Ejō's death, Keizan went to the nearby monastery of Hōkyōji and continued his studies under another disciple of Dōgen, Jakuen (1207–1299). At age twenty-eight, Keizan was invited as the founding abbot (kaisan; C. KAISHAN) of the monastery of Jōmanji in Awa (present-day Tokushima prefecture). The next year, Keizan briefly visited Eiheiji to train in the conferral of bodhisattva precepts (bosatsukai; PUSA JIE; see also BODHISATTVAŚĪLA) under the guidance of the abbot Gien (d. 1313). Keizan returned to Jōmanji the very same year and began to confer precepts. Several years later, Keizan joined Gikai once more at the latter's new temple of Daijōji in Ishikawa and became his disciple. Three years later, Keizan succeeded Gikai as abbot of Daijōji. In 1300, Keizan began his lectures on what would eventually come to be known as the DENKŌROKU. In 1311, while setting the regulations for Daijōji, Keizan composed the ZAZEN YŌJINKI and *Shinjinmei nentei*. He also entrusted Daijōji to his disciple Meihō Sotetsu (1277–1350) and established the monastery of Jōjūji in nearby Kaga. In 1317, Keizan established the monastery of Yōkōji on Mt. Tōkoku. Keizan also came into possession of a local temple known as Morookadera, which was renamed SŌJIJI. In 1322, Yōkōji and Sōjiji were sanctioned as official monasteries by Emperor Godaigo (r. 1318–1339). This sanction is traditionally considered to mark the official establishment of Sōtō as an independent Zen institution. Keizan later entrusted the monastery of Sōjiji to his disciple Gasan Jōseki (1276–1366) and retired to Yōkōji. In the years before his death, Keizan built a buddha hall, founder's hall, dharma hall, and monk's hall at Yōkōji.

**Kenchōji**. (建長寺). A monastery in Kamakura, Japan, which is currently headquarters (honzan) of the Kenchōji branch of the RINZAI ZEN tradition. Kenchōji was established in 1249 by the powerful regent Hōjō Tokiyori (1227–1263). The founding abbot (kaisan; C. KAISHAN) of Kenchōji was the émigré Chan master LANXI DAOLONG, whose lineage, known as the Daikakuha (along with WUXUE ZUYUAN's Bukkōha), came to dominate the abbacy of Kenchōji. In 1293, the monastery was destroyed in a conflagration following an earthquake. In 1300, the reconstruction of Kenchōji took place. Kenchōji continued to serve as the private worship grounds for the Kamakura shōguns. In 1385, Ashikaga Yoshimitsu (1358–1408) placed Kenchōji as first rank of the GOZAN system. Kenchōji went through several reconstructions during the Edo period.

**Kenninji**. (建仁寺). A monastery in Kyōto, Japan, which is currently headquarters (honzan) of the Kenninji branch of the RINZAI ZEN tradition. Kenninji was established in 1202 by the shōgun Minamoto Yoriie (1182–1204), who appointed MYŌAN EISAI (1141–1215) its abbot and founding patriarch (kaisan; C. KAISHAN). Kenninji was one of the first Zen monasteries to be established in Japan. Although Kenninji was devastated by fire in 1246, 1256, and 1258, the influential abbot ENNI BEN'EN (1202–1280) restored it back to glory. Throughout most of the fourteenth century, Kenninji remained a high-ranking monastery in the GOZAN system.

**Keqin**. (C) (克勤). See YUANWU KEQIN.

**Kern, Hendrik**. (1833–1917). Important Dutch scholar of Sanskrit and Buddhism. Born Johan Hendrik Caspar Kern to Dutch parents in the Dutch East Indies, his family returned to the Netherlands when he was six years old. Beginning in 1851, he studied Sanskrit at Leiden and then in Berlin (with Albrecht Weber) before returning to the Netherlands as a lecturer in Greek.

In 1863, he accepted an invitation to teach Sanskrit in Benares, returning in 1865 to become professor of Sanskrit at Leiden University, a position that he held until his retirement in 1903. He commanded a remarkable array of languages and published on a wide range of topics, mostly writing in his native Dutch. In 1884, he published the first English-language translation of the SADDHARMAPUṆḌARĪKASŪTRA ("Lotus Sūtra") as part of MAX MÜLLER's Sacred Books of the East series; a French translation of the sūtra by EUGÈNE BURNOUF had been published in 1852. Kern published an edition of the Nepalese manuscript in 1912. His chief contribution to Buddhist Studies was his two-volume *Geschiedenis van het Buddhisme in Indië* (*History of Buddhism in India*) published in 1882–1884, in which he put forward the view that the Buddha was a solar god, with the twelve NIDĀNAS, representing the twelve months, etc. In this work, he also argued for the influence of the Yoga school on early Buddhism.

**Kerouac, Jack**. (1922–1969). American novelist influenced by Buddhism. Kerouac was born in Lowell, Massachusetts, to a working-class Quebecois family. His first language was the Quebecois French dialect; he learned English from nuns at the local parish school. An outstanding student and athlete in high school, he accepted an athletic scholarship to Columbia University in 1940 and became a star football player, before a broken leg ended his career. Kerouac left the university and enlisted in the Navy but was discharged. He served as a merchant seaman before returning to Columbia in 1944, where he met ALLEN GINSBERG and began to gather a group of companions that Kerouac would later dub the "Beat Generation." His friend Neal Cassady's enthusiasm for the psychic Edgar Cayce (1877–1945) prompted Kerouac to want to learn something about Asian religions. Finding DWIGHT GODDARD's *A Buddhist Bible* in the public library in San Jose, California, he studied the book carefully and memorized sections of it. Although Kerouac considered himself to be a Roman Catholic throughout his life, his interest in Buddhism grew, in part due to the influence of the poet GARY SNYDER, whom he met in San Francisco. At Snyder's urging, Kerouac wrote a Buddhist scripture, *The Scripture of the Golden Eternity*, as well as a life of the Buddha. His best-known works, however, are *On the Road* (1957) and *The Dharma Bums* (1958). Kerouac died in his mother's home in Florida at the age of forty-seven of complications resulting from alcoholism.

**ketu**. (T. rgyal mtshan; C. chuang; J. dō; K. tang 幢). In Sanskrit and Pāli, "banner"; symbolizing the victory of a buddha's teachings and the vanquishing of Buddhism's ideological opponents. See FACHUANG.

**Kevaṭṭasutta**. (C. Jiangu jing; J. Kengokyō; K. Kyŏn'go kyŏng 堅固經). In Pāli, "Sermon to Kevaṭṭa" [alt. Kevaddhasuttanta]; eleventh sutta of the DĪGHANIKĀYA (a separate DHARMAGUPTAKA recension appears as the twenty-fourth sūtra in the Chinese translation of the DĪRGHĀGAMA), preached by the Buddha to the householder Kevaṭṭa [alt. Kevaddha] in the Pāvārika mango grove at NĀLANDĀ. According to the Pāli account, Kevaṭṭa approached the Buddha and asked him to order a monk disciple to perform a miracle in order to inspire faith among the Buddha's followers dwelling in Nālandā. The Buddha responded that there are three kinds of wonder, the wonder of supranormal powers (iddhipāṭihāriya), the wonder of manifestation (ādesanāpāṭihāriya), and the wonder of education (anusāsanīpāṭihāriya). The wonder of supranormal powers is composed of the ability to make multiple bodies of oneself, to become invisible, to pass through solid objects, to penetrate the earth, to walk on water, to fly through the sky, to touch the sun and moon, and to reach the highest heaven of BRAHMĀ. The wonder of manifestation is the ability to read the thoughts and feelings of others. The Buddha declared all these wonders to be trivial and disparages their display as vulgar. Far superior to these, he says, is the wonder of education, which leads to awakening to the teaching and entering the Buddhist order, training in the restraint of action and speech, observance of minor points of morality, guarding the senses, mindfulness, contentment with little, freedom from the five hindrances, joy and peace of mind, the four meditative absorptions, insight (ñāṇadassana; JÑĀNADARŚANA) into the conditioned nature and impermanence of body and mind, knowledge of the FOUR NOBLE TRUTHS (catvāry āryasatyāni), and the destruction of the contaminants (āsavakkhaya; S. ĀSRAVAKṢAYA).

**Kewen**. (C) (克文). See ZHENJING KEWEN.

**Kha ba dkar po**. (Kawagarbo). A famous mountain on the Tibetan plateau and the toponym of the deity embodied there; currently located in the Chinese province of Yunnan on the border with the Tibet Autonomous Region, close to Bde chen (Diqin). It is one of the eight famous mountains and mountain ranges, including Mount KAILĀSA in western Tibet and Dag pa shel ri (the Crystal Mountain) in the TSA RI, on the borders of eastern Nepal on the pilgrimage circuit (see GNAS SKOR BA). The mountain (22,113 ft) is an important site for a two-week pilgrimage circuit.

**Kha char gtsug lag khang**. (Kachar tsuklakang). A temple, known also as Kho char and Kho chags, built at the end of the tenth century near Spu rang (Purang), the eastern capital of the Tibetan GU GE kingdom. It was built by Kho re, a brother of YE SHES 'OD, and housed a special silver statue. Two other images were later added, which together were called "the three silver brothers" (dngul sku mched gsum). They were generally thought to be AVALOKITEŚVARA, MAÑJUŚRĪ, and VAJRAPĀṆI, although which was the original and central image is unknown. Kho re took over the kingdom after Ye shes 'od renounced the throne to take up the religious life in 988. The temple, the full name of which is Kha char Yid bzhin lhun gyi grub pa'i gtsug lag khang, was built during the same phase of temple building as TA PHO GTSUG LAG KHANG.

**khaḍgaviṣāṇa**. (P. khaggavisāṇa; T. bse ru; C. linjiao; J. ringaku; K. in'gak 麟角). In Sanskrit, "rhinoceros"; the solitary way of life pursued by the rhinoceros is a metaphor commonly found in the sūtras to refer to the life of solitude that monks should follow. The Buddha acknowledged the value of living together with a community of like-minded religious colleagues (KALYĀṆAMITRA), but rather than keep the company of "bad friends," it was instead preferable to live "like a rhinoceros" (KHAḌGAVIṢĀṆAKALPA). As but one of many examples in the literature, the *Khaggavisāṇasutta* ("Discourse on the Rhinoceros") in the SUTTANIPĀTA (I.13) is a series of verses that all end with the repeated refrain that monks should "wander alone, like a rhinoceros." Since the term khaḍga (P. khagga) by itself means a "rhinoceros," the Pāli commentaries parsed the compound khaḍgaviṣāṇa (khaggavisāṇa) to mean "rhinoceros horn," a rendering sometimes found in English translations, and the metaphor was then interpreted to mean "solitary" like the single horn of a rhinoceros. The standard Chinese translation for this term as "rhinoceros horn" (linjiao) also reflects this traditional understanding.

**khaḍgaviṣāṇakalpa**. (P. khaggavisāṇakappa; T. bse ru lta bu; C. linjiaoyu; J. ringakuyu; K. in'gagyu 麟角喩). In Sanskrit, "like a rhinoceros"; a metaphor for the life of solitude that monks should follow (see KHAḌGAVIṢĀṆA). The term is also used to refer to one of the two types of solitary buddhas (PRATYEKABUDDHA): the khaḍgaviṣāṇakalpa type, who live in solitude "like a rhinoceros," and the "congregators" (VARGACĀRIN).

**khakkhara**. (T. 'khar bsil; C. xizhang; J. shakujō; K. sŏkchang 錫杖). In Sanskrit, a "mendicant's staff" that monks carried during their itinerant wandering; written variously as khakharaka, khaṅkharaka, etc. The staff was one on a list of eighteen requisites (NIŚRAYA) of a monk, along with robes, alms bowl, etc. The mendicant carried the staff during his wanderings to scare away wild animals and to ward off any small animals in his path. It could also serve as a means of letting his presence be known to the laity when begging for alms (PIṆḌAPĀTA). This is because the staff was topped by a round metal cap usually made of brass, while the staff itself was made of wood or iron. As the onomatopoeic Sanskrit word suggests, the metal cap has small rings dangling from it that made a jingling sound when shaken. This cap was often decorated with symbols of the teachings and virtues of the Buddha, such as a CINTĀMAṆI, a dragon (NĀGA), a five-wheeled STŪPA (C. wulunta; J. gorinta; K. oryunt'ap 五輪塔), or a buddha triad. Depending on the number of rings that hung symmetrically from each side of the metal cap, the staff could also be referred to as a four-, six-, or twelve-ring staff. KṢITIGARBHA statues are often depicted holding such a staff; it is also one of the attributes of eleven-headed AVALOKITEŚVARA (EKĀDAŚAMUKHĀVALOKITEŚVARA).

**Khams sprul incarnations**. (Kamtrül). A revered Tibetan lineage of incarnate masters (SPRUL SKU) belonging to the 'BRUG PA BKA' BRGYUD sect of Tibetan Buddhism. The fourth, Bstan 'dzin chos kyi nyi ma (Tendzin Chökyi Nyima, 1730–1780), composed an important description of the sacred sites of the Kathmandu Valley. The lineage includes

1. Karma bstan 'phel (Karma Tenpel, 1598–1638)
2. Kun dga' bstan 'phel (Kunga Tenpel, 1639–1679)
3. Kun dga' bstan 'dzin (Kunga Tendzin, 1680–1729)
4. Bstan 'dzin chos kyi nyi ma (Tendzin Chökyi Nyima, 1730–1780)
5. Grub brgyud nyi ma (Drupgyü Nyima, 1781–1847)
6. Bstan pa'i nyi ma (Tenpe Nyima, 1848–1907)
7. Sangs rgyas bstan 'dzin (Sangye Tendzin, 1908–1929)
8. Don brgyud nyi ma (Dongyü Nyima, b. 1930)

**Khandhaka**. In Pāli "Collections"; the second major division of the Pāli basket of discipline (VINAYAPIṬAKA), which is subdivided between the MAHĀVAGGA ("Great Chapter") and the CŪḶAVAGGA ("Lesser Chapter"). This division covers the early history of the SAṂGHA and the institution of formal rules and procedures governing monastic life. Whereas the PRĀTIMOKṢA offers extensive sets of rules regarding the individual conduct of monks or nuns, the *Khandhaka* largely deals with their roles as members of the monastic community. See also SKANDHAKA.

**khanikasamādhi**. In Pāli, "momentary concentration"; a type of rudimentary concentration ancillary to UPACĀRASAMĀDHI and APPANĀSAMĀDHI, which is used with reference to meditators who are developing insight (vipassanā; S. VIPAŚYANĀ) practice. Although a meditator specializing in insight techniques may not be developing advanced forms of meditative absorption (JHĀNA; S. DHYĀNA), he still requires a modicum of concentration in order to maintain his intensive analysis of experience. Hence, the commentators posit that even insight practice requires "momentary concentration" in order to succeed.

**khapuṣpa**. (T. nam mkha'i me tog; C. konghua/xukonghua; J. kūge/kokūge; K. konghwa/hŏgonghwa 空華/虛空華). In Sanskrit, lit. "flower in the sky," a common metaphor in Buddhist texts for something illusory. Just as a person with macular degeneration might believe that the "flowers" he perceives floating in the sky are real, when in fact they are actually a symptom of his disease, so too might an ignorant sentient being believe that he possesses a perduring soul (ĀTMAN) or self-nature (SVABHĀVA) that exists in reality, when in fact this notion is simply a misperception of the reality of nonself (ANĀTMAN); or that the afflictions (KLEŚA) affecting his mind are real, when in fact they are a product of attachment and are thus emptiness (ŚŪNYATĀ).

**Kharoṣṭhī**. An ancient Indic script used in northwest India between the third century BCE and the third century CE to write

Sanskrit and GĀNDHĀRĪ. It was used in the GANDHĀRA region, as well as KUṢANA and SOGDIANA. Its alphabet follows the order of ARAPACANA. Several of the edicts of AŚOKA from northwest India are in Kharoṣṭhī script; these were deciphered by James Prinsep. In the late twentieth century, numerous birch-bark Buddhist manuscripts written in Kharoṣṭhī were discovered in Afghanistan; dating from as early as the first century CE, they represent the oldest extant Buddhist manuscripts.

**khaṭvāṅga**. (T. khri shing; C. chuangzu; J. shōsoku; K. sangjok 床足). In Sanskrit, lit. "the foot of a bedstead," a staff topped by a skull that was thought to be the weapon of Śiva. This type of staff was one of the requisites commonly carried by Indian ascetics, SIDDHAs, and tāntrikas.

**Khemā, Ayya**. (1923–1997). Prominent THERAVĀDA Buddhist nun, meditation teacher, and advocate of women's rights, born Ilse Ledermann to Jewish parents in Germany. In 1938, she fled from Nazi Germany to Scotland along with two hundred child refugees and two years later was reunited with her parents, who had escaped to Shanghai, China. The family was subsequently interned by the Japanese in World War II. She immigrated to the United States in 1949, where she married and had two children. In the early 1960s, she toured Asia with her husband and children, and it was at this time that she learned Buddhist meditation. She began teaching meditation in the 1970s and established Wat Buddha Dhamma, a Theravāda forest monastery near Sydney, Australia, in 1978. Soon thereafter, she was ordained a Buddhist nun by Nārada Mahāthera in Sri Lanka in 1979, receiving the name Khemā. In Colombo, she founded both the International Buddhist Women's Center as a training center for Sri Lankan nuns and the Parappuduwa Nuns' Island Hermitage at Dodanduwa. In 1987, Ayya Khemā organized the first international conference of Buddhist nuns held in BODHGAYĀ, India, and helped found Sakyadhita, the first global Buddhist women's organization. Also in 1987, she was the first Buddhist invited to address the United Nations. In 1989, she established Buddha Haus in Germany and served as its first director. A prolific writer, she authored over a dozen books on Buddhist meditation and teachings. She died in 1997 while in residence at Buddha Haus.

**Khóa Hư Lục**. (課虛錄). In Vietnamese, "Instructions on Emptiness," composed by Trần Thái Tông (1218–1277); the first prose work on Buddhism written in Vietnamese. It is a collection of sermons and essays, most of them fragmentary, on the philosophy and practice of Buddhism from the perspective of the three trainings in morality (ŚĪLA), concentration (SAMĀDHI), and wisdom (PRAJÑĀ). It also marks one of the earliest efforts to assimilate the worldview of the Southern school (NAN ZONG) of CHAN into Vietnamese Buddhism. The *Khóa Hư Lục* consists of two books. The first (lit. "upper") book includes twenty-one short essays, which can be classified as follows according to their literary styles: one "verse" on the FOUR NOBLE TRUTHS; two "general discourses" on the contemplation of the body and the Buddhist path; six "essays" on generating the thought of enlightenment (BODHICITTA), not taking life, not stealing, not indulging in sensual pleasures, not telling lies, and not using intoxicants; five "treatises" on the topics of morality, concentration, wisdom, receiving precepts, buddha-contemplation (NIANFO), sitting in meditation, and the mirror of wisdom; four "prefaces" to longer complete works (three of which are no longer extant), viz., "A Guide to the Chan School," "A Commentary on the VAJRASAMĀDHISŪTRA," "Liturgy of the Six-Period Repentance," and "An Essay on the Equality Repentance Liturgy"; "recorded encounter dialogues with disciples" that record dialogues between Trần Thái Tông and his students; a "verse commentary" on the ancient public cases (GONG'AN) of Chan; and an "afterword." The second (lit. "lower") book includes a complete essay entitled "Liturgy of the Six-Period Repentance," which offers a detailed instruction on the performance of the repentance liturgy.

**Khotan**. (C. Yutian; J. Uten; K. Ujŏn 于闐). Indo-European oasis kingdom at the southern edge of the Taklamakhan Desert in Central Asia, along the northern slope of the Kunlun Mountains, which served as a major center of Buddhism in Central Asia and an important conduit for the transmission of Buddhism from India to China. Buddhist sources claim that Khotan was colonized first by Indians, when Kuṇāla, the eldest son of King AŚOKA, is said to have left the northwest Indian city of TAKṢAŚILĀ (Taxila) for Khotan in the third century BCE. From at least the third through the tenth centuries CE, Khotan was a major Buddhist and trade center along the southern SILK ROAD through Central Asia, where MAHĀYANA traditions associated with northwestern Indian Buddhism predominated. Indeed, through about the tenth century CE, Khotan was essentially a bastion of Indian urban culture in the Tarim Basin, which used GĀNDHĀRĪ PRAKRIT (in the KHAROṢṬHĪ script) in much of its written communications until the relatively late rise in the use of indigenous vernacular Khotanese (probably sometime after the sixth century CE). The Khotanese language, which no longer survives, belonged to the Middle Iranian branch of the Indo-European language family, and fragments of Buddhist texts translated into Khotanese were discovered by SIR MARC AUREL STEIN (1862–1943) during his excavations in the region. Already by the third century CE, Chinese monks were traveling to Khotan to learn Buddhist doctrine and acquire Buddhist scriptures, and Khotanese scholars and monks were making their way to China to transmit and translate Buddhist texts (including such important Mahāyāna scriptures as the AVATAṂSAKASŪTRA, which was brought from Khotan early in the fifth century). The pilgrimage reports of FAXIAN and XUANZANG attest that Khotan was the home of at least four major monasteries and several smaller ones, with several tens of thousands of monks in residence. The Chinese occupied Khotan during both the first and seventh centuries CE, but throughout the first millennium they maintained close economic and cultural ties with the kingdom. By the eighth century, the continued incursions of Arabs, Turks, and Mongols inexorably led to the demise of Buddhism in the region and the people's conversion to Islam; Khotan was finally converted to Islam in 1004. Since the mid-eighteenth century, during the Qing dynasty (1644–1912), Khotan has been under the political control of China and currently is located in the Uighur Autonomous Region of Xinjiang province. See also KUCHA.

**Khra 'brug**. (Tradruk). The earliest of Tibet's great geomantic temples, after the JO KHANG in LHA SA, said to have been founded by king SRONG BTSAN SGAM PO near the town of Tsetang (Rtse thang). According to traditional accounts, it was erected on the left shoulder of a great supine demoness whose body splayed across Tibet, hindering the spread of Buddhist teachings. It is therefore counted as one of the four "edge-taming temples" or "edge-pinning temples" (MTHA' 'DUL GTSUG LAG KHANG). The site was later venerated as a royal monastery by kings KHRI SRONG LDE BTSAN and Mu ne btsan po in the late eighth and early ninth centuries. After the persecution of king GLANG DAR MA, Khra 'brug was renovated and expanded in 1351, and later by the fifth DALAI LAMA, NGAG DBANG BLO BZANG RGYA MTSHO, who added a golden roof. By the late eighteenth century, the site had become a complex of twenty-one temples. Although almost completely destroyed during the Chinese Cultural Revolution, reconstruction of the temple began in the 1980s.

**khregs chod**. (trekchö). In Tibetan, lit. "breaking through the hard" or "breakthrough"; one of the two main practices in the SNYING THIG tradition of RDZOGS CHEN, the other being THOD RGAL, "crossing the crest" or "leap over." Khregs chod is paired with the essential purity (ka dag) of awareness; the practice of khregs chod leads to thod rgal; it cuts through the stream of obscurations and reveals awareness (RIG PA) devoid of object–subject bifurcation (GRĀHYAGRĀHAKAVIKALPA). Sustaining this awareness uninterruptedly while involved in ordinary sense perception is the essence of the practice. It cuts the stream of past and future thought and uses the gap of the unfindable present to contact the primordial pure awareness. It is oriented toward the emptiness (ŚŪNYATĀ) aspect free from conceptual proliferation (NIṢPRAPAÑCA). Both thod rgal and khregs chod are concerned with the natural light ('od gsal; PRABHĀSVARA) of pure awareness; but whereas the former leads to the total dissolution of the body into light in a vision of transcendental consciousness (ye shes; JÑĀNA), the practice of the latter leaves the practitioner as a small particle of dust, as it were.

**Khri srong lde btsan**. (Trisong Detsen) (r. 754–799). A Tibetan ruler considered the second of three great religious kings (chos rgyal) during the Imperial Period, the other two being SRONG BTSAN SGAM PO and RAL PA CAN, and as a human incarnation of the BODHISATTVA AVALOKITEŚVARA. Inheriting the throne in 754 as the thirty-eighth monarch of the Yar klungs dynasty, Khri srong lde btsan directed several events that are considered milestones in Tibetan history. During the early years of his reign, he extended the boundaries of the Tibetan empire forged under his predecessors. In 763, the king's army occupied the imperial capital of Tang China at Chang'an (present-day Xi'an), an action commemorated on a stele that was erected in front of the PO TA LA Palace. However, Khri srong lde btsan is best remembered for his patronage of Buddhism and support in founding Tibet's first Buddhist monastery of BSAM YAS. Later chronicles record that he actively suppressed the native BON religion, as well as the aristocratic clans who were its benefactors, although he never entirely proscribed early Bon rituals. Khri srong lde btsan invited the renowned Indian Buddhist preceptor ŚĀNTARAKṢITA to oversee the project of building Bsam yas and to establish the first monastic order in Tibet. According to traditional accounts, local spirits inimical to Buddhism created obstacles that hindered the project, which prompted the Indian abbot to request Khri srong lde btsan to invite the powerful tantric master PADMASAMBHAVA to Tibet in order to aid in their subjugation, after which the establishment of the monastery was able to proceed. Khri srong lde btsan is said to have become a devotee of Padmasambhava, with one of his queens, YE SHES MTSHO RGYAL, becoming the yogin's consort and serving as scribe for many of his GTER MA teachings. Padmasambhava also revived the king's eight-year-old daughter PADMA GSAL after her death in order to bestow a special teaching. According to tradition, at the time of his death, ŚĀNTARAKṢITA warned in his final testament that a mistaken philosophical view would become established in Tibet and advised the king to invite KAMALAŚĪLA to come to Tibet in order to dispel it. The view was apparently that of the Northen Chan (BEI ZONG) monk Heshang Moheyan, who had developed a following at the Tibetan court. Kamalaśīla was invited and a debate was held between the Indian monk and the Chinese monk, with the king serving as judge. It is unclear whether a face-to-face debate took place or rather an exchange of documents. According to Tibetan sources, the king declared Kamalaśīla the winner, named MADHYAMAKA as the official philosophical school of his realm, and banished the Chinese party from his kingdom. (Chinese records describe a different outcome.) This event, variously known as the BSAM YAS DEBATE, the Council of Bsam yas, and the Council of Lhasa, is regarded as one of the key moments in the history of Tibetan Buddhism.

**Khro phu bka' brgyud**. (Trophu Kagyü). One of the four major and eight subsects of the Bka' brgyud sect of Tibetan Buddhism (BKA' BRGYUD CHE BZHI CHUNG BRGYAD), originating with Rgya tsha (Gyatsa, 1118–1195), Kun ldan ras pa (Kundenrepa, 1148–1217), and their nephew Khro phu lo tsā ba Byams pa dpal (Tropu lotsaba Jampapal, 1173–1228).

**Khruba Si Wichai**. (1878–1938). One of the most famous and revered Lānnā (northern Thai) monks of the twentieth century, who supervised the renovation of more than one hundred northern Thai monasteries; many of these projects were later criticized by art historians for their excessive use of cement and lack of attention to preserving authentic stylistic features. He also organized the construction of the road up the famous landmark mountain Doi Suthep, leading to the monastery of WAT PHRA THAT DOI SUTHEP. The road, which opened on April 10, 1935, is approximately 9.3 miles (fifteen kilometers) in length and took only slightly more than five months to complete through the labors of as many as five thousand volunteer workers. Khruba is an honorary title for a teaching monk in Thailand and usually implies that the monk is perceived to have strong charisma and sometimes supernatural powers. Statues of Khruba Si Wichai are found at Wat Phra That Doi Suthep and Wat Phra Singh.

**Khuddakanikāya**. (S. Kṣudrakapiṭaka; T. Phran tshegs sde; C. Xiaobu; J. Shōbu; K. Sobu 小部). In Pāli, "Miscellaneous Collection"; the fifth and last division of the PĀLI SUTTAPIṬAKA. Such miscellanies, or "mixed baskets" (S. kṣudrakapiṭaka), were known to have existed in several of the mainstream Buddhist schools, including the DHARMAGUPTAKA, MAHĀSĀṂGHIKA, and MAHĪŚĀSAKA, but none of these recensions are extant (and there is no specific analogue in the Chinese ĀGAMA translations). The Pāli miscellany is composed of fifteen independent books, some of them representing the earliest strata of the Pāli canon, others relatively late compositions. The works are generally in verse, including the KHUDDAKAPĀṬHA, DHAMMAPADA, UDĀNA, ITIVUTTAKA, SUTTANIPĀTA, VIMĀNAVATTHU, PETAVATTHU, THERAGĀTHĀ, THERĪGĀTHĀ, JĀTAKA, APADĀNA, BUDDHAVAṂSA, and CARIYĀPIṬAKA. The *Khuddhakanikāya* contains in addition a commentary on portions of the *Suttanipāta*, called the MAHĀNIDDESA and CŪḶANIDDESA, and one treatise, the PAṬISAMBHIDĀMAGGA, that conforms to the abhidhamma in style and content. The Burmese recension of the Pāli canon adds to the collection four other works: the MILINDAPAÑHA, *Suttasaṅgaha*, PEṬAKOPADESA, and NETTIPPAKARAṆA, making nineteen books in all.

**Khuddakapāṭha**. In Pāli, "Miscellaneous Readings"; first of the fifteen books contained in the KHUDDAKANIKĀYA of the Pāli SUTTAPIṬAKA and comprised of excerpts taken from earlier canonical texts. This late Pāli composition is mentioned as a canonical text only in the commentaries. The KHUDDAKAPĀṬHA appears in the Pali Text Society's English translation series as *The Minor Readings*.

**Khuông Việt**. (匡越) (933–1011). Prominent Vietnamese monk and royal advisor, a native of Thường Lạc (nowadays Thanh Hóa Province, in northern Vietnam). His personal name was Ngô Chân Lưu. According to the THIỀN UYỂN TẬP ANH, he was a descendent of Ngô Thuận Đế. As a young man, he studied Confucianism but later turned to Buddhism, receiving full ordination from CHAN Master Vân Phong. Khuông Việt was widely read in the Buddhist scriptures and diligently investigated the teachings of Chan. When he was in his forties, his fame reached the royal court, and King Đinh Tiên Hoàng (r. 968–979), the founder of the Đinh dynasty (968–980), summoned him to the capital city and honored him with the rank General Supervisor of Monks. The king also granted him the sobriquet Khuông Việt Thái Sư (Great Master Who Brings Order to Việt). King Lê Đại Hành (r. 980–1005), the founder of the former Lê dynasty (980–1009), invited him to participate in all military, administrative, and diplomatic affairs, and he was often appointed to receive Chinese envoys. Khuông Việt was particularly famed for his exchange of couplets and poems with the Song-dynasty envoy Li Jue, who reported favorably on Vietnam to the Song-dynasty Emperor.

**Khyung po rnal 'byor Tshul khrims mgon po**. (Kyungpo Naljor Tsultrim Gönpo) (c. tenth–eleventh centuries) A Tibetan scholar and adept considered the founder of the SHANGS PA BKA' BRGYUD sect of Tibetan Buddhism. Although his traditional biographies are somewhat ambiguous, it is known that he traveled to India and studied under several MAHĀSIDDHA including MAITRĪPA and two female masters, Sukha and NIGUMA. From the latter, who was said to have been the wife or sister of the Indian scholar NĀROPA, Khyung pa rnal 'byor received a collection of instructions known as the six doctrines of NIGUMA (Ni gu chos drug). These ranked with the better known doctrines of NĀROPA (NA RO CHOS DRUG) and became the seminal teachings of the Shangs pa bka' brgyud. Khyung po rnal 'byor returned to Tibet and, according to traditional accounts, founded 108 religious establishments in the region of Shangs, from which the Shangs pa bka' brgyud takes its name. Khyung po rnal 'byor established his main seat at Zhang zhong monastery (also called Zhang zhang and Zhong zhong) and attracted a great number of disciples from all parts of Tibet. Although the Shangs pa bka' brgyud never developed a strong centralized institution, the transmission of Khyung po rnal 'byor's distinctive teachings spread in many directions, eventually finding their way into nearly every sect of Tibetan Buddhism.

**Kihwa**. (己和) (1376–1433). Korean SŎN master of the Chosŏn dynasty, also known as Hamhŏ Tŭkt'ong and Mujun. Kihwa was a native of Ch'ungju in present-day North Ch'ungch'ŏng province. The son of a diplomat, Kihwa entered the Sŏnggyun'gwan academy and received a traditional Confucian education, although even there he already showed strong interests in Buddhism. In 1396, after the death of a close friend, Kihwa decided to become a monk, eventually becoming a disciple of the eminent Sŏn master MUHAK CHACH'O (1327–1405) at the monastery of Hoeamsa. After studying kanhwa Sŏn (see KANHUA CHAN) under Chach'o, Kihwa is said to have attained his first awakening at a small hut near his teacher's monastery. Kihwa devoted the next few years to teaching and lecturing at various monasteries around the Korean peninsula. In 1412, Kihwa began a three-year retreat at a small hermitage named Hamhŏdang near the monastery of Yŏnbongsa on Mt. Chamo in P'yŏngsan. In 1420, he made a pilgrimage to

Mt. Odae, and the following year he was invited to the royal monastery of Taejaŏch'al. In 1424, King Sejong (r. 1419–1450) forcibly consolidated the different schools of Korean Buddhism into the two branches of Sŏn (CHAN; Meditation) and KYO (Doctrine), reduced the number of officially recognized monasteries, and limited the number of monks allowed to ordain. Perhaps in reaction to this increasing persecution of Buddhism, Kihwa left the royal monastery that same year. In response to the growing criticisms of Buddhism by the Confucian scholars at court, Kihwa composed his HYŎNJŎNG NON. Kihwa also composed influential commentaries on the VAJRACCHEDIKĀPRAJÑĀPĀRAMITĀSŪTRA ("Diamond Sūtra") and the YUANJUE JING ("Perfect Enlightenment Sūtra"). In 1431, he began restorations on a monastery known as Pongamsa on Mt. Hŭiyang in Yongnam and died at the monastery two years later in 1433.

**Kim hwasang**. (K) (金和尚). See CHŎNGJUNG MUSANG.

**Kim Iryŏp**. (金一葉) (1896–1971). In Korean, Kim "single leaf," influential Korean Buddhist nun during the mid-twentieth century and part of the first generation of Korean women intellectuals, or "new women" (sin yŏsŏng), thanks to her preordination career as a leading feminist writer, essayist, and poet. Her secular name was Wŏnju, and her Buddhist names were Hayŏp and Paengnyŏn Toyŏp; Iryŏp is her pen name, which Yi Kwangsu (1892–1955?), a pioneer of modern Korean literature, gave her in memory of the influential Japanese feminist writer Higuchi Ichiyō (1872–1896) (J. Ichiyō = K. Iryŏp). Kim's early years were influenced by Christianity and her father even became a Protestant minister. Her mother died when Kim was very young and her father also passed away while she was still in her teens. Kim was educated at the Ihwa Haktang, a women's academy (later Ewha University), and later studied abroad in Japan. She and other Ihwa graduates participated in the first female-published magazine in Korea, "New Women" (*Sinyŏja*), which began and ended in 1920. Kim was a feminist intellectual who sought self-liberation and the elevation of women's status through her writing. After her first marriage ended in divorce, she continued to pursue her search for her "self" and was involved in much-publicized relationships with men such as Oda Seijo and Im Nowŏl, a writer of "art-for-art's sake." But Kim's ideal of female liberation based on individual self-identity appears to have undergone a profound transformation, thanks to her associations with Paek Sŏnguk (1897–1981), a Buddhist intellectual who worked to revitalize Korean Buddhism during the Japanese colonial period and eventually became a monk himself in 1929. Through her encounter with Buddhism, Iryŏp's pursuit of self-liberation seems to have shifted from an emphasis on a self-centered identity based on feminism to the release from the self (ANĀTMAN). After Paek Sŏnguk entered into the Diamond Mountains (KŬMGANGSAN) to become a monk, she again married, seemingly in an attempt both to keep her self-identity as a female and to realize the Buddhist release of self, by combining secular life with Buddhist practice. But a few years later, in 1933, she ultimately decided to become a nun under the tutelage of the Sŏn master MAN'GONG WŎLMYŎN (1871–1946) and became a long-time resident of SUDŎKSA. There, she became an outspoken critic of secularized Japanese-style Buddhism and particularly of its sanction of married monks and eating meat. But most notable were her writings on the pursuit of self-liberation, which she expressed as "becoming one body" (ilch'ehwa) with all people and everything in the universe. Iryŏp is credited for her contributions to popularizing Buddhism through her accessible writings in the Korean vernacular, as well as for elevating the position of nuns in Korean Buddhism.

**Kim Kyogak**. (K) (金喬覺). See CHIJANG.

**kiṃnara**. (P. kinnara; T. mi 'am ci; C. jinnaluo; J. kinnara; K. kinnara 緊那羅). A class of wondrous celestial musicians in the court of KUBERA, ranking below the GANDHARVA. In Sanskrit, the name lit. means "How could this be human?" They are said to have human bodies but the heads of horses, but they also are sometimes depicted as little birds with human heads. Kiṃnara are common decorative figures in Buddhist cave and temple art. The kiṃnara is one of the eight kinds of nonhumans (AṢṬASENĀ) who protect the dharma, and they often appear in the audience of Buddhist SŪTRAs. The other seven are the DEVA, ASURA, GANDHARVA, NĀGA, YAKṢA, GARUḌA, and MAHORĀGA.

**Kinkakuji**. (金閣寺). In Japanese, "Golden Pavilion monastery"; a Japanese temple located in northern Kyōto, the ancient capital city of Japan, formally known as Rokuonji (Deer Park temple, cf. MṚGADĀVA). It was originally built as a retirement villa for Ashikaga Yoshimitsu (1358–1408), the third shōgun of the Muromachi (1337–1573) shogunate. However, following his father's wishes, his son converted it to a ZEN temple of the RINZAI school after the shōgun's death in 1408. The temple inspired the building of Ginkakuji (Silver Pavilion monastery), which was constructed about sixty years later on the other side of the city. The name Kinkaku derived from the pavilion's extravagant use of gold leaf, typical of Muromachi style, which covers the entire top two stories of the three-story pavilion. The pavilion uses three different architectural styles on each floor: the first emulates the residential style of Heian aristocracy; the second, warrior aristocracy; the third, Chinese CHAN style. The second floor enshrines the image of the BODHISATTVA Kannon (AVALOKITEŚVARA), surrounded by the statues of the four heavenly kings (CĀTURMAHĀRĀJAN), the guardian divinities (DEVA) of Buddhism. The pavilion burned down several times, including twice during the Ōnin war (1467–1477) and most recently by arson in 1950; the present structure was reconstructed in 1955. Kinkakuji is currently a branch temple of the RINZAI Zen monastery of SHŌKOKUJI.

**kirigami**. (切紙). In Japanese, "secret initiation documents" (lit. "strips of paper"), ; secret instructions or formulas written on individual pieces of paper, which were used in the medieval Japanese traditions, including the SŌTOSHŪ, to transmit esoteric knowledge and monastic routines. Kirigami were a central pedagogical feature in many fields involving apprenticeships in medieval Japan and were used to transmit knowledge about acting, poetic composition, martial arts, and religious practice. Sōtō Zen kirigami were also elaborations of the broader Chinese monastic codes (shingi; see QINGGUI) and focused on the secret rituals that a Zen abbot would perform in private, including consecration, funerals, and transmission of precepts or a dharma lineage. Many kirigami also provide short, targeted instruction on individual Zen cases (kōan; C. GONG'AN), such as the correct sequence of questions and answers, or the appropriate "capping phrase" (JAKUGO), that would prove mastery of a specific kōan. Because kirigami were also kept hidden away in Sōtō monasteries and were known only to the abbots, access to them was a potent symbol of the abbots' enhanced religious authority.

**kiriyavāda**. In Pāli, lit. "teaching on deeds," the philosophical position that upholds the efficacy of deeds, specifically that a distinction should be drawn between merit (puñña, S. PUṆYA) and demerit (apuñña, S. apuṇya). The term is usually seen in conjuction with the related kammavāda, viz., one who accepts the efficacy of action (KARMAN) and its fruition (VIPĀKA).

**Kisā Gotamī**. (S. *Kṛśā Gautamī). In Pāli, "Gotamī the emaciated"; an eminent arahant (S. ARHAT) therī, who was declared by the Buddha to be foremost among his nun disciples in the wearing of coarse robes (lūkhacīvara). The story of Kisā Gotamī is found in several places in the Pāli canon and commentaries and is one of the most beloved narratives in the THERAVĀDA world for its poignancy. Born to a poor family in the city of Sāvatthi (S. ŚRĀVASTĪ), her personal name was Gotamī, and she received the epithet Kisā ("lean," or "emaciated") because she was so thin. She was fortunate to marry into a wealthy family, although she was not treated with respect until she bore a son. Her happiness was short lived, however, for her son died just as he became old enough to run around and play. Driven mad with grief, Kisā Gotamī wandered about carrying her son's body at her hip, seeking everywhere for medicine to restore him to life. She was mocked and driven away by everyone she approached, until a kind man finally took pity on her and directed her to the Buddha. In response to her pleas to revive her son, the Buddha told her he would do so if she would bring him a mustard seed from a household in which no one had died. Searching frantically from house to house and ultimately finding none that had not experienced the death of loved ones, she came to realize the inevitability of death and so was able finally to lay her child's body to rest in the charnel ground. Returning to the Buddha, she sought admission into the nun's order and was ordained. She promptly became a stream-enterer (sotāpanna; S. SROTAĀPANNA) and, soon afterward, an arahant (S. ARHAT). In a previous existence, she had witnessed Padumuttara Buddha declare one of his nuns foremost among those who wear coarse robes, and it was then that she vowed to one day earn that same title.

**Kissa yōjōki**. (喫茶養生記). In Japanese, "Record of Drinking Tea for Health," composed by the Japanese monk MYŌAN EISAI in 1211. After Eisai returned to Japan from his pilgrimage in China, he is said to have transplanted in Uji the tea seeds that he had brought back with him from the mainland. The *Kissa yōjōki* is a record of the method that he used to transplant and care for the tea plants. The names of different types of tea, the ideal time and techniques for harvesting the leaves, and the proper way of preparing tea are carefully explained. Eisai also discusses the health and spiritual benefits of drinking tea in the text. The *Kissa yōjōki* is a seminal text in the development of tea culture in Japan.

**Kiyomizudera**. (清水寺). In Japanese, "Pure Water Monastery"; an important monastery of the Japanese HŌSSŌ school of YOGĀCĀRA Buddhism, located in the Higashiyama (Eastern Mountains) District of Kyōto. The monastery claims to have been founded in 778 by a monk named Enchin and the general Sakanoue no Tamuramaro, who stopped on the site for a drink from a waterfall fed by a natural spring, where he met the monk. Together, they contracted to create a magnificent image of an eleven-faced and forty-armed Kannon (AVALOKITEŚVARA), which was enshrined in 798 in a temporary hall that was given the name Kiyomizudera. The monastery became a state shrine in 810 and a focus of state-protection Buddhism (see HUGUO FOJIAO) in Japan. The current buildings date from the latest reconstruction of the monastery in 1633. The monastery is perhaps best known for its long veranda that juts over the hillside in front of the main shrine hall; there is a folk tradition dating back to the Edo period that anyone who survives a plunge off the veranda is granted whatever one wishes. The monastery was designated a UNESCO World Heritage Site in 1994.

**Kiyozawa Manshi**. (清沢満之) (1863–1903). Meiji-era Japanese Buddhist leader in the HIGASHI-HONGANJIHA of JŌDO SHINSHŪ. Kiyozawa was born into a poor warrior class family in a small town east of Nagoya and ordained in 1878 as a Higashi-Honganji priest. After studying Western philosophy at college and graduate school in Tokyo, he served his sect as an educator. In 1888, he was appointed principal of a Higashi-Honganji middle school in Kyōto and taught Western philosophy at a Higashi-Honganji seminary. In 1890, however, Kiyozawa left his position as principal to lead a rigorous ascetic life, wearing Buddhist robes, separating himself from his family, and living on simple food. Around this time, Kiyozawa launched a reform movement within Higashi-Honganji to return the school to the spirit of its founder, SHINRAN (1173–1262), and to make its ecclesiastical structure conform better to modern secular society, such as by having its deacons elected democratically. However, his movement failed and he was excommunicated in 1897. After being reinstated a year later, Kiyozawa again played an important role in the sect's education, serving in 1901 and 1902 as a dean of Higashi-Honganji's newly founded college (present-day Ōtani University). He died at the age of forty from the tuberculosis he had contracted during his practice of asceticism. Kiyozawa is credited with popularizing the TANNISHŌ, a short collection of Shinran's sayings that previously were not widely known. Kiyozawa emphasized individual religious experience, in which the adherent's self-awareness of his or her incapacity for moral perfection would instead prompt the adept to realize the truth of salvation through absolute reliance on the infinite. Kiyozawa argued that such individual spiritual realization could contribute to the welfare of society at large. Although Kiyozawa's thought was not widely accepted during his own age, it influenced a younger generation of Higashi-Honganji scholars, such as Akegarasu Haya (1877–1967), Sōga Ryōjin (1875–1971), and Kaneko Dai'ei (1881–1976), who later became leading intellectual figures in the sect.

**Kizil**. [alt. Qizil]. A complex of some 230 Buddhist caves from the ancient Central Asian kingdom of KUCHA, located about seventy kilometers northwest of the present-day city of Kucha on the bank of the Muzat River in Baicheng County, in the Uighur Autonomous Region of China's Xinjiang province. The Kizil caves represent some of the highest cultural achievements of the ancient Indo-European petty kingdom of Kucha, an important oasis along the northern SILK ROAD connecting China to the bastions of Buddhist culture in the greater Indian cultural sphere. Construction at the site perhaps began as early as the third century CE and lasted for some five hundred years, until the region succumbed in the ninth century to Islamic control. Given the importance of the Kucha region in the development and transmission of Buddhism along the ancient Silk Road, scholars believe that the DUNHUANG murals were influenced by the art of Kizil. Although no statuary remains at the Kizil site, many wall paintings are preserved depicting events from the life of the Buddha; indeed, Kizil is second only to the Mogao caves of Dunhuang in the number of wall paintings it contains. The layout of many of the intact caves includes a central pillar, forming both a front chamber and a rear chamber, which often contains a PARINIRVĀṆA scene. The first modern studies of the site were conducted in the early twentieth century by the German explorers Alfred Grünwedel and Alfred von Le Coq. The nearby site of Kumtura contains over a hundred caves, forty of which contain painted murals or inscriptions. Other cave sites near Kucha include Subashi, Kizilgaha, and Simsim.

**kleśa**. (P. kilesa; T. nyon mongs; C. fannao; J. bonnō; K. pŏnnoe 煩惱). In Sanskrit, "afflictions," or "defilements"; mental factors that disturb the mind and incite unwholesome (AKUŚALA) deeds of body, speech, and/or mind. In order to be liberated from rebirth, the kleśa and the actions they incite must be controlled and finally eliminated. A typical standard list of kleśa includes the so-called three poisons (TRIVIṢA) of greed or sensuality (RĀGA or LOBHA), hatred or aversion (DVEṢA), and delusion (MOHA). According to the SARVĀSTIVĀDA school, there are six "fundamental afflictions" or "defiled factors of wide extent" (KLEŚAMAHĀBHŪMIKA) that are associated with all defiled thoughts: delusion (MOHA), heedlessness (PRAMĀDA), lassitude (KAUSĪDYA), lack of faith (ĀŚRADDHYA), sloth (STYĀNA), and restlessness (AUDDHATYA). There are similarly ten "defiled factors of limited extent" (upakleśaparīttabhūmika), which may be associated with defiled thoughts: anger (KRODHA), hypocrisy (MRAKṢA), selfishness (MĀTSARYA), envy (ĪRṢYĀ), agitation or competition (PRADĀSA), harmfulness (VIHIṂSĀ), enmity (UPANĀHA), trickery or guile (ŚĀṬHYA), and arrogance (MADA). In the YOGĀCĀRA school, there are typically enumerated six fundamental kleśa—greed (rāga), aversion (PRATIGHA), stupidity (mūḍhi), pride (MĀNA), skeptical doubt (VICIKITSĀ), and the five wrong views (DṚṢṬI), viz., (1) presuming that the five aggregates (SKANDHA) possess a self, (2) the two extreme views of eternalism and annihilationism, (3) rejection of the law of causality, (4) maintaining wrong views and presuming them superior to all other views, (5) misconceiving wrong types of conduct or morality to be conducive to enlightenment—and twenty derivative ones (UPAKLEŚA).

**kleśamahābhūmika**. (T. nyon mongs chen po'i sa; C. da fannaodi fa; J. daibonnōjihō; K. tae pŏnnoeji pŏp 大煩惱地法). In Sanskrit, "defiled factors of wide extent"; the six principal factors (DHARMA) that ground all afflictions (KLEŚA) or defiled activities, according to the SARVĀSTIVĀDA ABHIDHARMA: (1) confusion (MOHA), (2) heedlessness (APRAMĀDA), (3) lassitude (KAUSĪDYA), (4) lack of faith (ĀŚRADDHYA), (5) sloth (STYĀNA), and (6) restlessness (AUDDHATYA). See KLEŚA.

**kleśāvaraṇa**. (T. nyon mongs kyi sgrib pa; C. fannao zhang; J. bonnōshō; K. pŏnnoe chang 煩惱障). In Sanskrit, "afflictive obstructions," or, more literally, the obstructions that are the afflictions. This is the first of the two categories of obstructions (ĀVARAṆA), together with the cognitive or noetic obstructions (JÑEYĀVARAṆA), that the MAHĀYĀNA holds must be overcome in order to complete the BODHISATTVA path and achieve buddhahood. In the YOGĀCĀRA system, based on the mistakes in understanding generated by the cognitive obstructions, the individual engages in defiled actions, such as anger, envy, etc., which constitute the afflictive obstructions. The afflictive obstructions may be removed by followers of the ŚRĀVAKA, PRATYEKABUDDHA, and beginning BODHISATTVA paths, by applying various antidotes or counteragents to the afflictions (KLEŚA); overcoming these types of obstructions will lead to freedom from further rebirth (and specifically the PARICCHEDAJARĀMARAṆA, or "determinative birth-and-death"). The cognitive obstructions, however, can be overcome only by advanced bodhisattvas who aspire instead to achieve buddhahood.

**kliṣṭamanas**. [alt. kliṣṭamanovijñāna] (T. nyon yid; C. ranmona/mona shi; J. zenmana/manashiki; K. yŏmmalla/malla sik 染末那/末那識). In Sanskrit, "afflicted mentality"; refers to the seventh of the eight categories of consciousnesses set forth in the YOGĀCĀRA school and enumerated by ASAṄGA. The first six consciousnesses are the six sensory consciousnesses of eye, ear, nose, tongue, body, and mentality; the eighth is the foundational consciousness, the "storehouse consciousness" (ĀLAYAVIJÑĀNA), which serves as the repository of the seeds (BĪJA) of past actions. The seventh "afflicted mentality" observes the foundational consciousness and mistakenly conceives it to be the self. Upon the achievement of buddhahood, the afflicted mentality is transformed into the wisdom of equality (SAMATĀJÑĀNA).

**kliṣṭamanovijñāna**. (S). See KLIṢṬAMANAS.

**klong chen snying thig**. (longchen nyingtik). In Tibetan, the "Heart Essence of the Great Expanse," one of the most important cycles of "treasure texts" (GTER MA) of the RNYING MA sect of Tibetan Buddhism. They are RDZOGS CHEN teachings revealed by 'JIGS MED GLING PA in 1757. The teachings were a dgongs gter, or "mind treasure," discovered by him in his own mind. They are considered to embody the two major snying thig lineages, the BI MA SNYING THIG brought to Tibet by VIMALAMITRA and the MKHA' 'GRO SNYING THIG brought to Tibet by PADMASAMBHAVA. The revelation eventually encompassed three volumes, including dozens of individual treatises, SĀDHANAS, and prayers.

**Klong chen rab 'byams**. (Longchen Rabjam) (1308–1364). Also known as Klong chen pa (Longchenpa). An esteemed master and scholar of the RNYING MA sect of Tibetan Buddhism known especially for his promulgation of RDZOGS CHEN. Klong chen pa is believed to be the direct reincarnation of PADMA LAS 'BREL RTSAL, who revealed the *Rdzogs chen snying thig*, and also of PADMA GSAL, who first received those teachings from the Indian master PADMASAMBHAVA. Born in the central Tibetan region of G.yo ru (Yoru), he received ordination at the age of twelve. At nineteen, he entered GSANG PHU NE'U THOG monastery where he engaged in a wide range of studies, including philosophy, numerous systems of SŪTRA and TANTRA, and the traditional Buddhist sciences, including grammar and poetics. Having trained under masters as diverse as the abbots of Gsang phu ne'u thog and the third KARMA PA, RANG 'BYUNG RDO RJE, he achieved great scholarly mastery of numerous traditions, including the Rnying ma, SA SKYA, and BKA' BRGYUD sects. However, Klong chen pa quickly became disillusioned at the arrogance and pretension of many scholars of his day, and in his mid-twenties gave up the monastery to pursue the life of a wandering ascetic. At twenty-nine, he met the great yogin Kumārarāja at BSAM YAS monastery, who accepted him as a disciple and transmitted the three classes of rdzogs chen (rdzogs chen sde gsum), a corpus of materials that would become a fundamental part of Klong chen pa's later writings and teaching career. Klong chen pa lived during a period of great political change in Tibet, as the center of political authority and power shifted from Sa skya to the Phag mo gru pa hierarchs. Having fallen out of favor with the new potentate, TAI SI TU Byang chub rgyal mtshan (Jangchub Gyaltsen, 1302–1364), he was forced to spend some ten years as a political exile in the Bum thang region of Bhutan, where he founded eight monasteries including Thar pa gling (Tarpa ling). Among the most important and well-known works in Klong chen pa's extensive literary corpus are his redaction of the meditation and ritual manuals of the heart essence (SNYING THIG), composed mainly in the hermitage of GANGS RI THOD DKAR. Other important works include his exegesis on the theory and practice of rdzogs chen, such as the MDZOD BDUN ("seven treasuries") and the NGAL GSO SKOR GSUM ("Trilogy on Rest"). Klong chen pa's writings are renowned for their poetic style and refinement. They formed the basis for a revitalization of Rnying ma doctrine led by the eighteenth-century visionary and treasure revealer (GTER STON) 'JIGS MED GLING PA.

**klong sde**. (long de). In Tibetan, the "expanse class," one of the three classes of ATIYOGA in the RNYING MA sect of Tibetan Buddhism. The atiyoga or RDZOGS CHEN teachings are traditionally divided into three classes: the mind section (SEMS SDE), which emphasizes the luminosity of the mind (RIG PA) in its natural state; the expanse section, which emphasizes the expansive or spacious mind in its natural state; and the instruction section (MAN NGAG SDE), which emphasizes the indivisibility of luminosity and expansiveness. The root tantra of the klong sde is traditionally said to be the *Klong chen rab 'byams rgyal po'i rgyud*, a long text in which the term klong figures prominently. Some of the texts ascribed to this class may date from as early as the ninth century, but the genre seems to have taken shape in the twelfth century; an important tantra for this class is the *Rdo rje sems dpa nam mkha'i mtha' dang mnyam pa'i rgyud chen po*, where an important theme is the four signs (brda). According to tradition, klong sde is traced back to the late eighth-century Tibetan master VAIROCANA.

**klu**. (lu). A class of Tibetan pre-Buddhist subteranean deities associated with water and infectious diseases such as leprosy. With the arrival of Buddhism, the klu were subsumed with the Indian NĀGA. They have the head and torso of humans but the tails of snakes. The klu are possibly related to the Chinese long, or dragon: long fly in the air, klu remain submerged in subterranean lakes, but both are associated with water. The klu must be propitiated before the construction of monasteries and other buildings in Tibet, in rituals that involve both peaceful offerings and displays of violent power. The klu combine with other classes of Tibetan deities to create composite entities: klu bdud, klu sman, klu btsan, klu srin, and the like.

**Klu'i rgyal mtshan**. (Lui Gyaltsen). (fl. late eighth–early ninth century) A translator (LO TSĀ BA) during the early spread of Buddhism in Tibet. Perhaps a native of Spiti, his clan name is Cog ro. He is known for his collaboration with Jinamitra in translating basic VINAYA texts into Tibetan and for his collaboration with JÑĀNAGARBHA on a translation of BHĀVAVIVEKA'S PRAJÑĀPRADĪPA. See also YE SHES SDE; DPAL BRTSEGS.

**Klu khang**. (Lukang). In Tibetan, the "NĀGA Temple"; a small temple located in the middle of an artificial lake behind the PO TA LA Palace in LHA SA, Tibet, reached by a stone bridge. Its full name is Rdzong rgyab klu khang, the "Nāga Temple Behind the Fortress [i.e., the Po ta la]." According to legend, the regent of the fifth DALAI LAMA, SDE SRID SANGS RGYAS RGYA MTSHO, negotiated an agreement with the king of the nāgas at the time of construction of the Po ta la, receiving the king's permission to dig up the soil in return for building a temple in honor of the nāga king in the center of the lake that formed in the pit from groundwater. The temple was constructed around 1700 during the reign of the sixth Dalai Lama, who is said to have used the upper chamber for romantic assignations. The temple is a small three-storied pavilion in the shape of a MAṆḌALA, with doors in each of the cardinal directions. The temple was rebuilt by the eighth Dalai Lama in 1791 and restored by the thirteenth Dalai Lama, who used it as a retreat. The temple is renowned for a magnificent set of murals on the second and third floors. The murals depict the eighty-four MAHĀSIDDHAS, PADMASAMBHAVA and his chief disciples, illustrations of the human body drawn from Tibetan medicine, a wide arrary of RDZOGS CHEN practices, scenes from the life of the renowned treasure revealer (GTER STON) PADMA GLING PA, and the peaceful and wrathful deities of the BAR DO.

**koan**. Romanization of the Japanese term kōan, now entered into the English language to refer (not quite correctly) to an impenetrable or even nonsensical "question" or "paradox." See GONG'AN.

**Kōben**. (J) (高辨/弁). See MYŌE KŌBEN.

**Kōbō Daishi**. (J) (弘法大師). See KŪKAI.

**Ko brag pa Bsod nams rgyal mtshan**. (Godrakpa Sönam Gyaltsen) (1170–1249). A meditator of uncertain lineage, but best known for instruction manuals on the SA SKYA LAM 'BRAS (path and result) practice; his instructions are representative of the mo rgyud (female transmission) of the Ma gcig Zhwa ma (1062–1149) line; he is also known for a lineage of the KĀLACAKRATANTRA six-branched yoga (ṣaḍaṅgayoga). One of his teachers, Chos kyi gzi brjid (1164–1224), was a student of 'JIG RTEN MGON PO, the founder of the 'BRI GUNG BKA' BRGYUD subsect. He is known for his *Gegs sel ha dmigs rgya mtsho* and a collection of songs.

**Kōfukuji**. (興福寺). In Japanese, "Flourishing Merit Monastery"; an ancient monastery in Nara, Japan, which is currently the headquarters (honzan) of the Hossō (see YOGĀCĀRA) tradition. Kōfukuji was first established in Yamashina (present-day Kyōto) in 669 as the merit cloister of the Fujiwara clan and was moved to the old capital of Fujiwarakyō in 672. When the new capital Heijōkyō was established, Kōfukuji was moved to its current location in Nara. After the death of Fujiwara no Fuhito (659–720), maternal grandfather of Emperor Shōmu (r. 724–749), Kōfukuji was formally designated an official state monastery. Under Fujiwara patronage, Kōfukuji came to dominate the early Buddhist community in Japan and has been traditionally considered one of the six great temples of Nara. Kōfukuji was destroyed during the war between the Taira and Minamoto clans in the twelfth century, and there were periodic attempts to rebuild the temple. Following the Meiji persecution of Buddhism (HAIBUTSU KISHAKU), major restorations on the monasteries were made. Kōfukuji is famous for its exquisite five-story pagoda and ancient icons, which testify to the aesthetic glory of Nara Buddhism.

**Kōhō Kennichi**. (高峰顯日) (1241–1316). Japanese ZEN master of the RINZAI Zen tradition, who is known to have been the son of Emperor Gosaga (r. 1242–1246). Kennichi was ordained by the Japanese monk ENNI BEN'EN at the monastery of Tōfukuji. In 1260, when the émigré CHAN master Wu'an Puning (1197–1276) was appointed abbot of the monastery of KENCHŌJI in Kamakura, Kennichi visited the master and became his student. Later, his patrons built the monastery of Unganji in Nasu and invited him to serve as abbot. In 1279, he also visited the émigré Chan master WUXUE ZUYUAN and continued to study under him at Kenchōji. Kennichi eventually received transmission (YINKE) from Wuxue and inherited his Rinzai (LINJI ZONG) lineage. With the support of the powerful regents Hōjō Sadatoki (1271–1311) and Takatoki (1303–1333), Kennichi also came to serve as abbot of the influential monasteries Jōmyōji, Manjuji, and Kenchōji. See also MUGAI NYODAI.

**kokubunji**. (國分寺). In Japanese, lit. "nationally distributed monasteries"; a network of centrally controlled provincial monasteries established during the Nara and Heian periods in Japan. During the reign of Emperor Shōmu (r. 724–749), he ordered that monasteries be established in every province of Japan, which would each have seven-story pagodas enshrining copies of the SADDHARMAPUṆḌARĪKASŪTRA ("Lotus Sūtra"). In 741, these provincial monasteries were organized into a national network as a means of bringing local power centers under the control of a centralized state government. The nunneries or convents that were also established as part of this same strategy were known as kokubunniji. The first headquarters of this kokubunji system was DAIANJI, which was based on the capital of Nara; the headquarters later moved to the major Kegon (HUAYAN) monastery of TŌDAIJI, which was constructed at Shōmu's behest. By the time of Shōmu's death in 756, there were at least twenty of these provincial monasteries already established.

**Kondāne**. Early Buddhist monastic cave site located in western India, which dates from the early decades of the first century CE. The highly ornamented, four-story facade of its CAITYA hall has projecting balconies supported by curved brackets and deeply recessed windows with latticed screens. Although carved in stone, the architectural form is modeled after earlier wooden designs and accords well with the real woodwork of the main arch, fragments of which are still in situ. This style of architecture is related to the slightly earlier hall at BHĀJĀ. In the third row of balconies are panels depicting pairs of dancers, who display ease of movement and considerable rhythmic grace. In this cave, there is also an inscription in BRAHMĪ script that records the name of one Balaka, a student of Kanha (or Kṛṣṇa), who constructed the cave. The record is carved near the head of a statue that probably represents Balaka.

**kongji lingzhi**. (J. kūjaku ryōchi; K. kongjŏk yŏngji 空寂靈知). In Chinese, "void and calm, numinous awareness." See LINGZHI.

**kong jia zhong sanguan**. (C) (J. kū-ge-chū sangan; K. kong ka chung samgwan 空假中三觀). See SANGUAN.

**Kongmu zhang**. (J. Kumokushō; K. Kongmok chang 孔目章). In Chinese, "Items and Chapters"; the usual abbreviated title of the *Huayan jingnei zhangmendeng za kongmu zhang* composed by the HUAYAN master ZHIYAN. The *Kongmu zhang* is essentially a four-roll commentary on BUDDHABHADRA's sixty-roll translation of the AVATAṂSAKASŪTRA, which discusses over 140 items and chapters from the sūtra. Zhiyan's unique tenet classification schema (JIAOXIANG PANSHI) and his teachings on the one vehicle (C. yisheng; S. EKAYĀNA) in the *Kongmu zhang* have influenced other Huayan exegetes such as FAZANG.

**kongōkai**. (S. vajradhātu; T. rdo rje dbyings; C. jingang jie; K. kŭmgang kye 金剛界). In Japanese, "diamond realm" or "diamond world"; one of the two principal diagrams (MAṆḌALA) used in the esoteric traditions of Japan (see MIKKYŌ), along with the TAIZŌKAI ("womb realm"); the Sanskrit reconstruction for this diagram is *vajradhātumaṇḍala. The teachings of the kongōkai are said to derive in part from two seminal scriptures of the esoteric traditions, the MAHĀVAIROCANĀBHISAṂBODHISŪTRA and SARVATATHĀGATATATTVASAṂGRAHA, but its construction as a maṇḍala relies on no known written instructions and more likely evolved pictorially. KŪKAI (774–835), the founder of the SHINGONSHŪ, used the kongōkai maṇḍala in combination with the taizōkai maṇḍala in a variety of esoteric rituals designed to awaken the individual adept. However, Japanese TENDAI Buddhism as well as various SHUGENDŌ complexes also heavily incorporated their own rituals into the two maṇḍalas. ¶ The kongōkai consists of nine smaller, nearly square-shaped maṇḍalas, or "assemblies" (J. e), some of which are sometimes isolated for worship and visualized independently. It is said that, by visualizing the maṇḍala, the kongōkai ultimately demonstrates that the universe as a whole is coextensive with the body of the DHARMAKĀYA or cosmic buddha, Mahāvairocana (SEE VAIROCANA). In the center of the maṇḍala, Mahāvairocana sits on a lotus flower, surrounded by four female figures, who symbolize the four perfections. Immediately outside are four discs, each encompassing a directional buddha: AMITĀBHA to the west, AKṢOBHYA to the east, AMOGHASIDDHI to the north, and RATNASAMBHAVA to the south. Each is, in turn, surrounded by four BODHISATTVAS. This ensemble of buddhas, bodhisattvas, and female figures is repeated in the first four maṇḍala of outward trajectory and its structure repeated in the lower six. Below the center maṇḍala is the maṇḍala of physical objects, each representing the buddhas and bodhisattvas. The next one in outward trajectory are figures residing inside a three-pointed vajra, representing the sounds of the world. The fourth maṇḍala displays all figures (excluding buddhas) in their female form, each exhibiting specific bodily movements. Arriving next at the upper-left maṇḍala, the group is reduced to Mahāvairocana and four surrounding bodhisattvas. In the top-center maṇḍala sits only a large Mahāvairocana. The last three maṇḍalas in the outward spiral shift toward worldly affairs. The top right reveals passions and desire. In the next to last are horrific demons and deities. The last maṇḍala represents consciousness. ¶ Looking at the depictions in the kongōkai individually, the nine smaller maṇḍalas are arrayed in a clockwise direction as follows. (1) The perfected-body assembly (jōjinne) is the central assembly of the entire maṇḍala. In the center of this assembly sits Mahāvairocana, displaying the gesture (MUDRĀ) of the wisdom fist (BODHYAṄGĪMUDRĀ; J. chiken-in), surrounded by the four directional buddhas (Akṣobhya, Ratnasambhava, Amitābha, and Amoghasiddhi), who embody four aspects of Mahāvairocana's wisdom. Each of these buddhas, including Mahāvairocana, is in turn attended by four bodhisattvas. (2) The SAMAYA assembly (J. sammayae; S. samayamaṇḍala) replaces the buddhas and bodhisattvas with physical objects, such as VAJRAS and lotuses. (3) The subtle assembly (J. misaime; S. sūkṣmamaṇḍala) signifies the adamantine wisdom of Mahāvairocana. (4) In the offerings assembly (J. kuyō-e; S. pūjāmaṇḍala), bodhisattvas make offerings to the five buddhas. (5) The four-mudrās assembly (J. shiinne; S. caturmudrāmaṇḍala) depicts only Mahāvairocana and four bodhisattvas. (6) The single-mudrā assembly (J. ichiinne; S. ekamudrāmaṇḍala) represents Mahāvairocana sitting alone in the gesture of wisdom. (7) In the guiding-principle assembly (J. rishu-e; S. nayamaṇḍala), VAJRASATTVA sits at the center, surrounded by four female figures, representing craving, physical contact, sexual desire, and fulfillment. (8) In the assembly of the descent into the three realms of existence (J. gōzanze-e; S. trailokyavijayamaṇḍala), Vajrasattva assumes the ferocious appearance of Gōsanze (TRAILOKYAVIJAYA). (9) The samaya of the descent into the three-realms assembly (J. gōzanzesammayae; S. trailokyavijayasamaya maṇḍala) has the same structure as the previous one. ¶ In one distinctively Shingon usage, the maṇḍala was placed in the east and the kongōkai stood in juxtaposition across from it. The initiate would then invite all buddhas, bodhisattvas, and divinities into the sacred space, invoking all of their power and ultimately unifying with them. In SHUGENDŌ, the two maṇḍalas were often spatially superimposed over mountain geography or worn as robes on the practitioner while entering the mountain. See TAIZŌKAI.

**Kongōsan**. (J) (金剛山). In Japanese, "Diamond Mountain(s)"; the highest peak in the KATSURAGISAN region, on the border between the present-day Japanese prefectures of Nara and Ōsaka. The mountain was likely visited by EN NO OZUNU, the putative founder of the SHUGENDŌ school of Japanese esoterism, who spent three decades practicing in the Katsuragi mountains. Its name may refer to the belief that En no Ozunu was a manifestation of Hōki Bosatsu (DHARMODGATA), who resided in the Diamond Mountains (see KŬMGANGSAN), according to the account in the AVATAṂSAKASŪTRA.

**Kong sprul mdzod lnga**. (Kongtrül dzö nga). In Tibetan, lit. "five treasuries of Kong sprul"; the name for a collection of five encyclopedic works composed by the Tibetan author 'JAM MGON KONG SPRUL BLO GROS MTHA' YAS. Kong sprul himself classified his writings in more than ninety volumes into a scheme of five "treasuries," in order to preserve and systematize numerous teachings that were in danger of being forgotten or lost. These collections of works, which belonged primarily to the BKA' BRGYUD and RNYING MA sects of Tibetan Buddhism, are now regarded as a primary source for the so-called nonsectarian (RIS MED) movement of the late nineteenth century and as outstanding literary achievements. The five treasuries are (1) SHES BYA KUN KHYAB MDZOD ("Treasury Embracing All Knowledge"); (2) BKA' BRGYUD SNGAGS MDZOD ("Treasury of Bka' brgyud Mantra"); (3) RIN CHEN GTER MDZOD ("Treasury of Precious Treasure Teachings"); (4) GDAMS NGAG MDZOD ("Treasury of Practical Instructions"); and (5) THUN MONG MA YIN PA'I MDZOD ("Uncommon Treasury").

**Konjaku monogatarishū**. (今昔物語集). In Japanese, "Tales of Times Now Past"; a collection of Buddhist tales compiled by the Japanese monk Minamoto no Takakuni (1004–1077). The *Konjaku monogatarishū* is claimed to have originally been composed in thirty-one rolls, but rolls eight, eighteen, and twenty-one are not extant. Rolls one through five are Buddhist tales from India, six through ten from China, and eleven through twenty from Japan. The *Konjaku monogatarishū* contains stories about the life of the Buddha and the events that occurred after his PARINIRVĀṆA, the transmission of Buddhism to China, the merits that accrue from worshipping the three jewels (RATNATRAYA), and moralistic tales of filial piety and karmic retribution. The tales of Japan provide a narrative of the transmission of Buddhism and the various Chinese schools to Japan, SHŌTOKU TAISHI's support of Buddhism, the establishment of Buddhist monasteries, the merit of constructing Buddhist images and studying SŪTRAs, and the lives of eminent Japanese monks. Fascicles twenty-two to thirty-one deal with worldly tales about the Fujiwara clan, arts, battles, and ghosts.

**Koryŏguk sinjo taejang kyojŏng pyŏllok**. (高麗國新雕大藏校正別錄). In Korean, "Supplementary Record of Collation Notes to the New Carving of the Great Canon of the Koryŏ Kingdom"; a thirty-roll compilation of editorial notes to the carving of the second edition of the Korean Buddhist canon (see KORYŎ TAEJANGGYŎNG), compiled in 1247 by the monk-editor Sugi (d.u.) and his editorial team. See SUGI.

**Koryŏ taejanggyŏng**. (高麗大藏經). In Korean, "The Koryŏ [Dynasty] Scriptures of the Great Repository"; popularly known in Korean as the P'ALMAN TAEJANGGYŎNG ("The Scriptures of the Great Repository in Eighty Thousand [Xylographs]"); referring specifically to the second of the two xylographic canons produced during the Koryŏ dynasty (937–1392) and widely regarded as one of the greatest cultural achievements of the Korean Buddhist tradition. The first Koryŏ edition of the canon was carved between 1011 and c. 1087 but was destroyed in 1234 during the Mongol invasion of the Korean peninsula. The second edition was carved between 1236 and 1251 and included some 1,514 texts in 6,815 rolls, all carved on 81,258 individual woodblocks, which are still housed today in the Scriptural Repository Hall at the monastery of HAEINSA. This massive project was carried out at royal behest by its general editor SUGI (d.u.) and an army of thousands of scholars and craftsmen. The court supported this project because of the canon's potential value in serving as an apotropaic talisman, which would prompt the various buddhas, as well as the divinities (DEVA) in the heaven of the thirty-three [divinities] (TRĀYASTRIṂŚA), to ward off foreign invaders and bring peace to the kingdom. By protecting Buddhism through a state project to preserve its canonical teachings, therefore, Buddhism would in turn protect the state (viz., "state-protection Buddhism," K. hoguk pulgyo, C. HUGUO FOJIAO). Sugi left thirty rolls (kwŏn) of detailed collation notes about the editorial procedures he and his team followed in compiling the new canon, the KORYŎGUK SINJO TAÉJANG KYOJŎNG PYŎLLOK (s.v.). Sugi's notes make clear that the second Koryŏ edition followed the Song Kaibao and first Koryŏ xylographic canons in its style and format but drew its readings in large measure from the Khitan Buddhist canon compiled by the Liao dynasty in the north of China. The xylographs typically include twenty-three lines of fourteen characters apiece, with text carved on both sides of the block. The second Koryŏ canon is arranged with pride of place given to texts from the MAHĀYĀNA tradition:

1. Major Mahāyāna scriptures (K 1–548), beginning with the PRAJÑĀPĀRAMITĀ, followed by the RATNAKŪṬASŪTRA, and continuing through all the major Mahāyāna sūtras and sūtra collections, from the AVATAṂSAKA to the PARINIRVĀṆA, SAṂDHINIRMOCANA, and LAṄKĀVATĀRA

2. Mahāyāna śāstras and scriptural commentaries, beginning with the DAZHIDU LUN (*Mahāprajñāpāramitāśāstra*) (K 549–646)
3. ĀGAMA collections and "hīnayāna" sūtras (K 647–888)
4. VINAYA materials (K 889–937)
5. ABHIDHARMA texts (K 938–977)
6. AVADĀNA and JĀTAKA tales and miscellaneous materials (K 978–1034)
7. Biographies of individual monks, starting with AŚVAGHOṢA, NĀGĀRJUNA, etc. (K 1035–1049)
8. Rosters of numerical lists, scriptural catalogues (K 1050–1064)
9. Travelogues and Biographies of Eminent Monks anthologies (K 1065–1086)
10. Miscellaneous sūtras, DHĀRAṆĪ scriptures, and dhāraṇī anthologies (K 1087–1242)
11. Other miscellaneous sūtras (K 1243–1496)
12. References, Chan anthologies, and indigenous Korean works (K 1497–1514)

Because this second Koryŏ canon was renowned throughout East Asia for its scholarly accuracy, it was used as the basis of the modern Japanese TAISHŌ SHINSHŪ DAIZŌKYŌ ("New Edition of the Buddhist Canon Compiled during the Taishō Reign Era"), edited by TAKAKUSU JUNJIRŌ and Watanabe Kaikyoku, published using movable-type printing between 1924 and 1935, which has become the standard reference source for East Asian Buddhist materials. See also DAZANGJING.

**Kośala**. (P. Kosala; T. Ko sa la; C. Jiaosaluo guo; J. Kyōsatsura koku; K. Kyosalla kuk 憍薩羅國). Name of an important Indian kingdom during the Buddha's time, located to the northeast of the Indian subcontinent, in the foothills of modern-day Nepal; also spelled Kosala and Kauśala. Kośala was located to the south of the region of the ŚĀKYA tribe, the Buddha's native clan, and exerted some political influence over its smaller neighbor. Along with MAGADHA, Kośala was one of the two strongest kingdoms at the time of the Buddha and had its capital at ŚRĀVASTĪ. The Buddha spent much of his time teaching in Śrāvastī, especially in the JETAVANA monastery, which was located on its outskirts. The Kośala kingdom was eventually conquered by King AJĀTAŚATRU of Magadha. Kośala is also one of the twenty-four sacred sites associated with the CAKRASAṂVARATANTRA. See PĪṬHA.

**Kosambiyasutta**. (C. Changshou; J. Chōju; K. Changsu 長壽). In Pāli, "Discourse to the Kosambians"; the forty-eighth sutta contained in the MAJJHIMANIKĀYA (scholars had presumed that an unidentified recension, perhaps MAHĀSĀṂGHIKA or DHARMAGUPTAKA, appears in the Chinese translation of the EKOTTARĀGAMA, but this putative affiliation seems to be in error); delivered by the Buddha to a gathering of monks in Ghosita's park at Kosambī (S. Kauśāmbī). The monks living in Kosambī had fallen into dispute over trivial matters, and the Buddha admonishes them to make loving-kindness (mettā; S. MAITRĪ) the basis of their mutual relations. He describes six principles of cordiality that contribute to the cohesion, harmony, and unity of the SAṂGHA; viz., (1) bodily acts of loving-kindness, (2) verbal acts of loving-kindness, (3) mental acts of loving-kindness, (4) sharing and cooperation, (5) public and private virtue conducive to meditative concentration, and (6) public and private virtue conducive to enlightenment and liberation. The Buddha then describes seven knowledges possessed by the stream-enterer (sotāpanna; S. SROTAĀPANNA). The stream-enterer knows that (1) his mind is well prepared for awakening to the truth, and (2) his mind is serene; (3) the Buddha's teachings are not contained in the wrong views of other teachers, and (4) he confesses his misdeeds and makes amends for future restraint; and (5) he completes the work that is to be done for the holy life. Furthermore, he knows (6) the strength of one who adheres to right view and (7) that he possesses that strength.

**Kotani Kimi**. (小谷喜美) (1901–1971). Cofounder along with KUBO KAKUTARŌ (1892–1944) of the REIYŪKAI school of modern Japanese Buddhism, which derives from the teachings of the NICHIRENSHŪ school of Buddhism. Kotani Kimi was the wife of Kotani Yasukichi, Kubo's elder brother. She and her husband became two of the earliest and most active proponents of Reiyūkai. After her husband died, she became the first official president of the group in 1930, and after Kubo's death in 1944, she ran the organization successfully on her own, although many splinter groups formed in reaction to her leadership. Kotani focused on the SADDHARMAPUṆḌARĪKASŪTRA ("Lotus Sūtra"), but because ancestor worship was her primary religious practice, she used the sūtra rather idiosyncratically as a path to the spiritual realm. Kotani also focused the group's energies on social welfare programs, and especially youth education, for she felt that Japan's rapid modernization was neglecting the needs of the youth.

**koṭi**. (T. mtha'; C. juzhi; J. kutei; K. kuji 俱胝). In Sanskrit and Pāli, lit. the "end" of a scale and thus effectively referring to any large number; often translated by the Indian numerical term "crore," and variously numbering as one hundred thousand, ten million, one hundred million, or an infinity. Note this same sense of koṭi as "end" in various Sanskrit and Pāli compounds, such as BHŪTAKOṬI, lit. "end of reality," and thus "true end" or "ultimate state." The term can also have a negative connotation in the sense of "extreme," as in the case of practice or philosophical position far from the moderate. For its use in MADHYAMAKA philosophy, see CATUṢKOṬI.

**Kōtokuin**. (高德院). In Japanese, "High Virtue Cloister"; located in Kamakura, Kanagawa prefecture, Japan. Kōtokuin is best known as the home of the colossal buddha image of Kamakura (see KAMAKURA DAIBUTSU), a huge bronze statue of AMITĀBHA Buddha; as a consequence, the temple is often called

Daibutsuji. The temple is associated with the JŌDOSHŪ, or Pure Land sect. After one crosses the threshold of the entrance gate into the temple compound, the site appears more like a park dedicated to the colossal buddha image than a temple; in fact, the real Kōtokuin temple buildings are now located to the east of the image and are off-limits to most tourists. Toward the back of the temple is now located the Kangetsudō, or Moon-Viewing Hall, which was brought from Korea in 1934; it enshrines an Edo-period (1603–1868) statue of Kannon (AVALOKITEŚVARA). To the right of the Moon-Viewing Hall is a stone stele on which is inscribed a famous tanka poem by Akiko Yosano (1878–1942) describing her impression on first seeing the Kamakura Daibutsu (although she mistakenly presumes she is viewing ŚĀKYAMUNI, not Amitābha).

**kōun ryūsui**. (C. xingyun liushui; K. haengun yusu 行雲流水). In Japanese, "moving clouds and flowing water"; the phrase from which the term "clouds and water" (J. unsui; C. yunshui; K. unsu) derives, referring to an itinerant Zen monk in training. See YUNSHUI.

**Kounsa**. (孤雲寺). In Korean, "Solitary Cloud Monastery"; the sixteenth district monastery (PONSA) of the contemporary CHOGYE CHONG of Korean Buddhism, located on Mount Tŭngun in North Kyŏngsang province. The monastery was founded in 681 by great Hwaŏm (C. HUAYAN) master ŬISANG (625–702), during the reign of the Silla king Sinmun (r. 681–692). The original Chinese characters for Kounsa meant "High Cloud Monastery," but during the Unified Silla period, the monastery adopted the homophonous name "Solitary Cloud," after the pen name of the famous literatus Ch'oe Ch'iwŏn (b. 857). During the reign of King Hŏn'gang (r. 875–886), a famous stone image of BHAIṢAJYAGURU was enshrined at the monastery. During the Koryŏ dynasty, the monk Ch'ŏnhae (fl. c. 1018) is said to have seen a Kwanŭm (AVALOKITEŚVARA) statue in a dream; later, he found an identical image on Mount Taehŭng in Songdo and enshrined it in the Kŭngnak chŏn at Kounsa. The monastery was rebuilt and repaired several times during the Chosŏn period. The large-scale rebuilding project that began in 1695 and continued through the eighteenth century helped raise the monastery's overall status within the ecclesia. Kounsa suffered severe damage from fires that broke out in 1803 and 1835, but the monastery was soon reconstructed. During the Japanese colonial period (1910–1945), Kounsa became one of thirty-one head monasteries (ponsa) and managed fifty-four branch monasteries (MALSA).

**koutou Chan**. (J. kutōzen/kōtōzen; K. kudu Sŏn 口頭禪). In Chinese, lit. "mouth Chan"; the CHAN that is practiced only through words, referring to practitioners who are versed in Chan theory but have not comprehended that theory themselves through their meditation. This Chan Buddhist expression refers to those practitioners who have merely memorized the pithy sayings and GONG'AN dialogues of the patriarchs and masters (ZUSHI) of the Chan school without actually understanding them or putting them into practice. Cf. YINGWU CHAN.

**Kōyasan**. (高野山). In Japanese, "Mt. Kōya"; a Japanese sacred mountain in Wakayama prefecture. Currently, the monastery Kongōbuji on Mt. Kōya serves as the headquarters (honzan) of the Kōyasan SHINGONSHŪ sect of the Shingon tradition. While traveling through the lands southwest of Yoshino, the Japanese monk KŪKAI is said to have stumbled upon a flat plateau named Kōya (High Field) on a mountain. Kūkai determined that Kōya was an ideal site of self-cultivation, as it appeared to be an uninhabited area surrounded on four sides by high mountain peaks. It is said that the mountain was revealed to Kūkai by a hunter who was an incarnation of the god (KAMI) of the mountain, Kōya Myōjin. This deity is still worshipped on Mt. Kōya in his hunter form as Kariba Myōjin. In 816, Kūkai received permission from the emperor to establish a practice center dedicated to the study of MIKKYŌ ritual and doctrine at Kōya. Kūkai first sent his disciples Jitsue (786–847) and Enmyō (d. 851) to survey the entire area and went to the site himself in 818. Due to his activities at the official monastery, TŌJI, and his business at the monasteries Jingōji and Murōji, Kūkai's involvement with Mt. Kōya was limited. In 835, he retired to Mt. Kōya due to his deteriorating health and finally died there, purportedly while in a deep meditative state. Kūkai's body is housed in the mausoleum complex Okunoin near Kongōbuji. According to legend, he remains there in a state of eternal SAMĀDHI. As a result of the developing cult of Kūkai, who increasingly came to be worshipped as a bodhisattva, Mt. Kōya came to be viewed as a PURE LAND on earth. Later, as a result of political contestations, as well as several fires on the mountain in 994, Mt. Kōya entered a period of protracted decline and neglect. Through the efforts of Fujiwara and other aristocrats as well as the patronage of reigning and retired emperors, Mt. Kōya reemerged as a powerful monastic and economic center in the region, and became an influential center of pilgrimage and religious cultivation famous throughout Japan. In 1114, KAKUBAN took up residence on the mountain and assiduously practiced mikkyō for eight years. In 1132, he established the monasteries of Daidenbōin and Mitsugon'in on Mt. Kōya. Despite his efforts to refocus Mt. Kōya scholasticism around the doctrinal and ritual teachings of Kūkai, his rapid rise through the monastic ranks was met with great animosity from the conservative factions on the mountain. In 1288, the monk Raiyu (1226–1304) moved Daidenbōin and Mitsugon'in to nearby Mt. Negoro and established what came to be known as Shingi Shingon, which regarded Kakuban as its founder. In 1185, Myōhen, a disciple of HŌNEN, moved to Mt. Kōya to pursue rebirth in the pure land, a common goal for many pilgrims to Mt. Kōya. It is said that, around 1192, NICHIREN and Hōnen made pilgrimages to the mountain. MYŌAN EISAI's senior disciple Gyōyū established Kongōsanmaiin and taught Chinese RINZAI (LINJI) Zen on Mt. Kōya. Zen lineages developed between Mt. Kōya, Kyōto, and Kamakura around this time. In 1585, during the Warring States Period, the monk Mokujiki Ōgo was able to convince Toyotomi Hideyoshi not to burn down the mountain as Oda Nobunaga had done at HIEIZAN. As a result, Mt. Kōya preserves ancient manuscripts and images that would have otherwise been lost. Mt. Kōya's monastic structures shrank to less than a third of their original size during the Meiji persecution of Buddhism (HAIBUTSU KISHAKU). At that same time, Mt. Kōya lost much of its former land holdings, which greatly reduced its economic base. In the twentieth century, Mt. Kōya went through several modernization steps: the ban against women was lifted in 1905, its roads were paved, and Mt. Kōya University was built on the mountain. At present, Mt. Kōya is a thriving tourist, pilgrimage, and monastic training center.

**Kōzen gokokuron**. (興禪護國論). In Japanese, "Treatise on the Promulgation of Zen as Defense of the State"; written by MYŌAN EISAI in 1198 to legitimize the new ZEN teachings that he had imported from China. In ten sections, Eisai responds to the criticisms from the monks at HIEIZAN (see ENRYAKUJI and TENDAISHŪ) with extensive references to scriptures, Chan texts, and the writings of SAICHŌ, ENNIN, and ENCHIN. Eisai argued that the new teachings would protect the state and allow for the "perfect teachings" (see JIAOXIANG PANSHI) of Tendai to flourish.

**kriyātantra**. (T. bya rgyud). In Sanskrit, "action tantra"; the lowest of the traditional fourfold categorization of tantric texts, the others being (in ascending order) CARYĀTANTRA, YOGATANTRA, and ANUTTARAYOGATANTRA. According to traditional commentaries, this class of tantras is so called because they emphasize the performance of external action or ritual over the practice of meditation. Tantras classified in this group include the *SUSIDDHIKARASŪTRA and the SUBĀHUPARIPṚCCHĀTANTRA.

**krodha**. (P. kodha; T. khro ba; C. fen; J. fun; K. pun 忿). In Sanskrit, "anger," or "wrath." One of the forty-six mental factors (see CAITTA) according to the ABHIDHARMAKOŚABHĀṢYA, and one of the fifty-one according to the YOGĀCĀRA school. Krodha is the infuriation one feels toward unpleasant objects and is one possible way in which aversion (DVEṢA) manifests itself. Krodha is distinguishable from "enmity" (UPANĀHA) in that "anger" is a more potent but more quickly dissipated kind of emotion, whereas "enmity" is a long-term simmering grudge.

***Kṛśā Gautamī**. (S). See KISĀ GOTAMĪ.

**Kṛṣṇācārya**. [alt. Kṛṣṇā[cārya]-pāda/Kṛṣṇacārin/Kāṇha] (T. Nag po pa/Nag po spyod pa). Sanskrit proper name of one of the eighty-four MAHĀSIDDHAS. A number of tantric works by an author or authors whose name is usually rendered in Tibetan as Nag po pa (the dark-skinned one) are extant in Tibetan translation.

**kṛtsna/kṛtsnāyatana**. (S). See KASIṆA.

**kṛtyānuṣṭhānajñāna**. (T. bya ba sgrub pa'i ye shes; C. chengsuozuo zhi; J. jōshosachi; K. sŏngsojak chi 成所作智). In Sanskrit, "the wisdom of having accomplished what was to be done"; one of the four [alt. five] wisdoms of a buddha described in the YOGĀCĀRA school, which is created through the transmutation of the five sensory consciousnesses (VIJÑĀNA). This type of wisdom brings about perfection in all one's action, which benefits both oneself and others. This particular type of wisdom thus works on behalf of the welfare of all sentient beings and serves as the cause for the various emanations of a buddha.

**kṣaṇa**. (P. khaṇa; T. skad cig; C. chana; J. setsuna; K. ch'alla 刹那). In Sanskrit, "instant" or "moment"; the shortest possible span of time, variously measured as either the ninth part of a thought moment or the 4,500th part of a minute. The term figures prominently in mainstream Buddhist discussions of impermanence and epistemology (see KṢAṆIKAVĀDA). Physical objects and mental events that persist over time are posited in fact to be merely a collection of these moments. As a result of ignorance, these are falsely perceived as lasting more than one moment. For example, sense experience is composed entirely of the perception of these moments of a given object, but this is not noticed by ordinary sense consciousness, and thought mistakenly projects continuity onto sense experience. The term therefore appears commonly in expositions of impermanence (ANITYA). According to the VAIBHĀṢIKA school of abhidharma, ultimate truths (PARAMĀRTHASATYA) are only these indivisible instants of time and partless particles of matter (PARAMĀṆU); one of the MADHYAMAKA arguments concerning emptiness (ŚŪNYATĀ) is that even the apparently smallest units of time and matter have parts. ¶ As the "right moment," kṣaṇa also has the denotation of an "opportune birth" (KṢAṆASAṂPAD), referring specifically to birth at a time and place where a buddha or his teachings are present and with the faculties to be able to understand his teachings. This fortunate birth is contrasted with eight kinds of "inopportune births" (AKṢAṆA), where one by contrast will be born in a place or state where one is either incapable of learning anything from a buddha or, even if one could learn, no buddha is present in the world.

**kṣaṇasaṃpad**. (P. khaṇasampadā; T. dal 'byor; C. chana juzu; J. setsunagusoku; K. ch'alla kujok 刹那具足). In Sanskrit, lit. "fortunate moment," or an "auspicious moment," viz., "opportune birth" (see KṢAṆA), referring specifically to rebirth as a human being and under circumstances that permit access to the practice of the dharma. The Tibetan literally means "freedom and endowment" or "leisure and opportunity," referring to an auspicious human birth. Indian texts enumerate eight conditions of "nonleisure" (such as rebirth as an animal) and ten conditions of opportunity (such as rebirth in a land where the dharma is present). The absence of these eight conditions defines AKṢAṆA, "inopportune birth" (lit. "not a right moment"), referring specifically to a birth in which one will not be able to learn from a buddha. These are, when one is born (1) in one of the hells (NĀRAKA); (2) as an animal, (3) hungry ghost (PRETA), or (4) a long-lived divinity (DEVA); (5) in a border land or barbarian region; (6) with perverted views or heretical disposition; (7) stupid and unable to understand the teachings; or (8) at a time when no buddhas have appeared. An opportune birth (kṣaṇasaṃpad, kṣaṇa), by contrast, means to be born at a time and place where a buddha or his teachings are present and where one has the faculties to understand his teachings.

**kṣaṇika**. (T. skad cig ma; C. chana qing; J. setsunakei; K. ch'alla kyŏng 刹那頃). In Sanskrit, "momentary"; originally used in the sūtras in its literal sense of a very small fraction of time, the term has also been used synonymously with "impermanence" (ANITYA) to indicate the "momentary" (kṣaṇika) nature of all phenomena. Kṣanika acquired technical significance when the doctrine of impermanence (ANITYA) came to be elaborated and interpreted in the various mainstream Indian schools in their attempt to ground the Buddhist understanding of the processes governing compounded existence on a logically defensible basis. These developments led the SAUTRĀNTIKA school to advocate a "doctrine of momentariness" (KṢAṆIKAVĀDA), viz., that a dharma lasts only a single moment (KṢAṆA), in which is comprised both its genesis and its destruction.

**kṣaṇikavāda**. (T. skad cig ma smra ba; C. chanalun; J. setsunaron; K. ch'allaron 刹那論). In Sanskrit, "doctrine of momentariness"; a doctrinal position emblematic of the SAUTRĀNTIKA school of the mainstream Buddhist tradition. The doctrine of momentariness derives from attempts to elaborate the foundational Buddhist concept of impermanence (ANITYA): viz., how long exactly do causally created events or objects exist before their destruction? Some of the early mainstream schools of Buddhism, such as the SARVĀSTIVĀDA and STHAVIRANIKĀYA, presume that this process of existence, although extremely brief, could be differentiated into several specific moments. The Sarvāstivāda school, for example, assumed that events persisted through four moments (KṢAṆA), viz., the four marks (CATURLAKṢAṆA) of birth, subsistence, decay, and extinction; the Sarvāstivāda school posited that these marks were forces dissociated from thought (CITTAVIPRAYUKTASAṂSKĀRA), which exerted real power over compounded objects, carrying an object along from one force to another, until the force "extinction" extinguishes it. According to the Sthaviranikāya, all mental events include three moments of origination (uppāda), subsistence (ṭhiti), and dissolution (bhaṅga), which together constitute the present. The SAUTRĀNTIKA, by contrast, believed that the elements of existence (DHARMA) are momentary (KṢAṆIKA) appearances in the phenomenal world, which are disconnected in space and not linked by any pervading substance. They are also disconnected in time or duration, since they last only a single moment (kṣaṇa), a moment that includes both its genesis and its destruction. Unlike the Sarvāstivāda school, then, the Sautrāntikas assert that, because all conditioned dharmas are inherently destined to be extinguished, annihilation occurs spontaneously and simultaneously with origination, without the exertion of a specific "force."

**kṣānti**. (P. khanti; T. bzod pa; C. renru; J. ninniku; K. inyok 忍辱). In Sanskrit, "patience," "steadfastness," or "endurance"; alt. "forbearance," "acceptance," or "receptivity." Kṣānti is the third of the six (or ten) perfections (PĀRAMITĀ) mastered on the BODHISATTVA path; it also constitutes the third of the "aids to penetration" (NIRVEDHABHĀGĪYA), which are developed during the "path of preparation" (PRAYOGAMĀRGA) and mark the transition from the mundane sphere of cultivation (LAUKIKA-BHĀVANĀMĀRGA) to the supramundane vision (DARŚANA) of the FOUR NOBLE TRUTHS (catvāry āryasatyāni). The term has several discrete denotations in Buddhist literature. The term often refers to various aspects of the patience and endurance displayed by the bodhisattva in the course of his career: for example, his ability to bear all manner of abuse from sentient beings; to bear all manner of hardship over the course of the path to buddhahood without ever losing his commitment to liberate all beings from SAṂSĀRA; and not to be overwhelmed by the profound nature of reality but instead to be receptive or acquiescent to it. This last denotation of kṣānti is also found, for example, in the "receptivity to the fact of suffering" (duḥkhe dharmajñānakṣānti; see DHARMAKṢĀNTI), the first of the sixteen moments of realization of the four noble truths, in which the adept realizes the reality of impermanence, suffering, emptiness, and nonself and thus overcomes all doubts about the truth of suffering; this acceptance marks the inception of the DARŚANAMĀRGA and the entrance into sanctity (ĀRYA). Kṣānti as the third of the aids to penetration (nirvedhabhagīya) is distinguished from the fourth, highest worldly dharmas (LAUKIKĀGRADHARMA), only by the degree to which the validity of the four noble truths is understood: this understanding is still somewhat cursory at the stage of kṣānti but is fully formed with laukikāgradharma.

**kṣāntipāramitā**. (P. khantipāramī; T. bzod pa'i pha rol tu phyin pa; C. renru boluomi; J. ninnikuharamitsu; K. inyok paramil 忍辱波羅蜜). In Sanskrit, "perfection of patience." See KṢĀNTI.

**Kṣāntivādin**. (P. Khantivādī; T. Bzod pa smra ba; C. Renru xianren/Chanti xianren; J. Ninniku sennin/Sandai sennin; K. Inyok sŏnin/Sanje sŏnin 忍辱仙人/羼提仙人). Lit. "Teacher of Patience"; one of the more famous previous lives of the Buddha as recounted in the Sanskrit and Pāli JĀTAKA collections. Over the course of millions of lifetimes, the BODHISATTVA is said to accrue vast stores of merit (PUṆYA) through the practice of the six or ten perfections (PĀRAMITĀ). The story of Kṣāntivādin is the most famous story about the bodhisattva's practice of patience (KṢĀNTI). In the story, the bodhisattva is a brāhmaṇa who renounces the world and lives in a forest near Benaras. One day, the king comes into the forest accompanied by his female attendants, who entertain him. Exhausted by his indulgence in pleasure and drink, the king falls asleep. The women wander off, eventually coming upon Kṣāntivādin seated beneath a tree. They gather around him and he preaches to them. The king awakes to find the women gone and becomes enraged. When he finally locates them, he presumes that Kṣāntivādin has stolen them away. When he asks the ascetic what he teaches, Kṣāntivādin replies "patience." Seeking to test the ascetic's ability to remain free from anger when injured and abused, he tortures him, cutting off his limbs, his nose, and his ears in turn, at each point asking the ascetic whether he still teaches patience; the various versions differ as to the order in which the limbs are severed and whether they are severed by the king himself or by his executioner. Leaving the ascetic to die of his wounds, the king walks away, only to be swallowed by the earth and transported to the AVĪCI hell. It is said that the king was DEVADATTA in a former life and that his fate prefigured Devadatta's own demise.

**kṣapita**. (P. jhāpita; T. zad byed; C. chapi/tupi; J. dabi; K. tabi/tobi 荼毘/茶毘). In Sanskrit, "destroy" or "burn up"; the Chinese characters are simply a transcription of the Sanskrit. This term refers to the cremation of the corpse and is performed especially as part of the funerary rites for a monk or nun. Elaborate manuals of cremation ceremonies are available in many Buddhist traditions to guide the celebrants in the steps of preparing the pyre and cremating the corpse. Living within the precincts of a cremation site or charnel ground (ŚMAŚĀNA) is also considered to be one of the most powerful ascetic practices (DHUTAṄGA), which helps to vanquish lust and establish the mindfulness of death (see KAMMAṬṬHĀNA).

**kṣatriya**. (P. khattiya; T. rgyal rigs; C. chali; J. setsuri; K. ch'alli 刹利). In Sanskrit, "warrior" or "royalty"; the second of the four castes of traditional Indian society, along with priests (brāhmaṇa), merchants (vaiśya), and servants (śūdra). As the son of the Śākya king, ŚUDDHODANA, the soon-to-be buddha GAUTAMA belonged to the kṣatriya caste. Many of the leading figures in the ŚRAMAṆA movement, ascetic wanderers who stood in opposition to the brāhmaṇa priests of traditional Vedic religion, derived primarily from people of kṣatriya background. The Buddha's caste may also account for the frequent disparagement in the sūtras of the sacrificial activities of Vedic priests and the common topos in the sūtras of redefining the meaning of brahman (brāhmaṇa) in terms of meditative achievement and enlightenment (see KASSAPASĪHANĀDASUTTA; TEVIJJASUTTA), although it is also the case that brāhmaṇa priests were a chief rival of the early Buddhist community for patronage. The Buddhist and broader śramaṇa suspicions of the soteriological efficacy of the sacrifices performed by brāhmaṇas also appear in the dismissal of religious rites and rituals (ŚĪLAVRATAPARĀMARŚA) as one of the three coarser fetters (SAṂYOJANA) or wrong views (MITHYĀDṚṢṬI) that must be given up to attain stream-entry (SROTAĀPANNA). It is said that buddhas are only born into two castes, the brāhmaṇa and the kṣatriya, depending upon which is regarded most highly at the time of that buddha's birth.

**kṣayajñāna**. (T. zad pa shes pa; C. jinzhi; J. jinchi; K. chinji 盡智). In Sanskrit, "knowledge of cessation"; one of the two types of knowledge that accompanies liberation from rebirth (SAṂSĀRA). Kṣayajñāna is the understanding that one has eradicated the afflictions (KLEŚA), viz., greed, hatred, and delusion. Kṣayajñāna occurs at the point that the adept becomes an AŚAIKṢA (one who has no more need of religious training) and brings an end to the clinging to existence, thus eradicating the desire for continued rebirth. This type of knowledge is typically paired with the "knowledge of nonproduction" (ANUTPĀDAJÑĀNA), the awareness that the kleśas, once eradicated, will never arise again.

**Kṣemā**. (P. Khemā; T. Dge ma; C. Anwen; J. Annon; K. Anon 安穩). The chief of the Buddha's nun (BHIKṢUṆĪ) disciples and foremost among them in wisdom (PRAJÑĀ). According to Pāli sources, Khemā was born to the royal family of Sāgala and became the chief queen of King BIMBISĀRA. Known for her exceptional beauty, she was said to have a complexion the color of gold. When Khemā's husband became a lay disciple of the Buddha, he encouraged her to accompany him to listen to the Buddha's sermons, but she resisted, lest the great sage disparage her beauty to which she was greatly attached. Coaxed by court poets extolling the charms of the Veḷuvana (S. VEṆUVANA), or Bamboo Grove, where the Buddha was sojourning, Khemā finally agreed to visit him there. At her approach, the Buddha created an apparition of a celestial nymph that far exceeded in feminine beauty any human woman. He then caused the apparition to age and die in decrepitude before Khemā's eyes, filling the queen with dismay and disgust. With her mind thus prepared, the Buddha preached to her a sermon on the frailty of physical beauty and the vanity of lust; as she listened to his words, she attained arahantship (S. ARHAT). As an arahant, Khemā could no longer live the householder's life, and with the consent of her husband King Bimbisāra, she took ordination as a nun. During the lifetimes of the previous buddhas Kassapa (S. KĀŚYAPA), Kakusandha, and Konāgamana, she had great monasteries built for them and their disciples, and during the time of Vipassī (S. VIPAŚYIN) Buddha, she became a renowned preacher of dhamma. Once while staying at Toranavatthu, Khemā gave a discourse to King Pasenadi (S. PRASENAJIT) of Kosala (S. KOŚALA) on whether or not the Buddha exists after death, which allayed his doubts.

**kṣetraśuddhi**. [alt. kṣetraviśuddhi] (T. dag zhing). In Sanskrit, "pure [buddha] field"; a type of buddha-field (BUDDHAKṢETRA) created by a buddha as a result of his practice and which comes into existence at the time of that buddha's enlightenment. The nature of the purity is variously defined but typically means that in this world the realms of animals, ghosts, and hell beings do not exist; although songbirds may exist, they have been created by the buddha for the delight of the inhabitants of his buddha-field. The pure buddha-field is regarded as the outcome of the training (PRAYOGA) in purifying a buddha-field, one of the final practices of BODHISATTVAS set forth in the fourth chapter of the ABHISAMAYĀLAṂKĀRA's explanation of the PRAJÑĀPĀRAMITĀ SŪTRAs. The purification is brought about by the six perfections (PĀRAMITĀ): for example, perfect giving (DĀNAPĀRAMITĀ) brings about an external pure field (parallel to the BHĀJANALOKA) supplied with all the enjoyments of the deities, and so on. See also JINGTU.

**kṣīṇāsrava**. (P. khīnāsava; T. zag pa zad pa; C. loujin; J. rojin; K. nujin 漏盡). In Sanskrit, "contaminants destroyed" or "free from impurities"; an epithet of the ARHAT who has destroyed all of the contaminants (ĀSRAVA) and will enter NIRVĀṆA upon death. The term appears commonly in the opening passages of the MAHĀYĀNA SŪTRAS when describing the arhats who have gathered to hear the Buddha's teaching. In an example of the self-praise of the Mahāyāna sūtras at the expense of the arhat, the ŚŪRAṂGAMASAMĀDHISŪTRA declares that a man who has committed the five deeds of immediate retribution (ĀNANTARYAKARMAN) yet has heard the sūtra is superior to an arhat who has destroyed the contaminants; this is because the former may achieve buddhahood while the arhat is destined only for nirvāṇa. See also ĀSRAVAKṢAYA.

**Kṣitigarbha**. (T. Sa yi snying po; C. Dizang; J. Jizō; K. Chijang 地藏). In Sanskrit, lit. "Earth Store," an important BODHISATTVA who has the power to rescue beings who have the misfortune to be reborn in the hells. Although Kṣitigarbha is known in all Mahāyāna countries through his inclusion in the widely known grouping of eight great bodhisattvas (MAHOPAPUTRA; AṢṬAMAHOPAPUTRA), he was apparently not the object of individual cultic worship in India or Tibet. It was in East Asian Buddhism that Kṣitigarbha came into his own and became widely worshipped. In China, the cult of Kṣitigarbha (C. Dizang) gained popularity by at least the fifth century, with the translation of the *Dasheng daji Dizang shilun jing* ("Mahāyāna Mahāsannipāta Sūtra on Kṣitigarbha and the Ten Wheels"), first in the Northern Liang dynasty and subsequently again by XUANZANG in 651 CE. The eponymous KṢITIGARBHASŪTRA, translated at the end of the seventh century, specifically relates the bodhisattva's vow to rescue all beings in the six realms of existence before he would attain buddhahood himself and tells the well-known prior-birth story of the bodhisattva as a young woman, whose filial piety after the death of her heretical mother saved her mother from rebirth in the AVĪCI hell. It was his ability to rescue deceased family members from horrific rebirths that became Dizang's dominant characteristic in China, where he took on the role of the Lord of Hell, opposite the Jade Emperor of native Chinese cosmology. This role may possibly have resulted from Dizang's portrayal as the Lord of Hell in the apocryphal (see APOCRYPHA) *Foshuo Dizang pusa faxin yinlu shiwang jing* and reflects Buddhist accommodations to the medieval Chinese interest in the afterlife. This specialization in servicing the denizens of hell seems also to have evolved alongside the emergence of Dizang's portrayal as a monk, whom the Chinese presume to reside on the Buddhist sacred mountain of JIUHUASHAN in Anhui province. (See also CHIJANG; KIM KYUGAK.) Kṣitigarbha is easily recognizable in Chinese iconography because he is the only bodhisattva who wears the simple raiments of a monk and has a shaved head rather than an ornate headdress. In Japan, where Kṣitigarbha is known as Jizō, the bodhisattva has taken on a different significance. Introduced to Japan during the Heian period, Jizo became immensely popular as a protector of children, patron of travelers, and guardian of community thresholds. Jizō is typically depicted as a monk carrying a staff in his left hand and a chaplet or rosary in his right. The boundaries of a village beyond which children should not wander were often marked by a stone statue of Jizō. Japanese fisherman also looked to Jizō for protection; statues of the bodhisattva erected by early Japanese immigrants to Hawaii are still found today at many popular shoreline fishing and swimming sites in the Hawaiian Islands. In modern Japan, Jizō continues to be regarded as the special protector of children, including the stillborn and aborted. In memory of these children, and as a means of requesting Jizō's protection of them, statues of Jizō are often dressed in a bib (usually red in color), sometimes wearing a knit cap or bonnet, with toys placed nearby (see MIZUKO KUYŌ). Tibetan iconography typically has Kṣitigarbha seated on a lotus flower, holding a CINTĀMAṆI in his right hand and displaying the VARADAMUDRĀ with his left.

**Kṣitigarbhasūtra**. (C. Dizang pusa benyuan jing; J. Jizō bosatsu hongangyō; K. Chijang posal ponwŏn kyŏng 地藏菩薩本願經). In Sanskrit, "The Scripture on Kṣitigarbha," now extant only in a Chinese translation (which may be rendered as "Scripture on the Original Vows of Kṣitigarbha Bodhisattva") made by the Khotanese monk ŚIKṢĀNANDA between 695 and 700 CE. The Chinese recension is in a total of thirteen chapters, which are divided into three sections. The sūtra is presented as a dialogue between ŚĀKYAMUNI Buddha and KṢITIGARBHA before a congregation of buddhas, BODHISATTVAS, divinities, and ghosts. The sūtra describes Kṣitigarbha's vow to save all beings from SAṂSĀRA before becoming a buddha himself and offers various accounts of his prior births, during which he exhibited the uncanny ability to save beings from rebirth in the AVĪCI hell. For example, in one prior-birth story, the bodhisattva is portrayed as a young girl mourning the death of her non-Buddhist mother; through the girl's filial devotion, her mother was rescued from avīci hell and reborn in one of the heavens. Another chapter outlines the far-reaching effects of Kṣitigarbha's vows, by demonstrating that even beings suffering in different hells (the attributes of which are described in vivid detail in the sūtra) were rescued by various other transformations of Kṣitigarbha. Some chapters also detail proper religious behavior: for example, in one chapter, Śākyamuni Buddha outlines in detail the ways one should pray to Kṣitigarbha, while in another is delineated the appropriate actions for honoring and benefiting the dead and the dying.

**kṣuramārga**. (T. spu gri'i lam; C. daoren lu/jianshu diyu; J. tōjinro/kenjujigoku; K. toin no/kŏmsu chiok 刀刃路/劍樹地獄). In Sanskrit, "razor road"; the third of the four "neighboring hells" (PRATYEKANARAKA) located to the four sides of the eight hot hells (see NĀRAKA). This hell is a road made of sword blades, which the hell denizens must traverse before entering a razor forest (ASIPATTRAVANA) where blades fall from the trees and where they are forced to climb trees embedded with iron spikes (AYAḤŚĀLMALĪVANA).

**Kubera**. (T. Lus ngan po; C. Jufeiluo; J. Kubeira; K. Kup'yera 俱吠囉). In Sanskrit, the ancient Indian god of wealth and king of the YAKṢAS, related to VAIŚRAVAṆA and JAMBHALA. According to Hindu mythology, Kubera was the son of Viśrāva; hence, Vaiśravaṇa is his patronym. His abode is said to be in Sri Lanka, although prior to becoming the god of wealth he lived at Mount KAILĀSA. Kubera is especially popular in the Himalayan regions, where he is usually depicted as a rich man with a large potbelly and holding a mongoose, which vomits jewels when he squeezes it.

**Kubjottarā**. (P. Khujjuttarā; T. Rgur 'jog; C. Jiushouduoluo; J. Kujutara; K. Kusudara 久壽多羅). In Sanskrit, "Hunchbacked"; an eminent lay disciple best known from Pāli sources, whom the Buddha declared to be foremost among laywomen of wide learning (P. bahussuta; S. bahuśruta); she was the slave of Sāmāvatī (S. ŚYĀMĀVATĪ), the wife of Udena and queen of Kosambī (S. Kauśambī). Kubjottarā was hunchbacked, which was said to have been retribution for having once, in a previous existence, mocked a solitary buddha (paccekabuddha; S. PRATYEKABUDDHA) for having this same disfigurement. In another lifetime, she had made a nun do chores for her, which led to her rebirth as a slave. As the servant of Sāmāvatī, Kubjottarā was sent to the market every day with eight coins to purchase flowers, where she would spend four coins and pocket the rest. One day, she witnessed the Buddha preach and at once became a stream-enterer (sotāpanna; S. SROTAĀPANNA). Returning to the palace, she confessed her previous wrongdoing to Sāmāvatī, who immediately forgave her; the slave then related the contents of the Buddha's sermon. Fascinated, Sāmāvatī requested Kubjottarā to listen to the Buddha's sermons every day and tell her and her harem attendants the Buddha's message upon returning to the palace. Through Kubjottarā's instructions, Sāmāvatī and her attendants also became stream-enterers. Kubjottarā suggested that they pierce a hole in the walls of the harem so that they could watch as the Buddha passed in the street below and worship him. After her mistress's death, Kubjottarā spent her time in religious works, teaching and preaching the DHARMA. She was said to be extremely intelligent and to have memorized the entire canon (tipiṭaka; S. TRIPIṬAKA).

**Kubo Kakutarō**. (久保角太郎) (1892–1944). Cofounder along with KOTANI KIMI of the REIYŪKAI school of modern Japanese Buddhism, which derives from the teachings of the NICHIRENSHŪ school of Buddhism. Kubo Kakutarō was an orphan who by age thirteen was employed as a carpenter's apprentice in Tōkyō. He began to work for the Imperial Household Ministry, where he met Count Sengoku, a bureaucrat who sponsored Kubo's marriage to a woman from the aristocratic Kubo family; he then took the family's surname. His parents-in-law were followers of Nichiren. After learning of the possibility of self-ordination through the teachings of Toki Jonin, he founded Rei No Tomo Kai with Wakatsuki Chise; this group became known as Reiyūkai in 1924. Kubo also grew increasingly interested in ancestor veneration, a key component in the practice of the Reiyūkai school.

**Kucha**. (S. *Kucīna; C. Qiuzi; J. Kiji; K. Kuja 龜茲). Indo-European oasis kingdom at the northern edge of the Taklamakhan Desert, which served as a major center of Buddhism in Central Asia and an important conduit for the transmission of Buddhism from India to China; the name probably corresponds to *Kucīna in Sanskrit. Indian Buddhism began to be transmitted into the Kuchean region by the beginning of the Common Era; and starting at least by the fourth century CE, Kucha had emerged as a major Buddhist and trade center along the northern SILK ROAD through Central Asia. Both mainstream and MAHĀYĀNA traditions are said to have coexisted side by side in Kucha, although the Chinese pilgrim XUANZANG, who visited Kucha in 630, says that SARVĀSTIVĀDA scholasticism predominated. Xuanzang also reports that there were over one hundred monasteries in Kucha, with some five thousand monks in residence. The indigenous Kuchean language, which no longer survives, belongs to Tocharian B, one of the two dialects of TOCHARIAN, the easternmost branch of the western Indo-European language family. In the fourth and fifth centuries CE, many Kuchean monks and scholars began to make their way to China to transmit Buddhist texts, including the preeminent translator of Buddhist materials into Chinese, KUMĀRAJĪVA. To the west of Kucha are the KIZIL caves, a complex of some 230 Buddhist caves that represent some of the highest cultural achievements of Central Asian Buddhism. Construction at the site perhaps began as early as the third century CE and lasted for some five hundred years, until Kucha came under Muslim control in the ninth century. Since the mid-eighteenth century, during the Manchu Qing dynasty (1644–1912), Kucha has been under the political control of China, and the present-day city of Kucha is located along the banks of the Muzat River in Baicheng County, in the Uighur Autonomous Region of China's Xinjiang province. In East Asia, monks from Kucha were given the ethnikon Bo, the Chinese transcription of the surname of the reigning family of Kucha. See also Khotan.

**Kuiji**. (J. Kiki; K. Kyugi 窺基) (632–682). Scholar–monk of the Tang dynasty, commonly regarded as the founder of the Faxiang zong of Chinese Yogācāra Buddhism. Orphaned as a boy, Kuiji was ordained as a teenager and assigned to the imperial translation bureau in the Tang capital; there, he emerged as one of the principal disciples of Xuanzang, under whom he studied Sanskrit and Indian Buddhist abhidharma and Yogācāra scholasticism. He participated in Xuanzang's numerous translation projects and is closely associated with the redaction of the Cheng weishi lun, which included extensive selections from ten Indian commentaries. Kuiji played a crucial role in selecting and evaluating the various doctrinal positions that were to be summarized in the text. Kuiji subsequently wrote a series of lengthy commentaries on Dharmapāla's doctrinally conservative lineage of Vijñaptimātratā-Yogācāra philosophy. His elaborate and technical presentation of Yogācāra philosophy, which came to be designated pejoratively as Faxiang (Dharma Characteristics), contrasted markedly with the earlier Chinese Yogācāra school established by Paramārtha. Because he resided and eventually died at Daci'ensi, he is often known as Ci'en dashi (J. Jion daishi; K. Chaŭn taesa), the Great Master of Ci'en Monastery. Kuiji commentaries include the *Chengweishi lun shuji* and the Dasheng fayuan yilin zhang. See also Wŏnch'ŭk.

**Kūkai**. (空海) (774–835). In Japanese, "Sea of Emptiness"; monk who is considered the founder of the tradition, often referred to as the Shingonshū, Tōmitsu, or simply mikkyō. He is often known by his posthumous title Kōbō Daishi, or "Great Master Who Spread the Dharma," which was granted to him by Emperor Daigo in 921. A native of Sanuki province on the island of Shikoku, Kūkai came from a prominent local family. At the age of fifteen, he was sent to Nara, where he studied the Chinese classics and was preparing to become a government official. However, he seems to have grown disillusioned with this life. At the age of twenty, Kūkai was ordained, perhaps by the priest Gonsō, and the following year he took the full precepts at Tōdaiji. He is claimed to have experienced an awakening while performing the Kokūzō gumonjihō, a ritual dedicated to the mantra of the bodhisattva Ākāśagarbha. While studying Buddhist texts on his own, Kūkai is said to have encountered the Mahāvairocanābhisaṃbodhisūtra and, unable to find a master who could teach him to read its mantras, decided to travel to China to learn from masters there. In 804, he was selected as a member of a delegation to China that set sail in four ships; Saichō was aboard another of the ships. Kukai eventually traveled to the Tang capital of Chang'an, where he studied tantric mijiao Buddhist rituals and theory under Huiguo and Sanskrit under the Indian monk Prajña. Under the direction of his Chinese master, Kūkai was initiated into the two realm (ryōbu) maṇḍala lineages of Yixing, Śubhakarasiṃha, Vajrabodhi, and Amoghavajra. In 806, Kūkai returned to Japan; records of the texts and implements he brought with him are preserved in the *Shōrai mokuroku*. Little is known about his activities until 809, when he moved to Mt. Takao by imperial request. Kūkai described his new teachings as mikkyō, or "secret teachings," vajrayāna (J. kongōjō), and mantrayāna (J. shingonjō). At the core of Kūkai's doctrinal and ritual program was the belief that all acts of body, speech, and mind are rooted in, and expressions of, the cosmic buddha Mahāvairocana (see Vairocana), as the dharmakāya. Kūkai argued that the dharmakāya itself teaches through the artistic and ritual forms that he brought to Japan. Once his teachings gained some renown, Kūkai conducted several abhiṣeka ceremonies, including one for the Tendai patriarch Saichō and his disciples. However, Kūkai and Saichō's relationship soured when Kūkai refused to transmit the highest level of initiation to Saichō. In 816, Emperor Saga granted Kūkai rights to Kōyasan, to serve as a training center for his Shingon mikkyō tradition. In early 823, Kūkai was granted the temple of Tōji in Kyōto, which became a second center for the Shingon tradition. In the summer of 825, Kūkai built a lecture hall at Tōji, and in 827 he was promoted to senior assistant high priest in the Bureau of Clergy. In 829, he built an abhiṣeka platform at Tōdaiji. In early 834, he received permission to establish a Shingon chapel within the imperial palace, where he constructed a maṇḍala altar. Kūkai passed into eternal samādhi (J. nyūjō) in 835 on Mt. Kōya, and it is said that he remains in his mausoleum in meditation waiting for the bodhisattva Maitreya to appear. Kūkai authored a number of important texts, including the Benkenmitsu nikyōron, a treatise outlining the inherent differences of kengyō (revealed) and mikkyō (inner) teachings; *Sokushin jōbutsugi*, a treatise on the doctrine of attainment of buddhahood in "this very body" (J. sokushin jōbutsu); *Unjigi*, a text describing the contemplation of Sanskrit syllables (S. bīja, J. shuji); *Shōjijissōgi*, a text outlining Kūkai's theory of language in which all sounds and letters are themselves full embodiments of the dharmakāya's teachings; and his magnum opus, the Himitsu mandara jūjūshinron, in which Kūkai makes his case for recognizing Shingon mikkyō as the pinnacle of Buddhist wisdom. Kūkai was an accomplished calligrapher, poet, engineer, and sculptor and is also said to have invented kana, the Japanese syllabary.

**Kukkuṭapāda, Mount**. (T. Ri bo bya rkang; C. Jizushan; J. Keisokusen; K. Kyejoksan 鷄足山). In Sanskrit, "Cock's Foot"; a mountain located in the ancient Indian state of Magadha; also known as Gurupādaka (Honored Foot); the present Kurkihar, sixteen miles northeast of Bodhgayā. The mountain is renowned as the site where the Buddha's senior disciple, Mahākāśyapa, is said to be waiting in trance for the advent of the future buddha Maitreya. Once Maiteya appears, Mahākāśyapa will hand over to him the robe (cīvara) of

ŚĀKYAMUNI, symbolizing that Maitreya is his legitimate successor in the lineage of the buddhas. The Chinese monk–pilgrim FAXIAN visited the mountain on his sojourn in India in the fifth century CE, describing the mountain as home to many dangerous predators, including tigers and wolves.

**Kukkuṭārāma**. (T. Bya gag kun ra; C. Jiyuansi; J. Keionji; K. Kyewŏnsa 鷄園寺). Major Indian Buddhist monastery, located to the southeast of the Mauryan capital of PĀṬALIPUTRA (P. Pāṭaliputta, present-day Patna); founded by King AŚOKA in the third century BCE, with YAŚAS serving as abbot. The Chinese pilgrim XUANZANG visited the site of the monastery in the seventh century, but only the foundations remained. Aśoka is said to have often visited the monastery to make offerings, but Puṣyamitra, who founded the Śuṅga dynasty in 183 BCE, destroyed the monastery when he invaded Pāṭaliputra and murdered many of its monks. Next to the monastery was a large reliquary named the Āmalaka STŪPA, which is said to have been named after half an āmalaka fruit that Aśoka gave as his final offering to the SAṂGHA before his death; thanks, however, to the merit that accrued from the profound sincerity with which the king made even such a meager offering, Aśoka recovered from his illness, and the seeds of the fruit were preserved in this stūpa in commemoration of the miracle. The KAUKKUṬIKA school, one of the three main subgroups of the MAHĀSĀṂGHIKA branch of the mainstream Buddhist tradition, is said to have derived its name from this monastery.

**kukūla**. (T. me ma mur; C. tangwei zeng; J. tōezō; K. tangoejŭng 煻煨增). In Sanskrit, "heated by burning chaff"; the first of the four "neighboring hells" (PRATYEKANARAKA) located to the four sides of the eight hot hells (see NĀRAKA). This hell is a pit of hot ashes where the hell denizens are burned.

**kula**. (T. rigs; C. jiazu; J. kazoku; K. kajok 家族). In Sanskrit, lit. "family"; used metaphorically to refer to a community of practice. The term is particularly associated with tantric Buddhism and is used to categorize the various buddhas, BODHISATTVAS, other deities, and initiates into spiritual families, or groups. Early tantric texts utilize a threefold system of three buddha families, comprising the tathāgata family (TATHĀGATAKULA) associated with ŚĀKYAMUNI or VAIROCANA, the vajra family (VAJRAKULA) associated with VAJRAPĀṆI or AKṢOBHYA, and the lotus family (PADMAKULA) associated with AVALOKITEŚVARA or AMITĀBHA. Later tantric traditions employ a fivefold system, wherein initiates are divided into five buddha families based on their predominant affliction and the ability of a particular buddha to lead them to enlightenment. The five buddha families (PAÑCATATHĀGATA) are correlated with the five wisdoms (PAÑCAJÑĀNA) or aspects of enlightenment (BODHI) and are composed of the tathāgata family (Vairocana), the vajra family (Akṣobhya), the ratna family (RATNASAṂMBHAVA), the lotus family (Amitābha), and the action family (AMOGHASIDDHI).

**kuladuhitṛ**. (P. kuladhītā; T. rigs kyi bu mo; C. shannüren; J. zennyonin; K. sŏnyŏin 善女人). In Sanskrit, "daughter of good family," or "respectable family"; an Indian term of address used by teacher toward a female student; hence, in the sūtras, the Buddha typically addresses his "pupils" as kuladuhitṛ and "sons of good family" (KULAPUTRA). In the Mahāyāna sūtras, the term is often interpreted to mean a woman who belongs to the BODHISATTVA lineage.

**kuladūṣaka**. (P. kuladūsaka; T. khyim sun 'byin pa; C. wujia; J. wake; K. oga 汚家). In Sanskrit, "corruptor of good families." "Corrupting" refers to a monk (or nun) imposing on the services of a lay family with acts that, it was feared, might destroy the laity's religious faith in and respect for the institution of the SAMGHA. Such acts include giving flowers, garlands, fruits, powder, toiletries, etc., as gifts to the laity—presumably for the purpose of courting favor—or acting as a physician, messenger, or marriage go-between. A monk or nun who does any of these things is guilty of a suspension offense (S. SAṂGHĀVAŚEṢA; P. saṅghādisesa).

**kulaṃkula**. (T. rigs nas rigs su skye ba; C. jiajia; J. keke; K. kaga 家家). In Sanskrit, "one who goes from family to family"; a specific type of stream-enterer (SROTAĀPANNA); one of the twenty members of the ĀRYASAMGHA (see VIṂŚATIPRABHEDASAṂGHA). According to the ABHIDHARMAKOŚABHĀṢYA, the kulaṃakula has eliminated one or two of the nine sets of afflictions (KLEŚA) that cause rebirth in the sensuous realm (KĀMADHĀTU); these are the impediments to the first DHYĀNA that the mundane (LAUKIKA) path of cultivation (BHĀVANĀMĀRGA) removes prior to reaching the path of vision (DARŚANAMĀRGA). They will take two or even three rebirths among the humans or divinities of the sensuous realm before they reach the goal of ARHAT. They are called "family to family" because the two rebirths are of a similar class, for example, in the sensuous realm.

**kulaputra**. (P. kulaputta; T. rigs kyi bu; C. shannanzi; J. zennanshi; K. sŏnnamja 善男子). In Sanskrit, "son of good family," or "son of respectable family"; an Indian term of address used by a teacher toward a male student; hence in the sūtras, the Buddha typically addresses his "pupils" as kulaputra and "daughters of good family" (KULADUHITṚ). In the MAHĀYĀNA sūtras, the term was often interpreted to mean a man who belongs to the BODHISATTVA lineage.

**Kulatā**. (S). One of the twenty-four sacred sites associated with the CAKRASAṂVARATANTRA. See PĪṬHA.

**Kumano**. (熊野). In Japanese, lit. "Ursine Wilderness"; a mountainous region in Wakayama prefecture on the Kii Peninsula; Kumano is an important site in the history and development of SHUGENDŌ, a syncretistic tradition of mountain asceticism in Japan. Artifacts from the seventh century provide the earliest traces of Kumano's sacred roots, although worship there likely predated this time. Throughout the medieval period, the area developed ties with the powerful institutions of Japanese Tendai (TIANTAI), SHINGON, the Hossō monastery KŌFUKUJI, and the imperial family, with additional influences from PURE LAND Buddhism. By the eleventh century, its three major religious sites, collectively known as Kumano Sanzan (the three mountains of Kumano), were well established as centers of practice: the Hongū Shrine, home to Amida (AMITĀBHA); the Shingū Shrine, home to Yakushi (BHAIṢAJYAGURU); and Nachi Falls and its shrine, the residence of the thousand-armed BODHISATTVA Kannon (AVALOKITEŚVARA; see SĀHASRABHUJASĀHASRANETRĀVALOKITEŚVARA). Following the principle of HONJI SUIJAKU (buddhas or bodhisattvas appearing in the world as spirits), Buddhist deities were readily adopted into the local community of gods (KAMI). Hence, Amida took the form of the god Ketsumiko no kami, Yakushi manifested as Hayatama no kami, and Kannon appeared as Fusubi no kami. Kumano developed close ties with the aristocratic elite in Kyōto from the tenth through the twelfth centuries. After the ex-Emperor Uda's pilgrimage to Kumano in 907, a long line of monarchs, often retired, made one or multiple journeys to the sacred destination. In the early twelfth century, ex-Emperor Shirakawa granted Shōgoin—a Japanese Tendai (TIANTAI) monastery in Kyōto—to the monk Zōyō, whose appointment included responsibility for overseeing Kumano. Later in the Tokugawa Period (1600–1868), it was Shōgoin that regulated Tendai-affiliated Shugen centers around the country, consequently making a large impact on their doctrine and practice. The nearby Yoshino mountains of Kinbu and Ōmine, where Shugendō's semilegendary founder EN NO OZUNU regularly practiced, share much history with Kumano. A text known as the *Shozan Engi* (1180?) describes Kumano as the garbhadhātu (J. TAIZŌKAI, or "womb realm") MAṆḌALA and the northern Yoshino mountains as the vajradhātu (J. KONGŌKAI, or "diamond realm") maṇḍala. These two geographic maṇḍalas, now superimposed over the physical landscape, became the basis of the well-known Yoshino–Kumano pilgrimage route, which is still followed today. As the prestige and patronage of the court began to wane in the late twelfth century, revenue from visitors to the area became an important source of income for the local economy. In the following centuries, increasing numbers of pilgrims, including aristocrats, warriors, and ordinary people, undertook the journey, accompanying Kumano Shugen guides (sendatsu).

**kumārabhūta**. (T. gzhon nur gyur pa; C. tongzhen; J. dōshin; K. tongjin 童眞). In Sanskrit, lit. "youthful," and "in the form of a prince"; a name commonly used in Sanskrit sources as an epithet of the BODHISATTVA MAÑJUŚRĪ, who is considered to remain perennially youthful in appearance. The term may also be used to refer to either a novice monk (ŚRĀMAṆERA), in particular one between the ages of four or eight and twenty; an unmarried man over the age of eight; or BODHISATTVAS in general. ¶ In Korea, Tongjin is identified with either BRAHMĀ, the king of the BRAHMALOKA, the first DHYĀNA heaven in the realm of subtle materiality (RŪPADHĀTU), or Skandha (K. Wit'a; C. Weituo), the guardian deity who is one of the eight generals subordinate to VIRŪḌHAKA, one of the four heavenly kings (caturmahārāja; see LOKAPĀLA), who is the king of the southern quarter of the world. In both cases, Tongjin is described as a dharma protector (DHARMAPĀLA). His name is interpreted to mean a "youth" (tong), whose character is "authentic" (–jin). Hanging paintings (T'AENGHWA) of Tongjin and the SINJUNG ("host of spirits"; lokapāla) are often displayed on the right wall of the main shrine halls (TAEUNG CHŎN) in Korean monasteries. In these paintings, Tongjin is typically portrayed wearing a grand, feathered headdress accompanied by over a dozen associates, who aid him in protecting the religion. Tongjin's image also sometimes appears on the first and last pages of a Buddhist scripture, thus protecting its content.

**Kumārajīva**. (C. Jiumoluoshi; J. Kumarajū; K. Kumarajip 鳩摩羅什) (344–409/413). The most influential translator of Buddhist texts into Chinese. He is regarded by tradition as the founder of the Chinese SAN LUN ZONG or "Three Treatises" branch of the MADHYAMAKA school of MAHĀYĀNA philosophy. According to his hagiography, Kumārajīva was born in the Central Asian petty kingdom of KUCHA, where he was related to the royal family on his mother's side. In his youth, he studied SARVĀSTIVĀDA doctrine in Kashmir but was later converted to MAHĀYĀNA at the Central Asian oasis town of Kashgar by the monk BUDDHAYAŚAS. When the Chinese general Lü Guang conquered Kucha in 383, he took Kumārajīva back with him to Liangzong near the Chinese outpost of DUNHUANG as a prize, only to lose the eminent scholar–monk to Yaoxing (r. 394–416) when the Latter Qin ruler reconquered the region in 401. During his eighteen years as a hostage, Kumārajīva apparently learned to speak and read Chinese and seems to have been one of the first foreign monks able to use the language fluently. A year later in 402, Yaoxing invited Kumārajīva to the capital of Chang'an, where he established a translation bureau under Kumārajīva's direction that produced some of the most enduring translations of Buddhist texts made in Chinese. The sheer number and variety of the translations made by Kumārajīva and his team were virtually unmatched until XUANZANG (600/602–664 CE). Translations of some seventy-four texts, in 384 rolls, are typically attributed to Kumārajīva, including various sūtras, such as the PAÑCAVIṂŚATISĀHASRIKĀPRAJÑĀPĀRAMITĀSŪTRA, AṢṬASĀHASRIKĀPRAJÑĀPĀRAMITĀ, SADDHARMAPUṆḌARĪKASŪTRA, VIMALAKĪRTINIRDEŚA, SUKHĀVATĪVYŪHASŪTRA, and VAJRACCHEDIKĀPRAJÑĀPĀRAMITĀSŪTRA, and important śāstras such as the MŪLAMADHYAMAKAKĀRIKĀ, ŚATAŚĀSTRA, *Dvādaśamukhaśāstra*, and the DAZHIDU LUN. Because Kumārajīva was one of the first foreign monks to have learned Chinese well, he produced translations that were readily comprehensible as Chinese, and his translations remain the most widely read in East Asia of any translator's; indeed, where there are multiple translations of a scripture, it is almost inevitably

Kumārajīva's that remains part of the living tradition. The accuracy of his translations is said to be attested by the fact that his tongue remained unburned during his cremation. Along with his correspondences with the monk LUSHAN HUIYUAN found in the DASHENG DAYI ZHANG, these translations laid the foundation for Mahāyāna thought, and especially Madhyamaka philosophy, in China. His many famous disciples include DAOSHENG, SENGZHAO, Daorong, and Sengrui, who are known collectively as the "four sages."

**Kumāra-Kāśyapa**. (P. Kumāra-Kassapa; T. 'Od srung gzhon nu; C. Jiumoluo Jiashe; J. Kumara Kashō; K. Kumara Kasŏp 鳩摩羅迦葉). An ARHAT declared by the Buddha as foremost among his monk disciples in eloquence (PRATIBHĀNA) or versatile discourse (P. chittakathika). According to Pāli sources, his mother was a banker's daughter who had married after her father refused to give his consent for her to join the Buddhist order. But her new husband was sympathetic to her religious quest and granted her permission. Unbeknown to her, however, she was already pregnant when she was ordained and ended up giving birth to her son in the monastery. When her condition became known, Devadatta rebuked her as a PĀRĀJIKA, but the Buddha handed the case to UPĀLI for adjudication, who declared that there was no transgression. (In such cases, the VINAYA authorizes the nuns to care for the child until he is weaned, after which he should be given to a BHIKṢU and ordained as a novice, or ŚRĀMAṆERA, or else handed over to relatives to be raised. According to the MŪLASARVĀSTIVĀDA VINAYA, however, his parents Udāyin and Guptā were an ordained monk and nun, who conceived him—supposedly not through sexual intercourse but through the nun impregnating herself with the monk's semen—and then raised him in the monastery.) After his birth, the boy was raised by the king of ŚRĀVASTĪ and was ordained as a novice when he reached the minimum age of seven. He received the epithet kumāra (youth) because of his youth when he was ordained and his royal upbringing and because he was a favorite of the Buddha, who used to give him sweets. Kumāra-Kāśyapa attained arhatship by pondering fifteen questions put to him by a BRAHMĀ god, who was himself a nonreturner (ANĀGĀMIN) and had been the boy's companion in a previous life. Kumāra-Kāśyapa, in turn, assisted his mother in attaining insight. His mother was very attached to him and had wept for twelve years because she never saw him. When one day she happened upon him, she was so overwhelmed with emotion that she stumbled and milk flowed from her breasts. Realizing that her love for him was an impediment to her liberation, he harshly rebuked her to lessen her affections; that evening, she attained arhatship. Kumāra-Kāśyapa received higher ordination (UPASAṂPADĀ) as a monk prior to reaching the minimum age of twenty, as the VINAYA normally stipulates, when Buddha ruled that the ten months spent in the mother's womb could be included in determining the ordinand's age. During the time of a previous buddha, Kumāra-Kāśyapa was a brāhmaṇa who overheard a disciple of the Buddha being praised for his eloquence; it was then that he vowed to attain the same distinction under a future buddha.

**kumbhāṇḍa**. [alt. kumbhaṇḍa] (P. kumbhaṇḍa; T. grul bum; C. jiupantu; J. kuhanda; K. kubando 鳩槃荼). In Sanskrit, a type of evil spirit, and typically listed along with especially RĀKṢASA, but also PIŚĀCA, YAKṢA, and BHŪTA spirits. VIRŪḌHAKA (P. Virūḷhaka), one of the four world-guardians (LOKAPĀLA), who protects the southern cardinal direction, is usually said to be their overlord, although some texts give Rudra this role instead. The kumbhāṇḍa are also sometimes listed among the minions of MĀRA, evil personified.

**Kŭmgang sammaegyŏng non**. (C. Jingang sanmei jing lun; J. Kongō sanmaikyōron 金剛三昧經論). In Korean, "Exposition of the KŬMGANG SAMMAE KYŎNG" (*Vajrasamādhisūtra*); composed by the Korean monk WŎNHYO (617–686). The circumstances of the commentary's composition are provided in Wŏnhyo's biography in ZANNING's SONG GAOSENG ZHUAN. According to that account, an unidentified Silla king sent an envoy on a voyage to China in search of medicine that would cure his queen. On his way to China, however, the envoy was waylaid and taken to the dragon king's palace in the sea, where he was told that the queen's illness was merely a pretext in order to reintroduce the *Vajrasamādhi* into the world. The dragon king informed the envoy that the scripture was to be collated by an otherwise unknown monk named Taean (d.u.) and interpreted by Wŏnhyo, the most eminent contemporary scholar of the Korean Buddhist tradition. The commentary that Wŏnhyo wrote later made its way into China, where it was elevated to the status of a ŚĀSTRA (lun; K. non), hence the title *Kŭmgang sammaegyŏng non*. Wŏnhyo's commentary is largely concerned with the issue of how to cultivate "original enlightenment" (BENJUE), that is, how it is that the original enlightenment motivates ordinary sentient beings to aspire to become enlightened buddhas. Wŏnhyo discerns in the *Kŭmgang sammae kyŏng* a map of six sequential types of meditative practice, which culminate in the "contemplation practice that has but a single taste" (ilmi kwanhaeng). In Wŏnhyo's account of this process, the ordinary sensory consciousnesses are transformed into an "immaculate consciousness" (AMALAVIJÑĀNA), wherein both enlightenment and delusion are rendered ineluctable and all phenomena are perceived to have but the "single taste" of liberation. In Wŏnhyo's treatment, original enlightenment is thus transformed from an abstract soteriological concept into a practical tool of meditative training.

**Kŭmgang sammae kyŏng**. (S. *Vajrasamādhisūtra; C. Jingang sanmei jing; J. Kongō sanmaikyō 金剛三昧經). In Korean, "Adamantine Absorption Scripture," usually known in English by its reconstructed Sanskrit title **Vajrasamādhisūtra*. East Asian Buddhists presumed that the scripture was an anonymous Chinese translation of an Indian sūtra, but the text is now known to be an apocryphal scripture (see APOCRYPHA), which was composed in Korea c. 685 CE, perhaps by an early adept of the nascent SŎN (C. CHAN) school, which would make it the second oldest text associated with the emerging Chan movement. The sūtra purports to offer a grand synthesis of the entirety of MAHĀYĀNA doctrine and VINAYA, as the foundation for a comprehensive system of meditative practice. One of the main goals of the scripture seems to have been to reconcile the newly imported Chan teachings with the predominantly Hwaŏm (HUAYAN) orientation of Korean Buddhist doctrine (see KYO). The text also includes quotations from BODHIDHARMA's ERRU SIXING LUN and teachings associated with the East Mountain Teachings (DONGSHAN FAMEN) of the Chan monks DAOXIN and HONGREN, arranged in such a way as to suggest that the author was trying to bring together these two distinct lineages of the early Chan tradition. Unaware of the text's provenance and dating, WŎNHYO (617–686), in the first commentary written on the sūtra, the KŬMGANG SAMMAEGYŎNG NON, presumed that the sūtra was the scriptural source of the emblematic teaching of a treatise, the DASHENG QIXIN LUN ("Awakening of Faith According to the Mahāyāna"), that was written over a century earlier, viz., the one mind and its two aspects, true-thusness (ZHENRU; viz., S. TATHATĀ) and production-and-cessation (shengmie), which correspond respectively to ultimate truth (PARAMĀRTHASATYA) and conventional truth (SAṂVṚTISATYA), or the unconditioned (ASAṂSKṚTA) and conditioned (SAṂSKṚTA) realms. (For the traditional account of the putative "rediscovery" of the sūtra and the writing of its commentary, see KŬMGANG SAMMAEGYŎNG NON s.v.).

**Kŭmgangsan**. (C. Jingangshan; J. Kongōsan; 金剛山). In Korean, "Diamond (S. VAJRA) Mountains," Buddhist sacred mountains and important Korean pilgrimage site. The mountains are located in Kangwŏn Province, North Korea, on the east coast of the Korean peninsula in the middle of the Paektu Taegan, the mountain range that is regarded geographically and spiritually as the geomantic "spine" of the Korean peninsula. The mountains are known for their spectacular natural beauty, and its hundreds of individual peaks have been frequent subjects of both literati and folk painting. During the Silla dynasty, Kŭmgangsan began to be conceived as a Buddhist sacred site. "Diamond Mountains," also known by its indigenous name Hyŏllye, is listed in the *Samguk sagi* ("History of the Three Kingdoms") and SAMGUK YUSA ("Memorabilia of the Three Kingdoms") as one of the three mountains (samsan) and five peaks (o'ak) that were the objects of cultic worship during the Silla period; scholars, however, generally agree that this refers to another mountain closer to the Silla capital of KYŎNGJU rather than what are now known as the Diamond Mountains. The current Diamond Mountains have had several names over the course of history, including Pongnae, P'ungak, Kaegol, Yŏlban, Kidal, Chunghyangsŏng, and Sangak, with "Kŭmgang" (S. VAJRA) becoming its accepted name around the fourteenth century. The name "Diamond Mountains" appears in the AVATAṂSAKASŪTRA as the place in the middle of the sea where the BODHISATTVA DHARMODGATA (K. Pŏpki posal) resides, preaching the dharma to his congregation of bodhisattvas. The Huayan exegete CHENGGUAN (738–839), in his massive HUAYAN JING SHU, explicitly connects the *Avataṃsakasūtra*'s mention of the Diamond Mountains to Korea (which he calls Haedong, using its traditional name). The AṢṬASĀHASRIKĀPRAJÑĀPĀRAMITĀ also says that the Dharmodgata (K. Tammugal; J. Donmuketsu; C. Tanwujian) preaches the PRAJÑĀPĀRAMITĀ at GANDHAVATĪ (K. Chunghyangsŏng; C. Zhongxiangcheng; J. Shukōjō, "City of Multitudinous Fragrances"), one of the alternate names of the Diamond Mountains and now the name of one of its individual peaks. According to the Koryŏ-period *Kŭmgang Yujŏmsa sajŏk ki* by Minji (1248–1326), on a visit to the Diamond Mountains made by ŬISANG (625–702), the vaunt-courier of the Hwaŏm (C. Huayan) school in Korea, Dharmodgata appeared to him and told him that Kŭmgangsan was the place in Korea where even people who do not practice could become liberated, whereas only religious virtuosi would be able to get enlightened on the Korean Odaesan (cf. C. WUTAISHAN). For all these reasons, Pŏpki Posal is considered to be the patron bodhisattva of Kŭmgangsan. Starting in the late-Koryŏ dynasty, the Diamond Mountains became a popular pilgrimage site for Korean Buddhists. Before the devastation of the Korean War (1950–1953), it is said that there were some 108 monasteries located on Kŭmgangsan, including four primary ones: P'YOHUNSA, CHANGANSA, SIN'GYESA, and Mahayŏnsa. Mahayŏnsa, "Great Vehicle Monastery," was built by Ŭisang in 676 beneath Dharmodgata Peak (Pŏpkibong) and was considered one of the ten great Hwaŏm monasteries (Hwaŏm siptae sach'al) of the Silla dynasty. Currently, the only active monasteries are P'yohunsa and its affiliated branch monasteries, a few remaining buildings of Mahayŏnsa, and Sin'gyesa, which was rebuilt starting in 2004 as a joint venture of the South Korean CHOGYE CHONG and the North Korean Buddhist Federation. In the late twentieth century, the Diamond Mountains were developed into a major tourist site, with funding provided by South Korean corporate investors, although access has been held hostage to the volatile politics of the Korean peninsula. ¶ In Japan, Diamond Mountains (KONGŌSAN) is an alternate name for KATSURAGISAN in Nara, the principal residence of EN NO OZUNU (b. 634), the putative founder of the SHUGENDŌ school of Japanese esoterism, because he was considered to be a manifestation of the bodhisattva Dharmodgata.

**Kŭmsansa**. (金山寺). In Korean, "Gold Mountain Monastery," the seventeenth district monastery (PONSA) of the contemporary CHOGYE order of Korean Buddhism; located on Moak Mountain near Kimje in North Chŏlla province. The monastery was founded in 600 CE and grew quickly. The Silla monk CHINP'YO (fl. c. 800), one of the early figures associated with the transmission of the monastic regulations (VINAYA) to Korea, was responsible for a major expansion of the monastery that took place between 762 and 766. Chinp'yo dedicated the monastery to the BODHISATTVA MAITREYA and built a three-story main shrine hall, or TAEUNG CHŎN, which is dominated by the golden 39-ft. high statue of Maitreya, standing in the gesture of fearlessness (ABHAYAMUDRĀ) between two attendants who are both 29-ft. high. The south wall of the hall is decorated with a T'AENGHWA painting of Maitreya conferring the monastic rules (vinaya) on Chinp'yo. The monastery was expanded again in 1079 by the Koryŏ YOGĀCĀRA monk Hyedŏk Sohyŏn (1038–1096), who added several additional hermitages and sanctuaries; a STŪPA reputed to enshrine his ŚARĪRA is located on the monastery grounds. In 1596, the Japanese burned the monastery, whose monks had organized a 1,500-man force to resist the Hideyoshi invasion force. The oldest buildings currently on the site date to 1635, when the monastery was reconstructed under the leadership of the monk Sumun (d.u.). The scriptural repository (Taejang chŏn) at Kŭmsansa was built in 1652 but moved to its current site in 1922; inside can be found images of ŚĀKYAMUNI and the two ARHATs MAHĀKĀŚYAPA and ĀNANDA. The wooden building is quite ornate and is one of the best-preserved examples of its type from the Chosŏn period. There are various other items of note on the monastery campus, including a hexagonal stone pagoda made from slate capped by granite, another five-story pagoda, and a stone bell resembling those at T'ONGDOSA and Silluksa. Carvings on the bell date it to the Koryŏ dynasty and depict buddhas, dharma protectors (DHARMAPĀLA), and lotus flowers (PADMA).

**kuṇapa**. (T. ro myags 'dam; C. shifenzeng; J. shifunzō; K. sibunjŭng 屍糞增). In Sanksrit, "mud of corpses"; the second of the four "neighboring hells" (PRATYEKANARAKA) located to the four sides of the eight hot hells (see NĀRAKA). This hell is a swamp of rotting corpses.

**Kun byed rgyal po**. (Kun che gyalpo). In Tibetan, the "All-Creating King," an important tantra for the RNYING MA sect of Tibetan Buddhism, known for its exposition of RDZOGS CHEN. Within the tripartite division of ATIYOGA, it is placed in the SEMS SDE class. Although presented as an Indian text (in which case, its Sanskrit title would be *Kulayarāja*), the work is likely of Tibetan origin, dating from the late tenth century. A work in eighty-four chapters, it takes the form of a dialogue between the All-Creating King and Sattvavajra. Among its famous teachings are the "ten absences" (med pa bcu) that point to the special nature of primordial awareness, called BODHICITTA as well as the "all-creating king" in the text. The ten are as follows: no philosophical view on which to meditate, no vows to maintain, no method to seek, no MAṆḌALA to create, no transmission to receive, no path to traverse, no BHŪMI to achieve, no conduct to abandon or adopt, an absence of obstacles in the primordial wisdom, and spontaneous perfection beyond all hope and fear.

**Kun bzang bla ma'i zhal lung**. (Kunzang Lame Shelung). In Tibetan, "Words of My Perfect Teacher," a popular Buddhist text, written by the celebrated nineteenth-century Tibetan luminary DPAL SPRUL RIN PO CHE during a period of prolonged retreat at his cave hermitage above RDZOGS CHEN monastery in eastern Tibet. It explains the preliminary practices (SNGON 'GRO) for the KLONG CHEN SNYING THIG ("Heart Essence of the Great Expanse"), a system of RNYING MA doctrine and meditation instruction stemming from the eighteenth-century treasure revealer (GTER STON) 'JIGS MED GLING PA. The work is much loved for its direct, nontechnical approach and for its heartfelt practical advice. Dpal sprul Rin po che's language ranges from lyrical poetry to the vernacular, illustrating points of doctrine with numerous scriptural quotations, accounts from the lives of past Tibetan saints, and examples from everyday life—many of which refer to cultural practices specific to the author's native land. While often considered a Rnying ma text, the *Kun bzang bla ma'i zhal lung* is read widely throughout the sects of Tibetan Buddhism, a readership presaged by the author's participation in the RIS MED or so-called nonsectarian movement of eastern Tibet during the nineteenth century.

**Kuṇḍadhāna**. (C. Juntubohan; J. Kuntohakan; K. Kundobarhan 君屠鉢漢). In Sanskrit and Pāli, name of an ARHAT who is listed as one of the four great ŚRĀVAKAS (C. sida shengwen). According to Pāli sources, the Buddha declared him to be foremost among monks in receiving food-tickets (salākā; S. śalākā), small slips of wood used to determine which monks would receive meals from the laity, a distinction he was given because he was always the first of the Buddha's disciples to receive food-tickets when he accompanied the Buddha on invitations. Kuṇḍadhāna was a learned brāhmaṇa from Sāvatthi (S. ŚRĀVASTĪ) who knew the Vedas by heart. When he was already an old man, he heard the Buddha preach and decided to renounce the world and join the Buddhist order. However, beginning on the day of his ordination, an apparition of a young woman would follow him wherever he went, although he himself could not see her. This caused great amusement among the public, and he became a frequent butt of jokes that he could not comprehend. On alms rounds (PIṆḌAPĀTA), women would place two helpings of food in his bowl, remarking that the first was for him and the second for his lady friend. In the monastery, his fellow monks and even novices were relentless in their teasing, until one day he lost his temper and abused his tormentors. This outburst was duly reported to the Buddha, who admonished the old monk to be patient, as he was only suffering retribution from some past misdeed. King Pasenadi (PRASENAJIT) of Kosala (S. KOŚALA) heard of Kuṇḍadhāna's strange case and, after an inquiry that proved his innocence, supplied him with requisites so that he need no longer go into the city for alms. Free from the taunting, Kuṇḍadhāna was able to concentrate his mind and in due course became an arahant (S. ARHAT), whereupon the apparition disappeared. Kuṇḍadhāna's wrongdoing had occurred during the time of Kassapa (S. KĀŚYAPA) Buddha, when, as a sprite, he played a trick on two monks to test their friendship. Assuming the form of a maiden rearranging her clothes after a tryst, he caused one monk to accuse his companion of a violation. Because his mischief forever ended the friendship of the two monks, the sprite was reborn in hell for an eon and, in his last life, as the monk Kuṇḍadhāna, he was compelled to be followed around by this apparition of a maiden. He is also sometimes listed as one of the four great śrāvakas (C. sida shengwen); the lists vary widely but typically include either MAHĀKĀŚYAPA, PIṆḌOLA-BHĀRADVĀJA, and RĀHULA; or MAHĀMAUDGALYĀYANA, Mahākāśyapa, and ANIRUDDHA; or ŚĀRIPUTRA, Mahāmaudgalyāyana, Mahākāśyapa, and SUBHŪTI, etc.

**Kun dga' bzang po**. (Kunga Sangpo) (1382–1456). A Tibetan Buddhist master, better known as Ngor chen, "the great man of Ngor"; renowned as the founder of the Ngor subsect of the SA SKYA sect after the seat he founded at NGOR E WAM CHOS LDAN monastery in 1429 (alt. 1434) near Shigatse (Gzhis ka rtse) in Gtsang (Tsang). His collected works in four volumes include works on the LAM 'BRAS (path and result), and rituals and guidance texts for a wide range of tantric practices including HEVAJRA, GUHYASAMĀJA, VAJRABHAIRAVA, and CAKRASAṂVARA. Among his students are SHĀKYA MCHOG LDAN and GO BO RAB 'BYAMS PA BSOD NAMS SENG GE.

**Kun dga' dpal 'byor**. (Kunga Paljor) (1426/8–1476). The second "throne holder" ('Brug chen) of the 'BRUG PA BKA' BRGYUD sect of Tibetan Buddhism, after GTSANG PA RGYA RAS YE SHES RDO RJE, the founder of the 'Brug pa bka' brgyud. Prior to Kun dga' dpal 'byor (called Chos rje "dharma lord"), the line of 'BRUG CHEN INCARNATIONS passed down for twelve generations through Gtsang pa rgya ras's family; the line of incarnations is counted from Chos rje Kun dga' dpal 'byor, a great teacher and author. His collected works in two volumes include explanations of MAHĀMUDRĀ, tantric songs (mgur), and special instructions.

**kuṇḍikā**. (T. ril ba spyi blugs/ril tshags; C. jingping/junchi; J. jōbyō/gunji; K. chŏngbyŏng/kunji 淨瓶/軍持). In Sanskrit and Pāli, "water pot" or "water sprinkler"; also seen spelled as kuṇḍika or kuṇḍaka (there are similarly many variations in the Chinese transcriptions and translations); the vessel originally used by monks and nuns for carrying water, which later became a common ritual implement used in a wide variety of Buddhist ceremonies for sprinkling water for purification. The kuṇḍikā was one of the eighteen requisites (PARIṢKĀRA, NIŚRAYA) that monks and nuns were allowed to keep and could be used either as a canteen for drinking water or as a pot for carrying water to use at the latrine. The kuṇḍikā has a distinctive shape: the oval main vessel, which can typically hold over three liters of water has a separate short spout, which was used to fill the pot with water, and its long neck is topped with a long slender tube through which water was poured (although these functions were sometimes interchanged). The two spouts were capped with metal, bamboo, or even fabric so that insects and dirt would not foul the water. The vessels were commonly made from earthenware, porcelain, or bronze. Scores of metal kuṇḍikā that were used in rituals are found in East Asia from the seventh and eighth centuries. During the Koryŏ dynasty in Korea, such kuṇḍikā were widely used by nobility and commoners, monks, and laypersons for storing water. A particularly exquisite twelfth-century bronze kuṇḍikā, inlaid with silver willows and aquatic birds, is a Korean national treasure. The BODHISATTVA AVALOKITEŚVARA, especially his moon in the water form (SHUIYUE GUANYIN), is often depicted holding a kuṇḍikā capped by a willow twig and filled with the nectar of immortality (AMṚTA), which he used to alleviate the suffering of sentient beings.

**Kŭngsŏn**. (K) (亘璇). See PAEKP'A KŬNGSŎN.

**Kuo'an Shiyuan**. (J. Kakuan Shion; K. Kwagam Sawŏn 廓庵師遠). (d.u.). Chinese CHAN monk best known as author of one of the two classic depictions of the ten oxherding pictures (C. Shiniu tu) that eventually became normative within the Chan tradition. Shiyuan was a disciple of Dasui Yuanjing (d. 1135) in the YANGQI PAI of the LINJI ZONG but little else is known about his life or career. His set of ten oxherding pictures traces the development of the Chan student (the "herdsman") who seeks to tame the "ox" of his unchecked thoughts, so that he may put his enlightened mind to use in the service of all sentient beings. His images of each stage, accompanied with his own explanatory verses, spread widely across East Asia and became a staple of Chan pedagogy. See OXHERDING PICTURES, TEN.

**Kurukullā**. (T. Dbang gi lha mo). Sanskrit proper name of a form of TĀRĀ; Kurukullā appears in both peaceful and wrathful manner, generally red in color. Wrathful, she stands in ARDHAPARYAṄKA ĀSANA, one face with three eyes, wearing a crown of skulls and holding in her four hands a bow and arrow and snare (pāśa) and displaying the ABHAYAMUDRĀ. When peaceful, she is portrayed in seated posture and has eight arms. Kurukullā is propitiated in a rite of VAŚĪKARAṆA, by which men are bewitched. She is therefore considered the Tārā of love, propitiated by women seeking success in romance. Her mantra is oṃ kurukulle hrī svāhā.

**kuśala**. (P. kusala; T. dge ba; C. shan; J. zen; K. sŏn 善). In Sanskrit, "wholesome," "virtuous," "salutary," or "meritorious." Kuśala is the primary term used to identify salutary deeds of body, speech, and mind (often enumerated as ten) that result in favorable rebirths. A "wholesome" action generally refers to any volition (CETANĀ) or volitional action, along with the consciousness (VIJÑĀNA) and mental constructions (SAṂSKĀRA) associated with it, that is not motivated by the afflictions (KLEŚA) of greed (LOBHA), hatred (DVEṢA; P. dosa), or delusion (MOHA). Such volitional actions produce fortunate results for the actor and ultimately are the cause of the favorable rebirths in the destinies (GATI) of humans and divinities (DEVA). A list of ten wholesome courses of actions (kuśalakarmapatha; see KARMAPATHA), which are the opposite of the unwholesome (AKUŚALA) courses of action is typically given. These include, under the category of body, the avoidance of killing and instead sustaining life, the avoidance of stealing and instead giving, and the avoidance of sexual misconduct and instead maintaining sexual morality; under the category of speech, the avoidance of lying and instead speaking truthfully, the avoidance of slander and instead speaking harmoniously, the avoidance of offensive speech and instead speaking kindly, and the avoidance of prattle and instead speaking sensibly; under the category of mind, unselfishness, good will, and right views (SAMYAGDṚṢṬI).

**kuśalakarmapatha**. In Sanskrit, the ten "wholesome courses of action." See KARMAPATHA.

**kuśalamahābhūmika**. (T. dge ba'i sa mang; C. da shandi fa; J. daizenjihō; K. tae sŏnji pŏp 大善地法). In Sanskrit, "wholesome factors of wide extent"; the principal factors (DHARMA) that ground all wholesome activities. In the SARVĀSTIVĀDA ABHIDHARMA system, ten specific forces associated with mentality (CITTASAṂPRAYUKTASAṂSKĀRA) are identified as accompanying all wholesome activities and therefore are described as "wholesome factors of wide extent." These ten dharma are (1) "confidence" or "faith" (ŚRADDHĀ), (2) "heedfulness" or "vigilance" (APRAMĀDA), (3) "tranquillity" or "pliancy" (PRAŚRABDHI), (4) "equanimity" (UPEKṢĀ), (5) "sense of shame" (HRĪ), (6) "fear of blame" (APATRĀPYA), (7) "absence of craving" (ALOBHA), (8) "absence of ill will" (ADVEṢA), (9) "absence of harmful intentions" (AHIṂSĀ), (10) and "vigor" or "effort" (VĪRYA).

**kuśalamūla**. (P. kusalamūla; T. dge ba'i rtsa ba; C. shangen; J. zengon; K. sŏn'gŭn 善根). In Sanskrit, the term "wholesome faculties," or "roots of virtue," refers to the cumulative meritorious deeds performed by an individual throughout his or her past lives. Different schools offer various lists of these wholesome faculties. The most common list is threefold: nongreed (ALOBHA), nonhatred (ADVEṢA), and nondelusion (AMOHA)—all factors that encourage such wholesome actions (KARMAN) as giving (DĀNA), keeping precepts, and learning the dharma. These three factors thus will fructify as happiness in the future and will provide the foundation for liberation (VIMUKTI). These three wholesome roots are the converse of the three unwholesome faculties, or "roots of nonvirtue" (AKUŚALAMŪLA), viz., greed (LOBHA), hatred (DVEṢA), and delusion (MOHA), which lead instead to unhappiness or even perdition. In place of this simple threefold list, the VAIBHĀṢIKA school of ABHIDHARMA offers three separate typologies of kuśalamūlas. The first class is the "wholesome roots associated with merit" (puṇyabhāgīya-kuśalamūla), which lead to rebirth in the salutary realms of humans or heavenly divinities (DEVA). These include such qualities as faith, energy, and decency and modesty, the foundations of moral progress. Second are the "wholesome roots associated with liberation" (MOKṢABHĀGĪYA-kuśalamūla), which eventually lead to PARINIRVĀṆA. These are factors associated with the truth of the path (MĀRGASATYA) or various factors conducive to liberation. Third are the "wholesome roots associated with spiritual penetration" (NIRVEDHABHĀGĪYA-kuśalamūla), which are the four aspects of the direct path of preparation (PRAYOGAMĀRGA): heat (ŪṢMAN), summit (MŪRDHAN), receptivity (KṢĀNTI), and highest worldly dharmas (LAUKIKĀGRADHARMA). These nirvedhabhāgīyas open access to the path of vision (DARŚANAMĀRGA), where the first stage of sanctity, stream-entry (SROTAĀPANNA), is won. The nirvedhabhāgīya differ so markedly from the two previous categories of wholesome roots that they are often listed independently as the four wholesome faculties (catvāri kuśalamūlāni). The wholesome roots may be dedicated toward a specific aim, such as rebirth in a heavenly realm; toward the benefit of a specific person, such as a parent or relative; or toward the achievement of buddhahood for the sake of all sentient beings.

**Kuṣāṇa**. (S). See KUSHANA.

**Kusan Sŏnmun**. (九山禪門). In Korean, "Nine Mountains School of Sŏn," the major strands of the Korean SŎN (C. CHAN) school during the Unified Silla and early Koryŏ dynasties. Due to severe opposition from the exegetical traditions supported by the court, especially Hwaŏm (C. HUAYAN), Korean adepts who returned from China with the new teachings of Chan (pronounced Sŏn in Korean) established monasteries far away from the Silla capital of KYŎNGJU to propagate the new practice. At least nine such mountain monasteries appeared during the latter Unified Silla and early Koryŏ dynasty, which soon developed into independent lines of Sŏn. Each line was named after the mountain (san) on which the monastery of its founder was built. Toŭi is regarded as the founder of the Kajisan line of Sŏn, Hongch'ŏk of Silsangsan, Hyech'ŏl of Tongnisan, Muyŏm of Sŏngjusan, Pŏmil of Sagulsan, Toyun of Sajasan, Hyŏnuk of Pongnimsan, Iŏm of Sumisan, and Tohŏn of Hŭiyangsan. With the exception of Iŏm's Sumisan line of Sŏn, all these traditions traced themselves back to the HONGZHOU lineage of MAZU DAOYI. The earliest biographies of many of these founders of the Kusan Sŏnmun are found in the CHODANG CHIP ("Hall of the Patriarchs Record"), a tenth-century genealogical anthology and one of the earlier "lamplight histories" (denglu). Along with the other Buddhist traditions in Korea, the Nine Mountains Sŏn traditions were largely united and reorganized under the rubric of Sŏn (Meditation) and Kyo (Doctrine) by King Sejong (r. 1419–1450) in 1424.

**Kusan Sŏnp'a**. (九山禪派). In Korean, "Nine Mountains Lineage of Sŏn." See KUSAN SŎNMUN.

**Kushana**. (S. Kuṣāṇa). A northwest Indian kingdom (late first to third centuries CE) located adjacent to the GANDHĀRA region of the Indian subcontinent. The story of the Kushan king KANIṢKA's conversion to Buddhism is widely found in the literature, but it seems to belong to the realm of legend, not history.

Thanks to Kaniṣka's putative support, the Kushan kingdom has traditionally been assumed to have been an important conduit for the introduction of Buddhist materials into China via the Silk Roads of Central Asia. Recent evidence of the decline in west Central Asian trade during the Kushan period, however, may suggest instead that the Kushans were more of an obstacle than a help. Hence, it may not have been the Kushans who facilitated the transmission of Buddhism but their Indo-Scythian predecessors in the region, the Saka (S. Śaka) tribe. The Chinese tradition identifies several important early translators of Buddhist materials as hailing from the Kushan kingdom, including *LOKAKṢEMA, who was active in the last quarter of the second century. Monks who hailed from this region were given the ethnikon ZHI by the Chinese.

**Kuśinagarī**. [alt. Kuśinagara] (P. Kusinārā; T. Rtswa mchog grong; C. Jushinajieluo; J. Kushinagara; K. Kusinagera 拘尸那揭羅). The town in Uttar Pradesh where the Buddha entered into PARINIRVĀṆA among a grove of ŚĀLA trees. While he was sojourning in VAIŚĀLĪ, the Buddha had repeatedly hinted to his disciple ĀNANDA that it would be possible for him to live out the KALPA, if only Ānanda would make such a request. (See CĀPĀLACAITYA.) However, Ānanda did not understand what the Buddha was insinuating and neglected to make the request, so the Buddha renounced his will to live, saying that he would pass away three months hence. (Ānanda is said to have had to confess this mistake when the first Buddhist council was convened; see COUNCIL, FIRST.) After they had traveled to Kuśinagarī for the parinirvāṇa, Ānanda had asked the Buddha not to attain parinirvāṇa in such a "little mud-walled town, a back-woods town, a branch township," but the Buddha disabused him of this notion, telling him that Kuśinagarī had previously been the magnificent capital of an earlier CAKRAVARTIN king named Sudarśana (P. Sudassana). The Buddha passed away on a couch arranged between twin śāla trees. Following the Buddha's cremation, the brāhmaṇa DROṆA was called upon to decide the proper procedure for apportioning the Buddha's relics (ŚARĪRA). Droṇa divided the relics into eight parts that the disputing kings could carry back to their home kingdoms for veneration and built a reliquary STŪPA in Kuśinagarī to house the vessel that had temporarily held the relics. As the site of the Buddha's parinirvāṇa, Kuśinagarī became one of the four major Indian pilgrimage sites (MAHĀSTHĀNA) and is often depicted in Buddhist art.

**Kūṭadantasutta**. (C. Jiuluotantou jing; J. Kuradantōkyō; K. Kuradandu kyŏng 究羅檀頭經). In Pāli, "Discourse to Kūṭadanta"; the fifth scripture in the Pāli DĪGHANIKĀYA (a separate DHARMAGUPTAKA recension appears as the twenty-third SŪTRA in the Chinese translation of the DĪRGHĀGAMA). According to the Pāli recension of the scripture, the Buddha engages in a discourse with an accomplished brāhmaṇa teacher and debater named Kūṭadanta, who was living in the prosperous brāhmaṇa village of Khānumata in the country of MAGADHA. While Kūṭadanta was preparing to make a grand sacrifice of thousands of cattle, he consulted the Buddha on how properly to conduct the rite. The Buddha tells him a story of an earlier king, who conducted an exemplary sacrifice under the guidance of his wise court chaplain, in which all four castes took part. The king and his chaplain both were endowed with eight virtues suitable to their royal and priestly functions. Their sacrifice entailed the killing of no living creatures, and the labor for the sacrifice was not conscripted but offered voluntarily. The sacrifice was offered for the benefit of all and not just the king, and no regrets were felt during any stage of the rite. The Buddha then proceeds to describe even better kinds of sacrifice in increasing order of benefit, beginning with the serving and feeding of recluses; the building of monasteries (VIHĀRA) for the Buddhist order (SAṂGHA); taking refuge in the three jewels (RATNATRAYA) of the Buddha, the dharma, and the saṃgha; observing the precepts; renouncing the world to become a Buddhist monk; controlling the senses with mindfulness (sati; S. SMṚTI); cultivating the four meditative absorptions (JHĀNA; S. DHYĀNA); and developing the six higher knowledges or supernormal powers (abhiññā; S. ABHIJÑĀ), which culminate in enlightenment and liberation from the cycle of rebirth. Upon hearing the discourse, Kūṭadanda becomes a stream-enterer (sotāpanna; S. SROTAĀPANNA) and declares himself a disciple of the Buddha. Through this parable, the Buddha expresses his disapproval of blood rituals, highlighting the unnecessary cruelty and waste involved in such sacrifices. Through this lengthy discourse, he persuades Kūṭadanta of the correctness of these principles and converts him to Buddhism. The conversion of this respected brāhmaṇa is regarded as one of the great spiritual victories of the Buddha.

**kuti**. In Thai, "monk's residence," a small, simple, hut-like building, made of wood and/or bamboo, used as living quarters for a monk or at some monasteries for lay meditators in Thailand. A kuti is usually built on stilts in the traditional Southeast Asian style. The word can also be used to refer to a monk's room in a larger building.

**Kūya**. (空也) (903–972). Japanese monk and itinerant holy man (HIJIRI) renowned for his efforts to spread the practice of nenbutsu (C. NIANFO) or invocation of the name of the buddha AMITĀBHA among the common people. Little is known of his early life, but legends of his building bridges and roads and producing images of buddhas and BODHISATTVAS abound. He is also famous for preaching at the marketplace, for which he came to be known as the "holy man (hijiri) of the marketplace." Kūya is said to have received full ordination from the TENDAISHŪ monk Enshō (880–964) on HIEIZAN in 948. A famous statue of Kūya practicing nenbutsu is now housed at his temple Rokuharamitsuji. It shows the syllables of the nenbutsu emerging from this mouth in the form of buddhas.

**kwaebul**. (掛佛). In Korean, lit. "hanging buddha [image]." See T'AENGHWA.

**Kwallŭk**. (J. Kanroku 觀勒) (d.u.). Early seventh-century Korean monk from the kingdom of Paekche, who arrived in Japan in 602 CE and was instrumental in transmitting Buddhism and Sinitic civilization to the Japanese isles. According to the account in the *Nihon shoki*, Kwallŭk was a specialist in the MADHYAMAKA school of MAHĀYĀNA philosophy, who arrived in Japan also bringing documents on calendrics, astronomy, geometry, divination, and numerology to the Japanese court, which placed many students under his tutelage. Kwallŭk's interests were so diverse, in fact, that he was later chastised by the Japanese ruler for paying too much attention to astronomy and geography and confusing them with the "true vehicle" of Buddhism. Kwallŭk became arguably the most influential monk of his time and was eventually appointed in 624 by Queen Suiko (r. 593–628) to the new position of SŌJŌ (saṃgha primate), one of the earliest ecclesiastical positions created within the Japanese Buddhist church. His appointment to this position also indicates the prestige that monks from the Paekche kingdom enjoyed at the incipiency of Buddhism in Japan.

**Kwangmyŏngsa**. (廣明寺). In Korean, "Vast Radiance Monastery," a major SŎN (CHAN) monastery during the Koryŏ dynasty; located on Songak Mountain in the Koryŏ capital of Kaesŏng. The monastery was established in 922, when the founder of the Koryŏ dynasty, Wang Kŏn (T'aejo, 877–943/r. 918–943), donated his residence to the Buddhist order. With King Kwangjong's (r. 925–975) launching of an ecclesiastical examination system (SŬNGKWA), Kwangmyŏngsa was designated as the site for the selection examination for monks in the Sŏn (Meditation) school, with WANGNYUNSA (Royal Wheel Monastery) chosen to administer the Doctrinal (KYO) school examinations. During the military rule of the Ch'oe family during the late twelfth and thirteenth centuries, the monastery was also one of the major sites in the capital for the discussing Sŏn dharma assembly (tamsŏn pŏphoe), along with Pojesa (Universal Salvation Monastery) and Sŏpot'ongsa (Western Universal Penetration Monastery). A well located to the northeast of the monastery was associated with the legend of Chakchegŏn, the ancestor of the Koryŏ ruling family, who is said to have visited the Dragon King's palace. The monastery was the site of many Buddhist court ceremonies during the Koryŏ dynasty. King Ch'ungnyŏl (r. 1236–1308) visited the monastery in 1282 with his queen to meet the monk IRYŎN (1206–1289), writer of the SAMGUK YUSA, and a ceremony to speed the king's recovery from illness was held there in the following year. King Ch'ungnyŏl later held an *ULLAMBANA (K. Uranbunje) rite (1296) and a yonghwahoe (dragon flower assembly; 1301, 1302) at the monastery. In 1371, King Kongmin (1330–1374/r. 1351–1374) commanded NAONG HYEGŬN (1320–1376) to administer there the monastic training examination (kongbusŏn, see sŭngkwa), an advanced test taken by the monks from the two meditative and five doctrinal schools. Kwangmyŏngsa's close relationship with the royal family continued into the early Chosŏn dynasty, when, for example, King T'aejong (1367–1422/r. 1400–1418), granted grain and slaves to the monastery in 1405. The monastery was reassigned to the Kyo (Doctrinal) school after 1424 and subsequently drops from Korean Buddhist sources.

**Kwanŭmsa**. (觀音寺). In Korean, "AVALOKITEŚVARA monastery," the twenty-third parish monastery (PONSA) of the contemporary CHOGYE ORDER of Korean Buddhism, located on Halla Mountain on Cheju Island. Its foundation date is uncertain. The monastery was destroyed during the eighteenth century and rebuilt in 1912 by the laywoman Pong Yŏgwan (fl. c. 1907), who named it Pŏpchŏngam (Dharma Well Hermitage). While Pong was on a sea journey to Piyang Island in 1901, she felt she would have been lost at sea were it not for the saving grace of Avalokiteśvara, the bodhisattva of compassion. Pong subsequently was ordained as a nun (BHIKṢUṆĪ) in 1907 and returned to Cheju island to rebuild the monastery. As the monastery's following increased, it became known as Kwanŭmsa. The monastery's main buddha image and its hanging picture (T'AENGHWA) of the Buddha were brought from Kwangsansa and Yonghwasa. Kwanŭmsa currently manages approximately thirty branch temples (MALSA).

**kwāpā dya**. A Newari term for the image of the central, nontantric, deity located on the ground floor shrine in a Newar monastery (BĀHĀ), most often located directly across from the main entryway. The term is likely derived from the Sanskrit koṣṭhapāla, "guard," "watchman," and carries the meaning of "guardian of the SAṂGHA," although the image does not generally function as a "guardian or protector deity." The shrine of the kwāpā dya is generally open to the public, and, although visitors are not normally permitted inside, they may view the image from the gate and make offerings through the shrine's attendant.

**kyaung**. (Burmese). See VIHĀRA.

**Kyeyul chong**. (戒律宗). In Korean, "VINAYA school." See KYO.

**Kyo**. (C. jiao; J. kyō 敎). In Korean, "doctrine" or "teaching," generally referring to doctrinally oriented Buddhist schools and their tenets, as distinguished from meditation-oriented Buddhist schools and practices (SŎN; C. CHAN). While the Chinese and Japanese Buddhist traditions appear to have used the term doctrine only to describe one of two generic approaches to Buddhism, in Korea Buddhist schools have often been categorized as belonging to either the Doctrine (Kyo) or the Meditation (Sŏn) schools; indeed, during the period of Buddhist suppression under the Chosŏn dynasty, Kyo and Sŏn became the specific designations for the two officially sanctioned schools of the tradition. During the stable political environment of the

Unified Silla period (668–935), five major Kyo schools are traditionally presumed to have developed in Korean Buddhism: NIRVĀṆA (Yŏlban chong), VINAYA (Kyeyul chong), Dharma-nature (PŎPSŎNG CHONG), Hwaŏm [alt. Wŏnyung chong], and YOGĀCĀRA (Pŏpsang chong). Toward the end of the Unified Silla period, however, the newly imported Sŏn (C. Chan, Meditation) lineages, which were associated with local gentry on the frontier of the kingdom, began to criticize the main doctrinal school, Hwaŏm, that was supported by the old Silla aristocracy in the capital of KYŎNGJU; these schools came to be called the "Nine Mountains School of Sŏn" (KUSAN SŎNMUN). These various doctrine and meditation schools were collectively referred to as the "Five Doctrinal [Schools] and Nine Mountains [Schools of Sŏn]" (OGYO KUSAN). The Ogyo Kusan designation continued to be used into the succeeding Koryŏ dynasty (937–1392), which saw the first attempts to bring together these two distinct strands of the Korean Buddhist tradition. Attempts to find common ground between the Kyo and Sŏn schools are seen, for example, in ŬICH'ŎN's "cultivation together of scriptural study and contemplation" (kyogwan kyŏmsu) and POJO CHINUL's "cultivation in tandem of concentration [viz., Sŏn] and wisdom [viz., scripture]" (chŏnghye ssangsu). The Ch'ŏnt'ae (C. TIANTAI) and CHOGYE schools that are associated respectively with these two monks were both classified as Sŏn schools during the mid- to late-Koryŏ dynasty; together with the five previous Kyo schools, these schools were collectively called the "Five Kyo and Two [Sŏn] Traditions" (OGYO YANGJONG). This designation continued to be used into the early Chosŏn dynasty (1392–1910). The Confucian orientation of the new Chosŏn dynasty led to an increasing suppression of these Buddhist traditions. In 1407, King T'aejong (r. 1400–1418) restructured the various schools then current in Korean Buddhism into three schools of Sŏn and four of Kyo; subsequently, in 1424, King Sejong (r. 1418–1450) reduced all these remaining schools down to, simply, the "Two Traditions, Sŏn and Kyo" (SŎN KYO YANGJONG), a designation that continued to be used through the remainder of the dynasty. The modern Chogye order of Korean Buddhism claims to be a synthetic tradition that combines both strands of Sŏn meditation practice and Kyo doctrinal study into a single denomination.

**Kyōgyō shinshō**. (教行信証). In Japanese, "Teaching, Practice, Faith, and Realization," composed by the Japanese JŌDO SHINSHŪ teacher SHINRAN (1173–1263), also known as the *Ken jōdo shinjitsu kyōgyōshō monrui*. The *Kyōgyō shinshō* is considered one of the most important texts of the Jōdo Shinshū tradition. The exact dates of its compilation are unknown, but it seems to have gradually developed into its current shape over the first half of the thirteenth century. Several other similar works were also composed during this period by disciples of HŌNEN, largely in response to the monk MYŌE KŌBEN's criticism of exclusive nenbutsu (C. NIANFO), the hallmark of the Jōdo traditions. The *Kyōgyō shinshō* largely consists of citations of scriptural passages on the practice of nenbutsu or invocation of the name of the buddha AMITĀBHA. Perhaps the most important section of the *Kyōgyō shinshō* is that on faith (shinjin; C. XINXIN), where Shinran attempted to demonstrate that faith is based on the practice of nenbutsu and comes not from the effort made by the practitioner but from Amitābha himself (see TARIKI). Citing the SUKHĀVATĪVYŪHASŪTRA's teachings on the original vows (hongan) of the BODHISATTVA DHARMĀKARA (the future Amitābha), Shinran also emphasized the importance of the "single nenbutsu" (ICHINENGI) in attaining rebirth in the PURE LAND. He also sought to legitimize the practice of nenbutsu through recourse to the notion of the "final age of the DHARMA" (J. mappō, C. MOFA) when other types of Buddhist practice were ineffective.

**Kyojong sŏn**. (教宗選). In Korean, the "Doctrinal (KYO) School examination." See SŬNGKWA.

**Kyŏnghan**. (K) (景閑). See PAEGUN KYŎNGHAN.

**Kyŏnghŏ Sŏngu**. (鏡虛惺牛) (1849–1912). The preeminent Korean SŎN master of his generation, renowned for his efforts to revitalize Korean Buddhism at the end of the Chosŏn dynasty. Kyŏnghŏ lost his father at an early age, and his mother entrusted him to the monastery of Ch'ŏnggyesa in Kwangju, where he became a monk. He was tonsured by the monk Kyehŏ (d.u.) in 1857, but when Kyehŏ later renounced his vows, Kyŏnghŏ left for Tonghaksa, where he continued his studies under the monk Manhwa Kwanjun (1850–1919). Later, Kyŏnghŏ went to the hermitage Ch'ŏnjangam in Hongju and became the disciple of the monk Yongam (d.u.). For the next twenty years, Kyŏnghŏ taught at various places including Ch'ŏnjangam, Kaesimsa, and PUSŎKSA. In 1899, he settled down at the major monastery of HAEINSA, where he presided over the publication of Buddhist scriptures and the reopening of POJO CHINUL's SUSŎNSA. Kyŏnghŏ is presumed to be the author of the SŎNMUN CH'WARYO ("Selected Essentials from the Gate of Sŏn"), an anthology of the essential canon of the Korean Sŏn school. Kyŏnghŏ subsequently led the life of an itinerant monk until his death in 1912. Kyŏnghŏ was a strong advocate for the revitalization of GONG'AN meditation practice (kanhwa Sŏn; see KANHUA CHAN) and did much to reestablish what was then a moribund meditation tradition in Korean Buddhism. Among his disciples, MAN'GONG WŎLMYŎN (1871–1946) and HANAM CHUNGWŎN (1876–1951) are most famous. Largely through the influence of his disciples, many modern and contemporary Korean Sŏn monks came to trace their lineages back to Kyŏnghŏ.

**Kyŏngju**. (慶州). Ancient capital of the Korean Silla dynasty and location of hundreds of important Buddhist archeological sites—for example, South Mountain (NAMSAN) in central modern Kyŏngju. Among the many monasteries in Kyŏngju, HWANGNYONGSA (Yellow Dragon monastery) was one of the most renowned. It was built during the reign of King Chinhung

(r. 540–576), and its campus had seven rectangular courtyards, each with three buildings and one pagoda, covering an area of around eighteen acres; in 645, a 262 ft. high nine-story pagoda was added. Hwangnyongsa was destroyed during the Mongol invasion in 1238 and was never rebuilt. PULGUKSA (Buddha Land monastery) was built in 535 during the reign of the Silla King Pŏphŭng (r. 514–540). The main courtyard is dedicated to the buddha ŚĀKYAMUNI and includes on either end the highly decorative Pagoda of Many Treasures (Tabot'ap), resembling the form of a reliquary (ŚARĪRA) shrine and symbolizing the buddha PRABHŪTARATNA, and the Pagoda of Śākyamuni (Sŏkkat'ap). During a 1966 renovation of the Sŏkka t'ap, the world's oldest printed document was discovered sealed inside the stūpa: the MUGUJŎNGGWANG TAEDARANI KYŎNG (S. *Raśmivimalaviśuddhaprabhādhāraṇī*; "Great DHĀRAṆĪ Scripture of Immaculate Radiance"). The terminus ad quem for the printing of the Dhāraṇī is 751 CE, when the text was sealed inside the Sŏkkat'ap, but it may have been printed even earlier. Four kilometers up T'oham Mountain to the east of Pulguksa is its affiliated SŎKKURAM grotto temple, which was built in the late eighth century. In contrast to the cave temples of ancient India and China, the rotunda of Sŏkkuram was assembled with granite. The central image is a stone buddha (probably of Śākyamuni) seated cross-legged on a lotus throne, surrounded by BODHISATTVAS, ARHATS, and Indian divinities carved in relief on the surrounding circular wall. A miniature marble pagoda, which is believed to have stood in front of the eleven-faced Avalokiteśvara, disappeared in the early years of the Japanese occupation of the Korean peninsula in the early twentieth century.

**Kyōō gokokuji**. (J) (教王護国寺). See TŌJI.

**kyōsaku**. (C. jingce; K. kyŏngch'aek 警策). In Japanese, "admonition," also pronounced keisaku by the RINZAI ZEN tradition. The term kyōsaku came to refer to the long wooden stick used by the SŌTŌ Zen tradition for waking, alerting, and instructing monks during meditation sessions.

**Kyoto school**. An influential school of modern and contemporary Japanese philosophy that is closely associated with philosophers from Kyōto University; it combines East Asian and especially MAHĀYĀNA Buddhist thought, such as ZEN and JŌDO SHINSHŪ, with modern Western and especially German philosophy and Christian thought. NISHIDA KITARŌ (1870–1945), Tanabe Hajime (1885–1962), and NISHITANI KEIJI (1900–1991) are usually considered to be the school's three leading figures. The name "Kyoto school" was coined in 1932 by Tosaka Jun (1900–1945), a student of Nishida and Tanabe, who used it pejoratively to denounce Nishida and Tanabe's "Japanese bourgeois philosophy." Starting in the late 1970s, Western scholars began to research the philosophical insights of the Kyoto school, and especially the cross-cultural influences with Western philosophy. During the 1990s, the political dimensions of the school have also begun to receive scholarly attention. ¶ Although the school's philosophical perspectives have developed through mutual criticism between its leading figures, the foundational philosophical stance of the Kyoto school is considered to be based on a shared notion of "absolute nothingness." "Absolute nothingness" was coined by Nishida Kitarō and derives from a putatively Zen and PURE LAND emphasis on the doctrine of emptiness (ŚŪNYATĀ), which Kyoto school philosophers advocated was indicative of a distinctive Eastern approach to philosophical inquiry. This Eastern emphasis on nothingness stood in contrast to the fundamental focus in Western philosophy on the ontological notion of "being." Nishida Kitarō posits absolute nothingness topologically as the "site" or "locale" (basho) of nonduality, which overcomes the polarities of subject and object, or noetic and noematic. Another major concept in Nishida's philosophy is "self-awareness" (jikaku), a state of mind that transcends the subject–object bifurcation, which was initially adopted from William James' (1842–1910) notion of "pure experience" (J. junsui keiken); this intuition reveals a limitless, absolute reality that has been described in the West as God or in the East as emptiness. Tanabe Hajime subsequently criticized Nishida's "site of absolute nothingness" for two reasons: first, it was a suprarational religious intuition that transgresses against philosophical reasoning; and second, despite its claims to the contrary, it ultimately fell into a metaphysics of being. Despite his criticism of what he considered to be Nishida's pseudoreligious speculations, however, Tanabe's Shin Buddhist inclinations later led him to focus not on Nishida's Zen Buddhist-oriented "intuition," but instead on the religious aspect of "faith" as the operative force behind other-power (TARIKI). Inspired by both Nishida and such Western thinkers as Meister Eckhart (c. 1260–1327), Friedrich Nietzsche (1844–1900), and Martin Heidegger (1889–1976) (with whom he studied), Nishitani Keiji developed the existential and phenomenological aspects of Nishida's philosophy of absolute nothingness. Concerned with how to reach the place of absolute nothingness, given the dilemma of, on the one hand, the incessant reification and objectification by a subjective ego and, on the other hand, the nullification of reality, he argued for the necessity of overcoming "nihilism." The Kyoto school thinkers also played a central role in the development of a Japanese political ideology around the time of the Pacific War, which elevated the Japanese race mentally and spiritually above other races and justified Japanese colonial expansion. Their writings helped lay the foundation for what came to be called Nihonjinron, a nationalist discourse that advocated the uniqueness and superiority of the Japanese race; at the same time, however, Nishida also resisted tendencies toward fascism and totalitarianism in Japanese politics. Since the 1990s, Kyoto school writings have come under critical scrutiny in light of their ties to Japanese exceptionalism and pre-war Japanese nationalism. These political dimensions of Kyoto school thought are now considered as important for scholarly examination as are its contributions to cross-cultural, comparative philosophy.

**Kyunyŏ**. (均如) (923–973). Korean monk, exegete, poet, and thaumaturge during the Koryŏ dynasty, also known as Wŏnt'ong. According to legend, Kyunyŏ is said to have been so ugly that his parents briefly abandoned him at a young age. His parents died shortly thereafter, and Kyunyŏ sought refuge at the monastery of Puhŭngsa in 937. Kyunyŏ later continued his studies under the monk Ŭisun (d.u.) at the powerful monastery of Yŏngt'ongsa near the Koryŏ-dynasty capital of Kaesŏng. There, Kyunyŏ seems to have gained the support of King Kwangjong (r. 950–975), who summoned him to preach at the palace in 954. Kyunyŏ's successful performance of miracles for the king won him the title of great worthy (taedŏk) and wealth for his clan. Kyunyŏ became famous as an exegete of the AVATAṂSAKASŪTRA. His approach to this scripture was purportedly catalyzed by the deep split between the exegetical traditions associated with the Korean exegete WŎNHYO (617–686) and the Chinese-Sogdian exegete FAZANG (643–712). Kyunyŏ sought to bridge these two traditions of Hwaŏm (C. HUAYAN) exegesis in his numerous writings, which came to serve as the orthodox doctrinal standpoint for the clerical examinations (SŬNGKWA) in the Koryŏ-period KYO school, held at the royal monastery of WANGNYUNSA. In 963, Kyunyŏ was appointed the abbot of the new monastery of Kwibŏpsa, which the king established near the capital. Kyunyŏ's life and some examples of his poetry are recorded in the *Kyunyŏ chŏn*; the collection includes eleven "native songs," or hyangga, one of the largest surviving corpora of Silla-period vernacular poems, which used Sinographs to transcribe Korean. His Buddhist writings include the *Sŏk Hwaŏm kyobun'gi wŏnt'ong ch'o*, *Sŏk Hwaŏm chigwijang*, *Sipkujang wŏnt'ong ki*, and others.

# L

**Lakkhaṇasutta**. (C. Sanshi'er xiang jing; J. Sanjūnisōgyō; K. Samsibi sang kyŏng 三十二相經). In Pāli, "Discourse on the Marks," the thirtieth sutta of the DĪGHANIKĀYA (a separate SARVĀSTIVĀDA recension appears as the 115th SŪTRA in the Chinese translation of the MADHYAMĀGAMA). At ANĀTHAPIṆḌADA's (P. Anāthapiṇḍika) park in ŚRĀVASTĪ (P. Sāvatthi), the Buddha explained to his disciples the thirty-two physical marks of a great man (MAHĀPURUṢALAKṢAṆA) and explained how one endowed with these marks has only two possible destinies: becoming a wheel-turning monarch (CAKRAVARTIN) or a buddha. The Buddha then recounts the deeds he performed in his previous lives that engendered each of his own thirty-two physical marks.

**lakṣaṇa**. (P. lakkhaṇa; T. mtshan nyid; C. xiang; J. sō; K. sang 相). In Sanskrit, a polysemous term for a "mark," "characteristic," "attribute," or "sign"; used in a variety of contexts to indicate either the principal characteristic or defining quality of something. As a primary characteristic, lakṣaṇa refers to the distinguishing features of a factor (DHARMA), i.e., the factor "earth" (PṚTHIVĪ) may be characterized by its mark of "hardness," etc. ¶ The three defining characteristics (TRILAKṢAṆA) of all conditioned (SAṂSKṚTA) things are their impermanence (anityatā), unsatisfactoriness (DUḤKHA), and lack of a perduring self (ANĀTMAN). ¶ The four characteristics (CATURLAKṢAṆA) governing all conditioned objects (SAṂSKṚTALAKṢAṆA), as described in the SARVĀSTIVĀDA school, are "origination," or birth (JĀTI); "continuance," or maturation (STHITI); "senescence," or decay (JARĀ); and "desinence," or death (ANITYA). The Sarvāstivāda school treated these four as "forces dissociated from thought" (CITTAVIPRAYUKTASAṂSKĀRA), which exerted real power over compounded objects, escorting an object along from one force to another, until the force "desinence" extinguishes it; this rather tortured explanation was necessary in order to explain how factors that the school presumed existed in all three time periods (past, present, and future) nevertheless still appeared to undergo change. Some Sarvāstivāda ABHIDHARMA texts, however, accept only three characteristics, omitting continuance. ¶ The term lakṣaṇa is also used with reference to the thirty-two major marks (DVĀTRIṂŚADVARALAKṢAṆA) of a great man (see MAHĀPURUṢALAKṢAṆA), which appear on the physical body (RŪPAKĀYA) of either a buddha or on a wheel-turning monarch (CAKRAVARTIN); these are accompanied by eighty minor marks (ANUVYAÑJANA). ¶ The term lakṣaṇa is also used in the YOGĀCĀRA school to refer to the three intrinsic characteristics (trilakṣaṇa) of all phenomena, and in this context is equivalent to the three qualities or natures (TRISVABHĀVA), viz., imaginary (PARIKALPITA), dependent (PARATANTRA), and consummate (PARINIṢPANNA). ¶ In the MADHYAMAKA school, the term lakṣana is used to refer to the "signs" of intrinsic existence (SVABHĀVA) that are falsely perceived by the senses as the result of ignorance. Ignorance mistakenly regards each phenomenon as having its own defining characteristic (SVALAKṢAṆA). ¶ In Buddhist epistemology, the term lakṣaṇa is used for the specific or particular mark (svalakṣaṇa) and general or shared mark (SĀMĀNYALAKṢAṆA) of an object; the former is known only by nonconceptual knowledge; the latter is the object that appears when one thinks about something. See also NIMITTA.

**lakṣaṇaśāstra**. (T. mtshan nyid bstan bcos). In Sanskrit, lit. "marks treatise"; in Mahāyāna works, a pejorative designation for the pre-Mahāyāna ABHIDHARMA, which is portrayed as being obsessively concerned with generating exhaustive lists of factors (DHARMA) and their defining characteristics (LAKṢAṆA).

**lakṣaṇayāna**. (T. mtshan nyid theg pa). In Sanskrit, "vehicle of attributes," a term used in PRAJÑĀPĀRAMITĀ and tantric literature to refer to the SŪTRA (i.e., exoteric) paths of ŚRĀVAKAS, PRATYEKABUDDHAS, and BODHISATTVAS. In the TANTRAS, lakṣaṇayāna refers to the practices of bodhisattvas as delineated in the sūtras and their commentaries. In this context, it is a synonym of PĀRAMITĀYĀNA.

**Lakuṇṭaka Bhadrika**. (P. Lakuṇṭaka Bhaddiya; T. Snyan pa bzang ldan; C. Xianyan/Luoponabati; J. Ken'en/Rabanabadai; K. Hyŏnyŏm/Nabanabalche 賢鹽/羅婆那拔提). An ARHAT monk declared by the Buddha to be foremost among his monk disciples who were sweet in voice. According to Pāli sources, he was the son of a wealthy family from ŚRĀVASTĪ, handsome but very small in stature, hence his sobriquet lakuṇṭaka ("dwarf"). After listening to one of the Buddha's sermons, he was moved to enter the monastic order and eventually became a gifted preacher noted for his sweet voice. It was for this quality that he won preeminence and numerous stanzas in the SUTTAPIṬAKA are attributed to him. Despite his eventual eminence, his small size apparently made him the butt of many cruel jokes early in his vocation. It is said that novices used to tweak his ears, and a group of thirty village monks once pushed him about until the Buddha intervened. One instance of disrespect, however, prompted his enlightenment. A woman riding in a chariot saw the diminutive Bhadrika and laughed at him, showing her teeth. Bhadrika took her teeth as an object of foulness meditation (AŚUBHABHĀVANĀ) and quickly reached the third stage of sanctity, that of a nonreturner (ANĀGĀMIN). ŚĀRIPUTRA subsequently instructed him in mindfulness of the body (see KĀYĀNUPAŚYANĀ) and Bhadrika attained arhatship. The Buddha is reported to have been delighted to hear that Śāriputra's instructions proved so efficacious.

**lalanā**. (T. brkyang ma). In tantric physiology, the channel (NĀḌĪ) that runs in males from the right nostril to the base of the spine and in females from the left nostril to the base of the spine. It is one of the three main channels, together with the central channel (AVADHŪTĪ), and the right channel in females and the left channel in males (RASANĀ). According to some systems, 72,000 channels are found in the body, serving as the conduits for subtle energies or winds (PRĀṆA). The most important of these channels are the central channel (avadhūtī), the lalanā, and the rasanā. The central channel runs from the place between the eyebrows to the crown of the head and down in front of the spinal column, ending at the genitals. The right and left channels run parallel to the central channel on either side. These two channels wrap around the central channel at various points, of which as many as seven are enumerated. These points, called wheels or CAKRAs, are located between the eyes, at the crown of the head, at the throat, at the heart, at the solar plexus, at the base of the spine, and at the tip of sexual organ. In highest yoga tantra (ANUTTARAYOGATANTRA), especially in practices associated with the "stage of completion" (NIṢPANNAKRAMA), much emphasis is placed on loosening these knots in order to cause the winds to flow freely through the central channel.

**lalitāsana**. (T. rol pa'i 'dug stangs). In Sanskrit, "posture of relaxation," an iconographic posture (ĀSANA), in which the left leg is bent resting on the seat, and the right leg pendant, often with the knee slightly raised. Occasionally, the leg positions are reversed. This posture is common in BODHISATTVA images from the AJAṆṬĀ caves in India, as well as in Chinese representations of GUANYIN (AVALOKITEŚVARA), Korean depictions of MAITREYA, and Tibetan images of Green Tārā (ŚYĀMATĀRĀ). A common variant of this posture is the RĀJALĪLĀSANA. See also MAITREYĀSANA.

**Lalitavajra**. (S). See LĪLAVAJRA.

**Lalitavistara**. (T. Rgya cher rol pa; C. Puyao jing/Fangguang da zhuangyan jing; J. Fuyōkyō/Hōkō daishōgongyō; K. Poyo kyŏng/Panggwang taejangŏm kyŏng 普曜經/方廣大莊嚴經). In Sanskrit, lit. "Extensive Play," a relatively late treatment of the Buddha's life, in mixed prose and verse, probably dating from the third or fourth century CE. The work treats the current Buddha's last lifetime, from his time waiting in the TUṢITA heaven to take his final rebirth to the "first turning of the wheel of the dharma" (DHARMACAKRAPRAVARTANA) at SĀRNĀTH, when the Buddhist dispensation (ŚĀSANA) begins. The frame of the Buddha's life story is enhanced with exuberantly told tales of his thaumaturgic abilities and his numinous essence. For example, the infant Buddha, after emerging from his mother's right side, takes seven steps and then gives an extended discourse to ĀNANDA, predicting that there will be fools who will not believe the miracles surrounding his birth and will reject the *Lalitavistara*, and as a consequence, will be reborn in the AVĪCI hell. Some scholars have suggested the text's supernal portrayal of the Buddha may have influenced the development of the MAHĀYĀNA conception of the multiple bodies of a buddha (see TRIKĀYA). The work is attributed to the SARVĀSTIVĀDA school, but it has been extensively reworked along Mahāyāna lines (including allusions to such emblematic Mahāyāna terms as TATHĀGATAGARBHA), suggesting that it went through continued, even radical, embellishment after its initial composition. There are two translations corresponding to this text in Chinese, the *Puyao jing*, translated by DHARMARAKṢA in 308, and the *Fangguang da zhuangyan jing*, translated by Divākara in 683. The Newari Buddhist tradition of Nepal includes the *Lalitavistara* among its nine principal books of the Mahāyāna (NAVAGRANTHA; see NAVADHARMA).

**Lamaism**. An obsolete English term that has no correlate in Tibetan, sometimes used to refer to the Buddhism of Tibet. Probably derived from the Chinese term lama jiao, or "teachings of the lamas," the term is considered pejorative by Tibetans, as it carries the negative connotation that the Tibetan tradition is something distinct from the mainstream of Buddhism. The use of this term should be abandoned in favor of, simply, "Tibetan Buddhism."

**lam 'bras**. (lamdre). In Tibetan, lit. "path and result." The central tantric system of the SA SKYA sect of Tibetan Buddhism, derived from the HEVAJRATANTRA and transmitted to Tibet by 'BROG MI SHĀKYA YE SHES. The system was first set down in written form by the first of the five Sa skya hierarchs, SA CHEN KUN DGA' SNYING PO of the aristocratic 'Khon family. There are two exegetical traditions, first, the slob bshad (lopshe), or "explanation for disciples," was originally reserved for members of the 'Khon family, and the second, the tshogs bshad (tsokshe), or "explanation in the assembly," was for a wider audience. The preliminary practices of the lam 'bras are taught under the rubric of the snang ba gsum (nangwa sum) "three appearances" (impure, yogic, and pure) that systematize the topics found in the fundamental Sa skya teaching called "parting from the four attachments" (zhen pa bzhi bral) (see SA CHEN KUN DGA' SNYING PO). These topics are covered in other Tibetan sects under different such names as BSTAN RIM, LAM RIM ("stages of the path"), and so on. The second, the tantric part of the system, requires consecration and includes the practice of esoteric yogas. The practices convey to the practitioner the insight that the nature of the basis (gzhi), path (lam), and result ('bras bu) is the same, and that liberation through the practice of coemergent knowledge (lhan cig skyes pa'i ye shes)—i.e., the enlightened body, speech, and mind—is indivisible from the basis.

**Lamotte, Étienne**. (1903–1983). A Belgian Buddhologist and Roman Catholic monsignor, considered to be the principal successor of LOUIS DE LA VALLÉE POUSSIN in the Franco–Belgian school of European Buddhist Studies. After receiving his doctorate in 1930 (with a dissertation on the *Bhagavadgītā*), Lamotte taught for forty-five years (1932–1977) as a professor at the Université catholique de Louvain. In 1953, he was awarded the Francqui Prize, a prestigious Belgian prize awarded to scholars and scientists under the age of fifty. Making use of his knowledge of Sanskrit, Pāli, Tibetan, and Chinese, he made definitive French translations, all with extensive annotation, of a wide range of important Indian sūtra and treatises, including the ŚŪRAṂGAMASAMĀDHISŪTRA, VIMALAKĪRTINIRDEŚA, SAṂDHINIRMOCANASŪTRA, VASUBANDHU's KARMASIDDHIPRAKARAṆA, and ASAṄGA's MAHĀYĀNASAṂGRAHA. He was also the first to translate the lengthy prolegomenon to the **Mahāprajñāpāramitāśāstra*, a massive commentary on the "Great Perfection of Wisdom Sūtra" extant only in a Chinese recension known as the DAZHIDU LUN, which is attributed by the East Asian tradition to NĀGĀRJUNA. Lamotte's annotated translation of this text was published in five volumes between 1944 and 1980 but remained unfinished at the time of his death. Among his monographs, perhaps the most important is his comprehensive history of early Indian Buddhism published in 1958, *Histoire du Bouddhisme Indien: des origines à l'ère Śaka* (translated into English in 1988 as *History of Indian Buddhism: From its Origins to the Śaka Era*), which remains the most extensive such history yet produced in a Western language.

**Lampāka**. (S). One of the twenty-four sacred sites associated with the CAKRASAṂVARATANTRA. See PĪṬHA.

**Lamp for the Path to Enlightenment**. See BODHIPATHAPRADĪPA.

**lam rim**. In Tibetan, "stages of the path"; a common abbreviation for byang chub lam gyi rim pa (jangchup lamkyi rimpa), or "stages of the path to enlightenment," a broad methodological framework for the study and practice of the complete Buddhist path to awakening, as well as the name for a major genre of Tibetan literature describing that path. It is closely allied to the genre known as BSTAN RIM, or "stages of the doctrine." The initial inspiration for the instructions of this system is usually attributed to the Bengali master ATIŚA DĪPAṂKARAŚRĪJÑĀNA, whose BODHIPATHAPRADĪPA ("Lamp for the Path to Enlightenment") became a model for numerous later stages of the path texts. The system presents a graduated and comprehensive approach to studying the central tenets of MAHĀYĀNA Buddhist thought and is often organized around a presentation of the three levels of spiritual predilection, personified as "three individuals" (skyes bu gsum): lesser, intermediate, and superior. The stages gradually lead the student from the lowest level of seeking merely to obtain a better rebirth, through the intermediate level of wishing for one's own individual liberation, and finally to adopting the MAHĀYĀNA outlook of the "superior individual," viz., aspiring to attain buddhahood in order to benefit all living beings. The approach is most often grounded in the teachings of the sūtra and usually concludes with a brief overview of TANTRA. Although usually associated with the DGE LUGS sect, stages of the path literature is found within all the major sects of Tibetan Buddhism. One common Dge lugs tradition identifies eight major stages of the path treatises:

1. LAM RIM CHEN MO ("Great Treatise on the Stages of the Path")
2. LAM RIM CHUNG BA ("Short Treatise on the Stages of the Path")
3. LAM RIM BSDUS DON ("Concise Meaning of the Stages of the Path"); all by TSONG KHA PA BLO BZANG GRAGS PA
4. LAM RIM GSER ZHUN MA ("Stages of the Path [like] Refined Gold") by the third DALAI LAMA BSOD NAMS RGYA MTSHO
5. BDE LAM LAM RIM ("The Easy Path Stages of the Path") by the first PAṆ CHEN BLA MA BLO BZANG CHOS KYI RGYAL MTSHAN
6. LAM RIM 'JAM DPAL ZHAL LUNG ("Stages of the Path [which are] the Instructions of Mañjuśrī") by the fifth Dalai Lama NGAG DBANG BLO BZANG RGYA MTSHO
7. MYUR LAM LAM RIM ("The Quick Path Stages of the Path") by the second Paṇ chen Lama Blo bzang ye shes dpal bzang po (Losang Yeshe Palsangpo, 1663–1737)
8. LAM RIM SNYING GU ("Essential Stages of the Path") by Dwags po Ngag dbang grags pa (Dakpo Ngawang Drakpa, born c. 1450).

**Lam rim bsdus don**. (Lamrim Düdön). In Tibetan, "Concise Meaning of the Stages of the Path"; also called *Lam rim chung ngu* or "Brief Stages of the Path." The shortest of three major treatises on the stages of the path to awakening (LAM RIM) composed by the renowned Tibetan scholar TSONG KHA PA BLO BZANG GRAGS PA. The text is written in verse form, based upon the author's own meditative experiences. For that reason, it is often called the *Lam rim nyams mgur ma* or "Song of Experience of the Stages of the Path."

**Lam rim chen mo**. In Tibetan, "Great Treatise on the Stages of the Path"; the abbreviated title for one of the best-known works on Buddhist thought and practice in Tibet, composed by the Tibetan luminary TSONG KHA PA BLO BZANG GRAGS PA in 1402 at the central Tibetan monastery of RWA SGRENG. A lengthy treatise belonging to the LAM RIM, or stages of the path, genre of Tibetan Buddhist literature, the LAM RIN CHEN MO takes its inspiration from numerous earlier writings, most notably the BODHIPATHAPRADĪPA ("Lamp for the Path to Enlightenment") by the eleventh-century Bengali master ATIŚA DĪPAṂKARAŚRĪJÑĀNA. It is the most extensive treatment of three principal stages that Tsong kha pa composed. The others include (1) the LAM RIM CHUNG BA ("Short Treatise on the Stages of the Path"), also called the *Lam rim 'bring ba* ("Intermediate Treatise on the States of the Path") and (2) the LAM RIM BSDUS DON ("Concise Meaning of the Stages of the Path"), occasionally also referred to as the *Lam rim chung ngu* ("Brief Stages of the Path"). The latter text, which records Tsong kha pa's own realization of the path in verse form, is also referred to as the *Lam rim nyams mgur ma* ("Song of Experience of the Stages of the Path"). The LAM RIM CHEN MO is a highly detailed and often technical treatise presenting a comprehensive and synthetic overview of the path to buddhahood. It draws, often at length, upon a wide range of scriptural sources including the SŪTRA and ŚĀSTRA literature of both the HĪNAYĀNA and MAHĀYĀNA; Tsong kha pa treats tantric practice in a separate work. The text is organized under the rubric of the three levels of spiritual predilection, personified as "the three individuals" (skyes bu gsum): the beings of small capacity, who engage in religious practice in order to gain a favorable rebirth in their next lifetime; the beings of intermediate capacity, who seek liberation from rebirth for themselves as an ARHAT; and the beings of great capacity, who seek to liberate all beings in the universe from suffering and thus follow the bodhisattva path to buddhahood. Tsong kha pa's text does not lay out all the practices of these three types of persons but rather those practices essential to the bodhisattva path that are held in common by persons of small and intermediate capacity, such as the practice of refuge (ŚARAṆA) and contemplation of the uncertainty of the time of death. The text includes extended discussions of topics such as relying on a spiritual master, the development of BODHICITTA, and the six perfections (PĀRAMITĀ). The last section of the text, sometimes regarded as a separate work, deals at length with the nature of serenity (ŚAMATHA) and insight (VIPAŚYANĀ); Tsong kha pa's discussion of insight here represents one of his most important expositions of emptiness (ŚŪNYATĀ). Primarily devoted to exoteric Mahāyāna doctrine, the text concludes with a brief reference to VAJRAYĀNA and the practice of tantra, a subject discussed at length by Tsong kha pa in a separate work, the SNGAGS RIM CHEN MO ("Stages of the Path of Mantra"). The *Lam rim chen mo*'s full title is *Skyes bu gsum gyi rnyams su blang ba'i rim pa thams cad tshang bar ston pa'i byang chub lam gyi rim pa.*

**Lam rim chung ba**. (Lamrim Chungwa). In Tibetan, "Short Treatise on the Stages of the Path"; also called *Lam rim 'bring ba* ("Intermediate Treatise on the Stages of the Path"); the middle-length of three major treatises on LAM RIM, or stages of the path, composed by the renowned Tibetan luminary TSONG KHA PA BLO BZANG GRAGS PA. It is about half the size of the author's classic LAM RIM CHEN MO ("Great Treatise on the Stages of the Path"), and also less formal. He wrote this work in 1415, some thirteen years after *Lam rim chen mo*. Although the first sections of the text are largely a summary of what appears in *Lam rim chen mo*, the section on insight (VIPAŚYANĀ) is substantially different from what appears in Tsong kha pa's earlier and longer work, changing the order of the presentation and adding dozens of quotations from Indian works that he did not use in *Lam rim chen mo*. Perhaps the most important contribution of this later work is its discussion of the two truths (SATYADVAYA) found in the vipaśyanā section.

**Lam rim gser zhun ma**. (Lamrim Sershunma). In Tibetan, "Stages of the Path [like] Refined Gold"; a famous LAM RIM, or stages of the path, text composed by the third DALAI LAMA BSOD NAMS RGYA MTSHO constituting a "word commentary" (tshig 'grel) on TSONG KHA PA BLO BZANG GRAGS PA's LAM RIM BSDUS DON ("Concise Meaning of the Stages of the Path").

**Lam rim 'jam dpal zhal lung**. (Lamrim Jampal Shelung). In Tibetan, "Stages of the Path [which are] the Instructions of Mañjuśrī"; an important LAM RIM, or stages of the path, treatise composed by the fifth DALAI LAMA NGAG DBANG BLO BZANG RGYA MTSHO.

**Lam rim snying gu**. (Lamrim Nyingu). In Tibetan, "Essential Stages of the Path"; an important LAM RIM, or stages of the path, treatise composed by Dwags po Ngag dbang grags pa (Dakpo Ngawang Drakpa, born c. 1450).

**Lam rim thar pa'i lag skyang**. (Lamrim Tharpe Lakyang). In Tibetan, "Stages of the Path [which are like] Liberation in the Palm of One's Hand"; a well-known LAM RIM, or stages of the path, treatise written by the twentieth-century DGE LUGS scholar Pha bong ka Byams pa bstan 'dzin 'phrin las rgya mtsho (Pabongka Jampa Tendzin Trinle Gyatso, 1878–1941).

**Laṅkāvatārasūtra**. (T. Lang kar gshegs pa'i mdo; C. Ru Lengqie jing; J. Nyū Ryōgakyō; K. Ip Nŭngga kyŏng 入楞伽經). In Sanskrit, "Scripture on the Descent into Laṅka"; a seminal MAHĀYĀNA sūtra that probably dates from around the fourth century CE. In addition to the Sanskrit recension, which was discovered in Nepal, there are also three extant translations in Chinese, by GUṆABHADRA (translated in 443), BODHIRUCI (made in 513), and ŚIKṢĀNANDA (made in 700), and two in Tibetan. The text is composed as a series of exchanges between the Buddha and the BODHISATTVA Mahāmati, who asks his questions on behalf of Rāvaṇa, the YAKṢA king of Laṅka. Thanks to the wide-ranging nature of Mahāmati's questions, the text covers many of the major themes that were the focus of contemporary Indian Mahāyāna Buddhism, and especially the emerging YOGĀCĀRA school, including the theory of the storehouse consciousness (ĀLAYAVIJÑĀNA), the womb or embryo of the buddhas (TATHĀGATAGARBHA), and mind-only (CITTAMĀTRA); despite these apparent parallels, however, the sūtra is never quoted in the writings of the most famous figures of Indian Yogācāra, ASAṄGA (c. 320–390) and VASUBANDHU (c. fourth century CE). The sūtra also offers one of the earliest sustained condemnations in Buddhist literature of meat eating, a practice that was not proscribed within the mainstream Buddhist tradition (see JAINA; DHUTAṄGA). The *Laṅkāvatāra* purports to offer a comprehensive synthesis of the Mahāyāna, and indeed, its many commentators have sought to discover in it a methodical exposition of scholastic doctrine. In fact, however, as in most Mahāyāna sūtras, there is little sustained argumentation through the scripture, and the scripture is a mélange composed with little esprit de synthèse. ¶ The emerging CHAN school of East Asia retrospectively identified the *Laṅkāvatāra* as a source of scriptural authority; indeed, some strands of the tradition even claimed that the sūtra was so influential in the school's development that its first translator, Guṇabhadra, superseded BODHIDHARMA in the roster of the Chan patriarchal lineage, as in the LENGQIE SHIZI JI ("Records of the Masters and Disciples of the *Laṅkāvatāra*"). Rather than viewing the Chan school as a systematic reading of the *Laṅkāvatāra*, as the tradition claims, it is perhaps more appropriate to say that the tradition was inspired by similar religious concerns. The Newari Buddhist tradition of Nepal also includes the *Laṅkāvatāra* among its nine principal books of the Mahāyāna (NAVAGRANTHA; see NAVADHARMA).

**Lanxi Daolong**. (J. Rankei Dōryū; K. Nan'gye Toryung 蘭溪道隆) (1213–1278). Chinese CHAN monk in the Mi'an collateral branch of the LINJI ZONG. Lanxi was a native of Fujiang in present-day Sichuan province. At a young age, he became a monk at the nearby monastery of Dacisi in Chengdu and later visited the Chan masters WUZHUN SHIFAN (1178–1249) and Chijue Daochong (1169–1250). Lanxi eventually became the disciple of Wuming Huixing (1162–1237), who in turn was a disciple of the eminent Chan master Songyuan Chongyue (1132–1202). In 1246, Lanxi departed for Japan, eventually arriving in Hakata (present-day Kyūshū) with his disciple Yiweng Shaoren (1217–1281). At the invitation of the powerful regent Hōjō Tokiyori (1227–1263), Lanxi served as abbot of the monastery Jōrakuji in Kamakura. In 1253, Tokiyori completed the construction of a large Zen monastery named KENCHŌJI in Kamakura and appointed Lanxi its founding abbot (kaisan; C. KAISHAN). Lanxi soon had a large following at Kenchōji where he trained students in the new SAṂGHA hall (C. SENGTANG) according to the Chan monastic regulations (C. QINGGUI) that he brought from China. In 1265, he received a decree to take up residence at the powerful monastery of KENNINJI in Kyōto, but after three years in Kyōto, he returned to Kenchōji. Lanxi also became the founding abbot of the temple of Zenkōji in Kamakura. Retired emperor Kameyama (r. 1259–1274) bestowed upon him the title Zen Master Daikaku (Great Enlightenment); Lanxi's lineage in Japan thus came to be known as the Daikaku branch of the Japanese Rinzai Zen tradition (RINZAISHŪ).

**Laozi huahu jing**. (J. Rōshi kekokyō; K. Noja hwaho kyŏng 老子化胡經). In Chinese, "Scripture on Laozi's Conversion of the Barbarians," an indigenous Chinese scripture (see APOCRYPHA), of which only the first and tenth rolls are extant. The fragments of the text were discovered at the Central Asian cave site of DUNHUANG by the French Sinologist PAUL PELLIOT. A text known as the *Laozi huahu jing* is known to have been written by the Daoist priest Wang Fu (fl. c. third century CE) in the Western Jin dynasty, but the Dunhuang manuscript by the same title seems not to be Wang Fu's text; this assumption derives from the fact that the Dunhuang manuscript makes reference to Manichean thought, which was not introduced to China until later during the Tang dynasty. The *Laozi huahu jing* was written in China to advance the theory that the Daoist progenitor Laozi traveled to the West, where he became the Buddha. This theory appears as early as the year 166 in a petition submitted to the Emperor Huan (R. 146–168) of the Latter Han Dynasty. By positing a Chinese origin for the presumably imported religion of Buddhism, the *Laozi huahu jing* may have been written either to argue for the primacy of Daoism over Buddhism or to suggest that there was common ground between the imported tradition of Buddhism and indigenous Chinese religion. The Daoist canon contains a related text that similarly posits Laozi's identity as ŚĀKYAMUNI Buddha: the *Santian neijie jing* ("Inner Explanations of the Three Heavens"), which explains how Laozi left for KASHMIR in the ninth century BCE, where he converted both the king and his subjects to Daoism. After this success, he continued on to India, where he was subsequently reborn as Śākyamuni, thus demonstrating that Buddhism is nothing more than Daoism in foreign guise. Later, Daoist texts written during the thirteenth century provide descriptions of as many as eighty-one different incarnations of Laozi; several of these descriptions draw liberally from Buddhist sources.

**La phyi**. (Lapchi). Also La phyi gangs (Lapchi Gang) and 'Brog la phyi gangs kyi ra ba (Drok Lapchi Gangkyi Rawa). A preeminent sacred region in southern Tibet on the Nepalese border, considered by some Tibetan sources, especially those of the BKA' BRGYUD sect, to be one of the three most important Buddhist pilgrimage sites in Tibet, together with Mt. KAILĀSA and TSA RI. The central mountain of the region is considered the MAṆḌALA of CAKRASAṂVARA and VAJRAYOGINĪ, and the region is specifically identified as GODĀVARĪ, one of the twenty-four sacred sites (tīrtha; see PĪṬHA) according to the CAKRASAṂVARATANTRA. According to Tibetan tradition, the region was first made suitable for spiritual practice, through the taming of its local demons, by the eleventh-century yogin MI LA RAS PA, who established La phyi as one of his main centers for meditation practice. Central among the complex of retreat caves is Bdud 'dul phug (Dudulphuk), the Demon Vanquishing Cave.

**Larger Perfection of Wisdom Sūtra**. See PAÑCAVIṂŚATISĀHASRIKĀPRAJÑĀPĀRAMITĀSŪTRA.

**latent tendencies**. See VĀSANĀ; ANUŚAYA.

**Laughing Buddha**. See BUDAI; MAITREYA.

**laukika**. (P. lokiya; T. 'jig rten pa; C. shijian; J. seken; K. segan 世間). In Sanskrit, "mundane" or "worldly"; anything pertaining to the ordinary world or to the practices of unenlightened sentient beings (PṚTHAGJANA) in distinction from the noble ones (ĀRYA), who have directly perceived reality. The "worldly" embraces all the contaminated (SĀSRAVA) or conditioned (SAMSKṚTA) phenomena of the three realms of existence (LOKADHĀTU), since these are subject to impermanence (anityatā). In the context of the status of practitioners, laukika refers to ordinary sentient beings (pṛthagjana); more specifically, in the fifty-two-stage BODHISATTVA path, laukika usually indicates practitioners who are at the stage of the ten faiths (C. shixin), ten understandings (C. shijie), or ten practices (C. shixing), while "supramundane" (LOKOTTARA) refers to more enlightened practitioners, such as bodhisattvas who are on the ten stages (DAŚABHŪMI). But even seemingly transcendent dharmas can be considered mundane if they are changeable by nature, e.g., in the MADHYAMAKA (C. SAN LUN ZONG) exegete JIZANG's (549–623) *Shengman baoku* ("Treasure Store of the ŚRĪMĀLĀDEVĪSIṂHANĀDASŪTRA"); mind-made bodies (MANOMAYAKĀYA) produced by bodhisattvas on the eighth through the tenth bodhisattva stages (see BODHISATTVABHŪMI; DAŚABHŪMI) may still be designated "mundane" because they are subject to change. FAZANG's HUAYAN WUJIAO ZHANG ("Essay on the Five Teachings According to Huayan") parses these stages even more precisely: of the ten stages (daśabhūmi) of the path leading to buddhahood, stages one through three belong to the mundane (laukika); the fourth to the seventh stages are supramundane (lokottara) from the standpoint of the three vehicles (TRIYĀNA) of ŚRĀVAKA, PRATYEKABUDDHA, and BODHISATTVA; and the eighth to the tenth stages transcend even the supramundane and belong to the one vehicle (EKAYĀNA). In Indian YOGĀCĀRA and MADHYAMAKA works, and commonly in the Tibetan commentarial tradition, laukika and lokottara are used to differentiate paths in the mindstreams of noble (ĀRYA) beings in any vehicle (YĀNA), who have directly witnessed the true reality (TATTVA) of the FOUR NOBLE TRUTHS. The last instants before the lokottara stage are given the name LAUKIKĀGRADHARMA (highest worldly factors); this is the last stage of the PRAYOGAMĀRGA in the five path (PAÑCAMĀRGA) system. The ABHIDHARMASAMUCCAYA says that the first lokottaradharma, the first instant of the sixteen-instant path of vision (DARŚANAMĀRGA), happens in a single meditative sitting. Even after the supramundane awakening, all subsequent attainments (PṚṢṬHALABDHA) are mundane, with the exception of the knowledge in equipoise (SAMĀHITAJÑĀNA) when the initial vision is revisited in a process of habituation, leading to a union of subsequent states and equipoise in the final lokottara experience of full enlightenment.

**laukikabhāvanāmārga**. (S). See LAUKIKAMĀRGA.

**laukikāgradharma**. (T. 'jig rten pa'i chos kyi mchog; C. shidiyifa; J. sedaiippō; K. sejeilbŏp 世第一法). In Sanskrit, "highest worldly factors," the fourth of the "aids to penetration" (NIRVEDHABHĀGĪYA), which are developed during the "path of preparation" (PRAYOGAMĀRGA) and mark the transition from the mundane sphere of cultivation (LAUKIKAMĀRGA) to the supramundane vision (DARŚANA) of the FOUR NOBLE TRUTHS (catvāry āryasatyāni). This aid to penetration receives its name because these factors (DHARMA) constitute the highest mundane stage prior to the attainment of the first noble (ĀRYA) path, the "path of vision" (DARŚANAMĀRGA). There were rival definitions within MAINSTREAM BUDDHIST SCHOOLS and among VAIBHĀṢIKA teachers themselves about which factors constituted the laukikāgradharma; the orthodox view of the dominant Kashmiri branch was that the laukikāgradharma were those factors involving mind (CITTA) and mental concomitants (CAITTA) that immediately catalyze the abandonment of mundane stages of existence and induce "access to the certainty that one will eventually win liberation" (SAMYAKTVANIYĀMĀVAKRĀNTI). Emerging from the stage of laukikāgradharmas, there is a single moment of "acquiescence to the fact of suffering" (duḥkhe dharmajñānakṣānti) at the first (of the sixteen) moments of realization of the four noble truths, which then leads inexorably in the next instant to the path of vision (darśanamārga), which constitutes stream-entry (SROTAĀPANNA), the first of the four stages of sanctity. Thus, the laukikāgradharmas represent the final thought-moment of the ordinary person (PṚTHAGJANA) before one attains the "supreme" fruit of recluseship (ŚRĀMAṆYAPHALA). ¶ In the Mahāyāna reformulation of ABHIDHARMA in the perfection of wisdom (PRAJÑĀPĀRAMITĀ) tradition based on the ABHISAMAYĀLAṂKĀRA, the laukikāgradharma is divided into three parts, a smaller, middling, and final part, within a larger presentation of a path of vision (darśanamārga) that knows "the lack of self of phenomena" (DHARMANAIRĀTMYA), i.e., that even the knowledge of the four noble truths is itself without any essential ultimate truth. According to this Mahāyāna abhidharma presentation, the path counteracts not just the mistaken apprehension of the four noble truths of suffering, origination, cessation, and path but also a series of thirty-eight object and subject conceptualizations (GRĀHYAGRĀHAKAVIKALPA). The three parts of the bodhisattva's laukikāgradharma, each divided again into three, counteract the last set of nine "pure" subject conceptualizations of an essentialized liberated person who experiences a liberating vision.

**laukikamārga**. (T. 'jig rten pa'i lam; C. shijiandao; J. sekendō; K. segando 世間道). In Sanskrit, lit. "mundane path," those practices that precede the moment of insight (DARŚANAMĀRGA) and thus result in a salutary rebirth in SAṂSĀRA rather than liberation (VIMUKTI); also called laukikaBHĀVANĀMĀRGA (the mundane path of cultivation). In the five-stage soteriology of the SARVĀSTIVĀDA school, the mundane path corresponds to the first two stages, the path of accumulation (SAṂBHĀRAMĀRGA) and the path of preparation (PRAYOGAMĀRGA), because they do not involve the direct perception of reality that transforms an ordinary person (PṚTHAGJANA) into a noble one (ĀRYA). The mundane path is developed when a practitioner has begun to cultivate the three trainings (TRIŚIKṢĀ) of morality (ŚĪLA), concentration (SAMĀDHI), and wisdom (PRAJÑĀ) but has yet to eradicate any of the ten fetters (SAṂYOJANA) or to achieve insight (DARŚANA). The eightfold path (ĀRYĀṢṬĀṄGAMĀRGA) is also formulated in terms of the spiritual ascension from mundane (LAUKIKA) to supramundane (LOKOTTARA). For example, mundane right view (SAMYAGDṚṢṬI), the first stage of the eightfold path, refers to the belief in the efficacy of KARMAN and its effects and the reality of a next life after death, thus leading to better rebirths; wrong view (MITHYĀDṚṢṬI), by contrast, denies such beliefs and leads to unsalutary rebirths. After continuing on to cultivate the moral trainings of right speech, action, and livelihood based on this right view, the practitioner next devotes himself to right concentration (SAMYAKSAMĀDHI). Concentration then leads in turn to supramundane right view, which results in direct insight into the FOUR NOBLE TRUTHS and the removal of the initial fetters. ¶ In the MADHYĀNTAVIBHĀGA, a Mahāyāna work associated with the name of MAITREYA, the eightfold path is reformulated as a "worldly" path that a bodhisattva treads after the path of vision (darśanamārga), on the model of the Buddha's work for the world after his awakening beneath the BODHI TREE in BODHGAYĀ. The bodhisattva's supramundane vision, described by the seven factors of enlightenment (BODHYAṄGA), is an equipoise (SAMĀHITA) in which knowledge is beyond all proliferation (PRAPAÑCA) and conceptualization (VIKALPA); the states subsequent (pṛṣṭhalabdha) to that equipoise are characterized as the practice of skillful means (UPĀYA) to lead others to liberation, on the model of the Buddha's compassionate activities for the sake of others. The practice serves to accumulate the bodhisattva's merit collection (PUṆYASAMBHĀRA); there is no further vision to be gained, only a return to the vision in the supramundane stages characterized as the fundamental (maula) stages of the ten bodhisattva stages (BODHISATTVABHŪMI) or a supramundane cultivation (lokottarabhāvanā). All other acts are laukika ("worldly") skillful means.

**La Vallée Poussin, Louis de**. (1869–1938). Pioneering Belgian scholar of Buddhism, who is considered the founder of the Franco–Belgian school of European Buddhist Studies and one of the foremost European scholars of Buddhism during the twentieth century. La Vallée Poussin studied Sanskrit, Tibetan, and Chinese under SYLVAIN LÉVI at the Sorbonne in Paris and HENDRIK KERN at Leiden, before becoming a professor of comparative Greek and Latin grammar at the University of Ghent in 1895, where he taught for the next three decades. La Vallée Poussin became especially renowned for his multilingual approach to Buddhist materials, in which all available recensions of a text in the major canonical languages of the Buddhist tradition were carefully studied and compared. Indicative of this approach is La Vallée Poussin's massive French translation of VASUBANDHU's ABHIDHARMAKOŚABHĀṢYA (later translated into English in four volumes), which uses the Chinese recension (in an annotated Japanese edition) as the textus receptus but draws heavily on Sanskrit, Chinese, and Tibetan materials in order to present a comprehensive, annotated translation of the text, placed squarely within the broader context of the SARVĀSTIVĀDA ABHIDHARMA. La Vallée Poussin also published the first complete renderings in a Western language of DHARMAPĀLA/XUANZANG's CHENG WEISHI LUN (*Vijñaptimātratāsiddhi*) and ŚĀNTIDEVA's BODHICARYĀVATĀRA. He also published editions, translations, and studies of central YOGĀCĀRA, MADHYAMAKA, and tantric texts, in addition to a number of significant topical studies, including one on the Buddhist councils (SAṂGĪTI). In 1916, his Hibbert Lectures at Manchester College, Oxford, were published as *The Way to Nirvāṇa: Six Lectures on Ancient Buddhism as a Discipline of Salvation*. Of his many students, perhaps the most renowned was the Belgian ÉTIENNE LAMOTTE.

**Ldan kar ma**. (Denkarma). One of the earliest known catalogues of Tibetan Buddhist texts translated during the imperial period of the early dissemination (SNGA DAR) of Buddhism in Tibet; also spelled *Ldan dkar ma* or *Lhan kar ma*. The work, preserved in the BSTAN 'GYUR section of the Tibetan canon, was compiled in the early ninth century and catalogues more than seven hundred distinct texts. Its name is derived from the Ldan kar (Denkar) palace in which it was written. The work is an important aid for scholars in determining which Buddhist texts were known and available during this early period of Tibetan history. It also illustrates the development of early principles for categorizing Buddhist literature, prefiguring the formation of the modern canon with its BKA' 'GYUR and bstan 'gyur sections. MAHĀYĀNA sūtras are listed first, followed by HĪNAYĀNA sūtras, treatises (ŚĀSTRA), TANTRAS, DHĀRAṆĪs, praises (STOTRA), prayers (PRAṆIDHĀNA), auspicious verses (maṅgalagāthā), VINAYA texts, and works on logic (NYĀYA). The collection ends with a list of revisions and translations in progress. See also JINGLU.

**Ledi, Sayadaw**. (1846–1923). In Burmese, "Senior Monk from Ledi"; honorific title of the prominent Burmese (Myanmar) scholar-monk U Nyanadaza (P. Ñāṇadhaja), a well-known scholar of ABHIDHAMMA (S. ABHIDHARMA) and proponent of VIPASSANĀ (S. VIPAŚYANĀ) insight meditation. Born in the village of Saingpyin in the Shwebo district of Upper Burma, he received a traditional education at his village monastery and was ordained a novice (P. sāmaṇera; S. ŚRĀMAṆERA) at the age of fifteen. He took for himself the name of his teacher, Nyanadaza, under whom he studied Pāli language and the Pāli primer on abhidhamma philosophy, the ABHIDHAMMATTHASAṄGAHA. At the age of eighteen, he left the order but later returned to the monkhood, he said, to study the Brahmanical science of astrology with the renowned teacher Gandhama Sayadaw. In 1866, at the age of twenty, Nyanadaza took higher ordination (UPASAMPADĀ) as a monk (P. BHIKKHU; S. BHIKṢU) and the following year traveled to the Burmese royal capital of Mandalay to continue his Pāli education. He studied under several famous teachers and particularly excelled in abhidhamma studies. His responses in the Pāli examinations were regarded as so exceptional that they were later published under the title *Pāramīdīpanī*. In 1869, King MINDON MIN sponsored the recitation and revision of the Pāli tipiṭaka (S. TRIPIṬAKA) at Mandalay in what is regarded by the Burmese as the fifth Buddhist council (see COUNCIL, FIFTH). During the proceedings, Nyanadaza assisted in the editing of Pāli texts that were inscribed on stone slabs and erected at the Kuthodaw Pagoda at the base of Mandalay hill. Nyanadaza remained in the capital until 1882, when he moved to Monywa and established a forest monastery named Ledi Tawya, whence his toponym Ledi. It is said that it was in Monywa that he took up in earnest the practice of vipassanā meditation. He was an abhidhamma scholar of wide repute and an advocate of meditation for all Buddhists, ordained and lay alike. With the final conquest of Burma by the British and the fall of the monarchy in 1885, there was a strong sentiment among many Burmese monks that the period of the disappearance of the dharma (see SADDHARMAVIPRALOPA) was approaching. According to the MANORATHAPURĀṆĪ by BUDDHAGHOSA, when the dharma disappears, the first books to disappear would be the seven books of the abhidhamma. In order to forestall their disappearance, Ledi decided to teach both abhidhamma and vipassanā widely to the laity, something that had not been previously done on a large scale. He produced over seventy-five vernacular manuals on Buddhist metaphysics and insight meditation. He also wrote several treatises in Pāli, the best known of which was the *Pāramatthadīpanī.* He taught meditation to several disciples who went on to become some of the most influential teachers of vipassanā in Burma in the twentieth century. In recognition of his scholarship, the British government awarded Ledi Sayadaw the title Aggamahāpaṇḍita in 1911. Between 1913 and 1917, Ledi Sayadaw corresponded on points of doctrine with the British Pāli scholar CAROLINE A. F. RHYS DAVIDS, and much of this correspondence was subsequently published in the *Journal of the Pali Text Society.*

**Legs bshad gser 'phreng**. (Lekshe Sertreng). In Tibetan, "Golden Garland of Eloquence," TSONG KHA PA BLO BZANG GRAGS PA's explanation of the perfection of wisdom (PRAJÑĀPĀRAMITĀ) based on the commentaries of BU STON RIN CHEN GRUB and Nya dbon Kun dga' dpal. The text is composed in the GSANG PHU NE'U THOG commentarial tradition founded by RNGOG BLO LDAN SHES RAB, using the words of the ABHISAMAYĀLAṂKĀRA and Haribhadra's short commentary (ABHISAMAYĀLAṂKĀRAVIVṚTI) as a framework. *Legs bshad gser phreng* privileges the views of Indian YOGĀCĀRA and MADHYAMAKA writers, particularly Ārya VIMUKTISENA, and accords great respect to the work of RNGOG. It already reveals Tsong kha pa's antipathy for the distinctive GZHAN STONG ("emptiness of other") view of DOL PO PA SHES RAB RGYAL MTSHAN, but it eschews the strong sectarian tendencies that begin to appear after the death of Tsong kha pa in the early fifteenth century. As an early work of Tsong kha pa, some of the views it espouses were rejected by later DGE LUGS scholars.

**Leg bshad snying po**. (Lekshe Nyingpo). In Tibetan, "The Essence of Eloquence," by TSONG KHA PA BLO BZANG GRAGS PA; its full title in Tibetan is *Drang nges legs bshad snying po* ("Essence of Eloquence on the Provisional and Definitive"). It is the most famous of the five texts that Tsong kha pa wrote on the view of emptiness (ŚŪNYATĀ). In it, he explores the categories of the provisional (NEYĀRTHA) and the definitive (NITĀRTHA) as they are presented in the YOGĀCĀRA (CITTAMĀTRA), *SVĀTANTRIKA, and *PRĀSAṄGIKA schools. In 1402, at the age of forty-five, he completed LAM RIM CHEN MO, which concludes with a long and complex section on VIPAŚYANĀ. Five years later, when he was fifty, he began writing a commentary on NĀGĀRJUNA's MŪLAMADHYAMAKAKĀRIKĀ, entitled *Rigs pa'i rgya mtsho* ("Ocean of Reasoning"), at a hermitage above what would become SE RA monastery on the northern outskirts of LHA SA. While writing his commentary on the first chapter, he foresaw interruptions if he remained there and so moved to another hermitage nearby, called Rwa kha brag ("Goat-face Crag"). At this time, a representative of the Chinese emperor arrived in Lha sa bearing an invitation from the Ming emperor to come to teach the dharma at his court. Tsong kha pa left his hermitage in order to meet with him. Citing his advancing age and the wish to remain in retreat, Tsong kha pa sent images of the Buddha in his stead. Returning to his hermitage, he set aside for the time being his commentary on Nāgārjuna and began writing *Legs bshad snying po.* After completing it in 1408, he returned to his commentary on Nāgārjuna's text. In 1415, he wrote his medium length LAM RIM text, known as *Lam rim 'bring,* which contains a substantial exposition of vipaśyanā. At the age of sixty-one, one year before his death, he composed a commentary on CANDRAKĪRTI's MADHYAMAKĀVATĀRA. Among his works on Madhyamaka, *Legs bshad snying po* is considered the most daunting, called his iron bow and iron arrow. Just as it is hard to pull an iron bow to its full extent, but if one can, the arrow will travel far, in the same way, the words—not to mention the meaning—of this text are difficult to understand but, when understood, are said to yield great insight. It has been viewed by generations of Tibetan scholars as a work of genius, known for its often cryptic brevity, but yielding profound insight if pursued with analytical fortitude. (The metaphor of the iron bow may also be a polite allusion to the fact that the book is so abstruse and sometimes apparently self-contradictory that it takes considerable effort to attempt to construct a consistent account of Tsong kha pa's position.) Within the DGE LUGS sect, *Legs bshad snying po* is regarded as the foremost philosophical tome in the eighteen volumes of Tsong kha pa's collected works, presenting a particular challenge, both as an avenue to approach reality and as an elaborate exercise in constructing his thought.

**Legs pa'i shes rab**. (T). See RNGOG LEGS PA'I SHES RAB.

**Lei-kyun Man-aung Zedi**. A pagoda, or CAITYA (Burmese JEDI), located at the foot of the Sagaing Hills in Thotapan village in Upper Burma (Myanmar). Built in 1724 CE, the pagoda commemorates the spot where, according to local legend, the Buddha once vanquished ninety-nine ogres and converted them to Buddhism. The pagoda was built with eight faces to represent the Buddha's victory in all eight directions of the compass. It contains a shrine room with a twelve-foot buddha image, which is surrounded by figures of the ninety-nine ogres, all reverently listening to his preaching. There is an annual festival held here on the eighth day of the waxing moon in the Burmese lunar month of Tawthalin (September–October).

**lena**. [alt. leṇa] (S. layana; T. gnas; C. gui/zhu; J. ki/jū; K. kwi/chu 歸/住). In BUDDHIST HYBRID SANSKRIT and Pāli, "refuge" or "abode"; the term was used by extension to refer to a permanent dwelling place where a monk or group of monks remained in residence. In the early tradition, it appears that monks would rendezvous at specific places to spend the rains retreat (VARṢĀ) without those places becoming the permanent dwelling places for a specific monk or group of monks. The term lena was used for these more private and permanent dwelling places that developed for the use of a single resident SAṂGHA, as opposed to a seasonal settlement; visiting monks were welcome but only for a limited period. The CŪḶAVAGGA lists five kinds of lena, although the precise meaning of each is not entirely clear: (1) the VIHĀRA, which originally seemed to be either communal shelters or individual huts; (2) the aḍḍhayoga, a more permanent structure with eaves; (3) a pāsāda, a structure with one or more upper stories; (4) a hammiya, a structure with an upper story and an attic; and (5) a guha, a structure built into the side of a hill or mountain. Eventually, only two of these terms survived, with vihāra referring to a free-standing monastery and guha referring to a man-made cave monastery.

**Lengqie shizi ji**. (J. Ryōga shishiki; K. Nŭngga saja ki 楞伽師資記). In Chinese, "Records of the Masters and Disciples of the Laṅkāvatāra"; a genealogical anthology associated with the Northern school (BEI ZONG) of the early CHAN tradition, compiled by JINGJUE (683–c. 760). The *Lengqie shizi ji* contains the biographies and sayings of eight generations of masters (twenty-four in total), who received the "transmission of the lamp" (chuandeng) as patriarchs (ZUSHI) in the Chan school. The transmission narrative presented in this text differs markedly from that found in the LIUZU TAN JING ("Platform Sūtra"), which becomes normative in the mature Chan tradition. The recipients of the special transmission of the Chan teachings in the *Lenqi shizi ji* belong instead to the Northern school. Jingjue places GUṆABHADRA before BODHIDHARMA in the Chan patriarchal lineage (probably because of his role in translating the LAṄKĀVATĀRASŪTRA, an important scriptural influence in the early Chan school); in addition, SHENXIU is listed as the successor to the fifth Chinese patriarch, HONGREN, in place of HUINENG. The *Lenqie shizi ji* also contains a set of rhetorical questions and doctrinal admonitions known as zhishi wenyi (lit. "pointing at things and inquiring into their meaning") in the biographies of Guṇabhadra, Bodhidharma, Hongren, and Shenxiu. Jingjue quotes from numerous sources, including his teacher Xuanze's (d.u.) *Lengqie renfa zhi* ("Records of the Men and Teachings of the *Laṅkāvatāra*," apparently extant only in these embedded quotations in the *Lenqie shizi ji*), the DASHENG QIXIN LUN, the XIUXIN YAO LUN, Bodhidharma's ERRU SIXING LUN, and the *Rudao anxin yao fangpian famen* attributed to DAOXIN (which also seems to exist only as quoted, apparently in its entirety, in the *Lenqie shizi ji*). As one of the earliest Chan texts to delineate the transmission-of-the-lamplight theory as espoused by the adherents of the Northern school of Chan, the *Lenqie shizi ji* is an invaluable tool for understanding the development of the lineage of Chan patriarchs and the early history of the Chan school. See also CHUANDENG LU; LIDAI FABAO JI.

**Leshan dafo**. (樂山大佛). In Chinese, "Great Buddha of Leshan," the world's largest stone statue of the bodhisattva MAITREYA. See EMEISHAN.

**Lévi, Sylvain**. (1863–1935). Influential nineteenth-century European scholar of the YOGĀCĀRA school of Buddhism. Born in Paris to Alsatian parents, Lévi had a conservative Jewish education and held his first teaching position at a conservative seminary in Paris. Educated in Sanskrit at the University of Paris, Lévi became a lecturer at the École des Hautes Études in Paris in 1886. There, he taught Sanskrit until he became professor of Sanskrit language and literature at the Collège de France in 1894, a position that he would hold until 1935. Lévi went to India and Japan to carry out his research and also traveled extensively in Korea, Nepal, Vietnam, and Russia. He eventually became the director of the École des Hautes Études. In addition to Sanskrit, Lévi also read classical Chinese, Tibetan, and Kuchean and was one of the first Western scholars to study Indian Buddhism through translations that were extant only in those secondary canonical languages. Perhaps his most significant translations were of seminal texts of the YOGĀCĀRA school, including renderings of VASUBANDHU's twin synopses, the VIṂŚATIKĀ and TRIṂŚIKĀ (1925), and ASAṄGA's MAHĀYĀNASŪTRĀLAṂKĀRA, thus introducing the major writings of this important Mahāyāna scholastic school to the Western scholarly world. Lévi also published on classical Indian theater, the history of Nepal, and Sanskrit manuscripts from Bali. Together with TAKAKUSU JUNJIRŌ, Lévi was the cofounder of the joint Japanese–French *Hōbōgirin*, an encyclopedic dictionary of Buddhism, the compilation of which continues to this day.

**Lha btsun nam mkha' 'jigs med**. (Lhatsün Namka Jikme) (1597–1653). An adept of the RNYING MA sect of Tibetan Buddhism, renowned for his mastery of many Rnying ma doctrines and his great supernatural powers. Although ordained as a monk while a youth, he spent much of his life as a YOGIN, practicing meditation in retreat centers across the Tibetan countryside. He is best remembered for entering the region of Sikkim (T. 'Bras mo ljongs), in 1646, "opening" it as a place of pilgrimage and spiritual practice, and for founding the retreat center of Bkra shis lding (Tashiding).

**Lha btsun Rin chen rnam rgyal**. (Lhatsün Rinchen Namgyal) (1473–1557). A Tibetan Buddhist master famous for his literary compositions and publishing activities in southern Tibet. He was born into the ruling family of the Gung thang region of southwestern Tibet; the title lha btsun is generally applied to descendants of Tibet's royal dynastic aristocracy. Although his teachers represent a wide range of religious affiliations and intellectual currents of his time, Rin chen rnam rgyal's principal teacher is usually considered to be GTSANG SMYON HERUKA, the so-called mad YOGIN of Tsang. Following the example of his master, who edited and published a well-known biography and verse anthology of MI LA RAS PA, Rin chen rnam rgyal began a career of authoring, editing, and publishing a wide range of literary materials from his seat at the retreat complex of BRAG DKAR RTA SO. These works include biographies and verse anthologies of numerous BKA' BRGYUD masters. During the sixteenth century, Brag dkar rta so became one of Tibet's leading publishing centers.

**Lha lung**. A monastery located in the southern Tibetan region of LHO BRAG, founded in 1154 by the first KARMA PA DUS GSUM MKHYEN PA. It remained allied with the BKA' BRGYUD sect under the direction of the sixteenth-century scholar DPA' BO GTSUG LAG PHRENG BA but changed affiliation to the RNYING MA under the Gsung sprul (Sungtrul) lama, the speech incarnation of PADMA GLING PA. During the time of the fifth DALAI LAMA, NGAG DBANG BLO BZANG RGYA MTSHO, it was converted to the DGE LUGS sect. Although mostly demolished during the Chinese Cultural Revolution, Lha lung is architecturally unique, and an important collection of murals survived destruction.

**lha mo**. In Tibetan, lit. "the goddess"; the name for the classical theater of Tibet. These plays are drawn from Tibetan literature, often with Buddhist themes, and can last a full day when performed in their entirety. They are performed with a rich assortment of masks and costumes; the members of the lha mo troupe employ sung dialogue, chanted narration, stylized movement, and dancing. Satire and comic improvisation are also included. The tradition of lha mo is said to have begun with the famous saint THANG STONG RGYAL PO. See 'CHAM.

**Lha mo bla mtsho**. (Lhamo latso). An important oracular lake located in central Tibet, southeast of LHA SA. It is considered to be the receptacle for the life force (bla) of the DALAI LAMAS and considered sacred to the Buddhist protective deity DPAL LDAN LHA MO (Śrīdevī), protectress of the Dalai Lamas. Each Dalai Lama would try to visit the lake at least once during his life to receive visions on the water's surface regarding his future activities and death. The lake is also believed to display signs concerning the future rebirth of the Dalai and PAṆ CHEN LAMAS. Most recently, in 1933, the regent Rwa sgreng Rin po che saw visions in the lake that indicated the birthplace and circumstances of the fourteenth Dalai Lama.

**Lha sa**. In Tibetan, "place of the gods"; capital city of Tibet and location of some of the country's most important Buddhist institutions. According to traditional histories, the Tibetan king SRONG BTSAN SGAM PO moved his capital from the Yar klungs Valley to its current location when he founded the original edifice underlying the PO TA LA Palace in 637, a structure completed in its present form only during the seventeenth century under the direction of the fifth DALAI LAMA, NGA DBANG BLO BZANG RGYA MTSHO, and his regent. At about the same time, Srong bstan sgam po began work on the central JO KHANG temple. As goats were used as work animals during the construction, the area became known as Ra sa (lit. "place of the goats"). Following the temple's consecration in 647, it is said that the city's name was then changed to Lha sa ("place of the gods"). These two structures, together with the RA MO CHE temple, form the core of Lha sa's religious and sacred architecture. Over the centuries, many other institutions were added, including the medical college of Lcags po ri (Chakpori), the Dalai Lama's summer palace at the NOR BU GLING KHA, and numerous small monasteries, temples, and shrines. Around the city's periphery, a number of important monasteries were established, including the three great DGE LUGS monasteries of DGA' LDAN, 'BRAS SPUNGS, and SE RA (known collectively as the GDAN SA GSUM, or "three seats"), as well as GNAS CHUNG monastery, the seat of Tibet's state oracle. A series of three ritual circumambulation routes around the city's sacred centers developed: (1) the nang bskor (nangkor, "inner circuit"), skirting the Jo khang temple's inner sanctum; (2) the BAR BSKOR (barkor, "middle circuit"), circling the outer walls of the Jo khang and its neighboring buildings; and (3) the gling bskor (lingkor, "sanctuary circuit") circumnavigating the entire city, including the Po ta la Palace and Lcag po ri. Lha sa has long been considered the spiritual center of Tibet, and chief pilgrimage destination. Some devotees would travel the immense distance from their homeland to Lha sa while performing full-length prostrations, literally covering the ground with their bodies the entire way. Although the far eastern and western provinces of Tibet traditionally maintained a large degree of regional independence, after the seventeenth century Tibet's central government, the DGA' LDAN PHO BRANG, operated from Lha sa in the Po ta la Palace.

**Lho brag**. (Lhodrak). In Tibetan, lit. "the southern cliffs"; a region of alpine meadows and narrow gorges in southern Tibet on the border with Bhutan and location of numerous monasteries and retreat hermitages. The area was home to many translators and treasure revealers (GTER STON) of the RNYING MA and BKA' BRGYUD sects of Tibetan Buddhism during the early period of the later dissemination (PHYI DAR) of the DHARMA. Perhaps the most famous among them is the translator MAR PA CHOS KYI BLO GROS, who is often called Lho brag pa (Lhodrakpa), "The Man from Lhodrak," who established his seat at GRO BO LUNG. Other leading masters and their institutions include NYANG RAL NYI MA 'OD ZER who founded Smra bo rcog (Ma'ojok) monastery; Nam mkha'i snying po (Namke Nyingpo), Lo ras pa (Lorepa, 1187–1250), and PADMA DKAR PO, who established MKHAR CHU monastery; GURU CHOS KYI DBANG PHYUG, whose main seat was the Guru lha khang; and DPA' BO GTSUG LAG PHRENG BA, abbot of the monasteries at LHA LUNG and SRAS MKHAR DGU THOG.

**lho gter**. (lho ter). In Tibetan, "southern treasures," a term used to refer to the treasure texts (GTER MA) discovered by great seventeenth-century Rnying ma lama GTER BDAG GLING PA, which became the central texts studied at SMIN GROL GLING monastery.

**li**. (J. ri; K. i 理). In Chinese, "principle"; the fundamental "principle," general "pattern," or innate "quality" that governs reality. (The antiquated English rendering of li as "noumenon" is weighted down with Kantian connotations that are inappropriate in an East Asian philosophical context and is best avoided.) In ancient China, the term li was originally used as a noun to indicate the natural patterns that occurred on a piece of jade, although it could also be used as a verb referring to the carving that transforms a piece of raw jade into a refined cultural object. The term soon came to refer to the inner or outer patterns inherent in any kind of physical object. For example, in the section on "Jielao" ("Explaining Lao[zi]") from the *Hanfeizi*, compiled during the late second century BCE, li refers to either an object's overt quality or its hidden disposition to manifest certain qualities at a given time. XUANXUE (Dark Learning) scholars from the Wei-Jin period were among the first intellectuals to use the term in a philosophically meaningful way. In particular, Wang Bi (226–249) employed li as a synonym for his ontological concept of WU (nonbeing) to refer to a metaphysical principle that underlies all phenomena. Such usages of the term influenced early Buddhist thinkers in China. DAOSHENG (355–434), e.g., regarded li as an immutable, ultimate principle, often using it as a synonym for the buddhanature (FOXING) or the true self (zhenwo). During the Tang dynasty, Huayan Buddhism (HUAYAN ZONG) employed the term in a philosophically sophisticated manner, although with varying meanings. For DUSHUN, the putative founder of the Huayan school, li represents not a substance or thing but, instead, a proposition that expresses the true identity of the phenomenal world. For example, li could refer to the principle that all phenomena (SHI) are empty (ŚŪNYATĀ), a proposition that is only understandable through practice. His successors in the Huayan school, such as FAZANG and CHENGGUAN, imbued the term with additional ontological connotations. Fazang identified li with the mind as suchness (TATHATĀ; BHŪTATATHATĀ) described in the DASHENG QIXIN LUN ("Awakening of Faith According to the Mahāyāna"), which he considered to be synonymous with the TATHĀGATAGARBHA. Developing on Fazang's thought, Chengguan viewed li as the essential quality that pervades all four realms of reality (DHARMADHĀTU; SI FAJIE). During the Song dynasty, Neo-Confucian philosophers reinterpreted the term to fit a Confucian philosophical context. They interpreted li as an inherent principle within things that makes them what they are; when applied to human beings, li thus refers to the four inner moral essences of humaneness, righteousness, propriety, and wisdom. Some aspects of these Neo-Confucian interpretations of the term li appear in the writings of such Song-dynasty Chan masters as DAHUI ZONGGAO.

**Liang gaoseng zhuan**. (梁高僧傳). In Chinese, "Biographies of Eminent Monks [Compiled during the] Liang [Dynasty]." See GAOSENG ZHUAN.

**Liangjie**. (C) (良价). See DONGSHAN LIANGJIE.

**Lidai fabao ji**. (J. Rekidai hōbōki; K. Yŏktae pŏppo ki 歷代法寶記). In Chinese, "Record of the Dharma-Jewel throughout Successive Generations"; an influential genealogical history of the early CHAN tradition, composed by disciples of the Chan master BAOTANG WUZHU in the JINGZHONG ZONG. The history of the Chan school as related in the *Lidai fabao ji* begins with the arrival of Buddhism in China during the Han dynasty, which is followed by a brief discussion of the lineages of dharma transmission in the FU FAZANG YINYUAN ZHUAN and LENGQIE SHIZI JI. The *Lidai fabao ji* then provides the biographies of the six patriarchs (ZUSHI) of Chan in China: Bodhidharmatrāta [alt. BODHIDHARMA], Huike, Sengcan, Daoxin, Hongren, and Huineng. Each biography ends with a brief reference to the transmission of the purple monastic robe of Bodhidharma as a symbol of authority. The manner in which this robe came into the hands of Zhishen (609–702), a disciple of the fifth patriarch Hongren, is told following the biography of the sixth, and last, patriarch Huineng. According to the *Lidai fabao ji*'s transmission story, Huineng entrusted the robe to Empress WU ZETIAN, who in turn gave it to Zhishen during his visit to the imperial palace. Zhishen is then said to have transmitted this robe to Chuji [alt. 648–734, 650–732, 669–736], who later passed it on to his disciple CHŎNGJUNG MUSANG (C. Jingzhong Wuxiang). The robe finally came into the possession of Musang's disciple Baotang Wuzhu, whose teachings comprise the bulk of the *Lidai fabao ji*. After the *Lidai fabao ji* was translated into Tibetan, Wuzhu's teachings made their way to Tibetan plateau, where they seem to have exerted some influence over the early development of Tibetan Buddhism. The *Lidai fabao ji* was thought to have been lost until the modern discovery of several copies of the text in the manuscript cache at DUNHUANG. Cf. CHUANDENG LU; LENGQIE SHIZI JI.

**Lidai sanbao ji**. (J. Rekidai sanbōki; K. Yŏktae sambo ki 歷代三寶紀). In Chinese, "Record of the Three Jewels throughout Successive Dynasties," a private scriptural catalogue (JINGLU) composed by Fei Changfang (d.u.) in 597. The *Lidai sanbao ji* professes to be a history of the dissemination of the three jewels (RATNATRAYA) in China and provides lists of translated scriptures, indigenous works, or APOCRYPHA, and discussion of the circumstances of their compilation. The catalogue is in fifteen rolls, covering 2,268 texts in a total of 6,417 rolls. The first three rolls of the catalogue provide a chronology of the major events in the history of Buddhism from the Zhou through the Han dynasties. Rolls four through twelve detail the different translations of Buddhist scriptures made in China during different dynastic periods and present them in chronological order. Rolls thirteen and fourteen present a roster of the complete MAHĀYĀNA and HĪNAYĀNA TRIPIṬAKAS. Finally, the fifteenth roll provides an afterword, a table of contents of the *Lidai sanbao ji*, and a list of other scriptural catalogues that Fei consulted in the course of compiling his own catalogue. Fei's organizational principle is unique among the Chinese cataloguers and serves to legitimize specific scriptural translations by associating them with the Chinese dynastic succession. Fei's record is particularly important for its attention to scriptures translated in northern China and its attempt to authenticate the translation and authorship of certain apocryphal texts. Fei was especially concerned in his catalogue to reduce the number of scriptures that previously had been listed as anonymous, in order to quash potential questions about the reliability of the Buddhist textual transmission (a concern that Daoists at the Chinese court were then exploiting in their competition for imperial patronage). Fei thus blatantly fabricated scores of attributions for translations that previously had been listed as anonymous. These attributions were later adopted by the state-authorized *Da Zhou lu*, compiled in 695, which ensured that these scriptures would subsequently enter the mainstream of the Buddhist textual transmission. Fei's translator fabrications resulted in substantial numbers of Chinese Buddhist scriptures that were apocryphal and yet accepted as canonical; this list includes many of the most influential scriptures and commentaries in East Asian Buddhism, including the YUANJUE JING, RENWANG JING, and DASHENG QIXIN LUN.

**Liễu Quán**. (了觀) (1667–1742). Vietnamese monk who is considered the second patriarch of a branch of the Linji school (LINJI ZONG) of CHAN, which was brought to Vietnam by the Chinese Chan Master Nguyên Thiều (Yuanshao). He was born in Phú Yên Province (Central Vietnam), and his personal name was Lê Thiệt Diệu. When he was six years old, his father sent him at his request to Hội Tôn Monastery to study under the Venerable Tế Viên, a Chinese monk. After his teacher passed away, he went to Bảo Quốc Monastery in Huế to study under another Chinese monk, the Venerable Giác Phong. In 1695, he went to Huế to receive novice ordination under the Chinese Chan Master Thạch Liêm and received full ordination in 1697 from another Chinese monk, the Venerable Từ Lâm. In 1702, he traveled to Đông Sơn Monastery to receive instructions on the practice of Chan from the Chinese monk Tử Dung, an eminent Buddhist teacher of the time, and received the "mind seal" of the Chan transmission from him in 1708. In 1735, Liễu Quán returned to Huế and until 1735 presided over numerous precept ceremonies. He was invited to the royal court several times, but he declined each invitation. Liễu Quán founded the Thiền Tôn (Chan School) Monastery in Huế and was traditionally considered to be the thirty-fifth generation successor in the Linji lineage. Liễu Quán was particularly credited with reforming some of the Chinese Linji Chan rituals and practices, making them more palatable to Vietnamese Buddhists.

**li fajie**. (J. rihokkai; K. i pŏpkye 理法界). In Chinese, "dharma-realm of principle," the second of the four DHARMADHĀTU (realms of reality) according to the Huayan school (HUAYAN ZONG). The "dharmadhātu of principle" refers to the singular, all-pervasive truth of suchness (ZHENRU; see TATHATĀ) that unifies all individual phenomena (SHI). This sense of unity exists within the "sphere of dharma" (see dharmadhātu) because all phenomena share the same empty nature and derive from the same one mind (YIXIN). A common Huayan simile compares "principle" to the oceanic body of water in which waves (viz., "phenomena," shi) well up. Here, the "principle" is the creative, ontological source of all "phenomena." The five Huayan classes of teachings (HUAYAN WUJIAO) classify the dharmadhātu of principle under the "initial [Mahāyāna] teaching" (SHIJIAO) and the "sudden [Mahāyāna] teaching" (DUNJIAO), and their respective modes of meditative contemplation.

**Life of Milarepa**. See MI LA RAS PA'I RNAM THAR.

**Lihuo lun**. (理惑論). In Chinese, "Treatise on the Resolution of Doubts." See MOUZI LIHUO LUN.

**Līlavajra**. [alt. Līlāvajra, Lalitavajra] (T. Rol pa'i rdo rje). There is a disagreement in Tibetan lineage lists about whether this is the proper name of a single or multiple persons. In Sanskrit, both the words līlā and lalita denote joyful abandonment in a state of spontaneous play. According to Tibetan hagiographies, Līlavajra is one of the eighty-four MAHĀSIDDHAs, Indian tantric adepts who manifested eccentric, even antinomian, behavior and from whom Tibetan translators received the transmission of secret tantric instructions. He is found in the lineage of the CAKRASAṂVARA and GUHYASAMĀJA tantras but is associated in particular with the VAJRABHAIRAVA cycle (with the central figure given variously the name Kṛṣṇayamāri, Raktayamāri, YAMĀNTAKA, and Vajrabhairava), a wrathful form of MAÑJUŚRĪ, the embodiment of a buddha's wisdom. Līlavajra is the central figure in the lineage lists of five of the six early Vajrabhairava traditions in Tibet; he is the source of the RWA LO TSĀ BA RDO RJE GRAGS tradition that TSONG KHA PA BLO BZANG GRAGS PA learned while still young. Through him, the VAJRABHAIRAVATANTRA became a central practice in the DGE LUGS sect.

**li mi**. (理密). In Chinese, "esoteric as to principle." See ER MI.

**lineage**. See GOTRA; KULA; PARAṂPARĀ; CHUANDENG LU; FASI; ZUSHI.

**liṅga**. (T. mtshan/rtags; C. xiang/shengzhi; J. sō/shōshi; K. sang/saengji 相/生支). In Sanskrit and Pāli, "sign" or "mark," a polysemous term with three major denotations in Buddhist materials: (1) the distinguishing characteristic of a given phenomena, (2) the reason in a syllogism (PRAYOGA), and (3) a denominator of gender and specifically the male sexual organ. In the MAHĀYĀNA, in particular, the signs that a BODHISATTVA will not turn back (avaivartikaliṅga) on the path to full enlightenment are described in great detail; best known are the tears and horripilation that occur spontaneously in a true bodhisattva who hears a particular Mahāyāna SŪTRA for the first time, or when listening to an explanation of BODHICITTA and ŚŪNYATĀ. In a syllogism, according to DIGNĀGA, a true mark (liṅga) meets three prerequisites (trairūpya): it must be a property of the logical subject (PAKṢADHARMA), and there must be positive (anvaya) and negative concomitance (VYATIREKA). For example, in a standard syllogistic formulation, "sound (the logical subject) is impermanent because it is a product (the mark)," being a product is a property of the logical subject: there is positive concomitance between a product and impermanence (ANITYA), i.e., perishing in the next moment, and there is negative concomitance between being permanent and not being a product. As a denominator of gender, liṅga also refers to the gender of letters and words (male, female, and neuter). In TANTRA, liṅga refers to the gender of deities in MAṆḌALAs and defines their hand implements and the specific practices associated with the deities; in some cases, particularly in the RNYING MA VAJRAKĪLAYA tantras, as in Śaivism, liṅga refers specifically to the male sexual organ.

**lingyan**. (靈驗). In Chinese, "numinous attestation." See GANYING.

**lingying**. (靈應). In Chinese, "numinous response." See GANYING.

**Lingyinsi**. (靈隱寺). In Chinese, "Numinous Seclusion Monastery"; located in Zhejiang province northwest of Hangzhou. In 326 CE, an Indian monk with the Chinese name Huili (d.u.) is supposed to have come to Hangzhou, where he was awestruck by the sight of Feilai Feng (lit. "Peak that Flew Hither") and built a monastery there that he named Lingyin. The monastery is the largest of several that are located in the Wulin Mountains, which also features a large number of grottoes and religious rock carvings. The monastery was destroyed in 771 CE during the Tang dynasty and later rebuilt. In 1007 CE, during the Song dynasty, it was renamed Lingyin Chan Monastery but was subsequently destroyed as the result of war and rebuilt again. In 1359, during the Ming dynasty, it was given its present name of Lingyinsi.

**Lingyou**. (C) (靈祐). See GUISHAN LINGYOU.

**Ling Zhao**. (J. Rei Shō; K. Yŏng Cho 靈照). Daughter of the famous Tang-dynasty Chinese layman PANG YUN and a well-known lay adept of the CHAN school in her own right. See PANG YUN.

**lingzhi**. (J. ryōchi/reichi; K. yŏngji 靈知). In Chinese, "numinous awareness"; the quality of "sentience" common to all sentient beings, which constitutes their capacity both to experience the sensory realms in all their diversity and to attain enlightenment. Numinous awareness is both the inherent faculty that inspires sentient beings to seek enlightenment and the quality of mind perfected through meditative development. As the foundation of sentience, numinous awareness is what enables all sentient beings to see, hear, know, and experience their world and thus constitutes the capacity of the mind to remain "aware" of all sensory stimuli; hence, this "numinous awareness is never dark" (C. lingzhi bumei). This property of awareness is said to be itself "void and calm" (C. kongji) and is consequently able to adapt without limitation to the various inclinations of sentient beings; hence, the term is often known as the "void and calm, numinous awareness" (C. kongji lingzhi). Regardless of whether that particular sentient being's awareness inclines toward greed and hatred or toward wisdom and compassion, however, that sentience itself remains simply "aware." This numinous awareness is therefore equated in the CHAN school with enlightenment (BODHI), TATHĀGATAGARBHA, buddha-nature (BUDDHADHĀTU; C. FOXING), or one's "original face" (BENLAI MIANMU). The enlightenment inherent in the mind is naturally luminous, shining ever outward and allowing beings to experience their external world. This natural quality of luminosity is what is meant by "sentience," and the very fact that "sentient" beings are conscious is ipso facto proof that they are inherently enlightened. If the meditator can turn this radiance emanating from one's mind back to its source, one would rediscover that luminous core of the mind and be instantly enlightened. In CHAN meditation, the quality of introspection that allows the meditator to experience this numinous awareness directly is called "tracing back the radiance" (FANZHAO) or "seeing the nature" (JIANXING). The term receives particular attention in the works of the Chinese Chan/HUAYAN adept GUIFENG ZONGMI (780–841) and the Korean Sŏn master POJO CHINUL (1158–1210). See also RIG PA.

**lingzhi bumei**. (靈知不昧). In Chinese, "numinous awareness is never dark." See LINGZHI.

**Linh Mụ Tự**. (靈姥寺). In Vietnamese, "Numinous Matron Monastery"; also known popularly as the Chùa Linh Mụ or Linh Mụ Pagoda. See THIÊN MỤ TỰ.

**Linji lu**. (J. Rinzairoku; K. Imje nok 臨濟錄). In Chinese, "The Record of Linji," the discourse record (YULU) attributed to LINJI YIXUAN (d. 867), the putative founder of the eponymous LINJI ZONG of CHAN (J. Zen; K. Sŏn), and one of the most widely read and cited works within the Chan tradition; also known as the *Linji yulu* and the *Zhenzhou Linji Huizhao Chanshi yulu*. The *Linji lu* purports to provide a verbatim account of Linji's sermons, teachings, and his exchanges with disciples and guests. As with most texts in the discourse-record genre, however, the *Linji lu* was not compiled until long after Linji's death (the most popular recension was compiled in 1120, some 250 years after his death) and therefore provides a retrospective portrayal of how the mature Chan school assumed one of its quintessential masters would have taught and conducted himself. The record is in one roll and is divided into three sections: (1) formal discourses (e.g., SHANGTANG), many delivered at the request of local officials; (2) critical examinations (KANBIAN), viz., his encounters with monks, students, and lay visitors; and (3) a record of his activities (xinglu), which discusses his enlightenment under HUANGBO XIYUN (d. 850), his meetings with Chan masters early in his career, and concludes with an official biography taken from his stele inscription. The text is well known for its distinctive teachings, such as the "lump of raw flesh" (CHIROUTUAN), and his pedagogical technique called the Linji "shout" (he); see BANGHE.

**Linji Yixuan**. (J. Rinzai Gigen; K. Imje Ŭihyŏn 臨濟義玄) (d. 867). Chinese CHAN master of the Tang dynasty and putative founder of the eponymous LINJI ZONG. Linji was a native of Nanhua in present-day Shandong province. He is said to have begun his career as a monk by training in Buddhist doctrine and VINAYA, but he abandoned this scholastic path and headed south to study under the Chan master HUANGBO XIYUN (d. 850). Linji is also known to have visited Gao'an Dayu (d.u.) with whom he discussed the teachings of Huangbo. Having received certification of his attainment (see YINKE) from Huangbo, Linji returned north to Zhenzhou (in present-day Hebei province) and resided in a small hermitage near the Hutuo River that he named Linji'an, whence derives his toponym. There, with the help of the monk Puhua (d. 861), Linji was able to attract a large following. Linji is most famous for his witty replies and iconoclastic style of teaching. Like the Chan master DESHAN XUANJIAN's "blows" (bang), Linji was particularly famous for his "shouts" (he) in response to students' questions (see BANGHE). He was posthumously given the title Chan Master Huizhao (Illumination of Wisdom). The thriving descendents of Linji came to be known collectively as the Linji zong. Linji's teachings are recorded in his discourse record (YULU), the LINJI LU.

**Linji zong**. (J. Rinzaishū; K. Imje chong 臨濟宗). In Chinese, the "Linji school"; one of the so-called Five Houses and Seven Schools (WU JIA QI ZONG) of the mature Chinese CHAN school. Chan genealogical records (see CHUANDENG LU) describe a lineage of monks that can be traced back to the eponymous Tang-dynasty Chan master LINJI YIXUAN. Linji's lineage came to dominate the Chan tradition in the southern regions of China, largely through the pioneering efforts of his Song-dynasty spiritual descendants Fengxue Yanzhao (896–973), Fenyang Shanshao (947–1024), and Shishuang Chuyuan (986–1040). Shishuang's two major disciples, HUANGLONG HUINAN (1002–1069) and YANGQI FANGHUI (992–1049), produced the two most successful collateral lines within the Linji lineage: the HUANGLONG PAI and YANGQI PAI. Few monks had as significant an impact on the Chan tradition as DAHUI ZONGGAO, a successor in the Yangqi branch of the Linji lineage. Dahui continued the efforts of his teacher YUANWU KEQIN, who is credited with compiling the influential BIYAN LU ("Blue Cliff Record") and developed the use of Chan cases or precedents (GONG'AN) as subjects of meditation (see KANHUA CHAN). Dahui and his spiritual descendants continued to serve as abbots of the most powerful monasteries in China, such as WANSHOUSI (see GOZAN). During Dahui's time, the Linji lineage came into brief conflict with the resurgent CAODONG ZONG lineage over the issue of the latter's distinctive form of meditative practice, which Dahui pejoratively labeled "silent-illumination meditation" (MOZHAO CHAN). Other famous masters in the Linji lineage include WUZHUN SHIFAN, GAOFENG YUANMIAO, and ZHONGFENG MINGBEN. For the Korean and Japanese counterparts, see IMJE CHONG; RINZAISHŪ.

**lishi wu'ai fajie**. (J. rijimugehokkai; K. isa muae pŏpkye 理事無礙法界). In Chinese, "dharma-realm of the unimpeded interpenetration between principle and phenomena," the third of the four realms of reality (DHARMADHĀTU) according to the Huayan school (HUAYAN ZONG). A mere realization of the "principle" (LI) of the dharmadhātu, as is offered in the second of the four dharmadhātus (see LI FAJIE) is not a decisive insight, the Huayan school claims, because it does not take into account the dynamic interpenetration or unimpededness (wu'ai) between the singular "principle" of true suchness (ZHENRU; see TATHATĀ) and the myriad "phenomena" (SHI) of the external world. Since true suchness is an abstract entity without definable features or tangible substance of its own, it is only revealed and made accessible through "phenomena." Conversely, "phenomena" lose their ontological ground and epistemological coherence if they are not uniformly rooted in the "principle." Thus, the Buddhist practitioner must come to recognize that the vibrant functioning of the phenomenal aspects of reality is in fact the expression of the principle itself. Alternatively, some Huayan exegetes have equated "principle" with the imperturbable buddha-nature (S. BUDDHADHĀTU, C. FOXING) and "phenomena" with the active ĀLAYAVIJÑĀNA, the "storehouse consciousness." In this interpretation, these two factors "interpenetrate" because ālayavijñāna is taken to be grounded in the buddha-nature and, in response to activating conditions, the buddha-nature is transmuted into the ālayavijñāna. A common simile used to describe the relationship between "principle" and "phenomena" is that between the deep ocean and the waves welling up on its surface, the essence of each of those waves is the same "principle" of water, but each wave is a unique, discrete "phenomenon" in its own right. Traditionally, Huayan classifies the unimpeded interpenetration between principle and phenomena under the "final [Mahāyāna] teaching (zhongjiao)" in the five Huayan classes of teachings schema (HUAYAN WUJIAO).

**Li Tongxuan**. (J. Ri Tsūgen; K. Yi T'onghyŏn 李通玄) (635–730; alt. 646–740). Tang-dynasty lay exegete of the AVATAṂSAKASŪTRA (*Huayan jing*) and renowned thaumaturge. Li's life is the stuff of legend. He is claimed to have been related to the Tang imperial house but is known only as an elusive and eccentric lay scholar of Buddhism, who hid away in hermits' cells and mountain grottoes so as to devote himself entirely to his writing. Li's hagiographer says that he was able to work late into the night just from the radiance that issued forth from his mouth; his scholarship and health were sustained by two mysterious maidens who brought him paper, brushes, and daily provisions. The magnum opus of this life of scholarship is a forty-roll commentary to ŚIKṢĀNANDA's "new" 699 translation of the *Avataṃsakasūtra*; his commentary is entitled the *Xin Huayan jing lun* and was published posthumously in 774. In the mid-ninth century, Li's commentary was published together with the sūtra as the HUAYAN JING HELUN, and this compilation is the recension of Li's exegesis that is most widely used. Li also wrote a shorter one-roll treatise known usually by its abbreviated title of *Shiming lun* ("The Ten Illuminations"; the full title is *Shi Huayan jing shi'er yuansheng jiemi xianzhi chengbei shiming lun*), which discusses the *Huayan jing* from ten different perspectives on the doctrine of conditioned origination (PRATĪTYASAMUTPĀDA), and two other shorter works. Because Li Tongxuan was not associated with the mainstream of the Huayan lineage (HUAYAN ZONG), he was able to develop his own distinctive vision of the insights found in the *Avataṃsakasūtra*, a vision that often offered an explicit challenge to the interpretations of FAZANG and the mainstream tradition. Li stands outside the orthodox patriarchal lineage of the Huayan school by being a layperson, not a monk, and by being someone interested not just in the profound philosophical implications of the scripture but also its concrete, practical dimensions. In his commentary, Li focuses not on the description of the dimensions of the realm of reality (dharmadhātu; see SI FAJIE) as had Fazang, but instead on SUDHANA's personal quest for enlightenment in the final, and massive, GAṆḌAVYŪHA chapter of the sūtra. Li moved forward the crucial point of soteriological progress from the activation of the thought of enlightenment (BODHICITTOTPĀDA), which he places at the first stage of the ten abidings (shizhu), up to the first level of the ten faiths (shixin), what had previously been considered a preliminary stage of the Huayan path (MĀRGA). Since faith alone was sufficient to generate the understanding that one's own body and mind are identical to the dharmadhātu and are fundamentally equivalent to buddhahood, buddhahood could therefore be experienced in this very life, rather than after three infinite eons (ASAṂKHYEYAKALPA) of training. ¶ Although Li's writings seem to have been forgotten soon after his death, there was an efflorescence of interest in Li Tongxuan during the Song dynasty, when specialists in the Linji school of Chinese CHAN Buddhism (LINJI ZONG), such as JUEFAN HUIHONG (1071–1128) and DAHUI ZONGGAO (1089–1163), and their acquaintance, the scholar-official ZHANG SHANGYING (1043–1121), began to draw on Li's practical orientation toward the *Huayan jing* in order to clarify aspects of Chan practice. In particular, Li's advocacy of "nature origination" (XINGQI) in the *Huayan jing* (rather than conditioned origination of the dharmadhātu [FAJIE YUANQI]) seemed to offer an intriguing sūtra parallel to Chan's emphasis on "seeing the nature" in order to "achieve buddhahood" (JIANXING CHENGFO). In Korea, POJO CHINUL (1158–1210) was strongly influenced by Li Tongxuan's portrayal of Huayan thought, using it to demonstrate his claim that the words of the Buddha in the scriptural teachings of KYO and the mind of the Buddha transmitted by SŎN (C. Chan) were identical. Through Li, Chinul was able to justify his claim of an intrinsic harmony between Sŏn and Kyo. Chinul also wrote two treatises on Li's Huayan thought, including a three-roll abridgement of Li's *Xin Huayan jing lun*, entitled the *Hwaŏm non chŏryo*. In Japan, MYŌE KŌBEN (1173–1232) drew on Li's accounts of the radiance emanating from the Buddha himself, in conjunction with his readings of esoteric Buddhism (MIKKYŌ) and his own prophetic dreams and visionary experiences, to create a distinctive meditative technique called the SAMĀDHI of the Buddha's radiance (Bukkō zanmai). Thus, despite being outside the mainstream of the Huayan tradition, in many ways, Li Tongxuan proved to be its longest lasting, and most influential, exponent. PENG SHAOSHENG (1740–1796), in his JUSHI ZHUAN ("Biographies of [Eminent Laymen"), lists Li Tongxuan as one of the three great lay masters (SANGONG) of Chinese Buddhism, along with PANG YUN (740–803) and LIU CHENGZHI (354–410), praising Li for his mastery of scholastic doctrine (jiao).

**Liu Chengzhi**. (劉程之) (354–410). Chinese lay Buddhist known for his specialization in PURE LAND practice; his cognomen was Liu Yimin. Liu lived in the period between the Eastern Jin and Liu-Song dynasties. He lost his father at a very young age and is said to have waited on his mother with utmost filial piety. An accomplished scholar and civil servant, he eventually resigned his government post to live in solitude in the valleys and forests. Learning about the practice of reciting the Buddha's name (NIANFO) that was then occurring in the community of LUSHAN HUIYUAN (334–416) at DONGLINSI on LUSHAN, Liu Chengzhi moved there, eventually staying for eleven years, concentrating on the practice of reciting the Buddha's name. Eventually, he was able to achieve the samādhi of recitation (NIANFO sanmei), which provoked many spiritual responses. One day, for example, AMITĀBHA appeared before Liu, suffusing Liu with radiant light from his golden body. He subsequently dreamed about the water named Eight Kinds of Merit in the pond of the seven jewels in Amitābha's pure land. Hearing a voice telling him, "You may drink the water," he ingested only a small amount, after which he felt the cool refreshment spread throughout his chest and smelled unusual fragrance emanating from his entire body. The next day, he told Huiyuan that the time had come for him to be reborn in the western pure land and, soon afterwards, he passed away in serenity. PENG SHAOSHENG (1740–1796), in his JUSHI ZHUAN ("Biographies of [Eminent] Laymen"), lists Liu Chengzhi as one of the three great lay masters (SANGONG) of Chinese Buddhism, along with LI TONGXUAN (635–730) and PANG YUN (740–803), praising Liu for his mastery of pure land (JINGTU) practice.

**liuru**. (C) (六如). See LIUYU.

**liuxiang**. (J. rokusō; K. yuksang 六相). In Chinese, "six aspects," "characteristics," or "signs" (LAKṢAṆA) inherent in all DHARMAs, according to the Huayan school (HUAYAN ZONG). Based on their reading of the AVATAṂSAKASŪTRA, Huayan thinkers delineated six "aspects" to all things (with two alternate analogies given for each aspect): (1) The general or generic aspect (zongxiang), e.g., the aggregates (SKANDHA) together make up an individual person, which is the general sum of its parts; alt., being a sentient being is the generic aspect of a person. (2) The constituent or particular aspect (biexiang), e.g., the individual is constituted from the aggregates, which are the constituent parts that make up the sum of the person; alt., the fact that people may be differentiated as wise or fools is their particular characteristic. (3) The identity aspect (tongxiang), e.g., though distinct from one another, the aggregates are all part of this same person; alt., that each person possesses the identical wisdom of the buddhas is their characteristic of identity. (4) The differentiated aspect (yixiang), e.g., though they are of the same person, the aggregates are still distinct from one another; alt., that people have their unique attachments and vices is their characteristic of difference. (5) The collective, or integrated, aspect (chengxiang), e.g., the aggregates function collectively in interdependence one with another, thereby forming an integrated whole, which is the person; alt., that all beings are reborn in congruity with the actions they perform is their characteristic of integration. (6) The instantiated, or destructive, aspect (huaixiang), e.g., though forming a unitary whole in their function, each aggregate functions within its own laws and operational parameters; alt., that the mind ultimately does not abide anywhere is the characteristic of destruction. According to Huayan analysis, the first dyad pertains to the "essence" (TI) of things, the second to their "characteristics" (xiang), and the third to their "function" (YONG). Huayan exegetes argued that, in the enlightened vision of reality, these six aspects of things were seen simultaneously and not as contradictory facets. This vision of the "consummate interfusion" (YUANRONG) of the six aspects is said to occur on the first BHŪMI of the BODHISATTVA path (see BODHISATTVABHŪMI). See also SHISHI WU'AI FAJIE; FAJIE YUANQI.

**liuyu**. (J. rokuyu; K. yugyu 六喩). In Chinese, "six similes," referring to six analogies employed to illustrate the unreality and illusory nature of all DHARMAs, the locus classicus of which appears in the VAJRACCHEDIKĀPRAJÑĀPĀRAMITĀSŪTRA ("Diamond Sūtra"). The existence of all mundane and supramundane dharmas (including NIRVĀṆA and buddhahood) is said to be as evanescent as a "dream," a "phantasm," a "bubble," a "shadow," "morning dew," and "lightning." These similes appear frequently throughout MAHĀYĀNA Buddhist literature. See AṢṬAMĀYOPĀMA.

**liuyu**. (C) (六欲). See QIQING LIUYU.

**Liuzu tan jing**. (J. Rokuso dangyō; K. Yukcho tan kyŏng 六祖壇經). In Chinese, "Platform Sūtra of the Sixth Patriarch," the written transcription of the sermons of the sixth patriarch (LIUZU) HUINENG (638–713); the composition is attributed to the monk FAHAI; also known as the *Nan zong dunjiao zuishang dasheng mohe bore boluomi jing, Liuzu dashi fabao tan jing*, *Fabao tan jing*, or simply *Tan jing* ("Platform Sūtra"). The *Liuzu tan jing* is one of the most influential texts of the CHAN tradition. The text is ostensibly a record of the lectures delivered by the reputed sixth patriarch Huineng at the monastery of Dafansi in Shaozhou (present-day Guangdong province). The lectures contain the famous story of Huineng's verse competition with his rival SHENXIU, which wins Huineng the Chan patriarchy (see ZUSHI), in which Huineng distinguished his own "sudden teachings" (DUNJIAO) of a so-called Southern school (NAN ZONG) of Chan from the "gradual teachings" (jianjiao) of Shenxiu's Northern school (BEI ZONG). As Huineng defines the term later in this sermon, the "sudden teaching" involves an approach to Buddhist training that is free from all dualistic forms of practice (see ADVAYA) and that correspondingly rejects any and all expedient means (UPĀYA) of realizing truth. This sudden teaching comes to be considered emblematic of the so-called Southern school (Nan zong) of Chan, which retrospectively comes to be considered the mainstream of the Chan tradition. The teachings of the text also focus on the unity of concentration (SAMĀDHI) and wisdom (PRAJÑĀ), in which concentration is conceived to be the essence (TI) of wisdom and wisdom the functioning (YONG) of concentration; "no-thought" (WUNIAN), which the text defines as "not to think even when involved in thought"; seeing one's own nature (JIANXING); and the conferral of the formless precepts (WUXIANG JIE). Indeed, the "platform" in the title refers to the ordination platform (jietan; cf. SĪMĀ) where Huineng conferred these formless precepts. Although the *Liuzu tan jing* has been traditionally heralded as the central scripture of the Nan zong, and certainly is beholden to the teachings of the Southern-school champion HEZE SHENHUI, the text seems to have been influenced as well by the teachings of both the Northern and Oxhead schools (NIUTOU ZONG). Within the Chan tradition, a Yuan-dynasty edition of the *Liuzu tan jing*, which included an important preface by FORI QISONG, was most widely disseminated. SIR MARC AUREL STEIN's rediscovery in the DUNHUANG manuscript cache of a previously unknown, and quite different, recension of the text, dating to the mid-ninth century, did much to launch the modern scholarly reappraisal of the received history of the Chan school. See also DUNWU.

**lobha**. (T. chags pa; C. tan; J. ton; K. t'am 貪). In Sanskrit and Pāli, "craving," or "greed," a synonym of RĀGA ("sensuality" or "desire") and the opposite of "absence of craving" or "absence of greed" (ALOBHA). Lobha is one of the most ubiquitous of the defilements (KLEŚA) and is listed among six fundamental afflictions (KLEŚAMAHĀBHŪMIKA), ten fetters (SAṂYOJANA), ten proclivities (ANUŚAYA), five hindrances (ĀVARAṆA), three poisons (TRIVIṢA), and three unwholesome faculties (AKUŚALAMŪLA). Lobha is also one of the forty-six mental factors (see CAITTA) according to the VAIBHĀṢIKA school of SARVĀSTIVĀDA abhidharma, one of the fifty-one according to the YOGACĀRA school, and one of the fifty-two in the Pāli abhidhamma. When sensory contact with objects is made "without proper comprehension" or "without introspection" (ASAMPRAJANYA), craving (lobha), aversion (DVEṢA), and delusion (MOHA) arise. In the case of craving—which is a psychological reaction associated with the pursuing, possessing, or yearning for a pleasing stimulus and discontent with unpleasant stimuli—this greed could target a host of possible objects. Scriptural accounts list these objects of craving as sensual pleasures, material belongings, loved ones, fame, the five aggregates (SKANDHA), speculative views (DṚṢṬI), the meditative absorptions (DHYĀNA) of the "subtle-materiality" and "immaterial" realms (see TRILOKADHĀTU), the future "becoming" (BHAVA) of the "self" (S. bhavarāga), and the future "annihilation" of the "self" (S. abhavarāga), among other things. According to the ĀGAMAS and the ABHIDHARMAKOŚABHĀṢYA, craving is the self-imposed "yoking together" of the subject and its object, whereby the mind is "mired," "bonded," and "burdened" by desire. As one of the three unwholesome faculties (AKUŚALAMŪLA), craving is said to be the common ground or source of a variety of unwholesome mental states, such as possessiveness (MĀTSARYA) and pride (MADA).

**Lo chen Dharma Shri**. (1654–1717). Eminent scholar of the RNYING MA sect of Tibetan Buddhism. He was the younger brother of the founder of SMIN GROL GLING monastery, GTER BDAG GLING PA. More scholarly than his older brother, his collected works cover the entire range of traditional subjects, including astrology, VINAYA, and TANTRA, filling twenty volumes. Particularly important is his detailed explanation of Mnga' ris paṇ chen Padma dbang rgyal's (Ngari Panchen Pema Wangyel) SDOM GSUM RNAM NGES, his *Sdom pa gsum rnam par nges pa'i 'grel ba legs bshad ngo mtshar dpag bsam gyi snye ma*, the study of which forms the central part of the curriculum of many Rnying ma BSHAD GRWA (monastic schools).

**Lo chen sprul sku**. (Lochen tulku). A Tibetan title for the lineage of incarnations of the famed eleventh-century translator RIN CHEN BZANG PO, the main line of incarnate lamas at BKRA SHIS LHUN PO monastery after that of the PAṆ CHEN LAMA. The appellation is short for lo tsā ba chen po, "great translator" (see LO TSĀ BA).

**logic**. A term used to render Sanskrit YUKTI or NYĀYA, referring in general to the system of reasoning developed by DIGNĀGA and DHARMAKĪRTI that sets forth the constituents of correct reasoning and how such reasoning results in inference (ANUMĀNA). See also HETUVIDYĀ, LAKṢAṆA, LIṄGA.

**Lohapāsāda**. The ordination (P. uposatha; S. UPOṢADHA) hall of the MAHĀVIHĀRA monastery in ANURĀDHAPURA, Sri Lanka. Originally a small structure built by the Sri Lankan king DEVĀNAṂPIYATISSA in the third century BCE, King DUṬṬHAGĀMAṆĪ rebuilt it in the first century BCE, this time as a celebrated nine-story edifice with one hundred rooms on each floor, the four upper floors of which were reserved for ARHATS. The Lohapāsāda was restored and renovated numerous times. In the fourth century CE, King MAHĀSENA, under the advice of the heretical monk, Saṅghamitta, had the Lohapāsāda torn down and its materials reused for construction within the rival ABHAYAGIRI monastery. Mahāsena's son, Sirimeghavaṇṇa, in an effort to make amends for his father's misdeed, ordered the Lohapāsāda to be reconstructed on its original spot within the Mahāvihāra compound. BUDDHAGHOSA, the fifth-century commentator, describes the Lohapāsāda and its prominence as place of religious preaching and instruction. It was restored a final time in the twelfth century by King PARĀKRAMABĀHU I, after it had been sacked by Cōḷa invaders. Thereafter, the Lohapāsāda fell into ruin and has remained in that state until today. The site is marked by twelve hundred stone pillars which are believed to have supported the first terrace of the structure.

**Lohiccasutta**. (C. Luzhe jing; J. Roshakyō; K. Noch'a kyŏng 露遮經). In Pāli, "Discourse to Lohicca," the twelfth sutta of the Pāli DĪGHANIKĀYA (a separate DHARMAGUPTAKA recension appears as the twenty-ninth SŪTRA in the Chinese translation of the DĪRGHĀGAMA); preached by the Buddha to the brāhmaṇa Lohicca at the village of Sālavatikā in KOŚALA. According to the Pāli account, Lohicca holds the view that a sage who reaches certain wholesome states of mind should tell no one of it, for to do so would be to manifest craving and entangle him in new bonds. He puts this opinion to the Buddha who responds that, to the contrary, it would be selfish for such a person to remain silent if he had something of benefit to teach to others. The Buddha then describes three types of teachers who are worthy of blame. The first is one who, even though he himself has not attained true renunciation, teaches DHARMA and VINAYA to others but is rejected along with his teachings by his pupils. The second is one who, even though he himself has not attained true renunciation, is embraced along with his teachings by his pupils. The third is one who, even though he himself has attained true renunciation, is nevertheless rejected along with his teachings by his pupils. The Buddha then describes the teacher who is unworthy of blame as someone who awakens to the dharma and enters the Buddhist order, trains in the restraint of conduct and speech and observes minor points of morality, guards the senses, practices mindfulness, is content with little, becomes freed from the five hindrances (NĪVARAṆA), attains joy and peace of mind, cultivates the four meditative absorptions (DHYĀNA), develops insight (P. ñāṇadassana; JÑĀNADARŚANA) into the conditioned nature and the impermanence of body and mind, and gains knowledge of the FOUR NOBLE TRUTHS (CATVĀRY ĀRYASATYĀNI) and the destruction of the contaminants (ĀSRAVA). Lohicca is pleased by the sermon and becomes a lay disciple of the Buddha.

**loka**. (T. 'jig rten; C. shijie/shijian; J. sekai/seken; K. segye/segan 世界/世間). In Sanskrit and Pāli, "world," or "realm"; a polysemous term with a wide range of literal and figurative senses. Literally, loka is used to refer to a specific realm of various types of beings as well as more broadly to an entire world system (see LOKADHĀTU, TRAIDHĀTUKA), with Mount SUMERU at the center; the term can also refer collectively to the inhabitants of such a world. In a figurative sense, loka carries many of the connotations of "world" in English ("worldly," "mundane") to refer to SAṂSĀRA and its qualities, which, although attractive to the unenlightened, are subject to impermanence (ANITYA). Such a world is contrasted with what is, lit. "beyond the world" or LOKOTTARA, a term used to describe the "supramundane" aspirations and achievements of those seeking liberation.

**lokadharma**. (P. lokadhamma; T. 'jig rten gyi chos; C. shifa; J. sehō; K. sebŏp 世法). In Sanskrit, "worldly factors," a polysemous term that in its most general sense indicates mundane factors (DHARMA) that arise and cease according to causes and conditions (HETUPRATYAYA). The term also refers to worldly ways and principles, which can be summed up as the process of birth, decay, and death. However, in its most common usage, the term lokadharma is understood as referring to eight worldly conditions or states (AṢṬALOKADHARMA) that govern all of mundane life in this world: gain (lābha) and loss (alābha), fame (yaśas) and disgrace (ayaśas), praise (praśaṃsā) and blame (nindā), and happiness (SUKHA) and suffering (DUḤKHA). Each of these states will inevitably befall any sentient being trapped in the cycle of continued existence (SAṂSĀRA). In this schema, the lokadharma are understood as four complimentary pairs: gain (lābha) is the inevitable precursor of loss (alābha) and loss the inevitable outcome of gain; and so forth for the other three pairs. Learning to react with equanimity to each of these worldly conditions will lead to nonattachment and ultimately enlightenment.

**lokadhātu**. (T. 'jig rten pa'i khams; C. shijie; J. sekai; K. segye 世界). In Sanskrit and Pāli, "worldly realm" or "world system"; a cosmos within SAṂSĀRA that consists of the four continents, a central Mount SUMERU, etc. See AVACARA; TRAIDHĀTUKA.

***Lokakṣema**. (C. Zhi Loujiachan; J. Shi Rukasen; K. Chi Rugach'am 支婁迦讖) (c. 178–198 CE). A pioneering translator of Indic Buddhist materials into Chinese. Lokakṣema was an Indo-Scythian monk from the KUSHAN kingdom in the GANDHĀRA region of northwest India, who was active in China sometime in the last quarter of the second century CE, soon after the Parthian translator AN SHIGAO. His Sanskrit name is a tentative reconstruction of the Chinese transcription Loujiachan, and he is often known in the literature by the abbreviated form Zhi Chan (using the ethnikon ZHI). Lokakṣema is said to have arrived in the Chinese capital of Luoyang in 167 CE, where he began to render Indic Buddhist sūtras into Chinese. Some fourteen works in twenty-seven rolls are typically ascribed to him (although the numbers given in the literature vary widely), of which twelve are generally presumed to be authentic. The translations thought to be genuine include the first Chinese renderings of sūtras from some of the earliest strata of Indic MAHĀYĀNA literature, including the AṢṬASĀHASRIKĀPRAJÑĀPĀRAMITĀ (*Xiaopin bore jing*), the KĀŚYAPAPARIVARTA (*Yi rimonibao jing*), the PRATYUTPANNABUDDHASAṂMUKHĀVASTHITASAMĀDHISŪTRA (*Banzhou sanmei jing*), and the AKṢOBHYATATHĀGATASYAVYŪHA (*Achu foguo jing*). Given the time of his arrival in China, the Indic texts on which his translations were based must already have been in circulation in Kushan territory by at least 150 CE, giving a terminus ad quem for their composition. Rendered into a kind of pidgin Chinese, these "translations" may actually have targeted not Chinese readers but instead an émigré community of Kushan immigrants who had lost their ability to read Indic languages.

**lokapāla**. (T. 'jig rten skyong ba; C. si tianwang; J. shitennō; K. sa ch'ŏnwang 四天王). In Sanskrit, "world guardians" or "protectors of the world"; an alternate name for the four "great kings" (mahārāja) of heaven, who were converted by the Buddha and entrusted with protecting the inhabitants of the world. The world guardians reside in the first and lowest of the six heavens of the sensuous realm of existence (KĀMADHĀTU), the heaven of the four great kings (CĀTURMAHĀRĀJAKĀYIKA). They are vassals of ŚAKRA, the lord or king (INDRA) of the gods (DEVA) (ŚAKRO DEVĀNĀM INDRAḤ), who is lord of the heaven of the thirty-three devas (TRĀYASTRIṂŚA), the second of the six sensuous realm heavens, which is located at the summit of the world's central axis of Mount SUMERU. The world guardians' names are (1) DHṚTARĀṢṬRA, who guards the gate to the east at the midslope of Mount Sumeru, which leads to the continent of VIDEHA; (2) VIRŪḌHAKA in the south, who guards the gate that leads to JAMBUDVĪPA; (3) VIRŪPĀKṢA in the west, who guards the gate that leads to GODĀNĪYA; and (4) VAIŚRAVAṆA in the north, who guards the gate that leads to UTTARAKURU. Of the eight classes of demigods, who are subservient to the world guardians, Dhṛtarāṣṭra rules over the GANDHARVA and pūtana; Virūḍhaka over the KUMBHĀṆḌA and PRETA; Virūpākṣa over the NĀGA and PIŚĀCA; and Vaiśravaṇa over the YAKṢA and RĀKṢASA. The four world guardians began as indigenous Indian or Central Asian deities, who were eventually incorporated into Buddhism; they seem to have been originally associated with royal (KṢATRIYA) lineages, and their connections with royal warfare are evidenced in the suits of armor they come to wear as their cult is transmitted from Central Asia to China, Korea, and Japan.

**Lokātītastava**. (T. 'Jig rten las 'das par bstod pa). In Sanskrit, "In Praise of the Supramundane One"; an Indian philosophical work written in the form of a praise of the Buddha by the MADHYAMAKA master NĀGĀRJUNA. In the Tibetan tradition, there are a large number of such praises (called bstod tshogs or STAVAKĀYA), in contrast to the set of philosophical texts (called rigs tshogs or YUKTIKĀYA) attributed to Nāgārjuna, among which the ACINTYASTAVA, *Lokātītastava*, NIRAUPAMYASTAVA, and PARAMĀRTHASTAVA are extant in Sanskrit and generally accepted to be his work; these four works together are known as the CATUḤSTAVA. It is less certain that he is the author of the DHARMADHĀTUSTAVA ("Hymn to the Dharmadhātu") of which only fragments are available in the original. The *Lokātītastava* is a work in twenty-eight verses. The first part of the text refutes the independent existence of the aggregates (SKANDHA) that constitute the person; the second part of the text refutes the ultimate existence of the world; and the third part states that the knowledge of emptiness (ŚŪNYATĀ) leads to liberation. The content of the work accords with that of the MŪLAMADHYAMAKAKĀRIKĀ, although here, the Buddha is addressed directly and quoted in many of the stanzas.

**Lokāyata**. (T. 'Jig rten rgyang phan pa; C. Shunshi waidao; J. Junse gedō; K. Sunse oedo 順世外道). In Sanskrit and Pāli, "Naturalist" or "Worldly" school; one of the major early schools of the Indian movement of wandering religious (ŚRAMAṆA), which is mentioned occasionally in Buddhist scriptures. Its founding is attributed to the legendary figure Bṛhaspati, but during the Buddha's lifetime, its most prominent exponent was AJITA Keśakambala. The Lokāyata school is claimed to have taken a rigidly materialist perspective toward the world, in which everything in the universe, including consciousness, was composed only of the four elements (MAHĀBHŪTA) of earth, water, heat, and air. Since everything occurs spontaneously through the interaction of its inherent material properties, the Lokāyatas advocated a "natural," even laissez-faire, attitude toward conduct (yadṛcchāvāda), in which the summum bonum of existence was thought to be sensual pleasure (KĀMA). As a materialist school, the Lokāyatas also denied the efficacy of moral cause and effect because of its rejection of any prospect of transmigration or rebirth.

**lokeśvara**. (T. 'jig rten dbang phyug; C. shizizai; J. sejizai; K. sejajae 世自在). In Sanskrit, "lord of the world"; a polysemous term in a Buddhist context. Lokeśvara is one of the many titles of respect given to a buddha. The term also denotes several different divinities (DEVA) who are worshipped or called upon for favor; many of these gods were assimilated from the ancient Indian pantheon. Thus, the term can refer to any number of deities that are invoked by Buddhist practitioners. Lokeśvara is also one of the common variant names of the BODHISATTVA AVALOKITEŚVARA. Finally, LOKEŚVARARĀJA is the name of one of the fifty-three buddhas of the past mentioned in the SUKHĀVATĪVYŪHASŪTRA and the one who gave the prediction of future buddhahood to DHARMĀKARA, the eventual buddha AMITĀBHA.

**Lokeśvararāja**. (T. 'Jig rten dbang phyug rgyal po; C. Guanzizai wang rulai/Shizizai wang fo; J. Kanjizaiō nyorai/Sejizaiō butsu; K. Kwanjajae wang yŏrae/Sejajae wang pul 觀自在王如來/世自在王佛). Sanskrit proper name of one of the fifty-three buddhas of the past listed in the SUKHĀVATĪVYŪHASŪTRA (*Wuliangshou jing*); Lokeśvararāja is the one who displayed millions of buddha fields (BUDDHAKṢETRA) to DHARMĀKARA and who gave the monk the prediction of his future buddhahood (VYĀKARAṆA). Dharmakāra then selected the best qualities of each of these buddha lands and combined them into his conception of a single buddha field, which he described to Lokeśvararāja in terms of forty-eight vows. Dharmakāra subsequently completed the path of the bodhisattva to become the buddha AMITĀBHA, and his buddha field, or PURE LAND, became SUKHĀVATĪ.

**lokiyasamādhi**. (S. laukikasamādhi; T. 'jig rten pa'i ting nge 'dzin; C. shunshi sanmei; J. junse sanmai; K. sunse sammae 順世三昧). In Pāli, "mundane concentration," or "worldly concentration"; any type of mental concentration that is disassociated from the four paths (P. magga; S. MĀRGA) and four fruits (PHALA) of liberation. The term denotes all moments of concentration that are involved in ordinary mundane consciousness, whether virtuous or nonvirtuous, and states of meditative absorption (P. JHĀNA; S. DHYĀNA) cultivated through tranquillity meditation (P. samathabhāvanā; S. ŚAMATHA), which do not as yet involve insight or wisdom (P. paññā; S. PRAJÑĀ). See also LOKUTTARASAMĀDHI.

**lokottara**. (P. lokuttara; T. 'jig rten las 'das pa; C. chushijian; J. shusseken; K. ch'ulsegan 出世間). In Sanskrit, lit. "beyond the world"; "supramundane," "transcendent"; viz., something that is related to attaining liberation (VIMOKṢA) from SAṂSĀRA or that leads to such liberation. The term also can indicate a certain level of spiritual maturity, such as when the practitioner is no longer subject to the contaminants (ĀSRAVA). In the context of the status of practitioners, mundane (LAUKIKA) refers to ordinary beings; more specifically, in the fifty-two stage bodhisattva path, laukika usually indicates practitioners who are at the stage of the ten faiths (C. shixin), ten understandings (C. shijie), or ten practices (C. shixing), while "supramundane" (lokottara) refers to more enlightened practitioners, such as BODHISATTVAs who are on the ten stages (DAŚABHŪMI). FAZANG's HUAYAN WUJIAO ZHANG ("Essay on the Five Teachings according to Huayan") parses these stages even more precisely: of the ten stages (daśabhūmi) of the path leading to buddhahood, stages one through three belong to the mundane (laukika); the fourth to the seventh stages are supramundane from the standpoint of the three vehicles (TRIYĀNA) of ŚRĀVAKA, PRATYEKABUDDHA, and BODHISATTVA; and the eighth to the tenth stages transcend even the supramundane and belong to the one vehicle (EKAYĀNA). The LOKOTTARAVĀDA (Teaching of Transcendence), a subschool of the MAHĀSĀṂGHIKA school of mainstream Buddhism, took its name from its advocacy of the supramundane qualities of the Buddha and the univocality of the BUDDHAVACANA. The school's emblematic text, the MAHĀVASTU, claims that all the seemingly mundane acts of the Buddha are in fact supramundane; hence, although the Buddha may appear to eat and sleep, walk and talk like ordinary people, he in fact remains constantly in a state of meditation because he is free from all needs.

**Lokottaravāda**. (P. Lokuttaravāda; T. 'Jig rten 'das par smra ba; C. Shuochushibu; J. Setsushussebu; K. Sŏlch'ulsebu 說出世部). In Sanskrit, lit. "Teaching of Transcendence," meaning "Those Who Teach [that the Buddha and the BUDDHAVACANA] are Transcendent," the name of one of the three main branches of the MAHĀSĀṂGHIKA school of mainstream Buddhism; also known as the EKAVYAVAHĀRIKA ("Those Who Make a Single Utterance"). (Note that the Chinese translation suggests that the school should properly be called the Lokottaranikāya.) The name for the school comes from its distinguishing doctrine: that the Buddha articulates all of his teachings in a single utterance that is altogether transcendent or supramundane (LOKOTTARA). Later interpretations of the school also suggest that its name may derive from the fact that all the things of this world can be described in a single utterance because those phenomena are nothing more than mental constructions or have merely provisional reality. The Lokottaravāda position is in distinction to two rival schools that derive from the KAUKKUṬIKA branch of the Mahāsāṃghika: the BAHUŚRUTĪYA, who asserted that the buddhavacana includes both transcendent and provisional teachings; and the PRAJÑAPTIVĀDA, who asserted that the Buddha taught not only transcendent truths but also employed provisional designations (PRAJÑAPTI) and concepts to frame his teachings for his audience. The Lokottaravāda is now primarily known as the school that composed the MAHĀVASTU, a biography of the Buddha that is the earliest extant text of BUDDHIST HYBRID SANSKRIT. The *Mahāvastu* claims that all the seemingly mundane acts of the Buddha are in fact transcendent; hence, although the Buddha may appear to function like ordinary people, he in fact remains constantly in a state of meditation.

**lokuttaramagga**. (S. lokottaramārga; T. 'jig rten las 'das pa'i lam; C. chushi dao; J. shussedō; K. ch'ulse to 出世道). In Pāli, "supramundane path"; four stages of "attainment" along the noble path (S. ĀRYAMĀRGA) of enlightened persons (S. ĀRYAPUDGALA); viz., the path of stream-enterer (S. srotaāpattimārga), the path of once-returner (S. sakṛdāgāmimārga), the path of nonreturner (S. anāgāmimārga), and the path of the worthy (S. arhanmārga). The four supramundane paths are combined with four supramundane fruitions (LOKUTTARAPHALA) to make eight stages of holiness altogether.

**lokuttaraphala**. (S. lokottaraphala; T. 'jig rten las 'das pa'i 'bras bu; C. chushi guo; J. shusseka; K. ch'ulse kwa 出世果). In Pāli, "supramundane fruition"; four stages of "enjoyment" along the noble path (S. ĀRYAMĀRGA) of noble persons (S. ĀRYAPUDGALA); viz., the fruition of stream-enterer (S. srotaāpattiphala), fruition of once-returner (S. sakṛdāgāmiphala), fruition of nonreturner (anāgāmiphala), and fruition of the worthy one (S. arhatphala). The four supramundane fruitions are combined with four supramundane paths (LOKUTTARAMAGGA) to make a total of eight stages of sanctity. See ĀRYAMĀRGAPHALA; ĀRYAPUDGALA.

**lokuttarasamādhi**. (S. lokottarasamādhi; T. 'jig rten las 'das pa'i ting nge 'dzin; C. chushi sanmei; J. shusse sanmai; K. ch'ulse sammae 出世三昧). In Pāli, "supramundane concentration"; concentration associated with the attainment of any of the four paths (magga, S. MĀRGA) and/or four fruitions (PHALA) of enlightenment, which constitute collectively eight moments along the path to complete liberation from SAṂSĀRA. The eight moments in order of their occurrence are the (1) path and (2) fruition of a stream-enterer (S. SROTAĀPANNA), the (3) path and (4) fruition of a once-returner (S. SAKṚDĀGĀMIN), the (5) path and (6) fruition of a nonreturner (S. ANĀGĀMIN), and the (7) path and (8) fruition of a worthy one (S. ARHAT). All other forms of concentration not associated with the paths and fruits of enlightenment are deemed of this world or "mundane concentrations" (LOKIYASAMĀDHI). Supramundane concentration is also characterized by its singular object, NIRVĀṆA.

**Longchisi**. (龍池寺). In Chinese, "Monastery of the Dragon Pool"; located on ZHONGNANSHAN near the former Chinese capital of Chang'an (present-day Xi'an). According to DAOXUAN (596–667 CE), in 601 CE a Buddhist monk named Daopan (532–615 CE) assembled some disciples around a pond by Mt. Zhongnan, where they built this monastery. The name refers to the legend of a dragon king (see NĀGA), who flooded an entire kingdom so that he could use it as a pool in which to reside. He was later converted to Buddhism by MADHYĀNTIKA, one of ĀNANDA's two main disciples. In another account, it is said that the monastery already existed when Emperor Wen (r. 581–604 CE) of the Sui dynasty ordered its renovation in 587 CE, whereupon it was given the name Longchi Monastery. In this account, Daopan was already in residence at the monastery, which enjoyed the patronage of several influential court officials. Many eminent monks in addition to Daopan are buried here. They include Kongzang (569–642 CE), Huiman (589–642 CE), Jingxuan (569–611 CE), Huizan (536–607 CE), and Pukuang (548–620). It is also said that the HUAYAN master FAZANG (643–712 CE) was active at the monastery, where, at the behest of the Tang Emperor Ruizong (r. 684–690 CE and 710–712 CE), he famously performed a ritual to pray for snow in order to stave off a severe drought the region was experiencing. (There are conflicting accounts, however, as to whether this event occurred at Longchisi or WUZHENSI.)

**Longmen**. (龍門). In Chinese, lit. "Dragon Gate," an important Buddhist cave site located 7.5 miles south of the ancient Chinese capital of Luoyang in China's Henan province. Spanning over half a mile along a cliff above the Yi River, the Longmen grottoes contain some of the most spectacular examples of stone sculpture in China, together with the MOGAO KU near DUNHUANG, the YUNGANG grottoes at Datong, and the Dazu caves (DAZU SHIKE) outside the city of Chongqing. The first grotto at Longmen was excavated in 495 CE when the Northern Wei capital was moved from Datong to Luoyang. Construction at the site continued until the site was abandoned in 755 because of civil strife and reflects a period of intense Buddhist activity in China that lasted through the Tang and Northern Song dynasties. A total of 2,345 grottoes were excavated and carved, which include more than one hundred thousand Buddhist images, some three thousand inscribed tablets, and over forty pagodas. Although largely an imperial site, some of the individual caves and niches were commissioned by the local Buddhist laity. Fengxiansi, the largest of the Longmen grottoes, dates to the Tang dynasty. When that chapel was first constructed, a roof is thought to have enclosed the entire cliff face. Today, the roof no longer remains and the sculptures stand unprotected in the open air. In 2000, the Longmen grottoes were placed on the list of UNESCO World Heritage sites. See also BINGLINGSI.

**lo tsā ba**. (lotsawa). In Tibetan, "translator," used especially as an epithet for the Tibetan translators of the earlier dissemination (SNGA DAR) and later dissemination (PHYI DAR) of dharma in Tibet, who translated Buddhist texts from Sanskrit into Tibetan. The term may be a Tibetan phonetic rendering of the Sanskrit lokaścakṣus, "eye of the world." The title is often abbreviated simply as lo and appended at the beginning of the names of many of the early translators.

**lotus flower**. See PADMA.

**lotus posture**. See VAJRAPARYAṄKA; PADMĀSANA.

**Lotus Sūtra**. See SADDHARMAPUṆḌARĪKASŪTRA.

**lta ba nyon mongs can**. (S. dṛṣṭisaṃkleśa). In Tibetan, "defiled view" (see DṚṢṬI), a term for the fifth of the six ANUŚAYA ("proclivities") set forth as the basic afflictions or defilements (KLEŚA) in the ABHIDHARMAKOŚABHĀṢYA. It differentiates dṛṣṭi in the negative sense of "speculative opinions" from dṛṣṭi in the positive sense of "right view" (see SAMYAGDṚṢṬI). These defiled views are subdivided into five types of wrong views (pañcadṛṣṭi): SATKĀYADṚṢṬI (view that there is a perduring self), ANTAGRĀHADṚṢṬI (extreme views of permanence or annihilation), MITHYĀDṚṢṬI (fallacious views denying the efficacy of KARMAN, rebirth, and causality), DṚṢṬIPARĀMARŚA (clinging to one's own wrong views as being superior), and ŚĪLAVRATAPARĀMARŚA (belief in the efficacy of rites and rituals). All are eliminated by the path of vision (DARŚANAMĀRGA).

**Luang Prabang**. Ancient royal capital of the kingdom of Laos and one of the major historical centers of Laotian Buddhism. Originally named Muang Sua, the region was a frequent locus of political contestation and was periodically under the suzerainty of the Nanzhao kingdom in southern China, the Chams from Vietnam, the Khmer kingdom in Cambodia, and the Thais. In 1353, the city became the initial capital of the Lao Lan Xang kingdom (1353–1707) and after the demise of that state became the center of an independent Luang Prabang kingdom. After the French annexed Laos, Luang Prabang continued to be maintained as the royal residence. The city is a collection of districts, each of which is built around a central monastery. The city includes thirty-three major Buddhist monasteries (wat), which are built in a distinctive style, with tiered roofs, pillared porticos, and embellished from top to bottom with exceedingly elaborate ornamentation. One of the most important of the monasteries is Wat Xieng Thong, which was constructed in 1560 on the northern peninsula of the city and includes a rare image of a reclining buddha that is said to date from the monastery's founding. Luang Prabang was designated a UNESCO World Heritage Site in 1995 and has emerged as a major center of Buddhist tourism in Southeast Asia.

**Lumbinī**. (T. Lum bi'i tshal/Lum bi ni; C. Lanpini yuan; J. Ranbinion; K. Nambini wŏn 藍毘尼園). In Sanskrit and Pāli, the name of the Buddha's birthplace, now Rummindei in the Terai Region of modern Nepal. The Buddha's mother MĀYĀ was traveling from her home in KAPILAVASTU to her parents' home to give birth when she went into labor at Lumbinī. According to traditional accounts, she gave birth while standing between twin ŚĀLA trees. It is said that the Buddha stepped out of her right side and was born. (His conception had been similarly miraculous: the Buddha entered his mother's womb in the form of a white elephant.) The moment after the Buddha's birth, both mother and child were washed with water by divinities, the legendary origin of "bathing the infant Buddha" ceremonies that occur during the festival celebrating the Buddha's birth in numerous Buddhist cultures. As soon as he was born, he is claimed to have taken seven steps and declared that he was unrivalled on heaven and earth (see SIṂHANĀDA). As with all mothers of prospective buddhas, Māyā died seven days after the birth of her son. Queen Māyā's sister MAHĀPRAJĀPATĪ, another wife of his father King ŚUDDHODANA, would serve as the Buddha's wet nurse and foster mother and eventually become the founder of the order of nuns (BHIKṢUṆĪ). The mainstream MAHĀPARINIRVĀṆASŪTRA (P. MAHĀPARINIBBĀNASUTTA) recognizes Lumbinī as the first of the four principal pilgrimage sites (MAHĀSTHĀNA) Buddhists should frequent to recollect the achievements of the Buddha and to "arouse emotion in the faithful" along with BODHGAYĀ, where the Buddha attained enlightenment; the Deer Park (MṚGADĀVA) at ṚṢIPATANA (SĀRNĀTH), where he first "turned the wheel of the dharma" (DHARMACAKRAPRAVARTANA); and KUŚINAGARĪ, where he passed away into PARINIRVĀṆA. Lumbinī is still frequented today by Buddhist pilgrims from all over the world.

**luohan**. (J. rakan; K. nahan 羅漢). In Chinese, ARHAT, referring to groups of venerated disciples of the Buddha who in their popular forms served as objects of cultic worship in East Asia. Countless paintings and statues of arhats were created, and legends and miracle stories concerning them circulated throughout the East Asian region. The arhats were commonly worshipped in groups of sixteen, eighteen, and five hundred, the last two of which developed without a canonical basis. Especially important was the cult of sixteen (later sometimes expanded to eighteen) arhat disciples (see ṢOḌAŚASTHAVIRA), whom the Buddha ordered to forgo PARINIRVĀṆA and to continue to dwell in this world in order to preserve the Buddhist teachings until the coming of the future buddha, MAITREYA. Each of these arhats was assigned a residence and a retinue of disciples. Once Maitreya had advented on earth, the arhats would be charged with gathering the remaining relics of the current buddha ŚĀKYAMUNI and erecting one last STŪPA to hold them, after which they would finally pass into PARINIRVĀṆA. In China, arhat cults were popular particularly during the medieval period. Statues and paintings of arhats were enshrined throughout the land and Buddhists made offerings before those images. The Wuyue court even sponsored an annual summoning ritual of the five hundred arhats from the tenth century onward. The Song-dynasty court continued to sponsor the same ritual to pray for the welfare of the court and to ward off the evils. In Korea, the Koryŏ (918–1392) court performed a ritual for the five hundred arhats more than twenty-five times between 1053 and the end of the dynasty. The ritual was principally intended to pray for precipitation and protection from foreign invasion. This ritual even continued into the early Chosŏn (1392–1910) period. Still today, most of the larger Korean monasteries will have on their campus an arhat hall (nahan chŏn), which enshrines paintings and/or images, typically of the group of sixteen. In Japan, the arhat cults were especially connected with the ZEN school. In particular, many monasteries associated with the SŌTŌSHŪ have a hall dedicated to the arhats, which usually enshrines images of the sixteen, and the tradition engages in monthly and semiannual rituals dedicated to the arhats. In the Sōtō tradition, arhats are believed to play both salvific and apotropaic roles.

**Luoyang qielan ji**. (J. Rakuyō garanki; K. Nagyang karam ki 洛陽伽藍記). In Chinese, "Record of the Monasteries of Luoyang," written in 547 by Yang Xuanzhi (d.u.) of the Eastern Wei dynasty. (Qielan in the title is an abbreviated Chinese transcription of the Sanskrit term saṃghārāma or monastery; see ĀRĀMA.) This five-roll compilation is a record of forty-five great monasteries that flourished in or around the Chinese capital of Luoyang during the previous Northern Wei dynasty. The number of monasteries in the vicinity of Luoyang grew from forty-two during the Yongjia reign (307–313) of the Jin dynasty to 1,367 during the Northern Wei period; after the Wei moved its capital from Luoyang to Ye in 534, however, the number rapidly declined to 421. After witnessing the decline of Buddhism in the city during his visit in 547, Yang Xuanzhi decided to record in as much detail as he could the splendor of the monasteries that had once flourished in Luoyang. Yang provides a meticulous description of the founder, scenery, layout, and landscape of each of the great monasteries, as well as the icons and tablets housed inside the different basilicas and shrines on each monastic campus. Whenever possible, he also includes a brief account of ceremonies and services observed at the monasteries. The *Luoyang qielan ji* is an invaluable source of information on Northern Wei Buddhist institutions.

**Lushan**. (J. Rozan; K. Yŏsan 廬山). A Chinese sacred mountain located near Poyang Lake in present-day Jiangxi province. Lushan, or Cottage Mountain, is a scenic place that was long frequented by Daoist practitioners and known as the abode of Daoist perfected. AN SHIGAO, the early Parthian translator of Chinese Buddhist texts, is also said to have resided on the mountain during the Eastern Han dynasty. At the end of the fourth century CE, the Chinese monk DAO'AN is known to have established the monastery Xilinsi (Western Grove Monastery) on the mountain. A decade or so later, his famed disciple LUSHAN HUIYUAN also came to the mountain and established the influential monastery DONGLINSI (Eastern Grove Monastery). On a peak named the "PRAJÑĀ Terrace," Huiyuan enshrined an image of the buddha AMITĀBHA for worship and contemplation. Together with 123 colleagues, Huiyuan established the White Lotus Society (BAILIAN SHE), which was dedicated to Amitābha worship. Due especially to Huiyuan's influence, Lushan emerged as an important site for the cult of Amitābha and his PURE LAND (see SUKHĀVATĪ). During the Song dynasty, Lushan became the home of the CHAN master HUANGLONG HUINAN (1002–1069) and his disciples in the HUANGLONG PAI of the LINJI ZONG. In 1147, Donglin Changcong (1025–1091), one of Huanglong's chief disciples and recipient of the imperial purple robe, was appointed by the court to assume to abbotship of Donglinsi, which had been officially recognized as a public Chan cloister (chanyuan) in 1079. During his visit to Lushan, the renowned poet Su Shi (1037–1101) is said to have attained awakening under Changcong's guidance. In 1616, the Chan master HANSHAN DEQING established the monastery Fayunsi on Lushan's Wuru peak. Lushan continues to serve today as an important pilgrimage site for Chinese Buddhists.

**Lushan Huiyuan**. (J. Rozan Eon; K. Yŏsan Hyewŏn 廬山慧遠) (334–416). Chinese monk during the Six Dynasties period, who was an important early advocate of PURE LAND cultic practices. Huiyuan was a native of Yanmen in present-day Shanxi province. In 345, he is said to have visited the prosperous cities of Xuchang and Luoyang, where he immersed himself in the study of traditional Confucian and Daoist scriptures. In 354, Huiyuan met the translator and exegete DAO'AN on Mt. Heng (present-day Hebei province), where he was ordained, and became his student. Huiyuan seems to have primarily studied PRAJÑĀPĀRAMITĀ thought under Dao'an. In 381, Huiyuan headed south for LUSHAN, a mountain widely known as the abode of Daoist perfected and an ideal site for self-cultivation. There, he established the monastery DONGLINSI (Eastern Grove Monastery), which soon became the center of Buddhist activity in the south. Huiyuan is also known to have attracted a large lay following, consisting largely of educated members of the local gentry. He also began corresponding with the eminent monk KUMĀRAJĪVA to clarify certain issues (e.g., the nature of the DHARMAKĀYA) in MAHĀYĀNA doctrine. These correspondences were later edited together as the DASHENG DAYI ZHANG. In 402, together with 123 other monks and laymen, Huiyuan is said to have contemplated on an image of the buddha AMITĀBHA in order to seek rebirth in his pure land of SUKHĀVATĪ. This gathering is known as the beginning of the White Lotus Society (BAILIAN SHE). He should be distinguished from the commentator JINGYING HUIYUAN.

**lus med mkha' 'gro snyan brgyud chos skor dgu**. (lüme kadro nyengyu chökorgu). In Tibetan, "the nine teachings from the aural lineage of the formless ḌĀKINĪ"; a series of brief one-line instructions that the Indian SIDDHA TILOPA received from the formless display of reality. Tilopa passed these instructions to his disciple NĀROPA, who in turn passed them in part to his disciple MAR PA CHOS KYI BLO GROS and later, in full, to the Indian master TI PHU PA (said to be the miraculous reincarnation of his son). Mar pa transmitted four of the nine to his disciple MI LA RAS PA who then famously sent his disciple RAS CHUNG PA RDO RJE GRAGS to India in order to receive the remaining five from Ti phu pa. These instructions are understood to summarize the entire path of tantric practice and are foundational for many teachings of the BKA' BRGYUD sect of Tibetan Buddhism. The nine are:

1. maturation and liberation: sever the mind's tangled knots (smin grol sems kyi rgya mdud bshig)
2. commitments: look into your own mind, a mirror (dam tshig rang sems me long ltos)
3. channels and their energies: animate the networks and centers (rtsa rlung drwa mig 'khor lo bskor)
4. great bliss: keep the precious gem of speech (bde chen gsung gi rin chen zung)
5. pristine cognition: look with the lamp of primordial awareness (rig pa ye shes sgron me ltos)
6. self-liberation: attend to the great seal (rang grol phyag rgya chen po ltos)
7. sacramental substance: bask in realization's sun (dam rdzas rtogs pa'i nyi ma lde)
8. action: strike the water with a sword (spyod pa chu la ral gri rgyob)
9. equal-taste: gaze into the mirror of externals (ro snyoms phyi'i me long ltos).

**Lü zong**. (J. RISSHŪ; K. Yul chong 律宗). See NANSHAN LÜ ZONG; DONGTA LÜ ZONG; XIANGBU LÜ ZONG.

# M

**mada**. (T. rgyags pa; C. jiao; J. kyō; K. kyo 憍). In Sanskrit and Pāli, "conceit," "arrogance"; one of the forty-six mental factors (CAITTA) according to the VAIBHĀṢIKA school of SARVĀSTIVĀDA ABHIDHARMA and one of the fifty-one according to the YOGĀCĀRA school; it is listed among the twenty secondary afflictions (UPAKLEŚA). Conceit is considered to be a derivative of "passion" (RĀGA), since it entails an arrogant, self-absorbed state of mind that produces an air of superiority, invulnerability, and self-adoration. Some of the conditions that lead to conceit include: (1) one's youth or virility; (2) one's family lineage or social status; (3) one's wealth; (4) one's seemingly autonomous freedom in action; (5) one's apparent longevity and invulnerability to disease; (6) one's intelligence or knowledge; (7) one's virtue or charitable activities; (8) one's physical appearance or personal adornments.

**Madhupiṇḍikasutta**. (C. Miwanyu jing; J. Mitsugan'yukyō; K. Mirhwanyu kyŏng 蜜丸喻經). In Pāli, "Discourse on the Honey Ball," the eighteenth sutta in the MAJJHIMANIKĀYA (a separate SARVĀSTIVĀDA recension appears as the 115th SŪTRA in the Chinese translation of the MADHYAMĀGAMA, along with an untitled recension of unidentified affiliation in the EKOTTARĀGAMA). The Buddha addresses a prince named Daṇḍapāni, describing his teachings as avoiding discord with beings in this world, as indifference to perceptions, as abandoning doubts, and as not craving for existence. The disciple Mahākaccāna (S. MAHĀKĀTYĀYANA) then further explicates the sermon's meaning and the Buddha praises his erudition. The AṬṬHASĀLINĪ cites the *Madhupiṇḍikasutta* as an example of a scripture that, although preached by a disciple, still qualifies as the word of the Buddha (BUDDHAVACANA) because Mahākaccāna's exegesis is based on a synopsis given first by the Buddha. The *Madhupiṇḍikasutta* is best known for its discussion of how the process of sensory perception culminates in conceptual proliferation (P. papañca; S. PRAPAÑCA). Any sentient being will be subject to an impersonal causal process of perception in which consciousness (P. viññāṇa; S. VIJÑĀNA) occurs conditioned by a sense base and a sense object; the contact between these three brings about sensory impingement (P. phassa; S. SPARŚA), which in turn leads to sensation (VEDANĀ). At that point, however, the sense of ego intrudes and this process then becomes an intentional one, whereby what one feels, one perceives (P. saññā; S. SAṂJÑĀ); what one perceives, one thinks about (P. vitakka; S. VITARKA); and what one thinks about, one conceptualizes (papañca). However, by allowing oneself to experience sensory objects not as things-in-themselves but as concepts invariably tied to one's own point of view, the perceiving subject now becomes the hapless object of an inexorable process of conceptual subjugation: viz., what one conceptualizes becomes proliferated conceptually (P. papañcasaññāsaṅkhā; a term apparently unattested in Sanskrit) throughout all of one's sensory experience in the past, present, and future. The consciousness thus ties together everything that can be experienced in this world into a labyrinthine network of concepts, all tied to oneself and projected into the external world as craving (TṚṢṆĀ), conceit (MĀNA), and wrong views (DṚṢṬI), thus creating bondage to SAṂSĀRA. The goal of training is a state of mind in which this tendency toward conceptual proliferation is brought to an end (P. nippapañca; S. NIṢPRAPAÑCA).

**madhyamadeśa**. (P. majjhimadesa; T. yul dbus; C. zhongguo; J. chūgoku; K. chungguk 中國). In Sanskrit, "central land"; a term used to refer to the region of the Buddha's activities in what is today northeastern India, said to encompass an area some nine hundred leagues (YOJANA) in circumference. The term is also used more figuratively to refer to a civilized region, especially a region in which Buddhism has been established. Thus, it is considered to be fortunate not simply to be reborn as a human but to be reborn as a human in such a central region, where one will have ready access to the teachings of Buddhism. See KṢAṆASAṂPAD.

**Madhyamāgama**. (P. Majjhimanikāya; T. Dbu ma'i lung; C. Zhong ahan jing; J. Chūagongyō; K. Chung aham kyŏng 中阿含經). In Sanskrit, the "Medium [Length] Scriptures"; the division of the Sanskrit SŪTRAPIṬAKA corresponding closely to, but also substantially larger, than the MAJJHIMANIKĀYA of the Pāli canon. The *Madhyamāgama* collection is no longer extant in an Indic language but is preserved in its entirety in a Chinese translation made by Gautama Saṃghadeva between 397 and 398; a few fragments of a Sanskrit recension have been discovered (such as at TURFAN), and there are Tibetan translations of some individual sūtras from the collection. The extant Sanskrit fragments are ascribed to the SARVĀSTIVĀDA school; since these fragments correspond closely to the Chinese renderings, it is generally accepted that the Chinese translation of the *Madhyamāgama* represents the Sarvāstivāda school's recension of this collection. The *Madhyamāgama* contains 222 sūtras, eighty of which correspond to suttas in the Pāli AṄGUTTARANIKĀYA, eleven to suttas in the SAṂYUTTANIKĀYA, and twelve to suttas in the DĪGHANIKĀYA. Of the Pāli *Majjhimanikāya's* 152 suttas, ninety-eight have corresponding recensions in the *Madhyamāgama*. See also ĀGAMA.

**Madhyamaka**. (T. Dbu ma pa; C. San lun zong/Zhongguan; J. Sanronshū/Chūgan; K. Sam non chong/Chunggwan 三論宗/中觀). In Sanskrit, "Middle Way (school)"; a proponent or follower of the middle way" (MADHYAMAPRATIPAD); Buddhism is renowned as the middle way between extremes, a term that appears in the Buddha's first sermon (see P. DHAMMACAKKAPPAVATTANASUTTA) in which he prescribed a middle path between the extremes of self-indulgence and self-mortification. Thus, all proponents of Buddhism are in a sense proponents of the middle way, for each school of Buddhist philosophy identifies different versions of the two extremes and charts a middle way between them. The term Madhyamaka has however come to refer more specifically to the school of Buddhist philosophy that sets forth a middle way between the extreme of eternalism (ŚĀŚVATADṚṢṬI) and the extreme of annihilationism (UCCHEDADṚṢṬI). The Madhyamaka school derives from the works of NĀGĀRJUNA, the c. second century CE philosopher who is traditionally regarded as its founder. His major philosophical works, especially his MŪLAMADHYAMAKAKĀRIKĀ (a.k.a. MADHYAMAKAŚĀSTRA), as well as the writings of his disciple ĀRYADEVA, provide the locus classicus for the school (which only seems to have been designated the Madhyamaka school after Āryadeva's time). Commentaries on their works (by such figures as BUDDHAPĀLITA, BHĀVAVIVEKA, and CANDRAKĪRTI) provide the primary medium for philosophical expression in the school. Madhyamaka was highly influential in Tibet, where it was traditionally considered the highest of the four schools of Indian Buddhist philosophy (Madhyamaka, YOGĀCĀRA, SAUTRĀNTIKA, and VAIBHĀṢIKA). Tibetan exegetes discerned two branches in the Madhyamaka, the PRĀSAṄGIKA (associated with Buddhapālita and Candrakīrti) and the SVĀTANTRIKA (associated with Bhāvaviveka and ŚĀNTARAKṢITA). The works of Nāgārjuna and Āryadeva were also widely studied in East Asia, forming the basis of the "Three Treatises" school (C. SAN LUN ZONG; K. Sam non chong; J. Sanronshū), where the three treatises are the ZHONG LUN (the "Middle Treatise," or *Madhyamakaśāstra*), the SHI'ERMEN LUN ("Twelve Gate Treatise," or **Dvādaśamukhaśāstra*), and the BAI LUN ("Hundred Verses Treatise," *ŚATAŚĀSTRA), the latter two attributed to Āryadeva. The Madhyamaka school is most renowned for its exposition of the nature of reality, especially its deployment of the doctrines of emptiness (ŚŪNYATĀ) and the two truths (SATYADVAYA). Because of its central claim that all phenomena are devoid or empty (śūnya) of intrinsic existence (SVABHĀVA), its proponents are also referred to as ŚŪNYAVĀDA and Niḥsvabhāvavāda. The doctrine of emptiness has also led to the charge, going back to the time of Nāgārjuna and continuing into the contemporary era, that the Madhyamaka is a form of nihilism, a charge that Nāgārjuna himself deftly refuted. Central to Madhyamaka philosophy is the relation between emptiness and dependent origination (PRATĪTYASAMUTPĀDA). Dependent origination in its Madhyamaka interpretation refers not only to the twelvefold chain but more broadly to the fact that all phenomena arise in dependence on other factors. Hence, everything is dependent, and thus is empty of independent and intrinsic existence (NIḤSVABHĀVA). As Nāgārjuna states, "Because there are no phenomena that are not dependently arisen, there are no phenomena that are not empty." This analysis becomes key to the Madhyamaka articulation of the middle way: because everything is dependently arisen, the extreme of annihilation (UCCHEDĀNTA) is avoided; because everything is empty, the extreme of permanence (ŚĀŚVATĀNTA) is avoided. Although most of the major schools of Buddhist philosophy speaks of the two truths—the ultimate truth (PARAMĀRTHASATYA) and the conventional truth (SAṂVṚTISATYA)—this category is especially important for Madhyamaka, which must simultaneously proclaim the emptiness of all phenomena (the ultimate truth) while describing the operations of the world of cause and effect and the processes governing the path to enlightenment (all of which are deemed conventional truths). Although the true character of conventional truth is misperceived as a result of ignorance (AVIDYĀ), conventional truths themselves are not rejected; as Nāgārjuna states, "Without relying on the conventional, the ultimate cannot be taught; without understanding the ultimate, NIRVĀṆA is not attained." The precise nature of the two truths and their relation is explored in detail in the Madhyamaka treatises, most famously in the sixth chapter of Candrakīrti's MADHYAMAKĀVATĀRA. Although most renowned for its doctrine of emptiness, Madhyamaka is a MAHĀYĀNA school and, as such, also offers detailed expositions of the path (MĀRGA) to the enlightenment. These works that focus on soteriological issues include the SUHṚLLEKHA and RATNĀVALĪ of Nāgārjuna, the CATUḤŚATAKA of Āryadeva, the MADHYAMAKĀVATĀRA of Candrakīrti, the BODHICARYĀVATĀRA of ŚĀNTIDEVA, the BHĀVANĀKRAMA of KAMALAŚĪLA, and the BODHIPATHAPRADĪPA of ATIŚA DĪPAṂKARAŚRĪJÑĀNA.

**Madhyamakahṛdaya**. (T. Dbu ma'i snying po). In Sanskrit, "Essence of the Middle Way"; the major work of the sixth-century Indian MADHYAMAKA (and, from the Tibetan perspective, SVĀTANTRIKA) master BHĀVAVIVEKA (also referred to as Bhavya and Bhāviveka). The text is written in verse, accompanied by the author's extensive prose commentary, entitled the TARKAJVĀLĀ. The *Madhyamakahṛdaya* is preserved in both Sanskrit and Tibetan, the TARKAJVĀLĀ only in Tibetan. The work is in eleven chapters, the first three and the last two of which set forth the main points in Bhāvaviveka's view of the nature of reality and the Buddhist path, dealing with such topics as BODHICITTA, the knowledge of reality (tattvajñāna), and omniscience (SARVAJÑATĀ). The intervening chapters set forth the positions (and Bhāvaviveka's refutations) of various Buddhist and non-Buddhist schools, including the ŚRĀVAKA,

YOGĀCĀRA, Sāṃkhya, Vaiśeṣika, Vedānta, and Mīmāṃsā. These chapters (along with ŚĀNTARAKṢITA's TATTVASAṂGRAHA) are a valuable source of insight into the relations between Madhyamaka and the other Indian philosophical schools of the day. The chapter on the śrāvakas, for example, provides a detailed account of the reasons put forth by the mainstream Buddhist schools as to why the Mahāyāna SŪTRAs are not the word of the Buddha. Bhāvaviveka's response to these charges, as well as his refutation of Yogācāra in the subsequent chapter, are particularly spirited. He concludes by stating that the follower of the Buddha has compassion for those who hold mistaken philosophical views.

**Madhyamakālaṃkāra**. (T. Dbu ma rgyan). In Sanskrit, "Ornament of the Middle Way"; a verse work in ninety-seven stanzas by the eighth-century Indian master ŚĀNTARAKṢITA; it is accompanied by a prose commentary (vṛtti) by the author. Both the root text and commentary are lost in the original Sanskrit (although verses cited elsewhere remain) but preserved in Tibetan translation. Whereas Śāntarakṣita's other major work, the TATTVASAṂGRAHA, is valued largely for its detailed discussion of competing Buddhist and non-Buddhist schools of Indian philosophy, the *Madhyamakālaṃkāra*, which was composed later, is regarded as the foundational text of the YOGĀCĀRA–MADHYAMAKA synthesis that occurred in late Indian Buddhism, what Tibetan doxographers would dub YOGĀCĀRA–SVĀTANTRIKA–MADHYAMAKA. Śāntarakṣita argues that the proper method for gaining realization of reality is to first come to the Yogācāra understanding that external objects do not exist and then move to the Madhyamaka view that mind also is empty of self. The *Madhyamakālaṃkāra* famously states (at stanzas 92–93), "Through relying on mind-only, the nonexistence of external objects should be known. Relying on this [Madhyamaka] mode, it should be known that this [mind] also is completely selfless. Those who, having mounted the chariot of the two modes, grasp the reins of reasoning thereby attain the state of a Mahāyānist exactly as it is." Śāntarakṣita argues that anything that has intrinsic nature (SVABHĀVA) must be intrinsically either one or many. Whatever is neither intrinsically one nor many must lack intrinsic nature. He then goes on to subject a wide range of important philosophical categories to this reasoning in an effort to demonstrate that nothing is endowed with intrinsic nature. These categories include the conditioned (such as the elements of earth, water, fire, and wind), the unconditioned (NIRVĀṆA), the person (PUDGALA) asserted by the VĀTSĪPUTRĪYAs, and space (ĀKĀŚA). He continues on to apply this same reasoning to the major categories of consciousness of various Buddhist and non-Buddhist schools, focusing upon VAIBHĀṢIKA, SAUTRĀNTIKA, and the various subschools of VIJÑĀNAVĀDA. In the course of this section, he considers such important topics in Buddhist epistemology as whether or not the object casts an image or "aspect" (ĀKĀRA), toward the perceiving consciousness, and whether reflexivity (SVASAṂVEDANA) exists. He concludes that consciousness lacks intrinsic nature (NIḤSVABHĀVA). Roughly the last third of the text is devoted to an exposition of the two truths (SATYADVAYA).

**Madhyamakāloka**. (T. Dbu ma snang ba). In Sanskrit, "Illumination of the Middle Way"; the major independent (as opposed to commentarial) work of the late eighth-century Indian master KAMALAŚĪLA. The work is preserved only in Tibetan translation. While the MADHYAMAKĀLAṂKĀRA of Kamalaśīla's teacher, ŚĀNTARAKṢITA, is considered the foundational philosophical text of the YOGĀCĀRA–MADHYAMAKA synthesis, the *Madhyamakāloka* is its most important and detailed exposition. As such, it deals with a number of central epistemological and logical issues to articulate what is regarded as the defining tenet of the YOGĀCĀRA–SVĀTANTRIKA–MADHYAMAKA school: that major YOGĀCĀRA doctrines, such as "mind-only" (CITTAMĀTRA) and the three natures (TRISVABHĀVA), are important in initially overcoming misconceptions, but they are in fact only provisional (NEYĀRTHA) teachings for those who have not yet understood the Madhyamaka view. The *Madhyamakāloka* is also important for its exploration of such central MAHĀYĀNA doctrines as the TATHĀGATAGARBHA and the question of the EKAYĀNA. On this latter point, Kamalaśīla argues against the Yogācāra position that there are three final vehicles (ŚRĀVAKA, PRATYEKABUDDHA, and BODHISATTVA vehicles, with some beings excluded from any path to liberation; see SAMUCCHINNAKUŚALAMŪLA; ICCHANTIKA) in favor of the position that there is a single vehicle to buddhahood for all beings.

**Madhyamakaratnapradīpa**. (T. Dbu ma rin po che'i sgron ma). In Sanskrit, "Jeweled Lamp for the Middle Way"; a work of MADHYAMAKA philosophy attributed to Bhavya or BHĀVAVIVEKA. However, because the work contains references to CANDRAKĪRTI and DHARMAKĪRTI, who lived after Bhāvaviveka, some scholars do not consider it to be the work of the author of the PRAJÑĀPRADĪPA, but by a later scholar by that name, sometimes referred to as Bhavya II. The work begins with a discussion of the two truths (SATYADVAYA) and then goes on to offer criticisms of the positions of both non-Buddhist and Buddhist philosophical schools, with the latter including VAIBHĀṢIKA and SAUTRĀNTIKA, as well as YOGĀCĀRA. The text continues with a presentation and defense of the Madhyamaka interpretation of the two truths, followed by a presentation of the practices of the BODHISATTVA and of the three bodies (TRIKĀYA) of the Buddha. The text concludes with a paean to NĀGĀRJUNA and the benefits of following his teachings.

**Madhyamakārthasaṃgraha**. (T. Dbu ma'i don bsdus pa). In Sanskrit, "Summary of the Meaning of the Middle Way"; a brief text in verse attributed to BHĀVAVIVEKA. As the title suggests, it provides a brief outline of the basic topics of MADHYAMAKA philosophy, such as the middle way between the extremes of existence and nonexistence, Madhyamaka reasoning, and the two truths.

**Madhyamakaśāstra**. (T. Dbu ma'i bstan bcos; C. Zhong lun; J. Chūron; K. Chung non 中論). In Sanskrit, "Treatise on the Middle Way"; an alternative title of the magnum opus of the second-century Indian exegete NĀGĀRJUNA. See MŪLAMADHYAMAKAKĀRIKĀ.

**Madhyamakāvatāra**. (T. Dbu ma la 'jug pa). In Sanskrit, "Entrance to the Middle Way" (translated also as "Supplement to the Middle Way"); the major independent (as opposed to commentarial) work of the seventh-century Indian master CANDRAKĪRTI, who states that it is intended as an avatāra (variously rendered as "primer," "entrance," and "supplement") to NĀGĀRJUNA's MŪLAMADHYAMAKAKĀRIKĀ. The work is written in verse, to which the author provides an extensive prose commentary (bhāṣya). The work is organized around ten "productions of the aspiration to enlightenment" (BODHICITTOTPĀDA), which correspond to the ten stages (BHŪMI) of the bodhisattva path (drawn largely from the DAŚABHŪMIKASŪTRA) and their respective perfections (PĀRAMITĀ), describing the salient practices and attainments of each. These are followed by chapters on the qualities of the bodhisattva, on the stage of buddhahood, and a conclusion. The lengthiest (comprising approximately half of the work) and most important chapter of the text is the sixth, dealing with the perfection of wisdom (PRAJÑĀPĀRAMITĀ). This is one of the most extensive and influential expositions in Indian literature of Madhyamaka philosophical positions. In it, Candrakīrti provides a detailed discussion of the two truths—ultimate truth (PARAMĀRTHASATYA) and conventional truth (SAṂVṚTISATYA)—arguing that all things that have these two natures and that conventional truths (which he glosses as "concealing truths") are not in fact true because they appear falsely to the ignorant consciousness. He also discusses the crucial question of valid knowledge (PRAMĀṆA) among the unenlightened, relating it to worldly consensus (lokaprasiddha). The sixth chapter also contains one of the most detailed refutations of YOGĀCĀRA in MADHYAMAKA literature, treating such topics as the three natures (TRISVABHĀVA), the foundational consciousness (ĀLAYAVIJÑĀNA), and the statements in the sūtras that the three realms of existence are "mind-only" (CITTAMĀTRA). This chapter also contains Candrakīrti's most famous contribution to Madhyamaka reasoning, the sevenfold reasoning designed to demonstrate the absence of a personal self (PUDGALANAIRĀTMYA). Adding to and elaborating upon a fivefold reasoning found in Nāgārjuna's *Mūlamadhyamakakārikā*, Candrakīrti argues that the person does not intrinsically exist because of it: (1) not being the aggregates (SKANDHA), (2) not being other than the aggregates, (3) not being the basis of the aggregates, (4) not depending on the aggregates, (5) not possessing the aggregates, (6) not being the shape of the aggregates, and (7) not being the composite of the aggregates. He illustrates this reasoning by applying it to the example of a chariot, which, he argues, is not to be found among its constituent parts. The sixth chapter concludes with a discussion of the sixteen and the twenty forms of emptiness (ŚŪNYATĀ), which include the emptiness of emptiness (ŚŪNYATĀŚŪNYATĀ). The work was the most widely studied and commented upon Madhyamaka text in Tibet among all sects, serving, for example, as one of the "five texts" (ZHUNG LNGA) that formed the DGE LUGS scholastic curriculum. The work is preserved only in Tibetan, although a Sanskrit manuscript of verses has been discovered in Tibet.

**Madhyamakāvatārabhāṣya**. (S). See MADHYAMAKĀVATĀRA.

**madhyamapratipad**. (P. majjhimapaṭipadā; T. dbu ma'i lam; C. zhongdao; J. chūdō; K. chungdo 中道). In Sanskrit, "middle way"; a well-known description of the Buddhist path (MĀRGA), with two important denotations. As set forth by the Buddha in his first sermon, the "Setting in Motion the Wheel of the Dharma" (P. DHAMMACAKKAPPAVATTANASUTTA; S. DHARMACAKRAPRAVARTANASŪTRA), the middle way refers to a religious path between the two extremes of self-indulgence and self-mortification or extreme asceticism, extremes that the Buddha himself experienced prior to his enlightenment, the former during his youth as a prince, and the latter during his practice of self-mortification. In this first sermon, the Buddha identifies the middle way between these two extremes as the eightfold path (S. ĀRYĀṢṬĀṄGAMĀRGA). As expounded by NĀGĀRJUNA and his followers, the middle way is a philosophical position between the extremes of permanence (ŚĀŚVATĀNTA) and annihilation (UCCHEDĀNTA) (sometimes also called the extremes of existence and nonexistence; see ANTAGRĀHADṚṢṬI). Although the precise meaning of this interpretation of the middle way is widely discussed and debated, one interpretation identifies the extreme of permanence as the position that everything exists ultimately and the extreme of annihilation as the position that nothing exists even conventionally, with the middle way being the position that nothing exists ultimately but everything exists conventionally.

**Madhyāntavibhāga**. (T. Dbus mtha' rnam 'byed; C. Bianzhongbian lun; J. Benchūbenron; K. Pyŏnjungbyŏn non 辯中邊論). In Sanskrit, "Differentiation of the Middle Way and the Extremes"; one of the five works (together with the ABHISAMAYĀLAṂKĀRA, the MAHĀYĀNASŪTRĀLAṂKĀRA, the RATNAGOTRAVIBHĀGA, and the DHARMADHARMATĀVIBHĀGA) said to have been presented to ASAṄGA by the bodhisattva MAITREYA in the TUṢITA heaven. (More precisely, the title *Madhyāntavibhāga* refers to the *Madhyāntavibhāgakārikā* attributed to Maitreya; VASUBANDHU wrote a commentary to the text, entitled *Madhyāntavibhāgabhāṣya*, and STHIRAMATI wrote a commentary entitled *Madhyāntavibhāgaṭīkā*). Written in verse, it is one of the most important YOGĀCĀRA delineations of the three natures (TRISVABHĀVA), especially as they figure in the path to enlightenment, where the obstacles created by the imaginary (PARIKALPITA) are overcome ultimately by the antidote of the consummate (PARINIṢPANNA). The "middle way" exposed here is that of the Yogācāra, and is different from that of NĀGĀRJUNA, although the names of the two extremes to be avoided—the extreme of permanence (ŚĀŚVATĀNTA) and the extreme of annihilation (UCCHEDĀNTA)—are the same. Here the extreme of permanence is the existence of external objects, the imaginary nature (PARIKALPITASVABHĀVA). The extreme of annihilation would seem to include Nāgārjuna's emptiness of intrinsic nature (SVABHĀVA). The middle way entails upholding the existence of consciousness (VIJÑĀNA) as the dependent nature (PARATANTRASVABHĀVA) and the existence of the consummate nature (PARINIṢPANNASVABHĀVA). The work is divided into five chapters, which consider the three natures, the various forms of obstruction to be abandoned on the path, the ultimate truth according to YOGĀCĀRA, the means of cultivating the antidotes to the defilements, and the activity of the MAHĀYĀNA path. See also MAITREYANĀTHA.

**Madhyāntika**. (P. Majjhantika; T. Nyi ma gung pa; C. Motiandi; J. Matsudenchi/Madenchi; K. Malchŏnji 末田地). The third of the five teachers (dharmācārya) mentioned in Indian Sanskrit texts as the initial successors of the Buddha: viz., MAHĀKĀŚYAPA, ĀNANDA, Madhyāntika, ŚĀṆAKAVĀSIN, and UPAGUPTA. The AŚOKĀVADĀNA records that he lived a hundred years after the Buddha's death and, after becoming an ARHAT, was sent by his teacher Ānanda to disseminate Buddhism in Kashmir (see KASHMIR-GANDHĀRA). According to BUDDHAGHOSA's fifth-century CE VINAYA commentary, the SAMANTAPĀSĀDIKĀ, Madhyāntika was the preceptor of MAHINDA (S. Mahendra), the son of King Asoka (S. AŚOKA), who converted the Sinhalese king DEVĀNAṂPIYATISSA to Buddhism in the third century BCE, thus inaugurating Buddhism in Sri Lanka. According to that same text, after the third Buddhist council (see COUNCIL, THIRD), Madhyāntika traveled to Kashmir, where he led countless Kashmiris to enlightenment and ordained a thousand as novice monks (ŚRĀMAṆERA). He is also said to have tamed a malevolent NĀGA living in a lake there. The DA TANG XIYU JI by the Chinese pilgrim XUANZANG (600/602–664) records that the Buddha predicted before his PARINIRVĀṆA that Madhyāntika would travel to Udyāna in Kashmir to disseminate the dharma. Fifty years after the Buddha's death, Madhyāntika heard this prediction from his teacher Ānanda and set out on a successful mission to that region. Xuanzang reports that, in Udyāna, Madhyāntika supervised the carving of a hundred-foot-high wooden image of MAITREYA Buddha; Madhyāntika used his spiritual powers to send a sculptor directly to the TUṢITA heaven (on three separate occasions, according to the account) so he would be able to accurately model the image after the person of Maitreya himself. Sanskrit VINAYA materials, including those from the MAHĀSĀṂGHIKA and MŪLASARVĀSTIVĀDA schools, typically list Madhyāntika as the third successor of the Buddha. He is also subsequently listed as the third Indian patriarch (ZUSHI) in early Chinese records of dharma transmission (CHUANFA), such as the FU FAZANG YINYUAN ZHUAN and the CHU SANZANG JIJI, as well as in early Chan genealogical records, such as the CHUAN FABAO JI and the LIDAI FABAO JI. Later Chan lineage texts compiled after about the early ninth century, such as the BAOLIN ZHUAN and the JINGDE CHUANDENG LU, eliminate him from the roster and move Śāṇakavāsin up to the position of third patriarch.

**madhyendriya**. (T. dbang po 'bring; C. zhonggen; J. chūkon; K. chunggŭn 中根). In Sanskrit, "average faculties"; a term used to describe those disciples of the Buddha whose intellectual capacity is between that of the least intelligent (MṚDVINDRIYA) and the most intelligent (TĪKṢṆENDRIYA), and thus average. The term appears particularly in discussions of UPĀYA, the Buddha's ability to adapt his teachings to the intellects, interests, and aspirations of his disciples. Thus, in consideration of the abilities of his audience, the Buddha would teach different things to different people, sometimes extolling a particular practice to those of middling and lesser faculties, knowing that they were temporarily unable to practice the highest teaching. Precisely what constitutes the Buddha's highest teaching is a point of considerable disagreement over the course of Buddhist thought, with the advocates of one faction consigning the teaching held to be highest by another faction to the category of teachings intended for those of middling or lesser faculties.

**mae chi**. In Thai, "nun" (although not a novice ŚRĀMAṆERIKĀ or fully ordained BHIKṢUṆĪ) or the "order of nuns" in Thailand; those who are ordained as mae chi observe the eight precepts (SIKṢĀPADA; cf. AṢṬĀṄGASAMANVĀGATAṂ UPAVĀSAṂ, UPOṢADHA), dress in white robes similar in style to the saffron robes of the monks, shave their heads every fortnight, and spend much of their time in religious observances. However, because mae chi have not received a monastic ordination and are thus technically still laywomen (UPĀSIKĀ), they are not afforded the special legal status of fully ordained monks, and typically receive far less financial support from both the government and the laity. During the last two decades of the twentieth century, the number of mae chi increased substantially, particularly among college-educated women. Moreover, there was also an increased emphasis on practicing and teaching VIPASSANĀ (S. VIPAŚYANĀ) meditation, as well as on providing young women with opportunities for religious education, particularly those who were economically disadvantaged. The majority of women who ordain as nuns, however, continue to be middle aged and older, in sharp contrast to monks, most of whom ordain as either novices or as young men, and who often enter the monkhood for only a single rains retreat (Thai. pansa, P. vassa; S. VARṢĀ). In the late 1990s, there were around ten thousand nuns in Thailand, compared with almost two hundred thousand monks.

**Mae Thorani**. (Thai). See THORANI.

**Magadha**. (T. Yul ma ga dha; C. Mojietuo [guo]; J. Makatsuda[koku]; K. Magalta [kuk] 摩揭陀[國]). The largest of the sixteen states (MAHĀJANAPADA) that flourished in northern India between the sixth and third centuries BCE. As described in Pāli sources, its capital was Rājagaha (S. RĀJAGṚHA) and, during the lifetime of the Buddha was ruled by King BIMBISĀRA and his usurper son Ajātasattu (S. AJĀTAŚATRU), both of whom became patrons of Buddhism. The Ganges River (GAṄGĀNADĪ) was the border between Magadha and the powerful Licchavi federation. Beginning with Bimbisāra, the relative strength of Magadha vis-à-vis its neighbors rose steadily for several centuries. Ajātasattu annexed the kingdom of Kosala (S. KOŚALA) with the aid of the Licchavis after which he reduced the latter to vassals. The capital of Magadha was moved from Rājagaha to Pāṭaliputta (S. PĀṬALIPUTRA) sometime after Ajātasattu and subsequently became the seat of government for the Mauryan Empire. The height of Magadha's influence was reached in the third century BCE during the reign of the emperor Asoka (S. AŚOKA), when the authority of Pāṭaliputta extended across the north of the Indian subcontinent from Bengal in the east, to Afghanistan in the west and south to the borders of Tamil Nadu. Magadha has been described as the birthplace of Buddhism, and its language, the language of the Buddha. Buddhism in the region received its greatest impetus during the reign of Asoka, whose inscriptions indicate that he promoted the religion throughout his empire. Later depictions of Asoka that appear in Pāli sources portray him as exclusive in his patronage of Buddhism, although his own epigraphs indicate that he lent royal support to brāhmaṇas and non-Buddhist ŚRAMAṆA sects as well.

**Ma gcig lab sgron**. (Machik Labdrön) (c. 1055–1149). Female Tibetan Buddhist master who codified the important meditation tradition called "severance" (GCOD), classified as one of the so-called eight great conveyances that are lineages of achievement (SGRUB BRGYUD SHING RTA CHEN PO BRGYAD). Born in the southern Tibetan region of LA PHYI, Ma gcig lab sgron was recognized at a young age to be a prodigy. According to her traditional biographies, she had a natural propensity for the PRAJÑĀPĀRAMITĀ literature, spending much of her youth reading and studying its root texts and commentaries. She continued her religious education under the monk known as Grwa pa mngon shes (Drapa Ngönshe) and Skyo ston Bsod nams bla ma (Kyotön Sönam Lama) in a monastic setting where she was eventually employed to use her skills in ritual recitation and exegesis. She then took up the lifestyle of a tantric YOGINĪ, living as the consort of the Indian adept Thod pa Bhadra and giving birth to perhaps five children. Reviled in one source as "a nun who had repudiated her religious vows," Ma gcig lab sgron left her family and eventually met the figure who would become her root guru, the famed Indian yogin PHA DAM PA SANGS RGYAS who transmitted to her the instructions of "pacification" (ZHI BYED) and MAHĀMUDRĀ. She combined these with her training in prajñāpāramitā and other indigenous practices, passing them on as the practice of severance, principally to the Nepalese yogin Pham thing pa and her own son Thod smyon bsam grub (Tönyön Samdrup). Ma gcig lab sgron is revered as a ḌĀKINĪ, an emanation of the Great Mother (Yum chen mo, as the goddess PRAJÑĀPĀRAMITĀ is known in Tibetan), and the female bodhisattva TĀRĀ. Her reincarnations have also been recognized in contemporary individuals, including the former abbess of the important SHUG GSEB nunnery, Rje btsun Rig 'dzin chos nyid zang mo (Jetsun Rikdzin Chönyi Sangmo). Ma gcig lab sgron remains a source of visionary inspiration for new ritual cycles, as well as a primary Tibetan example of the ideal female practitioner. Her tradition of severance continues to be widely practiced by Tibetan Buddhists of all sectarian affiliations.

**maggacitta**. In Pāli, "path consciousness"; a term synonymous with "path knowledge" (maggañāṇa); the moment of consciousness that occurs upon accessing any one of the four supramundane or noble paths (P. ariyamagga; S. ĀRYAMĀRGA), viz., that of the stream-enterer (P. sotāpanna; S. SROTAĀPANNA), once-returner (P. sakadāgāmi; S. SAKṚDĀGĀMIN), nonreturner (P. anāgāmi; ANĀGĀMIN), and worthy one (P. arahant; S. ARHAT). It marks the attainment of what is called "purity of knowledge and vision" (ÑĀṆADASSANAVISUDDHI), which is the seventh and final purity (visuddhi; cf. S. VIŚUDDHI) that is developed along the path to liberation. Path consciousness is immediately preceded by GOTRABHŪÑĀṆA or "change-of-lineage knowledge," that point at which consciousness first takes the NIRVĀṆA element (P. nibbānadhātu) as its object, thereby freeing the practitioner from belonging to the lineage of ordinary worldlings (P. puthujjana; cf. S. PṚTHAGJANA). Path consciousness is immediately followed by two or three moments of "fruition consciousness" (PHALACITTA), after which the mind subsides into the subconscious continuum (BHAVAṄGASOTA). The difference between path consciousness and fruition consciousness may be described in the following way with reference to the stream-enterer: through the path of stream-entry, one "becomes" free of the first three fetters (SAṂYOJANA), whereas through fruition of stream-entry one "is" free of the first three fetters. Because path consciousness represents the first moment of entering of the path, it occurs only once to any given practitioner on each of the four paths. Fruition consciousness, on the other hand, is not so limited and thus may repeat itself innumerable times during a lifetime.

**maggāmaggañāṇadassanavisuddhi**. (S. *margāmargajñānadarśanaviśuddhi; C. dao feidao zhijian qingjing; J. dōhidōchikenshōjō; K. to pido chigyŏn ch'ŏngjŏng 道非道智見清淨). In Pāli, "purity of knowledge and vision of what is and is not the path." According to the VISUDDHIMAGGA, the fifth of seven "purities" (visuddhi; cf. S. VIŚUDDHI) to be developed along the path to liberation. This purity consists of the understanding that distinguishes between what is the right path and what is the wrong path. It requires as a prerequisite the cultivation of methodological insight (nayavipassanā) through contemplating the nature of the five aggregates (P. khandha; S.

SKANDHA). Through an understanding of the FOUR NOBLE TRUTHS and dependent origination (P. paṭiccasamuppāda; S. PRATĪTYASAMUTPĀDA), the practitioner realizes that the aggregates come into being and pass away from moment to moment, and that as a consequence they are insubstantial, unreliable, and empty, like a mirage. During this stage of purification, ten experiences arise, which, if the practitioner becomes attached to them, function as defilements of insight (vipassanūpakkilesa). These include: (1) radiant light (obhāsa), (2) knowledge (ñāṇa), (3) rapture (pīti), (4) tranquility (passaddhi), (5) pleasure (sukha), (6) determination (adhimokkha), (7) energy (paggaha), (8) awareness (upaṭṭhāna), (9) equanimity (upekkhā), and (10) delight (nikanti). These ten defilements may cause the practitioner to believe that he has attained liberation, when in fact he has not. They are overcome with continued practice, whereby the mind comes to regard them with indifference as mere concomitants of insight.

**Magoksa**. (麻谷寺). In Korean, "Hemp Valley Monastery"; the sixth district monastery (PONSA) of the contemporary CHOGYE CHONG of Korean Buddhism, located on T'aehwasan (Exalted Splendor Mountain) outside the city of Kongju in South Ch'ungch'ŏng province. The origins of the monastery and its name are obscure. One record claims that Magoksa was established by the Silla VINAYA master CHAJANG (fl. c. 590–658) in 643; because so many people attended Chajang's dharma lecture at the monastery's founding, the audience was said to have been "as dense as hemp stalks," so the Sinograph for "hemp" (ma) was given to the name of the monastery. This claim is, however, suspect since the monastery is located in what was then the territory of Silla's rival Paekche. A second theory is that the monastery was founded in 845 by Muju Muyŏm (799–888), founder of the Sŏngjusan school of the Nine Mountains school of Sŏn (KUSAN SŎNMUN). When Muyŏm returned to Silla in 845 from his training in China, he is said to have named the monastery after his Chinese CHAN teacher Magu Baoche (K. Magok Poch'ŏl; b. 720?). Finally, it is also said that the monastery's name simply derives from the fact that hemp was grown in the valley before the monastery's establishment. In 1172, during the Koryŏ dynasty, Magoksa was significantly expanded in scope by POJO CHINUL (1158–1210) and his disciple Suu (d.u.), who turned it into a major monastery in the region. Following the Japanese Hideyoshi invasions of 1592–1598, the monastery sat destroyed for some sixty years until several of its shrine halls were reconstructed by Kakch'ŏng (d.u.) in 1651 and the monastery returned to prominence. The Taegwang pojŏn (Basilica of Great Brightness) is Magoksa's central sanctuary and enshrines an image of the buddha VAIROCANA; the building was reconstructed in 1172 by Pojo Chinul and again in 1651. In front of the basilica is a juniper tree planted by the independence fighter Kim Ku (1876–1949), who later lived at the monastery as a monk. Magoksa's main buddha hall (taeung pojŏn; see TAEUNG CHŎN) enshrines a ŚĀKYAMUNI Buddha statue that is flanked by AMITĀBHA and BHAIṢAJYAGURU, and the calligraphy hanging outside this hall is reported to be that of Kim Saeng (711–790/791), one of Silla's most famous calligraphers. One of Magoksa's unique structures is its five-story, Koryŏ-era stone pagoda, which is built upon a two-story-high stone base; its bronze cap suggests Tibetan influences that may have entered Korea via the Mongol Yuan dynasty. It is one of only three STŪPAs of similar style known to exist worldwide. The Yŏngsan chŏn (Vulture Peak Hall) is decorated with paintings of the eight stereotypical episodes in the life of the Buddha (p'alsang; see C. BAXIANG); it is also called the Ch'ŏnbul chŏn, or Thousand Buddhas Hall, for the many buddha statues enshrined around the inside perimeter of the hall. The building, which was reconstructed by Kakch'ŏng in 1651, is today's Magoksa's oldest extant building, with a plaque that may display the calligraphy of King Sejo (r. 1455–1468).

**mahābhaya**. (T. 'jigs pa chen po; C. dakewei; J. daikai; K. taegaoe 大可畏). In Sanskrit, the "great fears"; things that are frightening and from which one may need the protection of either a BODHISATTVA or a specific text or practice. The great fears are often listed as eight, with various constituents. One common list is earth, water, fire, wind, snakes, elephants, thieves, and kings; another is lions, elephants, fire, snakes, thieves, violent waters (including floods and storms at sea), imprisonment, and demons.

**Mahābherīhārakaparivarta**. (T. Rnga bo che chen po'i le'u; C. Dafagu jing; J. Daihokkukyō; K. Taebŏpko kyŏng 大法鼓經). A Sanskrit MAHĀYĀNA sūtra translated into Chinese by GUṆABHADRA in the fifth century as the "Great Drum Sūtra"; it is considered one of the major sūtras for the exposition of the notion of the "embryo of the buddhas" (TATHĀGATAGARBHA). It is one of two texts (the other being the Mahāyāna AṄGULIMĀLĪYASŪTRA) that make specific reference to the TATHĀGATAGARBHASŪTRA, stating that only BODHISATTVA–MAHĀSATTVAs understand the nature of the tathāgatagarbha and thus preserve the *Tathāgatagarbhasūtra*. This sūtra also sets forth the doctrine of a single vehicle (EKAYĀNA), similar to that found in the SADDHARMAPUṆḌARĪKASŪTRA.

**mahābhūmika**. (T. sa chen po pa; C. dadi fa; J. daijihō; K. taeji pŏp 大地法). In Sanskrit, lit. "factors of wide extent"; "omnipresent mental factors" (DHARMA) that ground all conscious activity; also known as CITTAMAHĀBHŪMIKA. In the SARVĀSTIVĀDA ABHIDHARMA system, ten specific factors are said universally to accompany all consciousness activity and are therefore known as "omnipresent mental factors." The ten are: (1) "sensation" or "feeling" (VEDANĀ), (2) "volition" or "intention" (CETANĀ), (3) "perception" (SAṂJÑĀ), (4) "zest" or "desire to act" (CHANDA), (5) "sensory contact" (SPARŚA), (6) "discernment" (MATI), (7) "mindfulness" (SMṚTI), (8) "attention" (MANASIKĀRA), (9) "determination" (ADHIMOKṢA), (10) "concentration" (SAMĀDHI). To give but one example of how these factors are viewed as ubiquitous, even such mental states as distraction are still characterized by a relative "lack" of concentration, not a complete absence thereof; hence, "concentration" remains an omnipresent mental factor even amid distraction. There is also a list of six "fundamental afflictions" or "defiled factors of wide extent" (KLEŚA-mahābhūmika) that are associated with all defiled thoughts: delusion (MOHA), heedlessness (pramāda; see APRAMĀDA), lassitude (KAUSĪDYA), lack of faith (ĀŚRADDHYA), sloth (STYĀNA), and restlessness (AUDDHATYA). Finally, there are also two "unwholesome factors of wide extent" (AKUŚALA-mahābhūmika): lack of shame (ahrī; cf. HRĪ) and lack of dread (anapatrāpya; cf. APATRĀPYA).

**mahābhūta**. (T. 'byung ba chen po; C. dazhong/sida; J.daishu/shidai; K. taejong/sadae 大種/四大). In Sanskrit and Pāli, the "great elements"; or "major elementary qualities" of which the physical world of materiality or form (RŪPA) is composed. According to ABHIDHARMA analysis, these elements involve not only the common manifestations of earth (PṚTHIVĪ; P. paṭhavī), water (ĀPAS; P. āpo), fire (TEJAS; P. tejo), and wind (VĀYU; P. vāyu/vāyo), but also the fundamental qualities of the physical world that these elements represent. Thus, the quality of solidity is provided by earth, the quality of cohesion by water, the quality of heat or warmth by fire, and the quality of mobility by wind. All physical objects are said to possess of all four of the great elements, in greater or lesser proportion.

**mahābodhi**. (T. byang chub chen po; C. da puti/wushang puti; J. daibodai/mujōbodai; K. tae pori/musang pori 大菩提/無上菩提). In Sanskrit, "great enlightenment"; the enlightenment of a buddha and the enlightenment to which the BODHISATTVA aspires. In this sense, it is distinguished from the term BODHI, which can be used more broadly to describe both the enlightenment of a buddha as well as the enlightenment of an ARHAT. The term mahābodhi is thus synonymous with SAṂBODHI and ANUTTARASAMYAKSAṂBODHI, which are only used with reference to buddhas. Mahābodhi is also used to refer to both the BODHI TREE and to the monastery constructed at BODHGAYĀ, since those are the sites where ŚĀKYAMUNI achieved "great enlightenment." See also MAHĀBODHI TEMPLE.

**mahābodhinirmāṇakāya**. (T. byang chub chen po'i sprul sku). In Sanskrit, "emanation body of great enlightenment"; the familiar form assumed by a buddha in order to subdue the afflictions of sentient beings, which performed such deeds as going forth from the world, achieving enlightenment under the BODHI TREE, turning the wheel of the dharma (DHARMACAKRAPRAVARTANA), and passing into PARINIRVĀṆA. Among the three bodies of a buddha—the DHARMAKĀYA, the SAṂBHOGAKĀYA, and the NIRMĀṆAKĀYA—this body is a subtype of the last. It is also called a "supreme emanation body" (UTTAMANIRMĀṆAKĀYA) to distinguish it from other forms in which a buddha may appear in the world.

**mahābodhisattva**. (T. byang chub sems dpa' chen po; C. da pusa; J. daibosatsu; K. tae posal 大菩薩). In Sanskrit, "great bodhisattva"; a term that sometimes has the specific sense of a bodhisattva who has achieved the path of vision (DARŚANAMĀRGA). Such a bodhisattva is also called an āryabodhisattva.

**Mahābodhi Society**. An organization founded in 1891 by a group that included the Sinhalese nationalist and Buddhist leader, Anagārika Dharmapāla (1864–1933; see DHARMAPĀLA, ANAGĀRIKA). Dharmapāla had been shocked to read EDWIN ARNOLD's 1886 newspaper account of the sad condition of BODHGAYĀ, the site of the Buddha's enlightenment. Arnold described a dilapidated temple surrounded by hundreds of broken statues scattered in the jungle. The MAHĀBODHI TEMPLE itself had stood in ruins prior to renovations undertaken by the British in 1880. Also of great concern was the fact that the site had been under Śaiva control since the eighteenth century, with reports of animal sacrifice taking place in the environs of the temple. The society was established with the aim of restoring Bodhgayā as place of Buddhist worship and pilgrimage and it undertook a series of unsuccessful lawsuits to that end; a joint Hindu–Buddhist committee was eventually established in 1949 to oversee the site. The society also sought to return other neglected sites, such as KUŚINAGARĪ, the place of the Buddha's PARINIRVĀṆA, to places of Buddhist pilgrimage. Although the restoration of Indian Buddhist sites was the impetus for the founding of the Mahābodhi Society, this was not its only activity. It was the first organization of the modern period to seek to promote pan-Buddhist solidarity; Dharmapāla himself traveled widely on behalf of the society to North America, Japan, China, and Southeast Asia. The journal of the society, called *The Mahā Bodhi*, founded in 1892, has published articles and translations for more than a century.

**Mahābodhi Temple**. (T. Byang chub chen po; C. Daputisi; J. Daibodaiji; K. Taeborisa 大菩提寺). The "Temple of the Great Awakening"; proper name used to refer to the great STŪPA at BODHGAYĀ, marking the place of the Buddha's enlightenment, and hence the most important place of pilgrimage (see MAHĀSTHĀNA) in the Buddhist world. The Emperor AŚOKA erected a pillar and shrine at the site in the third century BCE. A more elaborate structure, called the VAJRĀSANA GANDHAKUṬĪ ("perfumed chamber of the diamond seat"), is depicted in a relief at Bodhgayā, dating from c. 100 BCE. It shows a two-storied structure supported by pillars, enclosing the BODHI TREE and the vajrāsana, the "diamond seat," where the Buddha sat on the night of his enlightenment. The forerunner of the present structure is described by the Chinese pilgrim XUANZANG. This has led scholars to speculate that the temple was built between the third and sixth centuries CE, with subsequent renovations. Despite various persecutions by Hindu kings, the site continued to receive patronage, especially during the Pāla period, from which many of the surrounding monuments date. The monastery fell into neglect after the Muslim invasions that began in the thirteenth century. British photographs from the nineteenth century show the monastery in ruins. Restoration of the site was ordered by the British governor-general of Bengal in 1880, with a small eleventh-century replica of the monastery serving as a model. There is a tall central tower some 165 feet (fifty meters) in height, with a high arch over the entrance with smaller towers at the four corners. The central tower houses a small shrine with an image of the Buddha. The structure is surrounded by stone railings, some dating from 150 BCE, others from the Gupta period (300–600 CE), which preserve important carvings. The area came under the control of a Śaiva mahant in the eighteenth century. In the late nineteenth century, the Sinhalese Buddhist activist Anagārika Dharmapāla (see DHARMAPĀLA, ANAGĀRIKA), was part of a group that founded the MAHĀBODHI SOCIETY and began an unsuccessful legal campaign to have control of the site returned to Buddhists. In 1949, after Indian independence, the Bodhgayā Temple Act was passed, which is established a joint committee of four Buddhists and four Hindus to oversee the monastery and its grounds.

**Mahābodhivaṃsa**. In Pāli, the "History of the Great Bodhi [Tree]"; a prose chronicle recounting the history of the BODHI TREE. It was composed in Sri Lanka by the monk Upatissa in the tenth or eleventh century CE. The work begins with an account of the buddha Dīpaṅkara (S. DĪPAṂKARA), the lives of the bodhisatta (BODHISATTVA) under previous buddhas, the life of Gotama (S. GAUTAMA) Buddha, his enlightenment under the Bodhi tree, his parinibbāna (PARINIRVĀṆA) and the distribution of his relics, and the three Buddhist councils in India. It then tells of MAHINDA's mission to Sri Lanka, the conversion of the island to Buddhism, the arrival of SAṄGHAMITTĀ with a branch of the Bodhi tree, and the commencement of pūjā in honor of the tree.

**mahābrahmā**. (T. Tshang pa chen po; C. Dafan tian; J. Daibonten; K. Taebŏm ch'ŏn 大梵天). In Sanskrit and Pāli, the "great BRAHMĀ"; the highest of the three heavens that constitute the first absorption (DHYĀNA) of the realm of subtle materiality (RŪPADHĀTU) in the Buddhist cosmological system. The term often appears in plural, as mahābrahmāṇaḥ (P. mahābrahmāno), suggesting that this heaven is not the domain of a single brahmā, of whom the divinities of the two lower heavens are his subjects and ministers, but rather that a number of mahābrahmā gods inhabit this heaven. However, it is typically a single Brahmā, often called Brahmā SAHĀṂPATI, who appears in the sūtras. In the BRAHMAJĀLASUTTA, the false belief in a creator god derives from the fact that the first mahābrahmā divinity to be reborn in this heaven at the beginning of world cycle falsely imagined himself to be the creator of the beings who were reborn after him in the brahmā heavens, with those beings in turn believing his claim and professing it on earth after they were reborn as humans. As with all the heavens of the realm of subtle materiality, one is reborn as a divinity there through achieving the same level of concentration (dhyāna) as the gods of that heaven during one's practice of meditation in a previous lifetime. See also BRAHMALOKA.

**Mahācakravāḍa**. (S). See CAKRAVĀḌA.

**mahādarśajñāna**. (S). See ĀDARŚAJÑĀNA.

**Mahādeva**. (T. Lha chen; C. Mohetipo; J. Makadaiba; K. Mahajeba 摩訶提婆). An Indian monk of questionable historicity, credited with the infamous "five theses" (pañcavastūni). Mahādeva appears in numerous accounts of the early centuries of the Buddhist order, but the various reports of dates, his affiliation, and his character are contradictory. Although extolled in some accounts, the ABHIDHARMAMAHĀVIBHĀṢĀ recounts that he had sexual relations with his mother; that he murdered his father, his mother, and several ARHATs; and that his cremation fire was fueled by dog excrement. Some accounts make him a participant at the second Buddhist council (see COUNCIL, SECOND), said to have occurred a century after the Buddha's death, which resulted in the schism of the SAṂGHA into the conservative STHAVIRANIKĀYA and the more liberal MAHĀSĀṂGHIKA. However, the chief point of controversy there seems to have been ten relatively minor rules of discipline, the most serious of which was the prohibition against monks and nuns handling gold or silver. If Mahādeva was a historical figure, it is more likely that he was involved in a later schism that occurred within the Mahāsāṃghika, as a result of which the followers of Mahādeva formed the CAITYA subsect. The theses attributed to Mahādeva challenge the authority of the arhat. Although there is a lack of consistency in the various renditions of the five theses, according to one widely repeated version, the five are (1) arhats are subject to erotic dreams and nocturnal emissions; (2) arhats retain a subtle form of ignorance, called the "unafflicted ignorance" (AKLIṢṬĀJÑĀNA), which prevents them from knowing the names of people, trees, grasses, and which road to take without being told; (3) arhats are therefore subject to doubt; (4) arhats thus must rely on others for corroboration, including on the question of whether they have achieved enlightenment; (5) entry into the path can be achieved simply by attaining the first DHYĀNA, becoming a stream-enterer (SROTAĀPANNA), and exclaiming "Oh suffering" (rather than by the more protracted method of the noble eightfold path). These theses, which are widely reported, reflect the Mahāsāṃghika attack on the arhat ideal, and presumably the Sthaviranikāya conception thereof. When these charges were leveled, and by whom, is unclear. In some accounts, Mahādeva was himself subject to each of these faults (reflecting on his transgression, he cried out "Oh suffering" in the night and later sought to deceive those who heard him by explaining that he had been contemplating the first of the FOUR NOBLE TRUTHS) and stated the five theses to protect his own claim to being an arhat.

**Mahādhammasamādānasutta**. (C. Shoufa jing; J. Juhōkyō; K. Subŏp kyŏng 受法經). In Pāli, the "Larger Discourse on Undertaking the DHARMA"; the forty-sixth sutta in the MAJJHIMANIKĀYA (a separate SARVĀSTIVĀDA recension appears as the 175th sūtra in the Chinese translation of the MADHYAMĀGAMA); preached by the Buddha to a gathering of monks in the JETAVANA grove at Sāvatthi (S. ŚRĀVASTĪ). The Buddha explains the different consequences that befall those who act with ignorance and those who act with wisdom. He then describes four ways of undertaking things in this life and the good and bad consequences that accrue to one who follows these ways. The first way is to live a painful life now, followed by a painful future existence; the second way is to live a pleasant life now, followed by a painful existence; the third way is to live a painful life now, followed by a pleasant existence; the fourth way is to live a pleasant life now, followed by a pleasant existence. The Buddha illustrates his points using the similes of a bitter gourd of poison, a bronze cup of a flavorful poisoned beverage, a medicine made from cow's urine, and a flavorful medicinal drink.

**Mahādukkhakkhandhasutta**. (C. Kuyin jing; J. Kuongyō; K. Koŭm kyŏng 苦陰經). In Pāli, the "Greater Discourse on the Mass of Suffering"; the thirteenth sutta in the MAJJHIMANIKĀYA (a separate SARVĀSTIVĀDA recension appears as the ninety-ninth SŪTRA in the Chinese translation of the MADHYAMĀGAMA); preached by the Buddha to his disciples at Sāvatthi (S. ŚRĀVASTĪ) to refute the claims of naked JAINA ascetics that their teachings were identical to the teachings of the Buddha. The Buddha explains the full implications of sensual pleasures, the advantages of renouncing them, and the path needed to escape from their influence. Finally he asserts that outside his teachings these truths are unknown, and that only a buddha and his disciples can teach of them.

**Mahāgopālakasutta**. (C. Fangniu pin; J. Hōgobon; K. Pangu p'um 放牛品). In Pāli, the "Greater Discourse on the Cowherd"; the thirty-third sutta in the MAJJHIMANIKĀYA (separate recensions appear in the Chinese translations of the SAṂYUKTĀGAMA and the EKOTTARĀGAMA); preached by the Buddha to an assembly of monks at the JETAVANA grove in the city of Sāvatthi (S. ŚRĀVASTĪ). The Buddha describes the conditions under which the teachings can prosper, using the example of the cowherd. Just as when a cowherd is equipped with the requisite skills in tending his cattle his herd can be expected to grow and prosper, so, too, when a monk is equipped with the requisite skills in leading the holy life, the teachings can be expected to grow and prosper.

**Mahāgosiṅgasutta**. (C. Niujiaosuoluolin jing; J. Gokakusarаringyō; K. Ugaksararim kyŏng 牛角娑羅林經). In Pāli, the "Greater Discourse in Gosiṅga Park"; the thirty-second sutta in the MAJJHIMANIKĀYA (a separate SARVĀSTIVĀDA recension appears as the 184th sūtra in the Chinese translation of the MADHYAMĀGAMA). On a beautiful moonlit night, while dwelling in the Gosiṅga woodland park, ŚĀRIPUTRA asks the eminent monks ĀNANDA, REVATA, ANIRUDDHA, MAHĀKĀŚYAPA, and MAHĀMAUDGALYĀYANA what kind of mendicant might adorn the park with their virtues. Each expresses his view, to which Śāriputra adds his own. The Buddha confirms their opinions, noting that each ideal in its own way would be an adornment to the Gosiṅga park.

**Mahāgovindasutta**. (C. Dianzun jing; J. Tensongyō; K. Chŏnjon kyŏng 典尊經). In Pāli, the "Great Discourse on Mahāgovinda"; the nineteenth sutta in the DĪGHANIKĀYA (a separate DHARMAGUPTAKA recension appears as the third sūtra in the Chinese translation of the DĪRGHĀGAMA). A celestial musician (gandhabba; GANDHARVA) named Pañcasikha recounts to the Buddha how the BRAHMĀ divinity Sanaṅkumāra once taught his fellow divinities a noble teaching acquired from a brāhmaṇa named Mahāgovinda. The Buddha reveals that he himself was that Mahāgovinda in a previous existence and that the teaching he set forth then as a bodhisatta (S. BODHISATTVA) could only lead to rebirth in the brahmā heavens. But now as a buddha, his teaching leads to the higher goals of the stream-enterer (P. sotāpanna; S. SROTAĀPANNA), once-returner (P. sakadagāmi; S. SAKṚDĀGĀMIN), nonreturner (P. anāgāmi; S. ANĀGĀMIN), and the highest goal of the arahant (ARHAT).

**Mahāhatthipadopamasutta**. (C. Xiangjiyu jing; J. Zōshakuyugyō; K. Sangjŏgyu kyŏng 象跡喻經). In Pāli, the "Greater Discourse on the Simile of the Elephant's Footprint"; the twenty-eighth sutta contained in the MAJJHIMANIKĀYA (a separate SARVĀSTIVĀDA recension appears as the thirtieth sūtra in the Chinese translation of the MADHYAMĀGAMA), preached by Sāriputta (S. ŚĀRIPUTRA) to an assembly of monks at the JETAVANA grove in the town of Sāvatthi (S. ŚRĀVASTĪ). Using the simile of the elephant's footprint, Sāriputta explains how just as the footprints of all animals can be contained in the footprint of an elephant, so all wholesome phenomena were contained in the FOUR NOBLE TRUTHS. He expounds on the four truths in terms of the four elements (MAHĀBHŪTA) of earth, water, fire, and air, and the dependent origination (P. paṭiccasamuppāda; S. PRATĪTYASAMUTPĀDA) of the five aggregates (P. khandha; S. SKANDHA).

**mahājanapada**. (T. grong khyer chen po; C. dacheng; J. daijō; K. taesŏng 大城). In Pāli, literally "great country." Sixteen mahājanapadas or states are mentioned in Pāli texts as flourishing in northern India at the time of the Buddha. They were Kāsi, Kosala (KOŚALA), Aṅga, MAGADHA, Vajji, MALLA, Cetiya, Vaṃsa, Kuru, Pañcāla, Maccha, Sūrasena, Assaka, AVANTI, GANDHĀRA, and Kamboja. Of these, the first fourteen are included in Majjhimadesa (the middle country), while the last two are in Uttarāpatha (the northern region).

**Mahākāla**. (T. Nag po chen po; C. Daheitian; J. Daikokuten; K. Taehŭkch'ŏn 大黑天). In Sanskrit, the "Great Black One"; one of the most important wrathful deities of tantric Buddhism.

He is a DHARMAPĀLA or "protector of the dharma," of the LOKOTTARA or "supramundane" variety; that is, one regarded as the manifestation of a buddha or bodhisattva. He is said to be the wrathful manifestation of AVALOKITEŚVARA, the bodhisattva of compassion. In the form of Avalokiteśvara with a thousand arms and eleven heads (see SĀHASRABHUJASĀHASRANETRĀVALOKITEŚVARA), the top head is that of Mahākāla. He has many aspects, including two-, four-, and six-armed forms, and appears in several colors, the most famous being black and white. He wears a crown of five skulls, symbolizing the transmutation of the five afflictions (KLEŚA) into the five wisdoms (PAÑCAJÑĀNA) of a buddha. One of his most popular forms in Tibet is as Pañjaranātha or "Protector of the Pavilion." In this form, which derives from the *Vajrapañjaratantra*, he is the protector of the HEVAJRATANTRA cycle. Here is depicted as a dwarf-like figure, holding a wooden staff across his arms. In Japan, where he is known as Daikokuten, Mahākāla is a less frightening figure and is one of the "seven gods of good fortune" (SHICHIFUKUJIN), extolled as a god of wealth and a god of the household.

**Mahākālika**. (S). See KĀLIKA.

**mahākalpa**. (P. mahākappa; T. bskal chen; C. dajie; J. daikō; K. taegŏp 大劫). In Sanskrit, "great eon"; one of the vast units of time in Buddhist cosmology, said to be equal in length to eighty KALPAS. A kalpa is traditionally said to be the length of time it would take to remove all the mustard seeds stored in a cube that was one YOJANA in height, length, and breadth, if one seed were removed each century. It is also said to be the length of time it would take to wear away a stone of similar size by wiping that stone with a piece of silk once every century. When it is said that a great kalpa is equal in length to eighty kalpas, a kalpa is sometimes referred to as an "intermediate eon" (ANTARAKALPA). When used to describe the duration of a particular world system, a great eon is divided into four periods: a period of nothingness, a period of creation, and period of subsistence, and a period of destruction, each twenty kalpas in length (see KALPA).

**Mahākapphiṇa**. (P. Mahākappina; T. Ka pi na chen po; C. Mohejiebinna; J. Makakōhinna; K. Mahagŏppinna 摩訶劫賓那). Sanskrit proper name of an eminent ARHAT deemed by the Buddha foremost among those who taught monks. According to Pāli accounts (where he is referred to as Mahākappina), he was older than the Buddha and had been the king of a frontier kingdom whose capital was Kukkutavatī. His wife was a princess from the city of Sāgala named Anojā. Mahākappina was endowed with a great intellect and every day he sent messengers from his city to inquire if scholars were traveling through his realm. One day, merchants from Sāvatthi (S. ŚRĀVASTĪ) visited Kukkutavatī and told the king about the Buddha and his teachings. On hearing the news, the king was overjoyed and, presenting the travelers with a gift of thousands of coins, resolved to meet the Buddha himself. Setting out for Sāvatthi with his retinue, Mahākappina found his path blocked by three rivers. These he crossed by means of an "asseveration of truth" (see SATYAVACANA), in which he declared, "If this teacher indeed be a perfect buddha, let not even the hooves of my horses get wet." When the royal delegation approached the Buddha, he preached to them, whereupon all of them attained arhatship and entered the order. When Anojā and the other royal wives heard the news, they resolved to follow their husbands and enter the order as nuns. When the Buddha preached to the women they all attained stream-entry (P. sotāpanna; S. SROTAĀPANNA) and took ordination. Mahākappina used to spend his time in the bliss of meditative absorption (P. JHĀNA; S. DHYĀNA) and was wont to exclaim, "Oh joy, Oh joy." While dwelling at the Maddakucchi Deer Park, he wondered whether he needed to attend the fortnightly confessional (P. UPOSATHA; S. UPOṢADHA). The Buddha, knowing his thoughts, appeared before him and instructed him to attend. Thinking Mahākappina too inactive, he instructed him to teach the dharma to others. Mahākappina complied, and by means of a single sermon a thousand recluses attained arhatship. In the Mahāyāna sūtras, where he is known by his Sanskrit name, Mahākapphiṇa, he is listed among the monks in audience for the preaching of the SUKHĀVATĪVYŪHASŪTRA.

**mahākaruṇā**. (T. snying rje chen mo; C. dabei; J. daihi K. taebi 大悲). In Sanskrit, "great compassion"; the compassion specific to BODHISATTVAS, viz., the wish to free all sentient beings from suffering. In expositions of the bodhisattva path, great compassion is distinguished from compassion (KARUṆĀ), often defined as the wish that others be free from suffering. "Great compassion" is distinguished both by its scope (all beings) and its agency (one oneself wishes to remove the suffering of others). Thus, it is said that compassion is possessed by both ŚRĀVAKAS and PRATYEKABUDDHAS who seek the state of the ARHAT, whereas great compassion is limited to bodhisattvas, who decide to seek buddhahood in order to fulfill the wish to liberate all beings from suffering. In this sense, great compassion is regarded as the precursor to BODHICITTA. Thirty-two specific types of a tathāgata's great compassion are listed in the MAHĀVYUTPATTI. Mahākaruṇā is also an epithet of AVALOKITEŚVARA, the bodhisattva of compassion (see MAHĀKARUṆIKA), and specifically to his manifestation as the "thousand-armed and thousand-handed AVALOKITEŚVARA" (S. SĀHASRABHUJASĀHASRANETRĀVALOKITEŚVARA).

**Mahākaruṇika**. (T. Thugs rje chen po; C. Dabeizhe; J. Daihisha; K. Taebija 大悲者). In Sanskrit, "Great Compassionate One"; an epithet of AVALOKITEŚVARA, the bodhisattva of compassion. The name Mahākaruṇika is also used specifically to refer to one of the more famous iconographic forms of the bodhisattva, his manifestation as the "thousand-armed and thousand-handed Avalokiteśvara" (S. SĀHASRABHUJASĀHASRANETRĀVALOKITEŚVARA). In some versions of this image, each of the hands has an eye in the palm, indicating its ability compassionately to see and offer assistance to suffering sentient beings.

In China, the esoteric code associated with Mahākaruṇika, the DABEI ZHOU (great compassion DHĀRAṆĪ), is often chanted at regular offices, especially in Chan monasteries, and is a common part of funeral ceremonies for monks and nuns. ¶ In the UPĀYAKAUŚALYASŪTRA, Mahākaruṇika is the name of the Buddha in his previous life as a ship captain. Learning that a bandit plans to murder a group of five hundred merchants also traveling on the ship, the ship captain kills the bandit in order to save the lives of the merchants and to prevent the bandit from committing himself the misdeed of murder. It is said that the ship captain did not suffer any negative results from this deed. This story is often cited as an example of justifiable homicide in Buddhism.

**Mahākāśyapa**. (P. Mahākassapa; T. 'Od srung chen po; C. Mohejiashe; J. Makakashō; K. Mahagasŏp 摩訶迦葉). Sanskrit name of one of the Buddha's leading disciples, regarded as foremost in the observance of ascetic practices (P. DHUTAṄGA; S. dhūtaguṇa). According to the Pāli accounts (where he is called Mahākassapa) his personal name was Pipphali and he was born to a brāhmaṇa family in MAGADHA. Even as a child he was inclined toward renunciation and as a youth refused to marry. Finally, to placate his parents, he agreed to marry a woman matching in beauty a statue he had fashioned. His parents found a match in Bhaddā Kapilānī (S. BHADRA-KAPILĀNĪ), a beautiful maiden from Sāgala. But she likewise was inclined toward renunciation. Both sets of parents foiled their attempts to break off the engagement, so in the end they were wed but resolved not to consummate their marriage. Pipphali owned a vast estate with fertile soil, but one day he witnessed worms eaten by birds turned up by his plowman. Filled with pity for the creatures and fearful that he was ultimately to blame, he resolved then and there to renounce the world. At the same time, Bhaddā witnessed insects eaten by crows as they scurried among sesame seeds put out to dry. Feeling pity and fear at the sight, she also resolved to renounce the world. Realizing they were of like mind, Pipphali and Bhaddā put on the yellow robes of mendicants and abandoned their property. Although they left together, they parted ways lest they prove a hindrance to one another. Realizing what had transpired, the Buddha sat along Pipphali's path and showed himself resplendent with yogic power. Upon seeing the Buddha, Pipphali, whose name thenceforth became Kassapa, immediately recognized him as his teacher and was ordained. Traveling to Rājagaha (S. RĀJAGṚHA) with the Buddha, Mahākassapa requested to exchange his fine robe for the rag robe of the Buddha. The Buddha consented, and his conferral of his own rag robe on Mahākassapa was taken as a sign that, after the Buddha's demise, Mahākassapa would preside over the convention of the first Buddhist council (see COUNCIL, FIRST). Upon receiving the Buddha's robe, he took up the observance of thirteen ascetic practices (dhutaṅga) and in eight days became an arahant (S. ARHAT). Mahākassapa possessed great supranormal powers (P. iddhi; S. ṚDDHI) and was second only to the Buddha in his mastery of meditative absorption (P. JHĀNA; S. DHYĀNA). His body was said to be adorned with seven of the thirty-two marks of a superman (MAHĀPURUṢALAKṢAṆA). So revered by the gods was he, that at the Buddha's funeral, the divinities would not allow the funeral pyre to be lit until Mahākassapa arrived and had one last chance to worship the Buddha's body. Mahākassapa seems to have been the most powerful monk after the death of the Buddha and is considered by some schools to have been the Buddha's successor as the first in a line of teachers (dharmācārya). He is said to have called and presided over the first Buddhist council, which he convened after the Buddha's death to counter the heresy of the wicked monk SUBHADRA (P. Subhadda). Before the council began, he demanded that ĀNANDA become an arhat in order to participate, which Ānanda finally did early in the morning just before the event. At the council, he questioned Ānanda and UPĀLI about what should be included in the SŪTRA and VINAYA collections (PIṬAKA), respectively. He also chastised Ānanda for several deeds of commission and omission, including his entreaty of the Buddha to allow women to enter the order (see MAHĀPRAJĀPATĪ), his allowing the tears of women to fall on the Buddha's corpse, his stepping on the robe of the Buddha while mending it, his failure to recall which minor monastic rules the Buddha said could be ignored after his death, and his failure to ask the Buddha to live for an eon or until the end of the eon (see CĀPĀLACAITYA). Pāli sources make no mention of Mahākassapa after the events of the first council, although the Sanskrit AŚOKĀVADĀNA notes that he passed away beneath three hills where his body will remain uncorrupted until the advent of the next buddha, MAITREYA. At that time, his body will reanimate itself and hand over to Maitreya the rag robe of ŚĀKYAMUNI, thus passing on the dispensation of the buddhas. It is said that the robe will be very small, barely fitting over the finger of the much larger Maitreya. ¶ Like many of the great arhats, Mahākāśyapa appears frequently in the MAHĀYĀNA sūtras, sometimes merely listed as a member of the audience, sometimes playing a more significant role. In the VIMALAKĪRTINIRDEŚA, he is one of the ŚRĀVAKA disciples who is reluctant to visit Vimalakīrti. In the SADDHARMAPUṆḌARĪKASŪTRA, he is one of four arhats who understands the parable of the burning house and rejoices in the teaching of a single vehicle (EKAYĀNA); later in the sūtra, the Buddha prophesies his eventual attainment of buddhahood. Mahākāśyapa is a central figure in the CHAN schools of East Asia. In the famous Chan story in which the Buddha conveys his enlightenment by simply holding up a flower before the congregation and smiling subtly (see NIANHUA WEIXIAO), it is only Mahākāśyapa who understands the Buddha's intent, making him the first recipient of the Buddha's "mind-to-mind" transmission (YIXIN CHUANXIN). He is thus considered the first patriarch (ZUSHI) of the Chan school.

**Mahākātyāyana**. (P. Mahākaccāna; T. Ka tya'i bu chen po; C. Mohejiazhanyan; J. Makakasen'en; K. Mahagajŏnyŏn 摩訶迦旃延). Also known as Kātyāyana (P. Kaccāna, Kaccāyana);

Sanskrit name of one of the Buddha's chief disciples and an eminent ARHAT deemed foremost among the Buddha's disciples in his ability to elaborate on the Buddha's brief discourses. According to the Pāli accounts, where he is known as Mahākaccāna, he was the son of a brāhmaṇa priest who served King Caṇḍappajjota of AVANTI. He was learned in the Vedas and assumed his father's position upon his death. He was called Kaccāna because of the golden hue of his body and because it was the name of his clan. Once, he and seven companions were sent by the king to invite the Buddha to Avanti, the capital city of Ujjenī (S. Ujjayinī). The Buddha preached a sermon to them, whereupon they all attained arhatship and entered the order. Mahākaccāna took up residence in a royal park in Ujjenī, where he was treated with great honor by the king. He was such an able preacher and explicator of doctrine that many persons joined the order, until, it is said, the entire kingdom of Avanti sparkled with yellow robes. He became most renowned for his discourses in the MADHUPIṆḌIKASUTTA, *Kaccāyanasutta*, and *Parāyanasutta*. In a previous life, Mahākaccāna was a thaumaturge (vijjādhara; S. VIDHYĀDHARA) during the time of the buddha Padumuttara. It was then that he first made the vow to win the eminence he eventually did under Gotama (S. Gautama) Buddha. Although living far away in Avanti, Mahākaccāna often went to hear the Buddha preach, and the assembled elders always left a place for him. He is said to have requested the Buddha to allow for special dispensation to ordain new monks in outlying regions without the requisite number of monastic witnesses. Mahākaccāna was noted for his ability to provide detailed exegeses of the Buddha's sometimes laconic instructions and brief verses, and several suttas in the Pāli canon are ascribed to him. According to tradition, he is the author of the NETTIPPAKARAṆA and the PEṬAKOPADESA, which seek to provide the foundational principles that unify the sometimes variant teachings found in the suttas; these texts are some of the earliest antecedents of commentarial exegesis in the Pāli tradition and are the only commentaries included in the suttapiṭaka proper. He is also said to be the author of the Pāli grammar, the *Kaccāyanavyākaraṇa*. According to the Sanskrit tradition, Mahākātyāyana was the initiator of the STHAVIRANIKĀYA branch of the mainstream Buddhist schools and traditional compiler of the ABHIDHARMA. The JÑĀNAPRASTHĀNA of the SARVĀSTIVĀDA ABHIDHARMAPIṬAKA is attributed to him, but it was certainly composed several hundred years later by an author of the same name. He is often depicted holding an alm's bowl (PĀTRA) or with his fingers interlaced at his chest. Like many of the great arhats, Mahākātyāyana appears frequently in the MAHĀYĀNA sūtras, sometimes merely as a member of the audience, sometimes playing a more significant role. In the VIMALAKĪRTINIRDEŚA, he is one of the ŚRĀVAKA disciples who is reluctant to visit the lay BODHISATTVA VIMALAKĪRTI. In the SADDHARMAPUṆḌARĪKASŪTRA, he is one of four arhats who understand the parable of the burning house and who rejoices in the teaching of the one vehicle (EKAYĀNA); later in the sūtra, the Buddha prophesies his eventual attainment of buddhahood.

**Mahākauṣṭhila**. (S). See KAUṢṬHILA.

**Mahālisutta**. In Pāli, the "Discourse to Mahāli"; the sixth sutta of the DĪGHANIKĀYA (there is no equivalent recension in the Chinese translations of the ĀGAMAS); preached by the Buddha to the Licchavi chief Mahāli at the Kūṭāgārasālā in Vesāli (S. VAIŚĀLĪ). Mahāli tells the Buddha that the ascetic Sunakkhatta claimed to be able to see heavenly forms but was not able to hear heavenly sounds. Mahāli asks whether such attainments are possible, whereupon the Buddha explains how through meditative absorption (P. JHĀNA; S. DHYĀNA) they indeed can be developed. He further explains to Mahāli that these supernatural powers are not the reason why people join the Buddhist order, but rather to attain the four degrees of sanctity, namely, those stream-enterer (P. sotāpanna; S. SROTAĀPANNA), once-returner (P. sakadagāmi; S. SAKṚDĀGĀMIN), nonreturner (P. anāgāmi; S. ANĀGĀMIN), and arahant (S. ARHAT). These are to be attained by following the noble eightfold path (P. ariyāṭṭhaṅgikamagga; see S. AṢṬĀṄGIKAMĀRGA). The question is then raised as to whether the soul and body are the same or different. This leads to another discussion of Buddhist practice and attainments, beginning with taking refuge in the three jewels, observing the precepts, renouncing the world to become a Buddhist monk, and controlling the senses with mindfulness (P. sati; S. SMṚTI), to cultivating the four meditative absorptions (P. jhāna; S. dhyāna), and developing the six superknowledges (P. abhiññā; S. ABHIJÑĀ), which culminate in enlightenment and liberation from the cycle of rebirth.

**Mahāmaudgalyāyana**. (P. Mahāmoggallāna; T. Mo'u 'gal gyi bu chen po; C. Mohemujianlian/Mulian; J. Makamokkenren/Mokuren; K. Mahamokkŏllyŏn/Mongnyŏn 摩訶目犍連/目連). An eminent ARHAT and one of the two chief disciples of the Buddha, often depicted together with his friend ŚĀRIPUTRA flanking the Buddha. Mahāmaudgalyāyana was considered supreme among the Buddha's disciples in supranormal powers (ṚDDHI). According to Pāli accounts, where he is called Moggallāna, he was older than the Buddha and born on the same day as Śāriputra (P. Sāriputta). Both he and Śāriputra were sons of wealthy families and were friends from childhood. Once, when witnessing a play, the two friends were overcome with a sense of the impermanence and the vanity of all things and decided to renounce the world as mendicants. They first became disciples of the agnostic Sañjaya Belaṭṭhiputta (SAÑJAYA VAIRĀṬĪPUTRA), although later they took their leave and wandered the length and breadth of India in search of a teacher. Finding no one who satisfied them, they parted company, promising one another that if one should succeed he would inform the other. Later Śāriputra met the Buddha's disciple, Assaji (S. AŚVAJIT), who recited for him a précis of the Buddha's teachings, the so-called YE DHARMĀ verse, which immediately prompted Śāriputra to attain the path of a stream-enterer (SROTAĀPANNA). He repeated the stanza to Mahāmaudgalyāyana, who likewise immediately became a stream-enterer.

The two friends thereupon resolved to take ordination as disciples of the Buddha and, together with five hundred disciples of their former teacher Sañjaya, proceeded to the Veḷuvana (S. VEṆUVANAVIHĀRA) grove where the Buddha was residing. The Buddha ordained the entire group with the formula ehi bhikkhu pabbajjā ("Come forth, monks"; see EHIBHIKṢUKĀ), whereupon all five hundred became arhats, except for Śāriputra and Mahāmaudgalyāyana. Mahāmaudgalyāyana attained arhatship seven days after his ordination, while Śāriputra reached the goal one week later. The Buddha declared Śāriputra and Mahāmaudgalyāyana his chief disciples the day they were ordained, noting that they had both strenuously exerted themselves in countless previous lives for this distinction; they appear often as the bodhisattva's companions in the JĀTAKAs. Śāriputra was chief among the Buddha's disciples in wisdom, while Mahāmaudgalyāyana was chief in mastery of supranormal powers. He could create doppelgängers of himself and transform himself into any shape he desired. He could perform intercelestial travel as easily as a person bends his arm, and the tradition is replete with the tales of his travels, such as flying to the Himālayas to find a medicinal plant to cure the ailing Śāriputra. Mahāmaudgalyāyana said of himself that he could crush Mount SUMERU like a bean and roll up the world like a mat and twirl it like a potter's wheel. He is described as shaking the heavens of ŚAKRA and BRAHMĀ to dissuade them from their pride, and he often preached to the divinities in their abodes. Mahāmaudgalyāyana could see ghosts (PRETA) and other spirits without having to enter into meditative trance as did other meditation masters, and because of his exceptional powers the Buddha instructed him alone to subdue the dangerous NĀGA, Nandopananda, whose huge hood had darkened the world. Mahāmaudgalyāyana's powers were so immense that during a terrible famine, he offered to turn the earth's crust over to uncover the ambrosia beneath it; the Buddha wisely discouraged him, saying that such an act would confound creatures. Even so, Mahāmaudgalyāyana's supranormal powers, unsurpassed in the world, were insufficient to overcome the law of cause and effect and the power of his own former deeds, as the famous tale of his death demonstrates. A group of naked JAINA ascetics resented the fact that the people of the kingdom of MAGADHA had shifted their allegiance and patronage from them to the Buddha and his followers, and they blamed Mahāmaudgalyāyana, who had reported that, during his celestial and infernal travels, he had observed deceased followers of the Buddha in the heavens and the followers of other teachers in the hells. They hired a group of bandits to assassinate the monk. When he discerned that they were approaching, the eighty-four-year-old monk made his body very tiny and escaped through the keyhole. He eluded them in different ways for six days, hoping to spare them from committing a deed of immediate retribution (ĀNANTARYAKARMAN) by killing an arhat. On the seventh day, Mahāmaudgalyāyana temporarily lost his supranormal powers, the residual karmic effect of having beaten his blind parents to death in a distant previous lifetime, a crime for which he had previously been reborn in hell. The bandits ultimately beat him mercilessly, until his bones had been smashed to the size of grains of rice. Left for dead, Mahāmaudgalyāyana regained his powers and soared into the air and into the presence of the Buddha, where he paid his final respects and passed into NIRVĀṆA at the Buddha's feet. ¶ Like many of the great arhats, Mahāmaudgalyāyana appears frequently in the MAHĀYĀNA sūtras, sometimes merely listed as a member of the audience, sometimes playing a more significant role. In the VIMALAKĪRTINIRDEŚA, he is one of the ŚRĀVAKA disciples who is reluctant to visit VIMALAKĪRTI. In the SADDHARMAPUṆḌARĪKASŪTRA, he is one of four arhats who understands the parable of the burning house and who rejoices in the teaching of the one vehicle (EKAYĀNA); later in the sūtra, the Buddha prophesies his eventual attainment of buddhahood. Mahāmaudgalyāyana is additionally famous in East Asian Buddhism for his role in the apocryphal YULANBEN JING. The text describes his efforts to save his mother from the tortures of her rebirth as a ghost (preta). Mahāmaudgalyāyana (C. Mulian) is able to use his supranormal powers to visit his mother in the realm of ghosts, but the food that he offers her immediately bursts into flames. The Buddha explains that it is impossible for the living to make offerings directly to the dead; instead, one should make offerings to the SAṂGHA in a bowl, and the power of their meditative practices will be able to save one's ancestors and loved ones from rebirths in the unfortunate realms (DURGATI).

**Mahāmāyā**. (S). See MĀYĀ.

**Mahāmāyātantra**. (T. Sgyu 'phrul chen mo'i rgyud). In Sanskrit, the "Great Illusion Tantra"; an important ANUTTARAYOGATANTRA of the "mother tantra" class, famous for its instructions on "dream yoga," one of the SIX YOGAS OF NĀROPA. It was translated into Tibetan during the earlier dissemination of the dharma (SNGA DAR) by VAIROCANA and GNUBS CHEN SANGS RGYAS YE SHES. It would later be counted as one of the five principal tantras of the SHANGS PA BKA' BRGYUD sect of Tibetan Buddhism.

**Mahāmāyūrī**. (T. Rma bya chen mo; C. Kongque mingwang; J. Kujaku myōō; K. Kongjak myŏngwang 孔雀明王). In Sanskrit, "Great Peacock"; one of the five female protectors (RAKṢĀ) of VAJRAYĀNA Buddhism, who frequently appear in MAṆḌALAs and remain important in the Newar Buddhism of Nepal. She is green in color and is sometimes depicted holding a peacock feather, à propos her name. She is considered the female emanation of the buddha AMOGHASIDDHI. Mahāmāyūrī has long been associated with curing snakebites. For example, in the *Mahāmāyūrīvidyārājñidhāraṇī* (T. Rma bya chen mo'i gzungs), an early Buddhist TANTRA, later classified as a KRIYĀTANTRA, a newly ordained monk named Svāti is bitten by a poisonous snake. ĀNANDA informs the Buddha, who imparts the DHĀRAṆĪ of Mahāmāyūrī which, when recited, cures snakebites.

**Mahāmeghasūtra**. (T. Sprin chen po'i mdo; C. Dafangdeng wuxiang jing/Dayun jing; J. Daihōdō musōkyō/Daiungyō; K. Taebangdŭng musang kyŏng/Taeun kyŏng 大方等無想經/大雲經). In Sanskrit, the "Great Cloud Sūtra"; it is also known in China as the *Dafangdeng wuxiang jing*. The *Mahāmeghasūtra* contains the teachings given by the Buddha to the bodhisattva "Great Cloud Secret Storehouse" (C. Dayunmizang) on the inconceivable means of attaining liberation, SAMĀDHI, and the power of DHĀRAṆĪs. The Buddha also declares that TATHĀGATAS remain forever present in the dharma and the SAṂGHA despite having entered PARINIRVĀṆA and that they are always endowed with the four qualities of NIRVĀṆA mentioned in the MAHĀPARINIRVĀṆASŪTRA, namely, permanence, bliss, purity, and selfhood (see GUṆAPĀRAMITĀ). The *Mahāparinirvāṇasūtra*'s influence on the *Mahāmeghasūtra* can also be witnessed in the story of the goddess "Pure Light" (C. Jingguang). Having heard the *Mahāparinirvāṇasūtra* in her past life, the goddess is told by the Buddha that she will be reborn as a universal monarch (CAKRAVARTIN). The sūtra is often cited for its prophecy of the advent of NĀGĀRJUNA, as well as for its injunctions against meat-eating. It was also recited in order to induce rain. In China, commentators on the *Mahāmeghasūtra* identified the newly enthroned Empress WU ZETIAN as the reincarnation of the goddess, seeking thereby to legitimize her rule. As Emperor Gaozong (r. 649–683) of the Tang dynasty suffered from increasingly ill health, his ambitious and pious wife Empress Wu took over the imperial administration. After her husband's death she exiled the legitimate heir Zhongzong (r. 683–684, 705–710) and usurped the throne. One of the many measures she took to gain the support of the people was the publication and circulation of the *Mahāmeghasūtra*. Two translations by ZHU FONIAN and DHARMAKṢEMA were available at the time. Wu Zetian also ordered the establishment of monasteries called DAYUNSI ("Great Cloud Monastery") in every prefecture of the empire.

**Mahāmeghavana**. In Pāli, "Great Cloud Grove"; a park in Sri Lanka donated to MAHINDA for use by the saṅgha (S. SAṂGHA) by King DEVĀNAṂPIYATISSA. The park was located on the southern outskirts of the Sinhalese capital, ANURĀDHAPURA, and received its name because a cloud appeared and rained upon the spot when the park was first laid out. The Mahāmeghavana was considered especially auspicious because it was said to have been visited by four of the five buddhas of the current auspicious eon (S. BHADRAKALPA; P. bhaddakappa), a fact Mahinda pointed out to the king after the park was donated to the saṅgha. The Mahameghavana came to be the site of many of the major monuments, shrines, and institutions of Sinhalese Buddhist history. These included the MAHĀVIHĀRA monastery, built for Mahinda, which became headquarters of the THERAVĀDA fraternity; the THŪPĀRĀMA monastery, which housed the first STŪPA or reliquary mound erected on the island; the southern branch of the BODHI TREE, brought to the island from India by Mahinda's sister, the elder nun SAṄGHAMITTĀ; and the MAHĀTHŪPA and LOHAPĀSĀDA built by King DUṬṬHAGĀMAṆI. Subsequently at the Mahāmeghavana were also built the ABHAYAGIRI monastery by King VAṬṬAGĀMAṆI ABHAYA and the JETAVANA monastery by King MAHĀSENA. These two monasteries became headquarters of rival fraternities that seceded from the Mahāvihāra.

**Mahāmoggallāna**. (P). See MAHĀMAUDGALYĀYANA.

**Mahāmucilinda**. (S). See MUCILINDA.

**mahāmudrā**. (T. phyag rgya chen po; C. dayin/dashouyin; J. daiin/daishuin; K. taein/taesuin 大印/大手印). In Sanskrit, "great seal"; an important term in tantric Buddhism, especially in the traditions that flourished in Tibet. In Tibet, although it is extolled by all sects, mahāmudrā is particularly associated with the BKA' BRGYUD sect and the lineage coming from TILOPA and NĀROPA to MAR PA and MI LA RAS PA. There, it is regarded as the crowning experience of Buddhist practice. It is a state of enlightened awareness in which phenomenal appearance and emptiness (ŚŪNYATĀ) are unified. It is also used to refer to the fundamental reality that places its imprint or "seal" on all phenomena of SAṂSĀRA and NIRVĀṆA. Mahāmūdrā literature exalts the ordinary state of mind as being both the natural and ultimate state, characterized by lucidity and simplicity. In mahāmudrā, the worldly mind is valued for its ultimate identity with the ordinary mind; every deluded thought contains within it the lucidity and simplicity of the ordinary mind. This identity merely needs to be recognized to bring about the dawning of wisdom, the realization that a natural purity pervades all existence, including the deluded mind. It is usually set forth in a threefold rubric of the basis (gzhi), path (lam), and fruition ('bras bu), with the first referring to the pure nature of the ordinary mind, the second referring to becoming aware of that mind through the practice of meditation, and the third referring to the full realization of the innate clarity and purity of the mind. There is some debate in Tibet whether mahāmudrā is exclusively a tantric practice or whether there is also a SŪTRA version, connected with TATHĀGATAGARBHA teachings. ¶ In tantric practice, mahāmudrā is also highest of the four seals, the others being the action seal (KARMAMUDRĀ), the pledge seal (SAMAYAMUDRĀ), and the wisdom seal (JÑĀNAMUDRĀ).

**Mahāmudropadeśa**. (T. Phyag rgya chen po'i man ngag). In Sanskrit, "Instructions on the Great Seal"; a text known primarily through its Tibetan translations. It records seminal instructions on the view and practice of MAHĀMUDRĀ, taught by TILOPA to his disciple NĀROPA on the banks of the Ganges River. Due to this setting, the works is commonly known in Tibet as the *Phyag chen gang gā ma* ("Ganges Mahāmudrā") or simply the *Gang gā ma*. Several versions are preserved in the Tibetan Buddhist canon and the writings of various Tibetan Buddhist masters.

**Mahāmuni**. (T. Thub pa chen po; C. Dasheng; J. Daishō; K. Taesŏng 大聖). In Sanskrit and Pāli, "Great Sage"; one of the common epithets of the Buddha, which figures in the Buddha's name MANTRA: oṃ muni muni Mahāmuni Śākyamuni svāhā. Mahāmuni is also the name of the most famous and venerated image of the Buddha in Burma; see ARAKAN BUDDHA.

**Mahānāman**. (P. Mahānāma; T. Ming chen; C. Mohenan; J. Makanan; K. Mahanam 摩訶男). The Sanskrit proper name of two significant disciples of the buddha. ¶ Mahānāman was one of the five ascetics (S. PAÑCAVARGIKA; P. pañcavaggiyā; alt. S. bhadravargīya) who was a companion of Prince SIDDHĀRTHA during his practice of austerities and hence one of the first disciples converted by the Buddha at the Deer Park (MṚGADĀVA) in ṚṢIPATANA following his enlightenment. Together with his companions, Mahānāman heard the Buddha's first sermon, the "Setting in Motion the Wheel of Dharma" (S. DHARMACAKRAPRAVARTANASŪTRA; P. DHAMMACAKKAPPAVATTANASUTTA), and he attained the state of a stream-enterer (SROTAĀPANNA) three days later. He and the others became ARHATs while listening to the buddha preach the ANATTALAKKHAṆASUTTA. Mahānāman later traveled to the town of Macchikāsaṇḍa, and, while he was out on alms rounds, the householder CITTA saw him. Citta was greatly impressed by Mahānāman's dignified deportment, and invited him to his house for an meal offering. Having served Mahānāman the morning meal and listened to his sermon, Citta was inspired to offer his pleasure garden Ambāṭakavana to Mahānāman as a gift to the SAṂGHA, and built a monastery there. ¶ Another Mahānāman was also an eminent lay disciple, whom the Buddha declared to be foremost among laymen who offer choice alms food. According to the Pāli account, Mahānāman was Anuruddha's (S. ANIRUDDHA) elder brother and the Buddha's cousin. It was with Mahānāman's permission that Anuruddha joined the order with other Sākiyan (S. ŚĀKYA) kinsmen of the Buddha. Mahānāman was very generous in his support of the order. During a period of scarcity when the Buddha was dwelling at Verañja, he supplied the monks with medicines for three periods of four months each. Mahānāman was keenly interested in the Buddha's doctrine and there are several accounts in the scriptures of his conversations with the Buddha. Once while the Buddha lay ill in the Nigrodhārāma, ĀNANDA took Mahānāman aside to answer his questions on whether concentration (SAMĀDHI) preceded or followed upon knowledge. Mahānāman attained the state of a once-returner (sakadāgāmi; S. SAKṚDĀGĀMIN), but his deception toward Pasenadi (S. PRASENAJIT), the king of Kosala (S. KOŚALA), precipitated the eventual destruction of the Sākiya (S. ŚĀKYA) clan. Pasenadi had asked Mahānāman for the hand of a true Sākiyan daughter in marriage, but the latter, out of pride, instead sent Vāsabhakkhattiyā, a daughter born to him by a slave girl. To conceal the treachery, Mahānāman feigned to eat from the same dish as his daughter, thus convincing Pasenadi of her pure lineage. The ruse was not discovered until years later when Viḍuḍabha, the son of Pasenadi and Vāsabhakkhattiyā, was insulted by his Sākiyan kinsmen who refused to treat him with dignity because of his mother's status as the offspring of a slave. Viḍuḍabha vowed revenge and later marched against Kapilavatthu (S. KAPILAVASTU) and slaughtered all who claimed Sākiyan descent. ¶ Another Mahānāma was the c. fifth century author of the Pāli MAHĀVAṂSA.

**Mahānidānasutta**. (C. Dayuan fangbian jing; J. Daien hōbengyō; K. Taeyŏn pangp'yŏn kyŏng 大緣方便經). In Pāli, the "Great Discourse on Causality"; the fifteenth sutta of the DĪGHANIKĀYA (a separate DHARMAGUPTAKA recension appears as the thirteenth sūtra in the Chinese translation of the DĪRGHĀGAMA); preached by the Buddha to ĀNANDA in the market town of Kammāsadhamma to dispel his wrong view that the doctrine of dependent origination (P. paṭiccasamuppāda; S. PRATĪTYASAMUTPĀDA) only appears to be profound. He then gives an exposition of dependent origination as a tenfold causal chain (rather than the typical twelvefold chain, dropping the first two links), explaining that those who do not fathom this truth, even if they be masters of meditative absorption (P. JHĀNA; S. DHYĀNA), will still be addicted to the notion of a self (P. atta; S. ĀTMAN) and hence bound to the cycle of rebirth.

**Mahāniddesa**. In Pāli, "Longer Exposition," first part of the *Niddesa* ("Exposition"), an early commentarial work on the SUTTANIPĀTA included in the Pāli SUTTAPIṬAKA as the eleventh book of the KHUDDAKANIKĀYA. The *Niddesa* is attributed by tradition to the Buddha's chief disciple, Sāriputta (S. ŚĀRIPUTRA), and is divided into two sections: the *Mahāniddesa* and the CŪḶANIDDESA ("Shorter Exposition"). The *Mahāniddesa* comments on the sixteen suttas (S. SŪTRA) of the AṬṬHAKAVAGGA chapter of the *Suttanipāta*; the *Cūḷaniddesa* comments on the sixteen suttas of the Parāyaṇavagga chapter and on the *Khaggavisānasutta* (see KHAḌGAVIṢĀṆA). The *Mahāniddesa* and *Cūḷaniddesa* do not comment on any of the remaining contents of the *Suttanipāta*, a feature that has suggested to historians that at the time of their composition the Aṭṭhakavagga and Parāyaṇavagga were autonomous anthologies not yet incorporated into the *Suttanipāta*, and that the *Khaggavisānasutta* likewise circulated independently. The exegesis of the *Suttanipāta* by the *Mahā-* and *Cūḷaniddesa* displays the influence of the Pāli ABHIDHAMMA (S. ABHIDHARMA) and passages from it are frequently quoted in the VISUDDHIMAGGA. Both parts of the *Niddesa* are formulaic in structure, a feature that appears to have been designed as a pedagogical aid to facilitate memorization. In Western scholarship, there has long been a debate regarding their dates of composition, with some scholars dating them as early as the third century BCE, others to as late as the second century CE. The *Mahā-* and *Cūḷaniddesa* are the only commentarial texts besides the SUTTAVIBHAṄGA of the VINAYAPIṬAKA to be included in the Sri Lankan and Thai recensions of the Pāli canon. In contrast, the Burmese canon includes two additional early commentaries, the NETTIPAKARAṆA and PEṬAKOPADESA, as books sixteen and seventeen in its recension of the *Khuddakanikāya*.

**Mahanikai**. (P. Mahānikāya). In Thai, "Great Congregation"; the predominant monastic fraternity of Thai Buddhism, to which the vast majority of Thai monasteries belong; sometimes also seen transcribed as Mahanikay, or by its Pāli equivalent, Mahānikāya. The current Mahanikai order traces its lineage back to the fifteenth century, when a group of Siamese monks were sent to Sri Lanka for reordination in order to revitalize and help preserve the Thai monastic tradition. The designation "Mahanikai," however, represents a synthesis of many Thai traditions that were all placed under this rubric in the nineteenth century by the Thai king Mongkut (RĀMA IV), who was a monk from 1824 to 1851. Mongkut was concerned with lax observance of the vinaya precepts within much of the Thai monastic community and used the term Mahanikai to refer to those monks who did not conform to his new "reform" order, the THAMMAYUT. Thus, any monks who did not reordain into the Thammayut order became by default Mahanikai monks. A similar situation occurred in Cambodia, when the Thammayut fraternity was introduced there later in the nineteenth century. In Mongkut's time, the two sects came to differ on many points of monastic practice, including the way robes were worn, how often monks could eat, and whether they could handle money. Thammayut monks were also encouraged to preach sermons in Thai vernacular language, while Mahanikai preached sermons grounded in Pāli. Many of these differences, and the tensions that surround them, still exist today. The largest and most important monastery of the Mahanikai order is WAT MAHATHAT, "Temple of the Great Relic," in Bangkok.

**Mahāpadānasuttanta**. (C. Daben jing; J. Daihongyō; K. Taebon kyŏng 大本經). In Pāli, the "Discourse on the Great Legend"; the fourteenth sutta of the Pāli DĪGHANIKĀYA (a separate DHARMAGUPTAKA recension is the first SŪTRA in the Chinese translation of the DĪRGHĀGAMA). The scripture was preached by the Buddha to a group of monks dwelling at the city of Sāvatthi (ŚRĀVASTĪ), wherein the Buddha recounts his encounters in his previous lives with the seven buddhas of antiquity (see SAPTABUDDHA). He describes the life of the buddha Vipassī (S. VIPAŚYIN), whose enlightenment story closely resembles his own. Vipassī is described as having attained liberation through insight (P. VIPASSANĀ; S. VIPAŚYANĀ) into dependent origination (P. paṭiccasamuppāda; S. PRATĪTYASAMUTPĀDA). Dependent origination is presented here as a tenfold causal chain rather than the standard twelvefold chain, suggesting that this sutta retains a version of the doctrine that predates its classical formulation. See also MAHĀVADĀNASŪTRA.

**mahāpadeśa**. (P. mahāpadesa; T. chen po bstan pa; C. dashuo; J. daisetsu; K. taesŏl 大說). In Sanskrit, "great authorities"; one of the categories employed in Buddhist hermeneutics to determine textual authority, that is, to judge after the Buddha's death, when he was no longer available as the final arbiter, whether a specific teaching was the authentic word of the Buddha (BUDDHAVACANA). According to this system of evaluation, someone might claim that a specific teaching is the word of the Buddha because of it having been heard from one of four possible authorities: (1) from the Buddha, (2) from a community (SAṂGHA) of senior monks, (3) from a smaller group of learned elder monks, and (4) from a single learned monk. When someone claims to have heard a teaching directly from one of these four sources, the saṃgha may determine whether it is the word of the Buddha by ascertaining whether it corresponds to the teachings of the SŪTRAs and is in agreement with the VINAYA. If it does, it is to be accepted as the word of the Buddha; if it does not, it is to be rejected. In the Pāli tradition, the four are set forth in the *Mahāpadesasutta*, which is found in the canon both as an independent text and as incorporated into the MAHĀPARINIBBĀNASUTTA. The Sanskrit versions of the topic, in both mainstream and MAHĀYĀNA materials, add a third criterion to this conformity with the sūtras and with the vinaya: that the words not go against "the way things are" (DHARMATĀ).

**Mahāpanthaka**. (S). See PANTHAKA; CŪḌAPANTHAKA.

**Mahāparākramabāhu-Katikāvata**. In Pāli, "The Great Law Code of Parākramabāhu"; a set of monastic regulations promulgated by the Sinhalese king PARĀKRAMABĀHU I (r. 1153–1186) as part of a monastic purification program (sāsanavisodhana) he inaugurated. This policy led to the abolition of the ABHAYAGIRI and JETAVANA fraternities and the ascendancy of the MAHĀVIHĀRA as the only recognized Buddhist fraternity on the island of Sri Lanka. His law code is classified as a sāsana-katikāvata; that is, a set of regulations binding on the entire saṅgha (S. SAṂGHA) of the kingdom, as opposed to a vihāra-katikāvata, or set of regulations binding only on the residents of a single monastery. As a document, the *Mahāparākramabāhu-Katikāvata* is laid out as a set of specific rules governing the life of the saṅgha, preceded by an historical introduction recounting purifications conducted in the past by notable kings such as Asoka (S. AŚOKA). The text was influential in Southeast Asia as both a blueprint for monastic revitalization movements and saṅgha organization, and as a model for the writing of Buddhist chronicles.

**Mahāparinibbānasuttanta**. (S. MAHĀPARINIRVĀṆASŪTRA; C. Youxing jing/Da banniepan jing; J. Yūgyōkyō/Daihatsunehangyō; K. Yuhaeng kyŏng/Tae panyŏlban kyŏng 遊行經/大般涅槃經). In Pāli, the "Discourse on the Great Decease" or the "Great Discourse on the Final Nirvāṇa"; the sixteenth sutta of the Pāli DĪGHANIKĀYA and longest discourse in the Pāli canon. (There were also either Sanskrit or Middle Indic recensions of this mainstream Buddhist version of the scripture, which should be distinguished from the longer MAHĀYĀNA recension of the scripture that bears the same title; see MAHĀPARINIRVĀṆASŪTRA.) There are six different Chinese translations of this mainstream version of the text, including a DHARMAGUPTAKA recension in the Chinese translation of the DĪRGHĀGAMA and an independent translation in three rolls by FAXIAN. This scripture recounts in six chapters the last year of Buddha's life, his passage into PARINIRVĀṆA, and his cremation. In the text, the Buddha and ĀNANDA travel from Rājagaha (S. RĀJAGṚHA) to Kusināra (S. KUŚINAGARĪ) in fourteen stages, meeting with different audiences to whom the Buddha gives a variety of teachings. The narrative contains numerous sermons on such subjects as statecraft, the unity of the SAṂGHA, morality, the FOUR NOBLE TRUTHS, and the four great authorities (MAHĀPADEŚA) for determining the authenticity of Buddhist doctrines following the Buddha's demise. The Buddha crosses a river using his magical powers and describes to the distraught where their deceased loved ones have been reborn. Becoming progressively more ill, the Buddha decides to spend his final rains retreat (P. vassa; S. VARṢĀ) with Ānanda meditating in the forest near VEṆUGRĀMAKA, using his powers of deep concentration to hold his disease in check. He is eighty years old and describes his body as being like an old cart held together by straps. When the Buddha expresses his wish to address the saṃgha, Ānanda assumes that there is a teaching that the Buddha has not yet taught. The Buddha replies that he was not one who taught with a "teacher's fist" (P. ācariyamuṭṭhi) or "closed fist," holding back some secret teaching, but that he has in fact already revealed everything. The Buddha also says that he is not the head of the saṃgha and that after his death each monk should "be an island unto himself" with the DHARMA as his island (P. dīpa; S. dvīpa) and his refuge. ¶ While meditating at the CĀPĀLACAITYA, the Buddha mentions to Ānanda three times that a TATHĀGATA has the power to live for an eon or until the end of an eon. (The Pāli commentaries take "eon" here to mean "his full allotted lifespan," not a cosmological period.) Ānanda, however, misses the hint and does not ask him to do so. MĀRA then appears to remind the Buddha of what he told him at the time of his enlightenment: that he would not enter nibbāna (NIRVĀṆA) until he had trained monks and disciples who were able to teach the dhamma (S. DHARMA). Māra tells the Buddha that that task has now been accomplished, and the Buddha eventually agrees, "consciously and deliberately" renouncing his remaining lifespan and informing Māra that he will pass away in three months' time. The earth then quakes, causing the Buddha to explain to Ānanda the eight reasons for an earthquake, one of which is that a tathāgata has renounced his life force. It is only at that point that Ānanda implores the Buddha to remain until the end of the eon, but the Buddha tells him that the appropriate time for his request has passed, and recalls fifteen occasions on which he had told Ānanda of this remarkable power and how each time Ānanda had failed to ask him to exercise it. The Buddha then explains to a group of monks the four great authorities (MAHĀPADEŚA), the means of determining the authenticity of a particular doctrine after the Buddha has died and is no longer available to arbitrate. He then receives his last meal from the smith CUNDA. The dish that the Buddha requests is called SŪKARAMADDAVA, lit., "pig's delight." There has been a great deal of scholarly discussion on the meaning of this term, centering upon whether it is a pork dish, such as mincemeat, or something eaten by pigs, such as truffles or mushrooms. At the meal, the Buddha announces that he alone should be served the dish and what was left over should be buried, for none but a buddha could survive eating it. Shortly after finishing the dish, the Buddha is afflicted with the dysentery from which he would eventually die. The Buddha then converts a layman named Pukkusa, who offers him gold robes. Ānanda notices that the color of the robes pales next to the Buddha's skin, and the Buddha informs him that the skin of the Buddha is particularly bright on two occasions, the night when he achieves enlightenment and the night that he passes away. Proceeding to the outskirts of the town of Kuśinagarī, the Buddha lies down on his right side between twin sāla (S. ŚĀLA) trees, which immediately bloom out of season. Shortly before dying, the Buddha instructs Ānanda to visit Cunda and reassure him that no blame has accrued to him; rather, he should rejoice at the great merit he has earned for having given the Buddha his last meal. Monks and divinities assemble to pay their last respects to the Buddha. When Ānanda asks how monks can pay respect to the Buddha after he has passed away, the Buddha explains that monks, nuns, and laypeople should visit four major places (MAHĀSTHĀNA) of pilgrimage: the site of his birth at LUMBINĪ, his enlightenment at BODHGAYĀ, his first teaching at ṚṢIPATANA (SĀRNĀTH), and his PARINIRVĀṆA at Kuśinagarī. Anyone who dies while on pilgrimage to one of these four places, the Buddha says, will be reborn in the heavens. Scholars have taken these instructions as a sign of the relatively late date of this sutta (or at least this portion of it), arguing that this admonition by the Buddha is added to promote pilgrimage to four already well-established shrines. The Buddha instructs the monks to cremate his body in the fashion of a CAKRAVARTIN. He says that his remains (ŚARĪRA) should be enshrined in a STŪPA to which the faithful should offer flowers and perfumes in order to gain happiness in the future. The Buddha then comforts Ānanda, telling him that all things must pass away and praising him for his devotion, predicting that he will soon become an ARHAT. When Ānanda laments the fact that the Buddha will pass away at such a "little mud-walled town, a backwoods town, a branch township," rather than a great city, the Buddha disabuses him of this notion, telling him that Kuśinagarī had previously been the magnificent capital of an earlier cakravartin king named Sudarśana (P. Sudassana). The wanderer SUBHADRA (P. Subhadda) then becomes the last person to be ordained by the Buddha. When Ānanda laments that the monks will soon have no teacher, the Buddha explains that henceforth the dharma and the VINAYA will be their teacher. As his last disciplinary act before he dies, the Buddha orders that the penalty of brahmadaṇḍa (lit. the "holy rod") be passed on CHANDAKA (P. Channa), his former charioteer, which requires that he be completely shunned by his fellow monks. Then, asking three times whether any of the five hundred monks present has a final question, and hearing none, the Buddha speaks his last words, "All conditioned things are subject to decay. Strive with diligence." The Buddha's mind then passed into the first stage of meditative absorption (P. JHĀNA; S. DHYĀNA) and then in succession through the other three levels of the subtle-materiality realm (RŪPADHĀTU) and then through the four levels of the immaterial realm (ĀRŪPYADHĀTU). He then passed back down through the same eight levels to the first absorption, then back up to the fourth absorption, and then passed away, at which point the earth quaked. Seven days later, his body was prepared for cremation. However, the funeral pyre could not be ignited until the arrival of MAHĀKĀŚYAPA (P. Mahākassapa), who had been away at the time of the Buddha's death. After he arrived and paid his respects, the funeral pyre ignited spontaneously. The relics (ŚARĪRA) of the Buddha remaining after the cremation were taken by the Mallas of Kuśinagarī, but seven other groups of the Buddha's former patrons also came to claim the relics. The brāhmaṇa DROṆA (P. Doṇa) was called upon to decide the proper procedure for apportioning the relics. Droṇa divided the relics into eight parts that the disputing kings could carry back to their home kingdoms for veneration. Droṇa kept for himself the urn he used to apportion the relics; a ninth person was given the ashes from the funeral pyre. These ten (the eight portions of relics, the urn, and the ashes) were each then enshrined in stūpas. At this point the scripture's narrative ends. A similar account, although with significant variations, appears in Sanskrit recensions of the *Mahāparinirvāṇasūtra*.

**Mahāparinirvāṇasūtra**. (T. Yongs su mya ngan las 'das pa chen po'i mdo; C. Da banniepan jing; J. Daihatsunehangyō; K. Tae panyŏlban kyŏng 大般涅槃經). In Sanskrit, "Discourse on the Great Decease" or the "Great Discourse on the Final Nirvāṇa"; also known in all languages simply as the *Nirvāṇa Sūtra*. As its title suggests, the SŪTRA describes the events and the Buddha's final instructions prior to his passage into PARINIRVĀṆA and is thus the Sanskrit retelling of the mainstream version of the text (see MAHĀPARINIBBĀNASUTTA). However, although some of the same events are narrated in both versions, the Sanskrit text is very different in content, providing one of the most influential sources for MAHĀYĀNA views of the true nature of the Buddha and his NIRVĀṆA, and of the buddha-nature (referred to in the sūtra as both BUDDHADHĀTU, or "buddha-element," and TATHĀGATAGARBHA). There appear to have been a number of Sanskrit versions of the sūtra, the earliest of which was likely compiled in Kashmir (see KASHMIR-GANDHĀRA) in the third century CE. One piece of internal evidence for the date of composition is the presence of prophecies that the dharma would fall into decline seven hundred years after the Buddha's passage into nirvāṇa. None of the Sanskrit versions is extant (apart from fragments), but several are preserved in Chinese and Tibetan translations. The earliest and shortest of these translations is in six rolls, translated into Chinese by FAXIAN (who brought the Sanskrit text to China from India) and BUDDHABHADRA, and completed in 418 CE. A second version was translated from Sanskrit into Tibetan at the end of the eighth century. The longest version, in forty rolls, was translated into Chinese by DHARMAKṢEMA and completed in 423. It is known as the "Northern Text." This version was later translated into Tibetan from the Chinese as the *Yongs su mya ngan las das pa chen po'i mdo*. Besides the Tibetan translation of the long Chinese version by Dharmakṣema, there is another version of the sūtra in Tibetan translation, a *Mahāparinirvāṇasūtra* in 3,900 ślokas, translated by Jinamitra, Dhyānagarbha, and Ban de btsan dra, as well as a few folios of a translation of the sūtra by Kamalagupta and RIN CHEN BZANG PO. The Faxian and Dharmakṣema Chinese versions were subsequently edited into a single work, in thirty-six rolls. Chinese scriptural catalogues (JINGLU) also refer to two other translations of the sūtra, made prior to that of Faxian, but these are no longer extant. There were significant differences between the versions of Faxian and Dharmakṣema (and hence apparently in the Sanskrit recensions that they translated), so much so that scholars speculate that the shorter version was composed in a non-Mahāyāna community, with Mahāyāna elements being added to what evolved into the longer version. The most famous of the differences between the versions occurs on the question of whether all beings, including "incorrigibles" (ICCHANTIKA), possess the buddha-nature; the shorter version says that they do not and they are therefore condemned to eternal damnation; the longer version says that they do and thus even they retain the capacity to achieve enlightenment. The shorter version of the sūtra describes the SAṂGHA as consisting of monks and nuns and preaches about the need to provide donations (DĀNA) to them; the longer version includes the laity among the saṃgha and preaches the need for charity to all persons. The longer version also recommends various forms of punishment, including execution, for those who denigrate the Mahāyāna. The sūtra also makes reference to other famous sūtras, such as the SADDHARMAPUṆḌARĪKASŪTRA, and is mentioned in other sūtras, such as the MAHĀMEGHASŪTRA. The *Mahāparinirvāṇasūtra*, like other important sūtras extolling tathāgatagarbha thought, such as the ŚRĪMĀLĀDEVĪSIṂHANĀDASŪTRA, plays on the classical doctrine of the four "inverted views" (VIPARYĀSA), according to which sentient beings mistakenly view that which is suffering as being pleasurable, that which is impermanent as permanent, that which is impure as pure, and that which is without self as having self. In this sūtra, by contrast, the four right views of suffering, impermanence, impurity, and no-self are proclaimed to be erroneous when describing the Buddha, his nirvāṇa, and the buddhadhātu; these are instead each said to be in fact blissful, permanent, pure, and endowed with self (see GUṆAPĀRAMITĀ). Thus, the Buddha did not pass into nirvāṇa, for his lifespan is incalculable. The Buddha's nirvāṇa—which is referred to in the sūtra as "great nirvāṇa" (mahānirvāṇa) or "great final nirvāṇa" (MAHĀPARINIRVĀṆA)—differs from that of the ARHAT. The nirvāṇa of the arhat is said to be merely the state of the absence of the afflictions (KLEŚA) but with no awareness of the buddhadhātu. The nirvāṇa of the buddha is instead eternal, pure, blissful, and endowed with self, a primordially existent reality that is only temporarily obscured by the kleśa; when that nirvāṇa and buddhadhātu are finally "recognized," buddhahood is then achieved. The Buddha reveals the existence of this nirvāṇa to bodhisattvas. Because the buddhadhātu is present within all sentient beings, these four qualities are therefore found not simply in the Buddha but in all beings. This implies, therefore, that the Buddha and all beings are endowed with self, in direct contradiction to the normative Buddhist doctrine of no-self (ANĀTMAN). Here, in this sūtra, the teaching of no-self is described as a conventional truth (SAṂVṚTISATYA): when the Buddha said that there was no self, what he actually meant was that there is no mundane, conditioned self among the aggregates (SKANDHA). The Buddha's true teaching, as revealed at the time of his nirvāṇa, is that there is a "great self" or a "true self" (S. mahātman; C. dawo), which is the buddhadhātu, in all beings. To assert that there is no self is to misunderstand the true dharma. The doctrine of emptiness (ŚŪNYATĀ) thus comes to mean the absence of that which is compounded, suffering, and impermanent. These teachings would become influential in Tibet, especially among the proponents of the doctrine of "other emptiness" (GZHAN STONG). See also GUṆAPĀRAMITĀ.

**Mahāprajāpatī**. (P. Mahāpajāpatī; T. Skye dgu'i bdag mo chen mo; C. Moheboshebotі; J. Makahajahadai; K. Mahabasabaje 摩訶波闍波提). An eminent ARHAT, the Buddha's stepmother and aunt, and the first woman to be ordained a Buddhist nun (S. BHIKṢUṆĪ; P. bhikkhunī). Mahāprajāpatī and the Buddha's mother, MĀYĀ, were sisters and both married to the bodhisattva's father, ŚUDDHODANA. When the bodhisattva's mother died seven days after his birth, Mahāprajāpatī raised him as her own son. According to the Pāli accounts, she became a lay disciple of the Buddha when he returned to the palace of his father and preached the *Mahādhammapāla-Jātaka*, becoming at that time a stream-enterer (SROTAĀPANNA). Upon the death of her husband, she resolved to renounce the world and follow the Buddha as a nun, but because there was no nuns' order, she had to request the Buddha to institute it. When, at the city of KAPILAVASTU, five hundred men of the ŚĀKYA clan entered the monastic order, Mahāprajāpatī together with the five hundred former wives of these men approached the Buddha and requested that they also be allowed to ordain and follow the religious life. The Buddha refused, warning that the presence of women in the order would speed the inevitable decline and demise of the dispensation. Despite his refusal, she and the five hundred Śākyan women shaved their heads and donned the yellow robes of Buddhist mendicants and followed the Buddha to the city of VAIŚĀLĪ. Again Mahāprajāpatī requested the Buddha to permit them to enter the order and again he refused. Finally, ĀNANDA, the Buddha's cousin and chief attendant, interceded on her behalf, asking the Buddha if women were capable of achieving enlightenment. He conceded that they were. Finally, the Buddha, acknowledging the debt he owed to his stepmother, granted ordination to her on the condition that she accept eight "heavy rules" (S. GURUDHARMA; P. garudhamma) that would guarantee the nuns' order's dependence on the monks' order and place it in an inferior rank. Her acceptance of these eight special rules served as her ordination. Mahāprajāpatī soon attained arhatship, as did her five hundred companions when they heard the *Nandakovādasutta* that the monk NANDAKA preached to them at the Buddha's request. (On the first hearing, the nuns attained stream-entry; when the Buddha had Nandaka repeat the same sermon the next day, they all achieved arahantship. Other sources say, however, that Mahāprajāpatī and her followers attained arahantship only moments before her death.) As the first bhikṣuṇī, Mahāprajāpatī is regarded as the mother of the nuns' order, and she was declared by the Buddha to be foremost among nuns in experience. She lived to be 120 years old, and when she died, her five hundred disciples passed into PARINIRVĀṆA with her. The miracles attending Mahāprajāpatī's cremation, including the duplication of the physical body (MAHĀPRĀTIHĀRYA) that the Buddha himself had performed, were said to have been second only to those of the Buddha himself.

***Māhaprājñāpāramitāśāstra**. [alt. *Mahāprajñāpāramitopadeśa]. See DAZHIDU LUN.

***Mahāprajñāpāramitāsūtra**. (T. Shes rab kyi pha rol tu phyin pa chen po'i mdo; C. Dabore boluomiduo jing; J. Daihannya haramittakyō; K. Taebanya paramilta kyŏng 大般若波羅蜜多經). In Sanskrit, the "Sūtra on the Great Perfection of Wisdom"; a massive compilation of PRAJÑĀPĀRAMITĀ scriptural literature said to have been preached by the Buddha in four different places to sixteen discrete assemblies. These sixteen assemblies correspond to sixteen separate perfection of wisdom sūtras, including such seminal works as the ŚATASĀHASRIKĀPRAJÑĀPĀRAMITĀSŪTRA ("Prajñāpāramitā in One Hundred Thousand Lines") and the VAJRACCHEDIKĀPRAJÑĀPĀRAMITĀSŪTRA ("Diamond Sūtra"), which are integrated in this text into a single narrative. This recension of the scripture is only extant in a Chinese translation made in six hundred rolls by XUANZANG and his translation team between the years 660 and 663. Xuanzang's recension is by far the largest of all the prajñāpāramitā scriptures in the Chinese Buddhist canon (DAZANGJING), constituting about a third of the entire prajñāpāramitā section. The *Mahāprajñāpāramitāsūtra* also often holds pride of place as the first sūtra found in many traditional East Asian Buddhist scriptural canons, such as the KORYŎ TAEJANGGYŎNG. (In Tibet, the ŚATASĀHASRIKĀPRAJÑĀPĀRAMITĀ in sixteen volumes comes at the start of the prajñāpāramitā section.) There has been speculation that the Chinese version of the well-known PRAJÑĀPĀRAMITĀHṚDAYASŪTRA ("Heart Sūtra"), which was also translated by Xuanzang, may be a redaction of sections of this Chinese recension of the *Mahāprajñāpāramitāsūtra*, made as a mneumonic encoding (DHĀRAṆĪ) of the massive perfection of wisdom literature.

**mahāprātihārya**. (P. mahāpāṭihāriya; T. cho 'phrul chen po; C. shenbianxiang; J. jinpensō; K. sinbyŏnsang 神變相). In Sanskrit, "great miracle." This and the "dual miracle" (YAMAKAPRĀTIHĀRYA) are two popular miracles that the Buddha performed during his career, frequently narrated in both canonical and commentarial literature and also widely depicted in Buddhist art. Both the mahāprātihārya and the yamakaprātihārya are generally understood to have taken place in the city of ŚRĀVASTĪ. In the mahāprātihārya, the Buddha creates duplicates of himself, his dopplegängers then appearing in various terrestrial and heavenly abodes. In one instance, the Buddha produces a doppelgänger that remains on earth while he then goes to the TUṢITA heaven to preach the dharma to his mother MĀYĀ. In another instance, the Buddha creates several duplicates of himself so that everyone present in his audience can interact with him privately.

**Mahāpratisarā**. (C. Dasuiqiu; J. Daizuigu; K. Taesugu 大隨求). One of the five female protectors (RAKṢĀ) of VAJRAYĀNA Buddhism, who remains important in the Newar Buddhism of Nepal. In the *Pañcarakṣāsūtra*, her DHĀRAṆĪ is said to provide protection from a variety of dangers and to bestow rebirth in heaven. In some accounts of the life of the Buddha, his son RĀHULA was conceived on the night that the prince left the palace, but was not born until six years later when his father became the Buddha; during her protracted pregnancy, the Buddha's wife, YAŚODHARĀ, is said to have been protected by Mahāpratisarā.

**Mahāpūrṇa**. (S). See PŪRṆA.

**mahāpuruṣa**. (P. mahāpurisa; T. skyes bu chen po; C. daren; J. dainin; K. taein 大人). In Sanskrit, lit., "great person," sometimes translated as "superman"; a being whose body is adorned with the "marks of a great person" (MAHĀPURUṢALAKṢAṆA), which include the thirty-two "major marks" (LAKṢAṆA) and the eighty secondary marks (ANUVYAÑJANA). A being with such physical marks is destined to become either a buddha or a CAKRAVARTIN. ¶ The term mahāpuruṣa is also used to indicate the highest rank in a threefold division of humans that occur in certain MAHĀYĀNA texts, notably ATIŚA's BODHIPATHAPRADĪPA: (a) beings of great capacity, who seek to free all beings from suffering; (b) beings of intermediate capacity, who seek to free themselves from suffering; and (c) beings of lesser capacity, who seek happiness within the cycle of rebirth. The Tibetan translation of this term, skyes bu chen po, is used widely in the LAM RIM literature as a designation for those practicing the Mahāyāna.

**mahāpuruṣalakṣaṇa**. (P. mahāpurisalakkhaṇa; T. skyes bu chen po'i mtshan; C. darenxiang; J. dainisō; K. taeinsang 大人相). In Sanskrit, "the marks of a great man," sometimes referred to in English as the "major marks"; a list of thirty-two marks (dvātriṃśadvaralakṣaṇa) possessed by both buddhas and "wheel-turning emperors" (CAKRAVARTIN); such beings possess in addition eighty minor marks (ANUVYAÑJANA). These marks are understood to be the karmic result of countless eons of effort on the path to either worldly or spiritual perfection (viz., ANUTTARASAMYAKSAṂBODHI). These are said to be fully present on the body of a buddha, especially in the SAṂBHOGAKĀYA, with similitudes of the marks found on the body of cakravartin. Each of the marks is said to result from the practice of a specific virtue in past lives, and elaborate commentary is provided on some of the marks, especially the UṢṆĪṢA and the ŪRṆĀ. Although the lists vary considerably, they typically include (1) supratiṣṭhitapāda—his feet stand firmly on the ground; (2) adhastāt pādatalayoś cakre jāte—he has thousand-spoked wheels on the palms of his hands and the soles of his feet; (3) āyatapādapārṣṇi—the heels of his feet are broad; (4) dīrghāṅguli—he has long fingers; (5) mṛdutaruṇahastapāda—his hands and feet are smooth; (6) jālahastapāda—his hands and feet are webbed; (7) ucchaṅkhapāda—his legs are long; (8) aiṇeyajaṅgha—he has thighs like an antelope; (9) sthitānavanata-pralambabāhu—his arms extend below the knees; (10) kośopagata-vastiguhya—his penis is retracted; (11) suvarṇavarṇa—his complexion is golden; (12) sūkṣmachavi—his skin is smooth (so that no dust clings to his body); (13) ekaikaroma—he has one hair in each pore of his body; (14) ūrdhvāgraroma—the hairs of his body point upward; (15) bṛhadṛju-gātra—his body is tall and straight; (16) saptotsada—the seven parts of his body are well-proportioned; (17) siṃhapūrvārdhakāya—the upper part of his body is like a lion's; (18) citāntarāṃsa—he has broad shoulders; (19) nyagrodhaparimaṇḍala—his body and limbs are perfectly proportionate and thus shaped like a fig tree; (20) susaṃvṛttaskandha—he has full, round shoulders; (21) rasarasāgra—he has an excellent sense of taste; (22) siṃhahanu—he has a jaw like a lion's; (23) catvāriṃśaddanta—he has forty teeth; (24) samadanta—his teeth are even; (25) aviraladanta—his teeth are evenly spaced; (26) suśukladaṃṣṭra—his teeth are white; (27) prabhūtajihva—his tongue is long and broad; (28) brahmasvara—his voice is like that of BRAHMĀ; (29) abhinīlanetra—his eyes are deep blue; (30) gopakṣma—his eyelashes are like those of a bull; (31) ūrṇā or ŪRṆĀKEŚA—he has a white tuft of hair between his eyebrows; and (32) uṣṇīṣaśīrṣa—he has a protrusion on the crown of the head. See also RĀṢṬRAPĀLAPARIPṚCCHĀ.

**mahārājan, four**. (CATURMAHĀRĀJA) (S). See LOKAPĀLA.

**Mahāratnakūṭasūtra**. (S). See RATNAKŪṬASŪTRA.

**Mahāraṭṭha**. (S. Mahārāṣṭra; T. Yul 'khor chen po; C. Mohelatuo guo; J. Makarata koku; K. Maharat'a kuk 摩訶剌侘國). One of nine adjacent lands (paccantadesa) converted to Buddhism by missionaries dispatched by the elder MOGGALIPUTTATISSA at the end of the third Buddhist council (see COUNCIL, THIRD) held in Pāṭaliputta (S. PĀṬALIPUTRA) during the reign of Asoka (S. AŚOKA) in the third century BCE. Mahāraṭṭha is identified with modern Maharashtra and was converted by Mahādhammarakkhita, who preached the *Mahānāradakassapa-Jātaka*. The third Buddhist council at Pāṭaliputta and the nine Buddhist missions are known only in Pāli sources and are first recorded in the fourth-century DĪPAVAṂSA.

**mahāraurava**. (P. mahāroruva; T. ngu 'bod chen po; C. dajiaohuan [diyu]; J. daikyōkan[jigoku]; K. taegyuhwan [chiok] 大叫喚[地獄]). In Sanskrit, "great screaming"; one of the eight hot hells in traditional Buddhist cosmology, the fifth in ascending order of suffering, so-called because the beings scream terribly there due to the torments they endure, torments greater than the hell above, which is merely called "screaming." This hell is said to be the destination of those who steal the property of others, especially that of divinities (DEVA), brāhmaṇas, and their teachers.

**Mahāriṭṭha**. The Pāli proper name of the nephew of the Sinhalese king DEVĀNAMPIYATISSA. Sent as an emissary to the court of King ASOKA, Mahāriṭṭha invited the arahant nun SAṄGHAMITTĀ to Sri Lanka in order to establish the BHIKKHUNĪ SAṂGHA on the island. Upon his return to the capital Anurādhapura, Mahāriṭṭha along with five hundred companions entered the BHIKKHU SAṂGHA, whereupon all of them attained arahantship. So that the religion would be firmly established on the island, Mahinda convened a SAṂGĪTI or rehearsal of scripture at the Thūpārāma in which he requested Mahāriṭṭa to recite the VINAYA. In the fourteenth-century chronicle, SADDHAMMASAṄGAHA, this recitation of vinaya by Mahāriṭṭha is deemed the fourth Buddhist council (see COUNCIL, FOURTH).

**Mahāsaccakasutta**. In Pāli, the "Great Discourse to Saccaka"; the thirty-sixth sutta contained in the MAJJHIMANIKĀYA (fragments are extant in Sanskrit, and portions corresponding to a untitled recension of uncertain affiliation are included in the Chinese translation of the EKOTTARĀGAMA); preached by the Buddha to the JAINA adherent Saccaka (S. MAHĀSATYANIRGRANTHA) in the Mahāvana forest in Vesāli (VAIŚĀLĪ). Saccaka asks about the proper method of cultivating the mind and the body in order to attain liberation. The Buddha explains the various methods of training mind and body he had tried during his own quest for liberation. Beginning with his renunciation of the householder's life, he tells of his training under two meditation masters, his rejection of meditation in favor of severe austerities, and his rejection of austerities for his own path midway between self-indulgence and extreme asceticism, which finally led to his enlightenment.

**Mahāsamayasuttanta**. (C. Dahui jing; J. Daiekyō; K. Taehoe kyŏng 大會經). In Pāli, the "Great Discourse to an Assembly [of Divinities]"; the twentieth sutta contained in the DĪGHANIKĀYA (a separate DHARMAGUPTAKA recension appears as the nineteenth SŪTRA in the Chinese translation of the DĪRGHĀGAMA). Once while the Buddha was dwelling in the Mahāvana grove with five hundred arahants, an assembly of DEVA and BRAHMĀ gods from ten thousand world systems (P. cakkavāḷa; S. CAKRAVĀḌA) gathered in order to hear verses recited by the Buddha. The Buddha proceeds to recount in verse the names of numerous divinities and concludes with an admonition that MĀRA, the evil one, will shrink back from those who are free from lust and fear.

**Mahāsāṃghika**. (T. Dge 'dun phal chen pa'i sde; C. Dazhongbu; J. Daishubu; K. Taejungbu 大衆部). In Sanskrit, "Great Congregation"; one of the major "mainstream" (i.e., non-MAHĀYĀNA) schools of Indian Buddhism. The Mahāsāṃghika came into existence in a dispute over monastic practice with the STHAVIRANIKĀYA, which occurred about a century after the Buddha's death, at the so-called second Buddhist council (SAṂGĪTI) held at VAIŚĀLĪ (see COUNCIL, SECOND). The Sthaviranikāya resolved that ten specific rules of the VINAYA must be observed, while another faction, which came to call itself the "Great Congregation" (Mahāsāṃghika), held that these rules could be ignored. The ten violations of monastic practice that the Sthaviranikāya sought to proscribe were (1) carrying salt in an animal horn, (2) eating when the shadow of the sundial is two fingerbreadths past noon, (3) after eating, traveling to another village on the same day to eat another meal, (4) holding several monastic assemblies within the same boundary (SĪMĀ) during the same fortnight, (5) making a monastic decision with an incomplete assembly and subsequently receiving the approval of the absent monks, (6) citing precedent as a justification to violate monastic procedures, (7) drinking whey after mealtime, (8) drinking unfermented wine, (9) using mats with fringe, and (10) accepting gold and silver. A rival group held that these did not constitute violations of the vinaya and, since those who held this view were apparently the larger faction, they then called themselves the "great congregation." Other sources state that a Mahāsāṃghika monk named MAHĀDEVA claimed that the Sthaviranikāya ARHATs were not free from certain failings, such as nocturnal emissions, although these charges may have been leveled at a subsequent point. Because of a paucity of sources, little is known of the doctrinal positions held by the school, although they seem to have emphasized the career of the bodhisattva and the supramundane nature of the Buddha, with his career as ŚĀKYAMUNI being only a display. They also taught that there was a root consciousness (MŪLAVIJÑĀNA) that serves as the support for the six sensory consciousnesses, just as the root of a tree is the basis of the leaves; this concept may have been the antecedent of the YOGĀCĀRA school's storehouse consciousness (ĀLAYAVIJÑĀNA). The famous biography of the Buddha, the MAHĀVASTU, is a product of the LOKOTTARAVĀDA, one of the three major branches of the Mahāsāṃghika; other major branches included the KUKKUṬĀRĀMA and the CAITYA. The school was found throughout India and present-day Afghanistan, but eventually died out as an ordination lineage.

**Mahāsaṃmata**. (T. Mang pos bkur pa; C. Dapingdeng wang; J. Daibyōdō ō; K. Taep'yŏngdŭng wang 大平等王). In Sanskrit and Pāli, "Greatly Revered" or "Great Consensus"; proper name of the first king of the current world system. After humans began to be reborn following the formation of this current world, wickedness arose, and it became necessary to select a king in order to bring order to society. One person was chosen to rule and he was called Mahāsaṃmata. In return for serving as king, he was allotted a portion of the harvest. He ruled compassionately without needing to resort to torture, fines, or exile. He is regarded as the progenitor of the KṢATRIYA caste, an ancient ancestor of the ŚĀKYA clan, and as a previous incarnation of the Buddha.

**Mahāsaṃnipātasūtra**. (T. 'Dus pa chen po'i mdo; C. Dafangdeng daji jing; J. Daihōdō daijukkyō; K. Taebangdŭng taejip kyŏng 大方等大集經). In Sanskrit, the "Great Compilation"; an anthology of texts that, along with the RATNAKŪṬASŪTRA, is one of the two major compendiums of MAHĀYĀNA sūtras. The collection consists of seventeen Mahāyāna sūtras, and was probably first compiled in the third century CE but did not reach its final form until the fifth century or later; the anthology was translated into Chinese by DHARMAKṢEMA c. 414 CE. The entire collection is only extant in Chinese, although individual sūtras in the collection are extant in Sanskrit and Tibetan. It includes such sūtras as the *Ākāśagarbhasūtra* and the CANDRAGARBHAPARIPṚCCHĀ, an important text on the decline of the dharma.

**Mahāsāropamasutta**. In Pāli, "Great Discourse on the Simile of the Heartwood"; the twenty-ninth sutta contained in the MAJJHIMANIKĀYA (a separate recension appears, but without title, in the Chinese translation of the EKOTTARĀGAMA); preached by the Buddha to an assembly of monks at Vulture Peak (GṚDHRAKŪṬAPARVATA) outside the town of Rājagaha (RĀJAGṚHA) to address DEVADATTA's secession from the Buddha's dispensation. Devadatta left because he was infatuated with the personal fame and profit he earned through his mastery of supernormal powers. The Buddha explained that the teachings were not spoken for the purpose of acquiring gain or profit, which were like the twigs and leaves of a tree, nor were they for mere morality (ŚĪLA), meditative concentration (SAMĀDHI), or supranormal powers (ABHIJÑĀ), which are like the inner and outer bark of a tree. Rather, the teachings were elucidated for the attainment of becoming a worthy one (ARHAT), which is like the heartwood of a tree.

**Mahāsatipaṭṭhānasuttanta**. (P). See SATIPAṬṬHĀNASUTTA.

**mahāsattva**. (T. sems dpa' chen po; C. dashi/mohesa; J. daiji/makasatsu; K. taesa/mahasal 大士/摩訶薩). In Sanskrit, "great being"; an epithet of a BODHISATTVA. Some commentators define mahāsattva as a bodhisattva who has attained the path of vision (DARŚANAMĀRGA), in which case the term would be synonymous with ĀRYABODHISATTVA. In the MAHĀYĀNA sūtras, however, the term does not seem always to carry this technical meaning and instead occurs as a standard epithet of an advanced bodhisattva, as in the PRAJÑĀPĀRAMITĀHṚDAYASŪTRA, where AVALOKITEŚVARA is referred to as "bodhisattva-mahāsattva."

**Mahāsatyanirgrantha**. (P. Saccaka; C. Dasazhenijianzi; J. Daisatsushanikenshi; K. Taesalch'anigŏnja 大薩遮尼犍子). A JAINA adherent and skilled debater, who was defeated in debate by the Buddha and became his disciple. See MAHĀSACCAKASUTTA.

**Mahāsena**. (C. Mohesina; J. Makashina; K. Mahasana 摩訶斯那) (r. 334–361 CE). A king of Sri Lanka, who, in the earlier part of his reign, looted the MAHĀVIHĀRA monastery and turned the spoils over to the ABHAYAGIRI monastery. On the advice of his advisor, the wicked monk Saṅghamitta, he forbade donations to the Mahāvihāra. He built the JETAVANA monastery within the boundaries of the Mahāvihāra. Later, he recanted and restored the confiscated property belonging to the Mahāvihāra. His is the last reign recorded in the DĪPAVAṂSA and MAHĀVAṂSA.

**mahāsiddha**. (T. grub thob chen po; C. dasheng; J. daishō; K. taesŏng 大聖). In Sanskrit, "great adept"; an epithet of a tantric YOGIN, used especially to refer to any one of a group of Indian tantric masters (in some renditions, numbering eighty or eighty-four; see "List of Lists"). These yogins, many of whom were historical figures (dating from between the seventh and twelfth centuries CE), were famous in India and Tibet and appear frequently in both hagiography and iconography. The most famous collection of hagiographies is the *CATURAŚĪTISIDDHAPRAVṚTTI by Abhayadatta. Just as the ARHAT is the ideal of mainstream Buddhism and the BODHISATTVA the ideal of the MAHĀYĀNA, the MAHĀSIDDHA is the ideal of Buddhist TANTRA in India. Although many of the hagiographies of the mahāsiddhas tell stories of princes who, like the Buddha, renounced the world, others tell of enlightened masters who are neither virtuous monks nor gentle bodhisattvas but are instead drawn from the most ignoble levels of Indian society: butchers, hunters, fishermen, blacksmiths, leathersmiths, pimps; i.e., those involved in professions that were considered to be sources of pollution. If this were not enough, they also engage in activities that break taboos: they eat meat, they meditate sitting on top of corpses, they copulate with low-caste girls. If the power of the monk derives from the purity he acquires through abstaining from the things that laymen do, the power of the tantric yogin derives from his transgression of purity, engaging in acts that both violate monastic vows as well as the prescriptions regarding purity and pollution of traditional Indian society. The mahāsiddhas also perform prodigious magical feats, such as flying through the air, turning base metals into gold, diving into the earth, and restoring amputated limbs. They are regarded as enlightened beings, using what is prohibited on the path, and transforming acts that would send others to hell into the deeds of a buddha. It is unclear how many of the mahāsiddhas were historical figures, and the accounts of their deeds are obviously rich in mythological detail. Their stories are replete with what we might regard as miracles, the performance of which the Buddha was said to have discouraged.

On a philosophical level, such miracles demonstrate that those who have insight into the true nature of reality are not bound by rules, their transgression of the conventions of society signifying their transcendence of the laws of nature. Those who understand the true nature of the world can manipulate it, unbound by the laws of either gravity or KARMAN. The stories of the mahāsiddhas also demonstrate the persistence of the worldly in the history of Buddhism. Tantric practice is said to produce two types of powers, called SIDDHIs. There are mundane (LAUKIKA) siddhis, such as the ability to turn base metals into gold, to find buried treasure, to gain the love of a woman, to curse an enemy, to paralyze an invading army, or to stop the sun from moving across the sky. These contrast with the supramundane (LOKOTTARA) siddhis of buddhahood. Much of the tantric literature that survives is designed to provide mundane siddhis, generally divided into four categories of deeds (CATURKARMAN): pacifying, increasing, controlling, and wrathful.

**Mahāsīhanādasutta**. (C. Shenmao xishu jing; J. Shinmōkijukyō; K. Sinmo hŭisu kyŏng 身毛喜豎經). In Pāli, the "Great Discourse on the Lion's Roar"; the twelfth sutta in the MAJJHIMANIKĀYA (Sanskrit fragments of small portions of the scripture are extant; no version is included in the Chinese translations of the ĀGAMAs, but there is an independent translation attributed to Weijing titled the *Shenmao xishu jing*, or "Horripilation Sūtra"); preached by the Buddha to Sāriputta (ŚĀRIPUTRA) in response to criticisms made by Sunakkhatta, a former disciple who charged that the Buddha was not endowed with supranormal powers. The Buddha states that because of his limited capacities, Sunakkhatta was unable to perceive the Buddha's ten powers, four kinds of self-confidence, and the nondecline of his omniscience. He then describes the meritorious deeds that give rise to these powers and the wrong views of the naked JAINA ascetics with whom Sunakkhatta had taken up residence. The Buddha declares that those who claim that the Buddha's insights are simply his own ideas and that he lacks supranormal powers will be reborn in the hells. ¶ A different *Mahāsīhanādasutta* also appears as the eighth sutta in the Pāli DĪGHANIKĀYA, where it is an alternate title for the KASSAPASĪHANĀDASUTTANTA ("Lion's Roar of Kassapa/Kaśyapa"); see KASSAPASĪHANĀDASUTTANTA.

**Mahasi, Sayadaw**. (1904–1982). In Burmese, "Senior Monk from Mahasi," also known as Sobhana Mahāthera; honorific title of U Thobana (P. Sobhana), a prominent Burmese (Myanmar) scholar-monk and influential promoter of insight meditation (VIPASSANĀ). He was born in Seikkhun village near Shwebo in Upper Burma to a prosperous peasant family. At the age of twelve, he was ordained as a novice (P. sāmaṇera; S. ŚRĀMAṆERA) at Pyinmana monastery in Saikkhun and in 1923 he took higher ordination (UPASAṂPADĀ) as a monk (P. BHIKKHU; S. BHIKṢU). Trained in Pāli and Buddhist scriptures at both Saikkhun and a number of monastic colleges in Mandalay, U Thobana alternated his own studies with teaching duties in Moulmien, Lower Burma, where he also encountered and trained under the meditation master Mingun Jetavan Sayadaw in the neighboring town of Thaton. U Thobana received his Dhammācāriya degree in 1941, just prior to the outbreak of World War II and the Japanese occupation of Burma. During the war, he returned to his native village in Upper Burma and settled in a monastery named Mahasi, whence his toponym. There he devoted himself to the practice and teaching of vipassanā meditation and wrote the *Manual of Vipassanā Meditation*, the first of his many treatises on the subject. In 1949, the Prime Minister of Burma, U Nu, invited Mahasi Sayadaw to head the newly founded Thathana Yeiktha (meditation hermitage) in Rangoon (Yangon). Since that time, affiliate branches of the Thathana Yeiktha headed by teachers trained in the Mahasi method of vipassanā have been established throughout the country and internationally, particularly in Thailand and Sri Lanka. Mahasi Sayadaw was an erudite scholar and the author of sixty-seven works on Buddhism in Burmese and Pāli. The Burmese government awarded him the title Aggamahāpaṇḍita for his scholarship in 1952. In 1954, he was appointed to the dual position of pucchaka (questioner) and osana (editor) in the sixth Buddhist Council (See COUNCIL, SIXTH) convened in Rangoon in 1954–56. Among other duties during the council, he oversaw the preparation of a new Burmese edition of the Pāli tipiṭaka (S. TRIPIṬAKA), its commentaries, and sub-commentaries for publication. Mahasi Sayadaw headed numerous Buddhist missions to countries in Asia, Europe, and America, and included among his disciples are many contemporary meditation teachers in Myanmar and internationally.

**mahāśmaśāna**. (S). See ŚMAŚĀNA.

**Mahāssapurasutta**. (C. Mayi jing; J. Meyūkyō; K. Maŭp kyŏng 馬邑經). In Pāli, the "Greater Discourse at Assapura"; the thirty-ninth sutta in the MAJJHIMANIKĀYA (a separate SARVĀSTIVĀDA recension appears as the 182nd sūtra in the Chinese translation of the MADHYAMĀGAMA, and another recension of unidentified affiliation in the EKOTTARĀGAMA); preached by the Buddha to a group of monks dwelling in the market town of Assapura in the Aṅga country. The people of Assapura were greatly devoted to the Buddha and were generous in their support of the monks. In recognition of their generosity, the Buddha admonished his disciples to strive ardently in their practice of the path to liberation by delivering a discourse on what makes one a true recluse. He describes the path in stages, beginning with the avoidance of evil deeds through the restraint of bodily and verbal actions, followed by the avoidance of evil thoughts through the mental restraint of meditation. This provides the foundation for the cultivation of four stages of meditative absorption (P. JHĀNA; S. DHYĀNA), which, in turn, facilitates the eradication of contaminants (P. āsava; S. ĀSRAVA) through the practice of insight (P. vipassanā; S. VIPAŚYANĀ) and the attainment of final liberation in NIRVĀṆA.

**Mahāsthāmaprāpta**. (T. Mthu chen thob; C. Dashizhi; J. Daiseishi; K. Taeseji 大勢至). In Sanskrit, "He who has Attained Great Power"; a BODHISATTVA best known as one of the two attendants (along with the far more popular AVALOKITEŚVARA) of the buddha AMITĀBHA in his buddha-field (BUDDHAKṢETRA) of SUKHĀVATĪ. Mahāsthāmaprāpta is said to represent Amitābha's wisdom, while Avalokiteśvara represents his compassion. According to the GUAN WULIANGSHOU JING, the light of wisdom emanating from Mahāsthāmaprāpta illuminates all sentient beings, enabling them to leave behind the three unfortunate destinies (APĀYA; DURGATI) and attain unexcelled power; thus, Mahāsthāmaprāpta is considered the bodhisattva of power or strength. There is also a method of contemplation of the bodhisattva, which is the eleventh of the sixteen contemplations described in the *Guan jing*. An adept who contemplates Mahāsthāmaprāpta comes to reside in the lands of all the buddhas, being relieved from innumerable eons of continued birth-and-death. In the ŚŪRAṂGAMASŪTRA, the bodhisattva advocates the practice of BUDDHĀNUSMṚTI. Mahāsthāmaprāpta also appears in the SADDHARMAPUṆḌARĪKASŪTRA ("Lotus Sūtra") as one of the bodhisattvas who assembled on Vulture Peak (GṚDHRAKŪṬAPARVATA) to hear the teachings of the buddha ŚĀKYAMUNI. Iconographically, the bodhisattva is rarely depicted alone; he almost always appears in a triad together with Amitābha and Avalokiteśvara. Mahāsthāmaprāpta can often be recognized by a small jar on his jeweled crown, which is believed to contain pure water to cleanse sentient beings' afflictions (KLEŚA). He is also often described as holding a lotus flower in his hand or joining his palms together in AÑJALI. Mahāsthāmaprāpta is one of the twenty-five bodhisattvas who protects those who recite Amitābha's name and welcomes them on their deathbed to the Buddha's PURE LAND. Serving as one of the thirteen bodhisattvas of the Japanese SHINGONSHŪ of esoteric Buddhism, Mahāsthāmaprāpta is believed to preside over the special ceremony marking the first year anniversary of one's death. He is also depicted in the Cloister of the Lotus Division (Rengebu-in) in the TAIZŌKAI MAṆḌALA.

**mahāsthāna**. (T. gnas chen; C. lingdi; J. reichi; K. yŏngji 靈地). In Sanskrit, lit. "great site"; a list of four or eight sites of Buddhist pilgrimage in India that were the scenes of famous events in the life of the Buddha. The four sites, as mentioned in the MAHĀPARINIBBĀNASUTTA, are the sites of (1) the miracle of his birth at LUMBINĪ, (2) the defeat of MĀRA and the achievement of buddhahood at BODHGAYĀ, (3) the first turning of the wheel of the dharma (DHARMACAKRAPRAVARTANA) at ṚṢIPATANA (SĀRNĀTH), (4) his passage into PARINIRVĀṆA at KUŚINAGARĪ. In the list of eight, between the third and fourth events are added the following sites of (5) the "twin miracles" (YAMAKAPRĀTIHĀRYA) performed at ŚRĀVASTĪ, (6) the descent from the TRĀYASTRIṂŚA heaven at SĀṂKĀŚYA, (7) the taming of the elephant NĀLĀGIRI at RĀJAGṚHA, (8) the receipt of the monkey's gift of honey at VAIŚĀLĪ. These sites became important places of pilgrimage in India and were ubiquitous stops during the sojourns of XUANZANG and other Chinese and Korean pilgrims on the subcontinent. These eight sites are found depicted in Indian sculpture dating from the Pāla period.

**Mahāsuddassanasuttanta**. (C. Dashanjian wang jing; J. Daizenkennōkyō; K. Taesŏn'gyŏn wang kyŏng 大善見王經). In Pāli, the "Great Discourse on King Suddassana"; the seventeenth sutta of the DĪGHANIKĀYA (a separate SARVĀSTIVĀDA recension appears as the fifty-eighth sūtra in the Chinese translation of the MADHYAMĀGAMA); preached by the Buddha to ĀNANDA in the town of Kusinārā (S. KUŚINAGARĪ) while he lay dying beneath twin sāla (S. ŚĀLA) trees in the grove of the Mallas. Ānanda begs the Buddha not to pass away in such an insignificant town, whereupon the Buddha recounts to him the former splendor of the place eons ago, when the city was governed by the CAKRAVARTIN Suddassana (S. Sudarśana). After recounting the king's virtues, the Buddha reveals that he himself had been Suddassana in a previous life while he was a BODHISATTVA. Thus, the Buddha concludes, Kusināra is indeed a suitable place for the final demise (parinibbāna; S. PARINIRVĀṆA) of a buddha.

**mahāsukha**. (T. bde ba chen po; C. dale; J. dairaku/tairaku; K. taerak 大樂). In Sanskrit, "great bliss"; an important term in Buddhist TANTRA, with a range of denotations, from orgasm to enlightenment. In a more technical usage, it refers to a special bliss consciousness generated during the practice of ANUTTARAYOGATANTRA by causing the winds (PRĀṆA) to enter the central channel (AVADHŪTĪ). This bliss consciousness is then to be used to perceive emptiness (ŚŪNYATĀ) directly, resulting in what is called the union of bliss and emptiness.

**Mahātaṇhāsaṅkhayasutta**. (C. Tudi jing; J. Dateikyō; K. Toje kyŏng 嗏帝經). In Pāli, the "Great Discourse on the Destruction of Craving"; the thirty-eighth sutta in the MAJJHIMANIKĀYA (a separate SARVĀSTIVĀDA recension appears as the 201st sūtra in the Chinese translations of the MADHYAMĀGAMA); preached by the Buddha at the JETAVANA grove in the town of Sāvatthi (S. ŚRĀVASTĪ) to the monk Sāti, who held the mistaken view that the Buddha taught that consciousness (P. viññāṇa; S. VIJÑĀNA) transmigrates from life to life. The Buddha reprimands Sāti, telling him he never taught such a view, but that consciousness arises only due to causes and conditions and never otherwise. He continues with a lengthy discourse on dependent origination (P. paṭiccasamuppāda; S. PRATĪTYASAMUTPĀDA) in which he describes how all worldly phenomena come into being and pass away according to the law of cause and effect.

**Mahāthūpa**. In Pāli, "great STŪPA"; the great reliquary mound built by the Sinhalese king DUṬṬHAGĀMAṆĪ in the first century BCE, erected after he had vanquished the Damiḷas and reunited the island kingdom under his rule. The Mahāthūpa was erected in the MAHĀMEGHAVANA grove near ANURĀDHAPURA at a spot visited by all four of the buddhas who had been born thus far in the present auspicious eon (P. bhaddakappa;

S. BHADRAKALPA). The monument, which was 120 cubits high and designed in the shape of a water drop, was crowned with a richly adorned relic chamber that housed physical relics (S. ŚARĪRA) of the Buddha acquired from the NĀGA MAHĀKĀLA. The arahant MAHINDA is said to have once indicated to King DEVĀNAṂPIYATISSA the site where the Mahāthūpa was to be built. Devānaṃpiyatissa wished to construct the shrine himself, but Mahinda informed him that that honor was to go the future king, Duṭṭhagāmaṇī. To commemorate that prophecy, Devānaṃpiyatissa had it inscribed on a pillar at the site. It was the discovery of that pillar that prompted Duṭṭhagāmaṇī to take up the task. Thousands of saints from various parts of the island and JAMBUDVĪPA (meaning India in this case) gathered at the Mahāmeghavana to celebrate the construction of the Mahāthūpa. Duṭṭhagāmaṇī fell ill and died just before the monument was completed. The royal umbrella was raised above the Mahāthūpa by his brother and successor, Saddhatissa.

**mahā-upaputra**. [alt. mahōpaputra] (T. nye ba'i sras chen brgyad; C. ba dapusa; J. hachidai bosatsu; K. p'al taebosal 八大菩薩). In Sanskrit, the "eight close sons"; a group of "eight great BODHISATTVAS" (which is the Chinese translation of the term). They are KṢITIGARBHA, ĀKĀŚAGARBHA, AVALOKITEŚVARA, VAJRAPĀṆI, MAITREYA, SARVANĪVARAṆAVIṢKAMBHIN, SAMANTABHADRA, and MAÑJUŚRĪ. These eight are often depicted flanking the buddhas ŚĀKYAMUNI or AMITĀBHA. This grouping is known throughout Asia, from northern India, where they appear in ELLORĀ, RATNAGIRI, and NĀLANDĀ, to Japan, as well as Indonesia—indeed, wherever MAHĀYĀNA and tantric Buddhism flourished. They figure as a group in TANTRAs of various classes, where the number of their arms corresponds to the main deity of the MAṆḌALA and their colors correspond to the direction in which they are placed. Textual evidence for the grouping is known from as early as the third century CE, with the Chinese translation of the *Ba jixiang shen jing* ("Eight Auspicious Spirits Scripture"). Their roles are laid out in the *Aṣṭamaṇḍalakasūtra*, where the aims of their worship are essentially mundane—absolution from evil, fulfillment of desires, and protection from ills. See also AṢṬAMAHOPAPUTRA.

**Mahāvadānasūtra**. (T. Rtogs par brjod pa chen po'i mdo; C. Daben jing; J. Daihongyō; K. Taebon kyŏng 大本經). In Sanskrit, the "Sūtra of the Great Legend"; a sūtra that exists in Pāli (where it is called the MAHĀPADĀNASUTTANTA) and is also extant in a DHARMAGUPTAKA recension that is the first SŪTRA in the Chinese translation of the DĪRGHĀGAMA. The scripture provides the biography of VIPAŚYIN (P. Vipassī), one of the buddhas of the past, from the time of his birth to the time of his enlightenment. The narrative closely mirrors that of the life of GAUTAMA SIDDHĀRTHA, but with the significant sites and persons having different names. The text notes that the life stories of all buddhas are the same. See also MAHĀPADĀNASUTTANTA.

**Mahāvagga**. In Pāli, "Great Chapter"; an important book in the Pāli VINAYAPIṬAKA, which provides the first systematic narrative of the early history of the SAṂGHA. The KHANDHAKA ("Collections"), the second major division of the Pāli vinaya, is subdivided between the *Mahāvagga* and the CŪḶAVAGGA ("Lesser Chapter"). The *Mahāvagga* includes ten khandhakas. The long, opening khandhaka narrate the events that immediately follow the Buddha's experience of enlightenment (BODHI) beneath the BODHI TREE, including the conversion of the first lay disciples, Tapussa (S. TRAPUṢA) and BHALLIKA (cf. TIWEI [BOLI] JING); his earliest teachings to the group of five (P. pañcavaggiyā; S. PAÑCAVARGIKA); the foundation of the order of monks; and the institution of an ordination procedure through taking the three refuges (P. tisaraṇa; S. TRIŚARAṆA) and the formula ehi bhikkhu pabbajjā ("Come, monks"; see S. EHIBHIKṢUKĀ). Much detail is provided also on the enlightenment experiences and conversion of his first major disciples, including Aññātakoṇḍañña (S. ĀJÑĀTAKAUṆḌINYA), Assaji (S. AŚVAJIT), and Uruvela-Kassapa (S. URUVILVĀ-KĀŚYAPA), as well as the two men who would become his two greatest disciples, Sāriputta (S. ŚĀRIPUTRA) and Moggallāna (see S. MAHĀMAUDGALYĀYANA). Subsequent khandhakas discuss the recitation of the rules of disciple (P. pāṭimokkha; S. PRĀTIMOKṢA) on the fortnightly retreat day (P. uposatha; S. UPOṢADHA), the institution of the rains retreat (P. vassa; S. VARṢĀ), medicines, the design of the monastic robes (CĪVARA), and the robe-cloth ceremony (KAṬHINA), and of the criteria for evaluating whether an action conforms to the spirit of the vinaya. The *Mahāvagga*'s historical narrative is continued in the *Cūḷavagga*, which relates the history of the saṃgha following the buddha's PARINIRVĀṆA.

**Mahāvairocana**. See VAIROCANA.

**Mahāvairocanābhisaṃbodhisūtra**. (T. Rnam par snang mdzad chen po mngon par rdzogs par byang chub pa rnam par sprul ba byin gyis rlob pa shin tu rgyas pa mdo; C. Da piluzhena chengfo shenbian jiachi jing/Dari jing; J. Daibirushana jōbutsu jinben kajikyō/Dainichikyō; K. Tae Pirojana sŏngbul sinbyŏn kaji kyŏng /Taeil kyŏng 大毘盧遮那成佛神變加持經/大日經). In Sanskrit, "The Discourse on the Enlightenment of Mahāvairocanā"; a scripture also known as the *Mahāvairocanasūtra* and the *Vairocanābhisaṃbodhitantra*; the full title of the work is *Mahāvairocanābhisaṃbodhivikurvitādhiṣṭhānavaipulyasūtra* ("Extensive Sūtra on the Enlightenment, Transformations, and Empowerment of MAHĀVAIROCANĀ"). This scripture is an early Buddhist TANTRA, which was probably composed sometime between the mid-sixth and seventh centuries, around the time that the MANTRAYĀNA was emerging as distinct strand of MAHĀYĀNA Buddhism; the text is later classified as both a YOGATANTRA and a CARYĀTANTRA. It was first translated into Chinese by ŚUBHAKARASIṂHA and YIXING in 724–725, and would become one of the two most important tantras for East Asian esoteric Buddhism (the other being the SARVATATHĀGATATATTVASAṂGRAHA). The text was translated into

Tibetan in the early ninth century; the Tibetan version contains an additional seven chapters, called the "continuation" (uttaratantra), that do not appear in the Chinese version. Among the commentaries to the text, the most important is that of BUDDHAGUYHA and that of the Chinese translators, Śubhakarasiṃha and Yixing. The tantra is set forth as a dialogue between VAJRAPĀṆI and the buddha Mahāvairocanā. The central topics of the text are BODHICITTA, KARUṆĀ, and UPĀYA, which the buddha VAIROCANA explains are respectively the cause, root, and culmination of his own omniscience. Much of the text deals with the traditional tantric topics of initiation (ABHIṢEKA), MANTRA recitation, MUDRĀ, visualization, and the description of the MAṆḌALA.

**Mahāvaṃsa**. In Pāli, the "Great Chronicle"; the most famous Pāli chronicle of Sri Lanka. Written in verse and attributed to Mahānāma Thera, it follows the outline of the earlier DĪPAVAṂSA in tracing the history of the Buddhist religion from its inception through the three Buddhist councils in India, to its introduction into Sri Lanka by MAHINDHA during the reign of DEVĀNAṂPIYATISSA, up to the reign of Mahāsena in the fourth century CE. Written most probably in the fifth century CE, the *Mahāvaṃsa* presents a more elaborate and coherent description of events than is found in the *Dīpavaṃsa*, although some material treated in the latter, such as the lineage of nuns, is omitted.

**Mahāvastu**. In Sanskrit, the "Great Chapter." Also known as the *Mahāvastu* AVADĀNA, this lengthy work is regarded as the earliest Sanskrit biography of the Buddha. The work describes itself as a book "of the VINAYAPIṬAKA according to the LOKOTTARAVĀDA, which is affiliated with the MAHĀSĀṂGHIKA." The work thus provides important insights into how the Buddha was understood by the Lokottaravāda, or "Proponents of the Supramundane," a branch of the Mahāsaṃghika, or "Great Community," which some scholars regard as a possible antecedent of the Mahāyāna. The placement of the work in the vinayapiṭaka suggests that the genre of biographies of the Buddha began as introductions to the monastic code, before becoming independent works. Indeed, it corresponds roughly to the MAHĀVAGGA portion of the KHANDHAKA in the Pāli vinayapiṭaka. The *Mahāvastu* is divided into three parts. The first part deals with the previous lives of the being who would become the buddha ŚĀKYAMUNI, recounting the virtuous deeds he performed and the BODHISATTVA vow he made to the buddha DĪPAṂKARA and other buddhas of the past. The second part begins in TUṢITA, when the bodhisattva decides where to take his final birth. It goes on to recount his birth, childhood and youth; departure from the palace; and search for enlightenment. It concludes with his defeat of MĀRA. The third section describes the first conversions and the foundation of the SAṂGHA. Like other early "biographies" of the Buddha, the narrative ends long before the Buddha's passage into PARINIRVĀṆA. Also like these other works, the *Mahāvastu* does not provide a simple chronology, but is interrupted with numerous teachings, avadānas, and JĀTAKAS, some of which do not have analogues in the Pāli. There are also interpolations: for example, there are two versions of the BODHISATTVA's departure, the first rather simple and the second more elaborate, containing the famous story of the chariot rides during which the prince encounters aging, sickness, and death for the first time (cf. CATURNIMITTA). The so-called proto-Mahāyāna elements of the *Mahāvastu* have been the subject of much debate. For example, the text includes a lengthy description of the ten bodhisattva BHŪMIS, often regarded as a standard Mahāyāna tenet, but their description differs in significant ways from that found in the Mahāyāna sūtras. Although clearly a work with many interpolations, linguistic elements suggest that portions of the text may date to as early as the second century BCE.

**Mahāvedallasutta**. (C. Dajuchiluo jing; J. Daikuchirakyō; K. Taeguch'ira kyŏng 大拘絺羅經). In Pāli, "Greater Discourse on Points of Doctrine"; the forty-third sutta in the MAJJHIMANIKĀYA (a separate SARVĀSTIVĀDA recension appears in the Chinese translation of the MADHYAMĀGAMA); expounded by Sāriputra (S. ŚĀRIPUTRA) to the monk Mahākoṭṭhita (S. KAUṢṬHILA) at Sāvatthi (S. ŚRĀVASTĪ) in the JETAVANA grove. Mahākoṭṭhita approached Śāriputra and questioned him concerning a number of points of doctrine preached by the Buddha. These included, what is wisdom (PRAJÑĀ); what is consciousness (VIJÑĀNA) and its relation to wisdom; what is sensation (VEDANĀ); what is perception (SAṂJÑĀ) and what is the relation between sensation, perception, and consciousness; what is knowable by the mind alone; what is existence and how many kinds of existence are there; what is the first meditative absorption (DHYĀNA); what are the five sense faculties (INDRIYA); and what are the various kinds of deliverance attained through meditation (VIMUKTI). Śāriputra answered all of questions put to him to Mahākoṭṭhiya's satisfaction.

**mahāvibhaṅga**. (S). See SŪTRAVIBHAṄGA.

**Mahāvibhāṣā**. (S). See ABHIDHARMAMAHĀVIBHĀṢĀ.

**Mahāvihāra**. (C. Mohepiheluo; J. Mahabihara/Makabikara; K. Mahabihara 摩訶毘訶羅). In Pāli, the "Great Monastery"; built in the third century BCE for the elder MAHINDA at ANURĀDHAPURA by the Sinhala king DEVĀNAṂPIYATISSA, following the king's conversion to Buddhism. The Mahāvihāra became the headquarters of the orthodox THERAVĀDA fraternity on the island, with many important shrines, such as the MAHĀTHŪPA, located on its grounds. Its authority was challenged by the ABHAYAGIRI and JETAVANA secessionist fraternities in the first century BCE and fourth century CE, respectively. Five hundred monks from Mahāvihāra were said to have participated in the first commitment to writing of a Buddhist canon, which occurred during the reign of VAṬṬAGĀMAṆI ABHAYA (the patron of Abhayagiri) in the last decades BCE. During the reign of Mahāsena, in the late third century CE, a royal decree forbade giving alms to the monks of the monastery, causing the monastery to be vacated for nine years; during this time, some of the buildings were destroyed, but they were eventually rebuilt. BUDDHAGHOSA composed his sutta commentaries while residing at the monastery. After the capital was moved from Anurādhapura to Pulatthipura, near the beginning of the ninth century, the monastery lost much of its influence and eventually fell into decay.

**Mahāvihāravāsin**. In Pāli, "Dweller in the Great Monastery"; the name of the monastic order and ordination lineage associated with the MAHĀVIHĀRA in Sri Lanka. Although originating in Sri Lanka, it established a presence in India, as indicated by inscriptions at NĀGĀRJUNAKOṆḌĀ. When FAXIAN traveled to Sri Lanka in 410 CE, he reported that there were three thousand monks belonging to the Mahāvihāravāsin. The commentarial tradition beginning with BUDDHAGHOSA, who compiled his sutta commentaries at the monastery, represents the Mahāvihāra positions on doctrine and practice. After a long period of decline, the Mahāvihāra fraternity was again made the sole monastic order on the island with the abolition of its rivals in the twelfth century CE during a purification program carried out by PARAKRĀMABĀHU I. It has been the dominant order in Sri Lanka during the modern period.

**Mahāvīra**. (T. Dpa' bo chen po; C. Daxiong; J. Daiyū/Daiō; K. Taeung 大雄). In Sanskrit and Pāli, "Great Victor"; the title of NIRGRANTHA JÑĀTĪPUTRA (P. Nigaṇṭha Nātaputta), also known as Vardhamāna (d. c. 488 BCE), leader of the JAINA tradition, a ŚRAMAṆA sect in northern India that the Buddhists listed among the TĪRTHIKA groups, the adherents of non-Buddhist religions, sometimes mistranslated as "heretics." Mahāvīra was considered to be the last in a long line of JINA ("victors" over ignorance) or tīrthaṃkaras going back through twenty-four generations to Pārśva. Mahāvira seems to have been an elder contemporary of the Buddha and figures prominently in Buddhist materials; indeed, he is one of the so-called six sectarian teachers criticized by the Buddha for their wrong views in such texts as the SĀMAÑÑAPHALASUTTA of the DĪGHANIKĀYA. See JAINA.

**Mahāvyutpatti**. (T. Bye brag tu rtogs par byed pa chen po; C. Fanyi mingyi daji; J. Hon'yaku myōgi taishū; K. Pŏnyŏk myŏngŭi taejip 翻譯名義大集). In Sanskrit, the "Great Detailed Explanation"; an important Sanskrit–Tibetan lexicon dating from the ninth century. In order to provide consistency in the translation of Indian SŪTRAs and ŚĀSTRAs, the Tibetan king RAL PA CAN convened a meeting of scholars in 821 and charged them with providing standard Tibetan equivalents for a wide range of terms encountered in Sanskrit Buddhist texts. The result was a lexicon known as the *Mahāvyutpatti*, which contains (in one version) 9,565 terms. The king is said to have instructed its compilers not to include tantric vocabulary. The work is organized into 283 categories, the purpose of some of which (the eighteen kinds of ŚŪNYATĀ, the ten virtuous actions, the thirty-two marks of a MAHĀPURUṢA) are more self-evident than others ("names of strange things," "various terms"). During the seventeenth century, Chinese, Mongolian, and Manchurian equivalencies were added to the lexicon so that the terms would be available in the four major languages used in the Qing empire (Manchu, Chinese, Tibetan, and Mongolian). The first English translation was made by ALEXANDER CSOMA DE KŐRÖS, but it was not published until long after his death. The *Mahāvyutpatti* continues to be consulted in editions produced by Japanese scholars that include additional Chinese equivalencies and various indexes.

**Mahāyāna**. (T. theg pa chen po; C. dasheng; J. daijō; K. taesŭng 大乘). In Sanskrit, "great vehicle"; a term, originally of self-appellation, which is used historically to refer to a movement that began some four centuries after the Buddha's death, marked by the composition of texts that purported to be his words (BUDDHAVACANA). Although ranging widely in content, these texts generally set forth the bodhisattva path to buddhahood as the ideal to which all should aspire and described BODHISATTVAs and buddhas as objects of devotion. The key doctrines of the Mahāyāna include the perfection of wisdom (PRAJÑĀPĀRAMITĀ), the skillful methods (UPĀYAKAUŚALYA) of a buddha, the three bodies (TRIKĀYA) of a buddha, the inherency of buddha-nature (BUDDHADHĀTU; TATHĀGATAGARBHA), and PURE LANDs or buddha-fields (BUDDHAKṢETRA). The term Mahāyāna is also appended to two of the leading schools of Indian Buddhism, the YOGĀCĀRA and the MADHYAMAKA, because they accepted the Mahāyāna sūtras as the word of the Buddha. However, the tenets of these schools were not restricted to expositions of the philosophy and practice of the bodhisattva but sought to set forth the nature of wisdom and the constituents of the path for the ARHAT as well. The term Mahāyāna often appears in contrast to HĪNAYĀNA, the "lesser vehicle," a pejorative term used to refer to those who do not accept the Mahāyāna sūtras as the word of the Buddha. Mahāyāna became the dominant form of Buddhism in China, Korea, Japan, Tibet, and Mongolia, and therefore is sometimes referred to as "Northern Buddhism," especially in nineteenth-century sources. Because of the predominance of the Mahāyāna in East Asia and Tibet, it is sometimes assumed that the Mahāyāna displaced earlier forms of Buddhism (sometimes referred to by scholars as "Nikāya Buddhism" or "MAINSTREAM BUDDHIST SCHOOLS") in India, but the testimony of Chinese pilgrims, such as XUANZANG and YIJING, suggests that the Mahāyāna remained a minority movement in India. These pilgrims report that Mahāyāna and "hīnayāna" monks lived together in the same monasteries and followed the same VINAYA. The supremacy of the Mahāyāna is also sometimes assumed because of the large corpus of Mahāyāna literature in India. However, scholars have begun to speculate that the size of this corpus may not be a sign of the Mahāyāna's dominance but rather of its secondary status, with more and more works composed but few gaining adherents. Scholars find it significant that the first mention of the term "Mahāyāna" in a stone inscription does not appear in India until some five centuries after the first Mahāyāna sūtras were presumably composed, perhaps reflecting its minority, or even marginal, status on the Indian subcontinent. The origins of the Mahāyāna remain the subject of scholarly debate. Earlier theories that saw the Mahāyāna as largely a lay movement against entrenched conservative monastics have given way to views of the Mahāyāna as beginning as disconnected cults (of monastic and sometimes lay members) centered around an individual sūtra, in some instances proclaimed by charismatic teachers called DHARMABHĀṆAKA. The teachings contained in these sūtras varied widely, with some extolling a particular buddha or bodhisattva above all others, some saying that the text itself functioned as a STŪPA. Each of these sūtras sought to represent itself as the authentic word of ŚĀKYAMUNI Buddha, which was more or less independent from other sūtras; hence, the trope in so many Mahāyāna sūtras in which the Buddha proclaims the supremacy of that particular text and describes the benefits that will accrue to those who recite, copy, and worship it. The late appearance of these texts had to be accounted for, and various arguments were set forth, most making some appeal to UPĀYA, the Buddha's skillful methods whereby he teaches what is most appropriate for a given person or audience. Thus, in the SADDHARMAPUṆḌARĪKASŪTRA ("Lotus Sūtra"), the Buddha famously proclaims that the three vehicles (TRIYĀNA) that he had previously set forth were in fact expedient stratagems to reach different audiences and that there is in fact only one vehicle (EKAYĀNA), revealed in the *Saddharmapuṇḍarīkasūtra*, the BUDDHAYĀNA, which had been taught many times in the past by previous buddhas. These early Mahāyāna sūtras seem to have been deemed complete unto themselves, each representing its own world. This relatively disconnected assemblage of various cults of the book would eventually become a self-conscious scholastic entity that thought of itself as the Mahāyāna; this exegetical endeavor devoted a good deal of energy to surveying what was by then a large corpus of such books and then attempting to craft the myriad doctrines contained therein into coherent philosophical and religious systems, such as Yogācāra and Madhyamaka. The authority of the Mahāyāna sūtras as the word of the Buddha seems to have remained a sensitive issue throughout the history of the Mahāyāna in India, since many of the most important authors, from the second to the twelfth century, often offered a defense of these sūtras' authenticity. Another influential strand of early Mahāyāna was that associated with the RĀṢṬRAPĀLAPARIPṚCCHĀ, KĀŚYAPAPARIVARTA, and UGRAPARIPṚCCHĀ, which viewed the large urban monasteries as being ill-suited to serious spiritual cultivation and instead advocated forest dwelling (see ARAÑÑAVĀSI) away from the cities, following a rigorous asceticism (S. dhutaguṇa; P. DHUTAṄGA) that was thought to characterize the early SAṂGHA. This conscious estrangement from the monks of the city, where the great majority of monks would have resided, again suggests the Mahāyāna's minority status in India. Although one often reads in Western sources of the three vehicles of Buddhism—the hīnayāna, Mahāyāna, and VAJRAYĀNA—the distinction of the Mahāyāna from the vajrayāna is less clear, at least polemically speaking, than the distinction between the Mahāyāna and the hīnayāna, with followers of the vajrayāna considering themselves as following the path to buddhahood set forth in the Mahāyāna sūtras, although via a shorter route. Thus, in some expositions, the Mahāyāna is said to subsume two vehicles, the PĀRAMITĀYĀNA, that is, the path to buddhahood by following the six perfections (PĀRAMITĀ) as set forth in the Mahāyāna sūtras, and the MANTRAYĀNA or vajrayāna, that is, the path to buddhahood set forth in the tantras.

**Mahāyānasaṃgraha**. (T. Theg pa chen po bsdus pa; C. She dasheng lun; J. Shōdaijōron; K. Sŏp taesŭng non 攝大乘論). In Sanskrit, the "Summary of the Great Vehicle"; an important treatise of the YOGĀCĀRA school, composed by the fourth-century master ASAṄGA. The text is lost in the original Sanskrit but is preserved in Tibetan and four Chinese translations, including those by such famous figures as PARAMĀRTHA and XUANZANG. The work is the most complete presentation of Yogācāra theory and practice, setting forth in detail the doctrines of the three natures (TRISVABHĀVA), as well as the foundational consciousness (ĀLAYAVIJÑĀNA), and the seeds (BĪJA) that reside there. It also sets forth practices for cultivating the wisdom derived from hearing (ŚRUTAMAYĪPRAJÑĀ), the wisdom derived from reflection (CINTĀMAYĪPRAJÑĀ), and the wisdom derived from meditation (BHĀVANĀMAYĪPRAJÑĀ), whereby the ālayavijñāna is destroyed and enlightenment attained. The lineage (GOTRA) of enlightenment and the nature of the DHARMAKĀYA are also elucidated. Both VASUBANDHU and ASVABHĀVA composed commentaries on the text, which were also translated into Chinese. The *Mahāyānasaṃgraha* served as the basis of the SHE LUN ZONG in China.

**Mahāyānasūtrālaṃkāra**. [alt. Sūtrālaṃkāra] (T. Theg pa chen po'i mdo sde'i rgyan; C. Dasheng zhuangyan jing lun; J. Daijō shōgongyōron; K. Taesŭng changŏmgyŏng non 大乘莊嚴經論). In Sanskrit, the "Ornament for the Mahāyāna Sūtras"; one of the five works (together with the ABHISAMAYĀLAṂKĀRA, the RATNAGOTRAVIBHĀGA, the MADHYĀNTAVIBHĀGA, and the DHARMADHARMATĀVIBHĀGA) said to have been presented to ASAṄGA by the bodhisattva MAITREYA in the TUṢITA heaven (see also MAITREYANĀTHA). Written in verse, the text offers a systematic presentation of the practices of the bodhisattva from the standpoint of the YOGĀCĀRA school and is one of the most important of the Indian Mahāyāna ŚĀSTRAS. Its twenty-one chapters deal with (1) the proof that the MAHĀYĀNA sūtras are the word of the Buddha; (2) taking refuge in the three jewels (RATNATRAYA); (3) the lineage (GOTRA) of enlightenment necessary to undertake the bodhisattva path; (4) the generation of the aspiration to enlightenment (BODHICITTOTPĀDA); (5) the practice of the BODHISATTVA; (6) the nature of reality, described from the Yogācāra perspective; (7) the attainment of power by the bodhisattva; (8) the methods of bringing oneself and others to maturation; (9) enlightenment and the three bodies of a buddha (TRIKĀYA);

(10) faith in the Mahāyāna; (11) seeking complete knowledge of the dharma; (12) teaching the dharma; (13) practicing in accordance with the dharma; (14) the precepts and instructions received by the bodhisattva; (15) the skillful methods of the bodhisattva; (16) the six perfections (PĀRAMITĀ) and the four means of conversion (SAṂGRAHAVASTU), through which bodhisattvas attract and retain disciples; (17) the worship of the Buddha; (18) the constituents of enlightenment (BODHIPĀKṢIKADHARMA); (19) the qualities of the bodhisattva; and (20–21) the consummation of the bodhisattva path and the attainment of buddhahood. There is a commentary (BHĀṢYA) by VASUBANDHU and a subcommentary by STHIRAMATI.

**Mahāyānottaratantraśāstra**. (S). See RATNAGOTRAVIBHĀGA.

**Mahāyānottaratantraśāstravyākhyā**. (S). See RATNAGOTRAVIBHĀGA.

**Mahayazawin-gyi**. In Burmese, "The Great Chronicle"; a voluminous Burmese YAZAWIN or royal chronicle written c. 1730 by U Kala. Historically, other Burmese (Myanmar) royal chronicles of the eighteenth and nineteenth centuries are based directly or indirectly on this text. Following the outlines of the DĪPAVAṂSA and MAHĀVAṂSA, the first part of U Kala's work traces the history of kings from the time of MAHĀSAṂMATA at the beginning of the present world-eon, through the Mauryan dynasty in India, to the history of kings in Sri Lanka. As in the Pāli chronicles upon which it is patterned, the *Mahayazawin-gyi* portrays the histories of the Buddhist religion and of Buddhist kingdoms as intertwined. The history of Burma, which occupies the majority of the text, is organized into periods according to the capital cities. It begins with the founding of Tagaung, the first Burmese capital, before the lifetime of the Buddha. The Tagaung period is followed in turn by the Sirīkhettarā, PAGAN, AVA, PEGU, and the second Ava periods. The most famous episode of the chronicle is the long account of the conversion of Pagan's king ANAWRAHTA (P. Anuruddha; S. Aniruddha; r. c. 1044–1077 CE) to Theravāda Buddhism through the efforts of the Mon saint, SHIN ARAHAN. This event allegedly precipitated Anawrahta's conquest of the neighboring Mon kingdom of Thaton in search of texts and relics, and in turn the founding of the first Burmese empire. U Kala's chronicle concludes with an account of the meritorious deeds of Tanin gan wei (r. 1714–1733), the king of Ava at the time the text was composed.

**mahāyoga**. (T. rnal 'byor chen po/ma hā yo ga). In Sanskrit "great yoga"; the seventh of the nine vehicles according to the RNYING MA sect of Tibetan Buddhism. Here, the system of practice described elsewhere as ANUTTARAYOGATANTRA is divided into three: mahāyoga, ANUYOGA, and ATIYOGA, with mahāyoga corresponding roughly to practices of the "stage of generation" (UTPATTIKRAMA), in which one visualizes oneself as a deity and one's environment as a MAṆḌALA. Its root text is the GUHYAGARBHATANTRA.

**Mahinda**. (S. Mahendra; T. Dbang chen; C. Moshentuo; J. Mashinda; K. Masinda 摩哂陀). Pāli proper name of the son of Asoka (S. AŚOKA), who converted the Sinhalese king, DEVĀNAṂPIYATISSA, to Buddhism in the third century BCE, thus inaugurating the Buddhist religion in Sri Lanka. The story of Mahinda is first recorded in the DĪPAVAṂSA (c. fourth century CE) and is elaborated in the MAHĀVAṂSA (c. fifth century CE) and BUDDHAGHOSA's VINAYA commentary, SAMANTAPĀSĀDIKĀ. In each of these works, Mahinda's story is preceded by a narrative that begins with the legend of Asoka's conversion to Buddhism, through the convention of the third Buddhist council (see COUNCIL, THIRD) under the direction of MOGGALIPUTTATISSA, to the dispatch of Buddhist missions to nine adjacent lands (paccantadesa). Mahinda was chosen to lead the mission sent to Sri Lanka. Mahinda, together with his sister SAṄGHAMITTĀ, was ordained at the age of twenty at the request of his father, Asoka. He attained arahantship immediately upon his ordination. Mahinda was swift in learning the doctrine, and was placed in charge of Moggaliputtatissa's one thousand disciples when the latter retired to Ahogaṅga due to a dispute within the SAṂGHA. Mahinda had been a monk for twelve years when the third Buddhist council was convened to celebrate the resolution of the dispute. Shortly thereafter, he was sent along with four other monks, a novice, and a layman to Sri Lanka for the purpose of converting its king. Mahinda preached the CŪḶAHATTHIPADOPAMASUTTA to Devānaṃpiyatissa, whereupon the king requested to be accepted as a lay disciple. The next day, he preached to the king's sister-in-law, Anulā, and five hundred women of the court, all of whom became stream-enterers. Preaching to them a second time, they became once-returners. When they asked be ordained, he said that monks could not ordain women, and suggested that his sister, the nun Saṅghamittā, be invited, which was done. She came to Sri Lanka, bringing with her a branch of the BODHI TREE. The king offered to Mahinda the MAHĀMEGHAVANA, a royal pleasure garden that was to be the future site of the MAHĀTHŪPA. In the garden, which was on the outskirts of the Sinhalese capital, ANURĀDHAPURA, Mahinda established the SĪMĀ boundary for the MAHĀVIHĀRA monastery, which thenceforth became the headquarters of the Theravāda fraternity on the island. At Mahinda's prompting, relics of the Buddha were received from Asoka and Sakka (S. ŚAKRA), king of the gods, which were interred in the Cetiyagiri and Thūpārāma. Under Mahinda's direction, a council was held where MAHĀRIṬṬHA, a native son of Sri Lanka, recited the vinaya. According to the *Samantapāsādikā*, this recital marked the firm establishment of the religion on the island. The *Saddhammasaṅgaha* reckons the recitation of the vinaya by Mahāriṭṭha as the fourth Buddhist council (see COUNCIL, FOURTH). Mahinda died at the age of sixty and was cremated and his ashes interred in a shrine near the Mahāthūpa.

**Mahisamaṇḍala**. (C. Moxisuomantuoluo [guo]; J. Makesamandara [koku]; K. Mahyesamandara [kuk] 摩醯娑慢陀羅[國]). One of nine adjacent lands (paccantadesa) converted to Buddhism by missionaries dispatched by the elder MOGGALIPUTTATISSA at the end of the third Buddhist council (SAṂGĪTI; see COUNCIL, THIRD) held in Pāṭaliputta (S. PĀṬALIPUTRA) during the reign of Asoka in the third century BCE. Mahisamaṇḍala has been identified with modern Mysore and was converted by the elder MAHĀDEVA, who preached the *Devadūtasutta*. The third Buddhist Council at Pātaliputta and the nine Buddhist missions are known only in Pāli sources and are first recorded in the c. fourth-century text, the DĪPAVAṂSA.

**Mahīśāsaka**. [alt. Mahiṃśāsaka] (P. Mahiṃsāsaka; T. Sa ston pa; C. Huadi bu; J. Kejibu; K. Hwaji pu 化地部). One of the eighteen traditional "mainstream" (i.e., non-MAHĀYĀNA) NIKĀYAS or schools of Indian Buddhism. The school may be named eponymously after its founder, whose name seems to mean "Governing the Land," a brāhmaṇa who had been a district governor before becoming an ARHAT. The school probably emerged some three centuries after the demise of the Buddha. Within the traditional division of schools into two groups, the MAHĀSĀṂGHIKA and the STHAVIRANIKĀYA, the Mahīśāsaka is placed among the latter. The school was an offshoot of the SARVĀSTIVĀDA and it may have spawned in turn the later DHARMAGUPTAKA school. Epigraphic evidence of the school has been found as far north as the Punjab and as far south as NĀGĀRJUNAKOṆḌĀ. The Chinese pilgrim FAXIAN came across its recension of the VINAYA in Sri Lanka. Like the other schools of the day, the Mahīśāsaka distinguished itself from its contemporaries through its position on a number of contested issues, including the question of which works should be included in the TRIPIṬAKA. In accordance with the Sarvāstivāda, it upheld that notion that dharmas function during all three time periods of past, present, and future. On the question of the whether or not there was an intermediate state (ANTARĀBHAVA) between death and rebirth, the Mahīśāsaka asserted that there was not, but that a subtle form of the aggregates (SKANDHA) was carried forward into the next lifetime. The Mahīśāsaka also asserted that the fourth noble truth of the path (MĀRGASATYA) was an unconditioned factor (ASAṂSKṚTADHARMA) like the third noble truth of cessation (NIRODHASATYA). The school also held that the Buddha is a member of the SAṂGHA, a question with important implications for the division of alms and monastic properties. The YOGĀCĀRA-exegete ASAṄGA is said to have been ordained in this school.

**mahopaputra**. (S). See AṢṬAMAHOPAPUTRA; MAHĀ-UPAPUTRA.

**mahorāga**. (T. lto 'phye chen po; C. mohouluojia; J. magoraga; K. mahuraga 摩睺羅迦). A type of demigod in the Buddhist pantheon, the mahorāga are huge subterranean serpents who lie on their sides and rotate in the earth, their rotations causing earthquakes and tremors. They are often propitiated prior to the construction of a shrine, STŪPA, or monastery. Iconographically, they are pictured like nāgas, with the head, arms, and torso of a human, and the lower body and tail of a serpent. The mahorāga are one of the eight kinds of nonhumans (AṢṬASENĀ) who protect the dharma, who often appear in the audience of Buddhist SŪTRAS; the other seven are the DEVA, ASURA, GANDHARVA, NĀGA, YAKṢA, GARUḌA, and KIṂNARA.

**Maijishan**. (J. Bakusekizan; K. Maekchŏksan 麥積山). In Chinese, "Haystack Mountain"; a cave monastery site located southeast of Tianshui in the northwest Chinese province of Gansu, located on a hill some 466 feet (142 meters) high. Situated on the edge of the Qinling Mountains, Maijishan was once an important stop along the ancient SILK ROAD. Based on an inscription dated to 407 CE in cave no. 76, construction of the Maijishan cave sites is presumed to have been initiated by the Yao Xin family (396–416) during the Later Qin dynasty and to have continued for centuries. Close to two hundred caves have been preserved, which include more than seven thousand terracotta sculptures and countless painted murals. Many of the caves and wooden structures at the site have been damaged or destroyed due to natural disasters. While the paintings at the site are heavily damaged, the sculptures are well preserved and feature smooth modeling and flat planes devoid of naturalism. The dignified facial expressions with foreign features (e.g., round, open eyes and pronounced noses) are similar to those of the BINGLINGSI images. The arrangement of cave no. 78 consists of three large seated buddhas, which probably represent the buddhas of the past, present, and future. Two small niches at the rear wall feature the pensive bodhisattva MAITREYA and SIDDHĀRTHA in the pensive pose (see MAITREYĀSANA).The two standing bodhisattvas in cave no. 74 are characterized by their smooth bodies and scarves that elegantly frame their bodies; these features, along with the three-disk crown, derive from the Silk Road cave site of KIZIL. The cave temple sites of Binglingsi and Maijishan reflect the artistic synthesis of different Central Asian styles, which heavily influenced the development of the later Northern Wei artistic styles at LONGMEN and YUNGANG. Both sites also display a range of iconographies derived from sūtras that were newly translated during the Liang and Qin dynasties, whose rulers used Buddhism to enhance their political prestige.

**Mināmati-Lalmai Range**. A low series of hills situated between the towns of Maināmati and Lalmai in the Comilla district of modern-day Bangladesh, where the ruins of a significant number of Buddhist monasteries have been discovered. The earliest ruins date from the sixth century CE, the latest, the thirteenth century CE. Among the more important sites are the Salban Vihāra with 115 monastic cells, the Kotila Mura, which has three STŪPAS, and the Charpatra Mura.

**mainstream Buddhist schools**. A neologism coined by modern scholars to refer to the non-MAHĀYĀNA traditions of Indian Buddhism, including DHARMAGUPTA, MAHĀSĀṂGHIKA,

MAHĪŚĀSAKA, SARVĀSTIVĀDA, SAUTRĀNTIKA, STHAVIRANIKĀYA, etc., which traditionally number eighteen (although over thirty different schools are named in the literature). These are also sometimes referred to as the NIKĀYA or ŚRĀVAKAYĀNA schools. The locution "mainstream Buddhist school" is to be preferred to the pejorative HĪNAYĀNA, or "lesser vehicle," a polemical term that the MAHĀYĀNA coined to refer to these schools, which (from their perspective) taught narrow and discredited perspectives on Buddhist practice. See List of Lists, "eighteen mainstream Buddhist schools," and individual entries for these schools.

**maithuna**. (T. 'khrig pa; C. jiaojie; J. kōsetsu; K. kyŏjŏp 交接). In Sanskrit, "coupling," "sexual intercourse"; a term that appears both in proscriptions in the monastic code as well as in prescriptions for certain forms of tantric practice. In the monastic codes (PRĀTIMOKṢA), there are discussions as to what constitutes the violation of the vow of celibacy (BRAHMACARYA), explaining that the misdeed has been committed if sexual penetration of an orifice to the depth of a mustard seed occurs. In tantric texts, especially of the ANUTTARAYOGA class, sexual union with a consort is prescribed as a technique for creating the great bliss (MAHĀSUKHA) necessary for the achievement of enlightenment.

**Maitreya**. (P. Metteya; T. Byams pa; C. Mile; J. Miroku; K. Mirŭk 彌勒). In Sanskrit, "The Benevolent One"; the name of the next buddha, who now abides in TUṢITA heaven as a BODHISATTVA, awaiting the proper time for him to take his final rebirth. Buddhists believed that their religion, like all conditioned things, was inevitably impermanent and would eventually vanish from the earth (cf. SADDHARMAVIPRALOPA; MOFA). According to one such calculation, the teachings of the current buddha ŚĀKYAMUNI would flourish for five hundred years after his death, after which would follow a one-thousand-year period of decline and a three-thousand-year period in which the dharma would be completely forgotten. At the conclusion of this long disappearance, Maitreya would then take his final birth in India (JAMBUDVĪPA) in order to reestablish the Buddhist dispensation anew. According to later calculations, Maitreya will not take rebirth for some time, far longer than the 4,500 years mentioned earlier. He will do so only after the human life span has decreased to ten years and then increased to eighty thousand years. (Stalwart scholiasts have calculated that his rebirth will occur 5.67 billion years after the death of Śākyamuni.) Initially a minor figure in early Indian Buddhism, Maitreya (whose name derives from the Indic MAITRĪ, meaning "loving-kindness" or "benevolence") evolved during the early centuries of the Common Era into one of the most popular figures in Buddhism across Asia in both the mainstream and MAHĀYĀNA traditions. He is also known as AJITA, although there are indications that, at some point in history, the two were understood to be different deities. As the first bodhisattva to become a figure of worship, his imagery and cult set standards for the development of later bodhisattvas who became objects of cultic worship, such as AVALOKITEŚVARA and MAÑJUŚRĪ. Worship of Maitreya began early in Indian Buddhism and became especially popular in Central and East Asia during the fifth and sixth centuries. Such worship takes several forms, with disciples praying to either meet him when he is reborn on earth or in tuṣita heaven so that they may then take rebirth with him when he becomes a buddha, a destiny promised in the SADDHARMAPUṆḌARĪKASŪTRA ("Lotus Sūtra") to those who recite his name. Maitreya is also said to appear on earth, such as in a scene in the Chinese pilgrim XUANZANG's account of his seventh-century travels to India: attacked by pirates as he sailed on the Ganges River, Xuanzang prayed to and was rescued by the bodhisattva. Maitreya also famously appeared to the great Indian commentator ASAṄGA in the form of a wounded dog as a means of teaching him the importance of compassion. Devotees across the Buddhist world also attempt to extend their life span in order to be alive when Maitreya comes, or to be reborn at the time of his presence in the world, a worldly paradise that will be known as ketumati. His earliest iconography depicts him standing or sitting, holding a vase (KUṆḌIKĀ), symbolizing his imminent birth into the brāhmaṇa caste, and displaying the ABHAYAMUDRĀ, both features that remain common attributes of his images. In addition, he frequently has a small STŪPA in his headdress, believed to represent a prophecy regarding his descent to earth to receive the robes of his predecessor from MAHĀKĀŚYAPA. Maitreya is also commonly depicted as a buddha, often shown sitting in "European pose" (BHADRĀSANA; see also MAITREYĀSANA), displaying the DHARMACAKRAMUDRĀ. He is said to sit in a chair in "pensive" posture in order to be able to quickly stand and descend to earth at the appropriate time. Once he is reborn, Maitreya will replicate the deeds of Śākyamuni, with certain variations. For example, he will live the life of a householder for eight thousand years, but having seen the four sights (CATURNIMITTA) and renounced the world, he will practice asceticism for only one week before achieving buddhahood. As the Buddha, he will first travel to Mount KUKKUṬAPĀDA near BODHGAYĀ where the great ARHAT Mahākāśyapa has been entombed in a state of deep SAMĀDHI, awaiting the advent of Maitreya. Mahākāśyapa has kept the robes of Śākyamuni, which the previous buddha had entrusted to him to pass on to his successor. Upon his arrival, the mountain will break open, and Mahākāśyapa will come forth from a stūpa and give Maitreya his robes. When Maitreya accepts the robes, it will only cover two fingers of his hands, causing people to comment at how diminutive the past buddha must have been. ¶ The cult of Maitreya entered East Asia with the initial propagation of Buddhism and reached widespread popularity starting in the fourth century CE, a result of the popularity of the *Saddharmapuṇḍarīkasūtra* and several other early translations of Maitreya scriptures made in the fourth and fifth centuries. The *Saddharmapuṇḍarīkasūtra* describes Maitreya's present abode in the tuṣita heaven, while other sūtras discuss his future rebirth on earth and his present residence in heaven. Three important texts belonging to the latter category were translated into Chinese, starting in the fifth century, with two differing emphases: (1) the *Guan Mile pusa shangsheng doushuo tian jing* promised sentient beings the prospect of rebirth in tuṣita heaven together with Maitreya; and (2) the *Guan Mile pusa xiasheng jing* and (3) the *Foshuo Mile da chengfo jing* emphasized the rebirth of Maitreya in this world, where he will attain buddhahood under the Dragon Flower Tree (Nāgapuṣpa) and save numerous sentient beings. These three texts constituted the three principal scriptures of the Maitreya cult in East Asia. In China, Maitreya worship became popular from at least the fourth century: DAO'AN (312–385) and his followers were among the first to propagate the cult of Maitreya and the prospect of rebirth in tuṣita heaven. With the growing popularity of Maitreya, millenarian movements associated with his cult periodically developed in East Asia, which had both devotional and political dimensions. For example, when the Empress WU ZETIAN usurped the Tang-dynasty throne in 690, her followers attempted to justify the coup by referring to her as Maitreya being reborn on earth. In Korea, Maitreya worship was already popular by the sixth century. The Paekche king Mu (r. 600–641) identified his realm as the world in which Maitreya would be reborn. In Silla, the hwarang, an elite group of male youths, was often identified with Maitreya and such eminent Silla monks as WŎNHYO (617–686), WŎNCH'ŬK (613–696), and Kyŏnghŭng (fl. seventh century) composed commentaries on the Maitreya scriptures. Paekche monks transmitted Maitreya worship to Japan in the sixth century, where it became especially popular in the late eighth century. The worship of Maitreya in Japan regained popularity around the eleventh century, but gradually was replaced by devotions to AMITĀBHA and KṢITIGARBHA. The worship of Maitreya has continued to exist to the present day in both Korea and Japan. The Maitreya cult was influential in the twentieth century, for example, in the establishment of the Korean new religions of Chŭngsan kyo and Yonghwa kyo. Maitreya also merged in China and Japan with a popular indigenous figure, BUDAI (d. 916)—a monk known for his fat belly—whence he acquired his now popular East Asian form of the "laughing Buddha." This Chinese holy man is said to have been an incarnation of the bodhisattva Maitreya (J. Miroku Bosatsu) and is included among the Japanese indigenous pantheon known as the "seven gods of good fortune"(SHICHIFUKUJIN). Hotei represents contentment and happiness and is often depicted holding a large cloth bag (Hotei literally means "hemp sack"). From this bag, which never empties, he feeds the poor and needy. In some places, he has also become the patron saint of restaurants and bars, since those who drink and eat well are said to be influenced by Hotei. Today, nearly all Chinese Buddhist monasteries (and many restaurants as well) will have an image of this Maitreya at the front entrance; folk belief has it that by rubbing his belly one can establish the potential for wealth.

**Maitreyanātha**. (T. Byams mgon; C. Cizun; J. Jison; K. Chajon 慈尊). In Sanskrit, the "Protector Maitreya"; an epithet of MAITREYA, the future buddha. The Sanskrit compound can also be read as "Protected by Maitreya," and scholars have presumed that this is the name of an Indian scholar and contemporary of ASAṄGA (fourth century CE), whom they credit with the authorship of some or all of the "five books of Maitreya," the ABHISAMAYĀLAṂKĀRA, the MAHĀYĀNASŪTRĀLAṂKĀRA, the RATNAGOTRAVIBHĀGA, the MADHYĀNTAVIBHĀGA, and the DHARMADHARMATĀVIBHĀGA; all of which, according to tradition, were presented to Asaṅga in the TUṢITA heaven by the BODHISATTVA Maitreya.

**Maitreyāsana**. (T. byams pa'i 'dug stangs; C. banjia siwei; J. hankashiyui; K. pan'ga sayu 半跏思惟). In Sanskrit, the "posture of MAITREYA"; a posture (ĀSANA) in which the figure sits on a raised seat, with either both legs hanging pendant to the ground or with one leg pendant to the ground, the other leg crossed over the opposite knee. This pose is common in early images of Maitreya in China, Korea, and Japan, where the posture is translated as the "pensive pose" or "contemplative pose" (C. siwei xiang), because in this form the right hand rests lightly on the right cheek, depicting Maitreya's musing over when he should take his final rebirth and reestablish the Buddhist dispensation. This posture was also adopted in Japan in representations of Nyoirin Kannon. This posture is also closely related to, and often synonymous with, the "auspicious pose" (BHADRĀSANA) and the "pendant leg posture" (PRALAMBAPĀDĀSANA).

**maitrī**. (P. mettā; T. byams pa; C. ci/cibei; J. ji/jihi; K. cha/chabi 慈/慈悲). In Sanskrit, "loving-kindness," "kindness"; often seen in Western literature in its Pāli form mettā. Loving-kindness is one of the four divine abidings (BRAHMAVIHĀRA) and the four immeasurables (APRAMĀṆA), and is defined as the wish for happiness; the other three divine abidings and immeasurables are KARUṆĀ, or compassion; MUDITĀ, or sympathetic joy; and UPEKṢĀ, or equanimity. Of the four divine abidings, loving-kindness, along with sympathetic joy and compassion, is capable of producing the first three of the four states of meditative absorption (DHYĀNA). Equanimity alone is capable of producing the fourth dhyāna. In the VISUDDHIMAGGA, loving-kindness is listed as one among forty meditative topics (KAMMAṬṬHĀNA). The text indicates that divine abidings, including loving-kindness, are only to be used for the cultivation of tranquility (P. samatha; S. ŚAMATHA), not insight (P. VIPASSANĀ; VIPAŚYANĀ). In the *Visuddhimagga*, BUDDHAGHOSA recommends that the practice of mettā (maitrī) begin with wishing for happiness for oneself, and then extending that wish to others. In other contexts, maitrī, as the wish for the happiness of others, is considered one of the factors that motivates the BODHISATTVA to seek to save all beings from suffering. See also METTĀSUTTA.

**Maitrīpa/Maitrīpāda**. (c. 1007–1085). A tantric adept and scholar from north India, especially associated with the transmission of instructions and songs of realization on the doctrine of MAHĀMUDRĀ. He is known by several names: the Tibetan form Maitrīpa or its Sanskrit original Maitrīpāda; as a Buddhist monk, Matrīgupta; as a tantric adept, Advayavajra and Avadhūtipāda. Born in Bengal, Maitrīpa began his training as a Brahmanical scholar but later converted to Buddhism after debating with the scholar NĀROPA. He then received ordination and studied at the Buddhist universities of NĀLANDĀ and VIKRAMAŚĪLA under such eminent masters as RATNĀKARAŚĀNTI. Maitrīpa is said to have become a great academician, but he was also practicing TANTRA in secret. According to some traditions, Maitrīpa was expelled when liquor and a female consort were found in his room, perhaps by ATIŚA DĪPAṂKARAŚRĪJÑĀNA, who was resident abbot of Vikramaśīla at the time. He then sought out the adept Śavaripa in south India and, after a series of trials, was accepted as his disciple, receiving various tantric instructions. Maitrīpa later returned to the north, marrying the king of Malabar's daughter and composing numerous treatises on tantric theory and practice, especially that of amanasikāra ("no mental activity"), which are preserved in the BSTAN 'GYUR portion of the Tibetan Buddhist canon. He was an important teacher of MAR PA.

**Majjhimanikāya**. (S. MADHYAMĀGAMA). In Pāli, "Collection of Middle [Length] Discourses"; the second of the five divisions of the Pāli SUTTAPIṬAKA, the others being the DĪGHANIKĀYA, SAṂYUTTANIKĀYA, AṄGUTTARANIKĀYA, and KHUDDAKANIKĀYA. The *Majjhimanikāya* contains 152 suttas (S. SŪTRA) divided into three major parts, with fifty suttas in each of the first two parts and fifty-two in the third. Each one of these parts is further subdivided into five sections (vagga). The suttas are not arranged in any particular order, although suttas with broadly related themes (e.g., the six sense faculties, or INDRIYA), similar styles (e.g., suttas that contain a shorter, and often verse, summary of doctrine followed by longer expositions) or target audiences (e.g., discourses to householders, monks, religious wanderers, or brāhmaṇas) are sometimes grouped together in the same section. The enlightenment cycle of Gotama (S. GAUTAMA) Buddha finds some of its earliest expressions in several suttas in this nikāya. For example, the ARIYAPARIYESANĀSUTTA does not include the famous story of the prince's chariot rides but says instead, "Later, while still young, a black-haired young man endowed with the blessing of youth, in the prime of life, though my mother and father wished otherwise and wept with tearful faces, I shaved off my hair and beard, put on the yellow robe, and went forth from the home life into homelessness." There is sometimes overlap between nikāyas; for example, the SATIPAṬṬHĀNASUTTA of the *Majjhimanikāya* appears as the first section of the *Mahāsatipaṭṭhānasutta* of the *Dīghanikāya*. Not all of the suttas are spoken by the Buddha; for example, ĀNANDA delivers the *Gopakamoggallānasutta* after the Buddha's passage into PARINIRVĀṆA. The Sanskrit counterpart of the *Majjhimanikāya* is the MADHYAMĀGAMA, which is the SARVĀSTIVĀDA school's recension of this collection. In the Chinese translation, ninety-eight of the *Madhyamāgama*'s 222 sūtras correspond to suttas found in the *Majjhimanikāya*, eighty appear in the *Aṅguttaranikāya*, twelve to the *Dīghanikāya*, and eleven to the *Saṃyuttanikāya*.

**major and minor marks**. See MAHĀPURUṢALAKṢAṆA.

**makara**. (T. chu srin; C. mojieyu; J. makatsugyo; K. magarŏ 摩竭魚). In Indian mythology, a kind of sea monster, depicted variously as either a crocodile, or a hybrid being with the body of a fish and the head of an elephant. In the twelve signs of the zodiac recognized in Indian astrology, makara corresponds to the constellation of Capricorn.

**Makiguchi Tsunesaburō**. (牧口常三郎) (1871–1944). Founder of SŌKA GAKKAI, a modern Japanese lay movement. Makiguchi was born in a small village in Niigata prefecture. Until 1928, he pursued a career as an educator and writer, serving as a teacher or a principal in several schools, and publishing articles on his educational philosophy, which focused on developing the creativity and personal experience of his students. Perhaps because of such personal misfortunes as the loss of four of his five children, Makiguchi converted in 1928 to NICHIREN SHŌSHŪ, an offshoot of Nichiren Buddhism, after finding that its teachings resonated with his own ideas about engendering social and religious values. Together with his disciple Toda Jōsei (1900–1958), Makiguchi founded in 1930 the Sōka Kyōiku Gakkai (Creating Educational Values), a lay organization under the umbrella of the Nichiren Shōshū, which focused on publicizing his pedagogical ideas, and led its first general meeting. The society subsequently began to take on a decidedly religious character, focusing on missionary work for Nichiren Shōshū. As the Pacific War expanded, Makiguchi and his followers refused to cooperate with state-enforced SHINTŌ practices, leading to a rift between them and TAISEKIJI, the head monastery of Nichiren Shōshū. As a result, Makiguchi was arrested in 1943 on charges of lèse-majesté and violations of the Public Order Act, and died in prison one year later. After Makiguchi's disciple Toda Jōsei was released from prison in July 1945, he took charge of the Sōka Kyōiku Gakkai organization and renamed it Sōka Gakkai in 1946, developing it into one of the largest lay Buddhist organizations in Japan.

**makuragyō**. (枕經). In Japanese, lit., "pillow scripture"; the deathbed recitation of Buddhist scriptures. In Japan, a monk is invited to offer prayers and recite scriptures for the recently deceased. Before the corpse is interred in the coffin, the makuragyō service is performed at the deceased's bedside or pillow, hence the service's name. Traditionally, the deathbed service was performed by a monk called the kasō, who chanted passages from the scriptures through the night.

**mala**. (T. dri ma; C. gou; J. ku; K. ku 垢). In Sanskrit, "taint," "stain," "maculation"; often used as a synonym for afflictions

(KLEŚA). Much of the discourse on the Buddhist path (MĀRGA) is expressed in terms of purity and pollution, with the path to liberation sometimes described as the gradual purification of the mind, in which various stains or taints are removed. What remains at the end of the process of purification is the subject of considerable discussion among the various Buddhist schools. For example, DHARMAKĪRTI declared in his PRAMĀṆAVĀRTTIKA, "The nature of the mind is clear light; its stains are adventitious." See also AMALAVIJÑĀNA.

**mālā**. (T. 'phreng ba; C. man; J. man; K. man 鬘). In Sanskrit and Pāli, lit. "garland" a "rosary," viz., a string of beads usually held in the right hand and used for counting the recitations of prayers or MANTRAs; also called a JAPAMĀLĀ. The number of beads on the rosary varies by tradition, with some rosaries in pure land traditions having twenty-seven beads, and rosaries in Tibetan Buddhism commonly having 108 or 111 beads. The rationale for 111 beads is as follows: it is assumed that in each set of ten repetitions, one repetition will be faulty and need to be redone. Thus ten beads are added for the first hundred beads and one bead is added for the additional ten beads. The significance of the more common number of 108 is less clear. One common interpretation is that this number refers to a list of 108 afflictions (KLEŚA); fingering all 108 beads in the course of a recitation would then be either a reminder to remain mindful of these afflictions or would constitute their symbolic purification. Alternatively, this 108 can refer to all of phenomenal existence, i.e., the eighteen elements (DHĀTU), viz., the six sense bases, six sense objects, and six sensory consciousnesses, in all of the six realms of existence (GATI) (18 × 6 = 108). See also JAPAMĀLĀ.

**Malalasekera, Gunapala Piyasena**. (1899–1973). One of the most influential Sinhalese scholars of the twentieth century. Born in Malamulla Panadura, Ceylon (Sri Lanka), Malalasekera entered the Ceylon Medical College in 1917. He attended the School of Oriental Studies at the University of London from 1923 to 1926, where he was a student of CAROLINE A. F. RHYS DAVIDS. He later taught Pāli and Buddhist civilization, Pāli language, Sanskrit, and Sinhalese at the University of Ceylon. Aside from an immense influence on at least two generations of Indologists and Buddhologists in Sri Lanka, Malalasekera was also a distinguished diplomat, serving as the Ceylonese ambassador to the then-Soviet Union, Poland, Czechoslovakia, and Romania. He served as the permanent representative for Ceylon at the United Nations from 1961 to 1963, and as the high commissioner in Great Britain for four years after that. He was the president of the All Ceylon Buddhist Congress from 1939 to 1957 and then again in 1967. He led the first conference of the WORLD FELLOWSHIP OF BUDDHISTS in 1950 and became editor-in-chief of the *Encyclopaedia of Buddhism* in 1956. Malalasekera published many books and articles, including *The Pāli Literature of Ceylon* and *A Dictionary of Pāli Proper Names*.

***Mālānanda**. (C. Moluonantuo; J. Marananda; K. Maranant'a 摩羅難陀). Reconstructed proper name of the Serindian monk who in 384 brought Buddhist scriptures and images to the Korean kingdom of Paekche (traditional dates 18 BCE–668 CE) from the Eastern Jin dynasty (265–420 CE) in China; his name is also reconstructed as *Kumāranandin. Mālānanda arrived in the Paekche capital via sea to an elaborate reception by the Paekche court and King Ch'imnyu (r. 384–385), suggesting that he came as part of an official mission from the Eastern Jin. In 385, under the auspices of the royal court, Mālānanda established a Buddhist monastery in the Paekche capital and ordained ten young men as monks, the first recorded instance of Buddhist ordination on the Korean peninsula.

**Malang fu**. (J. Merōfu; K. Marang pu 馬郎婦). In Chinese, "Mr. Ma's Wife"; also known as YULAN GUANYIN (Fish Basket Guanyin); a famous manifestation of the BODHISATTVA GUANYIN (AVALOKITEŚVARA). The story of Mrs. Ma is found in various Chinese miracle-tale collections. The basic outline of the story begins with a beautiful young woman who comes to a small town to sell fish. Many young men propose to her, but she insists that she will only marry a man who can memorize the "Universal Gateway" chapter of the SADDHARMAPUṆḌARĪKASŪTRA ("Lotus Sūtra") in one night. Twenty men succeed, so she then asks them to memorize the VAJRACCHEDIKĀPRAJÑĀPĀRAMITĀSŪTRA in one night. The ten men who succeed at that task are then asked to memorize the entire *Saddharmapuṇḍarīkasūtra*. One young man whose surname was Ma succeeds and he marries the beautiful fish seller. Unfortunately, she became ill on their wedding day and died the very same day. Later, a foreign monk visits the town to pay respects and informed Ma and the townsmen that this young fish seller was none other than the bodhisattva Guanyin in disguise.

**Mālava**. (S). One of the twenty-four sacred sites associated with the CAKRASAṂVARATANTRA. See PĪṬHA.

**Mallā**. (T. Gyad kyi yul; C. Moluo [guo]; J. Mara [koku]; K. Mara [kuk] 摩羅[國]). In the plural, the Sanskrit and Pāli name of the people in one of the sixteen countries (MAHĀJANAPADA) that flourished in northern India during the Buddha's lifetime. According to Pāli sources, the Mallā people were divided into two kingdoms, each with its own capital, Pāvā and Kusināra (S. KUŚINAGARĪ). The inhabitants of the former city were named Pāveyyakā Mallā, while those of the latter were named Kosinārakā. The Buddha is described as having inaugurated a new assembly hall in Pāvā by offering a sermon there for the populace. This hall was located in the Ambavana grove, which belonged to CUNDA, the blacksmith. Later, in the final year of his life, the Buddha would accept his last meal of SŪKARAMADDAVA (pork or possibly mushrooms) from Cunda, on account of which he would fall deathly ill with dysentery. From Cunda's residence in Pāvā, the Buddha made his way to Kusināra where, lying down between twin sāla (S. ŚĀLA) trees, he passed into parinibbāna (S. PARINIRVĀṆA). When Ānanda laments the fact that the Buddha will pass away at such a "little mud-walled town, a backwoods town, a branch township," rather than a great city, the Buddha disabused him of this notion, telling him that Kuśinagarī had previously been the magnificent capital named Kusāvatī of an earlier CAKRAVARTIN king named Sudarśana (P. Sudassana). The Buddha's body was cremated at the Makutabandhana shrine in Kuśinagarī, after which the relics were removed to the assembly hall. There, the brāhmaṇa Doṇa (S. DROṆA) distributed them among the many claimants from different kingdoms and clans that were demanding their share. The Buddha claimed many disciples from the Mallā country as did his rival, the JAINA leader, Nigaṇṭha Nātaputta (S. NIRGRANTHA-JÑĀTĪPUTRA). The Mallā belonged to the warrior caste (P. khattiya; S. KṢATRIYA), although they are depicted in Buddhist texts as living amicably with their neighbors. In Greek accounts, they are called Malloi, a people who for a time successfully resisted attack by Alexander's forces. If this identification is correct, it would place their country in the area of modern Punjab.

**Mallikā**. [alt. Mālikā] (P. Mallikā; T. Ma li ka; C. Moli; J. Matsuri/Mari; K. Malli 末利). In Sanskrit and Pāli, "Jasmine"; a prominent disciple of the Buddha and the wife of King PRASENAJIT of KOŚALA. She was the daughter of a lower-caste garland maker who one day offered the Buddha a basket of fermented rice, without knowing his identity. The Buddha predicted that day that she would become queen of Kośala, which indeed came true. Her faith in the Buddha led to her royal husband becoming a disciple of the Buddha, which occurred when she suggested that the king visit the Buddha to have him interpret some disturbing dreams he had had. Despite her lack of education, she gained extensive knowledge of the dharma from ĀNANDA, who visited the palace to teach. As queen, Mallikā was a generous supporter of the SAṂGHA, sponsoring the construction of a hall, lined with ebony, that was used for sermons. In the *Mallikāsutta*, she asks the Buddha why some women are beautiful and some ugly, some rich and some poor, some powerful and some powerless. The Buddha explains that beauty is the result of gentleness and calmness, wealth is the result of generosity, and power is the result of a lack of envy. The commentary to the DHAMMAPADA (DHAMMAPADAṬṬHAKATHĀ) relates a story in which Mallikā was mounted by her dog while drying herself after a bath. She allowed the dog to continue, not knowing that she was being observed by the king. When he accused her of bestiality, she lied, saying that the window in the bathhouse prevented one from seeing clearly. To prove her point, she told the king to go into the bathhouse. When he returned, she falsely accused him of having intercourse with a goat. As a result of these two misdeeds—the bestiality and the lie—after her death, she was reborn in the AVĪCI hell for seven days, a fact that the Buddha hid from her bereaved husband Prasenajit. After seven days, she was reborn in TUṢITA, at which point the Buddha informed the king that his wife had been reborn in a divine realm. In the ŚRĪMĀLĀDEVĪSIṂHANĀDASŪTRA, Queen Śrīmālā is the daughter of Mallikā and Prasenajit.

**malsa**. (末寺). In Korean, "branch monastery"; an affiliate monastery of one of the twenty-four "district monasteries" (PONSA) in the contemporary Korean CHOGYE CHONG. See PONSA.

**mamakāra**. (P. mamaṃkāra; T. bdag gir 'dzin pa; C. wosuo; J. gasho; K. aso 我所). In Sanskrit, lit. "mine-making"; the mistaken conception of "mine," or "possession." Mamakāra is a form of ignorance deriving from the conception of self or "I" (AHAṂKĀRA) in which objects (primarily the SKANDHAs) are mistakenly conceived to be the possessions of an autonomous person. Based on this false presumption, all manner of negative afflictions (KLEŚA) arise, including greed, jealousy, and hatred. Wisdom is often described as the abandonment of the conceptions of "I" and "mine." When it is understood that the person (PUDGALA) is merely a collection of impermanent and ever-changing physical and mental processes (SAṂTĀNA), one understands that there is no permanent, independent self among the constituents of materiality and mentality. If there is no autonomous self, then there can be no autonomous owner of the objects of experience. Thus, upon the abandonment of the conception of "I," the conception of "mine" is also abandoned.

**ma mo**. A class of indigenous Tibetan female spirits. They are generally hostile, known to carry disease sacks (nad rkyal). With the advent of Buddhism in Tibet, they came to be identified with the Indian deity Mātarī [alt. Mātṛkā]. DPAL LDAN LHA MO is considered their leader. PADMASAMBHAVA subdued all ma mo on a mountain named Chu bo ri. There are numerous groupings of ma mo who appear in various deities' retinues, such as Dpal ldan lha mo and YAMA, and who are invoked in rituals, called on both to cease their illness-causing activities and to inflict illnesses on enemies. They also figure in weather-making rituals, since they are able to withhold or send rain. They are depicted as ugly emaciated women with matted hair and withered breasts.

**māṃsacakṣus**. (P. maṃsacakkhu; T. sha'i spyan; C. rouyan; J. nikugen; K. yugan 肉眼). In Sanskrit, "fleshly eye"; one of the five eyes or five sorts of vision (PAÑCACAKṢUS), a list that overlaps with the five (or six) "clairvoyances" or superknowledges (ABHIJÑĀ). In Pāli texts, the "fleshly eye" is one of the five types of vision of a buddha. In Mahāyāna texts, the māṃsacakṣus refers to what would ordinarily be considered eyesight. It is said to be a VIPĀKAPHALA (maturation result) restricted in its range to the sight of the particular animal or deity that possesses it. In the case of vultures, for example, the fleshly eye may be able to see up to several miles, and in the case of certain divinities (DEVA) it may be the entire cosmos.

**māna**. (T. nga rgyal; C. man; J. man; K. man 慢). In Sanskrit and Pāli, "pride," "conceit"; also known as asmimāna, the "'I am' conceit." The eighth of ten "fetters" (SAṂYOJANA) that keep beings bound to the cycle of rebirth (SAṂSĀRA), pride arises from comparing oneself to others and manifests itself in three ways: viz., as the feeling that one is equal to, inferior to, or superior to others. Pride is a deep-seated and habitual affective response to other persons and continues to exist in subtle form in the minds of stream-enterers (SROTAĀPANNA), once-returners (SAKṚDĀGĀMIN), and nonreturners (ANĀGĀMIN) even though they have eliminated the "cognitive" fetter of personality belief (SATKĀYADṚṢṬI). Māna is permanently eliminated upon attaining the stage of worthiness (ARHAT), the fourth and highest degree of Buddhist sanctity (ĀRYAPUDGALA). According to the SARVĀSTIVĀDA ABHIDHARMA, there are seven kinds of conceit. The first kind is simply called "māna," which refers to a sense of superiority toward those who are inferior and a sense of pride in the idea of being equal to those who are equal. "Atimāna" is haughtiness, the insistence on one's superiority when in fact one is a mere equal to another person or the insistence on being equal to those who are in fact superior to oneself. "Mānātimāna" is "pride and conceit," the insistence on one's superiority when in fact the person to whom one is comparing oneself is superior. "Asmimāna" is the conceit "I am," the deriving of a sense of an enduring self from grasping onto external objects and the internal five aggregates (SKANDHA). "ADHIMĀNA" is the overestimation of or bragging about one's spiritual accomplishments. "ABHIMĀNA" has been variously interpreted as arrogance or "false humility," admitting of another's slight superiority when in fact he or she is vastly superior. "Mithyāmāna" is hypocrisy: posturing as a virtuous person when in fact one lacks virtue.

**manaḥsaṃcetanāhāra**. (T. yid la sems pa'i zas; C. sishi; J. shijiki; K. sasik 思食). In Sanskrit, "the sustenance (ĀHĀRA) that is mental volition (CETANĀ)"; a term used in YOGĀCĀRA materials to connote the support provided to the person by what might loosely be termed motivation. The term is said to refer to the mind (MANAS) in the sense of the sixth of six types of consciousness. See MANAS.

**Manam Chonghŏn**. (曼庵宗憲) (1876–1957). Korean monk and educator during the Japanese occupation and postwar periods; also known as Mogyang. After losing his parents at an early age, Manam became a monk and studied under HANYŎNG CHŎNGHO (1870–1948). In 1900, he devoted himself to the study of SŎN meditation at the monastery of Unmun Sŏnwŏn (UNMUNSA). In 1910, after Korea's annexation by Japan, Manam traveled throughout the southern regions of the peninsula and delivered lectures on Buddhism to the public until he settled down at the monastery of PAEGYANGSA in 1920 to serve as abbot. At a time when the Buddhist community was split over the issue of clerical marriage, Manam, for the first time, divided his monk-students between the celibate chŏngpŏp chung (proper-dharma congregation) and the married hobŏp chung (protecting-dharma congregation). Manam's actions were considered to be a formal recognition of clerical marriage and were heavily criticized by the rest of the Buddhist community led by YONGSŎNG CHINJONG (1864–1940) and Namjŏn Kwangŏn (1868–1936). In 1945, the Koburhoe organization that Manam established clashed with the General Administrative Committee of the Chosŏn Buddhist order over the issue of the laxity of Buddhist practice in Korea, with Manam arguing for a return to the strict and disciplined lifestyle of the past as a means of preventing the corruption of Buddhism. After the end of the Japanese occupation, Manam organized the Kobul Ch'ongnim gathering and initiated what later came to be called the "purification movement" (chŏnghwa undong) in Korean Buddhism. In 1952, he succeeded his teacher Hanyŏng and became head (kyojŏng) of the Chosŏn Buddhist order. As head, he gave the order a new name, the "Chogye Order of Korean Buddhism" (Taehan Pulgyo Chogye Chong; see CHONGYE CHONG), and created a new entry in its constitution, formally delineating the distinction between married monks (kyohwasŭng) and celibate monks (suhaengsŭng). He attempted to initiate a new plan for the organization of monasteries that would give priority to the celibate monks, but his plan was never put into practice. When President Syngman Rhee showed his support for the purification movement in May 1954, the monks of the Chogye order held a national convention and appointed Manam, Tongsan Hyeil (1890–1965), and Ch'ŏngdam Sunho (1902–1971) as the new leaders of the order and initiated a nationwide Buddhist reformation movement. Manam, however, was ultimately unable to mediate the different opinions of the representatives of the Buddhist community concerning the specific details and goals of the purification movement.

**mānāpya**. (S). See MĀNATVA.

**manas**. (T. yid; C. yi; J. i; K. ŭi 意). In Sanskrit and Pāli, "mind," or "mentation"; generally a synonym of such related terms as CITTA and VIJÑĀNA. In lists of the six internal sensory organs (INDRIYA), manas is the sixth, in which context it is also referred to as the mental faculty (MANENDRIYA). As such, it differs from the other five faculties (the eye, ear, nose, tongue, and bodily sense organs), all of which are associated with physical organs. The sixth consciousness, the mental consciousness (MANOVIJÑĀNA), however, can know any object, whether physical or nonphysical; hence its objects are phenomena (DHARMA). The mental consciousness does not rely directly on a physical sense organ, as in the case of the preceding five types of consciousness; hence its sense faculty (INDRIYA) is mental, and is identified as a previous moment of consciousness, which allows for either the next moment of mental cognition of a previous object or the first moment of cognition of a new object. In YOGĀCĀRA, manas is sometimes used as an abbreviation for KLIṢṬAMANAS.

**mānasapratyakṣa**. (S). See MANONUBHAVAPRATYAKṢA.

**manaskāra**. [alt. manasikāra] (P. manasikāra; T. yid la byed pa; C. zuoyi; J. sai; K. chagŭi 作意). In Sanskrit, "mental engagement," or "attention"; a general term for mental activity, concentration, or attention, with at least two technical senses: as one of the five omnipresent (SARVATRAGA) or seven universal (P. sabbacittasādhāraṇa) mental concomitants (CAITTA), it is the factor that directs the mind to a specific object; in the process of developing calmness or serenity (ŚAMATHA), there are four levels of increasingly powerful and continuous mental engagement with the object of concentration. See also AYONIŚOMANASKĀRA.

**manaskarman**. (P. manokamma; T. yid kyi las; C. yiye; J. igō; K. ŭiŏp 意業). In Sanskrit, "mental action"; thoughts that produce KARMAN. Virtuous and nonvirtuous actions are of three types: physical actions (those performed by the body), verbal actions (those expressed in words), and mental actions (thoughts). Physical actions of the nonvirtuous type would include killing, stealing, and sexual misconduct. Verbal actions of the nonvirtuous type would include lying, divisive speech, harsh speech, and senseless speech. Mental actions of the nonvirtuous type would include covetousness, harmful intent, and wrong view. (See also KARMAPATHA).

**Manasvin**. (T. Gzi can; C. Monasi; J. Manashi; K. Manasa 摩那斯). One of the eight great NĀGA kings who assembled to hear the Buddha preach the SADDHARMAPUṆḌARĪKASŪTRA.

**mānatva**. [alt. mānāpya] (P. mānatta; T. mgu bar bya ba; C. monatuo; J. manata; K. manat'a 摩那埵). In Sanskrit, a temporary period of "penance" imposed on a monk for a minor offense. According to the Pāli VINAYA, the mānatta penance is imposed on a monk who commits an offense requiring probation (P. saṅghādisesa; S. SAṂGHAVAŚEṢA) when that monk immediately confesses the infraction to another monk. The penance imposed in this circumstance is called "penance for unconcealed offenses" (apaṭicchannamānatta), which entails the loss of the usual privileges of monkhood for a set period of six nights. If a monk conceals a saṅghādisesa offense for a period of time before confessing it, he must undergo a "probationary penance" called either "probation" (PARIVĀSA) or "penance for concealed offenses" (paṭicchannamānatta). This probationary penance likewise entails the loss of privileges, but in this case that probation must last for as long as the offense was concealed. After the parivāsa penance is completed, the monk must then undergo mānatta penance for six nights. A monk undergoing mānatta punishment may not: (1) dwell under the same roof as another monk, (2) live where there is no other monk, (3) accept respect or praise from other monks or novices, (4) confer ordination (UPASAṂPADĀ) or provide "dependence" or guidance (P. nissaya; S. NIŚRAYA) to younger monks, (5) accept the services of a novice, (6) preach to nuns, (7) commit similar acts of wrongdoing, (8) criticize the act carried out against him, and (9) criticize the persons responsible for carrying out the act. After the six-night period of mānatta penance is finished, the monk is eligible to be readmitted into the SAṂGHA.

**manāyatana**. (T. yid kyi skye mched; C. yichu; J. isho; K. ŭich'ŏ 意處). In Sanskrit and Pāli, lit.,"mental source" or "mental base of cognition"; another term for MANAS, when it appears on the list of the twelve ĀYATANA, the sources of consciousness or bases of cognition. The twelve sources of consciousness are the six external sensory objects (form, sound, taste, odors, objects of touch, and phenomena) and the six internal sense faculties (eye, ear, nose, tongue, body, and mind). The five sense objects and the five sense faculties are necessarily physical, serving respectively as the causes of the first five types of sensory consciousnesses: visual, auditory, olfactory, gustatory, and tactile consciousnesses. The sixth consciousness, the mental consciousness (MANOVIJÑĀNA), however, can know any object, whether physical or nonphysical; hence its objects are phenomena (DHARMA). The mental consciousness does not rely directly on a physical sense organ; hence, its organ (INDRIYA) is mental, and is identified as a previous moment of consciousness.

**maṇḍa**. (T. snying po; C. tihu; J. daigo; K. cheho 醍醐). In Sanskrit and Pāli, "cream"; used figuratively to refer to something's "quintessence" or "supreme point." This usage is implicit, for example, in the compound term BODHIMAṆḌA (lit. "the supreme point of awakening," viz., "the seat of enlightenment"), the place where the buddha achieved complete, perfect enlightenment. Maṇḍa as representing the quintessence of the teachings of Buddhism is also found in the temporal taxonomy of the teachings (JIAOXIANG PANSHI) advocated by the Chinese TIANTAI ZONG, in which the "taste of ghee" (tihu wei) symbolizes the consummate teachings of Buddhism found in the SADDHARMAPUṆḌARĪKASŪTRA and MAHĀPARINIRVĀṆASŪTRA.

**maṇḍala**. (T. dkyil 'khor; C. mantuluo; J. mandara; K. mandara 曼荼羅). In Sanskrit, lit. "circle"; a polysemous term, best known for its usage in tantric Buddhism as a type of "circular diagram." Employed widely throughout South, East, and Central Asia, maṇḍala are highly flexible in form, function, and meaning. The core concept of maṇḍala originates from the Sanskrit meaning "circle," where a boundary is demarcated and increasing significance is accorded to areas closer to the center; the Tibetan translation (dkyil 'khor) "center periphery" emphasizes this general scheme. In certain contexts, maṇḍalas can have the broad sense of referring to circular objects ("maṇḍala of the moon") or a complete collection of constituent parts ("maṇḍala of the universe"). This latter denotation is found in Tibetan Buddhism, where a symbolic representation of the universe is offered to buddhas and bodhisattvas as a means of accumulating merit, especially as a preliminary practice (SNGON 'GRO). Maṇḍalas may have begun as a simple circle drawn on the ground as part of a ritual ceremony, especially for consecration, initiation, or protection. In its developed forms, a maṇḍala is viewed as the residential palace for a primary deity—located at the center—surrounded by an assembly of attendant deities. This portrayal may be considered either a symbolic representation or the actual residence; it may be mentally imagined or physically constructed. The latter constitutes a significant and highly developed contribution to the sacred arts of many Asian cultures. Maṇḍalas are often depicted two dimensionally by a pattern of basic geometric shapes and are most commonly depicted in paint or colored powders. These are thought of almost as architectural floor plans, schematic representations viewed from above of elaborate three-dimensional structures, mapping an ideal cosmos where every element has a symbolic meaning dependent upon the ritual context. Maṇḍalas are occasionally fashioned in three dimensions from bronze or wood, with statues of deities situated in the appropriate locations. When used in a private setting, such as in the Buddhist visualization meditation of deity yoga (DEVATĀYOGA), the practitioner imagines the entire universe as purified and transformed into the transcendent maṇḍala—often identifying himself or herself with the form of the main deity at the center. In other practices, the maṇḍala is visualized within the body, populated by deities at specific locations. In public rituals, including tantric initiations and consecration ceremonies, a central maṇḍala can be used as a common basis for the participation of many individuals, who are said to enter the maṇḍala. The maṇḍala is also understood as a special locus of divine power, worthy of ritual worship and which may confer "blessings" upon devotees. Religious monuments (BOROBUDUR in Java), institutions (BSAM YAS monastery in Tibet), and even geographical locations (WUTAISHAN in China) are often understood as maṇḍalas. Maṇḍalas have also entered the popular vocabulary of the West. Swiss psychologist Carl Jung developed theories of cognition incorporating maṇḍalas as an analytical model. The fourteenth DALAI LAMA has used the KĀLACAKRA maṇḍala as a means of spreading a message of peace throughout the world. See also KONGŌKAI; TAIZŌKAI.

**Mandalay**. The last royal capital of the Burmese Konbaung kingdom, prior to the British conquest of Burma (Myanmar). The city is situated on the eastern bank of the Irrawaddy River, twelve miles north of AVA (Inwa) and five miles north of AMARAPURA, both previous capitals of the Konbaung dynasty (1752–1885). Built in 1857 by MINDON MIN (r. 1853–1878) at the base of the eponymous Mandalay Hill, its construction was carried out at the place where the Buddha is said to have made a prophecy that a great Buddhist capital would arise on that spot in the 2,400th year after the parinibbāna. Very similar in plan to Amarapura, Mandalay is laid out in a grid pattern, at the center of which is a royal precinct in the shape of a perfect square surrounded by a wide moat and a brickwork defensive wall. The wall is pierced by twelve gates, three on each side, crowned with multistoried tiered pavilions (B. pyatthat), symbols of royal authority. Broad avenues run perpendicularly from the gates to the center of the royal compound where the palace and ancillary buildings are located. Destroyed during Allied bombing in World War II, these structures have recently been restored. The city's most famous shrine is the MAHĀMUNI pagoda, which houses the colossal bronze Mahāmuni image of Gotama Buddha (see ARAKAN BUDDHA). Originally housed in the palladium of Arakan, the Mahāmuni was seized by King Bodawpaya (r. 1782–1819) when he conquered that kingdom in 1785. As had been the case with the founding of earlier capitals, the construction of Mandalay was regarded as inaugurating a golden age wherein the religion, culture, and political fortunes of the Burmese kingdom would flourish. In connection with the prophecy, in 1868, Mindon Min summoned 2,400 learned monks to the capital from throughout the kingdom to revise the Pāli TIPIṬAKA in what came to be regarded by the Burmese as the fifth Buddhist council (see COUNCIL, FIFTH). In 1871, the revised Burmese canon was inscribed on 729 stone slabs that were erected, each in its own shrine, in concentric rings around the massive Kuthodaw pagoda (Pagoda of Great Merit). The entire complex occupies fourteen acres and is situated to the northeast of the fortified city at the base of Mandalay Hill. Nearby is the Sandamuni pagoda, constructed along a similar plan, which houses 1,171 slabs on which are inscribed the Pāli commentaries. Another monument constructed for the synod is the Kyauktawgyi pagoda modeled after the ANANDA TEMPLE at PAGAN, which contains a colossal seated statue of the Buddha. Commemorating Mandalay's foundation legend is the Shweyattaw temple, also built by Mindon Min and located halfway up a stairway leading to the top of Mandalay Hill. The structure houses a colossal standing image of the Buddha covered in gold leaf, whose outstretched arm points to the city center, marking the spot where the Buddha delivered his prophecy. In addition to its pagodas and temples, the city boasted numerous monasteries and colleges making it one of the major scholastic centers of the kingdom. Mandalay ceased to be the Burmese capital in 1885 when it fell to British troops at the conclusion of the Third Anglo–Burmese War.

**Mandāravā**. (T. Man da ra ba) (c. eighth century). A revered female Indian Buddhist master, renowned as a close disciple and consort of the tantric adept PADMASAMBHAVA. She was born the daughter of the king of Sahor, modern Rewalsar in Mandi District, Himachel Pradesh. According to traditional sources, Mandāravā rejected the marriage arrangements made by her father, wishing instead to renounce the world and practice religion. Padmasambhava accepted her as his disciple and the couple remained in a hilltop retreat. The king learned of their arrangement and, in a fit of anger, had Padmasambhava (or, according to some accounts, the couple) burned alive. As a dense cloud of smoke cleared, the adept appeared seated atop a lotus in the center of a large lake, miraculously unscathed. The king and his court were thus converted to Buddhism and became Padmasambhava's disciples. The lake became known in

Tibetan as Mtsho Padma (Lotus Lake) and has become a major site for pilgrimage and religious practice. Mandāravā accompanied Padmasambhava to MĀRATIKA cave in Nepal where they undertook the practice of longevity. Although Mandāravā remained most of her life in India, she was revered as a ḌĀKINĪ in Tibet, where she is believed to have appeared numerous times as a female teacher and YOGINĪ.

**mandorla**. See KĀYAPRABHĀ.

**manendriya**. (P. manindriya; T. yid kyi dbang po; C. yigen; J. ikon; K. ŭigŭn 意根). In Sanskrit, "mental faculty" or "mental dominant"; another term for MANAS as it appears in the list of the six INDRIYA or sensory faculties that provide the foundation for the six forms of consciousness. Each of the six consciousnesses—eye, ear, nose, tongue, body, mental—requires a sense faculty or indriya in order to function. For the five sense consciousnesses, this organ is the physical sense organ associated with the eye, ear, nose, tongue, or body. The mind or mental consciousness (MANOVIJÑĀNA) does not have a physical support in this sense. Thus, the mental faculty is identified as a previous moment of consciousness.

**maṅgala**. (T. bkra shis; C. jixiang; J. kichijō; K. kilsang 吉祥). In Sanskrit and Pāli, "auspiciousness," but having a wide range of connotations, including luck, good fortune, happiness, prosperity, welfare, good omen, and blessing. The term is also used to describe any number of social virtues, considered auspicious because they produce benefits in both this and future lifetimes. According to the Pāli MAṄGALASUTTA, for example, these virtues include not associating with fools, but associating instead with the wise; caring for parents, supporting wife and children, and following a salutary occupation; generosity, morality, helping relatives, and performing actions that are blameless; refraining from evil; abstaining from intoxicants; respect, humility, contentment, gratitude, learning the teachings (P. dhamma; S. DHARMA); obedience, ascetic practice, and so forth.

**Maṅgalasutta**. In Pāli, "Discourse on the Auspicious"; one of the best-loved and most frequently recited texts in the Southeast Asian Buddhist world. The Maṅgalasutta appears in an early scriptural anthology, the SUTTANIPĀTA; a later collection, the KHUDDAKAPĀṬHA; and in a postcanonical anthology of "protection texts," the PARITTA. The text itself is a mere twelve verses in length and is accompanied by a brief preface inquiring about what is true auspiciousness. The Buddha's response provides a straightforward recital of auspicious things, beginning with various social virtues and ending with the achievement of nibbāna (S. NIRVĀṆA). The *Maṅgalasutta*'s great renown derives from its inclusion in the *Paritta*, a late anthology of texts that are chanted as part of the protective rituals performed by Buddhist monks to ward off misfortunes; indeed, it is this apotropaic quality of the scripture that accounts for its enduring popularity. Paritta suttas refer to specific discourses delivered by the Buddha that are believed to offer protection to those who either recite the sutta or listen to its recitation. Other such auspicious apotropaic suttas are the RATANASUTTA ("Discourse on the Precious") and the METTĀSUTTA ("Discourse on Loving-Kindness"). These paritta texts are commonly believed in Southeast Asia to bring happiness and good fortune when chanted by the SAṂGHA. The *Maṅgalasutta* has been the subject of many Pāli commentaries, one of the largest of which, the *Maṅgalatthadīpanī*, composed in northern Thailand in the sixteenth century, is over five hundred pages in length and continues to serve as the core of the monastic curriculum in contemporary Thailand. The *Maṅgalasutta*'s twelve verses are: "Many divinities and humans, desiring well-being, have thought about auspiciousness; tell us what is the highest auspiciousness./ Not to associate with fools, to associate with the wise, to worship those worthy of worship—that is the highest auspiciousness./ To live in a suitable place and to have done good deeds before, having a proper goal for oneself—that is the highest auspiciousness./ Learning, craftsmanship, and being well-trained in discipline, being well-spoken—that is the highest auspiciousness./ Care for mother and father, supporting wife and children, and types of work that bring no conflict—that is the highest auspiciousness./ Generosity, morality, helping relatives and performing actions that are blameless—that is the highest auspiciousness./ Ceasing and refraining from evil, abstaining from intoxicants, diligence in morality—that is the highest auspiciousness./ Respect, humility, contentment, gratitude, listening to the dhamma at the proper time—that is the highest auspiciousness./ Patience, obedience, seeing ascetics and timely discussions of the dhamma—that is the highest auspiciousness./ Ascetic practice, the religious life, seeing the four noble truths, and the realization of nibbāna—that is the highest auspiciousness./ If someone's mind is sorrowless, stainless, secure, and does not shake when touched by the things of the world—that is the highest auspiciousness./ Having acted in this wise, unconquered everywhere they go to well-being everywhere—for them, this is the highest auspiciousness."

**Man'gong Wŏlmyŏn**. (滿空月面) (1871–1946). In Korean, "Replete in Emptiness, Moon-Face"; the cognomen and ordination name of an important SŎN (C. Chan) monk of the late Chosŏn and Japanese colonial periods. Man'gong was born in T'aein county, North Chŏlla province, and became a novice monk in 1884. After enlightenment experiences in 1895 and 1901, he became in 1904 a dharma heir of KYŎNGHŎ SŎNGU (1849–1912), the preeminent Sŏn master of his generation who was renowned for his efforts to revitalize Korean Sŏn practice. Like Kyŏnghŏ, Man'gong was also a well-known iconoclast, who practiced an "unconstrained practice" (K. muae haeng; C. WU'AI XING) that was not bound by the customary restrictions of monastic discipline. After 1905, Man'gong often resided at SUDŎKSA on Mt. Tŏksung in South Ch'ungch'ŏng province, and he and his lineage are closely associated with that monastery. Man'gong also collaborated with such contemporary Buddhist leaders as HAN YONGUN (1879–1944) and Sŏktu Pot'aek (1882–1954) in attempting to rejuvenate Korean Buddhist practice. Man'gong established the Sŏnhagwŏn (Cloister for Sŏn Learning) in 1921 in order to promote Korean Sŏn meditation training. Man'gong emphasized training in "questioning meditation" (K. kanhwa Sŏn; C. KANHUA CHAN), using the meditative topic (K. hwadu; C. HUATOU) "no" (K. mu; C. WU; see WU GONG'AN; GOUZI WU FOXING). Man'gong was also publicly critical of the Japanese colonial government. There is a well-known anecdote that, at a conference of abbots from the thirty-one Korean head monasteries (PONSA) in 1937, he chided the Japanese governor-general by telling him that only Korean Buddhists would be able to save him once he had fallen into hell for destroying their tradition. In his later years, Man'gong retreated to the hermitage of Chŏnwŏlsa, near Sudŏksa on Mt. Tŏksung. Man'gong had several renowned disciples who constitute the Tŏksung transmission lineage, including the monks Kobong (1890–1961), Ch'unsŏng (1891–1977), and Pyŏkch'o (1899–1986), and the nuns KIM IRYŎP (1896–1971) and Pŏphŭi (1887–1975); Sungsan Haengwŏn (1927–2004), a major propagator of the Korean Sŏn tradition in the West, was Man'gong's dharma successor through Kobong.

**Manhae**. (K) (萬海). See HAN YONGUN.

**maṇi**. (T. nor bu; C. moni/zhu; J. mani/shu; K. mani/chu 摩尼/珠). In Sanskrit and Pāli, "jewel"; one of the generic terms for a precious gem in Buddhist texts, appearing in such compounds as "wish-fulfilling jewel" (CINTĀMAṆI) and the famous MANTRA, OṂ MAṆI PADME HŪṂ. In this mantra and elsewhere, the term is particularly associated with the bodhisattva AVALOKITEŚVARA. The term occurs commonly in most strata of Buddhist texts, both literally in descriptions of the heavens and pure lands and figuratively as a metaphor for something beautiful, precious, and rare.

**Ma ṇi bka' 'bum**. In Tibetan, "One Hundred Thousand Pronouncements [Regarding] Maṇi"; a heterogenious compilation of texts traditionally attributed to the Tibetan king SRONG BTSAN SGAM PO. This large collection of works, usually published in two massive volumes, is generally understood as a treasure text (GTER MA), said to have been revealed by three individuals during the twelfth and thirteenth centuries: the SIDDHA Gngos grub (Ngödrup), the famed treasure revealer (GTER STON) NYANG RAL NYI MA 'OD ZER, and Shākya 'Od—a disciple in the Nyang ral lineage sometimes known as Shākya bzang po (Shākya Sangpo). The texts are organized into three parts or cycles (skor): (1) "The cycle of SŪTRAS" (mdo skor), containing many legendary accounts of the BODHISATTVA AVALOKITEŚVARA and Srong btsan sgam po; (2) "the cycle of sādhanas" (sgrub skor), containing various meditation manuals (SĀDHANA) based on different aspects of Avalokiteśvara; and (3) "the cycle of precepts" (zhal gdams kyi skor), a miscellany of texts, many of which relate to the bodhisattva of great compassion. The remaining texts are sometimes referred to as "the cycle of the disclosure of the hidden" (gab pa mngon phyung gi skor). The title of the collection refers to the famed six-syllable MANTRA of Avalokiteśvara, OṂ MAṆI PADME HŪṂ. The texts are an important early source for many of Tibet's key legends: the activities of Srong btsan sgam po, including the founding of the JO KHANG temple, and the status of Avalokiteśvara as the special protector of Tibet and the Tibetan people, incarnated in the person of Srong btsan sgam po himself. The *Ma ṇi bka' 'bum* also includes an account of a set of four statues (three or five according to some sources) in a form of AVALOKITEŚVARA (called the "Four Brother Statues of Avalokiteśvara") said to have spontaneously arisen by miraculous means from the trunk of single sandalwood tree. According to the Tibetan text, the Tibetan king Srong bstan sgam po dispatched a monk named Akaraśīla to southern Nepal, where he discovered the four images in the midst of a large sandalwood grove. Akaraśīla then "invited" the statues to reside in various locations in order to dispel misery and strife and serve as the basis for religious practice. These statues are considered some of the most sacred Buddhist images in Nepal and Tibet. In their most common reckoning, the four brothers are: (1) the white MATSYENDRANĀTH in Jana Bāhāl, Kathmandu, Nepal; (2) the red Matsyendranāth in nearby Patan; (3) the Ārya Lokeśvara in the PO TA LA Palace, LHA SA; (4) and the 'PHAGS PA WA TI in SKYID GRONG, southern Tibet (a part of which is now in possession of the Dalai Lama in exile). Sometimes a fifth image is included: the Minanāth in Patan.

**ma ṇi 'khor lo**. In Tibetan, lit. "MAṆI wheel," commonly rendered into English as a "prayer wheel"; a device for the repetition of a MANTRA, so-called because of its frequent use in conjunction with repetitions of the mantra OṂ MAṆI PADME HŪṂ. The device, commonly used in Tibetan Buddhism, is a hollow cylinder ranging in length from a few inches to a few feet, filled with a long scroll of paper on which a mantra has been printed thousands of times. The scroll is wrapped tightly around the central axis of the device and enclosed in the cylinder. Each turn of the wheel is considered the equivalent of one recitation of the mantra, multiplied by the number of times the mantra is printed on the scroll. Smaller prayer wheels are carried and spun in the left hand while a rosary (JAPAMĀLĀ) is counted in the right hand as the mantra is recited. Larger versions are often mounted in a series along walls; very large wheels may even fill a small temple, where they are turned by pushing handles at their base. There are also wheels that are turned by the wind, water, or convection.

**Mañjughoṣa**. (T. 'Jam pa'i dbyangs; C. Miaoyin pusa; J. Myōon bosatsu; K. Myoŭm posal 妙音菩薩). See MAÑJUŚRĪ.

**Mañjuśrī**. (T. 'Jam dpal; C. Wenshushili; J. Monjushiri; K. Munsusari 文殊師利). In Sanskrit, "Gentle Glory," also known as MAÑJUGHOṢA, "Gentle Voice"; one of the two most important BODHISATTVAs in MAHĀYĀNA Buddhism (along with AVALOKITEŚVARA). Mañjuśrī seems to derive from a celestial musician (GANDHARVA) named Pañcaśikha (Five Peaks), who dwelled on a five-peaked mountain (see WUTAISHAN), whence his toponym. Mañjuśrī is the bodhisattva of wisdom and sometimes is said to be the embodiment of all the wisdom of all the buddhas. Mañjuśrī, Avalokiteśvara, and VAJRAPĀṆI are together known as the "protectors of the three families" (TRIKULANĀTHA), representing wisdom, compassion, and power, respectively. Among his many epithets, the most common is KUMĀRABHŪTA, "Ever Youthful." Among Mañjuśrī's many forms, the most famous shows him seated in the lotus posture (PADMĀSANA), dressed in the raiments of a prince, his right hand holding a flaming sword above his head, his left hand holding the stem of a lotus that blossoms over his left shoulder, a volume of the PRAJÑĀPĀRAMITĀ atop the lotus. Mañjuśrī plays a major role in many of the most renowned Mahāyāna sūtras. Mañjuśrī first comes to prominence in the VIMALAKĪRTINIRDEŚA, which probably dates no later than the first century CE, where only Mañjuśrī has the courage to visit and debate with the wise layman VIMALAKĪRTI and eventually becomes the interlocutor for Vimalakīrti's exposition of the dharma. In the SADDHARMAPUṆḌARĪKASŪTRA, only Mañjuśrī understands that the Buddha is about to preach the "Lotus Sūtra." In the AVATAṂSAKASŪTRA, it is Mañjuśrī who sends SUDHANA out on his pilgrimage. In the *Ajātaśatrukaukṛtyavinodana*, it is revealed that Mañjuśrī inspired ŚĀKYAMUNI to set out on the bodhisattva path many eons ago, and that he had played this same role for all the buddhas of the past; indeed, the text tells us that Mañjuśrī, in his guise as an ever-youthful prince, is the father of all the buddhas. He is equally important in tantric texts, including those in which his name figures in the title, such as the MAÑJUŚRĪMŪLAKALPA and the MAÑJUŚRĪNĀMASAṂGĪTI. The bull-headed deity YAMĀNTAKA is said to be the wrathful form of Mañjuśrī. Buddhabhadra's early fifth-century translation of the *Avataṃsakasūtra* is the first text that seemed to connect Mañjuśrī with Wutaishan (Five-Terrace Mountain) in China's Shaanxi province. Wutaishan became an important place of pilgrimage in East Asia beginning at least by the Northern Wei dynasty (424–532), and eventually drew monks in search of a vision of Mañjuśrī from across the Asian continent, including Korea, Japan, India, and Tibet. The *Svayambhūpurāṇa* of Nepal recounts that Mañjuśrī came from China to worship the STŪPA located in the middle of a great lake. So that humans would be able worship the stūpa, he took his sword and cut a great gorge at the southern edge of the lake, draining the water and creating the Kathmandu Valley. As the bodhisattva of wisdom, Mañjuśrī is propiated by those who wish to increase their knowledge and learning. It is considered efficacious to recite his mantra "oṃ arapacana dhīḥ" (see ARAPACANA); Arapacana is an alternate name for Mañjuśrī.

**Mañjuśrīkīrti**. (T. 'Jam dpal grags pa). Eighth king of the mythical kingdom of ŚAMBHALA, and the first of the twenty-five so-called "kulika kings" of śambhala. The first seven kings of śambhala are known as dharmarājas, starting with Sucandra, who received the KĀLACAKRATANTRA from the Buddha and then propagated it in his kingdom. Mañjuśrīkīrti is said to have ascended to the throne of the kingdom 674 years after the Buddha entered PARINIRVĀṆA. He is credited with first preventing some three hundred thousand brāhmaṇas from leaving the kingdom and then converting them to Buddhism, turning all the inhabitants of śambhala into a single class, the VAJRAKULA, or "vajra family." This is one of the etymologies of the term "kulika king." His greatest achievement, however, was the composition of a summary of the *Kālacakratantra* received by Sucandra. This work is known as the *Mūlakālacakratantra*, or root *Kālacakratantra*, and alt., as the *Laghutantra*, or "short tantra." It is said that over the course of time, the original tantra was lost, so that the recension of the *Kālacakratantra* that exists today is the version composed by Mañjuśrīkīrti.

**Mañjuśrīmitra**. (T. 'Jam dpal bshes gnyen). An important, and possibly mythical, figure in the RDZOGS CHEN tradition of Tibetan Buddhism. According to some accounts, he was a king of Siṅghala (Sri Lanka). The rdzogs chen teachings are said to have originated from the primordial buddha SAMANTABHADRA, who transmitted them to his emanation (SAṂBHOGAKĀYA), the buddha VAJRASATTVA, who in turn transmitted them to his NIRMĀṆAKĀYA emanation, known by the Tibetan name DGA' RAB RDO RJE (perhaps Pramodavajra in Sanskrit), who finally transmitted them to Mañjuśrīmitra. He is said to have received these teachings in the form of 6,400,000 verses and organized them into the three categories of SEMS SDE, KLONG SDE, and MAN NGAG SDE. He in turn transmitted these teachings to Śrīsiṃha. Mañjuśrīmitra is the author of *Rdo la ser zhun*.

**Mañjuśrīmūlakalpa**. (T. 'Jam dpal gyi rtsa ba'i rgyud; C. Dafangguang pusazang wenshushili genben yigui jing; J. Daihōkō bosatsuzō Monjushiri konpongikikyō; K. Taebanggwang posalchang Munsusari kŭnbon ŭigwe kyŏng 大方廣菩薩藏文殊師利根本儀軌經). In Sanskrit "The Fundamental Ordinance of MAÑJUŚRĪ"; known in Tibetan as the "Fundamental Tantra of Mañjuśrī." The work is an early and important Buddhist TANTRA (marking a transition between the SŪTRA and tantra genres), dating probably from around the late sixth or early seventh centuries, which was later classed as a KRIYĀTANTRA. The text, which is in a compilation of fifty-five chapters, provides detailed instructions by the Buddha on the performance of rituals and consecrations, including the important jar or vase consecrations (KALAŚĀBHIṢEKA). The work is also among the first to introduce the notion of families (KULA) of divinities, in this case three families: the TATHĀGATAKULA, the PADMAKULA, and the VAJRAKULA. Like other tantric texts, it provides instruction on a wide range of topics, including the recitation of MANTRAs, the drawing of images and MAṆḌALAs, and the nature of the VIDYĀDHARA, as well as on astrology, medicine. Among the many prophecies in the text is the oft-cited prophecy concerning NĀGĀRJUNA, in which the Buddha states that four hundred years after his passage into PARINIRVĀṆA, a monk named Nāga will appear, who will live for six hundred years.

**Mañjuśrīnāmasaṃgīti**. (T. 'Jam dpal gyi mtshan yang dag par brjod pa; C. Sheng miaojixiang zhenshi ming jing; J. Shōmyōkichijō shinjitsumyōkyō; K. Sŏng myogilsang chinsil myŏng kyŏng 聖妙吉祥眞實名經). In Sanskrit, "Litany of the Names of MAÑJUŚRĪ"; one of the most popular liturgical works of late Indian Buddhism. The text dates from the late seventh or early eighth century CE and in its present form includes 167 verses and a lengthy prose section. It begins with a request to the Buddha from a disciple, in this case, the tantric deity VAJRADHARA, to set forth the names of Mañjuśrī. The Buddha offers extensive praise to Mañjuśrī in the form of multiple epithets and identifications, equating him with all that is auspicious, although special attention is paid to his identity with the myriad categories of Buddhist wisdom. In other verses, the Buddha provides syllables to be recited in order to visualize a variety of deities, all of whom are considered forms of Mañjuśrī. Mañjuśrī himself is identified with the letter A, the first letter of the Sanskrit alphabet, and hence the source of all other names and the deities they represent. The Buddha also describes the MAṆḌALA of Mañjuśrī. The prose section, like so many Mahāyāna sūtras, extols the virtues of its own recitation. Here, the Buddha declares that those who recite the *Mañjuśrīnāmasaṃgīti* three times daily will gain all manner of attainment and will also be protected by the Hindu gods, such as Viṣṇu (NĀRĀYAṆA) and Śiva (Maheśvara).

**man ngag sde**. (me ngak de). In Tibetan, "instruction class"; comprising the third of three main divisions of RDZOGS CHEN doctrine according to the RNYING MA sect of Tibetan Buddhism. The other two are SEMS SDE (mental class) and KLONG SDE (spatial class). The man ngag sde teachings, regarded as the highest of the three, have constituted the core of Rnying ma practice since the eleventh century. It is said that sems sde teaches the clarity/awareness side of enlightenment, klong sde teaches the spatial side of enlightenment, and man ngag sde combines the two. A wide range of practices are included in the man ngag sde, concerned above all with the presentation by the teacher of a "pure awareness" (RIG PA) that is free from dualistic conceptions, and the recognition and maintenance of that state by the student; the instructions on the BAR DO emerged from these texts. The most famous practices of man ngag sde are "cutting through" (KHREGS CHOD) and "leaping over" (THOD RGAL). The man ngag sde has a number of subcategories, the most famous of which is the SNYING THIG. The root tantras of the man ngag sde are said to be the seventeen tantras.

**manojalpa**. (T. yid la brjod pa; C. yiyan; J. igon; K. ŭiŏn 意言). In Sanskrit, lit., "mental talk" or "mental chatter"; a general term for thought (VIKALPA), often in the negative sense of a constant subconscious murmur of conceptions regarding sensory objects. In the YOGĀCĀRA school, the object of manojalpa is the imaginary (PARIKALPITA), defined as the falsely imagined nature of objects as separate from the consciousness that perceives them and naturally serving as the bases of their conceptual designations.

**manomayakāya**. (T. yid kyi rang bzhin gyi lus; C. yishengshen; J. ishōshin; K. ŭisaengsin 意生身). In Sanskrit and Pāli, "mind-made body"; a subtle body acquired during meditative practice, which can exercise psychical and magical powers (ṚDDHI), such as passing through solid objects, appearing in many places at once, or flying. This body is described as living on joy, not solid nutriment; lacking such characteristics of a physical body as solidity, cohesion, heat, and motion; and being invisible to normal sight. The SĀMAÑÑAPHALASUTTA refers to the manomayakāya as something achieved by the meditator who has mastered the fourth of the four meditative absorptions (P. JHĀNA; S. DHYĀNA) associated with the subtle-materiality realm (RŪPADHĀTU); this meditative body is created from one's current physical body, the sutta says, as if drawing a sword from its scabbard or a reed from its sheath. The LAṄKĀVATĀRASŪTRA lists three types of manomayakāya achieved by a BODHISATTVA: (1) a body obtained through the enjoyment of SAMĀDHI on the third, fourth, and fifth stages (BHŪMI) of the bodhisattva path; (2) a body obtained by recognizing the self-nature of the dharma itself, which is achieved on the eighth bhūmi; and (3) a body the bodhisattva assumes in accordance with the class of being he is seeking to edify. The manomayakāya is also analogous to the "transitional being" (GANDHARVA) that abides in the ANTARĀBHAVA, the intermediate state between death and rebirth. Existence in any of the four meditative (dhyāna) heavens of either the subtle-materiality realm (rūpadhātu) or the immaterial realm (ĀRŪPYADHĀTU) may also sometimes be designated as a heavenly mind-made body (divyo manomayaḥ kāyaḥ). Finally, the mind-made body is manifested by great bodhisattvas (vaśitāprāptabodhisattva) and other sanctified beings during their transfigurational births-and-deaths (PARIṆĀMIKAJARĀMARAṆA)—viz., the births-and-deaths that may occur even after enlightenment—one of the two categories of SAṂSĀRA, along with the determinative birth-and-death (PARICCHEDAJARĀMARAṆA) experienced by ordinary sentient beings within the three realms of existence (TRILOKADHĀTU). Mind-made bodies may be perceived only by the DIVYACAKṢUS, literally the "divine eye," one of the five (or six) superknowledges (ABHIJÑĀ) and three "knowledges" (TRIVIDYĀ). The term also figures in the development of the theories of the two, three, or four bodies of the Buddha (BUDDHAKĀYA). Early scholasts speak of the Buddha having both a physical body and a manomayakāya, or "emanation body" (NIRMĀṆAKĀYA), a second body that he used to perform miraculous feats such as visiting his mother in the TRĀYASTRIṂŚA heaven atop Mount SUMERU after her death.

**manonubhavapratyakṣa**. [alt. mānasapratyakṣa] (T. yid kyis myong ba'i mngon sum/yid kyi mngon sum; C. yishouxianliang; J. ijugenryō; K. ŭisuhyŏllyang 意受現量). In Sanskrit, "mental direct perception"; a form of perception (PRATYAKṢA). According to the ABHIDHARMA analysis, the mind (MANAS) is capable of directly perceiving an object without the intrusion of a process of thought, just as the five sense consciousnesses are capable of directly perceiving a sensory object. An experience of sensory direct perception is said to be followed by a single moment of mental direct perception. That moment, however, is so short that for ordinary beings it passes without being noticed. Other forms of mental direct perception include the various superknowledges, or ABHIJÑĀ, such as the ability to know the thoughts of others, the ability to remember one's own former lives, and the ability to hear and see things at a great distance. One element of the Buddhist path is the process of developing mental direct perception to the point that one can directly perceive with the mind (and without thought and imagination) the truths of impermanence, suffering, and nonself. When these truths are directly perceived at the level of a SAMĀDHI that unifies serenity (ŚAMATHA) and insight (VIPAŚYANĀ), the mental direct perception then becomes what is called yogic direct perception (YOGIPRATYAKṢA).

**Manorathapūraṇī**. In Pāli, the "Fulfiller of Wishes"; a Pāli commentary on the AṄGUTTARANIKĀYA written by BUDDHAGHOSA. Cf. SADDHARMAVIPRALOPA.

**manovijñāna**. (P. manoviññāṇa; T. yid kyi rnam par shes pa; C. yishi; J. ishiki; K. ŭisik 意識). In Sanskrit, "mental consciousness"; the sixth of the six consciousnesses (after the five sensory consciousnesses). Unlike the sense consciousnesses, all of which entail forms of direct perception (PRATYAKṢA), the mental consciousness is capable of both direct perception (pratyakṣa) and thought (KALPANĀ). Also, unlike the sensory consciousnesses, the mental consciousness is not limited by object: whereas the eye can only see visual objects, the ear can only hear auditory objects, etc., the objects of the mental consciousness are said to be all phenomena (DHARMA) because it is capable of thinking about anything that exists. The mental consciousness also differs from the five sense consciousnesses in terms of its precondition (PRATYAYA). For the five sense consciousnesses, the respective sense organ serves as the precondition; thus, each of these sense organs has a physical dimension (RŪPA). However, for the mental consciousness, the precondition is a previous moment of consciousness, which allows for either the next moment of mental cognition of a previous object or the first moment of cognition of a new object.

**Manpukuji**. (萬福寺). In Japanese, "Myriad Blessings Monastery"; located in Uji, outside Kyōto, Japan. Currently, Manpukuji is the headquarters (honzan) of the ŌBAKUSHŪ of the ZEN tradition. The monastery was founded by the émigré CHAN (Zen) master YINYUAN LONGXI with the support of the shōgun Tokugawa Ietsuna (1639–1680). Construction began in 1661 and the dharma hall was completed the next year with the help of the grand counselor Sakai Tadakatsu (1587–1662). In 1664, Yinyuan left his head disciple MU'AN XINGTAO in charge and retired to his hermitage at Manpukuji. Mu'an thus became the second abbot of Manpukuji and oversaw the construction of the buddha hall, the bell tower, the patriarchs' hall, and so forth. For several generations, émigré Chinese monks dominated the abbacy of Manpukuji. The construction of Manpukuji was modeled after Yinyuan's old monastery of Wanfusi (which is pronounced Manpukuji in Japanese) in Fuzhou (present-day Fujian province). The major icons were also prepared by émigré Chinese artists and, along with the famous portrait of Yinyuan, are now considered important cultural artifacts. Mu'an's disciple Tetsugen Dōkō (1630–1682) led a project to carve a complete set of xylographs of the Ming dynasty edition of the Buddhist canon, which is now housed at Manpukuji; this edition, commonly called the Ōbaku canon, is one of the few complete xylographic canons still extant in East Asia (cf. the second carving of the Korean Buddhist canon, KORYŎ TAEJANGGYŎNG).

**mantra**. (T. sngags; C. zhenyan; J. shingon; K. chinŏn 眞言). In Sanskrit, "spell," "charm," or "magic formula"; a syllable or series of syllables that may or may not have semantic meaning, most often in a form of Sanskrit, the contemplation or recitation of which is thought to be efficacious. Indian exegetes creatively etymologized the term with the paronomastic gloss "mind protector," because a mantra serves to protect the mind from ordinary appearances. There are many famous mantras, ranging in length from one syllable to a hundred syllables or more. They are often recited to propitiate a deity, and their letters are commonly visualized in tantric meditations, sometimes within the body of the meditator. Although mantras are typically associated with tantric texts, they also appear in the SŪTRAS, most famously in the PRAJÑĀPĀRAMITĀHṚDAYASŪTRA ("Heart Sūtra"). Numerous tantric SĀDHANAS require the recitation of a particular mantra a specific number of times, with the recitations counted on a rosary (JAPAMĀLĀ). In Tibetan Buddhism, mantras are also repeated mechanically by turning "prayer wheels" (MA ṆI 'KHOR LO). Perhaps the most famous of all such spells is the six-syllable mantra of the bodhisattva AVALOKITEŚVARA, OṂ MAṆI PADME HŪṂ, which is recited throughout the Tibetan Buddhist world. The Japanese SHINGONSHŪ takes its name from the Sinitic translation of mantra as "true word" (C. zhenyan; J. shingon).

**mantrayāna**. (T. sngags kyi theg pa; C. zhenyan sheng; J. shingonjō; K. chinŏn sŭng 眞言乘). In Sanskrit, "mantra vehicle"; often used as a synonym of VAJRAYĀNA, suggesting the central place of mantras in tantric practice. According to one popular paronomastic gloss, the term MANTRA means "mind protector," especially in the sense of protecting the mind from the ordinary appearances of the world. In this sense, the mantrayāna would refer not simply to the recitation of mantra but to the entire range of practices designed to transform the ordinary practitioner into a deity and his ordinary world into a MAṆḌALA. In Tibetan Buddhism, the Tibetan forms of the terms mantrayāna and guhyamantrayāna ("secret mantra vehicle") are used as commonly as vajrayāna and more commonly than TANTRAYĀNA.

**manuṣya**. (P. manussa; T. mi; C. ren; J. nin; K. in 人). In Sanskrit, "human"; one of the six realms of rebirth (GATI) in SAṂSĀRA, together with the realms of divinities, demigods, animals, ghosts, and hell denizens. Human rebirth (along with that of divinities and sometimes demigods) is considered a fortunate rebirth, unlike rebirth as an animal, ghost, or hell being, which are considered unfortunate (DURGATI; APĀYA). To achieve liberation from rebirth, human birth is considered the ideal state, because a human being is not so beset by suffering that one is unable to practice the path (as are the animals, ghosts, or hell denizens) or so intoxicated by pleasures (as are the divinities) that one is disinclined to do so. According to the theory of KARMAN, rebirth as a human is the result of having performed a virtuous deed, such as a keeping a vow, in a previous life. Among humans, some are more fortunate than others in terms of their access to the dharma and their opportunities for practice, described in a list of opportune births (KṢAṆA; KṢAṆASAṂPAD), such as birth at a time and place where a buddha exists and where one has the capability to understand his teachings. Rebirth as a human endowed with such prospects is said to be exceedingly rare and unlikely to occur again in the near future; therefore, every effort should be made either to achieve liberation in this lifetime or to accumulate the necessary merit (PUṆYA) to ensure rebirth as a human. In Buddhist cosmology, humans occupy the four island continents that surround Mount SUMERU in the cardinal directions. However, humans as they are commonly encountered are found only on the southern continent of JAMBUDVĪPA; the human inhabitants of the other three continents exceed them in both height and in life span.

**Manzan Dōhaku**. (卍山道白) (1636–1715). In Japanese, "Myriad Mountains, Purity of the Path"; ZEN master and scholar of the SŌTŌSHŪ. Manzan is said to have become a monk at the age of nine and to have experienced a deep awakening at sixteen. After his awakening, he left the following verse: "The night is deep and the clouds have cleared from the sky as if it had been washed; throughout the world, nowhere is the radiance of my eyes defiled or obstructed." In 1678, he met the Sōtō Zen master Gesshū Sōko (1618–1696) and inherited his dharma (shihō). Two years later Manzan took over the abbacy of the temple Daijōji from Gesshū and remained there for ten years. In 1700, Manzan went to the city of Edo (Tōkyō) in hopes of reforming the custom of IN'IN EKISHI, or "changing teachers according to temple." Instead, he called for a direct, face-to-face transmission (menju shihō) from one master to his disciple (isshi inshō). After several failed attempts he finally succeeded in persuading the bakufu government to ban the in'in ekishi and GARANBŌ ("temple dharma lineage") practice in 1703. Manzan was also a consummate scholar who is renowned for his efforts to edit Zen master DŌGEN KIGEN's magnum opus, SHŌBŌGENZŌ. He based his arguments for the abandonment of garanbō and in'in ekishi on his readings of the *Shōbōgenzō*. Manzan left many works. His *Zenkaiketsu* and *Taikaku kanna* offered a Zen perspective on the meaning of precepts. He also wrote the *Tōmon enyoshū*, which explains various matters related to Zen, including face-to-face transmission (menju shihō). His teachings can also be found in the *Manzan oshō gōroku*. His most eminent disciple was the Tokugawa reformer MENZAN ZUIHŌ (1683–1769).

**Māra**. (T. Bdud; C. Mo; J. Ma; K. Ma 魔). In Sanskrit and Pāli, lit., "Maker of Death"; the personification of evil in Buddhism and often referred to as the Buddhist "devil" or "demon"; he is in fact a powerful divinity of the sensuous realm (KĀMADHĀTU), devoted to preventing beings from achieving liberation from rebirth and thus conquering death. In the biographies of the Buddha, Māra figures as the Buddha's antagonist. According to the most elaborate accounts of the Buddha's enlightenment experience, when the BODHISATTVA SIDDHĀRTHA sat under the BODHI TREE, vowing not to rise until he attained liberation from SAṂSĀRA, he was approached by Māra, who sought to dissuade him from his quest. When he refused, Māra sent his minions to destroy him, but their weapons were transformed into flower blossoms. When he sent his daughters —Ratī (Delight), Aratī (Discontent), and Tṛṣṇā (Craving)—to seduce him, the bodhisattva remained unmoved, in some versions transforming them into hags and then restoring their beauty once they repented. When Māra questioned the bodhisattva's right to occupy his seat beneath the Bodhi tree, the bodhisattva declared that he had earned that right by accumulating merit over countless eons. When asked who could vouch for these deeds, the bodhisattva extended his right hand and touched the earth, thereby calling the goddess of the earth, STHĀVARĀ, to bear witness to his virtue; this gesture, called the BHŪMISPARŚAMUDRĀ ("earth-touching gesture"), is one of the most common iconographic depictions of the Buddha. The goddess bore witness to the bodhisattva's virtue by causing the earth to quake. In a Southeast Asian version, the goddess is called THORANI, and she wrung out from her hair all the water that the bodhisattva had offered in oblations over many lives. This created a great torrent, which washed Māra away. In all accounts, Māra is finally vanquished and withdraws, with the entire episode being referred to as the "defeat of Māra" (Māravijaya). Māra reappears shortly after the Buddha's enlightenment, urging him to immediately pass into PARINIRVĀṆA and not bother teaching others. His request is rejected, but he nevertheless extracts from the Buddha a promise to enter nirvāṇa when he has completed his teaching; near the end of the Buddha's life, Māra reappears at the CĀPĀLACAITYA to remind him of his promise. Māra also distracts the Buddha's attendant,

ĀNANDA, preventing him from requesting that the Buddha live until the end of the eon, a power that the Buddha possesses but must be asked to exercise. Ānanda is chided by the Buddha and later rebuked by the SAṂGHA for his oversight. Māra commonly appears in Buddhist literature when monks and nuns are about to achieve enlightenment, attempting to distract them. Māra would eventually figure in sectarian polemics as well. In the MAHĀYĀNA sūtras, those who claim that the Mahāyāna sūtras are not the authentic word of the Buddha are condemned as being possessed by Māra. In scholastic literature, Māra is expanded metaphorically into four forms. SKANDHAMĀRA, the māra of the aggregates (SKANDHA), is the mind and body of unenlightened beings, which serve as the site of death. Kleśamāra, the māra of the afflictions (KLEŚA), refers to such afflictions as greed, hatred, and delusion, which catalyze death and rebirth and which prevent liberation. MṚTYUMĀRA, the māra of death, is death itself, and DEVAPUTRAMĀRA, the deity Māra, is the divinity (DEVA) who attacked the Buddha and who seeks to prevent the defeat of the other three forms of Māra.

**maraṇa**. (T. 'chi ba; C. si; J. shi; K. sa 死). In Sanskrit and Pāli, "death." In ordinary parlance, death refers to the cessation of a living being's vital signs, marking the end of a single lifetime. This fact was apparently unknown to Prince SIDDHĀRTHA, such that his observation of a dead body during an excursion outside his palace served as one of the four signs or sights (CATURNIMITTA) that led him to renounce the world and seek a state beyond death. Death is common theme throughout Buddhist literature. Birth, aging, sickness, and death are often listed as four faults of SAṂSĀRA. The gods MĀRA and YAMA are closely associated with death. Throughout the Buddhist world, all manner of rituals are performed to forestall death, and there are numerous instructions on how to face death. Because death is certain to come, but its precise time is unknown, there are constant reminders to be prepared for death at any moment. Because the friends and possessions accumulated in this life cannot be taken to the next life, it is said that nothing is of benefit at the time of death except the dharma. The signs portending death in various levels of existence and the physical and psychological process of dying are described in detail in Buddhist literature. After death has occurred, rituals are typically performed to guide the consciousness of the deceased to rebirth in an auspicious realm. Together with "old age" or "senescence" (JARĀ), death constitutes the twelfth and final link in the cycle of dependent origination (PRATĪTYASAMUTPĀDA). From a philosophical perspective, death is also viewed as occurring constantly with the passage of each momentary combination of mind and matter (NĀMARŪPA) or the five aggregates (SKANDHA). Viewed from this perspective, an individual dies (and is reborn) moment after moment (see KṢAṆIKAVĀDA), physical death being merely the final specific instance thereof. The passing away of an enlightened person is described as a special kind of death, insofar as the conditions for future existence have been eliminated in that individual and as a consequence there will be no more rebirth for that person.

**maraṇānusmṛti**. (P. maraṇānussati; T. 'chi ba rjes su dran pa; C. niansi; J. nenshi; K. yŏmsa 念死). In Sanskrit, "recollection of death"; one of the most widely described forms of Buddhist meditation. This practice occurs as one of the forty objects of meditation (KAMMAṬṬHĀNA) for the development of concentration. One of the most detailed descriptions of the practice is found in the VISUDDHIMAGGA of BUDDHAGHOSA. Among six generic personality types (greedy, hateful, ignorant, faithful, intelligent, and speculative), Buddhaghosa states that mindfulness of death is a suitable object for persons of intelligent temperament. Elsewhere, however, Buddhaghosa says that among the two types of objects of concentration, the generically useful objects and specific objects, only two among the forty are generically useful: the cultivation of loving-kindness (P. mettā; S. MAITRĪ) and the recollection of death. In describing the actual practice, Buddhaghosa explains that the meditator who wishes to take death as his object of concentration should go to a remote place and repeatedly think, "Death will take place" or "Death, death." Should that not result in the development of concentration, Buddhaghosa provides eight ways of contemplating death. The first of the eight is contemplation of death as a murderer, where one imagines that death will appear to deprive one of life. Death is certain from the moment of birth; beings move progressively toward their demise without ever turning back, just as the sun never reverses its course through the sky. The second contemplation is to think of death as the ruin of all the accomplishments and fortune acquired in life. The third contemplation is to compare oneself to others who have suffered death, yet who are greater than oneself in fame, merit, strength, supranormal powers (P. iddhi; S. ṚDDHI), or wisdom. Death will come to oneself just as it has come to these beings. The fourth contemplation is that the body is shared with many other creatures. Here one contemplates that the body is inhabited by the eighty families of worms, who may easily cause one's death, as may a variety of accidents. The fifth contemplation is of the tenuous nature of life, that life requires both inhalation and exhalation of breath, requires a balanced alternation of the four postures (ĪRYĀPATHA) of standing, sitting, walking, and lying down. It requires moderation of hot and cold, a balance of the four physical constituents, and nourishment at the proper time. The sixth contemplation is that there is no certainty about death; that is, there is no certainty as to the length of one's life, the type of illness of which one will die, when one will die, nor where, and there is no certainty as to where one will then be reborn. The seventh contemplation is that life is limited in length. In general, human life is short; beyond that, there is no certainty that one will live as long as it takes "to chew and swallow four or five mouthfuls." The final contemplation is of the shortness of the moment, that is, that life is in fact just a series of moments of consciousness. Buddhaghosa also describes the benefits of cultivating mindfulness of death. A monk devoted to the mindfulness of death is diligent and disenchanted with the things of the world. He is neither acquisitive nor avaricious and is increasingly aware of impermanence (S. ANITYA), the first of the three marks of mundane existence. From this develops an awareness of the other two marks, suffering and nonself. He dies without confusion or fear. If he does not attain the deathless state of NIRVĀṆA in this lifetime, he will at least be reborn in an auspicious realm. Similar instructions are found in the literatures of many other Buddhist traditions.

**Māratajjanīyasutta**. (C. Xiangmo jing; J. Gōmakyō; K. Hangma kyŏng 降魔經). In Pāli, "Discourse on the Rebuke to Māra"; the fiftieth sutta in the MAJJHIMANIKĀYA (a separate SARVĀSTIVĀDA recension is the 131st sūtra in the Chinese translation of the MADHYAMĀGAMA; there are also two other independent translations); the scripture is an account of an encounter between MAHĀMAUDGALYĀYANA (P. Mahāmoggallāna) and the divinity MĀRA, the personification of evil. According to the Pāli recension, Mahāmoggallāna was in the Bhesakaḷā grove at Suṃsumāragiri in the Bhagga country when Māra entered his belly. Mahāmoggallāna coaxed Māra to stop vexing him by relating how in a previous life, during the time of Kakusandha Buddha, he had been Māra's uncle. He warns Māra of the dangers that befall those who create trouble for the Buddha and his disciples.

**Māratika**. (T. 'Chi ba mthar byed). A cave in eastern Nepal near the town of Rumjitar, called Haileshi in Nepali, believed by Tibetan Buddhists to be the site where PADMASAMBHAVA and his consort MANDĀRAVĀ undertook the practice of longevity for three months. According to traditional accounts, in a vision the couple received initiation and blessings directly from the buddha AMITĀYUS, and Padmasambhava attained the state of a VIDYĀDHARA with the power to control the duration of his life.

**māravijaya**. In Sanskrit, the "defeat of Māra." See MĀRA.

**mārga**. (P. magga; T. lam; C. dao; J. dō; K. to 道). In Sanskrit, "path"; a polysemous term in Sanskrit, whose root denotation is a road, track, way, or course. As one of the most important terms in Buddhism, it refers to the metaphorical route from one state to another, typically from suffering to liberation, from SAṂSĀRA to NIRVĀṆA. The term derives in part from the view that the means of achieving liberation from suffering have been identified by the Buddha, and he himself has successfully followed the route to that goal, leaving behind tracks or footprints that others can follow. Indeed, it is the Buddhist view that each of the buddhas of the past has followed the same path to enlightenment. However, in the interval between buddhas, that path becomes forgotten, and the purpose of the next buddha's advent in the world is to rediscover and reopen that same path. The term mārga occurs in the Buddha's first sermon (S. DHARMACAKRAPRAVARTANASŪTRA; P. DHAMMACAKKAPPAVATTANASUTTA) as the fourth constituent of the FOUR NOBLE TRUTHS (CATVĀRY ĀRYASATYĀNI), where it is identified as the eightfold path (ĀRYĀṢṬĀṄGAMĀRGA) between the two extremes of self-indulgence and self-mortification. Elsewhere, the path is associated with the threefold training (TRIŚIKṢĀ) in morality (ŚĪLA), concentration (SAMĀDHI), and wisdom (PRAJÑĀ). However, there are numerous delineations of the path to enlightenment. For example, both the mainstream Buddhist schools and the MAHĀYĀNA describe three paths: (1) the path of the ŚRĀVAKA, culminating in attainment of NIRVĀṆA as an ARHAT; (2) the path of the PRATYEKABUDDHA, also culminating in the nirvāṇa of an arhat; and (3) the path of the BODHISATTVA, culminating in the attainment of buddhahood. Each of these paths has its own stages, with a common system describing five (PAÑCAMĀRGA): (1) the path of accumulation (SAṂBHĀRAMĀRGA), (2) the path of preparation (PRAYOGAMĀRGA), (3) the path of vision (DARŚANAMĀRGA), (4) the path of cultivation (BHĀVANĀMĀRGA), and (5) the adept path, "where there is nothing more to learn" (AŚAIKṢAMĀRGA). In more technical descriptions, the path to enlightenment is described as a series of moments of consciousness in a process of purification, in which increasingly subtle states of contaminants (ĀSRAVA) and afflictions (KLEŚA) are permanently cleansed from the mind. The term "path" figures in the title of a number of highly important Buddhist works, such as the VISUDDHIMAGGA ("Path of Purification") by the Pāli commentator BUDDHAGHOSA. The Tibetan exegete TSONG KHA PA wrote of the "three principal aspects of the path" (lam rtso rnam gsum): renunciation, BODHICITTA, and correct view. See also DAO.

**mārgajñatā**. (T. lam shes; C. daozhi; J. dōchi; K. toji 道智). In Sanskrit, "knowledge of the paths"; one of the three knowledges (along with SARVĀKĀRAJÑATĀ and SARVAJÑATĀ, or VASTUJÑĀNA) set forth in the ABHISAMAYĀLAṂKĀRA. When explained from the perspective of the path that bodhisattvas have to complete in order to reach their goal of full enlightenment, the knowledge of paths is indicated by nine dharmas; these include its special causes (MAHĀKARUṆĀ, Mahāyāna GOTRA, and so on), the bodhisattva's paths of accumulation and preparation (called MOKṢABHĀGĪYA and NIRVEDHABHĀGĪYA), a special path of vision (DARŚANAMĀRGA), and a path of cultivation (BHĀVANĀMĀRGA) understood from the standpoints of UPĀYA (method) and PRAJÑĀ (wisdom). "Method" consists of zealous resolution (ADHIMOKṢA) regarding the merit (PUṆYA) that derives from the perfection of wisdom (PRAJÑĀPĀRAMITĀ) and its results; rejoicing (ANUMODANA) in that merit; and dedicating it to the goal of full enlightenment (PARIṆĀMANĀ). Wisdom consists in innate purity, and the purity that derives from the elimination of obscurations (ĀVARAṆA). When described from the perspective of the bodhisattva's actual practice, "knowledge of the paths" refers to the Mahāyāna path of bodhisattvas, including all the aspects (ĀKĀRA) of knowledge that are as yet uninformed by the full knowledge of a buddha (the sarvākārajñatā).

**mārgaphala**. (P. maggaphala; T. lam 'bras; C. daoguo; J. dōka; K. to kwa 道果). In Sanskrit, lit. "path and its fruition"; the eight stages of realization belonging to an ĀRYA, or "noble one." consisting of four supramundane paths (MĀRGA) and four supramundane fruits (PHALA). These are as follows: (1) realization of the path of stream-enterer (SROTAĀPANNA), and (2) the realization of the fruition of stream-enterer; (3) realization of the path of once-returner (SAKṚDĀGĀMIN), and (4) realization of the fruition of once-returner; (5) realization of the path of nonreturner (ANĀGĀMIN), and (6) realization of the fruition of nonreturner; and (7) realization of the path of the worthy ones (ARHAT); and (8) the realization of the fruition of worthy one. In Tibetan, the literal translation of mārgaphala as LAM 'BRAS refers to a central doctrine of the SA SKYA sect.

**mārgasatya**. (P. maggasacca; T. lam gyi bden pa; C. daodi; J. dōtai; K. toje 道諦). In Sanskrit, "the truth of the path"; the fourth of the so-called FOUR NOBLE TRUTHS (catvāry āryasatyāni) set forth by the Buddha in his first sermon (S. DHARMACAKRAPRAVARTANASŪTRA; P. DHAMMACAKKAPPAVATTANASUTTA) in the Deer Park (MṚGADĀVA) at SĀRNĀTH. In that sermon, the Buddha identified the truth of the path to the cessation of suffering to be the eightfold path (ĀRYĀṢṬĀṄGAMĀRGA). In later literature, the truth of the path is also described in terms of the three trainings (TRIŚIKṢĀ) in morality (SĪLA), concentration (SAMĀDHI), and wisdom (PRAJÑĀ). Like the three other truths, the truth of the path has four aspects. They are: (1) path (mārga), because the path leads to liberation from suffering and rebirth; stated more technically, it leads from the state of the ordinary person (PṚTHAGJANA) to the state of the noble one (ĀRYA); (2) suitability (nyāya), because the path contains the antidotes suitable to destroy suffering and the origin of suffering; (3) achievement (PRATIPATTI) because the path brings about liberation; and (4) deliverance (nairyāṇika), because wisdom destroys the afflictions (KLEŚA) and delivers one to a state of liberation.

**Marīcī**. (T. 'Od zer can ma; C. Molizhi; J. Marishi; K. Mariji 摩利支). In Sanskrit and Pāli, lit. "Shining," or "Mirage"; proper name of the Indian goddess of the morning sun, who was adopted into the Buddhist pantheon. Marīcī rides a chariot drawn by seven pigs; her charioteer is Rāhu. She is depicted with three faces and eight hands, either in her chariot or simply standing on the back of a sow. In tantric Buddhism, Marīcī is the consort of VAIROCANA, although she is rarely shown in sexual union with him. Due to her porcine steeds, in Nepal and Tibet she is sometimes confused with VAJRAVĀRĀHĪ. Under the name Aśokakāntā, she is also an attendant of TĀRĀ.

**Mar pa bka' brgyud**. (Marpa Kagyü). In Tibetan term, "Oral Lineage of Mar pa"; one of the so-called eight great conveyances that are lineages of achievement (SGRUB BRGYUD SHING RTA CHEN PO BRGYAD). The term refers generally to the teachings transmitted from such Indian masters as TILOPA, NĀROPA, and MAITRĪPA to the Tibetan teacher MAR PA CHOS KYI BLO GROS and subsequently to MI LA RAS PA, RAS CHUNG PA RDO RJE GRAGS, SGAM PO PA BSOD RNAM RIN CHEN, and the various BKA' BRGYUD subsects. It is generally synonomous with the term DWAGS PO BKA' BRGYUD. See also BKA' BRGYUD CHE BZHI CHUNG BRGYAD.

**Mar pa Chos kyi blo gros**. (Marpa Chökyi Lodrö) (1012?–1097). A renowned Tibetan translator and lay Buddhist master who played an important role in the later transmission (PHYI DAR) of Buddhism from India to Tibet. He is regarded as the Tibetan founder of the BKA' BRGYUD sect of Tibetan Buddhism, which traces its lineage to India and the MAHĀSIDDHAs TILOPA and NĀROPA. In his traditional biographies, Mar pa is generally regarded as a reincarnation of the Indian mahāsiddha DOMBĪ HERUKA. Mar pa was born to wealthy landowners in the southern Tibetan region of LHO BRAG and quickly proved to be a gifted child. As an adult, Mar pa was characterized as having a volatile temper, although ultimately compassionate. His parents sent their son to study Sanskrit and Indian vernacular languages with the translator 'BROG MI SHĀKYA YE SHES in western Tibet. Because resources for studying Buddhism in Tibet were limited as the so-called dark period between the earlier dissemination (SNGA DAR) and later dissemination (phyi dar) came to an end, Mar pa decided to make the harrowing journey to India to seek instruction from Buddhist masters. He would make three journeys there over the course of his life. He first spent three years in Nepal, acclimating to the new environment and continuing his study of local languages. There he met two Nepalese teachers, Chitherpa and Paiṇḍapa, who offered many religious instructions but also encouraged Mar pa to seek out the master who would become his chief guru, the great SIDDHA NĀROPA. According to tradition, Mar pa studied under Nāropa at the forest retreat of Pullahari, receiving initiations and teachings of several important tantric lineages, especially those of the BKA' 'BABS BZHI (four transmissions) that Nāropa had received from his principal teacher TILOPA. Despite the fame of this encounter, contemporary Tibetan sources indicate that Mar pa himself never claimed to have studied directly with Nāropa, who had already passed away prior to Mar pa's trip to India. Mar pa's other great master was the Indian siddha MAITRĪPA, from whom he received instruction in MAHĀMUDRĀ and the tradition of DOHĀ, or spiritual song. Mar pa received other tantric transmissions from Indian masters such as Jñānagarbha and Kukkurīpā. Upon his return to Tibet, Mar pa married several women, the most well known being BDAG ME MA, who figures prominently in the life story of MI LA RAS PA. He began his career as teacher and translator, while also occupying himself as landowner and farmer. He had intended to pass his dharma lineage to his son DARMA MDO SDE, for whom Mi la ras pa's famous tower was built, but the child was killed in an equestrian accident. Mar pa's accumulated instructions were later passed to four principal disciples: Ngog Chos sku rdo rje (Ngok Chöku Dorje), Mes tshon po (Me Tsönpo), 'Tshur dbang nge (Tsur Wangnge), and the renowned YOGIN and poet Mi la ras pa. At least sixteen works translated from Sanskrit by Mar pa are preserved in the Tibetan Buddhist canon. He is also known as Mar pa LO TSĀ BA (Marpa the Translator) and Lho brag pa (Man from Lhodrak). Among the biographies of Mar pa, one of the most famous is that by GTSANG SMYON HERUKA.

**Maru**. (S). One of the twenty-four sacred sites associated with the CAKRASAMVARATANTRA. See PĪṬHA.

**ma sanjin**. (J. masangin; K. ma samgŭn 麻三斤). In Chinese, "three catties of flax"; a CHAN expression that becomes a famous meditative topic (HUATOU) and is used in Chan "questioning meditation" (see KANHUA CHAN). The phrase appears in a case or precedent (GONG'AN) attributed to DONGSHAN SHOUCHU (910–990) in the YUNMEN ZONG: Once when Dongshan was asked, "What is the Buddha?," he replied, "Three catties of flax." This gong'an appears as case no. 18 in the WUMEN GUAN ("Gateless Checkpoint") and case no. 12 in the BIYAN LU ("Blue Cliff Record").

**Maskarin Gośālīputra**. (P. Makkhali Gosāla; T. Kun tu rgyu gnag lhas kyi bu; C. Moqieli Jushelizi; J. Magari Kusharishi; K. Malgari Kusarija 末伽梨拘賒梨子) (d. c. 488 BCE). In Sanskrit, "Maskarin, Who Was Born in a Cow Shed"; the name of an ĀJĪVAKA teacher (and the sect's founder, according to some sources) who was a contemporary of the Buddha. Because no Ājīvaka texts have survived, information about the school's doctrines must be derived from Buddhist and JAINA sources. According to Jaina accounts, Maskarin Gośālīputra was a disciple of MAHĀVĪRA but eventually left the Jaina fold. Maskarin Gośālīputra subsequently founded his own school of wandering religious (ŚRAMAṆA) called the Ājīvakas and was notorious for denying the doctrine of moral cause and effect (KARMAN). As his rivals describe his teachings, he asserted that there is no immediate or ultimate cause for the purity or depravity of beings; instead, beings are directed along their course by destiny or fate (niyati). Thus attainments or accomplishments of any kind are not a result of an individual's own action or the acts of others; rather, those beings experience ease or pain according to their positions within the various stations of existence. Maskarin Gośālīputra is portrayed as advocating a theory of automatic purification through an essentially infinite number of transmigrations (saṃsāraśuddhi), during which all beings would ultimately attain perfection. The Buddha is said to have regarded Makkhali Gośālīputra's views as the most dangerous of heresies, because they were capable of leading even the divinities (DEVA) to loss, discomfort, and suffering. He is one of the so-called six heterodox teachers (TĪRTHIKA) often mentioned in Buddhist sūtras and criticized by the Buddha. The other five are PŪRAṆA-KĀŚYAPA, AJITA KEŚAKAMBHALA, KAKUDA KĀTYĀYANA, SAÑJAYA VAIRAṬĪPUTRA, and NIRGRANTHA-JÑĀTĪPUTRA.

**Mathurā**. [alt. Madhurā] (T. Bcom rlag; C. Motouluo; J. Machūra; K. Mat'ura 摩偸羅). North central Indian city on the Yamunā River, located approximately thirty miles (fifty kms.) north of Agra, and renowned as the birthplace of Kṛṣṇa. During the time of the Buddha, it was the capital of Śurasena and was ruled by King Avantiputra. The Buddha seems to have visited the city but did not preach there. Indeed, he seems to have disliked it; in the *Madhurasutta*, he enumerates its five disadvantages: uneven ground, excessive dust, fierce dogs, bestial spirits (YAKṢA), and difficulty in obtaining alms. Buddhism gained favor there in later years, and Mathurā became one of the major scholastic centers of the SARVĀSTIVĀDA and/or MŪLASARVĀSTIVĀDA school; both FAXIAN and XUANZANG describe it as a flourishing Buddhist city.

**mati**. (P. mati; T. blo gros; C. hui; J. e; K. hye 慧). In Sanskrit and Pāli, "discernment" or "intelligence." This term is often used in ABHIDHARMA texts to mean "the proper discernment of DHARMAS," and, in this sense, mati is closely synonymous with PRAJÑĀ, or "wisdom." Mati in its denotation of "discernment" or "mentality" is used in the SARVĀSTIVĀDA ABHIDHARMA system to indicate one of the ten "omnipresent mental factors" (MAHĀBHŪMIKA) that are said to accompany all consciousness activity. In the "eight consciousnesses" model of the the YOGĀCĀRA school, mati refers to the seventh consciousness (KLIṢṬAMANAS). ¶ Mati is also used as a proper noun and serves as the name of a handful of figures in Buddhist literature, including a previous incarnation of ŚĀKYAMUNI Buddha.

**Mātṛceṭa**. (T. Ma khol; C. Moxilizhizha; J. Machiriseita; K. Majillijet'a 摩咥里制吒) (c. third century CE). An Indian monk regarded as one of the great Sanskrit poets of the Buddhist tradition. It is said that at the time of the Buddha he was an oriole who, upon seeing the Buddha, sang a beautiful song. Hearing the song, the Buddha predicted that the bird would be reborn as a great poet in the future. Mātṛceṭa was a Hindu poet and a devotee of Śiva. He was a skilled orator, defeating many Buddhists in debate. The monks of NĀLANDĀ monastery appealed to NĀGĀRJUNA for assistance and ĀRYADEVA volunteered to represent his teacher. Mātṛceṭa and Āryadeva engaged in a famous debate, with Āryadeva eventually defeating Mātṛceṭa and converting him to Buddhism. His most famous work is the *Śatapañcāśatakastotra* ("Praise in One Hundred Fifty Stanzas"), a work that praises the qualities and deeds of the Buddha in thirteen sections. A second work in praise of the Buddha is his *Catuḥśataka* ("Four Hundred Verses," also known as the *Varṇārhavarṇastotra*, not to be confused with the CATUḤŚATAKA by Āryadeva). YIJING, who visited India in the seventh century, reported that the two hymns were taught to all monks, whether HĪNAYĀNA or MAHĀYĀNA, immediately after ordination, and were regularly chanted at assemblies. Yijing translated the former work into Chinese. Mātṛceṭa is also known for his hymns in praise of TĀRĀ. In addition, he was the author of the *Mahārājakaniṣkalekha* ("Letter to King Kaniṣka"); he was invited to court by the king but, pleading old age, sent a letter of advice instead. If the reign of KANIṢKA is placed in the second century, it is possible that the letter is addressed to Kaniṣka II. In some Tibetan sources, Mātṛceṭa is identified with Āryaśura.

**mātṛkā**. (P. mātikā; T. phyi mo; C. modalijia; J. matarika; K. madalliga 摩怛理迦). In Sanskrit, lit. "matrix" and related etymologically to that English word; systematized "matrices" or "lists" of terms and topics appearing in the SŪTRAs, which served as the nucleus of the ABHIDHARMA literature. Important early disciples of the Buddha, including ŚĀRIPUTRA, MAHĀMAUDGALYĀYANA, and MAHĀKĀTYĀYANA, are said to have compiled such lists in order to systematize the disparate teachings found in the Buddha's discourses, using these rosters as mnemonic devices for teaching the DHARMA to their students. The earliest matrices may have been such common dharma lists as the five aggregates (SKANDHA), twelve sense spheres (ĀYATANA), and eighteen elements (DHĀTU). These relatively simple lists were gradually elaborated into complex matrices that were intended to provide a systematic overview of the full range of Buddhist spiritual development, such as an exhaustive matrix of twenty-two triads (such as wholesome, unwholesome, and indeterminate) and one hundred dyads that provides the exegetical framework for the DHAMMASAṄGAṆI, the first book in the Pāli ABHIDHAMMA. None of the early matrices of the SARVĀSTIVĀDA or YOGĀCĀRA schools are extant, but they can be reconstructed from culling the lists treated in their abhidharma literatures; these rosters closely follow those appearing in the Pāli abhidhamma. By tying together, expanding upon, and systematizing these various matrices, the different schools of abhidharma constructed scholastically meticulous and coherent exegeses of Buddhist doctrine and soteriology. The mātṛkā thus served as the forerunner of the adhidharma, and the abhidharma thus represents an elaboration and analysis of these lists. In some early accounts, in fact, a matrix was essentially synonymous with the abhidharma, and both terms are used in differing accounts of the initial recitation of the Buddhist canon following the Buddha's demise; indeed, the ABHIDHARMAPIṬAKA is sometimes even referred to as the mātṛkāpiṭaka.

**mātṛtantra**. (T. ma rgyud). In Sanskrit, lit., "mother tantra"; a term used in a twofold division of ANUTTARAYOGA tantric texts as mother tantras and father tantras (PITṚTANTRA). The former, also known as ḌĀKINĪ tantras, are traditionally said to emphasize wisdom (PRAJÑĀ) over method (UPĀYA), especially wisdom in the form of the mind of clear light (PRABHĀSVARACITTA). This designation may also derive from the fact that in these tantras, the majority (and in some cases, all) of the deities of the MAṆḌALA are female.

**mātsarya**. (P. macchariya; T. ser sna; C. qian/ji; J. ken/shitsu; K. kan/chil 慳/嫉). In Sanskrit, "selfishness," "miserliness"; one of the forty-six mental concomitants (see CAITTA) according to the SARVĀSTIVĀDA-VAIBHĀṢIKA school, one of the fifty-one according to the YOGĀCĀRA school, and one of the fifty-two according to the Pāli abhidhamma; it is listed among the secondary afflictions (UPAKLEŚA). Mātsarya is described as the inability to bear the good fortune of others because of one's attachment to objects. It is related to hatred (DVEṢA) and results in mental discomfort and unhappiness.

**Matsuo Bashō**. (松尾芭蕉) (1644–1694). A renowned Japanese Buddhist author of the Edo period. Although famous in the West especially for his haiku poetry, Bashō is also known for his renga, or linked verse, prose works, literary criticism, diaries, and travelogues, which also contain many famous poems. His most celebrated work is his travel diary, a work in mixed prose and verse entitled *Oku no Hosomichi* ("Narrow Road to the Deep North"), published posthumously in 1702. He was born in Iga Province (present-day Mie prefecture) to a family of the samurai class, but abandoned that life in favor of living as a Buddhist monk, much like the Heian period (794–1185) SHINGONSHŪ monk SAIGYŌ (1118–1190), with whom he is often compared. Bashō received instruction from the RINZAISHŪ master Butchō (1643–1715), and his work is commonly regarded as conveying a ZEN aesthetic, as in the famous haiku poem he wrote at his moment of awakening: "A timeless pond, the frog jumps, a splash of water" (J. furuike ya, kawazu tobikomu, mizu no oto).

**Matsyendranāth**. The Newar name given to several highly revered statues of AVALOKITEŚVARA, located in the Kathmandu Valley. See MA ṆI BKA' 'BUM.

**Maudgalyāyana**. (S). See MAHĀMAUDGALYĀYANA.

**māyā**. (T. sgyu ma; C. kuang; J. ō; K. kwang 誑). In Sanskrit, "deceit," "deception," "trickery," "fraudulence"; one of the forty-six mental concomitants (see CAITTA) according to the SARVĀSTIVĀDA–VAIBHĀṢIKA school of ABHIDHARMA and one of the fifty-one according to the YOGĀCĀRA school; it is classified among the secondary afflictions (UPAKLEŚA). Deceit includes such acts as feigning virtue and accomplishment, resorting to deceptive speech or underhanded subterfuge, and engaging in any of the inappropriate livelihoods (cf. SAMYAGĀJĪVA; ĀRYĀṢṬĀṄGAMĀRGA), such as divination or fortune-telling, when done with the intent to impress, trick, exploit, or manipulate others.

**Māyā**. [alt. Māyādevī; Mahāmāyā] (T. Sgyu 'phrul ma; C. Moye; J. Maya; K. Maya 摩耶). In Sanskrit and Pāli, "Illusion"; the mother of GAUTAMA Buddha. Her father was Añjana, king of Devadaha, and her mother was Yaśodharā. Māyā and her sister MAHĀPRAJĀPATĪ were both married to the Buddha's father ŚUDDHODANA, the king of KAPILAVASTU. Māyā was between forty and fifty when the future buddha was conceived. At that time, the future buddha was a BODHISATTVA residing in TUṢITA heaven, where he surveyed the world and selected his future parents. On the night of his conception, Māyā dreamed that four great gods transported her to the Himalayas, where goddesses bathed her in the waters of the Anotatta Lake and clad her in divine raiment. As she lay on a couch prepared for her, the future buddha, in the form of a white elephant holding a white lotus in its trunk, entered into her right side. After ten lunar months, during which time she remained chaste, Māyā set out to visit her parents in Devadaha. Along the way she stopped at the LUMBINĪ grove, where she gave birth to the prince and future buddha while holding onto a branch of a ŚĀLA tree; according to some accounts, he emerged from her right side. Seven days later, Māyā died. Varying reasons are provided for her demise, including that she died from joy at having given birth to the future buddha and that she died after seven days because she would have died from a broken heart when Prince SIDDHĀRTHA subsequently renounced the world at the age of twenty-nine. It is also said that the mothers of all buddhas die shortly after their birth because it is not suitable that any other child be conceived in the womb that had been occupied by a future buddha. Māyā was reborn as a male divinity named Māyādevaputra in the TUṢITA heaven. After her death, Māyā's sister Mahāprājāpatī raised the future buddha as her own child. Because his mother's death had prevented her from benefiting from his teachings, the Buddha once spent a rainy season in TRĀYASTRIṂŚA heaven atop Mount SUMERU, during which time he preached the ABHIDHARMA to his mother, who had come from tuṣita heaven to listen, along with the other assembled divinities. These teachings, which the Buddha later recounted to ŚĀRIPUTRA, would become the ABHIDHARMAPIṬAKA. The Buddha's descent from the heaven at SĀṂKĀŚYA at the conclusion of his teachings is one of the most commonly depicted scenes in Buddhist art. The entry of the future Buddha into his mother's womb, and by extension into the human realm of existence, is a momentous event in Buddhist history, and elaborate descriptions of that descent and of that womb appear in a number of texts. One of the most famous is found in the forty-fourth chapter of the GAṆḌAVYŪHA, a MAHĀYĀNA SŪTRA dating from perhaps the second century of the Common Era. In the sūtra, SUDHANA goes in search of enlightenment. During his journey, he encounters all manner of exalted beings, each of whom provides him with instruction. One of the teachers he meets is Māyā. She describes in elaborate detail how her son entered her womb, revealing that it was able to accommodate much more than a white elephant, without for a moment distorting her form. She reveals that it was not only the bodhisattva SIDDHĀRTHA who descended from the tuṣita and entered her womb; in fact, countless other bodhisattvas accompanied him to become buddhas simultaneously in millions of similar universes. She reveals as well that she is the mother not only of all the buddhas of the present, but of all the buddhas of the past and that she will also be the mother of the next buddha, MAITREYA.

**māyādeha**. (T. sgyu lus; C. huanshen; J. genshin; K. hwansin 幻身). In Sanskrit, "illusory body"; a polysemous term that, in its most general sense, refers to the fact that the body is insubstantial and thus like an illusion. The term is also the name of one of the so-called SIX YOGAS OF NĀROPA, where it encompasses a range of practices, including the contemplation of one's own reflection in a mirror and expressing praise and blame to the reflection as a means of overcoming attachment to one's body. In a more technical sense, the term refers to a body achieved through the practice of ANUTTARAYOGATANTRA, in which as a result of insight into the nature of reality and the control of the subtle energies that course through the CAKRAS, the yogin creates a subtle body created from the subtle wind (PRĀṆA) that serves as the conduit of the mind of clear light (PRABHĀSVARACITTA); this body appears in the form of the buddha that one will become.

**Māyājāla**. (T. Sgyu 'phrul dra ba). In Sanskrit, "Magical Net"; a class of TANTRAS. Certain Buddhist tantras from the eighth century onward described themselves as extractions from a massive, and probably mythological, urtext. In Tibet, and particularly within the RNYING MA sect, the Māyājāla ("Magical Net") became associated with the tantras of the MAHĀYOGA class. It is often said that there are eighteen Māyājāla tantras, although sources differ on which tantras should be included in the list. For the Rnying ma, the GUHYAGARBHATANTRA has been the most influential of the Māyājāla tantras, and its MAṆḌALA of one hundred deities (forty-two peaceful and fifty-eight wrathful deities) appears throughout the later Rnying ma ritual traditions. Some scholars have suggested that the similar group of VAJRAŚEKHARA tantras, also eighteen in number, represented a precursor to the Māyājāla group. The Vajraśekhara group played a larger role in East Asian tantric Buddhism. While the Vajraśekhara and Māyājāla groups share several titles in common, the Vajraśekhara tantras are generally associated with the YOGATANTRA class, of which the SARVATATHĀGATATATTVASAṂGRAHA is a particularly important member. See also GUHYAGARBHATANTRA.

**māyākāra**. (T. sgyu ma mkhan; C. huanshi; J. genshi; K. hwansa 幻師). In Sanskrit and Pāli, lit., "illusion-maker"; a term often translated as "magician," in the sense of someone who is able to conjure things that appear to be real but are in fact illusions. Given the consistent Buddhist claim of the fictive nature of ordinary sense experience, the magician figures prominently in illustrations of the false appearances of the world. In one example, a magician casts a spell on his audience, causing them to see what is in fact a small pebble as a beautiful woman. The magician also sees the woman but knows that she is not real. A person arriving late for the performance is unaffected by the spell and sees only the pebble. In this metaphor, the audience is likened to ordinary sentient beings, who both perceive false appearances and believe them to be true. The magician is likened to an ARHAT who perceives false appearances but is unaffected by them, knowing them to be false. The latecomer is like the Buddha who sees things as they truly are.

**māyopamasamādhi**. (T. sgyu ma lta bu'i ting nge 'dzin; C. ruhuan sanmei; J. nyogenzanmai; K. yŏhwan sammae 如幻三昧). In Sanskrit, lit. "illusion-like SAMĀDHI"; a meditative state that occurs after rising from the direct perception of emptiness (ŚŪNYATĀ). In this state, after having perceived the pure vacuity of emptiness, the objects of experience again appear to be real, but the meditator knows that they are like illusions, appearing to have intrinsic existence but in fact being empty thereof.

**Mazu Daoyi**. (J. Baso Dōitsu; K. Majo Toil 馬祖道一) (709–788). Chinese CHAN master of the Tang dynasty and retrospective patriarch of the HONGZHOU ZONG of the broader Chan tradition. Mazu was a native of Hanzhou in present-day Sichuan province. At an early age, he became a student of the Chan master Chuji (alt. 648–734, 650–732, 669–736) of Zizhou (also in present-day Sichuan province) and received the full monastic precepts later from the VINAYA master Yuan (d.u.) at nearby Yuzhou. Mazu is said to have later visited the sixth patriarch HUINENG's disciple NANYUE HUAIRANG (677–744), under whom he attained awakening. According to the famous story, which is frequently recited in Chan literature, Mazu was awakened when his teacher Nanyue likened Mazu's sitting in meditation to the act of polishing of a roof tile: just as a roof tile cannot be polished to make a mirror, sitting meditation, says Nanyue, cannot lead to buddhahood. In his thirties, Mazu began teaching at various monasteries in the southern regions of Fujian and Jiangxi province. In 769, he began his residence at the monastery of Kaiyuansi (also known as Youqingsi) in Zhongling (in present-day Jiangsu province) and attracted many students. Emperor Xianzong (r. 805–820) later gave him the posthumous title Chan Master Daji (Great Serenity). His teachings are recorded in the *Mazu Daoyi chanshi guanglu*. Mazu developed the idea of "original enlightenment" (BENJUE) from the DASHENG QIXIN LUN ("Awakening of Faith According to the Mahāyāna") in a radical direction. He asserted that "everyday mind is the way" (pingchangxin shi dao) and that "mind itself is the Buddha" (zixin shi fo), arguing that sentient beings have never in fact been deluded but have always been awakened buddhas. Although Mazu did not intend to advocate maintaining a deluded state of mind but wanted instead to recognize the value of the ordinary life as the ground of enlightenment, his emphasis on the inseparable relationship of enlightenment and ignorance drew severe criticisms, especially from GUIFENG ZONGMI (780–841), who believed that Mazu's teachings fostered antinomianism for suggesting that practice was not necessary in order to awaken.

**mchod rten**. (chöten). In Tibetan, lit., "basis for worship"; the Tibetan translation of the Sanskrit terms STŪPA and CAITYA. As in India, the Tibetan stūpa serves as a reliquary, and may contain the remains (ashes, hair, bones) of a prominent lama (BLA MA) or objects associated with an exalted being, such as the begging bowl or robe of a famous monk. In the case of a highly exalted personage, such as one of the DALAI LAMAS, the body is not cremated but is instead embalmed and then entombed inside a stūpa. They range greatly in size, from several inches high to hundreds of feet tall. In a standard ritual that precedes a teaching, the lama is offered a statue of the Buddha, a text, and a small stūpa, representing the body, speech, and mind of the Buddha, respectively. One of the most common forms of Buddhist practice in Tibet is to circumambulate a stūpa in a clockwise direction. There is a large literature in Tibetan devoted to the construction, consecration, and symbolism of the stūpa. Many different types of stūpas are described, one of the most famous rubrics being the eight types of stūpas, each with a different shape, which commemorate eight events in the life of the Buddha. These are: (1) the "heap of lotuses stūpa" (pad spungs mchod rten) commemorating the Buddha's birth, (2) the "enlightenment stūpa" (byang chub mchod rten) commemorating the Buddha's achievement of enlightenment beneath the BODHI TREE, (3) the "many auspicious doors stūpa" (bkra shis sgo mang mchod rten) commemorating the Buddha's turning of the wheel of the dharma, (4) the "display of miracles stūpa" (cho 'phrul mchod rten) commemorating the Buddha's display of miracles at ŚRĀVASTĪ, (5) the "divine descent stūpa" (lha babs mchod rten) commemorating the Buddha's descent from the TRĀYASTRIṂŚA heaven on the summit of Mount SUMERU to SĀṂKĀŚYA, (6) the "settling of disputes stūpa" (dbyen bsdums mchod rten) commemorating the Buddha's healing of a schism within the monastic community caused by his cousin DEVADATTA, (7) the "victory stūpa" (rnam rgyal mchod rten) commemorating the Buddha's extension of his life by three months, and (8) the "nirvāṇa stūpa" (myang 'das mchod rten) commemorating the Buddha's passage into PARINIRVĀṆA. See also BAXIANG.

**mchod yon**. (T). See YON MCHOD.

**Mchog gyur gling pa**. (Chokgyur Lingpa) (1829–1870). A Tibetan Buddhist visionary renowned for his activities as a treasure revealer (GTER STON) in Khams, eastern Tibet. His full name is often given as Mchog 'gyur bde chen zhig po gling pa (Chokgyur Dechen Shikpo Lingpa). At the age of thirteen, he had his first vision of PADMASAMBHAVA, who predicted that he would discover treasure texts (GTER MA). His early claims to be a gter ston were rejected and he was expelled from his monastery for having a consort. He eventually won the trust of 'JAM MGON KONG SPRUL and 'JAM DBYANGS MKHYEN BRTSE DBANG PO, and came to be regarded as an authentic revealer of treasure, discovering texts that he himself translated and for which he composed liturgies. He also discovered relics and images. With 'Jam mgon kong sprul and 'Jam dbyangs mkhyen brtse dbang po, he is considered an important figure in the RIS MED or nonsectarian movement in eastern Tibet during the nineteenth century.

**mchog zung**. (choksung). In Tibetan, "the two supreme attendants." In Tibetan Buddhist art, ŚĀKYAMUNI is typically depicted flanked by two ancillary companions, ŚĀRIPUTRA who is supreme in wisdom, and MAHĀMAUDGALYĀYANA who is supreme in ṚDDHI (magical attainment). See ER XIESHI.

**Mdo Mkhyen brtse Ye shes rdo rje**. (Do Kyentse Yeshe Dorje) (1800–1866). A Tibetan Buddhist master from the Mgo log (Golok) region of eastern Tibet, venerated as the body incarnation of the famous eighteenth-century treasure revealer (GTER STON) 'JIGS MED GLING PA and an important lineage holder of the "heart essence" (SNYING THIG) tradition of RDZOGS CHEN. He was the disciple of the first RDO GRUB CHEN, who instructed him to live the life of a lay tantric practitioner. He was known for his magical powers (SIDDHI), such as the ability to fly and to subjugate demons. Often known by the epithet 'Ja' lus pa chen po, "Great Rainbow-Body Man," his disciples included the second Rdo grub chen and DPAL SPRUL RIN PO CHE.

**Mdzod bdun**. (Dzö Dün). In Tibetan, lit. "seven great treasuries"; an important collection of texts compiled by the Tibetan master of the RNYING MA sect KLONG CHEN RAB 'BYAMS. The central theme of these works is the Rnying ma doctrine of RDZOGS CHEN. The seven texts are:

1. *Gnas lugs mdzod* ("Treasury of the Abiding Nature of Reality")
2. *Man ngag mdzod* ("Treasury of Instructions")
3. *Chos dbyings mdzod* ("Treasury of the DHARMADHĀTU")
4. *Grub mtha' mdzod* ("Treasury of Philosophical Systems")
5. *Theg mchog mdzod* ("Treasury of the Supreme Vehicle")
6. *Tshig don mdzod* ("Treasury of Word and Meaning")
7. *Yid bzhin mdzod* ("Wish-fulfilling Treasury")

**Me 'bar mtsho**. (Mebar Tso). In Tibetan, lit. "Lake of Blazing Fire"; an important Buddhist sacred site in the Bum thang region of central Bhutan, associated with the great Bhutanese treasure revealer (GTER STON) PADMA GLING PA. It is not an actual lake, but a wide pool amid a rock gorge, said to be the location from which Padma gling pa unearthed his first treasure (GTER MA). It takes its name from the well-known account of how Padma gling pa emerged from the river's depths with a butter lamp in his hand that remained burning.

**Medhaṅkara and Mahādhammagambhīra**. The names of two members of a delegation of twenty-five monks from the Thai kingdom of Lānnā (Chiangmai) who, in 1424 CE, together with a group of eight monks from Kamboja and six from Rāmañña (the Mon homeland in Lower Burma), were reordained in Sri Lanka at the Kalyāṇī river near Colombo. The delegation returned to Thailand in 1425, settling first in the kingdom of AYUTHAYA before proceeding to Chiangmai in 1430. The next king of Chiangmai, Tilokarājā (r. 1442–1487 CE), strongly promoted the reformist Sinhalese sect led by Mahāmedhaṅkara and Mahādhammagambhīra, making it the dominant Buddhist order throughout northern Thailand. This reformation occurred at the same time that the king consolidated and expanded the territories under his rule. Tilokarājā's patronage of the new Sinhalese order is celebrated in the sixteenth-century text JINAKĀLAMĀLĪ. In the PADAENG CHRONICLE, the leader of this reformist movement is given the name Ñāṇagambhīra.

**Medicine Buddha**. See BHAIṢAJYAGURU.

**meditation**. There is no single term in Buddhism that corresponds precisely to what in English is called "meditation." Some of its connotations are conveyed in such Buddhist terms as BHĀVANĀ; CHAN; DHYĀNA; JHĀNA; PAṬIPATTI; SAMĀDHI; ZUOCHAN.

**meditative absorption**. See DHYĀNA; JHĀNA; SAMĀPATTI.

**Menander**. See MILINDAPAÑHA.

**Menzan Zuihō**. (面山瑞方) (1683–1769). Japanese reformer of the SŌTŌSHŪ of ZEN during the Tokugawa period (1600–1867), who is largely responsible for establishing DŌGEN KIGEN (1200–1253) as the font of orthodoxy for the Sōtō school and, during the modern and contemporary periods, as an innovative religious thinker. Born in Higo province in the Kumamoto region, Menzan studied with MANZAN DŌHAKU (1636–1715) and later Sonnō Sōeki (1649–1705). At a thousand-day retreat Menzan led following Sonnō's death, Menzan read texts by Dōgen that had been neglected for centuries and subsequently used them as the scriptural authority from which he forged an entirely new vision of the Sōtōshū; he then deployed this revisioning of Dōgen to justify a reformation of long-held practices within the school. Menzan was a prolific author, with over a hundred works attributed to him, sixty-five of which have been published in modern Sōtō school collections; these works include everything from detailed philological commentaries to extended discussions of monastic rules and regulations. He remains best known for his *Shōbōgenzō shōtenroku*, an eleven-roll encyclopedic commentary to Dōgen's magnum opus, the SHŌBŌGENZŌ.

**merit**. See PUṆYA.

**merit cloister**. See GONGDE YUAN.

**Meru**. See SUMERU, MOUNT.

**method**. See UPĀYA.

**Mettāsutta**. (C. Ci jing; J. Jikyō; K. Cha kyŏng 慈經). In Pāli, the "Discourse on Loving-Kindness"; one of the best-loved and most frequently recited texts in the THERAVĀDA Buddhist world. According to the *Mettāsutta*'s framing narrative, a group of monks went into the forest during the rainy season to meditate. The tree deities of the forest were disturbed by the presence of the monks and sought to drive them away by frightening them during the night. The monks went to the Buddha and requested his assistance in quelling the disturbance. The *Mettāsutta* was the discourse that the Buddha then delivered in response, instructing the monks to meditate on loving-kindness (P. mettā; S. MAITRĪ), thinking, "May all beings be happy and safe. May they have happy minds. Whatever living beings there may be—feeble or strong, long, stout, or of medium size, short, small, large, those seen or those unseen, those dwelling far or near, those who are born as well as those yet to be born—may all beings have happy minds." Having radiated these thoughts throughout the forest, the monks were no longer troubled by the spirits. The *Mettāsutta* appears in an early scriptural anthology, the SUTTANIPĀTA, a later collection, the KHUDDAKAPĀṬHA, and in a postcanonical anthology of "protection texts," (PARITTA). (Separate recensions appear in the Chinese translations of the EKOTTARĀGAMA and the SAṂYUKTĀGAMA, the latter affiliated with the SARVĀSTIVĀDA school.) The *Mettāsutta*'s great renown derives from its inclusion among the paritta texts, which are chanted as part of the protective rituals performed by Buddhist monks to ward off misfortunes; indeed, it is this apotropaic quality of the scripture that accounts for its enduring popularity. Paritta suttas refer to specific discourses delivered by the buddha that are believed to offer protection to those who either recite the sutta or listen to its recitation. Other such auspicious apotropaic suttas are the MAṄGALASUTTA ("Discourse on the Auspicious") and the RATANASUTTA ("Discourse on the Precious"). These paritta texts are commonly believed to bring happiness and good fortune when chanted by the SAṂGHA. See also BRAHMAVIHĀRA.

**mianbi**. (C) (J. menpeki; K. myŏnbyŏk 面壁). See BIGUAN.

**Miaoshan**. (J. Myōzen; K. Myosŏn 妙善). In Chinese, "Sublime Wholesomeness"; a legendary Chinese princess who is said to have been an incarnation of the BODHISATTVA GUANYIN (S. AVALOKITEŚVARA). According to legend, Princess Miaoshan was the youngest of three daughters born to King Zhuangyan. As in the legend of Prince SIDDHĀRTHA, Miaoshan refused to fulfill the social expectations of her father and instead endured great privations in order to pursue her Buddhist practice. In frustration, Miaoshan's father banished her to a convent, where the nuns were ordered to break the princess's religious resolve. The nuns were ultimately unsuccessful, however, and in anger, the king ordered the convent set ablaze. Miaoshan escaped to the mountain of Xiangshan, where she pursued a reclusive life. After several years, her father contracted jaundice, which, according to his doctors' diagnosis, was caused by his disrespect toward the three jewels (RATNATRAYA). The only thing that could cure him would be a tonic made from the eyes and ears of a person who was completely free from anger. As fate would have it, the only person who fulfilled this requirement turned out to be his own daughter. When Miaoshan heard of her father's dilemma, she willingly donated her eyes and ears for the tonic; and upon learning of their daughter's selfless generosity and filiality, Miaoshan's father and mother both repented and became devoted lay Buddhists. Miaoshan then apotheosized into the goddess Guanyin, specifically her manifestation as the "thousand-armed and thousand-eyed Guanyin" (SĀHASRABHUJASĀHASRANETRĀVALOKITEŚVARA). Later redactions of the legend include Miaoshan's visit to hell, where she was said to have relieved the suffering of the hell denizens. The earliest reference to the Miaoshan legend appears in stele fragments that date from the early eleventh century, discovered at a site near Hangzhou. Other written sources include the *Xiangshan baojuan* ("Precious Scroll of Xiangshan Mountain"), which was revealed to a monk and then transmitted and disseminated by a minor civil servant. With the advent of the Princess Miaoshan legend, the Upper Tianzhu monastery, already recognized as early as the tenth century as a Guanyin worship site, became a major pilgrimage center. The earliest complete rendition of the Miaoshan legend dates from the early Song dynasty (c. twelve century). Thereafter, several renditions of the legend were produced up through the Qing dynasty.

**Mi bskyod rdo rje**. (Mikyö Dorje) (1507–1554). Tibetan Buddhist master recognized as the eighth KARMA PA, revered as one of the most dynamic teachers in his lineage. He was born in eastern Tibet and as a newborn child is said to have declared, "I am the Karma pa." Although a rival candidate was simultaneously promoted in A mdo, prominent BKA' BRGYUD lamas identified Mi bskyod rdo rje as the reincarnation of the seventh Karma pa. His enthronement took place on 1513 at RI BO CHE monastery. He received an invitation from the Chinese emperor Wuzong Zhengde (r. 1506–1522) who dispatched a military troop as an escort. The Karma pa declined the invitation, divining that the emperor would soon die. When the military escort returned to court, they found the emperor had indeed passed away. Mi bskyod rdo rje was famed as both a meditation master and scholar. He wrote dozens of works, including philosophical treatises on MADHYAMAKA and ABHIDHARMA, tantric commentaries, poetry, works on linguistics, SĀDHANAS, liturgies, and other ritual texts; his collected works comprise over thirty volumes. His artwork contributed to the establishment of a new painting style in eastern Tibet, known as the karma sgar bris, or "karmapa encampment" style.

**middha**. (T. gnyid; C. shuimian; J. suimen; K. sumyŏn 睡眠). In Sanskrit and Pāli, "torpor," or sometimes simply "sleep." In the SARVĀSTIVĀDA and YOGĀCĀRA dharma lists, middha is one of the four or eight "indeterminate" (ANIYATA) factors among the fifty-one mental constituents (CAITTA; P. cetasika) that, depending on the intention of the agent, may be virtuous, nonvirtuous, or neutral. Middha is defined as the unintended withdrawal of the senses' engagement with their objects. The term is often seen in compound with "sloth" or "laziness" (STYĀNA), which together constitute one of the five hindrances (NĪVARAṆA) to meditative absorption (DHYĀNA), specifically hindering the meditative factor (DHYĀNĀṄGA) of applied thought (VITARKA). This hindrance is countered by the spiritual faculty (INDRIYA) of effort (VĪRYA). Ways of countering sloth and torpor include memorizing the doctrine, developing the perception of light, or simply walking around in the open air. In the Pāli abhidhamma, middha is classified as an unvirtuous (akusala) state. In Sarvāstivāda and Yogācāra it is indeterminate because sleep may be virtuous, unvirtuous, or neutral based on one's state of mind when falling asleep.

**middle way**. See MADHYAMAPRATIPAD.

**Mihintale**. The Sinhala name of a mountain in Sri Lanka, located eight miles east of ANURĀDHAPURA; it is called Missakapabbata in Pāli. Mihintale is said to be the place where the monk MAHINDA, son of the emperor AŚOKA and recently arrived from India, first met the king of Sri Lanka, DEVĀNAṂPIYATISSA, teaching the king the dharma and thus introducing Buddhism to the island. The king was hunting in the area and, following a stag into the forest, encountered Mahinda and his companions. A STŪPA marks the site of their meeting. The mountain became an important place of pilgrimage, with numerous VIHĀRAs and shrines constructed over the centuries.

**Miidera**. (三井寺). A famous monastery in Ōtsu, Japan, which is currently the headquarters (honzan) of the Jimon branch of the TENDAISHŪ. In 858, the monk ENCHIN restored the dilapidated monastery of Onjōji, which was originally constructed by retired Emperor Kōbun's (r. 671–672) children as their clan temple in 686. Onjōji, which was renamed Miidera, thus became a subtemple of the powerful monastery of ENRYAKUJI on the nearby HIEIZAN. In 993, after a long period of conflict between the disciples of ENNIN and Enchin over the issue of succession, Enchin's followers moved to Miidera and eventually formed a separate branch of Tendai. For the next six hundred years, the monks of Miidera continued to contend for authority with the monks at Enryakuji, which came to be known as the Sanmon branch of the Tendaishū. Miidera suffered from a series of great fires from the eleventh to the fourteenth century, and further destruction was done to the monastery by the forces of Toyotomi Hideyoshi (1536–1598) in 1561. The golden hall (kondō) was rebuilt several decades later in 1598, and restoration efforts continued for several decades. Miidera is famous for its numerous treasures now designated important cultural properties.

**mijiao**. (J. mikkyō; K. milgyo 密教). In Chinese, "esoteric teachings"; a term used to describe a large body of literature and practices that included both MAHĀYĀNA rituals introduced from India and Central Asia into China beginning in the third and fourth centuries CE, as well as more specifically "tantric" teachings translated into Chinese in the eighth century. Rather than representing a specific independent school, mijiao refers more generically to a range of esoteric practices (including the recitation of MANTRAs and the creation of MAṆḌALAs), which came to be adopted by many of the Buddhist traditions of China. A more systematic form of mijiao appeared in the zhenyan zong (see SHINGONSHŪ), which flourished during the Tang dynasty, declining in influence after the Huichang persecution (see HUICHANG FANAN) of 842–845. Its adherents included the foreign masters ŚUBHAKARASIṂHA, VAJRABODHI, and AMOGHAVAJRA, each of whom held influential positions at court during the Tang, where the image of the divine king, as well as rituals to protect the state (HUGUO FOJIAO), found favor. Among the most important texts for mijiao were the MAHĀVAIROCANĀBHISAṂBODHISŪTRA and the SARVATATHĀGATATATTVASAṂGRAHA. See also MIKKYŌ.

**mikkyō**. (密教). In Japanese, lit. "esoteric teachings"; often translated as "esoteric Buddhism." The term mikkyō is used collectively today to refer to a large body of texts, liturgies, implements, and rituals that were imported from China to Japan during the Heian period (794–1185) by influential Japanese monk-pilgrims in the Japanese TENDAISHŪ and SHINGONSHŪ traditions. These new teachings and objects in turn were largely, but not exclusively, based on the teachings of late medieval Indian Buddhism (see TANTRA and VAJRAYĀNA) that had reached Central Asia and China. SAICHŌ (762–822) and KŪKAI (774–835) played the most notable roles in introducing esoteric Buddhism to the Japanese isles. Their trips to Tang-dynasty China (618–907) coincided with the height of esoteric practice on the continent. While Saichō's brief voyage to China in 804 focused on TIANTAI practice, he also learned a limited number of MANTRA practices toward the end of his stay, which he introduced to Japan. In 806, KŪKAI returned from a three-year stay in the Tang capital of Chang'an, bringing back with him the extensive training he had received in esoteric Buddhism from the prominent tantric master HUIGUO (746–805), as well as a large collection of esoteric texts and MAṆḌALAs. In the following years, Saichō and Kūkai's esoteric rituals quickly gained favor with the Japanese court, gradually becoming dominant among the political elite over the course of the Heian period. Alongside Kūkai's Shingon school of mikkyō (known as TŌMITSU), Tendai Buddhism increasingly developed its own set of tantric practices (known as TAIMITSU) under such successors of Saichō as ENNIN (794–864), ENCHIN (814–891), and ANNEN (b. 841). These practices were further adopted by the Nara Buddhist institutions and heavily influenced the growth and development of SHUGENDŌ. Many local cultic practices, now collectively referred to as SHINTŌ, also incorporated esoteric rituals. The primary deity of worship in mikkyō is the universal buddha MAHĀVAIROCANA. Concrete goals of esoteric practice included maintaining power, attaining good fortune, warding off evil, and becoming a buddha in one's very body (SOKUSHIN JŌBUTSU). Common ritual implements included maṇḍalas (see KONGŌKAI and TAIZŌKAI); icons, sometimes hidden, that were presented in the ritual hall (see HIBUTSU); and various ritual objects such as wands, bells, and the VAJRA.

**Mi la'i mgur 'bum**. (Mile Gurbum). In Tibetan, "The Hundred Thousand Songs of Milarepa", containing the collected spiritual songs and versified instructions of the eleventh-century Tibetan yogin MI LA RAS PA. Together with their brief narrative framing tales, the songs in this collection document the later period of Mi la ras pa's career, his life as a wandering hermit, his solitary meditation, subjugation of demons, and training of disciples. The work catalogues his songs of realization: expressions of his experiences as an awakened master, his reflections on the nature of the mind and reality, and his instructions for practicing the Buddhist path. The songs are composed in a vernacular idiom, abandoning the highly ornamental formal structure of classical poetry in favor of a simple and direct style. They are much loved in Tibet for their clarity, playfulness, and poetic beauty, and continue to be taught, memorized, and recited within most sects of Tibetan Buddhism. Episodes from the *Mi la'i mgur 'bum* have become standard themes for traditional Tibetan Buddhist plastic arts and have been adapted into theatrical dance performances (CHAMS). The number 100,000 is not literal, but rather a metaphor for the work's comprehensiveness; it is likely that many of the songs were first recorded by Mi la ras pa's own close disciples, perhaps while the YOGIN was still alive. The most famous version of this collection was edited and arranged by GTSANG SMYON HERUKA during the final decades of the fifteenth century, together with an equally famous edition of the MI LA RAS PA'I RNAM THAR ("The Life of Milarepa").

**Mi la ras pa**. (Milarepa) (1028/40–1111/23). The most famous and beloved of Tibetan YOGINS. Although he is associated most closely with the BKA' BRGYUD sect of Tibetan Buddhism, he is revered throughout the Tibetan cultural domain for his perseverance through hardship, his ultimate attainment of buddhahood in one lifetime, and for his beautiful songs. The most famous account of his life (the MI LA RAS PA'I RNAM THAR, or "The Life of Milarepa") and collection of spiritual songs (MI LA'I MGUR 'BUM, or "The Hundred Thousand Songs of Milarepa") are extremely popular throughout the Tibetan world. The themes associated with his life story—purification of past misdeeds, faith and devotion to the GURU, ardor in meditation and yogic practice, and the possibility of attaining buddhahood despite the sins of his youth—have inspired developments in Buddhist teaching and practice in Tibet. Mi la was his clan name; ras pa is derived from the single cotton robe (ras) worn by Tibetan anchorites, an attire Milarepa retained for most of his life. The name is therefore an appellation, "The Cotton-clad Mi la." Although his dates are the subject of debate, biographies agree that Mi la ras pa was born to a wealthy family in the Gung thang region of southwestern Tibet. He was given the name Thos pa dga', literally "Delightful to Hear." At an early age, after the death of his father, the family estate and inheritance were taken away by Mi la ras pa's paternal aunt and uncle, leaving Mi la ras pa, his mother, and his sister to suffer poverty and disgrace. At the urging of his mother, Mi las ras pa studied sorcery and black magic in order to seek revenge. He was successful in his studies, causing a roof to collapse during a wedding party hosted by his relatives, with many killed. Eventually feeling remorse and recognizing the karmic consequences of his deeds, he sought salvation through the practice of Buddhism. After brief studies with several masters, he met MAR PA CHOS KYI BLO GROS, who would become his root guru. Mar pa was esteemed for having traveled to India, where he received valuable tantric instructions. However, Mar pa initially refused to teach Mi la ras pa, subjecting him to all forms of verbal and physical abuse. He made him undergo various ordeals, including constructing single-handedly several immense stone towers (including the final tower built for Mar pa's son called SRAS MKHAR DGU THOG, or the "nine-storied son's tower"). When Mi la ras pa was at the point of despair and about to abandon all hope of receiving the teachings, Mar pa then revealed that the trials were a means of purifying the negative KARMAN of his black magic that would have prevented him from successfully practicing the instructions. Mar pa bestowed numerous tantric initiations and instructions, especially those of MAHĀMUDRĀ and the practice of GTUM MO, or "inner heat," together with the command to persevere against all hardship while meditating in solitary caves and mountain retreats. He was given the initiation name Bzhad pa rdo rje (Shepa Dorje). Mi la ras pa spent the rest of his life practicing meditation in seclusion and teaching small groups of yogin disciples through poetry and songs of realization. He had little interest in philosophical discourse and no tolerance for intellectual pretension; indeed, several of his songs are rather sarcastically directed against the conceits of monastic scholars and logicians. He was active across southern Tibet, and dozens of locations associated with the saint have become important pilgrimage sites and retreat centers; their number increased in the centuries following his death. Foremost among these are the hermitages at LA PHYI, BRAG DKAR RTA SO, CHU DBAR, BRIN, and KAILĀSA. Bhutanese tradition asserts that he traveled as far as the STAG TSHANG sanctuary in western Bhutan. Foremost among Milarepa's disciples were SGAM PO PA BSOD NAMS RIN CHEN and RAS CHUNG PA RDO RJE GRAGS. According to his biography, Mi la ras pa was poisoned by a jealous monk. Although he had already achieved buddhahood and was unharmed by the poison, he allowed himself to die. His life story ends with his final instructions to his disciples, the account of his miraculous cremation, and of how he left no relics despite the pleas of his followers.

**Mi la ras pa'i rnam thar**. (Milarepe Namtar). In Tibetan, "Life of Milarepa"; an account of the celebrated eleventh-century Tibetan yogin MI LA RAS PA. While numerous early Tibetan versions of the life story exist, including several that may date from his lifetime, the best-known account was composed in 1488 by GTSANG SMYON HERUKA, the so-called mad YOGIN of Tsang, based upon numerous earlier works. Its narrative focuses on Mi la ras pa's early wrongdoings, his subsequent training and meditation, and eventual death. It is a companion to the MI LA'I MGUR 'BUM ("The Hundred Thousand Songs of Milarepa"), also arranged and printed by Gtsang smyon Heruka, which records Milarepa's later teaching career through a compilation of his religious instruction and songs of realization. Gtsang smyon Heruka's version of the *Mi la ras pa'i rnam thar* is known and read throughout the Tibetan Buddhist cultural world and is widely accepted as a great literary achievement by Tibetans and Western scholars alike. The account of Milarepa's life profoundly affected the development of sacred biography in Tibet, a prominent genre in Tibetan Buddhist culture, and has influenced the way in which Tibet's Buddhism and culture have been understood in the West.

**Milarepa**. (T). See MI LA RAS PA.

**Milinda**. See MILINDAPAÑHA.

**Milindapañha**. (C. Naxian biqiu jing; J. Nasenbikukyō; K. Nasŏn pigu kyŏng 那先比丘經). In Pāli, the "Questions of Milinda"; a famous dialogical text that records the conversations of the ARHAT NĀGASENA and the Bactrian-Greek King Milinda (Menander) on various knotty points of Buddhist doctrine and ethics. The text was presumably composed in northern India in Sanskrit or Prakrit and later translated into Pāli, with the original composition or compilation probably occurring around the beginning of the Common Era. (There is an early Chinese translation made around the late fourth century, probably from a Central Asian recension in GĀNDHĀRĪ titled the **Nāgasenabhikṣusūtra*, which is named after the BHIKṢU Nāgasena rather than King Milinda.) It is uncertain whether such a dialogue ever in fact took place. There was indeed a famous king of BACTRIA named Menander (alt. Menandros; Milinda in Indian sources) who ruled over a large region that encompassed parts of modern India, Pakistan, and Afghanistan during the middle of the second century BCE. There is no evidence of Nāgasena's existence, however. Whatever the historical reality, the "Questions of Milinda" is one of the best-known texts of Pāli Buddhism. The text is structured as a series of questions by the king and answers by the monk on a wide range of topics, with each of the interlocutors displaying an impressive knowledge of Buddhist doctrine and literature. Nāgasena always provides a satisfying answer to each of the king's queries. His presentation of the dharma is so successful in fact that at the end of the dialogue King Milinda places his son upon the throne, enters the religious life, and becomes an arahant (S. arhat). The text was translated into Sinhalese in the eighteenth century by the elder Sumaṅgala. The *Milindapañha* is included in the Burmese recension of the Pāli TIPIṬAKA in the KHUDDAKANIKĀYA. Since its translation into English, it has become one of the more commonly anthologized of Pāli texts.

**mindfulness**. See SMṚTI; SMṚTYUPASTHĀNA.

**mindfulness of breathing**. See ĀNĀPĀNASMṚTI.

**mindfulness of the body**. See KĀYĀNUPAŚYANĀ; SMṚTYUPASTHĀNA.

**mind of clear light**. See PRABHĀSVARACITTA; PRABHĀSVARA.

**Mindon Min**. (r. 1853–1878). Tenth king of the Konbaung dynasty and penultimate Burmese king to rule Burma (Myanmar) before the imposition of complete British rule. His reign is known for its reforms and cultural renaissance. He usurped the throne from his brother Pagan Min (r. 1846–1853), during whose reign Great Britain declared war on Burma for a second time in 1852. Upon becoming king, Mindon Min sued for peace and was compelled to surrender Burma's remaining coastal provinces to Britain in exchange for a cessation of hostilities. In 1857 he built a new capital, MANDALAY, and sought to make it into a center for Buddhist learning. In 1871, he summoned scholar-monks from throughout the country to convene a Buddhist council for the purpose of revising the Pāli TIPIṬAKA and its commentaries. By Burmese reckoning, this conclave was the fifth Buddhist council (see COUNCIL, FIFTH). The revised texts were inscribed on stone tablets and erected in the Kuthodaw Pagoda compound at the base of Mandalay Hill, where they can still be seen today. In the secular sphere, Mindon promoted a number of reforms. He assessed a land tax and fixed the salaries for government officials. He standardized the country's weights and measures, built roads and a telegraph system, and was the first Burmese king to issue coinage. In 1872, he sent his chief minister, Kinwun Mingyi U Gaung, to London, Paris, and Rome to secure recognition of his kingdom as an independent country. Despite his efforts to revitalize his country culturally and politically, contemporary records indicate that many within the Burmese saṅgha (S. SAṂGHA) regarded British conquest of the Burmese kingdom as inevitable and imminent. Fundamentalist reform factions arose within the Burmese order that resisted the directives of the king's monastic council and organized themselves into independent self-governing congregations (see GAING). After the British destruction of the Burmese monarchy in 1885, these reformed congregations were to play an important role in shaping Burmese monastic culture in the twentieth century.

**mind-to-mind transmission**. See YIXIN CHUANXIN.

**Mingdi**. (J. Meitei; K. Myŏngje 明帝) (r. 58–76 CE). In Chinese, "Bright Emperor"; emperor during the Later Han dynasty, who is traditionally associated with the introduction of Buddhism into China. According to a famous legend found in the preface to the SISHI'ER ZHANG JING ("Sūtra in Forty-Two Sections"), in 67 CE, Emperor Ming had a dream of a radiant golden figure flying through the air. After he awoke and asked his vassals to interpret his dream, they told him he had seen the

Buddha. Emperor Ming subsequently sent envoys to the western regions (Xiyu, viz., Central Asia), where this divine being was known to reside. The envoys were said to have returned three years later with two foreign missionaries, KĀŚYAPA MĀTAṄGA and Zhu Falan (Dharmaratna), and many Buddhist scriptures, including a copy of the *Sishi'er zhang jing*. The emperor also ordered a monastery built on their behalves in the capital of Luoyang, which he called BAIMASI (White Horse Monastery), because the two Indian monks are said to have arrived in China with scriptures carried on white horses. Baimasi is, according to tradition, the first Buddhist monastery established on Chinese soil. Much of this legend is suspect. Buddhism probably had already begun to infiltrate into China at least fifty years prior to Mingdi's dream, since the emperor's vassals already knew who this golden figure was supposed to be. In addition, the *Sishi'er zhang jing*, the scripture thought to have been the first text translated by these two early missionaries, is now generally presumed to be an indigenous Chinese composition (see APOCRYPHA), not the translation of an originally Indian scripture.

**Mi pham 'Jam dbyangs rnam rgyal rgya mtsho**. (Mipam Jamyang Namgyal Gyatso) (1846–1912). A prominent Tibetan Buddhist scholar of the RNYING MA sect and a leading figure in the RIS MED or so-called nonsectarian movement of eastern Tibet. He is often known as Mi pham rgya mtsho or 'Ju Mi pham in reference to his clan name. As a young child he excelled at study—it is said that he composed his first text at age seven—and quickly mastered a broad range of traditional Buddhist learning, from MAHĀYĀNA sūtras to tantric rituals, as well as subjects such as logic, astrology, grammar, medicine, and the arts. His ease in learning a vast body of scriptures was ascribed to his devotion to the BODHISATTVA of wisdom MAÑJUŚRĪ. He is said to have read the entire BKA' 'GYUR seven times. He studied with and received transmission from many of the leading scholars of the day, including DPAL SPRUL RIN PO CHE and 'JAM MGON KONG SPRUL. His principal guru was the luminary 'JAM DBYANGS MKHYEN BRTSE DBANG PO. Unlike many other prominent Rnying ma lamas of his time, he was not actively involved in the discovery and revelation of treasure (GTER MA). He is especially renowned for his strikingly original, and often controversial, commentaries on important Indian treatises—scriptural exegesis of Indian works being relatively rare among his contemporary Rnying ma scholars. These works include his commentary on the ninth chapter of ŚĀNTIDEVA's BODHICARYĀVATĀRA and his commentary on ŚĀNTARAKṢITA's MADHYAMAKĀLAṂKĀRA. In other works, he sought to reveal the philosophical profundity of the RDZOGS CHEN teachings.

**Miram Ch'ungji**. (宓庵冲止) (1226–1292). Korean monk from the late Koryŏ dynasty and sixth-generation successor to the SUSŎNSA religious society (K. kyŏlsa; C. JIESHE) established by POJO CHINUL; also known as Pŏphwan. In 1244, Miram passed the highest-level civil examination at the age of nineteen. He was subsequently appointed to the Hallim academy, the king's secretariat, and was later sent to Japan as an emissary. When he heard that state preceptor (K. kuksa; C. GUOSHI) CH'UNGGYŎNG CH'ŎNYŎNG was residing at the nearby monastery of Sŏnwŏnsa in Kaegyŏng, he decided to become the master's disciple. In 1286, after Ch'unggyŏng passed away, Ch'ungji succeeded him as head of the Susŏnsa society. He later went to Yanjing (present-day Beijing) at the request of the Yuan emperor Shizong (r. 1260–1294). He passed away in 1292 at the age of sixty-seven, and was given the posthumous title and name State Preceptor Wŏn'gam. He was a talented poet and his poetry can be found in the *Tongmunsŏn*. His extant writings also include the *Chogye Wŏn'gam kuksa ŏrok*, *Haedong Chogye cheyukse Wŏn'gam kuksa kasong*, and *Haedong Chogye Miram hwasang chapchŏ*. A compendium of his writings, the *Wŏn'gam kuksa chip*, is no longer extant.

**Missakapabbata**. (P). See MIHINTALE.

**Misshaku Kongō**. (J) (密迹金剛). See NIŌ.

**mithyādṛṣṭi**. (P. micchādiṭṭhi; T. log par lta ba; C. ejian/xiejian; J. akuken/jaken; K. akkyŏn/sagyŏn 惡見/邪見). In Sanskrit, "wrong view," "mistaken view," or "perverse view"; a general term for misconceptions or a specific referent to erroneous philosophical positions, such as the belief in eternalism (ŚĀŚVATADṚṢṬI; ŚĀŚVATĀNTA) or annihilationism (UCCHEDADṚṢṬI; UCCHEDĀNTA) or the belief in a creator deity. The term is used more specifically as the last of the ten unwholesome actions (see KARMAPATHA)—viz., killing, stealing, sexual misconduct, lying, divisive speech, harsh speech, senseless speech, covetousness, harmful intent, and wrong views—in the context of which it refers to the mistaken belief that actions do not have effects and that former and future rebirths therefore do not occur. This particular wrong view is considered to be especially pernicious because one who holds such views would be inclined to engage in unwholesome deeds, falsely believing that they would be no consequences. (It is noteworthy in this context that in East Asia, one of the terms used to translate mithyādṛṣṭi is the same as that used for akuśaladṛṣṭi or "nonvirtuous view.") The term also appears as the fifth of five types of views (DṚṢṬI), which is a root affliction (MŪLAKLEŚA). The five are the view of the body as being real (SATKĀYADṚṢṬI); the view of holding to an extreme (ANTAGRĀHADṚṢṬI), that is eternalism or annihilationism; the holding of wrong views as being superior (DṚṢṬIPARĀMARŚA); the clinging to rites and rituals as being soteriologically efficacious (ŚĪLAVRATAPARĀMARŚA); and mithyādṛṣṭi. In this case as well, mithyādṛṣṭi includes the denial of cause and effect, the denial of the prospect of rebirth, or the denial of the possibility of liberation from rebirth.

**mithyājñāna**. (T. log pa'i shes pa; C. xiezhi; J. jachi; K. saji 邪智). In Sanskrit, "erroneous conceptions"; a consciousness that is mistaken with regard to its object of comprehension. Such knowledge may be nonconceptual, such as the perception of two moons by a person suffering from double vision, or conceptual, such as the belief that rebirth does not exist. This type of knowledge contrasts with the authentic knowledge of things as they are (yathārthajñāna), or the "knowledge and vision that accords with reality" (YATHĀBHŪTAJÑĀNADARŚANA). A common example of mithyājñāna offered by a variety of Indian traditions is mistaking a rope for a snake when the light is low: the presumed perception of a snake is completely erroneous, and the emotional reaction elicited by such a perception is entirely unwarranted. The most fundamental and deep-rooted of these misconceptions is the perception of the self (ĀTMAN) as an indivisible, unchanging, indestructible entity.

**mithyāsaṃvṛti**. (T. log pa'i kun rdzob). In Sanskrit, "false conventionality"; a term that occurs in MADHYAMAKA philosophy, where two types of conventionalities are enumerated: real conventionalities (TATHYASAṂVṚTI) and false conventionalities. A real conventionality is a conventional truth (SAṂVṚTISATYA) in the sense that it is not the object of an ultimate consciousness and is falsely imagined to possess SVABHĀVA, or intrinsic existence. Even though it may be falsely conceived, it is not however utterly nonexistent (like a false conventionality) because a real conventionality is capable of performing a function (ARTHAKRIYĀ) in accordance with its appearance. For example, the water in a lake would be a true conventionality because it can perform the function of water, whereas as the water in a mirage would be a false conventionality because it could not perform the function of a water. Only a real conventionality is a conventional truth; it is true in the sense that it can perform a function; a false conventionality is not a conventional truth because it does not exist even conventionally.

**Miyun Yuanwu**. (J. Mitsuun Engo; K. Mirun Wŏno 密雲圓悟) (1566–1642). Chinese CHAN master of the LINJI ZONG; also known as Tiantong. Miyun was a native of Changzhou prefecture in present-day Jiangsu province. He is said to have decided to become a monk after reading the LIUZU TAN JING and was formally ordained by Huanyou Zhengzhuan (1549–1614) at the age of twenty-eight. In 1602, Miyun followed Huanyou to the monastery of Longchiyuan in Changzhou and served as its prior (JIANYUAN). In 1611, Miyun received Huanyou's robes and bowls as a mark of transmission. Three years later, Miyun succeeded Huanyou's seat at Longchiyuan. In 1623, Miyun moved to the monastery Tongxuansi on TIANTAISHAN and again to Guanghuisi in Fuzhou prefecture (Zhejing province) a year later. In 1630, Miyun restored the monastery Wanfusi on Mt. Huangbo. He subsequently served as abbots of the monasteries Guanglisi on Mt. Yuwang, Jingdesi on Mt. Tiantong, and Dabao'ensi in Jinleng. His teachings are recorded in the *Miyun chanshi yulu*.

**mizuko kuyō**. (水子供養). In Japanese, lit., "offering to a child of the waters," viz., "ceremony for an aborted fetus"; a memorial ceremony performed by women and their families on behalf of the spirits of aborted, miscarried, and stillborn fetuses. Abortion is legal and widely practiced in contemporary Japan and this ceremony has become increasingly common since the 1970s as a way both to placate the potentially malevolent spirit of an aborted fetus and to comfort the woman who chose to undertake the procedure. Images of the BODHISATTVA Jizō (KṢITIGARBHA) in the form of a child are enshrined at temples, roadside shrines, or even family altars, and dedicated to the spirit of the fetus. In temples where this ceremony is common, small images of the bodhisattva are made available, which will then be typically garbed in either red bibs and caps or baby clothes so as to represent the fetus, with chanting performed and offerings made before the image. The mizuko kuyō ceremony was originally performed as an offering service to Jizō, the patron bodhisattva of children, but evolved during the Edo period in Japan into a ceremony for aborted fetuses or victims of infanticide, along the lines of other rituals performed for the ancestors of a family lineage. (Given the widespread famines of the time, some parents may have thought it better to offer children the prospect of a better rebirth than the suffering of continued starvation or unremitting sickness.) Because of this connection to Jizō, a hymn commonly sung at contemporary ceremonies is an indigenous Japanese Buddhist composition that calls on Jizō to protect the spirit of a deceased child and lead him or her to buddhahood. The mizuko kuyō may be performed at any time of the year but is especially prevalent on days dedicated to rituals for deceased ancestors, such as the Bon Festival in August.

**Mkha' 'gro snying thig**. (Kandro Nyingtik). In Tibetan, "Heart Essence of the ḌĀKINĪS"; an important set of treasure texts (GTER MA) of the RNYING MA sect of Tibetan Buddhism. These RDZOGS CHEN teachings are said to have been transmitted by PADMASAMBHAVA to Princess PADMA GSAL and to YE SHES MTSHO RGYAL. The treasure texts were discovered by PADMA LAS 'BREL RTSAL and were later included in the SNYING THIG YA BZHI, the fourfold collection of snying thig teachings by KLONG CHEN PA. He composed a commentary on the *Mkha' 'gro snying thig*, entitled *Mkha' 'gro yang thig*. The text and commentary together are known as the *Mkha' 'gro snying thig ma bu*, the "Mother and Son Heart Essence of the Ḍākinīs."

**Mkhar chu**. (Karchu). An important monastic center associated with both the RNYING MA and BKA' BRGYUD sects of Tibetan Buddhism, located in the LHO BRAG region of southern Tibet. The original site was established by the 'Brug pa bka' brgyud master Lo ras pa (1187–1250), but was later renovated and enlarged by famed 'Brug pa scholar and historian PADMA DKAR PO. The monastery and surrounding environs were a wealthy and active center for Buddhist practice, visited by numerous important masters. His disciple Nam mkha'i snying po stayed in a meditation retreat nearby, where he is said to have attained realization of MAHĀMUDRĀ. Mkhar chu later became a seat for

Nam mkha'i snying po's successive reincarnations. Other Rnying ma and Bka' brgud masters associated with Mkhar chu include NYANG RAL NYI MA 'OD ZER, RGOD TSHANG PA MGON PO RDO RJE, GURU CHOS KYI DBANG PHYUG, and Me long rdo rje (1234–1303).

**Mkhas grub Dge legs dpal bzang**. (Kedrup Gelek Palsang) (1385–1438). Also known as Mkhas grub rje, an early leader of the DGE LUGS sect of Tibetan Buddhism, who trained first under the influential scholar Red mda' ba Gzhon nu blo gros (Rendawa Shonu Lodro, 1349–1412). At the age of twenty-three he met TSONG KHA PA, who became his principal GURU. Mkhas grub rje excelled in his study of Buddhist logic and philosophy and his collected works contain numerous influential treatises on PRAMĀṆA, MADHYAMAKA, and TANTRA (especially the KĀLACAKRA); among his most famous works is the *Stong thun skal bzang mig 'byed*. At the age of forty-seven, he ascended the golden throne of DGA' LDAN monastery as the institution's abbot, replacing Tsong kha pa's other illustrious student RGYAL TSHAB DAR MA RIN CHEN (see DGA' LDAN KHRI PA). Mkhas grub rje was recognized posthumously as being first in the line of PAṆ CHEN LAMA incarnations. Mkhas grub rje is commonly depicted in paintings and statues called rje yab sras gsum, "the triumvirate of the foremost father and his [two] sons," showing Tsong kha pa flanked by Rgyal tshab and Mkhas grub. Here Mkhas grub can often be distinguished from Rgyal tshab by his younger visage and darker hair, and by his wild eyes, said to have been a result of his tantric practice.

**Mkhas pa'i dga' ston**. See CHOS 'BYUNG MKHAS PA'I DGA' STON.

**mkha' spyod**. (kachö). Literally, "sky-enjoyer"; a Tibetan translation of ḌĀKINĪ.

**Mkho mthing**. (Koting). In Tibet, one of the four "extra taming temples" or "extra pinning temples" (YANG 'DUL GTSUG LAG KHANG) said to have been constructed during the time of the Tibetan king SRONG BTSAN SGAM PO to pin down the limbs of the demoness (T. srin mo) in order to introduce Buddhism into Tibet. It is located in LHO BRAG and pins down her left elbow.

**mofa**. (J. mappō; K. malpŏp 末法). In Chinese, "final dharma" period. The dispensation of Buddhism, like all compounded things, is presumed to be impermanent and subject to decay and eventually dissolution. This process of eschatological decline was believed to occur in stages, often calculated at either five hundred or one thousand years at each stage (although there were many variations), and began with the passage of the Buddha into PARINIRVĀṆA. In East Asia, the notion of decline was formalized into an influential doctrinal system, consisting of three stages or periods named "true dharma" (zhengfa; see SADDHARMA), "semblance dharma" (XIANGFA), and "final dharma" (mofa). This tripartite system was not inherited from Indian Buddhism. The term mofa is not the translation of the Sanskrit SADDHARMAVIPRALOPA ("destruction of the dharma"), but is instead a neologism derived from moshi, the Chinese translation of term PAŚCIMAKĀLA ("latter time"). The notion of the period of the final dharma spawned a large and influential exegetical tradition in East Asia. The date of the onset of the final period was variously calculated (and was generally assumed to have already begun soon after Buddhism's introduction into East Asia). This assumption was widely employed as doctrinal justification for certain practices, such as the invocation of the name of the buddha AMITĀBHA (NIANFO) or the cult of the future buddha MAITREYA. In such contexts, it was claimed that during the period of the final dharma, beings lacked the capacity to successfully follow the standard path to liberation set forth by the Buddha and instead should rely on the efficacious powers of Amitābha or the prospect of an easier practice regimen after the advent of ŚĀKYAMUNI Buddha's successor, Maitreya. The notion of the age of the final dharma was espoused in many indigenous scriptures (see APOCRYPHA) written in East Asia. It also played an important role in the formation of such traditions as PURE LAND, JŌDOSHŪ, JŌDO SHINSHŪ, NICHIRENSHŪ, NICHIREN SHOSHŪ, and others. See also SADDHARMAVIPRALOPA.

**Mogao ku**. (莫高窟). In Chinese, "Peerless Caves." See DUNHUANG.

**Moggaliputtatissa**. (C. Mujianlianzidixu; J. Mokukenrenshiteishu; K. Mokkŏllyŏnjajesu 目犍連子帝須). According to Pāli sources, the monk who served as head of the third Buddhist council (SAṂGĪTI; see COUNCIL, THIRD) convened at Pāṭaliputta (S. PĀṬALIPUTRA) in the third century BCE. In a previous life, Moggaliputtatissa had been a divinity who, at the behest of a delegation of arahants (S. ARHAT), took human rebirth so that he could assist in the future purification of the Buddhist teaching. Fully trained in the TIPIṬAKA and its commentaries (AṬṬHAKATHĀ) as a novice, he became an arahant shortly after being ordained as a monk. King AŚOKA's lavish support of the Buddhist SAṂGHA prompted many non-Buddhist mendicants and brāhmaṇas to don the robes of Buddhist monks merely as a livelihood. With the orthodox saṃgha unable to forcibly remove the bogus monks from their midst, the ordination ceremony (P. uposatha; S. UPOṢADHA) was suspended. When this situation had persisted for seven years, Moggaliputtatissa, at Aśoka's request, taught the DHARMAVINAYA to the king so that he might intervene on behalf of the legitimate party. Aśoka interrogated the saṃgha and, drawing on the authority of the state (āṇācakka), defrocked those monks found to be improperly ordained. With the saṃgha thus purified of its corrupting influences, Moggaliputtatissa convened the third Buddhist council to rehearse the Buddha's teachings as preserved in the Pāli tipiṭaka and its commentaries. At that time Moggaliputtatissa composed the KATHĀVATTHU, the seventh and last book of the ABHIDHAMMAPIṬAKA, to refute heretical views. At the conclusion of the council, Moggaliputtatissa dispatched missionaries to nine adjacent lands (paccantajanapada) to propagate the newly purified teaching.

**Moggallāna**. (P). See MAHĀMAUDGALYĀYANA.

**Mogharāja**. (C. Mianwang [biqiu]; J. Men'ō [biku]; K. Myŏnwang [pigu] 面王[比丘]). The Sanskrit and Pāli proper name of an eminent ARHAT declared by the Buddha to be foremost among monks who wore coarse robes. According to Pāli sources, he was a brāhmaṇa ascetic who studied under Bāvarī, and one of sixteen students sent to defeat the Buddha in debate. When the Buddha answered the question posed by Mogharāja, he attained arahantship immediately. He became known for stitching his robes from coarse cloth discarded by tailors and dyers. Mogharāja suffered from various skin ailments and, believing his residence to be infested with insects, he slept on a straw bed laid out in the open, even during the winter. When the Buddha inquired how he fared, Mogharāja responded that he was happy even in the cold. The boils and sores that covered his body were a consequence of a misdeed performed in a previous life. During the time of Padumuttara Buddha he had blackened the floor of the Buddha's cloister with soot from a fire; for this transgression, he was compelled to suffer in hell for a thousand years and after that to endure skin disease for another five hundred lifetimes. It was during the lifetime of Padumuttara that Mogharāja heard him praise a disciple as foremost among those who wore coarse clothing, and he resolved to attain that preeminence during the dispensation of a future buddha.

**moha**. (T. gti mug; C. chi; J. chi; K. ch'i 癡). In Sanskrit and Pāli, "delusion," "confusion," "benightedness," "foolishness"; as a synonym of "ignorance" (AVIDYĀ), moha denotes a fundamental confusion concerning the true character of the conception of a person (PUDGALA) and the phenomenal world and is thus an affliction (KLEŚA) and cause of future suffering. Moha appears frequently in the sūtra literature as one of the "three poisons" (TRIVIṢA) or three unwholesome faculties (AKUŚALAMŪLA): viz., the kleśas of greed or sensuality (RĀGA or LOBHA), hatred or aversion (DVEṢA), and delusion (moha). Moha is also one of the forty-six mental concomitants (CAITTA) according to the SARVĀSTIVĀDA-VAIBHĀṢIKA school of ABHIDHARMA and is listed as the first of six "fundamental afflictions" or "defiled factors of wide extent" (kleśa-MAHĀBHŪMIKA) that are associated with all defiled thoughts, together with heedlessness (PRAMĀDA), lassitude (KAUSĪDYA), lack of faith (ĀŚRADDHYA), sloth (STYĀNA), and restlessness (AUDDHATYA). It also is listed as one of the fourteen unwholesome (akusala) mental states (CETASIKA) in the Pāli abhidhamma. Delusion is the opposite of nondelusion (AMOHA), one of the eleven wholesome factors (KUŚALADHARMA) in the YOGĀCĀRA list of one hundred dharmas (BAIFA).

**Moheyan**. See BSAM YAS DEBATE.

**Mohe zhiguan**. (J. Makashikan; K. Maha chigwan 摩訶止觀). In Chinese, "The Great Calming and Contemplation"; a comprehensive treatise on soteriological theory and meditation according to the TIANTAI ZONG; attributed to TIANTAI ZHIYI (538–597). The *Mohe zhiguan* is based on a series of lectures Zhiyi delivered in 594, which were transcribed and edited by his disciple GUANDING. Zhi (lit. "stopping") is the Chinese translation for ŚAMATHA (calmness, serenity) and guan (lit. "observation") is the Chinese for VIPAŚYANĀ (insight); the work as a whole seeks to establish a proper balance between meditative practice and philosophical insight. Zhi and guan practice are treated in three different ways in this treatise. Zhi in its denotation of "stopping" means calming the mind so that it is not buffeted by distracting thoughts; fixing the mind so that it stays focused on the present; and recognizing that distraction and concentration are both manifestations of a unitary, nondual reality. Guan in its denotation of "observation" means to illuminate the illusory nature of thought so that distractions are brought to an end; to have insight into the suchness (TATHATĀ) that is the ultimate nature of all phenomena in the universe; and to recognize that in suchness both insight and noninsight ultimately are identical. The original text of the *Mohe zhiguan* consists of ten chapters, but only the titles of the last three chapters survive. The last extant chapter, Chapter 7 on "Proper Contemplation," comprises approximately half of the entire treatise and, as the title suggests, provides a detailed description of the ten modes of contemplation and the ten spheres of contemplation. The first of the ten spheres of contemplation is called "the realm of the inconceivable" (S. ACINTYA). In his discussion of this realm in the first part of the fifth roll, Zhiyi covers one of the most famous of Tiantai doctrines: "the TRICHILIOCOSM in a single instant of thought" (YINIAN SANQIAN), which Zhiyi frames here as the "the trichiliocosm contained in the mind during an instant of thought" (sanqian zai yinian xin), viz., that any given thought-moment perfectly encompasses all reality, both temporally and spatially. By emphatically noting the "inconceivable" ability of the mind to contain the trichiliocosm, Zhiyi sought to emphasize the importance and mystery of the mind during the practice of meditation. This chapter, however, remains incomplete. The work also offers an influential presentation of the "four SAMĀDHIS," that is, the samādhis of constant sitting, constant walking, both sitting and walking, and neither sitting nor walking. Along with Zhiyi's FAHUA XUANYI and FAHUA WENJU, the *Mohe zhiguan* is considered to be one of the three most important treatises in the Tiantai tradition and is regarded as Zhiyi's magnum opus. The Tiantai monk ZHANRAN's MOHE ZHIGUAN FUXING ZHUANHONG JUE is considered to be the most authoritative commentary on the *Mohe zhiguan*.

**Mohe zhiguan fuxing zhuanhong jue**. (J. Makashikan bugyōdenguketsu; K. Maha chigwan pohaeng chŏnhong kyŏl 摩訶止觀輔行傳弘決). Often referred to in Chinese by its abbreviated title of *Zhuanhongjue*; a comprehensive commentary on ZHIYI'S MOHE ZHIGUAN composed by JINGXI ZHANRAN

(711–782). In the past, the *Mohe Zhiguan* and the *Zhuanhongjue* were frequently printed together; hence, the traditional interpretation of the *Mohe Zhiguan* has been heavily dependent upon Zhanran's commentary. It was largely through the exegetical efforts of Zhanran, in fact, that the *Mohe Zhiguan* was established as the foundation of Tiantai theory and practice. The commentary also provides Zhanran's own views regarding the teachings of other rival schools, such as the HUAYAN ZONG, CHAN ZONG, and FAXIANG ZONG. Zhanran also advocated the view that human nature was inherently evil (xing'e lun), and his views on human nature are elaborated in his commentary.

**mokṣa**. (P. mokkha; T. thar pa; C. jietuo; J. gedatsu; K. haet'al 解脫). In Sanskrit, "liberation," "freedom" or "release"; the state of liberation from suffering and rebirth, achieved via the path of the ŚRĀVAKA, PRATYEKABUDDHA, or BODHISATTVA and virtually interchangeable with the synonymous VIMOKṢA. The term is often used as a synonym for NIRVĀṆA. Buddhahood is the ultimate form of mokṣa, but it is possible to achieve liberation (as an ARHAT) without achieving buddhahood. Whether all beings will eventually achieve some form of mokṣa and whether all beings will eventually achieve buddhahood are points of controversy among Buddhist schools. The term is often paired with SVARGA ("heaven") as the two destinations that may result from practicing the Buddha's teachings. That is, by leading a virtuous life, one is reborn as a divinity (DEVA) in one of several heavenly realms. By understanding the nature of reality, one attains mokṣa, final liberation from all forms of rebirth. In this pairing, svarga is the lesser goal for those incapable of seeking the ultimate goal of mokṣa in the present lifetime.

**mokṣabhāgīya**. (T. thar pa cha mthun; C. shunjietuofen; J. jungedatsubun; K. sunhaet'albun 順解脫分). In Sanskrit, "aids to liberation"; abbreviation for the mokṣabhāgīya-kuśalamūla (wholesome faculties associated with liberation), the second of the three types of wholesome faculties (literally, "virtuous root") (KUŚALAMŪLA) recognized in the VAIBHĀṢIKA school of SARVĀSTIVĀDA ABHIDHARMA, along with the puṇyabhāgīya (aids to creating merit) and NIRVEDHABHĀGĪYA (aids to penetration). This type of wholesome faculty involves the intent to listen to (śruta) and reflect upon (cintā) the Buddhist teachings and then make the resolution (PRAṆIDHĀNA) to follow the DHARMAVINAYA to such an extent that all one's physical and verbal actions (KARMAN) will come into conformity with the prospect of liberation. The mokṣabhāgīyas are constituents of the path of preparation (PRAYOGAMĀRGA), the second segment of the five-path schema outlined in the Vaibhāṣika ABHIDHARMA system, which mark the transition from the mundane sphere of cultivation (LAUKIKA-BHĀVANĀMĀRGA) to the supramundane vision (viz., DARŚANAMĀRGA) of the FOUR NOBLE TRUTHS (catvāry āryasatyāni). In distinction to the nirvedhabhāgīyas, however, which are the proximate path of preparation, the mokṣabhāgīyas constitute instead the remote path of preparation and are associated only with the types of wisdom developed from learning (ŚRUTAMAYĪPRAJÑĀ) and reflection (CINTĀMAYĪPRAJÑĀ), not meditative practice (BHĀVANĀMAYĪPRAJÑĀ). The mokṣabhāgīyas are generally concerned with the temporary allayment of the influence of the three major afflictions (KLEŚA)—viz., greed (LOBHA), hatred (DVEṢA), and ignorance (MOHA)—by cultivating the three kuśalamūlas of nongreed (ALOBHA), nonhatred (ADVEṢA), and nondelusion (AMOHA). These factors are "conducive to liberation" by encouraging such salutary actions as giving (DĀNA), keeping precepts (ŚĪLA), and learning the dharma. The mokṣabhāgīya are associated with the development of the first twelve of the BODHIPĀKṢIKADHARMAS, or "thirty-seven factors pertaining to awakening." Among them, the first set of four develop SMṚTI (mindfulness) as described in the four SMṚTYUPASTHĀNA (applications of mindfulness), the second set of four develop VĪRYA (effort) as described in the four PRAHĀṆA (efforts or abandonments), and the third set of four develop SAMĀDHI (concentration) as described in the four ṚDDHIPĀDA (bases of psychic powers). According to a different enumeration, there are five mokṣabhāgīya: (1) faith (ŚRADDHĀ), (2) effort (VĪRYA), (3) mindfulness (SMṚTI), (4) concentration (SAMĀDHI), and (5) wisdom (PRAJÑĀ).

**mokṣamārga**. (T. thar lam; C. jietuodao; J. gedatsudō; K. haet'alto 解脫道). In Sanskrit, "path to liberation"; a path that leads to liberation from SAṂSĀRA, as opposed to a favorable rebirth within saṃsāra, such as in the heavens (SVARGA). In this case, the term would refer specifically to the five paths (PAÑCAMĀRGA): the path of accumulation (SAṂBHĀRAMĀRGA), the path of preparation (PRAYOGAMĀRGA), the path of vision (DARŚANAMĀRGA), the path of cultivation (BHĀVANĀMĀRGA), and the adept path where there is nothing more to learn (AŚAIKṢAMĀRGA). However, any virtuous practice that is motivated by the wish to achieve liberation from rebirth would also be qualified as a "path to liberation."

**mokt'ak**. (C. muduo; J. bokutaku 木鐸). In Korean, "wooden clacker"; a wooden percussion instrument that is used in Korean Buddhist monasteries to call monks and nuns to assembly and to keep time during religious services or meditation periods. The mokt'ak is abstractly carved in a shape that resembles a fish, and is thus the functional equivalent in Korea to the Chinese "wooden fish" (MUYU; see also DRUM). The instrument is constructed by carving wood (typically apricot, jujube, or birch) in the shape of a round bell with a handle grip. The bell shape of the wood is cut across the middle and the center hollowed out, producing a sound box. The sound resonates when it is struck by a small wooden mallet. The long, narrow cut in the mokt'ak represents the mouth of a fish, while the two small holes on each side of the "mouth" represent the eyes of a fish. Because a fish's eyes are always open day and night, the stylized mokt'ak version of the wooden fish is a subtle admonition to monks and nuns to remain ever vigilant about their practice. The term mokt'ak itself originates from ancient Chinese custom in which a government official would use a wooden or iron bell to summon people to the announcement of a new government ordinance. However, a Chinese wooden clacker is an iron bell with a wooden clapper inside, an instrument that is called a yoryŏng in Korean.

**monastery**. See VIHĀRA; CHŎL; TERA; DGON PA; entries on specific monasteries.

**Mongkut**. (Thai). See RĀMA IV.

**monk**. See BHIKṢU; ŚRAMAṆA; ŚRĀMAṆERA.

**monsan**. (門参). In Japanese, lit. "lineage instructions," probably an abbreviation of monto hissan (the secret instructions of this lineage); secret kōan (GONG'AN) manuals used in medieval Japanese SŌTŌSHŪ monasteries of the ZEN tradition, which provide detailed descriptions of the kōan curriculum taught in the various Sōtō lineages. As a record of the secret instructions transmitted in a particular lineage, the possession of these manuals often served as proof of the inheritance of that particular dharma lineage. The manuals contain names of kōans and a series of standardized questions and answers (WENDA) for each kōan. The monsan provide the required responses to the master's questions, which are in the form of Chinese verses and phrases known as AGYO and JAKUGO. The earliest extant monsan texts date from the sixteenth century, but they seem to represent long-established traditions within Zen lineages.

**moshi**. (J. masse; K. malse 末世). In Chinese, the "latter time"; a translation of the Sanskrit term PAŚCIMAKĀLA. The term commonly appears in the MAHĀYĀNA sūtras to refer to the time following the Buddha's passage into PARINIRVĀṆA. In China, this term seems to have served as the basis for the Chinese neologism MOFA, the more common term in East Asia to refer to the final period of the dharma.

**mother tantra**. See MĀTṚTANTRA.

**Mount Hiei**. See HIEIZAN.

**Mount Sumeru**. See SUMERU, MOUNT.

**Mouzi**. (J. Bōshi; K. Moja 牟子) (fl. c. third century CE?). A Chinese Buddhist layman who is the composer of the MOUZI LIHUO LUN, a text that is often known eponymously as simply the *Mouzi*. The author's family name was Mou and he is traditionally identified as Mou Rong of the Latter Han dynasty (25–220 CE), although this identification is no longer accepted by scholars. According to the preface to his treatise, Mouzi was a scholar-official from Cangwu in Jiaozhou, in the far southern reaches of the Chinese empire, where there seems to have been a flourishing Buddhist community that may date to the Latter Han dynasty. Mouzi's references to Buddhist monks wearing saffron robes, eating one meal a day, and living a celibate life suggest that he may have had contact with foreign monks who accompanied Indian traders arriving at southern Chinese seaports. Mouzi is said to have given up his administrative career after his mother's death so that he could devote himself to Buddhist scholarship and meditation for the rest of his life. Other than the attribution that he was the writer of this earliest extant Buddhist treatise written by a Chinese layman, however, nothing more is known about him.

**Mouzi lihuo lun**. (J. Bōshi riwakuron; K. Moja ihok non 牟子理惑論). In Chinese, "Treatise on the Resolution of Doubts," or "Treatise on the Disposition of Error"; the earliest extant Buddhist treatise written by a Chinese convert; often known by its abbreviated eponymous title, the *Mouzi*. The text is attributed to a Chinese Buddhist layman, MOUZI, who is claimed to have hailed from the south of China. The text is a polemical Buddhist defense of the faith, which responds to criticisms of Buddhism by rival religions in China. The text consists of a eulogistic preface, thirty-eight short dialogues between Mouzi and unnamed critic(s) of Buddhism, and a brief conclusion, in which the antagonist finally acquiesces to the rectitude of Buddhist positions. Stylistically, the work is written in Confucian commentarial form, thus making more palatable its putatively subversive idea, viz., that adherence to Buddhism is completely compatible with being a righteous and filial Chinese. Typically, criticisms deriving from Confucian beliefs are refuted using references from the *Laozi* and *Zhuangzi*, while Daoist criticisms are refuted with astute readings of both Daoist and Confucian texts. The *Mouzi* was thus successful not simply because it refuted the critiques of rival religions; in addition, by demonstrating the inherent inaccuracy and speciousness of their positions, the treatise was also able to prove the veracity, if not the superiority, of Buddhism itself. In one of the dialogues that argues that filiality is found not only in Confucianism but in Buddhism as well, the *Mouzi* compares the Buddhist monk to a son who saves his father from drowning by grabbing him and lifting him upside down back into the boat. Although the inelegant manner in which the son grabbed his father may initially seem disrespectful, since it saves his parent from drowning, the act would be acceptable even according to Confucius himself, who insisted that exigent circumstances justified adaptable demonstrations of filial piety. Similarly, the behavior of a Buddhist monk who leaves the home life may in fact be filial, even though initially it may not appear to be so. In another section, the *Mouzi* substantiates the filiality of Buddhism by pointing out that, since the Buddha protected his parents ŚUDDHODANA and MĀYĀ by showing them the path to their salvation, practicing Buddhism was indeed filial. In another dialogue concerning criticisms of the Buddhist teaching of rebirth, the *Mouzi* compares the spirit that is reborn to the seeds of a plant, which can grow into new plants even after the leaves and roots (viz., the physical body) have died. The composition date of the *Mouzi* has proven to be an intractable problem. Its preface claims that the text was written in the second century

CE, although current scholarly estimates of its date range from the second quarter of the third century through the fourth or even early fifth century. More likely, the text developed over time, with many accretions. The text was included in the (nonextant) *Fa lun* ("Collection on the Dharma"), compiled by Lu Cheng (425–494) around 465, which would be the terminus ad quem for its composition. The text that is extant today is the recension appearing in SENGYOU's (445–518) HONGMING JI ("Collection on the Propagation and Clarification [of Buddhism]"), the important anthology of Buddhist apologetics, compiled c. 515–518. Although some earlier scholars have questioned the authenticity of the text, it is now generally accepted to be in fact one of the earliest extant sources from the incipiency of indigenous Chinese Buddhism.

**mozhao Chan**. (J. mokushōzen; K. mukcho Sŏn 默照禪) In Chinese, "silent illumination meditation"; a form of Chan meditation attributed to the CAODONG ZONG (J. SŌTŌSHŪ), and specifically the masters HONGZHI ZHENGJUE (1091–1157) and his teacher Danxia Zichun (1064–1117). This practice builds upon the normative East Asian notion of the inherency of buddhahood (see TATHĀGATAGARBHA) to suggest that, since enlightenment is the natural state of the mind, there is nothing that needs to be done in order to attain enlightenment other than letting go of all striving for that state. Authentic Chan practice therefore entails only maintaining this original purity of the mind by simply sitting silently in meditation. Hongzhi's clarion call to this new Caodong-style of practice is found in his *Mozhao ming* ("Inscription on Silent Illumination"), which may have been written in response to increasingly vehement criticisms of the practice by the rival LINJI ZONG, although its dating remains uncertain. In Hongzhi's description of the practice of silent illumination, silence (mo) seems to correlate roughly with calmness (Ch. zhi, S. ŚAMATHA) and illumination (zhao) with insight (C. guan, S. VIPAŚYANĀ); and when both silence and illumination are operating fully, the perfect interfusion of all things is made manifest. Silent-illumination meditation thus seems to have largely involved prolonged sessions of quiet sitting (see ZUOCHAN) and the cessation of distracted thought, a state likened to dead wood and cold ashes or a censer in an old shrine. The Linji Chan adept DAHUI ZONGGAO deploys the term to denigrate the teachings of his Caodong contemporaries and to champion his preferred approach of practice, investigating meditative topics (see KANHUA CHAN) through Chan cases (C. GONG'AN), which demands a breakthrough to enlightenment, not simply what he claims is the passive sitting of the Caodong zong. After Dahui's obstreperous critique of mozhao, the term seems to have acquired such a pejorative connotation that it stopped being used even within the Caodong tradition. See also SHIKAN TAZA.

**mrakṣa**. (P. makkha; T. 'chab pa; C. fu; J. fuku; K. pok 覆). In Sanskrit "disparagement" or "hypocrisy." The term is typically interpreted to mean either concealing the achievements or wholesome qualities of others, or concealing one's own faults. Mrakṣa is one of the forty-six mental concomitants (see CAITTA) according to the SARVĀSTIVĀDA–VAIBHĀṢIKA school of ABHIDHARMA and the ABHIDHARMAKOŚABHĀṢYA and one of the fifty-one according to the YOGĀCĀRA school; it is classified among the secondary afflictions (UPAKLEŚA).

**mṛdvindriya**. (T. dbang po rtul ba; C. dungen; J. donkon; K. tun'gŭn 鈍根). In Sanskrit, "dull faculties"; the lowest of the "three capacities" (TRĪNDRIYA) used to describe those disciples of the Buddha whose intellectual and spiritual abilities are lesser than those with "average faculties" (MADYENDRIYA) and "sharp faculties" (TĪKṢṆENDRIYA). The "follower of faith" (ŚRADDHĀNUSĀRIN) who enters into practice more quickly than the "follower of dharma" (DHARMĀNUSĀRIN), without first investigating whether the practice will deliver the result, is the archetypal mṛdvindriya person. The term appears in discussions of UPĀYA, the Buddha's skill at adapting his teachings to the intellects, interests, and aspirations of his disciples. The Buddha offers the simplest teachings, such as that the practice of charity (DĀNA) and morality (ŚĪLA), which result in a favorable rebirth as a divinity or human, to those of lesser faculties, understanding that such disciples are initially incapable of understanding more sophisticated teachings. The term is also put to polemical use, describing the adherents of competing schools who mistakenly think that their understanding of the doctrine is the Buddha's highest teaching. In the MAHĀYĀNA, those with "dull faculties" do not gain the irreversible (AVAIVARTIKA) stage until a later stage of the path.

**Mṛgadāva**. [alt. Mṛgadāya] (P. Migadāya; T. Ri dwags kyi gnas; C. Luyeyuan; J. Rokuyaon; K. Nogyawŏn 鹿野苑). In Sanskrit, the "Deer Park" in the modern town of SĀRNĀTH, some four miles (six kms.) north of Vārāṇasī, where the Buddha preached his first sermon, the "Turning the Wheel of the Dharma" (S. DHARMACAKRAPRAVARTANASŪTRA; P. DHAMMACAKKAPPAVATTANASUTTA), following his enlightenment; the site was also known as ṚṢIPATANA. It was there that the Buddha encountered the "group of five" (S. PAÑCAVARGIKA; P. pañcavaggiyā), the five ascetics who had previously repudiated him for abandoning the practice of austerities, and it was to this group that the Buddha taught the FOUR NOBLE TRUTHS (catvāry āryasatyāni) and the eightfold path (ĀRYĀṢṬĀṄGAMĀRGA). A number of other important discourses were also delivered there. The Deer Park later became the site of a large monastery. According to the Chinese pilgrim XUANZANG, the place derived its name from the *Nigrodhamṛgajātaka*, which tells the story of when the bodhisattva was reborn as Nigrodha, king of the deer. When he offered himself in sacrifice, the king of Vārāṇasī was so moved that he established a sanctuary where deer could live unmolested by hunters.

**Mṛgāramātṛprāsāda**. (P. Migāramātupāsāda; T. Ri dwags 'dzin gyi ma'i khang bzang; C. Luzimu tang; J. Rokushimodō;

K. Nokchamo tang 鹿子母堂). In Sanskrit, "Hall of Mṛgāra's Mother"; the name of the monastery inside the Pūrvārāma (P. Pubbārāma), a park located outside the eastern city gate of ŚRĀVASTĪ, which was constructed for the Buddha by his foremost female lay disciple VIŚĀKHĀ, who was also known as "Mṛgāra's Mother." The monastic residence is said to have been two stories high, with five hundred rooms on each floor, and each room lavishly appointed. A golden water tower that could hold sixty pots of water rose from the roof. The Buddha is said to have spent the last twenty years of his life in Śrāvastī, dividing his time between this monastery built for him by Viśākhā and the JETAVANA monastery in ANĀTHAPIṆḌADA's park (S. Anāthapiṇḍadārāma) built for him by his foremost male lay disciple Anāthapiṇḍada, typically moving between both sites every day.

**mṛtyumāra**. (T. 'Chi bdag gi bdud; C. Simo; J. Shima; K. Sama 死魔). In Sanskrit, "māra of death"; one of the four metaphorical forms of MĀRA, the personification of evil, along with the māra of the afflictions (kleśamāra), the māra of the aggregates (SKANDHAMĀRA), and the deity Māra (DEVAPUTRAMĀRA). In this form, death itself is an aspect of Māra, since death brings an end to everything that one holds precious in this current life.

**mtha' 'dul gtsug lag khang**. (tadül tsuklakang). In Tibetan, the four "edge-taming temples" or "edge-pinning temples" of KHRA 'BRUG, 'GRAM, BKA' TSHAL, and GRUM PA RGYANG, said to have been constructed during the time of the Tibetan king SRONG BTSAN SGAM PO to pin down the limbs of the demoness (T. srin mo) in order to pacify Tibet to prepare it for the introduction of Buddhism. The LHA SA gtsug lag khang, also known as the JO KHANG, pins down her heart and the four edge taming temples her right and left shoulders and hips.

**Mtshur phu**. (Tsurpu). A Tibetan monastery that served as the seat of the KARMA PA, established in 1187 by the first KARMA PA DUS GSUM MKHYEN PA in the Stod lung (Tölung) valley, northwest of LHA SA. The monastery was actually a large complex of assembly halls, residences (including that of the MTSHUR PHU RGYAL TSHAB incarnations), retreat centers, and meditation caves that greatly expanded as the fame of the Karma pas grew. At its height, it housed over one thousand monks. The monastery was completely demolished during the Chinese Cultural Revolution but has been partially restored since the 1980s.

**Mtshur phu rgyal tshab incarnations**. (Tsurpu Gyaltsap). A line of incarnate lamas (SPRUL SKU) of the KARMA BKA' BRGYUD sect of Tibetan Buddhism, entrusted as the regents of MTSHUR PHU monastery and traditionally close to the KARMA PAS. The lineage includes:

1. Go shrī Dpal 'byor don grub (Goshri Paljor Döndrup, c. 1427–1489)
2. Bkra shis rnam rgyal (Tashi Namgyal, c. 1490–1518)
3. Grags pa dpal 'byor (Drakpa Paljor, c. 1519–1549)
4. Grags pa don grub (Drakpa Döndrup, c. 1550–1617)
5. Grags pa mchog dbyangs (Drakpa Chokyang, c. 1618–1658)
6. Nor bu bzang po (Norbu Sangpo, c. 1659–1698)
7. Dkon mchog 'od zer (Könchok Öser, c. 1699–1765)
8. Chos dpal bzang po (Chöpal Sangpo, c. 1766–1820)
9. Grags pa ye shes (Drakpa Yeshe, c. 1821–1876)
10. Bstan pa'i nyi ma (Tenpe Nyima, c. 1877–1901)
11. Grags pa rgya mtsho (Drakpa Gyatso, c. 1902–1959)
12. Karma Grags pa bstan pa yar 'phel, a.k.a. Bstan 'dzin phrin las chos kyi nyi ma (Tendzin Trinle Chökyi Nyima, b. 1960)

**mu kōan**. (無公案) (J). See GOUZI WU FOXING.

**Mu'an Xingtao**. (J. Mokuan Shōtō; K. Mogam Sŏngdo 木菴性瑫) (1611–1684). Chinese CHAN master, calligrapher, and pioneer of the ŌBAKUSHŪ in Japan. He was a native of Quanzhou in present-day Fujian province. After his novice ordination at the age of eighteen, Mu'an received the full monastic precepts from the monk Yongjue Yuanxian (1578–1657) on Mt. Gu (present-day Fujian province). Mu'an visited the eminent Chan master MIYUN YUANWU before he returned to Yongjue, under whom he is said to have attained awakening. Later, Mu'an continued his studies under FEIYIN TONGRONG and his disciple YINYUAN LONGQI at the monastery of Wanfusi on Mt. Huangbo (present-day Fujian province). Mu'an eventually became Yinyuan's disciple and inherited his lineage. In 1655, Mu'an arrived in Nagasaki, Japan, and began his residence at the monastery of Fukusaiji. In 1661, Mu'an followed Yinyuan to his new monastery of MANPUKUJI in Uji. Three years later, Mu'an succeeded Yinyuan as the abbot of the monastery, and the next year he oversaw the ordination of monks at the triple-precept platform ceremony (sandan kaie). In 1670, he received the purple robe, and later with the support of the shōgun Tokugawa Ietsuna (1639–1680), he established the monastery of Zuishōji in Edo. In 1675, he turned over the administration of Zuishōji to his disciple Tetsugyū Dōki (1628–1700) and that of Manpukuji to Huilin Xingji (1609–1681).

**muccitukamyatāñāṇa**. [alt. muñcitukamyatāñāṇa]. In Pāli, "knowledge arising from the desire for deliverance"; according to the VISUDDHIMAGGA, the sixth of nine total types of knowledge cultivated as part of "purity of knowledge and vision of progress along the path" (PAṬIPADĀÑĀṆADASSANAVISUDDHI). This latter category, in turn, constitutes the sixth and penultimate purity (P. visuddhi; S. VIŚUDDHI) to be developed along the path to liberation. Having cultivated aversion toward all conditioned formations (P. saṅkhāra; S. SAṂSKĀRA) and the mental and physical phenomena (NĀMARŪPA) comprising the individual and the universe, because of their frightful nature and fundamental unsatisfactoriness, the practitioner generates the desire to be free from them. The *Visuddhimagga* explains that, like a frog caught in a snake's mouth, a bird caught in a cage, or a deer caught in a hunter's snare, the practitioner, being fearful of, dissatisfied with, and taking no delight in any kind of becoming in any realm or abode of existence, wishes only for deliverance from the cycle of rebirth.

**Muchū mondō**. (夢中問答). In Japanese, "Questions and Answers in Dreams," a primer on ZEN (C. CHAN) training attributed to the RINZAISHŪ master MUSŌ SOSEKI (1275–1351). The *Muchū mondō* is a record of the answers given by Musō to the questions regarding Zen asked by Ashikaga Tadayoshi (1306–1352), the brother of the shōgun Ashikaga Takauji (1305–1358). In total, Tadayoshi and Musō exchanged ninety-three sets of questions and answers that covered a wide range of subjects, including everything from praying for merit to the study of kōans (C. GONG'AN) and the practice of seated meditation (J. zazen; C. ZUOCHAN). Due to its simple and clear discussion of topics relevant to a lay audience, the *Muchū mondō* has been widely read within the tradition and republished often.

**Mucilinda**. [alt. Mahāmucilinda] (P. Mucalinda; T. Btang bzung; C. Muzhenlintuo; J. Mokushinrinda; K. Mokchillinda 目眞隣陀). In Sanskrit, the name of a snake divinity (NĀGA) who is said to have sheltered GAUTAMA Buddha while he was meditating following his enlightenment. According to the Pāli account, Mucalinda (S. Mucilinda) was the eponymous name of the nāga king of the Mucalinda tree, which was located in URUVILVĀ, along the bank of the NERAÑJARĀ river near the BODHI TREE in BODHGAYĀ, the site of the Buddha's enlightenment. In the third week following his enlightenment, the Buddha was meditating there, experiencing the bliss of enlightenment, when a severe thunderstorm broke out. Seeing that the Buddha was in danger, the nāga king of the tree (whom the commentaries say lived in a pond next to the tree), coiled himself around the Buddha seven times and then spread his hood over him like an umbrella to protect him from the storm. In other accounts, the nāga king resides in the Mucilinda lake, which is located just south of the present-day site of the MAHĀBODHI TEMPLE at Bodhgayā, and the event occurs in the sixth week following the enlightenment. In some versions of the story, once the storm had passed, the nāga transformed himself into a youth who then paid his respects before the buddha. The scene is a frequent subject of Buddhist art, where Mucilinda is often depicted in multiheaded form (often with seven heads). The story of Mucilinda is also exuberantly told in the LALITAVISTARA as well as in various MAHĀYĀNA sources.

**muditā**. (T. dga' ba; C. xi; J. ki; K. hŭi 喜). In Sanskrit and Pāli, "joy" or "sympathetic joy"; the third of the four divine abidings (BRAHMAVIHĀRA) and four immeasurables (APRAMĀṆA). Sympathetic joy is the attitude of taking delight in the happiness and good fortune of others and is the opposite of jealousy and envy. The other three divine abidings and immeasurables are MAITRĪ (loving-kindness), KARUṆĀ (compassion), and UPEKṢĀ (equanimity). The divine abidings are used for the cultivation of tranquillity or serenity meditation (ŚAMATHA). Of the four divine abidings, sympathetic joy, along with loving-kindness and compassion, is capable of producing the first three of four states of meditative absorption (DHYĀNA). Equanimity alone is capable of producing the fourth dhyāna. In the VISUDDHIMAGGA, sympathetic joy is listed as one among forty possible meditative topics (KAMMAṬṬHĀNA). The text indicates that, along with the other three divine abidings, sympathetic joy is used only for the cultivation of tranquillity, not to cultivate insight (P. VIPASSANĀ; S. VIPAŚYANĀ).

**mudrā**. (P. muddā; T. phyag rgya; C. yin; J. in; K. in 印). In Sanskrit, lit., "seal," "mark," or "sign"; but in Buddhist contexts it often refers to hand and arm "gestures" made during the course of ritual practice or depicted in images of buddhas, bodhisattvas, tantric deities, and other Buddhist images. Mudrās commonly associated with figures of the Buddha, such as the "gesture of fearlessness" (ABHAYAMUDRĀ), the "earth-touching gesture" (BHŪMISPARŚAMUDRĀ), the "wheel of the dharma gesture" (DHARMACAKRAMUDRĀ), and the "gesture of meditation" (DHYĀNAMUDRĀ), are found in the earliest Indian representations of ŚĀKYAMUNI. With the development of MAHĀYĀNA and VAJRAYĀNA iconography, the number of mudrās depicted in Buddhist art proliferated, until they numbered in the hundreds. They are a prominent feature in the vajrayāna artwork of the Himalayan region (northern India, Nepal, Tibet, and Bhutan) as well as early tantric images from Southeast Asia and the esoteric traditions of East Asia. Mudrās are also dynamic hand movements performed during the course of tantric ritual practice, where they may symbolize material offerings, enact forms of worship, or signify relationships with visualized deities. ¶ In a more specifically tantric denotation, the term mudrā is used to refer to a sexual consort, of which there are two types: the JÑĀNAMUDRĀ (a visualized consort) and the KARMAMUDRĀ (an actual consort). The highest state of realization in certain tantric systems is called MAHĀMUDRĀ, the great seal. See also ABHAYAMUDRĀ; AÑJALIMUDRĀ; BHŪTAḌĀMARAMUDRĀ; BODHYAṄGĪMUDRĀ; DAINICHI KEN-IN; HŪṂKĀRAMUDRĀ; HŌSHU-IN; ONGYŌ-IN; TARJANĪMUDRĀ; VARADAMUDRĀ; VITARKAMUDRĀ.

**Mugai Nyodai**. (無外如大) (1223–1298). Influential nun, who became Japan's first female ZEN master. A daughter of the powerful Adachi clan, Mugai entered the cloister and became a student of émigré teacher WUXUE ZUYUAN (J. Mugaku Sogen, 1226–1286). Wuxue was a Chinese CHAN master in the LINJI ZONG (J. RINZAISHŪ), who reluctantly came to Japan in 1279 at the invitation of Hōjō Tokimune (1251–1284), the eighth regent of the Kamakura shogunate, to escape the depredations of the Mongol troops then invading China. Nyodai eventually became a dharma heir (J. hassu; C. FASI) in WUXUE's Rinzai lineage, together with the imperial scion and monk KŌHŌ KENNICHI (1241–1316). Nyodai later founded Keiaiji, a Rinzai

Zen convent in the Japanese capital of Kyōto, which eventually became the leading cloister of the five mountain convent system (amadera gozan), the nun's counterpart of the five mountain (GOZAN) monastery system of the Kamakura.

**Mugujŏnggwang taedarani kyŏng**. (S. Raśmivimalaviśuddhaprabhādhāraṇī; T. 'Od zer dri ma med pa rnam par dag pa'i 'od gzungs; C. Wugoujingguang datuoluoni jing; J. Mukujōkō daidaranikyō 無垢淨光大陀羅尼經). In Korean, "Great DHĀRAṆĪ Scripture of Immaculate Radiance"; the world's oldest extant printed text, printed c. 751 CE in Silla dynasty Korea. The woodblock printing of the text was rediscovered in 1966 during reconstruction of the Sŏkka t'ap (ŚĀKYAMUNI STŪPA) at the royal monastery of PULGUKSA in the ancient Silla capital of KYŎNGJU. The terminus ad quem for its printing is 751 CE, when the text was sealed inside the Sŏkka t'ap, but since the colophon to the *Dhāraṇī* states that it was translated into Chinese in 704 by *Mitraśānta, the printing may well have occurred decades earlier. The dhāraṇī was printed using xylographic (woodblock) technology, in which the Sinographs are carved on specially cured wood in mirror image, then an impression taken off the blocks with ink.

**Muhak Chach'o**. (無學自超) (1327–1405). A Korean SŎN monk and pilgrim during the transition from the Koryŏ to the Chosŏn dynasty; Muhak was a native of Samgi (present-day South Kyŏngsang province). After his ordination in 1344, Muhak traveled to different monasteries to study. In 1353, he went to China, where he met the Indian ĀCĀRYA ZHIKONG CHANXIAN (d. 1363; K. Chigong Sŏnhyŏn; S. *Śūnyadiśya-Dhyānabhadra) and studied under his Korean student NAONG HYEGŬN at the Yuan-dynasty capital of Yanjing. Muhak returned to Korea in 1356. When Naong returned two years later, Muhak continued his studies under him at the hermitage of Wŏnhyoam on Mt. Ch'ŏnsŏng. In 1392, shortly after the establishment of the Chosŏn dynasty, Muhak was invited to the palace as the king's personal instructor (wangsa) and given the title Venerable Myoŏm (Subtle Adornment). He was also asked to reside at the royal monastery of Hoeamsa. In 1393, Muhak assisted the Chosŏn-dynasty founder, King T'aejo (r. 1392–1398), in deciding on the location for the new capital in Hanyang (present-day Seoul). Among his writings, Muhak's history of the Korean Sŏn tradition, *Pulcho chongp'a chido*, is still extant.

**Mujaku Dōchū**. (無着道忠) (1653–1744). Japanese ZEN master and historian of the RINZAISHŪ. Mujaku was a native of Tajima in present-day Hyōgo prefecture. He entered the monastery at a young age and was ordained by the monk Jikuin Somon (d.u.) at the monastery of Ryūgein. At the age of twenty-two, Mujaku followed his teacher Jikuin to Daijōji, where the latter was invited as its founding abbot (kaisan; C. KAISHAN). Later that same year, Jikuin was invited to MYŌSHINJI as its abbot and again Mujaku followed. In 1707, Mujaku himself became the abbot of Myōshinji and served again as abbot in 1714. He retired to Ryūgein in 1722 and devoted much of his time to his writing. Mujaku was a prolific writer who is said to have composed more than 370 works. His works include commentaries on various scriptures and discourse records (YULU) of CHAN and Zen masters, monastic regulations for the Zen community (see QINGGUI), histories of temples and monasteries, and dictionaries of Zen terms and vernacular phrases. His work thus serves as an invaluable tool for studying the history, doctrine, ritual, daily behavior, and language of the Zen tradition.

**Mujū Ichien**. (無住一圓) (1227–1312). A Japanese monk during the Kamakura period; also known as Mujū Dōgyō. He was born into a warrior family and became a monk at the age of eighteen. Mujū studied the doctrines of various sects, including the Hossōshū, SHINGONSHŪ, TENDAISHŪ, and JŌDOSHŪ, and received ZEN training from the RINZAISHŪ monk ENNI BEN'EN (1202–1280). In 1262, Mujū built Chōboji (Matriarchal Longevity Monastery) in Owari (present-day Nagoya, a port city in the center of the main Japanese island of Honshū), where he spent the rest of his life. Although affiliated with the Rinzaishū, Mujū took an ecumenical approach to Buddhism, arguing that all the different teachings of Buddhism were skillful means of conveying the religion's ultimate goal; he even denounced NICHIREN (1222–1382) for his contemporary's exclusivist attitude toward his own eponymous sect. Mujū was also famous for his collections of Japanese folklore, such as the SHASEKISHŪ ("Sand and Pebbles Collection"), written between 1279 and 1283; his *Tsuma kagami* ("Mirror for Wives") of 1300; and his 1305 *Zōdanshū* ("Collection of Random Conversations"). In particular, in the *Shasekishū*, Mujū introduced the idea of the "unity of spirits and buddhas" (SHINBUTSU SHŪGŌ), describing the Japanese indigenous gods, or KAMI, as various manifestations of the Buddha.

**Mujun**. (K) (無準). See KIHWA.

**Mukai nanshin**. [alt. Bukai nanshin] (霧海南針). In Japanese, "A Compass on the Misty Sea"; a Japanese vernacular sermon (kana hōgo) written in 1666 for a lay woman by the Japanese ŌBAKUSHŪ monk CHŌON DŌKAI and published in 1672. The *Mukai nanshin* provides an explanation of ZEN practice with reference to the four great vows (SI HONGSHIYUAN) and the six perfections (PĀRAMITĀ) of the BODHISATTVA. The *Mukai nanshin* also contains criticisms of other contemporary teachings, especially that of Zen kōan (C. GONG'AN) training as then practiced in Japanese Zen. Both the RINZAISHŪ and SŌTŌSHŪ of the Zen school during the Tokugawa period relied heavily upon the rote memorization of kōans and capping phrases (JAKUGO) and tended to ignore the study of the literary content of the kōans due to their lack of formal training in classical Chinese. Ōbaku monks like Chōon, under the influence of their Chinese émigré teachers, began to criticize this tendency within the Zen community in Japan.

**Mukan Fumon**. (無關普門) (1212–1291). Japanese proper name of RINZAISHŪ monk and first abbot of NANZENJI; also known as Gengo. Mukan was born in Hoshina in Shinano province (present-day Nagano prefecture) and received the BODHISATTVA precepts around 1230 at a monastery affiliated with MYŌAN EISAI's (1141–1215) lineage. He became versed at Japanese exoteric and esoteric Buddhist teachings, and traveled around the eastern part of Japan, especially the Kantō and Tōhoku regions, to lecture. Between 1243 and 1249, Mukan studied under ENNI BEN'EN (1202–1280). Mukan traveled to China in 1251, where he received transmission from Duanqiao Miaolun (1201–1261), the tenth-generation master in the YANGQI PAI collateral lineage of the LINJI ZONG, before returning to Japan in 1263. Mukan became the third abbot of Tōhukuji in 1281 and was later appointed in 1291 by the cloistered Emperor Kameyama (r. 1260–1274) to be the founding abbot (J. kaisan; C. KAISHAN) of Nanzenji. There is a well-known story about his appointment as the Nazenji abbot. The monastery was originally built as a royal palace, but soon after the emperor moved there, ghosts began to haunt it. After several other monks failed to exorcise the ghosts, the emperor finally invited Mukan to try. Mukan succeeded in removing the ghosts by conducting Zen meditation with his disciples. In gratitude, the emperor turned the palace into a Rinzai monastery and appointed Mukan its abbot.

**mūla**. (T. rtsa; C. gen; J. kon; K. kŭn 根). In Sanskrit and Pāli, "root" or "faculty"; referring specifically to three unwholesome or nonvirtuous (AKUŚALA) and three wholesome or virtuous (KUŚALA) roots or faculties that determine the moral quality of volition and volitional action (CETANĀ), the latter being essentially equivalent to the catalyst of action (KARMAN). The three unwholesome roots are greed (LOBHA), hatred (DVEṢA) and delusion (MOHA). The three wholesome roots are nongreed (ALOBHA), nonhatred (ADVEṢA), and nondelusion (AMOHA). Greed encompasses everything from the mildest desire for something to the grossest form of lust and arises through unsystematic attention (AYONIŚOMANASKĀRA) to alluring objects. Hatred encompasses everything from the mildest dislike of something to the most intense feelings of rage and arises through unsystematic attention to unattractive objects. The expression "wholesome faculties" or "virtuous roots" (KUŚALAMŪLA) refers not only to the absence of such unwholesome states but also to the presence of virtuous states. Thus, for example, nongreed refers to liberality and generosity, nonhatred to kindness, and nondelusion to wisdom, etc. As an antidote to greed, the perception of impurity (AŚUBHA) in objects is to be cultivated. As an antidote to hatred, loving-kindness (MAITRĪ) is to be cultivated. As an antidote to delusion, wisdom (PRAJÑĀ) is to be cultivated. The term mūla is used sometimes to refer to these attitudes that produce wholesome or unwholesome actions, and sometimes to refer to the positive and negative actions themselves, including those performed in previous lives. See also KUŚALAMŪLA; MOKṢABHĀGĪYA; NIRVEDHABHĀGĪYA; SAMMUCCHINNAKUŚALAMŪLA.

**mūlakleśa**. (T. rtsa ba'i nyon mongs; C. genben fannao; J. konpon bonnō; K. kŭnbon pŏnnoe 根本煩惱). In Sanskrit, "root afflictions," "basic afflictions"; a subcategory of the forty-six mental concomitants (CAITTA) according to the SARVĀSTIVĀDA school of ABHIDHARMA and fifty-one according to the YOGĀCĀRA school. It comprises the fundamental negative mental states, enumerated as six: sensuality (RĀGA), anger (PRATIGHA), pride (MĀNA), ignorance (AVIDYĀ), doubt (VICIKITSĀ), and views (DṚṢṬI). They are called root afflictions because they are the sources of all other afflictions, and are distinguished from the "secondary afflictions" (UPAKLEŚA), which are narrower in applicability. The list is also closely related to the three poisons (TRIVIṢA) of sensuality or greed (rāga or LOBHA), hatred or aversion (DVEṢA), and delusion (MOHA).

**Mūlamadhyamakakārikā**. (T. Dbu ma rtsa ba'i tshig le'u byas pa; C. Zhong lun; J. Chūron; K. Chung non 中論). In Sanskrit, "Root Verses on the Middle Way"; the magnum opus of the second-century Indian master NĀGĀRJUNA; also known as the *Prajñānāmamūlamadhyamakakārikā* and the *Madhyamakaśāstra*. (The Chinese analogue of this text is the *Zhong lun*, which renders the title as MADHYAMAKAŚĀSTRA. This Chinese version was edited and translated by KUMĀRAJĪVA. Kumārajīva's edition, however, includes not only Nāgārjuna's verses but also Piṅgala's commentary to the verses.) The most widely cited and commented upon of Nāgārjuna's works in India, the *Mūlamadhyamakakārikā*, was the subject of detailed commentaries by such figures as BUDDHAPĀLITA, BHĀVAVIVEKA, and CANDRAKĪRTI (with Candrakīrti's critique of Bhāvaviveka's criticism of a passage in Buddhapālita's commentary providing the locus classicus for the later Tibetan division of MADHYAMAKA into *SVĀTANTRIKA and *PRĀSAṄGIKA). In East Asia, it was one of the three basic texts of the "Three Treatises" school (C. SAN LUN ZONG), and was central to TIANTAI philosophy. Although lost in the original Sanskrit as an independent work, the entire work is preserved within the Sanskrit text of Candrakīrti's commentary, the PRASANNAPADĀ (serving as one reason for the influence of Candrakīrti's commentary in the European reception of the *Mūlamadhyamakakārikā*). The work is composed of 448 verses in twenty-seven chapters. The topics of the chapters (as provided by Candrakīrti) are the analysis of: (1) conditions (PRATYAYA), (2) motion, (3) the eye and the other sense faculties (INDRIYA), (4) aggregates (SKANDHA), (5) elements (DHĀTU), (6) passion and the passionate, (7) the conditioned (in the sense of production, abiding, disintegration), (8) action and agent, (9) prior existence, (10) fire and fuel, (11) the past and future limits of SAṂSĀRA, (12) suffering, (13) the conditioned (SAṂSKĀRA), (14) contact (saṃsarga), (15) intrinsic nature (SVABHĀVA), (16) bondage and liberation, (17) action and effect, (18) self, (19) time, (20) assemblage (sāmagrī), (21) arising and dissolving, (22) the TATHĀGATA, (23) error, (24) the FOUR NOBLE TRUTHS, (25) NIRVĀṆA, (26), the twelve links of dependent origination (PRATĪTYASAMUTPĀDA), and (27) views. The tone of the work is set in its famous homage to the Buddha, which opens the work,

"I bow down to the perfect Buddha, the best of teachers, who taught that what is dependently arisen is without cessation, without production, without annihilation, without permanence, without coming, without going, without difference, without sameness, pacified of elaboration, at peace." The *Mūlamadhyamakakārikā* offers a relentless examination of many of the most important categories of Buddhist thought, subjecting them to an analysis that reveals the absurd consequences that follow from imagining any of them to be real in the sense of possessing an independent and intrinsic nature (SVABHĀVA). Nāgārjuna demonstrates repeatedly that these various categories only exist relationally and only function heuristically in a worldly and transactional sense; they do not exist ultimately. Thus, in the first chapter, Nāgārjuna examines production via causes and conditions, one of the hallmarks of Buddhist thought, and declares that a thing is not produced from itself, from something other than itself, from something that is both itself and other, or from something that is neither itself nor the other. He examines the four kinds of conditions, declaring each to lack an intrinsic nature, such that they do not exist because they do not produce anything. In the second chapter, Nāgārjuna examines motion, seeking to determine precisely where motion occurs: on the path already traversed, the path being traversed, or on the path not yet traversed. He concludes that motion is not to be found on any of these three. In the twenty-fifth chapter, he subjects nirvāṇa to a similar analysis, finding it to be neither existent, nonexistent, both existent and nonexistent, nor neither existent nor nonexistent. (These are the famous CATUṢKOṬI, the "four alternatives," or tetralemma.) Therefore, nirvāṇa, like saṃsāra and all worldly phenomena, is empty of intrinsic nature, leading Nāgārjuna to declare (at XXV.19), in one of his most famous and widely misinterpreted statements, that there is not the slightest difference between saṃsāra and nirvāṇa. The thoroughgoing negative critique or apophasis in which Nāgārjuna engages leads to charges of nihilism, charges that he faces directly in the text, especially in the twenty-fourth chapter on the four noble truths where he introduces the topic of the two truths (SATYADVAYA)—ultimate truth (PARAMĀRTHASATYA) and conventional truth (SAṂVṚTISATYA)—declaring the importance of both in understanding correctly the doctrine of the Buddha. Also in this chapter, he discusses the danger of misunderstanding emptiness (ŚŪNYATĀ), and the relation between emptiness and dependent origination ("That which is dependent origination we explain as emptiness. This is a dependent designation; just this is the middle path"). To those who would object that emptiness renders causation and change impossible, he counters that if things existed independently and intrinsically, there could be no transformation; "for whom emptiness is possible, everything is possible." There has been considerable scholarly discussion of Nāgārjuna's target audience for this work, with the consensus being that it is intended for Buddhist monks well versed in ABHIDHARMA literature, especially that associated with the SARVĀSTIVĀDA school; many of the categories to which Nāgārjuna subjects his critique are derived from this school. In the Sarvāstivāda abhidharma, these categories and factors (DHARMA) are posited to be endowed with a certain reality, a reality that Nāgārjuna sees as implying permanence, independence, and autonomy. He seeks to reveal the absurd consequences and hence the impossibility of the substantial existence of these categories and factors. Through his critique, he seeks a new understanding of these fundamental tenets of Buddhist philosophy in light of the doctrine of emptiness as set forth in the PRAJÑĀPĀRAMITĀ SŪTRAs. He does not cite these sūtras directly, however, nor does he mention the MAHĀYĀNA, which he extols regularly in other of his works. Instead, he seeks to demonstrate how the central Buddhist doctrine of causation, expressed as dependent origination (pratītyasamutpāda), necessarily entails emptiness (śūnyatā). The understanding of emptiness is essential in order to abandon false views (MITHYĀDṚṢṬI). Nāgārjuna therefore sees his purpose not to reject the standard categories of Buddhist thought but to reinterpret them in such a way that they become conduits for, rather than impediments to, liberation from suffering, in keeping with the Buddha's intent.

**Mūlamahāsāṃghika**. (T. Gzhi dge 'dun phal chen pa; C. Genben Dazhong bu; J. Konpon Daishubu; K. Kŭnbon Taejung pu 根本大衆部). In Sanskrit, the "Root" or "Fundamental Great Congregation"; one of the nine subdivisions of the MAHĀSĀṂGHIKA school of mainstream Buddhism. The other eight are EKAVYAVAHĀRIKA, LOKOTTARAVĀDA, KAUKKUṬIKA, BAHUŚRUTĪYA, PRAJÑAPTIVĀDA, CAITYA, Avaraśaila, and Uttaraśaila.

**Mūlapariyāyasutta**. (C. Xiang jing; J. Sōkyō; K. Sang kyŏng 想經). In Pāli, "Discourse on the Root Instruction" or the "Roots of Phenomena"; the first sutta in the MAJJHIMANIKĀYA (an untitled recension of uncertain affiliation appears in the Chinese translation of the EKOTTARĀGAMA; there is also a related SARVĀSTIVĀDA recension that appears as the 102nd SŪTRA in the Chinese translation of the MADHYAMĀGAMA). Preached to a gathering of monks in Ukkaṭṭhā, the Buddha explains the basis of all phenomena under twenty-four categories (e.g., the four material elements, the heavens, sensory cognition, etc.), noting that the nature of these phenomena is truly knowable only by a TATHĀGATA. The Buddha describes the different cognitive capacities of four types of persons: ordinary worldlings (PṚTHAGJANA), disciples engaged in higher training, worthy ones (ARHAT), and perfect buddhas (SAMYAKSAṂBUDDHA).

**Mūlasarvāstivāda**. (T. Gzhi thams cad yod par smra ba; C. Genben Shuoyiqieyou bu; J. Konpon Setsuissaiubu; K. Kŭnbon Sŏrilch'eyu pu 根本說一切有部). In Sanskrit, lit., "Root SARVĀSTIVĀDA"; a subsect of the SARVĀSTIVĀDA (lit. "Everything Exists"), one of the "mainstream" (i.e., non-Mahāyāna) schools (NIKĀYA) of Indian Buddhism. The differences between the Mūlasarvāstivāda and the Sarvāstivāda are not entirely clear, but they are differentiated less by doctrinal disagreements than by disputes over VINAYA. There is virtually no evidence in Indian inscriptions of the term "Mūlasarvāstivāda," suggesting that it did not have an independent sectarian identity; to the contrary, however, some Chinese pilgrims to India mention only the former term. The scholarly consensus is that the designation Mūlasarvāstivāda seems to have originated in a dispute over vinaya recensions between the Sarvāstivāda school of MATHURĀ in north-central India and the northwestern Sarvāstivāda school in the KASHMIR-GANDHĀRA region. By calling their vinaya recension the MŪLASARVĀSTIVĀDA VINAYA—the "root" or "source" of the Sarvāstivāda vinaya in one interpretation—the Mathurā sect was claiming its primacy over other strands of the Sarvāstivāda school, especially this northwest branch, and essentially asserting that the Kashmiri Sarvāstivāda school was an offshoot of the Mathurā community. After the northwestern school fell into decline, the Mathurā school may also have adopted this name to demonstrate its preeminence as the "original," "root," or "foundational" Sarvāstivāda school. Their Mūlasarvāstivāda vinaya proved to be extremely important in the history of Buddhism by providing the foundation for monastic practice in the mature Tibetan traditions of Buddhism.

**Mūlasarvāstivāda vinaya**. (T. Gzhi thams cad yod par smra ba'i 'dul ba; C. Genben Shuoyiqieyou bu pinaiye; J. Konpon Setsuissaiubu binaya; K. Kŭnbon Sŏrilch'eyubu pinaeya 根本說一切有部毘奈耶). In Sanskrit, the "Monastic Code of the MŪLASARVĀSTIVĀDA," or "Original Monastic Code of the SARVĀSTIVĀDA School"; one of the six extant recensions of the VINAYA. Divergences between their respective monastic codes were one of the principal differentiating characteristics of the various mainstream schools of Indian Buddhism. The attempt to differentiate the Mūlasarvāstivāda vinaya from the Sarvāstivāda vinaya (both of which are extant in Chinese translation) may well derive from a polemical claim by the MATHURĀ branch of the Sarvāstivāda school in north-central India that their tradition comprised the "root" or "foundational" monastic code of the school. Whatever the precise denotation of the term, the Mūlasarvāstivāda vinaya, is by far the longest of the extant vinayas—by some calculations some four times longer than any of its counterparts. The Mūlasarvāstivāda vinaya contains some material that suggests it may belong to one of the earliest strata of the vinaya literature. The text was composed in Sanskrit in the first or second centuries CE, but only a few Sanskrit fragments have been discovered at GILGIT. The code is preserved in full only in Tibetan translation, although there is also a partial (but still massive) Chinese translation made by YIJING (635–713) in the late seventh and early eighth centuries. The code details 253 rules and regulations for fully ordained monks (BHIKṢU) and 364 rules for fully ordained nuns (BHIKṢUNĪ) as well as precepts for male and female lay practitioners (UPĀSAKA and UPĀSIKĀ), male and female novices (ŚRĀMAṆERA and ŚRĀMAṆERIKĀ), and female probationers (ŚIKṢAMĀṆĀ). Because each rule requires an explanation of how it came to be established, the text is a vast source of stories (many of which do not appear in other codes) that provide essential insights into Buddhist monastic life at the time of its composition. The collection also includes discussions of areas of monastic life that receive short shrift in other recensions, such as how to escort images on procession through town or lend the SAṂGHA's money with interest to laypeople. The Mūlasarvāstivāda vinaya also includes many narratives (AVADĀNA) and stories, including one of the earliest Sanskrit accounts of the life of the Buddha, as well as SŪTRAs that in other mainstream traditions appear in the scripture section of the canon (SŪTRAPIṬAKA). Because of its eclectic content, the Mūlasarvāstivāda vinaya functions almost as proto-canon (TRIPIṬAKA). The Mūlasarvāstivāda vinaya is the monastic code still followed today in the Tibetan traditions of Buddhism, where it is studied primarily via the summary composed by GUṆAPRABHA, entitled the VINAYASŪTRA.

**Mūlasāsana**. In Pāli, the "Origin of the Religion"; a Pāli chronicle composed in northern Thailand during the early fifteenth century, prior to the CĀMADEVĪVAṂSA and JINAKĀLAMĀLĪ, both of which use it as a source. The work is written in the Tai-Yuan language, a dialect prevalent in the Lānnā Thai kingdom. The chronicle recounts how a reformed monastic tradition from Sri Lanka was introduced to Martaban (Muttama) in Lower Burma in the fourteenth century, and how this tradition was then spread to SUKHOTHAI and Chiengmai.

**mūlatantra**. (T. rtsa rgyud). In Sanskrit, "root tantra"; a term used to distinguish the foundational text in a given tantric cycle from the various addenda, commentaries, ritual texts, and SĀDHANAs connected with the TANTRA. Thus, one would speak, for example, of the root tantra of the GUHYASAMĀJA.

**mūlavijñāna**. (T. rtsa ba'i rnam shes; C. benshi; J. honjiki; K. ponsik 本識). In Sanskrit, lit. "root consciousness," "foundational consciousness"; a generic form of consciousness described within the MAHĀSĀṂGHIKA branch of the mainstream Buddhist schools, which was said to serve as the support for the six sensory consciousnesses, just as the root of a tree is the basis of the leaves. This concept of a root consciousness may have been the antecedent of the storehouse consciousness (ĀLAYAVIJÑĀNA) in the YOGĀCĀRA school; the term is sometimes used as an alternate name for that form of consciousness in Yogācāra materials.

**Müller, Friedrich Max**. (1823–1900). Arguably the most famous Indologist of the nineteenth century, born in Dessau, the capital of the duchy of Anhalt-Dessau, son of the famous Romantic poet Wilhelm Müller. He studied Sanskrit in Leipzig, receiving a doctorate in philology in 1843 at the age of twenty. In Berlin, he attended the lectures of Franz Bopp and Schelling. He went to Paris in 1846 where he studied with EUGÈNE BURNOUF, who suggested the project that would become his life's work, a critical edition of the *Ṛgveda*. In order to study the available manuscripts, he traveled to London and then settled in Oxford, where he would spend the rest of his life, eventually being appointed to a newly established professorship in comparative philology. Although best known for his work in philology, Indology, and comparative religion, Müller wrote essays and reviews on Buddhism throughout his career. Perhaps his greatest contribution to Buddhist studies came through his role as editor-in-chief of the Sacred Books of the East series, published between 1879 and 1910. Ten of the forty-nine volumes of the series were devoted to Buddhist works. Reflecting the opinion of the day that Pāli texts of the THERAVĀDA tradition represented the most accurate record of what the Buddha taught, seven of these volumes were devoted to Pāli works, with translations by THOMAS W. RHYS DAVIDS and HERMANN OLDENBERG, as well as a translation of the DHAMMAPADA by Müller himself. Among other Indian works, AŚVAGHOṢA's famous life of the Buddha appeared twice, translated in one volume from Sanskrit by E. B. Cowell and in another from Chinese by SAMUEL BEAL. HENDRIK KERN's translation of the SADDHARMAPUṆḌARĪKASŪTRA ("Lotus Sūtra") was included in another volume. The final volume of the series, entitled *Buddhist Mahāyāna Texts* (1894), included such famous works as the VAJRACCHEDIKĀPRAJÑĀPĀRAMITĀSŪTRA ("Diamond Sūtra"), the PRAJÑĀPĀRAMITĀHṚDAYASŪTRA ("Heart Sūtra"), and the three major PURE LAND sūtras, all Indian works (or at least so regarded at the time) but selected because of their importance for Japanese Buddhism. Müller's choice of these texts was influenced by two Japanese students: TAKAKUSU JUNJIRŌ and NANJŌ BUN'YŪ, both JŌDO SHINSHŪ adherents who had gone to Oxford in order to study Indology with Müller. Upon their return, they introduced to Japanese academe the philological study of Buddhism from Sanskrit and Pāli sources. The works in *Buddhist Mahāyāna Texts* were translated by Müller, with the exception of the GUAN WULIANGSHOU JING (**Amitāyurdhyānasūtra*), which was translated by Takakusu. In his final years, with financial support of the King of Siam, Müller began editing the Sacred Books of the Buddhists series, which was taken over by T. W. Rhys Davids upon Müller's death in 1900.

**Mun, Ajahn**. See AJAHN MUN BHŪRIDATTA.

**muni**. (T. thub pa; C. mouni/shengzhe; J. muni/shōja; K. moni/sŏngja 牟尼/聖者). In Sanskrit and Pāli, "sage"; used in India to refer various seers, saints, ascetics, monks, and hermits, especially those who have taken vows of silence. In Buddhism, the term is used in reference to both the Buddha and PRATYEKABUDDHAs, more rarely to ARHATs. It figures in two of the most common epithets of the Buddha: ŚĀKYAMUNI, or "Sage of the Śākya Clan," and MAHĀMUNI, or "Great Sage." The term also figures in the name MANTRA of the Buddha, "oṃ muni muni mahāmuni Śākyamuni svāhā."

**mūrdhagata**. (S). See MŪRDHAN.

**mūrdhan**. (T. rtse mo; C. ding; J. chō; K. chŏng 頂). In Sanskrit, "summit," or "peak," or "climax"; the second of the "aids to penetration" (NIRVEDHABHĀGĪYA); these aids are developed during the PRAYOGAMĀRGA (path of preparation) and mark the transition from the mundane path of cultivation (LAUKIKABHĀVANĀMĀRGA) to supramundane vision (viz., DARŚANAMĀRGA) on both the HĪNAYĀNA and MAHĀYĀNA paths. Mūrdhan is defined specifically in terms of faith in the validity of the FOUR NOBLE TRUTHS (catvāry āryasatāni), a faith that begins to develop at the level of ŪṢMAN (heat), the first of the aids to penetration, and reaches its "summit" or "climax" at the level of mūrdhan. This stage is called "summit," the ABHIDHARMAMAHĀVIBHĀṢĀ explains, because it is like the summit of a mountain, where one cannot tarry long: either you continue on to ascend another peak or you retreat back down the mountain. Therefore, if one has no difficulties, one will progress on to KṢĀNTI (forbearance); but if one meets with problems, one will retrogress back to ūṣman. Thus, mūrdhan and ūṣman, the first two of the nirvedhabhāgīyas, are still subject to retrogression and thus belong to the mundane path of cultivation (laukikabhāvanāmārga). Mūrdhan marks the end of the possibility of the wholesome faculties (KUŚALAMŪLA) created by past salutary deeds being destroyed by unwholesome mental states, such as anger. The kuśalamūla are no longer susceptible to destruction from this point on the path forward to the achievement of the state of the ARHAT or buddha.

**Musang**. (K) (無相). See CHŎNGJUNG MUSANG.

**muṣitasmṛti**. (P. muṭṭhassati; T. brjed nges; C. shinian; J. shitsunen; K. sillyŏm 失念). In Sanskrit, "inattentiveness," "negligence," or "forgetfulness"; one of the forty-six mental concomitants (CAITTA) according to the SARVĀSTIVĀDA school of ABHIDHARMA (where the term is also called smṛtināśa) and one of the fifty-one according to the YOGĀCĀRA school. Within this group, it falls into the category of the "secondary afflictions" (UPAKLEŚA). "Inattentiveness" refers to the lack of clarity caused by the failure to attend properly to and be mindful of either the present moment or an intended object of attention, or the failure to recollect what had transpired in the immediately preceding moments. It involves the inattentiveness to virtuous objects, thus leading to attention to nonvirtuous objects. The term is taken to be one of the possible derivative mental states of "ignorance" (AVIDYĀ), because it causes the mind to become distracted to the objects of the afflictions. It is the opposite of "attentiveness," "proper recollection," and "presence of mind" (SMṚTI).

**Musō Soseki**. (夢窓疎石) (1275–1351). Japanese ZEN master in the RINZAISHŪ. A native of Ise, he became a monk at a young age and studied the teachings of the TENDAISHŪ. Musō's interests later shifted toward Zen and he became the student of the Zen master KŌHŌ KENNICHI. After receiving dharma transmission from Kōhō, Musō led an itinerant life, moving from one monastery to the next. In 1325, he received a decree from Emperor Godaigo (r. 1318–1339) to assume the abbotship of the powerful monastery of NANZENJI in Kyōto. The following year, he went to Kamakura, where he served as abbot of the influential monasteries of Jōchiji, Zuisenji, and ENGAKUJI. Later, he returned to Nanzenji at the request of the emperor. In 1333, Emperor Godaigo triumphantly returned to Kyōto and gave Musō the monastery Rinsenji and the title of state preceptor (kokushi; C. GUOSHI). After the emperor's death in 1339, Musō established the new monastery of TENRYŪJI with the help of the shōgun Ashikakga Takauji (1305–1358) and became its founding abbot (J. kaisan; C. KAISHAN). In this manner, Musō came to serve as abbot of many of the top-ranking monasteries of the GOZAN system. His disciples came to dominate the medieval Zen community and played important roles in the rise of gozan culture. His teachings are recorded in the *Musōroku*, *Musō hōgo*, and MUCHŪ MONDŌ.

**Muyong Suyŏn**. (無用秀演) (1651–1719). Korean scholastic (KYO) monk of the Chosŏn dynasty. Muyong lost both parents at the age of thirteen and lived with his elder brother, until he decided in 1669 to become a monk at the monastery of SONGGWANGSA. Three years later, he went to the monastery of SŎNAMSA to continue his studies under Ch'imgoeng Hyŏnbyŏn (1616–1684). At Ch'imgoeng's recommendation, Muyong became a disciple of the eminent SŎN master PAEGAM SŎNGCH'ONG (1631–1700) at Songgwangsa. In 1680, Muyong held a public lecture at Sinsŏnam in the vicinity of Chinggwangsa. In order to accommodate the large number of people coming to his lectures, Muyong is said to have moved back to the larger monasteries of Sŏnamsa and Songgwangsa. Muyong at one point went into retreat to meditate, but he was forced to return to teaching at the request of all those people who wished to attend his lectures. He also assisted in Paegam's publication of Buddhist scriptures. After Paegam's death, he taught at the hermitage of Ch'ilburam. In 1719, when his disciple Yakt'an (1668–1754) organized a great assembly to study Hwaŏm (C. HUAYAN) doctrine and verse commentaries to the public cases (K. kongan; C. GONG'AN) of the Chan masters of old, Muyong was asked to preside. His essays, letters, and poems are collected in the *Muyongdang chip*.

**muyu**. (J. mokugyo; K. mogŏ 木魚). In Chinese, literally "wooden fish"; referring to a wooden percussion instrument carved in the shape of a fish, which is commonly used in Chinese Buddhist monasteries to summon monks and nuns to daily events and to mark time during rituals. It is one of the four percussion instruments (see DRUM), together with the Brahmā bell, dharma drum, and cloud-shaped gong. Various explanations are given for its fish-like shape. According to the BAIZHANG QINGGUI ("Baizhang's Rules of Purity"), since a fish's eyes are never closed, the wooden fish is a subtle admonition to monks and nuns to remain ever vigilant about their practice. The TIANTAI monastic code, *Jiaoyuan Qinggui* ("Rules of Purity for the Garden of the Teachings"), includes a story said to come from the ABHIDHARMAMAHĀVIBHĀṢĀ, about a monk who had been reborn as a fish with a tree growing out of his back, which was retribution for betraying his teacher and slandering the dharma in a prior lifetime. Whenever the tree swayed, the fish bled and felt great pain. One day, the monk's former teacher was crossing the sea in a boat and, seeing the fish, recognized it to be his former student. He performed the "rite of water and land" (C. SHUILU HUI), freeing the fish from its torment, and the fish repented for its past behavior. When his former student was again reborn, the tree was donated to a monastery, which carved it into the shape of a fish as a symbol of admonition. In a third story from a different source, the Chinese pilgrim XUANZANG was returning home from India and saved a wealthy man's three-year-old son from the stomach of a big fish. The man wanted to repay him for his deed, so Xuanzang instructed him to have a piece of wood carved in the shape of a fish and hung in the monastery for the benefit of the fish. Over time, the body depicted on the wooden fish began to take on more the look of a dragon, autochthonous water divinities in traditional China, with a dragon-like head with a talismanic pearl (MAṆI) in its mouth. In Korea, the muyu takes on the more abstract fish shape of the MOKT'AK (wooden clacker).

**Myōan Eisai**. (明庵榮西) (1141–1215). Japanese monk associated with the TENDAISHŪ (C. TIANTAI ZONG) and ZENSHŪ (C. CHAN ZONG) traditions; a successor in the HUANGLONG PAI collateral lineage of the Chinese LINJI ZONG, he was also the first monk to introduce the Chan school to Japan. Eisai became a monk at a young age and received the full monastic precepts on HIEIZAN, studying the Tendai teachings at the monastery of MIIDERA. In 1168, he left for China and made a pilgrimage to Mt. Tiantai and Mt. Ayuwang in present-day Zhejiang province. He returned to Japan that same year with numerous Tiantai texts of and made an effort to revitalize the Tendai tradition in Japan. In 1187, Eisai set out on another trip to China. This second time, he stayed for five years and studied under the Chan master Xu'an Huaichang (d.u.) on Mt. Tiantai. Eisai followed Xu'an to the monastery of Jingdesi on Mt. Tiantong when the latter was appointed its abbot in 1189. After receiving dharma transmission from Xu'an, Eisai returned to Japan in 1191. Eisai's efforts to spread the teachings of Zen was suppressed by his fellow Tendai monks of ENRYAKUJI despite his claim that the denial of Chan meant the denial of the teachings of SAICHŌ, the spiritual progenitor of Tendai. In 1198, Eisai composed his KŌZEN GOKOKURON, wherein he defended Zen and argued for its usefulness in governing the nation and protecting Japan from foreign invasion. In 1199, he traveled to Kamakura where he won the support of the new shogunate and became the founding abbot (J. kaisan; C. KAISHAN) of the monastery of Jufukuji. Three years later, the shōgun Minamoto Yoriie (1182–1204) established KENNINJI and appointed Eisai as its founding abbot. In 1214, he composed his treatise on tea, the KISSA YŌJŌKI, for Minamoto

Sanetomo (1192–1219) who suffered from ill health. At Kenninji, Eisai taught a form of Zen that reflected his training in the esoteric (MIKKYŌ) teachings of Tendai.

**Myoch'ŏng**. (妙淸) (d. 1135). Korean monk during the Koryŏ dynasty who used his geomantic prowess to exert political power and who eventually led a rebellion against the kingdom; also known as Chŏngsim. Myoch'ŏng was a native of Sŏgyŏng (lit. "Western Capital"; present-day P'yŏngyang). His teachings on geomancy and divination, known as TOCH'AM, were derived from the earlier geomantic theories of TOSŎN (827–898) and became widely influential in Korea, eventually leading to Myoch'ŏng becoming an advisor to the Koryŏ king in 1127. In an attempt to emphasize the independence of the Koryŏ kingdom from the Chinese Song dynasty, Myoch'ŏng also proposed that the king adopt the title emperor and advocated that Koryŏ invade the adjacent kingdom of Jin. Taking advantage of the political turmoil of his times, Myoch'ŏng also attempted (unsuccessfully) to persuade the king to move the Koryŏ capital from Kaesŏng to Sŏgyŏng, his own ancestral home, which he claimed was a more geomantically auspicious site. His suggestions were criticized by such conservative officials as Kim Pusik (1075–1151), the famous general and compiler of the Korean history *Samguk sagi*. His proposals to move the capital rebuffed, Myoch'ŏng and other sympathetic court officials rebelled against the state in 1135, establishing a new kingdom, Taewi, and declaring Sŏgyŏng its capital. Myoch'ŏng's troops were defeated by the royal army led by Kim Pusik, and Myoch'ŏng himself was eventually betrayed and killed by one of his own officers.

**Myōe Kōben**. (明慧高弁) (1173–1232). A Japanese SHINGONSHŪ monk who sought to revitalize the Kegonshū (C. HUAYAN ZONG) in Japan; commonly known as Myōe Shōnin. Kōben promoted traditional Buddhist values over the newer approaches of so-called Kamakura Buddhism. Against the prevailing tide of belief that the world was in terminal decline (J. mappō; C. MOFA), he took a positive stance on Buddhist practice by arguing that salvation could still be attained through traditional means. Kōben was born in Kii province (present-day Wakayama Prefecture) and orphaned at the age of eight when both parents died in separate incidents. He went to live under the care of his maternal uncle Jōgaku Gyōji, a Shingon monk at Jingoji on Mt. Takao, northwest of Kyōto. In 1188, at the age of sixteen, he was ordained by Jōgaku at TŌDAIJI. He took the ordination name Jōben and later adopted the name Kōben. After ordination, he studied Shingon, Kegon, and esoteric Buddhism (MIKKYŌ) at one of Tōdaiji's subtemples, Sonshōin. Kōben tried twice to travel on pilgrimage to India, first in the winter of 1202–1203 and second in the spring of 1205, but was unsuccessful. On his first trip, Kasuga, a spirit (KAMI) associated with the Fujiwara family shrine in Nara, is said to have possessed the wife of Kōben's uncle, Yuasa Munemitsu, and insisted that Kōben not leave Japan. In the second attempt, he fell ill before he set out on his trip. In both instances, Kōben believed that the Kasuga deity was warning him not to go, and he consequently abandoned his plans. These portents were supported by Fujiwara opposition to his voyage. In 1206, the retired emperor Gotoba gave Kōben a plot of land in Toganoo. Gotoba designated the temple there as Kegon, renamed it Kōzanji, and requested that Kōben revive the study of Kegon doctrine. A year later, Gotoba appointed him headmaster of Sonshōin with the hope of further expanding Kōben's promotion of the Kegon school. Despite this generous attention, Kōben focused little of his efforts on this mission. He initially built a hermitage for himself at Toganoo, and it was not until 1219 that he constructed the Golden Hall at Kōzanji. Kōben dismissed the newer schools of Buddhism in his day, particularly HŌNEN's (1122–1212) reinterpretation of pure land practice in the JŌDOSHŪ. In 1212, he denounced Hōnen's nenbutsu (C. NIANFO) practice in *Zaijarin* ("Refuting the False Vehicle"), a response to Hōnen's earlier work, *Senchaku hongan nenbutsu shū* ("Anthology of Selections on the Nenbutsu and the Original Vow"; see SENCHAKUSHŪ). In contrast to the Jōdoshū's exclusive advocacy of the single practice of reciting the Buddha's name, Kōben defended the traditional argument that there were many valid methods for reaching salvation. Kōben spent the last several decades of his life experimenting with ways to make Kegon doctrine accessible to a wider audience. In the end, however, his efforts were largely unsuccessful. He was unable to garner popular support, and his disciples never founded institutionally independent schools, as did the disciples of the other teachers of Kamakura Buddhism. Kōben was fascinated by his dreams and recorded many of them in a well-known text known as the *Yume no ki*, or "Dream Diary." Like most Japanese of his day, Kōben regarded many of these dreams to be portents coming directly from the buddhas, bodhisattvas, and gods.

**myōkōnin**. (妙好人). In Japanese, "sublimely excellent people"; a term used especially in the JŌDO SHINSHŪ tradition of Japanese PURE LAND Buddhism to refer to a devout practitioner of nenbutsu (C. NIANFO; recitation of the Buddha's name). The Chinese exegete SHANDAO (613–681) was the first to use the term myōkōnin (C. miaohaoren) in his commentary on the GUAN WULIANGSHOU JING ("Book of the Contemplation of the Buddha of Limitless Life"), where he explains that the SŪTRA uses the term lotus flower (PUṆḌARĪKA) to refer to a "sublimely excellent" nianfo practitioner; HŌNEN similarly used the term to refer to nenbutsu practitioners in general. But it was SHINRAN (1173–1263), the founder of Jōdo Shinshū, who adopted the term in such writings as his *Mattōshō* ("Lamp for the Latter Age"), to refer to Jōdo Shinshū adherents whose virtuous conduct, prompted by their sincere faith in the buddha AMITĀBHA, could serve as a model for their colleagues. The term was popularized during the mid-nineteenth century with the publication of the MYŌKŌNINDEN, edited by the NISHI HONGANJIHA priest Sōjun (1791–1872). This collection of tales about various myōkōnin demonstrates how the acceptance of Amitābha's grace leads to virtuous deeds that are worthy of emulation. The myōkōnin could be farmers, fishermen, merchants, warriors, doctors, or priests, but many of them were illiterate peasants. The Jōdo Shinshū tradition is somewhat ambivalent toward the myōkōnin: despite the myōkōnin's sincere faith in Amitābha, they did not necessarily accept the authority of the school's head or some of its doctrines. Hence, despite being pure expressions of pure land faith, the myōkōnin are not necessarily a proper model for Jōdo Shinshū followers and may even be heretical. Because many of myōkōnin were uneducated common people, few left any writings, with the prominent exception of the modern myōkōnin Asahara Saichi (1850–1932).

**Myōkōninden**. (妙好人傳). In Japanese, "Record of Sublimely Excellent People"; a Jōdo Shinshū collection of the biographies of the MYŌKŌNIN, viz., devoted practitioners of the practice of nenbutsu (C. NIANFO; recitation of the Buddha's name). The anthology was first compiled by a Nishi Honganjiha priest Gōsei (1721–1794) and edited by Gōsei's disciple Rizen (1753–1819). The Nishi Honganji priest Sōjun (1791–1872) made additional editorial changes to this earlier edition and first published the *Myōkōninden* in 1842. Sōjun's original edition collected the biographies of twenty-two myōkōnin, in two rolls. Sōjun added more biographies between 1843 and 1858, and eventually published four additional chapters, adding biographies of thirty-seven myōkōnin in 1843, nineteen in 1847, thirty-seven in 1856, and twenty-one in 1858. In 1852, Zō'ō (fl. nineteenth century) also published the *Zoku Myōkōninden* ("Supplement to the *Myōkōninden*") with additional biographies of twenty-three myōkōnin. The present version of the text was first published in 1898, combining in a single volume all six chapters (viz., Gōsei's original first chapter, Sōjun's four additional chapters, and Zō'ō's supplement). The myōkōnin featured in the collection comes from various social classes, although most of them are common people, such as peasants and merchants. The accounts of their lives emphasize such traditional social virtues as filial piety, loyalty, and generosity, as well as the rewards of exclusive nenbutsu practice and the dangers of KAMI (spirit) worship.

**myŏngbu chŏn**. (冥府殿). In Korean, "hall of the dark prefecture"; a basilica in Korean monasteries that is dedicated to the BODHISATTVA KṢITIGARBHA, the patron bodhisattva of the denizens of the hells (NĀRAKA), and the ten kings of hell (shiwang), the judges of the dead. This hall is where monks typically perform the forty-ninth day ceremony (K. sasipku [il] chae; C. SISHIJIU [RI] ZHAI), which sends the deceased being to the intermediate transitional state (ANTARĀBHAVA) and then on to the next rebirth. See also YAMA.

**Myŏngnang**. (明郎) (d.u.). Korean monk of the Silla dynasty and reputed founder of the sinin (divine seal), or esoteric Buddhist, tradition; also known as Kugyuk. His father was a high-ranking court official and his cousin was the VINAYA master CHAJANG. Myŏngnang traveled to China in 632 and returned four years later to propagate the new teachings of esoteric Buddhism. He established the monasteries of Kŭmgwangsa and Wŏnwŏnsa and made them centers of esoteric Buddhist activity in Korea. He also was one of the teachers of the influential Korean scholiast WŎNHYO (617–686). The monastery Sach'ŏnwangsa is known to have been built at the site where Myŏngnang prepared a MAṆḌALA and recited MANTRAS that spawned the typhoon that defeated the Tang Chinese invasion force. His teachings continued to flourish until the Koryŏ dynasty, when he came to be viewed retrospectively as the founder of the sinin tradition.

**Myōshinji**. (妙心寺). In Japanese, "Sublime Mind Monastery"; an influential ZEN monastery in Kyōto that is currently the headquarters (HONZAN) of the Myōshinji branch of the RINZAISHŪ. After the eminent Zen master Daitō's (see SŌHŌ MYŌCHŌ) death in 1337, Emperor Hanazono (r. 1308–1318) converted his country villa into a monastery, which he named Myōshinji, and installed Daitō's disciple KANZAN EGEN as its founding abbot (J. kaisan; C. KAISHAN). During the Muromachi period, Myōshinji was excluded from the powerful GOZAN ranking system and became the subject of harsh persecution during Ashikaga's rule. In the early half of the fifteenth century, the monk Nippō Sōshun (1358–1448) oversaw the restoration of Myōshinji, but the monastery was consumed in a conflagration during the Ōnin war (1467–1469). In 1477, with the support of Emperor Gotsuchimikado (r. 1464–1500) the monastery was restored once more under the supervision of its abbot Sekkō Sōshin (1408–1486). At the decree of Emperor Gokashiwabara (r. 1500–1526), Myōshinji was included in the gozan system and enjoyed the financial support of a high-ranking official monastery. Largely through its tight fiscal management and active proselytizing efforts, Myōshinji expanded quickly to control over fifty branch temples and became one of the most influential monasteries of the Rinzai Zen tradition. During the Edo period, a renowned Zen master of the Myōshinji lineage named HAKUIN EKAKU played an important role in the revitalization of the kōan (C. GONG'AN) training system.

**Myur lam lam rim**. (Nyurlam Lamrim). In Tibetan, "The Quick Path Stages of the Path"; an important LAM RIM, or "stages of the path," treatise composed by the second PAṆ CHEN LAMA Blo bzang ye shes dpal bzang po (Losang Yeshe Palsangpo, 1663–1737). The work's complete title is *Byang chub lam gyi rim pa'i dmar khrid thams cad mkhyen par bgrod pa'i myur lam*.

# N

**nabich'um**. (나비춤). In Korean, "butterfly dance," a CHAKPŎP ritual dance usually performed by Buddhist nuns during Korean Buddhist rituals, such as the YŎNGSANJAE. This dance is typically performed outdoors in the central campus of a monastery and is often accompanied by ritual chanting (PŎMP'AE; C. FANBAI) and traditional musical instruments. The pŏmp'ae chant requests the three jewels (RATNATRAYA) and protecting dragons (NĀGA) to attend the ceremony. Generally, the nabich'um is performed by two or four nuns in long, white robes with floor-length sleeves and yellow conical hats, thus resembling butterflies. The dance expresses a desire to transform oneself so as to lead all sentient beings to enlightenment. Nabich'um is quite slow, with subdued movements, and is performed without the feet of the dancer moving more than a step away from where the dance began. Nabich'um may also be performed as part of an offering of incense and flowers carried out by the dancers. Nabich'um is also sometimes performed without musical accompaniment.

**nāḍī**. (T. rtsa). In Sanskrit, "tube" or "pipe," in tantric physiognomy, the "channels" that run throughout the body serving as conduits for the winds (PRĀṆA) that serve as the "mounts" of consciousness. According to some systems, there are 72,000 channels in the body. These channels branch out from networks located along the central channel (AVADHŪTI) that runs from the base of the spine to the crown of the head. The central channel is paralleled and entwined by two vertical channels on the right and left, called the RASANĀ (right) and LALANĀ (left). At the points where the right and left channels wrap around the central channel, there are networks (called CAKRA, or "wheels") of smaller channels that radiate throughout the body. The number of these networks differs among various systems, but they are commonly said to be located along the central channel at the crown of the head, the point between the eyes, the throat, the heart, the navel, the base of the spine, and the tip of the sexual organ. Much tantric practice is devoted to techniques for loosening knots in the channels in order that the winds will flow smoothly through them, with advanced practices designed to cause the winds to enter the central channel. The system of channels also provides the basis for medical theories in both India and Tibet.

**Nadī-Kāśyapa**. (P. Nadī-Kassapa; T. Chu klung 'od srungs; C. Nati Jiashe; J. Nadai Kashō; K. Naje Kasŏp 那提迦葉). One of the three "Kāśyapa brothers" (together with URUVILVĀ-KĀŚYAPA and GAYĀ-KĀŚYAPA), also known in Pāli as the Tebhātika Jaṭilas. Prior to their encounter with the Buddha, the three brothers were matted-hair ascetics engaged in fire worship, living with their followers on the banks of the NAIRAÑJANĀ River. Nadī-Kāśyapa himself had three hundred followers. After his first teachings in the Deer Park (MṚGADĀVA) at SĀRNĀTH and in Vārāṇasī, the Buddha returned to URUVILVĀ, where he had practiced asceticism prior to this enlightenment. There, he encountered Uruvilvā-Kāśyapa, a famous ascetic (said to be 120 years old) who claimed to be enlightened. The Buddha spent the rains retreat (VARṢĀ) with him and his followers, performing some 3,500 miracles. When the Buddha eventually convinced Uruvilva-Kāśyapa that he was not enlightened and that the fire worship that he taught did not lead to enlightenment, Uruvilva-Kāśyapa requested ordination. Uruvilvā-Kāśyapa and his five hundred followers all cut off their long locks and threw them in the river, where the other two brothers and their followers saw them floating by. They came to investigate and also sought ordination. The Buddha taught them the so-called "Fire Sermon" (ĀDITTAPARIYĀYA), at which point they all became ARHATs. They all then traveled to RĀJAGṚHA, where, in the presence of King BIMBISĀRA, the new monks proclaimed their allegiance to the Buddha. The three brothers are often listed among the audience of MAHĀYĀNA sūtras.

**nadī vaitaraṇī**. (T. chu bo rab med; C. liehe zeng; J. retsugazō; K. yŏrhajŭng 烈河增). In Sanskrit, "river difficult to ford," the fourth of the four types of "neighboring hells" (PRATYEKANARAKA) located at the four sides of the eight hot hells (cf. NĀRAKA). This hell is a river of boiling water, which the hell denizens are forced to swim across. The river is an example of the common Buddhist practice of appropriating elements of Hindu cosmology. In Hinduism, this river is important in funerary rites, when a gift of a cow is to be given to a brāhmaṇa in order for the deceased to be ferried across the river to the realm of YAMA. The boatman asks the deceased if the gift of a cow has been given. If so, they are allowed to board; if not, they must swim across the horrific waters. In the *Mahābhārata*, the Pāṇḍavas must cross the river en route to heaven. In Buddhist cosmology, it becomes just one of the "neighboring hells," which all denizens of hell must swim across as they exit the hot hells.

**nāga**. (T. klu; C. long; J. ryū; K. yong 龍). In Sanskrit and Pāli, "serpent" or "dragon" (as in the Chinese), autochthonous beings said to inhabit bodies of water and the roots of great trees, often guarding treasures hidden there. They are depicted iconographically with human heads and torsos but with the tail and hood of a cobra. They inhabit an underwater kingdom filled with magnificent palaces, and they possess a range of magical powers, including the ability to masquerade as humans. Nāgas appear frequently in Buddhist literature in both benevolent and malevolent forms. They are said to be under the command of VIRŪPĀKṢA, the god of the west, and are guards of the TRĀYASTRIṂŚA heaven. They sometimes appear in the audience of Buddha, most famously in the twelfth chapter of the SADDHARMAPUṆḌARĪKASŪTRA ("Lotus Sūtra"), where an eight-year-old nāga princess offers a gem to the Buddha. She instantaneously transforms into a male, traverses the ten bodhisattva stages (BHŪMI), and achieves buddhahood. This scene is sometimes cited as evidence that women have the capacity to achieve buddhahood. In the story of the Buddha's enlightenment, the Buddha is protected during a rainstorm by the nāga MUCILINDA. The Buddha is said to have entrusted the ŚATASĀHASRIKĀPRAJÑĀPĀRAMITĀ ("Perfection of Wisdom in One Hundred Lines") to the safekeeping of the nāgas at the bottom of the sea, from whom NĀGĀRJUNA recovered it. Digging the earth is said to displease nāgas, who must therefore be propitiated prior to the construction of a building.

**Nāgabodhi**. (T. Klu'i byang chub; C. Longzhi; J. Ryūchi; K. Yongji 龍智) (d.u.). A south Indian MAHĀSIDDHA, possibly of the eighth century, counted among the traditional list of eighty-four mahāsiddhas. He is renowned in Tibet as a master of ATIYOGA. He is said to have been a thief who tried to steal from NĀGĀRJUNA and ended up becoming his disciple, receiving tantric instructions from Nāgārjuna, which he then passed on to two disciples, ŚUBHAKARASIṂHA at NĀLANDĀ and VAJRABODHI in Sri Lanka, each of whom transmitted these teachings in China. In East Asian Buddhism, Nāgabodhi is considered the fourth of the eight patriarchs of the Zhenyan and SHINGON schools.

**Nāgadīpa**. In Pāli, "Serpent Island," the ancient name for the Jaffna Peninsula at the northern tip of the island of Sri Lanka. According to the MAHĀVAMSA, the Buddha came here during his second visit to the island in order to settle a dispute between two NĀGAS. A number of important monasteries and pilgrimage sites are located there. According to one prophecy, at the time when the teachings of the Buddha are about to disappear from this world, his relics (ŚARĪRA) will reassemble from the various reliquaries (STŪPA) and travel to the Rājāyatanacetiya in Nāgadīpa before returning to BODHGAYĀ, where they will burst into flame.

**Naganuma Myōkō**. (長沼妙佼) (1889–1957). Cofounder, with NIWANO NIKKYŌ (1906–1999), of Risshō Kōseikai, a Japanese "new religion" associated with the REIYŪKAI and NICHIREN schools. See RISSHŌ KŌSEIKAI.

**Nagara**. (S). One of the twenty-four sacred sites associated with the CAKRASAṂVARATANTRA. See PĪṬHA.

**Nāgārjuna**. (T. Klu sgrub; C. Longshu; J. Ryūju; K. Yongsu 龍樹). Indian Buddhist philosopher traditionally regarded as the founder of the MADHYAMAKA [alt. Mādhyamika] school of MAHĀYĀNA Buddhist philosophy. Very little can be said concerning his life; scholars generally place him in South India during the second century CE. Traditional accounts state that he lived four hundred years after the Buddha's PARINIRVĀṆA. Some traditional biographies also state that he lived for six hundred years, apparently attempting to identify him with a later Nāgārjuna known for his tantric writings. Two of the works attributed to Nāgārjuna, the RATNĀVALĪ and the SUHṚLLEKHA, are verses of advice to a king, suggesting that he may have achieved some fame during his lifetime. His birth is "prophesied" in a number of works, including the LAṄKĀVATĀRASŪTRA. Other sources indicate that he also served as abbot of a monastery. He appears to have been the teacher of ĀRYADEVA, and his works served as the subject of numerous commentaries in India, East Asia, and Tibet. Although Nāgārjuna is best known in the West for his writings on emptiness (ŚŪNYATĀ), especially as set forth in his most famous work, the "Verses on the Middle Way" (MŪLAMADHYAMAKAKĀRIKĀ, also known as the MADHYAMAKAŚĀSTRA), Nāgārjuna was the author of a number of works (even when questions of attribution are taken into account) on a range of topics, and it is through a broad assessment of these works that an understanding of his thought is best gained. He wrote as a Buddhist monk and as a proponent of the Mahāyāna; in several of his works he defends the Mahāyāna sūtras as being BUDDHAVACANA. He compiled an anthology of passages from sixty-eight sūtras entitled the "Compendium of Sūtras" (SŪTRASAMUCCAYA), the majority of which are Mahāyāna sūtras; this work provides a useful index for scholars in determining which sūtras were extant during his lifetime. Among the Mahāyāna sūtras, Nāgārjuna is particularly associated with the "perfection of wisdom" (PRAJÑĀPĀRAMITĀ) corpus. According to legend, Nāgārjuna retrieved from the Dragon King's palace at the bottom of the sea the "Perfection of Wisdom in One Hundred Thousand Lines" (ŚATASĀHASRIKĀPRAJÑĀPĀRAMITĀSŪTRA), which the Buddha had entrusted to the undersea king of the NĀGAS for safekeeping. He also composed hymns of praise to the Buddha, such as the CATUḤSTAVA, and expositions of Buddhist ethical practice, such as the *Ratnāvalī*. (Later exegetes classify his works into a YUKTIKĀYA, or "logical corpus," and a STAVAKĀYA, or "devotional corpus.") Nāgārjuna's works are addressed to a variety of audiences. His philosophical texts are sometimes directed against logicians of non-Buddhist schools, but most often offer a critique of the doctrines and assumptions of Buddhist ABHIDHARMA schools, especially the SARVĀSTIVĀDA. Other works are more general expositions of Buddhist practice, directed sometimes to monastic audiences, sometimes to lay audiences. An overriding theme in his works is the bodhisattva's path to buddhahood, and the merit (PUṆYA) and wisdom (PRAJÑĀ) that the bodhisattva must accumulate over the course of that path in order to achieve enlightenment. By wisdom here, he means the perfection of wisdom (prajñāpāramitā), declared in the sūtras to be the knowledge of emptiness (ŚŪNYATĀ). Nāgārjuna is credited with rendering the poetic and sometimes paradoxical declarations concerning emptiness that appear in these and other Mahāyāna sūtras into a coherent philosophical system. In his first sermon, the DHARMACAKRAPRAVARTANASŪTRA, the Buddha had prescribed a "middle way" between the extremes of self-indulgence and self-mortification. Nāgārjuna, citing an early sūtra, spoke of a middle way between the extremes of existence and nonexistence, sometimes also referred to as the middle way between the extremes of permanence (ŚĀŚVATĀNTA) and annihilation (UCCHEDĀNTA). For Nāgārjuna, the ignorance (AVIDYĀ) that is the source of all suffering is the belief in SVABHĀVA, a term that literally means "own being" and has been variously rendered as "intrinsic existence" and "self-nature." This belief is the mistaken view that things exist autonomously, independently, and permanently; to hold this belief is to fall into the extreme of permanence. It is equally mistaken, however, to hold that nothing exists; this is the extreme of annihilation. Emptiness, which for Nāgārjuna is the true nature of reality, is not the absence of existence, but the absence of self-existence, viz., the absence of svabhāva. Nāgārjuna devotes his *Mūlamadhyamakakārikā* to a thoroughgoing analysis of a wide range of topics (in twenty-seven chapters and 448 verses), including the Buddha, the FOUR NOBLE TRUTHS, and NIRVĀṆA, to demonstrate that each lacks the autonomy and independence that are mistakenly ascribed to it. His approach generally is to consider the various ways in which a given entity could exist, and then demonstrate that none of these is tenable because of the absurdities that would be entailed thereby, a form of reasoning often described in Western writings as *reductio ad absurdum*. In the case of something that is regarded to be the effect of a cause, he shows that the effect cannot be produced from itself (because an effect is the product of a cause), from something other than itself (because there must be a link between cause and effect), from something that is both the same as and different from itself (because the former two options are not possible), or from something that is neither the same as nor different from itself (because no such thing exists). This, in his view, is what is meant in the perfection of wisdom sūtras when they state that all phenomena are "unproduced" (ANUTPĀDA). The purpose of such an analysis is to destroy misconceptions (VIKALPA) and encourage the abandonment of all views (DṚṢṬI). Nāgārjuna defined emptiness in terms of the doctrine of PRATĪTYASAMUTPĀDA, or "dependent origination," understood in its more generic sense as the fact that things are not self-arisen, but are produced in dependence on causes and conditions. This definition allows Nāgārjuna to avoid the claim of nihilism, which he addresses directly in his writings and which his followers would confront over the centuries. Nāgārjuna employs the doctrine of the two truths (SATYADVAYA) of ultimate truth (PARAMĀRTHASATYA) and conventional truth (SAṂVṚTISATYA), explaining that everything that exists is ultimately empty of any intrinsic nature but does exist conventionally. The conventional is the necessary means for understanding the ultimate, and the ultimate makes the conventional possible. As Nāgārjuna wrote, "For whom emptiness is possible, everything is possible."

**Nāgārjunakoṇḍā**. "Nāgārjuna's hill" (koṇḍā means "hill" in Telugu), an important archaeological site in southern India, in the modern state of Andhra Pradesh; it is the present name for Vijayapurī, the capital of the Ikṣvāku dynasty (c. 227–309) founded by Vāsiṣṭīputra Caṃtamūla after the decline of AMARĀVATĪ, the southern capital of the later Sātavāhana [alt. Śātavāhana] dynasty. In 1926, ruins were discovered of what was the most important monastic center in the Deccan. There is no archaeological evidence to support its traditional association with the philosopher NĀGĀRJUNA, although there are remains of Buddhist monasteries and reliquaries of at least four Buddhist schools. Each monastic unit consisted of a STŪPA, two CAITYA halls (one containing a stūpa, the other an image of the buddha), and a VIHĀRA (residential quarters). The stūpas at the site are designed in the shape of a wheel. Limestone panels and friezes have also been discovered at the site. Nāgārjunakoṇḍā and AMARĀVATĪ are particularly important for showing how Buddhist and Brahmanical structures were constructed at the same time, alongside each other, supported by different members of the same ruling families.

**Nāgasena**. (T. Klu sde; C. Naxian biqiu/Naqiexina; J. Nasen biku/Nagasaina; K. Nasŏn pigu/Nagasŏna 那先比丘/那伽犀那). The Sanskrit and Pāli name for an eminent ARHAT celebrated in the Pāli MILINDAPAÑHA and the Sanskrit *Nāgasenabhikṣusūtra* (which may derive from a Bactrian SARVĀSTIVĀDA textual lineage) for his discussions on Buddhist doctrine with the Bactrian Greek king Menander (P. Milinda). Although Nāgasena was not born into a Buddhist family, he was destined to come to the aid of the Buddha's religion in fulfillment of a promise he had made in his previous existence as a divinity in the TRĀYASTRIṂŚA heaven. Thus, according to the Pāli account, he was born into a brāhmaṇa family in the Himalayas and became well versed in the Vedas at an early age. King Milinda was harassing the Buddhist order by skillfully disputing points of doctrine and defeating Buddhist representatives in debate. To counter this threat, the elder Assagutta summoned the monk Rohana, and charged him with the task of converting Nāgasena, convincing him to join the order and training him so that he might vanquish King Milinda and convert him to Buddhism. Rohana visited Nāgasena's house for seven years and ten months before receiving so much as a greeting from his proud brāhmaṇa father. Finally, impressed by the monk's demeanor, Nāgasena's father became his patron and invited him daily for his morning meal. After Nāgasena was sufficiently educated in Vedic lore, Rohana engaged him in discussions and convinced him of the veracity of the Buddha's teachings. Nāgasena entered the order under Rohana who, as his preceptor, taught him

ABHIDHAMMA (S. ABHIDHARMA). One day, Nāgasena, having inherited his father's pride, questioned the intelligence of his teacher. Rohana, an arhat endowed with the power to read others' minds, rebuked Nāgasena for his arrogance. Nāgasena begged forgiveness, but Rohana would grant it only if Nāgasena defeated King Milinda in debate. Thereafter, Nāgasena was sent to the Vattaniya hermitage to train under Assagutta and while there achieved stream-entry (SROTAĀPANNA). He was then sent to PĀṬALIPUTRA to study under the elder Dhammarakkhita, where he attained arhatship. At the appropriate time, Nāgasena, who was then widely renowned for his erudition, was invited to Milinda's kingdom. There, in the Saṅkheyya hermitage, Nāgasena engaged King Milinda in discussion on various points of doctrine, at the end of which the king took refuge in the three jewels (RATNATRAYA) and became a lay disciple in the Buddha's religion. Scholars are uncertain whether such a dialogue ever took place. There was indeed a famous king named Menander (Milinda in Indian sources) who ruled over a large region that encompassed parts of modern India, Pakistan, and Afghanistan during the middle of the second century BCE. There is, however, no historical evidence of Nāgasena. The text itself was probably composed or compiled around the beginning of the Common Era and marks some of the earliest abhidharma-style exchanges found in the literature. ¶ A different Nāgasena (corresponding to the second of the two Chinese transcriptions in the entry heading) is also traditionally listed as twelfth of the sixteen ARHAT elders (ṢOḌAŚASTHAVIRA), charged by the Buddha with protecting his dispensation until the advent of the next buddha, MAITREYA. East Asian sources claim that he resides on Bandubo Mountain with twelve hundred disciples. He is often depicted in paintings as cleaning his ears, earning him the nickname "Ear-Picking Arhat" (Wa'er Luohan). In CHANYUE GUANXIU's standard Chinese depiction, Nāgasena sits leaning on a rock, with large nose and deep-set eyes, staring ahead in anger. He has a high forehead and a hump on his back. His mouth is open with his tongue exposed. He supports his chin with his fists.

**naiḥsargikapāyattika**. (P. nissaggiyapācittiya; T. spang ba'i ltung byed; C. sheduo; J. shada; K. sat'a 捨墮). In Sanskrit, "forfeiture offense," a category of monastic infraction in the PRĀTIMOKṢA that includes offenses committed by a monk or a nun pertaining to the improper acquisition or characteristics of the alms bowl (PĀTRA), robes (TRICĪVARA), and other kinds of requisites. Such an offense always entails the forfeiture of property (although in some cases it is later returned). The offense is rectified when the guilty party forfeits the objects in question and confesses the misdeed to a SAṂGHA composed of four or more monks, to a gaṇa composed of two or three monks, or to an individual monk. In the Pāli VINAYA, there are thirty rules in this category, falling under three categories: robes, silk (although the rules pertain to other materials as well), and bowls. As an example of the first category, if a monk is given robe cloth by a layperson who is unrelated to him, he may accept only enough cloth to make an upper robe (UTTARĀSAṂGA) and an under robe (NIVĀSANA). Any additional cloth must be forfeited, and it is a violation to horde it. As an example of the second category, if a monk receives gold or silver, it must be forfeited; it is a violation of the rule to keep it. As an example of the third category, it is a violation for a monk to be in possession of an additional undamaged and properly made alms bowl for more than ten days; after ten days, the extra bowl must be forfeited and the transgression confessed.

**Nairañjanā**. (P. Nerañjarā; T. Ne ran dza na; C. Nilianchanhe; J. Nirenzenga; K. Niryŏnsŏnha 尼連禪河). Ancient name of the present-day Lilaja River, a tributary of the Ganges, located in the modern Indian state of Bihar; site of the Buddha's austerities and enlightenment. During a six-year period, from the time of his departure from the palace to his achievement of buddhahood, the BODHISATTVA Prince SIDDHĀRTHA practiced austerities at URUVILVĀ along the banks of this river. It was while bathing in this river during a period of intense self-mortification that the bodhisattva swooned from hunger, after which he concluded that extreme asceticism was not a viable path to liberation from suffering and continued rebirth. Sitting under a tree on the bank of the river, he accepted a bowl of milk porridge from a young woman named SUJĀTĀ, who mistook his gaunt visage for a YAKṢA to whom the local village made offerings. He ate the meal and then cast the dish into the river, saying, "If I am to become a buddha today, may the dish float upstream." The plate floated upstream for some distance before disappearing into a whirlpool, descending down to the palace of a serpent king (NĀGA), where it landed on top of the bowls used by the previous buddhas, making a clicking sound. The bodhisattva spent the afternoon prior to the night of his enlightenment in a grove on the banks of the river. After his enlightenment, it was on the banks of this river that BRAHMĀ persuaded him to teach the dharma. The Buddha later converted the ascetic URUVILVĀ-KĀŚYAPA, whose hermitage was located along this Nairañjanā River.

**nairātmya**. (T. bdag med; C. wuwo; J. muga; K. mua 無我). In Sanskrit, "selflessness," referring to the absence of a perduring self. It is a later scholastic term synonymous with the canonical term ANĀTMAN, lit., "nonself"; here, the same notion is turned into an abstract noun, nairātmya, hence "selflessness." This translation should not be understood in its common English meaning as a personality trait that is the opposite of selfishness. Nairātmya instead is used philosophically to refer to the quality of an absence of self. The major Buddhist philosophical schools of India differ on the precise meaning of this selflessness, based on how they define "self" (ĀTMAN). They would all agree, however, that an understanding of nairātmya is the central insight of the Buddhist path (MĀRGA) leading to liberation from the cycle of rebirth. Two types of nairātmya are distinguished, based on what it is that lacks self. The first is called the selflessness of persons (PUDGALANAIRĀTMYA), which refers to the absence of a permanent and autonomous entity among the aggregates of mind and body (NĀMARŪPA) that transmigrates from lifetime to lifetime. The second type of nairātmya is called the selflessness of phenomena (i.e., phenomena other than persons), or DHARMANAIRĀTMYA, which refers to the absence of any kind of enduring element in the factors that make up the universe. Nairātmya is used in both HĪNAYĀNA and MAHĀYĀNA philosophical schools but receives particular emphasis in the Mahāyāna. In the MADHYAMAKA school, e.g., the selflessness of phenomena is defined as the absence of intrinsic nature, or SVABHĀVA; see NIḤSVABHĀVA. ¶ Nairātmyā (T. Bdag med ma; C. Wuwomu), or "Selfless," is also the name of the consort of HEVAJRA. In the HEVAJRATANTRA, she represents the overcoming of wrath.

**naiṣkramya**. (P. nekkhamma; T. nges 'byung; C. chuyaozhi/chuli; J. shutsuyōshi/shutsuri; K. ch'uryoji/ch'ulli 出要志/出離). In Sanskrit, "renunciation" (see also NIḤSARAṆA; NIRVEDA) especially in the sense of leaving mundane life and embarking on a religious vocation. The Buddha repeatedly exhorts monks to develop renunciation as a means of eliminating attachment to the pleasures of the senses. As such, in the cultivation of the path (MĀRGA), renunciation is associated with right intention (SAṂYAKSAṂKALPA) and is essential for all three trainings (TRIŚIKṢĀ) in morality (ŚĪLA), concentration (SAMĀDHI), and wisdom (PRAJÑĀ). In the Pāli tradition, renunciation constitutes the third perfection (P. pāramī; S. PĀRAMITĀ) mastered by the bodhisatta (S. BODHISATTVA) on the path leading to buddhahood. In the MAHĀYĀNA traditions, renunciation is lauded as a prerequisite to developing the aspiration for enlightenment (BODHICITTA), since it is impossible to develop a wish to liberate all beings from SAṂSĀRA unless one is dissatisfied with saṃsāra oneself. In order to develop renunciation, the adept is advised to contemplate the rarity of human birth (KṢAṆASAMPAD), the suffering inherent in the realms of saṃsāra, the cause and effect of actions (KARMAN), and the inevitability and unpredictability of death. See also ĀDĪNAVA; ANUPUBBIKATHĀ.

**naivasaṃjñānāsaṃjñāyatana**. (P. nevasaññānāsaññāyatana; T. 'du shes med 'du shes med min skye mched; C. feixiang feifeixiang chu; J. hisōhihisōjo; K. pisang pibisang ch'ŏ 非想非非想處). In Sanskrit, "sphere of neither perception nor nonperception," the fourth and highest of the four levels of the immaterial realm (ĀRŪPYADHĀTU) and the fourth of the four immaterial absorptions (ĀRŪPYĀVACARADHYĀNA). It surpasses the first three levels of the immaterial realm, viz., infinite space (AKĀŚĀNANTYĀYATANA), infinite consciousness (VIJÑĀNĀNANTYĀYATANA), and nothingness (ĀKIÑCANYĀYATANA), respectively. It is a realm of rebirth and a meditative state that is entirely immaterial (viz., there is no physical or material [RŪPA] component to existence) in which perception of all mundane things vanishes entirely, but perception itself does not. Beings reborn in this realm are thought to live as long as eighty thousand eons (KALPA). However, as a state of being that is still subject to rebirth, even the sphere of neither perception nor nonperception remains part of SAṂSĀRA. Like the other levels of both the subtle-materiality realm (RŪPADHĀTU) and the immaterial realm, one is reborn in this state by achieving the specific level of meditative absorption associated with that state in the previous lifetime. One of the most famous and influential expositions on the subject of these immaterial states comes from the VISUDDHIMAGGA of BUDDHAGHOSA, written in the fifth century. Although there are numerous accounts of Buddhist meditators achieving immaterial states of SAMĀDHI, they are also used polemically in Buddhist literature to describe the attainments of non-Buddhist YOGINs, who mistakenly identify these exalted, but still impermanent, states of existence as the permanent liberation from rebirth. See also DHYĀNASAMĀPATTI; DHYĀNOPAPATTI.

**Nakagawa Sōen**. (中川宋淵) (1907–1984). Japanese ZEN monk in the RINZAISHŪ who was influential in the early transmission of that Zen tradition to North America. Born in Taiwan to a Japanese military family, he graduated from Tōkyō Imperial University in 1931 and was ordained as a monk at Kogakuji in 1933. After hearing the MYŌSHINJI Zen master Yamamoto Genpo (1866–1961) speak at Ryūtakuji, he became his disciple and trained under him at the latter monastery, eventually becoming abbot there. In 1935, Nakagawa began corresponding with Nyogen Senzaki (1876–1958), a Rinzai missionary in California, and eventually traveled to San Francisco to visit Senzaki in 1949; he made ten more such visits over the next three decades. Nakagawa helped to establish the Zen Studies Society in New York in 1965 and the Daibosatsu Zendo in the Catskills in 1971.

**Nakchin**. (樂眞) (1045–1114). In Korean, "Enjoying Truth"; Korean scholar-monk during the mid-Koryŏ dynasty, also known as royal master (wangsa) Ogong T'onghye (Awakening to Emptiness, Penetrating Wisdom). Initially a student of the state preceptor (kuksa; see GUOSHI) Kyŏngdŏk Nanwŏn (999–1066), Nakchin passed the monk's examination (SŬNGKWA) and received the title "greatly virtuous" (taedŏk). After Nanwŏn's death, Nakchin became a close colleague of the state preceptor Taegak ŬICH'ŎN (1055–1101), the fifth son of the Koryŏ king Munjong (r. 1046–1083). After Ŭich'ŏn surreptitiously departed for China against his royal father's wishes, the king sent Nakchin after him, and they eventually studied together under the HUAYAN teacher Jinshui Jingyuan (1011–1088), at Huiyinsi in Hangzhou. After the two monks returned to Korea, Nakchin stayed with Ŭich'ŏn at Hŭngwangsa in the capital, where he assisted Ŭich'ŏn in establishing the large monastic library known as the Kyojang Togam and in publishing the massive *Koryŏ sokchanggyŏng* ("Koryŏ Supplement to the Canon"), which was especially important for its inclusion of a broad cross section of the indigenous writings of East Asian Buddhist teachers. Nakchin also served as an editor of Ŭich'ŏn's *Wŏnjong mullyu*. Nakchin eventually rose to the preeminent position of "SAṂGHA overseer" (K. sŭngt'ong;

C. SENGTONG) under King Sukchong (r. 1096–1105) and, in 1114, received the title royal master (wangsa).

**Nakula**. (S). See BAKKULA.

**Nakulapitṛ and Nakulamātṛ**. (P. Nakulapitā and Nakulamātā; T. Ne'u le'i pha, Ne'u le'i ma; C. Nayouluo fu, Nuoguluo zhangzhe mu; J. Naura fu, Nakora chōja mo; K. Naura pu, Nakkora changja mo 那憂羅父, 諾酤羅長者母). In Sanskrit, "Nakula's Father" and "Nakula's Mother"; lay followers of the Buddha, declared by him to be foremost among laypersons who are intimate companions. According to the Pāli account, they were a married couple who lived in the village of Suṃsumāragiri in Bhagga country. Once on a visit to their village, the Buddha was staying at a grove called Bhesakalāvana. The couple went to pay their respects and, upon seeing the Buddha, immediately fell at his feet, calling him their son and asking why he had been away so long. This spontaneous reaction was a consequence of their past existences: for five hundred lifetimes they had been the Buddha's parents, and for many more lives they were his close relatives. The Buddha preached to them, and they immediately became streamenterers (sotāpanna; S. SROTAĀPANNA). Once when Nakulapitā was gravely ill, he began to fret about the fate of his wife and family, should he die. Nakulamātā, noticing his condition, consoled him in such a way that his anxiety was removed and he recovered his health. Later, he recounted what had transpired to the Buddha, who congratulated him on his wife's good qualities. Nakulapitā's conversations with the Buddha are recorded in the Pāli SAṂYUTTANIKĀYA. The Buddha again visited their village many years later when the couple was old. They invited him to their home for his morning meal. There, they related to him their devotion to one another and asked for a teaching that would keep them together through their future lives. It was on the basis of this discussion that the Buddha declared Nakulapitā and Nakulamātā foremost among those who live intimately. In a former life, Nakulapitā had resolved to attain this type of preeminence: during the time of the buddha Padumuttara, as a householder in the city of Haṃsavatī, he overheard the Buddha praise a lay couple for their intimacy.

**Nālāgiri**. (T. Nor skyong; C. Hucai/Shoucai; J. Gozai/Shuzai; K. Hojae/Sujae 護財/守財). The Sanskrit and Pāli name of a ferocious elephant whom the Buddha tames, in a scene often depicted in Buddhist art. The elephant was so dangerous that the citizens of RĀJAGṚHA asked King AJĀTAŚATRU to have a bell put around his neck to warn people of his approach. In an attempt to assassinate the Buddha and take control of the SAṂGHA, the Buddha's cousin DEVADATTA bribed the king's elephant keeper to let loose the fierce elephant against the Buddha. After being given a large quantity of palm wine, the elephant was unleashed and rampaged through the city. Hearing the bell, the monks implored the Buddha not to collect alms in the city that day, but he ignored their pleas. A woman who was fleeing from the elephant dropped her child at the Buddha's feet. When the elephant charged, the Buddha spoke to him and suffused him with loving-kindness (MAITRĪ), causing the elephant to stop before him. When he stroked the elephant's head, it knelt at his feet and received teachings from the Buddha. The townspeople were so impressed by the miracle that they showered the elephant's body with jewelry; for this reason, the elephant was henceforth known as DHANAPĀLA, "Wealth Protector." In some sources, he is called Vasupāla.

**Nālandā**. (T. Na len dra; C. Nalantuosi; J. Narandaji; K. Narandasa 那爛陀寺). A great monastic university, located a few miles north of RĀJAGṚHA, in what is today the Indian state of Bihar. It was the most famous of the Buddhist monastic universities of India. During the Buddha's time, Nālandā was a flourishing town that he often visited on his peregrinations. It was also frequented by MAHĀVĪRA, the leader of the JAINA mendicants. According to XUANZANG (whose account is confirmed by a seal discovered at the site), the monastery at Nālandā was founded by King Śakrāditya of MAGADHA, who is sometimes identified as the fifth-century ruler Kumāragupta I (r. 415–455). It flourished between the sixth and twelfth centuries CE under Gupta and Pāla patronage. According to Tibetan histories, many of the greatest MAHĀYĀNA scholars, including ASAṄGA, VASUBANDHU, DHARMAKĪRTI, DHARMAPĀLA, ŚĪLABHADRA, and ŚĀNTIDEVA, lived and taught at Nālandā. Several MADHYAMAKA scholars, including CANDRAKĪRTI, are also said to have taught there. At its height, Nālandā was a large and impressive complex of monasteries that had as many as ten thousand students and fifteen hundred teachers in residence. During the reign of Harṣa, it was supported by a hundred neighboring villages, each with two hundred households providing rice, butter, and milk to sustain the community of monastic scholars and students. The library, which included a nine-story structure, is said to have contained hundreds of thousands of manuscripts. The university had an extensive curriculum, with instruction offered in the VAIBHĀṢIKA school of SARVĀSTIVĀDA ABHIDHARMA, SAUTRĀNTIKA, YOGĀCARA, and MADHYAMAKA, the Vedas and Hindu philosophical schools, as well as mathematics, grammar, logic, and medicine. Nālandā attracted students from across Asia, including the Chinese pilgrims YIJING and Xuanzang, who provided detailed reports of their visits. Both monks were impressed by the strict monastic discipline that was observed at Nālandā, with Xuanzang reporting that no monk had been expelled for a violation of the VINAYA in seven hundred years. In the eleventh century, NĀROPA held a senior teaching position at Nālandā, until he left in search of his teacher TILOPA. In 1192, Nālandā was sacked by Turkic troops under the command of Bakhtiyar Khilji, who may have mistaken it for a fortress; the library was burned, with the thousands of manuscripts smoldering for months. The monastery had been largely abandoned by the time of a Tibetan pilgrim's visit in 1235 CE, although it seems to have survived in some form until around 1400. Archaeological excavations began at Nālandā in the early twentieth century and have continued since, unearthing monasteries and monastic cells, as well as significant works of art in stone, bronze, and stucco.

**Na lan dra**. [alt. Na len dra]. A Tibetan monastery named after the famed Indian Buddhist university of NĀLANDĀ. Na lan dra was founded in 1435 by the renowned scholar RONG STON SMRA BA'I SENG GE. Located in the region of 'Phan yul (Penyul) north of LHA SA, the institution is often known as 'Phan po Na len dra (Penpo Nalendra). The monastery declined after its founder's death and was absorbed by the SA SKYA sect at the end of the fifteenth century.

**nāmarūpa**. (T. ming gzugs; C. mingse; J. myōshiki; K. myŏngsaek 名色). In Sanskrit and Pāli, lit. "name-and-form," "mind-and-matter," "mentality-and-materiality"; a term for the mental and physical constituents of the person, with "name" (nāma) subsuming the four mental aggregates (SKANDHA) of sensations (VEDANĀ), perception (SAṂJÑĀ), conditioning factors (SAMSKĀRA), and consciousness (VIJÑĀNA), and "form" (RŪPA) referring to the materiality aggregate, viz., the physical body. The term occurs most commonly as the fourth of the twelve links in the chain of dependent origination (PRATĪTYASAMUTPĀDA), where, in some interpretations, it refers to the five aggregates of a new lifetime at the moment of conception, when the consciousness (vijñāna) from the previous lifetime enters the womb; in this interpretation, "name" would be the consciousness that has arrived in the womb from the previous lifetime, and "form" would be the embryo that it inhabits. Name and form are said to rely upon each other, like a lame man (name) traveling on the shoulders of a blind man (form). Because of this reciprocal relationship, if consciousness (name) is not present, the form of the embryo will not develop and miscarriage will result. But consciousness (name) also cannot exist without the support that form provides, for it is only when there are physical sense bases (INDRIYA) that can come into contact with the external world that consciousness can be produced. Name and form are thus also compared to two bundles of reeds leaning against one another, neither of which can stand without the other. In addition to this sense of the term as the physical and psychical components of the person, the term is also used in a wider sense to refer to the entire world, since it is composed of mind (nāma) and matter (rūpa).

**nam Myōhōrengekyō**. (J) (南無妙法蓮華經). Alternate transcription of NAMU MYŌHŌRENGEKYŌ.

**Namo Buddha**. (T. Stag mo lus sbyin). Together with SVAYAṂBHŪ and BODHNĀTH, one of the three major STŪPAS of the Kathmandu Valley in Nepal. Located twenty-five miles (forty kilometers) southeast of Kathmandu, it is built at the putative site where a prince named Mahāsattva, a bodhisattva who was a previous rebirth of ŚĀKYAMUNI Buddha, sacrificed his life to feed a starving tigress. In some versions of the story, the prince came across a starving tigress and her hungry cubs and, in order to save their lives, jumped off a cliff, committing suicide so they could eat his flesh. In another version, commemorated on a rock carving near the stūpa, the prince cut off pieces of his flesh and fed them to the tigress until he finally died. The stūpa is said to be built over his bones, and the tigress's cave is nearby. The Tibetan name of the stūpa means, "Offering the Body to the Tigress." The Nepali name is said to derive from the fact that there were once many tigers in the area; the residents would therefore repeat "namo Buddha" ("homage to the Buddha") for protection.

**Namsan**. (南山). In Korean, "South Mountain," important Buddhist site located to the south of the ancient Silla-dynasty capital of KYŎNGJU. Namsan had been worshipped as a Korean sacred mountain since prehistoric times and was strongly embedded in local shamanic cults. With the advent of Buddhism, Namsan became the center of Buddhist worship in Korea as the representation of Mt. SUMERU, the axis mundi of the world in Buddhist cosmology. As a result, the whole area of Namsan is dotted with rock-cut reliefs, engravings, and stone images, all fine examples of Korean Buddhist art from the seventh through the fourteenth centuries, depicting among many others the buddhas ŚĀKYAMUNI, BHAIṢAJYAGURU, and AMITĀBHA. Most of these images date from the seventh and eighth centuries, when the political power of the Silla dynasty was at its height. Most noteworthy is the massive boulder in T'apkok (Pagoda Valley), which is carved with a rich tapestry of Buddhist images that depict the popular view of the Buddhist world during the Silla period. In the center of the boulder's northern face is a seated buddha image, which is flanked by two images of wooden pagodas. A mythical lion below the pagodas acts as a guardian to this scene. The eastern face expresses the belief in the PURE LAND. It depicts a narrative scene of Amitābha, flanked by two BODHISATTVAS, presumably AVALOKITEŚVARA and MAHĀSTHĀMAPRĀPTA, with accompanying images of flying beings (S. APSARAS) and monks who came to venerate this central figure. On the boulder's southern face, a buddha triad and an individual image of a bodhisattva are carved. Finally, on its western face is depicted an image of Śākyamuni at the moment of his awakening beneath two BODHI TREES. Other noteworthy Buddhist images at Namsan include the rock-cut reliefs of seven buddhas at Ch'ilburam (Seven Buddhas Rock), which is uniquely composed of two boulders, one with a buddha triad, the other one with four bodhisattvas; the seated stone statue of Śākyamuni at Mirŭkkok (Maitreya Valley), which is one of the best-preserved Buddhist stone statues from the eighth century; the seated image of a bodhisattva carved on the high cliff of Sinsŏnam (Fairy Rock); and the seated figure of Śākyamuni in Samnŭnggok (Samnŭng Valley), which was carved on a colossal rock twenty-three feet high and sixteen feet in width.

**namu Amidabutsu**. (C. namo Amituo fo; K. namu Amit'a pul 南無阿彌陀佛). In Japanese, "I take refuge in the buddha

AMITĀBHA." Chanting of the name of the buddha Amitābha as a form of "buddha-recollection" (J. nenbutsu; see C. NIANFO) is often associated with the PURE LAND traditions. In Japan, nenbutsu practice was spread throughout the country largely through the efforts of itinerant holy men (HIJIRI), such as KŪYA and IPPEN. With the publication of GENSHIN's ŌJŌ YŌSHŪ, the practice of nenbutsu and the prospect of rebirth in Amitābha's pure land came to play an integral role as well in the TENDAI tradition. HŌNEN, a learned monk of the Tendai sect, inspired in part by reading the writings of the Chinese exegete SHANDAO, became convinced that the nenbutsu was the most appropriate form of Buddhist practice for people in the degenerate age of the dharma (J. mappō; C. MOFA). Hōnen set forth his views in a work called *Senchaku hongan nenbutsushū* ("On the Nenbutsu Selected in the Primal Vow," see SENCHAKUSHŪ). The title refers to the vow made eons ago by the bodhisattva DHARMĀKARA that he would become the buddha Amitābha, create the pure land of bliss (SUKHĀVATĪ), and deliver to that realm anyone who called his name. To illustrate the power of the practice of nenbutsu, Hōnen contrasted "right practice" and the "practice of sundry good acts." "Right practice" refers to all forms of worship of Amitābha, the most important of which is the recitation of his name. "Practice of sundry good acts" refers to ordinary virtuous deeds performed by Buddhists, which are meritorious but lack the power of "right practice" that derives from the grace of Amitābha. Indeed, the power of Amitābha's vow is so great that those who sincerely recite his name, Hōnen suggests, do not necessarily need to dedicate their merit toward rebirth in the land of bliss because recitation will naturally result in rebirth there. Hōnen goes on to explain that each bodhisattva makes specific vows about the particular practice that will result in rebirth in their buddha-fields (BUDDHAKṢETRA). Some buddha-fields are for those who practice charity (DĀNA), others for those who construct STŪPAs, and others for those who honor their teachers. While Amitābha was still the bodhisattva Dharmākara, he compassionately selected a very simple practice that would lead to rebirth in his pure land of bliss: the mere recitation of his name. Hōnen recognized how controversial these teachings would be if they were widely espoused, so he instructed that the *Senchakushū* not be published until after his death and allowed only his closest disciples to read and copy it. His teachings gained popularity in a number of influential circles but were considered anathema by the existing sects of Buddhism in Japan because of his promotion of the sole practice of reciting the name. His critics charged him with denigrating ŚĀKYAMUNI Buddha, with neglecting virtuous deeds other than the recitation of the name, and with abandoning the meditation and visualization practices that should accompany the chanting of the name. Some years after Hōnen's death, the printing xylographs of the *Senchakushū* were confiscated and burned as works harmful to the dharma. However, by that time, the teachings of Hōnen had gained a wide following among both aristocrats and the common people. Hōnen's disciple SHINRAN came to hold even more radical views. Like Hōnen, he believed that any attempt to rely on one's own powers (JIRIKI) to achieve freedom from SAṂSĀRA was futile; the only viable course of action was to rely on the power of Amitābha. But for Shinran, this power was pervasive. Even to make the effort to repeat silently "namu Amidabutsu" was a futile act of hubris. The very presence of the sounds of Amitābha's name in one's heart was due to Amitābha's compassionate grace. It was therefore redundant to repeat the name more than once in one's life. Instead, a single utterance (ICHINENGI) would assure rebirth in the pure land; all subsequent recitation should be regarded as a form of thanksgiving. This utterance need be neither audible nor even voluntary; instead, it is heard in the heart as a consequence of the "single thought-moment" of faith (shinjin, see XINXIN), received through Amitābha's grace. Shinran not only rejected the value of multiple recitations of the phrase namu Amidabutsu; he also regarded the deathbed practices advocated by Genshin to bring about rebirth in the pure land as inferior self-power (jiriki). Despite harsh persecution by rival Buddhist traditions and the government, the followers of Hōnen and Shinran came to form the largest Buddhist community in Japan, known as the JŌDOSHŪ and JŌDO SHINSHŪ.

**Namuci**. (T. Grol med; C. Mowang [Boxun]; J. Maō [Hajun]; K. Mawang [Pasun] 魔王 [波旬]). In Sanskrit and Pāli, "Non-releaser," a cognomen of MĀRA, the anthropomorphized evil one, also sometimes known as PĀPĪYĀṂS. Namuci is the name of a devil killed by the king of the divinities, INDRA, and absorbed into the Buddhist pantheon as one of the evil ones (māra). Namuci is sometimes identified with the third of the four types of māras most commonly found in Buddhist literature: (1) kleśamāra (P. kilesamāra), the māra of afflictions; (2) SKANDHAMĀRA (P. khandhamāra), the māra of the aggregates; (3) MṚTYUMĀRA (P. maccumāra), the māra of death; and (4) DEVAPUTRAMĀRA (P. devaputtamāra), the divinity Māra. As the "personification of death" itself, Māra cum Namuci thus releases no one from his grasp.

**namu Myōhōrengekyō**. (C. namo Miaofa lianhua jing; K. namu Myobŏp yŏnhwa kyŏng 南無妙法蓮華經). In Japanese, lit. "Homage to the Lotus Flower of the Sublime Dharma Scripture," the phrase chanted as the primary practice of the various subtraditions of the NICHIRENSHŪ, including NICHIREN SHOSHŪ and SOKKA GAKKAI. The first syllable of the phrase, "namu," is a transcription of the Sanskrit term "namas," meaning "homage"; "Myōhōrengekyō" is the Japanese pronunciation of the title of KUMĀRAJĪVA's (344–413) Chinese translation of the influential SADDHARMAPUṆḌARĪKASŪTRA ("Lotus Sūtra"). The phrase is also known in the Nichiren tradition as the DAIMOKU (lit. "title"). Chanting or meditating on the title of the *Saddharmapuṇḍarīkasūtra* seems to have had a long history in the TENDAISHŪ (TIANTAI ZONG) in Japan. The practice was further developed and popularized by the Tendai monk NICHIREN, who placed this practice above all others. Relying on the FAHUA XUANYI, an important commentary on the

*Saddharmapuṇḍarīkasūtra* by the Chinese monk TIANTAI ZHIYI (538–597), Nichiren claimed that the essence of the scripture is distilled in its title, or daimoku, and that chanting the title can therefore lead to the attainment of buddhahood in this very body (SOKUSHIN JŌBUTSU). He also drew on the notion that the dharma was then in decline (J. mappō; see C. MOFA) to promote the chanting of namu Myōhōrengekyō as the optimal approach to enlightenment in this degenerate age. The ONGI DUDEN ("Record of the Orally Transmitted Teachings"), the transcription of Nichiren's lectures on the sūtra compiled by his disciple Nichikō (1246–1332), gives a detailed exegesis of the meaning of the phrase. In the Nichiren interpretation, namu represents the dedication of one's whole life to the essential truth of Buddhism, which is the daimoku Myōhōrengekyō. Myōhō refers to the "sublime dharma" of the nonduality of enlightenment and ignorance. Renge is the "lotus flower" (PUṆḌARĪKA), which, because it is able to bear seeds and yet bloom at the same time, symbolizes the simultaneity of cause and effect. Finally, kyō represents the voices and sounds of all sentient beings, which affirm the universal presence of the buddha-nature (C. FOXING). The chanting of the phrase is therefore considered to be the ultimate means to attain buddhahood, regardless of whether or not one knows its meaning. In addition to its soteriological dimension, the chanting of the phrase is believed by some to convey such practical benefits as good health and financial well-being.

**ñāṇadassanavisuddhi**. In Pāli, "purity of knowledge and vision"; according to the VISUDDHIMAGGA, the seventh and final of seven "purities" (P. visuddhi; cf. S. VIŚUDDHI) to be developed along the path to liberation. This purity consists of knowledge associated with the attainment of any of the four supramundane or noble (P. ariya; S. ĀRYA) paths, viz., that of the stream-enterer (P. sotāpanna; S. SROTAĀPANNA), once-returner (P. sakadāgāmi; S. SAKṚDĀGĀMIN), nonreturner (P. anāgāmi; S. ANĀGĀMIN), or worthy one (P. arahant; S. ARHAT). Entry into the path is preceded by what is called "change-of-lineage knowledge" (GOTRABHŪÑĀṆA), which arises immediately following the attainment of the conformity knowledge (ANULOMAÑĀṆA) that occurred as the culmination of the preceding (sixth) purity called PAṬIPADĀÑĀṆADASSANAVISUDDHI, or "purity of knowledge and vision of progress along the path." Change-of-lineage knowledge takes as its object the unconditioned NIRVĀṆA element (P. nibbānadhātu; S. NIRVĀṆADHĀTU) by virtue of which the practitioner ceases kinship with ordinary worldlings (P. puthujjana; S. PṚTHAGJANA) and becomes a noble one (ariya; ārya). Immediately thereafter, he or she enters the path by attaining what is called MAGGACITTA, or "path consciousness." It is this attainment of path consciousness that, technically speaking, constitutes the purity of knowledge and vision. If, at this time, the practitioner attains the path of a stream-enterer, which is the first and lowest of the four paths of sanctity, he or she permanently uproots the first three of ten fetters (SAṂYOJANA) that bind one to the cycle of existence, viz., (1) belief in the existence of a self in relation to the body (P. sakkāyadiṭṭhi; S. SATKĀYADṚṢṬI); (2) belief in the efficacy of rites and rituals (P. sīlabbataparāmāsa; S. ŚĪLAVRATAPARĀMARŚA); and (3) skeptical doubt about the efficacy of the path (P. vicikicchā; S. VICIKITSĀ). The sotāpanna will never again suffer a lower rebirth and is destined to attain full enlightenment (BODHI) and nibbāna in at most seven more lifetimes.

**nānādhātujñānabala**. (T. khams sna tshogs mkhyen pa'i stobs; C. zhongzhongjie zhili; J. shujukai chiriki; K. chonggyonggye chiryŏk 種種界智力). In Sanskrit, "power of knowing diverse elements," one of the ten special powers (BALA) of a buddha (S. tathāgatabala). One of the keys to the Buddha's extraordinary pedagogical skill was his telepathic ability to understand the level of spiritual development or capacity of each member of his audience, whereby he was able to teach what was most appropriate for a given person at a given time (see TRĪNDRIYA). Thus, it is said that the Buddha taught the goal of rebirth as a divinity in heaven (SVARGA) to those who lacked the capacity to seek liberation from rebirth, and the doctrine of the absence of a perduring self (ANĀTMAN) to those who lacked the capacity to understand the more profound doctrine of emptiness (ŚŪNYATĀ). Whereas the NĀNĀDHIMUKTIJÑĀNABALA reflects a buddha's ability to discern the predilections or personality of a disciple in a particular lifetime, the nānādhātujñānabala reflects a buddha's ability to discern the level of intelligence of a disciple in a particular lifetime. According to some conceptions of the Buddha, through his skillful methods (UPĀYAKAUŚALYA), the Buddha was able to give a single discourse (sometimes said to consist only of the letter "A"), and each member of the audience would hear a different teaching appropriate for him or her.

**nānādhimuktijñānabala**. (P. nānādhimuttikañāṇa; T. mos pa sna tshogs mkhyen pa'i stobs; C. zhongzhong shengjie zhili; J. shujushōge chiriki; K. chongjong sŭnghae chiryŏk 種種勝解智力). In Sanskrit, "power of knowing diverse aspirations," one of the ten special powers (BALA) of a buddha (S. tathāgatabala). One of the keys to the Buddha's extraordinary pedagogical skill was said to be his telepathic ability to understand the predilections or interests of each member of his audience, so that he could tailor his message to the aspirations of each individual. Thus, it is said that when the Buddha taught the practice of SAMĀDHI, he set forth forty different objects of concentration, each appropriate for a different personality. For those who were lustful, he taught meditation on the foulness of the human body; for those who were hateful, he taught meditation on loving-kindness; for those who were proud, he taught meditation on the twelve links of dependent origination; for those who were distracted, he taught meditation on the breath. Whereas the NĀNĀDHĀTUJÑĀNABALA reflects a buddha's ability to discern the level of intelligence of a disciple in a particular lifetime, the nānādhimuktijñānabala reflects a buddha's ability to discern the interests or personality of a disciple in a particular lifetime.

**Ñāṇagambhīra**. The name given to the great fifteenth-century reformer of Thai Buddhism in the PADAENG CHRONICLE. He is known as MEDHAṄKARA in the JINAKĀLAMĀLĪ.

**Ñāṇamoli, Bhikkhu**. (1905–1960). A distinguished British THERAVĀDA monk and translator from Pāli. Born Osbert Moore, he was educated at Exeter College, Oxford. During World War II, he served as a staff officer in Italy, where he became interested in Buddhism after reading Julius Evola's *The Doctrine of Awakening*. He joined the BBC after the war. In 1949, he traveled to Sri Lanka with his friend Harold Musson. Together, they received lower ordination (P. pabbajjā; cf. S. PRAVRAJITA) as novices (P. sāmaṇera; S. ŚRĀMAṆERA) at the Island Hermitage in Dodunduwa. They took higher ordination (UPASAṂPADĀ) as monks (P. bhikkhu; S. BHIKṢU) at Vajirarama Temple (Colombo) in 1950. Taking the ordination name Ñāṇamoli, Moore spent the remainder of his life living as a monk at the Island Hermitage, translating Pāli texts into English. His magnum opus was his renowned translation of BUDDHAGHOSA's VISUDDHIMAGGA, rendered as *The Path of Purification*, in 1956. Other translations include the NETTIPPAKARAṆA (published as *The Guide*) and the PAṬISAMBHIDĀMAGGA (published as *The Path of Discrimination*), as well as most of the suttas of the MAJJHIMANIKĀYA and several from the SAṂYUTTANIKĀYA. Other of his books include *The Life of the Buddha* and *A Thinker's Note Book*. He died suddenly of heart failure while on pilgrimage at Majo and was cremated at Vajirarama monastery.

**Ñāṇaponika Mahāthera**. (1901–1994). A distinguished German THERAVĀDA monk and scholar. Born Siegmund Feniger to a Jewish family in Hanau am Main, Germany, he first developed an interest in Buddhism through readings in his youth. His family moved to Berlin in 1922, where he met like-minded students of Buddhism and later formed a Buddhist study circle in the city of Konigsberg. He traveled to Sri Lanka in 1936 for further study and to escape Nazi persecution. That same year, he received lower ordination (P. pabbajjā; cf. S. PRAVRAJITA) as a novice (P. sāmaṇera; S. ŚRĀMAṆERA) under the German scholar-monk ÑĀṆATILOKA at his Island Hermitage in Dodunduwa. He took higher ordination (UPASAṂPADĀ) as a monk (P. bhikkhu; S. BHIKṢU) in 1937. During World War II, he was interned by the British at Dehra Dun along with with other German nationals, including Heinrich Harrer (who would escape to spend seven years in Tibet) and LAMA ANAGARIKA GOVINDA. After the war, he traveled to Burma with Ñāṇatiloka to participate in the sixth Buddhist council (see COUNCIL, SIXTH) that was held in Rangoon (Yangon). Ñāṇaponika was a delegate to several WORLD FELLOWSHIP OF BUDDHISTS conferences convened at Rangoon, Bangkok, and Phnom Penh, and served as vice-president of the organization in 1952. He resided at the Forest Hermitage in Kandy from 1958 to 1984. Ñāṇaponika was the founding editor of the Buddhist Publication Society and served as its president till 1988. An energetic teacher and prolific writer, his books include the influential *The Heart of Buddhist Meditation* and *Abhidhamma Studies*. For his many contributions and accomplishments, Ñāṇaponika was honored as one of four "Great Mentors, Ornaments of the Teaching" (mahāmahopadhyāyasāsanasobhana) in the AMARAPURA NIKĀYA, the monastic fraternity to which he belonged. He was for several decades the most senior Western Theravāda monk in the world, having completed his fifty-seventh rains retreat as a monk by the time of his death in 1994.

**Ñāṇatiloka Mahāthera**. (1878–1957). A distinguished German THERAVĀDA monk and scholar. Born Anton Walter Florus Gueth in Wiesbaden, Germany, in 1878, Ñāṇatiloka studied music at conservatories in Frankfurt and Paris and became a violinist. As a child, he became interested in religion, and, after attending a lecture on Theosophy in Berlin in 1899, he decided to travel to Asia. Traveling as a violinist, he toured Turkey, Egypt, and India. From India, he went to Sri Lanka and then to Burma. In 1903 he took ordination as a Buddhist novice (P. sāmaṇera; S. ŚRĀMAṆERA) in Rangoon (Yangon) from bhikkhu Ānanda Metteyya, apparently the first German ever to be ordained. In the following year he took higher ordination (UPASAṂPADĀ) as a monk (P. bhikkhu; S. BHIKṢU). After his ordination, Ñāṇatiloka moved to Sri Lanka in 1905. He traveled to Europe in 1910–1911, the first of many international tours, staying mostly in Switzerland, where he conducted the first Buddhist novice ordination (P. pabbajjā; cf. S. PRAVRAJITA) on European soil. In 1911, he returned to Sri Lanka and made his hermitage on an island infested with poisonous snakes in the middle of Ratgama Lake in southwestern Sri Lanka. When he arrived at the hermitage site, he was the only human on the island. People in the nearby town of Dodanduwa brought him offerings by boat every day. Soon, many Europeans came to be ordained by Ñānatiloka at what became known as Island Hermitage. He was interned by the British during World War I as an enemy alien. In 1916, he was given a passport to return to Germany via the United States. He traveled to Honolulu and then on to China but was arrested in Chungking (Chongqing) and imprisoned in Hankow (Hankou) until 1919, when he was exchanged by the International Red Cross and sent back to Germany. He was unable to return to Sri Lanka in 1920 and so went on to Japan, where he served as a professor at Komazawa University. In 1926, Ñāṇatiloka was finally able to return to Sri Lanka. Ñāṇatiloka was interned again with other German nationals (including his student ÑĀṆAPONIKA) during the Second World War and returned again to Sri Lanka in 1946. He was later naturalized as a Sri Lankan citizen. He founded the International Buddhist Union with LAMA ANAGARIKA GOVINDA, another student, to whom he gave his Buddhist name. Ñāṇatiloka was viewed by the Sinhalese as a great religious practitioner; upon Ñāṇatiloka's death in 1957, he received a cremation ceremony of the highest honor in Independence Square, with both the prime minister of Sri Lanka and the German ambassador attending. He published his most famous work, *The Word of the Buddha*, in 1906, as well as articles and books in both English and German, including *Buddhist Dictionary*, *Guide through the Abhidhamma-Piṭaka*, and *Path to Deliverance*.

**Nanatsudera**. (七寺). Japanese vernacular name of the monastery of Tōenzan Chōfukuji in downtown Nagoya; famous as the repository of a massive twelfth-century manuscript canon of East Asian Buddhist works that was designated an Important Cultural Property after World War II. The monastery, which is affiliated with the SHINGONSHŪ, was founded by GYŌGI in 735 and was originally named Shōgakuin. The monastery was destroyed in an air raid in March 1945, but its canon survived, stored in lacquered chests called karabitsu. In 1990, scholarly investigation of the 4,954 juan (3,398 in rolls, 1,556 in folded books) of Nantsudera's canon identified scores of juan of scriptures that were long believed to have been lost. Especially important were several previously unknown Chinese Buddhist APOCRYPHA, including seminal works of the proscribed SANJIE JIAO school. The Nanatsudera collection is considered by many scholars of East Asian Buddhism to be the most important discovery of Buddhist textual materials since the unearthing of the DUNHUANG cache in the early twentieth century.

**Nanda**. (T. Dga' bo; C. Nantuo; J. Nanda; K. Nanda 難陀). In Sanskrit and Pāli, "Joyful"; an ARHAT declared by the Buddha to be foremost among his monk disciples in self-control. Nanda was the son of ŚUDDHODANA and MAHĀPRĀJĀPATĪ and half brother of the Buddha. He was a few days younger than the Buddha, and Mahāprajāpatī handed him over to a wet nurse so that she could raise the bodhisattva as her own son when the latter's mother, MAHĀMĀYĀ, died. Nanda was extremely handsome (he is also known as Sundara Nanda, or "Handsome Nanda") and was said to have been vain about his looks. During the Buddha's sojourn at the ŚĀKYA capital of KAPILAVASTU after his enlightenment, he visited Nanda on the day his half-brother was to be married to a beautiful maiden named JANAPADAKALYĀṆĪ NANDĀ (also called Sundarī Nandā). Having wished his half brother well, the Buddha handed him his alms bowl (PĀTRA) to carry back to the monastery; the scene of Nanda holding the bowl, standing between the departing Buddha and his beckoning bride-to-be, is often depicted in Buddhist art. Once Nanda arrived at the monastery with the alms bowl, the Buddha asked Nanda to join the order, and only reluctantly, and out of deference to the Buddha, did he agree. But he longed for his fiancée and soon fell ill from his loneliness and depression, drawing pictures of her on rocks. Knowing Nanda's mind, the Buddha then flew with him to the TRĀYASTRIṂŚA heaven. Enroute, he pointed out an injured female monkey and asked Nanda whether Janapadakalyāṇī Nandā was more beautiful than the monkey; Nanda replied that she was. When they arrived in the heaven, the Buddha showed Nanda the celestial maidens attending the gods. Nanda was entranced with their loveliness, which far exceeded the beauty of Janapadakalyāṇī, saying that, compared to the celestial maidens, the beauty of his bride-to-be was like that of the monkey. The Buddha promised him one of these maidens as his consort in his next lifetime if he would only practice the religious life earnestly. Nanda enthusiastically agreed. Upon returning to the human world at JETAVANA grove, Nanda was criticized by ĀNANDA for his base motivation for remaining a monk. Feeling great shame at his lust, he resolved to overcome this weakness, practiced assiduously, and in due course became an ARHAT. In another version of the story, Nanda only overcomes his lust after a second journey: after going to heaven, the Buddha takes Nanda on a journey to hell, where he shows him the empty cauldron that awaits him after his lifetime in heaven. After his enlightenment, Nanda came to the Buddha to inform him of his achievement and to release the Buddha from his promise of celestial maidens. It was because of his great will to control his passions that Nanda was deemed foremost in self-control. Due to his previous attachment to women, however, it is said that even after he became an arhat, Nanda would stare at the beautiful women who attended the Buddha's discourses. The story of Nanda appears in a number of versions, including the poem SAUNDARANANDA by AŚVAGHOṢA.

**Nandaka**. (T. Dga' byed; C. Nantuojia; J. Nandaka; K. Nandaga 難陀迦). In Sanskrit and Pāli, "Pleasing"; an ARHAT declared by the Buddha to be foremost among monk disciples who preach to nuns. According to the Pāli account, Nandaka was born into a rich family of merchants dwelling in Sāvatthi (S. ŚRĀVASTĪ). He entered the order on the same day that Anāthapiṇḍika (S. ANĀTHAPIṆḌADA) donated the JETAVANA grove to the Buddha after hearing him preach. Nandaka practiced meditation and soon attained insight and became an ARHAT. Once, the Buddha requested that he preach to a large gathering of nuns, who had entered the order with Mahāpajāpatī (S. MAHĀPRAJĀPATĪ). He was hesitant when he recognized that they had been his wives in a previous life, when he had been a king. Fearing criticism from his fellows, he sent another monk as his substitute. The Buddha insisted that he preach, however, for he knew that only a sermon by Nandaka could lead the nuns to liberation. On the first day of his discourse, all in attendance became stream-enterers (P. sotāpanna; S. SROTAĀPANNA), and on the second day, five hundred became arhats. It was because of his great skill on this occasion that Nandaka earned a reputation for being preeminent in preaching. In one sermon attributed to him, Nandaka addressed a group of monks gathered in a waiting hall at Jetavana monastery. His voice attracted the Buddha, who listened the entire night from outside, because the door was locked. When he entered the hall the next morning, Nandaka begged forgiveness for having made him wait, but the Buddha only praised Nandaka for the quality of his sermon, stating that it was the duty of all good monks to give such exhortations.

**Nandimitra**. (T. Dga' ba'i bshes gnyen; C. Qingyou; J. Keiyū; K. Kyŏngu 慶友) (c. second century CE). An Indian ARHAT, presumed to have been born in Sri Lanka, who is traditionally regarded as the author the *Nandimitrāvadāna* (*Da aluohan Nantimiduoluo suoshuo fazhu ji*, abbr. *Fazhu ji*; "Record of the Duration of the Dharma Spoken by the Great Arhat Nandimitra"), the primary source for the cult of the sixteen (alt. eighteen) ARHAT, or LUOHAN. In this text, which was translated by XUANZANG in 654 CE, Nandimitra explains that, when the Buddha was on his deathbed, he entrusted his religion to sixteen great arhats (see ṢOḌAŚASTHAVIRA), who were charged with watching over and caring for the welfare of the laity and protecting the religious interests of Buddhism. These arhats were to remain in the world until the BODHISATTVA MAITREYA appears as the next buddha. They will then collect all the relics (ŚARĪRA) of ŚĀKYAMUNI and build a magnificent STŪPA to contain them. After paying homage to the stūpa, they will then vanish into PARINIRVĀṆA. Nandimitra gives the names of these sixteen arhats and identifies their domains and the size of their retinues.

**Nang Thorani**. (Laotian). See THORANI.

**Nanhai jigui neifa zhuan**. (J. Nankai kiki naihōden; K. Namhae kigwi naebŏp chŏn 南海寄歸内法傳). In Chinese, lit., "Tales of Returning from the South Seas with the Dharma," translated into English as *A Record of the Buddhist Kingdoms of the Southern Archipelago*; an important Buddhist travelogue by the Chinese monk YIJING (635–713) and a major source of information on monastic practice in the various places that he visited during his trip. Yijing dreamed of following in the footsteps of the renowned pilgrims FAXIAN and XUANZANG and, in 671, at the age of thirty-six, set out for India via the southern maritime route. After arriving in 673, he visited the major pilgrimage sites (see MAHĀSTHĀNA) on the subcontinent, before traveling to the monastic university at NĀLANDĀ, where he remained for the next ten years, studying Sanskrit texts especially associated with the VINAYA tradition. After departing from India in 685, Yijing stayed over in ŚRĪVIJAYA (Palembang in present-day Sumatra) and continued his studies for another four years. It is there that he composed this record of his travels and began his translation of the massive MŪLASARVĀSTIVĀDA VINAYA. After returning once to Guangdong (Canton) to retrieve more paper and ink, he returned to China for good in 695 CE. Yijing's four-roll long pilgrimage record is divided into forty sections, which provide a detailed description of the customs, rules, and regulations of the different Buddhist kingdoms and regions he visited. Unlike Xuanzang, Yijing is less concerned with describing the areas he visited and more with detailing the practice of Buddhism in the homeland of the religion. Yijing's interest in establishing an orthodox interpretation of vinaya that could be emulated by the Chinese can be readily observed in his detailed account of monastic rules and best practices governing ordination procedures, monastic residence during the rains retreat (VARṢĀ), worshipping a buddha image, cleaning, washing, caring for the sick, and performing funerals, to name but a few. Many of the texts that Yijing cites in corroboration of these practices are now lost; Yijing's record also serves as a valuable source for the study of the Buddhist literature of the period.

**Nanhuasi**. (南華寺). In Chinese, "Southern Florate Monastery"; located in present-day Guangdong province close to Nanhua Mountain and facing the Caoqi River. The monastery was built by an Indian monk in 502 CE during the Liang dynasty and was originally named Baolinsi (Bejeweled Forest Monastery). It went through several name changes until it was renamed Nanhuasi in 968 CE during the Song dynasty, and it has carried that name ever since. In 677 CE, during the Tang dynasty, HUINENG, the so-called sixth patriarch (LIUZU) of the CHAN school, is said to have come to Nanhuasi, where he founded the so-called "Southern school" (NAN ZONG) of Chan. From that point on, the monastery became an important center of the Chan school, and Huineng's remains are enshrined there, as are those of the Ming-dynasty Chan monk HANSHAN DEQING (1546–1623 CE). The monastery contains a stone slab that supposedly displays indentations left by Huineng's constant prostrations during his devotional services. The monastery is also famous for housing a bell named the Nanhua Bell, which weighs six tons and can be heard up to ten miles away.

**Nanjō Bun'yū**. (南条文雄) (1849–1927). Japanese Buddhist scholar who helped to introduce the modern Western discipline of Buddhist Studies to Japan; he is usually known in the West by his own preferred transcription of Nanjio Bunyiu. Nanjō was the third son of the abbot of a temple in the HIGASHI HONGANJIHA (see ŌTANIHA; HONGANJI) of JŌDO SHINSHŪ, and was eventually ordained as a priest in that sect. In 1876, the Higashi Honganjiha sent Nanjō to England, where he studied Sanskrit and other Buddhist canonical languages with FRIEDRICH MAX MÜLLER (1823–1900). After eight years overseas, he returned to Japan in 1884, teaching Sanskrit and Buddhism at Tōkyō Imperial University, where he was an important Japanese pioneer in Sanskrit pedagogy and the study of Indian Buddhist literature. He also held a succession of posts as professor and president of several Buddhist universities in Tōkyō, Kyōto, and Nagoya. Nanjō played a critical role in reviving the study of Buddhist literature in China. While he was in Oxford, Nanjō met YANG WENHUI (1837–1911; cognomen Yang Renshan) and later arranged to send Yang copies of some three hundred Chinese Buddhist texts that had been lost in China during the depredations of the Taiping Rebellion (1851–1865). Yang was able to reprint and distribute these scriptures from his personal publication house, the Jinling Sūtra Publishing Center, in Nanjing. Nanjō is best known in the West for publishing in 1883 the first comprehensive catalogue of the East Asian Buddhist canon, *A Catalogue of the Chinese Translation of the Buddhist Tripiṭaka, the Sacred Canon of the Buddhists in China and Japan, compiled by order of the Secretary of State for India.* This catalogue is especially important for making one of the first attempts to correlate the Chinese translations of Buddhist texts with their Sanskrit and Tibetan recensions. Nanjō also edited the Sanskrit recensions of such texts as the LAṄKĀVATĀRASŪTRA and the larger and smaller SUKHĀVATĪVYŪHASŪTRA (which he translated in collaboration with F. Max Müller) and assisted HENDRIK KERN in preparing his Sanskrit edition of the SADDHARMAPUṆḌARĪKASŪTRA.

**Nanpo Jōmyō**. [alt. Shōmyō] (南浦紹明) (1235–1308). Japanese ZEN master in the RINZAISHŪ; a native of Suruga in present-day Shizuoka Prefecture. He studied under the émigré Chinese Chan master LANXI DAOLONG (1213–1278) at the monastery of KENCHŌJI in Kamakura. In 1259, Nanpo left for China, where he studied with the LINJI ZONG Chan master XUTANG ZHIYU (1185–1269). Before returning to Japan, Nanpo is said to have received Xutang's seal of approval (see YINKE) and thus inherited Xutang's Linji lineage. In 1267, Nanpo returned to Japan and served his teacher Lanxi. Nanpo later moved to the monastery of Sūfukuji in Hakata (present-day Kyūshū), where he continued to reside for the next thirty-three years. In 1305, he was invited to the influential monastery of Manjuji in Kyōto and was installed as its abbot. Later, he served as abbot of his home monastery of Kenchōji. In 1309, he received the posthumous title State Preceptor Entsū Daiō (Perfect Penetration, Great Resonance). Among his disciples SŌHŌ MYŌCHŌ (1282–1337), also known as Daitō, is most famous. Currently, virtually all monks in the Rinzai Zen tradition trace their lineages back to Nanpo via HAKUIN EKAKU (1685–1769). The lineages that originated from Nanpo came to be known collectively as the Ōtōkan, which is a combination of Sinographs taken from the names of Dai-ō, Dai-tō, and Kan-zan (see KANZAN EGEN).

**Nanquan Puyuan**. (J. Nansen Fugan; K. Namch'ŏn Powŏn 南泉普願) (748–834). Chinese CHAN master in the HONGZHOU ZONG; a native of Xinzheng in present-day Henan province. In 777, Nanquan received the full monastic precepts from a certain VINAYA master Hao (d.u.) at the nearby monastery of Huishansi in Songyue. Along with studying such important MAHĀYĀNA scriptures as the LAṄKĀVATĀRASŪTRA and AVATAṂSAKASŪTRA, Nanquan also explored the major texts of the SAN LUN ZONG, the Chinese counterpart of the MADHYAMAKA school of Buddhist philosophy. He later became the disciple of the eminent Chan master MAZU DAOYI (709–788) and eventually one of his dharma successors. In 795, he began his long-time residence on Mt. Nanquan in Chiyang (present-day Anhui province), whence he acquired his toponym. He remained on the mountain for thirty years, where he devoted himself to teaching his students. Among his immediate disciples, ZHAOZHOU CONGSHEN (778–897) is most famous. Nanquan is renowned for his enigmatic sayings and antinomian behavior. Many of his noteworthy conversations with other masters are quoted in public case collections, such as the BIYAN LU and CONGRONG LU. Nanquan's teaching style is perhaps best captured in the (in)famous public case (GONG'AN) "Nanquan cuts the cat in two" (case no. 63 of the *Biyan lu*, case no. 14 in the WUMENGUAN). Monks from the eastern and western wings of the monastery were arguing over possession of a cat. Nanquan grabbed the cat and told the monks, "If anyone can say something to the point, you will save this cat's life; if not, I will kill it." No one replied, so Nanquan cut the cat in two. In the following gong'an in the *Biyan lu* (case no. 64), his disciple Zhaozhou Congshen returned to the monastery and heard the story. He immediately took off his straw sandals, placed them on his head, and walked away. Nanquan remarked, "If you had been here a moment ago, you could have saved that cat's life."

**Nanshan lü zong**. (J. Nanzan risshū; K. Namsan yulchong 南山律宗). In Chinese, the "South Mountain School of Discipline," the name for a loose affiliation of Chinese exegetes who traced their lineage back to the Chinese VINAYA master DAOXUAN (596–667). (The name Nanshan, or South Mountain, refers to Daoxuan's residence at ZHONGNANSHAN in present-day Shanxi province.) This tradition is largely concerned with the exegesis of the SIFEN LÜ ("Four-Part Vinaya") of the DHARMAGUPTAKA school. This VINAYA text, which came to be adopted widely throughout East Asia, was translated into Chinese in 405 by the Kashmīri monk BUDDHAYAŚAS (c. early fifth century CE) and is still followed today in the East Asian Buddhist traditions. It taught a code of discipline that involved 250 principal monastic precepts for monks, 348 for nuns. The central scripture of the Nanshan lü zong is Daoxuan's influential commentary on the *Sifen lü*, the *Sifen lü shanfan buque xingshi chao*, which was composed in 626. Although the Nanshan lü zong remained the dominant tradition of vinaya exegesis in China, other groups such as the DONGTA LÜ ZONG (East Pagoda) and Xiangbu (Xiang Region) vinaya schools also flourished. The interpretations of the Nanshan lü zong were introduced into Japan by the Chinese monk GANJIN (C. Jianzhen; 687–763), who helped established the School of Discipline (J. RISSHŪ), one of the six schools of the Nara tradition of early Japanese Buddhism (see NARA BUDDHISM, SIX SCHOOLS OF).

**Nanto shichidaiji**. (南都七大寺). In Japanese, "seven great monasteries of Nara," seven of the major Buddhist monasteries founded in the ancient Japanese capital of Nara. See individual entries for DAIANJI, GANGŌJI, HŌRYŪJI, KŌFUKUJI, SAIDAIJI, TŌDAIJI, and YAKUSHIJI.

**Nanyang Huizhong**. (J. Nan'yō Echū; K. Namyang Hyech'ung 南陽慧忠) (675?–775). Chinese CHAN master of the Tang dynasty; a native of Yuezhou in present-day Zhejiang province. He is said to have studied under the sixth patriarch (LIUZU) HUINENG (638–713) as a youth and to have eventually become one of his dharma successors. After Huineng's death, Nanyang led an itinerant life, traveling from one monastery to the next until he settled down on Mt. Baiya in Nanyang (present-day Henan province), whence he acquired his toponym. He is said to have remained in seclusion on the mountain for some forty years. In 761, he was invited to the palace by Emperor Suzong (r. 756–762), who honored Nanyang as his teacher. He took up residence at the monastery of Qianfusi, but later moved to Guangzhaisi at the request of Emperor Daizong (r. 762–779). Nanyang later established the monasteries of Yanchangsi and Changshousi and installed a copy of the Buddhist canon (DAZANGJING) at each site. Juizong lived during a period of great efflorescence in the Chan school, but he was not closely identified with any one school. He is, however, said to have been critical of the teachings of the Chan master MAZU DAOYI (709–788) and other HONGZHOU ZONG teachers in Sichuan in the south of China, who rejected the authority of the traditional Buddhist scriptures; he is also said to have criticized the Hongzhou interpretation of "mind is buddha" as being akin to the ŚREṆIKA HERESY, in which the body is simply an impermanent vessel for an eternal mind or soul. The notion that "inanimate objects can preach the dharma" (wujing shuofa) is also attributed to Nanyang.

**Nanyue Huairang**. (J. Nangaku Ejō; K. Namak Hoeyang 南嶽懷讓) (677–744). Chinese CHAN monk of the Tang dynasty, Huairang was a native of Jinzhou in present-day Shandong province. At an early age, Huairang is said to have gone to the monastery of Yuquansi in Jingzhou (present-day Hubei province) where he studied VINAYA under the vinaya master Hongjing (d.u.). Later, he visited SONGSHAN and continued his studies under Hui'an (also known as Lao'an or "Old An"; 582–709), a reputed disciple of the fifth patriarch HONGREN (601–674). Hui'an purportedly introduced Huairang to the sixth patriarch (LIUZU) HUINENG (638–713), from whom Huairang eventually received dharma transmission. In 713, Huairang began teaching at the monastery of Boresi on Mt. Nanyue (present-day Hunan province), whence his toponym. There, Huairang acquired his most famous disciple, MAZU DAOYI (709–788). As most of what is known of Huairang comes from the work of Mazu and Mazu's students, some scholars contend that the obscure figure of Huairang was used as a convenient means of linking Mazu's successful HONGZHOU ZONG line with the legendary sixth patriarch Huineng. The Chan lamplight records (CHUANDENG LU) trace the GUIYANG ZONG and LINJI ZONG, two of the traditional "five houses" (see WU JIA QI ZONG) of the mature Chan tradition, back to Nanyue Huirang.

**Nanyue Huisi**. (J. Nangaku Eshi; K. Namak Hyesa 南嶽慧思) (515–577). Chinese monk in the TIANTAI school and teacher of TIANTAI ZHIYI (538–597); also known as Great Master Nanyue and Great Master Si. Huisi was a native of Yuzhou in present-day Anhui province. According to his biography in the Liang-era GAOSENG ZHUAN, Huisi was obsessed with the prospect of death in his youth and assiduously pursued a means of attaining immortality. Studying with his teacher Huiwen (d.u.), about whom next to nothing is known, Huisi is said to have learned a meditative technique based on NĀGĀRJUNA's premise of the identity of emptiness, provisionality, and their mean (see SANDI), which he later taught to his own students. Monks who disagreed with his teachings tried to poison him, so Huisi left northern China for the south, but his popularity there prompted jealous monks to brand him a spy. This charge was rejected by the Chen-dynasty emperor, and Huisi continued to teach in the south, where he attracted many students, including the renowned Tiantai Zhiyi. Huisi's meditative teachings on the suiziyi sanmei ("cultivating SAMĀDHI wherever mind is directed," or "the samādhi of freely flowing thoughts") were recorded in Zhiyi's MOHE ZHIGUAN. In this type of meditation, the adept is taught to use any and all experiences, whether mental or physical, whether wholesome or unwholesome, as grist for the mill of cultivating samādhi. Huisi is credited with the compilation of several treatises, such as the *Dasheng zhiguan*, *Cidi chanyao*, *Fahua jing anle xingyi*, and others.

**Nanzenji**. (南禪寺). In Japanese, "Southern ZEN Monastery," major monastery in Kyōto, Japan, that is currently the headquarters (honzan) of the Nanzenji branch of the RINZAISHŪ. In 1264, Emperor Kameyama (r. 1259–1274) built a country villa, which he later converted to a Zen monastery named Nanzenji. He invited the monk Mukan Fumon (1212–1291), a disciple of ENNI BEN'EN (1202–1280), to serve as the monastery's founding abbot (J. kaisan; C. KAISHAN). After Fumon's departure, the monk Soen (1261–1313) succeeded Mukan and oversaw additional construction at the monastery. As the first Zen monastery constructed by an emperor, many eminent Zen masters were appointed to its abbacy. In 1325, Emperor Godaigo (r. 1318–1339) invited MUSŌ SŌSEKI (1275–1351) to serve as abbot of Nanzenji. After his triumphant return to Kyōto in 1334, Godaigo elevated Nanzenji to the first rank in the influential GOZAN system. Nanzenji maintained this rank, even after political power was handed over to the Ashikaga shogunate. During the Muromachi period, the abbacy of Nanzenji came to be restricted only to those who had already served as abbot of another gozan monastery. For this reason, Nanzenji became the center of gozan culture and Zen practice. The monastery suffered from a series of conflagrations in 1393, 1447, and 1467. Although the monastery never fully recovered from these fires, some restoration efforts were made by Toyotomi Hideyoshi (1536–1598).

**Nan zong**. (J. Nanshū; K. Nam chong 南宗). In Chinese, "Southern School," an appellation used widely throughout the Tang dynasty, largely due to the efforts of HEZE SHENHUI (684–758) and his lineage, to describe what they claimed to be the orthodox lineage of the CHAN ZONG; in distinction to the collateral lineage of the "Northern School" (BEI ZONG) of SHENXIU (606–706) and his successors. Heze Shenhui toured various provinces and constructed ordination platforms, where he began to preach that HUINENG (638–713), whom he claimed as his teacher, was the true sixth patriarch (LIUZU) of the Chan school. In 732, during an "unrestricted assembly" (WUZHE

DAHUI) held at the monastery of Dayunsi in Huatai, Shenhui engaged a monk by the name of Chongyuan (d.u.) and publicly criticized what he called the "Northern School" of Shenxiu's disciples PUJI (651–739), YIFU (661–736), and XIANGMO ZANG (d.u.) as being merely a collateral branch of BODHIDHARMA's lineage, which advocated an inferior gradualistic teaching. Shenhui argued that his teacher Huineng had received the orthodox transmission of Bodhidharma's lineage and the "sudden teaching" (DUNJIAO), which was the unique soteriological doctrine of Bodhidharma and his Chan school. Shenhui launched a vociferous attack on the Northern School, whose influence and esteem in both religious and political circles were unrivaled at the time. He condemned Shenxiu's so-called "Northern School" for having wrongly usurped the mantle of the Chan patriarchy from Huineng's "Southern School." Shenhui also (mis)characterized the teaching of the "Northern School" as promoting a "gradual" approach to enlightenment (JIANWU), which ostensibly stood in stark contrast to Huineng's and thus Shenhui's own "sudden awakening" (DUNWU) teachings. As a result of Shenhui's polemical attacks on Shenxiu and his disciples, subsequent Chan historians, such as GUIFENG ZONGMI (780–841), came to refer reflexively to a gradualist "Northern School" that was to be rigidly distinguished from a subitist "Southern School." Modern scholarship has demonstrated that, in large measure, the centrality of the "Southern School" to early Chan history is a retrospective creation. The Chan patriarchal lineage going back to Chan's putative founder, Bodhidharma, was still inchoate in the eighth century; indeed, contemporary genealogical histories, such as the LIDAI FABAO JI, CHUAN FABAO JI, LENGQIE SHIZI JI, and BAOLIN ZHUAN, demonstrate how fluid and fragile the notion of the Chan lineage remained at this early period. Because the lineages that eventually came to be recognized within the later tradition were not yet cast in stone, it was therefore possible for Shenhui to advocate that a semilegendary, and relatively unknown figure, Huineng, rather than the leading Chan figures of his time, was the orthodox successor of the fifth patriarch HONGREN and the real sixth patriarch (liuzu). While this characterization is now known to be misleading, subsequent histories of the Chan tradition more or less adopted Shenhui's vision of early Chan history. The influential LIUZU TAN JING played an important role in this process of distinguishing a supposedly inferior, gradualist Northern School from a superior, subitist Southern School. By the eleventh century, with the composition of the mature Chan genealogical histories, such as the CHODANG CHIP (C. ZUTANG JI) and JINGDE CHUANDENG LU, this orthodox lineage was solidified within the tradition and became mainstream. In these later "transmission of the lamplight" records (CHUANDENG LU), the "Southern School" was now unquestioned as the orthodox successor in Bodhidharma's lineage, a position it retained throughout the subsequent history of the Chan tradition. Despite Shenhui's virulent attacks against the "Northern School," we now know that Shenxiu and his disciples were much more central to the early Chan school, and played much more important roles in Chan's early growth and development, than the mature tradition realized.

**Naong Hyegŭn**. (懶翁慧勤) (1320–1376). In Korean, "Old Lazybones, Earnest in Wisdom," an eminent Korean SŎN master and pilgrim of the Koryŏ dynasty. Naong was a native of Yŏnghae in present-day North Kyŏngsang province and is said to have decided to become a monk after the traumatic death of a close friend in 1339. After his ordination by the monk Yoyŏn (d.u.) of the hermitage of Myojŏgam on Mt. Kongdŏk, Naong traveled from one monastery to the next until he settled down at the monastery of Hoeamsa in 1344. Four years later at Hoeamsa, Naong is said to have attained his first awakening. In 1347, he left for China where he met the Indian master ZHIKONG CHANXIAN (1289–1363; K. Chigong Sŏnhyŏn; S. *Śūnyadiśya-Dhyānabhadra) at the monastery of Fayuansi in the Yuan-dynasty capital of Yanjing; later, Naong would receive dharma transmission from Zhikong. After studying under Zhikong, Naong visited the Chan master Pingshan Chulin (1279–1361) at Jingcisi in Hangzhou (present-day Zhejiang province). Naong is said to have later received Pingshan's chowrie (FUZI; VĀLAVYAJANA) as a sign of his spiritual attainment. Before his return to the Yuan capital of Yanjing in 1355, Naong made a pilgrimage to MT. PUTUOSHAN, where he made offerings to the bodhisattva AVALOKITEŚVARA (GUANYIN). Upon his arrival back in Yanjing, he was appointed abbot of the monastery of Guangjisi by Emperor Xundi (r. 1333–1368). In 1358, Naong returned to Korea and three years later was invited to the royal palace, where he taught the king and queen. In 1370, Naong was appointed the royal preceptor (wangsa) and abbot of the influential monastery of SONGGWANGSA. Naong was viewed as a living buddha and eventually became the object of cultic worship: in the apocryphal *Ch'isŏng kwangmyŏng kyŏng* ("Book of Blazing Light"), which was widely disseminated in Korea in the sixteenth century, Naong is said to have been an emanation of ŚĀKYAMUNI Buddha himself. He spent the next few years revitalizing the community at his old monastery of Hoeamsa. Among his many disciples, MUHAK CHACH'O (1327–1405) is most famous.

**Nara Buddhism, Six Schools of**. A traditional grouping of six major scholastic schools of Japanese Buddhism active during the Nara period (710–794 CE): (1) Sanronshū (see SAN LUN ZONG), an East Asian counterpart of the MADHYAMAKA school; (2) Kegonshū (see HUAYAN ZONG), an East Asian exegetical tradition focused on the AVATAṂSAKASŪTRA; (3) RISSHŪ, or VINAYA exegesis; (4) Jōjitsushū (see CHENGSHI LUN) the TATTVASIDDHI exegetical tradition; (5) Hossōshū (see FAXIANG ZONG), an East Asian strand of YOGĀCĀRA; and (6) Kushashū, focused on ABHIDHARMA exegesis using the ABHIDHARMAKOŚABHĀṢYA. These six schools are presumed to have been founded during the initial phase of Buddhism's introduction into Japan, between c. 552 and the end of the Nara period in 794. These learned schools were eventually supplanted by the practice and meditative schools of TENDAISHŪ and SHINGONSHŪ, which were introduced during the succeeding Heian period (794–1185), and the later schools of the ZENSHŪ, the pure land schools of JŌDOSHŪ and JŌDO SHINSHŪ, and NICHIRENSHŪ of the Kamakura period (1185–1333).

**Nara daibutsu**. [alt. Birushana Nyorai] (奈良大佛/毘盧遮那如來). In Japanese, lit. "The Great Buddha of Nara"; a colossal image of the buddha VAIROCANA located at TŌDAIJI in the ancient Japanese capital of Nara. At about forty-eight feet (14.98 meters) high, this image is the largest extant gilt-bronze image in the world, and the Daibutsuden (Great Buddha Hall) where the image is enshrined is the world's largest surviving wooden building. Despite its massive size, however, the current Daibutsuden, which was reconstructed during the middle of the Edo period (1603–1867) to a height of 156 feet (forty-eight meters), is only two-thirds the size of the original structure. The Indian monk BODHISENA (J. Bodaisenchi) (704–760), who traveled to Japan in 736 at the invitation of Emperor Shōmu (r. 724–749), performed the "opening the eyes" (KAIYAN; NETRAPRATIṢṬHĀPANA) ceremony for the 752 dedication of the great buddha image. The bronze body of the image was restored in 1185, and the massive head (seventeen feet, or 5.3 meters, in size) was repaired in 1692. See also KAMAKURA DAIBUTSU.

**Nārada Mahāthera**. (1898–1983). A prominent modern Sri Lankan THERAVĀDA scholar and missionary monk (dhammaduta bhikkhu). Born in a Colombo suburb, he studied at the Roman Catholic St. Benedict's College (where the medium of instruction was English) and at the Buddhist Paramananda Vihāra Sunday school. He was ordained as a novice (P. sāmaṇera; S. ŚRĀMAṆERA) at the age of eighteen under the guidance of Pelene Vajirañāna Mahānāyaka Thera. He received a traditional monastic education in Pāli but also studied Western philosophy, logic, and ethics. He began missionary work with the Servants of the Buddha Society and took his first journey outside of Sri Lanka in 1929, to India. He later traveled widely in Southeast Asia and developed close ties with Buddhists in Indonesia and Vietnam. In the late 1940s, he was involved in the resumption of Theravāda missionary activity among the Newars of Kathmandu Valley in Nepal after the ban on religious propagation was lifted by the Rana regime. He also devoted himself to promoting Theravāda Buddhism in Australia and Western Europe and was elected president of the Buddhist Vihāra Society in London in 1948. Nārada Mahāthera was a prolific writer, and his publications ranged from Buddhist ethics and meditation to ABHIDHAMMA studies. His more popular books include *Buddhism in a Nutshell*, *The Buddha and His Teachings*, *The Buddhist Conception of Mind or Consciousness*, *The Buddhist Doctrine of Kamma and Rebirth*, *The Way to Nibbana*, *The Life of the Buddha*, and *An Elementary Pali Course*. His English translations include *The Dhammapada* and *Abhidhammathasaṅgaha: A Manual of Abhidhamma*.

**Naraen Kongō**. (J) (那羅延金剛). See NIŌ.

**nāraka**. (P. nerayika; T. dmyal ba; C. diyu [youqing/zhongsheng]; J. jigoku [ujō/shujō]; K. chiok [yujŏng/chungsaeng] 地獄[有情/衆生]). In Sanskrit, "hell denizen," the lowest of the six rebirth destinies (GATI) in the realm of SAṂSĀRA, followed by ghosts, animals, demigods, humans, and divinities. In Buddhist cosmography, there is an elaborate system of hells (naraka or niraya in Sanskrit and Pāli), and Buddhist texts describe in excruciating detail the torment hell denizens are forced to endure as expiation for the heinous acts that led to such baleful rebirths (cf. ĀNANTARYAKARMAN). According to one well-known system, the hells consist of eight hot hells, eight cold hells, and four neighboring hells (PRATYEKANARAKA), all located beneath the surface of the continent of JAMBUDVĪPA. The ground in the hot hells is made of burning iron. The ground in the cold hells is made of snow and ice; there is no sun or any source of light or heat. The eight hot hells, in descending order in depth and ascending order in suffering, are named reviving (SAṂJĪVA), black line (KĀLASŪTRA), crushed together (SAṂGHĀTA), crying (RAURAVA), great crying (MAHĀRAURAVA), hot (TĀPANA), very hot (PRATĀPANA), and interminable (AVĪCI). The eight cold hells, in descending order in depth and ascending order in suffering, are named blisters (arbuda), bursting blisters (nirarbuda), chattering teeth (aṭaṭa), moaning (hahava; translated into Tibetan as a chu zer ba, "saying 'achoo'"), moaning (huhuva), [skin split like a] blue lotus (utpala), [skin split like a] lotus (padma), and [skin split like a] great lotus (mahāpadma). The neighboring hells include (1) the pit of embers (KUKŪLA), (2) the swamp of corpses (KUṆAPA), (3) the road of razors (KṢURAMĀRGA), grove of swords (ASIPATTRAVANA), and forest of spikes (AYAḤŚĀLMALĪVANA), and (4) the river difficult to ford (NADĪ VAITARAṆĪ). Buddhist hells are places of rebirth rather than permanent postmortem abodes; there is no concept in Buddhism of eternal damnation. The life spans in the various hells may be incredibly long but they are finite; once the hell denizen's life span is over, one will be reborn elsewhere. In a diorama of the hells on display at the Chinese cave sites at DAZU SHIKE, for example, after systematic depictions of the anguish of the various hells, the last scene shows the transgressor being served a cup of tea, as a respite from his protracted torments, before being sent on to his next rebirth.

**Nara, seven great monasteries of**. See NANTO SHICHIDAIJI.

**Nārāyaṇa**. (T. Sred med kyi bu; C. Naluoyan tian; J. Naraenten; K. Narayŏn ch'ŏn 那羅延天). In ancient India, Nārāyaṇa was the son of the primordial person (puruṣa) and was later regarded as an avatar of the Hindu god Viṣṇu. He was adopted into Buddhism as one of the guardian deities (DHARMAPĀLA). His image is often seen standing at the entrance to a monastery, protecting its hallowed precincts from baleful influences. Because the divinity BRAHMĀ (alt. Mahābrahmā) was born from a lotus that blossomed from the navel of Nārāyaṇa, Nārāyaṇa is also sometimes identified as being the mother of

Brahmā, the presiding divinity in the third and highest of the three levels of the first DHYĀNA heaven in the subtle-materiality realm (RŪPADHĀTU). (Like Nārāyaṇa, Brahmā is also adopted into Buddhism as a dharmapāla.) Since Brahmā is regarded as the "father of creatures," Nārāyaṇa is in turn called the "Origin of Human Life" (C. Renshengben). Nārāyaṇa is said to dwell in the Diamond Grotto on WUTAISHAN in China, which leads directly to the pure land and was thought to be the site where MAÑJUŚRĪ and VIMALAKĪRTI discussed the MAHĀYĀNA teachings in the VIMALAKĪRTINIRDEŚA.

**Narendrayaśas**. (C. Naliantiliyeshe; J. Narendairiyasha; K. Naryŏnjeriyasa 那連提黎耶舍) (517–589). Sanskrit proper name of an Indian translator of primarily Mahāyāna Buddhist texts into Chinese. Born in OḌḌIYĀNA in northeastern India into the KṢATRIYA caste, Narendrayaśas was ordained at the age of seventeen and left on pilgrimage to the Buddhist sacred sites on the Indian subcontinent, his travels taking him as far as the Himalayas in the north and the island of Sri Lanka in the south. After residing at the VEṆUVANAVIHĀRA monastery in India for a decade, he eventually traveled north of the Himalayas to propagate Buddhism, before getting caught in the Turkic invasions that made it impossible for him to return home. Turning east through Central Asia, he ended up traveling along the SILK ROAD to China, arriving in the Northern Qi kingdom in 556. Residing at Tianpingsi at the request of Emperor Wenxuan (r. 550–559) and later at Daxingshansi in Chang'an, he translated some fourteen texts into Chinese, including the KARUṆĀPUṆḌARĪKA, SAMĀDHIRĀJA, and the MAHĀMEGHASŪTRA.

**Nā ro chos drug**. (Naro chödruk). The Tibetan name for a series of tantric practices, often translated into English as "the six yogas (or dharmas) of Nāropa," which are attributed to the eleventh-century Indian adept NĀROPA. These practices spread widely throughout Tibet, where they were transmitted among various Tibetan Buddhist traditions, including those of the SA SKYA and DGE LUGS. However, the Nā ro chos drug became a fundamental component in the meditation training of BKA' BRGYUD practitioners and continue to be practiced especially in the context of the traditional three-year retreat. Nāropa received several streams of tantric instruction from his GURU, the Indian SIDDHA TILOPA, including the BKA' BABS BZHI (four transmissions). According to tradition, he later codified these instructions and transmitted them to his Tibetan disciple MAR PA CHOS KYI BLO GROS, although Nāropa had died before Mar pa's first journey to India. However, Mar pa received these teachings from Nāropa's disciples and taught them in Tibet as the Nā ro chos drug. There are several slight variations in their presentation, but the most common enumeration of the Nā ro chos drug are (1) GTUM MO (tummo), literally "fierce woman," referring to the inner heat produced as an effect of manipulating the body's subtle energies; (2) sgyu lus (gyulu), "illusory body" (see MĀYĀDEHA), in which the meditator realizes the illusory nature of ordinary experiences; (3) rmi lam (milam), "dreams," referring to the practice of developing conscious awareness during dream states; (4) 'od gsal (ösel), "clear light" (see PRABHĀSVARA), referring to the luminous aspect of mind and its recognition; (5) BAR DO, "intermediate state," referring to the practice of mental control during the disorienting period between death in one lifetime and rebirth into another; (6) 'PHO BA (powa), "transference," which is the practice of ejecting the consciousness out of the body at the moment of death to take rebirth in a pure realm. The first four are generally believed to facilitate liberation in the present life, the last two at the time of death.

**Nāropa**. (1016–1100?). An Indian scholar and tantric master who holds an important place in the lineages of tantric Buddhism in Tibet. According to his traditional biography, Nāropa was a brāhmaṇa born in Bengal, who traveled to KASHMIR as a child. He was forced to marry at the age of seventeen, but the marriage ended by mutual consent after eight years. According to some sources, Nāropa's wife (or sister according to other sources) was NIGUMA, who became a famous tantric YOGINĪ. Nāropa was ordained as a Buddhist monk, entering NĀLANDĀ monastry in 1049. His talents as a scholar eventually led him to be selected to serve as abbot and as a senior instructor known by the name Abhayakīrti. In 1057, while at the monastery, he encountered an old hag (in reality a ḌĀKINĪ), who told him that he had understood the words of the texts he had studied but not their inner meaning. She urged him to go in search of her brother TILOPA. As a result of this encounter, Nāropa left the monastery to find Tilopa and become his disciple. Over the course of his journey, he encountered Tilopa in various forms but was unable to recognize him. Tilopa eventually revealed himself to Nāropa, subjecting him to a famous series of twelve greater and twelve lesser trials, involving serious physical injury and mental anguish. Tilopa eventually transferred his realization to Nāropa by striking him on the head with his shoe. Nāropa later compiled Tilopa's instructions and transmitted them to his own disciples. According to tradition, these students included the Tibetan translator MAR PA CHOS KYI BLO GROS, but in fact Nāropa had died before Mar pa made his first journey to India. Regardless, various instructions of Nāropa were transmitted to Tibet, the most famous of which are the NĀ RO CHOS DRUG, or "six doctrines (or yogas) of Nāropa." These practices became important for numerous Buddhist lineages but are especially associated with the BKA' BRGYUD sect, where Nāropa holds a central place in the lineage from VAJRADHARA to Tilopa to Nāropa to Mar pa to MI LA RES PA. Several works attributed to Nāropa are preserved in the Tibetan canon.

**nāśanīya**. (P. nāsana; T. bsnyil ba; C. binchu; J. hinzui; K. pinch'ul 擯出). In Sanskrit, lit. "removal"; an ecclesiastical procedure (KARMAN) that the SAṂGHA carries out against a novice (ŚRĀMAṆERA) or a nun (BHIKṢŪṆĪ), whereby certain privileges are withdrawn because of misconduct. According to the Pāli VINAYA, there are three kinds of nāśanīya (P. nāsana): (1)

liṅganāsana, or "removal of the sign," here meaning removing the robe or defrocking the guilty party; (2) saṃvāsanāsana, or removing the guilty party from association with other monastics; and (3) daṇḍakammanāsana, or the expulsion of a novice for an offense. There are ten occasions that may entail the application of nāsana to the novice, viz., (1) killing living creatures, (2) theft, (3) unchastity, (4) lying about spiritual attainments, (5) using intoxicants, (6–8) criticizing either the Buddha, the dharma, or the saṃgha, (9) heresy, and (10) seducing nuns.

**Nāsik**. A group of twenty-four Buddhist caves dating from the early second century CE, northeast of Mumbai (Bombay) in the Indian state of Maharastra. All the caves except cave 18 are VIHĀRA caves. The interiors of the caves are quite plain, in contrast to their highly ornamented exteriors, which include lithic carvings made to resemble wooden structures. The CAITYA cave has a pillared interior with a STŪPA in its apse, which is a characteristic feature of early Indian Buddhist cave temples. Figures and ornaments in its facade bear resemblance to similar motifs at SĀÑCĪ, suggesting artistic influence from that site.

**nāstika**. (P. natthika; T. med pa pa; C. zhiwu; J. shūmu; K. chimmu 執無). In Sanskrit, literally, "one who says 'is not'," that is, "nihilist," typically used in Buddhist materials to refer to specific ŚRAMAṆA religious groups, like the ĀJĪVAKA and some of the Cārvāka materialists, who either do not accept the validity of moral cause and effect (KARMAN) and hence REBIRTH, or reject the reality of sensory phenomena. In Hindu literature, the term is used to refer to those who reject the authority of the Vedas; in this latter sense, Buddhists (as well as the JAINA) are classed as nāstika.

**nat**. In Burmese, a generic term for a "spirit" or "god." Burmese (Myanmar) lore posits the existence of numerous species of nats, of both indigenous and Indian origin. Nats can range in temperament from benign to malevolent, including those who are potentially helpful but dangerous if offended. The most generally benevolent species of nats are the divinities (DEVA) of the Indian pantheon. This group includes such gods as Thakya Min (ŚAKRA) and Byama (BRAHMĀ). Nats of Indian origin are typically looked upon as servants of the Buddhist religion, which is how they are depicted in Burmese Pāli literature. Indigenous nats in the form of nature spirits are thought to occupy trees, hills, streams, and other natural sites, and may cause harm if disturbed. The guardian spirits of villages and of the home are also classified as nats. Certain nats guard medicinal herbs and certain minerals, and, when properly handled, aid alchemists in their search for elixirs and potions. One species of nat, the oktazaung, are ghosts who have been forced to act as guardians of pagoda treasures. These unhappy spirits are thought to be extremely dangerous and to bring calamity upon those who attempt to rob pagodas or encroach upon pagoda lands. The best-known group of nats is the "thirty-seven nats" of the Burmese national pantheon. For centuries, they have been the focus of a royal cult of spirit propitiation; the worship of national nats is attested as early as the eleventh century CE at PAGAN (Bagan). At the head of the pantheon is Thakya Min, but the remaining are all spirits of deceased humans who died untimely or violent deaths, mostly at the hands of Burmese monarchs. The number thirty-seven has remained fixed over the centuries, although many of the members of the pantheon have been periodically replaced. One of the nats who has maintained his position is Mahagiri Min, lord of the nat pantheon, occupying a position just beneath Thakya Min. Mahagiri dwells atop Mount Poppa and is also worshipped as the household nat in most Burmese homes. An annual nat festival of national importance is held in August at the village of Taungbyon near Mandalay. The festival is held in honor of Shwepyingyi and Shwepyinnge, two Muslim brothers who became nats as a consequence of being executed by King Kyanzittha of Pagan (r. 1084–1112) who feared their supernormal strength.

**navadharma**. In Sanskrit, the "nine dharmas," also known as the NAVAGRANTHA ("nine books"); nine MAHĀYĀNA SŪTRAS that are the object of particular devotion in the Newar Buddhist tradition of Nepal. The notion of a collection of nine books seems to have originated in the Newar community, although the nine sūtras are all of Indian origin. The nine are the AṢṬASĀHASRIKĀPRAJÑĀPĀRAMITĀ, SADDHARMAPUṆḌARĪKASŪTRA, LALITAVISTARA, LAṄKĀVATĀRASŪTRA, SUVARṆAPRABHĀSOTTAMASŪTRA, GAṆḌAVYŪHA, Tathāgataguhyasūtra, SAMĀDHIRĀJASŪTRA, and DAŚABHŪMIKASŪTRA. Of these nine, the *Aṣṭasāhasrikāprajñāpāramitā* is granted the highest esteem, having its own cult and its own deity, the goddess PRAJÑĀPĀRAMITĀ. These texts serve an important ritual function in Newar Buddhism, where they are said to represent the entire Mahāyāna corpus of SŪTRA, ŚĀSTRA, and TANTRA. These texts are often recited during the religious services of monasteries, and a recitation of all nine texts is considered to be particularly auspicious. Some Newar Buddhist rituals (vrata) include offerings to the three jewels (RATNATRAYA), in which a priest will make a MAṆḌALA for the GURU, the Buddha, the DHARMA, and the SAṂGHA. These sūtras of the nine dharmas are used in the creation of the dharmamaṇḍala, a powerful ritual symbol in Newar Buddhism. In this MAṆḌALA, the center space is occupied by the *Aṣṭasāhasrikāprajñāpāramitā*. The fact that there are nine of these texts may derive from the need to have nine elements in the maṇḍala. Different renditions of the dharmamaṇḍala indicate that the texts included in the navadharma may have changed over time; this particular set of nine sūtras seems to date from the fifteenth century. Although these texts are held in particularly high regard, they are not the only authoritative texts in Newar Buddhism.

**navagrantha**. (S). The "nine books." See NAVADHARMA.

**navaṅga[pāvacana].** (S. navāṅga; T. gsung rab yan lag dgu; C. jiubu jing; J. kubu kyō; K. kubu kyŏng 九部經). In Pāli, the "nine sections" or categories of the Buddha's teachings based on content, structure, or literary style. In the Pāli tradition and some BUDDHIST HYBRID SANSKRIT sources, the nine sections that are typically listed are discourses (P. sutta; S. SŪTRA), aphorisms in mixed prose and verse (P. geyya; S. GEYA), prophetic teachings or expositions (P. veyyākaraṇa; S. VYĀKARAṆA), verses (GĀTHĀ), utterance or meaningful expressions (UDĀNA), fables (P. ITIVUTTAKA; S. ITIUṚTTAKA), tales of previous lives (JĀTAKA), marvelous events (P. abbhutadhamma; S. ADBHUTADHARMA), and catechisms or works of great extent (P. vedalla; S. VAIPULYA). See also DVĀDAŚĀṄGA[PRAVACANA].

**navasaṃjñā.** (P. navasaññā; T. 'du shes dgu; C. jiuxiang guan; J. kusōkan; K. kusanggwan 九想觀). In Sanskrit, lit. "the nine perceptions," one of the so-called meditations on the impurity/foulness [of the body] (AŚUBHABHĀVANĀ), the objective of which is to facilitate understanding of impermanence (ANITYA), to develop disenchantment toward one's own and others' bodies, and/or to subdue lustful thoughts. In this meditation, the adept either mentally visualizes or physically observes the progressive decay of a corpse through nine specific stages: mottled discoloration of the corpse (vinīlakasaṃjñā), discharges of pus (vipūyakasaṃjñā), the decay of rotten flesh (vipadumakasaṃjñā), bloating and tumefaction (vyādhmātakasaṃjñā), the exuding of blood and the overflow of body fluids (vilohitakasaṃjñā), infestation of worms and maggots (vikhāditakasaṃjñā), the dissolution of flesh and exposure of bones and sinews (vikṣiptakasaṃjñā), the cremated remains (vidagdhakasaṃjñā), and the dispersed skeletal parts (asthisaṃjñā). These contemplations help to wean the meditator from the affliction of lust (RĀGA; LOBHA), but lead only to the first of the four levels of meditative absorption (DHYĀNA).

**Neichi Toin.** (1557–1629). Important Mongolian teacher who helped to spread Buddhism in Inner Mongolia; his traditional biography appears in a work entitled *Cindamani-yin erike*. Neichi Toin was the son of a Torghud noble. In order to comply with his father's wishes, he married and fathered a child, but left the family home in his late twenties and traveled to Tibet. He spent several years at BKRA SHIS LHUN PO monastery, where he studied with the first PAṆ CHEN LAMA, BLO BZANG CHOS KYI RGYAL MTSHAN, receiving tantric initiation from him. He excelled particularly in practices associated with YAMĀNTAKA. In the 1590s, he returned to Mongolia, first to the Khalka region and then to Hohhot, where he spent the next thirty years living as a yogin with a group of disciples. His biography, which seems to take the story of MI LA RAS PA as its model, describes his habitation in mountain caves, his practice of GTUM MO, his unconventional behavior, and his performance of various miracles. He is said to have worn blue and green robes and to have taken money intended for monasteries and given it to the poor. Around 1629, he went to Eastern Mongolia, where he sought to spread Buddhism, bringing him into conflict with local shamans. He secured the support of powerful nobles, leading to the founding of four monasteries in the region. Although a devotee of the DGE LUGS PA, he ran afoul of the fifth DALAI LAMA (NGAG DBANG BLO BZANG RGYA MTSHO), who criticized him for giving the YAMĀNTAKA initiation to those without the proper qualification and for claiming to be the incarnation of TSONG KHA PA. On a more political level, it appears that the Dalai Lama was concerned that a Mongol was developing a strong following outside the bounds of the Dge lugs hierarchy controlled from LHA SA. When a formal complaint was brought against Neichi Toin, the Manchu emperor deferred to the Dalai Lama, who declared that Neichi Toin did not have the necessary qualifications to be a high lama. He was therefore purged and his followers disbanded.

**nenbutsu.** [alt. nembutsu] (念佛). In Japanese, "recollection of the Buddha's name." See NIANFO; NAMU AMIDABUTSU; ICHINENGI; TANENGI.

**netrapratiṣṭhāpana.** (P. akkhipūjā; T. spyan dbye). In Sanskrit, "fixing the eyes," viz., "opening the eyes"; a consecration ceremony for a buddha image (BUDDHĀBHIṢEKA), which serves to vivify the inert statue or painting, rendering it a hypostatization of the buddha. There are many versions of the ritual. In Southeast Asia, after making offerings to such Brahmanical protective divinities as INDRA, AGNI, or YAMA and conducting a purification ritual, the eyes of the image are painted in as the final act of preparing for its installation in a shrine. The ritual concludes with the recitation of a series of protective chants (PARITTA). The entire ritual often runs through the entire night, with the eyes "opened" around sunrise as the climax of the ritual. The Pāli form akkhipūjā, lit. "ritual of [opening] the eyes," is attested by the late-fifth or early-sixth century, in the MAHĀVAṂSA and BUDDHAGHOSA's SAMANTAPĀSĀDIKĀ. In Mahāyāna texts, such image consecration by painting in the eyes appears in the RATNAGUṆASAṂCAYAGĀTHĀ, which dates prior to the fifth century CE. See also PRATIṢṬHĀ. For East Asian equivalents, see DIANYAN; KAIYAN.

**Nettippakaraṇa.** In Pāli, "The Guide," a paracanonical Pāli text dedicated to the exegesis of scripture, which is included in the longer Burmese (Myanmar) edition of the KHUDDAKANIKĀYA. The *Netti* (as it is often called) is traditionally ascribed to the Buddha's disciple Kaccāna (see KĀTYĀYANA; MAHĀKĀTYĀYANA), but was likely composed in India sometime around the beginning of the Common Era. Some scholars presume that the work is a revision of the closely related PEṬAKOPADESA, which it ultimately superseded. Both the *Netti* and the *Peṭakopadesa* develop an elaborate hermeneutical theory based on the broad rubrics of "interpretation" or "guidance" (netti; cf. Skt. netri) as to "sense" (byañjana; Skt. vyañjana) and interpretation as to "meaning" (attha; Skt. ARTHA). The *Netti* is divided into two major sections: an outline of the contents, and a longer systematic set of rubrics that describe specific techniques of interpretation, in three subsections. See also VYĀKHYĀYUKTI; SANFEN KEJING.

**neyārtha**. (P. neyyattha; T. drang don; C. buliaoyi; J. furyōgi; K. puryoŭi 不了義). In Sanskrit, "provisional," "conventional"; one of the two categories (along with NĪTĀRTHA, "definitive," "absolute") into which the teachings of the SŪTRAs may be classified. The terms neyārtha and nītārtha are among several sets of categories employed in the interpretation of scriptures, providing a means of accounting for statements that appear to contradict what is regarded as the Buddha's final position on a topic. The Indian schools differ on what constitutes a provisional statement, with some holding that any statement by the Buddha that cannot be accepted literally is provisional, with others holding instead that any statement that does not describe the final nature of reality is provisional. See also SATYADVAYA; ABHISAṂDHI; ABHIPRĀYA.

**Ngag dbang blo bzang rgya mtsho**. (Ngawang Losang Gyatso) (1617–1682). The fifth DALAI LAMA of Tibet, widely held to be one of the most dynamic and influential members of his lineage. He was the first Dalai Lama to formally wield both religious and secular power over the Tibetan state and is renowned for his diverse range of religious and political activities. Commonly referred to as "the great fifth" (lnga pa chen po), Ngag dbang blo bzang rgya mtsho established himself as a gifted teacher, accomplished tantric practitioner, prolific author, and skillful statesman. The fifth Dalai Lama was born to an aristocratic family in the region of 'Phyong rgyas (Chongye) near the burial grounds of the early Tibetan dynastic rulers. His family had close ties with the RNYING MA sect, although the Dalai Lama claimed in one of his autobiographies that his mother had been the tantric consort of the JO NANG master TĀRANĀTHA and that Tāranātha was his biological father. He was recognized as the fifth Dalai Lama in 1622 by BLO BZANG CHOS KYI RGYAL MTSHAN, although there was a rival candidate, Grags pa rgyal mtshan. The fifth Dalai Lama mastered the DGE LUGS curriculum but also had a strong interest in Rnying ma, SA SKYA, and BKA' BRGYUD. During this period, the Dge lugs was being persecuted by the kings of Gtsang, who were patrons of the KARMA BKA' BRGYUD. The fifth Dalai Lama cultivated a relationship with the Qoshot Mongols. This deepened a connection with the Mongols begun by the third Dalai Lama, BSOD NAMS RGYA MTSHO, and enhanced by the fourth Dalai Lama, YON TAN RGYA MTSHO. With the aid of the Qoshot Mongol ruler Gushri Khan (1582–1655), the fifth Dalai Lama and his Dge lugs sect prevailed after a period of bitter political rivalry against the Bka' brgyud and their supporters in the Gtsang court. In 1642, the Dalai Lama and his regent Bsod nams chos 'phel became the rulers of Tibet, although it took nearly a decade before their power was consolidated throughout the provinces of central Tibet and extended to parts of eastern and western Tibet. The relationship thus forged between the Dalai Lama and the Mongol ruler was based on the so-called priest-patron (YON MCHOD) model previously established between the Sa skya heirarch 'PHAGS PA BLO GROS RGYAL MTSHAN and Qubilai Khan. The Dalai Lama promoted the view that he and the previous Dalai Lamas were incarnations (SPRUL SKU) of the BODHISATTVA AVALOKITEŚVARA and that he himself was linked to the three great religious kings (chos rgyal) SRONG BTSAN SGAM PO, KHRI SRONG LDE BTSAN, and RAL PA CAN. In 1645, the fifth Dalai Lama began construction of the PO TA LA Palace on the site of Srong btsan sgam po's palace on Dmar po ri (Red Hill) in LHA SA. He named it after POTALAKA, the abode of Avalokiteśvara. The palace included his residence quarters and space for the Tibetan government, the DGA' LDAN PHO BRANG, both relocated from 'BRAS SPUNGS monastery. In 1652, at the invitation of the Qing emperor, the fifth Dalai Lama traveled to the Manchu imperial court in Beijing, where he was greeted with great ceremony, although he resented attempts by the Chinese to present him as a vassal of the Qing emperor rather than as an equal head of state. The Dalai Lama forced the conversion to Dge lugs of those monasteries he considered doctrinally heterodox or politically dangerous. These included numerous Bka' brgyud institutions and, famously, the monastery of Dga' ldan (formerly Rtag brtan) phun tshogs gling (see JO NANG PHUN TSHOGS GLING), whose Jo nang texts were ordered to be locked under state seal. The fifth Dalai Lama did, however, support the founding of new Rnying ma institutions, such as RDZOGS CHEN monastery and SMIN GROL GLING, and the renovation of RDO RJE BRAG. He himself was a "treasure revealer" (GTER STON), discovering several texts that are included in his collected works. His religious training was broad and eclectic; among teachers of the Dge lugs sect, he was particularly close to the first PAṆ CHEN LAMA, BLO BZANG CHOS KYI RGYAL MTSHAN, who had also been the teacher of the fourth Dalai Lama, and from whom the fifth Dalai Lama received both his novice vows in 1625 and his monastic vows in 1638. After the Paṇ chen Lama's death, the Dalai Lama identified his next incarnation, continuing the alternating relation of teacher and student between the two foremost lamas of the Dge lugs. He died in 1682, but his death was kept secret by his regent, SDE SRID SANGS RGYAS RGYA MTSHO, until 1697. He is entombed in a massize STŪPA in the Po ta la. The fifth Dalai Lama was a prolific and talented author, with his collected works comprising twenty-five volumes on a wide range of topics. Of particular note are his extensive autobiographies. Among his more strictly "religious" works, his LAM RIM teachings entitled LAM RIM 'JAM DPAL ZHAL LUNG is well known.

**Ngal gso skor gsum**. (Ngalso khorsum). In Tibetan, "Trilogy on Rest"; one of the major works by the Tibetan master KLONG CHEN RAB 'BYAMS. It is composed of three cycles of teachings, each of which contains a root text, summary, autocommentary, and essential instruction (don khrid), as well as additional texts, for a total of fifteen works. The three cycles of teachings are (1) Sems nyid ngal gso ("Resting in Mind

Itself'); (2) Sgyu ma ngal gso ("Resting in Illusion"); and (3) Bsam gtan ngal so ("Resting in Concentration [DHYĀNA]").

**Ngor e wam chos ldan**. [alt. Ngor e waṃ chos ldan] (Ngor Evam Chöden). A Tibetan monastery founded by Ngor chen ("the great man of Ngor") KUN DGA' BZANG PO in 1429 near Gzhis ka rtse (Shigatse) in Gtsang (Tsang); the seat of the head of the NGOR subsect of the SA SKYA sect. After the monastery of Sa skya, it is regarded as the second most important monastery of the Sa skya sect, especially famous as a center for the LAM 'BRAS (path and result) teachings. It had four branches (bla brangs): Klu sding, Thar rtse, Phan bde khang gsar, and Khang sar; the abbacy (three years in duration) alternated among them. Its extensive library contained a number of Sanskrit manuscripts. The TSHAR PA order is considered an offshoot of the Ngor subsect. Prominent among a network of monasteries associated with Ngor e wam chos ldan is the Lhun grub steng monastery in SDE DGE, the monastery most closely associated with the royal family and the location of the famous Sde dge printery.

**Nguyên Thiều**. (C. Yuanshao 元韶) (c. 1610–c. 1691). Chinese monk who is considered the founding patriarch of a Vietnamese branch of the Chinese LINJI ZONG of CHAN. Born in Guangdong (China), he became a monk at the age of nineteen. He arrived in Vietnam in 1665 accompanying Chinese merchants and settled in Bình Định province (central Vietnam). He eventually built the Thập Tháp Di Đà monastery and began to teach Chan. He also founded the Hà Trung monastery in Thuận Hóa and Quốc Ân monastery in Huế. After that, at the request of Lord Nguyễn Phúc Tần, he returned to China to bring back Buddhist materials and utensils and to invite other eminent monks to Vietnam. Among these monks was the Chan master Thạch Liêm. Nguyên Thiều was the first monk to teach Linji Chan in central Vietnam. The modern Vietnamese Buddhist claim of an affinity with Linji Chan derives from this transmission via Nguyên Thiều.

**Nhất Hạnh**. (V) (一行). See THÍCH NHẤT HẠNH.

**nianfo**. (J. nenbutsu; K. yŏmbul 念佛). In Chinese, "recollection, invocation, or chanting of [the name of] the Buddha." The term nianfo has a long history of usage across the Buddhist tradition and has been used to refer to a variety of practices. The Chinese term nianfo is a translation of the Sanskrit term BUDDHĀNUSMṚTI (recollection of [the qualities of] the Buddha), one of the common practices designed to help develop meditative absorption (DHYĀNA) in the mainstream traditions. Buddhānusmṛti is listed as the first of six fundamental contemplative practices, along with recollection of the DHARMA, SAṂGHA, giving (DĀNA), morality (ŚĪLA), and the divinities (DEVA). Buddhānusmṛti (P. buddhānussati) is also the first in the Pāli list of ten "recollections" (P. anussati; S. ANUSMṚTI), which are included among the forty meditative exercises (see KAMMAṬṬHĀNA) discussed in the VISUDDHIMAGGA. The meditator is instructed to reflect on the good qualities of the Buddha, often through contemplating a series of his epithets, contemplation that is said to lead specifically to "access concentration" (UPACĀRASAMĀDHI). In early Mahāyāna texts, the term seems to refer to the meditative practice of recollecting, invoking, or visualizing an image of a buddha or advanced BODHISATTVA, such as ŚĀKYAMUNI, MAITREYA, or AMITĀBHA. In East Asia, the term nianfo came to be used primarily in the sense of reciting the name of the Buddha, referring especially to recitation of the Chinese phrase namo Amituo fo (K. namu Amit'abul; J. NAMU AMIDABUTSU; Homage to the buddha Amitābha). This recitation was often performed in a ritual setting and accompanied by the performance of prostrations, the burning of incense, and the intonation of scriptures, all directed toward gaining a vision of Amitābha's PURE LAND of SUKHĀVATĪ, a vision that was considered proof that one would be reborn there in the next lifetime. New forms of chanting Amitābha's name developed in China, such as WUHUI NIANFO (five-tempo intonation of [the name of] the Buddha), which used leisurely and increasingly rapid tempos, and YINSHENG NIANFO (intoning [the name of] the Buddha by drawing out the sound). Nianfo practice was often portrayed as a relatively easy means of guaranteeing rebirth in Amitābha's pure land. Many exegetes referred to the vows of the bodhisattva DHARMĀKARA (the bodhisattva who became Amitābha) as set forth in the SUKHĀVATĪVYŪHASŪTRA, as evidence of the efficacy of nianfo practice in the degenerate age of the dharma (MOFA). In China, these various forms of nianfo were advocated by such famous monks as TANLUAN, DAOCHUO, and SHANDAO; these monks later came to be retroactively regarded as patriarchs of a so-called pure land school (JINGTU ZONG). In fact, however, nianfo was widely practiced across schools and social strata in both China and Korea and was not exclusively associated with a putative pure land tradition. In Japan, nenbutsu, or repetition of the phrase "namu Amidabutsu" (homage to Amitābha Buddha) became a central practice of the Japanese PURE LAND schools of Buddhism, such as JŌDOSHŪ, JŌDO SHINSHŪ, and JISHŪ. The practice spread rapidly among common people largely through the efforts of such itinerant holy men (HIJIRI) as KŪYA and IPPEN. Influential pure land teachers, such as HŌNEN and his disciple SHINRAN, also promoted the exclusive practice of chanting the phrase NAMU AMIDABUTSU and debated whether multiple recitations of the Buddha's name (TANENGI) were expected of pure land adherents or whether a single recitation (ICHINENGI) would be enough to ensure rebirth. Despite periodic suppressions of this movement, Hōnen and Shinran's schools, known as the Jōdoshū and Jōdo Shinshū, became the largest Buddhist communities in Japan.

**niangu**. (J. nenko; K. yŏmgo 拈古). In Chinese, "raising [and analyzing] ancient [cases]"; a "lettered Chan" (WENZI CHAN) literary style, which uses verse to comment on CHAN public cases (GONG'AN). See HUANGLONG PAI.

**nianhua weixiao**. (J. nenge mishō; K. yŏmhwa miso 拈花微笑) In Chinese, lit. "holding up a flower and smiling subtly"; a famous CHAN transmission story in which ŚĀKYAMUNI Buddha instructs the congregation nonverbally by simply holding up a flower. Only MAHĀKĀŚYAPA understands the Buddha's intent and he smiles back in recognition, making him the first recipient of the Buddha's "mind-to-mind transmission" (YIXIN CHUANXIN). Mahākāśyapa is thus considered the first patriarch (ZUSHI) of the Chan school. This story, also called the "World-Honored One holding up a flower" (Shizun nianhua), first appears in the 1036 imperially ratified Chan genealogical record, *Tiansheng Guangdeng lu*. There, the story also portrays the Buddha giving his disciple his robe as a token of transmission, but this event does not appear in the later versions of the story, such as in the 1093 *Zongmen tongyao ji* and the 1183 *Liandeng huiyao*. The same story is recorded also in the apocryphal Chinese sūtra *Da fantianwang wenfo jueyi jing* ("Mahābrahmā Questions the Buddha and Resolves His Doubts"), compiled sometime between the mid-twelfth and the late fourteenth centuries, probably in order to defend the historicity of the story, the authenticity of which was questioned even in Chan circles. The story became famous among not only Buddhist clerics but also literati. The tale eventually became a meditative topic within the Chan school and is recorded as the sixth case (GONG'AN) in the 1228 WUMEN GUAN ("Gateless Checkpoint"); there, it concludes by giving the Buddha's verbal confirmation that the transmission is complete: "I have this repository of the true dharma eye (ZHENGFAYANZANG), the sublime mind of NIRVĀṆA, the authentic quality (C. shixiang; S. TATTVA) that is free from all qualities, the subtle and sublime dharma gate that does not rely on words or letters (BULI WENZI) but is a special transmission outside of the scriptures (JIAOWAI BIECHUAN). This I entrust to Mahākāśyapa." In Western literature, this story has been dubbed the "Flower Sermon," but this designation is never used in Chan literature.

**niannian wuchang**. (C) (念念無常). See ER WUCHANG.

**nibbidānupassanāñāṇa**. In Pāli, "knowledge arising from the contemplation of disgust." According to the VISUDDHIMAGGA, the fifth of nine knowledges (ñāṇa; S. JÑĀNA) cultivated as part of "purity of knowledge and vision of progress along the path" (paṭipadāñāṇadassanavisuddhi). This latter category, in turn, constitutes the sixth and penultimate purity (visuddhi) to be developed along the path to liberation. The knowledge arising from the contemplation of disgust (P. nibbidā; S. NIRVEDA) refers to the sense of disillusionment that the adept feels toward the aggregates (khandha; S. SKANDHA) or the mental and material phenomena (NĀMARŪPA) comprising the individual and the universe; this response is prompted by the realization that all phenomena are frightening and dangerous because they are characterized by impermanence (P. anicca; S. ANITYA), suffering (P. dukkha; S. DUḤKHA), and nonself (P. anatta; S. ANĀTMAN). The practitioner thus becomes dissatisfied with the things of this world and takes no delight in the thought of any further becoming (BHAVA) in any realm of rebirth (GATI). The *Visuddhimagga* states that this fifth knowledge, arising from the contemplation of disgust, is in essence not different from the preceding two knowledges: "knowledge arising from the contemplation of terror" (BHAYATUPAṬṬHĀNAÑĀṆA) and "knowledge arising from the contemplation of danger" (ĀDĪNAVĀNUPASSANĀÑĀṆA; see also ĀDĪNAVA). The differences among the three are said to be only nominal.

**Nichiren**. (日蓮) (1222–1282). Japanese founder of the NICHIRENSHŪ, one of the so-called new schools of Kamakura Buddhism. Nichiren is said to have been born into a commoner family in present-day Chiba prefecture. At the age of twelve he entered the priesthood and was ordained at the age of sixteen. In 1239, he left his rural temple and went first to Kamakura and then to the capital of Kyōto to study at the great monasteries there. Although he draws heavily on TENDAI and TAIMITSU teachings in his own writings, Nichiren seems to have been acquainted with other traditions of Buddhism as well. During this period, Nichiren began to question what he perceived as inconsistencies in the doctrines of the various schools he was studying. In particular, Nichiren disagreed with the JŌDOSHŪ pure land tradition of HŌNEN (1133–1212), and the practice of reciting the buddha's name (NENBUTSU; C. NIANFO). Nichiren eventually concluded that the SADDHARMAPUṆḌARĪKASŪTRA ("Lotus Sūtra") contained the Buddha's ultimate teaching, relegating all other teachings to a provisional status. Armed with this new insight, Nichiren proclaimed in 1253 that people should place their faith in the *Saddharmapuṇḍarīkasūtra* by reciting its "title" (J. DAIMOKU), viz., NAMU MYŌHŌRENGEKYŌ (Homage to the *Saddharmapuṇḍarīkasūtra*), an act that he claimed was sufficient for gaining liberation in the time of the decline of the dharma, or mappō (C. MOFA). It was at this point that he adopted the name "Nichiren" ("Lotus of the Sun,": i.e., Japan) Although Nichiren was a controversial figure, he attracted a large number of followers in Kamakura. In 1260, he wrote the *Risshō Ankokuron* ("Treatise on Establishing the Right [Teaching] for Securing the Peace of Our Country"), a tract that encouraged the Kamakura military government (bakufu) to rely on the teachings of the *Saddharmapuṇḍarīkasūtra* in order to avert political disaster and social upheaval and, in turn, to patronize Nichiren's school over other Buddhist sects. As a result of his lobbying, and his challenge to the pure land tradition, Nichiren was arrested and exiled to Shizuoka prefecture in 1261 but was pardoned two years later. In 1271, a failed assassination plot against Nichiren hardened his resolve. He was arrested again in 1272 and banished to the island of Sado, where he wrote many of his most important treatises, including *Kaimokushō* ("Opening the Eyes") and *Kanjin no honzonshō* ("The Object of Devotion for Observing the Mind"). In 1274, he was once again pardoned and subsequently returned to Kamakura. Failing for a third time to convince the Kamakura bakufu to turn to the *Saddharmapuṇḍarīkasūtra* for protection and salvation, he retired to Mt. Minobu in Yamanashi prefecture. There, he devoted his time to educating his disciples and writing essays, including *Senjishō* "(On the Selection of the Time") and *Hō'onshō* ("Repaying Indebtedness"). Nichiren died at the age of sixty in the year 1282, leaving behind hundreds of works and divisive infighting for control of his legacy.

**Nichiren Shōshū**. (日蓮正宗). In Japanese, "Orthodox School of Nichiren"; one of the principal Japanese Buddhist schools based on the teachings of NICHIREN (1222–1282). Nichiren Shōshū is descended from Nichiren through Nichikō (1246–1332), the alleged sole heir of Nichiren among his six chief disciples. Nichikō was a loyal student and archivist of Nichiren's writings, who established in 1290 what was then called the Fuji school at TAISEKIJI, a monastery on Mt. Fuji in Shizuoka prefecture. Nichikō's school later divided into eight subbranches, known collectively as the Fuji Monryū (Fuji schools) or Nichikō Monryū (Nichikō schools). The monk Nichikan (1665–1726), a noted commentator and teacher, was instrumental in resurrecting the observance of Nichiren's teachings at Taisekiji. He was also the person who systematized and established many of the innovative features of the school, particularly the school's unique view that Nichiren was the Buddha (see below). The eight associated temples that remained in the Fuji school reunited in 1876 as the Komon sect, later adopting a new name, the Honmon. However, in 1899, Taisekiji split from the other temples and established an independent sect, renaming itself Nichiren Shōshū in 1912. In 1930, MAKIGUCHI TSUNESABURO and Toda Josei established the SŌKA GAKKAI (then called Sōka Kyōiku Gakkai), a lay organization for the promotion of Nichiren Shōshū thought, but quickly ran afoul of the Japanese government's promotion of the cult of state Shintōism. Makiguchi refused to comply with government promulgation of Shintō worship and was imprisoned for violating the Peace Preservation Law; he died in prison in 1944. Toda was eventually released, and he devoted himself after World War II to promoting Sōka Gakkai and Nichiren Shōshū, which at that time were closely connected. The two groups acrimoniously separated in 1991, Nichiren Shōshū accusing Sōka Gakkai of forming a personality cult around their leader IKEDA DAISAKU (b. 1928) and of improper modifications of Nichiren practice; Sōka Gakkai accusing the Nichiren Shōshū leader Abe Nikken of trying to dominate both organizations. The two groups now operate independently. Nichiren Shōshū has grown to over seven hundreds temples in Japan, as well as a few temples in foreign countries. Nichiren Shōshū distinguishes itself from the other Nichiren schools by its unique view of the person of Nichiren: it regards the founder as the true buddha in this current degenerate age of the dharma (J. mappo; C. MOFA), a buddha whom ŚĀKYAMUNI promised his followers would appear two thousand years in the future; therefore, they refer to Nichiren as daishōnin, or great sage. Other Nichiren schools instead regard the founder as the reincarnation of Jōgyō Bosatsu (the BODHISATTVA VIŚIṢṬACĀRITRA). Nichiren Shōshū's claim to orthodoxy is based on two documents, not recognized by other Nichiren schools, in which Nichiren claims to transfer his dharma to Nichikō, viz., the *Minobu sōjōsho* ("Minobu Transfer Document") and the *Ikegami sōjōsho* ("Ikegami Transfer Document"), which are believed to have been written in 1282 by Nichiren, the first at Minobu and the second on the day of his death at Ikegami. Nichiren Shōshū practice is focused on the dai-gohonzon maṇḍala, the ultimate object of devotion in the school, which Nichiren created. The DAI-GOHONZON (great object of devotion), a MAṆḌALA (here, a cosmological chart) inscribed by Nichiren in 1279, includes the DAIMOKU (lit., "title"), viz., the phrase "NAMU MYŌHŌRENGEKYŌ" (Homage to the SADDHARMAPUṆḌARĪKASŪTRA), which is considered to be the embodiment of Nichiren's enlightenment and the ultimate reason for his advent in this world. The gohonzon is placed in a shrine or on a simple altar in the homes of devotees of the sect. This veneration of the gohonzon to the exclusion of all other deities and images of the Buddha distinguishes Nichiren Shōshū from other Nichiren schools. The school interprets the three jewels (RATNATRAYA) of the Buddha, DHARMA, and SAṂGHA to refer, respectively, to Nichiren (the buddha); to namu Myōhōrengekyō and the gohonzon (the dharma); and to his successor Nichikō (the saṃgha). By contrast, other Nichiren schools generally consider Śākyamuni to be the Buddha and Nichiren the saṃgha, and do not include the gohonzon in the dharma, since they question its authenticity. All schools of Nichiren thought accept Nichiren's acknowledgment of the buddhahood that is latent in all creatures and the ability of all human beings of any class to achieve buddhahood in this lifetime.

**Nichirenshū**. (日蓮宗). In Japanese, "schools [associated with] Nichiren." There was and is no single "Nichiren School," but the term is used to designate all of the different schools that trace their origins back to the life and teachings of NICHIREN (1222–1282). At the time of his death, Nichiren left no formal institution in place or instructions for the formation of any such institution. Thus, a number of groups emerged, led by various of his disciples. These groups, which can collectively be referred to as Nichirenshū, disagreed on a number of important points of doctrine and theories of propagation. However, they all shared the fundamental convictions that the SADDHARMAPUṆḌARĪKASŪTRA ("Lotus Sūtra") was the highest of the Buddha's teachings; that during the degenerate age (J. mappo; C. MOFA) liberation could be achieved by chanting the title (DAIMOKU) of that scripture; that Nichiren was the true teacher of this practice and Japan its appropriate site; and that all other forms of Buddhist practice were ineffective in this degenerate age and thus should be repudiated. However, Nichiren's disciples and his followers disagreed on such questions as whether they should have any connections with other Buddhist groups; how aggressively they should proselytize Nichiren's teachings; and whether the two sections of the *Saddharmapuṇḍarīkasūtra*—the "SHAKUMON" (Chapters 1–14), or trace teaching, and the "HONMON"

(Chapters 15–28), or essential teaching—are of equal importance or whether the "Honmon" is superior. During the Meiji period, specific schools of Nichiren's teachings were recognized, with six different schools institutionalized in 1874. One of these, which called itself the Nichirenshū, declared the two parts of the sūtra to be of equal importance; the other five declared the superiority of the "Honmon." One of these five eventually became the NICHIREN SHŌSHŪ.

**nidāna**. (T. gzhi/gleng gzhi; C. yinyuan/nituona; J. innen/nidana; K. inyŏn /nidana 因緣/尼陀那). A polysemous term in Sanskrit and Pāli, meaning variously "cause," "motivation," "occasion," or "episode." The term has at least three important denotations: (1) a general term for cause, used especially in the context of the twelvefold chain of dependent origination (PRATĪTYASAMUTPĀDA), often referred to as the "twelve nidāna," or twelve "links" in this chain; (2) one of the traditional categories of Buddhist literature, devoted to narratives that describe the occasion for the Buddha's exposition of a particular point of doctrine or a specific monastic rule; and (3) the portion of a sūtra that describes the setting of the discourse, such as where the Buddha was residing, the audience members, etc. In the second of these meanings, it is one of the nine (NAVAṄGA) (Pāli) or twelve (DVĀDAŚĀṄGA) (Sanskrit) categories (AṄGA) of Buddhist scripture, distinguished according to their narrative structure or literary style.

**Nidānakathā**. In Pāli, "Account of Origins," the introduction to the JĀTAKA, the collection of stories of the Buddha's past lives, which form the fifth and final part of the SUTTAPIṬAKA, the KHUDDAKANIKĀYA; it is traditionally attributed to the great fifth-century Pāli scholar BUDDHAGHOSA. The text gives an account of the Buddha's previous lives as a bodhisatta (S. BODHISATTVA), continuing through his last birth, his enlightenment, and his early ministry. The work is divided into three sections: (1) The "Dūre Nidāna," or "Distant Epoch," begins with the bodhisatta's encounter, as the mendicant SUMEDHA, with the buddha DIPAṂKARA. Sumedha could become Dipaṃkara's disciple and achieve liberation as an arahant (S. ARHAT) in that life, but instead vows to become a buddha in the far distant future. Dipaṃkara predicts that he will indeed become a buddha (see P. veyyākaraṇa; S. VYĀKARAṆA). The ten perfections (P. pāramī; S. PĀRAMITĀ) that he must practice in order to achieve buddhahood are then described. This is followed by an account of subsequent buddhas who also prophesied his eventual attainment of buddhahood, and the identity of the bodhisatta on each of those occasions. Next comes a list of perfections and the jātaka story that best exemplifies it. The first section ends with his penultimate birth as a divinity in TUṢITA heaven. (2) The "Avidūre Nidāna," or "Not Remote Epoch," recounts his descent from tuṣita heaven, through his birth as the son of King Suddhodana (S. ŚUDDHODANA) and Queen MĀYĀ, his princely life and marriage, and his renunciation and penances, concluding with his achievement of enlightenment. (3) The "Santike Nidāna" or "Present Epoch," recounts the period from his decision to teach the dhamma, through the conversion of his early disciples, and ends with the dedication of the JETAVANA grove as a monastery by the wealthy merchant Anāthapiṇḍika (S. ANĀTHAPIṆḌADA). The *Nidānakathā* represents the earliest continuous narrative of the Buddha's life contained in Pāli sources, and it served as the basis of later expanded narratives, such as that found in the near-contemporary *Manorathavilāsinī*. It is important to note that these episodes do not provide a complete biography of the Buddha, beginning with his birth and ending with his death. Instead, they begin in the distant past with his vow to become a buddha, skip over his many births as a bodhisatta (which are contained in the jātaka stories to which the *Nidānakathā* serves as an introduction), and end with the donation of Jetavana, in the first years after his enlightenment. These Pāli accounts are all relatively late. Earlier biographies of the Buddha are found in Sanskrit works of other schools, such as the second-century CE BUDDHACARITA by AŚVAGHOṢA, the third-century MAHĀVASTU contained in the LOKOTTARAVĀDA VINAYA, and the third-century LALITAVISTARA.

**Niddesa**. In Pāli, "Exposition"; the eleventh book of the KHUDDAKANIKĀYA of the Pāli SUTTAPIṬAKA. It is a commentarial work on portions of the SUTTANIPĀTA and is divided into two parts, the CŪḶANIDDESA ("Lesser Exposition") and the MAHĀNIDDESA ("Longer Exposition"). The former comments on the *Khaggavisānasutta* (cf. S. KHAḌGAVIṢĀṆA) and *Parāyaṇavagga*, while the latter comments on the AṬṬHAKAVAGGA. The book is among the earliest examples of the commentarial genre of Buddhist literature—so early, in fact, that it was included within the suttapiṭaka itself. See CŪḶANIDDESA; MAHĀNIDDESA.

**nidhāna**. (T. gter; C. fuzang; J. fukuzō/bukuzō; K. pokchang 伏藏/腹藏). In Sanskrit, "depository" or "hidden container"; ritual container placed in the interior of a Buddhist sculpture or hung above a painting in order to ritually vivify the image or painting. Following the methods described in the "Instructions on Image Making and Iconometry" (S. Sambaddhabhāṣitapratimālakṣaṇavivaranī; T. Rdzogs pa'i sangs rgyas kyis gzungs pa'i sku gzugs kyi mtshan nyid kyi rnam 'grel; C. Zaoxiang liangdu jing; J. Zōzō ryōdo kyō; K. Chosang nyangdo kyŏng), the insertion of the container was, along with the eye-opening ceremony (KAIYAN; NETRAPRATIṢṬHĀPANA), an important part of the ritual of image consecration, which served as an agency for transforming the inert statue or painting into an object of worship. The contents of these intestinal depositories were often similar to those found in ŚARĪRA containers: viz., relic fragments, copies of DHĀRAṆĪ and SŪTRAs, and consecration certificates. But they also could be objects that would serve as a symbolic vivifying and spiritual force, e.g., viscera and entrails made from cloth, as well as five types of grain and five-colored threads. Although it is unknown when the tradition of sewing intestines to deposit in images began, the earliest extant East Asian example is a container found in the UDĀYANA image of ŚĀKYAMUNI Buddha at Seiryōji in Kyōto, which is dated to 988 CE.

**niepan ba wei**. (C) (涅槃八味). See BA WEI.

**Niepan xi**. (J. Nehan wa yū; K. Yŏlban sŏk 涅槃夕). In Chinese, "dusk [when] the MAHĀPARINIRVĀṆASŪTRA [was preached]"; the second part of an expression that describes the two major stages in the teaching career of the Buddha. According to Chinese legend, the Buddha preached this scripture just before his ultimate demise (PARINIRVĀṆA)—a period that was likened to the sun setting at dusk. This statement is typically preceded by HUAYAN ZHAO, "the morning [when] HUAYAN [was preached]," since, according to the HUAYAN ZONG, in the days immediately following his enlightenment, the Buddha initially preached the AVATAṂSAKASŪTRA, or *Huayan jing*. "Morning" refers to the earliest stage of the Buddha's preaching career, which was likened to the sun rising at dawn.

**Niepan zong**. (J. Nehanshū; K. Yŏlban chong 涅槃宗). In Chinese, "Nirvāṇa tradition," an eclectic Chinese lineage of scholiasts who dedicated themselves to exegesis and dissemination of the MAHĀYĀNA recension of the MAHĀPARNIRVĀṆASŪTRA ("Nirvāṇa Sūtra"). The Niepan zong did not exist in any formal sense; the term is instead used to designate a group of exegetes with analogous intellectual interests. Foremost among these exegetes is DAOSHENG (355–434), a member of KUMĀRAJĪVA's (343–413) translation team in Chang'an, whose views are emblematic of teachers in this lineage. Daosheng was strongly critical of statements appearing in the first Chinese translation of the *Mahāparnirvāṇasūtra*, made in 418 by FAXIAN and BUDDHABHADRA, which asserted that all sentient beings except the incorrigibles (ICCHANTIKA) are endowed with the buddha-nature (FOXING). Daosheng opposed this view, which at the time had the authority of received scripture; instead, he made the radical claim that even icchantikas must also retain the capacity eventually to attain enlightenment, thus calling into question the accuracy of these two eminent monks' scriptural edition. DHARMAKṢEMA's new translation of the text four years later did not include the controversial statement and thus vindicated Daosheng's position. Daosheng also explored the soteriological implications of the buddha-nature doctrine in the *Mahāparnirvāṇasūtra*. If the buddha-nature were inherent in all sentient beings, as the scripture claimed, then enlightenment was not something that would unfold through the mastery of a gradual series of steps, but would instead be experienced in a sudden moment of insight—a "re-cognition" of the enlightenment that has always been present. Hence, Daosheng claimed, buddhahood is in fact attained instantaneously (see DUNWU), not progessively. This position initiated an extended examination within East Asian Buddhism of sudden versus gradual theories of enlightenment that played out in many of the mature traditions, including the TIANTAI ZONG, HUAYAN ZONG, and CHAN ZONG. The teachings of the Niepan zong were also influential in promoting Chinese Buddhism's turn away from "apophatic" forms of discourse emblematic of MADHYAMAKA styles of argumentation, to the more "kataphatic" or positive forms of discourse that are typical of the later indigenous schools, including Tiantai, Huayan, and Chan. Following Daosheng, his disciple Daolang (d.u.) in his *Niepan jing yishu* ("Commentary to the 'Nirvāṇa Sūtra'") postulated congruencies between the buddha-nature and emptiness (ŚŪNYATĀ), which suggested how the seemingly "apophatic" notion of emptiness found in Indian materials could actually serve as a dynamic force revealing the truth that underlies all conventional existence in the world. Still other Niepan zong exegetes devoted themselves to the text of the *Mahāparnirvāṇasūtra* itself, producing a new edition of the scripture known as the Southern Edition (Nanben), which collated the two earlier renderings and restructured the chapter headings. By the beginning of the Tang dynasty, the tradition of *Mahāparnirvāṇasūtra* exegesis had become moribund, and its intellectual concerns were subsumed into the Tiantai zong, which derived much of its teachings from the "Nirvāṇa Sūtra" and the SADDHARMAPUṆḌARĪKASŪTRA ("Lotus Sūtra").

**Nigrodha**. (C. Nijutuo; J. Nikuda; K. Niguda 尼瞿陀). According to Pāli accounts, the name of the Buddhist novice who converted the Mauryan king Asoka (AŚOKA) to Buddhism. When Asoka ascended the throne, he is said to have continued his father's practice of each day feeding sixty thousand mendicants and brāhmaṇas at the palace, but was unsettled by their indecorous deportment. One day he saw the young novice Nigrodha, an ARHAT, and was pleased by the boy's dignity and calm demeanor. Nigrodha is said to have become an arhat upon his ordination at age seven. Nigrodha converted Asoka to Buddhism by preaching the *Appamādasutta*, whereupon the king ceased his benefactions to the sixty thousand mendicants and brāhmaṇas and gave undivided support instead to the Buddhist SAṂGHA. Although Pāli sources claim that Asoka became a staunch and exclusive supporter of the STHAVIRANIKĀYA, Asoka's own inscriptions indicate that his allegiance to Buddhism was less rigid and that he continued to respect and support brāhmaṇas and non-Buddhist mendicants throughout his reign.

**Niguma**. (T. Ni gu ma). An Indian tantric YOGINĪ of the eleventh century, said to be either the wife or the sister of NĀROPA. Her teachings are renowned as the "six doctrines (or yogas) of Niguma" (Ni gu chos drug). They are inner heat (GTUM MO), illusory body (sgyu lus; MĀYĀDEHA), dream yoga (rmi lam), clear light ('od gsal; PRABHĀSVARA), transference of consciousness ('PHO BA), and intermediate state (BAR DO), nominally the same as the more famous NĀ RO CHOS DRUG ("six yogas of Nāropa"), but with different emphases. She is said to have transmitted these teachings to her Tibetan disciple KHYUNG PO RNAL 'BYOR, who returned to Tibet to found the Shangs pa branch of the BKA' BRGYUD.

**niḥprapañca**. (S). See NIṢPRAPAÑCA.

**niḥsaraṇa**. (P. nissaraṇa; T. nges 'byung; C. li; J. ri; K. i 離). In Sanskrit, "escape" or "emergence," often a synonym for liberation from REBIRTH. The term can also refer to the sense of dissatisfaction with SAṂSĀRA and the wish to escape from it, as in the compounds bhavaniḥsaraṇa, "escape for mundane existence," jarāniḥsaraṇa, "escape from old age," and kleśaniḥsaraṇa, "escape from the afflictions." The wish to escape from rebirth is cultivated by contemplating such things as the relative rarity of rebirth as a human with access to the DHARMA, the uncertainty of the time of death, the cause and effects of actions, and the various sufferings inherent in the six realms of saṃsāra. See also NIRVEDA; NIRYĀṆA.

**niḥsargika-pātayantika**. (S). See PĀYATTIKA.

**niḥśreyasa**. (T. nges legs; C. zhishan; J. shizen; K. chisŏn 至善). In Sanskrit, "ultimate goodness," a term often used in Buddhist texts to refer to liberation from REBIRTH. The term commonly occurs in conjunction with ABHYUDAYA (lit., "elevation"), which refers to the worldly prosperity and temporal happiness that is achieved through rebirth as a prosperous human or divinity. Thus, abhyudaya and niḥśreyasa constitute the two benefits that accrue from practicing the dharma: those who maintain the precepts and offer charity to the SAṂGHA attain the "elevation" (abhyudaya) of a happy rebirth within SAṂSĀRA; those who follow the path to its conclusion achieve the ultimate goodness (niḥśreyasa) of liberation from rebirth.

**niḥsvabhāva**. (T. rang bzhin med pa; C. wuzixing/wuxing; J. mujishō/mushō; K. mujasŏng/musŏng 無自性/無性). In Sanskrit, lit., "lack of self-nature," "absence of intrinsic existence." According to the MADHYAMAKA school, the fundamental ignorance that is the root of all suffering is the misconception that persons and phenomena possess an independent, autonomous, and intrinsic identity, called SVABHĀVA, lit., "self-nature" or "own-nature." Wisdom is the insight that not only persons, but in fact all phenomena, lack such a nature. This absence of self-nature, or niḥsvabhāva, is the ultimate nature of reality and of all persons and phenomena in the universe. It is a synonym for emptiness (ŚŪNYATĀ). The Madhyamaka school is sometimes referred to as the niḥsvabhāvavāda, "proponents of the lack of intrinsic existence." The term also figures prominently in the YOGĀCĀRA school and its doctrine of the "three natures" (TRISVABHĀVA) as set forth in the SAMDHINIRMOCANASŪTRA, where each of the three natures is described as having a different type of absence of self-nature (triniḥsvabhāva). Thus, the imaginary (PARIKALPITA) is said to lack intrinsic nature, because it lacks defining characteristics (lakṣaṇaniḥsvabhāvatā). The dependent (PARATANTRA) is said to lack production (utpattiniḥsvabhāvatā), because it is not independently produced. The consummate (PARINIṢPANNA) is said to be the ultimate lack of nature (paramārthaniḥsvabhāvatā) in the sense that it is the absence of all differences between subject and object. See also NAIRĀTMYA; ANĀTMAN.

**nikāya**. (T. sde; C. bu; J. bu; K. pu 部). In Sanskrit and Pāli, lit. "group" or "collection," a term with two important denotations: (1) Any of the various collections of SŪTRAs, such as in the Pāli canon, e.g., the "Long Collection" (DĪGHANIKĀYA), "Middle-Length Collection" (MAJJHIMANIKĀYA), etc. The Sanskrit collections of sūtras tend be called instead ĀGAMA. Nikāya is also used as a general term for the collection or "canon." (2) Any of the various groups (in the sense of schools or sects) of "mainstream" (i.e., non-Mahāyāna) Indian Buddhism. Traditional lists enumerate eighteen such groups, although there were in fact more; the names of thirty-four schools have been identified in texts and inscriptions. These groups, divided largely according to which VINAYA they followed, are sometimes referred to collectively as Nikāya Buddhism, a term that more specifically refers to monastic Buddhism after the split that occurred between the MAHĀSĀṂGHIKA and STHAVIRA schools. Nikāya Buddhism is also sometimes used as a substitute for the pejorative term HĪNAYĀNA, although it appears that in India the term hīnayāna was sometimes used to refer collectively to all Nikāya schools and sometimes to refer to a specific school, such as the VAIBHĀṢIKA school of SARVĀSTIVĀDA ABHIDHARMA. See also MAINSTREAM BUDDHIST SCHOOLS.

**Nikyōron**. (J) (二教論). See BENKENMITSU NIKYŌRON.

**Nīlakaṇṭhakasūtra**. (S). See QIANSHOU JING.

**nimitta**. (T. mtshan ma; C. xiang/ruixiang; J. sō/zuisō; K. sang/sŏsang 相/瑞相). In Sanskrit and Pāli, "mark" or "sign," in the sense of a distinguishing characteristic, or a meditative "image." Among its several denotations, three especially deserve attention. (1) In Buddhist epistemology, nimitta refers to the generic appearance of an object, in distinction to its secondary characteristics, or ANUVYAÑJANA. Advertence toward the generic sign and secondary characteristics of an object produces a recognition or perception (SAṂJÑĀ) of that object, which may in turn lead to clinging or rejection and ultimately suffering. Thus nimitta often carries the negative sense of false or deceptive marks that are imagined to inhere in an object, resulting in the misperception of that object as real, intrinsically existent, or endowed with self. Thus, the apprehension of signs (nimittagrāha) is considered a form of ignorance (AVIDYĀ), and the perception of phenomena as signless (ĀNIMITTA) is a form of wisdom that constitutes one of three "gates to deliverance" (VIMOKṢAMUKHA), along with emptiness (ŚŪNYATĀ) and wishlessness (APRAṆIHITA). (2) In the context of THERAVĀDA meditation practice (BHĀVANĀ), as set forth in such works as the VISUDDHIMAGGA, nimitta refers to an image that appears to the mind after developing a certain degree of mental concentration (SAMĀDHI). At the beginning of a meditation exercise that relies, e.g., on an external visual support (KASIṆA), such as a blue circle, the initial mental image one recalls is termed the "preparatory image" (PARIKAMMANIMITTA). With the deepening of concentration, the image becomes more refined but is still unsteady; at that stage, it is called the "acquired image" or "eidetic image" (UGGAHANIMITTA). When one reaches access or neighborhood concentration (UPACĀRASAMĀDHI), a clear, luminous image appears to the mind, which is called the "counterpart image" or "representational image" (PAṬIBHĀGANIMITTA). It is through further concentration on this stable "representational image" that the mind finally attains "full concentration" (APPANĀSAMĀDHI), i.e, meditative absorption (P. JHĀNA; S. DHYĀNA). (3) The term also appears in CATURNIMITTA, the "four signs," "sights," or "portents," which were the catalysts that led the future buddha SIDDHĀRTHA GAUTAMA to renounce the world (see PRAVRAJITA) and pursue liberation from the cycle of birth and death (SAṂSĀRA): specifically, the sight of an old man, a sick man, a dead man, and a religious mendicant (ŚRAMAṆA).

**Nine Mountain Schools of Sŏn**. See KUSAN SŎNMUN.

**Ninnaji**. (仁和寺). In Japanese, "Monastery of Humane Peace," located in the ancient Japanese capital of Kyōto and affiliated with the SHINGONSHŪ. The construction of the monastery began in 886 under the patronage of Emperor Kōkō (r. 884–887) and continued through the reign of Emperor Uda (r. 887–897). The main hall was completed in 888 by Emperor Uda and today contains an important Amida (S. AMITĀBHA) triad that has been designated a national treasure. In 904, Emperor Uda established a residence for himself at Ninnaji and assumed control of the monastery. Monks of royal blood began serving thereafter as abbots of Ninnaji.

**niō**. (仁王/二王). In Japanese, "humane kings," a pair of muscular wrathful guardian deities, often depicted as massive wooden statues flanking a separate entrance gate, called the Niōmon in Japanese Buddhist monasteries. (In Korea, this gate is known as the Kŭmgangmun, or Vajra Gate.) They are also sometimes known as the "two kings" (niō), the Kongōjin, or the Kongōrikishi. They are considered to be manifestations of VAJRAPĀṆI. The first figure is known as either Naraen Kongō (see NĀRĀYAṆA) or Agyō; he is usually depicted with his mouth open and holding a VAJRA in his right hand. The second figure is called either Misshaku Kongō or Ungyō; he usually has his mouth closed and is either wielding a sword or has nothing in his hands.

**Niōzen**. [alt. Ninōzen] (J) (仁王禪/二王禪). See SUZUKI SHŌZAN.

**nirākāra**. (T. rnam pa med pa; C. wuxiang; J. musō; K. musang 無相). In Sanskrit, "without aspect," an epistemological term used to describe the process of sensory perception by those who assert that perception is direct cognition of the object itself, rather than of an image or "aspect" (ĀKĀRA) of the object. A point of contention among the Indian Buddhist schools (and Indian philosophical schools more generally) is whether sense perception is mediated or immediate. The proponents of the former position hold that even in "direct perception" (PRATYAKṢA), sensory objects are not perceived directly by the sense consciousnesses, but rather through the medium of an image or aspect, compared to a reflection cast by an object onto a mirror. Consciousness is thus affected by the object, which leaves its impression on the perceiving consciousness. Proponents of this theory of epistemology include the SAUTRĀNTIKA and YOGĀCĀRA, who are called "proponents of having an aspect" or "aspectarians" (sākāravāda). The contrary position is that the six sensory consciousnesses do in fact perceive their objects directly, without recourse to an image or aspect, hence the term nirākāra, or "without aspect." In this case, consciousness is not changed by the object it perceives; consciousness is instead like a light that reveals an object previously hidden in darkness. Proponents of this position include the VAIBHĀṢIKA, who are called "proponents of no aspect," or "nonaspectarians" (NIRĀKĀRAVĀDA).

**nirākāravāda**. (T. rnam pa med par smra ba). In Sanskrit, "proponents of no aspect," or "nonaspectarians." See NIRĀKĀRA.

**Niraupamyastava**. (T. Dpe med par bstod pa). In Sanskrit, "Hymn to the Peerless One"; one of the four hymns (CATUḤSTAVA) of NĀGĀRJUNA. The other three hymns are the LOKĀTĪTASTAVA, the ACINTYASTAVA, and the PARAMĀRTHASTAVA. All four hymns are preserved in Sanskrit and are cited by a wide range of Indian commentators, leaving little doubt about their authorship. The *Niraupamyastava* consists of twenty-four stanzas (plus a dedication of merit) in praise of the "Peerless One," i.e., the Buddha. The praise falls roughly into three categories: the first section is devoted to the qualities of the Buddha's mind, the second section is devoted to the qualities of the Buddha's body, and the concluding section explains the relationship between the Buddha's true body and the practice of the three vehicles (TRIYĀNA). Nāgārjuna explains that the Buddha has two bodies. The first is the DHARMAKĀYA, which is the Buddha's true body and which is not visible to the world. The second is his physical body (RŪPAKĀYA), which is perfect, without orifices, flesh, blood, or bones and free from hunger, thirst, and any form of impurity. However, in order to conform to the ways of the world, the Buddha displays these physical aspects and engages in worldly activities with this body. With regard to the three vehicles, Nāgārjuna explains that because the DHARMADHĀTU is undifferentiated, there are not different vehicles; however, the Buddha teaches three vehicles in order to prompt beings to enter the path.

**nirgrantha**. (P. nigaṇṭha; T. gcer bu pa; C. lixi/nijianzi; J. rike/nikenshi; K. igye/nigŏnja 離繫/尼揵子). In Sanskrit, "free from all ties," the term generally used in Buddhist texts to refer to the followers of NIRGRANTHA-JÑĀTĪPUTRA (P. Nigaṇṭha-Nātaputta), the Buddhist name for the leader of the JAINA religion, MAHĀVĪRA. As described in Pāli sources, this group followed the four restraints prescribed by their teacher: restraint regarding the use of water, restraint regarding evil deeds, cleansing themselves of evil, and realizing when evil is held at bay. They wore a single garment rather than going naked, and used it to prevent dirt and dust (which they regarded as living things) from entering their alms bowls. The Nigaṇṭhas were renowned for their extreme asceticism. They taught that the consequences of past deeds could only be eliminated through severe penance and that future consequences could only be eliminated through the complete suspension of action. The cessation of action, they believed, led to the cessation of suffering and sensation, by which means the individual would be freed from the cycle of REBIRTH. According to Pāli sources, the Nigaṇṭhas were influential during the Buddha's time and already well established by the time he began his ministry. Their main strongholds were at Vesāli (S. VAIŚĀLĪ) and NĀLANDĀ. Among the many renowned members of the Nigaṇṭha order were several nuns, some of whom, such as Bhaddā-Kundalakesā (S. BHADRA-KUṆḌALAKEŚĀ), later converted to Buddhism. The Nigaṇṭhas are frequently singled out for ridicule in early Buddhist literature. The Buddha describes them as unworthy in ten ways, viz., that they are without faith, unrighteous, without fear or shame, associate with evil friends, are puffed up and disparaging of others, greedy, stubborn, faithless, evil in thought, and are supporters of wrong views.

**Nirgrantha-Jñātīputra**. (P. Nigaṇṭha-Nātaputta; T. Gcer bu pa gnyen gyi bu; C. Nijiantuo Ruotizi; J. Nikenda'nyakudaishi; K. Nigŏnda Yajeja 尼揵陀若提子) (599–527 BCE). The name commonly used in Buddhist texts to refer to the leader of the JAINA group of non-Buddhists (TĪRTHIKA), also known by his title MAHĀVĪRA (Great Victor). In Pāli sources, Nātaputta (as he is usually called) is portrayed as the Buddha's senior contemporary. He teaches a practice called the fourfold restraint, enjoining his followers to be restrained regarding water, to be restrained regarding evil, to wash away evil, and to live in the realization that evil was held at bay; a person who could perfect the fourfold restraint was called free from bonds (P. nigaṇṭha; S. NIRGRANTHA). Like the Buddha and the leaders of many other renunciant (P. sāmana, S. ŚRAMAṆA) sects, Nātaputta claimed omniscience. According to Buddhist accounts, he taught that the consequences of past deeds could be eradicated only through severe penance. He also taught that the accrual of future consequences could be prevented only through the suspension of action. The cessation of action would lead to the cessation of suffering and feeling, and with this the individual would be freed from the cycle of rebirth. In Pāli materials, Nātaputta is portrayed in a most unfavorable light and his teachings are severely ridiculed, suggesting that in the early years of the Buddhist community the Jainas were formidable opponents and competitors of the Buddhists. Nātaputta is described as often declaring the postmortem fate of his deceased disciples, although he did not in fact know it. He is said to have been irritable and resentful, and unable to answer difficult questions. His disciple CITTA abandoned him for this reason and became a follower of the Buddha. In fact, Nātaputta is described as losing many followers to the Buddha, the most famous of whom was the householder UPĀLI. Nātaputta was convinced that Upāli could resist the Buddha's charisma and defeat him in argument. When he discovered that Upāli, too, had lost the debate and accepted the Buddha as his teacher, he vomited blood in rage and died soon thereafter. Buddhist sources claim that, on his deathbed, Nātaputta realized the futility of his own teachings and hoped that his followers would accept the Buddha as their teacher. In order to sow the discord that would result in their conversion, Nātaputta taught contradictory doctrines at the end of his life, teaching one disciple that his view was a form of annihilationism and another that his view was a form of eternalism. As a result, the Nigaṇṭha sect fell into discord and fragmented soon after his death. (This account, predictably, does not appear in Jaina sources.) News of Nātaputta's death prompted Sāriputta (S. ŚĀRIPUTRA) to recite a synopsis of the Buddha's teachings to the assembled SAṂGHA in a discourse titled SAṄGĪTISUTTA. Nātaputta is often listed in Buddhist texts as one of six non-Buddhist (tīrthika) teachers. See NIRGRANTHA; JAINA.

**nirmāṇakāya**. (T. sprul pa'i sku; C. huashen; J. keshin; K. hwasin 化身). In Sanskrit, "emanation body," or "transformation body"; according to the MAHĀYĀNA descriptions, one of the three bodies (TRIKĀYA) of a buddha, together with the DHARMAKĀYA and the SAṂBHOGAKĀYA. In accounts where a buddha is said to have two bodies, the dharmakāya constitutes one body and the RŪPAKĀYA constitutes the other, with the rūpakāya subsuming both the saṃbhogakāya and the nirmāṇakāya. The term nirmāṇakāya may have been employed originally to describe the doubles of himself that the Buddha is sometimes said to display in order to teach multiple audiences simultaneously. (Cf. MAHĀPRĀTIHĀRYA.) In the Mahāyāna, however, the emanation body became the only body of a buddha to appear to ordinary beings, implying that the "historical Buddha" was in fact a display intended to inspire the world; in the debates about whether the Buddha felt hunger or suffered physical pain, the Mahāyāna schools as well as several of the MAINSTREAM BUDDHIST SCHOOLS asserted that he did not, but rather appeared to do so in order to conform to worldly conventions. The nirmāṇakāya of a buddha is said to be able to appear in any form, including divinities, humans, animals, and inanimate objects; some texts even suggest that a buddha may appear as a bridge or a cooling breeze. The form of the nirmāṇakāya that appeared in India as Śākyamuni is called a "supreme emanation body" (UTTAMANIRMĀṆAKĀYA). All such nirmāṇakāyas are said to perform twelve deeds, from waiting in TUṢITA heaven for their last rebirth to entering PARINIRVĀṆA. Another type of nirmāṇakāya is the JANMANIRMĀṆAKĀYA, the "birth" or "created" emanation body, which is the form of a buddha when he appears as a divinity, human, or animal to benefit sentient beings, or as a beneficial inanimate object, such as a bridge. A third type is the ŚILPANIRMĀṆAKĀYA, an "artisan emanation body," in which a buddha appears in the world as an artisan or as a work of art. The Sanskrit term nirmāṇakāya is translated into Tibetan as SPRUL SKU, spelled in English as tulku.

**nirmāṇarati**. (P. nimmānarati; T. 'phrul dga'; C. huale tian; J. kerakuten; K. hwarak ch'ŏn 化樂天). In Sanskrit, "enjoying creations" or "enjoying emanations," the fifth (in ascending order) of the six heavens (SVARGA) of the sensuous realm (S. KĀMADHĀTU), located above Mount SUMERU and thirty-two thousand leagues (YOJANA) above the immediately preceding heaven, TUṢITA. The heaven receives its name because the divinities reborn there create their own magical emanations that they control. In this heaven, males and females experience sexual pleasure without engaging in physical contact but merely by smiling at each other. The children produced from their union have the appearance of nine-year-old children at birth. The life span in this heaven is said to be eight thousand years, in which each day is as long as eight hundred human years.

**nirmita**. (P. nimmita; T. sprul pa; C. hua; J. ke; K. hwa 化). In Sanskrit, "conjured," referring to something perceived by the sensory organs to be real but that is in fact illusory, like the moon on the surface of a lake or the water in a mirage. The term is often associated in Buddhist literature with the various doubles the Buddha conjures of himself in order to bring varying types of sentient beings to liberation (see NIRMĀṆAKĀYA).

**nirodha**. (T. 'gog pa; C. mie; J. metsu; K. myŏl 滅). In Sanskrit and Pāli, "cessation," "extinction," or "suppression," referring especially to the extinction of a specific affliction (KLEŚA) or group of afflictions. Because NIRVĀṆA is the cessation of all action (KARMAN) and affliction, it is thus a form of nirodha. The "truth of cessation," or NIRODHASATYA, is the third of the FOUR NOBLE TRUTHS articulated by the Buddha in his first sermon, "Setting in Motion the Wheel of Dharma" (P. DHAMMACAKKAPPAVATTANASUTTA; S. DHARMACAKRAPRAVARTANASŪTRA). Because nirodha is an absence and hence does not change from moment to moment, it is sometimes classified as a permanent factor (NITYADHARMA). Two types of nirodha are described in ABHIDHARMA literature. PRATISAṂKHYĀNIRODHA, or "analytical cessation," refers to a cessation that occurs as a result of meditative analysis of the real nature of phenomena; it is one of the uncompounded factors (ASAṂSKṚTADHARMA) recognized in both the SARVĀSTIVĀDA-VAIBHĀṢIKA and YOGĀCĀRA schools. APRATISAṂKHYĀNIRODHA, or "nonanalytical cessation," refers to a mere absence, such as the temporary absence of hunger after a meal, or to an uncompounded factor (asaṃskṛtadharma) that suppresses the production of all other dharmas, ensuring that they are restrained from ever again arising in the present. See also NIRODHASAMĀPATTI.

**nirodhasamāpatti**. (T. 'gog pa'i snyoms 'jug; C. miejin ding; J. metsujinjō; K. myŏlchin chŏng 滅盡定). In Sanskrit and Pāli, "equipoise of cessation," also known as "the cessation of perception and sensation" (SAṂJÑĀVEDAYITANIRODHA). Nirodhasamāpatti constitutes the ninth and highest level of meditative attainment in the mainstream Buddhist schools, achieved after the fourth meditative absorption of the immaterial realm (ĀRŪPYADHĀTU) and thus transcending the four subtle-materiality absorptions (RŪPĀVACARADHYĀNA) and four immaterial absorptions (ĀRŪPYĀVACARADHYĀNA). Nirodhasamāpatti engenders a state of suspended animation: the meditator remains alive, but all physical and mental activities cease for a fixed, but temporary, period of time. There is a great deal of discussion of this state in the ABHIDHARMA literatures, especially concerning the process by which the meditator returns to consciousness at the conclusion of the equipoise of cessation. Many stories are also told in the literature of monks in the state of nirodhasamāpatti who remain impervious to the dangers of raging conflagrations or passing tigers. Because even mentality (CITTA) is temporarily absent in this state, nirodhasamāpatti is classified as a "conditioned force dissociated from thought" (CITTAVIPRAYUKTASAṂSKĀRA) in both the VAIBHĀṢIKA school of SARVĀSTIVĀDA ABHIDHARMA, and in the hundred-dharmas (BAIFA) classification of the YOGĀCĀRA school. In Yogācāra schools that accept the storehouse consciousness (ĀLAYAVIJÑĀNA), all consciousness, including the KLIṢṬAMANAS, stops in nirodhasamāpatti; it is only the presence of the ālayavijñāna that keeps the meditator alive.

**nirodhasatya**. (P. nirodhasacca; T. 'gog pa'i bden pa; C. miedi; J. mettai; K. myŏlche 滅諦). In Sanskrit, "truth of cessation," the third of the so-called FOUR NOBLE TRUTHS (catvāry āryasatyāni) set forth by the Buddha in his first sermon, the "Setting in Motion the Wheel of the Dharma" (P. DHAMMACAKKAPPAVATTANASUTTA; S. DHARMACAKRAPRAVARTANASŪTRA). In a general sense, NIRODHA as "cessation" refers to NIRVĀṆA, which constitutes the cessation of all action (KARMAN) and afflictions (KLEŚA) and the suffering they induce (although the term nirvāṇa does not appear in the first sermon). In the ABHIDHARMA, the term is applied to the specific destruction of each of the kleśa associated with the three realms of existence (TRILOKA[DHĀTU]), the sensuous realm (KĀMADHĀTU), the subtle-materiality realm (RŪPADHĀTU), and the immaterial realm (ĀRŪPYADHĀTU) and the nine levels (the sensuous realm, the four meditative absorptions of the subtle-materiality realm, and the four absorptions of the immaterial realm). Such cessations are "true" (SATYA) in the sense that they are permanent; the particular kleśa is destroyed such that it will not occur again. The eradication of all the kleśas and contaminants (ĀSRAVAKṢAYA) results in the achievement of liberation from rebirth as an ARHAT. The four truths are not presented in the order of cause and effect, but rather effect and cause, with the first truth of suffering (DUḤKHASATYA) being the effect of the second truth of origin (SAMUDAYASATYA). In the same way, the third truth of cessation (nirodhasatya) is said to be the effect of the fourth truth of the path (MĀRGASATYA). However, nirodha is not an effect in the ordinary sense of the term because it is a permanent state; it is classified instead as a VISAṂYOGAPHALA, an effect that is a separation, i.e., the practice of the path results in the attainment of nirodha but does not produce nirodha as its effect.

Nirodhyasatya has four aspects (ĀKĀRA): suffering has stopped (nirodha); nirodha is a state of peace (śānta); it is sublime (praṇīta) because there is no state superior to it; and it is a definite escape (NIRYĀṆA).

**Nirṛti**. (T. Bden bral; C. Nielidi; J. Neritei; K. Yŏllijŏ 涅哩底). Sanskrit name of the lord of ogres and the divinity of death and destruction, who presides over the southwesterly direction. Nirṛti is often described as wearing armor, riding a lion, brandishing a sword in his right hand, and showing the sword MUDRĀ (C. daoyin) with his left, symbolizing the power of wisdom (PRAJÑĀ) and the destruction of the afflictions (KLEŚA). See RĀKṢASA.

**nirukti**. (P. nirutti; T. nges pa'i tshig; C. yanjiao; J. gonkyō; K. ŏn'gyo 言教). In Sanskrit, "clarification," often referring specifically to the ability to understand the etymology and linguistic usage of a word, phrase, or text. Nirukti is the third of four "analytical" or "unlimited knowledges" (PRATISAMVID), four types of knowledge with which a BODHISATTVA on the ninth of the ten bodhisattva stages (DAŚABHŪMI; daśabodhisattvavihāra) is endowed. Nirukti and the other three knowledges are treated at length in the MAHĀYĀNASŪTRĀLAṄKĀRA and the BODHISATTVABHŪMI, where nirukti is described as the ability to understand any and all languages, including those of divinities (DEVA) and demigods (YAKṢA, GANDHARVA, ASURA, GARUḌA, KIṂNARA, and MAHORĀGA). Thanks to this linguistic power, bodhisattvas are able to parse the full range of etymological or linguistic expressions attached to all phenomena and make use of this ability to preach the dharma to all potential audiences, with the highest degree of efficacy. This power of nirukti also makes their voices pleasant and understandable to anyone in the world.

**nirupadhiśeṣanirvāṇa**. (cf. P. anupādisesanibbāna; T. lhag ma med pa'i mya ngan las 'das pa; C. wuyu niepan; J. muyonehan; K. muyŏ yŏlban 無餘涅槃). In Sanskrit, "NIRVĀṆA without remainder" or "nirvāṇa without residue," the nirvāṇa achieved upon the death of an ARHAT or a buddha, in which there is no "remainder" of the aggregates of mind and body. It is synonymous with ANUPADHIŚEṢANIRVĀṆA (s.v.).

**nirvāṇa**. (P. nibbāna; T. mya ngan las 'das pa; C. niepan; J. nehan; K. yŏlban 涅槃). In Sanskrit, "extinction"; the earliest and most common term describing the soteriological goal of the Buddhist path (MĀRGA). Its etymology and meaning have been widely discussed by both traditional exegetes and modern scholars. Nirvāṇa is commonly interpreted as meaning "blowing out" (from the Sanskrit root √vā, "to blow," plus the prefix nir-, "out"), as "when a flame is blown out by the wind," to use the famous metaphor from the AṬṬHAKAVAGGA, and is thus sometimes glossed as the extinction of the flame of desire (RĀGA) or, more broadly, to the extinction of the "three poisons" (TRIVIṢA) or primary afflictions (KLEŚA) of greed/sensuality (RĀGA or LOBHA), hatred/aversion (DVEṢA), and delusion/ignorance (MOHA). In a more technical sense, nirvāṇa is interpreted as the cessation of the afflictions (kleśa), of the actions (KARMAN) produced by these afflictions, and eventually of the mind and body (NĀMARŪPA; SKANDHA) produced by karman, such that rebirth (SAṂSĀRA) ceases for the person who has completed the path. In the first sermon after his enlightenment, "Setting in Motion the Wheel of the Dharma" (P. DHAMMACAKKAPPAVATTANASUTTA; S. DHARMACAKRAPRAVARTANASŪTRA), the Buddha outlines the FOUR NOBLE TRUTHS (catvāry āryasatyāni), the third of which was the "truth of cessation" (NIRODHASATYA). This state of the cessation of suffering (DUḤKHA) and its causes (SAMUDAYA) is glossed as nirvāṇa. In one famous description of nirvāṇa, the Buddha explained, "There is that plane (ĀYATANA) where there is neither earth, water, fire, nor air [viz., the four MAHĀBHŪTA], neither the sphere of infinite space [ĀKĀŚĀNANTYĀYATANA] ... nor the sphere of neither perception nor nonperception [NAIVASAṂJÑĀNĀSAṂJÑĀYATANA], neither this world nor another nor both together, neither the sun nor the moon. Here, O monks, I say that there is no coming or going, no staying, no passing away or arising. It is not something fixed, it moves not on, it is not based on anything. This is indeed the end of suffering." Even though this is a thoroughly negative description of nirvāṇa, it is important to note that the passage opens with the certitude that "there is that plane...." Whether this state of cessation represents a form of "annihilation" is a question that preoccupied early scholarship on Buddhism. The Buddha described human existence as qualified by various forms of suffering, sought a state that would transcend such suffering, and determined that, in order to put an end to suffering, one must destroy its causes: unwholesome (AKUŚALA) actions (karman) and the negative afflictions (kleśa) that motivate them. If these causes could be destroyed, they would no longer have any effect, resulting in the cessation of suffering and thus nirvāṇa. Nirvāṇa, therefore, was not regarded as a place or state of existence, since by definition that would mean it was part of saṃsāra and thus subject to impermanence and suffering. Nirvāṇa is instead an absence, and it is often described in rigidly apophatic terms, as in the passage above, as if by describing what nirvāṇa was not, at least some sense of what it is could be conveyed. When the tradition attempts more positive descriptions, nirvāṇa is sometimes described as deathless (AMṚTA), imperishable (acyuta), uncreated (abhūta), peace (upaśama), bliss (SUKHA), etc. The concept of nirvāṇa may be somewhat more accessible if it is approached soteriologically, as the culmination of the Buddhist path of practice (mārga). At the upper reaches of the path, the adept must pass through three "gates to liberation" (VIMOKṢAMUKHA), which mark the transition from the compounded (SAṂSKṚTA) realm of saṃsāra to the uncompounded (ASAṂSKṚTA) realm of nirvāṇa. In approaching nirvāṇa, the adept first passes through the gate of emptiness (ŚŪNYATĀ), which reveals that nirvāṇa is empty of anything associated with a sense of self. Next comes the gate of signlessness (ĀNIMITTA), which reveals that nirvāṇa has nothing by which it may be perceived. Finally comes the gate of wishlessness (APRAṆIHITA), meaning that nirvāṇa can be achieved only when one no longer has any desire for, or attachment to, nirvāṇa. Exactly what persisted in the state of nirvāṇa was the subject of considerable discussion over the history of the tradition. The Buddha is said to have realized nirvāṇa when he achieved enlightenment at the age of thirty-five, thus eradicating the causes of future rebirth. After this experience, however, he continued to live for another forty-five years, and, upon his death, he entered nirvāṇa, never to be reborn again. Because of this gap between his initial experience of nirvāṇa and his final PARINIRVĀṆA, the scholastic tradition therefore distinguished between two types of nirvāṇa. The first type is the "nirvāṇa with remainder" (SOPADHIŚEṢANIRVĀṆA), sometimes interpreted as the "nirvāṇa associated with the kleśas." This is the state of nirvāṇa achieved prior to death, where the "remainder" refers to the mind and body of this final existence. This is the nirvāṇa achieved by the Buddha under the BODHI TREE. However, the inertia of the karman that had led to this present life was still operating and would continue to do so until his death. Thus, his mind and body during the remainder of his final lifetime were what was left over after he realized nirvāṇa. The second type is referred to as the "nirvāṇa without remainder" (ANUPADHIŚEṢANIRVĀṆA or NIRUPADHIŚEṢANIRVĀṆA), sometimes interpreted as the "nirvāṇa of the skandhas." This is the nirvāṇa achieved at death, in which the causes of all future existence have been extinguished, bringing the chain of causation of both the physical form and consciousness to an end and leaving nothing remaining to be reborn. This is also called "final nirvāṇa" (parinirvāṇa), and it is what the Buddha achieved at the time of his demise at KUŚINAGARĪ. These states were accessible to all adepts who followed the Buddhist path to its conclusion. In the case of the Buddha, some traditions also refer to the third type of nirvāṇa, the "final nirvāṇa of the relics" (śarīraparinirvāṇa), viz., the dissolution of the relics (ŚARĪRA) of the Buddha at a point in the distant future. According to Buddhist eschatology, there will come a time in the far distant future when the teachings of ŚĀKYAMUNI Buddha will disappear from the world, and his relics will no longer be honored. At that point, the relics that have been enshrined in reliquaries (STŪPA) around the world will be released from their shrines and be magically transported to BODHGAYĀ, where they will reassemble into the resplendent body of the Buddha, who will be seated in the lotus posture under the Bodhi tree, emitting rays of light that illuminate ten thousand world systems. The relics will be worshipped by the divinities (DEVA) one last time and then will burst into flames and disappear into the sky. Until that time, the relics of the Buddha are to be regarded as his living presence, infused with all of his marvelous qualities. With the rise of MAHĀYĀNA, the "nirvāṇa without remainder" came to be disparaged in some texts as excessively quietistic, and the Buddha's passage into parinirvāṇa was described as simply a display; the Buddha is instead said to be eternal, inhabiting a place that is neither in saṃsāra nor nirvāṇa and that is referred to as the "unlocated nirvāṇa" (APRATIṢṬHITANIRVĀṆA). The MADHYAMAKA philosopher NĀGĀRJUNA declared that there was not the slightest difference between saṃsāra and nirvāṇa, a statement taken to mean that both are equally empty of any intrinsic nature (NIḤSVABHĀVA). Madhyamaka texts also refer to a nirvāṇa that is "intrinsically extinguished" (PRAKṚTIPARINIRVṚTA); this quiescence that is inherent in all phenomena is a synonym of emptiness (ŚŪNYATĀ).

**nirvāṇadhātu**. (P. nibbānadhātu; T. mya ngan las 'das pa'i dbyings; C. niepanjie; J. nehankai; K. yŏlban'gye 涅槃界). In Sanskrit, "the nirvāṇa element," a term that is essentially synonymous with NIRVĀṆA and refers to the plane or state experienced through the liberation (VIMOKṢA) that derives from the extinction of suffering (DUḤKHA). In the VAIBHĀṢIKA school of SARVĀSTIVĀDA ABHIDHARMA, two types of nirvāṇadhātu are discussed. First is the nirvāṇadhātu with remainder (sopadhiśeṣanirvāṇadhātu, see SOPADHIŚEṢANIRVĀṆA), where the remainder is the residue of the aggregates (SKANDHA); this form is the nirvāṇa that is experienced while the body remains alive. Second is the nirvāṇadhātu without remainder (nirupadhiśeṣanirvāṇadhātu; see NIRUPADHIŚEṢANIRVĀṆA, ANUPADHIŚEṢANIRVĀṆA), the nirvāṇa achieved upon the death of an ARHAT or a buddha, in which there is no "remainder" of materiality and mentality (NĀMARŪPA); this type is synonymous with PARINIRVĀṆA.

**Nirvāṇa school**. See NIEPAN ZONG.

**Nirvāṇa Sūtra**. See MAHĀPARINIRVĀṆASŪTRA.

**nirveda**. (P. nibbidā; T. skyo ba; C. yan; J. en; K. yŏm 厭). In Sanskrit, "disgust," "disillusionment," "loathing"; a term used in Buddhist meditation theory to indicate the preliminary and conditional turning away from the things of this world and turning toward NIRVĀṆA, which serves as the crucial mental factor (DHARMA) in catalyzing the transition from an ordinary person (PṚTHAGJANA) to a noble one (ĀRYA). There has been considerable discussion in the literature on the precise meaning of nirveda, with connotations suggested that range from disgust to disappointment to indifference. As the meditator comes to recognize that all worldly objects that may be perceived through the senses are impermanent (ANITYA), he realizes that association with, let alone attachment to, them will inexorably lead to suffering (DUḤKHA). The recognition of the ubiquity of suffering leads the adept inevitably toward a sense of nirveda, the volition to distance oneself from these worldly objects and to seek the alternative that is nirvāṇa. As a by-product of the experience of YATHĀBHŪTAJÑĀNADARŚANA ("seeing things as they really are"), nirveda thus produces the mental factor VAIRĀGYA ("dispassion"), which ultimately leads to VIMOKṢA ("liberation").

**nirvedha**. (T. nges par 'byed pa; C. jueze; J. ketchaku; K. kyŏlt'aek 決擇). In Sanskrit, "penetration," referring specifically to the direct penetration into the nature of reality that occurs on the path of vision (DARŚANAMĀRGA). See NIRVEDHABHĀGĪYA.

**nirvedhabhāgīya**. (T. nges par 'byed pa'i cha dang mthun pa; C. shunjuezefen; J. junketchakubun; K. sun'gyŏlt'aekpum 順決

擇分). In Sanskrit, "aids to penetration," the constituent stages developed during the path of preparation (PRAYOGAMĀRGA), the second segment of the five-path schema outlined in the VAIBHĀṢIKA ABHIDHARMA system, which mark the transition from the mundane sphere of cultivation (LAUKIKA[BHĀVANĀ]MĀRGA) to the supramundane vision (DARŚANA) of the FOUR NOBLE TRUTHS (catvāry āryasatyāni); also called the "virtuous faculties associated with penetration" (nirvedhabhāgīya-KUŚALAMŪLA) or the "four virtuous faculties" (CATUṢKUŚALAMŪLA). The nirvedhabhāgīya are the third of the three types of virtuous faculties (KUŚALAMŪLA) recognized in the VAIBHĀṢIKA school, along with the puṇyabhāgīya and MOKṢABHĀGĪYA kuśalamūlas. In distinction to the mokṣabhāgīyas, however, which are the remote path of preparation, the nirvedhabhāgīyas constitute instead the proximate path of preparation and are associated specifically with the type of wisdom that is generated through one's own meditative experience (BHĀVANĀMĀYĪPRAJÑĀ). The four aids to penetration are (1) heat (ŪṢMAN [alt. ūṣmagata]), (2) summit (MŪRDHAN), (3) acquiescence or receptivity (KṢĀNTI), (4) and highest worldly dharmas (LAUKIKĀGRADHARMA). After accumulating the preliminary skills necessary for religious cultivation on the preceding path of accumulation (SAṂBHĀRAMĀRGA), the practitioner continues on to develop the mindfulness of mental constituents (dharma-SMṚTYUPASTHĀNA) on the path of preparation. This path involves the four aids to penetration, which mark successive stages in understanding the sixteen aspects of the four noble truths and are each subdivided into various categories, such as weak, medium, and strong experiences. While the first two of these NIRVEDHABHĀGĪYAS are subject to retrogression and thus belong to the worldly path of cultivation (laukikabhāvanāmārga), the latter two are nonretrogressive (AVAIVARTIKA) and lead inevitably to insight (DARŚANA). Mastery of the four aids to penetration culminates in the "unimpeded concentration" (ĀNANTARYASAMĀDHI), in which the meditator acquires fully all the highest worldly dharmas; this distinctive concentration provides access to the third stage of the path, the path of vision (DARŚANAMĀRGA), which marks the entrance into sanctity (ĀRYA) as a stream-enterer (SROTAĀPANNA). Thus the nirvedhabhāgīyas are the pivotal point in the progression of an ordinary person (PṚTHAGJANA) to the status of a noble one (ĀRYA). According to the ABHIDHARMAMAHĀVIBHĀṢĀ, disciples (ŚRĀVAKA) and solitary buddhas (PRATYEKABUDDHA) may develop the nirvedhabhāgīyas either before or during any of the four stages of the meditative absorptions (DHYĀNA), while bodhisattvas develop all four in one sitting during their final lifetimes.

**nirvikalpa**. (P. nibbikappa; T. rnam par rtog pa med pa; C. wu fenbie; J. mufunbetsu; K. mubunbyŏl 無分別). In Sanskrit, "nonconceptual," an adjective used to describe states of direct perception, either by the sensory consciousnesses or the mental consciousness. The sense consciousnesses are necessarily nonconceptual, but a state of nonconceptual mental consciousness is required for direct realization of the truth, and hence liberation. The nonconceptual state is therefore praised for its ability to perceive directly without the intercession of the distorting medium of thought. See also NIRVIKALPAJÑĀNA.

**nirvikalpajñāna**. (T. rnam par mi rtog pa'i ye shes; C. wu fenbie zhi; J. mufunbetsuchi; K. mu punbyŏl chi 無分別智). In Sanskrit, "nondiscriminative wisdom," "nonconceptual awareness"; the insight that is marked by freedom from the misconception that there is an inherent bifurcation between a perceiving subject (grāhaka) and its perceived objects (grāhya). In the YOGĀCĀRA school, this misconception is called the discrimination of object and subject (GRĀHYAGRĀHAKAVIKALPA). Overcoming this bifurcation leads to the nondiscriminative wisdom (nirvikalpajñāna), which, in the five-stage path (PAÑCAMĀRGA) system of the Yogācāra school, marks the inception of the path of vision (DARŚANAMĀRGA), where the adept sees reality directly, without the intercession of concepts, and realizes the inherent unity of objects and cognition (jñeya-jñāna). The MAHĀYĀNASAṂGRAHA explains that nirvikalpajñāna has as its nature the following five types of absences: (1) the absence of inattention (amanasikāra), such as occurs during sleep, (2) the absence of discursive thought (VITARKA) and sustained consideration (VICĀRA), (3) the quiescence of the cessation of perception and feeling (SAṂJÑĀVEDAYITANIRODHA), (4) the absence of materiality (RŪPA), and (5) the absence of analytical investigation regarding truthfulness. These attributes mean that nirvikalpajñāna (1) is not merely a lack of attention; (2) it is not just the second stage of DHYĀNA or higher, where discursive thought (vitarka) and investigation (vicāra) no longer pertain; (3) it is not the "equipoise of cessation" (NIRODHASAMĀPATTI), which no longer includes mind (CITTA) and mental concomitants (CAITTA), because wisdom (JÑĀNA) is not possible without mind and its concomitants; (4) it is free from any kind of discrimination; and (5) it cannot be an object of analytical investigation, since it transcends the relationship between the objects in any discursive analysis. This type of wisdom is therefore associated with knowledge (jñāna) that is supramundane (LOKOTTARA) and uncontaminated (ANĀSRAVA). The term nirvikalpajñāna also appears in MADHYAMAKA descriptions of the path (MĀRGA), despite the fact that Madhyamaka does not reject the conventional existence of external objects. Here, the term refers to the nonconceptual realization of emptiness (ŚŪNYATĀ) that occurs on the path of vision (DARŚANAMĀRGA) and above, where reality is directly perceived in an experience in which emptiness and the consciousness that realizes emptiness are said to be like "pure water poured into pure water." See also VIKALPA; TRIVIKALPA.

**niryāṇa**. (T. nges 'byung; C. chuli; J. shutsuri; K. ch'ulli 出離). In Sanskrit, lit. "departure" or "going out." In the context of the FOUR NOBLE TRUTHS (catvāry āryasatyāni), it is an aspect of the third "truth of cessation" (NIRODHASATYA), where niryāṇa means the definite "escape" from suffering when its cause has been eliminated. In the context of the MAHĀYĀNA path, niryāṇa involves the final stages of a bodhisattva's progress (PRATIPATTI) leading to full enlightenment; the ABHISAMAYĀLAṂKĀRA gives a list of eight niryāṇas based on aspects of the final destination. In some contexts, the term, like NIRVEDA and NIḤSARAṆA, can mean "renunciation," in the sense of the conviction to be liberated or to emerge from rebirth in SAṂSĀRA, whether one is following the path of the ŚRĀVAKA or PRATYEKABUDDHA in order to become an ARHAT, or is following the BODHISATTVA path in order to become a buddha. It is in this sense that the Tibetan translation of the term as "emergence" (nges 'byung) is deployed by TSONG KHA PA in his delineation of the "three principal aspects of the path" (LAM GTSO RNAM GSUM), where emergence is the first of the three aspects, followed by BODHICITTA and wisdom (PRAJÑĀ).

**Nishida Kitarō**. (西田幾太郎) (1870–1945). Influential Japanese philosopher of the modern era and founder of what came to be known as the KYOTO SCHOOL, a contemporary school of Japanese philosophy that sought to synthesize ZEN Buddhist thought with modern Western, and especially Germanic, philosophy. Nishida was instrumental in establishing in Japan the discipline of philosophy as practiced in Europe and North America, as well as in exploring possible intersections between European philosophy and such Buddhist ontological notions as the idea of nonduality (ADVAYA). Nishida was born in 1870, just north of Ishikawa prefecture's capital city of Kanazawa. In 1894, he graduated from Tōkyō Imperial University with a degree in philosophy and eventually took an appointment at Kyōto University, where he taught from 1910 until his retirement in 1927. At Kyōto University, Nishida attracted a group of students who would later become known collectively as the "Kyoto School." These philosophers addressed an array of philosophical concerns, including metaphysics, ontology, phenomenology, and epistemology, using Western critical methods but in conjunction with Eastern religious concepts. Nishida's influential 1911 publication *Zen no kenkyū* ("A Study of Goodness") synthesized Zen Buddhist and German phenomenology to explore the unity between the ordinary and the transcendent. He argued that, through "pure experience" (J. junsui keiken), an individual human being is able to come in contact with a limitless, absolute reality that can be described either as God or emptiness (ŚŪNYATĀ). In Nishida's treatment, philosophy is subsumed under the broader soteriological quest for individual awakening, and its significance derives from its effectiveness in bringing about this goal of awakening. Other important works by Nishida include *Jikaku ni okeru chokkan to hansei* ("Intuition and Reflection in Self-Consciousness," 1917), *Geijutsu to dōtoku* ("Art and Morality," 1923), *Tetsugaku no konpon mondai* ("Fundamental Problems of Philosophy," 1933), and *Bashoteki ronri to shūkyōteki sekaikan* ("The Logic of the Place of Nothingness and the Religious Worldview," 1945). Nishida's *Zen no kenkyū* also helped lay the foundation for what later became regarded as Nihonjinron, a nationalist discourse that advocated the uniqueness and superiority of the Japanese race. Prominent in Nishida's philosophy is the idea that the Japanese—as exemplified in their exceptional cultivation of Zen, which here can stand for both Zen Buddhism and the homophonous word for "goodness"—are uniquely in tune with this concept of "pure experience." This familiarity, in part influenced by his longtime friend DAISETZ TEITARO SUZUKI, elevates the Japanese race mentally and spiritually above all other races in the world. This view grew in popularity during the era of Japanese colonial expansion and remained strong in some quarters even after the end of World War II. Since at least the 1970s, Nishida's work has been translated and widely read among English-speaking audiences. Beginning in the 1990s, however, his writings have come under critical scrutiny in light of their ties with Nihonjinron and Japanese nationalism.

**Nishi Honganjiha**. [alt. Honganjiha] (西本願寺派). In Japanese, "Western Honganji school"; the largest subsect of JŌDO SHINSHŪ. After the death of SHINRAN in 1263, the HONGANJI institution emerged as the dominant subsect of Jōdo Shinshū, administered by the descendants of Shinran's patriarchal line. In the Tokugawa Period (1600–1868), the shōgun Tokugawa Ieyasu (1543–1616) grew suspicious of Honganji, which during the fifteenth and sixteenth centuries had grown not only to be the largest sect of Japanese Buddhism but also one of the largest landholding institutions in Japan. By involving himself in a succession dispute, the shōgun was successfully able to cause a split within the Honganji into East (higashi; see HIGASHI HONGANJIHA; ŌTANIHA) and West (nishi) factions, with Kyōnyo (1558–1614) heading the Higashi faction, and Junnyo (1577–1631) leading the Nishi faction. In 1639, Nishi Honganji established its own seminary college in Kyoto that was renamed Ryūkoku University in 1922. Important modern Nishi Honganji Buddhists include ŌTANI KŌZUI (1868–1948), the famed explorer and collector.

**Nishitani Keiji**. (西谷啓治) (1900–1990). Japanese philosopher and member of what came to be known as the KYOTO SCHOOL, a contemporary school of Japanese philosophy that sought to synthesize ZEN Buddhist thought with modern Western, and especially Germanic, philosophy. Nishitani was schooled in Ishikawa prefecture and Tōkyō and graduated from Kyōto University in 1924 with a degree in philosophy. A student of NISHIDA KITARŌ (1870–1945), the founder of the Kyoto School, Nishitani became a professor in the Department of Religion at Kyōto University in 1935 and from 1937 to 1939 studied with Martin Heidegger in Freiburg, Germany. He later chaired the Department of Modern Philosophy at Kyōto Prefectural University from 1955 to 1963. In such works as his 1949 *Nihirizumu* (translated in 1990 as *The Self-Overcoming of Nihilism*) and *Shūkyō to wa nani ka* ("What Is Religion?," 1961, translated in 1982 as *Religion and Nothingness*), Nishitani sought to synthesize German existentialism, Christian mysticism, and what he considered to be Zen experience. Where German philosophy, which is governed by logic and cognitive thinking, addressed ontological questions regarding the self, he argued that such means as Christian mysticism and Zen meditation could complement German philosophy in constructing a path to a complete realization of the self. Nishitani took issue with Nietzsche's nihilism by borrowing from the Buddhist concept of emptiness (ŚŪNYATĀ) to argue that recognition of the self as empty brings one to an understanding of things as they are (viz., the Buddhist concept of suchness, or TATHATĀ), and hence a true understanding and affirmation of oneself. Nishitani's philosophical justification of Japan's wartime activities, notably his contributions to the well-known journal *Chūōkōron* ("Central Review") in the early 1940s, has become a controversial aspect of his work.

**niṣīdana**. [alt. niṣadana] (P. nisīdana; T. gding ba; C. zuoju; J. zagu; K. chwagu 坐具). In Sanskrit, lit. "the act of sitting," any cloth, rug, or mat that is spread out over the ground and used for sitting or sleeping, thus a "sitting mat." In the Buddhist tradition, a niṣīdana is a sitting cloth used during seated meditation or during prostrations. A niṣīdana is one of the few basic requisites (NIŚRAYA; PARIṢKĀRA) that a monk or nun is allowed to possess. For this reason, the VINAYA literature includes extensive discussions on the appropriate characteristics of the niṣīdana—i.e., how large it can be, its color, proper use, and so on. Many of these rules appear in the NAIḤSARGIKAPĀYATTIKA (forfeiture offense) section of the PRĀTIMOKṢA. The term also comes to refer by extension to a stool.

**niṣpannakrama**. (T. rdzogs rim; C. yuanman cidi; J. enmanshidai; K. wŏnman ch'aje 圓滿次第). In Sanskrit, "stage of completion" (also called saṃpannakrama and utpannakrama); one of the two major phases of ANUTTARAYOGATANTRA practice, the other being the UTPATTIKRAMA, variously translated as the "stage of generation," "creation stage," or "development stage." The stage of generation is considered the preparation for the stage of completion. After having received initiation (ABHIṢEKA), during the stage of generation the practitioner engages in the practice of detailed visualization of himself or herself as a deity and the environment as a MAṆḌALA. Meditation on emptiness (ŚŪNYATĀ) is also involved. The central point of the practice is to vividly imagine oneself as the buddha one is going to become and thus simulate the process whereby this achievement will occur. The stage of completion is the period in which the actual achievement of buddhahood by the path of anuttarayogatantra occurs. Here, the meditator engages in practices that cause the winds (PRĀṆA) to enter the central channel (AVADHŪTĪ) and gather at the heart CAKRA, causing the mind of clear light (PRABHĀSVARA) to become manifest, at which point the three states of death, intermediate state (ANTARĀBHAVA), and rebirth are transformed respectively into the DHARMAKĀYA, SAṂBHOGAKĀYA, and NIRMĀṆAKĀYA of a buddha.

**Niṣpannayogāvalī**. (T. Rdzogs pa'i rnal 'byor gyi 'phreng ba). In Sanskrit, "Garland of Perfect Yoga," a compendium of tantric SĀDHANAS (with descriptions of MAṆḌALAS and deities) by the eleventh-century Indian master ABHAYĀKARAGUPTA.

**niṣprapañca**. [alt. niḥprapañca] (P. nippapañca; T. spros pa dang bral ba; C. buxilun; J. fukeron; K. purhŭiron 不戲論). In Sanskrit, "conceptual nonproliferation" or "absence of superimposition," the transcendent (LOKOTTARA) state of mind that is characteristic of the enlightened noble person (ĀRYA). Niṣprapañca refers to the absence of that which is fanciful, imagined, or superfluous, especially in the sense of the absence of a quality that is mistakenly projected onto an object. This false quality is called PRAPAÑCA, which has the sense of "diffusion" or "expansion," viz., "conceptual proliferation." Such "proliferation" typically takes the form of a chaotic onslaught of thoughts and associations at the conclusion of the apprehension of an object by one of the five sensory consciousnesses. Those thoughts and associations are then objectified, projecting a false reality onto the sense object. Such projections are thus described as operations of ignorance. Reality is free from such elaborations, and wisdom is the state of mind that perceives this reality. The goal of meditation practice is therefore sometimes described as the achievement of a state free from such conceptual proliferation, i.e., niṣprapañca. By systematic attention (YONIŚOMANASKĀRA) to the impersonal, conditioned character of sensory experience and through sensory restraint (INDRIYASAṂVARA), the tendency to project the notion of a perduring self (ĀTMAN) into the perceptual process is brought to an end. This state of "nonproliferation" frees perception from its subjugation to conceptualization, allowing it to see the things of this world as impersonal causal products that are inevitably impermanent (ANITYA), suffering (DUḤKHA), and nonself (ANĀTMAN), freeing the mind in turn from the attachment to SAṂSĀRA. The precise nature of conceptual nonproliferation is defined differently in the various Indian schools. In the Pāli MILINDAPAÑHA, NĀGASENA explains to the king that the four fruits of stream-enterer (SROTAĀPANNA), once-returner (SAKṚDĀGĀMIN), nonreturner (ANĀGĀMIN), and ARHAT are in fact nippapañca. In the YOGĀCĀRA school of Mahāyāna Buddhism, niṣprapañca refers to the absence of the misapprehension of sensory objects as separate from the perceiving consciousness, and in the MADHYAMAKA school it refers to the absence of perceiving objects as endowed with SVABHĀVA.

**niśraya**. (P. nissaya; T. brten; C. suoyi; J. shoe; K. soŭi 所依). In Sanskrit, "requisite," "reliance," "support," in the sense of a basic possession required of any monk or nun. Four basic requisites are allowed for use by all monks and nuns: (1) food acquired through alms gathering (see PIṆḌAPĀTA; P. piṇḍiyālopabhojana); (2) a robe (CĪVARA) made from collected rags (pāṃsukūlacīvara; P. paṃsukūlacīvara); (3) dwelling at the foot of a tree (vṛkṣamūlasenāsana; P. rukkhamūlasenāsana); and (4) using fermented urine as medicine (pūtimuktabhaiṣajya; P. pūtimuttabhesajja). During the ordination procedure, when new ordinands "go forth" (PRAVRAJITA) as novice monks

(ŚRĀMAṆERA) or nuns (ŚRĀMAṆERIKĀ), they will be apprised of these four requisites and encouraged to be content with them for the rest of their lives. In addition to these four basic reliances, the VINAYA does allow the use of other related things, such as constructed residences, meals offered by laypeople by invitation, robes made of cloth other than rags, and a mixture of honey, molasses oil, and butter as a medicine. See also PARIṢKĀRA. ¶ The term niśraya is also used in the sense of "guidance." A newly ordained monk or nun is required to live under the "guidance" of his or her preceptor (S. UPĀDHYĀYA; P. upajjhāya) for a minimum of five years. During this period, the preceptor is to instruct the new monk in the teachings (DHARMA) and train him in the monastic regulations (VINAYA). Only a monk who has at least ten years of seniority in the SAṂGHA and who is otherwise qualified may provide "guidance" to another monk. If the new monk has lost his preceptor, he must seek niśraya from a teacher.

**niṣṭhā**. (P. niṭṭhā; T. mthar phyin pa; C. jiujing; J. kukyō; K. kugyŏng 究竟). In Sanskrit, "the end," "completion." In mainstream Buddhist materials, the Buddha often described the consummation of religious training and the achievement of the state of either stream-enterer (SROTAĀPANNA) or ARHAT as "the end"; the term is synonymous with the "deathless" (AMṚTA) and thus "liberation" (VIMOKṢA). The term appears in a variety of contexts in both mainstream and MAHĀYĀNA traditions to mean "coming to the end" of practice, viz., to achieve spiritual perfection, as in the soteriological term "path of completion" (NIṢṬHĀMĀRGA).

**niṣṭhāmārga**. (T. mthar phyin pa'i lam; C. jiujingdao/wei; J. kukyōdō/i; K. kugyŏngdo/wi 究竟道/位). In Sanskrit, "path of completion," the fifth of the "five-path" (PAÑCAMĀRGA) schema described in both SARVĀSTIVĀDA ABHIDHARMA and the YOGĀCĀRA school of MAHĀYĀNA. With the consummation of the path of cultivation (BHĀVANĀMĀRGA), the adept achieves the "adamantine-like concentration" (VAJROPAMASAMĀDHI), which leads to the permanent destruction of even the subtlest and most persistent of the ten fetters (SAṂYOJANA), resulting in the "knowledge of cessation" (KṢAYAJÑĀNA) and in some presentations an accompanying "knowledge of nonproduction" (ANUTPĀDAJÑĀNA), viz., the knowledges that the fetters are destroyed and can never again recur. Because the adept now has full knowledge of the eightfold path (ĀRYĀṢṬĀṄGAMĀRGA) and has achieved liberation (VIMOKṢA), he no longer needs any further instruction; for this reason, this path is also described as the "path where there is nothing more to learn" (AŚAIKṢAMĀRGA). With the attainment of this path, the practitioner is freed from the possibility of any further rebirth due to the causal force of KARMAN.

**niṣyandaphala**. (T. rgyu mthun gyi 'bras bu; C. dengliu guo; J. tōruka; K. tŭngnyu kwa 等流果). In Sanskrit, lit. "flowing-forth-from effect," "correlative effect," or "uniform-emanation effect"; this is one of the five types of effects or fruitions (PHALA) enumerated in the SARVĀSTIVĀDA ABHIDHARMA and the YOGĀCĀRA system. The niṣyandaphala is described as an effect that "flows out from" or arises in similarity with, its corresponding cause (HETU)—in this case, specifically the "homogeneous cause" (SABHĀGAHETU) and "all-pervasive cause" (SARVATRAGAHETU)—and is generally described in one of two ways. In the first sense, the effect may correlate with the cause of the previous action. For example, as a result of giving a gift in a past life, a person might enjoy the act of charity in a future life; or, as a result of committing murder in a past life, a person might enjoy killing in a future life. In the second sense, the effect may accord with the experience resulting from the previous action. For example, as a result of being charitable in a past life, one may receive charity in a future life; or as a result of committing murder in a past life, one may be murdered in a future life.

**nītārtha**. (P. nītattha; T. nges don; C. liaoyi; J. ryōgi; K. yoŭi 了義). In Sanskrit, "definitive," one of the two categories into which statements in the sūtras may be classified, along with NEYĀRTHA, or "provisional." Nītārtha and neyārtha are among a number of categories employed in the interpretation of scripture, and provide a means of accounting for statements by the Buddha that appear to contradict the Buddha's presumed final position on a topic. The Indian schools differ on what constitutes a definitive statement. Some hold that any statement that can be accepted literally is definitive. Thus, for those MAHĀYĀNA schools that hold that all beings will eventually achieve buddhahood, the statement in the SADDHARMAPUṆḌARĪKASŪTRA ("Lotus Sūtra") that there is only one vehicle (EKAYĀNA) would be regarded as a definitive teaching. Based on a statement in the AKṢAYAMATINIRDEŚASŪTRA, others hold that only those statements that describe the ultimate nature of reality are definitive, playing on the literal sense of nītārtha as "definite object" or "definite meaning." Thus, a statement that wealth is the result of charity (DĀNA), while literally true, would be deemed provisional because it does not make reference to the final nature or emptiness (ŚŪNYATĀ) of wealth or the act of giving.

**Nittō guhō junrei gyōki**. (入唐求法巡禮行記). In Japanese, "Record of a Pilgrimage to China in Search of the Dharma"; a renowned travel diary, in four rolls, by the Japanese TENDAISHŪ monk ENNIN (794–864) of his nine years sojourning in Tang China. In 838, Ennin sailed to China with his companions Engyō (799–852) and Jōkyō (d. 866), arriving in Yangzhou (present-day Jiangsu province) at the mouth of the Yangzi River. The next year, he found himself at the monastery of Kaiyuansi, where he received the teachings and rituals of the various KONGŌKAI (vajradhātu) deities from the monk Quanya (d.u.). When adverse winds kept him from returning to Japan, he remained behind at the monastery of Fahuayuan on Mt. Chi in Dengzhou (present-day Shandong province). From there, Ennin made a pilgrimage to WUTAISHAN, where he studied TIANTAI ZONG doctrine and practice. In 840, Ennin arrived in the capital Chang'an, where he studied under the master

(ĀCĀRYA) Yuanzheng (d.u.) of the monastery of Daxingshansi. The next year, Ennin also studied the teachings of the TAIZŌKAI (garbhadhātu) and the SUSIDDHIKARASŪTRA under the ācārya Yizhen (d.u.) of the monastery of Qinglongsi. In 842, Ennin furthered his studies of the taizōkai under the ācārya Faquan (d.u.) at the monastery Xuanfasi, SIDDHAM under Yuanjian (d.u.) of Da'anguosi, and siddham pronunciation under the Indian ācārya Baoyue (d.u.). In 845, Ennin fled the Huichang persecution of Buddhism (HUICHANG FANAN) that was then raging in Chang'an, and arrived back in Japan in 847. Ennin's record includes not only detailed information on the routes he took between Japan and China, but also the procedures and expenses required in order to obtain travel permits. In addition, his diary contains detailed descriptions of the daily rituals followed at a Korean monastery in Shandong province where he (and other foreign travelers) stayed for some time. The *Nittō guhō junrei gyōki* is therefore an important source for studying the daily lives of travelers, merchants, officials, and monks in medieval China.

**nitya**. (P. nicca; T. rtag pa; C. chang; J. jō; K. sang 常). In Sanskrit, "permanent"; technically defined in some schools as the quality of being capable of lasting more than a single instant (KṢAṆA). According to the SARVĀSTIVĀDA school of ABHIDHARMA exegesis, all conditioned factors (SAṂSKṚTADHARMA) are impermanent (ANITYA); there are only three unconditioned factors (ASAṂSKṚTADHARMA) that may be viewed as permanent, because they are not subject to the forces of impermanence that govern the conditioned realm of existence. These are the analytical cessation (PRATISAṂKHYĀNIRODHA, which would include NIRVĀṆA); nonanalytical cessation (APRATISAṂKHYĀNIRODHA); and space (ĀKĀŚA). To perceive as permanent conditioned factors that are actually impermanent is a fundamental misconception and a primary cause of suffering (DUḤKHA). This mistaken view of permanence thus figures among the four "inverted views" (VIPARYĀSA): to see the painful as pleasurable, the impermanent as permanent, the impure as pure, and that which is without self as having a self.

**nityadharma**. (P. niccadhamma; T. rtag pa'i chos; C. changfa; J. jōhō; K. sangpŏp 常法). In Sanskrit, "permanent factors," one of two basic categories of phenomena in certain strands of ABHIDHARMA exegesis. Despite the centrality of the doctrine of impermanence in Buddhism, it is not the case that all phenomena are impermanent: conditioned factors (SAṂSKṚTADHARMA) are impermanent, but unconditioned factors (ASAṂSKṚTADHARMA) may instead be viewed as permanent. Permanent factors are typically enumerated as three: analytical cessation (PRATISAṂKHYĀNIRODHA, which would include NIRVĀṆA); nonanalytical cessation (APRATISAṂKHYĀNIRODHA); and space (ĀKĀŚA). Since each of these types of factors is uncompounded, and thus not subject to the forces of impermanence that govern the conditioned realm of existence, they may be viewed as "permanent factors."

**nityānta**. (S). See ŚĀŚVATĀNTA.

**Niutou Farong**. (J. Gozu Hōyū; K. Udu Pŏbyung 牛頭法融) (594–657). In Chinese, "Oxhead, Dharma Interfusion"; proper name of the founder of an early CHAN school often known in English as the "Oxhead school" (NIUTOU ZONG), after his toponym Niutou (Oxhead). Farong was a native of Yanling in present-day Jiangsu province. Little is known of his early years. He is said to have studied the teachings of MADHYAMAKA and to have spent twenty years in the mountains after his ordination by a certain dharma master Ling (d.u.). In 643, Farong entered the monastery of Youqisi on Mt. Niutou (in present-day Jiangsu province), whence he acquired his toponym. In 647, he gave a public lecture on the SADDHARMAPUṆḌARĪKASŪTRA, and six years later he lectured on the PAÑCAVIṂŚATISĀHASRIKĀPRAJÑĀPĀRAMITĀSŪTRA at the monastery of Jianchusi (see BAO'ENSI). The influential treatise JUEGUAN LUN ("Extinguishing Cognition Treatise") is attributed by tradition to BODHIDHARMA, the legendary founder of the Chan school, but it is now generally believed to have been composed by Farong or one of his students. Although Farong's official biography in the XU GAOSENG ZHUAN does not mention this event, later stele inscriptions and Chan genealogical histories (see CHUANDENG LU) report that DAOXIN, the putative fourth patriarch of the Chan school, instructed Farong in the sudden teaching (DUNJIAO); Farong's connections with Daoxin are, however, historically dubious. Some of the more unusual positions Farong took include the notion that even inanimate objects, such as rocks, rivers, and flowers, possess the buddha-nature (FOXING). Farong was also one of the earliest teachers in the Chan school to advocate the nonreliance on conceptual descriptions of Buddhism (see BULI WENZI).

**Niutou zong**. (J. Gozushū; K. Udu chong 牛頭宗). In Chinese, "Oxhead School"; a lineage of early Chan that traces itself to the Chan master NIUTOU FARONG (594–657), a reputed disciple of the fourth patriarch DAOXIN (580–651), although the connections between the two monks are tenuous. The monk Zhiwei (646–722) is often credited with the actual formation of the Niutou zong as a lineage that could claim independence from both the Northern school (BEI ZONG) and Southern school (NAN ZONG) of Chan. The school was active in the seventh through eighth centuries, but reached its zenith in the third quarter of the eighth century. The school's name is derived from Mt. Niutou (in present-day Jiangsu province), where Farong and his students are said to have taught a form of Chan distinct from that of the other lineages then current in China. The Chan historian GUIFENG ZONGMI characterizes the Niutou school as the "tradition (that believes) all things are to be cut off without support" (minjue wuji zong). The teachings of the Niutou tradition show a strong predilection toward the notion of emptiness (ŚŪNYATĀ) and PRAJÑĀPĀRAMITĀ, as exemplified in its influential treatise JUEGUAN LUN ("Extinguishing Cognition Treatise"), which uses a series of negative argumentations, derived from MADHYAMAKA antecedents, to open students to an experience of the pure wisdom that transcends all dualities. Oxhead writings also frequently employ a threefold rhetorical structure of an initial question by the teacher, followed by the student's hesitation in how to respond, culminating in understanding; this structure seems to have its antecedents in TIANTAI ZHIYI's teachings of the "three truths" (SANDI) of absolute, conventional, and mean. One of the enduring influences of the Niutou school is on the 780 CE composition of the LIUZU TAN JING ("Platform Sūtra of the Sixth Patriarch"), which deploys a similar threefold rheotic in developing its understanding of Chan.

**Nivāpasutta**. (C. Lieshi jing; J. Ryōshikyō; K. Yŏpsa kyŏng 獵師經). In Pāli, "Discourse on the Snare," the twenty-fifth sutta in the MAJJHIMANIKĀYA (a separate SARVĀSTIVĀDA recension appears as the 178th SŪTRA in the Chinese translation of the MADHYAMĀGAMA); preached by the Buddha to an assembly of monks at the JETAVANA grove in the town of ŚRĀVASTĪ (P. Sāvatthi). The Buddha speaks of the obstacles that can hinder monks along the path to liberation using a simile of a hunter, his entourage, a green pasture, and four herds of deer being hunted as prey. The hunter represents MĀRA, the personification of evil and death, who seeks to entrap beings in the cycle of rebirth (SAṂSĀRA). The hunter's entourage is Māra's hordes. The pastures are the bait of sensual pleasures that Māra uses to ensnare beings, and the four herds of deer are four types of brāhmaṇas and recluses whom Māra tempts. Progressively deeper levels of soteriological attainment, from the meditative absorptions (P. JHĀNA; S. DHYĀNA) to the extinction of the contaminants (P. ĀSAVAKHAYA; S. ĀSRAVAKṢAYA), render one free from Māra's grasp.

**nīvaraṇa**. [alt. nivaraṇa] (T. sgrib pa; C. gai; J. gai; K. kae 蓋). In Sanskrit and Pāli, "hindrance" or "obstruction," referring specifically to five hindrances to the attainment of the first meditative absorption of the subtle-materiality realm (RŪPĀVACARADHYĀNA). Each of these five hindrances specifically obstructs one of the five constituents of absorption (DHYĀNĀṄGA) and must therefore be at least temporarily allayed in order for absorption (DHYĀNA) to occur. The five are: (1) "sensual desire" (KĀMACCHANDA), which hinders one-pointedness of mind (EKĀGRATĀ); (2) "malice" or "ill will" (VYĀPĀDA), hindering physical rapture (PRĪTI); (3) "sloth and torpor" (STYĀNA-MIDDHA), hindering the initial application of thought (VITARKA); (4) "restlessness and worry" (AUDDHATYA-KAUKṚTYA), hindering mental ease (SUKHA); and (5) "skeptical doubt" (VICIKITSĀ), hindering sustained consideration (VICĀRA). Buddhist sūtras and meditation manuals, such as the VISUDDHIMAGGA, provide extensive discussion of various antidotes or counteragents (PRATIPAKṢA, see also KAMMAṬṬHĀNA) to these hindrances, such as the contemplation on the decomposition of a corpse (AŚUBHABHĀVANĀ) to counter sensual desire; the meditation on loving-kindness (MAITRĪ) to counter malice; the recollection of death to counter sloth and torpor; quietude of mind to counter restlessness and worry; and studying the scriptures to counter skeptical doubt. In addition, the five faculties or dominants (INDRIYA) are also specifically designed to allay the five hindrances: faith (ŚRADDHĀ) counters malice; effort (VĪRYA) counters sloth and torpor; mindfulness (SMṚTI) counters sensual desire; concentration (SAMĀDHI) counters restlessness and worry; and wisdom (PRAJÑĀ) counters skeptical doubt. A similar correlation is made between the seven factors of enlightenment (BODHYAṄGA) and the hindrances. These five hindrances are permanently eliminated at various stages of the noble path (ĀRYAMĀRGA): worry (kaukṛtya) and skeptical doubt are permanently overcome at the point of becoming a stream-enterer (SROTAĀPANNA); sensual desire and malice on becoming a nonreturner (ANĀGĀMIN); and sloth and torpor and restlessness (auddhatya) on becoming a worthy one (ARHAT).

**nivāsana**. (T. sham thabs; C. niepanseng/qun; J. nehanzō/kun; K. yŏlbansŭng/gun 涅槃僧/裙). In Sanskrit and Pāli, "undergarment," the lower robe or skirt worn by Buddhist monks and nuns. The nivāsana is a large piece of cloth that is wrapped around the torso and tied at the waist, in some traditions extending to the ankles; it is also called the antaravāsaka, or inner garment. According to the VINAYA, it is to be made of three panels of cloth. This skirt, together with the UTTARĀSAṂGA or upper robe and the SAṂGHĀṬĪ or outer robe, constitute the TRICĪVARA, or triple robe of the monk. See also KĀṢĀYA.

**Niwano Nikkyō**. (庭野日敬) (1906–1999). Cofounder of RISSHŌ KŌSEIKAI, a Japanese lay Buddhist organization that was an offshoot of REIYŪKAI and was strongly influenced by NICHIRENSHŪ doctrine. Niwano was born into a poor family in a small town in Nigata prefecture in northern Japan. After going to work in Tokyo in 1923, Niwano led a typical working-class life, running such small businesses as rice, charcoal, and Japanese-pickle shops, while also showing an intense interest in astrology, numerology, and divination. Niwano became an ardent adherent of Reiyūkai in 1934, when his nine-month-old daughter recovered from a serious illness after he followed the organization's practice of ancestor worship. Niwano soon became a leading evangelist for Reiyūkai, recruiting many new followers, one of whom was NAGANUMA MYŌKŌ (1899–1957). In 1938, Niwano and Naganuma left Reiyūkai and cofounded Risshō Kōseikai, together with about thirty other followers. According to Niwano, the group seceded because of Reiyūkai's overemphasis on the miraculous benefit, rather than the teachings, of the SADDHARMAPUṆḌARĪKASŪTRA ("Lotus Sūtra"), although others say that the split occurred because the leader of Reiyūkai publicly criticized Niwano's interest in divination. After establishing the organization, Naganuma served as a spirit medium, while Niwano focused on teaching and administration. After Naganuma's death in 1957, Niwano became the president of the million-member organization and declared the end of the organization's first era of "skillful means" (J. hōben; S. UPĀYAKAUŚALYA), which had been characterized by spirit mediumship and divine instructions, and the dawn of a new era of "manifesting the truth" (shinjitsu kengen). Niwano affirmed that henceforth the central objects of the organization's faith would be the *Saddharmapuṇḍarīkasūtra* and ŚĀKYAMUNI Buddha, which were eternal and universal. Based on his understanding of the sūtra, Niwano emphasized the spiritual development of individuals along the BODHISATTVA path, whose salvific efforts should be dedicated not just to one's own family and ancestors, but also to Japanese society and the world at large. Niwano also dedicated himself to promoting world peace through interreligious cooperation, one example of which was the establishment of the Niwano Peace Foundation in 1978. Niwano resigned from the presidency of Risshō Kōseikai in 1991 and was succeeded by his eldest son Niwano Nichiko (b. 1938).

**niyāma**. [alt. niyama] (T. nges par 'gyur ba; C. jueding; J. ketsujō; K. kyŏlchŏng 決定). In Sanskrit and Pāli, "constraint," "certainty," referring to the certainty of what is to come or the fixedness of things. Laws governing the universe are referred to as the five certainties (pañcaniyāma). According to the Pāli commentaries, these five certainties are (1) the certainty of the seasons (utuniyāma), which includes such aspects of the natural environment as the regular progression of the seasons, the rise and fall in temperature, etc.; (2) the certainty of seeds (bījaniyāma), which refers to botany, viz., that specific seeds produce specific plants, that certain fruits have certain flavors, and so on; (3) the certainty of action (kammaniyāma), which refers to the fact that virtuous actions lead to happiness in the future and nonvirtuous actions lead to suffering; (4) the certainty of mind (cittaniyāma), which includes the processes and constituents of consciousness; and (5) the certainty of the dharma (dhammaniyāma), which refers, among other things, to certain events that occur in the lives of all buddhas. ¶ In the MAHĀYĀNA, nyāma, a BUDDHIST HYBRID SANSKRIT word that is probably an alternate form of niyāma, has a different meaning, referring to the development of compassion that overcomes the faults of the HĪNAYĀNA and is unique to the bodhisattva path. It has been translated into English as "the fixed condition" of a bodhisattva or a bodhisattva's "distinctive way of salvation."

**niyatagotra**. (T. nges pa'i rigs; C. jueding zhongxing; J. ketsujō shushō; K. kyŏlchŏng chongsŏng 決定種性). In Sanskrit, "definite" or "fixed" "lineage," a term that appears in YOGĀCĀRA soteriological theories. According to some Yogācāra texts, sentient beings are endowed with a disposition that determines whether they will follow the path of a ŚRĀVAKA, PRATYEKABUDDHA, or BODHISATTVA and eventually achieve liberation from rebirth as an ARHAT or a buddha. This disposition, or lineage (GOTRA), according to some Yogācāra schools, is determined from time immemorial and cannot be altered. It is on the basis of this doctrine that the Yogācāra is said to assert the existence of three separate soteriological vehicles (TRIYĀNA). These Yogācāra schools do not therefore accept the famous declaration in SADDHARMAPUṆḌARĪKASŪTRA ("Lotus Sūtra") that all beings will eventually enter the MAHĀYĀNA and achieve buddhahood. In order to account for the possibility of beings who, prior to their entry into NIRVĀṆA, move from a HĪNAYĀNA path to the Mahāyāna path (or vice versa), the Yogācāra asserts that some beings are endowed with an "indefinite lineage" (ANIYATAGOTRA), allowing them to change vehicles based on various circumstances, usually before reaching the aids to penetration (NIRVEDHABHĀGĪYA) that precede the path of vision (DARŚANAMĀRGA). They also hold that some beings, called ICCHANTIKA (incorrigibles), belong to no spiritual lineage at all and thus are doomed never to achieve liberation. This doctrine of the presence and absence of particular lineages is associated with the Yogācāra exegete ASAṄGA and is identified in East Asian Buddhism with the FAXIANG ZONG. The majority of Yogācāra texts, however, say that those fixed in a ŚRĀVAKA and PRATYEKABUDDHA lineage are only fixed in that lineage until they reach their goal; later, roused to enter the Mahāyāna by reflecting on the compassion of the Buddha, they then enter the bodhisattva lineage at the level of the MOKṢABHĀGĪYA-KUŚALAMŪLA ("virtuous faculties that are aids to liberation") and achieve full awakening.

**niyatamicchādiṭṭhi**. (C. jueding xiejian; J. ketsujō jaken; K. kyŏlchŏng sagyŏn 決定邪見). In Pāli, lit. "fixed deluded views"; the three wrong views that lead to a fixed destiny in the next rebirth; viz., the view that existence is uncaused (ahetukadiṭṭhi) and controlled by fate; the view that neither virtuous nor nonvirtuous actions produce results (akiriyadiṭṭhi); and the nihilistic view that death is annihilation, after which nothing happens that is the result of a previous action (natthikadiṭṭhi).

**niyatapuggala**. In Pāli, "person with a fixed destiny," in the sense of having a definite place of rebirth, either salutary or unsalutary, in the immediately following lifetime. Such persons are of three types: one who has committed one of five heinous deeds that results in immediate retribution in the next life (P. ānantariyakamma, S. ĀNANTARYAKARMAN) of being reborn in the interminable hell (AVĪCI); one who follows one of the wrong views that leads to a specific unfortunate rebirth in the next lifetime (niyatamicchādiṭṭhi); and one who has attained one of the four stages of noble persons (P. ariyapuggala, S. ĀRYAPUDGALA) and thus will be reborn as either a human or a divinity (DEVA) in the next life, or who, in the case of an arahant (S. ARHAT), will not be reborn at all.

**noble persons**. See ĀRYAPUDGALA.

**nonattachment**. Despite its ubiquity in Western Buddhist literature, there is no precise equivalency in Indian Buddhist terminology for this English word. For some of the connotations of nonattachment, see ALOBHA; ANUPALABDHI; NIRVEDA; UPEKṢĀ; VIMOKṢA; VAIRĀGYA.

**nonduality**. See ADVAYA.

**Nōnin**. (J) (能忍). See DAINICHI(BŌ) NŌNIN.

**nonreturner**. See ANĀGĀMIN.

**nonself**. See ANĀTMAN; NAIRĀTMYA.

**Nor bu gling kha**. (Norbulingka). The summer residence of the DALAI LAMAS and the Tibetan government, located in the city of LHA SA, south of the PO TA LA Palace. The original foundations for the palace were laid by the seventh Dalai Lama, Skal bzang rgya mtsho, in 1755 at a medicinal spring, with the building completed in 1783 during the reign of the eighth Dalai Lama. Subsequent incarnations greatly expanded the grounds, adding numerous residential and administrative buildings as well an arboretum, gardens, and pools. Every Dalai Lama beginning with the eighth, together with his administration, would transfer to the Nor bu gling kha on the eighteenth day of the third lunar month, usually sometime in April. The palace grounds were also the site of the yearly grand Tibetan drama festival known as Zho ston (Shotön). On March 10, 1959, Tibetans numbering in the thousands held a mass demonstration against Chinese occupation outside the walls of the Nor bu gling kha, behind which the fourteenth Dalai Lama and his family were sequestered. On March 17, the Dalai Lama secretly escaped from the residence to go into exile in India.

**Northern school (of Chan)**. See BEI ZONG.

**novice**. See ŚRĀMAṆERA; ŚRĀMAṆERIKĀ.

**nṛtyāsana**. (T. gar byed pa/gar stabs/gar gyi tshul gyis gnas pa). In Sanskrit, lit., "dancing posture," a physical position in which the figure stands on a slightly bent left leg with the right leg bent and right foot resting on the opposite thigh or groin. The position of the feet may also be reversed. This position is commonly found among female ḌĀKINĪ images, such as VAJRAVĀRĀHĪ. See also ĀSANA.

**nun**. See BHIKṢUṆĪ; MAE CHI; ŚRĀMAṆERIKĀ.

**Nu, U**. (1907–1995). Burmese (Myanmar) political leader and patron of Buddhism. (U is a Burmese honorific.) As a young man, U Nu became active in anti-British agitation and in 1936 was expelled by British authorities from the University of Rangoon law school for his political activities. Thereafter, he became a leader of the Burmese nationalist movement, adopting the nationalist title "Thakin" (master), along with his comrades Aung San, Ne Win, and others. On the eve of the Japanese invasion of Burma in 1942, he was imprisoned by the British as a potential agent. He was released by the Japanese occupation forces and served as the foreign minister of their puppet regime. With growing disenchantment at Japanese mistreatment of Burmese citizens, U Nu helped to organize a clandestine guerilla resistance force that assisted the British when they retook Burma. At the conclusion of World War II, he participated in negotiations with the British for Burmese independence. He became Burma's first prime minister and served three terms in office (1948–1956, 1957–1958, 1960–1962). A devout Buddhist, he organized under government auspices national monastic curricula, promoted the practice of insight meditation (VIPASSANĀ), and, in 1956, sponsored the convention of the sixth Buddhist council (according to Burmese reckoning; see COUNCIL, SIXTH) in celebration of the 2,500th anniversary of the Buddha's parinibbāna (S. PARINIRVĀṆA). The council prepared a new Burmese edition of the Pāli canon (P. tipiṭaka; S. TRIPIṬAKA), together with its commentaries and sub-commentaries, which is currently used in Burmese monastic education. U Nu also attempted, unsuccessfully, to unite the several noncommensal fraternities (Burmese GAING) of the Burmese SAṂGHA into a single body. While achieving much in the religious sphere, U Nu proved unable to cope with the political crises confronting his government, and Burma descended into civil war. He resigned as prime minister in 1956, returned to office in 1957, abdicated civilian government to General Ne Win in 1958, returned to office in 1960, and finally was deposed and arrested by Ne Win in a coup d'état in 1962. U Nu was released in 1968, and a year later he organized a resistance army from exile in Thailand. A rapprochement between U Nu and Ne Win was reached in 1980, and he was allowed to return to Burma, where he devoted himself to religious affairs, in particular as director of a Buddhist translation bureau located at Kaba Aye in Rangoon (Yangon). He again entered politics during the democracy uprising of 1988, setting up a symbolic provisional government when the then-ruling Burmese Socialist government collapsed. He was placed under house arrest in 1989 by the State Law and Order Restoration Council (SLORC), a group composed of generals who succeeded Ne Win. He was released in 1992. A prolific writer on politics and Buddhism, his works include *Buddhism: Theory and Practice, Burma under the Japanese, Unite and March, Towards Peace and Democracy,* and his autobiography, *Saturday's Son.*

**Nyagrodhārāma**. (P. Nigrodhārāma; T. Nya gro dha'i kun dga' ra ba; C. Nijulü lin; J. Nikuritsurin; K. Niguyullim 尼拘律林). In Sanskrit, "Nyagrodha's Grove," a grove near KAPILAVASTU where the Buddha resided during his first visit to the city after his enlightenment. It was donated to the order by Nyagrodha, a member of the ŚĀKYA clan. It was in this grove that the Buddha performed the famous "dual miracle" (YAMAKAPRĀTIHĀRYA) for his kinsmen and related the VESSANTARA-JĀTAKA (S. Viśvaṃtarajātaka). The Buddha is said to have resided there on other occasions, and several rules of the VINAYA were promulgated in Nyagrodha's Grove.

**nyāma**. (BHS). See NIYĀMA.

**Nyanaponika Thera**. See ÑĀṆAPONIKA MAHĀTHERA.

**Nyanatiloka Thera**. See ÑĀṆATILOKA MAHĀTHERA.

**Nyang ral nyi ma 'od zer**. (Nyangral Nyima Öser) (1124–1196). A Tibetan Buddhist master considered the first of the "five kingly treasure revealers" (GTER STON RGYAL PO LNGA) and as a reincarnation of the Tibetan king KHRI SRONG LDE BTSAN. He is also sometimes counted as the first of the "three supreme emanations" (mchog gi sprul sku gsum); the others are GURU CHOS KYI DBANG PHYUG and RGOD LDEM CAN. Born in the southern Tibetan region of LHO BRAG, he received numerous visions of PADMASAMBHAVA, before commencing his illustrious career as a treasure revealer (GTER STON). His *Chos 'byung me tog snying po sbrang rtsi'i bcud* ("Nectar of the Honey in the Heart of the Flower: A History of the Dharma") is an important early history of the dharma, with special emphasis on the RNYING MA sect. Among his other well-known works are the *Bka' brgyad bde gshegs 'dus pa'i rgyud* ("Tantra of the Gathering of the Sugatas of the Eight Transmitted Precepts") and a biography of Padmasambhava entitled BKA' THANG ZANGS GLING MA ("Copper Island Chronicle").

**Nyar ma gtsug lag khang**. (Nyarma Tsuklakang). Also spelled Myar ma. A religious institution established in the late tenth century by the king of the western Tibetan GU GE region YE SHES 'OD and the translator RIN CHEN BZANG PO. It is located in Mar yul, currently Ladakh, in northwest India.

**Nyāyabindu**. (T. Rigs pa'i thigs pa). In Sanskrit, "Drop of Reasoning," one of the seven treatises of the great seventh-century logician DHARMAKĪRTI. This text summarizes Dharmakīrti's positions on topics set forth at greater length in his most important work, the PRAMĀṆAVĀRTTIKA, focusing upon the two forms of valid knowledge (PRAMĀṆA): direct perception (PRATYAKṢA) and inference (ANUMĀNA). The work is divided into three chapters, with the first chapter dealing with direct perception (pratyakṣa), that is, valid knowledge gained through the sense consciousnesses (and the mental consciousness) without mediation by thought. The second chapter deals with "inference for one's own purposes" (SVĀRTHĀNUMĀNA), the process by which thought arrives at a valid judgment. The third chapter deals with "inference for the purpose of others" (PARĀRTHĀNUMĀNA), the statement of syllogisms to an opponent in a debate. Among the several commentaries to the text, the most important is that by DHARMOTTARA.

***Nyāyānusāra**. (C. Shun zhengli lun; J. Junshōriron; K. Sun chŏngni non 順正理論). In Sanskrit, "Conformity with Correct Principle"; influential VAIBHĀṢIKA ABHIDHARMA treatise by SAṂGHABHADRA (c. fifth century CE). It is intended as a refutation of VASUBANDHU's popular ABHIDHARMAKOŚABHĀṢYA and its presentation of what it purports to be the orthodox positions of the SARVĀSTIVĀDA school. The **Nyāyānusāra* is both an exposition of the abhidharma philosophy of the Kashmiri Sarvāstivāda Vaibhāṣikas and a critical commentary on Vasubandhu's *Abhidharmakośabhāṣya*, which advocated many positions that critiqued the Kashmiri Vaibhāṣika school. The **Nyāyānusāra* is roughly three times its rival text's length and sought to defend the Vaibhāṣikas against Vasubandhu's portrayal of their doctrines. For this reason, XUANZANG (who translated the text into Chinese) says that the original title of the text was the **Kośakaraka* (C. Jushi bao lun) or "Hailstones upon the *Kośa*." As but one example of its criticisms, Saṃghabhadra's opening critique of Vasubandhu centers on the latter's assumption that abhidharma does not represent the teaching of the Buddha himself. To refute Vasubandhu's misinterpretations, Saṃghabhadra cites scriptural passages that prove the Vaibhāṣika position, drawn from scripture (SŪTRA) but also from the massive ABHIDHARMAMAHĀVIBHĀṢĀ compendium of abhidharma. In addition to scriptural citation, Saṃghabhadra also resorts to logical argumentation (YUKTI) to refute Vasubandhu's positions, both by exposing the contradictions explicit in Vasubandhu's own presentations of doctrine and by demonstrating how Vasubandhu's positions would undermine fundamental principles of Buddhist doctrine. In addition to his challenge of Vasubandhu, Saṃghabhadra also criticizes the positions of other Vaibhāṣika detractors, including the Dārṣṭāntika teacher Śrīlāta, and the SAUTRĀNTIKA master Sthavira; Saṃghabhadra's goal is thus clearly to defend Vaibhāṣika abhidharma against any and all comers. The **Nyāyānusāra* is only extant in Xuanzang's eighty-roll Chinese translation (the Sanskrit title is a reconstruction); portions of the original Sanskrit text have, however, been preserved in citations from other Indian texts, such as commentaries to the *Abhidharmakośabhāṣya* by STHIRAMATI, Pūrṇavardhana, and YAŚOMITRA.

**Nyāyapraveśa**. (T. Tshad ma rigs par 'jug pa'i sgo; C. Yinming ru zhengli lun; J. Inmyō nisshōriron; K. Inmyŏng ip chŏngni non 因明入正理論). In Sanskrit, "Primer on Logic," by the sixth century CE Indian philosopher and logician ŚAṂKARASVĀMIN, a student of DIGNĀGA. Some scholars have argued, based on the Tibetan tradition, that the *Nyāyapraveśa* was actually written by Dignāga, and that the version translated into Chinese and attributed to Śaṃkarasvāmin is actually Śaṃkarasvāmin's later edition of Dignāga's text. The *Nyāyapraveśa* provides an introduction to the logical system of Dignāga, covering such subjects as valid and invalid methods of proof, methods of refutation, perception, erroneous perception, inference, and erroneous inference. Although Śaṃkarasvāmin's work was not as extensive, detailed, or original as Dignāga's, it proved to be popular within the tradition, as attested by the many commentaries on it, including exegeses by non-Buddhists. Large parts of the work survive in the original Sanskrit.

# O

**Ōbakushū**. (黄檗宗). In Japanese, "Ōbaku school"; one of the three main ZEN traditions in Japan, along with the RINZAISHŪ and SŌTŌSHŪ. The émigré Chinese CHAN master YINYUAN LONGQI (1594–1673) is credited with its foundation. In 1654, Yinyuan fled the wars that accompanied the fall of the Ming dynasty and the establishment of the Manchu Qing dynasty, and arrived in Nagasaki, Japan, where he first served as abbot of the monastery of Kōfukuji. With the support of the shōgun Tokugawa Ietsuna (1639–1680) and Emperor Gomizunoo (r. 1611–1629), in 1661, Yinyuan traveled to a mountain he named Ōbaku (after Mt. Huangbo in China), where he began construction of a new monastery that he named MANPUKUJI (C. Wanfusi), after his old monastery in Fujian, China. The monastery and the broader Ōbaku tradition retained many of the exotic Chinese customs that Yinyuan and his Chinese disciples MU'AN XINGTAO, Jifei Ruyi (1616–1617), and Huilin Xingji (1609–1681) had brought with them from the mainland, including the latest monastic architecture and institutional systems, the use of vernacular Chinese as the official ritual language in the monastery, and training in Chinese artistic and literary styles. In addition, for thirteen generations after Yinyuan, Manpukuji's abbots continued to be Chinese, and only later began to alternate between Chinese and Japanese successors. These Chinese monastic customs that Yinyuan introduced were met with great ambivalence by such Japanese Rinzai leaders as Gudō Tōshoku (1577–1661) and later HAKUIN EKAKU. Although Yinyuan himself was affiliated with the YANGQI PAI in the Chinese LINJI ZONG, Chinese Chan traditions during this period had also assimilated the widespread practice of reciting of the Buddha's name (C. NIANFO; J. nenbutsu) by transforming it into a form of "questioning meditation" (C. KANHUA CHAN; J. kannazen): e.g., "Who is it who is reciting the Buddha's name?" Raising this question while engaging in nenbutsu was a technique that initially helped to concentrate the mind, but would also subsequently help raise the sense of doubt (C. YIQING; J. gijō) that was central to Linji school accounts of authentic Chan meditation. However, since buddha-recitation was at this time closely associated in Japan with pure land traditions, such as JŌDOSHŪ and JŌDO SHINSHŪ, this approach to Chan practice was extremely controversial among contemporary Japanese Zen adepts. The Chinese style of Zen that Yinyuan and his followers promulgated in Japan prompted their contemporaries in the Rinzai and Sōtō Zen traditions to reevaluate their own practices and to initiate a series of important reform movements within their respective traditions (cf. IN'IN EKISHI). During the Meiji period, Ōbaku, Rinzai, and Sōtō were formally recognized as separate Zen traditions (ZENSHŪ) by the imperial government. Currently, the monastery Manpukuji in Uji serves as the headquarters (honzan) of the Ōbaku school.

**Obermiller, Eugène**. (1901–1935). Noted Russian scholar of Indian and Tibetan Buddhism, born in St. Petersburg to a family devoted to music and the arts. He studied English, French, and German as a youth and was planning to become a musician. However, when he was eighteen years of age, he was stricken by syringomyelia, a disease of the spinal cord, which deprived him of the full use of his hands and fingers. After the Russian Revolution, he attended FYODOR IPPOLITOVICH STCHERBATSKY's lectures on Sanskrit at the University of Petrograd (later Leningrad and St. Petersburg) and studied Sanskrit, Tibetan, and Mongolian. He became Stcherbatsky's student, preparing Sanskrit-Tibetan and Tibetan-Sanskrit indexes to the NYĀYABINDU and assisting him in editing the Tibetan text of the ABHIDHARMAKOŚABHĀṢYA. Obermiller spent a great deal of time in Buryatia in the Transbaikal, studying at Mongolian monasteries of the DGE LUGS PA tradition, where he learned to speak Tibetan. In working closely with learned Buddhist monks, Obermiller anticipated what would become a common model of scholarship after the Tibetan diaspora that began in 1959. In 1928, Stcherbatsky formed the Institute of Buddhist Culture (later to become part of the Institute of Oriental Studies), and Obermiller was appointed as a research scholar. In 1929, the two colleagues published an edition of the ABHISAMAYĀLAṂKĀRA. Obermiller continued to suffer from syringomyelia throughout this period. By the age of thirty, he had become incapacitated to the point that he was not able to write and died four years later. Despite his debilitating illness, during his last years, he remained committed to his scholarship and published a number of pioneering translations, including BU STON's "History of Buddhism" (BU STON CHOS 'BYUNG) and the RATNAGOTRAVIBHĀGA (*Uttaratantra*) in 1932. In his articles (several of which have been republished), he focused especially on the PRAJÑĀPĀRAMITĀ exegetical literature, relying largely on Dge lugs expositions.

**Odantapurī**. (T. O tan ta pū ri). Sometimes called Uḍḍandapura, Odantapurī is thought to be the second oldest of India's large monastic universities. It was located some six miles from NĀLANDĀ, in modern Bihar State. It was founded during the seventh century CE by King Gopāla (660–705), who also served as its main patron. Gopāla was the first king of the Pāla dynasty, which would continue to support Buddhism in this region for centuries. Odantapurī reached its peak around the eighth century CE and, according to some Tibetan sources, had approximately twelve thousand students at its height. The monastery was highly influential in the larger Buddhist world; the architectural layout of BSAM YAS monastery in Tibet is believed to have been modeled on Odantapurī. Odantapurī flourished until the turn of the thirteenth century, when it and VIKRAMAŚĪLA were destroyed in the 1199 and 1200 CE invasion of the Ghurid Muslims, who were said to have mistaken the monasteries for fortresses. The Ghurid military governors erected their administrative headquarters for the region at the site where Odantapurī had stood.

**Oḍḍiyāna**. (T. O rgyan/U rgyan). Also spelled Oḍiyāna and Uḍḍiyāna; a region northeast of India known for its early tantric Buddhist activity, often identified by modern scholars with the Swat Valley of Pakistan. It is fabled as the birthplace of PADMASAMBHAVA and is the place of origin of numerous tantric texts and lineages, including the GUHYASAMĀJATANTRA. Several Tibetan masters wrote accounts of their travels through Oḍḍiyāna, including O RGYAN PA RIN CHEN DPAL, whose name literally means "the man of Oḍḍiyāna," as well as Stag tshang ras pa (Taktsangrepa), and Buddhagupta. Because the Tibetan name O rgyan is almost synonymous with Padmasambhava (who is often referred to in Tibetan as O rgyan rin po che, O rgyan chen po, O rgyan pa, O rgyan pad ma, etc.), O rgyan is found in the names of many Tibetan temples and monasteries.

**Oḍra**. (S). One of the twenty-four sacred sites associated with the CAKRASAṂVARATANTRA. See PĪṬHA.

**ogha**. (T. chu bo; C. baoliu; J. boru; K. p'ongnyu 暴流). In Sanskrit and Pāli, "floods," "currents"; forces whose pull is so strong that, like a flood or strong current, they overwhelm the hapless ordinary person (PṚTHAGJANA). A list of three is typically found in the literature: greed for sensual experience (KĀMARĀGA), greed for continuing existence (BHAVARĀGA), and ignorance (AVIDYĀ), with a fourth, views (DṚṢṬI), sometimes added.

**Ogyo Kusan**. (五教九山). In Korean, "Five Doctrinal [schools] and Nine Mountains [school of Sŏn]"; a designation for the five major doctrinal schools (KYO)—viz., Nirvāṇa (Yŏlban chong; see NIEPAN ZONG), Vinaya (Kyeyul chong; cf. NANSHAN LÜ ZONG), Dharma-Nature (Pŏpsŏng chong), Hwaŏm (alt. Wŏnyung chong; see HUAYAN ZONG), and Yogācāra (Pŏpsang chong; see FAXIANG ZONG)—and the Nine Mountains school of SŎN (KUSAN SŎNMUN); this designation is presumed to have been used from the late Silla through the mid-Koryŏ dynasties to refer to the major sectarian strands within the Korean Buddhist tradition. This is a retrospective designation; there is little evidence that all five of these doctrinal schools ever existed as independent traditions in Korea, or that they identified themselves as belonging to an independent and separate doctrinal strand of Korean Buddhism. See KUSAN SŎNMUN; KYO; OGYO YANGJONG; SŎN; SŎN KYO YANGJONG.

**Ogyo Yangjong**. (五教兩宗). In Korean, "Five Doctrinal [schools] and Two [Meditative] Traditions"; a designation used from the mid-Koryŏ through early Chosŏn dynasties to refer to the major strands of KYO and SŎN within the Korean Buddhist tradition. See KUSAN SŎNMUN; KYO; OGYO KUSAN; SŎN; SŎN KYO YANGJONG.

**Ōjō yōshū**. (C. Wangsheng yao ji 往生要集). In Japanese, "Collection of Essentials on Going to Rebirth" [in the pure land]; one of the most influential Japanese treatises on the practice of nenbutsu (C. NIANFO) and the soteriological goal of rebirth in the PURE LAND, composed by the Japanese TENDAISHŪ monk GENSHIN at the Shuryōgon'in at YOKAWA on HIEIZAN in 985. The *Ōjō yōshū* offers a systematic overview of pure land thought and practice, using extensive passages culled from various scriptures and treatises, especially the writings of the Chinese pure land monks DAOCHUO and SHANDAO. Genshin's collection is divided into ten sections: departing from the defiled realm, seeking (rebirth) in the pure land; evidence for (the existence of) SUKHĀVATĪ; the proper practice of nenbutsu methods for assisting mindfulness; special nenbutsu (betsuji nenbutsu); the benefits of nenbutsu; evidence for the results forthcoming from nenbutsu; the fruits of rebirth in the pure land; and a series of miscellaneous questions and answers. Genshin contends that the practice of nenbutsu is relatively easy for everyone and is appropriate for people during the degenerate age of the final dharma (J. mappō; see MOFA), especially as a deathbed practice. Genshin also recommended the chanting of the name of the buddha AMITĀBHA to those of lower spiritual capacity (a total of nine spiritual capacities are posited by Genshin; cf. JIUPIN), and he regarded this practice as inferior to the contemplative practices described in the GUAN WULIANGSHOU JING. Genshin's work was also famous for its description of SAṂSĀRA, especially its vivid depiction of the hells (cf. NĀRAKA); his description inspired lurid paintings of the hells on Japanese screens. The *Ōjō yōshū* became popular among the Heian aristocracy; the text's view of the degenerate age (J. mappō; cf. C. MOFA) may have provided an explanation for the social upheaval at the end of the Heian period. The text also exerted substantial influence over the subsequent development of the pure land movements in the Tendai tradition on Mt. Hiei. The *Ōjō yōshū* also played an important role in laying the groundwork for an independent pure land tradition in Japan a century later. Several important commentaries on the *Ōjō yōshū* were prepared by the Japanese JŌDOSHŪ monk HŌNEN. In addition, the *Ōjō yōshū* was one of the few texts written in Japan that made its way to China, where it influenced the development of pure land Buddhism on the mainland.

**Olcott, Henry Steel**. (1832–1907). Cofounder of the Theosophical Society and a key figure in the modern history of Buddhism in Sri Lanka. Born in Orange, New Jersey, to a Presbyterian family, Olcott developed an interest in spiritualism during his twenties. He served in the Union Army during the American Civil War and subsequently was appointed to the commission that investigated the assassination of Abraham Lincoln. Working as a journalist in New York City, he traveled to the Eddy Farm in Chittenden, Vermont, in 1874 to investigate paranormal events occurring in a farmhouse. While there, he met HELENA PETROVNA BLAVATKSY. Together, they founded the Theosophical Society in New York in 1875, an organization that was responsible for bringing the teachings of the Buddha, at least as interpreted by the Society, to a large audience in Europe and America. With the aim of establishing links with Asian teachers, they traveled to India, arriving in Bombay in 1879 and proceeding to Ceylon (Sri Lanka) the next year. Enthusiastically embracing his new Buddhist faith and shocked at what he perceived to be the ignorance of the Sinhalese about their own religion, Olcott took it upon himself to restore true Buddhism to Ceylon and to counter the efforts of Christian missionaries on the island. In order to accomplish this aim, he adopted some of the techniques of Protestant missionaries, founding lay and monastic branches of the Buddhist Theosophical Society to disseminate Buddhist knowledge (and later assisted in the founding of the Young Men's Buddhist Association), designing a Buddhist flag, and publishing in 1881 *A Buddhist Catechism*. The book was printed in some forty editions in twenty languages and was long used in schools in Sri Lanka. Buddhist leaders (including his former protégé, ANAGĀRIKA DHARMAPĀLA) eventually grew alarmed at his rejection of traditional devotional practices and feared that he was misappropriating Buddhism into a universalist Theosophy. In 1885, Olcott set out for Burma and Japan on a mission to heal the schism he perceived between "the northern and southern Churches," that is, between the Buddhists of Ceylon and Burma (southern) and those of China and Japan (northern). In subsequent years, Olcott was involved in often acrimonious debates within the Theosophical Society, failing to prevent a schism in 1895 into an American section and the international headquarters in Adyar, India.

**Oldenberg, Hermann**. (1854–1920). An important scholar in the early history of Buddhist Studies in the West. Oldenberg was born in Hamburg, Germany, the son of a Protestant minister. He studied Sanskrit and Indology in Berlin, receiving his doctorate in 1875. During his career, he held positions at Berlin, Kiel, and Gottingen University, teaching comparative philology and Sanskrit. He traveled to India for the first time in 1912 and also worked in the India Office in London. Oldenberg was arguably the most influential German scholar of Buddhism of the nineteenth century. He published an edition of the Pāli VINAYAPIṬAKA in five volumes between 1879 and 1883. He also published an edition of the DĪPAVAṂSA and collaborated with THOMAS W. RHYS DAVIDS in translating the pāṭimokkha (S. PRĀTIMOKṢA), MAHĀVAGGA, and CŪḶAVAGGA for FRIEDRICH MAX MÜLLER's "Sacred Books of the East" series. He also contributed translations of Vedic works to the same series. His most influential work, however, was his 1881 *Buddha: sein Leben, seine Lehre, seine Gemeinde*, published in English as *Buddha: His Life, His Doctrine, His Order*. In Oldenberg's view, the majority of the texts included in the Pāli canon had been compiled prior to the second Buddhist council (SAṂGĪTI) in Vesālī (S. VAIŚALĪ), said to have taken place c. 380 BCE (see COUNCIL, SECOND). He also believed that these texts had been accurately preserved in Sri Lanka. Oldenberg is therefore (together with THOMAS RHYS DAVIDS and CAROLINE RHYS DAVIDS) largely responsible for the view that the Pāli canon is the most accurate record of the Buddha and his teachings, and that it contains reliable historical information about the events in the Buddha's life. Paralleling the search for the historical Jesus, Oldenberg attempted to strip away the legends of that life, in order to offer a demythologized, historical portrayal of the Buddha. In this effort, his work is often contrasted with that of the French scholar ÉMILE SENART, who, working largely from Sanskrit texts, took a more mythological approach to the accounts of the Buddha's life. For Oldenberg, the Buddha of the later Sanskrit texts was a superhuman figure; the Buddha of the Pāli was historical and human. Oldenberg also disagreed with Senart on the nature of Buddhism, seeing its true religious significance only in the aspiration to achieve NIRVĀṆA; Senart saw Buddhism as largely a popular movement that emphasized achieving happiness in the world and rebirth in the heavens. Oldenberg was the first scholar seriously to compare Pāli and Sanskrit versions of texts, a project that EUGÉNE BURNOUF had planned but was unable to undertake due to his untimely death. Based on these studies, Oldenberg sought to identify the older (and thus, in his view, the more reliable) stratum of textual materials. Oldenberg's views on both the centrality of the Pāli canon and the nature of Buddhism have remained influential in modern presentations of the religion.

**Oldenburg, Sergey**. (1863–1934). Russian scholar of Buddhism, known especially as the founder of the Bibliotheca Buddhica, based in St. Petersburg. The series, published in thirty volumes between 1897 and 1936, was composed primarily of critical editions (and in some cases translations) by the leading European and Japanese scholars of some of the most important texts of Sanskrit Buddhism, including the ŚIKṢĀSAMUCCAYA, MŪLAMADHYAMAKAKĀRIKĀ, AVADĀNAŚATAKA, and ABHISAMAYĀLAṂKĀRA. The series also included indexes as well as independent works, such as FYODOR IPPOLITOVICH STCHERBATSKY's *Buddhist Logic*. In the 1890s, Oldenburg published Sanskrit fragments discovered in Kashgar, and he led Russian expeditions to Central Asia in 1909–1910 and 1914–1915 in search of Buddhist manuscripts and artifacts.

His research interests were wide-ranging; he published articles on Buddhist art, on JĀTAKA literature, and on the *Mahābhārata* in Buddhist literature.

**oṃ maṇi padme hūṃ**. (T. oṃ maṇi padme hūṃ; C. an mani bami hong; J. on mani padomei un; K. om mani panme hum 唵嘛呢叭彌吽). In Sanskrit, "homage to the Jewel-Lotus One"; the most famous of all Buddhist MANTRAS and important especially in Tibetan Buddhism, where it is the mantra most commonly recited and most often placed in prayer wheels; indeed, the Tibetan term rendered in English as "prayer wheel" is MA ṆI 'KHOR LO, or "MAṆI wheel." This phrase is the renowned mantra of the bodhisattva of compassion, AVALOKITEŚVARA. The mantra seems to appear first in the KĀRAṆḌAVYŪHA, a MAHĀYĀNA SŪTRA presumed to have been composed in KASHMIR sometime around the end of the fourth or the beginning of the fifth century CE. The sūtra exalts Avalokiteśvara and praises the mantra at length, referring to it as the "six-syllable spell" (ṢAḌAKṢARĪVIDYĀ). Contrary to the widespread view, the mantra does not refer to "the jewel in the lotus." Instead, it is a call (in the vocative case in Sanskrit) to Avalokiteśvara, using one of his epithets, Maṇipadma, "Jewel-Lotus One." The mantra receives extensive commentary in Tibetan Buddhism. For example, according to the MAṆI BKA' 'BUM, the six syllables correspond to the six rebirth destinies (ṢAḌGATI) of divinities, demigods, humans, animals, ghosts, and hell denizens, so that by reciting the mantra, one is closing the door for all sentient beings to any possibility of further rebirth. See also QIANSHOU JING.

**once-returner**. See SAKṚDĀGĀMIN.

**one-hand clapping kōan**. See SEKISHU KŌAN.

**one mind**. See YIXIN.

**Ŏn'gi**. (K) (彦機). See P'YŎNYANG ŎN'GI.

**Ongi kuden**. (御義口傳). In Japanese, "Record of the Orally Transmitted Teachings"; transcription of the lectures on the SADDHARMAPUṆḌARĪKASŪTRA ("Lotus Sūtra") by NICHIREN, compiled by his disciple Nichikō (1246–1333). See NAMU MYŌHŌRENGEKYŌ.

**Onjōji**. (J) (園城寺). See MIIDERA.

**opening the eyes ceremony**. See DIANYAN; KAIYAN; NETRAPRATIṢṬHĀPANA.

**order**. See SAṂGHA.

**ordination**. See PRAVRAJITA; UPASAṂPADĀ.

**O rgyan gling pa**. (Orgyen Lingpa) (1323–1360). A Tibetan treasure revealer (GTER STON) and master of the RNYING MA sect of Tibetan Buddhism. At the age of twenty-three he is said to have discovered treasure texts (GTER MA) at BSAM YAS monastery. He is credited with discovering numerous treasure cycles, including the "Five Chronicles" (BKA' THANG SDE LNGA). He is also responsible for revealing a well-known biography of PADMASAMBHAVA, the PADMA BKA' THANG YIG, also referred to as the "Crystal Cave Chronicle" (*Bka' thang shel brag ma*) due to its extraction from Padmasambhava's meditation site at "Crystal Cave" (Shel brag) in the Yar klungs valley of central Tibet.

**O rgyan pa Rin chen dpal**. (Orgyenpa Rinchenpal) (1229/30–1309). A Tibetan Buddhist master venerated as a lineage holder in the early BKA' BRGYUD tradition. Also known as Seng ge dpal, he was a disciple of the renowned "upper" (stod) 'BRUG PA BKA' BRGYUD teacher RGOD TSHANG PA MGON PO RDO RJE and became famous as a highly accomplished meditator; for this reason, Tibetan literature frequently refers to him as a MAHĀSIDDHA, or great adept. He is said to have made a journey to the fabled land of OḌḌIYĀNA (O rgyan), believed by some modern scholars to lie in the Swat region of modern-day Pakistan. He thus became known as O rgyan pa, "the man of Oḍḍiyāna," and he later authored a pilgrimage guide to the location, the *O rgyan lam yig*. Some Tibetan historians have identified a separate transmission lineage stemming from O rgyan pa: the Service and Attainment of the Three Vajras (Rdo rje'i gsum gyi bsnyen sgrub), frequently known as the O rgyan bsnyen sgrub. Rin chen dpal is also known for his transmission of practices relating to the six-branch yoga of the KĀLACAKRATANTRA, a system of instructions he is said to have received from the ḌĀKINĪ VAJRAYOGINĪ during his travels in Oḍḍiyāna. These traditions appear to have largely disappeared in Tibet several centuries after his death. O rgyan pa officially recognized the young RANG 'BYUNG RDO RJE as the third KARMA PA and then served as the hierarch's principal teacher.

**original enlightenment**. See BENJUE; HONGAKU.

**original face**. See BENLAI MIANMU.

**oshō**. (和尚). One of the common Japanese pronunciations of the Chinese term HESHANG, which in turn is derived from the Sanskrit term UPĀDHYĀYA, meaning "preceptor." The term is now used generally in the Japanese Buddhist tradition to refer to an abbot, teacher, or senior monk. The pronunciation of the term varies according to tradition. In the ZENSHŪ, the term is pronounced "oshō," in the TENDAISHŪ "kashō," in RISSHŪ, SHINGONSHŪ, and JŌDO SHINSHŪ "wajō." In the Zen context, oshō refers to those monks who have been in training for ten years or more. In the SŌTŌSHŪ of the Zen school, monks who have received formal dharma transmission are referred to as oshō.

**Ōtaniha**. (大谷派). Also known as Ōtanishū and Higashi Honganjiha, the second largest subsect of JŌDO SHINSHŪ in the

Japanese PURE LAND tradition. After SHINRAN's founding of Jōdo Shinshū, the HONGANJI emerged as the dominant subsect and was administered by the descendants of Shinran's patriarchal line. During the Tokugawa period (1600–1868), the shōgun Tokugawa Ieyasu (1543–1616) grew suspicious of Honganji, which during the fifteen and sixteenth centuries had not only grown to be the largest sect of Japanese Buddhism but also one of the largest landholding institutions in Japan. By involving himself in a succession dispute, the shōgun was successfully able to blunt its power by causing a schism within the Honganji into east (higashi) and west (nishi) factions, with Kyōnyo (1558–1614) heading the Higashi faction and Junnyo (1577–1631) leading the Nishi faction. Because the eastern faction maintained control of Shinran's mausoleum in the Ōtani area of Kyoto, HIGASHI HONGANJI has also come to be called the Ōtaniha. Ōtani University developed from the Higashi Honganji seminary, which was founded in 1665. Several of the most important Buddhist thinkers of the Meiji period were affiliated with the Ōtaniha, including NANJŌ BUN'YŪ (1849–1927), Inoue Enryō (1858–1919), and KIYOZAWA MANSHI (1863–1903). DAISETZ TEITARO SUZUKI (1870–1966) founded the journal *The Eastern Buddhist* at Ōtani University, and the author Kanamatsu Kenryō (1915–1986) was also affiliated with the Ōtaniha. See also NISHI HONGANJIHA.

**Ōtani Kōzui**. (大谷光瑞) (1876–1948). Modern Japanese explorer to Buddhist archeological sites in Central Asia, and especially DUNHUANG; the twenty-second abbot of the NISHI HONGANJIHA, one of the two main sub-branches of the JŌDO SHINSHŪ of the Japanese pure land tradition. Ōtani was sent to London at the age of fourteen by his father, the twenty-first abbot of Nishi Honganji in Kyōto, to study Western theology. Inspired by the contemporary expeditions to Central Asia then being conducted by European explorers such as SIR MARC AUREL STEIN (1862–1943) and Sven Hedin (1865–1952), Ōtani decided to take an overland route on his return to Japan so that he could survey Buddhist sites along the SILK ROAD. Ōtani embarked on his first expedition to the region in 1902, accompanied by several other Japanese priests from Nishi Honganji. While en route, Ōtani received the news of his father's death and returned to Japan to succeed to the abbacy; the expedition continued and returned to Japan in 1904. Even though his duties subsequently kept him in Japan, Ōtani dispatched expeditions to Chinese Turkestan in 1908–1909 and between 1910 and 1914. The artifacts recovered during these three expeditions include manuscripts, murals, sculpture, textiles, etc., and are known collectively as the "Ōtani collection." These materials are now dispersed in Japan, Korea, and China, but they are still regarded as important sources for the study of Central Asian Buddhist archeology.

**Ouyi Zhixu**. (J. Gōyaku/Gūyaku Chigyoku; K. Uik Chiuk 蕅益智旭) (1599–1655). One of the four eminent monks (si da gaoseng) of the late-Ming dynasty, along with YUNQI ZHUHONG (1535–1615), HANSHAN DEQING (1546–1623), and DAGUAN ZHENKE (1543–1604); renowned for his mastery of a wide swath of Confucian and Buddhist teachings, particularly those associated with the TIANTAI, PURE LAND, and CHAN traditions. In his youth, he studied Confucianism and despised Buddhism, even writing anti-Buddhist tracts. He had a change of heart at the age of seventeen, after reading some of Zhuhong's writings, and burned his previous screeds. According to his autobiography, Zhixu had his first "great awakening" at the age of nineteen while reading the line in the *Lunyu* ("Confucian Analects") that "the whole world will submit to benevolence" if one restrains oneself and returns to ritual. After his father's death that same year, he fully committed himself to Buddhism, reading sūtras and performing recollection of the Buddha's name (NIANFO) until he finally was ordained under the guidance of Xueling (d.u.), a disciple of Hanshan Deqing, at the age of twenty-four. At that time, he began to read extensively in YOGĀCĀRA materials and had another great awakening through Chan meditation, in which he experienced body, mind, and the outer world suddenly disappearing. He next turned his attention to the bodhisattva precepts and the study of vinaya. Following his mother's death when he was twenty-seven, Zhixu rededicated himself to Chan meditation, but after a serious illness he turned to pure land teachings. In his early thirties, he devoted himself to the study of Tiantai materials, through which he attempted to integrate his previous research in Buddhism and began to write commentaries and treaties on Buddhist scriptures and on such Confucian classics as the *Zhouyi* ("Book of Changes"). In the late-sixteenth century, Jesuit missionaries such as Michele Ruggieri (1543–1607) and Matteo Ricci (1552–1610) had reintroduced Christianity to China and sought "to complement Confucianism and to replace Buddhism." This emerging religious challenge led Zhixu to publish his *Bixie ji* ("Collected Essays Refuting Heterodoxy") as a critique of the teachings of Christianity, raising specifically the issue of theodicy (i.e., why a benevolent and omnipotent god would allow evil to appear in the world); Zhixu advocates instead that good and evil come from human beings and are developed and overcome respectively through personal cultivation. After another illness at the age of fifty-six, his later years were focused mostly on pure land teachings and practice. In distinction to Japanese pure land teachers, such as HŌNEN (1133–1212) and SHINRAN (1173–1262), who emphasized exclusively Amitābha's "other-power" (C. tali; J. TARIKI), Zhixu, like most other Chinese pure land teachers, advocated the symbiosis between the other-power of Amitābha and the "self-power" (C. jiri; J. JIRIKI) of the practitioner. This perspective is evident in his equal emphasis on the three trainings in meditation (Chan), doctrine (jiao), and precepts (lü) (cf. TRIŚIKṢĀ). Ouyi's oeuvre numbers some sixty-two works in 230 rolls, including treatises and commentaries on works ranging from Tiantai, to Chan, to Yogācāra, to pure land. His pure land writings have been especially influential, and his *Amituojing yaojie* ("Essential Explanations" on the AMITĀBHASŪTRA) and *Jingtu shiyao* ("Ten Essentials on the Pure

Land") are regarded as integral to the modern Chinese Pure Land tradition.

**ovādapāṭimokkha**. (S. *avavādaprātimokṣa). In Pāli, "admonitory discipline"; the designation in Pāli materials for a foundational disciplinary code (PRĀTIMOKṢA) handed down by the past buddha Vipassī (S. VIPAŚYIN), which is believed to summarize the teachings fundamental to all the buddhas: "Not doing anything evil, / Undertaking what is wholesome,/Purifying one's mind,/This is the teaching of the buddhas" (P. sabbapāpassa akaraṇaṃ/kusalassūpasampadā/sacittapariyodapanaṃ/etaṃ buddhāna sāsanaṃ) (MAHĀPADĀNASUTTANTA [DĪGHANIKĀYA no. 14]; DHAMMAPADA, v. 183). This verse has been widely incorporated into THERAVĀDA Buddhist rituals and ceremonies. See also AVAVĀDA.

**Oxhead School**. See NIUTOU ZONG.

**Oxherding Pictures, Ten**. (C. Shiniu tu; J. Jūgyūzu; K. Sibu to 十牛圖). A varied series of illustrations used within the CHAN (J. ZEN; K. SŎN, V. THIỀN) schools to depict the process of religious training, a process that leads ultimately to awakening and the perfect freedom of enlightenment. The series show a young herdsman who goes out into the wild in search of a wild ox that he can tame. The "herdsman" represents the religious adept who seeks to tame the "ox" of his unchecked thoughts, so that he may put his mind to use in the service of all sentient beings. There are several different versions of the oxherding pictures found in the literature, but two are best known. The first is by the Song-dynasty adept Puming (d.u.): (1) not yet found, (2) training begun, (3) disciplining, (4) turning its head, (5) tamed, (6) unimpeded, (7) wandering freely, (8) each forgotten, (9) moon shining alone, and (10) both disappear. A second set of ten pictures, which became normative within the Chan tradition, was made later by the Song-dynasty YANGQI PAI teacher KUO'AN SHIYUAN (d.u.): (1) searching for the ox; (2) seeing its footprints; (3) finding the ox; (4) catching the ox; (5) taming the ox; (6) riding the ox home; (7) ox forgotten, but not the person; (8) person and ox both forgotten; (9) returning to the origin and going back to the fount; and (10) entering the marketplace to bestow gifts. This second set of pictures is often found painted sequentially around the outside walls of the main shrine hall (TAEUNG CHŎN) in Korean monasteries.

# P

**paccavekkhaṇañāṇa**. In Pāli, "reviewing knowledge"; the recollection of any meditative absorption (P. JHĀNA, S. DHYĀNA) or object of concentration, the attainment of any of the four noble paths (P. magga, S. MĀRGA), or the fruition (PHALA) of a noble path. In the case of a noble attainment, reviewing knowledge arises in the following manner. According to the Pāli ABHIDHAMMA analysis, first, path consciousness (MAGGACITTA) gives rise to two or three moments of fruition consciousness (PHALACITTA), after which the mind subsides into the subconscious mental continuum or life stream (BHAVAṄGASOTA). The subconscious life stream continues until the mind adverts to the previous path moment for the purpose of reviewing it. This is followed by seven moments of mental excitation, called impulsion or advertence (javana), that take as their object the past path moment. Thereafter the mind again subsides into the subconscious life stream. The mind then adverts to previous moments of fruition for the purpose of reviewing them. This is followed by seven moments of mental excitation that take as their object the past fruition moments. In the same way that the practitioner reviews the path and fruition, he also reviews the afflictions (P. kilesa; S. KLEŚA) eradicated from his mind, those remaining to be eradicated, nibbāna (S. NIRVĀṆA) as an object, etc. He knows thereby what he has attained, what remains to be attained, and what he has experienced.

**Padaeng Chronicle**. "Chronicle of the Red Forest Monastery," a chronicle of uncertain date written in the Khun language of Kengtung valley of the Shan states of Burma (Myanmar). It records the history of the THERAVĀDA tradition from its inception to the founding of Wat Padaeng at Kengtung and the vicissitudes of the religion in the Shan states thereafter. It begins with a record of the life of the Buddha, through the three Buddhist councils (SAṂGĪTI) in India, to Buddhism's spread to Sri Lanka and the Mon kingdom of SUVAṆṆABHŪMI in Lower Burma. From that point, it describes the introduction of two reformed Sinhalese monastic sects at Martaban (Muttama) in Lower Burma, and the spread of reformed Sinhalese Buddhism from there to the Thai kingdoms of AYUTHAYA, SUKHOTHAI, and Chiangmai, following the narrative outline of the MŪLASĀSANA.

**Paddamya Taung**. A pagoda or JEDI (P. cetī/cetiya; S. CAITYA) located at the northernmost range of the Sagaing Hills along the Irrawaddy (Ayeyarvaddi) River in Upper Burma (Myanmar). Situated on a hill named Mani-kinzana Paddamya, the monument is claimed by local tradition to have been built by the Indian Mauryan emperor AŚOKA in 308 BCE, and to contain gems and buddha relics (P. sarīra; S. ŚARĪRA) that he donated. The pagoda derives its name from the surrounding area, which at one time was rich in rubies (Burmese, paddamya) and medicinal plants. It was restored in 1300 CE, while Sagaing was the capital of the Burmese kingdom, by the monk Thingayaza from Padu Village near the city. An annual festival is held there on the full moon day of the Burmese month of Tawthalin (September-October).

**padma**. (P. paduma; T. padma; C. lianhua/hong lianhua; J. renge/gurenge; K. yŏnhwa/hong yŏnhwa 蓮華/紅蓮華). In Sanskrit, "lotus," an aquatic plant that blossoms above the surface of the water and is the most commonly occurring flower in Buddhist art and literature. Because the lotus flower blooms above the muddy waters of stagnant ponds, the lotus is used as a symbol for the purity of mind that develops out of the pollution that is SAṂSĀRA but remains unsullied by it. In addition, the lotus is said to be the only plant that produces its flower and fruit simultaneously, indicating in some interpretations that the cause (the Buddha's teaching) and its effect (enlightenment) are not separate. Lotuses occur in a variety of colors, some of which have their own names, such as the PUṆḌARĪKA, or white lotus, which occurs in the title SADDHARMAPUṆḌARĪKASŪTRA ("Lotus Sūtra"). Lotuses are often depicted at the feet of the Buddha; buddhas and bodhisattvas are commonly seated in the middle of large lotus blossoms; deities often hold lotus blossoms in their hands. When the Buddha was born, he is said to have taken seven steps, with a lotus blossoming under his foot with each step. Lotuses play important symbolic roles in a number of texts. For example, in the SUKHĀVATĪVYŪHASŪTRA, those who in their previous lives accumulate merit but continue to have doubts about being reborn in the PURE LAND are born there within the calyx of a lotus, where they reside for five hundred years, until the flower opens and they are able to begin their training. In the TATHĀGATAGARBHASŪTRA, countless lotuses appear in the sky; their petals unfold to reveal a buddha seated within, and then the petals fade. This symbolizes the presence of the TATHĀGATAGARBHA within all beings, hidden within the afflictions (KLEŚA), which are then destroyed upon the attainment of buddhahood. In tantric Buddhism, the term padma is sometimes used to refer to the female genitals.

**Padma bka' thang yig**. (Pema gatangyik). In Tibetan, "Chronicle of the Lotus"; a treasure text (GTER MA) containing a well-known biography of PADMASAMBHAVA, discovered by the treasure revealer (GTER STON) O RGYAN GLING PA. Its complete title is: *O rgyan gu ru padma 'byung gnas kyi skyes rabs rnam par thar pa rgyas par bkod pa padma bka'i thang yig*. Because it was excavated from Shel brag (Sheldrak), or Crystal Cave, it is also known as the *Shel brag ma* ("Crystal Cave Version").

**Padma bkod**. (Pema kö). One of Tibet's foremost SBAS YUL, or "hidden lands," located in southern Tibet and partially in Arunachal Pradesh in India. It is the location of the so-called Gtsang po (Tsangpo) gorges, where the Gtsang po River of Tibet makes a 180-degree bend from east to west through steep cliffs and waterfalls before changing its name to the Brahmaputra River in India. The region is primarily associated with PADMASAMBHAVA and his twenty-five main disciples, who are said to have meditated in caves throughout the area. After spending time there in retreat, the Indian master prophesied that the locale would become a powerful center for religious practice. The treasure revealer (GTER STON) Bdud 'dul rdo rje (Dudul Dorje, 1615–1672) discovered a pilgrimage guide (gnas yig) to the site and identified its geographical features with the body of the goddess VAJRAVĀRĀHĪ. Padma bkod was formally "opened" as a pilgrimage site and place of practice by Sgam po O rgyan 'gro 'dul gling pa (Gampo Orgyan Drodul Lingpa, b. 1757), Rig 'dzin Rdo rje rtog med (Rikdzin Dorje Tokme, 1746–1797), and Chos gling Gar dbang 'chi med rdo rje (Chöling Garwang Chime Dorje, b. 1763). The remote region is famous for its forests and dense jungle wilderness, and the numerous ethnic tribal groups living there. It has served as a safe haven for those fleeing conflict as well as a site for tantric practice. According to a seventeenth-century account, it is associated especially with VAJRAYOGINĪ, with the river representing her central channel (AVADHŪTĪ).

**Padma dkar po**. (Pema Karpo) (1527–1592). A Tibetan Buddhist master and lineage holder of the 'BRUG PA BKA' BRGYUD tradition, renowned for his extensive and wide-ranging scholarship. Born in the Kong po region of southern Tibet, as a child he was already recognized as the fourth member in the line of 'BRUG CHEN INCARNATIONS. He became a fully ordained monk and studied widely in the Tibetan traditions of logic and TANTRA. Although famed for his experience in yogic practice and meditation, he also served as a skillful politician and religious administrator. He is perhaps most widely celebrated for his scholarly writings, which include extensive commentaries on traditional doctrinal topics as well as comprehensive historical works on the spread of Buddhism in Tibet, particularly his own 'Brug pa bka' brgyud sect. His followers referred to him by the title kun mkhyen, "the omniscient," a testament to his great learning. Padma dkar po was active at the monasteries of previous 'Brug chen incarnations, including the famed twelfth-century institution at RWA LUNG in Gtsang, but he also founded his own monastery Gsang sngags chos gling in 1574 at Rta dbang near the border with Bhutan. Following Padma dkar po's death, two candidates were pitted against one another as the master's authentic rebirth and the legitimate successor to the 'Brug chen throne. The outcome of the rivalry was eventually decided by the ruler of central Tibet, the Gtsang pa sde srid; the losing candidate, who had already been installed as the throne holder of Rwa lung Monastery, fled to Bhutan in 1616, where he established himself as the important Bhutanese religious figure ZHABS DRUNG NGAG DBANG RNAM RGYAL.

**Padma gling pa**. (Pema Lingpa) (1450–1521). An esteemed Bhutanese treasure revealer (GTER STON), famous for unearthing treasure in public and responsible for promulgating numerous important religious traditions, including forms of ritual monastic dance ('CHAM). He is counted as the fourth of the so-called five kingly treasure revealers (GTER STON RGYAL PO LNGA) and the last of the five pure incarnations of the royal princess PADMA GSAL. He is also regarded as the mind incarnation of the translator VAIROCANA and an incarnation of KLONG CHEN RAB 'BYAMS. Padma gling pa was born into a humble family of blacksmiths in the Bum thang region of Bhutan and studied the craft from the age of nine. Many examples of Padma gling pa's craftsmanship, in the form of swords and chain mail, still exist. Padma gling pa's life is somewhat unusual in that he did not undertake a traditional course of study with a spiritual master; it is recorded that he once declared, "I have no master and I am not a disciple." Rather, his religious training was achieved almost entirely through visionary revelation. At the age of twenty-six, he had a vision of PADMASAMBHAVA, who bestowed on him a roster of 108 treasure texts that he would unearth in the future. The next year, amid a large public gathering, he made his first treasure discovery at ME 'BAR MTSHO, a wide pool of water in a nearby river. Surrounded by a multitude of people gathered along the riverside, Padma gling pa dove in the waters holding a burning butter lamp in his hand. When he reemerged, he held a great treasure chest under his arm, and, to the crowd's amazement, the lamp in his hand was unextinguished; from that point on the pool was called "Burning Flame Lake." This feat marked the beginning of Padma gling pa's prolific career as treasure revealer and teacher. Between the years 1501 and 1505, he founded his seat at GTAM ZHING monastery in Bum thang. Padma gling pa composed a lengthy autobiography recording many of his activities in great detail. He was a controversial figure in his time (some of the treasure texts he discovered contain condemnations of those who doubted their authenticity), and the historicity of his deeds has been the subject of scholarly critique. However, Padma gling pa remains an important figure in the religious and cultural life of Bhutan, where he is considered both a saint and a national hero. He never received monastic ordination and fathered several sons who continued to transmit Padma gling pa's spiritual lineage, especially at SGANG STENG monastery in central Bhutan. Several incarnation lineages of Padma gling pa were also recognized, such as the gsung sprul ("speech incarnation") based at LHA LUNG Monastery in southern Tibet. Both the sixth DALAI LAMA TSHANGS DBYANGS RGYA MTSHO and the Bhutanese royal family are said to be descendants of Padma gling pa's familial lineage.

**Padma gsal**. (Pemasel) (fl. c. eighth century). The daughter of the Tibetan King KHRI SRONG LDE BTSAN, to whom PADMASAMBHAVA entrusted a lineage of RDZOGS CHEN instructions known as MKHA' 'GRO SNYING THIG. She died at the age of eight. When the Tibetan king brought her body before the Indian master at the Brag dmar ke'u tshang (Drakmar Ke'utsang) cave at CHIMS PHU, he asked why someone with the great merit to be both a princess and a disciple of Padmasambhava had to die while still a child. The Indian master revealed she had been a bee who stung one of the four brothers involved in the completion of the great BODHNĀTH STŪPA. Thereafter Padmasambhava miraculously revived her, transmitted the instructions of the Mkha 'gro snying thig, and prophesied that she would reveal the teachings as a treasure (GTER MA) in a future rebirth as PADMA LAS 'BREL RTSAL. Some traditions describe a lineage of five pure incarnations of the royal princess Padma gsal (lha lcam padma gsal gyi dag pa'i skye ba lnga), including several important lamas of the RNYING MA sect of Tibetan Buddhism:

1. Padma gsal
2. PADMA LAS 'BREL RTSAL
3. Spang sgang pa Rin chen rdo rje (Pang gangpa Rinchen Dorje)
4. KLONG CHEN RAB 'BYAMS
5. PADMA GLING PA

According to some Tibetan sources, however, Padma las 'brel rtsal was the secret name of Spang sgang pa Rin chen rdo rje.

**Padmakāra**. (S). See PADMASAMBHAVA.

**padmakula**. (T. padma'i rigs; C. lianhua bu; J. rengebu; K. yŏnhwa pu 蓮華部). In Sanskrit, "lotus family" or "lotus lineage"; one of the three, four, or five buddha families (see PAÑCATATHĀGATA) that occur in the Buddhist TANTRAS. In the lotus family, the chief buddha is AMITĀBHA and the chief bodhisattva is AVALOKITEŚVARA. In the three-family system, associated especially with KRIYĀTANTRA and CARYĀTANTRA, the other two families are the TATHĀGATAKULA and the VAJRAKULA. In the four-family system, associated with YOGATANTRA, the RATNAKULA is added; in the five-family system, associated with ANUTTARAYOGATANTRA, the KARMAKULA family is added. Each of the five families is associated with one of the five SKANDHAS, five wisdoms (JÑĀNA), five afflictions (KLEŚA), five elements, and five colors. For the padma family, these are the perception (SAṂJÑĀ) skandha, the wisdom of specific knowledge (PRATYAVEKṢAṆĀJÑĀNA), the affliction of desire, the element fire, and the color red.

**Padma las 'brel rtsal**. (Pema Ledreltsal) (1231/1248–1259/1315). The reincarnation of Princess PADMA GSAL, daughter of the Tibetan king KHRI SRONG LDE BTSAN, and the treasure revealer (GTER STON) who discovered the MKHA' 'GRO SNYING THIG. According to some Tibetan sources, Padma las 'brel rtsal was the secret name of Spang sgang pa Rin chen rdo rje. Other sources hold the latter to be Padma las 'brel rtsal's incarnation, followed by KLONG CHEN RABS 'BYAMS and PADMA GLING PA.

**Padmapāṇi**. (T. Phyag na pad mo; C. Lianhuashou; J. Rengeshu; K. Yŏnhwasu 蓮華手). In Sanskrit, "He Who Holds a Lotus in His Hand," one of the common forms of AVALOKITEŚVARA, the bodhisattva of compassion. He is a two-armed form of the bodhisattva, holding a lotus blossom (PADMA) or the stem of a lotus flower in one hand, and is often depicted standing. One of the most famous images of Padmapāṇi is found at AJAṆṬĀ.

**Padmasambhava**. (T. Padma 'byung gnas) (fl. eighth century). Indian Buddhist master and tantric adept widely revered in Tibet under the appellation Guru rin po che, "Precious Guru"; considered to be the "second buddha" by members of the RNYING MA sect of Tibetan Buddhism, who view him as a founder of their tradition. In Tibetan, he is also known as Padma 'byung gnas (Pemajungne), "the Lotus Born," which translates his Sanskrit name. It is difficult to assess the many legends surrounding his life and deeds, although the scholarly consensus is that he was a historical figure and did visit Tibet. The earliest reference to him is in the SBA BZHED (a work that purports to be from the eighth century, but is likely later), where he is mentioned as a water diviner and magician, suggesting that he may have been an expert in irrigation, which would have required the ability to subdue local spirits. Two texts in the Tibetan canon are attributed to him. The first is the *Man ngag lta ba'i phreng ba*, which is a commentary on the thirteenth chapter of the GUHYAGARBHATANTRA. The second is a commentary on the *Upāyapāśapadmamālā*, a MAHĀYOGA TANTRA. Regardless of his historical status and the duration of his stay in Tibet, the figure of Padmasambhava has played a key role in the narrative of Buddhism's arrival in Tibet, its establishment in Tibet, and its subsequent transmission to later generations. He is also venerated throughout the Himalayan regions of India, Bhutan, and Nepal and by the Newar Buddhists of the Kathmandu Valley. According to many of his traditional biographies, Padmasambhava was miraculously born in the center of a lotus blossom (PADMA) on Lake Danakośa in the land of OḌḌIYĀNA, a region some scholars associate with the Swat Valley of modern Pakistan. Discovered and raised by King Indrabodhi, he abandoned his royal life to pursue various forms of Buddhist study and practice, culminating in his training as a tantric adept. He journeyed throughout the Himalayan regions of India and Nepal, meeting his first consort MANDĀRAVĀ at Mtsho padma in Himachal Pradesh, and later remaining in prolonged retreat in various locations around the Kathmandu Valley including MĀRATIKA, YANG LE SHOD and the ASURA CAVE. His reputation as an exorcist led to his invitation, at the behest of the Indian scholar ŚĀNTARAKṢITA, to travel to Tibet in order to assist with the construction of BSAM YAS monastery. According to traditional accounts, Padmasambhava subdued and converted the indigenous deities inimical to the spread of Buddhism and, together with Śāntarakṣita and the Tibetan king KHRI SRONG LDE BTSAN, established the first Buddhist lineage and monastic center of Tibet. He remained in Tibet as a court priest, and, together with his Tibetan consort YE SHES MTSHO RGYAL, recorded and then concealed numerous teachings as hidden treasure texts (GTER MA), to be revealed by a later succession of masters spiritually linked to Padmasambhava. The Rnying ma sect preserves the corpus of instructions stemming from the master in two classes of materials: those revealed after his passing as treasure texts and those belonging to an unbroken oral tradition (BKA' MA). It is believed that Padmasambhava departed Tibet for his paradise known as the Glorious Copper-Colored Mountain (ZANGS MDOG DPAL RI), where he continues to reside. From the time of the later dissemination of the doctrine (PHYI DAR) in the eleventh century onwards, numerous biographies of the Indian master have been revealed as treasure texts, including the PADMA BKA' THANG YIG, BKA' THANG GSER 'PHRENG, and the BKA' THANG ZANGS GLING MA. Padmasambhava is the focus of many kinds of ritual activities, including the widely recited "Seven Line Prayer to Padmasambhava" (Tshig 'dun gsol 'debs). The tenth day of each lunar month is dedicated to Padmasambhava, a time when many monasteries, especially those in Bhutan, perform religious dances reverencing the Indian master in his eight manifestations. In iconography, Padmasambhava is depicted in eight forms, known as the guru mtshan brgyad, who represent his eight great deeds. They are Padma rgyal po, Nyi ma 'od zer, Blo ldan mchog sred, Padmasambhava, Shākya seng ge, Padmakara (also known as Sororuhavajra, T. Mtsho skyes rdo rje), Seng ge sgra sgrogs, and RDO RJE GRO LOD.

**padmāsana**. (T. padma'i gdan; C. lianhua zuo; J. rengeza; K. yŏnhwa chwa 蓮華坐). In Sanskrit, "lotus posture," a term for the seated posture in which the right foot rests on the left thigh and the left foot rests on top on the right thigh. It is a position predominantly used in Hindu forms of yoga, and in a Buddhist context is often confused with the VAJRAPARYAṄKA (vajra cross-legged posture), where the position of the feet is reversed. See also ĀSANA. ¶ The term padmāsana, in the denotation of "lotus seat," is also used to designate the lotus-flower base upon which many Buddhist deities stand or sit.

**Paegam Sŏngch'ong**. (栢庵性聰) (1631–1700). Korean scholar-monk and poet from the mid-Chosŏn dynasty. Born in 1631, he entered the SAṂGHA in 1645, at the age of sixteen, and received the precepts from the monk Ch'wiam (d.u.). He went to Mt. Pangjang (present-day CHIRISAN) and became a disciple of the eminent Sŏn master Ch'wimi Such'o (1590–1668). In 1660, Sŏngch'ong became a lecturer and subsequently traveled from one monastery to the next, including SONGGWANGSA, Chinggwangsa, and SSANGGYESA. He was also a renowned poet and is known to have befriended many famous poets of his time. In 1681, a boat containing more than 190 Buddhist texts, including the *Daming Fashu*, *Huixuan ji*, *Sidashisuo lu*, and *Jingtubao shu*, was found adrift near Imja Island. Sŏngch'ong was able to acquire these texts, and for the next fifteen years he made over five thousand copies of them. He passed away in 1700, while residing at the hermitage of Sinhŭngam in Ssanggyesa. Sŏngch'ong was also a prolific writer and left many works, including his *Ch'imun chip chu* ("Commentary on the ZIMEN JINGXUN"), *Chŏngt'obosŏ*, *Paegam chip*, and *Chihŏm ki*.

**Paegun Kyŏnghan**. (白雲景閑) (1299–1374). Korean SŎN master in the Imje (C. LINJI ZONG) lineage, who is known as one of the three great Sŏn masters of the late-Koryŏ dynasty, along with T'AEGO POU (1301–1376) and NAONG HYEGŬN (1320–1376). After entering the monastery at a young age, Kyŏnghan eventually traveled to Yuan-dynasty China in 1351, where he studied under the Chan master Shiwu Qinggong (1272–1352), a Linji-Chan teacher from whom he received dharma transmission, and under the Indian monk ZHIKONG CHANXIAN, who later came to live and teach in Korea. After awakening in 1353, Kyŏnghan returned to Korea, residing at An'guksa and Sin'gwangsa, both in Hwanghae province, and later at Ch'wiamsa in Yŏju, where he passed away in 1374. Kyŏnghan's record of dharma talks, *Paegun hwasang ŏrok* ("Discourse Records of the Master Paegun"), in two rolls, was compiled posthumously by his disciple Sŏkch'an. Kyŏnghan is also the author of the PULCHO CHIKCHI SIMCH'E YOJŎL, an anthology of the biographies and teachings of the Buddhist patriarchs and Sŏn masters.

**Paegyangsa**. (白羊寺). In Korean, "White Ram Monastery"; the eighteenth district monastery (PONSA) of the contemporary CHOGYE CHONG of Korean Buddhism, located on Paegam (White Cliff) Mountain in South Chŏlla province. The monastery was founded in 632 by the Paekche monk Yŏhwan (d.u.) and was originally called Paegamsa; it was renamed Chŏngt'osa after a reconstruction project during the Koryŏ dynasty in 1034. Its current name of Paegyangsa comes from a Koryŏ-era legend. Sometime during the reign of King Sŏnjo of the Chosŏn dynasty (r. 1567–1607), a teacher now known as Hwanyang (d.u., lit. "Goat Caller") was said to have been leading a recitation assembly on the SADDHARMAPUṆḌARĪKASŪTRA ("Lotus Sūtra"), when a white ram came down out of the mountains to listen to the monks recite the SŪTRA. Once the event was over, the ram appeared to Hwanyang in a dream and explained that he had been reborn as a ram for transgressions he had committed in heaven; after hearing the master's sermon, however, he was redeemed and was able to take rebirth once again as a divinity (DEVA). The next day the body of the ram was found on the monastery grounds, and Paegyangsa received the name by which it has been known ever since. Paegyangsa is guarded by the Gate of the Four Heavenly Kings (Sach'ŏnwang mun). The main shrine hall (TAEUNG CHŎN) is unusually located to the right of the gate, rather than centered in the compound, and an eight-story stone STŪPA is located behind the main hall, rather than in front of it. The oldest extant building on the campus is the Kŭngnak pojŏn, or SUKHĀVATĪ hall, the construction of which was sponsored by the queen-consort of the Chosŏn king Chungjong (r. 1506–1544). The main shrine hall, reconstructed in 1917 by the prominent Buddhist reformer MANAM CHONGHŎN (1876–1957), is dedicated to ŚĀKYAMUNI Buddha, and enshrines an image of Śākyamuni flanked by the bodhisattvas MAÑJUŚRĪ and SAMANTABHADRA. Much of the monastery burned in 1950 during the Korean War, and reconstruction extended into the 1990s. In 1996, Paegyangsa was elevated to the status of an ecumenical monastery (CH'ONGNIM), and is one of the five such centers in the contemporary Chogye order, which are expected to provide training in the full range of practices that exemplify the major strands of the Korean Buddhist tradition; the monastery is thus also known as the Kobul Ch'ongnim.

**Paekkok Ch'ŏnŭng**. (白谷處能) (1617–1680). Korean monk of the Chosŏn dynasty, also known as Sinsu. Ch'ŏnŭng received a traditional Confucian education from Ŭihyŏn (d.u.) and subsequently became a monk in 1631. He returned to Seoul a few years later and continued to study the Confucian classics from a Confucian scholar by the name of Sin Iksŏng. He later went to the monastery of SSANGGYESA in CHIRISAN and became the disciple of the Sŏn master PYŎGAM KAKSŎNG, under whom he studied for the next twenty-three years. In 1680, while lecturing at KŬMSANSA, he passed away at the age of sixty-four. Ch'ŏnŭng was particularly renowned for his writing and poetry, and maintained a close relationship with the leading Confucian scholars at the time. As a response to King Hyŏnjong's (r. 1660–1674) suppression of Buddhism, Ch'ŏnŭng submitted to the court the *Kanp'ye Sŏkkyo so* ("Remonstration against the Ruination of Śākyamuni's Teachings"), a critical response to the Confucian criticisms of Buddhism that were prevalent during that period. His writings can also be found in the *Paekkok chip* and *Imsŏngdang taesa haengjang*. The *Paekkok chip* is a collection of his poems and the biographies, stele inscriptions, and records of other monks. The *Kanp'ye Sŏkkyo so* can also be found in the *Paekkok chip*. He also authored the *Imsŏngdang taesa haengjang*, a record of the life of the Sŏn master Imsŏng Ch'ungŏn (1567–1638).

**Paekp'a Kŭngsŏn**. (白坡亘璇) (1767–1852). Korean SŎN master of the Chosŏn dynasty, also known as Kusan. Paekp'a was a native of Mujang in present-day North Chŏlla province. In 1778, he was ordained by a certain Sihŏn (d.u.) at the nearby monastery of Sŏnŭnsa. In 1790, he moved from his original residence at the hermitage of Yongmunam on Mt. Ch'o to the Yŏngwŏnam on Mt. Pangchang, where he studied under the renowned Hwaŏm chong (C. HUAYAN ZONG) master, Sŏlp'a Sangŏn (1707–1791). A year before Sangŏn passed away, Kŭngsŏn received the full monastic precepts from him. Paekp'a established himself at the famous hermitage of Unmunam and attracted many students. He studied the teachings of the renowned CHAN master XUEFENG YICUN at Mt. Yŏnggu and acquired the name Paekp'a. In order to practice Sŏn meditation, he returned to Yongmunam and revived POJO CHINUL's Samādhi and Prajñā Society (CHŎNGHYE KYŎLSA). He subsequently returned to Unmunam to compile his influential treatise *Sŏnmun sugyŏng* ("Hand Mirror of the Sŏn School"), which was later the subject of a famous critique by the Sŏn master CH'OŬI ŬISUN (1786–1866) in his *Sŏnmun sabyŏn manŏ* ("Prolix Words on Four Distinctive Types in the Sŏn School"). Paekp'a was a staunch promoter of Sŏn, who sought to resolve what he perceived to be a fundamental internal tension within the Sŏn tradition: the radical subitism of the Imje chong (LINJI ZONG), which advocated the simultaneity of sudden awakening (DUNWU) and cultivation (K. tono tonsu; C. dunwu dunxiu), and the more moderate subitism of the Heze zong and POJO CHINUL (1158–1210), which advocated sudden awakening followed by gradual cultivation (K. tono chŏmsu; C. DUNWU JIANXIU). Paekp'a's goal was to demonstrate how the subitist "questioning meditation" (K. kanhwa Sŏn; C. KANHUA CHAN) that became emblematic of both the Linji zong and the Korean Sŏn tradition after Chinul could be reconciled with Korean Buddhism's preferred soteriological schema of moderate subitism. By contrast, Ch'oŭi was more concerned with exploring deeper levels of accommodation between Sŏn practice and Buddhist doctrinal teachings (KYO), by demonstrating the fundamental unity of these two major strands of the religion. Their respective positions set the stage for subsequent debates during the late Chosŏn dynasty over whether Korean Buddhism was an exclusively Sŏn, or a broader ecumenical, tradition, an identity debate that continues into the present day. Kŭngsŏn's many writings also include the *Susŏn kyŏlsamun*, *T'aegoamga kwasŏk*, *Sikchisŏl*, *Ojong kangyo sagi*, *Sŏnyo ki*, and *Chakpŏp kwigam*.

**Paek Yongsŏng**. (K) (白龍城). See YONGSŎNG CHINJONG.

**Pagan**. (Bagan). Capital of the first Burmese (Myanmar) empire (1044–c. 1287), located near the confluence of the Irrawaddy (Ayeyarwady) and Chindwin rivers in the middle of Burma's dry zone. The center of a classic hydraulic civilization, Pagan supported a large population of peasant farmers, specialized laborers, and religious and political elites through maintenance of elaborate irrigation works in nearby Kyaukse. Also known as Arimaddanapura, or "Crusher of Enemies," Pagan began as a cluster of nineteen villages that coalesced into a fortified city-state by the ninth century. Pagan rose in importance in the vacuum left by the collapse of the Pyu kingdom of Śrīkṣetra, which succumbed to military pressure from Nanchao in 832 CE. Invigorated by the cultural and technological advancements brought by Pyu refugees, Pagan emerged as an empire in the eleventh century under the military leadership of King ANAWRAHTA (r. 1044–1077), who united Burma for the first time. His domain extended from the borders of Nanchao in the north to the maritime regions of Bassein, Thaton, and the Tenasserim peninsula in the south. Later chronicles credit Anawrahta with adopting THERAVĀDA Buddhism as the official religion of his empire, a religion he acquired as war booty from his conquest of the Mon kingdom of Thaton. While details of the account are doubtful, Pagan became a stronghold of the Pāli Buddhist tradition, whence it spread to other parts of Southeast Asia. Anawrahta began an extensive program of temple building that lasted till the Mongol invasion of 1287. Pagan's royalty and aristocracy built thousands of pagodas, temples, monasteries, and libraries within the environs of the city, of which 2,217 monuments survive, scattered across an area of approximately forty square miles. Like the Pyu kingdom before it, Pagan received cultural influences from South India, Bengal, and Sri Lanka, all of which are reflected in varying degrees in the city's architecture and plastic arts. Beginning in the twelfth century, Pagan extended patronage to the reformed Sinhalese Theravāda Buddhism imported from Sri Lanka, which flourished alongside the native "unreformed" Burmese Theravāda tradition until the end of the empire. Under later dynasties, reformed Theravāda Buddhism became the dominant religion of Burma, Thailand, Laos, and Cambodia. Theravāda scholarship flourished at Pagan. Major works of the period include the Pāli grammars *Saddanīti, Suttaniddesa* and *Nyāsa*, and treatises on ABHIDHAMMA such as *Saṅkhepavaṇṇanā, Nāmācāradīpanī, Mātikatthadīpanī, Visuddhimaggagaṇṭhi* and *Abhidhammatthasaṅgahaṭīkā*.

**pagoda**. Portuguese term adapted into English, probably derived from the Sanskrit BHAGAVAT ("blessed," "fortunate") or the Persian but kadah ("idol house"); the term was first used by Portuguese explorers to describe Indian temples in general. The term was subsequently adopted by the British and eventually came to take on the specific meaning of the multistoried tower found in Buddhist monastic complexes, especially those in East Asia. In fact, the "pagoda" is a STŪPA, or reliquary, housing a relic (DHĀTU; ŚARĪRA) of the Buddha or a Buddhist saint. In East Asia, the finial or decorative ornament atop the hemispherical Indian stūpa evolved into a more prominent and elongated form, until the stūpa itself became a tower several stories tall, in some cases each story having it own projecting roof. See also CAITYA.

**paired miracle**. See YAMAKAPRĀTIHĀRYA.

**paiśunya**. (P. pisuṇa; T. phra ma; C. lijianyu; J. rikengo; K. iganŏ 離間語). In Sanskrit, "slander," or "malicious speech" (and sometimes rendered as "backbiting"); one of the ten unwholesome courses of action (daśākuśalakarmapatha; see KARMAPATHA) that lead to suffering in the future; also written as paiśunyavāda (P. pisuṇavācā). These ten unwholesome actions are classified into three negative physical deeds, four negative verbal deeds, and three negative verbal deeds. Slander falls into the second category, together with lying (mṛṣāvāda), offensive or harsh speech (PĀRUṢYA), and frivolous prattle (SAṂBHINNAPRALĀPA). Slander is speech intended to cause dissension and divisiveness between two parties. It has the effect of creating dissension between friends or greater dissension between enemies. It may be motivated by greed, hatred, or ignorance.

**Pak Chungbin**. (朴重彬) (1891–1943). Founder of the Korean new religion of WŎNBULGYO; also known by his cognomen SOT'AESAN. He is said to have begun his quest to discover the fundamental principle of the universe and human life at the age of seven and continued ascetic training for about twenty years. Finally, in 1916 at the age of twenty-six, Sot'aesan is said to have attained a personal enlightenment, which is considered the founding year of his religion. Since Sot'aesan recognized compelling parallels between his own experience and the description of enlightenment in Buddhism, he first called his religious organization the Pulpŏp Yŏn'guhoe (Society for the Study of the BUDDHADHARMA); later, the religion adopted the formal name of Wŏnbulgyo (lit. Consummate Buddhism). He presented his enlightenment, which he symbolized with the "one circle image" (IRWŎNSANG), as the criterion of religious belief and practice by proclaiming the "cardinal tenet of one circle" (irwŏn chongji). Along with organizing his religion's fundamental tenets and building its institutional base, he and his followers also worked to improve the ordinary life of his followers, by establishing thrift and savings institutions and engaging in farming and land reclamation projects. The three foundational religious activities of edification (kyohwa), education (kyoyuk), and public service (chasŏn) continue to be emblematic of Wŏnbulgyo practice. Sot'aesan published in 1943 the *Wŏnbulgyo chŏngjŏn* ("Principal Book of Wŏn Buddhism"), a primer of the basic tenets of Wŏnbulgyo, which is one of the two representative scriptures of the religion, along with the *Taejonggyŏng* ("Discourses of the Founding Master"), the dialogues and teachings of Sot'aesan, published in 1962 by his successor Chŏngsan Song Kyu (1900–1962). Sot'aesan died in 1943 at the age of fifty-three, after delivering his last lecture, entitled "The Truth of Birth and Death" (Saengsa ŭi chilli).

**pakṣa**. (T. phyogs). In Sanskrit, "side" or "class"; a technical term in in Buddhist logic (HETUVIDYĀ) used to designate the "logical subject." Pakṣa is related to two other terms, SAPAKṢA (similar instance), and VIPAKṢA (dissimilar instance): for example, in the syllogism (PRAYOGA) "sound is impermanent because it is produced," sound is the pakṣa, or logical subject; a pot is sapakṣa (a similar instance or in the similar class), and space is vipakṣa (a dissimilar instance or in the dissimilar class). The word is also found in a number of compounds in its basic denotation of side or class, e.g. PRATIPAKṢA, PAKṢADHARMA, bodhipakṣa (see BODHIPĀKṢIKADHARMA). See also PRAYOGA.

**pakṣadharma**. (T. phyogs chos; C. zongfa; J. shūhō/shūbō; K. chongpŏp 宗法). In Sanskrit, lit. "property of the position," a term in Buddhist logic that designates one of the qualities of a correct syllogism (PRAYOGA). A syllogism is composed of three parts, the subject (dharmin), the property being proved (SĀDHYADHARMA), and the reason (HETU or LIṄGA). In the syllogism "Sound is impermanent because of being produced," the subject is sound, the property being proved is impermanence, and the reason is "being produced." In order for the syllogism to be correct, three relations must exist among the three components of the syllogism: (1) the reason must be a property (DHARMA) of the subject, also called the "position" (PAKṢA); (2) there must be a relationship of pervasion (VYĀPTI) between the reason and the property being proved, such that whatever is the reason is necessarily the property being proved; and (3) there must be a relationship of reverse pervasion between the property and the reason such that whatever is not the property is necessarily not the reason. In the example, the syllogism "Sound is impermanent because of being produced" is correct because the reason (being produced) is a quality of the subject (sound), there is pervasion in the sense that whatever is produced is necessarily impermanent, and there is reverse pervasion because whatever is permanent is necessarily not produced. In Tibetan oral debate, the defender of a position is traditionally allowed only three answers to a position stated by the opponent; the position is typically stated in the form of a consequence (PRASAṄGA) rather than a syllogism (prayoga), but the mechanics of the statement are the same. The defender may say, "I accept" ('dod), meaning that he agrees that the property being proved is a property of the subject. The defender may say, "There is no pervasion" (ma khyab), meaning that whatever is the reason is not necessarily the property being proved. Or he may say, "The reason is not established" (rtags ma sgrub), meaning that the reason is not in fact a property of the position.

**P'algwanhoe**. (八關會). In Korean, "Eight-Restrictions Festival," a Korean variant of the pan-Buddhistic BAGUAN ZHAI (eight-restrictions feast). The Korean form is a large winter festival of thanksgiving held over two days during full-moon day of the eleventh month, and has little to do with the baguan zhai's origins in the Buddhist UPOṢADHA observance. The Korean version of this festival was sponsored by the royal court and would begin with the king and his ministers exchanging formal greetings, followed by a series of plays that depicted legends of the Silla dynasty. The festival also propitiated some of the important heavenly deities and autochthonous spirits of the mountains and rivers. Spirits of deceased heroes of the state were also commemorated, a practice that seems to stem from the origins of this festival in an earlier Silla ritual to appease the spirits of fallen warriors. This festival therefore combined various aspects of indigenous Korean cultural practice with an imported Buddhist ritual targeting the laity.

**Pāli**. [alt. Pāḷi]. The term used to designate a dialect of Middle Indo-Aryan, which serves as the canonical language of the THERAVĀDA school of mainstream Buddhism. The term pāli does not, however, appear with this denotation in the Theravāda canon, where instead it refers to a canonical text or passage, in distinction to a commentary (AṬṬHAKATHĀ) on such a passage. By extension, then, in modern usage in both Southeast Asian nations and the West, Pāli has come to designate the language in which those passages and their commentaries are written. According to the tradition, the Buddha spoke Māgadhī, the dialect of the Indian state of MAGADHA. Although no specimens of Māgadhī survive from the period before AŚOKA, linguists have determined that it differed from Pāli. It appears that the Buddha did not teach in Sanskrit but instead spoke in the local dialects of the regions of northern India in which he preached, one dialect of which may have been Māgadhī. It is assumed that, after his death, his various teachings were gathered and then regularized into an ecclesiastical language that could be comprehended and recited by monastic groups across a wide region. It appears that, after the reign of King Aśoka, some Buddhist schools translated the Buddha's teachings into Sanskrit while others used Pāli, but later scholastic Pāli was also influenced by Sanskrit. According to Theravāda tradition, the Buddha's teachings were first recorded in writing in Pāli, in Sri Lanka rather than India, at the end the first century BCE. Although these texts do not survive, scholars speculate that the Pāli used in those recensions was generally equivalent to what is used in the canon as it is preserved today. Later Pāli incorporates variant vocabulary that derives in part from the local language—thus, for example, Pāli texts composed in Thailand often show the influence of Thai vernacular. There is no single script for Pāli, with the local script, including, for example, Old Mon, Khmer, Sinhalese, Burmese, Thai, and now Romanization, being employed to write the language.

**Pali Text Society**. An organization founded in 1881 by the British PĀLI specialist THOMAS WILLIAM RHYS DAVIDS (1843–1922), which, according to Rhys Davids' mission statement, sought "to foster and promote the study of Pali texts." The Pali Text Society (PTS) was one response to Buddhism's growing popularity in the West in the mid- to late-nineteenth century, and the society played an essential role in sponsoring both the production of critical editions of Pāli texts and their translation into English. With the help of scholars around the world, the PTS published critical, Romanized editions of most of the Pāli Canon over the first three decades of its existence; this massive project was followed with editions of important commentarial literature and an English translation series. The PTS also started the *Journal of the Pali Text Society*, which continues to publish articles on both Pāli Buddhism and broader topics in Buddhist Studies. The group also published primers for learning the Pāli language and such important reference works as the Society's *Pali-English Dictionary*, begun by Rhys Davids and finished by his student William Stede, which is now available in a searchable electronic format online. By the time of Rhys Davids' death in 1922, the PTS had published almost thirty thousand pages of Romanized and translated Pāli materials, as well as a host of articles and essays written by Western scholars. Over the years, presidents of the PTS have included such distinguished Pāli scholars as CAROLINE A. F. RHYS DAVIDS (1858–1942), ISALINE BLEW HORNER, and K. R. Norman. In 1994, the PTS began the Fragile Palm Leaves project to collect, identify, catalogue, preserve, and copy a number of rare Pāli manuscripts that survive in the Southeast Asian Buddhist traditions.

**Pallava dynasty**. A line of hereditary rulers who governed the southeastern coast of India from their capital Kāñcī (or Kāñcīpuram) from the fourth through the ninth centuries CE. The Pallavas maintained important maritime trade links with Sri Lanka and Southeast Asia and were strong patrons of the JAINA religion through the sixth century, after which they shifted their allegiance to Śaivism. The Pallava kings were patrons of the arts, and their kingdom is renowned for its literature, music, painting, sculpture, and architecture. The most notable building of the Pallava period is the sculptured stone Shore Temple at Mahabalipuram dedicated to Śiva. While the capital of an increasingly Hindu-oriented kingdom, Kāñcī remained throughout the Pallava period an important Buddhist center. Its monasteries supported various schools of Buddhism, including STHAVIRANIKĀYA and VĀTSĪPUTRĪYA, and exerted a particularly strong influence on the Buddhism of Śrīkṣetra, the contemporary Pyu kingdom of Burma. Excavations at Pyu sites uncovered numerous Pāli and Sanskrit inscriptions written in Pallava script. The YOGĀCĀRA masters DIGNĀGA and DHARMAPĀLA were from Kāñcī and its environs, and the Chinese pilgrim XUANZANG visited the city in 642 and described a large walled monastery to the south of the city, which contained an Aśokan STŪPA one hundred feet tall, marking the spot where the Buddha had defeated a non-Buddhist (TĪRTHIKA). A formidable military power, the Pallavas were regularly at war with the Chalukyas of Badami. In 897, they fell to the Cōḷas, whose rising empire was to dominate South India for the next several centuries.

**P'alman taejanggyŏng**. (K) (八萬大藏經). In Korean, "The Scriptures of the Great Repository in Eighty Thousand [Xylographs]," the popular name of the second Koryŏ edition of the Buddhist canon (K. taejanggyŏng; C. DAZANGJING), now housed at the monastery of HAEINSA. See KORYŎ TAEJANGGYŎNG.

**Palsim suhaeng chang**. (發心修行章). In Korean, "Arouse Your Mind and Practice," an edifying tract by the Buddhist exegete and propagator WŎNHYO (617–686), which remains one of the most widely read of all Korean Buddhist works. The *Palsim suhaeng chang* is a clarion call to Buddhist practice, which warns about the dangers of desire and the value of studying the dharma. Even those who cannot enter the mountains and cultivate the mind in solitude should still apply themselves to cultivating virtuous courses of action (KUŚALA-KARMAPATHA). The verses end with a lament about the inevitability of death and the need to practice now before age robs people of their vitality. This text exemplifies Wŏnhyo's personal commitment to disseminating Buddhism among the people of Silla Korea and was probably written sometime during his most active period of propagation, perhaps between 677 and 684. During the middle of the Chosŏn dynasty (1392–1910), the *Palsim suhaeng chang* was included in the CH'OBALSIM CHAGYŎNG MUN ("Personal Admonitions to Neophytes Who Have First Aroused Their Minds"), a primer of three short texts used to train Korean postulants (K. haengja; C. XINGZHE) and novices in the basics of Buddhist morality and daily practice.

**pañcabala**. (T. stobs lnga; C. wuli; J. goriki; K. oryŏk 五力). In Sanskrit and Pāli, "five powers," (1) faith (ŚRADDHĀ), (2) effort (VĪRYA), (3) mindfulness (SMṚTI), (4) concentration (SAMĀDHI), and (5) wisdom (PRAJÑĀ). These five are essential to progress on the path, serving as antidotes to unwholesome states of mind, and specifically to the five hindrances (NĪVARAṆA) that obstruct the five factors of meditative absorption (DHYĀNĀṄGA): faith serves as an antidote to ill will (VYĀPĀDA); effort serves as an antidote to sloth and torpor (STYĀNĀ–MIDDHA); mindfulness serves as an antidote to either heedlessness (APRAMĀDA) or sensual desire (KĀMACCHANDA); samādhi serves as an antidote to distraction or restlessness and worry (AUDDHATYA-KAUKṚTYA); and wisdom serves as an antidote to skeptical doubt (VICIKITSĀ). In the SAṂYUTTANIKĀYA, the Buddha explains that faith is faith in the Buddha's enlightenment; effort is effort at the four exertions (to prevent the arising of unwholesome states that have not yet arisen, to abandon unwholesome states that have already arisen, to create wholesome states that have not yet arisen, and to maintain wholesome states that have already arisen); mindfulness is the practice of the four foundations of mindfulness (P. SATIPAṬṬHĀNA, Skt. SMṚTYUPASTĀNA); concentration is achievement of the four dhyānas; and wisdom is discerning the FOUR NOBLE TRUTHS (catvāry āryasatyāni). The five powers constitute five of the thirty-seven aspects of enlightenment (BODHIPĀKṢIKADHARMA). In the PRAJÑĀPĀRAMITĀ literature, they are described as five states achieved on the forbearance (KṢĀNTI) and highest worldly dharmas (LAUKIKĀGRADHARMA) levels of the path of preparation (PRAYOGAMĀRGA; see NIRVEDHABHĀGĪYA). They are preceded on the heat (ŪṢMAN) and peak (MŪRDHAN) levels by the five same factors at a lesser stage of development; there they are called the "five faculties," or "dominants" (PAÑCENDRIYA).

**pañcacakṣus**. (P. pañcacakkhu; T. spyan lnga; C. wuyan; J. gogen; K. oan 五眼). In Sanskrit, "five eyes," referring to five specific sorts of vision. In Pāli texts they are all associated with the vision of a buddha; in MAHĀYĀNA texts, the five eyes open at higher and higher stages of practice; they overlap with the five (or six) superknowledges (ABHIJÑĀ). The MĀṂSACAKṢUS (fleshly eye) is a VIPĀKAPHALA (maturation result) restricted in its range to the sight of the particular human, animal, or deity that possesses it. (In the case of vultures, for example, it is up to a hundred miles or so; in the case of deities it may be the entire cosmos.) The DIVYACAKṢUS (heavenly eye) sees the death and rebirth of all beings; the PRAJÑĀCAKṢUS (wisdom eye) knows all conditioned (SAṂSKṚTA) and unconditioned (ASAṂSKṚTA) dharmas and is free from all projections; the DHARMACAKṢUS (dharma eye) knows the attainments of all noble persons, from stream-enterer (SROTAĀPANNA) up to buddha; and the BUDDHACAKṢUS (buddha eye) sees all dharmas in the full awakening of final enlightenment. In place of dharmacakṣus, Pāli lists have the samantacakkhu (all-seeing eye).

**pañcagati**. (T. 'gro ba lnga; C. wudao/wuqu; J. godō/goshu; K. odo/och'wi 五道/五趣). In Sanskrit, the "five destinies" or places of rebirth in SAṂSĀRA; in descending order: divinities (DEVA), humans (MANUṢYA), animals (TIRYAK), ghosts (PRETA), and hell denizens (NĀRAKA). In other expositions of the places of rebirth, a sixth is often added, that of the ASURA, or demigods. See GATI.

**pañcajina**. (T. rgyal ba lnga; C. wuzhi rulai; J. gochi nyorai; K. oji yŏrae 五智如來). In Sanskrit, "five conquerors," a synonym for the PAÑCATATHĀGATA, viz. VAIROCANA, AKṢOBHYA, RATNASAMBHAVA, AMITĀBHA, and AMOGHASIDDHI.

**pañcajñāna**. (T. ye shes lnga; C. wuzhi; J. gochi; K. oji 五智). In Sanskrit, "five wisdoms," "five knowledges"; five aspects of the perfect enlightenment (BODHI) of the buddhas, according to the MAHĀYĀNA tradition. They are (1) the wisdom of the DHARMADHĀTU (DHARMADHĀTUJÑĀNA), (2) the mirrorlike wisdom (ĀDARŚAJÑĀNA), (3) the wisdom of equality or impartiality (SAMATĀJÑĀNA), (4) the wisdom of specific knowledge (PRATYAVEKṢAṆAJÑĀNA), and (5) the wisdom of accomplishing what was to be done (KṚTYĀNUṢṬHĀNAJÑĀNA). They are important especially in YOGĀCĀRA, where it is said, for example, that the foundational storehouse consciousness (ĀLAYAVIJÑĀNA) is transformed into the mirrorlike wisdom, and the afflicted mind (KLIṢṬAMANAS) is transformed into the wisdom of equality. In tantric Buddhism, the five wisdoms are associated with the five buddhas (PAÑCATATHĀGATA): VAIROCANA, AKṢOBHYA, RATNASAMBHAVA, AMITĀBHA, and AMOGHASIDDHI, respectively. It is also said that, through the practice of the tantric path, the five KLEŚAS of delusion or obscuration (MOHA), hatred (DVEṢA), pride (MĀNA), desire (RĀGA), and jealousy (ĪRṢYĀ) are transformed into the five wisdoms in the order listed above.

**pañcakāmaguṇa**. (T. 'dod yon sna lnga; C. wumiaoyu; J. gomyōyoku; K. omyoyok 五妙欲). In Sanskrit and Pāli, the "five strands of desire," the five qualities of the sensuous realm (KĀMADHĀTU): viz., pleasing visual objects, sounds, fragrances, tastes, and tangible objects. It is through attachment to these five that beings are reborn in the sensuous realm and it is in turn by giving up these attachments that beings are able to develop meditative absorption (DHYĀNA) and be reborn in the subtle-materiality realm (RŪPADHĀTU) and the immaterial realm (ĀRŪPYADHĀTU).

**pañcakaṣāya**. (T. snyigs ma lnga; C. wuzhuo; J. gojoku; K. ot'ak 五濁). In Sanskrit, lit. "five turbidities," the "five degenerations" that are said to be signs of the degenerate age of the dharma (SADDHARMAVIPRALOPA). These five are said to mark the period in the cosmic cycle when the human life span is less than one hundred years and more than ten years. The five are (1) degeneration of life span (āyuḥkaṣāya) because the life span is short during this period; (2) degeneration of views (dṛṣṭikaṣāya) because wrong views (DṚṢṬI) are prevalent; (3) degeneration of afflictions (kleśakaṣāya) because the afflictions (KLEŚA) become worse; (4) degeneration of sentient beings (sattvakaṣāya) because those beings are mentally and physically inferior; and (5) degeneration of the eon (kalpakaṣāya) because the world and environment worsen. A buddha does not appear in the world during a period marked by the five degenerations.

**pañcakrama**. (T. rim lnga; C. wucidi; J. goshidai; K. och'aje 五次第). In Sanskrit, "five stages," the five stages of the completion stage (NIṢPANNAKRAMA) of the ANUTTARAYOGATANTRA path according to the GUHYASAMĀJATANTRA. The five stages are (1) vajra repetition (vajrājāpa), (2) purification of consciousness (cittaviśuddhi), (3) self-empowerment (svādhiṣṭhāna), (4) enlightenment (abhisaṃbodhi), and (5) union (yuganaddha). ¶ *Pañcakrama* is also the title of a text attributed to NĀGĀRJUNA on the five stages according to the *Guhyasamājatantra*. Scholars attribute this to the "tantric Nāgārjuna," and not to the MADHYAMAKA master, although, according to the Tibetan tradition, Nāgārjuna lived for six hundred years and thus composed works on tantra. Together with ĀRYADEVA's commentary, the *Caryāmelāpakapradīpa*, the pañcakrama provides one of the most influential interpretive systems for an anuttarayogatantra cycle.

**pañcakula**. (T. rigs lnga; C. wubu; J. gobu; K. obu 五部). In Sanskrit, "five lineages" or "five families"; referring to the five buddha families of tantric Buddhism. The five are the TATHĀGATA, VAJRA, PADMA, RATNA, and KARMAN families. The concept of buddha families began to be formulated with the onset of the MAHĀYĀNA, likely rooted in earlier Buddhist tendencies to divide practitioners, scripture, deities, and the like into different "families" (GOTRA or KULA). One of the earliest expressions of this was the TRIKULA system, in which VAJRASATTVA is the buddha of VAJRAKULA, VAIROCANA belongs to the TATHĀGATAKULA, and AVALOKITEŚVARA belongs to the PADMAKULA. In the fivefold system, VAIROCANA, AKṢOBHYA,

AMITĀBHA, RATNASAMBHAVA, and AMOGHASIDDHI are the buddhas of the tathāgata, vajra, padma, ratna and karman families, respectively. The five buddhas were seen as DHARMAKĀYA buddhas, with the number five providing a number of homologies, including with the five aggregates, the five poisons, the five wisdoms, the five colors, and the five elements. The number five was also important for the MAṆḌALA, with one buddha holding the central position, and the other four in the cardinal directions.

**pañcamārga**. (T. lam lnga; C. wuwei; J. goi; K. owi 五位). In Sanskrit, "five paths," the most common description of the path to enlightenment in Sanskrit Buddhism: (1) the path of accumulation (SAṂBHĀRAMĀRGA), (2) the path of preparation (PRAYOGAMĀRGA), (3) the path of vision (DARŚANAMĀRGA), (4) the path of cultivation (BHĀVANĀMĀRGA), and (5) the adept path, lit., "the path where there is nothing more to learn" (AŚAIKṢAMĀRGA). These five paths are progressive, moving the practitioner sequentially from ordinary existence towards enlightenment and complete liberation from suffering. This system is elaborated especially in SARVĀSTIVĀDA ABHIDHARMA materials, as well as in the YOGĀCĀRA school of the MAHĀYĀNA. Depending on the source in which it is discussed, the pañcamārga can therefore be deployed to describe the spiritual development culminating in the rank of ARHAT or culminating in the rank of buddha. The general features of each of the five stages are as follows. ¶ The first is the "path of accumulation" or "equipment" (saṃbhāramārga), wherein the practitioner develops a small degree of three prerequisite qualities for spiritual advancement: morality (ŚĪLA) by way of the basic precepts, merit (PUṆYA) by way of veneration, and concentration (SAMĀDHI). The path of accumulation marks the beginning of the religious life. ¶ In the second "path of preparation" (prayogamārga), the practitioner continues to cultivate those qualities developed in the first path, but also undertakes a more stringent cultivation of concentration (samādhi) through the practice of calmness (ŚAMATHA); he also begins the cultivation of wisdom (PRAJÑĀ) through the practice of insight (VIPAŚYANĀ). ¶ With the third path, the "path of vision" (darśanamārga), the practitioner comes to a direct perception of the true nature of reality as it is. This reality may be described in terms of the FOUR NOBLE TRUTHS (catvāry āryasatyāni) and/or emptiness (ŚŪNYATĀ). In the Yogācāra school, this path is understood as the realization that subject and object derive from the same source and a subsequent perception of phenomenal objects without the intervention of conventional labels. The darśanamārga is of particular importance because it typically marks the end of the mundane path of training and the beginning of the supramundane path of sanctity; thus, it is upon entering the path of vision that one becomes a noble person (ĀRYA). In abhidharma models, the path of vision corresponds to the stage of stream-entry (SROTAĀPANNA); in later Mahāyāna models, attainment of this path marks the first stage (BHŪMI) of the bodhisattva path. ¶ The fourth path, the "path of cultivation" or "development" (bhāvanāmārga), involves the reinforcement and deepening of the insights developed in the path of vision. This cultivation is accomplished by advanced stages of meditation, through which one eliminates the most subtle and deep-rooted afflictions (KLEŚA). The various schools delineate the meditative practices involved in this path in a variety of ways. The ABHIDHARMASAMUCCAYA, for example, schematizes this path both in terms of the nature or object of the meditation and in terms of the type of affliction that is abandoned during practice. ¶ Finally, the fifth stage, the adept path, lit., the "path where there is nothing more to learn" or the "path where no further training is necessary" (aśaikṣamārga), is synonymous with the soteriological goal, whether that is the state of an arhat or a buddha. With the consummation of the path of cultivation, the adept achieves the "adamantine-like concentration" (VAJROPAMASAMĀDHI), which leads to the permanent destruction of even the subtlest and most persistent of the ten fetters (SAṂYOJANA), resulting in the "knowledge of cessation" (KṢAYAJÑĀNA) and in some presentations an accompanying "knowledge of nonproduction" (ANUTPĀDAJÑĀNA), viz., the knowledges that the fetters were destroyed and could never again recur. With the attainment of this path, the practitioner has nothing more he needs to learn and is freed from the possibility of any further rebirth due to the causal force of KARMAN. This final path is also sometimes referred to as the NIṢṬHĀMĀRGA, or "path of completion." All those proceeding to a state of liberation (VIMOKṢA), whether as an arhat or as a buddha, are said to traverse these five paths. See also ĀNANTARYAMĀRGA; VIMOKṢAMĀRGA.

**pañcāmṛta**. (T. bdud rtsi lnga). In Sanskrit, the "five ambrosias," one of the more graphic examples of the inversion of purity and pollution in the Buddhist TANTRAs. The five ambrosias are feces, urine, semen, menstrual blood, and marrow. In the ANUTTARAYOGATANTRAs, it is said that an advanced YOGIN is able to transform these five polluting substances into five types of ambrosia, which represent the five buddhas (PAÑCATATHĀGATA): VAIROCANA, AKṢOBHYA, AMITĀBHA, RATNASAMBHAVA, and AMOGHASIDDHI. Once purified, the five ambrosias can then be ingested as a form of worshipping the five buddhas and as a means of speeding the attainment of the five wisdoms (PAÑCAJÑĀNA): (1) the wisdom of the DHARMADHĀTU (DHARMADHĀTUJÑĀNA), (2) the mirrorlike wisdom (ĀDARŚAJÑĀNA), (3) the wisdom of equality (SAMATĀJÑĀNA), (4) the wisdom of specific knowledge (PRATYAVEKṢAṆĀJÑĀNA), and (5) the wisdom of accomplishing activities (KṚTYĀNUṢṬHĀNAJÑĀNA).

**pañcānantarya**. (P. pañcānantariya; T. mtsham med lnga; C. wu wujian ye; J. gomukengō; K. o muganŏp 五無間業). In Buddhist Hybrid Sanskrit, "five acts of immediate consequence" (ĀNANTARYAKARMAN) or "five great misdeeds," the worst moral offenses that one can commit. The lists vary slightly from source to source, but typically include: (1) patricide, (2) matricide, (3) killing an ARHAT, (4) spilling the blood of a buddha, and (5) causing schism in the monastic community (SAṂGHABHEDA). Despite whatever wholesome actions one may perform afterwards, after death, these deeds result in the "immediate retribution" of rebirth in the AVĪCI hell. In the SĀMAÑÑAPHALASUTTA of the Pāli canon, King Ajātasattu (AJĀTAŚATRU) admits to killing his father, the former king BIMBISĀRA. The Buddha remarks that this action is what keeps King Ajātasattu from fully realizing the fruits of hearing the DHARMA. However, the most notorious of those who have committed these actions is DEVADATTA, the Buddha's own cousin, who is infamous for attempting to kill the Buddha (and in one case wounding him), murdering the arhat UTPALAVARṆĀ, and then causing a schism in the saṃgha. As a result of these deeds, the earth opened up and Devadatta fell into AVĪCI hell, where he is said to remain for one hundred thousand eons.

**pañcaniyata**. (T. nges pa lnga; C. wu jueding; J. goketsujō; K. o kyŏlchŏng 五決定). In Sanskrit, the "five certainties," five qualities describing a buddha's enjoyment body (SAṂBHOGAKĀYA), the body that appears in an ideal realm and is visible to BODHISATTVAS. The order and detail of these characteristics vary slightly from source to source. Generally, the enjoyment body will appear (1) as a definite body, adorned with the thirty-two major marks and the eighty minor marks of a great man (MAHĀPURUṢALAKṢAṆA); (2) in a definite place, such as the heavenly AKANIṢṬHA realm; (3) with a definite retinue, viz. bodhisattvas who have achieved the first stage (BHŪMI) or above or, according to some sources, the tenth stage; (4) expounding a definite teaching, the doctrines of the MAHĀYĀNA; and (5) in a definite time, until the end of the SAṂSĀRA.

**pañcāntaradhānāni**. (P). See ANTARADHĀNA.

**Pañcappakaraṇaṭṭhakathā**. In Pāli, "Commentary on the Five Books," a voluminous Pāli commentary attributed to BUDDHAGHOSA on the last five books of the ABHIDHAMMAPIṬAKA: the DHĀTUKATHĀ, PUGGALAPAÑÑATTI, KATHĀVATTHU, YAMAKA, and PAṬṬHĀNA. Thus Buddhaghosa produced a commentary for each of the seven books of the Pāli abhidhammapiṭaka—the AṬṬHASĀLINĪ, a commentary on the DHAMMASAṄGAṆI, the SAMMOHAVINODANĪ, a commentary on the VIBHAṄGA, and this PAÑCAPPAKARAṆAṬṬHAKATHĀ. The section of the *Pañcappakaraṇaṭṭhakathā* that comments on the *Dhātukathā*—called the *Dhātukathāṭṭhakathā*—contains fourteen divisions and offers a detailed analysis of such doctrinal categories as ĀYATANA, SKANDHA, and DHĀTU. The commentary that deals with the *Kathāvatthu* is of particular interest, because it identifies the specific mainstream Buddhist schools that hold the various wrong types of wrong views that are refuted in the *Kathāvatthu*. The commentary begins with an account of the eighteen MAINSTREAM BUDDHIST SCHOOLS that arose prior to the third Buddhist council (see COUNCIL, THIRD), as well six additional schools. The section on the *Paṭṭhāna*—called the *Paṭṭhānapakaraṇaṭṭhakathā*—may have been written by a monk named Cullabuddhaghosa at the request of Buddhaghosa. Like other Pāli commentaries, this commentary also calls itself an "Exposition on the Highest Matter" (P. *Paramatthadīpanī*); however, this title is very rarely used for the work, since there is a commentary by DHAMMAPĀLA on the CARIYĀPIṬAKA written around the same time that is also called the *Paramatthadīpanī*.

**pañcasarvatraga**. (S). See SARVATRAGA.

**pañcaśīla**. (P. pañcasīla; T. bslab pa lnga; C. wujie; J. gokai; K. ogye 五戒). In Sanskrit, the "five precepts," five rules of conduct or "steps in training" (ŚIKṢĀPADA) that form the foundation for Buddhist morality (ŚĪLA) for both lay and monastic followers. The five are (1) to abstain from killing living creatures (usually interpreted to mean not killing human beings); (2) to abstain from taking what is not given; (3) to abstain from engaging in sexual misconduct; (4) to abstain from lying (commonly defined as not to lie about the possession of high states of attainment or superhuman powers); and (5) to abstain from consuming intoxicants that cause heedlessness (PRAMĀDA). These rules are commonly administered as part of the ceremony of going for refuge (ŚARAṆA), which is the formal acknowledgment of becoming an adherent of Buddhism. Each of these precepts is administered in the formula, "I undertake the training rule (śikṣāpada) to abstain from killing living creatures," etc. The precepts are regarded as steps in training that are useful in prompting virtuous actions (KUŚALAKARMAN), in restraining unvirtuous deeds of body and speech, and in correcting the intention (CETANĀ) that prompts action. It is generally understood that the practitioner must become adept in maintaining the precepts before he can effectively engage in the cultivation of concentration (SAMĀDHI) and wisdom (PRAJÑĀ), the next two stages in the threefold training (TRIŚIKṢĀ). Taking the precepts is considered karmically efficacious, since an act will be more virtuous if one first takes a vow to desist from an unvirtuous activity and then does so, rather than desisting from the activity without having first taken such a vow. ¶ These five precepts also figure in other important moral formulas. Monks and nuns take the five precepts (with the third precept defined as celibacy), with violation of the first four bringing "defeat" (PĀRĀJIKA) and, in some traditions, expulsion from the SAṂGHA. These five precepts (with celibacy as the third) are augmented by three additional precepts to form a short-term code observed by lay disciples fortnightly on the new moon and full moon days (UPOṢADHA; P. uposatha); this code is known as the eight "retreat precepts" (S. upoṣadhaśīla; P. uposathasīla), a sort of temporary renunciation (see AṢṬĀṄGASAMANVĀGATAṂ UPAVĀSAṂ; BAGUAN ZHAI) that essentially turns the layperson into a monk for that day. The three additional precepts are (6) not to eat at an inappropriate time (generally interpreted to mean between noon and the following dawn); (7) not to dance, sing, play music, attend performances, or adorn one's body with garlands, perfumes, or cosmetics; and (8) not to sleep on high or luxurious beds. The same five precepts (with the third again defined as celibacy) are augmented by five additional rules that are kept by novice monks (ŚRĀMAṆERA) and nuns (ŚRĀMAṆERIKĀ) to constitute the "ten precepts" (DAŚAŚĪLA). The additional five are (6) not to eat at an inappropriate time; (7) not to dance, sing, play music, or attend performances; (8) not to adorn one's body with garlands, perfumes, and cosmetics; (9) not to sleep on high or luxurious beds; (10) not to handle gold and silver, viz. money. Fully ordained monks (BHIKṢU) and nuns (BHIKṢUṆĪ) observe in turn hundreds of specific training rules, all putatively promulgated by the Buddha himself, which are set out in great detail in the PRĀTIMOKṢA of various VINAYA traditions. See also ŚĪLA.

**pañcaskandha**. (P. pañcakhandha; T. phung po lnga; C. wuyun; J. goun; K. oon 五蘊). The "five aggregates" that are the objects of clinging. See SKANDHA.

**Pañcaskandhaprakaraṇa**. (T. Phung po lnga'i rab tu byed pa; C. Dasheng wuyun lun; J. Daijō gounron; K. Taesŭng oon non 大乘五蘊論). In Sanskrit, "Explanation of the Five Aggregates," the title of two different works. The earliest *Pañcaskandhaprakaraṇa* is a short work, now lost in the original Sanskrit, by the fourth or fifth century CE Indian master VASUBANDHU. According to tradition, Vasubandhu had both a "HĪNAYĀNA" and a MAHĀYĀNA period, beginning as an adherent of the SAUTRĀNTIKA school of the mainstream Buddhist tradition, before being converted to the Mahāyāna by his half brother ASAṄGA. Although his presentation of the five aggregates bears many similarities to that in his ABHIDHARMAKOŚABHĀṢYA (the chief work of his so-called hīnayāna period), this work derives from his Mahāyāna period; it begins with a homage to the bodhisattva MAÑJUŚRĪ and mentions the ĀLAYAVIJÑĀNA. In this work, Vasubandhu seems to be reworking the presentation of the five aggregates found in Asaṅga's ABHIDHARMASAMUCCAYA; he also sets forth and criticizes the positions of the MAHĪŚĀSAKA, the school in which Asaṅga was originally trained. ¶ There is also a *Pañcaskandhaprakaraṇa* by the seventh-century Indian MADHYAMAKA master CANDRAKĪRTI, discussing the factors (DHARMA) categorized under the headings of the five SKANDHA, the twelve ĀYATANA, and the eighteen DHĀTU.

**pañcatathāgata**. (T. de bzhin gshegs pa lnga; C. wuzhi rulai/wu fo; J. gochi nyorai/gobutsu; K. ojiyŏrae/obul 五智如來/五佛). In Sanskrit, "five tathāgatas," a grouping of five buddhas important in tantric Buddhism. They are also known as the "five conquerors" (PAÑCAJINA) and sometimes in English as the "five DHYĀNI BUDDHAS" (although the term dhyāni buddha is a Western neologism that does not appear in Buddhist texts). The members of the group vary across tantric texts and traditions, but the most common grouping is that derived from the SARVATATHĀGATATATTVASAṂGRAHA. They are VAIROCANA, AKṢOBHYA, AMITĀBHA, RATNASAMBHAVA, and AMOGHASIDDHI, the buddhas of the TATHĀGATAKULA, VAJRAKULA, PADMAKULA, RATNAKULA, and KARMAKULA families, respectively. The concept of buddha families began to be formulated with the rise of the MAHĀYĀNA, rooted in earlier Buddhist tendencies to divide practitioners, scripture, deities, and the like into different "families" (GOTRA or KULA). One of the earliest expressions of such a grouping was the trikula system, in which VAJRASATTVA is the buddha of the vajrakula, Vairocana belongs to the tathāgatakula, and AVALOKITEŚVARA belongs to the padmakula. The five buddhas were seen as DHARMAKĀYA buddhas, with the number five providing a number of possible homologies, including the five aggregates, the five poisons, the five wisdoms, the five colors, and the five elements. The number five was also important for the MAṆḌALA, with one buddha holding the central position, the other four in the cardinal directions. The five tathāgatas were also integrated into the separate and later concept of the ĀDIBUDDHA, or "primordial buddha," which would become especially important in Newari Buddhism.

**pañcavargika**. (P. pañcavaggiyā; T. lnga sde; C. wuqun [biqiu]; J. gogun [biku]; K. ogun [pigu] 五群[比丘]). In Sanskrit, the "group of five"; the five ascetics who practiced austerities with the BODHISATTVA prior to his enlightenment and to whom the Buddha preached his first sermon after his enlightenment, thus becoming the Buddha's first disciples. They are ĀJÑĀTAKAUṆḌIYA (or Kauṇḍinya), AŚVAJIT, VĀṢPA, MAHĀNĀMAN, and BHADRIKA. According to the Pāli account (where they are called Aññātakoṇḍañña or Koṇḍañña, Assaji, Vappa, Mahānāma, and Bhaddiya), Koṇḍañña had been present as one of the eight brāhmaṇas who attended the infant's naming ceremony, during which the prophesy was made that the prince would one day become either a wheel-turning monarch (P. cakkavatti, S. CAKRAVARTIN) or a buddha. The other four ascetics were sons of four of the other brāhmaṇas in attendance at the naming ceremony. When the prince gave up his practice of austerities and accepted a meal, the five ascetics abandoned him in disgust. After his enlightenment, the Buddha surveyed the world with his divine eye (S. DIVYACAKṢUS) and surmised that, of all people then alive, these five ascetics were most likely to understand the profundity of his message. When he first approached them, they refused to recognize him, but the power of his charisma was such that they felt compelled to show him the honor due a teacher. He preached to them two important discourses, the DHAMMACAKKAPPAVATTANASUTTA, in which he explained the FOUR NOBLE TRUTHS (S. catvāry āryasatyāni), and the ANATTALAKKHAṆASUTTA (S. *Anātmalakṣaṇasūtra*), in which he explained the doctrine of nonself (P. anatta, S. ANĀTMAN). Upon hearing and comprehending the first sermon, the five ascetics attained the dhammacakku (S. DHARMACAKṢUS) or the "dhamma eye," an attainment equated in the Pāli canon with that of the stream-enterer (P. sotāpanna, S. SROTAĀPANNA). The five then requested to be accepted as the Buddha's disciples and were ordained as the first Buddhist monks (P. bhikkhu, S. BHIKṢU), using the informal EHIBHIKṢUKĀ (P. ehi bhikkhu), or "come, monk," formula. Upon hearing the second sermon, the five were completely freed of the contaminants (P. āsava, S. ĀSRAVA), becoming thereby arahants (ARHAT) freed from the prospect of any further rebirth. With this experience, there were then six arahants in the world, including the Buddha. The Pāli story of the conversion of the group of five is recounted in the MAHĀVAGGA section of the Pāli VINAYAPIṬAKA. The group of five appears often in JĀTAKA stories of the previous lives of the Buddha, indicating their long karmic connections to him, which result in their remarkable fortune at being the first to hear the Buddha preach the dharma. In Sanskrit materials, this group of five is usually known as the bhadravargīya, or "auspicious group."

**pañcavidyā**. (T. rig gnas che ba lnga; C. wuming; J. gomyō; K. omyŏng 五明). In Sanskrit, the "five sciences"; the five traditional sciences of ancient India, which a bodhisattva is said to have mastery of; also known as the pañcavidyāsthāna. These are śabda, which includes grammar and composition; hetu or logic; cikitsā or medicine; śilpakarma, which includes the manual arts; and adhyātmavidyā, the "inner knowledge," which in the case of Buddhism was said to be knowledge of the TRIPIṬAKA and the twelve categories (AṄGA) of the word of the Buddha (BUDDHAVACANA).

**Pañcaviṃśatisāhasrikāprajñāpāramitāsūtra**. (T. Shes rab kyi pha rol tu phyin pa stong phrag nyi shu lnga pa; C. Mohe bore boluomi jing; J. Maka hannya haramitsukyō; K. Maha panya paramil kyŏng 摩訶般若波羅蜜經). In Sanskrit, "Perfection of Wisdom in Twenty-five Thousand Lines," one of the three most important of the "large" PRAJÑĀPĀRAMITĀ sūtras, together with the ŚATASĀHASRIKĀPRAJÑĀPĀRAMITĀSŪTRA ("Perfection of Wisdom in One-Hundred Thousand Lines") and the AṢṬASĀHASRIKĀPRAJÑĀPĀRAMITĀSŪTRA ("Perfection of Wisdom in Eight Thousand Lines"). The early prajñāpāramitā sūtras were named based upon their length. The scholarly consensus is that the earliest of the sūtras of this genre was the version in eight thousand lines. Although it is not strictly the case that the two larger sūtras are simply prolix expansions of the shorter sūtra, there is considerable repetition among the texts, with the larger sūtras increasing the number of categories to which various qualifications, including negations, were made. The prajñāpāramitā sūtras are said to have an explicit meaning and a hidden meaning: the former is the doctrine of emptiness (ŚŪNYATĀ), the latter is the structure of the bodhisattva's path (MĀRGA) to this enlightenment. This structure is set forth in the ABHISAMAYĀLAṂKĀRA attributed to MAITREYANĀTHA, one of the most widely commented upon of all Mahāyāna ŚĀSTRAs in India. Although the text does not explicitly say so, the *Abhisamayālaṃkāra* is said to derive its categories from the *Pañcaviṃśatisāhasrikā*. Ārya VIMUKTISENA, Bhadanta Vimuktisena, and HARIBHADRA each wrote commentaries on the *Abhisamayālaṃkāra*, in which they explicitly connect it with the *Pañcaviṃśatisāhasrikā*. The DAZHIDU LUN is also considered a commentary on this sūtra.

**pañcaviṣaya**. (T. yul lnga; C. wujing; J. gokyō; K. ogyŏng 五境). In Sanskrit, "five objects," the five external physical sensory objects of forms, sounds, odors, tastes, and tangible objects. See VIṢAYA.

**pañcendriya**. (P. pañcindriya; T. dbang po lnga; C. wugen; J. gokon; K. ogŭn 五根). In Sanskrit, the "five [sense] faculties," or "dominants"; the five internal visual, auditory, olfactory, gustatory, and tactile faculties associated with the physical sense organs. In the ABHIDHARMA literature, these faculties are said not to refer to the physical eye, ear, etc., but to subtle matter located in the eye, ear, nose, tongue, and body that provide the physical basis for sense experience. ¶ The pañcendriya are also a soteriological term, referring to five spiritual "dominants" or "faculties" that are crucial to development along the path: faith (ŚRADDHĀ), effort (VĪRYA), mindfulness (SMṚTI), concentration (SAMĀDHI), and wisdom (PRAJÑĀ). These are called the "five powers" (PAÑCABALA) at a higher stage of development. See INDRIYA.

**Paṇ chen Lama**. A Tibetan title given to members of an important line of incarnate lamas (SPRUL SKU), commonly identified as second in stature in Tibet after the DALAI LAMAS. Their seat is BKRA SHIS LHUN PO monastery in Gtsang in western Tibet. Paṇ chen is a common abbreviation for the mixed Sanskrit and Tibetan appellation "paṇḍita chen po" (literally "great scholar"), and is an honorific title granted to scholars of great achievement. It was also used as an epithet for the abbot of Bkra shis lhun po monastery, beginning with its founder and first abbot DGE 'DUN GRUB. The fifth Dalai Lama gave the abbacy of Bkra shis lhun po to his tutor, BLO BZANG CHOS KYI RGYAL MTSHAN. As abbot of the monastery, he was called Paṇ chen, but he came to receive the distinctive title "Paṇ chen Lama" when the fifth Dalai Lama announced that, upon his teacher's death, his teacher would reappear as an identifiable child-successor. Blo bzang chos kyi rgyal mtshan thus had conferred on him the title "Paṇ chen Lama." The Paṇ chen Lama is considered the human incarnation of the buddha AMITĀBHA, while the Dalai Lama is considered the human incarnation of the BODHISATTVA AVALOKITEŚVARA. Blo bzang chos kyi rgyal mtshan is traditionally viewed as the fourth member of the lineage, with his previous incarnations recognized posthumously, beginning with TSONG KHA PA'S disciple MKHAS GRUB DGE LEGS DPAL BZANG PO. For this reason, there is some confusion in the numbering of the lamas of the lineage; Blo bzang chos kyi rgyal mtshan is sometimes referred to as the fourth Paṇ chen Lama, but more commonly in Tibetan sources as the first. Blo bzang dpal ldan ye shes is sometimes referred to as the sixth Paṇ chen Lama, but more commonly in Tibetan sources as the third. (In the discussion below, the higher numerical designation will be employed, since it is used in the contemporary controversy over the identity of the Paṇ chen Lama.) The fifth Dalai Lama apparently hoped that the Dalai Lama and Paṇ chen Lama could alternate as teacher and student in lifetime after lifetime. This plan required, however, that each live a long life, which was not to be the case. Subsequent incarnations were recognized and installed at Bkra shis lhun po and eventually grew to wield considerable religious and political power, at times rivaling that of the Dalai Lama himself. This was particularly true in the nineteenth century, when few Dalai Lamas reached their majority. The sixth Paṇ chen Lama, Blo bzang dpal ldan ye shes (Losang Palden Yeshe, 1738–1780), was a skilled politician who secured Tibet's first relationship with a European power when he befriended George Bogle, British emissary to the East India Company under Warren Hastings. The ninth Paṇ chen Lama (1883–1937) did not enjoy close relations with the thirteenth Dalai Lama; the Dalai Lama felt that the Paṇ chen Lama was too close to both the British and the Chinese. They also disagreed over what taxes the Paṇ chen Lama owed the LHA SA government. The Paṇ chen Lama went to China in 1925, and his supporters became aligned with the nationalist Guomindang party. While in China, he gave teachings and performed rituals, including some intended to repulse the Japanese invaders then on the Chinese mainland. After the death of the thirteenth Dalai Lama, he served in an advisory capacity in the search for the fourteenth Dalai Lama and died shortly thereafter, while en route back to Tibet. His successor, the tenth Paṇ chen Lama 'Phrin las lhun grub chos kyi rgyal mtshan (Trinle Lhündrup Chökyi Gyaltsen, 1938–1989) was selected by the Chinese, with the Lha sa government providing only tacit support. He was drawn into the official Chinese administration as a representative of the Communist party and remained in China when the Dalai Lama fled into exile in 1959. In 1964, he was arrested and imprisoned for his outspoken opposition to the Communist party's harsh policies in Tibet, and was subjected to public humiliation and physical abuse. After fourteen years in prison, he was released in 1978, and played a key role in fostering the cultural reconstruction that helped to reestablish religious life in Tibet. Despite his role in the Communist administration, many Tibetans continue to view his life as a heroic struggle for the cause of liberalization in Tibet. His death led to the recognition of two child incarnations: one, Dge 'dun chos kyi nyi ma (Gendün Chökyi Nyima, b. 1989), chosen by the fourteenth Dalai Lama in exile and favored by the majority of Tibetan people, and another, Rgyal mtshan nor bu (b. 1990), installed by the Chinese government. The disappearance of the Dalai Lama's candidate in China has led to a significant increase in tension between the two factions. The lineage of Paṇ chen Lamas includes:

1. Mkhas grub Dge legs dpal bzang (1385–1438)
2. Bsod nams phyogs kyi glang po (Sönam Chokyi Langpo, 1439–1505)
3. Dben sa pa Blo bzang don grub (Wensapa Losang Döndrup, 1505–1566)

The three above were recognized posthumously.

4. Blo bzang chos kyi rgyal mtshan (1567–1662)
5. Blo bzang ye shes dpal bzang po (Losang Yeshe Palsangpo, 1663–1737)
6. Blo bzang dpal ldan ye shes (Losang Palden Yeshe, 1738–1780)
7. Blo bzang bstan pa'i nyi ma (Losang Tenpe Nyima, 1781–1854)
8. Blo bzang bstan pa'i dbang phyug dpal ldan chos kyi grags pa (Losang Tenpe Wangchuk Palden Chökyi Drakpa), 1855–1882)
9. Blo bzang thub bstan chos kyi nyi ma dge legs rnam rgyal (Losang Tupden Chökyi Nyima Gelek Namgyal, 1883–1937)
10. 'Phrin las lhun grub chos kyi rgyal mtshan (Trinle Lhundrup Chökyi Gyaltsen, 1938–1989)
11. Dge 'dun chos kyi nyi ma (Gendün Chökyi Nyima, b. 1989)

**Pang Hanam**. (K) (方漢岩). See HANAM CHUNGWŎN.

**Pang jushi**. (J. Hō koji; K. Pang kŏsa 龐居士). See PANG YUN.

**Pang jushi yulu**. (J. Hō koji goroku; K. Pang kŏsa ŏrok 龐居士語錄). In Chinese, "The Recorded Sayings of Layman Pang"; the discourse record of the lay Chan adept PANG YUN. See PANG YUN.

**Pang Yun**. (J. Hō On; K. Pang On 龐蘊) (740–808). One of the most famous lay adepts of the CHAN ZONG, commonly known within the tradition as "Layman Pang" (PANG JUSHI); also referred to as "VIMALAKĪRTI of the East" (Dongtu Weimo). PENG SHAOSHENG (1740–1796), in his JUSHI ZHUAN ("Biographies of Lay Buddhists"), lists Pang Yun as one of the three great lay masters (sangong) of Chinese Buddhism, along with LI TONGXUAN (635–730) and LIU CHENGZHI (354–410), praising Pang for his mastery of Chan practice. One of the famous anecdotes regarding Pang is that, in his middle age, he gave his house away to be used for a monastery and discarded all his personal possessions by loading them onto a boat and sinking them in a river. Subsequently, he is said to have earned his livelihood by making and selling bamboo utensils. He is presumed to have carried on religious practices at a hermitage separate from his residence. Pang was father to both a son and a daughter. The daughter, LING ZHAO, who also attained a deep understanding of Chan, seems to have had an especially close spiritual relationship with her father. Pang is presumed to have visited the Chan master SHITOU XIQIAN (710–790) about 785, whom he asked, "What man is it who does not accompany the ten thousand dharmas?" Shitou covered the layman's mouth with his hand and Pang Yun was instantly enlightened. The layman stayed with Shitou until 786, when he traveled to visit MAZU DAOYI (707–786), one of the most influential Chan masters of his time. When the layman asked Mazu the same question he had asked Shitou, Mazu is said to have replied:

"Wait till you've swallowed in one swig all the water of the West River, then I'll tell you," whereupon he attained great enlightenment. After staying with Mazu for two years, Pang Yun is believed to have started pilgrimages around central China, probably writing many verses that are extant now in materials such as the PANG JUSHI YULU ("Recorded Sayings of Layman Pang"), the posthumous records of Pang's later years compiled by his friend the prefect Yu Di. Perhaps the most famous saying attributed to Pang Yun is: "Supernatural powers and marvelous activities are drawing water and carrying firewood." Pang is said to have had a premonition of the time of his death. When he was about to die, he sat up cross-legged in his bed and told his daughter to report to him when it was noon, at which point he would pass away; she looked out and said, "The sun has just reached the zenith, but there is an eclipse." While the layman went out to look at the eclipse, his daughter sat down sat cross-legged on his bed and passed away herself. Seeing this, the layman said, "My daughter has anticipated me." He then postponed his death for seven days and died in the presence of his friend Yu Di, uttering these final words: "Please just regard as empty everything in existence, but beware of presuming that all nonexistence is real. Live comfortably in the world, where all is like shadows and echoes." Records pertaining to Layman Pang are also found in such major Chan texts as BIYAN LU, CHODANG CHIP, ZONGJING LU, and JINGDE CHUANDENG LU.

**panjiao**. (判教). In Chinese, "tenet classifications," "doctrinal taxonomies." See JIAOXIANG PANSHI.

**Paññāsajātaka**. In Pāli, "Fifty Birth Stories," and sometimes referred to in Western scholarship as the "Apocryphal Jātakas"; a collection of fifty JĀTAKA stories that are not included in the canonical jātaka collection of the Pāli TRIPIṬAKA. There are Thai, Cambodian, and Burmese recensions of these stories, the first two of which are quite similar in structure, the last of which differs in the selection and order of the stories. This Burmese (Myanmar) recension of this collection, called the ZIMMÈ PAÑÑĀSA, literally means the "Chiangmai Fifty," suggesting that the provenance for many of these stories may be in the northwest of Thailand near the city of Chiangmai. The dating and authorship are unknown, but the terminus ad quem for the collection is around the fifteenth century. Some of the fifty stories show clear connections to the Pāli jātaka collection; others are more similar to Sanskrit texts. Still other stories seem to have no connection to the available Pāli and Sanskrit literature and may derive from folk traditions; indeed, the grammar and syntax of the stories also seems to suggest local influences.

**Panthaka**. [alt. Mahāpanthaka] (P. Mahāpanthaka; T. Lam chen bstan; C. Bantuojia; J. Hantaka; K. Pant'akka 半託迦). An ARHAT known for his mastery of the four immaterial absorptions (ĀRŪPYADHYĀNA); according to Pāli sources, the Buddha declared him foremost in the ability to manipulate perception (saññāvivaṭṭakusalānaṃ). Panthaka was the elder of two brothers born to a merchant's daughter from RĀJAGṚHA who had eloped with a slave. After she became pregnant, she decided to return home to give birth, but the infant was born along the way. This happened again when she gave birth to her second child. Because both he and his younger brother, CŪḌAPANTHAKA, were born along the side of a road, they were given the names, "Greater" and "Lesser" Roadside. The boys were eventually taken to Rājagṛha and raised by their grandparents, who were devoted to the Buddha. Panthaka often accompanied his grandfather to listen to the Buddha's sermons and was inspired to ordain. He proved to be an able monk, skilled in doctrine, and eventually attained arhatship. He later ordained his younger brother Cūḍapanthaka but was gravely disappointed in his brother's inability to memorize even a single verse of the dharma. He treated Cūḍapanthaka with such contempt that the Buddha intervened on his behalf, giving the younger brother a simple technique by which he too attained arhatship. ¶ Panthaka is also traditionally listed as tenth of the sixteen ARHAT elders (ṢOḌAŚASTHAVIRA), who were charged by the Buddha with protecting his dispensation until the advent of the next buddha, MAITREYA; his younger brother Cūḍapanthaka is the sixteenth on that list. Panthaka resides in the TRĀYASTRIṂŚA heaven (the heaven of the thirty-three devas) with 1,300 disciples. Panthaka was good at arithmetic and an expert in chanting and music. When sitting in meditation, Panthaka often sat in half-lotus posture; and after his finished his sitting, he would raise both his hands and take a deep breath. For this reason, he was given the nickname "the Arhat who Reaches Out His Hands" (Tanshou Luohan). In CHANYUE GUANXIU's standard Chinese depiction, Panthaka has placed his sitting-cloth on a rock, where he sits in meditation, with a sash across his shoulders. Holding a scroll in both hands, he appears to be reading a SŪTRA.

**pāpa**. (T. sdig pa; C. e/zui; J. aku/zai; K. ak/choe 惡/罪). In Sanskrit and Pāli, "transgression"; an unsalutary, unwholesome, or nonvirtuous (AKUŚALA) deed that produces a correspondingly negative effect; thus, any knowingly wrongful, wicked, or immoral act of body, speech, or mind. Equivalent in meaning to AKUŚALAKARMAN, or "unsalutary action," pāpa leads to unfortunate and painful consequences in the form of physical or mental suffering for the agent of the deed, either in this or future lives; it may lead to rebirth as an animal (TIRYAK), ghost (PRETA), or hell denizen (NĀRAKA). Pāpa is the opposite of PUṆYA, meritorious deeds that lead to happiness in this or future lifetimes. The common translation of pāpa as "sin" is misleading because there is no divine being in Buddhism whose commandments can be broken. Rather, painful consequences of unsalutary actions befall the agent, according to the impersonal law of KARMAN and its retribution. According to classical karman theory, a person is literally defiled by the performance of unwholesome deeds and carries that stain until those deeds are either expiated through painful experience, or until the person attains liberation, whereupon the seeds of all former nonvirtuous deeds are destroyed. In practice, however, the Buddhist traditions are replete with practices designed to remove or minimize the effects of past nonvirtuous actions.

**pāpadeśanā**. [alt. pāpaśodhana] (P. pāpadesanā; T. sdig pa bshags pa; C. chanhui; J. sange; K. ch'amhoe 懺悔). In Sanskrit, "confession of transgressions," "atonement"; the confession of unvirtuous deeds, either privately in the presence of a real or visualized representation of a buddha, or communally as part of a confession ceremony, such as the fortnightly monastic confession (S. UPOṢADHA; P. uposatha). Such confession also figures as a standard component in many MAHĀYĀNA and tantric liturgies. The Mahāyāna also deployed a confessional ritual designed for people burdened with heavy karmic obstructions who wished swiftly to attain complete, perfect enlightenment (ANUTTARASAMYAKSAṂBODHI); this ritual involved chanting the names of thirty-five buddhas of the ten directions (daśadigbuddha, see DAŚADIŚ) and making offerings before images of them. Regardless of the setting, the tenor of confession practice is to make public something that has been hidden; there is no tradition in Buddhism of a priest offering absolution of sins. According to standard theory of KARMAN, the seeds of an unsalutary deed can be removed only through suffering the effects of that deed or through destroying the seed through wisdom (PRAJÑĀ). However, there is a general view in the Buddhist ethical systems that the strength of an unwholesome deed, especially one of a less heinous nature, can be diminished through its declaration and revelation.

**Papañcasūdanī**. In Pāli, "Destruction of Obstacles [to Progress]," a commentary on the MAJJHIMANIKĀYA by the fifth-century exegete BUDDHAGHOSA. According to the colophon to the commentary, Buddhaghosa wrote the commentary in response to a request of Buddhamitta, a monk from Mayūrapaṭṭana. The Papañcasūdanī is quoted in Buddhaghosa's commentary to the VINAYAPIṬAKA, the SAMANTAPĀSĀDIKĀ, suggesting that it antedates that work.

**pāpaśodhana**. (S). See PĀPADEŚANĀ.

**Pāpīyāṃs**. (P. Pāpimant; BHS. Pāpīmant; T. Sdig can; C. Mowang [Boxun]; J. Maō [Hajun]; K. Mawang [Pasun] 魔王 [波旬]). An epithet of MĀRA. See NAMUCI.

**pāra**. (T. pha rol; C. bi'an; J. higan; K. p'ian 彼岸). In Sanskrit and Pāli, "distant," "opposite"; often freely rendered into Buddhist languages as "the other shore," a common metaphor for the state of liberation, or NIRVĀṆA. The Buddhist path is often described metaphorically in Buddhist texts as a crossing from the near shore of SAṂSĀRA to the far shore of nirvāṇa, with the DHARMA serving as one's raft or ship. In other imagery, saṃsāra itself is the perilous ocean, and nirvāṇa the safe harbor.

**parach'um**. (바라춤). In Korean, "cymbal dance," a CHAKPŎP ritual dance performed by Buddhist monks during such Korean Buddhist rites as the YŎNGSANJAE, using a cymbal (para). This dance is supposedly performed in veneration of, and as an offering to, the Buddha. One of the types of parach'um is known as "thousand-handed cymbal dance" (ch'ŏnsu para) and is performed while other monks chant in honor of the thousand-armed form of the BODHISATTVA AVALOKITEŚVARA (see SĀHASRABHUJASĀHASRANETRĀVALOKITEŚVARA). This dance is considered to be extremely masculine, owing to its confident and strong motions, and thus is almost always performed by monks. In this dance, an even number of dancers (generally between two and ten), dressed in ceremonial robes with long sleeves, grasp with both hands the two cymbals, which are larger than dinner plates. The dancers raise and lower the cymbals, bringing them clashing together in front of their bodies and over their heads. This sound is intended to lead sentient beings towards the path to buddhahood. The tempo is quicker than that of the butterfly dance (NABICH'UM), and, as the dancers turn, they also manipulate the shiny cymbals so that they flash beautifully.

**paracittajñāna**. [alt. cetoparyāyābhijñāna] (P. cetopariyañāṇa; T. gzhan gyi sems shes pa; C. taxintong; J. tashintsū; K. t'asimt'ong 他心通). In Sanskrit, "knowledge of others' minds"; one of the five mundane (LAUKIKA) "superknowledges" or "supranormal powers" (ABHIJÑĀ) that are gained through refinement of the fourth stage of meditative absorption (DHYĀNA). The sixth "superknowledge," the knowledge of the extinction of the contaminants (ĀSRAVAKṢAYA; P. āsavakhaya) is supramundane (LOKOTTARA). One who has developed paracittajñāna knows when another's mind is greedy or free from greed, hateful or free from hate, deluded or undeluded, constrained or distracted, developed or undeveloped, surpassable or unsurpassable, concentrated or unconcentrated, and freed or unfreed.

**pārājika**. (T. phas pham pa; C. boluoyi; J. harai; K. parai 波羅夷). In Sanskrit and Pāli, "defeat," according to the monastic codes, those misdeeds that entail automatic (and, according to the Pāli recension of the VINAYA, permanent) expulsion from the SAṂGHA and reversion to the laity. There are four pārājika offenses for monks (BHIKṢU): (1) sexual intercourse through any of the orifices, (2) theft, (3) murder or abetting the murder of a human being, and (4) falsely claiming to have attained any degree of enlightenment, or to possess suprahuman powers (uttaramanuṣyadharma). Nuns (BHIKṢUṆĪ) have a list of eight pārājika offenses, which include the above four, plus (5) enjoying physical contact with a male between the collarbone and the knee, (6) concealing the pārājika offense of another nun, (7) becoming the follower of a monk (who is suspended), and (8) possessing eight dispositions tinged with sexuality (which include cases of a lascivious nun rejoicing at the arrival of a lecherous man, asking him to sit down, or stretching her body toward him). In the Pāli VINAYA, a monk or nun who commits a pārājika offense is compared to a person with his or her head cut off, to a withered leaf dropped from a branch, and to a stone split in two, etc., in that they may never return to their former monastic state, and may never again rejoin the saṃgha. Other vinaya traditions, such as the MŪLASARVĀSTIVĀDA, retain some possibility of redemption from this state of "defeat" by continuing to live in the monastery as a "pārājika penitent," or ŚIKṢĀDATTAKA.

**Parākramabāhu I**. [alt. Parakkamabāhu I] (r. 1153–1186). Also known as Sirisaṅghabodhi Parakkamabāhu, a Sinhalese king who abolished the ABHAYAGIRI and JETAVANA fraternities and unified the Sinhalese SAṂGHA under the banner of the MAHĀVIHĀRA fraternity. Emulating the example of King AŚOKA, the king first acquainted himself with the rules and regulations of the order so that he could discriminate between compliance and noncompliance with the monastic code. Monks were summoned to be examined by him and a council of elders. Unworthy monks were expelled and were assigned lucrative positions so that they would not reenter the order. Of the three fraternities, only the Mahāvihāra was judged to be in possession of a valid ordination ritual (UPASAMPADĀ), so monks of the Abhayagiri and Jetavana fraternities were forced to be reordained into the Mahāvihāra fraternity. The CŪLAVAṂSA states that those monks from the Abhayagiri and Jetavana not unfrocked for misconduct were received as novices (P. samaṇera; S. ŚRĀMAṆERA). At the end of the purification movement, in 1165 CE, the king had a committee of elders draw up a new monastic code on the basis of DHAMMAVINAYA, which was called the *Mahā-Parakkamabāhu-Katikāvata*. This law code was promulgated by the king and, citing Aśoka as a precedent, was made binding on the entire Sinhalese saṃgha. The reforms of Parākramabāhu I are recognized as having influenced (directly or indirectly) the Sinhalese fraternities established at PAGAN by Chapada Thera and his associates beginning in 1181 CE, as well as SUKHOTHAI Buddhism (fourteenth–fifteenth century), Mon Buddhism (fourteenth–fifteenth century) and the THUDHAMMA reformation of Burmese Buddhism (late eighteenth century). Later Buddhist historical writings borrowed directly from the *Mahā-Parakkamabāhu-Katikāvata*, including, e.g., *Saddhammasaṅgaha* (fourteenth century) and the KALYĀṆĪ INSCRIPTIONS (fifteenth century).

**Parākramabāhu VI**. [alt. Parakkamabāhu VI] (r. 1410–1468). A Sinhalese king, who, according to the CŪLAVAṂSA, arranged for repeated performances of the UPASAMPADĀ ordination ceremony. He promulgated a monastic code (katikāvata), which is only partially preserved. In 1423, during his reign, a delegation of thirty-nine Thai and Mon monks headed by either Medhaṅkara (according to JINAKĀLAMĀLĪ) or Ñāṇagambhīra (according to the PADAENG CHRONICLE) reached Sri Lanka, where they were trained. In 1424 they were laicized and reordained into the MAHĀVIHĀRA order at Kalyāṇī near Colombo. The "Padaeng Chronicle" has the delegation of monks headed by Ñāṇagambhīra arriving in Sri Lanka and receiving ordination in 1419, whence they were trained for five years before returning to the Thai kingdom of AYUTHAYA. In either case, this delegation is credited with inaugurating a second wave of Sinhalese-inspired monastic reforms in the Thai kingdoms. The "Padaeng Chronicle" (but not the *Jinakālamālī*) states explicitly that Ñāṇagambhīra sought training and reordination in Sri Lanka because of numerous deficiencies and heresies in the Thai Buddhist order that had been introduced by the earlier reformer, Sumana. The contested points concern ownership of property, use of money, the ordination procedure, and the setting up of proper SĪMĀ boundaries for monastic rituals and procedures.

**paramāṇu**. (T. rdul phra rab; C. jiwei; J. gokumi; K. kŭngmi 極微). In Sanskrit and Pāli, "particle" or "atom"; the smallest unit of matter. Buddhist schools take a variety of positions on the ontological status of such atoms, especially as to whether or not they were divisible or indivisible. Both the SAUTRĀNTIKA and the SARVĀSTIVĀDA schools of mainstream Buddhism, for example, held that each paramāṇu was an indivisible unit of matter, but differed on the exact nature of the objects formed through the coalescence of these particles. By contrast, the MADHYAMAKA school of MAHĀYĀNA philosophy rejected any such notion of particles, since it did not accept that there was anything in the universe that possessed independent existence (NIḤSVABHĀVA), and thus the notion of such atoms was simply a convenient fiction. Numerous Mahāyāna SŪTRAs, notably the AVATAṂSAKASŪTRA, extol the ability of a buddha to place entire world systems within a single particle without changing either's size. These Buddhist debates have parallels within both the JAINA and Hindu traditions. Modern Buddhists have also sought to suggest that apparent parallels between the notion of paramāṇu and modern atomic theory are evidence that Buddhism is consistent with science.

**Paramārtha**. (C. Zhendi; J. Shindai; K. Chinje 眞諦) (499–569). Indian Buddhist monk, translator, and exegete. Paramārtha is said to have been a native of Ujjayinī in western India. Little is known of his early career, but he became renowned in China after arriving at the capital of Jiangang (near present-day Nanjing) and the court of the Liang-dynasty Emperor Wu (r. 502–549) in 546 CE. Under the patronage of Emperor Wu, Paramārtha began translating the many scriptures that he is said to have brought with him from India. After a rebellion took the life of the emperor, Paramārtha headed south, where he continued his translation activities with the support of local rulers. His translations include the SUVARṆAPRABHĀSOTTAMASŪTRA (552), *Suixiang lun zhong shiliu di shu* (555–556), *Anuttarāśrayasūtra* (557), MADHYĀNTAVIBHĀGA (558?), and VIṂŚATIKĀ (563), among others; the apocryphal DASHENG QIXIN LUN is also said by tradition to have been translated (in 553) by Paramārtha. Another influential anthology attributed to Paramārtha is the *Wuxiang lun* (consisting of the treatises *Zhuanshi lun*, *San wuxing lun*, and *Xianshi lun*), which posits the existence of an immaculate ninth consciousness known as the AMALAVIJÑĀNA and contends that the eighth consciousness, or ĀLAYAVIJÑĀNA, is impure. These claims were further developed by his followers in the SHE LUN ZONG exegetical tradition, who based their claims on Paramārtha's influential translation of the MAHĀYĀNASAṂGRAHA. Paramārtha died in 569 while translating the ABHIDHARMAKOŚABHĀṢYA. Among his disciples, Huikai (518–568) and Fatai (d. 601) are most famous.

**paramārthabodhicitta**. (T. don dam byang chub kyi sems). In Sanskrit, the "ultimate aspiration to enlightenment." In Indian MAHĀYĀNA scholastic literature, this term is contrasted with the "conventional aspiration to enlightenment" (SAṂVṚTIBODHICITTA). This latter term is used to refer to bodhicitta in its more common usage, as the aspiration to achieve buddhahood for the sake of all sentient beings. It is the creation of this aspiration for enlightenment (BODHICITTOTPĀDA) that marks the beginning of the bodhisattva path and the Mahāyāna path of accumulation (SAṂBHĀRAMĀRGA). The ultimate aspiration or mind of enlightenment refers to the bodhisattva's direct realization of the ultimate truth. In the case of MADHYAMAKA, this would be the direct realization of emptiness (ŚŪNYATĀ). Such realization, and hence the ultimate aspiration to enlightenment, occurs beginning on the Mahayāna path of vision (DARŚANAMĀRGA) and is repeated on the path of cultivation (BHĀVANĀMĀRGA).

**paramārthasatya**. (P. paramatthasacca T. don dam bden pa; C. zhendi/diyiyi di; J. shintai/daiichigitai; K. chinje/cheirŭi che 眞諦/第一義諦). In Sanskrit, "ultimate truth," "absolute truth"; one of the two truths (SATYADVAYA), along with "conventional truth" (SAṂVṚTISATYA). A number of etymologies of the term are provided in the commentarial literature, based on the literal meaning of paramārthasatya as "highest-object truth." Thus, an ultimate truth is the highest-object truth because it is the object of wisdom (PRAJÑĀ), the highest form of consciousness. It is also the highest-object truth because it is the supreme of all factors (dharma). The term paramārtha is variously defined in the Buddhist philosophical schools but refers in general to phenomena that do not appear falsely when directly perceived and that are the objects of wisdom, that is, those dharmas the understanding of which leads to liberation. Thus, Buddhist philosophical schools do not speak simply of a single "ultimate truth" but of ultimate truths. For example, according to VAIBHĀṢIKA school of SARVĀSTIVĀDA ABHIDHARMA, an ultimate truth is anything that cannot be broken into parts, such as particles or atoms (PARAMĀṆU), and persists only for the shortest unit of time, an instant (KṢAṆA). The term paramārtha is especially associated with the MADHYAMAKA school, where the ultimate truth is emptiness (ŚŪNYATĀ); the object qualified by emptiness is a conventional truth (SAṂVṚTISATYA).

**Paramārthastava**. (T. Don dam par bstod pa). In Sanskrit, "Praise of the Ultimate One"; one of the four hymns (CATUḤSTAVA) of NĀGĀRJUNA, along with the LOKĀTĪTASTAVA, ACINTYASTAVA, and NIRAUPAMYASTAVA. All four hymns are preserved in Sanskrit and are cited by Indian commentators, leaving little doubt about their authorship. There is somewhat greater doubt in the case of this text, however, since the Indian commentators, such as ATIŚA DĪPAMKARAŚRĪJÑĀNA, are from a later period. However, it is very similar in style and content to the *Niraupamyastava*, which is cited by BHĀVAVIVEKA and other early commentators. The *Paramārthastava* is a brief work in eleven stanzas. It is a hymn of praise to the Buddha from the perspective of the ultimate, acknowledging the dilemma of using worldly conventions to praise the Buddha, who transcends linguistic expression and comparison; the Buddha is described as being without intrinsic nature (NIḤSVABHĀVA), duality, color, measure, or location. Thus, Nāgārjuna writes, "Thus praised, and praised again, what, indeed, has been praised? All dharmas are empty; who has been praised, and by whom has he been praised?"

**paramārthaviniścayadharmacakra**. (T. don dam rnam par nges pa'i chos 'khor). In Sanskrit, "the dharma wheel for ascertaining the ultimate," the third of three turnings of the wheel of the dharma (DHARMACAKRAPRAVARTANA). The SAMDHINIRMOCANASŪTRA describes three turnings of the wheel of the dharma by the Buddha: in the first, he taught the FOUR NOBLE TRUTHS (catvāry āryasatyāni); in the second, he taught emptiness (ŚŪNYATĀ); and in the third, he taught what was "well differentiated" (suvibhakta). The third of the three turnings of the wheel of the dharma was delivered in VAIŚĀLĪ. The sūtra identifies it as a teaching for BODHISATTVAs and classifies it as definitive (NĪTĀRTHA); this third turning of the wheel is the teaching of the *Saṃdhinirmocanasūtra* itself. According to the commentators, this third wheel accounts for the Buddha's provisional (NEYĀRTHA) statements in the first wheel of the dharma (see CATUḤSATYADHARMACAKRA), namely, that the four noble truths exist; and his apparently contradictory statement in his second wheel of the dharma in the PRAJÑĀPĀRAMITĀ SŪTRAs (perfection of wisdom sūtras) (see ALAKṢAṆADHARMACAKRA) that all dharmas are "unproduced, unceased, primordially peaceful, and naturally passed beyond sorrow." Here, in this third and definitive teaching, also called "the dharma wheel that makes a fine delineation" (*SUVIBHAKTADHARMACAKRA), he says that dharmas have three natures (TRISVABHĀVA), and each of those in its own way lacks an intrinsic nature (SVABHĀVA). The three natures are the PARIKALPITA or imaginary nature of dharmas, the PARATANTRA or dependently arisen nature of dharmas, and the PARINIṢPANNA or consummate nature of dharmas. In Tibet, there was a debate that extended over centuries as to whether the paramārthaviniścayadharmacakra, this third turning of the wheel, according to the *Saṃdhinirmocanasūtra*, was provisional or definitive. See RANG STONG GZHAN STONG.

**Paramatthadīpanī**. In Pāli, "Lamp on the Ultimate Truth" (S. PARAMĀRTHA), a commentary on the UDĀNA, ITIVUTTAKA, VIMĀNAVATTHU, PETAVATTHU, THERAGĀTHĀ and THERĪGĀTHĀ of the KHUDDAKANIKĀYA by the post-fifth-century CE exegete DHAMMAPĀLA; this exegesis is also called the Vimalavilāsinī. ¶ The *Paramatthadīpanī* is also the name of a modern critique of the *Porāṇaṭīkā* written in Pāli by LEDI SAYADAW.

**Paramatthajotikā**. In Pāli, "Illumination of the Ultimate Truth" (S. PARAMĀRTHA), a commentary on the KHUDDAKAPĀṬHA, DHAMMAPADA, SUTTANIPĀTA, and JĀTAKA of the KHUDDAKANIKĀYA, attributed to the great fifth-century exegete BUDDHAGHOSA.

**Paramatthamañjūsā**. In Pāli, "Container of the Ultimate Truth" (S. PARAMĀRTHA), a commentary on BUDDHAGHOSA's VISUDDHIMAGGA by the post-fifth-century scholar DHAMMAPĀLA. This commentary is also often referred to in the literature as the "Great Subcommentary" (*Mahāṭīkā*).

**paramatthasaṅgha**. (S. paramārthasaṃgha; T. don dam pa'i dge 'dun; C. shengyi seng; J. shōgisō; K. sŭngŭisŭng 勝義僧). In Pāli, "ultimate community"; a technical term used in the Pāli commentaries to answer the question of what precisely constitutes the SAṂGHA jewel among the three jewels (RATNATRAYA), as in the refuge (ŚARAṆA) formula, "I go for refuge to the saṃgha." That is, does the saṃgha constitute the larger community of the Buddhist faithful, only those who have been ordained as monks or nuns, or only those who achieved some level of enlightenment? According to the Pāli tradition, the paramatthasaṅgha consists of the seven and/or eight dakkhiṇeyyapuggala (S. dakṣiṇīyapudgala), or "person(s) worthy to receive gifts," described in the DĪGHANIKĀYA. In keeping with the canonical definition of noble persons (P. ariyapuggala; S. ĀRYAPUDGALA), the term paramatthasaṅgha thus refers specifically to ordained monks and nuns who have reached any of the four ĀRYA paths: that of (1) sotāpanna (S. SROTAĀPANNA), or stream-enterer, (2) sakkadāgāmi (S. SAKṚDĀGĀMIN), or oncereturner, (3) anāgāmi (S. ANĀGĀMIN), or nonreturner, and (4) arahant (S. ARHAT), or worthy one. Technically speaking, then, this advanced paramatthasaṅgha group constitutes the saṃgha jewel. The paramatthasaṅgha is contrasted in the Pāli commentaries with the SAMMUTISAṄGHA (S. saṃvṛtisaṃgha) or "conventional saṃgha," which is comprised of monks and nuns who are still puthujjanas (S. PṚTHAGJANA), or ordinary unenlightened persons. Since the paramatthasaṅgha refers only to those who are both enlightened and ordained, the term necessarily excludes all laymen, enlightened or otherwise, as well as any nonhuman beings (such as divinities, etc.) even if they are enlightened, for nonhuman beings are ineligible for ordination as monks or nuns. Also excluded are all BODHISATTVAs, since by definition in the Pāli tradition bodhisattvas remain unenlightened persons until the night that they attain buddhahood. Buddhas are also excluded from the paramatthasaṅgha because they comprise the buddha jewel among the three jewels. While novices technically are outside the saṃgha by virtue of not having yet received higher ordination (UPASAMPADĀ), enlightened novices are nevertheless included in the paramatthasaṅgha as objects of refuge.

**pāramitā**. (P. pāramī; T. pha rol tu phyin pa; C. boluomi; J. haramitsu; K. paramil 波羅蜜). In Sanskrit, "perfection," a virtue or quality developed and practiced by a BODHISATTVA on the path to becoming a buddha. The term is paranomastically glossed by some traditional commentators as "gone beyond" or "gone to the other side" (see PARA), although it seems in fact to derive from Skt. parama, meaning "highest" or "supreme." The best-known enumeration of the perfections is a group of six: giving (DĀNA), morality (ŚĪLA), patience or forbearance (KṢĀNTI), effort (VĪRYA), concentration (DHYĀNA), and wisdom (PRAJÑĀ). There are also lists of ten perfections. In the MAHĀYĀNA (specifically in the DAŚABHŪMIKASŪTRA), the list of ten includes the preceding six, to which are added method (UPĀYA), vow (PRAṆIDHĀNA), power (BALA), and knowledge (JÑĀNA), with the explanation that the bodhisattva practices the perfections in this order on each of the ten bodhisattva stages or grounds (BHŪMI). Thus, giving is perfected on the first bhūmi, morality on the second, and so on. In Pāli sources, where the perfections are called pāramī, the ten perfections are giving (dāna), morality (sīla), renunciation (nekkhamma; S. NAIṢKRAMYA), wisdom (paññā), effort (viriya), patience (khanti), truthfulness (sacca; S. SATYA), determination (adhiṭṭhāna; S. ADHIṢṬHĀNA), lovingkindness (mettā; S. MAITRĪ), and equanimity (upekkhā; S. UPEKṢĀ). The practice of these perfections over the course of the many lifetimes of the bodhisattva's path eventually fructifies in the achievement of buddhahood. The precise meaning of the perfections is discussed at length, as is the question of how the six (or ten) are to be divided between the categories of merit (PUṆYA) and wisdom (JÑĀNA). For example, according to one interpretation of the six perfections, giving, morality, and patience contribute to the collection of merit (PUṆYASAMBHĀRA); concentration and wisdom contribute to the collection of wisdom (JÑĀNASAṂBHĀRA), and effort contributes to both. Commentators also consider what distinguishes the practice of these six from other instances of the practice of giving, etc. Some MADHYAMAKA exegetes, for example, argue that these virtues only become perfections when the bodhisattva engages in them with an understanding of emptiness (ŚŪNYATĀ); for example, giving a gift without clinging to any conception of giver, gift, or recipient.

**pāramitāyāna**. (T. phar phyin theg pa). In Sanskrit, "perfection vehicle." In scholastic tantric literature, the MAHĀYĀNA is sometimes divided into the pāramitāyāna and the VAJRAYĀNA, with the former referring to the path of the BODHISATTVA, set forth in Mahāyāna sūtras and focused on the practice of the six perfections (PĀRAMITĀ). The vajrayāna is represented as a faster and more effective route, set forth in the tantras, to the same goal of buddhahood. In this way, the Mahāyāna is represented as having both exoteric and esoteric forms. The pāramitāyāna is also called the pāramitānaya, or "perfection mode."

**paraṃparā**. (T. rgyud pa; C. xiangcheng; J. sōjō; K. sangsŭng 相承). In Sanskrit and Pāli, "succession," "lineage"; a lineage of teachers and disciples (ācāryaparaṃparā), through which the specific teachings and practices of a teacher are transmitted down through successive generations of students. The term, also important in both Hindu and JAINA traditions, has the sense of instructions passed down orally from master to disciple over the generations. In Buddhism, paraṃparā refers most often to a transmission of teachings that can be traced from the present time and place back to India and to the Buddha. Although such transmission is particularly important in Buddhist TANTRA and in the CHAN traditions of East Asia, it is a dominant element throughout the Buddhist world, including the ordination lineages of monks and nuns. See also CHUANDENGLU; FASI; YINKE.

**paranirmitavaśavartin**. (P. paranimmitavasavatti; T. gzhan 'phrul dbang byed; C. tahuazizai tian; J. takejizaiten; K. t'ahwajajaech'ŏn 他化自在天). In Sanskrit, "controlling the emanations of others," the sixth and highest of the six heavens of the sensuous realm (KĀMADHĀTU). This heaven is so named because the divinities there not only control their own emanations or creations (as do the divinities of the heaven of the enjoyment of creation, or NIRMĀṆARATI), but also have the ability to control the emanations of other beings. They are the tallest and longest-lived of all divinities in the sensuous realm.

**paraprasiddhānumāna**. (T. gzhan la grags pa'i rjes dpag). In Sanskrit, lit. "inference familiar to another," a term in Buddhist logic, important especially in the MADHYAMAKA school of Indian Buddhist philosophy. Similar to the case of PARĀRTHĀNUMĀNA ("inference for others"), paraprasiddhānumāna refers not to the mental conclusion or an inference drawn from evidence but rather to a logical argument made to an opponent. In this case, "inference familiar to another" refers to an argument consisting of elements that (1) the person stating the argument does not accept and (2) that the opponent accepts (or does not reject). The argument is stated with the intention of causing the opponent to draw the correct conclusion, that is, a conclusion contrary to his own tenets. It is generally the case in Indian logic that all elements of the syllogism must be accepted by both parties in a debate; such a syllogism is referred to as an "autonomous syllogism" (SVATANTRĀNUMĀNA; SVATANTRAPRAYOGA). This is not the case with the inference familiar to another, in which the elements of the syllogism are accepted only by the opponent. In the Madhyamaka school, there was a controversy over whether such syllogisms were acceptable when a Madhyamaka adherent debated with a proponent of another school. The locus classicus of the controversy is the debate between BHĀVAVIVEKA and CANDRAKĪRTI concerning BUDDHAPĀLITA's commentary on the first chapter of NĀGĀRJUNA's MŪLAMADHYAMAKAKĀRIKĀ. It was Candrakīrti's position that the Madhyamaka should use only consequences (PRASAṄGA) or an inference familiar to others; to use an autonomous syllogism implied acceptance of intrinsically established relations among the elements of the syllogism. Bhāvaviveka had argued that it was necessary for the Madhyamaka to state an autonomous syllogism at the conclusion of a debate. Based on this controversy, the terms *SVĀTANTRIKA and *PRĀSAṄGIKA were coined retrospectively in Tibet to describe later developments within the Indian Madhyamaka school.

**parārtha**. (T. gzhan don; C. lita; J. rita; K. it'a 利他). In Sanskrit, "welfare of others," "benefiting others." As part of his training, a BODHISATTVA, out of his concern for the welfare of others, willingly relinquishes motivations and deeds that would lead to his own personal benefit. For example, in the JĀTAKA stories, the bodhisattva repeatedly sacrifices his own welfare, and often his own life, for the benefit of others. This compassionate motivation is contrasted with the more selfish motivation of "benefiting oneself" (SVĀRTHA). However, it is said that through the practice of the bodhisattva path, one achieves buddhahood in which both of these two aims (ARTHA) are fulfilled. The welfare of others is fulfilled because the bodhisattva becomes a buddha who teaches the dharma to sentient beings. The welfare of oneself (that is, the bodhisattva himself) is fulfilled because, by achieving buddhahood, the bodhisattva achieves omniscience and liberation from rebirth.

**parārthānumāna**. (T. gzhan don rjes dpag; C. tabiliang; J. tahiryō; K. t'apiryang 他比量). In Sanskrit, "inference for others," a key term in Buddhist logic. Two types of inference (ANUMĀNA) are set forth: inference for oneself (SVĀRTHĀNUMĀNA) and inference for others. The former generally refers to the mental process of inference whereby a conclusion is arrived upon based on evidence. In contrast, inference for others is not an inference in a technical sense but only metaphorically. It refers to the statement that would be made to another person, such as an opponent in a debate, in order for that person to arrive at the correct conclusion. Precisely what constitutes such a statement—especially how much and how little is to be said—is a major topic of Buddhist logic. For example, there is discussion of whether the actual conclusion that one wishes the other person to draw must be formally stated, or not. In a standard example of an inference for others, the conclusion would not be stated. Thus, to someone who thought that sound is permanent, one might say: "Whatever is produced is impermanent, such as a clay pot. Sound is produced." The fourth chapter of DHARMAKĪRTI's PRAMĀṆAVĀRTTIKA is devoted to the topic of inference for others. See PARAPRASIDDHĀNUMĀNA.

**parasaṃbhogakāya**. (C. ta shouyong shen; J. tajuyūshin; K. t'a suyong sin 他受用身). In Sanskrit, "body intended for others' enjoyment"; one of the four types of buddha bodies (BUDDHAKĀYA) discussed in the BUDDHABHŪMIŚĀSTRA (C.

*Fodijing lun*), the MAHĀYĀNASAṂGRAHA (C. *She dasheng lun*), and the CHENG WEISHI LUN (S. **Vijñaptimātratāsiddhi*), along with the "self-nature body" (SVABHĀVAKĀYA), "body intended for personal enjoyment" (SVASAṂBHOGAKĀYA), and "transformation body" (NIRMĀṆAKĀYA). This fourfold schema of buddha bodies derives from the better-known three bodies of a buddha (TRIKĀYA)—viz., dharma body (DHARMAKĀYA), reward body (SAṂBHOGAKĀYA), and transformation body (nirmāṇakāya)—but distinguishes between two different types of enjoyment bodies. The first, the svasaṃbhogakāya, derives from the countless virtues that originate from the accumulation of immeasurable merit and wisdom over a buddha's infinitely long career; this body is a perfect, pure, eternal, and omnipresent material body that enjoys the bliss of dharma (DHARMAPRĪTI) for oneself until the end of time. By contrast, the parasaṃbhogakāya is a subtle virtuous body deriving from the wisdom of equality (SAMATĀJÑĀNA), which resides in a PURE LAND and displays supernatural powers in order to enhance the enjoyment of the dharma by bodhisattvas at all ten stages of the bodhisattva's career (BODHISATTVABHŪMI).

**paratantra**. (T. gzhan dbang; C. yitaqi xing; J. etakishō; K. ŭit'agi sŏng 依他起性). In Sanskrit, lit., "other-powered," viz., "dependent"; the second of the three natures (TRISVABHĀVA), a central tenet of the YOGĀCĀRA school in which all phenomena are classified as having three natures: an imaginary (PARIKALPITA), dependent (paratantra), and consummate (PARINIṢPANNA) nature. In the Yogācāra system, external objects do not exist as materially distinct entities that are separate from the consciousness that perceives them. According to this school, the perception of forms, sounds, smells, and so on is produced not by an external sensory stimulus, but from the ripening of karmic seeds (BĪJA); i.e., from residual impressions (literally "perfumings"; see VĀSANĀ) left by earlier perceptions of a similar type. The paratantra is the category of dependently originated, impermanent phenomena that arise from seeds stored in the foundational consciousness (ĀLAYAVIJÑĀNA), seeds that fructify as states of consciousness. Sentient beings do not comprehend the paratantra nature because sense experience is distorted by subject-object bifurcation (see GRĀHYAGRĀHAKAVIKALPA), called the imaginary (parikalpita) nature. The paratantra category encompasses all impermanent phenomena, which are produced in dependence on causes and conditions. The SAṂDHINIRMOCANASŪTRA describes the paratantra as lacking any intrinsic nature of production (utpattiniḥsvabhāvatā); that is, no impermanent phenomenon can produce itself. They provide for the functioning of SAMSĀRA and the path to NIRVĀṆA and enlightenment (BODHI). However, they also serve as the basis of misconceptions (parikalpita) due to ignorance, which falsely imagines objects to be separate entities from the consciousness that perceives them. The absence of this falsely imagined separation with regard to dependent phenomena is called the consummate (parinispanna).

**parātmaparivartana**. (T. bdag gzhan brje ba). In Sanskrit, "exchange of self and other," a method for developing BODHICITTA, or the aspiration to achieve buddhahood in order to liberate all beings from suffering. As described by ŚĀNTIDEVA in the eighth chapter of his BODHICARYĀVATĀRA, the BODHISATTVA should take one's natural sense of self-cherishing and transfer that to others, while taking one's natural disregard for others and transfer that to oneself. In this way, one can then seek the welfare of others as one once sought one's own welfare, and abandon one's own welfare as one once abandoned the welfare of others. The goal is for the bodhisattva to develop the aspiration to give all of one's happiness to others and to take all of the sufferings of others upon oneself.

**parātmasamatā**. (T. bdag gzhan mnyam pa; C. zita pingdeng; J. jita byōdō; K. chat'a p'yŏngdŭng 自他平等). In Sanskrit, "equalizing self and other," a method for developing BODHICITTA, or the aspiration to achieve buddhahood in order to liberate all beings from suffering. In the eighth chapter of his BODHICARYĀVATĀRA, ŚĀNTIDEVA, drawing apparently on the *Tathāgataguhyasūtra*, explains that there is no reason to cherish oneself over others, because both oneself and others equally wish for happiness and equally wish to avoid suffering. If suffering is to be dispelled, it should be done without distinguishing whether that suffering is experienced by oneself or by another sentient being. This equalizing of self and other is considered a prerequisite for the "exchange of self and other" (PARĀTMAPARIVARTANA).

**paricchedajarāmaraṇa**. (C. fenduan shengsi; J. bundan shōji; K. pundan saengsa 分段生死). In Sanskrit, "determinative birth-and-death," one of the two categories of SAṂSĀRA as delineated in the CHENG WEISHI LUN (**Vijñaptimātratāsiddhi*), along with transfigurational birth-and-death (PARIṆĀMIKAJARĀMARAṆA); this is saṃsāra as experienced by ordinary sentient beings taking rebirth within the three realms of existence (TRAIDHĀTUKA). (In this compound, jarāmaraṇa does not mean only "old age and death," but is used as an abbreviation for the whole panoply of human experience, viz. "birth, old age, sickness, and death.") While the mind-made bodies (MANOMAYAKĀYA) of ARHATs or great BODHISATTVAs may undergo transfigurational birth-and-death (pariṇāmikajarāmaraṇa) and are thus able to change their appearance and life span at will, the physical bodies of ordinary sentient beings are restricted in their longevity, appearance, and size and are thus subject to determinative birth-and-death. The main causes and conditions that lead to determinative birth-and-death are contaminated action (SĀSRAVA-KARMAN) and the afflictive obstructions (KLEŚĀVARAṆA); transfigurational birth-and-death is instead conceived to result from uncontaminated action (ANĀSRAVA-KARMAN) and the cognitive obstructions (JÑEYĀVARAṆA) that still remain even after overcoming the afflictive obstructions.

**parihāṇi**. (P. parihāni; T. yongs su nyams pa; C. tui; J. tai; K. t'oe 退). In Sanskrit, lit., "diminution," "retrogression," or "backsliding" from virtuous states that had previously been cultivated or mastered. Parihāṇi refers specifically to the diminution of mental states that had been directed toward liberation (VIMUKTI), which allows mental disturbances to reappear and thus causes regression to previous habitual tendencies involving unwholesome or mundane thoughts and activities. The term often appears in debates concerning the issue of whether the noble persons (ĀRYAPUDGALA) are subject to backsliding. Such MAINSTREAM BUDDHIST SCHOOLS as the MAHĀSĀṂGHIKA, SARVĀSTIVĀDA, and SAṂMITĪYA argued, for example, that ARHATS were subject to backsliding because they were still prone to vestigial negative proclivities of mind (ANUŚAYA), even if those only manifested themselves while the monks were sleeping, e.g., nocturnal emissions. The STHAVIRANIKĀYA argued that arhats were not subject to backsliding since they had perfected all the necessary stages of training and were free from such proclivities. Related to this issue are discussions concerning the status of once-returners (SAKṚDĀGĀMIN) and nonreturners (ANĀGĀMIN): the majority of schools posited that once-returners and nonreturners could regress to the status of the stream-enterer (SROTAĀPANNA), the first level of sanctity, but that the status of the stream-enterer was not subject to retrogression and was thus inviolate. In the PURE LAND tradition, backsliding is a core rationale justifying the pure land teachings, since, in the world of SAṂSĀRA, backsliding is inevitable for all except the most resolute practitioners. According to the AMITĀBHASŪTRA, for example, sentient beings have accumulated karmic burdens since time immemorial and are invariably subject to backsliding; thus, they will never be able to escape from the endless cycle of birth-and-death on their own. For this reason, the buddha AMITĀBHA encourages them to seek rebirth in the pure land, instead, where they will have no hindrances to their eventual attainment of liberation. In the MAHĀYĀNA tradition, reaching the stage where there no longer is any prospect of regression is a crucial threshold on the path to liberation. Different scriptures place this point of nonbacksliding at different stages along the path. One of the most common explanations about which stage is "irreversible" (AVAIVARTIKA) appears in the DAŚABHŪMIKASŪTRA, which locates it on the eighth stage (BHŪMI), the "immovable" (ACALĀ), where further progress is assured and where there is no possible of retrogressing to a preceding stage. However, HARIBHADRA in his commentary on the ABHISAMAYĀLAṂKĀRA identifies two earlier points at which the bodhisattva becomes irreversible, one on the path of preparation (PRAYOGAMĀRGA) and one on the path of vision (DARŚANAMĀRGA).

**parikalpita**. (T. kun btags; C. bianji suozhi xing; J. henge shoshūshō; K. pyŏn'gye sojip sŏng 遍計所執性). In Sanskrit, "imputed," "imaginary," or "artificial," the first of the three natures (TRISVABHĀVA), a central tenet of the YOGĀCĀRA school, in which all phenomena are classified as having three natures: an imaginary (parikalpita), dependent (PARATANTRA), and consummate (PARINIṢPANNA) nature. The Yogācāra "mind only" (CITTAMĀTRA) system expounded in the YOGĀCĀRABHŪMI, MADHYĀNTAVIBHĀGA, MAHĀYĀNASŪTRĀLAṂKĀRA, and the commentaries of ASAṄGA and VASUBANDHU asserts that external objects do not exist as materially different entities, separate from the consciousness that perceives them; all ordinary appearances are distorted by subject-object bifurcation (see GRĀHYAGRĀHAKAVIKALPA). Forms, sounds, and so on are only seen by ordinary persons in their imaginary (parikalpita) nature. In this system, which denies the existence of external objects, the imaginary refers to the falsely perceived nature of objects as entities that exist separate from the consciousness that perceives them. Karmic seeds (BĪJA), classified as dependent (paratantra), fructify to produce both the perceiving consciousness and the perceived object. However, due to ignorance (AVIDYĀ), subject and object are imagined to be distant from each other, with objects constituting an external world independent of the consciousness that perceives it. The constituents of such an external world are deemed imaginary (parikalpita). The term parikalpita is also used by DHARMAKĪRTI and his Yogācāra followers, who assert that the grāhyagrāhakavikalpa distortion makes objects appear to be naturally the bases of the terms used to designate them although they in fact do not. The SAṂDHINIRMOCANASŪTRA describes the parikalpita as lacking the nature of characteristics (lakṣaṇaniḥsvabhāvatā).

**parikalpitakleśāvaraṇa**. (T. nyon sgrib kun btags; C. fenbie huo; J. funbetsuwaku; K. punbyŏl hok 分別惑). In Sanskrit, "imaginary" or "artificial" "afflictive obstructions," those obstructions (ĀVARAṆA) to liberation that derive from mistaken conceptions of self (ĀTMAN) generated through the study of flawed philosophical systems in the present lifetime. This type is in distinction to SAHAJAKLEŚĀVARAṆA, "innate afflictive obstructions," which derive from the mistaken conceptions of self generated and reinforced over the course of many lifetimes. In progressing along the path to liberation, the parikalpitakleśāvaraṇa are said to be easier to abandon than the sahajakleśāvaraṇa.

**parikalpitasvabhāva**. (T. kun brtags kyi mtshan nyid). See PARIKALPITA.

**parikalpitātmagraha**. (T. bdag 'dzin kun btags; C. fenbie wozhi; J. funbetsugashū; K. punbyŏl ajip 分別我執). In Sanskrit, "artificial conception of self," a term used to refer to the conception of self acquired during a human lifetime through the study of false systems of tenets, such as those that assert the existence of a permanent self or soul (ĀTMAN). It is contrasted with the "innate conception of self" (SAHAJĀTMAGRAHA), the deep-seated conception of self that is carried by all sentient beings from lifetime to lifetime. Those on the path to enlightenment abandon the artificial conception of self more easily than the innate conception of self.

**parikalpitāvidyā**. (T. kun btags ma rig pa; C. fenbie wuming; J. funbetsumumyō; K. punbyŏl mumyŏng 分別無明). In Sanskrit, "imaginary" or "artificial ignorance"; the form of ignorance that derives from the study and adoption of mistaken philosophical views during the present lifetime of a human being. It is thus more superficial and more easily overcome than the "innate ignorance" (SAHAJĀVIDYA) that is accumulated over the course of many lifetimes. Because of its more superficial nature, imaginary ignorance is not cited as the cause of cyclical existence; rebirth is instead said to be caused by innate ignorance. Imaginary ignorance is, however, understood to be the cause of the multitude of wrong views (MITHYĀDṚṢṬI) regarding the nature of the self.

**parikammanimitta**. In Pāli, "preparatory image" or "preliminary sign;" the first of the three major visualization signs experienced in tranquillity (P. samatha; S. ŚAMATHA) exercises, along with the UGGAHANIMITTA (eidetic image) and the PAṬIBHĀGANIMITTA (representational or counterpart image). Any object of attention, such as a visualization device (KASIṆA) that is used in the initial development of concentration, is termed a parikammanimitta. Generally, these devices involve visual objects such as fire, a circle of earth, or a particular color, though the breath may also be considered a parikammanimitta. These three signs and the meditative exercises employed to experience them are discussed in detail in BUDDHAGHOSA's VISUDDHIMAGGA, where they are listed sequentially according to the degree of concentration necessary for them to appear. In these exercises, the meditator attempts to convert a visual object of meditation, such as earth, fire, or a color, into a mental projection or conceptualization that is as clear as the visual image itself. The image the practitioner views with his eyes is called the parikammanimitta or "preparatory image," and the effort the practitioner makes is called parikammabhāvanā. When that parikammanimitta is equally clear when visualized in the mind, the practitioner is then said to have obtained the uggahanimitta (eidetic image). Even that image, however, still represents a relatively weak degree of concentration, and it must be enhanced until the paṭibhāganimitta, or "counterpart image," emerges, which marks the access to meditative absorption (P. JHĀNA, S. DHYĀNA).

**parikammasamādhi**. In Pāli, "preparatory concentration"; a preliminary degree of concentration established at the beginning of a meditative development; parikammasamādhi takes as its object an initial mental image called the PARIKAMMANIMITTA (preparatory image). The parikkamanimitta can be developed on the basis of any number of mental or physical objects used as supports. One such object could be, for example, a blue circle used as an external visualization device (KASIṆA). The preparatory image so generated is crude, weak, and unstable. With the deepening of concentration, however, the image becomes refined, at which point it is called an "eidetic image" (UGGAHANIMITTA). Through increased concentration, the uggahanimitta eventually is displaced by a clear luminous image called the "representational" or "counterpart" "image" (PAṬIBHĀGANIMITTA), at which point the mind enters the next stage of concentration, called UPACĀRASAMĀDHI or "access concentration," which may eventually develop into thoroughgoing "meditative absorption" (P. JHĀNA; S. DHYĀNA).

**pariṇāmanā**. (T. yongs su bsngo ba; C. huixiang; J. ekō; K. hoehyang 迴向). In Sanskrit, "dedication," the practice of mentally or ritually directing the merit (PUṆYA) produced from a virtuous (KUŚALA) deed or deeds (KARMAN) to a particular aim. Merit may be dedicated to the benefit of all sentient beings or to the benefit of a specific person or persons (such as a family member), but the term is used especially to refer to the dedication of the merit accumulated by a BODHISATTVA to the greater goal of achieving buddhahood so that one may be able to liberate all beings from suffering. Merit may also be dedicated toward the goal of a rebirth in a specific realm (such as a PURE LAND or the heavens) in the next lifetime. The dedication of merit is a standard element of Mahāyāna ritual (PŪJĀ) and meditative practices and is often praised as a means of protecting virtuous faculties (KUŚALAMŪLA) from being destroyed by unwholesome states of mind. See also PATTIDĀNA.

**pariṇāmikajarāmaraṇa**. [alt. pariṇāmikijarāmaraṇa] (C. bianyi shengsi; J. henyaku shoji; K. pyŏnyŏk saengsa 變易生死). In Sanskrit, "transfigurational birth-and-death," one of the two categories of SAṂSĀRA as delineated in the CHENG WEISHI LUN (*Vijñaptimātratāsiddhi*), along with determinative birth-and-death (PARICCHEDAJARĀMARAṆA); this is saṃsāra as experienced by an ARHAT or great BODHISATTVA (vaśitāprāptabodhisattva). (In this compound, jarāmaraṇa does not mean only "old age and death," but is used as an abbreviation for the whole panoply of human existence, viz. "birth, old age, sickness, and death.") Since these noble (ĀRYA) beings have already achieved some measure of enlightenment, when they undergo rebirth and death in the three realms of existence (TRAIDHĀTUKA), these occur as a "transfigurational birth-and-death" of the "mind-made body" (MANOMAYAKĀYA), not a "determinative birth-and-death" of the physical body. Although these beings have overcome the afflictive obstructions (KLEŚĀVARAṆA) that tie one to the cycle of saṃsāra (and specifically to paricchedajarāmaraṇa), they may still be subject to the cognitive obstructions (JÑEYĀVARAṆA) that block full understanding (JÑĀNA); thus, while they may still engage in actions, these are non-karma-producing actions (viz., "uncontaminated actions," or ANĀSRAVAKARMAN) that do not lead to a determinative rebirth. While such beings may then appear to be reborn, these rebirths are actually transfigurations of their mind-made bodies (manomayakāya), which may be manipulated at will to change their appearances or to extend their life spans indefinitely.

**parinirvāṇa**. (P. parinibbāna; T. yongs su mya ngan las 'das pa; C. banniepan; J. hatsunehan; K. panyŏlban 般涅槃). In Sanskrit, "final nirvāṇa" or "complete nirvāṇa," the final passage into NIRVĀṆA upon the death of a buddha or an ARHAT. The term is most widely associated with the passing away of the buddha Śākyamuni. Delineations of the Buddhist path set forth the experience of nirvāṇa in two phases. The first occurs when all of the causes for future rebirth have been destroyed, at which point one becomes an arhat or a buddha. However, the karmic seed that had fructified as the final lifetime has not yet run its full course, and thus the enlightened person does not instantly die and pass into nirvāṇa, but instead lives out the remainder of his or her lifetime. This type of nirvāṇa is sometimes called the "nirvāṇa with remainder" (sopadhiśeṣanirvāṇa). When the term of the last lifetime comes to an end, there is a total extinction of all conventional physical and mental existence because the adept has previously brought an absolute end to any propensity toward defilement (kleśa) and eradicated all the causes that would lead to any prospect of future rebirth. The nirvāṇa that is experienced at death is thus "without remainder" (anupadhiśeṣanirvāṇa), because there are no physical or mental constituents remaining that were the products of previous karman; the "nirvāṇa without remainder" is therefore synonymous with parinirvāṇa. The parinirvāṇa of the Buddha is one of the most important scenes in all of Buddhist art and literature. It is described at length in both the eponymous Pāli Mahāparinibbānasutta and Sanskrit Mahāparinirvāṇasūtra. Images of the "reclining buddha" depict the buddha at the time of his parinirvāṇa.

**parinispanna**. (T. yongs su grub pa; C. yuanchengshi xing; J. enjōjisshō; K. wŏnsŏngsil sŏng 圓成實性). In Sanskrit, "perfected" or "consummate," the third of the three natures (trisvabhāva), a central tenet of the Yogācāra school, in which all phenomena are classified as having three natures: an imaginary (parikalpita), dependent (paratantra), and consummate (pariniṣpanna) nature. Pariniṣpanna is the emptiness or lack of an imaginary external world (bāhyārtha) materially different from the consciousness that perceives it. The paratantra category encompasses the conventional truth (saṃvṛtisatya) of dependently originated impermanent phenomena that arise from seeds stored in the foundational consciousness (ālayavijñāna). The pariniṣpanna category is their ultimate truth (paramārthasatya). Thus pariniṣpannasvabhāva, the consummate nature, is an absence of an object that is different in nature from the consciousness that perceives it. The consummate (pariniṣpanna) is sometimes defined as the absence of the imaginary (parikalpita) in the dependent (paratantra). The consummate nature is the highest reality according to Yogācāra; the Samdhinirmocanasūtra describes it as paramārthaniḥsvabhāva, the "lack of intrinsic nature, which is the ultimate."

**pariniṣpannasvabhāva**. (S). See pariniṣpanna.

**pariṣad**. (P. parisā; T. 'khor; C. zhonghui; J. shue; K. chunghoe 衆會). In Sanskrit, "following," "assembly," or "congregation"; the followers of the buddha, said to consist of four groups: monks (bhikṣu), nuns (bhikṣuṇī), male lay disciples (upāsaka), and female lay disciples (upāsikā). The term is often used to designate the followers of the Buddha collectively, whereas the term saṃgha is generally used in a more limited sense to designate the ordained followers, or the enlightened ordained. See āryasaṃgha; paramārthasaṃgha.

**pariṣkāra**. (P. parikkhāra; T. yo byad; C. ziju/daoju; J. shigu/dōgu; K. chagu/togu 資具/道具). In Sanskrit, "requisites," "personal belongings," "equipment"; the minimal possessions of food, shelter, and clothing that Buddhist monks and nuns were permitted to possess as "requisites" for their physical survival. A list of four such requisites is commonly found in the vinaya literature: robes (cīvara; tricīvara); alms bowl (pātra); seat and bed (śayanāsana); and medicine to cure illness (glānapratyayabhaiṣajya). In the Pāli recension of the vinaya, there are eight requisites: (1) the three robes, consisting of the inner robe (antaravāsaka), the upper robe (uttarāsaṅga), and a cloak or shawl (saṃghāṭī); (2) a waist band or belt (kāyabandhana); (3) an alms bowl (P. patta; S. pātra); (4) a sitting mat (nisīdana); (5) a piece of cloth for filtering water to prevent the accidental death of insects (P. parissāvana; S. parisrāvaṇa); (6) a jug for collecting water (dhammakaraka); (7) sewing needles kept in a small box (sūcighara); and (8) a razor for shaving (vāsi). There is also a list of thirteen, one version of which includes the three robes, a mat, two undergarments, two garments for absorbing perspiration, a face towel, a towel for the body, a bandage, a cloth for catching hair when shaving, and a cloth bag for medicines. There are also lists of eighteen requisites. Perhaps reflecting the increasing needs of a large and mainly sedentary monastic community, longer lists also appear. The Mahāvyutpatti lists one hundred requisites of a śramaṇa, including various dining utensils and containers, shoes, mattresses, cushions, stools, brooms, a mosquito net, a hatchet, a hook for hanging things on the wall, and an iron chain. When not involving a specific list, pariṣkāra may also refer generically to anything that may appropriately be offered to a monk or nun. The term is also occasionally used in the sense of "spiritual requisites" or "equipment," as in a list of seven pariṣkāra, which refer to the first seven steps in the eightfold path (āryāṣṭāṅgamārga) that culminate in right samādhi. The rationale behind the pariṣkāra is that they demonstrate that a monk shuns luxury and lives only on the bare essentials that are absolutely necessary for survival. Inevitably, however, the list more often represents an ideal rather than the actual state of monastic affairs. See also niśraya.

**pariṣkāravaśitā**. (T. yo byad la dbang ba; C. caizizai; J. zaijizai; K. chaejajae 財自在). In Sanskrit, lit. "power of requisites" or "equipment"; one of the ten powers of an advanced bodhisattva, which are discussed in the Bodhisattvabhūmi. Pariṣkāravaśitā indicates the power of a bodhisattva miraculously to produce the requisites, or "equipment" of life (such as food, shelter, and clothing). The *Bodhisattvabhūmi* explains that, as with the other nine powers, pariṣkāravaśitā is acquired through merit accumulated through the practice of a variety of selfless acts.

**parisrāvaṇa**. (P. parissāvana; T. chu tshags; C. lushui nang; J. rokusuinō; K. noksu nang 漉水囊). In Sanskrit, "strainer" or "filter"; one of the requisites (PARIṢKĀRA) of a Buddhist mendicant, which was to be placed over a vessel as water is poured into it in order to avoid the accidental drowning of insects. Although according to Buddhist karmic theory, only the intentional killing of insects had negative karmic effects, Buddhist monks and nuns, like their JAINA counterparts, sought in this way to avoid harming insects while also providing some measure of purification for their drinking water.

**pariśuddha**. (T. yongs su dag pa; C. qingjing; J. shōjō; K. ch'ŏngjŏng 清淨). In Sanskrit, "purified" or "cleansed"; a state that is free from afflictions or defilements (KLEŚA). In the Buddhist tradition, the term can be applied in a number of ways. The body, speech, and mind of a buddha are described as pariśuddha, as are many of the SŪTRAs that contain his teaching. The buddha-fields (BUDDHAKṢETRA) or PURE LANDs of AMITĀBHA and AKṢOBHYA are also described as pariśuddha. In doctrinal developments such as those associated with the TATHĀGATAGARBHA tradition, pariśuddha is used to characterize the inherent, inviolable nature that underlies the reality of all beings. This term is also used to describe the conduct of those who adhere to the teachings, as in the formulation pariśuddhakāyasamācāra, or "purity in bodily conduct." Pariśuddha is often coupled with the related term paryavadāta, also meaning "clean" or "pure"; in compound, they are often translated as "bright (or white) and pure."

**pariśuddhabuddhakṣetra**. (T. sangs rgyas kyi shing yongs su dag pa; C. qingjing foguotu; J. shōjō bukkokudo; K. ch'ŏngjŏng pulgukt'o 清淨佛國土). In Sanskrit, "purified buddha-field." In the MAHĀYĀNA, when a buddha attains enlightenment, he not only achieves the three bodies (TRIKĀYA) of a buddha, but also creates a land in which he will preach the dharma. That land can be either pure, impure, or mixed. A pure buddha field may be one in which the inhabitants engage in only virtuous deeds and experience no suffering. The term is also used to describe a buddha-field that does not include the unfortunate realms (APĀYA; DURGATI) of animals, ghosts, and hell denizens. The buddha-field of Amitābha, SUKHĀVATĪ, is a pure field in these two senses (although the term pariśuddhabuddhakṣetra does not appear in the SUKHĀVATĪVYŪHASŪTRA). The term may also be used with regard to whether the inhabitants of the buddha-field are all BODHISATTVAs, or all ĀRYABODHISATTVAs, that is, those who have achieved at least the first BHŪMI. It is possible that the Chinese term JINGTU (the source of the English term "PURE LAND"), which does not appear to be a direct translation from Sanskrit, derives from pariśuddhabuddhakṣetra, perhaps as an abbreviation of it. In the ABHISAMAYĀLAṂKĀRA's explanation of the PAÑCAVIṂŚATISĀHASRIKĀPRAJÑĀPĀRAMITĀSŪTRA, the pariśuddhabuddhakṣetra is twofold, corresponding to the BHĀJANALOKA ("container world," referring to the wider environment or the physical or inanimate world) and the SATTVALOKA, the "world of sentient beings," who are the inhabitants of that "container." A degraded environment with treeless deserts, thornbushes, and so on is impure; when beings are sick and hungry, etc., the sattvaloka is impure. The perfect purity of a buddha-field comes about when a bodhisattva achieves the purity of those two worlds by counteracting their imperfections through the creation of an entirely pleasant environment, and through the supply of food, clothing, shelter, etc.

**paritta**. [alt. parittā] (BHS. parītta, T. yongs su skyob pa; C. minghu/minghu jing; J. myōgo/myōgokyō; K. myŏngho/myŏngho kyŏng 明護/明護經). In Pāli, "protection" (classical S. paritrāṇa); referring to both the practice of reciting a short passage from a SŪTRA in order to draw on the text's apotropaic powers, as well as to the passages themselves. The use of paritta are said to have been sanctioned by the Buddha: after a monk had died of a snake bite, the Buddha recited a text (the *Khandhaparitta*, or "Protection of the Aggregates") for the monks to repeat as protection, which states that loving-kindness (P. mettā; S. MAITRĪ) and the infinite power of the Buddha, DHARMA, and SAṂGHA would guard the monks from the finite power of snakes, scorpions, and other dangerous creatures. There were many specific instances that subsequently led the Buddha to deliver different paritta verses, including protection from evil spirits, the assurance of good fortune, exorcism, curing serious illness, and even safe childbirth. The power of these verses often is thought to derive from an asseveration of truth (S. SATYAVACANA; P. saccavacana, saccakiriyā), as in the famous paritta associated with AṄGULIMĀLA, who offered this statement to help ease a woman's labor pains: "Since I was born of āryan birth, O sister, I am not aware of having intentionally deprived any living being of its life. By this asseveration of truth, may you be well and may your unborn child be well." (There is intentional irony in this statement, since Aṅgulimāla was well known to have been a murderous highwayman before he became a monk; his "āryan birth" here refers to his ordination into the SAṂGHA.) ¶ Collections of paritta are particularly common in Southeast Asian Buddhism, and the texts included in these collections are among the most widely known of Buddhist scriptures among the laity. One of the most popular such Pāli anthologies is the *Catubhanavara* ("The Text of the Four Recitals"), which contains twenty-nine (or in some recensions twenty-four) Pāli suttas whose protective powers are thought to be particularly efficacious. (This text is widely used in Sri Lanka, where it is known as the *Pirit Potha*.) Scriptures commonly presumed to have apotropaic powers in Pāli Buddhism include the METTĀSUTTA ("Discourse on Loving-Kindness"), the MAṄGALASUTTA ("Discourse on the Auspicious"), the RATANASUTTA ("Discourse on the Precious"), and the ĀTĀNĀTIYASUTTA ("Discourse on the Ātānātiya Protective Spell"). The recitation of these texts accompanies all sorts of Buddhist ceremonies, from weddings to funerals to house blessings. In Southeast Asia, the monks performing a paritta-recitation ritual are sometimes connected to the congregation with a ritual string, through which blessings and protection are transferred to the participants. See also RAKṢĀ.

**parīttābha**. (P. parittābhā; T. 'od chung; C. shaoguang tian; J. shōkōten; K. sogwang ch'ŏn 少光天). In Sanskrit, "lesser radiance," the lowest of the three heavens of the second meditative absorption (DHYĀNA) associated with the subtle-materiality realm (RŪPADHĀTU). The divinities of this heaven are so named because their bodies emanate less light than those of the divinities of the upper realms of the second dhyāna. As with all the heavens of the subtle-materiality realm, one is reborn as a divinity there through achieving the same level of absorption (dhyāna) as the gods of that heaven during one's practice of meditation in a previous lifetime.

**parīttaśubha**. (P. parittasubhā; T. dge chung; C. shaojing tian; J. shōjōten; K. sojŏng ch'ŏn 少淨天). In Sanskrit, "lesser purity," the lowest of the three heavens of the third meditative absorption (DHYĀNA) of the subtle-materiality realm (RŪPADHĀTU). The divinities of this heaven are so named because the purity of their bliss is less than that of the gods of the other two levels of the third dhyāna. As with all the heavens of the subtle-materiality realm, one is reborn as a divinity there through achieving the same level of concentration (dhyāna) as the gods of that heaven during one's practice of meditation in a previous lifetime.

**Parivāra**. In Pāli, lit., "The Accessory"; an appendix to the three major divisions of the Pāli recension of the monastic disciplinary code (VINAYAPIṬAKA)—viz. the SUTTAVIBHAṄGA, KHANDHAKA, and CŪḶAVAGGA—the *Parivāra* provides a summary and classification of the rules of monastic conduct, as well as additional instructions regarding administrative procedures to be followed within the monastic community (P. saṅgha; S. SAṂGHA). The *Parivāra* consists of nineteen chapters summarizing the earlier sections of the vinaya, the content and structure of which vary slightly. For example, the first chapter is a series of catechisms regarding the monks' rules (PRĀTIMOKṢA), which are classified according to subject. The second offers the same treatment on the rules for nuns. Other chapters are composed of verses or numerical lists. The *Parivāra* also offers detailed procedures regarding the settlement of disagreements or disputes within the community. The text dictates that disputes must be heard and settled by a court of vinaya experts (vinayadhara). Because it contains references to Ceylonese monks, the work is likely of a later origin than the rest of the Pāli vinaya.

**parivāsa**. (T. spo ba; C. biezhu; J. betsujū; K. pyŏlchu 別住). In Sanskrit and Pāli, "probation," a disciplinary term used in the context of the VINAYA. In the monastic disciplinary rules (PRĀTIMOKṢA), parivāsa refers to the temporary period of probation imposed on a monk for concealing a SAṂGHĀVAŚEṢA (P. saṅghadisesa) offense. When a monk commits a saṃghāvaśeṣa offense, he is required to confess it immediately to another monk. If he does so, he is then required to observe six nights of MĀNATVA (P. mānatta), or penance, only. If instead he conceals his offense, he is required to observe the parivāsa probation for as many days as he concealed his offense, after which he must observe six nights of mānatva punishment. Like mānatva, parivāsa entails the temporary loss of privileges normally accorded a monk. The guilty party is required to observe ninety-four restrictions, of which three are most important: (1) he may not dwell under the same roof with another monk, (2) he must announce to monks visiting his monastery that he is observing parivāsa, and (3) when visiting other monasteries, he must inform the monks living there that he is observing parivāsa. In addition, he is not allowed to accept the respect customarily due to a monk, and he may not be served by a novice. The monk observing parivāsa may not serve as an UPĀDHYĀYA or ĀCĀRYA and may not preach to nuns. He must occupy the lowest seat in the monastery and dwell in the worst accommodations. He must give up his seat when approached by another monk and take the lower seat. He may not walk on the same paths as other monks. He may not ask others to bring him his meals to hide his punishment. He may not live alone in the forest or observe ascetic practices (DHUTAṄGA) as a means to hide his offense from others. If at any point in the observance of parivāsa, the guilty monk commits another saṃghāvaśeṣa offense, he must restart the observance from the beginning. After completing his parivāsa penance and his six nights of mānatva, the monk approaches the saṃgha, which in this case means a quorum of monks consisting of at least twenty members, and requests to be "called back into communion" (abbhāna). If the saṃgha agrees, the monk is declared free of the saṃghāvaśeṣa offense and is restored to his former status. ¶ The term parivāsa is also used for a four-month probationary period imposed on mendicants belonging to other religions who wish to join the Buddhist saṃgha. To undertake this parivāsa, the mendicant must first shave his head and beard and don the saffron robes of a monk and approach the SAṂGHA with his request. Having taken the three refuges (TRIŚARAṆA) three times, he declares that formerly he was the member of another sect but now wishes to receive higher ordination as a Buddhist monk. To prepare for ordination, the supplicant requests the saṃgha to grant him parivāsa. The Buddha exempted JAINA ascetics from this requirement, as well as members of his own ŚĀKYA clan.

**parivrājaka**. (P. paribbājaka; T. kun tu rgyu; C. youxingzhe; J. yugyōja; K. yuhaengja 遊行者). In Sanskrit, "wanderer" or "recluse," a wandering ascetic in ancient India. The term is sometimes used to refer to Buddhist monks and nuns, but is more commonly used to refer to non-Buddhist "mendicants," both male and female (S. parivrājikā, P. paribbājikā) of various affiliations, particularly those associated with the various ŚRAMAṆA groups. A catalogue of their views and practices, as well as their condemnation by the Buddha, appears in the BRAHMAJĀLASUTTA. Several of the Buddha's most prominent disciples, including ŚĀRIPUTRA and MAHĀMAUDGALYĀYANA, were originally parivrājakas before leaving their teachers to join the Buddhist SAṂGHA. According to the Pāli VINAYA, Buddhist monks and nuns are not allowed to offer services, food, or clothing to mendicants of other sects; to do so is a pācittiya (S. PĀYATTIKA) offense.

**pāriyātraka**. (T. yongs 'du sa brtol; C. yuanshengshu/bolizhiduoshu; J. enshōju/harishittaju; K. wŏnsaengsu/parijiltasu 圓生樹/波利質多樹). Also known as pārijāta, in Sanskrit, "wish-granting tree," a magical tree whose fruit takes the form of whatever one wishes for. Numerous such trees appear in Buddhist legends. Perhaps the most famous of them is said to grow on the slopes of Mount SUMERU: its trunk is rooted in the realm of the demigods (ASURA), but its leaves, branches, and fruit are located high above in the realm of the divinities (DEVA). Because the demigods are thus unable to enjoy the fruit of the tree that grows in their land, they became jealous of the divinities and fought against them. See also KALPAVṚKṢA.

**pariyatti**. (S. paryavāpti; C. tong; J. tsū; K. t'ong 通). In Pāli, lit. "mastery" or "comprehension" (of a body of scriptural literature), or (in later Pāli commentarial usage) the "scriptures" themselves as transmitted through an oral tradition; one of the two principal monastic vocations noted in the Pāli commentarial literature, along with PAṬIPATTI (meditative practice). The pariyatti monk serves an important role within the Buddhist tradition by continuing the transmission of a corpus of scriptural literature down to the next generation. Pariyatti monks thus performed the function of a bhāṇaka (reciter) or DHARMABHĀṆAKA (reciter of the dharma), who were typically assigned to memorize one specific subcategory of the canon, i.e., Mahjjhimabhāṇaka ("reciters of the MAJJHIMANIKĀYA"), Jātakabhāṇaka ("reciters of the JĀTAKA"), etc. Monks in the contemporary Southeast Asian traditions who study Pāli literature are now also referred to as pariyatti monks; thus the term has come to mean a "study monk." ¶ Pariyatti is also the first of three progressive kinds of religious mastery. In this context, pariyatti is understood as a thorough comprehension of the theories, terms, and texts that ground Buddhist doctrine and that are enumerated in the literature of the TRIPIṬAKA (the canon). The second is paṭipatti, or "practice" of the prescriptions encountered in one's study of pariyatti. The final stage is paṭivedha (S. PRATIVEDHA), direct "penetration" to truth. See also GANTHADHURA.

**parokṣa**. (T. lkog gyur; C. zhiwai; J. chige; K. chioe 智外). In Sanskrit, "hidden," a term used in the twofold classification of phenomena into the manifest (ABHIMUKHĪ), those things that are evident to sense perception, and the hidden (parokṣa), those things whose existence must be inferred through reasoning. The latter category includes such important matters as subtle impermanence, the existence of rebirth, and the existence of liberation. A third category of the "very hidden" (atyantaparokṣa) is sometimes added, comprising those things that are known only by a buddha, such as the specific deeds in a past life that produced specific consequences in the present. Because those things that are "very hidden" are not accessible to direct perception or inference, they are known through statements by the Buddha in the scriptures (ĀGAMA).

**Pārśva**. (T. Rtsibs logs; C. Xie; J. Kyō; K. Hyŏp 脇). A North Indian ĀBHIDHARMIKA associated with the SARVĀSTIVĀDA school, who may have lived during the second century CE. Some four hundred years after the death of the Buddha, the king KANIṢKA (r. 132–152) is said to have convened an assembly of five hundred ARHATs to redact the canon; according to XUANZANG, Pārśva presided over this assembly, which came to be known as the fourth Buddhist council (SAṂGĪTI; see COUNCIL, FOURTH). It was at that council that the ABHIDHARMAPIṬAKA of the Sarvāstivāda school was compiled, including its massive encyclopedic coverage of abhidharma scholastic debates, the ABHIDHARMAMAHĀVIBHĀṢĀ. Pārśva is also claimed to have been a great expert in debate, which led him to convert AŚVAGHOṢA, who became his disciple after Pārśva defeated him in a public debate. In Chinese texts, Pārśva is also called Nansheng ("Hard to Be Born," probably a translation of Durjāta), since according to legend he stayed in his mother's womb until the age of six (or sixty) because of misdeeds he performed in his previous life. Some of the Chinese transmission of the lamplight (CHUANDENG LU) literature states that Pārśva was a native of central India who lived during the fifth century BCE and lists Pārśva as the ninth (as in, for example, the FOZU TONGJI) or tenth Indian patriarch (C. ZUSHI; as in the *Zhiyuelu*). ¶ Pārśva is also the name of the predecessor of MAHĀVĪRA (a.k.a. NIRGRANTHA-JÑĀTĪPUTRA), the Buddha's contemporary in the rival JAINA school of the Indian ŚRAMAṆA movement. This Pārśva seems to have been a historical figure, who appears on a list of twenty-four JINA in the Jaina spiritual lineage.

**Parthia**. (C. Anxi guo; J. Ansoku koku; K. Ansik kuk 安息國). A region in Central Asia, southeast of the Caspian Sea, which the Roman geographers knew as Parthia; the Chinese is a transcription of the Parthian proper name Aršak or Arsakes (see ANXI GUO), referring to the Arsacid kingdom (c. 250 BCE–224 CE). Aršak was the name adopted by all Parthian rulers, and the Chinese employed it to refer to the lands that those rulers controlled. In the Marv oasis, where the old Parthian city of Margiana was located, Soviet archeologists discovered the vestiges of a Buddhist monastic complex that has been dated to the third quarter of the fourth century CE, as well as birch-bark manuscripts written in the BRĀHMĪ script that are associated with the SARVĀSTIVĀDA school of the mainstream Buddhist tradition. There is therefore archeological evidence of at least a semblance of Buddhist presence in the area during the fourth through sixth centuries. Parthian Buddhists who were active in China enable us to push this dating back at least two more centuries, for two of the important early figures in the transmission of Buddhist texts into China also hailed from Parthia: AN SHIGAO (fl. c. 148–180 CE), a prolific translator of mainstream Buddhist works, and An Xuan (fl. c. 168–189), who translated the UGRAPARIPṚCCHĀ with the assistance of the Chinese Yan Fotiao. (The AN in their names is an ethnicon referring to Parthia.) There is, however, no extant Buddhist literature written in the Parthian language and indeed little evidence that written Parthian was ever used for purposes other than government documents and financial records until the third century CE, when Manichaean texts written in Parthian begin to appear.

**pāruṣya**. (P. pharusavācā; T. tshig rtsub; C. ekou; J. akuku; K. akku 惡口). In Sanskrit, "harsh speech," one of the ten unsalutary ways of action (AKUŚALA-KARMAPATHA) that lead to suffering in the future. The ten are classified into three negative physical deeds, four negative verbal deeds, and three negative verbal deeds. Harsh speech falls into the second category, together with lying (mṛṣāvāda), slander (PAIŚUNYA) and senseless speech (SAṂBHINNAPRALĀPA). Harsh speech would include insults, abusive speech, and sarcasm intended to hurt another person. It may be directed against a living being or a physical object. Harsh speech is typically motivated by hatred, but it can also be motivated by jealousy or ignorance.

**paryudāsapratiṣedha**. (T. ma yin dgag). In Sanskrit, "affirming negative," or "implied negation," a term used in Buddhist logic (HETUVIDYĀ) to refer to a negative declaration or designation (PRATIṢEDHA) that is expressed in such a way that it implies something positive. For example, the term "non-cat" implies the existence of something other than a cat. The standard example provided in works on Buddhist logic is: "The corpulent Devadatta does not eat during the day," where the absence of his eating during the day implies that he eats at night. In MADHYAMAKA philosophy, emptiness (ŚŪNYATĀ), the nature of reality, is not a paryudāsapratiṣedha, that is, it does not imply something positive in place of the absence of intrinsic existence (SVABHĀVA). See also PRASAJYAPRATIṢEDHA.

**Pāsādikasutta**. (C. Qingjing jing; J. Shōjōkyō; K. Ch'ŏngjŏng kyŏng 清淨經). In Pāli, the "Delightful Discourse," the twenty-ninth sutta of the DĪGHANIKĀYA (a separate DHARMAGUPTAKA recension appears as the seventeenth SŪTRA in the Chinese translation of the DĪRGHĀGAMA); preached to ĀNANDA and CUNDA in the Vedhañña grove in the Sākiya (S. ŚĀKYA) country. Ānanda and Cunda relate to the Buddha the news of the death of Nigaṇṭha Nātaputta (S. NIRGRANTHA-JÑĀTĪPUTRA), the leader of the JAINA sect of wandering mendicants, and the strife that subsequently arose among his followers. The Buddha declares that such disputes naturally arise when the dharma is not well taught. He then elaborates on various wrong views (P. micchādiṭṭhi; S. MITHYĀDṚṢṬI) and prescribes four foundations of mindfulness (P. SATIPAṬṬHĀNA; S. SMṚTYUPASTHĀNA) as a means by which wrong views can be allayed.

**paścimakāla**. (T. phyi ma'i dus; C. moshi; J. masse; K. malse 末世). In Sanskrit, lit. "latter time," a term that occurs especially in the MAHĀYĀNA SŪTRAS to describe the time after the Buddha's passage into PARINIRVĀṆA. This term does not necessarily connote a final period of the disappearance of the Buddha's dharma, as does the term SADDHARMAVIPRALOPA, but more specifically the period after the Buddha's passing. Since the Mahāyāna sūtras were composed long after the Buddha passed away, the author of the sūtra will sometimes have the Buddha recommend it in "the latter time" is to suggest the Buddha's approval of the text. In China, the translation of this term, moshi, seems to have served as the basis for the Chinese neologism MOFA, a more common term that in East Asia came to evoke the final period of the dharma.

**past lives**. See JĀTISMARA; PŪRVANIVĀSĀNUSMṚTI.

**Paśupatināth**. A large temple complex in Kathmandu, Nepal, along the Bhagmati River, dedicated to the form of Śiva known as Paśupati, "Lord of the Beasts." Newar and Tibetan Buddhist traditions, however, understand Paśupatināth as having Buddhist connections as well. Newar Buddhists venerate the central image of the Guhyeśwarī shrine (understood by Hindus to be Kālī) as the deity NAIRĀTMYĀ, consort of HEVAJRA. Some Tibetans consider several caves along the river to have been occupied by the Indian Buddhist adepts TILOPA and NĀROPA, a tradition that other Tibetan scholars have refuted.

**Paṭācārā**. (C. Boluozhena; J. Harashana; K. Parach'ana 波羅遮那). In Sanskrit and Pāli, an eminent female ARHAT declared by the Buddha to be foremost among his nun disciples in mastery of the VINAYA. According to the Pāli account, she was born the daughter of a wealthy banker in Sāvatthi (S. ŚRĀVASTĪ), but when her parents tried to arrange a marriage with a suitable groom, she instead eloped with a servant with whom she had fallen in love. Even though she had disappointed her parents, she still wished to give birth at their home. But her husband protested, so while he was away collecting wood, she set off for her parents' house alone. Her husband followed, but on the way she gave birth to a son and they returned home together. She did the same when she was ready to give birth to her second child. Again, her husband followed and she gave birth on the road. This time a great storm broke out, and her husband went to gather branches and leaves to make a temporary shelter. She waited in the storm all night, huddled around her children, but her husband did not return; he had been bitten by a snake and had died. She discovered his body the next day and, filled with sorrow, set off across a swollen river to her parents' home. She could not carry both children at the same time, so she left her infant on a bed of leaves on the shore as she waded into the river with the older son. Midstream she looked back to see an eagle swoop down and snatch her infant, and in her excitement she dropped her son who was swept away by the current. Now, more miserable than before, she made her way to Sāvatthi, only to discover that her parents' house had also collapsed in the storm, killing her parents and brother. With no family left, she went mad with grief, wandering about until her clothes fell off. People drove her away until one day she happened upon the JETAVANA grove, where the Buddha was staying. His attendants tried to prevent her approach, but the Buddha bade her to come and tell her story. Consoling her in a gentle voice, he preached to her of the inevitability of death, and, as she was listening to his words, she attained stream-entry (S. SROTAĀPANNA). She requested and was given ordination on the spot. Some time after, while washing her feet, Paṭācārā noticed how water droplets would each roll off in a different direction, and she noted, "So too do beings die, some in childhood, adulthood, or old age." With this realization she attained arhatship. Paṭācārā became a famous teacher of the vinaya, with many female disciples, and was sought out by women who had suffered tragedies because of her wise and gentle advice. A similar story is told about UTPALAVARṆĀ.

**Pāṭaliputra**. (P. Pāṭaliputta; T. Pa ṭa la yi bu; C Huashi cheng; J. Keshijō; K. Hwassi sŏng 華氏城). Capital of the kingdom of MAGADHA and later of the Mauryan empire, ruins of which are located near (and beneath) the modern city of Patna in Bihar. The place is described as having been a village named Pāṭaligāma at the time of the Buddha who, upon visiting the site, prophesied its future greatness. At that time Magadha's capital city was RĀJAGṚHA. It is not known when the capital was transferred to Pāṭaliputra, but it probably occurred sometime after the reign of the Buddha's junior contemporary, King AJĀTAŚATRU. The city reached its greatest glory during the reign of the third Mauryan emperor, AŚOKA, whose realm extended from Afghanistan in the west to Bengal in the east, and to the border of Tamil Nadu in the south. According to the Pāli chronicles DĪPAVAṂSA and MAHĀVAṂSA, it was in the royal palace of Pāṭaliputra that Aśoka was converted to Buddhism by the seven-year-old novice Nigrodha. The same sources state that Pāṭaliputra was the site of the third Buddhist council (SAṂGĪTI; see COUNCIL, THIRD), whence Buddhist missions were dispatched to nine adjacent lands (paccantadesa). These reports are partially confirmed by Aśoka's own inscriptions. in which he describes his adoption and promotion of Buddhism and his dispatch of what appear to be diplomatic missions to several neighboring states. The city was known to the Greeks as Pālibothra and was described by Megasthenes, who dwelled there for a time. It continued to be the capital of Magadha after the fall of the Mauryans and served again as an imperial capital between the fourth and sixth centuries under the Gupta dynasty. By the time the Chinese pilgrim XUANZANG (600/602–664) visited India during the seventh century, Pāṭaliputra was mostly in ruins; what little remained was destroyed in the Muslim invasions of the twelfth century. See also MOGGALIPUTTATISSA.

**path**. See MĀRGA; PATHA; DAO.

**patha**. (T. lam; C. dao; J. dō; K. to 道). In Sanskrit and Pāli, "course" or "way"; a term closely synonymous with "path" (MĀRGA), as in the ten wholesome and unwholesome courses of action (KARMAPATHA). Patha often functions as a pleonastic suffix to create an abstract formation similar to the Sanskrit –tā, e.g., rāgapatha (sensuality). One of its most celebrated usages is in the compound "ways of speech" (vacanapatha, vādapatha), the locus classicus for which appears in the AṬṬHAKAVAGGA: "When all dharmas are abolished, all paths of speech are also abolished" (P. sabbesu dhammesu samūhatesu/samūhatā vādapathā pi sabbe ti).

**path of accumulation**. See SAṂBHĀRAMĀRGA.

**path of cultivation**. See BHĀVANĀMĀRGA.

**path of no further training**. See AŚAIKṢAMĀRGA.

**path of preparation**. See PRAYOGAMĀRGA.

**path of vision**. See DARŚANAMĀRGA.

**paṭibhāganimitta**. In Pāli, lit., "counterpart image," "representational image"; the third of the three major visualization signs experienced in tranquillity (P. samatha; S. ŚAMATHA) exercises, along with the PARIKAMMANIMITTA (preparatory image) and the UGGAHANIMITTA (eidetic image). These three images and the meditative exercises employed to experience them are discussed in detail in BUDDHAGHOSA's VISUDDHIMAGGA, where they are listed sequentially according to the degree of concentration necessary to develop them. These images are particularly associated with the use of the ten visualization devices (KASIṆA) that are used in the initial development of concentration. In these exercises, the meditator attempts to convert a visual object of meditation, such as soil, fire, or a color, into a mental projection or conceptualization that is as clear as the visual image itself. When the image the practitioner sees with his eyes (the so-called parikammanimitta or "preparatory image") is equally clear when visualized in the mind, the practitioner is said to have obtained the uggahanimitta (eidetic image). This image, however, still represents a relatively weak degree of concentration, and it must be strengthened until the paṭibhāganimitta, or "representational image," emerges, which marks the access to meditative absorption (P. JHĀNA, S. DHYĀNA). This representational image is said to be a purely abstract, conceptual form of the visualized image that appears to "break out" from the eidetic sign, e.g., with the fire kasiṇa, the representational image of the visualized flame appears motionless, like a piece of red cloth hanging in space, or like a golden fan.

**Pāṭikasutta**. (C. Anouyi jing; J. Anuikyō; K. Anui kyŏng 阿㝹夷經). In Pāli, "Discourse on the [Ascetic] Pāṭika[putta]," the twenty-fourth sutta of the DĪGHANIKĀYA (a separate DHARMAGUPTAKA recension appears as the fifteenth sūtra in the Chinese translation of the DĪRGHĀGAMA); a discourse by the Buddha on the display of supernatural powers addressed to the mendicant Bhaggavagotta. The Buddha relates how his former disciple, Sunakkhatta, lost faith in the Buddha because the latter refused to display magical powers or speculate on such questions as the origin of the universe as other teachers of the time were wont to do. The Buddha explains that such displays of magic are trivial, and speculation on such matters does not lead to liberation. He does, however, relate the story of his defeat of the JAINA naked ascetic Pāṭikaputta, who challenges the Buddha to a miracle-working contest, but when the Buddha answers the challenge, he is unable to rise from his seat.

**paṭipadāñāṇadassanavisuddhi**. In Pāli, "purity of knowledge and vision regarding progress along the path"; according to the VISUDDHIMAGGA, the sixth of seven "purities" (VISUDDHI; cf. S. VIŚUDDHI) to be developed along the path to liberation. This purity consists of eight kinds of insight knowledge regarding phenomena, together with a ninth kind of knowledge that adapts itself to the supramundane path (P. ariyamagga; S. ĀRYAMĀRGA) and elements pertaining to enlightenment (P. bodhipakkhiyadhamma; S. BODHIPĀKṢIKADHARMA). The nine kinds of knowledge are (1) knowledge arising from the contemplation of arising and passing away (UDAYABBAYĀNUPASSANĀÑĀṆA), (2) knowledge arising from the contemplation of dissolution (BHAṄGĀNUPASSANĀÑĀṆA), (3) knowledge arising from the awareness of terror (BHAYATUPAṬṬHĀNĀÑĀṆA), (4) knowledge arising from the contemplation of danger (ĀDĪNAVĀNUPASSANĀÑĀṆA), (5) knowledge arising from the contemplation of aversion (NIBBIDĀNUPASSANĀÑĀṆA), (6) knowledge arising from the desire for deliverance (MUCCITUKAMYATĀÑĀṆA), (7) knowledge arising from contemplation of reflection (PAṬISAṄKHĀNUPASSANĀÑĀṆA), (8) knowledge arising from equanimity regarding all formations of existence (SAṄKHĀRUPEKKHĀÑĀṆA), and (9) conformity knowledge (ANULOMAÑĀṆA).

**paṭipatti**. (S. pratipatti; T. sgrub pa; C. xiuxing; J. shugyō; K. suhaeng 修行). In Pāli, "practice"; one of the two principal monastic vocations noted in the Pāli commentarial literature, along with PARIYATTI (scriptural mastery). Paṭipatti is the application in practice of the teachings outlined in the scriptures, as distinguished from a purely theoretical understanding of the teachings. Monks in the contemporary Southeast Asian traditions who are primarily engaged in meditative practice, rather than study of the Pāli scriptures, are referred to as paṭipatti monks; thus the term means a "meditation monk." The paṭipatti monk serves the laity by providing them with a PUṆYAKṢETRA, or "field of merit": i.e., by supporting monks who are striving to fully realize the Buddha's teaching, the laity can plant the seeds of merit (PUṆYA), which will improve both this and future lives. ¶ Paṭipatti is also the second of three progressive kinds of religious mastery. In this context, paṭipatti is understood as "practice" of the prescriptions encountered in the first type, pariyatti, the mastery of Buddhist doctrine and textual literature. Paṭipatti results in paṭivedha (S. PRATIVEDHA), direct "penetration" to truth. See also PRATIPATTI; VIPASSANĀDHURA.

**Paṭisambhidāmagga**. In Pāli, "Path to Analytical Knowledge," the twelfth book of the KHUDDAKANIKĀYA. Its chief subject is the attainment of "analytical knowledge" (P. paṭisambhidā, S. PRATISAṂVID), this being the highest attainment available to the ARHAT. This work is scholastic in nature, borrowing long passages from the VINAYAPIṬAKA and the SUTTAPIṬAKA, suggesting that it is a work of a later date, despite its traditional attribution to Sāriputta (S. ŚĀRIPUTRA). The *Paṭisambhidāmagga* describes in detail the nature of wisdom, including the wisdom of the Buddha, in the style of an ABHIDHAMMA text, even though it is included in the SUTTAPIṬAKA. It also discusses a range of central topics in Buddhist soteriology, including mindfulness of the breath (P. ānāpānasati; S. ĀNĀPĀNASMṚTI), the FOUR NOBLE TRUTHS (P. cattāri ariyasaccāni; S. catvāry āryasatyāni), emptiness (P. suñña; cf. S. ŚŪNYATĀ), supranormal powers (P. iddhi; S. ṚDDHI), the foundations of mindfulness (P. SATIPAṬṬHĀNA; S. SMṚTYUPASTHĀNA), serenity or calmness (P. samatha; S. ŚAMATHA), and insight (P. VIPASSANĀ; S. VIPAŚYANĀ). According to the account in the DĪPAVAṂSA, the *Paṭisambhidāmagga* was one of the works rejected by the MAHĀSĀṂGHIKA school from inclusion in the canon.

**paṭisaṅkhānupassanāñāṇa**. In Pāli, "knowledge arising from contemplation of reflection"; according to the VISUDDHIMAGGA, the seventh of nine types of knowledge (ÑĀṆA) cultivated as part of "purity of knowledge and vision of progress along the path" (PAṬIPADĀÑĀṆADASSANAVISUDDHI). This latter category, in turn, constitutes the sixth and penultimate purity (VISUDDHI; cf. S. VIŚUDDHI) to be developed along the path to liberation. The practitioner cultivates this knowledge as a means of escape from the conditioned factors (P. saṅkhāra; S. SAṂSKĀRA) comprising the universe, having become desirous of deliverance from all forms of existence in the cycle of rebirth. He develops this by reflecting again upon the conditioned factors by noting how they are characterized by the three marks (P. tilakkhaṇa; S. TRILAKṢAṆA) of impermanence (P. anicca; S. ANITYA), suffering (P. dukkha; S. DUḤKHA) and nonself (P. anatta; S. ANĀTMAN). Seeing them as evanescent, temporary, limited by arising and passing away, perishable, unstable, formed, subject to annihilation and death, etc., the practitioner understands these formations to be impermanent.

Seeing them as oppressed, unbearable, the cause of pain, a disease, a tumor, a dart, a calamity, subject to birth, aging, illness, sorrow, lamentation, despair, etc., he understands these conditioned factors to be suffering. Seeing them as alien, empty, vain, void, ownerless and without a master, as neither "I" nor "mine" nor belonging to anyone else, etc., he understands them to be nonself.

**pātra**. (P. patta; T. lhung bzed; C. bo; J. hachi; K. pal 鉢). In Sanskrit, "begging bowl" or "alms bowl," the bowl that monks, nuns, female probationers, and male and female novices use for gathering alms food (PIṆḌAPĀTA). The bowl is one of the eight requisites (PARIṢKĀRA) allowed the monk, and (along with robes), is the most visible possession of a monk. Because of its ubiquity in Buddhist monasticism, the bowl is an object of high practical and symbolic value within the tradition and thus figures prominently in Buddhist practice, institutions, and literature. There are rules of what materials bowls may, and may not, be made of. They are usually made of iron or clay and may be of three sizes, large, medium, or small. Offering food to monks is one of the primary means by which the laity may earn religious merit, and the bowl is symbolic of the close bonds of mutual support that are at the heart of monastic-lay relations. One of the most severe penalties the SAṂGHA can administer to the laity, therefore, is to refuse their donations. This act of ultimate censure is called "overturning the bowl" (S. PĀTRANIKUBJANA), and is imposed on a layperson who has, for example, harmed the interests of the saṃgha, abused monks or nuns, or spoken disparagingly of the Buddha, dharma, or saṃgha. If the layperson makes amends, the saṃgha ends its boycott by "turning the bowl upright" and receiving gifts from him or her again. In all traditions of Buddhism, the bowls of past masters have functioned as relics (and were sometimes enshrined). In some traditions, most famously that of the CHAN school, the bowl was passed on from teacher to student as a symbol of lineage and as an insignia of authority. See also TAKUHATSU.

**pātranikubjana**. (P. pattanikkujjana; T. lhung bzed khas phub pa; C. fubo/fubo jiemo; J. fuhatsu/fuhatsu konma; K. pubal/pubal kalma 覆鉢/覆鉢羯磨). In Sanskrit, "overturning the bowl," a severe form of censure for laypeople. See PĀTRA.

**patriarch(s)**. See ZUSHI.

**Paṭṭhāna**. [alt. Paṭṭhānappakaraṇa]. In Pāli, lit. "Relations," or "Foundational Conditions"; the sixth of the seven books of the Pāli ABHIDHAMMAPIṬAKA (but also sometimes considered the last book of that canon). This highly abstract work concerns the twenty-four conditions (P. paccaya; S. PRATYAYA) that govern the interaction of factors (P. dhamma; S. DHARMA) in the causal matrix of dependent origination (P. paṭiccasamuppāda; S. PRATĪTYASAMUTPĀDA). According to the Pāli ABHIDHAMMA, these relations, when applied to all possible combinations of phenomena, describe the entire range of conscious experience. The *Paṭṭhāna* is organized into four main divisions based on four distinct methods of conditionality, which it calls the positive, or "forward," method (anuloma); the negative, or "reverse," method (paccanīya); the positive–negative method (anuloma-paccanīya); and the negative–positive method (paccanīya-anuloma). Each of these four is further divided into six possible combinations of phenomena, e.g., in triplets (tika) and pairs (duka): for example, each condition is analyzed in terms of the triplet set of wholesome (P. kusala; S. KUŚALA), unwholesome (P. akusala; S. AKUŚALA), and neutral (P. avyākata; S. AVYĀKṚTA). The four main sections are each further subdivided into six sections, giving a total of twenty-four divisions, one for each possible mode of conditionality. The twenty-four modes are as follows: root condition (hetupaccaya), object condition (ārammaṇapaccaya), predominance condition (adhipatipaccaya), continuity condition (anantarapaccaya), immediate continuity condition (samanantarapaccaya), co-nascence condition (sahajātapaccaya), mutuality condition (aññamaññapaccaya), dependence condition (nissayapaccaya), reliance condition (upanissayapaccaya), antecedence condition (purejātapaccaya), consequence condition (pacchājātapaccaya), repetition condition (āsevanapaccaya), volitional action condition (kammapaccaya), fruition condition (vipākapaccaya), nutriment condition (āhārapaccaya), governing faculty condition (indriyapaccaya), absorption condition (jhānapaccaya), path condition (maggapaccaya), association condition (sampayuttapaccaya), disassociation condition (vippayuttapaccaya), presence condition (atthipaccaya), absence condition (natthipaccaya), disappearance condition (vigatapaccaya), and continuation condition (avigatapaccaya). The *Paṭṭhāna* is also known as the "Great Composition" (*Mahāpakaraṇa*) because of its massive size: the Pāli edition in Burmese script is 2,500 pages in length, while the Thai edition spans 6,000 pages. An abbreviated translation of the *Paṭṭhāna* appears in the Pali Text Society's English translation series as *Conditional Relations.* ¶ In contemporary Myanmar (Burma), where the study of abhidhamma continues to be highly esteemed, the *Paṭṭhāna* is regularly recited in festivals that the Burmese call pathan pwe. Pathan pwe are marathon recitations that go on for days, conducted by invited ABHIDHAMMIKA monks who are particularly well versed in the *Paṭṭhāna.* The pathan pwe serves a similar function to PARITTA recitations, in that it is believed to ward off baleful influences, but its main designated purpose is to forestall the decline and disappearance of the Buddha's dispensation (P. sāsana; S. ŚĀSANA). The Theravāda tradition considers the *Paṭṭhāna* to be the Buddha's most profound exposition of ultimate truth (P. paramatthasacca; S. PARAMĀRTHASATYA) and, according to the Pāli commentaries, the *Paṭṭhāna* is the first constituent of the Buddha's sāsana that will disappear from the world as the religion faces its inevitable decline. The abhidhammikas' marathon recitations of the *Paṭṭhāna*, therefore, help to ward off the eventual demise of the Buddhist religion. See also ANULOMAPRATILOMA.

**pattidāna**. [alt. patti] (cf. S. prāpti; C. de; J. toku; K. tŭk 得). In Pāli, lit. "assigned gift," referring to merit (P. puñña,

S. PUṆYA) that has been obtained and then transferred (parivaṭṭa) to others; the term is thus often translated into English as the "transfer of merit." The "transfer of merit" is one of the most common practices in THERAVĀDA Buddhism, in which the merit from a particular virtuous deed can be directed toward another person specified by the agent. In doing so, the agent of the deed does not lose the karmic benefit of the virtuous deed and accumulates further virtue through the gift. In the *Tirokuḍḍasutta*, a number of ghosts (P. peta, S. PRETA) cause a commotion in the palace of BIMBISĀRA after he serves a meal to the Buddha and his monks. The Buddha explains that they are former kinsmen of the king who have been reborn as ghosts, who can only be satiated by receiving merit. The king then offers alms to the Buddha and his monks the next day, verbally offering it to his relatives at the same time. The ghosts, who had been invisible, become visible and are seen receiving food and drink. When the king offers robes to the monks, they also receive robes. The transfer of merit is a practice found throughout the Buddhist world, based on the belief that the dead cannot directly receive offerings; instead, those offerings must be made to virtuous recipients, such as the Buddha or the members of the SAṂGHA, with the merit of that deed then transferred to the departed. See also PARIṆĀMANĀ; PUṆYĀNUMODANA.

**Paurṇagiri**. (S). See PŪRṆAGIRI.

**pauṣṭika**. (T. rgyas pa'i las; C. zengyi; J. zōyaku; K. chŭngik 增益). In Sanskrit, "increase," one of the four types of deeds or powers (caturkarman) described in tantric texts. The others are the pacification of difficulties (ŚĀNTIKA), the control of negative forces (VAŚĪKARAṆA), and the destruction of enemies (ABHICĀRA). Tantric texts often contain rituals designed to bestow one of more of these powers. Rituals for pauṣṭika typically promise the ability to increase auspicious elements, both physical and spiritual. Thus, one finds rituals for increasing wealth and prosperity (sometimes through finding buried treasure), for increasing one's intelligence, life span, fame, and beauty, and for avoiding famine and disease.

**Pāyāsisutta**. (C. Bisu jing; J. Heishukukyō; K. P'yesuk kyŏng 弊宿經). In Pāli, "Discourse to Pāyāsi," the twenty-third sutta of the DĪGHANIKĀYA (a separate DHARMAGUPTAKA recension appears as the seventh SŪTRA in the Chinese translation of the DĪRGHĀGAMA); preached by the Buddha's disciple Kumārakassapa (S. KUMĀRA-KĀŚYAPA) to Pāyāsi, governor of the town of Setabyā in Kosala (S. KOŚALA) country. Pāyāsi held the wrong views that there is neither another world, nor life after death, nor consequences of good and bad actions. Kumārakassapa convinced him of his errors and converted him to Buddhism through the skillful use of similes. He then taught the governor the proper way to make offerings to the three jewels (S. RATNATRAYA) of the Buddha, the DHARMA, and the SAṂGHA so that they would bear the greatest fruition of merit.

**pāyattika**. [alt. prāyaścittika, pātayantika, etc.] (P. pācittiya; T. ltung byed; C. danduo; J. tanda; K. tant'a 單墮). In Sanskrit, lit. "requiring expiation," "transgression to be confessed," a lesser category of violations of the monastic code (PRĀTIMOKṢA). Transgressions fall under three major headings: (1) those that result in "defeat" (PĀRĀJIKA), (2) those that are expiated through penance and probation imposed by the SAṂGHA (SAṂGHĀVAŚEṢA), and (3) those that are expiated simply by being confessed to another monk. The pāyattika constitute this last category. In the Pāli VINAYA, there are ninety-two acts that fall under this category, comprising a wide range of offenses, ranging from lying to digging in the earth, damaging a plant, lying down in the same lodging with a woman, not putting away bedding, sewing the robe of a nun who is not a relative, drinking alcohol, swimming for pleasure, offering food to a naked ascetic, staying more than two or three consecutive nights with an army, and hiding another monk's bowl as a joke. The term also appears in another category of transgressions, called "forfeiture" (S. NAIḤSARGIKAPĀYATTIKA; P. nissaggiyapācittiya), in which a monk or nun possesses an object that is prohibited or has been wrongly acquired; in that case, the object must be forfeited and the deed confessed.

**Pegu**. [alt. Bago]. Former capital of the Mon (Talaing) kingdom of Rāmaññadesa (1287–1539) in Lower Burma; also called Hanthawaddi. Founded c. 825 CE on the coast of the Bay of Bengal, Pegu served as an important entrepôt, which had flourishing commercial and cultural links with Sri Lanka, India, and ports farther east. The port was made the Mon capital in 1353 when the Mon court was transferred there from the city of Muttama (Martaban). The kingdom of Rāmaññadesa had originally gained independence in 1287 with the collapse of its former suzerain, the Burmese empire of PAGAN (Bagan), and for much of the next two and a half centuries it was engaged in internecine warfare with Pagan's landlocked successor state, AVA, for control of the maritime province of Bassein on Pegu's western flank. As the capital of a wealthy trading kingdom, Pegu was filled with numerous Buddhist shrines and monasteries. These included the Kyaikpien, Mahazedi, Shwegugale, and Shwemawdaw pagodas, and the nearby Shwethalyaung, a colossal reclining buddha built in 994. The most important Mon king in the religious sphere to rule from Pegu was Dhammacedi (r. 1472–1492) who, in 1476, conducted a purification of the Mon sāsana along the lines of the reformed Sinhalese tradition. The purification is recorded in the KALYĀṆĪ INSCRIPTIONS erected in Pegu at site of Kalyāṇī Sīmā Hall. Pegu fell to the Burmese in 1539, who retained it as the capital of their new Burmese Empire until 1599. The beauty of Pegu was regularly extolled in the travelogues of European merchants and adventurers. Pegu again briefly became the capital of an independent Mon kingdom between 1747 and 1757, after which it was utterly destroyed by the Burmese king ALAUNGPAYA (r. 1752–1760), founder of the Konbaung empire (1752–1885). It was rebuilt and subsequently served as the

British capital of Lower Burma between 1852 and 1862 and is currently the capital of Bago District.

**Pe har rgyal po**. (Pehar Gyalpo). A god of the Tangut people (T. Mi nyag; C. Xixia), who was adopted into Tibetan Buddhism as the state oracle. According to Tibetan legend, at the completion of the BSAM YAS monastery at the end of the eighth century, the monastery was in need of a protector god. At that time, Pe har was in residence at a hermitage in Bhata hor, having come there from Bengal. In the early ninth century, the Tibetan king KHRI SRONG LDE BTSAN sent his nephew Prince Mu rug btsan po to conquer Mi nyag and destroy Bhata hor, which he did with the assistance of the god VAIŚRAVAṆA. Pe har fled, turning himself into a vulture to escape. A YAKṢA in Vaiśravaṇa's command shot him with an arrow, and brought him to Bsam yas, where PADMASAMBHAVA installed him as the monastery's protector. Other versions credit Padmasambhava with the actual capture of Pe har, and still others have GE SAR defeat Pe har. The kingdom of Mi nyag was finally destroyed by the Mongol Genghis Khan in the twelfth century, leading to an influx in Mi nyag refugees; this was a time when Pe har's legends were being developed. From that point, Pe har, as a captured deity made to serve the Tibetan state, is a figure much interwoven in the events of the history of Tibetan imperial expansion. Pe har is said to have resided at Bsam yas for some seven centuries before moving to the Gnas chung shrine below 'BRAS SPUNGS monastery outside of LHA SA at the time of the fifth DALAI LAMA. It is at GNAS CHUNG, a monastery with both RNYING MA and DGE LUGS PA affiliations, that he serves as the state oracle. The legends of his move involve an initial move to a Rnying ma monastery on the banks of the Skyid chu upriver from Lha sa. Pe har and the abbot of the monastery did not get along, and, after causing a fair amount of mischief, Pe har was locked in a wooden box that was thrown into the river. Various accounts relate how the box was retrieved by monks of 'Bras spungs, and how Pe har then escaped, alighting in the form of a white dove in a tree below Gnas chung monastery where Pe har subsequently took up residence. (See GNAS CHUNG ORACLE for Pe har's activities as the Tibetan state oracle.) Pe har has been fully integrated into native Tibetan spirit pantheons: he is the head of the worldly DHARMAPĀLA, chief of the three hundred sixty rgyal po spirits, and leader of a group of deities known as the rgyal po sku lnga, the "kings of the five bodies," who in addition to Pe har are Brgya byin, Mon bu pu tra, Shing bya can, and Dgra lha skyes gcig bu, all of whom are also seen as emanations of Pe har. His consort is named Bdud gza' smin dkar. In iconography Pe har is frequently pictured as white, with three faces and six arms riding a white lion, although he is also shown with one face and two hands. Finally, the spelling of his name varies considerably, including Dpe kar, Pe dkar, Spe dkar, Dpe dkar, Be dkar, Dpe ha ra, and Pe ha ra.

**Pelliot, Paul**. (1878–1945). French Sinologist, whose retrieval of thousands of manuscripts from DUNHUANG greatly advanced the modern understanding of Buddhism along the ancient SILK ROAD. A pupil of SYLVAIN LÉVI (1863–1935), Pelliot was appointed to the École Française d'Extrême-Orient in Hanoi in 1899. In 1906, Pelliot turned his attention to Chinese Central Asia, leading an expedition from Paris to Tumchuq and KUCHA, where he unearthed documents in the lost TOCHARIAN language. In Urumchi, Pelliot received word of the hidden library cave at Dunhuang discovered by AUREL STEIN and arrived at the site in February 1908. There, he spent three weeks reading through an estimated twenty thousand scrolls. Like Stein, Pelliot sent thousands of manuscripts to Europe to be studied and preserved. Unlike Stein, who knew no Chinese or Prakritic languages, Pelliot was able to more fully appreciate the range of documents at Dunhuang, selecting texts in Chinese, Tibetan, Khotanese, Sogdian (see SOGDIANA), and Uighur and paying particular attention to unusual texts, including rare Christian and Manichaean manuscripts. Today these materials form the Pelliot collection of Dunhuang materials in the Bibliothèque nationale in Paris. Ironically, it was Pelliot's announcement of the Dunhuang manuscript cache to scholars in Beijing in May 1908 that resulted in the immediate closing of the site to all foreigners. Pelliot returned to Paris in 1909, only to be confronted by the erroneous claim that he had returned with forged manuscripts. These charges were proved false only in 1912 with the publication of Stein's book, *Ruins of Desert Cathay*, which made clear that Stein had left manuscripts behind in Dunhuang. In 1911, Pelliot was made chair of Central Asian Languages at the Collège de France and dedicated the rest of his career to the study of both China and Central Asia. During the First World War, Pelliot served as French military attaché in Beijing. In the postwar years he was an active member of the Société Asiatique. In 1920, he succeeded Édouard Chavannes as the editor of the journal *T'oung Pao*. His vast erudition, combined with his knowledge of some thirteen languages, made him one of the leading scholars of Asia of his generation.

**Peng Shaosheng**. (彭紹升) (1740–1796). A Confucian literatus turned Buddhist adherent during the Qing dynasty (1683–1839); his cognomen was Peng Jiqing. Peng authored several important biographical collections of Chinese Buddhist adherents who were mostly ignored in the traditional collections of biographies of eminent monks (GAOSENG ZHUAN); these include a collection of biographies of laypeople, the JUSHI ZHUAN ("Record of [Eminent] Laymen") and the SHANNÜREN ZHUAN ("Record of [Eminent] Laywomen"), along with a c. 1783 collection of biographies of pure land figures titled *Jingtu shengxian lu* ("A Record of Pure Land Sages"). See JUSHI ZHUAN; SHANNÜREN ZHUAN.

**perfect and sudden teaching**. See YUANDUN JIAO.

**perfection of wisdom**. See PRAJÑĀPĀRAMITĀ.

**perfection of wisdom sūtras**. See PRAJÑĀPĀRAMITĀ.

**perfection(s)**. See PĀRAMITĀ.

**person**. See PUDGALA.

**perverted views**. See VIPARYĀSA.

**Peṭakopadesa**. In Pāli, "Piṭaka-Disclosure"; a paracanonical Pāli text dedicated to the interpretation of canonical texts, which is included in the longer Burmese edition of the KHUDDAKANIKĀYA. The work is traditionally ascribed to the Buddha's disciple Kaccāna (S. KĀTYĀYANA; MAHĀKĀTYĀYANA), but was likely composed in India as early as the second century BCE. A work in eight chapters, it is meant to assist those who are already versed in the dharma in the proper exegesis and explanation of specific passages, allowing them to rephrase a passage in such a way that it remains consistent in meaning with the teaching as a whole. In this way it offers an early guide to authors of commentaries. In the Pāli tradition, it was superseded by a somewhat later and similar text, the NETTIPPAKARAṆA. Both the *Netti* and the *Peṭakopadesa* develop an elaborate hermeneutical theory based on the broad rubrics of "interpretation" or "guidance" (P. netti; cf. S. netri) regarding "sense" (vyañjana) and interpretation regarding "meaning" (P. attha; S. ARTHA). See also SANFEN KEJING; VYĀKHYĀYUKTI.

**Petavatthu**. In Pāli, "Accounts of Ghosts," the seventh book of the KHUDDAKANIKĀYA of the Pāli SUTTAPIṬAKA. It consists of fifty-one stories of petas (S. PRETA, often translated as "ghosts" or "hungry ghosts") who are suffering the negative consequences of their unsalutary deeds in a previous life. The stories seem to have been intended to serve as cautionary tales for the laity; the *Petavatthu* describes the horrors that await the wicked, just as the VIMĀNAVATTHU describes the pleasures in the heavens that await the good. In most of the stories, a monk encounters a peta and asks how he or she has come to suffer this fate. The peta then recounts the negative deeds in a former life that led to the present sorrowful rebirth.

**Pha dam pa sangs rgyas**. (Padampa Sangye) (d. 1117). An Indian tantric master renowned in Tibet for his teachings on the practice of "pacification" (ZHI BYED). His name in Sanskrit is sometimes given as Paramabuddha, although Pha dam pa is also regarded as an affectionate title, "Excellent Father." According to traditional accounts, he was from a family of seafaring merchants on the southeast coast of India. After his father's death, he was ordained at VIKRAMAŚĪLA, with the ordination name Kamalaśīla, leading some Tibetan sources to claim that he was the great paṇḍita of the same name who participated in the BSAM YAS DEBATE several centuries earlier. Other sources give his Indian name as Kamalaśrī. He visited Tibet on numerous occasions (according to some sources, seven times). Referred to by Tibetans as the "little black Indian" (rgya gar nag chung), he attracted few disciples initially, gaining greater fame on subsequent visits. He spent much time in the region of Ding ri in central Tibet, especially around the village of GLANG 'KHOR, where he is still venerated for the earthy and practical advice he gave on how to practice Buddhism. The most famous of these teachings is his *Ding ri brgya tsa ma* ("Dingri One Hundred"). He dressed as an Indian ascetic and sometimes taught simply through gestures, although it is unclear whether this was his tantric mode of expression or was because he initially spoke little Tibetan. Pha dam pa sangs rgyas reportedly encountered the famous YOGIN MI LA RAS PA on a nearby mountain pass, where they exchanged teachings and acknowledged each other's spiritual attainment. He was known for including women among his disciples. Indeed, his most famous disciple, the great female adept MA GCIG LAB SGRON, based her practice tradition known as severance (GCOD) partly on his instructions. After leaving Tibet for the last time, he is said to have traveled to China; according to a Tibetan tradition, he was known in China as BODHIDHARMA.

**Phag mo gru pa Rdo rje rgyal po**. (Pakmodrupa Dorje Gyalpo) (1110–1170). A Tibetan scholar and adept who is counted as one of the great disciples of the key BKA' BRGYUD founder SGAM PO PA BSOD NAMS RIN CHEN, and is venerated as the source for many subsequent Bka' brgyud lineages. Born in the 'Bri lung rme shod region of eastern Tibet, Phag mo gru pa's parents died while he was still young. Receiving ordination as a novice Buddhist monk at the age of eight, he studied under a variety of teachers during the early part of his life. At eighteen, he traveled to central Tibet, receiving full ordination at the age of twenty-five. There he trained under a number of BKA' GDAMS pa teachers, and later, under the great SA SKYA master SA CHEN KUN DGA SNYING PO, from whom he received extensive instruction in the tradition of the path and its result (LAM 'BRAS). At the age of forty, he traveled to DWAGS LHA SGAM PO in southern Tibet, where he met Sgam po pa, who became his principal guru. Sgam po pa famously held up a half-eaten ball of parched barley flour mixed with tea and said to Phag mo gru pa, "This is greater than the results of all your previous meditation." After he demonstrated his humility by carrying stones to build a STŪPA, Sgam po pa gave Phag mo gru pa the transmission of instructions on MAHĀMUDRĀ meditation and, through their practice, is said to have attained great realization. In 1158, Phag mo gru pa established a simple meditation hut where he lived until his death in 1170; this location later served as the foundation for the influential monastery of GDAN SA MTHIL. Phag mo gru pa was renowned for his strict adherence to the VINAYA, even going on alms rounds, a rare practice in Tibet. Several individuals among his many followers established a number of important branch lineages, the so-called "eight minor Bka' brgyud subsects" (see BKA' BRGYUD CHE BZHI CHUNG BRGYAD) that collectively came to be known as the Phag gru Bka' brgyud.

**'Phags pa Blo gros rgyal mtshan**. (Pakpa Lodrö Gyaltsen) (1235–1280). An eminent scholar of the SA SKYA sect of Tibetan Buddhism, famed for the position of political power he held at the court of the Mongol emperor of Qubilai Khan (r. 1260–1294). He is also revered as one of the five great Sa skya forefathers (SA SKYA GONG MA RNAM LNGA). 'Phags pa's uncle, SA SKYA PAṆḌITA, was summoned to the court of the Mongol prince Godan in 1244, eventually meeting the prince in 1247. 'Phags pa and his younger brother accompanied their uncle during this journey. After Sa skya Paṇḍita cured Godan Khan of a disease and converted him to Buddhism, the khan appointed him as regent of Tibet under Mongol patronage, and the young 'Phags pa was invited to remain at the Mongol court. After the death of Godan Khan, Qubilai Khan summoned 'Phags pa to his court (at what would come to be called Shangdu), seeking to solidify Mongol rule over Tibet by controlling the politically powerful Sa skya leaders. En route, he gave teachings in eastern Tibet and converted the Rdzong gsar region from BON to Buddhism, establishing the Sa skya tradition there. According to some accounts, 'Phags pa arrived at Qubilai Khan's court in 1253. He soon impressed the emperor with his erudition and display of magical powers, which apparently outshone those of other religious figures at the Mongol court, defeating Daoist priests in debate. By 1258, 'Phags pa had so impressed his hosts, first the emperor's wife Chabi and then Qubilai himself, that he was asked to bestow tantric initiations and teachings, thus converting the imperial couple to Buddhism. According to an arrangement suggested by Chabi, 'Phags pa would sit in a lower position than the emperor during state rituals, and the emperor would sit in a lower position than 'Phags pa in religious rituals. 'Phags pa would later identify Qubilai Khan as an incarnation of MAÑJUŚRĪ and as a CAKRAVARTIN. In 1260, the year Qubilai ascended to the rank of Great Khan, 'Phags pa was given the official positions of imperial preceptor (C. dishi) and state preceptor (C. GUOSHI). In this latter position, he was the head of the Buddhist clergy of the entire empire, including Tibet, although he himself remained in China. A new office of dpon chen (great minister) was created for a Mongol-appointed Tibetan official who would serve as civil and military administrator for Tibet. In 1280, 'Phags pa died, allegedly having been poisoned by the dpon chen. The relationship between 'Phags pa and Qubilai is often cited as the model for the subsequent relationship between Tibet and China known as "patron and priest" (YON MCHOD). According to the Tibetan view, this relationship was formed between the leading lama of Tibet (a position later filled by the DALAI LAMAS) who acted as chief spiritual advisor and priest to the emperor, who in return acted as patron and protector of the lama and the dominion of the Buddhist realm, Tibet. 'Phags pa is often called by the honorific title chos rgyal, or "dharma king," and is also credited with creating in 1269 a new script for the pan-empire use of the Mongolian language. The square forms of the 'Phags pa script had been thought by some scholars to have been the model for the creation of the indigenous Korean alphabet of Han'gŭl in the mid-fifteenth century. However, it is now generally believed that the shapes of the Han'gŭl letters mimic the mouth's shape when articulating classes of consonants, although probably with some influence from the 'Phags pa forms.

**'Phags pa wa ti lha khang**. (Pakpawati Lhakhang). A Nepalese pagoda-style temple located in the southwest Tibetan village of Skyid grong (Kyirong). It is named after its principal image, the famed 'Phags pa wa ti, said to be one of FOUR BROTHER STATUES OF AVALOKITEŚVARA (alt. three or five according to some sources) miraculously formed from the trunk of a single sandalwood tree. The 'Phag pa wa ti of Skyid grong, also called the Skyid grong Jo bo (Kyirong Jowo), is a likeness of the bodhisattva Avalokiteśvara in the form known as Khasarpāṇi and is considered one of the most sacred Buddhist images in Tibet. Its praises have been sung by many of the country's leading masters. The image was secretly removed to India in 1959 by Tibetan guerilla fighters and currently resides in the private chapel of the present DALAI LAMA in DHARMAŚĀLĀ. The other brother statues have been identified as the 'Phags pa Lokeśvara of the PO TA LA palace and the white and red MATSYENDRANĀTH statues in the Kathmandu Valley.

**phala**. (T. 'bras bu; C. guo; J. ka; K. kwa 果). In Sanskrit and Pāli, lit. "fruition," and thus "effect" or "result"; the term has three principal denotations. First, in discussions of causation, phala refers to the physical or mental "effect" produced by a cause (HETU), such as a sprout produced from a seed, or a moment of sensory consciousness (VIJÑĀNA) produced through the contact (SPARŚA) between a sense base (INDRIYA) and a sense object (ĀYATANA; ĀLAMBANA). Second, in discussions of the path (MĀRGA), phala refers to the fruition of the four supramundane paths (ĀRYAMĀRGA), i.e., stream-enterer (SROTAĀPANNA), once-returner (SAKṚDĀGĀMIN), nonreturner (ANĀGĀMIN), and worthy one (ARHAT). Third, in discussions of the process of moral causality, the specific type of fruition called the VIPĀKAPHALA (retributive fruition) refers to the maturation of a deed (KARMAN). ¶ Given the centrality of theories of causation in Buddhist philosophy and practice, the notion of cause and effect is analyzed in detail in Buddhist literature, particularly in the ABHIDHARMA systems. In the SARVĀSTIVĀDA abhidharma and the YOGĀCĀRA system, five types of phala are enumerated. These are (1) NIṢYANDAPHALA, "correlative fruition," wherein the effect may correlate with the cause of the previous action, e.g., as a result of giving a gift in a past life, a person might either enjoy the act of charity or receive charity in a future life; or, as a result of committing murder in a past life, a person might enjoy killing or be murdered in a future life; (2) VIPĀKAPHALA or "retributive fruition," which refers to the ripening of past actions; (3) VISAṂYOGAPHALA, or "disconnection fruition," which refers to the state of absence of, or separation from, the afflictions (KLEŚA), e.g., NIRVĀṆA is an effect that is disconnected from the afflictions; (4) PURUṢAKĀRAPHALA, lit. "effect caused by a being," or "virile fruition," which would include such things as a pot produced by a potter and a level of attainment that results from the practice of meditation; (5) ADHIPATIPHALA, or "predominant fruition," which would include the effects of past deeds that take the form of one's present environment and resources. ¶ Finally, the term phala is also used as one of the epithets of Buddhist TANTRA, which is called the PHALAYĀNA or "fruition vehicle" because it incorporates the fruition of buddhahood into the practice of the path.

**phalacitta**. In Pāli, "fruition consciousness"; the moment or moments of consciousness following the practitioner's entry into any of the four noble paths (P. ariyamagga, S. ĀRYAMĀRGA) of stream-enterer (P. sotāpanna, S. SROTAĀPANNA), once-returner (P. sakadāgāmi, S. SAKṚDĀGĀMIN), nonreturner (P. anāgāmi, S. ANĀGĀMIN) or worthy one (P. arahant, S. ARHAT). These four paths are entered through attaining path consciousness (MAGGACITTA), and it is through the force of this moment of path consciousness that fruition consciousness (phalacitta) arises. Fruition consciousness continues for two or three moments, after which the mind subsides into the subconscious mental continuum (BHAVAṄGASOTA). The difference between path consciousness and fruition consciousness may be described in the following way with reference to the stream-enterer: through the path of stream-entry one *becomes* free of the first three fetters (SAṂYOJANA), whereas through the fruition of stream-entry one actually *is* free of the first three fetters. Because path consciousness represents the first moment of attaining the path, it occurs only once to any given practitioner for each of the four noble paths. Fruition consciousness, on the other hand, is not so limited in its definition and therefore may repeat itself innumerable times during a lifetime. A synonym of phalacitta is phalañāṇa, or "knowledge of the path."

**phalapratipannaka**. (P. phalapaṭipannaka; T. 'bras bu la zhugs pa; C. deguo; J. tokuka; K. tŭkkwa 得果). In Sanskrit, "one who has entered upon the fruition [of the path]"; a term used to describe four preparatory steps on the path to becoming a "noble one" (ĀRYA). For each of the four stages of stream-enterer (SROTAĀPANNA), once-returner (SAKṚDĀGĀMIN), nonreturner (ANĀGĀMIN), and worthy one (ARHAT), there are two steps: entering upon the fruition (phalapaṭipannaka) and abiding in the fruition (PHALASTHITA). These two steps are distinguished as (1) achieving one of the four stages of the path, followed by (2) the state of having achieved that step.

**phalasthita**. [alt. phalastha] (P. phalaṭhita; T. 'bras bu la gnas pa; C. zhuguo; J. jūka; K. chugwa 住果). In Sanskrit, "abiding in the fruition," a term used to describe four resultant steps on the path to becoming a "noble one" (ĀRYA). For each of the four stages of stream-enterer (SROTAĀPANNA), once-returner (SAKṚDĀGĀMIN), nonreturner (ANĀGĀMIN), and worthy one (ARHAT), there are two steps: entering upon the fruition (PHALAPAṬIPANNAKA) and abiding in the fruition (phalasthita). These two steps are distinguished as (1) achieving one of the four stages of the path, followed by (2) the state of having achieved that step.

**phalayāna**. (T. 'bras bu theg pa). In Sanskrit, "fruition vehicle"; one of the epithets of the VAJRAYĀNA. In this context, the "effect" or "fruition" (PHALA) refers to buddhahood, specifically the pure abode, body, resources, and deeds of a buddha. In tantric practice, one visualizes oneself as a buddha, in a MAṆḌALA palace, with the possessions of a buddha such as the VAJRA and bell, performing the deeds of a buddha such as purifying environments and the beings who inhabit them. This practice is referred to as bringing the fruition to the path; as a means of proceeding quickly on the path to buddhahood, one imagines that the fruition of buddhahood has already been achieved.

**Pháp Loa**. (法螺) (1284–1330). In Vietnamese, "Dharma Conch"; the second patriarch of the TRÚC LÂM school of Vietnamese Buddhism. His personal name was Đồng Kiên Cương and was a native of Nam Sách (in northern Vietnam). He met TRẦN NHÂN TÔNG for the first time in 1304 and became his disciple. He received full ordination from Trần Nhân Tông in 1305 and was given the dharma name Pháp Loa. In 1308, he was officially recognized as the second patriarch of the Trúc Lâm School. Buddhism prospered under his leadership. In support of Trần Nhân Tông's goal of a unified SAṂGHA, Pháp Loa established in 1313 a national monastic hierarchy, according to which all monks had to register and were under his jurisdiction. Every three years, he would organize a collective ordination ceremony. He also oversaw the construction of many monasteries. By 1314, some thirty-three monasteries had been built, several with large libraries. He was also a tireless teacher, who gave frequent lectures on Chan texts and Buddhist scriptures. This was a period when many aristocrats either entered the monastic order or received precepts as lay practitioners and donated vast tracts of land to Buddhist temples. Among his disciples were the kings Trần Anh Tông and Trần Minh Tông. In 1311, he oversaw the printing of the complete canon and other Buddhist manuals. He also composed several works, most now lost, including commentaries on several MAHĀYĀNA sūtras.

**phi**. In Thai, "spirit"; used to refer to a diverse group of entities believed to have power over humans and thus requiring propitiation. In some cases, they are local demigods; in others, they are reincarnations of the dead. The category also includes the ghosts of the prominent dead as well as those who died mysterious or violent deaths. Phi inhabit trees, hills, water, the earth, and certain animals. "Spirit houses" are constructed for the phi, to which offerings are made.

**'pho ba**. (powa). In Tibetan, "transferring consciousness," a tantric practice included among the "six yogas of NĀROPA" (NĀ RO CHOS DRUG) by which one is able to eject one's consciousness from one's body (through the aperture at the top of the skull) at the moment of death and send it into a pure realm, with SUKHĀVATĪ of the buddha AMITĀBHA generally the preferred destination. In order to gain this ability, the practitioner requires instruction and initiation. Although the practice is found in all sects of Tibetan Buddhism (as well as in BON), it is particularly associated with the BKA' BRGYUD, and within it the 'BRI GUNG. It is one of the few forms of meditation in Tibet that is practiced by laypeople and one of the few forms that is practiced in a group setting.

**phra**. In Thai, "holy" or "venerable"; an honorific prefix used when referring to the Buddha (see PHRA PHUTTHA JAO) and before the names of monks, monasteries, relics, buddha images (e.g., PHRA KAEW MORAKOT), Hindu deities, and members of the Thai royal family. It is also used as a generic designation for "monk."

**Phra Bodhirak** (Thai). See BODHIRAK, PHRA.

**Phra Buddhacharn Toh Phomarangsi**. (Thai). See SOMDEJ TOH.

**Phra Kaew Morakot**. In Thai, "The Emerald Buddha" (full name: Phra Phuttha Maha Mani Ratana Patimakorn; P. Buddhamahāmaṇiratnapaṭimā); this most sacred and venerated buddha image in Thailand is currently enshrined at WAT PHRA KAEW (Temple of the Emerald Buddha), an ornate temple located on the grounds of the royal palace in the Thai capital of Bangkok. The image, which is in the seated meditation posture, is 29.5 inches (forty-five centimeters) tall; despite its name, it is in fact not made of emerald, but is carved from a single block of a green stone thought to be either jasper or jade. Kaew is an indigenous Thai word for "glass" or "translucence"; morakot derives from the Sanskrit word for emerald (S. morakata). According to legend, the Emerald Buddha was the first buddha image ever made and was carved five hundred years after the Buddha's death out of a sacred gem that came from INDRA's palace. The image is said to have been made by NĀGASENA (c. 150 BCE), the interlocutor of the MILINDAPAÑHA, in the north Indian city of PĀṬALIPUTRA around 43 BCE. The image was then taken to Sri Lanka in the fourth century CE, and was on its way to Burma in 457, when the ship carrying it went off course and the image next appeared in Cambodia. The image eventually came into Thai hands and made its way to AYUTHAYA, Chiangrai, Chiangmai, and ultimately Bangkok. The image's actual provenance is a matter of debate. Some art historians argue that on stylistic grounds the Emerald Buddha appears to have been carved in northern Thailand around the fifteenth century, while others argue for a south Indian or Sri Lankan origin based on its meditative posture, which is uncommon in Thai buddha images. The Emerald Buddha first enters the historical record upon its discovery in 1434 CE, in the area that is now the northern Thai province of Chiangrai, when lightning struck a chedi (P. cetiya, S. CAITYA) and a buddha image made of stucco was found inside. As the stucco began to flake off, the image of the Emerald Buddha was revealed. At that time, Chiangrai was ruled by the Lānnā Thai kingdom, whose king attempted to bring the image back to his capital of Chiangmai. The chronicles relate that three times he sent an elephant to bring the Emerald Buddha to Chiangmai, but each time the elephant went to Lampang instead, so the king finally relented and allowed the image to remain there. In 1468, the new Chiangmai monarch, King Tiloka, finally succeeded in moving the image to Chiangmai and installed it in the eastern niche of a large STŪPA at Wat Chedi Luang. The image remained there until 1552, when it was taken to LUANG PRABANG, then the capital of Laos, by the Lao ruler, who was also ruling Chiangmai at the time. In 1564, the king then took the image to Vientiane, where he set up a new capital after fleeing the Burmese. The Emerald Buddha remained in Vientiane for 214 years, until 1778 when the Siamese general Taksin captured the city and took the Emerald Buddha to Thonburi, then the Siamese capital. In 1784, when Bangkok was established as the capital, the image was installed there, in Wat Phra Kaew, the Temple of the Emerald Buddha, as the palladium of the nation (then known as Siam). Because Wat Phra Kaew is located within the palace grounds, the temple is unique in Thai Buddhism for having no monastic residences; the grounds contain only sacred shrines, stūpas, and the main ubosoth (UPOṢADHA hall), where the Buddha resides. The image of the Emerald Buddha is always clothed in golden raiments, which are changed according to the seasons. King Rāma I (r. 1782–1809) had two seasonal costumes made for the statue: a ceremonial robe for the hot season and a monastic robe for the rainy season. King Rāma III (1824–1851) had another costume made for the cold season: a mantle of gold beads. The ruling monarch performs the ceremonial changing of the garments each season.

**Phra Malai**. (P. Māleyya). A legendary arahant (S. ARHAT) and one of the most beloved figures in Thai Buddhist literature. According to legend, Phra Malai lived on the island of Sri Laṅka and was known for his great compassion and supramundane abilities, including the power to fly to various realms of the Buddhist universe. On one of his visits to the hells, he alleviated the suffering of hell beings and then returned to the human realm to advise their relatives to make merit on their behalf. One day as he was on his alms round, he encountered a poor man who presented him with eight lotus blossoms. Phra Malai accepted the offering and then took the flowers to tāvatimsa (S. TRĀYASTRIṂŚA) heaven to present them at the Cūḷāmaṇi cetiya (S. caitya), where the hair relic of the Buddha is enshrined. Phra Malai then met the king of the gods, INDRA, and asked him various questions: why he had built the caitya, when the future buddha Metteya (S. MAITREYA) would come to pay respects to it, and how the other deities coming to worship had made sufficient merit to be reborn at such a high level. The conversation proceeded as one divinity after another arrived, with Indra's explanation of the importance of making merit by practicing DĀNA (generosity), observing the precepts and having faith. Eventually Metteya himself arrived and, after paying reverence to the chedi, asked Phra Malai about the people in the human realm. Phra Malai responded that there is great diversity in their living conditions, health, happiness, and spiritual faculties, but that they all hoped to meet Metteya in the future and hear him preach. Metteya in response told Phra Malai to tell those who wished to meet him to listen to the recitation of the entire VESSANTARA-JĀTAKA over the course of one day and one night, and to bring to the monastery offerings totaling a thousand flowers, candles, incense sticks, balls of rice, and other gifts. In the northern and northeastern parts of Thailand, this legend is recited in the local dialects (Lānnā Thai and Lao, respectively) as a preface to the performance or recitation of the *Vessantara-Jātaka* at an annual festival. In central and south Thailand, a variant of the legend emphasizing the suffering of the hell denizens was customarily recited at funeral wakes, a practice that is becoming less common in the twenty-first century.

**phra pa**. In Thai, "forest monk," referring to monks who live in the forests rather than in towns or villages. The monks practice meditation and perform certain permitted forms of physical labor, rather than devoting their efforts to studying texts and interacting with laypeople, as village monks do. In Thailand, the most influential of the forest monk traditions was the KAMMAṬṬHANA or "meditation" tradition begun by Ajahn (Ăčhān) Sao Kantisīla (1861–1941) and AJAHN MUN BHŪRIDATTA, which emphasized strict adherence to the VINAYA and the practice of meditation techniques derived from the Pāli canon. See also ARAÑÑAVĀSI, ĀRAṆYA.

**Phra Pathom Chedi**. In Thai, lit. "Noble First Shrine," said to be the tallest Buddhist CAITYA (P. cetī) in the world at over 394 feet (120 meters); located in the Thai town of Nakhon Pathom. The original stūpa, located in the region where the first Buddhist missionaries taught in Thailand, may date from the fourth century CE. The stūpa was rebuilt in the Khmer style in the eleventh century and eventually fell into ruins. These ruins were visited by Prince Mongkut (the future RĀMA IV) during his years as a monk. After Mongkut ascended the throne, he ordered that a new stūpa be constructed at the site, which was completed in 1870 after seventeen years of construction.

**Phra Phuttha Jao**. In Thai, "the Venerable Lord Buddha," the most common vernacular Thai term for Gotama (S. GAUTAMA) Buddha.

**Phra Phuttha Sihing**. A highly revered image of the Buddha (PHRA PHUTTHA JAO) in Thailand, second in importance only to the Emerald Buddha (PHRA KAEW MORAKOT). According to legend, the Phra Phuttha Sihing image was created in Sri Lanka, and was being transported across the ocean when the ship carrying it sank; the image next appeared in the southern Thai city of Nakhon Si Thammarat. Stylistically, the image, seated in the earth-touching posture (BHŪMISPARŚAMUDRĀ), with its broad chest, fleshy face, and open robe with a short flap on the left side, belongs to the Lānnā, or northern Thai school, which flourished around the fifteenth century. In addition to uncertainties concerning the image's origin, there are questions of authenticity; at least three sculptures in Thailand are identified as the Phra Phuttha Sihing: they are found in the Buddhaisawan Chapel in the Bangkok National Museum compound, in an eponymous chapel in Nakhon Si Thammarat, and at Wat Phra Singh in Chiangmai.

**Phra Sangkachai**. A figure depicted in Thai sculpture as a fat monk seated in meditation. He resembles the figure of BUDAI (d. 916), the "Laughing Buddha," found in East Asia, although he may represent Mahākaccāyana (MAHĀKĀTYĀYANA). He is believed to be of Mon origin.

**Phúc Điền**. (福田) (c. late-nineteenth century). Scholar-monk of the Nguyễn dynasty, considered one of the most important historians of Buddhism in premodern Vietnam. His biography is recorded in the *Thiền Uyển Truyền Đăng Lục* ("Recorded Transmission of the Lamplight in the CHAN Community"). According to this source, he was a native of Sơn Minh, Hà Nội province. His family name was Vũ. He left home to become a monk at the age of twelve and first studied under the Venerable Viên Quang of Thịnh Liệt Đại Bi Temple. After three years, Viên Quang passed away, and Phúc Điền went to study under the Venerable Từ Phong of Nam Dư Phúc Xuân Temple. When he was twenty years old Từ Phong passed away, and Phúc Điền moved to Pháp Vân Temple in Bắc Ninh province and received full ordination under the Venerable Từ Quang. Phúc Điền's biography shows that he was not only an author, translator, and historian, but also an activist who tirelessly built and repaired many monasteries. Besides reprinting, editing, translating (from classical Chinese into vernacular Nôm Vietnamese) numerous Buddhist texts, and recording detailed histories of various temples, he also left behind several independent works, the most important of which are the *Tam Giáo Nguyên Lưu* ("Sources of the Three Religions"), the *Đại Nam Thiền Uyển Truyền Đăng Tập Lục* ("Recorded Transmission of the Lamplight [in the Chan Community] of Vietnam"), and the *Thiền Uyển Truyền Đăng Lục* ("Transmission of the Lamplight in the Chan Community"). His extant writings include more works on history than on Buddhist doctrine. His aspiration was to collect all the extant materials regarding the origin and transmission of Vietnamese Buddhism. Because he was convinced that Vietnamese Buddhism was a continuation of the orthodox school of Chinese Buddhism (and specifically the CHAN ZONG), he implicitly accepted the hermeneutical strategies of Chinese Chan in constructing his view of Vietnamese Buddhist history. However, in addition to Chinese Chan documents, he also consulted Vietnamese sources, together with copious notes drawn from his own fieldwork at various temples. His writings, therefore, provide valuable sources for the understanding of Vietnamese Buddhist history.

**phur pa**. [alt. phur bu] (S. kīla). A Tibetan ritual dagger. Although the word is used colloquially for any form of stake driven into the ground, such as a tent peg, in the context of Tibetan Buddhism it refers to a ritual implement used in the performance of tantric ceremonies. In its most common design, the phur pa is shaped like a stake with a three-sided blade tapering to a point, while the shaft of its handle is frequently capped with three wrathful or semiwrathful faces and a half-VAJRA. They are fashioned from a variety of materials and may be carved in clay, wood, or bone and are regularly cast from metal alloys. In some instances, phur ba daggers revealed as treasure (GTER MA) are said to be formed from meteorites (rnam lcags). The phur pa is regularly used in rituals for the subjugation of harmful or obstructive forces, such as the "black hat dance" in which participants repeatedly strike an effigy believed to embody those forces. It is also associated with the tantric literature of Rdo rje phur ba (S. VAJRAKĪLAYA) attributed to PADMASAMBHAVA, in which the lower portion of the central deity takes the form of a ritual dagger.

**Phyag chen chos sku mdzub tshugs**. (Chakchen Chöku Dzuptsuk). In Tibetan, "MAHĀMUDRĀ: Pointing Out the DHARMAKĀYA"; the briefest of three major texts composed by the ninth KARMA PA DBANG PHYUG RDO RJE on the doctrine and practice of the great seal (mahāmudrā). See also PHYAG CHEN MA RIG MUN GSAL ("Mahāmudrā: Eliminating the Darkness of Ignorance") and PHYAG CHEN NGES DON RGYA MTSHO ("Mahāmudrā: Ocean of Definitive Meaning").

**Phyag chen ma rig mun gsal**. (Chakchen Marik Munsel). In Tibetan, "MAHĀMUDRĀ: Eliminating the Darkness of Ignorance"; the intermediate of three major texts composed by the ninth KARMA PA DBANG PHYUG RDO RJE on the doctrine and practice of the great seal (mahāmudrā). See also PHYAG CHEN CHOS SKU MDZUB TSHUGS ("Mahāmudrā: Pointing out the DHARMAKĀYA") and PHYAG CHEN NGES DON RGYA MTSHO ("Mahāmudrā: Ocean of Definitive Meaning").

**Phyag chen nges don rgya mtsho**. (Chakchen Ngedön Gyatso). In Tibetan, "MAHĀMUDRĀ: Ocean of Definitive Meaning"; the most extensive of three major texts composed by the ninth KARMA PA DBANG PHYUG RDO RJE on the doctrine and practice of the great seal (mahāmudrā). See also PHYAG CHEN CHOS SKU MDZUB TSHUGS ("Mahāmudrā: Pointing out the DHARMAKĀYA") and PHYAG CHEN MA RIG MUN GSAL ("Mahāmudra: Eliminating the Darkness of Ignorance").

**Phyag chen zla ba'i 'od zer**. (Chakchen Dawe Öser). In Tibetan, "Moonbeams of MAHĀMUDRĀ"; an encyclopedic treatise on the doctrine and practice of the great seal (mahāmudrā) composed by the sixteenth-century BKA' BRGYUD scholar DWAGS PO BKRA SHIS RNAM RGYAL. It is highly regarded as a sourcebook and meditation manual for the practice of mahāmudrā, offering many quotations from Indian and Tibetan sources. The work is divided into two major divisions: the first on the practice of ŚAMATHA and VIPAŚYANĀ, the second on the practice of mahāmudrā.

**phyi dar**. (chi dar). In Tibetan, "later dissemination." Tibetan historians have traditionally divided the dissemination of Buddhist teachings in Tibet into two periods. The "earlier dissemination" (SNGA DAR) began in the seventh century with the conversion of king SRONG BTSAN SGAM PO to Buddhism and continued with the arrival of the Indian masters ŚĀNTARAKṢITA and PADMASAMBHAVA and the founding of the first monastery at BSAM YAS during the reign of king KHRI SRONG LDE BTSAN. This period ended in 842 with the assassination of king GLANG DAR MA and the fall of the Tibetan monarchy. There ensued a "dark period" of almost two centuries, during which recorded contact between Indian and Tibetan Buddhists declined. The "later dissemination" commenced in earnest in the eleventh century. It is marked by patronage of Buddhism by king YE SHES 'OD in western Tibet and especially the work of the noted translator RIN CHEN BZANG PO, who made three trips to India to study and to retrieve Buddhist texts, as well as the work of RNGOG LEGS PA'I SHES RAB. The noted Bengali monk ATIŚA DĪPAṂKARAŚRĪJÑĀNA arrived in Tibet in 1042. The "later dissemination" was a period of extensive translation of Indian texts; these new (GSAR MA) translations of tantras became central to the so-called "new" sects of Tibetan Buddhism: BKA' GDAMS, SA SKYA, BKA' BRGYUD, and later DGE LUGS, with the RNYING MA ("ancient") sect basing itself on "old" translations from the earlier dissemination. Of particular importance during this later dissemination was the resurgence of monastic ordination, especially that of the MŪLASARVĀSTIVĀDA VINAYA. New artistic styles were also introduced from neighboring regions during this period.

**Phywa pa** [alt. Cha pa] **Chos kyi Seng ge**. (Chapa Chökyi Senge) (1109–1169). The sixth abbot of GSANG PHU NE'U THOG, a BKA' GDAMS monastery founded in 1073 by RNGOG LEGS PA'I SHES RAB. Among his students are included the first KARMA PA, DUS GSUM MKHYEN PA and the SA SKYA hierarch BSOD NAMS RTSE MO. His collected works include explanations of MADHYAMAKA and PRAJÑĀPĀRAMITĀ. With his influential *Tshad ma'i bsdus pa yid kyi mun sel rtsa 'grel* he continued the line of PRAMĀṆA scholarship started by RNGOG BLO LDAN SHES RAB, one that would later be challenged by SA SKYA PAṆḌITA. He is credited with originating the distinctively Tibetan BSDUS GRWA genre of textbook (used widely in DGE LUGS monasteries) that introduces beginners to the main topics in abhidharma in a peculiar dialectical form that strings together a chain of consequences linked by a chain of reasons. He also played an important role in the formation of the BSTAN RIM genre of Tibetan Buddhist literature, the forerunner of the more famous LAM RIM.

**pibo sat'ap sŏl**. (裨補寺塔說). In Korean, "reinforcing [the land] through monasteries and STŪPAs"; geomantic theory of the Korean monk TOSŎN (827–898), who proposed that building monasteries and pagodas at geomantically fragile locations around the Korean peninsula could correct adverse energy flows in the native geography and thus alleviate topological weaknesses, in much the same way that acupuncture could correct adverse energy flows within the physical body. This term pibo (lit. "assisting and supplementing," and thus "reinforcing," or "remediation") is not attested as a technical term in Chinese geomancy, but seems to have been coined by Tosŏn. Pibo also comes to be used as an official ecclesiastical category to designate important monasteries that had figured in the founding of the Koryŏ dynasty.

**pilgrimage**. See MAHĀSTHĀNA; GNAS SKOR BA; XINGJIAO.

**Pilindavatsa**. (P. Pilindavaccha; T. Pi lin da ba tsa; C. Bilingqie Pocuo; J. Hitsuryōgabasha; K. P'illŭngga Pach'a 畢陵伽婆蹉). An eminent ARHAT declared by the Buddha foremost among monk disciples who are beloved of the gods. According to the Pāli account, he was born to a brāhmaṇa family named Vaccha (S. Vatsa) in the city of Sāvatthi (S. ŚRĀVASTĪ); Pilinda was his personal name. Pilinda became a hermit and mastered the magical science called cūḷa (or "lesser") gandhāravijjā, which allowed him to make himself invisible and walk through walls. However, in the presence of the Buddha the science was ineffective. Believing the Buddha to have canceled out his power through a mastery of mahā (or "greater") gandhāravijjā (the ability to read the minds of others and fly through the air), he entered the order to learn the Buddha's science. The Buddha instructed him in meditation, by means of which Pilinda became an arhat. In a previous existence, Pilinda had been a righteous ruler who had led many of his subjects to a heavenly rebirth. As a consequence, many of his former subjects, now divinities (DEVA), waited upon Pilinda morning and evening in gratitude. It is for this reason that he earned distinction as the disciple most beloved of the gods. Pilinda had the unfortunate habit of addressing everyone he met with the derogatory epithet of vasala, meaning outcaste. The Buddha explained that this was because he had been born an outcaste for a hundred lives. Once Pilinda inquired of a passerby carrying a bowl of peppers, "What is in the bowl, vasala?" Insulted, the passerby said, "rat dung," whereupon the peppers turned to rat dung. The passerby begged Pilinda to return the contents to their original state, which he did using his powers. Pilinda used his extraordinary powers on several other occasions. Once, he created a crown of gold for an impoverished girl so that her family could partake of a feast day; on another occasion he rescued two girls who had been kidnapped by robbers and returned them to their family. The involvement with females prompted some of his fellow monks to blame him for impropriety, but the Buddha ruled that no misdeed had been committed. He figures in several MAHĀYĀNA sūtras, being mentioned as a member of the audience of the SADDHARMAPUṆḌARĪKASŪTRA and appearing in the *ŚŪRAṂGAMASŪTRA.

**piṇḍapāta**. (T. bsod snyoms; C. qishi; J. kotsujiki; K. kŏlsik 乞食). In Sanskrit and Pāli, "alms food" (or, according to other etymologies, "alms bowl"); the food received in the alms bowl (S. PĀTRA; P. patta) of a monk or nun; by extension, the "alms round" that monks and nuns make each morning to accept alms from the laity. There are numerous rules found in all Buddhist traditions concerning the proper ways of receiving and consuming alms food. In the Pāli VINAYA, for example, this food must be received and consumed between dawn and noon and may consist of five types: cooked rice, baked or roasted flour, pulse and rice, fish, and meat. The monk may not, on his own initiative, intimate to the donor that he desires food or a specific kind of food; indeed, the monk makes little if any acknowledgement of receiving the food, but simply accepts whatever is offered and continues along his route. In East Asia, and especially Japan, TAKUHATSU, lit., "carrying the bowl," is often conducted by a small group of monks who walk through the streets with walking staffs (KHAKKHARA) and bells that alert residents of their presence. Because East Asian Buddhism was generally a self-sufficient cenobitic tradition that did not depend on alms food for daily meals, monks on alms round would typically receive money or uncooked rice in their bowls as offerings from the laity. The alms round was one of the principal points of interaction between monastic and lay Buddhists, and theirs was a symbiotic relationship: monks and nuns would receive their sustenance from the laity by accepting their offerings, the laity would have the opportunity to generate merit (PUṆYA) for themselves and their families by making offerings (DĀNA) to the monastics. Indeed, one of the most severe penalties the SAṂGHA can administer to the laity is to refuse their donations; this act of censure is called "overturning the bowl" (see PĀTRANIKUBJANA).

**Piṇḍola-Bhāradvāja**. (T. Bha ra dhwa dza Bsod snyoms len; C. Bintoulu Poluoduo zunzhe; J. Binzuruharada sonja; K. Pinduro Pallat'a chonja 賓頭盧頗羅墮尊者). Sanskrit and Pāli proper name of a prominent monk-disciple of the Buddha, born as the son of a brāhmaṇa priest in the service of King Udāyana of Kauśāmbī. He was a successful teacher of the Vedas, first encountering the Buddha when his travels took him to RĀJAGṚHA. Gluttonous by nature, he was impressed by all the offerings the Buddha's disciples received and so resolved to enter the order. For this reason, he carried with him an exceptionally large alms bowl (PĀTRA) made from a gourd. After he was finally able to conquer his avarice, he became an ARHAT and uttered his "lion's roar" (SIṂHANĀDA) in the presence of the Buddha, for which reason he was declared the foremost lion's roarer (siṃhanādin) among the Buddha's disciples. In a famous story found in several recensions of the VINAYA, the Buddha rebuked Piṇḍola for performing the following miracle before a crowd. A rich merchant had placed a valuable sandalwood alms bowl (pātra) atop a pole and challenged any mendicant to retrieve it with a magical display. Encouraged by MAHĀMAUDGALYĀYANA, Piṇḍola entered the contest and used his magical powers to rise into the air and retrieve the bowl. The Buddha rebuked Piṇḍola for his crass exhibitionism, and ordered that the bowl be ground into sandalwood powder (presumably for incense). The incident was the occasion for the Buddha to pass the "rule of defeat" (PĀRĀJIKA), forbidding monks from displaying supernatural powers before the laity. Sanskrit sources state that the Buddha rebuked Piṇḍola for his misdeed and ordered him not to live in JAMBUDVĪPA, but to move to aparagodānīya (see GODĀNĪYA) to proselytize (where he is said to reside with a thousand disciples). The Buddha also forbade him from entering PARINIRVĀṆA so that he would remain in the world after the Buddha's demise and continue to serve as a field of blessings (PUṆYAKṢETRA) for sentient beings; for this reason, Piṇḍola is also known in Chinese as the "World-Dwelling Arhat" (Zhushi Luohan). This is the reason why some traditions still today invoke his name for protection and why he is traditionally listed as the first of the sixteen ARHAT elders (ṢOḌAŚASTHAVIRA), who are charged by the Buddha with protecting his dispensation until the advent of the next buddha, MAITREYA. According to the DIVYĀVADĀNA, Piṇḍola was given the principal seat at the third Buddhist council (SAṂGĪTI) called by Emperor AŚOKA (see COUNCIL, THIRD); at that point, he was already several hundred years old, with long white hair and eyebrows that he had to hold back in order to see. In China, DAO'AN of the Eastern Jin dynasty once had a dream of a white-haired foreign monk, with long, flowing eyebrows. Later, Master Dao'an's disciple LUSHAN HUIYUAN read the SARVĀSTIVĀDA VINAYA and realized that the monk whom his teacher had dreamed about was Piṇḍola. From that point on, Dao'an offered Piṇḍola food every day, and, for this reason, a picture or image of Piṇḍola is often enshrined in monastic dining halls in China. This is also why Piṇḍola was given another nickname in Chinese, the "Long-Browed Monk" (Changmei Seng). In CHANYUE GUANXIU's standard Chinese depiction of the sixteen arhats, Piṇḍola-Bharadvāja is portrayed as squatting on a rock, holding a staff in his left hand, leaning on a rock with his right, with a text placed on his knees. In Tibetan iconography Piṇḍola holds a pātra; other East Asian images depict him holding a text and either a chowrie (C. FUZI; S. VĀLAVYAJANA) or a pātra.

**pirit**. In Sinhalese, "protection." See PARITTA.

**piśāca**. (P. pisāca; T. sha za; C. pisheshe; J. bishaja; K. pisasa 毘舍闍). In Sanskrit, "flesh-eater," a class of ogres or goblins, similar to RĀKṢASA and YAKṢA, who eat human flesh. A female ogress is called a piśācinī (P. pisācinī). Among the six rebirth destinies (GATI), they are included in the realm of the ghosts (PRETA). The term is also used to refer to the people of the Paiśācī district, who spoke one of the vernacular PRAKRIT dialects used during the Buddha's lifetime.

**piṭaka**. (T. sde snod; C. zang; J. zō; K. chang 藏). In Sanskrit and Pāli, "basket" (in a figurative sense), or canonical "collection," viz. a collection of scriptures organized by category. (The Chinese translates piṭaka as "repository.") The use of the term piṭaka to refer to such collections of scriptures may derive from the custom of collecting in baskets the individual bark slips on which the pages of the scriptures were written. The VINAYA, SŪTRA, and ABHIDHARMA (alt. śāstra) piṭakas together constitute the TRIPIṬAKA (P. tipiṭaka), the "three baskets" of the Buddhist canon, a term that is employed in both the mainstream and MAHĀYĀNA schools. The various schools of Indian Buddhism differ, however, on precisely which texts are to be included in these collections. The abhidharma was likely added later, since early texts refer only to monks who are masters of the SŪTRAPIṬAKA and the VINAYAPIṬAKA. A number of the MAINSTREAM BUDDHIST SCHOOLS seem also to have had a bodhisattvapiṭaka, which included texts related to the past lives of the BODHISATTVA, such as the JĀTAKA. This term BODHISATTVAPIṬAKA was adopted in the MAHĀYĀNA, and it was used as the title of a single text, a specific set of Mahāyāna sūtras, as well as to refer to the Mahāyāna sūtras collectively. With the rise of tantric Buddhism, the term vidyādharapiṭaka, the piṭaka of the "keepers of knowledge" (VIDYĀDHARA), came to be used to refer collectively to the Buddhist TANTRAs. See also DAZANGJING.

**Pitalkhorā**. An early Buddhist monastic cave site in western India, around fifty miles southwest of the cave sites of AJAṆṬĀ and twenty-three miles northwest of ELLORĀ, which was connected to Pitalkhorā by an ancient caravan route. Most of the fourteen caves are in ruins today, due at least partly to the fact that the original excavators, when translating the forms of wooden architecture into stone, neglected the structural features necessary to support the stone's extra weight. Cave 3, a large sanctuary (CAITYA), is divided by octagonal pillars (but without either bases or capitals) into a nave and two aisles, with half-barrel-vaulted side aisles flanking the central space; it resembles a similar sanctuary at BHĀJĀ. The STŪPA in Cave 3 contained crystal reliquaries set into oblong sockets, which were then plugged with fitted stone slabs; their presence indicates the practice of relic (ŚARĪRA) enshrinement. Cave 4 is entered through a doorway that is flanked by two gently smiling door guardians (DVĀRAPĀLA) holding javelins and shields. Extending to the right of this entrance is a row of nine life-size carved elephants, who appear to be bearing the weight of the cave; the sculptures are remarkable for their realistic modeling and resemble those at the SĀÑCĪ stūpa.

**Pitāputrasamāgamasūtra**. (T. Yab dang sras mjal ba'i mdo; C. Pusa jianshi jing/Fuzi heji jing; J. Bosatsu kenjitsukyō/Fushi gōjūkyō; K. Posal kyŏnsil kyŏng/Puja hapchip kyŏng 菩薩見實經/父子合集經). In Sanskrit, "Sūtra on the Meeting of Father and Son," a MAHĀYĀNA scripture found in the RATNAKŪṬASŪTRA, often cited in MADHYAMAKA texts, especially for its expositions of emptiness (ŚŪNYATĀ) and the two truths

(SATYADVAYA). It is quoted in such famous works as NĀGĀRJUNA's SŪTRASAMUCCAYA and ŚĀNTIDEVA's ŚIKṢĀSAMUCCAYA. The *Pitāputrasamāgamasūtra* was translated into Chinese by Rajendrayaśas in 568 as the *Pusa jianshi jing* and was included in the massive *Dabaoji jing* (*Ratnakūṭasūtra*) compilation. It was subsequently retranslated in the eleventh century by Richeng and others as the *Fuzi heji jing*.

**pīṭha**. (T. gnas). In Sanskrit, "abode" or "seat," in tantric literature, a location where YOGINĪs congregate and hence a potent site for tantric practice. There are various lists of such locations, sometimes numbering twelve, twenty-four, or thirty-two; the number twenty-four is the most common, but the lists of twenty-four vary in the names and locations of the specific sites. The pīṭha figure prominently in yoginītantras such as the CAKRASAṂVARATANTRA and the HEVAJRATANTRA. They also appear commonly in scenes from the lives of the MAHĀSIDDHAS. Many of the sites can be linked to geographical locations on the Indian subcontinent, although some remain unidentified and the location of others shifts according to different traditions. They are considered, however, to form a network, both in the external world and inside the body of the tantric practitioner; the external sites are called bāhyapīṭha, and the internal sites are called nāḍīsthāna, that is, places where important energy channels (NĀḌĪ) are located according to tantric physiology. In both their external and internal forms, the pīṭha are presumed to form a MAṆḌALA. The pīṭha are said to be the abodes of tantric goddesses, called yoginī or ḌĀKINĪ, associated with a particular tantric cycle. They are described as places where male and female tantric practitioners congregate in order to engage in a variety of ritual practices, after having identified each other using secret codes. Tantric texts extol the benefits of visiting the pīṭha, either externally or internally, and Tibetan pilgrims have long sought to find the twenty-four sites. Based on the conquest and transformation of Maheśvara (Śiva) by the Buddhist deity VAJRAPĀṆI, the twenty-four names of the Cakrasaṃvara sacred sites are the four seats (pīṭha) Uḍḍiyāna, Jālandhara, Pullīramalaya, and Arbuda; four outer seats (upapīṭha) Godāvarī, Rāmeśvara, Devīkoṭa, and Mālava; two fields (kṣetra) Kāmarūpa and Oḍra; two outer fields (upakṣetra) Triśakuni and Kośala; two pleasing places (chandoha) Kaliṅga and Lampāka; two outer delightful places (upacchanda) Kāñci and Himālaya; two meeting places (melāpaka) Pretapuri and Gṛhadevatā; two outer meeting places (upamelāpaka) Saurāṣṭra and Suvarṇadvīpa; two cremation grounds (ŚMAŚĀNA) Nagara and Sindu; and two outer cremation grounds (upaśmaśāna) Maru and Kulatā. The twenty-four sites were later symbolically "transferred" to locations in Nepal and Tibet. To Newar Buddhists, the Kathmandu Valley conceptually mirrors the structure of the Cakrasaṃvara MAṆḌALA, and the twenty-four temples of different Cakrasaṃvara goddesses make the valley a sacred space. In Tibet, DAGS PA SHEL RI (Crystal Mountain) in the TSA RI region also mapped the Cakrasaṃvara maṇḍala. Every twelve years pilgrims would make the arduous pilgrimage around the sites mapped onto that sacred space.

**pitṛtantra**. (T. pha rgyud). In Sanskrit, "father tantra," one of the categories of ANUTTARAYOGATANTRA. This category is paired with "mother tantra" (MĀTṚTANTRA); in some cases a third category of "nondual" (ADVAYA) tantras is added. The father tantras are those that place particular emphasis on method (UPĀYA) over wisdom (PRAJÑĀ), especially as it pertains to the achievement of the illusory body (MĀYĀDEHA) on the stage of generation (UTPATTIKRAMA). The chief tantra of this category is the GUHYASAMĀJATANTRA.

**Platform Sutra of the Sixth Patriarch**. See LIUZU TAN JING.

**Pŏbun**. (K) (法雲). See CHINHŬNG WANG.

**Pohwa**. (普化) (1875–1958). Influential SŎN master and ecclesiastical leader in the modern Korean Buddhist tradition; also known as Sŏgu. In 1912, while he was studying the writings of POJO CHINUL (1158–1210) at the monastery of POMŎSA, he decided to become a monk and subsequently went to CHANGANSA, where he was ordained by Yŏndam Ŭngsin (d.u.). The same year Pohwa received the precepts from Tongsŏn Chŏngŭi (1856–1936) at YUJŎMSA. After spending twenty years at Yŏngwŏnsa, he subsequently moved to Ch'ilbul hermitage on CHIRISAN, established the Haegwan hermitage in Namhae, and taught at the major monastery of HAEINSA. In 1955, at the end of the Japanese colonial period (1910–1945), Pohwa was appointed the first supreme patriarch (CHONGJŎNG) of the new Korean Buddhist CHOGYE CHONG after it was reorganized by MANAM CHONGHŎN. During his three years as patriarch, he led a "purification movement" (chŏnghwa undong) that sought to purge the Chogye order of what were considered to be the vestiges of nontraditional practices foisted on Korean Buddhism during the Japanese colonial period, such as clerical marriage and meat eating. Pohwa passed away at TONGHWASA near Taegu at the age of eighty-four.

**poisons, three**. See TRIVIṢA.

**Pojo Chinul**. (C. Puzhao Zhine; J. Fushō Chitotsu 普照知訥) (1158–1210). In Korean, lit. "Shining Universally, Knowing Reticence"; the premier Korean SŎN master of the Koryŏ dynasty and one of the two most influential monks in the history of Korean Buddhism (along with WŎNHYO); he usually referred to himself using his cognomen Moguja (Oxherder). Chinul was a native of the Tongju district to the west of the Koryŏ capital of Kaesŏng (present-day Sŏhŭng in Hwanghae province). In 1165, he was ordained by the Sŏn master Chonghwi (d.u.) at Kulsansa on Mt. Sagul, one of the monastic centers of the so-called "Nine Mountains school of Sŏn" (see KUSAN SŎNMUN). In 1182, Chinul passed the Sŏn clerical examinations (SŬNGKWA) held at the monastery of Pojesa in the capital of Kaesŏng, but rather than take an ecclesiastical position he opted instead to form a retreat society (KYŎLSA) with some fellow monks. Chinul left the capital and headed south and began his residence at Ch'ŏngwŏnsa in Ch'angp'yŏng (present-day South Chŏlla province). There, Chinul is said to have attained his initial awakening while reading the LIUZU TAN JING. In 1185, Chinul relocated himself to Pomunsa on Mt. Haga (present-day North Kyŏngsang province), where he had his second awakening while reading LI TONGXUAN's HUAYAN JING HELUN ("Commentary to the AVATAṂSAKASŪTRA"). In 1188, Chinul and the monk Tŭkchae (d.u.) launched the first Samādhi and Prajñā Retreat Society (CHŎNGHYE KYŎLSA) at the monastery of Kŏjosa on Mt. Kong (present-day North Kyŏngsang province). Chinul subsequently moved the community to the Kilsangsa on Mt. Songgwang, which was later renamed SUSŎNSA, or the Sŏn Cultivation Community, by King Hŭijong (r. 1204–1211); this is the major monastery now known as SONGGWANGSA. On his way to establish the retreat society, Chinul is said to have briefly resided at the hermitage Sangmujuam on CHIRISAN, where he attained his final awakening while reading the recorded sayings (YULU) of the CHAN master DAHUI ZONGGAO. In addition to reciting the VAJRACCHEDIKĀPRAJÑĀPĀRAMITĀSŪTRA, the practice of the Sŏn Cultivation Community at Kilsangsa was purportedly based on the three principles of the concurrent practice of SAMĀDHI and PRAJÑĀ as taught in the *Liuzu tan jing*, faith and understanding of the perfect and sudden teachings (K. wŏndon kyo; C. YUANDUN JIAO) according to the *Avataṃsakasūtra*, and the shortcut method of "questioning meditation" (K. kanhwa Sŏn; C. KANHUA CHAN) developed by Dahui. Chinul is renowned for developing an ecumenical approach to Buddhist thought and practice, which sought to reconcile the insights of the "word of the Buddha"—viz., the scriptures, or KYO—with the "mind of the Buddha"—viz., Sŏn practice. He taught an approach to Buddhist practice that combined an initial sudden awakening followed by continued gradual cultivation (K. donŏ chŏmsu; C. DUNWU JIANXIU), which he saw as the optimal soteriological schema for most practitioners. Chinul also was the first to introduce "questioning meditation" (kanhwa Sŏn) into the Korean Sŏn tradition, and this type of meditation would hold pride of place in Korean Buddhism from that point forward. Chinul was later given the posthumous title Puril Pojo (Buddha-Sun That Shines Universally). His many works include the SUSIM KYŎL ("Secrets on Cultivating the Mind"), KANHWA KYŎRŬI RON ("Resolving Doubts About Observing the Meditative Topic"), WŎNDON SŎNGBUL NON ("The Complete and Sudden Attainment of Buddhahood"), and his magnum opus, the PŎPCHIP PYŎRHAENGNOK CHŎRYO PYŎNGIP SAGI ("Excerpts from the 'Dharma Collection and Special Practice Record' with Personal Notes"), which is included in the SAJIP ("Fourfold Collection").

**Polonnaruva**. [alt. Polonaruva; Polonnaruwa]. An ancient capital of Sri Lanka, it was declared the capital by King Vijayabāhu I after his defeat of the Cōḷa in 1070. The city's golden age occurred under King PARĀKRAMABĀHU I, the grandson of Vijayabāhu, during whose reign agriculture and trade flourished and numerous architectural projects were undertaken. The city remained the capital until the late thirteenth century. Polonnaruva was the site of several important monasteries and STŪPAs, the ruins of which remain today. The ancient city was declared a World Heritage Site in 1982. Perhaps its most famous site is the Gal Viharaya, where three large statues of the Buddha (standing, seated, and reclining) were cut from a single granite wall during the reign of Parākramabāhu I. A stone inscription at the site details the king's efforts to unite the saṅgha (S. SAṂGHA) under a single NIKĀYA tradition and sets forth his sāsana reforms of the dispensation (P. sāsana; S. ŚĀSANA).

**Pŏmnang**. (法朗) (fl. c. 632–646). The proper name of the Korean monk who is credited by tradition with having first transmitted the teachings of the SŎN school (C. CHAN ZONG) to the Korean peninsula. Pŏmnang is said to have studied the East Mountain Teachings (DONGSHAN FAMEN) under the fourth patriarch of Chan, DAOXIN (580–651), but there is no independent evidence supporting this assertion. After returning to Korea, Pŏmnang is claimed to have passed his teachings on to Sinhaeng (704–779), a vaunt-courier in the Hŭiyangsan Sŏn school, thus making Pŏmnang the ancestor of this oldest lineage in the Nine Mountains school of Sŏn (KUSAN SŎNMUN). Unfortunately, next to nothing is known about Pŏmnang's life and career, and he may have been introduced merely as a way of burnishing the luster of Sinhaeng's lineage.

**Pŏmŏsa**. (梵魚寺). In Korean, "BRAHMĀ Fish Monastery"; the fourteenth district monastery (PONSA) of the contemporary CHOGYE CHONG of Korean Buddhism, located on Kŭmjŏng (Golden Well) Mountain outside the southeastern city of Pusan. According to legend, Pŏmŏsa was named after a golden fish that descended from heaven and lived in a golden well located beneath a rock on the peak of Kŭmjŏng mountain. The monastery was founded in 678 by ŬISANG (625–702) as one of the ten main monasteries of the Korean Hwaŏm (C. HUAYAN) school, with the support of the Silla king Munmu (r. 661–680), who had unified the three kingdoms of the Korean peninsula in 668. Korea was being threatened by Japanese invaders, and Munmu is said to have had a dream that told him to have Ŭisang go to Kŭmjŏng mountain and lead a recitation of the AVATAṂSAKASŪTRA (K. *Hwaŏm kyŏng*) for seven days; if he did so, the Japanese would be repelled. The invasion successfully forestalled, King Munmu sponsored the construction of Pŏmŏsa. During the Koryŏ dynasty the monastery was at the peak of its power, with more than one thousand monks in residence, and it actively competed for influence with nearby T'ONGDOSA. The monastery was destroyed during the Japanese Hideyoshi invasions of the late-sixteenth century, but it was reconstructed in 1602 and renovated after another fire in 1613.

The only Silla dynasty artifacts that remain are a stone STŪPA and a stone lantern. Pŏmŏsa has an unusual three-level layout with the main shrine hall (TAEUNG CHŎN) located at the upper level and the Universal Salvation Hall (Poje nu) anchoring the middle level. The lower level has three separate entrance gates. Visitors enter the monastery through the One-Pillar Gate (Ilchu mun), built in 1614; next they pass through the Gate of the Four Heavenly Kings (Sach'ŏnwang mun), who guard the monastery from baleful influences; and finally, they pass beneath the Gate of Nonduality (Puri mun), which marks the transition from secular to sacred space. The main shrine hall was rebuilt by Master Myojŏn (d.u.) in 1614 and is noted for its refined Chosŏn-dynasty carvings and its elaborate ceiling of carved flowers. In 1684, Master Hyemin (d.u.) added a hall in honor of the buddha VAIROCANA, which included a famous painting of that buddha that now hangs in a separate building; and in 1700, Master Myŏnghak (d.u.) added another half dozen buildings. Pŏmŏsa also houses two important stūpas: a three-story stone stūpa located next to the Poje nu dates from 830 during the Silla dynasty; a new seven-story stone stūpa, constructed following Silla models, enshrines relics (K. sari; S. ŚARĪRA) of the Buddha that a contemporary Indian monk brought to Korea. After a period of relative inactivity, Pŏmŏsa reemerged as an important center of Buddhist practice starting in 1900 under the abbot Sŏngwŏl (d.u.), who opened several hermitages nearby. Under his leadership, the monastery became known as a major center of the Buddhist reform movements of the twentieth century. Tongsan Hyeil (1890–1965), one of the leaders of the reformation of Korean Buddhism following the Japanese colonial period (1910–1945), who also served as the supreme patriarch (CHONGJŎNG) of the CHOGYE CHONG from 1958 to 1961, resided at Pŏmŏsa.

**Pŏmŭmjong po**. (梵音宗譜). In Korean, "Lineage of the Brahmā's Voice School," a one-roll lineage record of Korean chanting (pŏmp'ae) monks, written by TAEHWI (fl. c. 1748) during the Chosŏn dynasty, which traces this distinctive "Indian-style" of chanting back to CHIN'GAM HYESO (774–850). See FANBAI.

**Pongsŏnsa**. (奉先寺). In Korean, "Respecting Ancestors Monastery"; the twenty-fifth district monastery (PONSA) of the contemporary CHOGYE CHONG of Korean Buddhism, located on Mount Unak in Kyŏnggi province. The monastery was constructed by T'anmun (d.u.) in 968, in the twentieth year of the reign of Koryŏ King Kwangjong (r. 949–975), and was originally named Unaksa, after the mountain on which it was built. In 1469, the first year of the reign of King Yejong (r. 1468–1469), Queen Chŏnghŭi (1418–1483) decided that the tomb of her deceased husband, King Sejo (r. 1445–1468), should be established on this mountain, and she therefore had the monastery renamed "Respecting Ancestors Monastery" (Pongsŏnsa). The monastery became the headquarters of the KYO school when the two schools of Kyo (Doctrine) and SŎN (Meditation) were restored in 1551, during the reign of the Chosŏn king Myongjong (r. 1545–1567). The monastery was repeatedly destroyed by fire during several wars, including the Japanese Hideyoshi invasions of the late-sixteenth century, the Manchu invasions of the seventeenth century, and the Korean War.

**Pongwan**. (K) (奉玩). See HAN YONGUN.

**Pongwŏnsa**. (奉元寺). In Korean, "Respecting Primacy Monastery"; the head monastery of the T'AEGO CHONG of Korean Buddhism. Pongwŏnsa was founded in 889 by state preceptor (K. kuksa; C. GUOSHI) TOSŎN (827–898) on the grounds of what is currently the campus of Yonsei University in Seoul. It was moved by the great masters (TAESA) Ch'anjŭp and Chŭngam up the hill overlooking the present-day sites of Yonsei and Ewha universities in 1748, during the reign of king Yŏngjo (r. 1724–1776). During the reign of the next king, Chŏngjo (r. 1776–1800), an institute to reform and police Buddhism was established at Pongwŏnsa. A signboard for the monastery shows the calligraphy of the noted Confucian scholar Chŏng Tojŏn (1337–1398). The monastery is arguably the most beautiful in Seoul, partially due to the now well-weathered reconstruction carried out in 1911 by abbot Yi Podam (1859–?). The present main shrine hall (TAEUNG CHŎN) was built in 1966. Today the monastery is well known for its association with Korean Buddhist art and culture. Not only is it the current home of the troupe of monks who perform and preserve the Buddhist rite YŎNGSANJAE, including the dances NABICH'UM, PARACH'UM, and PŎPKO CH'UM, and the chanting of pŏmp'ae (C. FANBAI), but it has also been home to the premier master of TANCH'ŎNG and other types of Buddhist painting. The monastery also houses the Okchŏn Buddhist Music College, which trains laity as well as monks and nuns from other sects of Buddhism in traditional Korean music.

**ponsa**. (C. bensi; J. honji 本寺). In Korean, lit. "foundational monastery"; the major district or parish monasteries of the CHOGYE CHONG of Korean Buddhism; also referred to as ponsan, or "foundational mountain [monastery]." The institution of ponsa was started by the Korean state as one means of exerting state control over the Buddhist ecclesiastical community. When the Chosŏn king T'aejong (r. 1400–1418) in 1407 combined the preexisting eleven Buddhist schools into seven, a ponsa was designated for each school, all of them located in the vicinity of the Chosŏn capital of Hanyang (Seoul). King Sejong (r. 1418–1450) reduced the number of schools again in 1424 to the two schools of Doctrine (KYO) and Meditation (SŎN) (SŎN KYO YANGJONG) and designated HŬNGCH'ŎNSA and HŬNGDŎKSA as the ponsa of the Kyo and Sŏn schools, respectively. The institution of ponsa was discontinued during the reign of the Chosŏn king Myŏngjong (r. 1545–1567) because of the abolition of the two schools of Kyo and Sŏn. The institution was revived in 1911 during the Japanese colonial period (1910–1945), when the "Monastery Act" (Sach'allyŏng) of the

Japanese government-general divided the colony into thirty districts, with a ponsa heading each of them. One more was added in 1924, creating a total of thirty-one ponsa. After Korea was liberated in 1945, the South Korean Buddhist community established an independent Chogye order, which organized the monasteries of the peninsula into twenty-four districts, each headed by a ponsa. Each district monastery loosely presides over several affiliated "branch monasteries" (MALSA), each located in the geographical vicinity of its ponsa. The twenty-five ponsa of the contemporary Chogye order are (1) CHOGYESA, (2) YONGJUSA, (3) SINHŬNGSA, (4) WŎLCH'ŎNGSA, (5) PŎPCHUSA, (6) MAGOKSA, (7) SUDŎKSA, (8) CHIKCHISA, (9) TONGHWASA, (10) ŬNHAESA, (11) PULGUKSA, (12) HAEINSA, (13) SSANGGYESA, (14) PŎMŎSA, (15) T'ONGDOSA, (16) KOUNSA, (17) KŬMSANSA, (18) PAEGYANGSA, (19) HWAŎMSA, [(20) SŎNAMSA (control ceded to the rival T'AEGO CHONG)], (21) SONGGWANGSA, (22) TAEHŬNGSA, (23) KWANŬMSA, (24) SŎNUNSA, and (25) PONGSŎNSA.

**ponsan**. (本山). In Korean, "foundational mountain [monastery]" an alternate name for the major district or parish monasteries of the CHOGYE order of Korean Buddhism. See PONSA.

**Pŏpchip pyŏrhaengnok chŏryo pyŏngip sagi**. (法集別行錄節要竝入私記). In Korean, "Excerpts from the 'Dharma Collection and Special Practice Record' with Personal Notes" (according to the traditional parsing of the title within the Korean commentarial tradition), and often known by its abbreviated title *Chŏryo* ("Excerpts"); the magnum opus of the mid-Koryŏ Sŏn master POJO CHINUL (1158–1210), which provides an exhaustive analysis of the sudden-gradual issue in East Asian Buddhist thought and practice. Chinul's treatise is constructed around excerpts from a lesser-known work of the Chinese CHAN and HUAYAN teacher GUIFENG ZONGMI (780–841), which compares the approach to practice in four different schools of early Chinese Chan Buddhism. Chinul used Zongmi's analysis as a foil for a wider exploration of the sudden-gradual issue. After examining in meticulous detail the various schemata of awakening and cultivation outlined by such Buddhist teachers as Zongmi, CHENGGUAN (738–839), and YONGMING YANSHOU (904–975), Chinul comes out strongly in favor of sudden awakening/gradual cultivation (K. donŏ chŏmsu; C. DUNWU JIANXIU), a soteriological approach championed by Zongmi. In this approach, the Buddhist path (MĀRGA) begins with an initial sudden "understanding-awakening" (JIEWU), in which one gains correct conceptual understanding of the Buddhist teachings and awakens to the fact that one is inherently a buddha. But simply knowing that one is a buddha is not enough to ensure that one is able always to act like a buddha. Only after continued gradual cultivation (jianxiu) following this initial understanding-awakening will one remove the habitual tendencies or predispositions (VĀSANĀ) that have suffused the mind for an essentially infinite amount of time, eventually integrating one's knowledge and conduct. That correspondence marks the final "realization-awakening" (ZHENGWU) and is the point at which the practitioner truly realizes the complete, perfect enlightenment of buddhahood (ANUTTARASAMYAKSAṂBODHI). This soteriological process is compared by Chinul to that of an infant who is born with all the faculties of a human being (sudden understanding-awakening) but who still needs to go through a long process of maturation (gradual cultivation) before he will be able to embody his full potential as an adult human being (realization-awakening). While Chinul also accepts the validity of a "sudden awakening/sudden cultivation" (K. tono tonsu; C. dunwu dunxiu) approach, in which all aspects of cultivation are perfected simultaneously with the awakening experience, he ultimately concludes that this approach targets only the most advanced of practitioners and is actually sudden awakening/gradual cultivation when viewed from the standpoint of multiple lifetimes: viz., awakening and cultivation can be perfected simultaneously only for someone who has already had an initial sudden understanding-awakening in a previous life and who has been continuing to cultivate that experience gradually over multiple past lives. Chinul's treatise is also important for being the first Korean work to advocate the practice of Sŏn "questioning meditation" (K. kanhwa Sŏn; C. KANHUA CHAN), a type of meditation that subsequently comes to dominate Korean Sŏn practice. The *Chŏryo* is included in the "Fourfold Collection" (SAJIP), the core of the Korean monastic curriculum since at least the seventeenth century.

**Pŏpchusa**. (法住寺). In Korean, "Monastery Where the Dharma Abides"; the fifth district monastery (PONSA) of the contemporary CHOGYE CHONG of Korean Buddhism, located at the base of Songni (Leaving Behind the Mundane) Mountain in North Ch'ungch'ŏng province. Pŏpchusa was founded in 553, during the reign of the Silla King Chinhŭng (r. 540–576), by the monk Ŭisin (d.u.) who, according to legend, returned from the "western regions" (viz. Central Asia and India) with scriptures and resided at the monastery; hence the monastery's name. In 1101, during the Koryŏ dynasty, ŬICH'ŎN (1055–1101) held an assembly to recite the RENWANG JING ("Scripture for Humane Kings") here for the protection of the state (see HUGUO FOJIAO), which is said to have been attended by thirty thousand monks. On entering the monastery, to the back and left of the front gate there are two granite pillars that date from the eleventh century, which were used to support the hanging paintings (KWAEBUL) that were unfurled on such important ceremonial occasions as the Buddha's birthday. A pavilion on the right houses a huge iron pot dated to 720 CE, which was purportedly once used to prepare meals for monks and pilgrims; off to the side is a water tank made of stone that would have held about 2,200 gallons (ten cubic meters) of water. There is also a lotus-shaped basin dating from the eighth century and a lion-supported stone lantern sponsored by the Silla monarch Sŏngdŏk (r. 702–737) in 720. The main shrine hall (TAEUNG CHŎN) houses images of VAIROCANA, ŚĀKYAMUNI, and Rocana buddhas. Behind these three statues are three paintings of the same buddhas, accompanied by BODHISATTVAs, a young ĀNANDA, and the elderly MAHĀKĀŚYAPA. In the paintings Śākyamuni and Rocana are surrounded by rainbows and Vairocana by a white halo. Pŏpchusa is especially renowned for its five-story high wooden pagoda, which dates from the foundation of the monastery in 553; it may have been the model for the similar pagoda at HŌRYŪJI in Nara, Japan. The current pagoda was reconstructed in 1624 and is the oldest extant wooden pagoda in Korea. The pagoda is painted with pictures of the eight stereotypical episodes in the life of the Buddha (see BAXIANG). Inside are four images of Śākyamuni: the east-facing statue is in the gesture of fearlessness (ABHAYAMUDRĀ); the west, in the teaching pose (DHARMACAKRAMUDRĀ); the south, in the touching-the-earth gesture (BHŪMISPARŚAMUDRĀ); and the north, in a reclining buddha posture, a rare Korean depiction of the Buddha's PARINIRVĀṆA. Around the four buddha images sit 340 smaller white buddhas, representing the myriad buddhas of other world systems. The ceiling inside is three stories high, and the beams, walls, and ceiling are painted with various images, including bodhisattvas and lotus flowers. Outside the pagoda is Pŏpchusa's most striking image, the thirty-three-meter (108-foot), 160-ton bronze statue of the bodhisattva MAITREYA. The original image is said to have been constructed by the Silla VINAYA master CHINP'YO (fl. eighth century), but was removed by the Taewŏn'gun in 1872 and melted down to be used in the reconstruction of Kyŏngbok Palace in Seoul. A replacement image was begun in 1939 but was never completed; another temporary statue was crafted from cement and installed in 1964. The current bronze image was finally erected in 1989. Near the base is a statue of a woman with a bowl of food, representing the laywoman SUJĀTĀ, who offered GAUTAMA a meal of milk porridge before his enlightenment.

**Pŏphae pobŏl**. (法海寶筏). In Korean, "Precious Raft on the Ocean of Dharma." See SŎNMUN CH'WARYO.

**pŏpkoch'um**. (法鼓춤). In Korean, "dharma drum dance"; a CHAKPŎP ritual dance performed by Buddhist monks during such Korean Buddhist rites as the YŎNGSANJAE. The dance is performed with a giant drum that has a head often almost as wide as a person's outstretched arms. The dance seeks to teach human beings about the prospect of rebirth in the heavens and to rescue the denizens of hell from their suffering. The dancer uses two drumsticks and beats the drum while drawing the Sinograph sim (mind). The actual dance is in two parts: the first part, called the pŏpkoch'um, begins before the drumming, when the drummer is dancing without sound; the second part, called the honggoch'um, begins when the drumming starts. Because the dance is performed in conjunction with pŏmp'ae (C. FANBAI) chanting, the dancer moderates his movements and the strength of the drumbeats in accordance with the chant. The beating of the drum is intended to awaken all sentient beings in order to deliver them from suffering. Just as in the cymbal dance (PARACH'UM), the monk performing the dance wears grey ceremonial robes with long sleeves. This dance is sometimes performed with one drummer and one dancer on opposite sides of the drum.

**pŏpsŏng chong**. (法性宗). In Korean, "dharma-nature school"; one of the five schools of Korean doctrinal Buddhism (KYO) that are traditionally presumed to have developed during the Silla dynasty (668–935). This school is most closely associated with the scholiast WŎNHYO (617–686) and his interest in the fundamental qualities that underlie all phenomenal existence, such as the TATHĀGATAGARBHA. See FAXING ZONG; KYO.

**poṣadha**. (S). See UPOṢADHA.

**posal**. (菩薩). In Korean, "BODHISATTVA." In addition to its use as a transcription of bodhisattva, the term posal is also used in Korean to designate female adherents, and especially lay residents of monasteries, who assist with the menial chores of cooking, preserving food, doing laundry, etc. These women have often been widows or divorcées, who work for the monastery in exchange for room and board for themselves and their children. The posal often serve the monastery permanently and may even end up retiring there. The compound posal is generally followed by the honorific suffix -nim and then pronounced posallim.

**postulant**. See XINGZHE.

**postures, four**. See ĪRYĀPATHA.

**Po ta la**. The most famous building in Tibet and one of the great achievements of Tibetan architecture. Located in the Tibetan capital of LHA SA, it served as the winter residence of the DALAI LAMAs and seat of the Tibetan government from the seventeenth century until the fourteenth Dalai Lama's flight into exile in 1959. It takes its name from Mount POTALAKA, the abode of AVALOKITEŚVARA, the bodhisattva of compassion, of whom the three Tibetan dharma kings (chos rgyal) and the Dalai Lamas are said to be human incarnations. The full name of the Potala is "Palace of Potala Peak" (Rtse po ta la'i pho brang), and it is commonly referred to by Tibetans simply as the Red Palace (Pho brang dmar po), because the edifice is located on Mar po ri (Red Hill) on the northwestern edge of Lha sa and because of the red palace at the summit of the white structure. In the early seventh century, the Tibetan king SRONG BTSAN SGAM PO is said to have meditated in a cave located on the hill; the cave is preserved within the present structure. The earliest structure to have been constructed there was an eleven-storied palace that he had built in 637 when he moved his capital to Lha sa. In 1645, three years after his installation as temporal ruler of Tibet, the fifth Dalai Lama NGAG DBANG BLO BZANG RGYA MTSHO began renovations of what remained of this original structure, with the new structure serving as his own residence, as well as the site of his government (known as the DGA' LDAN PHO BRANG), which he moved from the DGE LUGS PA monastery of 'BRAS SPUNGS, located some five miles outside the city. The exterior of the White Palace (Pho brang dkar po), which includes the apartments of the Dalai Lama, was completed in 1648 and the Dalai Lama took up residence in 1649. The portion of the Po ta la known as the Red Palace was added by the regent SANGS RGYAS RGYA MTSHO in honor of the fifth Dalai Lama after his death in 1682. Fearing that the project would cease if news of his death became known, Sangs rgyas rgya mtsho was able successfully to conceal the Dalai Lama's death for some twelve years (making use of a double who physically resembled the Dalai Lama to meet foreign dignitaries) until construction could be completed in 1694. The current structure is thirteen stories (approximately 384 feet) tall and is said to have over a thousand rooms, including the private apartments of the Dalai Lama, reception and assembly halls, temples, chapels containing the stūpas of the fifth and seventh through thirteenth Dalai Lamas, the Rnam rgyal monastery that performed state rituals, and government offices. From the time of the eighth Dalai Lama, the Po ta la served as the winter residence for the Dalai Lamas, who moved each summer to the smaller NOR BU GLING KHA. The first Europeans to see the Po ta la were likely the Jesuit missionaries Albert Dorville and Johannes Grueber, who visited Lha sa in 1661 and made sketches of the palace, which was still under construction at the time. During the Tibetan uprising against the People's Liberation Army in March 1959, the Po ta la was shelled by Chinese artillery. It is said to have survived the Chinese Cultural Revolution through the intervention of the Chinese prime minister Zhou Enlai, although many of its texts and works of art were looted or destroyed. In old Lha sa, the Po ta la stood outside the central city, with the small village of Zhol located at its foot. This was the site of a prison, a printing house, and residences of some of the lovers of the sixth Dalai Lama. In modern Lha sa, the Po ta la is now encompassed by the city, and much of Zhol has been destroyed. The Po ta la still forms the northern boundary of the large circumambulation route around Lha sa, called the gling bskor (ling khor). Since the Chinese opened Tibet to foreign access in the 1980s, the Po ta la has been visited by millions of Tibetan pilgrims and foreign tourists. The stress of tourist traffic has required frequent restoration projects. In 1994, the Po ta la was designated a UNESCO World Heritage site. See also PUTUOSHAN.

**Potalaka**. (T. Po ta la; C. Butuoluoshan; J. Fudarakusen; K. Pot'araksan 補陀落山). According to the GAṆḌAVYŪHASŪTRA, a mountain that is the abode of the bodhisattva of compassion, AVALOKITEŚVARA. The precise location of the mountain is the subject of considerable speculation. According to XUANZANG, it is located in southern India to the east of the Malaya Mountains. He describes it as a perilous mountain with a lake and a heavenly stone palace at the summit. A river flows from the summit, encircling the mountain twenty times before flowing into the South Sea. Those who seek to meet the bodhisattva scale the mountain, but few succeed. Xuanzang says that the bodhisattva appears to his devotees at the base the mountain in the form of Maheśvara (Śiva) or an ascetic sadhu covered in ashes. Modern scholarship has speculated that Xuanzang was describing the mountain called Potikai or Potiyil in Tamil Nadu. Other sources place the mountain on an island in the Indian Ocean. In East Asian Buddhism, it is called PUTUOSHAN and is identified as a mountainous island in the Zhoushan Archipelago, about sixty-two miles off the eastern coast of Zhejiang province. When the fifth DALAI LAMA constructed his palace in LHA SA, he named it PO TA LA, after this mountain identified with Avalokiteśvara, of whom he is considered the human incarnation.

**Potaliyasutta**. (C. Buliduo jing; J. Horitakyō; K. P'orida kyŏng 晡利多經). The "Discourse to Potaliya," the fifty-fourth sutta of the MAJJHIMANIKĀYA (a separate SARVĀSTIVĀDA recension appears as the 203rd sūtra in the Chinese translation of the MADHYAMĀGAMA); preached by the Buddha to the mendicant (P. paribbājaka, S. PARIVRĀJAKA) Potaliya at a grove in the town of Āpaṇa in the country of the Aṅguttarāpas. Potaliya had recently left the householder's life to cut off his involvement with the affairs of the world and had taken up the life of itinerant mendicancy. When the Buddha encounters him, Potaliya had not abandoned his ordinary layman's attire, so the Buddha addresses him as "householder," to which the new mendicant takes great offense. The Buddha responds by telling Potaliya that the noble discipline rests on the support of eight abandonments: the abandonment of killing, stealing, lying, maligning others, avarice, spite, anger, and arrogance. The Buddha then enumerates the dangers of sensual pleasure and the benefits of abandoning it. Having thus prepared the ground, the Buddha explains that the noble disciple then attains the three knowledges (P. tevijja, S. TRIVIDYĀ), comprised of (1) recollection of one's own previous existences (P. pubbenivāsānussati, S. PŪRVANIVĀSĀNUSMṚTI); (2) the divine eye (P. dibbacakkhu, S. DIVYACAKṢUS), the ability to see the demise and rebirth of beings according to their good and evil deeds; and (3) knowledge of the extinction of the contaminants (P. āsavakkhaya, S. ĀSRAVAKṢAYA). This, the Buddha explains, is true cutting off of the affairs of the world. Delighted and inspired by the discourse, Potaliya takes refuge in the three jewels (RATNATRAYA) and dedicates himself as a lay disciple of the Buddha.

**Poṭṭhapādasutta**. (C. Buzhapolou jing; J. Futabarōkyō; K. P'ot'abaru kyŏng 布吒婆樓經). In Pāli, "Discourse to Poṭṭhapāda," the ninth sutta of the DĪGHANIKĀYA (a separate DHARMAGUPTAKA recension appears as the twenty-eighth SŪTRA in the Chinese translation of the DĪRGHĀGAMA); preached by the Buddha to the mendicant (P. paribbājaka, S. PARIVRĀJAKA) Poṭṭhapāda in a hall erected in Mallika's park in Sāvatthi (S. ŚRĀVASTĪ). The Buddha is invited to the hall by Poṭṭhapāda to express his opinion on the attainment of the cessation of thought (abhisaññānirodha). Various theories advocated by other teachers are put to the Buddha, all of which he rejects as unfounded. The Buddha then explains the means by which this attainment can be achieved, beginning with taking refuge in the Buddha, the DHARMA, and the SAṂGHA, observing the precepts, renouncing the world to become a Buddhist monk, controlling the senses with mindfulness (P. sati, S. SMṚTI), cultivating the four meditative absorptions (P. JHĀNA, S. DHYĀNA), developing the four formless meditations (P. arūpāvacarajhāna, S. ĀRŪPYĀVACARADHYĀNA), and finally attaining the cessation of thought. Poṭṭhapāda then asks about the existence of the soul (ĀTMAN), and whether or not the universe is eternal. The Buddha responds that he holds no opinions on these questions as they neither relate to the holy life (P. brahmacariya; S. BRAHMACARYA) nor lead to NIRVĀṆA. Rather, he teaches only the FOUR NOBLE TRUTHS of suffering (P. dukkha; S. DUḤKHA), its cause (SAMUDAYA), its cessation (NIRODHA), and the path leading thereto (P. magga, S. MĀRGA). Some days later, Poṭṭhapāda approaches the Buddha with his friend CITTA, the elephant trainer's son, and inquires again about the soul. Pleased with the Buddha's response, he becomes a lay disciple. Citta enters the Buddhist order and in due time becomes an arahant (S. ARHAT).

**Pou**. (K) (普雨). See HŎŬNG POU.

**Pou**. (K) (普愚). See T'AEGO POU.

**Prabhākaramitra**. (C. Boluopojialuomiduoluo; J. Harahakaramitsutara; K. Parap'agaramiltara 波羅頗迦羅蜜多羅) (564–633). A monk from NĀLANDĀ monastery who traveled to China in 626, where he translated a number of important texts, including the MAHĀYĀNASŪTRĀLAMKĀRA of MAITREYANĀTHA and the PRAJÑĀPRADĪPA of BHĀVAVIVEKA.

**prabhākarībhūmi**. (T. 'od byed pa; C. faguang di; J. hokkōji; K. palgwang chi 發光地). In Sanskrit, "illuminating," the name of the third of the ten BODHISATTVA BHŪMI, as found in a list of ten stages (DAŚABHŪMI) enumerated in the DAŚABHŪMIKASŪTRA ("Sūtra on the Ten Stages"), a sūtra that is later subsumed into the massive scriptural compilation, the AVATAṂSAKASŪTRA. The first bhūmi coincides with the attainment of the path of vision (DARŚANAMĀRGA), the remaining nine to the path of cultivation (BHĀVANĀMĀRGA). Prabhākarībhūmi is so called because the light of the bodhisattva's wisdom burns brightly through the attainment of the four meditative absorptions (DHYĀNA) and the five superknowledges (ABHIJÑĀ). When the practice of the six (or ten) perfections (PĀRAMITĀ) is aligned with the ten bhūmi, the prabhākarībhūmi is especially an occasion for the practice of the perfection of patience (KṢĀNTIPĀRAMITĀ), where the bodhisattva's patience becomes so great that even if someone were to mutilate his body, he would not respond in anger. The bodhisattva remains on this bhūmi until he is able to abide consistently in the limbs of enlightenment (BODHIPĀKṢIKADHARMA).

**prabhāsvara**. (P. pabhassara; T. 'od gsal; C. guangming; J. kōmyō; K. kwangmyŏng 光明). In Sanskrit, "luminous," "resplendent"; referring to an effulgence of light and often used as a metaphor for either deep states of meditation or, especially, the nature of the mind. This notion of the innate effulgence of the mind has a long pedigree in Buddhism, and its locus classicus is the oft-quoted passage in the Pāli AṄGUTTARANIKĀYA: "The mind, O monks, is luminous (P. pabhassara), but is defiled by adventitious defilements" (pabhassaraṃ idaṃ bhikkave cittaṃ tañ ca kho āgantukehi upakkilesehi upakkiliṭṭhaṃ). A similar sentiment appears in the early MAHĀYĀNA scripture AṢṬASĀHASRIKĀPRAJÑĀPĀRAMITĀSŪTRA, where it states that the "thought of enlightenment is no thought, since in its essential original nature thought is transparently luminous." Through enlightenment, the mind's innate luminosity is restored to its full intensity so that it shines through all objects, revealing their inherent vacuity and lack of substance. This same strand eventually develops into TATHĀGATAGARBHA thought, which sees the mind as inherently enlightened, the defilements of mind as ultimately extrinsic to the mind (cf. ĀGANTUKAKLEŚA), and the prospect of buddhahood as innate in all sentient beings. The concept of the "mind of clear light" (see PRABHĀSVARACITTA) becomes particularly important in ANUTTARAYOGATANTRA, where it is described as the primordial and fundamental form of consciousness, which becomes manifest at particular moments, such as falling asleep, awaking from sleep, orgasm, and especially, at the moment of death. Many practices of the stage of completion (NIṢPANNAKRAMA) are devoted to making manifest this mind of clear light and using it to understand the nature of reality. As such, the practice of clear light is one of the six yogas of Nāropa (NA RO CHOS DRUG).

**prabhāsvaracitta**. [alt. ābhāsvaracitta] (T. 'od gsal gyi sems; C. guangmingxin; J. kōmyōshin; K. kwangmyŏngsim 光明心). In Sanskrit, "mind of clear light." According to the systems of ANUTTARAYOGATANTRA, this state of mind is the most subtle form of consciousness, which must be used to perceive reality directly in order to achieve buddhahood. There are various views as to the location and accessibility of this type of consciousness, with some asserting that it resides in an indestructible drop (BINDU) located at the center of the heart CAKRA in the central channel (AVADHŪTĪ), entering at the moment of conception and departing at the moment of death. Because the mind of clear light must be made manifest in order to achieve buddhahood, various practices are set forth to simulate the process of its manifestation at the moment of death, including sexual yogas. Other views hold that the mind of clear light is present in all moments of awareness and needs only to be recognized in order to achieve enlightenment. See also ĀGANTUKAKLEŚA; PRABHĀSVARA.

**prabhava**. (P. pabhava; T. rab tu skye ba). In Sanskrit, "successive production," or "series of causes," used especially in the context of the process by which action (KARMAN) and the afflictions (KLEŚA) constantly produce different forms of suffering in an unrelenting manner. As such, prabhava is one of the four aspects of the second of the FOUR NOBLE TRUTHS, the truth of origin (SAMUDAYA).

**Prabhūtaratna**. (T. Mthu ldan rin chen; C. Duobao rulai; J. Tahō nyorai; K. Tabo yŏrae 多寶如來). In Sanskrit, "Abounding in Jewels"; the name of a buddha who appears in chapter eleven of the SADDHARMAPUṆḌARĪKASŪTRA, the influential "Lotus Sūtra." In this chapter, the audience is surprised to see a magnificent jeweled STŪPA emerge from the earth and float in space. The Buddha explains that it is the stūpa of the buddha Prabhūtaratna, who resides in a buddha-field (BUDDHAKṢETRA) named ratnaviśuddha, or "bejeweled purity." Prabhūtaratna appears because, as a BODHISATTVA, he made a vow that he would appear in his bejeweled stūpa whenever the *Saddharmapuṇḍarīkasūtra* was taught by any TATHĀGATA, in any world system. At the invitation of Prabhūtaratna, ŚĀKYAMUNI Buddha enters the jeweled stūpa, and the two buddhas sit side by side. The audience also rises into the sky so that they can see the two buddhas. Although Prabhūtaratna never became an object of cultic worship, the image of the two buddhas sitting together was a frequent subject of Buddhist sculpture as early as the fifth century.

**pradakṣiṇa**. (P. padakkhiṇa; T. skor ba; C. yourao; J. unyō; K. uyo 右遶). In Sanskrit, "circumambulation" (lit. "moving to the right"); a common means of demonstrating reverence to a person, place, or sacred object in the Indian tradition, since it places the object of reverence at the center of one's worship activity. Traditionally, circumambulation was performed in a clockwise direction with the worshipper's right side facing the object (the left side being considered polluted because of Indian toilet practices). In Buddhism, adherents might circumambulate a relic (ŚARĪRA) or reliquary (STŪPA), a monastery, an image, or even an entire geographical location, such as a sacred mountain. Reliquary mounds were designed to facilitate this practice, as they are often surrounded by reliefs depicting important stereotypical episodes in the life of the Buddha (see BAXIANG), which worshippers would review and recollect as they circumambulated the stūpa. The custom of making ritual circumambulations around stūpas appears to have come into popularity early in the Buddhist tradition. See also GNAS SKOR BA.

**pradāsa**. [alt. pradāśa] (P. padāleti; T. 'tshig pa; C. nao; J. nō; K. noe 惱). In Sanskrit, "irritation," "maliciousness," "vexation," or "contentiousness"; one of the forty-six mental concomitants (CAITTA) according to the SARVĀSTIVĀDA-VAIBHĀṢIKA school of ABHIDHARMA and one of the fifty-one according to the YOGĀCĀRA school. "Irritation" appears in conjunction with envy (ĪRṢYĀ) and disparaging others' achievements or wholesome qualities (MRAKṢA), and may be viewed as one of the possible derivative emotions of hatred (DVEṢA) or aversion (PRATIGHA). "Irritation" is the compulsive resistance to letting anyone gain advantage over oneself. Irritation may also arise when one dwells compulsively on unpleasant events from the past or present and is closely associated with "remorse" (KAUKṚTYA), "worries," and "sadness."

**pradhānacitta**. (P. padhānacitta; T. gtso sems). In Sanskrit, "chief mind," a term used in Buddhist epistemology in the context of treatments of mind (CITTA) and mental concomitants (CAITTA). A "chief mind" would refer to any instance of the six consciousnesses (citta, here the functional equivalent of VIJÑĀNA)—visual, auditory, olfactory, gustatory, tactile, and mental consciousnesses. A moment of any one of these consciousnesses will be accompanied by a combination of various mental concomitants (caitta). These mental concomitants fall into five categories and include the omnipresent (SARVATRAGA), the determining (viṣayapratiniyama), the virtuous (KUŚULA), the root afflictions (MŪLAKLEŚA), the secondary afflictions (UPAKLEŚA), and the indeterminate (ANIYATA). The chief mind and the mental concomitants that accompany it are said to have five similarities. They have the same basis (ĀŚRAYA); in the case of sense perception, this would be the same organ. They have the same object (ĀLAMBANA). They are produced in the same aspect (ĀKĀRA) or image of the object. They occur at the same time (KĀLA). Finally, they are the same entity (DRAVYA), in the sense that the mind and its mental factors are produced, abide, and cease simultaneously.

**Pra dum rtse**. (Tradumtse). In Tibetan, one of the four "extra taming temples" or "extra pinning temples" (YANG 'DUL GTSUG LAG KHANG) said to have been constructed during the time of the Tibetan king SRONG BTSAN SGAM PO to pin down the limbs of the demoness (T. srin mo) in order to introduce Buddhism into Tibet. It is located in Byang (Jang) and pins down her left knee.

**Prāgbodhi(giri)**. (C. Qianzhengjueshan/Boluojiputishan; J. Zenshōgakusen/Haragōbodaisen; K. Chŏnjŏnggaksan/Pallagŭpporisan 前正覺山/鉢羅笈菩提山). Literally, "Before Enlightenment," or "Before Enlightenment Mountain," a mountain near BODHGAYĀ that ŚĀKYAMUNI is said to have ascended shortly before his enlightenment. In the account of his travels in India, XUANZANG recounts a story that does not seem to appear in Indian versions of the life of the Buddha. After accepting the meal of milk porridge from SUJĀTĀ, the BODHISATTVA climbed a nearby mountain, wishing to gain enlightenment there. However, when he reached the summit, the mountain began to quake. The mountain god informed the bodhisattva that the mountain was unable to bear the force of his SAMĀDHI, and if he practiced meditation there the mountain would collapse. As the bodhisattva descended the mountain he came upon a cave; he sat down there to meditate, but the earth began to tremble again. Deities then informed him that the mountain was not the appropriate place for him to achieve enlightenment and directed him to a pipal tree fourteen or fifteen leagues (li; approximately three miles) to the southwest. However, the dragon that lived in the cave implored him to stay and achieve enlightenment there. The bodhisattva departed, but left his shadow on the wall of the cave for the dragon; among the souvenirs that Xuanzang took back to China was a replica of this shadow. Based on Xuanzang's account, the story of the Buddha's ascent and descent of Prāgbodhi became popular in East Asia, and is the apparent source for the theme in poetry and painting of "ŚĀKYAMUNI Descending the Mountain."

**prahāṇa**. [alt. pradhāna] (P. padrāna; T. spang ba; C. duan/si zhengqin; J. dan/shishōgon; K. tan/sa chŏnggŭn 斷/四正勤). In Sanskrit, "abandonment," "relinquishment," "exertions," "right effort"; the effort that a practitioner must apply to ridding himself of the afflictions (KLEŚA) and wrong views (MITHYĀDṚṢṬI) that bind one to suffering (DUḤKHA). Because the term implies the abandonment of the causes that bring about suffering, prahāṇa can also mean something that heals, thus an "antidote." Prahāṇa is commonly used to indicate the practice of meditation, through which afflictions and wrong views are abandoned; in the context of the Abhisamācārikā Dharmāḥ, for instance, the term is used when explaining how meditation is to be performed. ¶ Prahāṇa also has a second denotation of "strenuous exertion" or "right effort." This denotation is seen in a common list of four "exertions" (catvari prahāṇāni), also called the four "right efforts" (SAMYAKPRADHĀNA), viz., the practitioner exerts himself (1) to bring about the nonproduction [in the future] of evil and unwholesome dharmas that have not yet been produced; (2) to eradicate evil and unwholesome dharmas that have already been produced; (3) to bring about the production of wholesome dharmas that have not yet been produced; (4) to enhance those wholesome dharmas that have already been produced.

**prahāṇaśālā**. (T. spong khang; C. chanfang; J. zenbō; K. sŏnpang 禪房/禪坊). In Sanskrit, lit. "hall for religious exertion"; a "meditation hall." Prescriptions as to how and why to build such a structure are found in various literary sources, but most often in the VINAYA. For example, in the MŪLASARVĀSTIVĀDA VINAYA, the Buddha orders a prahāṇaśālā built so that monks will have some degree of privacy during their meditative practice. In the Abhisamācārikā Dharmāḥ, the Buddha lists the prahāṇaśālā as an appropriate place for the bimonthly confession and recitation of precepts (UPOṢADHA) and explains how the hall is to be maintained from day to day. See also SENGTANG.

**prāhāṇika**. (P. padhānika; T. spong ba bsam gtan pa). In Sanskrit, lit. "characterized by religious exertion," viz., a "meditating monk." This term is used in the MULASARVĀSTIVĀDA VINAYA to refer to monks who specialize in meditation training or more generally to monks who are involved in ascetic practices (see DHUTAṄGA, DUṢKARACARYĀ).

**Prajāpatī**. (S). See MAHĀPRAJĀPATĪ.

**prajñā**. (P. paññā; T. shes rab; C. bore/hui; J. hannya/e; K. panya/hye 般若/慧). In Sanskrit, typically translated "wisdom," but having connotations perhaps closer to "gnosis," "awareness," and in some contexts "cognition"; the term has the general sense of accurate and precise understanding, but is used most often to refer to an understanding of reality that transcends ordinary comprehension. It is one of the most important terms in Buddhist thought, occurring in a variety of contexts. In Buddhist epistemology, prajñā is listed as one of the five mental concomitants (CAITTA) that accompany all virtuous (KUŚALA) states of mind. It is associated with correct, analytical discrimination of the various factors (DHARMA) enumerated in the Buddhist teachings (dharmapravicaya). In this context, prajñā refers to the capacity to distinguish between the faults and virtues of objects in such a way as to overcome doubt. Prajñā is listed among the five spiritual "faculties" (PAÑCENDRIYA) or "powers" (PAÑCABALA), where it serves to balance faith (ŚRADDHĀ) and to counteract skeptical doubt (VICIKITSĀ). Prajñā is also one of the three trainings (TRIŚIKṢĀ), together with morality (ŚĪLA) and concentration (SAMĀDHI). In this context, it is distinguished from the simple stability of mind developed through the practice of concentration and refers to a specific understanding of the nature of reality, likened to a sword that cuts through the webs of ignorance (see ADHIPRAJÑĀŚIKṢĀ). Three specific types of wisdom are set forth, including the wisdom generated by learning (ŚRUTAMAYĪPRAJÑĀ), an intellectual understanding gained through listening to teachings or reading texts; the wisdom generated by reflection (CINTĀMAYĪPRAJÑĀ), which includes conceptual insights derived from one's own personal reflection on those teachings and from meditation at a low level of concentration; and the wisdom generated by cultivation (BHĀVANĀMAYĪPRAJÑĀ), which is a product of more advanced stages in meditation. This last level of wisdom is related to the concept of insight (VIPAŚYANĀ). The term also appears famously in the term PRAJÑĀPĀRAMITĀ or "perfection of wisdom," which refers to the wisdom whereby bodhisattvas achieved buddhahood, as well as a genre of texts in which that wisdom is set forth.

**Prajña**. [alt. Prajñā] (C. Bore; J. Hannya; K. Panya 般若). The proper name of a northwest Indian monk who arrived in the Chinese capital of Chang'an during the middle of the ninth century. Prajña is best known for his forty-roll translation of the GAṆḌAVYŪHASŪTRA, the lengthy final chapter of the AVATAṂSAKASŪTRA; his rendering, which was finished in 798, is thus considered the third and final (though shortest) translation of the *Avataṃsakasūtra* made in China. Five other translations are also attributed to Prajña and collaborators. While in China, Prajña was also associated with the Japanese monk Kūkai (774–835), the founder of the Shingonshū of Japanese esoteric Buddhism.

**prajñācakṣus**. (P. paññācakkhu; T. shes rab kyi spyan; C. zhihui yan; J. chiegen; K. chihye an 智慧眼). In Sanskrit, "wisdom eye," one of the five eyes or five sorts of vision (pañcacakṣus), which are similar to the five (or six) "clairvoyances" or superknowledges (abhijñā). In Pāli texts, the wisdom eye is one of the five sorts of extraordinary vision of a buddha. In Mahāyāna sources, the wisdom eye knows all conditioned (saṃskṛta) and unconditioned (asaṃskṛta) dharmas and is free from all projections.

**prajñājñānābhiṣeka**. (T. shes rab ye shes kyi dbang). In Sanskrit, lit., "knowledge of the wisdom empowerment," with wisdom (prajñā) here referring to a tantric consort. It is the third of the four empowerments or initiations employed in the anuttarayogatantras, the other three being the vase empowerment (kalaśābhiṣeka) and the secret empowerment (guhyābhiṣeka) that precede it, and the fourth empowerment (caturthābhiṣeka), which follows it. Having received the vase empowerment, in the secret empowerment the disciple ingests a drop of fluid (called bodhicitta) that results from the sexual intercourse of his master and a consort. In the knowledge of the consort empowerment, the disciple engages in sexual union with the same consort, resulting in increasing levels of bliss, which is said to result as a drop (bindu) that ascends through the central channel (avadhūtī). Although later monastic exegetes would interpret these empowerments symbolically, it appears that they were originally practiced as the tantric systems developed in India, and they continued to be practiced among certain groups of adepts in Tibet.

**Prajñākaragupta**. (T. Shes rab 'byung gnas sbas pa) (c. 750–810?). Author of a long (16,200-verse) commentary, the *Pramāṇavārttikabhāṣya* (alt. title *Pramāṇavārttikālaṃkārabhāṣya*) on Dharmakīrti's Pramāṇavārttika. The work was translated into Tibetan by Skal ldan rgyal po and Blo ldan shes rab and was later revised by Kumāraśrī and 'Phags pa shes rab as *Tshad ma rnam 'grel gyi rgyan*. There are subcommentaries to the work by Jamāri and Jayanta, both of which are extant in Tibetan translation.

**Prajñākaramati**. (T. Shes rab 'byung gnas blo gros) (950–1030). Indian author of an important pañjikā (commentary) on Śāntideva's Bodhicaryāvatāra. He also wrote a short but influential summary of Haribhadra's Abhisamayālaṃkāravivṛti. Tibetan sources list him among the so-called six gatekeepers of Vikramaśīla, a monastery that flourished during the Pāla dynasty in northeast India. According to one account, the six gatekeepers were Ratnākaraśānti at the eastern gate, Vāgīśvarakīrti at the southern gate, Prajñākaramati at the western gate, Nāropa at the northern gate, and Ratnavajra and Jñānaśrī in the center.

**prajñāpāramitā**. (P. paññāpāramī; T. shes rab kyi pha rol tu phyin pa; C. bore boluomiduo/zhidu; J. hannya haramitta/chido; K. panya paramilta/chido 般若波羅蜜多/智度). In Sanskrit, "perfection of wisdom" or "perfect wisdom"; a polysemous term, which appears in Pāli accounts of the Buddha's prior training as a bodhisattva (P. bodhisatta), but is widely used in Mahāyāna Buddhism. ¶ Prajñāpāramitā refers to a level of understanding beyond that of ordinary wisdom, especially referring to the the wisdom associated with, or required to achieve, buddhahood. The term receives a variety of interpretations, but it is often said to be the wisdom that does not conceive of an agent, an object, or an action as being ultimately real. The perfection of wisdom is also sometimes defined as the knowledge of emptiness (śūnyatā). ¶ As the wisdom associated with buddhahood, prajñāpāramitā is the sixth of the six perfections (pāramitā) that are practiced on the bodhisattva path. When the practice of the six perfections is aligned with the ten bodhisattva bhūmis, the perfection of wisdom is practiced on the sixth bhūmi, called abhimukhī. ¶ Prajñāpāramitā is also used to designate the genre of Mahāyāna sūtras that sets forth the perfection of wisdom. These texts are considered to be among the earliest of the Mahāyāna sūtras, with the first texts appearing sometime between the first century BCE and the first century CE. Here, the title "perfection of wisdom" may have a polemical meaning, claiming to possess a wisdom beyond that taught in the mainstream Buddhist schools. In addition to numerous descriptions of, and paeans to, emptiness, the perfection of wisdom sūtras also extol the practice of the bodhisattva path as the superior form of Buddhist practice. Although emptiness is said to be the chief topic of the sūtras, their "hidden meaning" is said to be the detailed structure of the bodhisattva path. A number of later commentaries, most notably the Abhisamayālaṃkāra, extracted terminology from these sūtras in order to systematize the presentation of the bodhisattva path. There are numerous sūtras with prajñāpāramitā in their titles, the earliest of which are designated simply by their length as measured in ślokas, a unit of metrical verse in traditional Sanskrit literature that is typically rendered in English as "stanza," "verse," or "line." Scholars speculate that there was a core text, which was then expanded. Hence, for example, the prajñāpāramitā sūtra in eight thousand lines (Aṣṭasāhasrikāprajñāpāramitā) is often thought to be one of the earliest of the genre, later followed by twenty-five thousand lines (Pañcaviṃśatisāhasrikāprajñāpāramitāsūtra), and one hundred thousand lines (Śatasāhasrikāprajñāpāramitā), as well as compilations many times longer, such as Xuanzang's translation of the Mahāprajñāpāramitāsūtra. The texts known in English as the "Heart Sūtra" (Prajñāpāramitāhṛdayasūtra) and the "Diamond Sūtra" (Vajracchedikāprajñāpāramitā) are both much shorter versions of these prajñāpāramitā sūtras. ¶ Perhaps because the Sanskrit term prajñāpāramitā is in the feminine gender, Prajñāpāramitā also became the name of a goddess, referred to as the mother of all buddhas, who is the embodiment of the perfection of wisdom. ¶ In the traditional Tibetan monastic curriculum, prajñāpāramitā is one of the primary topics of study, based on the *Abhisamayālaṃkāra* of MAITREYANĀTHA and its commentaries.

**Prajñāpāramitāhṛdayasūtra**. (T. Shes rab kyi pha rol tu phyin pa'i snying po'i mdo; C. Bore boluomiduo xin jing; J. Hannya haramitta shingyō; K. Panya paramilta sim kyŏng 般若波羅蜜多心經). In English, the "Heart of the Perfection of Wisdom Sūtra" (or, in other interpretations, the "DHĀRAṆĪ-Sūtra of the Perfection of Wisdom"); a work known in English simply as the "Heart Sūtra"; one of only a handful of Buddhist SŪTRAS (including the "Lotus Sūtra" and the "Diamond Sūtra") to be widely known by an English title. The "Heart Sūtra" is perhaps the most famous, and certainly the most widely recited, of all Buddhist sūtras across all Mahāyāna traditions. It is also one of the most commented upon, eliciting more Indian commentaries than any Mahāyāna sūtra (eight), including works by such luminaries as KAMALAŚĪLA, VIMALAMITRA, and ATIŚA DĪPAṂKARAŚRĪJÑĀNA, as well as such important East Asian figures as FAZANG, KŪKAI, and HAKUIN EKAKU. As its title suggests, the scripture purports to be the quintessence or heart (hṛdaya) of the "perfection of wisdom" (PRAJÑĀPĀRAMITĀ), in its denotations as both supreme wisdom and the eponymous genre of scriptures. The sūtra exists in long and short versions—with the longer version better known in India and the short version better known in East Asia—but even the long version is remarkably brief, requiring only a single page in translation. The short version, which is probably the earlier of the two recensions, is best known through its Chinese translation by XUANZANG made c. 649 CE. There has been speculation that the Chinese version may be a redaction of sections of the Chinese recension of the MAHĀPRAJÑĀPĀRAMITĀSŪTRA (also translated by Xuanzang) as a mnemonic encoding (dhāraṇī) of the massive perfection of wisdom literature, which was then subsequently translated back into Sanskrit, perhaps by Xuanzang himself. Although there is as yet no scholarly consensus on the provenance of the text, if this argument is correct, this would make the "Heart Sūtra" by far the most influential of all indigenous Chinese scriptures (see APOCRYPHA). The long version of the text, set on Vulture Peak (GṚDHRAKŪṬAPARVATA) outside RĀJAGṚHA, begins with the Buddha entering SAMĀDHI. At that point, the BODHISATTVA AVALOKITEŚVARA (who rarely appears as an interlocutor in the prajñāpāramitā sūtras) contemplates the perfection of wisdom and sees that the five aggregates (SKANDHA) are empty of intrinsic nature (SVABHĀVA). The monk ŚĀRIPUTRA, considered the wisest of the Buddha's ŚRĀVAKA disciples, is inspired by the Buddha to ask Avalokiteśvara how one should train in the perfection of wisdom. Avalokiteśvara's answer constitutes the remainder of the sūtra (apart from a brief epilogue in the longer version of the text). That answer, which consists essentially of a litany of negations of the major categories of Buddhist thought—including such seminal lists as the five aggregates (skandha), twelve sense-fields (ĀYATANA), twelve links of dependent origination (PRATĪTYASAMUTPĀDA), and FOUR NOBLE TRUTHS—contains two celebrated statements. The first, made in reference to the first of the five aggregates, is "form (RŪPA) is emptiness (ŚŪNYATĀ); emptiness is form" (RŪPAṂ ŚŪNYATĀ ŚUNYATAIVA RŪPAM). This is one of the most widely quoted and commented upon statements in the entire corpus of Mahāyāna sūtras and thus is not easily amenable to succinct explication. In brief, however, the line suggests that emptiness, as the nature of ultimate reality, is not located in some rarified realm, but rather is found in the ordinary objects of everyday experience. The other celebrated statement is the spell (MANTRA) that concludes Avalokiteśvara's discourse—GATE GATE PĀRAGATE PĀRASAṂGATE BODHI SVĀHĀ—which, unlike many mantras, is amenable to translation: "gone, gone, gone beyond, gone completely beyond, enlightenment, svāha." This mantra has also been widely commented upon. The presence of the mantra in the sūtra has led to its classification as a TANTRA rather than a sūtra in some Tibetan catalogues; it also forms the basis of Indian tantric SĀDHANAS. The brevity of the text has given it a talismanic quality, being recited on all manner of occasions (it is commonly used as an exorcistic text in Tibet) and inscribed on all manner of objects, including fans, teacups, and neckties in modern Japan.

**Prajñāpāramitānayaśatapañcaśatikā**. (T. Shes rab kyi pha rol tu phyin pa'i tshul brgya lnga bcu pa; C. Bore liqu fen; J. Hannya rishubun; K. Panya ich'wi pun 般若理趣分). In Sanskrit, "Way of the Perfection of Wisdom in One Hundred Fifty Lines," a short PRAJÑĀPĀRAMITĀ SŪTRA in fifteen chapters of ten lines each, spoken by different buddhas, including VAIROCANA. The presence of such terms as VAJRA, guhya, and SIDDHI have caused some to classify it as "tantric." The scripture is cited by both CANDRAKĪRTI and HARIBHADRA and was translated into Chinese five different times, by XUANZANG, BODHIRUCI, VAJRABODHI, AMOGHAVAJRA, and DĀNAPĀLA.

**Prajñāpāramitāpiṇḍārtha**. (T. Shes rab kyi pha rol tu phyin pa don bsdus pa). In Sanskrit, "Summary of the Perfection of Wisdom," a commentary on the AṢṬASĀHASRIKĀPRAJÑĀPĀRAMITĀ attributed to DIGNĀGA; also known as the *Prajñāpāramitāpiṇḍārthasaṃgraha* and the *Prajñāpāramitāsaṃgrahakārikā*. It is a short work in fifty-eight lines, which summarize the perfection of wisdom under thirty-two headings, including the ten misconceptions (VIKALPA) and their antidotes, as well as the sixteen types of emptiness (ŚŪNYATĀ). The opening stanza of the text is widely quoted: "The perfection of wisdom is nondual wisdom; it is the TATHĀGATA. That term [is used] for texts and paths because they have that goal." The work provides a YOGĀCĀRA perspective on the PRAJÑĀPĀRAMITĀ, presenting a more systematic outline of doctrines than is typically found in the diffuse prajñāpāramitā literature. Doctrinally, the work is closely related to the MADHYĀNTAVIBHĀGA. It appears to have been widely known; HARIBHADRA quotes from it five times in his ABHISAMAYĀLAṂKĀRĀLOKĀ. The text was translated into Chinese in 980 and into Tibetan in the eleventh century. There is a commentary on the text, entitled *Prajñāpāramitāpiṇḍārthasaṃgrahavivaraṇa*, by Triratnadāsa, a student of VASUBANDHU.

**Prajñāpāramitāratnaguṇasaṃcayagāthā**. (S). See RATNAGUṆASAṂCAYAGĀTHĀ.

**Prajñāpāramitāsarvatathāgatamātā-Ekākṣarā**. (T. Shes rab kyi pha rol tu phyin pa de bzhin gshegs pa thams cad kyi yum yi ge gcig ma). In Sanskrit, "Perfection of Wisdom in One Letter, the Mother of All Tathāgatas." The shortest of all the PRAJÑĀPĀRAMITĀ sūtras, it reads in its entirety: "Thus have I heard. At one time, the Lord (BHAGAVAT) was dwelling on Vulture Peak (GṚDHRAKŪṬAPARVATA) with a great assembly of 1,250 monks and many millions of bodhisattvas. At that time, the Lord said this to the venerable ĀNANDA: 'Ānanda, keep this perfection of wisdom in one letter for the benefit and happiness of sentient beings. It is thus: A.' So spoke the Lord and everyone—Ānanda, the monks, the BODHISATTVA-MAHĀSATTVAS—having understood and admired the perfection of wisdom, praised what the Lord had said." "The Perfection of Wisdom in One Letter" thus refers to the letter "a," the first letter of the Indic alphabet. See also A; AJIKAN.

**Prajñāpradīpa**. (T. Shes rab sgron me; C. Boredeng lun shi; J. Hannyatōron shaku; K. Panyadŭng non sŏk 般若燈論釋). In Sanskrit, "Lamp of Wisdom," the commentary on NĀGĀRJUNA's MŪLAMADHYAMAKAKĀRIKĀ by the sixth-century master BHĀVAVIVEKA. The "Wisdom" in the title is a reference to Nāgārjuna's text, the full title of which is *Prajñānāmamūlamadhyamakakārikā*. In his commentary on the first chapter of Nāgārjuna's text, Bhāvaviveka criticized the earlier commentary by BUDDHAPĀLITA, saying that it is insufficient simply to employ consequences (PRASAṄGA) and that one must also use autonomous syllogisms (SVATANTRĀNUMĀNA). CANDRAKĪRTI, in his own commentary, the PRASANNAPADĀ, came to Buddhapālita's defense and attacked Bhāvaviveka. It is largely based on this exchange that later Tibetan scholars came to categorize Bhāvaviveka as a *SVĀTANTRIKA and Buddhapālita and Candrakīrti as *PRĀSAṄGIKA. In addition to its intrinsic interest as a major work of an important Mahāyāna philosopher, Bhāvaviveka's commentary is of historical interest because it makes specific reference to other commentators on Nāgārjuna, as well as the doctrines of various rival schools, both Buddhist and non-Buddhist. The text is lost in Sanskrit but is preserved in Chinese and Tibetan translations and has a lengthy commentary by AVALOKITAVRATA preserved in Tibetan translation.

**prajñapti**. (T. gdags pa/btags pa; C. jiaming; J. kemyō; K. kamyŏng 假名). In Sanskrit, "designation," "imputation," or "convention," a term used to describe those things that are not intrinsic, ultimate, or primary, with phenomena whose reality is merely imputed (prajñapti), often contrasted with substantial phenomena (see DRAVYASAT). The various philosophical schools differ in the definition, extent, and deployment of the category, with the MADHYAMAKA arguing that all factors (DHARMA) are merely designations that exist only through imputation (PRAJÑAPTISAT), and nothing in the universe, including the Buddha or emptiness (ŚŪNYATĀ) exists substantially (dravyasat). However, the fact that conditioned dharmas are mere imputations does not imply that they lack functionality as conventional truths (SAṂVṚTISATYA). According to a YOGĀCĀRA explanation in the CHENG WEISHI LUN (**Vijñaptimātratāsiddhi*), all dharmas are said to have only imputed existence because (1) "dharmas are insubstantial and are contingent on fallacious imagining" (wuti suiqing jia); and (2) "dharmas have real substance but are real only in a provisional sense" (youti shishe jia). The first reason is based on the Yogācāra argument that the diversity, duality, and reality of things are merely mental projections (see PARIKALPITA), and are therefore artificial and imagined, existing only as fallacious conceptions. The second reason is based on the Yogācāra tenet of PARATANTRA, the "dependent nature of things." Accordingly, although things are "real" or "substantial" in that they have viable efficacy and functions, they are ultimately transformations of "activated" karmic "seeds" (BĪJA) stored within the eighth storehouse consciousness (ĀLAYAVIJÑĀNA). They are therefore said to be "dependent" on the consciousness and thus have only a "conditional" nature.

**Prajñaptibhāṣya[pādaśāstra]**. [alt. Prajñaptiśāstra] (T. Gdags pa'i gtsug lag bstan bcos; C. Shishe lun; J. Sesetsuron; K. Sisŏl non 施設論). In Sanskrit, "Treatise on Designations," one of the earliest books of the SARVĀSTIVĀDA ABHIDHARMAPIṬAKA; it is traditionally listed as the fourth of the six ancillary texts, or "feet" (pāda), of the JÑĀNAPRASTHĀNA, which is the central treatise or body (śarīra) of the Sarvāstivāda abhidharma canon. The *Prajñaptibhāṣya* derives from the earliest stratum of Sarvāstivāda abhidharma literature, along with the DHARMASKANDHA and the SAṂGĪTIPARYĀYA. YAŚOMITRA and BU STON attribute authorship of the *Prajñaptibhāṣya* to MAHĀMAUDGALYĀYANA. Unlike the rest of the canonical abhidharma texts of the Sarvāstivāda school, there is not a complete translation of this text in Chinese; the entire text survives only in a Tibetan translation ascribed to Prajñāsena. Portions of the second section of the text are, however, extant in a late Chinese translation by Dharmarakṣa et al. made during the eleventh century. The Tibetan text is in three parts: (1) lokaprajñapti, which deals with the cosmogonic speculations similar to such mainstream Buddhist texts as the AGGAÑÑASUTTA; (2) kāraṇaprajñapti, which deals with the causes governing the various stereotypical episodes in a bodhisattva's career (see BAXIANG), from entering the womb for his final birth to entering PARINIRVĀṆA; and (3) karmaprajñapti, a general discourse on the theory of moral cause and effect (KARMAN).

**prajñaptisat**. (T. btags yod; C. jiaming you; J. kemyōyu; K. kamyŏngyu 假名有). In Sanskrit, "imputed existence," a term used by the Buddhist philosophical schools to describe the ontological status of those phenomena that exist as designations, imputations, or conventions. The term is often contrasted with DRAVYASAT, or "substantial existence," a quality of those phenomena that possess a more objective nature. The various school of Buddhist philosophy differ on the meaning and extension of the category of prajñaptisat. The VAIBHĀṢIKA school of SARVĀSTIVĀDA ABHIDHARMA held that the world is composed of indivisible particles of matter and indivisible moment of time, which are dravyasat, and that everything composed of an aggregation of those particles or moments is prajñaptisat. In MADHYAMAKA, all dharmas are prajñaptisat and no dharmas are dravyasat. See PRAJÑAPTI; DRAVYASAT.

**Prajñaptivāda**. (P. Paññattivādā; T. Btags par smra ba; C. Shuojiabu; J. Setsukebu/Sekkebu; K. Sŏlga pu 說假部). In Sanskrit, "Teaching of Designations"; one of the two schools of the KAUKKUṬIKA branch of the MAHĀSĀṂGHIKA school of mainstream Buddhism, along with the BAHUŚRUTĪYA; it may have split off as a separate school around the middle of the third century CE. The Prajñaptivāda posits a distinction between reality and the way that reality is perceived by ordinary sentient beings. Beings use the "provisional designations" (PRAJÑAPTI) of concepts in order to describe what is real, but those concepts are merely imputations of reality and have only conventional validity (PRAJÑAPTISAT). The Prajñaptivāda also claims that the Buddha inevitably was compelled to use such provisional designations in order to convey his teachings to ordinary beings, a position distinct from the LOKOTTARAVĀDA, one of the other major branches of the Mahāsāṃghika, which claims that the Buddha articulated the entirety of his teachings in a single utterance that was altogether transcendent (LOKOTTARA). Little is known about the regional center or geographic extent of the school.

**prajñāśikṣā**. (P. paññāsikkhā; T. shes rab kyi bslab pa; C. huixue; J. egaku; K. hyehak 慧學). In Sanskrit, the "training in wisdom," one of the three trainings (TRIŚIKṢĀ), together with the training in ethics (ŚĪLAŚIKṢĀ) and the training in meditation (SAMĀDHIŚIKṢĀ). See ADHIPRAJÑĀŚIKṢĀ and TRIŚIKṢĀ.

**prajñāvimukta**. (P. paññāvimutta; T. shes rab kyis rnam par grol ba; C. hui jietuo; J. egedatsu; K. hyehaet'al 慧解脫). In Sanskrit, "one who is liberated through wisdom." The term refers specifically to a person who has attained liberation through insight (VIPAŚYANĀ) into the three marks of existence: impermanence (ANITYA), suffering (DUḤKHA), and nonself (ANĀTMAN). Anyone who has attained any of the four stages of sanctity (ĀRYA)—stream-entry, once-returning, nonreturning, or arhatship—is said to have attained liberation through wisdom. Such liberation is equivalent to enlightenment (BODHI), results in the permanent eradication of the contaminants (ĀSRAVAKṢAYA), and leads to the cessation of REBIRTH. In the Pāli abhidhamma and Sarvāstivāda ABHIDHARMA, the person "liberated through wisdom" is the sixth of seven types of enlightened disciples (ārya); the other six are: (1) the saddhānusāri (S. ŚRADDHĀNUSĀRIN), or faith-follower; (2) dhammānusāri (S. DHARMĀNUSĀRIN); (3) saddhāvimutta (S. ŚRADDHĀVIMUKTA), or one liberated through faith; (4) diṭṭhippatta (S. DṚṢṬIPRĀPTA), or vision-attainer; (5) kāyasakkhī (S. KĀYASĀKṢIN), or witnessing with this very body; (6) ubhatobhāgavimutta (S. UBHAYATOBHĀGAVIMUKTA), or liberated in both ways. The prajñāvimukta who has attained liberation through the contemplation of no-self is contrasted with cetovimukta (P. cetovimutta; cf. CETOVIMUKTI), or "one liberated through mind," who has mastery of meditative absorptions (P. JHĀNA; S. DHYĀNA). The prajñāvimukta is also one of the VIṂŚATIPRABHEDASAṂGHA ("twenty varieties of the āryasaṃgha") based on the list given in the MAHĀVYUTPATTI.

**Prakaraṇapāda[śāstra]**. (T. Rab tu byed pa'i rkang pa; C. Pinlei zu lun; J. Honruisokuron; K. P'umnyu chok non 品類足論). In Sanskrit, "Exposition"; a book from the later stratum of the SARVĀSTIVĀDA ABHIDHARMA, which is traditionally listed as the first of the six ancillary texts, or "feet" (pāda), of the JÑĀNAPRASTHĀNA, the central treatise, or body (śarīra), of the Sarvāstivāda ABHIDHARMAPIṬAKA. The *Prakaraṇapāda* is attributed by tradition to Vasumitra and dates from c. 160 to 320 CE, probably following the compilation of the ABHIDHARMAMAHĀVIBHĀṢĀ. The treatise is extant only in a complete Chinese translation made by GUṆABHADRA and Bodhiyaśas between 435 and 443. The *Prakaraṇapāda* establishes the definitive Sarvāstivāda categorization of dharmas into a fivefold grouping: materiality (RŪPA), mentality (CITTA), mental concomitants (CAITTA or CAITASIKA), conditioned factors dissociated from thought (CITTAVIPRAYUKTASAṂSKĀRA), and uncompounded elements (ASAṂSKṚTADHARMA). This fivefold grouping is first employed in the ABHIDHARMAMAHĀVIBHĀṢĀ, whence it enters the mainstream of the Sarvāstivāda-VAIBHĀṢIKA analysis of dharmas and is subsequently adopted by several other Buddhist schools, including the SAUTRĀNTIKA, MADHYAMAKA, and YOGĀCĀRA (see BAIFA). The *Prakaraṇapāda* also adds a new listing of KUŚALAMAHĀBHŪMIKA, or factors always associated with wholesome states of mind. The *Prakaraṇapāda* was the first of the pādaśāstras to represent the mature synthesis of Sarvāstivāda doctrine, which was followed in later abhidharma manuals and primers. The text therefore represents a transitional point in Sarvāstivāda abhidharma writing between the pādaśāstras of the middle period and the commentarial writings of the later tradition.

**Prakrit**. (S. Prākṛta). A term that literally means "natural" in Sanskrit, used to designate a group of Indo-Āryan vernacular languages in ancient India. The term "Sanskrit" (saṃskṛta) has the sense both of "constructed," "perfected," or "refined," and thus describes a classical language that may not ever have been used for everyday verbal communication. The earliest extant written forms of Prakrit are found in the inscriptions of AŚOKA. The Buddha is said to have spoken the Prakritic dialect of Māgadhī, the vernacular language of the Indian state of MAGADHA. Also important for Buddhism is the GĀNDHĀRĪ form of Prakrit, from the GANDHĀRA region of northwest India. These Prakrit dialects eventually evolved into many of the modern Indian vernacular languages, such as Bengali, Gujarati, Oriya, and Hindi. Although some scholars do not consider PĀLI and BUDDHIST HYBRID SANSKRIT to be Prakrits in the technical sense, they are clearly influenced by various Prakrits current at the time of their formation.

**prakṛtiparinirvṛta**. (T. rang bzhin gyis yongs su mya ngan las 'das pa; C. zixing niepan; J. jishō nehan; K. chasŏng yŏlban 自性涅槃). In Sanskrit, "intrinsically extinguished"; a term used in a phrase common to the PRAJÑĀPĀRAMITĀ literature, in which all phenomena in the universe are described as being "unproduced (anutpanna, see ANUTPĀDA), unceasing (aniruddha), primordially at peace (ādiśānta), and intrinsically fully extinguished (prakṛtiparinirvṛta)." It refers to the state of quiescence in which all phenomena in the universe naturally abide. In the MADHYAMAKA school, the term is sometimes used as a synonym for emptiness (ŚŪNYATĀ). See also NIRVĀṆA.

**prakṛtisthagotra**. (T. rang bzhin gnas rigs; C. benxing zhu zhongxing; J. honshōjūshushō; K. ponsŏng chu chongsŏng 本性住種性). In Sanskrit, "naturally endowed lineage" or "intrinsic lineage." In certain strands of YOGĀCĀRA thought, it is believed that there are two kinds of "seeds" (BĪJA) that lead to future KARMAN. The first is newly acquired karmic seeds (xinxun zhongzi), which are activated as suitable conditions arise and will expire once their karmic efficacy is spent. Second, there are also certain primordial seeds (benyou zhongzi), which remain indestructible and, in a sense, forever determine one's spiritual tendency and potential. One such example is the "naturally endowed lineage" (prakṛtisthagotra) that determines if a person will ultimately become an ARHAT (via either the ŚRĀVAKA or PRATYEKABUDDHA paths), a buddha, or forever remain as an unenlightened "incorrigible" (ICCHANTIKA). That is, whether one will attain enlightenment or not, and what spiritual status one will ultimately reach, is "predetermined" by such a predisposition. In this controversial tenet, a person lacking the "primordial seed" necessary to qualify one as belonging to a MAHĀYĀNA "lineage" (GOTRA), for example, is forever deprived of the potential to cultivate the path to buddhahood. Together, and in contrast to, the "lineage that is conditioned by habits" (see SAMUDĀNĪTAGOTRA), they are known as "the two lineages: intrinsic and acquired" (xingxi er[zhong]xing). For the two kinds of karmic seeds, see ERZHONG ZHONGZI.

**prakṛtiviśuddhi**. (T. rang bzhin gyis rnam par dag pa; C. benxing jing; J. honshōjō; K. ponsŏng chŏng 本性淨). In Sanskrit, "intrinsic purity," a term used to describe the inherent purity and luminosity of the mind, with the implication that all afflictions (KLEŚA) are therefore adventitious and extrinsic to the mind's true nature.

**pralambapādāsana**. (T. rkang pa brkyangs pa'i 'dug stangs; C. chuizuzuo; J. suisokuza; K. sujokchwa 垂足坐). In Sanskrit, lit. "pendant leg posture"; a posture (ĀSANA) sometimes called the "seated" or "European" pose, where both legs of a figure hang pendant, feet on the ground, usually from a throne or seat. Tibetan images of MAITREYA are commonly found in this posture (and thus it is also known as the MAITREYĀSANA); he is said to sit in this pose so that he can easily stand in preparation for his descent to the world as the next buddha. This position is sometimes known as the BHADRĀSANA.

**pramāda**. (P. pamāda; T. bag med pa; C. fangyi; J. hōitsu; K. pangil 放逸). In Sanskrit, "heedlessness"; one of the forty-six mental concomitants (CAITTA) according to the SARVĀSTIVĀDA-VAIBHĀṢIKA school of ABHIDHARMA and one of the fifty-one according to the YOGĀCĀRA school, where it is listed among the twenty secondary afflictions (UPAKLEŚA). Heedlessness refers to a lack of vigilance in one's interaction with the external world so that one neglects salutary (KUŚALA) actions that will be conducive to the benefit of both oneself and others (see SVĀRTHA; PARĀRTHA) and instead engages in morally questionable behavior. Heedlessness is the opposite of "heedfulness" (APRAMĀDA), which is considered foundational to any kind of ethical or virtuous behavior—so much so, in fact, that the Buddha is said to have recommended it in his last words delivered on his deathbed: "Indeed, monks, I declare to you: decay is inherent in all compounded things; strive on with heedfulness." (P. handadāni bhikkhave amantayāmi vo: vayadhammā saṅkhārā; appamādena sampādetha.)

**pramāṇa**. (T. tshad ma; C. liang; J. ryō; K. yang 量). In Sanskrit, "means of knowledge," or "valid knowledge," defined technically as a consciousness that is not deceived with regard to its object. Many schools of Buddhism posit two forms of valid knowledge: direct perception (PRATYAKṢA) and inference (ANUMĀNA), with the former deriving from correct sense perception and the latter deriving from correct reasoning. Dharmakīrti states in his PRAMĀṆAVĀRTTIKA that there are two forms of valid knowledge (pramāṇa) because there are two objects of comprehension (prameya). The two types of objects are the manifest (ABHIMUKHĪ) and the hidden (PAROKṢA), with the former referring to objects that can be known through direct sense perception, the latter referring to those things that can be known only through inference. His limitation of forms of valid knowledge to only two is meant to distinguish Buddhist epistemology from that of the Hindu schools, where sound (śabda), especially in the sense of the sound of the Vedas, is counted as a valid form of knowledge. Discussions of these two forms of valid knowledge, especially as set forth in the works of DIGNĀGA and DHARMAKĪRTI, encompassed a range of topics in epistemology and logic that became very influential in medieval India (among both Buddhists and non-Buddhists), and then in Tibet; its influence was less strong in East Asia. Thus, although the term pramāṇa technically refers to one of these two valid forms of knowledge, it comes by extension to refer to medieval and late Indian Buddhist epistemology and logic, in the latter case, especially as it pertains to the formal statement of syllogisms (PRAYOGA) to an opponent.

**pramāṇabhūta**. (T. tshad ma'i skyes bu). In Sanskrit, "authoritative one"; an epithet of the Buddha, which has also been variously translated as "he who is [like] valid knowledge," and "he who has come into existence as [a form of] valid knowledge." The epithet is most famously ascribed to the Buddha by DIGNĀGA in his PRAMĀṆASAMUCCAYA, and is variously commented upon by later Buddhist logicians. According to some commentators, the Buddha, unlike various Hindu deities, is like a form of valid knowledge (PRAMĀṆA) because he is reliable, in the sense that he is not deceptive and because he makes known things that were not known before, such as the FOUR NOBLE TRUTHS.

**Pramāṇasamuccaya**. (T. Tshad ma kun btus; C. Jiliang lun; J. Jūryōron; K. Chimnyang non 集量論). In Sanskrit, "Compendium on Valid Knowledge"; the most famous work of DIGNĀGA, the great Buddhist logician of the late fifth and early sixth centuries, and considered the foundational text of Buddhist logic and epistemology. In it, Dignāga describes direct perception (PRATYAKṢA) as being free from thought (KALPANĀ), and distinguishes between the objects of direct perception and thought, with direct perception able to discern specific characteristics (SVALAKṢAṆA), while thought deals only with general characteristics (SĀMĀNYALAKṢAṆA). In discussing the five sense consciousnesses and the mental consciousness (MANOVIJÑĀNA), he asserted that the sense consciousnesses operate exclusively through direct perception, whereas the mental consciousness knows objects through both direct perception and inference (ANUMĀNA). In explaining the function of thought, Dignāga described thought as operating through the negative route of APOHA, whereby thought does not perceive its object directly, but instead through the conceptual elimination of everything that is not the object. In this work, Dignāga also examines the elements of a logical syllogism (PRAYOGA) and the relations that must pertain among its various constituents in order for that statement to result in a correct inference.

**pramāṇavāda**. (T. tshad ma smra ba). In Sanskrit, "proponent of valid knowledge," a term used to describe the tradition of Buddhist logic deriving especially from the work of DIGNĀGA and DHARMAKĪRTI. This tradition did not represent a self-conscious school of Buddhist philosophy, but rather an approach to issues in logic and epistemology that were central to SAUTRĀNTIKA, YOGĀCĀRA, and MADHYAMAKA. See PRAMĀṆA.

**Pramāṇavārttika**. (T. Tshad ma rnam 'grel). In Sanskrit, "Commentary on Valid Knowledge," the most famous work of the great Buddhist logician DHARMAKĪRTI. The "Pramāṇa" in the title of text is a reference to DIGNĀGA's PRAMĀṆASAMUCCAYA; Dharmakīrti's work is ostensibly a commentary on Dignāga's text, although in fact Dharmakīrti's work makes significant refinements in, and occasional departures from, Dignāga's views. The *Pramāṇavārttika* is written in verse, with a prose commentary by the author, in four chapters, dealing with inference for oneself (SVĀRTHĀNUMĀNA), the proof of valid knowledge (pramāṇasiddhi), direct perception (PRATYAKṢA), and inference for others (PARĀRTHĀNUMĀNA). The work was the subject of numerous commentaries in India, and later in Tibet, where it was studied by all sects and became one of the "five books" (zhung lnga) that provided the foundation for the DGE LUGS monastic curriculum.

**Pramāṇaviniścaya**. (T. Tshad ma rnam par nges pa). In Sanskrit, "Determination of Valid Knowledge," one of the seven treatises of the Indian master DHARMAKĪRTI, perhaps second in fame to his PRAMĀṆAVĀRTTIKA, for which it serves as something of a summary. Following its translation into Tibetan by RNGOG BLO LDAN SHES RAB, it was the main text for the study of PRAMĀṆA (T. tshad ma) in Tibet, until Sa skya Paṇḍita's TSHAD MA RIGS GTER that explained the *Pramāṇavārttika* in detail.

**pramuditā**. (T. rab tu dga' ba; C. huanxi di; J. kangiji; K. hwanhŭi chi 歡喜地). In Sanskrit, "joyous," the first of the ten bodhisattva BHŪMI, a list of ten stages (DAŚABHŪMI) deriving from the DAŚABHŪMIKASŪTRA ("Sūtra on the Ten Bhūmis"), a sūtra that is later subsumed into the massive scriptural compilation, the AVATAṂSAKASŪTRA. This first bhūmi coincides with the attainment of the path of vision (DARŚANAMĀRGA) and the remaining nine to the path of cultivation (BHĀVANĀMĀRGA). The first stage is called "joyous" because the bodhisattva rejoices at having seen reality for the first time, or because he feels joy at seeing that he is close to buddhahood, at which point he can achieve the aims of sentient beings. When the six perfections are aligned with the ten bhūmis, the pramuditā stage is an occasion for the bodhisattva to practice the perfection of giving (DĀNAPĀRAMITĀ) in particular and attracts disciples through the four means of gathering (SAṂGRAHAVASTU). The bodhisattva remains at this stage as long as he remains unaware of subtle ethical transgressions; morality (ŚĪLA) is fully perfected on the second stage. On the first bhūmi, it is said that a bodhisattva can (1) see one hundred buddhas, (2) be blessed by one hundred buddhas, (3) live for one hundred eons, (4) see the past and future in those one hundred eons with wisdom, (5) enter into and withdraw from one hundred SAMĀDHIS, (6) vibrate one hundred worlds, (7) illuminate one hundred worlds, (8) bring one hundred sentient beings to spiritual maturity using emanations, (9) go to one hundred pure buddha-fields (PARIŚUDDHABUDDHAKṢETRA), (10) open one hundred doors of doctrine,

(11) display one hundred versions of his own body, and (12) surround each of those bodies with one hundred bodhisattvas. These numbers multiply as the bodhisattva proceeds to subsequent stages.

**prāṇa**. (T. srog; C. bona; J. hana; K. pana 波那). In Sanskrit, "wind," "breath," or "vital force"; the winds that course through the network of channels (NĀḌĪ) in the body, according to tantric physiognomy. There are various types of winds that perform functions such as movement, digestion, respiration, sexual activity, and sustenance of the life force. Much tantric practice is devoted, first, to causing these winds to flow freely through the system of channels and, subsequently, to gathering the various winds into the central channel in order to induce deep states of bliss.

**prāṇāyāma**. (T. srog rtsol; C. tiaoxi; J. chōsoku; K. chosik 調息). In Sanskrit, lit., "restraint of breath," "restraint of wind"; a term used to encompass various practices of breath control. During his six years of practice of asceticism prior to his achievement of enlightenment, some traditions say that the Buddha became adept at the practice of holding his breath for extended periods of time but eventually abandoned it as a form of self-mortification. Nonetheless, elaborate practices of breath control are found throughout Buddhism, especially in Buddhist TANTRA. For example, at the beginning of a tantric meditative session, one is instructed to purify the breath by inhaling through one nostril and exhaling through the other by closing each nostril successively with the index finger. In the practice of ANUTTARAYOGATANTRA, the term is used broadly to refer to all forms of meditation, including the visualization of seed syllables (BĪJA) that are intended to cause the various winds to enter into the central channel (AVADHŪTĪ). Such practices are to be distinguished from "mindfulness of breathing" (ĀNĀPĀNASMṚTI), which involves mindful awareness of the natural process of inhalations and exhalations, rather than any attempt to control or restrain the breath.

**praṇidhāna**. (P. panidhāna; T. smon lam; C. yuan; J. gan; K. wŏn 願). In Sanskrit, "vow" or "aspiration"; a statement expressing the solemn wish that a specific aim be achieved. The most famous type of praṇidhāna is the vow the BODHISATTVA takes to become a buddha in order to liberate all sentient beings from suffering (see PŪRVAPRAṆIDHĀNA). Praṇidhāna is also listed as one of the ten perfections (PĀRAMITĀ) and as one of the ten powers (BALA) of a bodhisattva. A vow may take the form of an oath, in which one promises to achieve an aim, or the form of a prayer, in which one asks that an aim be fulfilled, often through dedicating merit toward that aim. The term occurs also in pūrvapraṇidhāna, or "prior vow," a vow made in the past that has either been fulfilled in the present or will be fulfilled in the future, typically in conjunction with the aspiration to attain buddhahood. The term pūrvapraṇidhāna is used specifically in the MAHĀYĀNA to denote the vow made in the past by a bodhisattva to become a buddha himself, often specifying the place, the time, and the retinue that will be associated with that event. Since the buddhas succeeded in achieving their goal of buddhahood, their prior vows are therefore all considered to have been fulfilled. The most famous of all pūrvapraṇidhāna are the forty-eight vows that the monk DHARMĀKARA made before the buddha LOKEŚVARARĀJA, which ultimately led to his becoming the buddha AMITĀBHA and creating the pure land of SUKHĀVATĪ; these vows are described in the SUKHĀVATĪVYŪHASŪTRA and are foundational to the PURE LAND traditions of East Asia.

**praṇidhānapāramitā**. (T. smon lam gyi pha rol tu phyin pa; C. yuan boluomi; J. ganharamitsu; K. wŏn paramil 願波羅蜜). In Sanskrit, "perfection of aspiration," "prayer," or "resolve"; the eighth of the traditional list of ten perfections (PĀRAMITĀ). According to the system of the ten bodhisattva BHŪMI, this perfection, which is a subset of the "perfection of wisdom" (PRAJÑĀPĀRAMITĀ), is practiced on the eighth bhūmi, called the ACALĀ (immovable). Here, all of the aspirations (PRAṆIDHĀNA; PŪRVAPRAṆIDHĀNA) made by the bodhisattva over the long path he has traversed leading up to buddhahood are considered to have been achieved.

**praṇidhicittotpāda**. (T. smon pa'i sems bskyed; C. yuan puti xin; J. ganbodaishin; K. wŏn pori sim 願菩提心). In Sanskrit, lit., "aspirational creation of the intention," where "intention" or "thought" (CITTA) refers to BODHICITTA, the intention to achieve buddhahood in order to liberate all sentient beings from suffering. This is the first of two types of bodhicitta, the second being the PRASTHĀNACITTOTPĀDA, lit., the "creation of the intention to set out." In his BODHICARYĀVATĀRA, ŚĀNTIDEVA compares the first type of bodhicitta to the decision to undertake a journey and the second type to actually setting out on the journey. In the case of the BODHISATTVA path, the first refers to the process of developing the aspiration to buddhahood for the sake of others, while the second refers to undertaking the various practices of the bodhisattva path, such as the six perfections (PĀRAMITĀ). These two forms of bodhicitta are meant to be developed in sequence.

**prapañca**. (P. papañca; T. spros pa; C. xilun; J. keron; K. hŭiron 戲論). In Sanskrit, lit. "diffusion," "expansion"; viz. "conceptualization" or "conceptual proliferation"; the tendency of the process of cognition to proliferate the perspective of the self (ĀTMAN) throughout all of one's sensory experience via the medium of concepts. The locus classicus for describing how sensory perception culminates in conceptual proliferation appears in the Pāli MADHUPIṆḌIKASUTTA. As that scripture explains, any living being will be subject to an impersonal causal process of perception in which consciousness (P. viññāṇa; S. VIJÑĀNA) occurs conditioned by an internal sense base (INDRIYA) and an external sense object (ĀYATANA); the contact among these three brings about sensory impingement or contact (P. phassa; S. SPARŚA), which in turn leads to the sensation (VEDANĀ) of that contact as pleasant, unpleasant, or neutral. At that point, however, the sense of ego intrudes and this process then becomes an intentional one, whereby what one feels, one perceives (P. saññā; S. SAṂJÑĀ); what one perceives, one thinks about (P. vitakka; S. VITARKA); and what one thinks about, one conceptualizes (P. papañca; S. prapañca). By allowing oneself to experience sensory objects not as things-in-themselves but as concepts invariably tied to one's own perspective, the perceiving subject then becomes the hapless object of an inexorable process of conceptual subjugation: viz., what one conceptualizes becomes proliferated conceptually (P. papañcasaññāsaṅkhā; a term apparently unattested in Sanskrit) throughout all of one's sensory experience. Everything that can be experienced in this world in the past, present, and future is now bound together into a labyrinthine network of concepts, all tied to oneself and projected into the external world as craving (TṚṢṆĀ), conceit (MĀNA), and wrong views (DṚṢṬI), thus creating bondage to SAṂSĀRA. By systematic attention (YONIŚOMANASKĀRA) to the impersonal character of sensory experience and through sensory restraint (INDRIYASAṂVARA), this tendency to project ego throughout the entirety of the perceptual process is brought to an end. In this state of "conceptual nonproliferation" (P. nippapañca; S. NIḤPRAPAÑCA), perception is freed from concepts tinged by this proliferating tendency, allowing one to see the things of this world as impersonal causal products that are inevitably impermanent (ANITYA), suffering (DUḤKHA), and nonself (ANĀTMAN). ¶ The preceding interpretation reflects the specific denotation of the term as explicated in Pāli scriptural materials. In a Mahāyāna context, prapañca may also connote "elaboration" or "superimposition," especially in the sense of a fanciful, imagined, or superfluous quality that is mistakenly projected on to an object, resulting in its being misperceived. Such projections are described as manifestations of ignorance (AVIDYĀ); reality and the mind that perceives reality are described as being free from prapañca (NIṢPRAPAÑCA), and the purpose of Buddhist practice in one sense can be described as the recognition and elimination of prapañca in order to see reality clearly and directly. In the MADHYAMAKA school, the most dangerous type of prapañca is the presumption of intrinsic existence (SVABHĀVA). In YOGĀCĀRA, prapañca is synonymous with the "seeds" (BĪJA) that provide the basis for perception and the potentiality for future action. In this school, prapañca is closely associated with false discrimination (VIKALPA), specifically the bifurcation of perceiving subject and perceived object (GRĀHYAGRĀHAKAVIKALPA). The goal of practice is said to be a state of mind that is beyond all thought constructions and verbal elaboration. ¶ The precise denotation of prapañca has been the subject of much perplexity and debate within the Buddhist tradition, which is reflected in the varying translations for the term in Buddhist canonical languages. The standard Chinese rendering xilun means "frivolous debate," which reflects the tendency of prapañca to complicate meaningful discussion about the true character of sensory cognition. The Tibetan spros ba means something like "extension, elaboration" and reflects the tendency of prapañca to proliferate a fanciful conception of reality onto the objects of perception.

**prāpti**. (T. 'thob pa; C. de; J. toku; K. tŭk 得). In Sanskrit, "possession," "acquisition"; the first of the fourteen "conditioned forces dissociated from thought" (CITTAVIPRAYUKTASAṂSKĀRA) listed in the SARVĀSTIVĀDA-VAIBHĀṢIKA ABHIDHARMA and in the YOGĀCĀRA system. The function of prāpti is to serve as a kind of glue that causes the various independent constituents of existence (DHARMA) to adhere in seemingly permanent constructs. The leap the Sarvāstivāda school made was to assert that this factor of "possession" was a real dharma (DRAVYADHARMA), in distinction to other schools, which asserted that the notion of possession was simply an imputed designation (PRAJÑAPTI). Prāpti is the conditioned force that attaches a specific affliction, action, or dharma to the mental continuum (SAṂTĀNA) of the individual, thus helping to maintain the semblance of the continuity of the person. Prāpti also receives and retains the effects of positive and negative volitional actions (KARMAN) and thus ensures karmic continuity. This same notion of prāpti is also deployed to clarify how the afflictions (KLEŚA) can be eradicated in a cognition of the FOUR NOBLE TRUTHS (catvāry āryasatyāni): viz., that cognition brings to an end the "possession" of the afflictions, thus ensuring that they may never arise again. This factor is the opposite of the related dissociated force of "dispossession" (APRĀPTI). The PRAJÑĀPĀRAMITĀ sūtras vehemently rejected any such notion of "possession," even of NIRVĀṆA itself, which they claimed could neither be attained nor possessed.

**prasāda**. (P. pasāda; T. dad pa/dang ba; C. chengjing; J. chōjō; K. chingjŏng 澄淨). In Sanskrit, "clarity," or "trust." As "clarity," the term is used to describe both the serene sense consciousnesses of someone whose mind is at peace as well as such a state of mind itself. As "trust," the term is central to Buddhism, where it is employed in explanations of the psychology of faith or belief (see ŚRADDHĀ); it leads to zest or "desire-to-act" (CHANDA) that in turn leads to the cultivation of ŚAMATHA (serenity or calmness). These meanings of prasāda overlap when the term denotes the serenity or joy that results from trust. In the theology of the JŌDO SHINSHŪ school of Japanese PURE LAND Buddhism, it refers to a serene acceptance of the grace of AMITĀBHA.

**prasajyapratiṣedha**. (T. med dgag). In Sanskrit, "nonaffirming negative," or "nonimplied negation," a negative declaration (PRATIṢEDHA) that is expressed in such a way that nothing positive is implied. The most famous such nonimplied negation is emptiness (ŚŪNYATĀ), which is the mere absence of intrinsic existence (SVABHĀVA). See also PARYUDĀSAPRATIṢEDHA.

**prasaṅga**. (T. thal 'gyur). In Sanskrit, "consequence"; in Buddhist logic, a statement made to an opponent that uses the opponent's assertions to demonstrate contradictions in the opponent's position. It is not necessary that the person who states the consequence accept the subject, predicate, and reason of the consequence. There is a difference of opinion as to whether the statement of the consequence is sufficient to bring about correct understanding in the opponent or whether an autonomous syllogism (SVATANTRAPRAYOGA) stating the correct position (that is, the position of the person who states the consequence) is also required. This was one of the points of disagreement that led to the designation of the *PRĀSAṄGIKA and *SVĀTANTRIKA branches of the MADHYAMAKA school.

***Prāsaṅgika**. (T. Thal 'gyur ba). In Sanskrit, "Consequentialist," one of the two main branches of the MADHYAMAKA school, so called because of its use of consequences (PRASAṄGA) rather than autonomous syllogisms (SVATANTRAPRAYOGA) in debates about the nature of reality. Its leading proponents include BUDDHAPĀLITA and CANDRAKĪRTI. The other branch of Madhyamaka is *SVĀTANTRIKA, represented by such figures as BHĀVAVIVEKA, JÑĀNAGARBHA, ŚĀNTARAKṢITA, and KAMALAŚĪLA. The designation "Prāsaṅgika" as a subschool of Madhyamaka does not occur in Indian literature; it was coined retrospectively in Tibet to describe the later developments of the Indian Madhyamaka school. In the doxographical literature of the DGE LUGS sect in Tibet, where *Prāsaṅgika is ranked as the preeminent school of Indian Buddhist philosophy, Prāsaṅgika differs from Svātantrika primarily on questions of the nature of emptiness (ŚŪNYATĀ) and the correct role of reasoning in understanding it, although other points of difference are also enumerated, including the question of whether the arhat must understand the selflessness of phenomena (DHARMANAIRĀTMYA) in order to achieve liberation.

**Prasannapadā**. (T. Tshig gsal). In Sanskrit, "Clear Words," the commentary on NĀGĀRJUNA's MŪLAMADHYAMAKAKĀRIKĀ by the seventh-century Indian master CANDRAKĪRTI; its full title is *Mūlamadhyamakavṛtti-Prasannapadā*. Among Candrakīrti's major works, it is regarded as second in importance only to his independent treatise, the MADHYAMAKĀVATĀRA, which was composed earlier. Apart from its importance as a commentary on Nāgārjuna's text, Candrakīrti's work is also important as the locus classicus for the division of Madhyamaka into the *SVĀTANTRIKA and *PRĀSAṄGIKA. Candrakīrti's was the third in an influential series of commentaries. The first was that of BUDDHAPĀLITA. The second was the PRAJÑĀPRADĪPA of BHĀVAVIVEKA, who criticized Buddhapālita's commentary on the first chapter of Nāgārjuna's text, specifically the section in which Buddhapālita refutes the Sāṃkhya position that an effect is produced from a cause that is the same nature as itself. In the *Prasannapadā*, Candrakīrti defended Buddhapālita and attacked Bhāvaviveka. It is based largely on these exchanges that later Tibetan scholars came to designate Buddhapālita and Candrakīrti as *Prāsaṅgikas and Bhāvaviveka as a *Svātantrika. Candrakīrti's commentary is also valued by scholars for its many citations from Mahāyāna sūtras. The *Prasannapadā* has attracted the attention of modern scholars, in part because, unlike the commentaries of Buddhapālita and Bhāvaviveka, for example, it has been preserved in Sanskrit.

**Prasenajit**. (P. Pasenadi; T. Gsal rgyal; C. Bosini wang; J. Hashinoku ō; K. Pasanik wang 波斯匿王). In Sanskrit, the proper name of the king of the region of KOŚALA during the time of GAUTAMA or ŚĀKYAMUNI Buddha. Prasenajit's capital was the city of ŚRĀVASTĪ, where the Buddha delivered many of his sermons. During his reign, Kośala was one of the two most powerful kingdoms in the Indian subcontinent, along with MAGADHA, and seems to have exerted political control over the neighboring ŚĀKYA kingdom, where the Buddha was born. According to the tradition, Prasenajit was born in the same year as the Buddha. Because of his dedication to the propagation, protection, and preservation of the Buddhist order (SAṂGHA), Prasenajit is often used as an example of Buddhist notions of proper kingship. In fact, several of the Buddha's sermons are given in response to a question asked by Prasenajit. Such devotion can also be seen in one particular distinction held by Prasenajit: legend has it that he was first person to have an image made of the Buddha. (Elsewhere, this distinction is given to King Udāyana or Rudrāyana; see UDĀYANA BUDDHA.) According to the thirteenth-century Sinhalese source, the *Kosalabimbavaṇṇanā* ("Laudatory Account of the Kosala Image"), Prasenajit was disappointed when he went to visit the Buddha but found that the Buddha was away from his residence. He therefore requested that an image of the Buddha be made that would function as his double; the Buddha answered that whoever might create such an image would accumulate immeasurable merit. This first image was said to have been made of sandalwood and to have displayed the thirty-two marks of a great man (MAHĀPURUṢALAKṢAṆA); when the Buddha first came to see the image that Prasenajit had commissioned, it rose to greet him. Many members of Prasenajit's family also played important roles in Buddhist literature. His wife, MALLIKĀ, was the person who initially encouraged him to become a follower of the Buddha. One of Prasenajit's sons was prince JETA, from whom the banker ANĀTHAPIṆḌADA (P. ANĀTHAPIṆḌIKA) purchased the JETAVANA (Jeta's grove) to donate to the Buddha; this was one of the Buddha's favorite residences and the place where many of his sermons were delivered. Prasenajit was the father of the princess Śrīmālādevī, the protagonist of the ŚRĪMĀLĀDEVĪSIṂHANĀDASŪTRA. He was also the father of VIRŪḌHAKA, who, when he learned that his mother was not of noble birth, made war on the ŚĀKYA clan. Prasenajit's sister was VAIDEHĪ, the wife of king BIMBISĀRA.

**Prasphuṭapadā**. (T. Tshig rab tu gsal ba). In Sanskrit, "The Clearly Worded," a work by the Indian scholiast Dharmamitra (c. ninth century); the full title of this text is *Abhisamayālaṃkārakārikāprajñāpāramitopadeśaśāstraṭīkā-prasphuṭapadā* or "The

Clearly Worded, Commentary on Treatise Setting Forth the Perfection of Wisdom, the Verses of the Ornament of Realization." The *Prasphuṭapadā* is a subcommentary on HARIBHADRA's ABHISAMAYĀLAṂKĀRAVIVṚTI, which is intended to clarify points on the ABHISAMAYĀLAṂKĀRA, one of five texts that were purportedly revealed to ASAṄGA by the BODHISATTVA MAITREYA in the fourth or fifth centuries CE. The *Prasphuṭapadā* was written shortly after the composition of the *Abhisamayālaṃkāravivṛti* in the early ninth century. In the *Prasphuṭapadā*, Dharmamitra seeks to clarify Haribhadra's views as they appear in the *Vivṛti*, rather than put forth his own ideas regarding the *Abhisamayālaṃkāra*. In his work, Dharmamitra explains a number of doctrinal elements that would have a great impact on later forms of Tibetan Buddhism, including the TATHĀGATAGARBHA doctrine and the theory of multiple buddha bodies (BUDDHAKĀYA). For instance, in the *Prasphuṭapadā*, Dharmamitra asserts that the enjoyment body (SAṂBHOGAKĀYA) is accessible only to a bodhisattva who has reached the tenth stage (BHŪMI) of the bodhisattva path (see BODHISATTVABHŪMI). Dharmamitra's text, together with the *Durbodhāloka*, the subcommentary on the *Abhisamayālaṃkāravivṛti* by DHARMAKĪRTIŚRĪ (the teacher of ATIŚA DĪPAṂKARAŚRĪJÑĀNA), is often cited in Tibetan PRAJÑĀPĀRAMITĀ commentaries.

**praśrabdhi**. (P. passaddhi; T. shin tu sbyang ba; C. qing'an; J. kyōan; K. kyŏngan 輕安). In Sanskrit, "serenity," "calm"; one of the forty-six mental concomitants (CAITTA) according to the SARVĀSTIVĀDA-VAIBHĀṢIKA school of ABHIDHARMA, one of the fifty-one according to the YOGĀCĀRA school, where it is listed among the salutary (KUŚALA) mental states and one of the fifty-two in the Pāli ABHIDHAMMA. Praśrabdhi refers to the state of mind associated with concentration (SAMĀDHI), referring especially to the serenity that brings pliancy to the mind and body that enables the adept to direct the mind and body toward wholesome actions.

**prasthānacittotpāda**. (T. 'jug pa'i sems bskyed; C. xing putixin; J. gyōbodaishin; K. haeng porisim 行菩提心). In Sanskrit, lit., "creation of the intention to set out," where "intention" or "thought" (CITTA) refers to BODHICITTA, the wish to achieve buddhahood in order to save all sentient beings from suffering. This is the second of two types of bodhicitta, the other being PRAṆIDHICITTOTPĀDA, lit., "the aspirational creation of the intention." In his BODHICARYĀVATĀRA, ŚĀNTIDEVA compares the first type to the decision to undertake a journey and the second type to actually setting out on the journey. In the case of the BODHISATTVA path, the first refers to the process of developing the aspiration to buddhahood for the sake of others, while the second refers to the undertaking the various practices of the bodhisattva path, such as the six perfections (PĀRAMITĀ). These two forms of bodhicitta are meant to be developed in sequence.

**pratāpana**. (P. mahātapa; T. rab tu tsha ba; C. dajiaore; J. daishōnetsu; K. taech'oyŏl 大焦熱). In Sanskrit, "very hot," one of the hot hells in Buddhist cosmology; its prefix distinguishes it from another hell, which is merely "hot" (TĀPANA). Pratāpana is the seventh of the eight hot hells in increasing order of horror, and is thus exceeded in this regard only by the worst hell of all, the "interminable" (AVĪCI). The sufferings of the pratāpana hell include being cast into a vast cauldron of molten metal and having one's body wrapped with rods of burning iron.

**pratibhāna**. (P. paṭibhāna; T. spobs pa; C. biancai; J. benzai; K. pyŏnjae 辯才). In Sanskrit, "eloquence," or "ready speech," referring typically to the ability to inspire others through one's words. Pratibhāna is included among the four types of analytical knowledge (PRATISAṂVID) that are mastered by BODHISATTVAs at the ninth BHŪMI. In the East Asian tradition, a bodhisattva is said to have, or is exhorted to attain, eight qualities of true eloquence when delivering Buddhist teachings. He should display eloquence that is (1) free of hectoring and bellowing (since an accomplished bodhisattva inherently possesses such majestic charisma that he does not need to inveigle his audience to pay attention); (2) unconfused and organized in his delivery; (3) confident and unfazed; (4) unconceited; (5) meaningful, wholesome, and conducive to skillfulness; (6) profound, interesting, and informed; (7) free from harshness; (8) seasonable, adaptive, and responsive to the conditions at hand.

**pratibhāsa**. (T. snang ba; C. xianxian; J. kengen; K. hyŏnhyŏn 顯現). A polysemous term in Sanskrit, whose denotations include "appearance" and "perception." The term is often used to describe what is perceived by consciousness (VIJÑĀNA), as opposed to the true nature of the object perceived. The term therefore often carries a negative connotation of something ephemeral and deceptive. Tantric literature describes a practice of "pure appearance" in which the ordinary world is visualized as a MAṆḌALA and one's own body is visualized as the body of a buddha.

**pratideśanā**. (P. paṭidesanā; T. so sor bshags pa; C. huiguo; J. keka; K. hoegwa 悔過). Often translated from Sanskrit as "confession," but meaning something closer to "disclosure" or "acknowledgment"; the practice of acknowledging one's misdeeds. It is the central practice of the fortnightly UPOṢADHA rites, where monks and nuns "disclose" or "confess" their transgressions of the PRĀTIMOKṢA precepts and is also an important part of MAHĀYĀNA liturgy, in which misdeeds are revealed during an additional recitation during the upoṣadha rites, or, in the absence of a community (SAṂGHA), to an image of the buddha or to visualized buddhas. In the prātimokṣa, the related term PRATIDEŚANĪYA refers specifically to four infractions that need only be acknowledged.

**pratideśanīya**. (P. pāṭidesanīya; T. so sor bshags par bya ba; C. duishou/boluotitisheni; J. taishu/haradaidaishani; K. taesu/parajejesani 對首/波羅提提舍尼). In Sanskrit, lit., "entailing acknowledgment" or "disclosure"; a group of four ecclesiastical offenses related to the receiving and eating of food, which are to be disclosed to, or confessed before, another monk. These offenses include (1) receiving food from an unrelated nun in an uninhabited area, (2) not dismissing a nun who is giving orders while monks are eating, (3) consuming food received from a "family in training," that is, a family too poor to provide alms, and (4) consuming unsolicited food received in one's own residence in the wilderness while one is not ill. In certain recensions of the PRĀTIMOKṢA, such as the Pāli and MŪLASARVĀSTIVĀDA, the offenses entailing acknowledgment form a separate category of transgressions from other misdeeds that require confession, in that the words used in acknowledging the violation are specifically prescribed for these four rules.

**pratigha**. (P. paṭigha; T. khong khro; C. chen; J. shin; K. chin 瞋). In Sanskrit, "aversion," "hostility," or "repulsion," one of the primary mental afflictions (KLEŚA) and closely synonymous with "ill will" (DVEṢA). In the VAIBHĀṢIKA school of SARVĀSTIVĀDA ABHIDHARMA, pratigha is listed as the second of the six fundamental afflictions (MŪLAKLEŚA), along with greed (RĀGA), ignorance (AVIDYĀ), conceit (MĀNA), doubt (VICIKITSĀ), and wrong views (DṚṢṬI). These six kleśas, along with bhavarāga (the desire for continued existence) constitute the latent afflictions (anusayakilesa) in the Pāli ABHIDHAMMA. The YOGĀCĀRA school also uses the same list of six fundamental kleśas, including pratigha but replacing māna with stupidity (mūḍhi). In Buddhist psychology, when contact with sensory objects is made "without introspection" (ASAṂPRAJANYA), aversion can arise. Since aversion is a psychological reaction that is associated with repulsion, resistance, and active dislike of a displeasing stimulus, it can also generate secondary mental afflictions (UPAKLEŚA) that have pratigha as their common foundation, including "anger" (KRODHA), "enmity" (UPANĀHA), "agitation" (PRADĀSA), "envy" (ĪRṢYĀ), and "harmfulness" (VIHIṂSĀ). Because pratigha includes both cognitive and affective dimensions, it is not removed through insight upon entry into the path of vision (DARŚANAMĀRGA), but is abandoned only after repeated training on the path of cultivation (BHĀVANĀMĀRGA).

**prātihārya**. (P. pāṭihāriya; T. cho 'phrul; C. shixian; J. jigen; K. sihyŏn 示現). In Sanskrit, "wonder" or "miracle," miraculous powers generally said to be exclusive to a buddha. In this sense, the term is sometimes distinguished from ṚDDHI, or "magical powers," which results from the attainment of states of DHYĀNA. Among the many miracles ascribed to the Buddha, two are particularly famous and are widely depicted in Buddhist iconography. Both took place at ŚRĀVASTĪ, where the Buddha defeated a group of TĪRTHIKAs. The first is the so-called "dual miracle" (YAMAKAPRĀTIHĀRYA) in which the Buddha caused both fire and water to emanate from his body. The second is the "great miracle" (MAHĀPRĀTIHĀRYA) in which the Buddha, seated on a great lotus, multiplied himself until the sky was filled with buddhas, some seated, some standing, some walking, some lying down, each teaching the dharma. Three categories of miracles (triprātihārya) are also enumerated. The first, the "miracle of magical power" (ṛddhiprātihārya) includes the myriad supranormal powers of the Buddha, including the power to fly and to appear and disappear. The second, the "miracle of foretelling" (ādeśanāprātihārya), refers to the Buddha's ability to know the thoughts of others. The third, the "miracle of instruction," is the Buddha's unique ability to teach the dharma. Eight deeds of the Buddha, sometimes referred to as miracles, are commonly depicted during the Pāla period. Taking place at the eight "great sites" (MAHĀSTHĀNA), the eight are (1) the miracle of his birth at LUMBINĪ, (2) the defeat of MĀRA and achievement of buddhahood at BODHGAYĀ, (3) the turning of the wheel of the dharma (DHARMACAKRA) at ṚṢIPATANA (SĀRNĀTH), (4) miracles performed at ŚRĀVASTĪ, (5) the descent from the TRĀYASTRIṂŚA heaven at SĀṂKĀŚYA, (6) the taming of the elephant NĀLĀGIRI at RĀJAGṚHA, (7) the receipt of the monkey's gift of honey at VAIŚĀLĪ, and (8) the passage into PARINIRVĀṆA at KUŚINAGARĪ. (See also BAXIANG).

**pratijñā**. (T. dam bca'; C. lizong; J. risshū; K. ipchong 立宗). In Sanskrit, lit., "promise," but used in Buddhist logic (HETUVIDYĀ) to mean "thesis" or "proposition," that is, the position that one is seeking to prove to an opponent. In this sense, it used synonymously with PAKṢA and SĀDHYA ("what is to be established"). A thesis is composed of a subject and a predicate; for example, "the mountain is on fire," or "sound is impermanent," with mountain and sound being the subject. There is considerable discussion in Buddhist logic on what constitutes a valid thesis. According to DIGNĀGA, a thesis is a proposition intended by its proponent as something to be stated alone (i.e., without reasons or examples) and whose subject is not contradicted by direct perception (PRATYAKṢA), inference (ANUMĀNA), valid authorities (PRAMĀṆA), or what is commonly accepted as true. In the works of Dignāga and DHARMAKĪRTI (and their commentators), there is also considerable discussion of whether, in debating with an opponent, one's own thesis needs to be explicitly stated, or whether it can be implied. The term pratijñā is also important in the MADHYAMAKA school, deriving from NĀGĀRJUNA's famous declaration in his VIGRAHAVYĀVARTANĪ that he has no thesis, which became in Tibet one of the most commented upon statements in Madhyamaka literature.

**prātimokṣa**. (P. pāṭimokkha; T. so sor thar pa; C. boluotimucha; J. haradaimokusha; K. parajemokch'a 波羅提木叉). In Sanskrit, "code" or "rules," referring to a disciplinary code of conduct (of which there are several versions) for fully ordained monks (BHIKṢU) and nuns (BHIKṢUṆĪ), or a text that sets forth that code, which probably constitutes the oldest part of the various Buddhist VINAYAs. The pre-Buddhist denotation of prātimokṣa is uncertain, and may perhaps mean a promise that is to be redeemed; the Buddhist etymologies seem to indicate a "binding obligation" and, by extension, a monastic regulation.

Indian Buddhist schools tended to define themselves in terms of the particular monastic code to which they adhered, and differences in the interpretation of the rules of conduct resulted in the convening of councils (SAṂGĪTI) to adjudicate such differences and, ultimately, in the schisms that produced the various mainstream Buddhist schools. Several different recensions of the prātimokṣa are extant, but there are three main lineages followed within the Buddhist tradition today: the THERAVĀDA pāṭimokkha followed in Sri Lankan and Southeast Asian Buddhism; the DHARMAGUPTAKA prātimokṣa followed in Chinese and Korean Buddhism; and the MŪLASARVĀSTIVĀDA prātimokṣa followed in Tibetan Buddhism. Despite divergences in the numbers of rules listed in these codes (the Theravāda, for example, has 227 rules for bhikṣus, the Dharmaguptaka 250, and the Mūlasarvāstivāda 253, and all have considerably more rules for bhikṣuṇī), there is substantial agreement among the prātimokṣa of the various mainstream Buddhist schools. They are all similarly structured, with separate codes for monks and nuns, enumerating a set of categories of transgressions: (1) PĀRĀJIKA transgressions of ethical expectations that were so serious as to bring "defeat" and in some vinaya traditions to require expulsion from the order, e.g., engaging in sexual intercourse and murder; (2) SAṂGHĀVAŚEṢA, transgressions entailing temporary suspension from the order, such as masturbation, acting as a go-between for sexual liaisons, or attempting to cause schism in the order (SAṂGHABHEDA); (3) ANIYATA, undetermined cases exclusive to monks who are found with women, which require investigation by the saṃgha; (4) NAIḤSARGIKAPĀYATTIKA, transgressions requiring confession and forfeiture of a prohibited object, such as hoarding excessive numbers of robes (CĪVARA), begging bowls (PĀTRA), and medicine, or keeping gold and silver; (5) PĀYATTIKA, transgressions that can be expiated through confession alone, such as lying; (6) PRATIDEŚANĪYA, minor transgressions to be acknowledged, related to receiving and eating food, which were to be confessed; (7) ŚAIKṢA, minor training rules governing monastic etiquette and deportment, such as not wearing robes sloppily or eating noisily, violations of which were called DUṢKṚTA, lit. "bad actions." Both the bhikṣu and bhikṣuṇī prātimokṣa also include (8) ADHIKARAṆAŚAMATHA, seven methods of resolving ecclesiastical disputes. Regardless of the school, the prātimokṣa was recited separately during the fortnightly UPOṢADHA ceremony by chapters of monks and nuns who gather inside a purified SĪMĀ boundary. All monks and nuns were expected to have confessed (see PĀPADEŚANĀ) to any transgressions of the rules during the last fortnight prior to the recitation of the code, thus expiating them of that transgression. At the conclusion of the recitation of each category of transgression, the reciter questions the congregation as to whether the congregation is pure; silence indicates assent.

**prātimokṣasaṃvara**. (T. so sor thar pa'i sdom pa; C. boluotimuchahu/biejietuo lüyi; J. haradaimokushago/betsugedatsu ritsugi; K. parajemokch'aho/pyŏrhaet'al yurŭi 波羅提木叉護/別解脫律儀). In Sanskrit, "restraint proffered by the disciplinary code" (PRĀTIMOKṢA); one of the three types of restraint (SAṂVARA) mentioned in the VAIBHĀṢIKA school of SARVĀSTIVĀDA ABHIDHARMA, which are associated with "unmanifest material force" or "hidden imprints" (AVIJÑAPTIRŪPA). In Sarvāstivāda literature, three types of restraint (saṃvara) against unwholesome (AKUŚALA) actions are mentioned: (1) the restraint proffered to a monk or nun when he or she accepts the disciplinary rules of the order (prātimokṣasaṃvara); (2) the restraint that is produced through mental absorption (dhyānasaṃvara); and (3) the restraint that derives from being free from the contaminants (anāsravasaṃvara). The restraint inherent in the disciplinary code creates a special kind of "force field" that automatically protects and dissuades monks and nuns from unwholesome activity, even when they are not consciously aware that they are following the precepts or when they are asleep. This specific type of restraint is what makes a person a monk or a nun, since just wearing robes and following an ascetic way of life would not in themselves be enough to instill in him or her the protective power offered by the prātimokṣa. This particular type of avijñaptirūpa thus creates an invisible and impalpable barrier that helps to protect the monk or the nun from unwholesome action. The prātimokṣasaṃvara is incorporated into later MAHĀYĀNA Buddhist and tantric Buddhist codes (see SDOM GSUM; TRISAṂVARA).

**Prātimokṣasūtra**. (T. So sor thar pa'i mdo; C. Jie ben; J. Kaihon; K. Kye pon 戒本). In Sanskrit, "Sūtra on the Code," a scripture that provides a separate listing of the code of conduct and monastic rules (PRĀTIMOKṢA) for monks (BHIKṢU) and for nuns (BHIKṢUṆĪ). Several of the mainstream Buddhist schools, including the MAHĀSĀṂGHIKA and MŪLASARVĀSTIVĀDA schools, had a separate text, called the *Prātimokṣasūtra*, that listed the prātimokṣa rules for monks and for nuns. There is no such separate text in the THERAVĀDA school, where the pāṭimokkha is included in the SUTTAVIBHAṄGA, the first major section of the Pāli VINAYAPIṬAKA, which includes the *mahāvibhaṅga* with the rules for monks and the *bhikkunīvibhaṅga* with the rules for nuns.

**pratinivāsana**. See NIVĀSANA.

**pratipakṣa**. (P. paṭipakkha; T. gnyen po; C. duizhi; J. taiji; K. taech'i 對治). In Sanskrit, lit., "opposite"; a "counteragent" or "antidote," a factor which, when present, precludes the presence of its opposite. In Buddhist meditation theory, an antidote may be a virtuous (KUŚALA) mental state (CAITTA) that is applied as a counteragent against a nonvirtuous (AKUŚALA) mental state. The Buddhist premise that two contrary mental states cannot exist simultaneously leads to the development of specific meditations to be used as such counteragents, sometimes called the five "inhibitory" contemplations (C. zhiguan, tingguan): (1) lust (RĀGA) is countered by the contemplations on impurity (AŚUBHABHĀVANĀ), e.g., the cemetery contemplations on the stages in the decomposition of a corpse; (2) hatred (DVEṢA) is countered by the divine abiding (BRAHMAVIHĀRA) of loving-kindness (MAITRĪ); (3) delusion (MOHA) is countered by contemplating the twelvefold chain of dependent origination (PRATĪTYASAMUTPĀDA); (4) ego-conceit (asmimāna) is countered by the contemplation on the eighteen sense-fields (DHĀTU); and (5) discursive thought (VITARKA) is countered by mindfulness of breathing (ĀNĀPĀNASMṚTI). Progress on the path to liberation is also described technically in terms of the abandonment of a specific afflictive state (KLEŚA) through the application of its specific antidote. Thus, afflictions and their antidotes are enumerated for the nine levels of SAṂSĀRA (the sensuous realm, or KĀMADHĀTU, the four levels of the subtle-materiality realm, or RŪPADHĀTU, and the four levels of the immaterial realm, or ARŪPYADHĀTU). In each case, the antidote is an increasingly powerful level of wisdom (PRAJÑĀ) that displaces increasingly subtle levels of the afflictions. Both the four types of noble persons (ĀRYAPUDGALA) and the ten stages (BHŪMI) of the bodhisattva are defined by which antidotes have been successfully applied to eradicate specific afflictions. Thus, the accumulation and application of various antidotes is one of the practices that a bodhisattva must learn to perfect. The Buddha is said to have taught 84,000 antidotes for the 84,000 afflictions.

**pratipatti**. (P. paṭipatti; T. sgrub pa; C. xiuxing; J. shugyō; K. suhaeng 修行). In Sanskrit, "practice," "progress"; one of four aspects of the truth of the path (MĀRGASATYA), the fourth of the so-called FOUR NOBLE TRUTHS (catvāry āryasatyāni). The other aspects are mārga (path), nyāya (correct method), and nairyāṇika (providing a definite escape). As a word descriptive of the path, pratipatti is a word for all the practices, from the beginning practices of neophytes up to the final practices of noble beings (ĀRYA). In all cases the practice avoids the extremes (see MADHYAMAPRATIPAD) of self-indulgence and self-mortification, or the extreme views of eternalism (ŚĀŚVATADṚṢṬI) and annihilationism (UCCHEDADṚṢṬI). See also PAṬIPATTI.

**pratirūpaka**. (S). See SADDHARMAPRATIRŪPAKA.

**pratisaṃkakṣikā**. (S). See SAṂKAKṢIKĀ.

**pratisaṃkhyānirodha**. (T. so sor brtags 'gog; C. zemie; J. chakumetsu; K. t'aengmyŏl 擇滅). In Sanskrit, "analytical cessation," the permanent elimination of an affliction (KLEŚA) that occurs as a result of meditative analysis of the true nature of phenomena; one of the uncompounded factors (ASAṂSKṚTA–DHARMA) recognized in both the VAIBHĀṢIKA school of SARVĀSTIVĀDA ABHIDHARMA and the YOGĀCĀRA schools. The "true cessations" or "truth of cessation" (NIRODHASATYA) that constitute the third of the four noble truths (see NIRODHASATYA) involve analytical cessations. Analytical cessations are permanent phenomena because they are the permanent absence of a specific kleśa, essentially serving as a kind of "place marker" that ensures that a kleśa, once eliminated, can never recur. Analytical cessations are distinguished from nonanalytical suppressions (APRATISAṂKHYĀNIRODHA), which are neither an object of knowledge nor the result of insight; they suppress the production of any kind of dharma, ensuring (in the Sarvāstivāda interpretation) that they remain positioned in future mode and are never again able to arise in the present. The state of the analytical cessation of all the kleśas is synonymous with NIRVĀṆA.

**pratisaṃlayana**. (P. paṭisallāna; T. nang du yang dag 'jog pa; C. yanmo/jimo; J. enmoku/jakumoku; K. yŏnmuk/chŏngmuk 宴默/寂默). In Sanskrit, "seclusion" or "retirement"; withdrawing to a secluded place, such as the proverbial "root of a tree," so that one may rest or, in its technical usage, so that one may train in meditation free of distractions. By extension, pratisaṃlayana refers also to the mental "isolation" or "seclusion" that accompanies meditative practice. Pratisaṃlayana is listed as one of the constituents of practice (yogāṅga) and is sometimes described as a specific type of meditative absorption (DHYĀNA) in its own right.

**pratisaṃvid**. (P. paṭisaṃbhidā; T. so sor yang dag par rig pa; C. wu'ai jie; J. mugege; K. muae hae 無礙解). In Sanskrit, "analytical knowledge," of which there are four kinds: knowledge of (1) factors or phenomena (DHARMA), viz., one makes no mistakes in understanding causes, conditions, or the relationships pertaining between objects; (2) meaning (ARTHA), viz., to have no limitations with regard to the content, meaning, and analysis of one's teachings; (3) etymology or language (NIRUKTI), viz., the ability to comprehend all languages, including those of the divinities (DEVA) and other nonhuman beings (YAKṢA, GANDHARVA, ASURA, GARUḌA, KIṂNARA, MAHORĀGA), and to penetrate the full range of etymological or linguistic expressions; and (4) eloquence (PRATIBHĀNA), viz., ease in offering explanations and/or the ability to inspire others with one's words. These four types of knowledge are associated with both the attainment of arhatship and the achievement of the ninth of the ten stages (DAŚABHŪMI) of the BODHISATTVA path. In Chinese, these were known as the "unconstrained knowledges" (wu'ai jie).

**pratisaraṇa**. [alt. pratiśaraṇa] (P. paṭisaraṇa; T. rton pa; C. yi; J. e; K. ŭi 依). In Sanskrit, "reliance," "support," or "point of reference"; four things to be relied upon in the interpretation of a given teaching. The four are (1) to rely on the meaning (ARTHA), not the mere "letter" (vyañjana) or words; (2) to rely on the teachings (DHARMA), not the person (PUDGALA) who delivers those teachings; (3) to rely on true gnosis or knowledge (JÑĀNA), not the unreliable testimony of the ordinary consciousnesses (VIJÑĀNA); (4) to rely on the definitive meaning (NĪTĀRTHA), not the provisional meaning (NEYĀRTHA).

**pratiṣedha**. (T. dgag pa; C. zhe; J. sha; K. ch'a 遮). In Sanskrit, "negative" or "negation," the refutation of an opponent's position. The term is also used to mean "negative phenomenon," that is, a phenomenon that is understood through the elimination of another factor. Examples would include ĀKĀŚA ("space," when defined as the lack of obstruction) and ANĀTMAN (nonself), the absence of a self. In Buddhist logic, there are two types of negation, the "affirming negation" (PARYUDĀSAPRATIṢEDHA), which negates something while implying the existence of something else, and the "nonaffirming negation" (PRASAJYAPRATIṢEDHA), which negates without such implication.

**pratiṣedhya**. (T. dgag bya). In Sanskrit, "object of negation," that factor which is eliminated through the process of understanding a particular negative phenomenon (PRATIṢEDHA). The term is used especially in the context of discussions of nonself (ANĀTMAN) and emptiness (ŚŪNYATĀ), where the precise nature of what is being negated (that is, the meaning of self) is of great importance. If self is defined too narrowly, the conception of self that is the root cause of suffering may not be eliminated; if self is defined too broadly, there is a danger of falling into nihilism by denying even the conventional existence of such things are rebirth, KARMAN, and the efficacy of the path (MĀRGA).

**pratiṣṭhā**. (P. patiṭṭhā; T. rab tu gnas pa; C. jianli; J. konryū; K. kŏllip 建立). In Sanskrit, lit. "establishment," or "installation," but often having the sense of "consecration," especially of a monastery, temple, or buddha-image. There are numerous forms of consecration ceremonies across the Buddhist world. In the case of the consecration of buddha images, these ceremonies seek to cause the buddha to "enter" into his physical representation. In some cases, this consecration is done by reciting the life story of the Buddha in the presence of the image; in other cases, the DHARMAKĀYA of the buddha is invoked and requested to enter into the image. See also DIANYAN; KAIYAN; BUDDHĀBHIṢEKA.

**pratiṣṭhitanirvāṇa**. (T. gnas pa'i mya ngan las 'das pa; C. zhu niepan; J. jūnehan; K. chu yŏlban 住涅槃). In Sanskrit, "static NIRVĀṆA" or "localized nirvāṇa," a term used in the MAHĀYĀNA, often pejoratively, to describe the nirvāṇa of the ARHAT, which is "static" or "located" in a state of isolated serenity that transcends SAṂSĀRA. This type of nirvāṇa is contrasted with the "unlocalized nirvāṇa" (APRATIṢṬHITANIRVĀṆA) of a buddha which is not localized in either saṃsāra or the isolation of the arhat, but is instead a dynamic state that allows him to participate in the world while remaining forever untainted by it.

**pratītyasamutpāda**. (P. paṭiccasamuppāda; T. rten cing 'brel bar 'byung ba; C. yuanqi; J. engi; K. yŏn'gi 緣起). In Sanskrit, "dependent origination," "conditioned origination," lit., "origination by dependence" (of one thing on another); one of the core teachings in the Buddhist doctrinal system, having both ontological, epistemological, and soteriological implications. The notion of the conditionality of all existence is foundational in Buddhism. According to some accounts of the Buddha's life, it constituted the fundamental insight on the night of his enlightenment. In other accounts, in the first seven days and nights following his enlightenment, he sat contemplating the significance of his experience; finally on the seventh night he is said to have contemplated the fully realized chain of dependent origination in both forward and reverse order. In one of the earliest summaries of the Buddha's teachings (which is said to have been enough to bring ŚĀRIPUTRA to enlightenment), the Buddha is said to have taught: "When this is present, that comes to be. / From the arising of this, that arises. / When this is absent, that does not come to be. / From the cessation of this, that ceases." (P. imasmiṃ sati idaṃ hoti/imasuppādā idaṃ uppajjati/imasmiṃ asati idaṃ na hoti/imassa nirodhā idaṃ nirujjhati). This notion of causality (idaṃpratyayatā) is normatively described in a sequence of causation involving twelve interconnected links (NIDĀNA), which are often called the "twelvefold chain" in English sources: (1) ignorance (AVIDYĀ, P. avijjā), (2) predispositions, or volitional actions (S. SAMSKĀRA, P. saṅkhāra), (3) consciousness (S. VIJÑĀNA, P. viññāṇa), (4) name and form, or mentality and materiality (NĀMARŪPA), (5) the six internal sense-bases (ĀYATANA), (6) sensory contact (S. SPARŚA, P. phassa), (7) sensation, or feeling (VEDANĀ), (8) thirst, or attachment (S. TṚṢṆĀ, P. taṇhā), (9) grasping, or clinging (UPĀDĀNA), (10) existence or a process of becoming (BHAVA), (11) birth or rebirth (JĀTI), and (12) old age and death (JARĀMARAṆA), this last link accompanied in its full recital by sorrow (śoka), lamentation (parideva), pain (DUḤKHA) grief (daurmanasya), and despair (upāyāsa). Some formulations of the chain, as in the MAHĀPADĀNASUTTANTA, include only ten links (skipping the first two), suggesting that the standard list of twelve links developed over time. (The commentary to the *Mahāpadānasuttanta* explains away this inconsistency by noting that the ten-linked chain does not take past lives into account but applies only to the current life.) Each link in this chain of causality is said to be the condition for the following link, thus: "dependent on ignorance, predispositions (S. avidyāpratyayāḥ saṃskārāḥ; P. avijjāpaccayā saṅkhārā), ... dependent on birth, old age and death (S. jātipratyayāṃ jarāmaraṇaṃ; P. jātipaccayā jarāmaraṇaṃ)." This chain of dependent origination stands as the middle way (MADHYAMAPRATIPAD) between the two "extreme views" (ANTAGRĀHADṚṢṬI) of eternalism (ŚĀŚVATADṚṢṬI)—viz., the view that there is a perduring soul that continues to be reborn unchanged from one lifetime to the next—and annihilationism (UCCHEDADṚṢṬI)—the view that the person ceases to exist at death and is not reborn—because it validates the imputed continuity (SAṂTĀNA) of the personality, without injecting any sense of a permanent substratum of existence into the process. Thus, when the Buddha is asked, "Who is it who senses?," he rejects the question as wrongly framed and rephrases it as, "With what as condition does sensation (vedanā) occur? By contact (sparśa)." Or when asked, "Who is it who is reborn?," he would rephrase the question as "With what as condition does birth (jāti) occur? By becoming (bhava)."

Accurate understanding of dependent origination thus serves as an antidote (PRATIPAKṢA) to the affliction of delusion (MOHA) and contemplating the links in this chain helps to overcome ignorance (AVIDYĀ). ¶ The twelvefold chain of dependent origination is generally conceived to unfold in what are referred to as the "forward" and "reverse" orders, although in fact both versions proceed through the chain in the same sequence. First, as a progressive process of ontological becoming (bhavānulomaparīkṣā), the forward version of the chain describes the process by which ignorance ultimately leads to birth and death and thus the full panoply of existence in the turning wheel of SAṂSĀRA; in forward order, the chain is therefore an elaboration of the second noble truth, the truth of the origin of suffering (SAMUDAYASATYA). Second, the reverse order of the chain describes a negative process of soteriological eradication (kṣayavyayānulomaparīkṣā), where the cessation of ignorance serves as the condition for the cessation of predispositions, and so on through the entire chain until even old age and death are eradicated and the adept is released from continued rebirth in saṃsāra; in reverse order, the chain is therefore an elaboration of the third noble truth, the truth of the cessation of suffering (NIRODHASATYA). As a chain of ontological becoming, some traditional commentators organize the twelve links as occurring during the course of a single lifetime. Other commentators instead divide the twelve links over three lifetimes to illustrate explicitly the process of rebirth: ignorance and predispositions are assigned to a previous lifetime; consciousness, name and form, sense-fields, contact, sensation, thirst, grasping, and becoming are assigned to the current lifetime; and this leads to future birth, and eventual old age and death, in the immediately following lifetime. According to this interpretation, ignorance does not refer to a primordial ignorance, but rather to a specific moment of unsystematic reflection on things (AYONIŚOMANASKĀRA) that prompts a volitional action (saṃskāra). The predispositions created by that action imprint themselves on consciousness, which refers here to the "linking consciousness" (pratisaṃdhivijñāna) that links the past and present lives, a consciousness that is reborn, developing into a body with internal sense organs and a mind with sensory consciousnesses, which come into contact with external sensory objects, giving rise to sensations that are pleasant, unpleasant, or neutral. Sensations of pleasure, for example, can give rise to attachment to those sensations and then clinging, an intensification of that attachment. Such clinging at the end of life sustains the process of becoming, which leads to rebirth in the next existence, where one once again undergoes aging and death. This sequence of dependent conditions has repeated itself since time immemorial and will continue on indefinitely until liberation from rebirth is achieved. To illustrate the role of pratītyasamutpāda in the cycle of rebirth, its twelve links are sometimes depicted around the perimeter of the "wheel of life" (BHAVACAKRA). ¶ In the *Upanisāsutta* of the SAṂYUTTANIKĀYA, the standard twelvefold chain of dependent origination is connected to an alternate chain that is designated the "supramundane dependent origination" (P. lokuttara-paṭiccasamuppāda; S. lokottara-pratītyasamutpāda), which explicitly outlines the process leading to liberation. Here, the last factor in the standard chain, that of old age and death (jarāmaraṇa), is substituted with suffering, which in turn becomes the first factor in this alternate series. According to the *Nettipakaraṇa*, a Pāli exegetical treatise, this chain of supramundane dependent origination consists of (1) suffering (P. dukkha; S. duḥkha), (2) faith (P. saddhā; S. ŚRADDHĀ), (3) delight or satisfaction (P. pāmojja; S. prāmodya), (4) rapture or joy (P. pīti; S. PRĪTI), (5) tranquillity or repose (P. passaddhi; S. PRAŚRABDHI), (6) mental ease or bliss (SUKHA), (7) concentration (SAMĀDHI), (8) knowledge and vision that accords with reality (P. yathābhūtañāṇadassana; S. YATHĀBHŪTAJÑĀNADARŚANA), (9) disillusionment (P. nibbidā; S. NIRVEDA), (10) dispassion (P. virāga; S. VAIRĀGYA), (11) liberation (P. vimutti; S. VIMUKTI), and (12) knowledge of the destruction of the contaminants (P. āsavakkhayañāṇa; S. āsravakṣayajñāna; see ĀSRAVAKṢAYA). The *Kimatthiyasutta* of the AṄGUTTARANIKĀYA gives a slightly different version of the first links, replacing suffering and faith with (1) observance of precepts (P. kusalasīla; S. kuśalaśīla) and (2) freedom from remorse (P. avippaṭisāra; S. avipratisāra). ¶ Another denotation of pratītyasamutpāda is a more general one, the notion that everything comes into existence in dependence on something else, with such dependence including the dependence of an effect upon its cause, the dependence of a whole upon its parts, and the dependence of an object on the consciousness that designates it. This second meaning is especially associated with the MADHYAMAKA school of NĀGĀRJUNA, which sees a necessary relation between dependent origination and emptiness (ŚŪNYATĀ), arguing that because everything is dependently arisen, everything is empty of independence and intrinsic existence (SVABHĀVA). Dependent origination is thus central to Nāgārjuna's conception of the middle way: because everything is dependent, nothing is independent, thus avoiding the extreme of existence, but because everything is originated, nothing is utterly nonexistent, thus avoiding the extreme of nonexistence. In East Asia, and specifically the HUAYAN ZONG, this second interpretation of dependent origination is also recast as the unimpeded (wu'ai) "dependent origination of the DHARMADHĀTU" (FAJIE YUANQI), in which all things throughout the entire universe are conceived as being enmeshed in a multivalent web of interconnection and interdependency.

**Pratītyasamutpādahṛdayakārikā**. (T. Rten cing 'brel bar 'byung ba'i snying po'i tshig le'ur byas pa; C. Shi'er yinyuan lun; J. Jūniinnenron; K. Sibi inyŏn non 十二因緣論). In Sanskrit, "Verses on the Essence of Dependent Origination," a work attributed to NĀGĀRJUNA by BHĀVAVIVEKA. The work seeks to reconcile the two major meanings of PRATĪTYASAMUTPĀDA: that of a twelvefold sequence of cause and effect and a more general sense of phenomena arising in dependence on causes, which he sets forth in his MŪLAMADHYAMAKAKĀRIKĀ. Nāgārjuna qualifies the twelve links in the chain of causation under three headings, with ignorance (AVIDYĀ), attachment (TṚṢṆĀ), and grasping (UPĀDĀNA) classified as afflictions (KLEŚA);

predispositions (SAṂSKĀRA) and existence (BHAVA) as action (KARMAN); and the remaining seven as forms of suffering (DUḤKHA). Those five that are classified as kleśa and karman are also causes; the remaining seven are effects. The "essence" of pratītyasamutpāda in the title is the lack of self in both the person (PUDGALA) and the aggregates (SKANDHA).

***Pratītyasamutpādaśāstra**. (C. Yuansheng lun; J. Enshōron; K. Yŏnsaeng non 緣生論). In Sanskrit, "Treatise on Dependent Origination," a work by Ullaṅgha in thirty verses, with a prose explanation. The work is lost in Sanskrit and was translated into Chinese by Dharmagupta in 607 during the Daye era (605–616) of the Sui dynasty.

**Pratītyasamutpādavibhaṅganirdeśasūtra**. (T. Rten cing 'brel bar 'byung ba dang po dang rnam par dbye ba bstan pa zhes bya ba'i mdo). In Sanskrit, "Sūtra Setting Forth the Divisions of Dependent Origination," also known as the *Pratītyasamutpādādivibhaṅganirdeśasūtra*, a work discovered inscribed on two bricks at NĀLANDĀ monastery. The sūtra was commented upon by VASUBANDHU in his *Pratītyasamutpādavyākhyā*, with a subcommentary by Guṇamati.

**prativedha**. (P. paṭivedha; T. khong du chud pa; C. tongda; J. tsūdatsu; K. t'ongdal 通達). In Sanskrit, "penetration," or "direct realization," signifying the direct realization of the truth. Commonly, this realization, or actualization, of the truth is contrasted with the textual study of descriptions of the truth (PARIYATTI), or the soteriological practice of it (PAṬIPATTI). Prativedha is the culmination and fulfillment of these two prior disciplines. Thus the dharma is to be first studied, then practiced, and ultimately realized. In Pāli sources, paṭivedha (S. prativedha) is stratified into four degrees of liberation, beginning with the attainment of a "stream-enterer" (P. sotāpanna, S. SROTAĀPANNA), then "once-returner" (P. sakadāgāmi, S. SAKṚDĀGĀMIN), "nonreturner" (P. anāgāmi, S. ANĀGĀMIN), and finally arahant (S. ARHAT). It is understood that the last of these four degrees of penetration into the truth frees one from suffering and the prospect of further rebirth.

**pratyakṣa**. (T. mngon sum; C. xianliang; J. genryō; K. hyŏllyang 現量). In Sanskrit, "direct perception," cognition that is unmistaken in the sense that it correctly apprehends qualities such as shape and color, and is nonconceptual, in the sense that it does not perceive its object through the medium of an image, as does thought (KALPANĀ). In Buddhist epistemology, direct perception is one of only two forms of valid knowledge (PRAMĀṆA), along with inference (ANUMĀNA). Four types of direct perception are enumerated. The first is sensory direct perception, in which the five external sense objects are perceived directly by the sense consciousnesses (VIJÑĀNA), in reliance on the five sense organs (INDRIYA). This form of direct perception is to be differentiated from SAṂJÑĀ, also sometimes translated as "perception." The latter term refers to the specific function of consciousness to apprehend the various characteristics of a given object or to differentiate between two objects. The second kind of direct perception is mental direct perception (MANONUBHAVAPRATYAKṢA), which, according to one interpretation, includes a brief and unnoticed moment of direct perception by the mind at the end of sensory direct perception, with that moment of mental direct perception inducing the conceptual cognition of the object. Mental direct perception also includes the five ABHIJÑĀ, which result from states of deep concentration. The third type is self-knowing direct perception (svasaṃvedana), a function of self-consciousness, which observes a consciousness apprehending its object. It is this form of direct perception that makes possible memory of former moments of consciousness. The fourth type is yogic direct perception (YOGIPRATYAKṢA), which occurs only on one of the noble paths (ĀRYAMĀRGA), where the truth is directly perceived through a union of ŚAMATHA and VIPAŚYANĀ.

**pratyālīḍha**. (T. g.yon brkyang ba; C. zhanzuo; J. tensa; K. chŏnjwa 展左). In Sanskrit, lit., "extended to the left"; a term used to describe the Buddhist iconographical posture (ĀSANA), in which the figure holds the left leg bent forward at the knee with the right leg extended back in a lunging posture. While the term generally refers to standing postures, it may also apply to seated poses, and is distinguished from ĀLĪḌHA, where the leg positions are reversed. In Tibetan tantric art, the pratyālīḍha posture is often found in deities of the PITṚTANTRA class. See also ĀSANA.

**pratyāstaraṇa**. (P. paccattharaṇa; T. gding ba; C. woju; J. gagu; K. wagu 臥具). A sheet or mat permitted as one of the possessions of a Buddhist monk. The Buddha initially had allowed monks to place their few belongings on a piece of cloth. When monks pointed out to the Buddha that their sitting mat (NIṢĪDANA) was too small for lying down, he allowed them to have a larger piece of cloth that they could spread on the ground or the floor of their cell where they could rest or sleep.

**pratyātmādhigama**. (T. so sor rang gis rig pa; C. neizheng; J. naishō; K. naejŭng 內證). In Sanskrit, "specific understanding" or "individual understanding," a term used to describe the personal realization of a buddha, which is entirely nonconceptual and inexpressible. It is this realization that a buddha then compassionately translates into concepts and words in order to teach the dharma to sentient beings.

**pratyavekṣaṇājñāna**. (T. so sor rtogs pa'i ye shes; C. miao guancha zhi; J. myōkanzatchi; K. myo kwanch'al chi 妙觀察智). In Sanskrit, "wisdom of specific knowledge" (the Chinese means "wisdom of sublime investigation"); one of the five wisdoms (PAÑCAJÑĀNA) of a buddha in the MAHĀYĀNA, and specifically in the YOGĀCĀRA school, which are said to be achieved when consciousness is purified of afflictions (KLEŚA); each of these wisdoms thus entails a transformation of the one or more of the eight consciousnesses. According to the CHENG WEISHI LUN, pratyavekṣaṇājñāna is a transformation of the sixth MANOVIJÑĀNA and is a buddha's direct understanding of the general and specific characteristics of all the phenomena in the universe.

**pratyaya**. (P. paccaya; T. rkyen; C. yuan; J. en; K. yŏn 緣). In Sanskrit, "condition"; referring generally to the subsidiary factors whose concomitance results in the production of an effect from a cause, especially in the compound HETUPRATYAYA ("causes and conditions"). For example, in the production of a sprout from a seed, the seed would be the cause (HETU), while such factors as heat and moisture would be conditions (pratyaya). Given the centrality of the doctrine of causality of Buddhist thought, detailed lists and descriptions of conditions appear in all strata of Buddhist literature. In the context of epistemology, in the case of the perception of a tree by a moment of visual consciousness (CAKṢURVIJÑĀNA), the prior moment of consciousness that leads to this specific visual consciousness is called the immediately antecedent condition (SAMANANTARAPRATYAYA), the tree is called the object condition (ĀLAMBANAPRATYAYA), and the visual sense organ is called the predominant condition (ADHIPATIPRATYAYA); the "cooperative condition" (SAHAKĀRIPRATYAYA) is the subsidiary conditions that must be present in order for an effect to be produced, such as for light to be present in order to generate visual consciousness, or the presence of heat and moisture for a seed to grow into a sprout. ¶ A much more detailed roster of these conditions occurs in a detailed list of twenty-four conditions enumerated in the PAṬṬHĀNA, the seventh book of the Pāli ABHIDHAMMAPIṬAKA, a work that applies twenty-four specific conditions to the mental and physical phenomena of existence and presents a detailed account of the Pāli interpretation of the doctrine of dependent origination (P. paṭiccasamuppāda; S. PRATĪTYASAMUTPĀDA). The twenty-four conditions are (1) the root condition (hetupaccaya), the condition upon which mental states entirely depend, such as a tree depending on its root. These root conditions are greed (LOBHA), hate (P. dosa, S. DVEṢA), and delusion (MOHA) in the case of unwholesome mental states, or greedlessness (alobha), hatelessness (adosa; DVEṢA), and undeludedness (amoha) in the case of wholesome mental states. Without these roots being present, the respective mental states cannot exist. (2) The object condition (ārammaṇapaccaya) is an object of perception and as such forms the condition for mental phenomena. External sense objects, such a sound, comprise the object conditions for the five physical sense consciousnesses, while mental objects such as thoughts, emotions, and memories comprise the object condition for the single internal sense consciousness of mind. (3) The dominant condition (adhipatipaccaya) gives rise to mental phenomena by way of predominance and can be one of four types: intention (chanda), energy (viriya), consciousness (citta), and investigation (vīmaṃsā). At any given time only one of the four conditions can predominate in a state of consciousness. (4) The proximate condition (anantarapaccaya) and (5) the immediately antecedent condition (samanantarapaccaya) refer to any stage in the process of consciousness that serves as the condition for the immediately following stage. For example, an eye consciousness that sees a visual object functions as the immediately antecedent condition for the arising in the next moment of the mental consciousness that receives the visual image. The mental consciousness, in turn, serves as the immediately antecedent condition for the mental consciousness that performs the function of investigating the object. (6) The cooperative condition (sahajātapaccaya) is any phenomenon or condition the arising of which necessitates the simultaneous arising of another thing; for example, any one of the four mental aggregates (P. khandha; S. SKANDHA) of feeling (vedanā), conception (P. saññā; S. SAMJÑĀ), conditioning factors (P. saṅkhāra; S. SAMSKĀRA), and consciousness (P. viññāṇa; S. VIJÑĀNA) functions as the cooperative condition for all the rest, since all four invariably arise together in the same moment. (7) The condition by way of mutuality (aññāmaññapaccaya) refers to the fact that all simultaneous phenomena, such as the mental aggregates mentioned above, are mutually supportive and so are also conditioned by way of mutuality; they arise and fall in dependence on one another. (8) The support condition (nissayapaccaya) is a preceding or simultaneous condition that functions as a foundation for another phenomenon in the manner of earth for a tree. An example is the five external sense organs (eye, ear, nose, tongue and body) and the one internal mental sense organ (mind), which are the preceding and simultaneous conditions for the six kinds of consciousness that arise when sense organs come into contact with their respective objects. (9) The decisive support condition (upanissayapaccaya) is anything that functions as a strong inducement to moral, immoral, or neutral mental or physical action. It is of three kinds: (a) by way of object (ārammaṇa), which can be any real or imaginary object of thought; (b) by way of proximity; and (c) by way of natural support (pakati), which includes such things as mental attitudes and associations with friends that can act as natural inducements to either wholesome or unwholesome behavior, or climate and food that induce health or illness of the body. (10) The prenascent condition (purejātapaccaya) is something previously arisen that forms a base for something arising later. An example is the five physical sense organs and the physical base of mind that, having already arisen, form the condition for the arising of consciousness through their operation. (11) The postnascent condition (pacchājātapaccaya) refers to consciousness arisen through the operation of the senses, because it serves as the necessary condition for the continued preservation of this already arisen body with its functioning senses. (12) The repetition condition (āsevanapaccaya) refers to impulsion moments of consciousness (javana) that arise in a series, each time serving as a condition for succeeding moments by way of repetition and frequency. (13) The action condition (kammapaccaya) refers to the KARMAN or karmic volitions (kammacetanā) of a previous birth that functioned to generate the physical and mental characteristics of an individual's present existence. (14) The karma-result condition (vipākapaccaya) refers to the five karmically resultant external sense consciousnesses that function as simultaneous conditions for other mental and physical phenomena. (15) The nutriment condition (āhārapaccaya) is of four kinds and refers to material food (kabalinkārāhāra), which is food for the body; sensory and mental contact (phassa), which is food for sensation (vedanā); mental volition (CETANĀ = karman), which is food for rebirth; and consciousness (viññāna), which is food for the mind-body complex (NĀMARŪPA) at the moment of conception. (16) The faculty condition (indriyapaccaya) refers to twenty of twenty-two faculties (INDRIYA) enumerated in the Pāli abhidhamma out of which, for example, the five external sense faculties form the condition for their respective sense consciousnesses. (17) The meditative-absorption condition (jhānapaccaya) refers to a list of seven jhāna factors as conditions for simultaneous mental and corporeal phenomena. They are thought (vitakka), imagination (vicāra), rapture (pīti), joy (sukha), sadness (domanassa), indifference (upekkhā), and concentration (samādhi). (18) The path condition (maggapaccaya) refers to twelve path factors that condition progress along the path. These are: wisdom (paññā), thought-conception (vitakka), right speech (sammavācā), right bodily action (sammakammanta), right livelihood (sammajīva), energy (viriya), mindfulness (sati), concentration (samādhi), wrong views (micchāditthi), wrong speech (micchāvācā), wrong bodily action (micchākammanta), and wrong livelihood (micchājīva). (19) The association condition (sampayuttapaccaya) refers to the four mental aggregates of feeling (vedanā), perception (saññā), mental formations (saṅkhāra), and consciousness (viññāṇa), which assist one another by association through sharing a common physical base, a common object, and arising and passing away simultaneously. (20) The dissociation condition (vippayuttapaccaya) refers to phenomena that assist other phenomena by virtue of not having the same physical base and objects. (21 and 24) The presence condition (atthipaccaya) and the nondisappearance condition (avigatapaccaya) refer to any phenomenon that through its presence is a condition for other phenomena. (22 and 23) The absence condition (natthipaccaya) and the disappearance condition (vigatapaccaya) refer to any phenomenon, such as a moment of consciousness, which having just passed away constitutes the necessary condition for the immediately following moment of the same phenomenon by providing an opportunity for it to arise. ¶ The SARVĀSTIVĀDA school also recognizes a list of four conditions, all of which appear in the preceding Pāli list and thus appear to have evolved before the separation of the SARVĀSTIVĀDA and STHAVIRANIKĀYA schools: (1) HETUPRATYAYA, or condition qua cause, corresponding to no. 1 in the Pāli list; (2) SAMANANTARAPRATYAYA, or immediately antecedent condition, corresponding to no. 5 in the Pāli list; (3) ĀLAMBANAPRATYAYA, or object condition, corresponding to no. 2 in the Pāli list; (4) ADHIPATIPRATYAYA, or predominant condition, corresponding to no. 3 in the Pāli list. These four pratyaya first appear in the first-century CE VIJÑĀNAKĀYA and antedate the related Sarvāstivāda list of six "causes" (HETU).

**pratyekabuddha**. (P. paccekabuddha; T. rang sangs rgyas; C. yuanjue/dujue; J. engaku/dokukaku; K. yŏn'gak/tokkak 緣覺/獨覺). In Sanskrit, "individually enlightened one" or "solitary buddha"; an ARHAT who becomes enlightened through his own efforts without receiving instruction from a buddha in his final lifetime. Unlike the "perfectly enlightened buddhas" (SAMYAKSAṂBUDDHA), the pratyekabuddha refrains from teaching others about his experience because he has neglected to develop the same degree of great compassion (MAHĀKARUṆĀ) that motivates the samyaksaṃbuddhas. Even though he does not teach others, he may still guide by example, or through the use of gestures. Pratyekabuddhas are also distinguished from those who achieve the goal of arhat via the ŚRĀVAKA ("disciple") path, because śrāvakas are unable to achieve enlightenment on their own and must be instructed in the principles of Buddhism in order to succeed in their practice. A pratyekabuddha is also distinguished from the śrāvaka by the duration of his path: the pratyekabuddha path is longer because he must accumulate the necessary amount of merit (PUṆYA) to allow him to achieve liberation without relying on a teacher in his final lifetime. A pratyekabuddha is said to achieve liberation through contemplation of the principle of dependent origination (PRATĪTYASAMUTPĀDA), which accounts for the Chinese translation of yuanjue ("awakening via conditionality"). Two types of pratyekabuddhas are commonly enumerated in the literature: those who wander alone "like a rhinoceros" (KHAḌGAVIṢĀṆAKALPA) and the "congregators" (VARGACĀRIN). According to the MAHĀYĀNA, the path of the pratyekabuddha, together with the path of the śrāvaka, constitutes the HĪNAYĀNA, or "lesser vehicle"; these two categories are also often referred to as the "two vehicles" (C. ER SHENG) and their followers as "two-vehicle adherents." These lesser "two vehicles" contrast with the third and highest vehicle, the BODHISATTVAYĀNA.

**pratyekabuddhayāna**. (T. rang rgyal gyi theg pa; C. yuanjue sheng; J. engakujō; K. yŏn'gak sŭng 緣覺乘). In Sanskrit, "pratyekabuddha vehicle"; one of the three vehicles (TRIYĀNA), along with the ŚRĀVAKAYĀNA and the BODHISATTAYĀNA. MAHĀYĀNA sūtras and treatises classify the pratyekabuddhayāna as a form of the HĪNAYĀNA. Like the śrāvakayāna, the path of the PRATYEKABUDDHA culminates in achieving the enlightenment of an ARHAT, although according to some sources the path of the pratyekabuddha takes longer because he must master that path on his own, without instruction from a buddha in his final lifetime. In the ABHISAMAYĀLAṂKĀRA, pratyekabuddhas are said to eliminate the misconception of objects (grāhyavikalpa), but to be unable to eliminate the misconception of a subject (grāhakavikalpa); see GRĀHYAGRĀHAKAVIKALPA.

**pratyekanaraka**. (P. paccekaniraya; T. nye 'khor ba'i dmyal ba; C. gu diyu; J. kojigoku; K. ko chiok 孤地獄). In Sanskrit, "neighboring hell" or "surrounding hell," a group of hells (S. naraka; cf. NĀRAKA). In traditional Buddhist cosmology the main hells are a system of eight hot hells and eight cold hells, located beneath the surface of the continent of JAMBUDVĪPA. According to the ABHIDHARMAKOŚABHĀṢYA, four neighboring hells are located on each of the four sides of the eight hot hells. It is said that, as the hell denizens exit one of the hot hells, they must pass through these four. The four are named: (1) KUKŪLA or "heated by burning chaff," a pit of hot ashes where the hell denizens are burned; seeing what appears to be water ahead, they plunge into (2) KUṆAPA, "mud of corpses," a swamp of rotting corpses; emerging from this, they set out on (3) KṢURAMĀRGA, "razor road," a road made of sword blades, which the hell denizens must walk before entering a grove of swords (ASIPATTRAVANA) where blades fall from the trees and where they are forced to climb trees embedded with iron spikes (AYAḤŚĀLMALĪVANA); finally they enter (4) NADĪ VAITARAṆĪ, "river difficult to ford," a river of boiling water in which the hell denizens are forced to swim.

**Pratyutpannabuddhasaṃmukhāvasthitasamādhisūtra**. (T. Da ltar gyi sangs rgyas mngon sum du bzhugs pa'i ting nge 'dzin gyi mdo; C. Banzhou sanmei jing; J. Hanju zanmaikyō; K. Panju sammae kyŏng 般舟三昧經). In Sanskrit, "Sūtra on the SAMĀDHI for Encountering Face-to-Face the Buddhas of the Present," often known by its abbreviated title *Pratyutpannasamādhisūtra*; one of the earliest MAHĀYĀNA SŪTRAS, and one of the very first Mahāyāna sūtras to be translated into Chinese, by the Indo-Scythian monk LOKAKṢEMA in 179 CE. (There are also three other Chinese translations, as well as Tibetan and Mongolian recensions.) The sūtra sets forth a meditation and visualization practice (which seems related to the traditional "recollection of the Buddha," or BUDDHĀNUSMṚTI), whereby one is able to come directly into the presence of the buddhas of the present in various world systems. An adept was to sit in meditation for up to seven days, facing the direction of his or her preferred buddha and visualizing that buddha's thirty-two major marks (MAHĀPURUṢALAKṢAṆA) and his eighty minor characteristics (ANUVYAÑJANA) until he had a vision of that buddha in his world system. Through this visualization, one could receive the teachings of one's preferred buddha, transmit those teachings to others, and then be reborn in that buddha's realm (BUDDHAKṢETRA). Because AMITĀBHA is used as an example of how to apply this technique, this sūtra is retrospectively associated in East Asia with PURE LAND traditions. The sūtra also contains expositions of the doctrine of emptiness (ŚŪNYATĀ), in which the insubstantiality of meditative experiences can be extended to all phenomena, a perspective that seems to adumbrate later YOGĀCĀRA views on the projection of external phenomena by the mind. Like many other early Mahāyāna sūtras, the text also extols both lay and monastic practice, the worship of STŪPAs, the making of buddha images, and the veneration of texts. Because the sūtra describes a technique for hearing (viz. learning) new Buddhist teachings even after ŚĀKYAMUNI Buddha has passed into PARINIRVĀṆA, this technique might have been employed to authenticate the production of new Mahāyāna sūtras.

**pravāraṇā**. (P. pavāraṇā; T. dgag phye; C. zizi; J. jishi; K. chaja 自恣). In Sanskrit, "invitation" or "presentation," the monastic ceremony that marks the end of the annual rains retreat (VARṢĀ). (The Tibetan translation denotes the "separation from prohibition" that accompanies the end of the rains retreat; the Chinese translation zizi has the connotation of "self-indulgence," suggesting that monks are then free to "follow their own bent.") The purity of the SAṂGHA is reaffirmed by each monk by asking the community whether he committed any infraction of the code of discipline (PRĀTIMOKṢA) during the period of the retreat. In the Southeast Asian traditions, the ceremony is held at the end of the rains retreat (varṣā) on the full-moon day of the seventh or eighth lunar month (usually between September and November), at which time each monk resident at a monastery invites the monastic community to point out any wrongs he may have committed that were either seen, heard, or suspected. The pravāraṇā must be performed at a single site by all eligible members of a given saṃgha, although if a monk is ill, he may dispatch his invitation through an intermediary. A monk guilty of an offense that has not been expiated may not participate. According to VINAYA strictures, the pravāraṇā ceremony may not be performed in the presence of the following kinds of persons: nuns, women in training to become nuns, male and female novices, persons who have seceded from the order, monastics guilty of a PĀRĀJIKA offense, monks who refuse to acknowledge their own wrongdoing (of three kinds), eunuchs, false monks who wear monastic attire without having been ordained, monks who have joined other religions, nonhumans, patricides, matricides, murderers of an ARHAT, seducers of nuns, schismatics, those who have shed the blood of a buddha, hermaphrodites, and laypersons. Traditionally on the pravāraṇā day, laypeople would come to the monastery and make offerings of necessary requisites to the monks throughout the day on behalf of their parents and deceased ancestors. The Chinese pilgrim YIJING (635–713) in his NANHAI JIGUI NEIFA ZHUAN describes pravāraṇā as an elaborate communal festival, with senior monks delivering protracted dharma lectures throughout the day and night; lamps were lit and flowers and incense offered as laypeople distributed gifts to the entire saṃgha.

**pravrājanīyakarman**. (P. pabbājanīyakamma; T. bskrad pa'i las; C. quchu jiemo; J. kushutsukonma; K. kuch'ul kalma 驅出羯磨). In Sanskrit, "eccclesiastial act of banishment," a temporary expulsion from full participation in the SAṂGHA, as a result of certain misdeeds. A monk may be subject to such banishment if he is guilty of corrupting good families (kuladūṣaka) or indulges in frivolous worldly behavior such as wearing garlands, playing, singing, or dancing; if he is quarrelsome or indiscreet in his behavior, or adheres to perverse doctrinal views; and if he criticizes any of the three jewels (RATNATRAYA) of the Buddha, the DHARMA, or the saṃgha, harms others through unwholesome speech and action, or engages in wrong livelihood. A monk against whom a pravrājanīyakarman has been passed must leave his monastery and take up residence elsewhere while observing a number of restrictions. He may not confer UPASAṂPADĀ ordination or offer guidance (NIŚRAYA) to, or accept the services of, a novice; he may not accept an invitation to preach to nuns or actually preach to nuns; he should not repeat the offense for which he was banished or any similar or more serious offense; he should not criticize the decision passed against him or criticize the person(s) responsible for the decision. He may not object to the presence of any other monk at the UPOṢADHA or PRAVĀRAṆĀ ceremonies or interrogate another monk about alleged offenses; he may not reprimand other monks or cause a quarrel among other monks. When the saṃgha is satisfied that he has been rehabilitated, it is enjoined to revoke the act of banishment and restore the monk to full membership in the saṃgha.

**pravrajita**. (P. pabbajjā; T. rab tu byung ba; C. chujia; J. shukke; K. ch'ulga 出家). In Sanskrit, lit. "going forth," to leave behind the household life of a layperson in order to enter the monastic community as a religious mendicant; also pravrajyā and other variations. The term is often seen translated into English as "gone forth into homelessness" (the Chinese translation literally means "leaving home"). Pravrajita/pravrajyā is a technical term that refers to the lower ordination of a person as a ŚRĀMAṆERA or ŚRĀMAṆERIKĀ, that is, as a male or female novice. Admission of a novice into the SAṂGHA is performed with a simple ceremony. According to the Pāli tradition, the candidate shaves his hair and beard and, attiring himself in a monk's robe (CĪVARA) received from a donor, he presents himself before an assembly of monks, or a single monk of ten years' standing or more. Squatting on his haunches and folding his hands, the candidate recites the refuge formula three times (TRIŚARAṆA), whereupon he is made a novice. In most VINAYA traditions, a novice must observe ten precepts (ŚIKṢĀPADA, ŚRĀMAṆERASAṂVARA): abstaining from (1) killing, (2) stealing, (3) sexual intercourse, (4) lying, (5) intoxicants, (6) eating after midday, (7) dancing, singing, music, and other unseemly forms of entertainment, (8) using garlands, perfumes, and unguents to adorn the body, (9) using high and luxurious beds and couches, and (10) accepting gold and silver. The MŪLASARVĀSTIVĀDA VINAYA (which is followed in Tibet) expands these ten precepts to thirty-six. After receiving the lower ordination, the novice is required to live under the guidance (NIŚRAYA) of a teacher until he or she receives higher ordination (UPASAṂPADĀ) as a fully ordained monk (BHIKṢU) or nun (BHIKṢUṆĪ). The novice may not attend the reading of the PRĀTIMOKṢA during the bimonthly UPOṢADHA (P. uposatha) ceremony, or participate in any formal acts of the order (SAMGHAKARMAN), such as giving ordination, and so on. At the beginning of his dispensation, the Buddha did not confer the lower ordination of a novice separately from the higher ordination, or upasaṃpadā, of a fully ordained monk. In all cases, candidates simply took the going forth as a fully ordained monk by taking the refuge formula. Later, "going forth" and higher ordination (upasaṃpadā) were made into separate ceremonies to initiate candidates into two hierarchically ranked institutions: the novitiate and full monkhood. The following types of persons may not be ordained as novices: branded thieves, fugitives from the law, registered thieves, those punished by flogging or branding, patricides, matricides, murderers of ARHATs, those who have shed the blood of a buddha, eunuchs, false monks, seducers of nuns, hermaphrodites, persons who are maimed, disabled, or deformed in various ways, and those afflicted with various communicable diseases.

**pravrajyā**. (S). See PRAVRAJITA.

**prāyaścittaka**. (S). See PĀYATTIKA.

**prayer flag**. See RLUNG RTA.

**prayer wheel**. See MA ṆI 'KHOR LO.

**prayoga**. (T. sbyor ba; C. jiaxing; J. kegyō; K. kahaeng 加行). In Sanskrit, "application," "preparation," "joining together," "exertion." The term is widely used in soteriological, tantric, and astrological literature. It also functions as a technical term in logic, where it is often translated as "syllogism" and refers to a statement that contains a subject, a predicate, and a reason. A correct syllogism is composed of three parts, the subject (dharmin), the property being proved (SĀDHYADHARMA), and the reason (HETU or LIṄGA). For example, in the syllogism "Sound is impermanent because of being produced," the subject is sound, the property being proved is impermanence, and the reason is being produced. In order for the syllogism to be correct, three relations must exist among the three components of the syllogism: (1) the reason must be a property (DHARMA) of the subject, also called the "position" (PAKṢA), (2) there must be a relationship of pervasion (VYĀPTI) between the reason and the property being proved (SĀDHYADHARMA), such that whatever is the reason is necessarily the property being proved, and (3) there must be a relationship of "exclusion" or reverse pervasion (vyatirekavyāpti) between the property being proved and the reason, such that whatever is not the property being proved is necessarily not the reason. ¶ In the PRAJÑĀPĀRAMITĀ exegetical tradition based on the ABHISAMAYĀLAṂKĀRA, prayoga is the word used for the fourth to seventh of the eight ABHISAMAYAS ("clear realizations"). According to Ārya VIMUKTISENA's commentary (*Vṛtti*), the first three chapters set forth the three knowledges (JÑĀNA) as topics to be studied and reflected upon (see ŚRUTAMAYĪPRAJÑĀ, CINTĀMAYĪPRAJÑĀ); the next four chapters set forth the practice of those knowledges, viz. the practice of the knowledge of a buddha. This practice is called prayoga. It is primarily at the level of meditation (BHĀVANĀMAYĪPRAJÑĀ), and it leads to the SARVĀKĀRAJÑATĀ, a buddha's omniscient knowledge of all aspects. The first prayoga is habituation to the perfect realization of all aspects (sarvākārābhisambodha); the second is learning to remain at the summit of the realization (mūrdhābhisamaya; cf. MŪRDHAN); the third is a further habituation to each aspect, one by one (anupūrvābhisamaya); and the fourth is the realization of all aspects in one single instant (ekakṣaṇābhisamaya). This is the moment prior to omniscience. This prayoga is first detailed in twenty subtopics beginning with the cryptic statement that the practice is no practice at all; the 173 aspects (ĀKĀRA) that together cover the entire range of a bodhisattva's practice are set forth at all the stages of development, through the paths of vision (DARŚANAMĀRGA) and cultivation (BHĀVANĀMĀRGA) up through the bodhisattva stages (BHŪMI) to the purification of the buddha-field (BUDDHAKṢETRA) and final instants of the path. Through the first of the four prayogas, the bodhisattva gains mastery over all the aspects; through the second, he abides in the mastery of them; with the third, he goes through each and makes the practice special; and with the fourth, he enters into the state of a buddha. See also PRAYOGAMĀRGA.

**prayogamārga**. (T. sbyor lam; C. jiaxing dao; J. kegyōdō; K. kahaeng to 加行道). In Sanskrit, "path of preparation," the second stage of the five-path (PAÑCAMĀRGA) soteriological schema, which follows the path of accumulation (SAṂBHĀRAMĀRGA) and precedes the path of vision (DARŚANAMĀRGA). It is said to provide the "preparation" for the direct perception of reality that will occur on the path of vision. The path of preparation begins with the attainment of an understanding of reality at a level of concentration that is equal to or exceeding the state of serenity (ŚAMATHA). This understanding corresponds to the "wisdom generated by meditation" (BHĀVANĀMAYĪPRAJÑĀ). The path of preparation has four levels (see NIRVEDHABHĀGĪYA): heat (ŪṢMAN), peak (MŪRDHA), forbearance (KṢĀNTI), and supreme worldly dharmas (LAUKIKĀGRADHARMA). Like the preceding path of accumulation, it is not a "noble path" (ĀRYAMĀRGA) because the direct perception of reality has not yet not occurred here. With the completion of the path of preparation and the attainment of the path of vision, one passes from the state of being an ordinary being (PṚTHAGJANA) to that of a noble person (ĀRYA).

**precepts**. See ŚĪLA.

**precepts, eight**. See AṢṬĀṄGASAMANVĀGATAM UPAVĀSAM; ŚĪLA.

**precepts, five**. See PAÑCAŚĪLA.

**precepts, three categories of**. See ŚĪLATRAYA.

**prediction [of future buddhahood]**. See VYĀKARAṆA.

**predispositions**. See VĀSANĀ.

**preliminary practices**. See SNGON 'GRO.

**preta**. (P. peta; T. yi dwags; C. egui; J. gaki; K. agwi 餓鬼). In Sanskrit, lit. "departed one" or "ghost"; typically translated into English as "hungry ghost" (reflecting the Chinese rendering egui). The realm of hungry ghosts is one of the three or four unfortunate realms of rebirth (APĀYA; DURGATI), along with hell denizens (NĀRAKA), animals (TIRYAK), and sometimes demigods or titans (ASURA). Ghosts are most commonly depicted as having distended abdomens and emaciated limbs, like a human suffering from extreme malnutrition. Some traditions also say that they have gullets the size of the eye of a needle, so they are never able to consume enough to satiate their appetite. (This depiction of pretas as big-bellied and small-mouthed does not appear in Pāli and Southeast Asian sources until some late cosmological texts that date to the second millennium CE, suggesting that this is a north Indian or Sanskritic tradition, not a Pāli development.) Pretas are said to have been reborn in their unfortunate condition as a consequence of greed and avarice in a previous life. They spend their existence wandering in a futile search for food and drink; when they approach a river to drink, the water turns into blood and pus, and when they find food, they are unable to digest it due to various impediments, such as knots in their throats, or suffer when it is swallowed, when food turns into spears and molten iron. Traditions vary as to the location of the realm of ghosts, but there are many stories of the Buddha and his monks encountering ghosts. Feeding these departed spirits is an important ritual for Buddhist monks in many societies (see FANG YANKOU). Stories of encounters with such ghosts, who typically recount the unwholesome past deeds that led them to rebirth in such an unfortunate state, are common in Buddhist literature, as in the Pāli PETAVATTHU. The realm of the pretas also includes other ogres and goblins, such as PIŚĀCA.

**Pretamukhāgnivālayaśarakāra**. (S). See FANG YANKOU.

**Pretapurī**. (S). One of the twenty-four sacred sites associated with the CAKRASAṂVARATANTRA. See PĪṬHA.

**pride**. See MADA.

**prīti**. (P. pīti; T. dga' ba; C. xi; J. ki; K. hŭi 喜). In Sanskrit, "rapture," "joy," "zest"; the third of the five factors of meditative absorption (DHYĀNĀṄGA) and the fourth of the seven factors of enlightenment (BODHYAṄGA); rapture helps to control the mental hindrances (NĪVARAṆA) of both malice (VYĀPĀDA) and sloth and torpor (STYĀNA–MIDDHA). A sustained sense of prīti is obstructed by malice (vyāpāda), the second of the five hindrances to DHYĀNA. Prīti refreshes both body and mind and manifests itself as physical and mental tranquillity (PRAŚRABDHI). The most elemental types of prīti involve such physical reactions as horripilation (viz., hair standing on end). As the experience becomes ever more intense, it becomes "transporting rapture," which is so uplifting that it makes the body seem so light as almost to levitate. Ultimately, rapture becomes "all-pervading happiness" that suffuses the body and mind, cleansing it of ill will and tiredness. As both a physical and mental experience, prīti is present during both the first and second of the meditative absorptions associated with the subtle-materiality realm (RŪPĀVACARADHYĀNA), but fades into equanimity (UPEKṢĀ). In the even subtler third dhyāna, only mental ease (SUKHA) and one-pointedness (EKĀGRATĀ) remain. Divinities in the ŚUDDHĀVĀSA realm (viz., the five "pure abodes," the upper five of the eight heavens associated with the fourth dhyāna) and the ĀBHĀSVARALOKA (heaven of universal radiance) divinities are said literally to "feed on joy" (S. prītibhakṣa; P. pītibhakkha), i.e., to survive solely on the sustenance of physical and mental rapture.

**prītijanana**. (P. pītijanana; T. dga' ba bskyed; C. faxi J. hōki; K. pŏphŭi 法喜). In Sanskrit, lit. "joy inducing," viz. "joy of dharma," referring to the uplifting feelings of rapture that derive from properly observing precepts (ŚĪLA, e.g., to be morally "blameless" and harboring no regrets or shame) and from hearing, understanding, or practicing the dharma. Depending on its intensity, this joy may manifest in different ways, ranging from a radiant complexion, horripilation, and goose bumps, to ecstatic physical levitation. In the context of meditative absorption (DHYĀNA), such rapture is said to be conducive to the development of concentration and tranquillity.

**priyavādita**. (S). See SAṂGRAHAVASTU.

**progressive instruction**. See ANUPUBBIKATHĀ.

**pṛṣṭhalabdhajñāna**. [alt. tatpṛṣṭhalabdhajñāna] (T. rjes thob ye shes; C. houde zhi; J. gotokuchi; K. hudŭk chi 後得智). In Sanskrit, "subsequent wisdom" or "subsequently obtained wisdom"; a term used to describe one of the states of the noble path (ĀRYAMĀRGA). The attainment of the path of vision (DARŚANAMĀRGA) marks the first achievement of meditative equipoise (SAMĀHITA) in which the meditator has a direct and nonconceptual vision of reality. When the meditator withdraws from that state of direct realization to again perceive various phenomena, this state is called "subsequent wisdom." Reality is no longer being directly and exclusively perceived, but the power of that vision is said to infuse one's subsequent experience of the world, so that while objects may once again appear to be real, the meditator does not assent to that false appearance. Following the attainment of the path of vision, the meditator continues to proceed along the path through periods of meditative equipoise and subsequent wisdom.

**pṛthagjana**. (P. puthujjana; T. so so skye bo; C. fanfu; J. bonbu; K. pŏmbu 凡夫). In Sanskrit, "ordinary being," or "common person"; sentient beings who are still bound by the ten fetters (SAṂYOJANA) and thus have not attained the path of a noble person (ĀRYAMĀRGA)—that is, they have not yet become a stream-enterer (SROTAĀPANNA) or achieved the path of vision (DARŚANAMĀRGA). The ordinary being is often compared (unfavorably) to the noble person (ĀRYA) in Buddhist texts. It is said, for example, that the FOUR NOBLE TRUTHS (catvāry āryasatyāni) are called "noble" because they are true for noble persons, not for ordinary beings. Elsewhere, it is said that the suffering (DUḤKHA) associated with conditionality itself (SAṂSKĀRADUḤKATĀ) is like a wisp of wool in the palm of the hand for an ordinary person, in the sense that it is easily unnoticed; for the noble person, however, it is like a wisp of wool in the eye: It is utterly impossible not to notice it, and immediate effort is made to remove it.

**pṛthivī**. [alt. pṛthivīdhātu] (P. paṭhavī; T. sa; C. dida; J. jidai; K. chidae 地大). In Sanskrit, lit. "earth" or "ground," viz., the property of "solidity"; one of the four "great elements" (MAHĀBHŪTA) or "major elementary qualities" of which the physical world comprised of materiality (RŪPA) is composed, along with wind (viz. motion, movement, VĀYU, P. vāyu/vāyo), water (viz. cohesion, ĀPAS, P. āpo), and fire (viz. temperature, warmth, TEJAS, P. tejo). "Earth" is characterized by hardness and firmness, and can refer to anything that exhibits solidity. Because earth has temperature (viz. fire) and tangibility (viz. water), and is capable of motion (viz. wind), the existence of the other three elements may also be inferred even in that single element. In the physical body, this element is associated with hair, bones, teeth, organs, and so on. ¶ Pṛthivī, "Earth," is also the proper name of the goddess of the earth, also known as STHĀVARĀ, or "Immovable," who played a crucial role in the story of GAUTAMA Buddha's enlightenment. When the BODHISATTVA's right to occupy the sacred spot beneath the BODHI TREE was challenged by MĀRA, Gautama touched the earth (BHŪMISPARŚAMUDRĀ) with his right hand, calling on the goddess of the earth to testify to his boundless meritorious deeds over his past lives. She responded by causing a mild earthquake or, in other versions of the story, emerging from the earth to bear witness. See also THORANI.

**Pucheng**. (C) (普成). Son of the early Chinese lay figure FU DASHI (497–569). See FU DASHI.

**puch'ŏ[nim]**. (K) (부처님). Standard term for "buddha" in Korean. The compound is composed of the transcription puch'ŏ (buddha), typically followed by the honorific suffix nim. See BUDDHA.

**pudgala**. (P. puggala; T. gang zag; C. ren/buteqieluo; J. nin/futogara; K. in/pot'ŭkkara 人/補特伽羅). In Sanskrit, "person." Although all Buddhist schools deny the existence of a perduring, autonomous self (ĀTMAN), some schools accepted the provisional existence of a person that is associated with one or more of the aggregates (SKANDHA). There is a wide range of opinion as to the precise status of the person. Most Buddhist schools hold that the person is a provisional designation (PRAJÑAPTI), but differ as to which among the constituents of mind and body could be designated by the term "person," with some schools asserting that all five aggregates are designated as the person, while others that only the mental consciousness (MANOVIJÑĀNA) is the person. The philosophical challenge faced by the Buddhist schools is to be able to uphold the continuity (SAṂTĀNA) of the accumulation and experience of KARMAN over the course of a single lifetime as well as potentially infinite lifetimes in both past and future, while simultaneously upholding the fundamental impermanence of mind and matter and the absence of a permanent self (ANĀTMAN). The VĀTSĪPUTRĪYA and the SAṂMITĪYA responded to the problem of accounting for personal continuity and rebirth when there is no perduring self by positing the existence of an "inexpressible" (S. avācya) "person" that is neither permanent nor impermanent and which is neither the same as nor different from the aggregates (skandha), but which is the agent of cognition and the bearer of action (KARMAN) from moment to moment and lifetime to lifetime. This position was criticized by other Buddhist schools, including in the ninth chapter of the ABHIDHARMAKOŚABHĀṢYA, where VASUBANDHU condemns this view as the heretical assertion of a permanent self or soul (ĀTMAN). Pudgala is more generically also used in a salutary sense in connection with noble persons (ĀRYAPUDGALA) who have achieved one of the four stages of sanctity. See also ŚREṆIKA HERESY.

**pudgalanairātmya**. (T. gang zag gi bdag med; C. renwuwo; J. ninmuga; K. inmua 人無我). In Sanskrit, "selflessness of the person," one of two types of nonself or selflessness, along with DHARMANAIRĀTMYA, the nonself or selflessness of phenomena. The absence of self (ANĀTMAN) is often divided into these two categories by MAHĀYĀNA philosophical schools, with the selflessness of persons referring to the absence of self among the five aggregates (SKANDHA) that constitute the person, and the selflessness of phenomena referring to the absence of self (variously defined) in all other phenomena in the universe, specifically the factors (DHARMA) that were posited to be real by several of the abhidharma traditions of mainstream Buddhism, and especially the SARVĀSTIVĀDA. Numerous meditation practices are set forth that are designed to lead the realization of the selflessness of the person, many of which involve the close mental examination of the constituents of mind and body to determine which might constitute, individually or collectively, an independent and autonomous agent of actions and the experiencer of their effects, that is, the referent of the "I" and for whom possessions are "mine." The central claim of Buddhism is that there is no such self to be found among the constituents of the person; thus, the realization of this fact constitutes a liberating knowledge that brings an end to suffering and the prospect of further rebirth. The relation between the selflessness of persons and the selflessness of phenomena is discussed at length in Buddhist philosophical literature. In some Mahāyāna systems, the selflessness of persons is considered to be less profound than the selflessness of phenomena, since an adept is able to achieve liberation as an ARHAT through cognition of the selflessness of persons alone, while cognition of the selflessness of phenomena is required of the BODHISATTVA in order to achieve buddhahood.

**pudgalātmagraha**. (T. gang zag gi bdag 'dzin; C. renwozhi; J. ningashū; K. inajip 人我執). In Sanskrit, lit.,"conception of a self of a person" or the "grasping at the personal self," a term that is used in combination with DHARMĀTMAGRAHA, the "conception of the self of phenomena." In the MAHĀYĀNA philosophical schools, the notion of self (ĀTMAN) is expanded beyond that of a permanent soul in each person, to a broader sense of independent existence or intrinsic existence (SVABHĀVA) that is falsely imagined to exist in all objects of experience. Sentient beings are thus said to falsely imagine the presence of such a self in two broad categories: persons (PUDGALA) and all other phenomena (DHARMA). Wisdom (PRAJÑĀ) entails understanding the lack of self in these two categories, referred to as the selflessness of persons (PUDGALANAIRĀTMYA) and the selflessness of phenomena (DHARMANAIRĀTMYA). Among the path theories of YOGĀCĀRA and MADHYAMAKA, there are differences of opinion as to whether the conception of the self of persons is more easily uprooted than the conception of the self of phenomena. In addition, although all agree that both forms of the conception of self must be eradicated by the BODHISATTVA in order to become a buddha, there are differences of opinion as to whether both must be eradicated by the ŚRĀVAKA and PRATYEKABUDDHA in order to become an ARHAT.

**pudgalavāda**. (P. puggalavāda; T. gang zag smra ba; C. buteqieluo lun; J. futogararon; K. pot'ŭkkara non 補特伽羅論). In Sanskrit, "proponents of a person" or "personalists," a term (not apparently employed by its adherents) used to refer to several mainstream (that is, non-MAHĀYĀNA) schools of Indian Buddhism (including the VĀTSĪPUTRĪYA and the SAṂMITĪYA) that responded to the problem of how to account for personal continuity and rebirth when there is no perduring self (ANĀTMAN) by positing the existence of an "inexpressible" (S. avācya) "person" that is neither permanent nor impermanent and which is neither the same as nor different from the aggregates (SKANDHA), but which is the agent of cognition and the bearer of action (KARMAN) from moment to moment and lifetime to lifetime. Although its adherents presumed that this position conformed to the Buddha's dictum that there was no self to be discovered among the aggregates, it was criticized by other Buddhist schools, including in the ninth chapter of the ABHIDHARMAKOŚABHĀṢYA, where it was seen as the heretical assertion of a permanent self or soul (ĀTMAN). Despite vehement opposition from rival mainstream Buddhist schools, Chinese pilgrims reported the prominence in India of schools that held pudgalavāda positions, although whether all the monks of a particular ordination lineage held all the philosophical positions associated with this tradition remains a question.

The problem of personal and karmic continuity from lifetime to lifetime without positing a perduring a self or soul is a persistent issue throughout the history of Buddhist thought, and it is addressed in the Mahāyāna, for example, through the YOGĀCĀRA school's doctrine of the foundational consciousness (ĀLAYAVIJÑĀNA). See also ŚREṆIKA HERESY.

**Puggalapaññatti**. In Pāli, lit., "Concept of the Person," "Analysis of Character Types"; the fourth of the seven books of the Pāli ABHIDHAMMAPIṬAKA. It is a classification of human personalities following the method of the AṄGUTTARANIKĀYA, grouping types of persons in categories of from one to ten elements, in ascending order. In the STHAVIRANIKĀYA, the person was seen not as a real phenomenon (P. dhamma, S. DHARMA), but was instead a mere designation or concept (P. paññati, S. PRAJÑAPTI), hence the title of the work. Some sections of the *Puggalapaññatti* are drawn nearly verbatim from the *Aṅguttaranikāya*, while others are taken from the SAṄGĪTISUTTA, a scripture in the DĪGHANIKĀYA that likewise uses the *Aṅguttara* method. Indeed, because the work draws much of its form and its content from discussions of the nature of the person in the SUTTAPIṬAKA, some scholars speculate that the *Puggalapaññatti* may be belong to the earliest stratum of Pāli ABHIDHAMMA materials.

**Puhyu Sŏnsu**. (浮休善修) (1543–1615). Korean Sŏn master of the Chosŏn dynasty. Sŏnsu was a native of Osu in present-day North Chŏlla province. In 1562, he went to CHIRISAN, where he became the student of a certain Sinmyŏng (d.u.) and later continued his studies under the Sŏn master Puyong Yŏnggwan (1485–1571). He was especially renowned for his calligraphy. Sŏnsu survived the Japanese Hideyoshi invasions from 1592 to 1598 and resided after the war at the monastery of HAEINSA. Sŏnsu and his disciple PYŎGAM KAKSŎNG were once falsely accused by another monk and were subsequently imprisoned; they were released later when the king learned of their innocence. In 1614, Sŏnsu went to the hermitage of Ch'ilburam at the monastery of SONGGWANGSA and passed away the next year after entrusting his disciples to Kaksŏng. He was given the posthumous title Honggak Tŭnggye (Expansive Enlightenment, Mastery of All). He left over seven hundred disciples, seven of whom became renowned Sŏn masters in their own right and formed separate branches of Sŏnsu's lineage. His writings can be found in the *Puhyudang chip*.

**pūjā**. (T. mchod pa; C. gongyang; J. kuyō; K. kongyang 供養). In Sanskrit, lit. "worship" and "offering"; any "ritual" at which offerings are made, or the offerings themselves. These offering rituals involve a number of standard liturgies, including those in three parts (TRISKANDHAKA) and seven parts (SAPTĀṄGAVIDHI). In the MAHĀYĀNA, many pūjās seem to derive from a simple three-part liturgy, which appeared in two forms. One form consisted of (1) the confession of transgressions (PĀPADEŚANĀ), (2) the admiration of others' virtues (ANUMODANA), and (3) the dedication of merit (PARIṆĀMANĀ). The other consisted of (1) the confession of transgressions, (2) the admiration of others' virtue, and (3) the request to the buddhas to turn the wheel of the dharma (DHARMACAKRAPRAVARTANA). This tripartite ritual was eventually expanded to include seven sections: obeisance, offering, confession, admiration, supplication to the buddhas and bodhisattvas to teach the dharma, entreaty not to pass into PARINIRVĀṆA, and dedication of any merit accrued by performing the preceding ritual to the enlightenment of all sentient beings. This sevenfold liturgy, presented most famously in the opening twelve stanzas of the BHADRACARĪPRAṆIDHĀNA ("Vow of SAMANTABHADRA's Deeds"), the last section of the GAṆḌAVYŪHA in the AVATAṂSAKASŪTRA, became a standard part of many MAHĀYĀNA practices, often serving as a prolegomenon to a meditation session. This sevenfold liturgy became a common element of tantric pūjās as well.

**Puji**. (J. Fujaku; K. Pojŏk 普寂) (651–739). In Chinese, "Universal Quiescence"; CHAN monk and disciple of SHENXIU (606?–706) in the so-called "Northern School" (BEI ZONG) of the early Chan tradition. In his youth, Puji is said to have studied a wide range of Buddhist scriptures before ordaining at the age of thirty-eight. Soon afterwards, he left to study with Shenxiu at Yuquansi (Jade Spring Monastery) on Mt. Dangyang in Jingzhou. As the best-known disciple of Shenxiu, Puji was one of the subjects of a series of polemical attacks by the HEZE SHENHUI (684–758) beginning in 732. Shenhui denounced Puji and other disciples of Shenxiu as representing a mere collateral branch of BODHIDHARMA's lineage and for promoting what Shenhui called a "gradual" (jian) approach to enlightenment. Shenhui instead promoted a "sudden teaching" (DUNJIAO), which he claimed derived from a so-called "Southern school" (NAN ZONG) founded by HUINENG (638–713), whom Shenhui claimed was the true successor of the fifth patriarch HONGREN (601–74). Later Chan historians such as GUIFENG ZONGMI (780–841) came to refer to a "Northern school" (Bei zong) of Chan to describe this lineage of Shenxiu's, to which Puji, Yifu (661–736), and XIANGMO ZANG (d.u.) were said to have belonged.

**Pujian**. (C) (普建). Son of the early Chinese lay figure FU DASHI (497–569). See FU DASHI.

**Pulcho chikchi simch'e yojŏl**. (佛組直指心體要節). In Korean, "Essential Excerpts of the Buddhas and Patriarchs Pointing Directly to the Essence of Mind," also known by the abbreviated titles *Chikchi simch'e yojŏl*, or simply *Chikchi*; the earliest surviving example from anywhere in the world of a text printed using movable metal type, predating Gutenberg's 1455 printing of the Bible by seventy-eight years. The two-roll lineage anthology of the CHAN school was compiled in 1372 by PAEGUN KYŎNGHAN (1299–1374), one of the three great Sŏn masters of the late-Koryŏ dynasty. This anthology was first printed in 1377 at Hŭngdŏksa (the ruins of which were located in 1985 in Unch'ŏndong, near the city of Ch'ŏngju in South Korea) using movable cast-metal type. This printing technology was known to have been in use in Koryŏ–period Korea prior to the Mongol invasions of 1231–1232, but no examples survive. The metal-type printing of the *Chikchi* is held in the collection of the Bibliothèque nationale in Paris, and its existence was first noted by Maurice Courant in 1901. The first roll of the anthology includes the enlightenment poems of the seven buddhas of antiquity (SAPTATATHĀGATA), the twenty-eight Indian patriarchs of the Sŏn school (starting with MAHĀKĀŚYAPA and ending with BODHIDHARMA), the six Chinese patriarchs (ZUSHI) of Chan, and several later Sŏn masters. The second roll is a collection of the poetry, epitaphs, discourse records, and seminal teachings of eminent masters of the Sŏn school, such as the fourteen "nondualities" (ADVAYA) of Kyŏnghan's Indian teacher ZHIKONG CHANXIAN (K. Chigong Sŏnhyŏn; S. *Dhyānabhadra). Like many of these lineage anthologies, the text is derivative, drawing on such earlier genealogical collections as the JINGDE CHUANDENG LU and the SŎNMUN YŎMSONG CHIP of CHIN'GAK HYESIM (1178–1234). Although the entire first roll and the first page of the second roll of the metal-type recension are lost, a complete xylographic edition of the anthology survives, which dates to 1378, one year later than the metal-type recension.

**Pulguksa**. (佛國寺). In Korean, "Buddha Land Monastery," located outside KYŎNGJU, the ancient capital of the Silla dynasty, on the slopes of T'oham Mountain; this Silla royal monastery is the eleventh district monastery (PONSA) of the contemporary CHOGYE CHONG of Korean Buddhism and administers over sixty subsidiary monasteries and hermitages. According to the SAMGUK YUSA ("Memorabilia of the Three Kingdoms"), Pulguksa was constructed in 751 by Kim Taesŏng (700–774), chief minister of King Kyŏngdŏk (r. 742–765), and completed in 774; it may have been constructed on the site of a smaller temple that dated from c. 528, during the reign of the Silla King Pŏphŭng (r. 514–539). Although it was a large complex, Pulguksa was not as influential within the Silla Buddhist tradition as other Kyŏngju monasteries, such as HWANGNYONGSA and PUNHWANGSA. The monastery has since been renovated numerous times, one of the largest projects occurring at the beginning of the seventeenth century, after the monastery was burned during the Japanese Hideyoshi invasions of 1592–1598. Pulguksa's temple complex is built on a series of artificial terraces that were constructed out of giant stone blocks and is entered via two pairs of stone "bridges" cum staircases, which are Korean national treasures in their own right and frequently photographed. The main level of the monastery centers on two courtyards: one anchored by the TAEUNG CHŎN, or the main shrine hall, which houses a statue of ŚĀKYAMUNI Buddha, the other by the kŭngnak chŏn, or hall of ultimate bliss (SUKHĀVATĪ), which houses an eighth-century bronze statue of the buddha AMITĀBHA. The taeung chŏn courtyard is graced with two stone pagodas, the Sŏkka t'ap (Śākyamuni STŪPA) and the Tabo t'ap (Prabhūtaratna stūpa), which are so famous that the second of them is depicted on the Korean ten-wŏn coin. The juxtaposition of the two stūpas derives from the climax of the SADDHARMAPUṆḌARĪKASŪTRA ("Lotus Sūtra"), where the buddha PRABHŪTARATNA (Many Treasures) invites Śākyamuni to sit beside him inside his bejeweled stūpa, thus validating the teachings Śākyamuni delivered in the scripture. The Sŏkka t'ap represents Śākyamuni's solitary quest for enlightenment; it is three stories tall and is notable for its bare simplicity. This stūpa is in marked contrast to its ornate twin, the Tabo t'ap, or Pagoda of the buddha Prabhūtaratna, which is modeled after a reliquary and has elaborate staircases, parapets, and stone lions (one of which was removed to the British Museum). During a 1966 renovation of the Sŏkka t'ap, the world's oldest printed document was discovered sealed inside the stūpa: the MUGUJŎNGGWANG TAEDARANI KYŎNG (S. *Raśmivimalaviśuddhaprabhādhāraṇī*; "Great DHĀRAṆĪ of Immaculate Radiance"). The terminus ad quem for the printing of the *Dhāraṇī* is 751 CE, when the text was sealed inside the Sŏkka t'ap, but it may have been printed even earlier. Other important buildings include the Piro chŏn (VAIROCANA Hall) that enshrines an eighth-century bronze statue of its eponymous buddha, which is presumed to be the oldest bronze image in Korea; the Musŏl chŏn (The Wordless Hall), a lecture hall located directly behind the taeung chŏn, which was built around 670; and the Kwanŭm chŏn (AVALOKITEŚVARA hall), built at the highest point of the complex. Two and a half miles (4 kms) up T'oham Mountain to the east of Pulguksa is its affiliated SŎKKURAM grotto temple. Pulguksa and Sŏkkuram were jointly listed in 1995 as a UNESCO World Heritage Site.

**Pullīramalaya**. (S). One of the twenty-four sacred sites associated with the CAKRASAṂVARATANTRA. See PĪṬHA.

**punarbhava**. (P. punabbhava; T. yang srid pa; C. houyou; J. gou; K. huyu 後有). In Sanskrit, lit. "re-becoming," one of the Sanskrit terms used for what in English is translated as "rebirth" or "reincarnation," along with PUNARJANMAN (and PUNARMṚTYU, or "redeath"). See REBIRTH.

**punarjanman**. (T. yang skye; C. zaisheng; J. saishō; K. chaesaeng 再生). In Sanskrit, lit. "birth again." See REBIRTH.

**punarmṛtyu**. (T. yang shi; C. zaisi; J. saishi; K. chaesa 再死). In Sanskrit, lit. "re-death." See REBIRTH.

**puṇḍarīka**. (T. padma dkar po; C. bailianhua/fentuoli hua; J. byakurenge/fundarike; K. paengnyŏnhwa/pundari hwa 白蓮華/芬陀利華). In Sanskrit, "white lotus" (Nelumbo nucifera), a specific species of lotus flower (PADMA), the ubiquitous flower appearing in Buddhist literature. The lotus is one of the most important symbols used in Buddhist literature and iconography. Because its spectacular flowers bloom above the muddy waters of stagnant ponds, the lotus is used as a symbol for the purity of mind that develops out of the pollution that is SAṂSĀRA. The puṇḍarīka lotus is especially famous in Buddhism as the "lotus" in the title of what is known in English as the "Lotus Sūtra"; the Sanskrit title is SADDHARMAPUṆḌARĪKASŪTRA, "White Lotus of the True Dharma." See also PADMA.

**Punhwangsa**. (芬皇寺). In Korean, "Fragrant [viz. Virtuous] Sovereign Monastery"; one of the four major monasteries located in the Silla-dynasty capital of Kyŏngju. The monastery was built in 634 at the command of Queen Sŏndŏk (r. 632–647) and, at its peak, its campus covered several acres. Like its neighbor HWANGNYONGSA, Punhwangsa was established with the support of the Silla royal family and was a center of rituals performed for the protection of the state (K. hoguk Pulgyo; C. HUGUO FOJIAO). Punhwangsa is perhaps best known for its massive stone pagoda, the oldest extant example from the Silla kingdom. The pagoda was erected following Chinese Tang-dynasty models, but was constructed with black andesite stone, rather than the fired bricks used in China. About 9,700 stone bricks remain from the pagoda, twenty-five percent of which are damaged or significantly weathered. The pagoda was once seven to nine stories tall with a hollow center, but only three stories remain, and the collapse of its upper stories has filled the center with debris. A partial restoration of the pagoda in 1915 revealed a reliquary box (K. sarigu; C. SHELIJU) hidden between the second and third stories. Gold ornaments, coins, scissors, and a needle were also found in the pagoda; these are thought to have once been owned by Queen Sŏndŏk herself. The pagoda is presumed to have had doorways on each of its four sides; two guardian figures flanked each doorway. Lion statues are placed at the four corners of the pagoda's foundation platform, and lotus blossoms are carved into the granite. The famous Silla artist Sol Kŏ (d.u.), who lived during the reign of King Chinhŭng (r. 540–575), painted a famous fresco of the bodhisattva AVALOKITEŚVARA at the monastery. In 755, King Kyŏngdŏk (r. 742–764) had a colossal standing image of BHAIṢAJYAGURU, the medicine buddha, cast for Punhwangsa, which was said to have weighed some 36,000 catties (kŭn). Punhwangsa was the residence of many of the most famous Korean monks of the Silla dynasty. When the VINAYA teacher CHAJANG (d.u.; fl. c. 590–658) returned in 643 from a sojourn in Tang China with a set of the Buddhist canon, as well as Buddhist banners, streamers, and other ritual items, he resided at Punhwangsa at the queen's request. The renowned monk-scholiast WŎNHYO (617–686) wrote many of his treatises and commentaries at Punhwangsa and was closely associated with the monastery. After he died, according to the SAMGUK YUSA ("Memorabilia of the Three Kingdoms"), his famous literatus son, Sŏl Ch'ong (c. 660–730), took Wŏnhyo's ashes and cast them into a lifelike image, which he enshrined at the monastery. When Sŏl Ch'ong prostrated beside it, the image is said to have turned its head to look at the son, a posture it retained from that point on. Little of Punhwangsa remains today, but it is still a functioning monastery.

**puṇya**. (P. puñña; T. bsod nams; C. fu; J. fuku; K. pok 福). In Sanskrit, "merit," the store of wholesome KARMAN created by the performance of virtuous deeds, which fructify in the form of happiness in the future. This merit may be accumulated (see PUṆYASAṂBHĀRA) over many lifetimes and dedicated toward a specific outcome (see PARIṆĀMANĀ), such as a favorable rebirth for oneself or another, or the achievement of buddhahood. The accumulation of merit, especially through charity (DĀNA) to the SAṂGHA, is one of the central practices of Buddhism across cultures and traditions, and numerous techniques for accumulating merit, increasing the store of merit, and protecting the store of merit from depletion or destruction are set forth in Buddhist texts. Pāli sources, for example, delineate three specific "grounds for producing merit" (puññakiriyavatthūni): giving (dāna), morality (P. sīla, S. ŚĪLA), and meditative practice (BHĀVANĀ). Merit can be dedicated toward a specific end, whether it is rebirth in the next lifetime, rebirth in the retinue of the future buddha MAITREYA, or the achievement of buddhahood for the welfare of all sentient beings.

**puṇyajñānasaṃbhāra**. (T. bsod nams dang ye shes kyi tshogs; C. fuzhi ziliang; J. fukuchi shiryō; K. pokchi charyang 福智資糧). In Sanskrit, "equipment" or "collection of merit and knowledge," a term that encompasses all the practices and deeds that a BODHISATTVA perfects along the path to buddhahood. It is said that a bodhisattva must amass both a collection of merit (PUṆYA) and a collection of knowledge (JÑĀNA) in order to achieve buddhahood; this is because merit will help to overcome the afflictions (KLEŚA), while knowledge will help to counter ignorance (AVIDYĀ). MAHĀYĀNA exegetes explain that the collection of merit fructifies as the material body (RŪPAKĀYA) of a buddha (which includes both the SAṂBHOGAKĀYA and the NIRMĀṆAKĀYA) and the collection of knowledge fructifies as the DHARMAKĀYA. As such, the collection of merit is associated with UPĀYA, or method, and the collection of knowledge is associated with PRAJÑĀ, or wisdom. Mahāyāna scholiasts have also explored the question of the relationship between the accumulation of these two collections and the practice of the six perfections (PĀRAMITĀ). Among various opinions set forth, a common one states that practice of the first three perfections—of giving (DĀNA), morality (ŚĪLA), patience (KṢĀNTI)—contributes to the collection of merit; the practice of the last two perfections—concentration (DHYĀNA) and wisdom (prajñā)—contributes to the collection of knowledge; and the perfection of effort (VĪRYA) contributes to both.

**puṇyakriyāvastu**. (P. puññakiriyāvatthu; T. bsod nams bya ba'i dngos po; C. fuye shi; J. fukugōji; K. pogŏpsa 福業事). In Sanskrit, "things that create merit," a term that appears in

ABHIDHARMA materials to describe three practices: giving (DĀNA), moral behavior (ŚĪLA), and meditation (BHĀVANĀ). Among forms of moral behavior, the five precepts (PAÑCAŚĪLA) of abstaining from killing, stealing, sexual misconduct, lying, and using intoxicants are considered to be especially productive of merit. Among forms of meditation, meditation on the four BRAHMAVIHĀRA of loving-kindness, compassion, joy, and equanimity are considered to be especially productive of merit.

**puṇyakṣetra**. (P. puññakkhetta; T. bsod nams kyi zhing; C. futian; J. fukuden; K. pokch'ŏn 福田). In Sanskrit, "field of merit," referring specifically to a recipient (a "field") that has a substantial potential to provide karmic compensation to a benefactor who "plants the seeds of merit" there by performing wholesome actions (KUŚALA-KARMAN), especially through acts of charity (DĀNA). Traditionally, the Buddha, the SAṂGHA as an institution, or individual monks and nuns were described as the primary fields of merit for the laity, and in this context these provide an "unsurpassed" (anuttara) "field of merit." By providing material support (dāna) such as food and robes' cloth (see KAṬHINA) to the monastic order and its members, the laity in return would reap spiritual rewards (i.e., receiving religious instructions from the renunciants) as well as karmic rewards (viz. good fortune in this life and better rebirth in the next). The use of the term eventually expanded, as in the Chinese SANJIE JIAO (School of the Third Stage), to include one's parents, the poor, the sick, the community of monks and nuns, and ultimately all sentient beings, since serving any of them involves acts of charity that would lead to the accumulation of merit. Several pairs of fields of merit are variously described in the literature. (1) The merit field of the trainee, or ŚAIKṢA (xueren tian), and the merit field of the accomplished adept, or AŚAIKṢA (wuxue ren tian). By making offerings to and supporting the spiritually accomplished (in this case, he who is "beyond training"—viz. an ARHAT), it is said that the merit accrued therefrom is greater than if the offering and support are given to someone less spiritually worthy. (2) The merit field associated with compassion (beitian) and the merit field associated with reverence (jingtian). In the Sanjie jiao school, for example, the former is exemplified by the act of giving (dāna) when it is undertaken with compassion (KARUṆĀ), such as in the case of helping the indigent; the latter is exemplified by the act of giving when it is undertaken with reverence, such as in the case of providing for the spiritually accomplished. (3) The merit field associated with anticipation (youzuo futian) and the merit field that is free from anticipation (wuzuo futian). The former refers to undertaking the act of giving with an active wish or anticipation of specific rewards; the latter is undertaken with no such wish or anticipation—and, since it is considered to stem from an unadulterated motive, will generate greater rewards. (4) The merit field associated with reverence (jingtian) and the merit field associated with (requiting) benefaction (en tian). The former is the act of giving directed toward the three jewels (RATNATRAYA); the latter, toward one's parents, teachers, and other benefactors.

**puṇyānumodana**. (T. bsod nams rjes su yi rang; C. suixifu; J. zuikifuku; K. suhŭibok 隨喜福). In Sanskrit, "taking delight in merit," "admiration of merit," or in some contexts, "accumulation of merit"; one of the ways of developing merit, according to which one admires and finds joy in (ANUMODANA) the meritorious deeds (PUṆYA) of others, often those of the SAṂGHA or of BODHISATTVAS. It is sometimes said that, by admiring the meritorious deed of another person, one accumulates as much merit as if one had performed the deed oneself. Taking delight in others' merit is therefore considered an especially efficient way of accumulating merit and functions as a standard component of many Buddhist rituals and prayers.

**puṇyaprasava**. (T. bsod nams skyes; C. fusheng tian; J. fukushōten; K. poksaeng ch'ŏn 福生天). In Sanskrit, "merit born," the second (lowest) of the eight heavens of the fourth concentration (DHYĀNA) of the subtle-materiality realm (RŪPADHĀTU). The divinities of this heaven are so called because of the great merit that resulted in their birth in the heaven. As with all the heavens of the subtle-materiality realm, one is reborn as a divinity there through achieving the same level of concentration (dhyāna) as the divinities of that heaven during one's practice of meditation in a previous lifetime. This heaven has no analogue in Pāli.

**puṇyasaṃbhāra**. (T. bsod nams kyi tshogs; C. fude ziliang; J. fukutoku shiryō; K. poktŏk charyang 福德資糧). In Sanskrit, "equipment" or "collection" "of merit," one of the two accumulations (along with the JÑĀNASAṂBHĀRA) amassed over the course of the BODHISATTVA path and required for the attainment of buddhahood. This type of collection refers to the myriad meritorious deeds performed by a bodhisattva over millions of lifetimes, deeds that are dedicated to the achievement of buddhahood for the welfare of all sentient beings. Between the two poles of skill in means (UPĀYA) and wisdom (PRAJÑĀ), the collection of merit is associated with upāya. Among the six perfections (PĀRAMITĀ), the first three perfections, of giving (DĀNA), morality (ŚĪLA), and patience (KṢĀNTI), are traditionally associated with the collection of merit. The collection of merit, resulting from the performance of limitless meritorious deeds, is said to fructify as the RŪPAKĀYA of a buddha. See also PUṆYAJÑĀNASAṂBHĀRA.

**Pūraṇa-Kāśyapa**. (P. Pūraṇa-Kassapa; T. 'Od srung rdzogs byed; C. Fulanna Jiashe; J. Furannakashō; K. Puranna Kasŏp 富蘭那迦葉). One of the so-called "six heterodox teachers" (TĪRTHIKA) often mentioned in Buddhist sūtras and criticized by the Buddha. (The other five are MASKARIN GOŚĀLĪPUTRA, AJITA KEŚAKAMBHALA, KAKUDA KĀTYĀYANA, SAÑJAYA VAIRĀṬĪPUTRA, and NIRGRANTHA JÑĀTĪPUTRA.) Pūraṇa-Kāśyapa is said to have propounded the view of akiriyavāda, literally "nonaction," a kind of antinomianism that denied the law of moral cause and effect (KARMAN). Pūraṇa claimed that, since there was no ultimate distinction between good and evil because actions did not have any effects, there was hence no harm in killing and stealing and no benefit in giving gifts and speaking truthfully. He also appears in accounts of the miracles the Buddha's performed at ŚRĀVASTĪ (i.e., the YAMAKAPRĀTIHĀRYA, or "dual miracle," and the MAHĀPRĀTIHĀRYA or "great miracle") as one of the heterodox teachers who challenges the Buddha to a miracle contest. After the Buddha defeats the tīrthikas, Pūraṇa-Kāśyapa withdraws in despair and is said to have drowned himself in Lake Anavatapta.

**pure land**. (C. jingtu; J. jōdo; K. chŏngt'o 淨土). An English term with no direct equivalent in Sanskrit that is used to translate the Chinese JINGTU (more literally, "purified ground"); the Chinese term may be related to the term PARIŚUDDHABUDDHAKṢETRA (although this latter term does not appear in the SUKHĀVATĪVYŪHASŪTRA, the text most closely aligned with pure land thought). The term "pure land" has several denotations in English, which have led to some confusion in its use. These include (1) a buddha-field (BUDDHAKṢETRA) purified of transgressions and suffering by a buddha and thus deemed an auspicious place in which to take rebirth; (2) the specific (and most famous) of these purified fields, that of the buddha AMITĀBHA, named SUKHĀVATĪ; (3) the tradition of texts and practices in MAHĀYĀNA Buddhism dedicated to the description of a number of buddha-fields, including that of Amitābha, and the practices to ensure rebirth there; (4) a tradition of texts and practice in East Asian and Tibetan Buddhism, associated specifically with the goal of rebirth in the purified buddha-field of Amitābha; (5) the JŌDOSHŪ and JŌDO SHINSHŪ schools of Japanese Buddhism, deriving from the teachings of HŌNEN and SHINRAN, which set forth a "single practice" for rebirth in sukhāvatī. It is important to note that, although the *Sukhāvatīvyūhasūtra* (and other sūtras describing other buddha-fields) originated in India, there was no "pure land school" in Indian Buddhism; rebirth in a buddha-field, and especially that of sukhāvatī, was one of the many generalized goals of Mahāyāna practice. Although there was an extensive tradition in China of scriptural exegesis of the major pure land sūtras, this was not enough in itself to constitute a self-consciously "pure land school"; indeed, techniques for rebirth in sukhāvatī became popular in many strands of Chinese Buddhism (see NIANFO), especially in light of theories of the disappearance of the dharma (see MOFA). Finally, it is important to note that the goal of rebirth in sukhāvatī was an important practice in Japan prior to the advent of Hōnen, and remained so in schools other than Jōdoshū and Jōdo Shinshū.

**pure land school**. See JINGTU ZONG; JISHŪ; JŌDOSHŪ; JŌDO SHINSHŪ; YŪZŪNENBUTSUSHŪ.

**Pūrṇa**. (P. Puṇṇa; T. Gang po; C. Fulouna; J. Furuna; K. Puruna 富樓那). In Sanskrit, "Fulfilled," a famous ARHAT and disciple of the Buddha, often known as Pūrṇa the Great (MAHĀPŪRṆA). There are various stories of his origins and encounter with Buddha, leading some scholars to believe that there were two important monks with this name. In some cases, he is referred to as Pūrṇa Maitrāyaṇīputra (P. Puṇṇa Mantāṇīputta) and appears in lists of the Buddha's ten chief disciples, renowned for his skill in preaching the DHARMA. In the SADDHARMAPUṆḌARĪKASŪTRA ("Lotus Sūtra"), Pūrṇa is listed among the SRĀVAKAS who understand the parable in the seventh chapter on the conjured city; in the eighth chapter of that sūtra, the Buddha predicts Pūrṇa's eventual attainment of buddhahood. According to Pāli accounts, where he is known as Puṇṇa, he was a brāhmaṇa from Kapilavatthu (S. KAPILAVASTU), the son of Mantāṇī, who was herself the sister of Aññā Koṇḍañña (ĀJÑĀTAKAUṆḌINYA), the first of five ascetics (P. pañcavaggiyā; S. PAÑCAVARGIKA) converted and ordained by the Buddha at the Isipatana (S. ṚSIPATANA) deer park (MṚGADĀVA) after his enlightenment. After preaching to the five ascetics, the Buddha traveled to Rājagaha (S. Rājagṛha); Aññā Koṇḍañña instead went to Kapilavatthu, where he proceeded to ordain his nephew Puṇṇa. Aññā Koṇḍañña retired to the forest while Puṇṇa remained in Kapilavatthu, devoting himself to the study of scripture and the practice of meditation, soon becoming an arahant (S. ARHAT). He gathered around him five hundred disciples, all of whom became monks, and taught them the ten bases of discourse he had learned. All of them became arahants. At Sāvatthi (ŚRĀVASTĪ), the Buddha taught the dhamma to Puṇṇa in his private chambers, a special honor. While Puṇṇa was dwelling at the Andhavana grove, Sāriputta (S. ŚĀRIPUTRA) visited him to question him on points of doctrine. Puṇṇa was able to answer all of Sāriputta's queries. It was while listening to Puṇṇa's explication of causality that Ānanda became a stream-enterer (P. sotāpanna; S. SROTAĀPANNA). ¶ Other stories, most famously the *Pūrṇāvadāna* of the DIVYĀVADĀNA, tell of a different Pūrṇa, known as Puṇṇa Suppāraka in Pāli sources. His father was a wealthy merchant in the seaport of Sūrpāraka in western India. The merchant became ill and was cured by a slave girl, who eventually bore him a son, named Pūrṇa, who became in turn a skilled merchant. During a sea voyage with some merchants from ŚRĀVASTĪ, he heard his colleagues reciting prayers to the Buddha. Overcome with feelings of faith, he went to see the Buddha and was ordained. After receiving brief instructions from the Buddha, he asked permission to spread the dharma among the uncivilized people of Śroṇāparāntaka, where he converted many and became an arhat in his own right. He later returned to his home city of Sūrpāraka, where he built a palace of sandalwood and invited the Buddha and his monks for a meal. Events from the story of Pūrṇa are depicted in cave paintings at AJAṆṬĀ in India and KIZIL in Central Asia along the SILK ROAD. A similar story of Pūrṇa's life as a merchant from a border region is recounted in still other Pāli accounts. After the Buddha preached the *Puṇṇovādasutta* to him, he is said to have joined the saṃgha and became an arahant. Puṇṇa won many disciples in his native land, who then wished to build a sandalwood monastery for the Buddha. The Buddha flew in celestial palanquins to Sunāparanta in the company of Puṇṇa and five hundred arahants in order to accept the gift. Along the way, the Buddha converted a hermit dwelling atop Mount Saccabandha and left a footprint (BUDDHAPĀDA) in the nearby Narmada River so that the NĀGA spirits might worship it. Sunāparanta of the Pāli legend is located in India, but the Burmese identify it with their homeland, which stretches from Middle to Upper Burma. They locate Mount Saccabandha near the ancient Pyu capital of Sirīkhettarā (Prome). The adoption of Puṇṇa as an ancient native son allowed Burmese chroniclers to claim that their Buddhism was established in Burma during the lifetime of the Buddha himself and therefore was older than that of their fellow Buddhists in Sri Lanka, who did not convert to Buddhism until the time of Asoka (S. AŚOKA) two and half centuries later.

**Pūrṇagiri**. In Sanskrit, "Mountain of Abundance" (sometimes also seen written as Paurṇagiri); one of the four major geographical centers in India in the development of both the Hindu and the Buddhist tantric traditions, located near the city of Pittoragarh in the modern state of Uttar Pradesh. Many tantric texts, such as the eighth-century HEVAJRATANTRA, identify Kāmākhyā, Śrīhaṭṭa, UḌḌIYĀNA, and Pūrṇagiri as being the places where the secrets of tantra were first revealed. These four areas thus came to be known as śaktipīṭhas, or "seats of Śakti." Mythologically, this claim means that Pūrṇagiri is one of the places where the body of the goddess Śakti landed when it fell from heaven after being carved up by the gods. Different tantric schools offer various explanations as to which part of Śakti fell to Pūrṇagiri: some say it was her navel, others her neck and shoulders, still others her nose. Pūrṇagiri remains a popular pilgrimage site.

**Pūrṇa-Maitrāyaṇīputra**. (S). See PŪRṆA.

**puruṣa**. (P. purisa; T. skyes bu; C. ren/shifu/shenwo; J. nin/jifu/jinga; K. in/sabu/sina 人/士夫/神我). In Sanskrit, "person" or "being," a common term for an individual being or self in Indian literature. In the non-Buddhist Indian philosophical schools, especially Sāṃkhya, the term often refers to the imperishable self that persists from lifetime to lifetime. However, in Buddhist scholastic literature, the term tends to function as a synonym for PUDGALA, that is, the person or being created in each lifetime, which is the product of past action (KARMAN) and devoid of any perduring self (ĀTMAN). In less philosophical contexts, the term commonly means simply "man" or "(human) male." Thus, the Buddha is called a MAHĀPURUṢA, "great man." One of the famous uses of the term in Buddhist literature is found in the BODHIPATHAPRADĪPA of ATIŚA DĪPAṂKARAŚRĪJÑĀNA. In this work, Atiśa divides all persons into three capacities (TRĪNDRIYA), based on their level of aspiration. Those who seek only happiness within SAṂSĀRA, whether in this life or a future life, are classified as beings of lesser capacity (MṚDVINDRIYA). Those who seek liberation from rebirth for themselves alone are classified as beings of intermediate capacity (MADYENDRIYA). Those who seek to liberate all beings in the universe from suffering are beings of great capacity (TĪKṢṆENDRIYA). This threefold division provided the structure for TSONG KHA PA's LAM RIM CHEN MO.

**puruṣakāraphala**. (T. skyes bu'i byed pa'i 'bras bu; C. shiyong guo; J. jiyūka; K. sayong kwa 士用果). In Sanskrit, "effect produced by a person," or "virile fruition"; this is one of the five effects (PHALA) enumerated in the SARVĀSTIVĀDA ABHIDHARMA and the YOGĀCĀRA system. The puruṣakāraphala is the fruition of the coexistent cause (SAHABHŪHETU) and conjoined cause (SAṂPRAYUKTAHETU) and refers to effects that are the result of human effort (rather than the result of the ripening of past KARMAN), whether that effort be virtuous (KUŚALA), unvirtuous (AKUŚALA), or neutral. In this sense, the action performed by the person himself or herself leads to a result that is conjoined with that person: thus, a pot made by a potter would fall into this category of phala, as would a meditator's attainment of one of the noble paths (ĀRYAMĀRGA).

**pūrvanivāsānusmṛti**. (P. pubbenivāsānussati; T. sngon gyi gnas rjes su dran pa; C. suzhu suinian; J. shukujūzuinen; K. sukchu sunyŏm 宿住隨念). In Sanskrit, lit. "recollection of former abodes," viz., "memory of past lives."; a cardinal teaching of all schools of Buddhism and an element of meditative attainment in many Buddhist traditions. The term occurs most commonly as a component of one or another list, such as the superknowledges (ABHIJÑĀ), knowledges (VIDYĀ), or powers (BALA). Although lists of five, six, and seven abhijñā appear in Buddhist literature, the most common listing is of six, with the memory of past lives being fourth. The same memory of former abodes is sometimes called the first of the three knowledges (TRIVIDYĀ) that are realized at the point of enlightenment, the other two being the divine eye (DIVYACAKṢUS) and the knowledge of the destruction of the contaminants (ĀSRAVAKṢAYA). In addition, the memory of former abodes occurs as the eighth of the ten powers (bala) of the TATHĀGATA. ¶ In situating the memory of former abodes within broader descriptions of the practice of the path (MĀRGA), one general account describes the path of an average monk, while in another the Buddha relates his own experience. In the SĀMAÑÑAPHALASUTTA of the Pāli DĪGHANIKĀYA, for example, the Buddha describes the benefits of the life of mendicancy, providing a chronological catalogue of the attainments of one who follows the path, starting from the occasion of first hearing the dharma and proceeding to the attainment of NIRVĀṆA. Among those attainments are the six abhiññā/abhijñā, including memory of past lives and culminating with the knowledge of the destruction of the contaminants. Yet another variety of the arhat path is described in great detail in the CŪLAHATTHIPADOPAMASUTTA of the MAJJHIMANIKĀYA. This account differs from that in the *Dīgha* with respect to the superknowledges, in that here, having attained the fourth meditative absorption (P. jhāna, S. DHYĀNA), the monk achieves only the last three of the abhiññā: the knowledge of former abodes, the divine eye, and the knowledge of the destruction of the contaminants. Elsewhere, these three experiences are referred to as the three types of knowledge. In the VISUDDHIMAGGA, BUDDHAGHOSA describes a regimen in which the meditator recalls his or her life in reverse order, beginning with the most recent act of sitting down to meditate, tracing the events of this life back to the moment of conception and back to the moment of death in the previous existence and so on through the eons. Non-Buddhists are said to be able to recollect as far back as forty eons, ordinary ŚRĀVAKAS one thousand eons, the eighty great śrāvakas one hundred thousand eons, ŚĀRIPUTRA and MAHĀMAUDGALYĀYANA an incalculable age plus one hundred thousand eons, PRATYEKABUDDHAS two incalculable eons plus one hundred thousand eons, and buddhas limitless past lives. In the more detailed "autobiographical" narratives of the Buddha's enlightenment in mainstream sources, the bodhisattva becomes the Buddha by gaining the three types of knowledge: in the first watch of the night, the knowledge of former abodes; in the second watch, the divine eye; and in the third watch of the night, the knowledge of the destruction of the contaminants. In the second watch, he remembers his name, his clan, his caste, his food, his pleasure and pain, and his life span for individual lives over the incalculable past. In general, the achievement of the knowledge of former lives is described as the product of deep states of concentration and, as such, is accessible also to non-Buddhist YOGINS; for this reason it is considered a worldly or mundane (laukika) knowledge. In the MAHĀYĀNA sūtras, similar descriptions of the six abhijñā and three vidyā are found. However, the memory of former lives also occurs simply as the product of a certain meritorious deeds. The memory of past lives typically causes the person to practice virtue in order to avoid an unfortunate rebirth. In the SUKHĀVATĪVYŪHASŪTRA, it is said that all beings reborn in AMITĀBHA's PURE LAND will be endowed with memory of their former abodes going back trillions of eons.

**pūrvapraṇidhāna**. (T. sngon gyi smon lam; C. benyuan; J. hongan; K. ponwŏn 本願). In Sanskrit, "prior vow," a vow made in the past that has either been fulfilled in the present or will be fulfilled in the future, typically in conjunction with the attainment of buddhahood. The term pūrvapraṇidhāna is used specifically in the MAHĀYĀNA to denote the vow made in the past by a BODHISATTVA to become a buddha himself, often specifying the place, the time, and the retinue that will be associated with that achievement. Since the buddhas have perforce succeeded in achieving their goal of buddhahood, their prior vows are therefore all considered to have been fulfilled. The most famous of all prior vows are the forty-eight vows described in the SUKHĀVATĪVYŪHASŪTRA, in which the bodhisattva DHARMĀKARA makes a series of forty-eight vows to create the PURE LAND of SUKHĀVATĪ. These vows are narrated by the Buddha, who explains that the bodhisattva fulfilled all the vows and became the buddha AMITĀBHA. The exegesis of the vows of Dharmākara was an important element of JŌDOSHŪ and JŌDO SHINSHŪ buddhology in Japan. (The Chinese translation of this term literally means "original vow," and this English rendering is commonly seen in Western translations of PURE LAND works.) The compound *pubbepaṇidhāna is unattested in Pāli sources, but the term paṇidhāna is used to refer to this aspiration made in a previous life.

**Pūrvaśaila**. (P. Pubbaseliya; T. Shar gyi ri bo; C. Dongshan; J. Tōzan; K. Tongsan 東山). In Sanskrit, "Eastern Hill," the name of one of the offshoots of the MAHĀSĀṂGHIKA, associated particularly with the CAITYA school centered in the Andhra region of southern India. The name of the school seems to derive from the location of its chief VIHĀRA on a hill to the east of the city of Dhānyakaṭaka; one finds reference to both schools called Uttaraśaila ("Northern Hill") and Aparaśaila ("Western Hill"). Like other branches of the Caitya, the school seems to have held the building and veneration of reliquaries (CAITYA) to be particularly efficacious forms of creating merit (PUṆYA). Like other branches of the Mahāsāṃghika, they also held that the enlightenment of a buddha was superior to that of an ARHAT. Much of what is known about their doctrinal positions derives from the reports of authors from other schools, such as BUDDHAGHOSA in his commentary to the KATHĀVATTHU, where it is claimed that they asserted the existence of forces dissociated from thought (CITTAVIPRAYUKTASAṂSKĀRA) and of an intermediate state (ANTARĀBHAVA) between death and rebirth.

**pūrvavideha**. (S). See VIDEHA.

**Pusa benye jing**. (J. Bosatsu hongōkyō; K. Posal ponŏp kyŏng 菩薩本業經). In Chinese, "Original Acts [alt. Basic Endeavors] of the Bodhisattvas"; translated by ZHI QIAN (fl. c. 220–252). This scripture offers one of the earliest accounts of the ten BODHISATTVA stages (S. daśavihāra, DAŚABHŪMI) translated into Chinese. This text combines the variant versions of the ten bodhisattva stages found in the GAṆḌAVYŪHA (viz. AVATAṂSAKASŪTRA) and the MAHĀVASTU. This translated scripture should be distinguished from the PUSA YINGLUO PENYE JING, an indigenous Chinese sūtra attributed to the translator ZHU FONIAN (fl. c. 390), which may have been inspired by this similarly named text. In the tradition, the *Pusa benye jing* is usually abbreviated as the *Benye jing*, while that indigenous text is typically known by its abbreviated title *Yingluo jing*. (To confuse things even more, Zhu Fonian is also said to have translated a *Pusa yingluo jing*, which may be how his name became associated with the apocryphal *Pusa yingluo benye jing*.)

**pusa jie**. (J. bosatsukai; K. posal kye 菩薩戒). In Chinese, "BODHISATTVA precepts"; a set of precepts unique to the MAHĀYĀNA tradition, which bodhisattvas follow on the path to buddhahood. These precepts are regarded as independent from monastic precepts and can be taken and kept by monks and nuns, as well as laypeople. There are various enumerations of the vows, the most famous of which in East Asia is a list of ten major and forty-eight minor Mahāyāna precepts that derives from the apocryphal FANWANG JING ("Book of Brahmā's Net"). See the extensive discussion in BODHISATTVAŚĪLA entry; see also BODHISATTVASAMVARA.

**Pusajie jing**. (S. *Bodhisattvaśīlasūtra; J. Bosatsukaikyō; K. Posalgye kyŏng 菩薩戒經). In Chinese, "Book of the Bodhisattva Precepts"; independent title given to the second roll of the FANWANG JING ("Book of Brahmā's Net"), which provides a list of ten major and forty-eight minor MAHĀYĀNA precepts. This text is often cited by its reconstructed, but unattested, Sanskrit title, the **Bodhisattvaśīlasūtra*. See FANWANG JING; BODHISATTVAŚĪLA.

**Pusa yingluo benye jing**. (J. Bosatsu yōraku hongōkyō; K. Posal yŏngnak ponŏp kyŏng 菩薩瓔珞本業經). In Chinese, "Book of the Original Acts that Adorn the Bodhisattva," in two rolls, translation attributed to ZHU FONIAN (fl. c. 390); a Chinese indigenous sūtra (see APOCRYPHA) often known by its abbreviated title of *Yingluo jing*. The *Yingluo jing* was particularly influential in the writings of CHAN and TIANTAI exegetes, including such seminal scholastic figures as TIANTAI ZHIYI, who cited the sūtra especially in conjunction with discussions of the BODHISATTVA MĀRGA and Mahāyāna VINAYA. The *Yingluo jing* is perhaps best known for its attempt to synthesize the variant schemata of the Buddhist path (mārga) into a comprehensive regimen of fifty-two BODHISATTVA stages: the ten faiths, the ten abidings, the ten practices, the ten transferences, and the ten grounds (see C. DAŚABHŪMI; BHŪMI); these then culminate in the two stages of buddhahood, virtual or equal enlightenment (dengjue) and sublime enlightenment (miaojue), which the *Yingluo jing* calls respectively the immaculate stage (wugou di, S. *amalabhūmi) and the sublime-training stage (miaoxue di). The *Yingluo jing* is one of the first texts formally to include the ten faiths in its prescribed mārga schema, as a preliminary level prior to the initiation onto the bodhisattva path proper, which is said to occur at the time of the first arousal of the thought of enlightenment (BODHICITTOTPĀDA) on the first level of the ten abidings. The text therefore adds an additional ten steps to the forty-two named stages of the path outlined in the AVATAMSAKASŪTRA (C. *Huayan jing*), providing a complete fifty-two-stage path, one of the most comprehensive accounts of the mārga to be found in East Asian Buddhist literature. The *Yingluo jing* also offers one of the most widely cited descriptions of the threefold classification of Buddhist morality (C. sanju jingji; S. ŚĪLATRAYA), a categorization of precepts found typically in YOGĀCĀRA-oriented materials. The *Yingluo jing* describes these as (1) the moral code that maintains both the discipline and the deportments (= S. SAMVARAŚĪLA) through the ten perfections (PĀRAMITĀ); (2) the moral code that accumulates wholesome dharmas (= S. kuśaladharmasamgrāhaka) through the eighty-four thousand teachings; and (3) the moral code that aids all sentient beings (= S. SATTVĀRTHAKRIYĀ), through exercising loving-kindness, compassion, sympathetic joy, and equanimity (viz. the four BRAHMAVIHĀRA). The *Yingluo jing* specifies that these three categories of precepts are the foundation of morality for all bodhisattvas. The provenance and authorship of the *Pusa yingluo benye jing* have long been matters of controversy. In the fifth-century Buddhist catalogue CHU SANZANG JI JI, the compiler Sengyou lists the *Pusa yingluo benye jing* among miscellaneous works by anonymous translators. In the 594 scriptural catalogue *Zhongjing mulu*, the scripture is ascribed to Zhu Fonian, while the LIDAI SANBAO JI instead claims that the text was translated by the dhyāna master Zhiyan in 427. Later cataloguers generally accept the attribution to Zhu Fonian, though some note that the translation style differs markedly from that found in other of his renderings. The attribution to Zhu Fonian is also suspect because it includes passages and doctrines that seem to derive from other indigenous Chinese sūtras, such as the RENWANG JING, FANWANG JING, etc., as well as passages that appear in earlier Chinese translations of the AVATAMSAKASŪTRA, PUSA BENYE JING, SHENGMAN JING, *Pusa dichi jing*, and DA ZHIDU LUN. Both internal and external evidence therefore suggests that the *Yingluo jing* is a Chinese apocryphon from the fifth century. ¶ The *Pusa yingluo benye jing* should be distinguished from the *Pusa benye jing* ("Basic Endeavors of the Bodhisattvas"), translated by ZHI QIAN (fl. c. 220–252), an authentic translation that offers one of the earliest accounts of the ten stages (S. daśavihāra, DAŚABHŪMI) translated into Chinese. (It is usually known by its abbreviated title of *Benye jing*.) This text seems to combine the accounts of the ten bodhisattva stages found in the GAṆḌAVYŪHA (viz., *Avatamsakasūtra*) and the MAHĀVASTU and may have been the inspiration for the composition of this indigenous Chinese sūtra. (Zhu Fonian also translated a *Pusa yingluo jing*, which may be how his name became associated with this apocryphal *Pusa yingluo benye jing*.)

**Pusŏksa**. (浮石寺). In Korean, "Floating Rock Monastery," located on Mt. Ponghwang, in North Kyŏngsang province; one of the major Silla HWAŎM (C. HUAYAN ZONG) monasteries established by ŬISANG (625–702), the founder of the Hwaŏm school in Korea. According to the monastery's foundation story in the SAMGUK YUSA ("Memorabilia of the Three Kingdoms"), while Ŭisang was studying in China, he stayed over at the home of a layman, whose daughter Sŏnmyo (C. Shenmiao) became enamored of the master. When the time came for Ŭisang to return to Silla, he went to see Sŏnmyo to let her know that he was leaving, but she was not at home, so he just left a note for her. After receiving the message, Sŏnmyo ran down to the waterfront, only to see that his ship had already disappeared over the horizon. In despair, she jumped into the sea and died, but was reborn as a dragon who protected Ŭisang on the voyage back to Silla. After returning home, Ŭisang tried to build a monastery on Mt. Ponghwang in order to establish the Hwaŏm teachings in Silla. There were, however, five hundred bandits living on the mountain at the time, who stopped Ŭisang from proceeding. The dragon woman Sŏnmyo frightened them away by transforming herself into a huge rock floating in the air. The monastery takes its name "Pusŏk" (Floating Rock) from this rock, which is believed to be the massive boulder that sits next to the main shrine hall. Sŏnmyo Pavilion is named after this female dharma protector. Many Silla and Koryŏ monks studied Hwaŏm doctrine at Pusŏksa, including the Silla SŎN masters Hyech'ŏl (785–861) and Muyŏm (801–888), and the Koryŏ state preceptors Kyŏrŭng (964–1053) and Hagil (1052–1144). Despite its close sectarian associations with the Hwaŏm school, the monastery's shrine halls are more directly linked to the PURE LAND teachings, reflecting Ŭisang's eclectic approach to Buddhist thought and practice. These pure land linkages include (1) the Anyang nu (Pavilion of Peaceful Nurturing) is an alternative name for the pure land of SUKHĀVATĪ; (2) Muryangsu chŏn (Hall of Immeasurable Life), the main shrine hall of the monastery, is dedicated to AMITĀBHA, rather than to the MAHĀVAIROCANA image that might be expected in a Hwaŏm monastery; (3) the statue of AMITĀBHA in the main hall faces east so that worshippers will face west, in the direction of the Amitābha's pure land, when worshipping in the hall; (4) after entering the Ilchu mun (One-Pillar Gate), the front entrance gate to the monastery grounds, the monastery is laid out over nine stone terraces, which is often interpreted as corresponding to the pure land theory of nine grades of the pure land (kup'um chŏngt'o; see C. JIUPIN), a sort of a soteriological outline of rebirth in the pure land, which ranges from the worst of the worst to the best of the best. Pusŏksa is currently a branch monastery (MALSA) of the sixteenth district monastery (PONSA) KOUNSA (Secluded Cloud Monastery), which was also founded by Ŭisang.

**Putuoshan**. (J. Fudasen; K. Pot'asan 普陀山/補陀山). In Chinese, "Mount POTALAKA"; a mountainous island in the Zhoushan Archipelago, about sixty-two miles off the eastern coast of Zhejiang province; also known as Butuoshan, Butuoluojiashan, Xiaobaihuashan, etc. Putuoshan is considered one of the four Buddhist sacred mountains in China, along with WUTAISHAN in Shanxi, EMEISHAN in Sichuan, and JIUHUASHAN in Anhui. Each of the mountains is said to be the residence of a specific BODHISATTVA, and Putuoshan is regarded as the sacred mountain of AVALOKITEŚVARA, known in Chinese as GUANYIN pusa, the revered "bodhisattva of compassion." There are many legends told about Putuoshan. During the Tang dynasty, an Indian monk is said to have come to Putuoshan and immolated his ten fingers, after which Avalokiteśvara appeared and preached the dharma to him. As this legend spread, Putuoshan gained fame as the sacred site of Avalokiteśvara. In 916 CE, a Japanese monk was bringing a statue of Avalokiteśvara back to Japan from Wutaishan, but was delayed on Putuoshan by fierce storms. He built a monastery for Avalokiteśvara on the island and named it Baotuo monastery, an abbreviated Chinese transcription for the Sanskrit word Potalaka, an Indian holy mountain that, according to the GAṆḌAVYŪHA of the AVATAṂSAKASŪTRA, is thought to be the abode of Avalokiteśvara. Since that sūtra said that Mt. Potalaka was an isolated mountainous island rising out of the ocean, the sacred geography seemed to match Putuoshan's physical geography. After the Southern Song dynasty, the scale of monasteries, nunneries, monks and nuns in Putuoshan increased significantly through donations from the imperial court and lay Buddhists. Many people came to Putuoshan, especially to pray for safe voyages. It was also popular for the emperor to perform religious rites on Putuoshan. In 1131, during the Southern Song dynasty, all Buddhist schools on Putuoshan were designated as CHAN monasteries. In 1214, Putuoshan was ordered to emphasize the worship of Avalokiteśvara. At the height of its prestige, there were as many as 218 monasteries on the island, housing more than two thousand monks and nuns. There are now three major monasteries on Putuoshan—Pujisi, Fayusi, and Huijisi—all affiliated with either the LINJI ZONG or the CAODONG ZONG of CHAN Buddhism, and seventy-two smaller temples. Pious pilgrims come to Putuoshan from all over China to worship Avalokiteśvara, and Putuoshan continues to be one of the most popular pilgrimage sites in China. See also POTALAKA; PO TA LA.

**Puyan**. (C) (普巖). See YUN'AN PUYAN.

**Pyŏgam Kaksŏng**. (碧巖覺性) (1575–1660). Korean SŎN master of the Chosŏn dynasty; also known as Chingwŏn. Kaksŏng was a native of Poŭn (in present-day North Ch'ungch'ŏng province). After losing his father at an early age, Kaksŏng became a monk under Sŏlmuk (d.u.) at the hermitage of Hwasanam. Kaksŏng received the full monastic precepts in 1588 from a certain Pojŏng (d.u.) and subsequently became the disciple of the eminent Sŏn master PUHYU SŎNSU, whom he accompanied from one mountain monastery to another. When Japanese troops stormed the Korean peninsula in 1592 during the Hideyoshi invasions, Kaksŏng served in the war in place of his teacher, who had been recommended earlier to the king by the eminent monk SAMYŎNG YUJŎNG. Kaksŏng launched a successful sea campaign against Japanese naval forces. Kaksŏng was once falsely accused of a crime and imprisoned, but was later released and appointed prelate (p'ansa) of both the Sŏn and KYO traditions and abbot of the monastery Pongŭnsa in the capital of Seoul. In 1624, he was appointed the supreme director of the eight provinces (p'alto toch'ongsŏp) and oversaw the construction of Namhansansŏng. Kaksŏng then spent the next few years in Chŏlla province, restoring the monasteries of HWAŎMSA, SONGGWANGSA, and SSANGGYESA, which had been burned during the Hideyoshi invasions. He also taught at HAEINSA, PAEGUNSA, and Sangsŏnam, but eventually returned to Hwaŏmsa, where he passed away in 1660. He produced many famous disciples, such as Ch'wimi Such'o (1590–1668), Paekkok Ch'ŏnŭng (1617–1680), Moun Chinŏn (1622–1703), and Hoeŭn Ŭngjun (1587–1672). Kaksŏng's lineage expanded into eight branches, and his influence on the subsequent development of Korean Sŏn rivalled that of CH'ŎNGHŎ HYUJŎNG, the preeminent Korean monk during the Chosŏn dynasty. Kaksŏng also composed many treatises, including the *Sŏnwŏnjipto chung kyŏrŭi*, *Kanhwa kyŏrŭi*, *Sŏngmun sangŭi ch'o*, and others.

**P'yohunsa**. (表訓寺). In Korean, "P'yohun's monastery"; one of the four major monasteries on the Buddhist sacred mountain of KŬMGANGSAN (Diamond Mountains), now in North Korea. The monastery is said to have been built in 598 during the Silla dynasty by Kwallŭk (d.u.) and Yungun (d.u.), and rebuilt in 675 by P'yohun (d.u.), one of the ten disciples of ŬISANG (625–702), the vaunt-courier of the Korean HWAŎM (C. HUAYAN) school. The present monastery was rebuilt after the Korean War (1950–1953) on the model of an earlier reconstruction project finished in 1778 during the late-Chosŏn dynasty. The main shrine hall of the monastery is named Panya Pojŏn (Prajñā Jeweled Basilica), rather than the typical TAEUNG CHŎN (basilica of the great hero [the Buddha]), and the image of the bodhisattva DHARMODGATA (Pŏpki Posal) that used to be enshrined therein was installed facing Dharmodgata Peak (Pŏpkibong) to the northeast of the hall, rather than toward the front. The relics (ŚARĪRA) of NAONG HYEGŬN (1320–1376), a late-Koryŏ period Sŏn monk who introduced the orthodox LINJI ZONG (K. IMJE CHONG) lineage to Korea from China, were enshrined at P'yohunsa. The monastery also was famous for its iron pagoda (STŪPA) with fifty-three enshrined buddha images, but these were lost sometime during the Japanese occupation of Korea (1910–1945), along with Naong's relics. Chŏngyangsa, one of the branch monasteries of P'yohunsa, is said to have been built at the spot where Dharmodgata and his attendant bodhisattvas appeared before the first king of the Koryŏ dynasty, Wang Kŏn, T'aejo (877–943; r. 918–943), on his visit to Kŭmgangsan. The peak where Dharmodgata made his appearance is named Panggwangdae (Radiant Terrace), and the spot where T'aejo prostrated himself before Dharmodgata is called Paejŏm (Prostration Hill). Podŏgam, a hermitage affiliated with P'yohunsa, is notable for its peculiar construction: for four hundred years it has been suspended off a cliff, supported by a single copper foundation pillar.

**P'yŏnyang Ŏn'gi**. (鞭羊彥機) (1581–1644). Korean SŎN master and renowned painter during the Chosŏn period. Ŏn'gi entered the SAṂGHA at the age of eleven and subsequently became a student of the Sŏn master CH'ŎNGHŎ HYUJŎNG. He taught at various monasteries and hermitages, including Ch'ŏndŏksa, Taesŏngsa on Mt. Kuryong, and Ch'ŏnsuam on Mt. Myohyang. He died at sixty-three, leaving behind some thirty disciples, the largest group among Hyujŏng's four direct lineages. His writings can be found in the *P'yŏnyangdang chip*.

# Q

**Qianfo dong**. (C) (千佛洞). In Chinese, "Caves of the Thousand Buddhas." See DUNHUANG.

**Qianshou jing**. (S. Nīlakaṇṭhakasūtra; T. Mgrin pa sngon po can [gyi mdo]; J. Senjūkyō; K. Ch'ŏnsu kyŏng 千手經). In Chinese, "Thousand Hands Sūtra"; in Sanskrit, "Blue-Throated [Avalokiteśvara] Sūtra"; an abbreviated title commonly used for the text that provides the scriptural foundation for the popular cult of Thousand-Armed and Thousand-Eyed AVALOKITEŚVARA (SĀHASRABHUJASĀHASRANETRĀVALOKITEŚVARA). There are several Chinese translations of the scripture, including Bhagavaddharma's (fl. c. seventh century) *Qianshou Qianyan Guanshiyin pusa guangda yuanman wu'ai dabeixin tuoluoni jing* ("Dhāraṇī-Sūtra of Thousand-Eyed and Thousand-Armed Bodhisattva Who Regards the World's Sounds and Feels Vast, Complete, Unimpeded Great Compassion"), translated between 650 and 661, and Zhitong's (fl. c. seventh century) *Qianyan Qianbi Guanshiyin pusa tuoluoni shenzhou jing* ("Dhāraṇī-Sūtra of Thousand-Eyed and Thousand-Armed Bodhisattva Who Regards the World's Sounds"), translated between 627 and 649. (There are additional translations by BODHIRUCI, made in 709; VAJRABODHI, made between 731 and 736; and AMOGHAVAJRA, made during the eighth century.) Each version differs in its content and structure, but most include a spell dedicated to Thousand-Armed Avalokiteśvara (C. GUANYIN), which is commonly called the Qianshou (Thousand-Handed/Armed) or Dabei (Great Compassion) DHĀRAṆĪ. There are at least eight different Chinese transcriptions of this dhāraṇī and two Tibetan transcriptions, suggesting that different Sanskrit recensions of the spell were in circulation. Bhagavaddharma's translation of the sūtra has been the most popular in the East Asia and the title *Qianshou jing* typically refers to his recension. According to Bhagavaddharma's translation of the text, innumerable eons ago, Avalokiteśvara received this dhāraṇī from a buddha named Qianguang Wangjing Zhu Rulai (Tathāgata Tranquil Abode who is King of the Thousandfold Radiance), and, after making ten vows to benefit all sentient beings, the bodhisattva came to be endowed with a thousand arms and a thousand eyes. The sūtra then explains the various benefits of keeping and reciting the dhāraṇī. Keeping the dhāraṇī ensures, for example, fifteen kinds of salutary rebirths, such as being born in a good country, living during a peaceful time, meeting good friends, having sufficient money and food, and being protected by the divinities; it also ensures that the adept will avoid fifteen kinds of painful deaths, such as from hunger, madness, drowning, conflagration, poison, and suicide. These various sets of benefits are only included in Bhagavadharma's version, which may partly account for the greater popularity of his translation. His version also forgoes the complex instructions on ritual matters found in Zhitong's version, such as the detailed rules of creating an image of Guanyin, which were probably intended for ritual specialists. Bhagavaddharma's text introduced the dhāraṇī and the names of forty gestures (MUDRĀ) and their particular benefits; Amoghavajra's (705–774) later recension includes illustrations of these mudrā. Due to the great popularity of Bhagavaddharma's early translation, Thousand-Armed and Thousand-Eyed Avalokiteśvara became identified specifically with Avalokiteśvara's manifestation as Great Compassion (C. Dabei; S. MAHĀKARUṆIKA). Based on the same version, the Song TIANTAI master SIMING ZHILI (960–1028) composed a manual for a repentance ritual using this scripture: the *Qianshou Qianyan Dabeixinzhou xingfa* ("Rules for Performing the Great Compassion Heart Dhāraṇī of the Thousand-Handed and Thousand-Eyed One"). A late-ninth-century abridgment of Bhagavaddharma's translation, the *Dabei qiqing* ("Great Compassion Invocation"), was also created, probably for use as a ritual manual. Bhagavaddharma's translation of the sūtra also became popular in Japan and Korea as well. In Korea, where the text is known as the *Ch'ŏnsu kyŏng*, another abridgment was made that included only the Thousand-Hands dhāraṇī and Avalokiteśvara's vows; it was probably intended as a type of ritual procedure. This version also cites materials that derive from a variety of different traditions, including HWAŎM (C. HUAYAN), SŎN (C. CHAN), CH'ŎNT'AE (C. TIANTAI), and PURE LAND. Starting in the eighteenth century, several manuals were written with procedures for the ritual dedicated to Thousand-Armed Kwanŭm (Guanyin), all based on the dhāraṇī and vows. The current form of the rite is recited in the daily ritual of many Chinese and Korean monasteries. See also OM MAṆI PADME HŪṂ.

**qiao**. (S. śarīre khāni; J. kyō; K. kyu 竅). In Chinese, the "bodily orifices," of which nine are listed: the two eyes, the two ears, the two nostrils, the mouth, the reproductive organ, and the anus. In one form of "foulness contemplation" (S. AŚUBHABHĀVANĀ), in which the impure aspects of the human body are concentrated upon in order to counter lust and excessive attachment to the body, practitioners focus on the way impurities (pus, blood, secretions, etc.) and odors are constantly being secreted through these nine orifices.

**qi miezheng fa**. (七滅諍法). In Chinese, "seven means of settling disputes" (SAPTĀDHIKARAṆAŚAMATHA). See also ADHIKARAṆAŚAMATHA.

**Qimingsi**. (齊明寺). In Chinese, "Brightness of Qi" convent, located in Yanguan county in Zhejiang province; the residence for several Qi-dynasty nuns listed in the BIQIUNI ZHUAN ("Lives of the Nuns") collection, including Dele (421–501 CE), SENGMENG (418–489 CE), Chaoming (438–498 CE), and Shi Faxuan (434–516 CE). Differing explanations of its foundation appear in the *Biqiuni zhuan*. The first story credits Sengmeng for founding the convent. It is said that when her mother became ill, Sengmeng returned to her home in Yanguan county to tend to her. While there, Sengmeng decided to turn her residence into a convent. It is said that she participated actively in the construction of the convent's various halls. The second account credits a devout layman named Yüan Jian for donating his residence to build the convent in 487 CE, during the Qi dynasty (479–502 CE). According to this version, the nun Dele was chosen as abbess of the convent because of her renowned lecturing skills and intellectual talent, her meditative expertise, and her ability to attract a wide following of both monks and nuns, including the aforementioned Shi Faxuan.

**qinggou**. (輕垢). In Chinese, "minor fault." See DUṢKṚTA.

**qinggui**. (J. shingi; K. ch'ŏnggyu 清規). In Chinese, lit. "rules of purity" or "rules for the pure (assembly)," a genre of monastic codes compiled by adherents within the CHAN tradition. According to such Song-period genealogical records as the JINGDE CHUANDENG LU, the Tang Chan master BAIZHANG HUAIHAI (720–814) composed the first such Chan code, entitled the BAIZHANG QINGGUI ("Baizhang's Rules of Purity"), in order to establish an independent Chan discipline distinct from the normative VINAYA tradition; his qinggui is not extant, however, and modern scholars doubt that it ever existed. There might have been some Chan monastic codes as early as the Tang dynasty, influenced by such Chinese codes as DAO'AN's (312–384) *Sengni guifan* ("Standards for Monks and Nuns") or DAOXUAN's (596–667) *Jiaojie xinxue biqiu xinghu lüyi* ("Exhortation on Manners and Etiquette for Novices in Training"). However, the oldest surviving Chan code is the CHANYUAN QINGGUI compiled by the YUNMEN ZONG master CHANGLU ZONGZE (d. c. 1107). These types of texts were typically composed by the founding abbots of monasteries and thus include their vision of how monks in their monasteries should conduct themselves. These codes deal with daily routines in the monastery, monthly schedules, annual festivals, titles and duties of the administrative monks in the monastery, and outlines of various religious services. They may also include monastic rules and regulations related to state policies regarding SAṂGHA administration, such as rules on travel permits and the election of abbots. The codes differed in content, since each monastery compiled its own in accord with its own needs, e.g., as to whether it was a public or private monastery. For this reason, the Yuan Emperor Shun (r. 1333–1368) eventually compiled a unified code based on the rules attributed to Baizhang, entitled the *Chixiu Baizhang qinggui*. Although the term qinggui originally referred to the monastic codes associated with the Chan school, it later came to be used as a general term for the monastic codes used by other schools, such as in the TIANTAI monk Ziqing's (fl. fourteenth century) *Jiaoyuan qinggui* ("Pure Rules for the Garden of Doctrine") compiled in 1347. See also BCA' YIG.

**Qingliang guoshi**. (清涼國師). See CHENGGUAN.

**Qingyuan Xingsi**. (J. Seigen Gyōshi; K. Ch'ŏngwŏn Haengsa 青原行思) (d. 740). A Chinese CHAN master of the Tang dynasty, Qingyuan is said to have been a native of Jizhou in present-day Jiangxi province. Little is known of his career besides the fact that he was ostensibly the student of the sixth patriarch (LIUZU) HUINENG. He later resided at the monastery of Jingjusi on Mt. Qingyuan (present-day Jiangxi province) and acquired many students, of whom SHITOU XIQIAN (700–790) is the most famous. Like many of the reputed disciples of Huineng (e.g., YONGJIA XUANJUE and NANYUE HUAIRANG), Qingyuan's relation with Huineng is dubious. Later, three major "houses" (jia) of the Chan tradition, YUNMEN, CAODONG, and FAYAN, traced their lineages back to Huineng via Shitou and his teacher Qingyuan (see WU JIA QI ZONG). Qingyuan was given the posthumous title Chan master Hongji (Universal Salvation).

**qini[zui]**. (J. shichigyaku[zai]; K. ch'iryŏk[choe] 七逆[罪]). In Chinese, "seven transgressions," a listing of major moral transgressions in the Mahāyāna school as outlined in the Chinese *Book of Brahmā's Net* (FANWANG JING). The seven are the following: inflicting injuries on the Buddha ("shedding the Buddha's blood"), patricide, matricide, killing a renunciant, killing a preceptor, killing an ARHAT, and causing schism within the monastic community (SAṂGHABHEDA). If any of the seven are committed, one will not be eligible to receive precepts of any kind nor attain any considerable spiritual fruition within this lifetime. See also ICCHANTIKA; SAMUCCHINNAKUŚALAMŪLA.

**qinli jue**. (J. shinrikaku; K. ch'illi kak 親里覺). In Chinese, lit. "affection for one's relatives and hometown" or "partiality and nostalgia for one's loved ones, relatives, or fellow townsmen," one of the so-called eight kinds of misplaced attention (see BA JUE). This emotion refers to one's identification with favoritism and nostalgia for loved ones, whether that be in the form of one's land and country (guotu), family and clan (zuxing), or the endearing circle of familiar individuals (as in the case of this qinli jue). Especially for a monk who has become a homeless renunciant (see PRAVRAJITA), such attachment could be a subtle spiritual obstacle. It is said that only ARHATs or advanced bodhisattvas have perfected their equanimity and are therefore completely impartial to both strangers and acquaintances (wu qingyuan xiang) and devoid of any dualistic concept of friends versus enemies.

**qiqi**. (J. shichishichi; K. ch'ilch'il 七七). In Chinese, "seven periods of seven days," viz., the forty-nine-day transitional period between rebirths. According to some Buddhist accounts, the forty-nine days following a person's death is of crucial importance in his or her karmic destiny. A deceased with strong and unambiguous karmic propensities is said to be reborn immediately into the appropriate realm. However, for those whose karmic composition is of mixed evil and good deeds and whose temperaments do not draw them so decidedly toward any one particular kind of existence, there would not be such clear-cut and swift propulsion into any particular realm of rebirth. They are said to reside in an "intermediate state" (ANTARĀBHAVA; see also BAR DO) for upward of forty-nine days, during which time the precarious equilibrium of their karmic indeterminacy is highly susceptible to conditions that would potentially tip the balance. These conditions might include a whimsical thought or emotion on the part of the intermediate-state being (GANDHARVA) or the intervening power of proper rituals and "transference of merits" (PARIṆĀMANĀ) performed on its behalf. For this reason, religious services of the latter sorts are widely performed in many Buddhist traditions during this "window of opportunity." Thus, "qiqi" refers either to the forty-nine-day period in which such services are held or to the services themselves.

**qiqi ji**. [alt. qiqi [ri] zhai] (J. shichishichi no ki/shichishichi [nichi]sai; K. ch'ilch'il ki/ch'ilch'il [il] chae 七七忌/七七[日]齋). In Chinese, lit. "seven-sevens service," the memorial services performed on the seven "seventh days" following a person's death, culminating in the forty-ninth-day ceremony (SISHIJIU [RI] ZHAI) that marks the official point of rebirth. (For a discussion of the transitional period between rebirths, see ANTARĀBHAVA; BAR DO; QIQI.) During this transitional period, intermediate-state beings (GANDHARVA) are presumed to be especially susceptible to the power of religious rituals, which transfers merit to them (PARIṆĀMANĀ) and thus potentially improves the quality of their next rebirth. For this reason, in many Buddhist traditions, but especially those in East Asia, the qiqi ji is performed weekly during this "window of opportunity," which culminates in the final "forty-ninth-day ceremony."

**qiqing**. (七情). In Chinese, "seven emotions." See QIQING LIUYU.

**qiqing liuyu**. (J. shichijō rokuyoku; K. ch'ilchŏng yugyok 七情六欲). In Chinese, "seven emotions and six desires." According to the DAZHIDU LUN, the seven emotions of joy, anger, sadness, horror, love, hate, and desire are directed to other people's (1) physical body (se), (2) appearance (xingmao), (3) comportment (weiyi), (4) voice (yanyu yinsheng), (5) delicateness or smoothness [of skin] (xihua), and (6) physical features (renxiang).

**qiqi [ri] zhai**. (七七[日]齋). In Chinese, "seven-sevens ceremony." See QIQI; SISHIJIU [RI] ZHAI.

**qishan**. (J. shichizen; K. ch'ilsŏn 七善). In Chinese, "seven excellences [of the Buddha's teaching]." They are the following: the excellence of its timing (shishan), meaning (yishan), language (i.e., its adaptiveness to regional dialects; yushan), singular goal [of attaining "NIRVĀṆA"] (dufa), completeness (juzu), melodiousness and edificatory properties (qingjing tiaorou), and conduciveness to living out the holy life (fanxing; see BRAHMACARYA).

**qisheng**. (C) (七生). See QIYOU.

**qishengshi**. (J. shichishōji; K. ch'ilsŭngsa 七勝事). In Chinese, "seven surpassing qualities [of the Buddha]": his physical marks (shensheng; see MAHĀPURUṢALAKṢAṆA), his abiding in or perfect conformity to the dharma (rufa zhu sheng), wisdom (zhisheng), perfections (juzu sheng; see PĀRAMITĀ), practices (xingchu sheng), ineffability (buke siyi sheng), and liberation (jietuo sheng).

**Qisong**. (C) (契嵩). See FORI QISONG.

**qixian**. (J. shichiken; K. ch'irhyŏn 七賢). In Chinese, lit. "seven sagacities," seven stages on the path of preparation (PRAYOGAMĀRGA) derived from the Chinese translation of the ABHIDHARMAKOŚABHĀṢYA. The first stage involves the cultivation of meditative "antidotes" (PRATIPAKṢA) such as the contemplation of foulness, the contemplation of loving-kindness, and the contemplation of the breath to counter, respectively, the excessive tendencies toward lust, ill will, and discursiveness. The second involves the practice of the so-called four foundations of mindfulness, which involves insight (VIPAŚYANĀ) into real-time experiences as they unfold in the body and mind. The third focuses on the contemplation of the three marks of existence (TRILAKṢAṆA), noticing the characteristics of impermanence, unsatisfactoriness, and selflessness in those psychophysical experiences. The fourth through seventh stages correspond to the "wholesome roots associated with the knowledge that penetrates reality" (NIRVEDHABHĀGĪYA-KUŚALAMŪLA): heat (ŪṢMAN), summit (MŪRDHAN), receptivity or acquiescence (KṢĀNTI), and highest worldly dharmas (LAUKIKĀGRADHARMA). These nirvedhabhāgīya open access to the path of vision (DARŚANAMĀRGA) where the first stage of sanctity, stream-entry (SROTAĀPANNA), is won.

**qixing**. (C) (七星). See BEIDOU QIXING.

**Qixin lun**. (C) (起信論). See DASHENG QIXIN LUN.

**qiyou**. (J. shichiu; K. ch'iryu 七有). In Chinese, "seven modes of existence": the six destinies (see GATI) and the "intermediate state" of the ANTARĀBHAVA.

**qizhi**. (J. shichichi; K. ch'ilchi 七知). In Chinese, "seven knowledges" or "seven discernments," the specific types of understanding that are indispensable in order to be an effective BODHISATTVA according to the MAHĀPARINIRVĀṆASŪTRA. These are (1) knowing the DHARMA (zhifa); (2) understanding the implicit meanings of the dharma (zhiyi); (3) knowing the timing of different kinds of practices (zhishi); (4) knowing contentment (zhizu); (5) knowing one's current level of spiritual capacity (zhizi); (6) a sense of the audience, viz., knowing how to adapt and cater to its specific backgrounds and abilities (zhizhong); and (7) realizing that reaching out to believers and nonbelievers requires different approaches and that there is a priority (zunbei) in saving oneself before one can save others (zhiren zunbei).

**qizhongshe**. (J. shichishu no sha; K. ch'ilchongsa 七種捨). In Chinese, "seven kinds of relinquishment." They are as follows: (1) an expansive, imperturbable equanimity (see UPEKṢĀ) that is devoid of attachments; (2) being impartial to all sentient beings, harboring no distinction between those who are endearing and those who are not; (3) not giving in to the effects of passion and enmity, craving, and ill will; (4) not harboring thoughts of anxiety, regret, or parsimony while one is overseeing the deliverance of sentient beings; (5) staying firmly anchored in the realization of emptiness (ŚŪNYATĀ) and relinquishing all clinging to the superficial and contingent characteristics of things; (6) willingly sharing with and giving to others, even if that means parting with what one loves and takes delight in; and (7) harboring no expectation for reciprocity, gratitude, or any other reward in one's acts of giving.

**qizhongyu**. (J. shichishugo; K. ch'ilchongŏ 七種語). In Chinese, the Buddha's "seven modes of speech." They are (1) yinyu, explanations of how a present cause will induce a specific future effect; (2) guoyu, explanations of how a present effect was a result of a specific past cause; (3) yinguo yu, explanations of the comprehensive principles and mechanisms of the operation of cause and effect; (4) yuyu, explanations through the use of parables, analogies, and illustrations; (5) buying [shuo] yu, a mode of speech that has been variously interpreted as either "enigmatic speech" ("buying" in this case is understood as "not connected with [logic or common sense or traditional tenets])" or "spontaneous speech" ("buying" in this case is understood as "[to speak] without responding [to specific questions]" and therefore is a "self-induced, spontaneous speech"); (6) shi liubu yu, explanations aimed at conforming and catering to worldly concerns, customs, or world views; in other words, these are mundane, provisional explanations not necessarily aimed at transmitting the highest truths; (7) ruyi yu, a mode of speech interpreted as either explanations made according to the likings and predilections of the audience ("ruyi" in this case means "conforming to the wishes" [of the audience]) or explanations that come from the Buddha's ultimate intent—i.e., these are the ultimate, "definitive" explanations ("ruyi" in this case means "conforming to [the Buddha's original] wish").

**Qizil**. See KIZIL.

**qizuisheng**. (J. shichisaishō; K. ch'ilch'oesŭng 七最勝). In Chinese, "the seven unsurpassed [qualities of the perfections]." According to the CHENG WEISHI LUN (S. **Vijñaptimātratāsiddhi*), the "perfections" (PĀRAMITĀ) of a BODHISATTVA are distinguished from other forms of virtuous and wholesome practices because of their seven unsurpassed qualities. They are the following: (1) being firmly anchored in the BODHISATTVA lineage (see GOTRA) (anzhu zuisheng); (2) being firmly founded on BODHICITTA, the bodhisattva's aspiration to lead all beings to deliverance (yizhi zuisheng); (3) being permeated with the intention to take pity in all sentient beings (yiguo zuisheng); (4) implementing all good deeds, not just a limited number (shiye zuisheng); (5) being compatible with all skillful means (see UPĀYA) and not constrained by just a limited number of them (qiaobian zuisheng); (6) ultimately leading to perfect BODHI (huixiang zuisheng); and (7) being undefiled by the two obstructions of KLEŚĀVARAṆA (afflictive obstructions) and JÑEYĀVARAṆA (cognitive obstructions) (qingjing zuisheng).

**quanshen sheli**. (J. zenshinshari; K. chŏnsin sari 全身舍利). In Chinese, "whole-body relics," the mummified remains of eminent masters. See ŚARĪRA.

**quan shi**. (J. gonjitsu; K. kwŏn sil 權實). In Chinese, "provisional versus definitive" or "conventional versus absolute," a bifurcation used in the TIANTAI school to refer to either the different grades of the Buddhist teachings or the different levels of truth to which the teaching points. In the former context, quan is equivalent to "provisional" as in "provisional teaching" (NEYĀRTHA), and shi is synonymous with "definitive" as in "definitive teaching" (NĪTĀRTHA). In the latter context, quan is equivalent to "conventional" as in the "conventional truth" (SAṂVṚTISATYA, e.g., the relative existence of a "self"), and shi is equivalent to "absolute" as in the "absolute truth" (PARAMĀRTHASATYA, e.g., all dharma lack a "self"). Used adjectivally, these two Sinographs modify a variety of other Chinese characters to form new compounds. See also FAXING ZONG.

**Questions of King Milinda**. See MILINDAPAÑHA.

# R

**Rabten, Geshe**. (1920–1986). A Tibetan monk-scholar of the DGE LUGS sect who played an important role in the transmission of Tibetan Buddhism in the West. He was born into a farming family approximately fifty miles south of Dar rgyas (Dargye) monastery in the Tre hor region of Khams. At the age of seventeen Geshe Rabten began his studies at SE RA monastery in LHA SA; he later became the teacher of the five-year-old incarnate lama Dgon gsar rin po che (Gonsar Rinpoche), who would remain his close disciple throughout Geshe Rabten's life. Geshe Rabten and Dgon gsar followed the DALAI LAMA into exile where he received his DGE BSHES lha ram pa degree in 1963 at the age of forty-three. He attracted many students, was appointed religious assistant (mtshan zhabs) to the DALAI LAMA, and began to teach Western students in 1969. He started Tharpa Chöling Center of Higher Tibetan Studies near Lausanne, Switzerland, later in 1977. His full name is Dge bshes Rta mgrin rab brtan (Geshe Tamdin Rabten).

**Rādha**. (C. Luotuo; J. Rada; K. Rada 羅陀). Sanskrit and Pāli proper name of an eminent ARHAT deemed by the Buddha to be foremost among his monk disciples who were able to inspire speech in others. According to the Pāli account, Rādha was an aging brāhmaṇa who was neglected by his children in his old age and sought to enter the order of monks (SAṂGHA) for refuge. He initially went to a monastery in RĀJAGṚHA, where he performed chores, but was refused ordination by the monks because of his advanced age. Out of disappointment, Rādha began to grow thin. The Buddha, realizing that Rādha had the potential to achieve arhatship, summoned the monks and asked if any of them remembered any act of kindness performed for them by Rādha. ŚĀRIPUTRA recalled once receiving a ladle of food from Rādha's meager meal while on alms rounds in Rājagṛha, so the Buddha ordered Śāriputra to ordain him and soon afterward, he became an arhat. Śāriputra was pleased with Rādha's gentle behavior and kept him as an attendant; he also served for a time as an attendant to the Buddha. It was during that time that he was recognized for preeminence in inspiring others. His power even influenced the Buddha, who said that whenever he saw Rādha, he felt inclined to speak on subtle aspects of doctrine because of Rādha's wealth of views and his constant faith.

**rāga**. (T. 'dod chags; C. tan; J. ton; K. t'am 貪). In Sanskrit and Pāli, "passion," or "desire," one of the six root afflictions (MŪLAKLEŚA) and typically listed along with aversion (DVEṢA) and ignorance (MOHA) as one of the three poisons (TRIVIṢA) that cause suffering. Rāga is defined as a mental factor that perceives an internal or external contaminated phenomenon to be pleasant and then seeks it. It is closely synonymous with "greed" (LOBHA). In this denotation, rāga is also sometimes called KĀMARĀGA. In Buddhist psychology, when contact with objects is made "without proper comprehension" or "without introspection" (ASAṂPRAJANYA), passion, aversion, and delusion arise. Passion—which is a psychological reaction that is associated with the pursuing, possessing, or yearning for a pleasing stimulus and with being discontent with unpleasant stimuli—may target a host of possible objects. Scriptural accounts list these objects of passion as sensual pleasures, material belongings, loved ones, fame, the five aggregates (SKANDHA), ideologies and views (DṚṢṬI), the meditative absorptions (DHYĀNA) of the "subtle materiality" and "immaterial" realms, the future "rebecoming" of the "self" (S. bhavarāga), and "nonexistence," viz., the future "annihilation" of the "self" (S. abhavarāga). It is noteworthy that the object of desire must be contaminated (SĀSRAVA), which in this context means that the object must be one whose observation results in an increase in such afflictions as hatred, ignorance, pride, and jealousy. This fact is relevant in light of the common question about whether the desire for enlightenment is a form of desire: it is not, because the object of that desire—NIRVĀṆA or buddhahood—is not a contaminated object. See also RŪPARĀGA.

**Rāhula**. (T. Sgra gcan 'dzin; C. Luohouluo; J. Ragora; K. Rahura 羅睺羅). In Sanskrit and Pāli, "Fetter"; proper name of the ARHAT who was the Buddha's only child, born on the day his father renounced the world. According to the Pāli account, as soon as Prince SIDDHARTHA learned of the birth of his son, he immediately chose to become a mendicant, for he saw his son as a "fetter" binding him ever more tightly to the household life. In a famous scene, the prince looks at his sleeping wife and infant son before departing from the palace to seek enlightenment. He wishes to hold his son one last time but fears that he will awaken his wife and lose his resolve. In the MŪLASARVĀSTIVĀDA VINAYA version of the story, Rāhula was conceived on the night of his father's departure from the palace and remained in gestation for a full six years, being born on the night that his father achieved buddhahood. After his enlightenment, when the Buddha accepted an invitation to visit his father's palace, Rāhula's mother (RĀHULAMĀTĀ) YAŚODHARĀ sent her son to her former husband to ask for his inheritance, whereupon the Buddha ordered ŚĀRIPUTRA to ordain the boy. Rāhula thus became the first novice (ŚRĀMAṆERA) to enter the order. Knowing Yaśodharā's grief at the loss of her son, the Buddha's father, King ŚUDDHODANA, requested that in the future no child should be ordained without the consent of his parents; the Buddha accepted his request and a question about parental consent was incorporated into the ordination procedure. Rāhula is described as dutiful and always in search of instruction. In one sermon to the young boy, the Buddha warns him never to lie, even in jest. Rāhula often accompanied the Buddha or Śāriputra on their alms rounds (PIṆḌAPĀTA). The meditation topic the Buddha assigned to Rāhula was intended to counter the novice's strong carnal nature. When his mind was ready, the Buddha taught him the *Cūḷa-Rāhulovādasutta*, at the end of which Rāhula attained arhatship. Rāhula was meticulous in his observation of the monastic regulations, and the Buddha declared him foremost among his disciples in his eagerness for training. According to Chinese sources, Rāhula was also renowned for his patience. One day in ŚRĀVASTĪ, he was harshly beaten and was bleeding badly from a head wound, but he bore his injury with composure and equanimity, which led the Buddha to praise him. Rāhula was also foremost in "practicing with discretion" (C. mixing diyi), meaning that he applied himself at all times in religious practice but without making a display of it. Rāhula passed away before both Śāriputra and the Buddha during a sojourn in TRĀYASTRIṂŚA heaven. In previous lives, Rāhula had many times been the son of the bodhisattva. He was called "lucky Rāhula" by his friends and Rāhula himself acknowledged his good fortune both for being the Buddha's son and for attaining arhatship. In the MAHĀYĀNA, Rāhula appears in a number of sūtras, such as the SADDHARMAPUṆḌARĪKASŪTRA, where his father predicts that he will become a buddha. Rāhula is also traditionally listed as eleventh of the sixteen ARHAT elders (ṢOḌAŚASTHAVIRA), who were charged by the Buddha with protecting his dispensation until the advent of the next buddha, MAITREYA. He is said to reside in Biliyangqu zhou (a Sanskrit transcription that supposedly means "land of chestnuts and grains") with 1,100 disciples. In CHANYUE GUANXIU's standard Chinese depiction, Rāhula is portrayed sitting on a rock in wide-eyed meditation, with his right finger held above his chest, pointing outward, and his left hand resting on his left knee.

**Rāhulamātā**. In Pāli, "Mother of RĀHULA," in the Pāli scriptures, a common term for Prince SIDDHĀRTHA's wife YAŚODHARĀ. See YAŚODHARĀ.

**rainbow body**. See 'JA' LUS.

**rains retreat**. See VARṢĀ.

**Rājagṛha**. (P. Rājagaha; T. Rgyal po'i khab; C. Wangshe cheng; J. Ōshajō; K. Wangsa sŏng 王舍城). Sanskrit name for the capital of the kingdom of MAGADHA during the time of the Buddha. Rājagṛha was known by several other names, including Girivraja, Vasumati, Bṛhadrathapura, Kuśāgarapura, Magadhapura, and Bimbisārapura. During the Buddha's lifetime, Rājagṛha was the capital city of King BIMBISĀRA, the ruler of Magadha and the first royal patron of the Buddha and his SAṂGHA. The Buddha's first visit occurred prior to his enlightenment, when he passed through the city shortly after his renunciation. He was watched on his alms round by Bimbisāra, who offered him half of his kingdom. The prince refused but promised to visit the city after he achieved his goal. When the Buddha returned to the city in the first year after his enlightenment, Bimbisāra donated a grove for the use of the Buddha and his monks during the rains retreat (VARṢĀ). It was called VEṆUVANAVIHĀRA, or "Bamboo Grove Monastery," and the Buddha spent several rains retreats after his enlightenment there (according to several sources, he spent his second, third, fourth, seventeenth, and twentieth rains retreat there). The Buddha received ŚĀRIPUTRA and MAHĀMAUDGALYĀYANA into the order in Rājagṛha. GṚDHRAKŪṬAPARVATA, or "Vulture Peak," the site where the PRAJÑĀPĀRAMITĀ sūtras, among many others, were delivered, was located outside the city. Together with ŚRĀVASTĪ, Rājagṛha was one of the two most important centers of the Buddha's activities. The Buddha made a final visit to the city shortly before his death. After his cremation, the city received a share of the Buddha's relics (ŚARĪRA) and AJĀTAŚATRU, Bimbisāra's son and successor, erected a STŪPA to house them. It is said that Ajātaśatru later gathered seven of the shares of the Buddha's relics and enshrined them in a single stūpa, from which AŚOKA later obtained the relics for the eighty-four thousand stūpas he is said to have erected. The first Buddhist council (see COUNCIL, FIRST) took place at Rājagṛha, during the first rains retreat immediately following the death of the Buddha. The great monastic university of NĀLANDĀ was located on the outskirts of Rājagṛha. Rājagṛha was in a dilapidated condition by the time the Chinese pilgrim XUANZANG visited the area in the seventh century CE.

**rājalīlāsana**. (T. rgyal po rol pa'i stabs). In Sanskrit, "posture of royal ease," a seated pose (ĀSANA) similar to LALITĀSANA, formed with the right knee bent vertically and left knee horizontally, with the heels lightly touching on the seat. The leg positions may be reversed and one arm often rests atop the lifted knee with the other pushing up from the ground. This pose is characteristically found in certain bodhisattva images of AVALOKITEŚVARA or MAÑJUŚRĪ, and in representations of the Tibetan religious kings. See also ĀSANA.

**rakṣā**. [alt. rākṣā] (P. rakkhā; T. srung ba; C. yonghu; J. ōgo; K. ongho 擁護). In Sanskirt, "protection," "safeguard," referring to ritual actions or practices that are intended to ward off baleful and impure influences. These protective acts are often performed as a preliminary step in constructing a MAṆḌALA, performing an initiation ritual (ABHIṢEKA), or cultivating meditative practices. The ritual is performed by inviting or imagining deities who purify the body, speech, and mind of the practitioner, and remove all inner and outer obstacles and evils; a common form of the Tibetan ritual utilizes a distinctive form of propitiatory offering (S. bali) called a GTOR MA (torma), small conical cakes. The officiating tantric master (VAJRĀCĀRYA) attracts the negative forces (T. gegs) to the offering, where they are propitiated or bound and led away from the assembly. Setting up a "wheel of protection" is an integral part of many ANUTTARAYOGATANTRA ritual practices (SĀDHANA) (see RAKṢĀCAKRA). A "protection cord" (rakṣāsūtra; T. srung skud) is ritually embued with protective power by a tantric master and given to each supplicant at the start of an initiation ritual; this is a piece of string or a narrow strip of cloth, usually red, that is tied around the neck, arm, or the wrist to protect the wearer. Tibetan religious figures often give visitors a "protection cord" as a gift. Small amulets (T. ga'u) housing protective buddhas, relics, or tightly rolled copies of ritual invocations or mantras believed to be particularly efficacious against harm are also carried on a belt or around the neck. See also PARITTA; RATANASUTTA.

**rakṣācakra**. (T. srung gi 'khor lo). In Sanskrit, "wheel of protection," a figurative wheel used to destroy internal and external evils during tantric rituals and meditative practices. The wheel is created through ritual actions or visualization as a preliminary step in constructing a MAṆḌALA, performing an initiation ritual (ABHIṢEKA), or cultivating meditative practices. The wheel has various intents, including maintaining the faithfulness of the disciple toward one's master, destroying the power of an enemy, preventing the intrusion of baleful influences, preventing infectious diseases, or averting a curse. For example, in the GUHYASAMĀJATANTRA, a practitioner visualizes a wheel with ten spokes, representing the ten directions (DAŚADIŚ). Each spoke is occupied by the ten wrathful deities (daśakrodha), who conquer enemies or inner hindrances, the names and the locations of which are as follows: YAMĀNTAKA (east), Prajñāntaka (south), Padmāntaka (west), Vighnāntaka (north), ACALA (northeast), Ṭakkirāja (southeast), Nīladaṇḍa (southwest), Mahābala (northwest), Uṣṇīṣacakravartin (zenith), and Sumbha (nadir). The practitioner then imagines demonic beings filling the areas between the spokes, so that, as the wheel turns, the spokes destroy the demons. In a more detailed explanation, the demons are also bound by ropes and put in well-like cells in the ground. This wheel is also called "wheel of the ten spokes" (daśacakra).

**rākṣasa**. [alt. rakṣas] (P. rakkhasa; T. srin po; C. luocha; J. rasetsu; K. rach'al/nach'al 羅刹). In Sanskrit, "ogre"; a species of demigod in Buddhist mythology (the female form is an "ogress," or rākṣasī) usually described as a flesh-eating demon that is able to fly, run like the wind, and possess superhuman strength during the night. According to numerous Buddhist texts, including the SADDHARMAPUṆḌARĪKASŪTRA ("Lotus Sūtra") and the ABHINIṢKRAMAṆASŪTRA, the island of Sri Lanka is inhabited by ogres, who are able to shape-shift and seduce human beings in order to eat them. In the MAHĀPARINIRVĀṆASŪTRA, the king of the gods, INDRA, is said to have assumed the form of a rākṣasa in order to test the spiritual resolve of a young ascetic—ŚĀKYAMUNI Buddha in one of his previous lifetimes. Rākṣasas are also described as horse- or ox-headed wardens of a hell, who torture the hell denizens (NĀRAKA); in this case, they are often identified with YAKṢA. In the Buddhist pantheon, there is a rākṣasadeva (C. luocha tian), or lord of the rākṣasa, who presides over the southwest as one of the twelve directional guardians; this deva is also called NIRṚTI. The deva appears on the outer perimeter of the two MAṆḌALAs, the VAJRADHĀTU and GARBHADHĀTU maṇḍalas, at the bottom right side, representing the southwesterly direction. In Tibetan Buddhist accounts of the early spread of Buddhism (SNGA DAR), the land of Tibet is described as the supine body of a female ogress (rākṣasī; T. srin mo) who has to be pinned down with a series of temples (MTHA' 'DUL GTSUG LAG KHANG) built over strategic places on her body.

**Ral pa can**. (Ralpachen) (r. 815–838). The name by which Khri gtsug lde btsan (Titsuk Detsen), the forty-first ruler of the Tibetan dynastic period, is best known. He is considered to be the third of three great religious kings (chos rgyal) of Tibet, together with his predecessors SRONG BTSAN SGAM PO and KHRI SRONG LDE BTSAN. All three are regarded as human incarnations of the bodhisattva AVALOKITEŚVARA. Ral pa can is remembered as an enthusiastic patron of Buddhism, especially for raising the position and prestige of monks by establishing a tax to sustain their needs. He was so devoted to the SAṂGHA that he is said to have allowed monks to sit on his long locks of hair; his sobriquet "ral pa can" means "having long locks." He patronized the translation of Buddhist texts from a wide range of materials, including TANTRAs and ŚĀSTRAs that were not transmitted to other countries in East or Southeast Asia. The first standard Sanskrit–Tibetan lexicon, the MAHĀVYUTPATTI, was also completed during his reign. In addition to his support for Buddhism, Ral pa can is known for his military conquests, which expanded the territory of the Tibetan empire to its largest extent, conquering regions of China, India, Nepal, Khotan, Turkestan, and Gansu. After Tibetan armies attacked Yanzhou in modern Shandong Province, the Chinese sued for peace. A peace treaty in 821 set the boundaries between the two countries, marking a period of peaceful relations along the border. Three great bilingual steles bearing the inscription of this treaty were fashioned. One, erected in 823, still stands in front of the JO KHANG temple. Ral pa can's Buddhist sympathies eventually garnered the resentment of the aristocracy. In 838, he was assassinated by his elder brother, GLANG DAR MA, thus ending the period of the religious kings and the early propagation (SNGA DAR) of Buddhism in Tibet. According to Buddhist accounts, his death initiated a period of persecution of Buddhism.

**Rāma IV**. (Mongkut) (1804–1868). Thai monarch who spent twenty-seven years as a monk before becoming king of Siam. As a monk between 1824 and 1851 (his ordination name was Vajirañāna), Mongkut's studies led him to conclude that the VINAYA was not being strictly observed by the Thai SAṂGHA and that many rituals performed by monks did not derive from the Buddha's teachings. In 1830, he organized a small group of reformist monks called the THAMMAYUT nikai (P. Dhammayuttikanikāya), "the group that adheres strictly to the dharma," in contrast to what came to be known as the MAHANIKAI (P. Mahānikāya), the "great congregation" of monks who continued to follow the then-normative practices of Thai Buddhism. To establish this new reform tradition of Thai Buddhism, Mongkut drew on what he considered to be a pure ordination lineage from the Mon people of Burma (Myanmar). Prince Mongkut also sought to produce an authentic recension of the Pāli canon after finding the extant editions deficient and incomplete. His new movement emphasized study of the tipiṭaka (S. TRIPIṬIKA) as the basis for understanding Buddhist doctrine and rejected as unorthodox many Buddhist texts popular in Thai Buddhism (such as the *Traiphumikatha* as well as the JĀTAKA tales). The Thammayut movement also stressed proper monastic discipline, particularly details such as the correct way of wearing the robes (TRICĪVARA) and carrying the alms bowl (PĀTRA), as well as the proper demarcation of monastic space (SĪMĀ). Mongkut's reforms began a trend that led to the SAṄGHA ADMINISTRATION ACT, passed in 1902, establishing uniform practices for all monks throughout the country. Mongkut had considerable interaction with Western missionaries and was sensitive to their bias regarding Christianity's supposed superiority over Buddhism because of its affinities for science and technology. In possible response to this European influence, Mongkut and the Thammayut movement also emphasized the rational aspects of Buddhism that sought to make their religion compatible with science and modernity. Mongkut eventually became abbot of WAT BOWONNIWET (Wat Bovoranives) in the Thai capital of Bangkok, which continues to be the headquarters of the Thammayut sect. After Mongkut ascended to the throne, the Thammayut continued to be closely associated with the royal court; the majority of Thai monks, however, have remained in the Mahanikai order. Rāma IV, to the chagrin of many Thais, is the historical (if fanciful) figure behind Anna Leonowens's memoir about her experience in the Thai court as tutor to Mongkut's children, which became the inspiration for Margaret Landon's book *Anna and the King of Siam* and the Rodgers and Hammerstein musical *The King and I*.

**Rāma V**. (Chulalongkorn) (1853–1910). Thai monarch revered for his efforts to modernize the country; credited with moving Thailand into the modern age and maintaining close relations with the European colonial powers, while protecting the independence of his kingdom. He was known in Thai as the Royal Buddha ("Phra Phutta Jao Luang"). Like his father, RĀMA IV, he was a strong patron of Buddhism. In 1893, he had the Pāli tipiṭaka (S. TRIPIṬAKA) published in thirty-nine volumes and distributed to five hundred monasteries of the kingdom. This was the first time that a Buddhist canon had been printed in codex form. In 1895, he sent sets to 260 academic institutions and libraries around the world. Rāma V founded both of Thailand's public Buddhist universities, Mahachulalongkornrajavidyalaya (affiliated with the MAHANIKAI fraternity) and Mahamakut Buddhist University (affiliated with the THAMMAYUT fraternity), in 1887 and 1893, respectively. Since the late 1980s, Rāma V has been the object of popular devotion. Books, portraits, amulets, and chanting of khatha (magic formulae) are among the manifestations of this reverence, which culminates on Chulalongkorn Day (October 23), a national holiday commemorating the monarch's death.

**Rāmañña Nikāya**. Pāli name of one of the three predominant monastic fraternities (P. NIKĀYA) within the Sinhalese THERAVĀDA SAṂGHA, the others being the majority SIYAM NIKĀYA and the AMARAPURA NIKĀYA. The Rāmañña Nikāya is the smallest of these three, their monastic population being a third that of the Siyam Nikāya and half that of the Amarapura Nikāya. The Rāmañña Nikāya was one of several reform schools that appeared in Sri Lanka in the mid-nineteenth century. At that time, the dominant Siyam Nikāya only ordained members of the elite Goyigama caste. The Goyigama caste was concentrated in the interior highlands of Sri Lanka, which was governed by the Kandyan king. The lower castes—comprised of toddy tappers and cinnamon peelers (salāgama), who formed the majority population in the British-controlled coastal lowlands—were at most given lower ordination (P. pabbajjā; see S. PRAVRAJITA) as novices (P. sāmaṇera; S. ŚRĀMAṆERA). This discrimination led to the formation of as many as thirty religious orders whose members came from lower or rising castes. Members of the cinnamon-peeler caste sponsored delegations of religious aspirants who traveled to Burma (Myanmar) in order to receive ordination in an established lineage, ordination they could not receive in Sri Lanka. One such aspirant from the salāgama caste was Ambagahawatte Saranankara, who was ordained on June 12, 1861, by Venerable Gneiyadharma Sangharāja of the Ratnapunna Vihāra in Burma. In 1864, Ambagahawatte Saranankara returned to Sri Lanka and established the Rāmañña Nikāya order. (Rāmañña is the Pāli name for the region of south-coastal Burma.) The Rāmañña Nikāya was established not only in response to caste discrimination but also as an attempt to reform the practices of the Sri Lankan saṃgha. Indeed, the Rāmañña Nikāya's official status as an institution that makes no distinction between castes is portrayed as a return to the Buddha's acceptance of all strata of the Indian caste system. The Rāmañña Nikāya is particularly strong in the southwestern coastal regions of Sri Lanka, where it was founded.

**Rāmeśvara**. (S). One of the twenty-four sacred sites associated with the CAKRASAṂVARATANTRA. See PĪṬHA.

**Ra mo che**. One of the two oldest and most important religious institutions of LHA SA, together with the JO KHANG temple. Constructed during the same period as the Jo khang, the Ra mo che temple was originally intended as the repository of the famed JO BO SHĀKYAMUNI statue brought to Tibet by King SRONG BTSAN SGAM PO's Chinese bride, WENCHENG. According to legend, when the statue was being transported into the city, the cart became stuck and the princess stated that the temple should be built at that spot. That statue was later moved to the Jo khang and replaced in Ra mo che by the statue that had originally been in the Jo khang, a statue of the Buddha called JO BO MI BSKYOD RDO RJE, which had been brought to Tibet by BHṚKUṬĪ, the Nepalese wife of Srong btsan sgam po. Prior to 1959, Ra mo che was the site of RGYUD STOD, a tantric college of the DGE LUGS sect.

**Rang 'byung rdo rje**. (Rangjung Dorje) (1284–1339). A Tibetan Buddhist master recognized as the third KARMA PA, renowned for his erudition and his knowledge of practice traditions based on both new translation (GSAR MA) and old translation (RNYING MA) tantras. He was born either in the Skyid rong Valley or in the western Tibetan region of Ding ri and, according to traditional sources, as a child, was known for his exceptional perspicacity. The DEB THER SNGON PO ("Blue Annals") records that as a five-year-old boy, he met O RGYAN PA RIN CHEN DPAL, his principal guru, who recognized the young boy as the reincarnation of his teacher KARMA PAKSHI when the child climbed up on a high seat that had been prepared for O rgyan pa Rin chen dpal and declared himself to have been Karma Pakshi in his previous life (this was before the institution of incarnate lamas was established in Tibet). Rang 'byung rdo rje trained first at MTSHUR PHU monastery. He also studied with teachers from GSANG PHU and JO NANG. His collected works include explanations of the major YOGĀCĀRA and MADHYAMAKA treatises and commentaries and rituals based on the CAKRASAṂVARA, HEVAJRA, GUHYASAMĀJA, and KĀLACAKRA tantras. According to his traditional biographies, while in retreat, he had a vision of VIMALAMITRA and PADMASAMBHAVA in which he received the complete transmission of the Rnying ma tantras. He received instructions on the RDZOGS CHEN doctrine from Rig 'dzin Gzhon nu rgyal po, and wrote short works on rdzogs chen. He also discovered a treasure text (GTER MA), known as the *Karma snying thig*. He was a renowned poet and wrote important works on GCOD practice. The third Karma pa was also a skilled physician and astrologer. He developed a new system of astrology known as Mtshur rtsi, or "Mtshur phu astrology," on the basis of which a new Tibetan calendar was formulated and promulgated at Mtshur phu monastery. In 1331, he was summoned to the court of the Yuan emperor Tugh Temür, but stopped enroute when he correctly interpreted portents that the emperor had died. He later traveled to the Mongol capital of Daidu (modern Beijing) during the reign of Togon Temür, for whom he procured an elixir of long life. After returning to Tibet, he was summoned once again to the Mongol capital, where he passed away while meditating in a three-dimensional Cakrasaṃvara MAṆḌALA. Rang 'byung rdo rje's writings include the influential tantric work *Zab mo nang don* ("Profound Inner Meaning"). It is said that his image appeared in the full moon on the evening of his death, and illustrations of the third Karma pa often portray him seated amid a lunar disk.

**Rang 'byung rig pa'i rdo rje**. (Rangjung Rikpe Dorje) (1924–1981). A renowned and influential Tibetan Buddhist master, recognized as the sixteenth Karma pa, principal leader of the KARMA BKA' BRGYUD sect of Tibetan Buddhism. He was born in 1924 in the SDE DGE area of Khams, eastern Tibet, to an aristocratic family, and was recognized as the incarnation of the fifteenth Karma pa by the eleventh TAI SI TU. At the age of eight, the Karma pa was enthroned by the Tai Si tu at DPAL SPUNGS monastery in Khams. Soon after, he went to MTSHUR PHU monastery in central Tibet, where he undertook his studies. In his early years, he received many important Bka' brgyud, SA SKYA, and RNYING MA teachings from eminent masters of the time. In his teenage years, the Karma pa divided his time between Mtshur phu and Dpal spungs monasteries, settling at Mtshur phu at the age of eighteen for several years of retreat. In 1947, the Karma pa took his first long pilgrimage and visited the holy sites of India, Nepal, and Sikkim. In 1954, he accompanied the fourteenth DALAI LAMA to Beijing in attempts to find a peaceful agreement between the nations of China and Tibet. The next year, the Karma pa returned to Khams, where he sought to mediate conflicts between Tibetan militias and the Chinese military, which was beginning to establish a presence in Tibet. By the spring of 1959, the Karma pa decided that it would be better for the preservation of his tradition's religious heritage to leave his homeland and move into exile. After informing the Dalai Lama of his decision, the Karma pa left for Bhutan with an entourage of one hundred fifty laypeople, incarnate lamas (SPRUL SKU), and monks. He soon moved to Rumtek (Rum theg) monastery in Sikkim, which had been founded previously by the ninth Karma pa DBANG PHYUG RDO RJE. By 1966, the sixteenth Karma pa and his followers had restored Rumtek and formed a new seat in exile for the Karma Bka' brgyud sect. Rang 'byung rig pa'i rdo rje was renowned for his erudition in Buddhist philosophy as well as his mastery of meditation and his ability to work miracles. Beginning in 1974, the sixteenth Karma pa undertook numerous journeys to Europe and North America, where he founded several important Karma bka' brgyud study and meditation centers. During this time, he traveled widely, attracting a great number of Western disciples. In 1981, the sixteenth Karma pa passed away in a hospital near Chicago. His attending physician attested to the fact that the Karma pa's body remained warm for three days after being pronounced dead. Rang 'byung rig pa'i rdo rje was succeeded by the seventeenth Karma pa, O rgyan 'phrin las rdo rje (Orgyan Tinle Dorje).

**rang rgyud shar gsum**. (rang gyu shar sum). In Tibetan, "the three [texts] of the eastern Svātantrikas," a term used to refer to three important works of the SVĀTANTRIKA MADHYAMAKA school of Indian Buddhism (although the appellation "*Svātantrika" was not used in India and was applied retrospectively by Tibetan doxographers) composed by authors from eastern India. The three works are the MADHYAMAKĀLAṂKĀRA by ŚĀNTARAKṢITA, the MADHYAMAKĀLOKA by KAMALAŚĪLA, and the SATYADVAYAVIBHAṄGA by JÑĀNAGARBHA.

**rang stong gzhan stong**. (rang dong shen dong). In Tibetan, lit. "self-emptiness, other-emptiness," an important and persistent philosophical debate in Tibetan Buddhism, dating to the fifteenth century. The opposing factions are the DGE LUGS sect on one side and the JO NANG sect on the other, with support from certain BKA' BRGYUD and RNYING MA authors. The debate concerns issues fundamental to their understanding of what constituted enlightenment and the path to its achievement. For the Dge lugs, the most profound of all Buddhist doctrines is that all phenomena in the universe are empty of an intrinsic nature (SVABHĀVA), that the constituents of experience are not naturally endowed with a defining characteristic. Emptiness (ŚŪNYATĀ) for the Dge lugs is the fact that phenomena do not exist in and of themselves; emptiness is instead the lack of intrinsic existence. The Dge lugs then, are proponents of "self-emptiness," and argue that the hypostatized factor that an object in reality lacks (i.e., is empty of) is wrongly believed by the unenlightened to be intrinsic to the object itself. Everything, from physical forms to the omniscient mind of the Buddha, is thus equally empty. This emptiness is described by the Dge lugs as a non-affirming or simple negation (PRASAJYAPRATIṢEDHA), an absence with nothing else implied in its place. From this perspective, the Dge lugs judge the sūtras of the second of the three turnings of the wheel of the dharma as described in the SAṂDHINIRMOCANASŪTRA, "the dharma wheel of signlessness" (ALAKṢAṆADHARMACAKRA), to contain the definitive expression of the Buddha's most profound intention. By contrast, the Jo nang look for inspiration to the third turning of the wheel, "the dharma wheel for ascertaining the ultimate" (PARAMĀRTHAVINIŚCAYADHARMACAKRA; see also *SUVIBHAKTADHARMACAKRA), especially to those statements that describe the nonduality of subject and object to be the consummate nature (PARINIṢPANNA) and the understanding of that nonduality to be the highest wisdom. They describe this wisdom in substantialist terms, calling it eternal, self-arisen, and truly established. This wisdom consciousness exists autonomously and is thus not empty in the way that emptiness is understood by the Dge lugs. Instead, this wisdom consciousness is empty in the sense that it is devoid of all afflictions and conventional factors, which are extraneous to its true nature. Hence, the Jo nang speak of the "emptiness of the other," the absence of extrinsic and extraneous qualities. The Dge lugs cannot deny the presence of statements in the MAHĀYĀNA canon that speak of the TATHĀGATAGARBHA as permanent, pure, blissful, and endowed with self. But they argue that such statements are provisional, another example of the Buddha's expedient means of attracting to the faith those who find such a description appealing. The true tathāgatagarbha, they claim, is the emptiness of the mind; it is this factor, present in all sentient beings, that offers the possibility of transformation into an enlightened buddha. This is the view of CANDRAKĪRTI, they say, whom they regard as the supreme interpreter of the doctrine of emptiness. The Jo nang do not deny that this is Candrakīrti's view, but they deny Candrakīrti the rank of premier expositor of NĀGĀRJUNA's thought. For them, Candrakīrti teaches an emptiness which is a mere negation of true existence, which they equate with nihilism, or else a preliminary stage of negation that precedes an understanding of the highest wisdom. Nor do they deny that such an exposition is also to be found in Nāgārjuna's philosophical corpus (YUKTIKĀYA). But those texts, they claim, do not represent Nāgārjuna's final view, which is expressed instead in his devotional corpus (STAVAKĀYA), notably the DHARMADHĀTUSTAVA ("Praise of the Sphere of Reality"), with its more positive exposition of the nature of reality. Those who would deny its ultimate existence, such as Candrakīrti, they classify as "one-sided Madhyamakas" (phyogs gcig pa'i dbu ma pa) as opposed to the "great Madhyamakas" (DBU MA PA CHEN PO), among whom they would include the Nāgārjuna of the four hymns and ĀRYADEVA, as well as thinkers whom the Dge lugs classify as YOGĀCĀRA or SVĀTANTRIKA-MADHYAMAKA: e.g., ASAṄGA, VASUBANDHU, MAITREYANĀTHA, and ŚĀNTARAKṢITA. The Dge lugs attempt to demonstrate that the nature of reality praised by Nāgārjuna in his hymns is the same emptiness that he describes in his philosophical writings.

**rasa**. (T. ro; C. wei; J. mi; K. mi 味). In Sanskrit and Pāli, "taste," sensory objects of the tongue; the contact (SPARŚA) between the gustatory sense organ (JIHVENDRIYA) and the gustatory sensory object leads to gustatory consciousness (JIHVĀVIJÑĀNA). Six types of taste are enumerated in the ABHIDHARMA: sweet, sour, salty, pungent, bitter, and astringent.

**rasanā**. (T. ro ma). In tantric physiology, the channel (NĀḌĪ) that runs from the left nostril to the base of the spine in males and from the right nostril to the base of the spine in females. It is one of three main channels, together with the central channel (AVADHŪTĪ) and the LALANĀ, the left channel in females and the right channel in males. According to some systems, seventy-two thousand channels are found in the body, serving as the conduits for subtle energies or winds (PRĀṆA). The most important of these channels are the avadhūti, the lalanā, and the rasanā. The central channel runs from the place between the eyebrows to the crown of the head and down in front of the spinal column, ending at the genitals. The right and left channels run parallel to the central channel on either side. These two channels wrap around the central channel at various points, of which as many as seven are enumerated. These points, called wheels (CAKRA), are located between the eyes, at the crown of the head, at the throat, at the heart, at the solar plexus, at the base of the spine, and at the tip of sexual organ. In ANUTTARAYOGATANTRA, especially in practices associated with the "stage of completion" (NIṢPANNAKRAMA), much emphasis is placed on loosening these knots in order to cause the winds to flow freely through the central channel.

**rasāyatana**. (T. ro'i skye mched; C. weichu; J. misho; K. mich'ŏ 味處). In Sanskrit, "taste sense field" or "gustatory sense field," i.e., tastes or flavors (RASA) as they occur in the list of twelve sense faculties or "bases of cognition" (ĀYATANA), which serve as the bases for the production of consciousness, viz., the six internal sense bases, or sense organs (eye, ear, nose, tongue, body, and mind), and the six external sense objects (forms, sounds, odors, tastes, tangible objects, and mental phenomena). In the case of taste, the contact (SPARŚA) between the gustatory sense organ (JIHVENDRIYA) and its gustatory sensory object leads to gustatory consciousness (JIHVĀVIJÑĀNA).

**Ras chung pa Rdo rje grags**. (Rechungpa Dorje Drak) (1083/4–1161). A close disciple of the Tibetan sage MI LA RAS PA and an early master of the BKA' BRGYUD sect of Tibetan Buddhism. He was born in the southwest Tibetan region of Gung thang and, while herding cattle at the age of eleven, met Mi la ras pa, who was meditating in a nearby cave. Much to the consternation of his family, Ras chung pa left his home to follow the YOGIN, subsequently spending many years serving and training under his GURU. As one of Milarepa's youngest disciples, he earned the name Ras chung pa, lit. "little cotton-clad one." He was later dispatched to India in order to retrieve several transmissions of the LUS MED MKHA' 'GRO SNYAN RGYUD CHOS SKOR DGU ("nine aural lineage cycles of the formless ḌĀKINĪs"); Mi la ras pa's teacher MAR PA CHOS KYI BLO GROS had only received five of these nine cycles during his own studies in India. Ras chung pa acquired these teachings from the brāhmaṇa-adept TI PHU PA in India and, returning to Tibet, spent many years in solitary meditation. He eventually taught numerous disciples of his own. Although Ras chung pa was not a central part of the Bka' brgyud sect's institutional development, a role played by Mi la ras pa's other well-known disciple SGAM PO PA BSOD NAMS RIN CHEN, he figures prominently in the MI LA'I MGUR 'BUM ("Hundred Thousand Songs of Milarepa"), the collected verse instructions of Mi la ras pa. He also transmitted an important tradition of tantric instructions that were redacted as the RAS CHUNG SNYAN BRGYUD (Aural Lineage of Ras chung). These teachings gained some importance over the next several centuries and were later revived during the fifteenth century by GTSANG SMYON HERUKA at a religious center founded at one of Ras chung pa's principal meditation caves, RAS CHUNG PHUG.

**Ras chung phug**. (Rechung puk). A Tibetan hermitage and monastic center founded around a principal retreat cave of RAS CHUNG PA RDO RJE GRAGS, after whom the cave and complex are named. Located near the Yar klungs and Chong gye valleys of central Tibet, Ras chung phug housed over one thousand monks at the height of its florescence, although it was completely destroyed during the Chinese Cultural Revolution. During the fifteenth century, GTSANG SMYON HERUKA, the so-called madman of Gtsang, spent time there and helped to revive the religious tradition of Ras chung pa known as the RAS CHUNG SNYAN BRGYUD (aural lineage of Ras chung).

**Ras chung snyan brgyud**. (Rechung nyengyu). In Tibetan, lit. "the aural lineage of Ras chung," referring to RAS CHUNG PA RDO RJE GRAGS, a principal disciple of the BKA' BRGYUD founder MI LA RAS PA. Although called an aural lineage (snyan brgyud), it comprises a system of liturgies, ritual manuals, and tantric commentaries, together with their oral instructions, based primarily on the CAKRASAṂVARATANTRA. The lineage began with the LUS MED MKHA' 'GRO SNYAN RGYUD CHOS SKOR DGU ("nine aural lineage cycles of the formless ḌĀKINĪs") promulgated by the Indian adepts TILOPA and NĀROPA. Five of these were subsequently transmitted in Tibet by the Bka' brgyud founders MAR PA CHOS KYI BLO GROS and Mi la ras pa. Ras chung pa received them from Mi la ras pa and then journeyed to India, where he obtained the remaining instructions from the tantric master TI PHU PA. The system of teachings that Ras chung pa subsequently passed on became known as the "aural lineage of Ras chung pa." The fifteenth-century YOGIN GTSANG SMYON HERUKA later codified these teachings, together with those of Mi la ras pa's other prominent disciples, SGAM PO PA BSOD NAM RIN CHEN and Ngan rdzongs ras pa (Ngendzong Repa), into the SNYAN BRGYUD SKOR GSUM ("three cycles of aural lineage instructions").

**Rāṣṭrapāla**. (P. Raṭṭhapāla; T. Yul 'khor skyong; C. Laizhaheluo; J. Raitawara; K. Noet'ahwara 賴吒和羅). In Sanskrit, an eminent ARHAT declared by the Buddha to be foremost among his monk disciples who renounced the world through faith. According to the Pāli account, he was born in Kuru as the son of a wealthy counselor who had inherited the treasure of a destroyed kingdom. He lived with his wives amid great luxury in his father's house in the township of Thullakoṭṭhita. He went to listen to the Buddha preach when the latter was visiting his city and decided at once to renounce the world and become a monk in the Buddha's dispensation. His parents refused to give their permission until he threatened to starve himself to death. They agreed on the condition that he return to visit their house as a monk. After his ordination, Rāṣṭrapāla accompanied the Buddha to ŚRĀVASTĪ (P. Sāvatthi) and there, through assiduous practice, attained arhatship. Having received the Buddha's permission, Rāṣṭrapāla resolved to fulfill his promise to his parents and returned to Thullakoṭṭhita, where he lived in the park of the Kuru king. On his alms round the next morning, he stopped at entrance of his parents' house. His father did not recognize him and mistook him for one of the monks who had enticed his son to abandon his home. He cursed Rāṣṭrapāla and ordered him away. But a servant girl recognized him and offered him the stale rice she was about to throw away and then announced his true identity to his father. His father, filled with joy and hope at seeing his son, invited him to receive his morning meal at his home the next day. When he returned at the appointed time, Rāṣṭrapāla's father tried to tempt him to return to the lay life with a vulgar display of the family's wealth and the beauty of his former wives. They taunted him about the celestial maidens for whose sake he had renounced the world. They fainted in disappointment when he addressed them as "sisters" in reply. At the end of his meal, he preached to his family about the impermanence of conditioned things, the uselessness of wealth, and the enticing trap of physical beauty. But even then they were not convinced, and it is said that Rāṣṭrapāla flew through the air to return to his abode after his father bolted the doors to keep him at home and had servants try to remove his robes and dress him in the garb of a layman.

**Rāṣṭrapālaparipṛcchā**. (T. Yul 'khor skyong gis zhus pa; C. Huguo pusahui [jing]; J. Gokoku bosatsue[kyō]; K. Hoguk posal hoe [kyŏng] 護國菩薩會[經]). In Sanskrit, "The Questions of RĀṢṬRAPĀLA," one of the earliest MAHĀYĀNA sūtras; the terminus ad quem for its composition is the third century CE, when DHARMARAKṢA (c. 233–310) translated the sūtra into Chinese (c. 270 CE), probably following a manuscript from the GANDHĀRA region in the KHAROṢṬHĪ script. (The extant Sanskrit recension is much later.) There are also two later Chinese translations, one made c. 585–600 by JÑĀNAGUPTA and other c. 980 by DĀNAPĀLA. The *Raṣṭrapāla* represents a strand of early MAHĀYĀNA (found also in such sūtras as the KĀŚYAPAPARIVARTA and the UGRAPARIPṚCCHĀ) that viewed the large urban monasteries as being ill-suited to serious spiritual cultivation because of their need for constant fund-raising from the laity and their excessive entanglements in local politics. The *Rāṣṭrapāla* strand of early Mahāyāna instead dedicated itself to forest dwelling (see ARAÑÑAVĀSI) away from the cities, like the "rhinoceros" (KHAḌGAVIṢĀṆA), and advocated a return to the rigorous asceticism (S. DHŪTAGUṆA; see P. DHUTAṄGA) that was thought to characterize the early SAṂGHA. To the *Rāṣṭrapāla* author(s), the Buddha's own infinitely long career as a bodhisattva was an exercise in self-sacrifice and physical endurance, which they in turn sought to emulate through their own asceticism. The physical perfection the Buddha achieved through this long training, as evidenced in his acquisition of the thirty-two major marks of the superman (MAHĀPURUṢALAKṢAṆA), receives special attention in the sūtra. This approach is in marked contrast to other early Mahāyāna sūtras, such as the AṢṬASĀHASRIKĀPRAJÑĀPĀRAMITĀ, which were suspicious of the motives of forest dwellers and supportive of cenobitic monasticism in the towns and cities, where monks and nuns would be in a better position to serve the laity by preaching the dharma to them.

**Ratanasutta**. In Pāli, "Discourse on the Precious," one of the best loved and most widely-recited Buddhist texts in the THERAVĀDA Buddhist world (there is no analogous recension in the Chinese translations of the ĀGAMAS). The *Ratanasutta* appears in an early scriptural anthology, the SUTTANIPĀTA, a later collection, the KHUDDAKAPĀṬHA, and in a postcanonical anthology of PARITTA ("protection texts"). The Pāli commentaries say that the discourse was first delivered to the Buddha's attendant ĀNANDA, who then went around the city of the Licchavis reciting the text and sprinkling holy water from the Buddha's own begging bowl (PĀTRA). Through this performance, the baleful spirits harassing the city were vanquished and all the people's illnesses were cured. The text itself consists of a mere seventeen verses, twelve of which recount the virtues of the three jewels (RATNATRAYA) of the Buddha, DHARMA, and SAṂGHA. The *Ratanasutta*'s great renown derives from its inclusion in the *Paritta* anthology, texts that are chanted as part of the protective rituals performed by Buddhist monks to ward off misfortunes; indeed, it is this apotropaic quality of the text that accounts for its enduring popularity. Paritta suttas refer to specific discourses delivered by the Buddha that are believed to offer protection to those who either recite the sutta or listen to its recitation. Other such auspicious apotropaic suttas are the MAṄGALASUTTA and the METTĀSUTTA. In Southeast Asia, these paritta texts are commonly believed to bring happiness and good fortune when chanted by the saṃgha. See also RAKṢĀ.

**Rathavinītasutta**. (C. Qiche jing; J. Shichishakyō; K. Ch'ilch'a kyŏng 七車經). In Pāli, the "Discourse on the Relay Chariots," the twenty-fourth scripture of the MAJJHIMANIKĀYA (a separate SARVĀSTIVĀDA version appears as the ninth sūtra in the Chinese translation of the MADHYAMĀGAMA, as well as a recension of uncertain affilation in the EKOTTARĀGAMA). This discourse recounts a dialogue between Sāriputta (S. ŚĀRIPUTRA) and Puṇṇa Mantāṇiputta (see PŪRṆA) concerning the seven stages of purification (see VISUDDHI) that must be traversed in order to attain final liberation in nibbāna (NIRVĀṆA), viz., the purification of (1) morality (SĪLAVISUDDHI); (2) mind (CITTAVISUDDHI); (3) views (DIṬṬHIVISUDDHI); (4) overcoming doubt (KAṄKHĀVITARAṆAVISUDDHI); (5) the purity of knowledge and vision of what is and is not the path (MAGGĀMAGGAÑĀṆADASSANAVISUDDHI); (6) knowledge and vision of progress along the path (PAṬIPADĀÑĀṆADASSANAVISUDDHI); (7) knowledge and vision itself (ÑĀṆADASSANAVISUDDHI). The seventh purification leads directly to final nibbāna. The seven stages are compared to a relay of seven chariots needed to transport the king of Kosala (KOŚALA) from his palace in Sāvatthi (ŚRĀVASTĪ) to his palace in Sāketa.

**ratna**. (P. ratana; T. rin chen/dkon mchog; C. zhenbao; J. chinbō; K. chinbo 珍寶). In Sanskrit, "jewel," "valuable," or "treasure," the most common term for a precious object in Buddhist texts and regularly used in Buddhist literature as a metaphor for enlightenment, since jewels represent purity, permanence, preciousness, rarity, etc. TATHĀGATAGARBHA texts often call the tathāgatagarbha or buddha-nature the jewel-nature, since the preciousness of a jewel is unaffected even when it is sullied by mud (defilements); the TATHĀGATAGARBHASŪTRA, for example, specifically compares the tathāgatagarbha to a jewel buried in the dirt (see also RATNAGOTRAVIBHĀGA). In the SADDHARMAPUṆḌARĪKASŪTRA ("Lotus Sūtra"), the buddha-nature is described in a simile as a jewel that a rich man (the Buddha) has surreptitiously sown into the robes of his destitute friend (sentient beings). Such CHAN masters as GUIFENG ZONGMI (780–840) and POJO CHINUL (1158–1210) use jewels as metaphors to explain their theories of the buddha-nature. A jewel is also used to represent the pristine nature of the realm of enlightenment: in the AVATAṂSAKASŪTRA, the bejeweled canopy of the king of the gods, INDRA (see INDRAJĀLA), is deployed to illustrate the mutual interdependence that pertains between all phenomena in the universe. Several different lists of jewels are found in Buddhist literature. The most important is the "three jewels" (RATNATRAYA; TRIRATNA) of the Buddha, DHARMA, and SAṂGHA; commentaries explain that these three are called jewels because they are difficult to find and, once found, are of great value. The Tibetan translation of "three jewels," dkon mchog gsum (könchok sum) (lit. "three rare excellences") reflects this meaning. There are also several different lists of "seven jewels" (saptaratna). One list describes the seven "valuables" that are essential to the successful reign of a wheel-turning monarch (CAKRAVARTIN): a wheel, elephant, horse, gems, a queen, an able minister or treasurer, and a loyal adviser. Another list of seven is of the jewels decorating SUKHĀVATĪ, the PURE LAND of AMITĀBHA; these are listed in the AMITĀBHASŪTRA (see also SUKHĀVATĪVYŪHASŪTRA) as gold, silver, lapis lazuli, crystal, agate, ruby, and carnelian. Finally, there are seven "moral" jewels listed in mainstream Buddhist literature, as in the Pāli list of morality (P. sīla; S. ŚĪLA), concentration (SAMĀDHI), wisdom (P. paññā; S. PRAJÑĀ), liberation (P. vimutti; S. VIMUKTI), the knowledge and vision of liberation (P. vimuttiñāṇadassana; S. vimuktijñānadarśana), analytical knowledge (P. paṭisambhidā; S. PRATISAṂVID), and the factors of enlightenment (P. bojjhaṅga; S. BODHYAṄGA).

**Ratnagiri**. (T. Rin chen ri bo). In Sanskrit, "Bejeweled Mountain," also known as Ratnagiri Mahāvihāra, or "the great monastery Ratnagiri"; the name of an ancient monastery located in the Jajapur district of the contemporary Indian state of Orissa. The site was discovered and excavated in the mid-twentieth century. Ratnagiri was established sometime around the fifth or sixth centuries CE and flourished until the twelfth century. Both textual and archaeological evidence indicates that Ratnagiri, like NĀLANDĀ, was a prosperous and influential center of MAHĀYĀNA philosophy. Furthermore, the monastery appears to have played a significant role in the rise of VAJRAYĀNA and tantric Buddhism in India. The excavation of this site revealed two main monastic complexes, one of which was two stories high. The main reliquary mound (STŪPA) is nearly twenty feet high and fifty feet across at the base. Hundreds of smaller STŪPAS surround it on the main campus. The remains are decorated by carved depictions of buddhas, BODHISATTVAS, and a variety of deities from the Mahāyāna pantheon.

**Ratna gling pa**. (Ratna Lingpa) (1403–1478). An important treasure revealer (GTER STON) of the RNYING MA sect of Tibetan Buddhism, credited with discovering twenty-five collections of treasure texts (GTER MA). As a youth, he was identified as the reincarnation of Lang gro Dkon mchog 'byung gnas, one of the twenty-five disciples of PADMASAMBHAVA. According to traditional sources, he is said to have uncovered in a single lifetime the treasures ordinarily discovered in three lifetimes, and therefore is known under three names: Zhig po gling pa (Shikpo Lingpa), 'Gro 'dul gling pa (Drodul Lingpa), and Ratna gling pa. The treasures included RDZOGS CHEN teachings, peaceful and wrathful guru SĀDHANAS, AVALOKITEŚVARA practices, and MAHĀMUDRĀ texts. He also searched extensively for ancient tantras and oral traditions and compiled an extensive RNYING MA'I RGYUD 'BUM, a compendium of the tantras and tantric exegetical literature of the Rnying ma sect; that compendium is no longer extant, but it served as the basis of the rnying ma'i rgyud 'bum of 'JIGS MED GLING PA.

**Ratnagotravibhāga**. [alt. Ratnagotravibhaṅga] (T. Dkon mchog gi rigs rnam par dbye ba; C. Jiujing yisheng baoxing lun; J. Kukyō ichijō hōshōron; K. Kugyŏng ilsŭng posŏng non 究竟一乘寶性論). In Sanskrit, "Analysis of the Lineage of the [Three] Jewels," a seminal Indian MAHĀYĀNA ŚĀSTRA on the doctrine of the "embryo of the tathāgatas" (TATHĀGATAGARBHA), probably dating from the fourth century CE. Its full title is *Ratnagotravibhāga-Mahāyāna-Uttaratantra* and the treatise is often referred to simply as the *Uttaratantra*, or "Sublime Continuation." The Sanskrit recension is extant, along with Chinese and Tibetan translations. (RATNAMATI's Chinese translation was finished in 508.) The Chinese tradition attributes the work to Sāramati (C. Jianyi), while the Tibetan tradition attributes the core verses of the text to MAITREYA/MAITREYANĀTHA and its prose commentary entitled the *Uttaratantravyākhyā* to ASAṄGA. It is one of the "five books of Maitreya," which, according to legend, were presented by the future buddha Maitreya to Asaṅga during the latter's visit to the TUṢITA heaven. The primary subject of the *Ratnagotravibhāga* is the tathāgatagarbha or buddha-nature; this is the element (DHĀTU) or lineage (GOTRA) of the buddhas, which is present in all beings. The text offers an extensive overview of the tathāgatagarbha doctrine as set forth in such sūtras as the TATHĀGATAGARBHASŪTRA and the ŚRĪMĀLĀDEVĪSIṂHANĀDASŪTRA. Like the *Śrīmālā Sūtra*, the treatise describes the tathāgatagarbha as being both empty (śūnya) of the afflictions (KLEŚA) but nonempty (aśunya) of the buddhas' infinite virtues. In ordinary beings, the tathāgatagarbha may be obscured by adventitious defilements, but when those defilements are removed, the state of enlightenment is restored. In proving this claim, the treatise examines in detail the "body of the tathāgata," an alternate name for the buddha-nature, which is said to have four perfect virtues (GUṆAPĀRAMITĀ): permanence, bliss, selfhood, and purity. Those who have not realized the buddha-nature make two fundamental mistakes about emptiness (ŚŪNYATĀ): either viewing emptiness as annihilation (see UCCHEDADṚṢṬI), assuming that the experience of NIRVĀṆA requires the extinction of the phenomenal world; or substantiating emptiness by presuming that it is something distinct from materiality (RŪPA). Instead, the *Ratnagotravibhāga* asserts that the tathāgatagarbha is free from all the various types of afflictions, but fully contains the myriad inconceivable attributes of a buddha. The treatise also examines the specific deeds the buddhas perform for the welfare of all sentient beings. See also FOXING.

**Ratnaguṇasaṃcayagāthā**. (T. Yon tan rin po che sdud pa tshigs su bcad pa; C. Fomu baodezang bore boluomi jing; J. Butsumo hōtokuzō hannya haramitsukyō; K. Pulmo podŏkchang panya paramil kyŏng 佛母寶德藏般若波羅蜜經). In Sanskrit, "Verses on the Collection of Precious Qualities," the longer title is *Prajñāpāramitāratnaguṇasaṃcayagāthā*, or "Verses on the Collection of the Precious Qualities of the Perfection of Wisdom." The *Ratnaguṇasaṃcayagāthā* epitomizes the early MAHĀYĀNA in its emphasis on the emptiness (ŚŪNYATĀ) of the aggregates (SKANDHA) and its praise of the path of the BODHISATTVA over that of the ARHAT. The text is considered to be of particular importance in the history of the Mahāyāna because many of its verses, particularly those that appear early in the text, may represent some of the earliest expressions of Mahāyāna philosophy and may date as far back as 100 BCE. Another indication of the text's antiquity is that it was translated into Chinese as early as the second century CE. The only extant Sanskrit version is that edited in the eighth century by HARIBHADRA to conform to the structure of the ABHISAMAYĀLAṂKĀRA, making the precise order of the original verses difficult to determine. Many Mahāyāna sūtras are composed of alternating verse and prose. The verses of the *Ratnaguṇasaṃcayagāthā* are written in an ancient meter, suggesting to some that they constitute part of an original sūtra, with the AṢṬASĀHASRIKĀPRAJÑĀPĀRAMITĀ ("Perfection of Wisdom in Eight Thousand Lines") supplying the prose section. However, because the verses that appear in the *Ratnaguṇasaṃcayagāthā* are not in all cases identical to those in the *Aṣṭasāhasrikā*, the *Ratnaguṇasaṃcayagāthā* may have originally been a separate work. It appears as the verse recapitulations in the Chinese translation of the *Aṣṭasāhasrikā* and as the eighty-fourth chapter of the *Aṣṭadaśasāhasrikāprajñāpāramitā* ("Perfection of Wisdom in Eighteen Thousand Lines") in its Tibetan translation.

**Ratnākaraśānti**. (T. Shān ti pa/Rin chen 'byung gnas zhi ba) (c. late-tenth to early-eleventh century). Sanskrit proper name of an Indian scholar philosophically affiliated with the YOGĀCĀRA school, who resided and later taught at the monastic university of VIKRAMAŚĪLA in the northern region of ancient MAGADHA (modern Bengal). At Vikramaśīla, he studied under RATNAKĪRTI and JITĀRI and eventually become a prolific scholar of enormous breadth, who wrote significant works on logic, MADHYAMAKA and PRAJÑĀPĀRAMITĀ, Yogācāra, and TANTRA. Ratnākaraśānti composed at least thirteen works in Sanskrit. His writings on tantra are particularly noteworthy for their attempt to present a systematic view of tantric philosophy and practice from the perspective of Buddhist scholasticism. His works on logic include the *Antarvyāptisamarthana*, on "pervasion" or "concomitance" (VYĀPTI). He wrote commentaries on the eight-thousand- and twenty-five-thousand-line PRAJÑĀPĀRAMITĀ SŪTRAS (entitled *Sārottamā* and *Śuddhamati*, respectively). His tantric works included commentaries on both the HEVAJRATANTRA and GUHYASAMĀJATANTRA, as well as a work on the three vehicles, the *Triyānavyavasthāna*. During his tenure as a teacher at Vikramaśīla, he held the position of eastern gatekeeper. He was a teacher of ATIŚA DĪPAṂKARAŚRĪJÑĀNA, and he offered instruction to Tibetan students, including the translator 'BROG MI SHĀKYA YE SHES, who transmitted the LAM 'BRAS (path and result) teachings to the 'Khon family, who founded the SA SKYA sect. Ratnākaraśānti's fame was so widespread that he was even invited by the Sinhalese king to travel to Sri Lanka and preach. In Tibetan sources, a Shānti pa (a common Tibetan abbreviation of the name Ratnākaraśānti) is reported to have been a student of the renowned tantric adept and scholar NĀROPA (1016–1100), and is listed as one of the eighty-four masters (SIDDHAS) in the CATURAŚĪTISIDDHAPRAVṚTTI ("History of the Eighty-Four Siddhas").

**Ratnakīrti**. (T. Dkon mchog grags pa). Eleventh-century YOGĀCĀRA logician and student of Jñānaśrīmitra at VIKRAMAŚĪLA monastery. He is the author of ten extant treatises on logic, including the *Apohasiddhi*, or "Proof of Exclusion." The work deals with the topic of APOHA, the theory that words refer to concepts rather than to objects in the world and that these concepts are the exclusion of their opposite, i.e., that one's idea of a table, for example, is not that of a specific table but rather a generic image of everything that is "non-nontable," i.e., not not a table. Buddhist logicians considered the question of the negative and positive aspects of the meaning of words as well as their sequence; Ratnakīrti argued that they are simultaneous. The *Ratnakīrtikalā*, a commentary to the ABHISAMAYĀLAṂKĀRA, is attributed to Ratnakīrti, but its author may be a different scholar of the same name.

**ratnakula**. (T. rin chen rigs; C. baobu; J. hōbu; K. pobu 寶部). In Sanskrit, "jewel family," one of the "five lineages" or "five families" (PAÑCAKULA; PAÑCATATHĀGATA) of tantric Buddhism. The five are usually given as the TATHĀGATAKULA, VAJRAKULA, PADMAKULA, ratnakula, and the KARMAKULA (different tantras have different lists of these families). Those in the ratnakula become enlightened in the form of the buddha RATNASAMBHAVA. Each of the five families is associated with one of the five aggregates (SKANDHA), five wisdoms (JÑĀNA), five afflictions (KLEŚA), five elements, and five colors. For the ratnakula, the skandha is sensation (VEDANĀ), the wisdom is the wisdom of equality (SAMATĀJÑĀNA); the affliction is pride, the color yellow, and the element earth.

**Ratnakūṭasūtra**. (T. Dkon mchog brtsegs pa'i mdo; C. Dabaoji jing; J. Daihōshakukyō; K. Taebojŏk kyŏng 大寶積經). In Sanskrit, "The Jewel-Heap Sūtra"; often known also as the *Mahāratnakūṭasūtra*, or "The Great Jewel-Heap Sūtra." Despite its title, this is actually not one SŪTRA but rather an early collection of forty-nine independent MAHĀYĀNA sūtras. The texts contained in this collection cover a broad range of important MAHĀYĀNA topics, including detailed discussions of emptiness (ŚŪNYATĀ), PURE LAND practices, skillful means (UPĀYA), the importance of cultivating both compassion (KARUṆĀ) and wisdom (PRAJÑĀ), and other significant subjects. Many of the texts embedded in the collection are seminal to the Mahāyāna tradition. In this collection, we find treated such influential figures as the buddhas AMITĀBHA and AKṢOBHYA, the BODHISATTVA MAÑJUŚRĪ, and the ARHAT MAHĀKĀŚYAPA. Its KĀŚYAPAPARIVARTA chapter was widely cited in MADHYAMAKA treatises. The collections also contain pure land texts, including the longer SUKHĀVATĪVYŪHASŪTRA as well as the AKṢOBHYATATHĀGATASYAVYŪHA on the pure land of Akṣobhya. The *Trisaṃvaranirdeśaparivarta* explains the bodhisattva VINAYA and how it differs from the vinaya of the ŚRĀVAKAS. Excerpts from the *Ratnakūṭasūtra* were translated into Chinese as early as the second century CE. While the entire collection is available in Chinese and Tibetan, only portions of it survive in Sanskrit. The *Ratnakūṭasūtra* occupies six volumes of the Tibetan canon (BKA' 'GYUR) (with fifty-two separate works in the SDE DGE edition, some with the same title but different content). In Chinese, the best-known recension of the *Ratnakūṭasūtra* is a massive 120-roll translation made by BODHIRUCI between 703 and 716 during the Tang dynasty; it incorporates in the collection some earlier translations of individual texts by DHARMARAKṢA, KUMĀRAJĪVA, ŚIKṢĀNANDA, etc. There are also two shorter renderings of portions of the text, one attributed to AN SHIGAO in the latter half of the second century CE, the second to Jñānagupta (523–600) in 595 CE, both in only one roll.

**Ratnamati**. (Rin chen blo gros; C. Lenamoti; J. Rokunamadai; K. Nŭngnamaje 勒那摩提) (fl. c. 508 CE). In Sanskrit, "Bejeweled Intelligence," name of an Indian scholar and Chinese translator who lived during the fifth and sixth centuries CE. He was especially renowned for his prodigious memory of a great many SŪTRA verses. In 508 CE, Ratnamati traveled from India to the Northern Wei capital of Luoyang, where he began to work on a translation of VASUBHANDU's "Treatise on the Ten Stages" (S. DAŚABHŪMIVYĀKHYĀNA; C. SHIDIJING LUN) with BODHIRUCI and Buddhaśānta (d.u.). However, disagreements between the collaborators over the nature of the ĀLAYAVIJÑĀNA (viz., whether it was pure, impure, or both) led them to produce different translations. Those who studied Bodhiruci's rendering came to be known as the Northern DI LUN ZONG, while the followers of Ratnamati's version were known as the Southern Di lun zong. The Southern Di lun school was represented by Ratnamati's foremost pupil, Huiguang (468–537), who advocated that the ālayavijñāna was an ultimate truth (PARAMĀRTHASATYA) and coextensive with the buddha-nature (FOXING), which thus was in fact innate. Ratnamati subsequently went on to collaborate with other scholars on the translation of other works, including the RATNAGOTRAVIBHĀGA, and the *Saddharmapuṇḍarīkopadeśa* attributed to VASUBANDHU. ¶ Ratnamati is also the name of a bodhisattva who appears in various MAHĀYĀNA sūtras.

**Ratnameghasūtra**. (T. Dkon mchog sprin gyi mdo; C. Baoyun jing; J. Hōungyō; K. Poun kyŏng 寶雲經). The "Cloud of Jewels," an important Mahāyāna sūtra, perhaps dating from the third or fourth century CE. It opens with the Buddha residing on the peak of Mt. Gayāśīrṣa when the BODHISATTVA SARVANĪVARAṆAVIṢKAMBHĪ approaches the Buddha and asks him more than one hundred questions ranging from the practice of giving (DĀNA) and the six perfections (PĀRAMITĀ) to the means of swiftly attaining ANUTTARASAMYAKSAMBODHI. The Buddha's answers to these questions are widely quoted in later ŚĀSTRAS. In China, during the Ming dynasty, there were charges that interpolations were made in the sūtra during the reign of the Empress WU ZETIAN in order to legitimize her usurpation of the throne. These interpolations included the story of Prince Moonlight (Yueguang tongzi), who received a prediction from the Buddha that he would later become a great queen in China.

**Ratnapāṇi**. (T. Lag na rin chen; C. Baoshou pusa; J. Hōshu bosatsu; K. Posu posal 寶手菩薩). In Sanskrit, lit. "Bejeweled Hand" i.e., "one whose hand holds a jewel"; the name of a BODHISATTVA who is most often associated with the buddha RATNASAṂBHAVA, one of the five TATHĀGATAS (PAÑCATATHĀGATA) who are associated with the SARVATATHĀGATATATTVASAṂGRAHA's VAJRADHĀTU and GARBHADHĀTU MAṆḌALAS. Ratnapāṇi is usually depicted as seated with his right hand in the "gesture of generosity" or "boon-granting gesture" (VARADAMUDRĀ); his left hand sits in his lap and holds a wish-fulfilling gem (CINTĀMAṆI).

**Ratnasambhava**. (T. Rin chen 'byung gnas; C. Baosheng rulai; J. Hōshō nyorai; K. Posaeng yŏrae 寶生如來). In Sanskrit, "Born of a Jewel," one of the PAÑCATATHĀGATAS. He is the buddha of the ratna family (RATNAKULA) and his pure land is located in the south. He is often accompanied by the bodhisattva RATNAPĀṆI and his NIRMĀṆAKĀYA is KĀŚYAPA. He is depicted as golden in hue, displaying the VARADAMUDRĀ with his right hand (often with jewels pouring forth), and a CINTĀMAṆI in his left hand; these jewels suggest his ability to both provide material wealth and to enrich one's knowledge of the dharma. He is sometime depicted riding a horse or a pair of lions. When depicted with a consort, it is either Locanā or Māmakī. The least developed of the five tathāgatas, Ratnasambhava is rarely depicted alone and does not seem to have become the object of cultic worship.

**ratnatraya**. [alt. triratna] (P. ratanattaya/tiratana; T. dkon mchog gsum; C. sanbao; J. sanbō; K. sambo 三寶). In Sanskrit, the "three jewels," also translated into English as the "triple gem" or the "three treasures"; the term is also often given as triratna. In the Buddhist tradition, RATNATRAYA refers to the three principal objects of veneration: the Buddha, the DHARMA, and the SAṂGHA. One of the most common practices that define a Buddhist is "taking refuge" (see ŚARAṆA) in the three jewels. This formula, which accompanies many lay and monastic rituals, involves a formal declaration that the practitioner "goes to" each of the three jewels for refuge (śaraṇa) or protection. The Sanskrit formula is as follows: "Buddhaṃ śaraṇaṃ gacchāmi. Dharmaṃ śaraṇaṃ gacchāmi. Saṃghaṃ śaraṇaṃ gacchāmi." meaning "I go to the Buddha for refuge. I go to the dharma for refuge. I go to the saṃgha for refuge." By repeating this formula three times, one identifies oneself as a Buddhist. (See also TRIŚARAṆA.) The precise meanings of these three terms, how they relate to one another, and exactly how each one is to be venerated are all subjects of extensive commentary within the tradition. The term buddha refers first, and most obviously, to the historical Buddha, GAUTAMA or ŚĀKYAMUNI, the sage of ancient India who realized and then taught the way to end all suffering. But the Buddha may also refer to any number of buddhas found in the extensive MAHĀYĀNA pantheon. In some varieties of the Mahāyāna, buddha may even refer to the inherent state of buddhahood that is the fundamental characteristic of all sentient beings. The term dharma refers to the teachings of a buddha, which can take a variety of possible forms including specific beliefs, texts, or practices; the dharma is sometimes divided into the scriptural dharma (ĀGAMADHARMA) and the realized dharma (ADHIGAMADHARMA). In the context of the three jewels, one is said to go for refuge in the latter. However, dharma may also refer to the pervasive, universal truth that is realized by a buddha, particularly as enshrined in the teaching of the FOUR NOBLE TRUTHS (catvāry āryasatyāni). Some commentators specify that in the context of the three jewels, the dharma refers to the third and fourth of the four truths, the truth of cessation (NIRODHASATYA) and the truth of the path (MĀRGASATYA), and most specifically to the truth of cessation. The term saṃgha refers to the community that seeks to realize and enact the teachings of a buddha for the sake of its own liberation and the liberation of others. Saṃgha is usually understood to include only those followers who have renounced the life of a householder (PRAVRAJITA) and taken up the life of a monk (BHIKṢU) or nun (BHIKṢUṆĪ). However, the saṃgha is also sometimes interpreted to include both laymen (UPĀSAKA) and laywomen (UPĀSIKĀ) as well. In the context of refuge, the saṃgha is generally said to refer to those members of the community who are ĀRYAPUDGALA. See ĀRYASAṂGHA.

**Ratnāvalī**. (T. Rin chen phreng ba; C. Baoxingwang zheng lun; J. Hōgyō ō shōron; K. Pohaengwang chŏng non 寶行王正論). In Sanskrit, "Garland of Jewels," a Sanskrit work by the MADHYAMAKA philosopher NĀGĀRJUNA. The work consists of five hundred verses arranged in five chapters. While the *Ratnāvalī* contains many of Nāgārjuna's fundamental philosophical ideas, grounded primarily in the notion of emptiness (ŚŪNYATĀ), the work is more focused on issues of ethics. The *Ratnāvalī* is addressed to King Gautamīputra of ĀNDHRA, a friend and patron of Nāgārjuna, and much of the text discusses the proper conduct of the laity, particularly those in administrative positions such as ministers and kings. In particular, the fourth chapter is devoted to an exploration of kingship and the proper management of a kingdom. The work also contains a defense of the Mahāyāna as the word of the Buddha (BUDDHAVACANA), an exposition of the collection of merit (PUṆYASAṂBHĀRA) and the collection of wisdom (JÑĀNASAṂBHĀRA), a description of the ten bodhisattva stages (BHŪMI) based on the DAŚABHŪMIKASŪTRA, and a correlation of the practice of specific virtues with the achievement of the thirty-two marks of a superman (MAHĀPURUṢALAKṢAṆA). There are complete versions of the work extant in Tibetan and Chinese translations, but only parts survive in the original Sanskrit.

**Raṭṭhapāla**. (P). See RĀṢṬRAPĀLA.

**raudracāra**. (T. drag po'i las). In Sanskrit, "wrathful action," a synonym for ABHICARA. See ABHICARA.

**raurava**. (P. roruva; T. ngu 'bod; C. jiaohuan [diyu]; J. kyōkan[jigoku]; K. kyuhwan [chiok] 叫喚[地獄]). In Sanskrit, "crying" or "weeping," the name of the fourth of the eight hot hells, described as a land of red-hot iron where the denizens constantly weep because of their horrendous suffering.

**ṛddhi**. (P. iddhi; T. rdzu 'phrul; C. shenli; J. jinriki; K. sillyŏk 神力). In Sanskrit, "psychic powers," any number of supernatural powers regarded as a by-product of deep states of meditation (DHYĀNA). When listed as one of the six supranormal powers (ABHIJÑĀ; see also ṚDDHIVIDHĀBHIJÑĀ), these psychic powers include: (1) the ability to replicate one's body and, having done so, to make it one again; (2) the ability to pass through solid objects, such as walls and mountains, as if they were air; (3) the ability to walk on water as if it were solid earth; (4) the ability to fly through the air like a bird, even with one's legs crossed; and (5) the ability to touch the sun and the moon with one's hand. Such powers may be attained by any YOGIN, whether Buddhist or non-Buddhist, and are not in themselves an indicator of enlightenment. The Buddha is said to have generally dissuaded his monks from the display of such powers, although Buddhist texts are replete with accounts of such displays, including by the Buddha himself.

**ṛddhipāda**. (P. iddhipāda; T. rdzu 'phrul gyi rkang pa; C. si shenzu; J. shijinsoku; K. sasinjok 四神足). In Sanskrit, "bases of psychic powers," the four qualities that are regarded as prerequisites for the attainment of magical power. They are aspiration (CHANDA), thought (CITTA), effort (VĪRYA), and analysis (mīmāṃsā).

**ṛddhividhābhijñā**. (P. iddhividhābhiññā; T. rdzu 'phrul mngon shes; C. shenjing zhizhengtong; J. jinkyōchishōtsū; K. sin'gyŏng chijŭngt'ong 神境智證通). In Sanskrit, "psychic supranormal powers," referring to a set of five mundane (LAUKIKA; P. lokiya) supranormal powers (ABHIJÑĀ; P. abhiññā) produced through the perfection of meditative absorption (DHYĀNA). These psychic powers (ṚDDHI) include (1) the ability to replicate one's body and, having done so, to make it one again; (2) the ability to pass through solid objects, such as walls and mountains, as if they were air; (3) the ability to walk on water as if it were solid earth; (4) the ability to fly through the air like a bird, even with one's legs crossed; and (5) the ability to touch the sun and the moon with one's hand. See also ṚDDHI.

**Rdo grub chen**. (Do Drupchen). An important monastic seat of the RNYING MA sect of Tibetan Buddhism. The first Rdo grub chen lama, 'Jigs med phrin las 'od zer (Jigme Tinle Öser, 1742–1821) founded the monastery of Yar klungs Padma bkod in the Mgo log region of A mdo in 1810. His successor, 'Jigs med phun tshogs (Jikme Puntsok), founded another monastery in the same region at Rdo stod. The third Rdo drub chen lama, 'Jigs med bstan pa'i nyi ma (Jikme Tenpe Nyima, 1865–1926), a student of the RIS MED masters 'JAM DBYANGS MKHYEN BRTSE'I DBANG PO and 'JAM MGON KONG SPRUL BLO GROS MTHA' YAS, constructed a seminary there, attracting a large number of students.

**Rdo grub chen incarnations**. (Do Drupchen). An important Tibetan Buddhist incarnation lineage associated with the transmission of the KLONG CHEN SNYING THIG tradition revealed by 'JIGS MED GLING PA. The incarnation lineage includes:

1. 'Jigs med phrin las 'od zer (1745–1821)
2. 'Jigs med phun tshogs 'byung gnas (1824–1863)
3. 'Jigs med bstan pa'i nyi ma (1865–1926)

4a. Rig 'dzin bstan pa'i rgyal mtshan (1927–1961)
4b. Thub bstan phrin las dpal bzang (b. 1927)

The first incarnation, 'Jigs med phrin las 'od zer (Jikme Tinle Öser), was born in the Rdo valley of Mgo log, in eastern Tibet, and for this reason was later known as Rdo grub chen, the "great adept (grub chen) of Rdo." Despite the fact that he was not recognized as an incarnate lama (SPRUL SKU) at a young age, his youth is described as having been filled with visionary experiences of his past lives. He spent his early life studying under numerous masters throughout eastern, central, and southern Tibet, although it was only at the age of forty-one that he met his principal GURU, 'Jigs med gling pa, from whom he received the entire RNYING MA transmissions of BKA' MA and GTER MA and by whom he was certified as the principal lineage holder of the klong chen snying thig tradition. His fame as a spiritual luminary spread and traveled widely among the great monastic communities of eastern Tibet, teaching many of the great Rnying ma masters of his day and establishing the monastic center of Yar klungs Padma bkod in eastern Tibet. The second incarnation, 'Jigs med phun tshogs 'byung gnas (Jikme Puntsok Jungne), was known for his ability to perform miraculous feats, and he continued many of the traditions of his predecessor. He also laid the foundations for what would later become the famed Rdo grub chen monastery. The third incarnation, 'Jigs med bstan pa'i nyi ma (Jikme Tenpe Nyima), was born into a prominent family in the Mgo log region of eastern Tibet: his father was Bdud 'joms gling pa (1835–1903), a famed treasure revealer (GTER STON), and his seven younger brothers were all recognized as incarnate lamas. He studied under many great Rnying ma masters, including DPAL SPRUL RIN PO CHE and 'JAM DBYANGS MKHYEN BRTSE DBANG PO. Two individuals were recognized as the fourth incarnation and were enthroned simultaneously at Rdo grub chen monastery in about 1930. They continued their education together until the age of twenty. The first, Rig 'dzin bstan pa'i rgyal mtshan, was imprisoned during the Chinese invasion of Tibet and died in a prison labor camp. In 1957, the second incarnation, Thub bstan phrin las dpal bzang, escaped into exile in Sikkim where he established a permanent residence. He later became a representative at the Sikkim Research Institute of Tibetology in Gangtok and traveled widely throughout Europe and the United States.

**Rdo rje brag**. (Dorje Drak). The monastic seat for the BYANG GTER or "Northern Treasure" tradition of the RNYING MA sect of Tibetan Buddhism, located on the Gtsang po (Tsangpo) River in central Tibet. The Byang gter tradition originated with the treasure revealer Dngos grub rgyal mtshan (Ngödrup Gyaltsen), better known as RGOD LDEM CAN. His subsequent reincarnations, called the Rdo rje brag rig 'dzin ("the VIDYĀDHARAS of Dorje Drak"), became the institution's principal teacher. Rdo rje brag monastery was established in its present location in the sixteenth century by the third Rdo rje brag rig 'dzin Ngag gi dbang po (Ngaki Wangpo, 1580–1639), together with his master Bkra shis stobs rgyal (Tashi Topgyal, 1550?–1603). It was greatly expanded by the fourth Rdo rje brag rig 'dzin Padma 'phrin las (Pema Trinle, 1641–1717), but was subsequently destroyed (and Padma 'phrin las himself killed) during the Dzungar Mongol invasion. It was again demolished during the Chinese Cultural Revolution and has since been rebuilt. The monastery takes its name, lit. "vajra cliffs," from the shape of the surrounding rock face, said to resemble the shape of a VAJRA. Rdo rje brag is one of the six major Rnying ma monasteries; besides SMIN GROL GLING in central Tibet, they are KAḤ THOG, ZHE CHEN, RDZOGS CHEN, and DPAL YUL in Khams.

**Rdo rje gling pa**. (Dorje Lingpa) (1346–1405). A Tibetan Buddhist master, identified as the third of the five kingly treasure revealers (GTER STON RGYAL PO LNGA), and considered to be an emanation of the Tibetan king KHRI SRONG LDE BTSAN. As a youth, he took monastic ordination and studied both the ancient (RNYING MA) and new (GSAR MA) traditions of the sūtras and tantras. At age thirteen he discovered his first treasure text (GTER MA) behind a miracle-performing image of TĀRĀ in the KHRA 'BRUG temple. He considered himself to be the incarnation of the translator VAIROCANA and was guided by visions of him. When doubts were raised about the authenticity of his treasures, he began discovering texts and sacred objects in public settings. In addition to his discoveries, he was famous for his eccentric behavior and spontaneous songs. Rdo rje gling pa is said to have unearthed forty-three sets of treasure, foremost of which was the *Bla rdzogs thugs gsum* ("Trio of the Guru, Great Perfection, and Great Compassionate One").

**Rdo rje grags ldan**. (Dorje Drakden). A Tibetan DHARMAPĀLA associated with PE HAR RGYAL PO as his "minister" (T. blon po) who also takes possession of Pe har's medium, the GNAS CHUNG chos rje (Nechung Chöje), the "state oracle" of Tibet. One version of the origin of the oracle is that Rdo rje grags ldan, wishing to rise above his present status, began to appear to the monks of Tshal gung thang. Rather than inviting the god to take up residence at the monastery, they trapped him in a box, which they threw into the river. This box made its way to Gnas chung, where he escaped. The monks there thought it appropriate to invite the chief deity of the emanation, and thus Pe har was brought to the monastery to serve as the oracle. Elsewhere, it is explained that because Pe har will soon attain enlightened status as a supramundane protector ('jig rten las 'das pa'i srung ma), he is increasingly reluctant to answer questions pertaining to mundane matters. For this reason, he occasionally sends Rdo rje grags ldan to speak for him through the Gnas chung cho rje.

**Rdo rje gro lod**. (Dorje Drolö). One of the eight forms of PADMASAMBHAVA, that in which he subdued harmful spirits at Spa ro stag tshang (Paro Taktsang) and established Buddhism in Bhutan. He is wrathful with one face with three eyes, holds a VAJRA and a dagger (PHUR PA), and rides a tiger.

**rdo rje gsum gyi bsnyen sgrub**. (dorje sumgyi nyendrup). A rare Tibetan Buddhist tradition, lit. "propitiation and achievement of the three adamantine states," closely related to the KĀLACAKRATANTRA. It was originally promulgated by the great Tibetan adept O RGYAN PA RIN CHEN DPAL, who is said to have received the instructions directly from VAJRAYOGINĪ while traveling through northwest India. O rgyan pa's disciples composed several commentaries on the teaching, but it seems to have since fallen into obscurity.

**Rdo rje legs pa**. (Dorje Lekpa). A Tibetan deity who was subdued by PADMASAMBHAVA at 'O yug bge'u tshang and became a DHARMAPĀLA. He is a member of the gter gyi srung ma sde bzhi, "the four guardians of treasure," who guard the treasures of the four quarters of the world; he occupies the southern quarter and guards gold. He is depicted riding a goat and wearing a broad-brimmed hat. His origin legends include being born from the union of two demons (BDUD) as well as being the spirit of a learned but sinful Indian monk from NĀLANDĀ. He is said to take possession of numerous mediums.

**Rdo rje shugs ldan**. (Dorje Shukden). A protector of the DGE LUGS sect of Tibetan Buddhism. According to his legend, he is the spirit of Grags pa rgyal mtshan (Drakpa Gyaltsen), an alternate candidate for the position of fifth DALAI LAMA and a distinguished scholar who later was either assassinated or committed suicide. Grags pa rgyal mtshan was himself said to be the reincarnation of Paṇ chen Bsod nams grags pa (Sönam Drakpa), an important abbot of 'BRAS SPUNGS monastery after the death of the third Dalai Lama. Following the death of Grags pa rgyal mtshan, numerous calamities struck the Tibetan capital and the person of the fifth Dalai Lama. The Tibetan government enlisted the aid of the abbot of SMIN SGROL GLING monastery, who successfully convinced the spirit to adopt the role of protector of the Dge lugs pa, in which role he is said to guard against the corrupting influences of other sects' teachings, specifically those of the RNYING MA sect. He resides outside GNAS CHUNG monastery below 'Bras spungs monastery, outside of LHA SA, where the east gate is always locked to keep him from entering and displacing the state oracle, PE HAR RGYAL PO. He is depicted riding a snow lion. He has one face and three eyes and is holding a khaḍga and skull cup (S. KAPĀLA), with a mongoose and a golden goad (aṅkuśa) held in his left arm. Since the early twentieth century, Rdo rje shugs ldan became a widely worshipped protector of the Dge lugs pa due largely to the prominent Dge lugs cleric Pha bong kha pa (1878–1943). Both the thirteenth and fourteenth Dalai Lamas outlawed his worship on the grounds that he is in fact a harmful spirit, with the proclamations of the fourteenth Dalai Lama generating opposition from within the Dalai Lama's own Dge lugs sect, especially from monks who had been close disciples of the Dalai Lama's junior tutor Khri byang rin po che. In 1997, the principal of the School of Buddhist Dialectics in DHARMAŚĀLĀ, India, DGE BSHES Blo bzang rgya mtsho (Geshe Losang Gyatso), a supporter of the Dalai Lama's position, was brutally murdered. The Indian authorities issued arrest warrants for six men, mainly from the Cha phreng region of eastern Tibet associated with a group supporting worship of Rdo rje shugs ldan.

**Rdo rje tshig rkang**. (Dorje Tsikang). In Tibetan, "VAJRA Verses," a text whose content is said to have originated with the Indian adept VIRŪPA. The work forms a scriptural basis for the SA SKYA tradition of tantric theory and practice known as LAM 'BRAS ("path and result"). The work presents a summary of the entire tantric path to enlightment, from the most basic points of doctrine to the consummate tantric meditative practices. The text is said to have been transmitted in purely oral form for at least eight generations. According to traditional accounts, Virūpa received the content of these teachings as a direct visionary transmission from the deity NAIRĀTMYĀ, on the basis of which he formulated the condensed instructions known as the *Rdo rje tshig khang*. Virūpa first taught the verses to his disciple Kāṇha, who taught them to Ḍāmarupa. They were passed to Avadhūti and then to the master Gayadhara (d. 1103), who traveled to Tibet in 1041 and transmitted the teachings to the great Sa skya founder and translator 'BROG MI SHĀKYA YE SHES. The latter taught the work orally in Tibetan (translated from the Indian dialect) and it was memorized and transmitted in this fashion until the prominent Sa skya master SA CHEN KUN DGA' SNYING PO promulgated them in written form.

**rdzogs chen**. (dzokchen). A Tibetan philosophical and meditative tradition, usually rendered in English as "great perfection" or "great completion." Developed and maintained chiefly within the RNYING MA sect, rdzogs chen has also been embraced to varying degrees by other Tibetan Buddhist sects. The non-Buddhist Tibetan BON religion also upholds a rdzogs chen tradition. According to legend, the primordial buddha SAMANTABHADRA (T. Kun tu bzang po) taught rdzogs chen to the buddha VAJRASATTVA, who transmitted it to the first human lineage holder, DGA' RAB RDO RJE. From him, rdzogs chen was passed to MAÑJUŚRĪMITRA and thence to ŚRĪSIṂHA, and the Tibetan translator Ba gor VAIROCANA, who had been sent to India by the eighth-century Tibetan King KHRI SRONG LDE BTSAN. In addition to Vairocana, the semimythical figures of VIMALAMITRA and PADMASAMBHAVA are considered to be foundational teachers of rdzogs chen in Tibet. Historically, rdzogs chen appears to have been a Tibetan innovation, drawing on multiple influences, including both non-Buddhist native Tibetan beliefs and Chinese and Indian Buddhist teachings. The term was likely taken from the GUHYAGARBHATANTRA. In the creation and completion stages of tantric practice, one first generates a visualization of a deity and its MAṆḌALA and next dissolves these into oneself, merging oneself with the deity. In the *Guhyagarbha* and certain other tantras, this is followed with a stage known as rdzogs chen, in which one rests in the unelaborated natural state of one's own innately luminous and pure mind. In the Rnying ma sect's nine-vehicle (T. THEG PA DGU) doxography of the Buddhist teachings, these three stages constitute the final three vehicles: the MAHĀYOGA, ANUYOGA, and ATIYOGA, or rdzogs chen. The rdzogs chen literature is traditionally divided into three categories, which roughly trace the historical development of the doctrine and practices: the mind class (SEMS SDE), space class (KLONG SDE), and instruction class (MAN NGAG SDE). These are collected in a group of texts called the RNYING MA'I RGYUD 'BUM ("treasury of Rnying ma tantras"). The mind class is comprised largely of texts attributed to Vairocana, including the so-called eighteen tantras and the KUN BYED RGYAL PO. They set forth a doctrine of primordial purity (ka dag) of mind (sems nyid), which is the basis of all things (kun gzhi). In the natural state, the mind, often referred to as BODHICITTA, is spontaneously aware of itself (rang rig), but through mental discursiveness (rtog pa) it creates delusion ('khrul ba) and thus gives rise to SAṂSĀRA. Early rdzogs chen ostensibly rejected all forms of practice, asserting that striving for liberation would simply create more delusion. One is admonished to simply recognize the nature of one's own mind, which is naturally empty (stong pa), luminous ('od gsal ba), and pure. As tantra continued to grow in popularity in Tibet, and new techniques and doctrines were imported from India, a competing strand within rdzogs chen increasingly emphasized meditative practice. The texts of the space class (klong sde) reflect some of this, but it is in the instruction class (man ngag sde), dating from the eleventh to fourteenth centuries, that rdzogs chen fully assimilated tantra. The main texts of this class are the so-called seventeen tantras and the two "seminal heart" collections, the BI MA SNYING THIG ("Seminal Heart of Vimalamitra") and the MKHA' 'GRO SNYING THIG ("Seminal Heart of the ḌĀKINĪ"). The seventeen tantras and the "Seminal Heart of Vimalamitra" are said to have been taught by Vimalamitra and concealed as "treasure" (GTER MA), to be discovered at a later time. The "Seminal Heart of the Ḍākinī" is said to have been taught by Padmasambhava and concealed as treasure by his consort, YE SHES MTSHO RGYAL. In the fourteenth century, the great scholar KLONG CHEN RAB 'BYAMS PA DRI MED 'OD ZER systematized the multitude of received rdzogs chen literature in his famous MDZOD BDUN ("seven treasuries") and the NGAL GSO SKOR GSUM ("Trilogy on Rest"), largely creating the rdzogs chen teachings as they are known today. With the man ngag sde, the rdzogs chen proponents made full use of the Tibetan innovation of treasure, a means by which later tantric developments were assimilated to the tradition without sacrificing its claim to eighth-century origins. The semilegendary figure of Padmasambhava was increasingly relied upon for this purpose, gradually eclipsing Vairocana and Vimalamitra as the main rdzogs chen founder. In subsequent centuries there have been extensive additions to the rdzogs chen literature, largely by means of the treasure genre, including the KLONG CHEN SNYING THIG of 'JIGS MED GLING PA and the *Bar chad kun gsal* of MCHOG GYUR GLING PA to name only two. Outside of the Rnying ma sect, the authenticity of these texts is frequently disputed, although there continue to be many adherents to rdzogs chen from other Tibetan Buddhist lineages. Rdzogs chen practitioners are commonly initiated into the teachings with "pointing-out instructions" (sems khrid/ngos sprod) in which a lama introduces the student to the nature of his or her mind. Two main practices known as KHREGS CHOD (breakthrough), in which one cultivates the experience of innate awareness (RIG PA), and THOD RGAL (leap over), elaborate visualizations of external light imagery, preserve the tension between the early admonition against practice and the appropriation of complex tantric techniques and doctrines. Extensive practices engaging the subtle body of psychic channels, winds, and drops (rtsa rlung thig le) further reflect the later tantric developments in rdzogs chen.

¶ RDZOGS CHEN is also used as the short name for one of the largest and most active Tibetan monasteries, belonging to the Rnying ma sect of Tibetan Buddhism, located in the eastern Tibetan region of Khams; the monastery's full name is Rus dam bsam gtan o rgyan chos gling (Rudam Samten Orgyan Chöling). It is a major center for both academic study and meditation retreat according to Rnying ma doctrine. At its peak, the monastery housed over one thousand monks and sustained more than two hundred branches throughout central and eastern Tibet. The institution was founded in 1684–1685 by the first RDZOGS CHEN INCARNATION Padma rig 'dzin (Pema Rikdzin) with the support of the fifth DALAI LAMA NGAG DBANG BLO BZANG RGYA MTSHO. Important meditation hermitages in the area include those of MDO MKHYEN RTSE YE SHE RDO RJE and MI PHAM 'JAM DBYANGS RNAM RGYAL RGYA MTSHO. DPAL SPRUL RIN PO CHE passed many years in retreat there, during which time he composed his great exposition of the preliminary practices of Tibetan Buddhism entitled the KUN BZANG BLA MA'I ZHAL LUNG ("Words of My Perfect Teacher").

**Rdzogs chen incarnations**. A lineage of incarnate lamas (SPRUL SKU) associated with RDZOG CHEN monastery. The first Rdzog chen incarnation, Rdzogs chen Padma rig 'dzin (Dzokchen Pema Rikdzin), founded the monastery at the behest of the fifth DALAI LAMA. The lineage comprises:

1. Rdzogs chen Padma rig 'dzin (1625–1697);
2. Rdzogs chen 'Gyur med theg mchog bstan 'dzin (Dzokchen Gyurme Tekchok Tendzin, 1699–1758);
3. Rdzogs chen Nges don bstan 'dzin bzang po (Dzokchen Ngedön Tendzin Sangpo, 1759–1792);
4. Rdzogs chen Mi 'gyur nam mkha'i rdo rje (Dzokchen Mingyur Namkhe Dorje, b. 1793);
5. Rdzogs chen Thub bstan chos kyi rdo rje (Dzokchen Tupten Chökyi Dorje, 1872–1935);
6. Rdzogs chen 'Jigs bral byang chub rdo rje (Dzokchen Jikdrel Jangchup Dorje, 1935–1959);
7. Rdzogs chen 'Jig med blo gsal dbang po (Jikme Losel Wangpo) (b. 1964).

**rdzogs chen sde gsum**. (dzokchen desum). Three major divisions of RDZOGS CHEN teachings in the Tibetan Buddhist tradition: the SEMS SDE (mental class), the KLONG SDE (space class), and the MAN NGAG SDE (instruction class). Of them, only the man ngag sde is now widely disseminated based on the tradition going back to KLONG CHEN PA.

**Rdzogs pa chen po klong chen snying thig**. See KLONG CHEN SNYING THIG.

**Rdzong gsar**. (Dzongsar). A Tibetan Buddhist monastery establised in 1253 by the illustrious SA SKYA hierarch 'PHAGS PA BLO GROS RGYAL MTSHAN in the SDE DGE region of eastern Tibet. It was greatly expanded during the nineteenth century by the great master 'JAM DBYANG MKHYEN BRTSE DBANG PO and his incarnation Rdzong gsar mkhyen brtse Chos kyi blo gros, who added a teaching institute (BSHAD GRWA). For the past several centuries, Rdzong gsar has been renowned as one of Tibet's premier centers for intellectual study. Its full name is Rdzong gsar bkra shis lha rtse (Dzongsar Tashi Lhatse).

**rebirth**. An English term that does not have an exact correlate in Buddhist languages, rendered instead by a range of technical terms, such as the Sanskrit PUNARJANMAN (lit. "birth again") and PUNARBHAVA (lit. "re-becoming"), and, less commonly, the related PUNARMṚTYU (lit. "redeath"). The Sanskrit term JĀTI ("birth") also encompasses the notion of rebirth. The doctrine of rebirth is central to Buddhism. It was not an innovation of the Buddha, being already common to a number of philosophical schools of ancient India by the time of his appearance, especially those connected with the ŚRAMAṆA movement of religious mendicants. Rebirth (sometimes called metempsychosis) is described as a beginningless process in which a mental continuum (see SAṂTĀNA) takes different (usually) physical forms lifetime after lifetime within the six realms (GATI) of SAṂSĀRA: divinities (DEVA), demigods (ASURA), humans (MANUṢYA), animals (TIRYAK), ghosts (PRETA), and hell denizens (NĀRAKA). The cycle of rebirth operates through the process of activity (KARMAN), with virtuous (KUŚALA) actions serving as the cause for salutary rebirths among the divinities and human beings, and unvirtuous (AKUŚALA) actions serving as the cause of unsalutary rebirths (DURGATI; APĀYA) among demigods, animals, ghosts, and hell denizens. The goal of the Buddhist path has been traditionally described as the cessation of the cycle of rebirth through the eradication of its causes, which are identified as the afflictions (KLEŚA) of greed, hatred, and ignorance and the actions motivated by those defilements. Despite this ultimate goal, however, much traditional Buddhist practice has been directed toward securing rebirth as a human or divinity for oneself and one's family members, while avoiding rebirth in the evil realms. The issue of how Buddhism reconciles the doctrine of rebirth with its position that there is no perduring self (ANĀTMAN) has long been discussed within the tradition. Some schools of mainstream Buddhism, such as the VĀTSĪPUTRĪYA or PUDGALAVĀDA, have gone so far as to posit that, while there may be no perduring "self," there is an "inexpressible" (avācya) "person" (PUDGALA) that is neither the same as nor different from the five aggregates (SKANDHA), which transmigrates from lifetime to lifetime. A more widely accepted view among the traditions sees the person as simply a sequence of mental and physical processes, among which is the process called consciousness (VIJÑĀNA). Consciousness, although changing every moment, persists as a continuum over time. Death is simply the transfer of this conscious continuum (SAṂTĀNA) from one impermanent mental and physical foundation to the next, just as the light from one candle may be transferred to the next in a series of candles. The exact process by which rebirth occurs is variously described in the different Buddhist traditions, with some schools asserting that rebirth occurs in the moments immediately following death, with other schools positing the existence of an "intermediate state" (ANTARĀBHAVA) between death in one lifetime and rebirth in another, with that period lasting as long as forty-nine days (see SISHIJIU [RI] ZHAI). This state, translated as BAR DO in Tibetan, became particularly important in Tibet in both funerary rituals and in tantric practice, especially that of the RNYING MA sect. The reality of rebirth is one of the cardinal doctrines of Buddhism, which the religion claims can be empirically validated through direct spiritual insight (see YOGIPRATYAKṢA). Indeed, understanding the validity of this cycle of rebirth is associated with two of the three types of knowledge (TRIVIDYĀ) that are experienced through the enlightenment of an ARHAT or a buddha: the ability to remember one's own former lives (PŪRVANIVĀSĀNUSMṚTI) in all their detail and insight into the future rebirth destinies of all other beings based on their own actions (S. CYUTYUPAPĀDĀNUSMṚTI). See also SAṂSĀRA.

**Record of Buddhist Kingdoms**. See FAXIAN ZHUAN.

**Record of the Western Regions**. See DA TANG XIYU JI.

**Red Hats**. (C. hongmao 紅帽). A popular designation in both European languages and Chinese for the BKA' BRGYUD and sometimes the RNYING MA sects of Tibetan Buddhism, whose lamas do indeed wear red hats. Although the term ZHWA DMAR, or "Red Hat," is used to designate an important lineage of incarnate lamas within the KARMA BKA' RGYUD sect, the Western and Chinese division of major Tibetan Buddhist sects into the YELLOW HATS, Red Hats, and BLACK HATS has no corollary within the Tibetan tradition and should be avoided.

**reigen**. (靈驗). In Japanese, lit. "numinous verification," a term used to refer to the miraculous efficacy of a prayer, vow, or religious praxis. The benefits are often understood as the result of the "sympathetic resonance" (C. GANYING) between buddhas and/or deities who are the objects of the prayer and the subject who engages in prayer. The term can also refer to the miraculous power and virtue of the buddhas and deities to respond to the prayers of people.

**reincarnation**. See REBIRTH, PUNARBHAVA, PUNARJANMAN, SPRUL SKU.

**Reiyūkai**. (霊友会/靈友會). In Japanese, lit. "Numinous Friends Society," or "Society of Friends of the Spirits"; a Japanese Buddhist lay organization, deriving from the teachings of the NICHIRENSHŪ. It was founded in 1925 by KUBO KAKUTARŌ (1892–1944) and KOTANI KIMI (1901–1971), the wife of Kubo's elder brother, who took over leadership of the organization and became president in 1944 upon Kubo's death. Kubo insisted that everyone keep a family death register and give posthumous names to venerated ancestors; these activities were formerly the domain of monks, who would be paid for their services. His other ideas included the classical directive to convert the world into a PURE LAND for Buddhism and the need to teach others the truth. He particularly emphasized the ability of each individual to improve him or herself. Kubo's ideas appealed to the poor and he began to attract converts quickly, including his brother Kotani Yasukichi and Kotani's wife, Kotani Kimi. In 1971 after Kotani Kimi died, Kubo's son Kubo Tsugunari took over as the leader of the group. For years he had prepared for this future, including studying Indian philosophy and Buddhism at Risshō University. Despite this preparation, Reiyūkai was rocked by what some viewed as his personal failings and political maneuverings and Kubo Tsugunari eventually lost his leadership post. More recent leaders have been elected democratically. Some noted activities in recent years include opening the Lumbinī International Research Institute in Nepal and the International College for Advanced Buddhist Studies in Tōkyō. The organization reached its peak during the years surrounding the Second World War, when it claimed some three million members, and was the source of numerous Nichiren-related new religious movements, of which the RISSHŌ KŌSEIKAI, founded in 1938, became the most prominent. Reiyūkai continues to be an active lay organization in both Japan and abroad. The Reiyūkai organization has no clergy and no formal affiliation with any other Buddhist school, but instead relies on volunteer lay teachers who lead informal group meetings and discussions. Reiyūkai focuses on the human capacity for lifelong self-cultivation in order to become ever more wise and compassionate. All its adherents must have a personal sponsor in order to join the order. The school stresses ancestor worship, believing that personal and social ills are the result of inadequate veneration of ancestor spirits who have been unable to attain buddhahood and instead became guardian spirits until the proper rites are performed so they may be liberated. Its followers believe that reciting the SADDHARMAPUṆḌARĪKASŪTRA ("Lotus Sūtra") in abridged form during daily morning and evening services or a group meeting transfers merit to their ancestors.

**relics**. See DHĀTU, ŚARĪRA, STŪPA, SUISHEN SHELI.

**reliquary**. See STŪPA, SHELIJU.

**Rennyo**. (蓮如) (1415–1499). In Japanese, "Lotus Suchness"; proper name of the Japanese monk who played a crucial role in the consolidation of JŌDO SHINSHŪ tradition. Rennyo was born at the monastery of HONGANJI in the Higashiyama district of Kyōto. He was the son of Zonnyo (1396–1457), himself a descendent of SHINRAN and the seventh abbot of Honganji. Despite some opposition from his stepmother and her son Nyojō (1412–1460), Rennyo succeeded his father as abbot of Honganji after his father's death in 1457. Rennyo began expanding his sphere of influence by proselytizing in the outskirts of Kyōto. In 1465, the monks of HIEIZAN (see ENRYAKUJI) destroyed Honganji in order to restrict the spread of Rennyo's influence in regions under TENDAI control. Rennyo was able to save the portrait of Shinran (goei) from destruction and installed it temporarily at the temple of MIIDERA. After the attack, Rennyo wandered from region to region until he settled down far away from Mt. Hiei in Hokuriku (present-day Echizen), where he acquired a large following (of mostly peasants) through active proselytizing and the writing of pastoral letters (ofumi). In 1475, Rennyo returned to Kyōto, where he began the construction of a new Honganji in the district of Yamashina the following year. Rennyo also restored the hōonko memorial service for Shinran and established the nenbutsu (C. NIANFO; see NAMU AMIDABUTSU) inscriptions as an important object of worship. In his writings, Rennyo also systematized the teachings of Shinran and criticized priestly corruption and "heretical" teachings that did not emphasize exclusive faith in the buddha AMITĀBHA and his name. Under Rennyo's tenure as abbot, the Honganji complex grew into one of the most powerful monasteries of its era, controlling a vast network of subtemples. This period is traditionally considered to represent the institutional formation of Jōdo Shinshū.

**rentian jiao**. (C) (人天教). See HUAYAN WUJIAO.

**Renwang baigaozuo hui**. (J. Ninnō hyakukōzae; K. Inwang paekkojwa hoe 仁王百高座會). In Chinese, lit., "Humane Kings assembly of one hundred high seats." See RENWANG JING; HUGUO FOJIAO.

**Renwang bore boluomi jing**. (C) (仁王般若波羅蜜經). See RENWANG JING.

**Renwang huguo bore boluomiduo jing**. (C) (仁王護國般若波羅蜜多經). See RENWANG JING.

**Renwang jing**. (J. Ninnōgyō; K. Inwang kyŏng 仁王經). In Chinese, "Scripture for Humane Kings"; an influential indigenous Chinese scripture (see APOCRYPHA), known especially for its role in "state protection Buddhism" (HUGUO FOJIAO) and for its comprehensive outline of the Buddhist path of practice (MĀRGA). Its full title (infra) suggests that the scripture belongs to the "perfection of wisdom" (PRAJÑĀPĀRAMITĀ) genre of literature, but it includes also elements drawn from both the YOGĀCĀRA and TATHĀGATAGARBHA traditions. The text's audience and interlocutors are not the typical ŚRĀVAKAS and BODHISATTVAS but instead kings hailing from the sixteen ancient regions of India, who beseech the Buddha to speak this sūtra in order to protect both their states and their subjects from the chaos attending the extinction of the dharma (MOFA; SADDHARMAVIPRALOPA). By having kings rather than spiritual mentors serve as the interlocutors, the scripture thus focuses on those qualities thought to be essential to governing a state founded on Buddhist principles. The text's concepts of authority, the path, and the world draw analogies with the "humane kings" of this world who serve and venerate the transcendent monks and bodhisattvas. The service and worship rendered by the kings turns them into bodhisattvas, while the soteriological vocation of the monks and bodhisattvas conversely renders them kings. Thus, the relationship between the state and the religion is symbiotic. The sūtra is now generally presumed to be an indigenous Chinese scripture that was composed to buttress imperial authority by exalting the benevolent ruler as a defender of the dharma. The *Renwang jing* is also known for including the ten levels of faith (ŚRADDHĀ) as a preliminary stage of the Buddhist path prior to the arousal of the thought of enlightenment (BODHICITTOTPĀDA). It is one of a number of Chinese Buddhist apocrypha that seek to provide a comprehensive elaboration of all fifty-two stages of the path, including the PUSA YINGLUO BENYE JING and the YUANJUE JING. The *Renwang jing* is not known in Sanskrit sources, but there are two recensions of the Chinese text. The first, *Renwang bore boluomi jing*, is purported to have been translated by KUMĀRAJĪVA and is dated to c. 402, and the latter, titled *Renwang huguo bore boluomiduo jing*, is attributed to AMOGHAVAJRA and dated to 765. The Amoghavajra recension is based substantially on the Kumārajīva text, but includes additional teachings on MAṆḌALA, MANTRA, and DHĀRAṆĪ, additions that reflect Amoghavajra's place in the Chinese esoteric Buddhist tradition. Furthermore, because Amoghavajra was an advisor to three Tang-dynasty rulers, his involvement in contemporary politics may also have helped to shape the later version. Chinese scriptural catalogues (JINGLU) were already suspicious about the authenticity of the *Renwang jing* as least as early as Fajing's 594 *Zhongjing mulu*; Fajing lists the text together with twenty-one other scriptures of doubtful authenticity (YIJING), because its content and diction do not resemble those of the ascribed translator. Modern scholars have also recognized these content issues. One of the more egregious examples is the RENWANG JING's reference to four different perfection of wisdom (prajñāpāramitā) sūtras that the Buddha is said to have proclaimed; two of the sūtras listed are, however, simply different Chinese translations of the same text, the PAÑCAVIṂŚATISĀHASRIKĀPRAJÑĀPĀRAMITĀSŪTRA, a blunder that an Indian author could obviously not have committed. Another example is the scripture's discussion of a three-truth SAMĀDHI (sandi sanmei), in which these three types of concentrations are named worldly truth (shidi), authentic truth (zhendi), and supreme-meaning truth (diyiyidi). This schema is peculiar, and betrays its Chinese origins, because "authentic truth" and "supreme-meaning truth" are actually just different Chinese renderings of the same Sanskrit term, PARAMĀTHASATYA. Based on other internal evidence, scholars have dated the composition of the sūtra to sometime around the middle of the fifth century. Whatever its provenance, the text is ultimately reclassified as an authentic translation in the 602 catalogue *Zongjing mulu* by Yancong and continues to be so listed in all subsequent East Asian catalogues. See also APOCRYPHA; SANDI.

**requisites**. [alt. four, eight, or eighteen]. See PARIṢKĀRA; NIŚRAYA.

**Revata**. (T. Nam gru; C. Lipoduo; J. Ribata; K. Ibada 離婆多). Sanskrit and Pāli proper name of an important ARHAT who was foremost among the Buddha's monk disciples in mastery of meditative absorption (DHYĀNA; P. JHĀNA). He is typically known as "doubting Revata" (KĀṄKṢĀ-REVATA; P. Kankhā-Revata), to distinguish him from several other Revatas who appear in the literature, because prior to his enlightenment he is said to have been troubled by doubt concerning what was permissible and what was not. According to the Pāli account, Revata was born into a wealthy family in the city of Sāvitthi (S. ŚRĀVASTĪ). One day he heard the Buddha preach in Kapilavatthu (S. KAPILAVASTU) and resolved to renounce the world and enter the order. He attained arhatship by relying on dhyāna, and his exceptional skill in these meditative states won him distinction. Revata had resolved to attain this distinction in a previous life as a brāhmaṇa when, during the time of the buddha Padmottara, he heard the Buddha describe one of his disciples as preeminent in his attainment of dhyāna. In another famous story, the mother of Uttara had been reborn as a hungry ghost (S. PRETA, P. peta) and after fifty-five years of wandering, encountered Revata and begged him for relief. He relieved her suffering by making various offerings to the SAṂGHA in her name. ¶ There was a later monk named Revata who played a major role at the second Buddhist council (SAṂGĪTI; see COUNCIL, SECOND) held at VAIŚĀLĪ. Some one hundred years after the death of the Buddha, the monk YAŚAS was traveling in Vaiśālī when he observed the monks there receiving alms in the form of gold and silver directly from the laity, in violation of the prohibition against monks' touching gold and silver. He also found that the monks had identified ten points in the VINAYA that were classified as violations but that they had determined were sufficiently minor to be ignored. Yaśas challenged the monks on these practices, but when he refused to accept their bribes to keep quiet, they expelled him from the order. Yaśas sought support of several respected monks in the west, including ŚĀṆAKAVĀSĪN and Revata, and together they traveled to Vaiśālī. Once there, Revata went to Sarvagāmin, the eldest monk of his era, who is said to have been a disciple of ĀNANDA, to question him about these ten points. At Revata's suggestion, a jury of eight monks was appointed to adjudicate, with four representatives selected from each party. Revata was selected as one of four from the party declaring the ten practices to be violations, and it was Revata who publically put the questions to Sarvagāmin. In each case, the senior monk said that the practice in question was a violation of the vinaya. Seven hundred monks then gathered to recite the vinaya. Those who did not accept the decision of the council held their own convocation, which they called the MAHĀSĀṂGHIKA, or "Great Assembly." This event is sometimes said to have led to the first "great schism" within the mainstream Buddhist tradition, between the STHAVIRANIKĀYA, or Fraternity of the Elders, and the Mahāsāṃghika.

**Revatī**. (T. Nam gru ma). In Sanskrit and Pāli, a laywoman whose story illustrates the unsalutary consequences of niggardliness toward monks and the salutary power of taking delight (MUDITĀ) in the virtue of others. According to the Pāli account, Revatī was the daughter of a householder of Vārāṇasī, who had no faith in the Buddha and was extremely uncharitable. Her husband was the wealthy lay patron of the Buddha, Nandiya, who had her partake in his meritorious deeds. When he went abroad, he asked his wife to continue his meritorious deeds toward the SAṂGHA. Revatī did so for seven days but then stopped and began to abuse the monks who came to her house for alms (PIṆḌAPĀTA). As a consequence of their respective actions, upon her death, Revatī was reborn in hell, while Nandiya was reborn as a divinity in the TRĀYASTRIṂŚA heaven. When he saw with his divine eye (DIVYACAKṢUS) that his wife had become a denizen of hell, he went to her and asked her to take delight in his meritorious deeds. As soon as she did so, Revatī became a divinity herself and resided with Nandiya in that same heaven. In Buddhist TANTRA, particularly in the SA SKYA and DGE LUGS sects of Tibet, Śrīmatī Revatī (T. Dmag zor ma) (rendered "magical weapon army") is a form of the protectress (T. srung ma) Śrīdevī (T. DPAL LDAN LHA MO).

**Rgod ldem can Dngos grub rgyal mtshan**. (Gödemchen Ngödrup Gyaltsen) (1337–1408). An important master and treasure revealer (GTER STON) of the RNYING MA sect of Tibetan Buddhism, often venerated with the title rig 'dzin (S. VIDYĀDHARA). According to traditional accounts, three vulture feathers miraculously grew from the crown of his head at the age of twelve; five more appeared when he turned twenty-four. For this reason he is known as Rgod ldem can, the "vulture quilled." He began his career as treasure revealer at twenty-nine, forming an important lineage known as the Northern Treasure (BYANG GTER) tradition. The Northern Treasures were eventually seated at RDO RJE BRAG monastery south of LHA SA, with Rgod ldem can's subsequent incarnations, known as the Rdo rje brag rig 'dzin lineage, serving as the institution's abbot.

**Rgod tshang pa Mgon po rdo rje**. (Götshangpa Gönpo Dorje) (1189–1258). A Tibetan Buddhist master revered as the founder of the upper (stod) branch of the 'BRUG PA BKA' BRGYUD sect of Tibetan Buddhism. He was born in the LHO BRAG region of southern Tibet, and as a child was known for his pleasing appearance and his beautiful singing voice. In his youth, he studied under a number of tutors and finally reached RWA LUNG monastery, where he met his principal guru, the 'Brug pa Bka' brgyud founder GTSANG PA RGYA RAS YE SHES RDO RJE, from whom he received monastic ordination and extensive instruction. In accordance with his master's advice, he spent much of his life as a wandering YOGIN, traveling across central, southern, and western Tibet and visiting numerous pilgrimage places including KAILĀSA, TSA RI, and Jālandhara (the modern Kangra Valley of Himachal Pradesh in northwest India).

He also established several important retreat centers where he passed many years in meditation, including Rgod tshang near modern-day Rtsib ri in Gtsang, Steng gro, Bde chen stengs, and Bar 'brogs Rdo rje gling.

**Rgya gar chos 'byung**. (Gyakar Chöjung). In Tibetan, "History of the Dharma in India," a detailed history of the development of Buddhism on the subcontinent written in 1608 by the Tibetan savant Kun dga' snying po (1575–1634), better known as TĀRANĀTHA. The work's complete title is *Dam pa'i chos rin po che 'phags pa'i yul du ji ltar dar ba'i tshul gsal bar ston pa dgos 'dod kun 'byung*. It is often consulted by Tibetan and Western scholars of Buddhism because of its judicious use of earlier traditional sources and its sense of the larger history of the subcontinent, perhaps fostered by the author's access to Indian informants, unusual for such a late period in Indian Buddhist history. The work restricts itself largely to the history of Buddhism in India and follows a chronology that can be loosely characterized as historical: it is based on five time periods between the time of AJĀTAŚATRU and AŚOKA, five time periods from there to the time of the third Buddhist council (see COUNCIL, THIRD), and remaining time periods covering the great MAHĀYĀNA masters, through the history of the Pāla dynasty. It ends with a history of Buddhism in different regions, a history of TANTRA, and of image making. Tāranātha's *Rgya gar chos 'byung* is supplemented by his histories of PADMASAMBHAVA, the KĀLACAKRATANTRA, the TĀRĀ and YAMĀNTAKA lineages, and by his BKA' 'BABS BDUN LDAN GYI RNAM THAR, "Biographies of the Seven Instruction Lineages."

**Rgyal rabs gsal ba'i me long**. (Gyalrab Salwe Melong). In Tibetan, "The Mirror Illuminating the Royal Genealogies," an important chronicle of the early Tibetan dynastic period, written in the fourteenth century by the SA SKYA hierarch BSOD NAMS RGYAL MTSHAN. Although its precise dating has long been in question, current scholarship suggests it was compiled in 1368. The work was regarded highly in Tibet and is often cited in later Tibetan literature.

**Rgyal tshab Dar ma rin chen**. (Gyaltsap Darma Rinchen) (1364–1432). One of the two principal disciples (together with MKHAS GRUB DGE LEGS DPAL BZANG) of the Tibetan Buddhist master TSONG KHA PA. Ordained and educated in the SA SKYA sect, Rgyal tshab (a name he would only receive later in life) studied with some of the great teachers of the day, including Red mda' ba gzhon nu blo gros. Rgyal tshab was already an established scholar, known especially for his expertise in PRAMĀṆA, when he first met Tsong kha pa at Rab drong around 1400. According to a well-known story, Rgyal tshab sought to debate Tsong kha pa and asked a nun, "Where is Big Nose?" (impertinently referring to Tsong kha pa's prominent proboscis). The nun rinsed out her mouth and lit a stick of incense before saying that the omniscient master Tsong kha pa was teaching in the temple. Rgyal tshab entered the temple and announced his presence, at which point Tsong kha pa interrupted his teaching and invited the great scholar to join him on the teaching throne. Rgyal tshab arrogantly accepted but as he listened to Tsong kha pa's teaching, he became convinced of his great learning and edged away from the master, eventually descending from the throne and prostrating before Tsong kha pa and taking his place in the assembly. From that point, he would become Tsong kha pa's closest disciple, credited with hearing and remembering everything that Tsong kha pa taught. He assisted Tsong kha pa in the founding of DGA' LDAN monastery and upon Tsong kha pa's death in 1419, Rgyal tshab assumed the golden throne of Dga' ldan, becoming the first DGA' LDAN KHRI PA or "Holder of the Throne of Dga' ldan," a position that would evolve into the head of the DGE LUGS sect. He was also called the "regent" (rgyal tshab) of Tsong kha pa, which became the name by which he is best known. He was a prolific author, known especially for his detailed commentaries on the works of DHARMAKĪRTI, as well as such important Indian texts as the ABHISAMAYĀLAṂKĀRA, BODHICARYĀVATĀRA, RATNĀVALĪ, CATUḤŚATAKA, and RATNAGOTRAVIBHĀGA. Rgyal tshab figures in the most common image in Dge lugs iconography, the rje yab sras gsum, or "the triumvirate, the lord father, and the sons," showing Tsong kha pa flanked by Rgyal tshab and Mkhas grub (with Rgyal tshab often shown with white hair). The collected works of these three scholars form something of a canon for the Dge lugs sect and are often printed together as the rje yab sras gsung 'bum or the "collected works of the lord father and the [two] sons."

**Rgyud smad**. (Gyume). In Tibetan, the "Lower Tantric College," one of two major DGE LUGS centers for tantric studies in LHA SA, together with RGYUD STOD. Prior to his death in 1419, TSONG KHA PA is said to have enjoined his disciple Rgyud Shes rab seng ge (1383–1445) to spread his tantric teachings. In 1432, he founded a tantric college in the Sras district of Gtsang called the Sras rgyud grwa tshang (the "tantric college of Se") or as the Gtsang stod rgyud (the "tantric [college] of Tsang, the upper [region]"). The term stod, lit. "upper" in Tibetan, also means "western" and is sometimes used as a synonym for Gtsang, the province to the west of the central province of Dbus. In 1433, he returned to Lha sa and founded Rgyud smad grwa tshang, or the "tantric college of lower [Tibet])." The term smad, literally "lower," also means "eastern." In 1474, Shes rab seng ge's disciple, Rgyud chen Kun dga' don grub, left Rgyud smad when he was not selected as the abbot. He later founded another tantric college in Lha sa, which he called Dbus stod 'Jam dpal gling grwa tshang or the "Garden of MAÑJUŚRĪ College of Upper Ü." It eventually became known as Rgyud stod. Shortly after its founding, it moved to the RA MO CHE temple in Lha sa. Hence, the the standard translations "lower tantric college" for Rgyud smad and "upper tantric college" for Rgyud stod have no implications of hierarchy or curricular gradation, but refer simply to the geographical locations of the institutions from which they evolved. Monks from the three great Dge lugs monasteries of Lha sa ('BRAS SPUNGS, SE RA, and DGA' LDAN) who had achieved one of the two higher DGE BSHES (geshe) degrees—the lha ram pa or the tshogs ram pa—could enter as a dge bshes bka' ram pa. Which of the two tantric colleges a geshe attended was determined by his birthplace. The curriculum of both of the tantric colleges involved study of the GUHYASAMĀJATANTRA, CAKRASAṂVARATANTRA, and VAJRABHAIRAVATANTRA systems. These were studied through memorization and debate, as in the sūtra colleges. Monks also received instruction in the performance of ritual, the use of MUDRĀ, the making of images, and the construction of MAṆḌALAs. Monks were also instructed in chanting; the deep chanting that has become famous in the West was taught at both Rgyud smad and Rgyud stod. Those who successfully completed the curriculum received the title of dge bshes sngags ram pa. Monks who were not already geshes of one of three monasteries could enter one of the tantric colleges to receive ritual instruction but received a lower degree, called bskyed rim pa. Becoming a dge bshes sngags ram pa and especially an officer of one of the tantric colleges (dge bskos or disciplinarian; bla ma dbu mdzad, lit. "chant leader" but the vice abbot; and mkhan po or abbot) was essential for holding positions of authority in the Dge lugs hierarchy. For example, the DGA' LDAN KHRI PA was required to be a former abbot of Rgyud smad or Rgyud stod. After the Chinese takeover of Tibet, Rgyud smad and Rgyud stod were reestablished in exile in India.

**Rgyud stod**. (Gyutö). In Tibetan, "Upper Tantric College." See RGYUD SMAD.

**rhinoceros [horn] simile**. See KHAḌGAVIṢĀṆA; KHAḌGAVIṢĀṆAKALPA.

**Rhys Davids, Caroline Augusta Foley**. (1857–1942). A prominent scholar of Pāli Buddhism and wife of THOMAS WILLIAM RHYS DAVIDS. Caroline Augusta Foley attended University College in London, where she studied Pāli language and literature. She later became a fellow at University College and worked as a Pāli reader at the School of Oriental and African Studies at the University of London. Known to be a brilliant Pāli scholar and teacher, Rhys Davids had many dedicated students when she lectured in Indian philosophy at Manchester University. In 1894, at the age of thirty-six, she married T. W. Rhys Davids. They had three children together. In 1922, Rhys Davids became the president of the PĀLI TEXT SOCIETY, which had been founded by her husband, and served as president for twenty years. Rhys Davids published more than twenty-five monographs and translations. Two of her most famous books are *Gotama the Man* and *Sakya or Buddhist Origins*.

**Rhys Davids, Thomas William**. (1843–1922). Preeminent British scholar of Pāli Buddhism, Thomas William Rhys Davids was born in Colchester, the son of a Congregationalist minister. He attended secondary school in Brighton and then went on to the University of Breslau in Germany, where he studied Sanskrit. He received a PhD from the University of Breslau before taking a position as a judge in the Ceylon Civil Service in 1864. He resigned from this position in 1872 and became a lawyer in 1877. Instead of practicing law, Rhys Davids turned to researching and writing about Pāli literature. His first book, *The Ancient Coins and Measures of Ceylon*, was published in 1877, after which he began to publish regularly in the *Journal of the Royal Asiatic Society*. In 1880, he translated the NIDĀNAKATHĀ. His 1881 Hibbert Lectures became quite famous, and at the second lecture, Rhys Davids announced the creation of the PALI TEXT SOCIETY, the first learned society in the West to focus on Pāli language and literature. In 1882, Rhys Davids became a professor of Pāli at University College, London. From 1885 to 1904, he also worked for the Royal Asiatic Society. In 1904, he became professor of comparative religion at Victoria University, Manchester. In 1894, Rhys Davids married Caroline August Foley (see RHYS DAVIDS, CAROLINE AUGUST FOLEY); the two worked and published together for the rest of their lives. Rhys Davids published many works, including a *Manual of Buddhism*, the first two volumes of the "Sacred Books of the Buddhists" series, and the first volume of a *Pāli-English Dictionary*. The Rhys Davidses together translated the DĪGHANIKĀYA between 1910 and 1921.

**Ri bo che**. (Riwoche). A branch monastic seat of the STAG LUNG subsect of the BKA' BRGYUD sect of Tibetan Buddhism, located near Chab mdo in eastern Tibet. Ri bo che's founder, Sangs rgyas dbon (Sangye Ön, 1250/1–1296) better known as Dbon po bla ma (Önpo Lama), previously served a brief period as abbot of Stag lung monastery, the subsect's main seat in central Tibet. According to traditional sources, Sangs rgyas dbon left central Tibet in order to fulfill the prophecy that he would construct an even greater monastic institution in the east. His departure, however, may have been hastened by political pressure exerted by Stag lung monastery's political patrons, who favored a rival abbot. Sangs rgyas dbon established Ri bo che in 1276, and while it originally served as a branch of Stag lung monastery, it later developed a strong, nearly independent tradition. With its grand, imposing structure, Ri bo che was renowned as one of the great centers of Buddhist learning in eastern Tibet, possessing an impressive library of religious works. Its monks were highly esteemed for their expertise in meditation.

**Ri bo dpal 'bar**. (Riwo Palbar). A mountain in Skyid grong (Kyirong) county of southwestern Tibet on the Nepalese border believed to have been a retreat location of both the Indian sage PADMASAMBHAVA and the Tibetan YOGIN MI LA RAS PA. According to the latter's biography, the village of Ragma at the mountain's base was home to many of the yogin's patrons and the site of his meditation cave called Byang chub rdzong (Jangchup Dzong), "The Fortress of Enlightenment." Near the summit lies a small chapel, now in partial ruins, housing the relics of the great RNYING MA scholar and historian KAḤ THOG RIG 'DZIN TSHE DBANG NOR BU.

**right action**. See SAMYAKKARMĀNTA.

**right concentration**. See SAMYAKSAMĀDHI.

**right effort**. See SAMYAGVYĀYĀMA.

**right intention**. See SAMYAKSAṂKALPA.

**right livelihood**. See SAMYAGĀJĪVA.

**right mindfulness**. See SAMYAKSMṚTI.

**right speech**. See SAMYAGVĀK.

**right view**. See SAMYAGDṚṢṬI.

**rig pa**. The standard Tibetan translation of the Sanskrit term VIDYĀ, or "knowledge." The Tibetan term, however, has a special meaning in the ATIYOGA and RDZOGS CHEN traditions of the RNYING MA sect of Tibetan Buddhism, where it refers to the most profound form of consciousness. Some modern translators of Tibetan texts into European languages consider the term too profound to be rendered into a foreign language, while others translate it as "awareness," "pure awareness," or "mind." Unlike the "mind of clear light" (PRABHĀSVARACITTA; 'od gsal gyi sems) as described in other tantric systems, rig pa is not said to be accessible only in extraordinary states, such as death and sexual union; instead, it is fully present, although generally unrecognized, in each moment of sensory experience. Rig pa is described as the primordial basis, characterized with qualities such as presence, spontaneity, luminosity, original purity, unobstructed freedom, expanse, clarity, self-liberation, openness, effortlessness, and intrinsic awareness. It is not accessible through conceptual elaboration or logical analysis. Rather, rig pa is an eternally pure state free from the dualism of subject and object (cf. GRĀHYAGRĀHAKAVIKALPA), infinite and complete from the beginning. It is regarded as the ground or the basis of both SAṂSĀRA and NIRVĀṆA, with the phenomena of the world being its reflection; all thoughts and all objects of knowledge are said to arise from rig pa and dissolve into rig pa. The ordinary mind believes that its own creations are real, forgetting its true nature of original purity. For the mind willfully to seek to liberate itself is both inappropriate and futile because rig pa is already self-liberated. Rig pa therefore is also the path, and its exponents teach practices that instruct the student how to distinguish rig pa from ordinary mental states. These practices include a variety of techniques designed to eliminate karmic obstacles (KARMĀVARAṆA), at which point the presence of rig pa in ordinary experience is introduced, allowing the mind to eliminate all thoughts and experiences itself, thereby recognizing its true nature. Rig pa is thus also the goal of the path, the fundamental state that is free from obscuration. Cf. LINGZHI.

**Rin chen bzang po**. [alt. Lo tsā ba chen po, Lo chen] (Rinchen Sangpo) (958–1055). A Tibetan translator of Sanskrit Buddhist texts who helped to initiate the revival of Buddhism in Tibet known as the later dissemination (PHYI DAR) of the dharma. He was born in the western Tibetan region of GU GE. According to traditional histories, at the age of seventeen, he was sent to India together with a group of twenty other youths by King YE SHES 'OD to study Sanskrit and Indian vernacular languages. Rin chen bzang po made several trips to India, spending a total of seventeen years in Kashmir and the monastic university of VIKRAMAŚĪLA before returning the Tibet. During the last years of his life, he collaborated with the Bengali master ATIŚA DĪPAṂKARAŚRĪJÑĀNA at THO LING monastery. Rin chen bzang po's literary career concentrated on new and revised translations of important Indian Buddhist works; he is credited with 178 translations spanning the SŪTRAs, TANTRAs, and commentarial literature. Apart from his literary activities, he also brought with him numerous artisans and craftsmen from Kashmir and, with their aid, was highly active in the construction of new monasteries, temples, and shrines across western Tibet. These institutions, and the artwork they house, were strongly influenced by the artistic styles and religious practices of northwest India and now serve as important records of a tradition otherwise nearly lost. Most important among these temples are Tho ling, KHA CHAR, and NYAR MA, although tradition ascribes him with founding 108 buildings in all. Rin chen bzang po is still considered a local hero in the regions of western Tibet, Ladakh, Lahul, Spiti, and Kinnaur, and the current reincarnation, LO CHEN SPRUL SKU, maintains his monastic seat at Kyi monastery in Spiti.

**rin chen gter mdzod**. (rinchen terdzö). In Tibetan, "treasury of precious treasure teachings"; a collection of root texts, liturgical and ritual works, meditation manuals (SĀDHANA), commentarial, and supplemental literature pertaining to the genre of discovered treasure teachings (GTER MA) of the RNYING MA sect of Tibetan Buddhism. The collection was compiled and edited by the nineteenth-century savant 'JAM MGON KONG SPRUL BLO GROS MTHA' YAS and forms one of his five treasuries (KONG SPRUL MDZOD LNGA). Kong sprul's motivation for this massive project, resulting in sixty-three volumes of literature (over one hundred in modern redactions), was complex. The compilation preserves many systems of instruction that were in danger of being lost or forgotten, but it also forms a canonical collection of authoritative treasure texts—one of the first projects of its kind.

**rin po che**. In Tibetan, lit. "of great value," hence "precious one"; most commonly an honorific added to the name of a Tibetan BLA MA (lama), which is also used as a term of respect for addressing and referring to one's own or another's lama or teacher. The term may be used for any lama, but the term is most commonly used for incarnate lamas (SPRUL SKU), in which case it is often affixed to the name of the lineage, for example, Rgyal ba rin po che (a common appellation of the DALAI LAMA), Paṇ chen rin po che (the PAṆ CHEN BLA MA), mkhan rin po che ("precious abbot"), and so on. In ordinary Tibetan parlance, to refer to someone as a rin po che means that he (rarely she) is a sprul sku (incarnate lama).

**Rinzaishū**. (臨濟宗). In Japanese, "Rinzai School"; one of the major Japanese ZEN schools established in the early Kamakura period. The various branches of the Japanese Rinzai Zen tradition trace their lineages back to the Chinese CHAN master LINJI YIXUAN (J. Rinzai Gigen) and his eponymous LINJI ZONG; the name Rinzai, like its Chinese counterpart, is derived from Linji's toponym. The tradition was first transmitted to Japan by the TENDAISHŪ monk MYŌAN EISAI (1141–1215), who visited China twice and received training and certification in the HUANGLONG PAI collateral line of the Linji lineage on his second trip. Eisai's Zen teachings, however, reflected his training in the esoteric (MIKKYŌ) teachings of the Tendai school; he did not really intend to establish an entirely new school. After Eisai, the Rinzai tradition was transferred through Japanese monks who trained in China and Chinese monks who immigrated to Japan. Virtually all of the Japanese Rinzai tradition was associated with the YANGQI PAI collateral line of the Linji lineage (see YANGQI FANGHUI), which was first imported by the Japanese vinaya specialist Shunjō (1166–1227). According to the early-Edo-period *Nijūshiryū shūgen zuki* ("Diagrammatic Record of the Sources of the Twenty-Four Transmissions of the Teaching"), twenty-four Zen lineages had been transmitted to Japan since the Kamakura period, twenty-one of which belonged to the Rinzai tradition; with the exception of Eisai's own lineage, the remaining twenty lineages were all associated with the Yangqi collateral line. Soon after its introduction into Japan, the Rinzai Zen tradition rose to prominence in Kamakura and Kyōto, where it received the patronage of shōguns, emperors, and the warrior class. The Rinzai teachers of this period included monks from Tendai and SHINGONSHŪ backgrounds, such as ENNI BEN'EN (1202–1280) and SHINCHI KAKUSHIN (1207–1298), who promoted Zen with an admixture of esoteric elements. Chinese immigrant monks like LANXI DAOLONG (J. Rankei Dōryu, 1213–1278) and WUXUE ZUYUAN (J. Mugaku Sogen, 1226–1286) also contributed to the rapid growth in the popularity of the Rinzai tradition among the Japanese ruling classes, by transporting the Song-style Linji Chan tradition as well as Song-dynasty Chinese culture more broadly. With the establishment of the Ashikaga shogunate in 1338, the major Zen temples were organized following the Song Chinese model into the GOZAN (five mountains) system, a tripartite state control system consisting of "five mountains" (gozan), "ten temples" (jissetsu), and several associated "miscellaneous mountains" (shozan). The powerful gozan monasteries located in Kamakura and Kyōto functioned as centers of classical Chinese learning and culture, and continued to influence the ruling classes in Japan until the decline of the Ashikaga shogunate in the sixteenth century. The disciples of Enni Ben'en and MUSŌ SOSEKI (1275–1351) dominated the gozan monasteries. In particular, Musō Soseki was deeply engaged in both literary endeavors and political activities; his lineage produced several famous gozan poets, such as Gidō Shūshin (1325–1388) and Zekkai Chūshin (1336–1405). Outside the official gozan ecclesiastical system were the RINKA, or forest, monasteries. DAITOKUJI and MYŌSHINJI, the two principal rinka Rinzai monasteries, belonged to the Ōtōkan lineage, which is named after its first three masters NANPO JŌMYŌ (1235–1309), SŌHŌ MYŌCHŌ (1282–1337), and KANZAN EGEN (1277–1360). This lineage emphasized rigorous Zen training rather than the broader cultural endeavors pursued in the gozan monasteries. After the decline of the gozan monasteries, the Ōtōkan lineage came to dominate the Rinzai Zen tradition during the Edo period and was the only Rinzai line to survive to the present. Despite the presence of such influential monks as TAKUAN SŌHŌ (1573–1645) and BANKEI YŌTAKU (1622–1693), the Rinzai tradition began to decline by the sixteenth and the seventeenth centuries. The monk credited with revitalizing the Rinzai tradition during the Edo period is the Myōshinji monk HAKUIN EKAKU (1685–1769). Hakuin systematized the KŌAN (see GONG'AN; KANHUA CHAN) method of meditation, which is the basis of modern Rinzai Zen practice; it is also through Hakuin and his disciples that most Rinzai masters of today trace their lineages. The Rinzai tradition is currently divided into the fifteen branches named after each of their head monasteries, which represents the influence of the head and branch temple system designed in the Edo period. Of the fifteen branches, the Myōshinji branch has largely eclipsed its rivals and today is the largest and most influential of all the Rinzai lines.

**ris med**. (ri me). In Tibetan, lit. "unbounded," "unlimited," or "impartial"; often translated as "nonsectarian" or "eclectic" in conjunction with a religious ideal that appears to have gained widespread currency in the early nineteenth century, most famously in the Khams SDE DGE kingdom in eastern Tibet. The origins of the movement are traced to the founding of DPAL SPUNGS monastery, established in 1727 by the eighth TAI SI TU CHOS KYI 'BYUNG GNAS, a great BKA' BRGYUD scholar, historian, and linguist, with support from Sde dge's ruler Bstan pa tshe ring (Tenpa Tsering, 1678–1738), who sponsored the carving and printing of the Sde dge edition of the Tibetan BKA' 'GYUR and BSTAN 'GYUR. Si tu revitalized the study of Sanskrit and stressed the importance of older traditions that had fallen into decline after the rise to power of the DGE LUGS sect. The revitalization of religious learning in Sde dge spread to the Bka' 'brgyud and RNYING MA institutions in the region and reached its peak in the middle of the nineteenth century. When the Dpal spungs-based revitalization began to disturb the traditional SA SKYA affilation of the Sde dge royal family (from the time of 'PHAGS PA,' 1235–1280), such leading figures as 'JAM MGON KONG SPRUL BLO 'GRO MTHA' YAS, 'JAM DBYANG MKHYEN BRTSE

DBANG PO, and MCHOG GYUR GLING PA responded to the danger of conflict among powerful Sde dge clans by using impartial liturgies that did not stress one tradition over another. There is some evidence that another great ris med lama, DPAL SPRUL RIN PO CHE, extended the spirit to include even Dge lugs traditions. The frequency of the occurrence of the term ris med in Tibetan literature from that era has given rise in the West to the notion that something akin to a "nonsectarian movement" occurred in eastern Tibet in the nineteenth century, one in which scholars of the Rnying ma, Bka' brgyud, and Sa skya sects not only read and benefited from each other's traditions (as had long been the case), but also studied the works of the politically more powerful Dge lugs sect, which had been at odds with both Rnying ma and Bka' brgyud at various points since the seventeenth century. This idea that such a "movement" occurred has been largely drawn from preliminary studies of 'Jam mgon kong sprul. This Bka' brgyud lama (who was born into a BON family and initially ordained into a Rnying ma monastery) achieved a remarkable breadth and depth in his scholarship. In several collections of liturgical texts and lengthy treatises, he set forth a vision of a nonsectarian ideal in which intersectarian exchanges were valued, yet strict separations between the multiple lineages and orders were carefully upheld. Still, the notion that 'Jam mgon kong sprul, 'Jam dbyang mkhyen brtse, and Dpal sprul Rin po che were at the center of a "nonsectarian movement," in the sense that there was a widespread institutional reformation in their lifetimes, is not historically accurate. It is perhaps better to speak of the nonsectarian ideal and their own lives as models of its expression. That model was indeed much imitated in the early twentieth century, and the ris med ideal appears to have become a standard motif for the social and political unification of the Tibetan exile community since 1959. The current DALAI LAMA, for example, is known to use the metaphor of the five-fingered hand (the four main Buddhist orders and the Bon religion) to describe a Tibetan society as fundamentally united yet respectful of its differences.

**Risshō Kōseikai**. (立正佼成会). In Japanese, "Society for Establishing Righteousness and Peaceful Relations," one of Japan's largest lay Buddhist organizations. Risshō Kōseikai was founded in 1938 by NIWANO NIKKYŌ (1906–1999), the son of a farming family in Niigata prefecture, and NAGANUMA MYŌKŌ (1889–1957), a homemaker from Saitama prefecture. In 2007, it claimed 1.67 million member households, with 239 churches in Japan and fifty-six churches in eighteen countries outside of Japan. Originally formed as an offshoot of REIYŪKAI, Risshō Kōseikai is strongly influenced by NICHIRENSHŪ doctrine, although it bears no organizational ties with the latter school. In terms of its ethos and organizational structure, it embodies many of the characteristics of Japan's so-called new religions. Risshō Kōseikai emphasizes worship of the SADDHARMAPUṆḌARĪKASŪTRA ("Lotus Sūtra") as a means for self-cultivation and salvation as well as for the greater good of humanity at large. Religious practice includes recitation of chapters from the *Saddharmapuṇḍarīkasūtra* every morning and evening and chanting of the Japanese title of the sūtra, or DAIMOKU, viz., NAMU MYŌHŌRENGEKYŌ. As is common among schools associated with worship of the *Saddharmapuṇḍarīkasūtra*, Risshō Kōseikai believes that people share karmic links with their ancestors. Through recitation of *Saddharmapuṇḍarīkasūtra* passages and its title, along with repentance for one's past transgressions, one can transfer merit to one's ancestors. This transference aims to subdue the troubled spirits of ancestors who did not attain buddhahood, as well as to eliminate any negative karmic bonds with them. Risshō Kōseikai is headquartered in Tōkyō. However, its organization is largely decentralized and it has no priesthood. This structure places more value and responsibility on its laity, who are presumed to be capable of transferring merit and conducting funerals and ancestral rites on their own. Group gatherings generally address counseling issues for individuals and families alongside the study of Buddhist doctrine. In contrast to Reiyūkai, which emphasizes devotional faith to the *Saddharmapuṇḍarīkasūtra* without the need for detailed doctrinal understanding of Buddhism, adherents of Risshō Kōseikai, in line with the school's founders, include the analytic study of doctrine as complementary to their faith.

**Risshū**. [alt. Ritsushū] (律宗). In Japanese, "School of Discipline," one of the so-called six schools of the Nara tradition of early Japanese Buddhism (see NARA BUDDHISM, SIX SCHOOLS OF); the term is also sometimes seen transcribed as RITSUSHŪ. Although its origins are uncertain, a decree by the Grand Council of State (J. Daijōkan) in 718 acknowledged Risshū as one of major schools of Buddhism in the Japanese capital of Nara. The school is dedicated to the exegesis and dissemination of the rules of Buddhist VINAYA, especially those associated with the SIFEN LÜ ("Four-Part Vinaya") of the DHARMAGUPTAKA school. Rather than an established religious institution, the Risshū, like the other contemporaneous schools of the Nara period (710–974), should instead be considered more of an intellectual tradition or school of thought. Risshū arose as an attempt to systematize monastic rules and practices on the basis of Chinese translations of Indian vinaya texts. Throughout the first half of the eighth century, Japanese monks relied on the Taihō Law Code (701), a set of government-mandated monastic regulations, to guide both their ordination ceremonies (J. jukai) and their conduct. Realizing that Japan lacked proper observance of the vinaya, Nara scholars who had studied monastic discipline in China sought the aid of GANJIN (C. Jianzhen; 687–763), a well-known Chinese master of the NANSHAN LÜ ZONG (South Mountain School of Discipline), the largest of the three vinaya traditions of China. Their attempts to use Ganjin to establish an orthodox ordination ceremony in Japan met with considerable resistance, first from the Chinese court, which did not want to part with Ganjin, and second with entrenched interests in Nara, which had grown accustomed to the Taihō regulations. After five failed attempts to travel to Japan at these monks' invitation, Ganjin finally arrived in Japan in 754. Then sixty-six and blind, Ganjin finally established an ordination platform that summer at the great Nara monastery of TŌDAIJI. Soon thereafter, two more ordination platforms were erected under the jurisdiction of Risshū: one at Yakushiji in Shimotsuke province (in present-day Tochigi prefecture), and one at Kanzeonji in Chikuzen province (in present-day Fukuoka prefecture). In his later years, Ganjin also founded the monastery of TŌSHŌDAIJI in Nara, where he trained monks according to his own codification of the rules. Risshū and the other Nara schools fell into a period of decline over the course of the Heian period (794–1185), which ultimately set the stage for a restoration of Risshū in the early Kamakura period (1185–1333). Under the leadership of the Tendai priest Shunjō (1166–1227), who had studied in China, a group of monks with interests in vinaya assembled at Sennyūji in Kyōto. They would later become identified as the Hokkyō, or "northern capital," branch of the Risshū school, in contrast to the Nankyō (southern capital) branch in Nara. Monks in Nara also attempted to restore Risshū, as exemplified by Kakujō's (1194–1249) move to Tōshōdaiji and the efforts of Eizon (1201–1290), who incorporated esoteric practice (see MIKKYŌ) in his restoration of Risshū at Saidaiji in Nara. Today, Risshū survives in the two monasteries of Tōshōdaiji and Saidaiji, although the latter was officially joined with the SHINGONSHŪ during the Meiji Restoration (1868–1912).

**Ritsu School**. (J). See RISSHŪ.

**Ritsushū**. (J) (律宗). See RISSHŪ; NANSHAN LÜ ZONG.

**rje**. (je). A Tibetan title or honorific, lit. "one to be followed," hence "leader." It is affixed at the beginning or the end of a name, to indicate the person's importance. The three founders of the DGE LUGS sect, for example, commonly have the title affixed to their names: Rje RIN PO CHE is TSONG KHA PA; Rgyal tshab rje is RGYAL TSHAB DAR MA RIN CHEN, and Mkhas grub rje is MKHAS GRUB DGE LEGS DPAL BZANG; this triumvirate is commonly referred to be the abbreviation rje yab sras gsum (je yabse sum) ("triumvirate of the lord father and the [two] sons"). See also RJE BSTUN; RJE BTSUN DAM PA.

**rje 'bangs nyer lnga**. (jebang nyernga). In Tibetan, lit. "the twenty-five, king and subjects," referring to the twenty-five chief disciples of the eighth-century Indian adept PADMASAMBHAVA during his activity in Tibet. The king refers to the Tibetan ruler KHRI SRONG LDE BTSAN, who was responsible for inviting Padmasambhava to Tibet to aid in the founding of BSAM YAS monastery. According to some lists, the remaining twenty-four disciples are:

1. Nam mkha'i snying po (Namke Nyingpo)
2. Sangs rgyas ye shes (Sangye Yeshe)
3. Rgyal ba mchog dbyangs (Gyalwa Chokyang)
4. Mkhar chen bza' (Karchensa)
5. Dpal gyi ye shes (Palgyi Yeshe)
6. Dpal gyi seng ge (Palgyi Senge)
7. Bai ro tsa na (VAIROCANA)
8. Gnyags Jñānakumāra (Nyak Jñānakumāra)
9. G.yu sgra snying po (Yudra Nyingpo)
10. Rdo rje bdud 'joms (Dorje Dudjom)
11. Ye shes dbyangs (Yeshe Yang)
12. Sog po Lha dpal (Sokpo Lhapal)
13. Zhang YE SHES SDE (Shang Yeshe De)
14. Dpal gyi dbang phyug (Palgyi Wangchuk)
15. Ldan ma rtse mang (Denma Tsemang)
16. Ska ba DPAL BRTSEGS (Kawa Paltsek)
17. Shud bu dpal gyi seng ge (Shubu Palgyi Senge)
18. Rgyal ba'i blo gros (Gyalwe Lodrö)
19. Khye'u chung lo (Khye'u Chunglo)
20. 'O bran Dpal gyi dbang phyug (Odran Palgyi Wangchuk)
21. Rma Rin chen mchog (Ma Rinchen Chok)
22. Lha lung Dpal gyi rdo rje (Lhalung Palgyi Dorje)
23. Lang gro Dkon mchog 'byung gnas (Langdro Könchok Jungne)
24. La gsum rgyal ba byang chub (Lasum Gyalwa Jangchub)

Other lists include Padmasambhava's female disciples MANDĀRAVĀ and YE SHES MTSHO RGYAL.

**rje btsun**. (jetsün). In Tibetan, "lord" or "reverend," a Tibetan honorific used especially for revered religious figures. The term is perhaps most commonly used to as a term of respect for MI LA RAS PA, so much so that the term rje btsun alone in Tibetan often refers to him. The word btsun (tsun) (S. and P. bhadanta) is usually reserved for monks, but by extension applies also to saintly persons; RJE means one to be followed. The feminine form of the term is rje btsun ma (jetsünma), often used to refer to TĀRĀ, or to saintly women; it is used as a prefix to show respect to nuns or prominent female teachers.

**Rje btsun dam pa**. (Jetsün Dampa). In Tibetan, "excellent lord," the Tibetan name of the Khalkha Jebtsundamba Khutuktu, the lineage of incarnate lamas who serve as head of the DGE LUGS sect in Mongolia, also known as Bogd Gegen. The lineage was established by the fifth DALAI LAMA, who, after his suppression of the JO NANG sect, declared that the renowned Jo nang scholar TĀRANĀTHA had been reborn in Mongolia, thus taking an important line of incarnations from a rival sect and transferring it to his own Dge lugs sect. The first Rje btsun dam pa was Blo bzang bstan pa'i rgyal mtshan (1635–1723), known in Mongolian as Bogdo Zanabazar or simply Zanabazar. He was the son of the Mongol prince Gombodorj, the Tosiyetu Khan, ruler of the Khan Uula district of Mongolia, and himself became the head of the Khalkha Mongols. He and the second Rje btsun dam pa lama were direct descendants of Genghis

Khan. Zanabazar was ordained at the age of five and recognized as the incarnation of Tāranātha, this recognition confirmed by the fifth Dalai Lama and first PAṆ CHEN LAMA. He spent 1649–1651 in Tibet where he received initiations and teachings from the two Dge lugs hierarchs. Zanabazar is remembered especially as a great sculptor who produced many important bronze images. He was also a respected scholar and a favorite of the Manchu Chinese Kangxi emperor. During the Qing dynasty, the Rje btsun dam pa was selected from Tibet, perhaps in fear that a Mongol lama would become too powerful. During the Qing, it was said that the Qing emperor, the Dalai Lama, and the Rje btsun dam pa were incarnations of MAÑJUŚRĪ, AVALOKITEŚVARA, and VAJRAPĀṆI, respectively. When northern Mongolia sought independence, the eighth Rje btsun dam pa (1869–1924) assumed the title of emperor of Mongolia, calling himself Boghda Khan (also "Bogd Khan"). He was the head of state until his death in 1924, after which the Communist government declared the end of the incarnation line. However, 'Jam dpal rnam grol chos kyi rgyal mtshan was recognized in LHA SA as the ninth Rje btsun dam pa; he fled into exile in India in 1959.

**rlung rta**. (lung ta). In Tibetan, the word for "luck," lit. "wind horse"; in its secondary meaning, it is commonly referred to in English as a "prayer flag." It is a colored square of cloth, usually about one foot square, and often imprinted with a prayer. These flags are then attached to poles, the rooftops of monasteries and dwellings, or are strung from the cairns found at the summits of mountain passes. The wind is said to carry the benefits requested by the prayer imprinted on the fluttering flag, both to the person who flies the flag as well as to all beings in the region. The prayer flag has in its center an image of a deity or auspicious symbol usually two or three inches square, set within a single-line frame; the female bodhisattva TĀRĀ is commonly depicted, as is the "wind horse" itself, a horse carrying a jewel on its back. The prayer itself (often a series of mantras) appears on the flag as if on a sheet of paper, with lines breaking in the middle of the flag to accommodate the central image. Prayer flags are made from a wooden block print. The block is inked and the piece of cloth then laid across it and pressed with a roller to transfer the words and picture onto the cloth. With many prayer flags, there is a brief statement after the prayer of the benefits that will accrue from its flying.

**Rma chen spom ra**. (Machen Pomra). A Tibetan mountain god whose seat is A MYES RMA CHEN in A mdo (today the Qinghai region of China) where he is the chief SA BDAG, or "earth lord," of the region. As with other pre-Buddhist Tibetan mountain deities, Rma chen spom ra was converted to Buddhism, in his case by PADMASAMBHAVA. The mountain was inserted into a Tibetan list of the twenty-four PĪṬHA from the CAKRASAṂVARATANTRA, and is further understood to be a three-dimensional Cakrasaṃvara MAṆḌALA. The cult of Rma chen spom ra was introduced to central Tibet by TSONG KHA PA, a native of the region; he made Rma chen spom ra the chief DHARMAPĀLA of DGA' LDAN monastery. That monastery used to remove his image from the monastery each night to a small shrine outside the walls: since the god is a layman and has a female consort, by the rules of the monastery he cannot sleep inside the walls. Later the practice was replaced with a formal daily request to the god to leave the monastery for the night. He is golden, wears a golden cuirass and a helmet, carries a lance with a flag, a sack made from the skin of a mongoose and rides a white horse. His consort is the sman mo (menmo) Gung sman ma (Gungmenma). The DGE LUGS sect considers the god Phying dkar ba (Chingkarwa) to be an emanation of Rma chen spom ra.

**Rme ru snying pa**. (Meru Nyingpa). A Tibetan monastery on the northeast side of the JO KHANG in the Tibetan capital of LHA SA; one of six institutions constructed by the Tibetan king RAL PA CAN, purportedly on the site where Thon mi Sambhoṭa (c. seventh century) developed the Tibetan script. The Indian master ATIŚA DĪPAṂKARAŚRĪJÑĀNA refurbished the monastery and it was later converted to the DGE LUGS sect in the sixteenth century under the third DALAI LAMA, BSOD NAMS RGYA MTSHO. Me ru rnying pa is dedicated primarily to RDO RJE GRAGS LDAN, one of Tibet's central protector deities and the spirit that possesses the medium of GNAS CHUNG, the state oracle of Tibet.

**rnam thar**. (namtar). In Tibetan, "complete liberation," translating the Sanskrit VIMOKṢA. In the Tibetan context, rnam thar refers to a widespread literary genre of sacred biography or autobiography. As its translation suggests, the term usually indicates an emphasis on the stereotypically Buddhist aspects of the subject's life, including his or her religious training, practice of meditation, and eventual liberation. Such works often incorporate elements of the fabulous and the fantastic and have parallels with the genre of hagiography. Three types of rnam thar are often enumerated: the "outer autobiography" (phyi'i rnam thar), which narrates the important events of daily life, including travels and meetings with prominent persons; the "inner autobiography" (nang gi rnam thar), which describes religious teachings received and relationships with teachers and disciples; and the "secret autobiography" (GSANG BA'I RNAM THAR), which describes religious experiences, with the author often writing from the perspective of a transcendental subject.

**Rngog Blo ldan shes rab**. (Ngok Loden Sherap) (1059–1110). A Tibetan scholar and translator, nephew of RNGOG LEGS PA'I SHES RAB. After studying under his uncle and participating in the "Council of THO LING" in GU GE, he left for India at the age of eighteen with a group of companions, including RWA LO TSĀ BA. He spent seventeen years pursuing the study of Buddhist texts, including the SŪTRAS, TANTRAS, and Buddhist sciences; his main teacher of PRAMĀṆA was the Kashmiri logician

Bhavyarāja. At the age of thirty-five, he returned to Tibet to become the second abbot of GSANG PHU NE'U THOG monastery near LHA SA. He translated numerous works still found in the BKA' 'GYUR and BSTAN 'GYUR sections of the Tibetan Buddhist canon. These include the PRAMĀṆAVINIŚCAYA of DHARMAKĪRTI, the five works of MAITREYA, and the major works of what would be dubbed the YOGĀCĀRA SVĀTANTRIKA school. He also composed a number of works himself, which do not seem to have survived. Along with RIN CHEN BZANG PO, he is often referred to as a "great translator" (lo chen); in later works sometimes simply as bdag nyid chen po (S. mahātma). Because of the influence of his translations and his own substantial writings, he is considered along with SA SKYA PAṆḌITA to be a founding figure of Tibetan Buddhist scholasticism.

**Rngog Legs pa'i shes rab**. (Ngog Lekpe Sherap) (fl. eleventh century). Tibetan scholar and translator venerated as an important founder of the BKA' GDAMS sect of Tibetan Buddhism. The exact year of his year of birth is unclear, although it is known that he was born in the western Tibetan region of GU GE. According to Tibetan histories, he was one of twenty-one young scholars sent to India by the region's king, YE SHES 'OD, to study Sanskrit, Buddhist philosophy, and TANTRA. He returned to Tibet and became an important disciple of the Bengali master ATIŚA DĪPAṂKARAŚRĪJÑĀNA. He also studied under and collaborated with the famed translator RIN CHEN BZANG PO. Together with Atiśa and 'BROM STON RGYAL BA'I 'BYUNG GNAS, Ngog Legs pa'i shes rab is considered an important Bka' gdams forefather. In 1073, he laid the foundations for an early monastic center for Buddhist learning, GSANG PHU NE'U THOG, south of LHA SA. He is also known as Rngog lo tsā ba (Ngog, the translator) and Rngog lo chung (Ngog, the junior translator) in distinction to Rin chen Bzang po, the great translator (lo chen).

**Rnying ma**. (Nyingma). In Tibetan, "Ancient," the name of one of the four major sects of Tibetan Buddhism. The name derives from the sect's origins during the "early dissemination" (SNGA DAR) of Buddhism in Tibet and its reliance on translations of TANTRAs made during that period; this is in distinction to the new (GSAR MA) sects of BKA' BRGYUD, SA SKYA, and DGE LUGS, all of which arose during the later dissemination (PHYI DAR) and make use of newer translations. The Rnying ma is thus "ancient" in relation to the new sects and only began to be designated as such after their appearance. The sect traces its origins back to the teachings of the mysterious figure of PADMASAMBHAVA, who visited Tibet during the eighth century and is said to have hidden many texts, called "treasures" (GTER MA), to be discovered in the future. In addition to the Buddhist canon accepted by all sects of Tibetan Buddhism, the Rnying ma adds another collection of tantras (the RNYING MA'I RGYUD 'BUM) as well as the discovered "treasure" (GTER MA) texts to their canonical corpus, works that in many cases the other sects regard as APOCRYPHA, i.e., not of Indian origin. Rnying ma identifies nine vehicles among the corpus of Buddhist teachings, the highest of which is known as ATIYOGA or, more commonly, the "great perfection" (RDZOGS CHEN). These teachings describe the mind as the primordial basis, characterized by qualities such as presence, spontaneity, luminosity, original purity, unobstructed freedom, expanse, clarity, self-liberation, openness, effortlessness, and intrinsic awareness. It is not accessible through conceptual elaboration or logical analysis. Rather, the primordial basis is an eternally pure state free from the dualism of subject and object, infinite and perfect from the beginning, and ever complete. The technique for the discovery of the ubiquitous original purity and self-liberation is to engage in a variety of practices designed to eliminate karmic obstructions, at which point the mind eliminates all thoughts and experiences itself, thereby recognizing its true nature. The rdzogs chen doctrine does not seem to derive directly from any of the Indian philosophical schools; its precise connections to the Indian Buddhist tradition have yet to be established. Some scholars have claimed an historical link and doctrinal affinity between rdzogs chen and the CHAN tradition of Chinese Buddhism, but the precise relationship between the two remains to be fully investigated. It is noteworthy that certain of the earliest extant rdzogs chen texts specifically contrast their own tradition with that of Chan. In comparison to the Dge lugs, Bka' brgyud, and Sa skya, the Rnying ma (with some important exceptions, notably at the time of the fifth DALAI LAMA) remained largely uninvolved in state politics, both within Tibet and in foreign relations. Although they developed great monasteries, such as SMIN GROL GLING, RDZOGS CHEN, and RDO RJE BRAG, the Rnying ma also maintained a strong local presence as lay tantric practitioners (sngags pa) who performed a range of ritual functions for the community. The Rnying ma produced many famous scholars and visionaries, such as KLONG CHEN RAB 'BYAMS, 'JIGS MED GLING PA, and MI PHAM. In the nineteenth century, Rnying ma scholars played a key role in the so-called nonsectarian movement (RIS MED) in eastern Tibet, which produced many important new texts.

**Rnying ma'i rgyud 'bum**. (Nyingme Gyübum). A compendium of the tantras and tantric exegetical literature of the RNYING MA sect of Tibetan Buddhism; considered apocryphal by the redactors of the Tibetan Buddhist canon (BKA' 'GYUR), the collection thus represents an alternative or supplementary Rnying ma canon of tantric scriptures. Numerous editions are extant, including the SDE DGE edition (twenty-six volumes), the Gting kye (twenty-six volumes), the Skyi rong (thirty-seven volumes), the Tsham brag (forty-six volumes), and the Vairo rgyud 'bum (eight volumes). All but the last divide the tantras into the standard Rnying ma doxographical categories of MAHĀYOGA, ANUYOGA, and ATIYOGA, although within those categories differences emerge (the Vairo rgyud 'bum, for example, includes only atiyoga). Further editions include those recently discovered in Kathmandu and the so-called Waddell edition, a close relative to the Gting kye. All but the Sde dge are manuscripts. Catalogues of Buddhist texts were made as far back as the eighth century, but the roots of the Rnying ma'i rgyud 'bum go back to the second propagation of Buddhism in Tibet (roughly the eleventh to thirteenth centuries). In opposition to the new translation sects (GSAR MA) that developed around newly imported tantras, adherents of the earlier translations coalesced into the Rnying ma, or "ancients," sect. There is evidence that 'Gro mgon Nam mkha' 'phel, the son of one of the earliest proponents of the Rnying ma sect, NYANG RAL NYI MA 'OD ZER, arranged a collection of early tantras in eighty-two volumes, which is no longer extant. The Vairo rgyud 'bum also may date as far back as the twelfth century, although its origins are unclear. When BU STON RIN CHEN GRUB edited the Tibetan Buddhist canon in the fourteenth century, he excluded the tantras found in the Rnying ma'i rgyud 'bum on the basis that he could find no Indic originals with which to authenticate them. Bu ston's position has been shown by Tibetan and Western scholars to have been partisan and inconsistent, and several tantras he excluded, such as the VAJRAKĪLAYA tantras, are accepted by other sects. Some excluded tantras do in fact appear to be early combinations of Indic and Tibetan material, while others, especially later revelatory scriptures (GTER MA) are entirely of Tibetan composition. An early version of the Rnying ma'i rgyud 'bum that may have influenced later editions was that of RATNA GLING PA, no longer extant. The Tshams brag appears to have been commissioned by Tsham brag bla ma Ngag dbang 'brug pa (1682–1748) and was based on a still earlier Bhutanese version. GTER BDAG GLING PA's edition later became the basis for that of 'JIGS MED GLING PA, in twenty-five volumes, which was produced in 1772, and is known as the Padma 'od gling edition. This in turn was the basis for the Sde dge block-print edition, carved between 1794 and 1798 and overseen by Dge rtse paṇ chen 'Gyur med mchog grub (1761–1829) of KAḤ THOG monastery.

**Rnying ma pa**. (Nyingmapa). A person affiliated with the RNYING MA sect of Tibetan Buddhism.

**Rōben**. (J) (良辨). See RYŌBEN.

**Roerich, George (Yuri)**. (1902–1960). George (Yuri) Nikolaevich Roerich was the son of Russian painter and mystic Nikolai Roerich and Helena Ivanova, a Theosophist who translated Madame Blavatsky's *The Secret Doctrine* into Russian. Roerich spent much of his childhood traveling the world. The family traveled to Urga, in the far western region of Siberia, and their journeys took them to Ladakh as well as later to Europe and America. He studied Asian languages at the University of London, at Harvard University, and at Paris, where he studied with SYLVAIN LÉVI. Nikolai Roerich believed that ŚAMBHALA was located in Central Asia, perhaps in the Gobi Desert, and from 1925 to 1928 he led an expedition through Chinese Turkestan, Mongolia, and Tibet, in search of evidence of the hidden kingdom of śambhala, the supposed abode of the mahātmas, the spiritual masters of all religions. In 1928, George and his father established the Urusvati Himalayan Research Institute in Darjeeling, India, moving later to the Kullu Valley in the western Himalayas. George Roerich was a scholar in Tibetology and Mongolian studies, later serving as the first director of the Buddhist Branch of the Institute of Oriental Studies in Moscow. Roerich played a significant role in reviving Russian Orientalism after returning from exile in 1957. Under Khrushchev's government, Roerich was able to revive the Biblioteca Buddhica Series, which had ceased publication in 1937. He worked with Bidiya Dandaron and GUNAPALA PIYASENA MALALASEKERA (1899–1973) and succeeded in printing the first Russian version of the DHAMMAPADA in 1960. He died suddenly from a heart attack that same year. Among his publications, his most important for Buddhist studies was his translation (with the assistance of DGE 'DUN CHOS 'PHEL) of the DEB THER SNGON PO ("Blue Annals") by 'Gos lo tsā ba Gzhon nu dpal.

**rōhatsu sesshin**. (臘八攝心). In Japanese, lit. "retreat on the eighth [day] of the last [month]," typically refering to an intensive week-long session of meditation (SESSHIN) that ends on the eighth day of the twelfth lunar month (rōhatsu), the reputed day of the Buddha's enlightenment according to the East Asian calendar. The retreat begins with a ceremony on the first of the twelfth lunar month and ends on the morning of the eighth with another ceremony, which usually consists of a lecture by the abbot known as the rōhatu jōdo, and offerings made to an image of ŚĀKYAMUNI emerging from the mountains (shussan Shaka). (Cf. PRĀGBODHI[GIRI].) The rōhatsu sesshin performed in the SAṂGHA hall (SENGTANG) at ZEN monasteries often entails nonstop meditative practice with little or no sleep. See also YONGMAENG CHŎNGJIN.

**Rong ston Smra ba'i seng ge**. (Rongtön Mawe Senge) (1367–1449). A Tibetan Buddhist master, especially revered within the SA SKYA sect, also known as Rong ston Shes bya kun rig Shākya rgyal mtshan (Rongton Sheja Kunrik Shākya Gyaltsen). Born into a BON family in Rgyal rong (Gyarong) in eastern Tibet, Rong ston traveled to the famed BKA' GDAMS institution of SANG PHU NE'U THOG, where he received ordination and studied all the major branches of Buddhist learning. He furthered his education under numerous masters across central Tibet and became renowned for his writings on PRAMĀṆA and PRAJÑĀPĀRAMITĀ. His two most famous students were SHĀKYA MCHOG LDAN and GO BO RAB 'BYAMS PA BSOD NAMS SENG GE, both prolific scholars known for polemical exchanges with early defenders of TSONG KHA PA. Rong ston founded NA LAN DRA monastery in 'Phan yul (Penyul), north of LHA SA, which later became an important Sa skya institution.

**Rong zom Chos kyi bzang po**. (Rongzom Chökyi Sangpo) (1012–1088). An important figure in the renaissance of the

RNYING MA tradition in Tibet. His collected works in two volumes include the *Rdzogs pa chen po'i lta sgom* ("Instructions on Cultivating the View of the Great Perfection") (see RDZOGS CHEN) and a seminal work on SDOM GSUM ("three codes") *Dam tshig mdo rgyas*. He was learned in the older traditions based on earlier translations and in the new traditions that spread after the return of the translators RIN CHEN BZANG PO and RNGOG LEGS PA'I SHES RAB. Traditionally, he is said to be the recipient of teachings deriving from Heshang MOHEYAN, VAIROCANA, and VIMALAMITRA—important figures of the early dissemination (SNGA DAR)—and it is said that upon meeting ATIŚA DĪPAṂKARAŚRĪJÑĀNA after his arrival in Tibet, Atiśa considered him a manifestation of his teacher Nag po pa (Kṛṣṇapāda). Rong zom instructed many important figures of the day, including the translator MAR PA, prior to his departure for India.

**rosary**. See JAPAMĀLĀ; MĀLĀ.

**rōshi**. (老師). In Japanese, lit. "old master," an honorific typically used with reference to a senior Buddhist teacher or monk, sometimes interpreted to be a contraction of the compound rōdaishūshi ("elder teacher of the tradition"). In the Japanese ZEN schools, rōshi is a technical term used to designate a senior teacher who is authorized to offer spiritual guidance and to hold higher ecclesiastical positions. Within the RINZAISHŪ, rōshi specifically refers to a Zen master who has received certification to teach (J. inka; C. YINKE) from another rōshi and who is thereafter authorized to sanction the awakening of others during private interviews known as sanzen. In the SŌTŌSHŪ, one becomes a rōshi through a shihō or series of ordination ceremonies with one's teacher, which acknowledge mastery of the precepts and receipt of dharma transmission, so that the recipient is then authorized to teach and receive appointment as abbot of a Sōtō monastery. Despite its literal denotation, the term rōshi may also be used as an honorary appellation for older monks who are not yet teachers, or even to refer to monks in general. Thus the term rōshi is not necessarily used to imply old age but rather respect or veneration.

**Ṛṣipatana**. (P. Isipatana; T. Drang srong lhung ba; C. Xianren duochu; J. Sennin dasho; K. Sŏnin t'ach'ŏ 仙人墮處). In Sanskrit, lit. "Place where Holy Men Descend"; referring specifically to the Ṛṣipatana (P. Isipatana) MṚGADĀVA (Deer Park), located just northeast of the city of Vārāṇasī, where the Buddha spoke his first sermon, the "Turning of the Wheel of the Dharma" (DHARMACAKRAPRAVARTANASŪTRA; P. DHAMMACAKKAPPAVATTANASUTTA); this site is also commonly known as the Deer Park (Mṛgadāva) in SĀRNĀTH. Explanations for the name Ṛṣipatana generally involve slight variations of a story set in the time of the previous buddha KĀŚYAPA. Just before the advent of Kāśyapa, five hundred PRATYEKABUDDHAs were said to be living in the hills of the park. When they heard of the coming of this Buddha, they flew into to the air, attained NIRVĀṆA, and manifested the fire element; the fire burned their material bodies, which fell as ashes to the park below. Thus, the site came to be called "the place where holy men descend." Others argue that Ṛṣipatana is instead a variation of Ṛṣipattana, meaning "gathering place of holy men."

**rtsod grwa**. (tsödra). In Tibetan, lit. "debating institution," particularly a large DGE LUGS monastery where a central part of the monastic complex is the chos ra (chöra), literally "fenced enclosure for dharma," hence "debate courtyard," often an enclosed open space close to the main assembly hall where monks who study scriptures assemble to debate points of doctrine. The term mtshan nyid grwa tsang (tsenyi dratsang) is often used in place of rtsod grwa. The origins of the rtsod grwa may go back to the model of study followed in BKA' GDAMS monasteries like GSANG PHU NE'U THOG, although such debate was also a part of the curriculum in the large monastic universities of northeast India, such as VIKRAMAŚĪLA, NĀLANDĀ, and ODANTAPURĪ. The rtsod grwa is sometimes contrasted with teaching institutes (BSHAD GRWA) and places given over to meditation (sgrub khang), although most monasteries have parts dedicated to those activities as well. The best-known rtsod grwa are the six great Dge lugs monasteries of pre-1959 Tibet where the calendar year had strict debating periods; debate was raised to a high level there, forming a central part of the curriculum. For a month during the winter, 'Jang phu monastery to the southwest of LHA SA was the site of an intensive debate called the 'Jang dgun chos (Janggünchö) attended by students from the major Dge lugs monasteries in the greater Lha sa area, where debate focused particularly on the PRAMĀṆAVĀRTTIKA of DHARMAKĪRTI.

**Ru fajie pin**. (S. *Dharmadhātupraveśanaparivarta; J. Nyūhokkaibon; K. Ip pŏpkye p'um 入法界品). In Chinese, "Chapter on 'Entering the DHARMADHĀTU.'" See GAṆḌAVYŪHA; AVATAṂSAKASŪTRA.

**rūpa**. (T. gzugs; C. se; J. shiki; K. saek 色). In Sankrit and Pāli, "body," "form," or "materiality," viz., that which has shape and is composed of matter. The term has two primary doctrinal denotations. More generally, rūpa refers to materiality, which serves as objects of the five sensory consciousnesses (VIJÑĀNA): visual, auditory, olfactory, gustatory, and tactile. This is the meaning of rūpa as the first of the five aggregates (SKANDHA), where it includes all the physical constituents of the person. The second sense is more limited; the colors and shapes that serve as objects of the visual consciousness (CAKṢURVIJÑĀNA) are designated as rūpa (and this accounts for the Chinese translation of the term as "color"); this second denotation is a subset of the first, and much more limited, referring only to the objects of the visual consciousness (CAKṢURVIJÑĀNA). It is in this second sense that rūpa is counted among the twelve ĀYATANA and eighteen DHĀTU. In formulations of the person as "name and form" (NĀMARŪPA), viz., an individual's mental and physical constituents, "name" (NĀMA) subsumes the four mental aggregrates

(SKANDHA) of sensation (VEDANĀ), perception (SAṂJÑĀ), conditioning factors (SAṂSKĀRA), and consciousness (VIJÑĀNA), while "form" (rūpa) refers to the materiality aggregate (RŪPASKANDHA), viz., the physical body. In some MAHĀYĀNA sūtras, rūpādi ("form, and so on") means all dharmas because form is the first in the all-inclusive list of SAṂKLIṢṬA and VYAVADĀNA dharmas that are declared to be empty of an essential identity (SVABHĀVA).

**rūpadhātu**. (T. gzugs khams; C. sejie; J. shikikai; K. saekkye 色界). In Sanskrit and Pāli, the "realm of subtle materiality" or "form realm," which together with the sensuous, or desire, realm (KĀMADHĀTU) and the immaterial, or formless, realm (ĀRŪPYADHĀTU) constitute the three realms (TRAIDHĀTUKA) of SAṂSĀRA; the term is synonymous with rūpāvacara. The subtle-materiality realm is located above the heavens of the sensuous realm, which are situated on and above Mount SUMERU. This realm is divided into four meditative heavens associated with the four meditative concentrations of the subtle-materiality realm (RŪPĀVACARADHYĀNA). These meditative heavens are places of rebirth in saṃsāra and are accessible only through mastery of a specific rūpāvacaradhyāna; the beings reborn there are classified as BRAHMĀ gods. Rebirth in these meditative heavens is the result of a specific kind of virtuous action, called an "immovable action" (S. ANIÑJYAKARMAN), in which the action has the definite and specific effect of bringing about rebirth in either the subtle-materiality or immaterial heavens. The immovable action that would result in rebirth in, for example, the second concentration of the subtle-materiality realm, is the achievement of that specific state of dhyāna as a human in the immediately preceding lifetime. This realm is called the "subtle-materiality realm" because the beings there are free of the desires of the sensuous realm yet retain at least some semblance of physicality, albeit extremely subtle, and have a vestigial attachment to form (RŪPA). Only three of the five sensory objects remain in the subtle-materiality realm: visual objects, auditory objects, and objects of touch; hence, the deities there have only three physical sense organs, of sight, hearing, and touch. Each of the four concentrations of the subtle-materiality realm has its own sublevels, with three levels in the the first heaven, three in the second, three in the third, and eight in the fourth, totaling seventeen. In each ascending level, the heaven is situated farther above Mount Sumeru, the height of its beings grows taller, and their life spans increase. Although the characteristics of the various heavens within the subtle-materiality realm are described in some detail, the greater emphasis in Buddhist literature is on the states of meditative absorption that characterize each, how they are achieved, and how they differ from each other, with particular attention paid to the highest of the four, the fourth dhyāna of the subtle-materiality realm. The first three absorptions are characterized by a feeling of physical rapture (PRĪTI) and mental ease or bliss (SUKHA), whereas the fourth and subtlest of these dhyānas is characterized by one-pointedness of mind (CITTAIKĀGRATĀ) and equanimity (UPEKṢĀ). It is therefore considered an ideal state from which to achieve NIRVĀṆA: for example, when the Buddha entered PARINIRVĀṆA, his mind passed through each of the four subtle-materiality and immaterial absorptions before passing into nirvāṇa directly from the fourth absorption. The fourth absorption also received particular attention as a place of rebirth. While the first three concentrations each have only three divisions, the fourth concentration has eight, with the additional five reserved for those beings who become ĀRYA, or noble beings, through direct insight into the nature of reality. In the fourfold division of noble persons (ĀRYAPUDGALA; viz., stream-enterer, once-returner, nonreturner, and ARHAT), the nonreturner (ANĀGĀMIN) is defined as that noble person who is never again reborn in the sensuous realm. Such a person may be reborn in the subtle-materiality realm, however, and the upper five heavens of the fourth absorption are a special place of rebirth called the pure abodes (ŚUDDHĀVĀSA) that are reserved just for such beings. See also DEVA.

**rūpakāya**. (T. gzugs sku; C. seshen; J. shikishin; K. saeksin 色身). In Sanskrit and Pāli, "physical body," a term that seems to have been used originally to refer to the physical body of the Buddha, as opposed to the body or corpus of the Buddha's marvelous qualities, which were referred to as the DHARMAKĀYA. In the MAHĀYĀNA tradition, the rūpakāya refers to two specific visible forms of a Buddha: the NIRMĀṆAKĀYA, or "emanation body," which is visible to ordinary beings, and the SAṂBHOGAKĀYA, or "enjoyment body," which appears only to advanced bodhisattvas. When texts refer to the two bodies of a buddha, these refer to the rūpakāya and the dharmakāya. When texts refer to the three bodies (TRIKĀYA) of a buddha, these refer to the two types of the rūpakāya—the nirmāṇakāya and the saṃbhogakāya—along with the dharmakāya.

**rūpaloka**. (S). See RŪPADHĀTU.

**rūpaṃ śūnyatā śunyataiva rūpam**. (T. gzugs stong pa'o stong pa nyid gzugs so; C. se jishi kong kong jishi se; J. shikisokuzekū kūsokuzeshiki; K. saek chŭksi kong kong chŭksi saek 色即是空空即是色). In Sanskrit, "form is emptiness, emptiness is form"; a famous line from PRAJÑĀPĀRAMITĀ sūtras, known particularly from the PRAJÑĀPĀRAMITĀHṚDAYASŪTRA ("Heart Sūtra"). The line is widely commented upon in India, Tibet, and East Asia, but is generally presumed to describe the relationship between the objects of ordinary experience (represented by "form," or RŪPA, the first of the five aggregates, or SKANDHA; see RŪPASKANDHA) and ultimate reality (here "emptiness," or ŚŪNYATĀ). Some Sanskrit editions of the sūtra read the first phrase as "form is empty," a reading reflected also in the Tibetan translation. In brief, the line might be interpreted to mean that the nature of the objects of ordinary experience is emptiness and that the ultimate truth *cum* emptiness is to be found in the objects of ordinary experience.

**rūparāga**. (T. gzugs la chags ba; C. se tan; J. shikiton; K. saek t'am 色貪). In Sanskrit and Pāli, "craving for existence in the subtle-materiality realm," the sixth of ten "fetters" (SAṂYOJANA) that keep beings bound to SAṂSĀRA. Rūparāga is the desire to be reborn as a divinity (DEVA) in the subtle-materiality realm (RŪPADHĀTU) where beings are possessed of refined material bodies, are free from physical passions, and have minds that are perpetually absorbed in the rapture, ease, and equanimity of meditative absorption (DHYĀNA). According to this interpretation, craving for subtle-material existence is permanently eliminated upon attaining the stage of an ARHAT, the fourth and highest degree of Buddhist sanctity (ĀRYAPUDGALA). Other schools of ABHIDHARMA use the name "free from attachment to form" (rūpavītarāga) to refer to a subset of nonreturners (ANĀGĀMIN) who eliminate all attachment to the subtle-materiality absorptions (RŪPĀVACARADHYĀNA) while in a sensuous-realm body, take rebirth in an immaterial state (ĀRŪPYADHĀTU), and go on to the BHAVĀGRA where they finally reach NIRVĀṆA.

**rūpaskandha**. (P. rūpakkhandha; T. gzugs kyi phung po; C. se yun; J. shikiun; K. saek on 色蘊). In Sanskrit, "materiality aggregate," the first of the five aggregates (SKANDHA). It includes all material elements of the body, including the five sense objects of visual forms, sounds, tastes, odors, and tangible objects, and the five sense organs (INDRIYA).

**rūpāvacaradhyāna**. (P. rūpāvacarajhāna; T. gzugs na spyod pa'i bsam gtan; C. sejie ding; J. shikikaijō; K. saekkye chŏng 色界定). In Sanskrit, "meditative absorption associated with the subtle-materiality realm"; in some Buddhist schools, one of the two main classifications of meditative absorption (DHYĀNA), along with ĀRŪPYĀVACARADHYĀNA, meditative absorption associated with the immaterial realm. In both cases, dhyāna refers to the attainment of single-pointed concentration of the mind on an object of meditation. The four absorptions of the subtle-materiality realm are characterized by an increasing attentuation of consciousness as one progresses from one stage to the next. By entering into any one of the dhyānas, the meditator temporarily allays the five hindrances (NĪVARAṆA) through the force of concentration, which puts in place the five constituents of absorption (DHYĀNĀṄGA). The five hindrances are (1) sensuous desire (KĀMACCHANDA), which hinders the constituent of one-pointedness of mind (CITTAIKĀGRATĀ); (2) malice (VYĀPĀDA), hindering physical rapture (PRĪTI); (3) sloth and torpor (STYĀNA-MIDDHA), hindering applied thought (VITARKA); (4) restlessness and worry (AUDDHATYA-KAUKṚTYA), hindering mental ease and bliss (SUKHA); and (5) skeptical doubt (VICIKITSĀ), which hinders sustained thought (VICĀRA). These hindrances thus specifically obstruct one of the factors of absorption (dhyānāṅga), and once they are allayed the first subtle-materiality dhyāna will be achieved. In the first subtle-materiality dhyāna, all five constituents of dhyāna are present; as concentration deepens, these gradually fall away, so that in the second dhyāna, both types of thought vanish and only prīti, sukha, and ekāgratā remain; in the third dhyāna, only sukha and ekāgratā remain; and in the fourth dhyāna, concentration is now so rarified that only ekāgratā is left. Mastery of the fourth rūpāvacaradhyāna is required for the cultivation of the supranormal powers (ABHIJÑĀ) and also provides the foundation for the cultivation of the four dhyānas of the immaterial realm (ĀRŪPYĀVACARADHYĀNA). Mastery of any of the subtle-materiality absorptions can result in rebirth as a BRAHMĀ god within the corresponding plane of the subtle-materiality realm (RŪPADHĀTU).

**rūpāyatana**. (T. gzugs kyi skye mched; C. sechu; J. shikisho; K. saekch'ŏ 色處). In Sanskrit and Pāli, "visual sense field," i.e., visible form (RŪPA) as it occurs in the list of twelve sense faculties or "bases of cognition" (ĀYATANA), which serve as the bases for the production of consciousness, viz., the six internal sense bases, or sense organs (eye, ear, nose, tongue, body, and mind) and the six external sense objects (forms, sounds, odors, tastes, tangible objects, and mental phenomena). In the case of form, the contact (SPARŚA) between the visual sense base (CAKṢURINDRIYA) and its corresponding visual sensory object (rūpa) leads to visual consciousness (CAKṢURVIJÑĀNA).

**Rwa lo tsā ba Rdo rje grags**. (Ra Lotsawa Dorje Drakpa) (1016–1128?). A prominent translator and YOGIN of the "later dissemination" (PHYI DAR) of Buddhism to Tibet. While still in his teens, he went to Nepal, where he received instructions and transmissions of a number of tantric cycles; he received the VAJRABHAIRAVA and VAJRAVĀRĀHĪ transmissions from the Nepalese master Bharo. Upon his return to Tibet, he attracted many students and received generous offerings from patrons, which he used for the support of the dharma; among his many projects was the rebuilding of BSAM YAS after it was destroyed by fire. He translated many tantric texts and is known especially for his translations of texts connected with YAMĀNTAKA. He also translated the KĀLACAKRATANTRA into Tibetan; the tradition deriving from his translation is known as the Rwa lugs. He was also a controversial figure, known to have little patience with those who opposed him; he is said to have used his tantric powers to "liberate" (i.e., kill) thirteen rivals, including according to some accounts, MAR PA's son DAR MA SDO SDE.

**Rwa lung**. (Ralung). A principal monastic seat of the 'BRUG PA BKA' BRGYUD sect of Tibetan Buddhism, located southwest of LHA SA. The monastery was established in 1180 by the 'Brug pa founder GTSANG PA RGYA RAS YE SHES RDO RJE on a site consecrated by his master GLING RAS PA. According to traditional accounts, the site takes its name from a sacred goat whose milk was accidentally splashed on a rock. When the milk dried, the mantra oṃ aḥ hūṃ was found miraculously inscribed on the rock face. Gling ras pa took this as an important omen and called the site Rwa lung, lit. "Goat's Omen." Rwa lung was first directed by Gtsang pa rgya ras and later, beginning in the fifteenth century, by his successive reincarnations (SPRUL SKU) known as the 'BRUG CHEN INCARNATIONS.

**Rwa sgreng**. (Reting). A principal monastery of the BKA' GDAMS sect in central Tibet, located in the region of 'Phan po north of LHA SA. The monastery was established in 1056 by 'BROM STON RGYAL BA'I 'BYUNG GNAS, foremost disciple of the Bengali master ATIŚA DĪPAṂKARAŚRĪJÑĀNA. The institution was greatly expanded under the direction of 'Brom ston pa's successors Rnal 'byor pa chen po and Po to ba (b. 1031), although it was sacked by Mongol invaders in 1240. In 1397, the eminent scholar TSONG KHA PA visited Rwa sgreng and experienced a vision of Atiśa, prompting him to compose his celebrated work LAM RIM CHEN MO there. The monastery subsequently became an important DGE LUGS institution. The monastery was severely damaged during the Chinese Cultural Revolution, but has since been partially rebuilt. From the time of the seventh DALAI LAMA, the abbots of Rwa sgreng became eligible to serve as regents during the interegnum between the Dalai Lama's death and his reincarnation's majority. The Rwa sgreng lamas served as regent two times: between the reigns of the eleventh and twelfth Dalai Lamas and between that of the thirteenth and fourteenth.

**Ryōanji**. [alt. Ryūanji] (龍安寺). In Japanese, "Dragon Peace Monastery," located in northwest Kyōto and famous for its dry landscape garden (J. karesansui). Originally an estate of the Fujiwara clan, the site was converted into a ZEN temple in 1450 by order of the military leader Hosokawa Katsumoto (1430–1473), a vassal of the Ashikaga shōgun. He installed Giten Genshō, the fifth abbot of MYŌSHINJI, as its founding religious leader (see KAISAN); since that time the monastery has been affiliated with the Myōshinji branch of the RINZAISHŪ of Zen Buddhism. The site of bloody fighting during the Ōnin civil war (1467–1477), Ryōanji had to be rebuilt by Hosokawa Katsumoto's son Hosokawa Masamoto between 1488 and 1499. Much of the monastery burned down in 1789 and was subsequently reconstructed. The monastery was a relatively obscure temple in the first half of the twentieth century, but the garden gained great fame in 1949 when it was used in a scene of Ozu Yasujirō's film *Banshun* (*Late Spring*). Beginning in the 1950s, the garden began to be described as a "Zen garden" and has since come to be considered one of Japan's cultural masterpieces. The garden has fifteen moss-covered boulders set in a sea of white pebbles. During the nineteenth century, the arrangement of the stones was called "tiger cubs crossing a river," referring to a Chinese folktale, although many other interpretations have been offered in more recent decades. The temple grounds are the burial site of seven Hosokawa lords. Ryōanji was listed as a UNESCO World Heritage Site in 1994.

**Ryōben**. [alt. Rōben] (良辨) (689–773). Founder of the Japanese Kegonshū (C. HUAYAN ZONG) during the Nara period (710–784) and the first abbot of TŌDAIJI, the major Kegon monastery and the headquarters of the KOKUBUNJI network of provincial temples. Ryōben originally studied the teachings of the Hossō (C. FAXIANG) school under Gien (d. 728) and resided at the monastery of Konshuji. Under the patronage of the emperor Shōmu (r. 724–749), Tōdaiji and its network of provincial temples was completed and the colossal NARA DAIBUTSU consecrated in 752; Ryōben was appointed the monastery's first abbot and he formally established the Kegon school at the site. The Kegon school, one of the six major scholastic traditions of Nara Buddhism (see NARA BUDDHISM, SIX SCHOOLS OF), is said to date from 740, when Ryōben invited the Korean monk SIMSANG (J. Shinjō, d. c. 744), a disciple of FAZANG (643–712), to Konshōji to lecture on the AVATAṂSAKASŪTRA to Emperor Shōmu. Simsang is therefore typically considered the first patriarch of the Kegon school and Ryōben the second.

**ryōbu**. (兩部). In Japanese, the "two groupings," also known as ryōkai ("two realms"); referring to the TAIZŌKAI and KONGŌKAI systems and their related MAṆḌALAS in the esoteric tradition (MIKKYŌ) of Japan. See TAIZŌKAI and KONGŌKAI.

**Ryōgen**. (良源) (912–985). In Japanese, "Virtuous Fount"; a tenth-century exponent of the TENDAISHŪ during the Heian Period, also known posthumously as Jie Daishi. Born in Ōmi province (present-day Shiga prefecture), Ryōgen became the eighteenth appointed head (zasu) of the Tendai school in 966 and spent the last nineteen years of his life at ENRYAKUJI reforming monastic discipline, promoting doctrinal studies, and writing works of his own. He used strategic political alliances to help what was then a marginalized Tendai school become the most powerful religious institution in Japan; in addition, he raised funds both to reconstruct burned monastic buildings on HIEIZAN and to construct new monasteries within its precincts. In response to escalating disputes among regional monastic communities, Ryōgen also established in 970 the first permanent fighting force to defend and serve the interests of the Mt. Hiei monks. While this move appears to contradict a set of reforms he had previously issued that forbade his monks from carrying weapons, it seems that his first troops may actually have been hired mercenaries rather than "monk soldiers" (J. SŌHEI). Among Ryōgen's disciples, perhaps the best known is GENSHIN (942–1017), the author of the influential ŌJŌ YŌSHŪ.

**ryōkai**. (J) (兩界). See RYŌBU.

**Ryōkan**. (良寬) (1758–1831). In Japanese, "Virtuous Liberality"; Edo-period ZEN monk in the SŌTŌSHŪ, often known as Ryōkan Taigu (lit. Ryōkan, the Great Fool). Ryōkan was associated with a reformist group within the contemporary Sōtō monastic community that sought to restore formal meditative practice and the study of the writings of DŌGEN KIGEN. Ryōkan grew up in Echigo province (present-day Niigata prefecture), the son of a SHINTŌ priest. He became a novice monk at age seventeen at the nearby Sōtō monastery of Kōshōji and was ordained when he turned twenty-one under a Sōtō monk named Kokusen (d. 1791). He left for Kokusen's monastery in the Bitchū province (present-day Okayama prefecture) and subsequently inherited the temple after Kokusen died. Soon afterward, however, he departed from the monastery, choosing instead to follow an itinerant lifestyle for the next several years. In 1804, he settled down for twelve years in a hut on Mt. Kugami, situated near his hometown. In 1826 Ryōkan met Teishin (d. 1872), a young nun who had been previously widowed, and the two remained close companions until Ryōkan's death. Ryōkan eventually chose for himself a radically simple existence, living much of his life as a hermit, owning few possessions and begging for alms. He was well regarded for his love of children and his compassion for people from all social strata, including prostitutes. His expression of compassion was so extreme that he is even said to have placed lice inside his robes so they would not get cold and to have exposed his legs to mosquitoes while he slept. Ryōkan was a renowned calligrapher and poet (in both Chinese and vernacular Japanese). Most of his verses are written as thirty-one-syllable tanka, although he also wrote ninety chōka (long poems) and at least twenty other verses in nonstandard form. Ryōkan's poetry addressed his common everyday experiences in the world in direct, humble terms. Ryōkan did not publish during his lifetime; rather, his verses were collected and published posthumously by his companion Teishin.

**Ryōnin**. (良忍) (1072–1132). In Japanese, "Virtuous Forbearance"; founder of the YŪZŪNENBUTSUSHŪ, an early PURE LAND school in Japan. Ryōnin traveled to HIEIZAN at the age of twelve to study the TENDAISHŪ (C. TIANTAI ZONG) teachings and was ordained at the age of fifteen. He retreated to Ōhara, a rural area north of Kyōto, in 1095, where he spent the next thirty years. There, Ryōnin at first studied the SADDHARMAPUṆḌARĪKASŪTRA and the AVATAṂSAKASŪTRA, but later concentrated on reciting the SUKHĀVATĪVYŪHASŪTRA. Through a revelation from the buddha AMITĀBHA that he received in 1117, Ryōnin began teaching his principle of YŪZŪNENBUTSU (perfect-interpenetration recitation of the Buddha's name), in which every individual benefits from both his own and others' chanting of the Buddha's name (J. nenbutsu; C. NIANFO) through a mutual transfer of merit. In 1124, Ryōnin began traveling throughout Japan to spread the practice. His decision to begin teaching evokes Śākyamuni Buddha's own life story: after realizing this principle, Ryōnin was content dwelling in solitude, but VAIŚRAVAṆA (J. Tabun tennō) appeared before Ryōnin to ask him to teach his revelation and disseminate the chanting practice among the people. As Ryōnin traveled around Japan, he carried with him a booklet in which he recorded the names of all the people who agreed to practice the chanting of the Buddha's name everyday. Soon after beginning his campaign, Ryōnin received the imperial bell from the retired monarch Toba (r. 1107–1123), who also added his name to this register of adherents: both the bell and the register are now housed at Dainenbutsuji, the headquarters of the Yūzūnenbutsu school. Such a sign of imperial support for Ryōnin's campaign attracted many new followers to his school. Ryōnin continued his evangelical efforts until his death in 1132 at Raigōin, one of the two cloisters (along with Jōrengein) that he established in Ōhara. Ryōnin also studied Buddhist "BRAHMĀ chanting" (J. bonbai; see C. FANBAI; K. pŏmp'ae) and founded his own lineage of bonbai chanting during his thirty years in Ōhara.

# S

**Sabbāsavasutta**. (C. Loujin jing; J. Rojingyō; K. Nujin kyŏng 漏盡經). In Pāli, "Discourse on All the Contaminants," the second sutta in the Pāli MAJJHIMANIKĀYA (a separate SARVĀSTIVĀDA recension appears as the tenth SŪTRA in the Chinese translation of the MADHYAMĀGAMA; there is also a recension of unidentified affiliation in the EKOTTARĀGAMA); preached by the Buddha to a gathering of monks in the JETAVANA grove in the town of Sāvatthi (S. ŚRĀVASTĪ). The Buddha describes the contaminants or outflows (ĀSRAVA) that afflict the minds of ordinary worldlings and keep them bound to the cycle of birth and death. He then prescribes seven methods for controlling and eradicating the contaminants: by correct vision (of the nature of the self), restraint (of the senses), usage (i.e, correct usage of the monastic requisites), endurance (e.g., bearing hunger, climate, physical pain), avoidance (e.g., bad friends, unsuitable residences), removal (e.g., of sensuality and ill will), and development (of the seven limbs of awakening).

**sa bdag**. (sadak). In Tibetan, lit. "lord of the earth" or "owner of the earth"; a term that encompasses a number of deities who are the rightful owners of particular sites, such as lakes, hills, mountains, and valleys, and who must be properly propitiated before using, and especially digging at, a site. If not properly propitiated, they may cause a wide range of maladies, including epidemics among humans and livestock. These deities can be of either Tibetan or Indian origin, the latter including such beings as NĀGAS.

**śabda**. (P. sadda; T. sgra; C. sheng; J. shō; K. sŏng 聲). In Sanskrit, "sound," or "auditory object"; the object of the auditory consciousness and one of the five sense objects, the others being visible forms (RŪPA), smells (GANDHA), tastes (RASA), and tangible objects (SPARŚA). Sounds are the object of the auditory sense organ (ŚROTRENDRIYA) and lead to the production of auditory consciousness (ŚROTRAVIJÑĀNA). In the ABHIDHARMAKOŚABHĀṢYA, sounds are categorized according to their source, being divided into those sounds caused by elements conjoined with consciousness (upāttamahābhūtahetuka) and sounds caused by elements not conjoined with consciousness (anupāttamahābhūtahetuka). The former would include the sound made by the clapping of hands or the vocalization of a human or animal; the latter would include sounds in the natural world, such as the sound of wind or water. Each of these two types is further subdivided into the articulate (sattvākhya, lit. "sentient being's utterance") and the inarticulate (asattvākhya, lit. "not a sentient being's utterance") based on whether or not the sound communicates meaning to a sentient being. Each of these is further divided into two types, the pleasant (yaśa) and the unpleasant (ayaśa), yielding eight types of sound. The nature of sound is an important point of controversy between Buddhist and Hindu thinkers in India, with Buddhists arguing that sound is impermanent (ANITYA) against Mīmāṃsakas who claim that the Vedas are eternal sounds that are not created by persons (apauruṣeya) and hence permanent.

**śabdasāmānya**. (T. sgra spyi). In Sanskrit, lit. "sound generality" or "sound universal"; a term that appears in Buddhist logic and epistemology in discussions of the operations of thought and the relations between thought and language. The term refers to the sound or phonetic component that appears to the mind, regardless of whether the meaning of that sound is understood. The referent, or semantic content, of the sound that appears to the mind is called arthasāmānya, literally "meaning generality" or "meaning universal." It is possible to have a sound generality independent of meaning generality, as in the case of hearing a word in a language that one does not understand. It is also possible to have a meaning generality alone, as in the case of seeing an object or hearing a description of an object, but not knowing its name. A conceptual consciousness (see KALPANĀ) is defined as one in which a sound generality and a meaning generality are suitable to be mixed, that is, for the name of the object to be associated with its mental image. The term appears in DIGNĀGA and is important in Tibetan Buddhist epistemology.

**śabdāyatana**. (P. saddāyatana; T. sgra'i skye mched; C. shengchu; J. shōsho; K. sŏngch'ŏ 聲處). In Sanskrit, "auditory sense-field," that is, sound (ŚABDA) as it occurs in the list of twelve sense faculties or "bases of cognition" (ĀYATANA), which serve as the bases for the production of consciousness: viz., the six internal sense bases, or sense organs (eye, ear, nose, tongue, body, and mind) and the six external sense objects (forms, sounds, odors, tastes, tangible objects, and mental phenomena). In the case of sound, the contact (SPARŚA) between the auditory sense base and its corresponding auditory sensory object leads to auditory consciousness (ŚROTRAVIJÑĀNA).

**sabhāgahetu**. (T. skal mnyam gyi rgyu; C. tonglei yin; J. dōruiin; K. tongnyuin 同類因). In Sanskrit, "homogeneous cause"; the fourth of the six types of causes (HETU) outlined in the JÑĀNAPRASTHĀNA, the central text of the SARVĀSTIVĀDA ABHIDHARMA, wherein a cause is always antecedent to its incumbent effect. This homogeneity can occur in a number of guises. In the case of physical causation, an apple seed would be a homogenous cause to the production of an apple. In the case of mental causation, a moment of wisdom that derives from what is heard (ŚRUTAMAYĪPRAJÑĀ) would be a homogenous cause to subsequent moments of the wisdom that derives from reflection (CINTĀMAYĪPRAJÑĀ). In the case of actions, a wholesome (KUŚALA) action (KARMAN) is a homogeneous cause to wholesome effects. This homogeneity extends throughout all of the three realms (TRAIDHĀTUKA) of SAṂSĀRA, viz., the sensuous realm (KĀMADHĀTU), the subtle-materiality realm (RŪPADHĀTU), and the immaterial realm (ĀRŪPYADHĀTU). In these cases, a cause may produce an effect that it superior to it, as long as the effect is produced in the same realm. For example, a moment of the wisdom that derives from what is heard (śrutamayīprajñā) in the sensuous realm might serve as a homogeneous cause for a moment of the wisdom that derives from reflection (cintāmayīprajñā) in the sensuous realm.

**sābhisaṃskāraparinirvāyin**. (T. mngon par 'du byed dang bcas pa yongs su mya ngan las 'das pa; C. youxing banniepan; J. ugyōhatsunehan; K. yuhaeng panyŏlban 有行般涅槃). In Sanskrit, "one who achieves NIRVĀṆA through effort"; a particular sort of nonreturner (ANĀGĀMIN), one of the twenty members of the ĀRYASAṂGHA (see VIṂŚATIPRABHEDASAṂGHA). According to the ABHIDHARMAKOŚABHĀṢYA, the sābhisaṃskāraparinirvāyin are nonreturners who, having achieved any of the sixteen birth states of the immaterial realm (ĀRŪPYADHĀTU), enter "nirvāṇa with remainder" (SOPADHIŚEṢANIRVĀṆA) at that support, but only after they have made a conscious effort and applied a little force. This differentiates them from the UPAPADYAPARINIRVĀYIN and the ANABHISAṂSKĀRAPARINIRVĀYIN.

**Saccaka**. (P). See MAHĀSACCAKASUTTA.

**Sa chen Kun dga' snying po**. (Sachen Kunga Nyingpo) (1092–1158). A great scholar and adept of the SA SKYA sect of Tibetan Buddhism, renowned especially for his writings on the tantric system of LAM 'BRAS, or "path and result." He is usually referred to simply as Sa chen, or "Great Master of Sa skya." Born the son of DKON MCHOG RGYAL PO, another important Sa skya master and first throne-holder of Sa skya monastery, he was a child prodigy. He first trained under the Sa skya hierarch Ba ri lo tsā ba Rin chen grags pa (Bari Lotsāwa Rinchen Drakpa, 1040–1111), from whom he received numerous transmissions of both SŪTRA and TANTRA. At the age of eleven he began a meditation retreat in which he had a visionary encounter with the bodhisattva MAÑJUŚRĪ. The bodhisattva spoke to him four lines that subsequently became a fundamental Sa skya teaching called the zhen pa bzhi bral ("parting from the four attachments"):

> If you are attached to this life, you are not a religious person.
> If you are attached to SAMSĀRA, you do not have renunciation.
> If you are attached to your own welfare, you do not have BODHICITTA.
> If grasping occurs, you do not have the view.

In 1111, at the age of twenty, he received the throne of Sa skya monastery from Ba ri lo tsā ba and became the institution's third abbot, a position he held for the remainder of his life. Beginning in 1120, Sa chen received the seminal Sa skya instructions on lam 'bras from Zhang ston chos 'bar (Shangtön Chöbar, 1053?–1135?), a YOGIN who initially claimed not to know anything about the topic. However, he eventually provided instruction to Sa chen for eight years, after which he instructed him not to teach lam 'bras for the next eighteen years. Sa chen then spent those eighteen years in retreat, practicing these instructions. During this time, he had a vision of the Indian adept VIRŪPA, founder of the lam 'bras lineage, who bestowed on him the lam 'bras teachings in their entirety. After completing his retreat, Sa chen put Virūpa's instructions on lam 'bras, known as the RDO RJE TSHIG RKANG ("Vajra Verses"), into writing for the first time, eventually composing eleven commentaries on them. Later, Sa chen was poisoned and went into a coma. When he regained consciousness, he had suffered complete memory loss. He thus went to his former teachers to receive instructions again. However, there was no one to provide the lam 'bras teachings and Zhang ston chos 'bar had passed away. Sa chen went into retreat, during which Zhang ston chos 'bar appeared to him and repeated his previous teachings. Among Sa chen's four sons, two became prominent Sa skya leaders: BSOD NAMS RTSE MO and Grags pa rgyal mtshan (Drakpa Gyaltsen, 1147–1216). Another of his sons, Dpal che 'od po (Palche Öpo, 1150–1204), was the father of SA SKYA PAṆḌITA KUN DGA' RGYAL MTSHAN, who would become one of Tibet's most influential religious figures. Kun dga' snying po and the most illustrious of his offspring over the next two generations (Grags pa rgyal mtshan, Bsod nams rtse mo, Kun dga' snying po, and 'PHAGS PA) are known as SA SKYA GONG MA LNGA (the five Sakya hierarchs) and as such have iconic status in Sa skya ritual.

**Sacred Books of the Buddhists**. A pioneering series of translations of Buddhist texts, initially edited by F. MAX MÜLLER and later by CAROLINE A. F. RHYS DAVIDS. After Müller had completed the Sacred Books of the East series (ten of whose forty-nine volumes were devoted to Buddhist works), he continued to receive requests to publish translations of more texts, especially Asian texts. He decided to start a new series for Buddhism, with financial support provided by the Thai king Chulalongkorn (RĀMA V). The first volume was published in 1895 by Oxford University Press. Publication was eventually taken over by the PALI TEXT SOCIETY. To date, some fifty volumes have been published in the series.

**ṣaḍakṣarī**. [alt. ṣaḍakṣarīvidyā] (T. yi ge drug pa'i rig sngags; C. liuzi daming/liuzi zhangju; J. rokujidaimyō/rokujishōku; K. yukcha taemyŏng/yukcha changgu 六字大明/六字章句). In Sanskrit, "six-syllable spell"; the renowned MANTRA associated with the BODHISATTVA of compassion, AVALOKITEŚVARA: viz., "OṂ MAṆI PADME HŪṂ." The mantra has six syllables and is used to call upon the bodhisattva, using his epithet Maṇipadma or "Jewel Lotus," a four-armed form who holds both a rosary of jewels (RATNA) and a lotus flower (PADMA). Hence, the mantra means "Oṃ, O Jewel-Lotus," not "jewel in the lotus," contrary to popular belief. The earliest textual source for this mantra is the KĀRAṆḌAVYŪHA [alt. Avalokiteśvaraguṇa-Kāraṇḍavyūha]. See OṂ MAṆI PADME HŪṂ.

**Sadāparibhūta**. (T. Rtag tu mi brnyas pa; C. Changbuqing pusa; J. Jōfukyō bosatsu; K. Sangbulgyŏng posal 常不輕菩薩). In Sanskrit, "Never Disparaging," the name of a BODHISATTVA described in the eponymous nineteenth or twentieth chapter (depending on the version) of the SADDHARMAPUṆḌARĪKASŪTRA ("Lotus Sūtra"). The Buddha explains that long ago there was a bodhisattva named Sadāparibhūta who did not study or recite the sūtras. Whenever he saw a monk (BHIKṢU), nun (BHIKṢUṆĪ), male lay disciple (UPĀSAKA), or female lay disciple (UPĀSIKĀ), he would say, "I dare not belittle you because you will all become buddhas." Arrogant monks, nuns, and male and female lay disciples began to sarcastically refer to him as "Never Disparaging." When the bodhisattva was about to die, he heard millions of verses of the *Saddharmapuṇḍarīkasūtra* in the sky and as a result his life span was increased by many eons, during which he taught the sūtra. Those who had mocked him were reborn in AVĪCI hell, but were eventually reborn as his disciples and later became the five hundred bodhisattvas in the assembly of the *Saddharmapuṇḍarīkasūtra*. The Buddha reveals that he had been the bodhisattva Sadāparibhūta in a previous life. The bodhisattva's famous statement, "I dare not belittle you because you will all become buddhas," came to be known as the "twenty-four character 'Lotus Sūtra'" because in KUMĀRAJĪVA's translation, the line is twenty-four Sinographs long. The chapter was especially important to the Japanese reformer NICHIREN, who noted the importance of developing even a negative relationship with the true teaching, as evidenced by the fact that those who slandered Sadāparibhūta eventually became bodhisattvas themselves.

**Sadāprarudita**. (T. Rtag tu ngu; C. Changti [pusa]; J. Jōtai [bosatsu]; K. Sangje [posal] 常啼[菩薩]). In Sanskrit, "Ever Weeping," the name of a BODHISATTVA whose story appears in the AṢṬASĀHASRIKĀPRAJÑĀPĀRAMITĀ. He sets out in search of a teacher who will teach him the perfection of wisdom (PRAJÑĀPĀRAMITĀ) but, unable to find one, is constantly crying. He eventually learns that the bodhisattva DHARMODGATA is teaching in a faraway city. He has nothing to offer his teacher and thus announces that he is willing to sell his body. ŚAKRA, the king of the gods, decides to test his commitment and takes the form of an old man who agrees to buy some of Sadāprarudita's flesh. He cuts off a piece of his thigh and gives it to the man. The man then asks for some bone marrow. Sadāprarudita is about to break his leg to extract the marrow when a wealthy merchant's daughter, impressed by his dedication, offers to provide the necessary gifts for Dharmodgata. Śakra then reveals his true form and heals Sadāprarudita's body. Sadāprarudita, the merchant's daughter, and her five hundred attendants then proceed to the city where Dharmodgata is residing and receive his teachings. The story is a famous example of DEHADĀNA, the "gift of the body" that bodhisattvas make out of their dedication to the welfare of others. It is also an important example of devotion to the teacher.

**ṣaḍāyatana**. (P. saḷāyatana; T. skye mched drug; C. liuchu; J. rokusho; K. yukch'ŏ 六處). In Sanskrit, "six bases of cognition"; the fifth link in the twelvefold chain of dependent origination (PRATĪTYASAMUTPĀDA), preceded by "name and form" (NĀMARŪPA) and followed by "contact" (SPARŚA). Here, the six bases of cognition refer to the six sense organs (INDRIYA): the eye, ear, nose, tongue, body, and mentality. In some interpretations of the twelvefold chain, the term refers specifically to the formation of the sense organs in the womb, on the basis of the prior link, "name and form" (nāmarūpa), which refers to the five aggregates (SKANDHA) directly after conception. The term "bases" or "sources" (ĀYATANA) more commonly refers to the twelve bases of cognition—the six sense organs and their six objects—but in the context of dependent origination, it refers specifically to the sense organs.

**Saddanīti**. In Pāli, the "Practice of Grammar," an important work on Pāli grammar and philology by the twelfth century Burmese monk Aggavaṃsa. Composed in 1154, it is considered the most important of the extant Pāli grammars. It draws both on the first known Pāli grammar, written by Kaccāyana, as well as Pāṇini's Sanskrit grammar. Its twenty-eight chapters contain a detailed morphology of Pāli and discussions of prefixes and particles.

**Ṣaḍdarśanasamuccaya**. In Sanskrit, "Compendium of the Six Views," a work by the eighth-century Indian scholar Haribhadra (or Haribhadra Sūri) of the Śvetāmbara school of Jainism. The six views refer to six schools of Indian philosophy: Buddhism, Jainism (see JAINA), and the four Hindu schools of Nyāya, Sāṃkhya, Vaiśeṣika, and Mīmāṃsā. The work also contains an appendix on the so-called "materialist" school, Cārvāka. The work remains useful to scholars of Buddhism for articulating how Buddhist doctrines were interpreted by non-Buddhist schools.

**Saddhammapajjotikā**. [alt. Saddhammaṭṭhitikā]. In Pāli, "Illumination of the True Dharma," a commentary on the

NIDDESA of the KHUDDAKANIKĀYA, written by UPASENA of Sri Lanka, probably in either 817 or 877 CE. The text borrows heavily from the VISUDDHIMAGGA of BUDDHAGHOSA.

**Saddhammappakāsinī**. In Pāli, "Explanation of the True Dharma," a commentary on the PAṬISAMBHIDĀMAGGA of the KHUDDAKANIKĀYA, attributed to Mahānāma of Sri Lanka. According to its colophon, the commentary was composed in the first half of the sixth century CE. The text contains numerous quotations from the VISUDDHIMAGGA of BUDDHAGHOSA.

**Saddhammasaṅgaha**. In Pāli, "Chronicle of the True Dharma," an ecclesiastical and literary history of THERAVĀDA Buddhism, written by Dhammakitti Mahāsāmī at the Thai capital AYUTHAYA during the reign of PARAMARĀJĀ I (1370–1388 CE); it is the earliest Buddhist chronicle composed in Southeast Asia. The author was inspired to write the history after his return from Sri Lanka, where he had participated in an ongoing purification and revival of Buddhism on the island. The work relies heavily on the DĪPAVAṂSA, MAHĀVAṂSA, and VINAYA commentary, SAMANTAPĀSĀDIKĀ, as well as on the historical introduction to the twelfth-century MAHĀPARĀKRAMABĀHU-KATIKĀVATA of PARĀKRAMABĀHU I. The work is divided into eleven chapters and concludes with an account of the benefits of listening to the preaching of the dharma. The *Saddhammasaṅgaha* was translated into English in 1941 by B. C. Law under the title, *A Manual of Buddhist Historical Traditions*.

**saddharma**. (P. saddhamma; T. dam pa'i chos; C. zhengfa; J. shōbō; K. chŏngpŏp 正法). In Sanskrit, "true dharma" or "right dharma" (and often translated as "true law" in the nineteenth century), a term for the teaching of the Buddha. The term appears widely in Buddhist literature, including the Pāli canon. The term DHARMA has many meanings in Indian literature in general and in Indian Buddhism in particular. Scholars speculate that SADDHARMA was coined to indicate specifically that the saddharma was "the teaching of the Buddha," in order to distinguish his doctrine from those of non-Buddhist teachers (whose doctrines were also termed dharma). It may have also been intended to imply a truer, in the sense of a more definitive, teaching within the teachings of the Buddha, as in the title of the "Lotus Sūtra," SADDHARMAPUṆḌARĪKASŪTRA, lit., "White Lotus of the True Dharma," where the Buddha explains that his teaching on the one vehicle (EKAYĀNA) supersedes his previous teaching of three vehicles (TRIYĀNA). Saddharma was also used to refer to that period after the PARINIRVĀṆA of a particular buddha, when his teaching remained complete and intact and its practice was faithful and virtuous; this period preceded their inevitable decline (see SADDHARMAPRATIRŪPAKA and SADDHARMAVIPRALOPA).

**saddharmapratirūpaka**. (T. dam pa'i chos kyi gzugs brnyan; C. xiangfa/xiangsi zhengfa; J. zōhō/zōjishōbō; K. sangpŏp/sangsajŏngpŏp 像法/像似正法). In Sanskrit, "semblance dharma," or "counterfeit dharma" (although this latter translation has a pejorative connotation in English that is not present in the Sanskrit); the term more literally means "a [mere] reflection of the true dharma." The term occurs most commonly in MAHĀYĀNA literature and is largely absent in the texts of the MAINSTREAM BUDDHIST SCHOOLS, suggesting that it came into use around the beginning of the Common Era. In its most general sense, it refers to the entire period during which the true dharma (SADDHARMA) of a given buddha exists in the world, i.e., from the time that the buddha passes into PARINIRVĀṆA to the time that his dharma finally vanishes completely. In some texts, this term refers specifically to the second of two periods in the duration of the dharma: the first is the saddharma, or true dharma, the second is the saddharmapratirūpaka, or reflection of the true dharma. In East Asian eschatological traditions, saddharmapratirūpaka came to refer to the second of three periods in the disappearance of the dharma from the world: there was a period of the true dharma (zhengfa), a period of "semblance dharma" (called XIANGFA in Chinese), and a period of final dharma (see MOFA, SADDHARMAVIPRALOPA). See also ANTARADHĀNA.

**Saddharmapuṇḍarīkasūtra**. (T. Dam pa'i chos padma dkar po'i mdo; C. Miaofa lianhua jing/Fahua jing; J. Myōhōrengekyō/Hokekyō; K. Myobŏp yŏnhwa kyŏng/Pŏphwa kyŏng 妙法蓮華經/法華經). In Sanskrit, "Sūtra of the White Lotus of the True Dharma," and known in English simply as the "Lotus Sūtra"; perhaps the most influential of all MAHĀYĀNA sūtras. The earliest portions of the text were probably composed as early as the first or second centuries of the Common Era; the text gained sufficient renown in India that a number of chapters were later interpolated into it. The sūtra was translated into Chinese six times and three of those translations are extant. The earliest of those is that made by DHARMARAKṢA, completed in 286. The most popular is that of KUMĀRAJĪVA in twenty-eight chapters, completed in 406. The sūtra was translated into Tibetan in the early ninth century. Its first translation into a European language was that of EUGÈNE BURNOUF into French in 1852. The *Saddharmapuṇḍarīkasūtra* is perhaps most famous for its parables, which present, in various versions, two of the sūtra's most significant doctrines: skill-in-means (UPĀYA) and the immortality of the Buddha. In the parable of the burning house, a father lures his children from a conflagration by promising them three different carts, but when they emerge they find instead a single, magnificent cart. The three carts symbolize the ŚRĀVAKA vehicle, the PRATYEKABUDDHA vehicle, and the BODHISATTVA vehicle, while the one cart is the "one vehicle" (EKAYĀNA), the buddha vehicle (BUDDHAYĀNA). This parable indicates that the Buddha's previous teaching of three vehicles (TRIYĀNA) was a case of upāya, an "expedient device" or "skillful method" designed to attract persons of differing capacities to the dharma. In fact, there is only one vehicle, the vehicle whereby all beings proceed to buddhahood. In the parable of the conjured city, a group of weary travelers take rest in a magnificent city, only to be told later that it is a magical creation. This conjured city symbolizes the NIRVĀṆA of the ARHAT; there is in fact no such nirvāṇa as a final goal in Buddhism, since all will eventually follow the bodhisattva's path to buddhahood. The apparently universalistic doctrine articulated by the sūtra must be understood within the context of the sectarian polemics in which the sūtra seems to have been written. The doctrine of upāya is intended in part to explain the apparent contradiction between the teachings that appear in earlier sūtras and those of the *Saddharmapuṇḍarīkasūtra*. The former are relegated to the category of mere expedients, with those who fail to accept the consummate teaching of the *Saddharmapuṇḍarīkasūtra* as the authentic word of the Buddha (BUDDHAVACANA) repeatedly excoriated by the text itself. In a device common in Mahāyāna sūtras, the sūtra itself describes both the myriad benefits that accrue to those who recite, copy, and revere the sūtra, as well as the misfortune that will befall those who fail to do so. The immortality of the Buddha is portrayed in the parable of the physician, in which a father feigns death in order to induce his sons to commit to memory an antidote to poison. The apparent death of the father is compared to the Buddha's entry into nirvāṇa, something which he only pretended to do in order to inspire his followers. Elsewhere in the sūtra, the Buddha reveals that he did not achieve enlightenment as the prince Siddhārtha who left his palace, but in fact had achieved enlightenment eons before; the well-known version of his departure from the palace and successful quest for enlightenment were merely a display meant to inspire the world. The immortality of the Buddha (and other buddhas) is also demonstrated when a great STŪPA emerges from the earth. When the door to the funerary reliquary is opened, ashes and bones are not found, as would be expected, but instead the living buddha PRABHŪTARATNA, who appears in his stūpa whenever the *Saddharmapuṇḍarīkasūtra* is taught. ŚĀKYAMUNI joins him on his seat, demonstrating another central Mahāyāna doctrine, the simultaneous existence of multiple buddhas. Other famous events described in the sūtra include the miraculous transformation of a NĀGA princess into a buddha after she presents a gem to Śākyamuni and the tale of a bodhisattva who immolates himself in tribute to a previous buddha. The sūtra contains several chapters that function as self-contained texts; the most popular of these is the chapter devoted to the bodhisattva AVALOKITEŚVARA, which details his ability to rescue the faithful from various dangers. The *Saddharmapuṇḍarīkasūtra* was highly influential in East Asia, inspiring both a range of devotional practices as well as the creation of new Buddhist schools that had no Indian analogues. The devotional practices include those extolled by the sūtra itself: receiving and keeping the sūtra, reading it, memorizing and reciting it, copying it, and explicating it. In East Asia, there are numerous tales of the miraculous benefits of each of these practices. The practice of copying the sūtra (or having it copied) was a particularly popular form of merit-making either for oneself or for departed family members. Also important, especially in China, was the practice of burning either a finger or one's entire body as an offering to the Buddha, emulating the self-immolation of the bodhisattva BHAIṢAJYARĀJA in the twenty-third chapter (see SHESHEN). In the domain of doctrinal developments, the *Saddharmapuṇḍarīkasūtra* was highly influential across East Asia, its doctrine of upāya providing the rationale for the systems of doctrinal taxonomies (see JIAOXIANG PANSHI) that are pervasive in East Asian Buddhist schools. In China, the sūtra was the central text of the TIANTAI ZONG, where it received detailed exegesis by a number of important figures. The school's founder, TIANTAI ZHIYI, divided the sūtra into two equal parts. In the first fourteen chapters, which he called the "trace teaching" (C. jimen, J. SHAKUMON), Śākyamuni appears as the historical buddha. In the remaining fourteen chapters, which Zhiyi called the "origin teaching" (C. benmen, J. HONMON), Śākyamuni reveals his true nature as the primordial buddha who achieved enlightenment many eons ago. Zhiyi also drew on the *Saddharmapuṇḍarīkasūtra* in elucidating two of his most famous doctrines: the three truths (SANDI, viz., emptiness, the provisional, and the mean) and the notion of YINIAN SANQIAN, or "the trichiliocosm in an instant of thought." In the TENDAISHŪ, the Japanese form of Tiantai, the sūtra remained supremely important, providing the scriptural basis for the central doctrine of original enlightenment (HONGAKU) and the doctrine of "achieving buddhahood in this very body" (SOKUSHIN JŌBUTSU); in TAIMITSU, the tantric form of Tendai, Śākyamuni Buddha was identified with MAHĀVAIROCANA. For the NICHIREN schools (and their offshoots, including SŌKA GAKKAI), the *Saddharmapuṇḍarīkasūtra* is not only its central text but is also considered to be the only valid Buddhist sūtra for the degenerate age (J. mappo; see C. MOFA); the recitation of the sūtra's title is the central practice in Nichiren (see NAMU MYŌHŌRENGEKYŌ). See also SADĀPARIBHŪTA.

**saddharmavipralopa**. (T. dam pa'i chos rab tu rnam par 'jig pa; C. mofa; J. mappō; K. malpŏp 末法). In Sanskrit, "disappearance of the true dharma," the predicted demise of the Buddha's dispensation (ŚĀSANA) from the world. Mainstream Buddhist doctrine holds that all evidence of the teaching of the previous buddha must vanish before the next buddha can appear in the world. The precise length of the duration of ŚĀKYAMUNI Buddha's dispensation is a persistent issue in Buddhist literature. The most common, and probably the oldest, of these predictions occurs in the accounts of the Buddha's decision to permit the ordination of women, where he says that if he had not ordained women, the true dharma (SADDHARMA) would have endured for one thousand years; however, because of his decision to ordain women, it will only last five hundred years (see MAHĀPRAJĀPATĪ). A variety of other predictions for the decline and disappearance of the dharma appear in various sūtras, with the period of the duration of the dharma ranging from as short as five hundred years to as long as twelve thousand years (in some Chinese sources); other figures include seven hundred, one thousand, one thousand five hundred, two thousand, two thousand five hundred, and five thousand years. The majority of periods involving one thousand years or more occur in MAHĀYĀNA sūtras. However, in BUDDHAGHOSA's MANORATHAPŪRAṆĪ, a chronology of five thousand years is provided, in which the dharma gradually disappears over five periods of one thousand years each. During the first millennium after the Buddha's demise, there will be a disappearance of the attainments (P. ADHIGAMA), at the end of which no disciple will have the capacity to attain the rank of stream-enterer (P. sotāpanna; S. SROTAĀPANNA). During the second millennium, there will be a disappearance of practice (P. PAṬIPATTI) at the end of which no disciple will be able to attain meditative states or maintain the precepts. During the third millennium, there will be a disappearance of learning (P. PARIYATTI), at the end of which all books of the tipiṭaka (S. TRIPIṬAKA) will be lost. During the fourth millennium, the indicators or signs (NIMITTA) of monastic life will begin to vanish, at the end of which all monks will stop wearing saffron robes and will return to lay life. During the fifth and final millennium, there will be a disappearance of the relics (DHĀTU, see ŚARĪRA), at the end of which the relics of the Buddha will reassemble and, after being worshipped by the divinities, will burst into flame and vanish. Buddhaghosa's five thousand-year timetable has become standard in the Pāli tradition. The doctrine of the disappearance of the dharma is central to the various East Asian theories of decline. See also MOFA; ANTARADHĀNA.

**Saddhatissa, Hammalawa**. (1914–1990). A prolific Pāli scholar, translator, social activist, and senior Buddhist monk. Born at Hammalawa in Satkorale province, Sri Lanka, he was ordained a BHIKṢU in 1926 and pursued his undergraduate studies in Sri Lanka at Vidyodaya Pirivena and Prachina Bhasopakara Samagama. He continued his studies in Benares in India, the School of Oriental and African Studies (SOAS) in London, and ultimately received his Ph.D. at Edinburgh in 1965. He was proficient in Pāli, Sanskrit, Prakrit, Sinhala, and Hindi and held numerous academic posts in Asia, Europe, and North America, including Professor of Pāli at Banaras Hindu University from 1956 to 1957, Lecturer in Sinhala at SOAS from 1958 to 1960, Professor of Buddhism and Pāli at the University of Toronto from 1966 to 1969, and Visiting Lecturer at Oxford in 1973. While holding these posts, he also conducted numerous lecture tours in Europe, the United States, and Japan. In 1956, he served as an advisor to Dr. BHIMRAO RAMJI AMBEDKAR (1891–1956) at Nagpur, India, during the organization of mass conversions of members of the Dalit caste (the so-called untouchables) to Buddhism. Between 1957 and 1985 he served as head of London Buddhist Vihara, and in 1966 revived the British MAHĀBODHI SOCIETY, which had been defunct since World War II, serving as its president. He also helped found the New London Buddhist Vihara in 1964; the Buddhist Center, Oakenholt, in Oxford in 1971; the Buddhist Research Library, in Nugegoda, Sri Lanka in 1984; and the Buddha Vihara, Handsworth, in Birmingham in 1986. He was appointed president of the Saṅgha Council of Great Britain in 1966, and the Sanghanayaka Thera of the United Kingdom in 1980. In 1984 he served as vice-president of the Pali Text Society. His English publications and critical editions and translations include *The Buddha's Way*, *Buddhist Ethics*, *The Birth-Stories of the Ten Bodhisattas and the Dasabodhisattuppattikathā*, *Sutta Nipāta*, *Upāsakajanālankāra*, *Handbook for Buddhists*, *Introduction to Buddhism*, and *The Life of the Buddha*.

**ṣaḍgati**. (P. *chagati; T. 'gro ba rigs drug; C. liuqu; J. rokushu; K. yukch'wi 六趣). In Sanskrit, "six destinies"; an expansion of the more common list of five rebirth destinies (PAÑCAGATI), adding demigods or titans (ASURA) to the usual five: divinities (DEVA; including those of the sensuous, subtle-materiality, and immaterial realms); asuras, humans (MANUṢYA), animals (TIRYAK), ghosts (PRETA), and hell beings (NĀRAKA). See GATI; PAÑCAGATI.

**sādhana**. (T. sgrub thabs; C. chengjiu fa; J. jōjuhō; K. sŏngch'wi pŏp 成就法). In Sanskrit, "method" or "technique," used especially in reference to a tantric ritual designed to receive attainments (SIDDHI) from a deity. Tantric sādhanas generally take one of two forms. In the first, the deity (which may be a buddha, BODHISATTVA, or another deity) is requested to appear before the meditator and is then worshipped in the expectation of receiving blessings. In the other type of tantric sādhana, the meditator imagines himself or herself to be the deity at this very moment, that is, to have the exalted body, speech, and mind of an enlightened being. Tantric sādhanas tend to follow a fairly set sequence, whether they are simple or detailed. More elaborate sādhanas may include the recitation of a lineage of GURUs; the creation of a protection wheel guarded by wrathful deities to subjugate enemies; the creation of a body MAṆḌALA, in which a pantheon of deities take residence at various parts of the meditator's body, etc. Although there are a great many variations of content and sequence, in many sādhanas, the meditator is instructed to imagine light radiating from the body, thus beckoning buddhas and bodhisattvas from throughout the universe. Visualizing these deities arrayed in the space, the meditator then performs a series of standard preliminary practices called the sevenfold service (SAPTĀṄGAVIDHI), a standard component of sādhanas. The seven elements are (1) obeisance, (2) offering (often concluding with a gift of the entire physical universe with all its marvels), (3) confession of misdeeds, (4) admiration of the virtuous deeds of others, (5) entreaty to the buddhas not to pass into NIRVĀṆA, (6) supplication of the buddhas and bodhisattvas to teach the dharma, and (7) dedication of the merit of performing the preceding toward the enlightenment of all beings. The meditator then goes for refuge to the three jewels (RATNATRAYA), creates the aspiration for enlightenment (BODHICITTA; BODHICITTOTPĀDA), the promise to achieve buddhahood in order to liberate all beings in the universe from suffering, and dedicates the merit from the foregoing and subsequent practices toward that end. The meditator next cultivates the four "boundless" attitudes (APRAMĀṆA) of loving-kindness (MAITRĪ), compassion (KARUṆĀ), empathetic joy (MUDITĀ), and equanimity or impartiality (UPEKṢĀ), before meditating on emptiness (ŚŪNYATĀ) and reciting the purificatory mantra, oṃ svabhāvaśuddhāḥ sarvadharmāḥ svabhāvaśuddho 'haṃ ("Oṃ, naturally pure are all phenomena, naturally pure am I"), understanding that emptiness is the primordial nature of everything, the unmoving world and the beings who move upon it. Out of this emptiness, the meditator next creates the maṇḍala. The next step in the sādhana is for the meditator to animate the residents of the maṇḍala by causing the actual buddhas and bodhisattvas, referred to as "wisdom beings" (JÑĀNASATTVA), to descend and merge with their imagined doubles, the "pledge beings" (SAMAYASATTVA). Light radiates from the meditator's heart, drawing the wisdom beings to the maṇḍala where, through offerings and the recitation of mantra, they are prompted to enter the residents of the maṇḍala. With the preliminary visualization now complete, the stage is set for the central meditation of the sādhana, which varies depending upon the purpose of the sādhana. Generally, offerings and prayers are made to a sequence of deities and boons are requested from them, each time accompanied with the recitation of appropriate MANTRA. At the end of the session, the meditator makes mental offerings to the assembly before inviting them to leave, at which point the entire visualization, the palace and its residents, dissolve into emptiness. The sādhana ends with a dedication of the merit accrued to the welfare of all beings.

**sādhana**. (T. sgrub pa; C. nengli; J. nōryū; K. nŭngnip 能立). In Sanskrit, "proof"; a term used in Indian logic in the sense of a proof statement or syllogism. The Indian Nyāya (Logic) school advocated that there were five necessary stages in syllogistic reasoning: (1) probandum or proposition (PRATIJÑĀ), viz., "The mountain is on fire"; (2) reason (HETU), "because there is smoke," (3) analogy (udāharaṇa), "Whatever is smoky is on fire, like a stove, but unlike a lake"; (4) application (upanaya), "Since this mountain is smoky, it is on fire"; (5) conclusion (nigamana), "The mountain is on fire." Using the same example, the Buddhist logician DIGNĀGA reduced the syllogism down to just three essential steps: (1) thesis or proposition (PAKṢA), "the mountain is on fire"; (2) reason (HETU), "because there is smoke"; (3) exemplification (dṛṣṭānta), "whatever is smoky is on fire, like a stove," and "whatever is not on fire is not smoky, like a lake," or, more simply, "like a stove, unlike a lake." See also LIṄGA; PRAYOGA.

**Sādhanamālā**. (T. Sgrub thabs rgya mtsho). In Sanskrit, "Garland of Methods," sometimes attributed to ABHAYĀKARAGUPTA; an important compendium of some three hundred individual tantric SĀDHANAS, the latest of which were composed around the twelfth century. In addition to the details its provides about tantric practice during this period, the detailed descriptions of the deities to be visualized are an important source of tantric Buddhist iconography. The version preserved in Tibetan is entitled *Sādhanasāgara*, "Ocean of Methods."

**sādhāraṇasiddhi**. (T. thun mong gi dngos grub). In Sanskrit, "common attainment," a term used, especially in the tantric context, to refer to various supranormal powers, such as the ability to fly, walk through walls, and find buried treasure, which can be attained through the recitation of MANTRAS and the propitiation of deities by both Buddhist and non-Buddhist YOGINS. It is contrasted with the "uncommon attainment" (asādhāraṇasiddhi), which is synonymous with "supreme attainment" (UTTAMASIDDHI), viz., the attainment of buddhahood.

**sādhumatī**. (T. legs pa'i blo gros; C. shanhui di; J. zen'eji; K. sŏnhye chi 善慧地). In Sanskrit, "auspicious intellect," the ninth of the ten bodhisattva BHŪMIS. A list of ten stages (DAŚABHŪMI) is most commonly enumerated, deriving from the DAŚABHŪMIKASŪTRA ("Sūtra on the Ten Bhūmis"), a sūtra that is later subsumed into the massive scriptural compilation, the AVATAMSAKASŪTRA. The first bhūmi coincides with the attainment of the path of vision (DARŚANAMĀRGA) and the remaining nine to the path of cultivation (BHĀVANĀMĀRGA). Together with the eighth and tenth bhūmis, this is one of the three "pure bhūmis," because at the end of the seventh bhūmi, the bodhisattva has abandoned all afflictions (KLEŚA), and is devoted to destroying the remaining obstructions (ĀVARAṆA). On this bhūmi, the bodhisattva practices the ninth of the ten perfections, the perfection of power (BALAPĀRAMITĀ). This stage is called "auspicious intellect" because at this stage the bodhisattva gains a special understanding of the dharma, which allows him to teach others without error. This special understanding comes from his attainment of the four analytical knowledges (PRATISAṂVID). By means of the analytical knowledge of phenomena or factors (dharmapratisaṃvid; see DHARMA), he gains a thorough knowledge of the specific characteristics of all phenomena. By means of the analytical knowledge of meanings (arthapratisaṃvid; see ARTHA), he gains a thorough knowledge of the categories of all phenomena. Through the analytical knowledge of etymology (niruktipratisaṃvid; see NIRUKTI) he gains perfect facility in language so that he can teach without confusing doctrines. With the analytical knowledge of eloquence (pratibhānapratisaṃvid; see PRATIBHĀNA), he is able to inspire others with his words. Another explanation says that through dharmapratisaṃvid, the bodhisattva knows the words in the twelve branches of the Buddha's teaching (dharma); through arthapratisaṃvid, he knows the content or meaning of the twelve branches of the Buddha's teaching (DVĀDAŚĀṄGA [PRAVACANA]); through niruktipratisaṃvid, he knows the languages of each region (nirukti); and through pratibhānapratisaṃvid, he possesses the above three knowledges and thus has confidence to teach others. The bodhisattva remains on this stage as long as he is unable to display the land, retinue, and emanations of a buddha, make full use of the qualities of a buddha, and bring sentient beings to spiritual maturity.

**sādhyadharma**. (T. sgrub bya'i chos; C. suoli/suochengli; J. shoryū/shojōryū; K. sorip/sosŏngnip 所立/所成立). In

Sanskrit, the "property being proven," a term in Buddhist logic that designates one of the elements of a correct syllogism or proof (PRAYOGA) leading to inference (ANUMĀNA). A syllogism is composed of three parts, the subject (dharmin), the property being proved (sādhyadharma), and the reason (HETU or LIṄGA). It is called sādhyadharma because the sādhya ("what is being proved") must be a dharma ("property") of the logical subject. For example, in the syllogism, "Sound is impermanent because of being produced," the subject is sound, the property being proved is impermanence, and the reason is being produced. In order for the syllogism to be correct, three relations must exist among the three components of the syllogism: (1) the reason must be a property (DHARMA) of the subject, also called the "position" (PAKṢA), (2) there must be a relationship of pervasion (VYĀPTI) between the reason and the property being proved, such that whatever is the reason is necessarily the property being proved, and (3) there must be a relationship of "exclusion" or reverse pervasion (vyatirekavyāpti) between the property being proved and the reason such that whatever is not the property being proved is necessarily not the reason. In the example, the syllogism "Sound is impermanent because of being produced," is correct because the reason (being produced) is a quality of the subject (sound), there is pervasion because whatever is produced is necessarily impermanent, and there is reverse pervasion because whatever is not impermanent is necessarily not produced. See ANUMĀNA; LIṄGA.

**sad mi bdun**. (se mi dün). In Tibetan, lit. "seven men who were tested"; the first seven Tibetans to be ordained as Buddhist monks at BSAM YAS monastery under the preceptor ŚĀNTARAKṢITA during the late seventh century. The seven were: (1) Sba khri gzigs (Ba Tisik), ordained as Śrīghoṣa (T. Dpal byangs); (2) Sba gsal snang (Ba Selnang), ordained as Jñānendra (T. Ye shes dbang po); (3) Sba khri bzher/bzhir (Ba Tisher); (4) Ba gor VAIROCANA, or Vairocanarakṣita; (5) Rma rin chen mchog (Ma Rinchen Chok); (6) Rgyal ba mchog dbyangs (Gyelwa Chokyang); and (7) 'Khon klu'i dbang po srung ba (Könlu Wangpo Sungwa) (Nāgendrarakṣita). Alternate lists occasionally include: Rtsang legs grub (Tsang Lekdrup), or La sum rgyal ba'i byang chub (La sum Gyelwe Jangchup).

**ṣaḍmūlakleśa**. (T. rtsa ba'i nyon mongs drug; C. liu genben fannao; J. roku konpon bonnō; K. yuk kŭnbon pŏnnoe 六根本煩惱). In Sanskrit, "six root afflictions," as outlined in the SARVĀSTIVĀDA ABHIDHARMA and in the YOGĀCĀRA list of dharmas (see BAIFA); the six unsalutary mental states that serve as the sources for all the other KLEŚA. They are: desire (RĀGA), anger (PRATIGHA), pride (MĀNA), ignorance (AVIDYĀ), doubt (VICIKITSĀ), and wrong view (DṚṢṬI). See ANUŚAYA; KLEŚAMAHĀBHŪMIKA; MŪLAKLEŚA; SAṂYOJANA.

**ṣaḍpāramitā**. (T. phar phyin drug; C. liu boluomi; J. ropparamitsu; K. yuk paramil 六波羅蜜). In Sanskrit, the "six perfections," the six bodhisattva perfections (PĀRAMITĀ) of giving (DĀNA), morality (ŚĪLA), patience (KṢĀNTI), effort (VĪRYA), meditative absorption (DHYĀNA), and wisdom (PRAJÑĀ). In the DAŚABHŪMIKASŪTRA, four additional perfections are added, such that one perfection is associated with each of the ten bodhisattva stages (BHŪMI). These additional four perfections are understood as additional elements of the sixth perfection, prajñāpāramitā. They are the perfection of expedient means (UPĀYAPĀRAMITĀ), the perfection of the vow (to attain buddhahood) (PRAṆIDHĀNAPĀRAMITĀ), the perfection of powers (BALAPĀRAMITĀ) and the perfection of knowledge (JÑĀNAPĀRAMITĀ). In Pāli materials, there is a different set of ten perfections (PĀRAMĪ) that are practiced by the bodhisattva. See PĀRAMITĀ and the specific types of perfections.

**ṣaḍvārgika**. (P. chabbaggiya; T. drug sde; C. liuqun [biqiu]; J. rokugun [biku]; K. yukkun [pigu] 六群[比丘]). In Sanskrit, the "group of six," a notorious group of six mischievous monks (BHIKṢU), whose misbehavior led to the promulgation of many rules of conduct for the Buddhist order. According to the tradition, the rules of the VINAYA were not formulated hypothetically. Instead, when a monk acted in an inappropriate way, the Buddha would then make a rule prohibiting that action in the future. Thus, for each infraction, the vinaya provides an account of the circumstances that led to its formulation. The names of these six monks, individually and collectively, figure prominently in an inordinate number of those accounts. They are also often portrayed as actively resisting the enforcement of the rules of discipline. The names of the members of this infamous group of malefactors differ in Sanskrit and Pāli sources. In Sanskrit, they are usually listed as Nanda, Upananda, Udāyin (alt. Kālodāyin), Chanda, Aśvaka, and Punarvasu. The Pāli typically gives instead Assaji, Punabhasu, Paṇḍuka, Lohitaka, Mettiya, and Bhummajaka. According to Pāli sources, prior to their ordination, they were acquaintances of each other, living in ŚRĀVASTĪ. Unable to earn a living, they decided to enter the order. Deciding that it was unwise to remain together, they divided into three groups of two (Assaji and Punabhasu, Paṇḍuka and Lohitaka, and Mettiya and Bhummajaka). Each pair attracted a following of five hundred monks. The followers of Paṇḍuka and Lohitaka, living at JETAVANA, were the most virtuous, remaining near the Buddha and accompanying him in his travels. Some sources also offer a salutary motivation behind their frequent transgressions: to provide a wide range of test cases leading to specific monastic rules, so that the SAṂGHA would be protected against future unscrupulous behavior.

**Sagaing**. One of five Burmese capitals that flourished in Upper Burma (Myanmar) after the fall of PAGAN between the fourteenth and nineteenth centuries, the others being Pinya, AVA (Inwa), Amarapura and MANDALAY. The city of Sagaing lies adjacent to the Sagaing Hills along the Irrawaddy (Ayeyarwady) River to the west of Mandalay in central Burma. The Irrawaddy flows from north to south as it passes Mandalay and then turns west for several miles. Sagaing is named for this point on the river, "the beginning of the bend." Following the collapse of the Pagan empire, Sagaing served as the capital city of a much reduced Burmese state between 1316 and 1364, after which the capital was moved across the river to Ava. Sagaing has been an important Buddhist center since Pagan times, and tradition claims the Buddha visited the site himself. The city and the surrounding hills contain hundreds of pagodas, monasteries, nunneries, and cave retreats, and many of Burma's most celebrated scholars hailed from Sagaing over the centuries. Sagaing retains its preeminence as one of the country's main centers of Buddhist scholarship and meditation practice.

**Sāgara**. (T. Rgya mtsho; C. Suojieluo/Suoqieluo; J. Shakara [alt. Shakatsura]/Shagara; K. Sagalla/Sagara 娑竭羅/娑伽羅). In Sanskrit, "Ocean"; one of the eight dragon kings (NĀGA) who served as guardians of the BUDDHADHARMA. His name appears alongside those of the other seven dragon kings who were in the audience when the Buddha taught the SADDHARMAPUṆḌARĪKASŪTRA. Sāgara is believed to be the dragon king of the ocean, who governs precipitation. He resides in a palace beneath the ocean that surrounds Mt. SUMERU. Sāgara occasionally appears as a flanking-attendant of the BODHISATTVA AVALOKITEŚVARA. In his palace, Sāgara is said to store a MAṆI jewel, which he sometimes offers to the bodhisattva. In the twelfth chapter of the *Saddharmapuṇḍarīkasūtra*, Sāgara also appears as the father of the eight-year-old nāga princess who, by offering a jewel to the Buddha, instantaneously turns into a male, traverses the ten bodhisattva stages (BHŪMI), and achieves buddhahood, evidence to some exegetes in the tradition that women have the capacity to achieve buddhahood.

**sāgaramudrāsamādhi**. (T. rgya mtsho'i phyag rgya ting nge 'dzin; C. haiyin sanmei; J. kaiin zanmai; K. haein sammae 海印三昧). In Sanskrit, "ocean-seal samādhi," or "oceanic reflection samādhi," a concentration (SAMĀDHI) often treated as emblematic of the HUAYAN ZONG's most profound vision of reality. "Ocean seal" is a metaphor for the pure and still mind that is able to reflect all phenomena while remaining perpetually unaffected by them, just as the calm surface of the ocean is said to be able to reflect all the phenomena in the universe. The AVATAṂSAKASŪTRA includes the sāgaramudrāsamādhi among several other types of samādhi that it mentions. In the "SAMANTABHADRA Bodhisattva Chapter" (Puxian pusa pin), the first of the ten samādhis taught by this bodhisattva is the sāgaramudrāsamādhi; through its power, a buddha is enabled to perform all types of works to rescue sentient beings, such as manifesting himself as a buddha and using numerous skillful means (UPĀYA) in order to guide them. The "Ten Bhūmis Chapter" (Shidi pin) mentions sāgaramudrāsamādhi as one of a list of eleven samādhis that occur to bodhisattvas who reach the tenth stage (BHŪMI) on the path. The "Manifestation of the Tathāgata Chapter" (Rulai chuxian pin) says that sāgaramudrāsamādhi is so named because it is like the ocean that reflects the images of all sentient beings. In the Huayan scholastic tradition, sāgaramudrāsamādhi is raised to pride of place within its doctrinal system. Sāgaramudrāsamādhi is considered to be the generic samādhi (zongding) that the Buddha enters prior to beginning the elucidation of the various assemblies recounted in the *Avataṃsakasūtra* itself; the seven subsequent samādhis that the Buddha enters as he preaches the teaching of the *Avataṃsakasūtra* at each of the eight assemblies (hui) (there is no samādhi prior to the second assembly) are regarded instead as specific types of samādhis (bieding). ZHIYAN (602–668), the second Huayan patriarch, associated sāgaramudrāsamādhi with the teaching of one vehicle (EKAYĀNA) in his KONGMU ZHANG, where he says that the common and distinctive teachings of the one vehicle (yisheng tongbie) are revealed through the "ocean-seal" samādhi, while the teachings of the three vehicles (TRIYĀNA) are revealed through the subsequently obtained wisdom (C. houde zhi; S. PṚṢṬHALABDHAJÑĀNA). FAZANG (643–712), the third Huayan patriarch, following his teacher Zhiyan's view, declares at the beginning of his HUAYAN WUJIAO ZHANG that his work was written to reveal the teaching of the one vehicle that the Buddha attained through the "ocean-seal" samādhi. It is Fazang who formalized the place of the sāgaramudrāsamādhi in the Huayan doctrinal system. In his XIU HUAYAN AOZHI WANGJIN HUANYUAN GUAN, Fazang noted that the "ocean-seal" samādhi and the Huayan samādhi (C. Huayan sanmei), both mentioned among the ten samādhis in the Xianshou pusa pin of the *Avataṃsakasūtra*, correspond to the "two functions" (er YONG): respectively, to the "function of the eternal abiding of all things reflected on the ocean" (haiyin senluo changzhu yong) and the "function of the autonomy of the perfect luminosity of the DHARMADHĀTU" (fajie yuanming zizai yong). Both of these types of functions were subordinated to the highest category of the "one essence" (yi TI), viz., the "essence of the pure and perfect luminosity of the self-nature" (*zixing qingjing yuanming ti*). The first type of function, which was associated with the sāgaramudrāsamādhi, was the perfect reflection of all things in the pure mind; like the unsullied ocean that reflected all phenomena, it also was freed from any type of delusion or falsity. For Fazang, "ocean seal" (haiyin) was interpreted to mean the "original enlightenment of true thusness" (ZHENRU BENJUE) by correlating this function with the "ocean of the thusness of the dharma nature" (faxing zhenru hai) as mentioned in the DASHENG QIXIN LUN ("Awakening of Faith According to the Mahāyāna"). In Fazang's *Huayan youxin fajie ji*, the "ocean-seal" samādhi was classified as a cause and the Huayan samādhi as a fruition. Elsewhere, in his HUAYAN JING TANXUAN JI, Fazang additionally differentiates the ocean-seal samādhi itself into two phases of cause and fruition: the stage of the cause is attained by the bodhisattva SAMANTABHADRA at the tenth of the ten stages of faith, while the fruition stage corresponds to the samādhi of a tathāgata. In addition to its importance in the *Avataṃsakasūtra* and the Huayan school, there are several other sūtras that also mention the sāgaramudrāsamādhi. For example, the MAHĀPRAJÑĀPĀRAMITĀSŪTRA says that the sāgaramudrāsamādhi incorporates all other samādhis. The RATNAKŪṬASŪTRA states that one should abide in sāgaramudrāsamādhi in order to obtain complete, perfect enlightenment

(ANUTTARASAMYAKSAMBODHI). Finally, the MAHĀSAMNIPĀTASŪTRA says that one can see all sentient beings' mental functions and gain the knowledge of all teaching devices (DHARMAPARYĀYA) through the sāgaramudrāsamādhi.

**sa ga zla ba**. (saga dawa). The name of the fourth Tibetan month, the holiest month of the year, when it is believed the results of wholesome actions increase a hundred thousand times; the fifteenth day of this month is particularly auspicious, commemorating the day when ŚĀKYAMUNI was born, enlightened, and entered NIRVĀṆA. See WESAK.

**sahabhūhetu**. (T. lhan cig 'byung ba'i rgyu; C. juyouyin; J. kuuin; K. kuyuin 俱有因). In Sanskrit, the "coexistent cause"; the second of the six types of causes (HETU) outlined in the JÑĀNAPRASTHĀNA, the central text of the SARVĀSTIVĀDA ABHIDHARMA. This type of cause refers to the fact that coexistent dharmas simultaneously condition one another, as with a great element (MAHĀBHŪTA) and its derivatives, or a specific dharma and its four conditioned characteristics (SAṂSKṚTALAKṢAṆA). This process is comparable to the coexistence of the three legs of a tripod: if any one leg is missing, the other two legs are unable to function; thus, these coexistent dharmas must all exist simultaneously, so that if one is missing, all are missing. In the case of perception, for example, the Sarvāstivāda claimed that a moment of visual perception required that the visual sense-faculty (viz., the eye; INDRIYA), the visual object, and visual consciousness all had to exist simultaneously. This interpretation of the coexistent cause is subsequently adapted as a crucial component of the YOGĀCĀRA theory of representation-only (VIJÑAPTIMĀTRATĀ).

**sahaja**. (T. lhan skyes; C. jushengqi; J. kushōki; K. kusaenggi 俱生起). A polysemous Sanskrit term, variously translated as "coemergence," "connate," "simultaneously arisen," and "the innate." This term is used frequently in the tantric Buddhist verses composed by the SIDDHAs of medieval north India such as SARAHA, Kāṇha, and TILOPA; these include collections of DOHĀ recorded in APABHRAṂŚA and Bengali compilations of caryāgīti (see CARYĀGĪTIKOṢA). In these contexts, sahaja refers most generally to the ultimate and innermost true nature, as well as to its realization through the spontaneous and uninhibited lifestyle and practice associated with tantric adepts. The term may be used as a noun for the ultimate state itself, or as an adjective describing a state or condition as natural and uncontrived. In the context of the YOGINĪ tantras such as the HEVAJRATANTRA, the term sahaja is used to refer to the highest of four states of ecstasy—innate ecstasy (sahajānanda)—which can be gained through the visualized or actual practice of sexual yoga, and through which one comes to realize the mind's luminosity and natural purity. Early twentieth-century authors—beginning with the Bengali scholars and translators who first published studies on the collections of tantric verses—described what they called the sahajayāna ("path of sahaja") and the sahajiyās who followed it, although neither term is found in traditional Indian Buddhist literature. The Tibetan form, lhan skyes (short for lhan cig tu skyes pa) appears widely in the subsequent literature of MAHĀMUDRĀ.

**sahajakleśāvaraṇa**. (T. nyon sgrib lhan skyes; C. jusheng fannao zhang/jusheng huo; J. kushō no bonnōshō/kushō no waku; K. kusaeng pŏnnoe chang/kusaeng hok 俱生煩惱障/俱生惑). In Sanskrit, "innate afflictive obstructions," those obstructions (ĀVARAṆA) to liberation that derive from mistaken conceptions of self (ĀTMAN) that are generated and reinforced over many lifetimes. This type is in distinction to PARIKALPITAKLEŚĀVARAṆA (T. nyon sgrib kun btags) or "artificial afflictive obstructions," which are mistaken conceptions of self that are generated through the study of flawed philosophical systems or ideologies in the present lifetime. The latter are understood to be more easily abandoned than the sahajakleśāvaraṇa.

**sahajātmagraha**. (T. bdag 'dzin lhan skyes; C. jusheng wuming; J. kushō no mumyō; K. kusaeng mumyŏng 俱生無明). In Sanskrit, "innate conception of self," a term used to refer to the deep-seated conception of self that is maintained by all sentient beings from lifetime to lifetime. It is contrasted with the artificial conception of self (PARIKALPITĀTMAGRAHA), which is acquired during a human lifetime through the study of false tenet systems, such as those that assert the existence of a perduring self (ĀTMAN). Those on the path to enlightenment abandon the artificial conception of self more easily than they do the innate conception of self.

**sahajāvidyā**. (T. lhan cig skyes pa'i ma rig pa; C. jusheng wuming; J. kushō no mumyō; K. kusaeng mumyŏng 俱生無明). In Sanskrit, "innate ignorance," a term used to refer to the deep-seated ignorance that is maintained by sentient beings from lifetime to lifetime. It is contrasted with artificial ignorance (PARIKALPITĀVIDYĀ), the ignorance acquired during a human lifetime through the study of false tenet systems, such as those that assert the existence of a perduring self (ĀTMAN). Those on the path to enlightenment abandon the artificial ignorance more easily than the innate ignorance.

**sahajayāna**. (T. lhan skyes theg pa). In Sanskrit, "innate vehicle" or "spontaneous vehicle." See SAHAJA.

**sahakāripratyaya**. (T. lhan cig byed pa'i rkyen; C. zhuyuan; J. joen; K. choyŏn 助緣). In Sanskrit, the "cooperative condition," referring to those subsidiary conditions that must be present in order for an effect to be produced, such as the presence of heat and moisture for a seed to grow into a sprout. In the context of epistemology, sahakāripratyaya is the last of four types of conditions (PRATYAYA) that must be present in order for consciousness to occur: for example, in the case of the perception of a tree by a moment of visual consciousness (CAKṢURVIJÑĀNA), the prior moment of consciousness that leads to this visual consciousness is called the immediately antecedent condition (SAMANANTARAPRATYAYA), the tree is called the object condition (ĀLAMBANAPRATYAYA), and the visual sense organ is called the predominant condition (ADHIPATIPRATYAYA); the cooperative condition would be the light that must be present in order to see.

**sahāloka**. (T. mi mjed kyi 'jig rten; C. suopo shijie; J. shaba sekai; K. saba segye 娑婆世界). In Sanskrit, lit. "world of endurance," in the MAHĀYĀNA, the name of the world system we inhabit where the buddha ŚĀKYAMUNI taught; the term may also be seen written as sahālokadhātu. The tradition offers at least two explanations for designating this realm as the sahāloka. First, it is called the "world of endurance" because of the suffering endured by the beings that populate it. Second, the Sanskrit term sahā can also mean "together with, conjointly," and in this sense the term is understood to indicate that in this realm karmic causes and their effects are inextricably bound together. There is a range of opinion concerning the extent of the sahā world. Some texts identify this land with the continent of JAMBUDVĪPA, some with all four continents of this world system, and some with the entire trichiliocosm (TRISĀHASRAMAHĀSĀHASRALOKADHĀTU). The sahāloka is the buddha-field (BUDDHAKṢETRA) of Śākyamuni, which is described as an impure field because it includes animals, ghosts, and hell denizens. In both the SADDHARMAPUṆḌARĪKASŪTRA and the VIMALAKĪRTINIRDEŚA, however, Śākyamuni indicates that while unenlightened beings may perceive it as a world of suffering and desire, the sahā world is in reality his pure buddha field, a fact that is fully perceived by those who have achieved enlightenment. The highest divinity (DEVA) in the sahāloka is BRAHMĀ, one of whose epithets is SAHĀṂPATI, "Lord of the Sahā World."

**Sahāṃpati**. (P. Sahampati; T. Mi mjed kyi bdag po; C. Suopo shijie zhu; J. Shabasekaishu; K. Saba segye chu 娑婆世界主). In Sanskrit, "Lord of the Sahā World," the epithet of a BRAHMĀ deity. The first concentration (DHYĀNA) of the realm of subtle materiality (RŪPADHĀTU; see RŪPĀVACARADHYĀNA) has three levels, called BRAHMAKĀYIKA, BRAHMAPUROHITA, and MAHĀBRAHMĀ. The most senior of the deities of this third and highest level within the first concentration is called Brahmā Sahāṃpati. He plays a crucial role in the inception of the Buddhist teaching (ŚĀSANA). After his enlightenment, the newly enlightened Buddha is said to have wondered whether there was anyone in this world who would be able to understand his teaching. Brahmā Sahāṃpati then appeared to him and implored him to teach, convincing him that there were persons "with little dust in their eyes" who would be able to understand his teachings. According to BUDDHAGHOSA, the Buddha had every intention to teach but feigned reluctance in order that Brahmā Sahāṃpati would make the request, knowing that if the most powerful divinity in the SAHĀLOKA implored the Buddha to teach, those who honored Brahmā would heed the Buddha's teachings. Brahmā Sahāṃpati also assured the Buddha that in their last lifetimes, none of the buddhas of the past had had a teacher other than the DHARMA they discovered themselves. According to some accounts, he is divinity not of the mahābrahmā realm but rather of the ŚUDDHĀVĀSA.

**Sāhasrabhujasāhasranetrāvalokiteśvara**. [alt. Sahasrabhujasahasranetrāvalokiteśvara] (T. Spyan ras gzigs phyag stong spyan stong; C. Qianshou Qianyan Guanyin; J. Senju Sengen Kannon; K. Ch'ŏnsu Ch'ŏnan Kwanŭm 千手千眼觀音). In Sanskrit, "Thousand-Armed and Thousand-Eyed AVALOKITEŚVARA"; one of the manifestations of the bodhisattva of compassion, Avalokiteśvara (C. GUANYIN). The iconographical representations of this manifestation are usually depicted in abbreviated form with forty arms, each of which has an eye on its palm, indicating its ability compassionately to see and offer assistance to suffering sentient beings. Every arm also holds a different instrument, such as an axe, a sword, a bow, an arrow, a staff, a bell, or blue, white, and purple lotuses, each symbolizing one of the bodhisattva's various skills in saving sentient beings. The forty arms and eyes work on behalf of the sentient beings in the twenty-five realms of existence, giving the bodhisattva a total of a thousand arms and eyes. The images also typically are depicted with eleven or twenty-seven heads, although images with five hundred heads are also found. The origin of this manifestation is uncertain; the prototype may be such Indian deities as Viṣṇu, INDRA, and Śiva, who are also sometimes depicted with multiple hands and eyes. Since no image of this form of the BODHISATTVA has been discovered in India proper, some scholars suggest that the form may have originated in Kashmir (See KASHMIR-GANDHĀRA) and thence spread north into Central and East Asia; this scenario is problematic, however, because the earliest such image found at DUNHUANG, the furthest Chinese outpost along the SILK ROAD, dates to 836, about two hundred years later than the first such image painted in China, which is said to have been made for the Tang emperor by an Indian monk sometime between 618 and 626. The Thousand-Armed and Thousand-Eyed Guanyin became popular in China through translations of the QIANSHOU JING ("Thousand Hands Sūtra"; *Nīlakaṇṭhakasūtra*) made between the mid-seventh and early-eighth centuries. Due to the great popularity of Bhagavaddharma's (fl. c. seventh century) early translation, which was rendered between 650 and 658, the Thousand-Armed and Thousand-Eyed Avalokiteśvara became identified specifically with Avalokiteśvara's manifestation as Great Compassion (C. Dabei; S. MAHĀKARUṆIKA), although the epithet is used also to refer to Avalokiteśvara more generally. The Guanyin cult was popular in Chang'an and Sichuan during the Tang period and became widespread throughout China by the Song period; this bodhisattva was subsequently worshipped widely in Korea, Japan, and Tibet, as well. The ritual of repentance offered to the bodhisattva was created by the TIANTAI monk ZHILI (960–1028); the ritual is still widely performed in Taiwan and China. By the twelfth century, the Thousand-Armed and Thousand-Eyed Guanyin also came to be identified with the legendary princess MIAOSHAN, who was so filial that she offered her own eyes to save her father's life. In Tibet, this form of Avalokiteśvara is called Sāhasrabhuja-ekādaśamukha Avalokiteśvara (Spyan ras gzigs phyag stong zhal bcu gcig), with one thousand arms (often depicted in a fan formation) and eleven heads. According to a well-known story, the bodhisattva of compassion had vowed that if he ever gave up his commitment to suffering sentient beings and sought instead his own welfare, his head would break into ten pieces and his body into a thousand. In a moment of despair at the myriad sufferings of the world, his head and body exploded. The buddha AMITĀBHA put his body back together, crafting one thousand arms and ten heads, placing a duplicate of his own head at the top. This form of Avalokiteśvara is therefore known as, "one thousand arms and eleven heads" (phyag stong zhal bcu gcig).

**Sahasrākṣa**. (P. Sahassākkha; T. Mig stong can; C. Qianyan; J. Sengen; K. Ch'ŏnan 千眼). In Sanskrit, "One-Thousand Eyes," an epithet of INDRA. In Sanskrit and Pāli sources, Indra is known by several names, the most frequent being ŚAKRO DEVĀNĀṂ INDRAḤ (P. Sakko devānām indo), meaning "ŚAKRA, king of the gods." A number of Indra's various epithets are explained in one section of the Pāli SAṂYUTTANIKĀYA; there, the name "One-Thousand Eyes" (P. Sahassākkha) is explained by saying that in one instant Indra can consider one thousand different matters. The broader Indian religious tradition, from which Buddhism appropriated the divinity Indra, also has a number of stories explaining why Indra is called "One-Thousand Eyes." In the most popular of these stories, Indra seduces the wife of a famous seer (ṛṣi). The ṛṣi punishes Indra with a curse—causing one thousand vulvas (S. bhaga) to appear on his body. The ṛṣi is later persuaded to remove the curse and he turns each one of the vulvas into an eye.

**sahā world**. (S). See SAHĀLOKA.

**Saichō**. (最澄) (767–822). In Japanese, "Most Pure"; the monk traditionally recognized as the founder of the TENDAISHŪ in Japan; also known as Dengyō Daishi (Great Master Transmission of the Teachings). Although the exact dates and place of Saichō's birth remain a matter of debate, he is said to have been born to an immigrant Chinese family in Ōmi province east of HIEIZAN in 767. At age eleven, Saichō entered the local Kokubunji and studied under the monk Gyōhyō (722–797), a disciple of the émigré Chinese monk Daoxuan (702–766). In 785, Saichō received the full monastic precepts at the monastery of TŌDAIJI in Nara, after which he began a solitary retreat in a hermitage on Mt. Hiei. In 788, he built a permanent temple on the summit of Mt. Hiei. After Emperor Kanmu (r. 781–806) moved the capital to Kyōto in 794, the political significance of the Mt. Hiei community and thus Saichō seem to have attracted the attention of the emperor. In 797, Saichō was appointed a court priest (naigubu), and in 802 he was invited to the monastery of Takaosanji to participate in a lecture retreat, where he discussed the writings of the eminent Chinese monk TIANTAI ZHIYI on the SADDHARMAPUṆḌARĪKASŪTRA. Saichō and his disciple GISHIN received permission to travel to China in order to acquire Tiantai texts. In 804, they went to the monastery or Guoqingsi on Mt. Tiantai and studied under Daosui (d.u.) and Xingman (d.u.), disciples of the eminent Chinese Tiantai monk JINGQI ZHANRAN. Later, they are also known to have received BODHISATTVA precepts (bosatsukai) from Daosui at Longxingsi. He is also said to have received tantric initiation into the KONGŌKAI and TAIZŌKAI (RYŌBU) MAṆḌALAS from Shunxiao (d.u.). After nine and a half months in China, Saichō returned to Japan the next year with numerous texts, which he catalogued in his *Esshūroku*. Emperor Kanmu, who had been ill, asked Saichō to perform the esoteric rituals that he had brought back from China as a therapeutic measure. Saichō received permission to establish the Tendai sect and successfully petitioned for two Tendai monks to be ordained each year, one for doctrinal study and one to perform esoteric rituals. After the death of Kanmu in 806, little is known of Saichō's activities. In 810, he delivered a series of lectures at Mt. Hiei on the *Saddharmapuṇḍarīkasūtra*, the SUVARṆAPRABHĀSOTTAMASŪTRA, and the RENWANG JING ("Scripture for Humane Kings"). In 812, Saichō also constructed a meditation hall known as the Hokkezanmaidō. Later, Saichō is also said to have received kongōkai initiation from KŪKAI at the latter's temple Takaosanji, but their relations soured after a close disciple of Saichō's left Saichō for Kūkai. Their already tenuous relationship was sundered completely when Saichō requested a tantric initiation from Kūkai, who replied that Saichō would need to study for three years with Kūkai first. Saichō then engaged the eminent Hossōshū (FAXIANG ZONG) monk Tokuitsu (d.u.) in a prolonged debate concerning the buddha-nature (see BUDDHADHĀTU, FOXING) and Tendai doctrines, such as original enlightenment (see HONGAKU). In response to Tokuitsu's treatises *Busshōshō* and *Chūhengikyō*, Saichō composed his *Shōgonjikkyō*, *Hokke kowaku*, and *Shugo kokkaishō*. Also at this time, Saichō began a prolonged campaign to have an independent MAHĀYĀNA ordination platform established at Mt. Hiei. He argued that the bodhisattva precepts as set forth in the FANWANG JING, traditionally seen as complementary to monastic ordination, should instead replace them. He argued that the Japanese were spiritually mature and therefore could dispense entirely with the HĪNAYĀNA monastic precepts and only take the Mahāyāna bodhisattva precepts. His petitions were repeatedly denied, but permission to establish the Mahāyāna ordination platform at Mt. Hiei was granted a week after his death. Before his death Saichō also composed the *Hokke shūku* and appointed Gishin as his successor.

**Saidaiji**. (西大寺). In Japanese, "Great Monastery to the West"; one of the seven major monasteries in the ancient Japanese capital of Nara ( J. NANTO SHICHIDAIJI); the headquarters of the True Word Precepts (SHINGON-Ritsu) school in Japan. As its name implies, Saidaiji is located in the western part of Nara and was first constructed in 765 in accordance with a decree from SHŌTOKU TAISHI (572–622). The monastery originally had two main halls, one dedicated to the buddha BHAIṢAJYAGURU and the other to the bodhisattva MAITREYA. After conflagrations in 846 and 860, the monastery began to decline, but revived when Eison (Kōshō bosatsu; 1201–1290) moved there in 1235 and made it the center of his movement to restore the VINAYA. After another major fire in 1502, the Tokugawa Shogunate supported a rebuilding project. The monastery enshrines four bronze statues of the four heavenly kings (CATURMAHĀRĀJA), dating to the Nara (710–794) period. The main hall is dominated by a statue of ŚĀKYAMUNI said to have been carved cooperatively by eleven sculptors in 1249. To its right is a statue of MAÑJUŚRĪ riding a lion, to its left, a statue of Maitreya dating from 1322.

**Saigyō**. (西行) (1118–1190). A Japanese Buddhist poet of the late Heian and early Kamakura periods, especially famous for his many waka poems, a traditional style of Japanese poetry; his dharma name literally means "Traveling West," presumably referring to the direction of the PURE LAND of AMITĀBHA. Born as Satō Norikiyo into a family of the warrior class, he served during his youth as a guard for the retired emperor Toba (r. 1107–1123) before becoming a monk at the age of twenty-two. Although relatively little is known about his life, Saigyō seems to have traveled around the country on pilgrimage before eventually settling in relative seclusion on KŌYASAN, the headquarters of the SHINGONSHŪ. Virtually all of his poems are written in the thirty-one-syllable waka form favored at court and cover most of the traditional topics addressed in such poems, including travel, reclusion, cherry blossoms, and the beauty of the moon in the night sky. His poetry also reflects the desolation and despondency that Japanese of his time may have felt was inevitable during the degenerate age of the dharma (J. mappō; C. MOFA). Saigyō's *Sankashū* ("Mountain Home Collection") includes some fifteen hundred poems written in the course of his career; ninety-four of these poems were included in the imperially sponsored waka collection, the *Shinkokinshū* ("New Collection of Ancient and Modern Times"), compiled in 1205, making him one of Japan's most renowned and influential poets.

**śaikṣa**. (P. sekha; T. slob pa; C. xueren; J. gakunin; K. hagin 學人). In Sanskrit, "neophyte," "acolyte," one who is undergoing religious training. The path to enlightenment is often divided into the path of training and the path of no further training (AŚAIKṢA), with the former including (1) the seven paths of enterer and abider in the stages of the stream-enterer, once-returner, and nonreturner, and the enterer in the stage of the arhat; and (2) the paths of accumulation, preparation, vision, and meditation. The adept path where no further training is necessary (AŚAIKṢAMĀRGA) is the state of an ARHAT or a buddha.

**śaikṣadharma**. (P. sekhiyadhamma; T. bslabs pa'i chos; C. zhongxue; J. shugaku; K. chunghak 衆學). In Sanskrit, lit., "qualities in which to be trained"; in the PRĀTIMOKṢA, a large set of rules to be followed in the course of daily monastic life, the violation of which entails no sanction beyond the need for confession. They are for the most part items of etiquette with regard to dress, accepting and eating food, teaching the dharma, and using the toilet. The number of these precepts varies by VINAYA recension, with the Chinese MAHĀSĀṂGHIKA having sixty-six and the Chinese SARVĀSTIVĀDA having 113. In the Pāli vinaya, the term refers to a group of seventy-five precepts found in the *Pāṭimokkha* divided into seven sections. The first two rules concern proper dress. The next twenty-four rules concern the proper way to enter villages and inhabited areas and interact with the laypeople there. A set of thirty rules concerns the proper way to take meals. The next fifteen rules concern the preaching of dharma, and the last three rules concern the use of the toilet. Śaikṣa rules are the same for monks and nuns. One who knowingly transgresses these rules is guilty of an "offense of wrongdoing" (S. DUṢKṚTA; P. dukkata).

**Sajip**. (四集). In Korean, "Fourfold Collection," a compilation of three Chinese CHAN and one Korean SŎN texts that has been used in Korean Buddhist seminaries (kangwŏn) since at least the eighteenth century as the core of the monastic curriculum. The four books in the collection provide monks and nuns with, first, a systematic overview of mature Korean Buddhist thought and soteriology, focusing on the accommodation between Buddhist doctrinal study (KYO)—specifically HUAYAN (K. Hwaŏm) thought—and CHAN (Sŏn) meditation practice and different schemata of awakening (C. WU; K. o) and cultivation (C. xiu; K. su); and second, extensive grounding in the theory and mode of practice of "questioning meditation" (K. kanhwa Sŏn; C. KANHUA CHAN), the predominant form of meditative practice in Korea since the middle of the Koryŏ dynasty. The books of the "Fourfold Collection" are, in their traditional order: (1) The "Letters of Dahui" (C. DAHUI PUJUE CHANSHI SHU, better known in Korea by its abbreviated title *Sŏjang*, C. SHUZHUANG), a collection of the correspondence between the Chinese LINJI master DAHUI ZONGGAO (1089–1163) and various of his lay and ordained students, which describe the specifics of kanhua Chan meditation; (2) The "Chan Prolegomenon" (CHANYUAN ZHUQUANJI DUXU, known in Korea by its abbreviated title of TOSŎ), by GUIFENG ZONGMI (780–841), which provides an overarching hermeneutical framework—drawing on a series of polarities such as sudden and gradual, emptiness and self-nature, true and provisional—through which to understand the relationships among the teachings of representative traditions of Chan and the various doctrinal traditions, leading to a vision of Buddhism that reconciles the scholastic schools and the Chan schools; (3) The "Essentials of Chan" (GAOFENG HESHANG CHANYAO, typically known in Korea as the SŎNYO), by GAOFENG YUANMIAO (1238–1295), which Koreans have considered one of the clearest expositions of kanhwa Sŏn in all of Sŏn literature and use as a primer on the technique; (4) The "Excerpts from the 'Dharma Collection and Special Practice Record' with Personal Notes" (PŎPCHIP PYŎRHAENGNOK CHŎRYO PYŎNGIP SAGI, usually known by its abbreviated title

CHŎRYO) by POJO CHINUL (1158–1210), which offers an exhaustive examination of the question of whether enlightenment is achieved via a sudden or gradual process of soteriological development, advocating as the optimal stratagem the approach of sudden awakening followed by gradual cultivation (K. tono chŏmsu; C. DUNWU JIANXIU), and first introducing to Korea the kanhwa Sŏn technique; through this examination, Chinul specifically correlates the path as described in the doctrinal teachings of Buddhism (Kyo) with the practice of Sŏn, an approach that subsequently becomes emblematic of Korean Buddhism. The four books of the *Sajip* are thus intended to provide monks and nuns with substantial grounding in the theory and practice of kanhwa Sŏn prior to their beginning intensive training in the meditation hall (Sŏnbang).

**sākāra**. (T. rnam bcas; C. youxiang; J. usō; K. yusang 有相). In Sanskrit, lit. "having aspects," a term used in Buddhist epistemological accounts of perception, which asserts that what is perceived in sensory perception is not the object itself, but the "aspect" (ĀKĀRA) of the object. Buddhist philosophical schools differ as to whether or not such an "aspect" is required in order for sense perception to occur. VAIBHĀṢIKAS are "nonaspectarians" (NIRĀKĀRAVĀDA), who hold that mind knows objects directly; SAUTRĀNTIKAS are "aspectarians" (SĀKĀRAVĀDA), who say mind knows its object through an image of the object that is taken into the mind. YOGĀCĀRA also holds that the mind knows its object through an image. However, there is an internal debate within the school as to whether the appearance is a true aspect (satyākāra) or a false aspect (alīkākāra). In the late eighth century in north India, in the MADHYAMAKĀLAMKĀRA of ŚĀNTARAKṢITA, and the commentaries on his work by his students KAMALAŚĪLA and HARIBHADRA, this terminology was central in a discussion of how the TATHĀGATA can be all-knowing (literally, "knowing all aspects," SARVĀKĀRAJÑATĀ) while possessing ADVAYAJÑĀNA (nondual knowledge). See ĀKĀRA.

**sākāravāda**. (T. rnam pa dang bcas par smra ba). In Sanskrit, "proponent of having aspects," or "aspectarians"; a position in Buddhist epistemology, according to which sensory perception is not of the object itself but of an "aspect" (ĀKĀRA) of the object. See ĀKĀRA; SĀKĀRA.

**Sāketa**. (T. Gnas bcas; C. Suozhiduo cheng; J. Shagita jō; K. Sagida sŏng 娑枳多城). In Sanskrit and Pāli, a town in KOŚALA regarded during the Buddha's time as one of the six great cities of India, said to be located six or seven leagues (YOJANA) from ŚRĀVASTĪ. The other cities are Kauśāmbī, Campā, Vārāṇasī, Śrāvastī, and RĀJAGṚHA. The city has been identified by some with Ayodhyā. The Buddha and his disciples visited the city often; it is the setting for the *Sāketa Jātaka* and the *Sāketasutta*.

**Sakkapañhasutta**. (C. Di-Shi suowen jing; J. Taishaku shomongyō; K. Che-Sŏk somun kyŏng 帝釋所問經). In Pāli, "Discourse on Sakka's Question"; the twenty-first sutta of the DĪGHANIKĀYA (there are three separate recensions in Chinese: an independent sūtra translated by FAXIAN; a SARVĀSTIVĀDA recension that appears as the fourteenth sūtra in the Chinese translation of the DĪRGHĀGAMA; and a SARVĀSTIVĀDA recension that appears as the 134th sūtra in the Chinese translation of the MADHYAMĀGAMA). The sūtra is preached to ŚAKRA (P. Sakka), king of the gods, by the Buddha while he dwelt in the Indraśāla [alt. Indraśaila] (P. Indasāla) cave near RĀJAGṚHA. Śakra inquired as to why there was so much hostility between beings. The Buddha explained that hostility is caused by selfishness; that selfishness is caused by likes and dislikes, and that likes and dislikes, in turn, are caused by desire. Desire is produced by mental preoccupations (S. VITARKA, P. vitakka) born from the proliferation of concepts (S. PRAPAÑCA, P. papañca) that gives rise to SAṂSĀRA. The Buddha then delineates a practice to be pursued and a practice to be abandoned for subduing this conceptual proliferation.

**Śakra**. (P. Sakka; T. Brgya byin; C. Di-Shi; J. Taishaku; K. Che-Sŏk 帝釋). Sanskrit name of a divinity who is often identified with the Vedic god INDRA (with whom he shares many epithets), although it is perhaps more accurate to describe him as a Buddhist (and less bellicose) version of Indra. Typically described in Buddhist texts by his full name and title as "Śakra, the king of the gods" (ŚAKRO DEVĀNĀM INDRAḤ), he is the divinity (DEVA) who appears most regularly in Buddhist texts. Śakra is chief of the gods of the heaven of the thirty-three (TRĀYASTRIṂŚA), located on the summit of Mount SUMERU. As such, he is a god of great power and long life, but is also subject to death and rebirth; the Buddha details in various discourses the specific virtues that result in rebirth as Śakra. In both the Pāli canon and the MAHĀYĀNA sūtras, Śakra is depicted as the most devoted of the divine followers of the Buddha, descending from his heaven to listen to the Buddha's teachings and to ask him questions (and according to some accounts, eventually achieving the state of stream-enterer), and rendering all manner of assistance to the Buddha and his followers. In the case of the Buddha, this assistance was extended prior to his achievement of buddhahood, both in his previous lives (as in the story of Vessantara in the VESSANTARA JĀTAKA) and in his last lifetime as Prince SIDDHĀRTHA; when the prince cuts off his royal locks and throws them into the sky, proclaiming that he will achieve buddhahood if his locks remain there, it is Śakra who catches them and installs them in a shrine in the heaven of the thirty-three. When the Buddha later visited the heaven of the thirty-three to teach the ABHIDHARMA to his mother MĀYĀ (who had been reborn there), Śakra provided the magnificent ladder for his celebrated descent to JAMBUDVĪPA that took place at SĀṂKĀŚYA. When the Buddha was sick with dysentery near the end of his life, Śakra carried his chamber pot. Śakra often descends to earth disguised as a brāhmaṇa in order to test the virtue of the Buddha's disciples, both monastic and lay, offering all manner of miraculous boons to those who pass the test. In the Pāli canon, a section of the SAṂYUTTANIKĀYA consists of twenty-five short suttas devoted to him.

**sakṛdāgāmin**. (P. sakadāgāmi; T. lan gcig phyir 'ong ba; C. yilai/situohan; J. ichirai/shidagon; K. illae/sadaham 一來/斯陀含). In Sanskrit, lit. "once-returner"; the second (in ascending order) of the four grades of noble person (ĀRYAPUDGALA), the others being the SROTAĀPANNA or "stream-enterer" (the first grade), the ANĀGĀMIN or "nonreturner" (the next grade above sakṛdāgāmin), and the ARHAT or "worthy one" (the highest grade). The sakṛdāgāmin is one who has completely put aside the first three of ten fetters (SAṂYOJANA) that bind one to the cycle of rebirth; namely, (1) belief in the existence of a self in relation to the body (SATKĀYADṚṢṬI), (2) doubt about the efficacy of the path (VICIKITSĀ), (3) belief in the efficacy of rites and rituals (ŚĪLAVRATAPARĀMARŚA); and in addition, he has made progress in substantially overcoming the fourth and fifth fetters, namely, (4) sensual craving (KĀMARĀGA), and (5) malice (VYĀPĀDA). Having put aside the first three fetters completely and mitigated the fourth and fifth fetters, the sakṛdāgāmin is destined to be reborn in the sensuous realm (KĀMADHĀTU) at most one more time, although he may be reborn in the realm of subtle materiality (RŪPADHĀTU) or the immaterial realm (ĀRŪPYADHĀTU) before attaining NIRVĀṆA. Both SAKṚDĀGĀMIPHALAPRATIPANNAKA and SAKṚDĀGĀMIPHALASTHA are once-returners. The sakṛdāgāmin is also one of the twenty members of the ĀRYASAṂGHA (see VIṂŚATIPRABHEDASAṂGHA). In this context sakṛdāgāmin is the name for candidates (pratipannaka) for the fruition of sakṛdāgāmin SAKṚDĀGĀMIPHALAPRATIPANNAKA). They may be either a follower through faith (ŚRADDHĀNUSĀRIN) or a follower through doctrine (DHARMĀNUSĀRIN) with either dull (MṚDVINDRIYA) or keen faculties (TĪKṢṆENDRIYA). In all cases they are those who, before reaching the path of vision (DARŚANAMĀRGA), have eliminated six or seven of the levels of afflictions (KLEŚA) that cause rebirth in the sensuous realm (KĀMADHĀTU) that the ordinary (LAUKIKA) path of meditation (BHĀVANĀMĀRGA) removes, but they will not have eliminated the eighth or ninth level. Were they to have done so, they would be called candidates for the third fruit of nonreturner (ANĀGĀMIPHALAPRATIPANNAKA).

**sakṛdāgāmiphalapratipannaka**. (P. sakadāgāmimagga; T. phyir 'ong zhugs pa; C. yilai xiang; J. ichiraikō; K. illae hyang 一來向). In Sanskrit, candidate for the fruit of once-returner. If they are VĪTARĀGAPŪRVIN (those who have already eliminated afflictions (KLEŚA) associated with the sensuous realm prior to reaching the path of vision) and ānupūrvin (those who reach the four fruits of the noble path in a series), they are SROTAĀPANNAPHALASTHA. See SAKṚDĀGĀMIPHALASTHA.

**sakṛdāgāmiphalastha**. (P. sakadāgāmiphala; T. phyir 'ong 'bras gnas; C. zheng yilai guo; J. shōichiraika; K. chŭng illae kwa 證一來果). In Sanskrit, "one who has reached, or is the recipient of, the fruit of once-returner"; this term is paired with the SAKṚDĀGĀMIPHALAPRATIPANNAKA, one who is a candidate for the fruit of once-returner. Both refer to the "once-returner" (SAKṚDĀGĀMIN), one of the four types of noble persons (ĀRYA); the sakṛdāgāmiphalapratipannaka has, however, only reached the ĀNANTARYAMĀRGA (unimpeded path), while the sakṛdāgāmiphalastha has reached the VIMUKTIMĀRGA (path of freedom). In general, according to the ABHIDHARMAKOŚABHĀṢYA, a noble person reaches the goal of ARHAT by becoming free of all the afflictions (KLEŚA) of the three realms, from the sensuous realm to the BHAVĀGRA, the highest level of the immaterial realm. There are nine levels to the three realms: the level of the sensous realm is counted as one, and each of the four meditative absorptions (DHYĀNA) of the realms of both subtle materiality and and immateriality are counted as one each. The path of vision (DARŚANAMĀRGA) has sixteen instants, eight ānantaryamārga and eight vimuktimārga. The first four instants (consisting of two pairs of ānantaryamārga and vimuktimārga) are focused on the truth of suffering as it pertains to the sensuous realm, and then to the remaining eight levels of the two upper realms. The second four instants are focused on the truth of origination as it pertains to the sensuous realm, and then to the remaining eight levels of the two upper realms (see DHARMAKṢĀNTI). In this way, during sixteen instants that systematize the path of vision, all the afflictions to be eliminated by the path of vision are removed. The sharpest people (TĪKṢṆENDRIYA), with the finest store of previous actions, like the Buddha, know all three realms are equally conditioned by suffering (SAṂSKĀRADUḤKHATĀ) and feel disgust for all of it equally as SAṂSĀRA; they enter into the path of vision, eliminate the fetters, and awaken as arhats. Others have gradations of good fortune, ranging from those who will reach the final goal after death, to those who spend many lives taking rebirth in different heavens in the upper two realms before finally reaching the goal of arhatship. Those whose prior store of actions is such that, prior to reaching the path of vision, they have eliminated all, some, or none of the nine sets of afflictions that specifically cause rebirth in the sensuous realm reach the intermediate fruits of nonreturner, once-returner, and stream-enterer, respectively, when they reach the path of vision. The number of births they will take, and the places they take them, give rise to an āryasaṃgha made up of twenty different persons (VIṂŚATIPRABHEDASAṂGHA). In the Mahāyāna didactic reformulations of ABHIDHARMA, sakṛdāgāmin is a name for celestial bodhisattvas who are in their last life before taking birth in the TUṢITA heaven prior to becoming complete and perfect buddhas (samyaksaṃbuddha).

**Śakro devānām indraḥ**. (P. Sakko devānām indo). In Sanskrit, "ŚAKRA, king of the gods." See ŚAKRA, INDRA.

**Śakulā**. (P. Sakulā; C. Shejuli; J. Shakuri; K. Saguri 奢拘梨). An eminent ARHAT nun declared by the Buddha as foremost among his nun disciples in mastery of the divine eye (S. DIVYACAKṢUS, P. dibbacakkhu). She was the daughter of a brāhmaṇa family in the city of ŚRĀVASTĪ (P. Sāvatthi), who became a lay follower of the Buddha when she witnessed him accept the gift of the JETAVANA grove offered by ANĀTHAPIṆḌADA. Once, while listening to an arhat monk preach, she became overwhelmed with a sense of the transience of worldly things and joined the order as a nun. Through cultivating insight, she eventually attained arhatship. One of the extraordinary powers (ABHIJÑĀ) she developed as a consequence of her practice was the divine eye, or the ability to perceive the past lives of other beings and to understand the karmic consequences of the actions that led them from one existence to the next. It was because of her exceptional ability that she was deemed foremost in this regard. During the time of Padmottara (P. Padumuttara) Buddha, she was the half-sister of the Buddha and overheard one of his nun disciples being called foremost in mastery of the divine eye. It was at that time that she resolved to attain that distinction during the dispensation of a future buddha.

**Śākya**. (P. Sākiya; T. Shākya; C. Shijia; J. Shaka; K. Sŏkka; V. Thích ca 釋迦). Name of an ancient north Indian tribe that flourished in the southern foothills of the Himālayas near what is now the border between Nepal and India. This tribe produced the historical buddha, called either GAUTAMA or ŚĀKYAMUNI, whose name means "Sage of the Śākya Clan." Unfortunately virtually no sources referring to the Śākyas can be found outside the Buddhist tradition. The origin of the name is uncertain, being variously described as synonymous with the Sanskrit term śākya, meaning "able," or as a derivative of the noun śāka, a kind of tree used by this clan in construction. Texts describe this clan as ruled by KṢATRIYAS, the military or administrative caste of the Indian social system. At the time of the Buddha, the Śākyas were ruled by his father, King ŚUDDHODANA. The Śākyas made KAPILAVASTU the capital of their region. Both the MAHĀVASTU and the BUDDHACARITA name the Śākyas as descendants of the legendary solar king Ikṣvāku; the ultimate progenitor of the Śākyas was MAHĀSAṂMATA, the first king of the present world system. In the time of the Buddha, the Śākyas, although they were self-governing, were subjects of the neighboring kingdom of KOŚALA. According to various accounts, VIRŪḌHAKA (P. Viḍūḍabha), the king of KOŚALA, annexed the territory of the Śākyas and killed most of its inhabitants after they insulted him by revealing that his mother, whom they had provided as a bride to his father PRASENAJIT, was a servant. Prior to their demise, the Buddha himself is said to have dissuaded Virūḍhaka from invading the territory of the Śākyas. In East Asian Buddhism after the fourth century CE, monks and nuns traditionally abandoned their family surnames and adopted instead the Buddha's clan name Śākya (C. Shi); see SHI.

**śākyabhikṣu**. (P. sākiyabhikkhu or sakkabhikkhu; T. shākya dge slong; C. shijia seng; J. shakasō; K. sŏkka sŭng 釋迦僧). Literally "ŚĀKYA monk," a term for a Buddhist monk that appears most frequently in Buddhist donor inscriptions, but also occasionally in non-Buddhist Indian sources. Śākya refers to the northern Indian clan into which was born the historical buddha, who is thus known as ŚĀKYAMUNI, or "Sage of the Śākya Clan." In its most general use, the term refers to any Buddhist monk, in distinction to mendicants of other Indian religious traditions, such as the JAINA. This figurative use of the term Śākya—i.e., all monks as members of the Śākya clan—is common in Buddhist texts. Often monks are described as kinsmen or sons of the Buddha or the Śākyas. In its more specific use, śākyabhikṣu refers to those monks who, like the Buddha, actually belonged to the Śākya clan. Some scholars have argued that, in the Indian context, the term śākyabhikṣu was used specifically and exclusively by MAHĀYĀNA monks. Many East Asian monastic traditions use their pronunciations of the Sinographic transcription of the name Śākya as the "clan name" for all their ordained members (see SHI).

**Śākyamuni**. (P. Sakkamuni; T. Shākya thub pa; C. Shijiamouni; J. Shakamuni; K. Sŏkkamoni 釋迦牟尼). In Sanskrit, "Sage of the ŚĀKYA Clan," one of the most common epithets of GAUTAMA Buddha, especially in the MAHĀYĀNA traditions, where the name ŚĀKYAMUNI is used to distinguish the historical buddha from the myriad other buddhas who appear in the SŪTRAs. The Śākyas were a tribe in northern India into which was born SIDDHĀRTHA GAUTAMA, the man who would become the historical buddha. According to the texts, the Śākya clan was made up of KṢATRIYAS, warriors or political administrators in the Indian caste system. The Śākya clan flourished in the foothills of the Himālayas, near the border between present-day Nepal and India. Following the tradition's own model, which did not seek to provide a single and seamless biography of Gautama or Śākyamuni until centuries after his death, this dictionary narrates the events of the life of the Buddha in separate entries about his previous lives, his teachings, his disciples, and the places he visited over the course of his forty-five years of preaching the dharma. In India, accounts of events in the life of the Buddha first appeared in VINAYA materials, such as the Pāli MAHĀVAGGA or the LOKOTTARAVĀDA school's MAHĀVASTU. Among the Pāli SUTTAs, one of the most detailed accounts of the Buddha's quest for enlightenment occurs in the ARIYAPARIYESANĀSUTTA. It is noteworthy that many of the most familiar events in the Buddha's life are absent in some of the early accounts: the miraculous conception and birth; the death of his mother, Queen MĀYĀ; his sheltered youth; the four chariot rides outside the palace where he beholds the four portents (CATURNIMITTA); his departure from the palace; and his abandonment of his wife, YAŚODHARĀ, and his newborn son, RĀHULA. Those stories appear much later, in works like AŚVAGHOṢA's beloved verse narrative, the BUDDHACARITA, from the second century CE; the SARVĀSTIVĀDA school's third- or fourth-century CE LALITAVISTARA; and the NIDĀNAKATHĀ, the first biography of the Buddha in Pāli, attributed to BUDDHAGHOSA in the fifth century CE, some eight centuries after the Buddha's passing. Even in that later biography, however, the "life of the Buddha" ends with ANĀTHAPIṆḌADA's gift of JETAVANA grove to the Buddha, twenty years after the Buddha's enlightenment and twenty-five years before his death. Other biographical accounts end even earlier, with the conversion of ŚĀRIPUTRA and MAHĀMAUDGALYĀYANA. Indeed, Indian Buddhist literature devotes more attention to the lives of previous buddhas and to the former lives (JĀTAKA) of Gautama or Śākyamuni than they do to biographies of his final lifetime (when biography is taken to refer to a chronological account from birth to death). And even there, the tradition takes pains to demonstrate the consistency of the events of his life with those of previous buddhas; in fact, all buddhas are said to perform the same eight or twelve deeds (see BAXIANG; TWELVE DEEDS OF A BUDDHA). The momentous events of his birth, renunciation, enlightenment under the BODHI TREE, and first turning of the wheel of the dharma (DHARMACAKRAPRAVARTANA) are described in detail in a range of works, and particular attention is given to his death, in both the Pāli MAHĀPARINIBBANASUTTA and the Sanskrit MAHĀPARINIRVĀṆASŪTRA. And all traditions, whether MAINSTREAM BUDDHIST SCHOOLS or the Mahāyāna, are deeply concerned with the question of the location of the Buddha after his passage into PARINIRVĀṆA.

**Śākyaprabha**. (T. Shākya 'od). (d.u.) Medieval Indian master of the VINAYA, renowned in Tibet, together with GUṆAPRABHA, as one of the "two supreme ones" (mchog gnyis). Apparently from KASHMIR, he was an expert in the MŪLASARVĀSTIVĀDA VINAYA. He is best known for his work *Śrāmaṇeratriśatakakārikā* ("Three Hundred Verses on the Novice"), to which he wrote an autocommentary entitled *Prabhāvatī*.

**Śākyaśrībhadra**. (T. Shākya shrī) (1127–1225). Also known as Śākyaśrī, a monk and scholar from KASHMIR who played an important role in the later dissemination (PHYI DAR) of Buddhism in Tibet, especially for the SA SKYA sect of Tibetan Buddhism. He served as abbot at both NĀLANDĀ and VIKRAMAŚĪLA monasteries. As the last abbot of Vikramaśīla monastery, he witnessed its destruction by Muslim troops. Declaring that Buddhism had been destroyed in India, he traveled to Tibet in 1204 (at the age of seventy-seven, if his birth year of 1127 is accurate) at the invitation of the Tibetan translator Khro phu lo tsā ba, in the company of nine Indian and Nepalese paṇḍitas. There, he gave teachings on PRAMĀṆA, ABHIDHARMA, VINAYA, the ABHISAMAYĀLAṂKĀRA, MADHYAMAKA, TANTRA, and Sanskrit grammar and poetics. His most famous Tibetan disciple was SA SKYA PAṆḌITA KUN DGA' RGYAL MTSHAN, whom he ordained as a BHIKṢU in 1208. It is said that Śākyaśrībhadra gave him the name Sa skya Paṇḍita ("Scholar from Sa skya") because of his ability to spontaneously translate Tibetan into Sanskrit. The two worked together on a new translation of DHARMAKĪRTI's PRAMĀṆAVĀRTTIKA, marking the beginning of Sa skya Paṇḍita's influence in the field of pramāṇa. Śākyaśrībhadra's ordination lineage, known as the Kha che lugs, or "Kashmiri system," would be adopted by the GSAR MA sects. Śākyaśrībhadra gave teachings at many monasteries in central and western Tibet, ordained many monks, translated Sanskrit texts, and established several monasteries. While at BSAM YAS, he discovered a manuscript of the GUHYAGARBHATANTRA and vouched for its authenticity. He is also credited with providing the Tibetans with a more accurate chronology of the life of the Buddha. In 1212, he consecrated a great statue of MAITREYA at Khro pu. After ten years in Tibet, he returned to his native Kashmir where he spent the last decade of his life. He is often referred to in Tibetan simply as Kha che paṇ chen, the "great paṇḍita from Kashmir."

**śāla**. (P. sāla; T. sā la; C. shaluoshu; J. saraju/sharaju; K. sarasu 沙羅樹). In Sanskrit, the "sal" tree (Shorea robusta, [alt. Vatica robusta]); a species of tree native to South Asia, which figures prominently in the Buddhist tradition. In India, the tree grows upwards of one hundred feet in height and provides both timber and fragrant resin, which is burned for incense. In several of his discourses, the Buddha uses the growth of the śāla tree as an analogy for the development of wholesome qualities (KUŚALA). This tree also is particularly significant in Buddhist hagiography because it was under this type of tree that the Buddha was born and died. Queen MĀYĀ, the Buddha's mother, is said to have given birth to the prince while clinging for support to the branches of a śāla tree that had bent itself down to help her. The Buddha chose a grove of śāla trees near the town of KUŚINAGARĪ as the site of his PARINIRVĀṆA. Different versions of the Buddha's demise represent these trees in various ways. One version says that the Buddha laid down between twin śāla trees and passed away. Another version says that the Buddha's deathbed was surrounded by pairs of śāla trees—two in each of the four cardinal directions—and at the moment of his death these trees blossomed out of season, rained petals upon him, and their trunks turned white. See also SIKU.

**Sāleyyakasutta**. In Pāli, the "Discourse to the Sāleyyakas"; the forty-first sutta contained in the MAJJHIMANIKĀYA (a separate SARVĀSTIVĀDA recension appears, but without title, in the Chinese translation of the SAṂYUKTĀGAMA); preached by the Buddha to a group of brāhmaṇa householders at the town of Sālā in the Kosala (S. KOŚALA) country. The Buddha describes for them the ten nonvirtuous actions that lead to unhappiness and unfortunate rebirths and the ten virtuous actions that lead to happiness and fortunate rebirths (see KARMAPATHA). The ten nonvirtuous actions are divided into three kinds of bodily misdeed: (1) killing, (2) stealing, (3) and sexual misconduct; four kinds of verbal misdeed: (4) lying, (5) divisive speech, (6) harsh speech, and (7) senseless prattle; and three kinds of mental misdeed: (8) covetousness, (9) harmful intent, and (10) wrong views. The ten virtuous actions are explained as the abstaining from the ten virtuous actions. The Buddha then describes the fortunate rebirths among humans and divinities that may be expected by those who perform virtuous deeds.

**Śālistambasūtra**. (T. Sā lu ljang pa'i mdo; C. Daogan jing; J. Tōkangyō; K. Togan kyŏng 稻稈經). In Sanskrit, the "Rice Seedling Sūtra," a MAHĀYĀNA SŪTRA noted for its detailed presentation of the doctrine of dependent origination (PRATĪTYASAMUTPĀDA). The sūtra begins with the Buddha gazing at a rice seedling and then declaring, "Monks, he who sees dependent origination sees the dharma. He who sees the dharma sees the Buddha." ŚĀRIPUTRA asks MAITREYA what this statement means, and the majority of the sūtra is devoted to his answer. This sūtra provides one of the most detailed treatments of the doctrine of dependent origination found anywhere in the scriptural literature. The doctrine had been set forth in various ways in previous sūtras, and the Śālistambasūtra appears to be something of a digest of these various presentations. The sūtra is widely quoted by Indian commentators in their own expositions of dependent origination, including MADHYAMAKA authors, although the sūtra does not connect dependent origination with emptiness (ŚŪNYATĀ). Indeed, the text is so widely quoted that, although the sūtra is lost in the original Sanskrit, approximately ninety percent of the Sanskrit text can be recovered from citations of it in various Indian treatises.

**Sallekhasutta**. (C. Zhouna wenjian jing; J. Shūna monkengyō; K. Chuna mun'gyŏn kyŏng 周那問見經). In Pāli, "Discourse on Effacement," the eighth sutta in the MAJJHIMANIKĀYA (a separate SARVĀSTIVĀDA recension appears as the ninety-first sūtra in the Chinese translation of the MADHYAMĀGAMA, as well as a recension of unidentified affiliation in the EKOTTARĀGAMA); preached by the Buddha to Mahācunda, a master of meditative absorption (P. JHĀNA, S. DHYĀNA) in the JETAVANA grove in the town of Sāvatthi (S. ŚRĀVASTĪ). The Buddha explains that pride and speculative views regarding self and the nature of the world cannot be overcome by mere meditative absorption, but only through insight into the Buddhist truths (insight that implicitly will lead to stream-entry). Furthermore, true austerity is nothing other than refraining from forty-four types of unwholesome qualities; one mired in sensuality cannot help bring another to purity.

**samādhi**. (T. ting nge 'dzin; C. sanmei; J. sanmai; K. sammae 三昧). In Sanskrit, "concentration"; a foundational term in Buddhist meditation theory and practice, which is related to the ability to establish and maintain one-pointedness of mind (CITTAIKĀGRATĀ) on a specific object of concentration. The SARVĀSTIVĀDA school of ABHIDHARMA and the YOGĀCĀRA school list samādhi as one of a group of five determinative (VINIYATA) mental concomitants (CAITTA), whose function is to aid the mind in ascertaining or determining its object. The five are: aspiration or desire-to-act (CHANDA), determination or resolve (ADHIMOKṢA), mindfulness or memory (SMṚTI), concentration (SAMĀDHI), and wisdom or cognition (PRAJÑĀ). According to ASAṄGA, these five determinative factors accompany wholesome (KUŚALA) states of mind, so that if one is present, all are present. In Pāli ABHIDHAMMA materials, concentration is one of the seven mental factors (P. cetasika) that are invariably associated with all moments of consciousness (CITTA, MANAS, or VIJÑĀNA). Concentration occurs in many other important lists, including as the second of the three trainings (TRIŚIKṢĀ), and the last stage of the eightfold path (ĀRYĀṢṬĀṄGAMĀRGA). Concentration is distinguished according to the quality of consciousness with which it is associated. "Right concentration" (SAMYAKSAMĀDHI, P. sammāsamādhi) is concentration associated with wholesome (KUŚALA) states of mind; it is listed not only as one element of the eightfold noble path, but as one of seven factors of enlightenment (BODHYAṄGA, P. bojjhaṅga), and, in an incipient state, as one of five powers (BALA) and the other categories that together make up the BODHIPĀKṢIKADHARMA (thirty-seven factors associated with awakening). High degrees of concentration can be developed through the practice of meditation (BHĀVANĀ). Concentration of such intensity receives the designation "one-pointedness of mind" (cittaikāgratā). When developed to its greatest degree, mental concentration leads to the attainment of DHYĀNA (P. JHĀNA), "meditative absorption." It is also the main mental factor defining the four magical powers (ṚDDHIPĀDA, P. iddhipāda). The cultivation of concentration for the purposes of attaining meditative absorption is called tranquillity meditation (ŚAMATHA). In the Pāli abhidhamma, three levels of concentration are distinguished in the practice of tranquility meditation: (1) preparatory concentration (PARIKAMMASAMĀDHI) is the degree of concentration established at the beginning of a meditation session. (2) Access or neighborhood concentration (UPACĀRASAMĀDHI) arises just as the practitioner approaches but does not enter the first level of meditative absorption; it is marked by the appearance in the mind of a representational image (PAṬIBHĀGANIMITTA) of the object of meditation. (3) "Attainment" or "full" concentration (APPANĀSAMĀDHI) is the level of concentration that arises upon entering and abiding in any of the meditative absorptions. In the MAHĀYĀNA sūtras, a wide variety of profound meditative experiences are described as samādhis and are mentioned as attainments of the bodhisattva as he ascends through the ten BHŪMIs. The MAHĀVYUTPATTI lists 118 different samādhis that are specified by name in the PRAJÑĀPĀRAMITĀ sūtras, such as candravimala (stainless moon), sarvadharmodgata (surpassing all dharmas), siṃhavikrīḍita (lion's play), anantaprabha (limitless light), and acala (immovable). See also YATHĀBHŪTAJÑĀNADARŚANA.

**Samādhirājasūtra**. (T. Ting nge 'dzin rgyal po'i mdo; C. Yuedeng sanmei jing; J. Gatttōsanmaikyō; K. Wŏltŭng sammae kyŏng 月燈三昧經). The "King of Concentrations Sūtra"; an important MAHĀYĀNA sūtra (also known as the *Candrapradīpa*) composed in India, probably in the fourth century CE, with the text undergoing expansion in subsequent centuries. The text is a mixture of poetry and prose, with the verse sections considered to be the older stratum. The sūtra is cited often in Mahāyāna śāstras, especially in the PRASANNAPADĀ of CANDRAKĪRTI and the ŚIKṢĀSAMUCCAYA of ŚĀNTIDEVA, and is also one of the foundational texts, or "nine dharmas" (see NAVAGRANTHA), of Newar Buddhism. A Chinese translation of the complete sūtra was made by Narendrayaśas in 557. The *Samādhirājasūtra* is composed of a dialogue between the Buddha and the bodhisattva Candragupta, and sets forth various forms of meditation for bodhisattvas, including the "king of concentrations" of the sūtra's title, which is defined as "the proclamation that all phenomena are of the same nature." The sūtra does not offer instructions for developing these samādhis, but instead provides their names and recounts their wondrous effects. The sūtra describes at some length the two (rather than three) bodies of a buddha, the DHARMAKĀYA and the RŪPAKĀYA, with the former identified with the "mind of clear light" (PRABHĀSVARACITTA).

**samādhiśikṣā**. (T. ting nge 'dzin gyi bslab pa). In Sanskrit, "training in meditation." See ADHISAMĀDHIŚIKṢĀ.

**samādhisūtra**. In Sanskrit, "meditation sūtra." See SANMEI JING.

**samāhita**. (T. mnyam bzhag; C. dengyin; J. tōin; K. tŭngin 等引). In Sanskrit and Pāli, "equipoise" (lit. "composed" or "collected"); a past passive participle formed from the Sanskrit root √dhā ("to place") with the prefixes sam ("fully") and ā ("from all sides") (and etymologically related to SAMĀDHI), in which the mind of the practitioner is linked to its object, in such a way that discursive thought no longer intrudes. A paranomastic gloss interprets it as linking (āhita) the mind to equanimity (sama). The term is sometimes contrasted with subsequent attainment (pṛṣṭhalabha), when discursiveness returns. The decision to include samāhita in the Buddhist narrative on meditation, but to emphasize instead samādhi, could be a reaction to brahmanical discourses on meditative states, which tend to emphasize samāhita over samādhi. In the Buddhist tradition, the notion of samāhita as an attainment is incorporated in different ways from one meditation model to another. In the YOGĀCĀRABHŪMIŚĀSTRA of the YOGĀCĀRA school, for example, samāhita is listed as the sixth of seventeen stages (BHŪMI) by which progress is made toward the state of a buddha. See also SAMĀPATTI.

**samāhitajñāna**. (T. mnyam bzhag ye shes; C. dengyin zhi; J. tōinchi; K. tŭngin chi 等引智). In Sanskrit, "wisdom of equipoise," the state of direct realization of reality in which the ultimate truth is perceived without mediation by thought in a state of yogic direct perception (YOGIPRATYAKṢA). In descriptions of the five paths (PAÑCAMĀRGA) to enlightenment, the attainment of such wisdom occurs on the path of vision (DARŚANAMĀRGA) and is repeated over the course of the path of cultivation (BHĀVANĀMĀRGA). It has two parts, the VIMUKTIMĀRGA and the ĀNANTARYAMĀRGA.

**samanantarapratyaya**. (P. samanantarapaccaya; T. de ma thag pa'i rkyen; C. dengwujian yuan; J. tōmuken'en; K. tŭngmugan yŏn 等無間緣). In Sanskrit, "immediate-antecedent condition"; the second of the four types of conditions (PRATYAYA) recognized in the VAIBHĀṢIKA school of SARVĀSTIVĀDA ABHIDHARMA and the YOGĀCĀRA school. Samanantarapratyaya is also listed as one of the twenty-four conditions (P. paccaya) in the massive Pāli ABHIDHAMMA text, the PAṬṬHĀNA. This type of condition refers to the immediately antecedent moment, which through its cessation enables a subsequent moment to arise; in the case of consciousness (VIJÑĀNA), it therefore refers to the prior moment of consciousness that is a necessary antecedent to the next moment of consciousness. All types of thought in the conditioned (SAṂSKṚTA) realm serve as immediate-antecedent conditions. The only exception is the final thought-moment in the mental continuum of an ARHAT: because the next thought-moment involves the experience of the unconditioned (ASAṂSKṚTA), no further thoughts from the conditioned realm can ever again recur. This type of condition is also called the "antecedent condition" (ANANTARAPRATYAYA); the VISUDDHIMAGGA explains that samanantarapratyaya and anantarapratyaya are essentially the same, except that the former emphasizes the immediacy of the connection between the two moments.

**samānapratibhāsadharmin**. (T. chos can mthun snang). In Sanskrit, lit. "subject that appears the same" or "commonly appearing subject," a term in Buddhist logic, particularly important in Tibetan Buddhism. This term refers to the common basis (T. gzhi mthun) that must be present in order for a reasonable and constructive debate to occur. In other words, if adherents of two different doctrinal systems try to debate, but employ only terms and ideas that are unique to their own systems, then no position can be effectively proven or refuted. Furthermore, the participants in a debate must have a common understanding of the subject that is being debated and a shared understanding of what constitutes a logical example. This term is also understood to mean that the participants in a debate must understand the scripture on which the debate is based. Some Buddhist philosophers, such as Jayānanda, refuted the notion that debate or inference (ANUMĀNA) was in any way constructive on the following general grounds: to the enlightened mind, all phenomena are devoid of substance or definition and therefore no phenomenon can serve as a samānapratibhāsadharmin. This is a central issue in MADHYAMAKA, where the proponent of emptiness (ŚŪNYATĀ) rejects the notion of anything that possesses its own nature (SVABHĀVA). This raises the question of whether there is a commonly appearing subject in a debate between a Madhyamaka and non-Madhyamaka; if there is, to what degree is the appearance "common"; and how does the Madhyamaka present his position under such circumstances.

**samānārthatā**. (P. samānattatā; T. don mthun pa; C. tongshi; J. dōji; K. tongsa 同事). In Sanskrit, "consistency"; viz., acting in accordance with one's own teachings, or demonstrating consistency between one's words and deeds. See SAṂGRAHAVASTU.

**Sāmaññaphalasutta**. (S. Śrāmaṇyaphalasūtra; C. Shamenguo jing; J. Shamongakyō; K. Samun'gwa kyŏng 沙門果經). In

Pāli, the "Discourse on the Fruits of Mendicancy," the second sutta of the DĪGHANIKĀYA (a separate DHARMAGUPTAKA recension appears as the twenty-seventh sūtra in the Chinese translation of the DĪRGHĀGAMA; another unidentified recension also is included in the Chinese translation of the EKOTTARĀGAMA). The patricide king AJĀTAŚATRU (P. Ajātasattu) and the physician JĪVAKA visit the Buddha dwelling at Jīvaka's mango grove, Ambavana. Impressed by the silence and discipline of the Buddha's disciples gathered there, Ajātaśatru thinks that it would be good if his own son, Udayabhadra (P. Udāyibaddha), were to join such an assembly of mendicants. He asks the Buddha about the benefits of mendicancy here and now, such that men would put aside worldly pursuits and join the Buddhist order. According to the Pāli recension, he states that he had already put this question to six other famous recluses of the day—namely, PŪRAṆA-KĀŚYAPA, MASKARIN GOŚĀLĪPUTRA, AJITA KEŚAKAMBALA, KAKUDA KĀTYĀYANA, NIRGRANTHA-JÑĀTĪPUTRA, and SAÑJAYA VAIRĀṬĪPUTRA (P. Pūraṇa Kassapa, Makkhali Gosāla, Ajita Kesakambala, Pakudha Kaccāyana, Nigaṇṭha Nātaputta and Sañjaya Belaṭṭiputta)—but received no satisfactory answer. In response to the king's query, the Buddha describes the immediate benefits of mendicancy from the most mundane to the most exalted. He notes that even a servant or householder who becomes a mendicant receives the honor of kings. Moreover, the mendicant is free of taxation and the burden of supporting a family and learns control of the senses, mindfulness (SMṚTI, P. sati) and contentment. Being content, the mendicant becomes glad and calm, which provide the foundation for attaining the four meditative absorptions (DHYĀNA, P. JHĀNA). Higher than any of these and on the basis of having mastered the four meditative absorptions, the mendicant can develop the six higher knowledges or supranormal powers (ABHIJÑĀ, P. abhiññā), which culminate in enlightenment and liberation from the cycle of rebirth. Upon hearing this discourse, Ajātaśatru expressed regret at having murdered his father and took refuge in the Buddha. After the king's departure, the Buddha noted to his disciples that were it not for the fact that the king had murdered his father, he would have attained the stage of stream-enterer (SROTAĀPANNA) then and there.

**Samantabhadra**. (T. Kun tu bzang po; C. Puxian; J. Fugen; K. Pohyŏn 普賢). The Sanskrit name of both an important bodhisattva in Indian and East Asian Buddhism and of an important buddha in Tibetan Buddhism. As a bodhisattva, Samantabhadra is a principal bodhisattva of the MAHĀYĀNA pantheon, who is often portrayed as the personification of the perfection of myriad good works and spiritual practices. He is one of the AṢṬAMAHOPAPUTRA, and an attendant of ŚĀKYAMUNI Buddha, standing opposite MAÑJUŚRĪ at the Buddha's side. In the PAÑCATATHĀGATA configuration, he is associated with the buddha VAIROCANA. Samantabhadra figures prominently in the AVATAṂSAKASŪTRA. In a chapter named after him, he sets forth ten SAMĀDHIs. In the GAṆḌAVYŪHA (the final chapter of the *Avataṃsakasūtra*), the bodhisattva SUDHANA sets out in search of a teacher, encountering fifty-two beings (twenty of whom are female), including the Buddha's mother Mahāmāyā (MĀYĀ), the future buddha MAITREYA, as well as AVALOKITEŚVARA and MAÑJUŚRĪ. His final teacher is the bodhisattva Samantabhadra, who sets forth the ten vows in his famous BHADRACARĪPRAṆIDHĀNA. In China, the center of Samantabhadra's worship is EMEISHAN in Sichuan province, which began to develop in the early Tang. According to legend, Samantabhadra arrived at the mountain by flying there on his white elephant, his usual mount. As a buddha, Samantabhadra is the primordial buddha (ĀDIBUDDHA) according to the RNYING MA sect of Tibetan Buddhism. He is depicted naked, blue, and in sexual union with his consort Samantabhadrī. He is embodiment of the original purity of all phenomena of SAṂSĀRA and NIRVĀṆA. Called the "primordial basis" (ye gzhi), he is regarded as the eternal union of awareness (RIG PA) and emptiness (ŚŪNYATĀ), of emptiness and appearance, and of the nature of the mind and compassion. As such he is the wellspring of the ATIYOGA teachings.

**Samantabhadracarī-praṇidhāna-rāja**. (S). See BHADRACARĪPRAṆIDHĀNA.

**Samantagandha**. (T. Kun tu dri bsung; C. Puxiang; J. Fukō; K. Pohyang 普香). In Sanskrit and Pāli, "Universal Fragrance." In the SADDHARMAPUṆḌARĪKASŪTRA ("Lotus Sūtra"), Samantagandha is listed as one of the many divinities (DEVA) who accompany ŚAKRA, the king of the gods, and are present from the outset of the Buddha's sermons. In other texts, such as the MAHĀVASTU, Samantagandha is listed as one of the divinities who appears on more than one occasion to honor the Buddha by scattering in the sky such articles as flowers (see KHAPUṢPA) and sandalwood powder. In the APADĀNA, a Pāli collection of hagiographical narratives found in the KHUDDAKANIKĀYA, Samantagandha is listed as a name for one of the hundreds of ARHATs whose prior births are recounted in the text. In the distant past, the ARHAT Pādapūjaka Thera was born thirteen times as a king under the name Samantagandha.

**sāmantaka**. (T. nyer bsdogs; C. jinfen; J. gonbun; K. kŭnbun 近分). In Sanskrit, "preparation," "neighboring state"; according to the YOGĀCĀRABHŪMI and the ABHIDHARMASAMUCCAYA, each of the four concentrations (DHYĀNA) and attainments (SAMĀPATTI) has two parts: maula (fundamental state) and sāmantaka (a neighboring part that is preparatory to that fundamental state). The fundamental state is ŚAMATHA (serenity, calmness) and the sāmantaka (preparation) is included under the heading of VIPAŚYANĀ (insight). Six or seven types of attentions (MANASKĀRA) are listed as preparations for the attainment of the first dhyāna. These include attention that contemplates marks (lakṣaṇapratisaṃvedīmanaskāra), arises from belief (ādhimokṣikamanaskāra), arises from separation (prāvivekyamanaskāra), contemplates joy and withdrawal (ratisaṃgrāhakamanaskāra), investigates (mīmāṃsakamanaskāra), is a final practice (prayoganiṣṭamanaskāra), and leads to the result of the final practice (prayoganiṣṭaphalamanaskāra). There are nine impediments (heya) between the fundamental stages of the first and second concentrations (dhyāna), for example. Attention is then paid to the marks of the lower as coarse (audārika) and the higher as delightful (śānta). The first attention identifies the impediments and focuses the mind on removing them; the second brings vigor or energy (VĪRYA); the third, fourth, and six actually counteract the three sets of three impediments; the fifth investigates to see whether the impediments have actually been eliminated. The seventh is the fundamental state. See also UPACĀRASAMĀDHI.

**Samantapāsādikā**. (C. Shanjianlü piposha; J. Zenkenritsubibasha; K. Sŏn'gyŏnyul pibasa 善見律毘婆沙). In Pāli, lit. "Entirely Pleasing"; the title of a fifth-century commentary on the VINAYAPIṬAKA, written in Sri Lanka by the renowned exegete BUDDHAGHOSA. The *Samantapāsādikā* contains a lengthy introduction called *Bāhiranidāna*, which recounts the early history of the dispensation from the death of the Buddha through the convocation of the first three Buddhist councils (see SAṂGĪTI) and to the recitation of the VINAYA in Sri Lanka by MAHĀRIṬṬHA during the reign of the Sinhalese king DEVĀNAṂPIYATISSA. A translation of the *Bahīranidāna* appears in the Pali Text Society's English translation series as *The Inception of Discipline.* The remainder of the *Samantapāsādikā* covers a broad array of topics, touching on many points of historical and geographical interest. The commentary makes reference to the specific locations of a host of Indian VIHĀRAS and CAITYAS (P. cetiya). It also offers details on the life and works of AŚOKA, BIMBISĀRA, AJĀTAŚATRU, and other Indian kings as well as information on the missionaries that Aśoka sent throughout South and Southeast Asia. The *Samantapāsādikā* includes an account of the life of the elder MOGGALIPUTTATISSA, compiler of the KATHĀVATTHU in the Pāli ABHIDHAMMAPIṬAKA. The three classifications of vinaya, SUTTA, and abhidhamma piṭakas are also explained by Buddhaghosa in this commentary.

**sāmānyalakṣaṇa**. (T. spyi mtshan; C. gongxiang; J. gūsō; K. kongsang 共相). In Sanskrit, "general characteristic," "generic quality," "shared mark"; a term used in contrast to SVALAKṢAṆA ("specific characteristic," "own mark") to describe qualities that are generic to a class of phenomena, as opposed to those qualities that are unique to a given object. In the SAUTRĀNTIKA school, sāmānyalakṣaṇa refers to the objects of thought (KALPANĀ) that must be apprehended through a mental image and thus lack the specificity of the impermanent objects of direct perception (PRATYAKṢA).

**samāpatti**. (T. snyom 'jug; C. dengzhi/zhengshou; J. tōji/shōju; K. tŭngji/chŏngsu 等至/正受). In Sanskrit and Pāli, "attainment" or "trance," a state of deep concentration produced through the practice of meditation; the term literally means "correct entrance." Specifically, samāpatti refers to eight levels of attainment, which correlate with the eight meditative absorptions (DHYĀNA), the four absorptions of the realm of subtle materiality (RŪPĀVACARADHYĀNA) and the four of the immaterial realm (ĀRŪPYĀVACARADHYĀNA). However, unlike the dhyāna model, samāpatti may also add a ninth attainment, called either the attainment of the cessation of perception and sensation (SAṂJÑĀVEDAYITANIRODHA) or the trance of cessation (NIRODHASAMĀPATTI). The four attainments of the realm of subtle materiality are named for the order in which they occur. Thus, in ascending order, they are the first concentration (prathamadhyāna, P. paṭhamajjhāna), the second concentration (dvitīyadhyāna, P. dutiyajjhāna), the third concentration (tṛtīyadhyāna, P. tatiyajjhāna), and the fourth concentration (caturthadhyāna, P. catutthajjhāna). The four levels of the immaterial realm are the attainment of the sphere of boundless space (ākāśānantyāyatanasamāpatti, P. ākāsānañcāyatanasamāpatti), attainment of the sphere of boundless consciousness (vijñānānantyāyatanasamāpatti, P. viññāṇāñcāyatanasamāpatti), attainment of the sphere of nothingness (ākiñcanyāyatanasamāpatti, P. ākiñcaññāyatanasamāpatti), and attainment of the sphere of neither perception nor nonperception (naivasaṃjñānāsaṃjñāyatanasamāpatti, P. nevasaññānāsaññāyatanasamāpatti). As indicated earlier, a ninth stage, the attainment of the cessation of perception and sensation (saṃjñāvedayitanirodha) or the attainment of cessation (nirodhasamāpatti), is often added to these latter four. These eight or nine states are also known as the "successive dwellings" (anupūrvavihāra). By achieving one of these states of absorption through the practice of meditation while still a human being, one will be reborn in the respective level of these realms of existence in the next lifetime. Similar samāpatti schemes, which present stratified levels of meditative attainment, also appear in non-Buddhist yogic systems. See also ASAṂJÑĀSAMĀPATTI.

**samāpattidhyāna**. (S). See DHYĀNASAMĀPATTI.

**samāropa**. (T. sgro 'dogs; C. zengyi; J. zōyaku; K. chŭngik 增益). In Sanskrit, "superimposition," "reification," or "erroneous affirmation"; the mistaken attribution to an object of a quality that the object does not in fact possess. The term samāropa is sometimes paired with APAVĀDA ("denigration" or "denial"), where samāropa would refer to the claim or belief that something that in fact does not exist, does exist, while apavāda would refer to the claim or belief that something that in fact does exist, does not exist (such as the FOUR NOBLE TRUTHS). In Buddhist philosophy, the most important of such erroneous superimpositions is the attribution of a perduring self (ĀTMAN) to the impermanent aggregates (SKANDHA). In MADHYAMAKA, samāropa refers to the false ascription of intrinsic nature (SVABHĀVA) to phenomena (DHARMA). The purpose of the Madhyamaka critique is to refute these false qualities that have been superimposed by ignorance onto the objects of experience; the conventionally existent objects that serve as the object of these false projections are not refuted. In YOGĀCĀRA, samāropa is often used to refer to the superimposition of objective existence to phenomena that are in fact of the nature of consciousness.

**samatājñāna**. (T. mnyam nyid ye shes; C. pingdengxing zhi; J. byōdōshōchi; K. p'yŏngdŭngsŏng chi 平等性智). In Sanskrit, "wisdom of equality" or "impartial wisdom"; one of the five wisdoms (PAÑCAJÑĀNA) of a buddha. Through the samatājñāna, a buddha sees beyond all superficial distinctions and differentiations and perceives the fundamental nature of all things as emptiness (ŚŪNYATĀ). Thus, a buddha makes no distinction between one sentient being and another, and no distinction between self and other; in addition, no ultimate difference is perceived between SAṂSĀRA and NIRVĀṆA. Such undifferentiated perception gives rise to equality, impartiality, and compassion for all beings. In YOGĀCĀRA theory, samatājñāna is understood to arise through the cessation of attachment to conceptions of self and pride. In TANTRA, among the five buddhas (PAÑCATATHĀGATA), this type of wisdom is associated with RATNASAMBHAVA.

**śamatha**. (P. samatha; T. zhi gnas; C. zhi; J. shi; K. chi 止). In Sanskrit, variously translated as "calmness," "serenity," "quiescence," or "tranquillity" (and sometimes as "stopping," following the Chinese rendering of the term); one of the two major branches of Buddhist meditative cultivation (BHĀVANĀ), along with insight (VIPAŚYANĀ). Calmness is the mental peace and stability that is generated through the cultivation of concentration (SAMĀDHI). Śamatha is defined technically as the specific degree of concentration necessary to generate insight (VIPAŚYANĀ) into reality and thus lead to the destruction of the afflictions (KLEŚA). Śamatha is a more advanced degree of concentration than what is ordinarily associated with the sensuous realm (KĀMADHĀTU) but not fully that of the first meditative absorption (DHYĀNA), viz., the first absorption associated with the subtle-materiality realm (RŪPĀVACARADHYĀNA). According to the YOGĀCĀRABHŪMI and the ABHIDHARMASAMUCCAYA, śamatha is the fundamental state (maula) of each of the four concentrations (dhyāna) and attainments (SAMĀPATTI), in distinction to a neighboring part that is preparatory to that fundamental state (see SĀMANTAKA), which is vipaśyanā. The process of meditative cultivation that culminates in calmness is described in one account as having nine stages. In the account found in the MADHYĀNTAVIBHĀGA, for example, there are eight forces that operate during these stages to eliminate five hindrances: viz., laziness, forgetting the object of concentration, restlessness and worry, insufficient application of antidotes (anabhisaṃskāra), and over-application of the antidotes (abhisaṃskāra). During the initial stage, when first placing the mind on its object, the first hindrance, laziness, is counteracted by a complex of four motivational mental factors: CHANDA (desire-to-do), vyāyāma (resolve), ŚRADDHĀ (faith), and PRAŚRABDHI (pliancy or readiness for the task). When the cultivation of calmness has reached a slightly more advanced stage, mindfulness (SMṚTI) counteracts the forgetfulness that occurs when concentration wanders away from the meditation object. When a stream of concentration is first achieved, a meta-awareness called introspection or clear comprehension (SAṂPRAJANYA) operates to counteract dullness and restlessness. Finally, in the last stages of the process, there is an application (abhisaṃskāra) in order to heighten the intensity of the concentration to the requisite level, and to avoid the subtle overexcitement that comes with feelings of great ease; and just prior to the attainment of śamatha, there is the setting aside of any application of conscious effort. At that point, calmness continues on its own as a natural stream of tranquillity, bringing great physical rapture (PRĪTI) and mental ease (SUKHA) that settles into the advanced state of serenity called śamatha. ¶ In the context of monastic discipline, śamatha, in its denotation as calming, is also used technically to refer to the formal settlement of monastic disputes. See ADHIKARAṆAŚAMATHA; SAPTĀDHIKARAṆAŚAMATHA.

**śamathavipaśyanā**. (P. samathavipassanā; T. zhi gnas lhag mthong; C. zhiguan; J. shikan; K. chigwan 止觀). In Sanskrit, "calmness and insight," a term used to describe a meditative state that combines the clarity and stability of ŚAMATHA with the understanding of the nature of reality associated with VIPAŚYANĀ. In Indian ŚĀSTRA literature, vipaśyanā is defined as insight into reality that is conjoined with śamatha and induced by analytical meditation. Thus, true vipaśyanā includes śamatha. The combination of śamatha and vipaśyanā marks the attainment of the wisdom arisen from reflection (CINTĀMAYĪPRAJÑĀ); and the combination of the two with emptiness (ŚŪNYATĀ) as their object marks the beginning of the path of preparation (PRAYOGAMĀRGA). In YOGĀCĀRA accounts, as in the YOGĀCĀRABHŪMI and the ABHIDHARMASAMUCCAYA, the four concentrations (DHYĀNA) and attainments (SAMĀPATTI) are said to have two parts: a fundamental state (maula), which is śamatha, and a neighboring part that is preparatory to that fundamental state (SĀMANTAKA), which is vipaśyanā; this explanation suggests the vital interconnection between these two terms. Samatha and vipassanā are known in Pāli, but chiefly in a later stratum of the suttas and in commentarial literature. The terms are also important in Chinese Buddhism, serving for example as the subject of the magnum opus of TIANTAI ZHIYI, the MOHE ZHIGUAN, or the "Great Calmness and Insight."

**samaya**. (T. dam tshig; C. sanmoye; J. sanmaya; K. sammaya 三摩耶). In Sanskrit and Pāli, "vow," "occasion," a polysemous term within the tradition. This term is especially important in tantric Buddhism, where it refers to a specific set of vows (see SAṂVARA) taken in conjunction with an initiation rite (ABHIṢEKA, dīkṣā). These vows are considered to represent a powerful bond between student and teacher and a commitment to maintain them is deemed essential to success in tantric practice. A breech of one's samaya vows is often said to have serious consequences, including rebirth in hell. Pledging to keep tantric practices secret and pledging never to bring harm to one's teacher are two examples of a samaya vow. A student of tantra will often take more and more of these vows as he or she progresses. In the Tibetan categorization of tantras into four sets, these vows are systematized into codes. In ANUTTARAYOGATANTRA, there is a set list of nineteen samayas associated with the PAÑCATATHĀGATA. The term samaya may also refer to the symbolic representation of a buddha, BODHISATTVA, or deity, such as with a VAJRA, a sword, or a lotus flower. These symbols may represent the divinity itself or more often an attribute of that divinity, such as a vow taken by a buddha or bodhisattva. ¶ In Sanskrit, samaya also indicates a general unit of time that is understood as one specific occasion or as a season of the year. The term samaya is often seen in ABHIDHARMA analyses of distinct chronological moments. For example, in the AṬṬHASĀLINĪ, a Pāli commentary on the DHAMMASAṄGAṆI, BUDDHAGHOSA analyzes the term samaya into five specific meanings related to the passage of time.

**Samayabhedoparacanacakra**. (T. Gzhung tha dad pa rim par bklag pa'i 'khor lo; C. Yibuzonglun lun; J. Ibushūrinron; K. Ibujongnyun non 異部宗輪論). In Sanskrit, "The Wheel of the Formations of Divisions of the Doctrine"; the title of an important historiographical text written by VASUMITRA, a prominent scholar of the SARVĀSTIVĀDA school, who wrote in KASHMIR sometime around the second century CE. The text records the Sarvāstivāda account of the evolution of the various schools (NIKĀYA) that arose in the mainstream Buddhist community in the years after the Buddha's death. Thus, it is an important source of information on the schools and subschools of mainstream Nikāya Buddhism in ancient India. In VASUMITRA's version, the divisions in the Buddhist sects occur roughly one hundred years later than they do in the Sinhalese Pāli records of the same events. According to Vasumitra, the major disagreement that led to the first major schism in the SAṂGHA was the result of five propositions put forward by the monk MAHĀDEVA concerning the nature and achievements of an ARHAT. The MAHĀSĀṂGHIKA agreed with Mahādeva's five theses, while the STHAVIRANIKĀYA did not, thus leading to the split.

**samayamudrā**. (T. dam tshig gi phyag rgya; C. sanmoye yin; J. sanmayain; K. sammaya in 三摩耶印). In Sanskrit, "seal of the vow," "seal of time," or "seal of the symbol," all three denotations related to objects of meditation in tantric Buddhism. The samayamudrā is usually listed as the third of four "seals" (MUDRĀ), "seal" here being used in the sense of a doorway through which one must pass in order to attain full realization; the other three are the KARMAMUDRĀ, the JÑĀNAMUDRĀ, and the MAHĀMUDRĀ. In the context of sexual yoga, the term is also used to refer to a tantric consort who maintains the tantric pledges, as opposed to a karmamudrā (a consort who does not maintain such pledges) and a jñānamudrā (a consort who is not a physical person but is visualized in meditation). As "seal of the vow," the samayamudrā involves sustained focus on one's intention to keep a specific set of vows received as part of one's initiation (ABHIṢEKA, dīkṣā) into tantric practice. As "seal of time," samaya carries its temporal denotation and the meditation involves an abandonment of past and future for the sake of a sustained experience of the present moment. As "seal of the symbol," the object of attention is a symbolic representation of various aspects of a buddha, BODHISATTVA, or deity.

**samayasattva**. (T. dam tshig sems dpa'; C. sanmeiye saduo; J. sanmayasatta; K. sammaeya salt'a 三昧耶薩埵). In Sanskrit, "pledge being," an important element in tantric visualization. Prior to inviting a deity to appear, the meditator visualizes the body of the deity. This visualized image is called the "pledge being." The actual deity, called the "wisdom deity" (JÑĀNASATTVA), is then invited to descend into and fuse with the visualized form. In this context, the term SAMAYA may be understood in two different ways. First, the term is synonymous with "conventional," indicating that the visualized body of the deity is not his or her actual body. The term samaya is also understood to indicate the practitioner's "vow" or "pledge" to undertake those practices that will evoke the actual presence of the deity. When the meditator visualizes himself or herself as the deity, the initial visualization is the "pledge being." In some tantric circles, the term samayasattva is also used to indicate one who has been newly initiated into esoteric practice.

**samayavimukta**. (T. dus kyis rnam par grol ba; C. shi jietuo; J. jigedatsu; K. si haet'al 時解脫). In Sanskrit, "one liberated dependent upon a specific occasion"; one of the twenty members of the ĀRYASAṂGHA (see VIṂŚATIPRABHEDASAṂGHA). The term refers to an ARHAT who is a ŚRADDHĀNUSĀRIN and who, because of weaker faculties, has limited periods of meditative concentration during which it is possible to achieve NIRVĀṆA.

**śambhala**. (T. bde 'byung). Often spelled Shambhala. In the texts associated with the KĀLACAKRATANTRA, the kingdom of śambhala is said to be located north of the Himālayan range. It is a land devoted to the practice of the *Kālacakratantra*, which the Buddha himself had entrusted to śambhala's king SUCANDRA, who had requested that the Buddha set forth the tantra. The kingdom of śambhala is shaped like a giant lotus and is filled with sandalwood forests and lotus lakes, all encircled by a massive range of snowy peaks. In the center of the kingdom is the capital, Kalapa, where the luster of the palaces, made from gold, silver, and jewels, outshines the moon; the walls of the palaces are plated with mirrors that reflect a light so bright that night is like day. In the very center of the city is the MAṆḌALA of the buddha Kālacakra. The inhabitants of the 960 million villages of śambhala are ruled by a beneficent king, called the Kalkin. The laypeople are all beautiful and wealthy, free of sickness and poverty; the monks maintain their precepts without the slightest infraction. They are naturally intelligent and virtuous, devoted to the practice of the VAJRAYĀNA, although all authentic forms of Indian Buddhism are preserved. The majority of those reborn there attain buddhahood during their lifetime in śambhala. The *Kālacakratantra* also predicts an apocalyptic war. In the year 2425 CE, the barbarians (generally identified as Muslims) and demons who have destroyed

Buddhism in India will set out to invade śambhala. The twenty-fifth Kalkin, Raudracakrin, will lead his armies out of his kingdom and into India, where they will meet the forces of evil in a great battle, from which the forces of Buddhism will emerge victorious. The victory will usher in a golden age in which human life span will increase, crops will grow without being cultivated, and the entire population of the earth will devote itself to the practice of Buddhism. Given the importance of the *Kālacakratantra* in Tibetan Buddhism, śambhala figures heavily in Tibetan Buddhist belief and practice; in the DGE LUGS sect, it is said that the PAṆ CHEN LAMAS are reborn as kings of śambhala. There is also a genre of guidebooks (lam yig) that provide the route to śambhala. The location of śambhala has long been a subject of fascination in the West. Śambhala plays an important role in the Theosophy of HELENA PETROVNA BLAVATSKY, and the Russian Theosophist Nicholas Roerich led two expeditions in search of śambhala. The name śambhala is considered the likely inspiration of "Shangri-La," described in James Hilton's 1933 novel *Lost Horizon*.

**saṃbhāra**. (T. tshogs; C. ziliang; J. shiryō; K. charyang 資糧). In Sanskrit, "equipment," requisite," "accumulation." This term is used to indicate those qualities that are necessary for the realization of some religious attainment, usually progress along the path to enlightenment. For example, in a common formulation of the stages of the path that successively lead one to enlightenment, the SAṂBHĀRAMĀRGA, or "path of accumulation," is the first of the five paths (PAÑCAMĀRGA). On this path, the practitioner attains a degree of three prerequisite qualities that must be developed before one can begin to undertake the religious life: morality (ŚĪLA), merit (PUṆYA), and concentration (SAMĀDHI). Similarly, MAHĀYĀNA literature cites merit (puṇya) and knowledge (JÑĀNA) as the saṃbhāra, or "equipment," of the BODHISATTVA. In this sense, the term saṃbhāra is also understood to indicate "accumulation" in that it is amassing these qualities that brings about progress on the path. See also BODHISAṂBHĀRA.

**saṃbhāramārga**. (T. tshogs lam; C. ziliang dao; J. shiryōdō; K. charyang to 資糧道). In Sanskrit, "path of accumulation" or "path of equipment"; the first of two parts of the preparatory adhimukticaryābhūmi, literally, "level of belief performance" (see ADHIMOKṢA); the first of the five paths (PAÑCAMĀRGA), which begins the accumulations of merit and wisdom necessary to achieve NIRVĀṆA or BODHI, respectively, on the ŚRĀVAKA, PRATYEKABUDDHA, or BODHISATTVA paths. The path of accumulation is said to begin with the authentic wish to achieve the goal of one's path, viz., with NIRVEDA (P. nibbidā) (i.e., disgust for SAṂSĀRA) in the case of those who wish for nirvāṇa, and with the development of BODHICITTA (the aspiration to enlightenment) in the case of those suited for the Mahāyāna. In the first pañcamārga model, the path of accumulation, like the path of preparation (PRAYOGAMĀRGA) that follows it, is not a noble path of a noble being (ĀRYA) because the direct perception of reality does not occur there. The saṃbhāramārga is subdivided into the three stages of small, middling, and large: at the first stage, the cultivation of the four applications of mindfulness (SMṚTYUPASTHĀNA) is primary, at the second the four resolves (PRAHĀṆA), and at the third the four legs of miraculous attainment (ṚDDHIPĀDA). In Mahāyāna ABHIDHARMA, the first level of the path of accumulation is exemplified by earth because it is the ground for all good qualities. The second level is exemplified by gold because from that time on the aspiration to reach enlightenment will not change to anything baser; a bodhisattva is no longer capable of retrogressing from the Mahāyāna and gains an initial capacity to hear the voice of an actual buddha through the achievement of the SROTO'NUGATO NĀMA SAMĀDHIḤ. On the third level of the path of accumulation, the bodhisattva is able to see the NIRMĀṆAKĀYA of buddhas directly and receive teachings from them.

**saṃbhinnapralāpāt prativirati**. (P. samphappalāpā paṭivirata; T. ngag 'khyal ba spong ba; C. bu qiyu; J. fukigo; K. pul kiŏ 不綺語). In Sanskrit, "[the monk] abstains from idle chatter," one of ten wholesome (KUŚALA) ways of action (see KARMAPATHA); it refers to the effort or vow to abstain from speech that is either nonsensical or unwholesome. As a moral offense, speaking idly or nonsensically is of greater or lesser severity depending upon how often one engages in it. According to the CŪḶAHATTHIPADOPAMASUTTA in the Pāli MAJJHIMANIKĀYA, one who abstains from idle chatter instead speaks at the right time (kālavādī), speaks only of facts (bhūtavādī), speaks of the goal (atthavādī), speaks of the teaching (dhammavādī), and speaks of religious discipline (vinayavādī).

**saṃbhogakāya**. (T. longs spyod rdzogs pa'i sku; C. baoshen; J. hōjin; K. posin 報身). In Sanskrit, "enjoyment body" or "reward body"; in the MAHĀYĀNA, the second of the three bodies of a buddha (TRIKĀYA), along with the body of reality (DHARMAKĀYA) and the transformation body (NIRMĀṆAKĀYA). The saṃbhogakāya is described as simultaneously a body for one's own enjoyment (C. zi shouyong shen), in which the buddha knows the joy that comes from experiencing the dharma for oneself; and a body for others' enjoyment (C. ta shouyong shen), in which advanced bodhisattvas experience the increasing magnificence of the buddha's grandeur as they continue to move up the bodhisattva path (MĀRGA). The saṃbhogakāya buddha is adorned with all the accoutrements that are received as rewards for his advanced spiritual experience, which are only visible to similarly advanced beings, specifically bodhisattvas at the first bodhisattva stage (BODHISATTVABHŪMI) and upwards who are dwelling in buddha-fields (BUDDHAKṢETRA). Lesser beings, such as humans, are only able to view the manifestation body (nirmāṇakāya) of a buddha, not his saṃbhogakāya. In bipartite divisions of the buddhas' bodies as a flesh body (RŪPAKĀYA) and a body of reality (dharmakāya), the saṃbhogakāya and nirmāṇakāya are subsumed within the rūpakāya. A saṃbhogakāya is defined by five certainties: it will always be in an AKANIṢṬHA heaven, it will always teach Mahāyāna doctrine, it will always last until the end of SAṂSĀRA, it will always be surrounded exclusively by bodhisattvas who have reached the bodhisattva bhūmis, and it will always be endowed with the thirty-two major and eighty minor marks of a great person (see MAHĀPURUṢALAKṢAṆA).

**saṃbodhi**. (T. rdzogs pa'i byang chub; C. zhengjue; J. shōgaku; K. chŏnggak 正覺). In Sanskrit, "complete enlightenment" or "full awakening," a synonym for buddhahood. See ANUTTARASAMYAKSAṂBODHI; MAHĀBODHI.

**sambo sach'al**. (三寶寺刹). In Korean, "three-jewel monasteries"; three major Korean monasteries that by tradition represent one of the three jewels (RATNATRAYA) of Buddhism: T'ONGDOSA, the Buddha jewel monastery (Pulbo sach'al), because of its ordination platform and the relics (K. sari; S. ŚARĪRA) of the Buddha enshrined behind its main shrine hall (TAEUNG CHŎN); HAEINSA, the DHARMA-jewel monastery (Pŏppo sach'al), because it preserves the xylographs of the Korean Buddhist canon (KORYŎ TAEJANGGYŎNG); and SONGGWANGSA, the SAṂGHA-jewel monastery (Sŭngbo sach'al), because of the series of state preceptors (K. kuksa; C. GUOSHI) during the Koryŏ dynasty who practiced at the monastery.

**Saṃcayagāthāprajñāpāramitā**. (S). See RATNAGUṆASAMCAYAGĀTHĀ.

**Saṃdhinirmocanasūtra**. (T. Mdo sde dgongs 'grel; C. Jieshenmi jing; J. Gejinmikkyō; K. Haesimmil kyŏng 解深密經). In Sanskrit, variously interpreted to mean the sūtra "Unfurling the Real Meaning," "Explaining the Thought," or "Unraveling the Bonds"; one of the most important Mahāyāna sūtras, especially for the YOGĀCĀRA school. The sūtra is perhaps most famous for its delineation of the three turnings of the wheel of the dharma (DHARMACAKRAPRAVARTANA), which would become an influential schema for classifying the teachings of the Buddha. The sūtra has ten chapters. The first four chapters deal with the nature of the ultimate (PARAMĀRTHA) and how it is to be understood. The fifth chapter discusses the nature of consciousness, including the storehouse consciousness (ĀLAYAVIJÑĀNA) where predispositions (VĀSANĀ) are deposited and ripen. The sixth chapter discusses the three natures (TRISVABHĀVA). In the seventh chapter, the division of the Buddha's teachings into the provisional (NEYĀRTHA) and the definitive (NĪTĀRTHA) is set forth. The eighth chapter explains how to develop ŚAMATHA and VIPAŚYANĀ. The ninth chapter describes the ten bodhisattva BHŪMIS and the final chapter describes the nature of buddhahood. Each of these chapters contains important passages that are cited in subsequent commentaries and treatises. ¶ Perhaps the most influential of all the sūtra's chapters is the seventh, which discusses the three turnings of the wheel of the dharma (dharmacakrapravartana). There, the bodhisattva Paramārthasamudgata explains that the first turning of the wheel had occurred at ṚṢIPATANA (the Deer Park at SĀRNĀTH), where the Buddha had taught the FOUR NOBLE TRUTHS to those of the ŚRĀVAKA ("listener, disciple") vehicle. This first turning of the wheel is called the CATUḤSATYADHARMACAKRA, the "dharma wheel of the four truths." The bodhisattva says, "This wheel of dharma turned by the Buddha is surpassable, an occasion [for refutation], provisional, and subject to dispute." Referring presumably to the perfection of wisdom (PRAJÑĀPĀRAMITĀ) sūtras, the bodhisattva then goes on to explain that the Buddha then turned the wheel of dharma a second time for those who had entered the Mahāyāna, teaching them the doctrine of emptiness (ŚŪNYATĀ), that phenomena are "unproduced, unextinguished, originally quiescent, and inherently beyond sorrow." Commentators would call this second turning of the wheel the ALAKṢAṆADHARMACAKRA, "the dharma wheel of signlessness." But this wheel also is provisional. The Buddha finally turned the wheel of doctrine a third time for those of all vehicles, clearly differentiating how things exist. "This wheel of doctrine turned by the BHAGAVAT is unsurpassed, not an occasion [for refutation], of definitive meaning; it is indisputable." Commentators would call this third turning of the wheel the PARAMĀRTHAVINIŚCAYADHARMACAKRA, "the dharma wheel for ascertaining the ultimate"; it is also called "the dharma wheel that makes a fine delineation" (*SUVIBHAKTADHARMACAKRA). The sūtra thus takes something of an historical perspective on the Buddha's teaching, declaring both that his first sermon on the four noble truths addressed to śrāvakas and his teaching of the perfection of wisdom addressed to bodhisattvas was not his final and most clearly delineated view. That consummate view, his true intention, is found in the third turning of the wheel of dharma, a wheel that includes, at very least, the *Saṃdhinirmocanasūtra* itself. The *Saṃdhinirmocanasūtra* was translated into Chinese four times: by GUṆABHADRA, BODHIRUCI, PARAMĀRTHA, and XUANZANG. Of these recensions, the translations by Bodhiruci and Xuanzang are complete renderings of the sūtra and circulated most widely within the East Asian tradition; the other two renderings were shorter digests of the sūtra.

**saṃdhyābhāṣyā**. (S). See SANDHYĀBHĀṢĀ.

**saṃgha**. (P. saṅgha; T. dge 'dun; C. sengqie; J. sōgya; K. sŭngga 僧伽). A BUDDHIST HYBRID SANSKRIT term, generally translated as "community" or "order," it is the term most commonly used to refer to the order of Buddhist monks and nuns. (The classical Sanskrit and Pāli of this term is saṅgha, a form often seen in Western writings on Buddhism; this dictionary uses saṃgha as the generic and nonsectarian Buddhist Hybrid Sanskrit form.) The term literally means "that which is struck together well," suggesting something that is solid and not easily broken apart. In ancient India, the term originally meant a "guild," and the different offices in the saṃgha were guild terms: e.g., ĀCĀRYA, which originally meant a "guild master," was adopted in Buddhism to refer to a teacher or preceptor of neophytes to the monastic community. The Buddhist saṃgha began with the ordination of the first monks, the "group of five" (PAÑCAVARGIKA) to whom the Buddha delivered his first sermon, when he turned the wheel of the dharma (DHARMACAKRAPRAVARTANA) at SĀRNĀTH. At that time, there was no formal ordination ceremony; the Buddha simply used the EHIBHIKṢUKĀ formula, lit. "Come, monk," to welcome someone who had joined the order. The order grew as rival teachers were converted, bringing their disciples with them. Eventually, a more formal ritual of ordination (UPASAṂPADĀ) was developed. In addition, as circumstances warranted, the Buddha slowly began making rules to organize the daily life of the community as a whole and its individual members (see VINAYA). Although it seems that in the early years, the Buddha and his followers wandered without fixed dwellings, donors eventually provided places for them to spend the rainy season (see VARṢĀ) and the shelters there evolved into monasteries (VIHĀRA). A saṃgha came to be defined as a group of monks who lived within a particular geographical boundary (SĪMĀ) and who gathered fortnightly (see UPOṢADHA) to recite the monastic code (PRĀTIMOKṢA). That group had to consist of at least ten monks in a central region and five monks in more remote regions. In the centuries after the passing of the Buddha, variations developed over what constituted this code, leading to the formation of "fraternities" or NIKĀYAs; the tradition typically recognizes eighteen such groups as belonging to the MAINSTEAM BUDDHIST SCHOOLS, but there were clearly more. ¶ There is much discussion in Buddhist literature on the question of what constitutes the saṃgha, especially the saṃgha that is the third of the three jewels (RATNATRAYA), to which Buddhists go for refuge (ŚARAṆA). One of the oldest categories is the eightfold saṃgha, composed only of those who have reached a certain level of spiritual attainment. The eight are four groups of two, in each case one who is approaching and one who has attained one of the four ranks of stream-enterer, or SROTAĀPANNA; once-returner, or SAKṚDĀGĀMIN; nonreturner, or ANĀGĀMIN; and worthy one, or ARHAT. This is the saṃgha of the saṃgha jewel, and is sometimes referred to as the ĀRYASAṂGHA, or "noble saṃgha." A later and more elaborate category expanded this group of eight to a group of twenty, called the VIṂŚATIPRABHEDASAṂGHA, or "twenty-member saṃgha," based on their different faculties (INDRIYA) and the ways in which they reach NIRVĀṆA; this subdivision appears especially in MAHĀYĀNA works, particularly in the PRAJÑĀPĀRAMITĀ literature. Whether eight or twenty, it is this group of noble persons (ĀRYAPUDGALA) who are described as worthy of gifts (dakṣiṇīyapudgala). Those noble persons who are also ordained are sometimes referred to as the "ultimate saṃgha" (PARAMĀRTHASAṂGHA) as distinguished from the "conventional saṃgha" (SAṂVṚTISAMGHA), which is composed of the ordained monks and nuns who are still ordinary persons (PṚTHAGJANA). In a still broader sense, the term is sometimes used for a fourfold group, composed of monks (BHIKṢU), nuns (BHIKṢUṆĪ), lay male disciples (UPĀSAKA), and lay female disciples (UPĀSIKĀ). However, this fourfold group is more commonly called PARIṢAD ("followers" or "congregation"), suggesting that the term saṃgha is more properly used to refer to the ordained community. In common parlance, however, especially in the West, saṃgha has come to connote any community of Buddhists, whether monastic or lay, or a combination of the two. In the long history of Buddhism, however, the presence or absence of the Buddhist dispensation (ŚĀSANA) has traditionally been measured by the presence or absence of ordained monks who virtuously maintain their precepts. In the history of many Buddhist lands, the establishment of Buddhism is marked by the founding of the first monastery and the ordination of the first monks into the saṃgha. See also SAṂGHABHEDA; SAMMUTISAṄGHA; ĀRYAPUDGALA; SŬNGT'ONG; SAṄGHARĀJA.

**Saṃgha Administration Act**. See SAṄGHA ADMINISTRATION ACT.

**Saṃghabhadra**. (T. 'Dus bzang; C. Zhongxian; J. Shugen; K. Chunghyŏn 衆賢) (c. fifth century CE). In Sanskrit, "Auspicious to the Community"; the proper name of an influential Indian master of the VAIBHĀṢIKA school of SARVĀSTIVĀDA ABHIDHARMA. Historical sources suggest that Saṃghabhadra hailed from KASHMIR and was a younger contemporary of his principal rival VASUBANDHU. The historical records of XUANZANG and PARAMĀRTHA agree that Saṃghabhadra publicly challenged Vasubandhu to debate, but his challenge was never accepted. Saṃghabhadra's most famous works include the *NYĀYĀNUSĀRA, or "Conformity with Correct Principle," and the **Abhidharmasamayapradīpikā* (C. Xianzong lun), or "Exposition of Accepted Doctrine." The **Nyāyānusāra* is both a clarification of the ABHIDHARMA philosophy of the Vaibhāṣika school and a critical commentary on the presentation found in Vasubandhu's ABHIDHARMAKOŚABHĀṢYA. The later *Samayapradīpikā* is a shorter explanation of the doctrines of the Vaibhāṣikas, which in large measure summarizes the positions explored in the **Nyāyānusāra*. Neither of these works survives in their Sanskrit originals but only in their Chinese translations. Saṃghabhadra's defense of Kashmir Sarvāstivāda-Vaibhāṣika positions ushered in the neo-Vaibhāṣika period of Sarvāstivāda thought, which took the **Nyāyānusāra* and the *Samayapradīpikā* as its main texts.

**saṃghabheda**. (P. saṅghabheda; T. dge 'dun gyi dbyen byed pa; C. poseng; J. hasō; K. p'asŭng 破僧). In Sanskrit, "splitting the community"; the act of causing a schism in the community of Buddhist monks and nuns (SAṂGHA). Technically, a schism occurs when nine or more fully ordained monks separate themselves from the order; a faction of less than nine monks constitutes a "dissension" (saṃgharāji) rather than a schism. These schisms may occur over disagreements in the teachings (DHARMA) or details of monastic life (VINAYA). The ABHIDHARMAMAHĀVIBHĀṢĀ distinguishes two different types of saṃghabheda, one in which there are two separate saṃghas established within a single SĪMĀ boundary, the second in which a group attempts to establish a new dispensation with a different teacher. The first and most infamous example of this latter type of schism is the one caused by Buddha's cousin DEVADATTA, who declared that he, and not GAUTAMA, was the real master and that his five practices were the correct dispensation. After failing in his attempts to take Gautama's life, Devadatta convinced a group of monks in the city of VAIŚĀLĪ that the asceticism advocated by Gautama and his followers was not rigorous enough; five hundred monks chose to enlist in Devadatta's new order. The act of causing or encouraging such a rift in the saṃgha is presented as the worst of the five "uninterrupted deeds" (ĀNANTARYAKARMAN) and is so heinous that it guarantees the perpetrator a KALPA-long lifetime in AVĪCI—the worst of the various Buddhist hells. According to the *Abhidharmamahāvibhāṣā*, the consequences of saṃghabheda are so odious that if the malefactor's sentence in hell has not been completed by the time of the annihilation accompanying the end of the kalpa, he will be reborn into another world-system's hell to complete his term. The seriousness of the saṃghabheda offense is also demonstrated by the fact that King AŚOKA himself warns against it in one of his rock edicts. Therein, he states that any monk who causes schism should be cast from the monastery and returned to the status of a layman. Despite this censure, the Buddhist tradition is full of instances of such divisions in the monastic community. As Buddhism spread through India, a host of different schools (NIKĀYA) emerged, some based on significant doctrinal distinctions, others on regional variations in monastic and ritual observances. Texts that document the proceedings of the third Buddhist council (SAṂGĪTI, see COUNCIL, THIRD), which occurred sometime around 250 BCE, list eighteen to twenty major schools.

**saṃghakarman**. (P. saṅghakamma; T. dge 'dun gyi las; C. seng jiemo; J. sōkonma; K. sŭng kalma 僧羯磨). In Sanskrit, an "ecclesiastical act," such as admission into the order as novices (PRAVRAJITĀ), full ordination of monks and nuns (UPASAMPADĀ); the fortnightly confession ceremony recitation of the PRĀTIMOKṢA (UPOṢADHA), the ceremony closing the rains retreat (PRAVĀRAṆĀ), giving cloth for robes (KAṬHINA), the adjudication of rules, the administration of punishments to transgressors of the precepts, and the settlement of disputes among the clergy. See KARMAN.

**saṃgharājan**. (S). See SAṄGHARĀJA.

**saṃghāta**. (P. saṅghāta; T. bsdus 'joms; C. zhonghe [diyu]; J. shugō[jigoku]; K. chunghap [chiok] 衆合[地獄]). In Sanskrit, lit. "crushing"; the name of the third of eight stratified hot hells that are detailed in many Buddhist cosmological models. The Sanskrit term saṃghāta has a variety of meanings and the exact nature and method of the torment experienced in this hell varies from source to source. One of its meanings is "crushing" and thus saṃghāta is often rendered in English as the "crushing hell." Creatures unfortunate enough to be reborn in this destiny are commonly described as being continually crushed together between mountain ranges. Alternatively, they may be crushed by iron rollers, plates, and even iron elephants that come at them from the four directions while they are trapped waist-deep in a thick sheet of iron. This form of the saṃghāta hell is most often associated with sexual misconduct. However, the *Sadgatikārikā* describes saṃghāta in altogether different terms. It takes the Sanskrit term saṃghāta as meaning "heap" or "collection," and beings reborn in that hell are piled into heaps and slaughtered together as punishment for having killed living creatures.

**saṃghāṭī**. (P. saṅghāṭi; T. snam sbyar; C. sengqieli/dayi; J. sōgyari/daie; K. sŭnggari/taeŭi 僧伽梨/大衣). In Sanskrit, "outer robe"; the largest of the "three robes" (TRICĪVARA) worn by a monk or nun, along with the "lower robe" or waistcloth (S. ANTARVĀSAS, P. antaravāsaka), and the upper robe (S. UTTARĀSAṂGA, P. uttarāsaṅga). This particular robe was in two layers and was required to be tailored in patches, numbering from nine up to twenty-five, depending on the account in the various VINAYA recensions. This use of patches of cloth is said to have been modeled after plots of farmland in MAGADHA that the Buddha once surveyed. See also CĪVARA; KĀṢĀYA.

**saṃghātiśeṣa**. (S). See SAṂGHĀVAŚEṢA.

**Saṃghavarman**. (C. Sengqiebamo; J. Sōgyabatsuma; K. Sŭnggabalma 僧伽跋摩) (fl. c. fifth century). Sanskrit proper name of an Indian monk who in 433 presided over the first ordination of nuns (BHIKṢUṆĪ) in China performed according to the correct ecclesiastical act (SAṂGHAKARMAN) of the VINAYA. At this time, SENGGUO and over three hundred other nuns were ordained with both an assembly of monks and an assembly of nuns in attendance, thereby officially instituting the monastic order for women in China. Saṃghavarman also translated DHARMATRĀTA II's SAṂYUKTĀBHIDHARMAHṚDAYA into Chinese. See SENGGUO.

**saṃghāvaśeṣa**. [alt. saṃghātiśeṣa] (P. saṅghādisesa; T. dge 'dun lhag ma; C. sengcanzui/sengcanfa; J. sōzanzai/sōzanhō; K. sŭngjanjoe/sŭngjanpŏp 僧殘罪/僧殘法). In Sanskrit, "probationary offense"; a category of offenses in the roster of monastic rules (PRĀTIMOKṢA) that require penance and/or probation. The saṃghāvaśeṣa offenses are the second most serious category of offense in the VINAYA, second only to the "defeats" (PĀRĀJIKA), which render a monk or nun "not in communion" (ASAṂVĀSA) with the community. A saṃghāvaśeṣa infraction requires either an open confession of the offense before a gathering of monks or else expulsion from the order (SAṂGHA) if the offender refuses to confess. According to one paranomastic gloss, because the remedy for these offenses requires the intervention of the saṃgha at both the beginning (ādi) and the end (śeṣa) of the expiation process, these offenses are known collectively as saṃghādiśeṣa. The probationary offender receives two different kinds of punishments: penance (MĀNATVA) and temporary probation (PARIVĀSA). The mānatva penance is imposed on a monk who commits a saṃghāvaśeṣa offense when that monk immediately confesses the infraction to another monk. In the Pāli vinaya, the penance imposed in this circumstance is called "penance for unconcealed offenses" (apaṭicchannamānatta), which entails the loss of the usual privileges of monkhood for a set period of six nights. If a monk instead conceals a saṃghāvaśeṣa offense for a period of time before confessing it, he must undergo a "probationary penance" called either parivāsa or, in Pāli, "penance for concealed offenses" (paṭicchannamānatta). This probationary penance likewise entails the loss of privileges, but in this case that probation must last for as long as the offense was concealed. After the parivāsa penance is completed, the monk must then undergo mānatta penance for six nights. These penances are similar in some vinaya traditions to those meted out to "pārājika penitents" (ŚIKṢĀDATTAKA). During his probationary period, the offender is stripped of his seniority and expected to observe certain social constraints. For example, the VINAYAPIṬAKA states that such offenders may not leave the monastery grounds without being accompanied by at least four monks (BHIKṢU) who are not themselves on probation. Also, every day of his probation, the offending monk must inform the other monks of the offense for which he is being punished. The exact number of precepts that fall under the category of saṃghāvaśeṣa varies somewhat among the different vinaya traditions; a typical list of thirteen rules for monks includes (1) willingly emitting semen, (2) engaging in lustful physical contact with a woman, (3) using sexually inappropriate language toward a woman, (4) praising sexual intercourse as a religious act, (5) acting as the liaison in the arrangement of a marriage, (6) building a personal hut that is larger than the prescribed dimensions, (7) building a monastery (VIHĀRA) for the community that does not meet the prescribed specifications, (8) falsely and maliciously accusing another monk of an infraction, (9) taking up an issue as a ploy to falsely accuse another monk of an infraction, (10) taking any action that may result in a schism within the community (SAṂGHABHEDA), (11) siding with or following a monk who has created a schism in the order, (12) refusing to acknowledge and to heed the admonishments of training given by other monks, and finally (13) corrupting families. Nuns are typically subject to seventeen rules, including a few additional restrictions enumerated in the *bhikṣuṇīprātimokṣa*. After completing the parivāsa penance and his six nights of mānatva, the monk approaches the saṃgha, which in this case means a quorum of monks consisting of at least twenty members, and requests to be "called back into community" (S. ABHYĀYANA, P. abbhāna). If the saṃgha agrees, the monk is declared free of the saṃghāvaśeṣa offense and is restored to his former status.

**saṃgīti**. (P. saṅgīti; T. bka' bsdu; C. jieji; J. ketsujū; K. kyŏlchip 結集). In Sanskrit, "chant," "recitation," and, by extension, "council." The term is used to refer to both the recitation of scripture and a communal gathering of monks held for the purpose of such recitation; for this reason, the term is often translated as "council," or "synod," such as the first council, second council, etc., following the death of the Buddha. These councils were held to resolve questions of orthodoxy and typically involved the recitation and redaction of the Buddhist canon (TRIPIṬAKA). At such Buddhist councils, the Buddhist canon was communally rehearsed, agreed upon, and codified; in the Pāli account, the same procedure was followed for redacting the exegetical commentaries, called AṬṬHAKATHĀ. In this same Pāli narrative, a saṃgīti was convened at the conclusion of a successful purification of the dispensation (P. sāsanavisodhana) in which false monks and heretics are expelled, schism healed, and the SAṂGHA reunified. A saṃgīti is conducted by representatives of that newly purified saṃgha, who in a public forum unanimously affirm the authority of a common canon. For a detailed description of the major councils, see COUNCIL (s.v.). ¶ The term saṃgīti may also be used to refer to the "recitation" of a specific scripture itself. A famous such text is the MAÑJUŚRĪNĀMASAṂGĪTI or "Recitation of the Names of Mañjuśrī."

**saṃgītikāra**. [alt. saṃgītikāraka] (T. bka' sdud pa po; C. jiejizhe; J. ketsujūsha; K. kyŏlchipcha 結集者). In Sanskrit, "rapporteur," the person who recites a discourse that they have heard spoken by the Buddha, e.g., the "I" in "thus have I heard" (EVAṂ MAYĀ ŚRUTAM). This person is typically identified as ĀNANDA (for the SŪTRAPIṬAKA) or UPĀLI (for the VINAYAPIṬAKA), but the identity of the saṃgītikāra became a topic of discussion in the MAHĀYĀNA, which asserted that the Buddha also delivered discourses outside the physical presence or mental comprehension of Ānanda. In those cases, the saṃgītikāra was usually a BODHISATTVA, such as MAÑJUŚRĪ.

**Saṃgītiparyāya[pādaśāstra]**. (T. 'Gro ba'i rnam grangs; C. Jiyimen zulun; J. Shūimonsokuron; K. Chibimun chok non 集異門足論). In Sanskrit, "Treatise on Pronouncements," one of the earliest books of the SARVĀSTIVĀDA ABHIDHARMAPIṬAKA; it is traditionally listed as the last of the six ancillary texts, or "feet" (pāda), of the JÑĀNAPRASTHĀNA, the central treatise, or body (śarīra), of the Sarvāstivāda abhidharmapiṭaka. The text is a commentary on the *Saṃgītisūtra* ("Discourse on Communal Recitation"; see SAṄGĪTISUTTA) and is attributed either to Mahākauṣṭhila (according to YAŚOMITRA and BU STON) or to ŚĀRIPUTRA (according to Chinese tradition). Following closely the structure of the *Saṃgītisūtra*, the author sets out a series of dharma lists (MĀTṚKĀ), given sequentially from ones to tens, to organize the Buddha's teachings systematically. The sets of twos, for example, cover name and form (NĀMARŪPA); the threes, the three unwholesome faculties (AKUŚALAMŪLA) of greed (LOBHA), hatred (DVEṢA), and delusion (MOHA); the fives, the five aggregates (SKANDHA), etc. Its ten sections (nipāta) cover a total of 203 sets of factors (DHARMA). Sanskrit fragments of the *Saṃgītiparyāya* were discovered at BĀMIYĀN and TURFAN, but the complete text is only extant in a Chinese translation made by XUANZANG and his translation team between 660 and 664. The *Saṃgītiparyāya* derives from the earliest stratum of Sarvāstivāda abhidharma literature, along with the DHARMASKANDHA and the PRAJÑAPTIBHĀṢYA. The *Saṃgītiparyāya*'s closest analogue in the Pāli ABHIDHAMMA literature is the DHAMMASAṄGAṆI.

**saṃgrahavastu**. (T. bsdu ba'i dngos po; C. si sheshi; J. shishōji; K. sa sŏpsa 四攝事). In Sanskrit, translated variously as "grounds for assembling," "means of conversion," or "articles of sympathy"; in the Mahāyāna sūtras, these are four methods by which bodhisattvas attract and retain students. The four are: (1) generosity (DĀNA), (2) kind words (priyavādita), (3) helpfulness, viz., teaching others to fulfill their aims (arthacaryā), and (4) acting in accordance with one's own teachings, viz., consistency between words and deeds, or perhaps even the "common good" (SAMĀNĀRTHATĀ). There is an extensive description of these four qualities in the sixteenth chapter of the MAHĀYĀNASŪTRĀLAṂKĀRA, an important Mahāyāna ŚĀSTRA said to have been presented to ASAṄGA by the bodhisattva MAITREYA in the TUṢITA heaven (see also MAITREYANĀTHA).

**Samguk yusa**. (三國遺事). In Korean, "Memorabilia of the Three Kingdoms"; a collection of historical records and legends from the Three Kingdoms period in Korea, attributed to the Korean monk IRYŎN (1206–1289), although the extant version may well have been expanded and emended by one of his disciples. The *Samguk yusa* was written c. 1282–1289, during the period of Mongol suzerainty over Korea, which began in 1259. In his miscellany, Iryŏn includes a variety of hagiographies of eminent monks in the early Korean Buddhist tradition, often drawing from local accounts of conduct (haengjang) rather than official biographies, and from stories of early Korean Buddhist miracles and anomalies drawn from regional lore. In its emphasis on local narrative, where Buddhism dominated, over official discourse, Iryŏn's *Samguk yusa* contrasts with Kim Pusik's (1075–1151) earlier *Samguk sagi* ("Historical Annals of the Three Kingdoms"), which included little information on Buddhism. The text is divided into nine sections, in five rolls: a dynastic chronology of early Korean kingdoms; "wonders" from the three kingdoms of Koguryŏ, Paekche, and Silla and their predecessor states; the rise of Buddhism; STŪPAs and images; exegetes; divine spells; miraculous responses of bodhisattvas; the lives of recluses; and expressions of filial piety. The dynastic chronology that appears at the beginning of the definitive 1512 edition of the text contains several discrepancies with information that appears later in the text and may be a later addition from the fourteenth century. The *Samguk yusa* also makes one of the earliest references to the Tan'gun foundation myth of the Korean state and contains many indigenous Korean songs known as hyangga.

**saṃjīva**. (P. sañjīva; T. yang gsos; C. denghuo [diyu]; J. tōkatsu [jigoku]; K. tŭnghwal [chiok] 等活[地獄]). In Sanskrit, "revival," or "repetition"; the name of one of the many hells in Buddhist cosmology, usually listed as the first of eight hot or burning hells. The exact punishment meted out on those unfortunate enough to be reborn in this hell varies depending on how the Sanskrit term saṃjīva is understood. First, saṃjīva may be interpreted as "reanimation" or "regeneration." Thus, beings born into this realm are injured—in some versions by each other—in a variety of cruel ways, e.g., mangled, stabbed, pounded, and crushed. After meeting their demise so cruelly, they are then brought back to life and their bodies revived by a cool wind that sweeps over the entire realm; the same tortures are then repeated. Second, the term saṃjīva may be understood as "repetition," and beings in this hell are understood to undergo the sufferings they inflicted upon others.

**saṃjñā**. (P. saññā; T. 'du shes; C. xiang; J. sō; K. sang 想). In Sanskrit, "perception," "discrimination," or "(conceptual) identification." The term has both positive and negative connotations. As one of the five omnipresent factors (SARVATRAGA) among the listings of mental concomitants (CAITTA, P. CETASIKA) in the VAIBHĀṢIKA school of SARVĀSTIVĀDA ABHIDHARMA and in the YOGĀCĀRA school, saṃjñā might best be translated as "discrimination," referring to the mental function of differentiating and identifying objects through the apprehension of their specific qualities. Saṃjñā perceives objects in such a way that when the object is perceived again it can be readily recognized and categorized conceptually. In this perceptual context, there are six varieties of saṃjñā, each derived from one of the six sense faculties. Thus we have perception of visual objects (rūpasaṃjñā), perception of auditory objects (śabdasaṃjñā), perception of mental objects (dharmasaṃjñā), and so on. As the third of the five aggregates (SKANDHA), saṃjñā is used in this sense, particularly as the factor that perceives pleasant or unpleasant sensations as being such, giving rise to attraction, aversion and other afflictions (KLEŚA) that motivate action (KARMAN). In the compound "equipoise of nonperception" (ASAṂJÑĀSAMĀPATTI), saṃjñā refers to mental activities that, when temporarily suppressed, bring respite from tension. Some accounts interpret this state positively to mean that the perception aggregate itself is no longer functioning, implying a state of rest with the cessation of all conscious thought. In other accounts, however, asaṃjñāsamāpatti is characterized as a nihilistic state of mental dormancy, which some non-Buddhist teachers had mistakenly believed to be the ultimate, permanent quiescence of the mind and to have become attached to this state as if it were final liberation. In Pāli materials, saññā may also refer to "concepts" or "perceptions" that may be used as objects of meditation. The Pāli canon offers several of these meditative objects, such as the perception of impermanence (aniccasaññā, see S. ANITYA), the perception of danger (ĀDĪNAVA-saññā), the perception of repugnance (paṭighasaññā, see PRATIGHA), and so on.

**saṃjñāvedayitanirodha**. (P. saññāvedayitanirodha; T. 'du shes dang tshor ba 'gog pa; C. xiangshou mie; J. sōjumetsu; K. sangsu myŏl 想受滅). In Sanskrit, lit. "the suppression (NIRODHA) of perception (SAṂJÑĀ) and sensation (vedayita)"; an experience specific to states of deep meditative attainment (e.g., SAMĀPATTI). The term refers to the last in a series of nine stratified meditative attainments (samāpatti), which involve the progressive suppression (S. anupūrvanirodha, P. anupubbanirodha) of subtle elements that constitute conscious experience. The series begins with the first DHYĀNA, in which the awareness of all sense objects is temporarily allayed, and culminates in a state "beyond" the last of the four immaterial absorptions (ĀRŪPYĀVACARADHYĀNA), where there is the cessation of all sensations and perceptions. Saṃjñāvedayitanirodha is understood to be an experience of consciousness in its purest form, without any attributes or objects to distort it. Despite being free of content and/or objects, however, consciousness is still said to persist in some form. In VASUBANDHU's *Mahāyānaśatadharmavidyādvāraśāstra* ("Mahāyāna Treatise on Entry into Knowledge of the Hundred Dharmas"), Vasubandhu lists saṃjñāvedayitanirodha as one of six unconditioned factors (ASAṂSKṚTADHARMA). See also NIRODHASAMĀPATTI.

**saṃkakṣikā**. (P. saṅkacchika; T. rngul gzan; C. sengzhizhi; J. sōgishi; K. sŭnggiji 僧祇支). In Sanskrit, "undershirt," "vest," or "waistcloth"; an article of clothing worn by Buddhist monks, which is a standard part of a monk's accoutrements in some, but not all, Buddhist monastic traditions. Although the exact function and details of the garment vary slightly, the saṃkakṣikā is generally described as a kind of undershirt that leaves one shoulder (usually the right one) bare. Often this garment is completely covered by other robes (see CĪVARA) that are worn over it, especially when monks and nuns are outside the precincts of the monastery. The Tibetan translation of this term, rngul gzan, literally means "shawl for sweat," and refers to a garment intended for use during the day; a "night sweatshirt" (rngul gzan gyi gzan, which is a translation of the Sanskrit term pratisaṃkakṣikā) is intended for use in the evening. In some traditions, the saṃkakṣikā is also known as the aṃsavaṭṭaka; in others, it is known as the UTTARĀSAṂGA.

**Śaṃkarasvāmin**. (T. Bde byed bdag po; C. Shangjieluozhu; J. Shōkarashu; K. Sanggallaju 商羯羅主) (c. sixth century CE). Sanskrit proper name of an Indian philosopher and logician, who was a student of the Indian logician DIGNĀGA. Śaṃkarasvāmin is credited with the authorship of the *Nyāyapraveśa*, or "Primer on Logic," which became an important work in many Asian schools. Some have argued, based on the Tibetan tradition, that the *Nyāyapraveśa* was actually written by Śaṃkarasvāmin's teacher Dignāga, and that the recension translated into Chinese is a version that Śaṃkarasvāmin later edited. The *Nyāyapraveśa* provides an introduction to the logical system of Dignāga, covering such subjects as valid and invalid methods of proof, methods of refutation, perception, erroneous perception, inference, and erroneous inference. Although Śaṃkarasvāmin's work was not as extensive, detailed, or original as Dignāga's, it proved to be popular within the tradition, as attested by its extensive commentarial literature, including exegeses by non-Buddhists. Large parts of the work survive in the original Sanskrit. See NYĀYAPRAVEŚA.

**Sāṃkāśya**. (P. Saṅkassa; T. Sang kha sa; C. Sengqieshi; J. Sōgyase; K. Sŭnggasi 僧伽施). City in northern India, near ŚRĀVASTĪ, renowned as the site where the Buddha descended to earth from the heaven of the thirty-three (TRĀYASTRIṂŚA), after spending the rains retreat (VARṢĀ) there teaching ABHIDHARMA to his mother, MĀYĀ; also known as Kapitha. At the time for his descent, ŚAKRA and BRAHMĀ made three ladders or staircases—one of gold, one of silver, and one of jewels—with the Buddha descending from heaven on the staircase of jewels, Śakra on the staircase of gold, and Brahmā on the staircase of silver. This descent is often depicted in Buddhist iconography and the city of Sāṃkāśya, said to be the place where all buddhas descend to earth from the heaven of the thirty-three, was one of the eight "great sites" (MAHĀSTHĀNA) and an important place of pilgrimage. The event is often referred to as the DEVĀVATĀRA, or "descent of the divinities," which is another alternate name for Sāṃkāśya.

**saṃkleśa**. (P. saṃkilesa; T. kun nas nyon mongs pa; C. ran; J. zen; K. yŏm 染). In Sanskrit, "impurity," "defilement," or "pollution," sometimes used interchangeably with the more frequent term "affliction" (KLEŚA). There are two basic kinds of impurities (saṃkleśa): craving (TṚṢṆĀ) and ignorance (AVIDYĀ). These impurities lead to a whole host of more specific impurities, such as the desire for sensual pleasure, and erroneous views, such as the views of eternalism and annihilationism. The goal of the Buddhist path is to cleanse the mind of these impurities. Saṃkleśa is frequently seen used in contrast to the term purity (VYAVADĀNA) and indicates a mode of causation that inevitably leads one to suffering. Beings are constantly engaged in the process of either purification (vyavadāna) or defilement (saṃkleśa), depending upon their actions and thoughts at any given moment. In some MAHĀYĀNA texts, it is understood that the ultimate result of the process of purification is the realization that all phenomena (DHARMA) are ultimately devoid of any distinction between pure and impure.

**saṃkliṣṭa**. [alt. saṃkleśika] (T. kun nas nyon mongs pa; C. bujing; J. fujō; K. pujŏng 不淨). In Sanskrit, "afflicted," "defiled," "soiled," a polysemous term used to describe the predominate characteristic of SAṂSĀRA, applied in a variety of contexts related to the cause and fact of suffering. More specifically, saṃkliṣṭa is used to describe the truth of suffering (DUḤKHASATYA) and the truth of origination (SAMUDAYASATYA). In the PRAJÑĀPĀRAMITĀ literature, dharmas are divided into two classes, the afflicted and the pure (viśuddha), often referred to by the abbreviation rūpādi ("form and so on"), where form is the first term in the list of the afflicted class, viz., the first of the five skandhas that are associated with suffering. The list includes the SKANDHAS, ĀYATANAS, DHĀTUS, the twelvefold chain of dependent origination (PRATĪTYASAMUTPĀDA), and so on, all of which are saṃkliṣṭa ("afflicted") dharmas. In the prajñāpāramitā, the list of dharmas goes on to the list of pure dharmas as well, ending with the fruits of the noble path, the unshared qualities of a buddha (ĀVEṆIKA[BUDDHA]DHARMA), and the knowledge of all aspects (SARVĀKĀRAJÑATĀ).

**Saṃkusumitarājendra**. (T. [Rgyal dbang] Me tog cher rgyas; C. Kaifuhua wang [rulai]; J. Kaifukeō [nyorai]; K. Kaebuhwa wang [yŏrae] 開敷華王[如來]). In Sanskrit, "Flowering [viz., Fully-Manifested] King," the name of a TATHĀGATA who is mentioned in the MAÑJUŚRĪMŪLAKALPA, an influential tantric text from India composed around the seventh century; also known as Saṃkusumitarājan. At one point in the *Mañjuśrīmūlakalpa*, the buddha ŚĀKYAMUNI enters into a deep state of concentration, and causes a ray of light to shoot from his head. The light travels to Kusumāvatī, where dwells the tathāgata Saṃkusumitarājendra with a host of BODHISATTVAS. MAÑJUŚRĪ sees the light and understands that it is a beacon from Śākyamuni. Saṃkusumitarājendra encourages Mañjuśrī to visit Śākyamuni, ostensibly to inquire about his well-being, which is a pretext for Mañjuśrī to learn a MANTRA from him. Saṃkusumitarājendra is one of the five buddhas who appears in the GARBHADHĀTUMAṆḌALA; he usually sits to the right of VAIROCANA, the cosmic buddha at the center of the MAṆḌALA. One interpretation of his name is that Saṃkusumitarājendra spreads virtue and compassion through the universe as if they were flowers.

**Sammādiṭṭhisutta**. In Pāli, "Discourse on Right View," the ninth sutta in the MAJJHIMANIKĀYA (a somewhat similar SARVĀSTIVĀDA recension appears as the twenty-ninth sūtra in the Chinese translation of the MADHYAMĀGAMA, although with a different title and interlocutor; there is also an untitled Sarvāstivāda recension in the Chinese translation of the SAṂYUKTĀGAMA); preached by ŚĀRIPUTRA (P. Sāriputta) to a group of monks in the JETAVANA grove in the town of ŚRĀVASTĪ (P. Sāvatthi). Śāriputra explains that when actions of body, speech, and mind are motivated by greed, hatred, and delusion they are deemed unwholesome (P. akusala; S. AKUŚALA). When they are motivated by nongreed, nonhatred and nondelusion they are deemed wholesome (P. kusala; S. KUŚALA). He further explains the significance of the FOUR NOBLE TRUTHS, the twelve links of dependent origination (P. paṭiccasamuppāda, S. PRATĪTYASAMUTPĀDA), and the afflictions.

**Saṃmitīya**. (T. Mang bkur ba; C. Zhengliang bu; J. Shōryōbu; K. Chŏngnyang pu 正量部). One of the "mainstream" (that is, non-Mahāyāna) schools of Indian Buddhism, a subsect of the VĀTSĪPUTRĪYA, and remembered primarily for its affirmation of the notion of a "person" (PUDGALA) that is neither the same as nor different from the aggregates (SKANDHA). Because of their assertion of such an "inexpressible" (avācya) person, the adherents of the school were dubbed PUDGALAVĀDA ("proponents of the person") and were criticized by other Buddhist schools for asserting the existence of a self, a position anathema to the mainstream Buddhist position of nonself (ANĀTMAN). Despite this apparent heresy, the school enjoyed considerable popularity in India; the seventh-century Chinese pilgrim XUANZANG describes it as the largest of the mainstream Buddhist schools in India, representing one quarter of all active monks. See VĀTSĪPUTRĪYA.

**Sammohavinodanī**. In Pāli, "The Dispeller of Delusion," a commentary by the influential Pāli scholar BUDDHAGHOSA on the VIBHAṄGA, the second book of the Pāli ABHIDHAMMAPIṬAKA. This work covers much of the same material found in Buddhaghosa's VISUDDHIMAGGA, which is thought to be the earlier of the two works. In his introduction to *Sammohavinodanī*, Buddhaghosa claims to have drawn his analysis from more ancient commentaries. The work is divided into eighteen sections, beginning with an exposition on the five aggregates (P. khandha, S. SKANDHA). Each subsequent section covers a different element of the *Vibhaṅga*'s content, including analyses of the sense spheres (ĀYATANA), elements (DHĀTU), stages of meditative absorption (P. JHĀNA, S. DHYĀNA), the path (P. magga, S. MĀRGA), rules of training (P. sikkhāpada, S. ŚIKṢĀPADA), and so on. This commentary is particularly well known for its analysis of conditioned origination (P. paṭiccasamuppāda, S. PRATĪTYASAMUTPĀDA), which offers perhaps the most detailed examination of this doctrine found in the Pāli abhidhamma; there, Buddhaghosa represents the entire chain of causes and effects as occurring in both an entire lifetime as well as in single moment of consciousness. The *Sammohavinodanī* itself became the subject of extensive exegesis in the Pāli tradition.

**sammutisaṅgha**. (S. saṃvṛtisaṃgha; T. kun rdzob pa'i dge 'dun; C. shisu seng; J. sezokusō; K. sesok sŭng 世俗僧). In Pāli, "conventional order"; the community of legally ordained monks and nuns. A technical term used in the Pali commentaries, the sammutisaṅgha is comprised of monks and nuns who are still puthujjana (S. PṚTHAGJANA), or ordinary unenlightened persons. This contrasts with the PARAMATTHASAṄGHA, or "ultimate order," comprised of noble (P. āriya, S. ĀRYA) monks and nuns.

**saṃnāha**. (T. go cha; C. beijia; J. hikō; K. p'igap 被甲). In Sanskrit, "armor"; a term that occurs especially in the tradition of the ABHISAMAYĀLAṂKĀRA, where the term "armor practice" (saṃnāhapratipatti) refers both to the bodhisattva path in general as well as to specific practices begun on the path of accumulation or equipment (SAṂBHĀRAMĀRGA). In the PRAJÑĀPĀRAMITĀ sūtras (which are termed the jinajananī, "mother of victors"), bodhisattvas are said to be armed with a great armor (saṃnaddhasaṃnāha), an equipment made out of the interwoven six perfections (PĀRAMITĀ); and to set out (prasthāna) for the difficult work (duṣkaracaryā) necessary to become "victors" (JINA). This "difficult work" involves activities done for the sake of others. Each of the perfections is said to subsume all the other perfections, so that, for example, when bodhisattvas engage in exceptional acts of giving away their wealth or limbs (DĀNA), the act is informed by the bodhisattva's morality (ŚĪLA); done with forbearance (KṢĀNTI) that can withstand the difficulty involved; propelled by perseverance (VĪRYA), and informed by concentration (SAMĀDHI), which enables the bodhisattva to stay focused on the aim of enlightenment while remaining tranquil and at ease; and is grounded on the wisdom (PRAJÑĀ) that understands that the act of giving, the carrying out of the act, and the donor are all interdependent and without any inherent nature (SVABHĀVA). When bodhisattvas are armed with this great armor, they do not become discouraged by the long and difficult task of looking after the welfare of others (PARĀRTHA) who are "numberless like the sands of the Ganges" (GAṄGĀNADĪVĀLUKĀ). Buckling on the armor (saṃnāha) and setting out (prasthāna) on their quest, bodhisattvas ultimately accumulate all their necessary equipment (SAṂBHĀRA) and go forth (niryāṇa) to the final goal of buddhahood.

**saṃpannakrama**. (S) (T. rdzogs rim). See NIṢPANNAKRAMA.

**Sampasādanīyasutta**. (C. Zihuanxi jing; J. Jikangikyō; K. Chahwanhŭi kyŏng 自歡喜經). In Pāli, "Discourse on Serene Faith"; the twenty-eighth sutta of the DĪGHANIKĀYA (a separate DHARMAGUPTAKA recension appears as the eighteenth SŪTRA in the Chinese translation of the DĪRGHAGĀMA; there is also a separate but untitled SARVĀSTIVĀDA recension in the Chinese translation of the SAṂYUKTĀGAMA); addressed to ŚĀRIPUTRA at NĀLANDĀ in Pāvārika's mango grove. Śāriputra declares that there has never been nor will there ever be anyone equal to the Buddha in wisdom. When questioned by the Buddha whether he had ever met a buddha of the past or had been able to fathom the Buddha's own mind, Śāriputra admits he had done neither but nevertheless proceeds to justify his faith on the basis of the Buddha's unsurpassable qualities. The Buddha approves of Śāriputra's explanation and advises him to preach it often to others.

**saṃprajanya**. (P. sampajañña; T. shes bzhin; C. zhengzhi; J. shōchi; K. chŏngji 正知). In Sanskrit, "clear comprehension," "circumspection," "introspection"; a term that is closely related to, and often appears in compound with, mindfulness (S. SMṚTI, P. sati). In descriptions of the practice of developing meditative absorption (DHYĀNA), smṛti refers to the factor of mindfulness that ties the mind to the object, while saṃprajanya is the factor that observes the mind to determine whether it has strayed from its object. Specifically, Pāli sources refer to four aspects of clear comprehension, which involve the application of mindfulness in practice. The first is purpose (P. sātthaka), viz., whether the action will be in the best interests of oneself and others; its principal criterion is whether it leads to growth in dharma. Second is suitability (P. sappāya): whether an action is in accord with the appropriate time, place, and personal capacity; its principal criterion is skillfulness in applying right means (P. upāyakosalla; S. UPĀYAKAUŚALYA). Third is the domain of meditation (gocara): viz., all experiences should be made a topic of mindful awareness. Fourth is nondelusion (asammoha): viz., recognizing that what seem to be the actions of a person are in fact an impersonal series of mental and physical processes; this aspect of saṃprajanya helps to counteract the tendency to view all events from a personal point of view. Saṃprajanya thus expands upon the clarity of thought generated by mindfulness by incorporating the additional factors of correct knowledge (JÑĀNA) or wisdom (PRAJÑĀ).

**saṃprayukta**. (T. mtshungs ldan; C. xiangying; J. sōō; K. sangŭng 相應). In Sanskrit, literally "yoked," "harnessed," "joined together." This term is used in the ABHIDHARMA in the sense of "concomitant" or "associated"; its nominal counterpart saṃprayoga may be translated as "concomitance." The term saṃprayukta is used to describe the relationship between mind (CITTA) and mental concomitants (CAITTA). This relationship is described as "concomitant" in that the origination and specific features of one are closely related to the origination and specific features of the other. The SARVĀSTIVĀDA enumerated five ways in which the mind and mental functions are concomitant by listing five features that they share: sense base (ĀŚRAYA), object (ĀLAMBANA), aspect of the object (ĀKĀRA), moment of arising (KĀLA), and substance (DRAVYA).

**saṃprayuktahetu**. (T. mtshungs ldan gyi rgyu; C. xiangying yin; J. sōōin; K. sangŭngin 相應因). In Sanskrit, "conjoined" or "associative" "cause"; the third of the six kinds of causes (HETU) outlined in the JÑĀNAPRASTHĀNA, the central text of the SARVĀSTIVĀDA ABHIDHARMA, which accounts for the fact that mental events cannot exist in isolation but instead mutually condition, or are "associated" with, one another. This type of cause is effectively a subsection of the coexistent cause (SAHABHŪHETU). Mind (CITTA) or consciousness (VIJÑĀNA) cannot exist in isolation; they are always conjoined with various related mental concomitants (CAITTA). Thus the conjoined causes exist in a relationship of mutuality or reciprocation, e.g., mind causes mental concomitants, but mental functions also cause mind. Because of this reciprocity, the functioning of the visual organ (viz., the eye) leads to an associated visual consciousness (CAKṢURVIJÑĀNA) and associated mental concomitants, such as visual sensations (VEDANĀ), perceptions (SAMJÑĀ), emotions that derive from those perceptions, and so forth.

**saṃprayuktasaṃskāra**. In Sanskrit, "forces conjoined [with thought]." See CITTASAṂPRAYUKTASAṂSKĀRA.

**Saṃpuṭa Tantra**. (S). See HEVAJRATANTRA.

**saṃsāra**. (T. 'khor ba; C. lunhui/shengsi lunhui; J. rinne/shōjirinne; K. yunhoe/saengsa yunhoe 輪迴/生死輪迴). In Sanskrit and Pāli, "wandering," viz., the "cycle of REBIRTH."

The realms that are subject to rebirth are typically described as composed of six rebirth destinies (GATI): divinities (DEVA), demigods or titans (ASURA), humans (MANUṢYA), animals (TIRYAK), ghosts (PRETA), and hell denizens (NĀRAKA). These destinies are all located within the three realms of existence (TRAIDHĀTUKA), which comprises the entirety of our universe (see also AVACARA; LOKADHĀTU). At the bottom of the sensuous realm (KĀMADHĀTU; kāmāvacara) are located the denizens of the hells (NĀRAKA), the lowest of which is named the interminable (AVĪCI). This most ill-fated of existences is followed by ghosts, animals, humans, demigods, and the divinities of the six heavens of the sensuous realm. Higher levels of the divinities occupy the upper two realms of existence, the subtle-materiality realm (RŪPADHĀTU) and the immaterial realm (ĀRŪPYADHĀTU). The bottom three destinies, of hell denizens, hungry ghosts, and animals, are referred to as the three evil bournes (DURGATI); these are destinies where suffering predominates because of the past performance of unwholesome (AKUŚALA) actions (KARMAN). In the various levels of the divinities, happiness predominates, because of the past performance of wholesome (KUŚALA) actions. By contrast, the human destiny is thought to be ideally suited for religious training, because it is the only bourne where both suffering and happiness can be readily experienced, allowing the adept to recognize more easily the true character of life as impermanent (ANITYA), suffering (DUḤKHA), and nonself (ANĀTMAN). Saṃsāra is said to have no beginning and to come to end only for those individuals who achieve liberation from rebirth through the practice of the path (MĀRGA) to NIRVĀṆA. Saṃsāra is depicted iconographically as a "wheel of existence" (BHAVACAKRA), which shows the six rebirth destinies, surrounding a pig, a rooster, and a snake, which symbolize ignorance (AVIDYĀ), desire (LOBHA), and hatred (DVEṢA), respectively. Around the edge of the wheel are scenes representing the twelve links of dependent origination (PRATĪTYASAMUTPĀDA). The relation between saṃsāra and nirvāṇa is discussed at length in Buddhist texts, with NĀGĀRJUNA famously declaring that there is not the slightest difference between them, because the true nature of both is emptiness (ŚŪNYATĀ).

**saṃskāra**. (P. saṅkhāra; T. 'du byed; C. xing; J. gyō; K. haeng 行). In Sanskrit, a polysemous term that is variously translated as "formation," "volition," "volitional action," "conditioned," "conditioning factors." In its more passive usage (see SAṂSKṚTA, P. saṅkhata), saṃskāra refers to anything that has been formed, conditioned, or brought into being. In this early denotation, the term is a designation for all things and persons that have been brought into being dependent on causes and conditions. It is in this sense that the Buddha famously remarked that "all conditioned things (saṃskāra) are impermanent" (anityāḥ sarvasamskārāḥ), the first of the four criteria that "seal" a view as being authentically Buddhist (see CATURNIMITTA). In its more active sense, saṃskāra as latent "formations" left in the mind by actions (KARMAN) refers to that which forms or conditions other things. In this usage, the term is equivalent in meaning to action. It is in this sense that saṃskāra serves as the second link in the twelvefold chain of dependent origination (PRATĪTYASAMUTPĀDA). There, saṃskāra refers specifically to volition (CETANĀ) and as such assumes the karmically active role of perpetuating the rebirth process; alternatively, in the YOGĀCĀRA school, saṃskāra refers to the seeds (BĪJA) left in the foundation or storehouse consciousness (ĀLAYAVIJÑĀNA). Saṃskāra is also the name for the fourth of the five aggregates (SKANDHA), where it includes a miscellany of phenomena that are both formed and in the process of formation, i.e., the large collection of factors that cannot be conveniently classified with the other four aggregates of materiality (RŪPA), sensation (VEDANĀ), perception (SAṂJÑĀ), and consciousness (VIJÑĀNA). This fourth aggregate includes both those conditioning factors associated with mind (CITTASAMPRAYUKTASAṂSKĀRA), such as the mental concomitants (CAITTA), as well as those conditioning forces dissociated from thought (CITTAVIPRAYUKTASAṂSKĀRA), such as time, duration, the life faculty, and the equipoise of cessation (NIRODHASAMĀPATTI).

**saṃskāraduḥkhatā**. (T. 'du byed kyi sdug bsngal; C. xingku; J. gyōku; K. haenggo 行苦). In Sanskrit, "suffering inherent in conditioning," the third of the three types of suffering, together with DUḤKHADUḤKHATĀ and VIPARIṆĀMADUḤKHATĀ. This is the most subtle and most pernicious of the three types of suffering, since it conditions all of SAṂSĀRA. Saṃskāraduḥkhatā is identified as neutral sensations and their objects, which, due to impermanence, can turn into sensations of pain in the next instant. It is said that this form of suffering generally goes unnoticed by ordinary beings (PṚTHAGJANA), where it is like a wisp of wool in the palm of the hand, but it cannot be ignored by noble beings (ĀRYAPUDGALA), where it is like a wisp of wool in the eye. An example for the three types of suffering is a burn: as a conditioned event, it is suffering just because of what it is (saṃskāraduḥkhatā); when soothed with a cooling ointment it feels better, but when the temporary relief ends it will inevitably become suffering again (vipariṇāmaduḥkhatā); and when jabbed, it causes excruciating pain (duḥkhaduḥkhatā).

**saṃskṛta**. (T. 'dus byas; C. youwei; J. ui; K. yuwi 有爲). In Sanskrit, "conditioned," a term that describes all impermanent phenomena, that is, all conditioned factors (saṃskṛtadharma) that are produced through the concomitance of causes and conditions; these phenomena are subject to the four characteristics (CATURLAKṢAṆA) governing all conditioned objects (SAṂSKṚTALAKṢAṆA), viz., "origination," or birth (JĀTI), "continuance," or maturation (STHITI), "senescence," or decay (JARĀ), and "desinence," or death (ANITYA). Saṃskṛta is contrasted with ASAṂSKṚTA, "unconditioned," a common adjective of NIRVĀṆA, but also a category that in some traditions includes space (ĀKĀŚA) and other types of absence and cessation. The fact that the objects of ordinary experience are conditioned is commonly cited as a reason why they are unreliable and thus should be abandoned, and why the unconditioned state should be sought. See also SAṂSKĀRA.

**saṃskṛtalakṣaṇa**. (T. 'dus byas kyi mtshan nyid; C. youwei xiang; J. uisō; K. yuwi sang 有爲相). In Sanskrit, "compounded characteristics"; according to the SARVĀSTIVĀDA ABHIDHARMA analysis of causality, four "forces dissociated from thought" (CITTAVIPRAYUKTASAṂSKĀRA) that govern conditioned existence: viz., origination or birth (JĀTI), continuance or maturation (STHITI), "senescence" or decay (JARĀ), and "desinence" or extinction, viz., death (ANITYA). See CATURLAKṢAṆA.

**saṃtāna**. (P. santāna; T. rgyud / rgyun; C. xiangxu; J. sōzoku; K. sangsok 相續). In Sanskrit, "continuum," a term used to designate an uninterrupted sequence of cause and effect, especially a sequence of mental moments. Because there is nothing permanent in the mind and body, but there is continuity in the ways in which they are made manifest, they are described as a continuum. The term is used most commonly to refer to the mental continuum, both within a single lifetime and as it extends over many lifetimes. In the VAIBHĀṢIKA school of SARVĀSTIVĀDA ABHIDHARMA, the "immediate-antecedent condition" (SAMANANTARAPRATYAYA) accounts for the immediately preceding moment in the saṃtāna, which by coming to an end, enables a subsequent moment of thought to arise. All types of thought in the conditioned (SAṂSKṚTA) realm serve as immediate-antecedent conditions that enable the mental continuum to persist. The only exception is the final thought-moment in the mental continuum of an ARHAT: the immediate-antecedent condition does not function at the specific moment, because the arhat's next thought-moment involves the experience of the unconditioned (ASAṂSKṚTA); thus, no further thoughts from the conditioned realm can ever again recur and the arhat is liberated from SAṂSĀRA. This notion of a mental continuum also serves to counter annihilationist interpretations (see UCCHEDAVĀDA, UCCHEDĀNTA) of the quintessential Buddhist doctrine of nonself (ANĀTMAN): there may be no permanent, underlying substratum of being that can be designated as a self or soul (ĀTMAN), but this fact does not controvert the continuity that pertains in the flow of moral cause and effect (KARMAN) or the possibility of REBIRTH.

**samucchinnakuśalamūla**. (T. dge rtsa bcad pa; C. duanshangen; J. danzengon; K. tansŏn'gŭn 斷善根). In Sanskrit, "those whose wholesome roots are eradicated," referring to beings who have performed the most heinous of acts, or who are unable to engage in even the most basic of wholesome activities. Their wholesome roots (KUŚALAMŪLA) being thereby eradicated, they are thus condemned to subsequent rebirth in the hells (see NĀRAKA), where they may spend an "indefinite" period. The samucchinnakuśalamūla is related to the MAHĀYĀNA term for the spiritual bereft, or incorrigibles (ICCHANTIKA), who also may be condemned to a virtual eternity in the hells. A person can become samucchinnakuśalamūla through lack of faith (ĀŚRADDHYA), wrong views (MITHYĀDṚṢṬI), or by being swayed by the afflictions (kleśasaṃyoga). It is said that the inability to engage in charity (DĀNA), the foundation of Buddhist ethical practice, is the determining factor that leads to a person becoming samucchinnakuśalamūla.

**samudācāra**. (T. kun tu spyod pa; C. xianxing; J. gengyō; K. hyŏnhaeng 現行). In Sanskrit, the term has two important denotations: "proper conduct," or "intention, purpose, habitual idea"; and "manifest action." Samudācāra designates religious action that is undertaken for the sake of attaining liberation for oneself and either liberation or an improved state of rebirth for others. Thus, the term can refer to a buddha's unceasing effort and the influence he exerts to help beings attain liberation. In its description of the first BHŪMI, the MAHĀVASTU lists eight types of samudācāra for a BODHISATTVA. These are generosity (tyāga), compassion (KARUṆĀ), relentlessness (aparikheda), humility (amāna), study of all the treatises (sarvaśāstrādhyāyitā), courage (vikrama), social skills (lokānujñā), and resolve (dhṛti). Deriving from its denotation of volitional impulse, samudācāra also comes to be used in the YOGĀCĀRA school to indicate the emergence of conditioned factors (saṃskṛtadharma) from the ĀLAYAVIJÑĀNA, since, once they have arisen and are no longer dormant, they influence conscious action. In the context of Yogācāra thought, then, samudācāra is often translated as "manifest action." The term is also used in the sense of the special qualities of the practice of bodhisattvas, who are habituated to the ultimate nature of things (TATHATĀ, literally, "suchness"). The dependent origination of an action and the ultimate way in which that action occurs are inseparable; hence samudācāra, and in particular actions prompted by the aspiration for enlightenment, are "manifest actions." In tantric literature, the term is used for the four types of activities, also known as the CATURKARMAN.

**samudānītagotra**. (T. yang dag par bsgrub pa'i rigs; C. xizhongxing; J. shūshushō; K. sŭpchongsŏng 習種性). In Sanskrit, "the [karmic] lineage that is conditioned by habits." In the YOGĀCĀRA school, a distinction is made between the indestructible, inherent "naturally endowed lineage" (PRAKṚTISTHAGOTRA) and this changeable, continuously acquired "lineage conditioned by habits" (samudānītagotra). In contrast to the former, which predetermines a person's orientation toward the two vehicles of either MAHĀYĀNA or HĪNAYĀNA, the latter allows for some leeway for personal adaptations and change through doctrinal study, practice, and exposure (these are what are meant by "habits"). According to this controversial Yogācāra tenet, whereas a person cannot effect change in terms of his highest spiritual potential and vehicular predisposition because of his "naturally endowed lineage," he can nevertheless influence the speed with which he is able to attain enlightenment, and other extrinsic variations within his predetermined "lineage." This flexibility is the lineage that is conditioned, and can be altered, by "habits." Together and in contrast with the "naturally endowed lineage," they are known as "the two lineages: intrinsic and acquired" (xingxi er[zhong]xing). ¶ In another interpretation based on the BODHISATTVABHŪMI and MAHĀYĀNASAMGRAHA, the naturally endowed (prakṛtistha) lineage is present since time immemorial (anādikālika) and is called śrutavāsanā (the residual impression left by listening). In Yogācāra, where there are no external objects, and the ĀLAYAVIJÑĀNA is the storehouse of all seeds (BĪJA), the śrutavāsanā is a seed planted in the deepest recesses of the ālaya (see AMALAVIJÑĀNA) and helps explains how those who first hear the different branches of the Buddha's doctrine thereby learn and reach the goal of full enlightenment. In this interpretation, the difference between the prakṛtisthagotra and the samudānītagotra is only one of time: when the lineage (understood on the analogy of a seed or capacity) is dormant it is the naturally endowed lineage; when, nutured by the practices leading up to the path of vision (DARŚANAMĀRGA), it comes closer to the ĀŚRAYAPARĀVṚTTI (fundamental transformation of the basis) on the eighth bodhisattva bhūmi, it is samudānītagotra.

**samudaya**. (T. kun 'byung; C. ji; J. jū; K. chip 集). In Sanskrit and Pāli, "origination" or "arising." In the *Samudayasutta*, the 132nd sutta of the twenty-second section of the Pāli SAṂYUTTANIKĀYA, samudaya refers to the origination of the five aggregates (P. khandha; S. SKANDHA), which is followed by their subsistence and passing away. In this basic sense, samudaya conveys the sense that the aggregates that make up a person are not miraculously there, or there permanently, but arise as the result of specific causes and conditions. The term is most widely used in the compound SAMUDAYASATYA ("truth of the origin [of suffering]") the second of the FOUR NOBLE TRUTHS. In the more detailed explanation of the truth of origination, samudaya is the second of four aspects (ĀKĀRA), each of which counteract a mistaken view about the origin of suffering (see SAMUDAYASATYA). It counteracts the view that suffering is created only once, in a single act by a creator god, because the skandhas arise continually in a stream or continuum (SAṂTĀNA).

**samudayasatya**. (P. samudayasacca; T. kun 'byung gi bden pa; C. jidi; J. jittai; K. chipche 集諦). In Sanskrit, "truth of origination"; the second of the so-called FOUR NOBLE TRUTHS (catvāry āryasatyāni) promulgated by the Buddha in his first sermon (see DHAMMACAKKAPPAVATTANASUTTA) in the Deer Park at SĀRNĀTH. In this context, SAMUDAYA refers to the origination or cause of the first truth, suffering (DUḤKHA; DUḤKHASATYA). The origination of suffering is identified as KARMAN and KLEŚA. Karman or past actions, in this case unwholesome (AKUŚALA) actions, are identified as the immediate cause of suffering, with negative deeds fructifying as experiences of mental and physical pain. The afflictions (kleśa), often enumerated in this context as greed, hatred, and delusion, are the mediate causes of suffering, motivating the nonvirtuous deeds that result in future suffering. Among these three, delusion, understood as the mistaken conception of a perduring self (ĀTMAGRAHA), is the root cause of suffering, and produces greed and hatred. The implication of the second truth is that if one can eliminate the cause or origin of suffering, one can then put an end to suffering itself. This truth of the origin of suffering has four aspects (ĀKĀRA): it is the cause (HETU), origination (SAMUDAYA), producer (saṃbhava), and condition (PRATYAYA). These four aspects counteract respectively the mistaken views that (1) suffering is arbitrary and has no cause, (2) there is only a single cause for suffering even though it is diverse and ongoing, (3) suffering is just the imaginary transformations of reality, and (4) suffering is the result of a particular mental focus, not the inexorable result of a mind governed by kleśa and karman. These four aspects of the truth of origination are like a disease (in the sense that kleśa and karman are the root cause of suffering), like a boil that is the origin of ongoing pain, like a thorn that produces intense suffering immediately, and like misfortune, in that the unbroken continuum (SAṂTĀNA) of the aggregates (SKANDHA) is the condition for a life that is governed by suffering.

**saṃvara**. (P. saṃvara; T. sdom pa; C. lüyi/sanbaluo; J. ritsugi/sanbara; K. yurŭi/samballa 律儀/三跋羅). In Sanskrit, "restraint," referring generally to the restraint from unwholesome (AKUŚALA) actions (KARMAN) that is engendered by observance of the monastic disciplinary code (PRĀTIMOKṢA), the BODHISATTVA precepts, and tantric vows. In the VAIBHĀṢIKA school of SARVĀSTIVĀDA ABHIDHARMA, three specific types of restraint (SAṂVARA) against unwholesomeness (akuśala) are mentioned, which are all associated with "unmanifest material force" or "hidden imprints" (AVIJÑAPTIRŪPA): (1) the restraint proffered to a monk or nun when he or she accepts the disciplinary rules of the order (PRĀTIMOKṢASAṂVARA); (2) the restraint that is engendered by mental absorption (dhyānajasaṃvara); and (3) the restraint that derives from being free from the contaminants (anāsravasaṃvara). The restraint inherent in the disciplinary code (prātimokṣasaṃvara) creates a special kind of protective force field that helps to dissuade monks and nuns from unwholesome activity, even when they are not consciously aware they are following the precepts or even when they are asleep. This specific type of restraint is what makes a person a monk, since just wearing robes or following an ascetic way of life would not in themselves be sufficient to instill in him the protective power offered by the prātimokṣa. The restraint engendered by DHYĀNA (dhyānajasaṃvara) refers to the fact that absorption in meditation was thought to confer on the monk protective power against physical harm: the literature abounds with stories of monks who discover tiger tracks all around them after withdrawing from dhyāna, thus suggesting that dhyāna itself was a force that provided a protective shield against accident or injury. Finally, anāsravasaṃvara is the restraint that precludes someone who has achieved the extinction of the contaminants (ĀSRAVA)—that is, enlightenment—from committing any action (karman) that would produce a karmic result (VIPĀKA), thus ensuring that their remaining actions in this life do not lead to any additional rebirths. ¶ In MAHĀYĀNA materials, such as the BODHISATTVABHŪMI, the first of three types of morality that together codify the moral training of a bodhisattva is called saṃvaraśīla ("restraining morality"); under this heading is included the different sets of rules for BHIKṢU, BHIKṢUṆĪ and so on in the prātimokṣa, taken as a whole; two further codifications of rules called the morality of collecting wholesome factors (kuśalasaṃgrāhakaśīla), and the morality that acts for the welfare of beings (sattvārthakriyāśīla; see ARTHAKRIYĀ); together, these three constitute the definitive and exhaustive explanation of bodhisattva morality, known as TRISAṂVARA, the "three restraints" or "triple code." The original meaning of saṃvara as "restraint" remains central in the *Bodhisattvabhūmi*'s account, but the text expands the scope of morality (ŚIKṢĀPADA) widely, incorporating all altruistic acts under the rubric of skillful means employed for the sake of others, in essence formulating a code for bodhisattvas who are committed to acting like buddhas. In Indian and Tibetan tantra, the meaning of trisaṃvara undergoes yet further expansion. Each of the five buddha KULA (in one list AKṢOBHYA, VAIROCANA, RATNASAMBHAVA, AMITĀBHA, and AMOGHASIDDHI) has a vowed morality, called SAMAYA. This tantric code is the third of the three codes, the other two being the prātimokṣa codes and the *Bodhisattvabhūmi*'s code for bodhisattvas. These three, then, are called the prātimokṣasaṃvara, the bodhisattvasaṃvara, and the guhyamantrasaṃvara ("secret mantra vows") (see SDOM GSUM RAB DBYE). ¶ In tantric literature, saṃvara also has the sense of "union," a meaning that is conveyed in the proper name of (CAKRA)SAṂVARA (see also HERUKA), a principal deity of the VAJRAYĀNA ANUTTARAYOGATANTRA tradition. A god named Saṃvara appears in the *Ṛg Veda* as an enemy of the gods who hoarded the precious soma (the divine nectar) and kept it from INDRA, who eventually destroyed Saṃvara's mountain fortress. The myth suggests the possibility that Saṃvara or Cakrasaṃvara began his existence as a pre-Vedic Indian deity preserved in Buddhist tantra in a subordinated position. With his adoption into the Buddhist pantheon, Saṃvara (likely the Buddhist version of Śiva) himself vanquishes the Vedic god—he is commonly depicted trampling BHAIRAVA (Śiva) and/or his consort. Alternate Indian names for him include Śambara and Paramasukha Cakrasaṃvara. The Tibetan Bde mchog, or "supreme bliss," is a translation of paramasukha. Tantric cycles connected to Saṃvara were introduced to Tibet by the translator MAR PA in the eleventh century CE. He is said to reside at the mountain of TSHA RI in Rdza yul, southern Tibet, as well as in the Bde mchog pho brang on Mount KAILĀSA, where the nearby Lake Manasarovar is sacred to him. His consort is VAJRAVĀRĀHĪ.

**saṃvartakalpa**. (P. saṃvaṭṭakappa; T. 'jig pa'i bskal pa; C. huaijie; J. ekō; K. koegŏp 壞劫). In Sanskrit, "eon of dissolution," one of the four periods in the cycle of the creation and destruction of a world system, according to Buddhist cosmology. These are: the eon of creation (VIVARTAKALPA); the eon of abiding (VIVARTASTHĀYIKALPA); the eon of dissolution (saṃvartakalpa); and the eon of nothingness (SAṂVARTASTHĀYIKALPA). According to the ABHIDHARMAKOŚABHĀṢYA, each of the four eons lasts twenty intermediate eons. After the complete dissolution of the previous world system, an eon of nothingness occurs, during which the universe remains in a state of vacuity, with the sentient beings who had populated that world system reborn in other worlds or in the second absorption (DHYĀNA) of the subtle-materiality realm (RŪPADHĀTU). The eon of creation begins when a wind begins to blow in space, impelled by the previous actions (KARMAN) of sentient beings. A circle of wind forms, followed by a circle of water, followed by a circle of golden earth. The entire world-system of the sensuous realm (KĀMADHĀTU) then forms, including Mount SUMERU, the four continents and their subcontinents, the heavens, and the hells. These are then populated by beings, reborn in the various realms as a result of their previous actions. When all realms of the world system have been populated, the eon of creation ends and the eon of abiding begins. At the beginning of the eon, the human life span is said to be "infinite" and decreases until it eventually reaches ten years of age. It then increases to eighty thousand years, before decreasing again to ten years. It takes one intermediate eon for the life span to go from ten years to eighty thousand years to ten years again. The eon of abiding is composed of twenty eons, beginning with the intermediate eon of decrease (in which the life span decreases from "infinite" to ten years), followed by eighteen intermediate eons of increase and decrease, and ending with an intermediate eon of increase, when the life span increases from ten years to eighty thousand years, at which point the next eon, the eon of dissolution begins. Buddhas only appear during periods of decrease. ŚĀKYAMUNI Buddha appeared when the life span was one hundred years. It is said that MAITREYA will come when the human life span next reaches eighty thousand years. The eon of dissolution begins when sentient beings are no longer reborn in the hell realms of that world system. After that point, the hell realms of that world then disappear. (Beings who subsequently commit deeds warranting rebirth in hell are reborn into the hell realms of other universes.) The realms of ghosts and animals then disappear. Through the practice of meditation, humans are reborn in the first DHYĀNA and then into the second dhyāna. When the karman that has caused beings to be reborn in that world is exhausted, such that the physical world is depopulated, seven suns appear in the sky and incinerate the entire world system, including Mount Sumeru and all of the first dhyāna. This is followed by another eon of nothingness. See also SATTVALOKA.

**saṃvartasthāyikalpa**. (P. saṃvaṭṭaṭṭhāyīkappa; T. stong pa'i bskal pa; C. kongjie; J. kūkō; K. konggŏp 空劫). In Sanskrit, "eon of nothingness"; one of the four periods in the cycle of the creation and destruction of a world system, according to Buddhist cosmology. These are: the eon of creation (VIVARTAKALPA); the eon of abiding (VIVARTASTHĀYIKALPA); the eon of dissolution (SAṂVARTAKALPA); and the eon of nothingness (saṃvartasthāyikalpa). According to the ABHIDHARMAKOŚABHĀṢYA, each of the four eons lasts twenty intermediate eons. After the complete dissolution of the previous world system, an eon of nothingness occurs in which the universe remains in a state of vacuity, with the sentient beings who had populated that world system reborn in other worlds or in the second concentration (DHYĀNA) of the realm of subtle materiality (RŪPADHĀTU). (For the remainder of this cosmology, see the preceding entry SAṂVARTAKALPA, s.v.) After successive eons of formation, abiding, and dissolution, the karma that had caused beings to be reborn into the world is exhausted, such that the physical world is depopulated; seven suns then appear in the sky and incinerate the entire world system, including Mount SUMERU and all of the first dhyāna. Thus begins a new eon of nothingness, a period of twenty intermediate eons of vacuity. See also BHĀJANALOKA.

**saṃvṛti**. (P. sammuti; T. kun rdzob; C. shisu/su; J. sezoku/zoku; K. sesok/sok 世俗/俗). In Sanskrit, "conventional" or "relative"; a term used to designate the phenomena, concepts, and understanding associated with unenlightened, ordinary beings (PṚTHAGJANA). Saṃvṛti is akin to the Sanskrit term LAUKIKA (mundane), in that both are used to indicate worldly things or unenlightened views, and is typically contrasted with PARAMĀRTHA, meaning "ultimate" or "absolute." In Sanskrit the term carries the connotation of "covering, concealing," implying that the independent reality apparently possessed by ordinary phenomena may seem vivid and convincing, but is in fact ultimately illusory and unreal. Much analysis and debate has occurred within the various philosophical schools regarding the questions of if, how, and in what way saṃvṛti or conventional phenomena exist. For example, in his PRASANNAPADĀ, the seventh-century scholar CANDRAKĪRTI lists the following three characteristics of saṃvṛti. First, they conceal reality (avacchādana). Second, they are mutually dependent (anyonyasamāśraya), meaning that saṃvṛti phenomena are dependent on causes and conditions. Finally, they are concerned with worldly activities or speech (lokavyavahāra). Buddhas and BODHISATTVAs use their understanding of conventional reality to help them convey the DHARMA to ordinary beings and lead them away from suffering. See also SAṂVṚTISATYA.

**saṃvṛtibodhicitta**. (T. kun rdzob byang chub kyi sems). In Sanskrit, "conventional (or relative) aspiration to enlightenment." In Indian MAHĀYĀNA scholastic literature, this term is contrasted with the "ultimate aspiration to enlightenment" (PARAMĀRTHABODHICITTA). The term saṃvṛtibodhicitta is used to refer to BODHICITTA in its more common usage, as the aspiration to achieve buddhahood for the sake of all sentient beings. It is the generation of this aspiration for enlightenment (BODHICITTOTPĀDA) that marks the beginning of the bodhisattva path and the Mahāyāna path of accumulation (SAṂBHĀRAMĀRGA). The ultimate aspiration or mind of enlightenment refers to the bodhisattva's direct realization of the ultimate truth (PARAMĀRTHASATYA). In the case of the MADHYAMAKA school's interpretation, this would be the direct realization of emptiness (ŚŪNYATĀ). Such realization, and hence the ultimate aspiration to enlightenment, occurs beginning on the Mahāyāna path of vision (DARŚANAMĀRGA) and is further developed on the path of cultivation (BHĀVANĀMĀRGA). These two types of bodhicitta explain how bodhicitta is present both during periods of concentration or equipoise (see SAMĀPATTI, SAMĀHITA) on the ultimate truth and during all the other stages of the path, called subsequent attainment (pṛṣṭhalabdha; cf. PṚṢṬHALABDHAJÑĀNA). These two terms inform the presentation of bodhicitta in the BODHICITTAVIVARAṆA, attributed to NĀGĀRJUNA, and are widely employed in Tibetan BLO SBYONG literature.

**saṃvṛtisaṃgha**. (S). See SAMMUTISAṄGHA.

**saṃvṛtisatya**. (P. sammutisacca; T. kun rdzob bden pa; C. shisu di/sudi; J. sezokutai/zokutai; K. sesok che/sokche 世俗諦/俗諦). In Buddhist Sanskrit, "conventional truth" or "relative truth"; the term carries the pejorative connotation of deception, concealment, and obscuration. Conventional truth (saṃvṛtisatya) and ultimate truth (PARAMĀRTHASATYA) constitute the "two truths" (SATYADVAYA), a philosophical bifurcation that is widely referenced and analyzed in Buddhism. All dharmas are said to be included in one of these two categories. Saṃvṛtisatya is variously defined by the Buddhist philosophical schools, but it is generally understood to refer to objects of ordinary experience that involve misperceptions tainted by ignorance, in distinction to the true or ultimate nature of those objects, which are ultimate truths (paramārthasatya). It is important to note that conventional truths, although misperceived, nonetheless exist conventionally or have conventional utility. The object of the most consequential misconception, a perduring self (ĀTMAN), is not a conventional truth because it is utterly nonexistent. Saṃvṛtisatya is also understood to mean the unavoidable domain through which sentient beings must navigate and communicate with one another in the mundane world. Thus buddhas and BODHISATTVAs use their knowledge of conventional truths to teach unenlightened beings and lead them away from suffering. Some Buddhist schools further subdivide saṃvṛtisatya into two categories: tathyasaṃvṛtisatya (correct conventional truth) and atathyasaṃvṛtisatya (or mithyāsaṃvṛtisatya, incorrect or false conventional truth), a distinction based upon whether or not the object can perform functions in accordance with their appearance. For example, a face would be a tathyasaṃvṛtisatya but a reflection of a face in a mirror would be a mithyāsaṃvṛtisatya.

**samyagājīva**. (P. sammājīva; T. yang dag pa'i 'tsho ba; C. zhengming; J. shōmyō; K. chŏngmyŏng 正命). In Sanskrit, "right livelihood" or "correct livelihood"; the fifth constituent of the noble eightfold path (ĀRYĀṢṬĀṄGAMĀRGA). "Right" (samyak) in this context is interpreted as "resulting in a decrease in the net suffering experienced by oneself and others." Of the three divisions of the eightfold path—morality (ŚĪLA), concentration (SAMĀDHI), and wisdom (PRAJÑĀ)—samyagājīva is the third of the three aspects of moral training. It involves abstention from engaging in occupations that are considered to be incompatible with morality because they bring harm to other beings, either directly or indirectly. Such inappropriate occupations include selling weapons, or working as a butcher, fisherman, or soldier. Right livelihood also involves abstention from any occupation that may cause oneself, or encourage others, to break precepts associated with right speech (SAMYAGVĀC) and right action (SAMYAKKARMĀNTA). For this reason, selling intoxicants is considered to be a breach of right livelihood. The tradition provides examples of wrong livelihoods for both monastics and the laity. In Pāli literature, the BRAHMAJĀLASUTTA and SĀMAÑÑAPHALASUTTA of the DĪGHANIKĀYA list several "wrong livelihoods" for monks. These include performing divination and astrology as well as casting spells. MAHĀYĀNA interpretations stress the absence of absolutes, and the relative merits or demerits of any occupation based on the situation at hand and its value to the larger goal of promoting the welfare of others. In the inversion of categories that is characteristic of much of tantric literature, many of the MAHĀSIDDHAs are involved in professions that do not constitute right livelihood according to mainstream Buddhist definitions.

**samyagdṛṣṭi**. (P. sammādiṭṭhi; T. yang dag pa'i lta ba; C. zhengjian; J. shōken; K. chŏnggyŏn 正見). Often translated as "right view" or "correct view," the first constituent of the noble eightfold path (ĀRYĀṢṬĀṄGAMĀRGA). It is described as the correct understanding of the FOUR NOBLE TRUTHS (catvāry āryasatyāni); namely, the truth of suffering, the truth of the cause of suffering, the truth of cessation of suffering, and the truth of the path leading to the end of suffering. The last truth is itself the same as the eightfold path. Right view is also identified as the correct understanding of nonself (ANĀTMAN). In the MADHYĀNTAVIBHĀGA, right view refers to the understanding of the vision of truth that has just been witnessed, the unique formulation of the inexpressible in the mind of the awakened one who has just emerged from equipoise (SAMĀHITA).

**samyagvāc**. (P. sammāvācā; T. yang dag pa'i ngag; C. zhengyu; J. shōgo; K. chŏngŏ 正語). In Sanskrit, "right speech" or "correct speech," the third constituent of the noble eightfold path (ĀRYĀṢṬĀṄGAMĀRGA), described as refraining from the four types of unwholesome verbal action: viz., lying, divisive speech, harsh speech, and frivolous prattle. See KARMAPATHA.

**samyagvyāyāma**. (P. sammāvāyāma; T. yang dag pa'i rtsol ba; C. zhengjingjin; J. shōshōjin; K. chŏngjŏngjin 正精進). In Sanskrit, "right effort" or "correct effort"; the sixth constituent of the noble eightfold path (ĀRYĀṢṬĀṄGAMĀRGA), which is divided into four progressive endeavors: (1) preventing the arising of unwholesome (AKUŚALA) mental states that have not yet arisen, (2) continuing to abandon unwholesome mental states that have already arisen, (3) generating wholesome (KUŚALA) mental states that have not yet arisen, and (4) continuing to cultivate wholesome mental states that have already arisen. These wholesome mental states are characterized by mindfulness (SMṚTI), energy (VĪRYA), rapture (PRĪTI), concentration (SAMĀDHI), and equanimity (UPEKṢĀ), with the emphasis on energy or vigor (vīrya), here called effort (vyāyāma). In a more technical sense, as the sixth constituent of the eightfold noble path as set forth in the MADHYĀNTAVIBHĀGA, MAHĀYĀNASŪTRĀLAṂKĀRA, and parts of the ABHIDHARMAKOŚABHĀṢYA, samyagvyāyāma is the right effort required to eliminate the specific sets of afflictions (KLEŚA) that are to be abandoned on the path of cultivation (BHĀVANĀMĀRGA). The same force, required right from the start of the development of the path to enlightenment, is systematized as the four pradhāna (effort) or PRAHĀṆA (abandonments). Like smṛti and samādhi (see ṚDDHIPĀDA), effort is singled out for special treatment because of its importance at all stages of the path. The word SAMYAKPRADHĀNA (correct effort) is synonymous with samyakvyāyāma when it describes pradhāna that is fully developed. See also SAMYAKPRADHĀNA.

**samyakkarmānta**. (P. sammākammanta; T. yang dag pa'i las kyi mtha'; C. zhengye; J. shōgō; K. chŏngŏp 正業). In Sanskrit, lit. "correct ends of actions," commonly translated as "right action" or "correct action" and is the fourth constituent of the noble eightfold path (ĀRYĀṢṬĀṄGAMĀRGA). Of the three divisions of the eightfold path—morality (ŚĪLA), concentration (SAMĀDHI), and wisdom (PRAJÑĀ)—samyakkarmānta is the second of the three types of moral training. It is described as refraining from the three unwholesome physical actions of killing, stealing, and sexual misconduct. Thus three of the five most fundamental Buddhist precepts (PAÑCAŚĪLA) are encompassed by samyakkarmānta (the other two being abstinence from false speech and abstinence from intoxicants). Action is considered to be particularly significant in the Buddhist tradition because it is understood to be a product of mental volition (CETANĀ). Various schools variously interpret the nuances of right action. For example, East Asian Buddhism has generally concluded that meat-eating inevitably causes animals to suffer and is therefore inconsistent with samyakkarmānta, even though meat-eating is not specifically proscribed in the mainstream Buddhist VINAYAS.

**samyakpradhāna**. (P. sammāpadhāna; T. yang dag par spong ba; C. zhengqin; J. shōgon; K. chŏnggŭn 正勤). In Sanskrit, "right effort" or "correct effort"; in Tibetan (which reads the term as PRAHĀṆA), "right abandonment." There are four right efforts, which are set forth within the presentation of the second set of dharmas making up the thirty-seven constituents of enlightenment (BODHIPĀKṢIKADHARMA). The four pradhānas (efforts or, as prahāṇa, abandonments) describe effort at incipient stages of the path or religious training; by contrast, right effort (SAMYAKVYĀYĀMA), the sixth constituent of the eightfold path (ĀRYĀṢṬĀṄGAMĀRGA), denotes the effort or abandonment that occurs during the path of vision (DARŚANAMĀRGA) or the path of cultivation (BHĀVANĀMĀRGA), when the path is more fully developed. Pradhāna involves the effort to abandon unwholesome (AKUŚALA) mental states—and their resulting actions via body, speech, and mind—that are conducive to suffering. Simultaneously, samyakpradhāna encompasses the effort to cultivate those wholesome (KUŚALA) mental states that are conducive to happiness for both oneself and others. These wholesome mental states are characterized by mindfulness (SMṚTI), energy (VĪRYA), rapture (PRĪTI), concentration (SAMĀDHI), and equanimity (UPEKṢĀ). At the first stage of practice, the focus is on SMṚTI, which, as the foundations of mindfulness (SMṚTYUPASTHĀNA), involves mindfulness of the FOUR NOBLE TRUTHS as applied to the body, sensations, states of mind, and wholesome and unwholesome dharmas. At the second stage of the practice, the focus is on the effort needed to develop samādhi. When fully developed in the mind of the awakened person, the practice of mindfulness is called right mindfulness; concentration, rapture, and equanimity are included under right concentration; and energy is called right effort (samyakvyāyāma).

**samyaksamādhi**. (P. sammāsamādhi; T. yang dag pa'i ting nge 'dzin; C. zhengding; J. shōjō; K. chŏngjŏng 正定). In Sanskrit, "right concentration" or "correct concentration," the eighth constituent of the noble eightfold path (ĀRYĀṢṬĀṄGAMĀRGA). It is defined generally as the concentration of the mind on wholesome objects. When fully developed, such concentration results in the attainment of the four levels of meditative absorption (DHYĀNA) associated with the realm of subtle materiality (RŪPADHĀTU). In this context, two types of samyaksamādhi are described. The first, called mundane, or LAUKIKA, is associated with all forms of ordinary concentration up to and including the four stages of dhyāna. The second type is associated with the attainment of the four supramundane (LOKOTTARA) paths of the stream-enterer, once-returner, nonreturner, and arhat.

**samyaksaṃbodhi**. (P. sammāsaṃbodhi; T. yang dag par rdzogs pa'i byang chub; C. zhengdengjue; J. shōtōgaku; K. chŏngdŭnggak 正等覺). In Sanskrit, "complete, perfect enlightenment." The term, along with its synonym, ANUTTARASAMYAKSAṂBODHI, is commonly used to refer to the enlightenment of a buddha, achieved under the BODHI TREE. Different schools of Buddhist thought distinguish this samyaksaṃbodhi from the simple enlightenment (BODHI) of an ARHAT in a variety of ways, with the MAHĀYĀNA schools asserting, for example, that a buddha has destroyed both the afflictive obstructions (KLEŚĀVARAṆA) and the obstacles to omniscience (JÑEYĀVARAṆA), while an arhat has only destroyed the former.

**samyaksaṃbuddha**. (P. sammāsaṃbuddha; T. yang dar par rdzogs pa'i sangs rgyas; C. zhengbianzhi; J. shōhenchi; K. chŏngp'yŏnji 正遍知). In Sanskrit, "complete and perfect buddha" or "complete and perfect enlightened one," a common epithet of a buddha, emphasizing that he has achieved the ultimate enlightenment, one that surpasses all others, including the enlightenment of the ARHAT.

**samyaksaṃkalpa**. (P. sammāsaṅkappa; T. yang dag pa'i rtog pa; C. zhengsiwei; J. shōshiyui; K. chŏngsayu 正思惟). In Sanskrit, "right attitude" or "right intention"; the second constituent of the noble eightfold path (ĀRYĀṢṬĀṄGAMĀRGA), described as the intention to avoid thoughts of attachment, hatred, and harmful intent, and to promote loving-kindness and nonviolence. Alternatively, it is the mental articulation or conceptualization (SAṂKALPA) of the content of the inexpressible vision of the FOUR NOBLE TRUTHS that occurs on the path of vision (DARŚANAMĀRGA) and that motivates one to teach it to others; SAMYAGDṚṢṬI (right view) is, by contrast, the nonconceptual understanding of that content.

**samyaksmṛti**. (P. sammāsati; T. yang dag pa'i dran pa; C. zhengnian; J. shōnen; K. chŏngnyŏm 正念). In Sanskrit, "right mindfulness" or "correct mindfulness," the seventh constituent of the noble eightfold path (ĀRYĀṢṬĀṄGAMĀRGA). It is defined as the full development of the cultivation of the four foundations of mindfulness (SMṚTYUPASTHĀNA) on the body (KĀYA; KĀYĀNUPAŚYANĀ), sensations (VEDANĀ), mind (CITTA), and various factors (DHARMA).

**samyaktvaniyāmāvakrānti**. (P. sammattaniyāma-okkanti; T. yang dag pa nyid skyon med pa la zhugs pa; C. zhengxing lisheng; J. shōshōrishō; K. chŏngsŏng isaeng 正性離生). In Sanskrit, "access to the certainty that one will eventually win liberation" or "entering the stage of certainty that one is destined for enlightenment." In the five-stage path structure (PAÑCAMĀRGA) of the SARVĀSTIVĀDA school of ABHIDHARMA, the third stage, the path of vision (DARŚANAMĀRGA), is marked by single thought-moments of realization regarding the FOUR NOBLE TRUTHS (catvāry āryasatyāni), divided into four insights for each of the four truths. The second of these sixteen moments involves the "knowledge of the fact of suffering" (duḥkhe dharmajñāna) with regard to the sensuous realm of existence (KĀMADHĀTU). This acceptance marks the access to the stage of certainty that one is destined for enlightenment (samyaktvaniyāmāvakrānti). This certainty is catalyzed by the highest worldly dharmas (LAUKIKĀGRADHARMA), the fourth and last of the four aids to penetration (NIRVEDHABHĀGĪYA). This process leads to stream-entry (SROTAĀPANNA), the first of the four stages of sanctity (ĀRYAMĀRGA).

**saṃyojana**. (T. kun tu sbyor ba; C. jie; J. ketsu; K. kyŏl 結). In Sanskrit and Pāli, "fetter." There are ten fetters that are commonly listed as binding one to the cycle of rebirth (SAṂSĀRA): (1) SATKĀYADṚṢṬI (P. sakkāyadiṭṭhi) is the mistaken belief in the existence of a self in relation to the five aggregates (SKANDHA). (2) VICIKITSĀ (P. vicikicchā) is doubt about the efficacy of the path (MĀRGA). Such skeptical doubt is also classified as one of five hindrances (NĪVARAṆA) that prevent the mind from attaining meditative absorption (DHYĀNA). (3) ŚĪLAVRATAPARĀMARŚA (P. sīlabbataparāmāsa), "attachment to rules and rituals," one of four kinds of clinging (UPĀDĀNA), is the mistaken belief that, e.g., purificatory rites, such as bathing in the Ganges River or performing sacrifices, can free a person from the consequences of unwholesome (AKUŚALA) actions (KARMAN). (4) KĀMARĀGA ("craving for sensuality"), or KĀMACCHANDA ("desire for sense gratification"), and (5) VYĀPĀDA ("malice"), synonymous with DVEṢA (P. dosa; "hatred"), are both also classified as hindrances to meditative absorption; along with greed (LOBHA) and ignorance (AVIDYĀ, P. avijjā; see the tenth fetter below), dveṣa is also one of the three unwholesome faculties (AKUŚALAMŪLA). (6) RŪPARĀGA ("craving for existence in the realm of subtle-materiality") is the desire to be reborn as a divinity in the realm of subtle materiality (RŪPADHĀTU), where beings are possessed of refined material bodies and are perpetually absorbed in the bliss of meditative absorption (dhyāna). (7) ĀRŪPYARĀGA ("craving for immaterial existence") is the desire to be reborn as a divinity in the immaterial realm (ĀRŪPYADHĀTU), where beings are comprised entirely of mind and are perpetually absorbed in the meditative bliss of the immaterial attainments (SAMĀPATTI). (8) MĀNA ("pride") arises from comparing oneself to others and manifests itself in three ways, in the feeling that one is superior to, equal to, or inferior to others. (9) AUDDHATYA (P. uddhacca) is the mental restlessness or excitement that impedes concentration. (10) AVIDYĀ is ignorance regarding the FOUR NOBLE TRUTHS whereby one sees what is not self as self, what is not profitable as profitable, and what is painful as pleasurable. The first three fetters vanish when one reaches the level of stream-enterer; there is a reduction in the other fetters when one reaches the level of once-returner and nonreturner; and all the fetters vanish when one reaches the stage of arhatship. See also ANUŚAYA; ĀRYAMĀRGAPHALA; ANĀGĀMIN.

**Samyŏng Yujŏng**. (四溟惟政) (1544–1610). Influential Korean SŎN master during the Chosŏn dynasty and important resistance leader during the Japanese Hideyoshi invasions of the late sixteenth century. Yujŏng was a native of Miryang in present-day South Kyŏngsang province. He was ordained by a monk named Sinmuk (d.u.) at the monastery of CHIKCHISA on Mt. Hwanghak (in present-day North Kyŏngsang province). In 1561, he passed the clerical examinations (SŬNGKWA) for Sŏn monks and was appointed the abbot of Chikchisa in 1573. He later became the disciple of the eminent Sŏn master CH'ŎNGHŎ HYUJŎNG (a.k.a. SŎSAN TAESA). When the Japanese invaded the Korean peninsula in 1592, Yujŏng took over his teacher Hyujŏng's place as leader of the monks' militia (ŭisŭnggun) against the invading troops. Leading several thousand monk-soldiers, Yujŏng's army played a crucial role in several battles where the Japanese were defeated. After the war ended, Yujŏng is also said to have gone to Japan as an emissary of the Korean king to negotiate peace with the new shōgun Tokugawa Ieyasu (1543–1616); he also helped to negotiate the release of some three thousand Korean hostages and prisoners of war taken during the invasion. For his valor during the war, Yujŏng was appointed prelate (p'ansa) of the SŎN (Meditation) and KYO (Doctrine) schools of the Chosŏn-dynasty ecclesia. By the eighteenth century, Yujŏng had become the object of a popular cult in Korea, and shrines to Yujŏng and his teacher Hyujŏng were erected around the country.

**Saṃyuktābhidharmahṛdaya**. (C. Za apitan xin lun; J. Zōabidon shinron; K. Chap abidam sim non 雜阿毘曇心論). In Sanskrit, "Heart of Abhidharma with Miscellaneous Additions"; the last of a series of expository treatises that summarized the SARVĀSTIVĀDA ABHIDHARMA as it was prevailing in BACTRIA and GANDHĀRA. The treatise was based on Dharmaśresthin's ABHIDHARMAHṚDAYA and includes material adapted from the ABHIDHARMAMAHĀVIBHĀṢĀ. The text is available only in a Chinese translation made by SAṂGHAVARMAN in the Liu Song capital of Jiankang in 434 CE; it is divided into eleven rolls, which correspond to separate chapters, on such topics as the elements (DHĀTU), conditioned factors (SAṂSKĀRA), KARMAN, etc. This treatise was composed during the early fourth century CE by the Sarvāstivāda ĀBHIDHARMIKA DHARMATRĀTA II (d.u.). The text was probably composed during a third major stage in the development of Sarvāstivāda abhidharma literature, following the JÑĀNAPRASTHĀNA and its six traditional ancillary treatises, or "feet" (pādaśāstra), and then the major *Vibhāṣā* exegeses; this stage eventually culminated in the composition of VASUBANDHU's celebrated ABHIDHARMAKOŚABHĀṢYA. This Dharmatrāta is often designated in the scholarly literature as Dharmatrāta II, to distinguish him from the Dārṣṭāntika Dharmatrāta I, who was one of the four great ābhidharmikas whom XUANZANG says participated in the fourth Buddhist council (SAṂGĪTI; see COUNCIL, FOURTH) convened by the KUSHAN king KANIṢKA (r. c. 127–151 CE). Dharmatrāta II also composed the *Pañcavastuvibhāṣā* (C. *Wushi piposha lun*; "Exposition of the Fivefold Classification"), a commentary on the first chapter of Vasumitra's PRAKARAṆAPĀDA, one of the seven major texts of the Sarvāstivāda ABHIDHARMAPIṬAKA, which was translated by Xuanzang in 663; it involves a discussion of the mature Sarvāstivāda school's fivefold classification system for dharmas: materiality (RŪPA), mentality (CITTA), mental concomitants (CAITTA), forces dissociated from thought (CITTAVIPRAYUKTA-SAṂSKĀRA), and the unconditioned (ASAMSKṚTA).

**Saṃyuktāgama**. (P. Saṃyuttanikāya; T. Yang dag par ldan pa'i lung; C. Za ahan jing; J. Zōagongyō; K. Chap aham kyŏng 雜阿含經). In Sanskrit, "Connected Discourses," a division of the ĀGAMAS corresponding roughly to the Pāli SAṂYUTTANIKĀYA. The collection was probably compiled sometime between 200 and 400 CE. Some Sanskrit fragments, especially of the nidānasaṃyukta section, were discovered in TURFAN, but the full collection is only preserved in a Chinese translation, in fifty rolls, made by GUṆABHADRA between 435 and 443 CE, with a second partial Chinese translation (in sixteen rolls) made by an anonym and a brief one-roll version (with only twenty-seven sūtras) apparently translated by AN SHIGAO. The longer Chinese translation is presumed to belong to the SARVĀSTIVĀDA school, with the shorter partial translation perhaps attributed to the KĀŚYAPĪYA school. The *Saṃyuktāgama* collects 1,362 sūtras (compared to 2,872 for the Pāli Saṃyuttanikāya), with some nascent attempts at a subject-matter arrangement, but nothing nearly as systematic as that found in the *Saṃyuttanikāya*. The Chinese translated title of *Za Ahan jing* (lit. "Miscellaneous Āgama") corresponds more closely to a Sanskrit **Kṣudrakāgama* (cf. P. KHUDDAKANIKĀYA), a "miscellaneous" collection of sūtras that is not known to have existed in the Sarvāstivāda school, although the content is more closely aligned with the *Saṃyuttanikāya*.

**Saṃyuttanikāya**. (S. Saṃyuktāgama; T. Yang dag par ldan pa'i lung; C. Za ahan jing; J. Zōagongyō; K. Chap aham kyŏng 雜阿含經). In Pāli, "Collection of Related Discourses" (or in its nineteenth-century translation *Book of Kindred Sayings*); the third of the five divisions of the Pāli SUTTAPIṬAKA and corresponds roughly to the SAṂYUKTĀGAMA of the SARVĀSTIVĀDA and KĀŚYAPĪYA schools, which is now extant only in its Chinese translations. The Pāli recension is comprised of some 2,872 individual suttas. Because of questions as to what constitutes a sutta in this case (some are only one sentence in length), enumerations of the number of suttas in the various saṃyutta/saṃyukta collections vary widely, from just under three thousand to over seven thousand (the longer of the two Chinese recensions contains 1,362 sūtras). The *Saṃyuttanikāya* is divided into five chapters, or vaggas, which are subdivided into fifty-six saṃyuttas, arranged largely by subject matter. The collection derives its title from this classificatory system. The five vaggas are devoted to: (1) verses (sagātha), suttas that in the majority of cases contain verses; (2) causation (NIDĀNA), suttas that deal primarily with epistemology and psychology; (3) the aggregates (P. khandha, S. SKANDHA) on the five aggregates; (4) the six sense-fields (P. saḷāyatana, S. ṢAḌĀYATANA), dealing with the six sources of consciousness; and (5) the great division (mahāvagga), which contains suttas on the noble eightfold path (ĀRYĀṢṬĀṄGAMĀRGA), the states of concentration (DHYĀNA), the establishments of mindfulness (SMṚTYUPASTHĀNA), and other important doctrines.

**Śāṇakavāsin**. (T. Sha na'i gos can; C. Shangnahexiu/Shangnuojiafusuo; J. Shōnawashu/Shōnyakabasha; K. Sangnahwasu/Sangnakkabaksa 商那和修/商諾迦縛娑). In Sanskrit, "Linen Wearer" [alt. Śāṇakavāsa]; the third (or fourth according to SARVĀSTIVĀDA sources) successor to the Buddha in some of the traditional dharma lineages preserved in Nepal, Tibet, and East Asia. His name derives from a legend that, from the moment he was born following a six-year-long period of gestation in his mother's womb, he was always dressed in linen garments. Before becoming a monk, he was a rich merchant in RĀJAGṚHA, who frequently offered alms to the SAṂGHA. He entered the religious order on the recommendation of ĀNANDA, and eventually succeeded him. After mastering all the canons, Śāṇakavāsin traveled around India, propagating Buddhism. He converted many people to the religion, including UPAGUPTA, who became his successor. He also played a role in the second Buddhist council (see COUNCIL, SECOND). He is believed to have died in MATHURĀ.

**Sanbōe**. (三宝絵). In Japanese, "The Three Jewels," a work composed by Minamoto Tamenori (d. 1011); also known as *Sanbōekotoba*. In this preface, Tamenori laments the fact that the world has now entered into the age of the final dharma (J. mappō; see C. MOFA) and speaks of the need to honor the DHARMA. Tamenori's text largely consists of three sections corresponding to the three jewels (RATNATRAYA), namely the Buddha, dharma, and saṃgha. In the buddha-jewel section, Tamenori provides JĀTAKA stories from various sources. In the dharma-jewel section, he describes the history of Buddhism in Japan from the rise of SHŌTOKU TAISHI (574–622) to the end of the Nara period. In the saṃgha-jewel section, Tamenori relies on many temple records and texts to speak of the representative ceremonies and rituals of Japanese Buddhism, their provenance, and the biographies of some important monks who carried out these events. The *Sanbōe* serves as a valuable source for studying the history of Buddhism during the Nara period.

**Sāñcī**. A famous STŪPA or CAITYA about six miles southwest of Vidiśā in the Indian state of Madhya Pradesh; often seen transcribed as Sanchi. The Sāñcī stūpa and its surrounding compound is one of the best-preserved Buddhist archeological sites in the world and is well known for its many monasteries, reliquaries, pillars, and stone relief carvings. Sāñcī was an active site of worship and pilgrimage in India between the third century BCE and the twelfth century CE. However, unlike other pilgrimage sites such as SĀRNĀTH and BODHGAYĀ, Sāñcī is not known to be a place that was associated with the historical Buddha and there are no records or stories of the Buddha himself ever visiting the site. The emperor AŚOKA is credited with laying the foundation of the compound by erecting a stūpa and a pillar on the site. Other stories mention a Vidiśā woman whom Aśoka married, called Vidiśā Devī, who was a devout Buddhist; according to tradition, she was the one who initiated construction of a Buddhist monastery at the site. When Aśoka ascended the throne at PĀṬALIPUTRA, she did not accompany him to the capital, but remained behind in her hometown and later became a nun. Sāñcī and the nearby city of Vidiśā were located near the junction of two important trading routes, and the city's wealthy merchants munificently supported its monasteries and religious sites. Structures erected during the rule of the Śuṅgas and the Śātavāhanas still stand today, and the area flourished after 400 CE during the reign of the Guptas. Sāñcī subsequently fell into a lengthy decline and seems to have been completely deserted at least by the end of the thirteenth century. The site was rediscovered in 1818 by a certain British General Taylor, who excavated the western section of the stūpa; his archeological work was continued by F. C. Maisay and Alexander Cunningham, who discovered relics (ŚARĪRA) believed to be those of the Buddha's two major disciples ŚĀRIPUTRA and

MAHĀMAUDGALYĀYANA in the center of the dome of the main stūpa. There was ongoing controversy within different divisions of the British colonial government over whether or not Sāñcī artifacts should be shipped to British museums; finally, in 1861, the Archeological Survey of India was established and the area was preserved and protected. See also NĀSIK.

**sandaihihō**. (三大秘法). In Japanese, "three great esoteric laws," three secret teachings that are presumed to have been hidden between the lines of the SADDHARMAPUṆḌARĪKASŪTRA ("Lotus Sūtra") until NICHIREN (1222–1282) discovered them and revealed them to the world. The three are: (1) the DAI-GOHONZON (J. honmon no honzon), the main object of worship in the NICHIREN SHŌSHŪ school, which is a cosmological chart (MAṆḌALA) of the universe surrounding an inscription of homage to the title of the "Lotus Sūtra" and Nichiren's own name; (2) the sanctuary (J. honmon no kaidan) where the dai-gohonzon is enshrined at Taisekiji, the head temple of Nichiren Shōshū; and (3) the teaching of NAM MYŌHŌRENGEKYŌ (J. honmon no DAIMOKU), "Homage to the 'Lotus Sūtra,'" the recitation that is central to Nichiren practice.

**sandao**. (J. sandō; K. samdo 三道). In Chinese, lit. "three destinies," in East Asian Buddhist iconography, the "triple fold" of skin at the base of the neck on images of the buddhas and bodhisattvas, which is intended to indicate the inevitability of rebirth and the operation of cause and effect. These three folds of skin are interpreted to represent the "three destinies" that inevitably accrue to life in the realm of SAṂSĀRA, viz., the afflictions (S. KLEŚA, C. fannao dao), actions (S. KARMAN, C. ye dao), and suffering (S. DUḤKHA, C. ku dao).

**sandhyābhāṣā**. [alt. saṃdhyābhāṣyā] (T. dgongs bshad/dgongs skad). In Sanskrit, "intentional language," often mistranslated as "twilight language"; a kind of secret or coded speech, used especially, but not exclusively, in TANTRA. The term is used in a broader hermeneutical sense to explain how a difficult or otherwise problematic text requires commentary in order to bring out its doctrinally consistent meaning. The term is also used in an exclusively tantric sense to refer to a secret linguistic code that is understood and used by initiates of a particular tantric circle: e.g., "frankincense" means "blood" and "camphor" means "semen." The *Pradīpoddyotana* commentary by the tāntrika Candrakīrti on the *Guhyasamājamūlatantra* explains sandhyābhāṣā with a scheme of six alternatives (ṣaṭkoṭi) in a series of four modes going from less to more profound. The six alternatives are provisional (NEYĀRTHA) and definitive (NĪTĀRTHA); requiring interpretation (ābhiprāyika) and not requiring interpretation (anābhiprāyika); and ayathāruta (when one cannot take words literally) and yathāruta (when one can take words literally). Complicated or obscure language (called VAJRA expression) that can be taken literally (yathāruta), or that can be taken at face value to convey meaning, provides a provisional meaning, i.e., a meaning that requires interpretation (neyārtha); this leads to what the statement does not say literally (ayathāruta), which is its definitive meaning (nītārtha). A passage about a topic not addressed in statements about lower stages of the tantric path, and therefore couched in words that are coded and apparently contradictory to other statements, in the sense that other passages about practices at lower stages of the tantric path contradict what it says, are ābhiprāyika, while straightforward statements about a topic that is not addressed at lower stages of the tantric path are anābhiprāyika; for example, direct statements about clear light (PRABHĀSVARA) and illusory bodies (māyākāya), the culminating attainments in the Guhyasamāja system. Finally, a statement couched in ordinary language about a topic that is relevant to both earlier and later stages of the tantric path is yathāruta (can be taken literally); statements using a specialized argot, using unusual words that are ordinarily meaningless, like some words in MANTRAs, are ayathāruta. See also ABHIPRĀYA; ABHISAṂDHI.

**sandhyābhāṣita**. (S). See SANDHYĀBHĀṢĀ.

**sandi**. (J. santai; K. samje 三諦). In Chinese, "three truths," "threefold truth," or "three judgments"; a tripartite exegetical description of reality as being empty, provisional, and their mean, used in both the SAN LUN ZONG and TIANTAI ZONG of Chinese Buddhist philosophy. The three truths are said to have been first taught by SŬNGNANG (c. 450–c. 520), whom tradition considers an important vaunt courier in the development of the Chinese San lun school, the Chinese counterpart of the MADHYAMAKA branch of Indian philosophical exegesis, and then developed by later thinkers in both the San lun and Tiantai traditions. This Chinese notion of three truths is said to derive from a verse appearing in the Chinese translation of NĀGĀRJUNA's MŪLAMADHYAMAKAKĀRIKĀ (C. *Zhong lun*): "All phenomena that are produced from causes and conditions,/ These in fact are empty. /They are also provisional names. /This as well is the meaning of the middle way." This account is then systematized by Chinese exegetes into: (1) the authentic truth of emptiness (kongdi), viz., all things are devoid of inherent existence and are empty in their essential nature: (2) the conventional truth of being provisionally real (jiadi), viz., all things are products of a causal process that gives them a derived reality; and (3) the ultimate truth of the mean (zhongdi), viz., all things, in their absolute reality, are neither real nor unreal, but simply thus. This three-truth schema may have been influenced by indigenous Chinese scriptures (see APOCRYPHA) such as the RENWANG JING and the PUSA YINGLUO BENYE JING. The *Renwang jing*, for example, discusses a three-truth SAMĀDHI (sandi sanmei), in which these three types of concentrations are named worldly truth (shidi), authentic truth (zhendi), and supreme-meaning truth (diyiyidi). In this treatment, worldly truth is the affirmation of the dualistic phenomena of ordinary existence, while authentic truth is presumed to be the denial of the reality of those phenomena; both are therefore aspects of what is typically called conventional truth (SAṂVṚTISATYA) in the two-truth schema (see SATYADVAYA). The supreme-meaning truth transcends all dichotomies, including affirmation and negation, to provide an all-embracing perspective and corresponds to ultimate truth (PARAMĀRTHASATYA). This schema is peculiar, and betrays its Chinese origins, because "authentic truth" and "supreme-meaning truth" are actually just different Chinese renderings of the same Sanskrit term, paramāthasatya. Zhiyi also interprets the statement "neither the same nor different" in the SADDHARMAPUṆḌARĪKASŪTRA ("Lotus Sūtra") as referring implicitly to the three-truth schema: "different" is the conventional truth of provisional reality, "same" is the authentic truth of emptiness, and the whole phrase is the ultimate truth of the mean. These presentations demonstrate that the Chinese were grappling with what they considered to be an unresolved internal tension in Indian presentations of conventional and ultimate truth and were exploring a three-truth schema as one means of resolving that tension.

**sanfen kejing**. (J. sanbunkakyō; K. sambun kwagyŏng 三分科經). In Chinese, "threefold division of a scripture," an exegetical technique developed by the pioneering scholiast and cataloguer DAO'AN (312–385) to analyze a specific SŪTRA's narrative structure. Dao'an's scriptural commentaries posited the following three major sections that were common to all sūtras: (1) the prefatory setting (C. xufen; S. nidāna), which specifies the time and place where the sūtra was delivered; (2) the "text proper" (zhengzongfen), viz., the main body of the sūtra, which relates the doctrines and practices that were the subject of the discourse; and (3) the "dissemination section" (liutongfen; S. parīndanā), which describes the confidence and insight the scripture inspired in its audience. This schema was frequently employed in subsequent scriptural exegesis of most of the major scholastic schools of East Asian Buddhism and is still widely used even today. See also NETTIPPAKARAṆA; PEṬAKOPADESA; VYĀKHYĀYUKTI; WUZHONG XUANYI.

**saṅgha**. Pāli and classical Sanskrit variant of "community." See also the BUDDHIST HYBRID SANSKRIT form SAṂGHA and its various compound forms.

**Saṅgha Administration Act**. A law enacted in Thailand in 1902 designed to bring the entire Buddhist order (P. saṅgha, S. SAṂGHA) of Thailand under a single administrative authority. It was primarily an initiative of Prince Wachirayān, brother of King Chulalongkorn (RĀMA V) and the son of King Mongkut (RĀMA IV). The law was initially applied only to royal monasteries and several other important monasteries, but in 1908 it was extended to encompass the entire northeast region. It established a single system for monastic education and standardized the ordination procedure. Under this act, all abbots in Thailand were appointed by government officials or the king. The act was revised in 1941 and in 1962. It has not met with universal acceptance or compliance, being challenged especially by the tradition of the forest monks (ARAÑÑAVĀSI).

**Saṅghamittā**. (S. Saṃghamitrā; C. Sengqiemiduo; J. Sōgyamitta; K. Sŭnggamilta 僧伽蜜多). In Pāli, "Friend of the Community," proper name of the nun (BHIKṢUṆĪ) who was the daughter of the Indian king Asoka (S. AŚOKA) and sister of MAHINDA (S. Mahendra). According to some accounts, Mahinda and Saṅghamittā were twins; others claim, instead, that Mahinda was one or two years her senior. According to Pāli sources, Saṅghamittā was born in Ujjeni (S. Ujjayinī) and married to Aggibrahmā (S. Agnibrahmā), with whom she had a son named Sumana. The most detailed account of her life comes to us in the MAHĀVAṂSA (c. fifth century CE). There, she is said to have been ordained when she was eighteen years old. When Mahinda went to Sri Lanka and converted King DEVĀNAṂPRIYATISSA, the king's daughter Anulā asked to be ordained. Mahinda replied that monks cannot ordain women, but that his sister was a nun and that she should be invited to come from India. Saṅghamittā traveled to the island kingdom, bringing along with her eleven other nuns in order to establish her ordination lineage in that new region, as well as a branch from the BODHI TREE. The *Mahāvaṃsa* tells us that during her voyage to Sri Lanka, nineteen NĀGAs threatened to use their magic to steal the bodhi tree, but Saṅghamittā defended it by taking the form of a GARUḌA (the natural enemy of the nāgas). Tradition holds that the bodhi tree she brought took root in ANURĀDHAPURA and it remains to this day an object of worship. Neither Mahinda nor Saṅghamittā returned to India. Upon her death, her body was cremated and her remains were enshrined in a STŪPA in Cittasālā, near the site of the bodhi tree.

**saṅgharāja**. In Pāli, lit. "ruler of the community," often rendered into English as "supreme patriarch"; a title used in the predominantly THERAVĀDA traditions of Sri Lanka, Thailand, and Cambodia. The title is given to one monk who serves as the head of a single monastic school (NIKĀYA), or the head of the entire national saṅgha (S. SAṂGHA). The procedure for appointing a saṅgharāja differs across traditions. At times, the title has been given to the most senior monk in the saṅgha, that is, the one who has been ordained the longest. At other times, designating a saṅgharāja has been the prerogative of the king, as was the case for the first saṅgharāja to be appointed in Southeast Asia: Mahākassapa, a forest-dwelling monk of Sri Lanka who, in the twelfth century, helped King PARĀKRAMABĀHU I reform the Ceylonese saṅgha. The duties of the saṅgharāja have varied widely. In some instances, the title is honorific and the office holder wields little or no administrative power; in such instances, the saṅgharāja serves as a figurehead and spokesman for the saṅgha. In other instances, such as with Mahākassapa, the saṅgharāja has the authority to enact dramatic changes in the order and structure of the Buddhist saṅgha. Another title related to the saṅgharāja is that of upasaṅgharāja, a deputy who is appointed to assist the saṅgharāja in carrying out his duties. The Burmese equivalent of saṅgharāja is thathanabaing. See also CHONGJŎNG.

**Saṅgītisutta**. (S. Saṃgītisūtra; C. Zhongji jing; J. Shushūkyō; K. Chungjip kyŏng 衆集經). In Pāli, "Discourse on

Communal Recitation," the thirty-third sutta of the DĪGHANIKĀYA (a separate DHARMAGUPTAKA recension appears as the ninth sūtra in the Chinese translation of the DĪRGHĀGAMA); preached by Sāriputta (S. ŚĀRIPUTRA) to a congregation of monks at Pāvā in Malla country. The followers of the JAINA leader Nigaṇṭha-Nātaputta (S. NIRGRANTHA-JÑĀTĪPUTRA) had begun to quarrel following the death of their master. Śāriputra related to the monks at Pāvā that this occurred because Jñātīputra was not enlightened and so his teachings were erroneous and not well taught, but the Buddha, by contrast, was enlightened and his teachings were well taught. Śāriputra suggested that the dharma be chanted by the congregation in unison as a means of preserving it. He then summarized the dharma under numerical classifications ranging from groups of ones to groups of tens as a device for memorization. This exegetical stratagem provides one of the first canonical recensions of the "matrices" (P. mātikā, S. MĀTṚKĀ) that are thought to mark the incipiency of the ABHIDHARMA, and its style of exposition is closely connected to that employed in the DASUTTARASUTTA (S. *Daśottarasūtra*); several of its exegetical categories are also reproduced in the SAṂGĪTIPARYĀYA of the SARVĀSTIVĀDA ABHIDHARMA.

**Saṅgītivaṃsa**. In Pāli, "Chronicle of the Councils"; a history of nine THERAVĀDA (i.e., STHAVIRANIKĀYA) Buddhist councils, or saṅgīti (S. SAMGĪTI), according to the Thai reckoning. Written in Pāli in Bangkok in 1789 by the monk Somdet Phra Wannarat, the text describes the three Buddhist councils held in ancient India, followed by an account of councils four through eight in Sri Lanka, and concludes with the ninth Buddhist council (see COUNCIL, NINTH) held in Bangkok under King Rāma I in 1788–1789. The work contains much information on the religion and polity of Thailand through the establishment of the Cakri dynasty (1782-present).

**sangong**. (三公). In Chinese, lit. "three gentlemen"; the three great lay masters of Chinese Buddhism recognized by PENG SHAOSHENG (1740–1796) in his JUSHI ZHUAN ("The Biographies of [Eminent] Laymen"): LIU CHENGZHI (354–410), for his mastery of PURE LAND (JINGTU) practice; LI TONGXUAN (635–730), for his scholarship on HUAYAN; and PANG YUN (740–803), for his practice of CHAN. See individual entries for the three.

**sang rgyas**. (sang gye). The Tibetan translation of buddha. In coining neologisms to render Buddhist terminology, Tibetan translators sometimes sought to evoke multiple meanings of a single Sanskrit term. In the case of buddha, they knew that the Sanskrit root √budh has the meaning of both "awaken" and "open" or "spread." They therefore translated buddha as "awakened" and "spread," meaning that a buddha has awakened from the sleep of ignorance and spread his mind to all objects of knowledge.

**Sangs rgyas gling pa**. (Sangye Lingpa) (1340–1396). Tibetan treasure revealer (GTER STON) and master of the RNYING MA sect of Tibetan Buddhism. He was born in the southern Tibetan region of Rkong po (Kongpo) and experienced visions of AVALOKITEŚVARA as a child. He was ordained as a BHIKṢU at Byang chub gling monastery on TSA RI. From the age of thirty-four onward, he is credited with discovering numerous treasure cycles, especially from the region of Rkong po. Foremost among these are the "six root tantras of the gathering intentions" (dgongs 'dus rtsa ba'i rgyud drug), which he later divided into thirteen volumes. These teachings were acclaimed by masters of varied sectarian affiliation including the fourth and fifth KARMA PAs, the latter transmitting them to the Ming emperor Yongle.

**sanguan**. (J. sangan; K. samgwan 三觀). In Chinese, "threefold contemplation"; several versions of such a threefold contemplation are elaborated in Chinese exegetical traditions, of which the most influential was the TIANTAI version outlined by TIANTAI ZHIYI in his MOHE ZHIGUAN. Zhiyi's version entails a system of contemplative practice that leads to the attainment of insight into the nature of reality. Zhiyi's "threefold contemplation" consists of the contemplations of the "three truths: (SANDI): emptiness, conventional existence, and their mean (C. kong jia zhong sanguan; J. kū ge chū sangan; K. kong ka chung samgwan). The first, "contemplation on emptiness" (kongguan), is the step of practice that advances beyond naïve realism by penetrating into the conditionally constructed, and therefore insubstantial, nature of all phenomena (see ŚŪNYATĀ). The second, the "contemplation on conventionality" (jiaguan), involves the reaffirmation of the conventional existence of all phenomena, whereby a bodhisattva actively engages the world in spite of his awareness of the reality of emptiness. The third, the "contemplation of their mean" (zhongguan), is understood as a dialectical transcendence of the previous two modes of practice. This transcendence has two aspects: it is transcendent because it is neither ("the middle that negates both," C. shuangfei zhi zhong) and because it affirms both ("the middle that illuminates both," C. shuangzhao zhi zhong). It is "neither" because the middle way is not fixed exclusively on either abiding in emptiness or on wallowing in mundane existence. It is "both" because it elucidates that "emptiness" and "conventionality" are not opposing realities but are in fact mutually validating. "The threefold contemplation" is understood variously as a gradual or a simultaneous practice ("two kinds of 'threefold contemplation,'" C. erzhong sanguan; J. nishu no sangan; K. ijong samgwan). The gradual practice of the "threefold contemplation" begins with the contemplation of emptiness, advances to that of conventional existence, and culminates in the contemplation of their mean. Tiantai exegetes variously labeled this approach "the threefold contemplation" by either "graduated stages" (C. cidi sanguan; J. shidai sangan; K. ch'aje samgwan) or "differentiation" (C. biexiang sanguan; J. bessō no sangan; K. pyŏlsang samgwan). As a simultaneous practice, all three aspects of the reality are to be contemplated simultaneously within any given instant of thought: a true understanding of "emptiness" is the same as the correct understanding of "conventional existence," for they are just different emphases of the same truth of conditionality; only an erroneous construction of "emptiness" and "conventional existence" would lead to the conclusion that they are separate, contradictory realities. This approach is variously referred to as "the threefold contemplation that does not involve graduated stages" (C. bucidi sanguan; J. fushidai sangan; K. pulch'aje samgwan), "the perfectly interfused threefold contemplation" (C. yuanrong sanguan; J. ennyū no sangan; K. wŏnyung samgwan), or "the threefold contemplation [that is to be conducted within] a single moment of thought" (C. yixin sanguan; J. isshin sangan; K. ilsim samgwan). See also SANZHI.

**sanimitta**. (T. mtshan bcas). In Sanskrit, literally "with marks" or "with signs," a term that has at least two principal denotations. In the context of MADHYAMAKA, sanimitta is a pejorative term, implying that one perceives the world via the chimeric signs or marks of intrinsic nature (SVABHĀVA). Because all phenomena are ultimately "signless" (ĀNIMITTA), to perceive them as having signs is a benighted form of ignorance. In the context of tantric meditation, however, the term has a more salutary meaning. Tantric texts and especially YOGATANTRAs, mention two forms of meditation, one called "yoga with signs" (SANIMITTAYOGA), the other "yoga without signs" (ANIMITTAYOGA). Yoga with signs refers to meditation in which one visualizes oneself as a deity, one's environment as a MAṆḌALA, etc. Yoga without signs refers to meditation in which one meditates on emptiness (ŚŪNYATĀ). In certain tantric SĀDHANAs, both forms of meditation are performed.

**sanimittayoga**. (T. mtshan bcas kyi rnal 'byor). Literally, "yoga with signs," a term that occurs in Buddhist tantric literature, and is especially associated with YOGATANTRA class of tantric texts. Yoga with signs refers to those meditation practices that entail dualistic appearances or "signs," in the sense that the meditator visualizes seed syllables (BĪJA) and deities. It is contrasted with ANIMITTAYOGA, or "yoga without signs," those meditation practices in which one meditates on emptiness (ŚŪNYATĀ) in such a way that there are no dualistic appearances or signs.

**Sañjaya Vairāṭīputra**. [alt. Saṃjayin Vairāṭīputra] (P. Sañjaya/Sañcaya Belaṭṭhiputta; T. Smra 'dod kyi bu mo'i bu yang dag rgyal ba can; C. Shansheye Piluozhizi; J. Sanjaya Birateishi; K. Sansaya Pirajija 刪闍耶毘羅胝子). One of the so-called "six heterodox teachers" often mentioned in Buddhist sūtras, whose views and/or practices were criticized by the Buddha, along with PŪRAṆA-KĀŚYAPA, MASKARIN GOŚĀLĪPUTRA, AJITA KEŚAKAMBALA, KAKUDA KĀTYĀYANA, and NIRGRANTHA-JÑĀTĪPUTRA. Sañjaya was a skeptic who doubted the possibility of knowledge and the validity of logic. On questions such as the presence of a world beyond the visible world, the nature of the postmortem condition, and whether actions done in this life had effects in the next, he found the four traditional answers—affirmation, negation, partial affirmation and partial negation, and neither affirmation or negative—to each be unacceptable, and therefore gave evasive answers when asked such speculative questions. The Buddha's two foremost disciples, ŚĀRIPUTRA and MAHĀMAUDGALYĀYANA, were originally disciples of Sañjaya before encountering the teachings of the Buddha. They are said to have each taken 250 of Sañjaya's followers with them when they abandoned him for the Buddha. Upon hearing the news of their departure, Sañjaya vomited blood and fainted.

**Sanjie jiao**. (J. Sangaikyō/Sankaikyō; K. Samgye kyo 三階教). In Chinese, often translated as the "Three Stages School," but more probably referring to the "School of the Third Stage." The Sanjie jiao was a Chinese religious movement that was inspired by the influential teachings of the Chinese monk XINXING (540–594). The community shared Xinxing's belief in the decline of the DHARMA (MOFA) and the concomitant decay of one's potential or capacity (genji) for attaining buddhahood. According to the Three Stages teachings, the capacities of sentient beings are roughly divided into the so-called three stages (sanjie). The first two stages, now past, are those of the one vehicle (YISHENG; cf. EKAYĀNA) or three vehicles (TRIYĀNA), during which correct views about Buddhism were still present in the world. The current "third stage" (i.e., the present) was characterized instead by the proliferation of false views and prejudices. Because people during this degenerate age of the dharma were inevitably mistaken in their perceptions of reality, it was impossible for them to make any correct distinctions, whether between right and wrong, good and evil, ordained and lay. To counter these inveterate tendencies toward discrimination, Sanjie jiao adherents were taught instead to treat all things as manifestations of the buddha-nature (FOXING), leading to a "universalist teaching" (pufa) of Buddhism that was presumed to have supplanted all the previous teachings of the religion. Xinxing advocated that almsgiving (DĀNA) was the epitome of Buddhist practice during the degenerate age of the dharma and that the true perfection of giving (DĀNAPĀRAMITĀ) meant that all people, monks and laypeople alike, should be making offerings to relieve the suffering to those most in need, including the poor, the orphaned, and the sick. In its radical reinterpretation of the practice of giving in Buddhism, even animals were considered to be a more appropriate object of charity than were buddhas, bodhisattvas, monks, or the three jewels (RATNATRAYA); members of the community were even said to bow down to dogs. As the only reliable practice during this degenerate third stage, the Sanjie jiao community institutionalized giving in the form of an "inexhaustible storehouse cloister" (WUJINZANG YUAN). Donations made to the inexhaustible storehouse established by the Three Stages community at the monastery Huadusi in Chang'an would be distributed again during times of famine. The offerings were also used to fund the restoration of monasteries and the performance of religious services (i.e., the reverence field of merit, C. jingtian), and to provide alms to the poor (i.e., the compassion field of merit, C. beitian; see PUṆYAKṢETRA). The inexhaustible storehouse also came to serve as a powerful money-lending institution. The Three Stages community was labeled a heresy during the persecution of Buddhism during the Tang dynasty and, in 713, the Tang emperor Xuanzong (r. 712–756) issued an edict closing the inexhaustible storehouse due to charges of embezzlement; its scriptures were eventually labeled spurious (see APOCRYPHA) and dropped out of circulation, only to be rediscovered in the DUNHUANG manuscript cache. Despite these persecutions, the school continued to be influential for several more centuries.

**sanju**. (J. sanku; K. samgu 三句). In Chinese, "three propositions," a unique set of precepts taught by CHŎNGJUNG MUSANG (680–756, alt. 684–762) in the JINGZHONG ZONG lineage of the early CHAN school. Musang sought to summarize the method of practice taught by the founder of Chinese Chan school, BODHIDHARMA, in three propositions, which he described as "no-recollection" (wuyi), which he equated with morality (ŚĪLA); "no-thought" (WUNIAN), which corresponded to concentration (SAMĀDHI); and "not-forgetting" (mowang), which was the equivalent of wisdom (PRAJÑĀ). In other Jingzhong zong texts, Musang's successor BAOTANG WUZHU later claims that he was in fact the creator of these three propositions and makes the explicit connection between them and the three trainings (TRIŚIKṢĀ) of mainstream Buddhism. GUIFENG ZONGMI later explains the first proposition, "no-recollection," as not tracing back the past; the second "no-thought," as not yearning for the future; and the third "not-forgetting" as "always conforming to this knowledge without confusion or mistake."

**Sanjūsangendō**. (三十三間堂). In Japanese, "Hall of Thirty-Three Bays"; a Buddhist temple in Kyōto, Japan, also known as "Hall of the Lotus King" (J. Rengeōin); it is part of the Myōhōin (Sublime Dharma Hall), a temple affiliated with the Japanese TENDAISHŪ. The number thirty-three refers to the belief that the BODHISATTVA Kannon (S. AVALOKITEŚVARA) saves humanity by transforming himself into thirty-three different figures. Taira no Kiyomori (1118–1181) completed the temple at the command of former emperor Goshirakawa (1127–1192) in 1164. After a fire destroyed the temple hall in 1249, the reconstruction of the building was completed in 1266 by former emperor Gosaga (1220–1272). The principal image of the temple is the "Eleven-Headed and Thousand-Armed Kannon" (see S. EKĀDAŚAMUKHĀVALOKITEŚVARA and SĀHASRABHUJASĀHASRANETRĀVALOKITEŚVARA). This deity was made of Japanese cypress in the yosegi zukuri style (viz., using several blocks of wood) by the artist Tankei (1173–1256) during the Kamakura period. It has eleven faces on its head and twenty-one pairs of arms that symbolize his one thousand arms. On both sides of the central seated statue are one thousand more standing images of the same type of Kannon, in five rows, each about five feet five inches in height, each said to be different from the other. Along with these statues, the school of Unkei (1151–1223) and Tankei also made twenty-eight statues of guardian deities. Additionally, flanking the right and left side of this arrangement are the statues of the Wind God (J. Fūjin) and the Thunder God (J. Raijin), respectively.

**saṅkhārupekkhāñāṇa**. In Pāli, "knowledge arising from equanimity regarding all formations"; according to the VISUDDHIMAGGA, the eighth of nine knowledges (P. ñāṇa, S. JÑĀNA) cultivated as part of "purity of knowledge and vision of progress along the path" (PAṬIPADĀÑĀṆADASSANAVISUDDHI). This latter category, in turn, constitutes the sixth and penultimate purity (P. visuddhi, S. VIŚUDDHI) to be developed along the path to liberation. Knowledge arising from equanimity regarding all formations arises as a consequence of understanding all conditioned formations (S. SAṂSKĀRA) that comprise the individual and the universe as being characterized by the three marks (S. TRILAKṢAṆA) of impermanence (S. ANITYA), suffering (S. DUḤKHA) and nonself (S. ANĀTMAN). This understanding is the product of the immediately preceding (seventh) knowledge called "knowledge arising from contemplation of reflection" (PAṬISAṄKHĀNUPASSANĀÑĀṆA). Understanding the formations to be void (see ŚŪNYATĀ) in this way, the practitioner abandons both terror and delight, and, regarding them as neither "I" nor "mine," he becomes indifferent and neutral towards them. The sixth, seventh, and eighth knowledges when taken together are called "insight leading to emergence" (vuṭṭhānagāmini vipassanā) because they stand at the threshold of liberation. The *Visuddhimagga* states that, at this stage in the practice, one can continue to contemplate the formations with equanimity, or, if the mind turns towards the nibbāṇa element (S. NIRVĀṆADHĀTU) as its object, one of three types of liberation (S. VIMUKTI) ensues. If liberation occurs while contemplating impermanence, it is called "signless liberation," if it occurs while contemplating suffering it is called "wishless liberation," and if it occurs while contemplating nonself it is called "empty liberation" (see VIMOKṢAMUKHA).

**San lun xuanyi**. (J. Sanron gengi; K. Sam non hyŏnŭi 三論玄義). In Chinese, "Profound Meaning of the Three Treatises," composed by the monk JIZANG sometime around 597. Although the title mentions the so-called "three treatises" (see SAN LUN ZONG), the *San lun xuanyi* is actually a commentary on four influential texts, namely the *Zhong lun* (cf. S. MŪLAMADHYAMAKAKĀRIKĀ), BAI LUN (S. *ŚATAŚĀSTRA), SHI'ERMEN LUN (S. **Dvādaśamukhaśāstra*), and DAZHIDU LUN (**Mahāprajñāpāramitāśastra*). The *San lun xuanyi* systematically presents the teachings of NĀGĀRJUNA and provides a succinct explanation of the notion of emptiness (ŚŪNYATĀ). Jizang's treatise consists of two main sections, which he terms the destruction of heresies and the elucidation of truth. His first section discusses the non-Buddhist teachings of India and the traditions of Zhuangzi, Laozi, and the *Zhouyi* in China. He also condemns ABHIDHARMA as HĪNAYĀNA teachings, the *TATTVASIDDHI as provisional MAHĀYĀNA, and the teachings of the five periods (see WUSHI BAJIAO) as a misleading attachment to MAHĀYĀNA. In the second section, Jizang explains the appearance of Nāgārjuna and the teachings of the *Zhong lun*, *Bai lun*, *Shi'ermen lun*, and *Dazhidu lun*. Jizang's explanations rely heavily upon the notion of the two truths (SATYADVAYA).

**San lun zong**. (J. Sanronshū; K. Sam non chong 三論宗). In Chinese, the "Three Treatises school," a Chinese analogue of the MADHYAMAKA school of Indian Buddhism philosophy; a largely exegetical tradition that focused on three important texts translated by KUMĀRAJĪVA, namely the *Zhong lun* ("Middle Treatise"), BAI LUN ("Hundred [Verse] Treatise"), and SHI'ERMEN LUN ("Twelve [Chapter] Treatise"). The *Zhong lun* is ostensibly a translation of NĀGĀRJUNA's MŪLAMADHYAMAKAKĀRIKĀ. Kumārajīva's translation (dated 409), however, also contains his own notes as well as a commentary on Nāgārjuna's text by Piṅgala (fl. c. 4 CE). The *Bai lun* (*ŚATAŚĀSTRA) is attributed to ĀRYADEVA and was translated into Chinese by Kumārajīva in 404. In this text, the author employs the apophatic language of the Madhyamaka school and refutes the arguments of rival traditions. The *Shi'ermen lun* (**Dvādaśamukhaśāstra*) is also attributed to Nāgārjuna and is purportedly an introductory manual to the *Zhong lun*. In this text, the author provides an interpretation of emptiness (ŚŪNYATĀ) in twelve chapters. No Sanskrit or Tibetan recensions of the *Bai lun* or *Shi'ermen lun* are extant. The "three treatises," however, exerted much influence in East Asia, where they functioned as the central texts for students of emptiness and Madhyamaka doctrine. JIZANG (549–623) wrote influential commentaries on the three treatises and came to be regarded as the systematizer of the San lun school. He retrospectively traces the school to two important vaunt couriers: SENGZHAO (374–414), an influential early Chinese exegete and cotranslator of the perfection of wisdom (PRAJÑĀPĀRAMITĀ) literature, whose writings helped to popularize the works of the Madhyamaka school in China; and SŬNGNANG (c. 450–c. 520), who is claimed to have taught the notion of "three truths" or "three judgments" (SANDI)—the truths of emptiness, provisional reality, and their mean—an exegetical schema that was influential in the subsequent development of both the San lun and TIANTAI schools. The writings of San lun exegetes were also influential in Korea during the Three Kingdoms period (where the tradition was known as Sam non) and during the Nara and Heian periods in Japan (where it was called Sanron).

**sanmei jing**. (S. samādhisūtra; J. sanmaikyō; K. sammae kyŏng 三昧經). In Chinese, "SAMĀDHI scriptures"; a category of MAHĀYĀNA sūtras that are primarily or exclusively concerned with the practice or experience of meditation (SAMĀDHI), or whose title contains the term sanmei. The earliest reference to sanmei jing as a scriptural category appears in the oldest extant Chinese scriptural catalogue, CHU SANZANG JIJI ("Compilation of Notices on the Translation of the TRIPIṬAKA"), compiled by SENGYOU (445–518) around 515; there, Sengyou remarks that Zhu Fahu (DHARMARAKṢA) translated several sanmei jings. The Chinese Buddhist canon (DAZANGJING) contains more than fifty sūtras that use the term sanmei in their titles. These include sanmei jings whose Sanskrit titles do not use the term samādhi and to which the term sanmei was added when these scriptures were translated into Chinese. There are also other scriptures of uncertain provenance whose titles in earlier Chinese translations did not contain the term sanmei. An examination of successive Chinese Buddhist scriptural catalogues (JINGLU) in fact reveals that there were several sūtras that circulated first with one title, and later with a revised title that added sanmei to the original. Furthermore, there are a number of indigenous Chinese Buddhist scriptures (see APOCRYPHA), that were not entered into the canon, which call themselves sanmei jing. This phenomenon began early in the history of Chinese Buddhism. DAO'AN's 374 CE scriptural catalogue (ZONGLI ZHONGJING MULU), which is no longer extant but portions of which are excerpted in Sengyou's *Chu sanzang jiji*, lists twenty-six scriptures of dubious authenticity; of these, six are titled sanmei jing. Several sanmei jings, such as the *Banzhou sanmeijing* (S. PRATYUTPANNABUDDHASAṂMUKHĀVASTHITASAMĀDHISŪTRA), offer instruction regarding the full range of practices involved in cultivating a specific samādhi technique. The majority of sanmei jings, however, are instead concerned with the various states of mind that the Buddha or BODHISATTVAs attained through samādhi, praising that samādhi, and/or emphasizing the merit gained through keeping and transmitting the text of the sanmei jing. The popularity of the sanmei jing genre in Chinese Buddhism can be at least partially attributed to Chinese Buddhists' faith and interest in the religious practice of copying and reciting scriptures, which most sanmei jings encourage as a means of attaining enlightenment. Higher meditative states like samādhi sometime seem ancillary to the topic of certain sanmei jings: the JINGDU SANMEI JING, for example, offers a detailed account of thirty separate levels of the hells and the incumbent punishments meted out there; in order to avoid the torments of hell, the scripture exhorts laypeople not to meditate, but instead to observe the five precepts (PAÑCAŚĪLA) and perform the "eight-restrictions fast" (BAGUAN ZHAI) on specific Chinese seasonal days.

**sanmi**. (三密). In Chinese, "three mysteries." See SANMITSU.

**sanmitsu**. (C. sanmi, K. sammil 三密). In Japanese, "three secrets" or "three mysteries"; an esoteric Buddhist teaching that posits that the body, speech, and mind of sentient beings, which are understood to be the source of the three forms of KARMAN in standard Buddhist doctrine, abide in a nondual relationship with the body, speech, and mind of MAHĀVAIROCANA, the DHARMAKĀYA buddha. All speech is therefore in actuality the speech of this buddha, all forms are his body, and all mental formations are at their root the mind of Mahāvairocana. The doctrine of the three mysteries appears in various strata of

Mahāyāna materials, but is featured most prominently in esoteric literature. In China, Tiantai thinkers such as Tiantai Zhiyi and Zhanran argued that the Buddha taught via his nirmāṇakāya, sambhogakāya, or dharmakāya, depending on the capacities of his audience. On another level, however, these three bodies of the Buddha were said to be nondual. In Japan, Kūkai argued that all beings had the capacity to experience the teaching of the dharmakāya directly, a position that later Japanese Tendai thinkers argued was implicit in the earlier Chinese Tiantai teachings on the three mysteries. Kūkai's sanmitsu theory held that ordinary beings may rapidly realize their buddhanature through abhiṣeka, or ritual initiation, and adhiṣṭhāna, or ritual empowerment, which allowed for the efficacious performance of mudrā, the chanting of mantra and dhāraṇī, and the contemplation of the maṇḍala of a chosen object of devotion. These forms of initiation and empowerment, when followed by these three modes of ritual comportment, were said to reveal that the sublime reality of buddhahood is alive within the mundane reality that beings ordinarily inhabit. Once the body, speech, and mind of beings and buddhas are recognized as nondual, an ordinary being is then able to acquire siddhi, or supernatural powers, which may be used to effect change in the world, up to and including achieving buddhahood in this very body (J. sokushin jōbutsu; C. jishen chengfo).

**Sansheng yuanrong guan**. (三聖圓融觀). In Chinese, "contemplation on the consummate interfusion of the Three Sages," viz., Vairocana Buddha and the two bodhisattvas Mañjuśrī and Samantabhadra. See treatment in yuanrong.

**Śāntarakṣita**. (T. Zhi ba 'tsho) (725–788). Eighth-century Indian Mahāyāna master who played an important role in the introduction of Buddhism into Tibet. According to traditional accounts, he was born into a royal family in Zahor in Bengal and was ordained at Nālandā monastery, where he became a renowned scholar. He is best known for two works. The first is the Tattvasaṃgraha, or "Compendium of Principles," a critical survey and analysis of the various non-Buddhist and Buddhist schools of Indian philosophy, set forth in 3,646 verses in twenty-six chapters. This work, which is preserved in Sanskrit, along with its commentary by his disciple Kamalaśīla, remains an important source on the philosophical systems of India during this period. His other famous work is the Madhyamakālaṃkāra, or "Ornament of the Middle Way," which sets forth his own philosophical position, identified by later Tibetan doxographers as Yogācāra-*Svātantrika-Madhyamaka, so called because it asserts, as in Yogācāra, that external objects do not exist, i.e., that sense objects are of the nature of consciousness; however, it also asserts, unlike Yogācāra and like Madhyamaka, that consciousness lacks ultimate existence. It further asserts that conventional truths (saṃvṛtisatya) possess their own character (svalakṣaṇa) and in this regard differs from the other branch of Madhyamaka, the *Prāsaṅgika. The Yogacāra-Madhyamaka synthesis, of which Śāntarakṣita is the major proponent, was the most important philosophical development of late Indian Buddhism, and the *Madhyamakālaṃkāra* is its locus classicus. This work, together with the Madhyamakāloka of Śāntarakṣita's disciple Kamalaśīla and the Satyadvayavibhaṅga of Jñānagarbha, are known in Tibet as the "three works of the eastern *Svātantrikas" (rang rgyud shar gsum) because the three authors were from Bengal. Śāntarakṣita's renown as a scholar was such that he was invited to Tibet by King Khri srong lde btsan. When a series of natural disasters indicated that the local deities were not positively disposed to the introduction of Buddhism, he left Tibet for Nepal and advised the king to invite the Indian tantric master Padmasambhava, who subdued the local deities. With this accomplished, Śāntarakṣita returned, the first Buddhist monastery of Bsam yas was founded, and Śāntarakṣita invited twelve Mūlasarvāstivāda monks to Tibet to ordain the first seven Tibetan monks. Śāntarakṣita lived and taught at Bsam yas from its founding (c. 775) until his death (c. 788) in an equestrian accident. Tibetans refer to him as the "bodhisattva abbot." The founding of Bsam yas and the ordination of the first monks were pivotal moments in Tibetan Buddhist history, and the relationship of Śāntarakṣita, Padmasambhava, and Khri srong lde btsan figures in many Tibetan legends, most famously as brothers in a previous life. Prior to his death, Śāntarakṣita predicted that a doctrinal dispute would arise in Tibet, in which case his disciple Kamalaśīla should be invited from India. Such a conflict arose between the Indian and Chinese factions, and Kamalaśīla came to Tibet to debate with the Chan monk Moheyan in what is referred to as the Bsam yas Debate, or the "Council of Lhasa."

**Santi Asoke**. A modern reform movement in Thailand that began under the leadership of Bodhirak (P. Bodhirakka), a monk who had a storied past as a television entertainer, spirit medium, and bhikkhu (S. bhikṣu). In 1975 he set up an independent saṅgha, ordaining monks and nuns himself, thereby ignoring the traditional requirement that a monk must have a minimum of ten years of seniority before ordaining others. For this reason, along with his violation of several other rules in the monastic code, Bodhirak was officially defrocked by the Supreme Saṅgha Council of Thailand. Santi Asoke emphasizes a semi-ascetic lifestyle for the laity and austerity for the monks, as opposed to what he criticized as the luxurious living conditions enjoyed by many popular monks around the country, some of whom live in modern buildings, travel in private cars, and have meals brought to their residences. Santi Asoke monks wear brown robes rather than the traditional saffron color commonly worn by many monks in Thailand, do not shave their eyebrows, and adhere to a strict vegetarian diet. Laypeople also observe vegetarianism and many observe the eight precepts (see śīla, aṣṭāṅgasamanvāgataṃ upavāsaṃ) in their daily lives. The group criticizes lavish merit-making as lacking in moral virtue, which it feels can be attained by working hard, avoiding unnecessary consumption, and sharing one's surplus with the rest of society. In addition to avoiding traditional metaphysical beliefs and practices, the group is also opposed to meditation. It views the concept of right concentration (SAMYAKSAMĀDHI), the eighth step of the eightfold path (ĀRYĀṢṬĀṄGAMĀRGA), as the culmination of the other steps, not as a separate stage of practice. Santi Asoke also differs from more mainstream forms of Buddhism in that its temples do not have any images of the Buddha, explaining that only the dharma can represent the Buddha. Its adherents view themselves as followers of "authentic Buddhism," as opposed to: (1) occult Buddhism, whose followers believe in superstition, fortune-telling, and the power of amulets; (2) capitalistic Buddhism, which Santi Asoke contends is composed of business people who practice meditation in order to become more competitive; and (3) hermetic Buddhism, which encourages asceticism and which the Asoke group criticizes as selfish. Santi Asoke affords a somewhat higher status to its female renunciants than does the mainstream Thai saṅgha, granting female monastics status and title equivalent to that of novice monks, rather than the mainstream's wholly lay MAE CHI designation. Bodhirak and scores of his followers were arrested in 1989 at the behest of Thailand's Supreme Saṅgha Council for committing the criminal act of impersonating monks. All were convicted, but given suspended sentences. While opposed by the federal government and the saṅgha, Santi Asoke maintains its existence and influence through the efforts of a small number of politically connected lay followers, most notably a former governor of Bangkok.

**śānticāra**. (S). See ŚĀNTIKA.

**Śāntideva**. (T. Zhi ba lha). Eighth-century Indian monk of NĀLANDĀ monastery, renowned as the author of two influential MAHĀYĀNA texts: the BODHICARYĀVATĀRA (a long poem on the practice of the bodhisattva path) and the ŚIKṢĀSAMUCCAYA (a compendium of passages from Mahāyāna sūtras corroborating the explanations given in the *Bodhicaryāvatāra*). Nothing is known of his life apart from legends. According to these tales, he was of royal birth but renounced the world before his investiture as king. At Nālandā monastery, he was known as an indolent monk. In order to humiliate him, his fellow monks challenged him to recite sūtras before the assembly. He asked whether they wished to hear something old or something new. When they requested something new, he recited the *Bodhicaryāvatāra*. When he reached the ninth chapter, on wisdom (PRAJÑĀ), he began to rise into the air and disappeared, never to return. For this reason, there is some controversy as to how the ninth chapter ends, and indeed, there are different recensions of the text, one longer and one shorter. Based on the contents of the *Bodhicaryāvatāra*'s ninth chapter, Tibetan doxographers count Śāntideva as a proponent of the *PRĀSAṄGIKA-MADHYAMAKA. The *Bodhicaryāvatāra* was very influential in Tibet; particularly noteworthy is the BKA' GDAMS tradition of dge bshes Po to ba, who lists it and the *Śikṣāsamuccaya*, along with the BODHISATTVABHŪMI, MAHĀYĀNASŪTRĀLAṂKĀRA, Āryaśūra's JĀTAKAMĀLĀ, and the UDĀNAVARGA, as the six fundamental treatises of the Bka' gdams tradition.

**śāntika**. (T. zhi ba'i las; C. xizai; J. sokusai; K. sikchae 息災). In Sanskrit, "pacifying activities," (also seen written as śānticāra); one of the four types of activities (CATURKARMAN) set forth in the Buddhist TANTRAs. The other three are: activities of increase (PAUṢṬIKA) to increase prosperity, lengthen life, etc.; control or subjugation (VAŚĪKARAṆA) of the unruly or unwilling; and violent or drastic measures (ABHICĀRA), such as killing and warfare. Pacifying activities involve those rituals that purify baleful influences that appear in such forms as hindrances and illness.

**sanyao**. (J. san'yō; K. samyo 三要). In Chinese, the "three essentials," of meditation practice in the CHAN school: (1) the faculty of great faith (da xingen; cf. ŚRADDHĀ and INDRIYA), (2) great ferocity or tenacity of purpose (da fenzhi), and (3) the sensation of great doubt (da YIQING). These essentials are specifically relevant to cultivation of the "Chan of observing the meditative topic" (KANHUA CHAN), or "questioning meditation." This list was first compiled by the Yuan-dynasty Chan monk GAOFENG YUANMIAO (1238–1295) in his *Gaofeng heshang chanyao*, better known as simply the CHANYAO ("Essentials of Chan"; K. Sŏnyo); the list figures prominently in the presentation of SŎN in the SŎN'GA KWIGAM by the Korean Sŏn monk CH'ŎNGHŎ HYUJŎNG (1520–1604), whence it enters into the Japanese ZEN tradition. As Gaofeng explains them, the faculty of great faith (śraddhendriya) refers to the steadfastness of belief in the inherency of the buddha-nature (FOXING) as the ground of enlightenment. Great ferocity means intense passion toward practice, which he compares to the emotions you would feel if you came across your father's murderer. Gaofeng describes the sensation of doubt (YIQING) regarding the intent behind Chan meditative topics (HUATOU) as like the anxiety and anticipation you feel when you are about to be exposed for some heinous act you committed. All three of these factors are essential, Gaofeng says, if the adept is to have any hope of mastering the kanhua Chan technique.

**sanzhi**. (J. sanshi; K. samji 三止). In Chinese, "threefold calming" or "threefold concentration"; a complement to the "threefold contemplation" (SANGUAN) taught by TIANTAI ZHIYI of the TIANTAI ZONG. These three types of calming or concentration are: (1) the "concentration that [leads to the] experience of reality" (tizhen zhi); (2) the "concentration that [leads to] expedient responses to conditions" (fangbian suiyuan zhi); and (3) the "concentration that [leads to the] cessation of the two discriminatory extremes" (xi erbian fenbie zhi). The first concentration corresponds to the "contemplation of emptiness" in the "threefold contemplation" scheme; this is because, by bringing to cessation the various forms of conceptual proliferation (PRAPAÑCA) and bringing the practitioner to a direct experience of emptiness (ŚŪNYATĀ), it generates an insight into the fact that all things are dependent for their existence on conditions and therefore lack a "self" or any abiding substance. The second mode of concentration corresponds to the "contemplation of conventional existence"; this is because, by abiding in this concentration, the bodhisattva understands emptiness without becoming stuck in inactivity or unresponsiveness to worldly phenomena, such as the suffering of other sentient beings. He is able to function dynamically in the world without becoming disquieted or contaminated by those conditions he is responding to or participating in. The third complements the "contemplation of the mean" in the "threefold contemplation" scheme, and brings an end to such dualistic concepts as SAMSĀRA and NIRVĀṆA. The "discriminatory extremes" are sometimes read as referring to the excesses that are potentially involved in practicing exclusively the first two modes of concentration.

**sanzhi sanguan**. (C) (三止三觀). See SANZHI and SANGUAN.

**sanzhong shijian**. (J. sanshuseken; K. samjong segan 三種世間). In Chinese, "the three types of world systems": the world of sentient beings (SATTVALOKA), the receptacle world (BHĀJANALOKA), and the world of the five aggregates (C. WUYUN SHIJIAN). See SATTVALOKA.

**sapakṣa**. (T. mthun phyogs; C. tongpin; J. dōhon; K. tongp'um 同品). In Sanskrit, "similar instance"; one of three related Sanskrit terms used in Buddhist logic (HETUVIDYĀ): viz., PAKṢA (logical subject), sapakṣa (similar instance), and VIPAKṢA (dissimilar instance). For example, in the syllogism (PRAYOGA) "sound is impermanent because it is produced," sound is the pakṣa; a pot is sapakṣa (similar instance or in the similar class), and space is vipakṣa (dissimilar instance or in the dissimilar class). The VYĀPTI (positive concomitance) is established based on the similar instance, i.e., the opponent's knowledge that a pot breaks because it is produced is extended to sound; the VYATIREKA (negative concomitance) is established based on the dissimilar instance, i.e., the opponent's knowledge that space is permanent because it is not produced is extended to exclude a sound from the dissimilar class because it is produced. See also PAKṢADHARMA, PRAYOGA.

**Sa pan**. (T). See SA SKYA PAṆḌITA KUN DGA' RGYAL MTSHAN.

**sap'ansŭng**. (事判僧). In Korean, "administrative monk," monks who are responsible for the administrative and financial affairs of a Korean monastery; one of the two major divisions of Korean monastic vocations, along with IP'ANSŬNG, practice monks who are engaged in scriptural study, meditative training, and ritual chanting. A large social organization like a monastery required a whole range of ecclesiastical positions to administer the monastic office, treasury, kitchen, etc.; the monks who occupied these offices are collectively referred to as sap'ansŭng. In the past, these monks would also have managed the various economic activities that took place in the monastery, including farming, book printing, paper making, and straw-sandal production. See also TOUSHOU; ZHISHI.

**saptabuddha**. (S). See SAPTATATHĀGATA.

**saptadhana**. (P. sattadhana; T. nor bdun; C. qi cai; J. shichizai; K. ch'il chae 七財). In Sanskrit, "seven kinds of riches [in the dharma]." They are: (1) faith or confidence (ŚRADDHĀ), (2) vigor or effort (VĪRYA), (3) virtue or moral restraint (ŚĪLA), (4) sense of shame (HRĪ) and fear of blame (APATRĀPYA), (5) listening to or learning the dharma (lit. "hearing," śruta), (6) relinquishment (PRAHĀṆA), and (7) the wisdom arising from meditative training (BHĀVANĀMAYĪPRAJÑĀ).

**saptādhikaraṇaśamatha**. (P. sattādhikaraṇasamatha; T. rtsod pa nye bar zhi ba bdun; C. qi miezheng fa; J. shichimetsujōhō; K. ch'il myŏlchaeng pŏp 七滅諍法). In Sanskrit, "seven methods of settling disputes." In confronting monastic members who have transgressed the rules and regulations of the order (see PRĀTIMOKṢA), or when there are disputes about meting out the appropriate sanctions for such infraction, the VINAYA outlines seven methods for dealing with the transgressors and resolving the differences, respectively. According to the CŪḶAVAGGA section of the Pāli pāṭimokkha (using the Sanskrit name for each section): (1) Saṃmukha-vinaya involves the appeal to scriptural and vinaya laws or to direct evidence of transgression. (2) Smṛti-vinaya relies on character witness, testimony of witness[es] of the infraction, and the memory of the transgressor himself if he or she has a clean record and is of trustworthy temperament. In the latter case, an otherwise trustworthy suspect who claims to have no memory of the infraction is presumed innocent. (3) Amūḍha-vinaya is resorting to insanity claims. "Temporary insanity" or the loss of judgment due to different causes at the time of the infraction is considered mitigating and even exculpatory. The transgressor is only brought to the monastic hearing when his sanity or consciousness is restored. (4) Tatsvabhāvaiṣīya-vinaya is the postponement of appropriate punishment after the transgressor has offered a voluntary confession. (5) Yadbhūyasikīya-vinaya is used when a suspect intransigently refuses to confess. It is the citing of contrary evidence to, and self-contradictions and variances in, the suspect's account. (6) Pratijñākāraka-vinaya is the verdict of the majority through voting. Typically elder monks of renowned virtue are assembled for the vote. (7) Tṛṇastāraka-vinaya is interpreted in two ways. One account explains this procedure as having the disputing parties each elect a senior representative to argue their respective cases. Another account has it that, in the case of ultimately irresolvable disputes, both parties should bow down to each other reverentially like "grass in the wind," offering apologies and divulging how oneself could have possibly been more culpable. The Tibetan translation (rtswa bkram pa lta bur 'os pa) suggests a procedure "that strews grass over it [as a covering]." See also ADHIKARAṆAŚAMATHA.

**saptakṛdbhavaparama**. (T. re ltar thogs na srid pa lan bdun pa; C. jiqi fanyou; J. gokushippon'u; K. kŭkch'il panyu 極七返有). In Sanskrit, "one who takes up to seven existences" before NIRVĀṆA; a specific type of stream-enterer (SROTAĀPANNA), one of the twenty members of the ĀRYASAṂGHA (see VIṂŚATIPRABHEDASAṂGHA).

According to the ABHIDHARMAKOŚABHĀṢYA, they are those who, on reaching the path of vision (DARŚANAMĀRGA), have not yet eliminated even one of the set of nine levels of afflictions (KLEŚA) that cause rebirth in the sensuous realm (KĀMADHĀTU), these being the impediments to the first DHYĀNA that the mundane (LAUKIKA) path of cultivation (BHĀVANĀMĀRGA) removes; they will therefore take up to a maximum of seven rebirths in the sensuous realm before they reach the goal of ARHAT.

**saptāṅgavidhi**. (T. yan lag bdun pa'i cho ga; C. qizhi zuofa; J. shichishisahō; K. ch'ilchi chakpŏp 七支作法). In Sanskrit, "seven-branched worship," a common component of MAHĀYĀNA Buddhist liturgy, often performed as a means of accumulating merit at the beginning of a Mahāyāna or tantric ritual or meditation session. The list may include more than seven items, but its standard form includes: obeisance (vandanā), offering (pūjana), confession of wrongdoing (PĀPADEŚANĀ), admiration or rejoicing (ANUMODANA), requesting the buddhas to turn the wheel of dharma (dharmacakrapravartanacodana), requesting the buddhas not to pass into PARINIRVĀṆA (aparinirvṛtādhyeṣaṇa), and the dedication of merit (PARIṆĀMANĀ). Obeisance includes reciting the three refuges (TRIŚARAṆA) formula and praising the excellent qualities of the Buddha, DHARMA, and SAṂGHA; the offering branch is expanded to include elaborate offerings to each of the senses, and, in tantric rituals, so-called inner and secret offerings. In the BHADRACARĪPRAṆIDHĀNA, the final part of the GAṆḌAVYŪHA (and itself the final chapter of the AVATAṂSAKASŪTRA), the bodhisattva SAMANTABHADRA reveals the worship in its fullest Mahāyāna formulation: he prefaces his famous ten vows with a version in which he imagines, on each atom in the universe, as many buddhas and bodhisattvas as there are atoms in the universe, and before each atom he imagines beings, as many as there are atoms in the universe, making obeisance, offering, confessing, and so on.

**Saptaśatikāprajñāpāramitā**. (T. Shes rab kyi pha rol tu phyin pa bdun brgya pa; C. Qibai song bore; J. Shichihyakuju hannya; K. Ch'ilbaek song panya 七百頌般若). In Sanskrit, the "Perfection of Wisdom in Seven Hundred Lines," a PRAJÑĀPĀRAMITĀ sūtra in which the interlocutors include the Buddha, MAÑJUŚRĪ, MAITREYA, ŚĀRIPUTRA, ĀNANDA, and Nirālambā Bhaginī. It sets forth such topics as the true nature of the TATHĀGATA, the ultimate nonexistence of enlightenment and the stages leading to it, and the samādhi of the "single array" (ekavyūhasamādhi, see YIXING SANMEI). Like the VAJRACCHEDIKĀPRAJÑĀPĀRAMITĀSŪTRA, it emphasizes the paradoxical nature of the teachings of the perfection of wisdom.

**saptatathāgata**. (P. sattatathāgata; T. de bzhin gshegs pa bdun; C. qifo/guoqu qifo; J. shichibutsu/kako shichibutsu; K. ch'ilbul/kwagŏ ch'ilbul 七佛/過去七佛). In Sanskrit, the "seven buddhas [of antiquity]"; a list of seven past buddhas bridging the last two cyclical periods of the universe, which include ŚĀKYAMUNI and the six buddhas who preceded him, i.e., VIPAŚYIN (P. Vipassin), Śikhin (P. Sikhī), Viśvabhū (P. Vessabhū), Krakucchanda (P. Kondañña), Kanakamuni (P. Konāgamana) and KĀŚYAPA (P. Kassapa). The first three buddhas are the last three of the one thousand buddhas who appeared in the preceding "glorious eon" (vyūhakalpa), the cyclic period of a universe just prior to the present "auspicious eon" (BHADRAKALPA), and the remaining four buddhas are the first four of the one thousand buddhas during the present bhadrakalpa. Śākyamuni will be succeeded by MAITREYA, the fifth buddha in the current cycle. The seven buddhas of antiquity are widely discussed in the ĀGAMA literature and in such texts as the BHADRAKALPIKASŪTRA, where their activities, lineages, parents, offspring, disciples, residences, and teachings are recorded in great detail. Initially depicted symbolically, such as at BHĀRHUT and SĀÑCĪ in the form of a row of seven BODHI TREEs, the seven tathāgatas were shown in human form by the time of the Kushan dynasty and are common in monastic art across Central and East Asia. The buddhas are often differentiated only by the MUDRĀs they display. MAITREYA is often added as an eighth figure, distinguished by his bodhisattva guise.

**Śāradvatīputra**. (S). See ŚĀRIPUTRA.

**Saraha**. (T. Sa ra ha; C. Shaluohe; J. Sharaka; K. Saraha 沙羅訶). An eighth-century Indian tantric adept, counted among the eighty-four MAHĀSIDDHAs and renowned for his songs of realization (DOHĀ); also known as Sarahapāda. There are few historical facts regarding Saraha, but according to traditional sources he was born into a Bengali brāhmaṇa family. He is often known by the appellation "Great Brāhmaṇa." In his youth he entered the Buddhist monastic order but later abandoned the clergy in favor of living as a wandering YOGIN. During a visionary experience, he was exhorted to train under a female arrowsmith, who, by means of symbolic instruction, taught Saraha the means for piercing through discursiveness and dualistic thought. Having realized the nature of MAHĀMUDRĀ, he earned the name Saraha, lit., "piercing arrow" or "he who has shot the arrow." Saraha is an important member in Tibetan lineages for the instructions on mahāmudrā. He also composed numerous spiritual songs (dohā) popular among Newari and Tibetan Buddhists. Originally recorded in an eastern Indian APABHRAṂŚA dialect, these songs were later collected and translated into Tibetan as the well-known DO HA SKOR GSUM ("Three Cycles of Songs").

**śaraṇa**. (P. saraṇa; T. skyabs; C. guiyi; J. kie; K. kwiŭi 歸依). In Sanskrit, "refuge," "shelter," or "haven"; referring specifically to the "three refuges" (TRIŚARAṆA) of the Buddha, DHARMA, and SAṂGHA, where Buddhists seek safe haven. The recitation of the three refuges is one of the foundational ritual practices in Buddhism: "I go for refuge to the Buddha (buddhaṃ śaraṇaṃ gacchāmi). I go for refuge to the dharma (dharmaṃ śaraṇaṃ gacchāmi). I go for refuge to the saṃgha (saṃghaṃ śaraṇaṃ gacchāmi)." Reciting this formula three times was one of the first ways supplicants gained admittance to the Buddhist community, which initially began with wandering monks and later expanded into different levels of both clergy and lay. Separate rituals for each level of ordination developed, but the triśaraṇa recitation is found in them all. In general, after identifying the three objects of refuge through their special features and unique qualities, supplicants are instructed to keep a set of rules; the most basic rule is associated with the dharma ("the actual refuge"), i.e., not willfully hurting any living being (AHIṂSĀ). It is not clear how the triśaraṇa recitation became associated with conversion (see AMBEDKAR, BHIMRAO RAMJI), although in modern contexts it is often the formula associated with that religious event. See TRIŚARAṆA; RATNATRAYA.

**Saraṇaṃkara**. (1698–1778). Sinhalese monk instrumental in the founding of the SIYAM NIKĀYA. At the time of his youth, the tradition of full ordination (UPASAMPADĀ) of monks had died out in Sri Lanka because there were not the requisite number of bhikkhus (S. BHIKṢU) on the island to ordain others. All monks were therefore novices (ŚRĀMAṆERA), many of whom do not wear saffron robes and had wives and children. Despite not having received a legitimate ordination, Saraṇaṃkara and a group of like-minded ascetics sought instead to live the life of the bhikkhu and maintain all 227 rules of the Pāli pāṭimokkha (S. PRĀTIMOKṢA). He eventually petitioned the king to allow monks from abroad to be invited so they could restore the tradition of full ordination (as had been done twice before in the previous five centuries) but his request was rejected and he was banished to a remote region of the island. Saraṇaṃkara eventually returned and became tutor to the next king. During the reign of the following king, Kīrti Śrī Rājasiṃha, a group of Thai monks, led by Upāli, was invited to Sri Lanka at the entreaty of Saraṇaṃkara, where they reestablished full ordination and began what became known as the Siyam Nikāya, since Upāli was from Siam (Thailand). Based at Kandy, it would become the largest of the Sinhalese monastic lineages. In 1760, Saraṇaṃkara was implicated in a plot to overthrow the Sinhalese king and install a Thai prince on the throne of Sri Lanka, but he was later cleared of any wrongdoing. Among his important writings is the *Sāratthadīpanī*.

**Sarasvatī**. (T. Dbyangs can ma; C. Biancaitian/Miaoyintian; J. Benzaiten/Myōonten; K. Pyŏnjaech'ŏn/Myoŭmch'ŏn 辯才天/妙音天). An Indian goddess revered in both Hinduism and Buddhism as the goddess of composition (including music and poetry) and of learning. She is often depicted playing a vīṇā lute and riding on a swan. She appears in a number of Buddhist sūtras, including the SUVARṆAPRABHĀSOTTAMASŪTRA. Because of that sūtra's articulation of a role for Buddhism in "state protection" (see HUGUO FOJIAO), Sarasvatī came to be regarded as important goddess in Japan, where, as Benzaiten, she was included among the "seven gods of good fortune" (SHICHIFUKUJIN).

**Sāratthappakāsinī**. In Pāli, "Revealer of Essential Meaning," a commentary on the SAṂYUTTANIKĀYA by BUDDHAGHOSA.

**sārdhavihārin**. (P. saddhivihārika [alt. saddhivihārī]; T. lhan cig gnas pa; C. gongxing dizi; J. gūgyō deshi; K. konghaeng cheja 共行弟子). In Sanskrit, lit. "one who lives with," or "one who lives in accord with," but often translated as "disciple" or "apprentice" (see ANTEVĀSIKA). Although the term can simply refer to one of the residents of a monastery, as "disciple" it refers to a novice or a monk who dwells with his UPĀDHYĀYA or preceptor for the purpose of receiving instruction in the dharma and training in the VINAYA. A disciple in residence with his preceptor is said to be under "guidance" (NIŚRAYA). The relationship of the sārdhavihārin and the upādhyāya is described as being like that of a son and a father. Accordingly, the disciple is required to serve the daily needs of his preceptor, by, for example, providing him with water, washing and preparing his robes and alms bowl, cleaning his residence, accompanying him on journeys, and attending him when he is sick. The sārdhavihārin requires the permission of the upādhyāya to attend others, to accompany others on alms rounds, to seek instruction from others, etc. The sārdhavihārin is required to seek pardon from his upādhyāya for any wrongdoing, and may be expelled for bad behavior. If he loses his upādhyāya while he is still in need of guidance, because the latter dies, goes away, secedes from the order, or changes religions, the disciple is to seek out a competent teacher (ĀCĀRYA) to serve in place of the upādhyāya. A fully ordained monk must remain under the guidance of either an upādhyāya or ācārya for a minimum of five years from the time of his ordination. A monk may be required to live under niśraya for a longer period, or for his whole life, if he is unable to become competent in dharma and vinaya.

**Śāriputra**. (P. Sāriputta; T. Shā ri bu; C. Shelifu; J. Sharihotsu; K. Saribul 舍利弗). In Sanskrit, "Son of Śārī"; the first of two chief disciples of the Buddha, along with MAHĀMAUDGALYĀYANA. Śāriputra's father was a wealthy brāhmaṇa named Tiṣya (and Śāriputra is sometimes called Upatiṣya, after his father) and his mother was named Śārī or Śārikā, because she had eyes like a śārika bird. Śārī was the most intelligent woman in MAGADHA; she is also known as Śāradvatī, so Śāriputra is sometimes referred to as Śāradvatīputra. Śāripūtra was born in Nālaka near RĀJAGṚHA. He had three younger brothers and three sisters, all of whom would eventually join the SAṂGHA and become ARHATs. Śāriputra and Mahāmaudgalyāyana were friends from childhood. Once, while attending a performance, both became overwhelmed with a sense of the vanity of all impermanent things and resolved to renounce the world together. They first became disciples of the agnostic SAÑJAYA VAIRĀṬĪPUTRA, although they later took their leave of him and wandered through India in search of the truth. Finding no solution, they parted company, promising one another that whichever one should succeed in finding the truth would inform the other. It was then that Śāriputra met the Buddha's disciple, AŚVAJIT, one of the Buddha's first five disciples (PAÑCAVARGIKA) and already an arhat. Śāriputra was impressed with Aśvajit's countenance and demeanor and asked whether he was a master or a disciple. When he replied that he was a disciple, Śāriputra asked him what his teacher taught. Aśvajit said that he was new to the teachings and could only provide a summary, but then uttered one of the most famous statements in the history of Buddhism, "Of those phenomena produced through causes, the TATHĀGATA has proclaimed their causes (HETU) and also their cessation (NIRODHA). Thus has spoken the great renunciant." (See YE DHARMĀ s.v.). Hearing these words, Śāriputra immediately became a stream-enterer (SROTAĀPANNA) and asked where he could find this teacher. In keeping with their earlier compact, he repeated the stanza to his friend Mahāmaudgalyāyana, who also immediately became a stream-enterer. The two friends resolved to take ordination as disciples of the Buddha and, together with five hundred disciples of their former teacher Sañjaya, proceeded to the VEṆUVANAVIHĀRA, where the Buddha was in residence. The Buddha ordained the entire group with the EHIBHIKṢUKĀ ("Come, monks") formula, whereupon all except Śāriputra and Mahāmaudgalyāyana became arhats. Mahāmaudgalyāyana was to attain arhatship seven days after his ordination, while Śāriputra reached the goal after a fortnight upon hearing the Buddha preach the *Vedanāpariggahasutta* (the Sanskrit recension is entitled the *Dīrghanakhaparivrājakaparipṛcchā*). The Buddha declared Śāriputra and Mahāmaudgalyāyana his chief disciples the day they were ordained, giving as his reason the fact that both had exerted themselves in religious practice for countless previous lives. Śāriputra was declared chief among the Buddha's disciples in wisdom, while Mahāmaudgalyāyana was chief in mastery of supranormal powers (ṚDDHI). Śāriputra was recognized as second only to the Buddha in his knowledge of the dharma. The Buddha praised Śāriputra as an able teacher, calling him his dharmasenāpati, "dharma general" and often assigned topics for him to preach. Two of his most famous discourses were the DASUTTARASUTTA and the SAṄGĪTISUTTA, which the Buddha asked him to preach on his behalf. Sāriputra was meticulous in his observance of the VINAYA, and was quick both to admonish monks in need of guidance and to praise them for their accomplishments. He was sought out by others to explicate points of doctrine and it was he who is said to have revealed the ABHIDHARMA to the human world after the Buddha taught it to his mother, who had been reborn in the TRĀYASTRIṂŚA heaven; when the Buddha returned to earth each day to collect alms, he would repeat to Śāriputra what he had taught to the divinities in heaven. Śāriputra died several months before the Buddha. Realizing that he had only seven days to live, he resolved to return to his native village and convert his mother; with this accomplished, he passed away. His body was cremated and his relics were eventually enshrined in a STŪPA at NĀLANDĀ. Śāriputra appears in many JĀTAKA stories as a companion of the Buddha, sometimes in human form, sometimes in animal form, and sometimes with one of them a human and the other an animal. Śāriputra also plays a major role in the MAHĀYĀNA sūtras, where he is a common interlocutor of the Buddha and of the chief BODHISATTVAs. Sometimes he is portrayed as a dignified arhat, elsewhere he is made the fool, as in the VIMALAKĪRTINIRDEŚA when a goddess turns him into a woman, much to his dismay. In either case, the point is that the wisest of the Buddha's arhat disciples, the master of the abhidharma, does not know the sublime teachings of the Mahāyāna and must have them explained to him. The implication is that the teachings of the Mahāyāna sūtras are therefore more profound than anything found in the canons of the MAINSTREAM BUDDHIST SCHOOLS. In the PRAJÑĀPĀRAMITĀHṚDAYA ("Heart Sūtra"), it is Śāriputra who asks AVALOKITEŚVARA how to practice the perfection of wisdom, and even then he must be empowered to ask the question by the Buddha. In the SADDHARMAPUṆḌARĪKASŪTRA, it is Śāriputra's question that prompts the Buddha to set forth the parable of the burning house. The Buddha predicts that in the future, Śāriputra will become the buddha Padmaprabha.

**śarīra**. (P. sarīra; T. lus/sku/ro/ring bsrel; C. sheli; J. shari; K. sari 舍利). In Sanskrit, a common term for "body" in both the literal and metaphoric sense (as in the "main body" of a text as opposed to a commentary). The term is also used to refer to a corpse, especially that of a monk or of the Buddha, both before and after cremation; in the latter case, the term is often translated as "relic" (śarīra). However, this is not always the meaning in the mortuary context, and the term śarīrapūjā, "worship of the śarīra," often seems to mean the funeral ceremony for the Buddha or a monk, rather than the worship of relics. Relics entombed in a STŪPA were indeed worshipped; in those contexts, the term generally appears in the plural. In general, relics include whole-body relics (C. QUANSHEN SHELI; J. zenshin shari; K. chŏnsin sari)—e.g., the mummified remains of eminent masters—and partial-body relics (C. SUISHEN SHELI; J. saishin shari; K. swaesin sari)—e.g., portions of the physical body, such as a finger bone, TOOTH RELIC, or crystalline substances that are presumed to be the condensation of the sanctified remains of an enlightened person that occurs during cremation. Such physical remains were believed to represent the Buddha's or the sages' ongoing presence and power and have been objects of worship since the time of the Buddha's own PARINIRVĀṆA. According to written sources, the śarīra left after the cremation of the Buddha were apportioned by the brāhmaṇa DROṆA, who divided the relics into eight shares and distributed them among the kingdoms of north India. Nevertheless, the "war of the relics" that was supposed to have broken out over the disposition of the relics—depicted on two friezes appearing on architraves on the southern and western gateways of the great STŪPA of SĀÑCĪ—probably never occurred. Emperor AŚOKA is said to have subsequently collected and redistributed these relics by erecting eighty-four thousand STŪPAs throughout his realm to enshrine them. Nineteen such stūpas were "discovered" in China before the Tang dynasty, among them one at Changgansi on Ayuwangshan and another on WUTAISHAN. Major śarīra like the finger bone of the buddha at FAMENSI also became the objects of fervent cults in medieval China. Buddhist scriptures, which were the "relics of the DHARMAKĀYA" (C. fashen sheli; J. hosshin shari; K. pŏpsin sari), also came to be enshrined in stūpas and Buddhists worshipped them just as they worshipped physical remains. See also DHARMAŚARĪRA; DHĀTU.

**Sārnāth**. The modern place name for a site approximately four miles outside of Vārāṇasī and the location of the Deer Park (MṚGADĀVA) in ṚṢIPATANA where the Buddha is said to have first "turned the wheel of dharma" (DHARMACAKRAPRAVARTANA), viz., delivered his first sermon. Sārnāth is thus considered one of the holiest sites in the Buddhist world and has long been an important place of pilgrimage. Seven weeks after the Buddha became enlightened at BODHGAYĀ, he started out for the Deer Park at Ṛṣipatana, where he met and preached to his five former ascetic companions, the PAÑCAVARGIKA. To these five men, the Buddha preached the FOUR NOBLE TRUTHS (catvāry āryasatyāni). Of the five, the first to become enlightened was ĀJÑĀTAKAUṆḌINYA, followed shortly thereafter by the other four. Soon after the Buddha began teaching, a young man named YAŚAS arrived from Vārāṇasī with fifty-four other people, who all asked to be ordained. Later, Emperor AŚOKA had a large STŪPA and other monuments erected at the spot. When FAXIAN visited Sārnāth during his fifth-century pilgrimage, the site was an active religious center, with two monasteries and four stūpas. The monastic community was still thriving during the seventh century when XUANZANG visited. Today, the Dhamek stūpa is the major surviving architectural structure, likely the restoration of a stūpa dating back to the Aśokan period. Ruins of the monastery are also visible, along with an important edict on an Aśokan pillar forbidding activities that might cause a schism in the order (SAṂGHABHEDA).

**Sarvadurgatipariśodhanatantra**. (T. Ngan song thams cad yongs su sbyong ba'i rgyud; C. Zuisheng foding tuoluoni jingchu yezhang zhou jing; J. Saishōbutchōdarani jōjogōshōjukyō; K. Ch'oesŭng pulchŏng tarani chŏngje ŏpchang chu kyŏng 最勝佛頂陀羅尼淨除業障呪經). In Sanskrit, "Tantra on the Complete Purification of All Negative Places of Rebirth," an important Indian tantra classified sometimes as a CARYĀTANTRA, but most commonly as a YOGATANTRA, associated with the SARVATATHĀGATATATTVASAṂGRAHA. In the text, ŚAKRA asks the Buddha ŚĀKYAMUNI about the fate of a deity named Vimalamaṇiprabha, who is no longer living in the TRĀYASTRIṂŚA heaven. The Buddha explains that he has been reborn in the AVĪCI hell. The gods then ask the Buddha how to avoid rebirth in the three "evil destinies" (DURGATI) of animals, ghosts, and hell denizens. The Buddha sets forth a variety of rituals, including rituals for the four kinds of activities (ŚĀNTIKA, PAUṢṬIKA, VAŚĪKARAṆA, ABHICĀRA) as well as rituals for the dead. The text was widely commented upon in Tibet, where it was a major source of rituals for the fortunate rebirth of the dead.

**sarvajñatā**. (P. sabbaññu; T. kun shes/thams cad mkhyen pa; C. yiqie zhi; J. issaichi; K. ilch'e chi 一切智). In Sanskrit, "all-knower," "all-knowledge," or "omniscience"; in early versions of the perfection of wisdom (PRAJÑĀPĀRAMITĀ) sūtras, the name for a buddha's knowledge; later, the term was used for the knowledge of a ŚRĀVAKA or PRATYEKABUDDHA, in contrast to a buddha's knowledge of all aspects (SARVĀKĀRAJÑATĀ), which is reached by cultivating a bodhisattva's knowledge of the paths (MĀRGAJÑATĀ). The "all" (sarva) means all the grounds (vastu) of the knowledge of defiled (SAṂKLIṢṬA) and pure (viśuddha, see VIŚUDDHI) dharmas systematized in the FOUR NOBLE TRUTHS. In the ABHISAMAYĀLAṂKĀRA and VIMUKTISENA's commentary to that text, sarvajñatā has both a positive and a negative meaning. In the opening verses of the *Abhisamayālaṃkāra*, for example, sarvajñatā is called the mother of the perfection of wisdom. In such cases it is a positive term for the part of a buddha's knowledge that is shared in common with śrāvakas, and so on. In the third chapter of the same work, sarvajñatā is a negative term used to identify the absence of skillful means (UPĀYA) and the lack of the total absence of subject-object conceptualization (GRĀHYAGRĀHAKAVIKALPA) in śrāvakas, in order to point clearly to the superiority of the BODHISATTVA path.

**sarvajñatājñāna**. (P. sabbaññutāñāṇa; T. thams cad mkhyen pa'i ye shes; C. yiqiezhi zhi; J. issaichichi; K. ilch'eji chi 一切智智). In Sanskrit, "omniscient knowledge"; a buddha's knowledge of all the grounds (vastu) of the knowledge of defiled (SAṂKLIṢṬA) and purified (viśuddha, see VIŚUDDHI) dharmas systematized in the FOUR NOBLE TRUTHS. In the ABHISAMAYĀLAṂKĀRA and its commentarial tradition, sarvajñatājñāna also refers to the knowledge of the four noble truths in the mental continuum of a bodhisattva or buddha. See SARVAJÑATĀ.

**sarvākārajñatā**. (T. rnam pa thams cad mkhyen pa; C. yiqiezhong zhi; J. issaishuchi; K. ilch'ejong chi 一切種智). In Sanskrit, "knowledge of all aspects," the preferred term in the ABHISAMAYĀLAṂKĀRA and its commentaries for the omniscience of a buddha, which simultaneously perceives all phenomena in the universe and their final nature. When explained from the perspective of the goal that bodhisattvas will reach, the knowledge of all aspects is indicated by ten dharmas, among which are cittotpāda (cf. BODHICITTOTPĀDA), defining all the stages of all the Buddhist paths; AVAVĀDA, defining all the instructions relevant to those stages, the stages leading to the elimination of the subject-object conceptualization (GRĀHYAGRĀHAKAVIKALPA) along the entire range of accomplishments up to and including the state of enlightenment itself (see also NIRVEDHABHĀGĪYA); the substratum (GOTRA), objective supports (ĀLAMBANA) and aims (uddeśa) of the practice; and the practices (PRATIPATTI) incorporating the full range of skillful means (UPĀYAKAUŚALYA) necessary to turn the wheel of the dharma (DHARMACAKRAPRAVARTANA) in all its variety. When described from the perspective of the bodhisattva's practice that leads to it, sarvākārajñatā has 173 aspects: twenty-seven aspects of a ŚRĀVAKA's knowledge of the four noble truths (SARVAJÑATĀ), thirty-six aspects of a BODHISATTVA's knowledge of paths (MĀRGAJÑATĀ) and one hundred ten aspects that are unique to a buddha. These are again set forth as the thirty-seven aspects of all-knowledge, thirty-four aspects of the knowledge of the paths, and the thirty-nine aspects of the knowledge of all aspects itself. See also ĀKĀRA.

**Sarvamaṇḍalasāmānyavidhiguhyatantra**. (T. Gsang ba spyi rgyud; C. Ruixiye jing; J. Suikiyakyō; K. Yuhŭiya kyŏng 蕤呬耶經). In Sanskrit, "Secret Tantra for the Common Ritual for all MAṆḌALAS"; a text that belongs, according to Tibetan categorization of tantras, to the KRIYĀTANTRA class.

**Sarvanīvaraṇaviṣkambhin**. (T. Sgrib pa thams cad rnam par sel ba; C. Chugaizhang pusa; J. Jogaishō bosatsu; K. Chegaejang posal 除蓋障菩薩). In Sanskrit, "Blocking all Hindrances"; a BODHISATTVA who is the interlocutor of the KĀRAṆḌAVYŪHA; in the GUHYASAMĀJATANTRA, he is listed as one of the eight great bodhisattvas (see AṢṬAMAHOPAPUTRA); he associated with the buddha AMOGHASIDDHI. See KĀRAṆḌAVYŪHA.

**Sarvāstivāda**. (T. Thams cad yod par smra ba; C. Shuo yiqieyou bu/Sapoduo bu; J. Setsuissaiubu/Satsubatabu; K. Sŏrilch'eyu pu/Salbada pu 說一切有部/薩婆多部). In Sanskrit, "Teaching that All Exists," one of the most influential of all the mainstream (that is, non-Mahāyāna) schools of Indian Buddhism, named after its doctrine that all conditioned factors (DHARMA) continue to exist (sarvam asti) throughout all three time periods (TRIKĀLA) of past, present, and future. The Sarvāstivāda had one of the most elaborate ABHIDHARMA canons (ABHIDHARMAPIṬAKA) in all of Buddhism and the school was especially known for its distinctive and influential dharma theory. The Sarvāstivāda identified seventy-five dharmas that the school held were substantially existent (dravyasat) and endowed with intrinsic nature (SVABHĀVA): viz., the five sense organs (INDRIYA), the five sense objects, nonmanifest materiality (AVIJÑAPTIRŪPA), mind (CITTA), forty-six mental concomitants (CAITTA), fourteen conditioned forces dissociated from thought (CITTAVIPRAYUKTASAṂSKĀRA), and three unconditioned (ASAṂSKṚTA) factors. Although the conditioned dharmas always existed, they still were impermanent and thus still moved between temporal periods because of specific "forces dissociated from thought" (CITTAVIPRAYUKTASAṂSKĀRA): the "compounded characteristics" (SAṂSKṚTALAKṢAṆA, CATURLAKṢAṆA) of origination (JĀTI), continuance (STHITI), "senescence" or decay (JARĀ), and "desinence," viz., extinction (ANITYATĀ). In the Sarvāstivāda treatment of causality, these four characteristics were forces that exerted real power over compounded objects, escorting those objects along the causal path until the force "desinence" finally extinguished them; this rather tortured explanation was necessary in order to explain how factors that the Sarvāstivāda school posited continued to exist in all three time periods yet still appeared to undergo change. Even after enlightenment, those dharmas still continued to exist, although they were then effectively "canceled out" through the force of the "nonanalytical suppressions" (APRATISAṂKHYĀNIRODHA), which kept in check the production of all types of dharmas, ensuring that they remained positioned in future mode forever and were never again able to arise in the present. This distinctive dharma theory of the Sarvāstivāda was probably what the MADHYAMAKA philosopher NĀGĀRJUNA was reacting against in his clarion call that all dharmas were devoid of intrinsic existence (NIḤSVABHĀVA) and thus characterized by emptiness (ŚŪNYATĀ). The Sarvāstivāda school's elaborate abhidharma was also the inspiration for the still more intricate "Mahāyāna abhidharma" of the YOGĀCĀRA school (see BAIFA), which drew much of its classification scheme and many of its specific dharmas directly from the Sarvāstivāda. In describing the path of the ARHAT, the Sarvāstivāda set forth a five-stage path system (PAÑCAMĀRGA, of accumulation/equipment, preparation, vision, cultivation, and no further learning) for the ARHAT and asserted that the BODHISATTVA practices six perfections (PĀRAMITĀ) in the course of his training. This five-stage path was also adopted by the Yogācāra in its own theory of the bodhisattva MĀRGA. The Sarvāstivāda developed an elaborate view of the Buddha and the events of his life, as represented in the famous LALITAVISTARA. In its view of death and rebirth, Sarvāstivāda accepted the reality of the "intermediate state" (ANTARĀBHAVA) between rebirths, which in the Sarvāstivāda analysis could range from instantaneous rebirth, to rebirth after a week, indeterminate duration, and as many as forty-nine days; the latter figure seems to have become dominant in later traditions, including Mahāyāna, after it was adopted by the ABHIDHARMAKOŚABHĀṢYA and the YOGĀCĀRABHŪMI. The Sarvāstivāda was one of the main subgroups of the STHAVIRANIKĀYA (School of the Elders), which split with the MAHĀSĀṂGHIKA in the first centuries following the Buddha's death. The Sarvāstivāda evolved as one of the three major subdivisions of the Sthaviranikāya, perhaps as early as a century or two following the first schism, but certainly no later than the first century CE. Sarvāstivāda was one of the most enduring and widespread of the mainstream Buddhist schools. It was especially important in northern India in such influential Buddhist regions as KASHMIR and GANDHĀRA and eventually along the SILK ROAD in some of the Indo-European petty kingdoms of the Tarim River basin, such as KUCHA. Its geographical location along the major overland trade routes also led to it becoming the major mainstream school known to East Asian Buddhism. The Sarvāstivāda school includes an important subgroup, the VAIBHĀṢIKA ("Followers of the Vibhāṣā"), who were the ĀBHIDHARMIKAS associated with the Sarvāstivāda school, especially in Kashmir in northwestern India but also in Gandhāra and even BACTRIA. Because these masters considered their teachings to be elaborations of doctrines found in the encyclopedic Sarvāstivāda abhidharma treatise, the

ABHIDHARMAMAHĀVIBHĀṢĀ, they typically referred to themselves as Sarvāstivāda-Vaibhāṣika or simply Vaibhāṣika. This group was later also distinguished from the MŪLASARVĀSTIVĀDA ("Root Sarvāstivāda"), a distinction that may have originated in a dispute over VINAYA recensions between the northwestern Sarvāstivāda-Vaibhāṣika school in Kashmir and Gandhāra and the Sarvāstivāda school of MATHURĀ in north-central India. The Mūlasarvāstivāda is best known for its massive MŪLASARVĀSTIVĀDA VINAYA, one of the oldest and by far the largest (by up to a factor of four) of the major monastic codes (see VINAYAPIṬAKA) of the mainstream Buddhist schools; because of its eclectic content, it functioned almost as a proto-canon. The Mūlasarvāstivāda vinaya is the monastic code still followed today in the Tibetan traditions of Buddhism. See also SAUTRĀNTIKA.

**Sarvatathāgatatattvasaṃgraha**. (T. De bzhin gshegs pa thams cad kyi de kho na nyid bsdus pa; C. Yiqie rulai zhenshishe dasheng xianzheng sanmei dajiaowang jing; J. Issainyorai shinjitsushō daijōgenshōzanmai daikyōōgyō; K. Ilch'e yŏrae chinsilsŏp taesŭng hyŏnjŭng sammae taegyowang kyŏng 一切如來眞實攝大乘現證三昧大教王經). In Sanskrit, "Compendium of Principles of All the Tathāgatas"; one of the most important Buddhist tantras, whose influence extended through India, China, Japan, and Tibet. Likely dating from the late seventh century, the text presented a range of doctrines, themes, and practices that would come to be regarded as emblematic of tantric practice. These include the the view that ŚĀKYAMUNI Buddha did not actually achieve enlightenment under the BODHI TREE but did so through ritual consecration. The commentaries to the *Sarvatathāgatatattvasaṃgraha* recount that Prince SIDDHĀRTHA was meditating on the banks of the NAIRAÑJANĀ River when he was roused by the buddha VAIROCANA and all the buddhas of the ten directions, who informed him that such meditation would not result in the achievement of buddhahood. He thus left his physical body behind and traveled in a mind-made body (MANOMAYAKĀYA) to the AKANIṢṬHA heaven, where he received various consecrations and achieved buddhahood. He next descended to the summit of Mount SUMERU, where he taught the YOGATANTRAs. Finally, he returned to the world, reinhabited his physical body, and then displayed to the world the well-known defeat of MĀRA and the achievement of buddhahood under the Bodhi tree. The tantra also includes the violent subjugation of Maheśvara (Śiva) by the wrathful bodhisattva VAJRAPĀṆI, suggesting competition between Hindu and Buddhist tantric practitioners at the time of its composition and the increasing importance of violent imagery in Buddhist tantra. Such important elements as the five buddha families (PAÑCATATHĀGATA) and the practice of visualizing oneself as a deity also appear in the text. The tantra is also important for the prominent role given to the buddha Vairocana. In East Asia, the *Sarvatathāgatatattvasaṃgraha* was particularly influential in the form of the VAJRAŚEKHARA, the reconstructed Sanskrit title derived from the Chinese translations of the first chapter of the *Sarvatathāgatatattvasaṃgraha* made by VAJRABODHI and AMOGHAVAJRA during the Tang dynasty. This would become a central text for the esoteric traditions of China and Japan. The full text of the *Sarvatathāgatatattvasaṃgraha* was not translated into Chinese until Dānapāla completed his version in 1015. Ānandagarbha (fl. c. 750) wrote an important commentary on the *Sarvatathāgatatattvasaṃgraha* called *Tattvālokakarī* ("Illumination of the Compendium of Principles Tantra"), and Śākyamitra (fl. c. 750) wrote a commentary called *Kosalālaṃkāra* ("Ornament of Kosala"). Ānandagarbha's maṇḍala ritual called *Sarvavajrodayamaṇḍalavidhi* is a ritual text based on the first chapter of the *Sarvatathāgatatattvasaṃgraha*. The tantra was very influential in Tibet during both the earlier dissemination (SNGA DAR) and the later dissemination (PHYI DAR) periods. Classified as a yogatantra, it was an important source during the later period, for example, for such scholars as BU STON RIN CHEN GRUB and TSONG KHA PA in their systematizations of tantra.

**sarvatraga**. (T. kun 'gro; C. bianxing; J. hengyō; K. p'yŏnhaeng 遍行). In Sanskrit, "all-pervasive" or "omnipresent"; referring specifically to the five omnipresent (sarvatraga) mental concomitants (CAITTA) that are present to varying degrees in all conscious states according to the analysis of the YOGĀCĀRA ABHIDHARMA. These five factors are: sensory contact (SPARŚA), sensation (VEDANĀ), volition (CETANĀ), perception or discrimination (SAMJÑĀ), and attention (MANASKĀRA). It is not possible to identify consciousness or mind (CITTA) except through these omnipresent factors; each has a specific mental function, and when these functions operate together they produce what is conventionally called a conscious state or mind. Thus manaskāra functions as a basic level of mental activity; cetanā functions to make consciousness nonarbitrary, giving consciousness intention relative to its object; sparśa functions to connect consciousness with its object; vedanā extends mere contact into the realm of sentient experience; and saṃjñā functions to differentiate and identify a particular object. These five factors are included among the ten MAHĀBHŪMIKA dharmas in the seventy-five dharmas of the SARVĀSTIVĀDA school. In the Pāli ABHIDHAMMA, there are seven mental factors (P. cetisika) that are associated with all states of consciousness, these five together with concentration (SAMĀDHI) and mental vitality (JĪVITA).

**sarvatragahetu**. (T. kun 'gro'i rgyu; C. bianxing yin; J. hengyōin; K. p'yŏnhaeng in 遍行因). In Sanskrit, "all-pervasive," or "universally active," "cause," the fifth of the six types of causes (HETU) outlined in the JÑĀNAPRASTHĀNA, the central text of the SARVĀSTIVĀDA ABHIDHARMA. This type of cause refers to the fact that the unwholesome proclivities (ANUŚAYA) of mind produce not only identical types of subsequent proclivities, but also serve as the root cause of all other types of afflictions, thus obstructing a person's capacity to understand the true nature of reality. The unwholesome cause and effect must occur in the same realm (such as the RŪPADHĀTU), but the cause and effect can be different types of unwholesome states, e.g., ignorance can produce attachment.

**Sarvodaya**. Also known as Sarvodaya Shramadana, a reform movement founded in Sri Lanka in 1958 by A. T. Ariyaratne. This lay Buddhist movement sought to promote, as its name suggests, "the welfare of all" through "the donation of labor," especially at the local level, through various public works and relief projects, such as building roads, digging wells, and bringing better healthcare and farming techniques to the village. Sarvodaya also sought to reestablish what it considered to be the traditional relationship between the village and its monastery.

**Sasaki, Ruth Fuller**. (1892–1967). An influential Western scholar of the CHAN (ZEN) Buddhist tradition. Ruth Fuller Everett had been married to Charles Everett, who died in 1940. She was introduced to Asian religions while living in Nyack, New York, and more specifically to Buddhism while on a world cruise that took her and her husband to Japan in 1930. There, she met DAISETZ TEITARO SUZUKI. Two years later, she returned to Japan and spent more than three months at the monastery of NANZENJI, where she was allowed to practice with the monks. She met ALAN WATTS when she traveled to London with her daughter Eleanor, who married Watts in 1938, the same year that Fuller joined Sokei-an, Shigetsu Sasaki's Buddhist Society of America, and began to edit the Society's Journal (*The Cat's Yawn*). Fuller and Sasaki translated the YUANJUE JING ("Perfect Enlightenment Sūtra") together. Sasaki was imprisoned in 1942 during the American internment of Americans of Japanese heritage in World War II. In prison, his health deteriorated. Fuller and Sasaki were married in 1944, but he died in 1945, at which time Fuller became the leader of the Zen Institute in New York City. She moved to Japan in 1949 in order to find a teacher for the Institute and finish translating her husband's work. Fuller was ordained in 1958, and traveled between Japan and the United States until her death in 1967. She published *Zen Dust* with Miura Isshū, and *Zen: A Method for Religious Awakening*.

**śāsana**. (P. sāsana; T. bstan pa; C. shengjiao; J. shōgyō; K. sŏnggyo 聖教). In Sanskrit, "dispensation," "teachings"; the Buddha's teachings especially as conceived historically as an institutionalized religion; a common term for the teachings of the Buddha, or what is typically known in the West as "Buddhism." The Pāli commentaries analyze the teachings of the Buddha according to both a twofold and threefold system of classification. The twofold dispensation is comprised of the "teaching for monks" (P. bhikkhusāsana) and "teaching for nuns" (P. bhikkhunīsāsana). The threefold dispensation is comprised of the "teaching on scriptural study" (P. pariyattisāsana), "teaching on practice" (P. paṭipattisāsana), and the "teaching on realization" (P. paṭivedhasāsana). According to this system, scriptural study constitutes the foundation of the Buddha's teaching, without which there can be no successful practice of the path (MĀRGA) and hence no realization of the Buddhist truths or of enlightenment. The same Pāli commentaries state that the teachings of GAUTAMA Buddha will last for five thousand years and propose a variety of scenarios as to how it will suffer gradual decline until its complete disappearance (see ANTARADHĀNA). According to the THERAVĀDA calculation, the śāsana reached its halfway point in 1956.

**Sāsanavaṃsa**. In Pāli, "Chronicle of the Dispensation," an ecclesiastical history written by the Burmese (Myanmar) scholiast Paññāsāmi at Mandalay in 1861. Written from the perspective of the royally sponsored THUDHAMMA Council, the text purports to record the history of the THERAVĀDA saṅgha from the time of the Buddha, through its introduction into Burma in ancient times, up to the author's own period. Based on the earlier Burmese-language Buddhist chronicle, *Thathanalinkara Sadan* (1831), the *Sāsanavaṃsa* was the last of a series of such chronicles, all representing the Thudhamma point of view, to be produced during the Konbaung dynasty (1752–1885). The text was edited for the PALI TEXT SOCIETY by Mabel Bode in 1897, and was translated as *The History of the Buddha's Religion* by B. C. Law in 1952.

**sāsanavisodhana**. In Pāli, "purification of the Buddha's teaching"; referring specifically to the expulsion of malefactors and heretics from the congregation of Buddhist monks and nuns (P. saṅgha; S. SAṂGHA). It is typically, but not necessarily followed by a communal recitation (SAṂGĪTI) of the Buddhist canon (P. tipiṭaka; S. TRIPIṬAKA) by the newly purified and reunited saṅgha. The monastic code (VINAYA) severely limits the ability of the saṅgha as a body or its leaders to force the secession of false monks, monks guilty of PĀRĀJIKA offenses, schismatics, or heretics. For this reason this authority has been ceded by historical precedent and tradition (but not by vinaya law) to the state, embodied ideally in the person of the pious Buddhist king. In the Pāli tradition, the ultimate paradigm for royal interventionism in saṅgha affairs is King Dhammāsoka (see AŚOKA), who is portrayed in the Pāli chronicles of Sri Lanka and the Pāli commentaries as having purged the saṅgha of malefactors at the behest of the saṅgha and under the guidance of the elder MOGGALIPUTTATISSA. After the saṅgha was purified, Moggaliputtatissa convened the third Buddhist council (see COUNCIL, THIRD) to rehearse and reaffirm the Buddha's true teachings. Cf. SIKKHĀPACCAKKHĀNA; ŚIKṢĀDATTAKA.

**Sa skya**. (Sakya). In Tibetan, lit. "gray earth"; a principal sect and monastery of the Tibetan tradition. The Sa skya was politically powerful during the thirteenth and fourteenth centuries and renowned for its scholastic training and emphasis on the tantric system of LAM 'BRAS, or "path and result." Its name is derived from the sect's original institution of Sa skya monastery (see infra), which was named after a place by that name, meaning "gray earth"; the monastery is painted with a distinctive gray-blue wash. Sa skya doctrinal history extends back to the Indian adept VIRŪPA, who is considered a primary source for the instructions on the HEVAJRATANTRA and lam 'bras, and the Tibetan translator 'BROG MI SHĀKYA YE SHES, who carried these teachings to Tibet. The founding of the Sa skya sect in Tibet is attributed to members of the ancient 'Khon family including DKON MCHOG RGYAL PO, a disciple of 'Brog mi. Dkon mchog rgyal po founded Sa skya monastery in 1073, with its tantric practice based on the new tantras that were then being brought from India; Sa skya is thus one of the "new translation" (GSAR MA) sects. His son SA CHEN KUN DGA' SNYING PO promulgated the seminal Sa skya instructions on the *Hevajratantra* and lam 'bras. In 1247 the acclaimed scholar SA SKYA PAṆḌITA KUN DGA' RGYAL MTSHAN fashioned an agreement with the Mongol ruler Godan Khan, in which the Tibetan monk was granted supreme political authority in Tibet. Later, Sa skya Paṇḍita's nephew, 'PHAGS PA BLO BROS RGYAL MTSHAN formed a similar agreement with Qubilai Khan, establishing Sa skya rule into the fourteenth century. The principal leaders of the Sa skya were traditionally chosen from among members of the 'Khon family and the position of SA SKYA KHRI 'DZIN, or "Sakya Throne Holder," continues to be a hereditary, as opposed to an incarnation-based, position. Beginning in the fifteenth century several branches of the Sa skya sect developed. The NGOR subsect was established by KUN DGA' BZANG PO, known as Ngor chen ("great man of Ngor"), who founded a seat at NGOR E WAM CHOS LDAN in 1429. Blo gsal rgya mtsho (Losel Gyatso, 1502–1566), called Tshar chen ("great man of Tshar"), established the Tshar Sa skya lineage. Also counted among the greatest Sa skya masters are the SA SKYA GONG MA RNAM LNGA, the so-called "five Sa skya forefathers." ¶ Sa skya is also the name of the monastery that is the monastic seat of the Sa skya sect of Tibetan Buddhism, located in Gtsang (Tsang) in central Tibet, and founded in 1073 by the Sa skya hierarch Sa chen kun dga' snying po. It served as the site of Tibetan political power during the period of Sa skya dominance in the thirteenth and fourteenth centuries. The central monastic complex is a massive, imposing structure, renowned for its extensive library.

**Sa skya gong ma rnam lnga**. (Sakya Gongma Namnga). In Tibetan, "five Sa skya forefathers," or "five hierarchs of Sa skya." Five great masters, the most illustrious scholar-saints of the aristocratic 'Khon family, revered as early founders and teachers of the SA SKYA sect of Tibetan Buddhism. They are:

1. SA CHEN KUN DGA' SNYING PO (1092–1158)
2. BSOD NAMS RTSE MO (1142–1182)
3. Grags pa rgyal mtshan (Drakpa Gyaltsen, 1147–1216)
4. SA SKYA PAṆḌITA KUN DGA' RGYAL MTSHAN (1182–1251)
5. 'PHAGS PA BLO GROS RGYAL MTSHAN (1235–1280)

Kun dga' snying po (called Sa chen) was instrumental in making the LAM 'BRAS tradition a central pillar of the Sa skya sect, Kun dga' rgyal mtshan (called Sa paṇ) was one of the greatest scholars Tibet has produced, and 'Phags pa (called Dharmarāja, T. Chos rgyal) forged an alliance with the Mongolian rulers of China and instituted Sa skya rule over much of Tibet in the thirteenth century. The different subsects of Sa skya all give the five an iconic role in their practices and rituals.

**Sa skya khri 'dzin**. (Sakya Tridzin). In Tibetan, lit. "throne holder of SA SKYA," used as a title for the principal religious leader of the Sa skya sect of Tibetan Buddhism. It is a hereditary position assumed by male members (often a son or nephew) of the ancient 'Khon family that traces its lineage back to 'Khon DKON MCHOG RGYAL PO, who founded Sa skya monastery in 1073. The forty-first holder of the Sa skya throne, Ngag dbang kun dga' theg chen dpal 'bar (Ngawang Kunga Tekchen Pelbar) (b. 1945), was born in southern Tibet. Following his enthronement at Sa skya monastery in 1959, he escaped the Chinese communist invasion by fleeing to India where he established a new seat near the former British hill station of Dehradun. He continues to travel throughout Asia, Europe, and North America, where he teaches to a wide audience.

**Sa skya pa**. An adherent of the SA SKYA sect of Tibetan Buddhism.

**Sa skya pa'i bka' 'bum**. (Sakya Kabum). In Tibetan, "Collected Works of the Sa skya"; the collected writings of the SA SKYA GONG MA RNAM LNGA, the first five great hierarchs of the SA SKYA tradition: SA CHEN KUN DGA SNYING PO, BSOD NAMS RTSE MO, Grags pa rgyal mtshan (Drakpa Gyaltsen, 1147–1216), SA SKYA PAṆḌITA KUN DGA' RGYAL MTSHAN, and 'PHAGS PA BLO GROS RGYAL MTSHAN. The standard edition of the collected works is in fifteen volumes carved on wood blocks at the SDE DGE printery in Khams in eastern Tibet in 1736.

**Sa skya Paṇḍita Kun dga' rgyal mtshan**. (Sakya Paṇḍita Kunga Gyaltsan) (1182–1251). Although associated primarily with the SA SKYA sect, Sa skya Paṇḍita is traditionally considered one of the greatest savants and religious luminaries in the history of Tibetan Buddhism. He authored a number of seminal philosophical treatises, and beyond his role as scholar and logician, played an instrumental role in forging a relationship with the Mongol court. The name Sa skya Paṇḍita is an honorific title, meaning "Scholar of Sa skya," often abbreviated as Sa paṇ. Born into a renowned family, he was the grandson of SA CHEN KUN DGA' SNYING PO and the nephew of the Sa skya BSOD NAMS RTSE MO and Grags pa rgyal mtshan (Drakpa Gyaltsen, 1147–1216), from whom he received teachings. Sa paṇ began his studies at a young age, and was quickly recognized as a prodigy. He studied extensively with the leading masters of his day, including scholars from the great centers of learning in India, such as ŚĀKYAŚRĪBHADRA, from whom he received BHIKṢU ordination in 1208. He excelled in all fields of Buddhist knowledge, especially Sanskrit grammar and poetics and the logical treatises on epistemology (PRAMĀṆA). In 1216, Grags pa rgyal mtshan passed away, and Sa paṇ became the principal religious master of Sa skya. The next twenty-eight years of his career were highly productive. It was during this time that he composed his pramāṇa masterpiece, TSHAD MA RIGS GTER ("Treasury of Logical Reasoning") circa 1219, and his great synthetic doctrinal tract, SDOM GSUM RAB DBYE ("Clear Differentiation of the Three Vows"), in about 1232. He was renowned as both a debater (famously defeating a renowned Hindu scholar) and a polemicist, composing works critical of various doctrines of the rival BKA' BRGYUD, RNYING MA, and JO NANG sects. In 1244 Sa paṇ received a summons to the court of the Mongol prince Godan for the purpose of negotiating the submission of Tibet to Mongol authority. Traveling slowly across Tibet together with his nephew and eventual successor 'PHAGS PA BLO GROS RGYAL MTSHAN, he reached the Mongol court and met with Godan in 1247. The prince was greatly impressed by Sa paṇ's erudition, as well as his magical and medical powers; the prince is said to have converted to Buddhism after Sa paṇ cured him of a skin disease. Tibet was subsequently spared Mongol occupation, and the Sa skya sect, with Sa paṇ as its chief prelate, was granted political authority within Tibet, a position that was later passed on to 'Phags pa by Qubilai Khan. The relation of Sa paṇ, and later 'Phags pa, with the Mongol ruler would be cited as the paradigm of the so-called "priest-patron" (YON MCHOD) relationship. Sa paṇ did not live to return to Tibet, passing away at the capital of Godan's court. Sa paṇ authored more than a hundred works and translated many texts from Sanskrit into Tibetan. Among his compositions, the five most famous are, including the two listed above: *Legs bshad* ("Elegant Sayings"), *Mkhas pa rnams 'jug pa'i sgo* ("Entrance Gate for the Wise"), and *Thub pa'i dgongs gsal* ("Elucidating the Intention of the Sage").

**sāsrava**. (P. sāsava; T. zag bcas; C. youlou; J. uro; K. yuru 有漏). In Sanskrit, lit. "with outflows," hence, "contaminated," "tainted." Just as a leaky roof lets in rain that destroys a residence and all its contents, the edifice of the five aggregates (SKANDHA) is a ruin dampened by the afflictions (KLEŚA) of greed, hatred, and delusion and riddled with the rot of KARMAN (viz., the formative forces left by the actions motivated by the afflictions). Sāsrava is similar in meaning to SAṂKLIṢṬA (defilement, affliction), although wider in application because unwholesome (AKUŚALA) and wholesome (KUŚALA) states are sāsrava if they lead to a future state with outflows, even if that is a fortunate state of happiness in this lifetime or the next. In this sense, sāsrava is a common designation for the aggregates (skandha) and refers to those objects that may serve as an occasion for the increase of kleśa. Thus, even an inanimate object can be considered "contaminated" in the sense that it can serve as a cause for the increase of the afflictions, such as greed. According to the ABHIDHARMAKOŚABHĀṢYA, only four dharmas are uncontaminated. Three of these are permanent: space (ĀKĀŚA), nonanalytical cessation (APRATISAṂKHYĀNIRODHA), and analytical cessation (PRATISAṂKHYĀNIRODHA), which would include NIRVĀṆA. The only impermanent dharma that is uncontaminated is the truth of the path or true path (MĀRGASATYA); technically, this would refer to the equipoise of nonperception (ASAṂJÑĀSAMĀPATTI) when absorbed in a perfect vision of the FOUR NOBLE TRUTHS, or, in the MAHĀYĀNA, in the perfect vision of the emptiness (ŚŪNYATĀ) of all dharmas. The SĀSRAVASKANDHA (contaminated aggregates) is the entire heap of dharmas that make up a person (PUDGALA), with the sole exception of the NIRVĀṆA element, or in Mahāyāna the pure element (DHĀTU) that locates the lineage (GOTRA) of all beings destined for the final perfect enlightenment. The ABHIDHARMASAMUCCAYA gives six meanings for sāsrava, which it says can be (1) a contaminant (ĀSRAVA) itself, i.e., an actual kleśa, (2) the other parts of the mind that are necessarily present when obscuration (ĀVARAṆA) is present, (3) the aggregates when kleśa is operating, (4) the future contaminated aggregates that arise from the earlier cause, (5) the higher stages of the path because, although not governed by kleśa, they are tied up with thought construction, and (6) even the very final stage of the bodhisattva path, because it is affected by residual impressions left by earlier contaminated states.

**sāsravaskandha**. (P. sāsavakhandha; T. zag bcas kyi phung po; C. youlou yun; J. uroun; K. yuru on 有漏蘊). In Sanskrit, "aggregates associated with the contaminants," the entire heap of dharmas, systematized as the "five aggregates that are the objects of clinging" (pañcopādānaskandha) that comprise the person (PUDGALA). See SĀSRAVA; SKANDHA.

**śāstṛ**. (P. satthar; T. ston pa; C. shi; J. shi; K. sa 師). In Sanskrit, "teacher"; referring to any teacher and a common epithet for the Buddha, who is often referred to as the "teacher of gods and men [or princes and people]" (śāstā devamanuṣyāṇām; see discussion in the conclusion to DEVA, s.v.). Among the various terms for a teacher in Buddhist literature, including GURU, ĀCĀRYA, and UPĀDHYĀYA, śāstṛ was a term of particular respect. In early Buddhist literature, it seems to have been reserved exclusively for the Buddha and past buddhas and not for disciples (ŚRĀVAKA) of the Buddha; thus, whenever the term "teacher" appears, it typically refers to the Buddha himself. To recognize the Buddha as the true teacher and to declare him as such is regarded as a central determinant of Buddhist identity. Outside the Buddhist community, the term was also used to refer to the so-called "six heterodox teachers," such as PŪRAṆA KĀŚYAPA.

**śāstra**. (T. bstan bcos; C. lun; J. ron; K. non 論). In Sanskrit, "treatise," a term used to refer to works contained in the various Buddhist canons attributed to various Indian masters. In this sense, the term is distinguished from SŪTRA, a discourse regarded as the word of the Buddha or spoken with his sanction. In the basic division of Buddhist scripture in the Tibetan canon, for example, the translations of śāstra (BSTAN 'GYUR) are contrasted with the words of the Buddha (or a buddha) called BKA' 'GYUR. A Buddhist śāstra can be in verse or prose, and of any length, and it includes the different Sanskrit compositional genres (vṛtti, vārttika, bhāṣya, ṭīkā, vyākhyā, pañjikā, and so on) often rendered by the single English word "commentary." In the Buddhist context, the genre is typically a form of composition that explains the words or intention of the Buddha. The word śāstra is found in the actual title of a number of works, for example, the *Prajñāpāramitopadeśaśāstrakārikā*, an alternate title of the ABHISAMAYĀLAṂKĀRA, and the *Mahāyānottaratantraśāstravyākhyā*, another name for the RATNAGOTRAVIBHĀGA.

**śāstṛsaṃjñā**. (T. ston par 'du shes; C. dashi xiang; J. daishisō; K. taesa sang 大師想). In Sanskrit, "recognition as the teacher," a term that appears especially in the MAHĀYĀNA sūtras in a variety of contexts. In addition to its denotation of recognizing the Buddha as the true teacher (ŚĀSTṚ), the Mahāyāna also claims that a bodhisattva should regard all other bodhisattvas as his teachers, as if they were the Buddha himself; one should regard as one's teacher the person from whom one hears the perfection of wisdom (PRAJÑĀPĀRAMITĀ); one should regard the text of the prajñāpāramitā itself as one's teacher; and one should regard all sentient beings as one's teacher.

***śāstrapiṭaka**. (C. lunzang; J. ronzō; K. nonjang 論藏). In Sanskrit reconstruction, "treatise basket," a more inclusive designation for the ABHIDHARMAPIṬAKA, the third "basket" of the Buddhist canon (TRIPIṬAKA), which expands this section of the canon to take in scholastic treatises (ŚĀSTRA) from the MAHĀYĀNA exegetical schools in addition to the ABHIDHARMA texts of the MAINSTREAM BUDDHIST SCHOOLS. The Sanskrit term appears in Western literature on the canon, but seems not to be attested in Indian sources (or in their Tibetan translation) and may be a back-translation from the Chinese locution lunzang. Since virtually the inception of Buddhism in China, the Mahāyāna tradition dominated. This allegiance is apparently why Chinese scriptural catalogues (JINGLU), since at least the time of the definitive KAIYUAN SHIJIAO LU (730), had listed Mahāyāna materials first in their respective rosters of SŪTRA and śāstra texts. This same order is subsequently followed in the traditional printed versions of the Chinese Buddhist canon (DAZANGJING; see also KORYŎ TAEJANGGYŎNG). To the Chinese, who proudly identified with the Mahāyāna, it must have seemed anathema to treat as canonical ABHIDHARMA works by the ARHAT-ĀBHIDHARMIKAS (such as KĀTYĀYANĪPUTRA or VASUMITRA) but not the scholastic treatises by the Indian BODHISATTVA-exegetes of Mahāyāna (such as NĀGĀRJUNA and VASUBANDHU) who were much more renowned to the Chinese. In order to give pride of place to the works of these influential Mahāyāna scholiasts, the Chinese listed them before abhidharma texts in the roster of śāstra materials collected in the Chinese Buddhist canon, and referred to this third basket more expansively as a "treatise basket" (lunzang) rather than merely an abhidharmapiṭaka.

**śāśvatadṛṣṭi**. (P. sassatadiṭṭhi; T. rtag lta; C. changjian; J. jōken; K. sanggyŏn 常見). In Sanskrit, "eternalism," one of the two "extreme views" (ANTAGRĀHADṚṢṬI), along with "annihilationism" (UCCHEDADṚṢṬI). Eternalism is the mistaken belief or view that a self (ĀTMAN) exists independently of the five aggregates (SKANDHA) and that it continues to exist eternally, transmigrating from one rebirth to the next. Annihilationism (ucchedadṛṣṭi) is, by contrast, the mistaken belief that the self is the same as the aggregates and that the continuum (SAṂTĀNA) of consciousness ceases to exist at death. See also ŚĀŚVATĀNTA.

**śāśvatānta**. (P. sassata; T. rtag pa'i mtha'; C. changbian; J. jōhen; K. sangbyŏn 常邊). In Sanskrit, "extreme of eternalism"; one of the two extremes (along with the extreme of annihilationism, or UCCHEDĀNTA) included in the ANTAGRĀHADṚṢṬI, or "extreme views." There are six root afflictions (MŪLAKLEŚA), according to the hundred-dharma list (BAIFA) of the YOGĀCĀRA ABHIDHARMA, the last of which is DṚṢṬI ([wrong] views); dṛṣṭi is further subdivided into five types of wrong views, which in turn include antagrāhadṛṣṭi. The "extreme view" refers specifically to the mistaken notion that (1) there is a perduring soul that continues to be reborn unchanged from one lifetime to the next, or (2) the continuum (SAṂTĀNA) of consciousness is annihilated at death and thus not subject to rebirth. The former view is called the extreme of eternalism (ŚĀŚVATADṚṢṬI; P. sassatadiṭṭhi); the latter, the extreme of annihilationism (UCCHEDADṚṢṬI; P. ucchedadiṭṭhi). The praise of the Buddha by NĀGĀRJUNA at the opening of his MŪLAMADHYAMAKAKĀRIKĀ says that the Buddha avoided these two and six other extremes (the extremes of cessation and production, coming and going, difference and sameness) by teaching that all dharmas are products of a process of dependent origination (PRATĪTYASAMUTPĀDA) and are thus free from any essential nature (SVABHĀVA). Although variously defined, the term sāśvānta is generally used in descriptions of the view that phenomena possess a greater degree of permanence and reality than they in fact do, a tenet that is often ascribed to non-Buddhist schools, such as Sāṃkhya. The various schools of Buddhist philosophy also deploy the term polemically to denigrate the tenets of a rival. The SAUTRĀNTIKA school, for example, could claim that the Sarvāstivāda position that dharmas exist throughout all three time periods represented a mistaken attachment to the extreme of permanence; the MADHYAMAKA school could claim that the YOGĀCĀRA assertion that all objects have the nature of consciousness represented a mistaken attachment to the extreme of permanence. The extremes (anta) are contrasted with the middle (madhyama) that defines freedom from SAṂSĀRA, or, in Mahāyāna works, freedom from the extremes of both SAṂSĀRA and NIRVĀṆA. The Buddhist middle way (MADHYAMAPRATIPAD) between these two extremes posits that there is no permanent, perduring soul (countering eternalism), and yet there is karmic continuity from one lifetime to the next (countering annihilationism). See also SATKĀYADṚṢṬI.

**śatadharma**. In Sanskrit, "hundred factors"; the normative roster of factors (DHARMA) recognized in the YOGĀCĀRA school's system of MAHĀYĀNA ABHIDHARMA. See BAIFA; and, for the full roster, the List of Lists.

**Śataka**. (S). See *ŚATAŚĀSTRA.

**Śatasāhasrikāprajñāpāramitāsūtra**. (T. Shes rab kyi pha rol tu phyin pa stong phrag brgya pa; C. Shiwansong bore; J. Jūmanju hannya; K. Simmansong panya 十萬頌般若). In Sanskrit, the "Perfection of Wisdom in One Hundred Thousand Lines," the longest of the PRAJÑĀPĀRAMITĀ sūtras. Some scholars regard the AṢṬASĀHASRIKĀPRAJÑĀPĀRAMITĀ (eight thousand lines) to be the earliest of the prajñāpāramitā sūtras, which was then expanded into the *Aṣṭadaśasāhasrikāprajñāpāramitāsūtra* (eighteen thousand lines) and the PAÑCAVIṂŚATISĀHASRIKĀPRAJÑĀPĀRAMITĀSŪTRA (twenty-five thousand lines). According to this explanation, the most extensive of the expansions is the *Śatasāhasrikāprajñāpāramitā*, sometimes referred to as the "great mother [of the victors]." The composition sequence of these different sūtras is not as clear as once thought, however, and there appear to be parts of the *Śātasāhasrikā* not found in the *Aṣṭa*, which may go back to very early material. The text is in three major sections, with the first two expanding on the contents of the *Aṣṭasāhasrikāprajñāpāramitā*. The third section, which seems to be an independent text, contains discussions of topics such as the nature of enlightenment, the Buddha's omniscience, the body of the Buddha, and the six perfections. Unlike the other two briefer expansions, the version in one hundred thousand lines omits four chapters that occur in the *Aṣṭasāhasrikāprajñāpāramitā*. It is said that after the Buddha taught the *Śatasāhasrikāprajñāpāramitā*, he entrusted it to the NĀGAs, who kept it in a jeweled casket in the bottom of the ocean, where it was eventually retrieved and brought to the human world by NĀGĀRJUNA.

***Śataśāstra**. (C. Bai lun [alt. Bo lun]; J. Hyakuron; K. Paek non 百論). In Sanskrit, lit., "The Hundred Treatise," a work attributed to the MADHYAMAKA master ĀRYADEVA, and counted as one of the "three treatises" of the SAN LUN ZONG of Chinese Buddhism, together with the *Zhong lun* ("Middle Treatise") and SHI'ERMEN LUN ("Twelve Gate Treatise"), both attributed to NĀGĀRJUNA. The *Zhong lun* is ostensibly a translation of Nāgārjuna's MŪLAMADHYAMAKAKĀRIKĀ; however, KUMĀRAJĪVA's translation (dated 409) also contains his own annotation and a commentary to Nāgārjuna's text by Piṅgala (fl. fourth century CE). The *Shi'ermen lun* (**Dvādaśamukhaśāstra*) is also attributed to Nāgārjuna and is purportedly an introductory manual to the *Zhong lun*. The *Śataśāstra* was translated into Chinese by Kumārajīva in 404. No Sanskrit or Tibetan recensions of the work are known to exist; the Sanskrit title is a reconstruction. Some have speculated that the work is an abbreviated version of Āryadeva's most famous work, the CATUḤŚATAKA. The two works consider many of the same topics, including the nature of NIRVĀṆA and the meaning of emptiness (ŚŪNYATĀ) in a similar fashion and both refute Sāṃkhya and Vaiśeṣika positions, but the order of their treatment of these topics and their specific content differ; the *Śatakaśāstra* also contains material not found in the *Catuḥśataka*. The *Śataśāstra* is therefore probably not a mere summary of the *Catuḥśataka*, but may instead represent Kumārajīva's interpretation of Āryadeva's text.

**śāṭhya**. (P. sāṭheyya; T. g.yo; C. kuang; J. ō; K. kwang 誑). In Sanskrit, "dissimulation" or "deception"; the sixth of the twenty secondary afflictions (UPAKLEŚA) in the SARVĀSTIVĀDA list of seventy-five dharmas. Śāṭhya is the attempt to conceal one's faults out of a desire to receive goods or services from others. Dissimulation is said to prevent one from meeting spiritual mentors (KALYĀṆAMITRA) in this or subsequent lives. Dissimulation differs from deceit (MĀYĀ) in that deceit is the pretension to have good qualities that one in fact lacks, while dissimulation is the concealment of faults that one possesses.

**sati**. (P). See SMṚTI.

**satipaṭṭhāna**. (P). See SMṚTYUPASTHĀNA.

**Satipaṭṭhānasutta**. (S. *Smṛtyupasthānasūtra; T. Dran pa nye bar bzhag pa'i mdo; C. Nianchu jing; J. Nenjogyō; K. Yŏmch'ŏ kyŏng 念處經). In Pāli, "Discourse on the Foundations of Mindfulness"; the tenth sutta in the MAJJHIMANIKĀYA (a separate SARVĀSTIVĀDA recension appears as the ninety-eighth SŪTRA in the Chinese translation of the MADHYAMĀGAMA; there is another unidentified recension in the Chinese translation of the EKOTTARĀGAMA). An expanded version of the same sutta, titled the "Great Discourse on the Foundations of Mindfulness" (MAHĀSATIPAṬṬHĀNASUTTANTA), which adds extensive discussion on mindfulness of breathing (P. ānāpānasati, S. ĀNĀPĀNASMṚTI), is the twenty-second sutta in the Pāli DĪGHANIKĀYA. This sutta is one of the most widely commented upon texts in the Pāli canon and continues to hold a central place in the modern VIPASSANĀ (S. VIPAŚYANĀ) movement. The sutta was preached by the Buddha to a gathering of disciples in the town of Kammāsadhamma in the country of the Kurus. The discourse enumerates twenty-one meditation practices for the cultivation of mindfulness (P. sati, S. SMṚTI), a term that refers to an undistracted watchfulness and attentiveness, or to recollection and thus memory. In the text, the Buddha explains the practice under a fourfold rubric called the four foundations of mindfulness (P. satipaṭṭhāna, S. SMṚTYUPASTHĀNA). The four foundations are comprised of "contemplation of the body" (P. kāyānupassanā, S. KĀYĀNUPAŚYANĀ); "contemplation of sensations" (P. vedanānupassanā, S. vedanānupaśyanā), that is, physical and mental sensations (VEDANĀ) that are pleasurable, painful, or neutral; "contemplation of mind" (P. cittānupassanā, S. cittānupaśyanā), in which one observes the broader state of mind (CITTA) as, e.g., shrunken or expanded, while under the influence of various positive and negative emotions; and "contemplation of phenomena" (P. dhammānupassanā, S. dharmānupaśyanā), which involves the contemplation of several key doctrinal categories, such as the five aggregates (P. khandha, S. SKANDHA) and the FOUR NOBLE TRUTHS. The first of the four, the mindfulness of the body, involves fourteen exercises, beginning with the mindfulness of the inhalation and exhalation of the breath (P. ānāpānasati, S. ĀNĀPĀNASMṚTI). Mindfulness of the breath is followed by mindfulness of the four physical postures (P. iriyāpatha, S. ĪRYĀPATHA) of walking, standing, sitting, and lying down. This is then extended to a full general awareness of all physical activities. Thus, mindfulness is something that is also meant to accompany all of one's actions in the course of the day, and is not restricted to formal meditation sessions. This discussion is followed by mindfulness of the various components of the body, an intentionally revolting list that includes fingernails, bile, spittle, and urine. Next is the mindfulness of the body as composed of the four great elements (MAHĀBHŪTA) of earth, water, fire, and air. Next are the "contemplations on the impure" (P. asubhabhāvanā, S. AŚUBHABHĀVANĀ), viz., contemplation of a corpse in nine successive stages of decomposition. The practice of the mindfulness of the body is designed to induce the understanding that the body is a collection of impure elements that arise and cease in rapid succession, utterly lacking any kind of permanent self. This insight into the three marks of existence—impermanence, suffering, and no-self—leads in turn to enlightenment. Mindfulness of the body is presented as the core meditative practice, with the other three types of mindfulness applied as the meditator's attention is drawn to those factors. The sutta calls the foundations of mindfulness the ekayānamagga, which in this context might be rendered as "the only path" or "the one way forward," and states that correct practice of the four foundations of mindfulness will lead to the stage of the worthy one (P. arahant, S. ARHAT), or at least the stage of the nonreturner (P. anāgāmi, S. ANĀGĀMIN), in as little as seven days of practice, according to some interpretations. See also ANUPASSANĀ.

**satkāyadṛṣṭi**. (P. sakkāyadiṭṭhi; T. 'jig tshogs la lta ba; C. youshenjian; J. ushinken; K. yusin'gyŏn 有身見). In Sanskrit, "[wrong] view of a real person," "view of a existent body"; the wrong view that the impermanent components of the body (KĀYA) are in fact real (sat). This wrong view is related to the (mis)conceptions of I (AHAṂKĀRA) and mine (MAMAKĀRA). It is classed as a type of afflicted view (kliṣṭadṛṣṭi), that is, a mistaken belief about a self in relation to the five aggregates (SKANDHA). In mainstream Buddhist materials, satkāyadṛṣṭi is listed as the first of ten fetters (SAṂYOJANA) that keep beings bound to the cycle of rebirth (SAṂSĀRA) and as the sixth of ten fundamental afflictions (MŪLAKLEŚA). Pāli materials delineate four types of satkāyadṛṣṭi for each of the five aggregates (P. khandha, S. SKANDHA), for a total of twenty varieties in all. The four types are: (1) the belief that the self is the same as the aggregates; i.e., the same as materiality (RŪPA), sensations (VEDANĀ), perception (SAṂJÑĀ), conditioning factors (SAṂSKĀRA), and consciousness (VIJÑĀNA); (2) the belief that the self is contained in the aggregates, (3) the belief that the self is different from the aggregates, and (4) the belief that the self is the owner of the aggregates. Satkāyadṛṣṭi is permanently eradicated by attaining the state of a stream-enterer (SROTAĀPANNA), the first of four degrees of sanctity (see ĀRYAPUDGALA).

**satori**. (悟). In Japanese, "awakening," "enlightenment." See WU; DUNWU; BODHI.

**sattva**. (P. satta; T. sems can; C. youqing/zhongsheng; J. ujō/shujō; K. yujŏng/chungsaeng 有情/衆生). In Sanskrit, "living being," commonly translated into English as "sentient being"; a generic term for any being in the cycle of rebirth (SAṂSĀRA), including the five or six rebirth destines (GATI) of divinities (DEVA), demigods or titans (ASURA), humans (MANUṢYA), animals (TIRYAK), ghosts (PRETA), and hell denizens (NĀRAKA). Buddhism, unlike the JAINA tradition, does not generally accept that plants are endowed with consciousness and thus does not typically include plant life among sentient beings (although this claim later becomes a matter of debate within the tradition, especially in East Asia). The term sattva technically does not include buddhas and ARHATs, because they are no longer subject to rebirth. In the word BODHISATTVA and MAHĀSATTVA, sattva may retain a meaning closer to its mainstream Indian usage as "spiritual essence," as in the Sāṃkhya school, where sattva is conceived as the spiritual, enlightening "strand" (guṇa) that interacts with tamas (dullness) and rajas (energy) to explain the dispositions of people and the changes that occur in the environment.

**sattvakaṣāya**. (T. sems can snyigs ma; C. zhongsheng zhuo; J. shujōjoku; K. chungsaeng t'ak 衆生濁). In Sanskrit, "degeneracy of beings," one of the five signs of the degeneration of a world system that, according to Buddhist cosmology, occur between the time when the average human life span is one hundred years and when it is ten years. The term sattvakaṣāya refers to the fact that the intelligence and moral character of the beings who populate the world deteriorate during this period. See KĀṢĀYA; SAṂVARTAKALPA.

**sattvaloka**. (P. sattaloka; T. sems can 'jig rten; C. zhongsheng shijian/youqing shijian; J. shujō seken/ujōseken; K. chungsaeng segan/yujŏng segan 衆生世間/有情世間). In Sanskrit, "world of sentient beings"; a term used to refer to the sentient beings (SATTVA) who are the inhabitants of the realms of SAṂSĀRA. The sattvaloka is used in distinction to, and in conjunction with, its companion term BHĀJANALOKA, the "receptacle world" that is the physical environment or "container" for those sentient beings. The inanimate bhājanaloka and the animate sattvaloka together make up the three realms of existence (TRILOKA[DHĀTU]). The bhājanaloka is formed during the first of the twenty intermediate-length eons (KALPA) that make up the one great eon (MAHĀKALPA), called the "kalpa of creation" (VIVARTAKALPA); the sattvaloka comes into existence during the remaining nineteen intermediate-length kalpas as sentient beings begin to be reborn in the bhājanaloka, beginning in the heavens and ending in the hells. The disappearance of the sattvaloka takes the form of a gradual depopulation of the bhājanaloka during the "kalpa of dissolution" (SAṂVARTAKALPA). This process begins with the cessation of those beings' rebirth in hell, which is followed by the dissolution of the hells themselves. (Those beings whose time in hell is not yet exhausted will be reborn in a hell in another universe.) The same twofold process then occurs for the realms of animals and ghosts. After that, seven suns appear in the sky, incinerating the remaining bhājanaloka, including Mount SUMERU, the four continents, and the subtle-materiality heavens of the first DHYĀNA. Beings in the first DHYĀNA who can achieve the second dhyāna escape destruction. When the kalpa of creation begins again, the bhājanaloka and the sattvaloka reappear due to the inertial force of the KARMAN of sentient beings. These two worlds and the world of the five aggregates (C. WUYUN SHIJIAN) together constitute the three types of world systems (C. SANZHONG SHIJIAN).

**sattvaparyaṅka**. (T. skyil krung). In Sanskrit, "heroic cross-legged posture," the sattvaparyaṅka is a seated pose formed with both legs bent horizontally with the shins lying flat on the seat and one foot lying slightly in front of the other. See also ĀSANA.

**sattvārdhaparyaṅka**. (T. skyil krung phyed pa). In Sanskrit, "heroic half cross-legged posture," the sattvārdhaparyaṅka is a seated pose similar to SATTVAPARYAṄKA, where one leg is bent horizontally with the shin lying flat on the seat and the other leg bent and hanging somewhat pendant. See also ĀSANA.

**sattvārtha**. (T. sems can gyi don; C. raoyi youqing; J. nyōyakuujō; K. yoik yujŏng 饒益有情). In Sanskrit, the "welfare of sentient beings," a term that occurs in Buddhist morality in the phrase sattvārthakriyāśīla, "the precept of acting for the welfare of sentient beings," the third of the bodhisattva's "three sets of pure precepts" (trividhāni śīlāni, see ŚĪLATRAYA) as systematized in the BODHISATTVABHŪMI. This set refers to practices that accrue to the welfare of others, in distinction to the saṃvaraśīla, or "restraining precepts," which refers to the HĪNAYĀNA rules of discipline (PRĀTIMOKṢA) that help adepts restrain themselves from all types of unwholesome conduct; and practicing all types of virtuous deeds (kuśaladharmasaṃgrāhakaśīla), which accumulates the various sorts of wholesome conduct. The welfare of sentient beings emphasizes a more active involvement in the lives of others through such deeds as nursing the sick, offering charity to the poor, protecting the helpless from harm, comforting the afflicted, and providing hospitality to travelers. It also includes more unusual forms of aid, such as using one's supranormal powers to reveal to potential transgressors the consequences of suffering in hell. The welfare of sentient beings is ultimately achieved by teaching them the dharma. In the case of the bodhisattva, sarvasattvārtha, the "welfare of all sentient beings," is one of the two goals that bodhisattvas have vowed to achieve, the other being buddhahood. It is said that by achieving buddhahood, the bodhisattva fulfills two aims or goals, his own welfare (SVĀRTHA) and the welfare of others (PARĀRTHA), the latter term being a synonym of sattvārtha. Of the three buddha bodies (BUDDHAKĀYA), the SAṂBHOGAKĀYA and NIRMĀṆAKĀYA are described as bodies that serve the welfare of others, and the DHARMAKĀYA is described as completing one's own aims or welfare.

**satya**. (P. sacca; T. bden pa; C. di; J. tai; K. che 諦). In Sanskrit, "truth," in the sense of that which is nondeceptive and exists as it appears. The term appears in two famous lists: the FOUR NOBLE TRUTHS (catvāry āryasatyāni) that were set forth in the Buddha's first sermon, the DHAMMACAKKAPPAVATTANASUTTA (S. DHARMACAKRAPRAVARTANASŪTRA); and the two truths (SATYADVAYA) discussed in the Buddhist philosophical schools and especially in MADHYAMAKA, viz., the conventional truth, or SAṂVṚTISATYA, and the ultimate truth, or PARAMĀRTHASATYA. In Madhyamaka, satya is also used in the compound satyasiddha, "truly existent" or "truly established," to refer to a false degree of truth or autonomy imagined by ignorance. It is also found in the compound SATYAVACANA ("statement of truth"), where magical powers derive from the truth inherent in one's words. In the MAHĀYĀNA, such solemn asseverations of truth reflect the power of a bodhisattva's aspiration to bring about the welfare of all sentient beings. See also SANDI.

**satyadvaya**. (P. saccadvaya; T. bden pa gnyis; C. erdi; J. nitai; K. ije 二諦). In Sanskrit, "the two truths," viz., "ultimate truth" (PARAMĀRTHASATYA) and "conventional truth" (SAṂVṚTISATYA). The two truths are central terms in Buddhist philosophy for categorizing the phenomena of the universe. Regardless of the school, the two truths are presumed to be exhaustive, with everything that exists, that is, all DHARMAs, falling into one of the two categories. This bifurcation is associated especially with the MADHYAMAKA school, but it occurs in other schools as well, with each providing its own view of what constitutes the two truths. In each case, however, conventional truths might be described as the objects of ordinary experience that tend to be misperceived by the unenlightened, by mistakenly ascribing to them a greater degree of reality than they in fact possess. Thus, despite being "truths," conventional truths are falsely perceived, as implied in the term saṃvṛti, with its connotation of deception. Ultimate truths, literally "supreme object truths," might be described as those realities that exist as they appear and whose direct perception can lead to liberation from rebirth. For the VAIBHĀṢIKA branch of SARVĀSTIVĀDA ABHIDHARMA, a conventional truth is any phenomenon that can be either physically or mentally broken down into parts; an ultimate truth is a partless particle of matter or an indivisible moment of consciousness. For the YOGĀCĀRA, conventional truths are dependent phenomena (PARATANTRA) as well as permanent phenomena such as space (ĀKĀŚA); ultimate truths are consummate natures (PARINIṢPANNA). In Madhyamaka, conventional truths are all phenomena other than emptiness (ŚŪNYATĀ), which is the ultimate truth. The Chinese SAN LUN ZONG

(Madhyamaka) master JIZANG (549–623) discusses the three stages of the two truths, in which each of these stages serves to correct any possible reification of Buddhist truth.

**Satyadvayavibhaṅga**. (T. Bden pa gnyis rnam par 'byed pa). In Sanskrit, "Distinction Between the Two Truths," a work by the eighth-century MADHYAMAKA master JÑĀNAGARBHA. According to Tibetan classification, the work belongs to the SVĀTANTRIKA-MADHYAMAKA, and within that, the SAUTRĀNTIKA-SVĀTANTRIKA-MADHYAMAKA. This work, together with the MADHYAMAKĀLAṂKĀRA by ŚĀNTARAKṢITA and the MADHYAMAKĀLOKA of KAMALAŚĪLA are known in Tibet as the "three works of the eastern *SVĀTANTRIKAS" (rang rgyud shar gsum) because the three authors were from Bengal. The *Satyadvayavibhaṅga* is composed in verses (kārikā) and includes a prose autocommentary (vṛtti) by the author. There is also a commentary (pañjikā) by Śāntarakṣita, who is said to have been a student of Jñānagarbha. The text presumably takes its title from Nāgārjuna's statement in his MŪLAMADHYAMAKAKĀRIKĀ: "Those who do not comprehend the distinction between these two truths do not know the nature of the profound doctrine of the Buddha." The ultimate truth (PARAMĀRTHASATYA) is nondeceptive; its nature accords not with appearance, but with valid knowledge gained through reasoning (nyāya). It is also free from discursive thought (NIRVIKALPA). The conventional truth (SAṂVṚTISATYA) includes ordinary appearances, or as the text says, "whatever appears even to cowherds and women." Within the category of the conventional, there are true and false conventions, which are distinguished based on their ability to perform a function (ARTHAKRIYĀ) in accordance with their appearance; thus water is a true convention and a mirage is a false convention. The work ends with a discussion of the three bodies (TRIKĀYA) of a buddha.

***Satyasiddhiśāstra**. (C. Chengshi lun; J. Jōjitsuron; K. Sŏngsil non 成實論). See CHENGSHI LUN; *TATTVASIDDHI.

**satyavacana**. (P. saccavacana, [alt. saccakiriyā]; T. bden pa'i ngag; C. shiyu; J. jitsugo; K. sirŏ 實語). In Sanskrit, "asseveration of truth," or "statement of truth"; a solemn declaration or oath in which the truth inherent in its words generates magical or protective powers (see PARITTA). For example, when Prince SIDDHĀRTHA first renounced the world and cut off his hair, he threw it into the air and said, "If I am to become a buddha, may it stay in the sky." Due to this asseveration of truth, his hair was caught by the chief of the gods ŚAKRA, who enshrined it in a CAITYA in the TRĀYASTRIṂŚA heaven. The Buddha's disciple AṄGULIMĀLA offered a well-known asseveration of truth to help ease a woman's labor pains: "Since I was born of āryan birth, O sister, I am not aware of having intentionally deprived any living being of its life. By this asseveration of truth, may you be well and may your unborn child be well." (There is intentional irony in this statement, since Aṅgulimāla was a murderer before he became a monk; his "āryan birth" here refers to his ordination into the SAṂGHA.) In Buddhist literature, miraculous events are said to be a result of an asseveration of truth. Often, when a bodhisattva has given away some body part as an act of DĀNA (see DEHADĀNA; SHESHEN) that body part is restored as a result of one's solemn declaration, as in the case of SADĀPRARUDITA. In the JĀTAKAMĀLĀ of Āryaśūra, Śakra appears in the form of a blind brāhmaṇa to test the generosity of King ŚIBI, one of the Buddha's previous lives. The king goes blind when he donates his eyes to the brāhmaṇa, but his sight is restored when he makes a solemn statement of truth that his charity is sincere, articulating, in effect, the bodhisattva's aspiration to seek the welfare of all beings (SATTVĀRTHA). According to another story, a young boy was bitten by a poisonous snake. The distraught parents stopped a passing monk and asked him to use his medical knowledge to save the child. The monk replied that the situation was so grave that the only possible cure was an asseveration of truth. The father said, "If I have never seen a monk that I did not think was a scoundrel, may the boy live." The poison left the boy's leg. The mother said, "If I have never loved my husband, may the boy live." The poison retreated to the boy's waist. The monk said, "If I have never believed a word of the dharma, but found it utter nonsense, may the boy live." The boy rose, completely cured. Such is the power of the truth.

**Saundarananda**. (T. Mdzes dga' bo). In Sanskrit, "Handsome Nanda," the Indian philosopher-poet AŚVAGHOṢA's verse recounting of NANDA's transformation from enamored husband, to ascetic, and finally to enlightened ARHAT, written c. second century CE. "Handsome Nanda" is the epithet of NANDA, the younger half brother of the Buddha. The first half of this ornate poem provides a elaborate retelling of Nanda's forced ordination into the Buddhist order, his humiliation due to his erotic attachments to both his wife Sundarī (a.k.a. JANAPADAKALYĀṆĪ NANDĀ) and various heavenly nymphs (APSARAS), and finally his decision to abandon carnality and seek enlightenment. In the second half of the poem, the Buddha offers Nanda instruction in moral and sensory restraint, leading up to the FOUR NOBLE TRUTHS, and finally the achievement of the "deathless," a synonym for NIRVĀṆA. The poem ends with the now-enlightened Nanda compassionately teaching to others the path to liberation. Aśvaghoṣa's elaborate kāvya version of this well-known tale of conversion is a classic of early Indian Buddhist literature. There is some controversy over its influence and popularity, however, since unlike most of Aśvaghoṣa's other works, there are no Indian commentaries, and the poem was never translated into either Chinese or Tibetan.

**Saurāṣṭra**. (S). One of the twenty-four sacred sites associated with the CAKRASAṂVARATANTRA. See PĪṬHA.

**Sautrāntika**. (T. Mdo sde pa; C. Jingliang bu; J. Kyōryōbu; K. Kyŏngnyang pu 經量部). In Sanskrit, "Followers of the Sūtras," one of the "mainstream" (that is, non-MAHĀYĀNA) schools of Indian Buddhism, which may have been a dissenting offshoot of the SARVĀSTIVĀDA school. Its name was apparently meant to distinguish this school from those ĀBHIDHARMIKAS who based themselves on ABHIDHARMA treatises, such as the ABHIDHARMAMAHĀVIBHĀṢĀ. The Sautrāntika were "Followers of the Sūtras" because they were said to have rejected the validity of the abhidharma as being the word of the Buddha (BUDDHAVACANA) and advocated a doctrine of momentariness (KṢAṆIKAVĀDA), in which (again in distinction to the Sarvāstivāda) only present activity exists. No texts of the school are extant, but its positions are represented in the ABHIDHARMAKOŚABHĀṢYA, which presents the SARVĀSTIVĀDA-VAIBHĀṢIKA positions in detail, and as deficient relative to a putative Sautrāntika position. According to Tibetan accounts, VASUBANDHU, the author of the *Abhidharmakośabhāṣya*, wrote from the perspective of the Sautrāntika position even while he himself was a YOGĀCĀRA adherent. Similarly, some of the chapters of the Yogācāra DHARMAKĪRTI's explanation of Dignāga's logical system are written from the Sautrāntika perspective. According to ŚĀNTARAKṢITA and his student KAMALAŚĪLA, one major difference between the Vaibhāṣika and Sautrāntika schools is their respective rejection or acceptance of SVASAṂVEDANA ("self-cognizing awareness"). Although both schools accept that atoms (PARAMĀṆU) build up to form external objects that are perceived by consciousness, the Vaibhāṣika say that the mind knows these objects directly, while the Sautrāntika position is that it knows them through images (ākāra). In late Indian and Tibetan classifications, the Sautrāntika and Vaibhāṣika are called the two ŚRĀVAKA schools (T. nyan thos sde pa), to distinguish them from the two Mahāyāna schools of YOGĀCĀRA and MADHYAMAKA.

**Sautrāntika-Svātantrika-Madhyamaka**. (T. Mdo sde spyod pa'i dbu ma rang rgyud pa). One of the two subschools (along with the YOGĀCĀRA-SVĀTANTRIKA-MADHYAMAKA) of the *SVĀTANTRIKA branch of MADHYAMAKA, as identified by Tibetan exegetes. This is the school of BHĀVAVIVEKA, his commentator AVALOKITAVRATA, and JÑĀNAGARBHA. Like other Svātantrikas, these three exegetes assert that phenomena exist conventionally by way of their own qualities (SVALAKṢAṆA). They thus declare that external objects exist conventionally and deny the existence of a self-cognizing awareness (SVASAṂVEDANA). With regard to the path, they contend that ŚRĀVAKAS and PRATYEKABUDDHAS understand the selflessness of the person (PUDGALANAIRĀTMYA) but not the selflessness of phenomena (DHARMANAIRĀTMYA), whereas BODHISATTVAS understand both kinds of nonself.

**sayadaw**. In Burmese, an honorific used for a respected monk. The term was originally used specifically to designate the senior monk (mahathera) who was selected to serve as royal preceptor, but it eventually came to be used more generically as a term of respect for any eminent monk.

**Sba bzhed**. (Bashe). In Tibetan, the "Annals of Sba," a ninth-century history of the early Tibetan dynastic period and the activities of King KHRI SRONG LDE BTSAN, traditionally attributed to the author Sba Gsal snang (Ba Salnang, c. late-eighth century)—a leading member of the Sba (Ba) clan and abbot of BSAM YAS monastery during the years leading up to the BSAM YAS DEBATE. The text thus discusses the founding of Bsam yas, the debate, and other events surrounding the establishment of Buddhism during the period. It contains the earliest reference to PADMASAMBHAVA, describing him as a water diviner. Modern scholarship tends to date the complete version of the work to the twelfth or even fourteenth century, although there are extant fragments that are likely earlier. The complete title is *Sba bzhed ces bya ba las sba gsal snang gi bzhed pa bzhugs*.

**sbas yul**. (beyul). In Tibetan, "hidden land," often translated as "hidden valley," a paradisaical land whose existence is not often known until the land is "opened" by a lama (BLA MA). Such lands are typically located in southern Tibet, northern Nepal, and Sikkim and are associated especially with the RNYING MA sect as sites where PADMASAMBHAVA hid treasure texts (GTER MA). After converting the local gods to Buddhism, Padmasambhava "sealed" the lands so that they could be discovered at a time in the future and serve as a refuge from the vicissitudes of the world; the weather is clement, the harvests are good, and there is no disease or conflict. They are special places for the practice of TANTRA during the degenerate age of the dharma, where an adept can make rapid progress on the path; in this regard, they are akin to Buddhist PURE LANDs, even though they are located on earth. Hidden lands are considered safe havens, inaccessible to the enemies of the dharma and of Tibet, where one may live a long and peaceful life. According to some traditions, there are 108 hidden lands. In addition to concealing treasure texts in the hidden lands, Padmasambhava also left guidebooks for their discovery. One of the most famous of the hidden lands is PADMA BKOD.

**scripture, nine/twelves divisions of**. See NAVAṄGA [PĀVACANA]; DVĀDAŚĀṄGA[PRAVACANA].

**Sde dge**. (Derge). A region on the Tibet-China border, which until the 1950s was one of the most famous kingdoms in Khams; now incorporated into China's Sichuan province. The kingdom with its twenty-five districts enjoyed the autonomy of an independent state throughout much of its existence. Included among its famous monasteries are DPAL SPUNGS, KAḤ THOG, RDZOGS CHEN, ZHE CHEN, and DPAL YUL. From the eighteenth century onward, its royal family supported a famous printery that became the repository of hundreds of thousands of woodblock prints. The printing of the entire BKA' 'GYUR and BSTAN 'GYUR edited by TAI SI TU Gstug lag chos kyi 'byung gnas (1700–1774) and of the foundational texts of the SA SKYA and RNYING MA sects, among others, were started there in 1729 and completed in 1744. In the nineteenth century, the region became the center of the Khams RIS MED (nonsectarian) movement; many of the modern traditions of Tibetan

Buddhism can be traced back to its founders 'JAM MGON KONG SPRUL, 'JAM DBYANGS MKHYEN BRTSE, and DPAL SPRUL RIN PO CHE.

**Sde srid Sangs rgyas rgya mtsho**. (Desi Sangye Gyatso) (1653–1705). The third and final regent of the fifth DALAI LAMA NGAG DBANG BLO BZANG RGYA MTSHO, serving as regent of Tibet from 1679 until his death. He successfully concealed the death of the fifth Dalai Lama in 1682 for some fifteen years, in part to allow for the completion of the PO TA LA Palace. During this time, he served as ruler of Tibet, overseeing (and keeping secret) the discovery of the sixth Dalai Lama, TSHANGS DBYANGS RGYA MTSHO. In addition to being a skilled politician, Sangs rgyas rgya mtsho was one of the most learned and prolific authors in the history of Tibet, composing important treatises on all manner of subjects, including statecraft, ritual, astrology and calendrics, poetics, architecture, and court etiquette. He had a special interest in medicine, composing his famous treatise entitled BAIḌŪRYA SNGON PO and founding a medical college on Lcag po ri near the Po ta la. His largest literary project was his seven-thousand page work on the life of the fifth Dalai Lama and his previous incarnations. More than any other author, he was responsible for solidifying the mythic identity of the Dalai Lama as an incarnation of the bodhisattva AVALOKITEŚVARA and establishing the line of incarnations over the centuries in India and Tibet, which culminated in the person of the fifth Dalai Lama. He was a staunch supporter and active promoter of the DGE LUGS sect, greatly increasing the number of its monasteries and the size of its monastic population. After the Mongol chieftain Lha bzang Khan claimed rulership over Tibet in 1700, Sangs rgyas rgya mtsho agreed to share power with him, but was soon deposed. Armed conflict occurred between the factions despite a series of truces. Sde srid Sangs rgyas rgya mtsho was captured and beheaded by Mongol troops in 1705.

**sdom gsum**. (domsum). In Tibetan, "three vows" or "three codes"; variously the three sets of vows or restraints (TRISAṂVARA) set forth in the śīlaparivarta (morality chapter) of the BODHISATTVABHŪMI; or (1) the seven sets of VINAYA rules that make up the PRĀTIMOKṢA code of the HĪNAYĀNA, (2) the three sets of vows or restraints defining bodhisattva morality in the BODHISATTVABHŪMI, and (3) the nineteen SAMAYAs that codify tantric morality, particularly as found in the Tibetan version of the VAJRAŚEKHARATANTRA. See also TRISAṂVARA, SAṂVARA, ŚĪLATRAYA.

**Sdom gsum rab dbye**. (Domsum Rapye). In Tibetan, "Clear Differentiation of the Three Vows," an important work by the Tibetan master SA SKYA PAṆḌITA KUN DGA' RGYAL MTSHAN. Composed in verse, around 1232, it deals with the three vows or codes: the PRĀTIMOKṢA vows, the BODHISATTVA vows, and the tantric vows (SAMAYA). In Tibet, it was considered possible, and in some cases ideal, for the Buddhist practitioner to receive and maintain all three sets of precepts: the monk's precepts (prātimokṣa), which from the Tibetan perspective derived from the HĪNAYĀNA; the bodhisattva precepts, which derived from the MAHĀYĀNA, and the tantric precepts, which derived from the VAJRAYĀNA. However, there was a wide range of opinion on the relation among these three and how to resolve contradictions among them. The "Clear Differentiation of the Three Vows" is not an exposition of the three sets of precepts, but rather a polemical work in which Sa skya Paṇḍita criticizes interpretations of the three then current in the other sects of Tibetan Buddhism. Sa skya Paṇḍita's own view, in brief, was that the prātimokṣa and the bodhisattva precepts provided the foundation for the tantric precepts, such that someone receiving tantric initiation should already hold the other two sets. The work provoked hostile responses from those whose views were criticized in the text, leading Sa skya Paṇḍita to reply to his critics in a series of letters. His text sparked the development in subsequent centuries of a genre of texts on the three vows or codes (SDOM GSUM).

**Sdom gsum rnam nges**. (Domsum Namnge). A work in the SDOM GSUM (three codes) genre by Mnga' ris paṇ chen Padma dbang rgyal (Ngari Panchen Pema Wangyel, 1487–1542). It is a work of the RNYING MA sect, but is influenced both by the SDOM GSUM RAB DBYE and by works on ethics by TSONG KHA PA. It became widely known through LO CHEN DHARMA SHRI's detailed explanation, which is a central part of the curriculum of many Rnying ma BSHAD GRWA (monastic schools).

**secession from the order**. See SIKKHĀPACCAKKHĀNA.

**seiban**. (西班). In Japanese, "west rank"; the offices of the prefects (C. TOUSHOU) at a CHAN or ZEN monastery. These offices are often located on the west side of the monastery and are hence referred to as the west rank. On the east are the stewards (C. ZHISHI), who are thus referred to as the east section or rank. The CHANYUAN QINGGUI, for instance, refers to the stewards as the east section (C. dongxu) and the prefects as the west section (C. xixu).

**Sekhasutta**. In Pāli, "Discourse on the Disciple in Higher Training," the fifty-third sutta in the MAJJHIMANIKĀYA (no precise equivalent appears in the Chinese translations of the ĀGAMAs, but the sūtra is cited in the DAZHIDU LUN, indicating it was known in other mainstream Buddhist traditions); preached by the Buddha's attendant ĀNANDA to the leader of the Sakiya (ŚĀKYA) tribe, Mahānāma, and his entourage in the meeting hall of the Sakiyans in the city of Kapilavatthu (S. KAPILAVASTU). Ānanda teaches them about the higher training practiced by the disciple who has entered the path. Such a disciple practices morality (P. sīla, S. ŚĪLA) which includes observance of the monastic code, guarding the sense faculties, moderation in all things, and wakefulness. He is further possessed of seven wholesome qualities, including faith, a sense of shame, fear of blame, learning, energy, mindfulness, and wisdom. He is master of the four meditative absorptions (P. JHĀNA, S. DHYĀNA) and possesses the three knowledges (P.

tevijja, S. TRIVIDYĀ). The three knowledges are comprised of (1) recollection of one's previous existences (P. pubbenivasanusati, S. PŪRVANIVĀSĀNUSMṚTI); (2) the divine eye (P. dibbacakkhu, S. DIVYACAKṢUS) or the ability to see the demise and rebirth of beings according to their good and evil deeds; and (3) knowledge of the extinction of contaminants (P. āsavakkhayañāna, S. ĀSRAVAKṢAYAJÑĀNA), which encompasses knowledge of the FOUR NOBLE TRUTHS and is equivalent to arhatship.

**sekishu kōan**. (隻手公案). In Japanese, "the case of one-hand [clapping]"; a famous kōan (C. GONG'AN) attributed to the Japanese RINZAI ZEN master HAKUIN EKAKU (1685–1769), in which he asks, "What is the sound of one hand [clapping]?" The kōan is included in his 1752 collection *Yabukōji*, along with Hakuin's autocommentary. The sekishu kōan came to be used within some Rinzai kanna Zen (see KANHUA CHAN) systems as the first case given to neophytes in Zen training and, along with the mu kōan (C. WU GONG'AN), continues to be one of the emblematic kōans used in Japanese Rinzai Zen circles.

**self-immolation**. See DEHADĀNA; SHESHEN; YŌNJI.

**sems sde**. (sem de). In Tibetan, literally "mind class," one of the three divisions of RDZOGS CHEN, together with KLONG SDE, or "expanse class," and the MAN NGAG SDE, or "instruction class." It appears that the three classes were created simultaneously rather than sequentially, probably dating to the PHYI DAR, or later period of the dissemination of Buddhism in Tibet, that began in the eleventh century. It is possible that the classification scheme was invented by members of the Zur clan, who were involved in codifying the RNYING MA texts that were circulating at that time. Within the threefold division, the texts classified do not necessarily share a single set of characteristics. However, it can be said that the works in the sems sde are often earlier than those in the other two classes. The root tantra of the sems sde is the KUN BYED RGYAL PO, where a number of short early-period rdzogs chen texts were gathered into a single new tantra. The sems sde works tend toward simple, evocative statements that deny the need for any practice or moral concerns.

**Senart, Émile**. (1847–1928). French Indologist who made significant contributions to the study of Indian Buddhism. His knowledge of Middle Indic languages allowed him to do important work on Indian epigraphy, most notably the edicts of AŚOKA, in his *Les inscriptions de Piyadasi*, first published in a series of articles in *Journal Asiatique* between 1881 and 1886. His research suggested that the Aśoka inscriptions represented a popular Buddhism in which following an ethical code led to rebirth in heaven, with less emphasis on NIRVĀṆA. His most famous and controversial work was on the biography of the Buddha, presented in his *Essai sur la légende du Buddha* (1882). There, he argued that the life of the Buddha was not a series of originally historical events that over time became encrusted with legendary elements, but rather that those mythological elements of the Buddha's life formed a coherent whole that was fully formed in India before the Buddha's birth, with the Buddha as a solar deity. His argument was famously opposed by HERMANN OLDENBERG. Senart also argued that a pre-classical version of Yoga played a significant role in the formation of Buddhist thought and practice. Senart also made major contributions through his editing of Buddhist texts. Among his editions, the most substantial was his three-volume edition of the MAHĀVASTU, published between 1882 and 1897. He was also among the first to study the KHAROṢṬHĪ fragments of the DHARMAPADA. See also DHAMMAPADA.

**Senchakushū**. (選擇集). In Japanese, "Collection of Selections," composed by the Japanese PURE LAND monk HŌNEN in 1198; also known as *Senjakushū* or *Senchaku hongan nenbutsushū* ("Collection of Selections on Nenbutsu and the Original Vow"). Hōnen's *Senchakushū* is one of the most influential texts in Japan on the practice of nenbutsu (see NIANFO), i.e., the invocation of the name of the buddha AMITĀBHA; it is also traditionally regarded as the founding scripture of the JŌDOSHŪ tradition of Japanese pure land. Relying on the three pure land sūtras (JINGTU SANBUJING, viz., the longer and shorter SUKHĀVATĪVYŪHASŪTRA and the GUAN WULIANGSHOU JING) and a number of important commentaries by SHANDAO and TANLUAN, Hōnen attempted to elucidate the importance of the practice of nenbutsu in the context of Amitābha's original vows as described in the *Sukhāvatīvyūhasūtra*. He first cites DAOCHUO's division of Buddhist practice into that of the sacred path (that is, the traditional Buddhist path) and the pure land path, and then cites SHANDAO's division into proper and miscellaneous. These divisions are used as an argument for the practice of exclusive nenbutsu. Hōnen then demonstrates that exclusive nenbutsu is the practice advocated by Amitābha in his original vows. In the next few sections of his text, Hōnen also mentions the benefits of exclusive nenbutsu and explains why this practice is most appropriate for those in the age of the final dharma (J. mappō; see MOFA). The other sections of the *Senchakushū* provide further scriptural evidence for the importance of nenbutsu and discuss the proper method for practicing it. At Hōnen's request, the work was not widely circulated until after his death. Numerous commentaries on this text exist in Japanese.

**Sengai Gibon**. (仙厓義梵) (1750–1837). Japanese ZEN monk in the RINZAISHŪ, known for his whimsical teachings, his poetry, and especially for his calligraphy and sumi-e paintings. His best-known work in the West is a simple ink drawing of a circle, triangle, and square. He spent much of his life at SHŌFUKUJI, where he served as abbot.

**Sengcan**. (J. Sōsan; K. Sŭngch'an 僧粲) (d. 606?). Chinese monk and reputed third patriarch of the CHAN tradition. Although the influential Chan poem XINXIN MING ("Faith in Mind") is attributed to Sengcan, little is actually known of this mysterious figure, and he may simply have been a later invention created to connect the BODHIDHARMA-HUIKE line of early Chan with the East Mountain teachings (DONGSHAN FAMEN) of DAOXIN (580–651) and HONGREN (602–675). Most of what is known of Sengcan is constructed retrospectively in such early Chan genealogical histories as the BAOLIN ZHUAN, LENGQIE SHIZI JI, CHUAN FABAO JI, and LIDAI FABAO JI, and in later Chan histories known as "transmission of the lamplight records" (CHUANDENG LU). Sengcan is claimed to have studied under Huike, the first Chinese disciple of the Chan founder, Bodhidharma, and the second patriarch of the Chan school. During Emperor Wu's (r. 502–549) persecution of Buddhism, Sengcan is said to have gone into hiding and later resided on Mt. Sikong in Shuzhou (present-day Anhui province). The *Lengqie shizi ji* and *Chuan fabao ji* claim that Daoxin became Sengcan's disciple sometime in the late-sixth century, but Daoxin's connection to this dubious figure is tenuous at best and most probably spurious. Sengcan was later given the posthumous title Chan Master Jingzhi (Mirror-like Wisdom).

**Sengguo**. (J. Sōka; K. Sŭngkwa 僧果) (b. 408). In Chinese, "Fruition of the Saṃgha"; a Buddhist nun from Xiuwu in northern China during the Liu-Song dynasty (420–479), the first of the four short-lived southern dynasties that formed during the Six Dynasties period. Her biography, contained in the BIQIUNI ZHUAN, exemplifies several prevalent characteristics of early Chinese Buddhist nuns' hagiographies. She engaged in a strict observance of the monastic rules (VINAYA), which inspired her disciples. Her contemplative practice, which began from a young age, was reputed to be so intense that it often produced trance states resembling death. She left secular life as an adult and practiced at a convent near the Song capital, where a number of Ceylonese nuns resided. Upon conversing with them, Sengguo discovered that while Chinese nuns had previously accepted monastic obligations from an assembly of monks (BHIKṢU), they had not received them from an assembly of nuns (BHIKṢUṆĪ), as was required by the VINAYA. After consulting with the Indian monk GUṆAVARMAN (367–431) on the issue, she resolved that she and her fellow nuns should be reordained. Thus in 433, in an ordination ceremony presided over by SAṂGHAVARMAN, Sengguo and over three hundred other nuns were ordained with both an assembly of monks and an assembly of nuns in attendance, thereby officially instituting the monastic order for women in China.

**Sengmeng**. (J. Sōmō; K. Sŭngmaeng 僧猛) (418–489). A Buddhist nun (BHIKṢUṆĪ) from Yanguan County in southeastern China during the Qi dynasty (479–502). As was common in the biographies collected in the BIQIUNI ZHUAN, she left secular life at a young age. Despite her family's long fealty to Daoism, Sengmeng alone rejected Daoism in favor of Buddhism, strictly adhering to the monastic precepts. Sengmeng demonstrated a penetrating grasp of scripture and was extremely diligent in her study. In addition, she could recite from memory extraordinary amounts of text, often after only a single reading. Sengmeng demonstrated her Buddhist compassion in many ways, including dramatic moments when she used her own body as a barricade to protects animals from predators, enduring pecks and bites as a result. Her exemplary deeds were cited as ideal models for Buddhist monastics and laity alike.

**sengtang**. (J. sōdō; K. sŭngdang 僧堂). In Chinese, the "SAṂGHA hall," or "monks' hall"; also known as the yuntang (lit. cloud hall; J. undō) or xuanfochang (site for selecting buddhas). The saṃgha hall was the center of monastic practice in the Chinese CHAN school. The hall, often large enough to hold hundreds of monks, was traditionally built on the west side of a Chan monastery. The foundation of the saṃgha hall is traditionally attributed to the Chan master BAIZHANG QINGGUI (749–814). According to Baizhang's CHANMEN GUISHI, Chan monks were obligated throughout the day and night to eat, sleep, and meditate in the saṃgha hall. There, they would sit according to seniority on a long platform. A similar description of the saṃgha hall is also found in the CHANYUAN QINGGUI of CHANGLU ZONGZE (d.u.; fl. c. late-eleventh to early-twelfth century). During the Song dynasty, the saṃgha hall became incorporated into the monastic plans of all large public monasteries (SHIFANG CHA) in China, regardless of sectarian affiliation. The saṃgha hall was introduced into Japan by the SŌTŌSHŪ master DŌGEN KIGEN (1200–1253), who built the first sōdō in 1236 at the monastery of Kōshōji; for this reason, the sōdō is most closely associated with the Sōtō tradition. Dōgen also wrote detailed instructions in his BENDŌHŌ ("Techniques for Pursuing the Way," 1246) on how to practice in the sōdō. Stemming from a practice initiated by DAO'AN, an image of the ARHAT PIṆḌOLA was usually placed in the middle of the saṃgha hall. Sometimes an image of MAÑJUŚRĪ, ĀJÑĀTAKAUṆḌINYA, or MAHĀKĀŚYAPA was installed in lieu of Piṇḍola. The Sōtō Zen tradition, for instance, often places a statue of Mañjuśrī in the guise of a monk in its saṃgha halls. The Japanese RINZAISHŪ chose to call their main monks' hall a zendō (meditation hall) rather than a saṃgha hall. Unlike the Sōtō sōdō, which was used for eating, sleeping, and meditating, the Rinzai zendō was reserved solely for meditation (J. ZAZEN). Japanese ŌBAKUSHŪ, following Ming dynasty (1368–1644) Chinese customs, also called their main hall a zendō. In Korea, the term sŭngdang is no longer used and the main meditation hall is typically known as a sŏnbang (lit. meditation room). See also PRAHĀṆAŚĀLĀ.

**Sengyou**. (J. Sōyū; K. Sŭngu 僧祐) (445–518). Early Chinese VINAYA teacher and scriptural cataloguer, whose career is indicative of early Chinese Buddhism's concerns to preserve the integrity of the dispensation and to transmit its beliefs and practices accurately. According to his biography in the GAOSENG ZHUAN ("Biographies of Eminent Monks"), Sengyou was born in Jianye (present-day Nanjing, Jiangsu province), the capital of the Liu-Song dynasty (420–479), the first of the four short-lived southern dynasties that formed during the Six Dynasties period. He became a monk at an early age, and studied under vinaya master Faying (416–482). Later, Sengyou himself gained a reputation as a vinaya master; the *Gaoseng zhuan* says that, whenever he was invited by the prince Wenxuan (406–494) of the Qi dynasty (479–502) to lecture on the vinaya, typically seven or eight hundred people would attend. During the Yongming era (483–493) of the Qi dynasty, Sengyou received an imperial order to travel to the Wu region (in present-day Jiangnan) to lecture on the *Shisong lü*, the SARVĀSTIVĀDA VINAYA, as well as to explain the methods for receiving the precepts. In addition to his vinaya-related activities, Sengyou also tried to establish an authoritative canon of Buddhist texts by compiling the CHU SANZANG JIJI ("Compilation of Notices on the Translation of the TRIPIṬAKA"), the earliest extant Buddhist scriptural catalogue (JINGLU). In his catalogue, Sengyou introduced three criteria for distinguishing an apocryphal scripture (see APOCRYPHA) from a genuine one: (1) the meanings and expressions found in a text were "shallow and coarse"; (2) a text did not come from "foreign regions"; (3) a text was not translated by a "Western guest." While the first criterion was a more subjective form of internal evidence, the latter two were important pieces of external evidence that all subsequent cataloguers adopted as objective standards for determining textual authenticity. Sengyou's other extant major works include the *Shijia pu* ("Genealogy of ŚĀKYAMUNI"), in five rolls, and the Buddhist apologetic HONGMING JI ("Collection for the Propagation and Clarification [of Buddhism]"), in fourteen rolls.

**Sengzhao**. (J. Sōjō; K. Sŭngjo 僧肇) (374–414). Influential early Chinese monk and exegete, whose writings helped to popularize the works of the MADHYAMAKA school in China. Sengzhao is said to have been born into an improverished family but was able to support himself by working as a copyist. Thanks to his trade, he was able to read through much of traditional Chinese literature and philosophy, including such Daoist classics as the *Zhuangzi* and *Laozi*, and is said to have resolved to become a monk after reading the VIMALAKĪRTINIRDEŚA. He later became a disciple of KUMĀRAJĪVA and served as the Chinese-language stylist for Kumārajīva's translations. After Yao Xing (r. 394–416) of the Latter Qin dynasty (384–417) destroyed the state of Liang in 401, Sengzhao followed his teacher to Chang'an, where he and his colleague Sengrui (352–436) were appointed as two of the main assistants in Kumārajīva's translation bureau there. Yao Xing ordered them to elucidate the scriptures Kumārajīva had translated, so Sengzhao subsequently wrote his BORE WUZHI LUN to explicate the PAÑCAVIṂŚATISĀHASRIKĀPRAJÑĀPĀRAMITĀSŪTRA that Kumārajīva and his team had translated in 404. This and other influential treatises by Sengzhao were later compiled together as the ZHAO LUN. Sengzhao's treatises and his commentary on the *Vimalakīrtinirdeśa* played a crucial role in the development of MAHĀYĀNA thought in China. Sengzhao is treated retrospectively as a vaunt courier in the SAN LUN ZONG, the Chinese analogue of the Madhyamaka school, which was formally established some two centuries later by JIZANG (549–623). The influential BAOZANG LUN is also attributed to Sengzhao, although that treatise is probably a later work of the early CHAN tradition.

**Sensōji**. (淺草寺). In Japanese, "Low Grass Monastery," located in the Asakusa (lit. Low Grass) district of Tōkyō; it is the oldest monastery in the current Japanese capital. Legend says that in 628 a statue of the BODHISATTVA Kannon (AVALOKITEŚVARA) was found by fishermen in the Sumida River and the village elder turned his home into a shrine for the image; this image remains an important object of veneration in Japanese Buddhism. Originally called Komagatadō, the current monastery was built in 645 and is the oldest in Tōkyō. Sensōji was formerly associated with the TENDAISHŪ (C. TIANTAI ZONG), but has been independent since after World War II. The monastery is entered through the Kaminarimon, or Thunder Gate, which is graced by a gigantic paper lantern that is vividly painted to evoke storm clouds and lightning. This gate was built by the governor of the Musashi District, Tairano Kinmasa, in 942, as was the inner Hōzō gate; both have subsequently been reconstructed following fires. The main Kannondō hall at Sensōji is devoted to Avalokiteśvara; it burned down during a World War II air raid but has been rebuilt. The monastery grounds also include a five-story pagoda, a beautiful garden, and many oracle stalls (omikuji). Next door is an important SHINTŌ shrine, the Asakusa Jinja, which may partially explain why Sensōji is the site of the biggest festival in Tōkyō, the Sanja Matsuri, which is held annually in the late spring.

**sensory restraint**. See INDRIYASAṂVARA.

**sentient beings**. See SATTVA.

**Se ra**. A large monastic complex counted among the "three seats" (GDAN SA GSUM) of the DGE LUGS sect of Tibetan Buddhism, located at the north end of the LHA SA valley. TSONG KHA PA wrote *Rtsa she ṭik chen rigs pa'i rgya mtsho*, his commentary on NĀGĀRJUNA's MŪLAMADHYAMAKAKĀRIKĀ, in a hermitage above the future site of the monastery and predicted that it would become a great seat of learning. Foundations for the complex were laid in 1419 by Byams chen chos rje Shākya ye shes (Jamchen Chöje Shākya Yeshe, 1354–1435), a disciple of Tsong kha pa. Begun as a center for tantric studies, four colleges were later established, which were later consolidiated into two: Se ra smad (Sera Me) and Se ra byes (Sera Je). Se ra byes, the larger of the two, was constructed by Kun mkhyen blo gros rin chen seng ge (Künkyen Lodrö Rinchen Senge, fl. fifteenth century), a disciple of both Tsong kha pa and Byams chen chos rjes. A third college, the Sngags pa drwa tshang (Ngakpa Dratsang) or tantric college, was established in the eighteenth century, most likely under the patronage of the Mongolian ruler Lha bzang Khan. Traditionally said to house 5,500 monks, Se ra was home to roughly eight thousand monks at its peak, with some thirty-five regional dormitories (khams tshan). Monks from Se ra participated in the 1959 uprising against the Chinese People's Liberation Army, which led to the monastery being closed and used as an army barracks. It also suffered significant damage during the Chinese Cultural Revolution. After that, it reopened as a monastery, but with a much smaller monastic population. Following the exodus of Tibetans into exile after 1959, a new Se ra monastery was also established in south India, near the town of Bylakuppe.

**Sesshū Tōyō**. (雪舟等楊) (1420–1506). A Japanese monk-painter of the Muromachi (1337–1573) period, best known for his use of realism in landscape painting. He was born to a warrior family in Bitchū province (present-day Okayama Prefecture, in the southwestern part of the main Japanese island of Honshū) and became a ZEN monk in the RINZAISHŪ tradition in 1431. From early in his monastic career, however, Sesshū (lit. Snow Boat) showed more interest in painting than in Zen training. Around 1440, he moved to SHŌKOKUJI, one of the GOZAN (five mountains) temples of Kyōto, where he received formal training in Chinese painting of the Song-dynasty (960–1279) style from Tenshō Shūbun (d. c. 1444–1450), the most famous monk-painter of his time. In 1467, Sesshū traveled to China, where he studied the emerging Ming style of painting. After returning to Japan in 1469, he established an atelier in present-day Ōita Prefecture in Kyūshū; subsequently, he moved to present-day Yamaguchi prefecture in the far west of Honshū in 1486. Using his "splashed-ink" (haboku) style, he established a style of realism in landscape painting, which included bold brush strokes and splashes of ink, with subtle tones. Many students gathered around him, later forming what became known as the Unkoku-rin (Cloud Valley) school, after the name of the monastery where Sesshū served as abbot. Sesshū's best-known works include his 1486 *Sansui chōkan* ("Long Landscape Scroll"), a fifty-foot-long scroll depicting the four seasons; *Haboku sansui* ("Splashed-Ink Landscape") of 1495; and the *Ama-no-Hashidate zu* ("View of Ama-no-Hashidate") of c. 1501–1505, which offers an unusual bird's-eye view of a picturesque sandbar, bay, and mountains in Tango province facing the Sea of Japan/East Sea. Sesshū is often judged to be the greatest of all Japanese painters.

**Sgam po pa Bsod nams rin chen**. (Gampopa Sönam Rinchen) (1079–1153). A principal disciple of the Tibetan YOGIN MI LA RAS PA and leading figure in the early formation of the BKA' BRGYUD sect of Tibetan Buddhism. At an early age, Sgam po pa trained as a physician but renounced his career and received monastic ordination at the age of twenty-five following the death of his wife and child. He is often known as Dwags po lha rje (Dakpo Lhaje), "the physician from Dakpo," because of his vocation. Sgam po pa initially trained in the BKA' GDAMS tradition under the master Snyug rum pa Brtson 'grus rgyal mtshan (Nyukrumpa Tsöndru Gyaltsen, b. eleventh century) as well as Po to ba Rin chen gsal. At the age of thirty-one, he heard three beggars discussing Mi la ras pa and experienced a strong feeling of faith. He asked permission of his Bka' gdams teachers to study with him, which they granted under the condition that he not renounce his monk's precepts. When he met Mi la ras pa in 1109, Sgam po pa offered him gold and tea, which he refused. Mi la ras pa offered him a skullcup full of wine, which Sgam po pa initially declined but then drank, even though it was a violation of his monk's vows. He received a number of teachings from Mi la ras pa, first concerning VAJARVĀRĀHĪ, and later the transmission of MAHĀMUDRĀ instructions and the "six yogas of Nāropa" (NĀ RO CHOS DRUG), stemming from the Indian MAHĀSIDDHAS TILOPA and NĀROPA. Later, Sgam po pa developed his own system of exposition, fusing elements of his Bka' gdams pa training with the perspectives and practices of mahāmudrā. This has been called the "confluence of the two streams of Bka' gdams pa and mahāmudrā" (bka' phyag chu bo gnyis 'dres). Unlike Mi la ras pa, he kept the practices of mahāmudrā and sexual yoga separate, teaching the latter only to select disciples. Sgam po pa remained a monk, founding his monastic seat at DWAGS LHA SGAM PO in southern Tibet and composing numerous works on Buddhist doctrine and practice. His work entitled THAR PA RIN PO CHE'I RGYAN ("Jewel Ornament of Liberation"), remains a seminal Bka' rgyud textbook. He also promulgated the controversial system of mahāmudrā instructions known as the DKAR PO CHIG THUB, or "self-sufficient white [remedy]." The lineage of Bka' brgyud masters and teachings following Sgam po pa came to be known collectively as the DWAGS PO BKA' BRGYUD. The division of the lineage into numerous subsects called the BKA' BRGYUD CHE BZHI CHUNG BRGYAD or "four major and eight minor Bka' brgyud subsects" stem from the disciples of Sgam po pa and his nephew Dwags po Sgom tshul (Dakpo Gomtsul, 1116–1169). Sgam po pa's principal disciples included the first KARMA PA DUS GSUM MKHYEN PA and PHAG MO GRU PA RDO RJE RGYAL PO.

**Sgam po pa'i chos bzhi**. (Gampope chöshi). In Tibetan, "the four dharmas of Sgam po pa," a series of brief instructions encompassing the entirety of the Buddhist path composed by the BKA' BRGYUD founder SGAM PO PA BSOD NAMS RIN CHEN. The instructions are often recited in the form of a prayer: Grant your blessings that my mind may turn toward the dharma. / Grant your blessings that the dharma may follow the path. / Grant your blessings that the path may clarify confusion. / Grant your blessings that confusion may arise as wisdom.

**Sgang steng**. (Gangteng). A monastery located in the Shar district of central Bhutan, founded by Padma 'phrin las (Pema Trinle, b. sixteenth century), son of the great treasure revealer PADMA GLING PA. It serves as the principal monastic seat for Padma gling pa's speech incarnation (gsung sprul) lineage.

**Sgrag yang rdzong**. (Drakyang Dzong). One of two labyrinthine cave complexes located near RDO RJE BRAG monastery, south of LHA SA in central Tibet; venerated as a site where the Indian adept PADMASAMBHAVA and his consort YE SHES MTSHO RGYAL remained in meditation retreat.

**Sgrol ma lha khang**. (Drölma Lhakhang). In Tibetan, "Tārā Temple," a temple in the central Tibetan region of Snye thang

(Nyetang) where the Bengali scholar ATIŚA DĪPAṂKARAŚRĪJÑĀNA lived for much of his time in Tibet, where he made his principal seat, and later died. The primary image is a statue of TĀRĀ (T. Sgrol ma), the female bodhisattva of compassion who served as Atiśa's personal protector, after which the temple takes its name. Constructed in the mid-eleventh century, it was spared major damage during the Chinese Cultural Revolution due to the intervention of officials from the Indian state of Bengal, which was ruled at the time by the Communist Left Front. Consequently, the temple still houses Atiśa's relics and original artwork of great value and beauty.

**sgrub brgyud shing rta chen po brgyad**. (drupgyü shingta chenpo gye). In Tibetan, literally "eight great conveyances that are lineages of achievement," referring to a system of classifying the various tantric traditions and transmission lineages in Tibet. This schema developed in about the thirteenth century, during the initial period of the later dissemination (PHYI DAR) of Buddhism, based upon the preeminence of individual masters, their regional affiliations, and especially their traditions of esoteric instruction. The classification of Tibetan tantric traditions into "eight great conveyances" was adopted by later Tibetan historians and exegetes, perhaps most famously by the Tibetan master 'JAM MGON KONG SPRUL BLO GROS MTHA' YAS in his GDAMS NGAG MDZOD ("Treasury of Practical Instructions"). According to his reckoning, the eightfold classification consists of the following categories:

1. SNGA' 'GYUR RNYING MA "Ancient Translation Tradition"
2. BKA' GDAMS "Tradition of Precepts and Instructions"
3. LAM 'BRAS "Tradition of the Path and Result"
4. MAR PA BKA' BRGYUD "Tradition of the Transmitted Precepts of Marpa"
5. SHANGS PA BKA' BRGYUD "Tradition of the Transmitted Precepts of the Shang Valley"
6. ZHI BYED GCOD "Traditions of Pacification and Severence"
7. RDO RJE'I RNAL 'BYOR "Tradition of Vajrayoga"
8. RDO RJE'I GSUM GYI BSNYEN SGRUB "Propitiation and Attainment of the Three Adamantine States."

**sgrub pa bka' brgyad**. (drup pa ka gye). In Tibetan, "eight transmissions for attainment," referring to the eight chief deities of the MAHĀYOGA class of RNYING MA doctrine together with their corresponding TANTRAS and SĀDHANAS. They are (1) 'Jam dpal sku, (2) Padma gsung, (3) Yang dag thugs, (4) Bdud rtsi yon tan, (5) Phur pa phrin las, (6) Ma mo rbod gtong, (7) Dmog pa drag snags, and (8) 'Jig rten mchod bstod.

**shakumon**. (C. jimen; K. chŏngmun 迹門). In Japanese, lit. "trace teaching," or "teaching involving traces"; the provisional teaching of the SADDHARMAPUṆḌARĪKASŪTRA ("Lotus Sūtra"), which appears in the first half of the twenty-eight chapters of the scripture; in distinction to HONMON (fundamental teaching), the definitive final fourteen chapters of the scripture. The term is especially important in both the TIANTAI (J. TENDAI) and NICHIREN-oriented schools of East Asian Buddhism. The Tiantai master TIANTAI ZHIYI (538–597) first applied the two terms to refer to these two distinctive parts of the *Saddharmapuṇḍarīkasūtra*, adapting the terms traces (C. ji, J. shaku) and root (C. ben, J. hon) that had originally been used by SENGZHAO (374–414), a disciple of KUMĀRAJĪVA (344–413), to explain the inconceivable relationship between skillful means (UPĀYA) and enlightened wisdom (PRAJÑĀ). Zhiyi made a distinction between the transient buddha who attained the buddhahood during his lifetime in India and the universal buddha who attained buddhahood infinite numbers of KALPAS ago. Zhiyi regarded shakumon to be the teaching of the transient buddha, and honmon the teaching of the universal buddha. The shakumon of the *Saddharmapuṇḍarīkasūtra* is also called the practice or causal section of the sūtra, since it details the stages of BODHISATTVA practices over countless lifetimes that serve as the prerequisites of future buddhahood. The shakumon thus emphasizes the various skillful means that lead to the one buddha vehicle (see YISHENG; EKAYĀNA).

**Shaku Sōen**. (釋宗演) (1859–1919). Influential early ZEN figure in the West. Ordained as a novice in the RINZAISHŪ at the age of twelve, Shaku Sōen studied under the Rinzai master Imakita Kōsen (1816–1892). Shaku Sōen trained under Kōsen at the famous ENGAKUJI monastery in Kamakura, receiving dharma transmission, and the authority to teach, at the age of twenty-four. He attended Keiō University and then traveled to Ceylon to study Pāli and live as a THERAVĀDA monk. Upon his return, he became chief abbot of Engakuji in 1892. He gave instruction in Zen meditation to laymen and laywomen, both in Kamakura and Tōkyō. One of his most influential students was DAISETZ TEITARO SUZUKI. In 1893, Shaku Sōen was chosen to represent the Zen tradition at the World's Parliament of Religions in Chicago. While in the United States, he met PAUL CARUS, and later arranged for D. T. Suzuki to work with Carus in LaSalle, Illinois. He served as Buddhist chaplain to the Japanese First Army Division after the outbreak of the Russo-Japanese War in 1904. He later lectured on Zen in Europe, America, India, and Ceylon. He spent the remainder of his life lecturing extensively on Zen to lay audiences. He served as president of Rinzai College of Hanazono University in Kyōto from 1914 to 1917, before returning as abbot of Engakuji. His 1906 *Sermons of a Buddhist Abbot* was the first book on Zen to appear in English.

**Shākya mchog ldan**. (Shākya Chokden) (1428–1507). A celebrated Tibetan scholar associated with the SA SKYA sect. A renowned scholar of MADHYAMAKA, he defended the GZHAN STONG ("other emptiness") view of the JO NANG. He was a student of the Sa skya master Rong ston Shes bya kun rig (Rongtön Sheja Künrik, 1367–1149). His explanation of the SDOM GSUM RAB DBYE was intended as a defense of SA SKYA PAṆḌITA's views, but later Sa skya writers rejected it as authoritative in favor of the works of his contemporary, the Sa skya master GO BO RAB 'BYAMS PA BSOD NAMS SENG GE. Shākya mchog ldan's collected works fill twenty-four volumes and are known for their consistently high quality of scholarship and erudition. He was particularly critical of the views of TSONG KHA PA, and engaged in a polemical exchange with Rje btsun pa Chos kyi rgyal mtshan (Jetsünpa Chökyi Gyeltsen, 1469–1546) whose works became the standard textbooks of the Byes (Je) college of SE RA monastery.

**Shambhala**. See ŚAMBHALA.

**Shamen bujing wangzhe lun**. (J. Shamon fukyōōsharon; K. Samun pulgyŏng wangja non 沙門不敬王者論). In Chinese, "The ŚRAMAṆA Does Not Pay Homage to the Ruler Treatise." In response to the anticlerical policy of the monarch Huanxuan (who reigned for less than three months as King of Chu in 404) LUSHAN HUIYUAN compiled this apologetical treatise in 404. It is preserved in the fifth roll of the HONGMING JI. The treatise is comprised of five sections. The first two sections, on householders and monks, detail the differences in their social status and way of life. The other three sections are concerned with more doctrinal and theoretical issues, which are presented in the form of a debate between imaginary opponents. In the third section, Huiyuan, as the "host," argues that monks, unlike householders including the worldly ruler, seek the "truth" and thus strive to free the "spirit" from the realm of worldly desires and emotions, or SAṂSĀRA. In the fourth section, the opponent argues that there is no truth beyond that which has been revealed by the sages of the past. In the last section, Huiyuan replies that these sages are merely manifestations of the Buddha, or the immortal spirit. Although the immortal spirit "mutually resonates" (GANYING) with SAṂSĀRA, it is not, Huiyuan explains, a worldly thing itself. The argument for the immortality of the spirit also appears in Zongbing's (375–443) *Mingfo lun* ("Treatise on Clarifying Buddhism)," the MOUZI LIHUO LUN, and various other treatises found in the *Hongming ji*.

**Shandao**. (J. Zendō; K. Sŏndo 善導) (613–681). In Chinese, "Guide to Virtue"; putative third patriarch of the Chinese PURE LAND tradition; also known as Great Master Zhongnan. At an early age, Shandao became a monk under a certain DHARMA master Mingsheng (d.u.), with whom he studied the SADDHARMAPUṆḌARĪKASŪTRA and the VIMALAKĪRTINIRDEŚA; he later devoted himself to the study of the GUAN WULIANGSHOU JING, which became one of his major inspirations. In 641, Shandao visited the monk DAOCHUO (562–645) at the monastery of Xuanzhongsi, where he is said to have cultivated vaipulya repentance (fangdeng canfa). Shandao also continued to train himself there in the visualization practices prescribed in the *Guan Wuliangshou jing*, which led to a profound vision of the buddha AMITĀBHA's PURE LAND (JINGTU) of SUKHĀVATĪ. Shandao subsequently eschewed philosophical exegesis and instead devoted himself to continued recitation of the Buddha's name (NIANFO) and visualization of the pure land as detailed in the *Guan jing*. After Daochuo's death, he remained in the Zongnan mountains before eventually moving to the Chinese capital of Chang'an, where he had great success in propagating the pure land teachings at the monastery of Guangmingsi. Shandao is also known to have painted numerous images of the pure land that appeared in his vision and presented them to his devotees. He was also famous for his continuous chanting of the AMITĀBHASŪTRA. Shandao's influential commentary on the *Guan Wuliangshou jing* was favored by the Japanese monk HŌNEN, whose teachings were the basis of the Japanese pure land tradition of JŌDOSHŪ.

**Shangs pa bka' brgyud**. (Shangpa Kagyü). In Tibetan, "Succession of the Transmitted Precepts of the Shang Valley"; a lineage of Tibetan Buddhism traced back to its founder KHYUNG PO RNAL 'BYOR TSHUL KHRIMS MGON PO who was active in the Shangs Valley of western Tibet. It is generally counted as one of the eight great conveyances that are lineages of attainment (SGRUB BRGYUD SHING RTA CHEN PO BRGYAD). The teachings and practice of the Shangs pa bka' brgyud are in many ways similar to those of the MAR PA BKA' BRGYUD and stem from two principal sources: (1) a tantric system of instruction known as the six doctrines of NIGUMA (Ni gu chos drug), similar to those associated with NĀROPA, of whom Niguma is said to have been the wife or sister; and (2) the MAHĀMUDRĀ text entitled PHYAG CHEN GA'U MA ("Amulet Box Mahāmudrā"). Few Shangs pa bka' brgyud institutions were ever constructed, and the sect has almost disappeared as an independent entity. However, the Shangs pa bka' brgyud was highly influential in Tibet and its most important instructions were also transmitted within the BKA' BRGYUD, DGE LUGS, SA SKYA, JO NANG, and RNYING MA sects. Shangs pa teachings have been especially promulgated in modern times by the late contemporary master KALU RINPOCHE.

**shangtang**. (J. jōdō; K. sangdang 上堂). In Chinese, lit. "ascending the hall"; a public lecture or sermon delivered by a CHAN, SŎN, or ZEN master at the dharma hall. The master, often the abbot of the monastery, would typically ascend the dais in the dharma hall to deliver his sermon, hence the term shangtang, or "ascending the hall." The dharma hall of a Chan monastery typically did not house any icons, for the master himself was considered a living buddha while he was preaching on the dais. These shangtang lectures came to be carefully recorded by the disciples of the master and were typically edited together with other minor sermons like the xiaocan into the "recorded sayings" (YULU) of the master. By the medieval period, shangtang became more formalized, taking place at regular intervals; thus there are several specific types of shangtang described in the literature. Those that occurred on a bi-monthly basis were called danwang shangtang, since the sermons were given on the first (dan) and the fifteenth (wang) of each lunar month. Those that took place on the fifth, tenth, fifteenth, twentieth, twenty-fifth of each lunar month were called wucan shangtang, because there were a total of five assemblies (wucan) each month. Those held once every three days were called jiucan shangtang, because there were approximately nine such assemblies (jiucan) each lunar month. Shangtang that occurred on the birthday of the reigning emperor were called shengjie (occasion of His Majesty) shangtang, while those that took place as funerary memorials and deliverance rituals for a recently deceased emperor were called daxing zhuiyan shangtang. Shangtang that occurred after the abbot of the monastery had returned from a begging round were called chudui (troupe on a mission) shangtang. Those that took place to resolve an ongoing issue in the monastic community, such as quarrels, disputes, or other emergencies, were called yinshi shangtang (ascending the hall due to an exigency). Those that occurred to honor monastery staff overseeing internal affairs were called xie bingfu shangtang, while shangtang to honor monastery staff overseeing external and financial affairs were called xie dusizhai shangtang.

**Shang Tianzhusi**. (上天竺寺). In Chinese, "Upper Tianzhu Monastery," located on Mt. Tianzhu in Hangzhou, along the southern coast of China. (TIANZHU is one of the common Sinographic transcriptions of Sindu, or India.) Founded by King Qian Liu (852–932 CE) of the Kingdom of Wuyue (907–978 CE) during the Five Dynasties and Ten Kingdoms period following the demise of the Tang dynasty. According to certain sources, before he became king, Qian Liu dreamed of a woman dressed in white robes, who promised to protect him and his descendants if he was compassionate and did not kill living creatures. She then informed him that she could be found on Mt. Tianzhu in Hangzhou twenty years hence. When Qian Liu ascended the throne, he dreamed once more of this white-robed woman, whom he realized was BAIYI GUANYIN (White-Robed AVALOKITEŚVARA). In this dream, she informed Qian Liu that she needed a residence, in return for which she would bestow her patronage on his kingdom. When the king discovered that, of all the monasteries on Mt. Tianzhu, only one housed a Baiyi Guanyin icon, he became its patron and named it the Tianzhu Kanjing Yuan (Tianzhu Center for Reading Scriptures). Later renamed Upper Tianzhu monastery, it became renowned as a GUANYIN pilgrimage site. The monastery is also known for its association with the Song-dynasty legend of Princess MIAOSHAN (first complete rendition 1100 CE) when Jiang Zhiqi (1031–1104 CE), prefect of Ruzhou in Henan province, was transferred to Hangzhou in 1104 CE. Upon his arrival, he had the Miaoshan legend inscribed on a stele to be enshrined in Upper Tianzhu monastery.

**Shanhui dashi**. (C) (善慧大士) (497–569). See FU DASHI.

**Shanjia Shanwai**. (J. Sange Sangai; K. San'ga Sanoe 山家山外). In Chinese, "On-Mountain, Off-Mountain"; two factions in a debate that engulfed the TIANTAI ZONG during the eleventh century over issues of the school's orthodoxy and orthopraxy. The Shanjia (On-Mountain) faction was led by the monk SIMING ZHILI (960–1028) and his disciples; they pejoratively referred to their opponents within the Tiantai school, such as Ciguang Wu'en (912–988), Yuanqing (d. 997), Qingzhao (963–1017), Zhiyuan (976–1022) and their disciples, as Shanwai (Off-Mountain), for drawing on non-Tiantai elements in their exegeses. The debate began over an issue of textual authenticity, but soon came to cover almost all major facets of Tiantai doctrine and practice. The On-Mountain faction criticized their rivals for attempting to interpret Tiantai doctrine using concepts borrowed from texts such as the DASHENG QIXIN LUN, which had not previously been an integral text in Tiantai exegesis, and from rival exegetical traditions, such as the HUAYAN ZONG. These Shanwai monks argued that the doctrine of the "TRICHILIOCOSM in an single instant of thought" (YINIAN SANQIAN) should be understood in the Huayan framework of the suchness that is in accord with conditions (zhenru suiyuan): in this understanding, an instant of thought is identified with the true mind that in its essence is pure, unchanging, and inherently enlightened; subsequently, by remaining in accord with conditions, that suchness in turn produces the trichiliocosm in all its diversity. From this perspective, they argued that the true mind should be the focus of contemplative practice in Tiantai. Shanjia masters feared such interpretations were a threat to the autonomy of the Tiantai tradition and sought to remove these Huayan elements so that the orthodox teachings of Tiantai would be preserved. Zhili, the major proponent of the Shanjia faction, argued that the Shanwai concept of suchness involved the principle of separation (bieli), since it excluded the afflicted and the ignorant, and only encompassed the pure and the enlightened. According to Zhili, suchness does not produce the trichiliocosm only when it is in accord with conditions, as the Huayan-influenced Shanwai exegetes asserted, because suchness is in fact identical to the trichiliocosm; therefore the instant of thought that encompasses all the trichiliocosm, including both its pure and impure aspects, should be the true focus of contemplative practice in Tiantai. Zhili's disciple Renyue (992–1064) and his fourth-generation successor Congyi (1042–1091) were subsequently branded the "Later Off-Mountain Faction," because they accepted some of the Shanwai arguments and openly rejected parts of Zhili's argument. Nevertheless, the Shanjia faction eventually prevailed, overshadowing their Shanwai rivals and institutionalizing Zhili's interpretations as the authentic teachings of the Tiantai tradition. Two Tiantai genealogical histories from the Southern Song dynasty, the *Shimen zhengtong* ("Orthodox Transmission of Buddhism") and the FOZU TONGJI ("Chronicle of the Buddhas and Patriarchs"), list Zhili as the last patriarch in the dharma transmission going back to the Buddha, thus legitimating the orthodoxy of the Shanjia faction from that point forward.

**Shannüren zhuan**. (善女人傳). In Chinese, lit., "Record of Good Women," "Record of [Eminent] Laywomen," by the Qing-dynasty author PENG SHAOSHENG (1740–1796), a Confucian literatus turned Buddhist layman; in two rolls. The "Record" is the only surviving collection in Chinese Buddhist literature of the biographies of exemplary laywomen disciples (UPĀSIKĀ). The collection compiles 138 biographies of Chinese Buddhist laywomen from the inception of Buddhism in China through the mid-Qing dynasty, including empresses, concubines, wives of officials, and commoners from various walks of life. The stories of these laywomen are characterized by their pious faith in the three jewels (RATNATRAYA) and their devout practice. Peng also explores the ways in which these exemplary Buddhist laywomen embodied such traditional Confucian values as filiality, chastity, and obedience to fathers, husbands, and eldest sons, in order to demonstrate how Buddhism was also concerned with women's broader social roles. Peng Shaosheng adapts the entries included in the anthology from such biographical, historical, and genealogical works as the GAOSENG ZHUANS, FAYUAN ZHULIN, CHUANDENG LU, *Wudeng huiyuan*, FOZU TONGJI, *Jingtu wen*, and *Mingxiang ji*, as well as various literary works. Prior to completing this record of female lay disciples of Buddhism, Peng also authored a parallel collection of the biographies of Buddhist laymen, the JUSHI ZHUAN. The *Shannüren zhuan* is also included as the last chapter of the *Moni zhukun jiyao* by the Qing-dynasty laywoman Shanyi.

**Shansuibu**. (C) (善歲部). The Suvarṣaka school. See KĀŚYAPĪYA.

**Shaolinsi**. (J. Shōrinji; K. Sorimsa 少林寺). In Chinese, "Small Grove Monastery"; located at the foot of SONGSHAN in Dengfeng county, Henan province. According to the XU GAOSENG ZHUAN ("Continued Biographies of Eminent Monks"), the Xiaowen emperor (r. 471–500 CE) of the Northern Wei dynasty built the monastery in 496 CE for the Indian monk Fotuo (d.u.). Shaolinsi initially was an important center of translation activities, and many famous monks, including BODHIRUCI, RATNAMATI, JINGYING HUIYUAN, and XUANZANG, resided at the monastery. But the monastery is best known in the East Asian tradition as the putative center of martial arts in China. Fotuo, the monastery's founder, is claimed to have had two disciples who displayed sublime acrobatic skills, perhaps a harbinger of later martial-arts exercises. Li Shimin (599–649; r. 626–649), second ruler and Taizong emperor of the Tang dynasty (618–907), is said to have used the Shaolin monks' martial talents, especially with the heavy cudgel, to help his father found their new dynasty. Within another century, Shaolinsi became associated with the legend of the Indian monk BODHIDHARMA (c. early fifth century), the putative founder of the CHAN school, who is said to have practiced wall-gazing meditation (BIGUAN) for nine years in a cave above the monastery; according to later traditions, Bodhidharma also taught himself self-defense techniques both to protect himself against wild animals and for exercise, which he transmitted to his disciples at the monastery. In subsequent years, the monastery continued to be renowned as a center of both martial arts and Chan Buddhism. In 1245, the Yuan emperor Shizu (r. 1260–1294) appointed the Chan master Xueting Fuyu (1203–1275) abbot of Shaolinsi, and under Xueting's guidance the monastery flourished. At least by the fifteenth century, the connection between Shaolinsi and the martial arts became firmly established in the Chinese popular imagination and "Shaolin monks" remain popular on the international performing-arts circuit.

**shaoshen**. (J. shōshin; K. sosin 燒身). In Chinese, "autocremation." See SHESHEN.

**Shasekishū**. (沙石集). In Japanese, "Sand and Pebbles Collection"; an anthology of edifying folkloric tales from the Kamakura period (1185–1333). The collection was compiled by a RINZAISHŪ monk named MUJŪ ICHIEN (1227–1312) between 1279 and 1283 and contains 150 stories in a total of ten rolls. After finishing his initial compilation, Mujū continued to add the stories to the collection, so there are different editions of varying length. The preface to the collection explains the title: "Those who search for gold extract it from sand; those who treasure jewels gather pebbles that they then polish." The collection, therefore, seeks to explain profound Buddhist truths as they are found in mundane affairs. Mujū demonstrates throughout the collection his belief in "crazy words and embellished phrases" (kyōgen kigo) as an expedient means of articulating ultimate religious goals. He even argues that the traditional waka style of Japanese poetry is in fact DHĀRAṆĪ, a mystic code that encapsulates the essence of Buddhist teachings. Most of the stories in the collection offer edifying lessons in such basic Buddhist beliefs as nonattachment and karmic retribution and in such ethical values as loyalty, filial piety, and fidelity. The idea of expedient means (UPĀYA) is also applied to the various Buddhist schools and to Japanese traditional religion: all the various teachings of Buddhism are depicted as expedient means of conveying the religion's beliefs, and Mujū denounces Buddhist practitioners who exclusively promote the teachings of only their own sects. The collection also introduced the idea of the "unity of SHINTŌ and Buddhism" (SHINBUTSU SHŪGŌ) by describing Japanese indigenous spirits, or KAMI, as various manifestations of the Buddha. The humorous tone of the collection attracted many readers during the Tokugawa period (1603–1868), when it was reprinted several times.

**She dasheng lun**. (J. Shōdaijōron; K. Sŏp taesŭng non 攝大乘論). See MAHĀYĀNASAṂGRAHA.

**sheliju**. (J. sharigu; K. sarigu 舍利具). In Chinese, a "reliquary container" containing the relics (ŚARĪRA) of the Buddha or a sage; also written as SHELIQI. The relics were deposited in a set of nested caskets and were placed inside or buried below the foundation of a STŪPA. A tiny glass bottle placed inside several layered caskets served as the innermost container for the crystalline relic-grains remaining after cremation. The shape of the caskets differed according to time and region, from a stūpa shape to the shape of a bowl or tube, and the caskets were made of gold, silver, gilt bronze, lacquered wood, porcelain, or stone.

The sides of the caskets were often incised with buddha images or guardian deities. In addition to the relic, the donors frequently deposited a multitude of objects of intrinsic or artistic value in the containers, including beads, pearls, jewelry, or coins. The earliest known reliquary is a steatite casket found in the stūpa of Piprāwā (fifth–fourth centuries BCE) in India. In China, the reliquary chamber excavated at the FAMENSI pagoda is the most widely researched. In contrast to most Chinese reliquary chambers, which were only accessible prior to the construction of a pagoda, the Famensi relic was escorted to and from the imperial palace. Further outstanding examples of reliquaries have been excavated at Songnimsa and Kamŭnsa in Korea. Both reliquaries date from the Silla period and show the refined amalgamation of foreign influences and native Silla craftsmanship. The center of the Songnimsa reliquary is a small green glass bottle, placed in a green glass cup decorated with twelve rings of coiled glass, which derives from Persian or Syrian prototypes. The Kamŭnsa reliquary contains a vessel in the shape of a miniature pavilion and an outer container decorated on each side with the four heavenly kings, pointing to the LOKAPĀLA cult that thrived in Silla society at that time.

**sheliqi**. (J. sharigu; K. sarigi 舍利器). In Chinese, "reliquary container." See SHELIJU.

**She lun zong**. (J. Shōronshū; K. Sŏp non chong 攝論宗). In Chinese, "School of the MAHĀYĀNASAṂGRAHA"; one of the early Chinese indigenous doctrinal schools, focusing on YOGĀCĀRA philosophy. The school has its origins in exegetical traditions that began with PARAMĀRTHA's (499–569) translation of ASAṄGA's *Mahāyānasaṃgraha* (C. *She Dasheng lun*). The school played a central role in early Chinese doctrinal controversies concerning the interpretation of consciousness in two different Indian Buddhist systems of thought: Yogācāra and TATHĀGATAGARBHA. The controversies revolved around the issue of the nature of the eighth storehouse consciousness (ĀLAYAVIJÑĀNA), based on VASUBANDHU's ambiguous position in the SHIDIJING LUN (DAŚABHŪMIVYĀKHYĀNA), a commentary on the DAŚABHŪMIKASŪTRA. In some passages, Vasubandhu implied that the ālayavijñāna was the tainted source from which SAṂSĀRA arises; in others, he implied instead that the ālayavijñāna was coextensive with suchness (TATHATĀ) and thus fundamentally pure. The northern branch of the DI LUN ZONG argued that the storehouse consciousness was impure; it is a tainted source that produces only defiled dharmas. By contrast, the southern branch argued that the ālayavijñāna was fundamentally pure but came to be adventitiously associated with impure elements: it was the functioning of suchness and thus was pure, but it also was subject to the same laws of conditioned origination (PRATĪTYASAMUTPĀDA) as the sensory consciousnesses and thus on that level was also impure. The She lun school sought to integrate these two interpretations by drawing on Paramārtha's concept of an immaculate consciousness (AMALAVIJÑĀNA). Paramārtha in his personal writings condemned the ālayavijñāna as being fundamentally impure, positing instead that only a ninth mode of consciousness, which he termed the immaculate consciousness, was pure. Following Paramārtha, She lun exegetes treated the ālayavijñāna as impure, and instead established the amalavijñāna as the pure ninth consciousness. They identified this new consciousness with suchness (tathatā) by using it as a synonym for PARINIṢPANNA, the perfected nature described in Yogācāra philosophy. In the She lun zong interpretation, amalavijñāna thus came to be regarded as the absolute basis for all previous eight types of consciousness; the eighth consciousness, the ālayavijñāna, was instead seen as the provisional basis of afflictions (KLEŚA). Several She lun masters advocated this admixture between ālayavijñāna and tathāgatagarbha thought, including Huikai (518–568), Daoni (fl. 590), Huikuang (534–613), and Tanqian (542–607). Tanqian was especially influential and was even invited by the Sui emperor Wendi (r. 581–604) to the imperial capital of Chang'an in 587 to preach the She lun teachings. The emperor later built the monastery of Chandingsi in the capital and appointed Tanqian as its first abbot, which became the center of the She lun zong. Sengbian (568–642), a She lun master from Daoni's lineage, was one of the teachers of the renowned Korean Yogācāra master WŎNCH'ŬK (613–696). Doctrinal positions held in the She lun zong were crucial in the evolution of the HUAYAN school of the mature Chinese tradition.

**shenguang**. (J. shinkō; K. sin'gwang 身光). In Chinese, lit. "body light"; a "mandorla" surrounding the body of holy figures in Buddhist painting and sculpture. See KĀYAPRABHĀ.

**Shenhui**. (C) (神會). See HEZE SHENHUI.

**Shenxiu**. (J. Jinshū; K. Sinsu 神秀) (606?–706). Chinese CHAN master of the Tang dynasty and putative founder of the "Northern school" (BEI ZONG) of early Chan Buddhism. Shenxiu was a native of Kaifeng in present-day Henan province. As an extraordinarily tall man with well-defined features, Shenxiu is said to have had a commanding presence. In 625, Shenxiu was ordained at the monastery of Tiangongsi in Luoyang, but little is known of his activities in the first two decades following his ordination. In 651, Shenxiu became a disciple of HONGREN (601–674), cofounder of the East Mountain Teachings (DONGSHAN FAMEN) and the monk later recognized as the fifth patriarch of the Chan school; indeed, by many early accounts, such as the CHUAN FABAO JI and LENGQIE SHIZI JI, Shenxiu became Hongren's legitimate successor. According to the famous story in the LIUZU TANJING ("Platform Sūtra of the Sixth Patriarch"), however, Shenxiu lost a verse-writing contest to the unlettered HUINENG (638–713), whom Hongren then in secret sanctioned as the sixth patriarch. However, it is unclear how long Shenxiu studied with Hongren. One source states that it was for a period of six years, in which case he would have left Hongren's monastery long before Huineng's arrival, making the famous poetry contest impossible. Regardless of the date of his departure, Shenxiu eventually left Hongren's monastery for Mt. Dangyang in Jingzhou (present-day Hubei province), where he remained for over twenty years and attracted many disciples. Shenxiu and his disciples were the subjects of a polemical attack by HEZE SHENHUI (684–758), who disparaged Shenxiu as representing a mere collateral branch of BODHIDHARMA's lineage and for promoting what Shenhui called a "gradual" (jian) approach to enlightenment. Shenhui instead promoted a "sudden teaching" (DUNJIAO), which he claimed derived from a so-called "Southern school" (NAN ZONG) founded by Huineng, another (and relatively obscure) disciple of Hongren, whom Shenhui claimed was Hongren's authentic successor and the true sixth patriarch (LIUZU). Later Chan historians such as GUIFENG ZONGMI (780–841) began to use the designation "Northern school" (Bei zong) to describe the lineage of Shenxiu and his disciples YIFU (661–736), PUJI (651–739), and XIANGMO ZANG (d.u.). While Shenhui's characterization of Shenxiu and his supposed "gradualism" is now known to be misleading, subsequent histories of the Chan tradition (see CHUANDENG LU) more or less adopted Shenhui's vision of early Chan; thus Huineng, rather than Shenxiu, comes to be considered the bearer of the orthodox Chan transmission. As one mark of Shenxiu's high standing within the Chan tradition of his time, in 700, Shenxiu was invited to the imperial palace by Empress WU ZETIAN, where the empress prostrated herself before the nonagenarian monk. She was so impressed with the aged Chan master that she decided to build him a new monastery on Mt. Dangyang named Dumensi. She also gave him the title of state preceptor (GUOSHI). Upon his death, he was given a state funeral. He is one of only three Buddhist monks whose biography is included in the *Tang shi* ("Tang Annals"). This is clearly not the profile of an imposter within the Chan lineage. Shenxiu's teachings are known to have focused on the transcendence of thoughts (linian) and the five expedient means (fangbian; S. UPĀYA); these teachings appear in "Northern school" treatises discovered at Dunhuang, such as the YUANMING LUN, *Guanxin lun*, and DASHENG WUSHENG FANGBIAN MEN. Shenxiu was an expert on the LAṄKĀVATĀRASŪTRA, a text favored by Hongren and the early Chan tradition, and is also thought to have written a substantial commentary on the AVATAṂSAKASŪTRA. Despite the uncomplimentary portrayal of the "Northern school" in mainstream Chan materials, it is now recognized that Shenxiu and his disciples actually played a much more important role in the early growth and development of the Chan school than the mature tradition acknowledged.

**Shes bya kun khyab mdzod**. (Sheja Kunkyap Dzö). In Tibetan, "Treasury Embracing All Knowledge"; the title of a multivolumed encyclopedic compendium of Tibetan Buddhist thought, composed by the Tibetan luminary 'JAM MGON KONG SPRUL BLO GROS MKTHA' YAS between 1862 and 1864. The work consists of a brief root text in verse together with an extensive prose autocommentary, and is one of the earliest examples of the author's place in the nonsectarian (RIS MED) movement. The work is one of five "treasuries" (KONG SPRUL MDZOD LNGA) written and edited by the master.

**sheshen**. (S. ātmaparityāga/dehadāna; T. rang gi lus yongs su gtong ba / lus kyi sbyin pa; J. shashin; K. sasin 捨身). In Chinese, lit. "relinquishing the body," viz., "self-immolation"; a whole complex of religiously motivated types of suicide in the MAHĀYĀNA tradition, of which "autocremation" (shaoshen) is best known but which may also include suicide by drowning, starvation, feeding oneself to wild animals, etc. (The Sanskrit ātmabhāvaparityāga means "giving up one's self," as soldiers might for their country, and by extension an act of extreme charity.) This practice is associated with the perfection of giving (DĀNAPĀRAMITĀ) that occurs on the first BHŪMI, PRAMUDITĀ (joyful), of the bodhisattva path, where the bodhisattva learns to abandon everything that is most precious to him, including his wealth, his wife and family, and even his own body. Self-immolation is a common trope in Indian Mahāyāna literature, where this "gift of the body" (DEHADĀNA) is performed as an ultimate act of self-sacrifice. One of best-known examples is BHAIṢAJYAGURURĀJA (Medicine King) in the SADDHARMAPUṆḌARĪKASŪTRA, who pays homage to the buddhas by burning himself alive. Self-immolation goes back to at least the late-fourth century in Chinese Buddhism but is perhaps best known today through the suicides of such Vietnamese monks as THÍCH QUẢNG ĐỨC (1897–1963), whose autocremation in 1963 at his residence of THIÊN MỤ TỰ drew attention to the persecution of Buddhists by the pro-Catholic Vietnamese government of Ngô Đình Diệm. The legitimacy of the act of self-immolation was a matter of continued debate within the Buddhist tradition, since suicide could be viewed as a form of attachment or passion (RĀGA), viz., the attachment to "nonexistence" (S. abhavarāga; C. wuyou ai). But there were also vehement supporters of self-immolation, who saw it as the consummate expression of asceticism (see DHUTAṄGA) and selflessness (ANĀTMAN). The Chinese term sheshen is used interchangeably with the synonyms wangshen (to lose the body) and yishen (to let go of the body); an analogous Sanskrit term is svadehaparityāga (abandoning the body). See also DEHADĀNA.

**Shes rab rgyal mtshan**. (Sherap Gyaltsen) (1356–1415). One of the most influential Tibetan masters of the BON religion. In 1405 he founded the monastery of SMAN RI in central Tibet, which became one of Tibet's premier Bon religious institutions. He is often known as Mnyam med (Nyame), "the Incomparable."

**shi**. (J. ji; K. sa 事). In Chinese, "phenomenon," "event," "object"; the specific elements of the empirical world as they are experienced conventionally. In East Asian Buddhism, shi is typically used in distinction to "principle" (LI): li refers to the fundamental pattern or principle that underlies all phenomena, thus representing the true nature of reality; shi by contrast refers to all the particular expressions of this li in the phenomenal world. This interrelationship thus implies the inherent presence of li within shi. Teachers within the TIANTAI ZONG were among the first to employ the two terms in their systematic analysis of Buddhist thought. TIANTAI ZHIYI (538–597), the systematizer of the Tiantai zong, applied the terms to refer not only to doctrinal but also to the practical dimensions of Buddhism. In the contexts of Buddhist practice, shi refers to such specific ritual and meditative activities as repentance, circumambulation, reciting the sūtras, and sitting meditation, which could lead to the realization of the principle of emptiness or the truth of the median (see SANDI). The term shi is especially crucial in HUAYAN doctrinal analysis, where it is deployed in the taxonomy of the four realms of reality (DHARMADHĀTU), four successively more profound levels of experience (see SI FAJIE). According to Huayan doctrine, because each and every individual phenomenon (shi) is pervaded by principle (li), all the various discrete phenomena pervade, and are in turn pervaded by, each and every other discrete phenomenon in the experience of what Huayan terms the "dharma-realm of the unimpeded interpenetration between phenomenon and phenomena" (SHISHI WU'AI FAJIE). As the individual products of dependent origination (PRATĪTYASAMUTPĀDA), shi thus represents the organic totality of reality, in which every phenomenon is in multivalent interaction with everything else in the universe, mutually creating, and being created by, all other things.

**Shi**. (J. Shaku; K. Sŏk; V. Thích 釋). The transcription of the first syllable of the Buddha's clan name, ŚĀKYA (C. Shijia), as found in the Buddha's appellation ŚĀKYAMUNI, "Sage of the Śākya Clan." In East Asian Buddhism since the time of DAO'AN (312–385), monks traditionally abandoned their family's surname and used in its place the Buddha's own clan name; hence, monks and nuns in premodern East Asia typically took the surname Shi. Before Dao'an, ordinands had adopted the surname of their preceptors, including using ethnikons in case their master was a foreigner, e.g., AN for monks and missionaries who hailed from PARTHIA, also known as Aršak or Arsakes (C. ANXI GUO)—viz., the Arsacid kingdom (c. 250 BCE–224 CE) southeast of the Caspian Sea; ZHU for Indians; ZHI for monks from KUSHAN (Yuezhi) in northwest India; YU for monks from KHOTAN; KANG for monks from SOGDIANA; and BO for monks from KUCHA. While Dao'an was resided in Xiangyang (in present-day Hubei province) between 365 and 379, he introduced the custom of adopting Shi as the monastic surname so that all Buddhist monks would have a common religious identity. The adoption of the Buddha's surname signified the monks' and nuns' severance of their ties with their natal families and worldly society, as well as the dedication of their lives to the lineage of the Buddha. The custom became general practice after 385, when there seemed to be textual justification for the practice in a translated passage from the *Zengyi ahan jing* (EKOTTARĀGAMA), which referred to "ŚRAMAṆAS who were sons of the Śākya" (C. shamen Shijiazi; S. śramaṇaśākyaputrīyāḥ). Zhu DAOSHENG (355–434) was one of the last influential Chinese monks to adopt the surname of his preceptor, rather than that of the Buddha. See also FAMING; ŚĀKYABHIKṢU.

**Shibei**. (C) (師備) (835–908). See XUANSHA SHIBEI.

**shi bushanye dao**. (C) (十不善業道). In Chinese, "ten unwholesome ways of action." See KARMAPATHA.

**shichidō garan**. (七堂伽藍). In Japanese, "seven-halled temple"; an early Japanese monastic layout consisting of seven main structures (shichidō). The oldest extant example of this layout in Japan can be seen in the Kudara (viz., the Korean Paekche) layout at HŌRYŪJI. The seven halls of the monasteries built in the Nara period (646–794) generally included the golden hall (kondō), pagoda (tō), lecture hall (kōdō), bell tower (shurō), scriptorium (kyōzō), monks' dormitories (sōbō), and refectory (jikidō). This term, however, does not seem to appear in any Chinese or Japanese materials predating its use by the Japanese monk Ichijō Kanera (1402–1481) to refer to the layout of ZEN monasteries. His list of the seven halls consists of the mountain gate (sanmon), buddha hall (butsuden), DHARMA hall (hattō), kitchen-office (kuin), SAṂGHA hall (sōdō; see SENGTANG), bathhouse (yokushitsu), and latrine (seijō or tōsu). The seven-hall design is now commonly laid out in anthropomorphic form, consisting of a central axis—the mountain gate (the privates), buddha hall (heart), and dharma hall (head)—flanked by two pairs of buildings, namely (1) the latrine (left leg) and bathhouse (right leg) and (2) the saṃgha hall (left arm) and kitchen-office (right arm).

**Shichifukujin**. (七福神). In Japanese, "Seven Gods of Good Fortune"; an assembly of seven deities dating from at least the fifteenth century, which gained popularity in Japan's folk religious setting and are still well known today. Those who have faith in the group are said to gain happiness and good fortune in their lives. Before their grouping, each of the individual gods existed independently and historically shared little in common. Of the seven, Ebisu is the only god with an identity linked to the Japanese islands. Daikokuten (C. Dahei tian; S. MAHĀKĀLA), Bishamonten (C. Pishamen tian; S. VAIŚRAVAṆA), and Benzaiten (C. Biancai tian; S. SARASVATĪ) originated in India, and Hotei (C. BUDAI, d. 917), Jurōjin (C. Shoulaoren), and Fukurokuju (C. Fulushou) come from the Chinese Buddho-Daoist traditions. Their grouping into seven gods of good fortune likely occurred in the Japanese Kansai region, with the commerce-affiliated Daikoku and Ebisu gaining initial popularity among merchants. Early mention of them appears in a reference from 1420, when they were said to have been escorted in procession through Fushimi, a southern ward of Kyōto, in imitation of a daimyō procession. ¶ Ebisu (a.k.a. Kotoshiro-nushi-no-mikoto, the abandoned child of Izanami and Izanagi) is the god of fishermen and the sea, commerce, good fortune, and labor. Among its etymological roots, the term "ebisu" traces back to the Ainu ethnic group of Hokkaidō, connecting them to fishermen who came from abroad. Ebisu is often depicted with a fishing rod in one hand and either a large red sea bream (J. tai) or a folding fan in the other. Since the inception of the Shichifukujin, he is often paired with Daikokuten as either son or brother. ¶ Daikokuten, or "Great Black Spirit," comes originally from India (where is he is called Mahākāla); among the Shichifukujin, he is known as the god of wealth, agriculture, and commerce. Typically portrayed as standing on two bales of rice, Daikokuten carries a sack of treasure over his shoulder and a magic mallet in one hand. He is also considered to be a deity of the kitchen and is sometimes found in monasteries and private kitchens. Prior to the Tokugawa period, he was called Sanmen Daikokuten (Three-Headed Daikokuten), a wrathful protector of the three jewels (RATNATRAYA). ¶ Bishamonten, also originally from India (where he is called Vaiśravaṇa), is traditionally the patron deity of the state and warriors. He is often depicted holding a lance in one hand and a small pagoda in the palm of his other hand with which he rewards those he deems worthy. Through these associations, he came to represent wealth and fortune. His traditional residence is Mt. SUMERU, where he protects the Buddha's dais and listens to the dharma. ¶ Benzaiten ([alt. Myōonten]; C. Miaoyin tian) is the Indian goddess Sarasvatī. She is traditionally considered to be a goddess of music, poetry, and learning but among the Shichifukujin, she also represents good fortune. She takes two forms: one playing a lute in both hands, the other with eight arms. ¶ Hotei is the Japanese name of Budai (d. 916), a Chinese thaumaturge who is said to have been an incarnation of the BODHISATTVA MAITREYA (J. Miroku bosatsu). The only historical figure among the Shichifukujin, Hotei represents contentment and happiness. Famous for his fat belly and broad smile, Hotei is often depicted holding a large cloth bag (Hotei literally means "hemp sack"). From this bag, which never empties, he feeds the poor and needy. In some places, he has also become the patron saint of restaurants and bars, since those who drink and eat well are said to be influenced by Hotei. ¶ Jurōjin and Fukurokuju, often associated with one another and said to share the same body, originated within the Chinese Daoist tradition. Jurōjin (lit. "Gaffer Long Life"), the deity of longevity within the Shichifukujin, is possibly a historical figure from the late eleventh through twelfth century. Depicted as an old man with a long, white beard, he is often accompanied by a crane or white stag. Fukurokuju (lit. "Wealth, Happiness, and Longevity") has an elongated forehead, a long, white beard and usually a staff in one hand; he is likely based on a mythical Daoist hermit from the Song period. ¶ This set of seven gods is most commonly worshipped in Japan. There are, however, other versions. Especially noteworthy is a listing found in the 1697 *Nihon Shichifukujinden* ("The Exposition on the Japanese Seven Gods of Good Fortune"), according to which Fukurokuju and Jurōjin are treated as a single god named Nankyoku rōjin and a new god, Kichijōten (C. Jixiang tian; S. Śrīmahādevī), the goddess of happiness or auspiciousness, is added to the group.

**Shide**. (J. Jittoku; K. Sŭptŭk 拾得) (d.u.). In Chinese, lit. "Picked Up"; a legendary layman of the Tang dynasty. The young Shide is said to have acquired his name from having been adopted or "picked up" by the hermit Fenggan (d.u.). Shide is known to have worked in the kitchen of the monastery of Guoqingsi on Mt. TIANTAI in present-day Zhejiang province. Shide became a favored subject in brushstroke art and was often depicted madly wielding his broom around the monastery, often together with the legendary poet HANSHAN. Fenggan, Hanshan, and Shide are collectively known as the "three hermits of Guoqing."

**Shidijing lun**. (T. Sa bcu'i rnam par bshad pa; J. Jūjikyōron; K. Sipchigyŏng non 十地經論). In Chinese, "Explanation of the DAŚABHŪMIKASŪTRA." See DAŚABHŪMIVYĀKHYĀNA; DI LUN ZONG.

**Shi'ermen lun**. (S. *Dvādaśamukhaśāstra, J. Jūnimonron; K. Sibimun non 十二門論). In Chinese, lit., "Twelve Gate Treatise," a Chinese translation of the **Dvādaśamukhaśāstra*, made by KUMĀRAJĪVA in 409. As one of the "three treatises" of the SAN LUN ZONG, the Chinese counterpart of the MADHYAMAKA school of Indian Buddhist philosophy, along with the BAI LUN (S. *ŚATAŚĀSTRA; "The Hundred Treatise") and the *Zhong lun* ("Middle Treatise"), the *Shi'ermen lun* is purportedly an introductory manual to NĀGĀRJUNA's MŪLAMADHYAMAKAKĀRIKĀ (C. *Zhong lun*), which was also translated by KUMĀRAJĪVA in the same year (409) as this text. No Sanskrit or Tibetan recensions of the *Shi'ermun lun* are known to have existed and the Sanskrit title is a tentative reconstruction. In this text, the putative author Nāgārjuna provides an interpretation of emptiness (ŚŪNYATĀ) in twelve chapters. Each chapter begins with an introductory verse, supplemented in some cases with additional exegetical verses; the text is thus composed of twenty-six verses in total. Prose exegeses follow, explaining each of the verses. All verses except the seven opening ones are quoted from the *Mūlamadhyamakakārikā* (seventeen verses) or the *Śūnyatāsaptatikārikā* (C. *Kong qishi lun*) (two verses), which is also attributed to Nāgārjuna. The authorship of this text has been questioned even within the tradition. The San lun exegete JIZANG (549–623), in his commentary to the text, the *Shi'ermun lun shu*, attributes the verses to Nāgārjuna and the prose part to Piṅgala (d.u.), the sixth patriarch of the Madhyamaka school.

**shi fajie**. (J. jihokkai; K. sa pŏpkye 事法界). In Chinese, "dharma-realm of phenomena," the first of the four DHARMADHĀTUS (see SI FAJIE), according to the HUAYAN ZONG. The "dharma-realm of phenomena" refers to the fact that all phenomena (SHI) are discrete events, created according to their own unique causal process and demonstrating their own distinctive function. They are characterized by a conditioned, and therefore illusory, nature, and stand as objects of cognizance that abide by rules of causality and conventional language.

A common Huayan simile compares the different phenomena to the waves on the ocean, each composed and sustained by different sets of causes and conditions. The Huayan school polemically designates this particular level of reality as belonging to the purview of the "HĪNAYĀNA teachings" (XIAOSHENG JIAO)—which is called the xiaojiao, or "lesser vehicle," in the Huayan school's fivefold taxonomy of the teachings (HUAYAN WUJIAO)—and specifically to the ABHIDHARMA, with its meticulous treatment of distinct factors (DHARMA), categories of dharmas, and the causal relations that pertain between them all.

**shi fajie**. (J. jippōkai; K. sip pŏpkye 十法界). In Chinese, "ten DHARMADHĀTUs"; the ten realms of reality according to Buddhist cosmology as described, e.g., in the Chinese TIANTAI ZONG: the realms of hell denizens (NĀRAKA), hungry ghosts (PRETA), animals (TIRYAK), demigods (ASURA), humans (MANUṢYA), and celestial divinities (DEVA) belong to the six destinies (GATI) of unenlightened beings, whereas the realms of ŚRĀVAKAS, PRATYEKABUDDHAS, BODHISATTVAS, and buddhas make up the four categories of enlightened beings. See also DAŚADHĀTU.

**shifang cha**. (J. jippōsetsu; K. sibang ch'al 十方刹). In Chinese, lit. "realms of the ten directions," referring to all the world systems or universes in existence. The "cha" in shifang cha is a transcription of the Sanskrit term KṢETRA, and means realm, world, land, etc.; thus, it may also refer to a universe consisting of three thousand large chiliocosms, thus a "trichiliocosm" (TRISĀHASRAMAHĀSĀHASRALOKADHĀTU). "Ten directions" (C. shifang; S. DAŚADIŚ) refers to the four cardinal directions (north, east, south, west), the four ordinal, or intercardinal, directions (northeast, southeast, southwest, northwest), plus the zenith and the nadir. By covering every possible direction, the "ten directions" therefore comes to be used by extension to mean "everywhere." Thus, shifang cha is similar in connotation to the expressions "worlds of the ten directions" (shifang shijie; daśadiglokadhātu) or "lands of the ten directions" (shifang chatu). ¶ Shifang cha is also used in Chinese to mean "monastery of the ten directions," referring to Song-dynasty public monasteries that adopted the "institution of the abbacy of the ten directions" (SHIFANG ZHUCHI ZHI). In this usage, "cha" is instead a transliteration of the first syllable of the Sanskrit term CAITYA, a reliquary cairn or STŪPA that often was placed in front of the main shrine hall in a monastery and thus by metonymy indicated the monastery itself. The abbacy of the ten directions referred to a system of monastic succession in which a monk of particular renown was invited to serve as abbot of the monastery, regardless of his personal connection to the lineage of the preceding abbot. Monasteries whose abbots were thus chosen from the broader "ten directions," rather than from within a single, narrow monastic or ordination lineage, were termed "monasteries of the ten directions" (shifang cha, alt. shifang conglin). Monasteries whose control was passed within a single monastic lineage were private monasteries, and called lit. "small temples" (XIAOMIAO).

**shifang conglin**. (十方叢林). In Chinese, "monasteries of the ten directions"; an alternate term for SHIFANG CHA.

**shifang zhuchi zhi**. (十方住持制). In Chinese, "institution of the abbacy of the ten directions." See SHIFANG CHA.

**shijiao**. (始教). In Chinese, "inception teaching" of the MAHĀYĀNA. See HUAYAN WUJIAO.

**Shijingshan**. (石經山). In Chinese, "Stone Scriptures Hill." See FANGSHAN SHIJING; YUNJUSI.

**shijue**. (J. shikaku; K. sigak 始覺). In Chinese, "acquired," or "actualized enlightenment," one of the two main subdivisions of enlightenment outlined in the DASHENG QIXIN LUN ("Awakening of Faith According to the Mahāyāna"), along with "original" or "inherent enlightenment" (BENJUE). As the *Dasheng qixin lun* explains, although enlightenment is in fact innate in the mind of any sentient being, that mind is still subject to "production-and-cessation" (shengmie), viz., the continual process of creation and passing away that is inevitable in the conditioned realm of existence (SAṂSĀRA). But because that production-and-cessation aspect of mind is itself grounded on the embryo of buddhahood (TATHĀGATAGARBHA), conventional states of mind inherently retain the capacity to be transformed into "true thusness" (ZHENRU), the ultimate state of reality. This transformation takes place through the process of "actualized enlightenment," that is, undertaking religious cultivation, which in the *Dasheng qixin lun* specifically means serenity and insight meditation (ZHIGUAN) and no-thought practice (WUNIAN). This process of actualizing enlightenment occurs over four stages of cultivation: (1) the "nonenlightenment" (bujue) of the ordinary worldling who has just entered the path at the level of the ten stages of faith (shixin); (2) the "apparent enlightenment" (xiangsijue) of two-vehicle adherents (ER SHENG) and beginning BODHISATTVAS on the stages of the "three worthies" (sanxian), that is, the ten abodes (shizhu), ten practices (shixing), and ten transferences or dedications (shihuixiang); (3) the "approximate enlightenment" (suifen jue) of DHARMAKĀYA bodhisattvas (fashen pusa) at the stage of the first BHŪMI and above; and (4) the "ultimate enlightenment" (jiujingjue), which occurs at the consummation of the ten bhūmis (pusa jindi). At the completion of this actualization process, however, one realizes that the enlightenment one has achieved through practice is in fact identical to the enlightened dharma-body (DHARMAKĀYA) that has always been innate; thus "actualized enlightenment" is no different from "original enlightenment." Any apparent differences between these two are but a matter of perspective: the innate luminosity and purity of the tathāgatagarbha and dharmakāya are seen as "original" (viz., "intrinsic") by the sage, but as something that must be "actualized" by the ordinary person.

**shikan taza**. (C. zhiguan dazuo; K. chigwan t'ajwa 祇/只管打坐). In Japanese, "just sitting"; a style of meditation emblematic of the Japanese SŌTŌSHŪ of ZEN, in which the act of sitting itself is thought to be the manifestation of enlightenment. The Sōtō school attributes the introduction of this style of practice to DŌGEN KIGEN (1200–1253), who claimed to have learned it from his Chinese CAODONG ZONG teacher TIANTONG RUJING (1162–1227). In this degenerate age of the dharma (J. mappō; C. MOFA), Sōtō claims, a radical simplification of practice was necessary. Rather than attempting to master the full range of meditative techniques used for concentrating the mind, such as counting the breaths (J. susokukan) or investigating a Zen question (J. kanna Zen; C. KANHUA CHAN), Dōgen is claimed to have advocated "just sitting" in the posture that had been used by the buddhas (e.g., ŚĀKYAMUNI's seven days beneath the BODHI TREE) and the patriarchs of Zen (e.g., BODHIDHARMA's "wall contemplation," C. BIGUAN). As the later Sōtō school interprets shikan taza, by maintaining this posture of "just sitting," the mind would also become stabilized and concentrated in a state of full clarity and alertness, free from any specific content (i.e., "with body and mind sloughed off," J. SHINJIN DATSURAKU). By adopting this posture of the buddhas and patriarchs, the student's own body and mind would thus become identical to the body and mind of his spiritual ancestors. Shikan taza is therefore portrayed as the most genuine form of meditation in which a Buddhist adept can engage. The Sōtō tradition also deploys shikan taza polemically against the rival RINZAISHŪ, whose use of kōans (C. GONG'AN) in meditation training was portrayed as an inferior, expedient attempt at concentration. In Dōgen's own writings, however, there is little of this later Sōtō portrayal of the psychological dimensions of "just sitting"; instead, Dōgen uses shikan taza simply as a synonym of "sitting in meditation" (zazen, C. ZUOCHAN), and may have spent most of his time while "just sitting" in the contemplation of kōans.

**shi mi**. (事密). In Chinese, "esoteric as to practices." See ER MI.

**Shin Arahan**. An eleventh-century Mon monk credited with bringing THERAVĀDA Buddhism to Burma (Myanmar). According to legend, Shin Arahan (in Pāli, Dhammadassi) was the reincarnation of a NAT, born to a brāhmaṇa virgin wife in the Thaton region in the south of Burma. He attained the state of ARHAT shortly after his ordination. He learned that the dharma was being practiced impurely in the "western regions" (viz., PAGAN [Bagan]) and proceeded there. In Pagan, monks called ari had polluted the dharma, proclaiming that murder was permissible if the proper spells (MANTRA) are recited. They also required that all virgins have intercourse with them before marriage. The newly ordained king ANAWRAHTA (Anuruddha, r. 1044–1077) recognized that these monks were corrupt but was unable to remove them from the order. When Shin Arahan arrived in Pagan, he was discovered by a hunter who had never seen a monk before. Mistaking him for a spirit, he took him to the king. Shin Arahan preached a sermon that impressed the king, who asked him where the Buddha was, how much of the dharma remained, and if there were other disciples of the Buddha. Shin Arahan recounted the history of the Buddha and his relics and described the Pāli canon and the monastic order. The king then adopted Theravāda as the practice of his kingdom and defrocked the ari monks. He asked the Mon king to send a copy of the tipiṭaka (S. TRIPIṬAKA) and some relics of the Buddha. When the Mon king refused, Anawrahta invaded Thaton in 1057, taking the Mon king and his family captive. He also took monks and skilled craftsmen, as well as Pāli scriptures, back with him to Pagan.

**shinbutsu bunri**. (神佛分離). In Japanese, lit. "separation of spirits and buddhas" (spirits here referring to the deities, or KAMI, associated with the indigenous Japanese religion now referred to as SHINTŌ); an official policy established at the beginning of the Meiji period (1868–1912) to dissociate all aspects of indigenous Japanese religion, or Shintō, from Buddhism. Prior to this separation, Buddhist temples (J. tera) and Shintō shrines (J. jinja) were intimately connected complexes (J. jingūji; see SHINBUTSU SHŪGŌ), as were the practice, beliefs, and vocations of the two traditions. The policy of shinbutsu bunri was based in part on an argument first broached by Nativist scholars during the Tokugawa period (1600–1868): viz., that Shintō reflected Japan's true spirit, while the "foreign" imports of Buddhism and Confucianism had corrupted Japanese culture and tainted Japanese indigenous religion. The Meiji government built its foundation on this rhetoric by making Shintō a state cult and asserting that the emperor was a descendant of the indigenous deities (kami) described in the *Kojiki* (712), an early historical collection. Shinbutsu bunri was a successful government policy in that it helped to strengthen Shintō and give the tradition its own identity independent from the Buddhist institutions that had been patronized by the earlier Tokugawa bakufu government. Moreover, shrines around the country were ranked in a national hierarchy and provided with state funding; all citizens were also required to register as adherents at these shrines. The policy, however, also had a damaging impact on both Shintō and Buddhism. By forcibly separating many practices that had previously been shared between Shintō and Buddhism, shinbutsu bunri ended up replacing many long-held traditions in local communities with a newly imposed set of national practices and beliefs. State-sponsored shrines were now expected to comply with nationally oriented ceremonies and carry out government-specific agendas. Many smaller Shintō shrines, which did not receive state sponsorship, were forced to merge with larger regional shrines, thus severely diminishing their presence in many communities. As for Buddhist institutions, the government remained silent as a wave of anti-Buddhist sentiment known as HAIBUTSU KISHAKU swept the country, leaving temples to face targeted violence and destruction. The mountain complexes of SHUGENDŌ, which had never differentiated between the two traditions, received the harshest treatment from the policy: all their established practices were abolished and Shugendō priests were forced either to laicize or to become Shintō priests.

**shinbutsu shūgō**. (神佛習合). In Japanese, "unity of spirits and buddhas" (spirits here referring to the KAMI associated with the indigenous Japanese religion now referred to as SHINTŌ). The practice of associating local gods and spirits with buddhas and BODHISATTVAS is documented as early as the late seventh century. By the eighth century, Shintō shrines (J. jinja) and Buddhist temples (J. TERA) were being jointly constructed beside one another. Over the course of the Heian period (794–1185), Buddhism gradually became ingrained deeply within local belief systems in communities across Japan, requiring some sort of accommodation between local and imported religions. As Buddhism became central to Japanese religious practice, the kami were sometimes either categorized as inferior beings subject to suffering who therefore needed the guidance of the Buddhist teachings, or tasked with guarding Buddhist temples and shrines. Ultimately, kami were redefined, using the principle of HONJI SUIJAKU, as local manifestations of the universal deities of the Buddhist religion. The development of temple-shrine complexes (J. jingūji), which did not differentiate between the two traditions, followed, although the shrine priests were generally subservient to their better educated, and politically and socially connected, Buddhist counterparts. During the Tokugawa period (1600–1868), tensions appeared as Nativist scholars began identifying "Shintō" as Japan's pure, indigenous religion, which they advocated should be decontaminated of so-called "foreign" elements like Buddhism and Confucianism. When the Meiji government took power in 1868, it instituted a policy known as SHINBUTSU BUNRI, which forcibly separated the putative native "Shintō" tradition from Buddhism. See also HAIBUTSU KISHAKU.

**Shinchi Kakushin**. (心地覺心) (1207–1298). Japanese ZEN teacher in the RINZAISHŪ, who is retrospectively regarded as the founder of the small FUKESHŪ branch of the Zen tradition; also known by his posthumous title HOTTŌ KOKUSHI. He became a monk at the age of fourteen in the SHINGONSHŪ esoteric tradition, and received full ordination at twenty-nine at TŌDAIJI in Nara, the ancient capital of Japan. Shinchi studied esoteric teachings at KŌYASAN, the headquarters of the Shingon school, and engaged in Zen training under the Rinzai master Taikō Gyōyū (1163–1241) and the SŌTŌSHŪ master DŌGEN KIGEN (1200–1253). Shinchi left for China in 1249 to study under the Chinese Linji master WUZHUN SHIFAN (1177–1249). Unfortunately, the master died before Shinchi arrived, so Shichi instead traveled to Hangzhou to study under WUMEN HUIKAI (1183–1260), in the YANGQI PAI of the LINJI ZONG. Wumen is said to have given Shinchi dharma transmission (CHUANFA) after just six months of training. Shinchi returned to Japan in 1254 with the master's robe and portrait, as well as a copy of the master's WUMEN GUAN, which was the first introduction of that famous GONG'AN (J. kōan) collection to the Japanese isles. In present-day Wakayama prefecture, Shinchi built a monastery called Saihōji, which was later renamed Kōkokuji. Shinchi resided there for the rest of his life, but often traveled to Kyōto to lecture on Buddhism before the retired monarchs Gofukakusa (r. 1246–1259), Kameyama (r. 1259–74) and Gouda (r. 1274–87). Kameyama granted him the honorary title "Hottō Zenji" (Zen Master Dharma Lamp). After his death, the Emperor Godaigo (r. 1318–1339) later bestowed on him the posthumous title of Hottō Enmyō Kokushi (State Preceptor Lamp of Dharma that is Perfectly Bright). Shinchi came to be regarded as the founder of the Fukeshū, a smaller secondary school of Japanese Zen, whose itinerant practitioners played the bamboo flute (shakuhachi) as a form of meditation and wore a distinctive bamboo hat that covered the entire face. The school was proscribed in 1871 and vanished from the scene.

**Shingonshū**. (眞言宗). In Japanese, lit. "True Word School." Shingon is the Japanese pronunciation of the Chinese term ZHENYAN (true word), which in turn is a translation of the Sanskrit term MANTRA. In Japan, Shingon has also come to serve as the name for the various esoteric (MIKKYŌ) traditions that traced their teachings back to the eminent Japanese monk KŪKAI. In his voluminous oeuvre, such as the HIMITSU MANDARA JŪJŪSHINRON, HIZŌ HŌYAKU, *Sokushin jōbutsugi*, and *Shōji jissōgi*, Kūkai laid the foundations of a new esoteric discourse that allowed the Buddhist institutions of the Heian period to replace Confucian principles as the ruling ideology of Japan. Kūkai was able to effect this change by presenting the court and the Buddhist establishment with an alternative conception of Buddhist power, ritual efficacy, and the power of speech acts. Through Kūkai's newly imported ritual systems, monks and other initiated individuals were said to be able to gain access to the power of the cosmic buddha Mahāvairocana, understood to be the DHARMAKĀYA, leading to all manner of feats, from bringing rain and warding off disease and famine, to achieving buddhahood in this very body (SOKUSHIN JŌBUTSU). Kūkai taught the choreographed ritual engagement with MAṆḌALA, the recitation of MANTRAS and DHĀRAṆĪ, and the performance of MUDRĀ and other ritual postures that were said to transform the body, speech, and mind of the practitioner into the body, speech, and mind of a particular buddha. Kūkai's ritual teachings grew in importance to the point that he was appointed to the highest administrative post in the Buddhist establishment (sōgō). From this position, Kūkai was able to establish ordination platforms at the major monasteries in Nara and the capital in Kyōto. Later, the emperor gave Kūkai both TŌJI in Kyōto and KŌYASAN, which subsequently came to serve as important centers of esoteric Buddhism. Kūkai's Shingon mikkyō lineages also flourished at the monasteries of Ninnaji and DAIGOJI under imperial support. Later, Tōji rose as an important institutional center for the study of Kūkai's esoteric Buddhist lineages under the leadership of the monk Kangen (853–925), who was appointed head (zasu) of Tōji, Kongōbuji, and Daigoji. The Mt. Kōya institution also grew with the rise of KAKUBAN, who established the monasteries of Daidenbōin and Mitsugonin on the mountain. Conflict brewed between the monks of Kongōbuji and Daidenbōin when Kakuban was appointed the head of both institutions, a conflict that eventually resulted in the relocation of Daidenbōin to nearby Mt. Negoro in Wakayama. The Daidenbōin lineage came to be known as the Shingi branch of Shingon esoteric Buddhism. Attempts to unify the esoteric Buddhist traditions that claimed descent from Kūkai were later made by Yūkai (1345–1416), who eradicated the teachings of the "heretical" TACHIKAWARYŪ from Mt. Kōya, and worked to establish a Kūkai-centered Shingonshū orthodoxy. By the late medieval period, the major monastic landholding institutions in Kyōto, Nara, and Mt. Kōya, many of which were profoundly influenced by the teachings of Kūkai, suffered economic hardship with the initiation of the Warring States period (1467–1573) and the growing popularity of the so-called "Kamakura Schools" (e.g., JŌDOSHŪ, JŌDO SHINSHŪ, ZENSHŪ, and NICHIRENSHŪ). In particular, Oda Nobunaga (1534–1582) had crushed the major Buddhist centers on HIEIZAN. However, Mt. Kōya, which was still a thriving center for the study of Kūkai's Shingon esoteric Buddhism, was spared the same fate because the monks resident at the mountain successfully convinced Toyotomi Hideyoshi (1536–1598) not to burn down their center. Thanks to the political stability of the Tokugawa regime, studies of esoteric Buddhism thrived until the harsh persecution of Buddhism by the Meiji government (see HAIBUTSU KISHAKU). As an effort to recover from the Meiji persecution, the disparate traditions of esoteric Buddhism came together under the banner of the Shingonshū, but after World War II, the various sub-lineages reasserted their independence.

**Shin hpyu Shin hla Pagoda**. Shin hpyu Shin hla Pagoda or Zedi (Pāli, cetī) was built by the famous king of PAGAN (Bagan), Alaung-sithu (r. 1112/3–1168). It is located in the Sagaing Hills, which lie along the Irrawaddy (Ayeyarwady) River in Upper Burma (Myanmar). The pagoda receives its name from the two images of the Buddha interred in it, named Shin hpyu and Shin hla. It is said that Alaung-sithu received these statues as a gift from the king of the gods Thagya Min (P. Sakka; S. ŚAKRA) when the latter descended from his abode in the heaven of the thirty-three (P. tāvatiṃsa; S. TRĀYASTRIMŚA). King Alaung-sithu was particularly beloved by his subjects and is regarded in Burmese chronicles as one of the few Burmese monarchs to have been a hpaya-laung (P. bodhisatta; S. BODHISATTVA). An annual festival is held at Shin hpyu Shin hla Pagoda on the new moon day of the Burmese month of Tawthalin (September-October).

**shinjin datsuraku**. (C. shenxin tuoluo; K. sinsim t'allak 身心脫落). In Japanese, lit. "body and mind sloughed off," the psychological state generated during the practice of "just sitting" (SHIKAN TAZA), a style of meditation emblematic of the Japanese SŌTŌSHŪ of ZEN. The Sōtō school attributes this term to DŌGEN KIGEN (1200–1253), who claimed to have learned it from his Chinese CAODONG teacher TIANTONG RUJING (1162–1227). During the practice of "just sitting," the adept should sit with "body and mind sloughed off," that is, with the body and mind stabilized and concentrated in a state of full clarity and alertness that is free from any specific content. Once all conception of body and mind had fallen away, the "original face" (J. honrai menmoku, C. BENLAI MIANMU) of inherent enlightenment will then appear. Dōgen is said to have achieved enlightenment through hearing his teacher Rujing describe practice as "the sloughing off of body and mind." This phrase is mentioned in only a single passage of Rujing's discourse record (YULU), however. Rujing's record also includes the homophonous phrase shinjin datsuraku (C. xinchen tuoluo), or "defilements of mind sloughed off." It is uncertain which form of the phrase Dōgen might have heard, but it seems to have had much more significance for Dōgen than for Rujing.

**Shinran**. (親鸞) (1173–1262). Japanese priest who is considered the founder of the JŌDO SHINSHŪ, or "True PURE LAND School." After the loss of his parents, Shinran was ordained at age nine by the TENDAISHŪ monk Jien (1155–1225) and began his studies at HIEIZAN. There, he regularly practiced "perpetual nenbutsu" (J. nenbutsu; C. NIANFO), ninety-day retreats in which one circumambulated a statue of the buddha AMITĀBHA while reciting the nenbutsu. In 1201, he left Mt. Hiei and became the disciple of HŌNEN, an influential monk who emphasized nenbutsu recitation. Shinran was allowed to copy Hōnen's most influential (and at that time still unpublished) work, the SENCHAKUSHŪ. When Hōnen was exiled to Tosa in 1207, Shinran was defrocked by the government and exiled to Echigo, receiving a pardon four years later. He did not see Hōnen again. Shinran would become a popular teacher of nenbutsu practice among the common people, marrying (his wife Eshinni would later write important letters on pure land practice) and raising a family (the lineage of the True Pure Land sect is traced through his descendants), although he famously declared that he was "neither a monk nor a layman" (hisō hizoku). While claiming simply to be transmitting Hōnen's teachings, Shinran made important revisions and elaborations of the pure land doctrine that he had learned from Hōnen. In 1214, he moved to the Kantō region, where he took a vow to recite the three pure land sūtras (J. Jōdo sanbukyō; C. JINGTU SANBU JING) one thousand times. However, he soon stopped the practice, declaring it to be futile. It is said that from this experience he developed his notion of shinjin. Although literally translated as "the mind of faith," as Shinran uses the term shinjin might best be glossed as the buddha-mind realized in the entrusting of oneself to Amitābha's name and vow. Shinran often would contrast self-power (JIRIKI) and other-power (TARIKI), with the former referring to the always futile attempts to secure one's own welfare through traditional practices such as mastering the six perfections (PĀRAMITĀ) of the bodhisattva path to buddhahood, and the latter referring to the sole source of salvation, the power of Amitābha's name and his vow. Thus, Shinran regarded the Mahāyāna practice of dedicating merit to the welfare of others to be self-power; the only dedication of merit that was important was that made by the bodhisattva DHARMĀKARA, who vowed to become the buddha Amitābha and establish his pure land of SUKHĀVATĪ for those who called his name. He regarded the deathbed practices meant to bring about birth in the pure land to be self-power; he regarded multiple recitations of NAMU AMIDABUTSU to be self-power. Shinran refers often to the single utterance that assures rebirth in the pure land. This utterance need not be audible, indeed not even voluntary, but is instead heard in the heart as a consequence of the "single thought-moment" of shinjin, received through Amitābha's grace. This salvation has nothing to do with whether one is a monk or layperson, man or woman, saint or sinner, learned or ignorant. He said that if even a good man can be reborn in the pure land, then how much more easily can an evil man; this is because the good man remains attached to the illusion that his virtuous deeds will somehow bring about his salvation, while the evil man has abandoned this conceit. Whereas Hōnen sought to identify the benefits of the nenbutsu in contrast to other teachings of the day, Shinran sought to reinterpret Buddhist doctrine and practice in light of Amitābha's vow. For example, the important Mahāyāna doctrine of the EKAYĀNA, or "one vehicle," the buddha vehicle whereby all sentient beings will be enabled to follow the bodhisattva path to buddhahood, is interpreted by Shinran to be nothing other than Amitābha's vow. Indeed, the sole purpose of ŚĀKYAMUNI Buddha's appearance in the world was to proclaim the existence of Amitābha's vow. These doctrines are set forth in Shinran's magnum opus, an anthology of passages from Buddhist scriptures, intermixed with his own comments and arranged topically, entitled KYŌGYŌ SHINSHŌ ("Teaching, Practice, Faith, and Realization [in Pure Land])," a work that he began in 1224 and continued to expand and revise over the next three decades. Shinran did not consider himself to be a master and did not establish a formal school, leading to problems of authority among his followers when he was absent. After he left Kantō for Kyōto, for example, problems arose among his followers in Kantō, leading a disciple to record a series of conversations, later collected as TANNISHŌ ("Lamentations on Divergences").

**Shintō**. (J) (神道). In Japanese, lit. "The Way of the Spirits (KAMI)"; modern designation used to refer to a supposedly indigenous religion of Japan distinct from Buddhism. Shintō (alt. jindō) was originally a Buddhist term that designated the realm or course (tō) of the local gods and spirits (shin), in distinction to tendō, the Indian divinities who populated the Buddhist celestial heavens (SVARGA). The term therefore referred to an amorphous complex of local beliefs, myths, and rituals that were focused on village and clan tutelary gods called KAMI. During the medieval period, this amorphous set of beliefs was gradually being systematized on a broader scale, but always in conjunction with, and under the strong influence of, Buddhism. It was only in 1868, with the start of the Meiji Restoration, that there was a forced separation of the kami and the buddhas (SHINBUTSU BUNRI), which artificially created two distinct and autonomous religions: the putatively autochthonous Japanese religion of Shintō and the imported traditions of Japanese Buddhism. See HAIBUTSU KISHAKU; HONJI SUIJAKU; KAMI; SHINBUTSU BUNRI; SHINBUTSU SHŪGŌ.

**Shin Upagot**. A semi-immortal ARHAT who, according to Burmese (Myanmar) and Thai popular tradition, dwells in a gilded palace beneath the southern ocean. Shin Upagot (P. Upagutta, S. UPAGUPTA) is endowed with extraordinarily long life and is destined to survive until the coming of the future buddha, MAITREYA. According to Burmese legend, Shin Upagot was ordered by the Buddha not to pass into PARINIRVĀṆA until Maitreya had appeared so that he might protect the Buddha's religion during times of crisis. Shin Upagot is renowned for assisting King AŚOKA to construct eighty-four thousand STŪPAS, and for vanquishing MĀRA and converting him to Buddhism. The earliest known record of the legend of Shin Upagot as it is known in Southeast Asia is found in the *Lokapaññatti*, a Pāli cosmological text said to have been written at Thaton in the twelfth century. That recension of the legend, in turn, is based on Sanskrit Buddhist antecedents found in such works as the AŚOKĀVADĀNA, all of which recount the exploits of the Upagupta. The legend of Shin Upagot is celebrated in the Burmese royal chronicles (yazawin), *Mahayazawin-gyi* (c. 1730) and *Hmannan Mahayazawin-daw-gyi* (1829), while the story is omitted from all Burmese ecclesiastical chronicles (thathanawin), presumably because it is not attested in Pāli sources. Shin Upagot is regarded as a protector of sailors, and because of his powers to control the weather, he is propitiated to prevent rainfall at inopportune times. He is depicted iconographically as a monk seated cross-legged, looking skyward, with his right hand reaching into his alms bowl.

**shi rushi**. (J. jūnyoze; K. sip yŏsi 十如是). In Chinese, the "ten suchnesses" (also known as the shiru); ten "suchlike" aspects of reality, as outlined in the SADDHARMAPUṆḌARĪKASŪTRA: all dharmas are of suchlike characteristics (xiang), nature (xing), essence (TI), efficacy (li), function (YONG), causes (yin), conditions (yuan), fruitions (guo), retributions (bao), and suchlike "equivalency ultimately from beginning and end" (benmuo jiujing deng; referring to all the nine previous "suchnesses"). The doctrinal significance of these "ten suchnesses" was interpreted and promoted by the TIANTAI ZONG. TIANTAI ZHIYI argued that by reading this passage with different emphases, it corresponds respectively to each of the three independent modes of contemplation in the "threefold contemplation" system (see SANGUAN). By emphasizing the term "suchness"—i.e., the characteristics of all dharmas are such (shixiang ru), the nature of all dharmas is such (shixing ru), etc.—this passage illuminates the "contemplation of emptiness," because emptiness (ŚŪNYATĀ) is the unifying principle for all ten aspects of reality and the term "empty" is synonymous with "suchness." By emphasizing the suchlike characteristics (rushi xiang), suchlike nature (rushi xing), etc., this same passage could instead illuminate the "contemplation of conventional existence," since existence is characterized by myriad distinct aspects that can be differentiated by such conventional categories as "characteristics," "nature," and "essence." Finally, by emphasizing "the suchness of characteristics" (xiang rushi), the "suchness of nature" (xing rushi), etc., the passage points out how this profound "suchness" contains and simultaneously affirms the aspects of both "emptiness" and "conventional existence," therefore corresponding to the "contemplation of the middle" in the "threefold contemplation" scheme. See also TATHATĀ.

**shi shenme**. (J. kore ikana; K. si simma 是甚麼). In Chinese, "What is it?"; the fundamental existential question (see GONG'AN, HUATOU) asked within the CHAN school, especially in association with the technique of "questioning meditation" (KANHUA CHAN). See also IMWŎTKO.

**shishi wu'ai fajie**. (J. jijimugehokkai; K. sasa muae pŏpkye 事事無礙法界). In Chinese, "dharma-realm of the unimpeded interpenetration between phenomenon and phenomena," the fourth of the four dharma-realms (DHARMADHĀTU), according to the HUAYAN ZONG. In this Huayan conception of ultimate reality, what the senses ordinarily perceive to be discrete and separate phenomena (SHI) are actually mutually pervading and mutually validating. Reality is likened to the bejeweled net of the king of the gods INDRA (see INDRAJĀLA), in which a jewel is hung at each knot in the net and the net stretches out infinitely in all directions. On the infinite facets of each individual jewel, the totality of the brilliance of the expansive net is captured, and the reflected brilliance is in turn re-reflected and multiplied by all the other jewels in the net. The universe is in this manner envisioned to be an intricate web of interconnecting phenomena, where each individual phenomenon owes its existence to the collective conditioning effect of all other phenomena and therefore has no absolute, self-contained identity. In turn, each individual phenomenon "creates" the universe as it is because the totality of the universe is inconceivable without the presence of each of those individual phenomena that define it. The function and efficacy of individual phenomena so thoroughly interpenetrate all other phenomena that the respective boundaries between individual phenomena are rendered moot; instead, all things are mutually interrelated with all other things, in a simultaneous mutual identity and mutual intercausality. In this distinctively Huayan understanding of reality, the entire universe is subsumed and revealed within even the most humble of individual phenomena, such as a single mote of dust, and any given mote of dust contains the infinite realms of this self-defining, self-creating universe. "Unimpeded" (wu'ai) in this context therefore has two important meanings: any single phenomenon simultaneously creates and is created by all other phenomena, and any phenomenon simultaneously contains and is contained by the universe in all its diversity. A common Huayan simile employs the image of ocean waves to describe this state of interfusion: because individual waves form, permeate, and infuse all other waves, they both define all waves (which in this simile is the ocean in its entirety), and in turn are defined themselves in the totality that is the ocean. The Huayan school claims this reputedly highest level of understanding to be its exclusive sectarian insight, thus ranking it the "consummate teaching" (YUANJIAO) in the scheme of the HUAYAN WUJIAO (Huayan fivefold taxonomy of the the teachings).

**Shitennōji**. (四天王寺). In Japanese, "Four Heavenly Kings Monastery," a Buddhist temple located in Ōsaka, Japan, which tradition presumes to be the oldest monastery in Japan. The *Nihon shoki* ("Chronicles of Japan"), compiled in 720, claims that the monastery was founded in 593 by the semilegendary figure Prince Shōtoku (SHŌTOKU TAISHI, 572–621) who made a vow that he would build a temple dedicated to the four heavenly kings (CĀTURMAHĀRĀJA), the guardian divinities (DEVA) of Buddhism, if his pro-Buddhist SOGA clan was able to defeat the anti-Buddhist Mononobe clan in battle in 587. At the time of its construction, as the monastery's name indicates, the four heavenly kings were enshrined as the main objects of veneration in the monastery; but from the Heian period (794–1185) onward, the bodhisattva Kannon (AVALOKITEŚVARA) replaced them as the main tutelary deity in the monastery. The temple was affiliated with the TENDAISHŪ until 1948, when it became nonsectarian. Shitennōji has been reconstructed several times during its history; the main basilica in the monastery was rebuilt in 1963.

**Shitou Xiqian**. (J. Sekitō Kisen; K. Sŏktu Hŭich'ŏn 石頭希遷) (700–790). In Chinese, "Rare Transformation Atop a Stone"; master in the Tang-dynasty CHAN ZONG, who was an important ancestor in the lineages of the CAODONG ZONG, YUNMEN ZONG, and FAYAN ZONG, three of the five major houses of the mature Song-dynasty Chan tradition (see WU JIA QI ZONG). Xiqian is claimed to have studied with the sixth patriarch (LIUZU) HUINENG (638–713) while still a youth and was present at the master's deathbed. He subsequently traveled to Qingyuanshan in modern-day Jiangxi province to study with a monk who was claimed to have been one of the sixth patriarch's most eminent disciples: QINGYUAN XINGSI (d. 740). Xingsi is said to have thought highly of his new disciple, famously calling him a unicorn among the other horned animals in his congregation, and eventually made Xiqian his principal dharma heir (FASI). In 742, after his teacher's death, he traveled to Mt. Nanyue (present-day Hunan province), where he lived in a hermitage built on top of a large boulder, hence his cognomen Shitou ("Atop a Stone"). In 762, he traveled to Tanzhou near present-day Changsha, before returning to Mt. Nanyue, where he passed away at the age of ninety. Although during his lifetime Xiqian seems to have been a fairly obscure teacher in a little-known regional lineage, he retrospectively came to be viewed as one of the two most influential teachers of the classical Chan period, along with MAZU DAOYI (709–788). This inflated appraisal is largely a result of the prominence of Xiqian's third–generation successor DONGSHAN LIANGJIE (807–869), one of the two teachers after whom the Caodong school is named. Xiqian is the author of the CANTONG QI, regarded by the Chinese Caodong zong and Japanese SŌTŌSHŪ as one of their foundational scriptures. Xiqian's short verse, in a total of 220 Sinographs, is highly regarded for its succinct and unequivocal expression of the teaching of nonduality.

**shiwang**. (J. jūō; K. siwang 十王). In Chinese, "ten kings" [of hell]. See YAMA.

**shi xuanmen**. (J. jūgenmon; K. sip hyŏnmun 十玄門). In Chinese, "the ten mysteries"; the systematic elaboration of the implications of causality (PRATĪTYASAMUTPĀDA) and existence in the doctrinal system of the HUAYAN ZONG. ZHIYAN (602–668), the second patriarch of the Huayan lineage, first elaborated the ten profound mysteries in order to outline ten specific perspectives on the "dependent origination of the DHARMADHĀTU" (FAJIE YUANQI), viz., the perspectives of: (1) the interrelationship between all things, (2) simile (i.e., of Indra's Net, INDRAJĀLA), (3) conditionality, (4) characteristics, (5) time, (6) practice, (7) principle, (8) function, (9) mind, and (10) wisdom. This original listing was elaborated by FAZANG (643–712), the third patriarch of the school, to explain instead the dharmadhātu of the unimpeded interpenetration between all phenomena (see SHISHI WU'AI FAJIE): viz., all dharmas simultaneously have a distinct, independent existence, and yet are still thoroughly pervaded by one other; they thus mutually define, yet do not impede the distinctiveness of, each other. Fazang's revised listing of the "ten mysteries" comes to be definitive within the school:

1. Simultaneity (tongshi juzu xiangying men): The mutual creation of any one thing and all things does not take place sequentially, but simultaneously.
2. Immensity (guangxia zizai wu'ai men): The relative size of any single thing is derived from that of all things, just as the immensity of all things is derived from any one thing.
3. Abundance (yiduo xiangrong butong men): The number "one" is meaningful only in distinction to "many," and vice versa. "One" and "many" thus define and pervade one another, and yet the distinctiveness of the two concepts is left intact.
4. Identity (zhufa xiangji zizai men): Any one thing is defined by all other things, and vice versa; there is no identity of any one thing beyond the contextual definition it derives from the totality of all things, and vice versa.
5. Manifestation (yinmi xianliao jucheng men): The revelation of any one thing relies on the concealment of all other things, just as the manifestation of all other things requires the concealment (e.g., the shifting of attention away from) of any one thing, and vice versa.
6. Diminutiveness (weixi xiangrong anli men): The smallest number encapsulates infinity, the smallest mote of dust contains the most immense of world-systems, and the shortest duration of time spans incalculable eons. Yet, number, size, and time retain their logical order of magnitude amidst this scheme of things.
7. Indra's Net (Yintuoluo wang fajie men): Just as with the reflective jewels at each knot of the infinitely expansive Indrajāla, any one phenomenon captures and reflects the images of all phenomena. The images of all phenomena are thus reflected infinitely in a single instant as they are redirected to, and multiplied within, all the facets of the myriad jewels that make up Indra's Net.
8. Analogy (tuoshi xianfa shengjie men): The abstruse can be made known by analogies that draw on the plain and the obvious. Although the abstruse and the plain are distinct in their relative profundity, the principle they thus evince is one and the same.
9. Time (shishi gefa yicheng men): Although time can be divided into past, present, and future, from the perspectives of each of the three temporal periods, different sets of the past, present, and future can be delineated. All of the nine temporal periods (viz., the past, present, and future of the past, present, and future) are in turn subsumed in one instant of thought, which together make a total of ten temporal periods. These ten thus mutually "enter" (ru), subsume, and define each other.
10. Centrality (zhuban yuanming jude men): Each of the aforementioned categories explains and validates all the others. When focus is directed at any particular category, all the others become subordinate, and the one at hand becomes predominant. Each category involves the same principle of being collectively substantiated by all categories together. The same is true with all phenomena: the relation between centrality and marginality is relative and mutually substantiating.

**Shiyuan**. (C) (師遠). See KUO'AN SHIYUAN.

**shizhong**. (C) (示衆). See CHUISHI.

**Shizun nianhua**. (J. Seson nenge; K. Sejon yŏmhwa 世尊拈花). In Chinese, "The World-Honored One holding up a flower." See NIANHUA WEIXIAO.

**Shōbōgenzō**. (正法眼藏). In Japanese, "Treasury of the True Dharma Eye"; the magnum opus of the Japanese ZEN master DŌGEN KIGEN (1200–1253); the title refers to the Zen (C. CHAN) school, which is considered to be the repository of the insights of the buddha ŚĀKYAMUNI himself, transmitted through the lineage of the CHAN patriarchs (ZUSHI) starting with MAHĀKĀŚYAPA. A work bearing the same title (C. ZHENGFAYANZANG) by the eminent Song-dynasty Chinese monk DAHUI ZONGGAO was probably the inspiration for Dōgen's own title. Dōgen's oeuvre contains two works with this title. The first is a collection of 301 kōan (C. GONG'AN) cases, composed in literary Chinese, known as the *Shinji Shōbōgenzō* or the *Mana*

*Shōbōgenzō*. The second is a collection of essays written in Japanese, known as the *Kana* [viz., "vernacular"] *Shōbōgenzō*, which is the better known of the two and which will be the focus of this account. The *Shōbōgenzō* is a collection of individual essays and treatises that Dōgen composed throughout his eventful career. Its earliest included treatise is the BENDŌWA composed in 1231 and the latest is the *Hachidainingaku* composed in 1253, the year of Dōgen's death. Although the *Shōbōgenzō* seems to have been all but forgotten after Dōgen's death, later successors in the Japanese Sōtō Zen tradition, such as MANZAN DŌHAKU (1636–1715), TENKEI DENSON (1648–1735), and MENZAN ZUIHŌ (1683–1769), and the layman Ōuchi Seiran (1845–1918) rediscovered the text and their influential commentaries on it helped to make Dōgen's magnum opus the central scripture of the Sōtō Zen tradition. Six different editions of the *Shōbōgenzō* are known to exist: the "original" volume edited by Dōgen in seventy-five rolls, the twelve-roll Yōkōji edition, the sixty-roll Eiheiji edition edited by Giun (1253–1333), the eighty-four roll edition edited by Bonsei (d. 1427) in 1419, the eighty-nine roll edition edited by Manzan Dōhaku (1636–1715) in 1684 at Daishōji, and the ninety-five roll edition edited by Kōzen (1627–1693) in 1690 at Eiheiji. The seventy-five roll edition is today the most widely consulted and cited. Many of the essays were originally sermons delivered by Dōgen, such that some are written by him and others were recorded by his disciples. Late in his life, he began to revise the essays, completing the revision of twelve of them before his death. The essays are renowned for their subtle and elliptical style, clever word play, and sometimes enigmatic meanings. Part of their difficulty arises from the fact that Dōgen quotes liberally from Buddhist sūtras and the works of Chinese masters, but also interprets these passages quite ingeniously. Dōgen also invented a number of Buddhist neologisms that were largely unique to him, including creative "mis"-readings of original Chinese passages. For example, in his famous essay "Uji" ("Being Time"), Dōgen reads the quotidian Chinese compound youshi ("at a certain time") to suggest the identity of "being" (C. you, J. u) and "time" (C. shi, J. ji): i.e., since impermanency governs all compounded things, those things are in fact time itself. The text includes extensive discussions of the foundations of Zen thought, the meaning and significance of awakening (SATORI), as well as detailed instructions on the ritual procedures for performing sitting meditation (J. ZAZEN; C. ZUOCHAN), as in the chapter FUKAN ZAZENGI. The *Shōbōgenzō* remains a source of great interest to scholars and practitioners of Zen. See also SŌTŌSHŪ.

**Shōbōgenzō zuimonki**. (正法眼藏隨聞記). In Japanese, lit., "Treasury of the Eye of the True Dharma, Record of What Was Heard," a work by Koun Ejō (1198–1280), a disciple of DŌGEN KIGEN. The book is essentially a collection of notes taken by Kuon on talks, instructions, and advice given by Dōgen. Kuon's notes circulated in manuscript form before finally being printed in 1651. The text is considered to be more practical and accessible than Dōgen's much larger and prolix SHŌBŌGENZŌ.

**Shōkokuji**. (相国寺). In Japanese, "Ministering to the State Monastery," an important ZEN Buddhist monastery located just adjacent to the old imperial grounds in the ancient Japanese capital of Kyōto. The monastery was built in 1382 by Ashikaga Yoshimitsu (1358–1408), the third shōgun of the Muromachi (1337–1573) shogunate. The Zen master Shunnoku Myōha (1311–1388) was supposed to be installed as the abbot of the new monastery, but he instead insisted that his own teacher, MUSŌ SOSEKI (1275–1351), an eminent Zen master associated with the RINZAISHŪ, be posthumously designated its founding abbot. The temple was listed as the second of the so-called GOZAN (five mountains) temples of Kyōto, and served as a center of Zen culture during the period. The monastery continued to be sponsored by the subsequent Tokugawa (1603–1868) shogunate. The temple structures often suffered serious damage, including the monastery's complete destruction during the Ōnin war (1467–1477), and has been repeatedly reconstructed. The temple now serves as the head monastery of the Shōkokuji branch of the contemporary Rinzai school and has nearly a hundred affiliated branch temples, including the famous Golden Pavilion (KINKAKUJI).

**Shōrai mokuroku**. (J) (請來目錄). In Japanese, "Catalogue of Items Brought from China"; a roster of esoteric scriptures and ritual implements that the Japanese SHINGONSHŪ founder KŪKAI brought back with him to Japan in the early ninth century. See KŪKAI.

**Shōshitsu rokumonshū**. (少室六門集). In Japanese, "Collection of Six Treatises from Small Caves," a Japanese anthology of works attributed to BODHIDHARMA, the legendary Indian monk and founder of the CHAN school. "Small caves" (shaoshi) refers to the western peak of SONGSHAN, where Bodhidharma purportedly spent nine years facing a wall in meditation (see BIGUAN) near the monastery of SHAOLINSI. The anthology includes the *Xinjing song* ("Panegyric to the 'Heart Sūtra'"), *Poxiang lun*, *Erzhong ru* (see ERRU SIXING LUN), *Anxin famen*, *Wuxing lun*, and XUEMO LUN. The *Shōshitsu rokumonshū* was published sometime during the late Kamakura period and was republished in 1647, 1667, and 1675.

**Shōtoku Taishi**. (聖德太子) (572–622). Japanese statesman of the Asuka period (593–710) and second son of Emperor Yōmei (r. 585–587), who is traditionally assumed to have played an important role in the early dissemination of Buddhism in Japan. He is also known as Umayado no Miko (Prince Stable Door), but by the eighth century, he became known as Shōtoku Taishi (lit. Prince Sagacious Virtue). Given that the earliest significant writings on the life of Shōtoku Taishi come from two early histories, the *Kojiki* (712) and *Nihon shoki* (720), which are both written nearly a century after his death, little can be said definitively about his biography. According to the traditional accounts in these two texts, Suiko (554–628), the aunt of Prince Shōtoku and the Japanese monarch, appointed her nephew regent in 593, giving him broad political powers. Thanks to his enlightened leadership, Prince Shōtoku is credited with numerous historical achievements. These include the promotion of Buddhism within the court under an edict he issued in 594; promulgation of the Seventeen-Article Constitution in 604, which stresses the importance of the monarchy and lays out basic Buddhist and Confucian principles; sponsorship of trade missions to China; construction of the monasteries of HŌRYŪJI and SHITENNŌJI; authorship of two chronological histories (*Tennōko* and *Kokki*); and composition of three of the earliest Buddhist commentaries in Japan, on the SADDHARMAPUṆḌARĪKASŪTRA ("Lotus Sūtra"), VIMALAKĪRTINIRDEŚA, and ŚRĪMĀLĀDEVĪSIṂHANĀDASŪTRA ("Lion's Roar of Queen Śrīmālā"), which demonstrate his deep familiarity with Mahāyāna Buddhist doctrine. The credibility of Prince Shōtoku's achievements as described in the *Kojiki* and *Nihon Shoki* is undermined by fact that both texts were commissioned by the newly empowered monarchy in an attempt to strengthen its political standing. Some scholars have thus argued that because the new royal family wanted to identify itself with the powerful instrument of the new religion, they selected the person of Prince Shōtoku, who shared their lineage, to serve as the first political patron of Buddhism in Japan. This historical narrative focused on Prince Shōtoku thus denigrated the importance of the defeated SOGA clan's extensive patronage of Buddhism. As early as the Nara period (710–794), Prince Shōtoku began taking on legendary, even mythical status, and was eventually transformed into one of Japan's greatest historical figures, representing the quintessence of Buddhist religious virtue and benevolent political leadership. Priests often dedicated temples to him or transferred the merit of religious enterprises to Shōtoku. Both SHINRAN (1173–1263) and NICHIREN (1222–82) dedicated written works to his name. Throughout the Heian (794–1185) and Kamakura (1185–1333) periods, what is now referred to as the cult of Shōtoku Taishi was widely popular and members of the aristocracy regularly venerated him (a practice referred to as Taishi shinkō, lit. devotion to the Prince).

**Shouduan**. (C) (守端) (1025–1072). See BAIYUN SHOUDUAN.

**Shousui**. (C) (守遂) (1072–1147). See DAHONG SHOUSUI.

**shouzuo**. (J. shuza; K. sujwa 首座). In Chinese, "chief seat," the title held by one of the six prefects (C. TOUSHOU) of a CHAN monastery. The chief seat is in charge of dealing with any infractions of the monastic code and notifying the appropriate authorities of any problems within the monastery. His primary role is to serve as a model of good behavior for the other monks in the SAṂGHA hall (SENGTANG). The chief seat, for instance, leads the assembly in various matters such as eating, chanting, and meditating.

**shuchao**. (J. shuchō/juchō; K. such'o 豎超). In Chinese, "the tortuous (lit. vertical) deliverance/escape." In PURE LAND polemics, it is claimed that if a practitioner strictly relies on one's own effort (see JIRIKI) to attain liberation, it would involve an arduous, "vertical" ascent through successive stages of ever-deeper meditative absorptions and ever-more-daunting spiritual fruitions. Pure land followers argue that an expeditious, "horizontal" shortcut (cf. HENGCHAO) is possible, by which one simply has to travel "westward" instead of "upward"—i.e., by being reborn into AMITĀBHA Buddha's western pure land (see SUKHĀVATĪ), one will be liberated from the rounds of rebirth in one fell swoop.

**Shugendō**. (修験道). In Japanese, lit. the "Way of Cultivating Supernatural Power," a Japanese esoteric tradition that is focused on an intensive ascetic regiment of training in the mountains. Its practitioners claim as their founder EN NO OZUNU ([alt. En no Gyōja], En the Ascetic) (b. 634), a semilegendary ascetic from the mountains of KATSURAGISAN on the border between present-day Nara and Ōsaka prefectures, who is venerated for his shamanic powers and for being the prototypical shugenja (lit. one who cultivates supernatural powers). Before it evolved into an independent religious entity, Shugendō was a wide-ranging set of religious practices that included elements drawn from many traditions, lineages, and institutions, including Japanese TENDAI (TIANTAI), SHINGON, Nara Buddhism, ZEN, PURE LAND movements, Daoism, and local indigenous beliefs. Its practitioners, who were known as YAMABUSHI (lit. those who lie down [or sleep] in the mountains), were largely itinerant, spending much of their time in the mountains, which Japanese regarded as numinous places that housed the spirits of the dead. Through severe austerities in the mountains, such as immersion under waterfalls, solitary confinement in caves, fasting, meditating, and the recitation of spells (MANTRA), practitioners strove to attain buddhahood in this very body (SOKUSHIN JŌBUTSU) and accumulate power that would benefit others. As Shugendō evolved into a distinctive tradition during the mid- to late-Heian period (794–1185), Shugendō mountain centers either became linked with Tendai and Shingon institutions or continued to operate and expand independently. Mountains that were especially important to Shugendō included the Yoshino peaks in Nara prefecture, KUMANO in Wakayama prefecture, Haguro in Yamagata prefecture, Hiko in Kyūshū, and Ishizuchi in Shikoku. During this period, the aristocratic nobility, including a long succession of monarchs and retired monarchs, patronized the Yoshino and Kumano mountains. Shugenja guided these visitors on pilgrimage and performed magical and religious rites for them. Pilgrimages became increasingly popular and became a significant source of revenue for many of these mountain centers. Under the temple regulations (J. jiin hatto) imposed by the shōgun Tokugawa Ieyasu (1543–1616) at the start of the Tokugawa period (1600–1868), Shugendō sites were forced to align with either the Tendai Shugen branch of Honzan, administered by the temple of Shōgoin, or the Shingon branch of Tōzan, administered by Sanbōin, both located in Kyōto. Itinerant practitioners largely settled down and began performing rituals and offering prayers in villages. Due to sectarian strife between the two schools, in 1707 the Tōzan branch named as its founder Shōbō (a.k.a. Rigen Daishi; 832–909), who had established Daigoji at Mt. Yoshino. Shugendō was proscribed in 1872 during the Meiji persecution of Buddhism, as the government tried to purge Shintō-affiliated traditions of their "foreign" elements. However, Shōgoinryū, the primary branch of the Honzan school, was returned to the religious rolls in 1892. When religious freedom was restored in postwar Japan, many Shugendō institutions resumed their former rituals and traditions, although not to the same extent as they had previously. While a multitude of indigenous gods (KAMI), buddhas, and bodhisattvas have been venerated historically at Shugendō sites around Japan, Kongō Zaō Gongen, a deity in the Ōmine mountains who was venerated by En no Ozunu, gradually became the central deity in Shugendō. Other significant objects of worship include En no Ozunu himself, who is thought to have manifested himself as Hōki Bosatsu (the bodhisattva DHARMODGATA); Shōbō, an incarnation of Nyoirin Kannon (Cintāmaṇicakra AVALOKITEŚVARA); and Fudō Myōō (ACALANĀTHA-VIDYĀRĀJA), a wrathful DHARMAPĀLA of the VAJRAYĀNA pantheon.

**shugenja**. (J) (修驗者). In Japanese, lit. "one who cultivates supernatural powers"; a shaman or, in specific contexts, a practitioner of SHUGENDŌ. See also YAMABUSHI.

**Shug gseb**. (Shuksep). A Tibetan nunnery located south of LHA SA on a site originally sanctified by the great female adept MA GCIG LAB SGRON. The nunnery and its connected retreat center were established by GYER SGOM TSHUL KHRIM SENG GE, founder of the SHUG GSEB BKA' BRGYUD subsect of Tibetan Buddhism. Due to its close proximity to GANGS RI THOD DKAR, a favored retreat site of RNYING MA master KLONG CHEN RAB 'BYAMS, the nunnery developed a close relationship with the Rnying ma sect from the fourteenth century onwards. The nunnery was home to an important female incarnate lama (SPRUL SKU), the Shug gseb Rje btsun ma (Shuksep Jetsunma).

**Shug gseb bka' brgyud**. (Shuksep Kagyü). One of the four major and eight minor subsects of the BKA' BRGYUD sect of Tibetan Buddhism (BKA' BRGYUD CHE BZHI CHUNG BRGYAD), considered to have been founded by GYER SGOM TSHUL KHRIM SENG GE, a disciple of the Bka' brgyud hierarch PHAG MO GRU PA RDO RJE RGYAL PO.

**Shūhō Myōchō**. (J) 宗峰妙超. See SŌHŌ MYŌCHŌ.

**shuilu hui**. (J. suirikue; K. suryuk hoe 水陸會). In Chinese, "water and land assembly," a Buddhist ritual intended for universal salvation, although it was also sometimes directed only to deceased next of kin; the ceremony was also performed for a variety of this-worldly purposes, such as state protection (see HUGUO FOJIAO) and rain-making. The name "water and land" derives from its intent to save living creatures who inhabit the most painful domains of SAṂSĀRA, whether in water or on land. The ceremony, which typically took seven days to complete, was held at two different sites, the inner altar and the outer altar. The main performance was held at the inner altar, which was divided into an upper hall and a lower hall. The enlightened beings—buddhas, BODHISATTVAs, ARHATs, and guardian deities of the three jewels (RATNATRAYA)—were invited and feted with offerings at the upper hall; the unenlightened beings, specifically beings subject to the six rebirth destinies (GATI), were invited and feted at the lower hall. Once summoned to the lower hall at the inner altar, the unenlightened assembly was divested of its afflictions (KLEŚA), asked to pay homage to the enlightened assembly, and received offerings of both food and the dharma, which sent them on their way to the PURE LAND. According to the earliest extant records of the ceremony, none of which predate the Song period, the shuilu hui was first performed in 505 by the monk BAOZHI (418–514) at the behest of Emperor Wu (r. 502–549) of the Liang dynasty, with the VINAYA master and scriptural cataloguer SENGYOU (445–518) serving as chief celebrant. The same Song-period sources claim that the ceremony was revived by a monk during the Xianheng era (670–674), after its sudden disappearance following the collapse of the Liang dynasty. It was not until the tenth century, however, that there is independent confirmation in non-Buddhist sources of actual performances of the ceremony and it was not until the eleventh century that it seems to have achieved widespread popularity. According to the monk Zunshi (964–1032), the larger monasteries in the southeast of China maintained separate halls, called either shuilu tang or shuilu yuan, which were devoted entirely to the performance of the ceremony. In the Southern Song period, many of the largest monasteries throughout the realm had a "water and land hall" on their grounds. In Korea, the suryuk hoe was first performed in 971 and became popular during the early Chosŏn dynasty, with the royal family being its main supporter. There are several Chinese and Korean manuals that provide directions for performing the ritual, including the *Shuilu yiwen* ("Ritual Text for the Water and Land Ceremony") in three rolls, written by a Song-dynasty layman in 1071. The canonical locus classicus for the practice is the story of Jalavāhana in the SUVARṆAPRABHĀSOTTAMASŪTRA.

**Shuiyue Guanyin**. (J. Suigatsu Kannon; K. Suwŏl Kwanŭm 水月觀音). In Chinese, "Moon in the Water AVALOKITEŚVARA"; a representation of the BODHISATTVA GUANYIN that is frequently depicted in East Asian art. The name of this bodhisattva derives from this image's most characteristic feature: a luminous disk that encircles the bodhisattva and evokes both a nimbus (see KĀYAPRABHĀ) and a full moon, effectively suggesting its power to dispel the darkness of the night. Another connotation is indicated in texts such as the DAZHIDU LUN (*Mahāprajñāpāramitāśāstra*), where the term "moon in the water" connotes that all phenomena are like reflections of the moon on the surface of the water, thereby signifying insubstantiality and impermanence. The origin of Shuiyue Guanyin and its iconography is said to be based on the GAṆḌAVYŪHA section of the AVATAṂSAKASŪTRA, which describes the quest for ultimate truth by the youth SUDHANA. During his pilgrimage, Sudhana encounters Guanyin at the latter's sacred island home of POTALAKA. Artists used this account of Potalaka as the basis for Shuiyue Guanyin images from the eighth century onwards. The first Shuiyue Guanyin is presumed to have been painted by Zhou Fang (active c. 780–810 CE), but the earliest extant depiction appears on a silk banner at DUNHUANG dated to 943: Shuiyue Guanyin appears in the lower right of a large painting of the thousand-armed and thousand-eyed Guanyin (SĀHASRABHUJASĀHASRANETRĀVALOKITEŚVARA). There, the deity is seated on a rock outcropping surrounded by water, posed in majestic ease, attired in beautiful robes and sashes with intricate details on his robes and jewelry. Behind him is a lush bamboo grove with sheer, mountainous cliffs. Further standard attributes of Shuiyue Guanyin are the image of the buddha AMITĀBHA in his crown as well as a willow branch and a KUṆḌIKĀ bottle placed to the figure's right. Water spread by means of a willow branch was thought to have a healing effect on the believer. The island of Potalaka was believed to be located somewhere in the ocean south of India, but by the late Tang dynasty the Chinese had identified it with PUTUOSHAN, an island offshore from Zhejiang province near the seaport of Ningbo. It is probably due to maritime contacts between Ningbo and the Korean peninsula that Shuiyue Guanyin depictions became popular during the Koryŏ dynasty in Korea. Koryŏ images of Shuiyue Guanyin are especially renowned for their splendor and this form of the bodhisattva remains common in Korean Buddhist painting.

**shuji**. (J. shoki; K. sŏgi 書記). In Chinese, "scribe." Also known as the SHUZHUANG (lit. "letters"); one of the six prefects (C. TOUSHOU) at a CHAN monastery. The "scribe" was in charge of writing all the letters, prayers, and documents for the monastic community.

**shumidan**. (C. xumi tan; K. sumi tan 須彌壇). In Japanese, "MT. SUMERU altar," also known as the shumiza, or Mt. Sumeru throne; the elevated altar or platform in a Japanese Buddhist shrine, on which the central icons are placed. The shumidan is so named because it was modeled after Mt. Sumeru, the central axis of the world in Buddhist cosmology. The altar's origins are found in a legend about the buddha ŚĀKYAMUNI, who was said to have gone away for several months to TRĀYASTRIṂŚA heaven, located at the peak of Mt. Sumeru, to preach to his mother, MĀYĀ. Due to his long absence, some of his adherents made images of the missing Śākyamuni (see UDĀYANA BUDDHA), which they placed on a model of the mountain. Typically constructed in either square or octagonal shape, the shumidan is usually made of wood, metal, or stone and is decorated with various symbols. The square shape may symbolize the four sides of Mt. Sumeru, which are made of four types of jewels, generally listed as silver in the east, crystal in the west, lapis lazuli in the south, and gold in the north. The octagonal shape, by contrast, is said to represent the eightfold path (ĀRYĀṢṬĀṄGAMĀRGA). The shumidan is composed of upper, middle, and lower tiers. The Kamakura-period shumidan is a square-shaped altar constructed in a sophisticated style rich with symbolic meaning: its middle level consists of one thick, but narrow, tier, along with sixteen thinner tiers that gradually widen out in each direction toward both the top and the bottom. According to Buddhist esoteric teachings, the sixteen tiers toward the top represent the sixteen great bodhisattvas in the wisdom gate (J. emon); the sixteen tiers toward the bottom represent the sixteen great bodhisattvas in the meditation gate (J. jōmon); the four jewels, represented by a square shape, symbolize the five wisdoms, because the four jewels as a group symbolize the "wisdom that is the essential nature of the dharma realm" (J. hokkai taishōchi) and each jewel symbolizes the remaining four of the five wisdoms. Finally, the total of these thirty-two square-shaped tiers symbolizes the beings depicted in the diamond realm (J. KONGŌKAI) MAṆḌALA. The shumidan as a whole represents the mind of awakening (J. bodaishin; S. BODHICITTA), with which all sentient beings are endowed. In CHAN and ZEN monasteries, a shumidan without any displayed icon is placed in the dharma hall for the abbot or master to ascend for such occasions as the SHANGTANG ceremony.

**shuzhuang**. (J. shojō; K. sŏjang 書狀). In Chinese, "letters." Epistolary exchanges between monks and their disciples seems to have been an important didactic technique in China, especially from the Song dynasty onwards. The most prominent monks were members of the lettered intelligentsia in China and letters were an important means of transmitting their teachings. Such didactic correspondence was typically not meant to be private and an eminent monk was well aware that the letters he wrote would circulate among his students and disciples. Such letters might be framed as an exchange with the recipient, but they typically remove the formulaic openings and conclusions common with personal letters and thus become virtually indistinguishable from essays. In addition to such didactic letters, a teacher's letters might also include formulaic ritual letters and personal notes between master and student or close acquaintances, which would typically not have circulated beyond the recipient. Chan masters in particular were well known for their wide-ranging epistolary exchanges with literatocrats (shidafu) and other monks. One of the most famous set of letters is the DAHUI PUJUE CHANSHI SHU, the letters of the LINJI ZONG CHAN teacher DAHUI ZONGGAO; of the sixty-two letters in Dahui's collection, sixty of them were written to laypeople and only two to fellow monks. ¶ The term shuzhuang can also refer to the "scribe" (SHUJI) at a Buddhist monastery, who was in charge of drafting all letters, announcement posters, and written prayers for the monastic community. See also SŎJANG; YULU.

**Shwedagon**. In Burmese, "Golden Dagon"; monumental golden pagoda (B. JEDI; S. STŪPA; P. thūpa) that dominates the skyline of Rangoon (Yangon), capital of Burma (Myanmar); named after Dagon, the ancient name of Rangoon. According to Burmese and Mon legend, the pagoda was built during the Buddha's lifetime to house eight hair relics given to TRAPUṢA and BHALLIKA, two merchants from Ukkala who are said to have been the first disciples of the Buddha. The original account, which appears in the Pāli canon, places Ukkala in what is most likely modern-day ĀNDHRA, on the eastern coast of India. Mon-Burmese recensions of the story locate Ukkala at Dagon, acknowledgement of which is retained in the names Myauk Okkala-pa (North Ukkala) and Daung Okkala-pa (South Ukkala) given to Rangoon's suburbs. The Shwedagon is situated atop a two hundred-foot high hill, whose summit was leveled to create the four-acre plaza or platform that now surrounds the base of the shrine. The pagoda platform is approached by four covered stairways facing the cardinal directions, at the base of which are ornate entrances flanked by colossal Chinthe lions. The pagoda itself was repeatedly expanded and embellished over the centuries, reaching its current height of 326 feet in the fifteenth century. Constructed of brickwork, it is in the classical Burmese pagoda form of an inverted bell rising from an octagonal pyramidal base. These elements support a graceful spire crowned with a hti, or finial umbrella, that is encrusted with diamonds, rubies, pearls, and other gems of inestimable value. The hti also has many wind chimes, which gently tinkle in the constant breeze. The base of the pagoda is more than a quarter-mile in circumference and the entire structure is covered in gold, the accumulated munificence of generations of royal donors. Sixty-four smaller pagodas surround the main structure at its base, and at the four cardinal directions are shrines containing colossal statues of the four buddhas who have appeared in the world during the present fortunate eon (P. bhaddakappa; S. BHADRAKALPA). (See SAPTATATHĀGATA.) At one corner of the platform is a miniature replica of the main shrine, no more than a hundred feet tall. The smaller pagoda is affectionately known as the Shwedagon's older brother, as it was the model upon which the current main pagoda was based. At each corner of the Shwedagon's octagonal base is an alabaster statue of the Buddha dedicated to one of the eight days of the Burmese week (Wednesday being counted as two days), where it is believed to be especially auspicious for people born on those days to pray. A broad circumambulatory walkway paved in white marble rings the Shwedagon, which in turn is flanked with hundreds of lesser shrines dating mostly from the colonial period. Many types of religious piety are performed individually and in groups on the platform of the pagoda, such as the giving of DĀNA, freeing captured animals, processing candidates for the novitiate (B. shin-pyu), sweeping the plaza, lustrating images, reciting PARITTA texts, taking precepts, silent prayer, and meditation (B. taya a-to; P. BHĀVANĀ).

**Shwegyin**. The second largest monastic fraternity (B. GAING; P. GAṆA) of modern Myanmar (Burmese) Buddhism comprising approximately five percent of the monastic population of the country. It is preceded in size by the majority THUDHAMMA GAING, which comprises 85–90% of the Burmese monkhood. The Shwegyin gaing was founded in the mid-nineteenth century and was one of three reformist monastic gaing to emerge during the reign of the Burmese king, MINDON (r.1853–1878), along with the DWAYA GAING and the Hngettwin gaing. The Shwegyin gaing takes its name from its founder, the first SHWEGYIN SAYADAW, U Zagara (P. Jāgara) (1822–1893), a renowned scholar-monk from the village of Shwegyin in Upper Burma. U Zagara was especially strict in his observance of VINAYA and insisted, as did the leaders of the other reformist gaing, that monks who scrupulously followed the vinaya were in no need of oversight by the royally appointed THUDHAMMA Council, an ecclesiastical body established to govern the Burmese saṅgha (S. SAṂGHA) throughout the kingdom. King Mindon granted U Zagara and his disciples autonomy (P. gaṇavimutti) from Thudhamma control in 1860, marking the beginning of the Shwegyin gaing as an independent self-governing monastic fraternity. The Shwegyin Sayadaw established a network of monasteries in Upper and Lower Burma that were uniform in practice and institutional structure and regulated by its own gaing-specific hierarchical leadership. The Shwegyin gaing thus replicated for itself a system of monastic governance that the Thudhamma Council had been designed to provide for the Burmese saṅgha as a whole. This internal organization, along with the fraternity's emphasis on monastic discipline and Buddhist scholarship, enabled the Shwegyin gaing to survive and even flourish during the dislocations brought about by British conquest in 1885, which led to the dissolution of the Thudhamma Council and disestablishment of Buddhism as the state religion. Shwegyin monks can be distinguished from monks of other gaing by minor points of outward deportment. They are required to cover both shoulders with the upper robe whenever leaving their monastic compound, for example, unlike Thudhamma monks who require this style of attire only on such formal occasions as alms rounds or giving sermons. Shwegyin monks are not allowed to smoke tobacco, use umbrellas, or handle money. Shwegyin monasteries are also distinguished from those of other gaing in that they do not require lay people to remove their footwear when entering the monastic compound.

**Shwegyin Sayadaw**. (1822–1893). In Burmese, "Senior Monk from Shwegyin," honorific title of U Zagara (P. Jāgara), a prominent nineteenth-century reformist scholar-monk and founder of the SHWEGYIN GAING, which today is the second largest monastic fraternity (B. GAING; P. GAṆA) in the Burmese saṅgha (S. SAṂGHA). U Zagara was born in Shwegyin village near

Shwebo in Upper Burma. As a novice (P. sāmaṇera; S. ŚRĀMAṆERA) and as a young monk (P. BHIKKHU; S. BHIKṢU) he studied under many of the prominent abbots of his time, and according to some sources was a colleague of the learned and ultra-orthodox Okpo Sayadaw, U Okkamwuntha (P. Okkaṃvaṃsa), founder of the DWAYA GAING, in British-occupied Lower Burma. Like the Okpo Sayadaw, U Zagara emphasized Pāli scholarship and scrupulous attention to monastic discipline (P. VINAYA) as the foundation of the Buddha's religion (P. sāsana; S. ŚĀSANA), qualities which brought him to the attention of the Burmese king, MINDON (r. 1853–1878). King Mindon, who had inaugurated a revival and reform of Buddhism throughout his kingdom, appointed U Zagara as a royal preceptor (B. SAYADAW) and built for him an elaborate monastic complex at the foot of Mandalay Hill. This attention soon brought U Zagara into conflict with the powerful THUDHAMMA Council, a royally appointed ecclesiastical body charged with governing the Burmese saṅgha of the kingdom. After a falling out with the Thudhamma patriarch (B. thathanabaing; P. SAṄGHARĀJĀ), U Zagara petitioned the king for autonomy (P. gaṇavimutti) from Thudhamma control, which the king granted. He and his disciples thus formed the nucleus of the new Shwegyin gaing. Some years after the death of the Thudhamma patriarch, during the reign of Burma's last king, Thibaw (1878–1885), U Zagara was invited along with another senior monk to jointly head the Thudhamma Council. U Zagara declined the offer, focusing his energies instead on expanding the reach of the Shwegyin gaing throughout Upper and Lower Burma. The strong emphasis placed by U Zagara and his successors on Buddhist scholarship, monastic discipline, and strict institutional organization of member monasteries allowed the Shwegyin gaing to successfully weather the tumultuous years following the British conquest of the Burmese kingdom in 1885, which saw the dissolution of the Thudhamma Council and disestablishment of Buddhism as the state religion.

**Śibi**. (P. Sivi; T. Shi bi; C. Shipi; J. Shibi; K. Sibi 尸毘). A king who is the protagonist of a famous JĀTAKA tale. There are two different stories associated with him. In the first, versions of which also appear in the Hindu epics, Śibi is a king renowned for his generosity. Seeking to test the limits of his charity, the divinities (DEVA) ŚAKRA and AGNI take the form of a hawk and a dove. Pursued by the hawk, the dove seeks shelter in the king's lap. The hawk agrees to spare the dove if the king will offer in exchange flesh equal to the weight of the dove. A scale is produced and the king cuts off a piece of his own flesh. However, the gods manipulate the scale so that no matter how much of his flesh the king cuts off and places on the scale, it never equals the weight of the dove. Eventually, the king is reduced to a skeleton, at which point the gods reveal their true identity and make the king whole again. In the second version of the story, which appears in the JĀTAKAMĀLĀ and other sources, Śakra, the king of the gods, hears of the king's generosity and seeks to test it. He takes the form of a blind brāhmaṇa, who goes to King Śibi and asks that the king give him his eyes. The king agrees and has his eyes removed and given to the blind man, restoring his sight. Again, the god reveals his true identity and returns the king's eyes. Both versions are famous examples of the BODHISATTVA's "gift of the body" (DEHADĀNA), which he makes as part of his practice of the perfection of giving (DĀNAPĀRAMITĀ). See also SHE SHEN.

**sidalingshan**. (C) (四大靈山). In Chinese, "four great numinous mountains"; the four major sacred mountains of Chinese Buddhism. See EMEISHAN; JIUHUASHAN; PUTUOSHAN; WUTAISHAN.

**siddha**. (T. grub thob). In Sanskrit, lit. "accomplished," viz., an "adept," referring especially in tantric literature to a person who is accomplished in tantric practice and has attained SIDDHI. The siddha began to emerge in India as a new kind of Buddhist saint as early as the fifth century, perhaps under the influence of Śaivism, and continuing through the decline of Buddhism in India. The siddha embodies an ideal that stands outside both the monastic context as well as that of conventional lay Buddhist practice. See MAHĀSIDDHA.

**Siddham**. (C. Xitan; J. Shittan; K. Siltam 悉曇). In Sanskrit, "Accomplished" or "Perfected"; a North Indian written script descended from BRAHMĪ and an ancestor of Devanāgarī, the script in which Sanskrit and Hindi are written today. The use of Siddham is preserved only in East Asian Buddhism, the script having been introduced to China in the eighth century in order to transcribe DHĀRAṆĪ and MANTRA. KŪKAI is said to have introduced the Siddham script to Japan from China in 806 CE. The script is closely associated with the esoteric Buddhist traditions of East Asia (J. MIKKYŌ), in which the writing system itself became an object of visualization and veneration, as a written representation of the sounds enunciated in mantra and dhāraṇī. Siddham is also said to have influenced the development of the indigenous Japanese kana writing system, which is associated with Kūkai. Often in traditional sources, when an East Asian monk is said to know "Sanskrit" (Fanwen), what is really meant is that he is able to read Siddham and to recite correctly passages written in that script.

**siddhānta**. (T. grub mtha'; C. zong; J. shū; K. chong 宗). In Sanskrit, "conclusion" or "tenet," the term is used to refer to the various schools of Indian philosophy (both Buddhist and non-Buddhist), to their particular positions, and to texts that set out those positions in a systematic fashion. The most important examples of Buddhist siddhānta texts in India are BHĀVAVIVEKA's [alt. Bhavya] autocommentary (called TARKAJVĀLĀ) on his MADHYAMAKAHṚDAYAKĀRIKĀ and ŚĀNTARAKṢITA's TATTVASAṂGRAHA; both set forth the positions of non-Buddhist and Buddhist philosophies in order to demonstrate the superiority of their respective MADHYAMAKA positions. They are paralleled in Indian non-Buddhist literature by

Śaṅkarācārya's *Brahmasūtrabhāṣya*, for example, that sets forth the views of nāstika (heterodox) and āstika (orthodox) schools and shows the weaknesses and strengths in each as a strategy to demonstrate the superiority of Śaṅkara's own Advaita Vedāṇta philosophy. None of these Indian works were written simply as informative textbooks about the tenets of different Indian schools of thought. They instead have clear polemical agendas: namely, demonstrating the superiority of their own position, and showing how the lesser philosophies are either a hindrance or a stepping stone to their own philosophy, as revealed by the Buddha in the case of Buddhist siddhānta, and by the Vedas in the case of non-Buddhists. The *Sarvadarśanasaṃgraha*, a medieval work written from the perspective of a later Advaita school based on Śaṅkara's model, was important during the early reception of Buddhism in Europe and America in the nineteenth century because it cites the works of different schools of philosophy, including YOGĀCĀRA and Madhyamaka writers that were otherwise unknown at the time. As a literary genre, siddhānta reaches its full development in Tibet, where ever more detailed classifications of Indian and later Chinese, Tibetan, and Mongolian schools of Buddhism are found. Of particular importance are works known by the names of their authors: Dbu pa blo gsal (Upa Losel) (fl, fourteenth century), the first 'JAM DBYANGS BZHAD PA (1648–1721), and Lcang skya Rol pa'i rdo rje (1717–1786). Customarily Tibetan Buddhist siddhāntas employ the following structure: under the rubric of non-Buddhist (T. phyi pa) philosophies, they discuss the positions of the six schools that include Nyāya, Vaiśeṣika, JAINA, Sāṃkhya, Yoga, and Mīmāṃsā. They are all dismissed as inferior, based on their assertion of the existence of a self (ĀTMAN) and a creator deity (īśvara), both positions that are refuted in Buddhism. The Buddhist schools are set forth in ascending order, starting with the HĪNAYĀNA schools of VAIBHĀṢIKA and SAUTRĀNTIKA, followed by the Mahāyāna schools of Yogācāra and Madhyamaka. A typical structure for the presentation of each school was a tripartite division into the basis (gzhi), which set forth matters of epistemology and ontology; the path (lam), which set forth the structure of the path according to the particular school; and the fruition ('bras bu), which set forth the school's understanding of the enlightenment of ARHATs and buddhas. In Tibet, the genre of siddhānta was later expanded to include works that set forth the various sects and schools of Tibetan Buddhism and Chinese Buddhism. Cf. JIAOXIANG PANSHI.

**Siddhārtha**. (P. Siddhattha; T. Don grub; C. Xidaduo; J. Shiddatta/Shittatta; K. Siltalta 悉達多). In Sanskrit, "He Who Achieves His Goal," the personal name of GAUTAMA Buddha, also known as ŚĀKYAMUNI. In some accounts of the life of the Buddha, after his royal birth as the son of King ŚUDDHODANA, the BODHISATTVA was given this name and is referred to by that name during his life as a prince and his practice of asceticism. In the LALITAVISTARA, he is named Sarvārthasiddha, "He Who Achieves the Welfare of All." After his achievement of buddhahood, Siddhārtha is instead known as Gautama, Śākyamuni, or simply the TATHĀGATA. The name is perhaps best known in English as the title of the 1922 novel by Hermann Hesse, in which the protagonist (who is not the Buddha) is named Siddhartha.

**siddhi**. (T. dngos grub; C. xidi/chengjiu; J. shijji/jōju; K. silchi/sŏngch'wi 悉地/成就). In Sanskrit, "attainment" or "success," a power attained through tantric practice, often through the propitiation of a deity and the recitation of MANTRAs. Two types are identified: (1) mundane attainments (S. SĀDHĀRAṆASIDDHI), which are magical powers such as the ability to fly, to paralyze an enemy, to attract a lover, and to find buried treasure; and (2) the supreme attainment (S. UTTAMASIDDHI), viz., the attainment of buddhahood.

**si fajie**. (J. shihōkai/shihokkai; K. sa pŏpkye 四法界). In Chinese, "four DHARMADHĀTUS"; four successively more profound levels of reality as outlined in the HUAYAN ZONG: (1) the dharmadhātu of phenomena (SHI FAJIE); (2) the dharmadhātu of principle (LI FAJIE); (3) the dharmadhātu of the unimpeded interpenetration between phenomena and principle (LISHI WU'AI FAJIE); (4) the dharmadhātu of the unimpeded interpenetration between phenomenon and phenomena (SHISHI WU'AI FAJIE). This understanding of four successive levels of reality is widely used in Huayan classificatory schemata (see JIAOXIANG PANSHI; HUAYAN WIJIAO) of Buddhist doctrines and is also employed as a justification for the different soteriological techniques prescribed by the various Buddhist schools. See also DHARMADHĀTU.

**Sifen lü**. (J. Shibunritsu; K. Sabun yul 四分律). In Chinese, "Four-Part VINAYA"; the Chinese translation of the DHARMAGUPTAKA vinaya, the most influential of the different vinaya translations in East Asia, so-named because of the four main divisions into which the text was divided: (1) bhikṣuvibhaṅga, (2) bhikṣuṇīvibhaṅga, (3) SKANDHAKA, which includes a life of the Buddha and the twenty skandhaka, and (4) two Appendices, of saṃyuktavarga and vinayaikottara. The collection probably derives from some time in the first century BCE. With the support of the ruler Yao Xing (r. 394–416), the Kashmiri monk BUDDHAYAŚAS (d.u.; fl. c. early fifth century) recited the text from memory and translated it into Chinese with the help of the Chinese monk ZHU FONIAN (d.u.). Their work was carried out in the Chinese capital of Chang'an between 408 and 413 and was completed in sixty rolls. The Chinese translation is especially important because the Sanskrit recension is no longer extant and the text was never translated into Tibetan. The "Four-Part Vinaya" first circulated in the Chinese metropolitan centers of Chang'an and Luoyang, eventually replacing the other vinayas then circulating in China to became the definitive monastic code in East Asia. Exegetical schools such as DAOXUAN's NANSHAN LÜ ZONG (South Mountain vinaya school) and HUAISU's DONGTA LÜ ZONG (East Pagoda vinaya school), as well as the Korean YUL CHONG and the Japanese RITSUSHŪ, all focused on the explication of the "Four-Part

Vinaya." Among the numerous commentaries on the "Four-Part Vinaya," DAOXUAN's *Sifen lü shanfan buque xingshi chao* came to be regarded as most authoritative.

**Sigālovādasutta**. (S. Śīgālovādasūtra; C. Shansheng jing; J. Zenshōkyō; K. Sŏnsaeng kyŏng 善生經). In Pāli, "Instructions to Sigāla" (also known as the *Siṅgālovādasutta* and *Sigālakasutta*); thirty-first discourse in the Pāli DĪGHANIKĀYA (several different recensions appear in Chinese translations, including a DHARMAGUPTAKA recension that is the sixteenth sūtra in the DĪRGHĀGAMA, a SARVĀSTIVĀDA recension that is the 135th sūtra in the MADHYAMĀGAMA, and other recensions as well in the EKOTTARĀGAMA and SAṂYUKTĀGAMA); often interpreted within the tradition to offer the outlines of a code of conduct (VINAYA) for the laity. The buddha preached this discourse at Rājagaha (S. RĀJAGṚHA) to Sigāla [alt. Siṅgāla], a young brāhmaṇa householder. Following the wishes of his deceased father, it was Sigāla's practice to worship the six cardinal directions of east, south, west, north, nadir and zenith. The Buddha explains to him that the directions so worshipped are actually meant to symbolize, respectively, parents, teachers, wife and children, friends and associates, servants and workmen, and finally religious mendicants (ŚRAMAṆA) and brāhmaṇas. True veneration thus consists of fulfilling one's incumbent responsibilities toward each of these six groups of people, responsibilities that should be reciprocated in turn by each group. For instance, students should minister to teachers by rising to greet them, waiting on them, paying intention to their instructions, serving them, and mastering what they are taught; teachers in turn should minister to their students by thoroughly instructing them, making sure they have understood, grounding them in essential skills, recommending them to colleagues, and offering them security. The Buddha also offers practical advice on how to follow a well-lived life as a layperson, such as avoiding six ways of squandering wealth (viz., alcoholism, wandering the streets at inappropriate times, attending fairs and shows, gambling, keeping bad company, laziness), each of which in turn has six dangers.

**sights, four**. See CATURNIMITTA.

**sign**. See LAKṢAṆA; NIMITTA.

**signless**. See ĀNIMITTA.

**Sīhaḷadīpa**. In Pāli, "Island of Sīhaḷa"; the modern nation of Sri Lanka. According to Pāli sources, the island received the name Sīhaḷadīpa after it was colonized in the sixth century BCE by the Āryan Sīhaḷa peoples from northern India, led by Vijaya. Sīhaḷadīpa was the destination of one of nine Buddhist missions dispatched during the reign of King AŚOKA from Pātaliputta (S. PĀṬALIPUTRA, modern Patna) by the elder MOGGALIPUTTATISSA after the third Buddhist council (see COUNCIL, THIRD) in the third century BCE. Aśoka's son, the elder MAHINDA (S. Mahendra), was sent to Sīhaḷadīpa as a missionary, and since that time the island has been one of the major bastions of Buddhism in the region. Another common name for the island was Tambapaṇṇīdīpa, "Copper Island," named after the first capital, Tambapaṇṇī, founded by Vijaya.

**siho**. (C. shihao; J. shigō 諡號). In Korean, lit. "posthumous title," honorific title and/or name granted posthumously to an especially eminent Buddhist monk by the king. In ancient China, the shihao was originally a commendatory (or in some cases derogatory) title that was given to members of the royal clan and high government officials in accordance with their deeds. In Korea, the posthumous title came to be used in Confucian, secular, and Buddhist contexts, but virtually always in a commendatory denotation; it could signify both a name and/or an honorific title, presumably depending on the hierarchical status of the person. Siho became extremely popular in Korea, especially during the Chosŏn period, when Chosŏn kings received two-Sinograph-long siho from the Chinese emperor, which then became their posthumous names; officials also received siho, which were posthumous honorific titles bestowed by the king. Since the Koryŏ period, renowned Korean monks were given honorific titles such as "state preceptor" (KUKSA) and "royal preceptor" (wangsa), sometimes combined with posthumous names, as in the case of Chinul (1158–1210), who received both the posthumous title kuksa and the posthumous name Puril Pojo (Buddha Sun that Shines Universally; see POJO CHINUL). See also TANGHO.

**si hongshiyuan**. (J. shiguzeigan/shikuseigan; K. sa hongsŏwŏn 四弘誓願). In Chinese, the "four capacious vows," commonly known in English as the "four great vows"; a specific set of vows (S. PRAṆIDHĀNA) an adept takes that mark his initiation into the BODHISATTVA path and outline his continuing aspiration to seek buddhahood. There are two different formulations. By far the most common is the following list: (1) However innumerable sentient beings may be, I vow to save them all; (2) However inexhaustible the afflictions (KLEŚA) may be, I vow to eradicate them all; (3) However immeasurable the teachings may be, I vow to study them all; (4) However unsurpassed the path to buddhahood may be, I vow to attain it. This version of the bodhisattva vows is generally presumed to have first been formulated by TIANTAI ZHIYI (538–597) in his MOHE ZHIGUAN. These four great bodhisattva vows are frequently recited at the conclusion of MAHĀYĀNA Buddhist rituals in East Asia targeting both ordained and lay adherents. There is also an alternate list, known in India and Tibet, which runs as follows: (1) Those who are yet to be saved, I will save; (2) Those who are frightened, I will soothe; (3) Those who are unenlightened, I will awaken; (4) Those who are not yet in NIRVĀṆA, I will bring to nirvāṇa.

**sihuo**. (J. shiwaku; K. sahok 思惑). In Chinese, "misapprehensions associated with [instinctive] mentation"; the afflictions with which a person is born, also called "misapprehensions that arise at birth (jusheng qi)." The "misapprehensions associated with mentation" are ingrained patterns of reacting to sensory stimuli that involve clinging, revulsion, restlessness, or confusion. In contrast to the related "misapprehensions associated with [wrong] views" (JIANHUO), which are misapprehensions acquired and developed through wrong views (MITHYĀDṚṢṬI) and fallacious ideologies in the postnatal environment, sihuo operate at a level that is more subtle and reflexive. Jianhuo must be eradicated first before one can proceed to attenuate, and eventually eradicate, sihuo on the path of cultivation (BHĀVANĀMĀRGA); for this reason, sihuo are also known as "afflictions [that are eradicated at the stage of] the path of practice" (xiuhuo/xiudao suoduan huo). See also PARIKALPITAKLEŚĀVARAṆA; SAHAJAKLEŚĀVARAṆA.

**sikkhāpaccakkhāna**. [alt. sikkhāpaccakkhāta] (S. śikṣāpratyākhyāna; T. bslab pa spong ba/bslab pa 'bul pa; C. shexuejie; J. shagakukai; K. sahakkye 捨學戒). In Pāli, lit "disavowing/abandoning the training"; "secession from the order," or more colloquially "disrobing." In the contemporary THERAVĀDA tradition, monks (P. BHIKKHU; S. BHIKṢU) are free to leave the SAṂGHA at any time and, upon secession are no longer bound by the monastic rules of conduct. However, a set procedure must be followed for that act to be considered valid. If that procedure is not followed, the person will still officially continue to be considered a monk, for whom the monastic code remains binding. According to the Pāli VINAYA, for the act of secession from the order to be valid for a monk or a nun, four conditions must be met. (1) The monk or nun must be sane, and not overwhelmed by pain, delirium, or intoxication, or be possessed by spirits. (2) The monk or nun must have the intention of leaving the saṃgha; the act does not count if it is performed in jest or is coerced. (3) The monk or nun must make a clear, definitive statement that he or she is leaving the order; this statement must be made in the present tense, not in a conditional or a future tense. (4) The monk or nun must make his or her declaration before a competent human witness, who must be conscious and sane and understand what the monk or nun is saying and doing; making the declaration before a nonhuman being or an image, etc., is not sufficient. In addition to these minimum requirements laid down in the vinaya, the various national traditions of Sri Lanka and Southeast Asia typically enjoin further steps in the procedure to solemnify the ritual aspects of the act. In the Theravāda tradition of Thailand, a monk is allowed to secede from the order and reordain a maximum of seven times.

**śikṣā**. (P. sikkhā; T. bslab pa; C. xue; J. gaku; K. hak 學). In Sanskrit, "training," a general term for the practice of the dharma. It occurs in two major contexts. The first is the three trainings (TRIŚIKṢĀ), three overarching categories of Buddhist practice. They are (1) the training in higher morality (ADHIŚĪLAŚIKṢĀ), which encompasses all forms of restraint of body and speech, including lay and monastic precepts that serve as the foundation for the cultivation of concentration and wisdom; (2) the training in higher meditation (ADHISAMĀDHIŚIKṢĀ, also called adhicittaśikṣā), which encompasses all forms of meditative practice directed toward the achievement of states of concentration; and (3) the training in higher wisdom (ADHIPRAJÑĀŚIKṢĀ), which includes all study and meditation directed toward developing insight into the nature of reality. The second major denotation appears in the VINAYA, where the term śikṣā refers to the proper conduct of a monk, nun, novice, or layperson. In this context, śikṣā means behavior that conduces to following enjoined conduct. For laymen (UPĀSAKA) and laywomen (UPĀSIKĀ), for example, behavior conducive to keeping the five lay precepts (PAÑCAŚĪLA) would include treating even old and discarded cloth from the robe of a monk or nun with respect, making offerings of food and other requisites to monks and nuns, and refraining from privileging any doctrine above the Buddha's teachings.

**śikṣādattaka**. (T. bslab pa sbyin pa; C. yuxue; J. yogaku; K. yŏhak 與學). In Sanskrit, lit. "one who has been given [penance] training," viz., a "pārājika penitent"; a monk (or nun) who had transgressed one of the major precepts that bring "defeat" (PĀRĀJIKA) but continues to live in the monastery as a lifelong penitent. A pārājika monk or nun, such as one who engaged in sexual intercourse, would be given the lifelong punishment of being "not in communion" (ASAṂVĀSA) with the monastic community. The monk who is asaṃvāsa is not permitted to participate in any of the official monastic proceedings or ecclesiastical acts (KARMAN), thus effectively ostracizing him from the formal activities of the monastery. But in almost all extant recensions of the VINAYA (including those associated with the SARVĀSTIVĀDA, MŪLASARVĀSTIVĀDA, MAHĀSĀṂGHIKA, DHARMAGUPTAKA, and MAHĪŚĀSAKA schools), monks who have received the asaṃvāsa punishment could continue to live in the monastery even after their transgressions in the special status of a śikṣādattaka (or śikṣādattā for a nun). (The Pāli vinaya of the THERAVĀDA school is apparently the only recension that does not recognize the status of a śikṣādattaka, although the term is known to the Pāli commentarial tradition.) The śikṣādattaka was superior in status to regular novices (ŚRĀMAṆERA), the subordinate members of the SAṂGHA, but inferior to the most junior of monks (BHIKṢU). The śikṣādattaka was assigned such menial daily tasks as serving food to the senior monks or cleaning the toilets, and his actions were severely restricted: he was forbidden from teaching others, making extended trips outside the monastery, accepting the types of salutations and respect that monks normally would receive, or, in some traditions, listening to the PRĀTIMOKṢA recitation. These penances are similar to those meted out to monks on temporary probation (PARIVĀSA and MĀNATVA) for committing the SAṂGHĀVAŚEṢA offenses. The lifelong penance of the śikṣādattaka could be rescinded and the penitent restored to good standing if he subsequently became an ARHAT.

**śikṣamāṇā**. (P. sikkhamānā; T. dge slob ma; C. shichamona; J. shikishamana; K. sikch'amana 式叉摩那). In Sanskrit, female "postulant," or "probationer"; one of the categories of ordained women. Prior to receiving the full ordination (UPASAMPADĀ) of a nun (BHIKṢUṆĪ), a female novice (ŚRĀMAṆERIKĀ) was required to undergo a concurrent two-year period of probationary postulancy. During this period, she was expected to observe six specific rules of training (ŚIKṢĀPADA): (1) abstention from killing, (2) abstention from stealing, (3) abstention from sexual activity, (4) abstention from false speech, (5) abstention from intoxicants, and (6) abstention from eating after midday. (As a śrāmaṇerikā, she would also be expected to follow the usual set of ten precepts, or DAŚAŚĪLA, for novices, which subsume these six rules.) Only after completing this period would a śrāmaṇerikā be allowed to take full ordination. This postulancy requirement was the sixth of the eight "weighty rules" (GURUDHARMA) that the Buddha imposed on nuns as a condition of establishing the nun's SAṂGHA. Male novices (ŚRĀMAṆERA) were not required to undergo such a probationary period of training.

**śikṣamāṇāsaṃvara**. (T. dge slob ma'i sdom pa; C. shichamona jie; J. shikishamanakai; K. sikch'amana kye 式叉摩那戒). In Sanskrit, "restraints for a probationer"; the VINAYA rules to be followed by a female postulant (ŚIKṢAMĀṆĀ) during the probationary period before a female novice (ŚRĀMAṆERIKĀ) received full ordination (UPASAMPADĀ) as a nun (BHIKṢUṆĪ). In conjunction with the typical set of ten precepts (DAŚAŚĪLA) taken by novices (subdivided into thirty-six separate rules in the MŪLASARVĀSTIVĀDA school), these are six specific rules of training (ŚIKṢĀPADA): (1) abstention from killing, (2) abstention from stealing, (3) abstention from sexual activity, (4) abstention from false speech, (5) abstention from intoxicants, and (6) abstention from eating after midday. This additional set of rules, which had to be followed for two years before full ordination was allowed, constituted the sixth of the eight "weighty rules" (GURUDHARMA) that the Buddha imposed on nuns as a condition of establishing the nun's SAṂGHA. Some commentators say their purpose was to ensure that a probationer was not pregnant at the time of full ordination.

**Śikṣānanda**. (C. Shichanantuo; J. Jisshananda; K. Silch'anant'a 實叉難陀) (652–710). A monk from KHOTAN (C. Yutian), who was an important translator of Buddhist texts into Chinese during the Tang dynasty. The Empress WU ZETIAN (r. 690–705) invited Śikṣānanda to the Chinese capital of Luoyang, asking him to bring from Khotan its Sanskrit recension of the AVATAṂSAKASŪTRA (alt. *Buddhāvataṃsakasūtra*; C. *Dafangguang Fo huayan jing*), which was longer and more comprehensive than the sixty-roll version then in use in China, which had previously been translated by the Indian monk BUDDHABHADRA (359–429). Śikṣānanda arrived in Luoyang in 695 and supervised a translation team in rendering this Khotanese recension into Chinese; his team included BODHIRUCI (693–727), YIJING (635–713), and WŎNCH'ŬK (613–696). Śikṣānanda and his team finished their translation in 699, after four years of work, in a total of eighty rolls. The translation that Śikṣānanda supervised is typically called within the tradition the "new" (xin) translation, in contrast to Buddhabhadra's "old" translation. (LI TONGXUAN's commentary to Śikṣānanda's new rendering of the text is, for example, called the *Xin Huayan jing lun*; see HUAYAN JING HELUN.) Śikṣānanda continued with his translation projects until 705, when he returned to Khotan to care for his aged mother. Some thirteen other translations are attributed to him, including the LAṄKĀVATĀRASŪTRA and several shorter DHĀRAṆĪ sūtras, as well as a version of the DASHENG QIXIN LUN ("Awakening of Faith According to the Mahāyāna"). Emperor Zhongzong (r. 705–710) invited Śikṣānanda to return once again to China in 708, but he died of illness in 710 at the age of fifty-nine without beginning any new translation work. It is reported that after his cremation, his tongue remained untouched by flames—an indication of his remarkable erudition.

**śikṣāpada**. (P. sikkhāpada; T. bslab pa'i gzhi; C. xuechu; J. gakusho; K. hakch'ŏ 學處). In Sanskrit, lit. "training step"; "training rules," "precepts," or "moral instructions"; viz., various rules of conduct incumbent on both lay and monastic adherents of Buddhism. Theoretically, the number of śikṣāpadas, in the sense of situations where it is incumbent on an adherent to maintain proper moral decorum, is infinite, but the number of rules a specific adherent was expected to follow depended on his or her level of commitment. All these moral instructions are administered in the formula, "I undertake the training rule (śikṣāpada) to abstain from..." Thus, the Buddhist moral codes are not regarded as commandments handed down from on high, but steps in training that are found to be useful in promoting wholesome actions (KUŚALA-KARMAN) and in weaning the individual from clinging and attachment. It is generally understood that the practitioner must become adept in following these basic rules of training before he or she can go on to higher levels of training: the effective engagement in the cultivation of concentration (SAMĀDHI), wisdom (PRAJÑĀ), and so on. The five basic rules of conduct required of all Buddhists, and specifically the laity, are the five precepts (PAÑCAŚĪLA), viz., "undertaking the training rule to abstain from": (1) killing, (2) stealing, (3) sexual misconduct, (4) false speech, and (5) intoxicants. On full- and new-moon days (S. UPOṢADHA, P. uposatha), the laity had the option of increasing the number of śikṣāpada for their training in morality and keeping an expanded set of eight precepts (P. uposathasīla, see AṢṬĀṄGASAMANVĀGATAṂ UPAVĀSAṂ) as a sort of temporary renunciation. These added three precepts to the preceding list of five, viz., abstaining from: (6) eating after midday, (7) dancing, singing, music, and other unseemly forms of entertainment, and using garlands, perfumes, and unguents (viz., cosmetics) to adorn the body, and (8) using high and luxurious beds and couches. Additionally on that day, the layperson was also expected to abstain from all sexual activity, rather than just sexual misconduct defined specifically for the lay person. Ordination as a male novice (ŚRĀMAṆERA) or female novice (ŚRĀMAṆERIKĀ) required the ordinand to increase the number of śikṣāpada (grounds for moral training) to ten (DAŚAŚĪLA) in the Pāli VINAYA, a number expanded to thirty-six in the MŪLASARVĀSTIVĀDA VINAYA. Fully ordained monks (BHIKṢU) and nuns (BHIKṢUṆĪ) observed, in turn, a greatly expanded set of śikṣāpada codified in hundreds of specific training rules, set out in great detail in the various vinaya traditions. In MAHĀYĀNA and tantric Buddhist traditions, the śikṣāpada are expanded to include various activities, even those that seem antithetical to morality, under the general rubric of skillful means (UPĀYA). See also ŚĪLA; SAṂVARA; PRĀTIMOKṢA.

**Śikṣāsamuccaya**. (T. Bslab pa kun las btus pa; C. Dasheng ji pusa xue lun; J. Daijōjū bosatsugakuron; K. Taesŭng chip posal hak non 大乘集菩薩學論). In Sanskrit, "Compendium of Training," a work by the eighth-century Indian MAHĀYĀNA master ŚĀNTIDEVA. It consists of twenty-seven stanzas on the motivation and practice of the BODHISATTVA, including BODHICITTA, the six perfections (PĀRAMITĀ), the worship of buddhas and bodhisattvas, the benefits of renunciation, and the peace derived from the knowledge of emptiness (ŚŪNYATĀ). The topic of each of the stanzas receives elaboration in the form of a prose commentary by the author as well as in illustrative passages, often quite extensive, drawn from a wide variety of Mahāyāna SŪTRAs. Some ninety-seven texts are cited in all, many of which have been lost in their original Sanskrit, making the *Śikṣāsamuccaya* an especially important source for the textual history of Indian Buddhism. These citations also offer a window into which sūtras were known to a Mahāyāna author in eighth-century India. The digest of passages that Śāntideva provides was repeatedly drawn upon by Tibetan authors in their citations of sūtras. Although Śāntideva's BODHICARYĀVATĀRA and *Śikṣāsamuccaya* both deal with similar topics, the precise relation between the two texts is unclear. Several of the author's verses appear in both texts and some of the sūtra passages from the *Śikṣāsamuccaya* also appear in the *Bodhicaryāvatāra*. One passage in the *Bodhicaryāvatāra* also refers readers to the *Śikṣāsamuccaya*, but this line does not occur in the DUNHUANG manuscript of the text and may be a later interpolation.

**siku**. (J. shiko; K. sago 四枯). In Chinese, "four witherings." When the Buddha passed into PARINIRVĀṆA, there were said to be four pairs of ŚĀLA trees surrounding his body in the four cardinal directions. At his passing, one tree in each pair blossomed and the other withered. The four witherings are said to represent the four inverted views (VIPARYĀSA) as they pertain to the Buddha. These four views are typically listed as to see that which is painful as pleasurable, to see that which is impermanent as permanent, to see that which is impure as pure, and to see that which is without self as having self. In some texts, such as the ŚRĪMĀLĀDEVĪSIṂHANĀDASŪTRA, the TATHĀGATAGARBHA is said to be endowed with the four perfect qualities (GUṆAPĀRAMITĀ) of blissfulness, permanence, purity, and selfhood; however, in the context of the "four witherings," it is said to be a mistake to view NIRVĀṆA as blissful, the DHARMAKĀYA as eternal, the body of the Buddha as pure, and the tathāgatagarbha as self.

**śīla**. (P. sīla; T. tshul khrims; C. jie; J. kai; K. kye 戒). In Sanskrit, "morality"; those practices whose aim is to restrain nonvirtuous deeds of body and speech, often in conjunction with the keeping of precepts. Morality constitutes one of the three trainings (TRIŚIKṢĀ), together with SAMĀDHI and PRAJÑĀ, and the second of the six perfections (PĀRAMITĀ). In the traditional organization of the constituents of the noble eightfold path (ĀRYĀṢṬĀṄGAMĀRGA) under the rubrics of the three higher trainings (adhiśikṣā), the "morality group" (śīlaskandha; see ADHIŚĪLAŚIKṢĀ) consists of right speech (S. SAMYAGVĀC; P. sammāvācā), right action (S. SAMYAKKARMĀNTA; P. sammākammanta), and right livelihood (S. SAMYAGĀJĪVA; P. sammājīva). The term also appears in the five precepts, or PAÑCAŚĪLA, the five precepts taken by the Buddhist laity: "I undertake the training rules (ŚIKṢĀPADA) to abstain from" (1) killing living creatures, (2) stealing, (3) sexual misconduct, (4) false speech, and (5) consuming intoxicants. On full- and new-moon days (UPOṢADHA), the laity had the option of taking a modified version of these precepts as a sort of temporary renunciation, which are termed the eight precepts (S. see AṢṬĀṄGASAMANVĀGATAṂ UPAVĀSAṂ; BAGUAN ZHAI). They are (1) not to kill living beings, (2) not to steal, (3) not to engage to sexual activity, (4) not to lie about spiritual attainments, (5) not to use intoxicants, (6) not to eat after twelve noon, (7) not to sing, dance, play music, or attend entertainments and not to wear perfumes, garlands, or cosmetics, (8) not to sleep on high beds. All male novices (ŚRĀMAṆERA) and female novices (ŚRĀMAṆERIKĀ) were required to follow as part of their training the ten precepts (DAŚAŚĪLA), which were an expansion and enhancement of the five lay precepts (pañcaśīla): "I undertake the training rule to abstain from" (1) killing, (2) stealing, (3) sexual activity, (4) false speech, (5) intoxicants, (6) eating after midday, (7) dancing, singing, music, and other unseemly forms of entertainment, (8) using garlands, perfumes, and cosmetics to adorn the body, (9) using high and luxurious beds and couches, (10) handling money. In the context of the bodhisattva's perfection of morality (ŚĪLAPĀRAMITĀ), the meaning of śīla is expanded to encompass the taking and keeping of the bodhisattva precepts (BODHISATTVASAṂVARA); see SAṂVARA; ŚĪLAPĀRAMITĀ; ŚĪLATRAYA.

**Śīlabhadra**. (T. Ngang tshul bzang po; C. Jiexian; J. Kaigen; K. Kyehyŏn 戒賢) (529–645). Indian YOGĀCĀRA monk who hailed from the NĀLANDĀ monastic university in India. A native of the Samataṭa kingdom in eastern India, he resided at Nālandā after meeting DHARMAPĀLA (530–561) there. Śīlabhadra is perhaps best known as the principal teacher of XUANZANG, the great Chinese pilgrim and translator. Through Xuanzang's contact with Śīlabhadra, Dharmapāla's scholastic lineage was brought back to China, where it served as the foundation of the Chinese FAXIANG ZONG, which was developed by Xuanzang and his two main disciples, WŎNCH'ŬK and KUIJI. It is recorded that Śīlabhadra was already 106 years old when Xuanzang came to Nālandā to study with him. FAZANG (643–712) in his *Dasheng qixinlun yiji* quotes Divākara (613–687, C. Rizhao), a monk from central India, who describes the controversy between Śīlabhadra, as the successor of Dharmapāla within the Indian Yogācāra tradition, and Jñānaprabha (d.u., C. Zhiguang), a successor of BHĀVAVIVEKA (c. 490–570) in the SVĀTANTRIKA-MADHYAMAKA tradition.

**Śīladharma**. (C. Shiluodamo/Jiefa; J. Shiradatsuma/Kaihō; K. Siradalma/Kyebŏp 尸羅達摩/戒法) (d.u., fl. c. eighth-ninth centuries). A translator-monk from KHOTAN (C. Yutian), who stayed at the monastery of Longxingsi in Beiting (present-day Inner Mongolia), during the Tang dynasty. Wukong (d. 812), a Chinese pilgrim who spent some forty years sojourning in India and Central Asia, arrived in Beiting in 789 with several Sanskrit manuscripts of Indian scriptures. Wukong asked Śīladharma to collaborate with him in translating two of the sūtras he brought back with him into Chinese: the DAŚABHŪMIKASŪTRA (*Foshuo shidi jing*) and the *Pariṇāmacakrasūtra* (*Huixianglun jing*). Upon completing the translations, Śīladharma accompanied Wukong to the Tang capital of Chang'an in 790, where they had an audience at the imperial court, after which Śīladharma returned to his home country.

**śīlapāramitā**. (P. sīlapāramī; T. tshul khrims kyi pha rol tu phyin pa; C. jie boluomi; J. kaiharamitsu; K. kye p'aramil 戒波羅蜜). In Sanskrit, "perfection of morality," the second of the six or ten "perfections" (PĀRAMITĀ) of the BODHISATTVA, along with the perfection of charity (DĀNAPĀRAMITĀ), forbearance (KṢĀNTIPĀRAMITĀ), effort (VĪRYAPĀRAMITĀ), meditation (DHYĀNAPĀRAMITĀ), and wisdom (PRAJÑĀPĀRAMITĀ); and, in the longer list, the perfection of expedients (UPĀYAPĀRAMITĀ), vow (PRAṆIDHĀNAPĀRAMITĀ), power (BALAPĀRAMITĀ), and knowledge (JÑĀNAPĀRAMITĀ). In the MAHĀYĀNA tradition, the perfection of morality is accomplished through the bodhisattva precepts, and specifically "three sets of pure precepts" (trividhāni śīlāni; C. sanju jingjie, see ŚĪLATRAYA): (1) the saṃvaraśīla (see PRĀTIMOKṢASAṂVARA), or "restraining precepts," which refers to the rules of discipline (PRĀTIMOKṢA) and deportment that help adepts restrain themselves from all types of unwholesome conduct; (2) the accumulation of wholesome qualities (kuśaladharmasaṃgrāhaka), which accumulates all types of wholesome conduct that give rise to the buddhadharmas; and (3) SATTVĀRTHAKRIYĀ, acting for the welfare of beings, which involve giving aid and comfort to sentient beings. Here, the first group corresponds to the preliminary "HĪNAYĀNA" precepts, while the second and third groups are regarded as reflecting a Mahāyāna position on morality. Thus, the perfection of morality, through the three sets of pure precepts, is conceived as a comprehensive description of Buddhist views on precepts, which incorporates both hīnayāna and Mahāyāna perspectives into an overarching system. According to the CHENG WEISHI LUN (**Vijñaptimātratāsiddhi*), each of the ten stages (BHŪMI) of the bodhisattva path leads to the attainment of one of the ten kinds of suchness (TATHATĀ), through practicing one of the ten perfections (pāramitā) and thus overcoming one of the ten types of obstructions (ĀVARAṆA). As the second perfection, śīlapāramitā is practiced on the second stage of the bodhisattva path, the VIMALĀ (immaculate, stainless) bhūmi, and leads to the attainment of supreme suchness (paramarthatathatā; C. zuisheng zhenru), by overcoming the obstruction of deluded conduct (mithyāpratipattyāvaraṇa; C. xiexing zhang).

**śīlatraya**. (T. tshul khrims gsum; C. sanju jingjie; J. sanju jōkai; K. samch'wi chŏnggye 三聚淨戒). In Sanskrit, "three categories of morality" (also called the trividhāni śīlāni); a categorization of moral codes found typically in YOGĀCĀRA-oriented materials, which also becomes especially popular in indigenous East Asian scriptures (see APOCRYPHA). They are: (1) the restraining precepts, which maintain both the discipline and the deportments (saṃvaraśīla; see PRĀTIMOKṢASAṂVARA); (2) the accumulation of wholesome qualities (kuśaladharmasaṃgrāhaka); and (3) acting for the welfare of beings (SATTVĀRTHAKRIYĀ). Here, the first group corresponds to the preliminary "HĪNAYĀNA" precepts, while the second and third groups are regarded as reflecting a Mahāyāna position on morality. Thus, the three sets of pure precepts are conceived as a comprehensive description of Buddhist views on precepts, which incorporates both hīnayāna and Mahāyāna perspectives into an overarching system; and it is these three categories that are said to constitute the perfection of morality (ŚĪLAPĀRAMITĀ). These three categories are explained in such Yogācāra materials as the BODHISATTVABHŪMI section of the YOGĀCĀRABHŪMIŚĀSTRA and in the MAHĀYĀNASŪTRĀLAṂKĀRA and in several East Asian apocryphal scriptures, including the FANWANG JING, PUSA YINGLUO BENYE JING, *VAJRASAMĀDHISŪTRA (KŬMGANG SAMMAE KYŎNG), and the ZHANCHA SHAN'E YEBAO JING. See also SAṂVARA; SDOM GSUM.

**śīlaviśuddhi**. (P. sīlavisuddhi; T. tshul khrims rnam par dag pa; C. jingjie; J. jōkai; K. chŏnggye 淨戒). In Sanskrit, "purity of morality." In Pāli sources, the "purity of morality" was the first of seven "purities" (P. VISUDDHI) that were to be developed along the path to liberation. According to the treatment in BUDDHAGHOSA's VISUDDHIMAGGA, purity of morality refers to the proper observance of morality by a monk and is of four kinds: (1) "Morality of restraint according to the monastic code" (P. pāṭimokkhasaṃvarasīla; see S. PRĀTIMOKṢASAṂVARA); here the monk is perfect in observance of the rules of discipline laid down in the VINAYA, seeing danger in even minor offenses. (2) "Morality of restraint of the senses" (INDRIYASAṂVARA-sīla); the monk guards his senses so that unwholesome states of mind do not arise. (3) "Morality of the purity of livelihood" (P. ājīvapārisuddhisīla); the monk refrains from means of support that are not allowed by the rules of discipline. (4) "Morality with regard to the requisites" (P. paccayasannissitasīla); the monk mindfully makes proper use of the four requisites (see NIŚRAYA; PARIṢKĀRA) allowed to the monk; namely, alms food (PIṆḌAPĀTA), robes (CĪVARA), dwelling places, and medicine. Alms food is to be consumed merely to support the body. Robes are to be used merely to protect the body from heat and cold. Dwelling places are to be used merely to protect the body from the elements and to encourage solitude. Medicine is to be used merely to alleviate symptoms of illness and pain so that the monk may pursue the religious life.

**śīlavrataparāmarśa**. (P. sīlabbataparāmāsa; T. tshul khrims dang brtul zhugs mchog tu 'dzin pa; C. jiejinqu jian; J. kaigonjuken; K. kyegŭmch'wi kyŏn 戒禁取見). In Sanskrit, "attachment to rites and rituals" or "clinging to faulty disciplinary codes and modes of conduct" (lit. "holding [mistaken] rites and conduct to be superior"); the third of ten fetters (SAṂYOJANA) that keep beings bound to the cycle of rebirth (SAṂSĀRA). This type of attachment is one of the first three fetters that are permanently abandoned upon becoming a stream-enterer (SROTAĀPANNA), along with belief in the existence of a perduring self (SATKĀYADṚṢṬI) and doubts about the efficacy of the path (VICIKITSĀ). This specific type of attachment constitutes the wrong view (DṚṢṬI) that certain purificatory rites, such as bathing in the Ganges River or performing ritual sacrifices, can free a person from the consequences of unmeritorious action (AKUŚALA-KARMAN). Attachment to rites and rituals thus often constitutes either a belief in non-Buddhist religious systems, or a clinging to those elements of non-Buddhist systems that run contrary to Buddhist doctrine. Attachment to rites and rituals is also one of the four kinds of clinging (UPĀDĀNA), along with clinging to sensuality (RĀGA), which is a strong attachment to pleasing sense objects; clinging to false views and speculative theories (DṚṢṬI); and clinging to mistaken beliefs in a perduring self (ĀTMAVĀDA), viz., the attachment to the transitory mind and body as a real I and mine.

**Silent Illumination Zen**. See MOZHAO CHAN.

**Silk Road**. (C. Silu 絲路; J. Shiruku rōdo シルクロード; K. Pidan kil 緋緞길). Term coined by the German geographer Baron Ferdinand von Richthofen in 1877 to describe the ancient caravan routes through Central Asia that connected China, India, Syria, and the Roman Empire; also called the Silk Route. (Translations or transcriptions of the English term are now widely used in Asian languages as well, as in the CJK examples above.) Because silk was among the most highly prized commodities in this East–West trade, von Richthofen chose it as the symbolic designation for these trade routes. Other commodities that were traded along these routes included spices, livestock, perfumes, precious metals, and ceramics. The term Silk Road does not refer to a single road, but rather to a network of major and minor trade routes running through Central Asia that connected East and West. Looked at broadly, the Silk Road ultimately extended as far west as the Mediterranean Sea and as far east as modern Guangzhou (Canton) in China. In addition to facilitating trade, these routes also served as a principal conduit for cultural and religious interaction between the peoples of the different regions of Asia. Thus, it was via the Silk Road that Buddhism migrated out of its Indian homeland and into Central and East Asia; over the centuries, adherents of other religions, such as Nestorian Christianity, Manichaeism, and eventually Islam, would follow the same routes into India and China. From the Indian subcontinent, the Silk Road led northwest through KASHMIR to the outpost of Kashgar; there, it split, with a western route leading to SOGDIANA and eventually Damascus in the Middle East, and an eastern route leading through Central Asia into China and the rest of East Asia. There were two main routes through the oasis kingdoms of Central Asia, both skirting the Takla Makan desert in the Tarim basin. Starting at the city of Kashgar in the west, the northern route moved along the oases kingdoms of KUCHA, TURFAN, and KIZIL along the Tian Mountains; the southern route traveled along the base of the Kunlun Mountains through Niya and KHOTAN, until both routes reconnected at DUNHUANG, often the farthest outpost of the Chinese empire. From Dunhuang the route continued east until it terminated in the Chinese co-capitals of Chang'an and Luoyang, whence it connected to domestic feeder routes spreading throughout East Asia. Many of these Central Asian city-states were populated by various Indo-European peoples. The only remaining evidence of the long-lost native languages of these peoples are inscriptions and fragments of religious and civil-government manuscripts, such as the Niya documents, Gandhāran texts in the KHAROṢṬHĪ script, documents written in the TOCHARIAN and Kuchean languages, and so on. Scores of these documents were discovered in the nineteenth and twentieth centuries. In missions that began shortly after the death of the Buddha, Indian Buddhist monks accompanied the trading caravans that plied the overland Silk Road. These missions lasted for centuries and changed the religious and cultural landscape of Asia. Buddhist inscriptions, sculptures, manuscripts, reliquary mounds (STŪPA), and paintings have been discovered along the Silk Road. From northwestern India, Buddhism was taken to Central Asia. We find a host of inscriptions, texts, and images in the regions of modern-day Pakistan, Afghanistan, Russia, and the Islamic states of the former Soviet Union. By the first century CE, there existed a network of Buddhist religious centers stretching from northwestern India, to the Tarim basin, and into China. Buddhism entered East Asia along the Silk Road as well. According to Chinese sources, interaction between Indian and Chinese culture began as early as the first century BCE, when an emperor of the Han dynasty—by some accounts Emperor Wu (156–87 BCE), by others Emperor Ming (MINGDI) (r. 58–76 CE)—is said to have sent an emissary to the west along the Silk Road in response to the expansion of the KUSHAN empire to gather evidence of the new religion of Buddhism. In the second century CE, monks from India and the oasis kingdoms along the

Silk Road began translating Indian and Central Asian Buddhist texts into Chinese. One of the earliest of these translators was AN SHIGAO, who translated dozens of Indian works into Chinese. In the centuries that followed, East Asian pilgrims such as FAXIAN, XUANZANG, YIJING, and HYECH'O used the Silk Road to make their way back and forth between East Asia and the Buddhist homeland of India. From India, these pilgrims brought back manuscripts, relics, and insights into proper religious practice. Today the travelogues of these East Asian monks provide invaluable information regarding the development of Buddhism in Asia. Of the regions along the Silk Road where Buddhism flourished, China, Tibet, and Mongolia are the only ones where Buddhism survived beyond the first millennium CE. This decline was the result of a number of historical factors, including the revival of brahmanical Hinduism in India and the expansion of Islam into Central Asia.

**śilpanirmāṇakāya**. [alt. śilpinirmāṇakāya] (T. bzo bo sprul sku). In Sanskrit, "artisan emanation body," one of the various of emanation bodies (NIRMĀṆAKĀYA) in which a buddha may appear to the world. As the name suggests, in this case, a buddha may appear as a skilled artisan. The example that is typically cited for this type of body is when the Buddha, shortly before his passage into NIRVĀṆA, took the form a celestial musician (GANDHARVA) and challenged Sunanda, the king of the celestial musicians, to a lute-playing competition. The Buddha defeated him by playing a beautiful melody on a lute that had no strings. It is said that an artisan emanation body may also take the form of a work of art that is inspiring or calming.

**sīmā**. (T. mtshams; C. jiejie; J. kekkai; K. kyŏlgye 結界). In Sanskrit and Pāli, lit. "boundary"; the line that marks the geographical area within which monks and nuns gather fortnightly to recite the PRĀTIMOKṢA and perform other required acts and duties, called collectively ecclesiastical acts (SAṂGHAKARMAN). The term is used by extension to refer to the area itself and the congregation that resides within it. The area encompassed by a sīmā boundary may vary in size and include more than one VIHĀRA or monastic residence within its perimeter. In order to establish a sīmā, the SAṂGHA enacts a JÑAPTIDVITĪYĀ KARMAVĀCANĀ, an ecclesiastical act comprised of a resolution and a proclamation, whereby the boundaries of the sīmā are marked. A marker (nimitta) may be a natural object or be man-made; possible markers include a mountain, a large stone, a grove, a tree, a road, an ant hill, a river, or an expanse of water. In some cases, sīmās are not demarcated with physical objects and do not require a resolution and proclamation to establish them. For example, when monks live near a village, the natural boundary of the village itself may be taken as the sīmā. When dwelling in a forest, an area encompassed by seven specific units of length could comprise the sīmā. When monks were on a boat in a river, lake, or the sea, the sīmā could be established by the distance a person of average strength could throw water in a perimeter around the boat. In tantric Buddhism, sīmā is used to describe the boundaries practitioners draw for themselves when they enter into a retreat (T. mtshams). The boundaries can be drawn (T. mtshams tho) narrowly when there are others to bring food and other requisites, or more widely as circumstances require.

**sīmāsamūhana**. (T. mtshams 'jig pa; C. shejie/jiejie; J. shakai/gekai; K. sagye/haegye 捨界/解界). In Sanskrit and Pāli, "abolition of a boundary"; an ecclesiastical act (P. saṅghakamma; S. SAṂGHAKARMAN) whereby an existing boundary (SĪMĀ) is either abolished or altered. The sīmāsamūha may be performed when the resident SAṂGHA determines that the existing sīmā boundaries are either too small or too large. Since the boundaries of separate sīmās may neither overlap nor encompass one another, it is customary (as, for example, in Burma) when preparing an area for a new sīmā to perform a sīmāsamūhana ceremony beforehand in order to remove any sīmā that might previously have been established at the spot. The MŪLASARVĀSTIVĀDA VINAYA describes five ways in which a sīmā boundary may be abolished (including by a complete sex change for the entire saṃgha).

**siṃhanāda**. (P. sīhanāda; T. seng ge'i nga ro; C. shizi hu; J. shishiku; K. saja hu 師子吼). In Sanskrit, "lion's roar," a phrase commonly used to describe the teaching of the Buddha or his disciples. It is said that when the lion roars in the forest, all other animals become silent and listen; in the same way, the Buddha's proclamation of the DHARMA silences all non-Buddhist teachers (TĪRTHIKA), who are afraid to challenge him. The Buddha is often compared to a lion, the king of beasts: "lion among men" (S. narasiṃha) is an epithet of the Buddha, the Buddha's seat is called the lion's throne (SIṂHĀSANA), and his walk is called the lion's gait (siṃhavikrānta). According to the Pāli commentaries, there are two kinds of lion's roar: that of the Buddha and that of his disciples. The former applies specifically to those cases in which the Buddha proclaims his own attainments or the power of the dharma. The latter refers to those cases when disciples announce their attainment of the rank of ARHAT and their subsequent inspiriational teachings. The Buddha declared that PIṆḌOLA-BHĀRADVĀJA was the foremost lion-roarer (siṃhanādin) among his disciples. These utterances are described as a lion's roar in the ĀGAMAs and Pāli NIKĀYAs because of their incontrovertible veracity, boundless self-confidence, and ability to inspire others to urgency in their practice. Just as the lion's roar may horrify other creatures, a lion's roar may also instill fear in lesser beings, such as teachings on impermanence that strike fear into the hearts of long-lived divinities (DEVA) who mistakenly presume they are immortal. One of the best-known siṃhanāda in the literature (as recorded, e.g., in the NIDĀNAKATHĀ), is the lion's roar that GAUTAMA is said to have uttered immediately after his birth. Pointing to heaven and earth, he took seven steps and said: "I am the chief of the world." The term figures prominently in Buddhist literature, as in the MAHĀSĪHANĀDASUTTA and the CŪḶASĪHANĀDASUTTA of the MAJJHIMANIKĀYA, and in the ŚRĪMĀLĀDEVĪSIṂHANĀDASŪTRA. It also occurs in the names of deities, such as Lokeśvara Siṃhanāda, a form of AVALOKITEŚVARA.

**siṃhāsana**. (P. sīhāsana; T. seng ge'i khri; C. shizi zuo; J. shishiza; K. saja chwa 師子座). In Sanskrit, "lion's throne," or "lion's seat"; the seat that a buddha or an enlightened master uses when delivering a discourse. One of the buddha's epithets is "lion among men" (narasiṃha, P. narasīha) and where he sits therefore comes to be called the "lion's throne," regardless of whether that seat is a high platform or the bare ground. Throughout the Buddhist tradition, images of lions are carved not only on the seats of buddha images but on various other Buddhist architectural structures, such as STŪPAs. The siṃhāsana is also one of two most prevalent platforms for a buddha image in East Asian Buddhism, along with the "lotus seat" (padmasaṃstha, C. lianhwa zuo).

**Siming shiyi shu**. (J. Shimei jūgisho; K. Samyŏng sibŭi sŏ 四明十義書). In Chinese, "Siming's Letters on Ten Issues"; a collection of letters compiled by the TIANTAI monk SIMING ZHILI (960–1028) and edited together in 1006. The *Siming shiyi shu* is a valuable source of information on the SHANJIA SHANWAI, or "Home-Mountain/Off-Mountain," debate within the Song-dynasty Tiantai school. Two recensions of TIANTAI ZHIYI's commentary on the SUVARṆAPRABHĀSOTTAMASŪTRA, an expanded and an abridged version, were known to have circulated during the late Tang and early Five Dynasties period. Zhili and the Shanjia faction, which later came to define Tiantai orthodoxy, defended the expanded recension when the monk Ciguang Wu'en (912–986) and others of the so-called Shanwai faction began questioning the authenticity of certain of its passages, particularly the ten modes of contemplation found in the text. The *Siming shiyi shu* speaks of Zhiyi's teachings on contemplation in ten general points: (1) not discerning the subject of contemplation, (2) not discerning the object of contemplation, (3) not distinguishing between inside and outside, (4) not constructing the duality of principle and phenomena, (5) not elucidating the workings of contemplation, (6) not lingering on the difficulties of the mind, (7) not knowing the levels of contemplation, (8) not collecting the meanings of contemplation, (9) not being skilled at collecting passages, (10) not being skilled at studying principle.

**Siming Zhili**. (J. Shimei Chirei; K. Samyŏng Chirye 四明知禮) (960–1028). Chinese monk of the TIANTAI tradition. Zhili was a native of Siming in present-day Zhejiang province. After losing his mother at an early age, Zhili resolved to become a monk and he received the full monastic precepts at age fifteen. He then studied the VINAYA and the scriptures of the Tiantai tradition. In 991, he became the abbot of Ganfusi, and four years later he began his residence at the monastery Bao'enyuan on Mt. Siming, whence his toponym. In 1009, he completed the restoration of Bao'enyuan and the following year his monastery received the official plaque renaming it Yanqingsi. Zhili later found himself at the center of the SHANJIA SHANWAI or "Home-Mountain/Off-Mountain" debate that racked the Song-dynasty Tiantai school. Zhili's Shanjia (Home Mountain) faction and the Tiantai monk Ciguang Wu'en's (912–986) Shanwai (Off Mountain) faction were split over the authenticity of one of TIANTAI ZHIYI's texts and the practice of contemplation, as well as the role and value of practices and concepts generated from outside the Tiantai tradition in explicating Tiantai doctrine. In response to this debate, Zhili composed a series of letters, which were edited together as the SIMING SHIYI SHU. Zhili also composed the *Shibu'er men zhiyao chao* and wrote extensively on various PURE LAND-related repentance rituals. Zhili's disciples later comprised three separate branches of the Chinese Tiantai tradition.

**Simsang**. (C. Shenxiang; J. Shinjō 審祥) (d. c. 744). Putative Korean disciple of FAZANG (643–712) in the Chinese HUAYAN ZONG. Simsang is considered the first transmitter of the Huayan teachings in Japan, and his Japanese disciple RYŌBEN (689–773) is considered the official founder of the Japanese Kegonshū during the Nara period.

**sin**. See PĀPA; AKUŚALA; AKUŚALAKARMAPATHA; KARMAN; KARMAPATHA.

**Sindu**. (S). One of the twenty-four sacred sites associated with the CAKRASAṂVARATANTRA. See PĪṬHA.

**Sin'gyesa**. (神溪寺). In Korean, "Divine Brook Monastery"; one of the major monasteries on the Korean sacred mountain of KŬMGANGSAN (Diamond Mountains), now in North Korea. The monastery is claimed to have been constructed in 519 during the Silla dynasty by the monk Poun (d.u.). Its original name, Sin'gyesa, "Silla Brook Monastery," uses instead the homophonous sin (lit. new), the first character in Silla (Sin-la), presumably in honor of the Silla dynasty. The monastery received its current name after the founding monk Poun is said to have used his magical powers (ṚDDHI) to move fish that people were trying to catch out of the brook next to the monastery, because he thought that fishing corrupted the sacred place. The monastery underwent frequent repairs and reconstructions, before being completely destroyed in 1950 during the Korean War (1950–1953). Sin'gyesa was reconstructed starting in 2004 through the cooperative efforts of the South Korean CHOGYE CHONG and the North Korean Buddhist Federation.

**Sinhŭngsa**. (神興寺). In Korean, "Divinely Flourishing Monastery"; the third district monastery (PONSA) of the contemporary CHOGYE CHONG of Korean Buddhism, located in Outer Sŏraksan (Snowy Peaks Mountain) near the town of Sokch'o. The monastery was founded in 652 by the Silla VINAYA master CHAJANG (d.u.; fl. c. mid-seventh century), who named it Hyangsŏngsa, or City of Fragrances [see GANDHAVATĪ] (monastery), but it has been nicknamed "Monastery of Frequent Changes" because it has changed its location, name, and school affiliation so many times over the centuries. When Hyangsŏngsa burned down in 698, the Silla Hwaŏm (C. HUAYAN) teacher ŬISANG (625–702) had it rebuilt three years later near its current site and renamed it Sŏnjŏngsa (Meditative Absorption Monastery). The monastery was damaged during the Japanese Hideyoshi invasions of 1592–1598 and burned to the ground in 1642. The three monks who remained after the conflagration each dreamed of a spirit who told them that relocating the monastery's campus would protect it from any future damage by fire, water, or wind. Following the spirit's recommendation, the monks moved the site ten leagues (K. i; C. li) below where the monastery was then located and renamed it Sinhŭngsa, the name it has kept ever since. Sinhŭngsa proper is built on a foundation of natural stone with four large cornerstones. The visitor reaches the monastery along a half-mile-long path that is flanked by reliquaries and memorial stele until reaching the Ilchumun (Single Pillar Gate). Sinhŭngsa's main shrine hall is the Kŭngnak pojŏn (SUKHĀVATĪ Basilica), which faces west and is decorated on the outside by the ten ox-herding paintings (see OXHERDING PICTURES, TEN). Inside, AMITĀBHA is enshrined together with his companion BODHISATTVAS, AVALOKITEŚVARA and MAHĀSTHĀMAPRĀPTA; they sit below a canopy of yellow dragons and in front of a painting of ŚĀKYAMUNI with an elderly KĀŚYAPA and a young-looking ĀNANDA. Right after entering the Ilchumun is found the 14.6-meter (48 foot) high T'ongil Taebul (Unification Great Buddha) sitting on a 4.3 meter (14 foot) pedestal. Casting of this bronze image started in 1987 and was finished ten years later; it is now the largest seated bronze buddha image in the world, larger even than the Japanese KAMAKURA DAIBUTSU (at 13.35 meters, or 44 feet, high). Its pedestal is decorated with images of the sixteen ARHAT protectors of Buddhism (see ṢOḌAŚASTHAVIRA). This monastery should be distinguished from the homophonous Sinhŭngsa (Newly Flourishing Monastery), located in the T'aebaek Mountains near the city of Samch'ŏk in Kangwŏn province; that temple is the fourth district monastery of the Chogye order.

**sinjung**. (C. shenzhong; J. shinshū 神衆). In Korean, "host of spirits"; referring to the LOKAPĀLAs, the protectors of the dharma (DHARMAPĀLA). The sinjung are often headed by KUMĀRABHŪTA (K. Tongjin), who appears in a grand, feathered headdress accompanied by over a dozen associates, who aid him in protecting the religion. Originally Hindu deities, the sinjung were adopted into Buddhism as guardian deities after being converted by the Buddha's teachings. In particular, BRAHMĀ (K. Pŏm Ch'ŏnwang), INDRA (K. Chesŏk ch'ŏn), the four heavenly kings (S. CATURMAHĀRĀJA; K. sa ch'ŏn wang), and WEITUO (K. Wit'a) were so popular that many statues and paintings were made of them. As the SUVARṆAPRABHĀSOTTAMASŪTRA gained popularity in East Asian Buddhism, the sinjung also came to be regarded as protectors of the state as well as the dharma. Imported to Korea along with Buddhism, the sinjung also came to be worshipped in state Buddhist services. During the Chosŏn dynasty, when Neo-Confucianism replaced Buddhism as the state religion, the role of the sinjung stretched into the personal realm as well, including protecting against disease. Many of the sinjung derive from such Buddhist sūtras as the AVATAṂSAKASŪTRA, the SADDHARMAPUṆḌARĪKASŪTRA ("Lotus Sūtra"), and the RENWANG JING ("Scripture for Humane Kings"), but there are also indigenous sinjung who originated from within the Chinese and Korean religious traditions. Hanging paintings (T'AENGHWA) of the sinjung are often displayed on the right wall of the main shrine halls (TAEUNG CHŎN) in Korean monasteries. These paintings vary widely, and the main figures include: (1) Chesŏk ch'ŏn (Indra), alone without associates; (2) Yejŏk Kŭmgang (the vajra-ruler who purifies unclean places), with Chesŏk ch'ŏn on his left side and Pŏm Ch'ŏnwang (Brahmā) on his right; (3) Wit'a (Weituo) with the same associates of Yejŏk Kŭmgang to his sides; (4) thirty-nine sinjung from the *Avataṃsakasūtra*; (4) 104 sinjung, including all the indigenous sinjung.

**Siri Sanga Bō**. (P. Saṅghabodhi). A Sri Lankan king (r. 252–254 CE) whose story of utter devotion to Buddhism is told in the MAHĀVAMSA. The king was said to have been so committed to the Buddha's teachings that he refused to execute criminals. When his prime minister led a rebellion against him, he could not bear the thought of the bloodshed that would result from putting down the rebellion, so he voluntarily abdicated and retired to the forest to live as an ascetic. The prime minister, now King Gathābhaya, fearing the return of the rightful king, offered a reward to anyone who would bring him the head of Siri Sanga Bō. One day, a poor peasant shared his meal with Siri Sanga Bō who, having nothing to give him in return, informed the man of his identity and offered him his head, decapitating himself. Siri Sanga Bō is regarded as a great Buddhist saint in Sri Lanka.

**Sishi'er zhang jing**. (J. Shijūnishōgyō; K. Sasibi chang kyŏng 四十二章經). In Chinese, "Scripture in Forty-two Sections," a short collection of aphorisms and pithy moralistic parables traditionally regarded as the first Indian Buddhist scripture to be translated into Chinese, but now generally presumed to be an indigenous scripture (see APOCRYPHA) that was compiled in either China or Central Asia. Most scholars believe that the "Scripture in Forty-Two Sections" began to circulate during the earliest period of Buddhism in China. According to tradition, the "Scripture in Forty-Two Sections" was translated at the behest of MINGDI of the Han dynasty (r. 58–75 CE). According to the earliest surviving account, Emperor Ming had a dream one evening in which he saw a spirit flying in front of his palace. The spirit had a golden body and the top of his head emitted rays of light. The following day the emperor asked his ministers to identify the spirit. One minister replied that he had heard of a sage in India called "Buddha" who had attained the way (dao) and was able to fly. The emperor presumed that this must have been the spirit he observed in his dream, so he dispatched a group of envoys led by Zhang Qian who journeyed to the Yuezhi region (Indo-Scythia) to search out this sage; he returned with a copy of the "Scripture in Forty-Two Sections." A fifth-century source reports that the envoys also managed to secure the famous image of the UDĀYANA BUDDHA, the first buddha-image. In fifth- and sixth-century materials, there is additionally mention of two Indian monks, KĀŚYAPA MĀTAṄGA (d. u.) and Dharmaratna (d. u.), who returned with the Chinese envoys. By the medieval period these monks are regularly cited as cotranslators of the scripture. According to a relatively late tradition, the Emperor Ming also built the first Chinese Buddhist temple—BAIMASI in Luoyang—as a residence for the two Indian translators. Early Buddhist catalogues refer to the text simply as "Forty-Two Sections from Buddhist Scriptures," or "The Forty-Two Sections of Emperor Xiao Ming." The text consists largely of snippets culled from longer Buddhist sūtras included in the Buddhist canon; parallel sections are found in the ĀGAMAS and NIKĀYAS, as well as the MAHĀVAGGA. The text also bears a number of Chinese stylistic features. The most obvious is the phrase "The Buddha said" which is used to introduce most sections, rather than the more common Buddhist opening "Thus have I heard" (EVAṂ MAYĀ ŚRUTAM). This opening is reminiscent of Confucian classics such as the *Xiaojing* ("Book of Filial Piety") and the *Lunyu* ("Analects"), where maxims and illustrative anecdotes are often prefaced with the phrase, "The master said." The terminology of the *Sishi'er zhang jing* borrows heavily from Daoism and the philosophical tradition known as XUANXUE (Dark Learning).

**sishijiu [ri] zhai**. (J. shijūku[nichi]sai; K. sasipku [il] chae 四十九[日]齋). In Chinese, "forty-ninth day ceremony," the final funeral service performed on the day when rebirth will have occurred. The "forty-ninth day ceremony" is the culmination of the funeral observances performed every seventh day for seven weeks after a person's death, lit. the "seven sevens [days] services" (C. QIQI JI/qiqi [ri] zhai; J. shichishichi no ki/shichishichi [nichi] sai; K. ch'ilch'il ki/ch'ilch'il [il] chae), a term that is also used as an alternate for "forty-ninth day ceremony." Many traditions of Buddhism believe that the dead pass through an "intermediate state" (ANTARĀBHAVA) that leads eventually to the next rebirth. The duration of this intermediate period is variously presumed to be essentially instantaneous, to one-week long, indeterminate, and as many as forty-nine days; of these, forty-nine days eventually becomes a dominant paradigm. Ceremonies to help guide the transitional being (GANDHARVA) through the rebirth process take place once each week, at any point of which rebirth might occur; these observances culminate in a "forty-ninth day ceremony" (SISHIJIU [RI] ZHAI), which is thought to mark the point at which rebirth certainly will have taken place. Since the transitional being in the antarābhava is released from the physical body, it is thought to be unusually susceptible to the influence of the dharma during this period; hence, the preliminary weekly ceremonies and the culminating forty-ninth day ceremony both include lengthy chanting of SŪTRAS and MANTRAS, often accompanied by the performance of MUDRĀS, in order to help the being understand the need to let go of the attachment to the previous life and go forward to at least a more salutary rebirth, if not to enlightenment itself. In Korea, the forty-ninth-day ceremony is usually performed in the Hall of the Dark Prefecture (MYŎNGBU CHŎN), the shrine dedicated to KṢITIGARBHA, the patron bodhisattva of the denizens of hell, and the ten kings of hell (SHIWANG; see YAMA), the judges of the dead.

**Sitātapatrā**. (T. Gdugs dkar; C. Baisangaifoding; J. Byakusangaibutchō; K. Paeksan'gae Pulchŏng 白傘蓋佛頂). In Sanskrit, "White Parasol," an important female bodhisattva in the MAHĀYĀNA and tantric pantheons. In some accounts, she is said to have emerged from the Buddha's crown protrusion (UṢṆĪṢA) and therefore is sometimes called Uṣṇīṣasitātapatrā. She has numerous forms, but the most famous has a thousand heads, a thousand arms, and a thousand feet, with three eyes in each head and an eye in each hand and foot. Sitātapatrā is regarded as a powerful deity, capable of destroying enemies and removing obstacles. During the Mongol Yuan dynasty, she was venerated by emperors because she was believed to be able to destroy armies and overcome disasters. She continues to be highly venerated in Tibetan Buddhism.

**Sitatārā**. (T. Sgrol dkar). In Sanskrit, "White Tārā," one of the two most significant forms of the goddess TĀRĀ, one of the most important female deities of late Indian Mahāyāna and an object of particular devotion in Tibet. Her other famous form is "Dark Tārā" or "Green Tārā" (ŚYĀMATĀRĀ). Sitatārā is white in color and is depicted seated in the lotus posture (PADMĀSANA). Her right hand makes the boon-granting gesture (VARADAMUDRĀ) and her left hand make the gesture of protection (ABHAYAMUDRĀ). She has seven eyes: her two eyes, a third eye in her forehead, and eyes in the palms of her hands and the soles of her feet. She has a somewhat more peaceful mien than Green Tārā, and is propitiated especially for health and long life. In the story of King SRONG BTSAN SGAM PO and his two wives, one Chinese and one Nepalese, the Chinese wife, Princess WENCHENG, is said to have been an incarnation of Sitatārā.

**Si tu incarnations**. See TAI SI TU INCARNATIONS.

**Sīvalī**. (C. Shipoluo; J. Shibara; K. Sibara 尸婆羅). In Sanskrit and Pāli, the proper name of an eminent ARHAT who was foremost among the Buddha's disciples in receiving gifts. According to the Pāli account, Sīvalī was the son of Princess Suppavāsā of Koḷiya (see SUPPAVĀSĀ-KOḶIYADHĪTĀ), who was pregnant with him for seven years. For another seven days she was in labor and, believing that she was about to die from the ordeal, she sent a gift to the Buddha to earn merit. The Buddha accepted the gift and blessed her, and immediately she gave birth to a son. Sīvalī was possessed of extraordinary powers from infancy. ŚĀRIPUTRA is said to have conversed with him on the day of his birth and ordained him with Suppavāsā's consent. He attained the stage of stream-enterer (SROTAĀPANNA) and once-returner (SAKṚDĀGĀMIN) during his ordination as a novice, and while dwelling alone in the jungle, subsequently attained arhatship by contemplating the reasons for his delayed birth. (Some accounts say that Sīvalī learned he had been compelled to stay in his mother's womb for so long in retribution for having once laid siege for seven days to the city of Vārāṇasī during a previous existence.) Sīvalī's good luck at receiving gifts was the result of generosity shown by him in previous lifetimes to previous buddhas and the resolution he made during the time of Padmottara (P. Padumuttara) Buddha to one day be preeminent in this regard. The Buddha took Sīvalī with him on his journey to visit Khadiravaniya Revata because he knew provisions were scarce along the way. When Sīvalī and five hundred others journeyed to the desolate Himālaya mountains, the gods provided him and his companions with everything they needed. In Burma, Sīvalī is believed never to have passed into PARINIRVĀṆA, but to still remain in the world today; he is worshipped for good fortune and is depicted as a standing monk, holding a fan and an alms bowl.

**sixteen arhats/sthaviras**. See ṢOḌAŚASTHAVIRA.

**sixth patriarch**. See LIUZU; HUINENG.

**six yogas of Nāropa**. See NĀ RO CHOS DRUG.

**Siyam Nikāya**. The largest of the monastic orders in Sri Lanka, dating from 1753, so named because it derives from an ordination lineage that came from Thailand (Siam); today approximately half of the monks in Sri Lanka belong to this order. In the preceding five centuries, the tradition of full ordination (UPASAMPADĀ) of BHIKṢUs had died out in Sri Lanka because there was not the requisite number of five fully ordained monks to ordain new monks. Thus, all Sri Lankan monks remained as novices (ŚRĀMAṆERA). The tradition of full ordination had been reintroduced twice before, but it had died out each time. In 1753, with the support of King Kīrti Śrī Rājasiṃha, the novice SARAṆAṂKARA invited the Thai elder Upāli to come to Sri Lanka to officiate at an ordination ceremony. The Siyam Nikāya is principally based around the city of Kandy and only accepts upper-caste males for full ordination.

**skandha**. (P. khandha; T. phung po; C. yun; J. un; K. on 蘊). In Sanskrit, lit. "heap," viz., "aggregate," or "aggregate of being"; one of the most common categories in Buddhist literature for enumerating the constituents of the person. According to one account, the Buddha used a grain of rice to represent each of the many constituents, resulting in five piles or heaps. The five skandhas are materiality or form (RŪPA), sensations or feeling (VEDANĀ), perception or discrimination (SAṂJÑĀ), conditioning factors (SAṂSKĀRA), and consciousness (VIJÑĀNA). Of these five, only rūpa is material; the remaining four involve mentality and are collectively called "name" (NĀMA), thus the compound "name-and-form" or "mentality-and-materiality" (NĀMARŪPA). However classified, nowhere among the aggregates is there to be found a self (ĀTMAN). Yet, through ignorance (AVIDYĀ or MOHA), the mind habitually identifies one or another in this collection of the five aggregates with a self. This is the principal wrong view (DṚṢṬI), called SATKĀYADṚṢṬI, that gives rise to suffering and continued existence in the cycle of rebirth (SAṂSĀRA).

**skandhaka**. (T. phung po; P. khandhaka; C. jiandu; J. kendo; K. kŏndo 犍度). In Sanskrit, "chapter," or "division," especially referring to a major section of the VINAYA. Whereas the PRĀTIMOKṢA largely deals with the conduct of individual monk or nuns, the skandhaka primarily deals with the conduct of monks and nuns in their capacity as collective members of the SAṂGHA. In the extant Sanskrit vinayas, this section is sometimes called the VINAYAVASTU. The Pāli vinaya has twenty-two sections (khandhaka). Most of the Sanskrit vinayas have twenty skandhaka, as follows. (1) pravrajyāvastu: this section deals with matters related to admission into the order as a novice (pravrajyā; see PRAVRAJITA), ordination as a fully ordained monk (UPASAṂPADĀ), admission of novices (ŚRĀMAṆERA), regulations for the interactions with the preceptor (UPĀDHYĀYA) or teacher (ĀCĀRYA), and circumstances that disqualify one from being admitted to the monastic order; (2) poṣadhavastu: this section deals with the UPOṢADHA, or confession ceremony, including a history of its origin and the rules for its performance. (3) varṣāvastu: this section deals with the annual rains retreat (VARṢĀ) and the rules to be observed during that period, including what kinds of dwelling are permitted. (4) pravāraṇāvastu: this section deals with the ceremony that marks the end of the annual rains retreat (PRAVĀRAṆĀ) and elimination of any disharmony that may have arisen during the retreat. (5) carmavastu: this section deals with leather and especially the usage of shoes. (6) bhaiṣajyavastu: this section deals with both medicine and food, setting forth which medicines are permitted and when they may be used; the rules concerning food set forth which foods may be accepted, how invitations from the laity should be treated; how food is to be prepared, and how the monastery storeroom should be utilized. (7) cīvaravastu: this section deals with robes (CĪVARA), including how may robes a monk may possess, how robes are to be received from the laity, how robes are to worn, and how robes are to sewn; (8) kaṭhinavastu: this section deals specifically with the cloth (KAṬHINA) that monks receive from the laity at the end of the rains retreat; (9) kośambakavastu: this section deals with the dispute that occurred between the Kauśāmbī monks and how it was resolved by the Buddha, who allowed an expelled monk to be reinstated upon confession. (10) karmavastu: this section deals with ecclesiastical acts (SAṂGHAKARMAN) taken by the community in various assemblies. (11) pāṇḍulohitavastu: this section deals with disciplinary measures that are taken when violations of the monastic code occur. (12) pudgalavastu: this section deals with SAṂGHĀVAŚEṢA infractions, the types of probationary periods (e.g., MĀNATVA; PARIVĀSA), and the procedure for reinstatement after probation. (13) pārivāsikavastu: this section describes the proper conduct of a monk during the probationary period. (14) poṣadhasthāpanavastu: this section sets forth the circumstances under which a monk may be excluded from the UPOṢADHA ceremony. (15) śamathavastu: this section deals with legal cases (ADHIKARAṆA) and their resolution. (16) saṃghabhedavastu: this section deals with the schisms in the saṃgha (SAṂGHABHEDA), including the schism caused by DEVADATTA. (17) śayanāsanavastu: this section deals with the various dwelling places of members of the saṃgha. (18) ācāravastu: this section deals with conduct, especially in interactions with others, including laity, visiting monks, and forest-dwelling monks. (19) kṣudrakavastu: this section deals with miscellaneous minor rules. (20) bhikṣuṇīvastu: this section deals with the rules specific to nuns. The skandhaka begins with a biography of the Buddha that includes his genealogy, his birth, and his life up to the conversion of ŚĀRIPUTRA and MAHĀMAUDGALYĀYANA. It concludes with the story of the Buddha's death and goes on to describe the first Buddhist council (SAṂGĪTI, see COUNCIL, FIRST) at RĀJAGṚHA and the second council (COUNCIL, SECOND) at VAIŚĀLĪ. In the Tibetan BKA' 'GYUR, the vinaya section includes the above materials in the following sections: 'dul ba'i gzhi (vinayavastu), so sor thar pa (prātimokṣa), 'dul ba rnam par 'byed pa (vinayavibhaṅga), dge slong ma'i so sor thar pa'i mdo (bhikṣuṇī prātimokṣasūtra), dge slong ma'i 'dul ba rnam par 'byed pa (bhikṣuṇī vinayavibhaṅga), 'dul ba phran tshegs (vinayakṣudraka), 'dul ba gzhung bla ma/dam pa (vinayottaragrantha).

**skandhamāra**. (T. phung po'i bdud; C. yunmo; J. unma; K. onma 蘊魔). In Sanskrit, "Māra of the aggregates," one of the four forms of the demon MĀRA, along with the Māra of the afflictions (kleśamāra), the Māra of death (MṚTYUMĀRA), and the divinity Māra (DEVAPUTRAMĀRA). The deity Māra refers to the demonic entity that attacked the Buddha on the night of his enlightenment; the other three are figurative forms, which are also called Māra to indicate their pernicious nature. Skandhamāra is said to have two forms. The coarse form is the five appropriated aggregates (UPĀDĀNASKANDHA) that arise in dependence on KARMAN. The subtle form is the mental body that arises as a result of the predispositions of ignorance (AVIDYĀ-VĀSANĀ).

**skill-in-means**. See UPĀYAKAUŚALYA.

**Sku 'bum**. (Kumbum). In Tibetan, literally "one hundred thousand images," referring to a general architectural style of elaborate, multistories CAITYAS, including the Rgyal rtse sku 'bum (Gyantse Kumbum), GCUNG RI BO CHE, Jo nang sku 'bum, and Rgyang 'bum mo che (Gyang Bumoche). ¶ Sku 'bum is also the name of a Tibetan monastery founded in 1560 by Rin chen brtson 'grus rgyal mtshan (d.u.) commemorating the birthplace of DGE LUGS founder TSONG KHA PA BLO BZANG GRAGS PA; it is situated near Lake Kokonor and close to Xining, the capital of Qinghai province (incorporating much of the Tibetan A mdo region) in China. In 1583, the third DALAI LAMA, BSOD NAMS RGYA MTSHO, expanded the site by adding a temple dedicated to MAITREYA (T. Byams pa), after which the complex became known as Sku 'bum Byams pa gling (Kumbum Jampa Ling). The institution is centered around a miraculous tree marking Tsong kha pa's actual birthplace. It is also the site where Tsong kha pa's mother is said to have fashioned a STŪPA in 1379. Unlike other Tibet sites with the name sku 'bum, the name of the monastery does not derive from its architectural style but rather from a white sandalwood tree that grew at the spot where Tsong kha pa's father planted his placenta (in other versions, it grew from a drop of blood from the umbilical cord). The tree is said to have one hundred thousand leaves, with each leaf bearing an image of the seed syllables (BĪJA) and hand implements of the buddha Siṃhanāda, the buddha whom Tsong kha pa will eventually become. Over the centuries, Sku 'bum developed into an enormous complex, one of the largest in the region, with thirty temples, over a thousand buildings, and some 3,600 monks. It had four colleges, one each for the study of doctrine, tantra, medicine, and the KĀLACAKRATANTRA. The monastery's hereditary abbot was the A skya Rin po che, considered the incarnation of Tsong kha pa's father. Sku 'bum is counted among the six great Dge lugs monasteries in Tibet, traditionally drawing large numbers of monks from Mongolia, as well as parts of eastern Tibet. Since 1959, the size of the monastic population has been drastically reduced and, since the 1990s, the monastery has become a popular destination for Han Chinese tourists.

**skull (cup)**. See KAPĀLA.

**Skyid grong**. (Kyirong). A village and surrounding region in southwestern Tibet, on the border with Nepal. Numerous religious centers and pilgrimage sites are located in the area including the 'PHAGS PA WA TI LHA KHANG, RI BO DPAL 'BAR, and the YOGIN MI LA RAS PA's hermitage BRAG DKAR RTA SO. Skyid grong was an important staging post on the foremost ancient trade route between Tibet and Nepal.

**śloka**. (P. siloka; T. tshigs bcad; C. ji/song; J. ge/ju; K. ke/song 偈/頌). In Sanskrit, "stanza," referring to a unit of metrical verse in traditional Sanskrit literature. Although the exact form of the verse may vary, the most common form of ŚLOKA is composed of four "feet" (pāda), each foot consisting of eight syllables, for a total of thirty-two; this form is called the anuṣṭubh. Other forms include the triṣṭubh, which has four feet of eleven syllables each, and the gāyatrī, which has three feet of eight syllables each. The form is widely used in Buddhist and non-Buddhist Indian literature, which is often composed in a mixture of prose and verse. The term is implied in the titles of the PRAJÑĀPĀRAMITĀ SŪTRAS: e.g., in the AṢṬASĀHASRIKĀPRAJÑĀPĀRAMITĀ, which is often translated as "The Perfection of Wisdom in Eight Thousand Lines," where lines refers to ślokas.

**Sman ri**. (Menri). One of the largest and most influential BON monasteries, founded in 1405 by SHES RAB RGYAL MTSHAN in central Tibet.

**Smar tshang bka' brgyud**. (Martsang Kagyü). One of the four major and eight minor subsects of the BKA' BRGYUD sect of Tibetan Buddhism (BKA' BRGYUD CHE BZHI CHUNG BRGYAD), originating with Smar pa Shes rab seng ge (Marpa Sherap Senge, d.u.), student of Bka' brgyud hierarch PHAG MO GRU PA RDO RJE RGYAL PO.

**śmaśāna**. (P. susāna; T. dur khrod; C. shilin/hanlin; J. shirin/kanrin; K. sirim/hallim 屍林/寒林). In Sanskrit, "charnel ground," "cemetery"; funerary sites in ancient India where corpses were left to decompose. The charnel ground was recommended as a site for monks to practice meditation in order to overcome attachment to the body. In the MAHĀSATIPAṬṬHĀNASUTTA, the Buddha recommends nine "charnel ground contemplations" (sīvathikā manasikāra). There is a set of "contemplations on the foul" (AŚUBHABHĀVANĀ) described in mainstream Buddhist literature that were to take place in the charnel grounds, where the monks would sit next to the dead and contemplate the nine or ten specific stages in the decomposition of a corpse; this meditation was a powerful antidote to the affliction of lust (RĀGA). The traditional list of thirteen authorized ascetic practices (S. dhūtaguṇa; P. DHUTAṄGA) also includes dwelling in a charnel ground (no. 11) and wearing only discarded cloth (no. 1), which typically meant to use funerary cloth taken from rotting corpses to make monastic raiments (CĪVARA), thus weaning the monk or nun from attachment to material possessions. The ideal charnel ground is described as a place where corpses are cremated daily, where there is the constant smell of decomposing corpses, and where the weeping of the families of the dead can be heard. The practice of meditation there is said to result in an awareness of the inevitability of death, the abandonment of lust, and the overcoming of attachment to the body. In India, the charnel ground was a frightful place not only because of the presence of corpses but also for the creatures, including wild animals and various demons, that frequented it at night. Thus, in tantric Buddhism, the charnel ground was considered to be inhabited by wrathful deities, ḌĀKINĪs, and MAHĀSIDDHAs, making it a potent place for the performance of ritual and meditation. Mahāsiddhas are sometimes depicted in charnel grounds, sitting on corpses and drinking from skull cups. ANUTTARAYOGATANTRA texts also refer to a set of "eight great charnel grounds" (S. AṢṬAMAHĀŚMAŚĀNA), which are also frequently depicted in tantric Buddhist art. While the eight sites are often equated with actual geographic locations in India, they also carry a deeper symbolism, referring to regions of tantric sacred geography, points on a MAṆḌALA or a deity's body, and elements of tantric physiology such as the channels (NĀḌĪ) in the subtle body of a meditating YOGIN. Their origin myth describes the defeat of the demon Rudra, after which the charnel grounds arose in the eight cardinal and intermediate directions, each from a piece of his dismembered body. They are described as wild and terrifying places, littered with human corpses and wild animals, each with their own trees, protectors, STŪPAs, NĀGAs, jewels, fires, clouds, mountains, and lakes. They are inhabited by a host of spirits and nonhuman beings, as well as meditating yogins and YOGINĪs. In general, charnel grounds and similar frightening locations are said to be efficacious for the practice of tantric meditation. The aṣṭamahāśmaśāna are also usually depicted as forming part of the outer protection wheel in maṇḍalas of anuttarayogatantra. There are varying lists of the eight great charnel grounds, one of which is: caṇḍogrā (most fierce), gahvara (dense thicket), vajrajvala (blazing vajra), endowed with skeletons (karaṅkin), cool grove (śītavana), black darkness (ghorāndhakāra), resonant with "kilikili" (kilikilārava), and cries of "ha ha" (aṭṭahāsa); Tibetan sources give the names of the eight great charnel grounds as gtum drag (caṇḍogra), tshang tshing 'khrigs pa (gahvara), rdo rje bar ba (vajrajvala), keng rus can (karaṅkin), bsil bu tshal (śītavana), mun pa nag po (ghorāndhakāra) ki li ki lir sgra sgrog pa (kilikilārava), and ha ha rgod pa (aṭṭahāsa).

**Smin grol gling**. (Mindroling). Largest monastery of the RNYING MA sect of Tibetan Buddhism in central Tibet; established in 1670 by GTER BDAG GLING PA, the brother of LO CHEN DHARMA SHRI, and a close associate and supporter of the fifth DALAI LAMA. It was founded on the site of an earlier structure built in the early eleventh century by Klu mes Shes rab tshul khrims (Lume Sherap Tsultrim, b. c. tenth century). Smin grol gling flourished as the center of the Southern Treasure tradition (LHO GTER), which originated with the teachings and revelations of Gter bdag gling pa. The monastic compound was severely damaged by the Dzungar army in the early eighteenth century and again during the Chinese Cultural Revolution, although it has since undergone significant restoration. The abbots of Smin grol gling became known as the Smin gling khri can (Throne Holder of Mindroling), a line of important masters descending in a familial lineage from Gter bdag gling pa. The lineage of Smin grol gling throneholders is

1. Gter bdag gling pa 'Gyur med rdo rje (1646–1714)
2. Padma 'gyur med rgya mtsho (Pema Gyurme Gyatso, 1686–1717)
3. Rin chen rnam rgyal (Rinchen Namgyal, 1694–1758)
4. 'Gyur med padma bstan 'dzin (Gyurme Pema Tendzin, b. eighteenth century.)
5. 'Phrin las rnam rgyal (Trinle Namgyal, 1765–1812)
6. Padma dbyang rgyal (Pema Wangyal, b. eighteenth century)
7. 'Gyur med sangs rgyas kun dga' (Gyurme Sangye Kunga, born c. late eighteenth/early nineteenth century)
8. Khri can Yid bzhin dbyang rgyal (Trichen Yishin Wangyal, d.u)
9. Bde chen chos grub (Dechen Chödrup, d.u.)
10. Kun dga' bstan 'dzin (Kunga Tendzin, d.u.)
11. Don grub dbang rgyal (Döndrup Wangyal, d.u.)
12. Kun bzang dbang rgyal (Kunzang Wangyal, b. 1931).

**Smon lam chen mo**. (Mönlam Chenmo). In Tibetan, "great prayer," the great prayer festival that took place in the Tibetan capital of LHA SA as part of the celebration of the Tibetan lunar New Year (and thus occurring in February and sometimes March). The festival was established by TSONG KHA PA, the founder of the DGE LUGS sect, in 1409, to commemorate the Buddha's defeat of the heretical teachers (TĪRTHIKA) at ŚRĀVASTĪ. Lasting until the twenty-fifth day of the first month of the new year, the festival included prayers performed three times each day at the JO KHANG, the chief temple of Lha sa, as well as rituals for the expiation of misdeeds committed during the previous year and a rededication to the principles of Buddhism for the coming year. During the festival, the city would be filled with pilgrims from all over Tibet as well as with monks from the three Dge lugs monasteries in the vicinity of Lha sa. Elaborate butter sculptures (GTOR MA) were made and 'CHAM dances were performed. The examinations for the granting of the DGE BSHES lha ram pa degree took place at this time. For the period of the festival, the lay officials of the city of Lha sa turned over civil authority to the monks of 'BRAS SPUNGS monastery. The festival was suspended after the Tibetan uprising in 1959, but began again in 1986 with the political liberalization that followed the death of Mao Zedong, but was banned again in 1990. In times of conflict it has served as a focus for Tibetan political and cultural identity.

**smṛti**. (P. sati; T. dran pa; C. nian; J. nen; K. yŏm 念). In Sanskrit, "mindfulness" or "memory" and often seen in Western sources in the Pāli equivalency sati; a polysemous term, but commonly used in meditative contexts to refer to the ability to remain focused on a chosen object without forgetfulness or distraction. The SARVĀSTIVĀDA school of ABHIDHARMA lists smṛti as one of a group of five determinative (VINIYATA) mental concomitants (CAITTA), whose function is to aid the mind in ascertaining or determining its object. The five are: aspiration or desire-to-act (CHANDA), determination or resolve (ADHIMOKṢA), mindfulness or memory (smṛti), concentration (SAMĀDHI), and wisdom or cognition (PRAJÑĀ). According to ASAṄGA, these five determinative factors accompany wholesome (KUŚALA) states of mind, so that if one is present, all are present. Mindfulness is crucial to all types of formal meditative practice because of its role in bringing clarity to the perceptual process; it leaves the mind in a purely receptive state that inhibits the unwholesome responses to sensory stimuli, such as greed, hatred, and delusion. Mindfulness also contributes to control of the mind, by eliminating distraction and helping the meditator gain mastery of his thought processes. Smṛti is also a catalyst of the related term "circumspection" or "introspection" (SAṂPRAJANYA) and ultimately of wisdom (PRAJÑĀ). As the third of the five spiritual faculties (PAÑCENDRIYA), smṛti helps to balance faith (ŚRADDHĀ) and wisdom (prajñā)—which could degenerate into blind faith or skepticism, respectively—as well as vigor (VĪRYA) and concentration (SAMĀDHI)—which could degenerate respectively into restlessness and indolence. Smṛti is thus the keystone that ensures the uniform development of all five faculties; for this reason, unlike the other four factors, there can never be too much mindfulness, because it cannot degenerate into a negative state. The emphasis on mindfulness is one of the most distinctive features of Buddhist meditation theory. Consequently, the term appears in numerous lists of virtuous qualities, especially in those pertaining to meditation. For example, in perhaps its most popular usage, right mindfulness (SAMYAKSMṚTI) is the seventh of the eight aspects of the noble eightfold path (ĀRYĀṢṬĀṄGAMĀRGA). Generally in this context, the cultivation of the "foundations of mindfulness" (SMṚTYUPASTHĀNA) is understood to serve as a basis for the development of liberating wisdom (prajñā). Thus, meditation exercises involving smṛti are often discussed in connection with those related to VIPAŚYANĀ, or "insight." In one of the most widely read discourses on mindfulness, the MAHĀSATIPAṬṬHĀNASUTTANTA, the Buddha offers four specific foundations of mindfulness training, namely, on the body (KĀYA), sensations (VEDANĀ), mental states (CITTA), and specific factors (P. dhamma; S. DHARMA). In his *Prajñāpāramitāhṛdayanāmaṭīkā*, a commentary on the PRAJÑĀPĀRAMITĀHṚDAYASŪTRA ("Heart Sūtra"), KAMALAŚĪLA lists mindfulness as the third of five "powers" (BALA) that are attained on the path of preparation (PRAYOGAMĀRGA). In another popular schema, smṛti is listed as the first of seven "limbs of awakening" or factors of enlightenment (BODHYAṄGA); these are seven factors that contribute to enlightenment. See also ANUSMṚTI; SMṚTYUPASTHĀNA; SATIPAṬṬHANASUTTA.

**smṛtyupasthāna**. (P. satipaṭṭhāna; T. dran pa nyer bzhag; C. nianchu; J. nenjo; K. yŏmch'ŏ 念處). In Sanskrit, "foundations of mindfulness," a meditative training in which one contemplates with mindfulness (SMṚTI): one's (1) body (KĀYĀNUPAŚYANĀ; P. kāyānupassanā), by mean of mindfulness of breathing, mindfulness of postures, full awareness of bodily actions, contemplation of bodily impurities, contemplation of elements, and nine cemetery meditations; (2) sensations (vedanānupaśyanā; P. vedanānupassanā), viz., pleasant, unpleasant, or neutral sensations (VEDANĀ); (3) mental states (cittānupaśyanā; P. cittānupassanā), such as whether the mind (CITTA) generally is elated or depressed, distracted or concentrated; and (4) factors (dharmānupaśyanā; P. dhammānupassanā), such as the five hindrances (NĪVARAṆA), the five aggregates (SKANDHA), the seven factors of enlightenment (BODHYAṄGA); the FOUR NOBLE TRUTHS, etc. The explanation of smṛtyupasthāna, as the first of the thirty-seven dharmas associated with enlightenment (bodhyaṅga) details the role of mindfulness in the eightfold noble path (ĀRYĀṢṬĀṄGAMĀRGA). See also SMṚTI; SATIPAṬṬHĀNASUTTA.

**Smṛtyupasthānasūtra**. In Sanskrit, "Discourse on the Foundations of Mindfulness." See SATIPAṬṬHĀNASUTTA.

**Snar thang**. (Nartang). A Tibetan monastery famous as the source for an important printed edition of the Buddhist canon, the BKA' 'GYUR and BSTAN 'GYUR. It was located a short distance west of Gzhis ka rtse (Shigatse). The monastery was founded in 1153 and was originally a BKA' GDAMS center. The edition of the canon produced there appears to derive from a manuscript edition prepared between 1312 and 1320. The engraving of the woodblocks was completed in 1730. The main buildings of the monastery, the woodblock collection, and many of its art treasures were destroyed in 1966 during the Chinese Cultural Revolution.

**snga dar**. (ngadar). In Tibetan, "earlier dissemination" or "first dissemination," the first of two historical periods when Buddhism was disseminated to Tibet. The beginning of the period is variously indicated, sometimes being traced as far back as the first (and likely legendary) Tibetan king, Gnya' khri btsan po, sometimes to the king Lha tho tho ri. However, it is agreed that the dissemination became well established during the reign of king SRONG BTSAN SGAM PO in the seventh century, with his marriage to a Chinese princess and a Nepalese princess, each a Buddhist and each of whom brought a statue of the Buddha with her to Tibet. It continued through the reign of King KHRI SRONG LDE BTSAN, during which ŚĀNTARAKṢITA and PADMASAMBHAVA came to Tibet, the first Tibetan monastery at BSAM YAS was founded, and the BSAM YAS DEBATE took place. Traditionally the end of the first dissemination is associated with the murder of the great patron of Buddhism, King RAL PA CAN, by his brother GLANG DAR MA in 838, who then seized the throne and instituted a suppression of Buddhism. The beginning of the second or later dissemination (PHYI DAR) is traditionally dated from the first journey of the translator RIN CHEN BZANG PO to India. Subsequent research has shown that the dissemination of Buddhism in general did not end with the death of Ral pa can, but that there was a decline in particular forms of monasticism that disadvantaged institutional forms of religious expression. See JO KHANG.

**Sngags rim chen mo**. (Ngak rim chenmo). In Tibetan, "Great Exposition of the Stages of MANTRA," an extensive theoretical work on the classes and stages of TANTRA, written by the DGE LUGS savant TSONG KHA PA BLO BZANG GRAGS PA. The work is regarded as the tantric companion to his most famous work, the LAM RIM CHEN MO, or "Great Exposition of the Stages of the Path." The work begins with an influential discussion of what distinguishes the MAHĀYĀNA from the HĪNAYĀNA, and within Mahāyāna, what distinguishes the perfection vehicle (PĀRAMITĀYĀNA, phar phyin theg pa) from the mantra vehicle (MANTRAYĀNA, sngags kyi theg pa), with Tsong kha pa arguing that the practice of "deity yoga" (DEVATĀYOGA, lha'i rnal 'byor) is the distinguishing feature of tantric practice. The text then goes on to set forth the principal practices of each of the four major divisions of tantras according to Dge lugs: KRIYĀTANTRA, CARYĀTANTRA, YOGATANTRA, and ANUTTARAYOGATANTRA, with the greater part of the text devoted to the last of these divisions, regarded as essential for the achievement of buddhahood.

**Snga 'gyur rnying ma**. (Ngagyur nyingma). A Tibetan term referring to the RNYING MA sect of Tibetan Buddhism, lit. "Early Translation Ancient Tradition," referring to the fact that the Rnying ma sect relies on translations, especially translations of TANTRAS, that were made prior to the later dissemination (PHYI DAR) of Buddhism to Tibet. In distinction, the other sects of Tibetan Buddhism are called "new" (GSAR MA).

**sngon 'gro**. (ngöndro). In Tibetan, lit "going before," viz., "preliminary practices"; referring generally to practices that are performed in order to establish proper motivation, to purify the mind of afflictions, and to remove obstacles before embarking upon tantric practice. Although present in all sects of Tibetan Buddhism, "preliminary practices" are especially associated with the RNYING MA and BKA' BRGYUD sects. One of the most famous presentations of the preliminary practices is found in the nineteenth-century Rnying ma pa work, the KUN BZANG BLA MA'I ZHAL LUNG ("Words of My Perfect Teacher") by DPAL SPRUL RIN PO CHE. The text first sets forth the "common preliminaries," reflections on central points of Buddhist doctrine, intended to turn one's interests away from SAṂSĀRA and toward the wish for liberation from rebirth. These are: (1) the rarity of human birth, (2) the uncertainty of the time of death, (3) the causes and effect of actions, (4) and the sufferings incumbent in the six rebirth destinies (GATI) of SAṂSĀRA. The "uncommon preliminary practice" entail the accumulation of a specific number (usually one hundred thousand) of specific practices. It is these practices that are intended to purify afflictions and remove obstacles. These are (1) recitation of the refuge formula while performing a hundred thousand prostrations; (2) cultivation of BODHICITTA (often in the form of a hundred thousand repetitions of a prayer); (3) recitation of the hundred-syllable MANTRA of the buddha VAJRASATTVA; (4) a hundred thousand offerings of a MAṆḌALA; (5) the practice of GURU yoga through a hundred thousand repetitions of the name mantra of the guru. In each case, these practices are to be performed with the appropriate visualization. In order to complete the uncommon preliminary practices, disciples would often go on retreat, during which they would devote all their time to the practices.

**snyan brgyud**. (nyen gyü). In Tibetan, "hearing lineage" or "aural lineage," a term used to refer to teachings, especially tantric teachings, that are not committed to writing but that are instead transmitted orally from master to disciple from one generation to the next.

**snyan brgyud skor gsum**. (nyen gyü kor sum). In Tibetan, "the three aural lineage cycles"; a compilation of instructions based on the CAKRASAṂVARATANTRA, including liturgies, ritual manuals, and commentarial works, together with their oral commentaries, stemming from MI LA RAS PA's three principal disciples: RAS CHUNG PA RDO RJE GRAGS, SGAM PO PA BSOD NAMS RIN CHEN, and Ngan rdzongs ras pa Byang chub rgyal po (Ngendzong Repa Jangchup Gyalpo). The three cycles are respectively known as the RAS CHUNG SNYAN BRGYUD, Dwags po snyan brgyud (Dakpo nyengyu), and Ngan rdzongs snyan brgyud (Ngendzong nyengyu). They were later edited and systematized by the adept GTSANG SMYON HERUKA during the fifteenth century. See also SNYAN BRGYUD.

**Snyder, Gary**. (1930–). American poet and prominent figure in Zen Buddhism in America. Gary Snyder was born in San Francisco and raised on a farm outside Seattle, Washington. He attended Reed College in Oregon, where he studied literature and anthropology. Inspired by DAISETZ TEITARO SUZUKI's *Essays in Zen Buddhism*, he taught himself to meditate, and devoted himself to the practice of Zen meditation while working as a fire lookout in Washington state. In 1952, he enrolled in the Department of Oriental Languages at the University of California, Berkeley, to study Chinese and Japanese. He met ALLEN GINSBERG and JACK KEROUAC in San Francisco and participated in the famous Six Gallery reading in 1955, where Ginsberg first read *Howl*. Snyder traveled to Japan in 1956, returning again in 1958 to spend seven years practicing Zen meditation at the monastery of DAITOKUJI. He returned to San Francisco in 1966. His work and his poetry have remained committed both to the exploration of Buddhist, especially Zen, practice and to the protection of the environment. Snyder served on the California Arts Council from 1974 to 1980 and taught at the University of California, Davis, where he helped found the Nature and Culture curriculum. He founded the Ring of Bone Zendo at his mountain farm in the northern Sierra Nevada range in California.

**snying thig**. (nyingtik). In Tibetan, "heart drop" or "heart essence" (an abbreviation of snying gi thig le), a term used to describe an important genre of texts of the RNYING MA sect of Tibetan Buddhism. The master ŚRĪSIṂHA is said to have divided the "instruction class" (MAN NGAG SDE) of the great completion (RDZOGS CHEN) teachings into four cycles: the outer, inner, secret, and the most secret unexcelled cycle (yang gsang bla na med pa). In Tibet, VIMALAMITRA organized the teachings of this fourth cycle into an explanatory lineage with scriptures and an aural lineage without scriptures and then concealed these teachings, which were later revealed as the BI MA'I SNYING THIG ("Heart Essence of Vimalamitra"). During his stay in Tibet, PADMASAMBHAVA concealed teachings on the most secret unexcelled cycle, called "heart essence of the ḌĀKINĪ" (MKHA' 'GRO SNYING THIG). In the fourteenth century, these and other teachings were compiled and elaborated upon by KLONG CHEN RAB 'BYAMS into what are known as the "four heart essences" (SNYING THIG YA BZHI): (1) the "heart essence of VIMALAMITRA" (Bi ma'i snying thig), (2) the "ultimate essence of the lama" (bla ma yang thig), (3) the "heart essence of the ḍākinī" (mkha' 'gro snying thig), and (4) two sections composed by Klong chen pa, the "ultimate essence of the ḍākinī" (mkha' 'gro yang thig) and the "ultimate essence of the profound" (zab mo yang thig). Although tracing its roots back to Padmasambhava and Vimalamitra in the eighth century, the snying thig texts and their practices likely derive from Tibetan reformulations of great completion teachings beginning in the eleventh century, when new translations of Indian tantras were being made in Tibet. A wide range of new meditative systems were added into the rdzogs chen corpus, which would prove to be essential to Tibetan Buddhist practice, especially in the RNYING MA and BKA' BRGYUD sects in subsequent centuries.

**snying thig ya bzhi**. (T). See SNYING THIG.

**Sobhana Mahāthera**. (1904–1982). See MAHASI SAYADAW.

**Śobhita**. (P. Sobhita; T. Mdzes pa; C. Guoyi; J. Kae; K. Kwaŭi 菓衣). An eminent ARHAT elder declared by the Buddha to be foremost among his monk disciples in remembering past births (PŪRVANIVĀSĀNUSMṚTI). He was born the son of a brāhmaṇa family and dwelled in the city of ŚRĀVASTĪ. Hearing the Buddha preach one day, he resolved to renounce the world and enter the order as a monk. After some time he attained arhatship. During the time of Padmottara (P. Padumuttara) Buddha, when he was a householder living in the city of Haṃsavatī, he heard the Buddha praise a monk disciple as foremost in his ability to recall previous lives. It was then that he resolved to earn that same distinction during the dispensation of a future buddha. During the time of Sumedha Buddha, Śobhita was a learned brāhmaṇa who was expert in the Vedas. He renounced the householder's life to observe piety as a hermit in the environs of the Himālaya mountains. When he heard a Buddha had appeared in the world, he rushed to Bandhumatī to sing the Buddha's praises.

**ṣoḍaśasthavira**. (T. gnas brtan bcu drug; C. shiliu zunzhe; J. jūrokusonja; K. simnyuk chonja 十六尊者). In Sanskrit, "the sixteen elders" (most commonly known in the East Asian tradition as the "sixteen ARHATS"); a group of sixteen venerated arhat (C. LUOHAN) disciples of the Buddha whom the Buddha orders to forgo NIRVĀṆA and to continue to dwell in this world in order to preserve the Buddhist teachings until the coming of the future buddha, MAITREYA. Each of these arhats is assigned an (often mythical) residence and a retinue of disciples. With Maitreya's advent, they will gather the relics of the current buddha ŚĀKYAMUNI and erect one last STŪPA to hold them, after which they will finally pass into PARINIRVĀṆA. The *Śāriputraparipṛcchā* ("Sūtra on Śāriputra's Questions"), which was translated at least by the Eastern Jin dynasty (317–420 CE) but may date closer to the beginning of the millennium, mentions four great monks (mahā-BHIKṢU) to whom the Buddha entrusted the propagation of the teachings after his death: MAHĀKĀŚYAPA, PIṆḌOLA, Kundovahan (C. Juntoupohan, "Holder of the Mongoose," apparently identical to BAKKULA), and RĀHULA. The MILE XIASHENG JING ("Sūtra on the Advent of Maitreya"), translated in 303 CE by DHARMARAKṢA, states instead that the Buddha instructed these same four monks to wait until after the buddhadharma of the current dispensation was completely extinct before entering PARINIRVĀṆA. The *Śāriputraparipṛcchā*'s account is also found in the FAHUA WENJU by TIANTAI ZHIYI (538–597) of the Sui dynasty. The *Mahāyānāvatāra* (C. *Ru dasheng lun*; "Entry into the Mahāyāna"), a treatise written by Sāramati (C. Jianyi) and translated into Chinese c. 400 CE by Daotai of the Northern Liang dynasty (397–439) first mentions "sixteen" great disciples (mahā-ŚRĀVAKA) who disperse throughout the world to preserve the Buddha's teachings after his death, but does not name them. Indeed, it is not until the Tang dynasty that the full list of sixteen disciples who preserve the buddhadharma is first introduced into the Chinese tradition. This complete list first appears in the *Nandimitrāvadāna* (*Da aluohan Nantimiduo luo suoshuo fazhu ji*, abbr. *Fazhu ji*, "Record of the Duration of the Dharma Spoken by the Great Arhat NANDIMITRA"), which was translated by XUANZANG in 654 CE. (Nandimitra [C. Qingyou zunzhe] was born in the second century CE in Sri Lanka.) This text tells the story of the Buddha's special charge to this group of elders and offers each of their names, residences, and numbers of disciples. JINGQI ZHANRAN's (711–782) *Fahua wenju ji*, a commentary to TIANTAI ZHIYI's (538–597) FAHUA WENJU, also cites an account from the apocryphal *Ratnameghasūtra* (*Bao yun jing*) that the Buddha charged sixteen "worthy ones" (S. arhat; C. luohan) with preserving the BUDDHADHARMA until the advent of Maitreya, after which they could then enter parinirvāṇa. Zhanran's citation of this sūtra gives the names of each of the sixteen arhats, along with their residence and the number of their followers; but while Piṇḍola's and Rāhula's names are included in the sixteen, Mahākāśyapa is not mentioned. According to the *Xuanhe huapu* ("The Xuanhe Chronology of Painting"), the earliest Chinese iconography showing a group of sixteen disciples probably dates to the Liang dynasty (502–557), when ZHANG SENGYAO (d.u.; fl c. 502–549) first painted a rendering of the ṣoḍaśasthavira. After the *Nandimitrāvadāna* was translated into Chinese in the middle of the seventh century, the group of sixteen elders became so universally revered within China that many verses, paintings, and sculptures were dedicated to them. As a group, they appear frequently in East Asian monastic art, each arhat specifically identified by his unique (and often wildly exaggerated) physical characteristics. The most renowned such painting was made at the end of the ninth century by the monk CHANYUE GUANXIU (832–912); his work became the standard presentation of the sixteen. His vivid portrayal of the arhats offers an extreme, stylized rendition of how the Chinese envisioned "Indians" (fan) or "Westerners" (hu). He gives each of his subjects a distinctive bearing and deportment and unique phrenological features and physical characteristics; these features are subsequently repeated routinely in the Chinese artistic tradition. The standard roster of arhats now recognized in the East Asian tradition, in their typical order, are (1) PIṆḌOLA BHĀRADVĀJA; (2) KANAKAVATSA; (3) KANAKA BHĀRADVĀJA; (4) SUBINDA [alt. Suvinda]; (5) BAKKULA [alt. Bākula, Nakula]; (6) BHADRA; (7) KĀLIKA [alt. Karīka]; (8) VAJRAPUTRA; (9) JĪVAKA; (10) PANTHAKA; (11) RĀHULA; (12) NĀGASENA; (13) AṄGAJA; (14) VANAVĀSIN; (15) AJITA; (16) CŪḌAPANTHAKA. Sometime before the Song dynasty, the Chinese occasionally added two extra arhats to the roster, possibly in response to Daoist configurations of teachers, giving a total of eighteen. The most common of these additional members were Nandimitra (the putative subject of the text in which the protectors are first mentioned by name) and Piṇḍola Bhāradvāja (another transcription of the arhat who already appears on the list), although Mahākāśyapa also frequently appears. The Tibetan tradition adds still other figures. In a standard form of the Tibetan ritual, the sixteen elders are listed as Aṅgaja, Ajita, Vanavāsin, Kālika, Vajraputra, Bhadra, Kanakavatsa, Kanaka Bhāradvāja, Bakkula, Rāhula, Cūḍapanthaka, Piṇḍola Bhāradvāja, Panthaka, Nāgasena, GOPAKA (Sbed byed), and Abheda (Mi phyed pa). They are visualized together with Śākyamuni Buddha whose teaching they have been entrusted to protect, their benefactor the layman (UPĀSAKA) Dharmatāla [alt. Dharmatāra, Dharmatrāta], and the four great kings (CATURMAHĀRĀJA) VAIŚRAVAṆA [alt. Kubera], DHṚTARĀṢṬRA, VIRŪḌHAKA, and VIRŪPĀKṢA. Each of the elders is described as having a particular scroll, begging bowl, staff, and so on, and in a particular posture with a set number of arhats. They come miraculously from their different sacred abodes, assemble, are praised, and worshipped with the recitation of the bodhisattva SAMANTABHADRA's ten vows in the BHADRACARĪPRAṆIDHĀNA. Then, with solemn requests to protect the dispensation by watching over the lives of the gurus, they are requested to return to their respective homelands. In other rituals, one finds BUDAI heshang (Cloth-Bag Monk, viz., AṄGAJA), the Buddha's mother, Queen MĀYĀ, and his successor, Maitreya; or the two ancient Indian Buddhist sages "Subduer of Dragons" (C. Xianglong) and "Subduer of Lions" (C. Fuhu). See also LUOHAN; and individual entries on each of the sixteen arhats/sthaviras.

**Soga**. (蘇我). A powerful clan (J. uji) in Japan from the sixth through the mid-seventh centuries and early patrons of Buddhism in the Japanese isles. The Soga may have been descendants of immigrants from the Korean peninsula, as suggested in part by their close ties with the Korean Paekche kingdom; Soga no Iname (d. 570) appears to have been one of the first supporters of Buddhism in Japan, learning about the tradition via Paekche. As no textual sources exist from this early period, ascertaining their role in the Yamato court remains a difficult task and a topic much debated among scholars. Not until the *Nihon shoki* ("Chronicles of Japan"; 720) do we arrive at a historical account of the clan. This text was commissioned by the lineage of Tenmu (r. 672–686), who may have wanted to cast the Soga in negative light. Nevertheless, it offers the following narrative. Beginning with Soga no Iname, four generations of the Soga clan served as chief ministers (J. ōomi) to the Yamato court. Two of Iname's daughters were married to the emperor Kinmei (r. 531 or 539?–571), and three of his grandchildren are purported in the *Nihon shoki* to have been monarchs: Yōmei (r. 585–587), Sushun (r. 587–592), and Suiko (r. 593–628). It is also asserted that Soga no Umako (d. 626), son of Iname, commissioned the construction of the monastery of ASUKADERA. Archeological evidence suggests that this monastery was the greatest temple of its time in size and influence, despite the fact that it receives little attention in the *Nihon shoki*. By the mid-seventh century, the Soga clan heads, notably Umako's son, Emishi (d. 645), and Emishi's son, Soga no Iruka (d. 645), appear to have been the most powerful members of the Yamato court. According to the *Nihon shoki*, in 643, Iruka made a successful attack on SHŌTOKU TAISHI's surviving son, Yamashiro no Ōe and others. Prince Naka no Ōe, later enthroned as Tenji (r. 661–672), counterattacked in 644, killing Iruka and other Soga family members. Emishi and much of the rest of the Soga clan are said to have been forced to commit suicide the following day. Soga no Akae (623–672?), grandson of Umako, survived the coup, serving as ōomi through the Taika Reform (645). With the massacre of most of the clan, however, its power was substantially diminished.

**Sogdiana**. A kingdom in Inner Asia (the Greek Transoxiana) centered on the Zeravshan River in modern Uzbekistan. The Sogdians dominated trade between China and India from the second through the tenth centuries CE. Their language, Sogdian (a branch of Indo-Iranian), was used along the SILK ROAD as a mercantile language and Buddhist texts from China were translated into Sogdian and used by Buddhists in this region. (There is no evidence that Buddhist texts in Indian languages were translated into Sogdian.) In East Asia, monks from the kingdom of Sogdiana were designated with the ethnikon KANG, as in the case of the early translator KANG SENGHUI (d. 280).

**sōhei**. (僧兵). In Japanese, "monks' militia." During the mid-Heian period, the major Buddhist monasteries near Nara and Kyōto, such as KŌFUKUJI, ENRYAKUJI, and Onjōji (later called MIIDERA), became large landholders and were deeply immersed in political activities. The monasteries maintained small armies of private warriors to protect their assets and promote their interests. Although these warriors wore Buddhist robes and lived inside the temple complexes, they were not formally ordained; on the battlefield, they also wore full armor, making them virtually indistinguishable from ordinary warriors. During this period, these warriors were called simply "members of the congregation" (shuto; daishu) or pejoratively referred to as "evil monks" (akusō); the term sōhei seems not to have been used until 1715, when it first appeared in the *Dainihon shi* ("The History of Great Japan"). These monks' militias were mustered against both rival temples and secular authorities. From the tenth to the twelfth centuries, monks' militias engaged in pitched battles with their rivals, as in the intrasectarian rivalry between the Tendai monasteries of Enryakuji and Onjōji, and the intersectarian rivalries between Kōfukuji and its two Tendai counterparts. During this same period, monks' militias also participated in the Genpei War of 1180–1185, which led to the establishment of the Kamakura shogunate. There were more than two hundred major violent incidents involving monks' militias between the late-tenth and early-sixteenth centuries. The monks' militia of Enryakuji also battled the temples established by the new schools of JŌDO SHINSHŪ and NICHIRENSHŪ, which gained popularity among commoners and local warlords during the fifteenth and sixteenth centuries: for example, Enryakuji sōhei attacked and destroyed the original HONGANJI in Ōtani (east of Kyōto) in 1465 and twenty-one Nichiren temples in Kyōto in 1536. However, the power of monks' militias diminished significantly after 1571, when the warlord Oda Nobunaga (1534–1582) massacred the Buddhist clerics and sōhei on HIEIZAN and burned down Enryakuji, which had threatened him with its military power. Monks' militias are not an exclusively Japanese phenomenon but are found across much of the Buddhist tradition. See also HUGUO FOJIAO.

**Sōhō Myōchō**. [alt. Shūhō Myōchō] (宗峰妙超) (1282–1337/8). Japanese ZEN master of the RINZAISHŪ; commonly known as DAITŌ KOKUSHI (State Preceptor Great Lamp). Daitō was a native of Harima in present-day Hyōgo prefecture. At the age of ten, he entered the nearby TENDAI monastery of Engyōji on Mt. Shosha and received Tendai training under a VINAYA master Kaishin (d.u.). Later, Daitō visited the Zen master KŌHŌ KENNICHI at the monastery of Manjuji in Kamakura and received the full monastic precepts. In 1304, Daitō began his training under NANPO JŌMYŌ at the temple of Tōkōan in Kyoto. He followed Nanpo to Manjuji in Kyōto and again to KENCHŌJI in Kamakura. At Kenchōji, Daitō had his first awakening. According to legend, Daitō is said to have been instructed by Nanpo to continue his post-SATORI (awakening) cultivation for another twenty years. During this period of training, Daitō is said to have once lived as a beggar underneath the Gojō Bridge in Kyōto. Shortly after his teacher's death in 1308, Daitō left for Kyōto where he did indeed live for twenty years in a hermitage known as Ungoan. Later, Daitō moved to the Murasakino district in Kyōto and established the monastery of DAITOKUJI. In 1323, he was summoned by retired Emperor Hanazono (r. 1308–1318) and was given the title State Preceptor Master Daitō. Daitō also received the patronage of Emperor Godaigo (r. 1318–1339). They elevated the status of Daitokuji to that of NANZENJI, then the most powerful GOZAN monastery in Kyōto. Daitō and Nanpo's lineage, now known as the Ōtōkan, came to dominate the Rinzai Zen tradition.

**sojae toryang**. (消災道場). In Korean, "calamities-solving ritual"; one of the four most important annual rituals performed at court during the Koryŏ dynasty (918–1392), second only to the YŎNDŬNGHOE (lantern ritual). The sojae toryang is a representative of the esoteric Buddhist rituals that became popular in Korea during the Koryŏ dynasty. The first record of the ritual's performance dates from 1046, the last from 1399, a short time after the demise of the dynasty. This ritual to prevent natural calamities probably derives originally not from Buddhist cosmology but from the theory of heavenly retribution that was foundational in traditional East Asian thought. Koryŏ's ritual system, modeled after that of Tang China, presumed that cosmological influences dominated human life and activities. Since droughts, floods, and epidemics were considered "calamities from Heaven" (Ch'ŏnjae), and indicated Heaven's dissatisfaction with the quality of terrestrial governance, the sojae toryang sought to draw on various religious and astral powers in order to ward off these threats and to enhance the longevity of its royal sponsors. Koryŏ kings lavished riches on the monasteries whose monks performed these rituals, particularly when Koryŏ was threatened by foreign invasion or occupation. This concern explains why the majority of the recorded performances of the sojae toryang occurred during the reigns of kings Kojong (1231–1259), Wŏnjong (1259–1274), and Ch'ungnyŏl (1274–1308), who all ruled during the period of Mongol domination in Korea. During King Wŏnjong's thirteen-year reign, for example, the sojae toryang was performed twenty-three times, or about three times every two years. Historical sources provide little information on how the ritual was actually performed, but its conduct can be inferred from esoteric Buddhist sources. These sources require the monks to establish a purified ritual venue, install a buddha image there, and then make offerings of incense, flowers, and lanterns; once the site is prepared, they are then to recite various codes or spells (DHĀRAṆĪ) in order to invoke the power of the BODHISATTVAS, the seven stars of the Big Dipper (see BEIDOU QIXING), the gods of the zodiacal mansions and the constellations, the sun and moon, etc., to overcome calamities and transform disasters into blessings. In the case of the Koryŏ dynasty, the ritual was always held at court, and the king himself was both participant and presider at the ritual, indicating the close association between court and the religion during this period in Korean history.

**Sōjiji**. (總持寺). In Japanese, "DHĀRAṆĪ Monastery"; one of the two main monasteries of the SŌTŌSHŪ of ZEN Buddhism, located in Tsurumi, Yokohama. This monastery was originally established on the Noto peninsula (present-day Ishikawa prefecture) in 740 as Morookadera by the monk GYŌGI (668–749), who also founded TŌDAIJI. In 1321, KEIZAN JŌKIN (1268–1325), the founding patriarch of the Sōtō Zen institution, came into possession of this local monastery, which he renamed Sōjiji. In 1322, Sōjiji were sanctioned as an official monastery by Emperor Godaigo (r. 1318–1339), an event that is traditionally considered to mark the official establishment of Sōtō as an independent Zen institution in Japan. Keizan later entrusted Sōjiji to his disciple Gasan Jōseki (1276–1366). Sōjiji was an important government-sponsored monastery during the Muromachi and Edo periods and its status rivaled that of the other main Sōtō monastery, EIHEIJI; in its heyday, the monastery is said to have had more than seventy buildings within its precincts. After burning to the ground in 1898, the monastery was rebuilt in Yokohama in 1911, because Sōtō Zen leaders calculated that a location near Tokyo would have strategic value for the growth of the sect. Sōjiji is entered through a gigantic copper-roofed gate (sanmon) that was built in 1969. The butsuden, or main buddha hall, was completed in 1915 and enshrines a statue of ŚĀKYAMUNI with his disciples MAHĀKĀŚYAPA and ĀNANDA. There is a founders' hall (taisodō) for Keizan Jōkin that displays statues of the major historical figures of the Sōtō Zen tradition and that also doubles as a lecture hall; in addition, there is a large SAṂGHA hall (daisōdō) for ordaining and training monks, which displays a statue of the BODHISATTVA MAÑJUŚRĪ. Other buildings at the monastery include additional living quarters for the monks, a hall for Emperor Godaigo, and a hōmotsukan, or treasure house, full of important cultural properties held at the monastery, including a hanging tapestry from the Edo period that originally served as a cover for the chair of senior monks delivering sermons, and several precious buddha images.

**sōjō**. (僧正). In Japanese, "SAṂGHA primate"; one of the two earliest ecclesiastical positions created within the Japanese Buddhist church. According to the *Nihon shoki* ("Chronicles of Japan"), the first person to hold this position was the early-seventh-century Korean monk KWALLŬK (d.u.). Kwallŭk came to Japan in 602 from the southwestern Korean kingdom of Paekche and was appointed as sōjō in 624, when the government, alarmed by a widespread lack of discipline among the monks, established the sōgō (office of monastic affairs) to supervise national ecclesiastical affairs. The sōjō was later divided into three sub-positions, each of which was appointed by the government on the recommendation of the Buddhist order. In the early-Heian period, monks from the Nara Buddhist establishment (see NARA BUDDHISM, SIX SCHOOLS OF) dominated the sōjō positions. By the middle of the ninth century, however, monks from the TENDAISHŪ and SHINGONSHŪ schools held most of the appointments, and during the Kamakura period, Zen and pure land monks also were appointed sōjō. By the time of the Tokugawa regime, almost all Buddhist sects, including Tendai, Shingon, PURE LAND, and NICHIRENSHŪ, had adherents who were appointed to the sōjō positions. Once the Meiji government in 1872 split Buddhist ecclesiastical positions off from official government posts, each sect then established its own sōjō positions, each with slightly different administrative systems.

**Sōka Gakkai**. (創價學會/創価学会). In Japanese, "Value-Creating Society," a Japanese Buddhist lay organization associated with the NICHIRENSHŪ, founded by MAKIGUCHI TSUNESABURO (1871–1944) and his disciple Toda Jōsei (1900–1958). Formerly a teacher, Makiguchi became a follower of Nichiren's teachings, finding that they supported his own ideas about engendering social and religious values, and converted to NICHIREN SHŌSHŪ in 1928. In 1930, he established a lay organization under the umbrella of the

Nichiren Shōshū, which initially called itself the Sōka Kyōiku Gakkai (Creating Educational Values Society), and led its first general meeting. After its inauguration, the society began to take on a decidedly religious character, focusing on missionary work for Nichiren Shōshū. As the Pacific War expanded, Makiguchi and his followers refused to cooperate with state-enforced SHINTŌ practices, leading to a rift between them and TAISEKIJI, the head monastery of Nichiren Shōshū. In 1943, the society almost disintegrated with the imprisonment of Makiguchi and Toda, along with twenty other leaders charged with lèse-majesté and violations of the Public Order Act, which required each family to enshrine a Shintō talisman in its home. Makiguchi died in 1944 in prison, but Toda survived and was released on parole in July 1945. After his release, Toda took charge of the organization, renaming it Sōka Gakkai in 1946. He successfully led a massive proselytization campaign that gained Sōka Gakkai and Nichiren Shōshū vast numbers of new converts and by the late 1950s, upwards of 750,000 families had become adherents. After Toda died in 1958, IKEDA DAISAKU (b. 1928) became its third president and the society grew even more rapidly in Japan during the 1960s and the 1970s. In 1975, Ikeda also founded Sōka Gakkai International (SGI), which disseminated the society's values around the world. Sōka Gakkai publishes numerous books and periodicals, as well as a daily newspaper in Japan. During this period, Sōka Gakkai also became involved in Japanese domestic politics, establishing its own political party, the Kōmeitō (Clean Government Party) in 1964, which became completely separate and independent from the Sōka Gakkai in 1970. The society also supported Taisekiji with massive donations, including raising the funds for a new main shrine hall for the monastery. Sōka Gakkai, like other groups in the Nichiren lineage, focuses on worship of the SADDHARMAPUṆḌARĪKASŪTRA ("Lotus Sūtra") and its adherents are expected to chant daily the title (DAIMOKU) of the sūtra, NAM MYŌHŌRENGEKYŌ, as well as recite the most important sections of the sūtra and study Nichiren's writings. Sōka Gakkai believes that all beings possess the capacity to attain buddhahood and emphasizes the ability of each person's buddha-nature to overcome obstacles and achieve happiness. Sōka Gakkai followers can accomplish these goals through a "human revolution" (the title of one of Ikeda's books) that creates a sense of oneness between the individual and the environment, thus demonstrating how each individual can positively affect the surrounding world. As tensions grew between the Nichiren Shōshū and its increasingly powerful lay subsidiary, Nikken (b. 1922), the sixty-seventh chief priest of Nichiren Shōshū, tried to bring its membership directly under his control. His efforts were ultimately unsuccessful and he excommunicated the Sōka Gakkai in 1991, forbidding Sōka Gakkai followers from having access to the holiest shrines associated with Nichiren. Sōkka Gakkai remains at the center of controversy because of its strong emphasis on recruitment and proselytization, its demonization of enemies, and a mentorship structure within the organization that some claim creates a cult of personality centered on Ikeda. Sōka Gakkai remains among the largest Buddhist organizations in the Western world.

**Sŏkkuram**. (石窟庵). In Korean, "Stone Grotto Hermitage"; a Silla-period, man-made grotto located high on Mt. T'oham behind the monastery of PULGUKSA, which houses what is widely considered to be the most impressive buddha image in Korea. According to the SAMGUK YUSA ("Memorabilia of the Three Kingdoms," written c. 1282–1289), the master builder Kim Taesŏng (d. 774), who also designed Pulguksa, constructed the cave as an expression of filial piety toward his deceased parents. However, because the grotto directly faces the underwater tomb of the Silla king Munmu (r. 661–680) in the East Sea/Sea of Japan, the site may be also have been associated with a funerary cult surrounding the Silla royal family or with state-protection Buddhism (K. hoguk Pulgyo; C. HUGUO FOJIAO). The construction of both monasteries began around 751 CE, during the reign of the Silla king Kyŏngdŏk (r. 742–764), and the grotto temple was completed a few years after Kim Taesŏng's death in 774 CE. The site was originally named SŎKPULSA, or "Stone Buddha Monastery." Since the Korean peninsula has no natural stone grottos like those found in India or Central Asia, the cave was excavated out of the mountainside, and some 360 large granite blocks in various shapes were used to create the ceiling of the shrine. In addition, granite carvings were attached to the inner walls. The result was what appears for all intents and purposes to be a natural cave temple. The finished grotto combines two different styles of Buddhist architecture, the domed rotunda design of the CAITYA halls of India and the cave-temple design of Central Asia and China as seen in DUNHUANG and others sites along the SILK ROAD. At the Sŏkkuram grotto, a rectangular antechamber with two guardians carved on either side leads into a short, narrow passageway that opens onto the thirty-foot-(nine m.) high domed rotunda. In the vestibule itself are carvings of the four heavenly kings as guardians of the dharma. The center of the rotunda chamber enshrines the Sŏkkuram stone buddha, a seated-buddha image in the "earth-touching gesture" (BHŪMISPARŚAMUDRĀ). This image is 10 ft. 8 in. (3.26 meters) in height and carved from a single block of granite; it sits atop a lotus-throne base that is 5 ft. 2 in. (1.58 meters) high. The image is generally accepted to be that of ŚĀKYAMUNI Buddha, although some scholars instead identify it as an image of VAIROCANA or even AMITĀBHA. In the original layout of the grotto, the morning sunshine would have cascaded through the cave's entrance and struck the jeweled ŪRṆĀKEŚA in the Buddha's forehead. On the inner walls surrounding the statue are thirty-nine carvings of Buddhist figures, including the Indian divinities BRAHMĀ and INDRA, the two flanking bodhisattvas SAMANTABHADRA and MAÑJUŚRĪ, and the buddha's ten principal ARHAT-disciples. On the wall directly behind the main image is a carving of the eleven-headed AVALOKITEŚVARA. The combination of exquisite architectural beauty and sophisticated design is widely considered to be the pinnacle of Silla Buddhist culture. Despite its fame and reputation during the Silla kingdom,

Sŏkkuram fell into disrepair during the suppression of Buddhism that occurred during the Chosŏn dynasty (1392–1910). Almost everyone except locals had forgotten the grotto until one rainy day in 1909, when a weary postman traveling over the ridge of Mt. T'oham accidentally rediscovered the grotto as he sought shelter from a sudden thunderstorm. He found a narrow opening to a small cave, and as his eyes adjusted to the dark, he was startled to see the massive stone image of the Buddha along with exquisite stone wall carvings. In 1913, the Japanese colonial government spent two years dismantling and repairing the structure, using cement and iron, which later collected moisture and began to decay, threatening the superstructure of the grotto. In 1920, the earth was removed in order to secure the foundation and tar and asphalt were used to waterproof the roof. No further renovations were made until a UNESCO survey team came to evaluate the cave temple and decided to aid the Korean government in further restoring the site between 1961 and 1964. Nowadays, visitors enter the grotto from the side, rather than its original front entrance, and must view the buddha image from behind a protective glass window. Sŏkkuram is Korean National Treasure No. 24 and was also added to the list of UNESCO World Heritage Sites in 1995.

**Sŏkpulsa**. (K) (石佛寺). See SŎKKURAM.

**sokushin jōbutsu**. (C. jishen chengfo; K. chŭksin sŏngbul 即身成佛). In Japanese, "attainment of buddhahood in this very body." This doctrine is generally first attributed to KŪKAI (774–835), the founder of the SHINGONSHŪ, who argued in a work entitled *Sokushin jōbutsugi* ("The Meaning of Attaining Buddhahood in This Very Body") that the ultimate goal of practice was to attain awakening in this lifetime. By strictly adhering to Kūkai's ritualization of the body (through gestures, or MUDRĀ), speech (through spells, or MANTRA) and mind (as a MAṆḌALA), one could therefore align oneself with the cosmic buddha, MAHĀVAIROCANA, and become a buddha in one's own right. Kūkai's contemporary, SAICHŌ (767–822) of the TENDAISHŪ, located the notion of sokushin jōbutsu in the exoteric teachings of the SADDHARMAPUṆḌARĪKASŪTRA ("Lotus Sūtra"). By following its teachings, he believed that anyone could achieve universal salvation and become a buddha. In contrast to Kūkai's esoteric interpretation of sokushin jōbutsu, however, Saichō presumed this process of achieving buddhahood would require several lifetimes to complete. Given the two models, it is easy to understand the appeal of Kūkai's esoteric version, which promised immediate transformation into buddhahood, over the traditional Tendai doctrine cited by Saichō. As the interest in esotericism increased among the aristocracy during the Heian period (794–1185), Tendai Buddhism became more associated with esoteric ritual and less with practice derived from the *Saddharmapuṇḍarīkasūtra*. This shift toward esoteric Buddhism was completed under the Tendai master ANNEN (841–889?), who asserted not only that sokushin jōbutsu was attainable in a single lifetime, but that it was central to the Tendai ordination procedure. Given that the two dominant institutions of Heian Buddhism relied heavily on the doctrine of sokushin jōbutsu, it is not surprising that SHUGENDŌ, a movement heavily influenced by both of these schools, would also develop its own interpretation of this doctrine. The means Shugendō advocated for attaining buddhahood, however, were quite varied, as most Shugen mountains operated independently up until the Tokugawa period. One common ritual performed in both the Yoshino/KUMANO region and on Mt. Haguro, for instance, was passage through the ten realms of being (J. jikkai, S. DAŚADHĀTU). Physical structures placed along a pilgrimage route, such as torii gates and steps, served as symbolic gateways through the realms. By progressing from the lowest realm of the hells (see S. NĀRAKA) to the highest realm of the buddhas, the pilgrim could ritually enact his journey toward his own attainment of buddhahood. Furthermore, the concept of mountain geography as a maṇḍala in Shugendō created a space through which one entered the sacred realm of buddhahood. By crossing the border separating the mundane from the sacred, the practitioner would undergo a spiritual transformation by directly encountering the Buddha and immediately awakening. In a more severe example, ascetics at Mt. Yudono known as isse gyōnin (lifetime ascetics) practiced sokushin jōbutsu during the Tokugawa period by undergoing strict austerities in the mountains for from one to three thousand days. Once this period ended, a handful of these gyōnin ascetics, following the alleged precedent of Kūkai, entered a nearly airtight, underground chamber to die. Soon afterward, they were mummified as buddhas "in this very body" and venerated by their followers. During the Kamakura period, NICHIREN (1222–1282), who, like Saichō, emphasized the superiority of the *Saddharmapuṇḍarīkasūtra*, further claimed that chanting the title (DAIMOKU) of the sūtra could lead to the attainment of buddhahood in this very body. Relying on the FAHUA XUANYI, an important commentary on the *Saddharmapuṇḍarīkasūtra* by the Chinese monk TIANTAI ZHIYI (538–597), Nichiren claimed that the essence of the sūtra was distilled in its title and that chanting the title (see NAMU MYŌHŌRENGEKYŌ) could therefore lead to the attainment of sokushin jōbutsu.

**solitary buddha**. See PRATYEKABUDDHA.

**Sŏltu Yuhyŏng**. (雪竇有炯) (1824–1889). Korean SŎN master of the Chosŏn dynasty, also known as Pongmun and Ponggi. In 1842, Sŏltu entered the monastery under the guidance of Chŏnggwan K'waeil (d.u.) on Mt. Paegyang, and the following year he received the precepts from Ch'immyŏng Hansŏng (1801–1876). Sŏltu studied at various places throughout the country before visiting the Sŏn master PAEKP'A KŬNGSŎN. In 1870, Sŏltu began restoration of the monastery of Pulgapsa on Mt. Moak. In 1889, he taught Sŏn meditation at the monastery of Ponginsa at the request of Hwanong Hwanjin (1824–1904). Sŏltu became ill shortly after his trip to Ponginsa, so he entrusted his robe and bowl to his disciple Sŏryu Ch'ŏmyŏng (1858–1903) and retired to the hermitage of Sorimgul, where he passed away in 1889. Sŏltu was a prolific writer whose works include the *Haejŏng nok*, *T'ongbang chŏngan*, *Sŏnwŏn soryu*, *Sŏltu sijip* and others. His *Sŏnwŏn soryu* was written as a response to CH'OŬI ŬISUN (1786–1866) and UDAM HONGGI (1822–1881) who criticized Paekp'a's influential treatise, *Sŏnmun sugyŏng* ("Hand Mirror of the Sŏn School").

**Somapura**. A large Buddhist monastery in northern Bangladesh, near the modern town of Ompur, probably built in the early-ninth century by the Pāla dynasty ruler Devapāla (r. 810–850 CE), the son of Dharmapāla, who had built VIKRAMAŚĪLA. Somapura was a mahāvihāra, or "great monastery," under royal supervision and was known as the Dharmapāla Mahāvihara of Somapura. The monastery, which had a unique architectural style, included 177 monks' cells organized on four floors around a courtyard. It was one of the largest monasteries of its day, probably housing some eight hundred monks at the apex of its influence. The most architecturally significant element of the monastery is the Pāhārpur Temple, which is unlike other Indian temples, Hindu or Buddhist. It has a cruciform base, a terraced structure with inset chambers, and a pyramid form, quite similar to Buddhist temples in Burma, Java, and Cambodia. It remains a matter of controversy whether Somapura monastery might have served as a model for Southeast Asian temple architecture. In the mid-eleventh century, the monastery was burned by a Hindu king, but seems to have been restored. It is said that ATIŚA DĪPAṂKARAŚRĪJÑĀNA stopped at Somapura on his way to Tibet, translating there BHĀVAVIVEKA's MADHYAMAKARATNAPRADĪPA into Tibetan.

**Somdej Toh**. [alt. Somdet Toh] (1788–1872). The popular name of Phra Buddhacharn Toh Phomarangsi, one of the most famous Thai monks of the nineteenth century. He was born in Kamphaeng Phet province and, according to some accounts, was the son of King Rāma II. After his ordination, he distinguished himself as a scholar of Pāli scriptures and was eventually appointed as preceptor to Prince Mongkut (later King RĀMA IV) when the prince was ordained as a novice. Somdej Toh retired to the forest shortly thereafter, returning to Bangkok when he was summoned by Mongkut after his coronation as king. He remained a mentor to the king throughout his life and many stories are told of their friendship. He served first as abbot of Wat Rakhang, across the river from the Thai royal palace. Somdej Toh was renowned for his eloquent sermons and his skills as a poet, as well as for being a meditation and VINAYA master. He also was famous as a maker of highly prized amulets. After his death, he became the object of a devotional cult, with mediums who claim to speak in his voice.

**Sŏn**. (禪). In Korean, "Meditation"; the Korean branch of the broader East Asian Chan school, which includes Chinese CHAN, Japanese ZEN, and Vietnamese THIỀN. Sŏn is the Korean pronunciation of the Chinese term CHAN, which in turn is a transcription of the Sanskrit term DHYĀNA, or meditative absorption. More specifically, Sŏn denotes the Korean Buddhist traditions that trace their origins back to the Chinese Chan school, or CHAN ZONG. Koreans such as CHŎNGJUNG MUSANG were important participants in the development of the new teachings of the Chan zong on the Chinese mainland; in addition, Korean pilgrims were bringing this tradition home to the peninsula no later than the early-ninth century during the Silla dynasty. At least nine of these pilgrims are known to have established their own Sŏn lineages, which are traditionally referred to as the Nine Mountains School of Sŏn (KUSAN SŎNMUN). Eight of these nine traditions were associated with the lineage of MAZU DAOYI and the HONGZHOU ZONG, which was known for its iconoclastic approach to Chan pedagogy. The Sŏn tradition flourished during the Koryŏ dynasty largely through the efforts of POJO CHINUL and his successor CHIN'GAK HYESIM, and the late-Koryŏ and early-Chosŏn figures T'AEGO POU, MUHAK CHACH'O, and NAONG HYEGŬN. During this period, the teachings of masters associated with the Chinese Imje chong (C. LINJI ZONG) lineage became especially influential in Korea, and Sŏn practice came to focus on the meditative technique of "observing the meditative topic," or "questioning meditation" (K. kanhwa Sŏn, C. KANHUA CHAN). The Sŏn schools, like all of the religion, suffered under the centuries-long suppression of Buddhism during the Chosŏn dynasty, which reduced all the different strands of Korean Buddhism to the "two traditions of Sŏn (Meditation) and Kyo (Doctrine)" (SŎN KYO YANGJONG). Even during this period of crisis, however, Korean Sŏn produced some of its most eminent teachers, including CH'ŎNGHŎ HYUJŎNG and his student SAMYŎNG YUJŎNG. Sŏn was revitalized during the late-nineteenth and early-twentieth centuries thanks to the efforts of such monks as KYŎNGHŎ SŎNGU and MAN'GONG WŎLMYŎN. Two of the dominant schools of contemporary Korean Buddhism, the CHOGYE CHONG and T'AEGO CHONG, both consider themselves predominantly Sŏn traditions.

**Soṇā**. (C. Shuna; J. Shuna; K. Suna 輸那). The Sanskrit and Pāli proper name of an eminent nun declared by the Buddha to be foremost among nuns in her capacity for effort. According to the Pāli account, she belonged to a clan from Sāvatthi (S. ŚRĀVASTĪ) and had ten sons and daughters, whence she acquired the epithet Bahuputtikā, meaning "possessed of many children." Her husband left home to become a mendicant, after which she distributed her estate among her children. Despite her generosity, her children neglected her in her old age, so she entered the nuns' order. She devoted herself to serving the other nuns by performing chores and menial tasks for them and in the evening she devoted herself to study. When the Buddha became aware of her efforts, he magically appeared before her to encourage her striving, whereupon she became an ARHAT. Since the other nuns had been in the habit of finding fault with Soṇā despite her services, Soṇā was concerned that they would accrue demerit if they continued to do so now that she had attained arhatship. She devised a display of magical power to demonstrate her superior attainment: in the morning when the nuns arrived at the refectory, she supplied them with water heated not with fire but with the supernatural power (ṚDDHI). Recognizing her attainment, the other nuns begged her forgiveness for their previous wrongdoing.

**Soṇa and Uttara**. [alt. Soṇuttara] (S. *Śroṇa; C. Xunajia; J. Shunaka; K. Sunaga 須那迦; S. Uttara; C. Yuduoluo; J. Uttara; K. Ultara 欝多羅). According to Pāli sources, two ARHAT elders dispatched as missionaries to SUVAṆṆABHŪMI (S. Suvarṇabhūmi) to convert its inhabitants to Buddhism; one of nine missions commissioned by the elder MOGGALIPUTTATISSA after the conclusion of the third Buddhist council (SAṂGĪTI; see COUNCIL, THIRD) to propagate the doctrine. When Soṇa and Uttara arrived in Suvaṇṇabhūmi, they subdued a group of ocean-dwelling ogres who used to devour the newborn sons of the king; in memory of this victory, all the princes of the royal house were thereafter named Soṇuttara. The elders then went on to convert sixty thousand inhabitants of Suvaṇṇabhūmi by preaching the BRAHMAJĀLASUTTA. In addition, five hundred noblemen became monks and fifteen hundred women became nuns. The Mons identify their homeland of Rāmaññadesa in Lower Burma as Suvaṇṇabhūmi and date the second foundation of their religion to the mission of Soṇa and Uttara. They attribute the first foundation of the dharma to the elder Gavaṃpati (S. GAVĀṂPATI), who first invited the Buddha to preach in Suvaṇṇabhūmi and who, after the Buddha's death, brought thirty-two tooth relics of the Buddha for interment in STŪPAS throughout the country.

**Soṇadaṇḍasutta**. (S. *Suvarṇadaṇḍasūtra; C. Zhongde jing; J. Shutokugyō; K. Chongdŏk kyŏng 種德經). In Pāli, "Sermon to Soṇadaṇḍa," the fourth sutta of the DĪGHANIKĀYA (a DHARMAGUPTAKA recension appears as the twenty-second sūtra in the Chinese translation of the DĪRGHĀGAMA); a discourse delivered by the Buddha to the learned and wealthy brāhmaṇa Soṇadaṇḍa (S. Suvarṇadaṇḍa) on what makes a person a true brāhmaṇa. Despite the protests of his fellow brāhmaṇas, Soṇadaṇḍa visited the Buddha while the latter sojourned in Campā on the banks of the Gaggarā lake. There, the Buddha convinces Soṇadaṇḍa that family lineage is of no consequence, and that only by virtue and moral action is one rightly called a brāhmaṇa. The Buddha describes how the mendicant refrains from evil deeds through the observance of morality and guards his senses (INDRIYASAṂVARA) with mindfulness (P. sati, S. SMṚTI) whereby he achieves contentment. He goes on to say that being content, the mendicant becomes glad and calm, whereby he can attain the four meditative absorptions (P. JHĀNA, S. DHYĀNA). Further, on the basis of having mastered the four meditative absorptions, the mendicant can develop the six higher knowledges or supranormal powers (P. abhiññā, S. ABHIJÑĀ), which culminate in enlightenment and liberation from the cycle of rebirth. Soṇadaṇḍa was pleased with the discourse and requests that the Buddha, together with a group of his monks, accept a meal from him. At the conclusion of the meal, Soṇadaṇḍa asks the Buddha to pardon him for not showing enough deference to him; the commentary explains that this was because Soṇadaṇḍa had been embarrassed to make obeisance to the Buddha in the presence of his brāhmaṇa colleagues.

**Soṇa-Kolivīsa**. (S. Śrona-Viṃśatikoṭi/Śrona-Koṭiviṃśa; T. Gro bzhin skyes bye ba nyi shu pa; C. Shoulongna/Ershiyi'er; J. Shurōna/Nijūokuni; K. Surongna/Isibŏgi 守籠那/二十億耳). Pāli name of an ARHAT declared by the Buddha to be foremost among his monk disciples in striving energetically. According to the Pāli account, he was born the son of a wealthy man in the country of Campā. Because he had given a precious ring to a PRATYEKABUDDHA (P. paccekabuddha) in a previous life, his body was the color of burnished gold. His hands and feet were delicate, and fine curly hair covered his feet. King BIMBISĀRA of MAGADHA wished to see the unusual markings of the youth and sent for him. While at the Magadha capital of RĀJAGṚHA, Soṇa and eighty thousand companions went to see the Buddha, who was preaching at that time in the city. Impressed by the miraculous powers displayed by Sāgata (S. SVĀGATA), the Buddha's attendant, Soṇa asked his parents to allow him to enter the order. After his ordination, the Buddha gave Soṇa a subject of meditation (KAMMAṬṬHĀNA), and Soṇa retired to the Sītavana grove to practice. Soṇa strove diligently, taking up walking meditation as his main practice; however, because he was interrupted by frequent visitors, he made little progress and grew despondent. His feet became blistered and bled, so much so that the meditation path (P. caṅkama, S. CAṄKRAMA) upon which he walked was soaked in blood like a slaughter house. Seeing this scene, the Buddha instructed Soṇa on how to temper his energy with tranquility, and in due time he attained arhatship. Because of his delicate feet, the Buddha is said to have given Soṇa dispensation to wear sandals of a single layer, even though monks and nuns were required to go barefoot. Soṇa declined the exemption, however, for he did not wish to be treated more leniently than his fellow monks. In response, the Buddha then gave permission to all his monks to use such sandals.

**Soṇa-Koṭikaṇṇa**. (S. Śroṇa-Koṭikarṇa; T. Gro bzhin skyes rna ba bye ba; C. Yi'er; J. Okuni; K. Ŏgi 億耳). Pāli name of an ARHAT declared by the Buddha to be foremost among monks in eloquence (S. PRATIBHĀNA; P. paṭibhāna). Soṇa's mother was Kālī Kuraragharikā and his father a wealthy merchant. He received the epithet Koṭikaṇṇa (S. Koṭikarṇa) because he wore an earring (kaṇṇa) worth a crore (KOṬI). Soṇa's mother had become a stream-enterer (SROTAĀPANNA) on the night he was born. The monk MAHĀKĀŚYAPA was a family friend and often visited the family in the town of Kuraraghara. As a young man, Soṇa once traveled with a caravan headed towards Ujjayinī

(P. Ujjeni), but along the way got left behind. Continuing the journey alone, he encountered a hungry ghost in the form of a man eating his own flesh. He learned that in an earlier existence the ghost had been a miserly merchant who cheated his customers. He then encountered two ghosts in the form of boys spitting up blood. In a previous life they had criticized their mother for feeding an arhat. Filled with misgiving, he returned to his home and related what he had seen to Mahākāśyapa, after which he requested permission to enter the order. Mahākāśyapa immediately ordained Soṇa as a novice and after three years gave him the UPASAMPADĀ higher ordination as a monk (P. bhikkhu, S. BHIKṢU). The delay was caused by the fact that in the outlying town of Kuraraghara it was difficult to gather the quorum of ten monks needed to perform the upasaṃpadā ceremony. Soṇa gained preeminence for perfectly reciting the AṬṬHAKAVAGGA for the Buddha, a text he had learned from Mahākāśyapa. To reward his skill, the Buddha granted Soṇa a boon. Soṇa requested to be allowed to ordain new monks using a quorum of only five rather than ten monks to facilitate the performance of the ritual procedure in outlying areas.

**Sŏnamsa**. (仙巖寺). In Korean, "Monastery of the Peaks of the Perfected," one of the main mountain monasteries of the T'AEGO CHONG of Korean Buddhism; located on the opposite side of CHOGYE Mountain from SONGGWANGSA, and near the city of Sunch'ŏn, in South Chŏlla province. The monastery claims to have been founded in 529 by the legendary Koguryŏ monk ADO. In 861, the monk TOSŎN (827–898) enlarged the monastery and gave it its current name Sŏnamsa. During the Koryŏ dynasty, the royal monk ŬICH'ŎN (1055–1101) expanded the monastery again, making it a center for ecumenical training in both Doctrine (KYO) and Meditation (SŎN). The monastery was destroyed during the Japanese Hideyoshi invasions of the late-sixteenth century; rebuilt, it burned again in the eighteenth century and was reconstructed by the monks Nuram Sikhwal (1752–1830) and Haebung Chollyŏng (d. 1826) during the reign of the Chosŏn King Sunjo (r. 1800–1834). During the Japanese colonial period (1910–1945), Sŏnamsa was one of the thirty-one major district monasteries (ponsan) of the Buddhist ecclesiastical administration. After the purification movement (chŏnghwa undong) that occurred in Korean Buddhism after the end of Japanese colonial rule and the Korean War, Sŏnamsa was the only major mountain monastery to remain under the control of the married monks in the T'aego order. The contemporary CHOGYE CHONG claims legal title to Sŏnamsa and lists it officially as the twentieth of its twenty-five parish monasteries (PONSA), but has ceded control to the T'aego order. In 1985, the T'aego order opened a center at Sŏnamsa to train a new generation of priests in its order. The entrance to Sŏnamsa is graced by two bridges, one of which, the Sŭngsŏn Bridge, is considered one of the most beautiful in Korea, especially when its view is combined with nearby Kangsŏllu Tower and a pond that includes a tree-studded island. Sŏnamsa also preserves one of the largest hanging pictures (see KWAEBUL, T'AENGHWA) in Korea, which depicts in intricate detail all the assemblies of the AVATAṂSAKASŪTRA (K. *Hwaŏm kyŏng*).

**Sŏn chong**. (禪宗). In Korean, "Sŏn school." See SŎN.

**Sŏn'ga kwigam**. (C. Chanjia guijian; J. Zenke kikan 禪家龜鑑). In Korean, "Mirror of the Sŏn House"; one of the most widely read SŎN texts not only in Korea but also in Japan and China, composed by the Chosŏn-period Sŏn master CH'ŎNGHŎ HYUJŎNG (1520–1604), a.k.a. SŎSAN TAESA, to whom most modern Korean Sŏn teachers trace their lineage. Hyujŏng composed the text around 1564 by adding his own commentary to excerpts he had culled from about fifty different Buddhist scriptures and CHAN and Sŏn texts. The text was originally written in literary Chinese, but was first published in a 1569 Korean vernacular (ŏnhae) edition. The first literary Chinese edition was published in 1579; the Chinese edition was introduced into China and Japan and has been frequently reprinted since in all three countries. The text is also included as the last section of Hyujŏng's *Samga kwigam* ("Mirror of the Three Houses" [of Confucianism, Daoism, and Buddhism]), but that version records only the excerpts without Hyujŏng's commentary. Hyujŏng wrote the *Sŏn'ga kwigam* as a concise primer of Korean Buddhist doctrines and practices for his students. According to Hyujŏng's preface and the postface of his disciple SAMYŎNG YUJŎNG (1544–1610), the primary motive for composing the text was to advocate the fundamental harmony between Sŏn and the scriptural teachings of Buddhism (KYO). While supporting the unity between these two major strands of the Buddhist tradition, Hyujŏng's treatment ultimately subordinates Kyo beliefs to Sŏn practices. This approach is adopted from that of the eminent Koryŏ state preceptor POJO CHINUL (1158–1210). In particular, the text proposes the practical model of "relinquishing Kyo and entering into Sŏn" (sagyo ipsŏn), by integrating doctrinal studies and the technique of "questioning meditation" (K. kanhwa Sŏn; C. KANHUA CHAN) into Chinul's preferred soteriological schema of sudden awakening/gradual cultivation (K. tono chŏmsu; C. DUNWU JIANXIU). In addition, the *Sŏn'ga kwigam* also offers the technique of reciting the name of the buddha AMITĀBHA (K. yŏmbul; C. NIANFO) as an alternative practice for those of inferior spiritual capacity who are not yet able to cultivate the kanhwa Sŏn technique. The text also outlines the styles and lineages of the "five houses" (see WU JIA QI ZONG) of the mature Chan school: in particular, the text promotes the LINJI ZONG as the true heir of the sixth patriarch (LIUZU) of Chan, HUINENG (638–713), and presents a different lineage from the traditional one by suggesting that the four Chan lineages of Linji zong, GUIYANG ZONG, FAYAN ZONG, and YUNMEN ZONG all originated from MAZU DAOYI (707–788). The text thus provides a basic framework for the doctrines and practices that most of the modern Korean tradition follows, and thus remains widely read and studied in Korea today.

**Sŏngch'ong**. (K) (性聰). See PAEGAM SŎNGCH'ONG.

**Song gaoseng zhuan**. (J. Sō kōsōden; K. Song kosŭng chŏn 宋高僧傳). In Chinese, "Biographies of Eminent Monks [compiled during the] Song dynasty"; a thirty-roll hagiographical collection compiled by the Buddhist historian and VINAYA master ZANNING (919–1001). The compilation of the text began in 980 by Song-dynasty imperial edict and was entered into the official canon (DAZANGJING) in 988. The text records the lives of monks who primarily were active during the period between the early Tang dynasty and the early Song, or some 340 years after the period covered by DAOXUAN's (596–667) XU GAOSENG ZHUAN ("Continued Biographies of Eminent Monks"). The *Song gaoseng zhuan* contains 531 major and 124 appended biographies, for a total of 655 biographies. The text offers valuable material on the Buddhist history of the Tang dynasty, including information that is not recorded in the official dynastic history. The collection is organized according to the ten categories of monastic expertise used in Daoxuan's collection: translators (yijing), exegetes (yijie), practitioners of meditation (xichan), specialists in vinaya (minglü), protectors of the DHARMA (hufa), sympathetic resonance (gantong), self-immolators (YISHEN), chanters (dusong), benefactors (xingfu), and miscellaneous (zake). What is noteworthy in comparison to its immediate predecessor is that the number of the monks categorized as exegetes (yijie) was reduced significantly from 246 in Daoxuan's collection to ninety-four in Zanning's. This traditional nonsectarian approach to Buddhist biographical writing was soon supplanted by genealogical collections, such as Daoyuan's (d.u.) 1004 JINGDE CHUANDENG LU, which organized the biographies of Chan monks according to explicit sectarian lineages, and ZHIPAN's (1220–1275) FOZU TONGJI, which did the same for the lineage of the TIANTAI ZONG. The *Song gaoseng zhuan* is not included in the Korean Buddhist canon (KORYŎ TAEJANGGYŎNG), but does appear in Chinese canons compiled during the Song, Yuan, and Ming periods. Unlike its two predecessor collections, the *Song gaoseng zhuan* is included in the Qing-dynasty imperial archive, the *Siku quanshu* ("Complete Library of the Four Repositories"), compiled between 1773 and 1782.

**songgu**. (J. juko; K. songgo 頌古). In Chinese, "[attaching] verses to ancient [cases]"; a "lettered Chan" (WENZI CHAN) literary style, which used verses to comment on the prose narratives of CHAN public cases (GONG'AN). See HUANGLONG PAI.

**Songgwangsa**. (松廣寺). In Korean, "Piney Expanse Monastery"; the twenty-first district monastery (PONSA) of the contemporary CHOGYE CHONG of Korean Buddhism, located on Mount Chogye in South Chŏlla province. Along with HAEINSA and T'ONGDOSA, Songgwangsa is one of the "three-jewel monasteries" (SAMBO SACH'AL), which represent one of the three jewels (RATNATRAYA) of Buddhism; Songgwangsa has traditionally been considered the "SAṂGHA-jewel monastery" (sŭngbo sach'al), because of the succession of sixteen state preceptors (K. kuksa; C. GUOSHI) who resided at the monastery during the Koryŏ dynasty. According to legend, Songgwangsa began as a small monastery named Kilsangsa, which was founded by a certain Hyerim (d.u.). In 1197, that monastery was restored and expanded by the eminent Sŏn master POJO CHINUL, who moved his SAMĀDHI and PRAJÑĀ Community (CHŎNGHYE KYŎLSA) to the Kilsangsa site. To commemorate the establishment of the expanded monastery, King Hŭijong (r. 1204–1211) renamed it SUSŎNSA, or Sŏn Cultivation Community, in 1208. (Still today, the meditation hall at the monastery uses the name Susŏnsa.) Chinul's reliquary STŪPA, the Kamno t'ap (Sweet Dew Reliquary), sits on a hill behind the meditation hall, overlooking the monastery he founded. During the Chosŏn dynasty, Songgwang, the original name of the mountain on which Susŏnsa was built, became the name of the monastery itself, and the mountain came to be known instead as Mt. Chogye. One of the most famous buildings at the monastery is the Kuksa chŏn (State Preceptors Hall), built in 1369 and now listed as Korean National Treasure no. 56, which enshrined early Chosŏn-period portraits (CHINYŎNG) of Chinul and the sixteen state preceptors at Songgwangsa. (The portraits were themselves collectively listed as cultural treasure no. 1043.) The portraits were stolen in 1995 in a brazen late-night heist and only three have been recovered. In 1969, Songgwangsa was elevated to the status of an ecumenical monastery (CH'ONGNIM), and is one of the five such centers in the contemporary Chogye order, which are all expected to provide training in the full range of practices that exemplify the major strands of the Korean Buddhist tradition. Songgwangsa is thus also known as the Chogye Ch'ongnim.

**Songshan**. (J. Sūzan; K. Sungsan 嵩山). In Chinese, "Lofty Mountain"; sacred mountain located in northern Henan province. Mt. Song, also known as Zhongyue (Middle Marchmount), belongs to what is known as the wuyue, or five marchmounts. Mt. Song is actually a mountain range consisting of two groups of peaks. To the east there are twenty-four peaks known collectively as Taishi, and to the west twenty-six peaks known as Shaoshi. Since ancient times, Mt. Song has been considered sacred. Emperors frequently made visits to the mountain and many who sought physical immortality found it to be an ideal dwelling place. Mt. Song has also been the home of many Buddhist monks. Sometime during the Han dynasty, a monastery known as Fawangsi (Dharma King Monastery) was built on Mt. Song. For centuries, the monastery received the support of many emperors, such as Emperor Wendi of the Sui dynasty, who renamed it Shelisi (ŚARĪRA Monastery), Emperor Taizong (r. 626–649) who renamed it Gongdesi (Merit Monastery), and Emperor Daizong (r. 762–779) who renamed it Wenshushili Guangde Bao'ensi (Mañjuśrī's Vast Virtue, Requiting Kindness Monastery). During the Song dynasty, the monastery was supported by Emperor Renzong (r. 1022–1063), who once again renamed it Fawangsi. Mt. Song was also the home of the famous monastery of SHAOLINSI, which is claimed to have been built on its Shaoshi peaks by a certain Indian monk named Fotuo (d.u.) in 496. Shaolinsi is perhaps best remembered as the home of the semilegendary Indian monk BODHIDHARMA, who is presumed to have dwelled in a cave nearby for nine years, engaged in BIGUAN (wall contemplation). To the west of Fawangsi, there was also a monastery by the name of Xianjusi (Tranquil Dwelling Monastery), which had once been the private villa of Emperor Xuanwudi (r. 499–515) of the Northern Wei dynasty. Xianjusi was the residence of the meditation master Sengchou (480–560), and also PUJI (651–739), the disciple of CHAN master SHENXIU, and his disciple YIXING. Other monasteries such as Yongtaisi, Fengchansi, and Qingliangsi were also built on Mt. Song.

**Sŏngu**. (K) (惺牛). See KYŎNGHŎ SŎNGU.

**Sōnirei**. (僧尼令). In Japanese, "Regulations for Monks and Nuns"; a decree issued in 701 by the Japanese imperial court to regulate the activities of Buddhist clerics; the extant twenty-seven-article recension of these regulations was codified within the *Yōrō ritsurei* ("Civil and Penal Codes of the Yōrō Era"), which was compiled in 718 and promulgated in 757. The *Sōnirei* is believed to be modeled after the Tang-dynasty code regulating the activities of Daoist and Buddhist clerics, the *Daoseng ge*. The *Sōnirei* was also based on the traditional Buddhist precepts of the Chinese translation of the DHARMAGUPTAKA VINAYA (C. SIFEN LÜ): for example, it stipulated that committing a PĀRĀJIKA transgression, the most serious category of monastic offense—viz., sexual intercourse, murder, grand theft, and false claims of spiritual achievement—required punishment in accord with civil law. The code also forbade monks from consuming alcohol, meat, and strong-smelling herbs, and prohibited a monk from entering a nun's cell, and vice versa. The *Sōnirei* also reflected the state's concern about the possible threat to its power from an unregulated Buddhist clergy, as shown in the example of GYŌGI (668–749), a Hossō (FAXIANG ZONG) monk who disseminated Buddhism among the commoners and gained widespread popularity as a charismatic teacher and thaumaturge. Many of the *Sōnirei* regulations targeted such maverick clerics: to give but a few examples, monks and nuns were prohibited from predicting good and bad fortunes based on heavenly portents; speaking against the state; studying military tactics; living outside the temples or building a Buddhist chapel off temple grounds; giving scriptures or buddha images to a layperson or teaching outside the monastery; or accumulating private property or wealth. The *Sōnirei* also required all monks and nuns to receive official permission before ordaining. However, violations of the *Sōnirei* were widespread and the regulations had lost much of their effectiveness by the middle of the Heian period.

**Sŏnjong sŏn**. (禪宗選). In Korean, the "Meditation (SŎN) School examination"; see SŬNGKWA.

**Sŏn Kyo yangjong**. (禪教兩宗). In Korean, "Two Traditions of SŎN (Meditation) and KYO (Doctrine)"; a Chosŏn-dynasty period designation for the two major strands of the Korean Buddhist tradition. See KUSAN SŎNMUN; KYO; OGYO KUSAN; OGYO YANGJONG; SŎN.

**Sŏnmun ch'waryo**. (禪門撮要). In Korean, "Selected Essentials from the Gate of Sŏn"; a Korean anthology of the essential canon of the Korean SŎN (CHAN) school, in two rolls. Although the *Sŏnmun ch'waryo* is often attributed to the late-Chosŏn-period Sŏn master KYŎNGHŎ SŎNGU (1849–1912), its authorship remains a matter of debate. The text uses as its primary source material the *Pŏphae pobŏl* ("Precious Raft on the Ocean of Dharma"), which was compiled in 1883 at Kamnosa. The *Sŏnmun ch'waryo* contains texts that are foundational to the Korean Sŏn tradition. The first roll consists of the writings of the Chinese Chan patriarchs and teachers: the *Xuemo lun* ("Treatise of the Blood Lineage"), the *Guanxin lun* ("Treatise of Contemplating the Mind," sometimes otherwise attributed to SHENXIU [606?–706]), and the ERRU SIXING LUN ("Treatise on the Two Accesses and Four Practices"), all attributed to the first Chan patriarch, BODHIDHARMA; the *Xiuxin yao lun* ("Treatise on the Essentials of Cultivating the Mind"), attributed to the fifth patriarch HONGREN (600–674); the *Wanleng lu* ("Wanleng Record") and the CHUANXIN FAYAO ("Essential Teachings on Transmitting the Mind"), attributed to HUANGBO XIYUN (d. 850); the *Mengshan fayu* ("Mengshan's Dharma Discourses") composed of eleven dharma-talks by five masters including Mengshan Deyi (1231–1308) and NAONG HYEGŬN (1320–1376); and an excerpt from the *Canchan jingyu* ("Words of Admonition on Investigating Chan") attributed to Boshan Wuyi (1575–1630). The second roll consists of the writings of eminent Korean Sŏn monks from the Koryŏ and Chosŏn periods: POJO CHINUL's (1158–1210) SUSIM KYŎL ("Secrets on Cultivating the Mind"), *Chinsim chiksŏl* ("Straight Talk on the True Mind"), *Kwŏnsu Chŏnghye kyŏlsa mun* ("Encouragement to Practice: The Compact of the Samādhi and Prajñā Community"), and KANHWA KYŎRŬI NON ("Resolving Doubts About Observing the Hwadu"); the SŎNMUN POJANG NOK ("Record of the Treasure Trove of the Sŏn Tradition") and the *Sŏnmun kangyo* ("Essentials of the Sŏn Gate"), both attributed to CH'ŎNCH'AEK (b. 1206); and the *Sŏn'gyo sŏk* ("Explication of Sŏn and Kyo") attributed to CH'ŎNGHŎ HYUJŎNG (1520–1604). The first roll of the *Sŏnmun ch'waryo* was published in 1907 at the monastery of Unmunsa and the second in 1908 at PŎMŎSA. Among the 118 total xylographs of the book, the seventy-eighth and 118th xylographs list the names of people involved in the publication of the text, such as proofreaders, transcribers, and engravers, as well the donors, government officials, and landed gentry who contributed to the cost of the publication.

**Sŏnmun pojang nok**. (禪門寶藏錄). In Korean, "Record of the Treasure Trove of the Sŏn Tradition"; an anthology, in three rolls, of stories excerpted from various Chinese CHAN and Korean SŎN texts. Although the preface of the *Sŏnmun pojangnok* was written in 1293 by the Koryŏ CH'ŎNTAE (Ch. TIANTAI) monk CH'ŎNCH'AEK (1206–?) to whom it is attributed, the exact authorship of the anthology is still a matter of some debate. The epilogue to the text was written in 1294 by the Koryŏ lay Buddhist literatus Yi Hon (1252–1312). The first roll, "The Gate That Compares Sŏn and Kyo" (Sŏn'gyo taebyŏn mun) advocates that Sŏn is distinct from, and surpasses, KYO (Doctrinal Teachings) because, unlike Kyo, Sŏn directly reveals Buddhist truth without relying on verbal explanation. The second roll, "The Gate through which all Kyo Lecturers Return and Yield" (Chegang kwibok mun) illustrates this superiority of Sŏn over Kyo by citing several examples in which Kyo monks were embarrassed, or guided to an authentic awakening, by Chan or Sŏn monks. The third roll, "The Gate Revered and Trusted by Kings and Vassals" (Kunsin sungsin mun) includes stories of kings and government officials respecting and honoring Chan and Sŏn monks. One of the most interesting stories collected in the *Sŏnmun pojang nok* relates to the otherwise-unknown Patriarch Chin'gwi (Chin'gwi chosa). The story is recited twice in the first roll and once in the third, excerpted respectively from the *Talma millok* ("Secret Record of Bodhidharma"), the *Haedong ch'iltae nok* ("Record of the Seven Generations of the Patriarchs of Haedong [Korea]"), and the *Wimyŏngje somun chegyŏng p'yŏn* ("Section on the Emperor Ming of Wei Inquires about the Sūtras"), none of which are extant. The story is extremely controversial, because it states that because ŚĀKYAMUNI Buddha's awakening under the BODHI TREE was still imperfect, he continued to wander looking for guidance, until he met a Chan patriarch in the Snowy Mountains (Himālaya) who was finally able to lead him to true awakening. Later, the renowned Chosŏn monk SŎNSAN HYUJŎNG also included the same story in his *Sŏn'gyo sŏk* ("Exposition of Sŏn and Kyo"), but cited it instead from the *Pŏmil kuksa chip* ("Collected Works of the State Preceptor Pŏmil"), which is also not extant. However, since neither the story itself nor even the titles of any of the three texts cited in the *Sŏnmun pojang nok* are found in any Chinese Buddhist sources, it is presumed that the story itself was fabricated in Korea sometime between the times of PŎMIL (810–889) and Ch'ŏnch'aek. The *Sŏnmun pojang nok* is now embedded in the SŎNMUN CH'WARYO and is also published in volume six of the *Han'guk Pulgyo chŏnsŏ* ("Collected Works of Korean Buddhism").

**Sŏnmun yŏmsong chip**. (禪門拈頌集). In Korean, "Collection of Analyses and Verses on [Ancient Precedents] of the Sŏn School," the first and largest indigenous Korean kongan (C. GONG'AN, J. kōan; public case) anthology, compiled in thirty rolls by CHIN'GAK HYESIM (1178–1234) in 1226. The collection covers 1,463 kongan, along with annotations (yŏm), verses (song), and variant explanations, such as responding on behalf of a figure who does not answer during the kongan exchange (tae, lit. on his behalf), responding in a different way from the response given in the kongan exchange (pyŏl, lit. differently), and inquiring about the exchange (ch'ŏng, lit. soliciting, or verifying). The first xylographic edition of the collection was destroyed in 1232, just six years after its publication, during the Mongol invasions of the Korean peninsula. The second woodblock edition was carved sometime between 1244 and 1248 as a part of the massive project to remake the entire Koryŏ Buddhist canon (KORYŎ TAEJANGGYŎNG). The postface to the second edition notes that 347 more kongan was added to the original for a total of 1,472; the current edition, however, includes only 1,463 kongan, a discrepancy that remains unexplained. The collection shows the influence of the Song gong'an literature, especially the *Chanzong songgu lianzhu tongji* ("Comprehensive Collection of the Chan School's Verses on Ancient [Precedents] That Are a String of Jewels"), compiled in 1179. The ancient cases (viz., the kongan) are arranged in the order of the three jewels (RATNATRAYA), i.e., the Buddha, dharma, and saṃgha. The first thirty-seven kongan are attributed to ŚĀKYAMUNI Buddha himself. The next set of twenty-four is derived from Buddhist sūtras, including the AVATAṂSAKASŪTRA, the SADDHARMAPUṆḌARĪKASŪTRA ("Lotus Sūtra"), the *ŚŪRAṂGAMASŪTRA, and the VAJRACCHEDIKĀPRAJÑĀPĀRAMITĀSŪTRA ("Diamond Sūtra"). The remaining 1,402 kongan are taken from stories of the Indian and Chinese Sŏn (Chan) patriarchs and teachers, along with a few unknown lay Sŏn masters. The *Sŏnmun yŏmsong chip* was one of the official textbooks used for the monastic examinations (SŬNGKWA) in the Sŏn school during the early Chosŏn dynasty. There are a few important Korean commentaries to the anthology, including the *Sŏnmun yŏmsong sŏrhwa* ("Tales about the Sŏn School's Analyses and Verses") in thirty rolls, by Hyesim's disciple Kagun (c. thirteenth century), IRYŎN's (1206–1289) *Sŏnmun yŏmsong sawŏn* ("Garden of Affairs on the Sŏn School's Analyses and Verses") in thirty rolls, and PAEKP'A KŬNGSŎN's (1767–1852) *Sŏnmun yŏmsong ki* ("Record of the Sŏn School's Analyses and Verses") in five rolls.

**Sŏnsu**. (K) (善修). See PUHYU SŎNSU.

**Sŏnunsa**. (禪雲寺). In Korean, "Cloud of Meditation Monastery"; the twenty-fourth district monastery (PONSA) of the contemporary CHOGYE CHONG of Korean Buddhism, located on Mount Tosol (TUṢITA) in North Chŏlla province. There are several conflicting narratives concerning its foundation, but the prevailing view is that the monastery was founded by the meditation master Kŏmdan (fl. c. 577) during the reign of the Paekche king Widŏk (r. 554–598). Sŏnunsa has a history of repeated destruction and reconstruction through the Koryŏ and Chosŏn periods. Most of the monastery's present structures, including its main shrine hall (TAEUNG CHŎN), were built during the reign of the Chosŏn-dynasty King Kwanghae (r. 1608–1623). The monastery is famous for its associations with worship of KṢITIGARBHA (K. Chijang posal) and is well known for its many camellia bushes, one of the few flowers that bloom during the harsh Korean winter.

**sopadhiśeṣanirvāṇa**. (P. sopādisesanibbāna; T. phung po lhag ma dang bcas pa'i mya ngan las 'das pa/lhag bcas myang 'das; C. youyu niepan; J. uyonehan; K. yuyŏ yŏlban 有餘涅槃). In Sanskrit, "nirvāṇa with remainder"; one of the two kinds of NIRVĀṆA, along with the "nirvāṇa without remainder" (ANUPADHIŚEṢANIRVĀṆA), "with remainder" here meaning the residue of the aggregates (SKANDHA). At the time of his enlightenment under the BODHI TREE, the Buddha achieved the nirvāṇa with remainder, because he had destroyed all causes for future rebirth, but the "remainder" of his mind and body, viz., a substratum (UPADHI) of existence, persisted. At the time of his death, there was nothing more of the skandhas remaining, thus producing the "nirvāṇa without remainder," a synonym for PARINIRVĀṆA. According to those MAHĀYĀNA schools which assert that there is only one vehicle (EKAYĀNA) and that all sentient beings will achieve buddhahood, ARHATs who appear to enter the nirvāṇa without remainder at death actually do not do so; for if they did, it would be impossible for them to enter the bodhisattva path. Instead, they enter the uncontaminated realm (ANĀSRAVADHĀTU), where they remain in states of deep concentration (inside lotus flowers according to some texts) until they are roused by the buddhas and exhorted to abandon their "unafflicted ignorance" (AKLIṢṬĀJÑĀNA) and proceed on the path to buddhahood. ¶ In a *PRĀSAṄGIKA-MADHYAMAKA interpretation, the vision of reality free from all elaborations (PRAPAÑCA) or dualistic subject-object conceptualization (GRĀHYAGRĀHAKAVIKALPA) in a state of absorption or equipoise (samāhitajñāna)—a state that occurs on the path of vision (DARŚANAMĀRGA) and the path of cultivation (BHĀVANĀMĀRGA)—is referred to as "nirvāṇa without remainder," because there is no appearance of any conventional reality (SAṂVṚTI) while the meditator is in that state. In the subsequent state (PṚṢṬHALABDHAJÑĀNA), conventional reality reappears; this state is called nirvāṇa with remainder. In this explanation, upadhi means any appearance of conventional reality.

**Sŏsan taesa**. (西山大師) (1520–1604). In Korean, "Great Master West Mountain." See CH'ŎNGHŎ HYUJŎNG.

**Soseki**. (J) (疎石) (1275–1351). See MUSŌ SOSEKI.

**Sot'aesan**. (K) (少太山) (1891–1943). Cognomen of the founder of the Korean new religion of WŎNBULGYO. See PAK CHUNGBIN.

**Sōtōshū**. (曹洞宗). One of the three major branches of the Japanese Zen tradition, along with the RINZAISHŪ and ŌBAKUSHŪ. The Sōtō tradition traces its lineage back to DŌGEN KIGEN (1200–1253), who is credited with transmitting to Japan the CAODONG ZONG line of the Chinese CHAN teacher TIANTONG RUJING (1162–1227). After returning from China in 1227, Dōgen settled in Kyōto and sought to create a new Zen community. Because of resistance from the TENDAI and Rinzai traditions that were already firmly entrenched in the capital (see ENNI BEN'EN), Dōgen and his followers eventually left for the rural area of Echizen (in the northern part of present-day Fukui prefecture), and founded EIHEIJI, which came to serve as the center of this new Zen institution. In Echizen, Dōgen devoted his time and energy to securing the doctrinal and institutional bases for his community. Dōgen's venture was aided by several adherents of the DARUMASHŪ, who joined the community. Among them were Koun Ejō (1198–1280), the editor of the seventy-five-roll version of Dōgen's magnum opus, the SHŌBŌGENZŌ, and Tettsū Gikai (1219–1309), whose lineage subsequently came to dominate the Sōtō school; these monks later served as the second and the third abbots of Eiheiji. Modern scholars believe that a dispute between Gikai and a fellow disciple of Koun Ejō named Gien (d. 1313) concerning the abbotship of Eiheiji prompted Gikai to move to Daijōji in Ishikawa. Gikai was succeeded by his disciple KEIZAN JŌKIN (1268–1325), who is honored as "the second patriarch" of Sōtō by the school's modern followers. Keizan revitalized the Sōtō community by synthesizing Zen practice with the worship of local gods (KAMI), thus appealing to the local populace. Keizan also established SŌJIJI, which along with Eiheiji came to serve as the headquarters (honzan) of the Sōtō tradition. Gazan Shōseki (1275–1365), a successor of Keizan, produced several disciples, including Taigen Sōshin (d. c. 1371) and Tsūgen Jakurei (1322–1391), who are credited with the Sōtō school's rapid expansion throughout Japan during the medieval period. Sōtō monks of this period, especially those belonging to Keizan-Gazan lines, proselytized in the rural areas of Japan, which had been largely neglected by the established Buddhist traditions at court, and attracted a following among commoners and local elites by engaging in such social activities as building bridges and irrigation systems, as well as by performing rituals that met their religious needs, such as funeral services and mass ordinations (jukai e). Each lineage of the Sōtō tradition also developed its own secret kōan manuals (monsan), only available to selected monks, which gave a received set of questions and answers regarding each kōan (C. GONG'AN). During the Tokugawa period, the Sōtō school developed into one of the largest Buddhist sects in Japan, with a stable financial base, thanks to the mandatory parish system (DANKA SEIDO) that the government launched, in which every household was required to register as a member of a local Buddhist temple and was responsible for the financial support for the temple. By the middle of the eighteenth century, there were more than 17,500 Sōtō temples across Japan. Although the religious life of the majority of the Sōtō monks and lay followers during this period was focused on practical religious benefits, such as faith healing and funeral services, a restoration movement eventually developed that sought to return to the putative "original teachings and practices" of the founder Dōgen. MANZAN DŌHAKU (1636–1714) opposed the custom of IN'IN EKISHI, or "changing teachers according to temple," which was widespread in the Sōtō tradition during the sixteenth and seventeenth centuries and was required in order to inherit the dharma lineage of a temple

(GARANBŌ). Instead, Manzan called for a direct, face-to-face transmission (menju shihō) from one master to his disciple (isshi inshō), which he claimed Dōgen had established for the Sōtō tradition. After several failed attempts, he finally succeeded in persuading the bakufu government to ban the in'in ekishi and garanbō practice in 1703. TENKEI DENSON (1648–1735) and MENZAN ZUIHŌ (1683–1769) also composed influential commentaries to Dōgen's magnum opus, the *Shōbōgenzō*, which led to a renaissance in Dōgen studies. After the Meiji reforms of 1868, the two head monasteries of Eiheiji and Sōjiji, which had remained rivals through the Tokugawa period, worked together to reform the school, issuing several standardizations of the rules for temple operation, ritual procedures, etc. In 1890, Azegami Baisen (d.1901) from Sōjiji and Takiya Takushū (d. 1897) from Eiheiji edited the layman Ōuchi Seiran's (1845–1918) introductory work on the *Shōbōgenzō* and distributed it under the title of the *Sōtō kyōkai shushōgi* ("Meaning of Practice and Realization in the Sōtō Sect"). This text played a major role in the popularization of the school's meditative practice of "just sitting" (SHIKAN TAZA), which fosters a psychological state in which "body and mind are sloughed off" (SHINJIN DATSURAKU); sitting practice itself is therefore regarded as the manifestation of the perfect enlightenment of buddhahood. The Sōtō school continues to thrive today, with the great majority of its more than fourteen thousand contemporary temples affiliated with Sōjiji.

**sotthika/sotthiya**. (P). See SVASTIKA.

**sound of one hand clapping**. See SEKISHU KŌAN.

**Southern School (of Chan)**. See NAN ZONG.

**sparśa**. (P. phassa; T. reg pa; C. chu; J. soku; K. ch'ok 觸). In Sanskrit, "contact," used technically as the sixth of the twelve links of dependent origination (PRATĪTYASAMUTPĀDA), referring to the sensory contact between a sense organ (INDRIYA) and a sense object (ĀLAMBANA), resulting in a corresponding sensory consciousness (VIJÑĀNA), with the function of distinguishing an object as pleasant, unpleasant, or neutral. Based on this contact, sensation or feeling (VEDANĀ), the next link in the chain (NIDĀNA), occurs. Thus, the term sparśa does not refer to the physical contact of the body and a physical object. It is instead the mental factor by which consciousness "touches" the object, setting in motion the process of cognition. The Buddha said that prior to his enlightenment, he sought to understand the nature of sensation, including its origin (SAMUDAYA) and its cessation (NIRODHA). He understood that sensation arose from contact, which in turn arose from the coming together of an object and one of the six sense organs (ṢAḌĀYATANA), such that if the six sense organs ceased, contact would cease, and sensation would cease. The six sense organs are sometimes referred to as the sparśāyatana, the "bases of contact" or "sources of contact."

**Spa tshab lo tsā ba Nyi ma grags**. (Patsap Lotsawa Nyima Drak) (1055–1145?). A Tibetan scholar of the eleventh and twelfth centuries who played a major role in establishing MADHYAMAKA in Tibet during the period of the second dissemination (PHYI DAR) of the dharma, through his translation of the two major works of CANDRAKĪRTI, the PRASANNAPADĀ and the MADHYAMAKĀVATĀRA, as well as ĀRYADEVA's CATUḤŚATAKA and Candrakīrti's commentary on it. At any early age, he made the arduous journey to Kashmir, where he spent the next twenty-three years, the first ten studying Sanskrit and the remaining years translating Madhyamaka works into Tibetan in collaboration with Kashmiri paṇḍitas at the monastery of Ratnaguptavihāra near modern-day Srinagar. His teachers and collaborators included Mahājana and Sūkṣmajana, the sons of the master Sajjana, as well as Mahāsumati, the disciple of Parahita. He eventually returned to Tibet, accompanied by two Kashmiri scholars: Kanakavarman and Tilakakalaśa. Basing himself at the RA MO CHE temple in LHA SA, he taught Madhyamaka and revised earlier translations of Madhyamaka texts. He thus played a major role in introducing what came to be known as *PRĀSAṄGIKA into Tibet and providing the texts upon which the distinction between Prāsaṅgika and *SVĀTANTRIKA could be made. Those terms were not names of branches of Madhyamaka school in India; rather, those designations were coined in Tibet, and Spa tshab may have been the first to use the term *Prāsaṅgika (thal 'gyur pa). He is credited by Tibetan historians as making the *Prāsaṅgika perspective, that is, the perspective of Candrakīrti, the prevailing interpretation of the works of Nāgārjuna and Āryadeva in Tibet.

**Sphuṭārthā**. (T. 'Grel pa don gsal). A common abbreviated title of the SPHUṬĀRTHĀ-ABHIDHARMAKOŚAVYĀKHYĀ by YAŚOMITRA (fl. sixth century?); also a mistaken Sanskrit reconstruction of the PRAJÑĀPĀRAMITĀ writer HARIBHADRA's short commentary (vivṛti) on the ABHISAMAYĀLAṂKĀRA, known in Tibetan sources (based on Haribhadra's description of his work) as *'Grel pa don gsal*; see ABHISAMAYĀLAṂKĀRAVIVṚTI.

**Sphuṭārthā-Abhidharmakośavyākhyā**. [alt. Abhidharmakośaṭīkā] (T. Chos mngon pa'i mdzod kyi 'grel bshad). A widely cited exegesis of Vasubandhu's ABHIDHARMAKOŚABHĀṢYA by YAŚOMITRA (fl. sixth century?). Written in Sanskrit, the title means "Clear Meaning Explanation of [Vasubandhu's] *Abhidharmakośabhāṣya*." Yaśomitra calls his work *Sphuṭārthā* ("in which the topics burst forth clearly") at the beginning of his text.

**spraṣṭavya**. (P. phoṭṭhabba; T. reg bya; C. suochu; J. shosoku; K. soch'ok 所觸). In Sanskrit, lit., "object of touch," or "tangible object," the object of tactile consciousness (KĀYAVIJÑĀNA) and one of the five sense objects (ĀLAMBANA), the others being visible form (RŪPA), sounds (ŚABDA), smells (GANDHA), and tastes (RASA). The contact (SPARŚA) between a tangible object and the tactile sense organ (KĀYENDRIYA) produce tactile consciousness (KĀYAVIJÑĀNA). In the ABHIDHARMA, tangible objects are divided into two main categories, the physical elements (BHŪTA; MAHĀBHŪTA) and those derived from the elements (BHAUTIKA). The four elements are earth, water, fire, and wind. The seven tangible objects derived from the elements are smoothness, roughness, heaviness, lightness, cold, hunger, and thirst.

**spraṣṭavyāyatana**. (P. phoṭṭhabbāyatana; T. reg bya'i skye mched; C. chuchu; J. sokusho; K. ch'okch'ŏ 觸處). In Sanskrit, "tactile sense-field," that is, tangible objects (SPRAṢṬAVYA) as they occur in the list of twelve sense faculties or "bases of cognition" (ĀYATANA), which serve as the bases for the production of consciousness: viz., the six internal sense bases, or sense organs (eye, ear, nose, tongue, body, and mind) and the six external sense objects (forms, sounds, odors, tastes, tangible objects, and mental phenomena). In the case of tangible objects, the contact (SPARŚA) between the tactile sense base and its corresponding tangible object leads to tactile consciousness (KĀYAVIJÑĀNA).

**sprul sku**. A Tibetan term often seen transcribed in English as "tulku"; it is the Tibetan translation of the Sanskrit term NIRMĀṆAKĀYA, the third of the three bodies of a buddha (TRIKĀYA), the "emanation body" that appears in the world for the benefit of sentient beings. Although the term retains this standard Buddhological meaning in Tibetan, sprul sku is used by extension to refer to an "incarnate lama," and the term is sometimes translated as such. It is not believed in every case that each incarnate lama is the emanation body of a buddha. However, the implication is that there is a difference in the processes whereby ordinary beings and incarnate lamas take birth in the world. For the former, rebirth is process over which one has no control, with a strong possibility that one's new life will be in the lower rebirth destinies (DURGATI) as an animal, hungry ghost, or hell denizen. The rebirth of an "emanation body" is instead considered to be a voluntary choice. The sprul sku are said to exercise control over their rebirth; a dying incarnation will often leave instructions for his disciples as to where to find his next rebirth. The practice of identifying children as the incarnations of deceased masters may date from as early as the eleventh or twelfth century. By the fifteenth century, all sects of Tibetan Buddhism had adopted the practice of identifying the successive rebirths of a great teacher, the most famous instance of which are the DALAI LAMAS. There were some three thousand lines of incarnation in Tibet (only several of whom are female). It was also the case that a single lama may have more than one incarnation; there were sometimes three, which were considered individual incarnations of the body, speech, and mind of the deceased master. The institution of the incarnate lama became a central component of Tibetan society, providing the means by which authority and charisma, both symbolic and material, was passed from one generation to another. The spread of Tibetan Buddhism can be traced by the increasingly large geographical areas in which incarnate lamas have been discovered. A variety of types and levels of sprul sku are identified. A mchog gi sprul sku (choki tulku) (UTTAMANIRMĀṆAKĀYA) is a buddha, such as ŚĀKYAMUNI, who appears in the world with a body adorned with the major and minor marks of a MAHĀPURUṢA. A skye ba'i sprul sku (kyewe tulku) (JANMANIRMĀṆAKĀYA) is the appearance of a buddha in the form of an animal, human, or divinity. Tibetan incarnate lamas would fall into this category. Also in this category would be those cases in which a buddha appears as an inanimate object that provides benefit to sentient beings, such as a bridge across a river, a path, a tree, or a cooling breeze. A bzo bo sprul sku (sowo tulku) (ŚILPANIRMĀṆAKĀYA) is an artisan or craftsman or a particular manifestation of artistic beauty that subdues the afflictions (KLEŚA). Within the the large DGE LUGS PA monasteries, a monk with the title of tshogs chen sprul sku (tsokchen tulku, "great assembly tulku") is excused from performing regular assembly duties. In Tibetan, an incarnate lama is addressed and referred to as RIN PO CHE (precious one), although that term is also used for abbots and other holders of high ecclesiastical office; it may also be used for one's teacher, even if he or she is not an incarnate lama. The term BLA MA (lama) is typically used to refer to incarnations but is also used widely for a teacher.

**śraddhā**. (P. saddhā; T. dad pa; C. xin; J. shin; K. sin 信). In Sanskrit, "faith" or "confidence," a term that encompasses also the sense of "belief." Faith has a wide range of meanings in Buddhism, ranging from a kind of mental clarity and positive disposition toward the Buddha (which is often attributed to an encounter with a buddha or with the bodhisattva in a former life), to a sense of conviction about the efficacy of the Buddhist path (MĀRGA), to a commitment to follow that path. In addition to its cognitive dimensions, which will be described more fully below, faith also has important conative and affective dimensions that are frequently recounted in Buddhist literature. The conative is suggested in the compulsion towards alms-giving (DĀNA), as described for example in encounters with previous buddhas in the Pāli APADĀNA, or in the pilgrim's encounter with an object of devotion. The affective can be seen, perhaps most famously, in Ānanda's affection-driven attachment to the Buddha, which is described as a result of his deep devotion to, and faith in, the person of the Buddha. These multiple aspects of faith find arguably their fullest expression in the various accounts of the story of the Buddha's ARHAT disciple VAKKALI, who is said to have been completely enraptured with the Buddha and is described as foremost among his monk disciples in implicit faith. In the ABHIDHARMA, faith is listed as the first of the ten major omnipresent wholesome factors (KUŚALAMAHĀBHŪMIKA) in the seventy-five dharmas list of the SARVĀSTIVĀDA school and as a virtuous (KUŚALA) mental factor (CAITTA) in the hundred-dharmas roster (BAIFA) of the YOGĀCĀRA school and in the Pāli abhidhamma. Faith is one of the foundational prerequisites of attainment, and its cognitive dimensions are described as a clarity of mind required for realization, as conviction that arises from the study of the dharma, and as a source of aspiration that encourages one to continue to develop the qualities of enlightenment. Faith is listed as the first of the five spiritual faculties (INDRIYA), together with diligence (VĪRYA), mindfulness (SMṚTI), concentration (SAMĀDHI), and wisdom (PRAJÑĀ). The faculty of faith is usually considered to be the direct counteragent (PRATIPAKṢA) of ill-will (DVEṢA), not of doubt (VICIKITSĀ), demonstrating its affective dimension. Faith generates bliss (PRĪTI), by which brings about serenity of mind and thought; in addition, faith also produces self-confidence, engendering the conative characteristic of diligence (vīrya). Faith and wisdom (prajñā) were to be kept constantly counterpoised by the faculty of mindfulness (smṛti). By being balanced via mindfulness, faith would guard against excessive wisdom, which could lead to skepticism, while wisdom would protect against excessive faith, which could lead to blind, uncritical acceptance. Thus faith, in the context of the spiritual faculties, is a tacit acceptance of the soteriological value of specific beliefs, until such time as those beliefs are verified through practice and understood through one's own insight. There are four main soteriological objects of faith: (1) the efficacy of moral cause and effect (viz., KARMAN) and the prospect of continued rebirth (PUNARJANMAN) based on one's actions; (2) the core teachings about the conditioned nature of the world, such as dependent origination (PRATĪTYASAMUTPĀDA) and the three marks of existence (TRILAKṢAṆA), viz., impermanence (ANIYATA), suffering (DUḤKHA), nonself (ANĀTMAN); (3) the three jewels (RATNATRAYA) of the Buddha, DHARMA, and SAṂGHA; and (4) the general soteriological outline of the path (MĀRGA) and the prospect of release from affliction through the experience of NIRVĀṆA.

**śraddhādhimukta**. (P. saddhādhimutta; T. dad pas lhag par mos pa; C. xinjie; J. shinge; K. sinhae 信解). In Sanskrit, "one who aspires through faith" or "one inclined to faith"; one of the twenty members of the ĀRYASAṂGHA (see VIṂŚATIPRABHEDASAṂGHA). In Sanskrit sources, the name is given to those with dull faculties (MṚDVINDRIYA) when they reach one of the first three results of the noble path (ĀRYAMĀRGA) or religious life (ŚRĀMAṆYAPHALA). They reach the result when they pass from the path of vision's (DARŚANAMĀRGA) uninterrupted path (ĀNANTARYAMĀRGA) to its path of freedom (VIMUKTIMĀRGA). While on the uninterrupted path, they are called ŚRADDHĀNUSĀRIN. Contingent on the number of sets of afflictions (KLEŚA) causing rebirth in the sensuous realm (KĀMADHĀTU) that they have already eliminated prior to reaching the uninterrupted path, they become either SROTAĀPANNAPHALASTHA, SAKṚDĀGĀMIPHALASTHA, or ANĀGĀMIPHALASTHA when they reach the path of liberation (VIMUKTIMĀRGA). Both the name śraddhānusārin and the śraddhādhimukta appear to have been borrowed from the list of noble persons (ĀRYAPUDGALA) found, for example, in the *Kīṭāgirisutta* of the MAJJHIMANIKĀYA. The name ŚRADDHĀVIMUKTA found in the list of seven noble persons is changed to śraddhādhimukta in the expanded list of twenty members of the āryasaṃgha. See ŚRADDHĀVIMUKTA.

**śraddhānusārin**. (P. saddhānusāri; T. dad pa'i rjes su 'brang ba; C. suixin xing; J. zuishingyō; K. susin haeng 隨信行). In Sanskrit, "follower of faith." The SARVĀSTIVĀDA (e.g., ABHIDHARMAKOŚABHĀṢYA) and Pāli (e.g., VISUDDHIMAGGA) traditions of mainstream Buddhism both recognize seven types of noble ones (ĀRYA, P. ariya): (1) follower of faith (S. śraddhānusārin; P. saddhānusāri); (2) follower of the dharma (S. DHARMĀNUSĀRIN, P. dhammānusāri); (3) one liberated through faith (S. ŚRADDHĀVIMUKTA; P. saddhāvimutta); (4) one who has formed right view (S. DṚṢṬIPRĀPTA; P. diṭṭhippatta), by developing both faith and wisdom; (5) the bodily witness (S. KĀYASĀKṢIN; P. kāyasakkhi), viz., through the temporary suspension of mentality in the equipoise of cessation (NIRODHASAMĀPATTI); (6) one who is freed by wisdom (S. PRAJÑĀVIMUKTA; P. paññāvimutta), by freeing oneself through analysis; and (7) one who is freed both ways (S. UBHAYATOBHĀGAVIMUKTA; P. ubhatobhāgavimutta), by freeing oneself through both meditative absorption and wisdom. A follower of faith is a person who has attained the fruit of stream-enterer (SROTAĀPANNA) and in whom the faculty (INDRIYA) of faith (ŚRADDHĀ) is predominant. Such a person will eventually become one who is freed through faith (ŚRADDHĀVIMUKTA). In the *Abhidharmakośabhāṣya*, there is a basic division of path types and personality types, where a faith-follower and a dharma-follower eliminate hindrances to goals all at once or in a series, and respectively either pass through the intermediate stages of once-returner and nonreturner, or else skip such stages completely, before finally becoming ARHATs. In general, dharma-followers are those who proceed based on knowledge of the FOUR NOBLE TRUTHS as it pertains to all three realms of existence; they eliminate hindrances to all goals all at once, while the achievements of faith-followers are more progressive. According to the Sarvāstivāda VAIBHĀṢIKA school of ABHIDHARMA, an ARHAT whose liberation is grounded in faith may be subject to backsliding from that state, whereas those who are dharmānusārin are unshakable (AKOPYA), because they have experienced the knowledge of nonproduction (ANUTPĀDAJÑĀNA), viz., that the afflictions (KLEŚA) can never occur again, the complement of the knowledge of extinction (KṢAYAJÑĀNA). In the MAHĀYĀNA interpretation of the terms, bodhisattvas who are dharma-followers have knowledge of emptiness (ŚŪNYATĀ), i.e., they have gained a knowledge of the way things are (TATTVA) even at early stages of the path and will never revert to the HĪNAYĀNA; the faith-followers are not irreversible (AVAIVARTIKA) in that way until higher levels of the path. The śraddhānusārin is also found in the list of the members of the saṃgha when it is subdivided into twenty (VIṂŚATIPRABHEDASAṂGHA). Among the śraddhānusārin, there are candidates for the fruit of stream-enterer (SROTAĀPANNAPHALAPRATIPANNAKA), once-returner (SAKṚDĀGĀMIPHALAPRATIPANNAKA), and nonreturner (ANĀGĀMIPHALAPRATIPANNAKA). The first has eliminated up to five of the nine sets of afflictions (KLEŚA) that cause rebirth in the sensuous realm (KĀMADHĀTU), the second all but the final set, and the last all of the afflictions. The first takes a number of births (never more than seven) in the sensuous realm before reaching nirvāṇa, the second has only one rebirth in the sensuous realm left, and the nonreturner will never again take rebirth in the sensuous realm prior to reaching nirvāṇa.

**śraddhāvimukta**. (P. saddhāvimutta; T. dad pas rnam par grol ba; C. xinshengjie; J. shinshōge; K. sinsŭnghae 信勝解). In Sanskrit, "liberated through faith." In the *Kīṭāgirisutta* of the MAJJHIMANIKĀYA, the Buddha describes seven types of noble persons (ĀRYAPUDGALA, P. ariyapuggala). They are: (1) the follower of faith (ŚRADDHĀNUSĀRIN, P. saddhānusāri), (2) the one liberated through faith (śraddhāvimukta), (3) the bodily witness (KĀYASĀKṢIN, P. kāyasakkhi), (4) the one liberated both ways (UBHAYATOBHĀGAVIMUKTA, P. ubhatobhāgavimutta), (5) the follower of the dharma (DHARMĀNUSĀRIN, P. dhammānusāri), (6) the one who has attained understanding (DṚṢṬIPRĀPTA, P. diṭṭhippatta), and (7), the one liberated through wisdom (PRAJÑĀVIMUKTA, P. paññāvimutta). A person liberated through faith is a noble person at any stage of the path, from the fruit of stream-enterer to the path of the arhat, who has understood the FOUR NOBLE TRUTHS and eliminated some of the defilements, but has not attained any of the DHYĀNA levels of the immaterial realm and who has a predominance of faith. Such a person may or may not have attained the levels of the subtle-materiality realm. The śraddhāvimukta is also found in the list of the members of the saṃgha when it is subdivided into twenty (VIṂŚATIPRABHEDASAṂGHA). There are three śraddhāvimukta: recipients of the fruit of stream-enterer (SROTAĀPANNAPHALASTHA), once-returner (SAKṚDĀGĀMIPHALASTHA), and nonreturner (ANĀGĀMIPHALASTHA). These parallel the three śraddhānusārin that are candidates for these same first three fruits of the noble path. See ĀRYAPUDGALA; ĀRYAMĀRGAPHALA.

**śramaṇa**. (P. samaṇa; T. dge sbyong; C. shamen; J. shamon; K. samun 沙門). In Sanskrit "renunciant," "mendicant," or "recluse," a term used in ancient India to refer to male religious of a number of different itinerant sects, including Buddhism, often associated with the warrior (KṢATRIYA) caste, which challenged the hegemony of the brāhmaṇa priests and mainstream Brahmanical religion deriving from the Vedas. Whereas the Brahmanical tradition traces itself back to a body of literature centered on the Vedas, the śramaṇa movements instead derive from historical persons who all flourished around the sixth century BCE. Six different śramaṇa groups are mentioned in the SĀMAÑÑAPHALASUTTANTA of the DĪGHANIKĀYA, each representing different trends in Indian thought, including antinomianism (PŪRAṆA-KĀŚYAPA); fatalism (MASKARIN-GOŚĀLĪPUTRA of the ĀJĪVAKA school); materialism (AJITA-KEŚAKAMBALA of the LOKĀYATA school); atomism (KAKUDA-KĀTYĀYANA); and agnosticism (SAÑJAYA-VAIRĀṬĪPUTRA); the sixth group is the JAINA tradition of NIRGRANTHA JÑĀTĪPUTRA, also known as MAHĀVĪRA, with which Buddhism shares many affinities. These six are typically referred to in Buddhist materials as the six "heterodox teachers" (TĪRTHIKA) and are consistently criticized by the Buddha for fostering wrong views (MITHYĀDṚṢṬI). Some scholars suggest that these groups were loosely associated with a third phase in the development of pan-Indian religion called the āraṇyaka (forest dwellers) movement, where the highly specialized fire rituals (HOMA) set forth in the *Brāhmaṇas* for the propitiation of Vedic gods gave way to a more internalized form of spiritual praxis. These itinerant asetics or wanders were also called PARIVRĀJAKA (P. paribbājaka; "those who go forth into homelessness"), in direct contrast to the householders (GṚHASTHA) whose behavior was governed by the laws set down in dharmaśāstras. Because so many of the beliefs and practices emblematic of the śramaṇa movement have no direct Vedic antecedents, however, other scholars have proposed that the śramaṇa groups may instead exemplify the resurfacing in Indian religion of aboriginal elements that had long been eclipsed by the imported rituals and beliefs that the Āryans brought with them to India. These doctrines, all of which have their parallels in Buddhism, include rebirth and transmigration (e.g., PUNARJANMAN); notions that actions have effect (e.g., KARMAN); asceticism (TAPAS, DHUTANGA) and the search for ways of behavior that would not bind one to the round of SAṂSĀRA; and liberation (MOKṢA, VIMOKṢA) as the goal of religious practice. In Buddhism, śramaṇa is also used generically to refer to all monks, including the Buddha, whose epithets include Śramaṇa Gautama and Mahāśramaṇa, "Great Renunciant." The term often occurs in the compound śramaṇabrāhmaṇa (P. samaṇabrāhmaṇa), "recluses and brāhmaṇas." This compound has a range of meanings. In some cases, it refers simply to those who practice and benefit from the Buddha's teachings. In other cases, it refers to non-Buddhist religious practitioners. In the edicts of AŚOKA, the term is used to refer to those who are worthy of respect and offerings, with śramaṇa taken to mean Buddhist monks (and possibly other ascetics) and brāhmaṇa taken to mean brāhmaṇa priests. The term śramaṇa should be carefully distinguished from ŚRĀMAṆERA (s.v.), a novice monk.

**śrāmaṇera**. (P. sāmaṇera; T. dge tshul; C. shami; J. shami; K. sami 沙彌). In Sanskrit "[male] novice"; a preliminary stage a man must pass through before he can be ordained as a fully ordained monk (BHIKṢU). The admission into the order (S. pravrajyā, P. pabbajjā; see PARIVRĀJAKA) of a novice is performed with a simple ceremony. The candidate shaves his hair and beard, attires himself in a monk's robe received from a donor, and presents himself before an assembly of monks, or a single monk of ten years' standing or more. Squatting on his haunches and folding his hands, he recites the three refuges (TRIŚARAṆA) formula three times, whereupon he is made a novice. According to the Pāli VINAYA, a novice must observe ten precepts (DAŚAŚĪLA) or "rules of training" (ŚIKṢĀPADA), viz., abstaining from: (1) killing, (2) stealing, (3) sexual misconduct, (4) false speech, (5) intoxicants, (6) eating after midday, (7) dancing, singing, music, and other unseemly forms of entertainment, (8), using garlands, perfumes, and cosmetics to adorn the body, (9) using high and luxurious beds and couches, and (10) accepting gold and silver. The MŪLASARVĀSTIVĀDA VINAYA expands these ten precepts to thirty-six. After receiving the lower ordination, the novice is required to live under the guidance (NIŚRAYA) of a teacher until he receives higher ordination (UPASAṂPADĀ) as a bhikṣu. The novice may not attend the reading of the PRĀTIMOKṢA during the bimonthly UPOṢADHA (P. uposatha) ceremony, or participate in any formal ecclesiastical acts (SAṂGHAKARMAN) such as giving ordination and so on. There are a variety of lists of persons who are not permitted to be ordained as novices: one list names branded thieves, fugitives from the law, registered thieves, those punished by flogging or branding, patricides, matricides, murderers of ARHATs, those who have shed the blood of a buddha, eunuchs, false monks, seducers of nuns, hermaphrodites, persons who are maimed, disabled, or deformed in various ways, and those afflicted with various communicable diseases.

**śrāmaṇerasaṃvara**. (P. sāmaṇerasaṃvara; T. dge tshul gyi sdom pa; C. qince lüyi; J. gonsakuritsugi; K. kŭnch'aek yurŭi 勤策律儀). In Sanskrit, "restraints for novices"; the ten precepts (DAŚAŚĪLA) that govern the conduct of a ŚRĀMAṆERA (male novice). The ten are framed in terms of training rules (ŚIKṢĀPADA): viz., "I undertake the training rule to abstain from": (1) killing, (2) stealing, (3) sexual activity, (4) false speech, (5) intoxicants, (6) eating after midday, (7) dancing, singing, music, and other unseemly forms of entertainment, (8) using garlands, perfumes, and cosmetics to adorn the body, (9) using high and luxurious beds and couches, (10) handling gold and silver (viz., money). On full- and new-moon days (UPOṢADHA), the laity had the option of taking all these precepts except no. 10; nos. 7 and 8 were then combined to give a set of eight precepts to be specially followed on these retreat days (see S. AṢṬĀṄGASAMANVĀGATAṂ UPAVĀSAṂ) as a sort of temporary renunciation. In the MŪLASARVĀSTIVĀDA VINAYA these ten precepts are expanded to thirty-six.

**śrāmaṇerikā**. [alt. śrāmaṇerī] (P. sāmaṇerī; T. dge tshul ma; C. shamini; J. shamini; K. samini 沙彌尼). In Sanskrit, [female] "novice"; also spelled śrāmaṇerakā. The rules of admission and observance as a female novice are the same as for the ŚRĀMAṆERA (male novice) with the exception that a female novice is required to practice as a ŚIKṢAMĀṆĀ ("postulant" or "trainee") for at least two years before being granted permission to receive the UPASAṂPADĀ higher ordination as a BHIKṢUṆĪ, or fully ordained nun. In addition, in the case of a woman, the higher ordination must be conferred twice instead of only once, first by the bhikṣuṇī SAṂGHA (nuns' order), and a second time by the BHIKṢU saṃgha.

**śrāmaṇerikāsaṃvara**. (T. dge tshul ma'i sdom pa; C. qince lüyi; J. gonsakuritsugi; K. kŭnch'aek yurŭi 勤策律儀). In Sanskrit, the restraints, or precepts, governing the conduct of a ŚRĀMAṆERIKĀ (female novice); see ŚRĀMAṆERASAṂVARA.

**śrāmaṇyaphala**. (P. sāmaññaphala; T. dge sbyong gi tshul gyi 'bras bu; C. shamen'guo; J. shamonka; K. samun'gwa 沙門果). In Sanskrit, "the fruit of recluseship," viz., "the beneficial effects of religious practice." "Fruit" in this compound refers to the benefits that come to fruition in a recluse's current or future life. The latter type includes both merit (PUṆYA) and a favorable rebirth. The former benefits are expounded by the Buddha in various versions of the *Śrāmaṇyaphalasūtra* (see SĀMAÑÑAPHALASUTTANTA). These benefits include respect from members of higher classes, sensory restraint, contentedness, abandonment of the hindrances, attainment of the four meditative absorptions, insight, supranormal powers, clairaudience, recollection of past lives, and so on. In regard to the progressive path to liberation, śrāmaṇyaphala refers to the four stages of sanctity that culminate in the realization of NIRVĀṆA: the fruits of the stream-enterer (SROTAĀPANNA), once-returner (SAKṚDĀGĀMIN), nonreturner (ANĀGĀMIN), and worthy one (ARHAT).

**Sras mkhar dgu thog**. (Sekar Gutok). In Tibetan, "Nine-Storied Son's Tower"; a tower purportedly constructed in the late eleventh century by the Tibetan saint MI LA RAS PA as part of his training under the master MAR PA CHOS KYI BLO GROS. Located in the LHO BRAG region of southern Tibet, on the bank of the Gsas River, the nine-storied tower was originally constructed as a memorial for Mar pa's son DAR MA MDO SDE, although because of its location it likely had strategic value as well. The building was renovated in the sixteenth century by DPA' BO GTSUG LAG PHRENG BA, who fashioned a golden roof and added a large monastic institution at the site. The tower remains an important pilgrimage site for Tibetan Buddhists.

**śrāvaka**. (P. sāvaka; T. nyan thos; C. shengwen; J. shōmon; K. sŏngmun 聲聞). In Sanskrit, lit. "listener"; viz., a direct "disciple" of the Buddha who "listened" to his teachings (and sometimes seen translated over-literally from the Chinese as "sound-hearer"). In the MAHĀYĀNA, the term was used to describe those who (along with PRATYEKABUDDHAS) sought their own liberation from suffering as an ARHAT by following the HĪNAYĀNA path (see ER SHENG), and was contrasted (negatively) to the BODHISATTVAs who seeks buddhahood for the sake of all beings. There is an issue in the Mahāyāna concerning whether śrāvakas will eventually enter the bodhisattva path and become buddhas, or whether arhatship is a final state where no further progress along the path (MĀRGA) will be possible (see ŚRĀVAKAGOTRA). The SADDHARMAPUṆḌARĪKASŪTRA, for example, declares that they will, and in the sūtra the Buddha makes prophecies about the future buddhahood of several famous śrāvakas. In many Mahāyāna sūtras, śrāvakas are often described as being in the audience of the Buddha's teaching, and certain śrāvakas, such as ŚĀRIPUTRA, play important roles as interlocutors. In the third chapter of the VIMALAKĪRTINIRDEŚA, a series of śrāvakas explain why they are reluctant to visit the bodhisattva VIMALAKĪRTI, because of the insurmountable challenge his profound understanding of the dharma will present to them.

**Śrāvakabhūmi**. (T. Nyan thos kyi sa; C. Shengwen di; J. Shōmonji; K. Sŏngmun chi 聲聞地). In Sanskrit, the "Stage of the Listener" or "Stage of the Disciple," a work by ASAṄGA included in the first and main section (Bahubhūmika/Bhūmivastu, "Multiple Stages") of his massive compendium, the YOGĀCĀRABHŪMI. The work, which also circulated as an independent text, deals with practices associated with the ŚRĀVAKA (disciples) and consists of four major sections (yogasthāna), which treat spiritual lineage (GOTRA), different types of persons (PUDGALA), preparation for practice (PRAYOGA), and the mundane path (LAUKIKAMĀRGA) and supramundane path (LOKATTARAMĀRGA). The first yogasthāna on spiritual lineage is divided into three parts. First, the stage of lineage (gotrabhūmi) discusses the spiritual potentiality or lineage (gotra) of the śrāvaka from four standpoints: its intrinsic nature, its establishment or definition (vyavasthāna), the marks (LIṄGA) characterizing the persons belonging to that lineage, and the classes of people in that lineage. Second, the stage of entrance (avatārabhūmi) discusses the stage where the disciple enters upon the practice; like the previous part, this section treats this issue from these same four standpoints. Third, the stage of deliverance (naiṣkramyabhūmi) explains the stage where the disciple, after severing the bonds of the sensual realm (KĀMADHĀTU), practices to obtain freedom from passion (VAIRĀGYA) by following either the mundane or supramundane path; this section subsequently discusses thirteen collections or equipment (saṃbhāra) necessary to complete both paths, such as sensory restraint, controlling food intake, etc. This stage of deliverance (naiṣkramyabhūmi) continues over the second through fourth yogasthānas to provide an extended treatment of śravāka practice. The second yogasthāna discusses the theoretical basis of śravāka practice in terms of persons (pudgala), divided into nineteen subsections on such subjects as the classes of persons who cultivate the śravāka path, meditative objects, descriptions of various states of concentration (SAMĀDHI), hindrances to meditation, etc. The third yogasthāna concerns the preliminary practices (prayoga) performed by these persons, describing in detail the process of training. This process begins by first visiting a teacher. If that teacher identifies him as belonging to the śrāvaka lineage, the practitioner should then cultivate in five ways: (1) guarding and accumulating the requisites of samādhi (samādhisaṃbhāra-rakṣopacaya), (2) selection (prāvivekya), (3) one-pointedness of mind (CITTAIKĀGRATĀ), (4) elimination of hindrances (ĀVARAṆA-viśuddhi), and (5) cultivation of correct mental orientation (MANASKĀRA-bhāvanā). Among these five, the section on cittaikāgratā contains one of the most detailed discussions in Sanskrit sources of the meditative procedures for the cultivation of ŚAMATHA and VIPAŚYANĀ. In the fourth yogasthāna, the practitioner, who has accomplished the five stages of application (prayoga), proceeds to either the mundane (laukika) or supramundane (lokottara) path. On the mundane path, the practitioner is said to be reborn into the various heavens of the subtle-materiality realm (RŪPADHĀTU) or the immaterial realm (ĀRŪPYADHĀTU) by cultivating the four subtle-materiality meditative absorptions (RŪPĀVACARADHYĀNA) or the four immaterial meditative absorptions (ĀRŪPYĀVACARADHYĀNA). On the supramundane path, the śravāka practices to attain the stage of worthy one (ARHAT) by relying on the insight of the FOUR NOBLE TRUTHS (catvāry āryasatyāni). See also BODHISATTVABHŪMI.

**śrāvakagotra**. (T. nyan thos kyi rigs; C. shengwen zhongxing; J. shōmon shushō; K. sŏngmun chongsŏng 聲聞種姓). In Sanskrit, "lineage of the disciples," a term that is used in the MAHĀYĀNA to describe a person who is predisposed toward the practice of the HĪNAYĀNA. Certain strands of the YOGĀCĀRA school advocated that there were five distinct spiritual lineages or destinies (PAÑCAGOTRA): (1) the TATHĀGATA lineage (GOTRA), for those destined to become buddhas; (2) the PRATYEKABUDDHA lineage, for those destined to become ARHATs via the pratyekabuddha path; (3) the ŚRĀVAKAYĀNA lineage, for those who will become arhats via the ŚRĀVAKA vehicle; (4) those of indefinite (ANIYATA) lineage, who may follow any of three vehicles; and (5) those without lineage (agotra), who are incapable of liberation, or who have lost the potential to achieve enlightenment by becoming incorrigibles (ICCHANTIKA). Persons are predisposed to follow the path of their lineage, with śrāvakas and pratyekabuddhas eventually achieving the enlightenment of the arhat and bodhisattvas achieving the enlightenment of a buddha, or tathāgata. A person of indeterminate lineage may become either an arhat or a buddha, and the icchantikas neither of the two.

**śrāvakayāna**. (T. nyan thos kyi theg pa; C. shengwen sheng; J. shōmonjō; K. sŏngmun sŭng 聲聞乘). In Sanskrit, "vehicle of the disciples," in MAHĀYĀNA treatments of the path, one of the two constituents (along with PRATYEKABUDDHAYĀNA) of the so-called "lesser vehicle" (HĪNAYĀNA). These two vehicles (C. ER SHENG), together with the third vehicle of the BODHISATTVA, are the "three vehicles" (TRIYĀNA) often mentioned in Mahāyāna sūtras. The proponents of the various Mahāyāna philosophical schools disagree as to whether or not the śrāvakayāna is an expedient stratagem (UPĀYA), with the MADHYAMAKA arguing that it is and that all beings, including ŚRĀVAKAs, will eventually enter the Mahāyāna and achieve buddhahood, and the some YOGĀCĀRA thinkers holding that śrāvakas will only become arhats and cannot go on to become buddhas.

**Śrāvastī**. (P. Sāvatthi; T. Mnyan yod; C. Shewei guo; J. Shae koku; K. Sawi kuk 舍衛國). Capital city of KOŚALA and one of the major cities of India at the time of the Buddha. The Pāli commentator BUDDHAGHOSA states implausibly that there were 5.7 million families living in Śrāvastī during the Buddha's lifetime. The Buddha spent many years there after he attained enlightenment, and he is reported to have passed twenty-five rains retreats (VARṢĀ) in the city. Śrāvastī was ruled by the Buddha's royal patron, King PRASENAJIT, and was home to his wealthiest patron, ANĀTHAPIṆḌADA, who offered to the Buddha the famous JETAVANA grove and its residences. Hundreds of sūtras are set in Śrāvastī. The city is also the site where the

Buddha (and, according to some accounts, all previous buddhas) performed two miracles: the "great miracle" (MAHĀPRĀTIHĀRYA), in which the Buddha creates various replicas of himself and appears simultaneously in various terrestrial and celestial abodes; and the "twin miracle" (YAMAKAPRĀTIHĀRYA) in which the Buddha, in response to a challenge from non-Buddhist YOGINs, rose into the air and simultaneously emitted fire and water from his body.

**Śrāvastī miracles**. See MAHĀPRĀTIHĀRYA; YAMAKAPRĀTIHĀRYA.

**Śreṇika heresy**. (C. Xianni waidao, J. Senni gedō, K. Sŏnni oedo 先尼外道). A heresy that originated with Śreṇika VATSAGOTRA, an ascetic wanderer (PARIVRĀJAKA) and contemporary of GAUTAMA Buddha, who claimed that the impermanent physical body was simply a temporary vessel for a permanent self (ĀTMAN); also known as the Senika heresy. In the *Aggi-Vacchagottasutta* ("Discourse to Vatsagotra on the [Simile of] Fire"), the seventy-second sutta in the Pāli MAJJHIMANIKĀYA, Vacchagotta (the Pāli equivalent of Vatsagotra) has a celebrated exchange with the Buddha concerning ten "indeterminate questions" (AVYĀKṚTA)—i.e., whether the world is eternal or not eternal, infinite or finite, what is the state of the TATHĀGATA after death, etc. The Buddha refuses to respond to any of the questions, since an answer would entangle him in an indefensible philosophical position. Instead, to convey some semblance of the state of the tathāgata after death, the Buddha uses the simile of extinguishing of fire: just as, after a fire has been extinguished, it would be inappropriate to say that it has gone anywhere, so after the tathāgata has extinguished each of the five aggregates (SKANDHA), they cannot be said to have gone anywhere. At the conclusion of the discourse, Vatsagotra accepts the Buddha as his teacher. (The *Ānandasutta* of the SAṂYUTTANIKĀYA explains that the Buddha kept silent in response to Vatsagotra's questions about the nature of the self in order to prevent him from falling into the extremes of either ŚĀŚVATAVĀDA, "eternalism," or UCCHEDAVĀDA, "annihilationism.") The DAZHIDU LUN (**Mahāprajñāpāramitāśāstra*) identifies the Vacchagotta of the Pāli suttas with Śreṇika Vatsagotra, the namesake of what in MAHĀYĀNA sources is termed the Śreṇika heresy. The locus classicus for this heresy appears in the MAHĀPARINIRVĀṆASŪTRA. There, when Śreṇika raises the question about whether there is a self or not, the Buddha keeps silent, so Śreṇika himself offers a fire simile, but with a radically different interpretation from what is found in the *Aggi-Vacchagottasutta.* He instead compares the physical body and the self to a house and its owner: even though the house may burn down in a fire, the owner is safe outside the house; thus, the body and its constituents (skandha) may be impermanent and subject to dissolution, but not the eternal self. The Śreṇika heresy is a frequent topic in the CHAN literature of East Asia. NANYANG HUIZHONG (675?–775), a successor of the sixth patriarch (LIUZU) HUINENG (638–713), is said to have criticized the "mind itself is buddha" (zixin shi fo) teaching of MAZU DAOYI (709–788) and other HONGZHOU ZONG teachers as being akin to the Śrenika heresy. The Japanese SŌTŌSHŪ ZEN master DŌGEN KIGEN (1200–1253), in his BENDŌWA and SHŌBŌGENZŌ, criticizes as equivalent to the Śreṇika heresy the view that the mind-nature is eternal (shinshō jōjū) even though the body perishes. There is much scholarly debate about whether Dōgen's criticism was directed at the "original enlightenment" (HONGAKU; cf. BENJUE) thought of the medieval TENDAISHŪ, or against the teachings of his rival Zen school, the DARUMASHŪ, whose similar declarations that the mind is already enlightened and that practice was not necessary opened it to charges of antinomianism.

**Śṛgālakamātṛ**. (P. Sigālakamātā; C. Shikeluoge zhangzhe mu; J. Shikaraka chōjamo; K. Silgaraga changja mo 室珂羅哥長者母). In Sanskrit, "Śṛgālaka's ("Jackal") Mother"; an eminent ARHAT declared by the buddha to be foremost among his nun disciples who aspire through faith (ŚRADDHĀDHIMUKTA, P. saddhādhimutta). According to the Pāli account, she was born into a wealthy merchant's family in Rājagaha (S. RĀJAGṚHA) and after marriage gave birth to a son named Sigālaka (S. Śṛgālaka), hence her epithet. Once she overheard the Buddha preach to her son concerning the brahmanical practice of worshipping the four directions and, immediately comprehending his words, she instantly became a stream-enterer (SROTAĀPANNA, P. sotāpanna). When later she renounced the world and entered the order (P. saṅgha; S. SAṂGHA), she was filled with faith and would gaze at the Buddha during his sermons, infatuated with his beauty. Knowing her nature, the Buddha preached to her in such a way that her infatuation would lead her to enlightenment. Many lifetimes before, during the time of Padmottara Buddha, she is said to have resolved to be foremost among those who aspire through faith. She was at that time the daughter of a minister and once accompanied him to hear the Buddha preach. Inspired by faith, she entered the order and, hearing the Buddha praise someone as foremost in faith, vowed to attain the same distinction in a future life.

**Śrīmālādevīsiṃhanādasūtra**. (T. Lha mo dpal phreng gi seng ge'i sgra'i mdo; C. Shengman shizihou yisheng da fangbian fangguang jing; J. Shōman shishiku ichijōdaihōben hōkōgyō; K. Sŭngman sajahu ilsŭng tae pangp'yŏn panggwang kyŏng 勝鬘師子吼一乘大方便方廣經). In Sanskrit, "Sūtra on the Lion's Roar of Queen Śrīmālā," one of the earliest TATHĀGATAGARBHA texts, composed about the third century CE, probably by MAHĀSĀṂGHIKA adherents in the ĀNDHRA region of southern India. The original Sanskrit has not survived, except in quotations in such texts as the RATNAGOTRAVIBHĀGA. The first translation of this sūtra into Chinese was made by the central Indian missionary DHARMAKṢEMA (d. 433) in the 420s, which was no longer extant by the Yuan dynasty. The second and most popular Chinese translation was made in 436 by GUṆABHADRA (394–468), also a native of central India. Although its full title is *Shengman shizihu yisheng da fangbian fangguang jing*, Guṇabhadra's title is abbreviated in six different ways in the

Chinese commentarial literature, the shortest and the best-known of which is simply as the *Shengman jing* (*Śrīmālā Sūtra*). A third translation was made in the early eighth century by BODHIRUCI (672–727), a native of southern India. The sūtra is exceptional in its distinctive stance on laypeople and laywomen. The chief character of the sūtra is Queen Śrīmālā, the daughter of King PRASENAJIT. The sūtra is considered one of the authoritative texts for the doctrine of tathāgatagarbha and buddha-nature (S. BUDDHADHĀTU; C. FOXING), even though the concept of tathāgatagarbha does not receive extensive treatment in the text. In the sūtra, the tathāgatagarbha is the basis of the one vehicle (EKAYĀNA); since all sentient beings share in the same tathāgatagarbha, they will all equally reach NIRVĀṆA. The *Śrīmālā Sūtra* criticizes rigidly apophatic interpretations of the doctrine of emptiness (ŚŪNYATĀ), maintaining that tathāgatagarbha is both empty (śūnya) and nonempty (aśūnya), because it simultaneously is empty of all afflictions (KLEŚA) but "nonempty" (viz., full) of all the Buddha's virtues. The sūtra explains the Buddha's virtues using kataphatic language, such as permanence (nitya) and selfhood (ĀTMAN). The *Śrīmālā Sūtra* was especially influential in East Asian Buddhism. Over twenty Chinese commentaries were composed, the most influential being those by JINGYING HUIYUAN (523–592), JIZANG (549–623), and KUIJI (632–682).

**Śrīmālā Sūtra**. (S). See ŚRĪMĀLĀDEVĪSIṂHANĀDASŪTRA.

**Śrīsiṃha**. (T. Shrī sing ha) (fl. eighth century). Sanskrit proper name of an important figure in the early dissemination (SNGA DAR) of Buddhism to Tibet, especially in the propagation of the RDZOGS CHEN teachings. According to some Tibetan accounts, he was born in China, although other sources identify his birthplace as Khotan or Kinnaur. At the age of eighteen, he is said to have traveled to Suvarṇadvīpa, often identified as the island of Sumatra. There he has a vision of AVALOKITEŚVARA, who advised him to go to India. Before doing so, he studied at "five-peak mountain," which some sources assume is WUTAISHAN in China. He next went to the Sosadvīpa charnel ground (ŚMAŚĀNA), where he studied with MAÑJUŚRĪMITRA for twenty-five years. After his teacher's death, he traveled to BODHGAYĀ, where he unearthed tantric texts hidden there by Mañjuśrīmitra. Śrīsiṃha is especially remembered in Tibet as the teacher of VAIROCANA, one of the most important figures in the earlier dissemination of Buddhism to Tibet. Vairocana was one of the first seven Tibetans (SAD MI BDUN) ordained as Buddhist monks by ŚĀNTARAKṢITA at the monastery of BSAM YAS, and he soon became an illustrious translator. He is said to have been a disciple of PADMASAMBHAVA and a participant on the Indian side in the BSAM YAS DEBATE. After Padmasambhava's departure from Tibet, the king required a fuller exposition of TANTRA and sent Vairocana to India to obtain further tantric instructions. After many trials, he arrived in India, where he was instructed by Śrīsiṃha. Fearing that other Indian masters would object to his imparting the precious esoteric teachings to a foreigner, Śrīsiṃha insisted that he study sūtras and less esoteric tantric texts with other teachers during the day, conveying the most secret teachings to him under the cover of darkness; these were the rdzogs chen teachings that Vairocana took back to Tibet and taught to king KHRI SRONG LDE BTSAN. Among other esoteric teachings that Vairocana gave to Śrīsiṃha is Śrīsiṃha's tantric commentary on the PRAJÑĀPĀRAMITĀHṚDAYASŪTRA.

**śrīvatsa**. (T. dpal be'u; C. jixiang haiyun; J. kichijōkaiun; K. kilsang haeun 吉祥海雲). In Sanskrit, literally, "beloved of Śrī," an epithet of Viṣṇu but used to describe a triangular pattern on the chest of Viṣṇu. The term is generally translated as "endless knot," and is considered to be one of the eight auspicious symbols (AṢṬAMAṄGALA) of Buddhism. Usually depicted as a closed design of intertwined lines at right angles, it is said to symbolize the endless wisdom and compassion of the Buddha. It is often listed as the last of the eighty secondary marks (ANUVYAÑJANA) of a superman (MAHĀPURUṢA), and is said to adorn the soles of a buddha's feet.

**Śrīvijaya**. (T. Dpal rnam par rgyal ba; C. Shilifoshi; J. Shitsuribussei; K. Sillibulsŏ 室利佛逝). A kingdom located on the island of Sumatra (in modern Indonesia) which was an important center of Buddhism from the seventh through the eleventh centuries. Located along the key maritime routes of Southeast Asia, it was a major political power in the region. The Chinese pilgrim YIJING (635–713 CE) made extended stays in the kingdom on both his trip to India and his return to China, stopping there first for six months to study Sanskrit, and then making a more lengthy stay beginning in 687, where he translated a number of texts, including much of the massive MŪLASARVĀSTIVĀDA VINAYA, and wrote an account of his journey, the NANHAI JIGUI NEIFA ZHUAN; because there was no paper and ink in Sumatra, Yijing made a short trip to China to retrieve these items before returning to Śrīvijaya to continue his work. He reported that in the city of Bhoga there were more than a thousand monks, whom he praised for their learning and their adherence to the vinaya, which he said was the same as that practiced in India. He advised Chinese monks to stop in Śrīvijaya for preparatory studies before proceeding to India. In the eleventh century, the Bengali monk ATIŚA DĪPAṂKARAŚRĪJÑĀNA may have visited Śrīvijaya to study with DHARMAKĪRTIŚRĪ; the sources say that he visited Suvarṇadvīpa, a term that seemed to encompass a larger region, which included Sumatra.

**Śroṇāparānta**. (P. Sunāparanta; C. Shuluna; J. Shurona; K. Surona 輸盧那). The region lying along the Narmadā River and traversing the present western Indian states of Rajasthan and Gujarat, most likely identical to Aparanta. The elder PŪRṆA (P. Puṇṇa) hailed from Śroṇāparānta. According to the Pāli legend, the elder Puṇṇa once invited the Buddha to accept the donation of a sandalwood monastery constructed by the inhabitants of Sunāparanta. The Buddha accepted this offer and traveled there by flying, accompanied by a host of 499 arhats. Along the way he descended to Saccabaddha (S. Satyabaddha) mountain and converted the sage dwelling there. The Burmese (Myanmar) identify Sunāparanta as a portion of their homeland named Sunāparanta-Tambdīpa along the northern reaches of the Irrawaddy (Ayeyarwady) river basin in Upper Burma. On the basis of the Puṇṇa legend, Burmese chroniclers also claim that Buddhism was established among the Burmese during the lifetime of the Buddha and therefore is older than the Buddhism of Sri Lanka. Later Burmese chroniclers also identify Sunāparanta with Aparanta, thus allowing them to claim that their homeland received the AŚOKA-era Buddhist mission of the Yavana (Greek) Dharmarakṣita (P. Yonaka Dhammarakkhita).

**Srong btsan sgam po**. (Songtsen Gampo) (r. c. 605–650). The thirty-third Tibetan religious king (chos kyi rgyal po) who reigned during the period of the Yar klungs dynasty; credited with establishing Buddhism as the predominant religion in Tibet. He is considered the first of three great religious kings, along with KHRI SRONG LDE BTSAN and RAL PA CAN. Although the historical facts of his life are somewhat murky, stories of Srong btsan sgam po's activities pervade Tibetan culture. His rule forged a cohesive national center and brought Tibet to the zenith of it military expansion, shaping an empire that rivaled any in Asia. During Srong btsan sgam po's reign, Tibet was surrounded by Buddhist currents to the south and west, which appear to have had a particularly profound effect on Tibetan civilization. According to traditional sources, the king and his two wives, the Nepalese BHṚKUTI and the Chinese WENCHENG, were instrumental in the early promulgation of Buddhist practice in his kingdom. An important Tibetan text, the MAṆI BKA' 'BUM ("One Hundred Thousand Instructions on the Maṇi"), describes the monarch as an earthly manifestation of AVALOKITEŚVARA, the BODHISATTVA of compassion, and his wives as forms of the female bodhisattva TĀRĀ. These accounts are at the heart of Tibet's Buddhist myth of origin and play a central role in how most Tibetans understand the history of their country and religion. After ascending the throne, Srong btsan sgam po moved his capital from the heartland of the Yar klungs Valley in the south to its modern location in LHA SA. With the support of their monarch, each queen established an important Buddhist temple to house a statue she had carried to Tibet: Bhṛkuti founding the JO KHANG temple for an image of ŚĀKYAMUNI called JO BO MI BSKYOD RDO RJE, Wencheng founding what is now the RA MO CHE temple for her statue of Śākyamuni called JO BO SHĀKYAMUNI or Jo bo rin po che. These images were later switched, and today the Jo bo Śākyamuni statue sits in the Jo khang, where it is venerated as Tibet's holiest Buddhist relic. According to legend, the Tang princess Wencheng also imported Chinese systems of geomancy and divination through which the Tibetan landscape was viewed as a supine demoness requiring subjugation in order for Buddhism to take root and flourish. Srong btsan sgam po purportedly constructed a series of "taming temples" that acted as nails pinning down the limbs of the demoness (T. srin mo), rendering her powerless. The Jo khang was constructed over the position of the demoness' heart. In addition to the Jo khang, traditional sources count twelve main taming (T. 'dul) temples spread across the Himalayan landscape, each pinning down a point on the demoness's body. These structures appear to be in concentric circles radiating out from her heart at Lha sa. Out from the heart are the "edge-pinning temples" (MTHA' 'DUL GTSUG LAG KHANG) of KHRA 'BRUG, 'GRUM, BKA' TSHAL, and GRUM PA RGYANG, said to pin down her right and left shoulders and right and left hips, respectively; and beyond that four "extra-pinning temples" (YANG 'DUL GTSUG LAG KHANG) BU CHU, MKHO MTHING, DGE GYES, and PRA DUM RTSE that pin down her right and left elbows and right and left knees, respectively. In 637, Srong btsan sgam po established an eleven-storied palace on the hill of northeast Lha sa called Mar po ri. While this structure was later destroyed by fire, it served as the foundation for the PO TA LA palace constructed in the seventeenth century under the direction of the fifth DALAI LAMA NGAG DBANG BLO BZANG RGYA MTSHO. The king is also said to have commissioned his minister Thon mi Saṃbhota to create a new script (what is now known as Tibetan) in order to translate Buddhist texts from Sanskrit. He also established what is known as the "great legal code" (gtsug lag bka' khrims chen po). While contemporary scholars now question the portrait of Srong btsan sgam po as a pious convert to Buddhism (it is known, for example, that he maintained close ties to the early BON religion), many of Tibet's most important Buddhist institutions were established during his time.

**srotaāpanna**. [alt. srotāpanna; śrotāpanna] (P. sotāpanna; T. rgyun du zhugs pa; C. yuliu [guo]/xutuohuan; J. yoru[ka]/shudaon; K. yeryu [kwa]/sudawŏn 預流[果]/須陀洹). In Sanskrit, "stream-enterer" or "stream-winner"; the first of four stages of sanctity (see ĀRYAPUDGALA) in mainstream Buddhism, followed by the once-returner (SAKṚDĀGĀMIN), non-returner (ANĀGĀMIN) and worthy one (ARHAT). These four stages are together referred to as "the fruits of recluseship" (ŚRĀMAṆYAPHALA), viz., "the effects of religious practice." The term srotaāpanna appears very often in the Buddhist sūtras, with members of the Buddha's audience said to have attained this stage immediately upon hearing him preach the dharma. The stage of stream-enterer begins with the initial vision of the reality of NIRVĀṆA, at which point one "enters the stream" leading to liberation. Because of this achievement, the srotaāpanna has abandoned completely the first three of ten fetters (SAṂYOJANA) that bind one to the cycle of rebirth (SAṂSĀRA): (1) belief in the existence of a self in relation to the body (SATKĀYADṚṢṬI), (2) doubt about the efficacy of the path (VICIKITSĀ), (3) belief in the efficacy of rites and rituals (ŚĪLAVRATAPARĀMARŚA). For this reason, after becoming a stream-enterer, the adept will never again be reborn into the unfortunate rebirth destinies (APĀYA, DURGATI) as a demigod, animal, ghost, or hell denizen and is destined to become an arhat in a maximum of seven more lifetimes (see SAPTAKṚDBHAVAPARAMA). There are two stages to stream-entry: SROTAĀPANNAPHALAPRATIPANNAKA, or one who is practicing, or is a candidate for, the fruition of stream-entry; and SROTAĀPANNAPHALASTHA, or one who has reached, or is the recipient of, the fruition of stream-entry. The srotaāpannaphalapratipannaka has only reached the ĀNANTARYAMĀRGA (unimpeded path), whereas the srotaāpannaphalastha has reached the VIMUKTIMĀRGA (path of freedom). In the five-path system (PAÑCAMĀRGA), stream-entry is equivalent to the path of vision (DARŚANAMĀRGA) on the ŚRĀVAKA and PRATYEKABUDDHA paths. The srotaāpanna is also one of the twenty members of the ĀRYASAṂGHA (see VIṂŚATIPRABHEDASAṂGHA). In this context srotaāpanna is the name for candidates (pratipannaka) for srotaāpanna (the first fruit of the noble path). They may be either a follower through faith (ŚRADDHĀNUSĀRIN) or a follower through doctrine (DHARMĀNUSĀRIN) with either dull (MṚDVINDRIYA) or keen faculties (TĪKṢṆENDRIYA). In all cases, they may have destroyed from none up to as many as five of the sets of afflictions (KLEŚA) that cause rebirth in the sensuous realm (KĀMADHĀTU) that the ordinary (LAUKIKA) path of meditation (BHĀVANĀMĀRGA) removes, but they will not have eliminated the sixth to the ninth sets. Were they to have removed the sixth set they would be called candidates for the second fruit of once-returner (sakṛdāgāmin), and were they to have removed the ninth set they would be called candidates for the third fruit of nonreturner (anāgāmin).

**srotaāpannaphalapratipannaka**. (P. sotāpattimagga; T. rgyun du zhugs pa'i 'bras bu la zhugs pa; C. yuliu xiang; J. yorukō; K. yeryu hyang 預流向). In Sanskrit, one who is practicing, or is candidate for the fruit of stream-enterer. Both the srotaāpannaphalapratipannaka and SROTAĀPANNAPHALASTHA (one who has reached, or is the recipient of the fruit of stream-enterer) are called "stream-enterer" (SROTAĀPANNA) and are noble persons (ĀRYA); the srotaāpannaphalapratipannaka has only reached the ĀNANTARYAMĀRGA (unimpeded path), the srotaāpannaphalastha has reached the VIMUKTIMĀRGA (path of freedom) of the path of vision (DARŚANAMĀRGA). The level of ordinary humans is the sensuous realm (KĀMADHĀTU), viz., the level where beings are dominated by sense pleasure (KĀMA). Those whose prior store of actions is such that, prior to reaching the path of vision, they have eliminated as many as five of the nine sets of afflictions (KLEŚA) that cause rebirth in the sensuous realm, are candidates for the fruit stream-enterer when they reach the path of vision's unimpeded path; and they are recipients of the fruit of stream-enterer when they reach the path of freedom. This is one of the VIṂŚATIPRABHEDASAṂGHA ("twenty varieties of the ārya saṃgha") based on the list given in the ABHISAMAYĀLAṂKĀRA; srotaāpannaphalapratipannaka is also included in the category of follower of faith (ŚRADDHĀNUSĀRIN).

**srotaāpannaphalastha**. (P. sotāpattiphala; T. rgyun du zhugs pa'i 'bras bu la gnas pa; C. zheng yuliu guo; J. shōyoruka; K. chŭng yeryu kwa 證預流果). In Sanskrit, one who has reached, or is the recipient of the fruit of stream-enterer, one of the eight ĀRYAPUDGALA ("noble persons") and one of the VIṂŚATIPRABHEDASAṂGHA ("twenty varieties of the āryasaṃgha") based on the list given in the ABHISAMAYĀLAṂKĀRA. The srotaāpannaphalastha is also included in the category of those who have aspired through faith (ŚRADDHĀDHIMUKTA). See SAKṚDĀGĀMIPHALASTHA.

**sroto'nugato nāma samādhiḥ**. (T. rgyun gyi rje su song ba zhes bya ba'i ting nge 'dzin/chos rgyun gyi ting nge 'dzin; C. suiliuxiang chanding; J. zuirukō zenjō; K. suryuhyang sŏnjŏng 隨流向禪定). In Sanskrit, "continuous instruction concentration"; a SAMĀDHI achieved on the path of accumulation (SAṂBHĀRAMĀRGA), in which a BODHISATTVA is able to magically receive continuous instruction (AVAVĀDA) in the dharma. The path of accumulation is subdivided into three sections, lesser, intermediate, and greater; when one reaches the intermediate stage, a bodhisattva is no longer capable of retrogressing from the MAHĀYĀNA and gains an initial capacity to hear the voice of an actual buddha. The bodhisattva hears instructions systematized in ten topics: practice (S. pratipatti, see PAṬIPATTI), FOUR NOBLE TRUTHS, three refuges (TRIŚARAṆA), nonattachment (asakti), indefatigability (apariśrānti), full acceptance (saṃparigraha) of infinite instructions from infinite buddhas, the five types of eyes (PAÑCACAKṢUS), the six supranormal powers (ABHIJÑĀ), the path of vision (DARŚANAMĀRGA), and the path of cultivation (BHĀVANĀMĀRGA).

**śrotravijñāna**. (P. sotaviññāṇa; T. rna ba'i rnam par shes pa; C. ershi; J. nishiki; K. isik 耳識). In Sanskrit, "auditory consciousness," or "ear consciousness," one of the five sensory consciousnesses (along with those of the eye, nose, tongue, and body) and one of the six sensory consciousnesses (adding the mental consciousness, or MANOVIJÑĀNA). The auditory consciousness perceives sounds (ŚABDA). Like the other sensory consciousnesses, auditory consciousness is produced through the contact (SPARŚA) between an auditory sensory object (śabda) and the auditory sense base (ŚROTRENDRIYA) and in dependence on three conditions (pratyaya): the object condition (ĀLAMBANAPRATYAYA), in this case, a sound; a dominant condition (ADHIPATIPRATYAYA), here, the ear sense organ (śrotrendriya); and the immediately preceding condition (SAMANANTARAPRATYAYA), a prior moment of consciousness. The auditory consciousness is counted as one of the six consciousnesses (VIJÑĀNA) and eighteen elements (DHĀTU).

**śrotrāyatana**. (P. sotāyatana; T. rna ba'i skye mched; C. erchu; J. nisho; K. ich'ŏ 耳處). In Sanskrit, "auditory sense-base," or "base of cognition"; the auditory sense base or ear sense organ (ŚROTRENDRIYA) as it occurs in the list of the twelve sense fields (ĀYATANA), which are called "bases of cognition" because each pair of sense-base and sense-object produces its respective sensory consciousness. In this case, the contact (SPARŚA) between an auditory sensory object (ŚABDA) and the auditory sense base (śrotrendriya) produces an auditory consciousness (ŚROTRAVIJÑĀNA).

**śrotrendriya**. (P. sotindriya; T. rna ba'i dbang po; C. ergen; J. nikon; K. igŭn 耳根). In Sanskrit, "auditory sense base," the physical organ located in the ear that makes it possible to hear auditory objects or "sounds" (ŚABDA). This sense base is not the ear itself, but a form of subtle materiality (RŪPA) located within the ear and invisible to the naked eye. It is said to be round in shape with many hollow openings, like a sheaf of hay that has been cut. If this sense organ is absent or damaged, hearing is not possible. The auditory sense organ serves as the dominant condition (ADHIPATIPRATYAYA) for the production of auditory consciousness (ŚROTRAVIJÑĀNA).

**śrutamayīprajñā**. (P. sutamayāpaññā; T. thos pa las byung ba'i shes rab; C. wenhui; J. mon'e; K. munhye 聞慧). In Sanskrit, "wisdom derived from hearing [viz., learning]," the first of the three types of wisdoms, which refers to understanding derived from listening to (and, by extension, reading and studying about) the dharma. This type of wisdom provides a grounding for the development of mental attention and concentration, which is crucial for meditative calmness (ŚAMATHA). It is not as profound as the second type of wisdom, which arises as a result of thinking about or reflecting on what one has learned (CINTĀMAYĪPRAJÑĀ); or the third type of wisdom, which is generated through meditation (BHĀVANĀMAYĪPRAJÑĀ) at the level of VIPAŚYANĀ.

**Ssanggyesa**. (雙溪[磎]寺). In Korean, "Twin Brooks Monastery"; the thirteenth district monastery (PONSA) in the contemporary CHOGYE CHONG of Korean Buddhism. Ssanggyesa was founded in 722 during the Silla dynasty by two monks, Taebi (d.u.) and Sampŏp (d.u.). The pair returned to Korea from Tang-dynasty China after having a dream that instructed them to enshrine the head of the sixth patriarch (LIUZU) HUINENG (638–713) of the Chinese CHAN school at a place where arrowroot flowers were blooming in the snow. Guided by a tiger (symbolizing the mountain spirit), they found the intended location on the mountain of CHIRISAN and constructed a monastery at the spot. The SŎN monk CHIN'GAM HYESO (774–850) rebuilt the monastery with the new name of Okch'ŏnsa (Jade Fount Monastery) after returning to Korea in 840 from studying Chan on the Chinese mainland. The name Ssanggyesa was eventually given to the monastery in 887 by the Silla king Chŏnggang (r. 886–887). Ssanggyesa is said to have been the site where Hyeso first introduced tea and tea culture to the Korean peninsula and the green tea grown in the mountains surrounding the monastery is still renowned in Korea for its quality. Ssanggyesa was burned to the ground during the Japanese Hideyoshi invasions (1592–1598) and the present monastery dates from the reconstruction spearheaded by PYŎGAM KAKSŎNG (1575–1660) in 1632.

**stage of completion**. See NIṢPANNAKRAMA.

**stage of generation**. See UTPATTIKRAMA.

**Stag lung**. (Taklung). The central Tibetan monastic seat of the STAG LUNG subsect of the BKA' BRGYUD sect of Tibetan Buddhism. Originally founded north of LHA SA in 1180 by STAG LUNG THANG PA BKRA SHIS DPAL, the monastery flourished under the guidance of his successors Sku yal ba Rin chen mgon po (Kuyalwa Rinchen Gönpo, 1191–1236) and Sangs rgyas yar byon (Sangye Yarjön, 1203–1272; also known as Prajñāguru). Under the latter's stewardship, Stag lung attained considerable power within the SA SKYA-Mongol political structure at the Yuan court. Together with his disciple and eventual successor Maṅgalaguru (T. Bkra shis bla ma, 1231–1297), he forged close ties with the Sa skya hierarch 'PHAGS PA BLO GROS RGYAL MTSHAN and towards the end of his life entrusted the monastery's welfare and security to the Sa skya prelate. Stag lung was renowned for its strict adherence to monastic discipline as well as for its prodigious atelier, which produced some of central Tibet's finest paintings of the period. During its peak, the monastic population grew to some seven thousand monks. At that time, the saying originated that monks of other monasteries were "unable to rival even a dog of Stag lung." After Sangs rgyas yar byon's death, the throne fell briefly to his nephew Sangs rgyas dbon (Sangye Wön, 1250/1–1296, better known as Dbon po bla ma). Sangs rgyas dbon was compelled to flee into exile after a single year, due to Maṅgalaguru's close ties with the politically powerful 'Phags pa Blo gros rgyal mtshan. In 1276, Sangs rgyas dbon established a new seat for the Stag lung bka' brgyud tradition at RI BO CHE monastery in the eastern Tibetan region of Khams. This eventually came to eclipse the original monastery in importance. From the sixteenth century onwards, Stag lung was increasingly influenced by officials from SE RA and 'BRAS SPUNGS monasteries in LHA SA. Stag lung monastery was completely destroyed during the Chinese Cultural Revolution.

**Stag lung bka' brgyud**. (Taklung Kagyü). One of the four major and eight minor subsects of the BKA' BRGYUD sect of Tibetan Buddhism (BKA' BRGYUD CHE BZHI CHUNG BRGYAD), founded by STAG LUNG THANG PA BKRA SHIS DPAL, a principal disciple of the Bka' brgyud hierarch PHAG MO GRU PA RDO RJE RGYAL PO. Its original seat was STAG LUNG monastery located north of LHA SA, although a branch institution was later founded in the eastern Tibetan region of Khams at RI BO CHE, which eventually eclipsed the former as a center of learning and formed a strong, nearly independent lineage.

**Stag lung Thang pa bkra shis dpal**. (Taklung Tangpa Tashipel) (1142–1210). Founder of the STAG LUNG BKA' BRGYUD, one of the four major and eight minor subsects of the BKA' BRGYUD. After being ordained as a novice, he studied the main texts of the BKA' GDAMS PA. In 1165, inspired by a vision, he went to meet the great Bka' brgyud hierarch PHAG MO GRU PA RDO RJE RGYAL PO, becoming his personal attendant and scribe. He received many teachings from him, including "the six yogas of Nāropa" (NĀ RO CHOS DRUG). He was ordained as a BHIKṢU in

1172. Stag lung thang pa was known for his commitment to monastic discipline; he was a vegetarian and did not enter the homes of laypeople. He would teach during the first half of the month and remain in retreat in the second half. He also maintained silence during each morning. He was also renowned for his tantric practice, especially MAHĀMUDRĀ and of the HEVAJRATANTRA. In 1180, he founded STAG LUNG monastery, which came to have more than three thousand monks in residence during his lifetime. He is also known as Stag lung thang pa chen po, "the Great Stag lung thang pa."

**Stag tshang**. (Taktsang). In Tibetan, "Tiger's Lair," a complex of meditation caves and temples located in Paro, Bhutan, considered one of the most important sacred Buddhist sites in the Himalayan region associated with the Indian adept PADMASAMBHAVA; also known as Spa gro Stag tshang (Paro Taktsang). Situated on a sheer cliff more than two thousand feet above the valley floor, the complex is the best known among numerous Stag tshang, or "Tiger's Lair," sites located across eastern Tibet. According to traditional accounts, Padmasambhava miraculously flew to the spot in wrathful form as RDO RJE DROD LO, seated on the back of a tigress believed to have been his consort YE SHES MTSHO RGYAL, and remained there for three months. In 853, one of Padmasambhava's twenty-five main disciples, Glang chen Dpal gyi seng ge (Langchen Palkyi Sengye), went to meditate in the main cave at Stag tshang, after which it became known as Stag tshang dpal phug, or "Pal's cave at Taktsang." Later, many great masters undertook meditation retreats there; these include PHA DAM PA SANGS RGYAS, MA GCIG LAB SGRON, THANG STONG RGYAL PO, and, according to one tradition, the great YOGIN MI LA RAS PA. The first buildings were likely erected in the fourteenth century. However, it was under the direction of the Bhutanese reformer ZHABS DRUNG NGAG DBANG RNAM RGYAL and later his regent Bstan 'dzin rab rgyas, that the modern structure was completed in 1692. In 1998, the complex was destroyed by fire.

**State-Protection Buddhism**. See HUGUO FOJIAO.

**stavakāya**. (T. bstod tshogs). In Sanskrit, "collection of hymns," or "corpus of hymns"; the devotional works attributed to NĀGĀRJUNA. There are traditionally four works in this group, known collectively as the CATUḤSTAVA. They are the LOKĀTĪTASTAVA, the NIRAUPAMYASTAVA, the ACINTYASTAVA, and the PARAMĀRTHASTAVA, although a number of other important hymns, including the DHARMADHĀTUSTAVA, are also ascribed to Nāgārjuna. This group of texts is often referred to in connection with YUKTIKĀYA, the "corpus of reasoning" or "collection of reasoning," a term used to refer collectively to six works that traditionally constitute NĀGĀRJUNA's philosophical oeuvre. Those six works are the MŪLAMADHYAMAKAKĀRIKĀ, the YUKTIṢAṢṬIKĀ, the ŚŪNYATĀSAPTATI, the VIGRAHAVYĀVARTANĪ, the VAIDALYASŪTRANĀMA, and the RATNĀVALĪ. In some versions, there are only five works in this corpus, with the *Ratnāvalī* eliminated. These two collections of Nāgārjuna's works figure prominently in the "self-emptiness, other-emptiness" (RANG STONG GZHAN STONG) debate in Tibetan Buddhism, where the parties disagree on the question of which corpus represents Nāgārjuna's definitive view. The proponents of the rang stong, or "self-empty" position, see a consistent philosophical view between the two collections, whereas the proponents of gzhan stong, or "other-emptiness," find a more substantialist position in the corpus of hymns and regard this as Nāgārjuna's true position.

**Stcherbatsky, Fyodor Ippolitovich**. (1866–1942). The leading Russian scholar of Buddhism of the early twentieth century; born in Kielce, Poland, to a Russian military family. Stcherbatsky was one of the first Russian Orientalists to study Buddhism; his main areas of scholarly interest were SARVĀSTIVĀDA and MAHĀYĀNA literature. He worked with EUGÈNE OBERMILLER (1901–1935), who was also his student, and knew SYLVAIN LÉVI (1863–1935) and other members of the French school of Buddhist Studies. Stcherbatsky conveyed messages between the Russian monk AGVAN DORZHIEV and the thirteenth DALAI LAMA, and traveled extensively in Mongolia and Trans-Baikalia. Stcherbatsky taught Sanskrit at St. Petersburg (Leningrad) University from 1900–1941. He was also the head of the Oriental Institute of the Imperial Russian Academy of Sciences. He often worked with Dorzhiev, and rescued him from jail on at least one occasion. He helped construct Dorzhiev's St. Petersburg Temple, which was consecrated in 1915, and was eventually entrusted with its care when the monks were forced to flee in 1918. He traveled to western Europe on a book-buying mission for the academy, and attended the First All-Russian Buddhist Congress in 1927. Because he supported the Bolshevik revolution, Stcherbatsky was not personally persecuted; his teacher, SERGE OLDENBURG, was a friend of Lenin. He remained an active scholar during the Soviet period, leading an expedition to acquire Tibetan manuscripts from Buryat monasteries in 1924. Along with other scholars, Stcherbatsky was evacuated from Leningrad to Khazakhstan in 1941, and died there the following year. Stcherbatsky's published works include *The Soul Theory of Buddhists* (1920), *The Central Conception of Buddhism and the Meaning of the Word Dharma* (1923), *The Conception of Buddhist Nirvana* (1927), and *Buddhist Logic* (1932).

**Stein, Sir Marc Aurel**. (1862–1943). Hungarian-born archaeologist who led four British expeditions through Central Asia to document and collect artifacts from the lost cultures of the ancient SILK ROAD. After receiving his doctorate in Sanskrit and Oriental religions under Rudolf von Roth at the University of Tübingen, Stein moved to England where he made use of the resources at the Ashmolean Museum, the Bodleian Library, the India Office Library, and the British Museum to further his study of Sanskrit. During his service in the Hungarian military, Stein learned both surveying and map-making, skills that would aid him in his career. Stein's greatest discovery was made at the

DUNHUANG caves in northwest China. There, he came across a hidden library cave (Cave 17) containing over forty thousand scrolls, many of which he sent back to England for study. The Stein collection at the British Library contains over thirty thousand manuscripts and printed documents in languages as varied as Chinese, Tibetan, Sanskrit, Mongolian, Tangut, Khotanese, Kuchean, Sogdian, and Uighur. The art objects Stein collected are now divided between the British Museum, the British Library, the Srinigar Museum, and the Indian National Museum at New Delhi. In addition, thousands of photographs taken by Stein dating from the 1890s to 1938 have been preserved, as well as several volumes published by Stein detailing his explorations. These items are critical to the study of the history of Central Asia generally and the spread of Buddhist art and literature. Stein died and was buried in Kabul, Afghanistan.

***sthāpyabhāvanā**. (T. 'jog sgom). In Sanskrit, "stabilizing meditation," the one-pointed concentration on a single object without discursive reflection. An example of such stabilizing meditation would be the concentration on the breath or the golden body of the Buddha, eventually resulting in a state of ŚAMATHA or DHYĀNA. The term is often paired with *VICĀRABHĀVANĀ, those forms of meditation that involve discursive reflection on points of Buddhist doctrine, such as the investigation of the constituents of mind and body. In instructions on meditation practice, advice is often given to alternate between these two forms of meditation, first arriving at a conclusion or conviction through analytical meditation and then focusing on that conclusion through stabilizing meditation, resulting in VIPAŚYANĀ.

**Sthāvarā**. (T. Sa'i lha mo; C. Anzhu dishen; J. Anjūjijin; K. Anju chisin 安住地神). In Sanskrit, "Immovable," the goddess of the earth, also known as PṚTHIVĪ. She plays an important role in the story of ŚĀKYAMUNI Buddha's enlightenment. After MĀRA and his armies were unable to unseat the BODHISATTVA, Māra challenged his right to occupy the space beneath the BODHI TREE, claiming that he, Māra, had a greater right since, as a god, he had greater merit; his army boisterously attested to Māra's claim. The bodhisattva responded that his merit was greater because he had practiced the ten perfections (PĀRAMITĀ) for many lifetimes. When Māra asked who would attest to the Bodhisattva's claim, he touched the earth with his right hand in the famous "earth-touching gesture" (BHŪMISPARŚAMUDRĀ), calling on the goddess of the earth to attest to the truth of his statement. She responded by causing a tremor; in some versions, she emerges from the earth to bear witness. In the GAṆḌAVYŪHA (the final chapter of the AVATAṂSAKASŪTRA), the bodhisattva SUDHANA sets out in search of a teacher, encountering fifty-two beings (twenty of whom are female), including the Buddha's mother MAHĀMĀYĀ, the future buddha MAITREYA, as well as AVALOKITEŚVARA and MAÑJUŚRĪ. The thirtieth being he encounters is Sthāvarā, whom he meets at BODHGAYĀ. She also bears witness to his practice of virtue and predicts that he will achieve buddhahood. See also THORANI.

**sthavira**. (P. thera; T. gnas brtan; C. shangzuo; J. jōza; K. sangjwa 上座). In Sanskrit, "elder," a term of respect for a senior monk, and typically one with at least a decade of seniority as a fully ordained monk or nun (BHIKṢU, BHIKṢUṆĪ), with seniority measured not by age but by the length of time since the monk or nun's full ordination (UPASAMPADĀ). One's years of ordination as a novice monk or nun (ŚRĀMAṆERA, ŚRĀMAṆERIKĀ) do not count in determining one's seniority within the order. The term also refers to sixteen (or in some lists, eighteen) ARHAT-disciples of the Buddha and were entrusted by him with preserving the teaching until the coming of the future buddha, MAITREYA. These monks became objects of devotion, especially in Tibet and East Asia; see ṢOḌAŚASTHAVIRA.

***Sthaviranikāya**. (T. Gnas brtan sde pa; C. Shangzuo bu; J. Jōzabu; K. Sangjwa pu 上座部). In Sanskrit, "School of the Elders"; one of the important "mainstream" (that is, non-MAHĀYĀNA) schools of Indian Buddhism, which later split into several other important MAINSTREAM BUDDHIST SCHOOLS. The Sthaviranikāya is thought to have come into existence in a dispute over monastic practice that occurred about a century after the Buddha's death, at the so-called second Buddhist council (SAṂGĪTI; see COUNCIL, SECOND) held at VAIŚĀLĪ. The Sthaviranikāya resolved that ten rules of the VINAYA must be observed, while another faction, which came to call itself the MAHĀSĀṂGHIKA ("Great Congregation") held that these rules could be ignored. The ten violations of monastic practice that the Sthaviranikāya sought to proscribe were: (1) carrying salt in an animal horn, (2) eating when the shadow of the sundial is two fingerbreadths past noon, (3) after eating, traveling to another village on the same day to eat another meal, (4) holding several monastic assemblies within the same boundary (SĪMĀ) during the same fortnight, (5) making an ecclesiastical decision with an incomplete assembly and subsequently receiving the approval of the absent monks, (6) citing precedent as a justification for violating monastic procedures, (7) drinking milk whey after mealtime, (8) drinking unfermented wine, (9) using mats with fringe, and (10) accepting gold and silver. A rival, and apparently larger, group of monks held that these actions did not constitute violations of the vinaya and thus called themselves the "Great Congregation." The other NIKĀYAs or schools subsequently branched off from the Sthaviranikāya and the Mahāsāṃghika strands of mainstream Buddhism. The Sthaviranikāya itself subsequently divided into three major branches. The earliest subgroup to evolve was the VĀTSĪPUTRĪYA or SAṂMITĪYA, commonly known as the PUDGALAVĀDA (Teaching of the Person), which advocated that the continuity of karmic experience and the prospect of rebirth demanded some sort of entity (the person, or PUDGALA) that was neither identical to, nor distinct from, the aggregates (SKANDHA). Despite the reproach the school received from virtually all other mainstream schools—which viewed this doctrine of the person as tantamount to a teaching about a perduring self (ĀTMAN), anathema to the quintessential Buddhist teaching of ANĀTMAN—the Pudgalavāda seems in fact to have been widespread and popular.

The second major school was the SARVĀSTIVĀDA (Teaching that All Exists), a highly influential school especially in the northwest regions of KASHMIR and GANDHĀRA, which developed one of the most elaborate ABHIDHARMA traditions in mainstream Buddhism, and which had a significant influence on the development of later MAHĀYĀNA scholasticism. The third was the VIBHAJYAVĀDA (Teaching of Differentiation), a broad designation for non-Sarvāstivāda strands of the Sthaviranikāya, which included such later mainstream schools as MAHĪŚĀSAKA, DHARMAGUPTAKA, and KĀŚYAPĪYA. The only surviving strand of the Sthaviranikāya is the THERAVĀDA. However, the Sanskrit form *Sthaviravāda, which would be the rendering for the Pāli term Theravāda, is not attested in any Indian source; attested Sanskrit forms (both very rare) include sthāvira or sthāvarīya ("followers of the elders"). In addition, the Tibetan and Sinographic renderings of the term would both be reconstructed in Sanskrit as *Sthaviranikāya, suggesting again that Sthaviravāda or Theravāda was not the traditional designation of this school. Scholars have therefore questioned the historical ties between the Sthaviranikāya and the Theravāda, especially given the rare use of the term Theravāda as a term of self-identification prior to the early twentieth century.

***Sthaviravāda**. See STHAVIRANIKĀYA; THERAVĀDA.

**Sthiramati**. (T. Blo gros brtan pa; C. Anhui; J. An'e/Anne; K. Anhye 安慧) (475–555). Indian Buddhist philosopher associated particularly with YOGĀCĀRA school. His dates are uncertain (leading one scholar to posit three figures with this name), but he is generally placed in the sixth century, although he is said to have been a disciple of both VASUBANDHU and Guṇamati. Sthiramati seems to have been primarily based in VALABHĪ, but may have also studied at NĀLANDĀ. He wrote a number of important commentaries on such Yogācāra works as the MAHĀYĀNASŪTRĀLAṂKĀRA and MADHYĀNTAVIBHĀGA of MAITREYANĀTHA and VASUBANDHU's TRIṂŚIKĀ.

**sthiti**. (P. ṭhiti; T. gnas pa; C. zhu; J. jū; K. chu 住). In Sanskrit, "continuance," "abiding," or "duration," one of the four characteristics (CATURLAKṢAṆA) governing all conditioned objects, along with origination or birth (JĀTI), "senescence" or decay (JARĀ), and "desinence" or extinction (ANITYA). Sthiti refers to the characteristic of impermanent things to remain for one moment prior to their senescence and ultimate extinction. In the SARVĀSTIVĀDA school, sthiti was treated as a "force dissociated from thought" (CITTAVIPRAYUKTASAṂSKĀRA): in this case, the force "continuance" remained in place until the object began to decay through the force of "senescence" and ultimately was extinguished through the force "desinence." This rather tortured explanation was necessary in order to explain how factors (DHARMA) that the school presumed continued to exist in all three time-periods nevertheless still appeared to undergo change. Some Sarvāstivāda ABHIDHARMA texts, however, accept only three characteristics, omitting continuance.

**sthūlātyaya**. (P. thullaccaya; T. nyes pa sbom po; C. toulanzhe; J. chūranja/chūransha; K. t'uranch'a 偸蘭遮). In Sanskrit, "grave offense" or "important fault"; a category of misdeed in the Buddhist VINAYA, it includes the most serious offenses that can be expiated through simple confession to another monk, rather than the more severe sanction of "defeat" (PĀRĀJIKA) or the sanction of confession at a formal meeting of the order (SAṂGHĀVAŚEṢA). The misdeeds that fall under this category generally involve a failed or lesser version of a misdeed that would otherwise entail a stronger sanction. Such transgressions would include, for example, attempting to kill someone but only inflicting injury, testing poison on a human being, killing a nonhuman being, such as a PRETA, NĀGA, or YAKṢA, stealing something of little or no value (defined in the Pāli vinaya as being worth more than one māsaka and less than five māsaka), touching the hem of a woman's garment with a lustful motivation, making lustful contact with an animal that one has mistaken for a woman, seeking to ejaculate but failing to do so, attempting to have sexual intercourse with a corpse, lustfully touching the genitals of cattle, making lascivious reference to a woman's private parts without her understanding the reference, performing two of the three deeds of a go-between (accepting the request, inquiring, reporting back), going naked, wearing a garment made of owls' wings, wearing a garment of bark, castrating oneself, eating human flesh, giving away a monastery, giving away a metal pot, causing a boat to rock in place although it does not move up or down stream, delivering the penultimate blow in chopping down a tree, causing an animal to move any of its feet, moving a boundary marker (SĪMĀ), causing an owner to give up attempts to regain possession of property, implying (although not stating explicitly) that one is endowed with supranormal powers, and unsuccessfully attempting to cause a schism in the order (SAṂGHABHEDA).

**storehouse consciousness**. See ĀLAYAVIJÑĀNA.

**stream-enterer**. See SROTAĀPANNA.

**stūpa**. (P. thūpa; T. mchod rten; C. ta; J. tō; K. t'ap 塔). In Sanskrit, "reliquary"; a structure, originally in the shape of a hemispherical mound, that contains the relics (ŚARĪRA) or possessions of the Buddha or a saint, often contained within a reliquary container. In the MAHĀPARINIBBĀNASUTTA, the Buddha says that after he has passed away, his relics should be enshrined in a stūpa erected at a crossroads, and that the stūpa should be honored with garlands, incense, and sandalwood paste. Because of a dispute among his lay followers after his death, his relics were said to be divided into ten portions and distributed to ten groups or individuals, each of whom constructed a stūpa to enshrine their share of the relics in their home region. Two of these sites were the Buddha's home city of KAPILAVASTU, and KUŚINAGARĪ, the place of his death, as well as RĀJAGṚHA and VAIŚĀLĪ. The original stūpas were later said to have been opened and the relics collected by the emperor AŚOKA in the third century BCE so that he could subdivide them for a larger number of stūpas in order to accumulate merit and protect his realm. Aśoka is said to have had eighty-four thousand stūpas constructed. The stūpa form eventually spread throughout the Buddhist world (and during the twentieth century into the Western hemisphere), with significant variations in architectural form. For example, the dagoba of Sri Lanka and the so-called "PAGODA" (derived from a Portuguese transcription of the Sanskrit BHAGAVAT ["blessed," "fortunate"] or the Persian but kadah ["idol house"]), which are so ubiquitous in East Asia, are styles of stūpas. The classical architectural form of the stūpa in India consisted of a circular platform surmounted by a hemisphere made of brick within which the relics were enshrined. At the summit of the hemisphere, one or more parasols were affixed. A walking path (see CAṄKRAMA) enclosed by a railing was constructed around the stūpa, to allow for clockwise circumambulation of the reliquary. Each of these architectural elements would evolve in form and eventually become imbued with rich symbolic meaning as the stūpa evolved in India and across Asia. The relics enshrined in the stūpa are considered by Buddhists to be living remnants of the Buddha (or the relevant saint) and pilgrimage to, and worship of, stūpas has long been an important type of Buddhist practice. For all Buddhist schools, the stūpa became a reference point denoting the Buddha's presence in the landscape. Although early texts and archeological records link stūpa worship with the Buddha's life and especially the key sites in his career, stūpas are also found at places that were sacred for other reasons, often through an association with a local deity. Stūpas were constructed for past buddhas and for prominent disciples (ŚRĀVAKA) of the Buddha. Indeed, stūpas dedicated to disciples of the Buddha may have been especially popular because the monastic rules stipulate that donations to such stūpas became the property of the monastery, whereas donations to stūpas of the Buddha remained the property of the Buddha, who continued to function as a legal resident of most monasteries. By the seventh century, the practice of enshrining the physical relics of the Buddha ceases to appear in the Indian archeological record. Instead, one finds stūpas filled with small clay tablets that have been stamped or engraved with a four-line verse (often known by its first two words YE DHARMĀ) that was regarded as conveying the essence of the Buddha's teaching: "For those factors that are produced through causes, the TATHĀGATA has set forth their causes (HETU) and also their cessation (NIRODHA). Thus has spoken the great renunciant." For the MAHĀYĀNA, the stūpa conveyed a variety of meanings, such as the Buddha's immortality and buddhahood's omnipresence, and served a variety of functions, such as a site of textual revelation and a center guaranteeing rebirth in a PURE LAND. Stūpas were also pivotal in the social history of Buddhism: these monuments became magnets attracting monastery building and votive construction, as well as local ritual traditions and regional pilgrimage. The economics of Buddhist devotion at these sites generated income for local monasteries, artisans, and merchants. The great stūpa complexes (which often included monasteries with endowed lands, a pilgrimage center, a market, and support from the state) were essential sites for the Buddhist polities of Asia. See CAITYA and entries for specific stūpas, including FAMENSI, RATNAGIRI, SĀÑCĪ, SHWEDAGON, SVAYAMBHŪ/SVAYAMBHŪNĀTH, THIÊN MỤ TỰ, THŪPĀRĀMA.

**styāna**. (P. thina; T. rmug pa; C. hunchen; J. konjin; K. honch'im 惛沉). In Sanskrit, "torpor," often paired with "sloth" (MIDDHA). As a compound, styānamiddha constitute the third of the five "hindrances" (NĪVARAṆA) to the attainment of the first meditative absorption (DHYĀNA), along with sensual desire (KĀMACCHANDA), malice or ill-will (VYĀPĀDA), restlessness and worry (AUDDHATYA-KAUKṚTYA), and skeptical doubt (VICIKITSĀ). Because of the laziness generated by this mental concomitant, styānamiddha specifically hinders the meditative constituent (DHYĀNĀṄGA) of applied thought (VITARKA). This hindrance is countered by the spiritual faculty (INDRIYA) of effort (VĪRYA). Ways of countering sloth and torpor include memorizing the doctrine, developing the perception of light, or simply walking around in the open air.

**Subāhuparipṛcchātantra**. (T. Dpung bzangs kyis zhus pa'i rgyud; C. Supohu tongzi qingwen jing; J. Sobakodōji shōmongyō; K. Sop'aho tongja ch'ŏngmun kyŏng 蘇婆呼童子請問經). In Sanskrit, "Tantra Requested by Subāhu," an important Buddhist TANTRA, translated into Chinese by ŚUBHAKARASIṂHA in 726. In the text, the bodhisattva VAJRAPĀṆI explains a range of tantric practices at the request of the youth Subāhu. It is one of the earliest tantras to set forth elements that would come to be considered standard in tantric practice, especially of the wrathful variety, including the performance of rituals to obtain magical powers (SIDDHI), the importance of cemeteries and charnel grounds (ŚMAŚĀNA) as a site for tantric practice, the use of human corpses in the MAṆḌALA, the use of bones, and the practice of sexual rites with semi-divine women (yakṣiṇī/yakṣī).

**Subhadra**. (T. Rab bzang; P. Subhadda; C. Xubatuoluo; J. Shubatsudara; K. Subaltara 須跋陀羅). The last person converted by the Buddha before he passed into PARINIRVĀṆA. According to some accounts, he was a 120-year-old brāhmaṇa, according to others, a young ascetic. Hearing that the Buddha would be passing away that night at KUŚINAGARĪ, Subhadra went to see the Buddha and asked ĀNANDA for permission to speak with him. Ānanda refused the request three times, saying that the Buddha was weary. The Buddha overheard their conversation and told Subhadra to come forward, saying, "Do not keep out Subhadra. Subhadra may be allowed to see the Tathāgata. Whatever Subhadra will ask of me, he will ask from a desire for knowledge, and not to annoy me, and whatever I may say in answer to his questions, that he will quickly understand." Subhadra began to ask the Buddha about the doctrines of various other teachers, but the Buddha cut him short, explaining that only one who knows the noble eightfold path (ĀRYĀṢṬĀṄGAMĀRGA) is a true ŚRAMAṆA. Subhadra then asked to be ordained. The Buddha replied that adherents of other sects first had to undergo a probationary period of four months before ordination. When Subhadra announced his willingness to do so, the Buddha waived the requirement and instructed Ānanda to shave the hair and beard of Subhadra. He was then escorted back to the Buddha who ordained him, making him the last person that Buddha personally ordained. The Buddha then gave him a subject of meditation. Walking up and down in the grove, he quickly became an ARHAT and came and sat by the Buddha. According to some accounts, Subhadra felt that he was unworthy to witness the passage of the Buddha into parinirvāṇa and thus asked the Buddha for permission to die first. The Buddha gave his permission. ¶ Subhadra is also the name of a former barber who entered the order late in life. He always carried a certain animus against the Buddha, because, while Subhadra was still a layman, the Buddha refused to accept a meal that he had prepared for him. After the Buddha's death, Subhadra told monks who were weeping at his passing that they should instead rejoice: since the Buddha would no longer be telling them what they could and could not do, monks would now be free to do as they pleased. MAHĀKĀŚYAPA overheard this remark and was said to have been so alarmed by it that he convened what came to be known as the first Buddhist council (SAṂGĪTI; see COUNCIL, FIRST) to codify the monastic rules and the Buddha's discourses.

**Śubhakarasiṃha**. (C. Shanwuwei; J. Zenmui; K. Sŏnmuoe 善無畏) (637–735). Buddhist ĀCĀRYA and Chinese translator, who played a major role in the introduction into China and translation of seminal Buddhist texts belonging to what is now known as the esoteric tradition, or MIJIAO (see MIKKYŌ; TANTRA); also known as Śubhakara. Śubhakarasiṃha's place of origin is unclear. Some sources say he hailed from the Indian kingdom of Oḍra, and others say MAGADHA or the Central Asian kingdom of Udyāna. According to his biography in the SONG GAOSENG ZHUAN, Śubhakarasiṃha was born into a royal family of Oḍra. A fratricidal feud over the throne led Śubhakarasiṃha to renounce the throne and become a monk. He later visited the famed monastic university of NĀLANDĀ and became the disciple of a certain Dharmagupta. His mastery of morality (ŚĪLA), concentration (DHYĀNA), and wisdom (PRAJÑĀ) under Dharmagupta earned him the title of TREPIṬAKA, and he later also gained fame as a thaumaturge. With Dharmagupta's permission, Śubhakarasiṃha left for China. Traveling north on the Central Asian trade routes, in 716, Śubhakarasiṃha arrived in the western capital of the Tang dynasty, Chang'an. The emperor invited him to stay at the monastery of Xingfusi. In 717, Śubhakarasiṃha began translating some of the Sanskrit texts that he had brought with him to China. In 724, he accompanied the emperor to the eastern capital of Luoyang, where he continued his translation work. During his stay in Luoyang, Śubhakarasiṃha translated the MAHĀVAIROCANĀBHISAṂBODHISŪTRA, a central scripture of the East Asian esoteric traditions. He was assisted by his Chinese disciple YIXING, who also composed an important commentary on the sūtra. In 726, Śubhakarasiṃha also translated the important *SUSIDDHIKARASŪTRA. Five years after his death, Śubhakarasiṃha's body was buried on the grounds of the monastery of Guanghuasi in LONGMEN. According to his biography, Śubhakarasiṃha's body did not decay (see ŚARĪRA) and thus became an object of fervent worship.

**śubhakṛtsna**. (P. subhakiṇṇā; T. dge rgyas; C. bianjing tian; J. henjōten; K. pyŏnjŏng ch'ŏn 遍淨天). In Sanskrit, "pervasive purity," the highest of the three heavens of the third absorption (DHYĀNA) of the realm of subtle materiality (RŪPADHĀTU). The divinities of this heaven are so-called because the radiance emanating from their bodies is of a steady brightness and does not occur in flashes. As with all the heavens of the realm of subtle materiality, one is reborn as a divinity there through achieving during one's practice of meditation in the preceding lifetime the same level of absorption as the divinities of that heaven. When the universe is destroyed by flood, the waters are said to rise to the level of this heaven.

**Subhasuttanta**. (C. Yingwu jing; J. Ōmukyō; K. Aengmu kyŏng 鸚鵡經). In Pāli, "Discourse to Subha"; tenth sutta of the DĪGHANIKĀYA (a related Pāli recension is included as the ninety-ninth sūtra of the MAJJHIMANIKĀYA and a separate SARVĀSTIVĀDA recension as the 152nd sūtra in the Chinese translation of the MADHYAMĀGAMA); preached by Ānanda at Sāvatthi (S. ŚRĀVASTĪ) to the brāhmaṇa Subha Todeyyaputta shortly after the Buddha's demise. In content that is very similar to the SĀMAÑÑAPHALASUTTANTA (S. Śrāmaṇyaphalasūtra), Subha invites Ānanda to tell him what things the Buddha extolled, what he inspired others to follow, and what he established others in. Ānanda responds that there were three bodies, or categories, of things which the Buddha extolled, inspired others to follow, and established them in. These were the noble body of morality (P. ariyasīlakkhandha, S. āryaśīlaskandha), the noble body of concentration (P. ariyasamādhikkhandha, S. āryasamādhiskandha), and the noble body of wisdom (P. ariyapaññākkhandha, S. āryaprajñāskandha). Under the noble body of morality (ŚĪLA), Ānanda enumerates the following points: the appearance of the Buddha in the world, understanding his teachings and entering the Buddhist order, training in the restraint of action and speech, and observance of minor points of morality, all of which leads to an absence of fear and a confidence of heart. Under the noble body of concentration (SAMĀDHI), he enumerates guarding the senses, mindfulness, contentment with little, freedom from the five hindrances, joy and peace of mind, and the four meditative absorptions (P. JHĀNA, S. DHYĀNA). Under the noble body of wisdom (PRAJÑĀ), he enumerates insight into the conditioned nature and impermanence of body and mind, the power to conjure up mind-made bodies (MANOMAYAKĀYA), knowledge of the FOUR NOBLE TRUTHS, and destruction of the contaminants (P. āsava, S. ĀSRAVA).

**Subhūti**. (T. Rab 'byor; C. Xuputi; J. Shubodai; K. Subori 須菩提). Sanskrit and Pāli proper name of an eminent ARHAT who was foremost among the Buddha's disciples in dwelling at peace in remote places and in worthiness to receive gifts. He was the younger brother of ANĀTHAPIṆḌADA and took ordination on the day the JETAVANA grove was dedicated, when he heard the Buddha preach. He mastered the ubhatovibhaṅga, the two collections comprising the VINAYAPIṬAKA, after which he retired to the forest to practice meditation. He attained arhatship on the basis of maitrīdhyāna (P. mettājhāna), meditative absorption cultivated through contemplation of loving-kindness (MAITRĪ). On his alms-rounds, Subhūti would cultivate loving-kindness at the door of every house where he stopped, thus expanding the amount of merit accrued by his donor. Subhūti taught the dharma without distinction or limitation, for which reason the Buddha singled him out for praise. Subhūti was widely revered for his holiness and was sought out as a recipient of gifts. King BIMBISĀRA once promised to build a cave dwelling for him in RĀJAGṚHA but later forgot. Without a dwelling place, Subhūti sat in the open air to practice meditation. Over time, this caused a drought in the region, for the clouds would not rain lest this disturb the saint's meditations. When Bimbisāra became aware of this issue, he built a grass hut for him, and as soon as Subhūti sat inside it, the clouds poured down rain. During the time of Padmottara Buddha, Subhūti had been a famous hermit named Nanda with forty thousand disciples. Once when the Buddha was visiting his hermitage, he directed one of his monks proficient in loving-kindness and foremost in worthiness to receive gifts to preach to his host. Upon hearing the sermon, all forty thousand disciples of Nanda became arhats, while Nanda, enthralled by the charisma of the preaching monk, resolved one day to earn the same distinction. Subhūti also plays a prominent role in a number of MAHĀYĀNA sūtras. The most famous of these roles is as the Buddha's chief interlocutor in PRAJÑĀPĀRAMITĀ sūtras like the VAJRACCHEDIKĀPRAJÑĀPĀRAMITĀSŪTRA. In the SADDHARMAPUṆḌARĪKASŪTRA, Subhūti is one the four ŚRĀVAKAS who understands the parable of the burning house; later his buddhahood is prophesied by the Buddha. In the VIMALAKĪRTINIRDEŚA, Subhūti is one of the arhats who is reluctant to visit Vimalakīrti. Among the Buddha's ten major disciples, he is said to have been foremost in the knowledge of insubstantiality.

**Subinda**. [alt. Suvinda] (C. Supintuo; J. Sobinda; K. Sobint'a 蘇頻陀). The Sanskrit name of the fourth of the sixteen ARHAT elders (ṢOḌAŚASTHAVIRA), according to the roster of arhats now recognized in the East Asian tradition; he is said to reside in UTTARAKURU with seven hundred disciples. Subinda is said to have been the last personal disciple of the Buddha and for this reason is shown holding a small STŪPA (symbolizing the Buddha), which he carried with him wherever he went; he is thus known in Chinese as the "Pagoda-Holding Arhat." Subinda has various portrayals in Chinese paintings. In the Mogao caves of DUNHUANG, he is shown sitting in full-lotus posture on a rock, with his right arm bent upwards and his left hand holding a water bottle in front of his chest. In CHANYUE GUANXIU's standard Chinese depiction, Subinda sits in meditation on a rock, with his robe worn across both his shoulders, his right fist holding fast to the front of his chest, and his left hand placed on his knee. He is not included in the Tibetan list of the sixteen.

**subitism**. See DUNWU; DUNWU JIANXIU.

**Sucandra**. (T. Zla ba bzang po). The king of ŚAMBHALA who requested the Buddha to deliver the KĀLACAKRATANTRA. According to legend, the king traveled to India from śambhala and asked that the Buddha set forth a teaching that would allow him to practice the dharma without renouncing the world. In response, the Buddha, while continuing to wear the robes of a monk on Vulture Peak (GṚDHRAKŪṬA) in RĀJAGṚHA, set forth the *Kālacakratantra* at Dhānyakaṭaka in southern India in the guise of the buddha Kālacakra. The king returned to śambhala, where he transcribed this tantra in twelve thousand verses. This text is referred to as the root tantra (mūlatantra) and is no longer extant. Sucandra also wrote a commentary in sixty thousand verses, now also lost. The king finally built a three-dimensional Kālacakra MAṆḌALA at the center of the kingdom, which was transformed into an ideal realm for Buddhist practice. The king, considered an incarnation of VAJRAPĀṆI, died two years after receiving the *Kālacakratantra* from the Buddha.

**suchness**. See TATHATĀ.

**Sudāna Jātaka**. (C. Xudana bensheng; J. Shudainu honjō; K. Sudaena ponsaeng 須大拏本生). An alternate name for the bodhisattva Viśvaṃtara and the popular *Viśvantara Jātaka* (P. VESSANTARA-JĀTAKA).

**sudarśana**. (P. sudassī; T. shin tu mthong ba; C. shanjian tian; J. zenkenten; K. sŏn'gyŏn ch'ŏn 善見天). In Sanskrit, "perfect vision," the name of the second highest of the eight heavens of the fourth meditative absorption (DHYĀNA) of the realm of subtle materiality (RŪPADHĀTU), and one of the five heavens that constitute the ŚUDDHĀVĀSA, the "pure abodes" where those who have attained the rank of ANĀGĀMIN become ARHATs. As with all the heavens of the realm of subtle materiality, one is reborn as a divinity there through achieving the same level of concentration (dhyāna) as the gods of that heaven during one's practice of meditation in a previous lifetime.

**Sudatta**. (T. Legs byin; C. Xuda; J. Shudatsu; K. Sudal 須達). The personal name of the Buddha's patron ANĀTHAPIṆḌADA. See ANĀTHAPIṆḌADA.

**sudden enlightenment**. See DUNWU; DUNWU JIANXIU.

**sudden-gradual issue**. See BSAM YAS DEBATE; DUNJIAO; DUNWU; DUNWU JIAOXIU; GUIFENG ZONGMI; KAMALAŚĪLA; POJO CHINUL.

**sudden teachings**. See DUNJIAO.

**śuddhāvāsa**. (P. suddhāvāsa; T. gnas gtsang; C. wujingju tian; J. gojōgoten; K. ojŏnggŏ ch'ŏn 五淨居天). In Sanskrit, "pure abodes," the term used to refer collectively to the five highest of the eight heavens that constitute the fourth meditative absorption (DHYĀNA) of the subtle-materiality realm (RŪPADHĀTU); the divinities residing there are called the śuddhāvāsakāyika gods. In some traditions, the śuddhāvāsa are said to be the abode of nonreturners (ANĀGĀMIN), the third of the four types of advanced adepts (ĀRYAPUDGALA), who are in their final rebirth before achieving arhatship (see ARHAT) and thus need never again to be reborn in, or return to, the sensuous realm (KĀMADHĀTU). Since nonreturners have removed the first five fetters (SAMYOJANA) associated with the sensuous realm, and weakened the latter five, they are "nonreturners" to the sensuous realm and are instead reborn into the pure abodes, whence they will complete their practice and attain enlightenment as an arhat. The pure abodes therefore serve as a kind of way station for advanced beings (ĀRYA) in their last lives before final liberation. In the ABHIDHARMAKOŚABHĀṢYA, the explanation of nonreturners differs; before they reach NIRVĀṆA they never take rebirth in the sensuous realm, but they may pass through each of the heavens before entering nirvāṇa, or skip over one or more heavens and enter into nirvāṇa from any heaven, depending on their aptitude. In certain Mahāyāna interpretations, such as in the ABHISAMAYĀLAṂKĀRA, the pure abodes are adjacent to the fourth dhyāna, like suburbs of that meditative absorption, and the AKANIṢṬHA heaven of the pure abodes is considered to be the abode of the enjoyment body (SAṂBHOGAKĀYA) of a buddha. Some say the pure abodes remain empty even for several eons (KALPA) when there are no buddhas. When a bodhisattva is in his last life before attaining buddhahood, it is said that the divinities of the pure abodes provide the four portents (CATURNIMITTA, viz., an old man, a sick man, and corpse, and a mendicant) that cause the bodhisattva to renounce the life of the householder and go forth to the homeless life. The five heavens that constitute the pure abodes are AVṚHA, ATAPA, SUDṚŚA, SUDARŚANA, and AKANIṢṬHA.

**śuddhāvāsakāyika**. (S; T. gnas gtsang ma'i ris; C. jingju tian; J. jōgoten; K. chŏnggŏ ch'ŏn 淨居天). Beings belonging to the ŚUDDHĀVĀSA, or "pure abodes," a region of the fourth dhyāna of the subtle-materiality realm (RŪPADHĀTU) where only noble beings (ĀRYA) are reborn.

**Śuddhipanthaka**. (S; C. Zhoulipante; J. Shurihandoku; K. Churibant'ŭk 周利槃特). See CŪḌAPANTHAKA.

**Śuddhodana**. (P. Suddhodana; T. Zas gtsang; C. Jingfan wang; J. Jōbon ō; K. Chŏngban wang 淨飯王). In Sanskrit, lit. "Pure Rice"; the royal father of GAUTAMA Buddha. Śuddhodana was the son of Siṃhahanu (P. Sīhahanu), a king of the ŚĀKYA clan, and ruled in KAPILAVASTU (P. Kapilavatthu) in the foothills of the Himālayas, in present-day Nepal. Śuddhodana's wife was MAHĀMĀYĀ, who died seven days after giving birth to prince Gautama. According to some accounts of the Buddha's life, Śuddhodana was also already married to, or subsequently married, MAHĀPRAJĀPATĪ, Māyā's sister and thus Gautama's aunt, who raised the infant and eventually became the first woman to be ordained as a Buddhist nun (BHIKṢUṆĪ). At the time of the bodhisattva's birth, his father asked eight priests to examine the child and predict his future. There are several versions of this event, but in the Pāli NIDĀNAKATHĀ, seven predict that he will become either a CAKRAVARTIN or a buddha, while one, Koṇḍañña (S. KAUṆḌINYA; see ĀJÑĀTAKAUṆḌINYA), predicts that it is certain that he will become a buddha, and will do so after seeing four portents (CATURNIMITTA)—viz., of a sick man, an old man, a corpse, and a religious mendicant. Koṇḍañña and the sons of four of the eight court priests would eventually become the group of five ascetics (S. PAÑCAVARGIKA, P. pañcavaggiyā) who would be the Buddha's first disciples. In order to prevent his son's exposure to the sufferings of life, the king built three palaces filled only with youth and beauty. His father paid homage to his young son on two occasions, first when the ascetic Asita bowed to the infant and second, when, during a ploughing festival, he saw his young son meditating under a tree; the sun had stopped its course across the sky in order that the child would remain in shadow of a jambu tree. Despite his attempts to distract his son with all manner of sensual pleasures in his three palaces, the king's efforts were ultimately in vain and the prince eventually determined to leave behind the household life (PRAVRAJITA) after witnessing each of the portents. His father sought unsuccessfully to dissuade him, saying that it was not the right time for the prince, now with a wife and child, to renounce the world. Years later, when Gautama returned to Kapilavastu as an enlightened buddha, Śuddhodana became a devoted follower of his son. However, he objected to the Buddha's ordination of his young son RĀHULA, causing the Buddha to promulgate a rule that in the future, parents must give permission before their son is ordained. The king became a stream-enterer (SROTAĀPANNA) himself, his success at meditation initially hindered by his excessive joy that his son was the Buddha. Shortly before his death, the king became an ARHAT.

**Sūden**. (J) (崇傳) (1569–1633). See ISHIN SŪDEN.

**Sudhana**. (T. Nor bzang; C. Shancai; J. Zenzai; K. Sŏnjae 善財). A youth who is the major protagonist of the GAṆḌAVYŪHA, the final section of the AVATAṂSAKASŪTRA. The story of Sudhana's search is related in the *Avataṃsakasūtra*'s massive final chapter, the "Entrance into the Dharmadhātu" (C. Ru fajie pin), which also circulated independently as the GAṆḌAVYŪHA. On the instructions of the BODHISATTVA MAÑJUŚRĪ, Sudhana sets out to the south in search of a spiritual mentor (KALYĀṆAMITRA), ultimately encountering fifty-two beings (sometimes counted as fifty-three, because Mañjuśrī is repeated) including the future buddha MAITREYA, as well as the bodhisattvas AVALOKITEŚVARA and Mañjuśrī; twenty of his teachers are female, including the Buddha's mother MAHĀMĀYĀ. His final teacher is the bodhisattva SAMANTABHADRA, who sets forth in the famous BHADRACARĪPRAṆIDHĀNA the ten vows he took to realize and access the DHARMADHĀTU, which thereby enable him to benefit sentient beings. After this encounter, Sudhana attains enlightenment and roams freely himself in the dharmadhātu. Sudhana's pilgrimage has been the inspiration for much East Asian Buddhist art and his statue often appears at the side of Buddhist altars as a boy bowing to the Buddha.

**Sudinna**. (T. Bzang byin; C. Xutina; J. Shudaina; K. Sujena 須提那). The Buddhist Hybrid Sanskrit and Pāli name of a disciple of the Buddha whose actions prompted the Buddha to formulate the first rule of the monastic code, the "defeat" offense (S. PĀRĀJIKA) forbidding sexual intercourse (abrahmacarya); his name is a Middle Indic form of the classical Sanskrit Sudatta. The monastic code (VINAYA; PRĀTIMOKṢA) was not formulated as a complete system. Rather, it is said that the Buddha formulated each rule in response to a specific misdeed by a monk, with the Buddha subsequently declaring a rule prohibiting that particular misdeed. Sudinna had been ordained with the grudging consent of his parents; he was their only child, was already married, and had not had a child at the time of his ordination. During a period of famine, he returned to his home region in order to beg for alms. When he was offered food at his parents' house, they, together with his wife, urged him to return to lay life. He refused, addressing his wife as "sister," which caused her to faint. His mother later visited him, imploring him to impregnate his wife so that his family would at least have an heir, thus preventing their property from being confiscated upon the death of his parents. Sudinna agreed and had intercourse with his wife three times, supposedly not out of lust but out of concern for the financial future of his family. He soon felt remorse for his deed. Upon learning of the reason for his remorse, his fellow monks informed the Buddha, who told him it would have been better for him to have inserted his penis into the mouth of a poisonous snake than to have placed it in a woman's vagina. The Buddha then established a rule of "defeat" (PĀRĀJIKA) forbidding monks from engaging in sexual intercourse, the first rule that the Buddha had ever had to promulgate in some twenty years of teaching. It was by no means the last: the monks' and nuns' codes of conduct (prātimokṣa) eventually included hundreds of specific rules of conduct.

**Sudŏksa**. (修德寺). In Korean, "Cultivating Merit Monastery"; the seventh district monastery (PONSA) of the contemporary CHOGYE CHONG of Korean Buddhism, located on the slopes of Tŏksung (Virtue Exalted) mountain in South Ch'ungch'ŏng province. According to Sudŏksa's monastic records, the monastery was first constructed at the end of the Paekche dynasty by Sungje (d.u.). During the reign of the Paekche king Mu (r. 600–641) the monk Hyehyŏn (d.u.) is said to have lectured there on the SADDHARMAPUṆḌARĪKASŪTRA ("Lotus Sūtra"). Alternate records state, however, that the monastery was founded by Chimyŏng (d.u.) during the reign of the Paekche king Pŏp (r. 599–600). The monastery was subsequently repaired by the renowned Koryŏ-dynasty Sŏn monk NAONG HYEGŪN (1320–1376), and since that time Sudŏksa has been one of the major centers of SŎN (C. CHAN) practice in Korea. Sudŏksa is best known for its TAEUNG CHŎN, the main shrine hall. The taeung chŏn was rebuilt in 1308 and is presumed to be the oldest wooden building in Korea, having been spared the conflagrations that struck many Korean monasteries during the Japanese Hideyoshi invasions (1592–1598). It was constructed in the Chusimp'o style, so that its support pillars are wider in the middle than they are at the bottom or top. The Tap'o-style bracketing, imported from Fujian during the Southern Song dynasty, is similar to other Koryŏ-era monasteries, such as Pongjŏngsa and PUSŎKSA. Inside the hall are images of three buddhas, ŚĀKYAMUNI, AMITĀBHA and BHAIṢAJYAGURU, and two bodhisattvas, MAÑJUŚRĪ and SAMANTABHADRA. Paintings depict KṢITIGARBHA, the ten kings of hell (see SHIWANG; YAMA), and some indigenous Korean divinities. Many of the oldest original wall paintings were damaged during the Korean War and have now been removed to the safety of the monastery's museum. The courtyard holds two STŪPAs, a three-story stone pagoda probably from the Koryŏ dynasty, and an older seven-story granite pagoda from the late Paekche dynasty, with typical upward curving corners. There is a thirty-three foot high statue of Maitreya a short walk up the mountain; the statue is unusual in that it is wearing Korean clothes, including a double cylindrical hat. It was erected by the Sŏn master MAN'GONG WŎLMYŎN (1872–1946), one of the renowned Sŏn teachers of the modern era who taught at Sudŏksa; other famous masters associated with the monastery include KYŎNGHŎ SŎNGU (1849–1912), the nun KIM IRYŎP (1869–1971), and Hyeam Hyŏnmun (1884–1985). Sudŏksa recently opened a museum near its entrance to hold the large number of important historical artistic and written works the monastery owns, such as the exquisite wall paintings that formerly were located in the taeung chŏn. In 1996, Sudŏksa was elevated to the status of an ecumenical monastery (CH'ONGNIM), and is one of the five such centers in the contemporary Chogye order, which are all expected to provide training in the full range of practices that exemplify the major strands of the Korean Buddhist tradition; the monastery is thus also known as the Tŏksung Ch'ongnim.

**sudṛśa**. (P. sudassā; T. gya nom snang ba; C. shanxian tian; J. zengenten; K. sŏnhyŏn ch'ŏn 善現天). In Sanskrit, "perfect form," or "skillful manifestation"; the name of the third highest of the eight heavens of the fourth meditative absorption (DHYĀNA) of the realm of subtle materiality (RŪPADHĀTU), and one of the five heavens that constitute the ŚUDDHĀVĀSA, the "pure abodes" where those who have attained the rank of ANĀGĀMIN become ARHATs. As with all the heavens of the realm of subtle materiality, one is reborn as a divinity there through achieving the same level of concentration (dhyāna) as the gods of that heaven during one's practice of meditation in a previous lifetime.

**sudurjayā**. (T. sbyang dka' ba; C. nansheng di; J. nanshōji; K. nansŭng chi 難勝地). In Sanskrit, "unconquerable," the name of the fifth of the ten bodhisattva stages (BHŪMI). A list of ten stages (DAŚABHŪMI) is most commonly enumerated, deriving from the DAŚABHŪMIKASŪTRA ("Sūtra on the Ten Bhūmis"), a sūtra that is later subsumed into the massive scriptural compilation, the AVATAṂSAKASŪTRA. The first bhūmi coincides with the attainment of the path of vision (DARŚANAMĀRGA) and the remaining nine to the path of cultivation (BHĀVANĀMĀRGA). This bhūmi is called "unconquerable" because, from this point on the path, the bodhisattva cannot be overcome by demons. On this bhūmi, the bodhisattva practices the perfection of meditative absorption (DHYĀNAPĀRAMITĀ), the fifth of the ten perfections (PĀRAMITĀ), achieving myriad forms of SAMĀDHI. Here, the bodhisattva also gains understanding of the subtle nature of the FOUR NOBLE TRUTHS. The bodhisattva remains on his stage as long as his distress deriving from his analysis of SAṂSĀRA prevents him entering into meditative equipoise (SAMĀHITA) on the signless (ĀNIMITTA).

**suffering**. See DUḤKHA.

**sugata**. (T. bde bar gshegs pa; C. shanshi; J. zenzei; K. sŏnsŏ 善逝). In Sanskrit and Pāli, lit., "well gone," one in a standard list of epithets of the Buddha. Su (cognate with Greek eu) is a prefix meaning good and gata is the past passive particle of "to go." Among other meanings, BUDDHAGHOSA says the Buddha is sugata because both the way he took (gata) is good (su) and where he has gone (gata) is good (su). The MAHĀYĀNA author HARIBHADRA also says the Buddha is sugata because he is one from whom all faults are totally (suṣṭhu) gone (gata), or into whom all good qualities have gone (gata) with none remaining (suparipūrṇa). It is customary to relate three denotations of sugata with three stages through which a buddha must pass in order to reach the goal of enlightenment: he has gone well beyond rebirth in SAṂSĀRA, he has gone well into NIRVĀṆA, and he has gone well into the state of perfect buddhahood (SAMYAKSAṂBUDDHA).

**sugatagarbha**. (T. bde bar gshegs pa'i snying po). In Sanskrit, "essence of the SUGATA," a synonym for TATHĀGATAGARBHA.

**sugati**. (T. bde 'gro; C. shanqu; J. zenshu; K. sŏnch'wi 善趣). In Sanskrit and Pāli, lit. "good destiny," a term used to refer to the realms of rebirth as a human or a divinity of either the sensuous realm (KĀMADHĀTU), the realm of subtle materiality (RŪPADHĀTU), or the immaterial realm (ĀRŪPYADHĀTU). This term contrasts with DURGATI, or "baleful destiny," which refers to the realms of rebirth as an animal, ghost, or hell denizen. One is reborn as a human or divinity as a result of virtuous practice in the past.

**Sugi**. (守其) (c. mid-thirteenth century). Korean monk during the Koryŏ dynasty who served as editor-in-chief of the second carving of the Korean Buddhist canon (KORYŎ TAEJANGGYŎNG). To supervise this massive editorial project, Sugi established a main editorial headquarters at Kanghwa Island, off the west-central coast of Korea, and a branch at Namhae in the far south of the Korean peninsula. Sugi gathered an army of scholars, first to collate the various editions of the scriptures and to establish the correct reading, and then to proofread meticulously the finished xylographs to ferret out any misprints. In editing this new canon, Sugi and his editorial team consulted principally three earlier canons: (1) the Chinese canon, carved during the Song-dynasty's Kaibao reign era between 971 and 983, which he called variously the Old Song edition (Ku-Song pon), Song edition (Song pon), etc.; (2) the Khitan Liao canon, printed c. 1031–1055, which he generally referred to as the Khitan edition (Tan pon); and (3) the first Koryŏ canon of 1011, which he usually called the State edition (Kuk pon). Foremost among these editions was the Liao canon of the Khitans, a complete copy of which Koryŏ had received in 1064. The xylographs of 1,514 texts in 6,815 rolls were carved between 1236 and 1251 in a total of 81,258 wood blocks—the oldest of the few complete xylographic canons still extant in East Asia. This second Koryŏ canon continues to be stored today in paired wooden archives at HAEINSA in Kyŏngsang province, as they have been since 1398. Sugi documented in remarkable detail the process he and his editorial team followed in compiling this new canon in his thirty-roll KORYŎGUK SINJO TAEJANG KYOJŎNG PYŎLLOK ("Supplementary Record of Collation Notes to the New Carving of the Great Canon of the Koryŏ Kingdom"), which was finished around 1247. In these notes, Sugi collated seventy-six passages from sixty-five different texts. In his textual analysis of a specific scripture, Sugi generally treated major issues of structure, translator attribution, textual lineage, and the like; he did not discuss minor variations in readings of a few Sinographs. In a typical entry for a specific text, Sugi lists the case character in the second Koryŏ canon where the work appears; the title of the text and the roll (K. kwŏn; C. quan) in which the disputed point appears; followed by the passage itself, generally indicated by kwŏn, scroll (p'ok) and line (haeng) numbers. The most common types of textual problems noted by Sugi in earlier canons were transpositions of passages (K. chŏnhu toch'ak) and dittographies (K. chungsa; chungch'ŏm). After evaluating the discrepancies in the different canonical editions, Sugi then indicated which reading he preferred and this reading was then entered into the second Koryŏ carving. Sugi also treated issues of textual authenticity in the course of editing his canon, especially in attempting to adjudicate the authenticity of some of the variant Chinese translations of Indic Buddhist scriptures. The information Sugi provides in his "Collation Notes" offers important information on how East Asian Buddhist scholars in the premodern era went about the task of collating and editing multiple recensions of thousands of scriptures into a definitive canonical collection.

Sugi's notes also help to document the textual genealogies of the various East Asian canons and provide definitive proof that, in style and format, the second Koryŏ canon imitated both the Chinese Kaibao and first Koryŏ canons, but its readings followed more closely those found in the Khitan Liao canon. Sugi's annotations are thus an extremely valuable source for detailing medieval Chinese xylographic lineages. In making editorial decisions, Sugi rejects such discredited techniques as following the reading of the majority of manuscripts—as when he rejects the readings of both the Kaibao and first Koryŏ canons—or following uncritically the "best" manuscript, as in the cases where he rejects the reading of the Khitan edition. Sugi's reputation for scholarly accuracy was such that Japanese scholars adopted the second Koryŏ canon as the textus receptus for the modern Taishō printed edition of the canon, the TAISHŌ SHINSHŪ DAIZŌKYŌ, compiled in Japan between 1922 and 1934.

**Suhṛllekha**. (T. Bshes pa'i spring yig; C. Longshu pusa quanjie wang song; J. Ryūju bosatsu kankaiōju; K. Yongsu posal kwŏn'gye wang song 龍樹菩薩勸誡王頌). In Sanskrit, "Friendly Letter," a famous work by the Madhyamaka exegete NĀGĀRJUNA. Like the RATNĀVALĪ, the work takes the form of advice to a king. In this case, scholars speculate that the king may be Gautamīputra Śatakarṇī of the Śātavāhana dynasty. The work is not concerned with philosophical doctrine but instead consists of advice to a Buddhist layperson on how to live an ethical life and accumulate merit (PUṆYA). It is clearly a MAHĀYĀNA work, mentioning AVALOKITEŚVARA and AMITĀBHA, but also contains numerous allusions to the Sanskrit ĀGAMAS.

**suishen sheli**. (J. saishinshari; K. swaesin sari 碎身舍利). In Chinese, "partial-body relics," crystalline substances that are the condensation of the remains of a holy person after death and cremation. See ŚARĪRA.

**Sujātā**. (T. Legs skyes ma; C. Xusheduo; J. Shujata; K. Susada 須闍多). The Sanskrit and Pāli proper name of a female lay disciple declared by the Buddha to be foremost among laywomen who had taken refuge in the three jewels (RATNATRAYA). According to the Pāli account, Sujātā was the daughter of a landowner named Senānī who lived in a village near Uruvelā. She had petitioned the spirit (YAKṢA) of a banyan tree for a son and when she gave birth to a boy she resolved to make an offering of rice milk to the spirit in gratitude. On the day of her offering, she sent her servant Puṇṇā to prepare a place beneath the tree. There, the servant encountered the bodhisattva SIDDHĀRTHA sitting in meditation, soon after he had decided to give up the practice of strict asceticism. Seeing the bodhisattva's emaciated body, the servant mistook him for the tree spirit and informed Sujātā of his physical presence. Sujātā prepared rice milk and offered it to the bodhisattva in a golden bowl. This offering was praised by the gods as important and praiseworthy, for it enabled the bodhisattva to regain his strength so that he could make the final push to achieve enlightenment as a perfect buddha (SAMYAKSAṂBUDDHA). One of Sujātā's sons was YAŚAS (P. Yasa), who became the Buddha's sixth convert after the enlightenment. Yaśas attained arhatship and was ordained, after which he received alms at his parents' house in the company of the Buddha. At that time, having listened to the Buddha's sermon, Sujātā and Yaśas' former wife became stream-enterers (SROTAĀPANNA) and took refuge in the three jewels, thus becoming the first female disciples to do so.

**sūkaramaddava**. (S. sūkaramārdava; C. zhantanshu'er; J. sendanjuni; K. chŏndansui 栴檀樹耳). In Pāli, lit., "soft pig," the last meal of the Buddha before his passage into PARINIRVĀṆA. According to the MAHĀPARINIBBĀNASUTTA, the Buddha and his disciples were invited to a meal by CUNDA, the son of a goldsmith. He served them sweet rice, cakes, and sūkaramaddava. The Buddha told Cunda to serve the sūkaramaddava only to him and to bury the rest in the ground because no one other than the Buddha would be able to digest it. The Buddha praised Cunda for the meal but shortly thereafter suffered an attack of dysentery. He proceeded to KUŚINAGARĪ, where he instructed ĀNANDA to visit Cunda and tell him that he should not feel remorse; he had in fact gained great merit by serving the Buddha his last meal. There has been much debate as to the meaning of sūkaramaddava. It is unclear whether this means something soft that is consumed by pigs, such as a type of mushroom or truffle, or perhaps bamboo shoots that had been trampled by pigs. The compound could also be the name of some kind of pork dish. The Indian and Sinhalese commentators prefer, although not unanimously, the latter interpretation. The Chinese rendering for the term means "sandalwood tree fungus," implying perhaps a kind of truffle, and the passage in the DĪRGHĀGAMA recension of the sūtra suggests that the dish was a delicate broth boiled with this ingredient. Some modern interpreters, trying to avoid the suggestion that the Buddha consumed pork, have insisted, following the Chinese, that it was a mushroom dish.

**sukha**. (T. bde ba; C. le; J. raku; K. nak 樂). In Sanskrit and Pāli, "bliss," "ease," or "joy"; the fourth of the five constituents of meditative absorption (DHYĀNĀṄGA). A sustained sense of sukha is obstructed by restlessness and worry (AUDDHATYA-KAUKṚTYA), the fourth of the five hindrances (NĪVARAṆA) to DHYĀNA. Sukha is the maturation of the physical and mental tranquillity (PRAŚRABDHI) that is associated with the coarser experience of physical "rapture" (PRĪTI). Sukha always appears in conjunction with prīti, but not necessarily the converse; whereas sukha is part of the perception aggregate (SAṂJÑĀ), prīti is instead grouped with the conditioning factors aggregate (SAṂSKĀRA). Sukha leaves one "feeling well" and catalyzes the development of expansive mental states. Sukha is present in the first, second, and third of the meditative absorptions (dhyāna) associated with the realm of subtle materiality (RŪPĀVACARADHYĀNA), but fades into equanimity (UPEKṢĀ) in the even subtler fourth dhyāna, wherein the meditator experiences neither pleasure nor pain and is left only with one-pointedness of mind (CITTAIKĀGRATĀ). The term sukha is also important in Buddhist TANTRA, especially ANUTTARAYOGATANTRA, where the movement of winds (PRĀṆA) and drops (BINDU) up and down the central channel generate various forms of bliss; the bliss created by the upward movement of the winds and drops are particularly powerful. In order to achieve buddhahood, the bliss consciousness is used to understand emptiness (ŚŪNYATĀ).

**sukhāvatī**. (T. bde ba can; C. jile jingtu; J. gokurakujōdo; K. kŭngnak chŏngt'o 極樂淨土). In Sanskrit, "blissful" or "full of happiness" (the Chinese translates the name as "ultimate bliss"); the name of the buddha-field (BUDDHAKṢETRA) or PURE LAND of the buddha AMITĀBHA as described in what are referred to in East Asia as the three pure land sūtras (JINGTU SANBUJING): the larger and smaller SUKHĀVATĪVYŪHASŪTRAs (see AMITĀBHASŪTRA) and GUAN WULIANGSHOU JING (*Amitāyurdhyānasūtra*). Although many buddha-fields are enumerated and described in the Mahāyāna sūtras, sukhāvatī is the most famous and is often referred to as "the western pure land" in East Asia. In India, rebirth in sukhāvatī appears to have been something of a generalized soteriological goal, disconnected from devotion to the buddha Amitābha; references to sukhāvatī appear in a number of important Mahāyāna sūtras, including the SAMĀDHIRĀJASŪTRA, which likely dates to the second century CE. The most detailed description of sukhāvatī appears in the larger *Sukhāvatīvyūhasūtra*, discussed in the next entry. See also PURE LAND and ANLE GUO.

**Sukhāvatīvyūhasūtra**. (T. Bde ba can gyi bkod pa'i mdo; C. Wuliangshou jing; J. Muryōjukyō; K. Muryangsu kyŏng 無量壽經). Literally, the "Sūtra Displaying [the Land of] Bliss," the title of the two most important Mahāyāna sūtras of the "PURE LAND" tradition. The two sūtras differ in length, and thus are often referred to in English as the "larger" and "smaller" (or "longer" and "shorter") *Sukhāvatīvyūhasūtra*s; the shorter one is commonly called the AMITĀBHASŪTRA. Both sūtras are believed to date from the third century CE. The longer and shorter sūtras, together with the GUAN WULIANGSHOU JING (*Amitāyurdhyānasūtra*), constitute the three main texts associated with the pure land tradition of East Asia (see JINGTU SANBUJING). There are multiple Sanskrit, Chinese, and Tibetan versions of both the longer and shorter sūtras, with significant differences among them. ¶ The longer *Sukhāvatīvyūhasūtra* begins with ĀNANDA noticing that the Buddha is looking especially serene one day, and so asks him the reason. The Buddha responds that he was thinking back many millions of eons in the past to the time of the buddha LOKEŚVARARĀJA. The Buddha then tells a story in the form of a flashback. In the audience of this buddha was a monk named DHARMĀKARA, who approached Lokeśvararāja and proclaimed his aspiration to become a buddha. Dharmākara then requested the Buddha to describe all of the qualities of the buddha-fields (BUDDHAKṢETRA). Lokeśvararāja provided a discourse that lasted one million years, describing each of the qualities of the lands of trillions of buddhas. Dharmākara then retired to meditate for five eons, seeking to concentrate all of the marvelous qualities of the millions of buddha-fields that had been described to him into a single pure buddha-field. When he completed his meditation, he returned to describe this imagined land to Lokeśvararāja, promising to create a place of birth for fortunate beings and vowing that he would follow the bodhisattva path and become the buddha of this new buddha-field. He described the land he would create in a series of vows, stating that if this or that marvel was not present in his pure land, may he not become a buddha: e.g., "If in my pure land there are animals, ghosts, or hell denizens, may I not become a buddha." He made forty-eight such vows. These included the vow that all the beings in his pure land will be the color of gold; that beings in his pure land will have no conception of private property; that no bodhisattva will have to wash, dry, or sew his own robes; that bodhisattvas in his pure land will be able to hear the dharma in whatever form they wish to hear it and whenever they wish to hear it; that any woman who hears his name, creates the aspiration to enlightenment (BODHICITTA), and feels disgust at the female form, will not be reborn as a woman again. Two of these vows would become the focus of particular attention. In the eighteenth vow (seventeenth in the East Asian versions), Dharmākara vows that when he has become a buddha, he will appear at the moment of death to anyone who creates the aspiration to enlightenment, hears his name, and remembers him with faith. In the nineteenth vow (eighteenth in the East Asian versions), he promises that anyone who hears his name, wishes to be reborn in his pure land, and dedicates their merit to that end, will be reborn there, even if they make such a resolution as few as ten times during the course of their life. Only those who have committed one of the five inexpiable transgressions bringing immediate retribution (ĀNANTARYAKARMAN, viz., patricide, matricide, killing an ARHAT, wounding a buddha, or causing schism in the SAṂGHA) are excluded. The scene then returns to the present. Ānanda asks the Buddha whether Dharmākara was successful, whether he did in fact traverse the long path of the bodhisattva to become a buddha. The Buddha replies that he did indeed succeed and that he became the buddha Amitābha (Infinite Light). The pure land that he created is called sukhāvatī. Because Dharmākara became a buddha, all of the things that he promised to create in his pure land have come true, and the Buddha proceeds to describe sukhāvatī in great detail. It is carpeted with lotuses made of seven precious substances, some of which reach ten leagues (YOJANA) in diameter. Each lotus emits millions of rays of light and from each ray of light there emerge millions of buddhas who travel to world systems in all directions to teach the dharma. The pure land is level, like the palm of one's hand, without mountains or oceans. It has great rivers, the waters of which rise as high or sink as low as one pleases, from the shoulders to the ankles, and vary in temperature as one pleases. The sound of the river takes the form of whatever auspicious words one wishes to hear, such as "buddha," "emptiness," "cessation," and "great compassion." The words "hindrance," "misfortune," and "pain" are never heard, nor are the words "day" and "night" used, except as metaphors. The beings in the pure land do not need to consume food. When they are hungry, they simply visualize whatever food they wish and their hunger is satisfied without needing to eat. They dwell in bejeweled palaces of their own design. Some of the inhabitants sit cross-legged on lotus blossoms while others are enclosed within the calyx of a lotus. The latter do not feel imprisoned, because the calyx of the lotus is quite large, containing within it a palace similar to that inhabited by the gods. Those who dedicate their merit toward rebirth in the pure land yet who harbor doubts are reborn inside lotuses where they must remain for five hundred years, enjoying visions of the pure land but deprived of the opportunity to hear the dharma. Those who are free from doubt are reborn immediately on open lotuses, with unlimited access to the dharma. Such rebirth would become a common goal of Buddhist practice, for monks and laity alike, in India, Tibet, and throughout East Asia. ¶ The "shorter" *Sukhāvatīvyūhasūtra* was translated into Chinese by such famous figures as KUMĀRAJĪVA and XUANZANG. It is devoted largely to describing this buddha's land and its many wonders, including the fact that even the names for the realms of animals and the realms of hell-denizens are not known; all of the beings born there will achieve enlightenment in their next lifetime. In order to be reborn there, one should dedicate one's merit to that goal and bear in mind the name of the buddha here known as AMITĀYUS (Infinite Life). Those who are successful in doing so will see Amitāyus and a host of bodhisattvas before them at the moment of death, ready to escort them to sukhāvatī, the land of bliss. In order to demonstrate the efficacy of this practice, the Buddha goes on to list the names of many other buddhas abiding in the four cardinal directions, the nadir, and the zenith, who also praise the buddha-field of Amitāyus. Furthermore, those who hear the names of the buddhas that he has just recited will be embraced by those buddhas. Perhaps to indicate how his own buddha-field (that is, our world) differs from that of Amitāyus, Śākyamuni Buddha concludes by conceding that it has been difficult to teach the dharma in a world as degenerate as ours.

**Sukhothai**. The first Thai polity in mainland Southeast Asia. Located in the central Menam valley, it began as a frontier outpost of the Khmer empire. In 1278 two local princes raised a successful rebellion to create a new kingdom with the city of Sukhothai as its capital. Under King Ramkhamhaeng (r. 1279–1298), Sukhothai brought several neighboring states under its sway and by the early 1300s enjoyed suzerainty over entire the Menam river basin, and westward across the maritime provinces of Lower Burma. Ramkhamhaeng established diplomatic and commercial relations with China and its envoys twice visited the Chinese capital on tributary missions to the emperor. Having won independence, the kings of Sukhothai chose a new cultural orientation to buttress their rule. The former Khmer overlords were votaries of Hinduism and MAHĀYĀNA Buddhism and the earliest CAITYAs in the city display the architectural features of traditional Khmer tower pyramids. The Thai ruling house abandoned these traditions in favor of Sinhalese-style Pāli Buddhism. In the 1330s a charismatic monk named Si Satha introduced a Sinhalese ordination lineage into the kingdom along with a collection of buddha relics around which was organized a state cult. The shift in religious affiliation is reflected in the lotus-bud and bell-shaped caityas built during the period, which have their prototypes in Sri Lanka. Sukhothai is upheld as a golden age in Thai cultural history. Known for its innovations in architecture and iconography, the kingdom also gave definitive form to the modern Thai writing system which is based on Mon and Khmer antecedents. By the mid-fourteenth century, with the rise of the kingdom of AYUTHAYA to its south, Sukhothai entered a period of decline from which it never recovered. In 1378, Ayuthaya occupied Sukhothai's border provinces, reducing it to the status of a vassal state. After unsuccessful attempts to break free from her southern overlord, Sukhothai was finally absorbed as a province of the Ayuthaya kingdom in the fifteenth century.

**sukkhavipassaka**. In Pāli, lit., "dry insight worker," i.e.,"one supported by insight alone." It refers to a person who has attained any of the four fruits of recluseship (ŚRĀMAṆYAPHALA)—stream-enterer (SROTAĀPANNA), once-returner (SAKṚDĀGĀMIN), nonreturner (ANĀGĀMIN), or ARHAT—by mere insight (P. VIPASSANĀ, S. VIPAŚYANĀ) without reliance on any of the meditative absorptions (P. JHĀNA, S. DHYĀNA). Some contemporary Burmese VIPASSANĀ meditation theory emphasizes this style of practice.

**Sule Paya**. A famous Burmese (Myanmar) pagoda complex located in the center of Rangoon (Yangon), with entrances in the four cardinal directions. It likely was first constructed by the Mon people, but has been restored and expanded repeatedly. The central STŪPA, which is octagonal in shape, is 152 feet tall, is said to contain one of the hairs that the Buddha gave to his first lay disciples, the merchants TRAPUṢA and BHALLIKA. The name Sule comes from a Burmese word for "gathering." The location of the pagoda is said to mark the place where divinities and humans gathered to ask an ancient NAT where the hairs of the Buddha should be enshrined. His answer led to construction of the pagoda of SHWEDAGON. When the British redesigned the surrounding city in the 1880s, they used the central pagoda as the center point of the grid design. The pagoda served as an important gathering place for monks during the uprisings of 1988 and 2007.

**Sumaṅgala**. (Venerable Hikkaduva Sri Sumaṅgala Nayaka Mahāthera) (1827–1911). Sumaṅgala, whose given name was Niclaus, was born in the town of Hikkaduwa in the Galle District of southern Sri Lanka. Sumaṅgala received his early education at the local village temple and, at age thirteen, began his monastic education at Totagamuwa. He received full ordination from the Malwatte chapter in Kandy in 1848. Sumaṅgala is considered to be one of the most influential Pāli scholars of his time. He took a significant role in the Sinhalese Buddhist revival, especially in Colombo. He helped GUṆĀNANDA prepare for the famous Panadura debate. An accomplished scholar, Sumaṅgala studied Buddhist history, arithmetic, and archeology; he also knew Sinhala, Pāli, Sanskrit, and English. In 1867 he received the title Sripada from the British government, making him the high priest of Adam's Peak (Mt. Sumanakūta). The principal and founder of Vidyodaya College, Sumaṅgala worked with Colonel HENRY STEEL OLCOTT and together they established Ananda College and Mahinda College in Colombo and Dharmaraja College in Kandy during the early 1890s. These schools helped to revitalize Buddhist education, which had dwindled under British colonialism. In 1891, Sumaṅgala became the president of the Bodh Gaya Maha Bodhi Society in Colombo. SUMAṄGALA was an inspirational figure for ANAGĀRIKA DHARMAPĀLA and the next generation of Sinhalese Buddhist scholars.

**Sumaṅgalavilāsinī**. A Pāli commentary on the DĪGHANIKĀYA written by BUDDHAGHOSA. It is quoted in the AṄGUTTARANIKĀYA commentary, MANORATHAPŪRAṆĪ.

**Sumedha**. [alt. Sumegha] (C. Shanhui; J. Zen'e; K. Sŏnhye 善慧). Sanskrit and Pāli name of the BODHISATTVA who would become GAUTAMA Buddha. He was an ascetic at the time of DĪPAṂKARA Buddha. Sumedha was born into a wealthy brāhmaṇa family of AMARĀVATĪ. Disenchanted with the vanities of the householders' life, he renounced the world and took up his abode in the Himalaya mountains as an ascetic. There, he practiced assiduously and ultimately gained great yogic power. Once, when flying over the town of Ramma Nagara, he saw a crowd. He landed and asked a member of the crowd why they had gathered and was told that Dīpaṃkara Buddha was approaching. When he heard the word "buddha," he was overcome with joy. Seeing that people of the town were festooning the road Dīpaṃkara would be using with decorations, Sumedha decided to prepare and decorate a portion of the road himself. The Buddha arrived before his work was completed and, seeing that the Buddha was walking toward a mud puddle, Sumedha lay facedown and spread his long matted locks over the mud. While lying in the mud, Sumedha realized that, were he to follow Dīpaṃkara's teachings, he could become an ARHAT in that very lifetime. However, he resolved instead to achieve enlightenment at a time when there was no other buddha in the world, vowing to become a fully enlightened buddha (SAMYAKSAṂBUDDHA) like Dīpaṃkara himself. Dīpaṃkara, using his supranormal powers, looked into the future and confirmed that Sumedha's vow (PŪRVAPRAṆIDĀNA) would be fulfilled and he would one day become GAUTAMA Buddha, the fourth of five perfect buddhas of the present age. It was with this vow, and with this confirmation by Dīpaṃkara Buddha, that the bodhisattva began the path to buddhahood, which, according to the Pāli tradition, he would complete four innumerable plus one hundred thousand eons later.

**Sumeru, Mount**. (T. Ri rab; C. Xumishan/Miaogaoshan; J. Shumisen/Myōkōsen; K. Sumisan/Myogosan 須彌山/妙高山). The central axis of the universe in Buddhist cosmology; also known as Mount Meru. Mount Sumeru stands in the middle of the world as its axis and is eight leagues (YOJANA) high. It is surrounded by seven mountain ranges of gold, each separated from the other by an ocean. At the foot of the seventh range, there is a great ocean, contained at the perimeter of the world by a circle of iron mountains (CAKRAVĀḌA). In this vast ocean, there are four island continents in the four cardinal directions, each flanked by two island subcontinents. The northern continent is square, the eastern semicircular, the southern triangular, and the western round. Although humans inhabit all four continents, the "known world" is the southern continent, named JAMBUDVĪPA, where the current average height is four cubits and the current life span is one hundred years. The four faces of Mount Sumeru are flat, and are each composed of a different precious stone: gold in the north, silver in the east, lapis lazuli in the south, and crystal in the west. The substance determines the color of the sky over each of the four continents. The sky is blue in the southern continent of Jambudvīpa because the southern face of the Mount Sumeru is made of lapis. The slopes of Sumeru are the abode of demigods (ASURA), and its upper reaches are the heavens of the four heavenly kings (see CĀTURMAHĀRĀJAKĀYIKA, LOKAPĀLA). At the summit of the mountain is the heaven of the thirty-three (TRĀYASTRIṂŚA), ruled by the king of the gods, ŚAKRA. Above Mount Sumeru are located the remaining heavens of the sensuous realm (KĀMADHĀTU). Different Buddhist traditions identify Mount Sumeru with different local mountains, including Mount KAILĀSA in the Indian and Tibetan traditions, NAMSAN in the Korean tradition, etc. See also SHUMIDAN.

**Sum rtags**. (Sumtak). In Tibetan, lit. "the Thirty and Signs"; a common abbreviation for two works on Tibetan grammar, the *Lung du ston pa rtsa ba sum cu pa* ("Root Grammar in Thirty Verses") and *Lung du ston pa rtags kyi 'jug pa* ("Grammatical Guide to Signs"). The former is often called simply *Sum cu pa* ("The Thirty") and the latter *Rtags 'jug* ("Guide to Signs"). These works are traditionally said to have been composed c. 650, and are the only two extant treatises of eight works on grammar attributed to Thon mi Saṃbhota, the scholar who, according to legend, was dispatched to India by the Tibetan king SRONG BTSAN SGAM PO in order to devise an alphabet and grammar for the Tibetan language. The remaining six works in his oeuvre are said to have been destroyed during the persecution of Buddhism under the Tibetan king GLANG DAR MA. Both texts are still included as a part of the Tibetan Buddhist curriculum. The traditional dating of the texts as we now have them has been called into question because neither appears in its present redaction until about the twelfth century.

**Sunakṣatra**. (P. Sunakkhatta; T. Legs pa'i skar ma; C. Shanxing; J. Zenshō; K. Sŏnsŏng 善星). The Sankrit proper name of the man who, according to some sources, was the Buddha's half-brother and personal attendant prior to that position being held by ĀNANDA. Despite his personal connection to the Buddha and his extensive knowledge of his teachings, Sunakṣatra had no respect for the Buddha, saying that in his twenty-four years of service to him, he saw no difference whatsoever between the Buddha and himself apart from the fact that the Buddha had a six-foot aura. One week after resigning from his position, he died and was reborn as a PRETA. His story is often told as a cautionary tale about disparaging one's teacher. He appears in several Pāli suttas, both before and after he left the order, living longer than seven days after disparaging the Buddha. There, he is described as a Licchavi prince from Vesāli (S. VAIŚĀLĪ), who served as the Buddha's personal attendant but then left the order to become a disciple of the naked ascetic Korakkhattiya, the "dog man" who walked on all fours, barked like a dog, and ate like a dog without using his hands. Sunakṣatra (P. Sunakkhatta) disparaged the Buddha and said that the dharma did not put an end to suffering, criticizing the Buddha for not performing miracles and showing the origin of things. The Buddha warned him that Korakkhattiya would die in seven days and be reborn as an ASURA, which in fact occurred. Sunakṣatra then became the disciple of another naked ascetic, who also died according to the Buddha's prediction. In the MAHĀPARINIRVĀṆASŪTRA, Sunakṣatra is described as a monk who achieved the four levels of DHYĀNA but later, under the influence of other teachers, came to lose faith in the Buddha.

**Sundarananda**. (T. Mdzes dga'; C. Suntuoluonantuo; J. Sondarananda; K. Sondaranant'a 孫陀羅難陀). In Sanskrit and Pāli, "Handsome Nanda," an epithet of NANDA, either the cousin or a younger half-brother of the buddha GAUTAMA. In the second century CE, the Indian poet AŚVAGHOṢA wrote a famous verse retelling of Nanda's journey from enamored paramour and fiancé to enlightened ascetic in his verse narrative SAUNDARANANDA. See NANDA.

**Sundarīnandā**. (T. Mdzes dga' mo; C. Suntuoli; J. Sondari; K. Sondari 孫陀利). In Pāli and Sanskrit, "Gorgeous Nandā"; one of three prominent nuns named Nandā mentioned in the Pāli canon (the others being ABHIRŪPĀ-NANDĀ and JANAPADAKALYĀṆĪ-NANDĀ), all of whom share similar stories. She is also called simply Sundarī. According to the Pāli account, she was an eminent ARHAT declared by the Buddha to be foremost among his nun disciples in meditative powers. She was the daughter of ŚUDDHODANA and MAHĀPRAJĀPATĪ and so the sister of the arhat NANDA and the half-sister of the Buddha. Most of her male and female relatives had joined the order of monks and nuns, and so out of loyalty to them rather than strong faith she also joined. She received the sobriquet Sundarī because of her extraordinary beauty. She was by nature extremely vain about her looks and so reluctant to visit the Buddha lest he rebuke her for her vanity. When finally one day she accompanied other nuns to hear the Buddha preach, he, knowing her disposition, created an apparition of a most beautiful woman fanning him. Sundarī was entranced by the beauty of the conjured female, whom the Buddha then caused to age, grow haggard, die, and rot. Having shocked her with this horrible vision, the Buddha then preached to her of the frailty of physical beauty, whereupon Sundarī became a stream-enterer (SROTAĀPANNA). He then gave her a suitable subject of meditation (P. KAMMAṬṬHĀNA) through which, after intense practice, she gained insight into the impermanence (ANITYA), suffering (DUḤKHA) and absence of self (ANĀTMAN) of all conditioned things and attained arhatship. She won preeminence through the strength of her meditation, a distinction she had resolved to earn during the time of Padmottara Buddha.

**Sundo**. (C. Shundao 順道) (c. late-fourth century). In Korean, "In Accordance with the Way"; proper name of the Chinese monk to whom Korean historical sources attribute the official introduction of Buddhism into the Korean peninsula. In 372, King Fu Jian (337–385) of the Former Qin dynasty (351–394) is said to have sent Sundo as his personal envoy to the court of King Sosurim (r. 371–384) of the northern Korean kingdom of Koguryŏ. Sundo's mission appears to have been an expression of gratitude for Koguryŏ's help in vanquishing their common foe, the Former Yan (337–370) state. Sundo is said to have brought Buddhist images and scriptures with him to Koguryŏ. We have no record of specifically which images or texts Sundo may have brought; however, since Fu Jian actively supported the dissemination of MAITREYA images throughout his realm, we may assume Sundo's gifts would probably have included such images. This hypothesis is also supported by the prevalence of Maitreya piety in the early Korean tradition. The scriptures he brought were probably early texts of the MAHĀYĀNA tradition, or perhaps SARVĀSTIVĀDA materials. The Former Qin kingdom had established hegemony over eastern Turkestan, which exposed northern China, and thus Koguryŏ, to influences from across the Asian continent. Three years after his arrival in Korea, Sundo is said to have collaborated with two other monks in founding a Buddhist monastery in the new Koguryŏ capital near present-day P'yŏngyang, the first such monastery established on Korean soil. See also ZHI DUN.

**sŭngkwa**. (C. sengke; J. sōka 僧科). In Korean, "ecclesiastical examinations," a clerical examination system used in Korea from the early Koryŏ through early Chosŏn dynasties to exert state control over the ecclesiastical institution, by selecting monks who would hold official monastic positions. The examination system was established in 958 during the reign of the Koryŏ king Kwangjong (r. 949–975) and the examinations were originally administered every three years. There is no direct Chinese analogue for this kind of selective examination system conducted at the state level and it seems to have been a distinctively Korean creation. There were two separate examinations to select official monks: the Doctrinal (KYO, C. Jiao) school selection (KYOJONG SŎN) and the Meditation (SŎN, C. CHAN) school selection (SŎNJONG SŎN). The selection examination for the Doctrinal (Kyo) school was held at WANGNYUNSA, one of the ten major monasteries built in the Koryŏ capital of Kaesŏng by Wang Kŏn (T'aejo, r. 918–943), the first king of the Koryŏ dynasty; the Meditation (Sŏn) exams were held at KWANGMYŎNGSA, also located in the capital. Monks who passed the examination were qualified to hold official ecclesiastical status. Monks in both the Kyo and Sŏn schools who passed the examinations were appointed, in ascending order, to the positions of taedŏk (great virtue), taesa (great master), ijungdaesa (second-grade great master), and samjungdaesa (third-grade great master). Beyond these positions common to both schools, there were two supreme positions exclusive to each school: sujwa (head seat) and SŬNGT'ONG for Kyo monks; and sŏnsa (Sŏn master) and taesŏnsa (great Sŏn master) for Sŏn monks. State preceptors (KUKSA) and royal preceptors (WANGSA), the highest ecclesiastical offices during the Koryŏ dynasty and the symbolic religious teachers to the state and the king, were appointed from monks who held the positions of sŭngt'ong or taesŏnsa. The subject matter for the Kyo examination was derived from the AVATAṂSAKASŪTRA (*Huayan jing*) and the DAŚABHŪMIVYĀKHYĀNA (SHIDIJING LUN); for the Sŏn examination, materials were taken from the JINGDE CHUANDENG LU and the SŎNMUN YŎMSONG CHIP. The examination system continued during the Chosŏn dynasty despite the state suppression of Buddhism, but was abolished during the reign of King Chungjong (r. 1506–1544). The monastic examinations were subsequently revived in 1550 during the reign of King Myŏngjong (r. 1545–1567), but again abolished in 1565.

**sŭngmu**. (僧舞). In Korean, "monk's dance"; a form of Korean Buddhist ritual dance that was originally performed by monks. During the Chosŏn dynasty (1392–1910), the sŭngmu gradually transformed into a dance performed primarily for artistic and entertainment purposes and is nowadays regarded as one of the major types of Korean traditional folk dance. The dance is typically performed to the accompaniment of a single drum. Modern professional solo dancers wear a white jacket with long and trailing sleeves, a white hood, a blue skirt, and a red sash crossing from shoulder to waist. The sophisticated gestures and delicate rhythmic sequences, as well as the mobile lines created by the long sleeve extension that cover the dancer's hands, create a peaceful yet dynamic composition. The delicate unison of dynamism and stillness in the sŭngmu is emblematic of Korean dance aesthetics. The T'AEGO CHONG of modern Korean Buddhism has sought to revive the sŭngmu as a specifically Buddhist dance form.

**Sŭngnang**. (C. Senglang; J. Sōrō 僧朗) (c. 450–c. 520). A monk putatively from the early Korean kingdom of Koguryŏ, whom JIZANG (549–623) credits with being an important vaunt courier in the development of the Chinese SAN LUN ZONG (K. Sam non chong), the Chinese counterpart of the MADHYAMAKA branch of Indian philosophical exegesis. Sŭngnang is claimed to have taught the notion of "three truths" or "three judgments" (SANDI)—the truths of emptiness, provisional reality, and their mean—an exegetical schema that was influential in the subsequent development of both the San lun and TIANTAI schools. It is uncertain whether Sŭngnang actually hailed from Koguryŏ, or was instead either a Koguryŏ hostage of the Northern Wei dynasty or a person of Chinese ancestry from the Liaodong region (which had been captured in 397 CE by the Koguryŏ king Kwanggaet'o).

**sŭngt'ong**. (僧統). In Korean, "SAṂGHA overseer," the highest ecclesiastical position that could be achieved by KYO (Doctrine) monks in the Korean monastic examination system (SŬNGKWA), especially during the Koryŏ dynasty. The position was first established in 551 by the Silla king Chinhŭng (r. 540–576) for the monk Hyeryang (c. sixth century). Initially, the appointee's major role was to help protect the court by hosting such national Buddhist services as the Inwang Paekkojwa hoe (Renwang Assembly of One-Hundred Seats) (see HUGUO FOJIAO). Later, as the Silla institution developed, the saṃgha overseer took actual charge of the national ecclesiastical affairs. During the Koryŏ dynasty, sŭngt'ong was the highest of the six positions that could be achieved by Kyo monks through the monastic examinations (sŭngkwa) (the equivalent in the Sŏn school of great Sŏn master, or taesŏnsa). The six Kyo positions in descending order were sŭngt'ong, sujwa (head seat), samjung taesa (third-grade great master), ijung taesa (second-grade great master), taesa (great master), and taedŏk (great virtue). Appointing an official national leader of the saṃgha became a long-standing Chinese tradition starting in the Six Dynasties period, when the Emperor Daowu (r. 386–409) of the Northern Wei dynasty appointed Faguo (fl. fourth century) as overseer of religion (daoren tong) probably around 396 and 397. During the Northern Dynasties, the position was called shamen tong (ŚRAMAṆA overseer) or zhaoxuan tong (luminous mystery overseer); under the Southern Dynasties, it was called sengzheng (saṃgha rectifier), sengzhu (saṃgha head), or daseng tong (great saṃgha overseer). Many later dynasties, including the Sui and Tang, had an equivalent ecclesiastical post.

**sŭnim**. (스님). In Korean, lit. "honored monastic"; a generic term used to refer to any ordained monk, nun, or novice. These different categories of the saṃgha are distinguished as pigu (BHIKṢU) sŭnim, piguni (BHIKṢUṆĪ) sŭnim, etc. Individual monastics in Korea are always referred to by their ordained names followed by sŭnim, thus Kusan sŭnim, Hyemyŏng sŭnim, etc. The term is a contraction of the Korean pronunciation of sŭng, the Sinograph that transcribes SAṂGHA (monastic congregation), plus the vernacular honorific suffix -nim.

**śūnyatā**. (T. stong pa nyid; C. kong; J. kū; K. kong 空). In Sanskrit, "emptiness"; the term has a number of denotations, but is most commonly associated with the perfection of wisdom (PRAJÑĀPĀRAMITĀ) sūtras and the MADHYAMAKA school of Mahāyāna philosophy. In its earlier usage, "emptiness" (as śūnya) is the third of the four aspects of the truth of suffering (DUḤKHASATYA), the first of the FOUR NOBLE TRUTHS: viz., the aggregates (SKANDHA) are (1) impermanent, (2) associated with the contaminants, (3) empty of cleanliness, and (4) nonself. There are a number of explanations of emptiness in this early usage, but most suggest the absence of cleanliness or attractiveness in the body that would lead to grasping at the body as "mine" (S. ātmīya, mama). This misapprehension is counteracted by the application of mindfulness with regard to the body (KĀYĀNUPAŚYANĀ), which demonstrates the absence or emptiness of an independent, perduring soul (ĀTMAN) inherent in the skandhas. In its developed usage in the Madhyamaka school, as set forth by NĀGĀRJUNA and his commentators, emptiness becomes an application of the classical doctrine of no-self (ANĀTMAN) beyond the person (PUDGALA) and the skandhas to subsume all phenomena (DHARMA) in the universe. Emptiness is the lack or absence of intrinsic nature (SVABHĀVA) in any and all phenomena, the final nature of all things (DHARMATĀ), and the ultimate truth (PARAMĀRTHASATYA). Despite its various interpretations among the various Madhyamaka authors, emptiness is clearly neither nothingness nor the absence of existence, but rather the absence of a falsely imagined type of existence, identified as svabhāva. Because all phenomena are dependently arisen, they lack, or are empty of, an intrinsic nature characterized by independence and autonomy. Nāgārjuna thus equates śūnyatā and the notion of conditionality (PRATĪTYASAMUTPĀDA). The YOGĀCĀRA school introduces the concept of the "three natures" (TRISVABHĀVA) to give individual meanings to the lack of intrinsic existence (NIḤSVABHĀVA) in the imaginary nature (PARIKALPITASVABHĀVA), the dependent nature (PARATANTRASVABHĀVA), and the consummate nature (PARINIṢPANNASVABHĀVA). Parinispanna in this Yogācāra interpretation is emptiness in the sense of the absence of a difference of entity between object and subject; it is the emptiness of the parikalpitasvabhāva or imagined nature in a paratantra or dependent nature. In Tibet, the question of the true meaning of emptiness led to the RANG STONG GZHAN STONG debate.

**Śūnyatāsaptati**. (T. Stong pa nyid bdun cu pa). In Sanskrit, "Seventy Stanzas on Emptiness"; one of the major works of NĀGĀRJUNA, and counted by Tibetans as part his philosophical corpus (YUKTIKĀYA). It is a work in seventy-three stanzas, which serves as a kind of appendix to the MŪLAMADHYAMAKAKĀRIKĀ, summarizing what is said there while adding some new topics. It declares that all phenomena, including the twelve links in the chain of dependent origination (PRATĪTYASAMUTPĀDA) exist only conventionally; the statement that everything is impermanent does not imply the existence of entities that have the property of impermanence. Reasoning (YUKTI) demonstrates that ultimately everything is unproduced (ANUTPANNA), including NIRVĀṆA. All entities (BHĀVA) are dependently arisen and empty (śūnya), including KARMAN and the five aggregates (SKANDHA). Ignorance (AVIDYĀ) disappears when it is understood that there is no self. The ultimate (PARAMĀRTHA) is emptiness (ŚŪNYATĀ) but this realization is gained through the conventional (SAṂVṚTTI); the person endowed with faith (ŚRADDHĀ) who investigates dependent origination with reasoning will achieve tranquility. There is an autocommentary (svavṛtti) to the text ascribed to Nāgārjuna. There is also a commentary by CANDRAKĪRTI, the *Śūnyatāsaptativṛtti*. The *Śūnyatāsaptati* is not included in the Chinese canon.

**śūnyatāśūnyatā**. (T. stong pa nyid kyi stong pa nyid; C. kongkong; J. kūkū; K. konggong 空空). In Sanskrit, lit. the "emptiness of emptiness," the most famous of the sixteen, eighteen, or twenty types of emptiness, indicating that emptiness is itself devoid of intrinsic nature (NIḤSVABHĀVA) and is therefore itself empty. YOGĀCĀRA-influenced interpretations of śūnyatāśūnyatā associate it with the emptiness of knowledge (jñānaśūnyatā). According to these interpretations, the first three in the list of emptinesses are inner (adhyātma) emptiness, outer (bahirdhā) emptiness, and the emptiness of both (ubhaya), where inner is a word for the six sense bases (INDRIYA), outer for their six sensory objects (VIṢAYA) and both for the physical receptacles (the physical eye and so on) of the six sense bases. Having understood the emptiness of all those elements, only the knowledge of emptiness remains; hence, the emptiness of that knowledge is called the emptiness of emptinesses, the fourth in the list.

**Śūnyavāda**. (T. Stong pa nyid smra ba; C. Kong zong; J. Kūshū; K. Kong chong 空宗). In Sanskrit, "Proponent of the Empty," another name for the MADHYAMAKA school, one usually used by the Buddhist and non-Buddhist opponents of Madhyamaka, who regarded the Madhyamaka view as a form of nihilism. However, it is important to note that CANDRAKĪRTI uses the term śūnyatādarśana, "the philosophical school of emptiness." The term also indicates that, although the terms śūnya and ŚŪNYATĀ are employed in all schools of Buddhist philosophy, they were associated particularly with the Madhyamaka.

**Suppavāsā-Koḷiyadhītā**. (S. Supravāsā-Koliyadhītṛ). The Pāli name of an eminent lay disciple of the Buddha declared by him to be foremost among laywomen who give choice alms food. According to the Pāli account, she was the daughter of the king of Koḷiya and was married to a Licchavi chieftain named Mahāli. She lived in the village of Sajjanela and later moved to ŚRĀVASTĪ. On a visit to Sajjanela, the Buddha once preached to her on the merits of giving alms food. She was always careful to give the best of foods to the Buddha and his monks, for which reason she attained preeminence in this regard, an honor she aspired to in a previous life during the time of Padmottara Buddha. She is praised along with the renowned donors ANĀTHAPIṆḌADA and VIŚĀKHĀ for her exceptional gifts, which were always welcomed by members of the order. Suppavāsā is most famous as the mother of the arhat SĪVALI.

She was pregnant with him for seven years and for seven days she was suffering through protracted labor. Believing that she would not survive the ordeal, she sent a gift to the buddha through her husband so that she could earn merit before her death. The buddha received the gift and she immediately gave birth to her son. Sīvali was compelled to stay in her womb for so long in retribution for having once laid siege to the city of Vārāṇasī for seven days while he was a prince in a previous existence. Suppavāsā had been his mother in that life as well.

**Supriyā**. (P. Suppiyā; T. Rab dga' ba; C. Xupiye nü; J. Shubiyanyo; K. Subiyanyŏ 須毘耶女). Sanskrit name of an eminent lay disciple (UPĀSIKĀ) of the Buddha, whom he declared foremost among laywomen who comfort the sick. Supriyā lived in Vārāṇasī with her husband Supriya. Both were devoted followers of the Buddha and generous patrons of the order. Once, while visiting a monastery, Supriyā encountered a sick monk in need of meat broth. She sent a servant to market to fetch some meat but none was to be had in all of Vārāṇasī. She therefore cut a piece of flesh from her thigh and gave it to her servant to make into broth, after which, ill from her injury, she lay on her bed. Her husband rejoiced at her piety and invited the Buddha to the morning meal the next day. When the Buddha was informed of her deed, he praised her for her generosity and through his supranormal powers magically healed her wounds. As a consequence of Supriyā's offering, however, the Buddha passed a rule forbidding monks to eat human flesh, even when it is freely given.

**Sūra Ambaṭṭha**. (S. Śūra Āmraṣtha; C. Yongjian zhangzhe; J. Yūken chōja; K. Yonggŏn changja 勇健長者). The Pāli name of an eminent lay disciple (UPĀSAKA) of the Buddha declared by him to be foremost among laymen in unwavering trust. Sūra Ambaṭṭha in Pāli means "hero who stays by the mango tree"; he was born into the family of a wealthy banker dwelling in ŚRĀVASTĪ. According to the Pāli account, he was originally the follower of a rival sect of recluses (ŚRAMAṆA). One day, the Buddha saw Sūra and, noting that he was ripe for conversion, went to his door for alms. Although his allegiance was to another teacher, out of deference Sūra invited the Buddha into his home to partake of his morning meal. When the Buddha spoke to him after the meal, Sūra became a stream-enterer (SROTAĀPANNA), thus marking his conversion. MĀRA, hoping to shake Sūra's newfound faith, appeared at his door in the guise of the Buddha. He said he had returned to correct a mistake he had made when preaching to him earlier. Believing Māra's conjured body to be the Buddha, Sūra let him in. Māra stated that whereas he had explained that all conditioned things were impermanent, he should have said that only some were impermanent. Since Sūra was already a stream-enterer, he easily saw through the ruse and promptly drove Māra from his house.

**śūraṃgamasamādhi**. (T. dpa' bar 'gro ba'i ting nge 'dzin; C. shoulengyan sanmei; J. shuryōgon zanmai; K. sunŭngŏm sammae 首楞嚴三昧). In Sanskrit, "heroic-march concentration," a SAMĀDHI in which the mind becomes free and unimpeded like the "march" (gama) of a "hero" (śūra), who "walks alone, fearlessly, like a lion." The śūraṃgama concentration (samādhi) as taught in the ŚŪRAṂGAMASAMĀDHISŪTRA, an eponymously titled early MAHĀYĀNA sūtra, not only enables BODHISATTVAS quickly to attain complete, perfect enlightenment (ANUTTARASAMYAKSAṂBODHI), but also ensures that even ŚRĀVAKAS, PRATYEKABUDDHAS, and ARHATS who benightedly believe themselves to be practicing correctly by following the HĪNAYĀNA are actually put on the right path leading to buddhahood. In addition, the śūraṃgamasamādhi also permits enlightened beings to manifest themselves in any variety of forms in order to teach sentient beings, so that ultimately anyone one encounters in life may in fact be an enlightened buddha. In the Chinese apocryphon, *Shoulengyan jing* (*ŚŪRAṂGAMASŪTRA), the Buddha also teaches a different version of the śūraṃgamasamādhi, where the concentration counters the false views about the aggregates (SKANDHA) and consciousness (VIJÑĀNA) and reveals the TATHĀGATAGARBHA that is inherent in all sentient beings. This tathāgatagarbha, or buddha-nature, is made manifest through the śūraṃgamasamādhi, which constitutes the "heroic march" forward toward enlightenment.

**Śūraṃgamasamādhisūtra**. (T. Dpa' bar 'gro ba'i ting nge 'dzin gyi mdo; C. Shoulengyan sanmei jing; J. Shuryōgon zanmaikyō; K. Sunŭngŏm sammae kyŏng 首楞嚴三昧經). In Sanskrit, "Sūtra on the Heroic-March Concentration," an early MAHĀYĀNA sūtra that explains how the mind becomes free and unimpeded like the "march" (gama) of a "hero" (śūra), who "walks alone, fearlessly, like a lion." (This translated sūtra should be distinguished from the *ŚŪRAṂGAMASŪTRA, a Chinese apocryphal scripture of similar name, which dates from the early eighth century.) The ŚŪRAṂGAMASAMĀDHI as taught in this sūtra not only enables BODHISATTVAS quickly to attain complete, perfect enlightenment (ANUTTARASAMYAKSAṂBODHI), but also ensures that even ŚRĀVAKAS, PRATYEKABUDDHAS, and ARHATS are put on the right path leading to buddhahood. In addition, the śūraṃgamasamādhi also permits enlightened beings to manifest themselves in any variety of forms in order to teach sentient beings. The sūtra also includes descriptions of the world systems of many other buddhas (BUDDHAKṢETRA), including ABHIRATI, the buddha-land of AKṢOBHYA. Although some fragments of the Sanskrit recension of the *Śūraṃgamasamādhisūtra* have survived, the full sūtra is extant only in an early-fifth-century translation attributed to the eminent Kuchean translator KUMĀRAJĪVA, in two rolls, and in an early-ninth-century Tibetan translation.

***Śūraṃgamasūtra**. (T. Dpa' bar 'gro ba'i mdo; C. Shoulengyan jing; J. Shuryōgongyō; K. Sunŭngŏm kyŏng 首楞嚴經). A Chinese indigenous scripture (see APOCRYPHA), usually known in the West by its reconstructed Sanskrit title *Śūraṃgamasūtra*, meaning "Heroic March Sūtra." Its full title is *Dafoding rulai miyin xiuzheng liaoyi zhu pusa wanxing Shoulengyan jing*; in ten rolls. (This indigenous scripture should be distinguished from an early-fifth century Chinese translation of the ŚŪRAṂGAMASAMĀDHISŪTRA, attributed by KUMĀRAJĪVA, in two rolls, for which Sanskrit fragments are extant.) According to the account in the Chinese cataloguer Zhisheng's *Xu gujin yijing tuji*, the *Śūraṃgamasūtra* was brought to China by a ŚRAMAṆA named Pāramiti. Because the *Śūraṃgamasūtra* had been proclaimed a national treasure, the Indian king had forbidden anyone to take the sūtra out of the country. In order to transmit this scripture to China, Pāramiti wrote the sūtra out in minute letters on extremely fine silk, then he cut open his arm and hid the small scroll inside his flesh. With the sūtra safely hidden away, Pāramiti set out for China and eventually arrived in Guangdong province. There, he happened to meet the exiled Prime Minister Fangrong, who invited him to reside at the monastery of Zhizhisi, where he translated the sūtra in 705 CE. Apart from Pāramiti's putative connection to the *Śūraṃgamasūtra*, however, nothing more is known about him and he has no biography in the GAOSENG ZHUAN ("Biographies of Eminent Monks"). Zhisheng also has an entry on the *Śūraṃgamasūtra* in his KAIYUAN SHIJIAO LU, but there are contradictions in these two extant catalogue accounts of the sūtra's transmission and translation. The *Kaiyuan Shijiao lu* merely records that the śramaṇa Huidi encountered an unnamed Western monk at Guangdong, who had with him a copy of the Sanskrit recension of this sūtra, and Huidi invited him to translate the scripture together. Since the names of this Western monk and his patron Fangrong are not mentioned, the authenticity of the scripture has been called into question. Although Zhisheng assumed the *Śūraṃgamasūtra* was a genuine Indian scripture, the fact that no Sanskrit manuscript of the text is known to exist, as well as the inconsistencies in the stories about its transmission to China, have led scholiasts for centuries to questions the scripture's authenticity. There is also internal evidence of the scripture's Chinese provenance, such as the presence of such indigenous Chinese philosophical concepts as yin-yang cosmology and the five elements (wuxing) theory, the stylistic beauty of the literary Chinese in which the text is written, etc. For these and other reasons, the *Śūraṃgamasūtra* is now generally recognized to be a Chinese apocryphal composition. The sūtra opens with one of the most celebrated stories in East Asian Buddhist literature: the Buddha's attendant ĀNANDA's near seduction by the harlot Mātaṅgī. With Ānanda close to being in flagrante delicto, the Buddha sends the bodhisattva MAÑJUŚRĪ to save him from a PĀRĀJIKA offense, by employing the śūraṃgama DHĀRAṆĪ to thwart Mātaṅgī's seductive magic. The Buddha uses the experience to teach to Ānanda and the congregation the ŚŪRAṂGAMASAMĀDHI, which counters the false views about the aggregates (SKANDHA) and consciousness (VIJÑĀNA) and reveals the TATHĀGATAGARBHA that is inherent in all sentient beings. This tathāgatagarbha, or buddha-nature, is made manifest through the śūraṃgamasamādhi, which constitutes the "heroic march" forward toward enlightenment. The *Śūraṃgamasūtra* was especially influential in the CHAN school during the Song and Ming dynasties, which used the text as the scriptural justification for the school's distinctive teaching that Chan "points directly to the human mind" (ZHIZHI RENXIN), so that one may "see the nature and achieve buddhahood" (JIANXING CHENGFO). Several noted figures within the Chan school achieved their own awakenings through the influence of the *Śūraṃgamasūtra*, including the Ming-dynasty master HANSHAN DEQING (1546–1623), and the sūtra was particularly important in the writings of such Ming-dynasty Chan masters as YUNQI ZHUHONG (1535–1615). The leading Chan monk of modern Chinese Buddhism, XUYUN (1840–1959), advocated the practice of the *Śūraṃgamasūtra* throughout his life, and it was the only scripture that he ever annotated. As a mark of the sūtra's influence in East Asian Buddhism, the *Śūraṃgamasūtra* is one of the few apocryphal scriptures that receives its own mention in another indigenous sūtra: the apocryphal *Foshuo fa miejin jing* ("The Sūtra on the Extinction of the Dharma") states that the first sūtra to disappear from the world during the dharma-ending age (MOFA) will in fact be the *Śūraṃgamasūtra*. The Tibetan translation of this Chinese apocryphon was produced during the Qianlong era (1735–1796) of the Qing dynasty; the scripture was apparently so important in contemporary Chinese Buddhism that it was deemed essential for it to be represented in the Tibetan canon as well.

***Susiddhikarasūtra**. (C. Suxidi jieluo jing; J. Soshijjikarakyō; K. Sosilchi kalla kyŏng 蘇悉地羯羅經). In Sanskrit, "Perfect Achievement Sūtra"; an important SŪTRA of the esoteric Buddhist traditions (see TANTRA and MIKKYŌ). No Sanskrit edition of the *Susiddhikarasūtra* is known to exist; the Sanskrit title is reconstructed from the Chinese translation (726) attributed to the Indian TREPIṬAKA ŚUBHAKARASIṂHA. The *Susiddhikaramahātantrasādhanopāyikapaṭala* found in the Tibetan canon is a translation in seventy-five folios (*Legs par grub par byed pa'i rgyud chen po las sgrub pa'i thabs rim par phye pa*) and is categorized by the editor BU STON as an important KRIYĀTANTRA. The Tibetan title means "SĀDHANA Section of the Susiddhikara Great Tantra." The *Susiddhikarasūtra*, along with the MAHĀVAIROCANĀBHISAṂBODHISŪTRA and the SARVATATHĀGATATATTVASAṂGRAHA, is considered one of the three central texts of the esoteric branch of the TENDAI tradition known as TAIMITSU.

**Susim kyŏl**. (C. Xiuxin jue 修心訣). In Korean, "Secrets on Cultivating the Mind," one of the most popular tracts on the practice of SŎN (C. CHAN), by the Korean Sŏn master POJO CHINUL (1158–1210); composed c. 1203–1205 at the newly established SUSŎNSA religious community. The tract provides a detailed outline of Chinul's preferred soteriological stratagem of "sudden awakening/gradual cultivation" (K. tono chŏmsu; DUNWU JIANXIU), that is, an initial sudden awakening to one's buddha-nature, followed by gradual cultivation of that awakening until one is able not only to be but also to act enlightened. Chinul also covers here the cultivation in tandem of concentration (SAMĀDHI) and wisdom (PRAJÑĀ), which treats these two meditative aids not as stages in a sequential series of meditative practices but instead as the calm and alert aspects of the mind-nature itself. The *Susim kyŏl* was lost in Korea following the Mongol invasions of the mid-thirteenth century and was not reintroduced to the peninsula (via a Northern Ming edition) until about two centuries later. It was translated into the Korean vernacular in 1467 and remains today one of the most widely read Korean Sŏn works.

**Susŏnsa**. (修禪社). In Korean, "Sŏn Cultivation Community"; the later name for the meditation retreat known originally as the Chŏngye Kyŏlsa or "Samādhi and Prajñā Community," established by the Korean Sŏn master Pojo Chinul (1158–1210) at the monastery of Kŏjosa on Mt. Kong in 1188. As the community grew, Chinul had to search for a more suitable location that would accommodate the large number of participants. In 1197, Chinul's disciple Suu (d.u.) began reconstruction of a small, dilapidated temple known as Kilsangsa on Mt. Songgwang. The community was relocated to the new site in 1200, but because a nearby monastery was also called Chŏnghyesa (Samādhi and Prajñā Monastery), Chinul was forced to seek another name for his community. King Hŭijong (r. 1204–1211) gave the community its new name of Susŏnsa, or Sŏn Cultivation Community. Largely through the efforts of Chinul's successor Chin'gak Hyesim, the Susŏnsa community became an influential Buddhist institution and remained so throughout the Koryŏ dynasty. Susŏnsa eventually became the influential monastery that has been known since the Chosŏn dynasty as Songgwangsa. The meditation hall at Songgwangsa is still called Susŏnsa.

**sūtra**. (P. sutta; T. mdo; C. jing; J. kyō; K. kyŏng 經). In Sanskrit, lit. "aphorism," but in a Buddhist context translated as "discourse," "sermon," or "scripture"; a sermon said to be delivered by the Buddha or delivered with his sanction. A term probably used originally to refer to sayings of the Buddha that were preserved orally by his followers (and hence called "aphorisms"), the sūtra developed into its own genre of Buddhist literature, with a fairly standard set of literary conventions. The most famous of these conventions was the phrase used to begin a sūtra, "Thus have I heard" (evaṃ mayā śrutam), intended to certify that what was to follow was the first-person report of the Buddha's attendant Ānanda (see saṃgītikāra) who was most often in the Buddha's presence and was renowned for his prodigious memory. Also standard was the nidāna, which describes the setting of the sūtra, noting where the Buddha was residing at the time, who was in the audience, who was the interlocutor, etc. According to tradition, the sūtras were first codified when Ānanda recited them at the first Buddhist council (see Council, First), shortly after the Buddha's death. This conceit of orality was maintained even for sūtras that were literary compositions, written long after the Buddha, most notably, the hundreds of Mahāyāna sūtras that began to appear in India starting some four hundred years after the Buddha's nirvāṇa. An important theme in these sūtras and their commentaries is the claim that they are indeed the word of the Buddha (buddhavacana). In the standard threefold division of the Buddha's teachings, sūtra indicates the contents of the sūtrapiṭaka, a grouping of texts that together with the vinaya and abhidharma together constitute the tripiṭaka, or "three baskets." In tantric literature, sūtra is used to refer to the exoteric teachings of the Buddha, in contrast to the tantras, his esoteric teachings. It is also one of the nine (navaṅga[pāvacana]) (Pāli) or twelve (dvādaśāṅga [pravacana]) (Sanskrit) categories (aṅga) of Buddhist scripture, according to structure or literary style.

**Sūtrālaṃkāra**. (S). See Mahāyānasūtrālaṃkāra.

**sūtrānta**. (P. suttanta; T. mdo sde). A synonym for sūtra, used also to designate the category of sūtras. In Pāli, suttanta is typically reserved for the longer suttas collected in the Dīghanikāya.

**sūtrapiṭaka**. (P. suttapiṭaka; T. mdo sde'i sde snod; C. jingzang; J. kyōzō; K. kyŏngjang 經藏). In Sanskrit, "basket of discourses," one of the three constituents of the tripiṭaka (together with the vinayapiṭaka and the abhidharmapiṭaka). This basket is a disparate collection of thousands of texts attributed to the Buddha (or said to be spoken with his sanction), varying in length from extended narrative accounts to short epigrams. The Pāli suttapiṭaka is divided into five groups, or nikāya. These are the Dīghanikāya, or "Long Group," comprising thirty-four lengthier sūtras; the Majjhimanikāya, or "Middle [Length] Group," comprising 152 sūtras; the Saṃyuttanikāya or "Related Group," comprising (by some counts) some seven thousand sūtras, organized largely by subject matter in fifty-six categories; the Aṅguttaranikāya, literally, the "Group Increasing by a Factor," or more generally, the "Numerical Group," an anthology of nearly ten thousand brief texts organized by the number of the subject, with the first group dealing with single things, the second dealing with pairs, the third dealing with things that occur in threes, up to things that occur in groups of eleven; and finally the Khuddakanikāya, or "Small Group," a diverse collection of miscellaneous texts, including such famous works as the Pāli Dhammapada. Although the *Khuddakanikāya* contains some early works, as an independent nikāya, it appears to have been the last to be added to the tipiṭaka and is not mentioned in early accounts. The suttapiṭaka seems to have been preserved orally for centuries, before being committed to writing in Sri Lanka at the end of the first century BCE. The sūtrapiṭakas of other Indian nikāyas (schools) translated from a number of Indian languages into Chinese and Tibetan use the word āgama (tradition) in place of nikāya (group) for the groupings of sūtras in their respective canons. In their Chinese translations, the Dīrghāgama or "Long Discourses," belonging to the Dharmaguptaka school, corresponds to the Pāli *Dīghanikāya*; the Madhyamāgama or "Middle-Length Discourses" of the Sarvāstivāda school corresponds to the Pāli *Majjhimanikāya*; the Saṃyuktāgama or "Connected Discourses," belonging to the Sarvāstivāda school (with a partial translation perhaps belonging to the KĀŚYAPĪYA school) corresponds to the Pāli *Saṃyuttanikāya*; and the EKOTTARĀGAMA or "Numerically Arranged Discourses," variously ascribed to the DHARMAGUPTAKAS, or less plausibly the MAHĀSĀṂGHIKA school or its PRAJÑAPTIVĀDA offshoot, corresponds to the Pāli *Aṅguttaranikāya*. Despite the similarities in the titles of these collections, there are substantial differences between the contents of the Sanskrit āgamas and the Pāli nikāyas. The Khuddakanikāya ("Miscellaneous Collection"), the fifth nikāya in the Pāli canon, has no equivalent in the extant Chinese translations of the āgamas; such miscellanies, or "mixed baskets" (S. kṣudrakapiṭaka), were however known to have existed in several of the mainstream Buddhist schools, including the Dharmaguptaka, Mahāsāṃghika, and MAHĪŚĀSAKA.

**Sūtrasamuccaya**. (T. Mdo kun las btus pa; C. Dasheng baoyaoyi lun; J. Daijō hōyōgiron; K. Taesŭng poyoŭi non 大乘寶要義論). In Sanskrit, "Compendium of Sūtras," a work attributed to NĀGĀRJUNA, an anthology of passages from sixty-eight mainly MAHĀYĀNA sūtras (or collections of sūtras), organized under thirteen topics. These topics extol the bodhisattva and the Mahāyāna path, noting the rarity and hence precious nature of such things as faith in the Buddha, great compassion, and laymen who are able to follow the bodhisattva path. The text is of historical interest because it provides evidence of the Mahāyāna sūtras that were extant at the time of Nāgārjuna. These include, in addition to various PRAJÑĀPĀRAMITĀ sūtras, such famous works as the LAṄKĀVATĀRASŪTRA, the DAŚABHŪMIKASŪTRA, the SADDHARMAPUṆḌARĪKASŪTRA, and the VIMALAKĪRTINIRDEŚA. The Chinese translation was made by Dharmarakṣa (c. 1018–1058) during the Northern Song dynasty and was among the last stratum of Indian materials to be entered into the Chinese Buddhist canon (C. DAZANGJING).

**sūtravibhaṅga**. (P. suttavibhaṅga; T. mdo rnam par 'byed pa; C. jingfenbie; J. kyōfunbetsu; K. kyŏngbunbyŏl 經分別). In Sanskrit, "analysis of the SŪTRAS," a section of the VINAYA that comments on the PRĀTIMOKṢA; also known as the VINAYAVIBHAṄGA. The prātimokṣa is a list of rules that monks and nuns must follow. The sūtravibhaṅga comments on each rule according to a fourfold structure. First, the text recounts the occasion for the formulation of the rule. According to the tradition, the Buddha did not initially impose rules on the SAṂGHA, but created the monastic code gradually as misconduct that required correction began to appear in the order. Thus, each rule was declared by the Buddha in a specific circumstance, only after a misdeed had occurred. The Buddha would then make a rule prohibiting that deed, without any retrospective sanction against the original perpetrator, since no rule was in place at the time of the misdeed. This section explains the circumstances that led to the Buddha's announcement of the rule and may include more than one story. (In the case of subcategories of a misdeed, the Buddha is not always mentioned.) This section of the text provides important insights into monastic life in India at the time. Second, the specific prātimokṣa rule is stated. Third, the text provides a word-for-word commentary on the rule as it is set forth in the prātimokṣa. Finally, accounts are provided of circumstances under which the rule might be violated without sanction or with reduced sanction. The sūtravibhaṅga is organized according to the eight sections of the prātimokṣa. There are separate versions of the text for BHIKṢUS and BHIKṢUṆĪS, with the former also being known as the mahāvibhaṅga. In most vinaya traditions, a prātimokṣa exists as a separate text, but in the Pāli vinaya, the pāṭimokkha is embedded within the SUTTAVIBHAṄGA.

**sutta**. In Pāli, "discourses." See SŪTRA.

**Suttanipāta**. In Pāli, "Sutta Collection"; the fifth book of the KHUDDAKANIKĀYA of the Pāli SUTTAPIṬAKA, which includes texts that derive from the earliest stratum of the Pāli canon. It is comprised of five VAGGAS or chapters, the *Uragavagga*, *Cūḷavagga*, MAHĀVAGGA, AṬṬHAKAVAGGA, and the *Pārāyaṇavagga*. The *Aṭṭhakavagga* and *Pārāyaṇavagga* are believed to have been early collections that circulated independently, as there is a canonical commentary on them, the NIDDESA, that ignores the other vaggas. They also include verse passages that metrical evidence places as among the most archaic in the canon.

**suttanta**. In Pāli, a synonym for SŪTRA, used also to designate the category of scriptural literature. In Pāli, suttanta is typically reserved for the longer suttas collected in the DĪGHANIKĀYA. See also SŪTRĀNTA.

**suttapiṭaka**. In Pāli, "basket of discourses," the first of the "three baskets" (P. TIPIṬAKA; S. TRIPIṬAKA) of the Buddhist canon. See SŪTRAPIṬAKA.

**suttavibhaṅga**. In Pāli, "analysis of the suttas"; the first major section of the Pāli VINAYAPIṬAKA. Embedded within the suttavibhaṅga is the pāṭimokkha (S. PRĀTIMOKṢA), a collection of 227 rules (311 for nuns) that were to be followed by fully ordained members of the Buddhist monastic community. The bulk of the suttavibhaṅga contains narratives and commentaries related to the promulgation of the pāṭimokkha rules, which explain the events that led to the Buddha's decision to establish a specific rule. Following the Buddha's pronouncement of the rule, the rule may be interpreted with word-for-word commentary and/or details that might justify an exception to the rule. In the suttavibhaṅga, these narrative and commentarial treatments are organized in the same way as the pāṭimokkha itself, that is, according to the category of offense. Thus, the suttavibhaṅga begins with the PĀRĀJIKA (defeat) offenses and works its way through the remaining sections of the pāṭimokkha. See also SŪTRAVIBHAṄGA.

**Suvaṇṇabhūmi**. (S. Suvarṇabhūmi). In Pāli, "The Golden Land," a territory generally identified with the Mon homeland of Rāmaññadesa in Lower Burma (Myanmar) lying along the coast of the Bay of Bengal from the Irrawaddy (Ayeyarwady) river delta in the west to Martaban in the east. Some chroniclers locate Suvaṇṇabhūmi to the east of the Isthmus of Kra along the southern Thai coast. According to Pāli sources, it was the destination of one of nine Buddhist missions dispatched during the reign of AŚOKA from Pātaliputta (S. PĀṬALIPUTRA, modern Patna) to adjacent lands by the elder MOGGALIPUTTATISSA after the convention of the third Buddhist council (see COUNCIL, THIRD) in the third century BCE. The elders SOṆA AND UTTARA were sent as missionaries to convert Suvaṇṇabhūmi. The third Buddhist council at Pātaliputta and the nine Buddhist missions are known only in Pāli sources and are first recorded in the fifth-century DĪPAVAṂSA.

**Suvarṇadvīpa**. (S). One of the twenty-four sacred sites associated with the CAKRASAṂVARATANTRA. See PĪṬHA.

**Suvarṇaprabhāsottamasūtra**. (T. Gser 'od dam pa'i mdo; C. Jinguangming zuishengwang jing; J. Konkōmyō saishōōkyō; K. Kŭmgwangmyŏng ch'oesŭngwang kyŏng 金光明最勝王經). In Sanskrit, "Sūtra of Supreme Golden Light," an influential MAHĀYĀNA sūtra, especially in East Asia. Scholars speculate that the text originated in India in the fourth century and was gradually augmented. It was translated into Chinese by YIJING in 703. The sūtra contains many DHĀRAṆĪ and is considered by some to be a proto-tantric text; in some editions of the Tibetan canon it is classified as a TANTRA. It is important in East Asian Buddhism for two main reasons. First was the role the sūtra played in conceptualizing state-protection Buddhism (HUGUO FOJIAO). The sūtra declares that deities will protect the lands of rulers who worship and uphold the sūtra, bringing peace and prosperity, but will abandon the lands of rulers who do not, such that all manner of catastrophe will befall their kingdoms. The sūtra was thus central to "state protection" practices in East Asia, together with the SADDHARMAPUṆḌARĪKASŪTRA and the RENWANG JING. Second, the sūtra provides the locus classicus for the "water and land ceremony" (SHUILU HUI), a ritual intended for universal salvation, but especially of living creatures who inhabit the most painful domains of SAṂSĀRA; the ceremony was also performed for a variety of this-worldly purposes, including state protection and rain-making. According to the sūtra, in a previous life, the Buddha was a merchant's son named Jalavāhana, who one day encountered a dried-up pond in the forest, filled with thousands of dying fish. Summoning twenty elephants, he carried bags of water from a river into the forest and replenished the pond, saving the fish. He then sent for food with which to feed them. Finally, recalling that anyone who hears the name of the buddha Ratnaśikhin will be reborn in the heavens, he waded into the pond and pronounced the Buddha's name, followed by an exposition of dependent origination. When the fish died, they were reborn in the TRĀYASTRIṂŚA heaven. Recalling the reason for their happy fate, they visited the world of humans, where each offered a pearl necklace to Jalavāhana's head, foot, right side, and left side. The sūtra also tells the story of Prince Mahāsattva who sees a starving tigress and her cubs. He throws himself off a cliff to commit suicide so that the tiger might eat his body (see NAMO BUDDHA). This is one of the most famous cases of DEHADĀNA, or gift of the body.

**Suvarṣaka**. (C. Shansui; J. Zensai; K. Sŏnse 善歲). In Sanskrit, the surname of the founder of the KĀŚYAPĪYA school, one of the eighteen traditional schools of mainstream Indian Buddhism. See KĀŚYAPĪYA.

***suvibhaktadharmacakra**. (T. legs par rnam par phye ba dang ldan pa'i chos 'khor; C. zhengzhuan falun; J. shōtenpōrin; K. chŭngjŏn pŏmnyun 證轉法輪). In Sanskrit, lit., "the dharma wheel that makes a fine delineation"; the third of the three turnings of the wheel of the dharma described in the SAṂDHINIRMOCANASŪTRA, said to have been delivered in VAIŚĀLĪ. It is also known as the PARAMĀRTHAVINIŚCAYADHARMACAKRA, or "the dharma wheel for ascertaining the ultimate," as the pravicayadharmacakra, or "the dharma wheel of investigation," and simply as the antyadharmacakra or "final wheel of the dharma." The sūtra identifies this as a teaching for bodhisattvas and classifies it as definitive (NĪTĀRTHA); this third turning of the wheel is the teaching of the *Saṃdhinirmocanasūtra* itself. According to the commentators, in this sūtra the Buddha, through his anamuensis Paramārthasamudgata, sets forth in clear and plain language what he means by his provisional statements in the first wheel of the dharma (see CATUḤSATYADHARMACAKRA), namely, that the FOUR NOBLE TRUTHS exist; and his statement in his middle wheel of the dharma in the PRAJÑĀPĀRAMITĀ SŪTRAS (perfection of wisdom sūtras) (see ALAKṢAṆADHARMACAKRA) that no dharmas exist. Both of the first two wheels are declared to be provisional (NEYĀRTHA). Here, in this definitive teaching called "the dharma wheel that makes a fine delineation," he says that dharmas have three natures (TRISVABHĀVA), and each of those in its own way lacks an intrinsic nature (SVABHĀVA). The three natures are the PARIKALPITA or imaginary nature, the PARATANTRA or dependent nature, and the PARINIṢPANNA or consummate nature. ¶ In Tibet there were different schools of interpretation of the three wheels of doctrine. The third Karma pa RANG 'BYUNG RDO RJE, DOL PO PA SHES RAB RGYAL MTSHAN, and the nineteenth-century RIS MED masters assert that the *Saṃdhinirmocanasūtra*'s third wheel of dharma is definitive and teaches a great MADHYAMAKA (DBU MA CHEN PO). They say this great Madhyamaka is set forth with great clarity in the ŚRĪMĀLĀDEVĪSIṂHANĀDASŪTRA and, particularly, in the RATNAGOTRAVIBHĀGA ("Delineation of the Jewel Lineage"; alt. title, *Uttaratantra*). They argue that in the second turning of the wheel, the prajñāpāramitā sūtras, the Buddha uses apophatic language to stress the need to eliminate KLEŚAs and false superimpositions. He does not clearly delineate, as he does in the third turning, the TATHĀGATAGARBHA, which is both empty (śūnya) of all afflictions (kleśa) and nonempty (aśūnya), viz., full of all the Buddha's virtues. Hence they assert that the third turning of dharma in the *Samdhinirmocanasūtra* sets forth the "great Madhyamaka" (dbu ma chen po), and is a definitive teaching that avoids both apophatic and kataphatic extremes. Others, most notably TSONG KHA PA, disagree, asserting that the *Saṃdhinirmocanasūtra*'s second turning of the wheel is the definitive teaching of the Buddha, and say that its third turning, i.e., the presentation of Buddhist tenets in the *Saṃdhinirmocanasūtra*, is a Yogācāra teaching intended for those temporarily incapable of understanding Madhyamaka.

**Suvikrāntavikrāmiparipṛcchāprajñāpāramitā**. (T. Rab kyi rtsal gyis rnam par gnon pas shus pa shes rab kyi pha rol tu phyin pa; C. Shengtian wang bore boluomi jing; J. Shōtennō hannya haramikkyō; K. Sŭngch'ŏn wang panya paramil kyŏng 勝天王般若波羅蜜經). In Sanskrit, the "Perfection of Wisdom Requested by Suvikrāntavikrāmin." A PRAJÑĀPĀRAMITĀ ("perfection of wisdom") sūtra in seven chapters, it is closely related to the first two chapters of the AṢṬASĀHASRIKĀPRAJÑĀPĀRAMITĀ in its themes, and displays a great familiarity with the various categories of the ABHIDHARMA, more so than other prajñāpāramitā sūtras. In the fourth chapter, it uses twelve similes for dharmas and the PRAJÑĀPĀRAMITĀ, including a reflection, a mirage, an echo, the pith of a banana tree, and a bubble (cf. LIUYU, AṢṬAMĀYOPĀMA). The PRAJÑĀPĀRAMITĀ is described as inaccessible and unestablished (apariniṣpannā) but pure and infinite. In the fifth chapter, ŚĀRIPUTRA asks SUBHŪTI to explain the dharma but Subhūti replies that there is nothing to explain.

**Suvinda**. (S). See SUBINDA.

**Suyŏn**. (K) (秀演). See MUYONG SUYŎN.

**Suzuki, Daisetz Teitaro**. (鈴木大拙[貞太郎]) (1870–1966). A Japanese scholar of Zen Buddhism, widely regarded as the person most responsible for introducing ZEN thought to the West. Born in Kanazawa, D. T. Suzuki, as he is usually known in Western writings, was the son of a physician. He taught English in primary schools before enrolling in what is now Waseda University in Tokyo. While he was a university student, he traveled to Kamakura to practice Zen meditation at the monastery of ENGAKUJI under the direction of the RINZAI master SHAKU SŌEN. He became Sōen's disciple and translated into English Sōen's lecture for the 1893 World's Parliament of Religions. Sōen subsequently arranged for Suzuki to travel to America to work with PAUL CARUS, author of *The Gospel of Buddha* and a leading proponent of Buddhism in America. Suzuki lived with Carus' family in LaSalle, Illinois from 1897 to 1908, producing translations and writing his first book in English, *Outlines of Mahayana Buddhism* (1907). He returned to Japan in 1909, where he taught English until 1921, when he accepted a chair in Buddhist philosophy at Ōtani University in Kyoto. In 1911, he married an American student of Buddhism, Beatrice Erskine Lane (1878–1939), who served as the coeditor of many of his books and published her own studies of Mahāyāna Buddhism. Suzuki remained in Japan during World War II, but in 1950, after the war, he returned to the United States and lectured on Zen Buddhism at a number of universities, including Columbia University, where he was a long-time visiting professor. Suzuki was a prolific author in both Japanese and English, and eventually came to be renowned in both academic traditions. Because Suzuki was something of an autodidact in Buddhism, he initially struggled to be accepted into the mainstream of Japanese academe, but his prodigious output (his writings in Japanese filled thirty-two volumes) and his emphasis on the Indian and Chinese foundations of Japanese Buddhism (at a time when Japanese nationalist interpretations of Buddhism were the order of the day) eventually brought him wide respect at home. In the West, he wrote on both Mahāyāna Buddhism and Zen. His writings on Mahāyāna Buddhism include his highly regarded English translation and study of the LAṄKĀVATĀRASŪTRA and a critical edition of the Sanskrit recension of the GAṆḌAVYŪHA. But Suzuki's most influential works in English scholarship are his voluminous writings on the Zen tradition, including his three-volume *Essays in Zen Buddhism*, *An Introduction to Zen Buddhism*, *The Training of a Zen Buddhist Monk*, and *Zen and Japanese Culture*. These books, for the first time, made Zen philosophy and history serious topics of Buddhological research, and also inspired many Zen popularizers, such as ALAN WATTS and JACK KEROUAC, whose works introduced the notion of "Zen" to the Western popular imagination. Suzuki also mentored many of the preeminent Western Buddhologists of the mid-twentieth century; even the notorious curmudgeon EDWARD CONZE gushed over Suzuki, such was his high regard for his Japanese colleague. Suzuki died in Tokyo at the age of ninety-six.

**Suzuki Shōzan**. [alt. Suzuki Shōsan] (鈴木正三) (1579–1655). Japanese ZEN monk of the Tokugawa period. Suzuki Shōzan was born into a samurai family in Mikawa, present-day Aichi prefecture. He is said to have fought under Tokugawa Ieyasu (1543–1616) at Sekigahara in 1600 and again at Ōsaka fourteen years later. He retired from lay life at the age of forty-one, and during this retirement he studied under various teachers such as DAIGU SŌCHIKU and GUDŌ TŌSHOKU of the RINZAISHŪ and Bannan Eishu (1591–1654) of the SŌTŌSHŪ. Whether he inherited the lineages of any of these figures is unclear. He established several temples throughout the country, which are now registered with the Sōtō Zen sect. At these temples, he taught a unique form of Zen called Niōzen or Ninōzen, which emphasized the fearsome cultivation of Zen in everyday life. He left many writings including the *Roankyō* ("Donkey-Saddle Bridge"), *Ninin bikuni* ("Two Nuns"), *Mōanjō* ("A Safe Staff for the Blind"), and *Banmin dokuyō* ("Right Action for All").

**Suzuki Shunryū**. (鈴木俊隆) (1904–1971). Japanese ZEN priest influential in American Buddhism during the mid-twentieth century. Suzuki Shunryū was born in a village forty miles southwest of Tokyo, the son of a poor Zen priest. After elementary school, he went to live at a temple run by a disciple of his father. He was ordained as a novice monk in 1917. After completing his secondary school education, where he excelled at English, he attended Komazawa University in Tokyo, the university affiliated with the Sōtō sect of Zen, graduating in 1930. He then went on to train at EIHEJI, the head temple of the SŌTŌSHŪ. In 1932, he took over as priest of his father's temple before moving on to serve as abbot at the larger temple of Rinsōin. He married in 1935. He spent the war years at Rinsōin and, unlike many Buddhist priests, did not actively support the war, although his temple was used to house soldiers, Korean laborers, and children displaced by the bombing of Tokyo. After the war, he engaged in a common occupation of Zen priests: performing services for the dead, while also opening a kindergarten. In 1959, he accepted a post offered by the headquarters of the Sōtō sect to serve as priest at a Japanese-American Zen temple in San Francisco, where he performed religious services for a community of some sixty families. He began to give lectures in English and to lead meditation retreats at the San Francisco temple. He continued to serve as priest to the Japanese community until 1969, when the tensions between his Japanese parishioners and his American disciples led him to resign from his original position. He then founded the San Francisco Zen Center, which eventually established both a residential center in the city, a mountain center in Tassajara, and a farm at Green Gulch. In 1970, an edited version of some of his lectures were published as *Zen Mind, Beginner's Mind*, a work that became a bestseller and classic of American Zen. Suzuki died in San Francisco in 1971.

**svabhāva**. (T. rang bzhin; C. zixing; J. jishō; K. chasŏng 自性). In Sanskrit, "self-nature," "intrinsic existence," or "inherent existence," the term has a general sense of "essence" or "nature," but is used in philosophical literature. It has at least three important, and different, usages, in MAHĀYĀNA Buddhist doctrine. In the MADHYAMAKA school, it refers to a hypostatized and reified nature that is falsely attributed to phenomena by ignorance, such that phenomena are mistakenly conceived to exist in and of themselves. In this sense, it is used as a synonym for ĀTMAN. Therefore, there is no svabhāva, nothing possesses svabhāva, and all phenomena are said to lack, or be empty of, svabhāva. This doctrine is sufficiently central to Madhyamaka that the school is also called NIḤSVABHĀVAVĀDA, the "Proponents of No Svabhāva." In YOGĀCĀRA, as represented in the SAṂDHINIRMOCANASŪTRA, all phenomena can be categorized into three natures (TRISVABHĀVA): the imaginary (PARIKALPITA), the dependent (PARATANTRA), and the consummate (PARINIṢPANNA). In the LAṄKĀVATĀRASŪTRA, seven forms of svabhāva or natures are enumerated to account for the functioning of phenomena: (1) samudayasvabhāva (C. jixing zixing), the nature of things that derives from the interaction between various conditions; (2) bhāvasvabhāva (C. xing zixing), the nature that is intrinsic to things themselves; (3) lakṣaṇasvabhāva (C. xiangxing zixing), the characteristics or marks (LAKṢAṆA) that distinguish one thing from another; (4) mahābhūtasvabhāva (C. dazhongxing zixing), the nature of things that derives from being constituted by the four physical elements (MAHĀBHŪTA); (5) hetusvabhāva (C. yinxing zixing), the nature of things that is derived from the "proximate causes" (HETU) that are necessary for their production; (6) pratyayasvabhāva (C. yuanxing zixing), the nature derived from the "facilitating conditions" (PRATYAYA); (7) niṣpattisvabhāva (C. chengxing zixing), the consummate, actualized buddha-nature that is the fundamental reality of things. See also NIḤSVABHĀVA.

**svabhāvakāya**. (T. ngo bo nyid sku; C. zixing shen; J. jishōshin; K. chasŏng sin 自性身). In Sanskrit, lit. "self-nature body," the buddha-body in its most elemental nature (also seen written as svābhāvikakāya); one of the four types of buddha bodies (BUDDHAKĀYA) discussed in the BUDDHABHŪMIŚĀSTRA (*Fodijing lun*), the MAHĀYĀNASAMGRAHA (*She dasheng lun*), and the CHENG WEISHI LUN (**Vijñaptimātratāsiddhiśāstra*), along with the "body intended for personal enjoyment" (SVASAṂBHOGAKĀYA), the "body intended for others' enjoyment" (PARASAṂBHOGAKĀYA), and the "transformation body" (NIRMĀṆAKĀYA). This type of buddha-body is functionally equivalent to the DHARMAKĀYA in the two or "three bodies" (TRIKĀYA) schema of buddha-bodies. ¶ A different understanding of the svabhāvakāya derives from the PRAJÑĀPĀRAMITĀ literature. The final chapter of the ABHISAMAYĀLAṂKĀRA sets forth an elliptic presentation of the svabhāvakāya that led to a number of different later interpretations. According to Ārya VIMUKTISENA's interpretation, the svabhāvakāya is not a separate buddha-body, but rather the ultimate nature (in essence, the emptiness or ŚŪNYATĀ) that locates or underpins the other three bodies (the dharmakāya, SAṂBHOGAKĀYA, and nirmāṇakāya). He proposes just three bodies. HARIBHADRA disagrees with this interpretation and proposes four bodies. Strongly influenced by YOGĀCĀRA thought, he privileges the dharmakāya and says it has two parts: a knowledge body (JÑĀNADHARMAKĀYA), which is a buddha's omniscient mind, and a svabhāvakāya, which is the ultimate nature of that mind. This controversy was widely debated in Tibet in the commentarial tradition.

**svabhāvaśūnya**. (T. rang bzhin gyis stong pa; C. zixing kong; J. jishōkū; K. chasŏng kong 自性空). In Sanskrit, "empty of intrinsic nature," a term used in the MADHYAMAKA school to specify that all persons and phenomena are empty of an intrinsic nature (SVABHĀVA). The term svabhāva is used in Madhyamaka to refer to a hypostatized and reified nature that is falsely attributed to phenomena by ignorance, such that phenomena are mistakenly conceived to exist in and of themselves. In this sense, it is used as a synonym for ĀTMAN. All phenomena are declared to lack, or be empty of, svabhāva and hence are svabhāvaśūnya. The term svabhāvaśūnyatā, "emptiness of intrinsic nature," is one in the list of emptinesses, sometimes as long as twenty, beginning with adhyātmaśūnyatā ("emptiness of the internal"), bahirdhāśūnyatā ("emptiness of the external"), ubhayaśūnyatā ("emptiness of both,"), and including abhāvaśūnyatā ("emptiness of nonbeing").

**svabhāvavikalpa**. (T. rang bzhin la rnam par rtog pa; C. zixing fenbie; J. jishō funbetsu; K. chasŏng punbyŏl 自性分別). In Sanskrit, "intrinsic discrimination"; the first of the three types of conceptual discrimination (VIKALPA). See TRIVIKALPA.

**Svāgata**. (P. Sāgata; T. Legs 'ongs; C. Shanlai; J. Zenrai; K. Sŏllae 善來). Sanskrit proper name of an eminent ARHAT elder declared by the Buddha to be foremost among his monk disciples in contemplation of the heat element (tejadhātu); also written in BUDDHIST HYBRID SANSKRIT as Sāgata. According to the Pāli account, Sāgata was the personal attendant of the Buddha when SOṆA KOLIVĪSA (S. Śrona-Viṃśatikoṭi/Śrona-Koṭiviṃśa) and eighty thousand companions visited RĀJAGṚHA at the request of King BIMBISĀRA. Sāgata appears to have been naturally endowed with supernatural powers (P. iddhi, S. ṚDDHI) and left such an impression on Soṇa Kolavīsa that he joined the order. At the king's request, Sāgata displayed numerous marvels in the sky and, when asked to show an even greater wonder, he fell at the Buddha's feet and declared him to be his teacher. In the hermitage of the Jaṭilas in Ambatittha (S. Āmratirtha), Sāgata dwelt in a powerful NĀGA's cave, angering him, yet he was easily able to defeat the creature. When the people of Kosambī (S. KAUŚĀMBĪ) heard of this feat, they resolved to honor Svāgata with a feast. The wicked chabbaggīyā (S. ṢAḌVĀRGIKA) monks, jealous of Sāgata's fame, were intent on his undoing, and so recommended to the citizens of Kosambī that they offer him liquor. Sāgata was offered liquor at every house until he fell unconscious and had to be carried back to the Buddha. Although he was laid down properly with his head facing the Buddha, he turned around and lay with his feet towards the Buddha. The Buddha used this occasion to preach about the heedlessness (PRAMĀDA) that arises from intoxication and passed a rule against the use of alcohol and other intoxicants. The next day when Sāgata awoke, he was informed of what had happened and begged the Buddha for forgiveness. After a short while, through diligent practice, he attained insight into the three marks of existence and became an arhat.

**svalakṣaṇa**. (T. rang mtshan; C. zixiang; J. jisō; K. chasang 自相). In Sanskrit, "own characteristic," or "specifically characterized," a term used in contrast to "general" or "generic" "characteristic" (SĀMĀNYALAKṢAṆA). In views that Tibetan doxographers have associated with the SAUTRĀNTIKA school, as set forth in the early chapters of DHARMAKĪRTI's PRAMĀṆAVĀRTTIKA, svalakṣaṇa is used to refer to impermanent things, which are objects of direct perception (PRATYAKṢA) and hence can be perceived in all of their specificity, as opposed to the objects of thought, which must be apprehended through the medium of mental images. For the *PRĀSAṄGIKA branch of MADHYAMAKA, svalakṣaṇa takes on the meaning of "established by means of it own characteristic," and thus is identified as a quality falsely ascribed to persons and phenomena by ignorance, a quality that all phenomena in the universe lack and of which they are empty. Thus, in Madhyamaka, nothing is svalakṣaṇasiddha, or "established by way of own nature." All phenomena lack this quality and are therefore described as SVALAKṢAṆAŚŪNYA.

**svalakṣaṇaśūnya**. (T. rang mtshan gyis stong pa; C. zixiang kong; J. jisōkū; K. chasang kong 自相空). In Sanskrit, "empty of own characteristic," a term is used in the perfection of wisdom (PRAJÑĀPĀRAMITĀ) literature to describe the fundamental truth of all phenomena. According to some ABHIDHARMA schools, the factors (DHARMA) that constitute physical and mental existence were real and were endowed with specific essential qualities (SVALAKṢAṆA). One of the major doctrinal developments present in prajñāpāramitā literature is the assertion that ultimate reality should be properly understood as devoid of such characteristics (svalakṣaṇaśūnya). The term svalakṣaṇa was used in the *PRĀSAṄGIKA branch of MADHYAMAKA to specify an intrinsic nature. In this context, the term svalakṣaṇa takes on the meaning of "established by means of it own characteristic," and thus is identified as a false quality imagined to exist by ignorance, a quality that all phenomena in the universe lack and of which they are empty; hence, they are svalakṣaṇaśūnya.

**Svalpākṣaraprajñāpāramitā**. (T. Shes rab kyi pha rol tu phyin pa yi ge nyung ngu; C. Shengfomu xiaozi bore boluomiduo jing; J. Shōbutsumo shōji hannya haramittakyō; K. Sŏngbulmo soja panya p'aramilta kyŏng 聖佛母小字般若波羅蜜多經). In Sanskrit, "Perfection of Wisdom in a Few Words"; also known as the *Alpākṣaraprajñāpāramitā*. Sometimes referred to in Western scholarship as the "Tantric Heart Sūtra," this brief PRAJÑĀPĀRAMITĀ sūtra that takes the form of a dialogue between the Buddha and AVALOKITEŚVARA, in which the buddha enjoins the bodhisattva to recite the "heart of the perfection of wisdom." The sūtra is directed to those beings of little merit and of limited intellectual capacity. The Buddha enters the SAMĀDHI called "liberation from all suffering" (sarvaduḥkhapramocana) and provides a MANTRA and DHĀRAṆĪ to his audience. The mantra is connected with an earlier buddha called Mahāśākyamuni. By reciting the mantra and the dhāraṇī, hindrances from past actions are extinguished and beings turn toward enlightenment.

**svarga**. (P. sagga; T. mtho ris; C. tianshang; J. tenjō; K. ch'ŏnsang 天上). In Sanskrit, "heaven," the realm of the divinities within the cycle of rebirth (SAṂSĀRA). The terms encompasses the six heavens of the sensuous realm (KĀMADHĀTU) as well as the heavens of the subtle-materiality realm (RŪPADHĀTU) and the immaterial realm (ĀRŪPYADHĀTU). Although sublime states, none of these are permanent abodes; the beings reborn there eventually die and are reborn elsewhere when the causes that led to their celestial births are exhausted. However, the Buddha repeatedly teaches the virtues that result in rebirth in heaven, and such rebirth has been one of the primary goals of Buddhist practice, especially among the laity, throughout the history of Buddhism. Rebirth as a divinity (DEVA) is presumed to be the reward of wholesome acts (KUŚALA-KARMAN) performed in previous lives and is thus considered a salutary, if provisional, religious goal. For example, in his typical "graduated discourse" (P. ANUPUBBIKATHĀ) the Buddha uses the prospect of heavenly rebirth, and its attendant pleasures, as one means of attracting laypersons to the religious life. Despite the many appealing attributes of these heavenly beings, such as their physical beauty, comfortable lives, and long life spans, even heavenly existence is ultimately unsatisfactory because it does not offer permanent release from the continued cycle of birth and death (SAṂSĀRA). Since devas are merely enjoying the rewards of their previous good deeds rather than performing new wholesome actions, they are considered to be spiritually stagnant, such that when the karmic effect of the deed that led to rebirth in heaven is exhausted, they are inevitably reborn in a lower realm of existence (GATI), perhaps even in one of the baleful destinies (DURGATI). For these reasons, Buddhist soteriological literature sometimes condemns religious practice performed solely for the goal of achieving rebirth in the heavens. It is only in certain higher level of the heavens, such as the those belonging to the five pure abodes (ŚUDDHĀVĀSA), that beings are not subject to further rebirth, because they have already eliminated all the fetters (SAṂYOJANA) associated with that realm and are destined to achieve ARHATship. ¶ In traditional Indian cosmology, the heavens of the sensuous realm are thought to rest on and extend far above the peak of Mt. SUMERU, the axis mundi of the universe. They are ranked according to their elevation, so the higher the heaven, the greater the enjoyments of their inhabitants. The lowest of these heavens is the heaven of the four heavenly kings (CĀTURMAHĀRĀJAKĀYIKA), who are protectors of the dharma (DHARMAPĀLA). The highest is the heaven of the divinities who have power over the creations of others, or the divinities who partake of the pleasures created in other heavens (PARANIRMITAVAŚAVARTIN), which is said to be the heaven where MĀRA resides. TUṢITA, the heaven into which ŚĀKYAMUNI was born as the divinity ŚVETAKETU in his penultimate life, is the fourth of the kāmadhātu heavens, in ascending order. ¶ The heavens of the subtle-materiality realm are grouped into four categories that correspond to the four stratified levels of DHYĀNA—states of profound meditative concentration. Thus, rebirth into any one of these heavens is dependent on the attainment of the dhyāna to which it corresponds in the immediately preceding lifetime. Each of the four dhyāna has various heavens. The lowest of these heavens is the heaven of brahmā's retainers (BRAHMAKĀYIKA), which corresponds to the first subtle-materiality absorption (RŪPĀVACARADHYĀNA), and the highest is the highest heaven (AKANIṢṬHA), which is also classified as one of the "pure abodes," or ŚUDDHĀVĀSA. ¶ The heavens of the immaterial realm similarly correspond to the four immaterial dhyānas (ĀRŪPYĀVACARADHYĀNA), beginning with the sphere of infinite space (ĀKĀŚĀNANTYĀYATANA) and so on up to the sphere of neither perception nor nonperception (NAIVASAṂJÑĀNĀSAṂJÑĀYATANA). As noted, despite their many enjoyments, none of these realms is eternal and all are thus understood to fall within the realm of saṃsāra. For a full account of all the heavens, see DEVA.

**svārtha**. (T. rang don; C. zili; J. jiri; K. chari 自利). In Sanskrit, "self-benefit," "benefitting oneself." The term is used in several contexts. First, it may refer to the goal of worldly actions that selfishly seek happiness but, because they are motivated by the afflictions (KLEŚA), in fact result in suffering. Second, the term may be used to describe the goal of the ŚRĀVAKA and PRATYEKABUDDHA, who seek their own welfare by becoming an ARHAT, in contrast to the BODHISATTVA who seeks the welfare of others (PARĀRTHA), willingly relinquishing motivations and deeds that would lead to his own personal benefit. In the case of the bodhisattva, it is said that by following the bodhisattva path to buddhahood, the bodhisattva fulfills both his own welfare (because he achieves the omniscience of a buddha) as well as the welfare of others (because he teaches the dharma so that others may also become buddhas).

**svārthānumāna**. (T. rang don rjes dpag; C. zibiliang; J. jihiryō; K. chabiryang 自比量). In Sanskrit, "inference for oneself," a term used in Buddhist logic to refer to what would generally be referred to as a correct inference, that is, a mental process of reasoning that results in a factual assumption about a particular state of affairs. Technically speaking, inference for oneself is a conceptual consciousness that discerns an object by means of a sign or reason (LIṄGA) that has the three qualities (trirūpa) of legitimate evidence. This refers to three relations that must obtain between the three elements of a syllogism: the subject, the predicate, and the reason. The three qualities are (1) the PAKṢADHARMA, that the reason is a quality of the subject; (2) the forward pervasion (anvayavyāpti), that whatever is the reason is necessarily the predicate; and (3) the "exclusion" or reverse pervasion (vyatirekavyāpti), that whatever is not the predicate is necessarily not the reason. DIGNĀGA contrasted the inference for oneself with the inference for others (PARĀRTHĀNUMĀNA), which is not an inference in a technical sense, but is used only metaphorically. Inference for others refers to a proof that would be stated to another person, such as an opponent in a debate, in order for that person to arrive at the correct conclusion that one oneself has understood. Because the proof serves as the cause of the other person's inference, it is called an inference for others.

**svasaṃbhogakāya**. (C. zi shouyong shen; J. jijuyūshin; K. cha suyong sin 自受用身). In Sanskrit, "body intended for personal enjoyment," in contrast to the PARASAṂBHOGAKĀYA, "body intended for others' enjoyment"; one of the four types of buddha bodies (BUDDHAKĀYA) discussed in the BUDDHABHŪMIŚĀSTRA (*Fodijing lun*), the MAHĀYĀNASAṂGRAHA (*She dasheng lun*), and the CHENG WEISHI LUN (**Vijñaptimātratāsiddhiśāstra*), along with the "self-nature body" (SVABHĀVAKĀYA or svābhāvikakāya), the "body intended for others' enjoyment" (parasaṃbhogakāya), and the "transformation body" (NIRMĀṆAKĀYA). This fourfold schema of buddha bodies derives from the better-known three bodies of a buddha (TRIKĀYA)—viz., dharma body (DHARMAKĀYA), reward body (SAṂBHOGAKĀYA), and transformation body (nirmāṇakāya)—but distinguishes between these two different types of reward bodies. The svasaṃbhogakāya derives from the countless virtues that originate from the accumulation of immeasurable merit and wisdom over a buddha's infinitely-long career; this body is a perfect, pure, eternal and omnipresent material body that enjoys the bliss of dharma (DHARMAPRĪTI) for oneself until the end of time. By contrast, the parasaṃbhogakāya is a subtle virtuous body deriving from the cognition of equality (SAMATĀJÑĀNA), which resides in a PURE LAND and displays supernatural powers in order to enhance the enjoyment of the dharma by bodhisattvas at all ten stages of the bodhisattva's career (BODHISATTVABHŪMI).

**svasaṃvedana**. (T. rang rig; C. zizheng/zijue; J. jishō/jikaku; K. chajŭng/chagak 自證/自覺). In Sanskrit, lit. "self-knowledge" or "self-awareness," also seen written as svasaṃveda, svasaṃvit, svasaṃvitti. In Buddhist epistemology, svasaṃvedana is that part of consciousness which, during a conscious act of seeing, hearing, thinking, and so on, apprehends not the external sensory object but the knowing consciousness itself. For example, when a visual consciousness (CAKṢURVIJÑĀNA) apprehends a blue color, there is a simultaneous svasaṃvedana that apprehends the cakṣurvijñāna; it is directed at the consciousness, and explains not only how a person knows that he knows, but also how a person can later remember what he saw or heard, and so on. There is disagreement as to whether such a form of consciousness exists, with proponents (usually YOGĀCĀRA) arguing that there must be this consciousness of consciousness in order for there to be memory of past cognitions, and opponents (MADHYAMAKA) propounding a radical form of nonessentialism that explains memory as a mere manipulation of objects with no more than a language-based reality. Beside the basic use of the term svasaṃvedana to explain the nature of consciousness and the mechanism of memory, the issue of the necessary existence of svasaṃvedana was pressed by the Yogācāra school because of how they understood enlightenment (BODHI). They argued that the liberating vision taught by the Buddha consisted of a self-reflexive act that was utterly free of subject-object distortion (GRĀHYAGRĀHAKAVIKALPA). In ordinary persons, they argued, all conscious acts take place within a bifurcation of subject and object, with a sense of distance between the two, because of the residual impressions or latencies (VĀSANĀ) left by ignorance. Infinite numbers of earlier conscious acts have been informed by that particular deeply ingrained ignorance. These impressions are carried at the foundational level of consciousness (ĀLAYAVIJÑĀNA). When they are finally removed by the process of BHĀVANĀ, knowledge (JÑĀNA) purified of distortion emerges in a fundamental transformation (ĀŚRAYAPARĀVṚTTI), thus knowing itself in a nondual vision. Such a vision presupposes self-knowledge. In tantric literature, svasaṃvedana has a less technical sense of a profound and innate knowledge or awareness. See also RIG PA.

**svastika**. (P. sotthika/sotthiya; T. bkra shis ldan/g.yung drung; C. wan/wanzi; J. man/manji; K. man/mancha 卍/萬字). In Sanskrit, lit. "well-being," "auspicious"; a mark of good fortune that is widely used in the Buddhist world as an auspicious symbol in both its right-facing and left-facing forms. It is one of the auspicious marks on the soles of a buddha's feet and it often appears on the chest of buddha images in East Asia (see ANUVYAÑJANA). It commonly appears as a pattern in Buddhist vestments and in various decorative patterns in works of art. Even in the most ancient of Indian art, where the Buddha is represented in aniconic rather that physical form, this symbol is sometimes used to indicate his presence. Although the symbol originated in India, it is subsequently transmitted throughout the Buddhist world and is commonly used as a decorative element on Buddhist temples and shrines. In East Asia, the symbol itself was even constituted as the Sinograph wan ("myriad"). In Tibet, it was translated as g.yung drung, a pre-Buddhist term meaning "eternal" or "unchanging." A variety of theories have been offered on the origin of the svastika symbol, one of the more widely accepted being that it was originally connected with solar worship. ¶ Svastika was also the name of the grass cutter who prepared a seat for the buddha beneath the BODHI TREE.

**svatantrānumāna**. (S). See SVATANTRAPRAYOGA.

**svatantraprayoga**. (T. rang rgyud kyi sbyor ba). In Sanskrit, "autonomous syllogism." Among the many meanings of the term PRAYOGA is its use as a technical term in logic, where it is often translated as "syllogism," and refers to a statement that contains a subject, a predicate, and a reason. A svatantraprayoga leads to a svatantrānumāna (T. rang rgyud rjes dpag), an "autonomous inference." The correct syllogism that gives rise to correct inference is composed of three parts, the subject (dharmin), the property being proved (SĀDHYADHARMA), and the reason (HETU or LIṄGA). For example, consider the syllogism "Sound is impermanent because of being produced." The subject is sound, the property being proved is impermanence, and the reason is being produced. For the syllogism to be correct, three relations must exist among its three components: (1) the reason must be a property (DHARMA) of the subject, also called the "position" (PAKṢA); (2) there must be a relationship of forward pervasion (anvayavyāpti) between the reason and the property being proved (SĀDHYADHARMA), such that whatever is the reason is necessarily the property being proved, and (3) there must be a relationship of "exclusion" or reverse pervasion (vyatirekavyāpti) between the property being proved and the reason such that whatever is not the property being proved is necessarily not the reason. In the example ("Sound is impermanent because of being produced"), the syllogism is correct because the reason ("being produced") is a quality of the subject ("sound"), there is forward pervasion in the sense that whatever is produced is necessarily impermanent, and there is reverse pervasion because whatever is not impermanent is necessarily not produced. It is generally the case in Indian logic that all elements of the syllogism must be accepted by both parties in a debate (see SAMĀNAPRATIBHĀSADHARMIN);

such a syllogism is referred to as an "autonomous syllogism" (svatantrānumāna or svatantraprayoga). In the Madhyamaka school of Indian Buddhist philosophy, there was a controversy over whether such syllogisms were acceptable when a Madhyamaka debated with a proponent of another school. The locus classicus of the controversy is the debate between BHĀVAVIVEKA and CANDRAKĪRTI concerning BUDDHAPĀLITA's commentary on the first chapter of NĀGĀRJUNA's MŪLAMADHYAMAKAKĀRIKĀ. It was Candrakīrti's position that the Madhyamaka should only use consequences (PRASAṄGA) or an inference familiar to others (PARAPRASIDDHĀNUMĀNA), i.e., that they should only draw out the unintended consequences in others' positions; to use an autonomous syllogism implied acceptance of intrinsically established relations among the elements of the syllogism. Bhāvaviveka had argued that it was necessary for the Madhyamaka to state an autonomous syllogism at the conclusion of a debate. Based on this controversy, the Tibetans coined the terms *SVĀTANTRIKA and *PRĀSAṄGIKA to designate these two positions.

***Svātantrika**. (T. rang rgyud pa). In Sanskrit, "Autonomist," one of the two main branches (together with the *PRĀSAṄGIKA or "Consequentialist") of the MADHYAMAKA school in India. It is important to note that the designation Svātantrika as a subschool of Madhyamaka does not occur in Indian literature and was coined retrospectively in Tibet to describe the developments of the Madhyamaka in India. The name *Svātantrika is derived from the insistence on the use of autonomous syllogisms (SVATANTRAPRAYOGA) in debates about the nature of reality, as set forth by BHĀVAVIVEKA and rejected by CANDRAKĪRTI in their respective commentaries on NĀGĀRJUNA's MŪLAMADHYAMAKAKĀRIKĀ. In the Tibetan doxographies, the leading proponents of the *Svātantrika include BHĀVAVIVEKA and ŚĀNTARAKṢITA; the former is regarded as the founder of the SAUTRĀNTIKA-SVĀTANTRIKA branch and the latter is considered the founder of the YOGĀCĀRA-SVĀTANTRIKA branch.

**Svayaṃbhū**. [alt. Svayaṃbhūnāth] (T. 'Phags pa shing kun). A large CAITYA complex located atop a hill at the western edge of the Kathmandu Valley, forming one of Nepal's most ancient and venerated Buddhist sites. The caitya of Svayaṃbhū, whose name literally means "self-arisen" or "self-created," is closely tied to the mythic origins of the Kathmandu Valley. According to legend, in prehistoric times the Kathmandu Valley formed a lake above which the summit of Svayaṃbhū hill rose. The buddha VIPAŚYIN, who is said to predate ŚĀKYAMUNI by several eons, cast a lotus seed into the waters. A lotus blossom grew from this seed, upon which appeared a spontaneously manifested (svayaṃbhū) crystalline caitya radiating five-colored rays of light. This light attracted the attention of the bodhisattva MAÑJUŚRĪ, who was residing at WUTAISHAN in China. Mañjuśrī traveled to Nepal where he miraculously drained the lake, thereby making the Kathmandu Valley an inhabitable land for the spread of Buddhism. The earliest Newar inscriptions at Svayaṃbhū date to the reign of the fifth-century Buddhist king Vṛṣadeva. Over the next 1,500 years, the stūpa and surrounding complex were renovated and expanded numerous times by Newar and Tibetan Buddhist priests. The complex of temples at Svayaṃbhū is under the guardianship of Newar Budddhist priests and it continues to play a central role in the religious lives of Newari and Tibetan Buddhists. According to some accounts, the Tibetan name (literally "Noble All Trees") stems from a legend recounting how the Buddhist sage NĀGĀRJUNA scattered his hair about Svayaṃbhū hill, from which many types of trees miraculously arose. Later Tibetan commentators have argued, however, that shing kun is likely a corruption of the Newar name Shinggu in use during the eighteenth century. According to Tibetan tradition, the Svayaṃbhū caitya is counted as one of Nepal's three great stūpas, along with BODHNĀTH and NAMO BUDDHA.

**Śvetaketu**. (P. Setaketu; T. Dam pa tog dkar po; C. Baijing/Baiying; J. Byakujō/Byakuei; K. Paekchŏng/Paegyŏng 白淨/白英). Proper name of ŚĀKYAMUNI when he was a divinity in the TUṢITA heaven, during his lifetime immediately preceding his attainment of buddhahood. He was a BODHISATTVA of the tenth BHŪMI, appointed as regent of tuṣita by the preceding buddha KĀŚYAPA. As Śvetaketu, he surveyed JAMBUDVĪPA to determine the proper time, place, caste, and family of his final lifetime. Upon his descent into the womb of Queen MĀYĀ, he appointed MAITREYA as regent. Depictions of Śvetaketu in heaven, alongside INDRA and BRAHMĀ, appear at a number of ancient Indian Buddhist sites, including NĀGĀRJUNAKOṆḌĀ and AMARĀVATĪ.

**Swam-oo Ponnya-shin Pagoda**. A gilded pagoda (Burmese, JEDI) located at the center of the Sagaing range of hills in Upper Burma (Myanmar). It is situated atop a prominence known as Dhammika Taung, or the "Hill of the Practitioners," because it has always been surrounded by monasteries suitable for study and meditation. The pagoda was built in 1332 by a royal minister named Ponnya (meaning "Brāhmaṇa") shortly after Sagaing was made the Burmese capital. The minister had neglected to seek the king's permission prior to the monument's construction, and because its foundation buried two earlier pagodas, the king ordered the minister to be drowned. At the last moment the execution order was rescinded, for which reason the pagoda received the name, "Ponnya-shin," meaning, "Ponnya lives." Ponnya made it a practice of donating his first offering of alms during the period of the Buddhist rains retreat (VARṢĀ) at this pagoda. For this reason it also became known as "Swam-oo," or "First alms-offering." To the present day, people pray at this pagoda to ward off any prospect of sudden death, and in Sagaing it is customary to make one's first donation of alms at the beginning of the Buddhist rains retreat season at this pagoda.

**Swāt**. A valley in present-day northern Pakistan, commonly identified with the ancient region known as OḌḌIYĀNA, Uḍḍiyāna, or Udyāna; an important center in the history of

Indian Buddhism. Buddhism moved into this area shortly after the time of King AŚOKA and flourished there in the periods that followed. Swāt contains many important archeological sites including STŪPAs and such relics as the footprints of the Buddha (BUDDHAPĀDA). Many of the first buddha images also come from this region. Swāt's geographical location between Central Asia and the Indian subcontinent made it an important trading and religious center. According to Chinese pilgrims, beginning with FAXIAN, who visited this region in the fifth century CE, this area was at one time home to five hundred Buddhist monasteries. This area is also fabled as the birthplace of PADMASAMBHAVA and the origin of numerous tantric texts and lineages, including the GUHYASAMĀJATANTRA. Several Tibetan masters also wrote accounts of their travels through Oḍḍiyāna, including O RGYAN PA RIN CHEN DPAL, whose name literally means "the man of Oḍḍiyāna," Stag tshang ras pa (Taktsangrepa), and BUDDHAGUPTA. Muslim armies began to moving into the region in the eighth century, which eventually led to the demise of Buddhism.

**Śyāmatārā**. (T. Sgrol ljang). In Sanskrit, "Dark Tārā"; in Tibetan "Green Tārā"; according to a widely held Tibetan myth, the goddess who consorted with a monkey (an emanation of AVALOKITEŚVARA) and gave birth to the Tibetan people. Later, she took the form of the princess BHṚKUṬĪ, Nepalese wife of King SRONG BTSAN SGAM PO. After Avalokiteśvara, Śyāmatārā is perhaps the most widely worshipped Buddhist deity in Tibet and the focus of the nonsectarian Tārā cult. The *Namas Tāre Ekaviṃśatistotra* ("Twenty-One Praises of Tārā") is one of the most widely known prayers in Tibet, and her MANTRA, oṃ tāre tuttāre ture svāha, is second in popularity only to OṂ MAṆI PADME HŪṂ, AVALOKITEŚVARA's mantra. Each Tibetan sect has its own tantric rituals (SĀDHANA) and ritual propitiations (VIDHI) for Green Tārā, who is considered particularly helpful to those building monasteries and other religious structures, and to those starting business ventures. Green Tārā is iconographically represented as sitting in LALITĀSANA with her left leg bent and resting on her lotus seat, her right leg pendant, with the knee slightly raised, the foot resting on a second smaller lotus. ATIŚA DĪPAṂKARAŚRĪJÑĀNA, an Indian Buddhist monk and scholar revered by Tibetan Buddhists as a leading teacher in the later dissemination (PHYI DAR) of Buddhism in Tibet, was a devotee of Green Tārā, and the temple commemorating his principal residence during his later years in central Tibet, in Snye thang (Nyethang), is the Sgrol ma lha khang (Drolma Lhakang) "Tārā Temple," which is widely believed by Tibetans to have a statue of Śyāmatārā that can speak. See also TĀRĀ.

**Śyāmāvatī**. (P. Sāmāvatī; T. Sngo bsangs can; C. Ganrong; J. Kon'yō; K. Kamyong 紺容). Lay disciple whom the Buddha declared to be foremost among laywomen who live in kindness. She was the daughter of a wealthy man from the city of Bhadravatī. When plague broke out in the city, she and her parents fled to Kauśāmbī (P. Kosambī) where her parents fell ill and died. She was adopted by two donors of alms to the poor, Mitra and Ghoṣaka, who noticed her virtue and intelligence. Śyāmāvatī was exceptionally beautiful and one festival day, Udāyana (P. Udena), the king of Kauśāmbī, noticed her on her way to the river to bathe and fell in love with her. Initially rebuffed in his advances, Udāyana eventually wed Śyāmāvatī and made her his chief queen. Śyāmāvatī's slave girl was Kṣudratārā (P. Khujjutarā) who each day was given eight coins to buy flowers from the market. Kṣudratārā was dishonest and would spend four coins on flowers and pocket the rest. One day on her way to the market, Kṣudratārā listened to the Buddha preach and at once became a stream-enterer (SROTAĀPANNA). She then confessed her thievery to Śyāmāvatī, who immediately forgave her, and she told her mistress about the Buddha's teachings. Enthralled, Śyāmāvatī asked Kṣudratārā to listen to the Buddha's sermons daily and report his message to her and her attendants. In this way, under Kṣudratārā's instruction, Śyāmāvatī and her attendants also became stream-enterers. On Kṣudratārā's advice, Śyāmāvatī had holes made in the walls of the women's quarters so that she and her attendants could watch the Buddha as he passed through the lane below. Śyāmāvatī had a wicked co-wife, Māgandiyā, who, out of jealousy of her and a hatred for the Buddha, sought her destruction. Śyāmāvatī survived three plots, which were eventually revealed, winning in compensation the boon to have ĀNANDA preach daily to her and her companions. Finally Māgandiyā had the palace set afire and Śyāmāvatī along with her attendants burned to death. The Buddha declared, however, that none of the deceased had attained less than the state of stream-enterer, while some had even reached the state of once-returners (SAKṚDĀGĀMIN) and nonreturners (ANĀGĀMIN).

**syllogism**. See PRAYOGA.

# T

**Tachikawaryū**. (立川流). A strand of Japanese esoteric Buddhism that is generally regarded as heterodox by the mainstream Shingonshū tradition because of its involvement in ritual sex and magical elements. The school was established in 1114 in the town of Tachikawa (Izu province) by Ninkan (1057–1123), who is known to have combined Daoist yin-yang cosmology with Shingon rituals and taught sexual union as a direct way of attaining buddhahood. Its teachings were subsequently systematized by Raiyu (1226–1304). The school sought to achieve buddhahood in this very body (sokushin jōbutsu) and taught that the loss of self that occurs through ritual sexuality was the most immediate approach to enlightenment; sexual climax, which the school termed the lion's roar (see siṃhanāda), constituted the moment of awakening. The Tachikawaryū was officially proscribed in the thirteenth century and its practices eliminated from the mainstream esoteric tradition through the efforts of the Shingon monk Yūkai (1345–1416). Although its scriptures were lost (except for a few that are said to have been sealed so that they would never be reopened), some of its practices are thought to have continued to circulate in secret in Shingon circles.

**Taegak Ŭich'ŏn**. (K) (大覺義天). See Ŭich'ŏn.

**T'aego chong**. (太古宗). In Korean, "T'aego Order"; an order of Korean married monks established in 1969, in response to the post–Korean War domination of Korean Buddhism by the Chogye chong of celibate monks. The name of the school is taken from the late Koryŏ-period monk T'aego Pou (1310–1382), who was presumed to have introduced the lineage of the Chinese Linji zong (K. Imje chong) to Korea at the end of the Koryŏ dynasty. The Korean monastic tradition had traditionally institutionalized celibacy throughout its history, but during the Japanese colonial period in Korea (1910–1945), the Japanese government-general had officially sanctioned clergy marriage along with many other reforms of Korean Buddhism that mirrored Japanese policies toward Buddhism in Japan during the Meiji Restoration. Following liberation from Japan in 1945, the celibate monks of Korea launched a purification movement (chŏnghwa undong) in 1955 to remove all vestiges of Japanese influence from Korean Buddhism, including the institution of clergy marriage. This campaign was supported by the Korean president Syngman Rhee, who issued a series of orders calling for the resignation of all "Waesaek sŭngnyŏ" (Japanized monks) from monastic positions. The married monks regarded these orders as the beginning of a pŏmnan (C. fanan), or persecution, of their way of life. The schism between the two sides deepened, often involving violent confrontations and continuing litigation. In 1961, a Korean Supreme Court ruling formally returned administrative control of virtually all the major monasteries to the celibate monks of the Chogye chong. In 1969, the remaining married monks who refused to leave their families split from the Chogye chong and, under the leadership of Taeryun (1884–1979), organized themselves into the T'aego chong. The T'aego chong is now the second largest Buddhist order in Korea, following the Chogye chong, which continues officially to observe celibacy. The major monasteries that remain under the control of the T'aego chong are T'aegosa and Pongwŏnsa in Seoul and Sŏnamsa in South Chŏlla province.

**T'aego Pou**. (太古普愚) (1301–1382). In Korean, "Grand Ancient, Universal Stupidity"; Sŏn master of the late Koryŏ dynasty, who is presumed to have introduced the lineage of the Linji zong (K. Imje chong) of the Chinese Chan school to Korea. T'aego was a native of Hongju in present-day South Ch'ungchŏng province. He is said to have been born into the prominent family of a court official and ordained as a youth in 1313 by the monk Kwangji (d.u.) at the monastery of Hoeamsa (Kyŏnggi province). T'aego later passed the clerical examinations (sŭngkwa) for specialists of the Hwaŏm (C. Huayan) school in 1329. While investigating the Chan case (gong'an) "the ten thousand dharmas return to one" (case 45 of the Biyan lu) in 1333, T'aego is said to have attained his first awakening at the monastery of Kamnosa in Sŏngsŏ (South Chŏlla province). Four years later, he is said to have had another awakening while investigating Zhaozhou Congshen's wu gong'an. In 1341, he built a hermitage near the monastery Chŭnghŭngsa on Mt. Samgak (Kyŏnggi province) named T'aegoam, whence he acquired his toponym. In 1346, T'aego headed for China, where he resided at the monastery of Daguangsi in the Yuan capital of Yanjing. T'aego is also said to have visited the eminent Chan master Shiwu Qinggong (1272–1352) and received his seal of transmission (C. yinke, K. in'ga) and thus an affiliation with Shiwu's Linji lineage. After T'aego returned to Korea in 1348, he retired to Miwŏn on Mt. Sosŏl (Kyŏnggi province). In

1356, he was summoned to the Koryŏ capital of Kaesŏng, where he taught at the influential monastery of Pongŭnsa. That same year he was appointed the king's personal instructor, or "royal preceptor" (wangsa), and abbot of the monastery KWANGMYŎNGSA, the major Sŏn monastery in the capital. T'aego continued to serve as the personal advisor to successive kings until his death on Mt. Sosŏl in 1382. His teachings are recorded in the *T'aego hwasang ŏrok*. ¶ In the last half of the twentieth century, attempts to trace the orthodox lineage of the contemporary Korean CHOGYE CHONG back to T'aego and his Chinese Linji lineage rather than to POJO CHINUL (1158–1210) caused a rift within the Korean Buddhist community. The focus of the critique is Chinul's putatively "gradualist" approach to Sŏn Buddhist soteriology (viz., his advocacy of tono chŏmsu, C. DUNWU JIANXIU) and Chinul's lack of an authentic dharma transmission from a recognized Chan or Sŏn master (he is known to have been an autodidact). T'aego was therefore credited with initiating true Sŏn orthodoxy in Korea, based on T'aego's transmission from Shiwu Qinggong, an authentic successor in the Chinese Linji school with its quintessentially "sudden awakening" (DUNWU) soteriology. This issue remains a matter of unremitting controversy in contemporary Chogye order politics. T'aego's name has also been adopted by the T'AEGO CHONG, a modern order of Korean married monks, in order to give a patina of orthodoxy to its school as well.

**Taehan Pulgyo Chogye Chong**. (大韓佛教曹溪宗). In Korean, "Chogye Order of Korean Buddhism"; full name of the largest contemporary order in the Korean Buddhist tradition. See CHOGYE CHONG.

**Taehŭngsa**. (大興寺). In Korean, "Monastery of Great Flourishing"; the twenty-second district monastery (PONSA) of the contemporary CHOGYE CHONG of Korean Buddhism, located on Turyun Mountain in near Haenam County in South Chŏlla province. According to memorial stele erected for early Koryŏ-dynasty monks, the monastery was founded some time before 900 CE, perhaps by either Chŏnggwan (fl. c. 426) or TOSŎN (827–898). During the Japanese Hideyoshi invasions of the late sixteenth century, the monk CH'ŎNGHŎ HYUJŎNG (1520–1604), also known as SŎSAN TAESA, led a monastic militia based at the monastery in fighting the Japanese. After the fighting ended in 1598, Sŏsan proclaimed that Taehŭngsa would never be touched by the "three disasters" (samjae) of flood, fire, or wind, and it was in part due to his efforts that Taehŭngsa became an important Buddhist center. Sŏsan requested that his personal belongings be kept there even after his death, and today his calligraphy, portrait, robe, and bowls can be seen in the monastery's museum. A famous resident was the Sŏn master CH'OŬI ŬISUN (1786–1866), the eighteenth-century reviver of the tea traditions of Korea, who developed the tea ceremony as a form of religious practice and is known for synthesizing the tea ceremony and Sŏn practice, as exemplified in his slogan ta Sŏn ilmi (tea and Sŏn are a single taste). The monastery's main shrine hall (TAEŬNG CHŎN) is approached by use of the Sinjin Bridge and enshrines images of ŚĀKYAMUNI, AMITĀBHA, and BHAIṢAJYAGURU. Taehŭngsa is also known for its Ch'ŏnbul chŏn, "Thousand-Buddha Hall," which enshrines a thousand miniature jade statues of the Buddha, all carved in Kyŏngju about 250 years ago. There is a story that the ship transporting the buddha images was hijacked by Japanese pirates, but the pirates later had a dream in which the Buddha severely admonished them and voluntarily returned the statues to Taehŭngsa. The grounds of the monastery also include a three-story stone pagoda from the Koryŏ dynasty, which is said to have held relics (K. sari; S. ŚARĪRA) of the Buddha brought to Korea by the VINAYA master CHAJANG (608–686). A five-inch (twelve-cm) high, seated bronze Buddha was found inside the base during repairs in 1967 to one of the other three-story pagodas, which appears to date back to the Silla dynasty. A seated MAITREYA Buddha is carved on a rock at Taehŭngsa, which is dated to the early Koryŏ dynasty. Taehŭngsa is also the home of a highly decorated bronze bell formerly owned by T'apsansa, which is held aloft by a hook shaped like a dragon.

**Taehwi**. (大煇) (fl. c. 1748). Renowned Korean chanting (pŏmp'ae) monk during the Chosŏn dynasty and author of the *Pŏmŭmjong po* ("Lineage of the Brahmā's Voice School"). See FANBAI.

**Taehyŏn**. [alt. T'aehyŏn] (C. Daxian/Taixian; J. Daiken/Taigen 大賢/太賢) (d.u.; fl. c. mid-eighth century). In Korean, "Great/Grand Sagacity"; Silla-dynasty monk during the reign of king Kyŏngdŏk (r. 742–765) and reputed founder of the Yuga (YOGĀCĀRA) tradition in Korea; also known as Ch'ŏnggu Samun ("Green Hill [viz., Korea] ŚRAMAṆA") and often referred to as Yuga cho, "Patriarch of Yogācāra," due to his mastery of that school's complex doctrine. As one of the three most productive scholars of the Silla Buddhist tradition, Taehyŏn is matched in his output only by WŎNHYO (617–686) and Kyŏnghŭng (fl. c. eighth century). Although renowned for his mastery of Yogācāra doctrine, his fifty-two works, in over one hundred rolls, cover a broad range of Buddhist doctrinal material, including Yogācāra, MADHYAMAKA, Hwaŏm (C. HUAYAN ZONG), and bodhisattva-precept texts. It is presumed that Taehyŏn was a disciple of WŎNCH'ŬK's (613–696) student Tojŭng (d.u.), and that his scholastic positions were therefore close to those of the Ximing school, a lineage of FAXIANG ZONG thought that derived from Wŏnch'ŭk; their connection remains, however, a matter of debate. Taehyŏn's *Sŏng yusik non hakki* ("Study Notes to the CHENG WEISHI LUN [**Vijñaptimātratāsiddhi-śāstra*]") (six rolls), the only complete Korean commentary on the *Cheng weishi lun* that is still extant, is particularly important because of its copious citation of the works of contemporary Yogācāra exegetes, such as KUIJI (632–682) and Wŏnch'ŭk. Taehyŏn appears to have been influenced by the preeminent Silla scholiast Wŏnhyo, since Taehyŏn accepts in his *Taesŭng kisin non naeŭi yak tamgi* ("Brief

Investigation of the Inner Meaning of the DASHENG QIXIN LUN") Wŏnhyo's ecumenical (HWAJAENG) perspective on the "Awakening of Faith According to the Mahāyāna." Although Taehyŏn never traveled abroad, his works circulated throughout East Asia and were commented upon by both Chinese and Japanese exegetes. His *Pŏmmang kyŏng kojŏkki* ("Record of Old Traces of the FANWANG JING"), for example, was widely consulted in Japan and more than twenty commentaries on Taehyŏn's text were composed by Japanese monks, including EISON (1201–1290) and GYŌNEN (1240–1321). Unfortunately, only five of Taehyŏn's works are extant; in addition to the above three texts, these are his *Yaksa ponwŏn kyŏng kojŏkki* ("Record of Old Traces of the BHAIṢAJYAGURUSŪTRA") and *Pŏmmang kyŏng posalgyebon chongyo* ("Doctrinal Essentials of the Bodhisattva's Code of Morality from the 'Sūtra of Brahmā's Net'").

**t'aenghwa**. (幀畫). In Korean, lit. "painting"; referring to the large "hanging paintings" painted on cloth or paper, which are hung on the inside walls of Korean shrine halls or behind buddha images on the altars. The term t'aenghwa may have been in use since the Koryŏ dynasty (918–1392), since a painting from 1306 includes the Sinograph t'aeng in its title. Because of their vulnerability to fire, most extant t'aenghwa date from the seventeenth century onward, the period following the depredations caused by the Japanese Hideyoshi invasions (1592–1598) of the Korean peninsula. T'aenghwa tend to depict different arrangements of various buddhas, BODHISATTVAS, and ARHATS, with guardians illustrated around the perimeter of the painting. Although t'aenghwa are usually painted in full color, it is possible to find them in various restrained formats such as gold and white on a black or red background; in this type, the lines are generally drawn in gold, while the skin is painted in white. There are no examples of this restrained type of t'aenghwa before the late 1800s. In main shrine halls, t'aenghwa tend to come in sets of three, with a main painting behind the central image and accompanying paintings on the walls to the left and right of the altar. Popular themes for such central t'aenghwa include the Buddha lecturing at Vulture Peak (GṚDHRAKŪṬAPARVATA), the PURE LAND of AMITĀBHA, the medicine buddha BHAIṢAJYAGURU with the twelve zodiacal signs, and stories from Buddhist history. The t'aenghwa on the right is usually the "host of spirits" (SINJUNG) hanging painting, and shows the LOKAPĀLAS, with the dharma protector KUMĀRABHŪTA (K. Tongjin) prominently featured. Kumārabhūta is typically portrayed wearing a grand, feathered headdress accompanied by over a dozen associates, who aid him in protecting the religion. The t'aenghwa on the left often commemorates the deceased and features the bodhisattva KṢITIGARBHA, who has vowed to rescue all beings from the hells. Sometimes monasteries with restricted budgets or space will use t'aenghwa without accompanying statues, especially for the t'aenghwas to the left and right. T'aenghwa in smaller shrine halls may include paintings of the mountain spirit (K. sansin), the guardian kings, and the seven star (ch'ilsŏng; see BEIDOU QIXING) spirits of the Big Dipper. ¶ Large hanging t'aenghwa, which were traditionally displayed outdoors during Buddhist ceremonies, are known as KWAEBUL. Kwaebul are generally twenty-five to forty feet (eight to twelve m.) high, although one at SSANGGYESA is fifty feet (fifteen m.) in height. Kwaebul with a depiction of a standing MAITREYA are common. The kwaebul are displayed on the Buddha's birthday and during rites such as YŎNGSANJAE, as well as for the funerals of important monks. Kwaebul are the equivalent of the Tibetan THANG KA and were especially popular in the seventeenth century.

**Taeryun**. (大輪) (1884–1979). In Korean, "Great Wheel"; founder of the T'AEGO CHONG of Korean Buddhism. In 1898, at the age of fifteen, he was ordained by Kwagun (d.u.) at the monastery of YUJŎMSA in the Diamond Mountains (KŬMGANGSAN), and later received the full BHIKṢU precepts from the VINAYA master Tongsŏn Chŏngŭi (1856–1936). In 1908, upon the completion of his studies at a Buddhist seminary (kangwŏn), Taeryun left for Seoul, where he served as the administrative director of the monastery of Kakhwangsa (present-day CHOGYESA) for six years. In 1915, he established a branch of Yujŏmsa in Pyongyang. He actively participated in the anti-Japanese and Buddhist reformation movements led by HAN YONGUN. In 1929, he established the monastery of Pŏmnyunsa in Sagandong, Seoul, and became the abbot of Yujŏmsa in 1945. In the 1950s, he served as both the chairman of the board of trustees of what is now Tongguk University and the chief of the general affairs bureau of the CHOGYE CHONG. As a result of an internal conflict between Korean monks over the issue of clerical marriage, he left the Chogye order in 1960 and established the T'aego chong of married monks in 1969.

**Taesŭng kisin non pyŏlgi**. (C. Dasheng qixin lun bieji; J. Daijō kishinron bekki 大乘起信論別記). In Korean, "Separate Record on the 'Awakening of Faith According to the Mahāyāna,'" written by WŎNHYO (617–686); a short commentary on the "Establishing the Meaning" (Liyi fen) and "Explanation" (Jieshi fen) chapters of the DASHENG QIXIN LUN. As Wŏnhyo himself explains, the *Taesŭng kisin non pyŏlgi* was meant to serve as personal notes for future reference, and the ideas broached in the *Taesŭng kisin non pyŏlgi* are expanded upon in detail in Wŏnhyo's longer commentary on the text, the TAESŬNG KISIN NON SO. There is also some evidence that the *pyŏlgi* may have been a transcription of his oral lectures on the *Dasheng qixin lun*, which was to be kept separate from Wŏnhyo's more formal commentary to the text.

**Taesŭng kisin non so**. (C. Dasheng qixin lun shu; J. Daijō kishinron sho 大乘起信論疏). In Korean, "Commentary on the 'Awakening of Faith According to the Mahāyāna'"; an influential commentary on the DASHENG QIXIN LUN composed by the eminent Korean monk WŎNHYO (617–686); also known as the *Haedong so* (lit. the "Korean commentary"). Wŏnhyo's commentary is traditionally regarded as one of the three great commentaries on the

"Awakening of Faith," along with FAZANG's (643–712) DASHENG QIXIN LUN YI JI and JINGYING HUIYUAN's (523–592) *Dasheng qixin lun yishu*. Wŏnhyo's exegesis was especially influential in Fazang's (643–712) understanding of the text. The *Taesŭng kisin non so* builds upon the ideas developed in Wŏnhyo's earlier work, the *Taesŭng kisin non pyŏlgi*, but provides an exhaustive line-by-line exegesis of the entire text. In this commentary, Wŏnhyo attempts to combine MADHYAMAKA and YOGĀCĀRA thought by demonstrating that the "one mind" (K. ilsim; see YIXIN) or TATHĀGATAGARBHA is the ground of all existence. He explains "mind as suchness" (K. sim chinyŏ; C. xin zhenru) and "mind that is subject to production-and-cessation" (K. sim saengmyŏl; C. xin shengmie) as being two aspects of the "one mind." Although Yogācāra and tathāgatagarbha materials formed the basis of his analysis of the *Dasheng qixin lun*, Wŏnhyo introduces Madhyamaka method as well into this commentary; for example, he uses the Madhyamaka tetralemma to explicate ineffable suchness. In distinction to Huiyuan, Wŏnhyo explains the ĀLAYAVIJÑĀNA as consisting of "three subtle characteristics," namely, the characteristic of KARMAN (K. ŏpsang; C. yexing), perceiving subject (K. nŭnggyŏn sang; C. nengjian xiang), and perceived objects (K. kyŏnggye sang; C. jingjie xing), which was adopted later by the Chinese Huayan master Fazang in his own commentary on the *Dasheng qixin lun*.

**taeung chŏn**. (大雄殿). In Korean, "basilica of the great hero"; the main worship hall in a Korean Buddhist monastery, where the main Buddha image of the monastery will be enshrined. The taeung chŏn is typically the largest shrine hall on the monastic campus and is intended to serve as the center of institutional life. Most of the monastery's residents will gather in this basilica for daily services in the early morning, before the noontime meal, and in the evening; other ceremonies and rituals that require the attendance of most of the monks will also be held in this hall. "Great hero" is an epithet for a buddha, and which "great hero" is enshrined in the hall will vary from monastery to monastery, although VAIROCANA and ŚĀKYAMUNI are most common. The taeung chŏn at T'ONGDOSA is unusual in Korea for having no enshrined image; instead, the back of the basilica is open and looks out on a STŪPA that is said to contain relics (K. sari; S. ŚARĪRA) of the Buddha himself; the relics thus represent the Buddha's presence in the monastery, rendering an image superfluous.

**taigong**. (C) (胎宮). See BIANDI.

**taimitsu**. (J) (台密). See MIKKYŌ.

**Taisekiji**. (大石寺). In Japanese, lit., "Great Stone Temple"; located on the lower slopes of Mount Fuji in Shizuoka Prefecture. The temple was originally named Daibō (Great Lodging) but takes its current name after Ōishigahara (Great Stone Field), the tract of land where it was first established. Taisekiji is the administrative head temple (sōhonzan) of the NICHIREN SHŌSHŪ school of Japanese Buddhism, and its abbot serves as the sect's leader. Taisekiji was founded in 1290 by NICHIREN's (1222–1282) principal successor Nichikō (1246–1333), who enshrined at the temple the DAI-GOHONZON (lit. great object of adoration), Nichiren's unique cosmological chart (MAṆḌALA) of the spiritual universe, along with his teacher's ashes and extant writings. The temple's Sanmon gate, built in 1717, is well known, as is the Mutsubō, most recently rebuilt in 1988. The Grand Reception Hall, Daikyakuden, was built in 1465 and rebuilt in 1995. Taisekiji's five-storied wooden pagoda, dating from 1749, faces toward the west rather than the usual south, signifying that Nichiren Buddhism would eventually spread back to the homeland of Buddhism. The Founders Hall, Mieidō, built in 1522, houses an image of Nichiren made in 1388, and Nichiren's autograph of the Dai-gohonzon is enshrined in the sanctuary (kaidan), known also as the Hōanden. Because the temple is the home of the sanctuary where the Dai-gohonzon is enshrined, Taisekiji has long been a major pilgrimage center for both Nichiren Shōshū and later SŌKA GAKKAI adherents; since the 1991 excommunication of the Sōka Gakkai lay organization from the Nichiren Shōshū, however, Sōka Gakkai members are barred from viewing the Dai-gohonzon.

**Taishō shinshū daizōkyō**. (大正新修大藏經). In Japanese, "The Taishō New Edition of the Buddhist Canon"; a modern Japanese edition of the East Asian Buddhist canon (DAZANGJING), edited by TAKAKUSU JUNJIRŌ and Watanabe Kaigyoku and published using movable-type printing between 1924 and 1935, during the Taishō reign era. This edition of the Buddhist canon has become the standard reference source for East Asian Buddhist materials; in Western sources, it is often referred to simply as "The Taishō"; in Korea, it is usually called the *Sinsu taejanggyŏng*. The Taishō canon includes 2,920 texts in eighty-five bound volumes (each volume is about one thousand pages in length), along with twelve volumes devoted to iconography, and three volumes of bibliography and scriptural catalogues, for a total of one hundred volumes. The Taishō's arrangement is constructed following modern scholarly views regarding the historical development of the Buddhist scriptural tradition, with scriptures of the MAINSTREAM BUDDHIST SCHOOLS opening the canon, followed by Indian MAHĀYĀNA materials, indigenous Chinese (and some Korean) writings, and finally Japanese writings:

1. ĀGAMA (vols. 1–2, nos. 1–151)
2. AVADĀNA (vols. 3–4, nos. 152–219)
3. PRAJÑĀPĀRAMITĀ (vols. 5–8, nos. 220–261)
4. SADDHARMAPUṆḌARĪKA (vol. 9, nos. 262–277)
5. AVATAṂSAKA/GAṆḌAVYŪHA (vols. 9–10, nos. 278–309)
6. RATNAKŪṬA (vols. 11–12, nos. 310–373)
7. MAHĀPARINIRVĀṆA (vol. 12, nos. 374–396)
8. MAHĀSAṂNIPĀTA (vol. 13, nos. 397–424)
9. Miscellaneous sūtras (vols. 14–17, nos. 425–847), e.g., YOGĀCĀRABHŪMI (nos. 602–620)

RATNAMEGHA (nos. 658–660)
SUVARṆAPRABHĀSA (nos. 663–665)
TATHĀGATAGARBHA (nos. 666–667)
LAṄKĀVATĀRA (nos. 670–672)
SAMDHINIRMOCANA (nos. 675–679)
BUDDHABHŪMI (no. 680)
GHANAVYŪHA (nos. 681–682)

10. Esoteric Buddhism (vols. 18–21, nos. 848–1420), e.g.,
SARVATATHĀGATATATTVASAṂGRAHA (vol. 18, no. 866)
MAHĀMĀYŪRĪ (vol. 19, nos. 982–988)
11. VINAYA (vols. 22–24, nos. 1421–1506), e.g.,
MAHĪŚĀSAKA (nos. 1421–1424)
MAHĀSĀṂGHIKA (nos. 1425–1427)
DHARMAGUPTAKA (nos. 1428–1434)
SARVĀSTIVĀDA (nos. 1435–1441)
MŪLASARVĀSTIVĀDA (nos. 1442–1459)
MAHĀYĀNA-BODHISATTVA (nos. 1487–1504)
12. Commentaries to Sūtras (vols. 24–26, nos. 1505–1535), e.g.,
Āgamas (nos. 1505–1508)
Mahāyāna sūtras (nos. 1509–1535)
13. ABHIDHARMA (vols. 26–29, nos. 1536–1563), e.g.,
JÑĀNAPRATHĀNA (nos. 1543–1544)
ABHIDHARMAMAHĀVIBHĀṢĀ (nos. 1545)
Vibhāṣā (nos. 1546–1547)
ABHIDHARMAKOŚABHĀṢYA (nos. 1558–1559)
14. MADHYAMAKA (vol. 30, nos. 1564–1578), e.g.,
MŪLAMADHYAMAKAKĀRIKĀ (no. 1564)
*ŚATAŚĀSTRA (no. 1569)
15. YOGĀCĀRA (vols. 30–31, nos. 1579–1627), e.g.,
YOGĀCĀRABHŪMIŚĀSTRA (no. 1579)
*VIJÑAPTIMĀTRATĀSIDDHIŚĀSTRA (Cheng weishi lun; no. 1585)
MAHĀYĀNASAṂGRAHA (nos. 1592–1598)
16. Treatises (vol. 32, nos. 1628–1692), e.g.,
SŪTRASAMUCCAYA (no. 1635)
ŚIKṢĀSAMUCCAYA (no. 1636)
DASHENG QIXIN LUN (nos. 1667–1668)
17. Chinese sūtra commentaries (vols. 33–39)
18. Chinese vinaya commentaries (vol. 40)
19. Chinese śāstra commentaries (vols. 40–44)
20. Chinese sectarian writings (vols. 44–48), e.g.,
HUAYAN school (vol. 45, nos. 1866–1890)
TIANTAI school (vol. 46, nos. 1911–1950)
PURE LAND school (vol. 47, nos. 1957–1984)
CHAN school (vols. 47–48, nos. 1985–2025)
21. Histories (vols. 49–52, nos. 2026–2120), e.g.,
FOZU TONGJI (vol. 49, no. 2035)
GAOSENG ZHUAN collections (vols. 50–51, nos. 2059–2066)
GUANG HONGMINGJI (vol. 52, no. 2103)
22. Encyclopedias and references (vols. 53–54, nos. 2121–2136), e.g.,
FAYUAN ZHULIN (vol. 53, no. 2122)
YIQIEJING YINYI (vol. 54, no. 2128)
23. Non-Buddhist schools (vol. 54, nos. 2137–2144), e.g.,
Saṃkhyakārikā (vol. 54, no. 2137)
24. Scriptural Catalogues (vol. 55, nos. 2145–2184), e.g.,
KAIYUAN SHIJIAO LU (vol. 55, no. 2152)
25. Japanese Buddhist writings (vols. 56–84)
26. Buddhist apocrypha and fragments (vol. 85)
27. Iconography (vols. 86–92)
28. Bibliography and catalogues (vols. 93–100).

The textus receptus for the Taishō was the second Korean xylographic edition of the Buddhist canon, the KORYŎ TAEJANGGYŎNG. This second Koryŏ canon enjoyed such a strong reputation for scholarly accuracy that the Japanese Taishō editors adopted its readings wholesale in preparing their canon—meaning that where there was a Koryŏ edition available for a text, the Taishō editors simply copied it verbatim, listing in footnotes any alternate readings appearing in other canonical editions. Although the Taishō is often considered to be the definitive East Asian canon, it is therefore not a true "critical edition" but, to a large extent, a modern typeset reprint of the xylographical Koryŏ canon, with an updated arrangement of its contents according to modern historiographical criteria. The standard format of the Taishō uses a page with three columns or registers, each register with twenty-nine lines of Sinographs; therefore, it is typical to cite texts included in the Taishō by sequential number in the canon, and/or volume number in the canon, followed by page, register (either a, b, or c) and line number, e.g., *Dafangguang fo huayan jing* (*Buddhāvataṃsakasūtra*) 23, *T* 278:9.542c27 = Chinese text name (Sanskrit name, where relevant), roll (juan) no. 23, *T*[*aishō* canon], sequential no. 278, volume no. 9, page no. 542, register c, line 27. (Note that sometimes the sequential number and the Taishō volume number are reversed, or the sequential number is dropped.) See also DAZANGJING; KORYŎ TAEJANGGYŎNG; SUGI; TRIPIṬAKA.

**Tai Si tu incarnations**. An influential incarnation (SPRUL SKU) lineage in the KARMA BKA' BRGYUD sect of Tibetan Buddhism. The Tai Si tu incarnations are traditionally venerated as emanations of the future buddha MAITREYA and, according to Tibetan sources, early members of the line include the Indian MAHĀSIDDHA ḌOMBĪ HERUKA and the Tibetans MAR PA CHOS KYI BLO GROS and TĀRANĀTHA. As one of the leading incarnate lamas of the Karma bka' brgyud, the Si tu incarnations traditionally maintained a close relationship with the KARMA PAS, the sect's spiritual leader; indeed, the two often alternated as guru and disciple. The first of the line, Chos kyi rgyal mtshan (Chökyi Gyaltsen, 1377–1448), trained under the fifth Karma pa and in 1407 received the honorary title from the Ming Emperor Yongle (r. 1403–1425). Perhaps most famous in the lineage is the eighth Si tu, CHOS KYI 'BYUNG GNAS, who is renowned for his erudition and literary accomplishments. The Tai Si tu lineage includes:

1. Chos kyi rgyal mtshan (1377–1448)
2. Bkra shis rnam rgyal (Tashi Namgyal, 1450–1497)

3. Bkra shis dpal 'byor (Tashi Paljor, 1498–1541)
4. Mi 'khrugs chos kyi go cha (Mitruk Chökyi Gocha, 1542–1585)
5. Chos kyi rgyal mtshan dge legs dpal bzang (Chökyi Gyaltsen Gelek Palsang, 1586–1657)
6. Mi pham phrin las rab brtan (Mipam Trinle Rapten, 1658–1682)
7. Legs bshad smra ba'i nyi ma (Lekshe Mawe Nyima, 1683–1698)
8. Chos kyi 'byung gnas (Chökyi Jungne, 1699–1774)
9. Padma nyin byed dbang po (Pema Nyinje Wangpo, 1774–1853)
10. Padma kun bzang (Pema Kunsang, 1854–1885)
11. Padma dbang mchog rgyal po (Pema Wangchok Gyalpo, 1886–1952)
12. Padma don yod nyin byed dbang po (Pema Dönyö Nyinje Wangpo, b. 1954)

**Taixu**. (太虛) (1889–1947). In Chinese, "Grand Voidness"; a leading figure in the Chinese Buddhist revival during the first half of the twentieth century. Taixu was ordained at the age of fourteen, purportedly because he wanted to acquire the supernatural powers of the buddhas. He studied under the famous Chinese monk, "Eight Fingers" (Bazhi Toutou), so called because he had burned off one finger of each hand in reverence to the Buddha, and achieved an awakening when reading a PRAJÑĀPĀRAMITĀ SŪTRA. In 1908, he joined a group of radicals, including other Buddhist monks, intent on revolution. In 1911, he organized the first of many groups (many of them short-lived) to revitalize Buddhism during this time of national crisis following the fall of the Qing dynasty. In 1912, he was involved in a failed attempt to turn the famous monastery of Chinshansi into a modern school for monks. After this disgrace, beginning in 1914, he went into retreat for three years, during which time he studied Buddhist scriptures and formulated plans to revitalize Buddhism, outlined in such works as his 1915 *Zhengli sengqie zhidu lun* ("The Reorganization of the SAṂGHA System"). He drafted a number of such plans over the remainder of his career, although none was ever implemented. In general, these plans called for improved and modernized education for monks and their participation in community and governmental affairs. He believed that Buddhism had become ossified in China and needed to be reformed into a force that would both inspire and improve society. In his view, for an effective reform of the monastic system to take place, Chinese Buddhists had to be educated according to the same standards as those in other Buddhist countries, beginning with Japan. For Taixu, the revival of Chinese Buddhism entailed starting a dialogue with the Buddhist traditions of other Asian countries; hence, a modern Buddhism had to reach out to these traditions and incorporate their intuitions and original insights. It was from these initial ideas that, during the 1920s, Taixu developed a strong interest in Japanese MIKKYŌ and Tibetan VAJRAYĀNA, as well as in the THERAVĀDA tradition of Sri Lanka. Taixu's participation in the "Revival of Tantra" (mijiao chongxing) debates with Wang Hongyuan (1876–1937), a Chinese convert to Japanese SHINGON, demonstrated his eclectic ideas about the reformation of Chinese Buddhism. The first of Taixu's activities after his return to public life was the founding of the Bodhi Society (Jueshe) in Shanghai in 1918. He was involved in the publication of a wide variety of Buddhist periodicals, such as "Masses Enlightenment Weekly," "Sound of Enlightenment," "Buddhist Critic," "New Buddhist Youth," "Modern Saṃgha," "Mind's Light," and the most enduring, "Sound of the Tides" (*Haichaoyin*). In 1922, he founded the Wuchang Buddhist Institute, where he hoped to produce a new generation of Buddhist leaders in China. In 1923, he founded the first of several "world Buddhist organizations," as a result of which he began to travel and lecture widely, becoming well known in Europe and America. He encouraged several of his students to learn the languages and traditions of Buddhist Asia. Among his students who went abroad in Tibet and Sri Lanka, FAZUN was the most accomplished in making several commentaries of late Indian Buddhism available to the Chinese public, thus fostering a comparison between the historical and doctrinal developments of Buddhism in China and in Tibet. In 1928 in Paris, Taixu donated funds for the establishment of the World Buddhist Institute, devoted to the unification of Buddhism and science; it would eventually be renamed Les Amis du Bouddhisme. He lectured in Sri Lanka and arranged an exchange program under which Chinese monks would study there. In 1929, he organized the Chinese Buddhist Society, which would eventually attract millions of members. During the Japanese occupation of China in the 1930s and 1940s, Taixu followed the Nationalist government into retreat in Sichuan. In this period, as a result of his efforts to internationalize Chinese Buddhism, Taixu founded two branches of the Wuchang Institute of Buddhist Studies specializing in Pāli and Tibetan Buddhism: the Pāli Language Institute in Xi'an, and the Sino-Tibetan Institute in Chongqing. In 1937, at the Sino-Tibetan Institute, in his famous essay "Wo de fojiao geming shibai shi" ("History of My Failed Buddhist Revolutions"), Taixu began an earnest self-reflection on his lifelong efforts to reform Chinese Buddhism, deeming them a failure in three domains: conceiving a Buddhist revolution, globalizing Buddhist education, and reorganizing the Chinese Buddhist Association. When the first global Buddhist organization, the WORLD FELLOWSHIP OF BUDDHISTS, was founded in 1950, Taixu, who had died three years earlier, was credited as its inspiration. His insights would eventually be developed and implemented by later generations of Buddhists in China and Taiwan. His collected works were published in sixty-four volumes. Several of the leading figures of modern and contemporary Chinese and Taiwanese Buddhism were close disciples of Taixu, including Fazun (1902–1980), Yinshun (1905–2005), Shengyan (1930–2009), and Xingyun (1927–).

**taizōkai**. (S. *garbhadhātu; C. taizang jie; K. t'aejang kye 胎藏界). In Japanese, "womb realm" or "womb world"; one of the two principal diagrams (MAṆḌALA) used in the esoteric traditions of Japan (see MIKKYŌ), along with the KONGŌKAI ("diamond realm"); this diagram is known in Sanskrit as the garbhadhātu maṇḍala. The taizōkai maṇḍala is believed to be based on instructions found in the MAHĀVAIROCANĀBHISAṂBODHISŪTRA (*Dainichikyō*); the term, however, does not actually appear in any Buddhist scripture and its pictorial form seems to have developed independently of any written documents. Although KŪKAI (774–835) is often recognized as introducing the taizōkai maṇḍala to Japan, in fact various versions developed over time. Use of the two maṇḍalas flourished during the Heian period, gradually becoming central to Japanese TENDAI Buddhism and SHUGENDŌ. The taizōkai consists of twelve cloisters, which contain various bodhisattvas and deities. At the very center of the maṇḍala is located the Cloister of the Central Dais with Eight Petals (J. Chūdaihachiyōin). There, the DHARMAKĀYA MAHĀVAIROCANA sits in the center of an eight-petaled lotus flower, with four companion buddhas and bodhisattvas sitting on its petals. In the four cardinal directions sit the buddhas Ratnaketu (J. Hōdō), Saṃkusumitarāja (J. Kaifukeō), AMITĀBHA (J. Muryōju), and Divyadundubhi-meghanirghoṣa (J. Tenkuraion). In the four ordinal directions sit the bodhisattvas SAMANTABHADRA (J. Fugen), MAÑJUŚRĪ (J. Monju), AVALOKITEŚVARA (J. Kanjizai; Kannon), and MAITREYA (J. Miroku). The central Buddha and the surrounding four buddhas and bodhisattvas represent the five wisdoms (PAÑCAJÑĀNA). ¶ Mahāvairocana's central cloister is surrounded by a series of cloisters in all the four directions. In the eastern section (the topside of the maṇḍala), there are three cloisters from the central cloister at the outside: (1) Cloister of Universal Knowledge (J. Henchiin), in which three deities sit on each side of a triangle; (2) Cloister of ŚĀKYAMUNI (J. Shakain), where Śākyamuni sits surrounded by his disciples, as a manifestation of Mahāvairocana in the phenomenal world; and (3) Cloister of Mañjuśrī (J. Monjuin), in which Mañjuśrī sits surrounded by many attendants. In the western section (the bottom of the maṇḍala), there are also three cloisters: (1) The Cloister of the Mantra Holders (J. Jimyōin) includes the bodhisattva Prajñā surrounded by the four VIDYĀRĀJA: ACALANĀTHA (Fudō), TRAILOKYAVIJAYA (Gōzanze), YAMĀNTAKA (Daiitoku), and an alternate manifestation of Trailokyavijaya. (2) The Cloister of ĀKĀŚAGARBHA (Kokūzōin) represents worldly virtue and merit in the form of Ākāśagarbha. (3) The Cloister of Unsurpassed Attainment (Soshitchiin) includes eight bodhisattvas, symbolizing the achievement of the various virtues through which Mahāvairocana benefits sentient beings. In the southern section (the right side of the maṇḍala), there are two cloisters: (1) Cloister of VAJRAPĀṆI (Kongōshuin); in this cloister, VAJRASATTVA is the main deity, representing the Buddha's wisdom inherent in all sentient beings; and (2) Cloister of Removing Obstacles (Jogaishōin), where sits the bodhisattva SARVANĪVARAṆAVIṢKAMBHIN, representing the elimination of the hindrances to enlightenment. In the northern section (the left side of the maṇḍala), there are also two cloisters: (1) Cloister of the Lotus Division (Rengebuin) where Avalokiteśvara is the central deity; and (2) Cloister of KṢITIGARBHA (Jizōin), dedicated to the bodhisattva who saves those suffering in hell. All of these eleven cloisters are then enclosed by the Cloister of Outer VAJRADHARAS (Ge Kongōbuin), where there are 205 deities, many of them deriving from Indic mythology. In one distinctively Shingon usage, the maṇḍala was placed in the east and the kongōkai stood in juxtaposition across from it. The initiate would then invite all buddhas, bodhisattvas, and divinities into the sacred space, invoking all of their power and ultimately unifying with them. In Shugendō, the two maṇḍalas were often spatially superimposed over mountain geography or worn as robes on the practitioner while entering the mountain.

**Takakusu Junjirō**. (高楠順次郎) (1866–1945). One of the leading Japanese scholars of Indian Buddhism of the early twentieth century, who played a leading role in establishing Japan as a major center of scholarship in Buddhist Studies. He was born, surnamed Sawai, in today's Hiroshima prefecture. He was raised in a JŌDO SHINSHŪ family belonging to the NISHI HONGANJIHA, and he remained a devout layman throughout his life. After primary school, he studied at the leading Jōdo Shinshū educational institution, today's Ryūkoku University, from 1885 to 1889, during which time, through Jōdo Shinshū connections, he was adopted into the Takakusu merchant house of Kōbe. With the support of his adoptive father, he spent the period from 1890 to 1897 in Europe. Through the introduction of the Jōdo Shinshū cleric NANJŌ BUN'YŪ, Takakusu was able to study Indology under FRIEDRICH MAX MÜLLER at Oxford University, receiving a B.A. in 1894 and an M.A. in 1896. While at Oxford, he assisted Müller with the Sacred Books of the East project. The final volume of the series, entitled *Buddhist Mahāyāna Texts* (1894), included the VAJRACCHEDIKĀPRAJÑĀPĀRAMITĀSŪTRA, the PRAJÑĀPĀRAMITĀHṚDAYA, and the three PURE LAND sūtras, all Indian works (or at least so regarded at the time) but selected because of their importance for Japanese Buddhism. Müller's choice of these texts was influenced by Takakusu and Nanjō Bun'yū. The works in *Buddhist Mahāyāna Texts* were translated by Müller, with the exception of the GUAN WULIANGSHOU JING, which was translated by Takakusu. Takakusu also studied in Paris with SYLVAIN LÉVI, with whom he would later collaborate on the *Hōbōgirin* Buddhist encyclopedia project. He returned to Japan in 1897 to lecture in Indian philosophy at Tokyo Imperial University, where he served as professor from 1899 to 1927, being appointed to the chair of Sanskrit studies in 1901. He was a devoted supporter of Esperanto and in 1906 was a founding member of the Japanese Esperantists Association. He supervised and contributed substantially to three monumental publishing projects: (1) the *Upanishaddo zensho*, a Japanese translation of the Upaniṣads (1922–1924); (2) the TAISHŌ SHINSHŪ DAIZŌKYŌ, a modern typeset edition of the East Asian Buddhist canon (see DAZANGJING) (1922–1934); and (3) the *Kokuyaku nanden* *daizōkyō*, a Japanese translation of the Pāli canon of what he called "Southern Buddhism" (1936–1941). For his work on editing the Taishō canon, he was awarded the Prix Stanislas Julien in Sinology from the Institut de France in 1929. Among his English-language publications, he is known especially for *A Record of the Buddhist Religion as Practised in India and the Malay Archipelago* (1896), which is his translation of YIJING's pilgrimage record (NANHAI JIGUI NEIFA ZHUAN), and *Essentials of Buddhist Philosophy* (1947). He died in Shizuoka Prefecture, outside Tokyo.

**Takṣaśilā**. (P. Takkasilā; T. Rdo 'jog; C. Shishi guo; J. Sekishitsu koku; K. Sŏksil kuk 石室國). Capital of GANDHĀRA (in the Punjab province of modern Pakistan), often known in the West by its Greek name Taxila; an important early center of Indian Buddhist learning and transcontinental trade. The city is mentioned frequently in the JĀTAKAS, but not in the Pāli suttas, although it is presumed that the Buddha's physician JĪVAKA studied there. AŚOKA is said to have built a dharmarājika STŪPA and monastery there, which were enlarged when the city was rebuilt following Scythian invasions. Takṣaśilā was a center for both Hindu and Buddhist scholarship, which flourished especially between the first and fifth centuries CE. Among the schools of Indian Buddhism, the SARVĀSTIVĀDA was especially strong in the city. Takṣaśilā was visited by the Chinese pilgrims FAXIAN and XUANZANG, who described it in their travel records.

**Takuan Sōhō**. (沢庵宗彭) (1573–1645). Japanese ZEN master in the RINZAISHŪ, especially known for his treatments of Zen and sword fighting. A native of Tajima in Hyōgo prefecture, he was ordained at a young age and later became a disciple of Shun'oku Sōon (1529–1611) at Sangen'in, a subtemple of the monastery DAITOKUJI, who gave him the name Sōhō. In 1599, Takuan followed Shun'oku to the Zuiganji in Shiga prefecture, but later returned to Sangen'in. In 1601, Takuan visited Itō Shōteki (1539–1612) and became his disciple. In 1607, Takuan was appointed first seat (daiichiza) at DAITOKUJI, but he opted to reside at Tokuzenji and Nanshūji, instead. Takuan was appointed abbot of Daitokuji in 1609, but again he quickly abandoned this position. Takuan later became involved in a political incident (the so-called purple-robe incident; J. shi'e jiken), which led to the forced abdication of Emperor Gomizunoo (r. 1611–1629) and in 1629 to Takuan's exile to Kaminoyama in Uzen (present-day Yamagata prefecture). Takuan had befriended Yagyū Munenori (1571–1646), the swordsman and personal instructor to the shōgun, and while he was in exile composed for him the FUDŌCHI SHINMYŌROKU ("Record of the Mental Sublimity of Immovable Wisdom"). This treatise on Zen and sword fighting draws on the concept of no-mind (J. mushin; C. WUXIN) from the LIUZU TAN JING ("Platform Sūtra of the Sixth Patriarch") to demonstrate the proper method of mind training incumbent on adepts in both the martial arts and Zen meditation. Takuan later returned to Edo (present-day Tōkyō) and, with the support of prominent patrons, became the founding abbot of Tōkaiji in nearby Shinagawa in 1638. He died at the capital in 1645.

**takuhatsu**. (C. tuobo; K. t'akbal 托鉢). In Japanese, lit. "lifting up the bowl," viz., "to seek alms"; the Japanese form of the traditional monastic practice of alms-round (PIṆḌAPĀTA). In Japan, takuhatsu is most commonly associated with the ZEN school and is typically conducted by a small group of monks who walk together through the streets with walking staffs (khakkhara) and bells that alert residents to their presence. Monks typically receive money or uncooked rice in their bowls as alms, rather than the cooked food received by monks in Southeast Asia. See also PĀTRA.

**Tambadīpa**. The region occupied by PAGAN and Sirīkhettarā (Prome) in Middle Burma (Myanmar), it is the southern portion of the Burmese homeland of Sunāparanta-Tambadīpa. The name is most probably derived from Tambapannidīpa, one of several names of Sri Lanka.

**tamnan**. In northern (Lānnā) Thai, "chronicle"; a genre of northern Thai historical writing combining local legends, myths, and Buddhist literary traditions, and written in Lānnā Thai, Mon, or Pāli; this genre flourished in the Lānnā kingdom between the fourteenth and seventeenth centuries. A tamnan generally begins with events in the life of Gotama (S. GAUTAMA) Buddha and continues on to the establishment of the dispensation (P. sāsanā; S. ŚĀSANA) at a specific location. Notable tamnan include the CĀMADEVĪVAMSA, the JINAKĀLAMĀLĪ, and the MŪLASĀSANA.

**tanch'ŏng**. (丹青). In Korean, "red and blue," or more literally "cinnabar and azure-green"; a style of painting colors and patterns on the wooden beams, rafters, and pillars of Korean Buddhist monastery buildings, as well as on palaces and other traditional-style wooden buildings. The five colors used in tanch'ŏng painting are red, azure-green, yellow, black, and white. These colors are related to the five Chinese elements (metal, wood, fire, water, earth) and the five directions (the four cardinal directions plus the center). The paint, made from a thick coating of minerals mixed with glue, protects the wood from burrowing insects and water damage and sets the monasteries and palaces apart from the buildings of private citizens, who were prohibited by law from using the same decorative techniques. Tanch'ŏng painting may date from early in the inception of Buddhism in Korea during the fourth or fifth centuries, and there is evidence of the use of tanch'ŏng during both the Koguryŏ and Silla kingdoms. There are various types of tanch'ŏng, which range from applying a utilitarian base coat, usually in azure-green, to protect the wood, to much more elaborate styles that uses all five colors in geometric patterns, sometimes interspersed with stylized flowers, water lilies, pomegranates, and bubbles. Tanch'ŏng is usually painted using stencils made from perforated paper dusted with chalk to imprint the pattern on the surface to be painted. After the painting is done, an oil coat is spread over the paint to protect and brighten the colors. Some of the best-known examples of tanch'ŏng can be found at the monasteries of Pusŏksa and Sudŏksa.

**tanengi**. (多念義). In Japanese, "the doctrine of multiple recitations," in the Japanese pure land traditions, the practice of multiple or even continuous recitations of the buddha Amitābha's name (J. nenbutsu; C. nianfo). The debate between multiple recitations and a single recitation (ichinengi) emerged in the early Jōdoshū movement of Hōnen (1133–1212). Hōnen himself emphasized faith, stating that even a single moment of faith would be sufficient to bring about rebirth in Amitābha's pure land of sukhāvatī. However, he himself practiced assiduously, chanting the nenbutsu tens of thousands of times a day. Hōnen's disciples Ryūkan (1148–1228) and Shōkōbō Benchō (1162–1238) are especially well known for promoting the tanengi position. Tanengi emphasized the value of a lifetime of practice, in which each moment of a disciple's life would come to be imbued with the power of the nenbutsu. It is said that, thanks to such constant practice, a disciple would gain the assurance of rebirth in sukhāvatī through a vision of Amitābha in the moments before death.

**Tang gaoseng zhuan**. (C) (唐高僧傳). See Gaoseng zhuan; Xu gaoseng zhuan.

**tangho**. (堂號). In Korean, lit. "hall epithet"; a new cognomen given to an especially eminent monk, which is bestowed by his teacher some twenty to thirty years after his ordination, often in conjunction with transmitting the master's lineage to his pupil; this name subsequently serves as the monk's funerary name. The name is typically selected to reflect the designated monk's spiritual attainments and/or the specific practices with which he is identified. For example, the monk Ch'ŏnghŏ Hyujŏng (1520–1604) was given the hall epithet Ch'ŏnghŏdang (Clear and Pure) in recognition of his enlightened understanding. The hall epithet of the monk Hwansŏng Chian (1664–1729), Hwansŏngdang (Calling [People] to Awake), refers to his efforts to disseminate the Buddhist teachings, while Nuram Sikhwal's (1725–1830) epithet Nuramdang (Reticent at the Hermitage) referred to the fact that he often meditated in seclusion deep in the mountains. The term originates from the designation of a person's dwelling and thus signifies the owner of a house. The term also is employed in both Confucian and secular contexts, but its usage in Buddhism seems to be unique to Korea, where it became customary to bestow such names from the late Koryŏ period onward. See also siho.

**tanju**. (短珠). In Japanese and Korean, "short rosary." See japamālā.

**Tanluan**. (J. Donran; K. Tamnan 曇鸞) (c. 476–542). Chinese monk and putative patriarch of the pure land traditions of East Asia. He is said to have become a monk at an early age, after which he devoted himself to the study of the Mahāsaṃnipātasūtra. As his health deteriorated from his intensive studies, Tanluan is said to have resolved to search for a means of attaining immortality. During his search in the south of China, Tanluan purportedly met the Daoist master Tao Hongjing (455–536), who gave him ten rolls of scriptures of the Daoist perfected. Tanluan is then said to have visited Bodhiruci in Luoyang, from whom he received a copy of the Guan Wuliangshou jing. Tanluan subsequently abandoned his initial quest for immortality in favor of the teachings of the buddha Amitābha's pure land (see sukhāvatī). He was later appointed abbot of the monasteries of Dayansi in Bingzhou (present-day Shaanxi province) and Xuanzhongsi in nearby Fenzhou. Tanluan is famous for his commentary on the Wuliangshou jing youpotishe yuansheng ji attributed to Vasubandhu.

**Tannishō**. (歎異抄). In Japanese, "Record of Lamentations on Divergences"; a short collection of the sayings of the Jōdo Shinshū teacher Shinran (1173–1263), compiled by his disciple Yuien (1222–1289). The work consists of eighteen short sections: the first ten sections are direct quotations of Shinran's sayings as recalled by the author; the remaining eight are Yuien's responses to what he considers misinterpretations of Shinran's teachings that arose after his death. The first part of the text, in particular, describes such characteristic teachings of Shinran as "evil people have the right capacity" (akunin shōki), i.e., that Amitābha's compassion is directed primarily to evildoers. The text was little known for centuries after its compilation, even to followers of Jōdo Shinshū, until it was popularized during the Meiji era by the Higashi Honganji reformer Kiyozawa Manshi (1863–1903).

**tantra**. (T. rgyud; C. tanteluo; J. dantokura; K. tant'ŭngna 檀特羅). In Sanskrit, lit. "continuum"; a term derived from the Sanskrit root √tan ("to stretch out," "to weave"), having the sense of an arrangement or a pattern (deployed not only in a ritual, but in military and political contexts as well). The term is thus used to name a manual or handbook that sets forth such arrangements, and is not limited to Buddhism or to Indian religions more broadly. Beyond this, the term is notoriously difficult to define. It can be said, however, that tantra does not carry the connotation of all things esoteric and erotic that it has acquired in the modern West. In Buddhism, the term tantra generally refers to a text that contains esoteric teachings, often ascribed to Śākyamuni or another buddha. Even this, however, is problematic: there are esoteric texts that do not carry the term tantra in their title (such as the Vajraśekharasūtra), and there are nonesoteric texts in whose title the term tantra appears (such as the Uttaratantra). Scholars therefore tend to define tantra (in the textual sense) based on specific sets of elements contained in the texts. These include mantra, maṇḍala, mudrā, initiations (abhiṣeka), fire sacrifices (homa), and feasts

(GAṆACAKRA), all set forth with the aim of gaining powers (SIDDHI), both mundane and supramundane. The mundane powers are traditionally enumerated as involving four activities: pacification of difficulties (ŚĀNTIKA), increase of wealth (PAUṢṬIKA), control of negative forces (VAŚĪKARAṆA), and destruction of enemies (ABHICĀRA). The supramundane power is enlightenment (BODHI). The texts called tantras began to appear in India in the late seventh and early eighth centuries CE, often written in a nonstandard (some would say "corrupt") Sanskrit that included colloquial elements and regional terms. These anonymous texts (including such famous works as the GUHYASAMĀJATANTRA, the CAKRASAṂVARATANTRA, and the HEVAJRATANTRA), typically provided mantras and instructions for drawing maṇḍalas, among a variety of other elements, but their presentation and organization were usually not systematic; these texts came to serve as the "root tantra" for a cycle of related texts. The more systematic of these were the SĀDHANA (lit. "means of achievement"), a ritual manual by a named author, which set forth the specific practices necessary for the attainment of siddhi. The standard form was to create a maṇḍala into which one invited a deity. The meditator would either visualize himself or herself as the deity or visualize the deity as appearing before the meditator. Various offerings would be made, mantras would be recited, and siddhis would be requested. Although scholars continue to explore the relation between the tantras and the MAHĀYĀNA sūtras, tantric exegetes viewed the tantras, like the Mahāyāna sūtras, as being the word of the Buddha (BUDDHAVACANA) and as setting forth forms of practice consistent with the bodhisattva vow and the quest for buddhahood, albeit more quickly than by the conventional path, via what came to be referred to as the VAJRA vehicle (VAJRAYĀNA). Thus, it was said that the Mahāyāna was divided into the pāramitānaya, the "mode of the perfections" set forth in the Mahāyāna sūtras, and the mantranaya, the "mode of the mantras" set forth in the tantras. These two are also, although less commonly, known as the sūtrayāna and the TANTRAYĀNA. In this context, then, the term "tantra" is often used by tantric exegetes in contrast to "sūtra," which is taken to mean the corpus of exoteric teachings of the Buddha. For those who accept the tantras as the word of the Buddha, the term "sūtras and tantras" would thus refer to the entirety of the Buddha's teachings. The corpus of tantras was eventually classified by late Indian Buddhist exegetes into a number of schemata, the most famous of which is the fourfold division into KRIYĀTANTRA, CARYĀTANTRA, YOGATANTRA, and ANUTTARAYOGATANTRA.

**tantrayāna**. In Sanskrit, "vehicle of the tantras"; see TANTRA.

**tantric vows**. (T. rig 'dzin gyi sdom pa; *vidyādharasaṃvara). Any of a number of vows taken as part of a tantric initiation and to be maintained as part of tantric practice. Many tantras list disparate sets of rules, the best known being that found in the *Rgyud rdo rje rtse mo* (the Tibetan version of the VAJRAŚEKHARASŪTRA, a SARVATATHĀGATATATTVASAṂGRAHA explanatory tantra). Such texts enumerate "restraints" or "vows" (SAṂVARA) and pledges (SAMAYA) connected with the five buddha families (BUDDHAKULA; PAÑCATATHĀGATA), and possibly an ordination and confession ceremony modeled on the PRĀTIMOKṢA. These disparate rules were later codified more systematically in a number of tantric texts: the so-called root infractions in the *Vajrayānamūlāpatti* attributed to AŚVAGHOṢA, and an even shorter list of secondary vows in the *Vajrayānasthūlāpatti* attributed to NĀGĀRJUNA. In addition, rules of deportment toward the guru were set forth in works such as the GURUPAÑCĀŚIKĀ ("Fifty Stanzas on the Guru"), also attributed to Aśvaghoṣa. In Tibet, these rules were codified and commented on at length in the "three vow" (SDOM GSUM) literature. The "root infractions" are the following: (1) to disparage the guru, (2) to overstep the words of the buddhas, (3) to be cruel to one's VAJRA siblings (disciples of the same guru), (4) to abandon love for sentient beings, (5) to abandon the two types of BODHICITTA, (6) to disparage the doctrines of one's own and others' schools, (7) to proclaim secrets to the unripened, (8) to scorn the aggregates, (9) to have doubts about the essential purity of all phenomena, (10) to show affection to the wicked, (11) to have false views about emptiness, (12) to disillusion the faithful, (13) not to rely on the pledges, and (14) to disparage women. It is noteworthy that, unlike the prātimokṣa, the infractions here involve attitudes and beliefs, in addition to transgressions of body and speech. It was generally said that receiving the bodhisattva vows was a prerequisite for receiving tantric vows; the prior receipt of prātimokṣa precepts was optional. In expositions of the "three vows," tantric vows are the third, after the prātimokṣa precepts and the bodhisattva precepts. Especially in Tibet there is extensive discussion of the compatibility of the three sets of vows. See also TRISAṂVARA.

**tao**. (C) (道). The obsolete Wade–Giles transcription for the Sinograph DAO (way, path).

**tāpana**. (T. tsha ba; yanre diyu; J. ennetsujigoku; K. yŏmyŏl chiok 炎熱地獄). In Sanskrit and Pāli, "heating"; one of the hot hells, usually identified as the sixth in descending order of depth beneath the continent of JAMBUDVĪPA and in ascending order of the suffering incumbent on denizens of that realm. According to some accounts, the denizens of this hell are burned in a great cauldron of molten metal; according to others, they are impaled on burning staves.

**tapas**. (P. tapa; T. dka' thub; C. kuxing; J. kugyō; K. kohaeng 苦行). In Sanskrit, "severe austerities"; mortification of the flesh, or other extreme forms of religious penance. The Buddha rejected self-mortification as a valid means of practice, after having practiced it himself, to no avail, prior to his enlightenment. For the authorized list of ascetic practices, see DHUTAṄGA.

**Ta pho gtsug lag khang**. (Tapo Tsuklakang). An important Tibetan Buddhist institution, also known as Ta pho chos 'khor, located at an altitude of ten thousand feet (3,050 m.)

along the Spiti River in the modern-day Lahoul and Spiti region of Himachal Pradesh in northwest India. It is situated along two of the former routes of travel between India and Tibet. Over its long existence, Ta pho has been an important center for both scholarship and artistic activity and remains an active Tibetan monastery, preserving many important Buddhist manuscripts, scroll paintings, statues, and murals. It was established in 996 by the king of the western Tibetan region of GU GE YE SHES 'OD and the translator RIN CHEN BZANG PO. According to traditional histories, at the age of seventeen, Rin chen bzang po was sent to India together with a group of twenty other youths by King Ye shes 'od to study Sanskrit and Indian vernacular languages. Rin chen bzang po made several trips to India, spending a total of seventeen years in Kashmir and the Buddhist monastic university of VIKRAMAŚĪLA before returning to Tibet. He is said to have founded 108 monasteries, among which was Ta pho. Among the many monasteries of western Tibet, it was second in importance only to THO LING and was the repository of a trove of old Tibetan texts that contributed to greater understanding of the formation of the Tibetan canon (BKA' 'GYUR). In 1996, the fourteenth DALAI LAMA gave the KĀLACAKRA initiation at Ta pho in commemoration of the one thousandth anniversary of the monastery's founding.

**Tārā**. (T. Sgrol ma; C. Duoluo; J. Tara; K. Tara 多羅). In Sanskrit, lit. "Savioress"; a female bodhisattva who has the miraculous power to be able to deliver her devotees from all forms of physical danger. Tārā is said to have arisen from either a ray of blue light from the eye of the buddha AMITĀBHA, or from a tear from the eye of the BODHISATTVA AVALOKITEŚVARA as he surveyed the suffering universe. The tear fell into a valley and formed a lake, out of which grew the lotus from which Tārā appeared. She is thus said to be the physical manifestation of the compassion of Avalokiteśvara, who is himself the quintessence of the compassion of the buddhas. Because buddhas are produced from wisdom and compassion, Tārā, like the goddess PRAJÑĀPĀRAMITĀ ("Perfection of Wisdom"), is hailed as "the mother of all buddhas," despite the fact that she is most commonly represented as a beautiful sixteen-year-old maiden. She is often depicted together with BHṚKUTĪ (one of her forms) as one of two female bodhisattvas flanking Avalokiteśvara. Tārā is the subject of much devotion in her own right, serving as the subject of many stories, prayers, and tantric SĀDHANAS. She can appear in peaceful or wrathful forms, depending on the circumstances, her powers extending beyond the subjugation of these worldly frights, into the heavens and into the hells. She has two major peaceful forms, however. The first is SITATĀRĀ, or White Tārā. Her right hand is in VARADAMUDRĀ, her left is at her chest in VITARKAMUDRĀ and holds a lotus and she sits in DHYĀNĀSANA. The other is ŚYĀMATĀRĀ, or Green Tārā. Her right hand is in varadamudrā, her left is at her chest in vitarkamudrā and holds an utpala, and she sits in LALITĀSANA. Her wrathful forms include KURUKULLĀ, a dancing naked YOGINĪ, red in color, who brandishes a bow and arrow in her four arms. In tantric MAṆḌALAS, she appears as the consort of AMOGHASIDDHI, the buddha of the northern quarter; together they are lord and lady of the KARMAKULA. But she is herself also the sole deity in many tantric SĀDHANAS, in which the meditator, whether male or female, visualizes himself or herself in Tārā's feminine form. Tārā is best-known for her salvific powers, appearing the instant her devotee recites her MANTRA, oṃ tāre tuttāre ture svāhā. She is especially renowned as Aṣṭabhayatrāṇatārā, "Tārā Who Protects from the Eight Fears," because of her ability to deliver those who call upon her when facing the eight great fears (mahābhaya) of lions, elephants, fire, snakes, thieves, water, imprisonment, and demons. Many tales are told recounting her miraculous interventions. Apart from the recitation of her mantra, a particular prayer is the most common medium of invoking Tārā in Tibet. It is a prayer to twenty-one Tārās, derived from an Indian TANTRA devoted to Tārā, the *Sarvatathāgatamātṛtārāviśvakarmabhavatantra* ("Source of All Rites to Tārā, the Mother of All the Tathāgatas"). According to some commentarial traditions on the prayer, each of the verses refers to a different form of Tārā, totaling twenty-one. According to others, the forms of Tārā are iconographically almost indistinguishable. Tārā entered the Buddhist pantheon relatively late, around the sixth century, in northern India and Nepal, and her worship in Java is attested in inscriptions dating to the end of the eighth century. Like Avalokiteśvara, she has played a crucial role in Tibet's history, in both divine and human forms. One version of the creation myth that has the Tibetan race originating from a dalliance between a monkey and an ogress says the monkey was a form of Avalokiteśvara and the ogress a form of Tārā. Worship of Tārā in Tibet began in earnest with the second propagation and the arrival of ATIŚA DĪPAṂKARAŚRĪJÑĀNA in the eleventh century; she appears repeatedly in accounts of his life and in his teachings. He had visions of the goddess at crucial points in his life, and she advised him to make his fateful journey to Tibet, despite the fact that his life span would be shortened as a result. His sādhanas for the propitiation of Sitatārā and Śyāmatārā played a key role in promoting the worship of Tārā in Tibet. He further was responsible for the translation of several important Indic texts relating to the goddess, including three by Vāgīśvarakīrti that make up the 'chi blu, or "cheating death" cycle, the foundation of all lineages of the worship of Sitatārā in Tibet. The famous Tārā chapel at Atiśa's temple at SNYE THANG contains nearly identical statues of the twenty-one Tārās. The translator Darmadra brought to Tibet the important ANUYOGA tantra devoted to the worship of Tārā, entitled *Bcom ldan 'das ma sgrol ma yang dag par rdzogs pa'i sangs rgyas bstod pa gsungs pa*. Tārā is said to have taken human form earlier in Tibetan history as the Chinese princess WENCHENG and Nepalese princess Bhṛkutī, who married King SRONG BTSAN SGAM PO, bringing with them buddha images that would become the most revered in Tibet. Which Tārā they were remains unsettled; however, some sources identify Wencheng with Śyāmatārā and Bhṛkutī with the goddess of the same name, herself said to be a form of Tārā. Others argue that the Nepalese princess was Sitatārā, and Wencheng was Śyāmatārā. These identifications, however, like that of Srong btsan sgam po with Avalokiteśvara, date only to the fourteenth century, when the cult of Tārā in Tibet was flourishing. In the next generation, Tārā appeared as the wife of King KHRI SRONG LDE BTSAN and the consort of PADMASAMBHAVA, YE SHES MTSHO RGYAL, who in addition to becoming a great tantric master herself, served as scribe when Padmasambhava dictated the treasure texts (GTER MA). Later, Tārā is said to have appeared as the great practitioner of the GCOD tradition, MA GCIG LAP SGRON (1055–1149). Indeed, when Tārā first vowed eons ago to achieve buddhahood in order to free all beings from SAMSĀRA, she swore she would always appear in female form.

**Tāranātha**. (1575–1634). The appellation of Kun dga' snying po (Kunga Nyingpo), a Tibetan scholar affiliated with the JO NANG tradition. Tāranātha was an author of exceptional scope, writing on a vast range of philosophical and doctrinal topics. Born in Drong, he was a precocious child, famously declaring himself to be an incarnate lama (SPRUL SKU) at the age of one, an identification that was eventually confirmed. He was installed at Chos lung rtse monastery at the age of four. By age fifteen, he had studied many tantric cycles, becoming adept at both the six yogas of NĀROPA (NA RO CHOS DRUG) and MAHĀMUDRĀ. He also developed an interest in Indian languages; several of his translations of Sanskrit works are included in the Tibetan canon. Tāranātha had a strong interest in India throughout his life, not simply its ancient past but also its contemporary present, chronicling events of the Mughal period. He even declared that he and the Mughal emperor Jahangir were emanations of the same person. He also had a strong interest in the SIDDHA tradition and studied with many Buddhist and non-Buddhist YOGINs. At the age of sixteen, Tāranātha met his most influential Indian teacher, Buddhaguptanātha, who had traveled throughout the Buddhist world and studied directly with some of the last remaining members of the siddha tradition. Tāranātha surveyed the Indian siddha lineages in his BKA' BABS BDUN LDAN GYI RNAM THAR ("Biographies of the Seven Instruction Lineages"). His most famous work, informally called the RGYA GAR CHOS 'BYUNG ("History of Indian Buddhism"), is highly regarded by later Tibetan historians. Tāranātha was a great master of the KĀLACAKRATANTRA and its surrounding topics, writing extensively about them. He restored the STŪPA built by the Jo nang founder DOL PO PA SHES RAB RGYAL MTSHAN. Tāranātha saw Dol po pa in many visions and strongly promoted his teachings, writing in support of the GZHAN STONG view. In 1615, with the patronage of the rulers of Gtsang, he began work on JO NANG PHUN TSHOGS GLING, northwest of Gzhis ka rtse (Shigatse) in central Tibet. It was completed in 1628. Renowned for its beautiful design and sumptuous artwork, the monastery would be his primary residence in the last years of his life. After his death, the fifth DALAI LAMA suppressed the Jo nang sect, converting the monastery into a DGE LUGS establishment. He also identified Tāranātha's incarnation in Mongolia as the first RJE BTSUN DAM PA, a line of incarnations who would serve as titular head of the Dge lugs sect in Mongolia until the twentieth century. The reasons for this identification are debated. The Dalai Lama claimed in one of his autobiographies that his mother had been the tantric consort of Tāranātha and that Tāranātha was his biological father. It was also the case that Tāranātha had been supported by the rulers of Gtsang, the opponents that the Dalai Lama's faction had defeated in the civil war that resulted in the Dalai Lama gaining political control over Tibet.

**tariki**. (C. tali; K. t'aryŏk 他力). In Japanese, "other power." The term tariki came to be used frequently by followers of SHINRAN and his JŌDO SHINSHŪ tradition. Tariki often appears in contast with JIRIKI, or "self-power." While tariki refers to the practitioner's reliance on the power or grace of the buddha AMITĀBHA, jiriki is often used in a pejorative sense to refer to practices requiring personal effort, such as keeping the precepts and cultivating the six PĀRAMITĀs. Reliance on jiriki was often condemned as a more difficult path than that based on tariki, such as reciting Amitābha's name (see NIANFO). The tariki and jiriki distinction is traditionally attributed to the Chinese monk TANLUAN and his commentary on the WULIANGSHOU JING YOUPOTISHE YUANSHENG JI. Basing his claims on the vows of Amitābha that appear in the SUKHĀVATĪVYŪHASŪTRA, Tanluan argued that true power belonged not to the practitioner but to Amitābha. While Tanluan himself did not condemn practices involving self-power, SHINRAN and his Japanese followers argued for exclusive faith in the power of Amitābha and denounced jiriki as inappropriate for the final age of the DHARMA (J. mappō; C. MOFA).

**tarjanīmudrā**. (T. sdigs mdzub phyag rgya; C. qike yin; J. kikokuin; K. kigŭk in 祈克印). In Sanskrit, "wrathful" or "threatening gesture." The tarjanīmudrā may be formed in several ways: with the index finger raised like a hook from the loosely closed fist of either hand, or with index and pinky fingers extended and remaining fingers closed lightly in a fist. This gesture is common in images of semiwrathful and wrathful deities, such as Acala and VAJRAPĀṆI, as well as dharma protectors (DHARMAPĀLA), and may be formed in combination with other hand gestures. See also MUDRĀ.

**tarjanīyakarman**. (P. tajjaniyakamma; T. bsdigs pa'i las; C. yinghe/lingbu; J. ōka/ryōfu; K. ŭngga/yŏngp'o 應訶/令怖). In Sanskrit, "act of censure" or "act of rebuke"; a formal and public criticism of a monk or nun for untoward behavior that does not require a formal punishment. Such behavior would include being quarrelsome, living among householders, and speaking disrespectfully about the Buddha, DHARMA, or SAṂGHA. A monk or nun who acknowledges such misbehavior may then request that the censure be rescinded.

**tarka**. (T. rtog ge; C. size; J. shichaku; K. sat'aek 思擇). In Sanskrit, "logic"; conceptual knowledge that relies on reasoning.

Although often used in this neutral sense, in some contexts the term is used pejoratively to refer to a pedantic logic that is unrelated, and in some cases detrimental, to progress on the path of enlightenment. In this latter sense, the term might be better translated as "sophistry."

**Tarkajvālā**. (T. Rtog ge 'bar ba). In Sanskrit, the "Blaze of Reasoning"; the extensive prose autocommentary on the MADHYAMAKAHṚDAYA, the major work of the sixth-century Indian MADHYAMAKA (and, from the Tibetan perspective, *SVĀTANTRIKA) master BHĀVAVIVEKA (also referred to as Bhavya and Bhāviveka). The *Madhyamakahṛdaya* is preserved in both Sanskrit and Tibetan; the *Tarkajvālā* only in Tibetan. It is a work of eleven chapters, the first three and the last two of which set forth the main points in Bhāvaviveka's view of the nature of reality and the Buddhist path, dealing with such topics as BODHICITTA, the knowledge of reality (tattvajñāna), and omniscience (SARVAJÑATĀ). The intervening chapters set forth the positions (and Bhāvaviveka's refutations) of various Buddhist and non-Buddhist schools, including the ŚRĀVAKA, YOGĀCĀRA, Sāṃkhya, Vaiśeṣika, Vedānta, and Mīmāṃsā. These chapters (along with ŚĀNTARAKṢITA's TATTVASAṂGRAHA) are an invaluable source of insight into the relations between Madhyamaka and the other Indian philosophical schools of the day. The chapter on the śrāvakas, for example, provides a detailed account of the reasons put forth by the śrāvaka schools as to why the MAHĀYĀNA sūtras are not the word of the Buddha (BUDDHAVACANA). Bhāvaviveka's response to these arguments, as well as his refutation of Yogācāra in the subsequent chapter, are particularly spirited.

**tārkika**. (T. rtog ge ba). In Sanskrit, "logician," but generally used in a pejorative sense of a sophist or pendant obsessed with argumentation and thus prevented from perceiving reality.

**tathāgata**. (T. de bzhin gshegs pa; C. rulai; J. nyorai; K. yŏrae 如來). In Sanskrit and Pāli, lit., "one who has thus come/gone," and generally translated into English as the "thus gone one." Tathāgata is, along with BHAGAVAT, one of the most common epithets of the Buddha and a term the Buddha commonly uses in the SŪTRAs to refer both to himself and to the buddhas of the past. The Sanskrit compound may be parsed to mean either "one who is thus gone" (tathā + gata), or "one who has thus come" (tathā + āgata), and for this reason the translations of the Sanskrit vary across languages. The Sanskrit root √gam is also used with prepositions in words that mean "understand," so a secondary denotation of the term is to "understand" things "as they are" (tathā). The Chinese settled on the translation "thus come one" (rulai). The Tibetan translation de bzhin gshegs pa reflects the ambiguity of the Sanskrit and can mean either "one who has thus gone" or "one who has thus come." The Pāli commentaries typically provide eight (and sometimes as many as sixteen) denotations of tathāgata, some of which may be of pre- or non-Buddhist origin, perhaps deriving from the JAINA tradition. In the early Pāli scriptures, the term seems to evoke the infinite knowledge of the Buddha, with little attempt to provide a clear etymology. Later commentators would offer a number of interpretations, among the most common of which are that the Buddha has "thus come" into the world like the other buddhas of the past, or that he has "thus gone" on to achieve NIRVĀṆA like the other buddhas of the past. Other explanations equate it with the word TATHATĀ.

**tathāgatabhūmi**. (T. de bzhin gshegs pa'i sa; C. rulai di; J. nyoraiji; K. yŏrae chi 如來地). The "stage of a thus gone one," the name given in the LAṄKĀVATĀRASŪTRA to an eleventh ground or stage (BHŪMI) of the BODHISATTVA path that constitutes the fruition of buddhahood (buddhaphala). The tenth BODHISATTVABHŪMI, DHARMAMEGHĀ, the culminating stage of the "path of cultivation" (BHĀVANĀMĀRGA), still contains both subtle remnants of the cognitive obstructions (JÑEYĀVARAṆA) as well as seeds of the afflictive obstructions (KLEŚĀVARAṆA). These obstructions will be completely eradicated through the diamond-like samādhi (VAJROPAMASAMĀDHI), which marks the transition to the "ultimate path" (NIṢṬHĀMĀRGA), or the "path where no further training is necessary" (AŚAIKṢAMĀRGA). This stage is the tathāgatabhūmi, which is also sometimes known as the "universally luminous" (samantaprabhā).

**tathāgatagarbha**. (T. de bzhin gshegs pa'i snying po; C. rulaizang; J. nyoraizō; K. yŏraejang 如來藏). In Sanskrit, variously translated as "womb of the TATHĀGATAs," "matrix of the tathāgatas," "embryo of the tathāgatas," "essence of the tathāgatas"; the term probably means "containing a tathāgatha." It is more imprecisely interpreted as the "buddha-nature," viz., the potential to achieve buddhahood that, according to some MAHĀYĀNA schools, is inherent in all sentient beings. The tathāgatagarbha is the topic of several important Mahāyāna sūtras, including the TATHĀGATAGARBHASŪTRA (with its famous nine similes about the state), the ŚRĪMĀLĀDEVĪSIṂHANĀDASŪTRA, the MAHĀPARINIRVĀṆASŪTRA, and the LAṄKĀVATĀRASŪTRA (where it is identified with the ĀLAYAVIJÑĀNA), as well as the important Indian ŚĀSTRA, the RATNAGOTRAVIBHĀGA (also known as the *Uttaratantra*), with a commentary by ASAṄGA. The concept is also central to such East Asian apocryphal scriptures as the DASHENG QIXIN LUN and the KŬMGANG SAMMAE KYŎNG. The concept of tathāgatagarbha seems to have evolved from a relatively straightforward inspiration that all beings are capable of achieving buddhahood to a more complex doctrine of an almost genetic determination that all beings would eventually become buddhas; the *Laṅkāvatāra* goes so far as to describe the tathāgatagarbha itself as possessing the thirty-two marks of a superman (MAHĀPURUṢALAKṢAṆA). Tathāgatagarbha thought seeks to answer the question of why ignorant beings are able to become enlightened by suggesting that this capacity is something innate in the minds of all sentient beings, which has become concealed by adventitious afflictions (ĀGANTUKAKLEŚA) that are extrinsic to the mind. "Concealment" (S. saṃdhi/abhisaṃdhi; C. yinfu) here suggests that the tathāgatagarbha is first, a passive object that is obscured by the presence of the afflictions; or, second, it is an active agent of liberation, which secrets itself away inside the minds of sentient beings so as to inspire them toward enlightenment. The former passive sense is more common in Indian materials; the latter sense of tathāgatagarbha as an active soteriological potency is more typical of East Asian presentations of the concept. Tathāgatagarbha thought could thus claim that enlightenment need involve nothing more rigorous than simply relinquishing the mistaken notion that one is deluded and accepting the fact of one's inherent enlightenment (see also BENJUE; HONGAKU). The notion of tathāgatagarbha was a topic of extensive commentary and debate in India, Tibet, and East Asia. It was not the case, for example, that all Mahāyāna exegetes asserted that all sentient beings possess the tathāgatagarbha and thus the capacity for enlightenment; indeed, the FAXIANG ZONG, an East Asian strand of YOGĀCĀRA, famously asserted that some beings could so completely lose all aspiration for enlightenment that they would become "incorrigible" (ICCHANTIKA) and thus be forever incapable of liberation. There was also substantial debate as to the precise nature of the tathāgathagarbha, especially because some of its descriptions made it seem similar to the notion of a perduring self (ĀTMAN), a doctrine that is anathema to most schools of Buddhism. The *Śrīmālādevīsiṃhanāda*, for example, described the tathāgatagarbha as endowed with four "perfect qualities" (GUṆAPĀRAMITĀ): permanence, purity, bliss, and self, but states that this "self" is different from the "self" (ĀTMAN) propounded by the non-Buddhists. In an effort to avoid any such associations, CANDRAKĪRTI explains that the tathāgatagarbha is not to be understood as an independent quality but rather refers to the emptiness (ŚŪNYATĀ) of the mind; it is this emptiness, with which all beings are endowed, that serves as the potential for achieving buddhahood. In Tibet, Candrakīrti's view was taken up by the DGE LUGS sect, while the more literal view of the tathāgatagarbha as an ultimately real nature obscured by conventional contaminants was asserted most famously by the JO NANG. Both the extensive influence of the doctrine and the controversy it provoked points to an ongoing tension in the Mahāyāna between the more apophatic discourse on emptiness, found especially in the PRAJÑĀPĀRAMITĀ sūtras, and the more substantialist descriptions of the ultimate reality implied by such terms as tathāgatagarbha, DHARMADHĀTU, and DHARMAKĀYA. The term is also central to the larger question of whether enlightenment is something to be achieved through a sequence of practices or something to be revealed in a flash of insight (see DUNWU). See also HIHAN BUKKYŌ.

**Tathāgatagarbhasūtra**. (T. De bzhin gshegs pa'i snying po'i mdo; C. Dafangdeng rulaizang jing; J. Daihōdō nyoraizōkyō; K. Taebangdŭng yŏraejang kyŏng 大方等如來藏經). In Sanskrit, "Discourse on the Embryo of the TATHĀGATAS"; also known by the longer title of *Tathāgatagarbhanāmavaipulyasūtra*, an influential Mahāyāna sūtra, and the earliest to set forth the doctrine of the womb or embryo of buddhahood (TATHĀGATAGARBHA). The sūtra, which is preserved only in Chinese and later Tibetan translations, was probably composed in the second half of the third century CE. The sūtra, set ten years after the Buddha's enlightenment, opens with the Buddha seated on Vulture Peak (GṚDHRAKŪṬAPARVATA) surrounded by one hundred thousand monks and bodhisattvas equal in number to the sands of the Ganges (GAṄGĀNADĪVĀLUKĀ). The Buddha causes myriad closed lotuses to fill the sky, each enclosing a buddha who is emitting rays of light. The petals of the lotuses open and then became wilted and finally rotten, but the buddhas seated upon them remain pristine. The bodhisattva Vajramati then asks the Buddha to explain what has occurred. In the most famous section of the sūtra, the Buddha then sets forth nine similes of the tathāgatagarbha. (1) Just as there was a buddha seated cross-legged within decaying lotus petals, so in each sentient being, there is a buddha encased in the sheaths of the afflictions. (2) Just as a honeycomb is surrounded by bees, so the buddhahood within each being is surrounded by afflictions and impurities; just as the beekeeper removes the bees, so the Buddha removes the afflictions and impurities of sentient beings. (3) Just as a kernel is encased in a husk, so buddhahood is encased by the afflictions. (4) Just as a piece of gold covered with excrement would be hidden until its presence was revealed by a god, so the buddha within each being, covered as he is by the filth of the afflictions, remains unknown until a buddha reveals his presence. (5) Just as a treasure buried deep beneath the house of a poor man would be unknown to him, leaving him to presume he was poor, so is the buddha-nature hidden deeply within all beings unknown to them, causing them to wander in SAṂSĀRA. The Buddha sees the body of a buddha within all beings and teaches them how to become treasures of the dharma. (6) Just as hidden within a fruit is a seed and sprout that will produce a tree, so the Buddha sees the body of a buddha within the sheaths of the afflictions. (7) Just as a jeweled image of the Buddha wrapped in putrid rags would lie unnoticed by the side of the road until its presence was revealed by a god, so the body of a buddha wrapped in afflictions inside even an animal is seen only by the Buddha. (8) Just as a poor and ugly woman who carried the embryo of a universal emperor (CAKRAVARTIN) in her womb would remain discouraged by her lot, so sentient beings who carry a buddha within them continue to be distressed by saṃsāra. (9) Just as a golden statue remains hidden within a blackened clay mold until the goldsmith breaks the mold with a hammer, so the knowledge of a buddha remains invisible within the afflictions until the Buddha uses the dharma to remove the afflictions.

**tathāgatagotra**. (T. de bzhin gshegs pa'i rigs; C. rulai xing; J. nyoraishō; K. yŏrae sŏng 如來性). In Sanskrit, "tathāgata lineage"; a term used to describe that element in the mental continuum (SAṂTĀNA) of a sentient being that makes it destined to achieve enlightenment as a buddha. In this sense, the term is roughly synonymous with TATHĀGATAGARBHA and BUDDHADHĀTU ("buddha element," or "buddha-nature"). The Mahāyāna schools differ on the question of whether all sentient beings are endowed with this lineage, with the MADHYAMAKA asserting that they are, while some followers of the YOGĀCĀRA argue that beings are endowed with different lineages, which will lead them to follow the paths of the ŚRĀVAKA or PRATYEKABUDDHA to become an ARHAT, and still other beings have no spiritual lineage at all (see ICCHANTIKA).

**tathāgatakula**. (T. de bzhin gshegs pa'i rigs; C. rulai bu; J. nyoraibu; K. yŏrae pu 如來部). In Sanskrit, the "tathāgata family"; one of the three families of the KRIYĀTANTRA, together with the VAJRAKULA (whose chief deity is VAJRASATTVA) and the PADMAKULA (whose chief deity is AVALOKITEŚVARA). The chief deity of the tathāgatakula is often ŚĀKYAMUNI. In the three-family schema, the tathāgatakula is considered the supreme of the three families, with initiates of this family allowed to perform the rituals of the other two. In the evolution to four and then five buddha families (with the addition of the RATNAKULA and then the KARMAKULA), the tathāgatakula remains supreme, with VAIROCANA then becoming the main deity of the tathāgatakula and holding the central position in many MAṆḌALAs. Each of the five families is associated with one of the five SKANDHAs, five wisdoms (JÑĀNA), five afflictions (KLEŚA), five elements, and five colors. For the tathāgata or buddha family, these are the form (RŪPA) skandha, the wisdom (JÑĀNA) of the DHARMADHĀTU (dharmadhātujñāna), the affliction of ignorance (AVIDYĀ), the element space (ĀKĀŚA), and the color blue. See PAÑCATATHĀGATA.

**Tathāgatoṣṇīṣasitātapatrā**. (T. De bzhin gshegs pa'i gtsug tor nas byung ba'i gdugs dkar po can). In Sanskrit, "She of the White Parasol [who arose from] the UṢṆĪṢA of the TATHĀGATA"; also known as Uṣṇīṣasitātapatrā. This goddess is a female protective deity, sometimes associated with TĀRĀ, who is propitiated to remove illness and other obstacles. Her most famous form is depicted with a thousand heads, a thousand hands, and a thousand feet.

**tathatā**. (T. de bzhin nyid/de kho na nyid; C. zhenru; J. shinnyo; K. chinyŏ 眞如). In Sanskrit, "suchness" or "thusness"; a term for ultimate reality, especially in the MAHĀYĀNA schools. Along with terms such as DHARMATĀ, DHARMADHĀTU, and BHŪTAKOṬI, it has a more "positive" connotation than emptiness (ŚŪNYATĀ), referring to the eternal nature of reality that is "ever thus" or "just so" and free of all conceptual elaborations. In YOGĀCĀRA/VIJÑĀNAVĀDA, the term refers to the ultimate wisdom that is free from the subject–object distinction (GRĀHYAGRĀHAKAVIKALPA). Buddhahood is sometimes described as tathatāviśuddhi, or "purity of suchness," that is, ultimate reality purified of all obstructions. In the MADHYAMAKA school, any attempt to substantiate the nature of reality is rejected, and tathatā is instead identified with emptiness and the cessation of all dichotomizing tendencies of thought. The Chinese equivalent, ZHENRU, is a seminal term in in East Asian Buddhist philosophy, figuring prominently, for example, in the DASHENG QIXIN LUN. See also TATTVA.

**tathyasaṃvṛti**. (T. yang dag pa'i kun rdzob). In Sanskrit, "real conventionality"; a term used in MADHYAMAKA philosophy in connection with MITHYĀSAṂVṚTI, "false conventionality." Real conventionality is a conventional truth (SAṂVṚTISATYA) in the sense that it is not the object of an ultimate consciousness and is falsely imagined to possess SVABHĀVA, or intrinsic existence. However, although it is falsely conceived, it is not utterly non-existent (like a false conventionality) because a real conventionality is capable of performing its function (ARTHAKRIYĀ). For example, a lake would be a true conventionality because it can perform the function of a lake, whereas a mirage would be a false conventionality because it could not perform the function of a lake. Only a real conventionality is a conventional truth; it is true in the sense that it can perform a function. A false conventionality is not a conventional truth because it does not exist even conventionally.

**tatpṛṣṭhalabdhajñāna**. (S). See PṚṢṬHALABDHAJÑĀNA.

**tattva**. (T. de nyid/de kho na nyid; C. shixiang; J. jissō; K. silsang 實相). In Sanskrit, lit., "thatness"; a term with two important denotations. First, it can mean "ultimate reality," a synonym of PARAMĀRTHA, the reality, free from all conceptual elaboration, that must be understood in order to be liberated from rebirth as well as the inexpressible reality that is the object of the Buddha's omniscient consciousness. Second, more prosaically, the term may be translated as "principle" and refer to the central doctrine of a particular philosophical school, as in the title of the works TATTVASAṂGRAHA or TATTVASIDDHI. When contrasted with TATHATĀ, tattva is the essential identity of a particular dharma, while tathatā is the common essential reality in which all dharmas partake.

**Tattvaratnāvalī**. (T. De kho na nyid rin po che'i phreng ba). In Sanskrit, the "Necklace of Principles"; a scholastic exposition of Buddhist TANTRA by Advayavajra, the apparent pen name of the Indian master Maitrīpāda, who flourished in the late tenth and early eleventh centuries CE. The work provides some insight into how Buddhism was understood in the late period of Indian Buddhism, dividing it into the three vehicles of the ŚRĀVAKAYĀNA, PRATYEKABUDDHAYĀNA, and MAHĀYĀNA, with the Mahāyāna further subdivided into the "way of the perfections" (pāramitānaya) and the "way of mantra" (mantranaya). The work also states that the Madhyamaka school is divided into the two, the Māyopamādvayavāda, or "Proponents of Illusion-like Nonduality," and the Sarvadharmāpratiṣṭhānavāda, or "Proponents That All Dharmas Are Nonabiding."

**Tattvasaṃgraha**. (T. De kho na nyid bsdus pa). In Sanskrit, the "Compendium of Principles"; one of the major works of the eighth-century Indian master ŚĀNTARAKṢITA. It is a massive work in 3,646 verses, in twenty-six chapters. The verses themselves are called the *Tattvasamgrahakārikā*; there is also an extensive prose commentary by Śāntarakṣita's student, KAMALAŚĪLA, entitled the

*Tattvasaṃgrahapañjikā*. The *Tattvasaṃgraha* is a polemical text, surveying the philosophical positions of a wide variety of non-Buddhist (and some Buddhist) schools on a number of topics or principles (TATTVA) and demonstrating their faults. These topics include matter (prakṛti), the person (PURUṢA), God (īśvara), the self (ĀTMAN), and valid knowledge (PRAMĀṆA), among many others. Among the schools whose positions are presented and critiqued are Sāṃkhya, Nyāya, Vaiśeṣika, Mīmāmsā, Advaita Vedānta, JAINA, and VĀTSĪPUTRĪYA. The work is of great value to scholars for its presentation (albeit polemical) of the tenets of these schools as they existed in eighth-century India. The commentary often provides the names and positions of specific philosophers of these schools. ¶ The term is also the abbreviated title of the *Sarvatathāgatatattvasaṃgraha*; see SARVATATHĀGATATATTVASAṂGRAHA.

**Tattvasiddhi**. [alt. Tattvasiddhi-nāma-prakaraṇa] (T. De kho na nyid grub pa zhes bya ba'i rab tu byed pa). In Sanskrit, "Proof of Reality"; a work of tantric philosophy, extant in Sanskrit, attributed to the eighth-century Indian master ŚĀNTARAKṢITA. The text presents a philosophical argument in support of the achievement of the states of yogic perception (YOGIPRATYAKṢA) and bliss (SUKHA) through tantric practice, citing a number of early tantras by name. In the work, the author argues that bodhisattvas endowed with PRAJÑĀ and UPĀYA are not bound by ethical conventions.

***Tattvasiddhi**. (C. Chengshi lun; J. Jōjitsuron; K. Sŏngsil non 成實論). In Sanskrit, the "Proof of Reality"; an important ABHIDHARMA text by HARIVARMAN, probably composed between 250 and 350 CE. (The Sanskrit reconstruction **Tattvasiddhi* is now generally preferred over the outmoded rendering **Satyasiddhi*.) The text was translated into Chinese by KUMĀRAJĪVA and was studied widely in China during the fifth and sixth centuries. The text is valued for its presentation of the abhidharma of the BAHUŚRUTĪYA school of Indian Buddhism and for its refutations of the positions of rival schools, which are organized in terms of ten points of controversy, including the person (PUDGALA), the status of past and present, and the existence of an intermediate state (ANTARĀBHAVA) between death and rebirth. See the extensive discussion in CHENGSHI LUN.

**Taung-hpila Pagoda**. A pagoda (Burmese, JEDI) built by King Thalun of AVA (r. 1629–1648) on the Taung-hpila spur of the Sagaing Hills in Upper Burma (Myanmar). Thalun also built a monastery at this locale, whose abbot came to be known as the royal preceptor, or "SAYADAW," of Taung-hpila. This first Taung-hpila Sayadaw wrote a famous commentary in Pāli on the five books of the VINAYA titled the *Vinayālaṅkāraṭīkā*. He also composed a bilingual Pāli–Myanmar commentary (nissaya) on the same five books, but when he discovered that another monk had already written such a treatise, Taung-hpila Sayadaw buried his own commentary in Thalun's pagoda. It was because of this act that the pagoda came to be known as Taung-hpila Pagoda. The works of Taung-hpila Sayadaw and other scholars of the Ava period were renowned throughout the THERAVĀDA world and were highly praised by the monks of Sri Lanka for their erudition.

**Taxila**. The Greek name for the Indian city of TAKṢAŚILĀ, an important center of Buddhist learning in the GANDHĀRA region (in Punjab province of modern Pakistan). See TAKṢAŚILĀ.

**Teishō**. (J) (提唱). In Japanese, "ZEN lecture." See TICHANG.

**Tejaprabha**. (C. Chishengguang rulai; J. Shijōkō nyorai; K. Ch'isŏnggwang yŏrae 熾盛光如來). In Sanskrit, "Effulgence"; proper name for a buddha who personifies the Pole Star as master of all asterisms, and especially the seven stars of the Big Dipper, viz., Ursa Major (see BEIDOU QIXING); this buddha is so named because light is said to stream out from every pore of his body. Tejaprabha was a popular figure within Chinese esoteric Buddhist circles after the eighth century, when the worship of the seven stars became well established during the Tang dynasty. While the cult of Tejaprabha Buddha gradually disappeared in China after the thirteenth century, the worship of the seven stars (K. ch'ilsŏng) was transmitted to Korea, where it continues even today. Starting in the twelfth century, during the Koryŏ dynasty, court rituals to the seven stars and Tejaprabha TATHĀGATA were frequently performed, and worship of the seven stars spread widely during the following Chosŏn dynasty (1392–1910). Chosŏn-period monasteries commonly included "seven-stars shrines" (ch'ilsŏnggak), inside of which were hung seven-stars paintings (T'AENGHWA), which typically depicted the seven-star tathāgatas, with Tejaprabha presiding at the center. There were also several comprehensive ritual and liturgical manuals compiled during the Chosŏn dynasty and Japanese colonial period in Korea, which include rituals and invocations to the seven stars and Tejaprabha Tathāgata, most dedicated to the prolongation of life.

**tejas**. [alt. tejodhātu] (P. tejo; T. me; C. huoda; J. kadai; K. hwadae 火大). In Sanskrit, lit. "fire," viz., the property of "temperature" or "luminosity"; one of the four "great elements" (MAHĀBHŪTA) or "major elementary qualities" of which the physical world of materiality (RŪPA) is composed, along with earth (viz., solidity, PṚTHIVĪ), water (viz., cohesion, ĀPAS), and wind (viz., motion, movement, VĀYU). "Fire" is understood to be that which gives light and provides the other elements with varying temperatures. Because fire, however, persists (viz., earth), has cohesion (viz., water), and moves (viz., wind), the existence of all the other three elements may also be inferred even in that single element. In the physical body, this element is associated with physical warmth, digestion, and maturation or aging.

**tejokasiṇa**. (S. tejaskṛtsnāyatana; T. me zad par gyi skye mched; C. huo bianchu; J. kahensho; K. hwa p'yŏnch'ŏ 火遍處).

In Pāli, "fire device"; one of the ten devices (KASIṆA) described in the PĀLI tradition for developing meditative concentration (P. JHĀNA, S. DHYĀNA); the locus classicus for their exposition is the VISUDDHIMAGGA of BUDDHAGHOSA. Ten kasiṇa are enumerated there: visualization devices that are constructed from the elements (MAHĀBHŪTA) of earth, water, fire, air; the colors blue, yellow, red, white; and light and empty space. In each case, the meditation begins by looking at the physical object; the perception of the device is called the "beginning sign" or "preparatory sign" (P. PARIKAMMANIMITTA). Once the object is clearly perceived, the meditator then memorizes the object so that it is seen as clearly in his mind as with his eyes. This perfect mental image of the device is called the "eidetic sign," or "learning sign" (P. UGGAHANIMITTA), and serves as the subsequent object of concentration. As the internal visualization of this eidetic sign deepens and the five hindrances (NĪVARAṆA) to mental absorption are temporarily allayed, a "representational sign" or "counterpart sign" (P. PAṬIBHĀGANIMITTA) will emerge from out of the eidetic image, as if, the texts say, a sword is being drawn from its scabbard or the moon is emerging from behind clouds. The representational sign is a mental representation of the visualized image, which does not duplicate what was seen with the eyes but represents its abstracted, essentialized quality. Continued attention to the representational sign will lead to all four of the meditative absorptions of the subtle-materiality realm (RŪPADHĀTU). In the case of the tejokasiṇa, the meditator begins by making a fire of dried heartwood, hanging a curtain of reeds, leather, or cloth in front of it, then cutting a hole four fingerwidths in size in the curtain. He then sits in the meditative posture and observes the flame (rather than the sticks or the smoke) through the hole, thinking, "fire, fire," using the perception of the flame as the preparatory sign. The eidetic sign, which is visualized without looking at the flame, appears as a tongue of flame and continually detaches itself from the fire. The representational sign is more steady, appearing motionless like a red cloth in space, a gold fan, or a gold column. With the representational sign achieved, progress through the various stages of absorption may begin. The tejokasiṇa figures prominently in the dramatic story of the passing away of the Buddha's attendant, ĀNANDA. According to FAXIAN, when Ānanda was 120 years old, he set out from MAGADHA to VAIŚĀLĪ in order to die. Seeking control of the saint's relics after his death, AJĀTAŚATRU followed him to the Rohīni River, while a group for Vaiśālī awaited him on the other side. Not wishing to disappoint either group, Ānanda levitated to the middle of the river in the meditative posture, preached the dharma, and then meditated on the tejokasiṇa, which caused his body to burst into flames, with his relics dividing into two parts, one landing on each side of the river.

**temple**. See VIHĀRA; CHŎL; TERA; DGON PA.

**Tendaishū**. (天台宗). In Japanese, "Platform of Heaven School," the Japanese counterpart of the Chinese TIANTAI ZONG, the name of the Chinese tradition from which Tendai derives. The pilgrim–monk SAICHŌ (767–822) is presumed to have laid the doctrinal and institutional foundations on which the Tendai tradition in Japan was eventually constructed. Like its Chinese counterpart, the Japanese Tendai tradition took the SADDHARMAPUṆḌARĪKASŪTRA ("Lotus Sūtra") and the commentaries on this sūtra by TIANTAI ZHIYI as its central scriptures. The Tendai tradition also came to espouse the doctrine of original or inherent enlightenment (HONGAKU). An important step in the development of an autonomous Japanese Tendai tradition was the establishment of a MAHĀYĀNA precepts platform (daijō kaidan). Saichō made numerous petitions to the court to have an independent Mahāyāna precepts platform established on HIEIZAN (see ENRYAKUJI), which would provide him with institutional autonomy from the powerful monasteries of the well-established Buddhist sects in Nara. Saichō's petition was finally granted after his death in 823. The following year, his disciple GISHIN (781–833) was appointed head (zasu) of the Tendai tradition, and several years later, a precepts platform was constructed at the monastery of Enryakuji on Mt. Hiei. The Tendai tradition prospered under the leadership of ENNIN (794–864) and ENCHIN (814–891). A controversy in 993 between the lineages of Enchin and Ennin over the issue of succession led to a schism between Ennin's Sanmon branch at Mt. Hiei and Enchin's Jimon branch at Onjōji (see MIIDERA). The Tendai tradition also produced important figures in the history of the PURE LAND movement in Japan, such as GENSHIN, RYŌNIN, HŌNEN, and SHINRAN. DŌGEN KIGEN, founder of the SŌTŌSHŪ of ZEN, began his career in the Tendai tradition, practicing as a monk at Mt. Hiei, as did NICHIREN. From the medieval period up through the Tokugawa era (1600–1868), Tendai was a dominant force in Japanese Buddhism. By extension, it had considerable political influence at the court in Kyōto and later with the Tokugawa Bakufu. In order to weaken the powerful Mt. Hiei institution, at the start of the Tokugawa era, the shogunate constructed Tō Eizan in the capital of Edo ("tō" means eastern, thus setting up a juxtaposition with the western Mt. Hiei), which received more funding and prestige than its western counterpart. A major factor in the success of the Tendai institution in Japan was its incorporation of esoteric Buddhism, or MIKKYŌ, beginning with a limited number of tantric practices that Saichō brought back with him from China. The extensive training that KŪKAI (774–835), the founder of the SHINGONSHŪ, received in esoteric Buddhism in China ultimately rivaled that of Saichō, a challenge that would eventually threaten Tendai's political sway at court. However, after Saichō's disciples Ennin, Enchin, and ANNEN (841–889?) returned from China with the latest esoteric practices, Tendai's preeminence was secured. This Tendai form of mikkyō, which Ennin called TAIMITSU, was considered equal to the teachings of the *Saddharmapuṇḍarīkasūtra*. Tendai also heavily influenced the esoteric practices of SHUGENDŌ centers around the country. During the Tokugawa era, many of these mountain practice sites became formally institutionalized under Tendai Shugendō (referred to as Honzan), and were administered by the monastery of Shōgoin in Kyōto. In addition,

Tendai monks were among those who made major efforts to incorporate local native spirits (KAMI) into Tendai practice, by acknowledging them as manifestations of the Buddha (see HONJI SUIJAKU).

**ten directions**. See DAŚADIŚ.

**Tenkei Denson**. (天桂傳尊) (1648–1735). Japanese ZEN master and scholar in the SŌTŌSHŪ. Tenkei was born in Kii (present-day Wakayama prefecture). He left home at an early age and served under various teachers during his youth. In 1677, he became the dharma heir of Gohō Kaion (d.u.) at the temple of Jōkoji in Suruga (present-day Shizuoka prefecture). He served as abbot of various other temples throughout his career. Tenkei is often remembered as the opponent of fellow Sōtō adept MANZAN DŌHAKU and his efforts to reform the practice of IN'IN EKISHI, or "changing teachers according to temple," whereby a monk would take the dharma lineage of the monastery where he was appointed abbot. Tenkei rejected Manzan's call for direct, face-to-face transmission (menju shihō) from a single master to a disciple (isshi inshō) and supported the in'in ekishi custom. The military bakufu favored Manzan's reforms and Tenkei's efforts were ultimately to no avail. Tenkei is also remembered for his extensive commentary to DŌGEN KIGEN's magnum opus SHŌBŌGENZŌ, entitled the *Shōbōgenzō benchū*.

**Ten Oxherding Pictures**. See OXHERDING PICTURES, TEN.

**tera**. (寺). Vernacular Japanese term for a Buddhist "temple" or "monastery"; synonymous with the Sino-Japanese reading of ji. The term is presumed to derive either from the vernacular Korean term CHŎL or the Pāli/Prakrit term THERA (elder).

**Tevijjasutta**. (C. Sanming jing; J. Sanmyōkyō; K. Sammyŏng kyŏng 三明經). In Pāli, "Discourse on the Three-fold Knowledge"; the thirteenth sutta of the DĪGHANIKĀYA (a DHARMAGUPTAKA recension appears as the twenty-sixth SŪTRA in the Chinese translation of the DĪRGHĀGAMA); preached by the Buddha to the two brāhmaṇa youths, Vāseṭṭha and Bhāradvāja, in a mango grove outside the village of Manasākaṭa in Kosala. Vāseṭṭha and Bhāradvāja request the Buddha to resolve their debate as to which path proposed by various brāhmaṇa teachers learned in the three Vedas truly leads to union with the god BRAHMĀ. The Buddha responds that since none of the brāhmaṇa teachers learned in the three Vedas themselves have attained union with Brahmā, none of the paths they teach can lead there. They are unable to attain this goal, he continues, because their minds are obstructed by the five hindrances (NĪVARAṆA) of sensuous desire (KĀMACCHANDA), malice (VYĀPĀDA), sloth and torpor (P. thīnamiddha, S. STYĀNA-MIDDHA), restlessness and worry (P. uddhaccakukkucca, S. AUDDHATYA-KAUKṚTYA), and doubt (P. vicikicchā, S. VICIKITSĀ) about the efficacy of the path. The Buddha then describes the true path by means of which a disciple may attain union with Brahmā as follows: the disciple awakens to the teaching, abandons the household life, and enters the Buddhist order, trains in the restraint of action and speech, and observes even minor points of morality, guards the senses, practices mindfulness, is content with little, becomes freed from the five hindrances and attains joy and peace of mind. Then the disciple pervades the four quarters with loving-kindness (P. mettā; S. MAITRĪ), then compassion (KARUṆĀ), sympathetic joy (MUDITĀ), and finally equanimity (P. upekkhā; S. UPEKṢĀ). In this way one attains union with Brahmā. Vāseṭṭha and Bhāradvāja are pleased with the discourse and become disciples of the Buddha. In adapting the term tevijja (S. TRIVIDYĀ), the Buddha is intentionally redefining the meaning of the three Vedas, contrasting his three knowledges with that of brāhmaṇa priests who have merely memorized the three Vedas.

**Thammakai**. (Thai). See DHAMMAKĀYA.

**Thammayut**. (P. Dhammayuttika). In Thai, "Adherents of the Dharma," the name of the "reformed" minority school (NIKĀYA) of the Thai tradition of Buddhism; sometimes also seen transcribed as Thommayut, or by its Pāli equivalency, Dhammayuttika. This fraternity was founded in 1830 by King RĀMA IV (Mongkut), who ruled from 1851 to 1868. From 1824 to 1851, before ascending the throne, Mongkut was a monk (P. BHIKKHU; S. BHIKṢU) in the Thai monastic community (P. SAṄGHA; S. SAṂGHA). Mongkut believed that superstition had corrupted the contemporary monastic community, obscuring the pure teachings of the tradition; he was also concerned that the monks of the predominate order, the MAHANIKAI (P. Mahānikāya), did not adhere strictly to the precepts of the PĀLI VINAYA. In response, Mongkut drew on an ordination lineage from the Mon people of Burma (Myanmar) to establish this new reform tradition of Thai Buddhism. Mongkut also emphasized the rational aspects of Buddhism that made it compatible with science and modernity. Mongkut eventually became abbot of WAT BOWONNIWET in the Thai capital of Bangkok, which continues to this day to be the headquarters of the Thammayut sect. After becoming king, Mongkut continued to promote and sponsor his new school. In the nineteenth century, the Thammayut movement was also introduced into both Cambodia and Laos. Thammayut monks are known for being strict constructionists in their understanding of the precepts and seek to adhere closely to both the word and the spirit of the vinaya. For example, Thammayut monks strictly adhere to the practice of eating nothing in the afternoon (and often eating only one meal a day), never wearing sandals outside the monastery grounds, and never handling money. Since the time of AJAHN MUN BHŪRIDATTA (1870–1949), the Thammayut tradition has also been closely associated with the Thai forest-dwelling tradition (see ARAÑÑAVĀSI), whose monks engage in ascetic practices (Thai, THUDONG, P. DHUTAṄGA) and meditation.

**thang ka**. In Tibetan, "scroll painting"; a Tibetan term for an image (usually of a deity or religious figure) drawn, painted, or sewn onto cloth (or sometimes paper), sewn into a border of silk brocade, and then mounted on dowels at the top and the bottom to allow the image to be rolled up and transported. It is the most common format for the presentation of Tibetan art. The term is also seen spelled as thang kha and thang ga. See also KWAEBUL; T'AENGHWA.

**Thang stong rgyal po**. (Tangtong Gyalpo) (1361–1485). A great adept famed throughout the Tibetan Buddhist world for his illustrious career as a YOGIN and teacher, as well as his many contributions to the fields of engineering, metallurgy, temple construction, and the performing arts. His biographies credit him with a life span of 124 years, during which he traveled widely throughout Tibet and the Himālayan regions, including India, Ladakh, Mongolia, China, and Bhutan. As a youth he studied under numerous masters and spent much of early life in meditation retreat. He received, and is said to have mastered, the corpus of teachings of the SHANG PA BKA' BRGYUD sect as well as the BYANG GTER (Northern Treasure) tradition of the RNYING MA. He is venerated as a treasure revealer (GTER STON) who extracted treasure teachings (GTER MA) from the CHIMS PHU retreat complex near BSAM YAS monastery, from STAG TSHANG in Bhutan, and the region of TSA RI in southern Tibet. His best known teachings include instructions on the system known as "severance" (GCOD) and a visionary meditation SĀDHANA based on the bodhisattva of compassion AVALOKITEŚVARA called *'Gro don mkha' khyab ma* ("The Benefit of Others, Vast as Space"), which continues to be practiced by Tibetan Buddhists of many sectarian affiliations. Thang stong rgyal po is also remembered for his construction of iron chain-link bridges throughout Tibet and Bhutan—an activity inspired directly by visions of Avalokiteśvara. For this reason, he is often called Lcags zam pa, literally the "Iron Bridge Man," and his lineage the "Iron Bridge" (lcags zam) tradition. He is most commonly depicted as holding links of iron chains in one hand. Thang stong rgyal po founded numerous geomantically important religious structures, including the great STŪPA of GCUNG RI BO CHE in western Tibet, which became an important seat of the master's tradition, and the ZLUM BRTSEGS temple in Bhutan. Thang stong rgyal po is also traditionally acknowledged as the father of the Tibetan performing arts, with his image commonly displayed prior to theatrical performances.

**Thảo Đường**. (草堂) (c. eleventh century). Vietnamese monk traditionally regarded as the founder of the third school of THIỀN in Vietnam. The THIỀN UYỂN TẬP ANH does not provide a full biography of Thảo Đường, giving only a list of the monks belonging to his school with a remark that he was the abbot of Khai Quốc monastery in the capital city of Thăng Long, and that he transmitted the lineage of the XUEDOU CHONGXIAN (980–1052) line of the YUNMEN ZONG of Chinese CHAN. The legend about Thảo Đường in the Vietnamese Buddhist tradition can be found in the *An Nam Chí Lược*. According to this source, Thảo Đường followed his teacher to live in Champa. King Lý Thánh Tông (1023–1072), in an expedition against Champa in 1069, captured him and gave him to a monk scribe as a servant. The king came to have great respect for Thảo Đường's virtue and learning and made him state preceptor.

**Thar pa rin po che'i rgyan**. (Tarpa rinpoche gyen). In Tibetan, "Jewel Ornament of Liberation"; a systematic presentation of Buddhist teachings and a seminal textbook for the BKA' BRGYUD sect of Tibetan Buddhism written by SGAM PO PA BSOD RNAM RIN CHEN. The text belongs to the genre of Tibetan literature known as LAM RIM, or "stages of the path," presenting an overview of the elementary tenets of MAHĀYĀNA doctrine through scriptural citation, philosophical reflection, and direct illustration. Its clear, concise, and unpedantic style has made it accessible to generations of readers. The doctrinal content reflects Sgam po pa's training in both the BKA' GDAMS sect and the tradition of MAHĀMUDRĀ, fusing Buddhist theory prevalent in both SŪTRA and TANTRA and presenting what has been called sūtra mahāmudrā—a tradition of mahāmudrā that does not rely on prerequisite tantric initiations and commitments. Sgam po pa thus transmits the underlying insights of tantric theory outside traditional methods of the VAJRAYĀNA. This system was later criticized by certain scholars such as SA SKYA PAṆḌITA KUN DGA' RGYAL MTSHAN. The work is also commonly known as the *Dwags po thar rgyan*, after the author's residence in the region of Dwags po (Dakpo).

**that**. In Thai, "a relic" (S. DHĀTU), typically of the Buddha; in Thailand there are numerous monasteries known as "Wat Phra That" or WAT MAHATHAT, which are said to house authentic relics of the Buddha. These monasteries are popular pilgrimage sites and have legends concerning their founding filled with descriptions of miraculous events and sometimes recounting the Buddha's visit to that site. See also ŚARĪRA.

**theg pa dgu**. In Tibetan, the "nine vehicles"; an important formulation of the Buddhist path, especially in the RNYING MA sect of Tibetan Buddhism. In this schema, the three vehicles of ŚRĀVAKAYĀNA, PRATYEKABUDDHAYĀNA, and BODHISATTVAYĀNA and the three vehicles of HĪNAYĀNA, MAHĀYĀNA, and VAJRAYĀNA are reorganized into nine, with three groups of three. The first group is called the "causal vehicle of characteristics" (rgyu mtshan nyid kyi theg pa) and consists of the śrāvakayāna, pratyekabuddhayāna, and bodhisattvayāna. The second group is called the "outer tantras" (phyi'i rgyud) and consists of KRIYĀTANTRA, CARYĀTANTRA (also called upatantra), and YOGATANTRA. The third group is called the "inner tantras" (nang gi rgyud) and consists of MAHĀYOGA, ANUYOGA, and ATIYOGA (also called RDZOGS CHEN). Although there are precedents for such a schema in Indian sources, this specific formulation appears to have originated in Tibet.

**Theragāthā**. In Pāli, "Verses of the [Male] Elders"; the eighth book of the KHUDDAKANIKĀYA of the Pāli SUTTAPIṬAKA, a collection of 1,279 verses ascribed to 264 elder monks (P. thera, S. STHAVIRA), organized by the number of verses in each poem. The *Theragāthā* contains verses said to have been composed by enlightened elder monks during the lifetime of the Buddha or shortly thereafter. In some instances, the verses recount the life stories of the elders, in others they record their spontaneous utterances of ecstasy at the moment of their enlightenments. Not all verses are said to have been recited by the monk in question; sometimes they are addressed to a particular monk or describe that monk. The dates of the verses are difficult to determine; according to tradition, the collection was recited at the first Buddhist council (see COUNCIL, FIRST), but some of its verses are said to have been recited at the second or third Buddhist councils (SAṂGĪTI), suggesting that the verses were composed over the course of several centuries. A large number of the verses describe the path to and attainment of enlightenment, while others take the form of religious instruction. The pervasive sense of ecstasy appearing in these verses belies the common Western scholarly portrayal of the ARHAT as apathetic, cool, and aloof.

**Theravāda**. (S. *Sthaviravāda/*Sthaviranikāya; T. Gnas brtan sde pa; C. Shangzuo bu; J. Jōzabu; K. Sangjwa pu 上座部). In Pāli, "Way of the Elders" or "School of the Elders"; a designation traditionally used for monastic and textual lineages, and expanded in the modern period to refer to the dominant form of Buddhism of Sri Lanka and Southeast Asia, which is associated with study of the Pāli Buddhist canon (P. tipiṭaka; S. TRIPIṬAKA). The denotation of the term Theravāda is fraught with controversy. Buddhaghosa's commentaries to the four Pāli NIKĀYAS typically refer to himself and his colleagues as MAHĀVIHĀRAVĀSIN (lit. "Dweller in the Great Monastery"), the name of the then dominant religious order and ordination lineage in Sri Lanka; in his fifth-century commentary to the Pāli VINAYA, the SAMANTAPĀSĀDIKĀ, Buddhaghosa uses the term Theravāda, but in reference not to a separate school but to a lineage of elders going back to the first Buddhist council (see SAṂGĪTI; COUNCIL, FIRST). According to some accounts, the term Theravāda is equivalent to the Sanskrit term *STHAVIRAVĀDA ("School of the Elders"), which is claimed to have been transmitted to Sri Lanka in the third century BCE. However, the term Sthaviravāda is not attested in any Indian source; attested forms (both very rare) include sthāvira or sthāvarīya ("followers of the elders"). In addition, the Tibetan and Sinographic renderings of the term both translate the Sanskrit term *STHAVIRANIKĀYA, suggesting again that Sthaviravāda or Theravāda was not the traditional designation of this school. By the eleventh century CE, what is today designated as the Theravāda became the dominant form of Buddhism in Sri Lanka, achieving a similar status in Burma in the same century, and in Cambodia, Thailand, and Laos by the thirteenth and fourteenth centuries. As a term of self-designation for a major branch of Buddhism, Theravāda does not come into common use until the early twentieth century, with ĀNANDA METTEYYA playing a key role. In the nineteenth century, the Buddhism of Sri Lanka and Southeast Asia was typically referred to in the West as "Southern Buddhism," in distinction to the "Northern Buddhism" of Tibet and East Asia. (See, e.g., EUGÈNE BURNOUF and TAKAKUSU JUNJIRŌ, whose treatments of Pāli materials described them as belonging to the "Southern tradition.") With increased interest in Sanskrit MAHĀYĀNA texts and the rise of Japanese scholarship on Buddhism, the term "Southern Buddhism" began in some circles to be replaced by the term HĪNAYĀNA ("lesser vehicle"), despite that term's pejorative connotations. Perhaps in an effort to forestall this usage, Pāli scholars, including THOMAS W. RHYS DAVIDS (who often referred to Pāli Buddhism as "original Buddhism"), began referring to what had been known as "Southern Buddhism" as Theravāda. The term has since come to be adopted widely throughout Sri Lanka and Southeast Asia. "Theravāda" had often been mistakenly regarded as a synonym of "hīnayāna," when the latter term is used to designate the many non-Mahāyāna schools of Indian Buddhism. In fact, to the extent that the Theravāda is a remnant of the Sthaviranikāya, it represents just one of the several independent traditions of what many scholars now call MAINSTREAM BUDDHIST SCHOOLS. In the 1950s, the WORLD FELLOWSHIP OF BUDDHISTS adopted a formal resolution replacing the pejorative term hīnayāna with the designation Theravāda in descriptions of the non-Mahāyāna tradition. This suggestion was reasonable as a referent for the present state of Buddhism, since the only mainstream Buddhist school that survives in the contemporary world is Theravāda, but it is not historically accurate. Despite the way in which scholars have portrayed the tradition, Theravāda is neither synonymous with early Buddhism, nor a more pristine form of the religion prior to the rise of the Mahāyāna. Such a claim suggests a state of sectarian statis or inertia that belies the diversity over time of doctrine and practice within what comes to be called the Theravāda tradition. In fact, the redaction of Pāli scriptures postdates in many cases the redaction of much of Mahāyāna literature. Even conceding this late coinage of the term Theravāda, it should still be acknowledged that many South and Southeast Asian Buddhists who self-identify as Theravāda do in fact regard the Pāli tipiṭaka (S. TRIPIṬAKA) as representing an earlier and more authentic presentation of the word of the Buddha (BUDDHAVACANA) than that found in other contemporary Buddhist traditions, in much that same way that many North and Northeast Asian Mahāyāna Buddhists hold that certain sūtras that most scholars identify as being of later date are authentically the teachings of the historical Buddha. Although Theravāda soteriological theory includes a path for the bodhisatta (S. BODHISATTVA), the bodhisattva is a much rarer sanctified figure here than in the Mahāyāna; the more common ideal being in Theravāda is instead the ARHAT. The difference between the Buddha and the arhat is also less pronounced in the Theravāda than in the Mahāyāna schools; in the Theravāda, the Buddha and the arhat achieve the same type of NIRVĀṆA, the chief difference between them being that the Buddha finds the path to nirvāṇa independently, while the arhat achieves his or her enlightenment by following the path set forth by the Buddha. (For other distinctive beliefs of the Theravāda tradition, see STHAVIRANIKĀYA.)

**Therīgāthā**. In Pāli, "Verses of the [Female] Elders"; the ninth book of the KHUDDAKANIKĀYA of the Pāli SUTTAPIṬAKA. It contains 522 verses in seventy-three poems, organized according to the number of verses in each poem, composed by approximately one hundred female elders (although one poem is said to have been uttered by thirty therīs, another by five hundred). It said to have been composed by enlightened therīs, or elder nuns, during the lifetime of the Buddha, including many of his most famous female disciples, such as his stepmother MAHĀPRAJĀPATĪ. According to tradition, the collection was recited at the first Buddhist council (SAṂGĪTI; see COUNCIL, FIRST) held shortly after the death of the Buddha, although some verses are clearly added later. In any case, it represents one of, if not the earliest record of women's religious experience. It corresponds to the THERAGĀTHĀ in content. The precise date and authorship of the verses is difficult to determine, although many of the poems are written from the women's points of view, describing the sufferings of childbirth, marriage, and the loss of a child, a husband, and physical beauty, experiences that lead the author to enter the SAṂGHA. The spontaneous ecstatic utterances that are said to have accompanied these women's experiences of enlightenment belie the common Western scholarly portrayal of the ARHAT as apathetic, cool, and aloof.

**Thích**. (V) (釋). The Vietnamese pronunciation of the Chinese transcription of the first syllable of the Buddha's clan name, ŚĀKYA. In East Asian Buddhism, monks traditionally have abandoned their family's surname and replaced it with the Buddha's own clan name. See also SHI; FAMING.

**Thích Minh Châu**. (釋明珠) (1918–2012). Vietnamese monk born in Quảng Nam (Central Vietnam), he received ordination in 1946 from Venerable Thích Tịnh Khiết at Tường Vân Temple in Huế. In 1951, he went to India to study Pāli and Buddhism at Nalanda University. He obtained a PhD in 1961 with a thesis entitled "A Comparative Study between the Pāli MAJJHIMA NIKĀYA and the Chinese MADHYAMA ĀGAMA." After returning to South Vietnam, he became a founding member of Vạn Hạnh University as well as its rector from 1964 until its disestablishment in 1975 when South Vietnam fell to communist forces from the North. A prolific writer and translator, Thích Minh Châu single-handedly translated into Vietnamese more than thirty works from the PĀLI canon. He also wrote a three-volume Pāli grammar. After the closing of Vạn Hạnh University, he founded the Vạn Hạnh Buddhist Institute, where he continued his research and translation. In 1989, he became president of the Vietnam Institute of Buddhist Studies and head of the Committee on the Translation of the Tripiṭaka. Many expatriate Vietnamese Buddhists regard Thích Minh Châu with some suspicion because of his alleged collaboration with the Communist government after 1975, while acknowledging his important contributions to Vietnamese Buddhist literature.

**Thích Nhất Hạnh**. (釋一行) (1926–). Internationally renowned Vietnamese monk and one of the principal propounders of "Engaged Buddhism." He was born in southern Vietnam, the son of a government bureaucrat. Nhất Hạnh entered a Buddhist monastery as a novice in 1942, where he studied with a Vietnamese Zen master, and received full ordination as a monk in 1949. His interests in philosophy, literature, and foreign languages led him to leave the Buddhist seminary to study at Saigon University. While teaching in a secondary school, he served as editor of the periodical "Vietnamese Buddhism," the organ of the Association of All Buddhists in Vietnam. In 1961, he went to the United States to study at Princeton University, returning to South Vietnam in December 1963 after the overthrow of the government of the Catholic president Ngô Đình Diem, which had actively persecuted Buddhists. The persecutions had led to widespread public protests that are remembered in the West through photographs of the self-immolation of Buddhist monks. Nhất Hạnh worked to found the Unified Buddhist Church and the Institute of Higher Buddhist Studies, which later became Vạn Hạnh University. He devoted much of his time to the School of Youth for Social Service, which he founded and of which he was the director. The school's activities included sending teams of young people to the countryside to offer various forms of social assistance to the people. He also founded a new Buddhist sect (the Order of Interbeing), and helped establish a publishing house, all of which promoted what he called Engaged Buddhism. A collection of his pacifist poetry was banned by the governments of both North and South Vietnam. While engaging in nonviolent resistance to the Vietnam War, he also sought to aid its victims. In 1966, Nhất Hạnh promulgated a five-point peace plan while on an international lecture tour, during which he met with Dr. Martin Luther King Jr. (who would later nominate him for the Nobel Peace Prize) and Thomas Merton in the United States, addressed the House of Commons in Britain, and had an audience with Pope Paul VI in Rome. The book that resulted from his lecture tour, *Vietnam: Lotus in a Sea of Fire*, was banned by the South Vietnamese government. Fearing that he would be arrested or assassinated if he returned to Vietnam after the lecture tour, his supporters urged him to remain abroad and he has lived in exile ever since, residing primarily in France. He founded a center called Plum Village in southern France, whence he has sought to assist Vietnamese refugees and political prisoners and to teach Engaged Buddhism to large audiences in Europe and the Americas. A prolific writer, he has published scores of books on general, nonsectarian Buddhist teachings and practices, some of which have become bestsellers. He has made numerous trips abroad to teach and lead meditation retreats. In his teachings, Nhất Hạnh calls for a clear recognition and analysis of suffering, identifying its causes, and then working to relieve present suffering and prevent future suffering through nonviolent action. Such action in bringing peace can only truly succeed when the actor is at peace or, in his words, is "being peace."

**Thích Quảng Đức**. (釋廣德) (1897–1963). Vietnamese monk who became internationally known for his self-immolation (see SHESHEN) to protest the oppression of Buddhism by the government of the partisan Catholic president Ngô Đình Diệm. Thích Quảng Đức was born in Khánh Hòa province (Central Vietnam) and his personal name was Lâm Văn Tức. He left home to become a monk at the age of seven and received full ordination at the age of twenty. Subsequently, he went to Mount Ninh Hòa to practice austerities and led the life of a mendicant monk for five years. In 1932, he was invited to be a preceptor at the Ninh Hòa branch of the An Nam Association of Buddhist Studies. In 1934, he moved to South Vietnam, working with Buddhist communities in various provinces for several years. He then traveled to Cambodia and lived there for three years, devoting himself to rebuilding monasteries and studying Pāli literature. In 1953, the Nam Việt Association of Buddhist Studies invited him to be the abbot of Phước Hòa Temple. The last temple he supervised was Quán Thế Âm Temple in Gia Định. On June 11, 1963, when the tension between Buddhism and the government reached a high point, he led a procession of more than one thousand monks through the streets of Saigon. At a crossroad, he calmly sat down in lotus posture, doused himself in gasoline, and set himself on fire. He is revered by Vietnamese Buddhists, who refer to him as Bodhisattva Quảng Đức.

**Thích Thiên Ân**. (釋天恩) (1926–1980). The first Vietnamese Buddhist monk to spread Buddhism in the West. He was born in 1926 in Huế (Central Vietnam) in a Buddhist family. He was ordained at age fourteen. In 1953, he went to Japan to study and earned a doctorate in literature at Waseda University in 1963. He returned to Vietnam and took a teaching position in the Department of Buddhist Studies at Vạn Hạnh University in 1964. In 1966 he was invited by the University of California, Los Angeles (UCLA), to be a visiting professor. At the urging of American students, he founded the International Buddhist Meditation Center (IBMC) in 1970 in Los Angeles, the first Vietnamese center to offer full monastic ordination to Westerners. In 1973 the College of Oriental Studies was established. After South Vietnam fell in 1975, many Vietnamese refugees relocated to Southern California and the IBMC became a shelter and residence for many of them. Eventually, it could no longer accommodate the increasing number of refugees who kept arriving in Southern California. Thích Thiên Ân purchased two houses in the same neighborhood and converted them into the Vietnamese Buddhist Temple and Amida Temple. These were the first Vietnamese Buddhist temples in North America. He was also the first Vietnamese monk to write books on Chan history and practice in Japanese and English.

**Thích Trí Quang**. (釋智光) (1923–). Vietnamese monk born into a Buddhist family in Đồng Hới (Central Vietnam). He became a monk at the age of thirteen in 1936. The following year he entered the Buddhist Studies Institute of the Huế Association of Buddhist Studies. He graduated in 1945 and received full ordination in 1946. In 1947, he joined the resistance movement against the French together with his three brothers. In 1949, he went to Huế to teach at the Báo Quốc Institute of Buddhist Studies. He traveled to Saigon for the first time in 1950. During his sojourn there he campaigned to found the Nam Việt Institute of Buddhist Studies and the Nam Việt Association of Buddhist Studies, and assumed editorship of the Buddhist periodical *Viên Âm*. He also contributed to the founding of the General Association of Vietnamese Buddhism, whose goal is to unify Vietnamese Buddhism. In 1956, two years after the French withdrew from Vietnam, he became director of the Association of Buddhist Studies and fought to change the term "Buddhist Studies" to "Buddhism" (during French rule, Buddhism was not recognized as a religion). Thích Trí Quang was one of the most eminent Buddhist figures in numerous protests against the oppression of Buddhism by the Ngô Đình Diệm and subsequent South Vietnamese regimes throughout the 1960s.

**Thiền**. (禪). In Vietnamese, "Meditation"; the Vietnamese strand of the broader East Asian Chan school, which includes Chinese CHAN, Japanese ZEN, and Korean SŎN. According to the THIỀN UYỂN TẬP ANH ("Outstanding Figures in the Thiền Garden"), one of the few primary sources of the school's history, Chan teachings were assumed to have been transmitted to Vietnam by VINĪTARUCI (d. 594), a South Indian brāhmaṇa who is claimed (rather dubiously) to have studied in China with the third Chan patriarch SENGCAN before heading south to Guangzhou and Vietnam. In 580, he is said to have arrived in Vietnam and settled at Pháp Vân monastery, where he subsequently transmitted his teachings to Pháp Hiền (d. 626), who carried on his Chan tradition. In addition to the Vinītaruci lineage, there are two other putative lineages of Vietnamese Thiền, both named after their supposed founders: VÔ NGÔN THÔNG (reputedly a student of BAIZHANG HUAIHAI), and THẢO ĐƯỜNG (reputedly connected to the YUNMEN ZONG in China). Much of this history is, however, a retrospective creation. The Thiền school is in reality a much more amorphous construct than it is in the rest of East Asia: in Vietnam, there is no obvious Chan monasticism, practices, or rituals as there were in China, Korea, and Japan. Thiền is instead more of an aesthetic approach or a way of life than an identifiable school of thought or practice. Some of the few recognizable influences of Thiền in Vietnam are the traces of Chan literary topoi in Vietnamese Buddhist literature. There is little else, whether physical sites, ecclesiastical institutions, or textual or praxis evidence, that points to a concrete school of Thiền in Vietnam. See also CHAN; CHAN ZONG.

**Thiên Mụ Tự**. [alt. Linh Mụ Tự] (天姥寺/靈姥寺). In Vietnamese, "Heavenly Matron Monastery"; important Vietnamese

Buddhist sacred site, located in Huế, the ancient capital of Vietnam; also commonly known as the Chùa Thiên Mụ, or Thiên Mụ Pagoda. The pagoda was the residence of THÍCH QUANG ĐỨC (1897–1963), the monk whose self-immolation (see SHESHEN) in 1963 drew attention to the persecution of Buddhists by the pro-Catholic Vietnamese government of Ngô Đình Diệm. The pagoda is sometimes known as the Numinous Matron monastery (Linh Mụ Tự), because it was built in 1601 by the governor of Huế, Nguyễn Hoàng (d.u.), after a vision in which an old woman told him that the site was rife with numinous power. Afterward, the site was renovated several times by the local governors or the kings of the Nguyễn dynasty (1802–1945). It consists largely of two parts: the Phúc Điền tower, a seven-story octagonal tower at the entrance to the site that was erected in 1884, and the main hall at the center. Since its construction, the Thiên Mụ Pagoda has been an important center of Buddhist religious and political activity in modern and contemporary Vietnam. In 1993, it was listed as a UNESCO World Heritage Site.

**Thiền Uyển Tập Anh**. (禪苑集英). In Vietnamese, "Outstanding Figures in the THIỀN Garden." Compiled by an unknown author around the third decade of the fourteenth century, this anthology is a collection of the biographies of eminent Thiền masters in Vietnam from the sixth to the thirteenth centuries, organized around the transmission of the three major Vietnamese Thiền schools: VINĪTARUCI, VÔ NGÔN THÔNG, and THẢO ĐƯỜNG. The *Thiền Uyển* purports to be a narrative history of Vietnamese Buddhism and as such is modeled upon the Chinese CHAN literary genre known as the "transmission of the lamplight" (CHUANDENG LU). According to the account presented in the *Thiền Uyển*, Vietnamese Buddhist history is a continuation of the development of the Chinese Chan tradition. In the same period during which the *Thiền Uyển* was compiled, there emerged a number of texts of the same genre, but only fragments of those are extant. The *Thiền Uyển* is the only such lineage history that appears to have been preserved in its entirety and is the only text that attempts to provide a cohesive narrative history of Vietnamese Buddhism. The *Thiền Uyển*, however, was all but forgotten for centuries until a later recension of the text was accidentally discovered by the scholar Trần Văn Giáp in 1927. Trần wrote a long article outlining the content of text, which accepts the record of the *Thiền Uyển* as veridical history. Since that time, the account of the order provided in the *Thiền Uyển* has been widely regarded as the official history of Vietnamese Buddhism.

**thirty-two major marks of a buddha**. See MAHĀPURUṢALAKṢAṆA.

**Thissa Zedi**. A pagoda located on a small hill named Hkamin-wei in the southern Sagaing Range in Upper Burma (Myanmar). It was built in 1108 CE by the king of PAGAN, Kyansittha (r. 1084–1112), in fulfillment of an oath (Burmese, thissa; P. sacca) he made while still a soldier (Burmese, sit-tha). The similarity of these two words has led to this pagoda receiving several names, viz., Thissa Zedi (Pagoda of the Oath), Sit-tha Hpaya (Pagoda of the Soldier), and Thissa-hpaya Zedi (a spoonerism based on "Sit-tha Hpaya" meaning, again, Pagoda of the Oath).

**thod rgal**. (tögel). In Tibetan, "crossing the crest" or "leap over" (in the sense of skipping over one or more of the stages in a sequence); a special practice of ATIYOGA and one of the two main practices in the SNYING THIG tradition of RDZOGS CHEN, the other being "breakthrough" (KHREGS CHOD). Falling specifically within the "instruction class" (MAN NGAG SDE) of rdzogs chen, thod rgal follows khregs chod, in which the experience of innate awareness or RIG PA is cultivated. With this foundation, in thod rgal, the meditator uses specific physical postures to induce visions that reveal the luminous nature of external phenomena. Whereas thod rgal signifies a type of cultivated spontaneous imagery culminating in visions of MAṆḌALAs of buddhas, and is paired with the spontaneous energy (lhun grub) of pure awareness (rig pa), khregs chod (literally, "breaking through the hard") is paired with the essential purity (ka dag) of awareness. It is said that thod rgal is a method of contemplating light that enables rdzogs chen practitioners to attain the 'JA' LUS (rainbow body) without leaving any bodily traces at death. The term also renders the Sanskrit vyutkrāntaka, described in the ABHIDHARMA as jumping at will from one meditative state (a DHYĀNA or SAMĀPATTI) to any other without having to go through the intermediate stages. Thod rgal ba is also used in Tibetan commentarial literature to describe a type of meditator who does not go sequentially through each of the four fruitions of the religious life, viz., the stream-enterer (SROTAĀPANNA), once-returner (SAKṚDĀGĀMIN), nonreturner (ANĀGĀMIN), and ARHAT, but rather jumps over the intermediate results to the final goal. Some sources suggest thod rgal may also be a translation of the pluta (sometimes rendered "floater"), a meditator who jumps over the intermediate heavens in the subtle-materiality and immaterial realms and proceeds directly to the AKANIṢṬHA and BHAVĀGRA heavens.

**Tho ling gtsug lag khang**. (Toling Tsuklakang). One of the principal religious institutions of the GU GE kingdom in the western Tibetan region of Mnga' ris, established in 996 by King YE SHE 'OD and translator RIN CHEN BZANG PO; also spelled Mtho lding, Tho gling, and 'Thon 'thing. It was the first residence of the Bengali scholar ATIŚA DĪPAṂKARAŚRĪJÑĀNA during his stay in Tibet, where he composed his famous treatise, the BODHIPATHAPRADĪPA. It also served as the seat for much of Rin chen bzang po's literary career. The main image in the central temple was of the buddha VAIROCANA.

**Thomas, Edward Joseph**. (1869–1958). British scholar of Pāli and Sanskrit Buddhism. He was the son of a Yorkshire gardener and worked as a gardener himself in his early life before studying at St. Andrews and then Cambridge, where he received his BA in 1905. He spent the remainder of his life at Cambridge, holding various positions at the university library, where he was renowned for his knowledge of languages (along with his work in Indian languages, he also published a book on Danish conversational grammar). He wrote both general works on Buddhist thought and translated Buddhist texts, including a collection of JĀTAKA stories from the Pāli. His most influential work was *The Life of the Buddha as Legend and History* (1927), in which he focused upon the structure of various biographical fragments and texts, and their role within the wider tradition. Thomas stressed the importance of studying all available language sources and the need to understand the mythic and fabulous elements of the religion as important traditions in their own right.

**Thomas, Frederick William**. (1867–1956). British scholar of Sanskrit and Tibetan who served as librarian at the India Office Library in London before being appointed Boden Professor of Sanskrit at Oxford, a position he held from 1927 to 1937. His research, some in collaboration with Jacques Bacot, included work on ancient Tibetan historical texts discovered at DUNHUANG. He catalogued the Tibetan manuscripts from SIR MARC AUREL STEIN's third expedition to Dunhuang.

**Thommayut**. (Thai). See THAMMAYUT.

**Thông Biện**. (通辨) (d. 1134). The first Vietnamese Buddhist author to write a history of Vietnamese Buddhism based on the model of the "transmission of the lamplight" (CHUANDENG) histories of the Chinese CHAN school. He was a native of Đan Phượng (which is now in Hà Tây province, North Vietnam). His family name was Ngô and he was born into a Buddhist family. He was respected by the Lý court and was bestowed the title *quốc sư* (state preceptor; C. GUOSHI). The THIỀN UYỂN TẬP ANH relates that in a lecture in 1096 he interpreted Vietnamese Buddhist history as the continuation of the transmission of both the scriptural school and the mind (or Chan) school of Chinese Buddhism. According to Thông Biện, the Scriptural School began with Mou Bo and Kang Senghui, and the Chan school was transmitted by BODHIDHARMA. He further claimed that Chan came to Vietnam through two streams, represented, respectively, by VINĪTARUCI (d. 594) and VÔ NGÔN THÔNG (d. 826). Vinītaruci and Vô Ngôn Thông thus were the ancestral teachers of the two streams of Chan that produced numerous side branches in Vietnam. Later in his life, Thông Biện founded a great teaching center and taught the SADDHARMAPUṆḌARĪKASŪTRA. His contemporaries referred to him as Ngộ Pháp Hoa (Awakened to the Lotus). Thông Biện's model of Vietnamese Buddhist history was subsequently adopted by Buddhist authors of later generations and thus exercised lasting influence on the traditional understanding of Vietnamese Buddhist history. Many modern Vietnamese Buddhist leaders still accept Thông Biện's views about the history of Buddhism in Vietnam.

**Thorani**. In Thailand and Laos, Phra Mae (Mother) Thorani or Nang (Lady) Thorani; a female deity depicted in mural depictions of the life of the Buddha. The name Thorani is the Thai and Lao pronunciation of the Sanskrit term DHĀRAṆĪ, which, in addition to its common Buddhist denotation of "code" or "spell," also means "the earth," "soil," or "ground." In a variation of the story of STHĀVARĀ, as the future Buddha sat in meditation about to attain enlightenment, he was attacked by MĀRA and his minions. Māra taunted him, saying that the bodhisattva had no one to attest to his worthiness of becoming a buddha, whereas his vast retinue was present to attest that he, Māra, should be acknowledged as the awakened one. The Buddha then touched the earth with his right hand and summoned the earth to bear witness to his meritorious acts (see BHŪMISPARŚAMUDRĀ), particularly acts of giving (DĀNA), that he had performed in past existences. Lady Thorani then appeared from out of the earth in the form of a beautiful woman with long wet hair. As she wrung out her hair, all the water that had accumulated on the earth each time the Buddha offered donative libations during his myriad past lives became such a torrential deluge that it swept away Māra and all his minions. (Pouring a ceremonial libation of water is a common way to conclude many ceremonies and offering rituals in Southeast Asian Buddhism.) In paintings, Lady Thorani stands beneath the VAJRĀSANA of the Buddha while Māra and his retinue are off to either side, caught in the floodwaters. Central city shrines to Lady Thorani can be found in both Laos and northeastern Thailand, and in the past, it was common for households in northeastern Thailand to have a small shrine dedicated to Lady Thorani in their household compounds.

**Thousand-Armed and Thousand-Eyed Avalokiteśvara**. See SĀHASRABHUJASĀHASRANETRĀVALOKITEŚVARA.

**three bodies (of the buddhas)**. See TRIKĀYA.

**three catties of flax (gong'an)**. See MA SANJIN.

**three doors/gates**. See TRIDVĀRA.

**three jewels**. See RATNATRAYA.

**three marks of existence**. See TRILAKṢAṆA.

**three natures**. See TRISVABHĀVA.

**three periods of the teachings**. See MOFA.

**three poisons**. See TRIVIṢA.

**three realms of existence**. See TRAIDHĀTUKA.

**three refuges**. See TRIŚARAṆA.

**Three Stages/Third Stage Sect**. See SANJIE JIAO.

**three trainings**. See TRIŚIKṢĀ.

**three turnings of the wheel of the dharma**. See SAṂDHINIRMOCANASŪTRA.

**three vehicles**. See TRIYĀNA.

**three vows**. See TRISAṂVARA.

**Thub bstan rgya mtsho**. (Tupten Gyatso) (1876–1933). The thirteenth DALAI LAMA of Tibet, remembered as a particularly forward-thinking and politically astute leader. Born in southeastern Tibet, he was recognized as the new Dalai Lama in 1878 and enthroned the next year. Surviving an assassination attempt (using black magic) by his regent, he assumed the duties of his office in 1895 during a period of complicated international politics between Britain, Russia, and China. British troops under the command of Col. Francis Younghusband entered Tibet in 1903. Before the British arrived in LHA SA the following year, the Dalai Lama fled to Mongolia and then continued to China, not returning to Lha sa until 1909. The following year, Chinese Manchu troops invaded Tibet and the Dalai Lama fled to India, returning in 1912. In 1912, the Manchu troops were expelled, and in 1913 the Dalai Lama declared Tibet's de facto independence. A progressive thinker, the thirteenth Dalai Lama made direct contact with Europe and the United States, and befriended Sir Charles Bell, the British political officer in Sikkim, Bhutan, and Tibet. He tried, unsuccessfully, to have Tibet admitted to the League of Nations, developed Tibet's first modern army, and sent the first young Tibetans to be educated in England. Most of his progressive plans, however, were thwarted by conservative religious and political forces within Tibet. The thirteenth Dalai Lama died in 1933, leaving behind a chilling prophecy, which read in part: "The monasteries will be looted and destroyed, and the monks and nuns killed or chased away. The great works of the noble dharma kings of old will be undone, and all of our cultural and spiritual institutions persecuted, destroyed, and forgotten. The birthrights and property of the people will be stolen. We will become like slaves to our conquerors, and will be made to wander helplessly like beggars. Everyone will be forced to live in misery, and the days and nights will pass slowly, with great suffering and terror."

**Thubten Yeshe**. (Thub bstan ye shes) (1935–1984). Influential teacher of Tibetan Buddhism in the West. Born to a farming family, in a village near LHA SA, Thubten Yeshe's first experience with monasticism began when, as a toddler, he was discovered to be an incarnation of the abbess of 'Chi med lung monastery. He displayed strong leanings toward the monastic life from a very early age and, when he was six, his parents put him in the care of an uncle at SE RA monastery outside Lha sa. He spent the next nineteen years at Se ra, where he studied diligently but was unable to complete his DGE BSHES (geshe) degree prior to fleeing Tibet at the time of the Lha sa uprising of 1959. He escaped to India with two of his brothers, going to the refugee camp in Buxador in northeast India. He began teaching Western students at Kopan monastery, near BODHNĀTH in Kathmandu, Nepal. He also traveled the world with his main disciple and fellow monk, Zopa Rinpoche. Together they created the Foundation for the Preservation of the Mahāyāna Tradition in 1975, along with Wisdom Publications, the Root Institute in BODHGAYĀ, the Tushita Dharma Center in DHARMAŚĀLĀ, India, and Nalanda monastery near Toulouse, France.

**Thudhamma**. (P. Sudhamma). The majority Buddhist monastic fraternity (B. GAING; P. gaṇa, cf. NIKĀYA) in contemporary Myanmar (Burma), comprising 85–90 percent of the monastic population of the country. The name derives from the Thudhamma Council, an ecclesiastical body appointed by royal decree in 1782, which was charged with reforming the Burmese saṅgha (S. SAṂGHA) and uniting its various factions into a single fraternity under Thudhamma leadership. The Thudhamma Council established a common monastic curriculum and in general promoted uniformity of doctrinal interpretation and VINAYA practice among the kingdom's monasteries. With the exception of a short hiatus in the 1810s, the council remained a permanent governing body of the Burmese saṅgha until the late nineteenth century, when it was dissolved following the British conquest of Upper Burma in 1885 and the deposition of the Burmese king. Even before that event, the authority of the council had declined in Lower Burma as a consequence of Britain's seizure of Burma's maritime provinces in 1824 and 1852. During the reign of MINDON MIN (1853–1878), Burmese monks living in British-controlled Lower Burma refused to recognize the authority of the Thudhamma Council and organized themselves into an independent fraternity called the DWAYA GAING (P. Dvāragaṇa). In the Burmese kingdom itself, the council's policies were not supported by ultra-orthodox monks who, because of their prominent disciplinary observances and scriptural expertise, gained popular support and royal patronage. From among these reformist monks, two prominent factions emerged, the SHWEGYIN and Hngettwin, both of which eventually organized themselves into independent fraternities with their own network of monasteries. After the disestablishment of Buddhism as the state religion of Burma by the British, all "unreformed" monasteries, which were the vast majority in the country, came to be designated Thudhamma by default, even though there was no longer an ecclesiastical umbrella under which they operated nor a hierarchy to which they were answerable. This allowed for the politicization of Thudhamma monks during the British colonial period, some of whom became leaders of the Burmese independence movement. In 1980, the Burmese government's Ministry of Religious Affairs recognized the Thudhamma gaing as one of nine officially sanctioned monastic fraternities comprising the Burmese saṅgha. Somewhat more relaxed in matters of outward deportment than especially the Shwegyin and Dwaya, the Thudhamma gaing is renowned for its scholarship and maintains major monastic colleges in Yangon (Rangoon), Mandalay, and Pakokku.

**thudong**. (P. dhutaṅga). In Thai, "ascetics"; the tradition of forest monks (P. ARAÑÑAVĀSI) who observe the strict set of thirteen austerities (DHUTAṄGA), such as eating only one meal a day, living in the forest or at the root of a tree, meditating in charnel grounds, eating only from the alms bowl, etc. In Thailand, the thudong tradition is strongest in the Northeast, near the Laotian border, and is particularly, but not exclusively, associated with the reformed THAMMAYUT (P. Dhammayuttika) order. The thudong tradition experienced a resurgence in the late nineteenth and twentieth centuries, when it was revitalized through the efforts of AJAHN MUN BHŪRIDATTA, Ajahn Sao Kantasīla (1861–1941), and, later, AJAHN CHAH BODHIÑĀṆA.

**Thun mong ma yin pa'i mdzod**. (Tunmong Mayinpe Dzö). In Tibetan, "The Uncommon Treasury"; an encyclopedic work written by the nineteenth-century Tibetan scholar 'JAM MGON KONG SPRUL BLO GROS MTHA' YAS. The text is counted among the five treasuries of Kongtrül (KONG SPRUL MDZOD LNGA). It preserves numerous tantric ritual and liturgical texts of the RNYING MA sect of Tibetan Buddhism, as well as works on philosophy, poetry, astrology, and descriptions of local Buddhist practices and sites.

**Thūpārāma**. In Pāli, "Monastery of the STŪPA"; a monastery situated to the south of the Sinhalese capital of ANURĀDHAPURA in the MAHĀMEGHAVANA grove. Built by King DEVĀNAṂPIYATISSA, the monastery derives its name from the thūpa reliquary mound located within its precincts. The thūpa houses the Buddha's collarbone and was the first shrine of its kind on the island. The spot where the thūpa stands is where Gotama (S. GAUTAMA) Buddha and other buddhas were thought to have once meditated. Also within the grounds of the Thūpārāma was planted a sapling taken from a branch of the BODHI TREE that had been brought to Sri Lanka by the nun SAṄGHAMITTĀ. Once, during the first century BCE, the monks of the Thūpārāma conspired with counselors to deny kingship to the island's rightful heir, the crown prince Lañjatissa, giving it instead to his younger brother, Thūlatthana. When Lañjatissa regained the throne, he chastised the saṅgha by causing its junior monks to be honored first, and its senior monks last—thus repaying them in kind. During the reign of King Mahāsena, the heretical monk, Saṅghamitta, planned to disassemble the Thūpārāma, but was assassinated before he could carry out the deed. The Thūpārāma has been restored and renovated numerous times and is richly ornamented with plates and bricks made of gold and silver.

**Thūpavaṃsa**. In Pāli, "Chronicle of the Thūpa"; a twelfth-century Pāli work in verse in sixteen chapters. (Thūpa is the Pāli term for S. STŪPA.) The text is attributed to Vācissara. The text includes accounts of the lives of previous buddhas, the life and parinibbāna (S. PARINIRVĀṆA) of Gotama (S. GAUTAMA) Buddha, the distribution of his relics, the meritorious deeds of AŚOKA, the dispatch of missions to Sri Lanka and other foreign lands, culminating with the construction of the MAHĀTHŪPA, or "Great Stūpa," by the Sinhala hero–king, DUṬṬHAGĀMAṆĪ, at ANURĀDHAPURA.

**ti**. (J. tai; K. ch'e 體). In Chinese, lit. "body," and by extension "essence," or "substance"; a term widely used in East Asian religious traditions, including Buddhism. "Essence" often constitutes a philosophical pair together with the term "function" (YONG). In early Confucian texts, such as the *Lunyu* ("Analects") and the *Mengzi*, ti simply referred to a "body" or the "appearance" of a person or a thing. It was Wang Bi (226–249), the founder of the "Dark Learning" (XUANXUE) school of Chinese philosophy, who imbued the term with philosophical implications, using ti as a synonym for the Daoist concepts of "nonbeing" (WU) or "voidness" (xu). However, ti, along with its companion yong, was not widely used until the Buddhists adopted both terms to provide a basic conceptual frame for reality or truth. For example, the Later Qin (384–417) monk SENGZHAO (384–414?) identified ti as the nature of calmness (ji) and advocated its unity with yong, which he defined as the function of illumination (zhao). The SAN LUN ZONG master JIZANG (549–623), in discussing the two-truth (SATYADVAYA) theory of MADHYAMAKA, argued that "neither ultimate nor conventional" (feizhen feisu) was the ti ("essence") of the two truths, while "both ultimate and conventional" (zhensu) were their yong ("function"). The LIUZU TAN JING ("Platform Sūtra of the Sixth Patriarch") associates ti and yong with two modes of meditation: concentration (SAMĀDHI) is the ti or essence of wisdom (PRAJÑĀ); wisdom is the yong or function of concentration. GUIFENG ZONGMI (780–841), the Tang master of both the HUAYAN ZONG scholastic and the Heze Chan traditions, systematized the Chinese discourse of the terms. Based on the DASHENG QIXIN LUN ("Awakening of Faith According to the Mahāyāna"), Zongmi interpreted ti as the unchanging essence of true thusness (ZHENRU), calling this absolute aspect of mind the "void and calm, numinous awareness" (KONGJI LINGZHI; see LINGZHI). Yong instead referred to the diverse functional aspects of true thusness, which corresponded to the "production-and-cessation" aspect of mind (shengmie). He also aligned ti and yong with other indigenous Chinese philosophical polarities such as, respectively, "nature" (XING) and "characteristics" (xiang), "principle" (LI) and "phenomena" (SHI), and "root" (ben) and "branches" (mo). Subsequently, Neo-Confucian thinkers, such as Cheng Yi (1033–1107) and Zhu Xi (1130–1200), adopted this paradigm into their own philosophical systems. In particular, Zhu Xi connected ti to the "nature bestowed by the heavenly mandate" (tianming zhixing) and yong to the "physical nature" (qizhi zhixing).

**Tiantai**. (C; J. Tendai; K. Ch'ont'ae 天台). See TIANTAI ZONG.

**Tiantai bajiao**. (J. Tendai hakkyō; K. Ch'ŏnt'ae p'algyo 天台八教). In Chinese, "The Eight [Classes of] Teachings according to the TIANTAI." According to the TIANTAI ZONG's system of doctrinal classification (JIAOXIANG PANSHI), the entirety of the Buddhist canon and its teachings can be divided into two groups of four teachings each. The first group of four was called "the four modes of transformative teachings" (huafa sijiao), which categorizes Buddhist teachings based on the content of their teachings and different doctrinal themes and their scriptural bases. The second group of four was called "the four styles of transformative edification" or "four modes of exposition" (huayi sijiao), which categorizes different strands of Buddhism primarily according to their means of conversion or pedagogical styles. ¶ The first group of four teachings, the transformative teachings (huafa sijiao), classifies Buddhism into four categories based on content: (1) zangjiao, the "TRIPIṬAKA teachings," the basic teachings that are foundational to the HĪNAYĀNA schools, such as the notions of impermanence, suffering, and no-self, and the imperative of attaining NIRVĀṆA; (2) tongjiao, the "joint" or "common teachings," a basic strand of MAHĀYĀNA teaching that shares many of the preceding doctrinal themes jointly with the "hīnayāna teachings," the main difference being that it additionally embraces the BODHISATTVA aspiration of helping others; (3) biejiao, the "distinct" or "separate teachings," so named because, unlike the previous category, this strand of Mahāyāna includes notions exclusive to that tradition and not shared with the "hīnayāna"; (4) yuanjiao, the "consummate" or "perfect teaching," which is the exclusive domain of the SADDHARMAPUṆḌARĪKASŪTRA, the main scripture the Tiantai school itself espouses. ¶ The second group of four teachings, the modes of exposition or conversion (huayi sijiao), contains the following divisions based on pedagogical style: (1) dunjiao, the "sudden teachings" or a direct pedagogical style. Epitomized by the AVATAṂSAKASŪTRA, this mode of teaching is characterized by a direct revelation of the stage of buddhahood, circumventing the gradual, and more conventional, stages of beginning bodhisattva practices and the "hīnayāna" tradition. (2) Jianjiao, the "gradual teachings" or pedagogical style. Representing these sequential, step-by-step soteriological approaches and pedagogical styles are the ĀGAMAs, the PRAJÑĀPĀRAMITĀ sūtras, and the VAIPULYA sūtras. (3) Budingjiao, the "indefinite teachings" or pedagogical style. The same utterance of the Buddha might be given without differentiation to various members of the audience, but the depth to which they were able to penetrate to that message, and the different interpretations they gave to it, varied depending on their spiritual maturity. (4) Mimijiao, the "esoteric teachings" or pedagogical style. Not to be confused with tantric teachings, "esoteric" here refers to the Tiantai belief that the Buddha sometimes preached in such a way that his same utterance resonated differently with various members within the audience, so that each received the instruction most suitable to his needs and temperament; with this pedagogical style, the Buddha essentially left members of the audience free to fathom an inexhaustibly elastic teaching and be benefited from it according to their unique conditions. See also WUSHI; CH'ŎNT'AE SAGYO ŬI.

**Tiantai sijiao**. (C) (天台四教). See TIANTAI BAJIAO.

**Tiantai wushi**. (J. Tendai goji; K. Ch'ŏnt'ae osi 天台五時). In Chinese, "the five periods [of the Buddha's teaching]"; the TIANTAI ZONG's temporal taxonomy of Buddhist doctrines, according to which the Buddha's teachings differ because he preached them at different points during his pedagogical career. The five are (1) Huayan (AVATAṂSAKASŪTRA), (2) ĀGAMA, (3) VAIPULYA, (4) PRAJÑĀPĀRAMITĀ, and (5) Lotus (SADDHARMAPUṆḌARĪKASŪTRA) and Nirvāṇa (MAHĀPARINIRVĀṆASŪTRA). See WUSHI; WUWEI.

**Tiantai xiaozhiguan**. (C) (天台小止觀). See XIUXI ZHIGUAN ZUOCHAN FAYAO.

**Tiantai Zhiyi**. (J. Tendai Chigi; K. Ch'ŏnt'ae Chiŭi 天台智顗) (538–597). One of the most influential monks in Chinese Buddhist history and de facto founder of the TIANTAI ZONG. A native of Jingzhou (in present-day Hunan province), Zhiyi was ordained at the age of eighteen after his parents died during the wartime turmoil that preceded the Sui dynasty's unification of China. He studied VINAYA and various MAHĀYĀNA scriptures, including the SADDHARMAPUṆḌARĪKASŪTRA ("Lotus Sūtra") and related scriptures. In 560, Zhiyi met NANYUE HUISI (515–577), who is later listed as the second patriarch of the Tiantai lineage, on Mt. Dasu in Guangzhou and studied Huisi's teachings on the suiziyi sanmei (cultivating SAMĀDHI wherever mind is directed, or the samādhi of freely flowing thoughts), the "four practices of ease and bliss" (si anle xing), a practice based on the *Saddharmapuṇḍarīkasūtra*, and the lotus repentance ritual. Zhiyi left Huisi at his teacher's command and headed for the southern capital of Jinling (present-day Jiangsu province) at the age of thirty (567) to teach the *Saddharmapuṇḍarīkasūtra* and the DAZHIDU LUN for eight years at the monastery of Waguansi. The *Shi chanboluomi cidi famen* [alt. *Cidi chanmen*] are his lecture notes from this period of meditation and teaching. In 575, he retired to Mt. Tiantai (present-day Zhejiang province), where he built a monastery (later named Xiuchansi by the emperor) and devoted himself to meditative practice for eleven years. During this time he compiled the *Fajie cidi chumen* and the *Tiantai xiao zhiguan*. After persistent invitations from the king of Chen, Zhiyi returned to Jinling in 585 and two years later wrote the FAHUA WENJU, an authoritative commentary on the *Saddharmapuṇḍarīkasūtra*. Subsequently in Yangzhou, Zhiyi conferred the bodhisattva precepts on the crown prince, who later became Emperor Yang (r. 604–617) of the Sui dynasty. Zhiyi was then given the title Great Master Zhizhe (Wise One). Zhiyi also established another monastery on Mt. Dangyang in Yuquan (present-day Hunan province), which Emperor Wen (r. 581–604) later named Yuquansi. Zhiyi then began lecturing on what became his masterpieces, the FAHUA

XUANYI (593) and the MOHE ZHIGUAN (594). At the request of the king of Jin, in 595 Zhiyi returned to Yangzhou, where he composed his famous commentaries on the VIMALAKĪRTINIRDEŚA, i.e., the *Weimojing xuanshou* and the *Weimojing wenshou*, before dying in 597. Among the thirty or so works attributed to Zhiyi, the *Fahua xuanyi*, *Fahuawenju*, and *Mohe zhiguan* are most renowned and are together known as the Tiantai san dabu (three great Tiantai commentaries).

**Tiantai zong**. (J. Tendaishū; K. Ch'ŏnt'ae chong 天台宗). In Chinese, "Terrace of Heaven School"; one of the main schools of East Asian Buddhism; also sometimes called the "Lotus school" (C. Lianhua zong), because of its emphasis on the SADDHARMAPUṆḌARĪKASŪTRA ("Lotus Sūtra"). "Terrace of Heaven" is a toponym for the school's headquarters on Mt. Tiantai in present-day Zhejiang province on China's eastern seaboard. Although the school retrospectively traces its origins back to Huiwen (fl. 550–577) and NANYUE HUISI (515–577), whom the school honors as its first and second patriarchs, respectively, the de facto founder was TIANTAI ZHIYI (538–597), who created the comprehensive system of Buddhist teachings and practices that we now call Tiantai. Zhiyi advocated the three truths or judgments (SANDI): (1) the truth of emptiness (kongdi), viz., all things are devoid of inherent existence and are empty in their essential nature; (2) the truth of being provisionally real (jiadi), viz., all things are products of a causal process that gives them a derived reality; and (3) the truth of the mean (zhongdi), viz., all things, in their absolute reality, are neither real nor unreal, but simply thus. Zhiyi described reality in terms of YINIAN SANQIAN (a single thought contains the TRICHILIOCOSM [TRISĀHASRAMAHĀSĀHASRALOKADHĀTU]), which posits that any given thought-moment perfectly encompasses the entirety of reality; at the same time, every phenomenon includes all other phenomena (XINGJU SHUO), viz., both the good and evil aspects of the ten constituents (DHĀTU) or the five sense organs (INDRIYA) and their respective objects and the three realms of existence (TRAIDHĀTUKA) are all contained in the original nature of all sentient beings. Based on this perspective on reality, Zhiyi made unique claims about the buddha-nature (FOXING) and contemplation (GUAN): he argued that not only buddhas but even sentient beings in such baleful existences as animals, hungry ghosts, and hell denizens, possess the capacity to achieve buddhahood; by the same token, buddhas also inherently possess all aspects of the unenlightened three realms of existence. The objects of contemplation, therefore, should be the myriad of phenomena, which are the source of defilement, not an underlying pure mind. Zhiyi's grand synthesis of Buddhist thought and practice is built around a graduated system of calmness and insight (jianzi ZHIGUAN; cf. ŚAMATHA and VIPAŚYANĀ), which organized the plethora of Buddhist meditative techniques into a broad, overarching soteriological system. To Zhiyi is also attributed the Tiantai system of doctrinal classification (panjiao; see JIAOXIANG PANSHI) called WUSHI BAJIAO (five periods and eight teachings), which the Koryŏ Korean monk CH'EGWAN (d. 970) later elaborated in its definitive form in his CH'ŎNT'AE SAGYO ŬI (C. *Tiantai sijiao yi*). This system classifies all Buddhist teachings according to the five chronological periods, four types of content, and four modes of conversion. Zhiyi was succeeded by Guanding (561–632), who compiled his teacher's works, especially his three masterpieces, the FAHUA XUANYI, the FAHUA WENJU, and the MOHE ZHIGUAN. The Tiantai school declined during the Tang dynasty, overshadowed by the newer HUAYAN and CHAN schools. The ninth patriarch JINGXI ZHANRAN (711–782) was instrumental in rejuvenating the school; he asserted the superiority of the Tiantai school over the rival Huayan school by adapting Huayan concepts and terminologies into the tradition. Koryŏ monks such as Ch'egwan and Ŭit'ong (927–988) played major roles in the restoration of the school by helping to repatriate lost Tiantai texts back to China. During the Northern Song period, Wu'en (912–988), Yuanqing (d. 997), Zhiyuan (976–1022), and their disciples, who were later pejoratively called the SHANWAI (Off-Mountain) faction by their opponents, led the resurgence of the tradition by incorporating Huayan concepts in the school's thought and practice: they argued that since the true mind, which is pure in its essence, produces all phenomena in accord with conditions, practitioners should contemplate the true mind, rather than all phenomena. Believing this idea to be a threat to the tradition, SIMING ZHILI (960–1028) and his disciples, who called themselves SHANJIA (On-Mountain), criticized such a concept of pure mind as involving a principle of separateness, since it includes only the pure and excludes the impure, and led a campaign to expunge the Huayan elements that they felt were displacing authentic Tiantai doctrine. Although Renyue (992–1064) and Congyi (1042–1091), who were later branded as the "Later Off-Mountain Faction," criticized Zhili and accepted some of the Shanwai arguments, the Shanjia faction eventually prevailed and legitimized Zhili's positions. The orthodoxy of Zhili's position is demonstrated in the FOZU TONGJI ("Comprehensive History of the Buddhas and Patriarchs"), where the compiler Zhipan (1220–1275), himself a Tiantai monk, lists Zhili as the last patriarch in the dharma transmission going back to the Buddha. Tiantai theories and practices were extremely influential in the development of the thought and practice of the Chan and PURE LAND schools; this influence is especially noticeable in the white-lotus retreat societies (JIESHE; see also BAILIAN SHE) organized during the Song dynasty by such Tiantai monks as Zhili and Zunshi (964–1032) and in Koryŏ Korea (see infra). After the Song dynasty, the school declined again, and never recovered its previous popularity. ¶ Tiantai teachings and practices were transmitted to Korea during the Three Kingdoms period through such Korean monks as Hyŏn'gwang (fl. sixth century) and Yŏn'gwang (fl. sixth century), both of whom traveled to China and studied under Chinese Tiantai teachers. It was not until several centuries later, however, that a Korean analogue of the Chinese Tiantai school was established as an independent Buddhist school. The foundation of the Korean CH'ŎNT'AE

CHONG is traditionally assumed to have occurred in 1097 through the efforts of the Koryŏ monk ŬICH'ŎN (1055–1101). Ŭich'ŏn was originally a Hwaŏm monk, but he sought to use the Ch'ŏnt'ae tradition in order to reconcile the age-old tension in Korean Buddhism between KYO (Doctrine) and SŎN (Meditation). In the early thirteenth century, the Ch'ŏnt'ae monk WŎNMYO YOSE (1163–1245) organized the white lotus society (PAENGNYŎN KYŎLSA), which gained great popularity especially among the common people; following Yose, the school was led by Ch'ŏn'in (1205–1248) and CH'ŎNCH'AEK (b. 1206). Although the Ch'ŏnt'ae monk Chogu (d. 1395) was appointed as a state preceptor (K. kuksa; C. GUOSHI) in the early Chosŏn period, the Ch'ŏnt'ae school declined and eventually died out later in the Chosŏn dynasty. The contemporary Ch'ŏnt'ae chong is a modern Korean order established in 1966 that has no direct relationship to the school founded by Ŭich'ŏn. ¶ In Japan, SAICHŌ (767–822) is credited with founding the Japanese TENDAISHŪ, which blends Tiantai and tantric Buddhist elements. After Saichō, such Tendai monks as ENNIN (793–864), ENCHIN (814–891), and ANNEN (b. 841) systematized Tendai doctrines and developed its unique forms, which are often called TAIMITSU (Tendai esoteric teachings). Since the early ninth century, when the court granted the Tendai school official recognition as an independent sect, Tendai became one of the major Buddhist schools in Japan and enjoyed royal and aristocratic patronage for several centuries. The Tendai school's headquarters on HIEIZAN became an important Japanese center of Buddhist learning: the founders of the so-called new Buddhist schools of the Kamakura era, such as HŌNEN (1133–1212), SHINRAN (1173–1263), NICHIREN (1222–1282), and DŌGEN KIGEN (1200–1253), all first studied on Mt. Hiei as Tendai monks. Although the Tendai school has lost popularity and patrons to the ZENSHŪ, PURE LAND, and NICHIRENSHŪ schools, it remains still today an active force on the Japanese Buddhist landscape.

**Tiantong Rujing**. (J. Tendō Nyojō; K. Ch'ŏndong Yŏjŏng 天童如净) (1162–1227). Chinese CHAN master in the CAODONG ZONG, also known as Jingchang (Pure Chang) and Changweng (Old Man Chang); he received his toponym Tiantong after the mountain where he once dwelled. Rujing was a native of Shaoxing in Yuezhou (present-day Zhejiang province) and was ordained at a local monastery named Tianyisi. Rujing later went to the monastery of Zishengsi on Mt. Xuedou to study under Zu'an Zhijian (1105–1192) and eventually became his dharma heir. Rujing spent the next few decades moving from one monastery to the next. In 1220, he found himself at Qingliangsi in Jiankang (Jiangsu province) and then at Rui'ansi in Taizhou and Jingcisi in Linan. In 1224, Rujing was appointed by imperial decree to the abbotship of the famous monastery of Jingdesi on Mt. Tiantong, where the Chan master HONGZHI ZHENGJUE had once resided. Rujing's teachings can be found in his recorded sayings (YULU), which were preserved in Japan. Although Rujing was a relatively minor figure in the history of Chinese Chan, he was profoundly influential in Japanese ZEN, due to the fact that the Japanese SŌTŌSHŪ founder DŌGEN KIGEN (1200–1253) considered himself to be Rujing's successor. Dōgen attributes many of the distinctive features of his own approach to practice, such as "just sitting" (SHIKAN TAZA) and "body and mind sloughed off" (SHINJIN DATSURAKU) to this man whom he regarded as the preeminent Chan master of his era. Little of this distinctively Sōtō terminology and approach actually appears in the records of Rujing's own lectures, however. Instead, he appears in his discourse record as a fairly typical Song-dynasty Chan master, whose only practical meditative instruction involves the contemplation of ZHAOZHOU's "no" (see WU GONG'AN). This difference may reflect the differing editorial priorities of Rujing's Chinese disciples. It might also derive from the fact that Dōgen misunderstood Rujing or received simplified private instructions from him because of Dōgen's difficulty in following Rujing's formal oral presentations in vernacular Chinese.

**Tiantong Zhengjue**. (C) (天童正覺). See HONGZHI ZHENGJUE.

**Tianxizai**. (J. Tensokusai; K. Ch'ŏnsikchae 天息災) (d. 1000). Kashmiri monk-translator, who arrived in China in 980. While residing at a cloister to the west of the imperial monastery of Taiping-Xingguosi in Yuanzhou (present-day Jiangxi province), he translated (sometimes working in collaboration with DĀNAPĀLA and Fatian) seventeen MAHĀYĀNA and prototantric scriptures into Chinese, including the BODHICARYĀVATĀRA, KĀRAṆḌAVYŪHA, *Alpākṣarāprajñāpāramitāsūtra*, *Āyuṣparyantasūtra*, *(Ārya) Tārābhaṭṭarikāyanāmāṣṭottaraśataka*, *Māricīdhāraṇī*, and the MAÑJUŚRĪMŪLAKALPA.

**Tianzhu**. (J. Tenjiku; K. Ch'ŏnch'uk 天竺). Early Chinese phonetic transcription of Sindhu, viz., India, which becomes the most common designation in Chinese sources for the Indian subcontinent. See also ZHU.

**Tibetan Book of the Dead**. See BAR DO THOS GROL CHEN MO.

**tichang**. (J. teishō; K. chech'ang 提唱). In Chinese, "lecture," a type of discourse associated especially with the CHAN ZONG and widely known in the West by its Japanese pronunciation teishō; also called tigang (J. teikō, K. chegang) or tiyao (J. teiyō, K. cheyo). Such lectures, which were often delivered in highly colloquial language, sought to point to the main purport of a Chan tradition, text, or "case" (GONG'AN) by drawing on the peculiar Chan argot and extensively citing Chan literature and Buddhist scriptures. Chan masters might also deliver a sequential series of lectures on each of the Chan cases in a larger gong'an collection, such as the BIYAN LU or the WUMEN GUAN. Such lectures were sometimes delivered in conjunction with the formal "ascending the hall" (SHANGTANG) procedure; the term may also refer to the master's expository comments regarding questions that visitors might raise in the course of listening to a formal lecture. The tichang lecture is the Chan counterpart of expositions of Buddhist teachings given by lecturers in doctrinal schools, but making more use of Chan rather than commentarial and scriptural materials. The term was widely used in the Chan tradition especially from the Song dynasty onward. Although the term appears only rarely in such Chan codes as the BAIZHANG QINGGUI ("Baizhang's Pure Rules") and the CHANYUAN QINGGUI ("Pure Rules of the Chan Garden"), these sources do describe the general procedures to be followed in delivering such a lecture. The forty-two roll *Liezu tigang lu* ("Record of the Lectures of Successive Patriarchs," using the alternate term tigang), compiled by the Qing-dynasty Chan master Daiweng Xingyue (1619–1684), collects about four hundred Chinese masters' lectures delivered at various special occasions, such as the reigning emperor's birthday or funeral, and in conjunction with daily services.

**tīkṣṇendriya**. (P. tikkhindriya; T. dbang po rnon po; C. ligen; J. rikon; K. igŭn 利根). In Sanskrit, "sharp faculties," the highest of the "three capacities" (TRĪNDRIYA), used to describe those disciples of the Buddha whose intellectual and spiritual abilities are greater than that of those of average (MADHYENDRIYA) and dull capacities (MṚDVINDRIYA). The term appears particularly in discussions of UPĀYA, the Buddha's ability to adapt his teachings to the intellects, interests, and aspirations of his disciples, with his highest teachings said to be reserved for disciples of sharp faculties. Thus the term is also often used polemically to describe one's preferred teaching as intended only for those of sharp faculties, while dismissing other competing teachings as intended for those of dull or average faculties. See also MAHĀPURUṢA; INDRIYA.

**Tilokaracha**. [alt. Tilokarat] (P. Tilokarājā) (r. 1441–1487). Thai name of an important Lānnā king of Chiangmai in northern Thailand who expanded the boundaries of the Lānnā kingdom militarily while promoting the reform Sinhalese monastic order led by Medhaṅkara throughout the territories under his domain. Tilokaracha promoted himself as a wheel-turning monarch (P. cakkavattin; S. CAKRAVARTIN), acting in emulation of AŚOKA. He constructed hundreds of monasteries and ordination halls throughout the kingdom, and directed that BODHI TREE saplings be planted at the sites. In 1445, built a replica of the MAHĀBODHI temple named Wat Photharam Maha Wihan (P. Bodhi-Ārāma Mahāvihāra), known also as Wat Chet Yot (Temple of the Seven Spires). In 1477, he convened a saṅgha (S. SAṂGHA) council at Wat Photharam for the editing of the Buddhist canon (P. tipiṭaka; S. TRIPIṬAKA), possibly also for the purpose of reconciling the new Sinhalese order with the older Sumana order. This meeting came to be recognized as an eighth Buddhist council by the Thais. In 1481, he restored the Wat Chedi Luang located in Chiangmai and installed the Emerald Buddha (PHRA KAEW MORAKOT) in its pinnacle. The political unification and religious and cultural integration of northern Thailand achieved under Tilokaracha laid the foundation for an efflorescence of Lānnā civilization during the reign of Phra Muang Kaew (r. 1495–1528), considered to be the golden age of Lānnā Buddhist scholarship.

**Tilopa**. (T. Ti lo pa) (988–1069). An Indian tantric adept counted among the eighty-four MAHĀSIDDHAS and venerated in Tibet as an important source of tantric instruction and a founder of the BKA' BRGYUD sect. Little historical information exists regarding Tilopa's life. According to his traditional biographies, Tilopa was born a brāhmaṇa in northeast India. As a young man he took the vows of a Buddhist monk, but later was compelled by the prophecies of a ḌĀKINĪ messenger to study with a host of tantric masters. He lived as a wandering YOGIN, practicing TANTRA in secret while outwardly leading a life of transgressive behavior. For many years Tilopa acted as the servant for the prostitute Barima (in truth a wisdom ḍākinī in disguise) by night while grinding sesame seeds for oil by day. The name Tilopa, literally "Sesame Man," derives from the Sanskrit word for sesamum. Finally, Tilopa is said to have received instructions in the form of a direct transmission from the primordial buddha VAJRADHARA. Tilopa instructed numerous disciples, including the renowned Bengali master NĀROPA, who is said to have abandoned his prestigious monastic position to become Tilopa's disciple, undergoing many difficult trials before receiving his teachings. Those teachings were later received by MAR PA CHOS KYI BLO GROS, who brought Tilopa's teachings to Tibet. As with many Indian siddhas, Tilopa's main instructions are found in the form of DOHĀ, or songs of realization. Many of his songs, together with several tantric commentaries and liturgical texts, are included in the Tibetan canon. Among the teachings attributed to him are the BKA' 'BABS BZHI ("four transmissions"), the LUS MED MKHA' 'GRO SNYAN RGYUD CHOS SKOR DGU ("nine aural lineage cycles of the formless ḍākinīs"), and the MAHĀMUDROPADEŚA.

**tingqian boshuzi**. (J. teizen no hakujushi; K. chŏngjŏn paeksuja 庭前柏樹子). In Chinese, "cypress tree in front of the courtyard"; a CHAN expression that becomes a popular meditative topic (HUATOU) and is used in Chan questioning meditation (KANHUA CHAN). The phrase appears in a GONG'AN exchange attributed to the Tang-dynasty monk ZHAOZHOU CONGSHEN (778–897): Once when Zhaozhou was asked, "Why did Bodhidharma come from the West?" (XILAI YI), he replied, "Cypress tree in front of the courtyard," suggesting that enlightenment, the reason that Bodhidharma traveled to China, is to be found in everyday experience. This gong'an appears as case no. 37 in the WUMEN GUAN ("Gateless Checkpoint"). See also XILAI YI.

**Ti phu pa**. "Pigeon Man," the Tibetan name for a twelfth-century Indian MAHĀSIDDHA in the lineage of NĀROPA who transmitted the LUS MED MKHA' 'GRO SNYAN RGYUD CHOS SKOR

DGU ("nine aural lineage cycles of the formless ḌĀKINĪS") to MI LA RAS PA's disciple RAS CHUNG PA during the latter's sojourn in India. Ti phu pa was said to be DAR MA MDO SDE, the son of MAR PA the Translator, according to the following story. Dar ma mdo sde was fatally injured for an equestrian accident, but before his death his father gave him instructions for "entering a corpse" (grong 'jug) whereby one can force one's consciousness to enter another body. Dar ma mdo sde was able to cause his consciousness to enter the body of a dead pigeon, which came back to life and flew across the Himālayas to India. There it entered the corpse of a sixteen-year-old boy who was about to cremated. He came back to life and put into practice the teachings he had received from Mar pa as Dar ma mdo sde, while also studying with other masters, including Nāropa, from whom he received the full transmission of the lus med mkha' 'gro snyan rgyud chos skor dgu ("nine aural lineage cycles of the formless ḍākinīs"). Nāropa's disciples had only taught five of these nine cycles to Mar pa during his visit to India, and hence Mi la ras pa had only received partial instruction. Mi la ras pa thus sent Ras chung pa to India to receive the full transmission of the lus med mkha' 'gro snyan rgyud chos skor dgu. Ras chung pa received that transmission from Ti phu pa.

**tiraścīna**. (S). See TIRYAK.

**tīrtha**. (S). See PĪṬHA.

**tīrthika**. (P. titthiya; T. mu stegs pa; C. waidao; J. gedō; K. oedo 外道). In Sanskrit, lit. "ford-maker"; referring specifically in Buddhist materials to "adherent of a non-Buddhist religion" and often seen translated as "heretic." Tīrthika is typically used to refer to a follower of one of the non-Buddhist Indian schools, such as ŚRAMAṆA schools of the ĀJĪVAKA and JAINA, which were contemporaries of the Buddha or the later Sāṃkhya tradition. The term probably referred originally to priests of temples near river crossings where travelers propitiated a deity before crossing, suggesting metaphorically that those teachings offered a ford across the raging river of SAṂSĀRA. See also ŚRAMAṆA.

**tiryak**. [alt. tiryaścīna, tiryañc] (P. tiracchāna; T. dud 'gro; C. chusheng; J. chikushō; K. ch'uksaeng 畜生). In Sanskrit, lit. "going horizontally" (i.e., not erect), viz., an animal; one of five or six rebirth destinies (GATI) in SAṂSĀRA. Among these, animals are classified as the one of the three (or four) unfortunate rebirth destinies (APĀYA; DURGATI), along with denizens of hell (NĀRAKA), ghosts (PRETA), and in some lists demigods or titans (ASURA). The category of animals includes both land and sea creatures, as well as insects. The specific kinds of suffering that animals undergo are frequently mentioned in Buddhist texts; these include the constant need to search for their own food while always seeking to avoid becoming food for others. Unlike humans, animals are generally killed not for some deed they have done but for the taste of their flesh or the texture of their skin. The possibility of achieving rebirth out of the realm of animals is said to be particularly difficult because of either the inevitable killing in which predators engage or because of animals' constant fear of becoming prey; neither mental state is conducive to higher rebirth. Despite this difficulty, there are many stories in Buddhist literature of predators who have willed themselves to stop killing (the first of the lay precepts) in order to create a karmic propensity that will be more conducive to rebirth out of the animal destiny. See also DAOTU.

**tiryañc**. (S). See TIRYAK.

**Tiwei [Boli] jing**. (提謂[波利]經). In Chinese, "Book of Trapuṣa [and Bhallika]"; an indigenous Chinese SŪTRA (see APOCRYPHA), written c. 460–464 during the Northern Wei dynasty, which praises the value of lay practice. The scripture is a retelling of the story of the encounter between the merchants TRAPUṢA and (in some versions) his brother BHALLIKA, who offered the Buddha his first meal after his enlightenment. Following the meal, the Buddha is said to have taught the brothers and transmitted to them the first two of the three refuges (see TRIŚARAṆA) (the SAṂGHA not yet existing at the incipiency of the religion), rendering them the first lay disciples (UPĀSAKA) of the Buddha. The Chinese text offers an extended account of what the Buddha taught during that first informal discussion of his experience. The Buddha's account of the dharma discusses the Buddhist value of keeping the five precepts (PAÑCAŚĪLA) and the lay practice of giving (DĀNA), but all set within a philosophical framework that draws heavily on indigenous Chinese concepts of the five phases or elements, the five viscera, etc., as well as the importance of karmic cause and effect.

**tōban**. (東班). In Japanese, lit. "east rank"; the offices of the six administrators or stewards (C. ZHISHI) at a Zen monastery, which were typically located to the east side of the monastery, hence the name. On the west are the prefects (C. TOUSHOU), who are thus referred to as the west rank. Similarly, the CHANYUAN QINGGUI refers to the stewards as the east section (C. dongxu) and the prefects as the west section (C. xixu).

**toch'am**. (圖讖). In Korean, "geomancy and divination"; a new theory of geomancy promulgated by the monk MYOCH'ŎNG (d. 1135), which was ultimately used to justify a rebellion against the Koryŏ dynasty. See MYOCH'ŎNG.

**Tocharian**. Generic term for Tocharian A (East Tocharian, or Turfanian) and Tocharian B (West Tocharian, or Kuchean), two related, but probably mutually unintelligible, Indo-European languages in which many Central Asian Buddhist texts from the Tarim River Basin along the SILK ROAD were composed. The languages were written in a variant of the BRAHMĪ script, which was first deciphered in 1908 by the German Indologists Emil Sieg and Wilhelm Siegling. Virtually all the extant Tocharian Buddhist manuscripts are translations of earlier Indian materials, many in bilingual editions that speeded the deciphering process. The languages were unknown until SIR MARC AUREL STEIN (1862–1943) discovered their manuscripts during his expeditions into the Tarim Basin. The name Tocharian derives from the Greek term for the people of this region. Texts in Tocharian A have been discovered in the oasis petty-kingdom of TURFAN and in the vicinity of Shorchuk/Yanqi. Tocharian B texts range much more widely across the Tarim Basin, but are especially prominent in the KUCHA region. Of the two languages, Tocharian B is the older of the two, with manuscripts ranging in age from the fifth through eighth centuries CE, and the most diverse linguistically. Tocharian A is more consistent linguistically and its manuscripts are later than those of its counterpart. The languages may have been spoken as late as the middle of the ninth century, when both became extinct; their peoples assimilated into the Uighurs who now populate the region in present-day Chinese Xinjiang.

**Tōdaiji**. (東大寺). In Japanese, "Great Monastery of the East"; a major monastery in the ancient Japanese capital of Nara affiliated with the Kegon (HUAYAN) school of Buddhism, listed as a UNESCO World Heritage site. The monastery was founded by the Hossōshū (FAXIANG ZONG) monk GYŌGI (668–749). The monastery is renowned for its colossal buddha image of VAIROCANA (J. Birushana nyorai), which is commonly known as the NARA DAIBUTSU; at forty-eight feet (fifteen meters) high, this image is the largest extant gilt-bronze image in the world and the Daibutsuden where the image is enshrined is the world's largest wooden building. The Indian monk BODHISENA (J. Bodaisenna) (704–760), who traveled to Japan in 736 at the invitation of Emperor Shōmu (r. 724–749), performed the "opening the eyes" (KAIYAN; NETRAPRATIṢṬHĀPANA) ceremony for the 752 dedication of the great buddha image. Tōdaiji was founded on the site of Konshūsenji by order of Emperor Shōmu and became the headquarters of a network of provincial monasteries and convents in the Yamato region. The first abbot, Ryōben (689–773), is commemorated in the kaisandō (founder's hall; see KAISHAN). Other halls include the inner sanctuary of the hokkedō (lotus hall), which was probably once Konshusenji's main hall. The hall enshrines the Fukūkensaku Kannon, a dry lacquer statue of the BODHISATTVA AVALOKITEŚVARA, which dates from 746. The monastery was renamed Konkōmyōji in 741 and, in 747 when major construction began on the large compound, it finally became known as Tōdaiji, the name it retains today. The Tōdaiji complex was completed in 798; monastery records state that 50,000 carpenters, 370,000 metal workers, and 2.18 million laborers worked on the compound, its buildings, and their furnishings, almost bankrupting the country. Entering the monastery through the Great Gate to the South (Nandaimon), itself a Japanese national treasure, a visitor would have passed through two seven-storied, 328-foot high pagodas to the east and west (both subsequently destroyed by earthquakes), before passing through the Inner Gate to the Daibutsuden. North of the Daibutsuden, which is flanked by a belfry and a SŪTRA repository, is the kōdō (lecture hall), which is surrounded on three sides by the monk's quarters. An ordination hall displays exceptional clay-modeled shitennō (four heavenly kings; see LOKAPĀLA) dating from the Tenpyō Era (729–749). Of the eighth-century buildings, only the tegaimon (the western gate) and the Hokkedō's inner sanctuary have survived. After a conflagration in 1180, then-abbot Chōgen (1121–1206) spearheaded a major reconstruction in a style he had seen in Southern Song-dynasty China. This style is exemplified by the south gate, which is protected by two humane-kings statues, both twenty-eight feet in height, carved in 1203. The Tokugawa Shogunate sponsored a second reconstruction after another fire in 1567 and the current Daibutsuden dates from about 1709. The Shōsōin repository at the monastery, itself a Japanese national treasure (kokuhō), contains over nine thousand precious ornamental and fine-art objects that date from the monastery's founding in the eighth century, including scores of objects imported into Japan via the SILK ROAD from all over Asia, including cut-glass bowls and silk brocade from Persia, Byzantine cups, Egyptians chests, and Indian harps, as well as Chinese Tang and Korean Silla musical instruments, etc. Every spring, the two-week long Omizutori (water-drawing) festival is conducted at Tōdaiji, which is thought to cure physical ailments and cleanse moral transgressions.

**Tōji**. (東寺). In Japanese, "Eastern Monastery," also known as Kyōō Gokokuji; a famous temple in Kyōto, Japan. Currently, Tōji is the headquarters (honzan) of the Tōji branch of the SHINGONSHŪ. Construction of Tōji and its sister temple Saiji (Western Monastery) began in 796, after the Japanese capital was moved from Nara to Kyōto and the capital divided into eastern and western precincts, following traditional Chinese city plans. The two monasteries seem to have been built for the purpose of protecting spiritually the southern borders of the new capital. In 812, construction of the golden hall (kondō) at the monastery was completed. In 823, the emperor bestowed the temple upon the eminent Japanese monk KŪKAI and the monastery was then named the Konkōmyō Shitennō Kyōō Gokokuji Himitsu Denbōin (Radiance of Golden Light, Four Heavenly Kings, King of Teachings, Protection of the State Temple, Esoteric Transmission of the Dharma Cloister). Sixteen years later, the central altar (SHUMIDAN) was completed and eyes of the central icons were opened (see KAIYAN). The famous five-story pagoda at Tōji, a national treasure (kokuhō), was completed in the second half of the ninth century. The pagoda was consumed in flames after it was struck by lightning in 1055, but with the support of the Edo bakufu, the pagoda was reconstructed to its current shape.

**Tokushō**. (J) (得勝) (1327–1387). See BASSUI TOKUSHŌ.

**Tominaga Nakamoto**. (富永仲基) (1715–1746). Important Japanese thinker during the Edo period. The third son of a soy sauce manufacturer in Ōsaka, Tominaga was raised in the merchant community. Tominaga's social position and subsequent education resulted in an eclectic and fairly impartial understanding of the varying schools of Confucian thought, Buddhism, and Daoism. Tominaga received a classical Confucian education at Kaitokudō, a private academy funded by his father and a few other Ōsaka manufacturers. He began his education at age nine, and eventually studied Buddhist scripture in great breadth and depth, even though he was never ordained. Tominaga was forced to leave Kaitokudō after writing a critical piece on competing Confucian schools of thought. The work, which is no longer extant, was called *Setsuhei*, or "A Critical Examination of [Confucian] Doctrine." Tominaga did the majority of his study of sūtras and MAHĀYĀNA Buddhism between 1730 and 1738. He published two titles that are still extant, *Shutsujō kōgo* ("Emerging from Meditation") (1745), and *Okina no fumi* ("Writings of an Old Man"), which was published six months after he died of lung disease in 1746. In these works, he took a historical approach that critiqued all claims to authenticity by the existing schools of Japanese religion, suggesting that the different sects of Buddhism evolved by reformations of preceding schools, reformations that were then justified by appeals to the authority of the Buddha himself. He even made the radical claim that the Buddha could not have taught the Mahāyāna sūtras because their language and teachings differed so dramatically from other types of Buddhist sūtras. Although he was vigorously criticized by the Buddhist ecclesia, his historical approach to Buddhism helped to establish the foundation for the Japanese scholarly study of Buddhism in the nineteenth and early twentieth centuries.

**tōmitsu**. (J) (東密). See MIKKYŌ.

**T'ongdosa**. (通度寺). In Korean, "Breakthrough Monastery" (lit. "Penetrating Crossing-Over Monastery"); the fifteenth district monastery (PONSA) in the contemporary CHOGYE CHONG of Korean Buddhism, located at the base of Yŏngch'uksan (S. GṚDHRAKŪṬAPARVATA, or Vulture Peak) in Yangsan, South Kyŏngsang province. Along with HAEINSA and SONGGWANGSA, T'ongdosa is one of the "three-jewel monasteries" (SAMBO SACH'AL) that represent one of the three jewels (RATNATRAYA) of Buddhism; T'ONGDOSA is the buddha-jewel monastery (pulbo sach'al), because of its ordination platform and the relics (K. sari; S. ŚARĪRA) of the Buddha enshrined in back of its main shrine hall (TAEUNG CHŎN). The oldest of the three-jewel monasteries, T'ongdosa has long been regarded as the center of Buddhist disciplinary studies (VINAYA) in Korea, and has been one of the major sites of ordination ceremonies since the Unified Silla period (668–935). Relics, reputed to be those of the Buddha himself, are enshrined at the monastery, and its taeung chŏn is famous for being one of four in Korea that does not enshrine an image of the Buddha; instead, a window at the back of the main hall, where the image ordinarily would be placed, looks out on the Diamond Ordination Platform (Kŭmgang kyedan), which includes a reliquary (STŪPA) that enshrines the Buddha's relics. This focus on vinaya and the presence of these relics, both of which are reminders of the Buddha, have led the monastery to be designated the buddha-jewel monastery of Korea. T'ongdosa is said to have been established by the vinaya master CHAJANG (608–686) in 646 to enshrine a portion of the relics that he brought back with him from his sojourn into China. While on pilgrimage at WUTAISHAN, Chajang had an encounter with the bodhisattva MAÑJUŚRĪ, who entrusted Chajang with a gold studded monk's robe (K. kasa; S. KAṢĀYA) wrapped in purple silk gauze, one hundred pieces of relics of the Buddha's skull bone and his finger joint, beads, and sūtras. One portion of the relics was enshrined together with the Buddha's robe in a bell-shaped stone stūpa at the center of the Diamond Ordination Platform; another portion was enshrined in the nine-story pagoda at HWANGNYONGSA in the Silla capital of Kyŏngju. Under Chajang's leadership, the monastery grew into a major center of Silla Buddhism and the monastery continued to thrive throughout the Silla and Koryŏ dynasties, until the whole monastery except the taeung chŏn was destroyed by invading Japanese troops in the late sixteenth century. In 1641, the monk Uun (d.u.) rebuilt the monastery in its current configuration. The Diamond Ordination Platform was periodically damaged during the sporadic Japanese invasions that occurred during the Chosŏn dynasty. In the fourth month of 1377, Japanese pirates invaded, seeking to plunder the śarīra; to keep them from falling into Japanese hands, the abbot went into hiding with the relics. Two years later, on the fifteenth day of the fifth month of 1379, the pirates came again, and the monks quickly whisked away the relics and hid them deep in the forest behind the monastery. The Japanese went in pursuit of the relics, but the abbot Wŏlsong (d.u.) took them to Seoul to keep them safe, returning with them once the danger had passed. During the Hideyoshi Invasions in the late sixteenth century, the relics were also removed in order to keep them safe. SAMYŎNG YUJŎNG, who was leading a monk's militia fighting the Japanese invaders, sent the relics to the Diamond Mountains (KŬMGANGSAN) in the north, where his teacher and the supreme commander, CH'ŎNGHŎ HYUJŎNG, was staying. Hyujŏng decided that the relics were no safer there than back at their home monastery, so he returned them to T'ongdosa. Yujŏng covered the hiding place of the relics with weeds and thorn bushes and, once the Japanese threat was rebuffed, he restored the site to its former glory and the relics were reenshrined in 1603. The platform was repaired again in 1653 and on a grand scale in 1705. The Diamond Ordination Platform remains the site where BHIKṢU and BHIKṢUṆĪ ordinations are held in Korea. In 1972, T'ongdosa was elevated to the status of an ecumenical monastery (CH'ONGNIM), and is one of the five such centers in the contemporary Chogye order, which are all expected to provide training in the full range of practices that exemplify the major strands of the Korean Buddhist tradition; the monastery is thus also known as the Yŏngch'uk Ch'ongnim.

**Tonghwasa**. (桐華寺). In Korean, "Paulownia Flower Monastery"; the ninth district monastery (PONSA) of the contemporary

CHOGYE CHONG of Korean Buddhism, located on Mount P'algong near the city of Taegu. The monastery was founded by the monk Kŭktal (d.u.) in 493, during of the reign of the Silla king Soji (r. 479–500), and was originally called Yugasa (Yoga monastery). When the royal preceptor (wangsa) Simji (d.u.) reconstructed the monastery in 832, Paulownia trees miraculously bloomed in the middle of the winter, so it was renamed Paulownia Flower monastery (Tonghwasa). The monastery was reconstructed several times: in 934, by a late-Silla monk; in 1190, by the mid-Koryŏ reformer POJO CHINUL (1158–1210); and in 1298 by the state preceptor (K. kuksa; C. GUOSHI) Hongjin (1228–1294). In 1606, following the depradations of the Japanese Hideyoshi invasions, the Sŏn master SAMYŎNG YUJŎNG (1544–1610) again reconstructed the monastery. The monastery contains many hermitages, including Kŭmdangam, Piroam, Naewŏnam, Pudoam, Yangjinam, and Yŏmburam. During the Japanese colonial period (1910–1945), Tonghwasa was designated one of the thirty-one head monasteries (PONSA) and it managed fifty-five branch temples (malsa). The monastery contains many cultural treasures, including the three-story pagodas at Piroam, the seated image of MAHĀVAIROCANA, and the seated image of the buddha carved into the cliff face. A more recent addition to the monastery campus is a massive fifty-five foot (seventeen meter) standing image of the healing buddha BHAIṢAJYAGURU.

**Tongrong**. (C) (通容) (1593–1661). See FEIYIN TONGRONG.

**tongxu**. (C) (通序). See ER XU.

**tonsure**. A somewhat antiquated term occasionally still found in discussions of East Asian and especially Japanese Buddhism, referring to the shaving of the head that occurs in conjunction with entering a monastery and taking ordination as a monk or nun. See PRAVRAJITA; UPASAṂPADĀ.

**tooth relic**. (S./P. dantadhātu). A left cuspid tooth presumed to be that of the buddha Gotama (S. GAUTAMA), which is the most sacred relic in Sri Lanka and one of the most famous Buddhist relics in the world. It is said that after the Buddha's cremation, the tooth relic was retrieved from the ashes of the funeral pyre by the monk Khema. It was passed down among several royal dynasties until coming into the possession of king Guhasīva of Kaliṅga in the fourth century CE. Fearing that the tooth would be destroyed by Hindus, he entrusted it to his daughter, Hemamālā, who hid the tooth in her hair. Together with her husband, prince Dantakumāra, they traveled to Sri Lanka and presented the relic to the king, who enshrined it in ANURĀDHAPURA. In 1280 it was captured by invaders and taken back to India but was returned shortly thereafter. In 1560, the tooth relic (in Jaffna at the time) was captured by the Portuguese viceroy of Goa, Dom Constantino de Braganza, and taken to Goa. There, he received word that the King of Pegu in Burma (Myanmar) would offer a huge sum as ransom for the tooth. The viceroy was inclined to accept, but the agreement was vetoed by the Archbishop of Goa who, in a public ceremony, ground the tooth to dust with a mortar and pestle, burned the dust in a brazier, and then cast the ashes into the sea. The Sinhalese later explained that this had not been the real tooth relic but was instead a replica; the real tooth was safe in Kandy. The relic is housed in the Dalada Maligawa Temple in the city of Kandy. Construction of the temple began in 1592, with the temple complex being enlarged by several kings during the seventeenth and eighteenth centuries. Possession of the tooth relic is said to confer the right to rule the island, so much so that when the British captured the tooth in 1815, this was interpreted as a sign of the legitimacy of their sovereignty. The authenticity of the tooth relic has been called into question at certain points in its history; HENRY STEEL OLCOTT declared it to be an animal bone, leading to his estrangement from the monastic authorities. The tooth relic remains an object of veneration and Dalada Maligawa Temple is an important place of pilgrimage in the South and Southeast Asian Buddhist world. See also DĀṬHĀVAṂSA.

**Tōshōdaiji**. (唐招提寺). In Japanese, "Monastery for a Tang Wanderer"; located in the ancient Japanese capital of Nara and the head monastery of the VINAYA school (J. Risshū). Tōshōdaiji was originally a residence for Prince Niitabe, who donated it to the Tang-Chinese monk GANJIN (C. Jianzhen; 688–763), the founder of the vinaya school (RISSHŪ) in Japan. Ganjin came to Japan in 759 at the invitation of two Japanese monks who had studied with him in China at his home monastery of Damingsi (J. Daimyōji) in present-day Yangzhou. Ganjin tried to reach Japan five times before finally succeeding; then sixty-six and blind, he established an ordination platform at TŌDAIJI before moving to Tōshōdaiji, where he passed away in 763. The monastery's name thus refers to Ganjin, a "wandering monk from Tang." The kondō, the golden hall that is the monastery's main shrine, was erected after Ganjin's death and finished around 781, followed three decades later by the monastery's five-story pagoda, which was finished in 810. The kondō is one of the few Nara-period temple structures that has survived and is one of the reasons why the monastery is so prized. It was built in the Yosemune style, with a colonnade with eight pillars, and enshrines three main images: the cosmic buddha VAIROCANA at the center, flanked by BHAIṢAJYAGURU, and a thousand-armed AVALOKITEŚVARA (see SĀHASRABHUJASĀHASRANETRĀVALOKITEŚVARA), only 953 of which remain today, with images of BRAHMĀ and INDRA at the sides and statues of the four heavenly king protectors of Buddhism standing in each corner. The kōdō, or lecture hall, was moved to the monastery from Heijō Palace and is the only extant structure that captures the style of a Tenpyō palace; it houses a statue of the bodhisattva MAITREYA. A kyōzō, or SŪTRA repository, holds the old library. The monastery also includes a treasure repository, a bell tower, and an ordination platform in the lotus pond. In 763, as Ganjin's death neared, he had a memorial statue of himself made and installed in his quarters at Tōshōdaiji. This dry-lacquer statue of a meditating Ganjin is enshrined today in the mieidō (image hall), but is brought out for display only on his memorial days of June 5–7 each year; it is the oldest example in Japan of such a memorial statue. Tōshōdaiji was designated a UNESCO World Heritage Site in 1998.

**Tosŏn**. (道詵) (827–898). Korean SŎN master during the Later Silla and the early Koryŏ kingdoms, who is said to have been the first Korean to combine geomancy (K. p'ungsu; C. fengshui) and Buddhism in order to assess and correct adverse energy flows in the indigenous Korean landscape. Tosŏn was probably a relatively little-known figure during his own lifetime, but he became the stuff of legend for supposedly predicting the rise to prominence of the founder of the Koryŏ dynasty, Wang Kŏn (r. 918–943), and using his geomatic prowess to locate the most auspicious site for the founding of its new capital, Kaesŏng. Tosŏn developed a theory of deploying Buddhist architectural sites as a palliative to geographic anomalies. This theory, called "reinforcing [the land] through monasteries and STŪPAS" (K. PIBO SAT'AP SŎL), proposed that building monasteries and pagodas at geomantically fragile locations could alleviate or correct weaknesses in the native topology, in much the same way that acupuncture could correct feeble energy flows within the physical body. His geomantic theory is unusual, because Chinese geomancy of the time focused more on the discovery of hidden propitious sites within the landscape, not correcting geomantic weaknesses. This term pibo (lit. "assisting and supplementing," and thus "reinforcing," or "remediation") is also unattested as a technical term in Chinese geomancy. The term may derive from similar terms used in the geomantic theories of the Chinese CHAN school and thence the Korean Nine Mountains Sŏn school (KUSAN SŎNMUN), with which Tosŏn was affiliated. The geomancy of Yang Yunsong (834–900) was popular in the Jiangxi region of China; this type of geomancy sought to interpret the lay of the land as a way of locating the most auspicious sites for constructing buildings. This tradition seems to have entered into the Chan lineages in that region, whence it might have been introduced in turn into Korea by the several Sŏn masters in the Nine Mountains school who studied in Jiangxi. The frequency with which late Silla and early Koryŏ period Sŏn monks located their monasteries following geomantic principles may well derive from the fact that seven of these nine early lineages of Korean Sŏn were associated with the Hongzhou school and the Jiangxi region. Some scholars instead propose that the source of Tosŏn's geomancy is to be found in esoteric Buddhism: Tosŏn viewed the country as a MAṆḌALA and, in order to protect the nation, proposed to situate monasteries at locations chosen through the ritual of demarcating a sacred site (sīmābandha). Finally, Korean indigenous religion and Togyo (Daoism) are also sometimes presented as sources of Tosŏn's geomantic teachings. Tosŏn's theory of geomancy also played a role in resituating the religious center of Korean Buddhism, which had previously been focused on the Silla capital of KYŎNGJU or such indigenous sacred mountains as the five marchmounts (o'ak). The Silla royal and aristocratic families founded monasteries around the capital of Kyŏngju based on the belief that this region had previously been a Buddha land (Pulgukt'o). Tosŏn's theory resulted in an expansion of the concept of "Buddha land" to take in the entire Korean peninsula, instead. After the establishment of the new Koryŏ dynasty in 918, Tosŏn's theory was appropriated as a means of integrating into the dynastic political structure local power groups and monasteries. In the posthumous "Ten Injunctions" (hunyo sipcho) attributed to Wang Kŏn, the Koryŏ founder is reputed to have instructed that monasteries should only be constructed at sites that had been specifically designated as auspicious by Tosŏn. For this reason, the term pibo later comes to be used as an official ecclesiastical category in Korea to designate important monasteries that had figured in the founding of the Koryŏ dynasty. Tosŏn's thought also subsequently became associated with the theory of geomancy and divination (TOCH'AM) taught by the diviner–monk MYOCH'ŎNG (d. 1135), who eventually led an unsuccessful rebellion against the Koryŏ dynasty.

**Toṭagamuwa, Śrī Rāhula**. (1408–1491). A Sinhalese monk of the fifteenth century and one of the most celebrated poets of Sri Lanka. His most famous works include *Selalihini Sandesa* ("The Bird Sela's Message") and *Kaviyasekera* ("The Crown of Poetry"). Despite his status as a monk, his verse includes many secular themes, such as the power of kings and the beauty of women. His erudition also secured him a reputation as a great debater. TOTAGAMUWA received much praise and support from the Sinhalese king PARĀKRAMABĀHU VI, who came to the throne in 1410.

**touguang**. (J. zōkō; K. tugwang 頭光). In Chinese, lit. "head light"; a "nimbus" encircling the head of holy figures in Buddhist painting and sculpture. See KĀYAPRABHĀ.

**toushou**. (J. chōshu; K. tusu 頭首). In Chinese, "prefect"; the prefects or chief officers at a CHAN monastery. Ideally, there are six prefects who govern different aspects of the daily activities of the monastic community. Because their offices were often located on the west side of the monastery, they were also often referred to as the west section or rank. The six prefects are the chief seat (C. SHOUZUO), scribe (C. SHUJI), library prefect (C. ZANGZHU), guest prefect (C. ZHIKE), bath prefect (C. ZHIYU), and hall prefect (C. ZHIDIAN). Cf. TŌBAN.

**Touzi Yiqing**. (J. Tōsu Gisei; K. T'uja Ŭich'ŏng 投子義青) (1032–1083). Chinese CHAN master in the CAODONG ZONG. Touzi was a native of Qingzhou prefecture in present-day Shandong province. He entered the monastery of Miaoxiangsi at the age of seven and was ordained at age fifteen. During this period, Touzi is said to have studied Buddhist doctrine and the AVATAṂSAKASŪTRA. Later, Touzi became a disciple of the LINJI ZONG master Fushan Fayuan (991–1067), from whom he received the portrait (DINGXIANG), leather shoes, and patched robes of the deceased DAYANG JINGXUAN, a Caodong lineage holder. Touzi thus became a holder not of his teacher Fushan's but of Dayang's Caodong lineage. In 1073, he began his residence at the Chan monastery of Haihui Chansi on Mt. Baiyun in Shuzhou prefecture, present-day Anhui province. Eight years later, he moved to the nearby Mt. Touzi, whence he acquired his toponym. His teachings are recorded in the *Shuzhou Touzi Qing heshang yulu* and *Touzi Qing heshang yuyao*.

**tracing back the radiance**. See FANZHAO.

**traidhātuka**. (P. tedhātuka; T. khams gsum; C. sanjie; J. sangai; K. samgye 三界). In Sanskrit, the "triple realm" or "three realms [of existence]"; the three realms of SAṂSĀRA, in which beings take rebirth: the sensuous, or desire, realm (KĀMADHĀTU); the subtle-materiality, or form, realm (RŪPADHĀTU); and the immaterial, or formless, realm (ĀRŪPYADHĀTU). See also AVACARA; LOKADHĀTU.

**trailokya**. (T. 'jig rten gsum; C. sanjie; J. sangai; K. samgye 三界). In Sanskrit, the "three realms." See TRILOKA[DHĀTU]; TRAIDHĀTUKA; AVACARA; LOKADHĀTU.

**Trailokyavijaya**. (T. Khams gsum rnam rgyal; C. Xiangsanshi mingwang; J. Gōzanze myōō; K. Hangsamse myŏngwang 降三世明王). In Sanskrit, "Victor of the Three Realms"; a wrathful deity, he is considered a wrathful form of VAJRAPĀṆI. He is depicted in Indian Buddhist iconography and plays an important role in the SARVATATHĀGATATATTVASAṂGRAHA. It is in the form of Trailokyavijaya that Vajrapāṇi conquers Maheśvara (the Hindu god Śiva). It was often the case that Buddhists gave Hindu deities Buddhist forms, especially in the tantras. In this case, Trailokyavijaya may have his antecedent in the Hindu god Tripurāntaka, "Destroyer of the Three [Demon] Cities," a form of Śiva whose worship was still current at the time the *Sarvatathāgatatattvasaṃgraha* was being formulated. Iconographic similarities as well as the Buddhist Trailokyavijaya's subjugation of the rival tradition's Maheśvara support the connection; a Hindu deity is appropriated by Buddhists, with the appropriated form then subduing the Hindu god. The cult of Trailokyavijaya entered China with the translations of the *Sarvatathāgatatattvasaṃgraha*, the MAHĀVAIROCANĀBHISAṂBODHISŪTRA, and several other texts translated by AMOGHAVAJRA in the second half of the eighth century, whence they quickly entered Japan. He is described as being terrible to behold, with four heads and eight arms, although in the GARBHADHĀTU MAṆḌALA, he has a single face with three eyes and two arms. He stands on prone figures of Śiva and Umā, whom he has thus subdued. His worship was largely replaced by that of HERUKA in the CAKRASAṂVARATANTRA cycles, who performs the same function in the taming of Maheśvara.

**Traiphum Phra Ruang**. In Thai, "The Three Worlds According to King Ruang"; the title of a Thai cosmological treatise written by Prince Lithai (d. 1374), before he became monarch of the central Thai kingdom of SUKHOTHAI. The treatise consists of descriptions of the three worlds or realms of existence (S. TRAIDHĀTUKA) into which beings are born, that is, the sensuous realm (KĀMADHĀTU), the realm of subtle materiality (RŪPADHĀTU), and the immaterial realm (ĀRŪPYADHĀTU). Each of the various places of rebirth within each of these realms is described, along with the deeds that lead to rebirth there. The treatise has played an important role in teaching Buddhist morals and values in Thai society and portions of it are often depicted in temple mural paintings.

**traividya**. (S). See TRIVIDYĀ.

**Trần Nhân Tông**. (陳仁宗) (1258–1308). The third king of the Vietnamese Trần dynasty (1225–1400) and the founding patriarch of the TRÚC LÂM (Bamboo Grove) school, the first authentic Vietnamese Thiền (CHAN) school. He was also the national hero who led Vietnam to victory over the Mongols in 1285 and 1288. In 1293, he abdicated, after being on the throne for fifteen years, to become thượng hoàng (retired emperor). When he was crown prince, he revered Buddhism and received instructions from eminent monks, including his uncle Huệ Trung Thượng Sĩ, an eminent Chan master of the time. In 1299 he went to Mount Yên Tử to become a monk and took the sobriquet Trúc Lâm Đại Sĩ. He was reverentially referred to as Trúc Lâm Điều Ngự or simply Điều Ngự. Even after taking residence in Yên Tử, he continued to travel to various temples to give instructions to monks, devoting himself to establishing a unified saṃgha. The *Tam Tổ Thực Lục* ("True Records on the Three Patriarchs") relates that he traveled extensively to shut down "depraved temples" and to encourage people to receive the ten precepts. Many eminent monks of the Trần were his disciples. According to historical records, Trần Nhân Tông left behind several treatises on Chan and a few collections of poems in both classical Chinese and Nôm (demotic script). Unfortunately, none of his writing are extant apart from a few poems collected in the *Việt Âm Thi Tập* in Chinese and two long poems in Nôm.

**transference of consciousness**. See 'PHO BA.

**transfer of merit**. See PUṆYĀNUMODANA.

**transmigration**. See REBIRTH; PUNARBHAVA; PUNARJANMAN; SPRUL SKU.

**transmission**. Many strands of Buddhism employ the concept of transmission to describe the dissemination of a particular doctrine or practice from teacher to student, with an unbroken dissemination line going back to the originator of the teaching (usually the Buddha) often considered essential for maintaining the authenticity and authority of the teaching and those who propound it. This line of transmission is often spoken of as the "lineage." Various forms of transmission are set forth in a number of Buddhist traditions, including the famous seal of transmission (YINKE) and "mind-to-mind transmission" (YIXIN CHUANXIN) of the East Asian CHAN schools, which is considered to be a "special transmission outside the teachings" (JIAOWAI BIECHUAN). In Tibetan Buddhism, reference is often made to the "aural transmission" (NYAN BRGYUD), the teachings received orally from a master as opposed to those derived from a text. The aural transmission often refers to practical instructions for meditation practice that have not been recorded in a text. See also CHUANDENG LU; CHUANFA; FASI; PARAṂPARĀ.

**transmission of the lamplight**. See CHUANDENG LU; JINGDE CHUANDENG LU.

**Trần Thái Tông**. (陳太宗) (1218–1277). Buddhist leader and literary figure of medieval Vietnam, who was also the founder of the Trần dynasty (1225–1400), one of the most illustrious dynasties in Vietnamese history. He ascended the throne as a child of eight after his uncle, Trần Thủ Độ, overthrew the Lý dynasty (1010–1225). During his youth he attempted to escape from the capital city to Mount Yên Tử to become a monk but was forced to return to court by his uncle. Trần Thái Tông related this incident and many events of his life in one of his writings, the preface to "A Guide to the Chan School." He reported that, even when he was a king, whenever he had free time he would gather together learned and virtuous monks to practice Chan and discuss the path of Buddhism. He also related that he often read the VAJRACCHEDIKĀPRAJÑĀPĀRAMITĀSŪTRA ("Diamond Sūtra") and that when he came across the phrase "one should not generate a mind based on any object," he gained realization. This and other incidents suggest that he interpreted his religious experience in accordance with that of HUINENG, the sixth patriarch (LIUZU) of Chinese Chan. In 1258, Trần Thái Tông abdicated and became thượng hoàng (retired emperor). From then until his death, he devoted himself to practicing Chan and studying Buddhist scriptures. It was during this period that he composed most of his works, including the KHÓA HƯ LỤC.

**Trapuṣa**. (P. Tapussa/Tapussu; T. Ga gon; C. Tiwei; J. Daii; K. Chewi 提謂). Sanskrit proper name of one of the two merchants (together with his brother BHALLIKA) who became the first lay Buddhists (UPĀSAKA). Following his enlightenment under the BODHI TREE, the Buddha remained in the vicinity for seven weeks, each week spent at a different site (see BODHGAYĀ). At the end of the seventh week (or in some versions the sixth), he sat under a Rājāyatana tree, where he continued his meditation. Two merchants, Trapuṣa and his younger brother Bhallika, who were leading a large trading caravan with some five hundred carts, saw him there. Realizing that he had not eaten for weeks (as many as seven weeks), upon the encouragement of a deity, the brothers offered the Buddha sweet rice cakes with butter and honey. The Buddha, however, did not have a bowl in which to receive the food and said it was inappropriate for him to receive the food directly into his hands. The divine kings of the four directions (LOKAPĀLA) then offered him bowls. (According to one account, he received four bowls and collapsed them into one, which is the origin of the "four-bowl" meals served in some East Asian monastic refectories.) In response to their act of charity (DĀNA), the Buddha spoke with them informally and they took refuge (ŚARAṆA) in the Buddha and the DHARMA (there being no third refuge, the SAṂGHA, at this early point in the dispensation), thus making them the first lay Buddhists. The Buddha is said to have given the two brothers eight strands of hair from his head, which they took back to their homeland and interred for worship as relics (ŚARĪRA) in a STŪPA. According to this account, it is interesting to note that the first thing the Buddha provided to another person after his enlightenment was not a teaching but a relic. In the account of the period of the Buddha's enlightenment in the NIDĀNAKATHĀ, this incident occurs immediately before the god BRAHMĀ descends from heaven and asks the Buddha to teach the dharma. According to Mon–Burmese legend, Trapuṣa and Bhallika were Mon natives, and their homeland of Ukkala was a place also called Dagon in the Mon homeland of Rāmañña in lower Burma. The stūpa they constructed at Ukkala/Dagon, which was the first shrine in the world to be erected over relics of the present Buddha, was to be enlarged and embellished over the centuries to become, eventually, the golden SHWEDAGON PAGODA of Rangoon. Because of the preeminence of this shrine, some Burmese chroniclers date the first introduction of Buddhism among the Mon in Rāmañña to Tapussa and Bhallika. Trapuṣa achieved the stage of "stream-enterer" (SROTAĀPANNA); Bhallika eventually ordained and became an ARHAT. The merchants were also the subject of a prototypical Chinese apocryphal text, the TIWEI [BOLI] JING, written c. 460–464, which praises the value of the lay practices of giving (dāna) and keeping the five precepts (PAÑCAŚĪLA).

**trāyastriṃśa**. (P. tāvatiṃsa; T. sum cu rtsa gsum pa; C. sanshisan tian/daoli tian; J. sanjūsanten/tōriten; K. samsipsam ch'ŏn/tori ch'ŏn 三十三天/忉利天). In Sanskrit, lit. "thirty-three"; the heaven of the thirty-three, the second lowest of the six heavens of the sensuous realm (KĀMADHĀTU), just above the heaven of the four heavenly kings (CĀTURMAHĀRĀJAKĀYIKA) and below the YĀMA heaven. Like all Buddhist heavens, it is a place of rebirth and not a permanent post-mortem abode. The heaven is situated on the flat summit of Mount SUMERU and is inhabited by thirty-three male divinities and their attendants, presided over by the divinity ŚAKRA, the king of the gods (ŚAKRO DEVĀNĀM INDRAḤ). The divinities live in palaces of gold among beautiful parks and have life spans of thirty million years. The heaven is commonly mentioned in Buddhist texts. In the seventh year after his enlightenment, after performing the ŚRĀVASTĪ MIRACLES, the Buddha magically traveled to the heaven of the thirty-three, where he spent the three months of the rains retreat (VARṢĀ) teaching the ABHIDHARMA to his mother MĀYĀ. (She had descended to meet him there from her abode in the TUṢITA heaven, where she had been reborn as a male deity after her death as Queen Māyā.) At the conclusion of his teaching, the Buddha made his celebrated return to earth from the heaven on a bejeweled ladder provided by Śakra, descending at the city of SĀṂKĀŚYA. MAHĀMAUDGALYĀYANA also made numerous visits to the heaven to learn from its inhabitants about the virtuous deeds they performed in the past that resulted in their rebirth there. It was said that when a human performed a particularly virtuous deed, a mansion for that person would appear in trāyastriṃśa for that person to inhabit upon being reborn there. When Prince SIDDHĀRTHA renounced the world, he cut off his hair with his sword and cast it into the sky; the hair was caught by Śakra in trāyastriṃśa, who enshrined it in a CAITYA that is worshipped by the gods. Scholars have noted the correspondence between the number of divinities in this heaven and the traditional number of thirty-three gods of the *Ṛgveda*, suggesting that this heaven represents an attempt by Buddhists to absorb the pre-Buddhistic Indian pantheon.

**trepiṭaka**. (P. tipeṭaka/tepiṭaka; T. sde snod gsum pa; C. sanzang fashi; J. sanzō hosshi; K. samjang pŏpsa 三藏法師). In Sanskrit, "a master of the canon"; an honorific title attached to the name of a renowned Buddhist teacher who is well versed in the three divisions of the Buddhist canon (TRIPIṬAKA), viz., the collection of monastic rules and regulations (VINAYAPIṬAKA; C. lü), the discourses collection (SŪTRAPIṬAKA; C. jing), and the treatise collection (ABHIDHARMAPIṬAKA, or *ŚĀSTRAPIṬAKA; C. lun). The Pāli form of this term appears first in the MILINDAPAÑHA, which is presumed to have been compiled around the beginning of the Common Era. In the East Asian Buddhist traditions, this term has been used as an honorific title for monks who mastered the Buddhist canon and were involved in translating Indic Buddhist literature into Chinese. Thus, such monks are also called "trepiṭaka who translate the scriptures" (YIJING SANZANG), or simply sanzang. There are many great translator-monks who carried this title of sanzang or sanzang fashi, including KUMĀRAJĪVA (344–413), PARAMĀRTHA (499–569), XUANZANG (600/602–664), and AMOGHAVAJRA (705–774). Later, this term was often commonly used to refer specifically to Xuanzang, as in the "Biography of the Master of the Buddhist Canon at the Beneficence of Great Compassion Monastery" (DACI'ENSI *sanzang fashi zhuan*), which is a biography of Xuanzang written by Huili (615–?). The Sanskrit of trepiṭaka is sometimes (mistakenly) reconstructed from the Chinese as *tripiṭakācārya.

**trichiliocosm**. See TRISĀHASRAMAHĀSĀHASRALOKADHĀTU; YINIAN SANQIAN.

**tricīvara**. (P. ticīvara; T. chos gos gsum; C. sanyi; J. san'e/sanne; K. samŭi 三衣). In Sanskrit, the "three robes" or "triple robe" worn by a monk or nun: the larger outer robe (S. SAṂGHĀṬĪ; P. saṅghāṭī), the upper robe (S. UTTARĀSAṂGA; P. uttarāsaṅga), and a lower robe or waist cloth (S. ANTARVĀSAS; P. antaravāsaka). According to the VINAYA account, the Buddha was concerned that too many monks had begun to hoard robes, which might cause them to "revert to luxury"; and after sitting through the cold one evening, he decided that the triple robe was sufficient to stay warm. The antarvāsas is the smallest of the three robes: normally made of one layer of cloth, it is worn around the waist and is intended to cover the body from the navel to the middle of the calf. The uttarāsaṃga is large enough to cover the body from the neck to the middle of the calf; it is also normally made of one layer of cloth. The saṃghāṭī or outer robe is the same size as the uttarāsaṃga but is normally made of two layers of cloth rather than one; it is worn over one or both shoulders, depending on whether one is inside or outside the monastery grounds. The saṃghāṭī was required to be tailored of patches, ranging in number from nine up to twenty-five, depending on the VINAYA recension; this use of patches of cloth is said to have been modeled after plots of farmland in MAGADHA that the Buddha once surveyed. All three robes must be dyed a sullied color, interpreted as anything from a reddish- or brownish-yellow saffron color to an ochre tone. For this reason, robes as also known as the KĀṢĀYA, or "dyed" (lit. "turbid-colored") robes, which were traditionally required to be sewn from pieces of soiled cloth and "dyed." Robes were one of the four major requisites (S. NIŚRAYA; P. NISSAYA) allowed to monks and nuns, along with such basics as a begging bowl (PĀTRA) and lodging, and were the object of the KAṬHINA ceremony, in which the monastics were offered cloth for making new sets of robes at the end of each rains retreat (S. VARṢĀ; P. vassa).

**tridhātu**. (S). See TRAIDHĀTUKA; AVACARA.

**tridvāra**. (P. dvārattaya; T. sgo gsum; C. sanmen; J. sanmon, K. sammun 三門). In Sanskrit, lit. "three doors" or "three gates"; referring to the body (KĀYA), speech (VĀK; see VĀKKARMAN), and mind (CITTA) as means for the performance of physical, verbal, and mental deeds (KARMAN). It is also understood that these are the three doors through which one may enter into the physical, verbal, and mental practice of the dharma. Since it is through these three doors that beings accumulate the fruits (VIPĀKA) of either negative or positive karman, the adept is taught to guard sense faculties (INDRIYASAṂVARA) throughout the activities of everyday life, in order to control the inveterate tendency toward craving. In tantric Buddhism, these three doors are known as the three mysteries (T. gsang ba gsum; J. SANMITSU), which are transformed into the three bodies of a buddha (TRIKĀYA) through tantric practice. The body is transformed into the emanation body (NIRMĀṆAKĀYA), speech into the enjoyment body (SAṂBHOGAKĀYA), and mind into the truth body (DHARMAKĀYA). Body, speech, and mind are said to be purified by the mantra oṃ āḥ hūṃ.

**trikāla**. (P. tikāla; T. dus gsum; C. sanshi; J. sanze; K. samse 三世). In Sanskrit, the "three times," used to refer collectively to the three time periods of past, present, and future; often mistakenly translated from the Chinese as "three worlds" (the Chinese term shi in this compound means an "age" or "generation"). The term often occurs in such phrases as trikāla-buddha, "the buddhas of the past, present, and future." Trikāla is also used to refer to the three periods of one day—dawn, daylight, and dusk. There are a range of views on the ontological status of the three temporal dimensions of the past, present, and future. One of the more common arguments is that, while the past no longer exists and the future does not yet exist, the present exists as an endless series of instances or moments in which a host of mental and physical constituents arise and cease instantaneously (see KṢAṆIKAVĀDA). On the other hand, the SARVĀSTIVĀDA school argued that dharmas exist, and can thus exert specific types of causal efficacy, in all three time periods, requiring a special set of "dissociated forces" (CITTAVIPRAYUKTASAṂSKĀRA) to account for the process of change (see CATURLAKṢAṆA; SAṂSKṚTALAKṢAṆA), essentially moving a dharma from past mode, to present and future modes.

**trikāya**. (T. sku gsum; C. sanshen; J. sanshin; K. samsin 三身). In Sanskrit, lit. "three bodies"; one of the central doctrines of MAHĀYĀNA buddhology. The three bodies refer specifically to three distinct bodies or aspects of a buddha: DHARMAKĀYA, the "dharma body" or "truth body"; SAṂBHOGAKĀYA, the "enjoyment body" or "reward body"; and NIRMĀṆAKĀYA, "emanation body" or "transformation body." The issue of what actually constituted the Buddha's body arose among the MAINSTREAM BUDDHIST SCHOOLS over such questions as the body he used on miraculous journeys, such as the one that he took to TRĀYASTRIṂŚA heaven to teach his mother MĀYĀ; the conclusion was that he had used a "mind-made body" (MANOMAYAKĀYA), also called a nirmāṇakāya, to make the trip. The notion of different buddha bodies was also deployed to respond to the question of the nature of the Buddha jewel (buddharatna), one of the three jewels (RATNATRAYA) or three refuges (TRIŚARAṆA) of Buddhism. Since the physical body of the Buddha was subject to decay and death, was it a suitable object of refuge? In response to this question, it was concluded that the Buddha jewel was in fact a body or group (kāya) of qualities (dharma), such as the eighteen unique qualities of a buddha (ĀVEṆIKA [BUDDHA]DHARMA). This "body of qualities," the original meaning of dharmakāya, was sometimes contrasted with the physical body of the Buddha, called the RŪPAKĀYA ("material body") or the vipākakāya, the "fruition body," which was the result of past action (KARMAN). With the development of Mahāyāna thought, the notion of dharmakāya evolved into a kind of transcendent principle in which all buddhas partook, and it is in this sense that the term is translated as "truth body." In the later Mahāyāna scholastic tradition, the dharmakāya was said to have two aspects. The first is the SVABHĀVIKAKĀYA, or "nature body," which is the ultimate nature of a buddha's mind that is free from all adventitious defilements (āgantukamala). The second is the jñānakāya, or "wisdom body," a buddha's omniscient consciousness. The dharmakāya was the source of the two other bodies, both varieties of the rūpakāya: the saṃbhogakāya and the nirmāṇakāya. The former, traditionally glossed as "the body for the enjoyment of others," is a resplendent form of the Buddha adorned with the thirty-two major and eighty minor marks (MAHĀPURUṢALAKṢAṆA), which appears only in buddha fields (BUDDHAKṢETRA) to teach the Mahāyāna to advanced bodhisattvas. Some śāstras, such as the BUDDHABHŪMIŚĀSTRA (*Fodijing lun*) and CHENG WEISHI LUN, distinguish between a "body intended for others' enjoyment" (PARASAṂBHOGAKĀYA) and a "body intended for personal enjoyment" (SVASAṂBHOGAKĀYA). In the trikāya system, the nirmāṇakāya is no longer a special body conjured up for magical travel, but the body of the Buddha that manifests itself variously in the world of sentient beings in order to teach the dharma to them. It also has different varieties: the form that manifests in the mundane world as the Buddha adorned with the major and minor marks is called the UTTAMANIRMĀṆAKĀYA, or "supreme emanation body"; the nonhuman or inanimate forms a buddha assumes in order to help others overcome their afflictions are called the JANMANIRMĀṆAKĀYA, or "created emanation body."

**trilakṣaṇa**. (P. tilakkhaṇa; T. mtshan nyid gsum/phyag rgya gsum; C. sanxiang; J. sansō; K. samsang 三相). In Sanskrit, the "three marks"; three characteristics of all conditioned phenomena in SAṂSĀRA: impermanence (ANITYA), suffering (DUḤKHA), and nonself (ANĀTMAN). According to the VISUDDHIMAGGA, realization of the truth and reality of the three marks constitutes enlightenment (BODHI), which eradicates belief in the existence of a perduring self (P. atta; S. ĀTMAN), otherwise called "personality belief" (P. sakkāyadiṭṭhi; S. SATKĀYADṚṢṬI), and delivers one to the noble path (P. ariyamagga; S. ĀRYAMĀRGA). Through this attainment, one becomes a stream-enterer (P. sotāpanna; S. SROTAĀPANNA) and is assured of becoming an ARHAT and entering NIRVĀṆA in at most seven lifetimes.

**triloka[dhātu]**. (P. tiloka; T. 'jig rten gsum; C. sanjie; J. sangai; K. samgye 三界). In Sanskrit, "three realms of existence"; a common Buddhist term for "everywhere" or "the whole world," glossed in one of two ways: (1) the three realms (TRAIDHĀTUKA), viz., the sensuous realm (KĀMADHĀTU), the realm of subtle materiality (RŪPADHĀTU), and the formless or immaterial realm (ĀRŪPYADHĀTU); (2) the three regions, viz., the region above the earth, the region on the surface of the earth, and the region below ground. See also TRISĀHASRAMAHĀSĀHASRALOKADHĀTU.

**Triṃśikā**. (T. Sum cu pa; C. Weishi sanshi lun song; J. Yuishiki sanjūronju; K. Yusik samsip non song 唯識三十論頌). In Sanskrit, lit., the "Thirty"; a work in thirty verses by the fourth or fifth century CE YOGĀCĀRA master VASUBANDHU; also known as the *Triṃśatikā* and the *Triṃśikāvijñaptimātratā*. Together with his VIṂŚATIKĀ (the "Twenty"), it is considered a classic synopsis of Yogācāra doctrine. In this work, which is extant in Sanskrit as well as in Chinese and Tibetan translations, Vasubandhu introduces the major categories of

Yogācāra thought, including the foundational consciousness or ĀLAYAVIJÑĀNA, and the mental concomitants (CAITTA) that accompany consciousness; the afflicted mental consciousness or KLIṢṬAMANAS (simply called MANAS in the text), which falsely perceives the ālayavijñāna as self; the three natures (TRISVABHĀVA); the three absences of intrinsic nature (NIḤSVABHĀVA); "consciousness-only" or "representation-only" (VIJÑAPTIMĀTRATĀ); and "revolution of the basis," or ĀŚRAYAPARĀVṚTTI. Among the commentaries on the text, the most influential is that by STHIRAMATI.

**trīndriya**. (T. dbang po gsum; C. sangen; J. sankon; K. samgŭn 三根). In Sanskrit, "three capacities," or "three faculties"; a division of disciples of the Buddha or of a particular teaching, based on relative levels of aptitude, understanding, or profundity. The three are as follows: those of dull faculties (MṚDVINDRIYA), those of intermediate faculties (MADHYENDRIYA), and those of sharp faculties (TĪKṢṆENDRIYA). The term is often used polemically to describe one's preferred teaching as intended only for those of sharp faculties, while dismissing other competing teachings as intended for those of dull or intermediate faculties. See also INDRIYA.

**triniḥsvabhāva**. (S.; T. ngo bo nyid med pa gsum). In Sanskrit, "three types of absence of intrinsic existence." See NIḤSVABHĀVA.

**tripiṭaka**. (P. tipiṭaka; T. sde snod gsum; C. sanzang; J. sanzō; K. samjang 三藏). In Sanskrit, "three baskets"; one of the most common and best known of the organizing schema of the Indian Buddhist canon. These three baskets were the SŪTRAPIṬAKA (basket of discourses), VINAYAPIṬAKA (basket of disciplinary texts) and ABHIDHARMAPIṬAKA [alt. *ŚĀSTRAPIṬAKA] (basket of "higher dharma" or "treatises"). The use of the term piṭaka for these categories is thought to come from the custom of storing the palm-leaf or wooden slips of written texts in baskets (S. piṭaka). (The Chinese translates piṭaka as a "repository," thus tripiṭaka is the "three repositories.") The various MAINSTREAM BUDDHIST SCHOOLS in India had their own distinctive version of each of the piṭakas; the Pāli version transmitted to Sri Lanka is the most complete to survive in an Indic language, although sections of those of other schools, such as the DHARMAGUPTAKA, SARVĀSTIVĀDA, and MŪLASARVĀSTIVĀDA, are preserved in Chinese, Tibetan, and in Sanskrit or Middle Indic fragments. Some schools used different organizing schema. The Dharmaguptaka school, for example, is said to have had five piṭakas; the usual three, plus a bodhisattvapiṭaka (on various doctrines and practices related to the BODHISATTVA) and a dhāraṇīpiṭaka (of DHĀRAṆĪ codes and spells). The MAHĀYĀNA sūtras were not organized under this rubric, although it is sometimes said that they can be when the three baskets are interpreted more figuratively, with the vinayapiṭaka including those teachings connected to the training in morality (ŚĪLA), the sūtrapiṭaka including those teachings connected to the training in meditation (SAMĀDHI), and the abhidharmapiṭaka including those teachings connected to the training in wisdom (PRAJÑĀ). The East Asian traditions arranged their own indigenous canons as a DAZANGJING (scriptures of the great repository), rather than a tripiṭaka; the two terms are not synonymous. See also BKA' 'GYUR; DAZANGJING; KORYŎ TAEJANGGYŎNG; TAISHŌ SHINSHŪ DAIZŌKYŌ.

***tripiṭakācārya**. (S). See TREPIṬAKA.

**triratna**. In Sanskrit, the "three jewels" of the BUDDHA, DHARMA, and SAṂGHA. See RATNATRAYA.

**trisāhasramahāsāhasralokadhātu**. (T. stong gsum gyi stong chen po'i 'jig rten gyi khams; C. sanqian daqian shijie; J. sanzendaisensekai; K. samch'ŏn taech'ŏn segye 三千大千世界). In Sanskrit, lit. "three-thousandfold great-thousandfold world system," but typically translated as "TRICHILIOCOSM"; the largest possible universe, composed of (according to some interpretations of the figure) one billion world systems, each of which have a similar geography, including a central axis at Mount SUMERU, four surrounding continents, etc. These worlds follow similar cosmic cycles of creation, abiding, disintegration, and annihilation. See YINIAN SANQIAN.

**Triśākuni**. (S). One of the twenty-four sacred sites associated with the CAKRASAṂVARATANTRA. See PĪṬHA.

**trisaṃvara**. (T. sdom gsum). In Sanskrit, "three vows" or "three restraints"; a collective term for three different sets of precepts. The *Trisaṃvaranirdeśaparivarta* of the RATNAKŪṬASŪTRA collection sets forth the three types of vows as the three types of bodhisattva morality found in the śīlaparivarta ("morality chapter") of the BODHISATTVABHŪMI. Usually, however, trisaṃvara refers to the three sets of precepts a practitioner of the VAJRAYĀNA may take: the prātimokṣasaṃvara or monastic precepts (see PRĀTIMOKṢA), the BODHISATTVASAṂVARA or bodhisattva precepts, and the guhyamantrasaṃvara ("secret mantra precepts") or tantric vows (SAṂVARA) or pledges (SAMAYA). The relations between and among these three types of precepts are the subject of an extensive, and often polemical, literature in Tibet, the most famous treatment being the SDOM GSUM RAB DBYE, or "Differentiation of the Three Vows," by SA SKYA PAṆḌITA. See also SAṂVARA; SDOM GSUM; PUSA JIE.

**triśaraṇa**. (P. tisaraṇa; T. skyabs gsum; C. sanguiyi; J. sankie; K. samgwiŭi 三歸依). In Sanskrit, the "three refuges" or the "triple refuge"; the three "safe havens" in which Buddhists seek refuge from the sufferings of SAṂSĀRA: the BUDDHA, the DHARMA, and the SAṂGHA. The recitation of the three refuges is one of the foundational Buddhist ritual practices: "I go for refuge to the Buddha (buddhaṃ śaraṇaṃ gacchāmi). I go for refuge to the dharma (dharmaṃ śaraṇaṃ gacchāmi). I go for refuge to the saṃgha (saṃghaṃ śaraṇaṃ gacchāmi)." Reciting these refuges three times is attestation that one is a Buddhist adherent; thus, the formula figures in a wide range of ceremonies across the Buddhist world. These three refuges are identical to the "three jewels" (RATNATRAYA).

**triśikṣā**. (P. tisikkhā; T. bslab pa gsum; C. sanxue; J. sangaku; K. samhak 三學). In Sanskrit, the "three trainings"; three overarching categories of Buddhist practice. First is the training in higher morality (ADHIŚĪLAŚIKṢĀ), which encompasses all forms of restraint of body and speech, including lay and monastic precepts that serve as the foundation for the cultivation of the succeeding stages of concentration and wisdom. Second is the training in higher concentration (ADHISAMĀDHIŚIKṢĀ, also called adhicitta), which encompasses all forms of meditative practice directed toward the achievement of states of concentration. Third is the training in higher wisdom (ADHIPRAJÑĀŚIKṢĀ), which includes all forms study and reflection that are directed toward developing insight into the true nature of reality. These three trainings are said to subsume all of the constituents of the noble eightfold path (ĀRYĀṢṬĀṄGAMĀRGA): adhiprajñāśikṣā comprises the first two constituents, viz., right views (SAMYAGDṚṢṬI) and right intention (SAMYAKSAṂKALPA); adhiśīlaśikṣā, the middle three constituents, viz., right speech (SAMYAGVĀC), right action (SAMYAKKARMĀNTA), and right livelihood (SAMYAGĀJĪVA); and adhisamādhiśikṣā, the last three constituents, viz., right effort (SAMYAGVYĀYĀMA), right mindfulness (SAMYAKSMṚTI), and right concentration (SAMYAKSAMĀDHI).

**triskandhaka**. (T. phung po gsum pa; C. sanju; J. sanju; K. samch'wi 三聚). In Sanskrit, lit. "three sections"; a three-part Mahāyāna liturgy that may have served as the foundation for more elaborate tantric liturgies (PŪJĀ), such as the sevenfold ritual (SAPTĀṄGAVIDHI). There are two versions of the three: (1) confession of transgressions (PĀPADEŚANĀ), (2) rejoicing in other's virtues (ANUMODANA), and (3) dedication of merit (PARIṆĀMANĀ). A second version is: (1) confession of transgressions, (2) appreciation of other's virtues, and (3) requesting the buddhas to turn the wheel of the dharma (dharmacakrapravartanacodana). See also PŪJĀ.

**trisvabhāva**. (T. mtshan nyid gsum/rang bzhin gsum; C. sanxing; J. sanshō; K. samsŏng 三性). In Sanskrit, "the three natures"; one of the central doctrines of the YOGĀCĀRA school. The three are PARIKALPITA, the "fabricated" or "imaginary" nature of things; PARATANTRA, literally "other-powered," their "dependent" nature; and PARINIṢPANNA, their "consummate" or "perfected" nature. The terms appear in several MAHĀYĀNA sūtras, most notably the sixth chapter of the SAṂDHINIRMOCANASŪTRA, and are explicated by both ASAṄGA and VASUBANDHU. Although the terms are discussed at length in Yogācāra literature, they can be described briefly as follows. The three natures are sometimes presented as three qualities that all phenomena possess. The parikalpita or imaginary nature is a false nature, commonly identified as the contrived appearance of an object as being a different entity from the perceiving consciousness. Since, in the Yogācāra analysis, objects do not exist independently from the perceiving subject, they come into existence in dependence upon consciousnesses, which in turn are produced from seeds that (according to some forms of Yogācāra) reside in the foundational consciousness, or ĀLAYAVIJÑĀNA. This quality of dependency on other causes and conditions for their existence, which is a characteristic of all objects and subjects, is the paratantra, or dependent nature. The nonduality between the consciousnesses and their objects is their consummate nature, the pariniṣpanna. Thus, it is said that the absence of the parikalpita in the paratantra is the pariniṣpanna.

**Trisvabhāvanirdeśa**. (T. Rang bzhin gsum nges par bstan pa). In Sanskrit, "Exposition of the Three Natures"; a work by the YOGĀCĀRA philosopher VASUBANDHU (fourth or fifth century CE). Possibly a late work of the author, it is less famous than several of his other works, in part because it lacks either an autocommentary or commentaries by subsequent figures in Indian Yogācāra. The work, extant in the original Sanskrit, consists of thirty-eight verses, dealing (as the title suggests) with the central Yogācāra doctrine of the three natures (TRISVABHĀVA): the PARIKALPITA or imaginary nature, the PARATANTRA or dependent nature, and the PARINIṢPANNA or consummate nature. According to this doctrine, briefly stated, objects do not exist apart from the perceiving consciousness. External objects are thus illusory and constitute the imaginary nature, the appearance of objects that arises in dependence on consciousness is the dependent nature, and the absence of duality between subject and object is the consummate nature. Among the most famous passages in the text is the metaphor of the magician's illusion, in which a magician recites a MANTRA over a piece of wood that causes the members of the audience to see an elephant in place of the wood. In explaining the metaphor, Vasubandhu says that the elephant seen by the audience is the imaginary nature, the appearance of the elephant through the conjuring trick is the dependent nature, and the actual nonexistence of the elephant is the consummate nature. He also likens the mantra to the foundational consciousness (MŪLAVIJÑĀNA, viz., ĀLAYAVIJÑĀNA) from which all appearances arise, and the wood to reality, or suchness (TATHATĀ).

**trividyā**. [alt. traividyā] (P. tevijjā; T. rig gsum; C. sanming; J. sanmyō; K. sammyŏng 三明). In Sanskrit, lit. "three knowledges"; three specific types of knowledge (VIDYĀ) that are the products of the enlightenment experience of an ARHAT or buddha, and a sequential set of insights achieved by the Buddha during the three watches of the night of his own enlightenment. They are: (1) the ability to remember one's own former lives (PŪRVANIVĀSĀNUSMṚTI; P. pubbenivāsānunssati) in all their detail, due to direct insight into the inexorable connection between action (KARMAN) and its fruition (VIPĀKA), viz., karmic cause and effect; (2) insight into the future rebirth destinies of all other beings (S. CYUTYUPAPATTIJÑĀNA [alt. cyutyupapādānusmṛti]; P. cutūpapātañāna), a by-product of the "divine eye" (DIVYACAKṢUS); (3) knowledge of the extinction of the contaminants (ĀSRAVAKṢAYA; P. āsavakhaya), which ensures complete liberation from the cycle of rebirth (SAṂSĀRA). The first and third types are also included in the superknowledges (ABHIJÑĀ; P. abhiññā). At various points in the literature of the MAINSTREAM BUDDHIST SCHOOLS (e.g., the Pāli ITIVUTTAKA), the Buddha describes the above list as the three knowledges of a true brāhmaṇa; in such accounts, the Buddha is intentionally contrasting his three knowledges (vidyā) with that of brāhmaṇa priests who have merely memorized the traditional three Vedas of Brahmanical religion. See also TEVIJJASUTTA.

**trivikalpa**. (T. rnam par rtog pa gsum; C. san fenbie; J. sanfunbetsu; K. sam punbyŏl 三分別). In Sanskrit, "three types of discrimination"; three aspects of the discriminative activities of mind, generally portrayed in the negative sense of fantasy and imagination. Three types are typically described in the literature. (1) Intrinsic discrimination (SVABHĀVAVIKALPA) refers to the initial advertence of thought (VITARKA) and the subsequent sustained thought or reasoning (VICĀRA) regarding a perceived object of the six sensory consciousnesses (VIJÑĀNA), i.e., the discrimination of present objects, as when visual consciousness perceives a visual object, etc. (2) Conceptualizing discrimination (ABHINIRŪPAṆĀVIKALPA) refers to discursive thought on ideas that arise in the sixth mental consciousness when it adverts toward a mental object that is associated with any of the three time periods (TRIKĀLA) of the past, present, or future. (3) Discrimination involving reflection on past events (ANUSMARAṆAVIKALPA) refers to discriminative thought involving the memory of past objects. It is said that there is no svabhāvavikalpa from the second stage of meditative absorption (DHYĀNA) onward, since vitarka and vicāra, the first two of the five constituents of dhyāna (DHYĀNĀṄGA), are then no longer present. There is no abhinirūpaṇāvikalpa from the first stage of dhyāna onward, since the mind is then temporarily isolated from any awareness of the passage of time. Only anusmaraṇavikalpa is involved in all three realms of existence (TRILOKADHĀTU), including both the subtle-materiality realm (RŪPADHĀTU) and the immaterial realm (ĀRŪPYADHĀTU).

**triviṣa**. (P. tivisa; T. dug gsum; C. sandu; J. sandoku; K. samdok 三毒). In Sanskrit, "three poisons"; the three primary afflictions (MŪLAKLEŚA) of sensuality, desire, or greed (RĀGA or LOBHA), hatred or aversion (DVEṢA), and delusion or ignorance (MOHA), regarded as poisons because of the harm they cause to those who ingest them or the way they poison the mind. This same list of three is also known as the three "unwholesome faculties" (AKUŚALAMŪLA), which will fructify as unhappiness in the future and provide the foundation for unfavorable rebirths (APĀYA). In the "wheel of existence" (BHAVACAKRA) that the Buddha is said to have instructed to be painted at the entrances of monasteries, showing the six realms of rebirth (ṢAḌGATI) as well as the twelve links of dependent origination (PRATĪTYASAMUTPĀDA), the three poisons are often depicted at the center of painting, suggesting their role as root causes of cycle of rebirth, with greed represented by a rooster, hatred by a snake, and delusion by a pig in a circle, each biting the tail of the other.

**triyāna**. (T. theg pa gsum; C. sansheng; J. sanjō; K. samsŭng 三乘). In Sanskrit, "three vehicles," three different means taught in Buddhist soteriological literature of conveying sentient beings to liberation. There are two common lists of the three: (1) the vehicles of the ŚRĀVAKA, PRATYEKABUDDHA (both of which lead to the state of an ARHAT), and BODHISATTVA (which leads to buddhahood); (2) the HĪNAYĀNA, MAHĀYĀNA, and VAJRAYĀNA, although the vajrayāna is considered by its adherents to be a form of the Mahāyāna; the vajrayāna would speak instead of the HĪNAYĀNA, PĀRAMITĀYĀNA, and VAJRAYĀNA. According to some Mahāyāna sūtras, most famously the SADDHARMAPUṆḌARĪKASŪTRA ("Lotus Sūtra"), the three vehicles (in the first sense above) are an expedient device (UPĀYA) developed by the Buddha to entice beings of differing spiritual capacities toward enlightenment; in fact, however, there is really only one vehicle (EKAYĀNA) by which all beings proceed to buddhahood. Thus, in the Mahāyāna philosophical schools, the question arises of whether or not there are "three final vehicles," that is, whether the state of the arhat is a permanent dead end or whether arhats would also eventually continue on to buddhahood. For example, the position that there are three separate and final vehicles is associated with the YOGĀCĀRA school of ASAṄGA and the Chinese FAXIANG ZONG. The position that there are not three, but instead a single decisive vehicle, is associated with the MADHYAMAKA school of NĀGĀRJUNA and CANDRAKĪRTI and the Chinese TIANTAI ZONG.

**tṛṣṇā**. (P. taṇhā; T. sred pa; C. ai; J. ai; K. ae 愛). In Sanskrit, lit. "thirst," or "craving," viz., the desire not to be separated from feelings of pleasure, the desire to be separated from feelings of pain, and the desire that feelings of neutrality not diminish. Typically, three types of craving are listed in the literature, such as the DHARMACAKRAPRAVARTANASŪTRA: craving for sensuality (KĀMA), craving for continued existence (BHAVA), and craving for nonexistence (vibhava). Craving is thus the cause or "origination" (SAMUDAYA) of suffering (DUḤKHA), viz., the second of the FOUR NOBLE TRUTHS. Craving is also the eighth link in the twelvefold chain of dependent origination (PRATĪTYASAMUTPĀDA), where it is a product of the preceding link of sensation (VEDANĀ) and leads to even stronger clinging or attachment (UPĀDĀNA). Tṛṣṇā thus manifests itself as the thirst for sensory experience of visual, auditory, olfactory, gustatory, tactile, and mental objects.

**Trúc Lâm**. (竹林). In Vietnamese, "Bamboo Grove"; the first indigenous Vietnamese school of THIỀN (C. CHAN), founded by TRẦN NHÂN TÔNG (1258–1308), the third king of the Trần dynasty (1225–1400). During the Trần period, Chan learning became established with the arrival of Chinese monks and Chan literature. Due to its literary bent (see WENZI CHAN), Chan was embraced by the Trần aristocratic circle, many of whom received instructions from Chan masters. Some Trần kings themselves would later in their lives be ordained and devote themselves to the practice of Chan. From the few extant writings of its three patriarchs, it is clear that Trúc Lâm Chan displays a conscious effort to emulate Chinese patriarchal Chan. There were also typical motifs that appear in Chinese Chan literature, including the use of dialogues (see WENDA) as an instructional tool, transmission directly from teacher to disciple, the construction of lineages, the teacher leaving behind instructional verses for his disciples, the teacher bequeathing his robe and begging bowl to his principal student as a mark of succession, the teacher publicly conferring precepts on both monks and laypeople, and so forth. The school died out after the death of its third patriarch Huyền Quang (1254–1334). Although the Trúc Lâm school was short-lived, it marked the first serious effort to establish a Buddhist community in medieval Vietnam, functioning essentially as a form of high-culture Buddhism for aristocrats. There were efforts among some Buddhist monks in the Later Lê (1428–1788) and Nguyễn (1802–1945) dynasties to connect themselves to Trúc Lâm Chan.

**Trungpa, Chögyam**. (Chos rgyam Drung pa) (1939–1987). One of the most influential Tibetan teachers of the twentieth century in introducing Tibetan Buddhism to the West. Chögyam Trungpa (his name, Chos rgyam Drung pa, is an abbreviation of chos kyi rgya mtsho drung pa) was born in Khams in eastern Tibet and identified while still an infant as the eleventh incarnation of the Drung pa lama, an important lineage of teachers in the BKA' BRGYUD sect, and was enthroned as the abbot of Zur mang monastery. He was ordained as a novice monk at the age of eight and received instruction from some of the leading scholars of the Bka' brgyud and RNYING MA sects. In 1958, he received the degrees of skyor dpon and mkhan po, as well as BHIKṢU ordination. After the Tibetan uprising against Chinese occupying forces in March 1959, he escaped across the Himalayas to India on horseback and on foot, accompanied by a group of monks. In 1963, he traveled to England to study at Oxford University. In 1967, he moved to Scotland, where he founded a Tibetan meditation center called Samye Ling. While there, he suffered permanent injury in a serious automobile accident and decided thereafter to give up his monastic vows and continue as a lay teacher of Buddhism. In 1969, he moved to the United States, where he established a meditation center in Vermont called Tail of the Tiger. Trungpa Rinpoche's extensive training in Tibetan Buddhism, his eclectic interests, and his facility in English combined to make him the first Tibetan lama (apart from the fourteenth DALAI LAMA) to reach a wide Western audience through his many books, including *Born in Tibet* (1966), *Meditation in Action* (1969), and *Cutting Through Spiritual Materialism* (1973). In 1974, he founded the Naropa Institute (now Naropa University) in Boulder, Colorado, a center devoted to the study of Buddhism, psychology, and the arts. He also developed a network of centers around the world called Dharmadhatus, as well as the Shambhala Training Program. He invited several important Tibetan lamas to the United States in the late 1970s and early 1980s, including DIL MGO MKHYEN BRTSE, BDUD 'JOMS RIN PO CHE, and the sixteenth KARMA PA. In 1986, he moved his headquarters to Halifax, Nova Scotia, and died there the following year.

**truths, three**. See SANDI.

**truths, two**. See SATYADVAYA.

**Tsa ri**. Also spelled Tsā ri; an important pilgrimage region in the sacred geography of Tibet, its central feature is the Pure Crystal Mountain (Dag pa shel ri). The BKA' BRGYUD sect, in particular, considers the site to be one of three quintessential pilgrimage destinations connected with the CAKRASAMVARATANTRA (together with KAILĀSA and LA PHYI). According to the *Cakrasaṃvaratantra* tradition, two of the twenty-four sacred lands (PĪṬHA), viz., Cārita and Devīkoṭa, are believed to be located in the region. Hunting and even cultivation are banned in some parts of the valley. Situated on the remote border between Tibet and Assam, Tsa ri is also one of the Himalayan region's most difficult and dangerous locations to access. The circumambulation trails skirting the mountain traverse high passes, deep ravines, and dense jungle. They also pass through territory controlled by tribal groups who are often unfriendly to outside visitors. For this reason, the state-sponsored pilgrimage season was traditionally preceded by government negotiations (and payments) in order to guarantee safe passage for pilgrims. The area is said to have been sanctified by visits from PADMASAMBHAVA and VIMALAMITRA, who are thought to have deposited there numerous treasure texts (GTER MA). Tsa ri later became primarily associated with the 'BRUG PA BKA' BRGYUD through the activity of GTSANG PA RGYA RAS YE SHES RDO RJE, who is often said to have "opened" the site as a powerful place for spiritual practice.

**Tshad ma rigs gter**. (Tsema Rikter). In Tibetan, "Treasure of Valid Knowledge and Reasoning"; an influential Tibetan work on logic and epistemology (PRAMĀṆA) by the renowned scholar SA SKYA PAṆḌITA KUN DGA' RGYAL MTSHAN, composed circa 1219. The *Tshad ma rigs gter* inaugurated a new period of pramāṇa studies in Tibet by focusing particularly on DHARMAKĪRTI's most famous work, the PRAMĀṆAVĀRTTIKA; prior to this time in Tibet, pramāṇa had been approached through summaries (bsdus pa) of the seven works of Dharmakīrti (see TSHAD MA SDE BDUN). Written in verse, the *Tshad ma rigs gter* seeks accurately to represent the positions of the late Indian traditions of logic and epistemology and to identify the errors of earlier Tibetan scholars, notably the summaries associated with GSANG PHU NE'U THOG monastery, especially the works of RNGOG BLO LDAN SHES RAB, PHYWA PA CHOS KYI SENG GE, and their disciples.

The *Tshad ma rigs gter* is said to have been so highly regarded that it was translated from Tibetan into Sanskrit and circulated in northern India.

**tshad ma sde bdun**. (tsema dedün). In Tibetan, "group of seven on valid knowledge"; the name for a collection of seven Indian treatises on logic and epistemology (PRAMĀṆA) written by the Indian scholar DHARMAKĪRTI. They are the PRAMĀṆAVĀRTTIKA, the PRAMĀṆAVINIŚCAYA, the NYĀYABINDU, the *Hetubindu*, the *Sambandhaparīkṣā*, the *Saṃtānāntarasiddhi*, and the *Vādanyāya*. The collection is also known as *tshad ma'i bstan bcos sde bdun*, or the "seven treatises on valid knowledge."

**Tshal pa bka' brgyud**. (Tshalpa Kagyü). One of the four major and eight minor subsects of the BKA' BRGYUD sect of Tibetan Buddhism (BKA' BRGYUD CHE BZHI CHUNG BRGYAD), originating with Zhang tshal pa Brtson grus grags pa (Shangtsalpa Tsöndrü Drakpa, 1123–1193), better known as BLA MA ZHANG, a disciple of Dwags po Sgom tshul (Dakpo Gomtsül, 1116–1169). In about 1175, Bla ma Zhang established Tshal Gung thang monastery near LHA SA, which served as a seat of the Tshal pa bka' brgyud.

**Tshangs dbyangs rgya mtsho**. (Tsangyang Gyatso) (1683–1706). The sixth DALAI LAMA, and among the most famous and beloved of the Dalai Lamas, but not for the same qualities of sanctity and scholarship for which several other members of the lineage are known. He was born into a RNYING MA family near the border with Bhutan. The fifth Dalai Lama had died in 1682 but his death was concealed until 1697 by his minister, SDE SRID SANGS RGYAS RGYA MTSHO, so that the construction of the PO TA LA palace could continue unabated. The sixth Dalai Lama was identified at the age of two, but his identification was kept secret; he and his family lived in seclusion in Mtsho na (Tsona) for twelve years. The death of the fifth Dalai Lama and the identity of the sixth were finally disclosed in 1697. In that year, the sixth Dalai Lama was brought to LHA SA, where he received the vows of a novice from the PAṆ CHEN LAMA. He received instructions in Buddhist doctrine and practice from the Paṇ chen Lama and other scholars for the next four years. In 1701, he was urged to take the percepts of a fully ordained monk (BHIKṢU). However, he refused to do so and also asked to give up his novice vows (which included the vow of celibacy), threatening to commit suicide if he were not permitted to do so. He gave up his vows and lived as a layman, with long hair, although he still remained in the position of Dalai Lama. He had liaisons with women in Lha sa; the houses he visited were said to have been painted yellow in his honor. He is credited with a series of famous love songs, some of which contain Buddhist references. In 1705, the Qoshot Mongol leader Lha bzang Khan declared himself king of Tibet and executed Sde srid Sang rgyas rgya mtsho. In 1706, Lha bzang Khan declared, with the support of the Manchu Kangxi emperor, that Tshangs dbyangs rgya mtsho was not the true Dalai Lama and sent him into exile in Beijing. He died en route, although a legend developed that he escaped death and lived in disguise for another forty years.

**Tshangs pa dkar po**. (Tsangpa Karpo). A Tibetan wrathful deity who figures frequently in the retinues of major DHARMAPĀLA, such as MAHĀKĀLA and PE HAR RGYAL PO, of whom Tshangs pa dkar po is an emanation. Although the name "Tshangs pa" was given to the Indian god BRAHMĀ, Tshangs pa dkar po was in all probability a native Tibetan deity, who lost his individual identity through associations with Brahmā and Pe har.

**Tshar chen Blo gsal rgya mtsho**. (T). See TSHAR PA.

**Tshar pa**. An offshoot of the NGOR subsect of the SA SKYA sect, established by Tshar chen Blo gsal rgya mtsho (Tsarchen Losal Gyatso, 1502–1567), founder of 'Dar Grang mo che (Dar Drangmoche) monastery. It represents a distinctive tradition of the LAM 'BRAS (path and result) teaching, including the distinction between the "assembly exegesis" (tshogs bshad) and "student exegesis" (slob bshad). It is said that the Ngor tradition became influential in the dissemination of the Sa skya tantric teachings, and the Tshar tradition in the esoteric transmission known as the slob bshad. Bco brgyad khri chen rin po che (Chogye Trichen Rinpoche, 1920–2007), a recent influential scholar of the Sa skya tradition, was head of the Tshar pa sect until his death.

**tshe lha rnam gsum**. (tshe lha nam sum). In Tibetan, the "three deities of long life"; three deities who are propitiated in order to extend one's life, especially in order to practice the dharma. They are the buddha AMITĀYUS and the female bodhisattvas white TĀRĀ (SITATĀRĀ) and Uṣṇīṣavijayā.

**tshe ring mched lnga**. (T). See BKRA SHIS TSHE RING MCHED LNGA.

**tshogs zhing**. (tsok shing). In Tibetan, "field of assembly" or "field of accumulation"; the assembly of buddhas, bodhisattvas, and other deities visualized in meditation practice (and represented in Tibetan scroll paintings, or THANG KA). The term is generally glossed to mean "the field for the collection of merit" because the assembly of deities are the objects of various virtuous practices through which the meditator accumulates merit. The most common practice performed in the presence of the field of assembly would be the sevenfold offering (SAPTĀṄGAVIDHI): obeisance (vandana), offering (pūjana), confession of transgressions (PĀPADEŚANĀ), rejoicing in others' virtues (ANUMODANA), requesting that the buddhas turn the wheel of the dharma (dharmacakrapravartanacodana), beseeching the buddhas not pass into NIRVĀṆA (aparinirvṛtādhyeṣaṇa), and the dedication (PARIṆĀMANĀ) of merit. In paintings of the field of assembly, the central figure is often depicted with previous figures in the lineage in a vertical line above, with various disciples on either side and protector deities at the bottom.

**Tsi'u dmar po**. (Tsi'u Marpo). The DHARMAPĀLA of BSAM YAS monastery; he succeeded PE HAR when the later moved to GNAS CHUNG outside of LHA SA. Tsi'u dmar is the leader of the BSTAN class of Tibetan spirits. His medium traditionally resided in the Tsi'u dmar lcog dbug khang at BSAM YAS, where each year the Lha sa glud 'gong would arrive bearing all the negative fortune of the city. Inside, Tsi'u dmar was said to sit in judgment of the dead, chopping up their spirits with such frequency that each year the chopping block would need to be replaced. According to legend, the deity Dza sa dmar po, the spirit of a nobleman who died of an illness caused by the Bsam yas protector, once defeated Tsi'u dmar, forcing the god to abandon his seat at Bsam yas. Dza sa dmar po later voluntarily left when he discovered he was unable to shoulder the burden of Tsi'u dmar po's helmet, and hence the responsibility of guarding Bsam yas; having established peaceful relations with the dharmapāla, he was installed by the monks at Bsam yas in his own protector temple at the monastery. In memory of the conflict, the mediums of Tsi'u dmar po begin their trance by thrusting their swords in the direction of Dza sa dmar po's temple.

**Tsong kha pa Blo bzang grags pa**. (Tsong kha pa Losang Drakpa) (1357–1419). A Tibetan scholar and teacher venerated as the founder of the DGE LUGS sect of Tibetan Buddhism; typically known simply as Tsong kha pa. Born in the Tsong kha region of A mdo in northeastern Tibet, he received his initial lay vows under the fourth KARMA PA and began his religious education in the BKA' GDAMS tradition. In 1372, he traveled to central Tibet for further study. He became a disciple of the SA SKYA scholar Red mda' ba Gzhon nu blo gros (Rendawa Shönu Lodrö, 1349–1412) but went on to study under many of the leading scholars of the day, including masters of various schools and sectarian affiliations. Another influential teacher was the lama Dbu ma pa (Umapa), from whom he received instructions on the KĀLACAKRATANTRA. He distinguished himself as a brilliant scholar and exegete of both SŪTRA and TANTRA. According to his traditional biographies, Tsong kha pa experienced visions of Indian masters such as NĀGĀRJUNA and BUDDHAPĀLITA, who helped to clarify difficult points of doctrine. He is also said to have maintained a special relationship with MAÑJUŚRĪ, the bodhisattva of wisdom, who appeared in visions throughout Tsong kha pa's life offering instruction and advice; Tsong kha pa is sometimes called 'Jam mgon, or "protected by Mañjuśrī." Tsong kha pa's biographies speak of four major deeds undertaken during his lifetime. The first, in 1399, was his restoration of an image of the future buddha, MAITREYA. The second was a council to reform the code of VINAYA, convened in 1403 and attended by monks representing all sects of Tibetan Buddhism. The third was the Great Prayer Festival (SMON LAM CHEN MO) inaugurated in 1409 at the JO KHANG in LHA SA, in which he offered the ornaments of a SAṂBHOGAKĀYA to the famous statue of JO BO SHĀKYAMUNI, celebrating the Buddha's performance of the ŚRĀVASTĪ MIRACLES. The festival became an important annual event, drawing thousands of participants from all quarters of the Tibetan Buddhist world. The fourth was the founding in 1409 of DGA' LDAN monastery, which would become one of principal religious institutions in the Lha sa region and seat of the leader of the Dge lugs sect. Tsong kha pa was an original and penetrating philosopher, who saw reason and intellectual development as key aspects of the path to enlightenment. Born during a period when the Tibetan Buddhist canon had been newly formulated, he sought a comprehensive explanation of the Buddhist path, with the PRĀSAṄGIKA-MADHYAMAKA of BUDDHAPĀLITA and CANDRAKĪRTI as the highest philosophical view. His works are marked with a concern with systematic consistency, whether it be between sūtra and tantra or PRAMĀṆA and MADHYAMAKA. A prolific author, Tsong kha pa's works fill eighteen volumes. Among his best known writings are the LAM RIM CHEN MO ("Great Treatise on the Stages of the Path to Enlightenment"), composed in 1402 at RWA SGRENG monastery, the SNGAGS RIM CHEN MO ("Great Treatise on the Stages of Mantra"), and the *Drang nges* LEGS BSHAD SNYING PO ("Essence of Eloquence on the Definitive and Interpretable"). Tsong kha pa called his system of religious practice the Bka' gdams gsar ma, or "New Bka' gdams," after the sect founded by the Bengali master ATIŚA DĪPAMKARAŚRĪJÑĀNA. His followers were later known as Dga' ldan pa (Gandenpa), "those of Dga' ldan," after the monastic seat established by Tsong kha pa. This was sometimes abbreviated as Dga' lugs pa, "those of the system of Dga' ldan," eventually evolving into the current name Dge lugs pa, "those of the system of virtue." Tsong kha pa's fame was greatly elevated through the political power of the Dge lugs sect after the establishment of the institution of the DALAI LAMA. His tomb at Dga' ldan became an important site of pilgrimage prior to its destruction during the Chinese Cultural Revolution. Tsong kha pa's fame in Tibet was sufficiently great that he is commonly known simply as Rje rin po che, the "precious leader."

**Tucci, Giuseppe**. (1894–1984). One of the leading European Tibetologists of the twentieth century. Born in Macerata, Italy, Guiseppe Tucci attended the University of Rome, where he later became professor of the religions and philosophies of India and the Far East. Between 1925 and 1930, he taught Italian, Chinese, and Tibetan in India at the University of Calcutta and the University of Santiniketan. During this time, he made numerous expeditions into Nepal and Tibet, gathering historical, religious, and artistic materials. In 1937, the Fascist government of Italy sent him to Japan in order to promote understanding between the two countries. In 1948, he was named president of the Italian Institute for the Middle and Far East. Over the next two decades, he led expeditions in Pakistan, Afghanistan, and Iran and remained an active scholar until shortly before his death. Tucci published extensively in Italian and English on a wide range of topics using Sanskrit, Chinese, and Tibetan sources. His works include *Indo-Tibetica* (published in seven volumes 1932–1942), *To Lhasa and Beyond* (1946), *Minor Buddhist Texts* (1956), and what many consider his magnum opus, *Tibetan Painted Scrolls* (1949).

**Tuệ Trung**. (V) (1230–1291). See HUỆ TRUNG.

**tulku**. (T). See SPRUL SKU.

**Turfan**. Central Asian petty kingdom located along the northern track of the SILK ROAD through the Takla Makhan desert, in what is now the Chinese province of Xinjiang. This and other oasis kingdoms in Central Asia served as crucial stations in the transmission of Buddhism from India to China. Buddhism had a strong presence in Turfan from the seventh century through the fourteenth century, with important texts being translated, cave temples built, and works of art produced. The oldest physical manuscripts of the Indian Buddhist tradition are manuscripts in the KHAROṢṬHĪ script (see GĀNDHĀRĪ), dated to the fourth to fifth centuries CE, which were discovered at Turfan. These and other discoveries were made by a team of German researchers led by Albert Grünwedel and Albert von Le Coq in a series of expeditions between 1902 and 1914. Turfan was also the locus where TOCHARIAN A (East Tocharian, or Turfanian) was used; manuscripts in Tocharian A date primarily from the eighth century. Western expeditions into the area led to the discovery of tens of thousands of textual fragments, in a variety of languages and scripts, which came to be known collectively as the "Turfan Collection." These texts belong to a variety of genres and schools, but the SARVĀSTIVĀDA is prevalent, leading to the conclusion that the school was prominent in Turfan. As with other locations in this region, the dry desert air helped to preserve the various materials on which these texts were written. In Turfan were found translations of Sanskrit and Chinese Buddhist texts, as well as some original Buddhist poetry and lay literature. Also discovered in Turfan were the Bezaklik rock caves, dating from around the ninth century, which contain the painted images of thousands of buddhas. Albert von le Coq removed many of these and transported them to Berlin, where many were destroyed by Allied bombing during the Second World War. Although this area was a melting pot of Indian, Chinese, and Central Asian traditions, Buddhist activity in the Turfan region saw a sharp rise in the ninth century, when the Uighur people moved from Mongolia into the Turfan region and many Turfan texts are recorded in the Uighur script. Buddhism seems to have survived in this region until as late as the fifteenth century.

**tuṣita**. (P. tusita; T. dga' ldan; C. doushuai tian; J. tosotsuten; K. tosol ch'ŏn 兜率天). In Sanskrit, "contentment"; in Buddhist cosmology, the fourth highest of six heavens within the sensuous realm (KĀMADHĀTU). This heaven is of particular importance to the Buddhist tradition because it is understood that BODHISATTVAs are born here before taking their final birth in the human world and attaining buddhahood. It was from this heaven that the deity ŚVETAKETU (the future ŚĀKYAMUNI) departed to enter MĀYĀ's womb for his final rebirth, and it is understood that the bodhisattva MAITREYA currently resides in the tuṣita heaven awaiting his own final rebirth when he will in turn achieve buddhahood. Consequently, many Buddhists throughout history have aspired for rebirth in the tuṣita heaven so that they may learn from Maitreya and accompany him when he takes his final birth as a buddha. Beings reborn in tuṣita enjoy unimaginable pleasure and live for hundreds of thousands of years. One day in this heaven is equal to four hundred earth years. In some texts, this heaven is described as having an inner and outer courtyard, the former of which is said to be utterly indestructible.

**twelve categories of scripture**. See AṄGA; DVĀDAŚĀṄGA [PRAVACANA].

**twelve deeds of a buddha**. (S. buddhakārya; T. sangs rgyas kyi mdzad pa). A list of twelve acts said to be performed or "displayed" by the "transformation body" (NIRMĀṆAKĀYA) of each buddha. Although the specific deeds in the list of twelve vary, the notion of the twelve deeds seems to have become popular during the Pāla dynasty in India, where it is often depicted. The *Dvādaśakāranāmanayastotra* (*Mdzad pa bcu gnyis kyi tshul la bstod pa*), "Praise of the Twelve Deeds of a Buddha," is extremely popular in Tibet and is often a part of a monastery's daily liturgy. One version of the list of deeds is (1) descent from TUṢITA, (2) entry into the womb (viz., conception), (3) taking birth in the LUMBINĪ Garden, (4) proficiency in the arts, (5) enjoyment of consorts, (6) renouncing the world, (7) practicing asceticism on the banks of the NAIRAÑJANĀ River, (8) seeking enlightenment in BODHGAYĀ, (9) subjugating MĀRA, (10) attaining enlightenment, (11) turning the wheel of the dharma (DHARMACAKRAPRAVARTANA), and (12) passing into PARINIRVĀṆA in KUŚINAGARĪ. Although the notion of twelve deeds seems to have developed in the MAHĀYĀNA, the idea of a specific set of actions common to all the buddhas is also found in the MAINSTREAM BUDDHIST SCHOOLS; for example, the Pāli tradition notes that thirty facts are common to all buddhas. For a similar East Asian list of eight stereotypical episodes in a buddha's life, see BAXIANG.

**twelve links of dependent origination/twelvefold chain of dependent origination**. See PRATĪTYASAMUTPĀDA.

**twin miracles**. See YAMAKAPRĀTIHĀRYA; MAHĀPRĀTIHĀRYA.

**two truths**. See SATYADVAYA.

**Tỳ Ni Đa Lưu Chi**. (V) (毗尼多流支). See VINĪTARUCI.

# U

**U Ba Khin**. (1899–1971). See BA KHIN, U.

**ubhayatobhāgavimukta**. (P. ubhatobhāgavimutta; T. gnyis ka'i cha las rnam par grol ba; C. ju jietuo; J. kugedatsu; K. ku haet'al 俱解脫). In Sanskrit, "liberated both ways." This is the type of liberation achieved by those noble persons (ĀRYA) who are liberated, first, by way of meditative absorption (DHYĀNA; P. JHĀNA), which is called "liberation of mind" (CETOVIMUKTI; P. cetovimutti), and second, "liberation through wisdom" (PRAJÑĀVIMUKTI; P. paññāvimutti), which involves insight by way of any of the four noble paths (ĀRYAMĀRGA), viz., the path of the stream-enterer (SROTAĀPANNA) to the path of the ARHAT. Liberation may be achieved via wisdom alone, but arhats enlightened in this manner, without any attainment of dhyāna, are in some materials pejoratively termed "dry insight workers" (P. SUKKHAVIPASSAKA); strands of contemporary Burmese VIPASSANĀ meditation theory, however, emphasize this focus on wisdom alone as a more subitist approach to enlightenment that does not require lengthy perfection of the dhyānas. Twofold liberation is thought to be a more complete experience, and all buddhas and their chief disciples are liberated in both these two ways. The ubhayatobhāgavimukta is also one of the VIṂŚATIPRABHEDASAṂGHA ("twenty varieties of the ĀRYASAṂGHA") based on the list given in the MAHĀVYUTPATTI.

**ucchedadṛṣṭi**. (P. ucchedadiṭṭhi; T. chad lta; C. duanjian; J. danken; K. tan'gyŏn 斷見). In Sanskrit, lit. the "[wrong] view of annihilationism"; one of the two "extreme views" (ANTAGRĀHADṚṢṬI) together with ŚĀŚVATADṚṢṬI, the "[wrong] view of eternalism." Ucchedadṛṣṭi is variously defined in the Buddhist philosophical schools but generally refers to the wrong view that causes do not have effects, thus denying the central tenets of KARMAN and rebirth (the denial of the possibility of rebirth was attributed to the Cārvāka school of ancient India). Among the divisions of the root affliction (MŪLAKLEŚA) of "wrong view" (DṚṢṬI), ucchedadṛṣṭi occurs in connection with SATKĀYADṚṢṬI, where it is defined as the mistaken belief or view that the self is the same as one or all of the five aggregates (SKANDHA) and that as such it ceases to exist at death. In this context, it is contrasted with ŚĀŚVATADṚṢṬI, the mistaken belief that the self is different from the aggregates and that it continues to exist eternally from one rebirth to the next. Annihilationism is thus a form of antagrāhadṛṣṭi, "[wrong] view of holding to an extreme," i.e., the view that the person ceases to exist at death and is not reborn (ucchedadṛṣṭi), in distinction to the view that there is a perduring soul that continues to be reborn unchanged from one lifetime to the next (śāśvatadṛṣṭi). The Buddhist middle way (MADHYAMAPRATIPAD) between these two extremes posits that there is no permanent, perduring soul (countering eternalism), and yet there is karmic continuity from one lifetime to the next (countering annihilationism). In the MADHYAMAKA school, ucchedadṛṣṭi is more broadly defined as the view that nothing exists, even at a conventional level. Thus, following statements in the PRAJÑĀPĀRAMITĀ SŪTRAS, the Madhyamaka school sets forth a middle way between the extremes of existence and nonexistence. In general, the middle way between extremes is able to acknowledge the insubstantiality of persons and phenomena (whether that insubstantiality is defined as impermanence, no-self, or emptiness) while upholding functionality, most importantly in the realm of cause and effect (and thus the conventional reality of karman and rebirth).

**ucchedānta**. (T. chad mtha'; C. duanbian; J. danhen; K. tanbyŏn 斷邊). In Sanskrit, "extreme of annihilation" or "extreme of nihilism"; along with the extreme of permanence (ŚĀŚVATĀNTA), one of the two extremes to be avoided in pursuit of the middle way (MADHYAMAPRATIPAD). Precisely how these two extremes are defined varies among the schools of Indian Buddhist philosophy. All Buddhist schools would consign the various non-Buddhist schools of Indian philosophy to one of the two extremes, with the Sāṃkhya, Vaiśeṣika, JAINA, Vedānta, Mīmāṃsaka, and Nyāya falling into the extreme of permanence (ŚĀŚVATĀNTA) and the Cārvāka falling into the extreme of nihilism (ucchedānta). The Buddhist schools each claim to avoid these two extremes, avoiding the extreme of permanence by denying the existence of a perduring, indivisible, and independent self, and avoiding the extreme of annihilation by upholding the existence of moral cause and effect (KARMAN) and of rebirth. Beyond this basic analysis, the various Buddhist schools refine the two extremes according to their specific tenets and charge their rivals with falling into one or the other of the two extremes. For example, the YOGĀCĀRA school claims that the MADHYAMAKA doctrine that all phenomena are devoid of intrinsic nature (NIḤSVABHĀVA) flirts with the extreme of nihilism, and the Madhyamaka claims that the Yogācāra emphasis on the autonomy of consciousness (VIJÑĀNA; VIJÑAPTIMĀTRATĀ) tends toward the extreme of permanence.

**ucchedavāda**. (T. chad par smra ba; C. duanjian lun; J. dankenron; K. tan'gyŏn non 斷見論). In Sanskrit and Pāli, "teaching on annihilationism," a synonym of UCCHEDADṚṢṬI.

**Udam Honggi**. (優曇洪基) (1822–1881). Korean SŎN monk of the late Chosŏn dynasty; his original dharma name was Uhaeng, and his sobriquet was Udam. A native of Andong, he lost his parents at an early age and entered the SAṂGHA in 1837. Honggi studied under the monks Chasin (d.u.) at the monastery of Hŭibangsa and Yŏnwŏl (d.u.) at the major monastery of SONGGWANGSA. Honggi also studied under Ch'immyŏng Hansŏng (1801–1876) and received the full monastic precepts from the VINAYA master Inp'a (d.u.). Honggi is most famous for his treatise, the *Sŏnmun chŭngjŏng nok* ("Record of Attesting to Orthodoxy in the Sŏn School"), a criticism of PAEKP'A KŬNGSŎN's magnum opus, the *Sŏnmun sugyŏng* ("Hand Mirror of the Sŏn School"). Honggi criticized Paekp'a for mistakenly positing three types of Sŏn, drawing heavily on CH'OŬI ŬISUN's arguments in his *Sŏnmun sabyŏnmanŏ* ("Prolix Words on Four Distinctive Types in the Sŏn School") to posit that there are, in fact, only two. SŎLTU YUHYŎNG (1824–1889), a second-generation successor in Paekp'a's lineage, responded to Honggi's critique by writing his own treatise, the *Sŏnwŏn soryu* ("Tracing the Source of Sŏn"), where he also criticizes Ch'oŭi Ŭisun's treatise *Sŏnmun sabyŏnmanŏ*. Ch'ugwŏn Chinha (1861–1926) criticized Paekp'a and Sŏltu from Ch'oŭi's standpoint in his short treatise, *Sŏnmun chaejŏng nok* ("Reconsidering Orthodoxy in Sŏn Writings"), written in 1890, arguing for the ultimate unity of all types of Sŏn.

**udāna**. (T. ched du brjod pa; C. youtuona; J. udana; K. udana 優陀那). In Sanskrit and Pāli, lit. "utterance," or "meaningful expression," a term with three important denotations. ¶ The *Udāna* is the third book of the Pāli KHUDDAKANIKĀYA and comprises eighty stories containing eighty utterances of the Buddha. The utterances are mostly in verse and are accompanied by prose accounts of the circumstances that prompted the Buddha to speak on those occasions. ¶ The name udāna is also given to a broader classification of texts within the Pāli canon as a whole, and in this usage it refers to a set of eighty-two suttas containing verses uttered out of joy. ¶ Finally, udāna are one of the standard sections in the division of the word of the Buddha (BUDDHAVACANA) into nine NAVAṄGA (Pāli) or twelve (DVĀDAŚĀṄGA) categories based on genre. In that context, udāna are defined as solemn utterances intended to convey an understanding of the dharma. Many of the Buddha's statements in the DHAMMAPADA are said to fall into this category.

**Udānavarga**. (T. Ched du brjod pa'i tshoms; C. Chuyao jing; J. Shutchōgyō; K. Ch'uryo kyŏng 出曜經). In Sanskrit, "Groups of Utterances," a Sanskrit text associated with the SARVĀSTIVĀDA school that corresponds to the DHAMMAPADA (S. Dharmapada) in the Pāli scriptural tradition. The *Udānavarga* collects some 1,050 verses in thirty-three groups, or vargas, and is therefore more than twice as long as the Pāli *Dhammapada*, which includes 423 verses in twenty-six vaggas. Approximately 360 verses appear to be shared by the two texts. There are four translations of varying recensions of the *Udānavarga* cum *Dharmapada* made into Chinese, the earliest of which was produced by ZHU FONIAN in 374 CE. The Tibetan translation (c. 900) of the *Udānavarga* is of an anthology compiled by Dharmatrāta (Chos skyob); it is included in both the BKA' 'GYUR and the BSTAN 'GYUR. There is also a Tibetan translation of a commentary by Prajñāvarman. The *Udānavarga* was one of the six basic texts (gzhung drug) of the BKA' GDAMS pa school.

**udayabbayānupassanāñāṇa**. In Pāli, "knowledge arising from the contemplation of arising and passing away"; the first of nine knowledges (P. ñāṇa) cultivated as part of the "purity of knowledge and vision of progress along the path" (P. PAṬIPADĀÑĀṆADASSANAVISUDDHI), according to the account in the VISUDDHIMAGGA. This latter category, in turn, constitutes the sixth and penultimate purity (P. visuddhi; S. VIŚUDDHI) to be developed along the path to liberation. Knowledge arising from the contemplation of arising and passing away refers to the clear comprehension of the arising, presence, and dissolution of material and mental phenomena (NĀMARŪPA). Through contemplating this process, the three universal marks of existence (P. tilakkhaṇa; S. TRILAKṢAṆA) become apparent, viz., (1) impermanence (ANITYA), (2) suffering (DUḤKHA), and (3) no-self (ANĀTMAN). Full comprehension of the three universal marks of existence is not possible so long as the mind is disturbed by attachment to any of the ten "defilements of insight" (P. vipassanūpakkilesa), which arise as concomitants of insight meditation (P. vipassanābhāvanā); these are (1) a vision of radiant light (obhāsa), (2) knowledge (ñāṇa), (3) rapture (pīti), (4) tranquillity (passaddhi), (5) happiness (sukha), (6) determination (adhimokkha), (7) energy (paggaha), (8) heightened awareness (upaṭṭhāna), (9) equanimity (upekkhā), and (10) delight (nikanti). The ten defilements are overcome by understanding them for what they are, as mere by-products of meditation. This understanding is developed through perfecting the "purity of knowledge and vision of what is and is not the path" (P. MAGGĀMAGGAÑĀṆADASSANAVISUDDHI), which is the fifth of seven "purities" (visuddhi) to be developed along the path to liberation.

**Udāyana Buddha**. (C. Youtian wang Shijia xiang; J. Uten'ō Shakazō; K. Ujŏn wang Sŏkka sang 優填王釋迦像). An Indian sandalwood image of ŚĀKYAMUNI Buddha that is purported to be the world's first Buddha image; supposedly commissioned by the VATSĀ king Udāyana (also called Rudrāyana in some versions) and hence named after him. While ancient Indian sources only mention a buddha image made for king PRASENAJIT, the story of this supposedly earlier image made for King Udāyana first appears in the 397 CE Chinese translation of the EKOTTARĀGAMA. XUANZANG later reports a legend about the image's production. According to this legend, when ŚĀKYAMUNI Buddha ascended to the TRĀYASTRIṂŚA (heaven of the thirty-three) to preach the DHARMA to his mother MĀYĀ, King Udāyana so missed his teacher that he asked MAHĀMAUDGALYĀYANA to transport an artist to the heaven to observe the Buddha's thirty-two bodily marks (MAHĀPURUṢALAKṢAṆA) and carve a sandalwood image of the master. Subsequent Indian rulers were unable to dislodge the miraculously powerful statue from its spot and therefore made copies of it for their own realms. FAXIAN and Xuanzang remark in their travel records that they saw a sandalwood image at the JETAVANA VIHĀRA in ŚRĀVASTĪ, which had been commissioned by King Prasenajit on the model of the Udāyana image. In addition, Xuanzang saw a Udāyana Buddha image enshrined in a large vihāra at Kauśāmbī, and mentions a third one, which was reputedly the original statue, that had flown north over the mountains to the Central Asian oasis kingdom of KHOTAN. Both KUMĀRAJĪVA and Xuanzang are claimed to have brought the Udāyana Buddha image to the Chinese capital of Chang'an. The Japanese pilgrim Chōnen (938–1016), during his sojourn in China, saw a replica of the allegedly original Indian statue at Qishenyuan in Kaifeng. He hired the artisans Zhang Yanjiao and Zhang Yanxi to make an exact copy of this replica. According to the legend, the original statue spoke to Chōnen in a dream, expressing its wish to go to Japan. Chōnen thus darkened the copy with smoke and took the original to Japan in 986. The tenth-century Chinese wooden sculpture is commonly known as the Seiryōji Shaka, since it was enshrined in 1022 in the monastery of Seiryōji. In February 1954, a group of Japanese scholars, including the renowned Buddhologist and Seiryōji abbot, Tsukamoto Zenryū (1898–1980), opened the cavity in the back of the image and discovered that it contained silk and brocade textiles, coins, mirrors, glass fragments, a small brass bell, textile intestines, wood-block prints of texts such as the VAJRACCHEDIKĀPRAJÑĀPĀRAMITĀSŪTRA ("Diamond Sūtra"), a Japanese manuscript of the SUVARṆAPRABHĀSOTTAMASŪTRA ("Sūtra of Golden Light") dated 804, as well as other handwritten documents, such as a vow written by Chōnen and Gizō dated 972, which they witnessed with the imprint of their hands in their own blood. The veneration of the Udāyana Buddha image reached its peak in thirteenth-century Japan, when further copies of the Seiryōji Shaka were made, for example, at SAIDAIJI (dated 1249) and TŌSHŌDAIJI (dated 1258) in Nara and at Gokurakuji (second half of the thirteenth century) in Kamakura.

**Udāyin**. (P. Udāyī; T. 'Char ka; C. Youtuoyi; J. Udai; K. Ut'ai 優陀夷). Sanskrit proper name of an eminent ARHAT disciple of the Buddha. According to the Pāli accounts, where he is known as Udāyī, he was a brāhmaṇa from Kapilavatthu (S. KAPILAVASTU), who first encountered the Buddha when the Buddha visited his native Sākiya (S. ŚĀKYA) clan who resided in the city. Attracted by the Buddha's charisma, he entered the order and later became an arhat. Udāyī once uttered sixteen verses, which compared the Buddha to a majestic elephant. Udāyī was a gifted preacher who attracted large, enthusiastic audiences; once, while staying at Todeyya's mango grove in Kāmandā, he converted a pupil of a brāhmaṇa belonging to the clan of Lady Verahaccāni. Hearing of his triumph, Verahaccāni invited Udāyī to her home several times to preach and eventually became a convert to the Buddha's teachings. In several suttas, Udāyī is described discussing points of doctrine with his fellow monks. In the *Udāyīsutta*, he asks ĀNANDA whether consciousness can also be deemed as lacking selfhood, and elsewhere he explains the concept of sensation (VEDANĀ) to the carpenter Pañcakaṅga. Ānanda reports this conversation to the Buddha, who confirms the accuracy of Udāyī's understanding. Udāyī requested instruction in the limbs of enlightenment (P. bhojjaṅga; S. BODHYAṄGA) from the Buddha, and later reported to him how he won liberation through their cultivation. Although an arhat, Udāyī was not without fault. Once he ridiculed Ānanda for not taking advantage of his close association with the Buddha to attain arhatship. The Buddha chastised Udāyī for his remark, pointing out to him that Ānanda was destined to become an arhat in that very life.

**Uḍḍandapura**. See ODANTAPURĪ.

**Uḍḍiyāna**. One of the twenty-four sacred sites associated with the CAKRASAṂVARATANTRA. See PĪṬHA; OḌḌIYĀNA.

**Udgata**. (P. Uggata; T. 'Phags pa; C. Yujiatuo; J. Utsukada; K. Ulgat'a 鬱伽陀). Lay disciple of the Buddha deemed to be foremost among laymen who served the order (SAṂGHA). According to the Pāli account, where he is known as Uggata, he was a wealthy householder living in the town of Hatthigāma. One day, while the Buddha was sojourning at the Nāgavanuyyāna garden in the town, Uggata visited the garden in a drunken state, accompanied by dancers, after a drinking binge that had lasted seven days. Seeing the Buddha, he was filled with shame and immediately sobered up. The Buddha preached to him, and he became a nonreturner (ANĀGĀMIN) on the spot. He dismissed the dancers and, from that time onward, devoted himself to serving the order. He used to receive visitations from the divinities, who told him of the attainments of various members of the order and suggested that he favor these above the rest. Uggata, however, treated all monks equally and showed no preference in his benefactions between those who had attained distinction as ĀRYAPUDGALA and those who were still unenlightened. When queried, Uggata said that there were eight wonderful things that happened to, and were done by, him in this life: he recovered his sobriety the very moment he saw the Buddha; he readily understood the Buddha's teaching of the FOUR NOBLE TRUTHS; when he took a vow of celibacy, he provided for his four wives even to the point of finding one of them a new husband of her choice; he shared his great wealth with persons of good conduct; he served monks wholeheartedly, listening to their sermons or preaching to them when they did not speak; he was equally generous to all monks without making distinctions; he was not prideful of his conversations with the divinities; and he did not worry about death, for the Buddha had assured him that he would not return to this world.

**Udraka Rāmaputra**. (P. Uddaka Rāmaputta; T. Rangs byed kyi bu lhag spyod; C. Yutoulanfu; J. Utsuzuranhotsu; K. Ulturambul 鬱頭藍弗). One of two teachers (the other being ĀRĀḌA KĀLĀMA) from whom Prince SIDDHĀRTHA received instruction in meditation after he renounced the world and before he achieved enlightenment. Both teachers are mentioned in the ARIYAPARIYESANĀSUTTA, one of the sparest accounts of the Buddha's quest that is considered by some scholars to be among the earliest. After having studied with Ārāḍa Kālāma and determining that his teachings did not lead to liberation, the BODHISATTVA next studied with Udraka Rāmaputra, whose father, Rāma, taught a form of meditation resulting in the state of neither perception nor nonperception (identified by commentators as the fourth immaterial DHYĀNA; see NAIVASAMJÑĀNĀSAMJÑĀYATANA). When the bodhisattva attained this state, Udraka Rāmaputra offered him the position of teacher of his disciples. Realizing that this state was not in fact liberation from rebirth, the bodhisattva declined and left Udraka Rāmaputra to practice austerities in URUVILVĀ. After his achievement of enlightenment, the Buddha determined that Ārāḍa Kālāma and Udraka Rāmaputra would be the most suitable recipients of his teachings, but both had recently died, so he proceeded to ṚṢIPATANA to teach the "group of five" (PAÑCAVARGIKA).

**udumbara**. (T. u dum bā ra; C. youtan hua; J. udonge; K. udam hwa 優曇華). In Sanskrit and Pāli, name of a flowering tree (the *Ficus glomerata*) that is said to bloom only once every one thousand or three thousand years. Because it blossoms so infrequently, Buddhist texts often use the udumbara in similes to indicate something exceedingly rare, such as the appearance of a buddha in the world or the chance of encountering the BUDDHADHARMA during one's lifetime.

**Udumbaragiri**. A mountain in Sri Lanka and legendary abode of demons (P. yakkha; S. YAKṢA), site of a monastery of forest-dwelling monks noted (according to the *Mahāvaṃsaṭikā*) for their scholarship and piety; also known as Udumbarapabbata, Dhūmarakkha, and Dimbulāgala. By the twelfth century CE, the Udumbaragiri monastery became the standard bearer of orthodoxy and played a central role in the monastic purifications of PARAKRĀMABĀHU I and his successors, Vijayabāhu III and Parakrāmabāhu II. The monastic reforms instituted by these three kings represented a watershed in Sinhalese Buddhist history, insofar as patterns of SAMGHA organization and saṃgha–state relations were established that were to remain essentially unchanged from that period onward. These reforms were transmitted in stages to Burma (Myanmar) beginning in the twelfth century. In the fourteenth and fifteenth centuries, the Udumbaragiri monastery was again the fountainhead of a major THERAVĀDA revival that was propagated into the Thai kingdoms of AYUTHAYA, SUKHOTHAI, and Chiangmai and the Mon kingdom of PEGU.

**Udumbarikasīhanādasutta**. (C. Santuona jing; J. Sandanagyō; K. Sandana kyŏng 散陀那經). In Pāli, the "Discourse on the Lion's Roar at Udumbarika Park," the twenty-fifth sutta of the DĪGHANIKĀYA (a DHARMAGUPTAKA recension appears as the eighth SŪTRA in the Chinese translation of the DĪRGHĀGAMA), preached by the Buddha to the ascetic Nigrodha and his followers at the Udumbarikā hermitage near RĀJAGṚHA. The Buddha explains to Nigrodha the relative merits of ascetic practices and the superiority of his own path that can lead to liberation in seven days. Infatuated with MĀRA's deceits, Nigrodha and his followers remain skeptical and do not heed the Buddha's message.

**uggahanimitta**. In Pāli, "eidetic image" or "learning sign," the second of the three major visualization signs experienced in calmness or tranquillity (P. samatha; S. ŚAMATHA) exercises, along with the PARIKAMMANIMITTA (preparatory image) and the PAṬIBHĀGANIMITTA (counterpart, or representational, image). The signs are listed sequentially according to the degree of concentration necessary for them to appear. These three visualization signs and the meditative exercises employed to experience them are discussed in detail in BUDDHAGHOSA's VISUDDHIMAGGA. These signs are particularly associated with the ten visualization devices (KASIṆA) that are used in the initial development of concentration. In these exercises, the meditator attempts to convert a visual object of meditation, such as earth, fire, or light, into a mental projection or conceptualization that is as clear as the visual image itself. When the image the practitioner sees with his eyes (the so-called parikammanimitta, or "preparatory image") is equally clear when visualized in the mind, the practitioner is said to have obtained the uggahanimitta. With the fire kasiṇa, for example, the eidetic image of the visualized flame appears like a detached flame, with any embers, ashes, or smoke that were present in the preparatory image still visible. This uggahanimitta, however, still represents a relatively weak degree of concentration, and it must be strengthened until the paṭibhāganimitta, or "counterpart/representational image," emerges, which marks the access to meditative absorption (P. JHĀNA; S. DHYĀNA).

**Ugra**. (P. Ugga; T. Drag shul can; C. Yuqie; J. Ikuga/Ikuka; K. Ukka 郁伽). An eminent lay disciple of the Buddha whom he declared to be foremost among laymen who give pleasant gifts. According to the Pāli accounts, where he is known as Ugga, he was a householder who lived in Vesāli (S. VAIŚĀLĪ). He became a stream-enterer (SROTAĀPANNA) when he saw the Buddha the first time and later became a nonreturner (ANĀGĀMIN). He vowed to give to the Buddha and his followers whatever they found most agreeable. The Buddha, reading his mind, appeared before him, whereupon he provided them with a sumptuous meal and communicated his intentions to the Buddha. The list of favorite things included rice cakes in the shape of sāla flowers, pork, and Kāsī cloth. He was possessed of six special qualities: steadfast confidence in the Buddha, his teachings, and the order, noble conduct, insight, and liberation. Ugga declared that there were eight wonderful things that happened to him and that he did in this life. The list is similar to what is found in the story of UDGATA and concludes with the freedom he achieved from the five lower fetters (SAṂYOJANA) that bind living beings to the cycle of existence: belief in the existence of the body as a real person (P. sakkāyadiṭṭhi; S. SATKĀYADṚṢṬI), doubt about the efficacy of the path (P. vicikicchā; S. VICIKITSĀ), clinging to the rules and rituals (P. sīlabbataparāmāsa; S. ŚĪLAVRATAPARĀMARŚA), sensuous craving (KĀMARĀGA), and ill will (VYĀPĀDA). When Ugga died, he was reborn in the realm of subtle materiality (RŪPALOKA) among the divinities who project mind-made bodies (MANOMAYAKĀYA). He visited the Buddha and informed him that he had attained arhatship in that existence.

**Ugraparipṛcchā**. (T. Drag shul can gyis zhus pa; C. Yuqie zhangzhe hui; J. Ikuga chōjae; K. Ukka changja hoe 郁伽長者會). In Sanskrit, "The Inquiry of Ugra," an influential MAHĀYĀNA SŪTRA, dating perhaps from the first century BCE, making it one of the earliest Mahāyāna sūtras. The text has not survived in any Indic-language version, but has been preserved in five translated versions: three in Chinese, one in Tibetan, and one in Mongolian. The sūtra is structured as a dialogue, mainly between the Buddha and the lay BODHISATTVA UGRA, whose inquiry prompts the Buddha to launch into a protracted discourse on the bodhisattva path (MĀRGA). Ugra is labeled a GṚHAPATI, a term that literally means "lord of the house" but that comes to refer to men belonging to the upper stratum of what would later be labeled as the vaiśya (often rendered as "merchant") caste. The sūtra is divided into two parts, one directed toward the lay bodhisattva and the other toward renunciants. In the oldest version of the sūtra, Ugra and his friends, after hearing the Buddha's discourse, ask for and receive ordination as monks; in later translations, this event takes place in the middle of the sūtra. In all versions, however, the overall message is that, although a lay practitioner may be capable of performing at least preliminary parts of the bodhisattva path, to attain the final goal of buddhahood he must become a monk. The Buddha declares, "For no bodhisattva who lives at home has ever attained supreme perfect enlightenment." Accordingly, the sūtra urges the lay bodhisattva to break the ties of affection that bind him to his family and, above all, to his wife; the condemnation of marriage and family life is striking. Moreover, he is urged to emulate the conduct of the monks in his local monastery even while he still lives at home—involving, among other things, complete celibacy. This sort of practice is congruent with what was required of the UPĀSAKA, the lay adherent who has taken the three refuges and the five or eight precepts and dresses in white as a sign of his semirenunciant status. The lay bodhisattva described in the *Ugraparipṛcchā* is repeatedly urged to seek ordination as soon as he possibly can. If the lay bodhisattva is portrayed as the best of all possible laymen, the renunciant bodhisattva is portrayed as the best of all possible monks. Not only does he follow the standard requirements of the monastic life, but he goes beyond them, spending large periods of time (ideally, his whole lifetime) performing strict ascetic practices in the wilderness. This is a reenactment of the biography of ŚĀKYAMUNI Buddha; it appears that aspiring bodhisattvas, both lay and monastic, took the stories of the Buddha's life—including his previous lives, described in the JĀTAKA stories—as prescriptive for those who wished to become buddhas themselves. The *Ugraparipṛcchā* never portrays any actual female practitioner, whether lay or monastic, as a bodhisattva. Apart from a formulaic reference to "sons and daughters of good lineage," which appears at the beginning and the end of the sūtra (and may have been added long after its initial composition), there is no indication that the authors of the sūtra believed that women were capable of embarking upon the bodhisattva path. The *Ugraparipṛcchā* was a highly influential sūtra in both India and East Asia, where it was widely quoted and commented upon and is regarded by scholars as an important and influential work in the formative period of Mahāyāna Buddhism.

**Uhaeng**. (K) (禹行/幸). See UDAM HONGGI.

**Ŭich'ŏn**. (C. Yitian 義天) (1055–1101). Korean prince, monk, and bibliophile, and putative founder of the CH'ŎNT'AE CHONG (C. TIANTAI ZONG) in Korea. Ŭich'ŏn was born the fourth son of the Koryŏ king Munjong (r. 1047–1082). In 1065, Ŭich'ŏn was ordained by the royal preceptor (WANGSA) Kyŏngdŏk Nanwŏn (999–1066) at the royal monastery of Yŏngt'ongsa in the Koryŏ capital of Kaesŏng. Under Nanwŏn, Ŭich'ŏn studied the teachings of the AVATAṂSAKASŪTRA and its various commentaries. In 1067, at the age of twelve, Ŭich'ŏn was appointed "saṃgha overseer" (K. sŭngt'ong; C. SENGTONG). Ŭich'ŏn is known on several occasions to have requested permission from his royal father to travel abroad to China, but the king consistently denied his request. Finally, in 1085, Ŭich'ŏn secretly boarded a Chinese trading ship and traveled to the mainland against his father's wishes. Ŭich'ŏn is said to have spent about fourteen months abroad studying under various teachers. His father sent his friend and colleague NAKCHIN (1045–1114) after Ŭich'ŏn, but they ended up studying together with the Huayan teacher Jingyuan (1011–1088) of Huiyinsi in Hangzhou. Ŭich'ŏn and Nakchin returned to Korea in 1086 with numerous texts that Ŭich'ŏn acquired during his sojourn in China. While residing as the abbot of the new monastery of Hŭngwangsa in the capital, Ŭich'ŏn devoted his time to teaching his disciples and collecting works from across East Asia, including the Khitan Liao kingdom. He sent agents throughout the region to collect copies of the indigenous writings of East Asian Buddhists, which he considered to be the equal of works by the bodhisattva exegetes of the imported Indian scholastic tradition. A large monastic library known as Kyojang Togam was established at Hŭngwangsa to house the texts that Ŭich'ŏn collected. In 1090, Ŭich'ŏn published a bibliographical catalogue of the texts housed at Hŭngwangsa, entitled *Sinp'yŏn chejong kyojang ch'ongnok* ("Comprehensive Catalogue of the Doctrinal Repository of All the Schools"), which lists some 1,010 titles in 4,740 rolls. The Hŭngwangsa collection of texts was carved on woodblocks and titled the *Koryŏ sokchanggyŏng* ("Koryŏ Supplement to the Canon"), which was especially important for its inclusion of a broad cross section of the writings of East Asian Buddhist teachers. (The one exception was works associated with the CHAN or SŎN tradition, which Ŭich'ŏn refused to collect because of their "many heresies.") Unfortunately, the xylographs of the supplementary canon were burned during the Mongol invasion of Koryŏ in 1231, and many of the works included in the collection are now lost and known only through their reference in Ŭich'ŏn's catalogue. In 1097, Ŭich'ŏn was appointed the founding abbot of the new monastery of Kukch'ŏngsa (named after the renowned Chinese monastery of Guoqingsi on Mt. Tiantai). There, he began to teach Ch'ŏnt'ae thought and practice and is said to have attracted more than a thousand students. Ŭich'ŏn seems to have seen the Tiantai/Ch'ŏnt'ae synthesis of meditation and doctrine as a possible means of reconciling the Sŏn and doctrinal (KYO) traditions in Korea. Ŭich'ŏn's efforts have subsequently been regarded as the official foundation of the Ch'ŏnt'ae school in Korea; however, it seems Ŭich'ŏn was not actually attempting to start a new school, but merely to reestablish the study of Ch'ŏnt'ae texts in Korea. He was awarded the posthumous title of state preceptor (K. kuksa; C. GUOSHI) Taegak (Great Enlightenment).

**Ŭisang**. (C. Yixiang; J. Gishō 義湘/相) (625–702). Influential Korean monk during the Silla dynasty, who was a leader in the Chinese HUAYAN ZONG and founder of the HWAŎM tradition in Korea. After ordaining at Hwangboksa in 644, Ŭisang left for China in 650 with his friend and colleague WŎNHYO (617–686) via the overland route, but was arrested by Koguryŏ border guards and forced to return to Silla. In 661, Ŭisang was able to reach China by sea and studied at Zhixiangsi on ZHONGNANSHAN under the guidance of ZHIYAN (602–668), the second patriarch in the Chinese Huayan school. In China, Ŭisang was a close colleague of FAZANG (643–712), a fellow student of Zhiyan's, who was eighteen years his junior; he is also said to have had associations with DAOXUAN (596–667), the founder of the NANSHAN LÜ ZONG, a major Chinese school of Buddhist discipline (VINAYA). According to some accounts, Ŭisang took over the leadership of Zhiyan's community after his master's death, but eventually returned to Korea in 671 to warn the Silla king Munmu (r. 661–681) of an impending Chinese invasion of Silla by the Tang emperor Gaozong (628–683). In gratitude, the Silla king provided munificent support for Ŭisang's Hwaŏm school and installed the master at the new monastery of PUSŎKSA near T'aebaeksan, where Ŭisang is said to have attracted more than three thousand students. Ŭisang is also presumed to have established a network of Hwaŏm monasteries around the peninsula, which included Mirisa, HWAŎMSA, and HAEINSA. Thanks to royal support, by the time of Ŭisang's death, the Hwaŏm school had emerged as the predominant scholastic tradition in Korean Buddhism. ¶ Even after his return to Korea, Ŭisang continued to exchange letters and to work with his Chinese colleague FAZANG. In 692, Fazang sent Ŭisang a copy of his HUAYAN JING TANXUAN JI, asking for his comments; this correspondence is still extant today. The most influential of Ŭisang's writings is the HWAŎM ILSŬNG PŎPKYE TO ("Diagram of the DHARMADHĀTU according to the One Vehicle of Hwaŏm"), which summarizes the gist of the Huayan school's interpretation of the AVATAṂSAKASŪTRA. His only other extant work is the *Paekhwa toryang parwŏn mun* ("Vow Made at the White Lotus Enlightenment Site"), a short paean to the bodhisattva AVALOKITEŚVARA (K. Kwanŭm); works attributed to Ŭisang that are no longer extant, most of which addressed aspects of Hwaŏm thought, include *Simmun kanpŏp kwan*, *Ip pŏpkye p'um ch'ogi*, and *Ilsŭng parwŏn mun*, as well as a commentary to the AMITĀBHASŪTRA (*So Amit'a ŭigi*).

**Ŭisun**. (K) (意恂). See CH'OŬI ŬISUN.

***ullambana**. (T. yongs su skyob pa'i snod; C. yulanben; J. urabon; K. uranbun 盂蘭盆). A hypothetical BUDDHIST HYBRID SANSKRIT, Middle Indic, or perhaps even Iranian reconstruction of the Chinese term yulanben and sometimes interpreted to correspond to the Sanskrit avalambana (lit. "hanging downward," "suspended"); the term would then refer to the "ghost festival," a ritual that sought the salvation of condemned beings who were "suspended" in hell. This interpretation of yulan is questionable, however, since this connotation of the Sanskrit term avalambana is unknown in Indian Buddhist contexts. The Tibetan translation of yulanben as yongs su skyob pa'i snod, or "vessel of complete protection," also does not correspond to any of the connotations of "hanging down"; the Tibetan rendering does, however, seem to better fit an alternate explanation of the derivation of yulan(ben) as the Buddhist Hybrid Sanskrit term ullumpana (sometimes wrongly transcribed as ullampana, ullambana, etc.), lit. "rescuing, extracting [from an unfortunate fate]." A more recent hypothesis concerning the transcription yulanben is that "yulan" is a transcription of the Sanskrit and Pāli term odana (cooked rice) and 'ben' a native word for bowl; the compound 'yulanben' is thus not a transcription of the hypothetical Sanskrit word *ullambana but actually means a "rice bowl," perhaps even a special kind of rice bowl for making offerings on the PRAVĀRAṆĀ day. The Japanese BON FESTIVAL (alt. Obon) derives from this term ullambana; it is celebrated in either mid-July or mid-August to honor the spirits of deceased ancestors. During this three-day period, family members return to their ancestral homes to make offerings to their ancestors (who are thought to return on those days) and to clean the family grave sites. On the last night, the celebrants light paper lanterns and float them down the river (J. tōrō nagashi) to help light the spirits' way back. See also YULANBEN; YULANBEN JING.

**Ulūka**. (T. 'Ug pa; C. Youlouqu; J. Urukya; K. Uruga 優樓佉). One of the non-Buddhist philosophers of India mentioned in Buddhist texts; he is identified with Kaṇāda of the Vaiśeṣika school. He is often listed as one of a group of three, the other two being Kapila and Ṛṣabha.

**U-min Ko-zei Pagoda**. A multitowered pagoda (Burmese, JEDI) located in the Sagaing Hills in Upper Burma (Myanmar). Its name means "ninety caves," and it was given this epithet in imitation of another famous shrine found in the Sagaing Hills called U-min Thon-zei, or the "Thirty Caves Shrine." U-min Ko-zei Pagoda is in actuality not comprised of ninety caves but is a freestanding structure with more than thirty entrances leading to an interior artificial cave. U-min Ko-zei Pagoda is one of four related pagodas originally built during the AVA period that are collectively known as Hsin-bo-lei Hpaya ("the four pagodas equal in value to an elephant"). This unusual name is explained by the following story. On one occasion, King Min-hkaung-gyi of Ava (r. 1481–1502) went by elephant to pay his respects to the monk Ariyawuntha, a famous scholar whose monastery was located between four hillocks. As it happened, while the king was meeting with this monk, his elephant ate leaves from the monastery's BODHI TREE and promptly fell unconscious. Luckily, the elephant was revived with medicinal herbs gathered from the four surrounding hills. In memory of this event, the king built a pagoda on each of the four hilltops, the total cost of which equaled the value of his elephant.

**U-min Thon-zei Zedi**. An artificial cave shrine (Burmese, u-min) located in the Sagaing Hills in Upper Burma (Myanmar), on the same mountain ridge as the Swam-oo Ponnya Shin Pagoda. It was built in 1366 CE by Padu Thinga-yaza, a monk from Padu Village. He was the royal preceptor (SAMGHARĀJAN) of the king of Sagaing, Tara-hpya Min-gyi, and was also venerated by Thato Min-hpaya, the king of AVA. Thinga-yaza built the cave with thirty entrances in memory of the Buddha's thirty moral perfections (P. pāramī; S. PĀRAMITĀ); hence, its name U-min Thon-zei, which means "thirty caves." This cave also contains forty-five statues of the Buddha in memory of the Buddha's forty-five-year teaching ministry.

**undō**. (J) (雲堂). In Japanese, "cloud hall." See SENGTANG.

**Ŭnhaesa**. (銀海寺). In Korean, "Silver Sea Monastery," the tenth district monastery (PONSA) of the contemporary CHOGYE CHONG of Korean Buddhism, located in Yŏngch'ŏn, near Taegu, on the slopes of P'algong Mountain. It was built by state preceptor (kuksa; C. GUOSHI) Hyech'ŏl (785–861) in 809 and was originally named Haeansa (Oceanic Eye Monastery), but was moved to the present site and received its new name in 1546. The monastery burned down in 1563 and was reconstructed in the following year. The monastery once again burned to the ground in 1861 and was substantially reconstructed under the supervision of the monks Palbong (d.u.) and Haewŏl (d.u.). Along with TONGHWASA, Ŭnhaesa is one of the representative monasteries on Mount P'algong and is known for the many hermitages that have been established in the surrounding mountains. The monastery's current site is near to Kŏjo Hermitage, which dates to approximately 738 and was once the main monastery in the area. The hermitage is noted for the Yŏngsan Chŏn (Vulture Peak Hall), built in 1375, which enshrines images of the Buddha and 526 stone ARHATs. Another hermitage, Unbuam, has a statue of a bodhisattva that is three-feet high, with a crown decorated with flames, flowers, and a bird of paradise. Paekhŭngam, a hermitage at Ŭnhaesa reserved for nuns, houses in its kŭngnak chŏn (hall of ultimate bliss) a pedestal called a sumidan (MT. SUMERU altar; J. SHUMIDAN) with a statue of the Buddha on top. The sumidan is also decorated with fine carvings of birds, animals, flowers, and demons. There are some ten buildings on the Ŭnhaesa grounds. The site is noted for its enshrined image of AMITĀBHA, and Ŭnhaesa is famous in Korea as a center of Amitābha worship. Ŭnhaesa is also home to one of the most recognized KWAEBUL, or giant hanging Korean religious art works (see also T'AENGHWA; T. THANG KA). Painted in 1750 on silk, it depicts the Buddha in a PURE LAND resplendent with birds and peonies.

**Unmuk**. (雲默) (d.u.; fl. late fourteenth century). Korean monk from the late Koryŏ dynasty, also known as Puam and Mugi. He entered the SAṂGHA and studied Ch'ŏntae (C. TIANTAI) philosophy under the state preceptor (KUKSA) Purin Chŏngjo (d.u.) at the White Lotus Society (see JIESHE) on Mandŏksan. After passing the monastic examinations (SŬNGKWA), he was appointed as the abbot of Kuramsa but soon left his post to travel throughout the country. He built a hermitage and settled down at Mt. Sihŭng, where he spent the next twenty years painting Buddhist images, copying scriptures, and chanting the SADDHARMAPUṆḌARĪKASŪTRA ("Lotus Sūtra"). He is the author of the two-roll *Sŏkka yŏrae haengjŏk song*, a verse retelling of the life of the Buddha, and the single-roll *Ch'ŏnt'ae marhak Unmuk hwasang kyŏngch'aek*, a book of his teachings and admonitions, which is only partially extant.

**unsui**. (雲水). In Japanese, lit. "clouds and water," referring to itinerant Buddhist monks, and especially monks in training. See YUNSHUI.

**upacārasamādhi**. In Pāli, "access concentration," "neighborhood concentration," or "threshold concentration"; the more elementary of the two broad types of concentration (SAMĀDHI) described in Pāli commentarial literature. Both of these two types of samādhi are used with reference to meditators who are specializing in calmness (P. samatha; S. ŚAMATHA) techniques. Upacārasamādhi precedes full meditative absorption (P. JHĀNA; S. DHYĀNA) and is the highest level of concentration that may be developed from the more discursive topics of meditation (KAMMAṬṬHĀNA), viz., the first eight of ten recollections (P. anussati; S. ANUSMṚTI), on the Buddha, dharma, SAṂGHA, morality, generosity, divinities, death, and peace, as well as the contemplation on the loathsomeness of food, and the analysis of the four material elements. Upacārasamādhi is characterized by the visualization in the mind of a luminous "counterpart" or "representational" "image" (PAṬIBHĀGANIMITTA) of the object of meditation. It is through further concentration on this stable representational image that the mind finally attains "full concentration" (APPANĀSAMĀDHI), which leads to jhāna. (See also KHANIKASAMĀDHI; SĀMANTAKA.) According to some THERAVĀDA accounts (e.g., in the modern VIPASSANĀ movement), concentration of at least the level of upacārasamādhi is said to be required for the achievement of the state of stream-enterer (P. sotāpanna; S. SROTAĀPANNA).

**upādāna**. (T. len pa; C. qu; J. shu; K. ch'wi 取). In Sanskrit and Pāli, "clinging," "grasping," or "attachment"; the ninth of the twelve links (NIDĀNA) of dependent origination (PRATĪTYASAMUTPĀDA), which is preceded by craving (TṚṢṆĀ) and followed by becoming (BHAVA). Clinging is regarded as a more intense form of craving, with craving defined as the desire not to separate from a feeling of pleasure, the desire to separate from a feeling of pain, or as a nondiminution of a neutral feeling. Upādāna is a stronger, and more sustained, type of attachment, which is is said to be of four types: (1) clinging to sensuality (RĀGA), which is strong attachment to pleasing sensory objects; (2) clinging to false views and speculative theories (DṚṢṬI); (3) clinging to faulty disciplinary codes and superstitious modes of conduct (ŚĪLAVRATAPARĀMARŚA); and (4) clinging to mistaken beliefs in a perduring self (ĀTMAVĀDA), viz., the attachment to the transitory mind and body as a real I and mine. In the context of dependent origination (PRATĪTYASAMUTPĀDA), craving (tṛṣṇā) leads to the clinging (upādāna) that nourishes the actions that will serve as the cause of "becoming" (bhava), viz., the next lifetime. Clinging that occurs near the moment of death is therefore particularly consequential.

**upādānakāraṇa**. (T. nyer len gyi rgyu; C. xianqu yin; J. genshuin; K. hyŏnch'wi in 現取因). In Sanskrit, "material cause" or "proximate cause"; the cause that produces an effect that is of the same substance (DRAVYA) as itself. For example, in the case of a sprout, the upādānakāraṇa is its seed; in the case of a pot, it is clay.

**upādānaskandha**. (P. upādānakandha; T. nyer len gyi phung po; C. quyun; J. shuun; K. ch'wion 取蘊). In Sanskrit, "aggregates that are the objects of clinging," "aggregates of attachment"; the five aggregates (SKANDHA), which are viewed as the foundational objects of clinging (UPĀDĀNA). In the FOUR NOBLE TRUTHS, the definition of the first noble truth, that of suffering (DUḤKHASATYA), specifies that "the five upādānaskandha themselves are suffering," which suggests that suffering is intrinsic to existence itself (see SAṂSKĀRADUḤKHATĀ), and that as long as one clings to continuing existence (BHAVA), the cycle of suffering within SAṂSĀRA will continue. The term upādānaskandha can also be translated as "appropriated aggregates," which suggests that the aggregates are caused, or appropriated, by KARMAN and KLEŚA and thus also serve in turn as the cause of future karman and kleśa. Again, the term may also be translated as "appropriating aggregates," which connotes that, although the skandhas are empty of a self or soul (ĀTMAN) that appropriates a new form of existence, they provide the locus for the karman and kleśa (viz., the clinging or grasping itself) that produce future forms of the aggregates and future suffering.

**upadeśa**. (P. upadesa; T. man ngag/gtan phab; C. youpotishe; J. upadaisha; K. ubajesa 優波提舍). In Sanskrit, "instruction," "teaching"; one of the nine (NAVAṄGA) (Pāli) or twelve (DVĀDAŚĀṄGA[PRAVACANA]) (Sanskrit) categories (AṄGA) of Buddhist scripture according to their structure or literary style, where it may refer to the subsequent elaboration by the great disciples of a sūtra that the Buddha had just spoken. In Mahāyāna treatises (ŚĀSTRA), upadeśa may suggest that the text is conveying something hidden or special in the Buddha's words (BUDDHAVACANA) that the student may not immediately realize is there. In Tibet, there was the question of whether a teacher's personal instructions (man ngag) to a student were superior to the explanation in a Buddhist text. The name BKA' GDAMS, literally, "those who take the words of the Buddha as instructions" (gdams ngag), may reflect a response to such a view. See also AṄGA.

**upadeśasaṃpramoṣa**. (T. gdams ngag brjed pa; C. wang shengyan; J. bōshōgon; K. mang sŏngŏn 忘聖言). In Sanskrit, lit. "loss of the instruction," a term that appears in instructions for developing SAMĀDHI, to describe the point in the early stages of developing concentration where the meditator loses focus upon the chosen object of concentration, thus allowing the mind to wander.

**upadhi**. (T. rdzas; C. yi; J. e; K. ŭi 依). In Sanskrit and Pāli, the "substratum" of rebirth or the "bonds" that bind one to continued existence in SAṂSĀRA. Upadhi is typically equated either with the five aggregates (SKANDHA) or with the afflictions (KLEŚA) of sensuality (RĀGA), ill will (DVEṢA), and delusion (MOHA). Less specifically, any of the ties that bind one to the world, whether family, possessions, or property are described as upadhi. In the NIDDESA of the Pāli KHUDDAKANIKĀYA, the upadhi were ultimately systematized into a list of ten bonds. ¶ In an Indian monastic context, upadhi also refers to the "material objects" held in common by the monastery, a meaning of the term unknown in Pāli. The "provost" or "guardian of the material objects" of a monastery was given the title upadhivārika.

**upādhyāya**. (P. upajjhāya; T. mkhan po; C. heshang; J. oshō/wajō/kashō; K. hwasang 和尚). In Sanskrit, a religious instructor or "preceptor." The upādhyāya is first and foremost a monk who confers the lower ordination (see PRAVRAJITA) to new novices (ŚRĀMAṆERA) and higher ordination (UPASAMPADĀ) to monks (BHIKṢU). To act as an upādhyāya, a monk must be qualified and competent and be of at least ten years standing in the order since his own higher ordination. The relationship of the preceptor to the disciple is described as being like that of father and son. The preceptor is enjoined to teach the DHARMA and VINAYA to his disciple and, as necessary, to supply him with requisites, such as robes and an alms bowl. He should tend to his disciple if he is ill and discipline him if he commits some wrongdoing. If the disciple should begin to entertain doubts about the religion, the preceptor should try to dispel them. If the disciple should commit a grave offense against the monastic rules and regulations, the preceptor is to prevail upon him to go before the SAṂGHA to seek expiation. If the disciple misbehaves or becomes disobedient, the preceptor is enjoined to expel him. But if the disciple shows remorse and asks forgiveness, the preceptor is to take him under guidance again. A monk ceases to be an upādhyāya when he goes away, dies, secedes from the order, changes religion, or expels his disciple. For the East Asian usage of the term, see also HESHANG.

**upādhyāyā**. (P. upajjhāyā; T. mkhan mo; C. heshangni; J. oshōni; K. hwasangni 和尚尼). In Sanskrit, a female religious instructor or "female preceptor." A qualified nun (BHIKṢUṆĪ) of at least twelve years standing may confirm the UPASAMPADĀ ordination on a female probationer (ŚIKṢAMĀṆĀ). The ordination can be performed only after formal agreement has been received from the bhikṣuṇī SAṂGHA. The newly ordained nun must live under the tutelage of the upādhyāyā as a disciple for a minimum of two years. The duties of the upādhyāyā and her disciple are the same as those for a male preceptor (UPĀDHYĀYA) and his disciple.

**Upagupta**. (T. Nyer sbas; C. Youpojuduo; J. Ubakikuta; K. Ubagukta 優婆毱多). An Indian ARHAT, said to have lived in the MATHURĀ region of India. Upagupta is unknown in Pāli canonical sources but appears frequently in the Sanskrit AVADĀNA literature, especially the AŚOKĀVADĀNA and the DIVYĀVADĀNA. Upagupta is famed for having tamed (and in some versions, converted) MĀRA by placing a garland of corpses around his neck. Upagupta was later invited to PĀṬALIPUTRA by King AŚOKA, and then conducted the monarch on a tour of the sacred sites (MAHĀSTHĀNA) associated with the life of the Buddha. The cult of Upagupta became popular in Southeast Asian Buddhist countries from the twelfth century onward, thanks to his prominent appearance in Sanskrit materials, and he eventually comes to be featured in noncanonical Pāli materials as well. Upagupta occupies pride of place in Burmese (Myanmar) Buddhism, where he is presumed to reside in a pavilion in the southern ocean, whence he is invited to rituals to protect the Burmese from Māra's interference. At the conclusion of the ceremonies, an image of Upagupta is placed on a raft and floated downstream. Upagupta is listed in SARVĀSTIVĀDA sources as the fifth of the Indian patriarchs who are said to have succeeded the Buddha as head of the SAṂGHA, following MAHĀKĀŚYAPA, ĀNANDA, MADHYĀNTIKA, and ŚĀṆAKAVĀSIN; the East Asian CHAN tradition typically lists him instead as the fourth patriarch. According to a Chinese account of the origins of the VINAYA, Upagupta had five major disciples who were said to have established their own schools based on their differing views regarding doctrine; these five also redacted separate editions of the vinaya, which the Chinese refer to as the "five vinaya recensions" (wubu lü).

**upakleśa**. (P. upakkilesa; T. nye ba'i nyon mongs; C. sui fannao; J. zuibonnō; K. su pŏnnoe 隨煩惱). In Sanskrit, "secondary afflictions" (as opposed to the "root afflictions," or MŪLAKLEŚA), or "subsidiary defilements"; a group of ten (according to the VAIBHĀṢIKA school of SARVĀSTIVĀDA ABHIDHARMA), sixteen (according to Pāli materials), or twenty (according to the YOGĀCĀRA school) mental afflictions, including anger (KRODHA), envy (ĪRṢYĀ), deceit (MĀYĀ), selfishness (MĀTSARYA), and enmity (UPANĀHA).

**upalabdhi**. (T. dmigs pa; C. suode; J. shotoku; K. sodŭk 所得). In Sanskrit, "observation" or "perception," i.e., "getting at" something, a common term for the cognition of an object. Upalabdhi is sometimes used in a pejorative sense to refer to the cognition of, or getting at, factors that do not exist in an object, notably, a perduring self. To be preferred to upalabdhi is cognition that that is "unascertainable" (ANUPALABDHI), viz., without any bifurcation between subject and object and thus freed from any kind of false dichotomization; this is the type of perception that occurs in enlightenment.

**Upāli**. (T. Nye bar 'khor; C. Youboli; J. Upari; K. Ubari 優波離). Sanskrit and Pāli proper name of an ARHAT who was foremost among the Buddha's disciples in his knowledge of the monastic code of discipline (VINAYA). According to Pāli accounts, Upāli was a barber from the city of Kapilavatthu (S. KAPILAVASTU) and was in the service of the Sākiya (S. ŚĀKYA) princes who ruled there. Upāli accompanied Anuruddha (S. ANIRUDDHA) and his cousins when they decided to renounce the world and take ordination from the Buddha in Anupiyā grove. They handed him all their clothes and ornaments in preparation, but Upāli refused the gift, asking instead to be allowed to take ordination with them. Anuruddha and the others requested the Buddha to confer ordination on Upāli first so that their barber would always be senior to them and thus quell their pride in their noble birth. The Buddha refused Upāli's request to be allowed to retire to the forest to practice meditation in solitude, realizing that, while Upāli had the qualities to attain arhatship through that course, he would as a consequence neglect the study of dharma. Following the Buddha's advice, Upāli practiced insight (P. VIPASSANĀ; S. VIPAŚYANĀ) and became an arhat without retiring to the forest, thus allowing the Buddha to teach him the entire VINAYAPIṬAKA. Upāli was frequently sought out to render decisions on matters of discipline, and he is frequently shown discussing with the Buddha the legal details of cases brought before him. Even during the Buddha's lifetime, monks frequently sought training in monastic discipline under Upāli; he was also regarded as a sympathetic guardian to monks facing difficulties. After the Buddha's demise, MAHĀKĀŚYAPA chose Upāli to recite the vinaya at the first Buddhist council (SAṂGĪTI; see COUNCIL, FIRST); ĀNANDA was chosen to recite the Buddha's sermons (SŪTRA). A succession of vinaya masters descended from Upāli, including MOGGALIPUTTATISSA, leader of the third Buddhist council (see COUNCIL, THIRD). Upāli's low status as a barber is often raised as evidence that the Buddha accepted disciples from all classes and castes in society and that all were capable of becoming arhats.

**Upālisutta**. (C. Youpoli jing; J. Ubarikyō; K. Ubari kyŏng 優婆離經). In Pāli, "Discourse to Upāli," the fifty-sixth sutta in the MAJJHIMANIKĀYA (a separate SARVĀSTIVĀDA recension appears as the 133rd SŪTRA in the Chinese translation of the MADHYAMĀGAMA); preached to the householder (P. gahapati; S. GṚHAPATI) Upāli, a wealthy lay disciple of Nigaṇṭha Nātaputta (S. NIRGRANTHA JÑĀTĪPUTRA; a.k.a. MAHĀVĪRA; see also JAINA) at the Pāvārika's mango grove in NĀLANDĀ. Nigaṇṭha Nātaputta dispatched his lay disciple Upāli to engage the Buddha in a debate on the nature of action (P. kamma; S. KARMAN). The Jaina leader held that, of the three types of action, physical, verbal, and mental, it is bodily action that is the most productive of consequences for the actor. The Buddha maintained, in contrast, that it is mental action that is the most productive of consequences for the actor, since it is the mental intention (CETANĀ) that initiates the physical action. Convinced of the Buddha's explanations, Upāli dedicated himself as a lay disciple of the Buddha. When Nigaṇṭha Nātaputta heard of Upāli's conversion, he was filled with rage and vomited blood.

**upanāha**. (T. 'khon du 'dzin pa; C. hen; J. kon; K. han 恨). In Sanskrit and Pāli, "enmity," "resentment," "malice," or "animosity"; one of the ten (according to the VAIBHĀṢIKA school of SARVĀSTIVĀDA ABHIDHARMA), sixteen (according to Pāli materials), or twenty (according to the YOGĀCĀRA school) secondary afflictions or subsidiary defilements (UPAKLEŚA). Upanāha is described as a pent-up anger that takes the form of a wish to harm others. Upanāha refers to a long-held grievance or bitterness and is one possible manifestation of aversion (PRATIGHA; DVEṢA). Upanāha is distinguishable from "anger" (KRODHA) in that anger is a more powerful but more quickly dissipated kind of emotion, whereas "enmity" is a longer-term, simmering grudge.

**Upananda**. (T. Nye dga' po; C. Youbonantuo; J. Upananda; K. Ubanant'a 優波難陀). Sanskrit and Pāli proper name of a monk disciple of the Buddha, who was regularly chastised for his greed. There are numerous stories in the VINAYA of his attempts to procure the best and most of all offerings made to monks, and especially of robes and food. The Buddha typically rebukes Upananda for his misconduct, and then goes on to promulgate a new rule of conduct in order to deter monks from committing such transgressions in the future.

**upapādukayoni**. (P. opapātikayoni/upapātikayoni; T. rdzus te skye ba; C. hua sheng; J. keshō; K. hwa saeng 化生). In Buddhist Hybrid Sanskrit, "metamorphic" or "spontaneous birth"; one of the four modes of birth (see YONI) of living beings in the three realms of existence, along with oviparous birth or birth from an egg (aṇḍajayoni), viviparous birth or birth from a womb (jarāyujayoni), and birth from moisture (saṃsvedajayoni). Beings born via this fourth mode are spontaneously generated and include divinities (DEVA), hungry ghosts (PRETA), denizens of hell (NĀRAKA), and those residing in the intermediate state (ANTARĀBHAVA). In addition, even beings that are generally classified under another mode of birth may in certain circumstances be spontaneously generated, such as human beings who are the first to be born at the beginning of an eon (KALPA) and certain animals, such as NĀGAs and GARUḌAs. Unlike the other three modes of birth, beings born via metamorphosis appear spontaneously at their rebirth destiny, are fully mature at the time of their birth, and leave no physical corpse behind at death. A spontaneously born being recognizes his appropriate rebirth destination at the moment of his death and generates a desire to appear in that specific destiny, even if that desire be directed toward a baleful place like the hells. Beings born into SUKHĀVATĪ are said to be born either spontaneously into a lotus flower in the PURE LAND, or, if they are not yet advanced enough to be born directly into the pure land, viviparously to other beings at the outer perimeter of that land. Beings born metamorphically are the most numerous of all the four modes of birth and are regarded as superior.

**upapadyaparinirvāyin**. [alt. utpattiparinirvāyin] (T. skyes nas yongs su mya ngan las 'das pa; C. sheng ban/sheng banniepan; J. shōhatsu/shōhatsunehan; K. saeng pan/saeng panyŏlban 生般/生般涅槃). In Sanskrit, "one who achieves NIRVĀṆA at birth," a particular sort of nonreturner (ANĀGĀMIN), one of the twenty members of the ĀRYASAṂGHA (see VIṂŚATIPRABHEDASAṂGHA). According to the ABHIDHARMAKOŚABHĀṢYA, the utpattiparinirvāyin are nonreturners who, having linked up with any of the sixteen birth states of the subtle-materiality realm (RŪPADHĀTU), enter the "nirvāṇa with remainder" (SOPADHIŚEṢANIRVĀṆA) on that support. They are those who make an effort, unlike the ANABHISAṂSKĀRAPARINIRVĀYIN, but to whom effort comes naturally, unlike the SĀBHISAṂSKĀRAPARINIRVĀYIN.

**upapadyavedanīyakarman**. (P. upapajjavedanīyakamma; T. skyes nas myong 'gyur gyi las; C. shunci shengshou ye; J. junjishōjugō; K. sunch'a saengsu ŏp 順次生受業). In Sanskrit, "action experienced upon birth," a category of deed whose karmic effect is experienced in the immediately following lifetime, as opposed to the present life or some other lifetime in the future.

**upaputra**. (T. nye sras). In Sanskrit, lit. "close sons," a group of eight BODHISATTVAS often depicted with the Buddha in MAHĀYĀNA iconography. They are MAÑJUŚRĪ, VAJRAPĀṆI, AVALOKITEŚVARA, KṢITIGARBHA, SARVANĪVARAṆAVIṢKAMBHIN, ĀKĀŚAGARBHA, MAITREYA, and SAMANTABHADRA.

**upāsaka**. (T. dge bsnyen; C. youposai; J. ubasoku; K. ubasae 優婆塞). In Sanskrit and Pāli, "[male] lay disciple," a lay Buddhist man who takes the three refuges (TRIŚARAṆA) and the five basic precepts (PAÑCAŚĪLA): (1) not to kill, (2) not to steal, (3) not to engage in sexual misconduct, (4) not to lie, and (5) not to use intoxicants. These precepts are taken permanently, with three other precepts observed on full-moon and new-moon days (S. UPOṢADHA; P. uposatha), for a total of eight lay precepts (aṣṭāṅgaśīla; see AṢṬĀṄGASAMANVĀGATAṂ UPAVĀSAṂ): (6) not to eat at an inappropriate time (generally interpreted to mean between noon and the following dawn), (7) not to dance, sing, play music, attend performances, or adorn one's body with garlands, perfumes, or cosmetics, and (8) not to sleep on high beds. Also, during the full-moon and new-moon days, the vow not to engage in sexual misconduct is interpreted to mean complete celibacy. The term is often translated simply as "layman," but given the level of religious commitment, "[male] lay disciple" is a more accurate rendering. See also ŚIKṢĀPADA; ŚĪLA.

**upāsakasaṃvara**. (T. dge bsnyen gyi sdom pa; C. jinshi lüyi; J. gonjiritsugi; K. kŭnsa yurŭi 近事律儀). In Sanskrit and Pāli, "restraints of a [male] lay disciple," any or all the five precepts (PAÑCAŚĪLA) taken by a lay disciple for life: (1) not to kill, (2) not to steal, (3) not to engage in sexual misconduct, (4) not to lie, and (5) not to use intoxicants. These precepts are meant to be observed every day, with three other precepts observed on full moon and new moon days (UPOṢADHA). The three additional precepts are (6) not to eat at an inappropriate time (generally interpreted to mean between noon and the following dawn); (7) not to dance, sing, play music, attend performances, or adorn one's body with garlands, perfumes, or cosmetics; and (8) not to sleep on high beds. Also, during the full-moon and new-moon days, the vow not to engage in sexual misconduct is interpreted to mean complete celibacy. See also ŚIKṢĀPADA; ŚĪLA.

**upasaṃpadā**. (P. upasampadā; T. bsnyen par rdzogs pa; C. shoujie; J. jukai; K. sugye 受戒). In Sanskrit, "ordination" or "higher ordination," the ecclesiastical ceremony whereby a male novice (ŚRĀMAṆERA) becomes a fully ordained monk (BHIKṢU) and a female postulant (ŚIKṢAMĀṆĀ) becomes a fully ordained nun (BHIKṢUṆĪ). Although there are some variations in the procedure according to the different VINAYAS, the ordination ceremony is largely the same; that described in the Pāli vinaya is outlined here. In the case of a male novice, the ordinand, who must be at least twenty years of age, must first shave his hair, moustache, and beard and be provided with a monk's robe and bowl. He must have chosen a preceptor (P. upajjhāya; S. UPĀDHYĀYA) who will confer ordination upon him. The upajjhāya must be an elder (P. thera; S. STHAVIRA) of at least ten years standing, who is qualified morally and intellectually to act as preceptor. The candidate will then be brought before an assembly comprising at least ten monks, if the ceremony is held within the Buddhist heartland of India; if not, a minimum of five monks is necessary to conduct a valid ordination. The ordination ritual must be conducted within the confines of a SĪMĀ, or consecrated ordination boundary, and proceeds as follows. Seated in a squatting position, the candidate requests the assembly three times to confer ordination upon him. The assembly then asks him a set of stock questions concerning his age, his sex, his health, his legal liabilities, his preceptor, whether he has received permission from his parents, etc. If the candidate passes the inquiry, a formal petition is then put before the assembly three times that the candidate be admitted to the SAMGHA. Silence from the assembly indicates approval, and the candidate is thereby ordained. Immediately upon receiving the higher ordination, the new monk is apprised of the four requisites (NIŚRAYA) of the monk, and of the four PĀRĀJIKAS or "defeats," these being grave misdeeds that would result in expulsion from the SAṂGHA. The following types of persons may not be ordained: branded thieves, fugitives from the law, convicted thieves; those punished by flogging or branding, patricides, matricides, murderers of arahants (S. ARHAT); those who have shed the blood of a buddha, eunuchs, false monks, seducers of nuns, hermaphrodites; those without an upajjhāya, persons who are maimed, disabled, or deformed in various ways; and those afflicted with various communicable diseases. In the case of a female postulant seeking higher ordination as a nun, the candidate is required to undergo a double ordination. First she is brought before the order of nuns (P. bhikkhuṇīsaṅgha, S. BHIKṢUṆĪSAṂGHA), where she is queried and, if found suitable, given the first upasaṃpadā. She is then brought before the order of monks, where she is given a second upasaṃpadā.

**Upasena**. (T. Nye sde; C. Youbosina; J. Upashina; K. Ubasana 優波斯那). Sanskrit and Pāli proper name of an eminent ARHAT declared by the Buddha to be foremost among his monk disciples in being altogether charming; also known in Pāli as Upasena Vaṅgantaputta. According to Pāli accounts, he was born into a brāhmaṇa family in Nālaka and was the younger brother of ŚĀRIPUTRA. His father was Vaṅganta, hence his name Vaṅgantaputta. Like his brother, Upasena was learned in the three Vedas. He was converted when he heard the Buddha preach and immediately entered the order. When he had been a monk for only one year, he ordained a new monk, for which offense he was severely rebuked by the Buddha. Chastened by the criticism, Upasena took up the practice of insight in earnest and attained arahantship. Upasena became a skilled and charismatic preacher who won many converts to the religion. He engaged in various ascetic practices (DHUTAṄGA) and convinced many followers to do likewise. Each of his followers was charming in his own way, with Upasena the most charming of all. Upasena had resolved to attain such preeminence during the time of the previous buddha Padumuttara, when, as a householder of Haṃsavatī, he overheard a monk so praised and wished the same for himself in the future. Upasena's death was attended by a miracle. He was sitting at the mouth of a cave after his morning meal, mending his robe amid a pleasant breeze. At that time two snakes were in the vines above the cave door when one fell on his shoulder and bit him. As the venom coursed through his body, he requested Śāriputra and other monks near him to carry him outside so that he could die in the open. In a few moments he died, and his body immediately scattered in the breeze like chaff.

**upāsikā**. (T. dge bsnyen ma; C. youpoyi; J. ubai; K. ubai 優婆夷). In Sanskrit and Pāli, "[female] lay disciple," a lay Buddhist woman who takes the three refuges (TRIŚARAṆA) and the five basic precepts (PAÑCAŚĪLA): (1) not to kill, (2) not to steal, (3) not to engage in sexual misconduct, (4) not to lie, and (5) not to use intoxicants. These precepts are meant to be observed every day, with three other precepts observed on full-moon and new-moon days (S. UPOṢADHA; P. uposatha). The three are (6) not to eat at an inappropriate time (generally interpreted to mean between noon and the following dawn); (7) not to dance, sing, play music, attend performances, or adorn one's body with garlands, perfumes, or cosmetics; and (8) not to sleep on high beds. Also, during the full-moon and new-moon days, the vow not to engage in sexual misconduct is interpreted to mean complete celibacy. The term is often translated simply as "laywoman," but given the level of religious commitment, "[female] lay disciple" is a more accurate rendering. See also MAE CHI; ŚIKṢĀPADA.

**upāsikāsaṃvara**. (T. dge bsnyen ma'i sdom pa; C. youpoyi jie; J. ubaikai; K. ubai kye 優婆夷戒). In Sanskrit and Pāli, "restraints of a [female] lay disciple"; any or all the five restraints taken by a lay disciple for life: (1) not to kill, (2) not to steal, (3) not to engage in sexual misconduct, (4) not to lie, and (5) not to use intoxicants. These precepts are meant to be observed every day, with three other precepts observed on full-moon and new-moon days (S. UPOṢADHA; P. uposatha), making a total of eight precepts (aṣṭāṅgaśīla; see AṢṬĀṄGASAMANVĀGATAṂ UPAVĀSAṂ). The three additional precepts are (6) not to eat at an inappropriate time (generally interpreted to mean between noon and the following dawn); (7) not to dance, sing, play music, attend performances, or adorn one's body with garlands, perfumes, or cosmetics; and (8) not to sleep on high beds. Also, during the full-moon and new-moon days, the precept not to engage in sexual misconduct is interpreted to mean complete celibacy. See ŚĪLA; ŚIKṢĀPADA.

**upavāsa**. (T. bsnyen gnas; C. jinzhu; J. gonjū; K. kŭnju 近住). In Sanskrit and Pāli, "fasting" or "abstinence," a term used to refer to the abstention practiced by lay disciples during the fortnightly UPOṢADHA observance. In this context, the term also refers to the eight precepts (AṢṬĀṄGAŚĪLA; see AṢṬĀṄGASAMANVĀGATAṂ UPAVĀSAṂ), also referred to as the "one-day precepts" observed by lay disciples at this time. They are the eight precepts: not to kill, steal, engage in sexual activity, lie, use intoxicants, eat after noon, adorn their bodies, or sleep on high beds.

**upavasatha**. (S). See UPOṢADHA.

**upāya**. (T. thabs; C. fangbian; J. hōben; K. pangp'yŏn 方便). In Sanskrit and Pāli, "stratagem," "method"; term with at least four important denotations: (1) as a synonym for "skillful means" (UPĀYAKAUŚALYA); (2) as a general term for the activities necessary for the attainment of buddhahood; and (3) as one of the two essential components of the path, along with "wisdom" (PRAJÑĀ). In this latter sense, method refers to the actions a BODHISATTVA takes on behalf of all sentient beings. In this formulation, the various deeds that fall under the rubric of upāya are said to fructify as the RŪPAKĀYA of a buddha, while the bodhisattva's development of prajñā is said to fructify as his DHARMAKĀYA. (4) In Buddhist tantra, the superiority of the esoteric path of the VAJRAYĀNA over the exoteric path in bringing about buddhahood is often attributed to the superior stratagems or methods set forth in the TANTRAS, compared to those found in the sūtras. In tantra, upāya is associated with the male and prajñā with the female.

**upāyakauśalya**. (P. upāyakosalla; T. thabs mkhas; C. fangbian shanqiao; J. hōbenzengyō; K. pangpy'ŏn sŏn'gyo 方便善巧). In Sanskrit, "skillful means," "skill-in-means," or "expedient means," a term used to refer to the extraordinary pedagogical skills of the buddhas and advanced BODHISATTVAS; indeed, upāyakauśalya is listed as one of the ten perfections (PĀRAMITĀ) mastered on the bodhisattva path. (The rare Pāli form refers specifically to the Buddha's teaching proficiency.) The notion of skillful means is adumbrated in the famous "simile of the raft" from the ALAGADDŪPAMASUTTA, where the Buddha compares his teachings to a makeshift raft that will help one get across a raging river to the opposite shore: after one has made it across that river of birth and death to the "other shore" of NIRVĀṆA, the teachings have served their purpose and may be abandoned; in one sense, therefore, all his teachings are merely an expedient. The notion of skill-in-means also suggests that the Buddha intentionally fashions different versions of his teachings to fit the predelictions and aptitudes of his audience. Because of a buddha's direct understanding of his disciples' abilities, he is able to teach what is most appropriate for each of them, like a doctor prescribing a treatment for a specific malady. Skillful means may also be used to justify why certain acts perceived as immoral by beings of lesser capacity become virtues when performed by a bodhisattva, who has their best interests at heart (see UPĀYAKAUŚALYASŪTRA). ¶ The Buddha's skill-in-means is often used to reconcile apparent contradictions in his teaching, since those teachings ultimately are provisional expressions of his realization. The notion of skillful means has also been put to polemical use, especially in the MAHĀYĀNA (and most famously in the SADDHARMAPUṆḌARĪKASŪTRA), when previous teachings of the Buddha, such as the three vehicles (TRIYĀNA), are declared by him to have been merely expedients that he employed to instruct disciples who were unable to comprehend the more profound teaching of the one vehicle (EKAYĀNA) of buddhahood. The concept of skillful means may thus also be deployed as a hermeneutical or polemical device to critique earlier, and implicitly inferior, formulations of Buddhist doctrine as expedient teachings given to those who are temporarily incapable of understanding and benefitting from the Buddha's more advanced teachings (as variously identified by different Buddhist schools).

**Upāyakauśalyasūtra**. (T. Thabs la mkhas pa'i mdo; C. Dasheng fangbian hui; J. Daijō hōben'e; K. Taesŭng pangp'yŏn hoe 大乘方便會). In Sanskrit, "Skillful Means Sūtra," an early MAHĀYĀNA sūtra included in the RATNAKŪṬASŪTRA collection, where it is also known as the *Jñānottarabodhisattvaparipṛcchā*. (In addition to the recension embedded in the 410 CE Chinese translation of the *Ratnakūṭa*, as transcribed above, there are also two other Chinese translations, one made in 285 CE, the other c. 980.) The first part of the sūtra extols the virtues of the practice of "skillful means" (UPĀYAKAUŚALYA), generally understood in this context to refer to the dedication of the merit from a virtuous deed, such as offerings made for the welfare and ultimate enlightenment of all beings. The sūtra goes on to explain how apparently nonvirtuous acts, such as sexual misconduct, become virtues when performed by a bodhisattva with skillful means, noting, "Something that sends other sentient beings to hell sends the bodhisattva who is skilled in means to rebirth in the world of BRAHMĀ." Also recounted is the famous story of the Buddha's previous life as a ship captain, when he kills a potential murderer in order to save others' lives. In the second part of the sūtra, the Buddha recounts the events of his life (see BAXIANG), from his entry into his mother's womb to his decision to teach the dharma as instances of his skillful means; none of these events are presented as the consequences of his own past nonvirtuous actions or indeed of any fault whatsoever on his part. For example, after his enlightenment, the Buddha has no hesitation to teach the dharma; nonetheless, he compels the god BRAHMĀ to descend from his heaven to implore the Buddha to teach. He forces this act so that beings who worship Brahmā will have faith in the Buddha and so that the myriad forms of the god Brahmā will generate BODHICITTA. The sūtra concludes with a discussion of ten cases in the life of the Buddha in which he apparently undergoes suffering (such as a headache, backache, and being pierced by a thorn) that had previously been ascribed to his nonvirtuous deeds in a past life; in each case, these are instead explained as being examples of the Buddha's skillful means.

**upekṣā**. (P. upekkhā; T. btang snyoms; C. she; J. sha; K. sa 捨). In Sanskrit, "equanimity," a term with at least four important denotations: (1) as a sensation of neutrality that is neither pleasurable nor painful; (2) as one of eleven virtuous mental concomitants (KUŚALA-CAITTA), referring to a state of evenness of mind, without overt disturbance by sensuality, hatred, or ignorance; (3) as a state of mental balance during the course of developing concentration, which is free from lethargy and excitement; and (4) one of the four "divine abidings" (BRAHMAVIHĀRA), along with loving-kindness (MAITRĪ), compassion (KARUṆĀ), and sympathetic joy (MUDITĀ). As a divine abiding, upekṣā indicates an even-mindedness toward all beings, regarding them with neither attachment nor aversion, as neither intimate nor remote; in some descriptions of the four "divine abidings," there is the additional wish that all beings attain such equanimity. In the VISUDDHIMAGGA, equanimity is listed as one of the meditative topics for the cultivation of tranquillity meditation (samathābhāvanā; see S. ŚAMATHA). Of the four divine abidings, equanimity is capable of producing all four levels of meditative absorption (P. JHĀNA; S. DHYĀNA), while the other divine abidings are capable of producing only the first three of four. The text indicates that, along with the other three divine abidings, equanimity is used only for the cultivation of tranquillity, not for insight training (P. vipassanābhāvanā; see S. VIPAŚYANĀ).

**upekṣāpramāṇa**. (P. upekkhāppamaññā; T. btang snyoms tshad med; C. she wuliangxin; J. shamuryōshin; K. sa muryangsim 捨無量心). In Sanskrit, "unlimited equanimity" or "boundless equanimity," a state of equanimity toward unlimited numbers of sentient beings, or the wish that unlimited sentient beings abide in a state of equanimity that is free from desire and hatred.

**upoṣadha**. [alt. poṣadha; upavasatha] (P. uposatha; T. gso sbyong; C. busa; J. fusatsu; K. p'osal 布薩). In Sanskrit, the fortnightly retreat (the term is generally left untranslated into English). It is the semimonthly ceremony (observed on the new moon and the full moon) in which monks and nuns are to assemble within a specified boundary (SĪMĀ) to recite the monastic rules of conduct set forth in the PRĀTIMOKṢA. The observance involves the confession of faults, following which the prātimokṣa is recited. The *bhikṣuprātimokṣa* is recited by fully ordained monks, the *bhikṣuṇīprātimokṣa* by fully ordained nuns; novices and laypeople are prohibited from participating in either observance. The purpose of the ceremony is for the SAṂGHA to purify itself of misdeeds through confession and to renew its commitment to moral conduct, thus helping to ensure harmony within the monastic community and between the clergy and the laity. Laypeople will often maintain eight precepts (AṢṬĀṄGASAMANVĀGATAṂ UPAVĀSAṂ) on this day, which essentially turn them into monks or nuns for a day: not to kill, steal, engage in sexual activity, lie, use intoxicants, eat after noon, adorn their bodies, or sleep on high beds. The term upoṣadha means to abide in a state of fasting or abstinence, a practice that was pre-Buddhist in origin; in Vedic times, it specifically referred to the day prior to a soma sacrifice. The practice seems to have been adopted from other religious sects in India during the Buddha's lifetime. There are several types of upoṣadha ceremony, the most common and important of which is the saṃgha upoṣadha, which is attended by four or more monks who recite the prātimokṣa and is held on the new- and full-moon days of the month. When three or fewer monks are present, the ceremony is held but the prātimokṣa is not recited. According to the Pāli vinaya, there are twenty-one types of persons in whose presence a monk's upoṣadha ceremony may not be held, viz., nuns, women in training to become nuns, male and female novices, persons who have seceded from the order, persons guilty of a PĀRĀJIKA offense, monks who refuse to acknowledge their own wrongdoing (of three kinds), eunuchs, ersatz monks who wear monastic attire without having been ordained, monks who have joined other religions, nonhumans, patricides, matricides, murderers of ARHATs, seducers of nuns, schismatics, hermaphrodites, laypersons, and those who have shed the blood of a buddha.

**ūrdhvasrotas**. (T. gong du 'pho ba; C. shangliu ban/shangliu banniepan; J. jōruhatsu/jōruhatsunehan; K. sangnyu pan/sangnyu panyŏlban 上流般/上流般涅槃). In Sanskrit, "one who goes higher" or "upstreamer"; a specific type of nonreturner (ANĀGĀMIN), one of the twenty members of the ĀRYASAṂGHA (see VIṂŚATIPRABHEDASAṂGHA). There are different accounts of the types of ūrdhvasrotas. According to Ārya VIMUKTISENA's explanation of the list of āryasaṃgha found in the ABHISAMAYĀLAṂKĀRAVṚTTI, based on the ABHIDHARMAKOŚABHĀṢYA, there are four: the pluta (those who leap over), ardhapluta (those who leap over half), sarvasthānacyuta (those who die in every place), and bhavāgraparama (those who journey to the summit of existence). All cultivate a meditation that enters and exits uncontaminated (ANĀSRAVA) states that cause them to take birth in the ŚUDDHĀVĀSA (pure abodes). This meditation allows them to jump at will from one meditative state (a DHYĀNA or SAMĀPATTI) to another without having to go through the intermediate stages. The pluta enters the first dhyāna, is reborn among the BRAHMAKĀYIKA divinities of the first meditative absorption and, through the force of earlier meditative development, emerges from that level of absorption, forsakes all levels in between, and is reborn in the pure abode region of the AKANIṢṬHA heaven of the highest divinities, where he enters NIRVĀṆA. The ardhapluta is similarly reborn among the brahmakāyika divinities of the first meditative absorption, also forsakes the levels in between the first and fourth absorption, and is reborn in the pure abodes, but not each in turn. Omitting some of them, he is then born in the AKANIṢṬHA heaven, where he enters nirvāṇa. The sarvasthānacyuta, as the name suggests, is born among the brahmakāyika divinities of the first meditative absorption and then goes through the process of taking birth in every other heaven in the subtle materiality and immaterial realms except the great Brahmā heaven until he enters nirvāṇa in the akaniṣṭha heaven. The bhavāgraparama are born as divinities in the heavens up to the level of the BṚHATPHALA (great fruition) heaven, forsake the pure abodes, and, having taken rebirths in stages in the immaterial realm (ĀRŪPYADHĀTU), enter nirvāṇa in the BHAVĀGRA (the summit of existence) heaven.

**ūrṇā**. (S). See ŪRṆĀKEŚA.

**ūrṇākeśa**. [alt. ūrṇākośa, ūrṇā] (P. uṇṇākesa; T. mdzod spu; C. baihao; J. byakugō; K. paekho 白毫). In Sanskrit, "hair treasure" or "tuft"; a spiral of hair said to be infinite in length located between the eyebrows of a buddha. It is frequently depicted as a gem inlaid between the eyebrows on buddha and BODHISATTVA images. In some lists, the ūrṇākeśa is the thirty-first of the thirty-two major marks of a superman (MAHĀPURUṢALAKṢAṆA) and is said to be endowed with a variety of magical powers. In many sūtras, the Buddha sometimes emits a ray of light from his ūrṇākeśa in order to illuminate distant worlds; see KĀYAPRABHĀ; TOUGUANG.

**Uruvilvā**. (P. Uruvelā; T. Lteng rgyas; C. Youloupinluo; J. Urubinra; K. Urubinna 優樓頻螺). In Sanskrit, said to mean "Great Bank of Sand," the name of an area, encompassing several villages, on the banks of the NAIRAÑJANĀ River in MAGADHA (today in the Indian state of Bihar), and the site of several important events in the life of the Buddha. It was in Uruvilvā that the BODHISATTVA practiced austerities for six years together with the group of five ascetics (PAÑCAVARGIKA). It was also there that he renounced the practice of asceticism, as a result of which he was repudiated by his five companions, who left him in Uruvilvā and departed for ṚSIPATANA. The bodhisattva then proceeded to the BODHI TREE, where he achieved enlightenment. In the forty-nine days after his enlightenment, the Buddha sat under various trees in Uruvilvā, where shrines were eventually established. It was also at Uruvilvā that BRAHMĀ SAHAṂPATĪ appeared before the Buddha and implored him to teach the dharma. After turning the wheel of the dharma (DHARMACAKRAPRAVARTANA) for the group of five in Ṛṣipatana, the Buddha returned to Uruvilvā, where he converted thirty young men, as well as the "Kāśyapa brothers," led by URUVILVĀ-KĀŚYAPA and their followers.

**Uruvilvā-Kāśyapa**. (P. Uruvela-Kassapa; T. Lteng rgyas 'od srung; C. Youloupinluo Jiashe; J. Urubinra Kashō; K. Urubinna Kasŏp 優樓頻螺迦葉). The chief of the three "Kāśyapa brothers" (together with NADĪ-KĀŚYAPA and GAYĀ-KĀŚYAPA), also known in Pāli as the Tebhātika Jaṭila. Prior to their encounter with the Buddha, the three brothers were matted-hair ascetics engaged in fire worship, living with their followers on the banks of the NAIRAÑJANĀ River. Uruvilvā-Kāśyapa himself is said to have had five hundred followers. After his first teachings in the Deer Park (MṚGADĀVA; ṚSIPATANA) at SĀRNĀTH, the Buddha returned to Uruvilvā, where he had practiced asceticism prior to this enlightenment. There he encountered Uruvilvā-Kāśyapa, who mistakenly believed that he was already an ARHAT and was liberated from the bonds of rebirth. Knowing that

Uruvilvā-Kāśyapa could be dissuaded from his false views by a display of yogic power, the Buddha spent the rains retreat with him, performing 3,500 magical feats to demonstrate his mastery of supernatural powers (S. ṚDDHI), including subduing a fire serpent (NĀGA) without being burned, a scene depicted in Indian rock carvings. Using his ability to read Kāśyapa's mind, the Buddha was able to convince the ascetic that he was not an arhat. When the Buddha told Uruvilvā-Kāśyapa that the fire worship that he taught did not lead to enlightenment, Uruvilvā-Kāśyapa requested ordination. Uruvilvā-Kāśyapa and his five hundred followers all cut off their long locks and threw them in the river. When the other two brothers and their followers saw the hair floating by, they came to investigate and in turn sought ordination. In one fell swoop, the Buddha's community of monks grew to over a thousand monks. The Buddha taught them the so-called "Fire Sermon" (ĀDITTAPARIYĀYA), at which point they all become arhats. They then traveled together to RĀJAGṚHA where, in the presence of King BIMBISĀRA, the new monks proclaimed their allegiance to the Buddha. The three brothers are often listed among the audience of MAHĀYĀNA sūtras.

**ūṣman**. [alt. ūṣmagata] (T. drod; C. nuan; J. nan; K. nan 煖). In Sanskrit, "heat"; the first of the "aids to penetration" (NIRVEDHABHĀGĪYA) that are developed during the "path of preparation" (PRAYOGAMĀRGA) and mark the transition from the mundane sphere of cultivation (LAUKIKA[BHĀVANĀ]MĀRGA) to the supramundane vision (viz., DARŚANAMĀRGA) of the FOUR NOBLE TRUTHS (CATVĀRY ĀRYASATYĀNI). This stage is called heat, the ABHIDHARMAMAHĀVIBHĀṢĀ says, because it "can burn all the fuel of the afflictions (KLEŚA)." Heat involves ardent faith (ŚRADDHĀ) regarding the DHARMAVINAYA: when that faith is conditioned by the noble truth of the path (MĀRGASATYA), it produces ardency regarding the right DHARMA; when it is faith conditioned by the noble truth of extinction (NIRODHASATYA), it produces ardency regarding the VINAYA. Ūṣman and summit (MŪRDHAN), the first two of the nirvedhabhāgīyas, are still subject to retrogression and thus belong to the worldly path of cultivation (laukikabhāvanāmārga).

**uṣṇīṣa**. (P. uṇhīsa; T. gtsug tor; C. foding/rouji; J. butchō/nikukei; K. pulchŏng/yukkye 佛頂/肉髻). In Sanskrit, lit. "turban," the protuberance appearing on the crown of a buddha's head, which is commonly depicted in buddha images. The MAHĀPADĀNASUTTANTA and LAKKHAṆASUTTANTA of the Pāli DĪGHANIKĀYA refer to the uṇhīsasīsa ("wearing a turban on the head") as one of the thirty-two major "marks of a superman" (P. mahāpurisalakkhaṇa; S. MAHĀPURUṢALAKṢAṆA). Many texts report that the uṣṇīṣa is endowed with a variety of magical powers. For example, it is said that, although the uṣṇīṣa is perfectly proportional to the Buddha's head, it cannot be measured. It is impossible to see the top of the uṣṇīṣa, and divinities (DEVA) are unable to fly above it. Many scriptures, including the *Uṣṇīṣavijayadhāraṇī*, also mention the Buddha radiating light from his uṣṇīṣa. Later Buddhist works in Sanskrit refer to this protuberance as the uṣṇīṣa-śiraskatā (lit. "head-bone"). The origin and precise interpretation of this unique feature of a Buddha remains in dispute. The Sanskrit term uṣṇīṣa is in fact a common word for turban. Some art historians have argued that the uṣṇīṣa originated as a topknot of hair, such as is found depicted in Graeco-Gandhāran Buddhist sculpture from northwestern India from around the first century CE; the interpretation of the uṣṇīṣa as a protuberance on the top of the skull subsequently evolved at MATHURĀ, where artists began to cover the uṣṇīṣa with little snail-curled hair, due to a misinterpretation of the wavy hairstyle of Gandhāran sculptures. The Chinese pilgrims FAXIAN and XUANZANG report seeing the "uṣṇīṣa bone" of the Buddha being worshipped at a monastery in Haḍḍa (in present-day Afghanistan).

**Uṣṇīṣasitātapatrā**. (S). See TATHĀGATOṢṆĪṢASITĀTAPATRĀ.

**utpāda**. (P. uppāda; T. skye ba; C. shengqi; J. shōki; K. saenggi 生起). In Sanskrit, "production," or "arising," the generation of a specific fruition or effect (PHALA) from a given cause (HETU). In generic Buddhist accounts of causality or etiology, hetu designates the main or primary cause of production, which operates in conjunction with various concomitant or subsidiary conditions (PRATYAYA); together, these two bring about the production (utpāda) of a specific "fruition" or result (phala). In the PRAJÑĀPĀRAMITĀ literature and the MADHYAMAKA school, the notion of production comes under specific criticism (see VAJRAKAṆĀ), with NĀGĀRJUNA famously asking, e.g., how an effect can be produced from a cause that is either the same as or different from itself. The prajñāpāramitā sūtras thus famously declare that all dharmas are actually ANUTPĀDA, or "unproduced."

**Utpalavarṇā**. (P. Uppalavaṇṇā; T. Ut pa la'i mdog; C. Lianhuase; J. Rengeshiki; K. Yŏnhwasaek 蓮華色). One of two chief nun disciples of the Buddha, the first being KṢEMĀ. According to Pāli accounts, where she is known as Uppalavaṇṇā, she was born into a banker's family in Sāvatthi (ŚRĀVASTĪ) and was renowned for her beauty. Her name, lit. "blue-lotus colored," refers to her skin complexion, which was dark like a blue lotus flower. Men of all ranks, royals and commoners, sought her hand in marriage. Her father, fearing to offend any of them, suggested to her that she renounce the world. Already inclined by nature to renunciation, Uppalavaṇṇā became a Buddhist nun. While sweeping an uposatha (S. UPOṢADHA) assembly hall, she attained meditative absorption (P. JHĀNA; DHYĀNA) by concentrating on the light of a candle, and soon became an ARHAT possessed of the analytical attainments (P. paṭisambhidā; S. PRATISAṂVID). Uppalavaṇṇā was renowned for her various supernatural powers born from her mastery of meditative absorption. The Buddha declared her to be chief among his nun disciples in supranormal powers (P. iddhi; S. ṚDDHI). After she had become a nun and an arhat, Uppalavaṇṇā was raped by her cousin Ānanda (not the Ānanda who was the Buddha's attendant), who had been enamored of her when she was a laywoman. Although he was swallowed by the earth for his heinous crime, the case raised the question within the monastic community as to whether arhats are capable of experiencing sensual pleasure and thus had sexual desire. The Buddha asserted categorically that arhats are immune to sensuality. Several verses of the THERĪGĀTHĀ are attributed to Uppalavaṇṇā. She and ŚĀRIPUTRA are also said to have been the first to greet the Buddha at SĀMKĀŚYA when he descended on ladders from the TRĀYASTRIṂŚA heaven, where he had been instructing his mother, MĀYĀ; in order to make her way through the large crowd that had gathered, she disguised herself as a CAKRAVARTIN. Among the many crimes of the Buddha's evil cousin DEVADATTA was beating her to death after she chastised him for attempting to assassinate the Buddha; he thus committed the deed of immediate retribution (ĀNANTARYAKARMAN) of killing an arhat. The commentary to the *Therīgāthā* and the Sanskrit VINAYAVIBHAṄGA provide differing accounts of how she became a nun. The first is briefer and has her come from Sāvatthi (S. ŚRĀVASTĪ); the latter is more extensive and has her come from TAKṢAŚILĀ (P. Taxila). In both accounts, she gives birth to two children by two different men and becomes separated from both children. Years later, she unknowingly marries her son, who then marries her daughter (whom Utpalavarṇā also does not recognize) as his second wife, making Utpalavarṇā husband to her son and co-wife to her daughter. In the Pāli account, her eventual recognition of this state of affairs is sufficient to cause her to renounce the world. In the Sanskrit account, she gives birth to a son by her first son and when she realizes this, she becomes a courtesan, who is hired to seduce MAHĀMAUDGALYĀYANA. She is unsuccessful, and his words convince her to renounce the world and become a nun.

**utpattikrama**. (T. bskyed rim; C. shengqi cidi; J. shōkishidai; K. saenggi ch'aje 生起次第). In Sanskrit, "stage of generation" or the "creation stage," one of the two major phases (along with the NIṢPANNAKRAMA or the "stage of completion") of ANUTTARAYOGATANTRA practice. The term encompasses a wide range of practices that commence after one has received initiation (ABHIṢEKA), generally involving the practice of the SĀDHANA of a particular deity with the aim of the "generation" or transformation of the body, environment, enjoyments, and activities of the practitioner into the body, environment, enjoyments, and activities of a buddha. This is done through the practice of deity yoga (DEVATĀYOGA), in which the meditator visualizes himself or herself as a buddha and the environment as a MAṆḌALA. In the RNYING MA sect of Tibetan Buddhism, MAHĀYOGA generally corresponds to the utpattikrama.

**uttamanirmāṇakāya**. (T. mchog gi sprul sku; C. shanghua shen; J. jōkeshin; K. sanghwa sin 上化身). In Sanskrit, "supreme emanation body," one of the forms of the emanation body (NIRMĀṆAKĀYA) of a buddha. A buddha may appear in any form in order to benefit sentient beings, including as an inanimate object. The form of a buddha that appears in the world and performs the twelve deeds or the eight episodes in the life of a buddha (BAXIANG), including achieving enlightenment, teaching the dharma, and passing into PARINIRVĀṆA, is called a "supreme emanation body." The "supreme emanation body" is a body adorned with the major and minor marks of a MAHĀPURUṢA and dressed in the robes of a monk, such as ŚĀKYAMUNI. This type of nirmāṇakāya is contrasted with the JANMANIRMĀṆAKĀYA, or "created emanation body," which are the nonhuman or inanimate forms a buddha assumes in order to help others overcome their afflictions. See also TRIKĀYA.

**uttamasiddhi**. (T. mchog gi dngos grub; C. zuishang daxidi; J. saijōdaishiji; K. ch'oesang taesilchi 最上大悉地). In Sanskrit, "supreme attainment"; a term used, especially in a tantric context, to refer to the attainment of buddhahood, in distinction to the common attainments (SĀDHĀRAṆASIDDHI), such as the ability to fly, walk through walls, and find buried treasure, which can be achieved through the recitation of MANTRA and the propitiation of deities.

**uttarakuru**. (T. sgra mi snyan; C. beijuluzhou; J. hokkurushū; K. pukkuro chu 北俱盧洲). Sanskrit and Pāli name of one of the four island continents located in the four cardinal directions surrounding Mount SUMERU, according to traditional Buddhist cosmology. Uttarakuru is the northern continent and is square in shape. Its inhabitants, classified as humans among the six types of beings who inhabit SAṂSĀRA, are said to be thirty-two cubits in height and to live for a thousand years. Their language is said to be very unpleasant to the ear.

**Uttaramūlanikāya**. A monastic fraternity in Sri Lanka, deriving from the ABHAYAGIRI sect. The main monastery of the group was the Uttarola VIHĀRA, built by King Mānavamma, and donated to the monks of the Abhayagiri Vihāra for having permitted his elder brother to be ordained, despite the fact that he had lost one eye and therefore would normally have been disqualified. The first head of the Uttarola monastery was the king's brother himself, whose duties included the supervision of the guardians of the TOOTH RELIC. The late-eleventh or early-twelfth century scholiast ANURUDDHA, author of the famous ABHIDHAMMA primer, ABHIDHAMMATTHASAṄGAHA, describes himself in a colophon as an elder of the Uttaramūlanikāya.

**Uttarā-Nandamātā**. An eminent laywoman declared by the Buddha to be foremost in the attainment of meditative power. According to Pāli accounts, she was the daughter of Puṇṇaka, a servant of the wealthy man Sumana of Rājagaha (S. RĀGAGṚHA). Uttarā's family was devoted to the Buddha and, on one occasion, while listening to a sermon he was preaching, Uttarā and her parents became stream-enterers (P. sotāpanna; S. SROTAĀPANNA). When Sumana requested that Uttarā be betrothed to his son, he was at first refused on the grounds that his family was not Buddhist. Agreement was reached when Sumana promised that Uttarā would be supplied with sufficient requisites to continue her daily devotions to the Buddha. Her new husband, however, reneged on the agreement and refused to allow her to observe the uposatha (S. UPOṢADHA) retreat day because she would have to refrain from intercourse for the night. In order that she could observe the uposatha, Uttarā requested money from her father-in-law so she could hire a courtesan named Sirimā to service her husband. According to legend, there subsequently ensued an incident that led to the enlightenment of the courtesan, her husband, and her father-in-law. It so happened that one day while Uttarā busied herself preparing a magnificent offering for the Buddha and his disciples, her husband was strolling hand in hand with Sirimā. Seeing his wife toiling, he smiled at her foolishness for not using her riches for herself. Uttarā saw her husband and likewise smiled at his foolishness for wasting his life in self-indulgence. Sirimā, misunderstanding their smiles, flew into a jealous rage and threw boiling oil at Uttarā. But through the power of Uttarā's compassion for Sirimā, the oil did not burn her, and, witnessing this miracle, Sirimā understood her mistake and begged forgiveness. Uttarā brought Sirimā to the Buddha, who preached to her, whereupon she became a once-returner (P. sakadāgamī; S. SAKṚDĀGĀMIN). Uttarā's husband and father-in-law, who also heard the sermon, became stream-enterers.

**uttarāsaṃga**. (P. uttarāsaṅga; T. bla gos; C. zhongjiayi; J. chūgee; K. chunggaŭi 中價衣). In Sanskrit, the "upper robe" or "cassock"; one of the three robes (TRICĪVARA) permitted for a monk or nun, along with the ANTARVĀSAS, or lower robe, and the SAṂGHĀṬĪ, or outer robe or waistcloth. The uttarāsaṃga is large enough to cover the body from the neck to the middle of the calf; it is normally made of one layer of cloth. See also CĪVARA; KĀṢĀYA.

**Uttaratantra**. (T. Rgyud bla ma). See RATNAGOTRAVIBHĀGA.

# V

**Vāgīsa**. (S). See VĀṄGĪŚA.

**vāgviveka**. (T. ngag dben). In Sanskrit, "isolation of speech"; one of the six stages of the completion state (NIṢPANNAKRAMA) in the ANUTTARAYOGATANTRA systems. In order to separate the mind from coarse conventional appearances and induce the dawning of the mind of clear light (PRABHĀSVARACITTA), the body, speech, and mind must be isolated from their ordinary forms. In the isolation of speech, the subtle wind (PRĀṆA) that is the root of speech is isolated from the ordinary movement of winds. That subtle wind is then combined with MANTRA.

**Vaibhāṣika**. (T. Bye brag smra ba; C. Piposha shi; J. Bibashashi; K. Pibasa sa 毘婆沙師). In Sanskrit, "Followers of the *Vibhāṣā*"; the ĀBHIDHARMIKAS associated with the SARVĀSTIVĀDA school of ABHIDHARMA, especially in KASHMIR-GANDHĀRA in northwestern India but even in BACTRIA. Because these masters considered their teachings to be elaborations of doctrines found in the Sarvāstivāda abhidharma treatise, the ABHIDHARMAMAHĀVIBHĀṢĀ, they typically referred to themselves as the Vaibhāṣika; hence, the Kashmiri strand of Sarvāstivāda may be called either Sarvāstivāda-Vaibhāṣika, or, simply, Vaibhāṣika. The root text of the Vaibhāṣika school is the *Abhidharmamahāvibhāṣā* (a.k.a. *Mahāvibhāṣā*), a massive encyclopedic compendium of Sarvāstivāda doctrine. The Vaibhāṣikas maintained that the *Mahāvibhāṣā* was originally spoken by the Buddha himself, and that the various interlocutors—including divinities, ŚĀRIPUTRA, and others—who facilitate the work's catechistic structure were summoned by the Buddha for the sake of the text's composition. The Gandhāran response to this and other claims made by the Vaibhāṣikas led to the formation of an offshoot that rejected the authority of this abhidharma literature. This offshoot called itself the SAUTRĀNTIKA, or "Those Who Adhere to the SŪTRAS." The Vaibhāṣika abhidharma system maintains the existence of seventy-five constituent factors (DHARMA). Seventy-two of these are conditioned (SAṂSKṚTA) and three are unconditioned (ASAṂSKṚTA). Like most other schools of Buddhism, the Vaibhāṣikas affirmed the selflessness (ANĀTMAN) of persons and the momentary (KṢAṆIKA) nature of conditioned dharmas. However, they maintained that these factors have their own real existence that endures in past, present, and future modes. They believed these factors to be both real and eternal—a view for which they generated many elaborate justifications. They also believed external objects to be composed of minute particles, like atoms (PARAMĀṆU). According to the Vaibhāṣikas, consciousness (VIJÑĀNA) or cognition has no form that is independent of its object; the Vaibhāṣika model of the relationship between consciousness and its objects is therefore sometimes referred to as "direct realism" (see ĀKĀRA). VASUBANDHU's ABHIDHARMAKOŚABHĀṢYA is mainly concerned with abhidharma theory as it was explicated in the Vaibhāṣika school; in comparison to the *Mahāvibhāṣā*, however, the *Abhidharmakośabhāṣya* presents a more systematic overview of Sarvāstivāda positions and, at various points in his expositions, Vasubandhu criticizes Sarvāstivāda doctrine from the standpoint of its more progressive Sautrāntika offshoot. This criticism elicited a spirited response from later Sarvāstivāda-Vaibhāṣika scholars, such as SAṂGHABHADRA in his *NYĀYĀNUSĀRA. The Vaibhāṣika disappeared as an independent school sometime around the seventh or eighth centuries CE.

**vaidalya**. (S) (P. vedalla). See VAIPULYA.

**Vaidalyaprakaraṇa**. (T. Zhib mo rnam par 'thag pa). In Sanskrit, "Extended" or "Woven" "Explanation"; a work now extant only in Tibetan, which is ascribed to NĀGĀRJUNA (although some modern scholarship has questioned the attribution). The treatise, also known as the *Vaidalyasūtra*, is listed in Tibet as one of Nāgārjuna's six works in his "logical corpus" (YUKTIKĀYA). The work is devoted to the refutation of sixteen principles (padārtha) set forth in the *Nyāyasūtra*, which is accomplished in seventy-three aphorisms, or sūtras. An autocommentary is also extant.

***Vaidalyasūtranāma**. (S) (T. Zhib mo rnam par 'thag pa zhes bya ba'i mdo). See VAIDALYAPRAKARAṆA.

**Vaidehī**. (P. Videhī; T. Lus 'phags ma; C. Weitixi; J. Idaike; K. Wijehŭi 韋提希). Sanskrit proper name of the queen of BIMBISĀRA, king of MAGADHA, and mother of AJĀTAŚATRU. According to some traditions, her name derives from the fact that she hailed from VIDEHA. When her son Ajātaśatru usurped the throne and imprisoned his father, no one was allowed to visit him except for Vaidehī. Although she was prohibited from bringing Bimbisāra food, she hid food in her clothes. When this was discovered, she hid food in her hair and then in her shoes. When these were discovered, she smeared her body with the four sweet substances, which the king licked for his sustenance. When this was discovered, the king lived on the energy from walking meditation, until his son had his feet lacerated, after which he died. The incident of Vaidehī's visit to the cell of Bimbisāra provides the setting for one of the three major sūtras of the East Asian PURE LAND traditions, the GUAN WULIANGSHOU JING (sometimes known by the hypothetical reconstructed Sanskrit title **Amitāyurdhyānasūtra*, or simply as the "Meditation Sūtra"). According to this sūtra, when Ajātaśatru discovers that his mother has been secretly feeding the king, he incarcerates her as well. Despite her sorrow, Vaidehī does not give up her faith in the Buddha and invokes his aid. The Buddha then appears before her, and she asks that he teach her about a place where there is no sorrow. The Buddha then teaches her how to visualize the SUKHĀVATĪ pure land of the buddha named "Infinite Life" (AMITĀYUS/AMITĀBHA). He next explains to her how one may be reborn in this wonderful paradise, which is a land without suffering, a world of endless bliss. At the end of the sūtra, Vaidehī is mentioned as one of many who were inspired by the Buddha's preaching.

**vaipulya**. [alt. vaidalya] (cf. P. vedalla; T. shin tu rgyas pa; C. fangdeng; J. hōdō; K. pangdŭng 方等). In Sanskrit, lit. "vast" or "extended," viz., "works of great extent"; a term that appears in the title of a number of MAHĀYĀNA sūtras meant to indicate their profundity, comprehensiveness, and stereotypically great length. Such sūtras will typically offer a more comprehensive overview of Buddhist thought and practice than shorter sūtras that may have a single, or more circumscribed, message. The term is used to name one of the nine (NAVAṄGA) (Pāli) or twelve (DVĀDAŚĀṄGA[PRAVACANA]) (Sanskrit) categories (AṄGA) of Buddhist scripture according to their structure or literary style. As one of the nine categories of scriptures organized by type or style, vaipulya corresponds to the Pāli category of vedalla (S. vaidalya), which refers to such catechetical texts as the SAKKAPAÑHASUTTANTA or the SAMMĀDIṬṬHISUTTA. In the twelve types of scripture used in Mahāyāna classifications, the vaipulyasūtras are listed as the eleventh category and especially refer to scriptures of massive size. Mahāyāna sūtras included in the vaipulya category include many of the seminal works of the tradition, including the PRAJÑĀPĀRAMITĀ sūtras, the RATNAKŪṬASŪTRA collection, and the AVATAṂSAKASŪTRA.

**vairāgya**. (P. virāga; T. chags bral; C. liran/liyu/wuyu; J. rizen/riyoku/muyoku; K. iyŏm/iyok/muyok 離染/離欲/無欲). In Sanskrit, "dispassion [toward the world]"; an important step in the soteriological process leading to NIRVĀṆA. In the ABHIDHARMAMAHĀVIBHĀṢĀ, vairāgya is said to correspond to "lack of greed" (S. ALOBHA; C. wutan), one of the three wholesome faculties (trīṇi kuśalamūlāni, see KUŚALAMŪLA), along with "lack of anger" (S. apratigha; C. wuchen) and "nondelusion" (S. amoha; C. wuchi). Vairāgya is an essential factor in reaching the state that is uncontaminated (ANĀSRAVA) by the afflictions (KLEŚA), a characteristic of the ARHAT path. Vairāgya is the tenth of the twelve links (NIDĀNA) in what is known in Pāli Buddhist literature as "supramundane dependent origination" (P. lokuttarapaṭiccasamuppāda; S. LOKOTTARA-PRATĪTYASAMUTPĀDA). This supramundane chain leads to liberation (P. vimutti; S. VIMUKTI), rather than continued rebirth in SAṂSĀRA, which is the end result of the more common mundane chain. In this "supramundane" chain, the twelve links are (1) suffering (P. dukkha; S. DUḤKHA), (2) faith (P. saddhā; S. ŚRADDHĀ), (3) delight or satisfaction (P. pāmojja; S. prāmodya), (4) physical rapture or joy (P. pīti; S. PRĪTI), (5) tranquillity or repose (P. passaddhi; S. PRAŚRABDHI), (6) mental ease or bliss (SUKHA), (7) concentration (SAMĀDHI), (8) knowledge and vision that accords with reality (P. yathābhūtañāṇadassana; S. YATHĀBHŪTAJÑĀNADARŚANA), (9) disillusionment (P. nibbidā; S. NIRVEDA), (10) dispassion (P. virāga; S. vairāgya), (11) liberation (P. vimutti; S. VIMUKTI), and (12) knowledge of the destruction of the contaminants (P. āsavakkhāya; S. ĀSRAVAKṢAYA). The **Āryaśāsanaprakaraṇa* (C. *Xianyang shengjiao lun*), a summary exposition of the YOGĀCĀRABHŪMIŚĀSTRA, also mentions vairāgya in a similar list of twelve links, the difference being that the first two links are replaced by "observance of precepts" (P. kusalasīla; S. kuśalaśīla), and "freedom from remorse" (P. avippaṭisāra; S. avipratisāra).

**Vairocana**. (T. Rnam par snang mdzad; C. Dari rulai/Piluzhena; J. Dainichi nyorai/Birushana; K. Taeil yŏrae/Pirojana 大日如來/毗盧遮那). In Sanskrit, "Resplendent"; one of the five buddhas (PAÑCATATHĀGATA) and the chief buddha of the TATHĀGATAKULA; he is also one of the major buddhas of East Asian Buddhism, where he is often conflated with MAHĀVAIROCANA. The origin of Vairocana can be traced back to the Hindu tradition, where he appears as a relatively minor deity associated with the Sun. ¶ Although the name Vairocana appears in some mainstream Buddhist and PRAJÑĀPĀRAMITĀ materials, it is not until the emergence of the AVATAṂSAKASŪTRA that Vairocana comes to be widely regarded as the buddha who is the personification of the universal truth of the religion. In its "Chapter on Vairocana," Vairocana is considered to be the main buddha of the sūtra, who is omnipresent as the DHARMAKĀYA. Vairocana is, however, also described in the sūtra as a buddha who mastered the BODHISATTVA path by making vows to attain buddhahood, performing all types of virtuous deeds, hearing the dharma, cultivating meditative practices, and realizing the truth of the dependent origination of the dharma realm (C. FAJIE YUANQI) in which each and every thing in existence is in multivalent interaction with all other things in a state of complete and perfect interfusion. In this case, Vairocana as the reward body (SAṂBHOGAKĀYA) is called ROCANA (C. Lushena) in order to distinguish him from Vairocana (C. Piluzhena) as the dharmakāya buddha. With the growing popularity of the *Avataṃsakasūtra*, Vairocana becomes one of the principal buddhas of East Asian Buddhism. Many Vairocana images were constructed in China starting in the sixth century, and colossal images of him were erected in the LONGMEN Grottoes near Luoyang in northern China and in TŌDAIJI in Nara, Japan. In Korea, Vairocana (as the dharmakāya buddha) often appeared at the center of a buddha triad, flanked by ŚĀKYAMUNI (as the NIRMĀṆAKĀYA) and ROCANA (as the saṃbhogakāya). Vairocana's popularity expanded with his appearance in the MAHĀVAIROCANASŪTRA, and, from this point on, Vairocana is generally regarded as the main buddha of the *Avataṃsakasūtra* and the HUAYAN ZONG, while Mahāvairocana is regarded as the main buddha of the MAHĀVAIROCANĀBHISAṂBODHISŪTRA and the ZHENYAN or SHINGON schools. ¶ Vairocana is also the central deity of the VAJRADHĀTU (J. KONGŌKAI) and the GARBHADHĀTU (J. TAIZŌKAI) MAṆḌALAS of YOGATANTRA associated with the SARVATATHĀGATATATTVASAMGRAHA, a highly influential tantric text in India, Tibet, and East Asia. He appears in the central assembly of the vajradhātu maṇḍala, displaying the MUDRĀ of wisdom (dainichi ken-in), surrounded by the four directional buddhas (AKṢOBHYA, RATNASAMBHAVA, AMITĀBHA, and AMOGHASIDDHI), each of whom embodies four aspects of Vairocana's wisdom. In the garbhadhātu maṇḍala, Vairocana is located at the center of the eight-petaled lotus in the central cloister of the maṇḍala, along with the four buddhas and four bodhisattvas sitting on the eight petals. Vairocana is typically depicted as white in color, holding the wheel of dharma (DHARMACAKRA) in his hands, which are in the gesture of teaching (VITARKAMUDRĀ). Vairocana is closely associated with the bodhisattva SAMANTABHADRA, and his consort is Vajradhātvīśvarī. The commentaries on the *Sarvatathāgatatattvasaṃgraha* recount that Prince SIDDHĀRTHA was meditating on the banks of the NAIRAÑJANĀ River when he was roused by Vairocana and the buddhas of the ten directions, who informed him that such meditation would not result in the achievement of buddhahood. He thus left his physical body behind and traveled in a mind-made body (MANOMAYAKĀYA) to the AKANIṢṬHA heaven, where he received various consecrations and achieved buddhahood. He next descended to the summit of Mount SUMERU, where he taught the yogatantras. Finally, he returned to the world, inhabited his physical body, and then displayed to the world the well-known defeat of MĀRA and the achievement of buddhahood. ¶ Vairocana is also the name of one of the chief figures in the earlier dissemination (SNGA DAR) of Buddhism to Tibet, where he is known by his Tibetan pronunciation of Bai ro tsa na. He was one of the first seven Tibetans (SAD MI BDUN) to be ordained as Buddhist monks by the Indian master ŚĀNTARAKṢITA at the first Tibetan monastery, BSAM YAS. According to Tibetan accounts, he was sent by King KHRI SRONG LDE BTSAN to India to study Sanskrit and to gather texts and teachings. He is said to have received teachings of the "mind class" (SEMS SDE) and the "expanse class" (KLONG SDE) at BODHGAYĀ, before traveling to OḌḌIYĀNA, where he met the master ŚRĪSIṂHA, who gave him exoteric teachings during the day and instructed him secretly in the great completeness (RDZOGS CHEN) practices at night. Returning to Tibet, he followed the same program, instructing the king secretly in the "mind class" teachings at night. This raised suspicions, which led to his banishment to eastern Tibet. He was later allowed to return, at the request of VIMALAMITRA. He is renowned as one of the three major figures (along with PADMASAMBHAVA and Vimalamitra) in the dissemination of the rdzogs chen teachings in Tibet and translated many texts from Sanskrit into Tibetan; the manuscripts of some of his translations have been discovered at DUNHUANG. See also JÑĀNAMUṢṬI.

**Vairocanābhisaṃbodhi**. (S). See MAHĀVAIROCANĀBHISAṂBODHISŪTRA.

**Vairocanābhisaṃbodhitantra**. (S). See MAHĀVAIROCANĀBHISAṂBODHISŪTRA.

**Vairocanadharma**. (T. rnam snang gi chos). In Sanskrit, "features of VAIROCANA"; seven constituents that constitute the ideal posture for meditation: sitting in the adamantine position (VAJRAPARYAṄKA), casting the eyes down toward the tip of the nose, keeping the backbone straight, keeping the shoulders level, tucking in the chin, placing the tongue against the back of the upper teeth, placing the hands in the position of equipoise. The Tibetan translator (LO TSĀ BA) MAR PA, teacher of MI LA RAS PA, was a strong proponent of this meditation posture.

**Vaiśālī**. (P. Vesāli; T. Yangs pa can; C. Pisheli; J. Bishari; K. Pisari 毘舍離). A town approximately twenty-five miles (forty km.) to the northwest of modern-day Patna, in the state of Bihar, India. During the Buddha's lifetime, this was the capital of the Licchavis, which was part of the Vṛji republic. The Buddha first visited the city in the fifth year after his enlightenment and spent his last rains retreat (VARṢĀ) in the vicinity of Vaiśālī. The Buddha preached a number of important sūtras and established several rules of discipline in the city. The Buddha accepted the gift of a mango grove (the Āmrapālīvana) from the city's famous courtesan ĀMRAPĀLĪ. When the Buddha was en route from KAPILAVASTU to Vaiśālī, his stepmother MAHĀPRAJĀPATĪ and five hundred women shaved their heads and followed him. Upon arriving in the city, they requested and eventually received ordination as nuns (BHIKṢUṆĪ). Before departing on the journey that would end at KUŚINAGARĪ with his passage into PARINIRVĀṆA, the Buddha is said to have turned his body like an elephant for one final look at the city. ¶ Vaiśālī was also the location of the second Buddhist council (SAṂGĪTI; see COUNCIL, SECOND), held approximately one hundred years after the Buddha's PARINIRVĀṆA. Some seven hundred monks were said to have attended the council at Vālukārāma monastery, although the number is probably more of a representation of the council's significance rather than an exact number of monks in attendance. The importance of the second council lies in the sectarian division that occurred within the SAṂGHA either at the time of that council or directly thereafter. According to the traditional account, the monk YAŚAS entered Vaiśalī to visit the monks there and found that they were engaging in what he believed to be ten violations of the VINAYA code of conduct. When Yaśas criticized the Vaiśalī monks for these violations, he was rebuked and expelled from the SAṂGHA. Yaśas later returned with the monk ŚĀṆAKAVĀSIN, at which point the monk REVATA called the council and presided over it. After the senior monks ruled in Yaśas's favor, the saṃgha split into the two groups, the STHAVIRANIKĀYA (the "Order of the Elders," which included Revata and Yaśas) and the MAHĀSĀṂGHIKA (the "Members of the Great Assembly," which included probably the majority of monks, who opposed the ruling). By the beginning of the Common Era, the saṃgha had split into what is commonly called the eighteen MAINSTREAM BUDDHIST SCHOOLS, in reference to the multiple traditions that developed following the second council at Vaiśālī.

**vaiśāradya**. (P. vesārajja; T. mi 'jigs pa; C. wusuowei; J. mushoi; K. musooe 無所畏). In Sanskrit, "self-confidence," or "fearlessness"; one of the qualities of all buddhas, generally enumerated (with some variants) as four: (1) the confidence that he is fully enlightened with regard to all phenomena, (2) the confidence that he has destroyed all contamination, (3) the confidence that he has correctly identified all obstacles to liberation, and (4) the confidence that all marvelous qualities are achieved through the path.

**Vaiśravaṇa**. (P. Vessavaṇa; T. Rnam sras/Rnam thos kyi bu; C. Duowen tian/Pishamen tian; J. Tamonten/Bishamonten; K. Tamun ch'ŏn/Pisamun ch'ŏn 多聞天/毘沙門天). One of the four LOKAPĀLA, the kings of the four directions who reside on the four faces of Mount SUMERU. He is king of the north, and the northern continent of UTTARAKURU, and resides on the northern face of the central mountain, where he commands armies of YAKṢAS. He is described in the Pāli canon as a stream-enterer (see SROTAĀPANNA), who was a devotee of the Buddha and a protector of his monks. Despite having a life span of ninety thousand years, Vaiśravaṇa, like all Buddhist divinities (DEVA), will eventually die and be reborn elsewhere, with another being reborn as his successor. Vaiśravaṇa is associated with the Indian gods of wealth KUBERA and Jambhala; the three were once individual deities who came to be identified with each other. Vaiśravaṇa may have originated as a Central Asian deity, perhaps in the kingdom of KHOTAN, where he was believed to have been the progenitor of the royal lineage. He is the main interlocutor in several chapters of the SUVARṆAPRABHĀSOTTAMASŪTRA, which sets forth the duties of the lokapāla to the virtuous king and his state. His cult does not seem to have taken hold in China until the ninth century, which is the date of the earliest Chinese images of the divinity. A legend relates that during an invasion of Tang China from ANXI (viz., PARTHIA), the Chinese emperor enlisted the aid of AMOGHAVAJRA, who called upon Vaiśravaṇa to guard the city wall. By the middle of the Tang, images of the god and the other lokapālas were commonly placed at city gates. The cult of Vaiśravaṇa entered Japan by the Heian period, where, despite his presence in the esoteric tradition there, he took on the appearance of local gods and is regarded as a form of HACHIMAN. In Tibet, the conflation of Vaiśravaṇa, Kubera, Jambhala, and Pañcika is more complete than in East Asia. As a lokapāla, Vaiśravaṇa wears armor, carries a banner of victory, and holds a mongoose that is vomiting jewels (hence his popularity as a god of wealth).

**vaiyāpṛtya(kara)**. [alt. vaiyāpatya(kara)] (P. veyyāvaccakara; T. zhal ta pa; C. zhishi/zhongzhu; J. shitsuji/shushu; K. chipsa/chungju 執事/衆主). In Sanskrit, lit. "one who performs service," viz., an "agent"; an administrative or supervisory officer who serves as "agent" for the SAṂGHA in accepting donations from the laity and supervising the use of the financial items and valuables received by the monastery; this officer may also serve as a kind of personal assistant to the monks. The term vaiyāpṛtyakara appears in connection with the tenth rule of the "offenses involving forfeiture" (NIḤSARGIKA-PĀTAYANTIKA; P. nissaggiyapācittiya), where the "agent" is solicited to accept robe cloth on behalf of a monk; that agent may be either a Buddhist layman (UPĀSAKA) or an unordained monastic employee (ārāmika). In this role, the vaiyāpṛtyakara is closely related to the KALPIKĀRAKA, a lay "steward" or "surrogate," who receives donations on behalf of monks and converts them into appropriate requisites. There are also, however, references to ordained agents (vaiyāpṛtyakarabhikṣu), who supervise the storage of offerings as robes and other gifts on behalf of the monks until they are ready to use them. DRAVYA MALLAPUTRA was singled out by the Buddha as preeminent among his monk disciples in providing such service to the community of monks (saṅghasya veyyāvacca), specifically in apportioning lodging and distributing meals.

**vaiyavadānika**. (T. rnam par byang ba; C. qingjing; J. shōjō; K. ch'ŏngjŏng 清淨). In Sanskrit, an adjective formed from VYAVADĀNA, "purification" or "cleansing," contrasted with sāṃkleśika (from SAṂKLEŚA), meaning impurity, defilement, stain, or pollution. Dharmas are understood to operate from two distinct and opposite modes of causation that condition one's future—sāṃkleśika (or SAṂKLIṢṬA) dharmas leading to suffering and vaiyavadānika dharmas leading to the end of suffering. In the perfection of wisdom (PRAJÑĀPĀRAMITĀ) sūtras, 108 types of phenomena are declared to be empty (śūnya); they are divided into two broad categories, purification (vaiyavadānika) and defilement (saṃkliṣṭa), or the pure and the defiled. Fifty-five phenomena of the pure class are enumerated in the MAHĀYĀNA, including, for example, the six perfections (PĀRAMITĀ), the eighteen types of emptiness (ŚŪNYATĀ), the thirty-seven factors of enlightenment (BODHIPĀKṢIKADHARMA), and the eighteen unshared qualities of a buddha (ĀVEṆIKA[BUDDHA]DHARMA). The defiled class includes, for example, the five aggregates (SKANDHA), the six sense organs (INDRIYA), the six consciousnesses (VIJÑĀNA), and the twelve links of dependent origination (PRATĪTYASAMUTPĀDA). See also VYAVADĀNA.

**Vajirañāṇavarorasa**. (Thai. Wachirayanwarorot) (1860–1921). One of the most influential Thai monks of the late-nineteenth and early-twentieth centuries; his name (given in its Pāli form here) is also rendered in the Thai vernacular as Wachirayanwarorot [alt. Wachirayan Warot]. The son of King Mongkut (RĀMA IV), after a youth spent in royal luxury, he was ordained as a monk in 1879. He distinguished himself as a scholar of the Buddhist scriptures and in 1892 became abbot of WAT BOWONNIWET [alt. Wat Bovoranives; P. Pavaranivesa], the leading monastery of the THAMMAYUT (P. Dhammayuttika) order. In 1893, he became patriarch of the order and served as supreme patriarch (saṅgharāja; S. SAṂGHARĀJAN) of the Thai saṅgha (S. SAṂGHA) from 1910 until his death. A distinguished scholar of Pāli, he was the author of many textbooks, including the definitive Thai primer on the Pāli VINAYA tradition, the *Vinayamukha* ("Gateway to the Discipline"), which he wrote in an (unsuccessful) attempt to bring together the two major sects of Thai Buddhism, the Thammuyut and the MAHANIKAI. Vajirañāṇavarorasa also designed the modern monastic curriculum and reorganized the Thai ecclesiastical hierarchy. As an advisor to King Chulalongkorn (RĀMA V), he also sought to extend modern education into the provinces. Vajirañāṇavarorasa's autobiography is considered the first work of the genre in Thai vernacular literature.

**Vajirapāṇi**. (P). In Pāli, the name of a yakkha (S. YAKṢA) who is also sometimes identified with INDRA. See VAJRAPĀṆI.

**vajra**. (T. rdo rje; C. jingang; J. kongō; K. kŭmgang 金剛). In Sanskrit, "adamant," "diamond," or "thunderbolt"; a magical weapon and common symbol of power, indestructibility, and immutability, especially in tantric Buddhism, which is known as the vajra vehicle (VAJRAYĀNA). The term is also employed to describe consummate meditative experiences, such as the VAJROPAMASAMĀDHI, the "SAMĀDHI that is like a vajra." ¶ Vajra is also the name of the ritual scepter commonly employed in tantric liturgies. When used in conjunction with a bell, the vajra symbolizes UPĀYA and the bell symbolizes PRAJÑĀ, with the vajra held in the right hand and the bell in the left hand. There are several types of vajras used in tantric rituals, varying in both size and the number of "points" or prongs, usually ranging from one to nine on each side. The elements that constitute the vajra are given rich symbolic value. For example, in the case of a five-pointed vajra, when held vertically, the five lower points are said to represent either the five aggregates (SKANDHA) of mind and body or the five afflictions of desire, anger, ignorance, pride, and jealousy. These five are transmuted through tantric practice into the five buddhas (PAÑCATATHĀGATA), represented by the five upper points. These are transmuted through the knowledge of emptiness, symbolized by the sphere that unites the upper and lower parts of the vajra. In some tantric texts, vajra is also a term for phallus.

**Vajrabhairava**. (T. Rdo rje 'jigs byed; C. Buwei Jingang; J. Fui Kongō; K. P'ooe Kŭmgang 怖畏金剛). In Sanskrit, "Indestructibly Frightening"; a tantric deity associated with YAMĀNTAKA; both deities are considered to be wrathful forms of the bodhisattva MAÑJUŚRĪ. Vajrabhairava likely derives from Śaiva sources; Śiva is also called Bhairava. Vajrabhairava is usually black or blue in color, and can be depicted with one or as many as nine faces, and thirty-two arms. The main Vajrabhairava root tantra, classified as a father tantra (PITṚTANTRA) of the ANUTTARAYOGATANTRA class, is the *Śrīmadmahāvajrabhairavatantra*, also known as the *Saptakalpa* ("Vajrabhairava Root Tantra in Seven Chapters"); it is three hundred stanzas long and explicitly sets forth legitimate transformations of violence for altruistic purposes. It is said to have been brought from UḌḌIYĀNA by one Lalitavajra. The Tibetan Skyo tradition also asserts that the *Gtam rgyud kyi rtog pa* ("Legend chapter") is a root tantra. Besides Lalitavajra, the adept Śrīdhara is closely associated with the practice and dissemination of the tantra. In Tibet there are six lineages originating from Cog gru Shes rab bla ma, RWA LO TSĀ BA RDO RJE GRAGS PA (the most widespread and influential tradition), Skyo ston 'Od 'byung (1126–1200), Gnyos lo tsā ba, Ba ri lo tsā ba, and Mal gyo lo tsā ba Blo gros grags. These are known as the Zhang, Rwa, Skyo, Gnyos, Ba ri, and Mal traditions. The cult of Vajrabhairava is common to the three new translation (GSAR MA) sects of Tibet. The SA SKYA sect considers Vajrabhairava to be one of the four principal tantric deities, alongside HEVAJRA, GUHYASAMĀJA, and CAKRASAṂVARA. He holds a similar position in the DGE LUGS sect, together with Guhyasamāja and Cakrvasaṃvara. The main lineages of his introduction to Tibet are traced to ATIŚA DĪPAṂKARAŚRĪJÑĀNA, Mal Lo tsā ba, and RWA LO TSĀ BA. See also YAMĀNTAKA.

**Vajrabhairavatantra**. (S). See VAJRABHAIRAVA.

**Vajrabodhi**. (C. Jingangzhi; J. Kongōchi; K. Kŭmgangji 金剛智) (671–741). Indian ĀCĀRYA who played a major role in the introduction and translation in China of seminal Buddhist texts belonging to the esoteric tradition or MIJIAO (see MIKKYŌ and TANTRA); also known as Vajramati. His birthplace and family background are uncertain, although one source says that he was a south Indian native whose brāhmaṇa father served as a teacher of an Indian king. At the age of nine, he is said to have gone to the renowned Indian monastic university of NĀLANDĀ, where he studied various texts of both the ABHIDHARMA and MAHĀYĀNA traditions. Vajrabodhi also learned the different VINAYA recensions of the eighteen MAINSTREAM BUDDHIST SCHOOLS. It is said that Vajrabodhi spent the years 701–708 in southern India, where he received tantric initiation at the age of thirty-one from NĀGABODHI (d.u.), a south Indian MAHĀSIDDHA of the VAJRAŚEKHARA (see SARVATATHĀGATATATTVASAṂGRAHA) line. He later traveled to Sri Lanka and then to ŚRĪVIJAYA before sailing to China, eventually arriving in the eastern Tang capital of Luoyang in 720. In 721, Vajrabodhi and his famed disciple AMOGHAVAJRA arrived in the western capital of Chang'an. Under the patronage of Emperor Xuanzong (r. 712–756), Vajrabodhi and Amoghavajra translated the VAJRAŚEKHARASŪTRA and other related texts. Vajrabodhi devoted his energy and time to spreading tantric Buddhism by establishing the ABHIṢEKA or initiation platforms and performing esoteric rituals. In particular, Vajrabodhi was popular as a thaumaturge; his performance of the rituals for rainmaking and curing diseases gained him favor at the imperial court; he even gave tantric initiation to the Tang emperor Xuanzong. During his more than twenty years in China, Vajrabodhi introduced about twenty texts belonging to the Vajraśekhara textual line. Vajrabodhi attracted many disciples; the Silla monk HYECH'O (704–87), known for his travel record WANG O CH'ŎNCH'UK KUK CH'ŎN ("Record of a Journey to the Five Kingdoms of India"), also studied with him. The Japanese SHINGONSHŪ honors Vajrabodhi as the fifth of the eight patriarchs in its lineage, together with Nāgabodhi and Amoghavajra.

**vajrācārya**. (T. rdo rje slob dpon; C. jingang asheli/jingangshi; J. kongōajari/kongōshi; K. kŭmgang asari/kŭmgangsa 金剛阿闍梨/金剛師). In Sanskrit, "VAJRA master"; referring to a tantric GURU (BLA MA) who has mastered the tantric arts, received the appropriate initiations, and is qualified to confer initiations and dispense tantric teachings. He is traditionally listed as having ten qualities. ¶ The title vajrācārya is also awarded to a person who has received a specific set of initiations (ABHIṢEKA) in the ANUTTARAYOGATANTRA systems. Although numerous variations occur, the main sequence of initiations in KRIYĀTANTRA, CARYĀTANTRA, and YOGATANTRA are (1) the water initiation (udakābhiṣeka), (2) the crown initiation (mukuṭābhiṣeka), (3) the VAJRA initiation (vajrābhiṣeka), (4) the bell initiation (ghaṇṭābhiṣeka), and (5) the name initiation (nāmābhiṣeka). One who has received these initiations is regarded as a vajrācārya. In the yogatantras, an additional initiation, called the vajrācārya initiation (vajrācāryābhiṣeka), is bestowed. In the anuttarayoga systems, this set of five or six is often condensed into one, becoming the first of four initiations, called the vajrācārya initiation or the vase initiation (KALAŚĀBHIṢEKA). ¶ In the Newar Buddhism of Nepal, the name vajrācārya is also used by an endogamous caste of lay priests who perform a wide variety of rituals for the Buddhist community, including life-cycle rites, fire rituals, temple rituals, protective rites. They also perform tantric initiation for high-caste members of the Newar community. According to the anuttarayoga systems, one becomes a vajrācārya as a result of a series of initiations; in the Newar community, however, it is a hereditary category.

**Vajracchedikāprajñāpāramitāsūtra**. (T. Rdo rje gcod pa shes rab kyi pha rol tu phyin pa'i mdo; C. Jingang jing; J. Kongōkyō; K. Kŭmgang kyŏng 金剛經). In Sanskrit, the "Diamond-Cutter Perfection of Wisdom Sūtra"; known in English as the "Diamond Sūtra" (deriving from its popular abbreviated Chinese title *Jingang jing*, as above), one of the most famous, widely read, and commented upon of all MAHĀYĀNA sūtras, together with two others that are also known by their English titles, the SADDHARMAPUṆḌARĪKASŪTRA ("Lotus Sūtra") and the PRAJÑĀPĀRAMITĀHṚDAYASŪTRA ("Heart Sūtra"). The "Diamond Sūtra" was composed in Sanskrit, probably sometime between the second and fourth centuries CE. Despite its fame, much of its meaning remains elusive, beginning with the title. In Sanskrit, it is *Vajracchedikāprajñāpāramitā*. The Sanskrit term VAJRA refers to a kind of magical weapon, sometimes described as a thunderbolt or a discus, and is said to be hard and unbreakable, like a diamond or adamant. Thus, the title might be rendered into English as "The Perfection of Wisdom That Cuts like a Diamond/Thunderbolt." The sūtra opens with the Buddha residing in the JETAVANA with 1,250 monks and a large number of bodhisattvas. After returning from his begging round (PIṆḌAPĀTA) and eating his meal, the Buddha is approached by the great ARHAT SUBHŪTI, who asks him about the practice of the BODHISATTVA. The Buddha says that a bodhisattva must vow to lead all beings in the universe into NIRVĀṆA, while fully recognizing that there are in fact no beings to be led into nirvāṇa. "If, Subhūti, a bodhisattva were to have the (mis)perception (SAṂJÑĀ) of a self (ĀTMAN), a being (SATTVA), a living entity (JĪVA), or a person (PUDGALA), he is not to be called 'a bodhisattva.'" This is one of many famous statements in the sūtra, regarded by commentators as setting forth the doctrine of emptiness (although the technical term ŚŪNYATĀ does not appear in the sūtra), i.e., that all phenomena are falsely imagined to have a self, a soul, and an "own-being," qualities that they, in fact, lack. Any meritorious deed, from the giving of a gift to the vow to free all beings, is not an authentic bodhisattva deed if it is tainted with the (mis)perception (saṃjñā) of a sign (NIMITTA) of selfhood: thus the perfection of the act of charity (DĀNAPĀRAMITĀ) means that true bodhisattva giving occurs when there is no conception of there being a donor, recipient, or gift—for that kind of giving would produce immeasurable merit. The Buddha asks Subhūti whether the Buddha is to be seen through the possession of the thirty-two physical marks of a superman (MAHĀPURUṢALAKṢAṆA) that adorn his body. Subhūti says that he is not, because what the Buddha has described as the possession of marks (LAKṢAṆA) is in fact the nonpossession of no-marks. This formula of question and response, with the correct answer being, "A is in fact not A, therefore it is called A" is repeated throughout the text. The sūtra is not simply a radical challenge to the ordinary conception of the world, of language, and of thought; it is also a polemical Mahāyāna sūtra, seeking, like other such sūtras, to declare its supremacy and to promise rewards to those who exalt it. It is noteworthy that here, as in many other perfection of wisdom (PRAJÑĀPĀRAMITĀ) sūtras, the Buddha's interlocutor is not a bodhisattva, but an arhat, the wise Subhūti, suggesting that even those who have completed the path to nirvāṇa still have more to learn. The Buddha predicts that this sūtra will be understood far into the future, even into the final five hundred years that the Buddha's teaching remains in the world. At that time, anyone who has even a moment of faith in this sūtra will be honored by millions of buddhas. Indeed, even now, long before this point in the distant future, anyone who would teach just four lines of this sūtra to others would earn incalculable merit. In a statement that appears in other perfection of wisdom sūtras, the Buddha declares, "On whatever piece of ground one will proclaim this sūtra, that piece of ground will become an object of worship. That piece of ground will become for the world together with its gods, humans, and demigods a true shrine to be revered and circumambulated." Scholars have seen in this statement the possibility that the perfection of wisdom sūtras were something of a "cult of the book," in which the sūtra itself was worshipped, serving as a substitute for more traditional sites of worship, such as reliquaries (STŪPA). The sūtra suggests that such practices were not always condoned by others; the Buddha goes on to say that those who worship the sūtra will be ridiculed for doing so, but by suffering ridicule they will destroy the great stores of negative KARMAN accumulated over many lifetimes. The Buddha's exhortations seem to have been taken to heart. The recitation and copying of the sūtra was widely practiced across Asia; many copies of the sūtra were discovered at DUNHUANG, and the earliest printed book in the world is a xylographic print of the Chinese translation of the *Vajracchedikāprajñāpāramitā* dated May 11, 868, that was found in the Dunhuang cache. On a rock cliff on the Chinese sacred mountain of Taishan, there is a massive carving of the *Vajracchedikāprajñāpāramitā* covering some 2,100 Sinographs in 21,000 square feet (2,000 sq. m.). Miracle tales of the benefits of reciting and copying the sūtra were also told across Asia. The *Vajracchedikāprajñāpāramitā* also played an important role in the CHAN traditions of East Asia: e.g., it was the scripture that the fifth patriarch HONGREN expounded to HUINENG, bringing him to enlightenment and enabling Huineng to be his successor as the sixth patriarch (LIUZU) of Chan.

**Vajraḍākatantra**. (T. Rdo rje mkha' 'gro rgyud). A YOGINĪTANTRA of the ANUTTARAYOGATANTRA class, named after the deity Vajraḍāka ("Vajra Hero"), a form of VAJRASATTVA with four faces and four arms. It is counted as one of the five explanatory tantras (S. vyākhyātantra; T. bshad rgyud) of the CAKRASAṂVARATANTRA. The text is employed in Tibet especially for its instructions on the performance of fire (HOMA) rituals.

**Vajradhara**. [alt. Vajradhāra] (T. Rdo rje 'chang; C. Jingangchi; J. Kongōji; K. Kŭmgangji 金剛持). "Vajra Holder"; an important buddha of the tantric systems, where he appears in some texts as an ĀDIBUDDHA (primordial buddha). He is closely related to VAJRAPĀṆI; indeed, Vajrapāṇi and Vajradhara may have originally been two names for the same deity (the Chinese translations of the two deities' names are the same). Vajradhara is the principal deity in many father-class tantras and is the chief buddha for the MAHĀMUDRĀ traditions. Vajradhara is said to have revealed the MAHĀMUDRĀ teachings to TILOPA; they were then transmitted in succession to NĀROPA, then to MAR PA, and then to MI LA RAS PA. Vajradhara is sometimes referred to as the sixth buddha, representing the quintessence of the five buddhas (PAÑCATATHĀGATA) and the five buddha families. In Tibetan Buddhism, he is one of two buddhas considered as both a primordial buddha (ādibuddha) and as a DHARMAKĀYA; the other is the buddha SAMANTABHADRA, the primordial buddha of RNYING MA. Vajradhara is the primordial buddha of the three new, or GSAR MA, sects, SA SKYA, BKA' BRGYUD, and DGE LUGS. Vajradhara is typically depicted as dark blue, with one head and two arms, dressed as a SAṂBHOGAKĀYA, seated in VAJRAPARYAṄKA, holding a VAJRA in each hand (or a vajra in his right and a bell in his left), which are crossed at his chest in the VAJRAHŪṂKĀRA pose. He is sometimes depicted surrounded by the eighty-four MAHĀSIDDHAs. When he is depicted with a consort, she is usually VAJRAVĀRĀHĪ. See also FEILAIFENG.

**vajradhātu**. (S). See KONGŌKAI.

**vajrahūṃkāra**. (T. rdo rje hūṃ mdzad). Sanskrit term for a position found in tantric iconography, sometimes called the "posture of embracing," in which the hands of the deity (often holding a VAJRA and a bell) are crossed at the chest. If the deity is in sexual embrace with a consort, the hands are crossed behind the consort, embracing her. If there is no consort, the hands are crossed over the chest of the deity.

**vajrakaṇā**. (T. rdo rje gzegs ma). In Sanskrit, lit. "diamond slivers"; a term used to describe one of the chief reasonings used by NĀGĀRJUNA in the MŪLAMADHYAMAKAKĀRIKĀ. A critique of production (UTPĀDA), it argues that a given thing does not intrinsically exist because of not being produced (1) from itself, (2) from something that is intrinsically different from itself, (3) from something that is both itself and intrinsically different from itself, or (4) without cause.

**Vajrakīlaya**. (T. Rdo rje phur pa). In Sanskrit, "Vajra Dagger," a tantric buddha worshipped primarily by the RNYING MA and BKA' BRGYUD sects of Tibetan Buddhism. He is the deification of the KĪLA (see PHUR PA), the ritual dagger used in tantric ceremonies. In the rituals involving the use of the kīla, the tantric dagger is typically used to subdue a ritual site, to subjugate the local demon by pinning him or her to the ground; the MAṆḌALA is thus planted and established on top of the offending demon. The dagger may be stabbed into a three-sided box, the triangle representing the violent tantric activity of liberation, or into an effigy. As a deity, Vajrakīlaya originally held the same duties as the ritual dagger: to protect the borders of ritual space and to pin down and destroy enemies, human or otherwise. This tradition may derive in part from the ancient Indian myth of Indrakīla, in which the serpent Vṛtra is pinned and stabilized by a mythic "peg" (kīla). Vajrakīlaya is found in the major early tantra systems as well as the GUHYASAMĀJATANTRA and the SARVATATHĀGATATATTVASAṂGRAHA, which contains his mantra and places him in the center of a MAṆḌALA, although throughout his status is inferior to that of the buddhas and bodhisattvas. It is only in the Vajrakīlaya tantras that the deity attains the status of a buddha. These texts are reputed to be eighth-century translations from Indic languages, transmitted in Tibet by PADMASAMBHAVA. The tantras form a substantial section of the RNYING MA'I RGYUD 'BUM, but BU STON rejected the Indian origin of the tantras and left them out of the BKA' 'GYUR. Defenders of the tradition cite the fact that 'BROG MI SHĀKYA YE SHES wrote that he saw the eight-syllable Vajrakīla MANTRA at the BODHGAYĀ STŪPA. In addition, SA SKYA PAṆḌITA discovered a Sanskrit fragment of the *Vajrakīlamūlatantrakhaṇḍa* at BSAM YAS, and ŚĀKYAŚRĪBHADRA confirmed that the cycle had existed in India. Although no East Asian tradition of Vajrakīlaya exists, some scholars have suggested an identification with Vajrakumāra; tantras concerning this deity were brought to China in the eighth century by AMOGHAVAJRA, but this identification is disputed. Vajrakīlaya is wrathful, with three faces with three eyes each, and six or more hands holding various instruments in addition to the kīla. He is said to dispel obstacles to progress on the path to enlightenment and to the swift attainment of both mundane and supramundane goals.

**vajrakula**. (T. rdo rje rigs; C. jingang bu; J. kongōbu; K. kŭmgang pu 金剛部). In Sanskrit, "VAJRA family" or "vajra lineage"; one of the three or five tantric lineages. In the three-lineage (TRIKULA) system, the lineages are the vajra lineage, the lotus lineage (PADMAKULA), and the buddha lineage (BUDDHAKULA). This system appears in such works as the MAHĀVAIROCANĀBHISAṂBODHISŪTRA and the SUSIDDHIKARASŪTRA. In the five-lineage (PAÑCAKULA) system, found in the GUHYASAMĀJA and other ANUTTARAYOGATANTRAS, the five are the vajra lineage, the lotus lineage, the jewel lineage (RATNAKULA), the action lineage (KARMAKULA), and the tathāgata lineage (TATHĀGATAKULA). The buddha associated with the vajra lineage is AKṢOBHYA or VAJRASATTVA. See also MAÑJUŚRĪKĪRTI; ŚAMBHALA. Each of the five families is associated with one of the five SKANDHAs, five wisdoms (JÑĀNA), five afflictions (KLEŚA), five elements, and five colors. For the vajra family, these are the consciousnss (VIJÑĀNA) skandha, the mirrorlike wisdom (ĀDARŚAJÑĀNA), the affliction of anger, the element water, and the color white.

**Vajrapāṇi**. (P. Vajirapāṇi; T. Phyag na rdo rje; C. Jingangshou pusa; J. Kongōshu bosatsu; K. Kŭmgangsu posal 金剛手菩薩). In Sanskrit, "Holder of the VAJRA"; an important bodhisattva in the MAHĀYĀNA and VAJRAYĀNA traditions, who appears in both peaceful and wrathful forms. In the Pāli suttas, he is a YAKṢA (P. yakkha) guardian of the Buddha. It is said that whoever refuses three times to respond to a reasonable question from the Buddha would have his head split into pieces on the spot; carrying out this punishment was Vajrapāṇi's duty. In such circumstances, Vajrapāṇi, holding his cudgel, would be visible only to the Buddha and to the person who was refusing to answer the question; given the frightening vision, the person would inevitably then respond. Vajrapāṇi is sometimes said to be the wrathful form of ŚAKRA, who promised to offer the Buddha protection if the Buddha would teach the dharma; he thus accompanies the Buddha as a kind of bodyguard on his journeys to distant lands. Vajrapāṇi is commonly depicted in GANDHĀRA sculpture, flanking the Buddha and holding a cudgel. In the early Mahāyāna sūtras, Vajrapāṇi is referred to as a yakṣa servant of the bodhisattvas, as in the AṢṬASĀHASRIKĀPRAJÑĀPĀRAMITĀ. In the SUVARṆAPRABHĀSOTTAMASŪTRA, he is called the "general of the yakṣas" (yakṣasenādhipati), and is praised as a protector of followers of the Buddha. In the SADDHARMAPUṆḌARĪKASŪTRA, AVALOKITEŚVARA explains that one of the forms that he assumes to convert sentient beings is as Vajrapāṇi. In later Mahāyāna and early tantric Buddhism, Vajrapāṇi becomes a primary speaker in important sūtras and tantras, as well as a principal protagonist in them, and comes to be listed as one of the "eight close sons" (*UPAPUTRA), the principal bodhisattvas. In the MAÑJUŚRĪMŪLAKALPA, as leader of the vajra family (VAJRAKULA), he flanks ŚĀKYAMUNI in the MAṆḌALA. In the SARVATATHĀGATATATTVASAṂGRAHA, his transition from "general of the yakṣas" to "the supreme lord of all tathāgatas" is played out through his subjugation of Maheśvara (Śiva). At the command of the buddha VAIROCANA, Vajrapāṇi suppresses all of the worldly divinities of the universe and brings them to the summit of Mount SUMERU, where they seek refuge in the three jewels (RATNATRAYA). Only Maheśvara refuses to submit to the Buddha. Through Vajarpāṇi's recitation of a MANTRA, Maheśvara loses his life, only to be reincarnated in another world system, where he eventually achieves buddhahood. Vajrapāṇi's yakṣa origins continue in his wrathful aspects, most common in Tibet, such as the three-eyed Caṇḍa Vajrapāṇi. It is in this form that he is part of a popular triad with Avalokiteśvara and MAÑJUŚRĪ known as the "protectors of the three families" (T. RIGS GSUM MGON PO). These three bodhisattvas are said to be the physical manifestation of the wisdom (Mañjuśrī), compassion (Avalokiteśvara), and power (Vajrapāṇi) of all the buddhas. Vajrapāni is also said to be the bodhisattva emanation of the buddha AKṢOBHYA and the chief bodhisattva of the vajra family. He himself has numerous forms and emanations, including Mahābāla (who may have developed from his early attendant Vajrapuruṣa), Vajrasattva, Vajradhara, Vajrahūṃkāra, Ucchuṣma, Bhūtaḍāmara, and Trailokyavijaya. Vajrapāṇi is closely related especially to VAJRADHARA, and indeed Vajradhara and Vajrapāṇi may have originally been two names for the same deity (the Chinese translations of the two deities' names are the same). Vajrapāṇi's MANTRA is oṃ vajrapāṇi hūṃ phaṭ. He is also known as Guhyakādhipati, or "Lord of the Secret." The secret (guhyaka) originally referred to a class of yakṣas that he commanded, but expanded in meaning to include secret knowledge and mantras. Vajrapāṇi is the protector of mantras and those who recite them, and is sometimes identified as the bodhisattva responsible for the collection, recitation, and protection of the VIDYĀDHARAPIṬAKA.

**vajraparyaṅka**. (T. rdo rje skyil krung; C. jingang jiafuzuo; J. kongōkafuza; K. kŭmgang kabujwa 金剛跏趺坐). In

Sanskrit, "VAJRA posture"; a seated position, often known (mistakenly) as the "lotus posture" in English (see discussion below), in which the left foot rests on the right thigh and the right foot rests on top on the left thigh. The Sanskrit name is said to derive from the stability and indestructibility of the posture, which is like a vajra. ŚĀKYAMUNI is said to have adopted this posture prior to his enlightenment experience under the BODHI TREE, and images of the historical buddha, as well as other enlightened figures, are commonly depicted in this position. Widely adopted as a basis for the practice of seated meditation throughout the Buddhist world, the vajraparyaṅka is occasionally known simply as the "meditation posture." It is often confused with the PADMĀSANA (lotus posture), where the positions of the left and right feet are reversed; this position is predominantly used in Hindu forms of yoga. See also ĀSANA.

**Vajraputra**. [alt. Vajrīputra] (T. Rdo rje mo'i bu; C. Fasheluofuduoluo; J. Batsujarahotsutara; K. Pŏlsarabultara 伐闍羅弗多羅). The Sanskrit name of the eighth of the sixteen ARHAT elders (ṢOḌAŚASTHAVIRA), who were charged by the Buddha with protecting his dispensation until the advent of the next buddha, MAITREYA. He resides in Bolanu zhou (the Sanskrit transcription of a region said to translate into Chinese as "reverence"), with 1,100 disciples. In the Chinese tradition, Vajraputra is said to have been a hunter who kept the precept against killing after he was ordained. Once he attained arhatship, two lion cubs came to him in appreciation for his efforts to stop the killing of animals. Vajraputra constantly brought the two cubs with him wherever he went after that, thus earning the nickname "Laughing Lions Arhat." Not long after the Buddha's PARINIRVĀṆA, Vajraputra is said to have attended a sermon ĀNANDA was delivering to some local villagers. As he listened to Ānanda speak, Vajraputra realized that Ānanda was not yet enlightened, and encouraged him to continue with his meditation deep in the forest. This goad was said to have been vital to Ānanda's spiritual growth. In CHANYUE GUANXIU's standard Chinese depiction, Vajraputra is portrayed with aquiline nose and deep-set eyes, sitting on a rock, his upper body bare, with both arms crossing over his left knee, and palms hanging down. He sits leaning slightly to the right, as if reading a sūtra that sits next to him on the rock.

**vajrasamādhi**. (S). See VAJROPAMASAMĀDHI.

***Vajrasamādhisūtra**. (S). See KŬMGANG SAMMAE KYŎNG.

**vajrāsana**. (T. rdo rje gdan; C. jingang zuo; J. kongōza; K. kŭmgangjwa 金剛座). In Sanskrit, "diamond seat," or "vajra throne." The term vajrāsana has three main denotations: the seat under the BODHI TREE where ŚĀKYAMUNI achieved enlightenment; a synonym for the VAJRAPARYAṄKA posture; and, especially in Tibetan texts, the designation for the site of Śākyamuni's enlightenment and hence, more generally, BODHGAYĀ. See BODHIMAṆḌA.

**Vajrasattva**. (T. Rdo rje sems dpa'; C. Jingang saduo; J. Kongōsatta; K. Kŭmgang sal'ta 金剛薩埵). In Sanskrit, lit. "VAJRA Being"; a tantric deity widely worshipped as both an ĀDIBUDDHA and a buddha of purification. Vajrasattva is sometimes identified as a sixth buddha in the PAÑCATATHĀGATA system, such as in the SARVATATHĀGATATATTVASAṂGRAHA, where he is also identical to VAJRAPĀṆI. Vajrasattva also occasionally replaces AKṢOBHYA in the same system, and so has been considered an emanation of that buddha. As an ādibuddha, he is identical with VAJRADHARA. He is also one of the sixteen bodhisattvas of the vajradhātumaṇḍala. In the trikula system, an early tantric configuration, Vajrasattva is the buddha of the VAJRAKULA, with VAIROCANA the buddha of the TATHĀGATAKULA and Avalokiteśvara the head of the PADMAKULA. East Asian esoteric Buddhism considers Vajrasattva to be the second patriarch of the esoteric teachings; VAIROCANA taught them directly to Vajrasattva, who passed them to NĀGĀRJUNA, who passed them to VAJRABODHI/VAJRAMATI, who taught them to AMOGHAVAJRA, who brought them to China in the eighth century. In Tibet, worship of Vajrasattva is connected to YOGATANTRA and ANUTTARAYOGATANTRA, such as the twenty-fifth chapter of the *Abhidhanottaratantra*, in which he is known as the Heruka Vajrasattva. He is particularly famous in Tibet for his role in a practice of confession and purification in which one repeats a hundred thousand times the hundred-syllable MANTRA of Vajrasattva. These repetitions (with the attendant visualization) are a standard preliminary practice (T. SNGON 'GRO) required prior to receiving tantric instructions. The mantra is: oṃ vajrasattva samayam anupālaya vajrasattva tvenopatiṣṭha dṛḍho me bhava sutoṣyo me bhava supoṣyo me bhava anurakto me bhava sarvasiddhiṃ me prayaccha sarvakarmasu ca me cittaṃ śreyaḥ kuru hūṃ ha ha ha ha hoḥ bhagavan sarvatathāgatavajra mā me muñca vajrī bhava mahāsamayasattva āḥ hūṃ. Unlike many mantras that seem to have no semantic meaning, Vajrasattva's mantra may be translated as: "Oṃ Vajrasattva, keep your pledge. Vajrasattva, reside in me. Make me firm. Make me satisfied. Fulfill me. Make me compassionate. Grant me all powers. Make my mind virtuous in all deeds. hūṃ ha ha ha ha ho. All the blessed tathāgatas, do not abandon me, make me indivisible. Great pledge being. āḥ hūṃ."

***Vajraśekharasūtra**. (T. Rdo rje rtse mo; C. Jingangding jing; J. Kongōchōkyō; K. Kŭmgangjŏng kyŏng 金剛頂經). In Sanskrit, "Sūtra on Vajra Peak"; also called the *Vajraśekharatantra*, the reconstructed Sanskrit title derived from the Chinese translations of the first chapter of the SARVATATHĀGATATATTVASAṂGRAHA made by VAJRABODHI and AMOGHAVAJRA during the Tang dynasty. The full text of the *Sarvatathāgatatattvasaṃgraha* was not translated into Chinese until Dānapāla completed his version in 1015 CE. In addition to these translations, a number of associated ritual manuals and commentaries containing the title "Vajraśekhara" are included in the Chinese Buddhist canon. The *Vajraśekhara* refers to a composite text of eighteen individual scriptures in a hundred thousand stanzas said to have been lost before it reached China. Based in part on a summary of the individual sūtras and tantras comprising the text that Amoghavajra composed, some scholars have speculated that the complete *Vajraśekhara*, in whatever form it originally took, represented the first esoteric Buddhist canon, beginning with the *Sarvatathāgatatattvasaṃgraha* and including the GUHYASAMĀJATANTRA, among other works. Other scholars have questioned the claim that the text ever existed at all. The *Vajraśekhara* is one of two (or three) central texts in the esoteric tradition (MIKKYŌ) of Japan. In Tibet, the title *Vajraśekaratantra* (*Rgyud rdo rje rtse mo*) is the name of an explanatory yoga tantra connected to the *Sarvatathāgatatattvasaṃgraha*, which is used as a major source in Tibetan delineations of the tantric vows.

**Vajravārāhī**. (T. Rdo rje phag mo). One of the most common forms of VAJRAYOGINĪ, an important female tantric deity associated especially with the CAKRASAṂVARATANTRA of the ANUTTARAYOGATANTRA class, popular in all sects of Tibetan Buddhism, where she is a consort of the central deity. Vārāhī means sow, referring to the goddess's characteristic porcine head protruding from the right side of her face. She likely derives from the Hindu goddess Vārāhī, depicted with a head of a boar; she is the counterpart of Vārāha, the incarnation of Viṣṇu who took the form of a boar. In the case of Vajravārāhī, she is typically (although not invariably) depicted with a human face but with a boar's head (sometimes quite small) visible on the right side of her face, contributing in part to her wrathful aspect. She is usually depicted as red in color, naked in a dancing pose, standing on the body of Bhairava. She holds a cleaver in her right hand and skull cup in her left, and is adorned with a garland of fifty severed heads. Beginning perhaps as one of a number of wrathful YOGINĪs situated as protectors on the outer circles of the MAṆḌALA, she moved toward the center as one of the consorts of the central deity in the HEVAJRATANTRA and became the main consort of HERUKA in the Cakrasaṃvara cycle, where she also appears without a consort as the "sole heroine" (ekavirā) in the center of the maṇḍala.

**Vajravidāraṇadhāraṇī**. (T. Rdo rje rnam par 'joms pa shes bya ba'i gzungs; C. Rangxiang jingang tuoluoni jing; J. Kongō saisai darani/Esō kongō daranikyō; K. Kŭmgang ch'oeswae tarani/Yangsang kŭmgang tarani kyŏng 金剛摧碎陀羅尼/壤相金剛陀羅尼經). Lit., "Dhāraṇī of the Adamantine Pulverizer"; a DHĀRAṆĪ scripture probably composed sometime between the late-seventh and early-eighth centuries, which enjoyed great popularity in India and Tibet. There are two late Chinese translations, one by Maitrībhadra (C. Cixian, fl. tenth century), the other by the central Asian monk Shaluoba (1259–1314). There are a few Tibetan commentaries on the text attributed to such Indian tantric Buddhist masters who went to Tibet as ŚĀNTARAKṢITA (725–788), Buddhaguhya (fl. eighth century), and PADMASAMBHAVA (fl. eighth century). The text states that VAJRAPĀṆI's wrathful form strikes fear into all sentient beings, which stops them from performing evil actions, destroys their ignorance and defilements, and protects them from any suffering. The text also lists various other practical benefits that accrue from reciting it, such as curing illness, longevity, and good fortune, and recommends reciting it between twenty-one and a hundred times. Due to its popularity, the *Vajravidāraṇadhāraṇī* itself became deified, and Vajravidāraṇa was worshipped as one of the manifestations of Vajrapāṇi.

**vajrayāna**. (T. rdo rje theg pa; C. jingang sheng; J. kongōjō; K. kŭmgang sŭng 金剛乘). In Sanskrit, "adamantine vehicle" or "thunderbolt vehicle"; a general term used to refer to tantric Buddhism, especially in distinction to HĪNAYĀNA and MAHĀYĀNA. The vajrayāna, however, is considered by its adherents to be not a separate vehicle but a form of the Mahāyāna; such adherents would speak instead of the three vehicles (TRIYĀNA) of hīnayāna, PĀRAMITĀYĀNA, and vajrayāna, with the latter two referring respectively to an exoteric and an esoteric path by which the bodhisattva achieves buddhahood, with the pāramitāyāna set forth in the Mahāyāna sūtras and the vajrayāna set forth in the tantras. Traditional etymologies of the term typically evoke the VAJRA to refer to the unbreakable and indivisible quality of two factors, typically method (UPĀYA) and wisdom (PRAJÑĀ). See TANTRA.

**vajrayoga**. (T. rdo rje rnal 'byor). In Sanskrit, "adamantine yoga"; a system of yogic practice associated with the KĀLACAKRATANTRA, as transmitted in Tibet by Gyi jo Lo tsā ba Zla ba'i 'od-zer, the tantra's earliest translator, during the eleventh century. It is counted as one of the "eight conveyances that are lineages of achievement" (sgrub brgyud shing rta chen po brgyad).

**Vajrayoginī**. (T. Rdo rje rnal 'byor ma). The most important of the ḌĀKIṆĪ in the VAJRAYĀNA, associated especially with the "mother tantras" (MĀTṚTANTRA) of the ANUTTARAYOGA class. She is also the most important of the female YI DAM. Her visualization is central to many tantric SĀDHANAs, especially in the practice of GURUYOGA, in which the meditator imagines himself or herself in the form of Vajrayoginī in order to receive the blessings of the GURU. She is also visualized in GCOD and GTUM MO practice. Her worship seems to originate with the CAKRASAṂVARATANTRA and is popular in all sects of Tibetan Buddhism. Vajrayoginī plays a special role in the "six yogas of NĀROPA" (NĀ RO CHOS DRUG), where she is known as Nā ro mkha' spyod ma (Kachöma). She is closely associated with VAJRAVĀRĀHĪ, the consort of CAKRASAṂVARA. In her most common form, she stands in the ĀLĪḌHA posture, holding a KAṬVĀṄGA and a skull cup.

**vajropamasamādhi**. (T. rdo rje lta bu'i ting nge 'dzin; C. jingang yu ding/jingang sanmei; J. kongōyujō/kongōzanmai/kongōsanmai; K. kŭmgang yu chŏng/kŭmgang sammae 金剛

喩定/金剛三昧). In Sanskrit, "adamantine-like concentration," sometimes called simply the "adamantine concentration" (VAJRASAMĀDHI); a crucial stage in both SARVĀSTIVĀDA ABHIDHARMA and MAHĀYĀNA presentations of the path (MĀRGA). The experience of vajropamasamādhi initiates the "path of completion" (NIṢṬHĀMĀRGA) or the "path where no further training is necessary" (AŚAIKṢAMĀRGA), the fifth and final stage of the five-path schema (PAÑCAMĀRGA). The arising of this concentration initiates a process of abandonment (PRAHĀṆA), which ultimately leads to the permanent destruction of even the subtlest and most persistent of the ten fetters (SAṂYOJANA), resulting in the "knowledge of cessation" (KṢAYAJÑĀNA) and, in some presentations, an accompanying "knowledge of nonproduction" (ANUTPĀDAJÑĀNA), viz., the knowledges that the fetters are destroyed and can never again recur. At that point, depending on the path that has been followed, the meditator becomes an ARHAT or a buddha. Because it is able to destroy the very worst of the fetters, this concentration is said to be "like adamant" (vajropama). The vajropamasamādhi thus involves both an "uninterrupted path" (ĀNANTARYAMĀRGA) and a path of liberation (VIMUKTIMĀRGA) and serves as the crucial transition point in completing the path and freeing oneself from SAṂSĀRA. In the MAHĀPARNIRVĀṆASŪTRA, this special type of concentration is closely associated with seeing the buddha-nature (BUDDHADHĀTU; FOXING) and achieving the complete, perfect enlightenment (ANUTTARASAMYAKSAṂBODHI) of the buddhas.

**Vakkali**. (S. *Vālkali?; C. Pojiali; J. Bakari; K. Pagari 婆迦梨). Pāli proper name of an eminent ARHAT declared by the Buddha to be foremost among his monk disciples who who aspire through faith (ŚRADDHĀDHIMUKTA, P. saddhādhimutta). According to the Pāli account, he was a learned brāhmaṇa from Sāvatthi (S. ŚRĀVASTĪ) who became a devoted follower of the Buddha from the very moment he saw him. Because of his extraordinary faith-cum-affection, Vakkali was so enraptured by the Buddha that he used to follow him around. He took ordination so that he could always remain close to the Buddha; when he was not in the Buddha's presence, he spent his time thinking about him. The Buddha admonished him not to be infatuated with the corruptible body of the Buddha, stating that he who sees the dharma, sees the Buddha. Vakkali could not be dissuaded, however, and finally the Buddha ordered him out of his presence, in an attempt to shock (saṃvega) Vakkali into awakening. Accounts differ as to what happened next. According to one story, Vakkali was greatly saddened and resolved to hurl himself from the top of Vulture Peak (GṚDHRAKŪṬA). Knowing this, the Buddha appeared to him and recited a stanza. Filled with joy, Vakkali rose into the air and attained arhatship. In another account, Vakkali retired to Vulture Peak to practice meditation but fell ill from his arduous, but ultimately unsuccessful, efforts. The Buddha visited him to encourage him, and Vakkali finally attained arhatship. The best-known account states that Vakkali fell ill on his way to visit the Buddha. The Buddha told Vakkali that he was assured of liberation and that there was therefore nothing for him to regret. The Buddha departed and proceeded to Vulture Peak, while Vakkali made his way to Kālasīla. At Vulture Peak, the divinities informed the Buddha that Vakkali was about to pass away. The Buddha sent a message telling him not to fear. Vakkali responded that he had no desire for the body or the aggregates, and committed suicide with a knife. When the Buddha saw his body, he declared that Vakkali had attained NIRVĀṆA and had escaped MĀRA's grasp. The commentary to the last account remarks that, at the moment of his suicide, Vakkali was in fact deluded in thinking he was already an ARHAT, hence his evil intention of killing himself. Even so, the pain of the blade so shocked his mind that in the moments just before his death he put forth the effort necessary to attain arhatship. See also ŚRADDHĀ.

**vākkarman**. (P. vacīkamma; T. ngag gi las; C. yuye; J. gogō; K. ŏŏp 語業). In Sanskrit, lit. "verbal action"; verbal deeds that create wholesome or unwholesome effects in the future. Speech (vāk) is one of the three conduits or "doors" (TRIDVĀRA) through which action (KARMAN) occurs, along with the body (KĀYA) and the mind (CITTA). According to the ABHIDHARMA, physical actions, words, and thoughts are all capable of producing karman that is either virtuous (KUŚALA) or unvirtuous (AKUŚALA). Unvirtuous verbal deeds include lying, divisive speech, harsh speech, and senseless speech. Virtuous verbal deeds include speaking truthfully, speaking harmoniously, speaking kindly, and speaking sensibly.

**Vakula**. (S). See BAKKULA.

**Valabhī**. [alt. Vallabhī]. Sanskrit name of a city in western India (in the modern state of Gujarat) that flourished under the Maitraka kings (475–775) and was the site of an important Buddhist monastery. Said to rival NĀLANDĀ in fame, Valabhī was known especially as a center of ŚRĀVAKAYĀNA learning, with each of the MAINSTREAM BUDDHIST SCHOOLS represented. However, the MAHĀYĀNA was also taught there, as were Brahmanical and secular subjects. Two important figures of the YOGĀCĀRA school, GUṆAMATI and STHIRAMATI, were said to have held prominent positions at Valabhī before they proceeded to Nālandā. In the late seventh century, XUANZANG found approximately six thousand monks residing there in about a hundred monastic buildings.

**vālavyajana**. (P. vījanī; T. rlung yab; C. fuzi; J. hossu; K. pulcha 拂子). In Sanskrit, "fly whisk" or "chowrie"; a yak-tail fan that Buddhist monks used to keep flies and mosquitoes away, also called a cāmara. The chowrie is presumed to have originally been used among adherents of the JAINA tradition to shoo away flies without injuring them, and it came to be used widely throughout India. In the Chinese CHAN tradition, the fly whisk (which in East Asia is usually made from a horse tail) became a symbol of the office or privilege of a Chan master and is one of the accoutrements he traditionally holds in formal portraits. "Taking up the fly whisk" (BINGFU) is, by metonymy, a term used to refer to a formal Chan sermon delivered by a master. See also FUZI.

**Vallabhī**. See VALABHĪ.

**Vallée Poussin, Louis de la**. See LA VALLÉE POUSSIN, LOUIS DE.

**Vammikasutta**. (C. Yiyu jing; J. Giyukyō; K. Ŭiyu kyŏng 蟻喩經). In Pāli, the "Anthill" or "Termite Mound Discourse," the twenty-third sutta (SŪTRA) contained in the MAJJHIMANIKĀYA (two separate SARVĀSTIVĀDA recensions appear in the Chinese translation of the SAṂYUKTĀGAMA, as well as an unidentified recension in the Chinese translation of the EKOTTARĀGAMA); preached by the Buddha at Sāvatthi (S. ŚRĀVASTĪ) in connection with a riddle presented to him by the monk Kumāra-Kassapa (S. KUMĀRA-KĀŚYAPA). Kumāra-Kassapa had been approached by a divinity (DEVA), who gave him a riddle comprising fifteen questions that he asked to be delivered to the Buddha for solution. The Buddha solved the riddle, identifying its cryptic elements as symbols and metaphors for points of Buddhist doctrine. The first riddle concerned an anthill that gave off fumes during the night and flames during the day. The anthill represents the body with its apertures. The flames it gives off during the day are bodily actions, while its fumes at night are the thoughts and worries about the day's activities that disturb one in the evening.

**vaṃsa**. In Pāli, lit. "lineage," but generally referring to a semihistorical "chronicle"; an important genre of Pāli literature that typically recounts the life of the Buddha, the establishment of the saṅgha (S. SAṂGHA), and the first Buddhist council (SAṂGĪTI; see COUNCIL, FIRST) after the Buddha's death. Depending upon the particular purpose of the chronicle, the work will then go on to describe such things as the transmission of the dharma to a particular place, the founding of a monastery, the tracing of a monastic lineage back to the first council, the enshrinement of a relic, and/or the patronage of the saṅgha by a pious king. The most famous Sinhalese chronicles include the MAHĀVAṂSA, or "Great Chronicle" (which has been periodically augmented since the fifth century); the DĪPAVAṂSA, or "Chronicle of the Island (of Sri Lanka)"; and the THŪPAVAṂSA, or "Chronicle of the STŪPA." Other important examples of the genre are the Thai JINAKĀLAMĀLĪ ("Garland of the Epochs of the Conqueror") and the Burmese SĀSANAVAṂSA ("Chronicle of the Dispensation").

**Vaṃśa**. (S). See VATSAGOTRA.

**Vanapatthasutta**. (C. Lin jing; J. Ringyō; K. Im kyŏng 林經). In Pāli, the "Discourse on Forest Dwelling"; the seventeenth sutta in the MAJJHIMANIKĀYA (a separate SARVĀSTIVĀDA recension appears as SŪTRA nos. 107–108 in the Chinese translation of the MADHYAMĀGAMA); preached by the Buddha to a gathering of monks in the JETAVANA grove in the town of Sāvatthi (S. ŚRĀVASTĪ). The Buddha describes the suitable conditions for a monk to practice meditation. Should he find a place suitable for neither material support (e.g., alms food, robes, lodgings) nor meditation practice, he should abandon that place. Should he find a place suitable for material support but not practice, he should abandon that place also. Should he find a place suitable for meditation practice but not for support, he should remain there. Should he find a place suitable for material support and meditation practice, he should take up lifelong residence there.

**Vanavāsi**. One of nine adjacent lands (paccantadesa) converted to Buddhism by missionaries dispatched by the elder MOGGALIPUTTATISSA at the end of the third Buddhist council (SAṂGĪTI; see COUNCIL, THIRD) held in Pāṭaliputta (S. PĀṬALIPUTRA) during the reign of AŚOKA in the third century BCE. Vanavāsi is located in south India and was converted by the elder Rakkhita, who preached the *Anamatagga-Saṃyutta* while floating in the air. The third Buddhist council at Pāṭaliputta and the nine Buddhist missions are known only in Pāli sources and are first recorded in the c. fourth-century DĪPAVAṂSA.

**Vanavāsin**. (P. Vanavāsī; T. Nags na gnas; C. Fanaposi zunzhe; J. Batsunabashi sonja; K. Pŏllabasa chonja 伐那婆斯尊者). Sanskrit proper name of the fourteenth of the sixteen ARHAT elders (ṢOḌAŚASTHAVIRA), who were charged by the Buddha with protecting his dispensation until the advent of the next buddha, MAITREYA. He abides on Habitable Mountain (C. Kezhushan) with 1,400 disciples. In the Chinese tradition, he was said to have been born during a heavy downpour, which made a racket as the raindrops hit the plantain leaves. After ordaining, he also often diligently studied under the plantain trees, thus earning him the nickname "Plantain Arhat" (Bajiao Luohan). In CHANYUE GUANXIU's standard Chinese depiction, Vanavāsin sits in meditation in a cave, with his eyes closed, wearing a robe across his shoulders with both hands hidden in the sleeves. East Asian images also portray him seated next to a vase, his hands together in AÑJALIMUDRĀ. In Tibetan iconography, he holds a chowrie (VĀLAVYAJANA).

**Vāṅgīśa**. [alt. Vāgīsa] (P. Vaṅgīsa; T. Ngag dbang; C. Poqishe; J. Bagisha; K. Pagisa 婆耆舍). Sanskrit proper name of an eminent ARHAT declared by the Buddha to be foremost among his monk disciples in eloquent expression (PRATIBHĀNA). According to Pāli sources, he was a learned brāhmaṇa proficient in the Vedas who became renowned for his ability to determine the destiny of the deceased by tapping his fingers on their skulls. Vaṅgīsa was much sought after and earned a great deal of money for his prognostications. One day he encountered Sāriputta (S. ŚĀRIPUTRA), who spoke to him of the Buddha's qualities. Intrigued, Vaṅgīsa resolved to meet the Buddha, much to the consternation of his associates. Knowing of Vaṅgīsa's fame as a prognosticator, the Buddha gave him the skull of an ARHAT and asked him to determine the dead saint's rebirth. Vaṅgīsa was unable to determine the deceased's whereabouts and, determined to discover the secret, joined the order as a monk. His preceptor was Nigrodhakappa. When his preceptor died, Vaṅgīsa asked the Buddha about his destiny, to which the Buddha replied that Nigrodhakappa had entirely passed away. Vaṅgīsa had been filled with doubt, for he knew that his preceptor had died with his hands curled up, which was not characteristic of an arhat; but in the case of Nigrodhakappa, this was due only to force of habit. Vaṅgīsa attained arhatship by contemplating the thirty-two impure parts of the body. Upon attaining his goal, he went to the Buddha and sang his praises in eloquent verse. From that time onward he became known as an exceptionally skilled poet, and for that won preeminence as foremost in eloquent expression (pratibhāna). There are several verses ascribed to him in the *Vaṅgīsa-Saṃyutta* of the SAṂYUTTANIKĀYA and in the THERAGĀTHĀ ("Verses of the Elders"): the verses describe his inner struggle against such obstacles as sensuality and conceit, as well as his praise of the Buddha and such eminent disciples as Śāriputra and MAHĀMUDGALYAYANA. According to the APADĀNA, a collection of biographical stories in the Pāli canon, he was given the name Vaṅgīsa because he was born in Vaṅga (modern Bengal) and also because he was a master (P. isi; S. ṛṣi) of the word (vacana).

**Vạn Hạnh**. (萬行) (d. 1025). An influential monk during the Vietnamese Lý dynasty (1010–1225); his family name was Nguyễn. Vạn Hạnh was a native of Cổ Pháp Village, Thiên Đức Prefecture, in northern Vietnam. The THIỀN UYỂN TẬP ANH reports that at the age of twenty-one, he left home to become a monk and served the monk Thiền Ông of Lục Tổ monastery. After Thiền Ông passed away, Vạn Hạnh devoted himself to the practice of DHĀRAṆĪ (spells or mnemonic codes) and SAMĀDHI. King Lê Đại Hành (r. 980–1005), founder of the Former Lê dynasty (980–1009), greatly revered him and relied on his prophecies in political and diplomatic matters. When Lê Ngọa Triều (r. 1005–1009), the last king of the Lê dynasty, appeared to be a cruel tyrant, Vạn Hạnh masterminded the overthrow of the latter and helped Lý Công Uẩn ascend the throne to establish the Lý dynasty (1010–1225). Vạn Hạnh remains the most beloved eminent monk among modern Vietnamese Buddhists. In his honor, in 1964, the first nonmonastic Buddhist university was established in Saigon and named after him. Vạn Hạnh University was the first Vietnamese university to be established following the model of an American liberal arts college.

**varadamudrā**. (T. mchog sbyin gyi phyag rgya; C. shiyuan yin; J. segan'in; K. siwŏn in 施願印). In Sanskrit, "gesture of generosity" or "gesture of granting boons"; a MUDRĀ usually formed with the right hand and commonly found in the iconography of peaceful deities. The varadamudrā is formed with the palm held outward with the fingers outstretched and pointing down. Occasionally, the thumb and index finger may touch lightly, forming a circle.

**vargacārin**. (T. tshogs spyod; C. buxing; J. bugyō; K. puhaeng 部行). In Sanskrit, lit. "congregator"; one of the two types of PRATYEKABUDDHAS, together with KHAḌGAVIṢĀṆAKALPA. Although pratyekabuddhas are renowned for living "solitary like a rhinoceros [horn]" (as indicated by the term khaḍgaviṣāṇakalpa), congregating pratyekabuddhas instead reside together with others in a community. Like all pratyekabuddhas, it is said that this type achieves enlightenment without relying on a teacher in their last lifetime, does not teach the dharma, and appears in the world only during a period when there is no buddha.

**varṣā**. [alt. varṣa, vārṣika] (P. vassa; T. dbyar gnas; C. anju; J. ango; K. an'gŏ 安居). In Sanskrit, "rains" and, by extension, "rains retreat"; a three-month period generally beginning the day after the full-moon day of the eighth lunar month (usually July) and concluding on the full moon of the eleventh lunar month (usually October), during which time monks are required to remain in residence in one place. According to tradition, the Buddha instructed monks to cease their peregrinations during the torrential monsoon period in order to prevent the killing of insects and worms while walking on muddy roads. However, the practice of observing a rains retreat was likely adopted from other mendicant ŚRAMAṆA sects in ancient India at the time of the Buddha. The residences established for use during the rains retreat are called varṣāvāsa or "rains abode," and the institution of the rains retreat (and the consequent need for more permanent shelter) probably led to the development of formal monasteries (VIHĀRA). During this three-month period, monks are expected to continue their studies and practice. They are not permitted to leave their monasteries except for essential tasks, and then for no more than seven nights. Occasions that permit the monk to be temporarily absent from his monastery include urgent personal matters, such as illness or death of one's parents; an invitation to preach the dharma; or the donation of a VIHĀRA or land or other property to the SAṂGHA or an individual monk. If for any reason the residence requirement is not kept, the monk is not eligible to receive a robe donation (KAṬHINA) at the end of the rains retreat. The varṣā is an important chronological marker, with monastic seniority measured by the number of rain retreats one has completed. In Thailand, where it is customary for all males to be ordained as novices for at least a brief period of their lives, the three months of the rains retreat is often chosen as a particularly auspicious time to undertake this commitment. The end of the retreat is marked by the kaṭhina, or "cloth" ceremony, in which laypeople present gifts to the monks, including cloth for new robes.

**vāsanā**. (T. bag chags; C. xunxi/xiqi; J. kunjū/jikke; K. hunsŭp/sŭpki 薰習/習氣). In Sanskrit, literally, "perfumings," hence "predispositions," "habituations," "latent tendencies," or "residual impressions" (and sometimes seen translated overliterally from the Chinese as "habit energies"); subtle tendencies created in the mind as a result of repeated exposure to positive or negative objects. Vāsanā are described as subtle forms of the afflictions (KLEŚA), which hinder the attainment of buddhahood. According to the DAZHIDU LUN (*Mahāprajñāpāramitāśāstra*), ARHATs remain subject to the influence of the vāsanā—for example, ŚĀRIPUTRA's anger and NANDA's staring at beautiful women—just as the scent of incense remains behind in a censer even after all the incense has burned away. Thus, only the buddhas have removed all such latent tendencies. In the YOGĀCĀRA system, the vāsanā "perfume" the "seeds" (BĪJA) of wholesome and unwholesome actions that are implanted in the storehouse consciousness (ĀLAYAVIJÑĀNA). The CHENG WEISHI LUN (*Vijñaptimātratāsiddhi*) lists the following three types of vāsanā: (1) linguistic predispositions (C. mingyan xiqi), the impressions created by concepts and expressions through which one evaluates his experience; (2) grasping-at-self predispositions (C. wozhi xiqi), impressions fostered by grasping at false notions of a perduring self (ĀTMAGRĀHA), which create an attachment to I and mine; and (3) cause-of-existence predispositions (C. youzhi xiqi), impressions that engender wholesome and unwholesome karmic retributions, which lead to continued rebirth in SAṂSĀRA.

**vaśīkaraṇa**. (T. dbang du bya ba/dbang po'i las). In Sanskrit, "controlling"; also called bhāgyacāra, "activities of control"; one of the four types of activities (CATURKARMA) set forth in the Buddhist tantras. The other three are activities of increase (PAUṢṬIKA) to increase prosperity, lengthen life, etc.; pacifying activities (ŚĀNTIKA) that purify the negativity that appears in such forms as hindrances and illness; and violent or drastic measures (ABHICĀRA) such as killing and warfare. Vaśīkaraṇa may be through physical force, but is more often done through MANTRAs or ritual; it brings control and influence over persons and situations.

**vaśitā**. (T. dbang bo; C. zizai; J. jizai; K. chajae 自在). In Sanskrit, "mastery," or "autonomy"; a list of ten types of mastery or autonomy developed by a BODHISATTVA, viz., of one's life span, action (KARMAN), necessities of life, determination, aspiration, magical powers, birth, dharma, mind, and wisdom.

**Vāṣpa**. (P. Vappa; T. Rlangs pa; C. Pofu; J. Bafu; K. Pabu 婆敷). Sanskrit proper name of one of the monks who belonged to the so-called group of five (PAÑCAVARGIKA; BHADRAVARGĪYA)—viz., KAUṆḌINYA [alt. Ājñāta-Kauṇḍiya], AŚVAJIT, VĀṢPA, MAHĀNĀMAN, and BHADRIKA—who were converted by the Buddha at the Deer Park (MṚGADĀVA) in SĀRNĀTH. When the sage ASITA predicted that the infant bodhisattva, SIDDHĀRTHA GAUTAMA, would one day become a buddha, Vāṣpa and four other brāhmaṇas headed by Kauṇḍinya became ascetics in anticipation of Siddhārtha's own renunciation. They practiced austerities with him for six years until Siddhārtha renounced asceticism. Dismayed with what they regarded as his backsliding, the five ascetics left him and took up residence in the Deer Park at ṚSIPATANA. After his enlightenment, the Buddha went there and preached to the five ascetics, and each of them attained enlightenment. The Pāli canon describes their enlightenment as proceeding in two stages: first, when the Buddha preached the DHAMMACAKKAPPAVATTANASUTTA (S. DHARMACAKRAPRAVARTANASŪTRA) ("Discourse Setting in Motion the Wheel of the Dharma"), Kauṇḍinya became a stream-enterer (SROTAĀPANNA) and in the subsequent days the other four did as well; and second, when the Buddha preached the (ANATTALAKKHAṆASUTTA; S. **Anātmalakṣaṇasūtra*) ("Discourse on the Mark of Nonself"), they all attained complete liberation as ARHATs.

**vastujñāna**. (T. gzhi shes; C. yiqiexiang zhi; J. issaisōchi; K. ilch'esang chi 一切相智). In Sanskrit, "knowledge of bases" (VASTU), in the PRAJÑĀPĀRAMITĀ literature, referring to knowledge that the bases (SKANDHA, ĀYATANA, DHĀTU, etc.) described in mainstream Buddhist sources lack any semblance of a personal self. It is one of the three knowledges (along with SARVĀKĀRAJÑATĀ and MĀRGAJÑATĀ) set forth in the ABHISAMAYĀLAṂKĀRA, a commentary on the PAÑCAVIṂŚATISĀHASRIKĀPRAJÑĀPĀRAMITĀSŪTRA that describe the MAHĀYĀNA path and result. In the *Abhisamayālaṃkāra*, the vastujñāna is more commonly called just SARVAJÑATĀ ("all-knowledge"). When it is not informed by skillful means (UPĀYA), that is, great compassion (MAHĀKARUṆĀ), it is understood negatively as the practice of a ŚRĀVAKA or PRATYEKABUDDHA that leads to their inferior goal of NIRVĀṆA and must be forsaken. When it is informed by skillful means, it is an essential component both of the practice of a bodhisattva (mārgajñatā), and of a buddha's knowledge (sarvākārajñatā). As an authentic knowledge of nonself gained through a direct understanding of the four noble truths, it is possessed by those who have reached the path of vision (DARŚANAMĀRGA).

**Vasubandhu**. (T. Dbyig gnyen; C. Shiqin; J. Seshin; K. Sech'in 世親) (fl. c. fourth or fifth centuries CE). One of the most influential authors in the history of Buddhism, and the only major figure to make significant contributions to both the MAINSTREAM BUDDHIST SCHOOLS and MAHĀYĀNA. In Tibetan Buddhism, Vasubandhu is counted as one of the "six ornaments" (T. rgyan drug), along with NĀGĀRJUNA, ĀRYADEVA, ASAṄGA, DIGNĀGA, and DHARMAKĪRTI. There has been considerable speculation about his dates, so much so that ERICH FRAUWALLNER proposed that there were two different Vasubandhus. This theory has been rejected, but there is still no consensus on his dates, with most scholars placing him in the fourth or fifth century CE. Vasubandhu is said to have been born in Puruṣapura in GANDHĀRA (identified with Peshawar in modern Pakistan), as the brother or half brother (with the same mother) of Asaṅga. He was ordained as a monk in a SARVĀSTIVĀDA school and studied VAIBHĀṢIKA ABHIDHARMA philosophy in KASHMIR–GANDHĀRA, as well as the tenets of the rival SAUTRĀNTIKA school. At the conclusion of his studies, he composed his first and what would be his most famous work, the *Abhidharmakośa*, or "Treasury of the Abhidharma." In over six hundred stanzas in nine chapters, he set forth the major points of the Vaibhāṣika system. He then composed a prose autocommentary, the ABHIDHARMAKOŚABHĀṢYA, in which he critiqued from a Sautrāntika perspective some of the Vaibhāṣika positions that he had outlined in the verses. These two texts would become two of the most influential texts on the abhidharma in the later history of Buddhism on the subcontinent and beyond, serving, for example, as the root texts for abhidharma studies in Tibet and as the foundational text for the Kusha (Kośa) school of early Japanese Buddhism. At some point after his composition of the *Kośa*, he encountered his half brother Asaṅga, author of at least some of the texts collected in the YOGĀCĀRABHŪMI, who "converted" him to the Mahāyāna. After his conversion, Vasubandhu became a prolific author on Mahāyāna materials, helping especially to frame the philosophy of the Yogācāra school. Major works attributed to him include the VIṂŚATIKĀ, or "Twenty [Stanzas]" and the TRIṂŚIKĀ, or "Thirty [Stanzas]," two works that set forth succinctly the basic philosophical positions of the Yogācāra. The *Triṃśikā* was, together with DHARMAPĀLA's commentary to the text, the basis of XUANZANG's massive commentary, the CHENG WEISHI LUN (**Vijñaptimātratāsiddhi*), which was the foundational text for the FAXIANG ZONG of East Asian Yogācāra. In his TRISVABHĀVANIRDEŚA, Vasubandhu also set forth the central doctrine of the Yogācāra, the "three natures" (TRISVABHĀVA), of imaginary (PARIKALPITA), dependent (PARATANTRA), and consummate (PARINIṢPANNA). His VYĀKHYĀYUKTI set forth principles for the exegesis of passages from the sūtras. He is also credited with commentaries on a number of Mahāyāna sūtras, including the AKṢAYAMATINIRDEŚA, the SADDHARMAPUṆḌARĪKASŪTRA, and the DAŚABHŪMIKASŪTRA (with his commentary serving as the basis of the DI LUN ZONG in China), as well as commentaries on three of the five treatises of MAITREYA, the MAHĀYĀNASŪTRĀLAṂKĀRA, the MADHYĀNTAVIBHĀGA, and the DHARMADHARMATĀVIBHĀGA. He also wrote a commentary on Asaṅga's MAHĀYĀNASAṂGRAHA. His KARMASIDDHIPRAKARAṆA, or "Investigation Establishing [the Correct Understanding] of KARMAN," examines the theory of action in light of the Yogācāra doctrine of the ĀLAYAVIJÑĀNA. The PAÑCASKANDHAPRAKARAṆA, or "Explanation of the Five Aggregates," presents a somewhat different view of the five aggregates (SKANDHA) than that found in his *Abhidharmakośabhāṣya* and thus probably dates from his Mahāyāna period; it is a reworking of the presentation of the five aggregates found in Asaṅga's ABHIDHARMASAMUCCAYA. In addition to the *Abhidharmakośabhāṣya* and the *Viṃśatikā*, a third text of his was highly influential in East Asia. It is a commentary on the larger SUKHĀVATĪVYŪHA, whose Sanskrit title might be reconstructed as the **Sukhāvatīvyūhopadeśa*. However, the work is known only in Chinese, as the JINGTU LUN, and its attribution to Vasubandhu has been called into question. Nonetheless, based on this traditional attribution, Vasubandhu is counted as an Indian patriarch of the PURE LAND schools of East Asia. ¶ In Tibet, a *bṛhaṭṭīkā* commentary on the ŚATASĀHASRIKĀPRAJÑĀPĀRAMITĀ and a *paddhati* on three PRAJÑĀPĀRAMITĀ sūtras (T. *Yum gsum gnod 'joms*) are attributed to Vasubandhu, although his authorship is disputed.

**Vasumitra**. (T. Dbyig bshes; C. Shiyou; J. Seu; K. Seu 世友) (d.u.). A prominent scholar of the SARVĀSTIVĀDA school in KASHMIR, possibly during the second century CE. His SAMAYABHEDOPARACANACAKRA is an important source of information on the various schools and subschools of mainstream Nikāya Buddhism in India. He is also credited with composing the PRAKARAṆAPĀDA, one of the "six feet" of the ABHIDHARMAPIṬAKA of the SARVĀSTIVĀDA, which first introduces the categorization of dharmas according to the more developed Sarvāstivāda lists of RŪPA, CITTA, CAITTA, CITTAVIPRAYUKTASAṂSKĀRA, and ASAṂSKṚTA dharmas; it also adds a new listing of KUŚALAMAHĀBHŪMIKA, or factors always associated with wholesome states of mind. Vasumitra is frequently cited in the ABHIDHARMAMAHĀVIBHĀṢĀ, the massive abhidharma exegesis of the VAIBHĀṢIKA school of the Sarvāstivāda, but it is unclear whether the scholar mentioned in the *Abhidharmamahāvibhāṣā* and the author of the texts mentioned earlier are the same figure. Vasumitra is also credited with composing a (now-lost) commentary to the ABHIDHARMAKOŚABHĀṢYA, which, if true, would move his dates forward into the fourth century.

**Vatsā**. [alt. Vaṃśā] (P. Vaṃsa; T. Gnas ma; C. Bacuo [guo]; J. Bassa[koku]; K. Palch'a [kuk] 跋蹉[國]). One of the sixteen great states (MAHĀJANAPADA) in ancient India, and one of three powerful kingdoms of the Gaṅgā (Ganges) river valley at the time of Buddha, together with MAGADHA and KOŚALA. Vatsā was located south of the Gaṅgā River, in what is today the Indian state of Uttar Pradesh, and had its capital at Kauśāmbī. During the time of the Buddha, Udayāna was king of Vatsā and a follower of the Buddha. See also UDĀYANA BUDDHA.

**Vatsagotra**. [alt. Vatsa, Vaṃśa] (P. Vacchagotta; C. Pocha; J. Basa; K. Pach'a 婆差). In Sanskrit, lit. "Calf Ancestry," an ARHAT and disciple of the Buddha. According to Pāli accounts, where he is known as Vacchagotta, he was a wandering mendicant of great learning who was converted and attained arhatship in a series of encounters with the Buddha. Numerous discourses in the Pāli SUTTAPIṬAKA concern metaphysical questions that Vacchagotta poses to the Buddha; an entire section of the SAṂYUTTANIKĀYA is devoted to these exchanges. In other suttas, he raises similar questions in conversations with such important disciples of the Buddha as Mahāmoggallāna (MAHĀMAUDGALYĀYANA) and ĀNANDA. Vacchagotta's gradual conversion is recorded in a series of discourses contained in the MAJJHIMANIKĀYA. In the *Tevijja-Vacchagottasutta*, he rejoices at the words of the Buddha. In the *Aggi-Vacchagottasutta*, Vacchagotta has a renowned exchange concerning ten "indeterminate questions" (AVYĀKṚTA)—is the world eternal or not eternal, infinite or finite, what is the state of the TATHĀGATA after death, etc. The Buddha refuses to respond to any of the questions, and instead offers the simile of extinguishing fire to describe the state of the tathāgata after death: just as after a fire has been extinguished, it would be inappropriate to say that it has gone anywhere, so too after the tathāgata has extinguished each of the five aggregates (P. khandha; S. SKANDHA), he cannot be said to have gone anywhere. At the conclusion of the discourse, Vacchagotta accepts the Buddha as his teacher. In the *Mahāvacchagottasutta*, he is ordained by the Buddha and attains in sequence all the knowledges possible for one who is not yet an arhat. The Buddha instructs him in the practice of tranquility (P. samatha; S. ŚAMATHA) and insight (VIPASSANĀ; S. VIPAŚYANĀ) whereby he can cultivate the six superknowledges (P. abhiññā; S. ABHIJÑĀ); Vacchagotta then attains arhatship. ¶ The DAZHIDU LUN (**Mahāprajñāpāramitā-śāstra*) identifies the Vacchagotta of the Pāli suttas with Śreṇika Vatsagotra, the namesake of what in MAHĀYĀNA sources is called the ŚREṆIKA HERESY. The locus classicus for this heresy appears in the MAHĀPARINIRVĀṆASŪTRA. There, when Śreṇika raises the question about whether there is a self or not, the Buddha keeps silent, so Śreṇika himself offers the fire simile, but with a very different interpretation than the Buddha's. He compares the physical body and the eternal self to a house and its owner: even though the house may burn down in a fire, the owner is safe outside the house; thus, the body and its constituents (SKANDHA) may be impermanent and subject to dissolution, but not the self. In other Sanskrit sources, Vatsagotra also seems to refer to the figure most typically known as Vatsa (T. Be'u) or Vaṃśa, a student of the ascetic Kāśyapa.

**Vātsīputrīya**. (P. Vajjiputtakā/Vajjiputtiyā; T. Gnas ma'i bu pa; C. Duzi bu; J. Tokushibu; K. Tokcha pu 犢子部). One of the traditional eighteen schools of "mainstream" (i.e., non-MAHĀYĀNA) Indian Buddhism, which takes its name from its leader, Vātsīputra. An offshoot of the SARVĀSTIVĀDA school, it is remembered primarily as one of the schools labeled by others as PUDGALAVĀDA, or "proponents of the person," that is, the apparently heretical position that there is a "person" (PUDGALA) with qualities that are "inexpressible" (avācya), which transmigrates from lifetime to lifetime. This position was criticized by exegetes in virtually all rival Buddhist schools, and earned a long critique in the ninth chapter of VASUBANDHU's ABHIDHARMAKOŚABHĀṢYA, where it was denigrated as the assertion of a permanent self or soul (ĀTMAN). In their defense, the Vātsīputrīyas argued that the pudgala was neither the same as nor different from the five aggregates (SKANDHA)—viz., that the pudgala was in an "indeterminate" relationship vis-à-vis the skandhas—thus conforming to the Buddha's dictum that there was no self to be discovered among the aggregates. For the Vātsīputrīyas, it was argued that it was necessary to posit the existence of the pudgala in order to account for personal continuity over the course of a single lifetime, karmic continuity over the course of multiple lifetimes, and, ultimately, so that there would be something that would attain NIRVĀṆA upon the cessation of the aggregates. However, recognizing the special nature of their view of the person, the Vātsīputrīya posited it as a fifth category of dharmas in addition to the standard four of the Sarvāstivāda school, viz., (1)–(3) conditioned factors (SAṂSKṚTADHARMA) belonging to the three time periods of past, present, and future; (4) an unconditioned factor (ASAṂSKṚTADHARMA), which for the Vātsīputrīyas, like the STHAVIRANIKĀYA, included only nirvāṇa; and (5) "inexpressible dharmas" (S. *avācyadharma; C. bukeshuo fa), a category exclusive to the Vātsīputrīyas, which included the notion of a pudgala. Despite the apparent heresy of this position, Chinese pilgrims reported the prominence in India of schools that held this view. The Vātsīputrīya spawned four additional mainstream schools: the Dharmottarīya, Bhadrayānīya, SAṂMITĪYA, and Ṣaṇṇagarika.

**Vaṭṭagāmaṇi Abhaya**. A Sinhalese king (r. 43 and 29–17 BCE) whose reign witnessed, tradition claims, a number of major developments in Sri Lankan Buddhism, including the first attempt to compile the Pāli canon (P. tipiṭaka; S. TRIPIṬAKA), and its Sinhalese commentaries (AṬṬHAKATHĀ) in written form; this event, which is said to have occurred at a cave named Ālokalena, is considered to mark the first written transcription of a complete Buddhist canon. The DĪPAVAṂSA and MAHĀVAṂSA state that a gathering of ARHATs had decided to commit the body of texts to writing out of fear that they could no longer be reliably memorized and passed down from one generation to the next. In the first year of his reign, Vaṭṭagāmaṇi Abhaya was deposed by a coalition of the forces of seven Damiḷa (Tamil) warriors and forced into exile for fourteen years. During that time, he was aided by a monk named Mahātissa. In gratitude for the assistance, when he regained the throne, Vaṭṭagāmaṇi sponsored the construction of the ABHAYAGIRI monastery, which he donated to the monk. But Mahātissa had been expelled from the MAHĀVIHĀRA for misconduct, so the disciples of Mahātissa then dwelling at the Abhayagiri monastery seceded from the Mahāvihāra fraternity and established themselves as a separate fraternity. The Abhayagiri fraternity that arose during the reign of Vaṭṭagāmaṇi flourished as a separate monastic sect in Sri Lanka until the twelfth century CE.

**Vatthūpamasutta**. (C. Shuijing fanzhi jing; J. Suijōbonjikyō; K. Sujŏng pŏmji kyŏng 水淨梵志經). In Pāli, the "The Simile of the Cloth Discourse"; the seventh sutta in the MAJJHIMANIKĀYA (a separate SARVĀSTIVĀDA recension appears as the ninety-third SŪTRA in the Chinese translation of the MADHYAMĀGAMA, as well as an unidentified recension in the Chinese translation of the EKOTTARĀGAMA); preached by the Buddha to a group of disciples in the JETAVANA grove in the town of Sāvatthi (S. ŚRĀVASTĪ). The Buddha describes the difference between a pure mind and a defiled mind by citing the example of cloth: just as only a clean cloth will absorb dye properly, so only a pure mind will be receptive to the dharma. The Buddha then lists a set of seventeen imperfections that defile the mind, which the monk must learn to abandon in order to gain confidence in the three jewels (RATNATRAYA) and ultimately liberation.

**vāyu**. [alt. vāyudhātu] (P. vāyu/vāyo; T. rlung; C. fengda; J. fūdai; K. p'ungdae 風大). In Sanskrit and Pāli, lit. "wind" or "air," viz., the property of "motion" or "movement"; one of the four major elements (MAHĀBHŪTA) or "principal elementary qualities" of which the physical world of materiality (RŪPA) is composed, along with earth (viz., solidity, PṚTHIVĪ; P. paṭhavī), water (viz., cohesion, ĀPAS; P. āpo), and fire (viz., temperature, warmth, TEJAS; P. tejo). "Wind" is defined as "that which is light and moving" and thus can refer not only to the wind, air, and breath but also to the general property of motion. Because wind also has the ability to convey things (viz., earth), has relative temperature (viz., fire), and has a certain tangibility (viz., water), the existence of all the other three elements may also be inferred even in that single element. In the physical body, the wind element is associated with the lungs and the intestinal system.

**vedalla**. (S. vaidalya). In Pāli, "extended" scriptures. See VAIPULYA.

**vedanā**. (T. tshor ba; C. shou; J. ju; K. su 受). In Sanskrit and Pāli, "sensation" or "sensory feeling"; the physical or mental sensations that accompany all moments of sensory consciousness. Sensations are always understood as being one of three: pleasurable, painful, or neutral (lit. "neither pleasant nor unpleasant"). Sensation is listed as one of the ten "mental factors of wide extent" (MAHĀBHŪMIKA) in the SARVĀSTIVĀDA ABHIDHARMA, one of the five "omnipresent" (SARVATRAGA) "mental constituents" (CAITTA) in the YOGĀCĀRA system, and one of the seven universal mental factors (lit. mental factors common to all) (sabbacittasādhāraṇa cetasika) in the Pāli ABHIDHAMMA. It is said universally to accompany all moments of sensory consciousness. Sensation is also listed as the second of the five aggregates (SKANDHA) and the seventh constituent in the twelvefold chain of dependent origination (PRATĪTYASAMUTPĀDA). The "contemplation of sensations" (S. vedanānupaśyanā, P. vedanānupassanā) is the second of the four foundations of mindfulness (S. SMṚTYUPASTHĀNA, P. satipaṭṭhāna) and involves being mindful (see S. SMṚTI, P. sati) of physical and mental sensations that are pleasurable, painful, and neutral.

**vehicle**. See YĀNA.

**Veṇugrāmaka**. (P. Beluvagāmaka/Veḷugāma; T. 'Od ma can gyi grong; C. Zhulincong; J. Chikurinsō; K. Chungnimch'ong 竹林叢). In Sanskrit, "Bamboo Town," near the city of VAIŚĀLĪ; remembered as the town where the Buddha spent his last rains retreat (VARṢĀ) prior to his passage into PARINIRVĀṆA. Because there was a famine in the region, making it difficult for the local population to support a large group of monks, the Buddha went to Veṇugrāmaka accompanied only by ĀNANDA. During their sojourn there, the Buddha, already eighty, became seriously ill. However, he did not want to die without addressing the SAṂGHA one last time, and, by using his powers of concentration (SAMĀDHI) to reduce the physical discomfort, the disease abated. It was while staying at Veṇugrāmaka that the Buddha made two famous statements to Ānanda. According to the Pāli MAHĀPARINIBBĀNASUTTANTA, when the Buddha expressed his wish to address the saṃgha, Ānanda assumed that the Buddha had a teaching he had not yet delivered to the monks. The Buddha replied that he was not one who taught with a "teacher's fist" (P. ācariyamuṭṭhi) or "closed fist," holding back some secret teaching, but that he had in fact revealed everything. The Buddha also said that he was not the head of saṃgha and that after his death each monk should "be an island unto himself, " with the DHARMA as his island and his refuge.

**Veṇuvanavihāra**. (P. Veḷuvanavihāra; T. 'Od ma'i tshal; C. Zhulin jingshe; J. Chikurin shōja; K. Chungnim chŏngsa 竹林精舍). In Sanskrit, "Bamboo Grove Monastery"; the name of a monastery in a grove of the kingdom of MAGADHA, to the north of the capital, RĀJAGṚHA, that King BIMBISĀRA offered to the Buddha as a residence for himself and his monks. The Veṇuvana was the first ĀRĀMA or park offered to the Buddha after his enlightenment, and the Buddha subsequently allowed monks to accept an ārāma offered by a layperson. It was during the Buddha's residence at Veṇuvana that ŚĀRIPUTRA and MAHĀMAUDGALYĀYANA entered the order. The Buddha is said to have passed his second, third, and fourth rains retreat there, in a VIHĀRA built by Kalandaka and offered to the Buddha. Veṇuvana is often mentioned in the scriptures as the location where the Buddha taught many sūtras, prescribed many rules of the VINAYA, and recounted many JĀTAKA tales. ĀNANDA is said to have lived at the Bamboo Grove after the Buddha's death.

**Verañjakasutta**. In Pāli, the "Discourse to the Verañjakas," the forty-second sutta in the Pāli MAJJHIMANIKĀYA (there is an untitled SARVĀSTIVĀDA recension included in the Chinese translation of the SAṂYUKTĀGAMA); preached by the Buddha to a group of brāhmaṇa householders from Verañja while he dwelt in the JETAVANA grove in the town of Sāvatthi (S. ŚRĀVASTĪ). The Buddha describes for them the ten demeritorious actions that lead to unhappiness and unfortunate rebirths and the ten virtuous actions that lead to happiness and fortunate rebirths. The ten unvirtuous actions are analyzed into three kinds of bodily misdeed: (1) killing and violence, (2) stealing, and (3) sexual misconduct; four kinds of verbal misdeed: (4) falsehood, (5) malicious gossip, (6) harsh speech, and (7) meaningless prattle; and three kinds of mental misdeed: (8) covetousness, (9) ill will, and (10) wrong views. The ten meritorious actions are explained as abstaining from the ten demeritorious actions. The Buddha then describes the fortunate rebirths among humans and the divinities that may be expected by those who live righteously and perform meritorious actions. The sutta is parallel in content to the SĀLEYYAKASUTTA, the forty-first sutta in the *Majjhimanikāya.*

**Vesākha**. (P). See WESAK.

**Vessantara**. (S. Viśvantara/Viśvaṃtara; T. Thams cad sgrol; C. Xudana; J. Shudainu/Shudaina; K. Sudaena 須大拏). Pāli name of a prince who is the subject of the most famous of all

JĀTAKA tales; he was the BODHISATTVA's final existence before he took rebirth in TUṢITA heaven, where he awaited the moment when he would descend into Queen MĀYĀ's womb to be born as Prince SIDDHĀRTHA and eventually become GAUTAMA Buddha. During his lifetime as Prince Vessantara, the bodhisattva (P. bodhisatta) fulfilled the perfection (P. pāramī; S. PĀRAMITĀ) of generosity (DĀNA; see also DĀNAPĀRAMITĀ). The story is found in Sanskrit in Āryaśura's JĀTAKAMĀLĀ and Kṣemendra's *Avadānakalpalatā*, with the same main features as in the Pāli version. The story enjoys its greatest popularity in Southeast Asia, so the Pāli version is described here. ¶ The bodhisattva was born as the crown prince of Siviraṭṭha, the son of King Sañjaya and Queen Phusatī of the kingdom of Jetuttara. On the day of his birth, a white elephant named Paccaya was also born, who had the power to make rain. When Vessantara was sixteen, he married a maiden named Maddī, with whom he had a son and a daughter, Jāli and Kanhajinā. Once, when Kaliṅga was suffering a severe drought, brāhmaṇas from that kingdom requested that Vessantara give them his white elephant to alleviate their plight. Vessantara complied, handing over to them his elephant along with its accessories. The citizens of Jetuttara were outraged that he should deprive his own kingdom of such a treasure and demanded his banishment to the distant mountain of Vaṅkagiri. His father, King Sañjaya, consented and ordered Vessantara to leave via the road frequented by highwaymen. Before his departure, Vessantara held a great almsgiving, in which he distributed seven hundred of every type of thing. Maddī insisted that she and her children accompany the prince, and they were transported out of the city on a grand carriage pulled by four horses. Four brāhmaṇas begged for his horses, which he gave. Gods then pulled his carriage until a brāhmaṇa begged for his carriage. Thereafter, they traveled on foot. Along the way crowds gathered, some even offering their kingdoms for him to rule, so famous was he for his generosity. At Vaṅkagiri, they lived in two hermitages, one for Vessantara and the other for his wife and children. These had been constructed for them by Vissakamma, architect of the gods. There, they passed four months until one day an old brāhmaṇa named Jūjaka arrived and asked for Jāli and Kanhajinā as slaves. Vessantara expected this to occur, so he sent his wife on an errand so that she would not be distressed at the sight of him giving their children away. Jūjaka was cruel, and the children ran away to their father, only to be returned so that Vessantara's generosity could be perfected. When Maddī returned, she fainted at the news. Then, Sakka (ŚAKRA), king of the gods, assumed the form of a brāhmaṇa and asked for Maddī; Vessantara gave his wife to the brāhmaṇa. The earth quaked at the gift. Sakka immediately revealed his identity and returned Maddī, granting Vessantara eight boons. In the meantime, Jūjaka, the cruel brāhmaṇa, traveled to Jetuttara, where King Sañjaya bought the children for a great amount of treasure, including a seven-storied palace. Jūjaka, however, died of overeating and left no heirs, so the treasure was returned to the king. Meanwhile, the white elephant was returned because the kingdom of Kaliṅga could not maintain him. A grand entourage was sent to Vaṅkagiri to fetch Vessantara and Maddī, and when they returned amid great celebration they were crowned king and queen of Siviraṭṭha. In order that Vessantara would be able to satisfy all who came for gifts, Sakka rained down jewels waist deep on the palace. When Vessantara died, he was born as a god in tuṣita heaven, where he awaited his last rebirth as Siddhattha Gotama, when he would become a buddha. ¶ As a depiction of the virtue of dāna, the story of Vessantara is one of the most important Buddhist tales in Thailand and throughout Southeast Asia and is depicted on murals throughout the region. Thai retellings of the *Vessantara-Jātaka*, known also as the *Mahāchat*, or "Great Jātaka," are found in the many Thai dialects and consist of thirteen chapters. The story is popular in Thailand's north and especially in the northeast, where virtually every monastery (excluding forest monasteries) holds a festival known as the Bun Phra Wet, usually in February or March, at which the entire story is recited in one day and one night. Laypeople assist in decorating their local monastery with trunks and branches of banana trees to represent the forest to which Vessantara was banished after giving away his kingdom's auspicious elephant. They also present offerings of flowers, hanging decorations, balls of glutinous rice, and money. The festival includes, among other things, a procession to the monastery that includes local women carrying long horizontal cloth banners on which the Vessantara story is painted. The merit earned by participating in the festival is linked to two beliefs: (1) that the participant will be reborn at the time of the future buddha, MAITREYA, known in Thai as Phra Si Ariya Mettrai (P. Ariya Metteyya), and (2) that the community, which remains primarily agricultural, will be blessed with sufficient rainfall.

**Vessantara-Jātaka**. See VESSANTARA.

**Vibhajyavāda**. (P. Vibhajjavāda; T. Rnam par phye ste smra ba; C. Fenbieshuo bu; J. Funbetsusetsubu; K. Punbyŏlsŏl pu 分別說部). In Sanskrit, "Distinctionist"; one of the "mainstream" (i.e., non-Mahāyāna) schools of Indian Buddhism. The Vibhajyavāda was one of the branches of the STHAVIRANIKĀYA, which, according to BUDDHAGHOSA, emerged at the time of the third Buddhist council (see COUNCIL, THIRD), around 240 BCE; the Sthaviranikāya also comprises a number of other schools, including the DHARMAGUPTAKA, whose VINAYA was predominant in East Asia; the THERAVĀDA of Sri Lanka and Southeast Asia traces itself to the Sthaviranikāya. Inscriptional evidence indicates that the Vibhajyavāda thrived in KASHMIR, GANDHĀRA, and BACTRIA, where the name may have been used to describe several of the branches of the Sthaviranikāya, including the Dharmaguptaka, MAHĪŚĀSAKA, and KĀŚYAPĪYA. Doctrinally speaking, the Vibhajyavāda's name derives from the distinction made between phenomena or factors (DHARMA) that exist and do not exist. The Sarvāstivāda ("those who hold that everything exists") asserted that dharmas exist in all three temporal modes of past, present, and future. In contrast, the Vibhajyavāda (and many other mainstream schools) made a distinction among past, present, and future dharmas, asserting that, while present dharmas obviously exist, no future dharmas exist, and the only past dharmas that exist are past actions that have yet to produce their karmic effects. Thus, the term vibhajyavāda is sometimes used in a more generic sense, referring not to a specific school, but to all mainstream schools that made a distinction among dharmas of the past, present, and future. In addition, the Vibhajyavāda is said to have held that thought is pure in its nature; that form (RŪPA) still occurs in the immaterial realm (ĀRŪPYADHĀTU); that there is no intermediate state (ANTARĀBHAVA) between death and rebirth; that PRATĪTYASAMUTPĀDA and the path (MĀRGA) are unconditioned (ASAṂSKṚTA); and that an ARHAT cannot retrogress on the path. The Pāli term Vibhajjavāda is sometimes used as a synonym for Theravāda, in the more general sense of those who hold that reality should be understood by discriminating between positive and negative positions. In the KATHĀVATTHU of the Pāli ABHIDHAMMAPIṬAKA, the venerable MOGGALIPUTTATISSA declared that the Buddha was a vibhajjavādī, or "teacher of analysis," since it is only through critical investigation and reasoning that an adept can begin to develop true insight, discriminating among positions rather than taking a one-sided position.

**Vibhaṅga**. [alt. Vibhaṅgappakaraṇa]. In Pāli, "Analysis"; the second of the seven books that together constitute the ABHIDHAMMAPIṬAKA of the Pāli canon. Since most of this book concerns subject matter introduced in the abhidhammapiṭaka's first book, the DHAMMASAṄGAṆĪ, the *Vibhaṅga* is often spoken of as a supplement to, or a commentary on, the *Dhammasaṅgaṇī*. The *Vibhaṅga*, however, applies different methods of analysis and includes a number of additional definitions and terms. The text is comprised of eighteen chapters (vibhaṅga), each of which presents a self-contained discourse on the following topics, in this order: the aggregates (P. khandha; S. SKANDHA), sense bases (ĀYATANA), elements (DHĀTU), truths (P. sacca; S. SATYA), faculties (INDRIYA), conditioned origination (P. paṭiccasamuppāda; S. PRATĪTYASAMUTPĀDA), foundations of mindfulness (P. SATIPAṬṬHĀNA; S. SMṚTYUPASTHĀNA), right effort (P. sammappadhāna; S. SAMYAKPRAHĀṆA), bases of psychic or supernatural powers (P. iddhipāda; S. ṚDDHIPĀDA), factors of enlightenment (P. bojjhaṅga; S. BODHYAṄGA), the eightfold path (P. magga; S. MĀRGA), mental absorption (P. JHĀNA; S. DHYĀNA), the boundless states (P. appammaññā; S. APRAMĀṆA), training rules (P. sikkhāpada; S. ŚIKṢĀPADA), analytical knowledges (P. paṭisambhidā; S. PRATISAṂVID), various types of knowledge (P. ñāṇa; JÑĀNA), minor topics (P. khuddhakavatthu), including an inventory of afflictions, and "the heart of the teaching" (P. dhammahadaya). Most, but not all, of these chapters are divided into three parts. First, they analyze the subject using the same method as the SUTTAs, often by simply quoting material directly from the suttas. Next, they analyze the subject using a typical ABHIDHARMA methodology—offering synonyms and numerical lists of categories, classes, and types of the phenomena. Finally, most treatments culminate in a catechistic series of inquiries (pañhāpucchaka). In this series of questions, the subject is analyzed by way of a set of "matrices" or "categories" (P. mātikā; S. MĀTṚKĀ) established in the *Dhammasaṅgaṇī*. Many commentaries have been written on the Pāli *Vibhaṅga*, the most popular of which is BUDDHAGHOSA's SAMMOHAVINODANĪ, which was written in the fifth century.

**vicāra**. (T. dpyod pa; C. si; J. shi; K. sa 伺). In Sanskrit and Pāli, "sustained thought," "sustained attention," "imagination," or "analysis"; one of the forty-six mental factors (CAITTA) according to the VAIBHĀṢIKA school of SARVĀSTIVĀDA ABHIDHARMA, one of the fifty-one according to the YOGĀCĀRA school, and one of the fifty-two in the Pāli ABHIDHAMMA. Although etymologically the term contains the connotation of "analysis," vicāra is polysemous in the Buddhist lexicon and refers to a mental activity that can be present both in ordinary states of consciousness and in meditative absorption (DHYĀNA). In ordinary consciousness, vicāra is "sustained thought," viz., the continued pondering of things. It is listed as an indeterminate mental factor (ANIYATA-CAITTA) because it can be employed toward either virtuous or nonvirtuous ends, depending on one's intention and the object of one's attention. Vicāra as a mental activity typically follows VITARKA, wherein vitarka is the "initial application of thought" and vicāra the "sustained thought" that ensues after one's attention has already adverted toward an object. In the context of meditative absorption, vicāra may be rendered as "sustained attention" or "sustained application of attention." With vitarka the practitioner directs his focus toward a chosen meditative object. When the attention is properly directed, the practitioner follows by applying and continuously fixing his attention on the same thing, deeply experiencing (or examining) the object. In meditative absorption, vicāra is one of the five factors that make up the first dhyāna (see DHYĀNĀṄGA). According to the VISUDDHIMAGGA, "applied thought" (P. vitakka; S. vitarka) is like a bee flying toward a flower, having oriented itself toward its chosen target, whereas "sustained attention" (vicāra) is like a bee hovering over that flower, fixating on the flower.

***vicārabhāvanā**. (T. dpyad sgom). In Sanskrit, "analytical meditation"; a general term for those forms of meditation that involve discursive reflection on points of Buddhist doctrine, as opposed to the focus of the mind upon a single object. An example of such analytical meditation would be the investigation of the constituents of mind and body in search of the self or systematic reflection on the certainty of death and the uncertainty of the time of death. The term is often paired with *STHĀPYABHĀVANĀ, "stabilizing meditation" (T. 'jog sgom), the one-pointed concentration on a single object without discursive reflection. In instructions on meditation practice, there is often advice to alternate these two forms of meditation, first arriving at a conclusion or conviction through analytical meditation and then focusing on that conclusion through stabilizing meditation, resulting eventually in VIPAŚYANĀ.

**vicikitsā**. (P. vicikicchā; T. the tshom; C. yi; J. gi; K. ŭi 疑). In Sanskrit, "doubt" or "skepticism"; classified as one of the six root afflictions (MŪLAKLEŚA) in the SARVĀSTIVĀDA school of ABHIDHARMA and the YOGĀCĀRA school, and one of the fourteen unwholesome mental factors (akusala-cetasika) in the Pāli abhidhamma, where it takes the form of doubt about such matters as the FOUR NOBLE TRUTHS, the effects of actions (KARMAN), or the efficacy of the path (MĀRGA). Doubt is also classified as the second of ten "fetters" (SAMYOJANA) that keep beings bound in SAṂSĀRA. It is also classified as one of five "hindrances" (NĪVARAṆA) that prevent the mind from attaining meditative absorption (DHYĀNA); skeptical doubt is the factor that hinders sustained thought (VICĀRA) among the five constituents of meditative absorption (DHYĀNĀṄGA). Doubt is a two-pointedness of mind that renders the mind unable to engage in virtuous action, just as one is unable to sew with a pronged needle. It is characterized by wavering and manifests itself as indecision. The counteragent (PRATIPAKṢA) to vicikitsā is wisdom (PRAJÑĀ), assisted by such specific practices as studying the scriptures. This state of doubt is temporarily allayed with the attainment of the first meditative absorption (dhyāna) and is permanently eliminated upon attaining the stage of stream-enterer (SROTAĀPANNA). Cf. YIJING.

**videha**. (T. lus 'phags po; C. pitihe; J. bidaika; K. pijeha 毘提訶). The Sanskrit and Pāli proper name of one of the four island continents arrayed according to traditional Buddhist cosmology in the four cardinal directions around Mount SUMERU; also referred to as pūrvavideha. Videha is the eastern continent and is semicircular in shape. Its inhabitants, classified as humans (MANUṢYA) among the six types of beings who inhabit SAṂSĀRA, are said to be twice as tall as the inhabitants of our southern continent of JAMBUDVĪPA and to have a life span of up to 250 years.

**vidhi**. (T. cho ga; C. yigui; J. giki; K. ŭigwe 儀軌). In Sanskrit, "rite"; a term that is used for Vedic and other rituals. In Buddhism, and in particular tantric Buddhism, vidhi is sometimes used interchangeably with PŪJĀ but can also refer to those elements of a SĀDHANA that are more overtly ceremonial, such as the making of offerings, the drawing of MAṆḌALA, the performance of MUDRĀ or of sacred dances, and the playing of music, as opposed to the more introspective elements of a sādhana, such as the practice of visualization, meditation, or the silent repetition of MANTRA.

**vidyā**. (P vijjā; T. rig pa/rig ma; C. ming; J. myō; K. myŏng 明). In Sanskrit, lit. "knowledge," a polysemous term with a wide range of denotations in Buddhist literature. Vidyā appears frequently in the sūtra literature of the MAINSTREAM BUDDHIST SCHOOLS (as in the title of the Pāli TEVIJJĀSUTTA), where it encompasses what might be called conventional knowledge of the world gained through investigation and analysis, as well as the salvific knowledge of the nature of reality gained through the practice of meditation (see TRIVIDYĀ). In Pāli commentarial literature, vidyā carries connotations of investigation, observation, and correct theories; thus, in some contexts, it is translated as "science" and appears in a number of important lists, such as the PAÑCAVIDYĀ. In tantric literature, it takes on a further meaning of esoteric and occult knowledge (and hence is sometimes translated as "spell"), as in the term VIDYĀDHARA. Vidyā is also used in tantric literature to refer to a sexual consort. Its negation, AVIDYĀ, lit., "non-knowledge," is the most common term for the fundamental ignorance that is the root cause of suffering.

**vidyādhara**. (P. vijjādhara; T. rig pa 'dzin pa; C. chiming; J. jimyō; K. chimyŏng 持明). In Sanskrit, lit. "keeper of knowledge." Knowledge (VIDYĀ) in this context has the denotation of knowledge of sacred lore and magic, such that a vidyādhara functions as a kind of sorcerer or thaumaturge. The term is used to refer to tantric deities as well as to human tantric masters, such as the MAHĀSIDDHAs, whose great powers derived from their knowledge of MANTRAs. As the repository of tantric knowledge, the tantric corpus was sometimes called the VIDYĀDHARAPIṬAKA. See also WEIKZA.

**vidyādharapiṭaka**. (T. rig 'dzin sde snod; C. chiming zang; J. jimyōzō; K. chimyŏng chang 持明藏). In Sanskrit, the "collection of the keepers of knowledge"; a term used to refer collectively to the Buddhist TANTRAs, which were said to have been collected by the tantric thaumaturges (VIDYĀDHARA). The tantras are said to constitute a fourth PIṬAKA—in addition to the SŪTRA, VINAYA, and ABHIDHARMA piṭakas—called the vidyādharapiṭaka.

**vidyāsthāna**. (P. vijjāṭṭhāna; T. rigs pa'i gnas; C. ming chu; J. myōsho; K. myŏng ch'ŏ 明處). In Sanskrit, lit. "abode of knowledge," but often translated as "science," especially in the context of the five traditional sciences of ancient India, which a BODHISATTVA is also expected to master. These five sciences (PAÑCAVIDYĀ) are śabda, which includes grammar and composition; hetu [alt. PRAMĀṆA], or logic; cikitsā, or medicine; śilpakarma, which includes the arts and mathematics; and adhyātmavidyā, the "inner science," which in the case of Buddhism was said to be knowledge of the TRIPIṬAKA and the twelve categories of scriptures (DVĀDAŚĀṄGA[PRAVACANA]).

**Vigrahavyāvartanī**. (T. Rtsod pa bzlog pa; C. Huizheng lun; J. Ejōron; K. Hoejaeng non 迴諍論). In Sanskrit, "Refutation of Objections"; one of the major works of NĀGĀRJUNA and considered as part of his philosophical corpus (YUKTIKĀYA). The work, which is preserved in Sanskrit, Tibetan, and Chinese, has seventy stanzas; there is also an autocommentary by the author. The work appears to have been composed after the MŪLAMADHYAMAKAKĀRIKĀ, responding to objections that might be raised to arguments in that text; hence, the title "Refutation of Objections." As in the case of the *Mūlamadhyamakakārikā*, the opponent is presumably an adherent of the ABHIDHARMA, although it is directed specifically to Naiyāyika-type arguments. Perhaps the most famous objection and response comes at the beginning of the text. In the first stanza of the work, the opponent states that, if it is true, as Nāgārjuna claims, that all things lack intrinsic nature (SVABHĀVA), then Nāgārjuna's own statement must also lack intrinsic nature, in which case the statement cannot deny the intrinsic nature of things. In the famous twenty-ninth stanza, Nāgārjuna responds, "If I had some thesis (PRATIJÑĀ), I would incur that fault; because I have no thesis, I am faultless." The autocommentary explains that there can be no thesis when all things are empty, utterly quiescent, and naturally pristine. Therefore, because he has no thesis, no mark of a thesis is entailed by his previous statement that all things lack intrinsic nature. The text is widely quoted by later commentators, both in India and in Tibet.

**vihāra**. (T. gtsug lag khang/dgon pa; C. zhu/jingshe; J. jū/shōja; K. chu/chŏngsa 住/精舍). In Sanskrit and Pāli, lit. "abode"; the term commonly used for a dwelling place for monks and nuns, and thus typically translated as "monastery." In the story of the life of the Buddha, in the early days of the saṃgha the monks had no fixed abode but wandered throughout the year. Eventually, the Buddha instructed monks to cease their peregrinations during the torrential monsoon period in order to prevent the killing of insects and worms while walking on muddy roads. The residences established for use during the rains retreat (VARṢĀ) are called varṣāvāsa or "rains abode," and the institution of the rains retreat (and the consequent need for more permanent shelter) probably led to the development of formal monasteries. According to the VINAYA, a vihāra must be donated to the SAṂGHA and, once accepted, it may never be given back, but remains in perpetuity the property of the order. There are various rules and recommendations concerning the layout of a vihāra. According to the Pāli VINAYA, a vihāra may be plastered and decorated, but never using figures of human beings. It may have three kinds of rooms, upper, large, and small. These rooms are typically arrayed around a central courtyard that often enshrined a sapling of a BODHI TREE or a STŪPA. The vihāra should have a refectory and a place for storing water, and it may be surrounded by a wall. It should be neither too near nor too far from a town or village and be suitable for gathering alms but secluded enough to be conducive to study and contemplation. A vihāra may be constructed for the use of the entire congregation of monks or nuns or for personal use. If a proposed vihāra for an individual monk is large or grand, permission for its construction must first be granted by the saṃgha. The Indian state of Bihar takes its name from the many Buddhist vihāras that were once scattered throughout the region. See also entries on specific monasteries.

**vihiṃsā**. (T. rnam par 'tshe ba; C. hai; J. gai; K. hae 害). In Sanskrit, lit. "harmfulness," sometimes translated as "injury," "cruelty," or "harmful intention"; one of the forty-six mental concomitants (CAITTA) according to the VAIBHĀṢIKA school of SARVĀSTIVĀDA ABHIDHARMA and one of the fifty-one according to the YOGĀCĀRA school. As the opposite of "harmlessness" or "nonviolence" (AHIṂSĀ), vihiṃsā is the ill will that wishes for, or causes, suffering to come to others. Vihiṃsā is listed among the fifth of the six categories of caitta, the secondary afflictions (UPAKLEŚA), which are not compatible with spiritual progress. Vihiṃsā is also considered to be one of the possible derivative emotions of "aversion" (DVEṢA) and cannot exist independently of that latter mental state. The antidote to this volition to bring harm to others is the development of loving-kindness (MAITRĪ).

**Vijaya**. The first Āryan king of Sri Lanka. According to the MAHĀVAṂSA, Vijaya led a band of seven hundred followers exiled from north India to Sri Lanka in the sixth century BCE. The capital he founded was named Tambapaṇṇi, whence one of the names for the island, Tambapaṇṇi Dīpa. Vijaya and his followers were known as Sīhaḷa, after an epithet of his father, Sīhabāhu or "lion-armed," who was the offspring of a lion and a human princess. For this reason, the island also came to be known as Sīhaḷa Dīpa or "Lion Island."

**vijñāna**. (P. viññāṇa; T. rnam par shes pa; C. shi; J, shiki; K. sik 識). In Sanskrit, "consciousness"; a term that technically refers to the six types of sensory consciousness (VIJÑĀNA): eye, or visual, consciousness (CAKṢURVIJÑĀNA); ear, or auditory, consciousness (ŚROTRAVIJÑĀNA); nose, or olfactory, consciousness (GHRĀṆAVIJÑĀNA); tongue, or gustatory, consciousness (JIHVĀVIJÑĀNA); body, or tactile, consciousness (KĀYAVIJÑĀNA); and mental consciousness (MANOVIJÑĀNA). These are the six major sources of awareness of the phenomena (DHARMA) of our observable universe. Each of these forms of consciousness is produced in dependence upon three conditions (PRATYAYA): the "objective-support condition" (ĀLAMBANAPRATYAYA), the "predominant condition" (ADHIPATIPRATYAYA), and the "immediately preceding condition" (SAMANANTARAPRATYAYA). When used with reference to the six forms of consciousness, the term vijñāna refers only to CITTA, or general mentality, and not to the mental concomitants (CAITTA) that accompany mentality. It is also in this sense that vijñāna constitutes the fifth of the five SKANDHAS, while the mental concomitants are instead placed in the fourth aggregate of conditioning factors (SAṂSKĀRA). The six forms of consciousness figure in two important lists in Buddhist epistemology, the twelve sense fields (ĀYATANA) and the eighteen elements (DHĀTU). With the exception of some strands of the YOGĀCĀRA school, six and only six forms of vijñāna are accepted. The Yogācāra school of ASAṄGA posits instead eight forms of vijñāna, adding to the six sensory consciousnesses a seventh afflicted mentality (KLIṢṬAMANAS), which creates the mistaken conception of a self, and an eighth foundational or storehouse consciousness (ĀLAYAVIJÑĀNA).

**Vijñānakāya[pādaśāstra]**. (T. Rnam shes kyi tshogs; C. Shishen zu lun; J. Shikishinsokuron; K. Siksin chok non 識身足論). In Sanskrit, "Collection on Consciousness"; a book from the middle stratum of the SARVĀSTIVĀDA ABHIDHARMAPIṬAKA, which is traditionally listed as the second of the six ancillary texts, or "feet" (pāda), of the JÑĀNAPRASTHĀNA, the central treatise or body (śarīra) of the Sarvāstivāda abhidharmapiṭaka. Authorship of the text is attributed to Devaśarman, and it is presumed to have been composed during the latter half of the first century CE. It is extant only in a complete translation into Chinese made by XUANZANG and his translation team at DACI'ENSI in 649. The *Vijñānakāya* is the only one of the six pādaśāstras that provides an elaborate proof of the veracity of the eponymous Sarvāstivāda position that dharmas exist in the past, present, and future, and its treatments are the foundation for the refinements of this position in later VAIBHĀṢIKA materials. The *Vijñānakāya* is also the only canonical Sarvāstivāda treatise that critiques the mistaken belief in a person (PUDGALA). The extensive refutation of the PUDGALAVĀDA position found in the appendix (chapter nine) to VASUBANDHU's ABHIDHARMAKOŚABHĀṢYA relies heavily on the *Vijñānakāya*'s content and approach. The *Vijñānakāya* also offers an elaborate analysis of fourteen types of causes (HETU); in addition, it provides the first listing of the four types of conditions (PRATYAYA), especially in connection with the arising of sensory consciousness. By bringing causation theory to the forefront of abhidharma philosophy, the *Vijñānakāya* occupies a crucial place in the evolution of the Sarvāstivāda abhidharma. The *Vijñānakāya*'s closest analogue in the Pāli ABHIDHAMMA literature is the DHĀTUKATHĀ.

**vijñānānantyāyatana**. (P. viññāṇañcāyatana; T. rnam shes mtha' yas skye mched; C. shi wubian chu; J. shikimuhenjo; K. sik mubyŏn ch'ŏ 識無邊處). In Sanskrit, "sphere of infinite consciousness"; the second (in ascending order) of the four levels of the immaterial realm (ĀRŪPYADHĀTU) and the second of the four immaterial absorptions (ĀRŪPYĀVACARADHYĀNA). It is "above" the first level of the immaterial realm, called infinites space (AKĀŚĀNANTYĀYATANA), and "below" the third and fourth levels, "nothingness" (ĀKIṂCANYĀYATANA) and "neither perception nor nonperception" (NAIVASAṂJÑĀNĀSAṂJÑĀYATANA). It is a realm of rebirth as well as a meditative state that is entirely immaterial (viz., there is no physical, or form [RŪPA], component to existence), in which the mind seems to expand to the point that it is essentially infinite. Beings reborn in this realm are thought to live as long as forty thousand eons (KALPA). However, as a state of being that is still subject to rebirth, even the realm of infinite consciousness remains part of SAṂSĀRA. Like the other levels of the realm of subtle materiality (RŪPADHĀTU) and the immaterial realm, one is reborn in this state by achieving the specific level of meditative absorption of that state in the previous lifetime. One of the most famous and influential expositions on the subject of these immaterial states comes from the VISUDDHIMAGGA of BUDDHAGHOSA, written in the fifth century. Although there are numerous accounts of Buddhist meditators achieving immaterial states of SAMĀDHI, they are also used polemically in Buddhist literature to describe the attainments of non-Buddhist YOGINs, who mistakenly identify these exalted states within saṃsāra as states of permanent liberation from rebirth. See also DHYĀNASAMĀPATTI; DHYĀNOPAPATTI.

**vijñānaskandha**. (P. viññāṇakhandha; T. rnam shes kyi phung po; C. shiyun/shiyin; J. shikiun/shikion; K. sigon/sigŭm 識蘊/識陰). In Sanskrit, the "consciousness aggregate"; the fifth of the five aggregates of being (SKANDHA). The vijñānaskandha refers to the six types of consciousness (VIJÑĀNA, viz., the visual, auditory, olfactory, gustatory, tactile, and mental consciousnesses) but not to the various mental concomitants (CAITTA) that accompany them, which are placed in the fourth aggregate, SAṂSKĀRA. See VIJÑĀNA.

**Vijñānavāda**. [alt. Vijñānavādin] (T. Rnam par shes pa smra ba; C. Weishi zong; J. Yuishikishū; K. Yusik chong 唯識宗). In Sanskrit, "Proponent of Consciousness"; an alternative designation for the YOGĀCĀRA school, emphasizing the central role of the exposition of consciousness (VIJÑĀNA) in the tenets of the school. The school's cardinal doctrine is that the objects of experience are of the nature of representation-alone (VIJÑAPTIMĀTRATĀ), also referred to as "mind only" (CITTAMĀTRA). See YOGĀCĀRA; FAXIANG ZONG.

**vijñapti**. (T. rnam par rig byed; C. shi; J. shiki; K. sik 識). In Sanskrit, "representation," "designation," or "imputation"; a term especially important in the YOGĀCĀRA school, where it indicates the subjective nature of the objects of experience, emphasizing the role of consciousness (VIJÑĀNA) in the identification, naming, and ontological status of the constituents of the external world. The term appears in the title of perhaps the most influential Indian Yogācāra treatise for East Asian Buddhism, the CHENG WEISHI LUN (*VIJÑAPTIMĀTRATĀSIDDHI; "Demonstration of Representation-Only"), which presents the philosophical positions of the sixth-century Yogācāra master DHARMAPĀLA (530–561).

**vijñaptimātratā**. (T. rnam par rig pa tsam nyid; C. weishi; J. yuishiki; K. yusik 唯識). In Sanskrit, "mere-representation" or "mere-designation"; the cardinal doctrine of the YOGĀCĀRA school, viz., that the objects of experience are mere projections of consciousness (VIJÑĀNA). Thus, all objects are mere representations and all categories are mere designations. No object is the natural basis of its name; rather, the mind itself instead designates the object. The term Vijñaptimātra is used as an alternative designation of the Yogācāra school, especially as represented in the works of VASUBANDHU, STHIRAMATI, and DHARMAPĀLA, with particular emphasis on the doctrine of the three natures (TRISVABHĀVA). Indeed, the term appears in the title of perhaps the most influential Indian Yogācāra treatise for East Asian Buddhism, the CHENG WEISHI LUN (S. **Vijñaptimātratāsiddhi*; "Demonstration of Representation-Only") by the sixth-century Yogācāra master DHARMAPĀLA (530–561). It is the Chinese translation of vijñaptimātratā (weishi) thought that became the primary source of Yogācāra philosophy in East Asia.

***Vijñaptimātratāsiddhi**. (S). See CHENG WEISHI LUN.

**vikalpa**. (P. vikappa; T. rnam par rtog pa; C. fenbie; J. funbetsu; K. punbyŏl 分別). In Sanskrit, "[false] discrimination," "imagining," or "conception"; the discriminative activities of mind, generally portrayed in the negative sense of fantasy and imagination, and often equivalent to "conceptual proliferation" (PRAPAÑCA). Vikalpa refers to the conceptual activities of the mental consciousness (MANOVIJÑĀNA), a mediated mental activity that operates through the medium of generic images (SĀMĀNYALAKṢAṆA). Vikalpa is often opposed to the immediate knowledge provided by direct perception (PRATYAKṢA). The direct perception of reality is therefore commonly described as NIRVIKALPA, or "free from thought." ¶ Three types of conceptual discrimination (TRIVIKALPA) are typically described in the literature. (1) Intrinsic discrimination (SVABHĀVAVIKALPA), which refers to the initial advertence of thought (VITARKA) and the subsequent sustained attention (VICĀRA) to a perceived object of the six sensory consciousnesses (VIJÑĀNA), that is, the discrimination of present objects, as when visual consciousness perceives a visual object. (2) Conceptualizing discrimination (ABHINIRŪPAṆĀVIKALPA), which refers to discursive thought on ideas that arise in the sixth mental consciousness when it adverts toward a mental object that is associated with any of the three time periods of past, present, or future. (3) Discrimination involving reflection on past events (ANUSMARAṆAVIKALPA), which refers to discriminative thought involving the memory of past objects. ¶ There is a wide range of opinion as to the value of vikalpa (in the sense of "thought" or "conception") in the soteriological progress. Some traditions would hold that the structured use of conceptual and logical analysis (and especially the use of inference, or ANUMĀNA) is a necessary prerequisite to reaching a state beyond all thought. Such a position is advocated in the Indian philosophical schools and in those that favor the so-called gradual path to enlightenment. In the stages of the path to enlightenment, all forms of meditation prior to the attainment of the path of vision (DARŚANAMĀRGA) are "conceptual" and thus entail vikalpa. Other schools radically devalue all thought as an obstacle to the understanding of the ultimate and would claim that the nonconceptual, described in some cases as "no-thought" (C. WUNIAN), is accessible at all times. Such an approach, most famously expounded in the CHAN traditions of Asia, is associated with the so-called sudden path to enlightenment (see DUNWU). ¶ In the YOGĀCĀRA school, vikalpa is described specifically as the "discriminative conception of apprehended and apprehender" (GRĀHYAGRĀHAKAVIKALPA), referring to the misconception that there is an inherent bifurcation between a perceiving subject (grāhaka) and its perceived objects (grāhya). This bifurcation occurs because of false imagining (ABHŪTAPARIKALPA), the tendency of the relative phenomena (PARATANTRA) to be misperceived as divided into a perceiving self and a perceived object that is external to it. By relying on these false imaginings to construct our sense of what is real, we inevitably subject ourselves to continued suffering (DUḤKHA) within the cycle of birth-and-death (SAṂSĀRA). Overcoming this bifurcation leads to the nondiscriminative wisdom (NIRVIKALPAJÑĀNA), which, in the five-stage path (PAÑCAMĀRGA) system, marks the inception of the path of vision (darśanamārga), where the adept sees reality directly, without the intercession of concepts. The elimination of grāhyagrāhakavikalpa proceeds from the less to the more subtle. It is easier to realize that a projected object is a projection than to realize that a projecting subject is as well; among projected objects, it is easier to realize that afflicted (SAṂKLIṢṬA) dharmas (the SKANDHAS and so on) are projections than to realize that purified (VYAVADĀNA) dharmas (the five paths and so on) are as well; and among subjects it is easier to realize that a material subject (a mental substratum and so on) is a projection than to realize that a nominally existing subject (a nominally existing self and so on) is. This explanation of vikalpa, common in the PRAJÑĀPĀRAMITĀ commentarial tradition, influenced the theory of the SAṂPANNAKRAMA (completion stage) in ANUTTARAYOGA (highest yoga) TANTRA, where prior to reaching enlightenment the four sets of vikalpas are dissolved with their associated PRĀṆAS in the central channel (AVADHŪTI).

**Vikramaśīla**. (T. Rnam gnon ngang tshul). A monastery and monastic university in the northern region of ancient MAGADHA, in the modern Bihar state of India, located along the Ganges River in the Bhagalpur District of Bihar, about 150 miles east of NĀLANDĀ. King Dharmapāla of the Pāla dynasty founded Vikramaśīla between the late eighth and early ninth centuries and appointed his teacher, Buddhajñānapāda, to be abbot of the monastic university. Throughout its existence, leaders of the Pāla dynasty supported the teachers, students, and maintenance of the institution. There were six areas of religious study, supplemented by such secular subjects as grammar, metaphysics, and logic. The two monastic universities of Vikramaśīla and Nālandā had a great deal of scholarly interaction, and, like Nālandā, Vikramaśīla served as a model for Tibetan monasteries. There were more foreign students at Vikramaśīla than at Nālandā, and the monastery is said to have been large enough to accommodate around ten thousand resident students, including specific dormitories for visiting Tibetan students. Vikramaśīla also housed a substantial library, where texts were both stored and recopied by students and teachers. By the tenth century CE, Vikramaśīla had outgrown even Nālandā, reaching its peak in the eleventh century, and offered a famous PRAJÑĀPĀRAMITĀ curriculum. The monastery became the focus of tantric scholarship during this period, and pilgrims came to study from many regions of Asia. During the reign of King Nayapāla, in the eleventh century, ATIŚA DĪPAṂKARAŚRĪJÑĀNA was considered the greatest scholar at the monastery. Other famous scholars also taught there, including JITĀRI, JÑĀNAŚRĪMITRA, NĀROPA (briefly), and RATNĀKARAŚĀNTI. Vikramaśīla was attacked by Muslim armies between 1199 and 1203 CE. During the same period, ODANTAPURĪ was also attacked, and the surviving scholars and students were forced to flee. Many scholars escaped to Nepal and Tibet, saving many texts from their libraries. ŚĀKYAŚRĪBHADRA was the last abbot of Vikramaśīla, and also the last to flee to Tibet from the monastery, arriving in 1204.

**vikṣepa**. (P. vikkhepa; T. rnam par g.yeng ba; C. sanluan; J. sanran; K. sallan 散亂). In Sanskrit, "distraction"; the movement of the mind away from the object of observation or a lack of mental balance that disturbs concentration. It is one of the forty-six mental concomitants (CAITTA) according to the VAIBHĀṢIKA school of SARVĀSTIVĀDA ABHIDHARMA and one of the fifty-one according to the YOGĀCĀRA school, which lists it as one of the twenty secondary afflictions (UPAKLEŚA).

**vimalā**. (T. dri ma med pa; C. ligou di; J. rikuji; K. igu chi 離垢地). In Sanskrit, "immaculate" or "stainless"; the name of the second of the ten bodhisattva stages, or BHŪMI. On this bhūmi, the bodhisattva engages in the perfection of morality (ŚĪLAPĀRAMITĀ) and is unstained by even subtle types of unwholesome actions performed by body, speech, or mind. It is said that from this bhūmi onward, the bodhisattva is untainted by killing, stealing, sexual misconduct, lying, divisive speech, harsh speech, senseless prattle, covetousness, harmful intent, or wrong views, even during dreams. He performs the ten virtues of protecting life, giving gifts, maintaining sexual ethics, speaking truthfully, speaking harmoniously, speaking kindly, speaking sensibly, nonattachment, helpful intent, and right views without the slightest taint of a conception of self (ĀTMAGRAHA). The bodhisattva remains on this stage until he is able to enter into all worldly forms of SAMĀDHI.

**Vimalakīrti**. (T. Dri med grags pa; C. Weimojie; J. Yuimakitsu; K. Yumahil 維摩詰). Sanskrit proper name of a mythical Indian Buddhist layman. He is the subject of an eponymous sūtra that describes his victories in debates with elite MAHĀYĀNA BODHISATTVAs. See VIMALAKĪRTINIRDEŚA.

**Vimalakīrtinirdeśa**. (T. Dri med grags pas bstan pa'i mdo; C. Weimo jing; J. Yuimagyō; K. Yuma kyŏng 維摩經). In Sanskrit, "Vimalakīrti's Instructions"; one of the most beloved Indian Mahāyāna sūtras, renowned especially for having a layman, the eponymous VIMALAKĪRTI, as its protagonist. The text probably dates from around the second century CE. Among the seven translations of the sūtra into Chinese, the most famous is that made by KUMĀRAJĪVA in 406. His translation seems to have been adapted to appeal to Chinese mores, emphasizing the worldly elements of Vimalakīrti's teachings and introducing the term "filial piety" into the text. The sūtra was also translated by XUANZANG in 650. The sūtra was translated into Tibetan twice, the more famous being that of Chos nyid tshul khrims in the ninth century. It has also been rendered into Sogdian, Khotanese, and Uighur. The original Sanskrit of the text was lost for over a millennia until a Sanskrit manuscript was discovered in the PO TA LA palace in Tibet in 2001. The narrative of the sūtra begins with the Buddha requesting that his leading ŚRĀVAKA disciples visit his lay disciple Vimalakīrti, who is ill. Each demurs, recounting a previous meeting with Vimalakīrti in which the layman had chastised the monk for his limited understanding of the dharma. The Buddha then instructs his leading bodhisattva disciples to visit Vimalakīrti. Each again demurs until MAÑJUŚRĪ reluctantly agrees. Vimalakīrti explains that his sickness is the sickness of all sentient beings, and goes on to describe how a sick bodhisattva should understand his sickness, emphasizing the necessity of both wisdom (PRAJÑĀ) and method (UPĀYA). A large audience of monks and bodhisattvas then comes to Vimalakīrti's house, where he delivers a sermon on "inconceivable liberation" (acintyavimokṣa). Among the audience is ŚĀRIPUTRA, the wisest of the Buddha's śrāvaka disciples. As in other Mahāyāna sūtras, the eminent śrāvaka is made to play the fool, repeatedly failing to understand how all dichotomies are overcome in emptiness (ŚŪNYATĀ), most famously when a goddess momentarily transforms him into a female. Later, a series of bodhisattvas take turns describing various forms of duality and how they are overcome in nonduality. Vimalakīrti is the last to be invited to speak. He remains silent and is praised for this teaching of the entrance into nonduality. The sūtra is widely quoted in later literature, especially on the topics of emptiness, method, and nonduality. It became particularly famous in East Asia because the protagonist is a layman, who repeatedly demonstrates that his wisdom is superior to that of monks. Scenes from the sūtra are often depicted in East Asian Buddhist art.

**Vimalamitra**. (T. Dri med bshes gnyen). An Indian master revered in Tibet as one of the chief figures in the transmission of the RDZOGS CHEN teachings of the RNYING MA sect, especially of the "heart drop" (SNYING THIG) tradition. He is said to have received rdzogs chen teachings from both Jñānasūra and ŚRĪSIṂHA. According to legend, Vimalamitra transmitted these teachings to Tibet when he was invited (when he was supposedly already two hundred years old) to come to Tibet by King KHRI SRONG LDE BTSAN, arriving either before or after the king's death in 799. He remained in Tibet for thirteen years, before leaving for China. While in Tibet, he collaborated in the translation of a number of texts from Sanskrit into Tibetan, including the GUHYASAMĀJATANTRA, the GUHYAGARBHATANTRA, and the PRAJÑĀPĀRAMITĀHṚDAYASŪTRA ("Heart Sūtra"). Vimalamitra is especially renowned for his transmission of the teachings of the "instruction class" (MANG NGAG SDE), which were gathered in a collection named after him, the BI MA SNYING THIG. He is also said to have concealed treasure texts (gter ma) at a hermitage above BSAM YAS monastery. The works attributed to him preserved in the Tibetan canons are all tantric in subject matter, with two exceptions, a commentary on the SAPTASĀHASRIKĀPRAJÑĀPĀRAMITĀSŪTRA ("Perfection of Wisdom in Seven Hundred Lines") and a commentary on the *Prajñāpāramitāhṛdayasūtra*. Both are straightforward exegetical works, which prompted the

Tibetan historian 'Gos lo tsā ba to report in his DEB THER SNGON PO ("Blue Annals") that these commentaries were not the product of the tantric master revered in Rnying ma, and that in fact there must have been two Vimalamitras.

**Vimalaprabhā**. (T. Dri med 'od). In Sanskrit, "Stainless Light," the most important commentary on the KĀLACAKRATANTRA. It is traditionally attributed to Puṇḍarīka, one of the kings of ŚAMBHALA.

**Vīmaṃsakasutta**. (C. Qiujie jing; J. Gugekyō; K. Kuhae kyŏng 求解經). In Pāli, "Discourse on Investigation"; the forty-seventh sutta in the MAJJHIMANIKĀYA (a separate SARVĀSTIVĀDA recension appears as the 186th SŪTRA in the Chinese translation of the MADHYAMĀGAMA); delivered by the Buddha to a gathering of monks in the JETAVANA grove at the town of Sāvatthi (ŚRĀVASTĪ). In this sutta, the Buddha describes specific means by which it may be determined whether or not the TATHĀGATA has in fact attained buddhahood. He directs the inquirer to rely on what he has seen and heard to determine whether the tathāgata possesses any defiled states, mixed states, or impure states; whether he possesses wholesome states; and whether he is free from the dangers of renown and fame, free from fear and sexual passion, and free from contempt for others due to their failings. Finally the Buddha states that the monk gains true confidence in the three jewels (RATNATRAYA) by learning the Buddha's teachings and confirming their truth through direct experience born of practice.

**Vimānavatthu**. In Pāli, "Accounts of the Celestial Abodes," the sixth book of the Pāli KHUDDAKANIKĀYA. The text contains accounts of the heavenly abodes (P. vimāna, lit. "mansion, palace") of various divinities (DEVA), which they acquired as rewards for meritorious deeds performed in previous lives. Its eighty-three stories were told to Moggallāna (MAHĀMAUDGALYĀYANA) and other saints during their sojourns in celestial realms, who in turn related them to the Buddha. The Vimānavatthu appears in the Pali Text Society's English translation series as *Stories of the Mansions*.

**vimokṣa**. (P. vimokkha; T. rnam par thar pa; C. jietuo; J. gedatsu; K. haet'al 解脫). In Sanskrit, "liberation" or "deliverance"; the state of freedom from rebirth, achieved by the ŚRĀVAKA, PRATYEKABUDDHA, or BODHISATTVA paths (MĀRGA). In mainstream Buddhist literature, this liberation is said to be of three types, corresponding to the three "doors to deliverance" (VIMOKṢAMUKHA): (1) emptiness (ŚUNYATĀ), (2) signlessness (ĀNIMITTA), and (3) wishlessness (APRAṆIHITA). Another set of eight grades of liberation (vimokṣa) is associated with the attainment of meditative absorption (DHYĀNA). In Pāli sources, these grades refer to eight levels in the extension of consciousness that accompany the cultivation of increasingly more advanced states of dhyāna (P. JHĀNA). The eight grades are (1) the perception of material form (RŪPA) while remaining in the subtle-materiality realm; (2) the perception of external material forms while not perceiving one's own form; (3) the development of confidence through contemplating the beautiful; (4) passing beyond the material plane with the idea of "limitless space," one attains the plane of limitless space (ĀKĀŚĀNANTYĀYATANA), the first level of the immaterial realm; (5) passing beyond the plane of limitless space with the idea of "limitless consciousness," one attains the plane of limitless consciousness (VIJÑĀNĀNANTYĀYATANA); (6) passing beyond the plane of limitless consciousness with the idea "there is nothing," one attains the plane of nothingness (ĀKIÑCANYĀYATANA); (7) passing beyond the plane of nothingness one attains the plane of neither perception nor nonperception (NAIVASAMJÑĀNĀSAMJÑĀYATANA); and (8) passing beyond the plane of neither perception nor nonperception one attains the cessation of consciousness (viz., NIRODHASAMĀPATTI). In the Mahāyāna ABHIDHARMA, it is said that the first two grades enable bodhisattvas to manifest different forms for the sake of others, the third controls their attitude toward those forms (by seeing that beauty and ugliness are relative), and the remaining five enable them to live at ease in order to help others.

**vimokṣamārga**. (S). See VIMUKTIMĀRGA.

**vimokṣamukha**. (P. vimokkhamukha; T. rnam par thar pa'i sgo; C. jietuo men; J. gedatsumon; K. haet'al mun 解脫門). In Sanskrit, "gates to deliverance," or "doors of liberation"; three points of transition between the compounded (SAṂSKṚTA) and uncompounded (ASAṂSKṚTA) realms, which, when contemplated, lead to liberation (VIMOKṢA) and NIRVĀṆA: (1) emptiness (ŚUNYATĀ), (2) signlessness (ĀNIMITTA), and (3) wishlessness (APRAṆIHITA). The three are widely interpreted. In mainstream Buddhist materials, emptiness (śunyatā) entails the recognition that all compounded (SAṂSKṚTA) things of this world are devoid of any perduring self (ĀTMAN) and are thus unworthy objects of clinging. By acknowledging emptiness, the meditator is thus able to turn away from this world and instead advert toward nirvāṇa, which is uncompounded (ASAṂSKṚTA). Signlessness (ānimitta) is a crucial stage in the process of sensory restraint (INDRIYASAṂVARA): as the frequent refrain in the SŪTRAs states, "In the seen, there is only the seen," and not the superimpositions created by the intrusion of ego (ĀTMAN) into the perceptual process. Signlessness is produced through insight into impermanence (ANITYA) and serves as the counteragent (PRATIPAKṢA) to attachments to anything experienced through the senses; once the meditator has abandoned all such attachments to the senses, he is then able to advert toward nirvāṇa, which ipso facto has no sensory signs of its own by which it can be recognized. Wishlessness is produced through insight into suffering (DUḤKHA) and serves as the counteragent (PRATIPAKṢA) to all the intentions (āśaya) and aspirations (PRAṆIDHĀNA) one has toward any compounded dharma. As the Buddha's famous simile of the raft also suggests, the adept must finally abandon even the attachment to the compounded religious system that is Buddhism in order to experience nirvāṇa, the summum bonum of the religion. Once the meditator has abandoned all such aspirations, he will then be able to advert toward nirvāṇa, which ipso facto has nothing to do with anything that can be desired (VAIRĀGYA). ¶ In the ABHIDHARMAKOŚABHĀṢYA, the three are explained in terms of three types of concentration (SAMĀDHI) on the sixteen aspects of the FOUR NOBLE TRUTHS. The four aspects of the first truth, of suffering (DUḤKHASATYA), are impermanence, misery, emptiness, and selflessness. The four aspects of the second truth, origination (SAMUDAYASATYA), are cause, origination, strong production, and condition. The four aspects of the third truth, cessation (NIRODHASATYA), are cessation, pacification, exaltedness, and emergence. The four aspects of the fourth truth, path (MĀRGASATYA), are path, suitability, achievement, and deliverance. According to the *Abhidharmakośabhāṣya*, the samādhi associated with signlessness observes the four aspects of cessation; the samādhi of emptiness observes emptiness and selflessness, two of the four aspects of suffering; and the samādhi of wishlessness observes the remaining ten aspects. ¶ In YOGĀCĀRA texts, such as the MAHĀYĀNASAṂGRAHA, emptiness, wishlessness, and signlessness are related to the three natures (TRISVABHĀVA) of the imaginary (PARIKALPITA), the dependent (PARATANTRA), and the consummate (PARINIṢPANNA), respectively. In the MAHĀYĀNASŪTRĀLAṂKĀRA, it is said that the samādhi of emptiness understands the selflessness of persons and phenomenal factors (DHARMA), the samādhi of wishlessness views the five aggregates (SKANDHA) as faulty, and the samādhi of signlessness views nirvāṇa as the pacification of the aggregates. Elsewhere in that text, the three are connected to the four seals (CATURMUDRĀ) that certify a doctrine as Buddhist. The statements "all compounded factors are impermanent" and "all contaminated things are suffering" are the cause of the samādhi of wishlessness. "All phenomena are devoid of a perduring self" is the cause of the samādhi of emptiness. "Nirvāṇa is peace" is the cause of the sāmadhi of signlessness. According to another interpretation, emptiness refers to the lack of a truly existent entity in phenomena, signlessness refers to the lack of a truly existent cause, and wishlessness refers to the lack of a truly existent effect.

**Viṃśatikā**. (T. Nyi shu pa; C. Weishi ershi lun; J. Yuishiki nijūron; K. Yusik isip non 唯識二十論). The "Twenty," also known as *Viṃśatikāvijñaptimātratāsiddhikārikā*, the "Twenty Stanzas Proving Representation-Only," one of the most influential independent (i.e., noncommentarial) works of the fourth- or fifth-century Indian master VASUBANDHU. A short work in twenty verses, it outlines the basic position of the YOGĀCĀRA regarding the status of external objects, arguing that such objects do not exist apart from the consciousness that perceives them. He argues, for example, that the fact that objects appear to exist in an external world is not proof of that existence, since an external world also appears to exist in dreams. Therefore, all external phenomena are merely projections of consciousness (VIJÑĀNA) and thus are representation-only (VIJÑAPTIMĀTRATĀ).

**viṃśatiprabhedasaṃgha**. (T. dge 'dun nyi shu; C. ershi sengqie/shengwen cidi; J. nijūsōgya/shōmonshidai; K. isip sŭngga/sŏngmun ch'aje 二十僧伽/聲聞次第). In Sanskrit, "the twenty varieties of the SAṂGHA" or "twenty members of the community"; a subdivision of the eight noble persons (AṢṬĀRYAPUDGALA) into twenty based on different faculties (INDRIYA) and the ways in which they reach NIRVĀṆA; a subdivision used in Mahāyāna works, particularly in the PRAJÑĀPĀRAMITĀ literature, as a template to further identify as many as forty-eight ĀRYA BODHISATTVAS. Only those who have reached the noble path (ĀRYAMĀRGA) or the religious life (śrāmaṇya) that begins with the path of vision (DARŚANAMĀRGA) are included in this idealized saṃgha. The twenty varieties are based on the eight noble persons, two for each of the four fruits of the noble path or religious life (ĀRYAMĀRGAPHALA; ŚRĀMAṆYAPHALA). The four fruits, from lowest to highest, are stream-enterer (SROTAĀPANNA), once-returner (SAKṚDĀGĀMIN), nonreturner (ANĀGĀMIN), and worthy one (ARHAT). For each there is one who enters (SROTAĀPANNAPRATIPANNAKA, etc.) and one who abides (SROTAĀPANNAPHALASTHA, etc.) in a particular fruition. This list also includes the seven noble persons (P. ariyapuggala; S. ĀRYAPUDGALA) as found in the MAJJHIMANIKĀYA. They are (1) the follower of faith (P. saddhānusāri; S. ŚRADDHĀNUSĀRIN); (2) the one liberated through faith (P. saddhāvimutta; S. ŚRADDHĀVIMUKTA); (3) the bodily witness (P. kāyasakkhi; S. KĀYASĀKṢIN); (4) the one liberated both ways (P. ubhatobhāgavimutta; S. UBHAYATOBHĀGAVIMUKTA); (5) the follower of the dharma (P. dhammānusāri; S. DHARMĀNUSĀRIN); (6) the one who has attained understanding (P. diṭṭhippatta; S. DṚṢṬIPRĀPTA); and (7) the one liberated through wisdom (P. paññāvimutta; S. PRAJÑĀVIMUKTA).

The list of the twenty according to the MAHĀVYUTPATTI is:

1. Stream-enterer (SROTAĀPANNA)
2. One who takes up to seven existences (SAPTAKṚDBHAVAPARAMA)
3. One who goes from family to family (KULAṂKULA)
4. Once-returner (SAKṚDĀGĀMIN)
5. One who has a single obstacle (EKAVICITA)
6. Nonreturner (ANĀGĀMIN)
7. One who achieves nirvāṇa in the intermediate state (ANTARĀPARINIRVĀYIN)
8. One who achieves nirvāṇa at birth (UPAPADYAPARINIRVĀYIN)
9. One who achieves nirvāṇa through effort (SĀBHISAṂSKĀRAPARINIRVĀYIN)
10. One who achieves nirvāṇa without effort (ANABHISAṂSKĀRAPARINIRVĀYIN)
11. One who goes higher (ŪRDHVASROTAS)
12. Bodily witness (KĀYASĀKṢIN)
13. Follower through faith (ŚRADDHĀNUSĀRIN)
14. Follower through doctrine (DHARMĀNUSĀRIN)

15. One who has aspired through faith (ŚRADDHĀDHIMUKTA)
16. One who attains through seeing (DṚṢṬIPRĀPTA)
17. One who is liberated dependent upon particular occasions (SAMAYAVIMUKTA).
18. One who is liberated regardless of occasion (ASAMAYAVIMUKTA)
19. One who is liberated through wisdom (PRAJÑĀVIMUKTA)
20. One who is liberated through both ways (UBHAYATOBHĀGAVIMUKTA)

Of these twenty, the first three are subdivisions of the first fruit, the next two of the second fruit, the sixth to twelfth of the third fruit, and the last two subdivisions of the fourth fruit of the ARHAT. The remaining are more general categories. For detailed explanations, see each individual entry.

**vimukti**. (P. vimutti; T. rnam par grol ba; C. jietuo; J. gedatsu; K. haet'al 解脫). In Sanskrit, "liberation." See VIMOKṢA.

**vimuktimārga**. (T. rnam par grol ba'i lam; C. jietuodao; J. gedatsudō; K. haet'alto 解脫道). In Sanskrit, "path of liberation"; a technical term that refers to the second of a two-stage process of abandoning the afflictions (KLEŚA). As one proceeds from the path of vision (DARŚANAMĀRGA) to the adept path where there is nothing more to learn (AŚAIKṢAMĀRGA), the kleśas are abandoned in sequence through repeated occasions of yogic direct perception (YOGIPRATYAKṢA), consisting of two moments. The first is called the ĀNANTARYAMĀRGA (uninterrupted path), in which the specific kleśa or set of kleśas is actively abandoned; this is followed immediately by the vimuktimārga [alt. vimokṣamārga], which is the state of having abandoned, and thus being liberated from, the kleśa.

**Vimuktisena**. [alt. Ārya Vimuktisena] (T. Grol sde). An Indian scholar-monk (likely from the sixth century CE) who is the author of the first extant commentary (vṛtti) on the ABHISAMAYĀLAṂKĀRA, a work associated with the name of MAITREYA or MAITREYANĀTHA, the most influential PRAJÑĀPĀRAMITĀ commentary for Indian and Tibetan Buddhism. Vimuktisena connects the *Abhisamayālaṃkāra* to the PAÑCAVIṂŚATISĀHASRIKĀPRAJÑĀPĀRAMITĀ ("Perfection of Wisdom in Twenty-five Thousand Lines"), making the otherwise cryptic *Abhisamayālaṃkāra* comprehensible. In scholastic Tibetan Buddhism his name is linked with the Yogācāra-Madhyamaka synthesis, but Vimuktisena's view is more closely aligned to MADHYAMAKA, without the distinctive terminology associated with the PRAMĀṆA school of DIGNĀGA and DHARMAKĪRTI.

***Vimuttimagga**. (T. Rnam grol gyi bstan bcos; C. Jietuodao lun; J. Gedatsudōron; K. Haet'alto non 解脫道論). In Pāli, "Treatise on the Path to Liberation"; an Indian ABHIDHARMA treatise attributed to Upatissa (S. *Upatiṣya). The *Vimuttimagga* was composed sometime prior to the fifth century, perhaps in northern India. It is no longer extant in its Indian recension, but was translated into Chinese in its entirety in 505; portions were also translated into Tibetan. The original language of the text is uncertain, and is usually known by its putative Pāli title (its Sanskrit reconstruction would be **Vimuktimārga*). It is clear that the work was known to the Pāli exegete BUDDHAGHOSA, who made use of it in composing his VISUDDHIMAGGA, although he does not cite it by name. Like the *Visuddhimagga*, the **Vimuttimagga* sets forth the path in terms of the three trainings in morality (P. sīla; S. ŚĪLA), meditation (SAMĀDHI), and wisdom (P. paññā; S. PRAJÑĀ). The **Vimuttimagga* is, however, a much shorter text, omitting the illustrative stories Buddhaghosa offers and including a more succinct section on prajñā. While the *Visuddhimagga* is regarded as a text delivering the doctrine of the conservative MAHĀVIHĀRA branch of the Sri Lankan Pāli tradition, the **Vimuttimagga* is thought to represent instead the views of the ABHAYAGIRI sect, a school that was influenced by MAHĀYĀNA thought.

**vinaya**. (T. 'dul ba; C. lü; J. ritsu; K. yul 律). In Sanskrit and Pāli, "discipline"; the corpus of monastic regulations, especially that directed at fully ordained monks (BHIKṢU) and nuns (BHIKṢUṆĪ). The term is used by extension for those texts in which these codes are set forth, which form the "basket of the discipline" (VINAYAPIṬAKA) in the Buddhist canon (TRIPIṬAKA). According to an account in the *Sifen lü kaizongji*, by the Chinese vinaya master DAOXUAN (596–667), UPAGUPTA, the fifth successor in the Buddha's lineage about a century following his death, had five major disciples, who were said to have established their own schools based on their differing views regarding doctrine; these five also redacted separate recensions of the VINAYA, which the Chinese refer to as "five recensions of the vinaya" (Wubu lü). These five vinayas are (1) the "Four-Part Vinaya" (C. SIFEN LÜ; S. **Cāturvargīyavinaya*) of the DHARMAGUPTAKA school; (2) the "Ten-Recitations Vinaya" (C. *Shisong lü*; S. **Daśādhyāyavinaya*; [alt. **Daśabhāṇavāravinaya*]) of the SARVĀSTIVĀDA school; (3) the "Five-Part Vinaya" (C. *Wufen lü*; S. **Pañcavargikavinaya*) of the MAHĪŚĀSAKA school and the **Prātimokṣavinaya* of the KĀŚYAPĪYA school; (4) the *MAHĀSĀṂGHIKA VINAYA of the MAHĀSĀṂGHIKA school; and (5) the MŪLASARVĀSTIVĀDA VINAYA. All five of these recensions are extant in Chinese translation, but the *Sifen lü* ("Four-Part Vinaya") of the Dharmaguptakas came to dominate the conduct of ecclesiastical affairs in East Asian Buddhism. The only vinaya to survive intact in an Indian language is the Pāli vinaya used in the STHAVIRANIKĀYA tradition; this vinaya compilation was unknown to the Chinese Tradition. The largest vinaya of them all, the Mūlasarvāstivāda vinaya, is a massive collection that is some four times longer than any of the other recensions. The entire collection is available in its Tibetan translation; portions of this vinaya were also translated in Chinese, and substantial fragments of its original Sanskrit version have survived. ¶ The vinayas are a rich source of Buddhist history because they describe the occasion surrounding the formulation of each of the myriads of rules of conduct and deportment promulgated by the Buddha. It is said that the Buddha made a new rule only after the commission of an infraction that would need to be prevented in the future, so the vinayas are careful to recount, in sometimes embarrassing detail, the specific events leading up to the Buddha's formulation of the rule. These accounts therefore provide important insights into issues facing the monastic institutions of India. The principal rules of monastic life are contained in the PRĀTIMOKṢA, which presents rosters of offenses of varying gravity, with penalties ranging from expulsion from the order for the most serious to mere confession for the more minor ones. The most serious offenses, called PĀRĀJIKA, or "defeat," and requiring expulsion according to some vinaya traditions, were four for monks: sexual misconduct (defined in the case of a monk as the penetration of an orifice to the depth of a mustard seed), theft, the killing of a living being, and lying about spiritual attainments. (Even for such serious misdeeds, however, some vinayas prescribe procedures for possible reinstatement; see ŚIKṢĀDATTAKA.) In the Mūlasarvāstivāda vinaya, there were 253 total rules to be followed by monks, 364 for nuns. The majority of these rules were matters of etiquette and decorum meant to ensure harmonious relations within the monastic institution and with lay patrons. The prātimokṣa was recited fortnightly in the UPOṢADHA ceremony. A second major part of the vinaya is the VIBHAṄGA, or explanation of each rule, explaining the circumstances of its formulation and the conditions under which a violation does and does occur. A third part was called the VINAYAVASTU or KHANDAKA, separate sections (ranging between seventeen and twenty in number) on various topics such as ordination, the rains retreats, bedding, robes, and the use of medicine. Although sometimes regarded simply as a collection of regulations, the various vinaya texts are an essential part of Buddhist literature. Many of the vinayas, but especially the Mūlasarvāstivāda vinaya, also include enormous numbers of narrative tales and ancillary materials, including texts that in other traditions would have been collected in the SŪTRAPIṬAKA.

**Vinayamūlasūtra**. Another name for GUṆAPRABHA's VINAYASŪTRA. See VINAYASŪTRA.

**vinayapiṭaka**. (T. 'dul ba'i sde snod; C. lüzang; J. ritsuzō; K. yulchang 律藏). In Sanskrit and Pāli, "basket of discipline" or the "collection of discipline"; one of the three "baskets" (TRIPIṬAKA), or divisions of Buddhist scripture, together with the SŪTRAPIṬAKA and the ABHIDHARMAPIṬAKA. Although typically presumed to include just the rules and regulations of monastic conduct, the vinayapiṭaka is actually one of the richest sources for understanding Buddhist practice and institutions in India. It is said that the Buddha instituted a new rule only after the commission of some form of misconduct that he sought to prevent in the future, so the vinayas are careful to recount in great detail the circumstances leading up to the Buddha's promulgation of the rule. The vinayapiṭaka is therefore composed largely of narratives, some of considerable length; one of the earliest biographies of the Buddha appears in the vinaya of the MŪLASARVĀSTIVĀDA school (see MŪLASARVĀSTIVĀDA VINAYA). According to tradition, the redaction of the vinayapiṭaka occurred at the first Buddhist council (SAṂGĪTI; see COUNCIL, FIRST), shortly after the Buddha's death, when a group of ARHATs assembled to recite the Buddha's teachings. There, the monk UPĀLI, considered an expert in the monastic code, was called upon to recite the vinaya. However, assuming that such a recitation occurred, disputes soon arose over what was allowable conduct according to the rules and regulations included in the vinayapiṭaka. At the time of his death, the Buddha told ĀNANDA that, after his death, the minor rules could be disregarded. At the first council, he was asked what those minor rules were, and Ānanda admitted that he had failed to ask. All rules were therefore retained, and his failure to ask was one of his errors requiring a confession of wrongdoing. The eventual division into the traditional eighteen MAINSTREAM BUDDHIST SCHOOLS often centered on questions of vinaya practice and conduct. There is, therefore, no single vinayapiṭaka, but a number of vinayapiṭakas, with the precise content determined by the specific Indian school. To give one example, the Pāli vinayapiṭaka, which was perhaps redacted around the first century CE, is composed of the following three major divisions: (1) SUTTAVIBHAṄGA (S. sūtravibhaṅga; cf. VINAYAVIBHAṄGA), which includes the pāṭimokkha (S. PRĀTIMOKṢA) code with explanations and commentary, including the mahāvibhaṅga with the rules for monks and the bhikkhuṇīvibhaṅga with the rules for nuns; (2) KHANDHAKA (S. skandhaka; cf. VINAYAVASTU), which is subdivided between the MAHĀVAGGA, which includes chapters on such topics as the procedure for the ordination of monks, the fortnightly observances (P. uposatha; S. UPOṢADHA), the rains retreat, the use of clothing, food, medicine, and so forth, and the CŪḶAVAGGA, which includes a variety of judicial rules, procedures for the ordination of nuns, and accounts of the first and second Buddhist councils; and (3) PARIVĀRA, an appendix that provides a summary and classification of the rules of monastic conduct. ¶ Numerous vinaya texts were translated into Chinese, including complete (or near-complete) vinayapiṭakas associated with five of the mainstream schools of Indian Buddhism. In the order of their translation dates, these five are (1) "Ten-Recitations Vinaya" (C. *Shisong lü*; C. **Daśabhāṇavāravinaya*; **Daśādhyāyavinaya*) of the SARVĀSTIVĀDA school, perhaps composed sometime between the first and third centuries CE and translated into Chinese between 404 and 409 CE; (2) DHARMAGUPTAKA vinaya, the renowned "Four-Part Vinaya" (SIFEN LÜ), translated between 410 and 412 CE, which becomes the definitive recension of the vinaya in the East Asian traditions and the focus of scholarship in the different East Asian vinaya schools (see NANSHAN LÜ ZONG, DONGTA LÜ ZONG, RISSHŪ); (3) MAHĀSĀṂGHIKA vinaya (*Mohesengji lü*), composed between 100 and 200 CE and translated between 416 and 418; (4) MAHĪṂŚĀSAKA vinaya, or the "Five-Part Vinaya" (*Wufen lü*), perhaps composed in the first century BCE and translated between 422 and 423; and (5) the MŪLASARVĀSTIVĀDA vinaya, perhaps composed in the fourth or fifth century CE and translated into Chinese between 703 and 713. (The complete Tibetan translation of this vinaya becomes definitive for Tibetan Buddhism). ¶ It is important to note that the texts contained in the vinayapiṭaka of any school have served as just one source of the monastic code. In China, no complete recension of any Indian vinaya was translated until the beginning of the fifth century. (Indeed, none of the surviving recensions of the vinayas of any Buddhist school can be dated prior to the fifth century CE.) When the Indian vinayas were translated into Chinese, for example, their regulations were viewed as being so closely tied to the customs and climate of India that they were sometimes found either incomprehensible or irrelevant to the Chinese. This led to the composition of indigenous Chinese monastic codes, called guishi ("regulations") or QINGGUI ("rules of purity"), which promulgated rules of conduct for monks and nuns that accorded more closely with the realities of life in East Asian monasteries. In Tibet, the VINAYASŪTRA by GUṆAPRABHA, a medieval Indian summary of the much larger Mūlasarvāstivāda vinaya, was the primary source for the monastic code, but each monastery also had its own regulations (BCA' YIG) that governed life there. See also PRĀTIMOKṢASŪTRA.

**Vinayasūtra**. (T. 'Dul ba'i mdo). In Sanskrit, "Discourse on Discipline"; a work on the monastic code by the Indian master GUṆAPRABHA, who is dated between the fifth and seventh century CE. Despite its title, the work is not a SŪTRA (in the sense of a discourse ascribed to the Buddha), but instead is an authored work composed of individual aphoristic statements (sūtras). The text offers a summary or condensation of the massive MŪLASARVĀSTIVĀDA VINAYA. At approximately one quarter the length of this massive vinaya collection, Guṇaprabha's abridgment seems to have functioned as a kind of primer on the monastic code, omitting lengthy passages of scripture and providing the code of conduct to which monks were expected to subscribe. In this sense, the text is an important work for determining what monastic practice may actually have been like in medieval India. The *Vinayasūtra* became the most important vinaya text for Tibetan Buddhism, being studied in all of the major sects. In the DGE LUGS, it is one of the five books (GZHUNG LNGA) that served as the basis of the monastic curriculum. The detailed commentaries on the *Vinayasūtra* by the Pāla dynasty writer Dharmamitra (early ninth century) and the BKA' GDAM PA master Tsho sna ba Shes rab bzang po's (b. thirteenth century) were widely studied.

**vinayavastu**. (T. 'dul ba'i gzhi; C. pinaiye shi; J. binayaji; K. pinaya sa 毘奈耶事). In Sanskrit, "foundation of the vinaya"; that section of the Sanskrit vinayas that corresponds to the KHANDHAKA (S. skandhaka) in the Pāli vinaya. This section consists of separate chapters (ranging in number from seventeen to twenty) on individual topics related to monastic life, including the procedures for ordination, the proper performance of the rains retreat, the KAṬHINA ceremony, and rules concerning the acquisition, use, and disposal of monastic robes (CĪVARA), foodstuffs, and medicines.

**vinayavibhaṅga**. (T. 'dul ba rnam par 'byed pa; C. Genben Shuoyiqieyoubu pinaiye; J. Konpon Setsuissaiubu binaya; K. Kŭnbon Sŏrilch'eyubu pinaya 根本說一切有部毘奈耶). In Sanskrit, lit. "Differentiation of the Discipline"; a major division of Sanskrit VINAYA literature, corresponding to the SUTTAVIBHAṄGA in the Pāli VINAYAPIṬAKA. The primary foci of such sections are the disciplinary rules for monks (PRĀTIMOKṢA), the exact number of which varies according to the tradition. The vinayavibhaṅga of the MŪLASARVĀSTIVĀDA vinaya (to which the Sinographs above correspond), for example, lists 253 such rules. Each rule is accompanied by a description of the appropriate response to its violation. These sanctions may range from possible expulsion from the order, as with the rules of "defeat" (PĀRĀJIKA), to simple confession of the misdeed during the fortnightly recitation of the rules (UPOṢADHA). The narrative form used to convey these rules follows that of most other vinaya literature, describing the circumstances that led to the Buddha's declaration of a particular rule. Just as the Pāli vinaya begins with a section of this type, the vinayas of the SARVĀSTIVĀDA and Mūlasarvāstivāda schools also begin with sections entitled vinayavibhaṅga. In both of these vinayas, a formal listing of the rules is followed by commentary and narratives that explain each rule more fully. These accounts provide important and often surprising insights into the concerns of Indian Buddhist monastic life.

**Vinītaruci**. (V. Tỳ Ni Đa Lưu Chi 毗尼多流支) (d. 594). The Sanskrit name of an Indian monk who is traditionally regarded as the founder of the first school of THIỀN (CHAN) in Vietnam. The Vietnamese genealogical history THIỀN UYỂN TẬP ANH records that Vinītaruci was a brāhmaṇa from south India who wandered throughout India as a young man searching for the essence of the Buddhist teaching. He is reputed to have arrived in China in 574, where he went to see the third Chan patriarch SENGCAN, who offered him instruction before advising him to go south. Vinītaruci then traveled to Zhizhi monastery in Guangzhou, where he remained for six years and translated many Buddhist texts. In 580, he arrived in Vietnam and settled at Pháp Vân monastery, where he subsequently transmitted the mind-seal (XINYIN) to Pháp Hiền (died 626), who carried on this Chan lineage associated with the third patriarch. He passed away sometime in 595. The Vinītaruci mentioned in the *Thiền Uyển Tập Anh* is undoubtedly the same Indian monk whose name is mentioned in Chinese Buddhist literature as a translator; however, it remains unclear whether Vinītaruci ever really came to Vietnam, as the Vietnamese Buddhist tradition reports. In any case, there are no historical grounds for the claim that he was the founding patriarch of a Chan lineage in Vietnam or to attribute to him the teaching style emblematic of the Southern school of Chan (NAN ZONG), which did not appear until centuries after his death.

**viniyata**. (T. yul nges; C. biejing [xinsuo]; J. betsukyō [no shinjo]; K. pyŏlgyŏng [simso] 別境[心所]). In Sanskrit, "determinative," or "object-specific"; the second of the six categories of mental concomitants (CAITTA) according to the hundred dharmas (BAIFA) schema of the YOGĀCĀRA school, along with the omnipresent (SARVATRAGA), the wholesome (KUŚALA), the root afflictions (MŪLAKLEŚA), the secondary afflictions (UPAKLEŚA), and the indeterminate (ANIYATA). There are five mental factors in the category of determinative mental concomitants; their function is to aid the mind in ascertaining or determining its object. The five are aspiration or desire-to-act (CHANDA), determination or resolve (ADHIMOKṢA), mindfulness (SMṚTI), concentration (SAMĀDHI), and wisdom (PRAJÑĀ). According to ASAṄGA, these five determinative factors accompany wholesome (kuśala) states of mind, so that if one is present, all are present.

**vipāka**. (T. rnam par smin pa; C. guobao/yishu; J. kahō/ijuku; K. kwabo/isuk 果報/異熟). In Sanskrit and Pāli, lit. "ripening," thus "maturation," "fruition," or "result"; referring specifically to the "maturation" of past deeds (KARMAN). Vipāka refers to any mental phenomenon that occurs as a result of a morally wholesome or unwholesome volitional action performed by body, speech, or mind, either in this or previous lives. Fruitions can be divided between those that occur during the lifetime in which the deed is performed, those that occur in the lifetime immediately following the lifetime in which the deed is performed, and those that occur two or more lifetimes later. Although the fruition is the result of a wholesome or unwholesome act, the vipāka itself is always morally neutral and manifests itself as something pleasant or painful that is either physical or mental. Vipāka is a subset of the related term "fruition" (PHALA); in the context of moral cause and effect, the ripening of moral causes is called the VIPĀKAPHALA, which is one of the five types of effects or fruitions (phala) described in the VAIBHĀṢIKA school of SARVĀSTIVĀDA ABHIDHARMA; in that context vipākaphala is limited to effects, such as the body and so on, that last from the first moment to the last moment of a life. In the MAHĀYĀNA in general, the term also appears (with other forms of the verbal root √pac, "to cook") in the sense of "maturation," to refer to the power of buddhas and BODHISATTVAs to "ripen" beings in their progress along the path (MĀRGA).

**vipākahetu**. (T. rnam smin gyi rgyu; C. yishu yin; J. ijukuin; K. isuk in 異熟因). In Sanskrit and Pāli, lit. "ripening cause"; the "retributive cause" that leads to either wholesome or unwholesome karmic retribution (VIPĀKAPHALA); one of the six types of causes (HETU) described in the VAIBHĀṢIKA school of SARVĀSTIVĀDA ABHIDHARMA and by VASUBANDHU in the ABHIDHARMAKOŚABHĀṢYA. The vipākahetu refers to the karmic seeds of either wholesome (KUŚALA) deeds (KARMAN) that are tainted by ignorance (AVIDYĀ), or of unwholesome (AKUŚALA) deeds; neutral actions cannot serve as retributive causes. These deeds have the potency to ripen, even at some point in the distant future, as vipākaphala, specifically as the aggregates (SKANDHA) of a future lifetime, producing the physical body (RŪPA), the six types of consciousness (VIJÑĀNA), and sensations (VEDANĀ). According to some schools, the retributive cause is essentially identical to volition (CETANĀ), since it is the force that initiates action. The goal of the eightfold path (ĀRYĀṢṬĀṄGAMĀRGA) is to end the generation of such causes and thereby exhaust the karmic forces that bind one to SAṂSĀRA.

**vipākaphala**. (T. rnam smin gyi 'bras bu; C. yishu guo; J. ijukuka; K. isuk kwa 異熟果). In Sanskrit, lit. "ripened fruit," viz., "retributive effect"; one of the five types of effects or fruitions (PHALA) described in the VAIBHĀṢIKA school of SARVĀSTIVĀDA ABHIDHARMA, as well as by VASUBANDHU in the ABHIDHARMAKOŚABHĀṢYA. These are karmic effects of either wholesome (KUŚALA) deeds (KARMAN) that are tainted by ignorance (AVIDYĀ), or of unwholesome (AKUŚALA) deeds; neutral actions do not produce ripened effects. These effects, the results of the VIPĀKAHETU, ripen, even at some point long after the performance of the specific deed, as the aggregates (SKANDHA) of a future lifetime, producing the physical body (RŪPA), the six types of consciousness (VIJÑĀNA), and sensations (VEDANĀ). The vipākaphala is the ultimate and inevitable effect of the "retributive cause" (vipākahetu): in a metaphor used in the tradition, the retributive cause is the seed that grows into the fruit-bearing tree that is the retributive effect.

**vipakṣa**. [alt. vipakṣabhūta] (T. mi mthun phyogs; C. yipin/suoduizhi; J. ihon/shotaiji; K. ip'um/sodaech'i 異品/所對治). In Sanskrit, "opposite class"; referring to a category that is the opposite of another category, such that one must be absent for the other to be present. The term appears especially in two contexts in Buddhist literature. First, in Buddhist logic (HETUVIDYĀ), vipakṣa is one of three terms: PAKṢA (logical subject), SAPAKṢA (similar instance), and vipakṣa (dissimilar instance). For example, in the syllogism (PRAYOGA) "sound is impermanent because it is produced," sound is the pakṣa. A pot would be an example or sapakṣa (a "similar instance" or "in the similar class;" knowledge that a pot breaks because it is produced can be extended to sound). Space would be a counterexample or vipakṣa (a dissimilar instance or in the dissimilar class; knowledge that it is not produced because it is permanent can be extended to exclude a sound from the dissimilar class because it is articulated and produced). Second, in Buddhist literature on the practice of the path (MĀRGA), vipakṣa is contrasted with PRATIPAKṢA ("counteracting force" or "antidote") to the afflictions (KLEŚA). For example, the opposing class of hatred (DVEṢA) is counteracted by loving-kindness (MAITRĪ), such that meditation on loving-kindness temporarily displaces hatred from the mind but does not permanently remove it, as does a pratipakṣa.

**vipariṇāmaduḥkhatā**. (P. vipariṇāmadukkha; T. 'gyur ba'i sdug bsngal; C. huaiku; J. eku; K. koego 壞苦). In Sanskrit, "suffering associated with change"; the second of the three types of suffering, along with DUḤKHADUḤKHATĀ ("physical and mental suffering") and SAṂSKĀRADUḤKHATĀ ("suffering intrinsic to conditioned existence itself"). This type of suffering is defined as feelings of mental and physical pleasure that inevitably turn into pain if the activity that produces them is continued indefinitely, such as overindulging in delicious food, staying out in the sun too long, or sitting in the same posture for hours on end. The Buddhist claim is that pain and pleasure are qualitatively different: painful feelings will continue to be painful unless some further action is taken to assuage the pain, whereas pleasurable feelings will become painful if one persists in engaging in the activity that produces the pleasure. For example, after walking for a long distance, walking becomes painful, at which point it is pleasurable to sit down. After sitting for a long period of time, sitting becomes painful, and it is pleasurable to stand up and walk. Feelings of pleasure are thus a type of suffering, because they will inevitably revert to pain. An example is pouring cold water on a burn; after a moment of relief, the burning sensation will return. In the same way, feelings of pleasure are merely a brief lessening of pain.

**viparyāsa**. (P. vipallāsa; T. phyin ci log; C. diandao; J. tendō; K. chŏndo 顚倒). In Sanskrit, lit. "inversion," but referring to "perverted," "corrupted," or "inverted" views (the Chinese translation diandao literally means "upside down") or simply "error." There is a standard list of four "inverted views" that cause sentient beings to remain subject to the cycle of rebirth (SAṂSĀRA). The four are (1) to view as pleasurable what is in fact painful or suffering (DUḤKHA), (2) to see as permanent what is in fact impermanent (ANITYA), (3) to see as pure what is in fact impure (AŚUBHA), and (4) to see as having self what is in fact devoid of self (ANĀTMAN). These four inversions are corrected through insight into the true nature of reality, which prompts the realization that the aggregates (SKANDHA) are in fact suffering, impermanent, impure, and devoid of self. In the TATHĀGATAGARBHA literature, these four putatively correct views are in turn said also to be inversions from the standpoint of the tathāgatagarbha, which is said to possess four perfect qualities (GUṆAPĀRAMITĀ): bliss, permanence, purity, and selfhood.

**vipassanā**. In Pāli, "insight" (see also S. VIPAŚYANĀ). Insight is defined as the direct intuition of the three marks (P. tilakkhaṇa; S. TRILAKṢAṆA) of existence that characterize all phenomena: P. aniccā (S. ANITYATĀ) or impermanence, dukkha (S. DUḤKHA) or suffering, and anatta (S. ANĀTMAN) or nonself. Insight associated with the attainment of any of the eight noble paths and fruits (P. ariyamaggaphala; S. ĀRYAMĀRGAPHALA) or associated with the attainment of cessation (NIRODHASAMĀPATTI) is classified as supramundane (P. lokuttara; S. LOKOTTARA); that which is not associated with the noble paths and fruits is classified as mundane (P. lokiya; S. LAUKIKA). The classical commentarial paradigm pairs vipassanā with samatha (S. ŚAMATHA), or tranquillity, these two together being described as the two wings of Buddhist meditative cultivation (BHĀVANĀ). Vipassanā, when fully developed, leads to enlightenment (BODHI) and nibbāna (S. NIRVĀṆA); samatha when fully developed leads to the attainment of JHĀNA (S. DHYĀNA), or meditative absorption, and the attainment of certain supranormal powers (P. abhiññā; S. ABHIJÑĀ). While the formal training in vipassanā meditation does not require the prior attainment of either jhāna or abhiññā, the mind must nevertheless have achieved a modicum of pacification through "threshold concentration" (UPACĀRASAMĀDHI) as a prerequisite for successful vipassanā practice. The VISUDDHIMAGGA lists eighteen main types of vipassanāñāṇa (S. vipaśyanājñāna), or insight knowledge, of (1) impermanence (aniccānupassanā), (2) suffering (dukkhānupassanā), (3) nonself (anattānupnupassanā), (4) aversion (nibbidānupassanā), (5) dispassion (virāgānupassanā), (6) extinction (nirodhānupassanā), (7) abandoning (paṭinissaggānupassanāā), (8) waning (khayānupassanā), (9) disappearing (vayānupassanā), (10) change (vipariṇāmānupassanā), (11) signlessness (animittānupassanā), (12) wishlessness (apaṇihitānupassanā), (13) emptiness (suññatānupassanā), (14) higher wisdom regarding phenomena (adhipaññādhammavipassanā), (15) knowledge and vision that accords with reality (YATHĀBHŪTAJÑĀNADARŚANA), (16) contemplation of danger (ādīnavānupassanā), (17) contemplation involving reflection (paṭisaṅkhānupassanā), and (18) turning away (vivaṭṭanānupassanā). While the terms samatha and vipassanā do appear in sutta discussions of meditative training—although far more often in the later KHUDDAKANIKĀYA sections of the canon—they figure most prominently in the ABHIDHAMMA and the later commentarial literature. The systems of vipassanā training taught today are modern constructs that do not antedate late-nineteenth century Burma (see LEDI SAYADAW; MAHASI SAYADAW); they are, however, derived from, or at least inspired by, commentarial or scriptural precedents. Two of the most successful vipassanā organizations outside Asia are the Insight Meditation Society and the loosely knit group of centers teaching S. N. Goenka's vipassana meditation; the former originates with AJAHN CHAH BODHIÑĀṆA (1917–1992) of the Thai forest tradition and the latter with the Burmese teacher U BA KHIN (1899–1971). See also YATHĀBHŪTAJÑĀNADARŚANA.

**vipassanādhura**. In Pāli, lit., "the burden of insight," in the sense of the obligation to develop insight through formal meditation training. The term is often contrasted with GANTHADHURA, "the burden of book," in the sense of the obligation to study. In the later THERAVĀDA tradition, these two duties have been seen as two vocations open to monks, viz., contemplative practice and doctrinal study. See also PAṬIPATTI.

**vipassanāñāṇa**. In Pāli, "insight knowledge"; see VIPASSANĀ.

**vipassanāñāṇikasamādhi**. In Pāli, "concentration of insight knowledge"; a commentarial term used to refer to a form of concentration that is developed through attending to the arising and passing away of the present thought-moment or object, when such concentration has successfully removed all distractions. It is equal in intensity to the "threshold concentration" (UPACĀRASAMĀDHI) that is cultivated in the course of practicing tranquillity meditation (P. samathabhāvanā; see ŚAMATHA). Vipassanāñāṇikasamādhi, when fully developed, leads to the attainment of the paths (P. magga; S. MĀRGA) and fruits (PHALA) of liberation, whereas upacārasamādhi, when fully developed, leads only to the attainment of "absorptive concentration" (APPANĀSAMĀDHI), which is synonymous with "meditative absorption" (P. JHĀNA; S. DHYĀNA).

**vipassanūpakkilesa**. In Pāli, "defilement of insight"; according to the VISUDDHIMAGGA, ten experiences that occur to the diligent practitioner of meditation as natural concomitants of insight training (VIPASSANĀ-BHĀVANĀ). If the practitioner should become attached to any of these experiences, they become a hindrance to further progress along the path to liberation and thus would be deemed defilements of insight. The ten experiences are (1) a vision of radiant light (P. obhāsa; S. avabhāsa), (2) knowledge (P. ñāṇa; S. JÑĀNA), (3) physical rapture (P. pīti; S. PRĪTI), (4) tranquillity (P. passaddhi; S. PRAŚRABDHI), (5) mental ease or bliss (SUKHA), (6) determination (P. adhimokkha; S. ADHIMOKṢA), (7) energy (P. paggaha; S. pragraha), (8) heightened awareness (P. upaṭṭhāna; S. upasthāna), (9) equanimity (P. upekkhā; S. UPEKṢĀ), and (10) delight (P. nikanti; S. nikānti). As long as the mind is disturbed through attachment to the ten defilements of insight, it will be unable to comprehend the three marks of existence (P. tilakkhaṇa; S. TRILAKṢAṆA) of impermanence P. (anicca; S. ANITYA), suffering (P. dukkha; S. DUḤKHA), and nonself (P. anatta; S. ANĀTMAN), the knowledge of which is the content of enlightenment (BODHI). These ten defilements may cause the practitioner to believe that he has already attained enlightenment as a stream-enterer (SROTAĀPANNA), a once-returner (SAKṚDĀGĀMIN), a nonreturner (ANĀGĀMIN), or a worthy one (ARHAT), when in fact he has not. Infatuation with the defilements is overcome by understanding them for what they are, as mere impermanent by-products of meditation. This understanding is developed through perfecting the "purity of knowledge and vision of what is and is not the path" (MAGGĀMAGGAÑĀṆADASSANAVISUDDHI), which is the fifth of seven "purities" (VISUDDHI) to be developed along the path to liberation.

**vipaśyanā**. (P. vipassanā; T. lhag mthong; C. guan; J. kan; K. kwan 觀). In Sanskrit, "insight"; a technical term for an understanding of reality (either conceptual or nonconceptual) at a level of mental concentration equal to or exceeding that of ŚAMATHA. The presence of vipaśyanā is the distinguishing feature of the wisdom that derives from meditation (BHĀVANĀMAYĪPRAJÑĀ). Such insight is required to destroy the various levels of afflictions (KLEŚA) and to proceed on the path to liberation (VIMOKṢA) from REBIRTH. See also VIPASSANĀ; MOHE ZHIGUAN; XIUXI ZHIGUAN ZUOCHAN FAYAO.

**Vipaśyin**. (P. Vipassī; T. Rnam gzigs; C. Piposhi fo; J. Bibashi-butsu; K. Pibasi pul 毘婆尸佛). Sanskrit proper name of the sixth of the seven buddhas of antiquity (SAPTATATHĀGATA), who directly precede ŚĀKYAMUNI; Vipaśyin is also listed as the nineteenth of twenty-five buddhas mentioned in the BUDDHAVAṂSA. In the Pāli tradition, his story is first recounted in the MAHĀPADĀNASUTTA in the DĪGHANIKĀYA. There, it is said that Vipassī's father was Bandhumā and his mother was Bandhumatī. He was born in the Khema park and belonged to the Kondañña clan. During his time, the human life span was eighty thousand years. He dwelt as a householder for eight thousand years and possessed three palaces named Nanda, Sunanda, and Sirmā, one for each of the three seasons. His wife's name was Sutanā, and he had a son named Samavattakkhandha. When he renounced the world, he left his house in a chariot, after which he practiced austerities for eight months. As with all BODHISATTVAs, Vipassī abandoned austerities as unprofitable when he realized that they did not lead to enlightenment. He attained buddhahood under a pāṭali (S. pātali) tree. In the description of his enlightenment, he is shown contemplating dependent origination (PRATĪTYASAMUTPĀDA), but in a chain of ten rather than the standard twelve links. He preached his first sermon in the Khema Deer Park to his brother Khandha and to Tissa, the son of his family's priest. These two became his chief monk disciples. His chief nun disciples were Candā and Candamittā, and his attendant was named Asoka. His chief lay disciples were the laymen Punnabbasummitta and Nāga, and the laywomen Sirimā and Uttarā. He died at the age of eighty thousand in the Sumittārāma, and over his relics was erected a reliquary (STŪPA) seven leagues high. The bodhisattva who was to become GAUTAMA Buddha was at that time a NĀGA king named Atula.

**viprayuktasaṃskāra**. (S). See CITTAVIPRAYUKTASAṂSKĀRA.

**vīra**. (T. dpa' bo; C. yongmeng; J. yūmyō; K. yongmaeng 勇猛). In Sanskrit and Pāli, "hero"; a common epithet of the Buddha. The word is also used for a bodhisattva skilled in tantric practices who accompanies a ḌĀKINĪ during the GAṆACAKRA (tantric feast) ritual. Ekavīra (T. Dpa' bo gcig pa), "Solitary Hero," is a form of YAMĀNTAKA widely practiced in Tibet and is used in general to describe the depiction of a male tantric deity without a consort.

**virati**. (T. spong ba; C. li; J. ri; K. i 離). In Sanskrit and Pāli, lit. "abstinence," "seclusion"; a polysemous term in both Sanskrit and Buddhist literature. In its Buddhist usages, virati generally refers to the separation or detachment from mental afflictions (KLEŚA) and false conceptualizations (VIKALPA); it may also indicate a desire to leave behind such afflictions. In Pāli literature, virati indicates three specific types of abstention, viz., from wrong speech, wrong action, and wrong livelihood. In SARVĀSTIVĀDA thought, virati results from a positive sense of perplexity about one's state in the world, and from it arises the soteriologically indispensable NIRVEDA, "disgust with the world" or "disillusionment." Two kinds of seclusion

(C. ERZHONG YUANLI) are also discussed in the Chinese tradition: physical seclusion (shen yuanli) and the seclusion of the mind (xin yuanli). Removing oneself from a distracting, unwholesome, and disquieting environment by leaving it behind constitutes physical seclusion. Seclusion of the mind usually refers to "guarding one's senses" (INDRIYASAṂVARA) with mindfulness so that the mind will neither cling to, not be repulsed by, sensory stimuli; it also refers to the "withdrawal" from sensory stimulations and the consolidation of attention during meditative states (see DHYĀNA).

**Virūḍhaka**. (P. Virūḷhaka [alt. Viḍūḍabha]; T. 'Phags skyes po; C. Zengzhang tian; J. Zōjōten; K. Chŭngjang ch'ŏn 增長天). Sanskrit proper name of one of the four LOKAPĀLA, the kings of the four directions who reside on the four sides of Mount SUMERU. He is king of the south and resides on the southern face of the central mountain, where he is lord of the kumbhaṇḍas. ¶ Virūḍhaka (corresponding to the Pāli transcription Viḍūḍabha) is also the proper name of a king of KOŚALA at the time of the Buddha; he was the son of the Buddha's patron, PRASENAJIT, and usurped his father's throne. When Prasenajit ascended the throne, he requested a wife from the ŚĀKYA tribe. The Śākyas instead sent a maidservant, claiming that she was from a noble family, and she eventually gave birth to Virūḍhaka. As a boy, he visited KAPILAVASTU and learned of his low birth. Realizing that his father had been deceived, he vowed to take revenge upon the Śākyas. After his father's death, he led an army against Kapilavastu, destroying the Śākya kingdom and slaughtering its inhabitants. A violent storm caused a flood during the night, and Virūḍhaka and his warriors, who were sleeping in the riverbed, were swept away. See also CĀTURMAHĀRĀJAKĀYIKA.

**Virūpa**. (Bi rū pa). Sanskrit proper name of one of the eighty-four MAHĀSIDDHAs, particularly revered in the SA SKYA sect of Tibetan Buddhism. Very little can be said with certainty about his life (whether he was a historical figure is open to question), but he may have lived at the end of the tenth century CE. He is said to have been a monk and a distinguished scholar of NĀLANDĀ monastery (in some sources, SOMAPURA), who was originally named Dharmapāla, devoting himself to scholastic study during the day and tantric practice at night. He recited the MANTRA of CAKRASAṂVARA for years, but, unable to make any progress in his practice, he threw his rosary into the latrine. That night, the goddess NAIRĀTMYĀ, appeared to him in a dream, instructing him to retrieve his rosary. Over the course of six nights, she conferred initiations and instructions that allowed him to attain the sixth bodhisattva BHŪMI. She also gave him a text, which is otherwise unknown in Sanskrit, whose Sanskrit title might be reconstructed as **Mārgaphalamūlaśāstra*, the "Root Treatise on the Path and Its Fruition." Dharmapāla subsequently began to engage openly in tantric practices and was expelled from the monastery and branded "deformed" or "ugly" (virūpa), whence he derived his name. Among the many stories told about him, perhaps the most famous tells of his stopping in a tavern to drink. When the tavern keeper demanded payment, he offered her the sun instead, using his ritual dagger to stop the sun in its course. The sun did not move for three days, during which time Virūpa consumed huge amounts of drink. In order to set the sun on its course, the king agreed to pay his bill. Virūpa eventually encountered two YOGINs who became his disciples: Ḍombiheruka and Kṛṣṇacārin. In the eleventh century, the Tibetan scholar SA CHEN KUN DGA' SNYING PO of the 'Khon clan is said to have had a vision of Virūpa in which he received transmission of the **Mārgaphalamūlaśāstra*. This became the foundation for the LAM 'BRAS teachings of the Sa skya sect, where Virūpa is regarded as a buddha, equal in importance to Nāropa for the BKA' RGYUD sect. His most famous work is his RDO RJE TSHIG RKANG ("Vajra Verses").

**Virūpākṣa**. (P. Virupakkha; T. Mig mi bzang; C. Guangmu tian; J. Kōmokuten; K. Kwangmok ch'ŏn 廣目天). One of the four LOKAPĀLA, the kings of the four directions who reside on the four sides of Mount SUMERU. He is king of the west and resides on the western face of the central mountain, where he is lord of the NĀGAS.

**vīrya**. (P. viriya; T. brtson 'grus; C. jingjin; J. shōjin; K. chŏngjin 精進). In Sanskrit, "energy," "effort"; an enthusiasm to perform virtuous acts, which serves as the antidote to laziness. Since, by definition, the term refers to a delight in virtue, striving for nonvirtuous ends would not be considered "energy." The connotations of the term include the willingness to undertake virtuous deeds, the delight in the performance of virtuous deeds, a lack of discouragement, a commitment to success, and a dissatisfaction with minimal virtues. Deemed essential to progress on the path, vīrya is a constituent of many numerical lists. Vīrya is the second of the five spiritual faculties (INDRIYA) and counters the hindrance (NĪVARAṆA) of sloth and torpor (STYĀNA-MIDDHA). It is counted as one of the eleven wholesome mental concomitants (KUŚALA-CAITTA) and constitutes the fourth of the six perfections (PĀRAMITĀ).

**vīryapāramitā**. (P. viriyapāramī; T. brtson 'grus kyi pha rol tu phyin pa; C. jingjin boluomiduo; J. shōjinharamita; K. chŏngjin paramilta 精進波羅蜜多). In Sanskrit, "the perfection of energy [alt. effort, vigor]"; the fourth of the six [alt. ten] perfections (PĀRAMITĀ) cultivated on the BODHISATTVA path. It is perfected on the fourth of the ten stages (DAŚABHŪMI) of the bodhisattva path, ARCIṢMATĪ (radiant), where the flaming radiance of the thirty-seven factors pertaining to enlightenment (BODHIPĀKṢIKADHARMA) becomes so intense that it incinerates all the obstructions and afflictions, giving the bodhisattva inexhaustible energy in his quest for enlightenment. When the six perfections are divided based on whether they are associated with the accumulation of merit (PUṆYASAṂBHĀRA) or of wisdom (JÑĀNASAṂBHĀRA), the perfection of energy is associated with both.

**Viśākha**. (P. Visākha; T. Sa ga; C. Pishequ; J. Bishakya; K. Pisagŏ 毗舍佉). A wealthy merchant of RĀJAGṚHA and husband of the female ARHAT DHAMMADINNĀ; he should be distinguished from VIŚĀKHĀ (s.v.), the foremost donor among laywomen. According to the Pāli account, Viśākha accompanied King BIMBISĀRA on a visit to the Buddha during the latter's first sojourn at Rājagaha (RĀJAGṚHA) after his enlightenment. Upon hearing the Buddha preach, Visākha became a stream-enterer (SROTAĀPANNA) and, subsequently, a once-returner (SAKṚDĀGĀMIN) and a nonreturner (ANĀGĀMIN). Once he became a nonreturner, his behavior toward his wife Dhammadinnā changed, and once she learned the reason, Dhammadinnā requested permission to renounce the world and enter the order as a nun. Impressed by his wife's piety, he informed Bimbisāra, who arranged for her to be carried to the nunnery on a golden palanquin. After Dhammadinnā attained arhatship, Visākha asked her questions pertaining to dharma, all of which she expertly answered. He reported this to the Buddha, who praised her for her skill in teaching. Visākha and Dhammadinnā were husband and wife during the time of Phussa (S. Puṣya) Buddha (the twenty-first of the thousand buddhas) when, as a treasurer, he had arranged an offering of alms for Phussa Buddha and his disciples. Visākha was a renowned teacher in his own right and is mentioned as one of seven lay disciples who each had five hundred followers.

**Viśākhā**. (P. Visākhā; T. Sa ga ma; C. Pishequmu/Luzimu; J. Bishakyamo/Rokushimo; K. Pisagŏmo/Nokchamo 毗舍佉母/鹿子母). Prominent female lay disciple of the Buddha (and to be distinguished from the Buddhist layman VIŚĀKHA); in the AṄGUTTARANIKĀYA, the Buddha declares her to be foremost among laywomen who minister to the order. According to the Pāli account, Visākhā was born into a wealthy family and was converted by the Buddha at the age of seven, when he visited her native city of Bhaddiya. Visākhā had been dispatched by her grandfather, Meṇḍaka, with five hundred chariots, five hundred companions, and five hundred slaves to approach the Buddha and listen to him preach. Upon hearing his sermon, Visākhā became a stream-enterer (SROTAĀPANNA). Later, Visākhā was married to the son of a wealthy merchant named Migāra, who dwelt in the city of Sāvatthi (ŚRĀVASTĪ) and was a follower of the Nigaṇṭhas (S. NIRGRANTHA; see JAINA). Although she was a dutiful wife and daughter-in-law, Visākhā was offended by the nakedness of the Nigaṇṭha ascetics and refused to show them respect. When criticized for her attitude, she threatened to return to her parents' house. Although sorely distressed by his daughter-in-law's behavior, Migāra consented to listen to a sermon by the Buddha if she would consent to remain in his family. Upon hearing the Buddha preach, Migāra became a stream-enterer (SROTAĀPANNA), and remained forever grateful to Visākhā, even giving her the sobriquet Migāramātā, "Migāra's Mother." Visākhā fed five hundred monks in her home daily, and was constant in her attentions to the monastic community in Sāvatthi. She fulfilled a long-held wish when she had a grand monastery built to the east of the city named Migāramātupāsāda (S. MṚGĀRAMṚTUPRĀSĀDA), which she visited with her children, grandchildren, and great grandchildren. The Buddha related how, in previous lives, Visākhā had ministered to the needs of the Buddhas Padumuttara (S. Padmottara) and Kassapa (S. KĀŚYAPA). Visākhā was said to have died at the age of 120, although she always looked to be a maiden of sixteen. She was endowed with phenomenal strength, and the people of Sāvatthi believed that she brought good fortune to their city. Visākhā is upheld by the tradition as the ideal laywoman.

**visaṃyogaphala**. (T. bral ba'i 'bras bu; C. liji guo; J. rikeka; K. igye kwa 離繫果). In Sanskrit, "separation effect"; a term used to describe liberation from rebirth and the reality of NIRVĀṆA. This is one of the five effects (PHALA) enumerated in the VAIBHĀṢIKA school of SARVĀSTIVĀDA ABHIDHARMA and the YOGĀCĀRA system. Liberation (VIMOKṢA) and nirvāṇa are forms of cessation (NIRODHA) and as such are unconditioned phenomena (ASAṂSKṚTADHARMA) and permanent (NITYA) because they do not change moment by moment. Specifically, they are classified as "analytical cessations" (PRATISAMKHYĀNIRODHA), that is, states of cessation that arise through the process of insight. In the Buddha's delineation of the FOUR NOBLE TRUTHS (catvāry āryasatyāni), the third truth of cessation (NIRODHASATYA) is followed by the fourth truth of the path (MĀRGASATYA). Later commentators would explain that cessation and path stand in a relationship of effect and cause, respectively. However, this is not possible in the literal sense, because an impermanent and conditioned phenomenon such as the path cannot serve as the cause for a permanent and unconditioned phenomenon such as cessation. In order to preserve this distinction but nonetheless acknowledge the role of religious practice in bringing about the state of nirvāṇa, the Vaibhāṣika school proposed the category of visaṃyogaphala, which is essentially an effect that has no cause. Thus, the practice of the path leads to a permanent separation from the KLEŚAS, and because that state of separation is permanent, it not formally the effect of a cause.

**viṣaya**. (P. visaya; T. yul; C. jing; J. kyō; K. kyŏng 境). In Sanskrit, lit. "sphere" or "object"; in epistemology, a general term for the object of a sensory consciousness (VIJÑĀNA). Various types of such objects are described in works on logic and epistemology, with distinctions made between the objects perceived by the five sensory consciousnesses and the objects perceived by the mental consciousness (MANOVIJÑĀNA).

**Viśiṣṭacāritra**. (C. Shangxing; J. Jōgyō; K. Sanghaeng 上行). In Sanskrit, "Exemplary Practices"; the leader of the four BODHISATTVAs of the earth to whom ŚĀKYAMUNI Buddha transfers the quintessence of the SŪTRA in the SADDHARMAPUṆḌARĪKASŪTRA ("Lotus Sūtra"). Viśiṣṭacāritra is said to represent the "true self" aspect of the buddha-nature (FOXING). Viśiṣṭacāritra has special significance for the Japanese NICHIRENSHŪ schools, because NICHIREN himself believed that his proselytization work had fulfilled the charge that Śākyamuni had given the bodhisattva. Thus, some Nichiren schools assume that their founder is the reincarnation of Viśiṣṭacāritra.

**viśuddhabuddhakṣetra**. (T. dag pa'i zhing khams; C. qingjing foguotu; J. shōjōbukkokudo; K. ch'ŏngjŏng pulgukt'o 清淨佛國土). In Sanskrit, lit. "purified buddha-field"; an important concept in Mahāyāna Buddhology and closely synonymous with some denotations of the East Asian term JINGTU ("PURE LAND"). According to certain MAHĀYĀNA texts, when a bodhisattva achieved buddhahood, the merit that he accumulated over the course of the path fructifies not only as the body, speech, mind, and activities of a buddha but also as the physical environment of that buddha as well. That physical environment is called a "buddha-field." These lands may be either "impure" or "pure," depending upon a number of factors, the most common of which is whether the land does or does not include three baleful destinies (DURGATI) of animals (TIRYAK), ghosts (PRETA), and hell denizens (NĀRAKA). The most famous of these pure buddha-fields is SUKHĀVATĪ, the land of the buddha AMITĀBHA. See also BUDDHAKṢETRA.

**viśuddhi**. [alt. viśuddha] (P. visuddhi; T. rnam par dag pa; C. qingjing; J. shōjō; K. ch'ŏngjŏng 清淨). In Sanskrit, "purity"; of which two types are enumerated: innate purity (prakṛti or svabhāvaviśuddhi) and purity free of temporary or adventitious stains (āgantukamalaviśuddhi). The former is the natural state of the mind (see PRABHĀSVARA) as in the Pāli AṄGUTTARANIKĀYA: "The mind, O monks, is luminous (P. pabhassara), but is defiled by adventitious defilements" (pabhassaraṃ idaṃ bhikkhave cittaṃ, tañ ca kho āgantukehi upakkilesehi upakkiliṭṭhaṃ). The latter is the mind when the path (MĀRGA) has cleansed it of hindrances (see NĪVARAṆA; ĀVARAṆA). In Pāli, there are seven purities (visuddhi) that must be developed along the path leading to liberation. The list of seven purities is first enumerated in the MAJJHIMANIKĀYA and forms the outline for both BUDDHAGHOSA's VISUDDHIMAGGA and Upatissa's earlier *VIMUTTIMAGGA. The seven purities are likened to seven carriages that one takes in sequence to reach seven progressive goals. Thus, (1) the purity of morality (P. sīlavisuddhi; see S. ŚĪLAVIŚUDDHI) leads to its goal of (2) the purity of mind (CITTAVISUDDHI), and the purity of mind leads to its goal of (3) purity of understanding or views (DIṬṬHIVISUDDHI). The purity of understanding leads to its goal of (4) purity of overcoming doubt (KAṄKHĀVITARAṆAVISUDDHI), and the purity of overcoming doubt leads to its goal of (5) the purity of knowledge and vision of what is and is not the path (MAGGĀMAGGAÑĀṆADASSANAVISUDDHI). The purity of knowledge and vision of what is and is not the path leads to its goal of (6) knowledge and vision of progress along the path (PAṬIPADĀÑĀṆADASSANAVISUDDHI), and knowledge and vision of progress along the path leads to its goal of (7) the purity of knowledge and vision (ÑĀṆADASSANAVISUDDHI). The goal of this last purity is liberation through the attainment of any of the four supramundane paths (P. ariyamagga; S. ĀRYAMĀRGA).

**Visuddhimagga**. In Pāli, "Path of Purity"; the definitive Pāli compedium of Buddhist doctrine and practice, written by the exegete BUDDHAGHOSA at the MAHĀVIHĀRA in ANURĀDHAPURA, Sri Lanka, in the fifth century CE. The work serves as a prolegomenon to the soteriological content of the entire Pāli canon in terms of the three trainings in morality (P. sīla; S. ŚĪLA), concentration (SAMĀDHI), and wisdom (P. paññā; S. PRAJÑĀ). These are the "three trainings" (P. tisikkhā; S. TRIŚIKṢĀ) or "higher trainings" (P. adhisikkhā; S. adhiśikṣā). In his use of this organizing principle for his material, Buddhaghosa is clearly following Upatissa's earlier *VIMUTTIMAGGA, which is now extant only in a Chinese translation. Buddhaghosa had originally come to Sri Lanka from India in order to translate the Sinhalese commentaries (AṬṬHAKATHĀ) to the Pāli canon back into the Pāli language. It is said that, in order to test his knowledge, the Mahāvihāra monks first gave him two verses and ordered him to write a commentary on them; the *Visuddhimagga* was the result. Legend has it that, after completing the treatise, the divinities hid the text so that he would be forced to rewrite it. After a third time, the divinities finally relented, and when all three copies were compared, they were found to be identical, testifying to the impeccability of Buddhaghosa's understanding of the doctrine. The commentaries that Buddhaghosa was then allowed to edit and translate make numerous references to the *Visuddhimagga*. The text contains a total of twenty-three chapters: two chapters on precepts, eleven on meditation, and ten on wisdom. In its encyclopedic breadth, it is the closest equivalent in Pāli to the ABHIDHARMAMAHĀVIBHĀṢĀ of the SARVĀSTIVĀDA school of ABHIDHARMA. The post-fifth century CE exegete DHAMMAPĀLA wrote a Pāli commentary to the *Visuddhimagga* titled the PARAMATTHAMAÑJŪSĀ ("Container of Ultimate Truth"), which is also often referred to in the literature as the "Great Subcommentary" (*Mahāṭīkā*).

**Viśvaṃtara**. (S). See VESSANTARA.

**Vitakkasaṇṭhānasutta**. (C. Zengshangxin jing; J. Zōjōshingyō; K. Chŭngsangsim kyŏng 增上心經). In Pāli, "Discourse on Removing Distracting Thoughts," the twentieth sutta in the MAJJHIMANIKĀYA (a separate SARVĀSTIVĀDA recension appears as the 101st SŪTRA in the Chinese translation of the MADHYAMĀGAMA); preached by the Buddha to an assembly of monks at the JETAVANA grove in the town of Sāvatthi (S. ŚRĀVASTĪ). The Buddha teaches five methods that can be used to overcome unwholesome, distracting thoughts (P. vitakka; S. VITARKA) that may arise during the course of meditation. These methods include replacing the unwholesome thought with a wholesome thought, contemplating the danger of the unwholesome thought, ignoring the unwholesome thought, progressively stilling the process of thought formation, and forcibly suppressing the unwholesome thought through the application of concentration. An analogous treatment of five methods of controlling thoughts also appears in the YOGĀCĀRABHŪMIŚĀSTRA.

**vītarāgapūrvin**. (T. chags bral sngon song; C. xian liyu ren; J. senriyokunin; K. sŏn iyok in 先離欲人). In Sanskrit, "one already free from attachment," that is, one who has eliminated the afflictions (KLEŚA) that cause rebirth in the sensual realm (KĀMADHĀTU) prior to reaching the path of vision (DARŚANAMĀRGA); a general designation used in ABHIDHARMA to describe a set of the twenty members of the ĀRYASAṂGHA (see VIṂŚATIPRABHEDASAṂGHA). The vītarāgapūrvin are said to be those who do not gain each of the four fruits of the noble path (ĀRYAMĀRGAPHALA) in a series, but leap over one or more before reaching NIRVĀṆA. See SROTAĀPANNAPHALAPRATIPANNAKA; SAKṚDĀGĀMIPHALASTHA.

**vitarka**. (P. vitakka; T. rtog pa; C. xun; J. jin; K. sim 尋). In Sanskrit, "thoughts," "applied thought," or "applied attention"; one of the forty-six mental concomitants (CAITTA) according to the VAIBHĀṢIKA school of SARVĀSTIVĀDA ABHIDHARMA, one of the fifty-one according to the YOGĀCĀRA school, and one of the fifty-two in the Pāli ABHIDHAMMA. Although etymologically the term contains the connotation of "investigation," vitarka is polysemous in the Buddhist lexicon and refers to a mental activity that could be present both in ordinary states of consciousness as well as during meditative absorption (DHYĀNA). Generically, vitarka can simply denote thoughts, and specifically "distracted thoughts," as in the VITAKKASAṆṬHĀNASUTTA. In ordinary consciousness, it is perhaps best translated as "applied thought" or "initial application of thought" and refers to the momentary advertence toward the chosen object of attention. Vitarka is listed in the ABHIDHARMA as an indeterminate mental factor (ANIYATACAITTA), because it can be employed toward either virtuous or nonvirtuous ends, depending on one's intentions and the object of one's attention. In meditative absorption, vitarka is one of the five constituents (DHYĀNĀṄGA) that make up the first DHYĀNA, and is perhaps best translated in that context as "applied attention" or "initial application of attention." In dhyāna, vitarka involves directing one's focus onto the single chosen meditative object. According to the Pāli VISUDDHIMAGGA, "applied attention" is like a bee flying toward a flower, having oriented itself toward its chosen target, whereas "sustained attention" (VICĀRA) is like a bee hovering over that flower, having closer contact with and fixing itself upon the flower.

**vitarkamudrā**. (C. anwei yin; J. anniin; K. anwi in 安慰印). In Sanskrit, "gesture of instruction" or "gesture of discussion." Vitarkamudrā is formed with a combination of gestures: the right palm faces outward, fingers up near the shoulder in the ABHAYAMUDRĀ, and the left palm faces out, fingers down by the knee in the VARADAMUDRĀ. Typically, the thumb and index finger of each hand also touch lightly, forming circles, while the rest of the fingers are splayed outward. This is a common gesture in Buddhist iconography, and the pose is often seen used with images of BHAIṢAJYAGURU, VAIROCANA, AMITĀBHA, MAÑJUŚRĪ, and even AVALOKITEŚVARA. This gesture is also sometimes called the vyākhyānamudrā, "the gesture of explanation."

**vivartakalpa**. (P. vivaṭṭakappa; T. chags pa'i bskal pa; C. chengjie; J. jōkō; K. sŏnggŏp 成劫). In Sanskrit, "eon of formation" or "eon of creation"; one of the four periods in the cycle of the creation and destruction of a world system, according to Buddhist cosmology. These are the eon of formation (vivartakalpa), the eon of abiding (VIVARTASTHĀYIKALPA), the eon of dissolution (SAṂVARTAKALPA), and the eon of nothingness (SAṂVARTASTHĀYIKALPA), According to the ABHIDHARMAKOŚABHĀṢYA, each of the four eons lasts for twenty intermediate eons. The eon of formation begins when a wind begins to blow in space, impelled by the KARMAN of sentient beings. A circle of wind forms, followed by a circle of water, followed by a circle of golden earth. The entire world system of the sensuous realm (KĀMADHĀTU) then forms, including Mount SUMERU, the four continents and their subcontinents, the heavens, and the hells (see BHĀJANALOKA). These are then populated by beings (see SATTVALOKA), reborn in the various realms as a result of their previous karman. When all realms of the world system have been populated, the eon of formation ends and the eon of abiding begins.

**vivartasthāyikalpa**. (P. vivaṭṭaṭṭhāyikappa; T. gnas pa'i bskal pa; C. zhujie; J. jūkō; K. chugŏp 住劫). In Sanskrit, "eon of abiding," or "eon of duration"; one of the four periods in the cycle of the creation and destruction of a world system, according to Buddhist cosmology. The others are: the eon of formation (VIVARTAKALPA), the eon of abiding (vivartasthāyikalpa), the eon of dissolution (SAṂVARTAKALPA), and the eon of nothingness (SAṂVARTASTHĀYIKALPA). According to the ABHIDHARMAKOŚABHĀṢYA, each of the four eons lasts twenty intermediate eons. The eon of formation begins when a wind begins to blow in space, impelled by the karman of sentient beings. A circle of wind forms, followed by a circle of water, followed by a circle of golden earth. The entire world system of the sensuous realm (KĀMADHĀTU) and the first DHYĀNA of the realm of subtle materiality (RŪPADHĀTU) then forms (see BHĀJANALOKA), which is then populated by beings (see SATTVALOKA) who are reborn there as a result of their previous KARMAN. When all realms of the world system have been populated, the eon of formation ends and the eon of abiding begins. At the beginning of the eon of abiding, the human life span is said to be "infinite" and decreases until it eventually reaches ten years of age. It then increases to eighty thousand years, before decreasing again to ten years. It takes one intermediate eon for the life span to go from ten years to eighty thousand years to ten years again. The eon of abiding is composed of twenty eons, beginning with the intermediate eon of decrease (in which the life span decreases from "infinite" to ten years), followed by eighteen intermediate eons of increase and decrease, and ending with an intermediate eon of increase, when the life span increases from ten years to eighty thousand years, at which point the next eon, the eon of dissolution, begins. ŚĀKYAMUNI Buddha appeared when the life span was one hundred years. It is said that MAITREYA will come when the human life span next reaches eighty thousand years.

**viveka**. (T. dben pa; C. yuanli; J. onri; K. wŏlli 遠離). In Sanskrit and Pāli, "seclusion," "aloofness," "solitude." In Buddhist meditative literature, viveka refers to the "aloofness" that occurs as a result of becoming increasingly focused on a meditative object and thus more "secluded" from the things of the sensual world. In the NIDDESA of the Pāli KHUDDAKANIKĀYA, three kinds of viveka are described: kāyaviveka, or "physical seclusion"; cittaviveka, or "mental seclusion;" and upadhiviveka, or "seclusion from the substrata of rebirth (UPADHI)," viz., the five aggregates (SKANDHA) and/or the afflictions (KLEŚA). Kāyaviveka is actual physical separation from family, friends, and distracting sense objects; cittaviveka is when meditative practitioners remain "aloof" or "secluded" from greed (RĀGA), hatred (DVEṢA), and delusion (MOHA). In some MAHĀYĀNA texts, the slavish pursuit of viveka is explained as a violation of the bodhisattva ideal, because the devotion to solitude impedes the bodhisattva's vow to save others from their suffering. In Buddhist tantras, such as the GUHYASAMĀJATANTRA, the practice of the three isolations of body (kāyaviveka), speech (VĀGVIVEKA), and mind (cittaviveka) precedes the practice of illusory body (MĀYĀKĀYA), clear light (PRABHĀSVARA), and union (YUGANADDHA).

**Vô Ngôn Thông**. (無言通) (d. 826). Vietnamese monk regarded by tradition as the founder of the second principal school of THIỀN (CHAN) in Vietnam. According to the Vietnamese genealogical history, THIỀN UYỂN TẬP ANH, Vô Ngôn Thông originally came from Guangzhou (China) and entered the Buddhist order at Shuanglinsi in Wuzhou. Because he was known for his ability to silently comprehend and realize the nature of things, his contemporaries called him "Wordless Realization" (V. Vô Ngôn Thông; C. Wuyantong). He is reputed to have studied under BAIZHANG HUAIHAI. In 820, Vô Ngôn Thông came to Kiến Sơ Monastery in northern Vietnam and took up residence there to practice Chan. He generally sat facing the wall (see BIGUAN), without uttering a word. A disciple, Cảm Thành, served him for many years and received the transmission of his full teaching.

**Vṛjiputraka**. (P. Vajjiputtakā; C. Baqizi; J. Batsugishi; K. Palgija 跋耆子). In Sanskrit, "Sons of Vṛji"; a group of monks condemned at the second Buddhist council (SAṂGĪTI; see COUNCIL, SECOND), the council at VAIŚĀLĪ, for what were judged to be ten violations of the VINAYA, the most serious of which was accepting gold and silver from the laity. Other violations included carrying a provision of salt, using a fringed sitting mat, eating after noon, eating meals from two different villages on the same day, and performing an ecclesiastical act (SAṂGHAKARMAN) without a sufficient number of monks being present. According to Pāli sources, after their condemnation, these monks seceded to form the MAHĀSĀṂGHIKA school. See also VĀTSĪPUTRĪYA; YAŚAS.

**Vulture Peak**. See GṚDHRAKŪṬAPARVATA.

**vyākaraṇa**. (P. veyyākaraṇa; T. lung bstan pa; C. shouji/piqieluo; J. juki/bigara; K. sugi/pigara 授記/毘伽羅). In Sanskrit, "prediction" or "prophecy"; a statement made by a buddha indicating the course of future events, especially regarding when, where, and with what name a BODHISATTVA will become a buddha. The most famous instance of such prophecy in the MAHĀYĀNA sūtras appears in the SADDHARMAPUṆḌARĪKASŪTRA ("Lotus Sūtra"), where the Buddha makes predictions that the great ARHATs, beginning with ŚĀRIPUTRA, will all eventually achieve buddhahood. ¶ Vyākaraṇa is also used to refer to one of the nine (NAVAṄGA) (Pāli) or twelve (DVĀDAŚĀṄGA [PRAVACANA]) (Sanskrit) categories (AṄGA) of Buddhist scripture according to their structure or literary style, where it refers to prophetic teachings or expositions. In the ninefold Pāli division, BUDDHAGHOSA defines veyyākaraṇa as something of a default category, which comprises the entire ABHIDHAMMAPIṬAKA, all suttas that do not contain verses, and any teaching of the Buddha that does not fall into any of the other eight categories.

**Vyākhyāyukti**. (T. Rnam par bshad pa'i rigs pa). In Sanskrit, "Principles of Exegesis," a treatise by VASUBANDHU preserved only in Tibetan translation. In the broadest sense, the text deals with scriptural interpretation, touching on a wide range of related issues, including the authenticity of the MAHĀYĀNA sūtras as the word of the Buddha (BUDDHAVACANA), which Vasubandhu upholds. The work is a companion to another work by Vasubandhu, the *Vyākhyāyuktisūtrakhaṇḍaśata* ("One Hundred Extracts from the Sūtras for the Principles of Exegesis"), a collection of 109 passages presented without identification and without comment, all of which derive from "mainstream" (that is, non-Mahāyāna) sources, in most cases from the canon of the MŪLASARVĀSTIVĀDA. These passages serve as the basis for the discussion in the *Vyākhyāyukti*, which states that sūtras are to be explained according to (1) their purpose, (2) their summarized meaning, (3) their sense, (4) their sequence, and (5) objections and responses. In discussing the sense or meaning of a sūtra passage, he considers thirteen terms that have multiple meanings, including DHARMA, RŪPA, and SKANDHA. In his explication of technical terminology, Vasubandhu explains four distinct aspects of "the meaning of the words" (padārtha): synonyms (paryāya), definition (lakṣaṇa), etymology (nirukti), and their subdivisions (prabheda; perhaps implying subsidiary meanings, or "connotations," in this context). In the course of the discussion, several Mahāyāna sūtras are quoted. The work was influential in late Indian scholastic circles, eliciting a commentary by Guṇamati; it was also cited by such scholars as HARIBHADRA. It was highly praised by such luminaries as SA SKYA PAṆḌITA and BU STON in Tibet, where it was used to establish principles for the translation of Buddhist texts from Sanskrit into Tibetan. See also NETTIPPAKARAṆA; PEṬAKOPADESA; SANFEN KEJING.

**vyāpāda**. (T. gnod sems; C. chen; J. shin; K. chin 瞋). In Sanskrit and Pāli, "malice" or "ill will"; the ninth of ten unwholesome courses of action (AKUŚALA-KARMAPATHA), referring to the hateful wish that harm will befall another. The ten courses of action are divided into three groups according to whether they are performed by the body, speech, or mind. Malice is classified as an unwholesome mental action (AKUŚALA-KARMAN), and forms a triad along with covetousness (ABHIDHYĀ) and wrong views (MITHYĀDṚṢṬI). Only extreme forms of defiled thinking are deemed an unwholesome course of mental action, such as the covetous wish to misappropriate someone else's property, the harmful intent to hurt someone, or the adherence to pernicious doctrines. Lesser forms of defiled thinking are still unwholesome (akuśala), but do not constitute a course of action. ¶ "Malice" is also listed as one of the five hindrances (NĪVARAṆA) to DHYĀNA, obstructing the dhyāna factor of rapture (PRĪTI). Malice is fostered by unwise attention (AYONIŚOMANASKĀRA) to objects causing aversion and is removed through frequent wise attention to loving-kindness (MAITRĪ), developing the meditation on loving-kindness, and recognizing the fact that every person's actions are his or her own and acknowledging the futility of anger. Malice is countered by faith (ŚRADDHĀ), the first of the five spiritual faculties (INDIYA), and by the enlightenment factors (BODHYAṄGA) of physical rapture (prīti) and equanimity (UPEKṢĀ). "Malice" is also included among the ten fetters (SAṂYOJANA) and is completely overcome only upon becoming an ARHAT.

**vyāpti**. (T. khyab pa; C. bian/bianzhi; J. hen/henshi; K. p'yŏn/p'yŏnji 遍/遍至). In Sanskrit, "pervasion" or "concomitance"; a term used in logic to indicate the relation that obtains between the reason and the predicate in a correct syllogism (PRAYOGA). There is positive concomitance (anvaya) and negative concomitance (VYATIREKA). For example, in order for the syllogism (PRAYOGA) "Sound is impermanent because of being produced" to be correct, it must be true that whatever is impermanent must necessarily be produced. That is, the category of the reason must either be coextensive with or subsume the category of the predicate. In Tibetan monastic debate, the term figures in one of three answers that the defender of a position may give. When presented with a syllogism or consequence (PRASAṄGA) by the challenger, the defender may (1) accept the thesis ('dod), (2) state that the reason is not a quality of the subject (rtags ma grub), or (3) state that there is no pervasion between the reason and the predicate (ma khyab).

**vyatireka**. (T. ldog pa; C. lizuofa; J. risahō; K. ijakpŏp 離作法). In Sanskrit, in Buddhist logic, "exclusion" or negative concomitance, as compared with positive concomitance (anvaya); in the syllogism (PRAYOGA) "Sound is impermanent because of being produced," the negative concomitance is whatever is permanent is not produced; the positive concomitance is whatever is produced is impermanent. The term also is used in the discussion of "reverse" (vyāvṛtta; T. ldog pa), a term that occurs in epistemology and logic treatises to describe how thought (as opposed to direct perception, viz., PRATYAKṢA) apprehends its object via a negative route, whereby, for example, the idea of "chair" is arrived at through the exclusion of everything that is "nonchair." This "non-nonchair" would be called the "reverse" (vyāvṛtta) of chair and the object of the concept of "chair." See also APOHA.

**vyavadāna**. (P. vodāna; T. rnam byang; C. jing; J. jō; K. chŏng 淨). In Sanskrit, "purification" or "cleansing"; often contrasted with SAṂKLEŚA, meaning impurity, defilement, stain, or pollution. This vyavadāna/saṃkleśa dichotomy is used in a variety of ways. These are understood to be two distinct and opposite modes of causation that condition one's future—one leading to suffering and other to the end of suffering. A being's consciousness (VIJÑĀNA) is constantly entering into either the process of purification (vyavadāna) or defilement (saṃkleśa), depending upon actions and thoughts at any given moment. The process of purification may be undertaken by way of morality (ŚĪLA), concentration (SAMĀDHI), or wisdom (PRAJÑĀ). Purification is evidenced by the resultant presence of tranquillity (PRAŚRABDHI). In some MAHĀYĀNA texts, it is emphasized that the ultimate result of the process of purification is the realization that all phenomena (DHARMA) are ultimately devoid of any distinction between pure and impure. The term vyavadāna may also be used independently of saṃkleśa, as, for example, where a BODHISATTVA's understanding of the DHARMA is said to be vyavadāna—pure and without blemish.

**vyavahāra**. (T. tha snyad; C. sudi/yanyu; J. zokutai/gongo; K. sokche/ŏnŏ 俗諦/言語). In Sanskrit, "convention" or "designation"; often with the connotation of something superficial. Generally, this term refers to matters involved with the mundane or worldly realm, as opposed to those of the sacred or supramundane realm. Vyavahāra has two general applications in a Buddhist context. First, it is used to indicate the established social conventions, experiences, and practices of the quotidian world. In Buddhism, these conventions are contrasted with the strict moral practices that conform to the ultimate truth (PARAMĀRTHASATYA) perceived by noble beings (ĀRYA). In this sense of a "conventional truth," vyavahārasatya is synonymous with SAṂVṚTISATYA. Second, and rather more commonly, this term is used in the context of language and discourse to indicate those conventional words used by ordinary, unenlightened beings to designate reality as they (mis)understand it. Here, again, the terms and the objects that they designate are merely conventional truths (saṃvṛtisatya); the term vyavahārasatya sometimes is used as a synonym. Since, according to the doctrine of emptiness (ŚŪNYATĀ), all phenomena are devoid of any inherent, unchanging nature, the linguistic expressions used to designate the things of this world are purely conventional designations and cannot contain or communicate the true nature of those phenomena. Through the power of their practice, buddhas and BODHISATTVAs have an inherent understanding of all such linguistic expressions (see NIRUKTI; PRATIBHĀNA) and use that knowledge to communicate the DHARMA to unenlightened beings. Buddhas and bodhisattvas, however, understand both the true and ineffable nature of the language they use, as well as the phenomena that language is meant to describe.

**Vyavahārasiddhi**. (T. Tha snyad grub pa). In Sanskrit, "Proof of Convention"; a work attributed to NĀGĀRJUNA; it is no longer extant, but six stanzas are cited by ŚĀNTARAKṢITA in his MADHYAMAKĀLAṂKĀRAVṚTTI. The verses state that a MANTRA is composed of letters just as a medicine is composed of ingredients, but the mantra and the medicine are neither the same as nor different from the elements of which they are comprised. Because they are dependently arisen, they cannot be said to be either existent or nonexistent; instead, they exist conventionally. This fact is true of all phenomena, including cessation (NIRODHA), which were set forth by the Buddha for specific purposes.

**vyaya**. (T. 'jig pa; C. mie; J. metsu; K. myŏl 滅). In Sanskrit and Pāli, "disintegration" or "destruction"; a close synonym of ANITYA, viz., "desinence" or "impermanence." In the SARVĀSTIVĀDA ABHIDHARMA, "disintegration" or "desinence" constitutes the final of the four characteristics (CATURLAKṢAṆA) of compounded phenomena (SAṂSKṚTADHARMA), along with production or origination (JĀTI), continuance or maturation (STHITI), and "senescence" or decay (JARĀ). Vyaya refers to the inevitable tendency of all compounded things to disintegrate, once the cause and conditions that sustain them vanish. The various abhidharma systems disagree as to whether these four conditioned characteristics are natural qualities inherent in all compounded things; or whether they are external factors that act upon those things, such as through "forces dissociated from thought" (CITTAVIPRAYUKTASAṂSKĀRA). They also disagree as to whether the four occur successively over a period of time or whether they are four perspectives on a single instant (KṢAṆA).

# W

**Wachirayanwarorot**. [alt. Wachirayan Warot] (Thai) (1860–1921). See VAJIRAÑĀṆAVARORASA.

**wajō**. (和上). An alternate Japanese transcription of the Sanskrit term UPĀDHYĀYA, or "preceptor," which is also pronounced kashō in the TENDAISHŪ. This term is often interchangeable with OSHŌ. See HESHANG.

**wall contemplation**. See BIGUAN.

**Wanfosi**. (J. Manbutsuji; K. Manbulsa 萬佛寺). In Chinese, "Monastery of Myriad Buddhas"; located outside the western gate of the old city wall of Chengdu in Sichuan province; currently only an archeological site. The monastery was founded during the Eastern Han period (25–220 CE) and survived through the end of the Ming dynasty (1368–1644), changing its name several times in the course of its history. It was known as Anpusi during the Liang dynasty (502–556), JINGZHONGSI during the Tang dynasty (618–907), Jingyinsi during the Song dynasty (960–1279), and Zhulinsi, Wanfusi, and, finally, Wanfosi, during the Ming dynasty (1368–1644), after which it fell into disrepair. Since the rediscovery of the site in 1882, some two hundred sculptures and other sacred objects have been uncovered during successive excavations, most of which are currently kept in the Sichuan Provincial Museum. The sculptures date mainly from the North–south Dynasties through the Tang periods. During the Tang, when the monastery was known as Jingzhongsi, it was the residence of the early CHAN monk CHŎNGJUNG MUSANG (680–756, alt. 684–762), a Korean monk from the Unified Silla dynasty (668–935), whose prosperous Sichuan Chan lineage came to be known as the JINGZHONG ZONG line. His toponym Chŏngjung (Jingzhong) comes from this monastery of Jingzhongsi.

**Wangnyunsa**. (王輪寺). In Korean, "Royal Wheel Monastery"; a major doctrinal (KYO) monastery located on Mt. Songak in the Koryŏ capital of Kaesŏng. It was one of the ten monasteries built in the capital in 919 by Wang Kŏn (T'aejo, r. 918–943), the first king of the Koryŏ dynasty, in conjunction with his policy to establish his new state on the foundations of the religious power of Buddhism. This monastery was the site for the ecclesiastical examinations (SŬNGKWA) for monks in the Doctrinal (Kyo) school, which were established during the reign of King Kwangjong (r. 949–975). Such important Koryŏ Kyo monks as the state preceptor (KUKSA) Chigwang Haerin (984–1067) and the royal preceptor (WANGSA) Hyedŏk Sohyŏn (1038–1096) were appointed to their positions after taking the examinations at Wangnyunsa. Although Wangnyunsa seems not to have been as heavily patronized by the royal family as some of the other monasteries in Kaesŏng, the *Koryŏsa* ("History of Koryŏ") notes a number of religious ceremonies that were held there during the dynasty. The monastery burned to the ground in 1236 during the Mongol invasion of the Korean peninsula and was subsequently rebuilt in 1275 by King Ch'ungnyŏl (r. 1274–1308). Wangnyunsa seems to have received special patronage during the reign of King Kongmin (r. 1351–1374). After his queen Noguk's (d. 1365) death, Kongmin sited her memorial hall of Inhŭi chŏn at Wangnyunsa; his own memorial hall, Hyemyŏng chŏn, was built in 1376 at the west of the campus, the last reference to the monastery to appear in Korean historical materials. See also KWANGMYŎNGSA.

**Wang o Ch'ŏnch'ukkuk chŏn**. (C. Wang wu Tianzhuguo zhuan 往五天竺國傳). In Korean, "Memoir of the Pilgrimage to the Five Regions of India"; composed by the Korean monk-pilgrim HYECH'O (d.u.; c. 704–780). After being ordained in Korea, Hyech'o left for China sometime around 721 and spent perhaps three years on the mainland before departing for India (the Ch'ŏnch'ukkuk of the title) via the southern sea route in 724. After landing on the eastern coast of the subcontinent, Hyech'o subsequently spent about three years on pilgrimage to many of the Buddhist sacred sites, including BODHGAYĀ, KUŚINAGARĪ, and SĀRNĀTH, and on visits to several of the major cities in north central India. He then traveled in both southern and western India before making his way toward the northwest, whence he journeyed on into KASHMIR, GANDHĀRA, and Central Asia. Making his way overland across the Central Asian SILK ROAD, Hyech'o arrived back in Chinese territory in December of 727, where he spent the rest of his life. Like other pilgrims before him, Hyech'o kept detailed notes of his pilgrimage, and his travelogue does not differ significantly in terms of style and content from the earlier and more famous records left by FAXIAN and XUANZANG; unfortunately, unlike their works, only fragments of his account survive. His text is largely organized according to the kingdoms, regions, and pilgrimage sites that Hyech'o visited. Hyech'o offers a general description of the geography, climate, economy, customs, and religious practices of each place he visited, and, when necessary, he clarifies whether MAHĀYĀNA, HĪNAYĀNA, or some combination of the two traditions was practiced at a specific site. Although Hyech'o is known to have been the disciple of VAJRABODHI and AMOGHAVAJRA, considered by some as patriarchs of esoteric Buddhism, he makes no mention in his travelogue of tantric texts or practices. Hyech'o does note the dilapidated state of some major STŪPAs and monasteries, the advance of the Turkic tribes into Buddhist areas, and the absence of any Buddhist practice in Tibet at that early date. In these and other respects, Hyech'o's memoir serves as a valuable resource for the study of Buddhism and regional history along the Silk Road.

**Wang Rixiu**. (王日休) (d. 1173). Chinese lay Buddhist during the Song dynasty (960–1279), who played an important role in revitalizing the PURE LAND (JINGTU) tradition, also known by his Buddhist name of Longshu. Although Wang was an accomplished Confucian scholar, he renounced all aspiration for civil office and instead devoted himself to pure land devotions, charitable activities, and a daily regimen of one thousand prostrations. Wang is best known as the author of *Longshu zhengguan jingtu wen* ("Longshu's Extended Writings on the Pure Land"), written in 1160, an extensive compendium of materials on the SUKHĀVATĪ pure land of AMITĀBHA, drawn from sūtras, commentarial writings, and biographical materials, with Wang's own exegeses. The collection offers practical instructions on how to have faith, and achieve rebirth, in the pure land, as well as a series of edifying tales about the successful rebirths and miracles that others generated through their own devotions.

**wangshen**. (J. bōshin; K. mangsin 亡身). In Chinese, lit., "loss of body," viz., "self-immolation." See SHESHEN.

**wangsheng**. (J. ōjō; K. wangsaeng 往生). In Chinese, "going to rebirth"; referring especially to rebirth in AMITĀBHA's PURE LAND of SUKHĀVATĪ. In its broadest sense, the term is sometimes used to refer to rebirth in either the three realms of existence (LOKADHĀTU) or other buddhas' or BODHISATTVAs' pure lands, such as the ABHIRATI pure land of the buddha AKṢOBHYA or the TUṢITA heaven of the bodhisattva MAITREYA. The term has a distinctive usage in the East Asian PURE LAND traditions, however, where it refers specifically to rebirth in sukhāvatī. The seminal pure land sūtra, the SUKHĀVATĪVYŪHASŪTRA, regards this kind of rebirth as the achievement of the stage of nonretrogression (S. AVAIVARTIKA), one of the stages of the BODHISATTVA path. The *Wangshenglun zhu*, a commentary by TANLUAN on VASUBANDHU's WULIANGSHOU JING YOUPOTISHE YUANSHENG JI (**Aparimitāyuḥsūtropadeśa*), says that rebirth in sukhāvatī is to be distinguished from the cycle of rebirth in the three realms of existence, because birth in the pure land frees one from any prospect of subsequent rebirths in SAṂSĀRA. In order to go to rebirth in sukhāvatī, the pure land tradition offered the simple practice of chanting the buddha Amitābha's name (C. NIAN FO; K. yŏmbul; J. NENBUTSU; see also NAMU AMIDABUTSU). Ritual practices associated with taking rebirth in the pure land also include the deathbed recitation of the name of Amitābha, which is introduced in the *Sukhāvatīvyūhasūtra* as the eighteenth of the forty-eight vows that DHARMĀKĀRA made before he attained enlightenment. According to this vow, a person may be reborn in sukhāvatī by sincerely calling out Amitābha's name a mere ten times. The quality of rebirth in the pure land will be dependent on the practitioner's level of achievement, viz., as superior, average, or inferior. Superior disciples are those who arouse the thought of enlightenment (BODHICITTA) and maintain mindfulness of Amitābha, while cultivating meritorious qualities. Average disciples are those who arouse the thought of enlightenment and maintain mindfulness of Amitābha, but who do not cultivate meritorious qualities to the same extent as do superior disciples. Inferior disciples are those who arouse the thought of enlightenment and maintain mindfulness of Amitābha, but who have not yet consistently begun to cultivate meritorious qualities. Several collections of testimonials regarding the efficacy of wangsheng practice exist in China, including the seventh-century *Wangsheng zhuan* by Jiacai (fl. c. 627) and the FAYUAN ZHULIN by Daoshi (d. 683).

**Wangsheng Jingtu zhuan**. (往生淨土傳). In Chinese, "Biographies of Those Who Have Gone to Rebirth in the Pure Land." See JINGTU ZHUAN.

**Wang Wei**. (J. Ō I; K. Wang Yu 王維) (701–761). Chinese poet, painter, and musician during the Tang dynasty and close associate of masters in the early CHAN school; his cognomen was Mojie. In 721, Wang Wei passed the imperial civil service examination and was appointed as assistant director of the Imperial Music Office. By 759, shortly after the An Lushan rebellion, he had risen to the high bureaucratic rank of right assistant director of the Department of State Affairs. Wang Wei is known to have maintained close relationships with several major figures in the thriving Chan tradition and wrote the funerary inscriptions for such monks as JINGJUE (683–c. 760), author of the LENGQIE SHIZI JI, and the sixth patriarch (LIUZU) HUINENG. Although there is no direct evidence of Buddhist influences in his writing, it is commonly asserted that his close relations with these Chan figures contributed to Wang Wei's subtle and reflective descriptions of nature in his landscape poetry.

**wangxiang**. (J. mōzō; K. mangsang 妄想). In Chinese, "deluded thoughts," "fantasies," viz., thoughts that arise from ignorance (AVIDYĀ), craving (TṚṢṆĀ), conceptualization (VIKALPA), or inverted views (VIPARYĀSA), which must be eliminated in order to achieve enlightenment. The Chinese term corresponds variously to such Sanskrit terms as PARIKALPITA (imaginary), VIKALPA (thought or conception), and KALPANĀ (conceptual construction). In Korean SŎN Buddhism, distracting thoughts or fantasies that arise during meditation practice, no matter how salutary, are denigrated as mangsang. The term has also entered vernacular Korean to mean "daydreaming," "flights of fancy," or even "paranoia."

**Wangyal, Geshe**. (1901–1983). Tibetan monk-scholar of the DGE LUGS sect who played an important role in the transmission of Tibetan Buddhism to the United States. He was born in the region of Kalmykia of Czarist Russia, whose Mongol population practiced Tibetan Buddhism, and became a novice monk at the age of six. He was selected by AGVAN DORZHIEV to continue his studies in LHA SA, enrolling at the Sgo mang college of 'BRAS SPUNGS monastery in 1922. After nine years of study, he traveled to Beijing and then to Calcutta, where he was hired to serve as translator for Sir Charles Bell (1870–1945), British political officer for Sikkim, Bhutan, and Tibet, during his travels in China and Manchuria. In India, he met the British mountaineer Marco Pallis, with whom he spent four months in England in 1937. With the Chinese invasion of Tibet, he left Tibet for India, coming to the United States in 1955 at the invitation of the Kalmyk community of New Jersey. In 1958, he founded the Lamaist Buddhist Monastery of America, known in Tibetan as the Bslab gsum bshad grub gling (Labsum Shedrup Ling), in Freewood Acres, New Jersey, the first Tibetan Buddhist monastery in the United States. At the monastery and subsequently at Retreat House (later named Tibetan Buddhist Learning Center) in Howell, New Jersey, he brought a number of monks to the United States and gave teachings to a large number of students, several of whom went on to become scholars of Buddhism. His full name was Dge bshes Ngag dbang dbang rgyal.

**Wanshan tonggui ji**. (J. Manzen dōkishū; K. Mansŏn tonggwi chip 萬善同歸集). In Chinese, "The Common End of Myriad Good Practices," in three rolls; a primer of Buddhist thought and practice composed by the Song-dynasty CHAN master YONGMING YANSHOU (904–975). Written largely in catechistic style, the *Wanshan tonggui ji* relies heavily upon scriptural quotations to answer questions raised concerning everything from meditation and making offerings of flowers to reciting the name of the buddha AMITĀBHA (see NIANFO). The overall message of the text is that all practices done properly return to the "true mark" of reality (shixiang), and this message is often interpreted as supporting the notion of "the unity of Chan and the teachings" (Chan jiao yizhi) and that of "sudden awakening (followed by) gradual cultivation" (DUNWU JIANXIU).

**Wanshousi**. (萬壽寺). In Chinese, "Long Life Monastery"; located on Mt. Jing, Hangzhou prefecture, in present-day Zhejiang province of China; the first of the so-called "five mountain" (wushan, cf. GOZAN) monasteries of the CHAN tradition in China. Wanshousi, also known as Jingshansi, was established by the Chan master FAQIN during the Tianbao reign (742–756) of the Tang dynasty. During the Song dynasty, the monastery was designated as a public monastery, or "monastery of the ten directions" (SHIFANG CHA), and was renamed on several occasions as Chengtian Chanyuan (Upholding Heaven Chan Cloister), Nengren Chansi (Śākyamuni Chan Monastery), and Xingsheng Wanshou Chansi (Flourishing of Holiness, Long Life Chan Monastery). Wanshousi attracted many eminent abbots, such as DAHUI ZONGGAO and WUZHUN SHIFAN, and flourished under their supervision. The famous Japanese pilgrims DŌGEN KIGEN and ENNI BEN'EN also studied at Wanshousi. The monastery was destroyed in a conflagration at the end of the Yuan dynasty but was reconstructed during the Hongwu era (1368–1398) of the Ming dynasty. Largely through the efforts of the abbot Nanshi Wenxiu and others, Wanshousi regained some of its past glory.

**Wanthadipani**. (P. Vaṃsadīpanī). In Burmese, "Lamp on the History [of the Religion]"; the first of four Burmese thathanawin, or Buddhist chronicles, that were composed in Burma (Myanmar) during the Konbaung dynasty (1752–1885). Written c. 1799 in the Burmese language by the monk Mehti SAYADAW, the text records the history of the THERAVĀDA saṅgha (S. SAṂGHA) from its inception during the lifetime of the Buddha, through cycles of decline and restoration in ancient India, Sri Lanka, and Burma, up through a reformation of the Burmese saṅgha begun at the capital AMARAPURA in 1784, of which Mehti Sayadaw himself was a leader. The text relies heavily on the Pāli chronicles SAMANTAPĀSĀDIKĀ and MAHĀVAṂSA for its account of the ancient tradition in India and Sri Lanka. It takes its material for the history of Buddhism in Burma among the Pyu, Myamma (ethnic Burmans), and Mon peoples from a variety of indigenous sources, including the KALYĀṆĪ INSCRIPTIONS (1479), the YAZAWIN-KYAW (1502), and U Kala's MAHAYAZAWIN-GYI (c. 1730). The text concludes with an account of Mehti Sayadaw's missionary activities in the city of Taungoo, where he was dispatched to propagate the new monastic reforms among the local saṅgha.

**Warren, Henry Clarke**. (1854–1899). One of the first American scholars of Buddhism, known for his translations from the Pāli; born in Boston, Massachusetts, in 1854. Warren suffered a crippling injury as a result of a childhood fall that left him with permanent spinal damage and excruciating physical pain throughout his life. After graduating from Harvard University in 1879, Warren studied with the eminent Sanskrit scholar Charles Lanman at Johns Hopkins University and, together with Lanman, founded the Harvard Oriental Series. Warren visited Oxford in 1884, where he met T. W. RHYS-DAVIDS and joined the PĀLI TEXT SOCIETY around the time of its foundation; he also made a substantial financial donation to the organization. Warren's best known work is an extensive anthology of Pāli materials, *Buddhism in Translations*, published in 1896 as the third volume in the Harvard Oriental Series. He also published an edition of BUDDHAGHOSA's VISUDDHIMAGGA as volume 41 in that series. Warren died in Cambridge,

Massachusetts, at the age of forty-five as a result of his debilitating spinal injury.

**wat**. In Thai, Khmer, and Lao, the most common term for a VIHĀRA or monastic complex. Wat is derived from the Pāli term vatta, meaning "practice, function, observance," which by extension comes to be interpreted as a "place where practice is performed," and thus a "monastery" (wat). Although Pāli regulations technically require a complex to have at least three monks in residence to be classified as a vihāra, the term wat is used in Thailand to refer to the deserted ruins of monasteries as well as to Hindu temples and Christian churches.

**Wat Arun**. In Thai, "Monastery of the Dawn," deriving from the Sanskrit and Pāli Aruṇa, the personification of dawn; located in Bangkok on the west bank of the Chao Phraya River. After defeating the Burmese in 1767, King Taksin (Boromrāja IV) is said to have arrived at the Wat Makok ("Olive Monastery") at dawn and renamed it Wat Jaeng ("Bright Monastery"). King RĀMA IV bestowed on the monastery its present name. The monastery is best known today for its tall prang, or Khmer-style tower, which was constructed during the reigns of kings Rāma II and Rāma III. The central tower is 250 feet tall and symbolizes Mount SUMERU. The temple was briefly the seat of the Emerald Buddha (see PHRA KAEW MORAKOT) before the image was moved to WAT PHRA KAEW in 1784.

**Wat Benchamabophit**. In Thai, "Monastery of the Fifth King," deriving from the Sanskrit Pañcamapavitra, with pañcama (Thai, benchama) meaning fifth, and pavitra (Thai, bophit/bophitra) meaning holy or benificent one, a synonym for "king"; the monastery is commonly known in English as the "Marble Temple." Located in Bangkok, it is one of the most renowned modern monasteries in Thailand. Construction began in 1900 at the request of the eponymous RĀMA V (Chulalongkorn), and the complex is built from Italian marble. It houses a large bronze statue of the Buddha called Phra Phuttha Chinnarat (Buddhajinarāja), which is a replica of the original. The ashes of Rāma V are enshrined under the image.

**Wat Bowonniwet**. [alt. Wat Bovoranives]. In Thai, "Monastery of Excellent Abode" (P. Pavaranivesa); the royal monastery that is the Bangkok headquarters of the THAMMAYUT sect of Thai Buddhism. Built in 1829, it is most famous as the monastery where Prince Mongkut, the future king RĀMA IV and leader of the Thammayut reform movement, served as abbot, beginning in 1836, before he ascended the throne in 1851. The future king lived as a monk (his ordination name was Vajirañāṇa) for twenty-seven years, fourteen of which he spent as abbot of this monastery, before he returned to lay life in order to assume the throne of the Chakri dynasty. Subsequent members of the royal family have served the traditional period of temporary ordination as monks of this monastery; his son, the eminent scholar-monk VAJIRAÑĀṆAVARORASA (1860–1921), was the long-time abbot of the monastery. The main temple enshrines the buddha image called Phra Phuttha Chinnasi (Buddhajinaśrī), said to date from 1357. Wat Bowonniwet is also the home of Mahamakut Buddhist University, one of Thailand's two public Buddhist universities.

**Water and Land Ceremony**. See SHUILU HUI.

**Wat Mahathat**. In Thai, "Monastery of the Great Relic" (P. Mahādhātu); the abbreviated name of several important Thai monasteries. ¶ Wat Mahathat in the ancient Thai capital of AYUTHAYA was constructed in 1374 and served as the seat of the SAṄGHARĀJA of the Kamavasi (P. Gāmavāsi, lit. "city-dweller") sect. The temple complex was expanded and restored several times before the city was sacked by the Burmese in 1767; it remains in ruins. Excavations in 1956 unearthed relics. ¶ Wat Phra Mahathat Woromaha Vihan (P. Mahādhātuvaramahāvihāra), located in Nakhon Si Thammarat and thus also known as WAT PHRA THAT NAKHON SI THAMMARAT, was founded c. 757 CE and was originally a ŚRĪVIJAYA MAHĀYĀNA Buddhist monastery. Its famous STŪPA, modeled on the MAHĀTHŪPA in Sri Lanka, was built in the early thirteenth century to house a tooth relic of the Buddha brought back from the island. ¶ The best-known of the contemporary wats with this name, Wat Mahathat Yuwaraja Rangsarit Raja Woramaha Wihan (P. Mahādhātuyuvarāja [Thai, Rangsarit] Rājavaramāhavihāra), dates from the Ayuthaya period (when it was called Wat Salak), and was named the relic temple for Bangkok in 1803. Because of its location near the palaces, it has often been used for royal ceremonies. Mahachulalongkornrajavidyalaya, Thailand's largest Buddhist university, was located on its grounds until 2008, when the main campus was moved to Wangnoi, Ayuthaya.

**Wat Pho**. In Thai, "Monastery of Awakening" (P. BODHI); also known as Wat Phra Chetuphon (P. JETAVANA); the oldest and largest monastery in Bangkok, constructed in the sixteenth century and occupying twenty acres of land. It was extensively rebuilt in 1781 by King Rāma I and renovated in the first half of the nineteenth century by King Rāma III. The site also houses Thailand's largest reclining buddha image and the largest number of buddha images in the country. The reclining buddha image, constructed in the reign of King Rāma III, is 153 feet (forty-six meters) long and fifty feet (fifteen meters) high. Modeled out of plaster around a brick core, the image is finished in gold leaf, with mother-of-pearl inlay in the eyes. The feet display the 108 different auspicious characteristics of a buddha. In all, the monastery contains over a thousand buddha images, many from the ruins of the former capitals of AYUTHAYA and SUKHOTHAI, and a total of ninety-five STŪPAS of various sizes. Other features are a series of 152 marble slabs depicting the second half of the epic Rāmakian story (the Thai version of the Hindu epic the *Rāmāyaṇa*), as well as numerous chapels, rock gardens, statues, and bell towers. Sometimes referred to as Thailand's first university, Wat Pho also contains an encyclopedic collection of engravings and paintings dealing with astrology, botany, herbal medicine, massage, and yoga. The wat is still a center for teaching traditional Thai massage.

**Wat Phra Kaew**. [alt. Wat Phra Kaeo]. In Thai, "Temple of the Emerald Buddha," perhaps the most famous Buddhist temple in Thailand, located on the grounds of the royal palace in Bangkok. Much of the construction had been completed when Rāma I moved the Thai capital to Bangkok in 1785. It is a large-walled complex, containing dozens of golden pagodas, many shrines, and two libraries. Unlike most other Buddhist temples in Thailand, the complex does not include monastic quarters because of its location inside the palace grounds. The temple is best known as the site of the Emerald Buddha, or PHRA KAEW MORAKOT, the most sacred buddha image in Thailand; Kaew is an indigenous Thai word for "glass" or "translucent"; morakot derives from the Sanskrit word for emerald (S. marakata).

**Wat Phra Pathom Chedi**. (P. Paṭhamacetī). In Thai, "Temple of the First Reliquary"; the monastery built at the site of what is said to be the tallest Buddhist CAITYA (P. cetī) in the world at over 394 feet (120 meters); located in the Thai town of Nakhon Pathom. See PHRA PATHOM CHEDI.

**Wat Phra Phutthabat**. In Thai, "Monastery of the Buddha's Footprint" (P. BUDDHAPĀDA); a Thai monastery located in Saraburi province. In the seventeenth century, a hunter encountered a large puddle of water that appeared to be a footprint of the Buddha (buddhapāda). Once this identification was verified, a monastery was built to enshrine the footprint. Visiting this monastery is considered a source of great merit, and it is traditional for the Thai king to make an annual pilgrimage to the site to pay homage to the relic.

**Wat Phra Thammakai**. (Thai). See DHAMMAKĀYA.

**Wat Phra That Doi Suthep**. In Thai, "Monastery of the Relic at Mt. Sudeva" ('That' is the Thai word for relic [P. dhātu], Suthep is the Thai pronunciation of the Pāli proper name Sudeva, and Doi is a non-Thai northern word for mountain). A famous mountain monastery in northern Thailand, built on a site that has long been considered sacred and the home of guardian spirits. According to legend, the site was chosen in 1371 CE by a white elephant that was sent out by local monks to find an auspicious location for enshrining a relic (DHĀTU; ŚARĪRA). The site has been expanded several times with the addition of buildings, murals, bells, and parasols. See also KHRUBA SI WICHAI.

**Wat Phra That Nakhon Si Thammarat**. In Thai, "Monastery of the Relic (P. Dhātu) in Nakhon Si Thammarat" (P. *Nagara-Sīri-Dhammarāja), also known as Wat Phra Mahathat Woramaha Wihan (Mahādhātuvaramahāvihāra); the oldest and most revered Buddhist site in southern Thailand. The monastery dates to 757 CE and was originally a ŚRĪVIJAYA MAHĀYĀNA Buddhist monastery. Its famous STŪPA, modeled on the MAHĀTHŪPA in Sri Lanka, was built in the early thirteenth century to house a tooth relic brought back from the island. See also WAT MAHATHAT.

**Wat Phra That Phanom**. In Thai, "Monastery of the Relic (P. DHĀTU) in the city of Phanom" (Phanom is the Lao and Khmer term for mountain); the most revered Buddhist shrine in northeast Thailand, located in the town of Nakhon Phanom. The STŪPA on the site has a history dating back some fifteen hundred years, according to some local traditions, while other legends claim that it was originally built in 535 BCE, eight years after the death of the Buddha, as a reliquary for his breastbone. The structure is Lao in style, with a square base surmounted by slender tapering vertical columns in the shape of an elongated lotus bud. Its present appearance dates from 1977, after its predecessor collapsed under heavy rains in 1975, and is modeled after WAT THAT LUANG in Vientiane, Laos.

**Wat Phu**. [alt. Wat Phou; Vat Phu]. In Lao, "Mountain Monastery"; an important Khmer monastery complex located in Champassak province on the Mekong River in southern Laos. The first monastery was probably constructed in the fifth century CE, although the surviving structures (now largely in ruins) date from the eleventh through the thirteenth centuries. Originally a Śaiva temple, the ruins contain a shrine to Śiva's bull Nandin, as well as pediments depicting INDRA, Kṛṣṇā, and Viṣṇu. The temple complex was converted to Buddhist use in the thirteenth century, with Buddhist images added to many of the shrines. In 2001, the site was designated a UNESCO World Heritage Site.

**Wat Suthat Thepwararam**. [alt. Wat Suthat]. In Thai, "Beautiful Noble Garden of the Devas" (P. Sudassanadevavarārāma); an important Thai monastery in Bangkok, founded by King Rāma I in 1807. It houses an image of the Buddha seated in the "earth-touching" (BHŪMISPARŚAMUDRĀ) pose. The image, known as Phra Sisakayamuni (derived from Śrī-ŚĀKYAMUNI), is considered the largest (over twenty-five feet tall) and oldest bronze buddha image in Thailand; it was brought from SUKHOTHAI by boat. The monastery is also known for its intricately carved wooden doors, created during the reign of Rāma II (r. 1809–1824) and now housed in the National Museum, and its murals of the Buddha's previous lives, from the reign of Rāma III (r. 1824–1851). The large ordination hall of the monastery is considered one of the most beautiful in Thailand. The temple grounds also contain twenty-eight pagodas, representing the twenty-eight buddhas of the auspicious eon. The temple is the traditional seat of the brāhmaṇa priest who oversees important Thai royal ceremonies, such as the annual plowing ceremony. In front of the monastery is a giant swing, once used in an annual festival in which young men tried to swing high enough to retrieve a sack of gold suspended at a height of seventy-five feet. The festival was banned in the 1930s because of the number of deaths that resulted from the competition.

**Wat That Luang**. In Lao, "Monastery of the Royal STŪPA"; located in the Laotian capital of Vientiane, it is one of the most important Buddhist sites in Laos. According to legend, the original monastery was founded by monks sent by AŚOKA in the third century BCE. Relics from the early twelfth century have been uncovered, although these may derive instead from a site in modern-day northern Thailand. The prestige of That Luang may have been enhanced due to its proximity to earlier Buddhist sites. The present monastery was constructed on a small hill south of the city in 1818 during the reign of King Manthaturat (r. 1817–1836). It is said to have been built partially from branches of a BODHI TREE located near Wat Keo Fa. The large bronze and gilded buddha in the nave was transferred from the now defunct Wat Aham Mungkhun, located a short distance from That Luang. That Luang has long been one of the important ritual sites in Laos for Buddhist, folk, and royal ceremonials. There are two large STŪPAS on the grounds. The golden funerary stūpa in front of the main hall contains the ashes of the popular and last crowned Laotian king, Sisavang Vong (r. 1904–1959). The grand stūpa, which towers over the rear of the main hall, dates from 1818 and is said to contain relics (DHĀTU; ŚARĪRA) of the Buddha. The wat also contains a number of smaller stūpas that contain ashes of kings, other members of the royal family, and a variety of other dignitaries. The wat has one of Vientiane's larger communities of monks and novices.

**Wat Traimit**. In Thai, "Monastery of the Three Friends" (S. Traimitra), so named because it was founded by three friends who emigrated from southern China; its full name is Wat Traimit Wittayaram Wora Wihan (S. Traimitravidyārāmavaravihāra). This monastery is located in the Thai capital of Bangkok and is commonly known in English as "The Temple of the Golden Buddha." It contains what is said to be the world's largest gold buddha image, named Phra Phuttha Maha Suwan Patimakon (P. Buddhamahāsuvaṇṇapaṭimā), seated in the "earth-touching" (BHŪMISPARŚAMUDRĀ) pose. The image itself is almost ten feet tall and is claimed to be composed of over five tons of solid gold. The statue, in the SUKHOTHAI style, is believed to have been originally installed in the ancient Thai capital of Sukhothai, perhaps in the thirteenth century. In order to protect it from being plundered by Burmese invaders, it was covered with a layer of plaster. The plastered statue was eventually installed in Wat Phraya Krai during the reign of King Rāma III (r. 1824–1851). When that monastery fell into disrepair around 1931, the image was placed in storage. When it was being moved to its present location in the mid-1950s, the plaster cracked, revealing the golden buddha image inside.

**Watts, Alan**. (1915–1973). A widely read British Buddhist writer. Born in Kent, Watts was inspired to study Buddhism after reading such works as W. E. Holmes' *The Creed of the Buddha*. At the age of fifteen, he declared himself a Buddhist and wrote to the Buddhist Lodge of the Theosophical Society in London, becoming a student and protégé of the head of the Lodge (later the Buddhist Society), CHRISTMAS HUMPHREYS. At the age of nineteen, Watts wrote his first book, *The Spirit of Zen*, largely a summary of the writings of DAISETZ TEITARO SUZUKI. Shortly thereafter, he assumed the editorship of the journal *Buddhism in England* (later to become *The Middle Way*). In 1938, he married the American Eleanor Everett, the daughter of Ruth Fuller Everett (later, RUTH FULLER SASAKI). They immigrated to the United States during World War II (Watts, a pacifist, did not serve) and lived in New York, where Watts studied briefly with Shigetsu Sasaki, a Japanese artist and Zen practitioner known as Sokei-an. Watts gave seminars in New York and published a book entitled *The Meaning of Happiness*. Shortly after his wife had a vision of Christ, Watts decided to become a priest and entered Seabury-Western Theological Seminary near Chicago. He became an Episcopal priest and served for five years as chaplain at Northwestern University, ultimately resigning from the priesthood shortly after his wife had their marriage annulled. He later worked for six years at the newly founded American Academy of Asian Studies in San Francisco. He published *The Way of Zen* in 1957, followed by *Nature, Man, and Woman* in 1958, and *Psychotherapy East and West* in 1961. He supported himself as a popular author and speaker and played a leading role in popularizing Buddhism and Zen until his death in 1973.

**weikza**. [alt. weikza-do]. In Burmese, a "wizard," deriving from the Pāli vijjādhara (S. VIDYĀDHARA). In Burmese popular religion, the weikza is portrayed as a powerful thaumaturge possessed of extraordinarily long life, whose abilities derive from a mastery of tranquillity meditation (P. samatha; S. ŚAMATHA) and a variety of occult sciences such as alchemy (B. ekiya), incantations (P. manta; S. MANTRA), and runes (B. ing, aing). Collectively, these disciplines are called weikza-lam or "the path of the wizard." Training in this path is esoteric, requiring initiation by a master (B. saya), and votaries typically are organized into semisecret societies called weikza-gaing (P. vijjāgaṇa). Although concerned with the acquisition of supernatural powers and an invulnerable body, these attributes are ultimately dedicated to the altruistic purpose of assisting good people in times of need and protecting the Buddha's religion from evil forces. In this regard, weikza practitioners often act as healers and exorcists, and in the modern era weikza-sayas with large followings are among the country's notables, who have built monumental pagodas and restored national shrines. The perfected weikza has the ability to live until the advent of the future buddha Metteya (S. MAITREYA), at which time he can choose to pass into nibbāna (S. NIRVĀṆA) as an enlightened disciple (P. sāvaka arahant; S. ŚRĀVAKA ARHAT), vow to become himself a solitary buddha (P. paccekabuddha; S. PRATYEKABUDDHA) or a perfect buddha (P. sammāsambuddha; S. SAMYAKSAṂBUDDHA), or simply continue living as a weikza. Weikza practitioners typically eschew the practice of insight meditation (P. VIPASSANĀ; S. VIPAŚYANĀ) on the grounds that this might cause them to attain nibbāna too quickly. Although largely domesticated to the prevailing worldview of Burmese THERAVĀDA orthodoxy, weikza practice and orientation ultimately derive from outside the Pāli textual tradition and show striking similarities to the Buddhist MAHĀSIDDHA tradition of medieval Bengal.

**Weimojie suoshuo jing zhu**. (J. Yuimakitsu shosetsukyōchū; K. Yumahil sosŏl kyŏng chu 維摩詰所說經註). An influential commentary on the VIMALAKĪRTINIRDEŚA. The commentary is attributed to KUMĀRAJĪVA, but it was actually written by his disciple SENG ZHAO, who recorded the interpretations of his teacher and combined them with those offered by other of Kumārajīva's disciples, such as DAOSHENG and Daorong. The commentary offers a paragraph-by-paragraph analysis of the sūtra and follows the order of Kumārajīva's Chinese translation of the sūtra. It is the first of the many commentaries on this famed rendering of the *Vimalakīrtinirdeśa* and is still the most frequently cited.

**weinuo**. [alt. weina] (S. *karmadāna/*karmādāna; T. las su bsko ba; J. ina/ino; K. yuna 維那/唯那). In Chinese, "rector"; a term designating either the process of overseeing, or the specific supervisor of, such crucial monastic activities as apportioning dwellings, managing the refectory, arranging sleeping quarters, cleaning the monastery grounds, etc. According to various VINAYA codes and Chinese pilgrimage accounts such as YIJING'S NANHAI JIGUI NEIFA ZHUAN, it was the rector's duty to strike instruments, such as gongs or chimes (GHAṆṬA), to remind others of the monastic schedule. Assemblies, meals, and services were conducted with the help of the rector's announcements. Because of his formal role in maintaining the monastic schedule, the rector may have thus come to serve as the principal supervisor or manager of daily activities in the monastery. The Sanskrit term *karmadāna does not appear in the extant corpus of Indian Buddhist literature, although it is attested in the MAHĀVYUTPATTI Sanskrit-Tibetan lexicon, and the reconstruction is confirmed in Chinese transcriptions. In India, however, karmadāna may not necessarily have referred to a specific monastic office, but rather to the general act of "assigning" (lit. giving, DĀNA) "duties" (lit. action, viz., KARMAN) within the monastery. The Chinese term weinuo, however, clearly refers to a monastic office. The term is typically parsed as a combination of a lexical translation and phonetic transcription, and means something like "regulating (wei) the [dā]na," an interpretation related to the literal sense of the Sanskrit term as "assigning duties," and becomes used in East Asian Buddhism as the specific title of a monastic administrator who delegates responsibilities within the monastery—and thus a "rector." According to the Chinese monastic codes (QINGGUI), the rector was responsible for all matters regarding the SAṂGHA and especially the saṃgha hall (SENGTANG). The rector not only was in charge of the physical maintenance of the hall itself, but he also was called upon to settle issues, such as the determination of relative seniority or the appropriate punishment for transgressions committed by residents of the saṃgha hall. The rector had the responsibility for appointing various low-ranking positions within the monastery, such as attendants, and conducted the tea ceremony. The weinuo also was in charge of leading the formal chanting at daily services, which involved much use of gongs and percussion instruments; weinuo is thus sometimes translated as functionally equivalent to the Western monastic office of "precentor," the leader of the monastic choir. In Korean monasteries, the yuna serves as a "rector" in that he has formal responsibility for enforcing discipline, making work assignments, and arranging the time for group work; in addition, however, he also serves as nominal head of the meditation compound in the monastery and spiritual advisor to the meditation monks.

**Weishan jingce**. (J. Isan Kyōsaku [alt. Keisaku]; K. Wisan Kyŏngch'aek 潙山警策). See GUISHAN JINGCE.

**Weishan Lingyou**. (J. Isan Reiyū; K. Wisan Yŏngu 潙山靈祐) (771–853). Alternate Chinese pronunciation of GUISHAN LINGYOU, cofounder of the GUIYANG ZONG [alt. Weiyang zong] of the mature CHAN tradition. See GUISHAN LINGYOU.

**Weituo tian**. (J. Idaten; K. Wit'a ch'ŏn 韋馱天). A Buddhist guardian deity, who is especially popular in East Asia, where he is often designated as a BODHISATTVA (pusa) or divinity (DEVA; C. tian). Weituo is connected to the god Kārtikeya, also known as Skanda, whom the Buddhist tradition appropriated from the Hindu pantheon. Kārtikeya, the six-headed son of Śiva, is a Hindu god of war who helps defend the gods; in Buddhism, he became one of the many guardian deities who protect the dispensation, its sacred objects, and its sacred spaces. Weituo is the spirit commander of the thirty-two divine generals subordinate to the four heavenly kings (CATURMAHĀRĀJA; see LOKAPĀLA), as well as one of the eight generals under VIRŪḌHAKA, the heavenly king of the southern quarter of the world. He is also identified with KUMĀRABHŪTA (C. Dongzhen). His East Asian name "Weituo" is apparently a mistaken Sinographic transcription from "Sijiantuo" or "Jiantuo tian," both Chinese transcriptions of Skanda. Weituo's role as a dharma protector (DHARMAPĀLA) is reflected in a story from the *Daoxuan lüshi gantong lu* ("Preceptor Daoxuan's Record of Miraculous Stories," c. seventh century), written by the Chinese VINAYA master DAOXUAN (596–667), which relates that Weituo was instructed by the dying Buddha to protect the dharma whenever it was disturbed by demonic forces (MĀRA). From the Tang dynasty onward in China, Weituo was considered the guardian of monasteries and Buddhist practitioners, as well as a symbol of fierce determination in spiritual training. One of Weituo's specific roles was to protect the STŪPAS that enshrine the Buddha's relics (ŚARĪRA). In a popular story involving Weituo, a group of malevolent demons steals one of the Buddha's tooth relics immediately following his death and cremation. Weituo battles the demons, saves the relic, and thereby earns a reputation as a fierce protector of the dharma. Weituo is typically depicted as a young man in full armor, with the headgear of a Chinese general. He is also often shown leaning on his weapon, sometimes a sword, but usually a VAJRA. In many East Asian monasteries, Weituo's image is found to one side of, and facing, the Buddha image in the main shrine hall (TAEŬNG CHŎN). Weituo is also seen in the company of, and sometimes back to back with, AVALOKITEŚVARA and MAITREYA. His visage also frequently appears at the end of Chinese editions of the SŪTRAS, as a reminder of his role in protecting the dharma.

**Weixin jue**. (J. Yuishinketsu; K. Yusim kyŏl 唯心訣). In Chinese, "Essentials of Mind Only"; an exposition on CITTAMĀTRA by the CHAN master YONGMING YANSHOU. In this short treatise, Yongming launched a critique of more than 120 differing Buddhist positions, and argued instead that these variant views are but manifestations of a single, true mind. By cutting through to this mind, Yongming argued that all conceptual dichotomies (e.g., gain and loss, right and wrong, sudden and gradual) would be brought to an end and an inconceivable awakening would be attained.

**weixin jingtu**. (J. yuishin no jōdo; K. yusim chŏngt'o 唯心淨土). In Chinese, "the mind-only PURE LAND"; an interpretation of the pure land influential in the PURE LAND, CHAN, HUAYAN, TIANTAI, and esoteric schools; synonymous with the phrase "AMITĀBHA Buddha of one's own nature/mind" (zixing Mituo/weixin Mituo/jixin Mituo). Rather than seeing Amitābha's pure land of SUKHĀVATĪ as a physical land located to the west of our world system, this interpretation suggests that the pure land is actually identical to, or coextensive with, the mind itself. One understanding of this interpretation is that the concept of "pure land" is simply a metaphor for the innate brilliance and eternality of one's own mind. In this case, "the mind-only pure land" stands in distinction to the idea of the pure land as an objective reality, and many pure land exegetes rejected this interpretation for implying that the pure land existed only metaphorically. In other interpretations, a pure land is understood to manifest itself differently to beings of different spiritual "grades." In this case, "mind-only pure land" is the highest level, which is accessible or visible only to those enlightened to the true nature of the mind; by contrast, the objectively real pure land is an emanation of the true pure land that manifests itself to unenlightened practitioners, but nonetheless is still a literal realm into which one could be reborn. In this case, "the mind-only pure land" is one level of the pure land, which does not, however, negate the reality of an external pure land. Such an interpretation was more amenable to pure land devotees and was sometimes incorporated into their exegetical writings.

**Weiyang zong**. (J. Igyōshū; K. Wiang chong 潙仰宗). Alternate Chinese pronunciation of the GUIYANG ZONG, one of the so-called "five houses" (wu jia; see WU JIA QI ZONG), or distinct lineages, that developed within the mature CHAN tradition during the late-Tang dynasty. See GUIYANG ZONG.

**Wencheng**. (T. Rgya mo bza' kong jo, C. Wencheng gongzhu 文成公主) (d. 680). The Tang-dynasty Chinese princess who married the Tibetan king SRONG BTSAN SGAM PO. Although she was in fact a person of little historical significance, she figures prominently in competing Tibetan and Chinese versions of the introduction of Buddhism into Tibet and of Sino-Tibetan relations. According to Tibetan sources, she was given in marriage to the Tibetan king under threat of invasion and became one of the king's five wives: three Tibetans, one Nepalese, and one Chinese. The Nepalese and Chinese brides were Buddhists and converted their husband to the faith. Each also brought a buddha image as part of their dowry. Princess Wencheng brought the JO BO SHĀKYAMUNI, eventually housed in the JO KHANG in LHA SA, and considered the most sacred buddha image in Tibet. The Nepalese princess BHṚKUTĪ brought the JO BO MI BSKYOD RDO RJE, housed at RA MO CHE. The journey of the Chinese princess and her statue was fraught with difficulties, as the giant demoness (srin mo), whose supine body is the landscape of Tibet, tried to impede their progress. As a result, the king built a series of temples to pin down her body (MTHA' 'DUL GTSUG LAG KHANG). Later sources would identify the Chinese princess as an incarnation of the bodhisattva TĀRĀ. Chinese sources depict the princess as a kind of cultural ambassador, helping to introduce Han culture into the wilds of Tibet and convincing her husband to abandon a variety of barbaric customs. This view of Princess Wencheng has been promoted in various Chinese media (including martial arts films) since the Chinese invasion of Tibet in 1950. Contrary to both versions, it appears that Princess Wencheng arrived at the Tibetan court as a twelve-year-old girl, intended as the bride of Srong btsan sgam po's son, who had died by the time that she arrived. Srong btsan sgam po, by then an old man, made her one of his wives, dying himself a few years later. She did not produce a royal heir and does not seem to have played a significant role at court.

**wenda**. (J. mondō; K. mundap 問答). In Chinese, lit. "question and answer"; pedagogical technique used in the CHAN (J. ZEN; K. SŎN) school that involves an "exchange" or "dialogue" between a Chan master and a disciple regarding the Buddhist teachings. The exchange often consists of questions from the disciple and the master's response, but sometimes the master would also question the disciple to check his or her level of understanding and attainment. The master's answers are typically not a theoretical or discursive response to the question, but instead will employ logical contradiction, contextual inappropriateness, and illocutionary uses of language in order to challenge the understanding of the student. The master's answer might not even be a verbal response at all but might instead employ "the stick and the shout" (BANGHE) as a way of goading the student out of his conventional ways of comprehension. The ultimate goal is to prompt not mere intellectual understanding but an experience of awakening (C. WU; J. SATORI). The recorded sayings (YULU) of eminent Chan masters often include a section on their wenda. These wenda constitute a major part of the GONG'AN literature of the Chan tradition, and the practice of wenda is itself performed using phrases drawn from the gong'an texts. During the Song dynasty in China, Chan monks were appointed to monastic positions, such as "interrogating monk" (wenseng) or "Chan receptionist" (chanke), whose responsibility was to ask questions of the master on behalf of the congregation, transforming wenda into a formal, ritualized occasion.

**Wenyan**. (C) (文偃). See YUNMEN WENYAN.

**Wenyi**. (C) (文益). See FAYAN WENYI.

**wenzi Chan**. (J. monjizen; K. muncha Sŏn 文字禪). In Chinese, "lettered Chan"; a designation coined by JUEFAN HUIHONG (1071–1128) during the Northern Song dynasty (960–1127) to refer to a literati style of Chan exegesis that valorized belle lettres, and especially poetry, in the practice of CHAN. Huihong himself traces the origins of "lettered Chan" to the "five ranks" (WUWEI) of CAOSHAN BENJI (840–901), although Caoshan himself attributes the five ranks to his teacher DONGSHAN LIANGJIE (807–869); in these ranks, Huihong finds the first evidence within the Chan tradition that the manipulation of language in the analysis of the sayings attributed to the ancient Chan masters can bring about awakening. This style of Chan is especially emblematic of monks in the HUANGLONG PAI collateral lineage of the LINJI ZONG.

**Wesak**. (S. Vaiśākha; P. Vesākha; T. Sa ga zla ba). A modern rendering of Vesākha, the Pāli name for the fourth lunar month of the traditional Indian calendar (thus corresponding to April–May in the solar calendar); by extension, the term refers to the important event(s) in the life of the Buddha that occurred during that month and to their annual commemoration. According to the THERAVĀDA and Tibetan traditions, it was on the full moon of the fourth lunar month that the Buddha was born, was enlightened, and passed into PARINIRVĀṆA. This date is therefore the most important in the Buddhist calendar of many traditions. Wesak is widely celebrated across much of the Buddhist world, but especially in Southeast Asia, where it is considered an especially important time to perform meritorious deeds. According to many East Asian traditions, the full moon of the fourth lunar month marks only the date of the Buddha's birth, with his enlightenment and passage into PARINIRVĀṆA occurring in the twelfth and eleventh lunar months, respectively; Wesak is therefore not nearly as important in the East Asian calendar as it is in Southeast Asia and Tibet.

**wheel of dharma**. See DHARMACAKRA.

**wheel of life**. See BHAVACAKRA.

**White Lotus Society**. See BAILIAN SHE.

**Wild Goose Pagoda**. See DACI'ENSI.

**wisdom**. See PRAJÑĀ.

**wisdom derived from cultivation/meditation**. See BHĀVANĀMAYĪPRAJÑĀ.

**wisdom derived from hearing/learning**. See ŚRUTAMAYĪPRAJÑĀ.

**wisdom derived from reflection/analysis**. See CINTĀMAYĪPRAJÑĀ.

**Wŏlchŏngsa**. (月精寺). In Korean, "Lunar Essence Monastery"; the fourth district monastery (PONSA) of the contemporary CHOGYE CHONG of Korean Buddhism, located on Odaesan (see WUTAISHAN) in Kangwŏn province. The monastery's history is closely linked to the VINAYA master CHAJANG (fl. c. 590–658). While Chajang was on pilgrimage at Wutaishan in China, he came across a mysterious old monk who interpreted a prophetic dream he had had and gave him relics (K. sari; S. ŚARĪRA) of the buddha to take back to Korea with him. Seven days later, a dragon told him to return to Odaesan in Korea to build a monastery; in 643, Chajang arrived at Odaesan, where he eventually constructed Wŏlchŏngsa. Wŏlchŏngsa's main shrine hall, Chŏkkwang chŏn (Calm Radiance Hall), enshrines an image of ŚĀKYAMUNI as well as a mysterious statue that was found in the diamond pond south of the monastery. This statue, delicately carved in a style common to the eleventh century, is believed to be of BHAIṢAJYAGURU. In front of the main hall is a nine-story octagonal pagoda, fifty feet (15.2 meters) high, that was constructed in the tenth century. Skillfully carved and multiangled, it is representative of Koryŏ-era STŪPAS. In front of the stūpa is a seated BODHISATTVA, perhaps MAÑJUŚRĪ, making an offering. The statue has been carved with detailed attention to ornamental accessories and clothing. The Chŏngmyŏl pogung (Precious Basilica of Calm Extinction) houses the relics of the Buddha that Chajang brought back to Korea and is one of four major shrine halls in Korea that does not enshrine a buddha image (the relics take the place of an image). One of Wŏlchŏngsa's most famous residents during the twentieth century was the monk HANAM CHUNGWŎN (1876–1951), who helped save some of its buildings from soldiers who had been ordered to burn them down during the Korean War (seventeen buildings were unfortunately burned and had to be reconstructed). Sangwŏnsa, one of Wŏlchŏngsa's branch monasteries (MALSA), is famous among Korean monasteries for its spectacular scenery and is a popular tourist stop.

**Wŏlmyŏn**. (K) (月面). See MAN'GONG WŎLMYŎN.

**womb maṇḍala**. See TAIZŌKAI.

**Wŏnbulgyo**. (圓佛教). In Korean, "Wŏn Buddhism" or "Consummate Buddhism"; a modern Korean new religion, founded in 1916 by PAK CHUNGBIN (1891–1943), later known by his sobriquet SOT'AESAN. Based on his enlightenment to the universal order of the "one-circle image" (IRWŎNSANG), Sot'aesan sought to establish an ideal world where this universal order could be accomplished in and through ordinary human life, rather than the specialized institution of the monastery. After perusing the scriptures of various religions, Sot'aesan came to regard the teachings of Buddhism as the ultimate source of his enlightenment and in 1924 named his new religion the Pulpŏp Yŏn'gu hoe (Society for the Study of the Buddhadharma); this organization was later renamed Wŏnbulgyo in 1947 by Sot'aesan's successor and the second prime Dharma master of the religion, Chŏngsan, a.k.a. Song Kyu (1900–1962). Since the tenets and institutions of Wŏnbulgyo are distinct from those of mainstream Buddhism in Korea, the religion is usually considered an indigenous Korean religion that is nevertheless closely aligned with the broader Buddhist tradition. Sot'aesan used the "one-circle image" as a way of representing his vision of the Buddhist notion of the "DHARMAKĀYA buddha" (pŏpsinbul), which was reality itself; since this reality transcended all possible forms of conceptualization, he represented it with a simple circle, an image that is now displayed on the altar at all Wŏnbulgyo temples. Sot'aesan's religious activities were also directed at improving the daily lot of his adherents, and to this end he and his followers established thrift and savings institutions and led land reclamation projects. Wŏnbulgyo has focused its activities on the three pillars of religious propagation (kyohwa), education (kyoyuk), and public service (chasŏn): for example, the second prime master Chŏngsan established temples for propagation, schools such as Wŏn'gwang University for education, and social-welfare facilities such as hospitals and orphanages. These activities, along with international proselytization, were continued by his successors Taesan, Kim Taegŏ (1914–1998), who became the third prime master in 1962, Chwasan, Yi Kwangjŏng (b. 1936), who became the fourth prime master in 1994, and Kyŏngsan, Chang Ŭngch'ŏl (b. 1940), who became the fifth prime master in 2006. The two representative scriptures of Wŏnbulgyo are the *Wŏnbulgyo chŏngjŏn* ("Principal Book of Wŏn Buddhism"), a primer of the basic tenets of Wŏnbulgyo, which was published by Sot'aesan in 1943, and the *Taejonggyŏng* ("Scripture of the Founding Master"), the dialogues and teachings of Sot'aesan, published in 1962 by his successor Chŏngsan. Wŏnbulgyo remains an influential religious tradition in Korea, especially in the Chŏlla region in the southwest of the peninsula; in addition, there currently are over fifty Wŏnbulgyo temples active in over fourteen countries.

**Wŏnch'ŭk**. (T. Wen tsheg; C. Yuance; J. Enjiki 圓測) (613–695). In Korean, "Consummate Keenness"; Silla-dynasty monk renowned for his expertise in Sanskrit and YOGĀCĀRA doctrine, who was influential in Chinese and in later Tibetan Buddhism. Wŏnch'ŭk is said to have left for Tang-dynasty China at the age of fifteen, where he studied the writings of PARAMĀRTHA and the *She lun*, or MAHĀYĀNASAMGRAHA, under Fachang (567–645). Wŏnch'ŭk later became the disciple of the Chinese pilgrim-translator XUANZANG who, in accordance with the new Yogācāra teachings of DHARMAPĀLA that he had brought back from India (see FAXIANG ZONG), denounced the existence of the ninth "immaculate consciousness" (AMALAVIJÑĀNA), which Paramārtha had advocated, and taught instead the innate impurity of the eighth "storehouse consciousness" (ĀLAYAVIJÑĀNA). These crucial doctrinal issues are said to have caused a split between the major disciples of Xuanzang: Wŏnch'ŭk and his followers came to be known as the Ximing tradition in honor of Wŏnch'ŭk's residence, XIMINGSI, and was said to have been more open to positions associated with the earlier SHE LUN ZONG; and the lineage of his fellow student and major rival KUIJI (632–682), which came to be known as the Ci'en tradition after Kuiji's monastery, Da CI'ENSI, and honed more rigidly to Xuanzang and Dharmapāla's positions. Wŏnch'ŭk's famed *Haesimmilgyŏng so* (C. *Jieshenmi jing shu*), his commentary on Xuanzang's translation of the SAṂDHINIRMOCANASŪTRA, includes traces of Wŏnchŭk's earlier training in She lun zong thought and Paramārtha's expositions on the controversial notion of amalavijñāna. Wŏnchŭk regarded the amalavijñāna as simply another name for the inherent purity of the ālayavijñāna, but, unlike Xuanzang, he considered the ālayavijñāna to be essentially pure in nature. He also disagreed with Xuanzang's contention that the ICCHANTIKA could not attain buddhahood. Hence, his work seems to be an attempt to reconcile the divergences between the old Yogācāra of Paramārtha and the new Yogācāra of Xuanzang. Wŏnch'ŭk's commentary to the *Saṃdhinirmocanasūtra* was extremely popular in the Chinese outpost of DUNHUANG, where CHOS GRUB (Ch. Facheng; c. 755–849) translated it into Tibetan during the reign of King RAL PA CAN (r. 815–838). Only nine of the ten rolls of the commentary are still extant in Chinese; the full text is available only in its Tibetan translation, which the Tibetans know as the "Great Chinese Commentary" (Rgya nag gi 'grel chen) even though it was written by a Korean. Five centuries later, the renowned Tibetan scholar TSONG KHA PA drew liberally on Wŏnch'ŭk's text in his major work on scriptural interpretation, LEGS BSHAD SNYING PO. Wŏnch'ŭk's views were decisive in Tibetan formulations of such issues as the hermeneutical stratagem of the three turnings of the wheel of the dharma (DHARMACAKRAPRAVARTANA), the nine types of consciousness (VIJÑĀNA), and the quality and nature of the ninth "immaculate" consciousness (amalavijñāna). Exegetical styles subsequently used in all the major sects of Tibetan Buddhism, with their use of elaborate sections and subsections, may also derive from Wŏnch'ŭk's commentary. Consequently, Wŏnch'ŭk remains better known and more influential in Tibet than in either China or Korea. Wŏnch'ŭk also wrote a eulogy to the PRAJÑĀPĀRAMITĀHṚDAYASŪTRA, and commentaries to the RENWANG JING and Dharmapāla's *VIJÑAPTIMĀTRATĀSIDDHI, the latter of which is no longer extant.

**Wŏndon sŏngbul non**. (圓頓成佛論). In Korean, "The Perfect and Sudden Attainment of Buddhahood"; posthumous publication on the convergence of HWAŎM (C. HUAYAN) and SŎN (C. CHAN) thought and practice by the mid-Koryŏ reformer POJO CHINUL (1158–1210). The *Wŏndon sŏngbul non* is said to have been found in a wooden box belonging to Chinul after his death and published posthumously by his disciple CHIN'GAK HYESIM. The text provides Chinul's most sustained presentation of his views on Hwaŏm thought and practice, which were profoundly influenced by LI TONGXUAN'S (635–730) idiosyncratic commentary on the AVATAṂSAKASŪTRA, the HUAYAN JING HELUN. Chinul seeks to demonstrate that the sudden understanding-awakening (K. haeo; C. JIEWU; viz., knowing that one is a buddha) is attained at the first level of the ten stages of faith (sipsin), which were usually thought to be a preliminary stage of training, rather than at the first arousing of the thought of enlightenment (BODHICITTOTPĀDA), which occurred at the first of the ten stages of abiding (sipchu). Chinul supports this argument by drawing on the Hwaŏm concept of "nature origination" (XINGQI), which he finds superior to the alternative Hwaŏm theory of the conditioned origination of the dharmadhātu (FAJIE YUANQI). This Hwaŏm understanding at the very inception of practice that one is endowed with the fundamental nature of buddhahood is compared to the CHAN and SŎN notion of "seeing one's nature and attaining buddhahood" (JIANXING CHENGFO). But because Chan/Sŏn does not sanction the prolix conceptual descriptions of this experience that are found in the Hwaŏm school, it is the true "perfect and sudden" school. See also YUANDUN JIAO.

**Wŏn'gam Kuksa**. (K) (圓鑑國師). See MIRAM CH'UNGJI.

**Wŏn'gwang**. (C. Yuanguang 圓光) (542–640). In Korean, "Consummate Brilliance"; Silla-dynasty monk known as an early exponent of the VINAYA tradition in Korea. Wŏn'gwang went to the Chinese kingdom of Chen and studied various texts such as the *TATTVASIDDHI and the MAHĀPARINIRVĀṆASŪTRA. After the fall of the Chen dynasty, Wŏn'gwang traveled to Chang'an, where he attended lectures on ASAṄGA'S MAHĀYĀNASAṂGRAHA delivered by the monk Tanqian (542–607). Wŏn'gwang returned to Korea in 600 and devised a set of lay precepts known as the "five secular injunctions" (Sesok ogye) at the request of two "flower youths" (hwarang) named Kwisan (d.u.) and Ch'uhang (d.u.). These injunctions adapted Confucian and Buddhist moral codes to the needs of a militant society involved in the ongoing peninsular reunification wars. The five are (1) loyalty, (2) filial piety, (3) trust, (4) not killing wantonly, and (5) not retreating in battle. According to his biography in the HAEDONG KOSŬNG CHŎN, Wŏn'gwang was also a renowned thaumaturge and tamer of autochthonous spirits. He passed away at the royal monastery of HWANGNYONGSA. Two commentaries on the TATHĀGATAGARBHASŪTRA, the *Taebangdŭng yŏraejanggyŏng so* and *Yŏraejanggyŏng sagi*, are attributed to Wŏn'gwang, but neither is extant.

**Wŏnhyo**. (C. Yuanxiao; J. Gangyō 元曉) (617–686). In Korean, "Break of Dawn"; famous monk of the Silla dynasty and probably one of the two most important monks in all of Korean Buddhist history, who was renowned for both his scholastic achievements and his efforts to propagate Buddhism among the common people. He is reputed to have written over one hundred commentaries, of which some twenty are extant. According to the hagiographical accounts of Wŏnhyo in the SONG GAOSENG ZHUAN and the SAMGUK YUSA, Wŏnhyo tried, but failed, to travel to China with his friend ŬISANG in order to study with the Chinese translator and YOGĀCĀRA exegete XUANZANG. While on the road, Wŏnhyo is said to have attained enlightenment after a traumatic experience in which he discovered that the earthen sanctuary in which the two travelers had taken refuge one stormy night was in fact a tomb. This experience prompted his awakening that all things are created by mind, which led Wŏnhyo to realize that he did not need to continue on to China in order to understand Buddhism. (Ŭisang did travel to the mainland, where he studied with the early HUAYAN exegete ZHIYAN.) As the legends about Wŏnhyo's enlightenment experience evolve, this story becomes even more horrific: Wŏnhyo is said to have discovered that the sweet water he drank in the tomb to slake his thirst was actually offal rotting in a skull, a traumatic experience that immediately prompted his realization that the mind creates all things. Wŏnhyo spent much of his life writing commentaries to the many new translations of Buddhist scriptures then being introduced into the Korean peninsula. A brief affair with the widowed princess of Yosŏk palace led to the birth of a son, who would grow up to become the famous literatus, Sŏl Ch'ong (c. 660–730), the creator of Idu ("clerical writing"), the earliest Korean vernacular writing system. After the affair, Wŏnhyo changed into lay clothes and traveled among the peasantry, singing and dancing with a gourd he named Unhindered (Muae) and practicing "unconstrained conduct" (K. muae haeng; C. WU'AI XING). ¶ In Wŏnhyo's many treatises, he pioneered a hermeneutical technique he called "reconciling doctrinal controversies" (HWAJAENG), which seeks to demonstrate that various Buddhist doctrines, despite their apparent differences and inconsistencies, could be integrated into a single coherent whole. This "ecumenical" approach is pervasive throughout Wŏnhyo's works, although its basic principle is explained chiefly in his *Simmun hwajaeng non* ("Ten Approaches to the Reconciliation of

Doctrinal Controversy," only fragments are extant), TAESŬNG KISILLON SO ("Commentary to the 'Awakening of Faith According to the Mahāyāna'"), and KŬMGANG SAMMAEGYŎNG NON ("Exposition of the VAJRASAMĀDHISŪTRA"). Wŏnhyo was versed in the full range of Buddhist philosophical doctrines then accessible to him in Korea, including MADHYAMAKA, YOGĀCĀRA, Hwaŏm, and TATHĀGATAGARBHA thought, and hwajaeng was his attempt to demonstrate how all of these various teachings of the Buddha were part of a coherent heuristic plan within the religion. Since at least the twelfth century, Wŏnhyo's hwajaeng exegesis has come to be portrayed as characteristic of a distinctively Korean approach to Buddhist thought.

**wŏnju**. (C. yuanzhu; J. inju 院主). In Korean, lit. "chief of the campus"; the preferred term in Korean monasteries for the "prior." See JIANYUAN.

**Wŏnmyo Yose**. (圓妙了世) (1163–1240). In Korean, "Consummate Sublimity, Knower of the World"; monk during the mid-Koryŏ dynasty, who is considered an influential figure in the revitalization of the Korean CH'ŎNT'AE (C. TIANTAI) tradition. Yose also played a major role in the popularization of a movement known as the PAENGNYŎN KYŎLSA, or White Lotus retreat society (see also JIESHE; BAILIAN SHE). Yose was ordained by the monk Kyunjŏng (d.u.) at the monastery of Ch'ŏllaksa in present-day Hapch'ŏn. In 1185, he passed the clerical examinations (SŬNGKWA) and led a retreat at a monastery known as Changyŏnsa on Mt. Yŏngdong. The eminent SŎN monk POJO CHINUL is known to have sent Yose a letter with a poem at that time, inviting Yose to his "Samādhi and Prajñā retreat society" (CHŎNGHYE KYŎLSA) at Kŏjosa. Yose subsequently joined the society and practiced Sŏn meditation with Chinul, but left the society when Chinul moved the society to the monastery of Kilsangsa (present-day SONGGWANGSA). With the support of some prominent lay followers, Yose restored a group of dilapidated buildings on Mt. Mandŏk and established a White Lotus Society there in 1211. Yose continued to reside at the site after the restoration was completed five years later in 1216. He was posthumously awarded the title of state preceptor (K. kuksa; C. GUOSHI) and given the funerary name Wŏnmyo. He is the reputed author of the *Samdaebu chŏryo*, which is no longer extant.

**Wŏnyung chong**. (圓融宗). In Korean, "Consummate Interfusion school"; an alternate name for the Hwaŏm (C. HUAYAN) school in Korea. See KYO.

**World Fellowship of Buddhists**. The first international Buddhist organization, founded in Colombo, Sri Lanka, in 1950, by representatives from twenty-seven countries, and headed by GUNAPALA PIYASENA MALALASEKERA (1899–1973). Although most Buddhist traditions around the world are actively involved in the organization, THERAVĀDA Buddhists of Southeast Asia have traditionally played a central role: all its previous and current headquarters have been located in countries where the Theravāda tradition predominates (e.g., Sri Lanka, Myanmar, and Thailand) and all its presidents have also come from those countries. The WFB has more than 130 regional centers in over thirty countries, including India, Australia, the United States, Korea, Japan, and some African and European countries. The organization aims to promote the teachings of the Buddha, strengthen collegiality among Buddhists of different national traditions, and contribute to world peace by participating in social, educational, and humanitarian activities. The current headquarters is located in Bangkok, Thailand.

**wu**. (J. satori; K. o 悟) In Chinese, "awakening," "enlightenment"; one of the common Chinese translations for the Sanskrit term BODHI (awakening); often seen in English through its indigenous Japanese pronunciation of SATORI. The precise content of this awakening differs according to the various schools of Buddhism. In the East Asian tradition, wu could typically involve a gradual awakening (JIANWU), but it is more commonly associated with "sudden awakening" (DUNWU), especially in the CHAN ZONG (J. ZEN; K. SŎN). Sudden awakening refers to the view that the mind is inherently enlightened (cf. "buddha-nature," or FOXING) and thus does not need to be purified of its afflictions (KLEŚA) in order for that buddha-nature to be realized. Gradual awakening, by contrast, refers to the view that enlightenment is the result of a process of purifying the mind of its afflictions over a series of stages, which may take several lifetimes to complete. The Chan scholiasts GUIFENG ZONGMI and POJO CHINUL, following earlier taxonomies of awakening in the HUAYAN ZONG, distinguish between two kinds of awakening: an initial sudden understanding-awakening (JIEWU), i.e., the instant when one first comes to know that one is innately a buddha; and, following a lengthy period of gradual cultivation (jianxiu), a final realization-awakening (ZHENGWU), when one is able fully to act on the potential inherent in one's initial awakening and not only *be* a buddha but also *act* like one. This description of the soteriological process is called sudden awakening followed by gradual cultivation (see DUNWU JIANXIU). Chan authors discuss many other possible permutations in this awakening and cultivation binary, including gradual cultivation/gradual enlightenment, sudden awakening/sudden cultivation, etc. Although the SUDDEN-GRADUAL ISSUE is most commonly associated with the CHAN school, there are precedents in Indian Buddhism. The so-called BSAM YAS DEBATE, or Council of Lha sa, that took place in Tibet at the end of the eighth century is said to have pitted the Indian monk KAMALAŚĪLA against the Chan monk Heshang MOHEYAN in a debate over the issue of whether enlightenment occurs gradually or suddenly.

**wu**. (J. mu; K. mu 無). In Chinese, a Sinograph meaning "not have," "without," "no," and, as a philosophical term, "nonbeing," "nothingness." Exegetes in the Dark Learning (XUANXUE) school of Chinese philosophy, which was influential in early Chinese Buddhist thought, first explored the philosophical implications of the term wu. Based on their reading of the *Daode jing* ("The Way and Its Power"), a seminal Daoist classic traditionally attributed to the legendary Laozi, they interpreted wu as meaning either (1) "nonexistence" or "nonbeing," in distinction to the Sinograph you, viz., "existence," or "being"; or (2) the metaphysical substratum of the universe, viz., "nothingness," which transcended the dichotomy of you and wu. Wu in this second denotation did not indicate simply voidness or negation; it rather referred to the source of the DAO itself or the principle underlying all existence. In this sense, wu was inseparable from you, the phenomenal expressions of the dao. This wu was termed "original nothingness" (benwu), because it served as the ultimate foundation of the myriad of existing things in the universe, and thus represented a preconceptual reality that transcended dichotomous existence (you). Wang Bi (226–249), traditionally regarded as the founder of Xuanxue, defined a person who attained wu as a sage (shengren). ¶ Early Chinese Buddhist thinkers, such as DAO'AN (312–385) and Zhu Fatai (320–387), drew on this Xuanxue concept of benwu to render the Buddhist concept of emptiness (ŚŪNYATĀ); SENGZHAO (374–414) in his ZHAO LUN also equates the original nothingness (benwu) with the dharma-nature (DHARMATĀ). As Chinese Buddhists gradually refined their understanding of the Buddhist notion of emptiness, prompted especially by the influence of KUMĀRAJĪVA's translations of the PRAJÑĀPĀRAMITĀ texts, this rendering of śūnyatā as wu was ultimately replaced by the new term kong (emptiness). ¶ In the context of the CHAN ZONG, wu was often used to emphasize the mental state of nonattachment. However, ever since the character wu (pronounced mu in Japanese and Korean) was singled out by Chan master DAHUI ZONGGAO as a meditative topic (HUATOU) in Chan practice, Chan adepts began to use "wu" as an aid in their "questioning meditation" (KANHUA CHAN). This meditative topic was derived from a popular GONG'AN (KŌAN) attributed to ZHAOZHOU CONGSHEN: "Does a dog have buddha nature, or not?" Zhaozhou answered, "wu" ("no," lit. "it does not have it"). The Sinograph wu was also a frequent subject of monochrome brushstroke calligraphy, which was and is still often hung on the walls of the abbot's quarters (FANGZHANG) in Chan monasteries. See WU GONG'AN; GOUZI WU FOXING.

**wu'ai xing**. (J. mugegyō; K. muae haeng 無礙行). In Chinese, "unhindered action" or "unconstrained conduct"; one of the types of practice of a BODHISATTVA-MAHĀSATTVA, as expounded especially in the AVATAṂSAKASŪTRA, referring to a conduct that is not constrained by the restrictions of customary morality or mundane societal expectations. Other related terms that are described as unhindered include "unhindered physicality" (wu'ai shen), "unhindered SAMĀDHI" (wu'ai sanmei), "unhindered wisdom" (wu'ai zhi), "unhindered dharma" (wu'ai fa), "unhindered path" (wu'ai dao), etc. The actions of a bodhisattva-mahāsattva conform to those of the buddhas themselves and any merit forthcoming from them are freely transferred (huixiang) to other sentient beings to help them with their salvation; for this reason, their actions are free from any kinds of hindrances. The MAHĀYĀNASAṂGRAHA (*She Dasheng lun*) also explains "unhindered action" as the merit of a buddha, which is obtained through the purest of wisdom. Unhindered action sometimes refers to a particular stage or practice of a bodhisattva-mahāsattva: the BODHISATTVABHŪMI (*Pusa shanjie jing*) presents it as the tenth of the twelve conducts of a bodhisattva-mahāsattva, along with such advanced practices as the signless practice, untainted practice, practice-less practice, and contented practice. In this context, unhindered action refers to the stage where a bodhisattva cultivates the realm of reality (DHARMADHĀTU) that transcends all discrimination and teaches the true dharma (SADDHARMA) for the sake of innumerable sentient beings. This status is said to correspond specifically to the ninth of the ten bodhisattva stages (DAŚABHŪMI), and the bodhisattva on this stage is described as being endowed with four types of analytical knowledges (PRATISAṂVID), which in Chinese were known as the four "unhindered knowledges" (C. si wu'ai jie): i.e., unhindered knowledge of (1) phenomena (DHARMA), viz., one makes no mistakes in one's teachings; (2) meaning (ARTHA), viz., to be unhindered with regard to the content and meaning of one's teachings; (3) etymology or language (NIRUKTI), viz., the ability to comprehend all languages; and (4) eloquence (PRATIBHĀNA), viz., ease in offering explanations. CHENGGUAN (738–839) states in his massive HUAYAN JING SHU ("Commentary to the AVATAṂSAKASŪTRA") that the bodhisattva is able to abide in unhindered action (lit. "unhindered abiding") because he no longer has any cognitive obstructions (JÑEYĀVARAṆA). The practice of unconstrained conduct has been a prominent, if controversial, feature of Korean Buddhism throughout its history. Several eminent Korean monks were known as practitioners of unconstrained conduct, including WŎNHYO (617–686), Chinmuk (1562–1633), and KYŎNGHŎ SŎNGU (1849–1912), and they followed ways of life that disregarded the standards of conduct typically incumbent upon ordained monks.

**Wubai wenlun shiyi**. (C) (五百問論釋疑). See FAHUA WUBAI WENLUN.

**wuchong xuanyi**. (J. gojūgengi; K. ojung hyŏnŭi 五重玄義). In Chinese, "five layers of profound meaning" according to the TIANTAI school. See FAHUA WUCHONG XUANYI.

**wudao song**. (J. godōju; K. odo song 悟道頌). In Chinese, lit. "hymn on awakening to the way (DAO)"; an "enlightenment hymn." See YIJI.

**wufa**. (J. gohō; K. obŏp 五法). In Chinese, "the five [aspects of] dharmas." According to various Chinese scholastic traditions, deriving from translations of the LAṄKĀVATĀRASŪTRA and YOGĀCĀRA materials, these five delineate the full ontological and epistemological range of all dharmas: phenomena (SHI), characteristics (xiang), conceptual discrimination (fenbie), correct knowledge of the way things are (zhengzhi), and suchness (ZHENRU). The first three aspects are called "factors associated with delusion/unenlightenment" (mifa) because the multiplicity, duality, and reality of "phenomena" and "characteristics" are merely "imagined" and "superimposed" by the discriminatory property of the unenlightened mind (which is covered by the third aspect, fenbie, viz., PARIKALPITA). In contrast, the last two aspects are called "factors associated with enlightenment" (wufa), with "knowledge" being the ability to discern the true "suchness" of things without conceptual superimpositions.

**wu gong'an**. (J. mukōan; K. mu kongan 無公案). In Chinese, "the case 'no'"; an influential CHAN case or precedent (GONG'AN) associated with the Tang-dynasty Chan master ZHAOZHOU CONGSHEN (778–897). In this exchange, once a student came to Zhaozhou and asked, "Does a dog have the buddha-nature (FOXING), or not?" Zhaozhou answered, "No" (lit., "It does not have it"). The complete exchange from which this gong'an is drawn continues: "Everything has buddha-nature, from the buddhas above, to the ants below. Why wouldn't a dog have it?" Zhaozhou replied: "Because he has the nature of karmically conditioned consciousness." This response seems to be associated with Chan debates concerning the Sinitic Buddhist doctrine of the "buddha-nature of the insentient" (wuqing foxing), which presumed that all insentient things, including rocks and tiles, trees, and grass, were also endowed with the buddha-nature; thus, if even rocks have the buddha-nature, why not dogs? Since the answer to the student's question should unequivocally be "Yes, a dog does have the buddha-nature," Zhaozhou's enigmatic response, which Wumen calls a "checkpoint of the patriarchs," seems to challenge one of the foundational beliefs of East Asian Buddhism; in so doing, it engenders a question in the student's mind, which will help to foster inquiry and ultimately a sense of doubt (YIQING). This answer "WU" ("no") became a popular meditative topic (HUATOU) in the Chan meditation practice of "questioning meditation" (KANHUA CHAN) and is one of the most important gong'ans used in kanhua Chan training, especially in the Chinese LINJI ZONG and Japanese RINZAISHŪ lineages, as well as in the Korean CHOGYE CHONG. The wu gong'an is the first case collected in the gong'an anthology WUMEN GUAN ("Gateless Checkpoint"), and its use in kanhua practice was popularized by the Chinese Linji teacher DAHUI ZONGGAO (1089–1163). See also GOUZI WU FOXING.

**wuhui nianfo**. (J. goe nenbutsu; K. ohoe yŏmbul 五會念佛). In Chinese, "five-tempo intonation of [the name of] the buddha" (see NIANFO). A method of intoning the name of the buddha AMITĀBHA devised by the Tang-dynasty monk FAZHAO (d.u.). While in SAMĀDHI, Fazhao is said to have received instructions for the wuhui nianfo technique directly from Amitābha himself. The practice seems to be based on the larger SUKHĀVATĪVYŪHASŪTRA, which speaks of the bejeweled trees that produce music in five tempos when swayed by the wind. The first tempo is a leisurely chant performed in a high tone (ping). The second tempo is a high and rising tone (pingshang). The third tempo is neither leisurely nor rapid, and the fourth gradually becomes rapid. The fifth tempo is a rapid and repetitious recitation of the four characters "A-mi-tuo-fo," the Chinese pronunciation of Amitābha. According to Fazhao, the practical aim of this practice is to focus on the three jewels (RATNATRAYA) until one attains "no-thought" (WUNIAN) and nonduality (ADVAYA). Fazhao recommends wuhui nianfo for both clergy and lay who wish to rid themselves of the five types of suffering and the five hindrances, or to purify the five sense organs (INDRIYA) and attain the five powers (BALA). The ultimate purpose of the practice is to attain rebirth in the PURE LAND of SUKHĀVATĪ. Two manuals by Fazhao detailing the practice of wuhui nianfo, the *Jingtu wuhui nianfo lüefa shiyi canben* ("Praise for the Abbreviated Ritual Manual of the Pure Land Five-Tempo Intonation of [the Name of] the Buddha") and the *Jingtu wuhui nianfo songjing guanxing yi* ("Rite for Intoning the Buddha's Name, Reciting Scripture, and Performing Meditation According to the Five Tempos of the Pure Land"), were recovered in the DUNHUANG manuscript cache.

**wujiao**. (C) (五教). In Chinese, the "fivefold taxonomy of the teachings" according to the Huayan school. See HUAYAN WUJIAO.

**Wujiao zhang**. (C) (五教章). See HUAYAN WUJIAO ZHANG.

**wu jia qi zong**. (J. goke shichishū; K. oga ch'ilchong 五家七宗). In Chinese, "five houses and seven schools." According to the traditional historical narratives of the CHAN tradition, the lineages of the sixth patriarch (LIUZU) HUINENG's two major disciples NANYUE HUAIRANG and QINGYUAN XINGSI grew into five houses and eventually seven schools. The five houses refer to the lineages of the GUIYANG [alt. Weiyang] ZONG, LINJI ZONG, CAODONG ZONG, YUNMEN ZONG, and FAYAN ZONG of the Tang dynasty. Each of these "houses" (jia) is said to have had its own unique teaching style (jiafeng) and was respectively named after its purported founder or "patriarch": the Guiyang was named after GUISHAN LINGYOU and his disciple YANGSHAN HUIJI, the Linji after LINJI YIXUAN, the Caodong after DONGSHAN LIANGJIE and his disciple CAOSHAN BENJI, the Yunmen after YUNMEN WENYAN, and the Fayan after FAYAN WENYI. Among these houses, the Linji became predominant during the Song dynasty, when it further split into two separate lineages known as the HUANGLONG PAI (named after HUANGLONG HUINAN) and the YANGQI PAI (named after YANGQI FANGHUI). These two Song-dynasty lineages, together with the original listing of five houses, constitute the so-called seven schools. According to the Chan historian GUIFENG ZONGMI, the early Chan lineages known as the NIUTOU ZONG, Heze zong (see HEZE SHENHUI), JINGZHONG ZONG, BAOTANG ZONG, BEI ZONG, and NAN ZONG were eventually supplanted by the flourishing lineages of Nanyue's disciple

MAZU DAOYI (i.e., the Guiyang and Linji) and Qingyuan's disciples SHITOU XIQIAN (i.e., the Caodong and Yunmen) and XUEFENG YICUN (i.e., the Fayan).

**wujinzang yuan**. (J. mujinzōin; K. mujinjang wŏn 無盡藏院). In Chinese, "inexhaustible storehouse cloister"; the emblematic institution of the Third Stage Sect (SANJIE JIAO), a major school of Buddhism during the Tang dynasty. The wujinzang yuan was established at Huadusi (Propagation and Salvation Monastery) in the capital Chang'an early in the Tang dynasty, probably between 618 and 627. The institution was based on the concept of "merit-sharing," i.e., that one could enter into the universal inexhaustible storehouse of the dharma realm, as articulated by the sect's founder XINXING (540–594), by offering alms to the wujinzang yuan on behalf of all sentient beings. By 713, when the Tang emperor Xuanzong (r. 712–756) issued an edict closing it due to charges of embezzlement, the wujinzang yuan had served as a major agency for promoting the sect for almost a century. Drawing on the AVATAṂSAKASŪTRA and the VIMALAKĪRTINIRDEŚA, the sect interpreted the Sinographs wujin (inexhaustible) to mean that both the field of reverence—viz., the three jewels (RATNATRAYA)—and the field of compassion—viz., sentient beings—were inexhaustible. The wujinzang yuan, therefore, was the place where the sect's sixteen kinds of almsgiving (DĀNA) were to be practiced, through offerings made to (1) the buddha, (2) the dharma, (3) the saṃgha, and (4) all sentient beings; (5) works that serve to ward off evil; (6) works that serve to do good; and offerings of (7) incense, (8) lamps, (9) the monks' baths, (10) bells and chants, (11) clothing, (12) dwellings, (13) beds and seats, (14) receptacles for food, (15) coal and fire, and (16) food and drink. There were two kinds of offerings made to the wujinzang yuan: (1) regular offerings collected in the form of a daily levy and (2) offerings received at particular times of the year. A Sanjie jiao text discovered at DUNHUANG says that a person is expected to offer one fen (a hundredth of a tael) of cash or one ge (a tenth of a pint) of grain per day, or thirty-six qian (a tenth of a Chinese ounce) or 3.6 dou (pecks) of grain per annum. However, the offerings were mostly made at specific times of the year, such as on the fourth day of the first lunar month, the day commemorating Xinxing's death, and the ULLAMBANA festival on the fifteenth day of the seventh lunar month. For those adherents who could not make offerings directly at Huadu monastery, the sect would temporarily open local branches, called "merit offices" (gongde chu), especially at the time of the Ullambana festival. The assets of the wujinzang yuan consisted for the most part of such tangible assets as money, cloth, gold and silver, and jade. The offerings were used, for example, to fund the restoration of monasteries and the performance of religious services (i.e., the reverence field of merit, jingtian), and to provide alms to the poor (i.e., the compassion field of merit, beitian; see PUṆYAKṢETRA). People could also receive loans from the wujinzang, a function comparable to today's microloans made to help raise people out of poverty. During the reign of Empress Wu, Fuxiansi in Luoyang was for a brief time also the site of a wujinzang yuan. See also XIANGFA JUEYI JING.

**Wuliangshou jing**. (J. Muryōjukyō; K. Muryangsu kyŏng 無量壽經). In Chinese, "Sūtra of Infinite Life." See SUKHĀVATĪVYŪHASŪTRA.

**Wuliangshou jing lun**. (C) (無量壽經論). See WULIANGSHOU JING YOUPOTISHE YUANSHENG JI.

**Wuliangshou jing youpotishe yuansheng ji**. (J. Muryōjukyō upadaisha ganshōge; K. Muryangsugyŏng ubajesa wŏnsaeng ke 無量壽經優婆提舍願生偈). In Chinese, "Verses on the Wish for Rebirth and the Exposition of the Limitless Life Scripture"; also known as the *Wuliangshou jing lun* ("Commentary on the Limitless Life Scripture"), *Jingtu lun* ("Treatise on the Pure Land"), *Wangsheng lun* ("Treatise on Rebirth"), and *Yuansheng ji* ("Verses on the Wish for Rebirth"). The *Wuliangshou jing youpotishe yuansheng ji* is attributed to VASUBANDHU and was translated into Chinese by BODHIRUCI at the monastery of YONGNINGSI in 529. The text is largely a commentary on the larger SUKHĀVATĪVYŪHASŪTRA and is comprised of a twenty-four-line verse and prose commentary. The verse section begins with an exhortation to be reborn in the country of peace and happiness (ANLEGUO) or PURE LAND (JINGTU) of the buddha AMITĀBHA, which it subsequently describes in detail, and ends with the dedication of merit (PARIṆĀMANĀ). The prose commentary explains the ritual means of rebirth in terms of "five gates of recollection" (wu nianmen). These five gates are veneration (libai), praise (cantan), vow (zuoyuan), discernment (guancha), and dedication (huixiang). The text came to be held in high regard in China and Japan after the eminent Chinese monk TANLUAN composed an influential commentary on the text. Along with the shorter and longer *Sukhāvatīvyūhasūtras* and the GUAN WULIANGSHOU JING, the Japanese monk HŌNEN recognized the *Wuliangshou jing youpotishe yuansheng ji* as a central scripture of the school now known as the JŌDOSHŪ. See also JINGTU LUN.

**Wuliang yi jing**. (J. Muryōgikyō; K. Muryang ŭi kyŏng 無量義經). In Chinese, "Sūtra of Immeasurable Meanings," one of the "Three [Sister] Sūtras of the 'Lotus'" (FAHUA SANBU [JING]), along with the SADDHARMAPUṆḌARĪKASŪTRA ("Lotus Sūtra") itself and the GUAN PUXIAN PUSA XINGFA JING ("Sūtra on the Procedures for Contemplating the Practices of the Bodhisattva SAMANTABHADRA"). The *Wuliang yi jing*, is presumed to be the prequel to the influential *Saddharmapuṇḍarīkasūtra*, while the *Guan Puxian pusa xingfa jing* is usually considered its sequel. The extant version of the scripture, in one roll, is attributed to the Indian translator *Dharmāgatayaśas of the Southern Qi dynasty (479–502), and is claimed to have been translated in 481; the LIDAI SANBAO JI scriptural catalogue also refers to a second, nonextant translation. There is, however, no evidence that a scripture with this title ever circulated in India, and no such text is ever cited in Indian sources. In addition, there are issues with the biography of the alleged translator (*Dharmāgatayaśas is otherwise unknown and this is his only attributed translation), and peculiar events in the transmission of the scripture, which suggest that attempts were made to obscure its questionable provenance. The scripture also includes unusual transcriptions and translations of Buddhist technical terminology, and peculiar taxonomies of Indian doctrinal concepts. Because of these problematic issues of provenance and content, the sūtra is now suspected of being an indigenous Chinese composition (see APOCRYPHA). Such Chinese exegetes as Huiji (412–496) and TIANTAI ZHIYI (538–597) presumed that this scripture was the otherwise-unknown MAHĀYĀNA sūtra titled "Immeasurable Meanings" that is mentioned in the prologue to the *Saddharmapuṇḍarīkasūtra*, which the Buddha is said to have preached just prior to beginning the "Lotus Sūtra" proper. The *Wuliang yi jing* is in three chapters (pin). The first chapter is the prologue, where the bodhisattva "Great Adornment" (Dazhuangyan pusa) offers a long verse paean describing the Buddha's many virtues. The second chapter is the sermon itself, where the Buddha explains the doctrine of immeasurable meanings as being the one teaching that will enable bodhisattvas to quickly attain complete, perfect enlightenment (ANUTTARASAMYAKSAṂBODHI). This doctrine reveals that all phenomena (DHARMA) are void and calm in both their natures and their characteristics and thus are empty and nondual (ADVAYA). Hence, the immeasurable meanings of all descriptions of dharmas derive from the one dharma that is free from characteristics. The final chapter is the epilogue, which describes the ten kinds of merit that accrue from hearing the sūtra.

**Wumen guan**. (J. Mumonkan; K. Mumun kwan 無門關). In Chinese, lit., "Gateless Checkpoint," or "Wumen's Checkpoint"; compiled by the CHAN master WUMEN HUIKAI, after whom the collection is named, also known as the *Chanzong Wumen guan* ("Gateless Checkpoint of the Chan Tradition"). Along with the BIYAN LU ("Blue Cliff Record"), the *Wumen guan* is considered one of the two most important GONG'AN (J. kōan; K. kongan) collections of the Chan tradition. In the summer of 1228, at the request of the resident monks at the monastery of Longxiangsi, Wumen lectured on a series of forty-eight cases (gong'an) that he culled from various "transmission of the lamplight" (CHUANDENG LU) histories and the recorded sayings (YULU) of previous Chan masters. His lectures were recorded and compiled that same year and published with a preface by Wumen in the following year (1229). Another case (case 49), composed by the layman Zheng Qingzhi, was added to the *Wumen guan* in 1246. The *Wumen guan* begins with a popular case attributed to ZHAOZHOU CONGSHEN, in which Zhaozhou replies "WU" (no) to the question, "Does a dog have buddha nature, or not?" (see WU GONG'AN). Wumen himself is known to have struggled with this case, which was given to him by his teacher Yuelin Shiguan (1143–1217). The Japanese monk SHINICHI KAKUSHIN, who briefly studied under Wumen in China, brought the *Wumen guan* to Japan. Although the collection was once declared to be heretical by the SŌTŌSHŪ in the mid-seventeenth century, many Japanese commentaries on the *Wumen guan* were composed at the time, testifying to its growing influence during the Edo period.

**Wumen Huikai**. (J. Mumon Ekai; K. Mumun Hyegae 無門慧開) (1183–1260). In Chinese, "Gateless, Opening of Wisdom"; CHAN master in the LINJI ZONG; author of the eponymous WUMEN GUAN ("Gateless Checkpoint"), one of the two most important collections of Chan GONG'AN (J. kōan; K. kongan). A native of Hangzhou prefecture in present-day Zhejiang province, Huikai was ordained by the monk "One Finger" Tianlong (d.u.), who also hailed from Hangzhou (see also YIZHI CHAN). Wumen later went to the monastery of Wanshousi in Jiangsu province to study with Yuelin Shiguan (1143–1217), from whom Huikai received the WU GONG'AN of ZHAOZHOU CONGSHEN; Huikai is said to have struggled with this gong'an for six years. In 1218, Huikai traveled to Baoyinsi on Mt. Anji, where he succeeded Yuelin as abbot. He subsequently served as abbot at such monasteries as TIANNINGSI, Pujisi, Kaiyuansi, and Baoningsi. In 1246, Huikai was appointed as abbot of Huguo Renwangsi in Hangzhou prefecture, and it is here that the Japanese ZEN monk SHINICHI KAKUSHIN studied under him. Emperor Lizong (r. 1224–1264) invited Huikai to provide a sermon at the Pavilion of Mysterious Virtue in the imperial palace and also to pray for rain. In honor of his achievements, the emperor bestowed upon him a golden robe and the title Chan master Foyan (Dharma Eye).

**wunian**. (T. bsam pa med pa; J. munen; K. munyŏm 無念). In Chinese, "no-thought"; a Chinese meditative term that appears in the sixth-century DASHENG QIXIN LUN but finds its locus classicus in the eighth-century CHAN classic, the LIUZU TAN JING. The putative author of the *Liuzu tan jing*, the sixth patriarch (LIUZU) HUINENG, defines "no-thought" as "not to think even when involved in thought." Thought, therefore, is not the issue, but rather the attachment to thought, which would encourage the proliferation of conceptualization throughout all of one's sensory experience and thus render one a hapless victim of the conceptualizing tendency (cf. PRAPAÑCA). The *Liuzu tan jing* also explains no-thought in terms of "non-form" (wuxian) and "non-abiding" (wuzhu) and parses the term as follows: wu ("no") refers to the absence of duality and nian ("thought") to thinking about thusness (TATHATĀ). HEZE SHENHUI used the term "no-thought" to criticize the teaching of the "transcendence of thoughts" (linian) espoused by SHENXIU and his followers in the so-called Northern school (BEI ZONG). According to Shenhui, whereas the "transcendence of thoughts" (linian) emphasized the progressive wiping away of afflictions (KLEŚA) and conceptual thinking, "no-thought" (wunian) by contrast implied that there was no need for such effort since one had only to "see one's nature" (JIANXING) in order to attain enlightenment. Thus, wunian became a central feature of those who espoused a "sudden" theory of enlightenment (see DUNWU). In some radical cases, the notion of wunian was used as theoretical justification for the abandonment of all ritual and practice, including meditation and the conferral of monastic precepts. This extreme form of "no-thought" doctrine played an important role in the LIDAI FABAO JI and the antinomian teachings of the Sichuan early-Chan lineages of the JINGZHONG ZONG and BAOTANG ZONG, the latter of which may have had some influence in the development of RDZOGS CHEN thought in Tibet.

**Wunian dahui**. (C) (五年大會). See WUZHE HUI.

**wushi**. (J. goji; K. osi 五時). In Chinese, "the five periods [of the Buddha's teaching]"; the TIANTAI school's temporal taxonomy of Buddhist doctrines (JIAOXIANG PANSHI), according to which the Buddha's teachings differ because he preached them at different points during his pedagogical career. The initial account of his awakening that the Buddha taught immediately after his enlightenment was described in the AVATAṂSAKASŪTRA; this stage is thus termed the HUAYAN period (huayan shiqi). This account of the experience of buddhahood was, however, so unadulterated and sublime that many ŚRĀVAKA disciples were utterly unable to comprehend its message. The Buddha therefore began his teaching anew in a second period that was termed Luyuan shiqi (after the Deer Park, MṚGADĀVA, where many of the ĀGAMA scriptures were taught) or ahan shiqi (after the āgamas, which were the compilation of the Buddha's words from this period). This period was said to be an explicit attempt on the part of the Buddha to accommodate those disciples who were confounded during the first period, by teaching his insights in their most elementary form. The third period is called fangdeng (VAIPULYA) shiqi, where the "HĪNAYĀNA" teachings of the second period were superseded by teaching the aspiration for the MAHĀYĀNA. Various sūtras that explicitly compare Mahāyāna favorably to "hīnayāna"—such as the ŚRĪMĀLĀDEVĪSIṂHANĀDASŪTRA and the VIMALAKĪRTINIRDEŚA—were supposedly products of this period. The fourth period is termed the bore shiqi, after its eponymous sūtras, the PRAJÑĀPĀRAMITĀ. This was the stage of the Buddha's teaching career where he began to remove the boundaries separating Mahāyāna and "hīnayāna" by leading his audience from the presumption that there were two separate vehicles to instead a common realization of emptiness (ŚŪNYATĀ). The final period is called Fahua Niepan shiqi, after its two representative sūtras, the SADDHARMAPUṆḌARĪKASŪTRA and the MAHĀPARINIRVĀṆASŪTRA. The teachings associated with this period are described as the "consummate" or "perfect" teachings (YUANJIAO) because they espouse the idea of one vehicle (or the one buddha vehicle; C. YISHENG; S. EKAYĀNA), which Tiantai claimed was the truest form of the Buddha's original intention (benyuan; see PŪRVAPRAṆIDHĀNA). The Tiantai school also compares these five stages of the teachings to the five stages in the clarification of milk (see WUWEI, "five tastes"). See also TIANTAI BAJIAO.

**wushi bajiao**. (J. goji hakkyō; K. osi p'algyo 五時八教). In Chinese, "five periods and eight teachings"; a classification of teachings (PANJIAO) attributed to the TIANTAI systematizer TIANTAI ZHIYI. A detailed explanation of the wushi bajiao is found in the text by the Korean exegete CH'EGWAN, the CH'ŎNT'AE SAGYO ŬI (C. *Tiantai sijiao yi*). The five periods correspond to what is believed to be the five major chronological periods (WUSHI) of the Buddha's teaching career (represented by the name of a SŪTRA or group of sūtras preached during each period), namely, (1) Huayan (AVATAṂSAKASŪTRA), (2) ĀGAMA, (3) VAIPULYA, (4) PRAJÑĀPĀRAMITĀ, and (5) Lotus (SADDHARMAPUṆḌARĪKASŪTRA) and Nirvāṇa (MAHĀPARINIRVĀṆASŪTRA). According to Zhiyi, the Buddha also employed different techniques of conversion or pedagogical modes (huayi) for audiences of varying capacities, which are broadly divided into four: the sudden, gradual, indeterminate, and secret. The sudden and gradual teachings are distinguished by their variant uses of skillful means (UPĀYA), and indeterminate refers to the differing levels of the understanding of individuals. Zhiyi's contribution to these well-established categories was his further division of the indeterminate teachings into "secret" and "manifest" based on the awareness of the presence of others in the assembly. The content of the Buddha's teachings (huafa) is further described in terms of the four categories of TRIPIṬAKA, common, distinct, and consummate. This division is based on whether the teachings are that of TRIPIṬAKA (viz. HĪNAYĀNA), MAHĀYĀNA (distinct), both (joint), or neither (consummate). Zhiyi referred to the central sūtra of his own Tiantai school, the *Saddharmapuṇḍarīkasūtra*, as consummate. Zhiyi's own classification system is based on those of earlier exegetical traditions of the north (wujiao shizong) and south (sanjiao), which he sought to unite and ultimately transcend. See TIANTAI BAJIAO.

**wushi jiao**. (C) (五時教). See WUSHI.

**Wutaishan**. (五臺山). In Chinese, "Five-Terraces Mountain"; a sacred mountain located in northern Shanxi province, which, together with EMEISHAN, PUTUOSHAN, and JIUHUASHAN, is one of the "four great mountains" (sidamingshan) of Buddhism in China. The name Wutai is derived from its five treeless, barren peaks (one in each cardinal direction and the center) that resemble terraces or platforms. During the Northern Wei dynasty (424–532), Wutaishan came to be identified with the mythic Mt. Qingliang (Clear and Cool) of the AVATAṂSAKASŪTRA, which speaks of a mountain to the northeast where the bodhisattva MAÑJUŚRĪ is said to be constantly preaching the DHARMA. From the time of the identification of Mount Wutai as Mt. Qingliang, numerous testimonies to the manifestation of Mañjuśrī on the mountain have been reported. Mt. Wutai thus came to be known as the primary abode and place of worship for Mañjuśrī and for this reason drew pilgrims from across the continent, including South Asia and, later, Tibet. Numerous monasteries and hermitages of both Buddhists and Daoists occupy its peaks. The first Buddhist monastery on Wutaishan, Da Futu Lingjiusi (Great Buddha Vulture Monastery), is claimed to have been built by KĀŚYAPA MĀTAṄGA (d.u.) and Dharmaratna (d.u.) sometime during the first century (see also BAIMASI and SISHI'ER ZHANG JING). The name of the monastery was changed to Xuantongsi and then to (Da) Huayansi during the Tang dynasty to reflect its role as the center of HUAYAN studies. The Huayan patriarch CHENGGUAN (738–839) composed his great HUAYANJING SHU at this monastery. The esoteric monk AMOGHAVAJRA also assisted in the establishment of another monastery on Mt. Wutai, which was given the name Jingesi (Gold Pavilion Monastery) in 770 after its gilded tiles. Emperor Daizong (r. 762–779) declared Jingesi as an important center for the new esoteric teachings (MIJIAO) brought to China by Amoghavajra. The monk FAZHAO also established the monastery of Zhulinsi (Bamboo Grove Monastery) on the model of a majestic monastery that Mañjuśrī had revealed to him in a vision. The monasteries Qingliangsi, Beishansi, Manghaisi, and Da Wenshusi are also located on the mountain. During a pilgrimage to Wutaishan by the Korean monk CHAJANG (d.u., c. mid-seventh century), he had a vision in which Mañjuśrī guided him to a Korean analogue of the mountain; that mountain is now known as Odaesan (the Korean pronunciation of Wutaishan) and is itself a major pilgrimage center of Korean Buddhism. During the Qing dynasty, Wutaishan was also the major center for the study of Tibetan Buddhism in China.

**wuwei**. (J. mui; K. muwi 無爲). In Chinese, lit., "nonaction," "effortless action," in later contexts "uncompounded"; a key term that appears in early Chinese classics such as the *Lunyu* ("Analects of Confucius"), the *Daode jing* ("The Way and Its Power"), and the *Zhuangzi*. "Nonaction" suggests action that takes place naturally or without artifice; thus variously interpreted as "effortless action," "unattached action," etc. Nonaction thus refers to the ideal mode of behavior for a sage, in which the sage "does nothing and yet there is nothing not done" (wuwei er wu buwei). Rather than acting by fiat, the sage acts by establishing a "sympathetic resonance" (GANYING) with the natural movements of heaven, which brings everything naturally to perfection, just as a tree grows naturally without making any effort to grow. The term is frequently used in indigenous Chinese texts in the context of good governance, where wuwei thus refers to the ultimate type of "soft power": by "practicing nonaction," a ruler creates an appropriate environment in which "the people are able to look after themselves" (*Daode jing*, chapter 49); he does not impose his point of view but instead allows common cause with his constituency to develop naturally. In certain Chinese contexts, wuwei could also connote something that was "unproduced," and the early Chinese Buddhists drew on this connotation to translate the seminal Sanskrit term NIRVĀṆA and nirvāṇa's putative "inactivity"; this misleading translation was eventually abandoned in favor of the phonetic transcription niepan. The Buddhists did however retain the term wuwei in this denotation to translate the concept of "uncompounded" or "unconditioned" factors (ASAṂSKṚTADHARMA), such as nirvāṇa and in some schools space (ĀKĀŚA), which are not conditioned (SAṂSKṚTA) and are thus not subject to the inevitable impermanence (ANITYA) to which all conditioned dharmas are subject.

**wuwei**. (J. goi; K. owi 五位). In Chinese, lit., "five ranks"; a doctrinal formula generally attributed to the CHAN master DONGSHAN LIANGJIE (807–869), the putative cofounder of the CAODONG ZONG of the mature Chan tradition. The antecedents of these five ranks are traced to SHITOU XIQIAN's CANTONG QI, which discusses the mutual "turning back on one other" (huihu) of the terms brightness and darkness. This dichotomy is eventually generalized as "relative" (pian), lit., "askew" or "partial," referring to that which is bright, conceivable, effable, and phenomena (SHI); and absolute (zheng), lit., "upright," correlating with what is dark, inconceivable, ineffable, and principle (LI). Although these two valences of relative and absolute may be discrete, they are interconnected, interdependent, and mutually defining, thus constantly "turning back on one other." The five ranks are systematized by Dongshan in his "Verses on the Five Ranks" (*Wuwei song*) as follows. (1) The relative within the absolute (zhengzhong pian): this valence suggests that the ordinary person constantly abides in original enlightenment (BENJUE), but is unaware of it. (2) The absolute within the relative (pianzhong zheng): the practitioner may have become aware of the reality of original enlightenment, but still treats it as an object to be understood conceptually, rather than directly experienced. (3) [The relative] emerging from the absolute (zhengzhong lai): as the Chan practitioner experiences the pervasiveness of emptiness, that emptiness turns back on itself and transforms into a more dynamic and luxuriant way of experience of reality. (4) [The relative and the absolute] jointly accessible (jianzhong zhi): as the reality of each and every independent phenomenon (shi) is experienced, the reality of principle (li) is simultaneously accessed. (5) Integration of the absolute and the relative, or lit. "arriving within together" (jianzhong dao): the bifurcations between relative and absolute, the experiencing subject and the object experienced, the realizer and the realized, etc., all drop away, so that the practitioner continues to practice but now without practicing anything, and seeks buddhahood while understanding that there is no buddhahood to be sought. In some interpretations, the first two ranks evoke the famous passage in the PRAJÑĀPĀRAMITĀHṚDAYASŪTRA: "form is emptiness, emptiness is form" (see RŪPAṂ ŚŪNYATĀ ŚUNYATAIVA RŪPAM). The third rank implies the bodhisattva practice of returning to the world after his or her attainment of enlightenment (BODHI). Similarly, the fourth and fifth ranks imply the bodhisattva vow to save all living beings so that they may all access NIRVĀṆA together.

Despite the use of the term "rank," a systematic progression is not necessarily implied, and some commentators suggest that all five ranks may be experienced simultaneously in a moment of sudden awakening (DUNWU); thus, the five ranks may be an attempt to demonstrate how gradual and sequential outlines of Buddhist soteriology can be integrated with the more subitist soteriologies that become emblematic of the mature Chan tradition. The five ranks are also sometimes correlated with the five wisdoms (PAÑCAJÑĀNA) of a buddha in the MAHĀYĀNA, and specifically in the YOGĀCĀRA school. Dongshan's "five ranks" were frequently used in East Asian GONG'AN collections as a means of checking a student's level of understanding. In one of the modern Japanese RINZAISHŪ systematizations of kōan training, the final stage in the practice that follows initial sudden awakening (J. SATORI, C. dunwu) also involves mastery of the five ranks (J. goi).

**wuwei**. (J. gomi; K. omi 五味). In Chinese, lit. "five tastes"; an originally Indian list of the five stages in the clarification of milk that is derived from the MAHĀPARINIRVĀṆASŪTRA: milk, cream, curds, butter, and ghee. This list was used in the TIANTAI ZONG as a simile for the five chronological periods (WUSHI) in the Buddha's preaching of the dharma. According to this school's taxonomy of the teachings (JIAOXIANG PANSHI), the various teachings of Buddhism may be categorized according to these five "tastes": milk symbolizes the AVATAṂSAKASŪTRA period; cream, the ĀGAMA period; curds, the VAIPULYA period; and butter, the PRAJÑĀPĀRAMITĀ period; the subtlest and more clarified form of milk, the flavor of ghee (tihuwei; see MAṆḌA), is finally compared to the "consummate" period of the SADDHARMAPUṆḌARĪKASŪTRA and the MAHĀPARINIRVĀṆASŪTRA.

**Wuwei sanzang chanyao**. (J. Mui sanzō zen'yō; K. Muoe samjang sŏnyo 無畏三藏禪要). In Chinese, "Essentials of Meditation by the TREPIṬAKA ŚUBHAKARASIṂHA"; a relatively short treatise that purportedly records a sermon that the esoteric master Śubhākarasiṃha prepared for a debate he had with CHAN master SHENXIU's disciple Jingxuan (660–723) sometime after 716. The sermon is largely concerned with the conferral of the BODHISATTVA precepts, repentance, the threefold pure precepts (SANJU JINGJIE; see ŚĪLATRAYA), and what Śubhākarasiṃha calls the secret essentials of meditation. Śubhākarasiṃha critiques Jingxuan and other fellow practitioners of meditation for their adherence to the doctrine of "no-thought" (WUNIAN) and offers instead a meditation technique that involves uttering a series of DHĀRAṆĪs, gesturing in a series of MUDRĀs, mindful breathing, and visualizing a lunar disk.

**wuwei zhenren**. (J. mui no shinnin; K. muwi chinin 無位眞人). In Chinese, "true man of no rank"; a CHAN expression attributed to LINJI YIXUAN (d. 867), which is used to refer to the sentience, or "numinous awareness" (LINGZHI), of the mind, that constantly moves through the sense faculties, thus enabling sensory experience; equivalent to the buddha-nature (FOXING). Linji contrasts this true man of no rank with the "lump of red flesh" (CHIROUTUAN), the physical body that is constantly buffeted by sensory experience. The term zhenren is also used within the Daoist tradition to refer to a Daoist "perfected," who has realized perfect freedom both mentally and physically by achieving immortality and transcending all dichotomies. See also GANSHIJUE.

**Wuxiang**. (C) (無相). See CHŎNGJUNG MUSANG.

**wuxiang jie**. (J. musōkai; K. musang kye 無相戒). In Chinese, "formless precepts"; a type of precept mentioned in the LIUZU TAN JING, where they are said to help constrain practitioners so that they are able to gain enlightenment. The formless precepts reflect the early CHAN community's effort to offer its own understanding of the MAHĀYĀNA precepts. Although no clear explanation of exactly what these precepts are is provided in the text, the wuxiang jie are said to be the premier type of precepts, which are superior to the usual types of constraints taught in earlier types of Buddhism, which sought to develop wholesome ways of action and deter unwholesome actions. The conferral of these precepts appears to have occurred at the start of a kind of initiation ceremony, which subsequently followed with acceptance of the four great vows (SI HONGSHIYUAN), repentance (chan), the three refuges (TRIŚARAṆA), and PRAJÑĀPĀRAMITĀ.

**wuxin**. (J. mushin; K. musim 無心). In Chinese, lit. "no-mind." The term wuxin appears in the Chinese classic the *Zhuangzi* and was adapted by the early Chinese Buddhists exegetes of PRAJÑĀPĀRAMITĀ literature as a gloss on the Madhyamaka notion of ŚŪNYATĀ or "emptiness." These exegetes were collectively known as the "school of the nonexistence of mind" (xinwu zong) and belonged to the larger tradition known as "Dark Learning" (XUANXUE). In later Buddhist treatises, most notably those belonging to the CHAN tradition, "no-mind" came to refer ambiguously either to a state in which all mental activity had ceased or one in which the mind was free of all discrimination, making it effectively equivalent to nonconceptualization (see NIṢPRAPAÑCA). In this latter sense, the term is closely synonymous with "no-thought" (WUNIAN). See also WUXIN LUN.

**Wuxin lun**. (J. Mushinron; K. Musim non 無心論). In Chinese, "Treatise on No-Mind"; an early CHAN treatise attributed by tradition to the legendary monk BODHIDHARMA, which, in both content and style, resembles NIUTOU FARONG'S JUEGUAN LUN. As the title indicates, the treatise is concerned with the notion of WUXIN, or "no-mind," which the text attempts to elucidate by enumerating a long list of dichotomies, such as visible and invisible, bright and dark, and differentiated and undifferentiated. The treatise argues largely in catechistic format that the attainment of no-mind engenders a state that is unmarred by the myriad afflictions (KLEŚA), birth and death, and even NIRVĀṆA. The treatise was largely unknown until its rediscovery in the manuscript cache at the DUNHUANG caves at the end of the nineteenth century.

**Wuxue Zuyuan**. (J. Mugaku Sogen; K. Muhak Chowŏn 無學祖元) (1226–1286). Chinese CHAN master in the LINJI ZONG, who was the founder of the influential monastery of ENGAKUJI in Kamakura, Japan; also known as Ziyuan. On the advice of his brother, Wuxue entered the Chinese monastery of Jingcisi, where he was ordained by Beijian Jujian (1164–1246). Wuxue later became the student of the Linji Chan master WUZHUN SHIFAN (1178–1249) and received his seal of transmission (YINKE). Wuxue also studied under XUTANG ZHIYU (1185–1269) and Wuchu Daguan (1201–1268) and spent the next few decades residing at various monasteries in Zhejiang prefecture. In 1275, Wuxue left for Nengrensi to avoid the invading Mongol troops of the Yuan dynasty. In 1279, at the invitation of Hōjō Tokimune (1251–1284), the eighth regent of the Kamakura shogunate, Wuxue reluctantly left China for Japan. Upon his arrival in Kamakura, Wuxue was appointed abbot of KENCHŌJI, succeeding the third abbot LANXI DAOLONG. In 1282, Tokimune established Engakuji to commemorate the defeat of the invading Mongol troops and installed Wuxue as its founding abbot (J. kaisan; C. KAISHAN). Serving as administrator of the two most powerful Buddhist institutions in Japan at the time, Wuxue established a firm foundation for the success of the RINZAISHŪ in Japan. Wuxue was given the posthumous title state preceptor (J. kokushi, C. GUOSHI) Bukkō (Buddha Radiance). His students included Japan's first female Zen master, MUGAI NYODAI (1223–1298), and KŌHŌ KENNICHI (1241–1316), the son of Emperor Gosaga (r. 1242–1246) and the teacher of MUSŌ SOSEKI. Wuxue's teachings appear in his *Bukkō kokushi goroku*.

**wuyun shijian**. (J. goun seken; K. oon segan 五蘊世間). In Chinese, "the world of the five aggregates." See SATTVALOKA.

**Wu Zetian**. (J. Bu Sokuten; K. Mu Ch'ŭkch'ŏn 武則天) (624–705). Chinese concubine and empress who was an important patron of Buddhism during the Tang dynasty and the short-lived Zhou-dynasty interregnum (684–704). Wu Zetian entered the palace as a concubine of Emperor Taizong (r. 626–649) while she was still in her teens. After the emperor's death, she became a Buddhist nun, but was summoned again to the palace as a concubine of Taizong's successor and son, the Gaozong emperor (r. 649–683). She bore Gaozong a son in 652 and began to exert much influence in court. Despite fierce opposition from court officials, Gaozong enthroned Wu Zetian as the new empress in 655. Wu Zetian quickly exiled all her foes in court and had the former empress Wang killed. In 657, she reinstated Luoyang as the cocapital of the empire and permanently moved the entire court there after Gaozong's death in 683. She subsequently exiled the Zhongzong emperor (r. 683–684, 705–710) and established her own dynasty named Zhou (684–704). Wu Zetian was an ardent supporter of Buddhism. She associated with such eminent monks as XUANZANG, SHENXIU, FAZANG, and YIJING. In an attempt to legitimize her reign, Wu Zetian also ordered the circulation of the MAHĀMEGHASŪTRA ("Great Cloud Sūtra"), which described a female reincarnation of MAITREYA and her rule over the whole world. She also arranged for the construction in every prefecture of the empire of monasteries all known as DAYUNSI (Great Cloud Monastery). In 705, she abdicated the throne to the restored Emperor Zhongzong.

**wuzhe hui**. (J. mushae; K. much'a hoe 無遮會). In Chinese, "unrestricted assembly"; an assembly hosted by the reigning monarch to make offerings to clergy and laity regardless of their status or station in life. The assembly was typically held every five years and is therefore also known as the "five-year great assembly" (C. wunian dahui; S. pañcavārṣikapariṣad). The first such assembly is attributed to King AŚOKA. Emperor Wu of the Liang dynasty (LIANG WUDI) is known to have held a wuzhe dahui in 529 for an assembly said to have numbered fifty thousand. The famous pilgrim XUANZANG also witnessed an unrestricted assembly during his travels along the SILK ROAD. In 596, Empress Suiko (554–628) held the first reported unrestricted assembly in Japan. In 732, HEZE SHENHUI organized an unrestricted great assembly (wuzhe dahui) at the monastery of DAYUNSI in Henan prefecture, where he attacked SHENXIU and his followers.

**Wuzhensi**. (悟眞寺). In Chinese, "Awakening to Truth Monastery"; located in the Wuzhen Valley of ZHONGNANSHAN near the capital of Chang'an (present-day Xi'an). The monastery is comprised of two compounds, known as the upper and lower monasteries. The upper monastery is also named Zhulinsi, or Bamboo Grove Monastery, because of the bamboo forest surrounding it. Wuzhen Monastery was founded by the Sui-dynasty Buddhist monk Jingye (564–616), who stayed there from 595 to 608. He was accompanied by other eminent monks including Huichao (546–622), a disciple of the TIANTAI master HUISI (515–568), and Facheng (563–640). The latter was instrumental in expanding the monastery by building the Huayan Hall and another hall to enshrine images of a hundred buddhas. He also inscribed Buddhist verses on cliffs surrounding the monastery and along its roads. Due to his efforts, Wuzhen monastery became renowned during the Tang dynasty for its majesty and became a favorite haunt of literati. Eminent SAN LUN ZONG monks such as HUIYUAN (523–592), Baogong (542–621), and Huiyin (539–629) also either resided here or were affiliated with the monastery. It was either at Wuzhensi or LONGCHISI that the HUAYAN master FAZANG (643–712), at the behest of the Ruizong emperor of Tang (r. 684–690, 710–712), is said to have famously performed a ritual to pray for snow in order to stave off a severe drought the region was experiencing. During the Song dynasty, the monastery was renamed CHONGFASI, or Monastery of the Esteemed Dharma.

**wuzhong xuanyi**. (J. goshu no gengi; K. ojong hyŏnŭi 五種玄義). In Chinese, "five categories of profound meaning"; a list of five general hermeneutical issues that should be addressed prior to undertaking an in-depth exegesis of any SŪTRA, attributed to TIANTAI ZHIYI (538–597) and emblematic of scriptural exegesis in the TIANTAI SCHOOL. These five are (1) explicating the meaning of the text's title (shiming), (2) analyzing the fundamental intent of the sūtra (bianben), (3) clarifying its principal themes or doctrines (mingzong), (4) expounding the sūtra's "function" or impact on its audience (lunyong), and (5) classifying the sūtra (PANJIAO), viz., delineating its place within the entire corpus of sūtras expounded by the Buddha. These five issues typically would be addressed by the commentator prior to beginning the exegesis of the sūtra proper. See also SANFEN KEJING; JIAOXIANG PANSHI.

**Wuzhu**. (C) (無住) (714–774). See BAOTANG WUZHU.

**Wuzhun Shifan**. (J. Bujun Shihan/Bushun Shiban/Mujun Shihan; K. Mujun Sabŏm 無準師範) (1178–1249). Chinese CHAN master in the LINJI ZONG. After his ordination in the winter of 1194, Wuzhun studied under a series of famed Chan masters, including FOZHAO DEGUANG and Po'an Zuxian. Wuzhun eventually attained awakening under Po'an and succeeded his lineage. During his illustrious career at such important monasteries as WANSHOUSI on Mt. Jing, Wuzhun also taught the Japanese pilgrims Hōshin (d.u.), Dōyū (1201–1258), and the famed ENNI BEN'EN, who is now regarded as the first exponent of ZEN in Japan. Wuzhun was later summoned by Emperor Lizong (r. 1224–1264) to provide a public lecture at the Pavilion of Benevolent Illumination in the imperial palace. The emperor later bestowed upon him the title Chan master Fojian (Buddha Mirror). Wuzhun left many famous disciples such as WUXUE ZUYUAN and Mu'an Puning, both of whom went to Kamakura in Japan and served as abbots of the powerful monastery of KENCHŌJI.

**Wuzu Fayan**. (J. Goso Hōen; K. Ojo Pŏbyŏn 五祖法演) (d. 1104). Chinese CHAN master in the LINJI ZONG. Wuzu was a native of Mianzhou prefecture in present-day Sichuan province. After being ordained at the age of thirty-four, Fayan studied YOGĀCĀRA doctrine in his home province, but later went south where he studied under Huilin Zongben (1020–1099), Fushan Fayuan (991–1067), and BAIYUN SHOUDUAN. Fayan eventually became Baiyun's disciple and inherited his Linji lineage. After staying at various monasteries in Anhui province, Fayan moved to Mt. Wuzu (also known as East Mountain) in Hubei province, where he acquired his toponym. The mountain itself received its name, Wuzu (fifth patriarch), from its most famous past resident, the fifth patriarch of Chan, HONGREN. Mt. Wuzu thus became an important center for the Linji lineage, and it was there that Fayan taught his famous disciples YUANWU KEQIN, Taiping Huiqin (1059–1117), and Foyan Qingyuan (1067–1120), known collectively as the "three Buddhas of East Mountain." Wuzu's teachings are recorded in the *Wuzu Fayan chanshi yulu*.

# X

**xiala**. (C) (夏臘). See JIELA.

**xiangdai miao**. (C) (相待妙). See DAIJUE ERMIAO.

**xiangfa**. (J. zōhō; K. sangpŏp 像法). In Chinese, "semblance dharma" or "counterfeit dharma"; a term related to the Sanskrit SADDHARMAPRATIRŪPAKA. The Sanskrit term has a range of uses, including as a designation for the BUDDHADHARMA after the buddha has passed into PARINIRVĀṆA. In the East Asian context, xiangfa came to designate the second and middle period of a buddha's teaching. The first period, that of the SADDHARMA (C. zhengfa), is the period of the true dharma after a buddha's passage into parinirvāṇa, during which time it is still possible to achieve enlightenment by following his teachings. The second period, of xiangfa, is a time during which the achievement of enlightenment is still possible, but the practice of the dharma has generally been reduced to rote repetition of the teachings and practices; there are also signs of laxity in both monastic and lay practice developing during this period. The third period, that of MOFA (cf. SADDHARMAVIPRALOPA), or the final dharma, is a time of degeneration and decline, during which the practice of the dharma is no longer efficacious, due largely to the diminished capacities of humans. This division into three periods of the dharma seems to have originated in China and was widely influential in East Asian Buddhism.

**Xiangfa jueyi jing**. (J. Zōbō ketsugikyō; K. Sangpŏp kyŏrŭi kyŏng 像法決疑經). In Chinese, the "Scripture on Resolving Doubts Concerning the Semblance Dharma"; an indigenous Chinese Buddhist scripture (see APOCRYPHA), dating from the mid-sixth century. The *Xiangfa jueyi jing* is set against the background of the Buddha's PARINIRVĀṆA. At the request of a BODHISATTVA named Changshi (Constant Giving), the Buddha offers instructions on the practice of giving (DĀNA), in which he declares charity to be the most appropriate practice during the age of the semblance dharma (XIANGFA; SADDHARMAPRATIRŪPAKA). The semblance-dharma period is characterized as an age of degeneration, during which both clergy and laity begin to transgress the precepts and slander the Buddha's teaching. The *Xiangfa jueyi jing* emphasizes the importance of collective rather than individual giving during this age, and especially giving to the impoverished and underprivileged, rather than just to the three jewels (RATNATRAYA) of Buddhism. These and other ideas from the *Xiangfa jueyi jing* were especially influential in the teachings of the Third-Stage school (SANJIE JIAO) and that school's emblematic institution, the WUJINZANG YUAN (inexhaustible storehouse cloister). Such eminent monks as TIANTAI ZHIYI, JIZANG, and HŌNEN also held the *Xiangfa jueyi jing* in high regard.

**Xiangguosi**. (相國寺). In Chinese, "Minister of the State Monastery"; located in eastern Henan in the city of Kaifeng. Originally built in 555 CE and named Jianguosi, it was subsequently destroyed during a battle. It then became a private residence and garden; but later, when a monk named Huiyun saw a reflection of a monastery in its garden pool, he collected enough subscriptions to buy the residence and turn it back into a monastery in 711. It was renamed Xiangguosi by the Ruizong emperor of the Tang (r. 684–690, 710–712). The monastery was well supported by Tang and Song emperors, as evidenced by the campus's extensive grounds and the lavish materials used in its accoutrements, such as using gold dust to decorate images, icons, and paintings. It is well known for its layout, including its use of twin pagodas (STŪPA). Xiangguosi also became famous for its frescoes, painted by famous contemporary artists from the neighboring region. Artists at the Song Painting Academy painted much of the Buddhist imagery at this monastery. Xiangguosi reached the zenith of its influence during the Song dynasty, when it became an outpost for foreign monks visiting China.

**xiangjiao**. (J. zōkyō; K. sanggyo 像教). In Chinese, "teaching [viz., religion] of images"; a pejorative term coined by Confucians to refer to Buddhism, derived from the emphasis in Buddhism on bowing before images during rituals and ceremonies. Confucianism, in turn, was called the "teaching [viz., religion] of names" (mingjiao), to demonstrate by contrast that it was based on intellectual inquiry and the "rectification of names" (zhengming) rather than on worship of images of Confucius and the teachers within the tradition.

**Xiangmo Zang**. (T. Bdud 'dul snying po; J. Gōma Zō; K. Hangma Chang 降魔藏) (d.u.). In Chinese, "Demon-Subduer Zang." Chinese monk and leading disciple of the CHAN master SHENXIU, in the Northern school (BEI ZONG). At an early age, Xiangmo Zang acquired the nickname "demon-subduer" (xiangmo) by dwelling in deserted houses and open fields. Later, he learned to recite the SADDHARMAPUṆḌARĪKASŪTRA and studied the VINAYA after he became a monk. He is said to have had an awakening experience after listening to a lecture on the "theories of the Southern school" (NAN ZONG lun) and, abandoning his scriptural studies, became a student of Shenxiu. As Shenxiu's disciple, Xiangmo Zang became the target of HEZE SHENHUI'S polemical attack on the Northern school of Chan. Xiangmo Zang also appears in the BSAM GTAN MIG SGRON by GNUBS CHEN SANGS RGYAS YE SHES along with a certain Wolun (d.u.) and MOHEYAN and others of the Northern school, whose teachings may have exerted some influence on MAHĀYOGA in Tibet.

**Xiangshansi**. (香山寺). In Chinese, "Fragrant Mountain Monastery"; located on SONGSHAN in Ruzhou, Henan province. It is not known when the monastery was first established, but it is thought to have been built c. 516 CE during the Northern Wei dynasty (386–584). One source credits the founding of a Xiangshan monastery in Xiangzhou to a certain general named Liu Qingzhi, but no further mention is made of either the general or the monastery. The current Xiangshansi underwent a major renovation around 1068 during the Northern Song dynasty, and special attention was paid to restoring its Dabei ta (Great Compassion pagoda), which still stands today; housed in the pagoda is a thousand-armed and thousand-eyed form of GUANYIN (SĀHASRABHUJASĀHASRANETRĀVALOKITEŚVARA). Xiangshansi, like SHANG TIANZHUSI, is known for being a major pilgrimage site for Guanyin (AVALOKITEŚVARA) worship. It became associated with the Princess MIAOSHAN incarnation of Guanyin, whose legend is inscribed on a stele at the monastery. The stele was commissioned in 1100 by a minor civil servant, Jiang Zhiqi (1031–1104), who was the prefect of Ruzhou. Jiang had the legend reinscribed on another stele at the Shang Tianzhusi when he moved to Hangzhou four years later.

**xiangxu wuchang**. (C) (相續無常). See ER WUCHANG.

**Xiangyan Zhixian**. (J. Kyōgen Chikan; K. Hyangŏm Chihan 香嚴智閑) (d. 898). Chinese CHAN master in the GUIYANG ZONG of the Chan tradition. Zhixian entered the monastery under BAIZHANG HUAIHAI and later became a student of YANGSHAN HUIJI. Zhixian dwelled for a long time at Mt. Xiangyan, whence his toponym. One day while he was sweeping the garden, Zhixian is said to have attained awakening when he heard the bamboo brush against the roof tiles. He is best known for the GONG'AN case "Xiangyan Hanging from a Tree": A man is dangling by his mouth from the branch of a tall tree, his hands tied behind his back and nothing beneath his feet. Someone comes under the tree branch and asks, "Why did BODHIDHARMA come from the West?" If he keeps his mouth clenched and refuses to answer, he is rude to the questioner; but if he opens his mouth to answer, he will fall to his death. How does he answer? Upon Zhixian's death, he was given the posthumous title Chan master Xideng (Inheritor of the Lamplight).

**xiang zong**. (J. sōshū; K. sang chong 相宗). In Chinese, "characteristics school"; also known as the FAXIANG ZONG or "Dharma Characteristics" school. Both these names were used polemically by rival scholiasts to polarize certain trends in Buddhist thought. In distinction to the XING ZONG, or "nature" school, FAZANG in the HUAYAN ZONG uses the term xiang zong to refer to those monk-scholars whose scholarship focused on the changing form of phenomena and reality. Monks of the Faxiang or YOGĀCĀRA tradition tended to be categorized as this characteristics school. Maintaining a strict distinction between the xing and the xiang trends was called xingxiang juepan (differentiation of nature and characteristics), while a scholastic approach that attempted to harmonize the two trends was characterized as xingxiang ronghui (harmonizing nature and characteristics).

**Xianzong ji**. (J. Kenshūki; K. Hyŏnjong ki 顯宗記). In Chinese, "Notes on Revealing the Cardinal Principle," attributed to HEZE SHENHUI; also known as the *Heze dashi xianzong ji* ("Notes on Revealing the Cardinal Principle of Great Master Heze") and *Xianzong lun* ("Treatise on Revealing the Cardinal Principle"). A simpler version of the *Xianzong ji*, entitled *Dunwu wusheng bore song* ("Verses on Sudden Enlightenment, the Unborn, and Prajñā"), was also discovered at DUNHUANG. As the title of the Dunhuang version makes clear, in this treatise Shenhui expounds on the notions of no-thought (WUNIAN), the unborn, or nonarising (ANUTPĀDA), and wisdom (prajñā), which all seem to function as synonyms for emptiness (ŚŪNYATĀ). Shenhui also mentions the Indian patriarch BODHIDHARMA'S transmission of this "secret teaching" to China and his conferral of the patriarchal robe as a mark of transmission. The *Xianzong ji* was later included in the genealogical history of the Chan tradition, the JINGDE CHUANDENG LU.

**Xiaodao lun**. (J. Shōdōron; K. Sodo non 笑道論). In Chinese, "Laughing at the Dao Treatise"; an anti-Daoist polemical treatise composed by Zhen Luan (d.u.) and presented to Emperor Wu (r. 560–578) of the Northern Zhou dynasty in 570. In response to the Daoist contentions in the LAOZI HUAHU JING that the Chinese sage Laozi went to India and became ŚĀKYAMUNI Buddha in order to convert the Western barbarians, the *Xiaodao lun* attempts to expose the inconsistencies in Daoist thought, cosmological perspectives, practice, and ritual, and to demonstrate that the Daoists actually borrowed heavily from Buddhism. The treatise so displeased the emperor that he is said to have immediately ordered the text burned.

**xiaoguo**. (C) (小過). In Chinese, "minor misdeed." See DUṢKṚTA.

**xiaomiao**. (小廟). In Chinese, lit. "small temple"; a Song-dynasty term for private monasteries whose control was passed within a single monastic lineage. The term is used in distinction to the large public monasteries, or "monasteries of the ten directions" (SHIFANG CHA).

**xiaosheng jiao**. (C) (小乘教). See HUAYAN WUJIAO.

**xiayu**. (C) 下語. See AGYO.

**Xiao zhiguan**. (C) (小止觀). See XIUXI ZHIGUAN ZUOCHAN FAYAO.

**xilai yi**. (J. seiraii; K. sŏrae ŭi 西來意). In Chinese, lit. "the meaning of coming from the west"; in CHAN literature, a common allusion to the question "What was the meaning of [Bodhidharma's] coming from the west?" (xilai yi ruohe), i.e., "Why did BODHIDHARMA, the founding patriarch of Chan, come from India to propagate Chan?" This question was commonly asked in Chan GONG'AN exchanges to test the spiritual depth of a teacher or disciple and as a meditative topic in "questioning meditation" (KANHUA CHAN). The phrase is found in HUANGBO XIYUN's (d. c. 850) CHUANXIN FAYAO, and the use of the question is well displayed in a famous exchange involving MAZU DAOYI (709–788) and his disciple Hongzhou Shuiliao (d.u.): when Shuiliao asks Mazu this question, Mazu encourages him to come closer, whereupon he kicks him to the ground, and Shuiliao immediately jumps up, enlightened. ZHAOZHOU CONGSHEN'S (778–897) answer to this question is the famous gong'an: "Cypress tree in front of the courtyard" (TINGQIAN BOSHUZI). Some of the other answers that appear in Chan literature include "sitting for a long time is a bother" (BIYAN LU, case no. 17), "there is no meaning in Bodhidharma's coming from the west" (*Biyan lu*, case no. 20), and "Zang's head is white, Hai's head is black" (*Biyan lu*, case no. 73).

**xilai yi ruohe**. (C) (西來意若何). See XILAI YI.

**Ximingsi**. (西明寺). In Chinese, "Luminosity of the West Monastery," located in the Tang capital of Chang'an (present-day Xi'an). There are two founding narratives. The first credits the Gaozong emperor (r. 649–683) with establishing the monastery at his old residence in 658 and installing DAOXUAN (596–667), founder of the Nanshan VINAYA school (NANSHAN LÜ ZONG), as its abbot. It is there that Daoxuan is said to have compiled the DA TANG NEIDIAN ("Great Tang Catalogue of Inner [viz., Buddhist] Classics") as an inventory of scriptures for the newly established library at the monastery. Daoxuan also assisted XUANZANG (600/602–664) in translating preceptive texts, collaborated with his brother Daoshi (d. c. 683) in publishing VINAYA texts, and wrote his collection of essays in defense of Buddhism entitled the GUANG HONGMING JI. A second narrative instead credits Xuanzang with founding the monastery. According to this story, the grounds were originally the residence of an imperial prince, and at first it was proposed to build both a Buddhist and a Daoist monastery there. After Xuanzang surveyed the site, he pronounced the site too small for two establishments, and thus only a Buddhist monastery was built. When Xuanzang settled there, the Gaozong emperor (r. 649–683) is said to have donated land, silk, and cotton to sustain it. ¶ Regardless of which account is correct, Ximingsi quickly became a major center of Buddhist scholarship and housed the most comprehensive library of Buddhist texts in the country. The monastery is said to have been built to match the dimensions of JETAVANA in India and, at one point, housed sixty-four cloisters. Because of its location in the Tang capital, several eminent monks resided and worked there. For example, the Tang emperor Xuanzong (r. 713–756) is said to have invited ŚUBHAKARASIṂHA to stay at Ximingsi, where YIXING (683–727) assisted him in his translation work. YIJING (635–713) also translated there the Sanskrit manuscripts he brought back with him from his pilgrimage to India. The Korean monk WŎNCH'ŬK (613–695) worked with Xuanzang at Ximingsi (to the point that his lineage of scholastic interpretation is sometimes called the Ximing lineage, see XIMING XUEPAI), and the Japanese monk KŪKAI (774–835) is also known to have studied at the monastery.

**Ximing xuepai**. (C) (西明學派). In Chinese, "the Ximing scholastic lineage" of the FAXIANG ZONG, associated with WŎNCH'ŬK. See FAXIANG ZONG.

**xindi**. (S. cintābhūmikā; J. shinji; K. simji 心地). In Chinese, lit. "mind-ground" or "mind as ground"; a common metaphor used in MAHĀYĀNA literature to suggest that mind or thought is the source, or "ground," of all phenomena. The *Dasheng bensheng xindi guan jing* ("Sūtra on the Great-Vehicle Contemplation of the Innate Mind Ground"), for example, metaphorically refers to the minds of the sentient beings of the three realms of existence as a "mind-ground," since all phenomena—whether mundane (LAUKIKA) or supramundane (LOKOTTARA), and including all virtuous and nonvirtuous dharmas, as well as the five rebirth destinies (GATI) and the states of a PRATYEKABUDDHA, BODHISATTVA, or even a buddha—are generated from the mind of sentient beings, just as all grains and fruits are generated from soil. A commentary to the MAHĀVAIROCANĀBHISAṂBODHISŪTRA (*Dari jing shu*) says that the mind is also metaphorically referred to as a "ground," since the practice of bodhisattvas relies on the mind, just as activities of ordinary people rely on the ground. In the FANWANG JING ("Brahmā's Net Sūtra"), the mind-ground refers to the bodhisattva precepts (PUSA JIE), which help to restrain the activities of body, speech, and mind; the precepts are the mind-ground because the activities of mind, or thought, are the basis for actions performed via body and speech. The buddha Vairocana says in the sūtra that he achieved complete, perfect enlightenment (SAMYAKSAṂBODHI) only after cultivating the mind-ground over a hundred incalculable eons (ASAṂKHYEYAKALPA). The Korean monk WŎNHYO (617–686), in his *Pŏmmanggyŏng Posal kyebon sagi* ("Personal Exposition on the Bodhisattva Precepts Text of the 'Brahmā's Net Sūtra'"), described three different denotations of mind-ground in terms of the abider and the ground on which that abider resides. These are (1) the fifty stages of the bodhisattva path (the ten BODHISATTVABHŪMI, plus the forty stages preliminary to the bhūmis), which is the ground on which the thought of enlightenment (BODHICITTA) of the bodhisattva abides; (2) the three categories of precepts (ŚĪLATRAYA), which is the ground on which the enlightened mind abides; and (3) the realm of reality (DHARMADHĀTU), which is the ground on which the practitioner abides. In the CHAN ZONG, the mind that was transmitted by BODHIDHARMA, the putative founder of Chan, is termed the mind-ground, and his teaching of the one (enlightened) mind is called the dharma teaching of the mind-ground (xindi famen). HUANGBO XIYUN (d. 850) says in his CHUANXIN FAYAO that the "dharma teaching of the mind-ground means that all dharmas are constructed depending upon this mind." Finally, GUIFENG ZONGMI in his CHANYUAN CHUCHUANJI TUXU ("Prolegomenon to the Comprehensive References to the Fountainhead of Chan Collection") equates mind-ground with the buddha-nature (FOXING): "the originally enlightened true nature of sentient beings is called both buddha-nature and mind-ground."

**xingjiao**. (J. angya; K. haenggak 行脚). In Chinese, lit., "wandering on foot," i.e., "pilgrimage"; a term used especially in the CHAN tradition to refer to a pilgrimage, often performed by a young monk who is in search of a teacher. Traditionally, this pilgrimage is made to numerous monasteries, most often located deep in the mountains, in hopes of having an interview with the resident master. In Japan, angya nowadays refers to the trip that young monks (known as unsui; see YUNSHUI) who have just completed their initial training at a provincial temple make to a major Zen training monastery, where they can continue their studies with a senior teacher (RŌSHI).

**xingju shuo**. (J. shōgusetsu; K. sŏnggu sŏl 性具說). In Chinese, the "nature-replete theory"; also known as liju sanqian, or "principle is replete with the trichiliocosm (TRISĀHASRAMAHĀSĀHASRALOKADHĀTU)." According to TIANTAI doctrine, everything within the three realms of existence (TRAIDHĀTUKA) is all contained within the original nature of all sentient beings. This theory is said to be based on TIANTAI ZHIYI'S notion of YINIAN SANQIAN, or "the trichiliocosm in a single thought." During the SHANJIA SHANWAI debate of the eleventh-century Tiantai community, the xingju theory came to connote the trichiliocosm that was replete within myriad phenomena and was distinguished from the HUAYAN doctrine of XINGQI.

**xingli**. (J. anri; K. haengni 行履). In Chinese, lit., "practice hidden"; a contraction of qiongxing lijian, which literally means "assiduous practice and hidden conduct." In the CHAN traditions, xingli generally refers to the daily conduct of a monk, which includes a whole gamut of activities from walking, sitting, and keeping silence to drinking tea and eating food. As such, the term can also refer to the progress of a monk's training or to the history of his activities.

**xingqi**. (J. shōki; K. sŏnggi 性起). In Chinese, "nature origination"; an important HUAYAN soteriological and ontological theory, which emphasizes the common ground of all phenomenal appearances in the true nature of the mind. The term xingqi probably derives from the "Baowang rulai xingqi pin" ("Chapter on the 'Nature Origination' of the Tathāgata Jeweled King"), the thirty-second chapter of BUDDHABHADRA'S (359–429) sixty-roll translation of the AVATAṂSAKASŪTRA, which seems to translate the Sanskrit term tathāgatagotrasaṃbhava (the arising of the lineage of the tathāgata). Its philosophical origins lie in the TATHĀGATAGARBHA corpus of literature, which maintains that all sentient beings are fundamentally identical to the buddhas, since they share the same buddha-nature (FOXING), and the term finds its antecedents in such earlier theories as the "conditioned origination of the true nature" (zhenxing yuanqi) proposed by the Southern DI LUN ZONG master JINGYING HUIYUAN (523–592). ¶ The term "nature origination" was coined by the second Huayan patriarch ZHIYAN (602–668), and its implications were elaborated by the "third patriarch" FAZANG (643–712) in his HUAYANJING TANXUAN JI and especially the "fifth patriarch" GUIFENG ZONGMI (780–841). In Zhiyan's soteriological interpretation of the xingqi, as elucidated in his influential treatise, HUAYAN JING NAIZHANGMEN DENG ZA KONGMU ZHANG, "nature" (xing) refers to the "essence" (TI) and "origination" (qi) to the appearance of that essence in the "mind-ground" (XINDI). Zhiyan explicitly contrasts nature origination with the soteriological formulations of dependent origination (C. yuanqi; S. PRATĪTYASAMUTPĀDA): unlike dependent origination, which explains the specific conditions through which the experience of enlightenment occurs—and thus inevitably distinguishes the ordinary realm of SAṂSĀRA from the enlightened realm of NIRVĀṆA—nature origination operates entirely on the level of fruition to explain how enlightenment can "originate" only from within the very "nature" of this world itself. Enlightenment is therefore not something that needs to be produced, for it is the inherent nature of the mind itself. Zongmi subsequently provides a more ontological explanation of the xingqi, by explaining that "nature" refers to the one mind (YIXIN) as discussed in the DASHENG QIXIN LUN ("Awakening of Faith According to the Mahāyāna") and "origination" refers to the process by which that nature is made manifest in the world at large. Thus, in distinction to the "conditioned origination of the DHARMADHĀTU" (FAJIE YUANQI), which explains how all phenomena in the universe are mutual conditioning, and conditioned by, all other phenomena, "nature origination" instead clarifies that all those phenomena simultaneously derive from the common ground that is the nature. Nature origination thus provides a description of causality from the standpoint of the "dharmadhātu of the unimpeded interpenetration of principle and phenomena" (LISHI WU'AI FAJIE).

**Xingsi**. (C) (行思). See QINGYUAN XINGSI.

**Xingtao**. (C) (性瑫). See MU'AN XINGTAO.

**xingzhe**. (J. anja; K. haengja 行者). In Chinese, "postulant." According to the *Shishi yaolan*, a postulant refers to an unordained lay practitioner, a minimum of sixteen years of age, who works in a monastery until he or she is formally ordained. Within the CHAN traditions of East Asia, the sixth patriarch (LIUZU) HUINENG (638–713) is usually presumed to have been a postulant at the time he achieved enlightenment and received transmission from the fifth patriarch HONGREN. In premodern China, a postulant referred to a layperson who lived and worked in the monastic compounds before ordination; the postulant was still permitted to grow his or her hair and might in some cases even have a spouse. Postulants were expected to observe the five lay precepts (C. wujie; S. PAÑCAŚĪLA), but with the third precept against improper sexual conduct strengthened to require celibacy. In Korea, postulants (haengja) work in the monastery for at least six months before being allowed to ordain as novices. In Japan, a postulant (anja) may or may not be expected to ordain and works under the guidance of the administrative monks (yakusō) at the monastery or temple. ¶ The term xingzhe may also be used generically to refer to anyone who studies or practices Buddhism.

**xing zong**. (J. shōshū; K. sŏng chong 性宗). In Chinese, the "school of the nature"; also known as the FAXING ZONG, or "Dharma Nature" school. In distinction to the XIANG ZONG, or "characteristics school," which mainly involved the analysis of phenomena, the xing school refers to those Buddhist intellectual traditions that studied the underlying essence or "nature" of reality. While the xiang school, i.e., the FAXIANG or "Dharma Characteristics" school, was a pejorative term referring to the Chinese YOGĀCĀRA school established on the basis of the new Yogācāra texts introduced from India by XUANZANG (600/602–664) and elaborated by his lineage, the name "xing zong" was used polemically to refer to the MADHYAMAKA teachings of the SAN LUN ZONG, the TATHĀGATAGARBHA teachings, or the last three of the five teachings in the HUAYAN school's hermeneutical taxonomy (see JIAOXIANG PANSHI): the advanced teachings of Mahāyāna (Dasheng zhongjiao), i.e., the sudden teachings (DUNJIAO) and the perfect teachings (YUANJIAO). Maintaining a strict differentiation between the xing and xiang tendencies was called xingxiang juepan (differentiation between nature and characteristics); a scholastic approach that sought to harmonize the two trends was characterized as xingxiang ronghui (harmonizing nature and characteristics).

**Xin Huayan jing lun**. (C) (新華嚴經論). See HUAYAN JING HELUN.

**xinman chengfo**. (C) (信滿成佛). See YUANRONG.

**xinxin**. (J. shinjin; K. sinsim 信心). In Chinese, "mind of faith" or "faith in mind"; the compound is typically interpreted to mean either faith in the purity of one's own mind or else a mind that has faith in the three jewels (RATNATRAYA) and the principle of causality. The "mind of faith" is generally considered to constitute the inception of the Buddhist path (MĀRGA). In the elaborate fifty-two stage path schema outlined in such scriptures as the AVATAṂSAKASŪTRA, the RENWANG JING, and the PUSA YINGLUO BENYE JING, "mind of faith" (xinxin) constitutes the first of the ten stages of faith (shixin), a preliminary level of the BODHISATTVA path generally placed prior to the generation of the thought of enlightenment (BODHICITTOTPĀDA) that occurs on the first of the ten abiding stages (shizhu). The MAHĀPARINIRVĀṆASŪTRA also says that the buddha-nature (FOXING) can be called the "great mind of faith" (da xinxin) because a bodhisattva-mahāsattva, through this mind of faith, comes to be endowed with the six perfections (PĀRAMITĀ). ¶ In the PURE LAND traditions, the mind of faith typically refers to faith in the vows of the buddha AMITĀBHA, which ensures that those who have sincere devotion and faith in that buddha will be reborn in his pure land of SUKHĀVATĪ. SHANDAO (613–681) divided the mind of faith into two types: (1) faith in one's lesser spiritual capacity (xinji), which involves acceptance of the fact that one has fallen in a state of delusion during myriads of rebirths, and (2) faith in dharma (xinfa), which is faith in the fact that one can be saved from this delusion through the vows of Amitābha. SHINRAN (1173–1262) glosses the mind of faith as the buddha-mind realized by entrusting oneself to Amitābha's name and vow. ¶ The term xinxin is also used as a translation of the Sanskrit ŚRADDHĀ (faith), which is one of the five spiritual faculties (INDRIYA), and of ADHYĀŚAYA (lit. "determination," "resolution"), which is used to describe the intention of the bodhisattva to liberate all beings from suffering. See also XINXIN MING.

**Xinxing**. (J Shingyō; K. Sinhaeng 信行) (540–594). In Chinese, "Practice of Faith"; founder of the "Third-Stage Sect" (SANJIE JIAO), a school of popular Buddhism that flourished during the Tang dynasty. Born in Ye in present-day Henan province, Xinxing ordained as a novice monk by the age of seventeen, after which he wandered the country, studying Buddhism and reading such Buddhist scriptures as the SADDHARMAPUṆḌARĪKASŪTRA ("Lotus Sūtra"), VIMALAKĪRTINIRDEŚA, and MAHĀPARINIRVĀṆASŪTRA. Feeling guilty for accepting from the laity offerings that he did not believe he deserved, Xinxing eventually abandoned monastic life, participating in various state labor projects and cultivating ascetic practices. He is also known to have bowed to all he met on the street, following the teachings of the SADĀPARIBHŪTA chapter of the *Saddharmapuṇḍarīkasūtra*. It is uncertain exactly when Xinxing established the Third-Stage Sect, but it was probably sometime around 587. In 589, at the behest of Emperor Wendi, he entered Chang'an, the capital city of the Sui dynasty, and stayed at Zhenjisi (Authentic Quiescence Monastery, later renamed Huadu monastery), where he promoted actively the teachings of the school until his death in 594. Xinxing had about three hundred followers, including Sengyong (543–631) and Huiru (d. c. 618). Due to the proscription of the sect during the Tang dynasty, only a few fragments of Xinxing's writings are extant. These include the *Sanjie fofa* ("Buddhadharma during the Third Stage"), in four rolls, and sections of the *Duigen qixing fa* ("Principles on Practicing in Response to the Sense-Bases") and the *Ming Dasheng wujinzang fa* ("Clarifying the Teaching of the Mahāyāna's Inexhaustible Storehouse"). ¶ Xinxing's teachings derive from the doctrines of the degenerate dharma (MOFA) and the buddha-nature (FOXING); they emphasize almsgiving (S. DĀNA) as an efficient salvific method, which contributed to the development of the school's distinctive institution, the WUJINZANG YUAN (inexhaustible storehouse cloister). Because people during the degenerate age (mofa) were inevitably mistaken in their perceptions of reality, it was impossible for them to make any meaningful distinctions, whether between right and wrong, good and evil, or ordained and lay. Instead, adherents were taught to treat all things as manifestations of the buddha-nature, leading to a "universalist" perspective on Buddhism that was presumed to have supplanted all the previous teachings of the religion. Xinxing asserted that almsgiving was the epitome of Buddhist practice during the degenerate age of the dharma and that the true perfection of giving (DĀNAPĀRAMITĀ) meant that all people, monks and laypeople alike, should be making offerings to relieve the suffering of those most in need, including the poor, the orphaned, and the sick. In its radical reinterpretation of the practice of giving in Buddhism, even animals were considered to be a more appropriate object of charity than were buddhas, bodhisattvas, monks, or the three jewels (RATNATRAYA). Particularly significant were offerings made to the inexhaustible storehouse cloister (Wujinzang yuan), which served the needs of the impoverished and suffering in society—especially offerings made on the anniversary of Xinxing's death. See also XIANGFA JUEYI JING.

**Xinxin ming**. (J. Shinjinmei; K. Sinsim myŏng 信心銘). In Chinese, "Inscription on the Mind of Faith" (or "Faith in Mind"); attributed to the dubious third patriarch of the CHAN tradition, the otherwise-unknown SENGCAN. The *Xinxin ming* is a relatively short poem that praises nonduality and the method for attaining that experience. The last stanza, for instance, states that "faith and mind" (xinxin) are not two, and nonduality (lit. "not two") is the "perfected mind" (xinxin). According to the *Xinxin ming*, the method of attaining nonduality largely involves the cultivation of detachment, especially from words and thoughts. Along with the ZHENGDAO GE, CANTONG QI, and BAOJING SANMEI, the *Xinxin ming* has been regarded as one of the seminal statements of the Chan understanding of the dharma. Numerous commentaries on the poem were composed in East Asia. The *Xinxin ming* is still recited aloud in some Chan and ZEN monasteries.

**xinxun zhongzi**. (C) (新薰種子). In Chinese, "newly acquired seeds." See BĪJA.

**Xiqian**. (C) (希遷). See SHITOU XIQIAN.

**Xitan ziji**. (J. Shittan jiki; K. Siltam chagi 悉曇字記). In Chinese, "Notes on the SIDDHAM Syllabary," by the Chinese monk Zhikuang (d.u.); an influential primer of the Indian Siddham writing system. The *Xitan ziji* is said to be based on the teachings of a certain South Indian monk named Prajñābodhi. The main purpose of the *Xitan ziji* is to explain briefly the morphological operation of combining vowels and consonants. Zhikuang begins by discussing short and long syllables (e.g., a and ā). He then provides a detailed explanation of each vowel, their pronunciations, their various inflections, and their names. His coverage then extends to the syllables formed from the combination of consonants and vowels.

**Xiuxin yao lun**. (J. Shushin yōron; K. Susim yo non 修心要論). In Chinese, "Treatise on the Essentials of Cultivating the Mind," attributed to the fifth patriarch of the CHAN school, HONGREN; an important text on meditative practice in the early Chan tradition. The edition of the *Xiuxin yao lun* used within the Chan school was published at the Korean monastery of Ansimsa in 1570 during the Chosŏn dynasty under the title CH'OESANGSŬNG NON ("Treatise on the Supreme Vehicle") and again in 1907 as part of an edited volume of SŎN materials known as the SŎNMUN CH'WARYO. With the recent discovery of some earlier versions of the text at DUNHUANG, a more nuanced history of the *Xiuxin yao lun* has emerged. Overall, the different recensions all seem to share the common goal of establishing "guarding the mind" (shouxin) as an authentic and effective practice in Chan. Largely written in dialogic format, the *Xiuxin yao lun* emphasizes the inherent purity of the mind, which the author likens to suchness (TATHATĀ). The practice of "guarding the mind" seems to be related to or even derived from the fourth patriarch DAOXIN'S "guarding the one" (shouyi), a practice that Daoxin probably borrowed from indigenous Chinese materials. The *Xiuxin yao lun* also emphatically notes the superiority of shouxin over the popular practice of reciting the buddha's name (NIANFO) and a (misguided) experience of SAMĀDHI, suggesting a polemical context for its composition.

**Xiuxi zhiguan zuochan fayao**. (J. Shujū shikan zazenhōyō; K. Susŭp chigwan chwasŏn pŏbyo 修習止觀坐禪法要). In Chinese, "Essentials for Sitting in Meditation and Cultivating Calmness and Contemplation"; also known as the *Tongmeng zhiguan* ("Calming and Contemplation for Neophytes") and the (*Tiantai*) *Xiao zhiguan* ("Shorter Calming and Contemplation of [Tiantai]"). The monk TIANTAI ZHIYI, the systematizer of the TIANTAI ZONG, is known to have composed this treatise as a guide for training his brother Zhen Zhen. The treatise was composed sometime after his *Shi chan boluomi cidi chanmen* (571) and MOHE ZHIGUAN (594). Despite its popular designation as the *Xiao zhiguan*, the relatively short *Xiuxi zhiguan zuochan fayao* borrows heavily from the *Shi chan boluomi cidi chanmen* and seems to have no direct relation to Zhiyi's massive *Mohe zhiguan*. A preface to the *Xiuxi zhiguan zuochan fayao* was prepared by the monk Yuanzhao (1048–1116) and was published together with the treatise in 1095. The treatise is divided into ten chapters: (1) necessary conditions, (2) rebuking desires, (3) discarding obstructions, (4) regulation, (5) expedient methods (UPĀYA), (6) proper cultivation, (7) manifestation of the (roots of) virtue (KUŚALAMŪLA), (8) recognizing MĀRA, (9) healing ailments, and (10) attainment of fruits. The practice of meditation outlined in the treatise is based on the twenty-five preparatory expedient methods of the DAZHIDU LUN and the *Shi chan boluomi cidi chanmen*. As the title makes clear, the general purpose of the treatise is to provide the essentials for the concurrent practice of calming (ŚAMATHA) and insight (VIPAŚYANĀ). The treatise is still widely used in various Buddhist traditions as a practical manual for beginning meditators.

**Xiyu ji**. (C) (西域記). See DA TANG XIYU JI.

**Xiyun**. (C) (希運). See HUANGBO XIYUN.

**Xuanhe huapu**. (宣和畫譜). In Chinese, "The Xuanhe Chronology of Painting." See ṢOḌAŚASTHAVIRA.

**Xuanjian**. (C) (宣鑑). See DESHAN XUANJIAN.

**Xuanjue**. (C) (玄覺). See YONGJIA XUANJUE.

**xuanmen**. (C) (玄門). See SHI XUANMEN.

**Xuansha sanbing**. (J. Gensha sanbyō; K. Hyŏnsa sambyŏng 玄沙三病). In Chinese, "Xuansha's Three Infirmities"; a famous sermon attributed to the CHAN master XUANSHA SHIBEI. Different versions of the sermon are found in the BIYAN LU (case 88), JINGDE CHUANDENG LU (roll 18), KAIAN KOKUGO (roll 6), etc. One day, Xuansha asked the assembly what they would do should a blind, mute, and deaf person come to them for teaching, since the blind cannot see them raise their whisk, the mute cannot reply, and the deaf cannot hear. On a different occasion, the Chan master YUNMEN WENYAN demonstrated how this could be done. When a monk stepped back as Yunmen was about to hit him, the master whimsically noted that the monk was not blind. When the monk approached at his bidding, Yunmen then noted that the monk was not deaf. Finally, Yunmen asked the monk if he understood, and when the monk gave him a negative reply, Yunmen declared that he was not mute.

**Xuansha Shibei**. (J. Gensha Shibi; K. Hyŏnsa Sabi 玄沙師備) (835–908). Chinese CHAN master in the lineage of QINGYUAN XINGSI (d. 740) and a predecessor in the FAYAN ZONG of the classical Chan school; he was a native of Min (present-day Fujian province). Xuansha left home to study with the Chan master Lingxun (d.u.) on Mt. Furong and later received the monastic precepts in 864 from the VINAYA master Daoxuan (d.u.) at the monastery KAIYUANSI in Jiangxi province. Two years later, he visited the Chan master XUEFENG YICUN and became his disciple. Xuansha's adherence to the precepts is said to have been so strict that he was given the nickname Bei Doutuo, or "DHUTAṄGA Bei." He subsequently left Xuefeng's side and established a cloister on Mt. Sheng (also known as Mt. Xuansha) in Fujian province, named Xuansha (Sublime Sand). In 898, he was summoned to live in the cloister of Anguoyin in Fujian by the king of Min. Emperor Zhaozong (r. 888–904) gave Xuansha the title of Great Master Zongyi (Tradition's Best). Luohan Kuichen (867–928) was one of his disciples. His sayings were published in the *Xuansha guanglu* and *Xuansha Shibei chanshi yulu*, and sporadic references to some of his more popular sayings (e.g., XUANSHA SANBING) can also be found in the BIYAN LU.

**Xuansu**. (C) (玄素). See HELIN XUANSU.

**Xuanxue**. (J. Gengaku; K. Hyŏnhak 玄學). In Chinese, "Dark Learning," or "Profound Learning"; a Chinese philosophical movement of the third through sixth centuries CE, which provided a fertile intellectual ground for the emergence of early Chinese forms of Buddhism. It is sometimes known as "Neo-Daoism," although the target audience of Xuanxue literati was fellow elite rather than adherents of the new schools of religious Daoism that were then developing in China. The social and political upheaval that accompanied the fall of the Han dynasty (206 BCE–220 CE) prompted many Chinese intellectuals to question the traditional foundations of Chinese thought and society and opened them to alternative worldviews. Buddhism, which was just then beginning to filter into Chinese territories, found a receptive audience among these groups of thinkers. Xuanxue scholars critiqued and reinterpreted the normative Chinese teachings of Confucianism by drawing on the so-called "three dark [treatises]" (sanxuan), i.e., the *Yijing* ("Book of Changes"), *Daode jing* ("The Way and Its Power"), and the *Zhuangzi*. Xuanxue designates a broad intellectual trend that sought a new way of understanding the "way" (DAO). Xuanxue philosophers explored the ontological grounding of the changing and diverse world of "being" (C. you) on a permanent and indivisible substratum called "nothingness" or "nonbeing" (C. WU). Xuanxue thinkers such as Wang Bi (226–249), who is regarded as the founder of the movement, and Guo Xiang (d. 312), who is often considered to represent its apex, explored how this ontological stratum of nothingness still was able to produce the world of being in all its diversity. This process was clarified by adopting the mainstream Chinese philosophical bifurcations between (1) the ineffable "substance" or "essence" (TI) of things and the ways in which that substance "functions" (YONG) in the phenomenal world; and (2) the "patterns" or "principles" (LI) that underlie all things and their phenomenal manifestations (SHI). These distinctions between ti/yong and li/shi proved to be extremely influential in subsequent Chinese Buddhist exegesis. Also according to Xuanxue interpretation, the sage (shengren) is one who understands this association between being and nothingness but realizes that their relationship is fundamentally inexpressible; nevertheless, in order to make it intelligible to others, he feels "compelled" to describe it verbally. This emphasis on the inadequacy of language resonated with Buddhist treatments of the ineffability of spiritual experience and the necessity to deploy verbal stratagems (UPĀYA) in order to make that experience intelligible to others. The sage was able to manifest his understanding in the phenomenal world not by conscious intent but as an automatic "response" (ying) to "stimuli" (gan); early Chinese Buddhist thinkers deploy the compound "stimulus and response" (GANYING) to explain the Buddhist concepts of action (KARMAN) and of grace (i.e., the "response" of a buddha or BODHISATTVA to a supplicant's invocation, or "stimulus"). Xuanxue thinkers also began to explore parallels between their ideas of "nonbeing" (wu) and the notion of emptiness (ŚŪNYATĀ) in the PRAJÑĀPĀRAMITĀ corpus, which was just then being translated into Chinese. Xuanxue exegesis has often been described in the scholarly literature as a "matching concepts" (GEYI) style of interpretation, where Buddhist concepts were elucidated by drawing on indigenous Chinese philosophical terminology, though this interpretation of geyi has recently been called into question. Although Xuanxue vanished as a philosophical movement by the early sixth century, its influence was profound on several pioneering Chinese Buddhist thinkers, including ZHI DUN (314–366) and SENGZHAO (374–414), and on such early philosophical schools of Chinese Buddhism as the SAN LUN ZONG and DI LUN ZONG, and eventually on the TIANTAI ZONG and HUAYAN ZONG of the mature Chinese tradition.

**Xuanzang**. (J. Genjō; K. Hyŏnjang 玄奘) (600/602–664). Chinese monk, pilgrim, and patriarch of the Chinese YOGĀCĀRA tradition (FAXIANG ZONG) and one of the two most influential and prolific translators of Indian Buddhist texts into Chinese, along with KUMĀRAJĪVA (344–413); in English sources, his name is seen transcribed in a variety of ways (now all outmoded), including Hsüan-tsang, Hiuen Tsiang, Yuan Chwang, etc. Xuanzang was born into a literati family in Henan province in either 600 or 602 (although a consensus is building around the latter date). In 612, during a state-supported ordination ceremony, Xuanzang entered the monastery of Jingtusi in Luoyang where his older brother was residing as a monk. There, Xuanzang and his brother studied the MAHĀPARINIRVĀṆASŪTRA and various MAHĀYĀNA texts. When the Sui dynasty collapsed in 618, they both fled the capital for the safety of the countryside. In 622, Xuanzang was given the complete monastic precepts and was fully ordained as a monk (BHIKṢU). By this time Xuanzang had also studied earlier translations of the MAHĀYĀNASAṂGRAHA, JÑĀNAPRASTHĀNA, and *TATTVASIDDHI under various teachers but came to doubt the accuracy of those translations and the veracity of their teachings. In order to resolve his doubts, Xuanzang embarked on an epic journey to India in 627, in flagrant disregard of the Taizong emperor's (r. 626–629) edict against traveling abroad. His trek across the SILK ROAD and India is well known, thanks to his travel record, the DA TANG XIYU JI, his official biography, and the famous Ming-dynasty comic novel based on Xuangzang's travels, XIYU JI ("Journey to the West"). (See "Routes of Chinese Pilgrims" map.) According to these sources, Xuanzang visited the various Buddhist pilgrimage sites of the subcontinent (see MAHĀSTHĀNA) and spent years at NĀLANDĀ monastery mastering Sanskrit, including fifteen months studying the texts of the Indian Yogācāra tradition under the tutelage of the 106-year-old ŚĪLABHADRA. In 645, Xuanzang returned to the Tang capital of Chang'an with over six hundred Sanskrit manuscripts that he had acquired in India, along with images, relics, and other artifacts. (These materials were stored in a five-story stone pagoda, named the DAYAN TA, or Great Wild Goose Pagoda, that Xuanzang later built on the grounds of the monastery of DA CI'ENSI; the pagoda is still a major tourist attraction in Xi'an.) The Taizong and Gaozong emperors (r. 649–683) honored Xuanzang with the title TREPIṬAKA (C. sanzang fashi; "master of the Buddhist canon") and established a translation bureau (yijing yuan) in the capital for the master, where Xuanzang supervised a legion of monks in charge of transcribing the texts, "rectifying" (viz., clarifying) their meaning, compiling the translations, polishing the renderings, and certifying both their meaning and syntax. Xuanzang and his team developed an etymologically precise set of Chinese equivalencies for Buddhist technical terminology, and his translations are known for their rigorous philological accuracy (although sometimes at the expense of their readability). While residing at such sites as HONGFUSI, Da ci'ensi, and the palace over an eighteen-year period, Xuanzang oversaw the translation of seventy-six sūtras and śāstras in a total of 1,347 rolls, nearly four times the number of texts translated by Kumārajīva, probably the most influential of translators into Chinese. (Scholars have estimated that Xuanzang and his team completed one roll of translation every five days over those eighteen years of work.) Xuanzang's influence was so immense that he is often recognized as initiating the "new translation" period in the history of the Chinese translation of Buddhist texts, in distinction to the "old translation" period where Kumārajīva's renderings hold pride of place. Among the more important translations made by Xuanzang and his translation team are the foundational texts of the Yogācāra school, such as the CHENG WEISHI LUN (*Vijñaptimātratāsiddhi*), ASAṄGA's MAHĀYĀNASAṂGRAHA, and the YOGĀCĀRABHŪMIŚĀSTRA, and many of the major works associated with the SARVĀSTIVĀDA school of ABHIDHARMA, including definitive translations of the *Jñānaprasthāna* and the encyclopedic ABHIDHARMAMAHĀVIBHĀṢĀ, as well as complete translations of VASUBANDHU's ABHIDHARMAKOŚABHĀṢYA and SAṂGHABHADRA's *NYĀYĀNUSĀRA. He translated (and retranslated) many major Mahāyāna sūtras and śāstras, including the massive MAHĀPRAJÑĀPĀRAMITĀSŪTRA, in six hundred rolls; this translation is given a place of honor as the first scripture in the East Asian Buddhist canons (see DAZANGJING; KORYŎ TAEJANGGYŎNG). Also attributed to Xuanzang is the Chinese translation of the famed PRAJÑĀPĀRAMITĀHṚDAYASŪTRA, or "Heart Sūtra," probably the most widely read and recited text in East Asian Buddhism. Because Xuanzang himself experienced a palpable sense of the Buddha's absence while he was sojourning in India, he also translated the *Nandimitrāvadāna* (*Da aluohan Nantimiduo luo suoshuo fazhu ji*, abbr. *Fazhu ji*, "Record of the Duration of the Dharma Spoken by the Great Arhat NANDIMITRA"), the definitive text on the sixteen ARHAT protectors (see ṢOḌAŚASTHAVIRA) of Buddhism, which became the basis for the LOUHAN cult in East Asia.

**Xuanzhong ming**. (J. Genchūmei; K. Hyŏnjung myŏng 玄中銘). In Chinese, "Inscription on the Center of Mystery," by the Chinese CHAN master DONGSHAN LIANGJIE. In this poem, Dongshan sings of the "mystery" of subtle reciprocation (huihu wanzhuan), simultaneous illumination of phenomena and principle (SHI LI shuangming), and the unimpededness of essence and function (TI YONG wuzhi), which he likens to the activities of a sage. The *Xuanzhong ming* is found in Dongshan's recorded sayings, the *Dongshan yulu*.

**Xuedou Chongxian**. (J. Setchō Jūken; K. Sŏltu Chunghyŏn 雪竇重顯) (980–1052). Chinese CHAN master in the YUNMEN ZONG of the mature Chan tradition; also known as Yinzhi. Xuedou was a native of Sichuan province. After his ordination under Renxian (d.u.) of the cloister of Pu'anyuan, Xuedou received doctrinal training from Yuanying (d.u.) of Dacisi and Guyin Yuncong (965–1032) of Shimen. During his travels in the south, Xuedou visited the Yunmen master Zhimen Guangzuo (d.u.) in Hubei province and became his leading disciple. Xuedou later resided on Cuiwei peak near Tongting Lake and the monastery of Zishengsi on Mt. Xuedou in Zhejiang province, whence he acquired his toponym. During his residence in Zishengsi, Xuedou acquired more than seventy students and composed his famed collection of one hundred old cases (guce, viz., GONG'AN) known as the *Xuedou songgu*, which in turn formed the basis of Chan master YUANWU KEQIN's influential BIYAN LU. Xuedou also composed the *Tongting yulu*, *Xuedou kaitang lu*, *Puquan ji*, *Zuying ji*, and various other texts. Xuedou's successful career as a teacher is often considered a period of revitalization of the Yunmen tradition.

**Xuefeng Yicun**. (J. Seppō Gison; K. Sŏlbong Ŭijon 雪峰義存) (822–908). Chinese CHAN master in the lineage of QINGYUAN XINGSI (d. 740); a native of Min (present-day Fujian province). He was ordained at the age of seventeen and given the dharma name Yicun, but temporarily returned to lay clothing during the severe persecution of the HUICHANG FANAN and studied under Furong Lingxun (d.u.). After a brief stay with DONGSHAN LIANGJIE, Xuefeng left at Dongshan's direction to study with DESHAN XUANJIAN (780/2–865). Xuefeng then embarked on a journey with his colleagues Yantou Quanhuo (828–887) and Qinshan Wensui (d.u.). With the help of Yantou, Xuefeng is said to have had his first awakening experience during a snowfall on Mt. Ao in Hunan. Xuefeng and Yantou became Deshan's leading disciples. Xuefeng later established a monastery with the support of the king of Min on what came to be known as Mt. Xuefeng in Fujian province. The mountain was originally known as Mt. Xianggu (Elephant Bone) but acquired its new name after a famous exchange at the mountain between the king of Min and the monk Xuefeng. Xuefeng's monastery was given the name Chongshengsi and Yingtian Xuefeng Chanyuan. In 882, Emperor Xizong (r. 873–888) bestowed upon him the title Great Master Zhenjue (Authentic Enlightenment) and the purple robe. His disciples include YUNMEN WENYAN (the founder of the YUNMEN ZONG of the classical Chan school), XUANSHA SHIBEI (whose students eventually would go on to establish the FAYAN ZONG), Changjing Huileng (854–932), Baofu Congzhan (d. 928), and Gushan Shenyan (d. 943). His teachings are recorded in his *Xuefeng Zhenjue chanshi yulu*.

**Xuemo lun**. [alt. Xuemai lun] (J. Kechimyakuron; K. Hyŏlmaek non 血脈論). In Chinese, "Treatise on the Blood-Vessel." This short treatise has been traditionally attributed to the legendary Indian monk BODHIDHARMA and is also referred to as the *Damo dashi xuemo lun* ("Great Master [Bodhi]dharma's Treatise on the Blood-Vessel"). Judging from its style of argumentation and doctrinal content, the treatise was most probably composed by a CHAN adept of the HONGZHOU ZONG or NIUTOU ZONG sometime during the ninth century, long after Bodhidharma's death. The treatise begins with the claim that the three realms of existence (TRAIDHĀTUKA) return to the "one mind" (YIXIN), which was transmitted from one buddha to another without recourse to words or letters (BULI WENZI). From beginning to end, the treatise consistently underscores the importance of the inherent purity of the mind (xin) and claims that the mind is none other than the buddha, DHARMAKĀYA, BODHI, and NIRVĀṆA. The treatise also polemically contends that the practice of chanting and being mindful of the buddha AMITĀBHA'S name (NIANFO), reading scriptures, and upholding the precepts may guarantee a better rebirth and intelligence but do not ensure the achievement of buddhahood. According to the treatise, only the practice of seeing one's own nature (JIANXING) can lead to buddhahood (see JIANXING CHENGFO). The first known edition of the *Xuemo lun* was first published in Korea in 1473 and was republished on several subsequent occasions. It is often anthologized in larger compilations such as the SŎNMUN CH'WARYO and SHŌSHITSU ROKUMON.

**Xu gaoseng zhuan**. (J. Zoku kōsōden; K. Sok kosŭng chŏn 續高僧傳). In Chinese, "Supplement to the Biographies of Eminent Monks," compiled by the VINAYA master DAOXUAN; also known as the *Tang gaoseng zhuan*. As the title suggests, the *Xu gaoseng zhuan* "supplements" or "continues" the work of HUIJIAO's earlier GAOSENG ZHUAN and records the lives of monks who were active in the period between Huijiao's composition during the Liang dynasty and Daoxuan's own time. The *Xu gaoseng zhuan* contains 485 major and 219 appended biographies, neatly categorized under translators (yijing), exegetes (yijie), practitioners of meditation (xichan), specialists of VINAYA (minglü), protectors of the DHARMA (hufa), sympathetic resonance (GANTONG), sacrifice of the body (YISHEN), chanters (dusong), benefactors (xingfu), and miscellaneous (zake). Although Daoxuan generally followed Huijiao's earlier categorizations, he made several changes. In lieu of Huijiao's divine wonders (shenyi), viz., thaumaturgists, Daoxuan opted to use the term sympathetic resonance, instead; he also subsumed Huijiao's hymnodists (jingshi) and propagators (changdao) under the "miscellaneous" category. Daoxuan also introduced the new category of protectors of the dharma order to leave a record of disputes that occurred at court with Daoists. These adjustments seem to reflect ongoing developments within Chinese Buddhism in how to conceive of, and write, history. Other related biographical collections include ZANNING's SONG GAOSENG ZHUAN, Shi Baochang's BIQIUNI ZHUAN, the Korean HAEDONG KOSŬNG CHŎN, and the Japanese HONCHŌ KŌSŌDEN.

**Xutang Zhiyu**. (J. Kidō Chigu; K. Hŏdang Chiu 虛堂智愚) (1185–1269). Chinese CHAN master in the LINJI ZONG; also known as Xijingsou. Xutang was ordained at age sixteen by Shiyun (d.u.) of Pumingsi and later became the disciple of YUN'AN PUYAN (1156–1226). He continued to visit various teachers throughout the country until he became the abbot of the monastery of Xingshengsi in 1229. Xutang also served as abbot of many other important Chan monasteries throughout his illustrious career, including BAOLINSI and WANSHOUSI. The emperors Lizong (r. 1224–1264) and Duzong (r. 1264–1274) honored Xutang as their teacher. Among his disciples is the Japanese monk NANPO JŌMYŌ (1235–1308), to whom the abbots of DAITOKUJI and MYŌSHINJI trace their lineage. The eminent Japanese monk and abbot of Daitokuji, IKKYŪ SŌJUN, even went so far as to consider himself to be a reincarnation of Xutang and had numerous portraits of himself drawn in the likeness of Xutang.

**Xuyun**. (虛雲) (1840–1959). In Chinese, "Empty Cloud"; CHAN monk of the modern period, renowned as one of the major reformers of modern Chinese Buddhism, especially of the Chan school; also known as Deqing. Xuyun was a native of Xiangxiang in Hunan province. He entered the monastery at the age of nineteen and received the precepts a year later from the monk Miaolian (d.u.). He then embarked on a long pilgrimage to famous mountains in China and to such distant sites as Tibet, India, and Sri Lanka, where he studied with teachers in a variety of Buddhist traditions. At the age of forty-three, Xuyun climbed WUTAISHAN, where he is said to have had a vision of the resident bodhisattva MAÑJUŚRĪ. His awakening experience came at the drop of a teacup at the age of fifty-six. Xuyun was particularly renowned for his austerities and longevity. He became an important exponent of the convergence of "questioning meditation" (KANHUA CHAN) and recitation of the Buddha's name (NIANFO), who was noted for using the meditative topic (HUATOU) "Who is reciting the Buddha's name?" Xuyun spent the rest of his career propagating Buddhism throughout China until his death on Mt. Yunju in Jiangxi province at the advanced age of 120. See also TAIXU; YINGUANG.

# Y

**yab yum**. A Tibetan term, literally meaning "father-mother," referring to the theme common in VAJRAYĀNA iconography, especially that of ANUTTARAYOGATANTRA, viz., male and female deities in sexual union. The deities are depicted either standing face-to-face or sitting, with the male deity in the VAJRĀSANA and the female deity seated on the male deity's lap, with her legs wrapped around his back, their arms embracing each other. Although interpreted in numerous ways, the male figure is generally understood to represent compassion (KARUṆĀ) and method (UPĀYA) and the female figure wisdom (PRAJÑĀ). Their union represents the indivisibility of these two qualities in the state of buddhahood. Although often described in such symbolic terms, numerous SĀDHANAs associated with the anuttarayogatantras include the practice of sexual union.

**yakṣa**. (P. yakkha; T. gnod sbyin; C. yecha; J. yasha; K. yach'a 夜叉). In Indian mythology, a class of nature spirit, commonly serving as local guardians of the earth and of trees and the treasures hidden there. They possess supernatural powers—including the ability to fly, to change their appearance, and to disappear—which they can employ for good or for evil. They appear often in Buddhist texts, sometimes serving as benevolent protectors of and messengers for the Buddha and his disciples. The most famous of them is VAJRAPĀṆI, who accompanies the Buddha as his bodyguard. They are commonly listed among the audience of the Buddha's sermons, with some attaining the rank of stream-enterer. There are also demonic yakṣas, especially the female yakṣas or yakṣiṇī, who devour infants and corpses and must be subdued by the Buddha, an ARHAT, or a BODHISATTVA. The continent of UTTARAKURU and the island of Sri Lanka were considered to be abodes of the yakṣas.

**Yakushiji**. (藥師寺). In Japanese, "Medicine Buddha Monastery." One of the seven great monasteries of Nara, Japan. Yakushiji is currently the headquarters (daihonzan) of the Hossō (C. FAXIANG ZONG) tradition. In 680, Emperor Tenmu (r. 673–686) ordered the construction of a statue of the Medicine Buddha (BHAIṢAJYAGURU) and a new monastery to pray for the recovery of his ill consort, who later succeeded him as Empress Jitō (r. 687–697). Due to the emperor's death and the lack of sufficient funds, construction began under Empress Jitō's reign in the old capital of Fujiwarakyō in present-day Kashihara city. Construction was completed in 697, but the monastery was physically relocated to the new capital Heijōkyō in 718 after the transfer of the capital in 710. The monastery originally consisted of two pagodas to the east and the west flanking a central golden hall (kondō) and a lecture hall (kōdō) behind it. After a great fire in 973, only the pagodas and the golden hall remained. The hall collapsed during a typhoon in 1445 and the west pagoda was lost to fire during a war in 1528. Reconstruction of the monastery took place during most of the late twentieth and early twenty-first centuries. The golden hall houses the famed Medicine Buddha triad from the Hakuhō period (645–710), now designated a national treasure.

**Yama**. (T. Gshin rje; C. Yanmo wang; J. Enma ō; K. Yŏmma wang 閻魔王). In the Buddhist pantheon, the lord of death and the king of hell. Among the six rebirth destinies (ṢAḌGATI), Yama is considered a divinity (DEVA), even though his abode is variously placed in heaven (SVARGA), in the realm of the ghosts (PRETA), and in the hells (see NĀRAKA). Birth, old age, sickness, and punishment are said to be his messengers, sent among humans to remind them to avoid evil deeds and to live virtuously. Since KARMAN functions as a natural law, with suffering resulting from unvirtuous actions and happiness from virtuous actions, the process of moral cause and effect should proceed without the need for a judge to mete out rewards and punishments. However, in Indian sources, Yama is sometimes described as the judge of the dead, who interrogates them about their deeds and assigns the wicked to the appropriate hell. This role of Yama was expanded in China, where he oversaw a quintessentially Chinese infernal bureaucracy: Yama is said to have organized the complex array of indigenous "subterranean prisons" (C. diyu) into a streamlined system of ten infernal courts, each presided over by a different king who would judge the incoming denizens. These judges were known collectively as the ten kings of hell (C. SHIWANG) and are the subject of the eponymous *Shiwang jing*, a Chinese indigenous scripture (see APOCRYPHA). See also KṢITIGARBHA.

**yāma**. (T. 'thab bral; C. yemo tian; J. yamaten; K. yama ch'ŏn 夜摩天). In Sanskrit and Pāli, proper name of a heaven in the sensuous realm (KĀMADHĀTU); also known as suyāma ("where the seasons are always good"). The yāma heaven is the third from the bottom of the six heavens located in the sensuous realm above Mount SUMERU, between TRĀYASTRIṂŚA below and

TUṢITA above. Like all Buddhist heavens, it is a place of rebirth and not a permanent post-mortem abode. Because this heaven is located in the sky, the divinities who inhabit it do not need to engage in combat with the ASURAs who dwell on the slopes of Mount Sumeru, hence the Tibetan interpretation of the name as "free from conflict." (The Chinese is a Sinographic transcription of the Sanskrit.) The life span in this heaven is said to be two thousand years, with each day lasting two hundred human years.

**yamabushi**. (山伏). In Japanese, lit. "those who lie down [or sleep] in the mountains"; itinerant mountain ascetics associated with the SHUGENDŌ (way of cultivating supernatural power) tradition; also known as shugenja, or "those who cultivate supernatural powers." Records reveal that as early as the Nara period (although possibly before), yamabushi practiced a variety of severe austerities in the mountains, which were thought to be numinous places that housed the spirits of the dead. Thanks to the special powers accumulated through this training, such adepts were able to mediate with the realm of the dead, convert baleful spirits, and provide healing services. During this early period, the yamabushi were not formally ordained but instead operated independently, drawing freely from Buddhism, Daoism, and indigenous religious beliefs. In the mid to late Heian period (794–1185), such Shugendō sites as the mountains of Yoshino and KUMANO became affiliated with Japanese Tendaishū (TIANTAI) and SHINGONSHŪ institutions, and yamabushi increasingly incorporated esoteric Buddhism into their training, whereby they strove to attain buddhahood (SOKUSHIN JŌBUTSU) through severe asceticism, such as immersion under waterfalls, solitary confinement in caves, fasting, meditating, and the recitation of spells (MANTRA). In addition, yamabushi guided people on pilgrimages through their mountain redoubts and performed powerful rites for the aristocratic nobility and royal court. During the Tokugawa period (1600–1868), they were forced because of temple regulations (J. jin hatto) to adopt permanent residences. While higher-ranking practitioners stayed at the mountain centers, many others settled down in villages, where they performed shamanic rituals and offered healing and prayers. Later in the Tokugawa period, many of these practices would provide the foundation for Japan's so-called new religions. When Shugendō was proscribed in 1872, yamabushi were forced to join either Buddhist or Shintō institutions and to forgo many of their former practices. When this ban was lifted in the late 1940s following World War II, yamabushi at some centers, including Mt. Haguro and Kumano, resumed their former practice, which continues to the present.

**Yamaka**. In Pāli, "Pairs"; one of the principal books of the Pāli abhidhammapiṭaka (see ABHIDHARMAPIṬAKA), which has no precise analogue in the abhidharmas of other MAINSTREAM BUDDHIST SCHOOLS. The text belongs to the second stratum of Pāli abhidhamma works and is traditionally dated to the time of the third Buddhist council (see COUNCIL, THIRD) (c. third–second century BCE). The *Yamaka* is divided into ten chapters: (1) nine kinds of faculties or roots (mūla), for example, the three wholesome faculties (see KUŚALAMŪLA), the three unwholesome faculties (see AKUŚALAMŪLA), and the three neutral faculties; (2) five aggregates (see SKANDHA); (3) six sensory bases (ĀYATANA); (4) eighteen elements (DHĀTU); (5) the FOUR NOBLE TRUTHS; (6) conditioning factors (see SAṂSKĀRA) created via body, speech, and mind; (7) the proclivities (see ANUŚAYA); (8) mind (CITTA); (9) factors (see DHARMA); and (10) faculties (INDRIYA). Each of these chapters is organized into three sections: (1) delimitation of terminology, viz., the precise denotation of the terms covered in a chapter; (2) process, viz., discussions of how the terms are deployed in the course of abhidhamma analysis; and (3) penetration, viz., what understandings are generated through this analysis. The coverage proceeds through series of paired exchanges. An example is the opening discussion of the truth of suffering (P. dukkhasacca; S. DUḤKHASATYA). Exchange A asks: "Are painful sensations (P. dukkha; S. DUḤKHA) always included in the truth of suffering? Yes." Exchange B asks: "Does the truth of suffering always refer to painful sensations? No, the truth of suffering involves other types of suffering apart from physical and psychological suffering." Through this exchange, the text clarifies that the term dukkha cannot be limited solely to physical or psychological pain (see DUḤKHADUḤKHATĀ), but suggests that it may also involve the suffering caused by change (see VIPARIṆĀMADUḤKHATĀ) and in fact lies at the very root of conditioning itself (see SAṂSKĀRADUḤKHATĀ). Perhaps because its format of paired exchanges does not readily lend itself to systematic analysis, the *Yamaka* has the dubious distinction of being probably the least read of all the works in the Pāli abhidhammapiṭaka.

**yamakaprātihārya**. (P. yamakapāṭihāriya; T. cho 'phrul ya ma zung; C. shuangshenbian; J. sōjinpen; K. ssangsinbyŏn 雙神變). In Sanskrit, "paired miracle" or "twin miracle"; this and the MAHĀPRĀTIHĀRYA are the two most famous of the miracles performed by the Buddha during his career, which are frequently narrated in both canonical and commentarial literature and widely depicted in Buddhist art. Both types are generally understood to have taken place in the city of ŚRĀVASTĪ and thus are often referred to collectively in the literature as the ŚRĀVASTĪ MIRACLES. The yamakaprātihārya involved the manifestation of the contrasting physical elements (MAHĀBHŪTA) of fire and water. After the Buddha established a rule preventing monks from displaying miraculous powers, he was challenged by a group of non-Buddhist yogins to a display of his own supranormal powers. As a buddha, he was exempt from this prohibition, so he accepted their challenge and stated that he would perform a miracle at the foot of a mango tree. To keep him from proceeding, his opponents uprooted all the mango trees in the vicinity, leading the Buddha to cause a great tree to grow spontaneously from a mango seed. At the appointed time, the Buddha created a bejeweled walkway in the sky and then proceeded back and forth on it, causing flames to emerge from the upper part of his body and streams of water from the lower part, then water from the upper part and flames from the lower part, then flames from the right side and water from the left side, then from his front and back, right eye and left eye, right ear and left ear, etc. He then created a double of himself (see MANOMAYAKĀYA), with whom he conversed. It is because of the simultaneous presence of fire and water (and perhaps because of his creation of his doppelgänger) that the event is called the "paired miracle." After performing the miracle and preaching for sixteen days, the Buddha departed for the heaven of the thirty-three (TRĀYASTRIṂŚA), where he spent the rains retreat (VARṢĀ) teaching the ABHIDHARMA to his mother MĀYĀ (who had been reborn as a divinity in the TUṢITA heaven). This miracle is said to be performed by all buddhas (and only by a buddha) and always in Śrāvastī.

**Yamāntaka**. (T. Gshin rje gshed; C. Yanmandejia/Daweide mingwang; J. Enmantokuka/Daiitoku myōō; K. Yŏmmandŏkka/Taewidŏk myŏngwang 焰曼德迦/大威德明王). In Sanskrit, "Destroyer of Death" (lit. "he who brings an end (antaka) to death (yama)"), closely associated with BHAIRAVA ("The Frightening One") and VAJRABHAIRAVA; one of the most important tantric deities. In Tibetan Buddhism, he was one of the three primary YI DAM of the DGE LUGS sect (together with GUHYASAMĀJA and CAKRASAṂVARA). Yamāntaka is considered to be a fully enlightened buddha, who appears always in a wrathful form. He is depicted both with and without a consort; the solitary depiction, called "sole hero" (ekavīra), is particularly popular. Bhairava also appears in the Hindu tantric pantheon as a wrathful manifestation of the god Śiva. According to Buddhist mythology, MAÑJUŚRĪ, the bodhisattva of wisdom, took the form of the terrifying bull-headed deity in order to destroy the Lord of Death (YAMA) who was ravaging the country; hence the epithet Yamāntaka (Destroyer of Death). Yamāntaka has nine heads, thirty-four arms, and sixteen legs, each arm holding a different weapon or frightening object, and each foot trampling a different being. Each of these receives detailed symbolic interpretation in ritual and meditation texts associated with Yamāntaka. Thus, his two horns are said to represent the two truths (SATYADVAYA) of MADHYAMAKA philosophy: ultimate truth (PARAMĀRTHASATYA) and conventional truth (SAṂVṚTISATYA). His nine heads represent the nine categories (NAVAṄGA[PĀVACANA]) of Buddhist scriptures. His thirty-four arms, together with his body, speech, and mind, symbolize the thirty-seven "factors pertaining to awakening" (BODHIPĀKṢIKADHARMA). His sixteen legs symbolize the sixteen emptinesses (ŚŪNYATĀ). The humans and animals that he tramples with his right foot represent the attainment of the eight accomplishments, viz., supernatural abilities acquired through tantric practice, including the ability to fly, to become invisible, and travel underground. The birds that he tramples with his left foot represent the attainment of the eight powers, another set of magical abilities, including the ability to travel anywhere in an instant and the power to create emanations. His erect phallus represents great bliss, his nakedness means that he is not covered up with obstacles, and his hair standing on end symbolizes his passage beyond all sorrow (DUḤKHA). The Yamāntaka root tantras are the *Sarvatathāgatakāyavāgcittakṛṣṇayamāritantra* ("Body, Speech, and Mind of All Tathāgatas: Black Enemy of Death Tantra") in eighteen chapters; *Sarvatathāgatakāyavāgcittaraktayamāritantra* ("Red Enemy of Death Tantra," in large part, a different version of the same tantra in nineteen chapters); and the important *Kṛṣṇayamārimukhatantra*, also called the "Three Summaries Tantra" (T. *Rgyud sdom gsum*) because it has no chapters. Also included in the cycle is the *Yamāntakakrodhavijayatantra* ("Victorious Wrathful Yamāntaka Tantra"), a CARYĀTANTRA. Based on these three works, in Tibet, the three varieties of Yamāntaka are called the "red, black, and the frightening" (T. dmar nag 'jigs gsum) derived from Raktayamāri (Red Enemy of Death), Kṛṣṇayamāri (Black Enemy of Death), and Vajrabhairava.

**yāna**. (T. theg pa; C. sheng; J. jō; K. sŭng 乘). In Sanskrit, "vehicle," "conveyance"; a common Sanskrit term for any means of transportation (in Pāli materials and in many of the MAINSTREAM BUDDHIST SCHOOLS, the term is generally used in this literal sense). In MAHĀYĀNA literature, the term takes on great significance in the metaphorical sense of a mode of transportation along the path to enlightenment, becoming a constituent of the term Mahāyāna ("Great Vehicle") itself. In Mahāyāna SŪTRAS and ŚĀSTRAS, this rhetorical sense of the term is often put to polemical use, with the followers of the Buddha being placed into three or two vehicles. The three vehicles are the BODHISATTVAYĀNA or Mahāyāna, the PRATYEKABUDDHAYĀNA, and the ŚRĀVAKAYĀNA. The two vehicles are the Mahāyāna and the HĪNAYĀNA (the "lesser vehicle," or even more disparagingly, "base vehicle" or "vile vehicle"), which subsumes the pratyekabuddhayāna and the śrāvakayāna. Other uses of the term yāna include the BUDDHAYĀNA and the EKAYĀNA ("one vehicle"), whose precise relationship to the bodhisattvayāna and the Mahāyāna is discussed in the scholastic literature. Among the Mahāyāna sūtras, the most celebrated expression of the rhetoric of the yānas occurs in the SADDHARMAPUṆḌARĪKASŪTRA ("Lotus Sūtra") where, in the parable of the burning house, a father promises to reward his children with three different carriages (yāna) when in fact there is only a single magnificent carriage. With the rise of tantric Buddhism, the Mahāyāna itself is divided into two, the PĀRAMITĀYĀNA or "perfection vehicle," referring to the path to buddhahood involving successive mastery of the perfections (PĀRAMITĀ) as set forth in the sūtras, and the MANTRAYĀNA or "mantra vehicle," referring to the path to buddhahood as set forth in the TANTRAS (although some scholars have argued that the proper term here is not yāna, but naya, meaning "mode" or "principle"). The tantric teachings are also variously referred to as the GUHYAMANTRAYĀNA ("secret mantra vehicle"), the PHALAYĀNA ("fruition vehicle"), and, most famously, as the VAJRAYĀNA ("diamond vehicle" or "thunderbolt vehicle").

**yang 'dul gtsug lag khang**. (yangdul tsuklakang). In Tibetan, the four "extra-taming temples" or "extra-pinning temples" of

Bu chu, Mkho mthing, Dge gyes, and Pra dum rtse said to have been constructed during the time of the Tibetan king Srong btsan sgam po to pin down the limbs of the demoness (T. srin mo) who was impeding the introduction of Buddhism into Tibet. The Lha sa temple (gtsug lag khang) pins down her heart and the four extra taming temples pin down her right and left elbows and right and left knees.

**Yang le shod**. (Yangleshö). An important pilgrimage site south of the Kathmandu Valley in Nepal, sacred to Tibetan and Newar Buddhists as well as to Hindus, although the source and meaning of the name are unclear. According to traditional Buddhist accounts, Padmasambhava practiced meditation in a cave here, subdued nāga demons through the practice of Vajrakīlaya, and attained realization of mahāmudrā. Hindus relate the site to the avatāra of Viṣṇu called Śeṣa Nārāyaṇa.

**Yangqi Fanghui**. (J. Yōgi Hōe; K. Yanggi Panghoe 楊岐方會) (992–1049). Chinese Chan master and patriarch of the Yangqi pai collateral line of the Linji zong; one of the two major Linji sublineages, along with the Huanglong pai. Yangqi was a native of Yuanzhou prefecture in present-day Jiangxi province. After studying under various teachers, he visited the Chan master Shishuang Chuyuan (986–1039), himself a successor of Fenyang Shanzhao (947–1024), and became one of Shishuang's leading disciples. Yangqi was later invited to serve as abbot of the monastery Putong Chanyuan on Mt. Yangqi in his hometown of Yuanzhou, whence he acquired his toponym. In 1046, he moved his residence to the monastery of Haihuisi on Mt. Yung'ai. Among his many talented disciples, the most famous is Baiyun Shouduan (1025–1072). His teachings are recorded in the *Yangqi Fanghui chanshi yulu*, *Yangqi Fanghui chanshi houlu*, and *Yangqi Hui chanshi yuyao*. See also wu jia qi zong.

**Yangqi pai**. (J. Yōgiha; K. Yanggi p'a 楊岐派). One of the two major branches of the Linji zong of the Chan school, which is listed among the five houses and seven schools (wu jia qi zong) of the mature Chinese Chan tradition. The school is named after its founder, Yangqi Fanghui (995–1049), who taught at Mt. Yangqi in what is now Yuanzhou province. Yangqi was a disciple of Shishuang Chuyuan (986–1039), a sixth-generation successor in the Linji school, who also taught Huanglong Huinan (1002–1069), the founder of the Huanglong pai sublineage of the Linji school. The Yangqi lineage flourished under its third-generation successors, Fojian Huiqin (1059–1117), Foyan Qingyuan (1067–1120), and Yuanwu Keqin (1063–1135), who promoted it among the literati, and it became one of the dominant schools of Song-dynasty Buddhism thanks to the decisive role played by Yuanwu's disciple Dahui Zonggao (1089–1163). It was especially within this lineage that the meditative technique of the Chan of investigating the meditative topic or questioning meditation (kanhua Chan) flourished. The Yangqi masters took a different approach to gong'an (public case) training, criticizing "lettered Chan" (wenzi Chan), a style of Chan developed by Yunmen and Huanglong masters, which gained popularity among the literati officials in the Northern Song period with its polished language and elegant verse explanations of the meaning of the gong'an. Dahui in particular presented the gong'an as a meditative tool for realizing one's innate enlightenment, not to demonstrate one's talent in clever repartee or one's literary prowess; at the same time, he critiqued the approaches of rival Chan schools, criticizing such Huanglong masters as Juefan Huihong (1071–1128) for clinging to intellectual and literary endeavors and such Caodong zong masters as Hongzhi Zhengjue (1091–1157) for clinging to tranquillity and simply waiting for one's innate enlightenment to manifest itself. The school also produced many gong'an collections, including the Biyanlu ("Blue Cliff Record"), complied by Yuanwu Keqin, and the Wumen guan ("Gateless Checkpoint"), compiled by the seventh-generation successor Wumen Huikai (1183–1260). The Yangqi lineage was formally introduced to Korea by T'aego Pou (1301–1382), who studied with the eleventh-generation Yangqi teacher Shiwu Qinggong (1272–1352); some modern Korean monks and scholars argue that the contemporary Korean Sŏn tradition should be traced back to T'aego and his Yangqi lineage, rather than to Pojo Chinul (1158–1210). The Yangqi school reached Japan in the thirteenth century through pilgrim monks, including Shunjō (1166–1227), who studied with the Yangqi teacher Meng'an Yuancong (1126–1209), and Nanpo Jōmyō (1235–1309), better known by his imperially bestowed title Entsū Daiō Kokushi ("state preceptor," see guoshi), who studied with the ninth-generation teacher Xutang Zhiyu (1185–1269). All Linji lineages in contemporary Japan are affiliated with the Yangqi pai.

**Yangshan Huiji**. (J. Gyōzan/Kyōzan Ejaku; K. Angsan Hyejŏk 仰山慧寂) (807–883). Chinese Chan master and patriarch of the Guiyang zong [alt. Weiyang zong]. Yangshan was a native of Shaozhou prefecture in present-day Guangdong province. According to his biography, Yangshan's first attempt to enter the monastery at age fifteen failed because his parents refused to give their required permission. Two years later he cut off two of his fingers as a sign of his resolve to become a monk and became a śrāmaṇera under the guidance of Chan master Tong (d.u.) of Nanhuasi. After he received his monastic precepts, Yangshan studied the vinayapiṭaka. Yangshan is said to have received the teachings of the circle diagrams from Danyuan Yingzhen (d.u.), and he later became a disciple of Chan master Guishan Lingyou after serving him for fifteen years. He later moved to Mt. Yang in Yuanzhou prefecture (present-day Jiangxi province), whence he acquired his toponym, and established a name for himself as a Chan master. Yangshan later moved to Mt. Dongping in his hometown of Shaozhou, where he passed away in the year 883 (alternative dates for his death are 916 and

891). He was posthumously honored with the title Dengxu dashi (Great Master Clear Vacuity) and a purple robe. He was also named Great Master Zhitong (Penetration of Wisdom). His teachings are recorded in the *Yuanzhou Yangshan Huiji chanshi yulu*. The names of the mountains on which Yangshan and his teacher Guishan resided were used in compound to designate their lineage, the Guiyang.

**Yangs pa can**. (Yangpachen). The monastic residence of the ZHWA DMAR incarnations in Tibet, founded under the direction of the fourth Zhwa dmar Chos kyi grags pa (Chökyi Drakpa, 1453–1524) and located near MTSHUR PHU monastery west of LHA SA; it was also known as Thub bstan Yangs pa can (Tupten Yangpachen). After the tenth Zhwa dmar was found guilty of treason, the monastery was converted to DGE LUGS and renamed Kun bde gling.

**Yang Wenhui**. (J. Yō Bunkai; K. Yang Munhoe 楊文會) (1837–1911). Chinese Buddhist layman at the end of the Qing dynasty, renowned for his efforts to revitalize modern Chinese Buddhism. A native of Anhui province, Yang fled from the Taiping Rebellion to Hangzhou prefecture. In 1862, he serendipitously acquired a copy of the DASHENG QIXIN LUN ("Awakening of Faith According to the Mahāyāna") and became interested in Buddhism. In 1878, he traveled to England, where he served at the Chinese Embassy in London, befriending the Japanese Buddhist scholar NANJŌ BUN'YŪ (1849–1927), who helped him to acquire Chinese Buddhist texts that had been preserved in Japan. After his return to China, Yang established a publishing press called the Jingling Kejing Chu and published more than three thousand Buddhist scriptures. In 1893, ANAGĀRIKA DHARMAPĀLA visited Yang in Shanghai. In 1894, Yang and the British missionary Timothy Richard translated the DASHENG QIXIN LUN into English. In 1907, the Jingling Kejing Chu began to publish primers of Buddhism in various languages. In 1910, Yang also founded the Fojiao Yanjiu Hui (Buddhist Research Society), where he regularly lectured until his death in 1911.

**Yanshou**. (C) (延壽). See YONGMING YANSHOU.

**yantra**. (T. 'khrul 'khor; C. tuxiang; J. zuzō; K. tosang 圖像). In Sanskrit, "diagram" or "instrument." Although the term can have many meanings in Sanskrit, within the Buddhist tradition it is most commonly used to refer to a picture made of images and/or geometric shapes, usually triangles, which are repeated in such a way that they form a pattern. Such magical diagrams are used in tantric rituals and meditations to depict in visual form the power of the invoked deities, representing the universe, or certain spiritual or cosmological powers in the universe. A yantra is commonly understood as rendering through lines and colors the sacred sound of a MANTRA. Yantras are used for such purposes as gaining magical protection, worshipping tantric deities, or facilitating meditation. The term is in some cases interchangeable with a MAṆḌALA, although there are some differences: a yantra is typically small in size while a maṇḍala is variously sized and may even be large enough for a practitioner to enter during the rituals; a yantra, except for those under temple statues, is often portable, while a maṇḍala is not; and deity figures rarely appear on a yantra, while they are common on a maṇḍala. A yantra can be two- or three-dimensional and may range from such simple geometric designs as dots or triangles to more elaborate temple structures. Some texts suggest that merely seeing a maṇḍala or drawing or imagining a yantra also brings benefits. Yantra tattooing (Thai, yak sant) is a common practice in Southeast Asia among both monks and laity. It is generally performed by specialist monks using traditional needles.

**yaoshi**. (J. yakuseki; K. yaksŏk 藥石). In Chinese, lit. "herbal medicine (yao) and stone probes" (shi); "medicine stone," the Chinese Buddhist euphemism for "supper." The VINAYA restricts monks and nuns from eating after noon; anytime afterwards is an "improper time." There are waivers allowed for certain types of "medicine," however, which may legally be consumed. To circumvent this prohibition against eating after noon, the Chinese referred to food consumed after noon as "medicine," and an evening meal therefore euphemistically came to be referred to as a "medicine stone."

**Yaśas**. (P. Yasa; T. Grags pa; C. Yeshe; J. Yasha; K. Yasa 耶舍). An early ARHAT disciple of the Buddha. The son of a wealthy merchant of Vārāṇasī, Yaśas was brought up in luxury. He had three mansions, one for the winter, one for the rainy season, and one for the summer, and was attended by a troupe of female musicians. Once, he happened to awake in the middle of the night and witnessed his attendants sleeping in an indecorous manner. Greatly disturbed, he put on a pair of golden sandals and wandered in the direction of the Deer Park (MṚGADĀVA) where the Buddha was dwelling, exclaiming, "Alas, what distress, what danger." The Buddha saw him approach and, knowing what he was experiencing, called out to him, "Yaśas, come. Here there is neither distress nor danger." Yaśas approached the Buddha, took off his golden sandals, and sat down beside him. The Buddha preached a graduated discourse (ANUPUBBIKATHĀ) to him, at the conclusion of which Yaśas became a stream-enterer (SROTAĀPANNA). He thus became the Buddha's sixth disciple and the first who had not known him prior to his achievement of enlightenment (as had his first five disciples, the bhadravargīya or PAÑCAVARGIKA). Yaśas was also the first person to become an enlightened lay disciple (UPĀSAKA), although he ordained a few minutes later. Later, Yaśas's father, who had come searching for his son, arrived at the Buddha's residence. The Buddha used his magical powers to make Yaśas invisible and, inviting his father to sit, preached a discourse to him. Yaśas's father also became a stream-enterer, while Yaśas, who overheard the sermon from his invisible state, became an arhat. When the Buddha made Yaśas visible to his father, he informed him that, since his son was now an arhat, it would be impossible for him to return home to a householder's life and he would have to become a monk. Yaśas thus became the sixth member of the Buddha's monastic order. Yaśas accompanied the Buddha to his father's house the next day to receive the morning meal. After the meal, the Buddha preached a sermon. Yaśas's mother, SUJĀTĀ, and other members of the household became stream-enterers, his mother thus becoming the first female disciple (UPĀSIKĀ) of the Buddha and the first woman to become a stream-enterer. At that time, fifty-four of Yaśas's friends also were converted and entered the order of monks, swelling its ranks to sixty members. It was at this time that the Buddha directed his disciples to go forth separately and preach the dharma they had realized for the welfare and benefit of the world. ¶ There was a later monk, also named Yaśas, whose protest led to the second Buddhist council (COUNCIL, SECOND), held at VAIŚĀLĪ. Some one hundred years after the Buddha's death, Yaśas was traveling in Vaiśālī when he observed the monks there receiving gold and silver as alms directly from the laity, in violation of the VINAYA prohibition against monks touching gold and silver. He also found that the monks had identified ten points in the vinaya that were identified as violations but that they felt were sufficiently minor to be ignored. The ten violations in question were: (1) carrying salt in an animal horn; (2) eating when the shadow of the sundial was two fingerbreadths past noon; (3) after eating, traveling to another village to eat another meal on the same day; (4) holding several assemblies within the same boundary (SĪMĀ) during the same fortnight; (5) making a monastic decision with an incomplete assembly and subsequently receiving the approval of the absent monks; (6) citing precedent as a justification to violate monastic procedures; (7) drinking milk whey after mealtime; (8) drinking unfermented wine; (9) using mats with a fringe; and (10) accepting gold and silver. Yaśas told the monks that these were indeed violations, at which point the monks are said to have offered him a share of the gold and silver they had collected. When he refused the bribe, they expelled him from the order. Yaśas sought the support of several respected monks in the west, including Sambhūta, ŚĀṆAKAVĀSIN, and REVATA. Together with other monks, they went to Vaiśālī, where they convened a council (SAṂGĪTI) at which Revata submitted questions about each of the disputed points to Sarvagāmin, the eldest monk of the day, who is said to have been a disciple of ĀNANDA. In each case, he said that the practice in question was a violation of the vinaya. Seven hundred monks then gathered to recite the vinaya. Those who did not accept the decision of the council held their own convocation, which they called the MAHĀSĀṂGHIKA or "Great Assembly," the rival group coming to be called the STHAVIRANIKĀYA, or "School of the Elders." This event is sometimes referred to as "the great schism," since it marks the first permanent schism in the order (SAṂGHABHEDA).

**Yasenkanna**. [alt. Yasenkanwa] (夜船閑話). In Japanese, "Idle Talk on a Night Boat"; a short meditative text composed by the ZEN master HAKUIN EKAKU in the RINZAISHŪ, and his most popular piece. The *Yasenkanna* was first published in 1757 and has remained in print ever since. The title seems to be an allusion to the popular saying, "night boat on the Shirakawa River" (Shirakawa yasen), which refers to the story of a man from the countryside and the lies he tells about his trip to Kyōto. Hakuin wrote the *Yasenkanna* to offer beginners of meditation an expedient technique for overcoming "Zen illness" (zenbyō) and fatigue. The *Yasenkanna* details Hakuin's own bout with this illness and his miraculous recovery with the help of a secret technique known as inner discernment or visualization (naikan), which he purports to have learned from the obscure hermit Hakuyū. Different versions of this story also appear in Hakuin's other writings, such as the *Kanzanshi sendai kimon*, *Orategama*, and *Itsumadegusa*.

**Yaśodharā**. (P. Yasodharā; T. Grags 'dzin ma; C. Yeshutuoluo; J. Yashudara; K. Yasudara 耶輸陀羅). The Sanskrit proper name of wife of the prince and BODHISATTVA, SIDDHĀRTHA GAUTAMA, and mother of his son, RĀHULA (she is often known in Pāli sources as Rāhulamātā, Rāhula's Mother); she eventually became an ARHAT, who was declared by the Buddha to be foremost among nuns possessing the six superknowledges (ABHIJÑĀ; P. abhiññā). According to Pāli accounts, she was born on the same day as Prince Gautama and had skin the color of gold, hence another of her epithets, Bhaddā Kaccānā. She is also referred to in Pāli commentaries as Bimbā. Yaśodharā married the prince when she was sixteen, after he had proved his superior skill in archery and other manly arts. She was chief consort in a harem of forty thousand women. On the day her son, Rāhula, was born, the prince renounced the world and abandoned his wife, child, and palace to become a mendicant. According to another version of the story, Rāhula was conceived on the night of the prince's departure and was not born until the night of the prince's enlightenment, six years later. Yaśodharā was so heartbroken at her husband's departure that she took up his ascetic lifestyle, eating only one meal per day and wearing the yellow robes of a mendicant. When the Buddha returned to his former palace in KAPILAVASTU after his enlightenment, Yaśodharā was allowed the honor of worshipping him in the manner she saw fit. After seven days, as the Buddha was about to depart, Yaśodharā instructed her son Rāhula to ask for his inheritance. In response, the Buddha instructed ŚĀRIPUTRA to ordain his son. As Rāhula was the first child to be admitted to the order, he became the first Buddhist novice (ŚRĀMAṆERA). Yaśodharā and Rāhula's grandfather ŚUDDHODANA were greatly saddened at losing the child and heir to the order; hence, at Śuddhodana's request, the Buddha passed a rule that, thenceforth, no child should be ordained without the consent of its parents. When later the Buddha allowed women to enter the order, Yaśodharā became a nun (BHIKṢUṆĪ) under MAHĀPRAJĀPATĪ, who was chief of the nuns' order and the Buddha's stepmother. Yaśodharā cultivated insight and became an arhat with extraordinary supranormal powers. She could recall her past lives stretching back an immeasurable age and one hundred thousand eons without effort. The JĀTAKA records numerous occasions when Yaśodharā had been the wife of the bodhisattva in earlier existences. Also mentioned as the wife of the Buddha is Gopā, although it is unclear whether this refers to another wife or is another name for Yaśodharā.

**Yaśomitra**. (T. Grags pa bshes gnyen) (fl. c. late sixth century). Indian ĀBHIDHARMIKA scholastic, probably affiliated with the SAUTRĀNTIKA school, and author of the SPHUṬĀRTHĀ-ABHIDHARMAKOŚAVYĀKHYĀ, an important commentary on VASUBANDHU'S ABHIDHARMAKOŚABHĀṢYA. His commentary is noted for its detail and clarity, and for its attempt to identify the adherents of the various doctrinal positions mentioned by Vasubandhu. The text is preserved in both Sanskrit and Tibetan. Yaśomitra's text was among the first ABHIDHARMA works to be studied in Europe; it was one of the Sanskrit manuscripts send by BRIAN HOUGHTON HODGSON from Kathmandu to Paris, where it was read by EUGÈNE BURNOUF, who discusses it in his *Introduction à l'histoire du Buddhisme indien* (1844).

**Yasutani Hakuun**. (安谷白雲) (1885–1973). Japanese ZEN teacher in the SŌTŌSHŪ, who was influential in the West. Born in Japan, Yasutani attended public school until he entered a Sōtō Zen seminary at the age of thirteen. Yasutani was trained as a teacher and taught elementary school. He was married at the age of thirty and raised five children before turning to a life dedicated to the work of a Sōtō priest. He met Sogaku Harada in 1924 while lecturing in Tōkyō. Yasutani began intensive study with Harada roshi and dedicated his life to teaching the dharma to laypeople. Yasutani organized a group called the Sanbō Kyodan (Fellowship of the Three Jewels), which became independent of the Sōtō school in 1954. Yasutani was the teacher of PHILIP KAPLEAU, who studied with him for eight years, and maintained a close relationship with him until 1967. Kapleau's *The Three Pillars of Zen* was based heavily on Yasutani's teachings. Yasutani traveled to the United States for the first time at the age of seventy-seven, three years after SHUNRYŪ SUZUKI arrived. For seven years, Yasutani taught Zen to many laypeople in the USA and, although he had prepared to live somewhat permanently in the country, a tuberculosis test prevented him from receiving a permanent visa. In his later years, Yasutani continued to travel in the United States as well as in India. He preferred to teach Zen in a nonmonastic environment. He died in Kamakura in 1973.

**Yatana Htut-hkaung zedi**. The Yatana Htut-hkaung Pagoda (Burmese, JEDI; P. cetī; S. CAITYA) is located on Minwun Hill in the northern part of the Sagaing Hills in Upper Burma (Myanmar). It was built in 1315 CE by Princess Soe Min-gyi, the daughter of Sagaing's founder, King Athinkaya Saw-yun. Over the course of time, the neighboring village, along with its monastery and line of SAYADAWS (abbots), came to be known as Htut-hkaung. One such abbot was Htut-hkaung Sayadaw, who flourished in the nineteenth century, was greatly respected by King MINDON (r. 1853–1878) for his learning and piety. The king built for the sayadaw a famous monastery named Mahādhammika Kyaung where he taught scripture and meditation to many hundreds of monks and nuns. This sayadaw was a prolific writer, and his catechisms are famous in Burmese literature. He received many titles from the King Mindon and was believed by some to have been an arahant (S. ARHAT).

**yathābhūtajñānadarśana**. (P. yathābhūtañāṇadassana; C. rushi zhijian; J. nyojitsu chiken; K. yŏsil chigyŏn 如實知見). In Sanskrit, "knowledge and vision that accord with reality"; a crucial insight leading to deliverance (VIMUKTI), which results in dispassion toward the things of this world because of seeing things as they actually are: i.e., as impermanence (ANITYA), suffering (DUḤKHA), and nonself (ANĀTMAN). "Knowledge and vision (jñānadarśana)" is usually interpreted to suggest the direct insight into things "as they are" (yathābhūta), meaning these three marks of existence (TRILAKṢAṆA), or sometimes the FOUR NOBLE TRUTHS. Yathābhūtajñānadarśana is presumed to be closely related to wisdom (PRAJÑĀ), but with one significant difference: yathābhūtajñānadarśana is the first true insight, but it is intermittent and weak, while prajñā is continuous and strong. Seeing things as they are, however, is intense enough that the insight so gleaned is sufficient to transform an ordinary person (PṚTHAGJANA) into an ĀRYA. ¶ In the *Upanisāsutta* of the SAṂYUTTANIKĀYA, the standard twelvefold chain of dependent origination (PRATĪTYASAMUTPĀDA) is connected to an alternate chain that is designated the "supramundane dependent origination" (P. lokuttara-paṭiccasamuppāda; S. lokottara-pratītyasamutpāda), which outlines the process leading to liberation and prominently includes the knowledge and vision that accord with reality. Here, the last factor in the standard chain, that of old age and death (JARĀMARAṆA), is substituted with suffering (P. dukkha; S. DUḤKHA), which in turn becomes the first factor in this alternate series. According to the *Nettipakaraṇa*, a Pāli exegetical treatise, this chain of supramundane dependent origination consists of: (1) suffering (P. dukkha; S. duḥkha), (2) faith (P. saddhā; S. ŚRADDHĀ), (3) delight or satisfaction (P. pāmojja; S. prāmodya), (4) rapture or joy (P. pīti; S. PRĪTI), (5) tranquility or repose (P. passaddhi; S. PRAŚRABDHI), (6) mental ease or bliss (SUKHA), (7) concentration (SAMĀDHI), (8) knowledge and vision that accord with reality (P. yathābhūtañāṇadassana; S. yathābhūtajñānadarśana), (9) disgust (P. nibbidā; S. NIRVEDA), (10) dispassion (P. virāga; S. VAIRĀGYA), (11) liberation (P. vimutti; S. VIMUKTI), and (12) knowledge of the destruction of the contaminants (P. āsavakkhayañāṇa; S. āsravakṣayajñāna; see ĀSRAVAKṢAYA). The *Kimatthiyasutta* of the AṄGUTTARANIKĀYA gives a slightly different version of the first links, replacing suffering and faith with (1) observance of precepts (P. kusalasīla; S. kuśalaśīla) and (2) freedom from remorse (P. avippaṭisāra; S. avipratisāra). In both formulations, yathābhūtajñānadarśana arises as a result of the preceding factor of meditative concentration (samādhi); it is regarded as the specific awareness (JÑĀNA) of the nature of reality, which is seen (DARŚANA) vividly and directly. In this context, yathābhūtajñānadarśana is essentially synonymous with insight (VIPAŚYANĀ). As this chain of transcendental dependent origination is sometimes interpreted, the stage of faith (P. saddhā; S. śraddhā) is made manifest through generosity (DĀNA) and observing precepts (ŚĪLA), which frees the mind from feelings of remorse and guilt (avipratisāra). The stage of delight or satisfaction (prāmodya) refers to a satisfied or relaxed state of mind, which is freed from any mental disturbances that might prevent concentration. The stages of rapture (prīti), bliss (sukha), and concentration (samādhi) are factors associated with the four levels of meditative absorption (DHYĀNA). The knowledge and vision that accord with reality arise in dependence on the preceding samādhi; it is able to destroy the afflictions (KLEŚA), rather than simply suppress them, as occurs in the state of concentration, and thus leads to liberation from SAṂSĀRA. The fact that samādhi provides a basis for seeing things "as they are," which generates an insight that can bring about liberation, demonstrates the explicitly soteriological dimensions of concentration in a Buddhist meditative context. ¶ In Pāli sources, such as the VISUDDHIMAGGA, yathābhūtajñānadarśana is the fifteenth of eighteen principal types of superior insight (P. mahāvipassanā), which liberate the mind from delusions regarding the world and the self. The eighteen insights are contemplations of: (1) impermanence (aniccānupassanā); (2) suffering (dukkhānupassanā); (3) nonself (anattānupassanā); (4) aversion (nibbidānupassanā); (5) dispassion (virāgānupassanā); (6) extinction (nirodhānupassanā); (7) abandoning (paṭinissaggānupassanā); (8) waning (khayānupassanā); (9) disappearing (vayānupassanā); (10) change (vipariṇāmānupassanā); (11) signlessness (animittānupassanā); (12) wishlessness (appaṇihitānupassanā); (13) emptiness (suññatānupassanā); (14) advanced understanding into phenomena (adhipaññādhammavipassanā); (15) knowledge and vision that accord with reality (yathābhūtañāṇadassana); (16) contemplation of danger (ādīnavānupassanā); (17) contemplation involving reflection (paṭisaṅkhānupassanā); and (18) contemplation of turning away (vivaṭṭanānupassanā). The counterparts which are overcome through these eighteen insights are: (1) the idea of permanence, (2) the idea of pleasure, (3) the idea of self, (4) delighting, (5) greed, (6) origination, (7) grasping, (8) the idea of compactness, (9) the accumulation of action (kamma), (10) the idea of lastingness, (11) signs, (12) desire, (13) misinterpretation, (14) misinterpretation due to grasping, (15) misinterpretation due to confusion, (16) misinterpretation due to reliance, (17) nonreflection or thoughtlessness, (18) misinterpretation due to entanglement.

**yathābhūtaparijñāna**. (T. ji lta ba mkhyen pa'i ye shes). An alternate term for YATHĀVADBHĀVIKAJÑĀNA (knowledge of the mode).

**yathāvadbhāvikajñāna**. (T. ji lta ba mkhyen pa'i ye shes; C. ruli zhi; J. nyorichi; K. yŏri chi 如理智). In Sanskrit, lit. "knowledge of the mode"; a buddha's knowledge of the single mode of being of the universe. This type of knowledge is typically mentioned in conjunction with the "knowledge of the multiplicities" (YĀVADBHĀVIKAJÑĀNA), a buddha's knowledge of each of the phenomena of the universe in its specificity. Only a buddha possesses these two knowledges and possesses them simultaneously; thus, only he is able to perceive all of the various phenomena of the universe as well as their ultimate nature. This joint awareness is referred to as the simultaneous knowledge of the two truths (SATYADVAYA).

**yāvadbhāvikajñāna**. (T. ji snyed pa mkhyen pa'i ye shes; C. ruliang zhi; J. nyoryōchi; K. yŏryang chi 如量智). In Sanskrit, lit., "knowledge of the multiplicities" or "knowledge of the varieties"; a buddha's knowledge of each of the phenomena of the universe in its specificity. This type of knowledge is typically mentioned in conjunction with a buddha's "knowledge of the mode" (YATHĀVADBHĀVIKAJÑĀNA), which understands the single mode of being of the universe. Only a buddha possesses these two knowledges and possesses them simultaneously; thus, only he is able to perceive all of the various phenomena of the universe as well as their ultimate nature. This joint awareness is referred to as the simultaneous knowledge of the two truths (SATYADVAYA).

**yavana**. (T. yol ba; C. biandi; J. henji; K. pyŏnji 邊地). In Sanskrit (from Greek Ionian), "peripheral" or "outlying regions"; referring to the regions beyond the civilizing influences of Buddhism and higher spiritual culture. The term was used to designate Greeks (Ionians) and later even Arab Muslims. In Buddhist cosmology, the term was used to designate regions north and west of India proper, which are inhabited by illiterate, barbaric peoples hostile to Buddhism. The birth into a "peripheral region" is considered to be one of the "insuperable difficulties" (see AKṢAṆA) to the attainment of enlightenment in the present lifetime. See also BIANDI.

**Yazawin-kyaw**. In Burmese, "Celebrated Chronicle"; the traditional title given to the MAHĀSAMMATAVAṂSA, the oldest extant yazawin, or Burmese (Myanmar) royal chronicle. It was completed in two installments by the monk MAHĀSĪLAVAṂSA of AVA, the first completed in 1502, the second in 1520. The chronicle is written in mixed Burmese and Pāli and contains the earliest surviving examples of the Burmese nissaya (Pāli to Burmese word-by-word translation) style of writing. The text follows roughly the outline of the MAHĀVAṂSA and devotes most of its coverage to the history of Buddhist dynasties in India and Sri Lanka. Only the last seventh of the work concerns the history of Burma from the time of the Buddha through the PAGAN (Bagan) and Ava periods. The text contains the assertion that the Buddhism of Burma was established by the elder Mahāpuṇṇa during the lifetime of the Buddha and hence is older and longer-lived than that of Sri Lanka. The Yazawin-kyaw concludes with an account of the meritorious deeds of Shwenan-kyaw-shin (r. 1502–1527), the king of Ava at the time the work was composed.

**ye dharmā**. In Sanskrit, lit. "those phenomena..."; the opening words of perhaps the most famous synopsis of the teachings of Buddhism; the full declaration in Sanskrit is "ye dharmā hetuprabhavā hetuṃ teṣāṃ tathāgato hy avadat teṣāṃ ca yo nirodha, evaṃ vādī mahāśramaṇaḥ": "Of those phenomena produced through causes, the TATHĀGATA has proclaimed their causes (HETU) and also their cessation (NIRODHA). Thus has spoken the great renunciant (ŚRAMAṆA)." This statement plays a central role in the story of ŚĀRIPUTRA'S conversion. Śāriputra, who was a disciple of the agnostic teacher SAÑJAYA VAIRĀṬĪPUTRA, encountered one of the Buddha's five original disciples (PAÑCAVARGIKA), AŚVAJIT. Noticing Aśvajit's serene countenance, Śāriputra asked him who his teacher might be, to which Aśvajit replied that his teacher was the Buddha. When Śāriputra asked what it was that the Buddha taught, Aśvajit demurred, explaining that he had only recently renounced the life of a householder and was unable to present the teaching in full. Śāriputra asked Aśvajit to give him the gist of the Buddha's teaching. Aśvajit replied with this famous ye dharmā line. Immediately upon hearing these words, Śāriputra is said to have gained the rank of stream-enterer (SROTAĀPANNA), the first stage of sanctity (ĀRYAMĀRGA). He then asked the whereabouts of the Buddha and was ordained, going on to become the disciple most renowned for his wisdom. Aśvajit's précis points to the central importance of causality in the Buddha's teachings and provides a kind of summary of the FOUR NOBLE TRUTHS. The Buddha has identified the causes (such as KARMAN and KLEŚA) of those things that have causes (such as suffering, S. DUḤKHA), and he has also identified their cessation in the experience of NIRVĀṆA. What may therefore have begun as a simple statement to mollify an eager questioner eventually became a slogan and ultimately a MANTRA, the very recitation of which was said to produce apotropaic powers. Like a mantra, the words of the ye dharmā slogan were often transcribed phonetically, rather than translated, into various languages across Asia. These words were also often written on strips of paper and enshrined in STŪPAS; they thus became a dharma-verse relic (ŚARĪRA), serving as a substitute for a bodily relic of the Buddha.

**Yellow Hats**. (C. huangmao 黃帽). A popular designation in both European languages and Chinese for the DGE LUGS sect of Tibetan Buddhism, whose monks do indeed wear yellow hats. Although the term zhwa gser, or "yellow hat," does occur occasionally in Tibetan as a term of self-appellation for the Dge lugs, the Western and Chinese division of major Tibetan sects into Yellow Hats, RED HATS, and BLACK HATS has no corollary in Tibetan Buddhism and should be avoided.

**Yel pa bka' brgyud**. (Yelpa Kagyü). One of the four major and eight minor subsects of the BKA' BRGYUD sect of Tibetan Buddhism (BKA' BRGYUD CHE BZHI CHUNG BRGYAD), originating with Ye shes brtsegs pa (b. 1134), a student of Bka' brgyud hierarch PHAG MO GRU PA RDO RJE RGYAL PO. After a period of decline, it was revived by CHOS KYI 'BYUNG GNAS but was latter absorbed into KARMA BKA' BRGYUD.

**ye shes**. (yeshe). In Tibetan, lit. "primordial knowledge," with ye meaning "original" or "primordial." The term renders the Sanskrit JÑĀNA; in the RNYING MA sect of Tibetan Buddhism, it refers to the originally pure mind. See RIG PA; JÑĀNA.

**Ye shes mtsho rgyal**. (Yeshe Tsogyal) (c. 757–817). A renowned female Tibetan Buddhist master, generally regarded as a wisdom ḌĀKINĪ and venerated especially as consort and disciple of the Indian adept PADMASAMBHAVA. Ye shes mtsho rgyal was born into an aristocratic family in central Tibet, south of LHA SA. According to traditional biographical accounts, a nearby lake miraculously swelled at the time of her birth and she was thus given the name "victor of the lake" (mtsho rgyal). This lake, near the cave complex of SGRAG YANG RDZONG, is believed to still hold Ye shes mtsho rgyal's life essence (bla). Her remarkable beauty even at a young age drew numerous suitors, but rather than submit to a marriage arranged by her father, she fled in order to undertake religious practice. She spent a brief period of time in the court of the Tibetan ruler KHRI SRONG LDE BTSAN (perhaps as one of his wives), after which she met Padmasambhava and was accepted as one of his chief disciples. In addition to receiving and practicing numerous tantric instructions, Ye shes mtsho rgyal helped to conceal many of Padmasambhava's treasure teachings (GTER MA), many of which are said to be her transcriptions of Padmasambhava's teachings. She is regarded as the first Tibetan to achieve buddhahood in a single lifetime. As a wisdom ḍākinī, she is also known as Bde chen rgyal mo ("Great Bliss Queen").

**Ye shes 'od**. (Yeshe Ö) (947–1024). A Tibetan king of the western region of GU GE credited with inspiring a revival of Buddhism that initiated the latter dissemination (PHYI DAR) of Buddhism in Tibet. He decried the state of Tibetan Buddhist practice, especially the practice of TANTRA, in a famous ordinance (bka' shog), complaining that people were engaging in murder and illicit sex under the guise of the tantric practices of "liberation" (grol) and "union" (sbyor). According to a famous story, Ye shes 'od was captured by a Gar log Turk chieftain while seeking to raise the capital necessary to invite ATIŚA DĪPAṂKARAŚRĪJÑĀNA to Tibet. He then sacrificed his own life by commanding his grandnephew BYANG CHUB 'OD to use whatever gold had been accumulated not as a ransom for his own release, but rather as an offering to the Indian scholar. Atiśa was so moved by the king's act of selflessness that, despite his previous declinations, he agreed to make the journey north. Traditional accounts also suggest that Ye shes 'od sponsored a group of twenty-two young scholars to study Indian languages and tantric literature in Kashmir (see KASHMIR-GANDHĀRA), of whom only two survived: the translators RIN CHEN BZANG PO and RNGOG LEGS PA'I SHES RAB. Both the story of his noble death for the sake of Atiśa's invitation and the story of his sponsorship of Rin chen bzang po present difficulties in chronology, suggesting that they are embellishments. He is also credited with inspiring the establishment of numerous religious institutions, including THO LING, NYAR MA, and TA PHO. He is also known as Lha bla ma (Lha Lama).

**Ye shes sde**. (Yeshe De) (fl. late eighth/early ninth century). A Tibetan translator (LO TSĀ BA) during the early dissemination (SNGA DAR) of Buddhism in Tibet; a native of Ngam shod of the Sna nam clan, also referred to by the clan name Zhang. He is said to have been a disciple of both PADMASAMBHAVA and ŚRĪSIṂHA, from whom he received tantric instructions, especially in the SEMS SDE (mind class) of RDZOGS CHEN. He collaborated with some fifteen Indian scholars, among them Jinamitra, Śīlendrabodhi, and Dānaśīla, on the translation of as many as 347 different works, if the later canonical records are correct. His translations includes upwards of 163 Mahāyāna sūtras, among them the PRAJÑĀPĀRAMITĀ, AVATAṂSAKASŪTRA, and RATNAKŪṬASŪTRA collections, translations of the YOGĀCĀRABHŪMI and other basic MADHYAMAKA and YOGĀCĀRA treatises, as well as a number of works by his contemporaries ŚĀNTARAKṢITA and KAMALAŚĪLA. He is also credited with the translation of tantric works that would come to be known as the "old translations" used by the RNYING MA sect. He is said to have been a practitioner of the VAJRAKĪLAYA tantras. He is also author of a number of original compositions, among them the *Lta ba'i khyad par* ("Differences in Views"), preserved in both a BSTAN 'GYUR and DUNHUANG version, which divides the Madhyamaka school into Sautrāntika-Madhyamaka and Yogācāra-Madhyamaka. See also DPAL BRTSEGS; KLU'I RGYAL MTSHAN.

**yi bao**. (C) (依報). See ER BAO.

**yi dam**. In Tibetan, a term often translated as "meditational deity" or "tutelary deity." In the practice of Buddhist tantra, it is the enlightened being, whether male or female, peaceful or wrathful, who serves as the focus of one's SĀDHANA practice. One is also to visualize one's tantric teacher (VAJRĀCĀRYA) as this deity. The term is of uncertain origin and does not seem to be a direct translation of a Sanskrit term, although iṣṭadevatā is sometimes identified with the term. The etymology that is often given sees the term as an abbreviation of yid kyi dam tshig, meaning "commitment of the mind." Traditionally, the yi dam is selected by throwing a flower onto a MAṆḌALA, with the deity upon whom the flower lands becoming the "chosen deity." However, when one receives a tantric initiation, the central deity of that tantra typically becomes the yi dam, with daily practices of offering and meditation often required. Through the propitiation of the deity and recitation of MANTRA, it is said that the deity will bestow accomplishments (SIDDHI). In the practice of DEVATĀYOGA, one meditates upon oneself as that deity in order to achieve buddhahood in the form of that deity. The yi dam is considered one of the three roots (rtsa gsum) of tantric practice, together with the GURU and the ḌĀKINĪ: the guru is considered to be the source of blessings; the yi dam, the source of accomplishments; and the ḍākinī, the source of activities. These three roots are considered the inner refuge, with the Buddha, DHARMA, and SAṂGHA being the outer refuge, and the channels (NĀḌĪ), winds (PRĀṆA), and drops (BINDU) being the secret refuge.

**yidashi**. (一大事). In Chinese, the "one great matter." See DASHI.

**Yifu**. (J. Gifuku, K. Ŭibok 義福) (661–736). Chinese CHAN master associated with the Northern school (BEI ZONG) of the early Chan tradition. Yifu was a native of Luzhou prefecture in present-day Shanxi province, who became a student of the lay master DU FEI (d.u.), the author of the CHUAN FABAO JI, at Fuxiansi in Luoyang. After Yifu received the full monastic precepts in 690, he went to the monastery of YUQUANSI in Jingzhou prefecture to study with the eminent Chan master SHENXIU. Yifu became Shenxiu's close disciple and continued to study under him probably until his master's death. Later, Yifu moved to the monastery of Huagansi on ZHONGNANSHAN, where he lived for about twenty years. During his stay at Huagansi, Yifu attracted a large following. In 722, he moved again to the grand monastery of DACI'ENSI in Chang'an, where he was patronized by the upper echelons of Tang Chinese society. At the request of Emperor Xuanzong (r. 712–756), Yifu returned once again to Luoyang and resided at the monasteries of Fuxiansi and Nanlongxingsi. He received the posthumous title Chan Master Dazhi (Great Wisdom).

**yi ge brgya pa**. (yi ge gyapa). In Tibetan, "hundred-syllable MANTRA"; term used to describe a number of lengthy MANTRAS, most commonly that of VAJRASATTVA, recited as part of a Tibetan tantric confession and purification practice. This is one of the preliminary practices (SNGON 'GRO) of the RNYING MA sect of Tibetan Buddhism, involving one hundred thousand repetitions of the Vajrasattva mantra.

**yiji**. (J. yuige; K. yuge 遺偈). In Chinese, "bequeathed verse" or "death verse"; a verse (C. ji; lit. S. GĀTHĀ) left by eminent monks and nuns, especially in the CHAN school, just before the moment of death, as a final expression of their enlightenment experience; also called a "taking leave of the world hymn" (cishi song) or, especially in the Korean tradition, a "moment of death gāthā" (imjongge). The verse may be either recited or written and is left as the master's last bequeathed teaching immediately before he passes away, often delivered as part of a final sermon. The final instructions of a buddha or a monk for the edification of his disciples are referred to as a "bequeathed teaching" (yijiao; see also YIJIAO JING), and the tradition of specifically bequeathing a verse as part of this final instruction is thought to have originated in the Tang-dynasty Chan tradition. Such bequeathed verses usually consisted of four lines of four, five, or seven Sinographs per line and thus are similar in format to other types of verses found within the Chan tradition, such as an "enlightenment hymn" (C. wudao song), the verse recited by a student upon achieving enlightenment, and "dharma-transmission gāthā" (C. chuanfa ji), the verse bestowed on a dharma successor as an authorization to teach. As an example of such a bequeathed verse, HONGZHI ZHENGJUE (1091–1157), a well-known teacher in the CAODONG ZONG, is said to have written the following gāthā just before his death: "An illusory fantasy and a flower in the sky (KHAPUṢPA),/ Are these sixty-seven years,/ A white bird fades into the mist,/ The autumnal waters merge with the sky." Not all renowned Chan masters left yiji and others derided the practice. The yiji of DAHUI ZONGGAO (1089–1163), the influential LINJI ZONG master and a contemporary of Hongzhi, expressed ironically his indifference to yiji: "Birth is thus,/ Death is thus,/ Verse or no verse,/ What's the fuss?" In Japan, handwritten death verses were treasured as precious calligraphic art and a virtual relic of the deceased master. They were thus often hung in the abbot's quarters (J. hōjō, C. FANGZHANG) or in the retirement cloisters.

**Yijiao jing**. (J. Yuikyōgyō; K. Yugyo kyŏng 遺教經). In Chinese, "Scripture on the Bequeathed Teachings"; also known as *Foshuo banniepan jiaojie jing* ("Scripture on the Admonishments Taught by the Buddha [before] his PARINIRVĀṆA") and *Fo yijiao jing* ("Scripture on the Teachings Bequeathed by the Buddha"). Sanskrit and Tibetan versions of this text are not known to have existed. The Chinese translation of this text is attributed to KUMĀRAJĪVA, but the text is now widely assumed to be an indigenous Chinese Buddhist scripture (see APOCRYPHA). The sūtra is set against the backdrop of the Buddha's parinirvāṇa, when he imparts his final instructions to the gathered disciples. The Buddha instructs his disciples to uphold the precepts and regard them as their teacher after his entry into parinirvāṇa. He then instructs them to control sensuality (KĀMA) and cultivate serenity and DHYĀNA. Finally, the Buddha asks the assembly if they have any questions regarding the FOUR NOBLE TRUTHS. When no one replies, the Buddha succinctly expounds upon impermanence and the need to seek liberation (VIMOKṢA). This sūtra bears striking resemblances in style and content to the MAHĀPARINIBBĀNASUTTA and AŚVAGHOṢA's BUDDHACARITA. Along with the SISHI'ER ZHANG JING and GUISHAN JINGCE, the *Yijiao jing* has been cherished by the CHAN tradition for its simple and clear exposition. Sometime during the late Tang and early Song dynasties, the three texts were edited together as the *Fozu sanjing* ("The Three Scriptures of the Buddhas and Patriarchs") and recommended to Chan neophytes.

**yijing**. (C) (疑經). In Chinese, lit. "suspicious scriptures" or "scriptures of doubtful [provenance]." See APOCRYPHA.

**Yijing**. (J. Gijō; K. Ŭijŏng 義淨) (635–713). Chinese Buddhist monk and pilgrim. Ordained at the age of twenty, Yijing dreamed of following in the footsteps of the renowned pilgrims FAXIAN and XUANZANG. He eventually set out for India in 671 via the southern maritime route. After visiting the major Indian pilgrimage sites (see MAHĀSTHĀNA), Yijing traveled to the monastic university at NĀLANDĀ, where he remained for the next ten years. On his return trip to China, Yijing stopped at ŚRĪVIJAYA (Palembang in Sumatra) to continue his studies. He praised the monks there for their high level of learning, describing them as primarily HĪNAYĀNA in affiliation. It was in Śrīvijaya that he began to compose his record of his travels, the NANHAI JIGUI NEIFA ZHUAN, which remains an important source on the practice of Buddhism in the many regions where he traveled and for understanding the various NIKĀYA affiliations of the period. It was also during his time in Śrīvijaya that Yijing began his translation of the massive MŪLASARVĀSTIVĀDA VINAYA. When he ran out of paper and ink, he made a brief trip back to China in 689 to retrieve more writing supplies and then returned to Śrīvijaya. After a thirty-year sojourn overseas, Yijing finally returned to China in 695 with some four hundred Sanskrit texts and three hundred grains of the Buddha's relics (ŚARĪRA). Yijing was warmly welcomed in the capital of Luoyang by Empress WU ZETIAN, who appointed him to the monastery of Foshoujisi. Later, from 695 to 699, Yijing participated in ŚIKṢĀNANDA's new translation of the AVATAṂSAKASŪTRA and devoted the next decade or so to the translation of the scriptures that he had brought back with him from India. In addition to the Mūlasarvāstivāda vinaya, his translations also include several important YOGĀCĀRA treatises and TANTRAS. His writings also include a collection of the biographies of renowned East Asian Buddhist pilgrims to India, the DA TANG XIYU QIUFA GAOSENG ZHUAN.

**yijing sanzang**. (J. yakukyō sanzō; K. yŏkkyŏng samjang 譯經三藏). In Chinese, lit. "master of the three repositories, translator of scriptures." See TREPIṬAKA.

**Yingluo jing**. (C) (瓔珞經). See PUSA YINGLUO BENYE JING.

**Yinguang**. (J. Inkō; K. In'gwang 印光) (1862–1940). Chinese monk renowned for his efforts to revitalize modern Chinese Buddhism, especially of the PURE LAND tradition; also sometimes referred to as the thirteenth patriarch of the Chinese JINGTU school and as Chang Cankui Seng (Forever Ashamed Monk). Yinguang was a native of Geyang in Shaanxi province. At a young age, Yinguang suffered from an eye ailment, probably conjunctivitis, which he is said to have cured by studying the Buddhist scriptures. He was formally ordained later at the monastery of Xing'an Shuangqisi in his home province. Yinguang's interest in pure land thought and practice is said to have been catalyzed by his encounter with the writings of the CHAN master Jixing Chewu (1741–1810), who came to be known as the twelfth patriarch of the pure land tradition in

China. For more than twenty years, he resided in isolation at the monastery of Fayusi on the sacred mountain of PUTUOSHAN, where he studied the scriptures and practiced the recitation of the name of the buddha AMITĀBHA (NIANFO; cf. NAMU AMIDABUTSU). Yinguang's reputation grew with the publication of his private correspondences and his collected essays known as *Jingtu jueyi lun* ("Treatise on Resolving Doubts about the Pure Land"). His writings were often critical of Chan and emphasized the efficacy of pure land practice instead. Yinguang also worked to restore monasteries and to republish important pure land writings until his death in 1940. See also TAIXU; XUYUN.

**yingwu Chan**. (J. ōmuzen; K. aengmu Sŏn 鸚鵡禪). In Chinese, lit. "parrot Chan"; a CHAN Buddhist expression referring to the way some practitioners merely parrot with their mouths the pithy sayings and GONG'AN dialogues of the patriarchs and masters (ZUSHI), but fail to realize their true message and attain enlightenment for themselves. This pejorative description is also applied to pundits of the traditional Buddhist scholastic schools (C. jiao, see K. KYO), whose intellectual erudition and doctrinal prowess were caricatured as "parrot Chan," in contrast to the Chan school's supposed subitist spiritual approach that did not rely on mere intellectual understanding (see BULI WENZI). These pundits are likened to parrots in that they also mimic other people's understanding through their doctrinal exegeses, but without comprehending it themselves. Cf. KOUTOU CHAN.

**yingyan**. (應驗). In Chinese, "responsive attestation." See GANYING.

**yinian sanqian**. (J. ichinen sanzen; K. illyŏm samch'ŏn 一念三千). In Chinese, lit. "the TRICHILIOCOSM in a single instant of thought"; a TIANTAI teaching that posits that any given thought-moment perfectly encompasses the entirety of reality both spatially and temporally. An instant (KṢAṆA) of thought refers to the shortest period of time and the trichiliocosm (TRISĀHASRAMAHĀSĀHASRALOKADHĀTU) to the largest possible universe; hence, according to this teaching, the microcosm contains the macrocosm and temporality encompasses spatiality. Thus, whenever a single thought arises, there also arise the myriad dharmas; these two events occur simultaneously, not sequentially. Any given thought can be categorized as belonging to one of the ten realms of reality (DHARMADHĀTU). For example, a thought of charity metaphorically promotes a person to the realm of the heavens at that instant, whereas a subsequent thought of consuming hatred metaphorically casts the same person into the realm of the hells. Tiantai exegetes also understood each of the ten dharmadhātus as containing and pervading all the other nine dharmadhātus, making one hundred dharmadhātus in total (ten times ten). In turn, each of the one hundred dharmadhātus contains "ten aspects of reality" (or the "ten suchnesses"; see SHI RUSHI) that pervade all realms of existence, which makes one thousand "suchnesses" (qianru, viz., one hundred dharmadhātus times ten "suchnesses"). Finally the one thousand "suchnesses" are said to be found in the categories of the "five aggregates" (SKANDHA), "sentient beings" (SATTVA), and the physical environment (guotu). These three latter categories times the one thousand "suchnesses" thus gives the "three thousand realms," which are said to be present in either potential or activated form in any single moment of thought. This famous dictum is attributed to the eminent Chinese monk TIANTAI ZHIYI, who spoke of the "trichiliocosm contained in the mind during an instant of thought" (sanqian zai yinian xin) in the first part of the fifth roll of his magnum opus, MOHE ZHIGUAN. Zhiyi's discussion of this dictum appears in a passage on the "inconceivable realm" (ACINTYA) from the chapter on the proper practice of ŚAMATHA and VIPAŚYANĀ. Emphatically noting the "inconceivable" ability of the mind to contain the trichiliocosm, Zhiyi sought through this teaching to emphasize the importance and mystery of the mind during the practice of meditation. Within the context of the practice of contemplation of mind (GUANXIN), this dictum also anticipates a "sudden" theory of awakening (see DUNWU). TIANTAI exegetes during the Song dynasty expanded upon the dictum and applied it to practically every aspect of daily activity, such as eating, reciting scriptures, and ritual prostration. See also SHANJIA SHANWAI.

**yinke**. (J. inka; K. in'ga 印可). In Chinese, lit. "seal of/in approval," "certification" and often seen in Western sources in its Japanese pronunciation inka; a seal of approval, certification, or transmission, which is given by masters in the various CHAN traditions across East Asia to practitioners who, in their estimation, have attained a satisfactory level of awakening or maturity of understanding to serve as public exponents of their lineage. Because these lineages are presumed to trace back to BODHIDHARMA, the founder of the Chan school, and ultimately to the person of the Buddha himself, the person who receives such certification is considered to be qualified to speak for the current generation of Chan adepts on behalf of the Chan patriarchs, masters, and even the Buddha, to accept and train students, and to give them certification in turn once their training is complete. The manner of certification differs within traditions. Certification often entails admission into the master's lineage; the conferral of such symbols of religious authority and memorial worship as robes, bowls, chowries (BINGFU), or portraits; and the right to serve in high ecclesiastical office in a sectarian monastery. In the modern ZEN traditions of Japan, certification is offered by a RŌSHI, a teacher who has himself been previously certified. Especially in the Japanese traditions, receiving inka need not necessarily be testimony to the profundity of a person's enlightenment experience, but may simply be public recognition that a student has sufficient maturity and ability to serve as abbot or hold other high ecclesiastical office in the monasteries and temples of a specific sectarian lineage. In some cases, yinke is an abbreviation for yinke zhengming, or "certification via seal of approval." Certification is also known as yinding (seal of meditation), renke (acceptance and approval), and yinzheng (seal and certify). See also CHUANFA; FASI.

**yinke zhengming**. (J. inka shōmyō; K. in'ga chŭngmyŏng 印可證明). In Chinese, "certification via a seal of approval." See YINKE.

**yinsheng nianfo**. (J. inshō nenbutsu/inzei nenbutsu; K. insŏng yŏmbul 引聲念佛). In Chinese, "intoning [the name of] the Buddha by drawing out the sound" (see NIANFO); one of the "five-tempo intonations of [the name of] the Buddha" (WUHUI NIANFO) devised by FAZHAO. Yinsheng nianfo involves the long, drawn-out intonation of the name of the buddha AMITĀBHA. Even before Fazhao, the practice of yinsheng nianfo is known to have been practiced by the CHAN master CHŎNGJUNG MUSANG (680–756 [alt. 684–762]), who recommended this practice for those who wished to attain "no recollection" (wuyi), "no thought" (WUNIAN), and "no forgetting" (mowang).

**Yinyuan Longxi**. (J. Ingen Ryūki 隱元隆琦) (1592–1673). Chinese CHAN master and founding patriarch of the Japanese ŌBAKUSHŪ. Yinyuan was a native of Fuzhou, in present-day Fujian province. He began his training as a monk in his early twenties on PUTUOSHAN and was formally ordained several years later at Wanfusi on Mt. Huangbo. Yinyuan continued his training under the Chan master MIYUN YUANWU and, while serving under the Chan master FEIYIN TONGRONG at Wanfusi Yinyuan, was formally recognized as an heir to Feiyin's lineage in 1633. Seven years later, in 1640, Yinyuan found himself at the monastery of Fuyansi in Zhejiang province and at Longquansi in Fujian province in 1645. The next year, in 1646, he returned to Mt. Huangbo and revitalized the community at Wanfusi. In 1654, at the invitation of Yiran Xingrong (1601–1668), the abbot of the Chinese temple of Kōfukuji in Nagasaki, Yinyuan decided to leave China to escape the succession wars and political turmoil that had accompanied the fall of the Chinese Ming dynasty. He was to be accompanied by some thirty monks and artisans. Due to political issues, however, Yinyuan was only allowed to enter Japan a year later in 1655. That same year, largely through the efforts of the Japanese monk Ryōkei Shōsen (1602–1670), the abbot of MYŌSHINJI, Yinyuan was allowed to stay at Ryōkei's home temple of Fumonji under virtual house arrest. The next year when Yinyuan expressed his wishes to return to China, Ryōkei arranged a visit to Edo and an audience with the young shōgun. At the end of 1658, Yinyuan made the trip to Edo and won the patronage of the shōgun and his ministers. With their support, Yinyuan began the construction of MANPUKUJI in Uji in 1661. The site came to be known as Mt. Ōbaku, the Japanese pronunciation of his mountain home of Huangbo, and served as the center for the introduction of Ming-dynasty Chan into Japan. Yinyuan's teachings, especially those concerning monastic rules, catalyzed institutional and doctrinal reform among the entrenched Japanese ZEN communities. In 1664, Yinyuan left his head disciple MU'AN XINGTAO in charge of all administrative matters involving the monastery and retired to his hermitage on the compounds of Manpukuji. Nine years later Emperor Gomizunoo (r. 1611–1629) bestowed upon him the title state preceptor (J. kokushi, C. GUOSHI) Daikō Fushō (Great Radiance, Universal Illumination). He died shortly thereafter. Yinyuan brought many texts and precious art objects with him from China, and composed numerous texts himself such as the *Huangbo yulu*, *Hongjie fayi*, *Fushō kokushi kōroku*, *Ōbaku oshō fusō goroku*, *Ingen hōgo*, and *Ōbaku shingi*.

**Yiqiejing yinyi**. (J. Issaikyō ongi; K. Ilch'egyŏng ŭmŭi 一切經音義). In Chinese, "Pronunciation and Meaning of All the Scriptures"; a specialized Chinese glossary of Buddhist technical terminology. As more and more Indian and Central Asian texts were being translated into Chinese, the use of Sanskrit and Middle Indic transcriptions and technical vocabulary increased, leading to the need for comprehensive glossaries of these abstruse terms. Because of the polysemous and sacred character of such Buddhist doctrinal concepts as BODHI, NIRVĀṆA, and PRAJÑĀ, many Chinese translators also preferred to transcribe rather than translate such crucial terms, so as not to limit their semantic range to a single Chinese meaning. The Indian pronunciations of proper names were also commonly retained by Chinese translators. Finally, the spiritual efficacy thought to be inherent in the spoken sounds of Buddhist spells (MANTRA) and codes (DHĀRAṆĪ) compelled the translators to preserve as closely as possible in Chinese the pronunciation of the Sanskrit or Middle Indic original. By the sixth century, the plethora of different transcriptions used for the same Sanskrit Buddhist terms led to attempts to standardize the Chinese transcriptions of Sanskrit words, and to clarify the obscure Sinographs and compounds used in Chinese translations of Buddhist texts. This material was compiled in various Buddhist "pronunciation and meaning" (yinyi) lexicons, the earliest of which was the twenty-five-roll *Yiqiejing yinyi* compiled by the monk Xuanying (fl. c. 645–656). Xuanying, a member of the translation bureau organized in the Chinese capital of Chang'an by the renowned Chinese pilgrim, translator, and Sanskritist XUANZANG (600/602–664), compiled his anthology in 649 from 454 of the most important MAHĀYĀNA, ŚRĀVAKAYĀNA, VINAYA, and ŚĀSTRA materials, probably as a primer for members of Xuanzang's translation team. His work is arranged by individual scripture, and includes a roll-by-roll listing and discussion of the problematic terms encountered in each section of the text. For the more obscure Sinographs, the entry provides the fanqie (a Chinese phonetic analysis that uses paired Sinographs to indicate the initial and final sounds of the target character), the Chinese translation, and the corrected transcription of the Sanskrit, according to the phonologically sophisticated transcription system developed by Xuanzang. Xuanying's compendium is similar in approach to its predecessor in the secular field, the *Jingdian shiwen*, compiled during the Tang dynasty in thirty rolls by Lu Deming (c. 550–630). The monk Huilin (783–807) subsequently incorporated all of Xuanying's terms and commentary into an expanded glossary that included difficult terms from more than 1,300 scriptures; Huilin's expansion becomes the definitive glossary used within the tradition. Still another yinyi was compiled later during the Liao dynasty by the monk Xilin (d.u.). In addition to their value in establishing the Chinese interpretation of Buddhist technical terms, these "pronunciation and meaning" glossaries also serve as important sources for studying the Chinese phonology of their times.

**yiqing**. (J. gijō; K. ŭijŏng 疑情). In Chinese, lit. the "sensation of doubt," or simply "doubt"; a feeling of puzzlement and sense of questioning that is a crucial factor in the meditation technique of "questioning meditation" (KANHUA CHAN) as systematized by DAHUI ZONGGAO (1089–1163). In the kanhua technique, doubt refers to the puzzlement and perplexity that the meditator feels when trying to understand the conundrum that is the GONG'AN (public case) or HUATOU (meditative topic). This doubt arises from the inability to understand the significance of the huatou through rational thought. This loss of confidence in one's conceptual and intellectual faculties releases the mind from the false sense of security engendered through habitual ways of thinking, creating a feeling of frustration that is often compared to "a mosquito trying to bite an iron ox." The meditator's sense of self ultimately becomes so identified with the huatou that the intense pressure created by the doubt "explodes" (C. po), freeing the mind from the personal point of view that is the self. Hence, by cutting off conceptualization and producing a state of intense concentration, the sensation of doubt helps to impel meditation forward toward the experience of awakening (WU). The term "sensation of doubt" was not coined by Dahui. One of its earliest usages is in the enlightenment poem of Luohan Guichen (867–928), the teacher of FAYAN WENYI (885–958), which describes enlightenment as shattering the "ball of doubt" (YITUAN). Dahui's grandteacher, WUZU FAYAN (d. 1104), also taught his students to keep the great ball of doubt. But it was Dahui who put doubt at the core of his interpretation of kanhua Chan meditation; for him, the sensation of doubt becomes an effective antidote to conceptual thinking as well as the force that drives the student forward toward enlightenment. The Chinese term yi is also used as the translation for the Sanskrit term VICIKITSĀ, or skeptical doubt, which was one of the five hindrances (NĪVARAṆA) to meditative absorption (DHYĀNA). But rather than being viewed as it had been in India as a hindrance, in Dahui's interpretation doubt instead plays a crucial role in the meditative process.

**Yishan Yining**. (J. Issan Ichinei; K. Ilsan Illyŏng 一山一寧) (1247–1317). Chinese CHAN master in the LINJI ZONG; a native of Taizhou prefecture in present-day Zhejiang province. At a young age, Yishan became a student of a certain Wudeng Rong (d.u.) at the monastery of Hongfusi on Mt. Fu near his hometown in Taizhou. He was later ordained at the monastery of Puguangsi in Siming in Zhejiang province and continued to study VINAYA at Yingzhensi and TIANTAI thought and practice at Yanqingsi. Yishan then began his training in Chan under several teachers. He eventually became a disciple of Wanji Xingmi (d.u.), a disciple of the Chan master CAOYUAN DAOSHENG. In 1299, the Yuan emperor Chengzong (r. 1294–1307) bestowed upon him the title Great Master Miaoci Hongji (Subtle Compassion, Universal Salvation) and an official post as the overseer of Buddhist matters in Zhejiang. That same year, he was sent to Japan as an envoy of the court, but was detained temporarily at the temple of Shūzenji in Izu by the Kamakura shogunate. When the Hōjō rulers learned of Yishan's renown in China, Yishan was invited to reside as abbot of the powerful monasteries of KENCHŌJI, ENGAKUJI, and Jōchiji in Kamakura. In 1313, Yishan was invited by the retired Emperor Gouda (r. 1274–1287) to reside as the third abbot of the monastery NANZENJI in Kyōto. Yishan had many students in Japan including the eminent Japanese monk MUSŌ SOSEKI. Yishan became ill and passed away in the abbot's quarters (J. hōjō; C. FANGZHANG) of Nanzenji in 1317. The emperor bestowed upon him the title state preceptor (J. kokushi; C. GUOSHI) Issan (One Mountain). Yishan is also remembered for his calligraphy and for introducing to Japan the new commentaries written by the great Neo-Confucian scholar Zhu Xi (1130–1200) to Japan. He and his disciples, such as Shiliang Rengong (1266–1334), Mujaku Ryōen (d.u.), Monkei Ryōsō (d. 1372), and Tōrin Yūkyū (d. 1369), contributed much to the development of GOZAN culture in Japan.

**yishen**. (J. yuishin; K. yusin 遺身). In Chinese, lit., "to let go of the body," viz., "self-immolation." See SHESHEN.

**Yisheng xianxing jiao**. (C) (一乘顯性教). See HUAYAN WUJIAO.

**yituan**. (J. gidan; K. ŭidan 疑團). In Chinese, "ball of doubt"; also referred to as dayituan, or "great ball of doubt." Although the term appears in a verse recorded in the JINGDE CHUANDENG LU that is attributed to Luohan Guichen (867–928), the teacher of FAYAN WENYI, it was the CHAN master DAHUI ZONGGAO who systematized and popularized its use. Dahui probably inherited the notion of a ball of doubt from his teacher YUANWU KEQIN, whose teacher WUZU FAYAN also mentions a ball of doubt in his teachings. Dahui described the arousal of the sensation of doubt (YIQING) or the ball of doubt as an important tool in his meditative approach called KANHUA CHAN, or investigation of the meditative "topic" (HUATOU).

**yixin**. (S. ekacitta; J. isshin; K. ilsim 一心). In Chinese, "one mind"; the ground of being and the principle (LI) foundational to all phenomena (SHI). The LAṄKĀVATĀRASŪTRA and the DASHENG QIXIN LUN ("Awakening of Faith According to the Mahāyāna"), both central texts in the TATHĀGATAGARBHA corpus of literature, treat the "one mind" as a central doctrine. The *Laṅkāvatārasūtra* states that the "calm extinction [of NIRVĀṆA] is called the one mind, and this one mind is called the tathāgatagarbha." The *Dasheng qixin lun* presents all of Buddhism in terms of the one mind and its two aspects: the mind's true-thusness aspect (xin zhenru men) and production-and-cessation aspect (xin shengmie men). The *Dasheng qixin lun*, arguably the most influential tathāgatagarbha text within the East Asian Buddhist tradition, has long been considered the principal treatise outlining the doctrine of the one mind and its associations with the YOGĀCĀRA theory of consciousness and tathāgatagarbha thought. ¶ The exegeses to the *Dasheng qixin lun* by JINGYING HUIYUAN (523–592), WŎNHYO (617–686), and FAZANG (643–712), which the tradition has regarded as its three major commentaries (san dashu), have each elucidated in considerable detail the foundational role that the notion of the one mind plays in that text. Fazang, for example, glossed the one mind of the *Dasheng qixin lun* as the "one tathāgatagarbha mind" and thus identified the one mind with the tathāgatagarbha; the two aspects of the one mind, true thusness and production-and-cessation, were correlated, respectively, with either MADHYAMAKA and YOGĀCĀRA or principle (li) and phenomena (shi). Fazang thus places tathāgatagarbha thought above both the SAN LUN ZONG (the Chinese analogue of the Madhyamaka school) and the FAXIANG ZONG (Yogācāra) teachings in his doctrinal taxonomy (panjiao; see JIAOXIANG PANSHI). By contrast, Huiyuan's commentary treats the one mind within the context of the nine-consciousnesses theory of the SHE LUN ZONG, an early Yogācāra-oriented strand of Chinese Buddhist thought. In his analysis of the two aspects of the one mind, Huiyuan correlates the true-thusness aspect of the one mind with the ninth "immaculate consciousness" (AMALAVIJÑĀNA); he correlates the production-and-cessation aspect of the one mind with the eighth "storehouse consciousness" (ĀLAYAVIJÑĀNA). Unlike Fazang's interpretation, tathāgatagarbha is here not identified with the one mind but is instead viewed as the production-and-cessation aspect of the mind. In Wŏnhyo's case, rather than seeking as Fazang did to distinguish the Faxiang teachings of Yogācāra from tathāgatagarbha thought, he sought instead to reconcile the Faxiang perspective on consciousness with the *Dasheng qixin lun*'s analysis of mind. Like Huiyuan, Wŏnhyo identified the tathāgatagarbha with the production-and-cessation aspect of the one mind. ¶ The one mind is also a central theme of the ZONGJING LU, an encyclopedic CHAN anthology compiled by YONGMING YANSHOU (904–976) in the FAYAN ZONG, which seeks to unify the various Chinese schools of Buddhism, including HUAYAN, Yogācāra, and TIANTAI, and to demonstrate the compatibility of doctrinal teachings and meditative practice. Yanshou draws on the doctrinal classification schema of GUIFENG ZONGMI (780–841), the Chan scholiast who was also the fifth patriarch of the Huayan school, in positing three broad strands of Buddhist teaching: dharma characteristics (Faxiang zong), destruction of characteristics (Poxiang), dharma nature (FAXING ZONG). Yanshou states that the Faxing (dharma nature) teachings, which include both the Huayan and Chan schools and which are based on tathāgatagarbha thought, treat both aspects of true thusness or the one mind, that is, the aspect of "immutability" (bubian) and "adaptability" (lit., "according to conditions," suiyuan); the Faxiang (dharma characteristics) teachings, by contrast, only treat the aspect of "adaptability." ¶ In the TIANTAI school, one mind or sometimes one thought (yinian) is said to be the ground of all things in existence in both their tainted and pure manifestations, a notion expressed in the aphorism "one thought [contains] the TRICHILIOCOSM" (YINIAN SANQIAN), one of the main doctrines of the school. The Tiantai teaching that "one mind," viz., a single instance of thought, contains all three "viewpoints" (yixin sanguan) also expresses how the three inseparable aspects of phenomena (SANDI)—viz., the truth of emptiness (kongdi), the truth of being only provisionally real (jiadi), and the truth of the mean (zhongdi)—are each contained in one thought moment. In the PURE LAND tradition, one mind generally refers to single-minded recollection (NIANFO) of, especially, the buddha AMITĀBHA, and is a synonym of one-pointedness of mind.

**yixin chuanxin**. (J. ishin denshin; K. isim chŏnsim 以心傳心). In Chinese, "mind-to-mind transmission." An oft-repeated phrase used mainly by the East Asian CHAN traditions to refer to a special transmission of the "mind" of the Buddha from master to disciple in a "telepathic" way that does not rely on words or letters (see JIAOWAI BIECHUAN and BULI WENZI). In an attempt to distinguish itself from the other Buddhist traditions that sought the teachings of the Buddha in sūtras and commentaries, the burgeoning Chan tradition of the eighth and ninth centuries emphasized the nonverbal transmission of the Buddha's teachings. The notion of mind-to-mind transmission has thus served as an important trope in the self-fashioning of the Chan tradition. Mind-to-mind transmission is often explained by reference to a famous Chan legend that first appears in the *Tiansheng guangdeng lu*. While at Vulture Peak (GṚDHRAKŪṬAPARVATA), the Buddha is said to have raised a flower in front of a large assembly, whereupon the elder MAHĀKĀŚYAPA smiled in response. The Buddha then announced that he had thereby entrusted his "treasury of the true dharma eye" (ZHENGFAYANZANG) to Mahākāśyapa, thus recognizing him as the Buddha's successor and first patriarch (ZUSHI). For this legend, see NIANHUA WEIXIAO.

**Yixing**. (J. Ichigyō; K. Irhaeng 一行) (683–727). In Chinese, "Single Practice"; a famous student of CHAN and master of esoteric Buddhism (MIJIAO), translator, and distinguished astronomer. Yixing was a native of Julu prefecture in present-day Hebei province. He became a monk under the eminent Chan master PUJI (651–739) in the Northern school (BEI ZONG) of the early Chan tradition and also studied the VINAYA under a monk by the name of Huizhen (d.u.). Having made a name for himself at the monastery of Guoqingsi on Mt. Tiantai, in 717, Yixing was invited by Emperor Xuanzong (r. 712–756) to the palace in Luoyang. While residing at the palace, Yixing became a disciple of the TREPIṬAKA ŚUBHAKARASIṂHA and, together, they translated the MAHĀVAIROCANĀBHISAṂBODHISŪTRA. Based on Śubhakarasiṃha's oral interpretations provided in the course of preparing their translation, Yixing also composed an important commentary on the sūtra, the *Darijing shu*. In 727, Yixing's reputation in astronomy and calendrics prompted the emperor to have him devise a new calendar, which is known as the Dayan li. Yixing also devised an elaborate celestial globe, which used hydraulic power to portray the precise movements of the sun, moon, and constellations across the firmament. After his death, he was bestowed the posthumous title Chan master Dahui (Great Wisdom).

**yixing sanmei**. (S. ekavyūhasamādhi; J. ichigyō zanmai; K. irhaeng sammae 一行三昧). In Chinese, "single-practice SAMĀDHI." The term yixing sanmei seems to first appear in a passage in the Chinese translation of the SAPTAŚATIKĀPRAJÑĀPĀRAMITĀSŪTRA: "The DHARMADHĀTU has only a single mark; to take the dharmadhātu as an object is called one-practice samādhi." Two practices are then recommended by the text for cultivating yixing sanmei, viz, the perfection of wisdom (PRAJÑĀPĀRAMITĀ) and recollection of the Buddha's name (S. BUDDHĀNUSMṚTI; C. NIANFO). The concept of yixing sanmei was later incorporated into the apocryphal Chinese treatise DASHENG QIXIN LUN and the influential meditation manual MOHE ZHIGUAN. TIANTAI ZHIYI, the author of the *Mohe Zhiguan*, identified the practice of constant sitting, the first of the so-called four kinds of samādhi (sizhong sanmei), with yixing sanmei. Famous teachers of the early CHAN community, such as DAOXIN, HUINENG, and HEZE SHENHUI, also emphasized the importance of yixing sanmei, which they identified with seated meditation (ZUOCHAN) and the cultivation of prajñāpāramitā. According to the LIUZU TANJING ("Platform Sūtra of the Sixth Patriarch"), Huineng interpreted yixing sanmei as the maintenance of a straightforward mind (yizhi xin) while walking, standing, sitting, and lying. Shenhui identified yixing sanmei with "no mind" (WUXIN; see also WUNIAN).

**Yixuan**. (C) (義玄). See LINJI YIXUAN.

**yizhi Chan**. (J. isshi no zen; K. ilchi sŏn 一指禪). In Chinese, "one-finger Chan"; the famous pedagogical technique used by the CHAN master Juzhi Yizhi (c. ninth century) and his teacher Hangzhou Tianlong (d.u.) in the lineage of MAZU DAOYI. "One-finger Chan" refers to Juzhi's propensity to answer any question he was asked by simply raising one finger, so as not to allow any conceptual understanding of Buddhism to arise in the student's mind. The phrase appears in Case 19 of the BIYAN LU and Case 3 of the WUMEN GUAN, and is frequently cited in Chan sources. In one well-known Chan case (GONG'AN), Juzhi is said to have cut off the finger of a boy who mimicked him without understanding the meaning of the gesture.

**yizi guan**. (J. ichijikan; K. ilcha kwan 一字關). In Chinese, "one-word checkpoint" or "one-word barrier"; a pedagogical device developed by YUNMEN WENYAN (864–949), the founder of the YUNMEN ZONG of the classical CHAN tradition, which used only a single utterance to respond to a student's question. For example, once a monk asked him, "When you kill your parents, you repent before the Buddha. But when you kill the buddhas and patriarchs, to whom do you repent?" Yunmen answered, "Lu" ("exposed"). Another time a monk asked him, "What is the treasury of the true dharma eye (ZHENGFAYANZANG)?" Yunmen answered, "Pu" ("universal"). Such terse answers offered no basis for conceptual understanding, instead demanding that students have a direct realization of truth. These one-word checkpoints were highly praised by DAHUI ZONGGAO for fostering especially close concentration during KANHUA CHAN meditation: "Once you enter into the gate of the one-word GONG'AN, even nine oxen wouldn't be able to pull you out."

**yoga**. (T. sbyor ba/rnal 'byor; C. xiu/xiuxing/xiuxi/yuqie; J. shu/shugyō/shujū/yuga; K. su/suhaeng/susŭp/yuga 修/修行/修習/瑜伽). In Sanskrit, "bond," "restraint," and by extension "spiritual discipline"; in Buddhism, a generic term for soteriological training or contemplative practice, including tantric practice.

**Yogabhāvanāmārga**. [alt. Bhāvanāyogamārga; Yogabhāvanāpatha] (T. Rnal 'byor bsgom pa'i lam). In Sanskrit, "Path of Yogic Cultivation"; a work on the BODHISATTVA path usually attributed to the eighth-century Indian master Jñānagarbha, who is known as the teacher of ŚĀNTARAKṢITA (c. 725–788) and a disciple of Śrīgupta. It is presumed that the *Yogabhāvanāmārga* is an example of the later MADHYAMAKA school's attention to the theme of the stages of meditative cultivation (BHĀVANĀ), as best exemplified by KAMALAŚĪLA's three BHĀVANĀKRAMAS. There are two Jñānagarbhas known to the tradition, one from the early ninth century and the other from the eleventh century. Some scholars suggest that the commentary to the Maitreya chapter of the SAṂDHINIRMOCANASŪTRA should be attributed to the first Jñānagarbha, while authorship of the *Yogabhāvanāmārga* should be ascribed to the second. The *Yogabhāvanāmārga*, along with Jñānagarbha's two other works, the *Satyadvayavibhaṅga* ("Analysis of the Two Truths") and its autocommentary *Satyadvayavibhaṅgavṛtti* ("Commentary on Analysis of the Two Truths"), are only extant in Tibetan translation.

**Yogācāra**. (T. Rnal 'byor spyod pa; C. Yuqiexing pai; J. Yugagyōha; K. Yugahaeng p'a 瑜伽行派). In Sanskrit, "Practice of YOGA"; one of the two major MAHĀYĀNA philosophical schools (along with MADHYAMAKA) in India, known especially for its doctrines of "mind-only" (CITTAMĀTRA) or "representation-only" (VIJÑAPTIMĀTRATĀ), the TRISVABHĀVA, and the ĀLAYAVIJÑĀNA. In addition, much of the exposition of the structure of the Mahāyāna path (MĀRGA) and of the Mahāyāna ABHIDHARMA derives from this school. The texts of the school were widely influential in Tibet and East Asia. Although several of the terms associated with the school occur in such important Mahāyāna sūtras as the DAŚABHŪMIKASŪTRA, the LAṄKĀVATĀRASŪTRA, and especially the SAṂDHINIRMOCANASŪTRA, the exposition of the key doctrines was largely the work of two

Indian scholastics of the fourth to fifth centuries CE, the half brothers ASAṄGA and VASUBANDHU and their commentators, especially STHIRAMATI and DHARMAPĀLA. Asaṅga's major works include the central parts of the YOGĀCĀRABHŪMI, the MAHĀYĀNASAṂGRAHA, and the ABHIDHARMASAMUCCAYA. Vasubandhu's most famous Yogācāra works are the VIṂŚATIKĀ and the TRIṂŚIKĀ (his most famous work of all, the ABHIDHARMAKOŚABHĀṢYA, is said to have been composed prior to his conversion to the Mahāyāna). Among the "five books of MAITREYA" (see BYAMS CHOS SDE LNGA), three are particularly significant in Yogācāra: the MADHYĀNTAVIBHĀGA, the DHARMADHARMATĀVIBHĀGA, and the MAHĀYĀNASŪTRĀLAṂKĀRA. Important contributions to Yogācāra thought were also made by the logicians DIGNĀGA and DHARMAKĪRTI. Although Yogācāra and Madhyamaka engaged in polemics, in the latter phases of Buddhism in India, a synthesis of Yogācāra and Madhyamaka took place in the works of such authors as ŚĀNTARAKṢITA and KAMALAŚĪLA; Tibetan doxographers dubbed this synthesis YOGĀCĀRA-SVĀTANTRIKA-MADHYAMAKA. ¶ Yogācāra authors offered detailed presentations and analyses of virtually all of the important topics in Buddhist thought and practice, built upon an edifice deriving from meditative experience. The school is perhaps most famous for the doctrines of "mind-only" (cittamātra) and "representation-only" (vijñaptimātra), according to which the conception of the objects of experience as existing external to and independent of the consciousness perceiving them was regarded as the fundamental ignorance and the cause of suffering. Instead of the standard six consciousnesses (VIJÑĀNA) posited by other Buddhist schools (the five sensory consciousnesses and the mental consciousness), some Yogācāra texts described eight forms of consciousness: these six, plus the seventh "afflicted mind" (KLIṢṬAMANAS), which mistakenly generates the false notion of a perduing self (ĀTMAN), and the eighth foundational, or "storehouse," consciousness (ālayavijñāna). This foundational consciousness is the repository of seeds (BĪJA) or imprints (VĀSANĀ) produced by past actions (KARMAN) that fructify as experience, producing simultaneously consciousness and the objects of consciousness. The afflicted mind mistakenly regards the foundational consciousness as a permanent and independent self. The doctrine of the three natures (trisvabhāva), although variously interpreted, is also often explained in light of the doctrine of representation-only. The imaginary nature (PARIKALPITA) refers to misconceptions, such as the belief in self and in the existence of objects that exist apart from consciousness. The dependent nature (PARATANTRA) encompasses impermanent phenomena, which are products of causes and conditions. The consummate nature (PARINIṢPANNA) is reality, classically defined as the absence of the imaginary nature in the dependent nature. By removing these latent predispositions from the ālayavijñāna and overcoming the mistaken bifurcation of experience between a perceiving subject and perceived objects (GRĀHYAGRĀHAKAVIKALPA), a transformation of consciousness (ĀŚRAYAPARĀVṚTTI) occurs which turns the deluded mind of the sentient being into the enlightenment cognition of the buddhas (BUDDHAJÑĀNA), with the ālayavijñāna being transformed into the mirrorlike wisdom (ĀDARŚAJÑĀNA). In the realm of soteriology, much of what would become the standard Mahāyāna elaboration of the five paths (PAÑCAMĀRGA) and the bodies (KĀYA, e.g., TRIKĀYA) of a buddha is found in works by Yogācāra authors, although there are important differences between Yogācāra and Madhyamaka on a number of key soteriological questions, including whether there is one vehicle (EKAYĀNA) or three final vehicles (TRIYĀNA), that is, whether all beings are destined for buddhahood, or whether some, such as the ARHATs of the mainstream Buddhist schools, are stuck in a soteriological dead end. ¶ Not all the scholastics regarded as Yogācāra exegetes adhered to all of the most famous doctrines of the school. The most common division of the school is into those who do and do not assert the existence of eight consciousnesses (and hence the ālayavijñāna). The former, who include Asaṅga and Vasubandhu, are called "followers of scripture" (āgamānusārin), and the latter, who include the famous logicians DIGNĀGA and DHARMAKĪRTI, are called "followers of reasoning" (nyāyānusārin). Yogācāra strands of Buddhism were extremely influential in the development of indigenous East Asian schools of Buddhism, including the mature schools of HUAYAN and even CHAN. For specifically East Asian analogues of Yogācāra, see FAXIANG ZONG, XIANG ZONG, DI LUN ZONG, and SHE LUN ZONG.

**Yogācārabhūmiśāstra**. [alt. Yogācārabhūmi] (T. Rnal 'byor spyod pa'i sa'i bstan bcos; C. Yuqieshidi lun; J. Yugashijiron; K. Yugasaji non 瑜伽師地論). In Sanskrit, "Treatise on the Stages of Yogic Practice"; an encyclopedic work that is the major treatise (ŚĀSTRA) of the YOGĀCĀRA school of Indian Buddhism. It was widely influential in East Asia and Tibet, being translated into Chinese by XUANZANG between 646 and 648 and into Tibetan circa 800. Authorship is traditionally ascribed to ASAṄGA (or, in China, to MAITREYA), but the size and scope of the text suggest that it is the compilation of the work of a number of scholars (possibly including Asaṅga) during the fourth century CE. The work is divided into five major sections. The first and longest, comprising approximately half the text, is called the "Multiple Stages" (Bahubhūmika or Bhūmivastu) and sets forth the stages of the path to buddhahood in seventeen sections. The two most famous of these sections (both of which are preserved in Sanskrit and which circulated as independent works) are the ŚRĀVAKABHŪMI and the BODHISATTVABHŪMI, the latter providing one of the most detailed discussions of the bodhisattva path (MĀRGA) in Indian literature. In this section, many of the central doctrines of the Yogācāra school are discussed, including the eight consciousnesses, the ĀLAYAVIJÑĀNA, and the three natures (TRISVABHĀVA). The structures and practices of the paths of the ŚRĀVAKA, PRATYEKABUDDHA, and BODHISATTVA are presented here in the form that would eventually become normative among MAHĀYĀNA scholasts in general (not just adherents of Yogācāra). The second section, "Compendium of Resolving [Questions]" (Viniścayasaṃgrahaṇī), considers controversial points that arise in the previous section. The third section, "Compendium of Interpretation" (Vyākhyānasaṃgrahaṇī), examines these points in light of relevant passages from the sūtras; it is interesting to note that the majority of the texts cited in this section are Sanskrit ĀGAMAs rather than Mahāyāna sūtras. The fourth, called "Compendium of Synonyms" (Paryāyasaṃgraha) considers the terms mentioned in the sūtras. The fifth and final section, "Compendium of Topics" (Vastusaṃgraha), considers central points of Buddhist doctrine, including PRATĪTYASAMUTPĀDA and BODHI. This section also contains a discussion of VINAYA and (in the Chinese version) ABHIDHARMA.

**Yogācāra-Svātantrika-Madhyamaka**. (T. Rnal 'byor spyod pa'i dbu ma rang rgyud pa). According to Tibetan exegetes, who coined the term, one of the two branches of the SVĀTANTRIKA school of MADHYAMAKA, together with the SAUTRĀNTIKA-SVĀTANTRIKA-MADHYAMAKA. Its main proponents include ŚĀNTARAKṢITA and KAMALAŚĪLA. Like YOGĀCĀRA, the school holds that external objects do not exist and that objects are of the nature of consciousness. Like MADHYAMAKA, the school holds that consciousness is empty of true existence. In its presentation of the three vehicles (TRIYĀNA), it correlates each vehicle with a different wisdom, thus bringing together the views of the HĪNAYĀNA, Yogācāra, and Madhyamaka. In order to achieve liberation from rebirth as an ARHAT, the ŚRĀVAKA must understand that a perduring self (ATMAN) does not exist. A PRATYEKABUDDHA must understand that objects, and hence the external world, do not exist separately from the consciousnesses that perceive them, thereby abandoning the GRĀHYAGRĀHAKAVIKALPA, the misconception of there being a bifurcation between subject and object. In order to achieve buddhahood, the BODHISATTVA must understand the emptiness (ŚŪNYATĀ) of all phenomena.

**yogatantra**. (T. rnal 'byor rgyud). One of the four traditional Indian categories of tantric texts. In a late Indian categorization of Buddhist TANTRA, a hierarchy was established that placed texts into one of four categories, in descending order: ANUTTARAYOGATANTRA, yogatantra, CARYĀTANTRA, and KRIYĀTANTRA. The precise meaning of these categories, their parameters, and their contents were widely discussed, especially in Tibet. In one influential description, yogatantra was said to emphasize internal yoga over external ritual practice and therefore did not employ the practice of sexual union. An examination of texts included in this category shows, however, that this description is somewhat arbitrary. Important texts classed as yogatantras include the SARVATATHĀGATATATTVASAṂGRAHA, the MAÑJUŚRĪMŪLAKALPA, the SARVADURGATIPARIŚODHANATANTRA, and the VAJRAŚEKHARA. MAṆḌALAs with the buddha VAIROCANA as the central deity occur often in the yogatantras.

**yogin**. (T. rnal 'byor pa; C. xiuxing ren; J. shugyōnin; K. suhaeng in 修行人). A male practitioner of YOGA (generally in the generic sense of meditative practice) who has gained some level of attainment in his practice. The term can be used to refer to any advanced Buddhist practitioner, although it refers especially to advanced practitioners of Buddhist TANTRA.

**yoginī**. (T. rnal 'byor ma). A female practitioner of YOGA, or contemplative practice, but used especially to refer to female adepts of Buddhist TANTRA, particularly those who engage in tantric rituals (including sexual rituals) with tantric YOGINs. The term is sometimes synonymous with ḌĀKINĪ.

**yoginītantra**. (T. rnal 'byor ma'i rgyud). Also known as "mother tantras" (MĀTṚTANTRA) and "wisdom tantras" (T. shes rab kyi rgyud), one of the two categories into which the ANUTTARAYOGATANTRAs are divided, the other being "father tantras" (PITṚTANTRA). Developing in India from the SIDDHA tradition, the yoginītantras apparently receive this name because the majority (and in some cases all) of the deities in the tantra's MAṆḌALA are female. According to a traditional explanation, these tantras emphasize wisdom (PRAJÑĀ), especially the mind of clear light (PRABHĀSVARACITTA), while father tantras emphasize method (UPĀYA), especially the illusory body (MĀYĀDEHA). See CAKRASAṂVARATANTRA.

**yogipratyakṣa**. (T. rnal 'byor mngon sum; C. dingguan zhi; J. jōkanchi; K. chŏnggwan chi 定觀知). In Sanskrit, "yogic direct perception"; a specific variety of direct perception (PRATYAKṢA) that is typically presumed to derive from meditative practice (BHĀVANĀ; YOGA). A direct intuition of the real obtained through meditative practice, this type of understanding was accepted as a valid means of knowledge by most of the traditional Indian religious schools. In Buddhism, the psychological analysis of the notion of yogipratyakṣa and the related yogijñāna (yogic knowledge or cognition) was undertaken by DHARMAKĪRTI (c. 600–670) in his PRAMĀṆAVĀRTTIKA and NYĀYABINDU, as well as by his commentators. Dharmakīrti's predecessor DIGNĀGA (c. 480–540) had posited that there were only two reliable sources of knowledge (PRAMĀṆA): direct perception (PRATYAKṢA) and logical inference (ANUMĀNA). Dharmakīrti, however, subdivided direct perception (pratyakṣa) into four subtypes, viz., sensory cognition (indriyajñāna), mental discrimination (MANOVIJÑĀNA), self-awareness (SVASAṂVEDANA), and yogic cognition (yogijñāna). In Dharmakīrti's analysis, yogic cognition (yogijñāna) is a form of yogic perception (yogipratyakṣa), because it fulfills the two conditions of perception (pratyakṣa): (1) it is devoid of conceptual construction (KALPANĀ); and (2) it is a cognition that is "nonerroneous" (abhrānta), viz., real. The treatment of yogipratyakṣa in the literature thus focuses on how yogipratyakṣa fulfills these two conditions of perception. Yogic knowledge is devoid of conceptual construction (kalpanā), Dharmakīrti maintains, because it is nonconceptual (akalpa; NIRVIKALPA) and thus "vivid" or "distinct" (spaṣṭa). This type of perception is therefore able to perceive reality directly, without the intercession of mental images or concepts. Since yogic cognition is said to be devoid of conceptual construction, this raises the issue of its second condition, its lack of error. Why is meditatively induced perception true and reliable? How does a meditator's yogic perception differ from the hallucinations of the deranged, since both of them presume they have a vivid cognition of an object? The reason, Dharmakīrti maintains, is that the objects of yogic knowledge are "true" or "real" (bhūta; sadbhūta), whereas hallucinations are "false" or "unreal" objects (abhūta; asadbhūta). The only true objects of yogic knowledge offered by Dharmakīrti are the FOUR NOBLE TRUTHS: that is, the perception of these truths is true and reliable because they enable one to reach the goal of enlightenment, not because they involve a perception of an ultimate substance. In this sense, Dharmakīrti's understanding of yogijñāna is more focused on the direct realization of the soteriological import of the four noble truths than on extraordinary sensory ability. Therefore, yogic direct perception is qualitatively different from the various forms of clairvoyance that are the byproducts of deep states of concentration that may be achieved by both Buddhist and non-Buddhist practitioners. Yogipratyakṣa is a form of insight (VIPAŚYANĀ) posssessed only by noble persons (ĀRYAPUDGALA); and among the five paths it occurs only on the path of vision (DARŚANAMĀRGA) and above. See also DARŚANA.

**yojana**. (T. dpag tshad; C. youxun; J. yujun; K. yusun 由旬). In Sanskrit, a "league"; a standard measure of distance in ancient India, and often used in Buddhist texts; it is said to be the distance a yoked team of oxen could travel in one day. Modern estimates of this distance vary widely, with the figure of eight miles often provided as an approximation, although estimates of from four to ten miles (six to sixteen kilometers) are also found.

**Yōkan**. (永観) (1032–1111). Japanese VINAYA master of the Sanronshū (C. SAN LUN ZONG); also known as Eikan. Yōkan wrote two important works on PURE LAND doctrine known as the *Ōjōjūin* and the *Ōjōkōshiki*. In contrast to the TENDAISHŪ and SHINGONSHŪ interpretation of the practice of NENBUTSU (C. NIANFO) as the contemplation of the buddha AMITĀBHA, Yōkan emphasized instead the efficacy of the vocal recitation of name of Amitābha (NAMU AMIDABUTSU). Doctrinally, Yōkan supported the view that enlightenment and afflictions, like buddhas and human beings, are not two but of a single essence. Yōkan or Eikan is also well known for the monastery in Kyōto that took his name, Eikandō, which is also called Zenrinji.

**Yokawa**. (横川). The northern of the three main subcomplexes of the TENDAISHŪ (C. TIANTAI ZONG) monastery ENRYAKUJI on HIEIZAN in Japan. In 848, the Japanese pilgrim-monk ENNIN established the Shūryōgon'in complex in Yokawa; subsequent expansion projects were undertaken by the monks RYŌGEN and GENSHIN. The Yokawa complex is famous for its central hall, now known as the Yokawa chūdō, also founded in 848, and the Eshin'in (or Eshindō) established by Genshin, which came to function as a special hall for practicing nenbutsu (C. NIANFO).

**Yona**. One of nine adjacent lands (P. paccantadesa) converted to Buddhism by missionaries dispatched by the elder MOGGALIPUTTATISSA at the end of the third Buddhist council (see COUNCIL, THIRD), which was held in PĀṬALIPUTRA during the reign of AŚOKA in the third century BCE. The region is generally identified as located in northwest India, homeland of the Bactrian Greeks, and is also known as Yonakā or YAVANA. Yona was converted by the elder Mahārakkhita, who preached the *Aggikkhandhopamasutta*. The third Buddhist council at Pāṭaliputra, and the nine Buddhist missions are known only in STHAVIRANIKĀYA sources and are first recorded in the fifth-century DĪPAVAMSA.

**Yŏndam Yuil**. (蓮潭有一) (1720–1799). Korean SŎN master and exegete during the Chosŏn dynasty; also known as Mui. Shortly after his parents' death in 1737, Yŏndam became a student of the monk Sŏngch'ŏl (d.u.) at the monastery of Pŏpch'ŏnsa on Mt. Sŭngdal and received the monastic precepts the next year from the VINAYA master Anbin (d.u.). In 1739, he began scriptural studies under the Sŏn master Pyŏkha Taeu (1676–1763), which he continued under Yongam Ch'ejo (1714–1779) and Sŏlp'a Sangŏn (1707–1791). In 1741, Yŏndam began training in Sŏn meditation under Hoam Ch'ejŏng (1687–1748) and eventually became his disciple. Yŏndam established himself as a talented exegete of Sŏn materials and was installed as the abbot of the monastery of Sŏbongsa in 1779. He left many writings, including the *Imha nok*, *Chabo haengŏp*, *Tosŏ kwamok pyŏngip sagi*, *Sŏnyo sagi*, *Sŏjang sagi*, *Wŏn'gak sagi*, *Simsŏng non*, and others. In his influential *Imha nok*, Yŏndam addressed the anti-Buddhist polemics of the Confucian scholars. His "personal notes" (sagi) on the CHANYUAN ZHUQUANJI DUXU, DAHUI SHUZHUANG, CHANYAO, and YUANJUE JING are still widely used in Korean monastic seminaries, or kangwŏn.

**yŏndŭng hoe**. (燃燈會). In Korean, "lantern-lighting ceremony"; a Korean Buddhist celebration that originated sometime during the Koryŏ dynasty. To celebrate the lunar New Year, lanterns were lit on the fifteenth day of the first lunar month and kept lit for two nights. Although King Sŏngjong (r. 982–997) banned the ceremony, the ban was lifted in the first year of King Hyŏnjong's (r. 1010–1031) reign and the ceremony was held again on the fifteenth day of the second lunar month and continued to be held on the second month from that point onward. In 1352, the celebration of the yŏndŭng hoe took place in the palace on the traditional East Asian date of the Buddha's birthday (the eighth day of the fourth lunar month) with one hundred monks in attendance, and the event was subsequently held on the Buddha's birthday throughout the remainder of the Chosŏn dynasty. This custom of lighting lanterns to celebrate the Buddha's birthday continues today in Korea.

**yong**. (J. yū; K. yong 用). In Chinese, "function," or "application"; a term often deployed in the East Asian religious traditions, including Buddhism, as a philosophical pair with "essence" (TI). Chinese Daoist and "Dark Learning" (XUANXUE) texts first imbued the term with philosophical implications: the *Daode jing* refers to yong as the "attributes" of the way, and the *Daodejing zhu*, Wang Bi's (226–249) commentary to the text, employs the term to indicate the functions or attributes of "nonbeing" (WU) or "voidness" (xu). However, yong, along with its companion ti, was not widely used until the Buddhists adopted both terms to provide a basic conceptual frame for reality or truth. For example, the SAN LUN ZONG master JIZANG (549–623) used ti and yong to explicate his theory of the middle way (MADHYAMAPRATIPAD). He connected the middle (zhong) to ti, which he described as "neither ultimate nor conventional" (feizhen feisu), and the provisional (jia) to yong, which he described as "ultimate and conventional" (zhensu). The ti and yong pair was often used in the HUAYAN, TIANTAI, and CHAN traditions. GUIFENG ZONGMI (780–841), a Tang-dynasty master of both the HUAYAN ZONG and Heze Chan traditions, provided a systematic explanation for yong and ti, based on the DASHENG QIXIN LUN ("Awakening of Faith According to the Mahāyāna"). In particular, he distinguished between two different types of function in his theory of mind: the "inherent function of the self-nature" (zixing benyong), which he called "numinous awareness" (LINGZHI), and the responsive functions that accord with conditions (suiyuan yingyong), which he described as the various mental functions that derive from the inherent function of the mind. Many Chinese and Korean Neo-Confucian thinkers, such as Cheng Yi (1033–1107), Zhu Xi (1130–1200), and Yi Hwang (1501–1570), applied Zongmi's interpretation of this pair to their own philosophical systems.

**Yongjia Xuanjue**. (J. Yōka Genkaku; K. Yŏngga Hyŏn'gak 永嘉玄覺) (675–713). Chinese CHAN monk renowned for his writings on meditation, also known as Mingdao, Yishujue, and Great Master Zhenjue (True Awakening); Yongjia is his toponym, the name of his hometown in Zhejiang province. Yongjia made a name for himself at a young age as an expert on meditation and the TIANTAI practices of calmness and insight (see ŚAMATHA and VIPAŚYANĀ). He is said to have later received a seal of approval (YINKE) from the sixth patriarch (LIUZU) of Chan, HUINENG, after studying under the master for only one day and a night; hence, his cognomen Yishujue (Single-Night Enlightened, or Overnight Guest). His teachings are primarily known through the influential works attributed to him, such as the ZHENGDAO GE and *Yongjia ji*. Yongjia was given the posthumous title Great Master Wuxiang (No Marks).

**Yongjusa**. (龍珠寺). In Korean, "Dragon Pearl Monastery"; the second district monastery (PONSA) of the contemporary CHOGYE CHONG of Korean Buddhism, located on Mt. Hwa in Kyŏnggi province. The temple was constructed in 854 and originally named Karyangsa. It was rebuilt in 1790 to serve as the royal tomb of Prince Sado (1735–1762), the father of King Chŏngjo (r. 1776–1800). During the Japanese colonial period (1910–1945), Yongjusa became one of thirty-one head monasteries (PONSA) and it managed forty-nine branch temples (malsa) in several regions. A monks' training school was established in 1955, followed by a meditation hall in 1969. Yongjusa's main shrine hall (TAEUNG CHŎN) was constructed in 1790 and enshrines images of the buddhas ŚĀKYAMUNI, BHAIṢAJYAGURU, and AMITĀBHA. Other cultural properties at the site include the main temple bell, bronze censers, and a hanging painting of the Buddha (KWAEBUL).

**yongmaeng chŏngjin**. (S. ārabdhavīrya; T. brtson 'grus rtsom pa, C. yongmeng jingjin; J. yūmyōshōjin 勇猛精進). In Korean, "ferocious effort"; an especially rigorous period of practice performed during a SŎN (C. CHAN) meditative retreat (K. kyŏlche; C. JIEZHI) in Korea. The term most commonly refers to a one-week period during the winter retreat and leading up to the enlightenment day of the Buddha (Puch'ŏnim sŏngdo il) on the eighth day of the twelfth lunar month (usually in early January), during which all the monks (or nuns) in the meditation hall will undertake the ascetic practice (see DHUTAṄGA) of constantly sitting and never lying down to sleep (K. CHANGJWA PURWA) for the entire seven days. This practice is a ritual reenactment of the Buddha's own final fervent effort to awaken. The phrase has also come to refer more generally to an intense session of meditation carried out by a small group of elite monks during a three-year retreat (samnyŏn kyŏlsa). See also SESSHIN; RŌHATSU SESSHIN.

**Yongming Yanshou**. (J. Yōmei Enju; K. Yŏngmyŏng Yŏnsu 永明延壽) (904–975). Chinese CHAN master in the FAYAN ZONG during the Five Dynasties and Song dynasty periods; also known as Chongxuan and Baoyizi. Yongming was a native of Lin'an prefecture in Zhejiang province. At the age of twenty-seven, Yongming left his post as a minor official to become a monk under Cuiyan Lingcan (d.u.), a disciple of the Chan master XUEFENG YICUN (822–908); he subsequently studied under TIANTAI DESHAO (891–972) and inherited his Fayan lineage. Beginning in 952, Yongming served as abbot of a series of different monasteries, including Zishengsi on Mt. Xuedou, Lingyinsi (at the request of the king of Wuyue), and Yongmingsi, whence he acquired his toponym. Yongming was renowned for his advocacy of the simultaneous cultivation of Chan meditation and NIANFO (recitation of the Buddha's name) and for his magnum opus ZONGJING LU, a massive Chan genealogical history, in one hundred rolls. His writings also include the famous WANSHAN TONGGUI JI and the WEIXIN JUE. Although Yongming's Fayan lineage declined in China during the Song dynasty, thirty-six envoys sent by the Koryŏ king to study under Yongming returned with his teachings to Korea, where the line continued to flourish. Yongming was posthumously given the title Chan master Zhijue (Wise Awakening).

**Yongningsi**. (J. Eineiji; K. Yŏngnyŏngsa 永寧寺). In Chinese, "Eternal Peace monastery"; one of the most important monasteries in the Northern Wei capital of Luoyang. After the Wei rulers moved the Chinese capital to Luoyang, Empress

Dowager Ling, the birth mother of Emperor Xiao Mingdi (r. 515–528), began construction of Yongningsi in 516. According to the LUOYANG QIELAN JI, Yongningsi was a grand complex that could house more than a thousand monks and was located to the west of the imperial highway and south of the Changhe gate. In the northern precinct of the monastery was a buddha hall, which housed various golden images, and to the south, a triple-gated tower more than two hundred feet in height. A nine-story pagoda that rose a thousand feet supported a tall golden pole with golden disks to collect the dew. Golden bells were also hung from the pagoda. Since it overlooked the palace, only Emperor Xiao Mingdi and the Empress Dowager were allowed to climb the pagoda to gaze at the entire capital. All the scriptures and paintings from foreign countries available at the time are said to have been stored at the monastery. The eminent translator BODHIRUCI also translated many scriptures while in residence at Yongningsi. The monastery was devastated by a fire and was left in ruins after the capital was moved again to Ye. Several restorations were made during the Sui and Tang dynasties, but the monastery remains in ruins today.

**Yŏngsanjae.** (靈山齋). In Korean, "Vulture Peak Ceremony"; a Korean Buddhist rite associated with the SADDHARMAPUṆḌARĪKASŪTRA ("Lotus Sūtra"), which has been performed in Korea since the mid to late Koryŏ dynasty (918–1392). This elaborate ritual is a loose reenactment of the *Saddharmapuṇḍarīkasūtra* and is intended to depict the process by which all beings, both the living and the dead, are led to enlightenment. Its performance often occurs in conjunction with the forty-ninth day ceremony (K. sasipku [il] chae; C. SISHIJIU [RI] ZHAI), which sends a deceased being in the intermediate transitional state (ANTARĀBHAVA) on to the next rebirth. The Yŏngsanjae is renowned for including the most complete repertoire of Buddhist chant and dance preserved in the Korean tradition. The rite may last for between one day and a week, although it is rare nowadays to see it extend beyond a single day; briefer productions lasting a couple of hours are sometimes staged for tourists. The Yŏngsanjae is protected through the Korean Cultural Property Protection Law as an intangible cultural asset (Muhyŏng Munhwajae, no. 50), and the group responsible for protecting and preserving the rite for the future consists of monks at the monastery of PONGWŎNSA in Seoul, the headquarters of the T'AEGO CHONG. The monks at the monastery also train monks and nuns from other orders of Buddhism, as well as laypeople, in different components of the rite. In recent years, the dominant CHOGYE CHONG of Korean Buddhism has also begun to perform the Yŏngsanjae again, thanks to training from the Pongwŏnsa specialists in the tradition. ¶ The Yŏngsanjae is held in front of a large KWAEBUL (hanging painting) scroll depicting ŚĀKYAMUNI teaching at Vulture Peak (GṚDHRAKŪṬAPARVATA), delivering the *Saddharmapuṇḍarīkasūtra* to his followers. A day-long version of the ceremony starts with bell ringing and a procession escorting the attending spirits in a palanquin, which then proceeds to a ceremonial raising of the kwaebul. The rest of the day is made up of the following sequence of events: chanting spells (DHĀRAṆĪ) to the bodhisattva AVALOKITEŚVARA (K. Kwanseŭm posal); the cymbal dance, or PARACH'UM, as monks chant the *Ch'ŏnsu kyŏng* (C. QIANSHOU JING) dedicated to the thousand-handed incarnation of Avalokiteśvara (see SĀHASRABHUJASĀHASRANETRĀVALOKITEŚVARA); PŎMP'AE; purification of the ritual site (toryanggye), during which the butterfly dance, or NABICH'UM, is performed to entice the dead to attend the ceremony while the pŏmp'ae chants entreat the three jewels (RATNATRAYA) and dragons (NĀGA) to be present; the dharma drum dance, or PŎPKOCH'UM, during which a large drum is beaten to awaken all sentient beings; a group prayer to the Buddha and bodhisattvas, where everyone in attendance has the chance to take refuge in the three jewels (ratnatraya); an offering of flowers and incense (hyanghwagye) to the Buddha and bodhisattvas is made by the nabich'um dancers, followed by offering chants; a chant hoping that the food offerings on the altar will be sufficient as the parach'um is performed again together with four dhāraṇī chants; placing the offerings on the altar while chanting continues; culminating in a transfer of merit (kongdŏkkye) to all the people in attendance, including sending off the spiritual guests of the ceremony. The siktang chakpŏp, an elaborate ceremonial meal, is then consumed. A recitation on behalf of the lay donors who funded the ceremony (hoehyang ŭisik) concludes the rite.

**Yongsŏng Chinjong.** (龍城震鐘) (1864–1940). Korean monk during the Japanese colonial period (1910–1945), also known as Paek Yongsŏng; leader of a conservative group of monastic reformers, and one of the thirty-three signatories to the Korean Declaration of Independence in 1919. Ordained at the monastery of HAEINSA in 1879, he received full monastic precepts five years later and became a disciple of Taeŭn Nango (1780–1841) at the hermitage of Ch'ilburam. Later, he had a great awakening while he was studying the JINGDE CHUANDENGLU at the monastery of SONGGWANGSA, where he became a disciple of the SŎN master HWANSŎNG CHIAN. One year after Korea was annexed by Japan, he established the monastery of Taegaksa and a Sŏn center (Sŏnhagwŏn) in Seoul in an attempt to propagate Buddhism among a wider public. On March 1, 1919, he signed the Korean Declaration of Independence as a representative of the Buddhist community and was consequently incarcerated by the Japanese colonial government for eighteen months. During his year and a half in prison, he translated many sūtras (such as the voluminous AVATAṂSAKASŪTRA, or *Hwaŏmgyŏng*) from literary Chinese into han'gŭl, the Korean vernacular script, in order to make more Buddhist texts accessible to ordinary Koreans. After his release from prison in March 1921, he established a community known as the Taegakkyo (Teaching of Great Awakening) and a translation center called Samjang Yŏkhoe (Society for Translating the TRIPIṬAKA), and devoted most of his time to the translation of Buddhist scriptures. In 1928 he published the journal *Mua* ("No Self") and with HANYŎNG CHŎNGHO also published the journal *Puril* ("Buddha Sun"). In May 1929, he and 127 other monks submitted a petition to the Japanese colonial government asking for the restoration of the tradition of celibacy in the Buddhist monasteries. Because of his interest in ensuring the continuance of the BHIKṢU and BHIKṢUṆĪ traditions, Yongsŏng personally established many ordination platforms and transmitted the complete monastic precepts (kujokkye) several times during his career. He also stressed the need for monasteries to be self-sustaining economically. In accordance with his plan for self-sustenance, he participated in the management of a mine in Hamgyŏng province, and in 1922, he bought some land in Manchuria and ran a farm on the compounds of a branch of the Taegakkyo. He also started a Ch'amsŏn Manil Kyŏlsahoe (Ten-Thousand Day Meditation Retreat Society) at the monastery of Ch'ilbulsa and attracted many followers from other monasteries. Yongsŏng was a prolific writer who left behind many works, including his famous *Kwiwŏn chŏngjong* ("The Orthodox Teaching that Returns to the Source"), a tract that compared Buddhism to Confucianism, Daoism, and Christianity, a modern twist on the old "three teachings" syncretism of medieval East Asian philosophy. This work was one of the first attempts by Buddhists to respond to the inroads made by Christianity in modern Korea. In his treatment, he suggests that Confucianism presented a complete moral doctrine but was deficient in transcendental teachings; Daoism was deficient in moral teachings but half-understood transcendental teaching; Christianity was fairly close to the Buddhist ch'ŏn'gyo ("teachings of [humans] and divinities"), which taught the kinds of meritorious actions that would lead to rebirth in heavenly realms but was completely ignorant of the transcendental teaching. Only Buddhism, Yongsŏng concluded, presented all facets of both moral and transcendental teachings. Yongsŏng's other works include his *Kakhae illyun*, *Susim non*, and *Ch'ŏnggong wŏnil*. See also IMWŎTKO.

**Yongzhong**. (C) (J. Eichū; K. Yŏngchung 永中) (d.u.). Yuan-dynasty CHAN master in the LINJI ZONG, also known as Jueji Yongzhong, and author of the ZIMEN JINGXUN.

**yoni**. (T. skye gnas; C. sheng; J. shō; K. saeng 生). In Sanskrit and Pāli, "modes of birth"; four modes by which sentient beings are born into the three realms of existence (TRAIDHĀTUKA): (1) oviparous birth (aṇḍajayoni), viz., beings born from eggs, such as birds, reptiles, fish, and insects; (2) viviparous birth (jarāyujayoni), viz., beings born from a womb, such as mammals and human beings; (3) moisture-born (saṃsvedajayoni), viz., beings such as maggots generated by rotten meat or mosquitoes born from swamp water, which are understood to be born as the result of the combination of heat and moisture; (4) metamorphic birth (UPAPĀDUKAYONI), viz., spontaneously generated beings, such an divinities (DEVA), hungry ghosts (PRETA), denizens of hell (NĀRAKA), and those residing in the intermediate state (ANTARĀBHAVA). In some interpretations, even beings generally classified in one category may in certain circumstances be born through other modes. For example, although human beings are viviparously born, the five hundred sons of the king of Pañcāla, one of the sixteen ancient kingdoms of India, are said to have been born from eggs, King Māndhātṛ was born from moisture, and the first humans to appear at the beginning of the KALPA are born by metamorphosis. Among animals, although the first three modes of birth are most common, there are also some animals born by metamorphosis, such as NĀGAs and GARUḌAs. Finally, among beings that are born through metamorphosis, there are certain types of preta who are said to be born viviparously.

**yoniśomanaskāra**. [alt. yoniśomanasikāra] (P. yonisomanasikāra; T. tshul bzhin yid la byed pa; C. ruli zuoyi/zheng siwei; J. nyorisai/shōshiyui; K. yŏri chagŭi/chŏng sayu 如理作意/正思惟). In Sanskrit, "systematic attention"; attention directed to an object or a phenomenon purposely and thoroughly, without becoming entranced by its external marks (LAKṢAṆA) and secondary characteristics (ANUVYAÑJANA). The term is used in the context of meditation to refer to the thoroughgoing reflection in which one traces an object or a phenomenon back to its cause or origin, so that one perceives how it arises and perishes in accordance with conditions. Thus, yoniśomanaskāra ultimately refers to attention directed to the FOUR NOBLE TRUTHS, which reveals that the things of this compounded world are fundamentally impermanent (ANITYA), suffering (DUḤKHA), and nonself (ANĀTMAN). While unsystematic attention (AYONIŚOMANASKĀRA) to the characteristics of sensory objects creates false views, craving, and eventually subjection to the objective order of SAṂSĀRA, systematic attention instead brings this unsystematic attention to an end so that the practitioner perceives the true nature of things. Thus, because of systematic attention, as yet unarisen erroneous views (MITHYĀDṚṢṬI) do not arise, already arisen ones cease, unarisen right views arise (SAMYAGDṚṢṬI), and already arisen ones increase. Systematic attention is thus foundational to the path that leads to liberation from saṃsāra. See also YUKTI.

**yŏnji**. (C. ranzhi; J. nenshi 燃指). In Korean, "finger burning." Although not officially sanctioned by the Korean Buddhist SAṂGHA, the ascetic practice of finger burning is sometimes performed by a handful of devoted Korean monks and nuns. Unlike a similar Chinese practice, the practice of finger burning is not performed in the context of ordination, and is held in high regard. The rationale for such a practice is often traced to the self-immolation of the bodhisattva BHAIṢAJYARĀJA in the SADDHARMAPUṆḌARĪKASŪTRA and the bodhisattva SADĀPRARUDITA's self-mutilation in the AṢṬASĀHASRIKĀPRAJÑĀPĀRAMITĀ. See also DEHADĀNA; SHESHEN.

**yon mchod**. [alt. mchod yon] (yön chö). In Tibetan, "priest-patron," a term used to describe the relationship between various Tibetan Buddhist hierarchs and Mongol, Manchu, and Chinese rulers. The compound is composed of abbreviations of two terms. The first, "yon bdag," connotes a powerful benefactor or patron, often a political or military leader. The second "mchod gnas" connotes a religious official, such as a court chaplain. The relationship between Tibetan hierarchs and Mongol rulers is traced to the meeting of SA SKYA PAṆḌITA and Godan Khan (1206–1251, the grandson of Genghis Khan). When Mongol troops invaded Tibet, Sa skya Paṇḍita led a delegation to the Mongol court in 1247, during which he cured Godan Khan of an illness and offered him religious instruction. Subsequently, Godan Khan became his disciple, sparing Tibet from further invasion and granting control of central Tibet to Sa skya Paṇḍita. The classic example of the "priest-patron" relationship occurred when Sa skya Paṇḍita's nephew 'PHAGS PA BLO GROS RGYAL MTSHAN served as religious preceptor and close advisor to Qubilai Khan. Other Tibetan Buddhist hierarchs would serve in similar roles during the Ming and Qing dynasties. As often invoked in Tibetan sources, in the "priest-patron" relationship, the Tibetan Buddhist lama provides religious instruction and spiritual protection (through the performance of tantric rituals) to the Mongol, Manchu, or Chinese chieftain and in return the Mongol, Manchu, or Chinese ruler provides material support and military protection, while allowing Tibet to remain independent.

**Yon tan rgya mtsho**. (Yöntan Gyatso) (1589–1616). In Tibetan, "Ocean of Good Qualities"; the fourth DALAI LAMA. The DGE LUGS monk BSOD NAMS RGYA MTSHO, later recognized as the third Dalai Lama, visited the court of the Mongol ruler, the Altan Khan, in 1578. It was the Altan Khan who first used the term "Dalai Lama" to refer to this leader of the Dge lugs sect. The third Dalai Lama soon returned to Tibet but came back to Mongolia after the death of the Altan Khan, spending the next five years giving Buddhist teachings and founding monasteries before dying in 1588. His incarnation was identified by the Mongols among their own people, as the grandson of Altan Khan's successor. He was given the name Yon tan rgya mtsho. He was thus the only Dalai Lama who was not ethnically Tibetan. The Dge lugs hierarchy in Tibet did not immediately recognize the Mongol as the incarnation of Bsod nams rgya mtsho. To assuage their concerns, a Mongolian delegation was sent to Tibet in 1600 to invite a group of Dge lugs dignitaries to come to Mongolia and administer the traditional tests to determine the boy's identity. After the tests convinced the Tibetan delegation that he was indeed the fourth Dalai Lama, they took the boy back to LHA SA in 1602, where he was ordained as a novice at the JO KHANG. He received BHIKṢU ordination in 1614 from his tutor BLO BZANG CHOS KYI RGYAL MTSHAN, who would later become the first (or according to a different reckoning, the fourth) PAṆ CHEN LAMA. Tibet was on the brink of civil war, with the king of Gtsang, a patron of the KARMA BKA' RGYUD, seeking to control central Tibet, where the Dge lugs were in power with the support of the Mongols. Although the young fourth Dalai Lama appears not to have been involved in politics, the fact that he was a foreigner seems to have been resented in some quarters. He died of uncertain causes in 1616 at the age of twenty-seven. The close relations that developed between the Mongols and the Dge lugs sect as a result of his selection as Dalai Lama would be an important factor in the eventual political ascendancy of his successor, the fifth Dalai Lama, NGAG DBANG BLO BZANG RGYA MSHO, in 1642.

**Yōsai**. (J) (榮西). See MYŌAN EISAI.

**Yose**. (K) (了世). See WŎNMYO YOSE.

**Yu**. (J. U; K. U 于). Ethnikon used in China for monks who hailed from KHOTAN (transcribed as Yutian in Chinese), an Indo-European oasis kingdom at the southern edge of the Takla Makhan desert in Inner Asia, along the northern slope of the Kunlun mountains. Khotan was a major center of Buddhism in Central Asia and an important conduit for the transmission of Buddhism from India to China along the SILK ROAD.

**Yuandeng**. (C) (圓澄). See ZHANRAN YUANDENG.

**yuandun jiao**. (J. endongyō; K. wŏndon kyo 圓頓教). In Chinese, "perfect and sudden teaching"; one of the highest levels of the various doctrinal taxonomies (panjiao; see JIAOXIANG PANSHI) deployed in the TIANTAI ZONG, HUAYAN ZONG, and sometimes the CHAN ZONG. The Tiantai school first introduced the term to refer to the highest form of the teachings. In the Tiantai analysis, "perfect" refers to "perfect teaching" or "consummate teaching" (YUANJIAO), the last of the four types of teachings according to content (huafa sijiao), while "sudden" refers to the "sudden teaching" (DUNJIAO), the first of the four modes of exposition (huayi sijiao) (see TIANTAI BAJIAO). The compound "perfect and sudden teaching" thus refers to the consummate vision of the ultimate truth of Buddhism that is expounded all at once without any provisional or gradual expedients. In the Tiantai zong, this "perfect and sudden teaching" may refer either to (1) the teachings of the Tiantai school itself, which provide an approach to Buddhist soteriology in which every stage, condition, and thought, whether defiled or pure, becomes the basis of enlightenment since it represents the perfect median truth (see SANDI); or (2) the teachings of the AVATAṂSAKASŪTRA, in which the Buddha expounded his consummate and unadulterated vision of reality immediately after his enlightenment without any consideration of the ability of his audience to understand that vision. The Huayan school follows closely the Tiantai concept of yuandun jiao. The Huayan and CHAN teacher GUIFENG ZONGMI (780–841), for example, refers to the perfect and sudden teaching as the "huayi dun" (sudden teaching according to the method of exposition), correlating it with the teaching of the dharma-realm of the mutual and unobstructed interpenetration between phenomenon and phenomena (SHISHI WU'AI FAJIE). The Korean SŎN (Chan) master POJO CHINUL (1158–1210), based on the works of LI TONGXUAN (635–730), interpreted the term as referring to the perfect and sudden enlightenment to the truth of nature origination

(XINGQI), which occurs through understanding Huayan doctrine from a Sŏn perspective. In the Chan tradition, therefore, the "perfect and sudden teaching" may refer to the highest form of the Buddhist teachings rather than to the teachings of any specific scholastic school (KYO). See also WŎNDON SŎNGBUL NON.

**yuanjiao**. (圓教). In Chinese, "perfect/consummate teaching." See HUAYAN WUJIAO.

**Yuanjue jing**. (J. Engakukyō; K. Wŏn'gak kyŏng 圓覺經). In Chinese, "Scripture of Perfect Enlightenment"; also known as *Dafangguang yuanjue xiuduoluo liaoyi jing*; an influential indigenous Chinese sūtra (see APOCRYPHA). The *Yuanjue jing* was purportedly translated by a certain Buddhatrāta (d.u.) at the monastery of BAIMASI in 693, but no Sanskrit or Tibetan equivalent is known to have existed and the scripture is now recognized as being an apocryphon. While in a special SAMĀDHI named "great illuminating repository of spiritual penetration" (shentong daguang mingzang), the Buddha is requested by twelve bodhisattvas including MAÑJUŚRĪ, SAMANTABHADRA, and MAITREYA to explain perfect enlightenment (yuanjue), the originally pure mind as its cause, and the different ways to cultivate it. The scripture focuses on ŚAMATHA, SAMĀPATTI, and DHYĀNA as the primary means of cultivation, and divides the spiritual capacity of sentient beings into three levels. The TATHĀGATAGARBHA and original-enlightenment (BENJUE) theories of the apocryphal DASHENG QIXIN LUN seem to have influenced the composition of the *Yuanjue jing*. The scripture was especially influential in the writings of the CHAN historian GUIFENG ZONGMI, who wrote several commentaries and subcommentaries on the text, including his *Yuanjue jing lueshu*, *Yuanjue jing lüeshu chao*, *Yuanjue jing daochang xiuzheng yi*, *Yuanjue jing dashu*, and *Yuanjue jing dashu chao*. Zongmi also wrote manuals, no longer extant, on the use of the *Yuanjue jing* in repentance rituals. The *Yuanjue jing* is one of a number of Chan-related texts that were translated into Uighur Turkish in the TURFAN region.

**Yuanmiao**. (原妙). See GAOFENG YUANMIAO.

**Yuanming lun**. (J. Enmyōron; K. Wŏnmyŏng non 圓明論). In Chinese, "Treatise on Perfect Illumination"; attributed to AŚVAGHOṢA, but almost certainly a transcription of a lecture by a teacher associated with the Northern school (BEI ZONG) in the nascent Chinese CHAN tradition. Several copies of this text have been discovered at DUNHUANG, and a private copy is extant in Japan. The treatise consists of nine chapters written largely in catechistic format. The treatise elucidates the causes and results of the path, the nature of the DHARMADHĀTU as the manifestation of one's own mind, false and correct views, the importance of UPĀYA, and the practice of meditation. The *Yuanming lun* serves as an important source on the teachings of the early Chan tradition before its coalescence around the mythology of the "sixth patriarch" (LIUZU) HUINENG and the so-called Southern school (NAN ZONG).

**Yuanren lun**. (J. Genninron; K. Wŏnin non 原人論). In Chinese, "Treatise on the Origin of Humanity"; by the eminent HUAYAN and CHAN scholiast GUIFENG ZONGMI. A preface to this relatively short treatise was prepared by Zongmi, as was another by his lay disciple Pei Xiu (787?–860). The treatise largely consists of four chapters: exposing deluded attachments, exposing the partial and superficial, directly revealing the true source, and reconciling root and branches. In his critique of deluded attachments, Zongmi offers a response to the different Confucian and Daoist theories of the way (DAO), spontaneity (ziran), primal pneuma (yuanqi), and the mandate of heaven (tianming). Zongmi then briefly summarizes the teachings of the different vehicles of Buddhism, such as HĪNAYĀNA and MAHĀYĀNA, and expounds their different approaches to reality. Relying on the teachings of the AVATAṂSAKASŪTRA, Zongmi finally offers a Buddhist alternative to the theories of the Confucian and Daoist critics: the TATHĀGATAGARBHA as the origin of humanity.

**yuanrong**. (J. ennyū; K. wŏnyung 圓融). In Chinese, "consummate interfusion," "perfectly interfused"; a term used in the HUAYAN and TIANTAI traditions to refer to the ultimate state of reality wherein each individual phenomenon is perceived to be perfectly interfused and completely harmonized with every other phenomena. Yuanrong is contrasted with "separation" (GELI), the understanding of reality in terms of the discriminative phenomena of the conventional realm. ¶ The concept of yuanrong is deployed soteriologically as one of the two modes of describing the bodhisattva path in the Huayan tradition, viz., the "approach of consummate interfusion" (yuanrong men), also known as the "approach of consummate interfusion and mutual conflation" (YUANRONG XIANGSHE MEN); this mode is contrasted with the "approach of sequential practices" (CIDI XINGBU MEN). The approach of sequential practices refers to the different stages in the process of religious training, which progress through the fifty-two stages of the bodhisattva path (MĀRGA). By contrast, the yuanrong men focuses instead on the principle of equivalency (pingdeng) and indicates the way in which any one stage of training subsumes all stages of the path, or how the inception of the path is in fact identical to its consummation. According to this mode of description, then, the completion of the ten stages of faith (shixin), a preliminary stage of the mārga in the Huayan tradition, is often stated to be identical to the achievement of buddhahood (XINMAN CHENGFO). In the Huayan school's fivefold taxonomy of the teachings (HUAYAN WUJIAO) as systematized by FAZANG (643–712), the three vehicles are considered to represent the xingbu men, while the "consummate teaching" (YUANJIAO), the final and highest level of teaching in this schema, corresponds to the yuanrong men. ¶ Yuanrong is also used in accounts of contemplation practice in the Huayan school, as, for example, in the "contemplation on the consummate interfusion of the three sages" (sansheng yuanrong guan), which was treated by both CHENGGUAN (738–839) and LI TONGXUAN (635–730). In this Huayan meditation, the bodhisattvas MAÑJUŚRĪ and

SAMANTABHADRA represent the causal aspects of practice (yinfen), and the buddha VAIROCANA, the fruition aspect (guofen); the consummate interfusion of the causal and effect aspects of practice thus indicates enlightenment. Samantabhadra and Mañjuśrī are juxtaposed as, respectively, the DHARMADHĀTU as the object of faith (suoxin) and the mind as the subject of faith (nengxin), as practice (xing) and understanding (jie), and as principle (LI) and wisdom (zhi). When these juxtaposed aspects are perfectly interfused with each other, the causal aspect is consummated and becomes perfectly interfused with the effect aspect. Thus Samantabhadra as the "empty TATHĀGATAGARBHA" (kong rulaizang) and Mañjuśrī as the "nonempty tathāgatagarbha" (bukong rulaizang) are interfused with Vairocana Buddha's "comprehensive tathāgatagarbha" (zong rulaizang). ¶ In the Tiantai tradition, the "consummate interfusion of the three truths" (yuanrong sandi) is one of the two ways of interpreting the three truths (SANDI), viz., of emptiness (kongdi), provisionally real (jiadi), and the mean (zhongdi). The yuanrong sandi, also termed the "nonsequential three truths" (BU CIDI SANDI), refers to the notion that each truth (di) is endowed with all three of these truths together, and thus the particular and the universal are not separate from one another. This mode is distinguished from the "differentiated three truths" (GELI SANDI), also known as the "sequential three truths" (cidi sandi), where each truth is treated independently; in this mode, the first two truths represent the aspect of phenomena, while the last truth, of the mean, refers to the aspect of principle. In the Tiantai doctrinal taxonomy (see TIANTAI BAJIAO; WUSHI BAJIAO), geli sandi and yuanrong sandi are said to correspond, respectively, to the "distinct teaching" (biejiao) and the "consummate teaching" (yuanjiao), the third and fourth of the "four types of teaching according to their content" (huafa sijiao) in the Tiantai doctrinal classification. ¶ In both the Huayan and Tiantai traditions, yuanrong is also employed as a defining characteristic of the "dharma realm" (fajie; S. dharmadhātu). The term "consummate interfusion of the dharma realm" (fajie yuanrong) describes both the infinitely interdependent state of the Huayan "dharmadhātu of the unimpeded interpenetration of phenomenon with phenomena" (SHISHI WU'AI FAJIE), as well as the Tiantai doctrine of "intrinsic inclusiveness" (xingju), in which each individual phenomenon is said to be endowed with the TRICHILIOCOSM (SANQIAN DAQIAN SHIJIE; see TRISĀHASRAMAHĀSĀHASRALOKADHĀTU), which represents the entirety of existence in the Tiantai cosmology. The Huayan "dharmadhātu of the unimpeded interpenetration of phenomenon with phenomena" is systematized in the doctrine of the Huayan version of causality, the "conditioned origination of the dharmadhātu" (FAJIE YUANQI), and this Huayan causality of the dharmadhātu is also explained as the "consummate interfusion of the six aspects" (LIUXIANG yuanrong).

**yuanrong sanguan**. (圓融三觀). In Chinese, "three contemplations of consummate interfusion." See SANGUAN.

**yuanrong xiangshe men**. (圓融相攝門). In Chinese, "approach of consummate interfusion and mutual conflation." See YUANRONG.

**Yuanwu Keqin**. (J. Engo Kokugon; K. Wŏno Kŭkkŭn 圜悟克勤) (1062–1135). Chinese CHAN master in the LINJI ZONG; also known as Wuzhuo and Foguo. Yuanwu was a native of Chongning, Pengzhou prefecture, in present-day Sichuan province (northwest of the city of Chengdu). Little is known about his early career, but Yuanwu eventually became a disciple of the Chan master WUZU FAYAN. According to legend, Yuanwu became ill after leaving Wuzu's side, and returned as Wuzu had predicted. Yuanwu then inherited Wuzu's Linji lineage. While traveling in the south, Yuanwu befriended the statesman ZHANG SHANGYING (1043–1122) and also won the support of other powerful local figures, such as the governor of Chengdu. At their request, Yuanwu served as abbot of several monasteries, including Jiashansi and Daolinsi, where he lectured on the *Xuedou gonggu* by XUEDOU CHONGXUAN. These lectures were later edited together as the BIYAN LU ("Blue Cliff Record"), an influential collection of Chan cases (GONG'AN). Yuanwu was honored with several titles: Emperor Huizong (r. 1100–1125) gave him the title Chan master Foguo (Buddha Fruition) and Gaozong the title Chan master Yuanwu (Consummate Awakening). The title Chan master Zhenjue (True Enlightenment) was also bestowed upon him. Among his hundred or so disciples, DAHUI ZONGGAO, the systematizer of the KANHUA CHAN method of meditation, is most famous. Yuanwu's teachings are recorded in the *Yuanwu Foguo chanshi yulu* and *Yuanwu chanshi xinyao*.

**yuganaddha**. (T. zung 'jug; C. shuangru/shuangyun; J. sōnyū/sōun; K. ssangip/ssangun 雙入/雙運). In Sanskrit and Pāli, lit., "yoked together," sometimes translated as "union" or "joining." The term is especially important in tantric literature, where it often refers to the union of two things, resulting in a state of nonduality (ADVAYA). However, the term appears in a variety of contexts where two elements are conjoined, including serenity (ŚAMATHA) and insight (VIPAŚYANĀ), wisdom (PRAJÑĀ) and method (UPĀYA), SAṂSĀRA and NIRVĀṆA, male and female, and subject and object. In Pāli literature, the term appears especially in the context of treatments of samatha and vipassanā, both in practices in which the meditator alternates between the two and practices in which the two are unified.

**Yuimae**. (C. Weimo hui; K. Yuma hoe 維摩會). In Japanese, "VIMALAKĪRTI ceremony." One of the three great ceremonies (Nankyō san[n]e) held in the ancient Japanese capital of Nara. In 656, when the senior courtier Nakatomi no Kamatari (an ancestor of the Fujiwara clan) became seriously ill, the Paekche nun Pŏmmyŏng (J. Hōmyō) advised Empress Saimei to sponsor a reading of the "Inquiry about Illness" chapter of the VIMALAKĪRTINIRDEŚA in order to speed his recovery. The reading was successful and, out of gratitude, Kamatari and his family subsequently sponsored a lecture on the sūtra in 658 to commemorate the construction of the new monastery of Sankaiji. This ceremony was transferred to the Hossōshū (C. FAXIANG ZONG) monastery of KŌFUKUJI in Nara in 712, where it was held periodically every two to five years; it is now observed annually on the tenth day of the tenth lunar month. For seven days, a lecture on the *Vimalakīrtinirdeśa* is offered to the public and offerings are made to the SAṂGHA.

**Yujŏmsa**. (楡岾寺). In Korean, "Elm Hillock Monastery"; one of the four major monasteries located in the Diamond Mountains (KŬMGANGSAN) in present-day North Korea, and best known traditionally for its fifty-three buddha images. Yujŏmsa claims to be one of the oldest monasteries on the Korean peninsula. According to its historical record, *Kŭmgangsan Yujŏmsa sajŏkki*, written in 1297 by the Koryŏ official and diplomat Min Chi (1248–1326), icons of fifty-three buddhas drifted to the Silla seashore in the year 4 CE through the intercession of an Indo-Scythian [alt. Yuezhi, Rouzhi] king from the northwestern region of India. These images were originally cast by MAÑJUŚRĪ in the Indian city of ŚRĀVASTĪ and enshrined inside a large bell. After landing in Korea, the bell containing these fifty-three icons magically traveled inland and was eventually discovered in a branch of an elm tree by a Korean local official. To house these icons, the Silla king Namhae Ch'ach'aung (r. 4–24 CE) ordered the construction of this monastery, which he named after the elm tree in which the bell was discovered. Despite this legend of the monastery's origins, however, the main construction work at Yujŏmsa could not have begun before 1168. In the thirteenth century, during the late Koryŏ period, the monastery enjoyed the patronage of the Mongol–Korean court, which raised its political status and importance. The fifty-three buddhas of Yujŏmsa remained a popular destination for both literati tourists and Buddhist pilgrims to the Diamond Mountains throughout the Chosŏn dynasty. When the site was surveyed in 1912 by the Japanese scholar Sekino Tadashi (1867–1935), only fifty small gilt bronze icons were displayed in the Nŭngin pojŏn on a unique screen altar that was ornamented with meandering tree branches. In contrast to Min Chi's description of the iconography, various other images, including bodhisattvas and monastic figures, were included along with the buddha icons. Stylistically, forty-three individual figures could be dated to the Unified Silla period, and the remaining seven were determined to be post-Koryŏ products. This incongruent mixture of styles is due to continuous devastations of the images by fire and theft and their subsequent restorations. Yujŏmsa burned to the ground during the Korean War (1950–1953) and the current whereabouts of the fifty-three icons are unknown.

**Yujŏng**. (K) (惟政). See SAMYŎNG YUJŎNG.

**yukti**. (P. yutti; T. rigs pa; C. daoli; J. dōri; K. tori 道理). In Sanskrit, "reasoning" or "argumentation"; the process of analytical reflection that results in correct understanding. The term often appears in conjunction with ĀGAMA (scripture), as criteria or tools deployed to verify a particular point of doctrinal correctness. Yukti is usually presumed to have two denotations in the literature, viz., "reasoning" and "rational principles," although sometimes it is difficult to differentiate between these two senses in a particular text. ¶ The MAHĀYĀNASŪTRĀLAṂKĀRA, for instance, refers to yukti as one of the four types of provisional establishment (prajñaptivyavasthāna), that is, provisional establishment of dharma (dharmaprajñaptivyavasthāna), truth (satyaprajñaptivyavasthāna), reasoning (yuktiprajñaptivyavasthāna), and vehicle (yānaprajñaptivyavasthāna). Yukti is itself subdivided into four types, that is, the yukti of reference (apekṣāyukti), defined as systematic attention (YONIŚOMANASKĀRA); efficacy (kāryakāraṇayukti), defined as right view together with its fruits (samyagdṛṣṭiḥ phalānvitā); valid proof (upapattisādhanayukti), defined as analysis by means of correct cognition (pramāṇavicaya); and reality (DHARMATĀ-yukti), defined as the inconceivable (ACINTYA). ¶ In such texts as the YOGĀCĀRABHŪMI, the SAṂDHINIRMOCANASŪTRA, and the ABHIDHARMASAMUCCAYA, the four types of yukti are described as tools or means for investigating Buddhist teachings and yukti thus carries the denotation of "rational principles" (see VYĀKHYĀYUKTI). In these scriptures, the principle of dependence (apekṣāyukti) is defined as the principle of dependent origination (PRATĪTYASAMUTPĀDA); thus, in dependence on the seed, the shoot emerges. The principle of efficacy (kāryakāraṇayukti) is defined as the way in which particular causes are associated with specific effects; thus, visual consciousness affects vision but not hearing. The principle of valid proof (upapattisādhanayukti) is defined as the three types of valid knowledge (PRAMĀṆA), that is, direct perception (PRATYAKṢA), logical inference (ANUMĀNA), and scripture (āgama). The principle of reality (dharmatā-yukti) is defined as the generic properties and natures of dharmas, such as the property of water falling downward, or the sun rising in the east. The *Saṃdhinirmocanasūtra*'s emphasis on the third yukti of valid proof ultimately led to a narrowing of the term to refer to the three types of valid knowledge (pramāṇa). After DIGNĀGA (c. 480–540), who accepted only two pramāṇas—that is, direct perception (pratyakṣa) and logical inference (anumāna), but not scripture (āgama)—yukti is subsequently confined to only these two types of pramāṇas. In the ABHIDHARMAKOŚABHĀṢYA, Vasubandhu advocates that the wisdom obtained through reflection (CINTĀMAYĪPRAJÑĀ), the second of the three modes of wisdom (prajñā) (along with the wisdom obtained through listening/learning [ŚRUTAMAYĪPRAJÑĀ] and the wisdom obtained through meditative practice [BHĀVANĀMAYĪPRAJÑĀ]) is produced from investigation by means of yukti (yuktinidhyānajā). Since Vasubandhu presents all three modes of wisdom as arising from meditative concentration (SAMĀDHI), yukti in this context seems to have been understood in relation to meditative practice, not purely intellectual reasoning. ¶ The Pāli equivalent yutti, which appears in the NETTIPPAKARAṆA, is presented as one of the sixteen categories (hārā) of scriptural exposition, referring to (logical) fitness, right construction, or correctness of meaning.

**yuktikāya**. (T. rigs tshogs). In Sanskrit, literally "corpus of reasoning," or "collection of reasoning"; a term used in the Indian and Tibetan traditions to refer collectively to six works that traditionally constitute NĀGĀRJUNA's philosophical oeuvre. The six works are the MŪLAMADHYAMAKAKĀRIKĀ, YUKTIṢAṢṬIKĀ, ŚŪNYATĀSAPTATI, VIGRAHAVYĀVARTANĪ, VAIDALYAPRAKARAṆA, and RATNĀVALĪ. (Some versions list only five works in the corpus, eliminating the *Ratnāvalī*; others substitute the AKUTOBHAYĀ in place of the *Ratnāvalī* as the sixth work). This group of texts is often referred to in connection with the STAVAKĀYA, or "corpus of hymns," the devotional works attributed to Nāgārjuna. There are traditionally four works in this group of hymns, known collectively as the CATUḤSTAVA: the LOKĀTĪTASTAVA, NIRAUPAMYASTAVA, ACINTYASTAVA, and PARAMĀRTHASTAVA, although a number of other important hymns are also ascribed to Nāgārjuna. These two collections of Nāgārjuna's works figure prominently in the "self-emptiness, other emptiness" (RANG STONG GZHAN STONG) debate in Tibetan Buddhism, where the parties disagree on the question of which corpus represents Nāgārjuna's final view.

**Yuktiṣaṣṭikā**. (T. Rigs pa drug cu pa; C. Liushisong ruli lun; J. Rokujūju nyoriron; K. Yuksipsong yŏri non 六十頌如理論). In Sanskrit, "Sixty Stanzas of Reasoning"; one of the most famous and widely cited works attributed to NĀGĀRJUNA, traditionally counted as one of the texts in his "corpus of reasoning" (YUKTIKĀYA). Although lost in the original Sanskrit, the work is preserved in both Tibetan and Chinese; a number of the Sanskrit stanzas have however been recovered as citations in other works. Sixty-one stanzas in length, the work is a collection of aphorisms generally organized around the topic of PRATĪTYASAMUTPĀDA. It begins with the famous homage to the Buddha, "Obeisance to the King of Sages who proclaimed dependent origination, this mode by which production and disintegration are abandoned." The work argues throughout that the world that is subject to production and disintegration is an illusion created by ignorance and that the path taught by the Buddha is the means to destroy this illusion and the suffering it creates. Individual stanzas are quoted by such commentators as BHĀVAVIVEKA, CANDRAKĪRTI, and ŚĀNTARAKṢITA in support of some of the central debates in MADHYAMAKA, such as whether ARHATS must understand the Madhyamaka conception of emptiness (ŚŪNYATĀ) in order to be liberated from rebirth and whether Nāgārjuna held that external objects do not exist (the thirty-fourth stanza can be read to suggest that he held this view).

**Yuktiṣaṣṭikāvṛtti**. (T. Rigs pa drug cu pa'i 'grel pa). "Commentary on [NĀGĀRJUNA's] Sixty Stanzas of Reasoning," by CANDRAKĪRTI. See YUKTIṢAṢṬIKĀ.

**Yulan Guanyin**. (C) (魚藍觀音). See MALANG FU.

**yulanben**. (T. yongs su skyob pa'i snod; J. urabon; K. uranbun 盂蘭盆). In Chinese, lit. "yulan vessel," referring to the "ghost festival." The Sinographs "yulan" have typically been interpreted by scholars to be a transcription of a hypothetical BUDDHIST HYBRID SANSKRIT, Middle Indic, or perhaps even Iranian form *ULLAMBANA, which is presumed to correspond to the Sanskrit avalambana (lit. "hanging downward," "suspended"); the term refers to the "Ghost Festival," a ritual that sought the salvation of beings condemned to the unfortunate fate of being "suspended" in hell. This explanation of yulan is questionable, however, since this connotation of the Sanskrit term avalambana is unknown in Indian Buddhist contexts. The Tibetan translation of yulanben as yongs su skyob pa'i snod, or "vessel of complete protection," also does not fit any connotations of "hanging down"; the Tibetan rendering does, however, seem to fit better an alternate explanation of the derivation of yulan(ben) as the Buddhist Hybrid Sanskrit term ullumpana (sometimes mistakenly transcribed as ullumpana, ullumbana, etc.), lit. "rescuing, extracting [from an unfortunate fate]." The Sinograph "ben" ("bowl") is less problematic: it refers to the bowl in which offerings are placed during the PRAVĀRAṆĀ festival in order to rescue one's ancestors from their unfortunate destinies. A more recent hypothesis is that "yulan" is a transcription of the Sanskrit and Pāli term odana (cooked rice) and "ben" a native word for bowl; the compound "yulanben" is thus not a transcription of the hypothetical Sanskrit word ullambana but actually means a "rice bowl," perhaps even a special kind of rice bowl for making offerings on the pravāraṇā day. The term yulanben is now used to refer to the "ghost festival," a popular ceremony in medieval China, Korea, and Japan, when offerings were made to the SAṂGHA of the ten directions (DAŚADIŚ) on behalf of one's ancestors. A bowl was filled with all kinds of flavorful foods and fruits and offered on behalf of seven generations of one's deceased parents and ancestors. The festival was held on the full moon of the seventh lunar month, when the saṃgha performed the pravāraṇā ceremony, ending the summer rains retreat (VARṢĀ). The origin myth and practices associated with the ghost festival are found in various sources, including popular stories known as BIANWEN and such Buddhist apocryphal scriptures as the YULANBEN JING and BAO'EN FENGBEN JING ("Sūtra for Offering Bowls to Repay Kindness"). The Japanese BON FESTIVAL (alt. Obon) derives from this term; it is celebrated in either mid-July or mid-August in order to honor the spirits of one's deceased ancestors.

**Yulanben jing**. (T. 'Phags pa yongs su skyobs pa'i snod ces bya ba'i mdo; J. Urabongyō; K. Uranbun kyŏng 盂蘭盆經). In Chinese, "Book of the Yulan Vessel"; an influential indigenous Chinese Buddhist scripture (see APOCRYPHA), often known in English as the *Ullambana Sūtra* or simply the *Yulanben Sūtra*. Along with the BAO'EN FENGBEN JING ("Scripture for Offering Bowls to Repay Kindness"), the *Yulanben jing* details the practice of the ghost festival (YULANBEN) and its origin myth. Little is known about the provenance of either text. Both are now generally presumed to be indigenous Chinese works, although some scholars continue to maintain that they are of Indian or Central Asian origin. They are thought to have been composed sometime between the fourth and fifth centuries and were included in the Chinese Buddhist canon as early as the sixth century. The origin myth recounted in the scripture describes the pious efforts of Mulian (S. MAHĀMAUDGALYĀYANA), one of the two main disciples of the Buddha, to save his mother from the tortures of her rebirth as a hungry ghost (PRETA). The Buddha explains to Mulian that it is impossible for an individual on his own to save his ancestors from their suffering; instead, one should place offerings in a bowl for the entire SAṂGHA of the ten directions, and these offerings will be sufficient to liberate up to seven generations of one's parents and ancestors from their unfortunate rebirths. At least six commentaries were written on the *Yulanben jing*, although only two survive, including an influential exegesis by GUIFENG ZONGMI. The Tibetan translation of the scripture, made in the Chinese outpost of DUNHUANG sometime in the early ninth century by 'GOS CHOS GRUB (C. Facheng; c. 755–849), is rendered directly from the Chinese recension and is extant in only three manuscript editions of the Tibetan canon (BKA' 'GYUR). See also YULANBEN.

**yulu**. (J. goroku; K. ŏrok 語録). In Chinese, "discourse records" or "recorded sayings," also known as yuben (lit. "edition of discourses") or guanglu ("extensive records"); compilations of the sayings of CHAN, SŎN, and ZEN masters. This genre of Chan literature typically involved collections of the formal sermons (SHANGTANG), exchanges (WENDA), and utterances of Chan masters, which were edited together by their disciples soon after their deaths. The yulu genre sought to capture the vernacular flavor of the master's speech, thus giving it a personal and intimate quality, as if the master himself were in some sense still accessible. Often the recorded sayings of a master would also include his biography, poetry, death verse (YIJI), inscriptions, letters (SHUZHUANG), and other writings, in addition to the transcription of his lectures and sayings. For this reason, Chan discourse records are the Buddhist equivalent of the literary collections (wenji) of secular literati. The term first appears in the SONG GAOSENG ZHUAN, and the genre is often associated particularly with the Chan master MAZU DAOYI (709–788) and his HONGZHOU line of Chan. Among the more famous recorded sayings are the *Mazu yulu (*a.k.a. *Mazu Daoyi chanshi guanglu)*, LINJI YIXUAN's LINJI LU, and HUANGBO XIYUN's CHUANXIN FAYAO. Recorded sayings written in Japanese vernacular are also often called a hōgo (dharma discourse).

**Yum bu bla sgang**. (Yumbu Lagang). A palace and adjacent tower purported to be Tibet's oldest building, established according to legend by the first Tibetan king Gnya' khri btsan po (Nyatri Tsenpo) in central Tibet's Yar klungs (Yarlung) Valley. It may have served as the residence for the earliest Tibetan rulers and was likely renovated by the twenty-eighth king, Lha Tho tho ri gnyan btsan (Lha Tothori Nyentsen, b. 433) during the mid-fifth century. Legends state that this king received the first Buddhist scriptures while residing at the Yum bu bla sgang as they miraculously descended from the sky, heralding the eventual religious conversion of the country. According to one early Tibetan historian, however, the texts were actually transported by the Indian cleric Buddharakṣita; the king, unable to read the Indic script, declared their miraculous descent in order to keep secret their foreign origins. The texts were therefore called the gnyan po gsang ba, "the sacred secret," and indeed remained a secret until the advent of king SRONG BTSAN SGAM PO in the seventh century.

**Yum chen mo**. In Tibetan, lit., "great mother"; a Tibetan epithet for a goddess who is the deified embodiment of the PRAJÑĀPĀRAMITĀ, or perfection of wisdom. The term is also used to refer to the ŚATASĀHASRIKĀPRAJÑĀPĀRAMITĀ ("Perfection of Wisdom in One Hundred Thousand Lines"), or to any other prajñāpāramitā sūtra. Finally, Yum chen mo is also an honorific term used to refer to the mother of the DALAI LAMA.

**Yun'an Puyan**. (J. Unnan Fugan; K. Unam Poam 運庵普巖) (1156–1226). Chinese CHAN master in the LINJI ZONG; a native of Siming in present-day Sichuan province. After studying under Shigu Xiyi (d.u.) and Wuyong Jingquan (1137–1207) following his ordination, Yun'an traveled to the monastery of Zhengzhao Chanyuan on Mt. Yang in 1184 and continued his training under the Chan master Songyuan Chongyue (1132–1202), who early in his vocation had been a student of DAHUI ZONGGAO. When Songyuan was moved to Guangxiao Chansi in Jiangsu province and again to Shiji Chanyuan in Anhui province, Yun'an followed and continued to serve the master for eighteen years. Yun'an eventually became Songyuan's successor. In 1202, after Songyuan's death, Yun'an was invited to reside in a new hermitage established by the master's brother in Yun'an's hometown in Siming. This hermitage was named Yun'an, whence he acquired his toponym. In 1206, Yun'an moved to Dasheng Puzhao Chansi in Jiangsu province, where he trained many eminent disciples, such as XUTANG ZHIYU. His disciples edited his sayings together in the *Yun'an Puyan chanshi yulu*.

**Yungang**. (J. Unkō; K. Un'gang 雲崗). A complex of some fifty-three carved Buddhist caves located at the southern foot of Mt. Wuzhou some ten miles west of the city of Datong, in the Chinese province of Shaanxi. The Yungang grottoes extend roughly half a mile from east to west and were carved over a fifty-year period between the fifth and sixth centuries CE under the patronage of the Northern Wei dynasty (386–534) court. The caves themselves contain roughly fifty thousand Buddhist sculptures, which are noted for their rich variety. The grottoes at Yungang are divided into eastern, western, and central zones. Most of the best-preserved grottoes are found in the western zone, although Grotto No. 1 in the eastern section still contains numerous sculptures in relief. Grotto No. 5, located inside the entrance to the site, contains a giant buddha statue. Grottoes

16–20 are especially renowned for their five colossal buddha images. The iconographical features of the sculptures preserved at the Yungang caves are similar to those found in the contemporaneous cave complex at DUNHUANG; unlike Dunhuang, however, the Yungang caves contain no paintings. Since their completion, the Yungang grottoes have fallen victim to both war and natural disasters. After the People's Republic of China was founded in 1949, the Chinese government took an interest in the site, officially placing it under state protection in 1961. In December 2001, the Yungang grottoes were listed as a UNESCO World Heritage site.

**Yunjusi**. (雲居寺). In Chinese, "Cloud Dwelling Monastery"; monastery that is the home of the FANGSHAN SHIJING (stone scriptures). The monk Jingwan (?–639) allegedly founded this monastery in 631, but a stone inscription dated to 669 is the earliest written record of its existence. The monastery was also known as Xiyusi (Western Valley or Western Region Monastery), and in the seventh-century *Mingbaoji* ("Records of Miraculous Retribution") it is called Zhichuansi (Fount of Wisdom Monastery). On the nearby hill of Shijingshan (Stone Scriptures Hill) just to the east of Yunjusi, nine cave libraries stored the Fangshan lithic canon: its total of 14,278 lithic blocks of 1,122 Buddhist scriptures represent textual lineages that derive from recensions that circulated during the Tang and Khitan Liao dynasties. The carving of the lithic scriptures started during the Sui dynasty under the monk Jingwan with the support of Empress Xiao (r. 604–617), and continued through the late Ming dynasty. The monastery itself is famous for its pagodas, which were closely associated with the engraving of the lithographs. Seven stone pagodas date from the Tang, of which the single-story one at the top of Stone Scriptures Hill, with an inscription dated to 898, is noted for both its architecture and carved decorations. Two of the five pagodas from the Liao are especially significant. Built in 1117, the octagonal Southern Pagoda has eleven stories and pointed eaves and includes a depository of Buddhist scriptures beneath it. The Northern Pagoda is uniquely shaped: the bottom half is octagonal with bracketed eaves and carved niches, while the upper half is cone-shaped and decorated with nine circular bands. Its surface is decorated with more than thirty groups of brick reliefs depicting scenes of dancing and singing, the most interesting example of which is a goddess strumming a three-stringed instrument, one of the rare extant examples for the study of Liao musical culture. The Northern Pagoda is surrounded by smaller stone pagodas dating from the Tang dynasty, several of which resemble the Xiaoyanta (Small Wild Goose Pagoda; see DACI'ENSI) in the ancient Chinese capital of Chang'an (modern Xi'an).

**Yunmen Wenyan**. (J. Unmon Bun'en; K. Unmun Munŏn 雲門文偃) (864–949). Chinese CHAN monk and founder of the YUNMEN ZONG, one of the so-called five houses and seven schools (WU JIA QI ZONG) of the classical Chinese Chan tradition. Yunmen was a native of Jiaxing in present-day Zhejiang province. He was ordained at the age of sixteen by the VINAYA master Zhideng (d.u.) of the monastery Kongwangsi and two years later received the full monastic precepts at the precept platform in Piling (present-day Jiangsu province). After his full ordination, Yunmen returned to Kongwangsi and studied the DHARMAGUPTAKA vinaya (SIFEN LÜ) under Zhideng. Later, Yunmen visited Muzhou Daoming (d.u.), a prominent disciple of the eminent Chan master HUANGBO XIYUN, and continued his studies of Chan under XUEFENG YICUN. Yunmen eventually became Xuefeng's disciple and inherited his lineage. Taking his leave of Xuefeng, Yunmen continued to visit other Chan masters throughout the country, and in 911 he visited the funerary STŪPA of the sixth patriarch (LIUZU) HUINENG on CAOXISHAN. Yunmen then visited Lingshu Rumin (d. 918), a famed disciple of the Chan master Fuzhou Da'an (793–883), at his monastery of Lingshu Chanyuan in Shaozhou (present-day Guangdong province) and continued to study under Lingshu until his death in 918. Yunmen was then asked by the ruler of the newly established Nan Han state (917–971), Liu Yan (r. 917–942), to succeed Lingshu's place at Lingshu Chanyuan. In 923, he established a monastery on Mt. Yunmen in the region, whence he acquired his toponym. He continued to reside on Mt. Yunmen for thirty years and frequently visited the palace of the Nan Han state to preach. In 938, Liu Cheng (943–958), monarch of the Nan Han, bestowed on him the title Great Master Kuangzhen (Genuine Truth). According to his wishes, no funerary stūpa was prepared for Yunmen and his body was left in his abbot's quarters (FANGZHANG). Yunmen was especially famous for his so-called one-word barriers (YIZI GUAN), in which he used a single utterance to respond to a student's question. For example, once a monk asked him, "When you kill your parents, you repent before the Buddha. But when you kill the buddhas and patriarchs, to whom do you repent?" Yunmen answered, "Lu" ("exposed"). Eighteen of Yunmen's most famous Chan cases (GONG'AN) are collected in the BIYAN LU ("Blue Cliff Record"); his extended teachings are recorded in the *Yunmen Kuangzhen chanshi guanglu*.

**Yunmen zong**. (J. Unmonshū; K. Unmun chong 雲門宗). In Chinese, "Cloud Gate school"; one of the so-called five houses and seven schools (WU JIA QI ZONG) of the mature Chinese CHAN tradition. It is named after the mountain, located in Shaozhou (present-day Guangdong province), where its founder YUNMEN WENYAN (864–949) taught. Yunmen Wenyan was famous for his "one-word barriers" or "one-word checkpoints" (YIZI GUAN), in which he responded to his students' questions by using only a single word. The school became one of the dominant Chan traditions in the Five Dynasties (Wudai) and early Song dynasty, producing such prominent masters as DONGSHAN SHOUCHU (910–990), Dongshan Xiaocong (d. 1030), XUEDOU ZHONGXIAN (980–1052), and Tianyi Yihuai (992–1064). Yunmen masters played a major role in the development of classical Chan literature. Xuedou Zhongxian's earlier collection of one hundred old cases (guce, viz., GONG'AN), known as the

*Xuedou songgu*, served as the basis for the famous Biyan lu ("Blue Cliff Record"), which added the extensive commentaries and annotations of the Linji master Yuanwu Keqin (1063–1135) to Zhongxian's original compilation. Several Yunmen masters were closely associated with the Song-dynasty intelligentsia. Dajue Huailian (1009–1090), for example, was as personal friend of the Song literocrat (shidafu) and poet Su Shi (1036–1101). Fori Qichong (1007–1072) asserted the fundamental harmony of Confucianism and Buddhism, explaining Confucian philosophical concepts using Buddhist terminology. Changlu Zongze (fl. c. late eleventh to early twelfth century) institutionalized the practice of reciting the name of the Buddha (nianfo) into the routine of Chan monastic life and wrote an influential text on Chan monastic regulations or "rules of purity" (qinggui), the Chanyuan qinggui ("Pure Rules for the Chan Grove"). The Yunmen school survived for about two centuries before it was eventually absorbed into the Linji zong.

**Yunqi fahui**. (雲棲法彙). In Chinese, "Anthology of the Teachings of Yunqi." See Yunqi Zhuhong.

**Yunqi Zhuhong**. (J. Unsei Shukō; K. Unsŏ Chugoeng 雲棲袾宏) (1535–1615). Chinese Chan master of the Linji zong and one of the so-called four great monks of the Ming dynasty, along with Hanshan Deqing (1546–1623), Daguan Zhenke (1543–1603), and Ouyi Zhixu (1599–1655); also known as Fohui and Lianchi. Yunqi was a native of Renhe, Hangzhou prefecture (present-day Zhejiang province). In 1566, Yunqi abandoned his family and his life as a Confucian literatus and was ordained by Xingtianli (d.u.) of West Mountain. Yunqi wandered throughout the country in search of prominent teachers and attained his first awakening at Dongchang in present-day Shandong province. In 1571, he arrived at Mt. Yunqi in Hangzhou, whence he acquired his toponym. There, he was able to restore Yunqi monastery with the help of local followers. His reputation grew after he successfully brought rain and drove tigers from the area. Yunqi remained on the mountain and composed over thirty major works. With the help of his Confucian background, Yunqi was able to draw a large public to his Chan teachings, and he also promoted the practice known as nianfo Chan in what was at the time the largest lay society in China. His influential works, such as the Changuan cejin, *Zizhi lu* ("Record of Self-Knowledge"), *Sengxun riji*, and *Zimen chongxing lu*, were edited together as the *Yunqi fahui* ("Anthology of the Teachings of Yunqi Zhuhong").

**yunshui**. (J. unsui; K. unsu 雲水). In Chinese, lit. "clouds and water"; a term abbreviated from the phrase "moving clouds and flowing water" (C. xingyun liushui; J. kōun ryūsui; K. haengun yusu), which is used to refer to an itinerant Buddhist practitioner who, like clouds or water, is always on the move and never settles down. The term is especially associated with the Chan (K. Sŏn; J. Zen) school, where it refers to a Chan monk in training. The term implies that a novice monk is expected to travel to various monasteries and learn from different teachers as part of his training, rather than remaining attached to one specific monastery or teaching. In contemporary Japanese Zen usage, unsui refers to neophyte priests who undergo training as novices and live in a sōdō (saṃgha hall, see sengtang) at a Zen training center. A "cloud robe" (J. unnō), by extension, refers to a monk's robe that is worn and ragged from following an itinerant lifestyle. During the Edo period (1600–1868), the term unsui became popularized to mean liberated, blissful travel, as exemplified in the novel, *Tōkaidōchū hizakurige* ("Traveling the Eastern Highway on a Chestnut Pony") by Jippensha Ikku (1765–1831). Unsui is also contrasted with the term "dragons and elephants" (C. longxiang; J. ryūzō; K. yongsang; see S. hastināga), which is commonly found in Chan texts to refer to an advanced adept of Chan.

**yuntang**. (雲堂). In Chinese, "cloud hall"; a monastic residential hall. See sengtang.

**Yuquansi**. (玉泉寺). In Chinese, "Jade Spring Monastery"; important meditative center located on Mt. Yuquan in Jingzhou prefecture (present-day Hubei province). During the Daye reign period (605–617) of the Sui dynasty, a name plaque for the monastery was prepared by the King of Jin, and the eminent monk Tiantai Zhiyi lectured there on his Fahua xuanyi and Mohe zhiguan. Yuquansi soon became a prominent center for meditators in China. The monastery became even more famous when the Chan master Shenxiu of the Northern school (Bei zong) took up residence at the site sometime in the last quarter of the seventh century. The famed Chan master Nanyue Huairang is also said to have ordained at Yuquansi.

**Yu sim allak to**. (C. Youxin anledao; J. Yūshin anrakudō 遊心安樂道). In Korean, "Wandering the Path to Mental Peace and Bliss"; traditionally attributed to the Korean monk Wŏnhyo, its authorship remains a matter of debate. No early references to this text are found in Korean canonical catalogues, and the earliest extant version was found in the library of the Raigōin in Kyōto, Japan. The prevailing scholarly view is that the text was composed in tenth-century Japan, perhaps by an adherent of the Tendaishū, with the first half of the work taken virtually verbatim from Wŏnhyo's *Muryangsugyŏng chongyo* ("Doctrinal Essentials of the Sukhāvatīvyūhasūtra"). The *Yu sim allak to* was influential in Japan, especially during the Kamakura period, when it was quoted in such texts as the *Kōmyō shingon dosha kanjinki* by Myōe Kōben, *An'yōshū* by Minamoto Takakuni (1004–1077), *Ketsujō ōjōshū* by Chinkai (1087–1165), and the Senchaku hongan nenbutsushū by Hōnen. The *Yu sim allak to* consists of seven sections: (1) the central tenet (i.e., the benefits of rebirth), (2) the whereabouts of the land of peace and happiness (anleguo, viz., sukhāvatī), (3) clarification of doubts and concerns, (4) the various causes and conditions of rebirth in the pure land, (5) the nine grades (jiupin) of rebirth, (6) the ease and difficulty of rebirth in the different buddha-fields (BUDDHAKṢETRA), (7) and the rebirth of women, those with dull faculties, and sinners. The last section also contains a MANTRA from the *Amoghapāśakalparājāsūtra* and an empowerment (ADHIṢṬHĀNA) ritual.

**Yu-Sŏk chirŭi non**. (儒釋質疑論). In Korean, "Treatise on Queries and Doubts concerning Yu (C. Ru, viz., Confucius) and Sŏk (C. Shi, ŚĀKYAMUNI)"; a Buddhist "defense of the faith" against Neo-Confucian criticisms, written during the early Chosŏn period. Although the authorship of this text remains a mystery, the style and content of the treatise resemble the HYŎNJŎNG NON by KIHWA (1376–1433), and it is clear that its Buddhist author was well versed in both Confucian and Daoist thought. The *Yu-Sŏk chirŭi non* is written in catechetic style and consists of nineteen questions and answers, which largely address misleading views that Confucian scholars hold regarding Buddhism. Following a syncretic approach that seeks to reconcile the teaching of Confucianism, Buddhism, and Daoism, this work generally argues that these three teachings each have their own distinctive roles to play in people's lives and need not be in conflict. Buddhism, Confucianism, and Daoism are explained as corresponding, respectively, to (1) nature (K. sŏng, C. XING), mind (K. sim, C. XIN), and pneuma (K. ki, C. qi); (2) truth (K. chin, C. zhen), its traces (K. chŏk, C. ji), and the connection between them; and so on. The treatise claims that these three teachings are ultimately in accord with one another because of their identical basis in the mind. The text also treats such traditional aspects of Chinese thought as yin-yang cosmology and the five phases (K. ohaeng, C. wuxing) (viz., the five traditional Chinese elements), as well as astrological and cosmological issues.

**yūzūnenbutsu**. (融通念佛). In Japanese, lit. "consummate-interfusion recitation of the Buddha's name"; a method of chanting Amida (S. AMITĀBHA) Buddha's name (J. nenbutsu; C. NIANFO), devised by the founder of the YŪZŪNENBUTSU school, RYŌNIN (1072–1132). The principle of yūzūnenbutsu is derived from Kegonshū (C. HUAYAN ZONG) and TENDAISHŪ (C. TIANTAI ZONG) philosophy, especially the Kegon teachings of "comsummate interfusion" (J. yūzū, C. YUANRONG) and the unobstructed interpenetration of all phenomena (J. jiji muge; see C. SHISHI WU'AI FAJIE) and the Tendai teaching of the mutual inclusion of the ten dharma-realms (J. jikkai goku; C. shijie huju). The principle of yūzūnenbutsu builds upon this sense that each and every phenomenon is perfectly interfused with all other phenomena to propose that the merit coming from one person's chanting of Amitābha's name is transferred to all other persons and vice versa. When more people chant the Buddha's name, more merit is thus transferred to all people, and the merit derived from these cooperative efforts reaches not only the dharma-realm (DHARMADHĀTU) in which it is created but also all other dharma-realms as well. Therefore, all things in all realms of existence receive benefit from any one individual's practice of chanting the Buddha's name. The practice of yūzūnenbutsu thus has two major characteristics: (1) the individual's burden to practice is relieved because salvation is due not just to one's own merit but to everyone's merit; (2) the notion of "other power" (TARIKI) in this form of pure land means both the power of one's fellow beings and the power deriving from Amitābha Buddha's vow of compassion.

**Yūzūnenbutsushū**. (融通念佛宗). In Japanese, "School of Consummate-Interfusion Recitation of the Buddha's Name"; one of the first Japanese PURE LAND schools. The school was founded by the TENDAISHŪ monk RYŌNIN (1072–1132), who claimed to have a direct revelation from the buddha Amida (S. AMITĀBHA) regarding the principle of YŪZŪNENBUTSU, in which every individual benefits from both his own and other's chanting of the Buddha's name (J. nenbutsu; C. NIANFO) through a mutual transfer of merit. Ryōnin traveled around Japan to teach the practice and spread the school, keeping a register of new adherents as he traveled. Indeed, carrying this register of adherents became a privilege of the leader of the school. Ryōnin also made Dainenbutsuji (Great Recitation of the Buddha's Name Temple), in the Ōsaka area, the center for his campaign in 1127. ¶ The Yūzūnenbutsu school declined after six generations. When the sixth patriarch of the school Ryōchin (d. 1182) died without a successor, the register of adherents was entrusted to the Iwashimizu Hachiman shrine, in the hopes that the HACHIMAN KAMI cum BODHISATTVA resident there would select the next patriarch of the school. About 140 years later, the Yūzūnenbutsu school was revitalized through the efforts of Hōmyō (1279–1349), who claimed to have received a revelation from Hachiman. After becoming Ryōnin's seventh successor in 1321, Hōmyō restored Dainenbutsuji and several other branch temples that had long been neglected. He also received imperial patronage from the monarch Godaigo (r. 1318–1339), who added his name and the names of many government officials to the school's register of adherents. After Hōmyō's death, the school declined again as other pure land schools gained popularity, until 1689, when Daitsū (1649–1716) became the forty-sixth patriarch of the school. Daitsū rejuvenated the school, ardently propagating the school's teachings and the practice of chanting the Buddha's name. Daitsū systematized the school's teachings: he established an academic institute and wrote two treatises, the *Yūzū enmonshō* ("Essay on the Complete Teachings of Perfect Interpenetration [*Yūzū*]") and the *Yūzūnenbutsu shingeshō* ("Essay on Faith and Understanding in the *Yūzūnenbutsu*"). In the former text, Daitsū lists five classifications of the Buddhist teachings in ascending order (the teaching of humans and divinities, HĪNAYĀNA, gradual, sudden, and consummate teachings) and classified Yūzūnenbutsu teachings in the fifth category of the "consummate teachings" (see YUANJIAO); he also discusses the school's daily practice of chanting Amida Buddha's name ten times while facing west. The Yūzūnenbutsu school remains active today at its head temple of Dainenbutsuji, although it is relatively small in size compared to the major Japanese pure land schools of JŌDOSHŪ and JŌDO SHINSHŪ. The AVATAṂSAKASŪTRA and the SADDHARMAPUṆḌARĪKASŪTRA are the principal scriptures of the school, with the three major pure land sūtras (JINGTU SANBUJING) of secondary importance.

# Z

**Zanabazar (Mongolian)**. See Rje btsun Dam pa.

**Zangs mdog dpal ri**. (Sangdok Palri). In Tibetan, the "Glorious Copper-Colored Mountain"; the abode of Padmasambhava. It is located on the island of Cāmara, one of the two "subcontinents" flanking the island of Jambudvīpa; Cāmara is sometimes identified as Sri Lanka. After leaving Tibet, Padmasambhava is said to have departed for the Copper-Colored Mountain. The island was inhabited by ogres (rakṣasa), whom he first had to subdue. He then constructed an octagonal palace, called "Lotus Light" (Padma 'od), at the summit of the mountain, where he will abide until the end of saṃsāra. In Tibetan Buddhism, Copper-Colored Mountain came to function as a pure land, although it is located on earth, and is not flat as pure lands are supposed to be. There are numerous prayers for rebirth on the Copper-Colored Mountain and numerous accounts of devotees being transported there in dreams and visions. Among the most common depictions of Padmasambhava in Tibetan painting are those of him enthroned on the Copper-Colored Mountain.

**zangzhu**. (J. zōshu/zōsu; K. changju 藏主). In Chinese, "library prefect." One of the six prefects (C. toushou) at a Chan monastery. The library prefect is in charge of the scriptures at the monastery. According to the Chanyuan qinggui, the library prefect prepares the reading desks and tea for those who wish to study the scriptures at the library or scriptorium.

**Zanning**. (J. Sannei; K. Ch'annyŏng 贊寧) (919–1001). Chinese vinaya master and historian. Zanning was a native of Bohai in present-day Hebei province. Sometime between 926 and 930, he was ordained at the monastery of Xiangfusi in Hangzhou, Zhejiang province, and received his monastic precepts on Mt. Tiantai. Zanning then studied the "Four-Part Vinaya" (Sifen lü) of the Dharmaguptaka school and became an expert in the South Mountain vinaya lineage (Nanshan Lü zong). He thus came to be known as Lühu or "Vinaya Tiger," and was given the title Great Master Mingyi (Bright Righteousness). In 978, he also received the title Great Master Tonghui (Penetrating Wisdom) and was invited to the monastery of Tianshousi. Upon the Emperor's decree, Zanning compiled the influential Buddhist biographical record, the Song gaoseng zhuan, which was completed and entered into the official canon (dazangjing) in 988. He also composed the Da Song seng shi lüe, one of the earliest attempts to provide a comprehensive account of the history of Buddhism throughout Asia. His other writings include the *Neidian ji*, *Jiuling shengxian lu*, and *Shichao yinyi zhigui*.

**Zaō gongen**. (藏王權現). In Japanese, "Provisional Manifestation of the Matrix King," also known as Zaō, Zaō bosatsu, and Kongō Zaō; proper name of a tutelary deity revered largely by followers of the Japanese Shugendō and Shingonshū traditions. Zaō gongen is said to have revealed himself to the legendary Japanese ascetic En no Gyōja, the reputed founder of Shugendō, on Mt. Kinbu in Nara. Zaō gongen is considered to be a bodhisattva who quells demons, as well as a nirmāṇakāya of the Buddha. Offerings and worship for Zaō gongen are conducted at the hall of Zaōdō on Mt. Kinbu. This wrathful deity is often depicted with three fearsome heads, with a three-pronged vajra in his right hand and his right leg suspended in the air.

**Zaya Paṇḍita**. [alt. Jaya Paṇḍita] (1599–1662). An important Mongolian monk of the Dge lugs sect of Tibetan Buddhism. Born as the fifth son in a noble family of the Qoshot tribe, in 1615 he was selected by its leader to become a monk. He was sent to Tibet where he became a disciple of the first (also counted as the fourth) Paṇ chen Lama, Blo bzang chos kyi rgyal mtshan, studying both the scholastic curriculum and the tantric curriculum. In 1639, after twenty-two years in Tibet, on the instructions of the Paṇ chen Lama and the fifth Dalai Lama, he returned to his homeland, serving as a missionary among the Qoshot. During this period, he invented the todorxoi üzüg (clear script) for the transcription of the Oirad language. In 1650, he returned to Tibet to make offerings to the Dalai Lama and to visit the Paṇ chen Lama, and then continued his missionary work, going as far west as the Kalmyk region of the Volga. Zaya Paṇḍita died while en route back to Tibet in 1662. He was a distinguished translator, translating 177 works from Tibetan into the Oirad language. The title of Zaya Paṇḍita was given to masters of the five traditional sciences; there were at least two other important Mongolian monks who bore the title and had lines of incarnation. The monk described here can be distinguished by his Tibetan name, Nam kha'i rgya mtsho.

**zazen**. (J) (坐禪). See zuochan.

**Zazen wasan**. (坐禪和讚). In Japanese, "Praise of Seated Meditation"; a short song by the Japanese ZEN master HAKUIN EKAKU in the RINZAISHŪ, which is probably his most popular work. The *Zazen wasan* is still printed in manuals for scripture recitation and is chanted at many Rinzai temples and monasteries today. In his song, Hakuin extols as the supreme virtues original enlightenment (J. HONGAKU; C. BENJUE), seated meditation (J. zazen; C. ZUOCHAN), and seeing one's own nature (J. kenshō; C. JIANXING).

**Zazen yōjinki**. (坐禪用心記). In Japanese, "Notes on Employing the Mind during Seated Meditation," by the ZEN master KEIZAN JŌKIN in the SŌTŌSHŪ; published in 1680. Following the model of his teacher DŌGEN KIGEN and his meditation manual FUKAN ZAZENGI, Keizan composed this relatively short treatise of his own on seated Zen (J. zazen; C. ZUOCHAN) for the edification of clergy and laity alike. The *Zazen yōjinki* delineates the purpose, method, and technique of seated meditation, with an emphasis on what kinds of mental states should be maintained during practice. Sitting meditation is explained as being a technique designed to set aside all attachments and concerns so that one will be able to abide serenely in one's true nature, or original face. Keizan also speaks of the specific impediments to meditative practice, such as deluded visions and sloth and torpor, and suggests some practical techniques for mitigating such problems.

**zedi**. (Burmese). See JEDI.

**Zen**. (禪). In Japanese, "Meditation"; the Japanese strand of the broader East Asian CHAN school, which includes Chinese Chan, Korean SŎN, and Vietnamese THIỀN. Zen is the Japanese pronunciation of the Chinese term Chan, which in turn is a transcription of the Sanskrit term DHYĀNA, or meditative absorption. More specifically, Zen denotes the Japanese Buddhist traditions that trace their origins back to the Chinese Chan school, or CHAN ZONG. Currently three major traditions in Japan, RINZAISHŪ, SŌTŌSHŪ, and ŌBAKUSHŪ, refer to themselves as Zen schools, and are thus known collectively as the Zen tradition (J. ZENSHŪ; C. CHAN ZONG). The Rinzaishū was first transmitted to Japan in the late twelfth century by MYŌAN EISAI (1141–1215), who visited China twice and received training and certification in the Chinese LINJI ZONG. By the end of the Kamakura period, some twenty-one different Rinzai lineages had been transmitted to Japan. The Rinzai school came to be associated with the meditative practice of contemplating Zen "cases" (J. kōan; C. GONG'AN; see also J. kanna Zen; C. KANHUA CHAN). The foundation of the Sōtōshū is attributed to DŌGEN KIGEN (1200–1253), who is credited with transmitting the CAODONG ZONG of the Chinese CHAN teacher TIANTONG RUJING (1162–1227). Dōgen is said to have taught the technique of "just sitting" (SHIKAN TAZA), through which the mind would become stabilized and concentrated in a state of full clarity and alertness, free from any specific content. During the Tokugawa period, the Sōtō school developed into one of the largest Buddhist sects in Japan through the mandatory parish system (DANKA SEIDO), in which every household was required to register as a member of a local Buddhist temple. By the middle of the eighteenth century, there were more than 17,500 Sōtō temples across the country. The Ōbakushū was founded by the émigré Chinese CHAN master YINYUAN LONGXI (J. Ingen Ryūki; 1592–1673), who traveled to Japan in 1654/1655 to escape the succession wars and political turmoil that had accompanied the fall of the Ming dynasty. The Ōbaku school introduced exotic contemporary Chinese customs and monastic practices to the Japanese Zen Buddhism of the time. Although it remained much smaller than the Rinzai and Sōtō Zen traditions, the presence of the Ōbaku school compelled the monks of its two larger rivals to reevaluate their own practices and to initiate a series of important reform movements within their respective traditions (see IN'IN EKISHI). In the modern era, largely through the efforts of such towering intellectual figures as DAISETZ TEITARO SUZUKI (1870–1966), NISHIDA KITARŌ (1870–1945), and NISHITANI KEIJI (1900–1991), the term Zen has also come to connote a "pure experience" (junsui keiken) that transcends language and thought, which is sometimes argued to be the unique property of the Japanese people and their culture (cf. KYOTO SCHOOL). The cavalier way in which the term Zen is now deployed in generic Western writings (e.g., the myriad "Zen in the Art of" books) often has little to do with the traditional perspectives of the Zen tradition found in either Japan or the rest of East Asia. As in the case of Chan, in more common parlance, Zen can also denote the particular teaching style of a Zen master and is often expressed as "so-and-so's Zen." See also entries on the SŌTŌSHŪ, RINZAISHŪ, and ŌBAKUSHŪ and on specific Japanese Zen masters and monasteries.

**zendō**. (禪堂). In Japanese, "meditation hall." See SENGTANG.

**Zenkōji**. (善光寺). In Japanese, "Monastery of the Radiance of Goodness"; located in modern-day Nagano. According to the *Zenkōji engi*, the monastery was built at the beginning of the seventh century by a certain Honda Yoshimitsu to enshrine a famous Amida (AMITĀBHA) triad. In the ancient Indian kingdom of VAIŚĀLĪ, a merchant by the name of Somachattra is said to have warded off epidemic demons and cured his daughter by invoking the name of the buddha Amitābha ten times. Somachattra was so moved by the appearance of Amitābha and his two attendants AVALOKITEŚVARA and MAHĀSTHĀMAPRĀPTA in the sky that he asked the Buddha for an icon to be made in their likeness. The triad was then forged with special gold from the dragon king's palace and worshipped as a living manifestation of Amitābha and his attendants. Somachattra was later reborn as King Sŏng (r. 523–553) of the Korean kingdom of Paekche. The triad first traveled to Paekche to aid King Sŏng, after which it was taken to Japan. Honda Yoshimitsu is said to have discovered the triad in the Naniwa Canal and enshrined it in his house, which was later transformed into a magnificent buddha hall by Empress Kōgyoku (r. 642–645). With support from the Hōjō bakufu, a Zenkōji cult proliferated especially during the Kamakura period and onwards, and numerous replicas of the "original" (Shinano) Zenkōji triad were made and enshrined in Shin ("New") Zenkōji temples. For centuries, the (Shinano) Zenkōji in Nagano remained under the control of another powerful TENDAISHŪ monastery known as MIIDERA. Zenkōji was devastated by fire in 1179, but legendary accounts testify to the miraculous escape of the "original" triad, which now remains as a secret buddha (HIBUTSU) image largely unavailable for public viewing. After the Japanese monk IPPEN's visit to Zenkōji, several Shin Zenkōji temples also came to be associated with his tradition, the JISHŪ.

**Zenrin kushū**. (禪林句集). In Japanese, "Phrase Collection of the ZEN Grove"; a lengthy collection of more than four thousand Zen phrases—specifically capping phrases (JAKUGO) or appended phrases (AGYO)—culled from Buddhist SŪTRAS, discourse records (YULU), kōan collections (see C. GONG'AN), and various Chinese belletristic classics. The collection was edited by a certain Ijūshi in 1688. Ijūshi's collection is based on a shorter phrase book entitled the *Kuzōshi*, compiled by the Zen master Tōyō Eichō (1428–1504) of the MYŌSHINJI lineage of the RINZAISHŪ. Beginning with single-character phrases, the Zen phrases in the *Zenrin kushū* are sequentially organized according to their number of Sinographs. The *Zenrin kushū* is one of the most commonly used collections in Japanese kōan training today.

**Zenrin shōkisen**. (禪林象器箋). In Japanese, "A Composition on the Images and Utensils of the Zen Grove"; compiled by the ZEN historian MUJAKU DŌCHŪ in the RINZAISHŪ; a comprehensive catalogue of regulations, events, utensils, and accoutrements used by the Zen (C. CHAN) tradition. The preface was prepared by Mujaku in 1741. More than just a simple catalogue, Mujaku's *Zenrin shōkisen* also meticulously notes the possible origin and history of each catalogued item and also expounds upon the significance of its implementation during his day, making it an invaluable tool for the study of Zen in practice. His research is based on an exhaustive list of sources (a total of 488 selections) beginning with sūtras and commentaries to Chinese and Japanese classics, lamplight histories (see CHUANDENG LU), and poetry. A handwritten copy of the text is currently housed at MYŌSHINJI in Kyōto.

**Zenshū**. (J) (禪宗). In Japanese, the school, lineage, or tradition of CHAN. See ZEN.

**Zetawun Pagoda**. In Burmese, "Prince Jeta's Grove" (P. JETAVANA); regarded as the oldest shrine in Sagaing. Zetawun Pagoda commemorates the Buddha's legendary first visit to Burma (Myanmar) in the company of ĀNANDA. According to tradition, the site was occupied by ninety-nine ogres (Burmese, bilu), the leader of whom was named Zeta. When they encountered the Buddha and Ānanda, the ogres welcomed them and, in return for their piety, the Buddha preached the dharma to them for seven days. All ninety-nine ogres became stream-enterers (P. sotāpanna; S. SROTAĀPANNA) while listening to these sermons. The Zetawun Pagoda purportedly contains the lower robe or waist cloth (P. antaravāsaka; S. ANTARVĀSAS) of the Buddha, which he is said to have presented to the ogres upon their entreaty to leave a token of his visit as an object of worship. The name Zetawun honors the ogre chief Zeta and recalls the fact that at the time of the Buddha's visit this spot was covered by forests (Burmese, wun). To commemorate the spiritual attainment of the ogres, the village that grew up around the site became known as Thotapan Ywa or Sotāpanna Village. An annual pagoda festival is held in the village on the new moon day of the Burmese month of Waso (July–August). Adjacent to the Zetawun can also be found an ordination hall said to have been established by the Mon saint, Shin Arahan.

**Zhabs dkar tshogs drug rang grol**. (Shapkar Tsokdruk Rangdröl) (1781–1851). One of the most revered Tibetan preachers and saints of the nineteenth century. He was born in the Reb kong region of A mdo in the northeast of the Tibetan cultural domain. During his youth, he received instruction in RDZOGS CHEN and various treasure (GTER MA) cycles of the RNYING MA sect. He undertook a one-year retreat at the age of sixteen and was ordained at the age of twenty at Rdo bis, a DGE LUGS monastery. He maintained his monastic vows throughout his life but wore his hair long and piled on the top of his head in the manner of a tantric YOGIN. His main teacher was Chos rgyal Ngag gi dbang po, but he studied with a variety of teachers, including those of the Dge lugs sect. He also studied traditional painting. An adept, pilgrim, and poet of the Rnying ma sect, he traveled throughout Tibet, undertaking retreats at such famous sites as Rma chen spom ra, TSA RI, and Mount KAILĀSA, including in a number of caves where MI LA RAS PA is said to have meditated. He became known as Zhabs dkar, or "white footprint," because he meditated at Mount Kailāsa, where the Buddha is said to have left his footprints (BUDDHAPĀDA). He also traveled to Kathmandu, where he offered gold for the spire of the BODHNĀTH STŪPA. He gained fame among all social classes through his wide-ranging activities as a Buddhist teacher and his enormous personal generosity and charisma. His autobiography, entitled *Snyigs dus 'gro ba yongs kyi skyabs mgon zhabs dkar rdo rje 'chang chen po'i rnam par thar pa rgyas par bshad pa* (translated as *The Life of Shabkar*) is regarded as one of the masterworks of that genre of Tibetan literature.

**Zhabs drung Ngag dbang rnam rgyal**. (Shapdrung Ngawang Namgyal) (1594–1651). A Tibetan Buddhist figure noted for unifying Bhutan as a Buddhist state. At a young age, Ngag dbang rnam rgyal was installed as the eighteenth successor to the throne of RWA LUNG monastery, seat of the 'BRUG PA BKA' BRGYUD sect of Tibetan Buddhism in central Tibet and its leaders, the 'BRUG CHEN INCARNATIONS. In 1616, at the age of twenty-three, he was forced to flee to Bhutan in a political dispute over his recognition as the reincarnation of the fourth 'Brug chen master, PADMA DKAR PO. Ngag dbang rnam rgyal initially gained control over the western region, with his forces eventually defeating his rivals and uniting the various regions into a single country under his leadership. He later successfully repelled an invasion of Bhutan by Tibetan forces mustered by the fifth DALAI LAMA. His title Zhabs drung (literally "at the feet") refers to his great stature as a Buddhist master. He is famed for establishing a religious and political system of monastic and administrative centers called rdzong (fortress), which are still in use today in Bhutan. Ngag dbang rnam rgyal is also considered the first master of a prominent Bhutanese incarnation lineage, the Zhabs drung incarnations.

**zhai**. (J. sai; K. chae 齋). A polysemous Chinese term that means "fast," "purify," "make offerings to monks," "festival," or "vegetarian feast" (and often seen translated as "maigre feast"); it is also used to translate the Sanskrit term UPOṢADHA. The traditional PRĀTIMOKṢA prohibition against monks and nuns eating after noon was referred to in Chinese as zhai, hence its translation as "fast." In China, zhai came to refer generally to meals offered at Buddhist rituals and events and more specifically to vegetarian feasts held at monasteries throughout the country. Monasteries often maintained special funds to be used for such purposes. These vegetarian feasts and festivals served as one of the primary means through which the laity made offerings to the monastic community. One of the most famous of such festivals in East Asia was the "Ghost Festival" (YULANBEN).

**Zhancha shan'e yebao jing**. (J. Senzatsu zen'aku gōhōkyō; K. Chŏmch'al sŏnak ŏppo kyŏng 占察善惡業報經). In Chinese, "Scripture of Divining the Requital of Good and Evil Actions"; an indigenous Chinese Buddhist scripture (see APOCRYPHA) compiled sometime during the late sixth century. The scripture seems to have been used by a community in Guangdong that was deemed heretical and whose practice of divination and repentance was banned in 593. The first roll of this scripture is largely concerned with the practice of divination, which is made possible through repentance. The scripture emphasizes the need for faith in this dharma-ending age (MOFA); the method of cultivating this faith is offered by the bodhisattva KṢITIGARBHA. This method largely involves the use of various spinning tops (lit. "wheels") on which the possible fate and fortune of the client is written. A total of 189 possible fates are offered. The repentance rite in the *Zhancha shan'e yebao jing* seems to have been influenced by the *Upāsakaśīlasūtra* translated by DHARMAKṢEMA. The second roll of the scripture has been a subject of controversy, for it provides an early version of the monistic "one mind" (YIXIN) and TATHĀGATAGARBHA doctrine that came to dominate in the East Asian schools of Buddhism. Comparisons are often made between this second roll and the influential DASHENG QIXIN LUN.

**Zhang Sengyao**. (C) (張僧繇) (d.u.; fl c. 502–549). The first Chinese artist to paint a rendering of the sixteen ARHAT protectors of Buddhism. See ṢOḌAŚASTHAVIRA.

**Zhang Shangying**. (J. Chō Shōei; K. Chang Sangyŏng 張商英) (1043–1122). Influential Chinese Buddhist layman and statesman; also known as Tinajue and Wujin jushi (Layman Infinite). Born to a prominent literati family in Xinjin (present-day Sichuan province), Zhang Shangying began his illustrious career in 1065 after receiving his jinshi degree. He first made a name for himself through military expeditions against neighboring barbarian tribes in Yuzhou, after which he was given a high metropolitan post by the powerful grand councilor Wang Anshi (1021–1086). Zhang thus became a supporter of Wang's administrative and fiscal reform attempts known as the "new policies" (xinfa). Even after Wang's fall from power, Zhang maintained his support for reform, which eventually allowed him to become grand councilor himself in 1111. Due to political battles at court and his complaints regarding Emperor Huizong's (r. 1100–1125) support of the Daoists' anti-Buddhist polemics, Zhang's tenure at court was cut short, and he spent the rest of his life in retirement. During this period of retirement, Zhang Shangying devoted much of his time to Buddhism. Throughout his life, Zhang befriended and studied under the most respected CHAN masters of his day, such as Dantang Wenzhun (1061–1115), Doushuai Congyue (1044–1091), Huitang Zuxin (1025–1100), ZHENJING KEWEN, YUANWU KEQIN, DAHUI ZONGGAO, and JUEFAN HUIHONG, and exchanged correspondence with many of them, some of which are still extant. Zhang was particularly fond of the AVATAṂSAKASŪTRA and commentaries on the text composed by the famous Tang dynasty layman LI TONGXUAN; emulating Li, Zhang made a pilgrimage to WUTAISHAN. He also wrote a treatise entitled *Hufa lun* ("Arguments in Defense of the Dharma)" as a rebuttal to the growing anti-Buddhist polemics among the Daoists at court.

**Zhanran**. (C) (湛然). See JINGXI ZHANRAN.

**Zhanran Yuandeng**. (J. Tannen Enchō; K. Tamyŏn Wŏnjing 湛然圓澄) (1561–1626). Chinese CHAN master in the CAODONG ZONG; also known as Sanmu daoren. Zhanran was a native of Huiji prefecture in Zhejiang province. In his early twenties, Zhanran became the student of the monk Miaofeng (d.u.) on Mt. Tianhuang and later received monastic precepts from the Chan master YUNQI ZHUHONG, one of the most eminent Chan teachers of the Ming dynasty. In 1591, Zhanran became the disciple of Cizhou Fangnian (d. 1594) and inherited his Caodong lineage. Zhanran first made a name for himself while residing at the monastery of Shouxingsi and subsequently served as abbot of the monasteries WANSHOUSI on Mt. Jing, and Xianshengsi in his hometown of Huiji, as well as several other monasteries in different regions of Zhejiang province. Zhanran composed the ZONGMEN HUOMEN, an influential treatise on

Chan meditation, and his other teachings are recorded in the *Zhanran Yuandeng chansi yulu*.

**zhao'er changji**. (C) (照而常寂). See JI ER CHANGZHAO.

**Zhao lun**. (J. Jōron; K. Cho non 肇論). In Chinese, "(Seng) zhao's Treatise"; an influential work by the eminent Chinese monk SENGZHAO (374–414), one of the major disciples of the important Kuchean translator KUMĀRAJĪVA (344–413). The *Zhao lun* was compiled sometime between 384 and 414 and brings together Sengzhao's four major works. The first, *Wubuqian lun* ("On the Immutability of Things"), explores the irrelevancy of time in explaining dharmas that are not subject to production and cessation. The second, *Buzhenkong lun* ("Emptiness of the Unreal"), explains how dharmas can simultaneously appear as both real and unreal. The BORE WUZHI LUN ("The Nescience of Prajñā") explains that because wisdom (PRAJÑĀ) is quiescent, empty, and lacking a perduring essence, any conscious awareness of it, or emanating from it, is impossible. Finally, "Niepan wuming lun" ("The Anonymity of Nirvāṇa") demonstrates that NIRVĀṆA is fundamentally ineffable and therefore nameless. A chapter entitled "Zong benyi" ("Fundamental Meaning of the Major Tenets") appears at the beginning of the *Zhao lun* and offers a succinct explanation of some important doctrinal matters, such as original nothingness (benwu), the true mark of reality (shixiang), dharma nature (faxing), and the emptiness of nature (xingkong). Letters exchanged between Sengzhao and the layman Liu Yimin (d. 410) of LUSHAN are appended at the end of the *Zhao lun*. Numerous commentaries on this text exist across the East Asian traditions.

**Zhaozhou Congshen**. (J. Jōshū Jūshin; K. Choju Chongsim 趙州從諗) (778–897). One of the most renowned Chinese CHAN teachers of the Tang dynasty; his toponym Zhaozhou derives from the Zhaozhou region in Hebei province, where he spent much of his later teaching career. Zhaozhou was ordained in his youth at Hutongyuan in his hometown of Caozhou (in present-day Shandong province). At the age of eighteen, he met NANQUAN PUYUAN (748–835), a successor of MAZU DAOYI (709–788), and studied under him for several decades until that teacher's death. Then in his fifties, Zhaozhou began to travel throughout China, visiting prominent Chan masters such as HUANGBO XIYUN (d. 850) and Daowu Yuanzhi (760–835). Having served as abbot of various monasteries on Mt. Huangbo, Baoshou, and Jia, Zhaozhou settled at the age of eighty in Guanyinyuan (AVALOKITEŚVARA Cloister) in Zhaozhou, and taught a small group of monks there for the next forty years. Zhaozhou did not use the iconoclastic pedagogical techniques, such as shouting and beating (BANGHE), made famous by other teachers of his era, but used his words to challenge his students and lead them to self-realization. The Song-dynasty Chan master YUANWU KEQIN (1063–1135) described this characteristic of Zhaozhou's teachings when he said, "Zhaozhou's Chan lies on the lips." Zhaozhou is frequently cited in the collections of Chan GONG'AN (public cases), including five of the forty-eight gong'ans collected in the WUMEN GUAN ("Gateless Checkpoint") and twelve of the one hundred in the BIYAN LU ("Blue Cliff Record"). The most influential gong'an associated with Zhaozhou is the first case collected in the *Wumen guan*, the so-called WU GONG'AN: "'Does a dog have the buddha-nature (FOXING) or not?' 'No.'" Zhaozhou's "WU" (no; lit. "it does not have it"), became one of the most oft-cited statements in all of Chan, SŎN, and ZEN literature. Due in large part to the efforts of Chan master DAHUI ZONGGAO and his followers, Zhaozhou's wu came to be used as one of the meditative topics (HUATOU) in the Chan meditation practice of "questioning meditation" (KANHUA CHAN). Although Zhaozhou had thirteen dharma heirs, his lineage soon died out. He posthumously received the title "Zhenji dashi" (Great Master Apex of Truth). The record of his teachings is contained in the three rolls of the *Zhenji dashi yulu* ("Discourse Record of Zhenji Dashi") and in his *Zhaozhou lu*.

**Zhe chen**. (Shechen). One of the four main RNYING MA monasteries in eastern Tibet, the others being KAḤ THOG, RDZOGS CHEN, and DPAL YUL; founded in 1735 by the second ZHE CHEN RAB 'BYAMS incarnation, 'Gyur med kun bzang rnam rgyal (Gyurme Kunsang Namgyel, 1710–1769). Zhe chen then became the seat for his subsequent incarnations, who all served as abbot, and a principal institution of the Rnying ma sect of Tibetan Buddhism. The monastery, comprised of several main temples and surrounding structures, was at times also governed by a line of regent lamas, the Zhe chen rgyal tshab (Shechen Gyaltsap) incarnations. The fourth Zhe chen rgyal tshab, Padma rnam rgyal (Pema Namgyel, 1871–1926), formally recognized the young twentieth-century luminary DIL MGO MKHYEN BRTSE as one of five reembodiments of 'JAM DBYANG MKHYEN BRTSE DBANG PO, a leading figure of the nineteenth-century RIS MED, or nonsectarian movement. The institution's full name is Zhe chen bden gnyis dar rgyas gling (Shechen Dennyi Dargyeling).

**Zhe chen rab 'byams**. (Shechen Rapjam). An important line of Tibetan incarnate lamas. The first Zhe chen rab 'byams, Bstan pa'i rgyal mtshan (Tenpe Gyaltsen, 1650–1709), was a disciple of the fifth DALAI LAMA, NGAG DBANG BLO BZANG RGYA MTSHO, and Padma rig 'dzin (Pema Rikdzin, 1625–1697)—the latter being the first RDZOGS CHEN INCARNATION and founder of RDZOGS CHEN monastery. The second Zhe chen rab 'byams, 'Gyur med kun bzang rnam rgyal (Gyurme Kunsang Namgyel, 1710–1769), founded Zhe chen monastery in 1735. Subsequent incarnations served as the abbots of Zhe chen monastery.

**zheng bao**. (J. shōhō; K. chŏngbo 正報). In Chinese "retribution proper," the actions, or KARMAN, directly affect the individual, conditioning one's physical body and psychological makeup. See ER BAO.

**Zhengdao ge**. (J. Shōdōka; K. Chŭngdo ka 證道歌). In Chinese, "Song of the Attainment of the Way"; attributed to YONGJIA XUANJUE (675–713); also known as the *Chanmen biyao jue* ("Secret Essentials of the Chan Tradition"). Along with the XINXIN MING, the *Zhengdao ge* is cherished by the CHAN tradition as one of the classic verse expressions on the process of meditation and the experience of enlightenment. Its contents purport to convey Yongjia's awakening after only a single day and night of tutelage under the sixth patriarch (LIUZU) HUINENG, whence Yongjia's cognomen Ishujue ("Single-Night Enlightened," or "Overnight Guest"). The poem consists of fewer than two thousand Sinographs and follows a traditional regulated-verse style. The verse describes enlightenment as the realization that the true nature of all things is in fact the buddha-nature (FOXING), which is emptiness itself, transcending all the dichotomies of existence or nonexistence or truth and falsity. This enlightenment is said to occur suddenly, "in a snap of the fingers" (danzhi), the verse says, and it is this sudden enlightenment (DUNWU) that has been transmitted through the twenty-eight Indian and six Chinese patriarchs (ZUSHI) of the Chan tradition. Aspects of the style and vocabulary used in the poem, which seem to antedate the eighth century, have led to questions about the authenticity of its attribution to Yongjia. Several copies of this text were found at DUNHUANG, and numerous commentaries of this text are extant, dating from the Song dynasty. The Song-dynasty teacher DAHUI ZONGGAO claimed that the verse was held in such high esteem that it had even been back-translated into Sanskrit.

**Zhengfayanzang**. (J. Shōbōgenzō; K. Chŏngpŏbanjang 正法眼藏). In Chinese, "Treasury of the Eye of the True Dharma," in three rolls, edited by the CHAN master DAHUI ZONGGAO and his lay disciples in 1147. The Zhengfayanzang is largely a collection of 661 cases or GONG'AN with Dahui's prose commentary (pingchang), annotations (C. zhuoyu/zhuyu; see J. JAKUGO), and instructions for the assembly. The zhengfayanzang of the title is a term used within Chan to indicate the school's special repository of the "eye" or "mind" of the BUDDHADHARMA, which is independent from the scriptural tradition. (See JIAOWAI BIECHUAN). The exchanges between masters and disciples that Daohui covers in his collection are described as being the transmission of this eye. His *Zhengfayanzang* thus records the exchanges of a number of renowned Tang and Northern Song Chan masters and their disciples, including ZHAOZHOU CONGSHEN, DESHAN XUANJIAN, and XUEFENG YICUN, as well as the sermons of masters associated especially with the LINJI ZONG, including LINJI YIXUAN, YANGQI FANGHUI, and HUANGLONG HUINAN. Dahui strings together typically between three and six exchanges or sermons and, at the end of each section, adds his own brief prose commentary, often about twenty Sinographs in length, most starting with "Miaoxi says." (Miaoxi is one of Daihui's cognomens.) The *Zhengfayanzang* seems to have exerted some influence on the compilation of the ZONGMEN LIANDENG HUIYAO, by Dahui's third-generation successor Huiweng Wuming (d.u.). The SHŌBŌGENZŌ, the magnum opus of the Japanese SŌTŌSHŪ monk DŌGEN KIGEN, bears the same title but in its Japanese pronunciation.

**Zhengjue**. (C) (正覺). See HONGZHI ZHENGJUE.

**Zhengnian**. (C) (正念). See DAXIU ZHENGNIAN.

**zhengwu**. (J. shōgo; K. chŭngo 證悟). In Chinese, "realization-awakening"; the most advanced of the two types of enlightenment (WU; BODHI) discussed in some CHAN schools, equivalent to the achievement of buddhahood. This type of awakening is achieved at the consummation of the ten stages (BHŪMI) of the bodhisattva path, rendering one a buddha in fact as well as in principle. The initial "seeing the nature" (JIANXING) of buddhahood catalyzes the "understanding-awakening" (JIEWU), in which the Chan adept comes to know that he is not a deluded sentient being but a buddha. This initial sudden awakening is not in itself sufficient, however, to bring an end to the habituations (VĀSANĀ) that have been engrained in the mind for an essentially infinite amount of time. It is only after a period of gradual cultivation (jianxiu) that these habitual tendencies will be removed and one's actions will finally correspond with one's understanding. That point where knowledge and action are fully integrated marks the final "realization-awakening" (ZHENGWU) and thus constitutes the complete, perfect enlightenment of buddhahood (ANUTTARASAMYAKSAṂBODHI). This two-tiered approach to awakening is the hallmark of the sudden awakening/gradual cultivation (DUNWU JIANXIU) path (MĀRGA) schema of certain Chan masters, such as GUIFENG ZONGMI (780–841) in the Chinese Hoze school of Chan, and POJO CHINUL (1158–1210) of the Korean Sŏn tradition.

**Zhenjing Kewen**. (J. Shinjō Kokubun; K. Chinjŏng Kŭngmun 眞浄克文) (1025–1102). Chinese CHAN master in the HUANGLONG PAI collateral line branch of the LINJI ZONG; also known as Yun'an, Baofeng, and Letan. Zhenjing was a native of Shanfu in present-day Henan province. He became a student of a certain master Guang of the North Pagoda in Fuzhou (present-day Hubei province) and was given the name Kewen. After receiving the monastic precepts at age twenty-four, Zhenjing began studying the sūtras and commentaries, but left for the South to seek out teachers of Chan. In 1065, Zhenjing spent a summer retreat on Mt. Dawei and had his first awakening experience upon hearing the words of the Chan master YUNMEN WENYAN from another monk. Zhenjing eventually became a disciple of the eminent Chan master HUANGLONG HUINAN (1002–1069) in Jicui and inherited his Linji lineage. At the request of the local king, Zhenjing moved to Jinleng, where he became the founding abbot of a monastery named Baoningsi. Zhenjing later retired to Gao'an, where he built a small hermitage named Toulao'an. Six years later, he moved to the monastery of Guizongsi on LUSHAN and again to Letan at the request of the famed statesman ZHANG SHANGYING. Along with his colleagues Huanglong Zuxin (1025–1100) and Donglin Changcong (1025–1091), Zhenjing helped to build their teacher Huanglong Huinan's lineage into one of the most prosperous in China. He retired to the hermitage of Yun'an, where he passed away in 1102. Zhenjing left numerous disciples and students, many of whom were statesmen and officials from Jiangxi province. His teachings can be found in the *Yun'an Zhenjing chanshi yulu*.

**Zhenke**. (C) (眞可). See DAGUAN ZHENKE.

**zhenru**. (J. shinnyo; K. chinyŏ 眞如). In Chinese, "true thusness" or "true suchness"; the Chinese translation of the Sanskrit terms BHŪTATATHATĀ or TATHATĀ, which comes to play its own important role in indigenous Chinese Buddhist thought. According to the Chinese scholastic tradition, deriving from translations of the LAṄKĀVATĀRASŪTRA and YOGĀCĀRA sources, ZHENRU is, along with right knowledge (chengzhi), one of the two "factors associated with enlightenment" (wufa), true thusness being what is seen by correct knowledge when perception is freed from conceptual superimpositions. True thusness (zhenru) is described in the DASHENG QIXIN LUN ("Awakening of Faith According to the Mahāyāna") as one of two distinct, but complementary, aspects of the one mind (YIXIN), along with production and cessation (shengmie). True thusness and production and cessation correspond, respectively, to ultimate truth (PARAMĀRTHASATYA) and conventional truth (SAṂVṚTISATYA), or the unconditioned (ASAMSKRTA) and conditioned (SAṂKṚTA) realms. Since the mind that is subject to production and cessation (which the *Dasheng qixin lun* identifies with ĀLAYAVIJÑĀNA) remains always grounded on the mind of true thusness (which the treatise identifies with TATHĀGATAGARBHA), the mind may therefore be simultaneously described as both deluded and enlightened. The bifurcation between this enlightened essence of the mind as "true thusness" and its various temporal manifestations as "production and cessation" also aligns with the "essence" (TI) and "function" (YONG) distinction that Buddhism imported from indigenous Chinese philosophy.

**zhenyan**. (J. shingon; K. chinŏn 眞言). In Chinese, lit. "true word." See MANTRA; SHINGONSHŪ.

**Zhi**. (J. Shi; K. Chi 支). Ethnikon used in China for monks from Scythia (C. Yuezhi) or its successor state, the KUSHAN kingdom, in the northwest of India.

**zhi byed**. (shije). In Tibetan, lit. "pacification"; a Tibetan Buddhist tradition of meditation practice traced back to the eleventh-century Indian adept PHA DAM PA SANGS RGYAS, who for many years taught at the small temple of GLANG SKOR, near Ding ri in western Tibet. The name derives from the goal of the practice, which is the "pacification" of all suffering, transforming negative states into positive states through the practice of the six perfections (PĀRAMITĀ), especially the perfection of wisdom (PRAJÑĀPĀRAMITĀ). The practice is also said to extend one's life. Together with the related tradition of GCOD, or "severance," promulgated by Pha dam pa sangs rgyas's female disciple MA GCIG LAB SGRON, pacification is frequently counted as one of eight major streams of Buddhist practice found in Tibet, the so-called eight great conveyances that are lineages of achievement (SGRUB BRGYUD SHING RTA CHEN PO BRGYAD). Unlike the tradition of severance, however, the practice of pacification as a unique system had largely died out by the nineteenth century, when great Tibetan scholars of the nonsectarian (RIS MED) movement attempted to preserve its transmission.

**zhidian**. (J. chiden; K. chijŏn 知殿). In Chinese, lit., "to know the halls," a "hall prefect"; one of the six prefects (C. TOUSHOU) at a CHAN or ZEN monastery. The hall prefect is in charge of cleaning and preparing the shrine halls and the ritual objects placed therein.

**Zhi Dun**. [alt. Zhi Daolin] (J. Shi Ton/Shi Dōrin; K. Chi Tun/Chi Torim 支遁/支道林) (314–366). An early exegete of the perfection of wisdom (PRAJÑĀPĀRAMITĀ) literature in the southern part of China and leader of an influential group of early Buddhist philosophers associated with the "Dark Learning" (XUANXUE) school. Zhi is especially important for his crucial reinterpretation of the Chinese philosophical term LI, which previously had meant the "pattern" or natural order of things. Zhi instead reinterprets li in light of perfection of wisdom thought as an absolute "principle," which later came to be contrasted with the manifestations of that principle in the world as various "phenomena" (SHI). This distinction between principle and phenomena later occupied a crucial position in the thought of many of the indigenous schools of Chinese Buddhism, including the TIANTAI ZONG and the HUAYAN ZONG. Zhi Dun is also known for the earliest communication to a certain monk from the Korean Koguryŏ Kingdom, at least one decade before the official introduction of Buddhism to the peninsula, suggesting earlier Buddhist contacts between China and Korea than the extant evidence indicates.

**zhike**. (J. shika; K. chigaek 知客). In Chinese, "guest prefect"; one of the six prefects (C. TOUSHOU) at a CHAN monastery. The guest prefect is in charge of receiving and accommodating important visitors and guests. In modern Japanese ZEN, the guest prefect plays an important role in the training of young monks on pilgrimage (J. ANGYA; see C. XINGJIAO) as they engage each other in the elaborate ritual of receiving permission to enter the monastery.

**zhi khro**. (shi dro). In Tibetan, "peaceful and wrathful"; a term used to refer to assemblies (especially in a MAṆḌALA) of peaceful and wrathful (also known as khrag 'thung or "blood drinking") deities. For example, in the so-called *Tibetan Book of the Dead*, known in Tibetan as the BAR DO THOS GROL CHEN MO or the *Karma zhi khro* ("The Peaceful and Wrathful Deities of

KARMA GLING PA"), a maṇḍala of forty-two peaceful deities and fifty-eight wrathful deities appears during the chos nyid bar do, the second of the three bardos (ANTARĀBHAVA).

**Zhikong Chanxian**. (J. Shikū Zenken; K. Chigong Sŏnhyŏn; S. *Śūnyadiśya-Dhyānabhadra 指空禪賢) (1289–1363). In Chinese, "Pointing to Emptiness, Meditative Worthy," an Indian monk who taught first in China, but later came to live and teach in Korea at the end of the Koryŏ dynasty, where his influence was especially important; his Chinese name is sometimes reconstructed into Sanskrit as *DHYĀNABHADRA, and this is how he is often known in the literature. According to his memorial stele written by the Korean literatus Yi Saek (1328–1396), Zhikong was born as the third son of the ruler of a small state in the MAGADHA region of northeastern India around 1235. He entered the monastic life at the age of eight and is said to have studied at the famous NĀLANDĀ monastic university under the guidance of Vinayabhadra (C. Lüxian). He claimed to have traveled to Sri Lanka at the age of nineteen to study under Samantaprabhāsa (C. Puming), the 107th patriarch in a putative "Chan" lineage starting from MAHĀKĀŚYAPA, which probably means some sort of meditative lineage quite distinct from the East Asian CHAN lineages. After receiving transmission from Samantaprabhāsa, Zhikong became the 108th patriarch in that lineage. Around 1324, Zhikong traveled via Tibet to the Yuan dynasty and then went on to Koryŏ in 1326 at the invitation of King Ch'ungsuk (1294–1339; r. 1313–1330, 1332–1339), whom he had met in Beijing at the Mongol court. During his stay in Koryŏ, Zhikong went on pilgrimage to many important Buddhist sites, including the famous Diamond Mountains (KŬMGANGSAN). He also founded Hoeamsa (Fir Tree Cliff Monastery) in 1328 in what is now Kyŏnggi province, which is said to have been modeled after Nālandā monastery. He returned to the Yuan in 1328, where he was visited by many Korean students, including the late Koryŏ monks NAONG HYEGŬN (1320–1376) and MUHAK CHACH'O (1327–1405), on whom he had great influence. He died in 1363, and because of the reverence in which he was held by King Kongmin (r. 1351–1374), some of his relics were sent to Koryŏ. The relics were first housed in the royal palace and later enshrined in a reliquary at Hoeamsa. Zhikong was supposed to have been well versed in literature of PRAJÑĀPĀRAMITĀ, VINAYA, and TANTRA. In Korea, there survives a collection of his teachings, the *Chigong hwasang Sŏnyo nok* ("Master Zhigong's Essentials of Sŏn Record"), and his putative sūtra, the *Munsusari posal ch'oesangsŭng musaenggye kyŏng* ("Sūtra on the Ultimate Nonproduction (ANUTPĀDA) Precepts of the Bodhisattva MAÑJUŚRĪ"), which is supposed to have been translated from a Sanskrit original by his disciple Naong.

**Zhili**. (C) (知禮). See SIMING ZHILI.

**Zhi Qian**. (J. Shi Ken; K. Chi Kyŏm 支謙) (fl. c. 220–252). Prolific earlier translator of Buddhist texts into Chinese. A descendant of an Indo-Scythian émigré from the KUSHAN kingdom in the KASHMIR-GANDHĀRA region of northwest India, Zhi Qian is said to have been fluent in six languages. Although never ordained as a monk, Zhi Qian studied under the guidance of Zhi Liang (d.u.), a disciple of the renowned Indo-Scythian translator LOKAKṢEMA (fl. c. 178–198 CE). Zhi Qian fled northern China in the political chaos that accompanied the collapse of the Han dynasty (206 BCE–220 CE), eventually migrating to the Wu Kingdom in the south. There, he settled first in Wuchang and later in the Wu capital of Jianye, which was where the majority of his translations appear to have been made. Zhi Qian was known to have been artistically talented, and many of his translations were noted for their fluent style that did not strive to adhere to the exact meaning of each word and phrase, but instead sought to convey the insights of the text in an accessible fashion for a Chinese audience. The fifty-three translations that are attributed to Zhi Qian range widely between ĀGAMA and didactic materials and early MAHĀYĀNA scriptural literature, but also include many spurious later attributions (see APOCRYPHA). Among the translations that may with confidence be ascribed to Zhi Qian are early renderings of the VIMALAKĪRTINIRDEŚA, the PUSA BENYE JING, the SUKHĀVATĪVYŪHASŪTRA, the AṢṬASĀHASRIKĀPRAJÑĀPĀRAMITĀ, and a primitive recension of the AVATAṂSAKASŪTRA. Zhi Qian is also presumed to be one of the first Buddhist commentators in the East Asian tradition: DAO'AN (314–385) states in his scriptural catalogue ZONGLI ZHONGJING MULU (now embedded in the CHU SANZANG JIJI) that Zhi Qian wrote a commentary to the ŚĀLISTAMBASŪTRA (C. Liaoben shengsi jing) while preparing its translation. Late in his life, Zhi Qian retired to Mt. Qionglong, where he is said to have passed away at the age of sixty.

**zhishi**. (J. chiji; K. chisa 知事). In Chinese, lit., "to know or manage affairs"; a "steward" at a CHAN monastery. Ideally, there are six stewards who oversee the administration and finances of the monastic community. Because their offices were often located on the east side of the monastery, they were also often referred to as the east section or rank. The influential CHANYUAN QINGGUI mentions only four stewards, the prior (C. JIANYUAN), rector (C. WEINUO), cook (C. DIANZUO), and overseer (C. ZHISUI). Later, the prior came to be referred to as the DUSI, and a comptroller (C. JIANSI) and assistant comptroller (C. FUSI) were added to the list of four.

**zhisui**. (J. shissui; K. chikse 直歲). In Chinese, "overseer"; one of the six stewards (C. ZHISHI) at a CHAN monastery. The zhisui supervises the manual labor conducted in the monastery, including everything from large construction projects, repairs, and the cultivation of land to patrolling the monastery grounds.

**Zhixu**. (J. Chigyoku; K. Chiuk 智旭) (C). See OUYI ZHIXU.

**Zhiyan**. (J. Chigon; K. Chiŏm 智儼) (602–668). Putative second patriarch of the Chinese HUAYAN tradition. Zhiyan was a native of Tianshui in present-day Gansu province. While still a boy, Zhiyan is said to have become a student of the monk DUSHUN at the monastery of Zhixiangsi on ZHONGNANSHAN. He was ordained at age fourteen and received the full monastic precepts at age twenty, at which time he began studying the "Four-Part Vinaya" (SIFEN LÜ) of the DHARMAGUPTAKA school, as well as the *TATTVASIDDHI, DAŚABHŪMIKASŪTRA, BODHISATTVABHŪMI, and MAHĀPARINIRVĀṆASŪTRA. Zhiyan also studied the MAHĀYĀNASAMGRAHA under Fachang (567–645). While studying under Jinglin (565–640), Zhiyan came across a copy of the AVATAṂSAKASŪTRA and, at age twenty-seven, composed his influential commentary on the *Avataṃsakasūtra*, the HUAYAN JING SOUXUAN JI. He also composed the KONGMU ZHANG (viz., *Huayan jingnei zhangmendeng za kongmu zhang*), *Shi xuan men*, *Huayan wushi yao wenda*, *Jingang jing lüeshu*, and others. Zhiyan began to make a name for himself by preaching the *Avataṃsakasūtra* to the rural populace and eventually counted among his many supporters the Emperor Gaozong (r. 649–683) himself. Zhiyan is closely associated with the doctrine of "nature origination" (XINGQI), which explains how enlightenment can be "originated" only from within the very "nature" of this world; enlightenment is therefore not something that needs to be created, for it derives from the inherent nature of the mind itself. ZHIYAN's teachings on the *Avataṃsakasūtra* were extremely influential in East Asian Buddhism and were developed further by his disciples ŬISANG and FAZANG. The Korean monk WŎNHYO was also heavily influenced by Zhiyan's writings. Because Zhiyan resided at his teacher's monastery Zhixiangsi, he later came to be called Great Master Zhixiang.

**Zhiyi**. (C) (智顗) (538–597). See TIANTAI ZHIYI.

**zhiyu**. (J. chiyoku; K. chiyok 知浴). In Chinese, the "bath prefect"; one of the six prefects (C. TOUSHOU) at a CHAN monastery. The bath prefect is in charge of cleaning the bathhouse, heating the water for use, and preparing necessities such as towels, incense, and tea. Usually, the bath prefect prepares the bath according to a strict monthly schedule.

**zhizhi renxin**. (J. jikishi ninshin; K. chikchi insim 直指人心). In Chinese, "directly point to the human mind"; a famous aphorism summarizing the soteriological approach of the CHAN school. The phrase appears for the first time in HUANGBO XIYUN's CHUANXIN FAYAO, where it is followed by the line JIANXING CHENGFO ("see one's own nature and become a buddha"). Subsequently, these two phrases appear together with two other phrases, BULIWENZI ("not establishing words or letters") and JIAOWAI BIECHUAN ("a special transmission outside the teachings"), in the ZUTING SHIYUAN compiled in 1108. These four phrases subsequently became a normative teaching for Chan practice and also the foundation on which the Chan, SŎN, and ZEN traditions created their own self-identity as a separate school of East Asian Buddhism.

**Zhongfeng Mingben**. (J. Chūhō Myōhon; K. Chungbong Myŏngbon 中峰明本) (1263–1323). Chinese CHAN master in the LINJI ZONG and one of the most influential monks of the Yuan dynasty; also known by the toponym Huanzhu (Illusory Abode). Zhongfeng was a native of Qiantang in Hangzhou prefecture (present-day Zhejiang province). While still a youth, Zhongfeng left home to study under the Chan master GAOFENG YUANMIAO of Mt. Tianmu, from whom he eventually received his monastic precepts at age twenty-four. After he left Gaofeng, Zhongfeng maintained no fixed residence and would on some occasions dwell on a boat. As his reputation grew, he came to be known as the Old Buddha of the South (Jiangnan Gufo). Mingben was an especially eloquent advocate of "questioning meditation" (KANHUA CHAN); his descriptions of the meaning and significance of Chan cases (GONG'AN) and meditative topics (HUATOU) and the processes and experience of kanhua practice are widely cited in the literature. In 1318, he was given a golden robe and the title Chan master Foci Yuanzhao Guanghui (Buddha's Compassion, Perfect Illumination, Broad Wisdom) from Emperor Renzong (r. 1311–1320). Zhongfeng also served as teacher of the next emperor Yingzong (r. 1320–1323). Emperor Wenzong (r. 1329–1332) also bestowed upon him the posthumous title Chan master Zhijue (Wise Enlightenment). Five years later, Emperor Shundi (r. 1333–1367) entered Zhongfeng's discourse records (YULU), the *Zhongfeng guanglu*, into the Chinese Buddhist canon (DAZANGJING), a signal honor for an indigenous author (few of whom are represented in the official canon); Shundi also bestowed on him the title State Preceptor Puying (Universal Resonance). Zhongfeng also composed his own set of monastic rules (QINGGUI) titled the *Huanzhu'an qinggui*.

**Zhongguan lun shu**. (J. Chūgan ronsho; K. Chunggwan non so 中觀論疏). In Chinese, "Commentary on the MŪLAMADHYAMAKAKĀRIKĀ"; composed by the Chinese SAN LUN ZONG monk JIZANG in 608. Jizang begins with his observations on Sengrui's (378–444?) preface to their teacher KUMĀRAJĪVA's translation of the *Mūlamadhyamakakārikā*. He then analyzes the twenty-seven chapters of the *Mūlamadhyamakakārikā* in a manner consistent with other scholars of the San lun tradition. Jizang contends that the middle way is a path traversed by the buddhas and BODHISATTVAS and explains its contents in terms of conventional truth (SAṂVṚTISATYA), absolute truth (PARAMĀRTHASATYA), and neither conventional nor absolute truth. (See also SANDI.) Jizang supports his arguments by citing numerous sūtras, commentaries, and theories of other teachers. For his analysis of emptiness (ŚŪNYATĀ), Jizang frequently makes recourse to the MAHĀPARINIRVĀṆASŪTRA.

**zhongjiao**. (C) (終教). See HUAYAN WUJIAO.

**Zhongnanshan**. (J. Shūnanzan; K. Chongnamsan 終南山). In Chinese, "Southernmost Mountain"; also called Nanshan, Mt. Taibai, Mt. Difei, and Mt. Zhounan. Zhongnanshan is located west of the former Chinese capital of Chang'an (present-day Xi'an) and occupies a section of the Qinling Mountain range that stretches through southern Shaanxi province. Because of its proximity to the capital, Zhongnanshan became an important practice site in both the Buddhist and Daoist traditions. Two Buddhist monasteries were built on the mountain, and they attracted many eminent Buddhist monks throughout the dynasties. DAOXUAN, the founder of the Nanshan branch of the Chinese VINAYA school (LÜ ZONG) studied there; because of his long association with the mountain, his tradition of monastic discipline came also to be known as the NANSHAN LÜ ZONG. FAZANG is also said to have begun his study of the AVATAṂSAKASŪTRA on Zhongnanshan and to have performed a Buddho-Daoist prayer ritual on the mountain at the behest of Emperor Ruizong in order to relieve a drought. The syncretic character of the ritual he performed symbolizes the way in which Zhongnanshan straddles the two religious traditions. Sources differ as to whether the monastery where he performed the ritual was Longchisi (Monastery of the Dragon Pool) or Wuzhensi (Awakening to Truth Monastery).

**Zhongxiangcheng**. (J. Shūkōjō; K. Chunghyangsŏng 衆香城). In Chinese, "City of Multitudinous Fragrances"; according to the AṢṬASĀHASRIKĀPRAJÑĀPĀRAMITĀ, the city where the BODHISATTVA DHARMODGATA lived and taught the perfection of wisdom (PRAJÑĀPĀRAMITĀ); an alternate name for the Korean "Diamond Mountains." See also GANDHAVATĪ, KŬMGANGSAN.

**Zhu**. (J. Jiku; K. Ch'uk 竺). Ethnikon typically used in China for monks who hailed from India (C. TIANZHU).

**Zhuanhong jue**. (C) (傳弘決). See MOHE ZHIGUAN FUXING ZHUANHONG JUE.

**zhuchi**. (J. jūji; K. chuji 住持). In Chinese, "abbot" of a Buddhist monastery. The term literally means "dwelling and holding," from the sense that the abbot occupies his own monastery and maintains the Buddha's dispensation in the current generation, serving as a "holding vessel" so that the Buddha's lineage can never be extinguished. The zhuchi dwells in the "abbot's quarters" (FANGZHANG), a term that in some contexts comes by metonymy to refer to the abbot himself, as is the case in certain Korean monasteries.

**Zhu Daosheng**. (C) (竺道生). See DAOSHENG.

**Zhu Fonian**. (J. Jiku Butsunen; K. Ch'uk Pullyŏm 竺佛念) (d.u.). A prolific early Chinese translator, who was active between the latter fourth and early fifth centuries. A native of Liangzhou, he collaborated with BUDDHAYAŚAS in the translation of the DĪRGHĀGAMA, with Dharmanandin in the translation of the EKOTTARĀGAMA, and the "Four-Part Vinaya" (SIFEN LÜ), the DHARMAGUPTAKA recension of the VINAYA, which eventually becomes the definitive version of the vinaya in the Sinitic tradition. He was also involved in the translation of such texts as the AṢṬASĀHASRIKĀPRAJÑĀPĀRAMITĀ, the UDĀNAVARGA, a SARVĀSTIVĀDA anthology of aphorisms, and the JÑĀNAPRASTHĀNA, the central treatise of the Sarvāstivāda ABHIDHARMA. Some indigenous Chinese scriptures (see APOCRYPHA), such as the PUSA YINGLUO BENYE JING, are also attributed to him.

**Zhuhong**. (C) (袾宏). See YUNQI ZHUHONG.

**Zhujing yao ji**. (J. Shokyō yōshū; K. Chegyŏng yo chip 諸經要集). In Chinese, "Collection of the Essentials of the Various Scriptures," edited by the Chinese monk Daoshi (d. 683); also known as the *Shan'e yebao lun* ("Treatise on Good and Evil Karmic Retribution"). As the title implies, the *Zhujing yao ji* is a collection of what Daoshi considered to be essential passages from more than two hundred primary sources, including various sūtras, VINAYAS, and commentaries. Many of the passages that were chosen by Daoshi for inclusion in his collection are concerned with the issue of KARMAN and retribution, hence the text's alternative title. The entire collection is comprised of a total of thirty sections: (1) the three jewels (RATNATRAYA), (2) worshiping STŪPAS, (3) controlling thoughts, (4) entering the way, (5) praises and chants, (6) lighting incense, (7) receiving requests, (8) receiving vegetarian feasts (ZHAI), (9) breaking fast, (10) wealth, (11) poverty, (12) leading others, (13) repaying debt to others, (14) releasing living beings, (15) the flourishing of merit, (16) choosing friends, (17) staying alert, (18) six classifications of beings (GATI), (19) cause of karman, (20) desire and defilements, (21) four types of birth, (22) retributions, (23) ten evils, (24) deception, (25) laziness, (26) wine and meat, (27) divination, (28) hell, (29) mortuary customs, and (30) miscellaneous matters.

**zhung lnga**. (shung nga). [alt. gzhung chen bka' pod lnga/gzhung chen pod lnga]. In Tibetan, "the five books," five Indian treatises that provided the foundation for the monastic curriculum of the DGE LUGS sect. The five works are the ABHISAMAYĀLAṂKĀRA of MAITREYA, the MADHYAMAKĀVATĀRA of CANDRAKĪRTI, the PRAMĀṆAVĀRTTIKA of DHARMAKĪRTI, the ABHIDHARMAKOŚABHĀṢYA of VASUBANDHU, and the VINAYASŪTRA of GUṆAPRABHA.

**zhuoyu**. (著語). In Chinese, "annotation," or "capping phrase." See JAKUGO.

**zhurengong**. (J. shujinkō; K. chuin'gong 主人公). In Chinese, literally "master" or "owner"; a term used within the CHAN tradition to refer to "buddha-nature" (C. FOXING) or "true mind" (C. zhenxin), sometimes seen also as the variant "old master" (zhurenweng). The ZIMEN JINGXUN ("Admonitions for the Dark-[Robed]"), an influential Buddhist primer compiled in 1313 by the CHAN monk Yongzhong (d.u.), specifically refers to the variant zhurenweng as a designation for "true mind." The

WUMEN GUAN ("Gateless Checkpoint"), the eponymous GONG'AN collection of WUMEN HUIKAI (1183–1260), includes a gong'an on zhurengong attributed to Ruiyan Shican (850–910), a second-generation successor of DESHAN XUANJIAN (782–865): Ruiyan would call to himself every day, "Master (zhurengong)!" And he would respond, "Yes." Then he would say, "Be clear!" "Yes." "Any time and any day, don't be fooled by anything." "I won't be." Yaun Kagu's (fl. c. 1376) CHAGYŎNG MUN ("Self-admonitions"), one of the three texts included in the Korean monastic primer CH'OBALSIM CHAGYŎNG MUN, opens with an admonition to postulants and novices: "Master (chuin'gong)! Listen to my words! How can you continue to transmigrate through the realms of suffering when so many people have realized the way through the gateway of emptiness?" The Korean Sŏn community uses the concept of chuin'gong as a generic "meditative topic" (hwadu; C. HUATOU) in kanhwa Sŏn (C. KANHUA CHAN), or "questioning meditation."

**Zhwa dmar incarnations**. (Shamar). An influential incarnation (SPRUL SKU) lineage in the KARMA BKA' BRGYUD sect of Tibetan Buddhism, regarded as a human incarnation of AMITĀBHA. The first incarnation, Grags pa seng ge (Drakpa Senge, 1283–1349), was a disciple of the third KARMA PA, who offered him a red crown (zhwa dmar), from which the name of the line of incarnations derives. Subsequent Zhwa dmar embodiments had close relationships with the Karma pa line, in many cases alternately serving as GURU and pupil to the BKA' BRGYUD hierarch. Grags pa seng ge founded a seat at GNAS NANG monastery in central Tibet, later moved to YANGS PA CAN monastery under the direction of the fourth incarnation, Chos grags ye shes (Chödrak Yeshe, 1453–1524). Several Zhwa dmar incarnations spent considerable time in Nepal, including the sixth, Gar dbang Chos kyi dbang phug (Garwang Chökyi Wangchuk, 1584–1630), who composed a detailed description of his travels. The lineage was interrupted for nearly a century when the tenth incarnation, Chos grub rgya mtsho (Chödrup Gyatso, 1741–1791), was accused of forging a treasonous alliance with the Gorkha army during a Tibetan conflict with Nepal, during which BKRA SHIS LHUN PO monastery was sacked. The tenth Zhwa dmar died in prison, by either suicide or murder. The Tibetan government seized Yangs pa can monastery and converted it into a DGE LUGS monastery. It also banned recognition of new Zhwa dmar embodiments, a proscription that lasted more than a century. In the interim, several incarnations were found but never officially installed. The incarnation lineage includes:

1. Grags pa seng ge (Drakpa Senge, 1283–1349)
2. Mkha' spyod dbang po (Kachö Wangpo, 1350–1405)
3. Chos dpal ye shes (Chöpal Yeshe, 1406–1452)
4. Chos grags ye shes (Chödrak Yeshe, 1453–1524)
5. Dkon mchog yan lag (Könchok Yanlak, 1525–1583)
6. Gar dbang Chos kyi dbang phyug (Garwang Chökyi Wangchuk, 1584–1630)
7. Ye shes snying po (Yeshe Nyingpo, 1631–1694)
8. Dpal chen chos kyi don grub (Palchen Chökyi Döndrup, 1695–1732)
9. Dkon mchog dge ba'i 'byung gnas (Könchok Gewe Jungne, 1733–1740)
10. Chos grub rgya mtsho (Chödrup Gyatso, 1741–1792) [interruption of lineage]
11. 'Jam dbyangs Rin po che (Jamyang Rinpoche, 1892–1946)
12. 'Phrin las kun khyab (Trinle Kunkyap, 1948–1950)
13. Mi pham smra ba'i go cha (Mipam Mawe Gocha, b. 1952)

**Zhwa lu**. (Shalu). A modest but important monastery near the Tibetan city of Gzhis ka tse (Shigatse), famous as the seat of fourteenth-century polymath BU STON RIN CHEN GRUB, and renowned for its unusual architectural features. The earliest foundations were laid circa 997 by Lo ston Rdo rje dbang phyug (Lotön Dorje Wangchuk, b. tenth century), an active teacher during the outset of the later dissemination (PHYI DAR) of Buddhism in Tibet. His disciple, Lce btsun Shes rab 'byung gnas (Chetsün Sherap Jungne, d.u.), established a larger structure in 1027, having promised his master to construct a temple "as large as a small hat," from which its name is derived. The project was completed just prior to a visit of the illustrious Bengali scholar ATIŚA DĪPAṂKARAŚRĪJÑĀNA. During the thirteenth century, Zhwa lu formed close ties with the ruling SA SKYA hierarchs and their Mongol patrons. In 1306, the Yuan emperor Temür (1265–1307) appointed Grags pa rgyal mtshan (Drakpa Gyaltsen, d.u.) as prelate, under whom the institution flourished. Bu ston's rise to the abbacy in 1320 is traditionally viewed as the beginning of a new lineage, the so-called Zhwa lu pa ("Those of Zhwa lu") or Bu lugs tshul ("Tradition of Bu [ston]"). It was at Zhwa lu that Bu ston famously redacted the several hundred volumes that would comprise his influential edition of the Tibetan Buddhist canon. The monastery is equally famous for its unique blend of Tibetan and Chinese architecture (most notably, its pagoda-style roof of glazed turquoise tiles) and murals executed under the direction of Newar artist-disciples of the master Newari artisan Arniko.

**Zibo**. (C) (紫柏) (1543–1603). See DAGUAN ZHENKE.

**Zimen jingxun**. (J. Shimon kyōkun/Shimon keikun; K. Ch'imun kyŏnghun 緇門警訓). In Chinese, "Admonitions for Those in the Dark-(Robed) School"; an important Buddhist primer, in nine rolls, compiled in 1313 by the CHAN monk YONGZHONG (d.u.) in the LINJI ZONG lineage of ZHONGFENG MINGBEN. Yongzhong's text is an expansion of an earlier one-roll primer entitled *Zilin baoxun* ("Precious Admonitions to the Forest of the Dark-[Robed]"), by the Song-dynasty monk Zexian (d.u.). In 1474, the monk Rujin (d.u.) of the monastery of Zhenrusi added some additional work of his own to Yongzhong's text and published the compilation as *Zimen* *jingxun*, in a total of ten rolls. The text contains 170 anecdotes, instructions, admonitions, and suggestions to neophytes, derived from eminent monks who lived between the Northern Song and the Ming dynasties. The author admonishes Chan students to observe the Buddhist precepts and to exert themselves in the study of Buddhism. Citing such Confucian classics as the *Lunyu* ("Analects of Confucius") and the *Shijing* ("Book of Poetry"), Yongzhong admonishes students to be diligent in their learning, even encouraging them to study Confucianism and Daoism in order better to promote Buddhism, just as ancient eminent masters had done. He provides several masters' detailed instructions on Chan meditation, including proper physical posture, and offers instructions on the proper way of reading Buddhist scriptures. Finally, Yongzhong includes the instructions of many renowned Chan masters, as conveyed in their sermons (SHANGTANG) and letters (SHUZHUANG). Rujin's edition of Yongzhong's work continues to be widely used today to instruct novices and neophytes. In Korea, Yongzhong's nine-roll version has been republished several times since T'AEGO POU (1301–1381) imported it to the peninsula during the Koryŏ period.

**Zimmè Paññāsa**. In Burmese, lit. "Chiangmai Fifty"; the Burmese recension of the *Paññāsajātaka*, or "Fifty [Apocryphal] Birth Stories." See PAÑÑĀSAJĀTAKA.

**Zlum brtsegs lha khang**. (Dumtsek Lhakang). A large, three-floored STŪPA constructed in 1421 by the renowned Tibetan adept THANG STONG RGYAL PO (Tangtong Gyalpo), located in Bhutan's Spa gro (Paro) Valley. According to traditional biographies, the master erected this structure at a geomantically powerful location in order to restrain a malignant demoness dwelling in the region. It was restored and enlarged in 1841 by the twenty-fifth head abbot (rje mkhan po) of Bhutan, Shes rab rgyal mtshan (Sherap Gyaltsen, served 1836–1839).

**zong**. (J. shū; K. chong 宗). A polysemous term in Chinese, which can refer to the "core teaching," "cardinal doctrine," or central "axiom" of a text or scholastic philosophy, or to a "school," "tradition," or even "lineage." Because of the denotation of zong as a cardinal doctrine, the term is used to translate the Sanskrit SIDDHĀNTA, an "axiom" or principal "tenet" of the various schools of Indian philosophy (both Buddhist and non-Buddhist). Although commonly translated as "school" ("sect" is incorrect in a Chinese Buddhist context), this rendering is only appropriate for those scholastic and practice traditions that trace themselves back through an unbroken lineage of ancestors to a specific founding "patriarch" (ZUSHI), such as the TIANTAI ZONG, HUAYAN ZONG, and CHAN ZONG. Commentarial traditions focused upon the exegesis of a specific text, such as the DI LUN (DAŚABHŪMIKASŪTRA), SHE LUN (MAHĀYĀNASAṂGRAHA), or CHENGSHI LUN (*TATTVASIDDHI), do not qualify as true schools of Chinese Buddhism, since they neither claim to derive from a single founder nor posit an exclusive lineage of successors; they might more correctly be termed "scholastic traditions."

**Zongjing lu**. (J. Sugyōroku; K. Chonggyŏng nok 宗鏡録). In Chinese, "Records of the Mirror of the Source"; composed c. 961 by the Song-dynasty CHAN master YONGMING YANSHOU (904–975), in one hundred rolls; also called "Records of the Mirror of the Mind" (*Xinjing lu*). The "source" (zong), Yanshou says in the preface to the *Zongjing lu*, refers to the "one mind" (YIXIN), which functions like a mirror that is able to reflect all dharmas. This comprehensive collection offers an exhaustive elaboration of the Chan teaching of "one mind" by systematizing the doctrinal and meditative positions of the various Chan traditions of past and present. The *Zongjing lu* consists of three main sections: exemplifications of the source (biaozong zhang), questions and answers (wenda chang), and citations (yinzheng chang). The first section, which comprises much of the first roll, offers a general overview of the treatise, focusing on Chan's "source" in the one mind. The massive second section, corresponding to the second half of the first roll through the ninety-third roll, offers various explanations on the one mind through a question raised at the beginning of each section, followed by Yanshou's detailed response. His explanations are typically accompanied by extensive citations from various sūtras and commentaries, such as the YUANJUE JING and the DAZHIDU LUN. Throughout this exhaustive survey and explanation of doctrinal matters, Yanshou underscores the importance of the one mind or one dharma as the underlying source of all external phenomena. The third and final section, which comprises the last seven rolls of the collection, validates the previous explanations through quotations of hundreds of scriptures and sayings of eminent Chan masters; its aim is to help those of inferior spiritual capacity give rise to faith. Many of these quotations are from materials that are no longer extant, thus providing an important overview of Chan during Yanshou's time. Yanshou's goal throughout this work is to present his distinctive vision of Chan as a pansectarian tradition that subsumes not only the different Chan lineages, but also such doctrinal traditions as TIANTAI, HUAYAN, and FAXIANG. Much of the source material that Yanshou compiled in the *Zongjing lu* may derive from GUIFENG ZONGMI's similarly massive *Chanyuan ji* ("Chan Collection"), only the prolegomenon to which survives (see CHANYUAN ZHUQUANJI DUXU). The collection was influential not only in China, but also in Koryŏ-period Korean SŎN and the five mountain (GOZAN) schools of Ashikaga-period Japanese ZEN.

**Zongli zhongjing mulu**. (J. Sōri shūkyō mokuroku; K. Chongni chunggyŏng mongnok 綜理衆經目錄). A scriptural catalogue (JINGLU) compiled by the Eastern Jin monk DAO'AN (312–385); often referred to by its abbreviated title, *An lu*, or "An's Catalogue." The complete catalogue is no longer extant, but is partially preserved within the CHU SANZANG JIJI. The catalogue covers texts translated between the Han dynasty to the year 374 and provides the titles, translators's names, and the dates of the translations, wherever possible. As one of the first such scriptural catalogues compiled in East Asia, Dao'an's compilation served as the model for all future such endeavors.

**Zongmen huomen**. (J. Shūmon wakumon; K. Chongmun hongmun 宗門或問). In Chinese, "Some Inquiries into the [Chan] Tradition," composed by the CHAN master ZHANRAN YUANDENG in the CAODONG ZONG. In 1605, Zhanran replied to inquiries he had received from Chan neophytes about the school's distinctive teachings and practices and edited together fifty-two of these exchanges as the *Zongmen huomen*. (The zongmen of the title is a common designation for the CHAN ZONG, especially in Song-dynasty and later materials.) As Zhanran explains in his preface, he wrote this text because it is difficult for neophytes to understand Chan since there are so many different Chan teachings and practices. For example, to the question of what is most essential in Chan meditation and how one should begin in Chan practice, Zhanran answers that one must aspire to investigate the matter of birth-and-death. As to how to investigate the matter of birth-and-death, he answers that one has to arouse three states of mind: (1) the mind of great faith; (2) the mind of ferocious effort (cf. YONGMAENG CHŎNGJIN) and nonretrogression; and (3) the mind of great doubt (see YIQING). (Cf. SANYAO). In the course of his exposition, Zhanran also covers other Buddhist practices, including recitation of the Buddha's name (NIANFO), but he is adamant that Chan is the best and most direct way to enlightenment. In addition to the series of exchanges, Zhanran also appends the following related texts to the *Zongmen huomen*: the *Canchan shinan* ("Difficulties in Investigating Chan"), *Huomen* ("Some Inquiries"), *Buyi* ("Appended Sayings"), *Daming Dingzi men* ("Clear Replies to Dingzi's Inquiries"), and the *Daguan heshang zhaoyang zhuan* ("Tale of the Monk Daguan's Invitation to Disaster"), a fervent defense of the renowned Chan master DAGUAN ZHENKE (a.k.a. ZIBO), who died amid political intrigue at court.

**Zongmen liandeng huiyao**. (J. Shūmon rentōeyō; K. Chongmun yŏndŭng hoeyo 宗門聯燈會要). In Chinese, "Essential Collection of the Lamplight Connections within the [Chan] Tradition"; composed by Huiweng Wuming (d.u.), a third-generation disciple of the CHAN master DAHUI ZONGGAO, in 1183. This work is a collection of anecdotes and teachings culled from the biographies and discourse records (YULU) of over six hundred patriarchs and teachers (ZUSHI) of the Chan tradition. Huiweng begins the collection with the seven buddhas of the past (SAPTABUDDHA), the twenty-eight Indian patriarchs, and the six patriarchs of China (see CHUANDENG LU). His collections also include the various lineages and collateral lines that split off from the sixth patriarch (LIUZU) HUINENG's disciples QINGYUAN XINGSI (up to the seventeenth generation) and NANYUE HUAIRANG (up to the fifteenth generation). In addition to its role as a genealogical history, the *Zongmen liandeng huiyao* was favored by many followers of Chan as a reliable and convenient collection of Chan cases (GONG'AN).

**Zongmen shigui lun**. (J. Shūmon jikkiron; K. Chongmun sipkyu non 宗門十規論). In Chinese, "Treatise on the Ten Rules of the [Chan] Tradition," composed by CHAN master FAYAN WENYI (885–958); also known as the *Fayan chanshi zongmen shigui lun*, *Jinghui Fayan chanshi zongmen shigui lun*, and simply *Shigui lun*. The *Zongmen shigui lun* warns against ten maladies to which those in the Chan tradition are succeptible, viz., (1) assuming the role of teacher without first purifying one's own mind, (2) sectarian disputes, (3) positing the main points of Chan without knowing the specific contexts, (4) answering without consideration of time and situation, (5) failure to distinguish defiled from pure, (6) baseless interpretations of the sayings of the masters of old, (7) memorizing slogans and not being able to use them at the right moment, (8) miscitations by not mastering the canon, (9) improperly composing songs and verses before one's understanding has matured, and (10) defending one's own shortcomings and indulging in disputes. The *Zongmen shigui lun* is also the first text to mention the names of the five houses (see WU JIA QI ZONG) of the mature Chan tradition.

**Zongmi**. (C) (宗密). See GUIFENG ZONGMI.

**Zongze**. (C) (宗賾). See CHANGLU ZONGZE.

**Zuihō**. (J) (瑞方) (1683–1769). See MENZAN ZUIHŌ.

**zuishangsheng Chan**. (J. saijōjōzen; K. ch'oesangsŭng Sŏn 最上乘禪). In Chinese, lit. "supreme vehicle Chan," referring to one of the styles of practice and pedagogy associated with the CHAN school; often considered to be equivalent to "unconventional Chan" (GEWAI CHAN). Supreme vehicle Chan is one of the five categories of Chan listed by GUIFENG ZONGMI (780–841) in his CHANYUAN ZHUJUAN JI DUXU ("Prolegomena to the Source of Chan Collection"). According to Zongmi's treatment, "supreme vehicle Chan" refers to meditation practices that rely on sudden approaches to awakening (DUNWU) and generate an initial insight into the true nature of mind, i.e., the original purity of mind that is shared by both sentient beings and buddhas. The text equates this form of Chan with the "pure Chan of the TATHĀGATAS" (rulai qingjing Chan), also known by its abbreviated name, tathāgata Chan (rulai Chan); it also is said to be equivalent to "single-practice SAMĀDHI" (YIXING SANMEI) and the "samādhi of suchness" (zhenru sanmei), since "supreme vehicle Chan" is the root of all kinds of samādhi. The text also defines supreme vehicle Chan as the "Chan transmitted from BODHIDHARMA"; this latter form of Chan is subsequently named "patriarchal Chan" (zushi Chan) in the Song-dynasty Chan collections, such as the JINGDE ZHUANDENG LU ("Record of the Transmission of the Lamplight Published during the Jingde Era") and Puji's (1179–1253) *Wudeng huiyuan* ("Collected Essentials of the Five Lamplight Histories"), which in turn redefines "tathāgata Chan" as subordinate to "patriarchal Chan."

**zuochan**. (J. zazen; K. chwasŏn 坐禪). In Chinese, "seated meditation." Zuochan is a combination of the Chinese term "to sit" (zuo) and the character CHAN, a transcription of the Sanskrit term DHYĀNA (meditation); often referred to in English-language sources by the Japanese pronunciation zazen. As its etymology implies, zuochan refers to sitting with legs folded on top of each other and eyes slightly closed in meditation. This meditative practice may be generically considered to be directed at samādhi, one of the three trainings (C. sanxue; S. śikṣātraya), along with morality (ŚĪLA) and wisdom (PRAJÑĀ), or alternatively at dhyāna, one of the six PĀRAMITĀs emblematic of BODHISATTVA practice, along with charity (DĀNA), precepts (śīla), forbearance (KṢĀNTI), effort (VĪRYA), and wisdom (prajñā). Sitting has long held pride of place within the Buddhist tradition as the archetypal position (ĪRYĀPATHA) most suited to sustained meditation training. The prototype for zuochan is the Buddha's own seated meditation under the BODHI TREE, as well as the legendary Indian monk BODHIDHARMA's "wall gazing" (BIGUAN) for nine years in a cave. Because of these associations with both the Buddha and Bodhidharma, the founder of the Chan school, zuochan was widely considered to be the primary practice within the CHAN, SŎN, and ZEN traditions. In China, zuochan came to be viewed as such a stereotypical aspect of the Chan school, broadly conceived, that Chan teachers began to critique its necessity and importance; these critiques suggested instead that Chan practice was not to be confined just to zuochan, but should also be conducted throughout the three other standard deportments of walking, standing, and lying down. For example, the LIUZU TANJING ("Platform Sūtra"), attributed to the sixth patriarch HUINENG, includes such a rectification of the meaning of zuochan when it says that "'seated' means, externally, to refrain from generating thoughts related to wholesome or unwholesome objects; 'meditation' means, internally, to see that the self-nature is unmoving." In this redefinition, zuochan means not just "seated meditation" but instead encompasses a way of understanding that is to be carried through all aspects of one's experience.

**Zur chung pa**. (Zur chung Shes rab grags pa) (1014–1074). A RNYING MA master, the disciple of ZUR PO CHE (Shākya 'byung gnas, 1002–1062) and father of Zur Shākya seng ge (also known as Sgro sbug pa, 1074–1135). Because he was a poor novice, Zur po che encouraged him to marry the daughter of a wealthy patron, which he reluctantly did. He is said to have spent thirteen years meditating in a cave. His most famous work is his final testament, the *Zhal gdams brgyad cu pa* ("Eighty Oral Instructions").

**Zur po che**. ([alt. Zur chen] Shākya 'byung gnas) (1002–1062). A RNYING MA master of the Zur clan. His disciple ZUR CHUNG PA, and Zur Shākya seng ge (also known as Sgro sbug pa, 1074–1135) are known with him as the three Zur (Zur rnam pa gsum), with Zur po che as the founding figure. He was a disciple of Nyang Ye shes 'byung gnas and was renowned especially for his practice and teaching of the "magical net" (MĀYĀJĀLA) class of TANTRAs, the *Dgongs pa 'dus pa'i mdo*, and the SĀDHANA of VAJRAKĪLAYA. As such, he holds an important place in the transmission of RDZOGS CHEN and SEMS SDE teachings. He was ordained by the famous VINAYA master Bla chen Dgongs pa rab gsal and also studied extensively with GNUBS CHEN SANGS RGYAS YE SHES. During the time of the later dissemination of Buddhism to Tibet, he is credited with organizing the Rnying ma tantras in such a way that a particular tantra, its commentaries, sādhanas, and ritual manuals were grouped together. He identified the *Dgongs pa 'dus pa'i mdo* as the root tantra of ANUYOGA, the GUHYAGARBHA as the root tantra of MAHĀYOGA, and the KUN BYED RGYAL PO as the root tantra of ATIYOGA. He is also credited with the fundamental division of the Rnying ma teachings in BKA' MA (words) and GTER MA (treasures). He founded the monastery of 'Ug pa lung (Owl Land) located to the east of Gzhis ka rtse (Shigatse).

**zushi**. (J. soshi; K. chosa 祖師). In Chinese, "patriarch" (lit. "ancestral teacher"), referring to eminent teachers in lineages that are claimed to trace back to ŚĀKYAMUNI Buddha or even earlier buddhas. Indian Sanskrit texts dating from the 2nd century CE onward refer to a tradition of five "masters of the dharma" (dharmācārya) who succeeded the Buddha as head of the SAṂGHA: MAHĀKĀŚYAPA, ĀNANDA, MADHYĀNTIKA, ŚĀṆAKAVĀSIN, and UPAGUPTA. Later sources expand this list into a roster of nine eminent masters who "handed down the lamplight of wisdom successively through the generations." Often, these genealogies were extended as far back as the seven buddhas of antiquity (SAPTATATHĀGATA). It is widely presumed that this notion of dharma-transmission lineages developed from the earlier VINAYA concept of the "preceptor" (UPĀDHYĀYA), a senior monk who confers the lower ordination (pravrajyā, see PRAVRAJITA) to new novices (ŚRĀMAṆERA) and higher ordination (UPASAṂPADĀ) to monks (BHIKṢU). This personal connection between preceptor and disciple created incipient ordination families connected to specific preceptors, connections that later could be extended to dharma transmission as well. ¶ In East Asia, these lists of Indian dharma masters continued to be expanded and elaborated upon so that they also included the preeminent indigenous figures within each lineage, thus connecting the Chinese patriarchs of each lineage with their Indian predecessors. Most of the indigenous traditions of East Asian Buddhism, including the CHAN ZONG, TIANTAI ZONG, JINGTU ZONG, and HUAYAN ZONG, draw their legitimacy at least partially from their claims that their teachings and practices derive from an unbroken lineage of authoritative teachers that can be traced back geographically to India and temporally to the person of the Buddha himself. The specific names and numbers of patriarchs recognized within each lineage typically change over time and vary widely between the different traditions. Of these lists, the list of patriarchs recognized in the Chan school has received the lion's share of scholarly attention in the West. This Chan list varies widely, but a well-established roster includes twenty-eight Indian and six Chinese patriarchs. These six Chinese patriarchs (liu zu)—BODHIDHARMA, HUIKE, SENGCAN, DAOXIN, HONGREN, and HUINENG—are credited by the classical tradition with the development and growth of Chan in China, but early records of the Chan school, such as the LENGQIE SHIZU JI and LIDAI FABAO JI, reveal the polemical battles fought between disparate contemporary Chan communities to place their own teachers on this roster of patriarchal orthodoxy. It is important to note that all of these various lists of patriarchs, in all the different traditions, are created retrospectively as a way of legitimizing specific contemporary lineages or teachers and verifying the authenticity of their teachings; thus their accounts of the chronology and history of their lineages must be used critically. The compound zushi can mean either "patriarch" (lit., ancestral teacher) or in other contexts "patriarchs and teachers," as in the stock phrase "all the buddhas of the three time-periods and patriarchs and teachers throughout successive generations" (sanshi zhufo lidai zushi), which explicitly traces a school's ancestral lineage from the past to the present and into the future. Some modern Buddhists, especially in the West, deplore the sexism inherent in the term "patriarch," preferring instead to render it with the gender-neutral term "ancestor." See also CHUANDENG LU; FASI; PARAṂPARĀ; YINKE.

**Zutang ji**. (J. Sodōshū; K. Chodang chip 祖堂集). In Chinese, "Anthology of the Patriarchs' Hall." See CHODANG CHIP.

**Zuting qianchui lu**. (J. Sotei kantsuiroku; K. Chojŏng kyŏmch'u nok 祖庭鉗鎚錄). In Chinese, "Record of Forceps and Hammers of the Patriarchs' Hall," edited by the CHAN master FEIYIN TONGRONG (1593–1661) of the LINJI ZONG during the late Ming dynasty. This collection includes over fifty anecdotes considered to be essential for the training of students. These anecdotes focus on the enlightenment stories of several renowned Tang- and Song-dynasty LINJI ZONG masters, such as LINJI YIXUAN, Shoushan Shengnian (926–993), Fenyang Shanzhao (947–1024), Shishuang Chuyuan (986–1039), YUANWU KEQIN, and DAHUI ZONGGAO, but also include a few stories concerning renowned masters in the YUNMEN ZONG and CAODONG ZONG. Most of these stories are excerpted from Chan texts published during the Song dynasty, especially Puji's (1179–1253) *Wudeng huiyuan* ("Collected Essentials of the Five Lamplight Histories"). Each story is accompanied by Feiyin's own short prose commentary (pingchang). Four additional exchanges between a certain master Wang Jing and the monk Fohui Faquan (d.u.) concerning the history of the Chan tradition are included as an appendix.

**Zuting shiyuan**. (J. Sotei jion; K. Chojŏng sawŏn 祖庭事苑). In Chinese, "Garden of Matters from the Patriarchs' Hall," edited in eight rolls by Mu'an Shanxiang (d.u.) in 1108; the oldest encyclopedia of the Chinese CHAN tradition. This collection includes over 2,400 items related to Chan pedagogy, culled from Buddhist and secular stories, proverbs, numerological lists, personal names, local dialects, and so forth. Mu'an is said to have embarked on this project in response to the growing number of monks who were unable to understand the rich content and context of the many GONG'AN exchanges found in Chan literature. Mu'an's material is drawn from over twenty important Chan sources, such as the discourse records (YULU) of YUNMEN WENYAN, XUEDOU CHONGXIAN, and FAYAN WENYI, and YONGJIA XUANJUE's popular ZHENGDAO GE. The encyclopedia functions as a glossary for these works, offering explanations for their difficult technical terms and obscure names (which are not necessarily Chan or Buddhist in origin), and drawing his explanations from Buddhist, Confucian, and Daoist materials, as well as such secular sources. For example, the first roll of the encyclopedia provides a glossary of the *Yunmen lu*, which discusses the author Yunmen Wenyan, offers definitions of terms and explanations of names appearing in the text, drawing on sources ranging from the *Shiji* ("Book of History") to the AGAMA SŪTRAS, and fills out the myriad numerical lists that appear in the text, such as the three vehicles (C. sansheng; S. TRIYĀNA), the three baskets of the canon (C. sanzang; S. TRIPIṬAKA), the eight teachings of Tiantai (see WUSHI BAJIAO), etc. Mu'an's exhaustive collection meticulously traces the source of each item and provides a detailed commentary on each. The *Zuting shiyuan* was republished in 1154, and numerous editions were published during the Tokugawa period in Japan.

# List of Lists

This roster provides some of the most important numerical lists used in the Buddhist traditions. Generally, we include the equivalencies only in Sanskrit, Tibetan, and Chinese, since in most cases these will be adequate to trace the terms back to the relevant entries in the dictionary. In instances where there are several variations of a list, we seek to provide only one common form. In addition, the various languages often provide different interpretations of a particular term, making it difficult to provide a single English translation. For ease in tracing terms back to their main dictionary entries, the numeric elements in the foreign-language names of each list have not been provided; the exceptions are those lists in which numerals are included in the main dictionary entries (for example, daśabhūmi).

## ONES

**one vehicle**. (S. ekayāna; T. theg pa gcig pa; C. yisheng 一乘)

## TWOS

**two accesses/entrances**. (C. er ru 二入)

1. access of principle (C. liru 理入)
2. access of practice (C. xingru 行入)

**two accumulations/equipments**. (S. saṃbhāra; T. tshogs; C. ziliang 資糧)

1. accumulation/equipment of merit (S. puṇyasaṃbhāra; T. bsod nams kyi tshogs; C. fuziliang 福資糧)
2. accumulation/equipment of wisdom (S. jñānasaṃbhāra; T. ye shes kyi tshogs; C. zhiziliang 智資糧)

**two aspects of esoteric Buddhism**. (C. er mi 二密)

1. esoteric as to principle (li mi 理密)
2. esoteric as to practices (shi mi 事密)

**two attainments**. (S. siddhi; T. dngos grub; C. chengjiu/xidi 成就/悉地)

1. mundane attainments (S. sādhāraṇasiddhi; T. thun mong gi dngos grub; C. gongtong chengjiu/xidi 共同成就/悉地)
2. supreme attainment (S. uttamasiddhi; T. mchog gi dngos grub; C. zuishang chengjiu/xidi 最上成就/悉地)

**two benefits**. (S. artha; T. don; C. li 利)

1. benefitting oneself (S. svārtha/ātmahita; T. rang don; C. zili 自利)
2. benefitting others (S. parārtha/parahita; T. gzhan don; C. lita 利他)

**two bodies (of a buddha)**. (S. kāya; T. sku; C. shen 身)

1. truth body (S. dharmakāya; T. chos sku; C. fashen 法身)
2. physical body (S. rūpakāya; T. gzugs sku; C. shengshen 生身)

**twofold generation of the aspiration to enlightenment**. (S. bodhicittotpāda; T. byang chub kyi sems bskyed; C. fa putixin 發菩提心)

1. attitude of aspiration (S. praṇidhicittotpāda; T. smon pa'i sems bskyed; C. yuan putixin 願菩提心)
2. attitude of undertaking (S. prasthānacittotpāda; T. 'jug pa'i sems bskyed; C. xing putixin 行菩提心)

**two karmic retributions**. (C. er bao 二報)

1. retribution proper [viz. one's own actions] (zheng bao 正報)
2. adjunct retribution [viz. environmental factors] (yi bao 依報)

**two means of knowledge**. (S. pramāṇa; T. tshad ma; C. liang 量)

1. direct perception (S. pratyakṣa; T. mngon sum; C. xianliang 現量)
2. inference (S. anumāna; T. rjes dpag; C. biliang 比量)

**two obstructions**. (S. āvaraṇa; T. sgribs pa; C. zhang 障)

1. afflictive obstructions (S. kleśāvaraṇa; T. nyon mongs pa'i sgrib ba; C. fannao zhang 煩惱障)
2. cognitive or noetic obstructions [to omniscience] (S. jñeyāvaraṇa; T. shes bya'i sgrib ba; C. suozhi zhang 所知障)

**two stages**. (S. krama; T. rim pa; C. cidi 次第)

1. stage of generation (S. utpattikrama; T. bskyed rim; C. shengqi cidi 生起次第)
2. stage of completion (S. niṣpannakrama; T. rdzogs rim; C. yuanman cidi 圓滿次第)

**two supreme ones.** (T. mchog gnyis)

1. Nāgārjuna
2. Asaṅga

OR

1. Guṇaprabha
2. Śākyaprabha

**two truths.** (S. satyadvaya; T. bden pa gnyis; C. er di 二諦)

1. conventional truth (S. saṃvṛtisatya; T. kun rdzob bden pa; C. sudi/shisu di 俗諦/世俗諦)
2. absolute truth/ultimate truth (S. paramārthasatya; T. don dam bden pa; C. zhendi/shengyi di/diyiyi di 真諦/勝義諦/第一義諦)

**two types of nonself.** (S. nairātmya; T. bdag med; C. wuwo 無我)

1. nonself of the person (S. pudgalanairātmya; T. gang zag gi bdag med; C. ren wuwo 人無我)
2. nonself of phenomena (S. dharmanairātmya; T. chos kyi bdag med; C. fa wuwo 法無我)

**two vehicles.** (S. yānadvaya; T. theg pa gnyis; C. er sheng 二乘)

1. vehicle of disciples (S. śrāvakayāna; T. nyan thos kyi theg pa; C. shengwen sheng 聲聞乘)
2. vehicle of solitary buddhas (S. pratyekabuddhayāna; T. rang rgyal gyi theg pa; C. yuanjue sheng 緣覺乘)

OR

1. great vehicle (S. mahāyāna; T. theg pa chen po; C. dasheng 大乘)
2. lesser vehicle (S. hīnayāna; T. theg pa dman pa; C. xiaosheng 小乘)

## THREES

**three actions.** (S. karman; T. las; C. ye 業)

1. wholesome/virtuous (S. kuśala; T. dge ba; C. shan 善)
2. unwholesome/unvirtuous (S. akuśala; T. mi dge ba; C. bushan 不善)
3. neutral/indeterminate (S. avyākṛta; T. lung ma bstan; C. wuji 無記)

**three afflictions.** (S. kleśa; T. nyon mongs; C. fannao 煩惱)

1. desire/greed (S. rāga; T. 'dod chags; C. tan 貪)
2. hatred/aversion (S. dveṣa; T. zhe sdang; C. chen 瞋)
3. delusion (S. moha; T. gti mug; C. chi 癡)

**three baleful destinies.** (S. apāya/durgati; T. ngan song; C. equ 惡趣)

1. animals (S. tiryak; T. dud 'gro; C. chusheng 畜生)
2. ghosts (S. preta; T. yi dwags; C. egui 餓鬼)
3. hell denizens (S. nāraka; T. dmyal ba; C. diyu 地獄)

**three baskets of the canon.** (S. tripiṭaka; T. sde snod gsum; C. sanzang 三藏)

1. basket of discourses (S. sūtrapiṭaka; T. mdo sde'i sde snod; C. jingzang 經藏)
2. basket of discipline (S. vinayapiṭaka; T. 'dul ba'i sde snod; C. lüzang 律藏)
3. basket of abhidharma/scholastic exegesis (S. abhidharmapiṭaka/*śāstrapiṭaka; T. chos mngon pa'i sde snod; C. lunzang 論藏)

**three becomings.** (S. bhava; T. srid pa; C. you 有)

1. becoming in the sensual realm (S. kāmabhava; T. 'dod pa'i srid pa; C. yuyou 欲有)
2. becoming in the realm of subtle materiality (S. rūpabhava; T. gzugs kyi srid pa; C. seyou 色有)
3. becoming in the immaterial realm (S. ārūpyabhava; T. gzugs med kyi srid pa; C. wuseyou 無色有)

**three bodies [of a buddha].** (S. trikāya; T. sku gsum; C. san shen 三身)

1. truth body (S. dharmakāya; T. chos sku; C. fashen 法身)
2. enjoyment body (S. saṃbhogakāya; T. longs spyod rdzogs pa'i sku; C. baoshen 報身)
3. emanation body (S. nirmāṇakāya; T. sprul pa'i sku; C. huashen 化身)

**three classes of atiyoga.** (T. rdzogs chen sde gsum)

1. mental class (T. sems sde)
2. instruction class (T. man ngag sde)
3. expanse class (T. klong sde)

**three contaminants.** (āsrava; T. zag pa; C. lou 漏)

1. contaminant of sensuality (S. kāmāsrava; T. 'dod pa'i zag pa; C. yu lou 欲漏)
2. contaminant of becoming (S. bhavāsrava; T. srid pa'i zag pa; C. you lou 有漏)
3. contaminant of ignorance (S. avidyāsrava; T. ma rig pa'i zag pa; C. wuming lou 無明漏)

**three enlightenments.** (S. bodhi; T. byang chub; C. puti 菩提)

1. enlightenment of the disciples (S. śrāvakabodhi; T. nyan thos kyi byang chub; C. shengwen puti 聲聞菩提)
2. enlightenment of the pratyekabuddhas (S. pratyekabodhi; T. rang rgyal gyi byang chub/rang sangs rgyas kyi byang chub; C. yuanjue puti 緣覺菩提)
3. complete perfect enlightenment [of the buddhas] (S. anuttarasamyaksaṃbodhi; T. bla na med pa yang dag par rdzogs pa'i byang chub; C. anouduoluo sanmiao sanputi 阿耨多羅三藐三菩提)

**three families, lords of**. (S. trikulanātha; T. rigs gsum mgon po; C. sanbu huzhu 三部護主)

1. Avalokiteśvara (T. Spyan ras gzigs; C. Guanshiyin 觀世音)
2. Mañjuśrī (T. 'Jam dpal; C. Wenshu 文殊)
3. Vajrapāṇi (T. Phyag na rdo rje; C. Jingangshou 金剛手)

**threefold contemplation**. (C. sanguan 三觀)

1. contemplation of emptiness (C. kongguan 空觀)
2. contemplation of conventional existence (C. jiaguan 假觀)
3. contemplation of their mean (C. zhongguan 中觀)

**three gates**. [viz. types of karmic activity] (S. dvāra; T. sgo; C. men 門)

1. body (S. kāya; T. lus; C. shen 身)
2. speech (S. vāc; T. ngag; C. kou 口)
3. mind (S. manas; T. yid; C. yi 意)

**three gates to deliverance**. (S. vimokṣamukha; T. rnam thar sgo; C. jietuo men 解脫門)

1. emptiness (S. śūnyatā; T. stong pa nyid; C. kong 空)
2. signlessness (S. ānimitta; T. mtshan ma med pa; C. wuxiang 無相)
3. wishlessness (S. apraṇihita; T. smon pa med pa; C. wuyuan/wuzuo 無願/無作)

**three inner tantras**. (T. nang rgyud sde gsum)

1. mahāyoga (T. rnal 'byor chen po)
2. anuyoga (T. rjes su rnal 'byor)
3. atiyoga (T. shin tu rnal 'byor)

**three jewels**. (S. ratnatraya; T. dkon mchog gsum; C. sanbao 三寶)

1. the buddha (T. sang rgyas; C. fo/fotuo 佛/佛陀)
2. the teachings (S. dharma; T. chos; C. fa/damo 法/達磨)
3. the community (S. saṃgha; T. dge 'dun; C. seng/sengqie 僧/僧伽)

**three knowledges**. (S. trividyā; T. rig pa gsum; C. sanming 三明)

1. recollection of past lives (S. pūrvanivāsānusmṛti; T. sngon gyi gnas rjes su dran pa; C. suzhu suinian/suming ming 宿住隨念/宿命明)
2. "the divine eye"/clairvoyance (S. divyacakṣus; T. lha'i mig; C. tianyan ming 天眼明)
3. the extinction of the contaminants (S. āsravakṣaya; T. zag pa zad pa shes pa; C. loujin ming 漏盡明)

**three means of knowledge**. (S. pramāṇa; T. tshad ma; C. liang 量)

1. direct perception (S. pratyakṣa; T. mngon sum; C. xianliang 現量)
2. inference (S. anumāna; T. rjes dpag; C. biliang 比量)
3. scripture (S. āgama; T. lung; C. shengyan liang/shengjiao liang 聖言量/聖教量)

**three natures**. (S. trisvabhāva; T. mtshan nyid gsum/ngo bo nyid gsum/rang bzhin gsum; C. sanxing 三性)

1. imaginary/imputed (S. parikalpita; T. kun btags; C. pianji suozhi xing 遍計所執性)
2. dependent (S. paratantra; T. gzhan dbang; C. yitaqi xing 依他起性)
3. perfected/consummate (S. pariniṣpanna; T. yongs su grub pa; C. yuanchengshi xing 圓成實性)

**three poisons**. (S. triviṣa; T. dug gsum; C. sandu 三毒)

1. desire/greed (S. rāga; T. 'dod chags; C. tan 貪)
2. hatred/aversion (S. dveṣa; T. zhe sdang; C. chen 瞋)
3. delusion (S. moha; T. gti mug; C. chi 癡)

**three realms**. [of existence] (S. traidhātuka; T. khams gsum; C. san jie 三界)

1. sensuous realm/desire realm (S. kāmadhātu; T. 'dod khams; C. yu jie 欲界)
2. realm of subtle materiality/form realm (S. rūpadhātu; T. gzugs khams; C. se jie 色界)
3. immaterial realm/formless realm (S. ārūpyadhātu; T. gzugs med khams; C. wuse jie 無色界)

**three refuges**. (S. triśaraṇa; T. skyabs gsum; C. san gui/san guiyi 三歸/三歸依)

1. the buddha (T. sang rgyas; C. fo/fotuo 佛/佛陀)
2. the teachings (S. dharma; T. chos; C. fa/damo 法/達磨)
3. the community (S. saṃgha; T. dge 'dun; C. seng/sengqie 僧/僧伽)

**three roots**. (S. mūla; T. rtsa ba)

1. teacher (S. guru; T. bla ma)
2. tutelary deity ( T. yi dam)
3. ḍākinī (S. ḍākinī; T. mkha' 'gro ma)

**three sages of Huayan**. (C. Huayan sansheng 華嚴三聖)

1. Vairocana Buddha (C. Piluzhena zunfo 毗盧遮那尊佛)
2. Samantabhadra bodhisattva (C. Puxian pusa 普賢菩薩)
3. Mañjuśrī bodhisattva (C. Wenshu pusa 文殊菩薩)

**three sufferings**. (S. duḥkha; T. sdug bsngal; C. ku 苦)

1. suffering of [physical and mental] pain (S. duḥkhaduḥkhatā; T. sdug bsngal gyi sdug bsngal; C. kuku 苦苦)
2. suffering inherent in change (S. vipariṇāmaduḥkatā; T. 'gyur ba'i sdug bsngal; C. huaiku 壞苦)
3. suffering inherent in conditionality (S. saṃskāraduḥkhatā; T. 'du byed kyi sdug bsngal; C. xingku 行苦)

**three times**. (S. trikāla; T. dus gsum; C. sanshi 三世)

1. past (S. atīta; T. 'das pa; C. guoqushi 過去世)
2. present (S. vartamāna; T. da lta ba; C. xianzaishi 現在世)
3. future (S. anāgata; T. ma 'ongs pa; C. weilaishi 未來世)

**three trainings**. (S. triśikṣā; T. bslab pa gsum; C. sanxue 三學)

1. morality/higher morality (S. śīla/adhiśīlaśikṣā; T. tshul khrims/lhag pa'i tshul khrims kyi bslab pa; C. jie/zengshangjie xue 戒/增上戒學)
2. concentration/higher concentration (S. samādhi/adhisamādhiśikṣā; T. ting nge 'dzin/lhag pa'i ting nge 'dzin gyi bslab pa; C. ding/zengshangxin xue 定/增上心學)
3. wisdom/higher wisdom (S. prajñā/adhiprajñāśikṣā; T. shes rab/lhag pa'i shes rab kyi bslab pa; C. hui/zengshanghui xue 慧/增上慧學)

**three truths/judgments**. [of the Tiantai school] (C. sandi 三諦)

1. truth of emptiness (C. kongdi 空諦)
2. truth of being provisionally real (C. jiadi 假諦)
3. truth of the mean (C. zhongdi 中諦)

**three turnings of the wheel of the law**. (S. dharmacakrapravartana; T. chos 'khor rim pa; C. zhuan falun 轉法輪)

1. the dharma-wheel of the four noble truths (S. catuḥsatyadharmacakra; T. bden pa bzhi'i chos 'khor; C. sidi falun 四諦法輪)
2. the dharma-wheel of the absence of defining characteristics (S. alakṣaṇadharmacakra; T. mtshan nyid med pa'i chos 'khor; C. wuxiang falun 無相法輪)
3. the dharma-wheel of thorough delineations (S. *suvibhaktadharmacakra/pravicayadharmacakra; T. legs par rnam par phye ba'i chos 'khor; C. [shan] fenbie falun/shan bian falun [善]分別法輪/善辯法輪)

**three vehicles**. (S. triyāna; T. theg pa gsum; C. san sheng 三乘)

1. śrāvakayāna (T. nyan thos kyi theg pa; C. shengwen sheng 聲聞乘)
2. pratyekabuddhayāna (T. rang sangs rgyas kyi theg pa; C. yuanjue sheng/pizhi fo sheng 緣覺乘/辟支佛乘)
3. bodhisattvayāna (T. byang chub sems dpa'i theg pa; C. pusa sheng 菩薩乘)

**three restraints**. (S. saṃvara; T. sdom pa; C. lüyi/sanbaluo 律儀/三跋羅)

1. the disciplinary rules of a monk or nun (S. prātimokṣasaṃvara; T. so so thar pa'i sdom pa; C. boluotimuchahu/biejietuo lüyi 波羅提木叉護/別解脫律儀)
2. the restraint that is engendered by meditative absorption (S. dhyānajasaṃvara; T. bsam gtan skyes pa'i sdom pa; C. chanlüyi 禪律儀)
3. the restraint that derives from being free from the contaminants (S. anāsravasaṃvara; T. zag pa med pa'i sdom pa; C. wuloulüyi 無漏律儀).

OR

**three vows**. (S. trisaṃvara; T. sdom gsum; C. san lüyi 三律儀)

1. the disciplinary rules of a monk or nun (S. prātimokṣasaṃvara; T. so so thar pa'i sdom pa; C. boluotimuchahu/biejietuo lüyi 波羅提木叉護/別解脫律儀)
2. bodhisattva vows (S. bodhisattvasaṃvara; T. byang sems kyi sdom pa; C. pusa lüyi 菩薩律儀)
3. secret mantra vows (S. guhyamantrasaṃvara; T. gsang sngags kyi sdom pa; C. mizhou lüyi 密咒律儀)

**three wisdoms**. (S. prajñā; T. shes rab; C. hui 慧)

1. wisdom derived from learning (S. śrutamayīprajñā; T. thos pa las byung ba'i shes rab; C. wenhui 聞慧)
2. wisdom derived from reflection (S. cintāmayīprajñā; T. bsam pa las byung ba'i shes rab; C. sihui 思慧)
3. wisdom derived from cultivation (S. bhāvanāmayīprajñā; T. bsgoms pa las byung ba'i shes rab; C. xiuhui 修慧)

## FOURS

**four absorptions**. (S. dhyāna; T. bsam gtan; C. chan/ding 禪/定)

1. first absorption (S. prathamadhyāna; T. bsam gtan dang po; C. chuchan 初禪)
2. second absorption (S. dvitīyadhyāna; T. bsam gtan gnyis pa; C. erchan 二禪)
3. third absorption (S. tṛtīyadhyāna; T. bsam gtan gsum pa; C. sanchan 三禪)
4. fourth absorption (S. caturthadhyāna; T. bsam gtan bzhi pa; C. sichan 四禪)

**four activities**. (S. karman; T. las; C. shiye 事業)

1. pacification (S. śāntika; T. zhi ba'i las; C. xizai 息災)
2. enrichment (S. pauṣṭika; T. rgyas pa'i las; C. zengyi 增益)
3. control (S. vaśīkaraṇa; T. bdang gi las; C. huai'ai 懷愛)
4. wrath (S. abhicāra; T. drag po mngon spyod; C. xiangfu 降伏)

**four aids to penetration**. (S. nirvedhabhāgīya; T. nges par 'byed pa'i cha mthun; C. shunjuezefen 順決擇分)

1. heat (S. ūṣman; T. drod; C. nuan 煖)
2. summit (S. mūrdhan; T. rtse mo; C. ding 頂)
3. receptivity/acquiescence (S. kṣānti; T. bzod pa; C. ren 忍)
4. supreme worldly dharmas (S. laukikāgradharma; T. 'jig rten pa'i chos kyi mchog; C. shi diyi fa 世第一法)

**four analytical knowledges**. (S. pratisaṃvid; T. so so yang dag par rig pa; C. wu'ai jie/wu'ai bian 無礙解/無礙辯)

1. of factors (S. dharma; T. chos; C. fa 法)
2. of meaning (S. artha; T. don; C. yi 義)

3. of etymology or language (S. nirukti; T. nges pa'i tshig; C. ci/ci 詞/辭)
4. of eloquence (S. pratibhāna; T. spobs pa; C. leshuo 樂說)

**four baleful destinies**. (S. apāya/durgati; T. ngan song; C. equ 惡趣)

1. demigods (S. asura; T. lha ma yin; C. axiuluo qu 阿修羅趣)
2. animals (S. tiryak; T. dud 'gro; C. chusheng qu 畜生趣)
3. ghosts (S. preta; T. yi dwags; C. egui qu 餓鬼趣)
4. hell denizens (S. nāraka; T. dmyal ba; C. diyu qu 地獄趣)

**four bases of psychic power**. (S. ṛddhipāda; T. rdzu 'phrul gyi rkang pa; C. shenzu/ruyizu 神足/如意足)

1. aspiration (S. chanda; T. 'dun pa; C. yu 欲)
2. vigor/effort (S. vīrya; T. brtson 'grus; C. qin 勤)
3. thought/concentration (S. citta; T. bsam pa; C. xin 心)
4. analysis (S. mīmāṃsā; T. dpyod pa; C. siwei/guan 思惟/觀)

**four bodies [of a buddha]**. (S. kāya; T. sku; C. shen 身)

1. dharma body (S. dharmakāya; T. chos sku; C. fashen 法身)
2. enjoyment body (S. saṃbhogakāya; T. longs spyod rdzogs pa'i sku; C. baoshen 報身)
3. emanation body (S. nirmāṇakāya; T. sprul pa'i sku; C. huashen 化身)
4. essence body (S. svābhāvikakāya; T. ngo bo nyid kyi sku; C. zixing shen 自性身)

**four bonds/fetters**. (S. grantha/saṃyojana; T. 'ching ba; C. jie/fu 結/縛)

1. covetousness (S. abhidhyā; T. brnab sems; C. yu'ai 欲愛)
2. ill-will (S. vyāpāda; T. gnod sems; C. chenhui 瞋恚)
3. attachment to rules and rituals (S. śīlavrataparāmarśa; T. tshul khrims dang brtul zhugs mchog tu 'dzin pa; C. jiejinqu 戒禁取)
4. attachment to views/dogmatic fanaticism (S. dṛṣṭiparāmarśa/idaṃsatyābhiniveśa; T. lta ba mchog tu 'dzin pa; C. wojianqu 我見取)

**four boundless states/immeasurables**. (S. apramāṇa; T. tshad med; C. wuliang xin 無量心)

1. loving-kindness (S. maitrī; T. byams pa; C. ci 慈)
2. compassion (S. karuṇā; T. snying rje; C. bei 悲)
3. empathetic joy (S. muditā; T. dga' ba; C. xi 喜)
4. equanimity (S. upekṣā; T. btang snyoms; C. she 捨)

**four characteristics of all conditioned objects**. (S. saṃskṛtalakṣaṇa/caturlakṣaṇa; T. 'dus byas kyi mtshan nyid/mtshan nyid bzhi; C. youwei xiang/sixiang 有爲相/四相)

1. origination/birth (S. jāti; T. skye ba; C. sheng 生)
2. maturation/continuance (S. sthiti; T. gnas pa; C. zhu 住)
3. senescence/decay/aging (S. jarā; T. rga ba; C. yi 異)
4. desinence/extinction (S. anitya [alt. anityatā]; T. mi rtag pa; C. mie 滅)

**four conditions**. (S. pratyaya; T. rkyen; C. yuan 緣)

1. causal condition (S. hetupratyaya; T. rgyu rkyen; C. yin yuan 因緣)
2. immediate antecedent condition (S. samanantarapratyaya; T. de ma thag pa'i rkyen; C. dengwujian yuan 等無間緣)
3. objective-support condition (S. ālambanapratyaya; T. dmigs rkyen; C. suoyuan yuan 所緣緣)
4. predominant condition (S. adhipatipratyaya; T. bdag rkyen; C. zengshang yuan 增上緣)

**four contaminants**. (S. āsrava; T. zag pa; C. lou 漏)

1. contaminant of sensuality (kāmāsrava; T. 'dod pa'i zag pa; C. yu lou 欲漏)
2. contaminant of becoming (bhavāsrava; T. srid pa'i zag pa; C. you lou 有漏)
3. contaminant of ignorance (avidyāsrava; T. ma rig pa'i zag pa; C. wuming lou 無明漏)
4. contaminant of views (dṛṣṭyāsrava; T. lta ba'i zag pa; C. jian lou 見漏)

**four continents**. (S. dvīpa; T. gling; C. [da][bu]zhou [大][部]洲)

1. videha [east] (T. lus 'phags; C. dong shengshen zhou 東勝身洲)
2. Jambudvīpa [south] (T. 'dzam bu gling; C. nan Shanbu zhou 南贍部洲)
3. godānīya [west] (T. ba glang spyod; C. xi niuhuo zhou 西牛貨洲)
4. uttarakuru [north] (T. sgra mi snyan; C. bei julu zhou 北俱盧洲)

**four "defeat" offenses**. (S. pārājika; T. phas pham pa; C. poluoyi 波羅夷)

1. sexual intercourse (S. abrahmacarya; T. mi tshangs pa spyod pa; C. yin 淫)
2. theft (S. adattādāna; T. ma byin par len pa; C. dao 盜)
3. killing [of a human being] (S. vadha; T. gsod pa; C. sha 殺)
4. lying about one's higher spiritual achievements (S. uttaramanuṣyadharmapralāpa; T. mi'i chos bla mar smra ba; C. wang 妄)

**four deportments/postures**. (S. īryāpatha; T. spyod lam; C. weiyi 威儀)

1. walking (S. caṅkrama; alt. gamana; T. 'chag pa; C. xing 行)
2. standing (S. sthāna; sthita; T. 'greng ba; C. zhu 住)
3. sitting (S. niṣaṇṇa; T. 'dug pa; C. zuo 坐)
4. lying down (S. śayana; T. nyal ba; C. wo 臥)

**four divine abidings**. (S. brahmavihāra; T. tshang pa'i gnas; C. fanzhu 梵住)

1. loving-kindness (S. maitrī; T. byams pa; C. ci 慈)
2. compassion (S. karuṇā; T. snying rje; C. bei 悲)
3. empathetic joy (S. muditā; T. dga' ba; C. xi 喜)
4. equanimity (S. upekṣā; T. btang snyoms; C. she 捨)

**four empowerments**. (S. abhiṣeka; T. dbang; C. guanding 灌頂)

1. vase empowerment (S. kalaśābhiṣeka; T. bum dbang; C. baoping guanding 寶瓶灌頂)
2. secret empowerment (S. guhyābhiṣeka; T. gsang dbang; C. mimi guanding 秘密灌頂)
3. wisdom–knowledge empowerment (S. prajñājñānābhiṣeka; T. shes rab ye shes kyi dbang; C. zhihui guanding 智慧灌頂)
4. word empowerment (S. śabdābhiṣeka; T. tshig dbang/dbang bzhi pa; C. mingci guanding 名詞灌頂)

**four fearlessnesses/self-confidences**. (S. vaiśāradya; T. mi 'jigs pa; C. wusuowei 無所畏)

The Tathāgata's self-confidence derives from:

1. his knowledge of all phenomena (S. sarvadharmābhisaṃbodhivaiśāradya; T. chos thams cad mkhyen pa la mi 'jigs pa; C. zhufa xiandengjue wuwei 諸法現等覺無畏)
2. his knowledge that all the contaminants are destroyed (S. sarvāsravakṣayajñānavaiśāradya; T. zag pa zad pa thams cad mkhyen pa la mi 'jigs pa; C. yiqie loujinzhi wuwei 一切漏盡智無畏)
3. his correct identification of all the obstacles to liberation (S. antarāyikadharmānanyathātvaniścitavyākaraṇavaiśāradya; T. bar du gcod pa'i chos rnams bzhan du mi 'gyur bar nges pa'i lung bstan pa la mi 'jigs pa; C. zhangfa buxu jueding shouji wuwei 障法不虛決定授記無畏)
4. his realization of all the marvelous qualities that are to be achieved through completing the path to liberation (S. sarvasampadadhigamāyanairyāṇikapratipattathātvavaiśāradya; T. phun sum tshogs pa thams cad thob par 'gyur bar nges par 'byung ba'i lam de bzhin du gyur ba la mi 'jigs pa; C. weizheng yiqie juzu chudao ruxing wuwei 為證一切具足出道如性無畏)

**four floods**. (S. ogha; T. chu bo; C. puliu 瀑流)

1. craving for sensuality (S. kāmarāga; T. 'dod pa la 'dod chags; C. yu'ai 欲愛)
2. craving for continued existence (S. bhavarāga; T. srid pa'i 'dod chags; C. you'ai 有愛)
3. ignorance (S. avidyā; T. ma rig pa; C. wuming 無明)
4. views (S. dṛṣṭi; T. lta ba; C. jian 見)

**four foundations of mindfulness**. (S. smṛtyupasthāna; T. dran pa'i nyer bzhag; C. nianchu 念處)

1. mindfulness of the body (S. kāyasmṛtyupasthāna; T. lus dran pa nye bar bzhag pa; C. shen nianchu 身念處)
2. mindfulness of sensations (S. vedanāsmṛtyupasthāna; T. tshor ba dran pa nye bar bzhag pa; C. shou nianchu 受念處)
3. mindfulness of mental states (S. cittasmṛtyupasthāna; T. sems dran pa nye bar bzhag pa ; C. xin nianchu 心念處)
4. mindfulness of phenomena (S. dharmasmṛtyupasthāna; T. chos dran pa nye bar bzhag pa; C. fa nianchu 法念處)

**four fruitions**. [of sanctity] (S. phala; T. 'bras bu; C. guo [zheng/wei] 果[證/位])

1. stream-enterer (S. srotaāpanna; T. rgyun du zhugs pa; C. yuliu guo/xutuohuan guo 預流果/須陀洹果)
2. once-returner (S. sakṛdāgāmin; T. lan cig phyir 'ong ba; C. yilai guo/situohan guo 一來果/斯陀含果)
3. non-returner (S. anāgāmin; T. phyir mi 'ong ba; C. buhuan guo/anahan guo 不還果/阿那含果)
4. worthy one (S. arhat; T. dgra bcom pa; C. wuxue guo/aluohan guo 無學果/阿羅漢果)

**four graspings**. (S. upādāna; T. nyer len; C. qu 取)

1. of sensuality (S. kāmopādāna; T. 'dod pa nye bar len pa; C. yuqu 欲取)
2. of wrong views (S. dṛṣṭyupādāna; T. lta ba nye bar len pa; C. jianqu 見取)
3. of rules and rituals (S. śīlavratopādāna; T. tshul khrims dang brtul zhugs mchog 'dzin nye bar len pa; C. jie[jin] qu 戒[禁]取)
4. of the concept "self" (S. ātmavādopādāna; T. bdag lta nye bar len pa; C. woyu qu 我語取)

**four great elements**. (S. mahābhūta; T. 'byung ba chen po; C. da 大)

1. earth/solidity (S. pṛthivī; T. sa; C. di 地)
2. water/cohesion (S. āpas; T. chu; C. shui 水)
3. fire/warmth (S. tejas; T. me; C. huo 火)
4. air/mobility (S. vāyu; T. rlung; C. feng 風)

**four guardian kings**. (S. mahārājan/lokapāla; T. rgyal chen; C. [hushi] tianwang/huguo tianwang [護世]天王/護國天王)

1. Dhṛtarāṣṭra; in the east (T. Yul 'khor srung; C. Chiguo 持國)
2. Virūḍhaka; in the south (T. 'Phags skyes po; C. Zengzhang 增長)
3. Virūpākṣa; in the west (T. Spyan mi bzang; C. Guangmu 廣目)
4. Vaiśravaṇa; in the north (T. Rnam thos sras; C. Duowen 多聞)

**four immaterial absorptions**. (S. ārūpyāvacaradhyāna; T. gzugs med pa'i snyoms 'jug; C. wuse ding 無色定) See FOUR IMMATERIAL REALMS (s.v.).

**four immaterial realms**. (S. ārūpyadhātu; T. gzugs med khams pa'i gnas; C. wuse jie 無色界)

1. infinite space (S. ākāśānantyāyatana; T. nam mkha' mtha' yas skye mched; C. kong wubian chu 空無邊處)

2. infinite consciousness (S. vijñānānantyāyatana; T. rnam shes mtha' yas skye mched; C. shi wubian chu 識無邊處)
3. nothingness (S. ākiñcanyāyatana; T. ci yang med pa'i skye mched; C. wu suoyou chu 無所有處)
4. neither perception nor nonperception (S. naivasaṃjñānā-saṃjñāyatana; T. 'du shes med 'du shes med min skye mched; C. feixiang feifeixiang chu 非想非非想處)

**four intentions**. (S. abhiprāya; T. dgongs pa; C. yiqu/miyi 意趣/密意)

1. intention directed towards sameness (S. samatābhiprāya; T. mnyam pa nyid la dgongs pa; C. pingdeng yiqu 平等意趣)
2. intention directed towards other meanings (S. arthāntar-ābhiprāya; T. don gzhan la dgongs pa; C. bieyi yiqu 別義意趣)
3. intention directed towards other times (S. kālāntar-ābhiprāya; T. dus gzhan la dgongs pa; C. bieshi yiqu 別時意趣)
4. intention directed towards other individuals (S. pudgalān-tarābhiprāya; T. gang zag gzhan la dgongs pa; C. bute-qieluo yiyao yiqu 補特伽羅意樂意趣)

**four intermediate states**. (S. antarābhava; T. bar do)

1. intermediate state of the birth (S. jātyantarābhava; T. skye gnas kyi bar do)
2. intermediate state of the moment of death (S. mumūrṣān-tarābhava; T. 'chi kha'i bar do)
3. intermediate state of dharmatā (S. dharmatāntarābhava; T. chos nyid bar do)
4. intermediate state of rebirth (S. bhavāntarābhava; T. srid pa bar do)

**four Māras**. (S. māra; T. bdud; C. mo 魔)

1. Māra of the aggregates (S. skandhamāra; T. phung po'i bdud; C. yinmo 陰魔)
2. Māra of the afflictions (S. kleśamāra; T. nyon mongs pa'i bdud; C. fannao mo 煩惱魔)
3. Māra of death (S. mṛtyumāra; T. 'chi bdag gi bdud; C. simo 死魔)
4. Māra the deity (S. Devaputramāra; T. Lha'i bu bdud; C. Tianzimo 天子魔)

**four means of conversion**. (S. saṃgrahavastu; T. bsdu dngos; C. sheshi; shefa 攝事/攝法)

1. generosity (S. dāna; T. sbyin pa; C. bushi 布施)
2. kind words (S. priyavādita; T. snyan par smra ba; C. aiyu 愛語)
3. helpfulness; viz. teaching others to fulfill their aims (S. arthacaryā; T. don spyod pa; C. lixing 利行)
4. consistency between words and deeds (S. samānārthatā; T. don mthun pa; C. tongshi 同事)

**four modes of birth**. (S. yoni; T. skye gnas rigs; C. sheng 生)

1. oviparous birth (S. aṇḍaja; T. sgo nga las skye ba; C. luansheng 卵生)
2. viviparous birth (S. jarāyuja; T. mngal nas skye ba; C. taisheng 胎生)
3. moisture-born (S. saṃsvedaja; T. drod sher las skye ba; C. shisheng 濕生)
4. metamorphic or transformative birth; viz. spontaneous generation [as of divinities] (S. upapāduka; T. brdzus te skye ba; C. huasheng 化生)

**four noble ones**. (S. ārya; T. 'phags pa; C. sheng 聖)

1. śrāvaka (T. nyan thos; C. shengwen 聲聞)
2. pratyekabuddha (T. rang rgyal; C. yuanjue 緣覺)
3. bodhisattva (T. byang chub sems dpa'; C. pusa 菩薩)
4. buddha (T. sang rgyas; C. fo 佛)

**four noble persons**. (S. āryapudgala; T. 'phags pa'i gang zag; C. xiansheng 賢聖)

1. stream-enterer (S. srotaāpanna; T. rgyun du zhugs pa; C. yuliu guo/xutuohuan guo 預流果/須陀洹果)
2. once-returner (S. sakṛdāgāmin; T. lan cig phyir 'ong ba; C. yilai guo/situohan guo 一來果/斯陀含果)
3. non-returner (S. anāgāmin; T. phyir mi 'ong ba; C. buhuan guo/anahan guo 不還果/阿那含果)
4. worthy one (S. arhat; T. dgra bcom pa; C. wuxue guo/aluohan guo 無學果/阿羅漢果)

**four noble truths**. (S. āryasatya; T. 'phags pa'i bden pa; C. shengdi 聖諦)

1. truth of suffering (S. duḥkhasatya; T. sdug bsngal gyi bden pa; C. kudi 苦諦)
2. truth of origination (S. samudayasatya; T. kun 'byung gi bden pa; C. jidi 集諦)
3. truth of cessation (S. nirodhasatya; T. 'gog pa'i bden pa; C. miedi 滅諦)
4. truth of the path (S. mārgasatya; T. lam gyi bden pa; C. daodi 道諦)

**four persons**. (S. pudgala; T. gang zag; C. buteqieluo 補特伽羅)

1. ordinary persons (S. pṛthagjana; T. so so skye bo; C. fanfu 凡夫)
2. disciples (S. śrāvaka; T. nyan thos; C. shengwen 聲聞)
3. solitary buddhas (S. pratyekabuddha; T. rang rgyal; C. yuanjue 緣覺)
4. bodhisattvas (T. byang chub sems dpa'; C. pusa 菩薩)

**four perverted views**. (S. viparyāsa; T. phyin ci log; C. diandao 顛倒)

1. to view as permanent what is actually impermanent (S. nityaviparyāsa; T. mi rtag pa la rtag par 'dzin pa; C. chang diandao 常顛倒)

2. to view as pleasurable what is actually suffering (S. sukhaviparyāsa; T. sdug bsngal ba la bde bar 'dzin pa; C. le diandao 樂顛倒)
3. to view as pure what is actually tainted (S. śuciviparyāsa; T. mi gtsang ba la gtsang bar 'dzin pa; C. jing diandao 淨顛倒)
4. to view as self what is actually non-self (S. ātmaviparyāsa; T. bdag med pa la bdag tu 'dzin pa; C. wo diandao 我顛倒)

**four philosophical systems**. (S. siddhāntabheda; T. grub mtha' smra ba)

1. Vaibhāṣika [Sarvāstivāda] (T. Bye brag tu smra ba; C. Piposha bu 毘婆沙部)
2. Sautrāntika (T. Mdo sde pa; C. Jingliang bu 經量部)
3. Vijñānavāda/Cittamātra (T. Rnam shes su smra ba/Sems tsam pa; C. Weishi 唯識)
4. Madhyamaka (Dbu ma pa; C. Zhongguan 中觀)

**four realms of reality [dharmadhātu]**. (C. si fajie 四法界)

1. dharmadhātu of phenomena (C. shi fajie 事法界)
2. dharmadhātu of principle (C. li fajie 理法界)
3. dharmadhātu of the unimpeded interpenetration between principle and phenomena (C. lishi wu'ai fajie 理事無礙法界)
4. dharmadhātu of unimpeded interpenetration of phenomenon and phenomena (C. shishi wu'ai fajie 事事無礙法界)

**four reliances**. (S. pratisaraṇa; T. rton pa; C. yi 依)

1. reliance on the meaning rather than the words (S. arthapratisaraṇena bhavitavyaṃ na vyañjanapratisaraṇena; T. don la rton par bya yi tshig 'bru la rton par mi bya; C. yiyi buyi yu 依義不依語)
2. reliance on the teaching rather than on the person [who delivers the teaching] (S. dharmapratisaraṇena bhavitavyaṃ na pudgalapratisaraṇena; T. chos la rton par bya yi gang zag la rton par mi bya; C. yifa buyi ren 依法不依人)
3. reliance on wisdom rather than [ordinary] consciousnesses (S. jñānapratisaraṇena bhavitavyaṃ na vijñānapratisaraṇena; T. ye shes la rton par bya yi rnam shes la rton par mi bya; C. yizhi buyi shi 依智不依識)
4. reliance on the definitive meaning rather than the provisional meaning (S. nītārthasūtrapratisaraṇena bhavitavyaṃ na neyārthasūtrapratisaraṇena; T. nges don la rton par bya yi drang don la rton par mi bya; C. yiliaoyi buyi buliaoyi 依了義不依不了義)

**four right efforts**. (S. samyakpradhāna/samyakprahāṇa; T. spong pa; C. zhengqin 正勤)

1. to bring about the (future) non-production of evil and unwholesome dharmas that have not yet been produced (S. anutpannānāṃ pāpakānām akuśalānāṃ dharmāṇām anutpādāya cchandaṃ janayati/anutpannānāṃ akuśalānāṃ saṃrakṣaṇaṃ; T. mi dge ba ma skyes pa mi bkyed pa; C. weisheng e ling busheng 未生惡令不生)
2. the abandonment of those evil and unwholesome dharmas that have been produced (S. utpannānāṃ pāpakānām akuśalānāṃ dharmāṇāṃ prahāṇāya cchandaṃ janayati/utpannānāṃ akuśalānāṃ prahāṇaṃ; T. mi dge ba skyes pa spong ba; C. yisheng e ling yongduan 已生惡令永斷)
3. the production of wholesome dharmas that have not yet been produced (S. anutpannānāṃ kuśalānāṃ dharmāṇām utpādāya cchandaṃ janayati; T. dge ba ma skyes pa bskyed pa; C. weisheng shan ling sheng 未生善令生)
4. the increase of those wholesome dharmas that have been produced (S. utpannānāṃ kuśalānāṃ dharmāṇāṃ sthitaye bhūyobhāvāya asaṃpramoṣāya paripūraṇāya cchandaṃ janayati/anutpannānāṃ punarutpāda; T. dge ba skyes pa spel ba; C. yisheng shan ling zengzhang 已生善令增長)

**four seals**. (S. mudrā; T. phyag rgya; C. yin 印)

1. pledge seal (S. samayamudrā; T. dam tshig phyag rgya; C. sanmoye yin 三摩耶印)
2. dharma seal (S. dharmamudrā; T. chos kyi phyag rgya; C. fa yin 法印)
3. action seal (S. karmamudrā; T. las kyi phyag rgya; C. jiemo yin 羯磨印)
4. great seal (S. mahāmudrā; T. phyag rgya chen po; C. da yin 大印)

**four seals indicative of the Buddhist view**. (S. caturmudrā/dṛṣṭinimittamudrā; T. phyag rgya bzhi/bka' rtags kyi phyag rgya; C. siyin/fayin 四印/法印)

1. all that is compounded is impermanent (S. sarvasaṃskārā anityatāḥ; T. 'dus byas thams cad mi rtag pa; C. zhuxing wuchang 諸行無常)
2. all that is contaminated is suffering (S. sarvasaṃskārā duḥkhāḥ; T. zag cas thams cad sdug bsngal ba; C. yiqie jie ku 一切皆苦)
3. all phenomena are without self (S. sarvadharmā anātmānaḥ; T. chos thams cad bdag med pa; C. zhufa wuwo 諸法無我)
4. nirvāṇa is peace (S. nirvāṇaśānta; T. mya ngan las 'das pa zhi ba; C. niepan jijing 涅槃寂靜)

**four tantra classes**. (S. tantra; T. rgyud sde)

1. action tantra (S. kriyātantra; T. bya ba'i rgyud)
2. performance tantra (S. caryātantra; T. spyod pa'i rgyud)
3. yoga tantra (S. yogatantra; T. rnal 'byor gyi rgyud)
4. unexcelled yoga tantra (S. anuttarayogatantra; T. rnal 'byor bla na med pa'i rgyud)

## FIVES

**five acts that bring immediate retribution**. (S. ānantaryakarman; T. mtshams med pa; C. wujian ye [nizui/zhongzui] 無間業 [逆罪/重罪])

1. matricide (S. mātṛghāta; T. ma gsod pa; C. hai mu/sha mu 害母/殺母)
2. patricide (S. pitṛghāta; T. pha gsod pa; C. hai fu/sha fu 害父/殺父)
3. killing an arhat (S. arhadghāta; T. dgra bcom pa gsod pa; C. hai aluohan/sha aluohan 害阿羅漢/殺阿羅漢)
4. maliciously spilling a buddha's blood (S. tathāgatasyāntike duṣṭacittarudhirotpādanam; T. de bzhin gshegs pa'i sku la ngan sems kyis khrag 'byin pa; C. [exin] chu foshen xie [惡心]出佛身血)
5. creating a schism in the order (S. saṃghabheda; T. dge 'dun gyi dbyen byas pa; C. poseng 破僧)

**five aggregates**. (S. skandha; T. phung po; C. yun/yin 蘊/陰)

1. aggregate of materiality (S. rūpaskandha; T. gzugs kyi phung po; C. se yun/se yin 色蘊/色陰)
2. aggregate of sensation (S. vedanāskandha; T. tshor ba'i phung po; C. shou yun/shou yin 受蘊/受陰)
3. aggregate of perception (S. saṃjñāskandha; T. 'du shes kyi phung po; C. xiang yun/xiang yin 想蘊/想陰)
4. aggregate of conditioning factors (S. saṃskāraskandha; T. 'du byed kyi phung po; C. xing yun/xing yin 行蘊/行陰)
5. aggregate of consciousness (S. vijñānaskandha; T. rnam shes kyi phung po; shi yun/shi yin 識蘊/識陰)

**five aids to liberation**. (S. mokṣabhāgīya; T. thar pa cha mthun; C. shunjietuofen 順解脱分)

1. faith (S. śraddhā; T. dad pa; C. xin 信)
2. effort (S. vīrya; T. brtson 'grus; C. jingjin/qin 精進/勤)
3. mindfulness (S. smṛti; T. dran pa; C. nian 念)
4. concentration (S. samādhi; T. ting nge 'dzin; C. ding 定)
5. wisdom (S. prajñā; T. shes rab; C. hui 慧)

**five buddha families**. (S. pañcakula; T. rigs lnga; C. wu bu/jia 五部/家)

1. tathāgata family (S. tathāgatakula; T. de bzhin gshegs pa'i rigs; C. rulai bu 如來部)
2. vajra family (S. vajrakula; T. rdo rje'i rigs; C. jingang bu 金剛部)
3. jewel family (S. ratnakula; T. rin chen rigs; C. bao bu 寶部)
4. lotus family (S. padmakula; T. padma rigs; C. lianhua bu 蓮華部)
5. action family (S. karmakula; T. las kyi rigs; C. ye bu 業部)

**five buddhas**. (S. pañcatathāgata; T. de bzhin gshegs pa lnga; C. wuzhi rulai/wu fo 五智如來/五佛)

1. Vairocana (T. Rnam par snang mdzad; C. Dari rulai/Piluzhena 大日如來/毗盧遮)
2. Akṣobhya (T. Mi bskyod pa; C. Achu fo 阿閦佛)
3. Ratnasambhava (T. Rin chen 'byung gnas; C. Baosheng rulai 寶生如來)
4. Amitābha (T. 'Od dpag med; C. Amituo fo/Wuliangshou fo 阿彌陀佛/無量壽佛)
5. Amoghasiddhi (T. Don yod grub pa; C. Bukong Chengjiu rulai fo 不空成就如來佛)

**five destinies** [of rebirth]. (S. gati; T. 'gro ba; C. qu/dao 趣/道)

1. divinities (S. deva; T. lha; C. tian 天)
2. humans (S. manuṣya; T. mi; C. ren 人)
3. animals (S. tiryak; T. dud 'gro; C. chusheng 畜生)
4. ghosts (S. preta; T. yi dwags; C. egui 餓鬼)
5. hell denizens (S. nāraka; T. dmyal ba; C. diyu 地獄)

**five effects**. (S. pañcaphala; T. 'bras bu lnga; C. wu guo 五果)

1. correlative effect (S. niṣyandaphala; T. rgyu mthun gyi 'bras bu; C. dengliu guo 等流果)
2. retributive effect (S. vipākaphala; T. rnam smin gyi 'bras bu; C. yishu guo 異熟果)
3. separation effect (S. visaṃyogaphala; T. bral ba'i 'bras bu; C. liji guo 離繫果)
4. effect caused by human action (S. puruṣakāraphala; T. skyes bus byed pa'i 'bras bu; C. shiyong guo 士用果)
5. predominant effect (S. adhipatiphala; T. bdag po'i 'bras bu; C. zengshang guo 增上果)

**five elements**. (S. mahābhūta/dhātu; T. 'byung po chen po; C. da[zhong] 大[種])

1. earth/solidity (S. pṛthivī; T. sa; C. di 地)
2. water/cohesion (S. āpas; T. chu; C. shui 水)
3. fire/warmth (S. tejas; T. me; C. huo 火)
4. air/mobility (S. vāyu; T. rlung; C. feng 風)
5. space (S. ākāśa; T. nam mkha'; C. kong 空)

**five eyes**. (S. cakṣus; T. spyan; C. yan 眼)

1. fleshly eye (S. māṃsacakṣus; T. sha'i spyan; C. rouyan 肉眼)
2. divine eye/clairvoyance (S. divyacakṣus; T. lha'i spyan; C. tianyan 天眼)
3. wisdom eye (S. prajñācakṣus; T. shes rab kyi spyan; C. huiyan 慧眼)
4. dharma eye (S. dharmacakṣus; T. chos kyi spyan; C. fayan 法眼)
5. buddha eye (S. buddhacakṣus; T. sangs rgyas kyi spyan; C. foyan 佛眼)

**five factors of meditative absorption**. (S. dhyānāṅga; T. bsam gtan gyi yan lag; C. chanzhi/dingzhi 禪支/定支)

1. applied thought/initial application of attention (S. vitarka; T. rtog pa; C. xun 尋)
2. sustained thought/sustained attention (S. vicāra; T. dpyod pa; C. si 伺)
3. physical rapture (S. prīti; T. dga' ba; C. xi 喜)
4. mental ease (S. sukha; T. bde ba; C. le 樂)
5. one-pointedness (S. cittaikāgratā; T. sems rtse gcig pa; C. xin yijing xing 心一境性)

**five faculties/dominants**. (S. indriya; T. dbang po; C. gen 根)

1. faith (S. śraddhā; T. dad pa; C. xin 信)
2. effort (S. vīrya; T. brtson 'grus; C. jingjin/qin 精進/勤)
3. mindfulness (S. smṛti; T. dran pa; C. nian 念)
4. concentration (S. samādhi; T. ting nge 'dzin; C. ding 定)
5. wisdom (S. prajñā; T. shes rab; C. hui 慧)

**five hindrances [to dhyāna]**. (S. nīvaraṇa; T. sgrib pa; C. gai 蓋)

1. sensual desire (S. kāmacchanda; T. 'dod pa la 'dun pa ; C. tanyu 貪欲)
2. malice (S. vyāpāda; T. gnod sems; C. chenhui 瞋恚)
3. sloth and torpor (S. styānamiddha; T. rmugs pa dang gnyid; C. shuimian/huanchen 睡眠/昏沈)
4. restlessness and worry (S. auddhatyakaukṛtya; T. rgod pa dang 'gyod pa; C. diaoju/sanluan/ezuo/hui 掉舉/散亂/惡作/悔)
5. skeptical doubt (S. vicikitsā; T. the tshom; C. yi 疑)

**Five Huayan classifications of the teachings**. (C. Huayan wujiao 華嚴五教)
*Earlier division, according to Dushun and Fazang:*

1. hīnayāna teachings/śrāvakayāna teachings (C. xiaosheng jiao/shengwensheng jiao 小乘教/聖聞乘教)
2. elementary teachings [of Mahāyāna] (C. shijiao 始教)
3. advanced/final teachings [of Mahāyāna] (C. zhongjiao 終教)
4. sudden teachings (C. dunjiao 頓教)
5. perfect teachings/consummate teachings C. yuanjiao 圓教)

*Later division, according to Guifeng Zongmi:*

1. teachings for divinities and humans (C. rentian jiao 人天教)
2. hīnayāna teachings (C. xiaosheng jiao 小乘教)
3. dharma-characteristics teachings of Mahāyāna (C. dasheng faxiang jiao 大乘法相教)
4. characteristics-negating teachings of Mahāyāna (C. dasheng poxiang jiao 大乘破相教)
5. The nature-revealing teaching of the one vehicle (C. yisheng xianxing jiao 一乘顯性教)

**five lineages**. (S. gotra; T. rigs pa; C. zhongxing 種姓/性)

1. tathāgata lineage (S. tathāgatayānābhisamayagotra; T. de bzhin gshegs pa'i theg pa mngon par rtogs pa'i rigs; C. rulai sheng zhongxing 如來乘種性)
2. pratyekabuddha lineage (S. pratyekabuddhayānābhisamayagotra; T. rang rgyal gyi theg pa mngon par rtogs pa'i rigs; C. dujue sheng zhongxing 獨覺乘種性)
3. śrāvakayāna lineage (S. śrāvakayānābhisamayagotra; T. nyan thos kyi theg pa mngon par rtogs pa'i rigs; C. shengwen sheng zhongxing 聲聞乘種性)
4. uncertain lineage (S. aniyatagotra; T. ma nges pa'i rigs; C. buding zhongxing 不定種性)
5. no lineage [viz. icchantika] (S. agotraka; T. rigs med pa; C. wu zhongxing 無種性)

**five nectars**. (S. amṛta; T. bdud rtsi; C. ganlu 甘露)

1. semen (S. bodhicitta; T. byang sems; C. nanjing 男精)
2. blood (S. rakta; T. rak ta; C. nüxie 女血)
3. urine (S. mūtra; T. dri chu; C. niao 尿)
4. excrement (S. purīṣa; T. dri chen; C. shi 屎)
5. flesh (S. māṃsa; T. sha; C. gusui 骨髓)

**five paths**. (S. pañcamārga; T. lam lnga; C. wuwei 五位)

1. path of equipment/accumulation (S. saṃbhāramārga; T. tshogs lam; C. ziliang wei 資糧位)
2. path of preparation (S. prayogamārga; T. sbyor lam; C. jiaxing wei 加行位)
3. path of vision (S. darśanamārga; T. mthong lam; C. jiandao wei 見道位)
4. path of cultivation (S. bhāvanāmārga; T. bsgom lam; C. xiudao wei 修道位)
5. adept path (where there is nothing more to learn) (S. aśaikṣamārga; T. mi slob lam; C. wuxue wei 無學位)

**five periods and eight teachings**. [according to the Tiantai school] (C. wushi bajiao 五時八教)
*The five major chronological periods of the Buddha's teaching* (C. wushi 五時)*:*

1. Huayan period (C. Huayan shiqi 華嚴時期)
2. āgamas/Deer Park period (C. ahan shiqi 阿含時期/Luyuan shiqi 鹿苑時期)
3. expansive (vaipulya) Mahāyāna period (C. Fangdeng shiqi 方等時期)
4. perfection of wisdom (prajñāpāramitā) period (C. bore shiqi 般若時期)
5. Lotus (*Saddharmapuṇḍarīkasūtra*) and Nirvāṇa (*Mahāparinirvāṇasūtra*) scriptures period (C. Fahua Niepan shiqi 法華涅槃時期)

*Fourfold division of the teaching according to means of conversion* (C. huayi sijiao 化儀四教):

1. sudden [Huayan jing] (C. dunjiao 頓教)
2. gradual [āgamas, vaipulya, prajñāpāramitā] (C. jianjiao 漸教)

3. indeterminate (C. puding jiao 不定教)
4. secret/esoteric (C. mimi jiao 祕密教)

*Fourfold division of the teaching according to content* [*and based on the capacity of the audience*] (C. huafa sijiao 化法四教):

1. tripiṭaka, viz., hīnayāna (C. sanzang jiao 三藏教)
2. common/shared [by both hīnayāna and Mahāyāna] (C. tongjiao 通教)
3. distinct/separate [Mahāyāna] (C. biejiao 別教)
4. perfect/consummate [Lotus and Nirvāṇa sutras] (C. yuanjiao 圓教)

**five powers**. (S. bala; T. stobs; C. li 力)

1. power of faith (S. śraddhābala; T. dad pa'i stobs; C. xin li 信力)
2. power of effort (S. vīryabala; T. brtson 'grus kyi stobs; C. jingjin li/qin li 精進力/勤力)
3. power of mindfulness (S. smṛtibala; T. dran pa'i stobs; C. nian li 念力)
4. power of concentration (S. samādhibala; T. ting nge 'dzin gyi stobs; C. ding li 定力)
5. power of wisdom (S. prajñābala; T. shes rab kyi stobs; C. hui li 慧力)

**five precepts**. [of the laity] (S. pañcaśīla; T. tshul khrims lnga; C. wujie 五戒)

1. to abstain from killing living creatures (S. prāṇātipāta-virati; T. srog gcod pa spong ba; C. bu shasheng/li shasheng 不殺生/離殺生)
2. to abstain from taking what is not given (S. adattādāna-virati; T. ma byin par len pa spong ba; C. bu toudao/li buyu qu 不偷盜/離不與取)
3. to abstain from engaging in sexual misconduct (S. kāmamithyācāra-virati; T. 'dod pas log par g.yem pa spong ba; C. bu xieyin/li yu xiexing 不邪婬/離欲邪行)
4. to abstain from lying (often explained as lying about the possession of high states of attainment or superhuman powers) (S. mṛṣāvāda-virati; T. rdzun du smra ba spong ba; C. bu wangyu/li xukuang yu 不妄語/離虛誑語)
5. to abstain from intoxicants (S. madyapāna-virati; T. myos par 'gyur ba'i btung ba spong pa; C. bu yinjiu/li yinjiu 不飲酒/離飲酒)

**five pure abodes**. (S. śuddhāvāsa; T. gtsang gnas; C. jing jutian 淨居天)

1. free from afflictions (S. avṛha; T. mi che ba; C. wufan tian 無煩天)
2. not burning/without torment (S. atapa; T. mi gdung ba; C. wure tian 無熱天)
3. perfect form (S. sudṛśa; T. gya nom snang ba; C. shanxian tian 善現天)
4. perfect vision (S. sudarśana; T. shin tu mthong ba; C. shanjian tian 善見天)
5. highest (S. akaniṣṭha; T. 'og min; C. se jiujing tian 色究竟天)

**five royal treasure revealers**. (T. gter ston rgyal po lnga)

1. Nyang ral Nyi ma 'od zer
2. Guru Chos kyi dbang phyug
3. Rdo rje gling pa
4. Pad ma gling pa
5. 'Jam dbyang mkhyen brtse dbang po

**five sciences**. (S. pañcavidyā; T. rig pa lnga; C. wuming 五明)

1. manual arts (S. śilpakarma[vidyā]; T. bzo gnas kyi rig pa; C. gongqiao ming 工巧明)
2. grammar (S. śabdavidyā; T. sgra'i rig pa; C. shengming 聲明)
3. medicine (S. cikitsāvidyā; T. gso ba'i rig pa; C. yifangming 醫方名)
4. logic (S. hetuvidyā; T. gtan tshigs kyi rig pa; C. yinming 因明)
5. inner knowledge (S. adhyātmavidyā; T. nang gi rig pa; C. neiming 內明)

**five supranormal powers**. (S. abhijñā; T. mngon shes; C. shentong 神通)

1. psychic powers (S. ṛddhividhābhijñā; T. rdzu 'phrul gyi bya ba shes pa; C. shenjing zhizheng tong 神境智證通)
2. "the divine eye"/clairvoyance (S. divyacakṣus; T. lha'i mig; C. tianyan 天眼)
3. "the divine ear"/clairaudience (S. divyaśrotra; T. lha'i rna ba; C. tian'er 天耳)
4. knowledge of others' minds (S. paracittajñāna; T. pha rol gyi sems shes pa; C. taxin tong 他心通)
5. knowledge of past lives (S. pūrvanivāsānusmṛti; T. sngon gyi gnas rje su dran pa; C. suzhu suinian/suming tong 宿住隨念/宿命通)

**five turbidities/degenerations**. (S. kaṣāya; T. snyigs ma; C. zhuo 濁)

1. turbidity of the lifespan (S. ayuḥkaṣāya; T. tshe'i snyigs ma; C. min zhuo 命濁)
2. turbidity of views (S. dṛṣṭikaṣāya; T. lta ba'i snyigs ma; C. jian zhuo 見濁)
3. turbidity of afflictions (S. kleśakaṣāya; T. nyon mongs kyi snyigs ma; C. fannao zhuo 煩惱濁)
4. turbidity of sentient beings (S. sattvakaṣāya; T. sems can gyi snyigs ma; C. zhongsheng zhuo 衆生濁)
5. turbidity of the age (S. kalpakaṣāya; T. dus kyi snyigs ma; C. jie zhuo 劫濁)

**five wheels/cakras**. (S. cakra; T. 'khor lo; C. lun 輪)

1. great bliss wheel [at the forehead] (S. mahāsukhacakra; T. spyi bde chen gyi 'khor lo; C. dalelun/dinglun 大樂輪/頂輪)

2. enjoyment wheel [at the throat] (S. sambhogacakra; T. mgrin pa longs spyod kyi 'khor lo; C. baolun/shouyonglun/houlun 報輪/受用輪/喉輪)
3. dharma wheel [at the heart] (S. dharmacakra; T. snying ka chos kyi 'khor lo; C. falun/xinlun 法輪/心輪)
4. emanation wheel [at the navel] (S. nirmāṇacakra; T. lte ba sprul pa'i 'khor lo; C. huanhualun/qilun 幻化輪/臍輪)
5. bliss protecting wheel [at the perineum] (S. sukhapālacakra; T. bde skyong gi 'khor lo; C. hulelun 護樂輪)

**five wisdoms/knowledges**. (S. pañcajñāna; T. ye shes lnga; C. wuzhi 五智)

1. wisdom of the dharmadhātu (S. dharmadhātujñāna; T. chos dbyings kyi ye shes; C. fajie tixing zhi 法界體性智)
2. mirror-like wisdom/great perfect mirror wisdom (ādarśajñāna/mahādarśajñāna; T. me long gi ye shes; C. da yuanjing zhi 大圓境智)
3. wisdom of equality/knowledge of impartiality (S. samatājñāna; T. mnyam nyid kyi ye shes; C. pingdeng xing zhi 平等性智)
4. wisdom of specific knowledge (S. pratyavekṣaṇājñāna; T. so sor rtog pa'i ye shes; C. miao guancha zhi 妙觀察智)
5. wisdom of having accomplished what was to be done (S. kṛtyānuṣṭhānajñāna; T. bya ba grub pa'i ye shes; C. cheng suozuo zhi 成所作智)

## SIXES

**six aspects** [of all phenomena in Huayan]. (C. liuxiang 六相)

1. generic/universal aspect (C. zongxiang 總相)
2. constituent/particular aspect (C. biexiang 別相)
3. identity/similarity aspect (C. tongxiang 同相)
4. differentiated aspect (C. yixiang 異相)
5. integrated/collective aspect (C. chengxiang 成相)
6. disintegration/instantiated aspect (C. huaixiang 壞相)

**six causes**. (S. ṣaḍhetu; T. rgyu drug; C. liu yin 六因)

1. efficient cause (S. kāraṇahetu; T. byed pa'i rgyu; C. nengzuo yin 能作因)
2. coexistent cause (S. sahabhūhetu; T. lhan cig 'byung ba'i rgyu; C. juyou yin 俱有因)
3. conjoined cause (S. saṃprayuktahetu; T. mtshungs ldan gyi rgyu; C. xiangying yin 相應因)
4. homogeneous cause (S. sabhāgahetu; T. skal mnyam gyi rgyu; C. tonglei yin 同類因)
5. all-pervasive cause (S. sarvatragahetu; T. kun gro'i rgyu; C. bianxing yin 遍行因)
6. retributive cause (S. vipākahetu; T. rnam smin gyi rgyu; C. yishu yin 異熟因)

**six consciousnesses**. (S. vijñāna; T. rnam par shes pa; C. shi 識)

1. visual consciousness (S. cakṣurvijñāna; T. mig gi rnam shes; C. yanshi 眼識)
2. auditory consciousness (S. śrotravijñāna; T. rna ba'i rnam shes; C. ershi 耳識)
3. olfactory consciousness (S. ghrāṇavijñāna; T. sna'i rnam shes; C. bishi 鼻識)
4. gustatory consciousness (S. jihvāvijñāna; T. lce'i rnam shes; C. sheshi 舌識)
5. tactile consciousness (S. kāyavijñāna; T. lus kyi rnam shes; C. shenshi 身識)
6. mental consciousness (S. manovijñāna; T. yid kyi rnam shes; C. yishi 意識)

**six destinies**. [of rebirth] (S. gati; T. 'gro ba; C. dao/qu 道/趣)

1. divinities (S. deva; T. lha; C. tian 天)
2. demigods (S. asura; T. lha ma yin; C. axiuluo 阿修羅)
3. humans (S. manuṣya; T. mi; C. ren 人)
4. animals (S. tiryak; T. dud 'gro; C. chusheng 畜生)
5. ghosts (S. preta; T. yi dwags; C. egui 餓鬼)
6. hell denizens (S. nāraka; T. dmyal ba; C. diyu 地獄)

**six doctrines of Nāropa**. (S. Nādapādadharma; T. Nā ro chos drug)

1. inner heat (S. caṇdaliyoga; T. gtum mo)
2. illusory body (S. māyākāyayoga; T. sgyu lus)
3. dreams (S. svapanayoga; T. rmi lam)
4. clear light (S. prabhāsvarayoga; T. 'od gsal)
5. intermediate state (S. antarābhavayoga; T. bar do)
6. transference (S. saṃkrāntiyoga; T. 'pho ba)

**six elements**. (S. dhātu; T. khams; C. da/jie 大/界)

1. earth/solidity (S. pṛthivī; T. sa; C. di 地)
2. water/cohesion (S. āpas; T. chu; C. shui 水)
3. fire/warmth (S. tejas; T. me; C. huo 火)
4. wind/mobility (S. vāyu; T. rlung; C. feng 風)
5. space (S. ākāśa; T. nam mkha'; C. kong 空)
6. consciousness (S. vijñāna; T. rnam shes; C. shi 識)

**six heavens of the sensuous realm**. (S. kāmadhātu-deva; T. 'dod pa'i khams kyi lha; C. Yujie tian 欲界天)

1. four great kings (S. cāturmahārājika; T. rgyal chen rigs bzhi; C. siwang tian 四王天)
2. divinities of the thirty-three (S. trāyastriṃśa; T. sum cu rtsa gsum; C. daoli tian/sanshisan tian 忉利天/三十三天)
3. free from conflict (S. yāma; T. 'thab bral; C. yemo tian 夜摩天)
4. contented (S. tuṣita; T. dga' ldan; C. doushuai[tuo] tian 兜率[陀]天)
5. enjoyment of creation (S. nirmāṇarati; T. 'phrul dga'; C. huale tian 化樂天)

6. divinities who have power over the creations of others/divinities who partake of the pleasures created in other heavens (S. paranirmitavaśavartin; T. gzhan 'phrul dbang byed; C. tahua zizai tian 他化自在天)

**six intermediate states**. (S. antarābhava; T. bar do)

1. intermediate state of the present lifetime (S. jatyantarābhava; T. skye gnas rang bzhin gyi bar do)
2. intermediate state of absorption (S. samādhyantarābhava; T. bsam gtan gyi bar do)
3. intermediate state of dreams (S. svapanāntarābhava; T. rmi lam gyi bar do)
4. intermediate state of the moment of death (S. mumūrṣāntarābhava; T. 'chi kha'i bar do)
5. intermediate state of dharmatā (S. dharmatāntarābhava; T. chos nyid bar do)
6. intermediate state of existence (S. bhavāntarābhava; T. srid pa bar do)

**six-limbed yoga** [of the *Kālacakratantra*]. (S. ṣaḍaṅgayoga; T. sbyor drug)

1. retraction (T. sor sdud)
2. concentration (T. bsam gtan)
3. breath control (T. srog 'dzin)
4. retention of the complete deity (T. sku ril bur 'dzin pa)
5. recollection (T. rjes su dran pa)
6. contemplation (T. ting nge 'dzin)

**six non-Buddhist teachers**. (S. tīrthika-śāstṛ; T. mu stegs can gyi ston pa; C. waidaoshi 外道師)

1. Pūraṇa-Kāśyapa (T. 'Od srung rdzogs byed; C. Fulanna jiashe 富蘭那迦葉)
2. Maskarin Gośālīputra (T. Kun tu rgyu gnag lhas kyi bu; C. Moqieli jusheli/Moqieli jushelizi 末伽梨拘舍梨/末伽梨拘賒梨子)
3. Ajita Keśakambala (T. Mi pham sgra'i la ba can; C. Aqiduo chishe qinpoluo 阿耆多翅舍欽婆羅)
4. Kakuda Kātyāyana (T. Ka tya'i bu nog can; C. Jialuo jiutuo jiazhanyan 迦羅鳩馱迦旃延)
5. Nirgrantha-Jñātīputra (T. Gcer bu pa gnyen gyi bu; C. Nijiantuo Ruotizi 尼乾陀若提子/尼揵陀若提子)
6. Sañjaya Vairāṭīputra (T. Smra 'dod kyi bu mo'i bu yang dag rgyal ba can; C. Shanduye pilyu zhizi 珊闍耶毗羅胝子)

**six ornaments of the world**. (T. 'dzam gling rgyan drug)

1. Nāgārjuna (T. Klu sgrub)
2. Āryadeva (T. 'Phags pa lha)
3. Asaṅga (T. Thogs med)
4. Vasubandhu (T. Dbyig gnyen)
5. Dignāga (T. Phyogs glang)
6. Dharmakīrti (T. Chos kyi grags pa)

**six perfections**. (S. pāramitā; T. pha rol tu phyin pa; C. du/boluomi 度/波羅蜜)

1. giving/generosity (S. dāna, T. sbyin pa; C. bushi/tan 布施/檀)
2. morality (S. śīla; T. tshul khrims; C. chijie/shiluo 持戒/尸羅)
3. patience/forbearance (S. kṣānti; T. bzod pa; C. renru/chanti 忍辱/羼提)
4. effort/vigor (S. vīrya; T. brtson 'grus; C. jingjin/piliye 精進/毗梨耶)
5. meditative absorption (S. dhyāna; T. bsam gtan; C. jinglü/chan 靜慮/禪)
6. wisdom (S. prajñā; T. shes rab; C. zhihui/bore 智慧/般若)

**six recollections**. (S. anusmṛti; T. rjes su dran pa; C. nian 念)

1. recollection of the buddha (S. buddhānusmṛti; T. sangs rgyas rjes su dran pa; C. nianfo 念佛)
2. recollection of the dharma (S. dharmānusmṛti; T. chos rjes su dran pa; C. nianfa 念法)
3. recollection of the saṃgha (S. saṃghānusmṛti; T. dge 'dun rjes su dran pa; C. nianseng 念僧)
4. recollection of morality (S. śīlānusmṛti; T. tshul khrims rjes su dran pa; C. nianjie 念戒)
5. recollection of charity (S. tyāgānusmṛti; T. gtong ba rjes su dran pa; C. nianshi 念施)
6. recollection of the divinities (S. devatānusmṛti; T. lha rjes su dran pa; C. niantian 念天)

**six sense faculties/sense bases**. (S. indrya; T. dbang po; C. gen 根)

1. visual faculty (S. cakṣurindriya; T. mig gi dbang po; C. yangen 眼根)
2. auditory faculty (S. śrotrendriya; T. rna ba'i dbang po; C. ergen 耳根)
3. olfactory faculty (S. ghrāṇendriya; T. sna'i dbang po; C. bigen 鼻根)
4. gustatory faculty (S. jihvendriya; T. lce'i dbang po; C. shegen 舌根)
5. tactile faculty (S. kāyendriya; T. lus kyi dbang po; C. shengen 身根)
6. mental faculty (S. manendriya; T. yid kyi dbang po; C. yigen 意根)

**six superknowledges/supramundane powers**. (S. abhijñā; T. mngon par shes pa; C. shentong 神通)

1. psychic powers (S. ṛddhividhi; T. rdzu 'phrul gyi bya ba shes pa'i mngon shes; C. shenjing/shenzu [zhizheng] tong 神境/神足[智證]通)
2. "the divine eye"/clairvoyance (S. divyacakṣus; T. lha'i mig gi mngon shes; C. tianyan [zhizheng] tong 天眼[智證]通)

3. "the divine ear"/clairaudience (S. divyaśrotra; T. lha'i rna ba'i mngon shes; C. tian'er [zhizheng] tong 天耳[智證]通)
4. knowledge of other's minds (S. paracittājñāna; T. pha rol gyi sems shes pa'i mngon shes; C. taxin [zhizheng] tong 他心[智證]通)
5. knowledge of past lives (S. pūrvanivāsānusmṛti; T. sngon gyi gnas rje su dran pa'i mngon shes; C. suzhu suinian zhizheng tong/suming [zhizheng] tong 宿住隨念[智證]通/宿命[智證]通)
6. knowledge of the extinction of the contaminants (S. āsravakṣayajñāna; T. zag pa zad pa'i mngon shes; C. loujin [zhizheng] tong 漏盡[智證]通)

**six tantras**. (T. rgyud sde drug; C. dateluo 怛特羅)

1. kriyātantra (T. bya rgyud)
2. caryātantra (T. spyod rgyud)
3. yogatantra (T. rnal 'byor rgyud)
4. mahāyogatantra (T. rnal 'byor chen po'i rgyud)
5. anuyogatantra (T. rje su rnal 'byor rgyud)
6. atiyogatantra (T. shin tu rnal 'byor rgyud)

## SEVENS

**seven-branch service**. (S. saptāṅgavidhi; T. yan lag bdun pa; C. qizhi zuofa 七支作法)

1. obeisance (S. vandanā; T. phyag 'tshal ba; C. lijing zhufo 禮敬諸佛)
2. offerings (S. pūjana; T. mchod pa phul ba; C. guangxiu gongyang 廣修供養)
3. confession of transgressions (S. pāpadeśanā; T. sdig pa bshags pa; C. chanhui yezhang 懺悔業障)
4. admiration/joy (S. anumodana; T. rjes su yi rang ba; C. suixi gongde 隨喜功德)
5. request [to turn the wheel of dharma] (S. saṃcodana; T. bskul ba; C. qing zhuan falun 請轉法輪)
6. request [to remain in the world] (S. prārthanā; T. gsol ba; C. qingfo zhushi 請佛住世)
7. dedication of merit (S. pariṇāmanā; T. bsngo ba; C. pujie huixiang 普皆迴向)

**seven buddhas [of the past]**. (S. saptatathāgata; T. sangs rgyas rabs bdun; C. qifo 七佛)

1. Vipaśyin (T. Rnam gzigs; C. Piposhi[fo] 毘婆尸[佛])
2. Śikhin (T. Gtsug gtor can; C. Shiqi[fo] 尸棄[佛])
3. Viśvabhū (T. Kun skyobs; C. Pishepo[fo] 毘舍婆[佛])
4. Krakucchanda (T. Log pa dang sel; C. Juliusun[fo] 拘留孫[佛])
5. Kanakamuni (T. Gser thub; C. Junahanmouni[fo] 拘那含牟尼[佛])
6. Kāśyapa (T. 'Od srung; C. Jiashe[fo] 迦葉[佛]
7. Śākyamuni (T. Shākya thub pa; C. Shijiamouni 釋迦牟尼)

**seven factors of enlightenment/limbs of awakening**. (S. bodhyaṅga; T. byang chub yan lag; C. juezhi/putifen 覺支/菩提分)

1. mindfulness (S. smṛti; T. dran pa; C. nian 念)
2. investigation of states (S. dharmapravicaya; T. chos rab tu rnam par 'byed pa; C. zefa 擇法)
3. perseverance/energy (S. vīrya; T. brtson 'grus; C. jingjin 精進)
4. rapture/bliss (S. prīti; T. dga' ba; C. xi 喜)
5. tranquility (S. praśrabdhi; T. shin yu sbyangs pa; C. qingan 輕安)
6. concentration (T. samādhi; T. ting nge 'dzin; C. ding 定)
7. equanimity (S. upekṣā; T. btang snyoms; C. she 捨)

**seven jewels [of a cakravartin]**. (S. ratna; T. rin chen; C. [lunwang]bao [輪王]寶)

1. wheel [chariot] (S. cakraratna; T. 'khor lo rin po che; C. lunbao 輪寶)
2. precious jewel (S. maṇiratna; T. nor bu rin po che; C. [moni]zhubao [末尼]珠寶)
3. queen (S. strīratna; T. btsun mo rin po che; C. nübao 女寶)
4. minister (S. pariṇāyakaratna; T. blon po rin po che; C. jushi bao/zhuzang bao 居士寶/主藏寶)
5. elephant (S. hastiratna; T. glang po rin po che; C. xiangbao 象寶)
6. general (S. senāpatiratna; T. dmag dpon rin po che; C. zhubingchen bao/jiangjun bao 主兵臣寶/將軍寶)
7. horse (S. aśvaratna; T. rta mchog rin po che; C. mabao 馬寶)

**seven men who were tested**. (T. sad mi mi bdun)
The first monks ordained in Tibet:

1. Sba khri gzigs, ordained as Śrīghoṣa (Dpal dbyangs)
2. Sba gsal snang, ordained as Jñānendra (Ye shes dbang po)
3. Sba khri bzher/bzhir
4. Ba gor Vairocana, or Vairocanarakṣita
5. Rma rin chen mchog
6. Rgyal ba mchog dbyangs
7. 'Khon Klu'i dbang po srung ba, or Nāgendrarakṣita

**seven-point posture of Vairocana**. (T. Rnam snang gi chos bdun)

1. legs in the vajra posture (T. rkang ba skyil krung)
2. hands in the positions of equipoise (T. lag pa mnyam bzhag)
3. spine straight (T. sgal tshigs drang por bsrang ba)
4. neck slightly bent (T. mgrin cung zad gug pa)
5. shoulders spread like the wings of a vulture (T. dpung ba rgod gshog ltar brkyangs pa)
6. gaze resting at the tip of the nose (T. mig sna rtser phabs pa)
7. tongue touching the palate (T. lce ya rkan la sbyar ba)

**seven riches/prizes**. (S. saptadhana; T. 'phags pa'i nor bdun; C. qi cai 七財)

1. faith/confidence (S. śraddhā; T. dad pa; C. xin 信)
2. vigor/effort (S. vīrya; T. brtson 'grus; C. jingjin 精進)
3. morality (S. śīla; T. tshul khrims; C. jie 戒)
4. shame and fear of blame/decency and modesty (S. hrī-apatrāpya; T. ngo tsha shes pa khrel yod pa; C. cankui 慚愧)
5. learning (S. śruta; T. thos pa; C. wen 聞)
6. relinquishment/renunciation (S. prahāṇa/tyāga; T. spang ba/gtong ba; C. duan/shi 斷/施)
7. wisdom (S. prajñā; T. shes rab; C. hui 慧)

## EIGHTS

**eight classes of non-human beings**. (S. aṣṭasenā; T. lha srin sde brgyad/mi ma yin; C. tianlong babu 天龍八部)

1. divinities (S. deva; T. lha; C. tian 天)
2. serpents (S. nāga; T. klu; C. long 龍)
3. demons (S. yakṣa; T. gnod sbyin; C. yecha 夜叉)
4. demigods (S. asura; T. lha ma yin; C. axiuluo 阿修羅)
5. divine musicians (S. gandharva; T. dri za; C. gantapo 乾闥婆)
6. mythical birds (S. garuḍa; T. khyung, mkha' lding; C. jialouluo 迦樓羅
7. half-horse, half-human beings (S. kiṃnara; T. mi 'am ci; C. jinnaluo 緊那羅)
8. great snakes (S. mahorāga; T. lto 'phye chen po; C. mohouluojia 摩睺羅迦)

**eight close sons**. See EIGHT GREAT BODHISATTVAS.

**eight common accomplishments**. (S. sādhāraṇasiddhi; T. thun mong gi dngos grub; C. gongtong chenjiu 共同成就)

1. medicinal pills (S. gulikā; T. ril bu; C. miaodan 妙丹)
2. eye medicine (S. añjana; T. mig sman; C. yanyao 眼藥)
3. swift-footedness (S. jaṅghākara; T. rkang mgyogs; C. tuzu 塗足)
4. going beneath the earth (S. pātāla; T. sa 'og; C. tuxing 土行)
5. enchanted sword (S. khaḍga; T. ral gri; C. baojian 寶劍)
6. traveling through the sky (S. khecara; T. rnam mkha' phur ba; C. kongxing 空行)
7. invisibility (S. antardhāna; T. mi snang ba; C. yinxing 隱形)
8. immortality (S. amṛta; T. 'chi med; C. busi 不死)

**eight consciousnesses**. (S. vijñāna; T. rnam shes; C. shi 識)

1. visual consciousness (S. cakṣurvijñāna; T. mig gi rnam shes; C. yanshi 眼識)
2. auditory consciousness (S. śrotravijñāna; T. rna ba'i rnam shes; C. ershi 耳識)
3. olfactory consciousness (S. ghrāṇavijñāna; T. sna'i rnam shes; C. bishi 鼻識)
4. gustatory consciousness (S. jihvāvijñāna; T. lce'i rnam shes; C. sheshi 舌識)
5. tactile consciousness (S. kāyavijñāna; T. lus kyi rnam shes; C. shenshi 身識)
6. mental consciousness (S. manovijñāna; T. yid kyi rnam shes; C. yishi 意識)
7. afflicted mental consciousness (S. kliṣṭamanas; T. nyon yid; C. mona shi 末那識)
8. storehouse consciousness (S. ālayavijñāna; T. kun gzhi'i rnam shes; C. alaiye shi 阿賴耶識)

**eight episodes in the life of a buddha**. (S. aṣṭabuddhakārya, T. sangs rgyas kyi mdzad pa brgyad; C. baxiang 八相)

1. descending from tuṣita heaven (T. dga' ldan gyi gnas nas 'pho ba; C. doushuai jiangshi 兜率降世)
2. entry into the womb (T. lhums su zhugs pa; C. rutai 入胎)
3. birth (T. sku bltams pa; C. chutai 出胎)
4. renouncing the world (T. rab tu byung ba; C. chujia 出家)
5. subjugating Māra (T. bdud btul ba; C. xiangmo 降魔)
6. attaining enlightenment (T. mngon par rdzogs par sangs rgyas pa; C. chengdao 成道)
7. turning the wheel of the dharma (dharmacakrapravartana) (T. chos kyi 'khor lo bskor ba; C. zhuan falun 轉法輪)
8. passing into parinirvāṇa (T. mya ngan las 'das pa; C. ru niepan 入涅槃)

**eightfold noble path**. (S. āryāṣṭāṅgamārga; T. lam yan lag brgyad; C. bazhengdao/bashengdao 八正道/八聖道)

1. right views (S. samyagdṛṣṭi; T. yang dag pa'i lta ba; C. zhengjian 正見)
2. right intention (S. samyaksaṃkalpa; T. yang dag pa'i rtog pa; C. zhengzhi/zhengsiwei 正志/正思維)
3. right speech (S. samyagvāk; T. yang dag pa'i ngag; C. zhengyu 正語)
4. right action (S. samyakkarmānta; T. yang dag pa'i las kyi mtha'; C. zhengye 正業)
5. right livelihood (S. samyagājīva; T. yang dag pa'i 'tsho ba; C. zhengming 正命)
6. right effort (S. samyagvyāyāma; T. yang dag pa'i rtsol ba; C. zhengqin/zheng jingjin 正勤/正精進)
7. right mindfulness (S. samyaksmṛti; T. yang dag pa'i dran pa; C. zhengnian 正念)
8. right concentration (S. samyaksamādhi; T. yang dag pa'i ting nge 'dzin; C. zhengding 正定)

**eight great bodhisattvas**. (S. mahā-upaputra; T. nye sras; C. bada suifo dizi/bada fozi 八大隨佛弟子/八大佛子)

1. Mañjuśrī (T. 'Jam dpal; C. Wenshu pusa 文殊菩薩)
2. Vajrapāṇi (T. Phyag na rdo rje; C. Jingan shou pusa 金剛手菩薩)

3. Avalokiteśvara (T. Spyan ras gzigs dbang phyug; C. Guanyin pusa 觀音菩薩)
4. Kṣitigarbha (T. Sa'i snying po; C. Dizang pusa 地藏菩薩)
5. Sarvanīvaraṇaviṣkambhin (T. Sgrib pa thams cad rnam par sel ba; C. Chu gaizhang pusa 除蓋障菩薩)
6. Ākāśagarbha (T. Nam mkha'i snying po; C. Xukongzang pusa 虛空藏菩薩)
7. Maitreya (T. Byams pa; C. Mile pusa 彌勒菩薩)
8. Samantabhadra (T. Kun tu bzang po; C. Puxian pusa 普賢菩薩)

**eight great chariots of the practice lineage**. (T. sgrub brgyud shing rta chen po brgyad)

1. ancient translation tradition (T. sna' 'gyur rnying ma)
2. tradition of precepts and instructions (T. bka' gdams)
3. tradition of the path and result (T. lam 'bras)
4. tradition of the transmitted precepts of Marpa (T. Mar pa bka' brgyud)
5. tradition of the transmitted precepts of the Shang Valley (T. Shangs pa bka' brgyud)
6. traditions of pacification and severence (T. zhi byed gcod)
7. tradition of vajrayoga (T. rdo rje'i rnal 'byor)
8. propitiation and attainment of the three adamantine states (T. rdo rje gsum gyi bsnyen sgrub)

**eight great charnel grounds**. (S. mahāśmaśāna, śmaśāna; T. dur khrod chen po; C. da shilin/ da hanlin 大尸林/大寒林)

1. most fierce (S. caṇḍogrā; T. gtum drag; C. baonue hanlin 暴虐寒林)
2. dense thicket (S. gahvara; T. tshang tshing 'khrigs pa; C. micong hanlin 密叢寒林)
3. blazing vajra (S. vajrajvala; T. rdo rje bar pa; C. jingangyan hanlin 金剛焰寒林)
4. endowed with skeletons (S. karaṅkin; T. keng rus can; C. gusuo hanlin 骨鎖寒林)
5. cool grove (S. śītavana; T. bsil bu tshal; C. hanlin 寒林)
6. black darkness (S. ghorāndhakāra; T. mun pa nag po; C. youan hanlin 幽暗寒林)
7. resonant with "kilikili" (S. kilikilārava; T. ki li ki lir sgra sgrog pa; C. jiujiu hanlin 啾啾寒林)
8. cries of "ha ha" (S. aṭṭahāsa; T. ha ha rgod pa; C. kuangxiao hanlin 狂笑寒林)

**eight great fears**. (S. mahābhaya; T. 'jigs pa chen po; C. nan 難)

1. lions (S. siṃha; T. seng ge; C. shi nan 獅難)
2. elephants (S. hastināga; T. glang po che; C. xiang nan 象難)
3. fire (S. agni; T. me; C. huo nan 火難)
4. snakes (S. sarpa; T. sbrul ; C. duchong nan 毒蟲難)
5. thieves (S. taskara; T. rkun po; C. zei nan 賊難)
6. violent waters (S. jalārṇava; T. chu bo; C. shui nan 水難)
7. imprisonment (S. nigaḍa; T. lcags sgrog; C. lao[yu] nan 牢[獄]難)
8. demons (S. piśāca; T. sha za; C. feiren nan/mo nan 非人難/魔難)

**eight liberations**. (S. vimokṣa; T. rnam thar ; C. jietuo/beishe 解脫/背捨)

1. embodied, one sees forms [of the realm of subtle materiality] (S. rūpī rūpāṇi paśyati; T. gzugs can gzugs rnams la lta ba'i rnam thar; C. neiyou sexiang guan zhuse 內有色想觀諸色)
2. without perceiving inward form [viz., one's own physical body], one sees outward forms [of the realm of subtle materiality] (S. adhyātmarūpasamjñī bahirdhā rūpāṇi paśyati; T. nang gzugs med par 'du shes las phyi rol gyi gzugs rnams la lta ba'i rnam thar; C. nei wusexiang guan waise 內無色想觀外色)
3. one develops determination by contemplating the beautiful/one becomes resolved on what is lovely (S. śubham ity evādhimukto bhavati; T. sdug pa'i rnam thar; C. jing jietuo shenzuozheng juzu zhu 淨解脫身作證具足住)
4. the sphere of infinite space (S. ākāśānantyāyatana; T. nam mkha' mtha' yas skye mched kyi rnam thar; C. ru wubiankong kong wubianchu juzu zhu/kong wubianchu juzu zhu 入無邊空空無邊處具足住/空無邊處具足住)
5. the sphere of infinite consciousness (S. vijñānāntyāyatana; T. rnam shes mtha' yas skye mched kyi rnam thar; C. ru wubian shi shiwubian chu juzu zhu/shi wubianchu juzu zhu 入無邊識識無邊處具足住/識無邊處具足住)
6. the sphere of nothingness (S. ākiñcanyāyatana; T. ci yang med pa'i skye mched kyi rnam thar; C. ru wusuoyou wu suoyouchu juzu zhu/wusuoyouchu juzu zhu 入無所有無所有處具足住/無所有處具足住)
7. the sphere of neither perception nor nonperception (S. naivasaṃjñānāsaṃjñāyatana; T. 'du shes med 'du shes med min skye mched kyi rnam thar; C. ru feixiang feifeixiangchu juzu zhu/feixiang feifeixiangchu juzu zhu 入非想非非想處具足住/非想非非想處具足住)
8. the cessation of perception and sensation (S. samjñāvedayitanirodha; T. 'du shes dang tshor ba 'gog pa'i rnam thar; C. ru shouxiangmie shenzuozheng juzu zhu/miexiangshouding juzu zhu 入受想滅身作證具足住/滅想受定具足住)

**eight manifestations of the Guru [Rin po che]**. (T. guru mtshan brgyad)

1. Padmākara
2. Padmasambhava
3. Blo ldan mchog sred
4. Shākya Seng ge
5. Seng ge sgra grogs
6. Padma rgyal po
7. Rdo rje gro lod
8. Nyi ma 'od zer

**eight noble persons**. (S. aṣṭāryapudgala; T. 'phags pa'i gang zag brgyad; C. baxiansheng 八賢聖)

1. candidate for the fruit of stream-enterer (S. srotaāpanna-phalapratipannaka; T. rgyun du zhugs pa'i 'bras bu la zhugs pa; C. yuliu xiang 預流向)
2. recipient of the fruit of stream-enterer (S. srotaāpanna-phalastha; T. rgyun du zhugs pa'i 'bras bu la gnas pa; C. zheng yuliu guo 證預流果)
3. candidate for the fruit of once-returner (S. sakṛdāgāmi-phalapratipannaka; T. phyir 'ong gi 'bras bu la zhugs pa; C. yilai xiang 一來向)
4. recipient of the fruit of once-returner (S. sakṛdāgāmi-phalastha; T. phyir 'ong gi 'bras bu la gnas pa; C. zheng yilai guo 證一來果)
5. candidate for the fruit of non-returner (S. anāgāmiphala-pratipannaka; T. phyir mi 'ong gi 'bras bu la zhugs pa; C. buhuan xiang 不還向)
6. recipient of the fruit of non-returner (S. anāgāmi-phalastha; T. phyir mi 'ong gi 'bras bu la gnas pa; C. zheng buhuan guo 證不還果)
7. candidate for worthy one (S. arhatphalapratipannaka; T. dgra bcom pa'i 'bras bu la zhugs pa; C. aluohan xiang 阿羅漢向)
8. worthy one (S. arhat; T. dgra bcom pa; C. zheng aluohan guo 證阿羅漢果)

**eight opportune births**. (S. kṣaṇa; T. dal ba; C. yuanli banan/yuanli ba wuxia 遠離八難/遠離八無暇)

Freedom from rebirth:

1. as a denizen of the hells (S. nāraka; T. dmyal ba; C. zai diyu nan 在地獄難)
2. as a ghost (S. preta; T. yi dwags; C. zai egui nan 在餓鬼難)
3. as an animal (S. tiryak; T. dud 'gro; C. zai chusheng nan 在畜生難)
4. as a long-lived divinity (S. dīrghāyurdeva; T. lha tshe ring bo; C. zai changshou tian nan 在長壽天難)
5. in a border region (S. pratyantajanapada; mtha' 'khob kyi mi; C. zai biandi zhi yudanyue nan 在邊地之鬱單越難)
6. with impaired sense faculties (S. indriyavaikalya; T. dbang po ma tshang ba; C. manglong yinya nan 盲聾瘖瘂難)
7. holding erroneous views (S. mithyādarśana; T. log par lta ba; C. shizhi congbian nan 世智聰辯難)
8. in a land where a tathāgata has not appeared (S. tathā-gatānutpāda; T. de bzhin gshegs pa ma byung ba; C. shengzai foqian fohou nan 生在佛前佛後難)

**eight precepts**. [of the laity on upoṣadha days] (S. aṣṭāṅgasa-manvāgatam upavāsam/poṣadhaśīla; T. bsnyen gnas yan lag brgyad; C. baguan zhai jie/ba zhaijie/ba guan zhai/ba jiezhai 八關齋戒/八齋戒/八關齋/八戒齋)

1. not to kill living beings (S. prāṇātipāta-virati; T. srog gcod pa spong ba; C. li shasheng 離殺生)
2. not to steal (S. adattādāna-virati; T. ma byin par len pa spong ba; C. li buyu qu 離不與取)
3. not to engage to sexual activity (S. abrahmacarya-virati; T. mi tshangs par spyod pa spong pa; C. li feifanxing 離非梵行)
4. not to lie [about spiritual attainments] (S. mṛṣāvāda-virati; T. rdzun du smra ba spong ba; C. li xukuangyu 離虛誑語)
5. not to use intoxicants (S. madyapāna-virati; T. myos par 'gyur ba'i btung ba spong pa; C. li yin zhujiu 離飲諸酒)
6. not to eat at improper times [viz. after twelve noon] (S. vikālabhojana-virati; T. dus ma yin pa'i kha zas spong pa; C. li feishi shi 離非時食)
7. not to use perfumes, garlands, or cosmetics and not to sing, dance, play music, or attend entertainments (S. gandhamālyavilepanavarṇakadhāraṇa-virati [nṛtyagīta-virati]; T. spos dang kha dog dang byug pa dang phreng ba thogs pa spong pa [glu gar spong pa]; C. li tushi xingman[li gewu guanting] 離塗飾香鬘[離歌舞觀聽])
8. not to sleep on high and luxurious beds (S. uccaśayana-mahāśayana-virati; T. khri stan mthon po dang khri stan chen po spong pa; C. li yanzuo gaoguang yanli chuangzuo 離眼坐高廣嚴麗牀座)

**eight similes of illusion**. (S. aṣṭamāyopamā; T. sgyu ma'i dpe brgyad; C. ruhuan yu 如幻喻)

Dharmas lack inherent nature (svabhāva), because they are like a:

1. dream (S. svapna; T. rmi lam; C. meng 夢)
2. illusion (S. māyā; T. sgyu ma; C. huanjing 幻景)
3. optical illusion (S. pratibhāsa; T. mig yor; C. guangying 光影)
4. mirage (S. marīci; T. smig rgyu; C. yangyan 陽燄)
5. reflection of the moon in water (S. udakacandra; T. chu zla; C. shui zhong yue 水中月)
6. echo (S. pratiśabda; T. brag cha; C. yuxiang 谷響)
7. city of the gandharvas (S. gandharvanagara; T. dri za'i grong khyer; C. xunxiang cheng/gantapo cheng 尋香城/乾闥婆城)
8. phantom (S. nirmita; T. sprul pa; C. huashen 化身)

**eight stūpas**. (S. stūpa; T. mchod rten; C. dalingta 大靈塔)

1. heap of lotuses stūpa (T. pad spungs mchod rten), commemorating the Buddha's birth at Lumbinī
2. enlightenment stūpa (T. byang chub mchod rten) at Bodhgayā
3. many auspicious doors stūpa (bkra shis sgo mang mchod rten), commemorating the first turning of the wheel of the dharma at Ṛṣipatana/Sārnāth

4. display of miracles stūpa (T. cho 'phrul mchod rten), commemorating the Buddha's display of the paired miracles at Śrāvastī
5. divine descent stūpa (T. lha babs mchod rten), commemorating the Buddha's descent from the trāyastriṃśa heaven at Saṃkāśya.
6. settling of disputes stūpa (T. dbyen bsdums mchod rten), commemorating the Buddha's healing of the schism caused by Devadatta
7. victory stūpa (T. rnam rgyal mchod rten), commemorating the Buddha's extension of his life by three months at the Cāpālacaitya
8. nirvāṇa stūpa (T. myang 'das mchod rten), commemorating the Buddha's passage into parinirvāṇa at Kuśinagarī.

**eight sufferings**. (S. aṣṭaduḥkha; T. sdug bsngal rgyad; C. baku 八苦)

1. birth (S. jāti; T. skye ba; C. shengku 生苦)
2. aging (S. jarā; T. rga ba; C. laoku 老苦)
3. sickness (S. vyādhi; T. na ba; C. bingku 病苦)
4. death (S. maraṇa; T. 'chi ba; C. siku 死苦)
5. separation from what is dear (S. priyaviprayoga; T. sdug pa dang bral ba; C. ai bieli ku 愛別離苦)
6. encountering what is not dear (S. apriyasaṃprayoga; T. mi sdug pa dang phrad pa; C. yuanzeng hui ku 怨憎會苦)
7. not finding what one seeks (S. yad apīcchayā paryeṣamāṇo na labhate; T. 'dod pa btshal gyang ma rnyed pa; C. qiu bude ku 求不得苦)
8. the five aggregates that are objects of clinging (S. pañcopādānaskandha; T. nye bar len pa'i phung po; C. wu quyun ku 五取蘊苦)

**eight vidyādharas**. (T. rig 'dzin brgyad)

1. Vimalamitra
2. Hūṃkara
3. Mañjuśrīmitra
4. Nāgārjuna
5. Padmasambhava
6. Dhanasaṃskṛta
7. Rambuguhya-Devacandra
8. Śāntigarbha

**eight worldly concerns**. (S. lokadharma; T. 'jig rten chos; C. [shi]feng [世]風)

1. gain (S. lābha; T. rnyed pa; C. li 利)
2. loss (S. alābha; T. ma rnyed pa; C. shuai 衰)
3. pleasure (S. sukha; T. bde ba; C. le 樂)
4. pain (S. duḥkha; T. sdug bsnyal; C. ku 苦)
5. fame (S. yaśas; T. snyan grags; C. yu 譽)
6. disgrace (S. ayaśas; T. ma grags pa; C. hui 毀)
7. praise (S. praśaṃsā; T. bstod pa; C. cheng 稱)
8. blame (S. nindā; T. smad pa; C. ji 譏)

## NINES

**nine attainments of successive stations of equipoise**. (S. anupūrvavihārasamāpatti; T. mthar gyis gnas pa'i snyoms par 'jug pa; C. ru jiujing chan/cidi ding 入究竟禪/次第定)

(1–4) the four absorptions of the realm of subtle materiality (S. dhyāna/rūpāvacaradhyāna; T. bsam gtan bzhi; C. sichan/ding 四禪/定)
(5–8) the four absorptions of the immaterial realm (S. ārūpyāvacaradhyāna; T. gzhugs med bzhi; C. si wuse ding 四無色定)
(9) attainment of the cessation of perception and sensation/equipoise of cessation (S. saṃjñāvedayitanirodha/alt. nirodhasamāpatti; T. 'gog pa'i snyoms par 'jug pa; C. xiangshou mie[jin] ding/ shouxiang mie[jin] ding 想受滅[盡]定/受想滅[盡]定)

**nine categories of scripture**. (BHS. navāṅga[pravacana]; T. gsung rab yan lag dgu; C. jiu bu jing 九部經)

1. discourses (S. sūtra; T. mdo; C. qijing/changhang 契經/長行)
2. aphorisms in mixed prose and verse (S. geya; T. dbyangs bsnyad; C. yingsong 應頌)
3. prophetic teachings (S. vyākaraṇa; T. lung bstan; C. jibie/shouji 記別/授記)
4. verses (S. gāthā; T. tshig bcad; C. fengsong/guqi 諷頌/孤起)
5. utterances/meaningful expressions (S. udāna; T. ched du brjod pa; C. zishuo 自說)
6. framing stories (S. nidāna/itivṛttaka; T. gleng gzhi; C. yinyuan 因緣)
7. expanded teachings (S. vaipulya; T. shin tu rgyas pa; C. fangguang 方廣)
8. tales of previous lives (S. jātaka; T. skyes rabs; C. bensheng 本生)
9. marvelous events (S. adbhutadharma; T. rmad du byung ba; C. xifa 希法)

**nine foulness contemplations/nine contemplations on the impure**. (S. aśubhabhāvanā/aśubhasaṃjñā; T. mi sdug pa'i 'du shes; C. bujing guan/bujing xiang 不淨觀/不淨想)
Contemplation of:

1. a swollen corpse [bloating and tumefaction] (S. vyādhmātakasaṃjñā; T. rnam par bam pa'i 'du shes; C. zhangxiang 脹想)
2. a worm-eaten, rotting corpse (S. vipadumakasaṃjñā; T. rnam par 'bus gzhig pa'i 'dus shes; C. huaixiang 壞想)
3. a festering corpse [discharging pus] (S. vipūyakasaṃjñā; T. rnam par rnags pa'i 'dus shes ; C. nonglan xiang 膿爛想)
4. a bloody corpse (S. vilohitakasaṃjñā; T. rnam par dmar ba'i 'du shes; C. xietu xiang 血塗想)

5. a blueish corpse [mottled discoloration] (S. vinīlakasaṃjñā; T. rnam par bsngos pa'i 'du shes; C. qingyu xiang 青瘀想)
6. a corpse being devoured by worms and maggots (S. vikhāditakasaṃjñā; T. rnam par zos ba'i 'du shes; C. danxiang 噉想)
7. a scattered corpse [dissolution of flesh and exposure of bones and sinews] (S. vikṣiptakasaṃjñā; T. rnam par mthor ba'i 'du shes; C. sanxiang 散想)
8. a burned corpse [cremated remains] (S. vidagdhakasaṃjñā; T. rnam par tshig pa'i 'du shes; C. shaoxiang 燒想)
9. a skeleton (S. asthisaṃjñā; T. rus gong gi 'du shes; C. guxiang 骨想)

**nine similes [for the presence of the tathāgatagarbha].** (S. navodāharaṇāni; T. dpe dgu; C. jiu yu 九喻)

The tathāgatagarbha is present:

1. like a statue of the buddha in a soiled lotus (S. buddhaḥ kupadme; T. sangs rgyas pad ngan; C. weihua zhong zhufo 萎華中諸佛)
2. like honey in beehives (S. madhu makṣikāsu; T. sbrang rtsi sbrang ma la; C. zhongfeng zhong meimi 衆蜂中美蜜)
3. like kernels in husks (S. tuṣeṣu sārāṇi; T. sbun pa snying po; C. pi deng zhong shi 皮等中實)
4. like gold in filth (S. aśucau suvarṇam; T. mi gtsang nang na gser; C. fenhui zhong zhenjin 糞穢中真金)
5. like treasure under the ground (S. nidhiḥ kṣitau; T. sa la gter; C. di zhong zhenbao zang 地中珍寶藏)
6. like the stages beginning with the sprout in a tiny seed (S. alpaphale 'ṅkurādi; T. myug sogs 'bras chung; C. zhu guozi zhong ya 諸果子中芽)
7. like a conqueror's body in sodden clothes (S. praklinnavastreṣu jinātmabhāvaḥ; T. gos hrul nang na rgyal ba'i sku; C. xiugu bihuai yi changuo zhenjin xiang 朽故弊壞衣纏裹真金像)
8. like royalty in the womb of a common woman (S. jaghanyanārījaṭhare nṛpatvaṃ; T. bud med ngan ma'i lto na mi bdag; C. pinjian choulou nü huai zhuanlun shengwang 貧賤醜陋女懷轉輪聖王)
9. like a precious image buried in the mud (S. mṛtsu ca ratnabimbam; T. sa la rin chen gzugs; C. jiaohei nimo zhong youshang miaobao xiang 焦黑泥模中有上妙寶像)

**nine vehicles.** (S. yāna; T. theg pa dgu)

1. śrāvakayāna (T. nyan thos kyi theg pa)
2. pratyekabuddhayāna (T. rang rgyal gyi theg pa)
3. bodhisattvayāna (T. byang sems kyi theg pa)
4. kriyātantra (T. bya rgyud kyi theg pa)
5. caryātantra (T. spyod pa'i rgyud kyi theg pa)
6. yogatantra (T. rnal 'byor gyi rgyud kyi theg pa)
7. mahāyogatantra (T. rnal 'byor chen po'i rgyud kyi theg pa)
8. anuyogatantra (T. rjes su rnal 'byor gyi rgyud kyi theg pa)
9. atiyogatantra (T. shin tu rnal 'byor gyi rgyud kyi theg pa)

## TENS

**ten dharma activities.** (S. dharmacarya; T. chos spyod; C. faxing 法行)

1. writing (S. lekhana; T. yi ge 'bri pa; C. shuxie 書寫)
2. worship (S. pūjā; T. mchod pa; C. gongyang 供養)
3. charity (S. dāna; T. sbyin pa; C. shita 施他)
4. listening/learning (S. śravaṇa; T. nyan ba; C. tingwen 聽聞)
5. reading (S. vācana; T. klog pa; C. pidu 披讀)
6. comprehending (S. udgrahaṇa; T. 'dzin pa; C. shouchi 受持)
7. instructing (S. prakāśana; T. rab tu ston pa; C. kaiyan 開演)
8. reciting (S. svādhyāya; T. kha 'don byed pa; C. fengsong 諷誦)
9. contemplation (S. cintana; T. sems pa; C. siwei 思惟)
10. meditation (S. bhāvanā; T. sgom pa; C. xiuxi 修習)

**ten directions.** (S. daśadiś; T. phyogs bcu; C. shifang 十方)

1. east (S. pūrvā; T. shar; C. dong 東)
2. southeast (S. pūrvadakṣiṇā; T. shar lho; C. dongnan 東南)
3. south (S. dakṣiṇā; T. lho; C. nan 南)
4. southwest (S. dakṣiṇapaścimā; T. lho nub; C. xinan 西南)
5. west (S. paścimaḥ; T. nub; C. xi 西)
6. northwest (S. paścimōttarā; T. nub byang; C. xibei 西北)
7. north (S. uttaraḥ; T. byang; C. bei 北)
8. northeast (S. uttarapūrvā; T. byang shar; C. dongbei 東北)
9. zenith (S. ūrdhvam; T. bla ma; C. shang 上)
10. nadir (S. adhaḥ; T. 'og; C. xia 下)

**ten endowments.** (T. 'byor ba bcu)

One has taken rebirth:

1. as a human (T. mi)
2. in a central land (T. yul dbus)
3. with complete sense faculties (T. dbang po tshang ba)
4. not engaging in mistaken actions (T. las kyi mtha' ma log pa)
5. having faith (T. gnas la dad pa)

and when:

1. a buddha has appeared in the world (T. sangs rgyas 'jig rten du byon pa)
2. he has taught the dharma (T. des dam pa'i chos ston pa)
3. his teaching remains (T. bstan pa gnas pa)

4. it has followers (T. de'i rjes su 'jug pa)
5. they kindly act on behalf of others (T. gzhan phyir snying brtse ba)

**ten fetters.** (S. saṃyojana; T. kun tu sbyor ba; C. jie 結)

1. view of a perduring self (S. satkāyadṛṣṭi; T. 'jig lta; C. shenjian 身見)
2. attachment to rules and rituals (S. śīlavrataparāmarśa; T. tshul khrims brtul zhugs mchog 'dzin; C. jiejin qu 戒禁取)
3. skeptical doubt (S. vicikitsā; T. the tshom; C. yi 疑)
4. craving for sensual gratification (S. kāmacchanda; T. 'dod pa'i 'dun pa; C. tanyu 貪欲)
5. malice (S. vyāpāda; T. zhe sdang; C. chenhui 瞋恚)
6. craving for the realm of subtle materiality (S. rūparāga; T. gzugs kyi sred pa; C. seai 色愛)
7. craving for the immaterial realm (S. ārūpyarāga; T. gzugs med pa na spyod pa'i sred pa; C. wuseai 無色愛)
8. conceit (S. māna; T. nga rgyal; C. man 慢)
9. delusion (S. moha; gti mug; C. wuming 無明)
10. restlessness (S. auddhatya; T. rgod pa; C. diaoju 掉舉)

**ten fundamental afflictions.** (S. mūlakleśa; T. rtsa nyon; C. shi/huo/genben fannao 使/惑/根本煩惱)

1. sensuality/greed (S. rāga; T. 'dod chags; C. tan 貪)
2. anger (S. pratigha; T. khong khro; C. chen 瞋)
3. conceit (S. māna; T. nga rgyal; C. man 慢)
4. ignorance (S. avidyā; T. ma rig pa; C. wuming 無明)
5. skeptical doubt (S. vicikitsā; T. the tshom; C. yi 疑)
6. view of a perduring self (S. satkāyadṛṣṭi; T. 'jig lta; C. shenjian 身見)
7. extreme views (S. antagrāhadṛṣṭi; T. mthar lta; C. bianjian 邊見)
8. attachment to one's own point of view (S. dṛṣṭiparāmarśa; T. lta ba mchog 'dzin; C. jianqu jian 見取見)
9. wrong views (S. mithyādṛṣṭi; T. log lta; C. xiejian 邪見)

**ten masteries.** (S. vaśitā; T. dbang; C. zizai 自在)

1. lifespan (S. āyuḥ; T. tshe; C. ming zizai 命自在)
2. actions (S. karman; T. las; C. ye zizai 業自在)
3. necessities of life (S. pariṣkāra; T. yo byad; C. cai zizai 財自在)
4. determination (S. adhimukti; T. mos pa; C. shengjie zizai 勝解自在)
5. aspiration (S. praṇidhāna; T. smon lam; C. yuan zizai 願自在)
6. psychic powers (S. ṛddhi; T. rdzu 'phrul; C. shentong zizai 神通自在)
7. birth (S. upapatti; T. skye ba; C. sheng zizai 生自在)
8. phenomena/teachings (S. dharma; T. chos; C. fa zizai 法自在)
9. mind (S. citta; T. sems; C. xin zizai 心自在)
10. wisdom (S. jñāna; T. ye shes; C. zhi zizai 智自在)

**ten meanings [of unimpeded interpenetration in the Huayan school].** (C. Huayan shiyi 華嚴十義)

1. teachings and their meanings/significance (C. jiaoyi 教義)
2. principle and phenomena (C. lishi 理事)
3. understanding and implementation (C. jiexing 解行)
4. causes and fruitions (C. yinguo 因果)
5. the "persons" who expound the dharma and the "dharma" they expound (C. renfa 人法)
6. the "distinction" and "unity" between discrete things (C. fenqi jingwei 分齊境位)
7. the "teacher," his "disciple," the "dharma" that is imparted, and the "wisdom" that the disciple develops (C. shidi fazhi 師弟法智)
8. the "dominant" and "subordinate," "primary" and "secondary" relations that pertain between things (C. zhuban yizheng 主伴依正)
9. the enlightened sages who "respond" to the spiritual maturity of their audiences and the audiences whose spiritual maturity "solicited" the appearance of the enlightened sages in the world (C. suishenggen yushixian 遂生根欲示現)
10. "autonomy" with regard to spiritual "obstacles" and their "antidotes," the "essence" of phenomena and their "functions" (C. nishun tiyong zizai 逆順體用自在).

**ten perfections.** (S. pāramitā; T. pha rol tu phyin pa; C. du/boluomi 度/波羅蜜)

1. perfection of generosity/giving (S. dānapāramitā; T. sbyin pa'i pha rol tu phyin pa; C. [bu]shi [布]施)
2. perfection of morality (S. śīlapāramitā; T. tshul khrims kyi pha rol tu phyin pa; C. [chi]jie [持]戒)
3. perfection of patience/forbearance (S. kṣāntipāramitā; T. bzod pa'i pha rol tu phyin pa; C. ren[ru] 忍[辱])
4. perfection of effort/vigor (S. vīryapāramitā; T. brtson 'grus kyi pha rol tu phyin pa; C. jinjing 精進)
5. perfection of meditative absorption (S. dhyānapāramitā; T. bsam gtan gyi pha rol tu phyin pa; C. chan[ding] 禪[定])
6. perfection of wisdom (S. prajñāpāramitā; T. shes rab kyi pha rol tu phyin pa; C. bore 般若)
7. perfection of skillful means (S. upāyapāramitā; T. thabs kyi pha rol tu phyin pa; C. fangbian 方便)
8. perfection of aspiration (S. praṇidhānapāramitā; T. smon lam gyi pha rol tu phyin pa; C. yuan 願)
9. perfection of powers (S. balapāramitā; T. stobs kyi pha rol tu phyin pa; C. li 力)
10. perfection of knowledge (S. jñānapāramitā; T. ye shes kyi pha rol tu phyin pa; C. zhi 智)

**ten powers of a bodhisattva.** (S. bala; T. byang chub sems dpa'i stobs; C. pusa li 菩薩力)

1. power of reflection (S. āśayabala; T. bsam pa'i stobs; C. shenxin li/zhixin li 深心力/直心力)

2. power of superior aspiration (S. adhyāśayabala; T. lhag bsam pa'i stobs; C. zengshang shenxin li 增上深心力)
3. power of application (S. prayogabala; T. sbyor ba'i stobs; C. fangbian li 方便力)
4. power of wisdom (S. prajñābala/jñānabala; T. shes rab/ye shes stobs; C. zhi[hui] li 智[慧]力)
5. power of their vow (S. praṇidhānabala; T. smon lam gyi stobs; C. yuanli 願力)
6. power of vehicle (S. yānabala; T. theg pa'i stobs; C. shengli 乘力)
7. power of conduct (S. caryābala; T. spyod pa'i stobs; C. xingli 行力)
8. power of transformation (S. vikurvaṇabala; T. rnam par 'phrul pa'i stobs; C. shenbian li/youxi shentong li 神變力/遊戲神通力)
9. power of enlightenment (S. bodhibala; T. byang chub kyi stobs; C. puti li 菩提力)
10. power of turning the wheel of the dharma (S. dharmacakrapravartanabala; T. chos kyi 'khor lo bskor ba'i stobs; C. zhuan falun li 轉法輪力)

**ten powers of a tathāgata**. (S. tathāgatabala; T. de bzhin gshegs pa'i stobs; C. rulai li 如來力)

1. power of knowing the positive and negative contingencies of things (S. sthānāsthānajñānabala; T. gnas dang gnas ma yin pa mkhyen pa'i stobs; C. chu feichu zhili 處非處智力)
2. power of knowing the maturation of deeds (S. karmavipākajñānabala; T. las kyi rnam smin mkhyen pa'i stobs; C. ye yishou zhili 業異熟智力)
3. power of knowing diverse aspirations (S. nānādhimuktijñānabala; T. mos pa sna tshogs mkhyen pa'i stobs; C. zhongzhong shengjie zhili 種種勝解智力)
4. power of knowing diverse dispositions (S. nānādhātujñānabala; T. khams sna tshogs mkhyen pa'i stobs; C. zhongzhong jie zhili 種種界智力)
5. power of knowing those who are of superior acumen and those who are not (S. indriyaparāparajñānabala; T. dbang po mchog dang mchog ma yin pa mkhyen pa'i stobs; C. gen shangxia zhili 根上下智力)
6. power of knowing the paths going everywhere (S. sarvatragāmanīpratipajjñāna; T. thams cad du 'gro ba'i lam mkhyen pa'i stobs; C. bianquxing zhili 遍趣行智力)
7. power of knowing absorption, liberation, concentration, trance, affliction, purification, and acquisition (S. sarvadhyānavimokṣasamādhisamāpattisaṃkleśavyavadānavyutthānajñānabala; T. bsam gtan dang rnam thar dang ting nge 'dzin dang snyoms par 'jug pa dang kun nas nyon mongs pa dang rnam par byang ba dang ldan pa thams cad mkhyen pa'i stobs; C. jinglü jietuo dengchi dengzhi zhili 靜慮解脫等持等至智力)
8. power of recollecting past lives (S. pūrvanivāsānusmṛtijñānabala; T. sngon gyi gnas rjes su dran pa mkhyen pa'i stobs; C. suzhu suinian zhili/suming zhili 宿住隨念智力/宿命智力)
9. power of knowing death and rebirth (S. cyutyupattijñānabala; T. 'chi 'pho bo dang skye ba mkhyen pa'i stobs; C. sisheng zhili 死生智力)
10. power of knowing the cessation of the contaminants (S. āsravakṣayajñānabala; T. zag pa zad pa mkhyen pa'i stobs; C. loujin zhili 漏盡智力)

**ten precepts**. [of novices] (*daśaśīla/śrāmaṇerasaṃvara; T. dge tshul gyi sdom pa; C. [shami] shijie [沙彌]十戒)

1. not to kill living beings (S. prāṇātipāta-virati; T. srog gcod pa spong ba; C. bu shasheng jie 不殺生戒)
2. not to steal (S. adattādāna-virati; T. ma byin par len pa spong ba; C. bu toudao jie 不偷盜戒)
3. not to engage in sexual activity (S. kāmamithyācāra-virati/abrahmacarya-virati; T. 'dod pas log par g.yem pa spong ba/mi tshangs par spyod pa spong pa; C. bu xieyin jie/li fei fanxing jie 不邪婬戒/離非梵行戒)
4. not to lie [about spiritual attainments] (S. mṛṣāvāda-virati; T. rdzun du smra ba spong ba; C. bu wangyu jie 不妄語戒)
5. not to use intoxicants (S. madyapāna-virati; T. myos par 'gyur ba'i btung ba spong pa; C. bu yinjiu jie 不飲酒戒)
6. not to eat at improper times [after twelve noon] (S. vikālabhojana-virati; T. dus ma yin pa'i kha zas spong pa; C. bu feishi shi jie 不非時食戒)
7. not to use perfumes, garlands, or cosmetics (S. gandhamālyavilepanavarṇakadhāraṇa-virati; T. spos dang kha dog dang byug pa dang phreng ba thogs pa spong pa; C. bu tushi xiangman jie 不塗飾香鬘戒)
8. not to sing, dance, play music, or attend entertainments (S. nṛtyagīta-virati; T. glu gar spong pa; C. bu gewu guanting jie 不歌舞觀聽戒)
9. not to sleep on high and luxurious beds (S. uccaśayanamahāśayana-virati; T. khri stan mthon po dang khri stan chen po spong pa; C. bu zuo gaoguang dachuang jie 不坐高廣大牀戒)
10. not to handle gold and silver/money (S. jātarūparajatapratigrahaṇa-virati; T. gser dang dngul la reg pa spong pa; C. bu xu jinyinbao jie 不蓄金銀寶戒)

**ten realms of reality [dharmadhātu]**. (C. shi fajie 十法界)

1. divinities (S. deva; T. lha; C. tian 天)
2. demigods (S. asura; T. lha ma yin; C. axiuluo 阿修羅)
3. humans (S. manuṣya; T. mi; C. ren 人)
4. animals (S. tiryak; T. dud 'gro; C. chusheng 畜生)
5. ghosts (S. preta; T. yi dwags; C. egui 餓鬼)

6. hell denizens (S. nāraka; T. dmyal ba; diyu 地獄)
7. disciples (S. śrāvaka; T. nyan thos; C. shengwen 聲聞)
8. solitary buddhas (S. pratyekabuddha; T. rang rgyal; C. yuanjue 緣覺)
9. bodhisattvas (T. byang chub sems dpa'; C. pusa 菩薩)
10. buddhas (T. sang rgyas; C. fo 佛)

**ten recollections**. (S. anusmṛti; T. rjes su dran pa; C. nian/suinian 念/隨念)

1. the Buddha (T. sangs rgyas rjes su dran pa; C. nianfo/fo suinian 念佛/佛隨念)
2. the dharma (T. chos rjes su dran pa; C. nianfa/fa suinian 念法/法隨念)
3. the saṃgha (T. dge 'dun rjes su dran pa; C. nianseng/seng suinian 念僧/僧隨念)
4. morality (S. śīla; T. tshul khrims rjes su dran pa; C. nianjie/jie suinian 念戒/戒隨念)
5. renunciation/generosity (S. tyāga; T. gtong ba rjes su dran pa; C. nianshi/shi suinian 念施/施隨念)
6. the divinities (S. devatā; T. lha rjes su dran pa; C. niantian/tian suinian 念天/天隨念)
7. breathing (S. ānāpāna; T. dbugs phyi nang du rgyu ba rjes su dran pa; C. nian anban/ruchuxi suinian 念安般/入出息隨念)
8. disgust (S. udvega; T. skyo ba rjes su dran pa; C. yan sui nian 厭隨念)
9. death (S. maraṇa; T. 'chi ba rjes su dran pa; C. niansi/si suinian 念死/死隨念)
10. what concerns the body (S. kāyagatā; T. lus kyi rnam pa rjes su dran pa; C. nianshen/shen suinian 念身/身隨念)

**ten stages [of the bodhisattva path]**. (S. daśabhūmi; T. sa bcu; C. shidi 十地)

1. joyful (S. pramuditā; T. rab tu dga' ba; C. jixidi/huanxi di 極喜地/歡喜地)
2. immaculate/stainless (S. vimalā; T. dri ma med pa; C. ligou di/wugou di 離垢地/無垢地)
3. luminous (S. prabhākarī; T. 'od byed pa; C. faguang di 發光地)
4. radiant (S. arciṣmatī; T. 'od 'phro ba; C. yanhui di 焰慧地)
5. invincible (S. sudurjayā; T. sbyang dka' ba; C. [ji] nansheng di [極]難勝地)
6. immediacy/coming face-to-face (S. abhimukhī; T. mngon du byed pa; C. xianqian di 現前地)
7. far-reaching/transcendent (S. dūraṅgamā; T. ring du song ba; C. yuanxing di 遠行地)
8. immovable/steadfast (S. acalā; T. mi g.yo ba; C. budong di 不動地)
9. eminence/auspicious intellect (S. sādhumatī; T. legs pa'i blo gros; C. shanhui di 善慧地)
10. cloud of dharma (S. dharmameghā; T. chos kyi sprin pa; C. fayun di 法雲地)

**ten unwholesome courses of action**. (S. akuśala-karmapatha; T. mi dge ba; C. e yedao 惡業道)

1. killing (prāṇātipāta; T. srog bcod pa; C. sha[sheng] 殺[生])
2. stealing (S. adattādāna; T. ma byin par len pa; C. [tou] dao [偷]盜)
3. sexual misconduct (kāmamithyācāra; T. 'dod pas log par g.yem pa; C. xieyin 邪淫)
4. lying (S. mṛṣāvāda; T. rdzun du smra ba; C. wangyu 妄語)
5. malicious speech (paiśunyavāda; T. phra ma; C. liangshe 兩舌)
6. verbal abuse (pārūṣyavāda; T. tshig rtsub; C. ekou 惡口)
7. frivolous prattle/idle gossip (saṃbhinnapralāpa; T. ngag 'khyal ba; C. qiyu 綺語)
8. covetousness (S. abhidhyā; T. brnab sems; C. tan[yu]/qiantan 貪[欲]/慳貪)
9. malice/ill-will (S. vyāpāda; T. gnod sems; C. chen[hui] 瞋恚)
10. wrong views (S. mithyādṛṣṭi; T. log lta; C. xiejian/yuchi 邪見/愚痴)

**ten visualization devices**. (S. *kṛtsnāyatana; P. kasiṇa; T. zad par gyi skye mched; C. bianchu 遍處)

1. earth (S. pṛthivī; T. sa; C. di 地)
2. water (S. āpas; T. chu; C. shui 水)
3. fire (S. tejas; T. me; C. huo 火)
4. wind (S. vāyu; T. rlung; C. feng 風)
5. empty-space (S. ākāśa; T. nam mkha'; C. kong 空)
6. blue (S. nīla; T. sngon po; C. qing 青)
7. yellow (S. pīta; T. ser po; C. huang 黄)
8. red (S. lohita; T. dmar po; C. chi 赤)
9. white (S. avadāta; T. dkar po; C. bai 白)
10. light (S. āloka/tejas; T. 'od/me; C. guangming/huo 光明/火)/[alt.] consciousness (S. vijñāna; T. rnam shes; C. shi 識)

**ten wholesome courses of action**. (S. kuśala-karmapatha; T. dge ba bcu; C. shanyedao 善業道) Abstention from the TEN UNWHOLESOME COURSES OF ACTION (s.v.).

## ELEVENS

**eleven cognitions**. (S. jñāna; T. shes pa; C. zhi 智)

1. of suffering (S. duḥkhajñāna; T. sdug bsngal shes pa; C. kuzhi 苦智)
2. of origination (S. samudayajñāna; T. kun 'byung ba shes pa; C. jizhi 集智)
3. of cessation (S. nirodhajñāna; T. 'gog pa shes pa; C. miezhi 滅智)
4. of the path (S. mārgajñāna; T. lam shes pa; C. daozhi 道智)
5. of extinction (S. kṣayajñāna; T. zad pa shes pa; C. jinzhi 盡智)

6. of nonproduction (S. anutpādajñāna; T. mi skye ba shes pa; C. wusheng zhi 無生智)
7. of factors (S. dharmajñāna; T. chos shes pa; C. fazhi 法智)
8. of subsequent cognition (S. anvayajñāna; T. rjes su rtogs par shes pa; C. leizhi 類智)
9. of worldly conventions (S. saṃvṛtijñāna; T. kun rdzob shes pa; C. shisu zhi 世俗智)
10. of others' minds (S. paracittajñāna; T. gzhan gyi sems shes pa; C. taxin zhi 他心智)
11. of things-as-they-are (S. yathābhūtajñāna; T. yang dag pa ji lta ba bzhin du yongs su shes pa; C. rushi zhi 如實智)

## TWELVES

**twelve ascetic practices**. (S. dhūtaguṇa; P. dhutaṅga; T. sbyangs pa'i yon tan; C. shi'er toutuo xing 十二頭陀行)

1. wears rag clothing from dust-heaps (S. pāṃśukūlika; T. phyag dar khrod pa; C. zhuo fensao yi/zhuo bina yi 著糞掃衣/著弊納衣)
2. possesses only three robes (S. traicīvarika; T. chos gos gsum pa; C. dan sanyi 但三衣)
3. does not eat after midday (S. khalupaścādbhaktika; T. zas phyis mi len pa; C. zhonghou bude yinjiang 中後不得飲漿)
4. eats only alms (S. paiṇḍapātika; T. bsod snyoms pa; C. cidi qishi 次第乞食)
5. eats one meal in a single sitting (S. aikāsanika; T. stan gcig pa; C. shou yishi fa 受一食法)
6. restricts the amount of food consumed (S. nāmantika; T. 'phyings pa pa; C. jieliang shi 節量食)
7. dwells in isolation in the forest (S. āraṇyaka; T. dgon pa ba; C. alanruo chu zhu 阿蘭若處住)
8. dwells at the foot of a tree (S. vṛkṣamūlika; T. shing drung pa; C. shuxia zhi 樹下止)
9. dwells in open, unsheltered places (S. ābhyavakāśika; T. bla gab med pa; C. ludi zuo 露地坐)
10. dwells in charnel grounds (S. śmāśānika; T. dur khrod pa; C. zhongjian zhu 塚間住)
11. never lies down to sleep (S. naiṣyadika; T. cog bu pa; C. changzuo buwo 長坐不臥)
12. does not omit any house on the almsround (S. yathāsaṃstarika; T. gzhi ji bzhin pa; C. changxing qishi 常行乞食)

**twelve categories of scripture**. (S. dvādaśāṅga[pravacana]; T. gsung rab yan lag bcu gnyis; C. shi'erbu jing/shi'erfen jiao 十二部經/十二分教)

1. discourses (S. sūtra; T. mdo; C. qijing/changhang 契經/長行)
2. aphorisms in mixed prose and verse (S. geya; T. dbyangs bsnyad; C. yingsong 應頌)
3. prophecies (S. vyākaraṇa; T. lung bstan; C. jibie/shouji 記別/授記)
4. verses (S. gāthā; T. tshig bcad; C. fengsong/guqi 諷頌/孤起)
5. utterances/meaningful expressions (S. udāna; T. ched du brjod pa; C. zishuo 自說)
6. framing stories (S. nidāna; T. gleng gzhi; C. yinyuan 因緣)
7. expanded teachings (S. vaipulya; T. shin tu rgyas pa; C. fangguang 方廣)
8. tales of previous lives (S. jātaka; T. skyes rabs; C. bensheng 本生)
9. marvelous events (S. adbhutadharma; T. rmad du byung; C. xifa 希法)
10. narratives (S. avadāna; T. rtogs pa brjod pa; C. piyu 譬喻)
11. fables (S. itivṛttaka; T. de lta bu byung ba; C. benshi 本事)
12. instructions (S. upadeśa; T. gtan phab; C. lunyi 論議)

**twelve deeds of a buddha**. (S. dvādaśabuddhakārya; T. sangs rgyas kyi mdzad pa bcu gnyis; C. shi'er xiang chengdao 十二相成道)

1. descent from tuṣita heaven (T. dga' ldan gyi gnas nas 'pho ba; C. doushuai jiangshi 兜率降世)
2. entry into the womb (T. lhums su zhugs pa; C. rutai 入胎)
3. taking birth (T. sku bltams pa; C. chutai 出胎)
4. proficiency in the arts (T. bzo yi gnas la mkhas pa; C. shanxian jiyi 善嫻技藝)
5. enjoyment of consorts (T. btsun mo'i 'khor dgyes rol ba; C. shouyong feijuan 受用妃眷)
6. renouncing the world (T. rab tu byung ba; C. chujia 出家)
7. practicing asceticism (T. dka' ba spyad pa; C. xiu kuxing 修苦行)
8. going to the bodhimaṇḍa (T. byang chub snying por gshegs pa; C. qu jingang zuo 趨金剛座)
9. subjugating Māra (T. bdud btul ba; C. xiangmo 降魔)
10. attaining enlightenment (T. mngon par rdzogs par sangs rgyas pa; C. chengdao 成道)
11. turning the wheel of the dharma (S. dharmacakra-pravartana; T. chos kyi 'khor lo bskor ba; C. zhuan falun 轉法輪)
12. passing into parinirvāṇa (T. mya ngan las 'das pa; C. ru niepan 入涅槃)

**twelvefold chain of dependent origination**. (S. pratītyasamutpāda; T. rten cing 'brel bar 'byung ba; C. yuanqi 緣起)

1. ignorance (S. avidyā; T. ma rig pa; C. wuming 無明)
2. predispositions/habituations (S. saṃskāra; T. 'du byed; C. xing 行)
3. consciousness (S. vijñāna; T. rnam shes; C. shi 識)

4. name and form/mentality and materiality (S. nāmarūpa; T. ming gzugs; C. mingse 名色)
5. six sense-bases (S. ṣaḍāyatana; T. skye mched drug; C. liuru 六入)
6. sensory contact (S. sparśa; T. reg pa; C. chu 觸)
7. sensations (S. vedanā; T. tshor ba; C. shou 受)
8. craving/thirst (S. tṛṣṇā; T. sred pa; C. ai 愛)
9. clinging (S upādāna; T. len pa; C. qu 取)
10. existence/process of becoming (S. bhava; T. srid pa; C. you 有)
11. [re]birth (S. jāti; T. skye ba; C. sheng 生)
12. old age and death (S. jarāmaraṇa; T. rga shi; C. laosi 老死)

**twelve sense-fields/bases of cognition**. (S. āyatana; T. skye mched; C. ru/chu/ruchu 入/處/入處)

1. the sense-field of the visual sense-base (S. cakṣurāyatana; T. mig gi skye mched; C. yan 眼)
2. the sense-field of visual objects (S. rūpāyatana; T. gzugs kyi skye mched; C. se 色)
3. the sense-field of the auditory sense-base (S. śrotrāyatana; T. rna ba'i skye mched; C. er 耳)
4. the sense-field of auditory objects (S. śabdāyatana; T. sgra'i skye mched; C. sheng 聲)
5. the sense-field of the olfactory sense-base (S. ghrāṇāyatana; T. sna'i skye mched; C. bi 鼻)
6. the sense-field of olfactory objects (S. gandhāyatana; T. dri'i skye mched; C. xiang 香)
7. the sense-field of the gustatory sense-base (S. jihvāyatana; T. lce'i skye mched; C. she 舌)
8. the sense-field of gustatory objects (S. rasāyatana; T. ro'i skye mched; C. wei 味)
9. the sense-field of the tactile sense-base (S. kāyāyatana; T. lus kyi skye mched; C. shen 身)
10. the sense-field of tactile objects (S. spraṣṭavyāyatana; T. reg bya'i skye mched; C. chu 觸)
11. the sense-field of the mental sense-base (S. manāyatana; T. yid kyi skye mched; C. yi 意)
12. the sense-field of mental objects (S. dharmāyatana; T. chos kyi skye mched; C. fa 法)

## FOURTEENS

**fourteen indeterminates/unanswerable questions**. (S. avyākṛta; T. lung du ma bstan pa'i chos; C. wuji 無記)

1. Is the world eternal? (S. śāśvato lokaḥ; T. 'jig rten rtag pa; C. shi chang 世常)
2. Is the world not eternal? (S. aśāśvato lokaḥ; T. 'jig rten mi rtag pa; C. shi wuchang 世無常)
3. Is the world both eternal and not eternal? (S. śāśvataś cāśāsvataś ca; T. 'jig rten rtag kyang rtag la mi rtag kyang mi rtag pa; C. shi yi chang yi wuchang 世亦常亦無常)
4. Is the world neither eternal nor not eternal? (S. naiva śāśvato nāśāśvataś ca; T. 'jig rten rtag pa yang ma yin mi tag pa yang ma yin; C. shi feichang feiwuchang 世非常非無常)
5. Is the world endless (viz. infinite)? (S. antavānlokaḥ; T. 'jig rten mtha' yod pa; C. shi youbian 世有邊)
6. Is the world not endless (viz. finite)? (S. anantavānlokaḥ; T. 'jig rten mtha' yod pa ma yin; C. shi wubian 世無邊)
7. Is the world both endless and not endless? (S. antavāṃś cānantavānlokaś ca; T. 'jig rten mtha' yod kyang yod la mtha' med kyang med; C. shi yi youbian yi wubian 世亦有邊亦無邊)
8. Is the world neither endless nor not endless? (S. naivāntavān nānantavāṃś ca; T. 'jig rten mtha' yod pa yang ma yin med pa yang ma yin; C. shi feiyoubian feiwubian 世非有邊非無邊)
9. Does the tathāgata exist after death? (S. bhavati tathāgataḥ paraṃ maranāt; T. de bzhin gshegs pa zhi nas yod; C. rulai sihou weiyou 如來死後爲有)
10. Does the tathāgata not exist after death? (S. na bhavati tathāgataḥ paraṃ maraṇāt; T. de bzhin gshegs pa zhi nas med; C. rulai sihou feiyou 如來死後非有)
11. Does the tathāgata both exist and not-exist after death? (S. bhavati ca na bhavati ca tathāgataḥ paraṃ maraṇāt; T. de bzhin gshegs pa zhi nas yod kyang yod la med kyang med; C. rulai sihou yi you yi feiyou 如來死後亦有亦非有)
12. Does the tathāgata neither exist nor not-exist after death? (S. naiva bhavati na na bhavati tathāgataḥ paraṃ maraṇāt; T. de bzhin gshegs pa zhi nas yod pa yang ma yin med pa yang ma yin; C. rulai sihou feiyou fei feiyou 如來死後非有非非有)
13. Are the life-force and the body identical? (S. sa jīvas tac charīram; T. srog de lus yin; C. mingzhe jishen 命者卽身)
14. Are the life-force and the body different? (S. anyo jīvo 'nyac charīram; T. srog kyang gzhan la lus kyang gzhan; C. mingzhe yishen 命者異身)

**fourteen root violations of the tantric commitments**.

1. contradicting one's guru
2. contradicting or denigrating the teachings of the Buddha or one's guru
3. quarreling with others on the same path
4. violating the bodhisattva vows (in action, word, or thought)
5. violating the sacred drops in the heart cakra through illicit sexual activity
6. denigrating the teachings and paths of other systems
7. revealing secrets to non-initiates or those not ready to receive them
8. viewing the five aggregates that compose the psycho-physical continuum as impure
9. doubting one's entrance into the path

10. having the ability to perceive the mental continuum of others and recognizing that someone will commit great harm to others, but not taking action
11. holding either of the extreme views of eternalism or annihilationism
12. refusing to teach someone who asks for teachings and is qualified to receive those teachings
13. superficial or dualistic clinging to appearances of pure/impure; good/bad, etc.
14. verbally or mentally denigrating women

## SIXTEENS

**sixteen arhats**. (S. ṣoḍaśasthavira; T. gnas brtan bcu drug; C. shiliu luohan 十六羅漢)

According to the East Asian tradition:

1. Piṇḍola Bhāradvāja (T. Bha ra dhwa dza bsod snyoms len; C. Bintoulu Baluoduo 賓頭盧跋羅墮)
2. Kanakavatsa (T. Gser gyi be'u; C. Jianuojiafacuo 迦諾迦伐蹉)
3. Kanaka Bhāradvāja (T. Bha ra dhwa dza gser can; C. Jianuojiabaliduoshe 迦諾迦跋釐墮闍)
4. Subinda [alt. Suvinda]/Abheda (T. Mi phyed pa; C. Supintuo 蘇頻陀)
5. Bakkula [alt. Nakula/Vakula] (T. Ba ku la; C. Bojuluo 薄拘羅)
6. Bhadra (T. Bzang po; C. Batuoluo 跋陀羅)
7. Kālika [alt. Karīka] (T. Dus ldan; C. Jialijia 迦里迦)
8. Vajraputra (T. Rdo rje mo'i bu; C. Fasheluofuduoluo 伐闍羅弗多羅)
9. Jīvaka (T. 'Tsho byed; C. Qipo/Shubojia 耆婆/戍博迦)
10. Panthaka [alt. Mahāpanthaka] (T. Lam chen bstan; C. Bantuojia 半託迦)
11. Rāhula (T. Sgra gcan 'dzin; C. Luohouluo 羅睺羅)
12. Nāgasena (T. Klu sde; C. Naqiexina 那伽犀那)
13. Aṅgaja (T. Yan lag 'byung; C. Yinjietuo 因揭陀)
14. Vanavāsin (T. Nags na gnas; C. Fanaposi 伐那婆斯)
15. Ajita (T. Ma pham pa; C. Ayiduo 阿逸多)
16. Cūḍapanthaka [alt. Cūḷapantha] (T. Lam phran bstan; C. Zhutubantuojia 注荼半托迦)

**sixteen aspects of the four noble truths**. (S. ākāra; T. bden bzhi'i rnam pa; C. xingxiang 行相)

1. impermanence (S. anitya; T. mi rtag pa; C. wuchang 無常)
2. suffering (S. duḥkha; T. sdug bsngal ba; C. ku 苦)
3. emptiness (S. śūnyatā; T. stong pa nyid; C. kong 空)
4. selflessness (S. anātmaka; T. bdag med pa; C. wuwo/feiwo 無我/非我)
5. origination (S. samudaya; T. kun 'byung ba; C. ji 集)
6. production/process (S. prabhava; T. rab tu skye ba; C. sheng 生)
7. cause (S. hetu; T. rgyu; C. yin 因)
8. conditions (S. pratyaya; T. rkyen; C. yuan 緣)
9. cessation (S. nirodha; T. 'gog pa; C. mie 滅)
10. serenity (S. śānta; T. zhi ba; C. jing 靜)
11. sublimity (S. praṇīta; T. gya nom pa; C. miao 妙)
12. deliverance (niḥsaraṇa; T. nges par 'byung ba; C. li 離)
13. path (S. mārga; T. lam; C. dao 道)
14. correctness (S. nyāya; T. rigs pa; C. ru 如)
15. achievement (S. pratipatti; T. sgrub pa; C. xing 行)
16. release (S. nairyāṇika; T. nges par 'byin pa; C. chu 出)

**sixteen elders**. (S. ṣoḍaśasthavira; T. gnas brtan bcu drug; C. shiliu zunzhe 十六尊者). See SIXTEEN ARHATS.

**sixteen emptinesses**. (S. śūnyatā; T. stong pa nyid; C. kong 空)

1. emptiness of the internal (S. adhyātmaśūnyatā; T. nang stong pa nyid; C. nei kong 內空)
2. emptiness of the external (S. bahirdhāśūnyatā; T. phyi stong pa nyid; C. wai kong 外空)
3. emptiness of both the internal and external (S. adhyātmabahirdhāśūnyatā; T. phyi nang stong pa nyid; C. neiwai kong 內外空)
4. emptiness of emptiness (S. śūnyatāśūnyatā; T. stong pa nyid stong pa nyid; C. kongkong 空空)
5. emptiness of the great (S. mahāśūnyatā; T. chen po stong pa nyid; C. dakong 大空)
6. emptiness of the ultimate (S. paramārthaśūnyatā; T. don dam pa stong pa nyid; C. shengyi kong 勝義空)
7. emptiness of the compounded (S. saṃskṛtaśūnyatā; T. 'dus byas stong pa nyid; C. youwei kong 有爲空)
8. emptiness of the uncompounded (S. asaṃskṛtaśūnyatā; T. 'dus ma byas stong pa nyid; C. wuwei kong 無爲空)
9. emptiness of the infinite (S. atyantaśūnyatā; T. mtha' las 'das pa stong pa nyid; C. bijing kong 畢竟空)
10. emptiness of the beginningless and endless (S. anavarāgraśūnyatā; T. thog ma dang mtha' ma med pa stong pa nyid; C. wuji kong 無際空)
11. emptiness of what cannot be repudiated (S. anavakāraśūnyatā; T. dor ba med pa stong pa nyid; C. wusan kong 無散空)
12. emptiness of essential nature (S. prakṛtiśūnyatā; T. rang bzhin stong pa nyid; C. benxing kong 本性空)
13. emptiness of all dharmas (S. sarvadharmaśūnyatā; T. chos thams cad stong pa nyid; C. yiqiefa kong 一切法空)
14. emptiness of intrinsic marks (S. lakṣaṇaśūnyatā; T. mtshan nyid stong pa nyid; C. zixiang kong 自相空)
15. emptiness of the unobservable (S. anupalambhaśūnyatā; T. mi dmigs pa stong pa nyid; C. bu kede kong 不可得空)
16. emptiness of the nature of nonexistence (S. abhāvasvabhāvaśūnyatā; T. dngos po med pa'i ngo bo nyid stong pa nyid; C. wuzixing zixing kong 無自性自性空)

**sixteen moments of the path of vision**. (S. darśanamārgakṣaṇa; T. mthong lam shes bzod skad cig ma; C. [jiandao wei] shiliu xin [見道位]十六心)

1. acquiescence to the cognition of dharma with regard to suffering in the sensuous realm (S. duḥkhe dharmajñānakṣāntiḥ; T. sdug bsngal chos bzod; C. kufa ren 苦法忍)
2. cognition of dharma with regard to suffering in the sensuous realm (S. duḥkhe dharmajñānam; T. sdug bsngal chos shes; C. kufa zhi 苦法智)
3. acquiescence to the subsequent cognition with regard to suffering in the subtle-materiality and immaterial realms (S. duḥkhe 'nvayajñānakṣāntiḥ; T. sdug bsngal rjes bzod; C. kulei ren 苦類忍)
4. subsequent cognition with regard to suffering in the subtle-materiality and immaterial realms (S. duḥkhe 'nvayajñānam; T. sdug bsngal rjes shes; C. kuleizhi 苦類智)
5. acquiescence to the cognition of dharma with regard to origination in the sensuous realm (S. samudaye dharmajñānakṣāntiḥ; T. kun 'byung chos bzod; C. jifa ren 集法忍)
6. cognition of dharma with regard to origination in the sensuous realm (S. samudaye dharmajñānam; T. kun 'byung chos shes; C. jifa zhi 集法智)
7. acquiescence to the subsequent cognition of origination in the subtle-materiality and immaterial realms (S. samudaye 'nvayajñānakṣāntiḥ; T. kun 'byung rjes bzod; C. jilei ren 集類忍)
8. subsequent cognition of origination in the subtle-materiality and immaterial realms (S. samudaye 'nvayajñānam; T. kun 'byung rjes shes; C. jilei zhi 集類智)
9. acquiescence to the cognition of dharma with regard to cessation in the sensuous realm (S. nirodhe dharmajñānakṣāntiḥ; T. 'gog pa chos bzod; C. miefa ren 滅法忍)
10. cognition of dharma with regard to cessation in the sensuous realm (S. nirodhe dharmajñānam; T. 'gog pa chos shes; C. miefa zhi 滅法智)
11. acquiescence to subsequent cognition with regard to cessation in the subtle-materiality and immaterial realms (S. nirodhe 'nvayajñānakṣāntiḥ; T. 'gog pa rjes bzod; C. mielei ren 滅類忍)
12. subsequent cognition with regard to cessation in the subtle-materiality and immaterial realms (nirodhe 'nvayajñānam; T. 'gog pa rjes shes; C. mielei zhi 滅類智)
13. acquiescence to the cognition of dharma with regard to the path in the sensuous realm (S. mārge dharmajñānakṣāntiḥ; T. lam chos bzod; C. daofa ren 道法忍)
14. cognition of dharma with regard to the path in the sensuous realm (S. mārge dharmajñānam; T. lam chos shes; C. daofa zhi 道法智)
15. acquiescence of subsequent cognition with regard to the path in the subtle-materiality and immaterial realms (S. mārge 'nvayajñānakṣāntiḥ; T. lam rjes bzod; C. daolei ren 道類忍)
16. subsequent cognition with regard to the path in the subtle-materiality and immaterial realms (S. mārge 'nvayajñānam; T. lam rjes shes; C. daolei zhi 道類智)

## SEVENTEENS

**seventeen heavens of the realm of subtle materiality**. (S. rūpadhātunivāsa; T. gzugs khams gnas ris; C. sejie shiqi tian 色界十七天)

FIRST DHYĀNA:

1. Brahmā's retainers (S. brahmakāyika; T. tshangs ris; C. fanzhong tian 梵衆天)
2. Brahmā's ministers (S. brahmapurohita; T. tshangs pa mdun na 'don; C. fanfu tian 梵輔天)
3. Great Brahmā (S. mahābrahmā; T. tshangs pa chen po; C. dafan tian 大梵天)

SECOND DHYĀNA:

1. lesser radiance (S. parīttābha; T. 'od chung; C. shaoguang tian 少光天)
2. immeasurable radiance (S. apramāṇābha; T. tshad med 'od; C. wuliangguang tian 無量光天)
3. ultimate radiance (S. ābhāsvara; T. 'od gsal; C. guangyin tian/jiguangjing tian 光音天/極光淨天)

THIRD DHYĀNA:

1. lesser purity (S. parīttaśubha; T. dge chung; C. shaojing tian 少淨天)
2. immeasurable purity (S. apramāṇaśubha; T. tshad med dge; C. wuliangjing tian 無量淨天)
3. pervasive purity (S. śubhakṛtsna; T. dge rgyas; C. bianjing tian 遍淨天)
4. cloudless (S. anabhraka; T. sprin med; C. wuyun tian 無雲天)
5. meritorious birth (S. puṇyaprasava; T. bsod nams 'phel; C. fusheng tian 福生天)
6. extensive fruition (S. bṛhatphala; T. 'bras bu che; C. guangguo tian 廣果天)

FOURTH DHYĀNA (THE FIVE PURE ABODES, ŚUDDHĀVĀSA):

1. free from afflictions (S. avṛha; T. mi che ba; C. wufan tian 無煩天)
2. not burning/without torment (S. atapa; T. mi gdung pa; C. wure tian 無熱天)
3. perfect form (S. sudṛśa; T. gya nom snang ba; C. shanxian tian 善現天)
4. perfect vision (S. sudarśana; T. shin tu mthong ba; C. shanjian tian 善見天)
5. highest (S. akaniṣṭha; T. 'og min; C. sejiujing tian 色究竟天)

## EIGHTEENS

**eighteen elements/bases of cognition**. (S. dhātu; T. khams bco brgyad; C. jie 界)

1. visual sense-base (S. cakṣurdhātu; T. mig gi khams; C. yan 眼)
2. visual sense-object (S. rūpadhātu; T. gzugs kyi khams; C. se 色)

3. visual consciousness (S. cakṣurvijñānadhātu; T. mig gi rnam par shes pa'i khams; C. yanshi 眼識)
4. auditory sense-base (S. śrotradhātu; T. rna ba'i khams; C. er 耳)
5. auditory sense-object (S. śabdadhātu; T. sgra'i khams; C. sheng 聲)
6. auditory consciousness (S. śrotravijñānadhātu; T. rna ba'i rnam par shes pa'i khams; C. ershi 耳識)
7. olfactory sense-base (S. ghrāṇadhātu; T. sna'i khams; C. bi 鼻)
8. olfactory sense-object (S. gandhadhātu; T. dri'i khams; C. xiang 香)
9. olfactory consciousness (S. ghrāṇavijñānadhātu; sna'i rnam par shes pa'i khams; C. bishi 鼻識)
10. gustatory sense-base (S. jihvādhātu; T. lce'i khams; C. she 舌)
11. gustatory sense-object (S. rasadhātu; T. ro'i khams; C. wei 味)
12. gustatory consciousness (S. jihvāvijñānadhātu; T. lce'i rnam par shes pa'i khams; C. sheshi 舌識)
13. tactile sense-base (S. kāyadhātu; T. lus kyi khams; C. shen 身)
14. tactile sense-object (S. spraṣṭavyadhātu; T. reg bya'i khams; C. chu 觸)
15. tactile consciousness (S. kāyavijñānadhātu; T. lus kyi rnam par shes pa'i khams; C. shenshi 身識)
16. mental sense-base (S. manodhātu; T. yid kyi khams; C. yi 意)
17. mental sense-object (S. dharmadhātu; T. chos kyi khams; C. fa 法)
18. mental consciousness (S. manovijñānadhātu; T. yid kyi rnam par shes pa'i khams; C. yishi 意識)

**eighteen emptinesses**. (S. śūnyatā; T. stong pa nyid bco brgyad; C. kong 空)

1. emptiness of the internal (S. adhyātmaśūnyatā; T. nang stong pa nyid; C. nei kong 內空)
2. emptiness of the external (S. bahirdhāśūnyatā; T. phyi stong pa nyid; C. wai kong 外空)
3. emptiness of both the internal and external emptiness (S. adhyātmabahirdhāśūnyatā; T. phyi nang stong pa nyid; C. neiwai kong 內外空)
4. emptiness of emptiness (S. śūnyatāśūnyatā; T. stong pa nyid stong pa nyid; C. kongkong 空空)
5. emptiness of the great (S. mahāśūnyatā; T. chen po stong pa nyid; C. dakong 大空)
6. emptiness of the ultimate (S. paramārthaśūnyatā; T. don dam pa stong pa nyid; C. shengyi kong 勝義空)
7. emptiness of the compounded (S. saṃskṛtaśūnyatā; T. 'dus byas stong pa nyid; C. youwei kong 有爲空)
8. emptiness of the uncompounded (S. asaṃskṛtaśūnyatā; T. 'dus ma byas stong pa nyid; C. wuwei kong 無爲空)
9. emptiness of the infinite (S. atyantaśūnyatā; T. mtha' las 'das pa stong pa nyid; C. bijing kong 畢竟空)
10. emptiness of the beginningless and endless (S. anavarāgraśūnyatā; T. thog ma dang mtha' ma med pa stong pa nyid; C. wuji kong 無際空)
11. emptiness of what cannot be repudiated (S. anavakāraśūnyatā; T. dor ba med pa stong pa nyid; C. wusan kong 無散空)
12. emptiness of essential nature (S. prakṛtiśūnyatā; T. rang bzhin stong pa nyid; C. benxing kong 本性空)
13. emptiness of all dharmas (S. sarvadharmaśūnyatā; T. chos thams cad stong pa nyid; C. yiqiefa kong 一切法空)
14. emptiness of intrinsic marks (S. lakṣaṇaśūnyatā; T. mtshan nyid stong pa nyid; C. zixiang kong 自相空)
15. emptiness of the unobservable (S. anupalambhaśūnyatā; T. mi dmigs pa stong pa nyid; C. bu kede kong 不可得空)
16. emptiness of the nature of nonexistence (S. abhāvasvabhāvaśūnyatā; T. dngos po med pa'i ngo bo nyid stong pa nyid; C. wuxing zixing kong 無性自性空)
17. emptiness of existence (S. bhāvaśūnyatā; T. dngos bo'i stong pa nyid; C. youxing kong 有性空)
18. emptiness of nonexistence (S. abhāvaśūnyatā; T. dngos po med pa'i stong pa nyid; C. wuxing kong 無性空)

**eighteen mainstream Buddhist schools**. (S. aṣṭadaśanikāya; T. sde pa bco brgyad; C. shiba bupai 十八部派)

1. Sarvāstivāda (T. Thams cad yod par smra ba; C. Shuo yiqie you bu 說一切有部)
   1. Mūlasarvāstivāda (T. Gzhi thams cad yod par smra ba'i sde; C. Genben shuo yiqie you bu 根本說一切有部)
   2. Kāśyapīya (T. 'Od srung pa'i sde; C. Yinguang bu 飲光部)
   3. Mahīśāsaka (T. Sa ston sde; C. Huadi bu 化地部)
   4. Dharmaguptaka (T. Chos srung sde; C. Fazang bu 法藏部)
   5. Bahuśrutīya (T. Mang du thos pa'i sde; C. Duowen bu 多聞部)
   6. Tāmraśāṭīya (T. Gos dmar sde; C. Tongxie bu 銅鍱部)
   7. Vibhajyavādin (T. Rnam par phye ste smra ba'i sde; C. Fenbieshuo bu 分別說部)
2. Saṃmitīya (T. Kun gyis bkur ba; C. Zhengliang bu 正量部)
   1. Kaurukullaka (T. Sar sgrog rigs kyi sde; C. Julujuluo bu/Xuandi bu 拘屢拘羅部/宣地部)
   2. Avantaka (T. Bsrung ba pa'i sde; C. Bukeqi bu 不可棄部)
   3. Vātsīputrīya (T. Gnas ma bu pa'i sde; C. Duzi bu 犢子部)
3. Mahāsāṃghika (T. Dge 'dun phal chen; C. Dazhong bu 大衆部)
   1. Pūrvaśaila (T. Shar gyi ri bo'i sde; C. Dongshanzhu bu 東山住部)
   2. Aparaśaila (T. Nub kyi ri bo'i sde; C. Xishanzhu bu 西山住部)
   3. Haimavata (T. Gang ri bo'i sde; C. Xueshan bu 雪山部)

4. Lokottaravāda (T. 'Jig rten 'das smra'i sde; C. Shuo chushi bu 說出世部)
5. Prajñaptivāda (T. Btags par smra ba'i sde; C. Shuojia bu 說假部)

4. *Sthaviranikāya (T. Gnas brtan sde; C. Shangzuo bu 上座部)
    1. Mahāvihāravāsa (T. Gtsug lag khang chen gnas sde; C. Dasizhu bu 大寺住部)
    2. Jetavanīya (T. Rgyal byed tshal gnas pa'i sde; C. Zhiduolin zhu bu 祇多林住部)
    3. Abhayagirivāsa (T. 'Jigs med ri gnas sde; C. Wuweishan zhu bu 無畏山住部)

**eighteen sciences**. (S. vidyāsthāna; T. rig gnas)

1. music (S. gandharva; T. rol mo)
2. erotic arts (S. vaiśika; T. 'khrig thabs)
3. livelihood (S. vārttā; T. 'tsho chas)
4. accounting (S. saṃkhya; T. grangs can)
5. grammar (S. śabda; T. sgra)
6. medicine (S. cikitsitā; T. gso dpyad)
7. law (S. nīti; T. chos lugs)
8. the arts (S. śilpa; T. bzo)
9. archery (S. dhanurveda; T. 'phong dpyad)
10. reasoning (S. hetu; T. gtan tshigs)
11. yoga (T. rnal 'byor)
12. learning (S. śruti; T. thos pa)
13. memorization (S. smṛti; T. dran pa)
14. astronomy (S. jyotiṣa; T. skar ma'i dpyad)
15. astrology (S. gaṇita; T. rtsis)
16. magic (S. māyā; T. mig 'phrul)
17. legend (S. purāṇa; T. sngon gyi rabs)
18. history (S. itihāsaka; T. sngon byung)

**eighteen unshared factors [distinct attributes] of the buddhas**. (S. āveṇikabuddhadharma; T. sangs rgyas kyi chos ma 'dres pa bco brgyad/ma 'dres pa'i chos; C. bugong[fo]fa 不共[佛]法)

1. their actions are without error (S. nāsti [tathāgatasya] skhalitam; T. 'khrul pa med pa; C. shen wushi 身無失)
2. their speech is not noisy (S. nāsti ravitam; T. ca co med pa; C. kou wushi 口無失)
3. they are never forgetful (S. nāsti muṣitasmṛtitā; T. bsnyel ba med pa; C. nian wushi 念無失)
4. their mind is never not in equipoise (S. nāsty asamāhitacittam; T. sems mnyam par ma gzhag pa med pa; C. wu yixiang 無異想)
5. their perception is free from discursiveness (S. nāsti nānātvasaṃjñā; T. tha dad pa'i 'du shes med pa; C. wu buding 無不定)
6. their equanimity is not due to a lack of discernment (S. nāsty apratisaṃkhyāyopekṣā; T. so sor ma rtogs pa'i btang snyoms med pa; C. wu buzhi she 無不知捨)
7. they do not regress in their zeal (S. nāsti cchandasya hāniḥ; T. 'dun pa nyams pa med pa; C. yu wumie 欲無滅)
8. they do not regress in their effort (S. nāsti vīryasya hāniḥ; T. brtson 'grus nyams pa med pa; C. jingjin wumie 精進無滅)
9. they do not regress in their recollection (S. nāsti smṛtihāniḥ; T. dran pa nyams pa med pa; C. nian wumie 念無滅)
10. they do not regress in their concentration (s. nāsti samādhihāniḥ; T. ting nge 'dzin nyams pa med pa; C. ding wumie 定無滅)
11. they do not regress in their wisdom (S. nāsti prajñāhāniḥ; T. shes rab nyams pa med pa; C. hui wumie 慧無滅)
12. they do not regress in their liberation (S. nāsti vimuktihāniḥ; T. rnam par grol ba nyams pa med pa; C. jietuo zhijian wumie 解脱知見無滅)
13. all their physical actions are preceded by gnosis and remain in conformity with gnosis (S. sarvakāyakarmajñānapūrvagamaṃ jñānānuparivarti; T. lus kyi las thams cad ye shes kyi sngon du 'gro shing ye shes kyi rjes su 'brang ba; C. yiqie shenye sui zhihui xing 一切身業隨智慧行)
14. all their verbal actions are preceded by gnosis and remain in conformity with gnosis (S. sarvavākkarmajñānapūrvagamaṃ jñānānuparivarti; T. ngag gi las thams cad ye shes kyi sngon du 'gro shing ye shes kyi rjes su 'brang ba; C. yiqie kouye sui zhihui xing 一切口業隨智慧行)
15. all their mental actions are preceeded by gnosis and remain in conformity with gnosis (S. sarvamanaḥkarmajñānapūrvagamaṃ jñānānuparivarti; T. yid kyi las thams cad ye shes kyi sngon du 'gro shing ye shes kyi rjes su 'brang ba; C. yiqie yiye sui zhihui xing 一切意業隨智慧行)
16. they enter into the perception of gnosis that is unobstructed and unimpeded with respect to the past (S. atīte 'dhvany asaṅgam apratihataṃ jñānadarśanaṃ pravartate; T. 'das pa'i dus la ma chags ma thogs pa'i ye shes gzigs par 'jug pa; C. zhihui zhi guoqushi wu'ai 智慧知過去世無礙)
17. they enter into the perception of gnosis that is unobstructed and unimpeded with respect to the future (S. anāgate 'dhvany asaṅgam apratihataṃ jñānadarśanaṃ pravartate; T. ma 'ongs pa'i dus la ma chags ma thogs pa'i ye shes gzigs par 'jug pa; C. zhihui zhi weilaishi wu'ai 智慧知未來世無礙)
18. they enter into the perception of gnosis that is unobstructed and unimpeded with respect to the present (S. pratyutpanne 'dhvany asaṅgam apratihataṃ jñānadarśanaṃ pravartate; T. da ltar gyi dus la ma chags ma thogs pa'i ye shes gzigs par 'jug pa; C. zhihui zhi xianzaishi wu'ai 智慧知現在世無礙)

## TWENTIES

**twenty-eight classes of divinities**. (S. deva; T. lha; C. tian 天)

SENSUOUS REALM (KAMADHĀTU):

1. four great kings (S. cāturmahārājakāyika; T. rgyas chen rigs bzhi; C. siwang tian 四王天)
2. divinities of the thirty-three (S. trāyastriṃśa; T. sum cu rtsa gsum; C. daoli tian/sanshisan tian 忉利天/三十三天)
3. free from conflict (S. yāma; T. 'thab bral; C. yemo tian 夜摩天)
4. contented (S. tuṣita; T. dga' ldan; C. doushuai[tuo] tian 兜率[陀]天)
5. enjoyment of creation (S. nirmāṇarati; T. 'phrul dga'; C. huale tian 化樂天)
6. divinities who have power over the creations of others/ divinities who partake of the pleasures created in other heavens (S. paranirmitavaśavartin; T. gzhan 'phrul dbang byed; C. tahua zizai tian 他化自在天)

REALM OF SUBTLE MATERIALITY (RŪPADHĀTU):

FIRST DHYĀNA:

1. Brahmā's retainers (S. brahmakāyika; T. tshangs ris; C. fanzhong tian 梵衆天)
2. Brahmā's ministers (S. brahmapurohita; T. tshangs pa mdun na 'don; C. fanfu tian 梵輔天)
3. Great Brahmā (S. mahābrahmā; T. tshangs pa chen po; C. dafan tian 大梵天)

SECOND DHYĀNA

1. lesser radiance (S. parīttābha; T. 'od chung; C. shaoguang tian 少光天)
2. immeasurable radiance (S. apramāṇābha; T. tshad med 'od; C. wuliang guang tian 無量光天)
3. ultimate radiance (S. ābhāsvara; T. 'od gsal; C. guangyin tian/jiguangjing tian 光音天/極光淨天)

THIRD DHYĀNA

1. lesser purity (S. parīttaśubha; T. dge chung; C. shaojing tian 少淨天)
2. immeasurable purity (S. apramāṇaśubha; T. tshad med dge; C. wuliangjing tian 無量淨天)
3. pervasive purity (S. śubhakṛtsna; T. dge rgyas; C. bianjing tian 遍淨天)
4. cloudless (S. anabhraka; T. sprin med; C. wuyun tian 無雲天)
5. meritorious birth (S. puṇyaprasava; T. bsod nams 'phel; C. fusheng tian 福生天)
6. extensive fruition (S. bṛhatphala; T. 'bras bu che; C. guangguo tian 廣果天
7. nonperception (S. asaṃjñisattva; T. 'du shes med pa'i lha; C. wuxiang tian 無想天) [Note: This heaven is sometimes added to the list of seventeen heavens of the realm of subtle materiality and is included on this list for comprehensiveness.]

FOURTH DHYĀNA (THE FIVE PURE ABODES, ŚUDDHĀVĀSA)

1. free from afflictions (S. avṛha; T. mi che ba; C. wufan tian 無煩天)
2. without torment (S. atapa; T. mi gdung pa; C. wure tian 無熱天)
3. perfect form (S. sudṛśa; T. gya nom snang ba; C. shanxian tian 善現天)
4. perfect vision (S. sudarśana; T. shin tu mthong ba; C. shanjian tian 善見天)
5. highest (S. akaniṣṭha; T. 'og min; C. sejiujing tian 色究竟天)

IMMATERIAL REALM (ĀRŪPYADHĀTU)

1. infinite space (S. ākāśānantyāyatana; T. nam mkha' mtha' yas skye mched; C. kong wubian chu tian 空無邊處天)
2. infinite consciousness (S. vijñānānantyāyatana; T. rnam shes mtha' yas skye mched; C. shi wubian chu tian 識無邊處天)
3. nothingness (S. ākiñcanyāyatana; T. ci yang med pa'i skye mched; C. wusuoyou chu tian 無所有處天)
4. neither perception nor nonperception (S. naivasamjñānāsamjñāyatana; T. 'du shes med 'du shes med min skye mched; C. feixiang feifeixiang tian 非想非非想天)

**twenty varieties of the saṃgha**. (S. viṃśatiprabhedasaṃgha; T. dge 'dun nyi shu; C. ershi sengqie/shengwen cidi, 二十僧伽/聲聞次第)

1. srotaāpanna (T. rgyun du zhugs pa; C. yuliu [guo]/ xutuohuan 預流[果]/須陀洹)
2. one who takes up to seven existences (S. saptakṛdbhavaparama; T. re ltar thogs na srid pa lan bdun pa; C. jiqi fanyou 極七返有)
3. one who goes from family to family (S. kulaṃkula; T. rigs nas rigs su skye ba; C. wang tianshang/jiajia 往天上/家家)
4. once-returner (S. sakṛdāgāmin; T. lan gcig phyir 'ong ba; C. yilai/situohan 一來/斯陀含)
5. one who has a single obstacle (S. ekavīcika; T. bar chad gcig pa; C. yijian, 一間)
6. non-returner (S. anāgāmin; T. phyir mi 'ong ba; C. bu huan/bu lai/anahan 不還/不來/阿那含)
7. one who achieves nirvāṇa in the intermediate state (S. antarāparinirvāyin; T. bar ma dor yongs su mya ngan las 'das ba; C. zhong ban/zhong banniepan 中般/中般涅槃)
8. one who achieves nirvāṇa at birth (S. upapadyaparinirvāyin; T. skyes nas yongs su mya ngan las 'das ba; C. sheng ban/sheng banniepan 生般/生般涅槃)
9. one who achieves nirvāṇa through effort (S. sābhisaṃskāraparinirvāyin; T. mngon par 'du byed dang bcas pas yongs su mya ngan las 'das ba; C. youxing ban/youxing banniepan 有行般/有行般涅槃)

10. one who achieves nirvāṇa without effort (S. anabhisaṃskāraparinirvāyin; T. mngon par 'du byed pa med par yongs su mya ngan las 'das ba; C. wuxing ban/wuxing banniepan 無行般/無行般涅槃)
11. one who goes higher/upstreamer (S. ūrdhvasrotas; T. gong du 'pho ba; C. shangliu ban/shangliu banniepan 上流般/上流般涅槃)
12. bodily witness (S. kāyasākṣin; T. lus kyi mngon sum du byed pa; C. shenzheng 身證)
13. follower through faith (S. śraddhānusārin; T. dad pa'i rjes su 'brang ba; C. suixin xing 隨信行)
14. follower through doctrine (S. dharmānusārin; T. chos kyi rjes su 'brang ba; C. suifa xing 隨法行)
15. one who aspires through faith (S. śraddhādhimukta; T. dad pas lhag par mos pa; C. xinjie 信解)
16. one who attains through seeing (S. dṛṣṭiprāpta; T. mthong bas thob pa; C. jianzhi/jiande 見至/見得)
17. one who is liberated dependent upon a specific occasion (S. samayavimukta; T. dus dang sbyor bar rnam par grol ba; C. shi jietuo 時解脫)
18. one who is liberated regardless of occasion (S. asamayavimukta; T. dus dang mi sbyor bar rnam par grol ba; C. bushi jietuo 不時解脫)
19. one who is liberated through wisdom (S. prajñāvimukta; T. shes rab kyis rnam par grol ba; C. hui jietuo 慧解脫)
20. one who is liberated both ways (S. ubhayatobhāgavimukta; T. gnyis ga'i cha las rnam par grol ba; C. ju jietuo 俱解脫)

## THIRTIES

**thirty-two marks of a great man.** (S. mahāpuruṣalakṣaṇa; T. skyes bu chen po'i mtshan sum bcu rtsa gnyis/mtshan bzang so gnyis; C. daren xiang 大人相)

1. his feet stand firmly on the ground (S. supratiṣṭhitapāda; T. zhabs shin tu gnas pa; C. zu shan anzhu xiang 足善安住相)
2. he has thousand-spoked wheels on the palms of his hands and the soles of his feet (S. cakrāṅkitahastapādatala; T. phyag dang zhabs kyi mthil 'khor lo'i mtshan dang ldan pa; C. shouzu lunxiang 手足輪相)
3. the heels of his feet are broad (S. āyatapādapārṣṇi; T. zhabs kyi mthil rting pa yangs pa; C. zugen fuchang xiang 足跟趺長相)
4. he has long fingers (S. dīrghāṅguli; T. sor mo ring ba; C. xianzhang zhi xiang 纖長指相)
5. his hands and feet are smooth (S. mṛdutaruṇahastapāda; T. phyag dang zhabs kyi mthil 'jam shing gzhon sha chags pa; C. shouzu xiruan xiang 手足細軟相)
6. his hands and feet are webbed (S. jālahastapāda; T. phyag dang zhabs dra bas 'brel ba; C. shouzu wangman xiang 手足網縵相)
7. his legs are long [alt. his ankles are not prominent] (S. utsaṅgapāda; T. zhabs kyi long bu mi mngon pa; C. zufu gaoman xiang 足趺高滿相)
8. he has thighs like an antelope (S. aiṇeyajaṅgha; T. byin pa ri dwags e na ya'i 'dra; C. yiniye chuai xiang 毉泥耶踹相)
9. his arms extend below the knees (S. sthitānavanatapralambabāhu; T. bzhengs bzhin du ma btud par phyag pus mor slebs pa; C. lishou moxi xiang 立手摩膝相)
10. his penis is retracted (S. kośopagata-vastiguhya; T. 'doms kyi sba ba sbubs su nub pa; C. shifeng zangmi xiang 勢峰藏密相)
11. his brow is broad and even (S. samalalāta; T. dpral ba'i dbyes mnyams pa; C. e guangping qi 額廣平齊)
12. his skin is smooth and golden (S. sūkṣmasuvarṇacchavi; T. pags pa srab cing mdog gser 'dra ba; C. pifu xihua xiang 皮膚細滑相)
13. he has one hair in each pore of his body (S. ekaikaroma; T. spu re re nas skyes shing g.yas su 'khyil ba; C. shenzhu maokong yiyi maosheng xiang 身諸毛孔一一毛生相)
14. the hairs of his body stand erect (S. ūrdhvāgraroma; T. sku'i spu gyen du phyogs pa; C. shenmao shangmi xiang 身毛上靡相)
15. his thighs are well rounded (S. suvartitoru; T. brla legs par zlum pa; C. tui meiyuan xiang 腿美圓相)
16. the seven parts of his body are well-proportioned (S. saptotsada; T. bdun mtho ba; C. qichu jieman xiang 七處皆滿相)
17. the upper part of his body is like a lion's (S. siṃhapūrvārdhakāya; T. ro stod seng ge'i 'dra ba; C. shen shang ban ru shiziwang xiang 身上半如師子王相)
18. he has broad shoulders (S. citāntarāṃsa; T. thal gong rgyas pa; C. bojian chongshi xiang 髆間充實相)
19. his body and limbs are perfectly proportionate and thus shaped like a fig tree (S. nyagrodhaparimaṇḍala; T. shing nya gro dha ltar chu zheng gab pa; C. shenxiang yuanman runuojutuo 身相圓滿如諾瞿陀)
20. he has full, round shoulders (S. susaṃvṛttaskandha; T. dpung mgo shin tu zlum pa; C. jianshan yuanman xiang 肩善圓滿相)
21. he has an excellent sense of taste (S. rasarasāgra; T. ro bro ba'i mchog dang ldan pa; C. yu zhuwei zhong de zui shangwei 於諸味中得最上味)
22. he has a jaw like a lion's (S. siṃhahanu; T. 'gram pa seng ge'i 'dra ba; C. han ru shizi xiang 頷如師子相)
23. he has forty teeth (S. catvāriṃśaddanta; T. tshems bzhi bcu mnga' ba; C. jusishichi 具四十齒)
24. his teeth are even (S. samadanta; T. thems mnyam pa; C. chi qiping 齒齊平)
25. his teeth are evenly spaced (S. aviraladanta; T. tshems thags bzang ba; C. chi wuxi 齒無隙)
26. his teeth are white (S. suśukladanta; T. tshems shin tu dkar ba; C. chi xianbai 齒鮮白)

27. his tongue is long and broad (S. prabhūtatanujihva; T. ljags shin tu ring zhing srab pa; C. she guangbo 舌廣薄)
28. his voice is like Brahmā's (S. brahmasvara; T. tshangs pa'i dbyangs; C. da fanyin 大梵音)
29. his eyes are deep blue with eyelashes like a bull (S. abhinīlanetragopakṣma; T. spyan mthon mthing la ba'i rdzi ma lta bu; C. mu ganqing jie ru niuwang 目紺青睫如牛王)
30. he has a white tuft of hair between his eyebrows (S. ūrṇākeśa; T. mdzod spu; C. meijian baihao xiang 眉間白毫相)
31. the hair on his head turns to the right (S. pradakṣiṇāvarttakeśa; T. dbu skra g.yas su 'khyil ba; C. toufa youxuan 頭髮右旋)
32. he has a protrusion on the crown of the head (S. uṣṇīṣaśīrṣa; T. dbu gtsug tor dang ldan pa; C. dingshang xian wusenisha 頂上現烏瑟膩沙)

**thirty-seven wings of enlightenment/factors pertaining to awakening**. (S. bodhipākṣikadharma; T. byang chub kyi phyogs kyi chos; C. daopin/puti fen 道品/菩提分)

1. four applications of mindfulness (S. smṛtyupasthāna; T. dran pa nye bar bzhag pa bzhi; C. si nianchu 四念處)
2. four right efforts (S. samyakpradhāna/samyakprahāṇa; T. yang dag par spong ba bzhi; C. si zhengqin 四正勤)
3. four bases of psychic power (S. ṛddhipāda; T. rdzu 'phrul gyi rkang pa bzhi; C. si shenzu/si ruyi zu 四神足/四如意足)
4. five [spiritual] faculties/dominants (S. indriya; T. dbang po lnga; C. wugen 五根)
5. five powers (S. bala; T. stobs lnga; C. wuli 五力)
6. seven factors of enlightenment (S. bodhyaṅga; T. byang chub yan lag bdun; C. qi puti fen/qi juezhi 七菩提分/七覺支)
7. eightfold [noble] path (S. āryāṣṭāṅgamārga; T. 'phags lam yan lag brgyad; C. ba zhengdao 八正道)

## FIFTIES

**fifty-one/fifty-two mental concomitants**. (S. caitta; P. cetasika; T. sem byung lnga bcu rtsa gcig; C. xin suoyou fa 心所有法). See EIGHTY-TWO DHAMMAS OF THE STHAVIRANIKĀYA/THERAVĀDA SCHOOL; ONE-HUNDRED DHARMAS OF THE YOGĀCĀRA SCHOOL.

## SEVENTIES

**seventy-five dharmas of the Sarvāstivāda school**. (S. pañcasaptatidharma; T. chos don lnga; C. qishiwu fa 七十五法)

1. eleven material factors (S. rūpa; T. gzugs; C. sefa 色法)
   1. visual faculty (S. cakṣurindriya; T. mig gi dbang po; C. yangen 眼根)
   2. auditory faculty (S. śrotrendriya; T. rna ba'i dbang po; C. ergen 耳根)
   3. olfactory faculty (S. ghrāṇendriya; T. sna'i dbang po; C. bigen 鼻根)
   4. gustatory faculty (S. jihvendriya; T. lce'i dbang po; C. shegen 舌根)
   5. tactile faculty (S. kāyendriya; T. lus kyi dbang po; C. shengen 身根)
   6. visual objects (S. rūpa; T. gzugs; C. se 色)
   7. sound (S. śabda; T. sgra; C. sheng 聲)
   8. scent (S. gandha; T. dri; C. xiang 香)
   9. flavor (S. rasa; T. ro; C. mei 味)
   10. contact (S. spraṣṭavya; T. reg bya; C. chu 觸)
   11. unmanifest materiality (S. avijñaptirūpa; T. rnam par rig byed ma yin pa'i gzugs; C. wubiao se 無表色)
2. mind (S. citta; T. sems; C. xinwang 心王)
3. forty-six mental concomitants (S. caitta; T. sems byung; C. xin suoyou fa 心所有法)
   1. ten omnipresent mental factors (S. mahābhūmika; T. sems kyi sa mang; C. dadi fa 大地法)
      1. sensation (S. vedanā; T. tshor ba; C. shou 受)
      2. perception (S. saṃjñā; T. 'du shes; C. xiang 想)
      3. volition/intention (S. cetanā; T. sems pa; C. si 思)
      4. sensory contact (S. sparśa; T. reg pa; C. chu 觸)
      5. zeal/desire-to-act (S. chanda; T. 'dun pa; C. yu 欲)
      6. discernment (S. mati; T. shes rab; C. hui 慧)
      7. mindfulness/memory (S. smṛti; T. dran pa; C. nian 念)
      8. attention (S. manaskāra; T. yid la byed pa; C. zuoyi 作意)
      9. determination (S. adhimokṣa; T. mos pa; C. shengjie 勝解)
      10. concentration (S. samādhi; T. ting nge 'dzin; C. ding 定)
   2. ten omnipresent wholesome factors (S. kuśalamahābhūmika; T. dge ba'i sa mang; C. da shan di fa 大善地法)
      1. faith (S. śraddhā; T. dad pa; C. xin 信)
      2. heedfulness/vigilance (S. apramāda; T. bag yod pa; C. bu fangyi 不放逸)
      3. tranquillity/serenity (S. praśrabdhi; T. shin tu sbyangs pa; C. [qing] an [輕]安)
      4. equanimity (S. upekṣā; T. btang snyoms; C. xingshe 行捨)
      5. shame/decency/propriety (S. hrī; T. ngo tsha shes pa; C. can 慚)
      6. fear of blame/modesty (S. apatrāpya; T. khrel yod pa; C. kui 愧)
      7. absence of craving (S. alobha; T. ma chags pa; C. wu tan 無貪)
      8. absence of ill-will (S. adveṣa; T. zhe sdang med pa; C. wu chen 無瞋)
      9. absence of harmful intentions (S. avihiṃsā; T. rnam par mi 'tshe ba; C. bu hai 不害)
      10. effort/vigor (S. vīrya; T. brtson 'grus; C. qin/jingjin 勤/精進)

3. six omnipresent afflicted factors (S. kleśamahābhūmika; T. nyon mongs chen po'i sa mang; C. da fannao di fa 大煩惱地法)
   1. delusion (S. moha; T. ma rig pa; C. chi 癡)
   2. heedlessness (S. pramāda; T. bag med pa; C. fangyi 放逸)
   3. lassitude (S. kausīdya; T. le lo; C. xiedai 懈怠)
   4. lack of faith (S. āśraddhya; T. ma dad pa; C. bu xin 不信)
   5. sloth (S. styāna; T. rmugs pa; C. [hun]shen [惛]沈)
   6. restlessness (S. auddhatya; T. rgod pa; C. diaoju 掉舉)
4. two major omnipresent unwholesome factors (S. akuśalamahābhūmika; T. mi dge ba'i sa mang; C. da bushan di fa 大不善地法)
   1. lack of shame/decency/propriety (S. āhrīkya; T. ngo tsha med pa; C. wucan 無慚)
   2. lack of fear of blame/lack of modesty (S. anapatrāpya; T. khrel med pa; C. wukui 無愧)
5. ten minor afflicted factors of wide extent (S. parīttakleśabhūmika; T. nyon mongs chung ngu'i sa mang; C. xiao fannao di fa 小煩惱地法)
   1. anger (S. krodha; T. khro ba; C. fen 忿)
   2. disparagement/hypocrisy/concealing (S. mrakṣa; T. 'chab pa; C. fu 覆)
   3. selfishness/stinginess (S. mātsarya; T. ser sna; C. qian 慳)
   4. envy (S. īrṣyā; T. phrag dog; C. ji 嫉)
   5. vexation (S. pradāśa; T. 'tshig pa; C. nao 惱)
   6. hostility (S. vihiṃsā; T. rnam par 'tshe ba; C. hai 害)
   7. enmity/resentment (S. upanāha; T. 'khon 'dzin; C. hen 恨)
   8. deception (S. śāṭhya; T. g.yo; C. chan 諂)
   9. deceit (S. māyā; T. sgyu; C. kuang 誑)
   10. arrogance (S. mada; T. rgyags pa; C. jiao 憍)
6. eight indeterminate mental factors (S. aniyata; T. gzhan 'gyur; C. buding 不定)
   1. applied thought (S. vitarka; T. rtog pa; C. xun 尋)
   2. sustained thought (S. vicāra; T. dpyod pa; C. si 伺)
   3. worry (S. kaukṛtya; T. 'gyod pa; C. ezuo 惡作)
   4. torpor (S. middha; T. gnyid; C. shuimian 睡眠)
   5. sensuality (S. rāga; T. 'dod chags; C. tan 貪)
   6. hatred (S. pratigha; T. khong khro; C. chen 瞋)
   7. pride (S. māna; T. nga rgyal; C. man 慢)
   8. skeptical doubt (S. vicikitsā; T. the tshom; C. yi 疑)

4. fourteen conditioned forces dissociated from thought (S. cittaviprayuktasaṃskāra; T. ldan min 'du byed; C. xin bu xiangying xing fa 心不相應行法)
   1. possession (S. prāpti; T. 'thob pa; C. de 得)
   2. nonpossession (S. aprāpti; T.'thob pa med pa; C. feide 非得)
   3. homogeneity (S. sabhāgatā/nikāyasabhāga; T. rigs 'thun pa; C. zhong tongfen 衆同分)
   4. state of nonperception (S. āsaṃjñika; T. 'du shes med pa; C. wuxiang guo/wuxiang bao/wuxiang shi 無想果/無想報/無想事)
   5. equipoise of nonperception (S. asaṃjñāsamāpatti; T. 'du shes med pa'i snyoms 'jug; C. wuxiang ding 無想定)
   6. equipoise of cessation (S. nirodhasamāpatti; T. 'gog pa'i snyoms 'jug; C. mie jin ding 滅盡定)
   7. vitality (S. jīvitendriya; T. srog gi dbang po; C. ming gen 命根)
   8. origination/birth (S. jāti; T. skye ba; C. sheng 生)
   9. continuance/maturation (S. sthiti; T. gnas pa; C. zhu 住)
   10. senescence/decay (S. jarā; T. rga ba; C. yi/lao 異/老)
   11. desinence/extinction (S. anityatā; T. mi rtag pa; C. mie/wuchang 滅/無常)
   12. name set (S. nāmakāya; T. ming gi tshogs; C. ming shen 名身)
   13. phrase set (S. padakāya; T. tshig gi tshogs; C. ju shen 句身)
   14. syllable set (S. vyañjanakāya; T. yi ge'i tshogs; C. wen shen 文身)

5. three uncompounded factors (S. asaṃskṛta; T. 'dus ma byas kyi chos; C. wuwei [fa] 無爲[法])
   1. space (S. ākāśa; T. nam mkha'; C. xukong 虛空)
   2. analytical cessation (S. pratisaṃkhyānirodha; T. so sor brtags 'gog pa; C. zemie 擇滅)
   3. nonanalytical suppression (S. apratisaṃkhyānirodha; T. so sor brtags min gyi 'gog pa; C. feizemie 非擇滅)

## EIGHTIES

**eighty secondary marks [of a mahāpuruṣa].** (S. anuvyañjana; T. dpe byad bzang po; C. bashi zhong hao 八十種好)

1. copper-colored nails (S. ātāmranakhaḥ; T. sen mo zangs kyi mdog lta bu; C. zhizhao hongtong xiang/zhizhao chitong se 指爪紅銅相/指爪赤銅色)
2. glossy nails (S. snigdhanakhaḥ; T. sen mo mdog snum pa; C. zhise huaze 指色滑澤)
3. raised nails (S. tuṅganakhaḥ; T. sen mo mtho ba; C. zhizhao gao 指爪高)
4. rounded fingers and toes (S. vṛttāṅguliḥ; T. sor mo rnams zlum pa; C. zhuzhi yuanxiang/zhichang xianyuan 諸指圓相/指長纖圓)
5. tapered fingers and toes (S. anupūrvāṅguliḥ; T. sor mo byin gyis phra ba; C. zhuzhi xirou (xiang)/zhuzhi jianxi 諸指細柔(相)/諸指漸細)
6. full fingers and toes (S. citāṅguliḥ; T. sor mo rnams rgyas pa; C. zhuzhi fengman xiang 諸指豊滿相)
7. veins are not visible (S. nigūḍhaśiraḥ; T. rtsa mi mngon pa; C. maijin bulou 脈筋不露)
8. veins are free from knots (S. nirgranthiśiraḥ; T. rtsa mdud med pa; C. erwu maijie/jinmai wujie 而無脈結/筋脉無結)

9. anklebones do not protrude (S. gūḍhagulphaḥ; T. long bu mi mngon pa; C. zu buxian gu/huai buxian 足不顯骨/踝不現)
10. feet [and hands] do not differ in size (S. aviṣamapādaḥ; T. zhabs mi mnyam pa med pa; C. zu wubuping/shouzu ruyi 足無不平/手足如意)
11. walks with the stride of a lion (S. siṃhavikrāntagāmī; T. seng ge'i stabs su gshegs pa; C. xing ru shizi/weiyi ru shizi 形如獅子/威儀如獅子)
12. walks with the stride of an elephant (S. nāgavikrāntagāmī; T. glang po che'i stabs su gshegs pa; C. xingan ru xiang/jinzhi ru xiangwang 形安如象/進止如象王)
13. walks with the stride of a goose (S. haṃsavikrāntagāmī; T. ngang pa'i stabs su gshegs pa; C. xing ru e/xingfa ru ewang 形如鵝/行法如鵝王)
14. walks with the stride of a bull (S. vṛṣabhavikrāntagāmī; T. khyu mchog gi stabs su gshegs pa; C. xing ru shengqun/jinzhi ru niuwang 形如勝群/進止如牛王)
15. walks turning toward the right side (S. pradakṣiṇāvartagāmī; T. g.yas phyogs su ldog cing gshegs pa; C. xiangyou/huishen gushi bijie youxuan 向右/回身顧視必皆右旋)
16. walks elegantly (S. cārugāmī; T. mdzes par gshegs pa; C. weimiao xiang/xingxiang mei/xingbu yansu 微妙相/行相美/行步嚴肅)
17. walks without swaying (S. avakragāmī; T. mi g.yo bar gshegs pa; C. bu waixie/xingbu duanzheng 不歪邪/行步端正)
18. well-rounded body (S. vṛttagātraḥ; T. sku 'khril bag chags pa; C. shen zhongxi/shen zichi weiyi 身重習/身自持逶迤)
19. cleansed body (S. mṛṣṭagātraḥ; T. sku byi dor byas pa; C. shen guangze ru diaozhuo/guangze ming ligou 身光澤如彫琢/光澤明離垢)
20. well-proportioned body (S. anupūrvagātraḥ; T. sku rim par 'tsham pa; C. shen jubei/shenti xiangcheng 身具備/身體相稱)
21. clean body (S. śucigātraḥ; T. sku gtsang ba; C. shen jiejing/shenti qingjie 身潔淨/身體清潔)
22. supple body (S. mṛdugātraḥ; T. sku 'jam pa; C. shen rouruan 身柔軟)
23. pure body (S. viśuddhagātraḥ; T. sku rnam par dag pa; C. qingjing shen/shen qingjing 清淨身/身清淨)
24. has perfect genitals (S. paripūrṇavyañjanaḥ; T. mtshan yong su rdzogs pa; C. juzu xiang/shen manzu 具足相/身滿足)
25. broad and magnificent frame (S. pṛthucārumaṇḍalagātraḥ; T. sku kho lag yangs shing bzang ba; C. shenzhi qimiao/shen runze/miao guangxia xiangcheng 身肢奇妙/身潤澤/妙廣狹相稱)
26. walks with an even pace (S. samakramaḥ; T. gom pa snyoms pa; C. xingbu zhengzhi 行步正直)
27. youthful body (S. sukumāragātraḥ; T. sku shin tu gzhon mdog can; C. shense nenruan/rongyan qimiao changruo shaonian 身色嫩軟/容顏奇妙常若少年)
28. unimpaired body (S. adīnagātraḥ; T. sku zhum pa med pa; C. shen wu tuiqu/shenti buqu 身無退屈/身體不曲)
29. broad body (S. unnatagātraḥ; T. sku rgyas pa; C. shen fengman/ruyi fengman 身豐滿/如意豐滿)
30. firm body (S. susaṃhitagātraḥ; T. sku shin tu grims pa; C. shenzhi anshang buqing/zhuchu wu nengdong zhe/shenzhi jianshi 身肢安上不傾/住處無能動者/身肢堅實)
31. limbs and features are well-proportioned (S. suvibhaktāṅgapratyaṅgaḥ; T. yan lag dang nying lag shin tu rnam par 'byed pa; C. zhijie junping/gujie ru gousuo 支節均平/骨節如鉤鎖)
32. sight is free from disease and clear (S. vitimiraviśuddhālokaḥ; T. gzigs pa rab rib med cing rnam par dag pa; C. mu qingjing wu buming 目清淨無不明)
33. round belly (S. vṛttakukṣiḥ; T. dku zlum pa; C. fu yuan 復圓)
34. clean belly (S. mṛṣṭakukṣiḥ; T. dku skabs phyin pa; C. shen wu buxiu 身無不修)
35. belly is free from defects (S. abhugnakukṣiḥ; T. dku ma rnyongs pa; C. fu wu aotu 服無凹凸)
36. flat belly (S. kṣāmodaraḥ; T. phyal phyang nge ba; C. fu yuanxiang 復圓相)
37. deep navel (S. gaṃbhīranābhiḥ; T. lte ba zab pa; C. qi shen/qi shen yuanhao 臍深/臍深圓好)
38. navel turns to the right (S. pradakṣiṇāvartanābhiḥ; T. lte ba g.yas phyogs su 'khyil ba; C. qi youxuan 臍右旋)
39. beautiful from all sides (S. samantaprāsādikaḥ; T. kun nas mdzes pa; C. guan wuyan zu 觀無厭足)
40. conduct is pure (S. śucisamācāraḥ; T. kun tu spyod pa gtsang ba; C. xingshi jiejing 行事潔淨)
41. body has no black moles (S. vyapagatatilakakālagātraḥ; T. sku la sme ba dang gnag bag med pa; C. shen wu zhidian 身無痣點)
42. hands are soft like cotton (S. tūlasadṛśasukumārapāṇiḥ; T. phyag shing bal ltar shin tu 'jam pa; C. shouruan ru mian 手軟如綿)
43. lustrous lines on his hands (S. snigdhapāṇilekhaḥ; T. phyag gi ri mo mdangs yod pa; C. shouwen juguang[se] 手文具光[色])
44. deep lines on his hands (S. gambhīrapāṇilekhaḥ; T. phyag gi ri mo zab pa; C. shouwen sheshen 手文甚深)
45. long lines on his hands (S. āyatapāṇilekhaḥ; phyag gi ri mo ring ba; C. shouwen chang 手文長)
46. face is not too long (S. nātyāyatavadanaḥ; T. shal ha cang yang mi ring ba; C. mian bu changda 面不長大)
47. lips the color of a bimba fruit (S. bimboṣṭhi; T. mchu bim ba ltar dmar ba; C. chun hong ru xiangxiangsi guo 唇紅如相想思果)
48. supple tongue (S. mṛdujihvaḥ; T. ljags mnyen pa; C. she ruanmei/she meiruan 舌軟美/舌美軟)
49. slender tongue (S. tanujihvaḥ; T. ljags srab pa; C. she ruan/she boguang 舌軟/舌薄廣)

50. red tongue (S. raktajihvaḥ; T. ljags dmar ba; C. she xianhong/she sechi 舌鮮紅/舌色赤)
51. voice resonates like an elephant and like thunder (S. gajagarjitajīmūtaghoṣaḥ; T. glang po che'i nga ro dang 'brug gi sgra dang ldan pa; C. ju xiangyu leiyin/xiangsheng longyin 具象語雷音/象聲龍音)
52. sweet, pleasing, and gentle voice (S. madhuracārumañjusvaraḥ; T. gsung snyan cing mnyen la 'jam pa; C. yinyun meihao/yinyun hechang 音韻美好/音韻和暢)
53. round canine teeth (S. vṛttadaṃṣṭraḥ; T. mche ba zlum pa; C. ya yuan 牙圓)
54. sharp canine teeth (S. tīkṣṇadaṃṣṭraḥ; T. mche ba rno ba; C. ya kuaili 牙快利)
55. white canine teeth (S. śukladaṃṣṭraḥ; T. mche ba dkar ba; C. ya bai 牙白)
56. even canine teeth (S. samadaṃṣṭraḥ; T. mche ba mnyam pa; C. ya fang/ya pingzheng 牙方/牙平正)
57. tapered canine teeth (S. anupūrvadaṃṣṭraḥ; T. mche ba byin gyis phra ba; C. ya jianxi 牙漸細)
58. high nose (S. tuṅganāsaḥ; T. shangs mtho ba; C. bi gao/bikong buxian 鼻高/鼻孔不現)
59. clean nose (S. śucināsaḥ; T. shangs gtsang pa; C. bi qingjing 鼻清淨)
60. clear eyes (S. viśuddhanetraḥ; T. spyan rnam par dag pa; C. mu qingjing 目清淨)
61. wide eyes (S. viśālanetraḥ; T. spyan yangs pa; C. mu guang 目廣)
62. thick eyelashes (S. citrapakṣmāḥ; T. rdzi ma stug pa; C. yanmao meihao 眼毛美好)
63. the iris and sclera of his eyes contrast like the petals and stamen of a blue lotus (S. sitāsitakamaladalaśakalanayanaḥ; T. spyan dkar nag 'byes shing pad ma'i 'dab ma'i mdangs pa lta bu; C. mu heibai fenqingmei ru lianhua xingxiang/mu heibai mei ru lianhua xingxiang 目黑白分清美如蓮華形相/目黑白美如蓮華形相)
64. long eyebrows [like a young crescent moon] (S. āyatabhrūḥ; T. smin tshugs ring ba; C. meimao xiuchang/mei ru chuyue 眉毛修長/眉如初月)
65. soft eyebrows (S. ślakṣṇabhrūḥ; T. smin ma 'jam pa; C. shuangmei nenruan 雙眉嫩軟)
66. eyebrows with even hairs (S. samaromabhrūḥ; T. smin ma spu mnyam pa; C. meimao pingqi 眉毛平齊)
67. lustrous eyebrows (S. snigdhabhrūḥ; T. smin ma snum pa; C. meimao run 眉毛潤)
68. full and long ears (pīnāyatakarṇaḥ; T. snyan shal stug cing ring ba; C. er hou xiuchang 耳厚修長)
69. even ears (S. samakarṇaḥ; T. snyan mnyam pa; C. er qiping 耳齊平)
70. unimpaired sense of hearing (S. anupahatakarṇendriyaḥ; T. snyan gyi dbang po ma nyams pa; C. ergen pingjun 耳根平均)
71. well-developed forehead (S. supariṇatalalāṭaḥ; T. dpral ba legs par dbyes pa; C. e guang yuanman 額廣圓滿)
72. broad forehead (S. pṛthulalāṭaḥ; T. dpral ba dbyes che ba; C. e kuan pingzheng 額寬平正)
73. large head (S. suparipūrṇa-uttamāṅgaḥ; T. dbu shin tu rgyas pa; C. tou ru motuona guo 頭如摩陀那果)
74. hair on the head is black as a bee (S. bhramarasadṛśakeśaḥ; T. dbu skra bung ba ltar gnag pa; C. fa se ganqing ru fengwang 髮色紺青如蜂王)
75. thick hair on the head (S. citakeśaḥ; T. dbu skra stug pa; C. fa mei 髮美)
76. soft hair on the head (S. ślakṣṇakeśaḥ; T. dbu skra 'jam pa; C. fa nenruan 髮嫩軟)
77. hair on the head is not disheveled (S. asaṃlulitakeśaḥ; T. dbu skra ma 'dzings pa; C. fa buluan 髮不亂)
78. hair on the head is not rough (S. aparuṣakeśaḥ; T. dbu skra mi gshor ba; C. shoufa zhengqi 首髮整齊)
79. fragrant hair on the head (S. surabhikeśaḥ; T. dbu skra dri zhim pa; C. shoufa xiangfu 首髮香馥)
80. hands and feet are adorned with such auspicious symbols as the śrīvatsa [endless knot]; svastika [swastika]; and nandyāvarta [elaborated swastika form] (S. śrīvatsasvastikanandyāvartalalitapāṇipādaḥ; T. phyags dang zhabs dpal gyi be'u dang bkra shis g.yung drung 'khyil bas brgyan pa; C. shouzu youru xiangdu jiangu/shouzu jixiang dexiang miaohao juzu 手足猶如祥犢堅固/手足吉祥德相妙好具足)

**eighty-two dhammas of the *Sthaviranikāya/Theravāda school**.

1. twenty-eight material factors (P. rūpa)
   1. four primary elements (P. mahābhūta)
      1. earth/solidity (P. paṭhavī[dhātu] )
      2. water/cohesion (P. āpo[dhātu])
      3. fire/heat (P. tejo[dhātu])
      4. air/mobility (P. vāyo[dhātu])
   2. twenty-four types of derived materiality (P. upādārūpa)
      1. eye/visual faculty (P. cakkhu)
      2. ear/auditory faculty (P. sota)
      3. nose/olfactory faculty (P. ghāna)
      4. tongue/gustatory faculty (P. jivhā)
      5. body/tactile faculty (P. kāya)
      6. visual objects (P. rūpa)
      7. sound (P. sadda)
      8. scent (P. gandha)
      9. flavor (P. rasa)
      10. femininity (P. itthindrya)
      11. masculinity (P. purisindriya)
      12. [physical] vitality/life-force (P. jīvita, [rūpa]jīvitindriya)
      13. heart [as the physical basis of mentality] (P. hadaya [vatthu])
      14. bodily intimation (P. kāyaviññatti)
      15. verbal intimation (P. vacīviññatti)
      16. limitation/space element (P. pariccheda, ākāsadhātu)

        17. lightness/buoyancy (P. lahutā)
        18. malleability (P. mudutā)
        19. wieldiness (P. kammaññatā)
        20. birth/development (P. upacaya)
        21. continuity (P. santati)
        22. senescence/decay (P. jaratā)
        23. desinence/extinction/impermanence (P. aniccatā)
        24. nutriment (P. āhāra)
2. mind (citta)
    1. mind/consciousness/mentality (P. citta, viññāṇa, manas)
3. fifty-two mental concomitants (P. cetasika)
    1. thirteen morally indeterminate (P. avyākata)
        1. seven general/universal (P. sabbacittasādhāraṇa)
            1. contact (P. phassa)
            2. sensation (P. vedanā)
            3. perception (P. saññā)
            4. intention (P. cetanā)
            5. one-pointedness (P. ekaggatā)
            6. [mental] vitality/life-force (P. jīvita, [nama] jīvitindriya)
            7. attention (P. manasikāra)
        2. six secondary (P. pakiṇṇaka)
            1. applied thought (P. vittaka)
            2. sustained thought (P. vicāra)
            3. determination/resolution (P. adhimokkha)
            4. energy (P. viriya)
            5. rapture (P. pīti)
            6. zeal (P. chanda)
    2. twenty-five wholesome (P. kusala)
        1. nineteen sobhanasādhāraṇa (universal splendid mental factors)
            1. faith/confidence (P. saddhā)
            2. mindfulness (P. sati)
            3. shame/propriety/decency (P. hiri)
            4. fear of blame/modesty (P. ottappa)
            5. nongreed (P. alobha)
            6. nonhatred (P. adosa)
            7. equanimity (P. tatramajjhattatā)
            8. tranquillity of mental body (P. kāyapassaddhi)
            9. tranquillity of consciousness (P. cittapassaddhi)
            10. lightness of mental body (P. kāyalahutā)
            11. lightness of consciousness (P. cittalahutā)
            12. malleability of mental body (P. kāyamudutā)
            13. malleability of consciousness (P. cittamudutā)
            14. wieldiness of mental body (P. kāyakammaññatā)
            15. wieldiness of consciousness (P. cittakammaññatā)
            16. proficiency of mental body (P. kāyapāguññatā)
            17. proficiency of consciousness (P. cittapāguññatā)
            18. rectitude of mental body (P. kāyujjukatā)
            19. rectitude of consciousness (P. cittujjukatā)
        2. three abstinences (virati)
            1. abstinence from physical misconduct (P. kāyaduccaritavirati); alt. right action (P. sammākammanta)
            2. abstinence from verbal misconduct (P. vacīduccaritavirati); alt. right speech (P. sammāvācā)
            3. abstinence from mental misconduct (P. manoduccaritavirati); alt. abstinence from wrong livelihood (P. ājīvaduccaritavirati), viz. right livelihood (P. sammājīva)
        3. two illimitables (appamañña)
            1. compassion (P. karuṇā)
            2. empathetic joy (P. muditā)
        4. one wisdom faculty (P. paññindriya)
            1. wisdom (P. paññā)
    3. fourteen unwholesome (P. akusala)
        1. delusion (P. moha)
        2. lack of shame or lack of decency (P. ahirika)
        3. lack of fear of blame or lack of modesty (P. anottappa)
        4. restlessness (P. uddhacca)
        5. greed (P. lobha)
        6. wrong view (P. diṭṭhi)
        7. pride/conceit (P. māna)
        8. hatred (P. dosa)
        9. envy (P. issā)
        10. selfishness/stinginess (P. macchariya)
        11. worry/remorse (P. kukkucca)
        12. sloth (P. thīna)
        13. torpor (P. middha)
        14. skeptical doubt (P. vicikicchā)
4. uncompounded (P. asaṅkhata)
    1. nirvāṇa (P. nibbāna)

**eighty-four mahāsiddhas.** (T. grub thob brgyad bcu rtsa bzhi)

*When the Tibetan is not provided, the Tibetan typically transliterates the Indic name.*

1. Lūyipa (T. Nya'i rgyu ma za ba)
2. Līlapa (T. Sgeg pa)
3. Virūpa
4. Ḍombipa
5. Śavaripa
6. Saraha (T. Mda' snun)
7. Kankaripa
8. Mīnapa (T. Nya bo pa)
9. Gorakṣa (T. Ba glang bsrung)
10. Caurāṅgi (T. Chom rkun gyu yan lag)
11. Vīnapa (T. Pi vang pa)
12. Śāntipa
13. Tantipa (T. Thags mkhan)
14. Camaripa (T. Lham mkhan)
15. Khaḍgapa (T. Ral gri pa)
16. Nāgārjuna (T. Klu sgrub)
17. Kāṇhapa (T. Nag po spyod pa)
18. Karṇaripa/Āryadeva ('Phags pa lha)
19. Thagnapa (T. Rdzun smra ba)
20. Nāropa (T. Rtsa bshad pa)
21. Śalipa (T. Spyan ki pa)

22. Tilopa (T. Snum pa)
23. Catrapa
24. Bhadrapa (T. Bzang po)
25. Dhukhandi (T. Gnyis gcig tu byed pa)
26. Ajokipa (T. Le lo can)
27. Kalapa (T. Smyon pa)
28. Dhombipa (T. Khrus khan)
29. Kaṅkana (T. Gdu bu can)
30. Kambala (T. Lwa ba pa)
31. Ṭeṅgipa (T. ’Bras rdung ba)
32. Bhandhepa (T. Nor la ’dzin pa)
33. Tandhepa (T. Cho lo pa)
34. Kukkuripa
35. Kucipa (T. Ltag lba can)
36. Dharmapa (T. Thos pa’i shes rab bya ba)
37. Mahipa (T. Ngar rgyal can)
38. Acinta (T. Bsam mi khyab pa)
39. Babhahi (T. Chu las ’o ma len)
40. Nalina (T. Pad ma’i rtsa ba)
41. Bhusuku (T. Zhi lha)
42. Indrabhūti (T. Dbang po’i blo)
43. Mekopa
44. Koṭali (T. Tog rtse zhabs)
45. Kaṃparipa (T. Mgar pa)
46. Jālandhari (T. Dra ba ’dzin pa)
47. Rāhula
48. Dharmapa (T. Chos pa)
49. Dhokaripa (T. Rdo ka ri)
50. Medhina (T. Thang lo pa)
51. Paṅkaja (T. ’Dam skyes)
52. Ghaṇḍhapa (T. Dril pu pa)
53. Yogipa
54. Caluki
55. Gorura (T. Bya ba)
56. Lucika
57. Niguṇa (T. Yon tan med pa)
58. Jayānanda (T. Rgyal ba mtha’ med)
59. Pacari (T. ’Khur ba ’tsong ba)
60. Campaka
61. Bhikṣana (T. So gnyis pa)
62. Telopa (T. Mar nag ’tshong mkhan)
63. Kumaripa (T. Rdza mkhan)
64. Caparipa
65. Maṇibhadrā
66. Mekhalā
67. Kanakhalā
68. Kalakala (T. Ku co can)
69. Kantali (T. Tshem bu pa)
70. Dhahuli (T. Rtswa thag can)
71. Udheli (T. Phur pa)
72. Kapalapa (T. Thod pa can)
73. Kirava (T. Rnam rtog spang ba)
74. Sakara (T. Mtsho skyes)
75. Sarvabhakṣa (T. Thams cad za ba)
76. Nāgabodhi (T. Klu’i byang chub)
77. Dārika (T. Smad ’tshong can)
78. Putali (T. Rgyan slang ba)
79. Panaha (T. Mchil lham can)
80. Kokali (T. Ko la la’i skad du chags)
81. Anaṅga
82. Lakṣmīnkarā (Legs smin kara)
83. Samudra (T. Rgya mtsho nas nor bu len mkhan)
84. Vyali

## HUNDREDS

**one-hundred dharmas of the Yogācāra school**. (S. śatadharma; T. chos brgya; C. baifa 百法)

1. eight consciousnesses (S. vijñāna; T. rnam par shes pa; C. xinfa/shi 心法/識)
   1. visual consciousness (S. cakṣurvijñāna; T. mig gi rnam par shes pa; C. yanshi 眼識)
   2. auditory consciousness (S. śrotravijñāna; T. rna ba’i rnam shes pa; C. ershi 耳識)
   3. olfactory consciousness (S. ghrāṇavijñāna; T. sna’i rnam par shes pa; C. bishi 鼻識)
   4. gustatory consciousness (S. jihvāvijñāna; T. lce’i rnam par shes pa; C. sheshi 舌識)
   5. tactile consciousness (S. kāyavijñāna; T. lus kyi rnam par shes pa; C. shenshi 身識)
   6. mental consciousness (S. manovijñāna; T. yid kyi rnam par shes pa; C. yishi 意識)
   7. afflicted mental consciousness (S. kliṣṭamanas; T. nyon yid rnam par shes pa; C. mona shi 末那識)
   8. storehouse consciousness (S. ālayavijñāna; T. kun gzhi rnam shes pa; C. alaiye shi 阿賴耶識)
2. fifty-one mental concomitants (S. caitta; T. sem byung; C. xin suoyou fa 心所有法)
   1. five omnipresent mental functions (S. sarvatraga; T. kun ’gro; C. bianxing[xinsuo] 遍行[心所])
      1. sensation (S. vedanā; T. tshor ba; C. shou 受)
      2. perception (S. saṃjñā; T. ’du shes; C. xiang 想)
      3. volition (S. cetanā; T. sems pa; C. si 思)
      4. attention (S. manaskāra; T. yid la byed pa; C. zuoyi 作意)
      5. sensory contact (S. sparśa; T. reg pa; C. chu 觸)
   2. five specific mental concomitants (S. viniyata; T. yul nges; C. biejing[xinsuo] 别境[心所])
      1. zeal/desire-to-act (S. chanda; T. ’dun pa; C. yu 欲)
      2. determination (S. adhimokṣa; T. mos pa; C. shengjie 勝解)
      3. mindfulness/recollection/memory (S. smṛti; T. dran pa; C. nian 念)
      4. concentration (S. samādhi; T. ting nge ’dzin; C. ding 定)
      5. wisdom/cognition (S. prajñā; T. shes rab; C. hui 慧)
   3. eleven wholesome mental comcomitants (S. kuśala; T. dge ba; C. shan 善)

1. faith (S. śraddhā; T. dad pa; C. xin 信)
2. shame/decency/propriety (S. hrī; T. ngo tsha shes pa; C. can 慚)
3. fear of blame/modesty (S. apatrāpya; T. khrel yod pa; C. kui 愧)
4. lack of craving (S. alobha; T. ma chags pa; C. wu tan 無貪)
5. lack of ill-will (S. adveṣa; T. zhe sdang med pa; C. wu chen 無瞋)
6. lack of delusion (S. amoha; T. gti mug med pa; C. wu chi 無癡)
7. vigor (S. vīrya; T. brtson 'grus; C. qin/jingjin 勤/精進)
8. tranquillity/serenity (S. praśrabdhi; T. shin tu sbyangs pa; C. [qing] an [輕]安)
9. vigilance (S. apramāda; T. bag yod pa; C. bu fangyi 不放逸)
10. equanimity (S. upekṣā; T. btang snyoms; C. xingshe 行捨)
11. absence of harmful intentions (S. avihiṃsā; T. rnam par mi 'tshe ba; C. bu hai 不害)

4. six root afflictions (S. mūlakleśa; T. rtsa nyon; C. genben fannao 根本煩惱)
   1. sensuality/lust (S. rāga; T. 'dod chags; C. tan 貪)
   2. anger (S. pratigha; T. khong khro; C. chen 瞋)
   3. ignorance (S. avidyā; T. ma rig pa; C. chi/wuming 癡/無明)
   4. pride (S. māna; T. nga rgyal; C. man 慢)
   5. skeptical doubt (S. vicikitsā; T. the tshom; C. yi 疑)
   6. wrong views (S. dṛṣṭi; T. lta ba nyon mongs can; C. jian 見)
5. twenty secondary afflictions (S. upakleśa; T. nye nyon; C. sui fannao 隨煩惱)
   1. anger (S. krodha; T. khro ba; C. fen 忿)
   2. resentment (S. upanāha; T. 'khon 'dzin; C. hen 恨)
   3. vexation/maliciousness (S. pradāśa; T. 'tshig pa; C. nao 惱)
   4. disparagement/hypocrisy (S. mrakṣa; T. 'chab pa; C. fu 覆)
   5. deception (S. māyā; T. sgyu; C. kuang 誑)
   6. deceit (S. śāṭhya; T. g.yo; C. chan 諂)
   7. arrogance (S. mada; T. rgyags pa; C. jiao 憍)
   8. hostility (S. vihiṃsā; T. rnam par 'tshe ba; C. hai 害)
   9. envy (S. īrṣyā; T. phrag dog; C. ji 嫉)
   10. selfishness/stinginess (S. mātsarya; T. ser sna; C. qian 慳)
   11. lack of shame/decency/propriety (S. āhrīkya; T. ngo tsha med pa; C. wucan 無慚)
   12. lack of fear of blame/lack of modesty (S. anapatrāpya; T. khrel med pa; C. wukui 無愧)
   13. lack of faith (S. āśraddhya; T. ma dad pa; C. bu xin 不信)
   14. lassitude (S. kausīdya; T. le lo; C. xiedai 懈怠)
   15. heedlessness (S. pramāda; T. bag med pa; C. fangyi 放逸)
   16. sloth (S. styāna; T. rmugs pa; C. hunchen 惛沈)
   17. restlessness (S. auddhatya; T. rgod pa; C. diaoju 掉舉)
   18. forgetfulness (S. muṣitasmṛtitā; T. brjed nges pa; C. shinian 失念)
   19. lack of circumspection (S. asaṃprajanya; T. shes bzhin ma yin pa; C. bu zhengzhi 不正知)
   20. distraction (S. vikṣepa; T. rnam par g.yeng ba; C. sanluan 散亂)
6. four indeterminate factors (S. aniyata; T. gzhan 'gyur; C. buding [fa] 不定[法])
   1. torpor/drowsiness (S. middha; T. gnyid; C. shuimian 睡眠)
   2. worry/remorse (S. kaukṛtya; T. 'gyod pa; C. ezuo 惡作)
   3. applied thought (S. vitarka; T. rtog pa; C. xun 尋)
   4. sustained thought (S. vicāra; T. dpyod pa; C. si 伺)

3. eleven material factors (S. rūpa; T. gzugs; C. shiyi sefa 色法)
   1. visual faculty (S. cakṣurindriya; T. mig gi dbang po; C. yangen 眼根)
   2. auditory faculty (S. śrotrendriya; T. rna ba'i dbang po; C. ergen 耳根)
   3. olfactory faculty (S. ghrāṇendriya; T. sna'i dbang po; C. bigen 鼻根)
   4. gustatory faculty (S. jihvendriya; T. lce'i dbang po; C. shegen 舌根)
   5. tactile faculty (S. kāyendriya; T. lus kyi dbang po; C. shengen 身根)
   6. visual objects (S. rūpa; T. gzugs; C. se 色)
   7. sound (S. śabda; T. sgra; C. sheng 聲)
   8. scent (S. gandha; T. dri; C. xiang 香)
   9. flavor (S. rasa; T. ro; C. mei 味)
   10. contact (S. spraṣṭavya; T. reg bya; C. chu 觸)
   11. materiality associated with the sphere of mental factors [e.g.; materiality generated in meditative states] (S. dharmāyatanarūpa; T. chos kyi skye mched pa'i gzugs; C. fachu suoshe se 法處所攝色)
4. twenty-four conditioned forces dissociated from thought (S. cittaviprayuktasaṃskāra; T. ldan min 'du byed; C. xin bu xiangying xing fa 心不相應行法)
   1. possession (S. prāpti; T. 'thob pa; C. de 得)
   2. vitality (S. jīvitendriya; T. srog gi dbang po; C. ming gen 命根)
   3. homogeneity (S. nikāyasabhāga; T. rigs 'thun pa; C. zhong tongfen 衆同分)
   4. nature of ordinary people (S. pṛthagjanatva; T. so so skye bo nyid; C. yisheng xing 異生性)
   5. equipoise of nonperception (S. asaṃjñāsamāpatti; T. 'du shes med pa'i snyoms 'jug; C. wuxiang ding 無想定)

6. equipoise of cessation (S. nirodhasamāpatti; T. 'gog pa'i snyoms 'jug; C. mie jin ding 滅盡定)
7. state of nonperception (S. āsaṃjñika; T. 'du shes med pa; C. wuxiang guo/wuxiang bao/wuxiang shi 無想果/無想報/無想事)
8. name set (S. nāmakāya; T. ming gi tshogs; C. ming shen 名身)
9. phrase set (S. padakāya; T. tshig gi tshogs; C. ju shen 句身)
10. syllable set (S. vyañjanakāya; T. yi ge'i tshogs; C. wen shen 文身)
11. origination/birth (S. jāti; T. skye ba; C. sheng 生)
12. continuance/maturation (S. sthiti; T. gnas pa; C. zhu 住)
13. senescence/decay (S. jarā; T. rga ba; C. yi/lao 異/老)
14. desinence/extinction (S. anityatā; T. mi rtag pa; C. mie/wuchang 滅/無常)
15. continuity (S. pravṛtti; T. 'jug pa; C. liuzhuan 流轉)
16. distinction (S. pratiniyama; T. so sor nges pa; C. dingyi 定異)
17. association (S. yoga; T. 'byor 'grel; C. xiangying 相應)
18. instantaneity (S. jāva; T. 'gyogs pa; C. shisu 勢速)
19. order (S. anukrama; T. go rim; C. cidi 次第)
20. direction/area (S. deśa; T. yul; C. fang 方)
21. time (S. kāla; T. dus; C. shi 時)
22. number (S. saṃkhyā; T. grangs; C. shu 數)
23. complete assemblage [of the causes and conditions that lead to the production of dharmas] (S. sāmagrī; T. tshogs pa; C. hehe xing 和合性)
24. incomplete assemblage (S. asāmagrī; T. ma tshogs pa; C. bu hehe xing 不和合性)

5. six uncompounded factors (S. asaṃskṛtadharma; T. 'dus ma byas kyi chos; C. wuwei fa 無爲法)
   1. space (S. ākāśa; T. nam mkha'; C. xukong 虛空)
   2. analytical cessation (S. pratisaṃkhyānirodha; T. so sor brtags 'gog pa; C. zemie 擇滅)
   3. nonanalytical suppression (S. apratisaṃkhyānirodha; T. so sor brtags min gyi 'gog pa; C. feizemie 非擇滅)
   4. motionlessness (S. āniñjya; T. mi g.yo ba; C. budong 不動)
   5. cessation of perception and sensation (S. saṃjñāvedayitanirodha; T. 'du shes dang tshor ba 'gog pa; C. xiangshou mie 想受滅)
   6. suchness (S. tathatā; Tib. de bzhin nyid; C. zhenru 眞如)

# Chinese Cross-References

## A

**Abanti [guo]** 阿般提[國]. *See* Avanti

**abi diyu** 阿鼻地獄. *See* avīci

**abiluoti** 阿比羅提. *See* abhirati

**Achamo pusa jing** 阿差末菩薩經. *See* Akṣayamatinirdeśa

**Achufo** 阿閦佛. *See* Akṣobhya

**Achu foguo jing** 阿閦佛國經. *See* Akṣobhyatathāgatasyavyūha

**Adiquduo** 阿地瞿多. *See* Atikūṭa

**afudi** 阿嚩底. *See* avadhūtī

**ahan jing** 阿含經. *See* āgama

**ai** 愛. *See* tṛṣṇā

**alaiyeshi** 阿賴耶識. *See* ālayavijñāna

**[a]lanruo** [阿]蘭若. *See* āraṇya

**Alizha jing** 阿梨吒經. *See* Alagaddūpamasutta

**aluohan** 阿羅漢. *See* arhat

**aluohan xiang** 阿羅漢向. *See* arhatpratipannaka

**Aluoluojialan** 阿羅邏迦蘭. *See* Ārāḍa Kālāma

**Amituo fo** 阿彌陀佛. *See* Amitābha

**Amituo jing** 阿彌陀經. *See* Amitābhasūtra

**amoluo shi** 阿摩羅識. *See* amalavijñāna

**anahan** 阿那含. *See* anāgāmin

**Analü** 阿那律. *See* Aniruddha

**Anan[tuo]** 阿難[陀]. *See* Ānanda

**Anhui** 安慧. *See* Sthiramati

**anju** 安居. *See* ango or varṣā

**an mani bami hong** 唵嘛呢叭彌吽. *See* oṃ maṇi padme hūṃ

**Annabannanian** 安那般那念. *See* Ānāpānsatisutta

**anouduoluo sanmiao sanputi** 阿耨多羅三藐三菩提. *See* anuttarasamyaksaṃbodhi

**Anouyi jing** 阿㝹夷經. *See* Pāṭikasutta

**Anpoluonü** 菴婆羅女. *See* Āmrapālī

**anshi** 庵室. *See* anjitsu

**anwei yin** 安慰印. *See* vitarkamudrā

**Anwen** 安穩. *See* Kṣemā

**Anzhu dishen** 安住地神. *See* Sthāvarā

**apidamo** 阿毘達磨. *See* Abhidharma

**apidamo dalunshi** 阿毘達磨大論師. *See* ābhidharmika

**Apidamo dapiposha lun** 阿毘達磨大毘婆沙論. *See* Abhidharmamahāvibhāṣā

**Apidamo fayun zu lun** 阿毘達磨法蘊足論. *See* Abhidharmadharmaskandha[pādaśāstra], Dharmaskandha [pādaśāstra]

**Apidamo fazhi lun** 阿毘達磨發智論. *See* Abhidharmajñānaprasthāna, Jñānaprasthāna

**Apidamo Jieshen zu lun** 阿毘達磨界身足論. *See* Abhidharmadhātukāya[pādaśāstra], Dhātukāya[pādaśāstra]

**Apidamo jushe lun** 阿毘達磨俱舍論. *See* Abhidharmakośabhāṣya

**Apitan xin lun** 阿毘曇心論. *See* *Abhidharmahṛdaya

**apotuona** 阿波陀那. *See* avadāna

**Aruojiaochenru** 阿若憍陳如. *See* Ājñātakauṇḍinya

**asengqi** 阿僧祇. *See* asaṃkhya

**asengqi jie** 阿僧祇劫. *See* asaṃkhyeyakalpa

**Asheli** 阿闍梨. *See* ācārya

**Asheshi wang** 阿闍世王. *See* Ajātaśatru

**Ashuoshi** 阿說示. *See* Aśvajit

**Asituo** 阿私陀. *See* Asita

**atuona shi** 阿陀那識. *See* ādānavijñāna

**aweishe** 阿尾奢. *See* āveśa

**axiuluo** 阿修羅. *See* asura

**Ayiduo** 阿逸多. *See* Ajita

**Ayu wang** 阿育王. *See* Aśoka

**Ayu wang zhuan** 阿育王傳. *See* Aśokāvadāna

## B

**babu** 八不. *See* AṢṬĀNTA, EIGHT NEGATIONS

**Bacheng jing** 八城經. *See* AṬṬHAKANĀGARASUTTA

**Bacuo [guo]** 跋蹉[國]. *See* VATSĀ

**Ba da pusa** 八大菩薩. *See* AṢṬAMAHOPAPUTRA

**bai** 白. *See* JÑAPTI

**baihao** 白毫. *See* ŪRṆĀKEŚA

**baijiemo** 白羯磨. *See* KARMAVĀCANĀ

**Baijing** 白淨. *See* ŚVETAKETU

**bailianhua** 白蓮華. *See* PUṆḌARĪKA

**Bai lun** [alt. Bo lun] 百論. *See* *ŚATAŚĀSTRA

**Baisangaifoding** 白傘蓋佛頂. *See* SITĀTAPATRĀ

**Baiying** 白英. *See* ŚVETAKETU

**ba jietuo** 八解脫. *See* AṢṬAVIMOKṢA

**baku** 八苦. *See* DUḤKHA

**ban jiafuzuo** 半跏趺坐. *See* ARDHAPARYAṄKA, ARDHAPADMĀSANA

**banjia siwei** 半跏思惟. *See* MAITREYĀSANA

**ban lianhua zuo** 半蓮華坐. *See* ARDHAPADMĀSANA, ARDHAPARYAṄKA

**banniepan** 般涅槃. *See* PARINIRVĀṆA

**Bantuojia** 半託迦. *See* PANTHAKA

**Banzhou sanmei jing** 般舟三昧經. *See* PRATYUTPANNABUDDHASAṂMUKHĀVASTHITASAMĀDHISŪTRA

**baobu** 寶部. *See* RATNAKULA

**baoliu** 暴流. *See* OGHA

**baoping guanding** 寶瓶灌頂. *See* KALAŚĀBHIṢEKA

**baoshen** 報身. *See* SAṂBHOGAKĀYA

**Baosheng rulai** 寶生如來. *See* RATNASAṂBHAVA

**Baoshou pusa** 寶手菩薩. *See* RATNAPĀṆI

**Baoxingwang zheng lun** 寶行王正論. *See* RATNĀVALĪ

**Baoyun jing** 寶雲經. *See* RATNAMEGHASŪTRA

**Baqizi** 跋耆子. *See* VṚJIPUTRAKA

**Bati** 跋提. *See* BHADDIYA-KĀḶIGODHĀPUTTA

**Batuoboluo** 跋陀波羅. *See* BHADRAPĀLA

**Batuo Juntuoluojuyiguo** 拔陀軍陀羅拘夷國. *See* BHADDĀ-KUṆḌALAKESĀ

**Batuolou zunzhe** 跋陀羅尊者. *See* BHADRA

**Batuoluo Jiabeiliye** 跋陀羅迦卑梨耶. *See* BHADRA-KAPILĀNĪ

**bazhaijie** 八齋戒. *See* AṢṬĀṄGASAMANVĀGATAṂ UPAVĀSAṂ

**bazhengdao** 八正道. *See* ĀRYĀṢṬĀṄGAMĀRGA

**bei** 悲. *See* KARUṆĀ

**Beihua jing** 悲華經. *See* KARUṆĀPUṆḌARĪKA

**beijia** 被甲. *See* SAṂNĀHA

**Beijuluzhou** 北俱盧洲. *See* UTTARAKURU

**benchu fo** 本初佛. *See* ĀDIBUDDHA

**Benmen** 本門. *See* HONMON

**bensheng jing** 本生經. *See* JĀTAKA

**benshi** 本識. *See* MŪLAVIJÑĀNA, ĀLAYAVIJÑĀNA

**bensi** 本寺. *See* PONSA

**benxing jing** 本性淨. *See* PRAKṚTIVIŚUDDHI

**benxing zhu zhongxing** 本性住種性. *See* PRAKṚTISTHAGOTRA

**benyuan** 本願. *See* PŪRVAPRAṆIDHĀNA

**bi'an** 彼岸. *See* PĀRA

**bian** 遍. *See* VYĀPTI

**biancai** 辯才. *See* PRATIBHĀNA

**Biancaitian** 辯才天. *See* SARASVATĪ, SHICHIFUKUJIN

**bianchu** 遍處. *See* KASIṆA

**bianjian** 邊見. *See* ANTAGRĀHADṚṢṬI

**bianjing tian** 遍淨天. *See* ŚUBHAKṚTSNA

**bianji suozhi xing** 遍計所執性. *See* PARIKALPITA

**bianxing** 遍行. *See* SARVATRAGA

**bianxing yin** 遍行因. *See* SARVATRAGAHETU

**bianyi shengsi** 變易生死. *See* PARIṆĀMIKAJARĀMARAṆA

**bianzhi** 遍至. *See* VYĀPTI

**Bianzhongbian lun** 辯中邊論. *See* MADHYĀNTAVIBHĀGA

**bichu** 鼻處. *See* GHRĀṆĀYATANA

**biejietuo lüyi** 別解脫律儀. *See* PRĀTIMOKṢASAṂVARA

**biejing [xinsuo]** 別境[心所]. *See* VINIYATA

**biexiang sanguan** 別相三觀. *See* SANGUAN

**biezhu** 別住. *See* PARIVĀSA

**bigen** 鼻根. *See* GHRĀṆENDRIYA

**biliang** 比量. *See* ANUMĀṆA

**Bilingqie Pocuo** 畢陵伽婆蹉. *See* PILINDAVATSA

**binchu** 擯出. *See* NĀŚANĪYA

**Bintoulu Poluoduo zunzhe** 賓頭盧跋羅墮尊者. *See* PIṆḌOLA-BHĀRADVĀJA

**biqiu** 比丘. *See* BHIKṢU

**biqiuni** 比丘尼. *See* BHIKṢUṆĪ

**Biqiu qing jing** 比丘請經. *See* ANUMĀNASUTTA

**biqiu weiyi** 比丘威儀. *See* ABHISAMĀCĀRIKĀ[ŚĪLA]

**bishi** 鼻識. *See* GHRĀṆAVIJÑĀNA

**Bisu jing** 弊宿經. *See* PĀYĀSISUTTANTA

**bo** 鉢. *See* PĀTRA

**Bojuluo** 薄拘羅. *See* BAKKULA

**Boli** 波利. *See* BHALLIKA

**bolizhiduoshu** 波利質多樹. *See* PĀRIYĀTRAKA

**Bo lun** 百論. *See* *ŚATAŚĀSTRA

**Boluojiputishan** 鉢羅笈菩提山. *See* PRĀGBODHI(GIRI)

**boluomi** 波羅蜜. *See* PĀRAMITĀ

**Boluopojialuomiduoluo** 波羅頗迦羅蜜多羅. *See* PRABHĀKARAMITRA

**boluotimucha** 波羅提木叉. *See* PRĀTIMOKṢA

**boluotimuchahu** 波羅提木叉護. *See* PRĀTIMOKṢASAṂVARA

**boluotitisheni** 波羅提提舍尼. *See* PRATIDEŚANĪYA

**boluoyi** 波羅夷. *See* PĀRĀJIKA

**Boluozhena** 波羅遮那. *See* PAṬACĀRĀ

**bona** 波那. *See* PRĀṆA

**bore boluomiduo** 般若波羅蜜多. *See* PRAJÑĀPĀRAMITĀ

**Bore boluomiduo xin jing** 般若波羅蜜多心經. *See* PRAJÑĀPĀRAMITĀHṚDAYASŪTRA

**Boredeng lun shi** 般若燈論釋. *See* PRAJÑĀPRADĪPA

**Bore liqu fen** 般若理趣分. *See* PRAJÑĀPĀRAMITĀNAYAŚATAPAÑCĀŚATIKĀ, ADHYARDHAŚATIKĀPRAJÑĀPĀRAMITĀSŪTRA

**Bosini wang** 波斯匿王. *See* PRASENAJIT

**boyi jiemo** 白一羯磨. *See* JÑAPTIDVITĪYĀ KARMAVĀCANĀ

**bu** 部. *See* NIKĀYA

**bucidi sanguan** 不次第三觀. *See* SANGUAN

**buding** 不定. *See* ANIYATA

**buding zhongxing** 不定種姓/種性. *See* ANIYATAGOTRA

**budong** 不動. *See* AKOPYA

**budong di** 不動地. *See* ACALĀ

**Budong mingwang** 不動明王. *See* ACALANĀTHA-VIDYĀRĀJA

**budong ye** 不動業. *See* ANIÑJYAKARMAN

**budongzuo** 不動坐. *See* ACALĀSANA

**bu'er** 不二. *See* ADVAYA

**bu'erzhi** 不二智. *See* ADVAYAJÑĀNA

**bufangyi** 不放逸. *See* APRAMĀDA

**bugong[fo]fa** 不共佛法. *See* ĀVEṆIKA[BUDDHA]DHARMA

**bugongzhu** 不共住. *See* ASAṂVĀSA

**buhai** 不害. *See* AHIṂSĀ

**buhuan** 不還. *See* ANĀGĀMIN

**buhuan xiang** 不還向. *See* ANĀGĀMIPHALAPRATIPANNAKA

**bujing** 不淨. *See* SAṂKLIṢṬA

**bujing guan** 不淨觀. *See* AŚUBHABHĀVANĀ

**bujing wu** 不淨物. *See* AKALPIKAVASTU

**bukede** 不可得. *See* ANUPALABDHI

**bukesiyi** 不可思議. *See* ACINTYA

**Bukong** 不空. *See* AMOGHAVAJRA

**Bukong Chengjiu rulai fo** 不空成就如來佛. *See* AMOGHASIDDHI

**Bukong Juansuo** 不空羂索. *See* AMOGHAPĀŚA

**bulai** 不來. *See* ANĀGĀMIN

**buliaoyi** 不了義. *See* NEYĀRTHA

**Bulìduo jing** 晡利多經. *See* POTALIYASUTTA

**bumie** 不滅. *See* ANIRUDDHA

**bu qiyu** 不綺語. *See* SAṂBHINNAPRALĀPĀT PRATIVIRATI

**buran wuzhi** 不染無知. *See* AKLIṢṬĀJÑĀNA

**busa** 布薩. *See* UPOṢADHA

**bushan** 不善. *See* AKUŚALA

**bushi** 布施. *See* DĀNA

**bushi boluomi** 布施波羅蜜. *See* DĀNAPĀRAMITĀ

**bushi jietuo** 不時解脫. *See* ASAMAYAVIMUKTA

**buteqieluo** 補特伽羅. *See* PUDGALA

**buteqieluo lun** 補特伽羅論. *See* PUDGALAVĀDA

**butuizhuan** 不退轉. *See* AVAIVARTIKA

**Butuoluoshan** 補陀落山. *See* POṬALAKA

**buwei** 不爲. *See* ABHABBAṬṬHĀNA

**Buwei** 怖畏. *See* BHAIRAVA

**Buwei Jingang** 怖畏金剛. *See* VAJRABHAIRAVA

**buxilun** 不戲論. *See* NIṢPRAPAÑCA

**buxin** 不信. *See* ĀŚRADDHYA

**buxing** 部行. *See* VARGACĀRIN

**Buzeng bujian jing** 不增不減經. *See* ANŪNATVĀPŪRṆATVANIRDEŚA

**Buzhapolou jing** 布吒婆樓經. *See* POṬṬHAPĀDASUTTA

**buzheng siwei** 不正思惟. *See* AYONIŚOMANASKĀRA

**buzhengzhi** 不正知. *See* ASAṂPRAJANYA

## C

**caishi** 財施. *See* ĀMIṢADĀNA

**caizizai** 財自在. *See* PARIṢKĀRAVAŚITĀ

**can** 慚. *See* HRĪ

**chali** 刹利. *See* KṢATRIYA

**chana** 刹那. *See* KṢAṆA

**chana juzu** 刹那具足. *See* KṢAṆASAMPAD

**chanalun** 刹那論. *See* KṢAṆIKAVĀDA

**chana qing** 刹那頃. *See* KṢAṆIKA

**chanding** 禪定. *See* DHYĀNA

**chanfang** 禪房/禪坊. *See* PRAHĀṆAŚĀLĀ

**chang** 常. *See* NITYA

**Chang Ahan jing** 長阿含經. *See* DĪRGHĀGAMA

**changbian** 常邊. *See* ŚĀŚVATĀNTA

**Changbuqing pusa** 常不輕菩薩. *See* SADĀPARIBHŪTA

**changfa** 常法. *See* NITYADHARMA

**changjian** 常見. *See* ŚĀSVATADṚṢṬI

**Changshou** 長壽. *See* KOSAMBIYASUTTA

**Changti [pusa]** 常啼[菩薩]. *See* SADĀPRARUDITA

**changzuo buwo** 長坐不臥. *See* CHANGJWA PURWA

**chanhui** 懺悔. *See* PĀPADEŚANA

**Chanjia guijian** 禪家龜鑑. *See* SŎN'GA KWIGAM

**Chanti xianren** 羼提仙人. *See* KṢĀNTIVĀDIN

**chanzhi** 禪支. *See* DHYĀNĀṄGA

**chapi** 茶毘. *See* KṢAPITA

**chen** 瞋. *See* DVEṢA, PRATIGHA, VYĀPĀDA

**chengjie** 成劫. *See* VIVARTAKALPA

**chengjing** 澄淨. *See* PRASĀDA

**chengjiu fa** 成就法. *See* SĀDHANA

**chengsuozuo zhi** 成所作智. *See* KṚTYĀNUṢṬHĀNAJÑĀNA

**Cheni** 車匿. *See* CHANDAKA

**Chenna** 陳那. *See* DIGNĀGA

**chi** 癡. *See* MOHA

**Chiguo tian** 持國天. *See* DHṚTARĀṢṬRA

**chiming** 持明. *See* VIDYĀDHARA

**chiming zang** 持明藏. *See* VIDYĀDHARAPIṬAKA

**Chishengguang rulai** 熾盛光如來. *See* TEJAPRABHA

**chu** 除. *See* APOHA

**chu** 處. *See* ĀYATANA

**chu** 觸. *See* SPARŚA

**chuang** 幢. *See* KETU

**chuangzu** 床足. *See* KHAṬVĀṄGA

**chuchu** 觸處. *See* SPRAṢṬAVYĀYATANA

**chudi yin** 觸地印. *See* BHŪMISPARŚAMUDRĀ

**Chugaizhang pusa** 除蓋障菩薩. *See* SARVANĪVARAṆAVIṢKAMBHIN

**chuizuzuo** 垂足坐. *See* PRALAMBAPĀDĀSANA

**chujia** 出家. *See* PRAVRAJITA

**chuli** 出離. *See* NAIṢKRAMYA, NIRYĀṆA

**chusheng** 畜生. *See* TIRYAK

**chusheng dasheng** 出生大乘. *See* EKAYĀNA

**chushi dao** 出世道. *See* LOKUTTARAMAGGA

**chushi guo** 出世果. *See* LOKUTTARAPHALA

**chushijian** 出世間. *See* LOKOTTARA

**chushi sanmei** 出世三昧. *See* LOKUTTARASAMĀDHI

**Chuyao jing** 出曜經. *See* UDĀNAVARGA

**chuyaozhi** 出要志. *See* NAIṢKRAMYA

**ci** 慈. *See* MAITRĪ

**cibei** 慈悲. *See* maitrī

**cidi sanguan** 次第三觀. *See* sanguan

**cidi shuofa** 次第說法. *See* anupubbikathā

**cidi yuan** 次第緣. *See* anantarapratyaya

**Ci jing** 慈經. *See* Mettāsutta

**Cizun** 慈尊. *See* Maitreyanātha

## D

**Da banniepan jing** 大般涅槃經. *See* Mahāparinirvāṇasūtra, cf. Mahāparinibbānasuttanta

**Dabaoji jing** 大寶積經. *See* Ratnakūṭasūtra

**dabei** 大悲. *See* mahākaruṇā

**Dabei kongzhi jingang dajiao wang yigui jing** 大悲空智金剛大教王儀軌經. *See* Hevajratantra/Hevajraḍākinījālasambaratantra

**Dabeizhe** 大悲者. *See* Mahākaruṇika

**Daben jing** 大本經. *See* Mahāpadānasuttanta, Mahāvadānasūtra

**Dabore boluomiduo jing** 大般若波羅蜜多經. *See* *Mahāprajñāpāramitāsūtra

**da bushandi fa** 大不善地法. *See* akuśalamahābhūmika

**dacheng** 大城. *See* mahājanapada

**dadi fa** 大地法. *See* mahābūmika

**Dafagu jing** 大法鼓經. *See* Mahābherīhārakaparivarta

**Dafangdeng daji jing** 大方等大集經. *See* Mahāsaṃnipātasūtra

**Dafangdeng rulaizang jing** 大方等如來藏經. *See* Tathāgatagarbhasūtra

**Dafangdeng wuxiang jing** 大方等無想經. *See* Mahameghasūtra

**Dafangguang fo huayan jing** 大方廣佛華嚴經. *See* Avataṃsakasūtra, Gaṇḍavyūha

**Dafangguang pusazang Wenshushili genben yigui jing** 大方廣菩薩藏文殊師利根本儀軌經. *See* Mañjuśrīmūlakalpa

**da fannaodi fa** 大煩惱地法. *See* kleśamahābhūmika

**Dafan tian** 大梵天. *See* Mahābrahmā

**Da foding rulai miyin xiuzheng liaoyi zhupusa wanxing shoulengyan jing** 大佛頂如來密因修證了義諸菩薩萬行首楞嚴經. *See* *Śūraṃgamasūtra

**Daheitian** 大黑天. *See* Mahākāla, Shichifukujin

**Dahui jing** 大會經. *See* Mahāsamayasuttanta

**dajiaohuan [diyu]** 大叫喚[地獄]. *See* mahāraurava

**dajiaore** 大焦熱. *See* pratāpana

**dajie** 大劫. *See* mahākalpa

**Dajuchiluo jing** 大拘絺羅經. *See* Mahāvedallasutta

**dakewei** 大可畏. *See* mahābhaya

**dale** 大樂. *See* mahāsukha

**Damoduoluo** 達摩多羅. *See* Dharmatrāta

**Damojiduo** 達摩笈多. *See* Dharmagupta

**danduo** 單墮. *See* pāyattika

**dao** 道. *See* patha

**daodi** 道諦. *See* mārgasatya

**dao feidao zhijian qingjing** 道非道智見清淨. *See* maggāmaggañāṇadassanavisuddhi

**Daogan jing** 稻稈經. *See* Śālistambasūtra

**daoguo** 道果. *See* mārgaphala

**daoju** 道具. *See* pariṣkāra

**daoli** 道理. *See* yukti

**daoli tian** 忉利天. *See* trāyastriṃśa

**daoren lu** 刀刃路. *See* kṣuramārga

**daozhi** 道智. *See* mārgajñatā

**Da piluzhena chengfo shenbian jiachi jing** 大毘盧遮那成佛神變加持經. *See* Mahāvairocanasūtra

**Dapingdeng wang** 大平等王. *See* Mahāsammata

**da pusa** 大菩薩. *See* mahābodhisattva

**da puti** 大菩提. *See* mahābodhi

**Daputisi** 大菩提寺. *See* Mahābodhi Temple

**daren** 大人. *See* mahāpuruṣa

**darenxiang** 大人相. *See* mahāpuruṣalakṣaṇa

**Dari jing** 大日經. *See* Mahāvairocanasūtra

**Dari rulai** 大日如來. *See* Vairocana

**Dasazhenijianzi** 大薩遮尼犍子. *See* Mahāsatyanirgrantha

**da shandi fa** 大善地法. *See* kuśalamahābūmika

**Dashanjian wang jing** 大善見王經. *See* Mahāsuddassanasuttanta

**Dasheng** 大聖. *See* MAHĀMUNI

**Dasheng** 大乘. *See* MAHĀYĀNA

**Dasheng Apidamo ji lun** 大乘阿毘達磨集論. *See* ABHIDHARMASAMUCCAYA

**Dasheng baoyaoyi lun** 大乘寶要義論. *See* SŪTRASAMUCCAYA

**Dasheng chengye lun** 大乘成業論. *See* KARMASIDDHIPRAKARAṆA

**Dasheng fangbian hui** 大乘方便會. *See* UPĀYAKAUŚALYASŪTRA

**Dasheng ji pusa xue lun** 大乘集菩薩學論. *See* ŚIKṢĀSAMUCCAYA

**Dasheng miyan jing** 大乘密嚴經. *See* GHANAVYŪHA

**Dasheng qixin lun bieji** 大乘起信論別記. *See* TAESŬNG KISIN NON PYŎLGI

**Dasheng qixin lun shu** 大乘起信論疏. *See* TAESŬNG KISIN NON SO

**Dasheng wuyun lun** 大乘五蘊論. *See* PAÑCASKANDHAPRAKARAṆA

**Dasheng zhuangyan baowang jing** 大乘莊嚴寶王經. *See* KĀRAṆḌAVYŪHA

**Dasheng zhuangyan jing lun** 大乘莊嚴經論. *See* MAHĀYĀNASŪTRĀLAṂKĀRA

**dashi** 大士. *See* MAHĀSATTVA

**dashi xiang** 大師想. *See* ŚĀSTṚSAṂJÑĀ

**Dashizhi** 大勢至. *See* MAHĀSTHĀMAPRĀPTA

**dashouyin** 大手印. *See* MAHĀMUDRĀ

**dashuo** 大說. *See* MAHĀPADEŚA

**Dasuiqiu** 大隨求. *See* MAHĀPRATISARĀ

**Daweide mingwang** 大威德明王. *See* YAMĀNTAKA

**Daxian** 大賢. *See* TAEHYŎN

**Daxiong** 大雄. *See* MAHĀVĪRA

**dayi** 大衣. *See* SAṂGHĀṬĪ

**dayin** 大印. *See* MAHĀMUDRĀ

**Dayuan fangbian jing** 大緣方便經. *See* MAHĀNIDĀNASUTTA

**dayuanjing zhi** 大圓鏡智. *See* ĀDARŚAJÑĀNA

**Dayun jing** 大雲經. *See* *MAHĀMEGHASŪTRA

**dazhong** 大種. *See* MAHĀBHŪTA

**Dazhongbu** 大衆部. *See* MAHĀSĀṂGHIKA

**de** 得. *See* PATTIDĀNA

**de** 得. *See* PRĀPTI

**Deguang** 德光. *See* GUṆAPRABHA

**deguo** 得果. *See* PHALAPRATIPANNAKA

**denghuo [diyu]** 等活[地獄]. *See* SAṂJĪVA

**dengliu guo** 等流果. *See* NIṢYANDAPHALA

**dengwujian yuan** 等無間緣. *See* SAMANANTARAPRATYAYA

**dengyin** 等引. *See* SAMĀHITA

**dengyin zhi** 等引智. *See* SAMĀHITAJÑĀNA

**dengzhi** 等至. *See* SAMĀPATTI

**di** 地. *See* BHŪMI

**di** 諦. *See* SATYA

**diandao** 顛倒. *See* VIPARYĀSA

**Dianzun jing** 典尊經. *See* MAHĀGOVINDASUTTA

**diao** 掉. *See* AUDDHATYA

**Dichi lun** 地持論. *See* BODHISATTVABHŪMI

**dida** 地大. *See* PṚTHIVĪ

**Di lun** 地論. *See* DAŚABHŪMIVYĀKHYĀNA, DI LUN ZONG

**ding** 頂. *See* MŪRDHAN

**dingguan zhi** 定觀知. *See* YOGIPRATYAKṢA

**Di-Shi** 帝釋. *See* ŚAKRA, INDRA

**Di-Shi suowen jing** 帝釋所問經. *See* SAKKAPAÑHASUTTA

**Di-Shi wang** 帝釋網. *See* INDRAJĀLA

**disi guanding** 第四灌頂. *See* CATURTHĀBHIṢEKHA

**diyiyi di** 第一義諦. *See* PARAMĀRTHASATYA

**diyu [youqing/zhongsheng]** 地獄[有情/衆生]. *See* NĀRAKA

**Dizang** 地藏. *See* KṢITIGARBHA

**Dizang pusa benyuan jing** 地藏菩薩本願經. *See* KṢITIGARBHASŪTRA

**Dongshan** 東山. *See* PŪRVAŚAILA

**doushuai tian** 兜率天. *See* TUṢITA

**duan** 斷. *See* PRAHĀṆA

**duanbian** 斷邊. *See* UCCHEDĀNTA

**duanjian** 斷見. *See* UCCHEDADṚṢṬI

**duanjian lun** 斷見論. *See* UCCHEDAVĀDA

**duanshangen** 斷善根. *See* SAMUCCHINNAKUŚALAMŪLA

**ducan** 獨參. *See* DOKUSAN

**duifa** 對法. *See* ABHIDHARMA

**duifa zhushi** 對法諸師. *See* ĀBHIDHARMIKA

**duishou** 對首. *See* PRATIDEŚANĪYA

**duizhi** 對治. *See* PRATIPAKṢA

**Dujimu** 獨髻母. *See* EKAJAṬĀ

**dujue** 獨覺. *See* PRATYEKABUDDHA

**dulou qi** 髑髏器. *See* KAPĀLA

**Dumu** 度母. *See* TĀRĀ

**dungen** 鈍根. *See* MṚDVINDRIYA

**Duobao rulai** 多寶如來. *See* PRABHŪTARATNA

**Duoluo** 多羅. *See* TĀRĀ

**Duowenbu** 多聞部. *See* BAHUŚRUTĪYA

**Duowen tian** 多聞天. *See* VAIŚRAVAṆA

**Duzi bu** 犢子部. *See* VĀTSĪPUTRĪYA

## E

**e** 惡. *See* PĀPA

**egui** 餓鬼. *See* PRETA

**ejian** 惡見. *See* AKUŚALADṚṢṬI, MITHYĀDṚṢṬI

**ekou** 惡口. *See* PĀRUṢYA

**equ** 惡趣. *See* DURGATI

**erchu** 耳處. *See* ŚROTRĀYATANA

**erdi** 二諦. *See* SATYADVAYA

**ergen** 耳根. *See* ŚROTRENDRIYA

**ershi** 耳識. *See* ŚROTRAVIJÑĀNA

**ershi sengqie** 二十僧伽. *See* VIṂŚATIPRABHEDASAṂGHA

**Ershiyi'er** 二十億耳. *See* SOṆA KOLIVĪSA

**erzhong sanguan** 二種三觀. *See* SANGUAN

**eshuo** 惡說. *See* DURBHĀṢITA

**ezuo** 惡作. *See* DUṢKṚTA

## F

**fa** 法. *See* DHARMA

**Facheng** 法成. *See* CHOS GRUB

**Facheng** 法稱. *See* DHARMAKĪRTI

**fachu** 法處. *See* DHARMĀYATANA

**faguang di** 發光地. *See* PRABHĀKARĪBHŪMI

**fahu** 法護. *See* DHARMAPĀLĀ

**Fahua jing** 法華經. *See* SADDHARMAPUṆḌARĪKASŪTRA

**fajie** 法界. *See* DHARMADHĀTU

**fajie tixingzhi** 法界體性智. *See* DHARMADHĀTUSVABHĀVAJÑĀNA

**Faji jing** 法集經. *See* DHARMASAṂGĪTI

**Faju jing** 法句經. *See* DHAMMAPADA, UDĀNA

**Fale biqiuni** 法樂比丘尼. *See* DHARMADINNĀ

**Fale biqiuni jing** 法樂比丘尼經. *See* CŪḶAVEDALLASUTTA

**falü** 法律. *See* DHARMAVINAYA

**falun** 法輪. *See* DHARMACAKRA

**famen** 法門. *See* DHARMAPARYĀYA

**Fanaposi zunzhe** 伐那婆斯尊者. *See* VANAVĀSIN

**Fandong jing** 梵動經. *See* BRAHMAJĀLASUTTANTA

**fanfu** 凡夫. *See* PṚTHAGJANA

**fanfu tian** 梵輔天. *See* BRAHMAPUROHITA

**fangbian** 方便. *See* UPĀYA

**fangbian shanqiao** 方便善巧. *See* UPĀYAKAUŚALYA

**fangdeng** 方等. *See* VAIPULYA

**Fangguang da zhuangyan jing** 方廣大莊嚴經. *See* LALITAVISTARA

**Fangniu pin** 放牛品. *See* MAHĀGOPĀLAKASUTTA

**fangyi** 放逸. *See* PRAMĀDA

**Fanjie** 梵界. *See* BRAHMALOKA

**fannao** 煩惱. *See* KLEŚA

**fannaozhang** 煩惱障. *See* KLEŚĀVARAṆA

**Fantian** 梵天. *See* BRAHMĀ

**Fantian qing fo jing** 梵天請佛經. *See* BRAHMANIMANTANIKASUTTA

**fanxing** 梵行. *See* BRAHMACARYA

**Fanyanna** 梵衍那. *See* BĀMIYĀN

**Fanyi mingyi daji** 翻譯名義大集. *See* MAHĀVYUTPATTI

**fanzhong tian** 梵衆天. *See* BRAHMAKĀYIKA

**fanzhu** 梵住. *See* BRAHMAVIHĀRA

**fa puti xin** 發菩提心. *See* BODHICITTOTPĀDA

**Faqi pusa** 法起菩薩. *See* DHARMODGATA

**faren** 法忍. *See* DHARMAKṢĀNTI

**Fasheluofuduoluo** 伐闍羅弗多羅. *See* VAJRAPUTRA

**fashen** 法身. *See* DHARMAKĀYA

**fashi** 法施. *See* DHARMADĀNA

**fawang** 法王. *See* DHARMARĀJAN

**fawozhi** 法我執. *See* DHARMĀTMAGRAHA

**fawuwo** 法無我. *See* DHARMANAIRĀTMYA

**faxi** 法喜. *See* DHARMAPRĪTI

**faxing** 法性. *See* DHARMATĀ

**fayan** 法眼. *See* DHARMACAKṢUS

**fayin** 法印. *See* DHARMAMUDRĀ

**fayun di** 法雲地. *See* DHARMAMEGHĀ

**Fayun zu lun** 法蘊足論. *See* DHARMASKANDHA[PĀDAŚĀSTRA]

**Fazang biqiu** 法藏比丘. *See* DHARMĀKARA

**Fazangbu** 法藏部. *See* DHARMAGUPTAKA

**Fazhi lun** 發智論. *See* JÑĀNAPRASTHĀNA

**feide** 非得. *See* APRĀPTI

**feijia** 非家. *See* ANAGĀRIKĀ

**feili zuoyi** 非理作意. *See* AYONIŚOMANASKĀRA

**Feixiang feifeixiang chu** 非想非非想處. *See* NAIVASAṂJÑĀNĀSAṂJÑĀYATANA

**feizemie** 非擇滅. *See* APRATISAṂKHYĀNIRODHA

**fen** 分. *See* BHĀGA

**fen** 忿. *See* KRODHA

**fenbie** 分別. *See* KALPANĀ, VIKALPA

**fenbie huo** 分別惑. *See* PARIKALPITAKLEŚĀVARAṆA

**fenbie wozhi** 分別我執. *See* PARIKALPITĀTMAGRAHA

**Fenbieshuo bu** 分別說部. *See* VIBHAJYAVĀDA

**fenbie wuming** 分別無明. *See* PARIKALPITĀVIDYĀ

**fenduan shengsi** 分段生死. *See* PARICCHEDAJARĀMARAṆA

**fengda** 風大. *See* VĀYU

**fentuoli hua** 芬陀利華. *See* PUṆḌARĪKA

**fo** 佛. *See* BUDDHA; FO

**Fo benxing ji jing** 佛本行集經. *See* ABHINIṢKRAMAṆASŪTRA

**foboyin** 佛鉢印. *See* BUDDHAPĀTRAMUDRĀ

**focha** 佛刹. *See* BUDDHAKṢETRA

**Fodi jing** 佛地經. *See* BUDDHABHŪMISŪTRA

**Fodijing lun** 佛地經論. *See* BUDDHABHŪMIŚĀSTRA

**foding** 佛頂. *See* UṢṆĪṢA

**fofa** 佛法. *See* BUDDHADHARMA

**Fohu** 佛護. *See* BUDDHAPĀLITA

**foji** 佛紀. *See* BUDDHAVARṢA

**Fomu baodezang bore boluomi jing** 佛母寶德藏般若波羅蜜經. *See* RATNAGUṆASAṂCAYAGĀTHĀ

**foshen** 佛身. *See* BUDDHAKĀYA

**fo sheng** 佛乘. *See* BUDDHAYĀNA

**Fosuoxing zan** 佛所行讃. *See* BUDDHACARITA

**Fotuobatuoluo** 佛陀跋陀羅. *See* BUDDHABHADRA

**Fotuoduoluo** 佛陀多羅. *See* BUDDHATRĀTA

**Fotuomiduoluo** 佛陀蜜多羅. *See* BUDDHAMITRA

**Fotuonanti** 佛陀難提. *See* BUDDHANANDI

**Fotuoyeshe** 佛陀耶舍. *See* BUDDHAYAŚAS

**foyan** 佛眼. *See* BUDDHACAKṢUS

**foyu** 佛語. *See* BUDDHAVACANA

**fozu** 佛足. *See* BUDDHAPĀDA

**fu** 覆. *See* MRAKṢA

**fu** 福. *See* PUṆYA

**fubo** 覆鉢. *See* PĀTRANIKUBJANA

**fubo jiemo** 覆鉢羯磨. *See* PĀTRANIKUBJANA

**fude ziliang** 福德資糧. *See* PUṆYASAṂBHĀRA

**Fulanna Jiashe** 富蘭那迦葉. *See* PŪRAṆA-KĀŚYAPA

**Fulouna** 富樓那. *See* PŪRṆA

**Fulushou** 福祿壽. *See* SHICHIFUKUJIN

**fusheng tian** 福生天. *See* PUṆYAPRASAVA

**futian** 福田. *See* PUṆYAKṢETRA

**fuye shi** 福業事. *See* PUṆYAKRIYĀVASTU

**fuzang** 腹藏/伏藏. *See* NIDHĀNA

**fuzhi ziliang** 福智資糧. *See* PUṆYAJÑĀNASAṂBHĀRA

**Fuzi heji jing** 父子合集經. *See* PITĀPUTRASAMĀGAMA SŪTRA

## G

**gai** 蓋. *See* NĪVARAṆA

**ganlu** 甘露. *See* AMṚTA

**Ganrong** 紺容. *See* ŚYĀMĀVATĪ

**gantapo** 乾闥婆. *See* GANDHARVA

**gantapo cheng** 乾闥婆城. *See* GANDHARVANAGARA

**gen** 根. *See* INDRIYA, MŪLA

**Genben Dazhong bu** 根本大衆部. *See* MŪLAMAHĀSĀṂGHIKA

**genben fannao** 根本煩惱. *See* MŪLAKLEŚA

**Genben Shuoyiqieyou bu** 根本說一切有部. *See* MŪLASARVĀSTIVĀDA

**Genben Shuoyiqieyoubu pinaiye** 根本說一切有部毘奈耶. *See* MŪLASARVĀSTIVĀDA VINAYA, VINAYAVIBHAṄGA

**genlüyi** 根律儀. *See* INDRIYASAṂVARA

**gongde** 功德. *See* ANUŚAṂSA, GUṆA

**gongde boluomi** 功德波羅蜜. *See* GUṆAPĀRAMITĀ

**gongxiang** 共相. *See* SĀMĀNYALAKṢAṆA

**gongxing dizi** 共行弟子. *See* SADDHIVIHĀRIKA

**gongyang** 供養. *See* PŪJĀ

**gou** 垢. *See* MALA

**gu** 鼓. *See* DRUM

**guan** 觀. *See* VIPAŚYANĀ

**guanding** 灌頂. *See* ABHIṢEKA

**guanding yin** 灌頂印. *See* ABHIṢEKAMUDRĀ

**guangbei** 光背. *See* KĀYAPRABHĀ

**Guang Bolun ben** 廣百論本. *See* CATUḤŚATAKA

**guangguo tian** 廣果天. *See* BṚHATPHALA

**guangming** 光明. *See* PRABHĀSVARA

**guangmingxin** 光明心. *See* PRABHĀSVARACITTA

**Guangmu tian** 廣目天. *See* VIRŪPĀKṢA

**Guanshiyin** 觀世音. *See* GUANYIN

**Guan suoyuanyuan lun** 觀所緣緣論. *See* ĀLAMBANAPARĪKṢĀ

**Guanzizai wang rulai** 觀自在王如來. *See* LOKEŚVARARĀJA

**gu diyu** 孤地獄. *See* PRATYEKANARAKA

**gui** 鬼. *See* BHŪTA

**gui** 歸. *See* LENA

**guiyi** 歸依. *See* ŚARAṆA

**Guizimushen** 鬼子母神. *See* HĀRĪTĪ

**guo** 果. *See* PHALA

**guo** 過. *See* PRASAṄGA, DOṢA

**guobao** 果報. *See* VIPĀKA

**guohuan** 過患. *See* ĀDĪNAVA

**guoqu qifo** 過去七佛. *See* SAPTATATHĀGATA

**Guoyi** 菓衣. *See* ŚOBHITA

## H

**hai** 害. *See* VIHIṂSĀ

**haiyin sanmei** 海印三昧. *See* SĀGARAMUDRĀSAMĀDHI

**hanlin** 寒林. *See* ŚMAŚĀNA

**hao** 好. *See* ANUVYAÑJANA

**haoyu** 好欲. *See* KĀMACCHANDA

**heimao** 黑帽. *See* BLACK HATS

**heisheng diyu** 黑繩地獄. *See* KĀLASŪTRA

**Helibamo** 訶梨跋摩. *See* HARIVARMAN

**hen** 恨. *See* UPANĀHA

**Henghe** 恒河. *See* GAṄGĀNADĪ

**Henghesha** 恒河沙. *See* GAṄGĀNADĪVĀLUKĀ

**heshangni** 和尚尼. *See* UPĀDHYĀYĀ

**hezhang** 合掌. *See* AÑJALI[MUDRĀ]

**hezheng** 和諍. *See* HWAJAENG

**hong lianhua** 紅蓮華. *See* PADMA

**houde zhi** 後得智. *See* PṚṢṬHALABDHAJÑĀNA

**houyou** 後有. *See* PUNARBHAVA

**hua** 化. *See* NIRMITA

**Huadi bu** 化地部. *See* MAHĪŚĀSAKA

**huai jie** 壞劫. *See* SAṂVARTAKALPA

**huaiku** 壞苦. *See* VIPARIṆĀMADUḤKHATĀ

**huale tian** 化樂天. *See* NIRMĀṆARATI

**huanshen** 幻身. *See* MĀYĀDEHA

**huanshi** 幻師. *See* MĀYĀKĀRA

**huanxi di** 歡喜地. *See* PRAMUDITĀ

**huashen** 化身. *See* NIRMĀṆAKĀYA

**hua sheng** 化生. *See* upapādukayoni

**Huashi cheng** 華氏城. *See* Pāṭaliputra

**Huayan jing** 華嚴經. *See* Avataṃsakasūtra

**Huayan yisheng fajie tu** 華嚴一乘法界圖. *See* Hwaŏm ilsŭng pŏpkye to

**Hucai** 護財. *See* Dhanapāla, Nālāgiri

**Hufa** 護法. *See* Dharmapāla

**Huguo pusahui [jing]** 護國菩薩會[經]. *See* Rāṣṭrapālaparipṛcchā

**hui** 悔. *See* kaukṛtya

**hui** 慧. *See* mati, prajñā

**Huichao** 慧超. *See* Hyech'o

**huiguo** 悔過. *See* pratideśanā

**hui jietuo** 慧解脫. *See* prajñāvimukta

**Huipin jing** 穢品經. *See* Anaṅgaṇasutta

**huixiang** 迴向. *See* pariṇāmanā

**huixue** 慧學. *See* prajñāśikṣā

**Huizheng lun** 迴諍論. *See* Vigrahavyāvartanī

**humo** 護摩. *See* homa

**hunchen** 惛沉. *See* styāna

**huo bianchu** 火遍處. *See* tejokasiṇa

**huoda** 火大. *See* tejas

**Huoshen** 火神. *See* Agni

## J

**ji** 嫉. *See* īrṣyā, mātsarya

**ji** 集. *See* samudaya

**ji** 偈. *See* śloka

**jiachi** 加持. *See* adhiṣṭhāna

**jiachinayi** 迦絺那衣. *See* kaṭhina

**Jiaduoyannizi** 迦多衍尼子. *See* Kātyāyanīputra

**Jialijia** 迦梨迦. *See* Kālī Kururagharikā

**Jialijia zunzhe** 迦里迦尊者. *See* Kālika

**Jialuojiutuo Jiazhanyan** 迦羅鳩馱迦旃延. *See* Kakuda Kātyāyana

**jialouluo** 迦樓羅. *See* garuḍa

**Jialupinqie niao** 迦陸頻伽鳥. *See* kalaviṅka

**jiaming** 假名. *See* prajñapti; prajñaptisat

**jiaming you** 假名有. *See* prajñaptisat

**jian** 見. *See* darśana

**jian** 見. *See* dṛṣṭi

**jiandao** 見道. *See* darśanamārga

**jiande** 見得. *See* dṛṣṭiprāpta

**jiandu** 犍度. *See* skandhaka

**jian fannao** 見煩惱. *See* lta ba nyon mongs can

**Jiangliangyeshe** 畺良耶舍. *See* Kālayaśas

**Jiangu jing** 堅固經. *See* Kevaṭṭasutta

**jianguyi** 堅固衣. *See* kaṭhina

**Jianisejia wang** 迦膩色迦王. *See* Kaniṣka

**jianli** 建立. *See* pratiṣṭhā

**jianqu** 見取. *See* dṛṣṭiparāmarśa

**jianshu diyu** 劍樹地獄. *See* kṣuramārga

**jiansi erhuo** 見思二惑. *See* jianhuo and sihuo

**Jiantuoluo** 健馱羅. *See* Gandhāra

**Jianuojiabaliduoshe** 迦諾迦跋釐墮闍. *See* Kanaka Bharadvāja

**Jianuojiafacuo** 迦諾迦伐蹉. *See* Kanakavatsa

**jianwei shuofa** 漸爲說法. *See* anupubbikathā

**Jianye lin** 劍葉林. *See* Asipattravana

**jianzhi** 見至. *See* dṛṣṭiprāpta

**jianzhi** 犍稚. *See* ghaṇṭā

**Jianzhi** 犍陟. *See* Kaṇṭhaka

**jiao** 教. *See* Kyo

**jiao** 憍. *See* mada

**jiaodaolun** 教導論. *See* avavāda

**jiaofa** 教法. *See* āgamadharma

**Jiaofanboti** 憍梵波提. *See* Gavāṃpati

**jiaohuan [diyu]** 叫喚[地獄]. *See* raurava

**jiaojie** 交接. *See* maithuna

**jiaopan** 教判. *See* jiaoxiang panshi

**Jiaosaluo guo** 憍薩羅國. *See* Kośala

**Jiashe Moteng** 迦葉摩騰. *See* Kāśyapa Mātaṅga

**Jiaoshijia** 憍尸迦. *See* Kauśika

**Jiapiluowei** 迦毘羅衛. *See* Kapilavastu

**Jiapimoluo** 迦毘摩羅. *See* Kapimala

**jiasha** 袈裟. *See* kaṣāya

**Jiashe** 迦葉. *See* Kāśyapa

**Jiasheyibu** 迦葉遺部. *See* Kāśyapīya

**jiaxing** 加行. *See* prayoga

**jiaxing dao** 加行道. *See* prayogamārga

**Jiazhanyan** 迦旃延. *See* Kātyāyana

**jiazu** 家族. *See* kula

**jidi** 集諦. *See* samudayasatya

**jidu fenbie** 計度分別. *See* abhinirūpaṇāvikalpa

**jie** 界. *See* dhātu

**jie** 偈. *See* gāthā

**jie** 劫. *See* kalpa

**jie** 結. *See* saṃyojana

**jie** 戒. *See* śīla

**Jie ben** 戒本. *See* Prātimokṣasūtra

**jie boluomi** 戒波羅蜜. *See* śīlapāramitā

**jiebobei** 劫波杯. *See* kapāla

**jiedi jiedi boluojiedi boluosengjiedi puti sapohe** 揭帝揭帝波羅揭帝波羅僧揭帝菩提薩婆訶. *See* gate gate pāragate pārasaṃgate bodhi svāhā

**Jiefa** 戒法. *See* Śīladharma

**jieji** 界繫. *See* avacara

**jieji** 結集. *See* saṃgīti

**jiejie** 結界. *See* sīmā

**jiejie** 解界. *See* sīmāsamūhana

**jiejinqu jian** 戒禁取見. *See* śīlavrataparāmarśa

**jiejizhe** 結集者. *See* saṃgītikāra

**Jielingqie** 羯陵伽. *See* Kalinga

**jiemo** 羯磨. *See* karman

**jiemo bu** 羯磨部. *See* karmakula

**Jieshen lun** 界身論. *See* Dhātukāya[pādaśāstra]

**Jieshenmi jing** 解深密經. *See* Saṃdhinirmocanasūtra

**jietai** 懈怠. *See* kausīdya

**jietuo** 解脫. *See* mokṣa, vimokṣa

**jietuodao** 解脫道. *See* mokṣamārga, vimuktimārga

**Jietuodao lun** 解脫道論. *See* Vimuttimagga

**jietuo men** 解脫門. *See* vimokṣamukha

**Jiexian** 戒賢. *See* Śīlabhadra

**jiguangjing tian** 極光淨天. *See* ābhāsvarāloka

**Jigudu zhangzhe** 給孤獨長者. *See* Anāthapiṇḍada

**Jile jingtu** 極樂淨土. *See* Sukhāvatī

**Jiliang lun** 集量論. *See* Pramāṇasamuccaya

**Jimen** 迹門. *See* Shakumon

**jimo** 寂默. *See* pratisaṃlayana

**jinfen** 近分. *See* sāmantaka

**jing** 經. *See* sūtra

**jing** 境. *See* viṣaya

**jing** 淨. *See* vyavadāna

**jingang** 金剛. *See* vajra

**jingang asheli** 金剛阿闍梨. *See* vajrācārya

**Jingangchi** 金剛持. *See* Vajradhara

**Jingang cuisui tuoluoni** 金剛摧碎陀羅尼. *See* Vajravidāraṇadhāraṇī

**Jingangding jing** 金剛頂經. *See* Vajraśekharasūtra

**jingang jia** 金剛家. *See* vajrakula

**jingang jiafuzuo** 金剛跏趺坐. *See* vajraparyaṅka

**Jingang jie** 金剛界. *See* kongōkai

**Jingang jing** 金剛經. *See* Vajracchedikāprajñāpāramitāsūtra

**Jingang saduo** 金剛薩埵. *See* Vajrasattva

**jingang sanmei** 金剛三昧. *See* vajropamasamādhi

**Jingang sanmei jing** 金剛三昧經. *See* Kŭmgang sammae kyŏng

**Jingang sanmei jing lun** 金剛三昧經論. *See* Kŭmgang sammaegyŏng non

**Jingangshan** 金剛山. *See* Kŭmgangsan

**jingang sheng** 金剛乘. *See* vajrayāna

**jingangshi** 金剛師. *See* vajrācārya

**Jingangshou pusa** 金剛手菩薩. *See* Vajrapāṇi

**jingang yu ding** 金剛喻定. *See* vajropamasamādhi

**Jingangzhi** 金剛智. *See* Vajrabodhi

**Jingang zuo** 金剛座. *See* vajrāsana

**jingce** 警策. *See* kyōsaku

**jingfa** 敬法. *See* gurudharma

**Jingfan wang** 淨飯王. *See* Śuddhodana

**Jing fenbie** 經分別. *See* Sūtravibhaṅga

**jingjie** 淨戒. *See* śīlaviśuddhi

**jingjin** 精進. *See* vīrya

**jingjin boluomiduo** 精進波羅蜜多. *See* vīryapāramitā

**jingju tian** 淨居天. *See* śuddhāvāsakāyika

**Jingliang bu** 經量部. *See* Sautrāntika

**jinglü boluomiduo** 靜慮波羅蜜多. *See* dhyānapāramitā

**jingping** 淨瓶. *See* kuṇḍikā

**jingren** 淨人. *See* kalpikāraka

**jingshe** 精舍. *See* vihāra

**Jinguangming jing** 金光明經. *See* Suvarṇaprabhāsottamasūtra

**Jinguangming zuishengwang jing** 金光明最勝王經. *See* Suvarṇaprabhāsottamasūtra

**jingxing** 經行. *See* caṅkrama

**Jingzang** 經藏. *See* Sūtrapiṭaka

**Jingzhong Wuxiang** 淨衆無相. *See* Chŏngjung Musang

**Jin heshang** 金和尚. *See* Chŏngjung Musang

**jinnaluo** 緊那羅. *See* kiṃnara

**jinshi lüyi** 近事律儀. *See* upāsakasaṃvara

**jinzhi** 盡智. *See* kṣayajñāna

**jinzhu** 近住. *See* upavāsa

**jinzhu dizi** 近住弟子. *See* antevāsika

**jiqi fanyou** 極七返有. *See* saptakṛdbhavaparama

**jishen chengfo** 即身成佛. *See* sokushin jōbutsu

**Jishi Yuanguang** 寂室元光. *See* Jakushitsu Genkō

**jiubu jing** 九部經. *See* navaṅga[pāvacana]

**jiujing** 究竟. *See* niṣṭhā

**jiujing dao/wei** 究竟道/位. *See* niṣṭhāmārga

**Jiujing yisheng baoxing lun** 究竟一乘寶性論. *See* Ratnagotravibhāga

**Jiuluotantou jing** 究羅檀頭經. *See* Kūṭadantasutta

**Jiumoluo Jiashe** 鳩摩羅迦葉. *See* Kumāra-Kāśyapa

**Jiumoluoshi** 鳩摩羅什. *See* Kumārajīva

**Jiumoluoshi fashi dayi** 鳩摩羅什法師大義. *See* Dasheng dayi zhang

**Jiupantu** 鳩槃荼. *See* kumbhāṇḍa

**Jiushouduoluo** 久壽多羅. *See* Kubjottarā

**jiuxiang guan** 九想觀. *See* navasamjñā

**jiwei** 極微. *See* paramānu

**jixiang** 吉祥. *See* maṅgala

**jixiang haiyun** 吉祥海雲. *See* śrīvatsa

**Jiyimen zu lun** 集異門足論. *See* Saṃgītiparyāya[pādaśāstra]

**Jiyin bu** 鷄胤部. *See* Kaukkuṭika

**Jiyuansi** 鷄園寺. *See* Kukkuṭārāma

**Jizushan** 鷄足山. *See* Kukkuṭapāda

**Juchiluo** 拘絺羅. *See* Kauṣṭhila

**jue** 覺. *See* bodhi

**jueding** 決定. *See* niyāma

**jueding xiejian** 決定邪見. *See* niyatamicchādiṭṭhi

**jueding zhongxing** 決定種性. *See* niyatagotra

**jueze** 決擇. *See* nirvedha

**juezhi** 覺支. *See* bodhyaṅga

**Jufeiluo** 俱吠囉. *See* Kubera

**ju jietuo** 俱解脫. *See* ubhayatobhāgavimukta

**Junabolapo** 瞿拏鉢剌婆. *See* Guṇaprabha

**junchi** 軍持. *See* kuṇḍikā

**Juntubohan** 君屠鉢漢. *See* Kuṇḍadhāna

**jusheng fannao zhang** 俱生煩惱障. *See* sahajakleśāvaraṇa

**jusheng fazhi** 俱生法執. *See* er fazhi

**jusheng huo** 俱生惑. *See* sahajakleśāvaraṇa

**jushengqi** 俱生起. *See* sahaja

**jusheng wozhi** 俱生我執. *See* sahajātmagraha; er wozhi

**jusheng wuming** 俱生無明. *See* sahajāvidyā

**jushi** 居士. *See* gṛhapati

**Jushinajieluo** 拘尸那揭羅. *See* Kuśinagarī

**jushou** 具壽. *See* āyuṣman

**Jutan** 瞿曇. *See* Gautama

**juyouyin** 俱有因. *See* sahabhūhetu

**juzhi** 俱胝. *See* koṭi

## K

**Kaifuhua wang [rulai]** 開敷華王[如來]. *See* Saṃkusumitarājendra

**kechen fannao** 客塵煩惱. *See* āgantukakleśa

**kong** 空. *See* śūnyatā

**konghua** 空華. *See* khapuṣpa

**kong jia zhong sanguan** 空假中三觀. *See* sanguan

**kongjie** 空劫. *See* saṃvartasthāyikalpa

**kongkong** 空空. *See* śūnyatāśūnyatā

**Kong wubian chu** 空無邊處. *See* Ākāśānantyāyatana

**ku** 苦. *See* duḥkha

**kuang** 誑. *See* māyā, śāṭhya

**kudi** 苦諦. *See* duḥkhasatya

**kui** 愧. *See* apatrāpya

**kuku** 苦苦. *See* duḥkhaduḥkhatā

**kuxing** 苦行. *See* dhutaṅga, duṣkaracaryā, tapas

**Kuyin jing** 苦陰經. *See* Cūḷadukkhakkhandhasutta, Mahādukkhakkhandhasutta

## L

**Laizhaheluo** 賴吒惒羅. *See* Rāṣṭrapāla

**Lanpini yuan** 藍毘尼園. *See* Lumbinī

**Lanqi Daolong** 蘭溪道隆. *See* Lanxi Daolong

**lao** 老. *See* jarā

**laosi** 老死. *See* jarāmaraṇa

**le** 樂. *See* sukha

**Lenamoti** 勒那摩提. *See* Ratnamati

**leqiu** 樂求. *See* abhilāṣa

**li** 力. *See* bala

**li** 離. *See* niḥsaraṇa, virati

**liang** 量. *See* pramāṇa

**liangbu** 兩部. *See* ryōbu

**lianhua** 蓮華. *See* padma

**lianhua bu** 蓮華部. *See* padmakula

**Lianhuase** 蓮華色. *See* Utpalavarṇā

**Lianhuashou** 蓮華手. *See* Padmapāṇi

**lianhua zuo** 蓮華坐. *See* padmāsana

**liaoyi** 了義. *See* nītārtha

**li boluomi** 力波羅蜜. *See* balapāramitā

**Liehe zeng** 烈河增. *See* Nadī Vaitaraṇī

**Lieshi jing** 獵師經. *See* Nivāpasutta

**ligen** 利根. *See* tīkṣṇendriya

**ligou di** 離垢地. *See* vimalā

**lijianyu** 離間語. *See* paiśunya

**lijiguo** 離繫果. *See* visaṃyogaphala

**lingbu** 令怖. *See* tarjanīyakarman

**lingdi** 靈地. *See* mahāsthāna

**linjiao** 麟角. *See* khaḍgaviṣāṇa

**linjiaoyu** 麟角喻. *See* khaḍgaviṣāṇakalpa

**Lin jing** 林經. *See* Vanapatthasutta

**liran** 離染. *See* vairāgya

**lita** 利他. *See* parārtha

**liuboluomi** 六波羅蜜. *See* ṣaḍpāramitā

**liuchu** 六處. *See* ṣaḍāyatana

**liu genben fannao** 六根本煩惱. *See* ṣaḍmūlakleśa

**liuqu** 六趣. *See* ṣaḍgati

**Liuqun biqiu** 六群比丘. *See* Ṣaḍvārgika

**Liushisong ruli lun** 六十頌如理論. *See* Yuktiṣaṣṭikā

**liuzi daming** 六字大明. *See* ṣaḍakṣarī

**liuzi damingzhou** 六字大明咒. *See* ṣaḍakṣarī

**liuzi zhangju** 六字章句. *See* ṣaḍakṣarī

**Lixi** 離繫. *See* Nirgrantha

**lixilun** 離戲論. *See* niṣprapañca

**liyi** 利益. *See* anuśaṃsa, arthakriyā

**liyu** 離欲. *See* vairāgya

**lizong** 立宗. *See* pratijñā

**lizuofa** 離作法. *See* vyatireka

**long** 龍. *See* nāga

**Longshu** 龍樹. *See* Nāgārjuna

**Longshu pusa quanjie wang song** 龍樹菩薩勸誡王頌. *See* Suhṛllekha

**longxiang** 龍象. *See* hastināga

**Longzhi** 龍智. *See* Nāgabodhi

**lou** 漏. *See* ĀSRAVA, ĀSAVA

**loujin** 漏盡. *See* KṢĪṆĀSRAVA, ĀSRAVAKṢAYA

**Loujin jing** 漏盡經. *See* SABBĀSAVASUTTA

**loujin[zhi]** 漏盡[智]. *See* ĀSRAVAKṢAYA

**lü** 律. *See* VINAYA

**luanshi** 亂識. *See* BHRĀNTIJÑĀNA

**lun** 輪. *See* CAKRA

**lun** 論. *See* ŚĀSTRA, BHĀṢYA

**lunhui** 輪迴. *See* SAṂSĀRA

**lunzang** 論藏. *See* ABHIDHARMAPIṬAKA, *ŚĀSTRAPIṬAKA

**luocha** 羅刹. *See* RĀKṢASA

**Luohouluo** 羅睺羅. *See* RĀHULA

**Luomo jing** 羅摩經. *See* ARIYAPARIYESANĀSUTTA

**Luoponabati** 羅婆那拔提. *See* LAKUṆṬAKA BHADRIKA

**Luotuo** 羅陀. *See* RĀDHA

**Luoxing fanzhi jing** 倮形梵志經. *See* KASSAPASĪHANĀDASUTTA

**lushui nang** 漉水囊. *See* PARISRĀVAṆA

**Luyeyuan** 鹿野苑. *See* MṚGADĀVA

**lüyi** 律儀. *See* SAṂVARA

**lüzang** 律藏. *See* VINAYAPIṬAKA

**Luzhe jing** 露遮經. *See* LOHICCASUTTA

**Luzimu** 鹿子母. *See* VIŚĀKHĀ

**Luzimu tang** 鹿子母堂. *See* MṚGĀRAMĀTṚPRĀSĀDA

## M

**Maming** 馬鳴. *See* AŚVAGHOṢA

**man** 慢. *See* ABHIMĀNA, MĀNA

**man** 鬘. *See* MĀLĀ

**mantuluo** 曼荼羅. *See* MAṆḌALA

**Matou Guanyin** 馬頭觀音. *See* HAYAGRĪVA

**Mayi jing** 馬邑經. *See* CŪḶĀSSAPURASUTTA, MAHĀSSAPURASUTTA

**Mianwang [biqiu]** 面王[比丘]. *See* MOGHARĀJA

**Miaofa lianhua jing** 妙法蓮華經. *See* SADDHARMAPUṆḌARĪKA

**Miaogaoshan** 妙高山. *See* SUMERU, MOUNT

**miao guancha zhi** 妙觀察智. *See* PRATYAVEKṢAṆĀJÑĀNA

**miaoxi** 妙喜. *See* ABHIRATI

**Miaoyin pusa** 妙音菩薩. *See* MAÑJUŚRĪ

**Miaoyintian** 妙音天. *See* SARASVATĪ, SHICHI FUKUJIN

**mie** 滅. *See* NIRODHA

**miedi** 滅諦. *See* NIRODHASATYA

**miejin ding** 滅盡定. *See* NIRODHASAMĀPATTI

**miezhengfa** 滅諍法. *See* ADHIKARAṆAŚAMATHA

**Mile** 彌勒. *See* MAITREYA

**mimi guanding** 秘密灌頂. *See* GUHYĀBHIṢEKA

**ming** 明. *See* VIDYĀ

**ming chu** 明處. *See* VIDYĀSTHĀNA

**Minggen** 命根. *See* JĪVITA

**minghu** 明護. *See* PARITTA

**minghu jing** 明護經. *See* PARITTA

**mingse** 名色. *See* NĀMARŪPA

**Miwanyu jing** 蜜丸喻經. *See* MADHUPIṆḌIKASUTTA

**miyi** 密意. *See* ABHISAṂDHI

**Mo** 魔. *See* MĀRA

**modalijia** 摩怛理迦. *See* MĀTṚKĀ

**Mohe bore boluomi jing** 摩訶般若波羅蜜經. *See* PAÑCAVIṂŚATISĀHASRIKĀPRAJÑĀPĀRAMITĀSŪTRA

**Moheboshebоti** 摩訶波闍波提. *See* MAHĀPRAJĀPATĪ

**Mohejiashe** 摩訶迦葉. *See* MAHĀKĀŚYAPA

**Mohejiazhanyan** 摩訶迦旃延. *See* MAHĀKĀTYAYANA

**Mohejiebinna** 摩訶劫賓那. *See* MAHĀKAPPHIṆA

**Mohelatuo guo** 摩訶剌佗國. *See* MAHĀRAṬṬHA

**Mohemujianlian** 摩訶目犍連. *See* MAHĀMAUDGALYĀYANA

**Mohenan** 摩訶男. *See* MAHĀNĀMAN

**Mohepiheluo** 摩訶毘訶羅. *See* MAHĀVIHĀRA

**mohesa** 摩訶薩. *See* MAHĀSATTVA

**Mohesina** 摩訶斯那. *See* MAHĀSENA

**Mohetipo** 摩訶提婆. *See* MAHĀDEVA

**mohouluojia** 摩睺羅迦. *See* MAHORĀGA

**Mojietuo [guo]** 摩揭陀[國]. *See* MAGADHA

**mojieyu** 摩竭魚. *See* MAKARA

**Moli** 末利. *See* MALLIKĀ

**Molizhi** 摩利支. *See* Marīci

**Moluo [guo]** 摩羅[國]. *See* Mallā

**Moluonantuo** 摩羅難陀. *See* *Mālānanda

**mona shi** 末那識. *See* kliṣṭamanas

**Monasi** 摩那斯. *See* Manasvin

**monatuo** 摩那埵. *See* mānatva

**moni** 摩尼. *See* maṇi

**Moqieli Jushelizi** 末伽梨拘賒梨子. *See* Maskarin Gośāla

**Motiandi** 末田地. *See* Madhyāntika

**Motouluo** 摩偸羅. *See* Mathurā

**Moulipoqunna jing** 牟犁破群那經. *See* Kakacūpamasutta

**mouni** 牟尼. *See* muni

**Mowang [Boxun]** 魔王[波旬]. *See* Namuci, Pāpīyāms

**Moxilizhizha** 摩咥里制吒. *See* Mātṛceṭa

**Moxisuomantuoluo [guo]** 摩醯娑慢陀羅[國]. *See* Mahisa Maṇḍala

**Moye** 摩耶. *See* Māyā

**muduo** 木鐸. *See* mokt'ak

**Mujianlianzidixu** 目犍連子帝須. *See* Moggaliputtatissa

**Mulian** 目連. *See* Mahāmaudgalyāyana

**Muzhenlintuo** 目眞隣陀. *See* Mucilinda

## N

**Nalantuosi** 那爛陀寺. *See* Nālandā

**Naliantiliyeshe** 那連提黎耶舍. *See* Narendrayaśas

**Naluoyan tian** 那羅延天. *See* Nārāyaṇa

**namo Amituo fo** 南無阿彌陀佛. *See* Amitābha, namu Amidabutsu

**Namo Miaofa lianhua jing** 南無妙法蓮華經. *See* Namu Myōhōrengekyō

**nanchu** 難處. *See* akṣaṇa

**nansheng di** 難勝地. *See* sudurjayā

**Nantuo** 難陀. *See* Nanda

**Nantuojia** 難陀迦. *See* Nandaka

**nao** 惱. *See* pradāsa

**Naqiexina** 那伽犀那. *See* Nāgasena

**Nati Jiashe** 那提迦葉. *See* Nadī-Kāśyapa

**Naxian** 那先. *See* Nāgasena

**Naxian biqiu** 那先比丘. *See* Nāgasena

**Naxian biqiu jing** 那先比丘經. *See* Milindapañha

**Nayouluo fu** 那憂羅父. *See* Nakulapitṛ and Nakulamātṛ

**neiming** 内明. *See* adhyātmavidyā

**neiyi** 内衣. *See* antarvāsas

**neizheng** 内證. *See* pratyātmādhigama

**nengli** 能立. *See* sādhana

**nengzuo yin** 能作因. *See* kāraṇahetu

**nian** 念. *See* anusmṛti, smṛti

**nianchu** 念處. *See* smṛtyupasthāna

**Nianchu jing** 念處經. *See* Satipaṭṭhānasutta

**niansi** 念死. *See* maraṇānusmṛti

**niansong** 念誦. *See* japa

**nianzhu** 念珠. *See* japamālā

**Nielidi** 涅哩底. *See* Nirṛti

**niepan** 涅槃. *See* nirvāṇa

**niepanjie** 涅槃界. *See* nirvāṇadhātu

**Niepan jing** 涅槃經. *See* Mahāparinibbānasuttanta, Mahāparinirvānasūtra

**niepanseng** 涅槃僧. *See* nivāsana

**Nijiantuo Ruotizi** 尼揵陀若提子. *See* Nirgrantha-Jñātīputra

**Nijianzi** 尼揵子. *See* Nirgrantha

**Nijulü lin** 尼拘律林. *See* Nyagrodhārāma

**Nijutuo** 尼瞿陀. *See* Nigrodha

**Nilianchanhe** 尼連禪河. *See* Nairañjanā

**nituona** 尼陀那. *See* nidāna

**Niujiaosuoluolin jing** 牛角娑羅林經. *See* Cūḷagosiṅgasutta, Mahāgosiṅgasutta

**Niuzhu** 牛主. *See* Gavāṃpati

**nuan** 煖. *See* ūṣman

**Nuoguluo zhangzhe mu** 諾酤羅長者母. *See* Nakulamātṛ

## P

**Pantoudaduo** 槃頭達多. *See* Bandhudatta

**Pijuzhi** 毘俱胝. *See* Bhṛkutī

**Piluzhena** 毗盧遮那. *See* VAIROCANA

**Pinaiye shi** 毘奈耶事. *See* VINAYAVASTU

**pingdengxing zhi** 平等性智. *See* SAMATĀJÑĀNA

**Pinlei zu lun** 品類足論. *See* PRAKARAṆAPĀDA[ŚĀSTRA]

**Pinposuoluo** 頻婆娑羅. *See* BIMBISĀRA

**Pipan Fojiao** 批判佛教. *See* HIHAN BUKKYŌ

**Piposha shi** 毘婆沙師. *See* VAIBHĀṢIKA

**Piposhi fo** 毘婆尸佛. *See* VIPAŚYIN

**piqieluo** 毘伽羅. *See* VYĀKARANA

**Pishamen tian** 毘沙門天. *See* VAIŚRAVAṆA

**Pisheli** 毘舍離. *See* VAIŚĀLĪ

**Pishequ** 毗舍佉. *See* VIŚĀKHA

**Pishequmu** 毗舍佉母. *See* VIŚĀKHĀ

**pisheshe** 毘舍闍. *See* PIŚĀCA

**Pitihe** 毘提訶. *See* VIDEHA

**piyu** 譬喻. *See* AVADĀNA

**Pocha** 婆差. *See* VATSAGOTRA

**Pofu** 婆敷. *See* VĀṢPA

**Pojiali** 婆迦梨. *See* VAKKALI

**Poqishe** 婆耆舍. *See* VAṄGĪSA

**poseng** 破僧. *See* SAṂGHABHEDA

**Poxijia** 婆呬迦. *See* BĀHIYA-DĀRUCĪRIYA

**pusa** 菩薩. *See* BODHISATTVA

**Pusa benshengman lun** 菩薩本生鬘論. *See* JĀTAKAMĀLĀ

**pusa di** 菩薩地. *See* BODHISATTVABHŪMI

**Pusa dichi jing** 菩薩地持經. *See* BODHISATTVABHŪMI

**Pusa jianshi jing** 菩薩見實經. *See* PITĀPUTRASAMĀGAMASŪTRA

**pusa sheng** 菩薩乘. *See* BODHISATTVAYĀNA

**pusa yuan** 菩薩願. *See* BODHISATTVAPRAṆIDHĀNA

**Pusazang jing** 菩薩藏[經]. *See* BODHISATTVAPIṬAKA

**puti** 菩提. *See* BODHI

**Putidamo** 菩提達磨. *See* BODHIDHARMA

**puti fen** 菩提分. *See* BODHIPĀKṢIKADHARMA

**puti ju** 菩提具. *See* BODHISAṂBHĀRA

**Putiliuzhi** 菩提流支. *See* BODHIRUCI

**puti shu** 菩提樹. *See* BODHI TREE

**Putixianna** 菩提僊那. *See* BODHISENA

**putixin** 菩提心. *See* BODHICITTA

**Putixing jing** 菩提行經. *See* BODHICARYĀVATĀRA

**puti ziliang** 菩提資糧. *See* BODHISAṂBHĀRA

**Puti ziliang lun** 菩提資糧論. *See* BODHISAṂBHĀRA

**Puxian** 普賢. *See* SAMANTABHADRA

**Puxiang** 普香. *See* SAMANTAGANDHA

**Puxian pusa xingyuan zan** 普賢菩薩行願讚. *See* BHADRACARĪPRAṆIDHĀNA

**Puyao jing** 普曜經. *See* LALITAVISTARA

**Puzhao Zhine** 普照知訥. *See* POJO CHINUL

## Q

**qian** 慳. *See* MĀTSARYA

**Qianshou Qianyan Guanyin** 千手千眼觀音. *See* SĀHASRABHUJASĀHASRANETRĀVALOKITEŚVARA

**Qianyan** 千眼. *See* SAHASRĀKṢA

**Qianzhengjueshan** 前正覺山. *See* PRĀGBODHI(GIRI)

**Qibai song bore** 七百頌般若. *See* SAPTAŚATIKĀPRAJÑĀPĀRAMITĀ

**qi cai** 七財. *See* SAPTADHANA

**Qiche jing** 七車經. *See* RATHAVINĪTASUTTA

**Qielan jing** 伽藍經. *See* KĀLĀMASUTTA

**Qieye Jiashe** 伽耶迦葉. *See* GAYĀ-KĀŚYAPA

**qifo** 七佛. *See* SAPTATATHĀGATA

**qijuezhi** 七覺支. *See* BODHYAṄGA

**qike yin** 祈克印. *See* TARJANĪMUDRĀ

**qi miezheng fa** 七滅諍法. *See* SAPTĀDHIKARAṆAŚAMATHA

**qince lüyi** 勤策律儀. *See* ŚRĀMAṆERASAṂVARA

**qing'an** 輕安. *See* PRAŚRABDHI

**Qingbian** 清辯. *See* BHĀVAVIVEKA

**qingjing** 清淨. *See* PARIŚUDDHA, VAIYAVADĀNIKA

**qingjing foguotu** 清淨佛國土. *See* PARIŚUDDHABUDDHAKṢETRA

**Qingjing jing** 清淨經. *See* PĀSĀDIKASUTTA

**Qingyou** 慶友. *See* NANDIMITRA

**Qipo** 耆婆. *See* JĪVAKA

**qishi** 乞食. *See* PIṆḌAPĀTA

**qishijian** 器世間. *See* BHĀJANALOKA

**Qiufa jing** 求法經. *See* DHAMMADĀYĀDASUTTA

**Qiujie jing** 求解經. *See* VĪMAṂSAKASUTTA

**Qiunabamo** 求那跋摩. *See* GUṆAVARMAN

**Qiunabatuoluo** 求那跋陀羅. *See* GUṆABHADRA

**Qiuzi** 龜茲. *See* KUCHA

**qiye** 祇夜. *See* GEYA

**qizhi zuofa** 七支作法. *See* SAPTĀṄGAVIDHI

**qu** 趣. *See* GATI

**qu** 取. *See* UPĀDĀNA

**quchu jiemo** 驅出羯磨. *See* PRAVRĀJANĪYAKARMAN

**qun** 裙. *See* NIVĀSANA

**Qutuoni** 瞿陀尼. *See* GODĀNĪYA

**quyun** 取蘊. *See* UPĀDĀNASKANDHA

## R

**ran** 染. *See* SAṂKLEŚA

**Rangxiang jingang tuoluoni jing** 壤相金剛陀羅尼經. *See* VAJRAVIDĀRAṆADHĀRAṆĪ

**ranmona** 染末那. *See* KLIṢṬAMANAS

**Ranshao** 燃燒. *See* ĀDITTAPARIYĀYASUTTA

**ranzhi** 燃指. *See* YŎNJI

**raoyi youqing** 饒益有情. *See* SATTVĀRTHA

**ren** 人. *See* MANUṢYA, PUDGALA, PURUṢA

**renru** 忍辱. *See* KṢĀNTI

**renru boluomi** 忍辱波羅蜜. *See* KṢĀNTIPĀRAMITĀ

**Renru xianren** 忍辱仙人. *See* KṢĀNTIVĀDIN

**renwozhi** 人我執. *See* PUDGALĀTMAGRAHA

**renwuwo** 人無我. *See* PUDGALANAIRĀTMYA

**Renxian** 仁賢. *See* BHADRIKA

**Rizhong** 日種. *See* ĀDITYABANDHU

**rouji** 肉髻. *See* UṢṆĪṢA

**rouyan** 肉眼. *See* MĀṂSACAKṢUS

**ruhuan sanmei** 如幻三昧. *See* MĀYOPAMASAMĀDHI

**ruhuan yu** 如幻喻. *See* AṢṬAMĀYOPĀMA

**ruixiang** 瑞相. *See* NIMITTA

**Ruixiye jing** 蕤呬耶經. *See* SARVAMAṆḌALASĀMĀNYAVIDHIGUHYATANTRA

**rulai** 如來. *See* TATHĀGATA

**rulai di** 如來地. *See* TATHĀGATABHŪMI

**rulai jia** 如來家. *See* TATHĀGATAKULA, BUDDHAKULA

**rulai xing** 如來性. *See* TATHĀGATAGOTRA

**rulaizang** 如來藏. *See* TATHĀGATAGARBHA

**Ru Lengqie jing** 入楞伽經. *See* LAṄKĀVATĀRASŪTRA

**ruliang zhi** 如量智. *See* YĀVADBHĀVIKAJÑĀNA

**ruli zhi** 如理智. *See* YATHĀVADBHĀVIKAJÑĀNA

**ruli zuoyi** 如理作意. *See* YONIŚOMANASKĀRA

**rushi wowen** 如是我聞. *See* EVAṂ MAYĀ ŚRUTAṂ

**rushi zhijian** 如實知見. *See* YATHĀBHŪTAJÑĀNADARŚANA

**ruyi baozhu** 如意寶珠. *See* CINTAMĀṆI

## S

**sanbaluo** 三跋羅. *See* SAṂVARA

**sanbao** 三寶. *See* RATNATRAYA

**sandu** 三毒. *See* TRIVIṢA

**san fenbie** 三分別. *See* TRIVIKALPA

**sangen** 三根. *See* TRĪNDRIYA

**sanguiyi** 三歸依. *See* TRIŚARAṆA

**sanjie** 三界. *See* TRAIDHĀTUKA, TRAILOKYA, TRILOKA

**sanju** 三聚. *See* TRISKANDHAKA

**sanju jingjie** 三聚淨戒. *See* ŚĪLATRAYA

**sanluan** 散亂. *See* VIKṢEPA

**sanmei** 三昧. *See* SAMĀDHI

**sanmeiye saduo** 三昧耶薩埵. *See* SAMAYASATTVA

**sanmen** 三門. *See* TRIDVĀRA

**sanming** 三明. *See* TRIVIDYĀ

**Sanming jing** 三明經. *See* TEVIJJASUTTA

**sanmoye** 三摩耶. *See* SAMAYA

**sanmoye yin** 三摩耶印. *See* SAMAYAMUDRĀ

**sanqian daqian shijie** 三千大千世界. *See* TRISĀHASRAMAHĀSĀHASRALOKADHĀTU

**sanshen** 三身. *See* TRIKĀYA

**sansheng** 三乘. *See* TRIYĀNA

**sanshi** 三世. *See* TRIKĀLA

**sanshi'er xiang** 三十二相. *See* DVĀTRIṂŚADVARALAKṢAṆA, MAHĀPURUṢALAKṢAṆA

**Sanshi'er xiang jing** 三十二相經. *See* LAKKHAṆASUTTA

**sanshiqi daopin** 三十七道品. *See* BODHIPĀKṢIKADHARMA

**sanshisan tian** 三十三天. *See* TRĀYASTRIṂŚA

**Santuona jing** 散陀那經. *See* UDUMBARIKASĪHANĀDASUTTA

**sanxiang** 三相. *See* TRILAKṢAṆA

**sanxing** 三性. *See* TRISVABHĀVA

**sanxue** 三學. *See* TRIŚIKṢA

**sanyi** 三衣. *See* TRICĪVARA

**sanzang** 三藏. *See* TRIPIṬAKA

**sanzang fashi** 三藏法師. *See* TREPIṬAKA

**Sapoduo bu** 薩婆多部. *See* SARVĀSTIVĀDA

**se** 色. *See* RŪPA

**sechu** 色處. *See* RŪPĀYATANA

**sejie** 色界. *See* RŪPADHĀTU

**sejie ding** 色界定. *See* RŪPĀVACĀRADHYĀNA

**se jishi kong kong jishi se** 色即是空空即是色. *See* RŪPAṂ ŚŪNYATĀ ŚUNYATAIVA RŪPAṂ

**sejiujing tian** 色究竟天. *See* AKANIṢṬHA

**sengcan fa/zui** 僧殘法/罪. *See* SAṂGHĀVAŚESA

**seng jiemo** 僧羯磨. *See* SAṂGHAKARMAN

**sengke** 僧科. *See* SŬNGKWA

**Senglang** 僧朗. *See* SŬNGNANG

**sengqie** 僧伽. *See* SAṂGHA

**Sengqiebamo** 僧伽跋摩. *See* SAṂGHAVARMAN

**sengqieli** 僧伽梨. *See* SAṂGHĀṬĪ

**Sengqiemiduo** 僧伽蜜多. *See* SAṄGHAMITTĀ

**Sengqieshi** 僧伽施. *See* SĀṂKĀŚYA

**sengzhizhi** 僧祇支. *See* SAṂKAKṢIKĀ

**seshen** 色身. *See* RŪPAKĀYA

**se tan** 色貪. *See* RŪPARĀGA

**se yun** 色蘊. *See* RŪPASKANDHA

**Shaluohe** 沙羅訶. *See* SARAHA

**shaluoshu** 沙羅樹. *See* ŚĀLA

**shamen** 沙門. *See* ŚRĀMAṆA

**shamenguo** 沙門果. *See* ŚRĀMAṆYAPHALA

**Shamenguo jing** 沙門果經. *See* SĀMAÑÑAPHALASUTTA

**shami** 沙彌. *See* ŚRĀMANERA

**shamini** 沙彌尼. *See* ŚRĀMAṆERIKĀ

**shan** 善. *See* KUŚALA

**Shancai** 善財. *See* SUDHANA

**shangen** 善根. *See* KUŚALAMŪLA

**shanghua shen** 上化身. *See* UTTAMANIRMĀṆAKĀYA

**Shangjieluozhu** 商羯羅主. *See* ŚAṂKARASVĀMIN

**shangliu ban** 上流般. *See* ŪRDHVASROTAS

**shangliu banniepan** 上流般涅槃. *See* ŪRDHVASROTAS

**Shangnahexiu** 商那和修. *See* ŚĀṆAKAVĀSIN

**Shangnuojiafusuo** 商諾迦縛娑. *See* ŚĀṆAKAVĀSIN

**Shangxing** 上行. *See* VIŚIṢṬACĀRITRA

**shangzuo** 上座. *See* STHAVIRA

**Shangzuo bu** 上座部. *See* STHAVIRANIKĀYA

**Shanhui** 善慧. *See* SUMEDHA

**shanhui di** 善慧地. *See* SĀDHUMATĪ

**Shanjianlü piposha** 善見律毘婆沙. *See* SAMANTAPĀSĀDIKĀ

**shanjian tian** 善見天. *See* SUDARŚANA

**Shanlai** 善來. *See* SVĀGATA

**shanlai bichu** 善來苾芻. *See* EHIBHIKṢUKĀ

**shannanzi** 善男子. *See* KULAPUTRA

**shannüren** 善女人. *See* KULADUHITṚ

**shanqu** 善趣. *See* SUGATI

**Shansheng jing** 善生經. *See* SIGĀLOVĀDASUTTA

**Shansheye Piluozhizi** 刪闍耶毘羅胝子. *See* SAÑJAYA VAIRĀṬĪPUTRA

**shanshi** 善逝. *See* SUGATA

**Shansui** 善歲. *See* SUVARṢAKA

**Shanwuwei** 善無畏. *See* ŚUBHAKARASIṂHA

**Shanxian** 善賢. *See* BHADRIKA

**shanxian tian** 善現天. *See* SUDṚŚA

**Shanxing** 善星. *See* SUNAKṢATRA

**Shanye jing** 善夜經. *See* Bhadrakārātrī

**shanzhishi** 善知識. *See* kalyāṇamitra

**shaoguang tian** 少光天. *See* parīttābha

**shaojing tian** 少淨天. *See* parīttaśubha

**she** 捨. *See* upekṣā

**shechu** 舌處. *See* jihvāyatana

**She dasheng lun** 攝大乘論. *See* Mahāyānasaṃgraha

**sheduo** 捨墮. *See* naiḥsargika pāyattika

**shegen** 舌根. *See* jihvendriya

**shejie** 捨界. *See* sīmāsamūhana

**Shejuli** 奢拘梨. *See* Sakulā

**sheli** 舍利. *See* śarīra

**Shelifu** 舍利弗. *See* Śāriputra

**shen** 身. *See* kāya

**Shenajueduo** 闍那崛多. *See* Jñānagupta

**shenbianxiang** 神變相. *See* mahāprātihārya

**shenchu** 身處. *See* kāyāyatana

**sheng** 聖. *See* ārya

**sheng** 生. *See* jāti

**sheng** 聲. *See* śabda

**sheng** 乘. *See* yāna

**sheng** 生. *See* yoni

**sheng ban** 生般. *See* upapadyaparinirvāyin

**sheng banniepan** 生般涅槃. *See* upapadyaparinirvāyin

**shengchu** 勝處. *See* abhibhvāyatana

**shengchu** 聲處. *See* śabdāyatana

**shengdao** 聖道. *See* āryamārga

**shengdaoguo** 聖道果. *See* āryamārgaphala

**shengde ding** 生得定. *See* dhyānopapatti

**shengdi** 聖諦. *See* four noble truths

**shengen** 身根. *See* kāyendriya

**Shengfomu xiaozi bore boluomiduo jing** 聖佛母小字般若波羅蜜多經. *See* Svalpākṣaraprajñāpāramitā

**shengjiao** 聖教. *See* śāsana

**shengjie** 勝解. *See* adhimokṣa

**Shengman shizihou yisheng da fangbian fangguang jing** 勝鬘師子吼一乘大方便方廣經. *See* Śrīmālādevīsiṃhanādasūtra

**Sheng miaojixiang zhenshi ming jing** 聖妙吉祥眞實名經. *See* Mañjuśrīnāmasaṃgīti

**shengqi** 生起. *See* utpāda

**shengqi cidi** 生起次第. *See* utpattikrama

**shengseng** 聖僧. *See* āryasaṃgha

**shengsheng** 勝生. *See* abhyudaya

**shengsi lunhui** 生死輪迴. *See* saṃsāra

**shengsizhi** 生死智. *See* cyutyupapattijñāna

**Shengtian wang bore boluomi jing** 勝天王般若波羅蜜經. *See* Suvikrāntavikrāmiparipṛcchāprajñāpāramitā

**shenguan** 身觀. *See* kāyānupaśyanā

**shengwen** 聲聞. *See* śrāvaka

**shengwen cidi** 聲聞次第. *See* viṃśatiprabhedasaṃgha

**Shengwen di** 聲聞地. *See* Śrāvakabhūmi

**shengwen sheng** 聲聞乘. *See* śrāvakayāna

**shengwen zhongxing** 聲聞種姓. *See* śrāvakagotra

**shengyi seng** 勝義僧. *See* paramārthasaṃgha

**shengzhe** 聖者. *See* muni

**shengzhi** 生支. *See* liṅga

**shengzhong** 聖種. *See* āryavaṃśa

**Shenisha jing** 闍尼沙經. *See* Janavasabhasuttanta

**shenjing zhizhengtong** 神境智證通. *See* ṛddhividhābhijñā

**shenli** 神力. *See* ṛddhi

**Shenmao xishu jing** 身毛喜豎經. *See* Mahāsīhanādasutta

**shenshi** 身識. *See* kāyavijñāna

**shentong** 神通. *See* abhijñā

**shenwo** 神我. *See* puruṣa

**Shenxiang** 審祥. *See* Simsang

**shenxin tuoluo** 身心脫落. *See* shinjin datsuraku

**Shen xiyou jing** 甚希有經. *See* Adbhutadharmaparyāyasūtra

**shenzheng** 身證. *See* kāyasākṣin

**Shenzhong** 神衆. *See* Sinjung

**sheru dasheng** 攝入大乘. *See* Ekayāna

**sheshi** 舌識. *See* jihvāvijñāna

**Shewei guo** 舍衛國. *See* Śrāvastī

**she wuliangxin** 捨無量心. *See* upekṣāpramāṇa

**shexuejie zhe** 捨學戒者. *See* SIKKHĀPACCAKKHĀNA

**shi** 食. *See* ĀHĀRA

**shi** 師. *See* GURU

**shi** 師. *See* ŚĀSTṚ

**shi** 識. *See* VIJÑĀNA, VIJÑAPTI

**shichamona** 式叉摩那. *See* ŚIKṢAMĀṆĀ

**shichamona jie** 式叉摩那戒. *See* ŚIKṢAMĀṆĀSAMVARA

**Shichanantuo** 實叉難陀. *See* ŚIKṢĀNANDA

**shidi** 十地. *See* DAŚABHŪMI

**Shidijing lun** 十地經論. *See* DAŚABHŪMIVYĀKHYĀNA, DI LUN ZONG

**shidiyifa** 世第一法. *See* LAUKIKĀGRADHARMA

**shi'erbu jing** 十二部經. *See* DVĀDAŚĀṄGA[PRAVACANA]

**Shi'er yinyuan lun** 十二因緣論. *See* PRATĪTYASAMUTPĀDAHṚDAYAKĀRIKĀ

**shifa** 世法. *See* LOKADHARMA

**shifang** 十方. *See* DAŚADIŚ

**Shifenzeng** 屍糞增. *See* KUṆAPA

**shifu** 士夫. *See* PURUṢA

**shihao** 謚號. *See* SIHO

**Shihu** 施護. *See* DĀNAPĀLA

**shiji** 實際. *See* BHŪTAKOṬI

**Shijia** 釋迦. *See* ŚĀKYA, cf. SHI

**Shijiamouni** 釋迦牟尼. *See* ŚĀKYAMUNI

**shijian** 世間. *See* LAUKIKA, LOKA

**shijia seng** 釋迦僧. *See* ŚĀKYABHIKṢU

**shijie** 十界. *See* DAŚADHĀTU

**shijie** 十戒. *See* DAŚAŚĪLA

**shijie** 世界. *See* LOKA

**shijie** 世界. *See* LOKADHĀTU

**shi jietuo** 時解脫. *See* SAMAYAVIMUKTA

**Shikeluoge zhangzhe mu** 室珂羅哥長者母. *See* ŚṚGĀLAKAMĀTṚ

**shili** 十力. *See* BALA, DAŚABALA

**Shilifoshi** 室利佛逝. *See* ŚRĪVIJAYA

**shilin** 屍林. *See* ŚMAŚĀNA

**shiliu luohan** 十六羅漢. *See* ṢODAŚASTHAVIRA

**shiliu zunzhe** 十六尊者. *See* ṢODAŚASTHAVIRA

**Shiluodamo** 尸羅達摩. *See* ŚĪLADHARMA

**shinian** 失念. *See* MUṢITASMṚTI

**Shiniu tu** 十牛圖. *See* OXHERDING PICTURES, TEN

**Shipi** 尸毘. *See* ŚIBI

**Shipoluo** 尸婆羅. *See* SĪVALI

**Shiqin** 世親. *See* VASUBANDHU

**Shishang jing** 十上經. *See* DASUTTARASUTTA

**Shishe lun** 施設論. *See* PRAJÑAPTIBHĀṢYA[PĀDAŚĀSTRA]

**Shishen zu lun** 識身足論. *See* VIJÑĀNAKĀYA[PĀDAŚĀSTRA]

**shishi** 實事. *See* DRAVYA

**Shishi guo** 石室國. *See* TAKṢAŚILĀ

**shisu** 世俗. *See* SAṂVṚTI

**shisu di** 世俗諦. *See* SAṂVṚTISATYA

**shisu seng** 世俗僧. *See* SAMMUTISAṄGHA

**Shiwansong bore** 十萬頌般若. *See* ŚATASĀHASRIKĀPRAJÑĀPĀRAMITĀ

**Shi wubian chu** 識無邊處. *See* VIJÑĀNĀNANTYĀYATANA

**shi wuwei** 施無畏. *See* ABHAYADĀNA

**shiwuwei yin** 施無畏印. *See* ABHAYAMUDRĀ

**shixian** 示現. *See* PRĀTIHĀRYA

**shixiang** 實相. *See* TATTVA

**Shixiang bore boluomi jing** 實相般若波羅蜜經. *See* ADHYARDHAŚATIKĀPRAJÑĀPĀRAMITĀSŪTRA/ PRAJÑĀPĀRAMITĀNAYAPAÑCAŚATIKĀ

**shiye** 始業. *See* ĀDIKARMIKA

**Shiyimian Guanyin** 十一面觀音. *See* EKĀDAŚAMUKHĀVALOKITEŚVARA

**shiyin** 識陰. *See* VIJÑĀNASKANDHA

**shiyong guo** 士用果. *See* PURUṢAKĀRAPHALA

**shi you** 實有. *See* DRAVYASAT

**Shiyou** 世友. *See* VASUMITRA

**shiyu** 實語. *See* SATYAVACANA

**shiyuan yin** 施願印. *See* VARADAMUDRĀ

**shiyun** 識蘊. *See* VIJÑĀNASKANDHA

**shizhu** 施主. *See* DĀNAPATI

**Shizhu jing** 十住經. *See* DAŚABHŪMIKASŪTRA

**shizihou** 師子吼. *See* siṃhanāda

**Shizihou jing** 師子吼經. *See* Cūḷasīhanādasutta

**Shizizai** 世自在. *See* Lokeśvara

**Shizizai wang fo** 世自在王佛. *See* Lokeśvararāja

**shizi zuo** 師子座. *See* siṃhāsana

**shizun** 世尊. *See* Bhagavat

**shou** 受. *See* vedanā

**Shoucai** 守財. *See* Dhanapāla, Nālāgiri

**Shoufa jing** 受法經. *See* Cūḷadhammasamādānasutta, Mahādhammasamādānasutta

**shouji** 授記. *See* vyākaraṇa

**shoujie** 受戒. *See* upasaṃpadā

**Shoulaoren** 壽老人. *See* Shichifukujin

**Shoulengyan jing** 首楞嚴經. *See* *Śūraṃgamasūtra

**Shoulengyan sanmei** 首楞嚴三昧. *See* śūraṃgamasamādhi

**Shoulengyan sanmei jing** 首楞嚴三昧經. *See* Śūraṃgamasamādhisūtra

**Shoulongna** 守籠那. *See* Soṇa Kolivīsa

**shoumenren** 守門人. *See* dvārapāla

**shouming** 壽命. *See* jīvita

**shuangru** 雙入. *See* yuganaddha

**shuangshenbian** 雙神變. *See* yamakaprātihārya

**shuangyun** 雙運. *See* yuganaddha

**Shubojia** 戍博迦. *See* Jīvaka

**shuida** 水大. *See* āpas [alt. āpodhātu]

**Shuijing fanzhi jing** 水淨梵志經. *See* Vatthūpamasutta

**shuimian** 睡眠. *See* middha

**Shuluna** 輸盧那. *See* Śroṇāparānta

**Shuna** 輸那. *See* Soṇā

**shunci shengshou ye** 順次生受業. *See* upapadyavedanīyakarman

**Shundao** 順道. *See* Sundo

**shunni** 順逆. *See* anulomapratiloma

**shunjietuofen** 順解脫分. *See* mokṣabhāgīya

**shunjuezefen** 順決擇分. *See* nirvedhabhagīya

**shunshi sanmei** 順世三昧. *See* lokiyasamādhi

**Shunshi waidao** 順世外道. *See* Lokāyata

**Shun zhengli lun** 順正理論. *See* *Nyāyānusāra

**Shuochushibu** 說出世部. *See* Lokottaravāda

**shuofashi** 說法師. *See* dharmabhāṇaka

**Shuojiabu** 說假部. *See* Prajñaptivāda

**Shuo yiqieyou bu** 說一切有部. *See* Sarvāstivāda

**shuxi guan** 數息觀. *See* ānāpānasmṛti

**shuzhu** 數珠. *See* japamālā

**si** 思. *See* cetanā

**si** 死. *See* maraṇa

**si** 伺. *See* vicāra

**sida** 四大. *See* mahābhūta

**sidi** 四諦. *See* catvāry āryasatyāni, four noble truths

**sidi falun** 四諦法輪. *See* catuḥsatyadharmacakra

**si fanzui men** 四犯罪門. *See* *caturāpattidvāra

**sihui** 思慧. *See* cintāmayīprajñā

**siju fenbie** 四句分別. *See* catuṣkoṭi

**Silu** 絲路. *See* Silk Road

**Simo** 死魔. *See* Mṛtyumāra

**si shangen** 四善根. *See* catuṣkuśalamūla

**si sheng** 四生. *See* yoni, catvāro yonayaḥ

**si shengdi** 四聖諦. *See* four noble truths

**si shenzu** 四神足. *See* ṛddhipāda

**si sheshi** 四攝事. *See* saṃgrahavastu

**sishi** 思食. *See* manaḥsaṃcetanāhāra

**sitianwang** 四天王. *See* lokapāla

**sitianwang tian** 四天王天. *See* cāturmahārājakāyika

**situohan** 斯陀含. *See* sakṛdāgāmin

**siwei** 思惟. *See* buddhi

**si wu'ai jie** 四無礙解. *See* pratisaṃvid

**sixiang** 四相. *See* caturlakṣaṇa, caturnimitta

**siyin** 四印. *See* caturmudrā

**size** 思擇. *See* tarka

**si zhengqin** 四正勤. *See* prahāṇa

**song** 頌. *See* śloka

**su** 俗. *See* saṃvṛti

**sudi** 俗諦. *See* SAṂVṚTISATYA, VYAVAHĀRA

**sui fannao** 隨煩惱. *See* UPAKLEŚA

**suifaxing** 隨法行. *See* DHARMĀNUSĀRIN

**suiliuxiang chanding** 隨流向禪定. *See* SROTO'NUGATO NĀMA SAMĀDHIḤ

**suimian** 隨眠. *See* ANUŚAYA

**suinian fenbie** 隨念分別. *See* ANUSMARAṆAVIKALPA

**suiwen** 隨聞. *See* ANUŚRAVA

**suixi** 隨喜. *See* ANUMODANA

**suixifu** 隨喜福. *See* PUṆYĀNUMODANA

**suixin xing** 隨信行. *See* ŚRADDHĀNUSĀRIN

**suming** 宿命. *See* JĀTISMARA

**sunjian** 損減. *See* APAVĀDA

**Suntuoli** 孫陀利. *See* SUNDARĪNANDĀ

**Suntuoluonantuo** 孫陀羅難陀. *See* SUNDARANANDA

**suochengli** 所成立. *See* SĀDHYADHARMA

**suochu** 所觸. *See* SPRAṢṬAVYA

**suode** 所得. *See* UPALABDHI

**suoduizhi** 所對治. *See* VIPAKṢA

**Suojieluo** 娑竭羅. *See* SĀGARA

**suoli** 所立. *See* SĀDHYADHARMA

**Suopo** 娑婆. *See* SAHĀLOKA

**Suopo shijie** 娑婆世界. *See* SAHĀLOKA

**Suopo shijie zhu** 娑婆世界主. *See* SAHĀṂPATI

**Suoqieluo** 娑伽羅. *See* SĀGARA

**suoqu nengqu fenbie** 所取能取分別. *See* GRĀHYAGRĀHAKAVIKALPA

**suoyi** 所依. *See* ĀŚRAYA, NIŚRAYA

**suoyuan** 所緣. *See* ĀLAMBANA

**suoyuan yuan** 所緣緣. *See* ĀLAMBANAPRATYAYA

**Suozhiduo cheng** 娑枳多城. *See* SĀKETA

**suozhizhang** 所知障. *See* JÑEYĀVARAṆA

**Supintuo** 蘇頻陀. *See* SUBINDA

**Supohu tongzi qingwen jing** 蘇婆呼童子請問經. *See* SUBĀHUPARIPṚCCHĀTANTRA

**Suxidi jieluo jing** 蘇悉地羯羅經. *See* *SUSIDDHIKARASŪTRA

**suzhu suinian** 宿住隨念. *See* PŪRVANIVĀSĀNUSMṚTI

# T

**ta** 塔. *See* STŪPA

**tabiliang** 他比量. *See* PARĀRTHĀNUMĀNA

**tahuazizai tian** 他化自在天. *See* PARANIRMITAVAŚAVARTIN

**taixian** 太賢. *See* T'AEHYŎN

**taizang jie** 胎藏界. *See* TAIZŌKAI

**tali** 他力. *See* TARIKI

**tan** 貪. *See* ABHIDHYĀ, LOBHA, RĀGA

**Tangwei zeng** 煻煨增. *See* KUKŪLA

**Tanmotina biqiuni** 曇摩提那比丘尼. *See* DHARMADINNĀ

**tanteluo** 檀特羅. *See* TANTRA

**Tanwuchen** 曇無讖. *See* DHARMAKṢEMA

**Tanwudebu** 曇無德部. *See* DHARMAGUPTAKA

**Tanwujian** 曇無竭. *See* DHARMODGATA

**tanyue** 檀越. *See* DĀNAPATI

**Tapomoluo** 沓婆摩羅. *See* DRAVYA MALLAPUTRA

**ta shouyong shen** 他受用身. *See* PARA-SAṂBHOGAKĀYA

**taxintong** 他心通. *See* PARACITTAJÑĀNA

**tian** 天. *See* DEVA

**tian'ai** 天愛. *See* DEVĀNĀṂ PRIYAḤ

**tianjie** 天界. *See* DEVALOKA

**tianlong babu** 天龍八部. *See* AṢṬĀSENA

**tiannü** 天女. *See* APSARAS

**tianshang** 天上. *See* DEVALOKA, SVARGA

**tianshen** 天神. *See* DEVATĀ

**tianshijie** 天世界. *See* DEVALOKA

**Tiantai sijiao yi** 天台四教儀. *See* CH'ŎNT'AE SAGYO ŬI

**tianwang** 天王. *See* DEVARĀJAN

**tianxiachu** 天下處. *See* DEVĀVATĀRA

**tianxialai** 天下來. *See* DEVĀVATĀRA

**tian zhong tian** 天中天. *See* DEVĀTIDEVA

**tiaoxi** 調息. *See* PRĀṆĀYĀMA

**Tiduojia** 提多迦. *See* DHṚTAKA

**Tieci lin** 鐵刺林. *See* AYAḤŚĀLMALĪVANA

**Tiewei shan** 鐵圍山. *See* CAKRAVĀḌA

**tigang** 提綱. *See* TICHANG

**tihu** 醍醐. *See* MAṆḌA

**Tipo** 提婆. *See* ĀRYADEVA

**Tipodaduo** 提婆達多. *See* DEVADATTA

**Tiwei** 提謂. *See* TRAPUṢA

**tiyao** 提要. *See* TICHANG

**tong** 通. *See* PARIYATTI

**tongda** 通達. *See* PRATIVEDHA

**tonglei yin** 同類因. *See* SABHĀGAHETU

**tongpin** 同品. *See* SAPAKṢA

**tongshi** 同事. *See* SAMĀNĀRTHATĀ

**Tongzhen** 童眞. *See* KUMĀRABHŪTA

**Tudi jing** 嗏帝經. *See* MAHĀTAṆHĀSAṄKHAYASUTTA

**tui** 退. *See* PARIHĀṆI

**tujiluo** 突吉羅. *See* DUṢKṚTA

**tuobo** 托鉢. *See* TAKUHATSU; cf. PIṆḌAPĀTA

**tuoluoni** 陀羅尼. *See* DHĀRAṆĪ

**tupi** 荼毘. *See* KṢAPITA

**tuxiang** 圖像. *See* YANTRA

**tuzhini** 荼枳尼. *See* ḌĀKINĪ

## W

**wai** 外. *See* BAHIRDHĀ

**waidao** 外道. *See* TĪRTHIKA

**waijing** 外境. *See* BĀHYĀRTHA

**wan** 卍 [alt. 萬字]. *See* SVASTIKA

**Wangshe cheng** 王舍城. *See* RĀJAGṚHA

**wang shengyan** 忘聖言. *See* UPADEŚASAMPRAMOṢA

**Wangsheng yao ji** 往生要集. *See* ŌJŌ YŌSHŪ

**Wang wu Tianzhuguo zhuan** 往五天竺國傳. *See* WANG O CH'ŎNCH'UKKUK CHŎN

**wanzi** 萬字. *See* SVASTIKA

**wei** 味. *See* RASA

**Weicengyou jing** 未曾有經. *See* ADBHUTADHARMAPARYĀYASŪTRA

**weichu** 味處. *See* RASĀYATANA

**weijing** 僞經. *See* APOCRYPHA

**Weimo hui** 維摩會. *See* YUIMAE

**Weimojie** 維摩詰. *See* VIMALAKĪRTI, VIMALAKĪRTINIRDEŚA

**Weimo jing** 維摩經. *See* VIMALAKĪRTINIRDEŚA

**weishen** 威神. *See* ANUBHĀVA

**weishi** 唯識. *See* VIJÑAPTIMĀTRATĀ

**Weishi ershi lun** 唯識二十論. *See* VIṂŚATIKĀ

**Weishi sanshi lun song** 唯識三十論頌. *See* TRIṂŚIKĀ

**Weitixi** 韋提希. *See* VAIDEHĪ

**weixin** 唯心. *See* CITTAMĀTRA

**weiyi** 威儀. *See* ĪRYĀPATHA

**Wencheng gongzhu** 文成公主. *See* WENCHENG

**wenhui** 聞慧. *See* ŚRUTAMAYĪPRAJÑĀ

**Wenshushili** 文殊師利. *See* MAÑJUŚRĪ

**wo** 我. *See* ĀTMAN

**woju** 臥具. *See* PRATYĀSTARAṆA

**woman** 我慢. *See* AHAṂKĀRA

**wosuo** 我所. *See* MAMAKĀRA

**woyu** 我語. *See* ĀTMAVĀDA

**wozhi** 我執. *See* ĀTMAGRĀHA, AHAṂKĀRA

**wubiaose** 無表色. *See* AVIJÑAPTIRŪPA

**wubu** 五部. *See* PAÑCAKULA

**wuchang** 無常. *See* ANITYA

**wuchi** 無癡. *See* AMOHA

**wuchen** 無瞋. *See* ADVEṢA

**wucidi** 五次第. *See* PAÑCAKRAMA

**wudao** 五道. *See* PAÑCAGATI

**wufan tian** 無煩天. *See* AVṚHA

**wu fenbie** 無分別. *See* NIRVIKALPA

**wu fenbie zhi** 無分別智. *See* NIRVIKALPAJÑĀNA

**Wu fo** 五佛. *See* PAÑCATATHĀGATA

**wugen** 五根. *See* PAÑCENDRIYA

**Wugoujingguang datuoluoni jing** 無垢淨光大陀羅尼經. *See* MUGUJŎNGGWANG TAEDARANI KYŎNG

**wugou shi** 無垢識. *See* AMALAVIJÑĀNA

**wuji** 無記. *See* AVYĀKṚTA

**wujia** 汚家. *See* KULADŪṢAKA

**wujian dao** 無間道. *See* ĀNANTARYAMĀRGA

**wujian ding** 無間定. *See* ĀNANTARYASAMĀDHI

**wujian diyu** 無間地獄. *See* AVĪCI

**wujian ye** 無間業. *See* ĀNANTARYAKARMAN

**wujie** 五戒. *See* PAÑCAŚĪLA

**wujifa** 無記法. *See* AVYĀKṚTADHARMA

**wujing** 五境. *See* PAÑCAVIṢAYA

**wujingju tian** 五淨居天. *See* ŚUDDHĀVĀSA

**Wujinyi pusa** 無盡意菩薩. *See* AKṢAYAMATI

**Wujinyi pusa pin** 無盡意菩薩品. *See* AKṢAYAMATINIRDEŚA

**wu jueding** 五决定. *See* PAÑCANIYATA

**wuli** 五力. *See* PAÑCABALA

**wuliangguang tian** 無量光天. *See* APRAMĀṆĀBHA

**wuliangjing tian** 無量淨天. *See* APRAMĀṆAŚUBHA

**Wuliangshou fo** 無量壽佛. *See* AMITĀYUS, AMITĀBHA

**Wuliangshou jing** 無量壽經. *See* SUKHĀVATĪVYŪHASŪTRA

**wuliangxin** 無量心. *See* APRAMĀṆA

**wulou** 無漏. *See* ANĀSRAVA

**wulou jie** 無漏界. *See* ANĀSRAVADHĀTU

**wuming** 無明. *See* AVIDYĀ

**wuming** 五明. *See* PAÑCAVIDYĀ

**wuqu** 五趣. *See* PAÑCAGATI

**wuqun [biqiu]** 五群[比丘]. *See* PAÑCAVARGIKA

**wure** 無熱. *See* ATAPA

**wure tian** 無熱天. *See* ATAPA

**wuse jie** 無色界. *See* ĀRŪPYADHĀTU

**wusejie ding** 無色界定. *See* ARŪPĀVACARADHYĀNA

**wuse tan** 無色貪. *See* ĀRŪPYARĀGA

**wushang puti** 無上菩提. *See* MAHĀBODHI

**wushang zhengdeng jue** 無上正等覺. *See* ANUTTARASAMYAKSAṂBODHI

**wusheng** 無生. *See* ANUTPĀDA

**wushengfaren** 無生法忍. *See* ANUTPATTIKADHARMAKṢĀNTI

**wusheng zhi** 無生智. *See* ANUTPĀDAJÑĀNA

**wusuowei** 無所畏. *See* VAIŚĀRADYA

**wu suoyou chu** 無所有處. *See* ĀKIÑCANYĀYATANA

**wutan** 無貪. *See* ALOBHA

**wuwei** 無爲. *See* ASAṂSKṚTA

**wuwei** 五位. *See* PAÑCAMĀRGA

**wuwei [bu]shi** 無畏[布]施. *See* ABHAYADĀNA

**wuweifa** 無爲法. *See* ASAṂSKṚTADHARMA

**wuwo** 無我. *See* ANĀTMAN, NAIRĀTMYA

**Wuwo** 無我. *See* ANATTALAKKHAṆASUTTA

**wu wujian ye** 五無間業. *See* PAÑCĀNANTARĪYA

**wuxiang** 無相. *See* ĀNIMITTA, NIRĀKĀRA

**wuxiang ding** 無想定. *See* ASAṂJÑĀSAMĀPATTI

**wuxiang falun** 無相法輪. *See* ALAKṢAṆADHARMACAKRA

**wuxiang tian** 無想天. *See* ASAṂJÑIKA

**wuxing** 無性. *See* NIḤSVABHĀVA

**wuxing ban** 無行般. *See* ANABHISAṂSKĀRAPARINIRVĀYIN

**wuxing banniepan** 無行般涅槃. *See* ANABHISAṂSKĀRAPARINIRVĀYIN

**wuxue** 無學. *See* AŚAIKṢA

**wuxuedao** 無學道. *See* AŚAIKṢAMĀRGA

**wuyan** 五眼. *See* PAÑCACAKṢUS

**wuyu** 無欲. *See* VAIRĀGYA

**wuyuan** 無願. *See* APRAṆIHITA

**wuyun** 五蘊. *See* PAÑCASKANDHA, SKANDHA

**wuyu niepan** 無餘涅槃. *See* ANUPADHIŚEṢANIRVĀṆA

**wuyun tian** 無雲天. *See* ANABHRAKA

**Wuzhao** 無著. *See* ASAṄGA

**wuzhi** 五智. *See* PAÑCAJÑĀNA

**Wuzhi rulai** 五智如來. *See* PAÑCATATHĀGATA, PAÑCAJINA

**wuzhu niepan** 無住涅槃. *See* APRATIṢṬHITANIRVĀṆA

**wuzhuo** 五濁. *See* PAÑCAKAṢĀYA

**Wuzi baoqie jing** 無字寶篋經. *See* ANAKṢARAKARAṆḌAKA [VAIROCANAGARBHA] SŪTRA

**wuzixing** 無自性. *See* NIḤSVABHĀVA

# X

**xi** 喜. *See* MUDITĀ, PRĪTI

**xiancheng gong'an** 現成公案. *See* GENJŌ KŌAN

**xiang** 香. *See* GANDHA

**xiang** 相. *See* LAKṢAṆA, LIṄGA, NIMITTA

**xiang** 想. *See* SAṂJÑĀ

**xiangcheng** 相承. *See* PARAMPARĀ

**xiangchu** 香處. *See* GANDHĀYATANA

**Xiang jing** 想經. *See* MŪLAPARIYĀYASUTTA

**Xiangjiyu jing** 象跡喻經. *See* CŪḶAHATTHIPADOPAMASUTTA, MAHĀHATTHIPADOPAMASUTTA

**xianglu** 香爐. *See* GANDHAGHAṬIKĀ

**Xiangmo jing** 降魔經. *See* MĀRATAJJANĪYASUTTA

**Xiangsanshi mingwang** 降三世明王. *See* TRAILOKYAVIJAYA

**xiang sanshi yin** 降三世印. *See* BHŪTAḌĀMARAMUDRĀ

**xiangshi** 香室. *See* GANDHAKUṬĪ

**xiangshou mie** 想受滅. *See* SAṂJÑĀVEDAYITANIRODHA

**xiangsi zhengfa** 像似正法. *See* SADDHARMAPRATIRŪPAKA, XIANGFA

**xianguan** 現觀. *See* ABHISAMAYA

**Xiangxing poluomen** 香姓婆羅門. *See* DROṆA

**xiangxu** 相續. *See* SAṂTĀNA

**xiangxu shi** 相續識. *See* ĀDĀNAVIJÑĀNA

**xiangying** 相應. *See* SAṂPRAYUKTA

**xiangying yin** 相應因. *See* SAṂPRAYUKTAHETU

**Xianhu** 賢護. *See* BHADRAPĀLA

**xianjie** 賢劫. *See* BHADRAKALPA

**xianjie jing** 賢劫經. *See* BHADRAKALPIKASŪTRA

**xianliang** 現量. *See* PRATYAKṢA

**xian liyu ren** 先離欲人. *See* VĪTARĀGAPŪRVIN

**Xianni waidao** 先尼外道. *See* ŚREṆIKA HERESY

**xianqian [di]** 現前[地]. *See* ABHIMUKHĪ

**xianqu yin** 現取因. *See* UPĀDĀNAKĀRAṆA

**Xianren duochu** 仙人墮處. *See* ṚṢIPATANA

**xiansheng** 賢聖. *See* ĀRYAPUDGALA

**xianxian** 顯現. *See* PRATIBHĀSA

**xianxing** 現行. *See* SAMUDĀCĀRA

**Xianyan** 賢鹽. *See* LAKUṆṬAKA BHADRIKA

**Xiaobu** 小部. *See* KHUDDAKANIKĀYA

**xiaojiao** 小教. *See* HUAYAN WUJIAO

**Xiaopin bore jing** 小品般若經. *See* AṢṬASĀHASRIKĀPRAJÑĀPĀRAMITĀ

**xiaosheng** 小乘. *See* HĪNAYĀNA

**Xiaoxian** 小賢. *See* BHADRIKA

**Xiaoyuan jing** 小緣經. *See* AGGAÑÑASUTTA

**xiashi** 下士. *See* ADHAMAPURUṢA

**Xidaduo** 悉達多. *See* SIDDHĀRTHA

**xidi** 悉地. *See* SIDDHI

**Xie** 脇. *See* PĀRŚVA

**xiejian** 邪見. *See* AKUŚALADṚṢṬI, MITHYĀDṚṢṬI

**xieming waidao** 邪命外道. *See* ĀJĪVAKA

**xieyin** 邪淫. *See* KĀMAMITHYĀCĀRA

**xiezhi** 邪智. *See* MITHYĀJÑĀNA

**Xilujia** 呬嚕迦. *See* HERUKA

**xilun** 戲論. *See* PRAPAÑCA

**xin** 心. *See* CITTA

**xin** 信. *See* ŚRADDHĀ

**xin buxiangying fa** 心不相應法. *See* CITTAVIPRAYUKTASAṂSKĀRA

**xing** 行. *See* SAṂSKĀRA

**xingku** 行苦. *See* SAṂSKĀRADUḤKHATĀ

**xing putixin** 行菩提心. *See* PRASTHĀNACITTOPĀDA

**xingxiang** 行相. *See* ĀKĀRA

**xin xiangying fa** 心相應法. *See* CITTASAMPRAYUKTASAṂSKĀRA

**xingyun liushui** 行雲流水. *See* KŌUN RYŪSUI

**Xinhui jing** 心穢經. *See* CETOKHILASUTTA

**xinjie** 信解. *See* ŚRADDHĀDHIMUKTA

**xin jietuo** 心解脫. *See* CETOVIMUKTI

**xinshengjie** 信勝解. *See* ŚRADDHĀVIMUKTA

**xinsuo** 心所. *See* CAITTA

**xin xiangxu** 心相續. *See* CITTASANTĀNA

**xin yijing xing** 心一境性. *See* CITTAIKĀGRATĀ

**xiqi** 習氣. *See* VĀSANĀ

**xitan** 悉曇. *See* SIDDHAṂ

**xiu** 修. *See* YOGA

**xiudao** 修道. *See* BHĀVANĀMĀRGA

**xiude ding** 修得定. *See* DHYĀNASAMĀPATTI

**xiuhui** 修慧. *See* BHĀVANĀMAYĪPRAJÑĀ

**xiuxi** 修習. *See* BHĀVANĀ, YOGA

**Xiuxin jue** 修心. *See* Susim kyŏl

**xiuxing** 修行. *See* paṭipatti, yoga

**xiuxing ren** 修行人. *See* yogin

**xizai** 息災. *See* śānticāra

**xizhang** 錫杖. *See* khakkhara

**xizhongxing** 習種性. *See* samudānītagotra

**Xubatuoluo** 須跋陀羅. *See* Subhadra

**Xuda** 須達. *See* Sudatta

**Xudana** 須大拏. *See* Vessantara

**Xudana bensheng** 須大拏本生. *See* Sudāna Jātaka

**xue** 學. *See* śikṣā

**xuechu** 學處. *See* śikṣāpada

**xueren** 學人. *See* śaikṣa

**Xueshanbu** 雪山部. *See* Haimavata

**xukong** 虛空. *See* ākāśa

**xukonghua** 虛空華. *See* khapuṣpa

**Xukongzang pusa** 虛空藏菩薩. *See* Ākāśagarbha

**Xumishan** 須彌山. *See* Sumeru, Mt

**xumi tan** 須彌壇. *See* shumidan

**xun** 尋. *See* vitarka

**Xunajia** 須那迦. *See* Soṇa and Uttara

**xunguan** 循觀. *See* anupaśyanā

**xunxi** 薰習. *See* vāsanā

**Xupiye nü** 須毘耶女. *See* Supriyā

**Xuputi** 須菩提. *See* Subhūti

**Xusheduo** 須闍多. *See* Sujātā

**Xutina** 須提那. *See* Sudinna

**xutuohuan** 須陀洹. *See* srotaāpanna

**xuwang fenbie** 虛妄分別. *See* abhūtaparikalpa

## Y

**yan** 眼. *See* cakṣus

**yan** 厭. *See* nirveda

**yanchu** 眼處. *See* cakṣurāyatana

**Yanfuti** 閻浮提. *See* Jambudvīpa

**yangen** 眼根. *See* cakṣurindriya

**Yangjuemoluo** 央掘摩羅. *See* Aṅgulimāla

**Yangjuemoluo jing** 央掘摩羅經. *See* Aṅgulimālīyasūtra

**yanhui di** 焰慧地. *See* arciṣmatī

**yanjiao** 言教. *See* nirukti

**Yanmandejia** 焰曼德迦. *See* Yamāntaka

**yanmo** 宴默. *See* pratisaṃlayana

**Yanmo wang** 閻魔王. *See* Yama

**yanre diyu** 炎熱地獄. *See* tāpana

**yanshi** 眼識. *See* cakṣurvijñāna

**yanyu** 言語. *See* vyavahāra

**Yaoshi benyuan jing** 藥師本願經. *See* Bhaiṣajyagurusūtra

**Yaoshi rulai** 藥師如來. *See* Bhaiṣajyaguru

**Yaowang pusa** 藥王菩薩. *See* Bhaiṣajyarāja

**ye** 業. *See* karman

**yecha** 夜叉. *See* yakṣa

**yedao** 業道. *See* karmapatha

**Yemo Tian** 夜摩天. *See* Yāma

**Yeshe** 耶舍. *See* Yaśas

**Yeshutuoluo** 耶輸陀羅. *See* Yaśodharā

**yezhang** 業障. *See* karmāvaraṇa

**yi** 義. *See* abhisaṃdhi, artha

**yi** 衣. *See* cīvara

**yi** 意. *See* manas

**yi** 依. *See* pratisaraṇa, upadhi

**yi** 疑. *See* vicikitsā

**Yibuzonglun lun** 異部宗輪論. *See* Samayabhedoparacanacakra

**yichanti** 一闡提. *See* icchantika

**yicheng** 疑城. *See* biandi

**yichu** 意處. *See* manāyatana

**Yi'er** 億耳. *See* Soṇa-Koṭikaṇṇa

**yigen** 意根. *See* manendriya

**yigui** 儀軌. *See* vidhi

**yijian** 一間. *See* ekavīcika

**yijing** 疑經. *See* apocrypha

**yilai** 一來. *See* sakṛdāgāmin

**yilai xiang** 一來向. *See* sakṛdāgāmiphalapratipannaka

**yin** 因. *See* hetu

**yin** 印. *See* mudrā

**yinggong** 應供. *See* arhat

**yinghe** 應訶. *See* tarjanīyakarman

**Yinguangbu** 飲光部. *See* Kāśyapīya

**Yingwu jing** 鸚鵡經. *See* Subhasuttanta

**Yinjietuo** 因揭陀. *See* Aṅgaja

**Yinming ru zhengli lun** 因明入正理論. *See* Nyāyapraveśa

**Yintuoluo** 因陀羅. *See* Indra

**Yintuoluo wang** 因陀羅網. *See* Indrajāla

**yinyuan** 因緣. *See* nidāna

**yin yuan** 因緣. *See* hetupratyaya

**yipin** 異品. *See* vipakṣa

**Yiqie rulai jingang sanye zuishang mimi dajiaowang jing** 一切如來金剛三業最上秘密大教王經. *See* Guhyasamājatantra

**Yiqie rulai zhenshishe dasheng xianzheng sanmei dajiaowang jing** 一切如來眞實攝大乘現證三昧大教王經. *See* Sarvatathāgatatattvasaṃgraha

**yiqiexiang zhi** 一切相智. *See* vastujñāna

**yiqie zhi** 一切智. *See* sarvajñatā

**yiqiezhi zhi** 一切知智. *See* sarvajñatājñāna

**yiqiezhong zhi** 一切種智. *See* sarvākārajñatā

**yiqu** 意趣. *See* abhiprāya

**Yiri monibao jing** 遺日摩尼寶經. *See* Kāśyapaparivarta

**yisheng** 一乘. *See* ekayāna

**yishengshen** 意生身. *See* manomayakāya

**yishi** 意識. *See* manovijñāna

**yishouxianliang** 意受現量. *See* manonubhavapratyakṣa

**yishu** 異熟. *See* vipāka

**yishu guo** 異熟果. *See* vipākaphala

**Yishuobu** 一說部. *See* Ekavyavahārika

**yishu yin** 異熟因. *See* vipākahetu

**yitaqi xing** 依他起性. *See* paratantra

**Yitian** 義天. *See* Ŭich'ŏn

**Yixiang** 義湘/相. *See* Ŭisang

**yixin sanguan** 一心三觀. *See* sanguan

**yiyan** 意言. *See* manojalpa

**yiye** 意業. *See* manaskarman

**Yiyu jing** 蟻喩經. *See* Vammikasutta

**Yizu jing** 義足經. *See* Aṭṭhakavagga

**yonghu** 擁護. *See* rakṣā

**Yongjian zhangzhe** 勇健長者. *See* Sūra Ambaṭṭha

**yongmeng** 勇猛. *See* vīra

**yongmeng jingjin** 勇猛精進. *See* yongmaeng chŏngjin

**you** 有. *See* bhava

**Youboli** 優波離. *See* Upāli

**Youboluose** 優波羅色. *See* Utpalavarṇā

**Youbonantuo** 優波難陀. *See* Upananda

**Youbosina** 優波斯那. *See* Upasena

**youbotishe** 優波提舍. *See* upadeśa

**youda** 有大. *See* bhautika

**youding tian** 有頂天. *See* bhavāgra

**youlou** 有漏. *See* sāsrava

**Youloupinluo** 優樓頻螺. *See* Uruvilvā

**Youloupinluo Jiashe** 優樓頻螺迦葉. *See* Uruvilvā-Kāśyapa

**Youlouqu** 優樓佉. *See* Ulūka

**youlou yun** 有漏蘊. *See* sāsravaskandha

**youlun** 有輪. *See* bhavacakra

**Youpojuduo** 優婆毱多. *See* Upagupta

**Youpoli jing** 優婆離經. *See* Upālisutta

**youposai** 優婆塞. *See* upāsaka

**youpoyi** 優婆夷. *See* upāsikā

**youpoyi jie** 優婆夷戒. *See* upāsikāsaṃvara

**youqing** 有情. *See* sattva

**youqing shijian** 有情世間. *See* sattvaloka

**yourao** 右遶. *See* pradakṣiṇa

**youshenjian** 有身見. *See* satkāyadṛṣṭi

**youtan hua** 優曇華. *See* udumbara

**Youtian wang Shijia xiang** 優塡王 釋迦像. *See* Udāyana Buddha

**youtuona** 優陀那. *See* udāna

**Youtuoyi** 優陀夷. *See* Udāyin

**youwei** 有爲. *See* SAṂSKṚTA

**youwei xiang** 有爲相. *See* SAṂSKṚTALAKṢAṆA

**Youxian** 有賢. *See* BHADRIKA

**youxiang** 有相. *See* SĀKĀRA

**Youxin anledao** 遊心安樂道. *See* YU SIM ALLAK TO

**youxing banniepan** 有行般涅槃. *See* SĀBHISAṂSKĀRAPARINIRVĀYIN

**Youxing jing** 遊行經. *See* MAHĀPARINIBBĀNASUTTANTA

**youxingzhe** 遊行者. *See* PARIVRĀJAKA

**youxun** 由旬. *See* YOJANA

**youyu niepan** 有餘涅槃. *See* SOPADHIŚEṢANIRVĀṆA

**yu** 欲. *See* KĀMA, CHANDA

**yuan** 園. *See* ĀRĀMA

**yuan** 願. *See* PRAṆIDHĀNA

**yuan** 緣. *See* PRATYAYA

**yuan boluomi** 願波羅蜜. *See* PRAṆIDHĀNAPĀRAMITĀ

**Yuance** 圓測. *See* WŎNCH'ŬK

**yuanchengshi xing** 圓成實性. *See* PARINIṢPANNA

**Yuan'er Bianyuan** 圓爾辨圓. *See* ENNI BEN'EN

**Yuanguang** 圓光. *See* WŎN'GWANG

**Yuan jing** 願經. *See* ĀKAṄKHEYYASUTTA

**yuanjue** 緣覺. *See* PRATYEKABUDDHA

**yuanjue sheng** 緣覺乘. *See* PRATYEKABUDDHAYĀNA

**yuanli** 遠離. *See* VIVEKA

**yuanman cidi** 圓滿次第. *See* NIṢPANNAKRAMA

**yuan puti xin** 願菩提心. *See* PRAṆIDHICITTOPĀDA

**yuanqi** 緣起. *See* PRATĪTYASAMUTPĀDA

**Yuanren** 圓仁. *See* ENNIN

**yuanrong sanguan** 圓融三觀. *See* SANGUAN

**Yuansheng lun** 緣生論. *See* *PRATĪTYASAMUTPĀDAŚĀSTRA

**yuanshengshu** 圓生樹. *See* PĀRIYĀTRAKA, KALPAVṚKSA

**Yuanxiao** 元曉. *See* WŎNHYO

**yuanxing di** 遠行地. *See* DŪRAṄGAMĀ

**yuanzhu** 院主. *See* WŎNJU

**Yuduoluo** 鬱多羅. *See* SOṆA AND UTTARA

**Yuedeng sanmei jing** 月燈三昧經. *See* SAMĀDHIRĀJASŪTRA

**Yuezang fen** 月藏分. *See* CANDRAGARBHAPARIPṚCCHĀ

**yujie** 欲界. *See* KĀMADHĀTU

**yuliu [guo]** 預流[果]. *See* SROTAĀPANNA

**yuliu xiang** 預流向. *See* SROTAĀPANNAPHALAPRATIPANNAKA

**yun** 蘊. *See* SKANDHA

**Yunmo** 蘊魔. *See* SKANDHAMĀRA

**yunshui** 雲水. *See* UNSUI

**Yuqie** 郁伽. *See* UGRA

**yuqie** 瑜伽. *See* YOGA

**Yuqieshidi** 瑜伽師地. *See* YOGĀCĀRABHŪMI

**Yuqieshidi lun** 瑜伽師地論. *See* YOGĀCĀRABHŪMIŚĀSTRA

**Yuqietuo** 鬱伽陀. *See* UDGATA

**Yuqiexing pai** 瑜伽行派. *See* YOGĀCĀRA

**Yuqie zhangzhe hui** 郁伽長者會. *See* UGRAPARIPṚCCHĀ

**yutan** 欲貪. *See* KĀMARĀGA

**Yutian** 于闐. *See* KHOTAN

**yutong** 愚童. *See* BĀLA

**Yutoulanfu** 鬱頭藍弗. *See* UDRAKA RĀMAPUTRA

**yuxue** 與學. *See* ŚIKṢĀDATTAKA

**yuye** 語業. *See* VĀKKARMAN

## Z

**Za ahan jing** 雜阿含經. *See* SAṂYUKTĀGAMA, SAṂYUTTANIKĀYA

**Za apitan xin lun** 雜阿毘曇心論. *See* SAṂYUKTĀBHIDHARMAHṚDAYA

**zaijia** 在家. *See* GṚHASTHA

**zaisheng** 再生. *See* PUNARJANMAN, REBIRTH

**zaisi** 再死. *See* PUNARMṚTYU, REBIRTH

**Zan fajie song** 讚法界頌. *See* DHARMADHĀTUSTAVA

**zang** 藏. *See* PIṬAKA

**zangshi** 藏識. *See* ĀLAYAVIJÑĀNA

**zemie** 擇滅. *See* PRATISAṂKHYĀNIRODHA

**zengshangding xue** 增上定學. *See* ADHISAMĀDHIŚIKṢĀ

**zengshangguo** 增上果. *See* ADHIPATIPHALA

**zengshanghui xue** 增上慧學. *See* ADHIPRAJÑĀŚIKṢĀ

**zengshangjie xue** 增上戒學. *See* ADHIŚĪLAŚIKṢĀ

**zengshangman** 增上慢. *See* ADHIMĀNA

**Zengshangxin jing** 增上心經. *See* VITAKKASAṆṬHĀNASUTTA

**zengshang yuan** 增上緣. *See* ADHIPATIPRATYAYA

**zengyi** 增益. *See* SAMĀROPA

**Zengyi ahan jing** 增壹阿含經. *See* EKOTTARĀGAMA, AṄGUTTARANIKĀYA

**zengzhang tian** 增長天. *See* VIRŪḌHAKA

**zhang** 障. *See* ĀVARAṆA

**Zhang Sengyao** 張僧繇. *See* ṢOḌAŚASTHAVIRA

**zhangzhe** 長者. *See* GṚHAPATI

**zhantanshu'er** 栴檀樹耳. *See* SŪKARAMADDAVA

**zhantuoli** 旃陀利. *See* CAṆḌĀLĪ

**zhanzuo** 展左. *See* PRATYĀLĪḌHA

**zhe** 遮. *See* PRATIṢEDHA

**zhenbao** 珍寶. *See* RATNA

**zhengbianzhi** 正遍知. *See* SAMYAKSAṂBUDDHA

**zheng buhuan guo** 證不還果. *See* ANĀGĀMIPHALASTHA

**zheng yilai guo** 證一來果. *See* SAKṚDĀGĀMIPHALASTHA

**zheng yuliu guo** 證預流果. *See* SROTAĀPANNAPHALASTHA

**Zhendi** 眞諦. *See* PARAMĀRTHA

**zhendi** 眞諦. *See* PARAMĀRTHASATYA

**zheng** 證. *See* ADHIGAMA

**zhengdengjue** 正等覺. *See* SAMYAKSAṂBODHI

**zhengding** 正定. *See* SAMYAKSAMĀDHI

**zhengfa** 證法. *See* ADHIGAMADHARMA

**zhengfa** 正法. *See* SADDHARMA

**zhengjian** 正見. *See* SAMYAKDṚṢṬI

**zhengjingjin** 正精進. *See* SAMYAGVYĀYĀMA

**zhengjue** 正覺. *See* SAṂBODHI

**Zhengliang bu** 正量部. *See* SAṂMITĪYA

**zhengming** 正命. *See* SAMYAGĀJĪVA

**zhengnian** 正念. *See* SAMYAKSMṚTI

**zhengqin** 正勤. *See* SAMYAKPRADHĀNA

**zhengshi** 諍事. *See* ADHIKARAṆA

**zhengshou** 正受. *See* SAMĀPATTI

**zhengsiwei** 正思惟. *See* SAMYAKSAṂKALPA, YONIŚOMANASKĀRA

**zhengsong** 諍訟. *See* ADHIKARAṆA

**zhengxing lisheng** 正性離生. *See* SAMYAKTVANIYĀMĀVAKRĀNTI

**zhengye** 正業. *See* SAMYAKKARMĀNTA

**zhengyu** 正語. *See* SAMYAGVĀC

**zhengzhi** 正知. *See* SAṂPRAJANYA

**zhengzhi xin** 正直心. *See* ADHYĀŚAYA

**zhengzhuan falun** 證轉法輪. *See* *SUVIBHAKTADHARMACAKRA

**zhenru** 眞如. *See* BHŪTATATHATĀ, TATHATĀ

**zhenyan** 眞言. *See* MANTRA, SHINGONSHŪ

**zhenyan sheng** 眞言乘. *See* MANTRAYĀNA

**zhenying** 眞影. *See* CHINYŎNG

**Zhepoluo ta** 遮婆羅塔. *See* CĀPĀLACAITYA

**zhi** 支. *See* AṄGA

**zhi** 智. *See* JÑĀNA

**zhi** 止. *See* ŚAMATHA

**zhidu** 智度. *See* PRAJÑĀPĀRAMITĀ

**Zhiduoshanbu** 制多山部. *See* CAITYA

**zhiguan** 止觀. *See* ŚAMATHAVIPAŚYANĀ

**zhiguan dazuo** 祇/只管打坐. *See* SHIKAN TAZA

**zhihui yan** 智慧眼. *See* PRAJÑĀCAKṢUS

**zhijian** 知見. *See* JÑĀNADARŚANA

**Zhiju** 智聚. *See* JÑĀNASAṂBHĀRA

**Zhi Loujiachan** 支婁迦讖. *See* LOKAKṢEMA

**Zhine** 知訥. *See* POJO CHINUL

**zhiquan yin** 智拳印. *See* BODHYAṄGĪMUDRĀ, JÑĀNAMUṢṬI

**zhishan** 至善. *See* NIḤŚREYASA

**zhishi** 執事. *See* VAIYĀPṚTYA(KARA)

**Zhishu Jigudu yuan** 祇樹給孤獨園. *See* JETAVANA

**zhiti** 支提. *See* CAITYA

**Zhituo taizi** 祇陀太子. *See* JETA

**zhiwai** 智外. *See* PAROKṢA

**zhiwu** 執無. *See* NĀSTIKA

**Zhong ahan jing** 中阿含經. *See* MADHYAMĀGAMA, MAJJHIMANIKĀYA

**zhong ban** 中般. *See* ANTARĀPARINIRVĀYIN

**zhong banniepan** 中般涅槃. *See* ANTARĀPARINIRVĀYIN

**zhongdao** 中道. *See* MADHYAMAPRATIPAD

**Zhongde jing** 種德經. *See* SOṆADAṆḌASUTTA

**zhonggen** 中根. *See* MADYENDRIYA

**Zhongguan** 中觀. *See* MADHYAMAKA

**zhongguo** 中國. *See* MADHYAMADEŚA

**zhonghe [diyu]** 衆合[地獄]. *See* SAṂGHĀTA

**zhonghui** 衆會. *See* PARIṢAD

**zhongjiayi** 中價衣. *See* UTTARĀSAṂGA

**Zhongji jing** 衆集經. *See* SAṄGĪTISUTTA

**Zhong lun** 中論. *See* MŪLAMADHYAMAKAKĀRIKĀ, MADHYAMAKAŚĀSTRA

**zhongsheng** 衆生. *See* SATTVA

**zhongsheng shijian** 衆生世間. *See* SATTVALOKA

**zhongsheng zhuo** 衆生濁. *See* SATTVAKAṢĀYA

**Zhongxian** 衆賢. *See* SAṂGHABHADRA

**zhongxing** 種性. *See* GOTRA

**zhongxue** 衆學. *See* ŚAIKṢADHARMA

**zhongyin** 中陰. *See* ANTARĀBHAVA

**zhongyou** 中有. *See* ANTARĀBHAVA

**zhongyun youqing** 中蘊有情. *See* GANDHARVA

**zhongzi** 種子. *See* BĪJA

**zhongzhongjie zhili** 種種界智力. *See* NĀNĀDHĀTUJÑĀNABALA

**zhongzhong shengjie zhili** 種種勝解智力. *See* NĀNĀDHIMUKTIJÑĀNABALA

**zhongzhu** 衆主. *See* VAIYĀPṚTYA(KARA)

**Zhoulipante** 周利槃特. *See* ŚUDDHIPANTHAKA

**Zhouna wenjian jing** 周那問見經. *See* SALLEKHASUTTA

**zhouyuan** 咒願. *See* ANUMODANA

**zhu** 珠. *See* MAṆI

**zhu** 住. *See* LENA, STHITI, VIHĀRA

**zhuan falun** 轉法輪. *See* DHARMACAKRAPRAVARTANA

**Zhuan falun jing** 轉法輪經. *See* DHAMMACAKKAPPAVATTANASUTTA

**zhuan falun yin** 轉法輪印. *See* DHARMACAKRAMUDRĀ

**Zhuanji baiyuan jing** 撰集百緣經. *See* AVADĀNAŚATAKA

**Zhuanlun shengwang xiuxing jing** 轉輪聖王修行經. *See* CAKKAVATTISĪHANĀDASUTTA

**zhuanlun wang** 轉輪王. *See* CAKRAVARTIN

**zhuanyi** 轉依. *See* ĀŚRAYAPARĀVṚTTI

**Zhu Fahu** 竺法護. *See* DHARMARAKṢA

**zhuguo** 住果. *See* PHALASTHITA

**zhujie** 住劫. *See* VIVARTASTHĀYIKALPA

**Zhulincong** 竹林叢. *See* VEṆUGRĀMAKA

**Zhulin jingshe** 竹林精舍. *See* VEṆUVANAVIHĀRA

**zhu niepan** 住涅槃. *See* PRATIṢṬHITANIRVĀṆA

**Zhunti** 准提. *See* CUNDĪ

**Zhuntuo** 準陀. *See* CUNDA

**zhuo** 濁. *See* KAṢĀYA

**zhuoyu** 著語. *See* JAKUGO

**Zhutubantuojia** 注荼半托迦. *See* CŪḌAPANTHAKA

**zhuyuan** 助緣. *See* SAHAKĀRIPRATYAYA

**zibiliang** 自比量. *See* SVĀRTHĀNUMĀNA

**Zihuanxi jing** 自歡喜經. *See* SAMPASĀDANĪYASUTTA

**ziju** 資具. *See* PARIṢKĀRA

**zijue** 自覺. *See* SVASAṂVEDANA

**zili** 自力. *See* JIRIKI

**zili** 自利. *See* SVĀRTHA

**ziliang** 資糧. *See* SAṂBHĀRA

**Ziliang dao** 資糧道. *See* SAṂBHĀRAMĀRGA

**zi shouyong shen** 自受用身. *See* SVASAṂBHOGAKĀYA

**zita pingdeng** 自他平等. *See* PARĀTMASAMATĀ

**zixiang** 自相. *See* SVALAKṢAṆA

**zixiang kong** 自相空. *See* SVALAKṢAṆAŚŪNYA

**zixing** 自性. *See* SVABHĀVA

**zixing fenbie** 自性分別. *See* SVABHĀVAVIKALPA

**zixing kong** 自性空. *See* SVABHĀVAŚŪNYA, SVABHĀVAŚŪNYATĀ

**zixing niepan** 自性涅槃. *See* PRAKṚTIPARINIRVṚTA

**zixing shen** 自性身. *See* SVABHĀVAKĀYA, SVABHĀVIKAKĀYA

**zizai** 自在. *See* AIŚVARYA, VAŚITĀ

**zizi** 自恣. *See* PRAVĀRAṆĀ

**zongchi** 總持. *See* DHĀRAṆĪ

**zongfa** 宗法. *See* PAKṢADHARMA

**zui** 罪. *See* PĀPA

**zuishang daxidi** 最上大悉地. *See* UTTAMASIDDHI

**zuisheng** 最勝. *See* JINA

**Zuisheng foding tuoluoni jingchu yezhang zhou jing** 最勝佛頂陀羅尼淨除業障呪經. *See* SARVADURGATIPARIŚODHANATANTRA

**zuishengzi** 最勝子. *See* JINAPUTRA

**zuo** 座. *See* ĀSANA

**zuofa** 坐法. *See* ĀSANA

**zuoju** 坐具. *See* NIṢĪDANA

**zuoyi** 作意. *See* MANASIKĀRA

# Japanese Cross-References

## A

**abatei** 阿嚩底. *See* AVADHŪTĪ

**abidatsuma** 阿毘達磨. *See* ABHIDHARMA

**Abidatsuma daibibasharon** 阿毘達磨大毘婆沙論. *See* ABHIDHARMAMAHĀVIBHĀṢĀ

**abidatsuma daironshi** 阿毘達磨大論師. *See* ĀBHIDHARMIKA

**Abidatsuma hotchiron** 阿毘達磨發智論. *See* ABHIDHARMAJÑĀNAPRASTHĀNA, JÑĀNAPRASTHĀNA

**Abidatsuma hōunsokuron** 阿毘達磨法蘊足論. *See* ABHIDHARMADHARMASKANDHA[PĀDAŚĀSTRA], DHARMASKANDHA[PĀDAŚĀSTRA]

**Abidatsuma kaishinsokuron** 阿毘達磨界身足論. *See* ABHIDHARMADHĀTUKĀYA[PĀDAŚĀSTRA], DHĀTUKĀYA[PĀDAŚĀSTRA]

**Abidatsuma kusharon** 阿毘達磨俱舍論. *See* ABHIDHARMAKOŚABHĀṢYA

**Abidon shinron** 阿毘曇心論. *See* *ABHIDHARMAHṚDAYA

**abijigoku** 阿鼻地獄. *See* AVĪCI

**abiradai** 阿比羅提. *See* ABHIRATI

**abisha** 阿尾奢. *See* ĀVEŚA

**adanashiki** 阿陀那識. *See* ĀDĀNAVIJÑĀNA

**agongyō** 阿含經. *See* ĀGAMA

**ahadana** 阿波陀那. *See* AVADĀNA

**Ahandai[koku]** 阿般提[國]. *See* AVANTI

**ai** 愛. *See* TṚṢṆĀ

**Aiku ō** 阿育王. *See* AŚOKA

**Aiku ō den** 阿育王傳. *See* AŚOKĀVADĀNA

**Aitta** 阿逸多. *See* AJITA

**ajari** 阿闍梨. *See* ĀCĀRYA

**Ajase ō** 阿闍世王. *See* AJĀTAŚATRU

**Ajikuta** 阿地瞿多. *See* ATIKŪṬA

**aku** 惡. *See* PĀPA

**akuken** 惡見. *See* AKUŚALADṚṢṬI, MITHYĀDṚṢṬI

**akuku** 惡口. *See* PĀRUṢYA

**akusa** 惡作. *See* DUṢKṚTA

**akusetsu** 惡說. *See* DURBHĀṢITA

**akushu** 惡趣. *See* DURGATI

**amarashiki** 阿摩羅識. *See* AMALAVIJÑĀNA

**Amidabutsu** 阿彌陀佛. *See* AMITĀBHA

**Amida kō** 阿彌陀講. *See* ŌJŌ KŌ

**Amida kuhon'in** 阿彌陀九品印. *See* AMITUO JIUPIN YIN

**Amidakyō** 阿彌陀經. *See* AMITĀBHASŪTRA

**anagon** 阿那含. *See* ANĀGĀMIN

**Anan** 阿難. *See* ĀNANDA

**Anaritsu** 阿那律. *See* ANIRUDDHA

**Anbaranyo** 菴婆羅女. *See* ĀMRAPĀLĪ

**An'e/Anne** 安慧. *See* STHIRAMATI

**angya** 行脚. *See* XINGJIAO

**anja** 行者. *See* XINGZHE

**anjin** 安心. *See* ANXIN

**Anjūjijin** 安住地神. *See* STHĀVARĀ

**Annahannanen** 安那般那念. *See* ĀNĀPĀNASMṚTI, ĀNĀPĀNASATISUTTA

**anniin** 安慰印. *See* VITARKAMUDRĀ

**Annon** 安穩. *See* KṢEMĀ

**annyōkai** 安養界. *See* ANYANG JIE

**anokutara-sanmyaku-sanbodai** 阿耨多羅三藐三菩提. *See* ANUTTARASAMYAKSAṂBODHI

**Anpanshuikyō** 安般守意經. *See* ANBAN SHOUYI JING

**anrakukoku** 安樂國. *See* ANLEGUO, SUKHĀVATĪ

**anri** 行履. *See* XINGLI

**An Seikō** 安世高. *See* AN SHIGAO

**Ansoku koku** 安息國. *See* ANXI GUO; PARTHIA

**Anuikyō** 阿㝹夷經. *See* PĀṬIKASUTTA

**Anyakyōjinnyo** 阿若憍陳如. *See* ĀJÑĀTAKAUṆḌINYA

**apadana** 阿波陀那. *See* avadāna

**arakan** 阿羅漢. *See* arhat

**arakankō** 阿羅漢向. *See* arhatpratipannaka

**[a]rannya** [阿]蘭若. *See* araṇya

**Ararakaran** 阿羅邏迦蘭. *See* Ārāḍa Kālāma

**arayashiki** 阿賴耶識. *See* ālayavijñāna

**Aritakyō** 阿梨吒經. *See* Alagaddūpamasutta

**Asamatsu bosatsukyō** 阿差末菩薩經. *See* Akṣayamatinirdeśa

**Asetsuji** 阿說示. *See* Aśvajit

**Ashida** 阿私陀. *See* Asita

**Ashuku bukkokukyō** 阿閦佛國經. *See* Akṣobhyatathāgatasyavyūha

**Ashukubutsu** 阿閦佛. *See* Akṣobhya

**ashura** 阿修羅. *See* asura

**asōgi** 阿僧祇. *See* asaṃkhya

**asōgikō** 阿僧祇劫. *See* asaṃkheyakalpa

## B

**Badai** 婆提. *See* Bhadrika

**Bafu** 婆敷. *See* Vāṣpa

**Bagisha** 婆耆舍. *See* Vaṅgīsa

**Bakari** 婆迦梨. *See* Vakkali

**Bakika** 婆呬迦. *See* Bāhiya-Dārucīriya

**Bakusekizan** 麥積山. *See* Maijishan

**Banzudatta** 槃頭達多. *See* Bandhudatta

**Basa** 婆差. *See* Vatsagotra

**Baso Dōitsu** 馬祖道一. *See* Mazu Daoyi

**Bassa[koku]** 跋蹉[國]. *See* Vatsā

**Batō Kannon** 馬頭觀音. *See* Hayagrīva

**Batsuda Gundarakuikoku** 拔陀軍陀羅拘夷國. *See* Bhaddā-Kuṇḍalakesā

**Batsudahara** 跋陀波羅. *See* Bhadrapāla

**Batsudai** 跋提. *See* Bhaddiya-Kāḷigodhāputta

**Batsudara Kahiriya** 跋陀羅迦卑梨耶. *See* Bhadra-Kapilānī

**Batsudara sonja** 跋陀羅尊者. *See* Bhadra

**Batsugishi** 跋耆子. *See* Vṛjiputraka

**Batsujarahotsutara** 伐闍羅弗多羅. *See* Vajraputra

**Batsunabashi sonja** 伐那婆斯尊者. *See* Vanavāsin

**Benchūbenron** 辯中邊論. *See* Madhyāntavibhāga

**Benshōron** 辯正論. *See* Baizheng lun

**benzai** 辯才. *See* pratibhāna

**Benzaiten** 辯才天. *See* Sarasvatī, Shichifukujin

**bessō no sangan** 別相三觀. *See* sanguan

**betsugedatsu ritsugi** 別解脫律儀. *See* prātimokṣasaṃvara

**betsujū** 別住. *See* parivāsa

**betsukyō [no shinjo]** 別境[心所]. *See* viniyata

**Bibashashi** 毘婆沙師. *See* Vaibhāṣika

**Bibashibutsu** 毘婆尸佛. *See* Vipaśyin

**Bidaika** 毘提訶. *See* Videha

**bigara** 毘伽羅. *See* vyākaraṇa

**bikon** 鼻根. *See* ghrāṇendriya

**biku** 比丘. *See* bhikṣu

**biku igi** 比丘威儀. *See* abhisamācārikā[śīla]

**bikuni** 比丘尼. *See* bhikṣuṇī

**Bikuniden** 比丘尼傳. *See* Biqiuni zhuan

**Bikushōkyō** 比丘請經. *See* Anumānasutta

**Bikutei** 毘俱胝. *See* Bhṛkuṭī

**Binayaji** 毘奈耶事. *See* Vinayavastu

**Binbashara** 頻婆娑羅. *See* Bimbisāra

**Binzuruharada sonja** 賓頭盧頗羅墮尊者. *See* Piṇḍola-Bhāradvāja

**Birushana** 毗盧遮那. *See* Vairocana

**bishaja** 毘舍闍. *See* piśāca

**Bishakya** 毗舍佉. *See* Viśākha

**Bishakyamo** 毗舍佉母. *See* Viśākhā

**Bishamonten** 毘沙門天. *See* Vaiśravaṇa, Shichifukujin

**Bishari** 毘舍離. *See* Vaiśālī

**bishiki** 鼻識. *See* ghrāṇavijñāna

**bisho** 鼻處. *See* ghrāṇāyatana

**bodai** 菩提. *See* bodhi

**bodaibun** 菩提分. *See* bodhipākṣikadharma

**Bodaidaruma** 菩提達磨. *See* Bodhidharma

**bodaigu** 菩提具. *See* bodhisaṃbhāra

**Bodaigyōkyō** 菩提行經. *See* Bodhicaryāvatāra

**bodaiju** 菩提樹. *See* Bodhi tree

**Bodairushi** 菩提流支. *See* Bodhiruci

**Bodaisenna** 菩提僊那. *See* Bodhisena

**bodaishin** 菩提心. *See* bodhicitta

**bodaishiryō** 菩提資糧. *See* bodhisaṃbhāra

**bōkatsu** 棒喝. *See* banghe

**bokutaku** 木鐸. *See* mokt'ak

**bon** 盆. *See* yulanpen

**bonbai** 梵唄. *See* fanbai

**bonbu** 凡夫. *See* pṛthagjana

**Bondōkyō** 梵動經. *See* Brahmajālasuttanta

**Bon'enna** 梵衍那. *See* Bāmiyān

**bongyō** 梵行. *See* brahmacarya

**bonhoten** 梵輔天. *See* brahmapurohita

**bonjū** 梵住. *See* brahmavihāra

**Bonkai** 梵界. *See* Brahmaloka

**Bonmōkyō** 梵網經. *See* Fanwang jing

**bonnō** 煩腦. *See* kleśa

**bonnōshō** 煩腦障. *See* kleśāvaraṇa

**bonshuten** 梵衆天. *See* brahmakāyika

**bonsō** [alt. bossō] 凡僧. *See* bonze

**Bonten** 梵天. *See* Brahmā

**Bonten shōbutsukyō** 梵天請佛經. *See* Brahmanimantanikasutta

**boru** 暴流. *See* ogha

**bosatsu** 菩薩. *See* bodhisattva

**bosatsugan** 菩薩願. *See* bodhisattvapraṇidhāna

**Bosatsu hongōkyō** 菩薩本業經. *See* Pusa benye jing

**Bosatsu honjōmanron** 菩薩本生鬘論. *See* Jātakamālā

**bosatsuji** 菩薩地. *See* bodhisattvabhūmi

**Bosatsujijikyō** 菩薩地持經. *See* Bodhisattvabhūmi

**bosatsujō** 菩薩乘. *See* bodhisattvayāna

**bosatsukai** 菩薩戒. *See* bodhisattvasaṃvara, bodhisattvaśīla, pusa jie

**Bosatsukaikyō** 菩薩戒經. *See* Pusajie jing

**Bosatsu kenjitsukyō** 菩薩見實經. *See* Pitāputrasamāgamasūtra

**Bosatsu yōraku hongōkyō** 菩薩瓔珞本業經. *See* Pusa yingluo benye jing

**Bosatsuzōkyō** 菩薩藏經. *See* Bodhisattvapiṭaka

**Bōshi** 牟子. *See* Mouzi

**bōshin** 亡身. *See* wangshen

**Bōshi riwakuron** 牟子理惑論. *See* Mouzi lihuo lun

**bōshōgon** 忘聖言. *See* upadeśasaṃpramoṣa

**bossō** [alt. bonsō] 凡僧. *See* bonze

**bu** 部. *See* nikāya

**budda** 佛陀. *See* fo

**bugyō** 部行. *See* vargacārin

**Bujun Shihan** 無準師範. *See* Wuzhun Shifan

**bukuzō** 伏藏. *See* nidhāna

**Bumo onjūgyō** 父母恩重經. *See* Fumu enzhong jing

**bun** 分. *See* bhāga

**bundanshōji** 分段生死. *See* fenduan shengsi, paricchedajarāmaraṇa

**Bun'en** 文偃. *See* Yunmen Wenyan

**buppatsuin** 佛鉢印. *See* buddhapātramudrā

**buppō** 佛法. *See* buddhadharma

**Bushun Shiban** 無準師範. *See* Wuzhun Shifan

**Bu Sokuten** 武則天. *See* Wu Zetian

**bussetsu** 佛刹. *See* buddhakṣetra

**busshin** 佛身. *See* buddhakāya

**Busshinshū** 佛心宗. *See* Foxin zong

**busshō** 佛性. *See* buddhadhātu, foxing

**Busshōron** 佛性論. *See* Foxing lun

**Busshō Tokkō** 佛照德光. *See* Fozhao Deguang

**busso** 佛祖. *See* fozu

**bussoku** 佛足. *See* buddhapāda

**Busso sangyō** 佛祖三經. *See* Fozu sanjing

**Busso tōki** 佛祖統紀. *See* Fozu tongji

**butchō** 佛頂. *See* uṣṇīṣa

**butsu** 佛. *See* buddha, fo

**Butsudabatsudara** 佛陀跋陀羅. *See* Buddhabhadra

**Butsudamitsutara** 佛陀蜜多羅. *See* Buddhamitra

**Butsudanandai** 佛陀難提. *See* Buddhanandi

**Butsudatara** 佛陀多羅. *See* Buddhatrāta

**Butsudayasha** 佛陀耶舍. *See* Buddhayaśas

**butsugen** 佛眼. *See* buddhacakṣus

**butsugo** 佛語. *See* buddhavacana

**Butsuhongyōjukkyō** 佛本行集經. *See* Abhiniṣkramaṇasūtra

**Butsujikyō** 佛地經. *See* Buddhabhūmisūtra

**Butsujikyōron** 佛地經論. *See* Buddhabhūmiśāstra

**butsujō** 佛乘. *See* buddhayāna

**butsuki** 佛紀. *See* Buddhavarṣa

**Butsumo hōtokuzō hannya haramitsukyō** 佛母寶德藏般若波羅蜜經. *See* Ratnaguṇasaṃcayagāthā

**Butsunichi Kaisū** 佛日契嵩. *See* Fori Qisong

**Butsushogyōsan** 佛所行讃. *See* Buddhacarita

**Butsutochō** 佛圖澄. *See* Fotudeng

**Buttochō** 佛圖澄. *See* Fotudeng

**byaku** 白. *See* jñapti

**Byakuei** 白英. *See* Śvetaketu

**Byakue kannon** 白衣觀音. *See* Baiyi Guanyin

**byakugō** 白毫. *See* ūrṇākeśa

**byakuichikonma** 白一羯磨. *See* jñaptidvitīyā karmavācanā

**Byakujō** 白淨. *See* Śvetaketu

**byakukonma** 白羯磨. *See* karmavācanā

**byakurenge** 白蓮華. *See* puṇḍarīka

**Byakurensha** 白蓮社. *See* Bailian she

**Byakusangaibutchō** 白傘蓋佛頂. *See* Sitātapatrā

**byōdōshōchi** 平等性智. *See* samatājñāna

## C

**chakumetsu** 擇滅. *See* pratisaṃkhyānirodha

**chi** 智. *See* jñāna

**chi** 癡. *See* moha

**chiden** 知殿. *See* zhidian

**chido** 智度. *See* prajñāpāramitā

**chiegen** 智慧眼. *See* prajñācakṣus

**chige** 智外. *See* parokṣa

**Chigi** 智顗. *See* Tiantai Zhiyi

**Chigon** 智儼. *See* Zhiyan

**Chigyoku** 智旭. *See* Zhixu

**chiji** 知事. *See* zhishi

**chiju** 智聚. *See* jñānasaṃbhāra

**chiken** 知見. *See* jñānadarśana

**chiken'in** 智拳印. *See* bodhyaṅgīmudrā, jñānamuṣṭi

**Chikurin shōja** 竹林精舍. *See* Veṇuvanavihāra

**Chikurinsō** 竹林叢. *See* Veṇugrāmaka

**chikushō** 畜生. *See* tiryak

**chinbō** 珍寶. *See* ratna

**chinzō** 頂相. *See* dingxiang

**Chitotsu** 知訥. *See* Pojo Chinul

**chiyoku** 知浴. *See* zhiyu

**chō** 頂. *See* mūrdhan

**Chōgen** 超元. *See* Daozhe Chaoyuan

**chōja** 長者. *See* gṛhapati

**chōjō** 澄淨. *See* prasāda

**Chōju** 長壽. *See* Kosambiyasutta

**Chōkan** 澄觀. *See* Chengguan

**Chōro Sōsaku** 長蘆宗賾. *See* Changlu Zongze

**Chō Shōei** 張商英. *See* Zhang Shangying

**chōshu** 頭首. *See* toushou

**chōsoku** 調息. *See* prāṇāyāma

**Chūagongyō** 中阿含經. *See* Madhyamāgama, Majjhimanikāya

**Chūdahantaka** 注荼半托迦. *See* Cūḍapanthaka

**chūdō** 中道. *See* madhyamapratipad

**Chūgan** 中觀. *See* Madhyamaka

**Chūgan ronsho** 中觀論疏. *See* Zhongguan lun shu

**chūgee** 中價衣. *See* uttarāsaṃga

**chūgoku** 中國. *See* MADHYAMADEŚA

**chūhatsu** 中般. *See* ANTARĀPARINIRVĀYIN

**chūhatsunehan** 中般涅槃. *See* ANTARĀPARINIRVĀYIN

**Chūhō Myōhon** 中峰明本. *See* ZHONGFENG MINGBEN

**chūin** 中陰. *See* ANTARĀBHAVA

**chūkon** 中根. *See* MADYENDRIYA

**chūranja/chūransha** 偸蘭遮. *See* STHŪLĀTYAYA

**Chūron** 中論. *See* MŪLAMADHAYAMIKAKĀRIKĀ, MADHYAMAKAŚĀSTRA

**chūu** 中有. *See* ANTARĀBHAVA

**chūun'ujō** 中蘊有情. *See* GANDHARVA

## D

**dabi** 荼毘[alt. 荼毘]. *See* KṢAPITA

**Daiba** 提婆. *See* ĀRYADEVA

**Daibadatta** 提婆達多. *See* DEVADATTA

**Daibirushana jōbutsu jinben kajikyō** 大毘盧遮那成佛神變加持經. *See* MAHĀVAIROCANASŪTRA

**daibodai** 大菩提. *See* MAHĀBODHI

**Daibodaiji** 大菩提寺. *See* MAHĀBODHI TEMPLE

**daibonnōjihō** 大煩惱地法. *See* KLEŚAMAHĀBHŪMIKA

**Daibonten** 大梵天. *See* MAHĀBRAHMĀ

**daibosatsu** 大菩薩. *See* MAHĀBODHISATTVA

**Daibyōdō ō** 大平等王. *See* MAHĀSAṂMATA

**Daichidoron** 大智度論. *See* DAZHIDU LUN

**daie** 大衣. *See* SAṂGHĀṬĪ

**Daie** 大慧. *See* DAHUI ZONGGAO

**Daie Fukaku zenji sho** 大慧普覺禪師書. *See* DAHUI PUJUE CHANSHI SHU

**Daie Fukaku zenji shūmon muko** 大慧普覺禪師宗門武庫. *See* DAHUI PUJUE CHANSHI ZONGMEN WUKU

**Daien hōbengyō** 大緣方便經. *See* MAHĀNIDĀNASUTTA

**Daiekyō** 大會經. *See* MAHĀSAMAYASUTTANTA

**daienkyōchi** 大圓鏡智. *See* ĀDARŚAJÑĀNA

**Daie Sōkō** 大慧宗杲. *See* DAHUI ZONGGAO

**daifuzenjihō** 大不善地法. *See* AKUŚALAMAHĀBHŪMIKA

**daigidan** 大疑團. *See* YITUAN

**daigo** 代語. *See* DAIYU

**daigo** 醍醐. *See* MAṆḌA

**Daihannya haramittakyō** 大般若波羅蜜多經. *See* MAHĀPRAJÑĀPĀRAMITĀSŪTRA

**Daihatsunehangyō** 大般涅槃經. *See* MAHĀPARINIRVĀṆASŪTRA, cf. MAHĀPARINIBBĀNASUTTANTA

**Daihatsunehangyō juge** 大般涅槃經集解. *See* DA BANNIEPAN JING JIJIE

**daihi** 大悲. *See* MAHĀKARUṆĀ

**Daihiju** 大悲咒. *See* DABEI ZHOU, QIANSHOU JING

**Daihi kūchi kongō daikyōō gikikyō** 大悲空智金剛大教王儀軌經. *See* HEVAJRATANTRA/HEVAJRAḌĀKINĪJĀLASAMBARATANTRA

**Daihisha** 大悲者. *See* MAHĀKARUṆIKA

**Daihōdō daijukkyō** 大方等大集經. *See* MAHĀSAṂNIPĀTASŪTRA

**Daihōdō musōkyō** 大方等無想經. *See* MAHĀMEGHASŪTRA

**Daihōdō nyoraizōkyō** 大方等如來藏經. *See* TATHĀGATAGARBHASŪTRA

**Daihokkukyō** 大法鼓經. *See* MAHĀBHERĪHĀRAKAPARIVARTA

**Daihōkō bosatsuzō Monjushiri konpongikikyō** 大方廣菩薩藏文殊師利根本儀軌經. *See* MAÑJUŚRĪMŪLAKALPA

**Daihōkō Butsu kegongyō** 大方廣佛華嚴經. *See* AVATAṂSAKASŪTRA, GAṆḌAVYŪHA

**Daihongyō** 大本經. *See* MAHĀPADĀNA SUTTANTA, MAHĀVADĀNASŪTRA

**Daihōshakukyō** 大寶積經. *See* RATNAKŪṬASŪTRA

**Daii** 提謂. *See* TRAPUṢA

**daiichigitai** 第一義諦. *See* PARAMĀRTHA SATYA

**daiin** 大印. *See* MAHĀMUDRĀ

**Daiitoku myōō** 大威德明王. *See* YAMĀNTAKA

**daiji** 大事. *See* DASHI

**daiji** 大士. *See* MAHĀSATTVA

**daijihō** 大地法. *See* MAHĀBŪMIKA

**Daijionji** 大慈恩寺. *See* DACI'ENSI

**daijō** 大城. *See* MAHĀJANAPADA

**Daijō** 大乘. *See* MAHĀYĀNA

**Daijō Abidatsuma jūron** 大乘阿毘達磨集論. *See* ABHIDHARMASAMUCCAYA

**Daijō daigishō** 大乘大義章. *See* Dasheng dayi zhang

**Daijō genron** 大乘玄論. *See* Dasheng xuanlun

**Daijō gishō** 大乘義章. *See* Dasheng yi zhang

**Daijō gounron** 大乘五蘊論. *See* Pañcaskandhaprakaraṇa

**Daijō hōben'e** 大乘方便會. *See* Upāyakauśalyasūtra

**Daijō hōon girinjō** 大乘法苑義林章. *See* Dasheng fayuan yilin zhang

**Daijō hōyōgiron** 大乘寶要義論. *See* Sūtrasamuccaya

**Daijō jōgōron** 大乘成業論. *See* Karmasiddhiprakaraṇa

**Daijō jūbosatsugakuron** 大乘集菩薩學論. *See* Śikṣāsamuccaya

**Daijō kishinron** 大乘起信論. *See* Dasheng qixin lun

**Daijō kishinron bekki** 大乘起信論別記. *See* Taesŭng kisin non pyŏlgi

**Daijō kisihinron giki** 大乘起信論義記. *See* Dasheng qixin lun yi ji

**Daijō kishin ron sho** 大乘起信論疏. *See* Taesŭng kisin non so

**Daijō mitsugongyō** 大乘密嚴經. *See* Ghanavyūha

**Daijō mushō hōbenmon** 大乘無生方便門. *See* Dasheng wusheng fangbian men

**Daijō shōgon hōōgyō** 大乘莊嚴寶王經. *See* Kāraṇḍavyūha

**Daijō shōgongyōron** 大乘莊嚴經論. *See* Mahāyānasūtrālaṃkāra

**Daiju Ekai** 大珠慧海. *See* Dazhu Huihai

**daikai** 大可畏. *See* mahābhaya

**Daiken** 大賢. *See* Taehyŏn

**daikō** 大劫. *See* mahākalpa

**Daikō Hōon** 大洪報恩. *See* Dahong Bao'en

**Daikokuten** 大黒天. *See* Mahākāla, Shichifukujin

**Daikō Shusui** 大洪守遂. *See* Dahong Shousui

**Daikuchirakyō** 大拘絺羅經. *See* Mahāvedallasutta

**daikyōkan[jigoku]** 大叫喚[地獄]. *See* mahāraurava

**Daikyū Shōnen** 大休正念. *See* Daxiu Zhengnian

**Dainichikyō** 大日經. *See* Mahāvairocanasūtra

**Dainichikyō gishaku** 大日經義釋. *See* Dari jing yishi

**Dainichikyōsho** 大日經疏. *See* Dari jing shu

**Dainichi nyorai** 大日如來. *See* Vairocana

**dainin** 大人. *See* mahāpuruṣa

**daininsō** 大人相. *See* mahāpuruṣalakṣaṇa

**Daiō** 大雄. *See* Mahāvīra

**dairaku** 大樂. *See* mahāsukha

**Daisatsushanikenshi** 大薩遮尼犍子. *See* Mahāsatyanirgrantha

**Daiseishi** 大勢至. *See* Mahāsthāmaprāpta

**daisetsu** 大說. *See* mahāpadeśa

**daishi kanjō** 第四灌頂. *See* caturthābhiṣekha

**daishisō** 大師想. *See* śāstṛsaṃjñā

**Daishō** 大聖. *See* Mahāmuni

**daishōnetsu** 大焦熱. *See* pratāpana

**daishu** 大種. *See* mahābhūta

**Daishubu** 大衆部. *See* Mahāsāṃghika

**daishuin** 大手印. *See* mahāmudrā

**Dai Sō sōshiryaku** 大宋僧史略. *See* Da Song seng shi lüe

**Daitaka** 提多迦. *See* Dhṛṭaka

**daitoku** 大德. *See* dade

**Dai Tō naitenroku** 大唐内典録. *See* Da Tang Neidian lu

**Dai Tō Saiiki guhō kōsōden** 大唐西域求法高僧傳. *See* Da Tang Xiyu qiufa gaoseng zhuan

**Dai Tō Saiiki ki** 大唐西域記. *See* Da Tang Xiyu ji

**Daiungyō** 大雲經. *See* *Mahāmeghasūtra

**Daiyū** 大雄. *See* Mahāvīra

**daizenjihō** 大善地法. *See* kuśalamahābūmika

**Daizenkennōkyō** 大善見王經. *See* Mahāsuddassanasuttanta

**Daizōkyō** 大藏經. *See* Dazangjing

**Daizuigu** 大隨求. *See* Mahāpratisarā

**dakini** 荼枳尼. *See* ḍākinī

**dan** 斷. *See* prahāṇa

**danhen** 斷邊. *See* ucchedānta

**danken** 斷見. *See* ucchedadṛṣṭi

**dankenron** 斷見論. *See* ucchedavāda

**dan'otsu** 檀越. *See* dānapati, danna

**dantokura** 檀特羅. *See* TANTRA

**danzengon** 斷善根. *See* SAMUCCHINNAKUŚALAMŪLA

**darani** 陀羅尼. *See* DHĀRAṆĪ

**Daruma** 達摩. *See* BODHIDHARMA

**Darumagyūta** 達摩笈多. *See* DHARMAGUPTA

**Darumatara** 達摩多羅. *See* DHARMATRĀTA

**Darumatara zenkyō** 達摩多羅禪經. *See* DAMADUOLUO CHAN JING

**Dateikyō** 嗏帝經. *See* MAHĀTAṆHĀSAṄKHAYASUTTA

**denbōge** [alt. denpōge] 傳法偈. *See* CHUANFA JI, YIJI

**Denbōhōki** 傳法寶紀. *See* CHUAN FABAO JI

**Denbōshōshūki** 傳法正宗記. *See* CHUANFA ZHENGZONG JI

**denpōge** [alt. denbōge] 傳法偈. *See* CHUANFA JI, YIJI

**Denshin hōyō** 傳心法要. *See* CHUANXIN FAYAO

**dentōroku** 傳燈録. *See* CHUANDENG LU

**dō** 道. *See* DAO, MĀRGA, PATHA

**dō** 幢. *See* KETU

**Dōan** 道安. *See* DAO'AN

**dōchi** 道智. *See* MĀRGAJÑĀTĀ

**dōgu** 道具. *See* PARIṢKĀRA

**dōhidōchikenshōjō** 道非道智見清淨. *See* MAGGĀMAGGAÑĀṆADASSANAVISUDDHI

**dōhon** 同品. *See* SAPAKṢA

**Do issaishobutsukyōgai chigongyō** 度一切諸佛境界智嚴經. *See* SARVABUDDHAVIṢAYĀVATĀRAJÑĀNĀLOKĀṂKĀRASŪTRA

**Dōitsu** 道一. *See* MAZU DAOYI

**dōji** 同事. *See* SAMĀNĀRTHATĀ

**dōjō** 道場. *See* DAOCHANG

**dōka** 道果. *See* MĀRGAPHALA

**Dōkai** 道楷. *See* FURONG DAOKAI

**dokukaku** 獨覺. *See* PRATYEKABUDDHA

**Dokukeimo** 獨髻母. *See* EKAJAṬĪ

**dokuroki** 髑髏器. *See* KAPĀLA

**Dōkyō gisū** 道教義樞. *See* DAOJIAO YISHU

**dōnin** 道人. *See* DAOREN

**donkon** 鈍根. *See* MṚDVINDRIYA

**Donmadaina bikuni** 曇摩提那比丘尼. *See* DHARMADINNĀ

**Donmukatsu** 曇無竭. *See* DHARMODGATA

**Donmusen** 曇無讖. *See* DHARMAKṢEMA

**Donmutokubu** 曇無德部. *See* DHARMAGUPTAKA

**Donran** 曇鸞. *See* TANLUAN

**dōri** 道理. *See* YUKTI

**dōruiin** 同類因. *See* SABHĀGAHETU

**Dōryū** 道隆. *See* LANXI DAOLONG

**Dōsha Chōgen** 道者超元. *See* DAOZHE CHAOYUAN

**Dōshaku** 道綽. *See* DAOCHUO

**Dōshin** 道信. *See* DAOXIN

**Dōshin** 童眞. *See* KUMĀRABHŪTA

**Dōshō** 道生. *See* CAOYUAN DAOSHENG

**dōtai** 道諦. *See* MĀRGASATYA

**dōtsū** 道通. *See* DAOTONG

## E

**e** 衣. *See* CĪVARA

**e** 慧. *See* MATI, PRAJÑĀ

**e** 依. *See* PRATISARAṆA, UPADHI

**Ebongyō** 穢品經. *See* ANAṄGAṆASUTTA

**Echū** 慧忠. *See* NANYANG HUIZHONG

**egaku** 慧學. *See* PRAJÑĀŚIKṢĀ

**egedatsu** 慧解脫. *See* PRAJÑĀVIMUKTA

**ehō** 依報. *See* ER BAO

**Eichū** 永中. *See* YONGZHONG

**Eineiji** 永寧寺. *See* YONGNINGSI

**eji** 依止. *See* NIŚRAYA

**Ejō** 懷讓. *See* NANYUE HUAIRANG

**Ejōron** 迴諍論. *See* VIGRAHAVYĀVARTANĪ

**Eka** 慧可. *See* HUIKE

**Ekai** 慧海. *See* DAZHU HUIHAI

**Ekai** 慧開. *See* WUMEN HUIKAI

**ekō** 迴向. *See* PARIṆĀMANĀ

**ekō** 壞劫. *See* SAṂVARTAKALPA

**ekō henjō** 回光返照. *See* HUIGUANG FANZHAO

**eku** 壞苦. *See* VIPARIṆĀMADUḤKHATĀ

**en** 厭. *See* NIRVEDA

**en** 緣. *See* pratyaya

**Enan** 慧南. *See* Huinan

**Enbudai** 閻浮提. *See* Jambudvīpa

**Enchō** 圓澄. *See* Zhanran Yuandeng

**endongyō** 圓頓教. *See* yuandun jiao

**engaku** 緣覺. *See* pratyekabuddha

**engakujō** 緣覺乘. *See* pratyekabuddhayāna

**Engakukyō** 圓覺經. *See* Yuanjue jing

**engi** 縁起. *See* pratītyasamutpāda

**Engo Kokugon** 圜悟克勤. *See* Yuanwu Keqin

**Enichi** 慧日. *See* Cimin Huiri

**Enjiki** 圓測. *See* Wŏnch'ŭk

**enjōjisshō** 圓成實性. *See* pariniṣpanna

**Enju** 延壽. *See* Yongming Yanshou

**Enma ō** 閻魔王. *See* Yama

**enmanshidai** 圓滿次第. *See* niṣpannakrama

**Enmantokka** 焰曼德迦. *See* Yamāntaka

**enmoku** 宴默. *See* pratisaṃlayana

**Enmyōron** 圓明論. *See* Yuanming lun

**Enneji** 焰慧地. *See* Arciṣmatī

**ennetsujigoku** 炎熱地獄. *See* tāpana

**ennyū** 圓融. *See* yuanrong

**ennyū no sangan** 圓融三觀. *See* sanguan

**Enō** 慧能. *See* Huineng

**enshōju** 圓生樹. *See* pariyatra, kalpavṛksa

**Enshōron** 緣生論. *See* *Pratītyasamutpādaśāstra

**Eon** 慧遠. *See* Lushan Huiyuan

**Eshi** 慧思. *See* Nanyue Huisi

**Esō kongō daranikyō** 壞相金剛陀羅尼經. *See* Vajravidāraṇadhāraṇī

**etakishō** 依他起性. *See* paratantra

## F

**fuda** 浮屠. *See* fo

**fūdai** 風大. *See* vāyu[dhātu]

**Fu daishi** 傅大士. *See* Fu dashi

**Fudarakusen** 補陀落山. *See* Poṭalaka

**Fudasen** 普陀山/補陀山. *See* Putuoshan

**fudō** 不動. *See* akopya

**fudōgō** 不動業. *See* aniñjyakarman

**Fudōji** 不動地. *See* acalābhūmi

**Fudō myōō** 不動明王. *See* Acalanāthavidyārāja

**fudōza** 不動坐. *See* acalāsana

**fugai** 不害. *See* ahiṃsā

**Fugan** 普願. *See* Nanquan Puyuan

**Fugan** 普巖. *See* Yun'an Puyan

**fugen** 不還. *See* anāgāmin

**Fugen** 普賢. *See* Samantabhadra

**Fugen bosatsu gyōgansan** 普賢菩薩行願讚. *See* Bhadracarīpraṇidhāna

**fugenkō** 不還向. *See* anāgāmiphalapratipannaka

**fugūbuppō** 不共佛法. *See* āveṇika[buddha]dharma

**fugūhō** 不共法. *See* āveṇika[buddha]dharma

**fugūjū** 不共住. *See* asaṃvāsa

**fuhatsu** 覆鉢. *See* pātranikubjana

**fuhatsu konma** 覆鉢羯磨. *See* pātranikubjana

**fuhōitsu** 不放逸. *See* apramāda

**Fuhōzō innenden** 付法藏因緣傳. *See* Fu fazang yinyuan zhuan

**fui** 不爲. *See* abhabbaṭṭhāna

**fui** 怖畏. *See* bhairava

**Fui Kongō** 怖畏金剛. *See* Vajrabhairava

**Fujaku** 普寂. *See* Puji

**fujigedatsu** 不時解脫. *See* asamayavimukta

**fujō** 不定. *See* aniyata

**fujō** 不淨. *See* saṃkliṣṭa

**fujōkan** 不淨觀. *See* aśubhabhāvanā

**fujōmotsu** 不淨物. *See* akalpikavastu

**fujōshushō** 不定種姓/種性. *See* aniyatagotra

**fukashigi** 不可思議. *See* acintya

**fukatoku** 不可得. *See* anupalambha

**fukeron** 不戲論. *See* niḥprapañca

**fukigo** 不綺語. *See* saṃbhinnapralāpāt prativirati

**Fukō** 普香. *See* Samantagandha

**fuku** 覆. *See* mrakṣa

**fuku** 福. *See* puṇya

**Fukū** 不空. *See* Amoghavajra

**fukuchi shiryō** 福智資糧. *See* puṇyajñānasaṃbhāra

**fukuden** 福田. *See* puṇyakṣetra

**fukugōji** 福業事. *See* puṇyakriyāvastu

**Fukū jōju nyoraibutsu** 不空成就如來佛. *See* Amoghasiddhi

**Fukū kenjaku** 不空羂索. *See* Amoghapāśa

**fukushōten** 福生天. *See* puṇyaprasava

**fukutoku shiryō** 福德資糧. *See* puṇyasaṃbhāra

**fukuzō** 腹藏. *See* nidhāna

**fukuzōmotsu** 腹藏物. *See* fuzangwu

**fumetsu** 不滅. *See* aniruddha

**fun** 忿. *See* krodha

**funbetsu** 分別. *See* vikalpa or kalpanā

**funbetsugashū** 分別我執. *See* parikalpitātmagraha

**funbetsumumyō** 分別無明. *See* parikalpitāvidyā

**Funbetsusetsubu** 分別說部. *See* Vibhajyavāda

**funbetsuwaku** 分別惑. *See* parikalpitakleśāvaraṇa

**fundarike** 芬陀利華. *See* puṇḍarīka

**funi** 不二. *See* advaya

**funichi** 不二智. *See* advayajñāna

**furai** 不來. *See* anāgāmin

**Furannakashō** 富蘭那迦葉. *See* Pūraṇa-Kāśyapa

**Furuna** 富樓那. *See* Pūrṇa

**furyōgi** 不了義. *See* neyārtha

**furyūmonji** 不立文字. *See* buli wenzi

**fusatsu** 布薩. *See* upoṣadha

**fuse** 布施. *See* dāna

**fuseharamitsu** 布施波羅蜜. *See* dānapāramitā

**fusetsu** 普說. *See* pushuo

**fushidai sangan** 不次第三觀. *See* sanguan

**Fushi gōjūkyō** 父子合集經. *See* Pitāputrasamāgamasūtra

**fushin** 不信. *See* āśraddhya

**fushōchi** 不正知. *See* asaṃprajanya

**Fushō Chitotsu** 普照知訥. *See* Pojo Chinul

**fushōshiyui** 不正思惟. *See* ayoniśomanaskāra

**fūsu** 副司. *See* fusi

**Futabarōkyō** 布吒婆樓經. *See* Poṭṭhapādasutta

**futaiten** 不退轉. *See* avaivartika

**futogara** 補特伽羅. *See* pudgala

**Futogara ron** 補特伽羅論. *See* Pudgalavāda

**Fuyō Dōkai** 芙蓉道楷. *See* Furong Daokai

**Fuyōkyō** 普曜經. *See* Lalitavistara

**fuzen** 不善. *See* akuśala

**fuzenkon** 不善根. *See* akuśalamūla

**fuzen muchi** 不染無知. *See* akliṣṭājñāna

**Fuzōfugengyō** 不增不減經. *See* Anūnatvāpūrṇatvanirdeśa

## G

**ga** 我. *See* ātman

**gago** 我語. *See* ātmavāda

**gagu** 臥具. *See* pratyāstaraṇa

**gai** 蓋. *See* nīvaraṇa

**gai** 害. *See* vihiṃsā

**gaki** 餓鬼. *See* preta

**gaku** 學. *See* śikṣā

**gakunin** 學人. *See* śaikṣa

**gakusho** 學處. *See* śikṣāpada

**gaman** 我慢. *See* ahaṃkāra

**gan** 願. *See* praṇidhāna

**ganbodaishin** 願菩提心. *See* praṇidhicittopāda

**Gangyō** 願經. *See* Ākaṅkheyyasutta

**Gangyō** 元曉. *See* Wŏnhyo

**ganharamitsu** 願波羅蜜. *See* praṇidhānapāramitā

**Garankyō** 伽藍經. *See* Kālāmasutta

**gasho** 我所. *See* mamakāra

**gashū** 我執. *See* ātmagrāha, ahaṃkāra

**gasshō** 合掌. *See* añjali

**Gatsuzōbun** 月藏分. *See* Candragarbhaparipṛcchā

**Gattōsanmaikyō** 月燈三昧經. *See* Samādhirājasūtra

**Gaya Kashō** 伽耶迦葉. *See* Gayā-Kāśyapa

**ge** 外. *See* bahirdhā

**ge** 偈. *See* gāthā, śloka

**gedatsu** 解脱. *See* mokṣa, vimokṣa

**gedatsudō** 解脱道. *See* mokṣamārga, vimokṣamārga

**Gedatsudōron** 解脱道論. *See* Vimuttimagga

**gedatsumon** 解脱門. *See* vimokṣamukha

**gedō** 外道. *See* tīrthika

**gego** 解悟. *See* jiewu

**Gejinmikkyō** 解深密經. *See* Saṃdhinirmocanasūtra

**gekai** 解界. *See* sīmāsamūhana

**gekyō** 外境. *See* bāhyārtha

**gen** 眼. *See* cakṣus

**Genchūmei** 玄中銘. *See* Xuanzhong ming

**gendatsubajō** 乾闥婆城. *See* gandharvanagara

**Gengaku** 玄學. *See* Xuanxue

**gengō** 賢劫. *See* bhadrakalpa

**Gengōgyō** 賢劫經. *See* Bhadrakalpikasūtra

**gengyō** 現行. *See* samudācāra

**Genjō** 玄奘. *See* Xuanzang

**Genkaku** 玄覺. *See* Yongjia Xuanjue

**genkan** 現觀. *See* abhisamaya

**genkon** 眼根. *See* cakṣurindriya

**Genninron** 原人論. *See* Yuanren lun

**genryō** 現量. *See* pratyakṣa

**Gensha sanbyō** 玄沙三病. *See* Xuansha shanbing

**Gensha Shibi** 玄沙師備. *See* Xuansha Shibei

**genshi** 幻師. *See* māyākāra

**genshiki** 眼識. *See* cakṣurvijñāna

**genshin** 幻身. *See* māyādeha

**gensho** 眼處. *See* cakṣurāyatana

**genshuin** 現取因. *See* upādānakāraṇa

**genzen[chi]** 現前[地]. *See* abhimukhī

**geshi** 下士. *See* adhamapuruṣa

**gi** 義. *See* abhisaṃdhi, artha

**gi** 愧. *See* apatrāpya

**gi** 疑. *See* vicikitsā

**Giba** 耆婆. *See* Jīvaka

**gidan** 疑團. *See* yituan

**Gida taishi** 祇陀太子. *See* Jeta

**Gifuku** 義福. *See* Yifu

**Gijō** 義淨. *See* Yijing

**gijō** 疑情. *See* yiqing

**Gijugikkodokuon** 祇樹給孤獨園. *See* Jetavana

**giki** 儀軌. *See* vidhi

**Gikkodoku chōja** 給孤獨長者. *See* Anāthapiṇḍada

**Gikyō** 疑經/僞經. *See* apocrypha

**Gisei** 義青. *See* Touzi Yiqing

**Gishō** 義湘/相. *See* Ŭisang

**Gisokukyō** 義足經. *See* Aṭṭhakavagga

**giya** 祇夜. *See* geya

**Giyukyō** 蟻喩經. *See* Vammikasutta

**gō** 業. *See* karman

**gobu** 五部. *See* pañcakula

**gobutsu** 五佛. *See* pañcatathāgata

**gochi** 五智. *See* pañcajñāna

**gochi nyorai** 五智如來. *See* pañcatathāgata, pañcajina

**gōdō** 業道. *See* karmapatha

**godō** 五道. *See* pañcagati

**godōju** 悟道頌. *See* wudao song, yiji

**goe nenbutsu** 五會念佛. *See* wuhui nianfo

**Gōga** 恒河. *See* Gaṅgānadī

**Gōgasha** 恒河沙. *See* Gaṅgānadīvālukā

**gogen** 五眼. *See* pañcacakṣus

**gogō** 語業. *See* vākkarman

**gogun [biku]** 五群[比丘]. *See* bhadravargīya, pañcavargika

**gohō** 五法. *See* wufa

**Gohō** 護法. *See* Dharmapāla

**goi** 五位. *See* pañcamārga

**goji** 五時. *See* wushi

**goji hakkyō** 五時八教. *See* WUSHI BAJIAO

**gojōgoten** 五淨居天. *See* ŚUDDHĀVĀSA

**gojoku** 五濁. *See* PAÑCAKAṢĀYA

**gojū gengi** 五重玄義. *See* FAHUA WUCHONG XUANYI

**gokai** 五戒. *See* PAÑCAŚĪLA

**Gokakusararingyō** 牛角娑羅林經. *See* CŪḶAGOSIṄGASUTTA, MAHĀGOSIṄGASUTTA

**Goke shichishū** 五家七宗. *See* WU JIA QI ZONG

**goketsujō** 五決定. *See* PAÑCANIYATA

**Gokoku bosatsue[kyō]** 護國菩薩會[經]. *See* RĀṢṬRAPĀLAPARIPṚCCHĀ

**gokoku bukkyō** 護國佛教. *See* HUGUO FOJIAO

**gokon** 五根. *See* PAÑCENDRIYA

**gokukōjōten** 極光淨天. *See* ĀBHĀSVARĀLOKA

**gokumi** 極微. *See* PARAMĀNU

**Gokuraku** 極樂. *See* JILE

**gokuraku jōdo** 極樂淨土. *See* SUKHĀVATĪ

**gokushichihen'u** 極七返有. *See* SAPTAKṚDBHAVAPARAMA

**gokushippon'u** 極七返有. *See* SAPTAKṚDBHAVAPARAMA

**gokyō** 五境. *See* PAÑCAVIṢAYA

**Gokyōshō** 五教章. *See* HUAYAN WUJIAO ZHANG

**goma** 護摩. *See* HOMA

**Gōmakyō** 降魔經. *See* MĀRATAJJANĪYASUTTA

**Gōma Zō** 降魔藏. *See* XIANGMO ZANG

**gomi** 五味. *See* WUWEI

**gomukengō** 五無間業. *See* PAÑCĀNANTARĪYA

**gomyō** 五明. *See* PAÑCAVIDYĀ

**gomyōyoku** 五妙欲. *See* PAÑCAKĀMAGUṆA

**gonbun** 近分. *See* SĀMANTAKA

**gongo** 言語. *See* VYAVAHĀRA

**gonjiritsugi** 近事律儀. *See* UPĀSAKASAṂVARA

**gonjitsu** 權實. *See* QUAN SHI

**gonjū** 近住. *See* UPAVĀSA

**gonjū deshi** 近住弟子. *See* ANTEVĀSIKA

**gonkyō** 言教. *See* NIRUKTI

**gonsakuritsugi** 勤策律儀. *See* ŚRĀMANERASAṂVARA

**goriki** 五力. *See* PAÑCABALA

**goroku** 語録. *See* YULU

**goshidai** 五次第. *See* PAÑCAKRAMA

**gōshō** 業障. *See* KARMĀVARAṆA

**goshu** 五趣. *See* PAÑCAGATI

**Goshu** 牛主. *See* GAVĀṂPATI

**goshu no gengi** 五種玄義. *See* WUZHONG XUANYI

**Goso Hōen** 五祖法演. *See* WUZU FAYAN

**gosshō** 業障. *See* KARMĀVARAṆA

**gotokuchi** 後得智. *See* PṚṢṬHALABDHAJÑĀNA

**gou** 後有. *See* PUNARBHAVA

**goun** 五蘊. *See* SKANDHA

**goun seken** 五蘊世間. *See* WUYUN SHIJIAN

**Gozai** 護財. *See* DHANAPĀLA, NĀLĀGIRI

**gōzanzein** 降三世印. *See* BHŪTAḌĀMARAMUDRĀ

**Gōzanze myōō** 降三世明王. *See* TRAILOKYAVIJAYA

**Gozu Hōyū** 牛頭法融. *See* NIUTOU FARONG

**Gozushū** 牛頭宗. *See* NIUTOU ZONG

**gudō** 愚童. *See* BĀLA

**gūfugūgō** 共不共業. *See* GONG BUGONG YE

**Gugekyō** 求解經. *See* VĪMAṂSAKASUTTA

**gūgyō deshi** 共行弟子. *See* SADDHIVIHĀRIKA

**Guhōgyō** 求法經. *See* DHAMMADĀYĀDASUTTA

**guju** 具壽. *See* ĀYUṢMAN

**Gumyōshū** 弘明集. *See* HONGMING JI

**Gunabaddara** 求那跋陀羅. *See* GUṆABHADRA

**Gunabatsuma** 求那跋摩. *See* GUṆAVARMAN

**Gunin** 弘忍. *See* HONGREN

**gunji** 軍持. *See* KUṆḌIKĀ

**gurenge** 紅蓮華. *See* PADMA

**gūsō** 共相. *See* SĀMĀNYALAKṢAṆA

**gusokukai** 具足戒. *See* UPASAṂPADĀ

**gyatei gyatei haragyatei harasōgyatei boji sowaka** 揭帝揭帝波羅揭帝波羅僧揭帝菩提薩婆訶. *See* GATE GATE PĀRAGATE PĀRASAṂGATE BODHI SVĀHĀ

**gyō** 行. *See* SAṂSKĀRA, CARITA

**gyōbodaishin** 行菩提心. *See* PRASTHĀNACITTOPĀDA

**gyōgu** 樂求. *See* ABHILĀṢA

**gyōku** 行苦. *See* SAṂSKĀRADUḤKHATĀ

**Gyoran Kannon** 魚藍觀音. *See* MALANG FU

**Gyōshi** 行思. *See* QINGYUAN XINGSI

**gyōsō** 行相. *See* ĀKĀRA

**Gyōzan Ejaku** 仰山慧寂. *See* YANGSHAN HUIJI

## H

**hachi** 鉢. *See* PĀTRA

**hachidai bosatsu** 八大菩薩. *See* AṢṬAMAHOPAPUTRA, MAHOPAPUTRA

**hachidai jizaiga** 八大自在我. *See* BA DA ZIZAI WO

**hachidainin** 八大人. *See* AṢṬĀRYAPUDGALA

**hachigedatsu** 八解脱. *See* AṢṬAVIMOKṢA

**Hachijōkyō** 八城經. *See* AṬṬHAKANĀGARASUTTA

**hachikaku** 八覺. *See* BA JUE

**hachikichijō** 八吉祥. *See* AṢṬAMAṄGALA

**hachimi** 八味. *See* BA WEI

**hakkaku** 八覺. *See* BA JUE

**hakkansai** 八關齋. *See* BAGUAN ZHAI

**hakku** 八苦. *See* DUḤKHA

**Haku** 帛. *See* BO

**Hakubaji** 白馬寺. *See* BAIMASI

**Hakukura** 薄拘羅. *See* BAKKULA

**Haku Kyoi** 白居易. *See* BO JUYI

**Hakuun Shutan** 白雲守端. *See* BAIYUN SHOUDUAN

**hana** 波那. *See* PRĀṆA

**Hanjuzanmaikyō** 般舟三昧經. *See* PRATYUTPANNABUDDHASAṂMUKHĀVASTHITASAMĀDHISŪTRA

**hankafuza** 半跏趺坐. *See* ARDHAPARYAṄKA, ARDHAPADMĀSANA

**hankashiyui** 半跏思惟. *See* MAITREYĀSANA

**hannya** 般若. *See* PRAJÑĀ

**Hannya haramitta** 般若波羅蜜多. *See* PRAJÑĀPĀRAMITĀ

**Hannya haramitta shingyō** 般若波羅蜜多心經. *See* PRAJÑĀPĀRAMITĀHṚDAYASŪTRA

**Hannya muchiron** 般若無知論. *See* BORE WUZHI LUN

**Hannya rishubun** 般若理趣分. *See* ADHYARDHAŚATIKĀPRAJÑĀPĀRAMITĀSŪTRA, PRAJÑĀPĀRAMITĀNAYAŚATAPAÑCĀŚATIKĀ

**Hannyatōronshaku** 般若燈論釋. *See* PRAJÑĀPRADĪPA

**hanrengeza** 半蓮華坐. *See* ARDHAPADMĀSANA, ARDHAPARYAṄKA

**Hantaka** 半託迦. *See* PANTHAKA

**happu** 八不. *See* AṢṬĀNTA, EIGHT NEGATIONS

**haradaidaishani** 波羅提提舍尼. *See* PRATIDEŚANĪYA

**haradaimokusha** 波羅提木叉. *See* PRĀTIMOKṢA

**haradaimokushago** 波羅提木叉護. *See* PRĀTIMOKṢASAṂVARA

**Haragōbodaisen** 鉢羅笈菩提山. *See* PRĀGBODHI(GIRI)

**Harahakaramitsutara** 波羅頗迦羅蜜多羅. *See* PRABHĀKARAMITRA

**harai** 波羅夷. *See* PĀRĀJIKA

**haramitsu** 波羅蜜. *See* PĀRAMITĀ

**Harashana** 波羅遮那. *See* PAṬACĀRĀ

**Hari** 波利. *See* BHALLIKA

**harishittaju** 波利質多樹. *See* PARIYATRA

**Hashinoku ō** 波斯匿王. *See* PRASENAJIT

**hasō** 破僧. *See* SAṂGHABHEDA

**hassaikai** 八齋戒. *See* AṢṬĀṄGASAMANVĀGATAṂ UPAVĀSAṂ

**hasshōdō** 八正道. *See* ĀRYĀṢṬĀṄGAMĀRGA, EIGHTFOLD PATH

**hassō** 八相. *See* BAXIANG

**hassu** [alt. hōshi] 法嗣. *See* FASI

**hatsunehan** 般涅槃. *See* PARINIRVĀṆA

**Heireiji** 炳靈寺. *See* BINGLINGSI

**Heishukukyō** 弊宿經. *See* PĀYĀSISUTTANTA

**Hekiganroku** 碧巖録. *See* BIYAN LU

**hekikan** 壁觀. *See* BIGUAN

**hen** 遍. *See* VYĀPTI

**henge shoshūshō** 遍計所執性. *See* PARIKALPITA

**hengyō** 遍行. *See* SARVATRAGA

**hengyōin** 遍行因. *See* SARVATRAGAHETU

**henji** 邊地. *See* BIANDI or YAVANA

**henjōten** 遍淨天. *See* ŚUBHAKṚTSNA

**henken** 邊見. *See* ANTAGRĀHADṚṢṬI

**hennyaku shōji** 變易生死. *See* PARIṆĀMIKAJARĀMARAṆA

**henshi** 遍至. *See* VYĀPTI

**henshō** 返照. *See* FANZHAO

**hensho** 遍處. *See* KASIṆA

**hi** 悲. *See* KARUṆĀ

**hichakumetsu** 非擇滅. *See* APRATISAṂKHYĀNIRODHA

**higan** 彼岸. *See* PĀRA

**Hiin Tsūyō** 費隱通容. *See* FEIYIN TONGRONG

**hike** 非家. *See* ANAGĀRIKĀ

**Hikekyō** 悲華經. *See* KARUṆĀPUṆḌARĪKA

**hikō** 被甲. *See* SAṂNĀHA

**himitsukanjō** 秘密灌頂. *See* GUHYĀBHIṢEKA

**hinpotsu** 秉拂. *See* BINGFU

**hinshutsu** 擯出. *See* NĀSANA

**Hiraihō** 飛来峰. *See* FEILAIFENG

**hiri no sai** 非理作意. *See* AYONIŚOMANASKĀRA

**hiryō** 比量. *See* ANUMĀṆA

**hisōhihisōjo** 非想非非想處. *See* NAIVASAṂJÑĀNĀSAṂJÑĀYATANA

**hitoku** 非得. *See* APRĀPTI

**Hitsuryōgabasha** 畢陵伽婆蹉. *See* PILINDAVATSA

**hiyu** 譬喻. *See* AVADĀNA

**hō** 法. *See* DHARMA

**hōben** 方便. *See* UPĀYA

**hōbenzengyō** 方便善巧. *See* UPĀYAKAUŚALYA

**hōbu** 寶部. *See* RATNAKULA

**hōbyōkanjō** 寶瓶灌頂. *See* KALAŚĀBHIṢEKA

**hōdō** 方等. *See* VAIPULYA

**hōdō** 法幢. *See* FACHUANG

**Hōe** 方會. *See* YANGQI FANGHUI

**Hōenkō** 放焰口. *See* FANG YANKOU

**hōgashū** 法我執. *See* DHARMĀTMAGRAHA

**hōgen** 法眼. *See* DHARMACAKṢUS

**Hōgen** 法眼. *See* FAYAN

**Hōgen Mon'eki** 法眼文益. *See* FAYAN WENYI

**Hōgenshū** 法眼宗. *See* FAYAN ZONG

**hōgo** 法護. *See* DHARMAPĀLA

**hōgo** 法語. *See* YULU

**Hōgobon** 放牛品. *See* MAHĀGOPĀLAKASUTTA

**Hōgyōō shōron** 寶行王正論. *See* RATNĀVALĪ

**Hōhōyō** 奉法要. *See* FENGFA YAO

**hōin** 法印. *See* DHARMAMUDRĀ

**hōitsu** 放逸. *See* PRAMĀDA

**hōjin** 報身. *See* SAṂBHOGAKĀYA

**hōjō** 方丈. *See* FANGZHANG

**hōjō** 放生. *See* FANGSHENG

**hōjōe** 放生會. *See* FANGSHENG HUI

**Hōjūkyō** 法集經. *See* DHARMASAṂGĪTI

**Hōkai** 法海. *See* FAHAI

**Hōkekyō** 法華經. *See* SADDHARMAPUṆḌARĪKASŪTRA

**Hokekyō giki** 法華經義記. *See* FAHUA JING YI JI

**Hokekyō ryakusho** 法華經略疏. *See* FAHUA JING LÜESHU

**Hōken** 法顯. *See* FAXIAN

**hōke nishin** 報化二身. *See* BAOHUA ERSHEN

**hōki** 法器. *See* FAQI

**hōki** 法喜. *See* DHARMAPRĪTI

**Hōki bosatsu** 法起菩薩. *See* DHARMODGATA

**Hōkin** 法欽. *See* FAQIN

**hokkai** 法界. *See* DHARMADHĀTU

**hokkai engi** 法界緣起. *See* FAJIE YUANQI

**hokkai kaji** 法界加持. *See* FAJIE JIACHI

**hokkai taishōchi** 法界體性智. *See* DHARMADHĀTUSVABHĀVAJÑĀNA

**Hokke anrakugyōgi** 法華安樂行義. *See* FAHUA ANLE XINGYI

**Hokke den[ki]** 法華傳[記]. *See* FAHUA ZHUAN[JI]

**Hokke gengi** 法華玄義. *See* FAHUA XUANYI

**Hokke genzan** 法華玄贊. *See* FAHUA XUANZAN

**Hokke gohyakumonron** 法華五百問論. *See* FAHUA WUBAI WENLUN

**Hokke gojūgengi** 法華五重玄義. *See* FAHUA WUCHONG XUANYI

**Hokke mongu** 法華文句. *See* FAHUA WENJU

**Hokke sanbu[kyō]** 法華三部[經]. *See* FAHUA SANBU [JING]

**Hokke senbō** 法華懺法. *See* FAHUA CHANFA

**Hokken** 法顯. *See* FAXIAN

**Hokken den** 法顯傳. *See* FAXIAN ZHUAN

**Hokkōji** 發光地. *See* PRABHĀKARĪBHŪMI

**Hokkugyō** 法句經. *See* DHAMMAPADA

**hokkurushū** 北俱盧洲. *See* UTTARAKURU

**Hōkō daishōgongyō** 方廣大莊嚴經. *See* LALITAVISTARA

**Hō koji** 龐居士. *See* PANG YUN

**Hō koji goroku** 龐居士語錄. *See* PANG JUSHI YULU

**Hokushū** 北宗. *See* BEI ZONG

**Hokuto Shichishō** 北斗七星. *See* BEIDOU QIXING

**Hōkyōsanmai** 寶鏡三昧. *See* BAOJING SANMEI

**hōmon** 法門. *See* DHARMAPARYĀYA

**hōmuga** 法無我. *See* DHARMANAIRĀTMYA

**hōmyō** 法名. *See* FAMING

**hōnan** 法難. *See* FANAN

**hongan** 本願. *See* PURVAPRAṆIDHĀNA

**hōnin** 法忍. *See* DHARMAKṢĀNTI

**Honjaku** 本寂. *See* CAOSHAN BENJI

**honji** 本寺. *See* PONSA

**honjiki** 本識. *See* MŪLAVIJÑĀNA

**honrai no menmoku** 本來面目. *See* BENLAI MIANMU

**Honruisokuron** 品類足論. *See* PRAKARAṆAPĀDA[ŚĀSTRA]

**honshobutsu** 本初佛. *See* ĀDIBUDDHA

**honshōjō** 本性淨. *See* PRAKṚTIVIŚUDDHI

**honshōjūshushō** 本性住種性/姓. *See* PRAKṚTISTHAGOTRA

**honshōkyō** 本生經. *See* JĀTAKA

**Hon'yaku myōgi taishū** 翻譯名義大集. *See* MAHĀVYUTPATTI

**honzai** 本際. *See* BENJI, KOṬI

**hōō** 法王. *See* DHARMARĀJA

**Hō On** 龐蘊. *See* PANG YUN

**Hōon** 報恩. *See* DAHONG BAO'EN

**Hōonbubongyō** 報恩奉盆經. *See* BAO'EN FENGBEN JING

**Hōon jurin** 法苑珠林. *See* FAYUAN ZHULIN

**Hōraku bikuni** 法樂比丘尼. *See* DHARMADINNĀ

**Hōraku bikunikyō** 法樂比丘尼經. *See* CŪḶAVEDALLASUTTA

**hōrin** 法輪. *See* DHARMACAKRA

**Hōrinden** 寶林傳. *See* BAOLIN ZHUAN

**Horitakyō** 哺利多經. *See* POTALIYASUTTA

**hōritsu** 法律. *See* DHARMAVINAYA

**hōrō** 法臘. *See* FALA

**hōse** 法施. *See* DHARMADĀNA

**hōshari** 法舍利. *See* DHARMAŚARĪRA

**hōshi** 法子. *See* FAZI

**Hōshi** 保誌 [alt. 寶誌]. *See* BAOZHI

**hōsho** 法處. *See* DHARMĀYATANA

**Hōshō** 法稱. *See* DHARMAKĪRTI

**Hōshō** 法照. *See* FAZHAO

**Hōshō nyorai** 寶生如來. *See* RATNASAṂBHAVA

**hōshu** 法主. *See* FAZHU

**hōshū** 法執. *See* FAZHI

**Hōshu bosatsu** 寶手菩薩. *See* RATNAPĀṆI

**hosshi** 法子. *See* FAZI

**hosshin** 法身. *See* DHARMAKĀYA

**hosshinshari** 法身舍利. *See* DHARMAŚARĪRA

**hossho** 法處. *See* DHARMĀYATANA

**hosshō** 法性. *See* DHARMATĀ

**Hosshōshū** 法性宗. *See* FAXING ZONG

**hosshu** 法主. *See* FAZHU

**hosshū** 法執. *See* FAZHI

**Hossō** 法相. *See* YOGĀCĀRA

**Hossōshū** 法相宗. *See* FAXIANG ZONG

**hossu** 拂子. *See* FUZI, VĀLAVYAJANA

**hossū** 法數. *See* FASHU

**Hotei** 布袋. *See* BUDAI, SHICHI FUKUJIN

**hotoke** 佛. *See* BUDDHA

**Hotō Mujū** 保唐無住. *See* BAOTANG WUZHU

**Hotōshū** 保唐宗. *See* BAOTANG ZONG

**hotsubodaishin** 發菩提心. *See* BODHICITTOTPĀDA

**hōugamushū** 法有我無宗. *See* FAYOU WOWU ZONG

**Hōungyō** 寶雲經. *See* RATNAMEGHASŪTRA

**Hōunji** 法雲地. *See* DHARMAMEGHĀ

**Hōunsokuron** 法蘊足論. *See* DHARMASKANDHA[PĀDAŚĀSTRA]

**Hōyū** 法融. *See* NIUTOU FARONG

**Hōzō** 法藏. *See* FAZANG

**Hōzō biku** 法藏比丘. *See* DHARMĀKARA

**Hōzōbu** 法藏部. *See* DHARMAGUPTA

**Hōzōron** 寶藏論. *See* BAOZANG LUN

**Hyakujō Ekai** 百丈懷海. *See* BAIZHANG HUAIHAI

**Hyakujō shingi** 百丈清規. *See* BAIZHANG QINGGUI

**Hyakuron** 百論. *See* ŚATAŚĀSTRA

**hyappō** 百法. *See* BAIFA

## I

**i** 意. *See* MANAS

**Ibushūrinron** 異部宗輪論. *See* SAMAYABHEDOPARACANACAKRA

**Ichigyō** 一行. *See* YIXING

**ichigyōzanmai** 一行三昧. *See* YIXING SANMEI

**ichijikan** 一字關. *See* YIZI GUAN

**ichijō** 一乘. *See* EKAYĀNA

**ichinen sanzen** 一念三千. *See* YINIAN SANQIAN

**ichirai** 一來. *See* SAKṚDĀGĀMIN

**ichiraikō** 一來向. *See* SAKṚDĀGĀMIPHALAPRATIPANNAKA

**Idaike** 韋提希. *See* VAIDEHĪ

**Idaten** 韋馱天. *See* WEITUO TIAN

**igi** 威儀. *See* ĪRYĀPATHA

**igō** 意業. *See* MANASKARMAN

**igon** 意言. *See* MANOJALPA

**Igyōshū** 潙仰宗. *See* GUIYANG ZONG

**ihon** 異品. *See* VIPAKṢA

**ijin** 威神. *See* ANUBHĀVA

**ijugenryō** 意受現量. *See* MANONUBHAVAPRATYAKṢA

**ijuku** 異熟. *See* VIPĀKA

**ijukuin** 異熟因. *See* VIPĀKAHETU

**ijukuka** 異熟果. *See* VIPĀKAPHALA

**ikken** 一間. *See* EKAVĪCIKA

**ikon** 意根. *See* MANENDRIYA

**Ikuga chōjae** 郁伽長者會. *See* UGRAPARIPṚCCHĀ

**Ikuga/Ikuka** 郁伽. *See* UGRA

**in** 因. *See* HETU

**in** 印. *See* MUDRĀ

**ina** [alt. ino] 維那. *See* WEINUO

**Indara** 因陀羅. *See* INDRA

**Indaramō** 因陀羅網. *See* INDRAJĀLA

**Ingen Ryūki** 隠元隆琦. *See* YINYUAN LONGQI

**injō/inzei nenbutsu** 引聲念佛. *See* YINSHENG NIANFO

**inju** 院主. *See* WŎNJU

**inka** 印可. *See* YINKE

**inka shōmyō** 印可證明. *See* YINKE ZHENGMING, YINKE

**Inkatsuda** 因揭陀. *See* AṄGAJA

**Inkō** 印光. *See* YINGUANG

**Inmyō nisshōriron** 因明入正理論. *See* NYĀYAPRAVEŚA

**innen** 因緣. *See* HETUPRATYAYA, NIDĀNA

**Isan Kyōsaku** [alt. Keisaku] 潙山警策. *See* GUISHAN JINGCE

**Isan Reiyū** 潙山靈祐. *See* GUISHAN LINGYOU

**ishiki** 意識. *See* MANOVIJÑĀNA

**ishin denshin** 以心傳心. *See* YIXIN CHUANXIN

**isho** 意處. *See* MANĀYATANA

**ishōshin** 意生身. *See* MANOMAYAKĀYA

**ishu** 意趣. *See* ABHIPRĀYA

**issaichi** 一切智. *See* SARVAJÑATĀ

**issaichichi** 一切知智. *See* SARVAJÑATĀJÑĀNA

**Issaikyō ongi** 一切經音義. *See* YIQIE JING YINYI

**Issainyorai kongōsangōsaijōhimitsu daikyōōgyō** 一切如來金剛三業最上秘密大教王經. *See* GUHYASAMĀJATANTRA

**Issainyorai shinjitsushō daijōgenshōzanmai daikyōōgyō** 一切如來眞實攝大乘現證三昧大教王經. *See* SARVATATHĀGATA-TATTVASAṂGRAHA

**issaishuchi** 一切種智. *See* SARVĀKĀRAJÑATĀ

**issaisōchi** 一切相智. *See* vastujñāna

**Issan Ichinei** 一山一寧. *See* Yishan Yining

**issendai** 一闡提. *See* icchantika

**Issetsubu** 一說部. *See* Ekavyavahārika

**isshin** 一心. *See* yixin

**isshin sangan** 一心三觀. *See* sanguan

## J

**jachi** 邪智. *See* mithyājñāna

**jain** 邪淫. *See* kāmamithyācāra

**jaken** 邪見. *See* akuśaladṛṣṭi, mithyādṛṣṭi

**jakumoku** 寂默. *See* pratisaṃlayana

**jakunijōshō** 寂而常照. *See* ji er changzhao

**jamyō gedō** 邪命外道. *See* Ājīvaka

**Janakutta** 闍那崛多. *See* Jñānagupta

**Janishakyō** 闍尼沙經. *See* Janavasabhasuttanta

**ji** 地. *See* bhūmi

**ji** 慈. *See* maitrī

**ji** 事. *See* shi

**jidai** 地大. *See* pṛthivī

**jifu** 士夫. *See* puruṣa

**jigedatsu** 時解脫. *See* samayavimukta

**jigen** 示現. *See* prātihārya

**Jigoku hen[sō]** 地獄變[相]. *See* Diyu bian[xiang]

**jigoku [ujō/shujō]** 地獄[有情/衆生]. *See* nāraka

**jihi** 慈悲. *See* maitrī

**jihiryō** 自比量. *See* svārthānumāna

**jihokkai** 事法界. *See* shi fajie

**jijimugehokkai** 事事無礙法界. *See* shishi wu'ai fajie

**Jijiron** 地持論. *See* Bodhisattvabhūmi

**jijuyūshin** 自受用身. *See* sva-saṃbhogakāya

**jikaku** 自覺. *See* svasaṃvedana

**Jikangikyō** 自歡喜經. *See* Sampasādanīyasutta

**jiki** 食. *See* āhāra

**jikishi ninshin** 直指人心. *See* zhizhi renxin

**jikkai** 十界. *See* daśadhātu

**jikkai** 十戒. *See* daśaśīla

**jikke** 習氣. *See* vāsanā

**Jikokuten** 持國天. *See* Dhṛtarāṣṭra

**Jiku** 竺. *See* Zhu

**Jiku Hōgo** 竺法護. *See* Dharmarakṣa

**Jikyō** 慈經. *See* Mettāsutta

**Jimin Enichi** 慈愍慧日. *See* Cimin Huiri

**jimyō** 持明. *See* vidyādhara

**jimyōzō** 持明藏. *See* vidyādharapiṭaka

**jin** 尋. *See* vitarka

**jinchi** 盡智. *See* kṣayajñāna

**jinga** 神我. *See* puruṣa

**Jinkeukyō** 甚希有經. *See* Adbhutadharmaparyāyasūtra

**jinkyōchishōtsū** 神境智證通. *See* ṛddhividhābhijñā

**Jinna** 陳那. *See* Dignāga

**jinpensō** 神變相. *See* mahāprātihārya

**jinriki** 神力. *See* ṛddhi

**Jinshū** 神秀. *See* Shenxiu

**jinzū** 神通. *See* abhijñā

**Jion daishi** 慈恩大師. *See* Kuiji

**jippō** 十方. *See* daśadiś

**jippōkai** 十法界. *See* shi fajie

**jippōsetsu** 十方刹. *See* shifang cha

**jiri** 自利. *See* svārtha

**Jironshū** 地論宗. *See* Di lun zong

**jiseiju** 辭世頌. *See* cishi song, yiji

**jishi** 自恣. *See* pravāraṇā

**jishō** 自性. *See* svabhāva

**jishō funbetsu** 自性分別. *See* svabhāvavikalpa

**jishōkū** 自性空. *See* svabhāvaśūnya, svabhāvaśūnyatā

**jishō nehan** 自性涅槃. *See* prakṛtiparinirvṛta

**jishōshin** 自性身. *See* svabhāvakāya, svabhāvikakāya

**jisō** 自相. *See* svalakṣaṇa

**jisōkū** 自相空. *See* svalakṣaṇaśūnya

**Jison** 慈尊. *See* Maitreyanātha

**jissai** 實際. *See* bhūtakoṭi

**Jisshananda** 實叉難陀. *See* Śikṣānanda

**jissō** 實相. *See* tattva

**Jissō hannya haramitsukyō** 實相般若波羅蜜經. *See* Adhyardhaśatikāprajñāpāramitāsūtra/Prajñāpāramitānayapañcaśatikā

**jita byōdō** 自他平等. *See* parātmasamata

**jitsugo** 實語. *See* satyavacana

**jitsuji** 實事. *See* dravya

**jitsuu** 實有. *See* dravyasat

**jittai** 集諦. *See* samudayasatya

**Jittoku** 拾得. *See* Shide

**jiyūka** 士用果. *See* puruṣakāraphala

**jizai** 自在. *See* aiśvarya, vaśitā

**Jizō** 地藏. *See* Kṣitigarbha

**Jizō bosatsu hongangyō** 地藏菩薩本願經. *See* Kṣitigarbhasūtra

**jo** 除. *See* apoha

**jō** 掉. *See* auddhatya

**jō** 常. *See* nitya

**jō** 淨. *See* vyavadāna

**jō** 乘. *See* yāna

**Jōagongyō** 長阿含經. *See* Dīrghāgama

**Jōbon ō** 淨飯王. *See* Śuddhodana

**jōbyō** 淨瓶. *See* kuṇḍikā

**Jōdo** 浄土. *See* pure land

**jōdō** 上堂. *See* shangtang

**Jōdoden** 淨土傳. *See* Jingtu zhuan

**Jōdo gungiron** 浄土群疑論. *See* Jingtu qunyi lun

**Jōdohen** 淨土變. *See* Jingtu bian

**Jōdo jūgi[ron]** 淨土十疑[論]. *See* Jingtu shiyi [lun]

**Jōdo no goso** 淨土五祖. *See* Jingtu wuzu

**Jōdoron** 浄土論. *See* Jingtu lun

**Jōdo sanbukyō** 浄土三部經. *See* Jingtu sanbujing

**Jōdosanmaikyō** 淨度三昧經. *See* Jingdu sanmei jing

**Jōdo sanshō** 淨土三聖. *See* Jingtu sansheng

**Jōdo zuiōden** 浄土瑞應傳. *See* Jingtu ruiying zhuan

**joen** 助緣. *See* sahakāripratyaya

**Jōfukyō bosatsu** 常不輕菩薩. *See* Sadāparibhūta

**Jogaishō bosatsu** 除蓋障菩薩. *See* Sarvanīvaraṇaviśkambhin

**jōgoten** 淨居天. *See* śuddhāvāsakāyika

**Jōgyō** 上行. *See* Viśiṣṭacāritra

**jōhen** 常邊. *See* śāśvatānta

**jōhō** 常法. *See* nityadharma

**jōji** 諍事. *See* adhikaraṇa

**jōjitsu** 成實. *See* satyasiddhi

**Jōjitsuron** 成實論. *See* Chengshi lun

**Jōjitsushū** 成實宗. *See* Chengshi zong, Chengshi lun

**jōjū** 常住. *See* changzhu

**jōjuhō** 成就法. *See* sādhana

**jōkai** 淨戒. *See* śīlaviśuddhi

**Jōkaku** 淨覺. *See* Jingjue

**jōkanchi** 定觀知. *See* yogipratyakṣa

**jōken** 常見. *See* śāsvatadṛṣṭi

**jōkeshin** 上化身. *See* uttamanirmāṇakāya

**jōkō** 成劫. *See* vivartakalpa

**Jōkō nyorai** 定光如來. *See* Dīpaṃkara

**joku** 濁. *See* kaṣāya

**jōnin** 淨人. *See* kalpikāraka

**Jōron** 肇論. *See* Zhao lun

**jōruhatsu** 上流般. *See* ūrdhvasrotas

**jōruhatsunehan** 上流般涅槃. *See* ūrdhvasrotas

**jōryoharamita** 靜慮波羅蜜多. *See* dhyānapāramitā

**jōshō** 諍訟. *See* adhikaraṇa

**jōshosachi** 成所作智. *See* kṛtyānuṣṭhānajñāna

**Jōshū Jūshin** 趙州從諗. *See* Zhaozhou Congshen

**Jōshū Musō** 淨衆無相. *See* Chŏngjung Musang

**Jōshūshū** 淨衆宗. *See* Jingzhong zong

**Jōtai [bosatsu]** 常啼[菩薩]. *See* Sadaprarudita

**Jōyō Eon** 浄影慧遠. *See* Jingying Huiyuan

**Jōyuishikiron** 成唯識論. *See* Cheng weishi lun, Vijñaptimātratāsiddhi

**Jōyuishikiron jukki** 成唯識論述記. *See* Cheng weishi lun shu ji

**jōza** 上座. *See* STHAVIRA

**Jōzabu** 上座部. *See* STHAVIRANIKĀYA

**jōza fuga** 長坐不臥. *See* CHANGJWA PURWA

**jū** 集. *See* SAMUDAYA

**ju** 頌. *See* ŚLOKA

**jū** 住. *See* STHITI, VIHĀRA, LENA

**ju** 受. *See* VEDANĀ

**Jubaka/Jubakuka** 戍博迦. *See* JĪVAKA

**juchō** 竪超. *See* SHUCHAO

**jūfuzengōdō** 十不善業道. *See* KARMAPATHA

**jūgenmon** 十玄門. *See* SHI XUANMEN

**Jūgyūzu** 十牛圖. *See* OXHERDING PICTURES, TEN

**Juhōkyō** 受法經. *See* CŪḶADHAMMASAMĀDĀNASUTTA, MAHĀDHAMMASAMĀDĀNASUTTA

**Jūichimen Kannon** 十一面觀音. *See* EKĀDAŚAMUKHĀVALOKITEŚVARA

**jūji** 十地. *See* DAŚABHŪMI

**jūji** 住持. *See* ZHUCHI

**Jūjikyōron** 十地經論. *See* DAŚABHŪMIVYĀKHYĀNA

**Jūjōkyō** 十上經. *See* DASUTTARASUTTA

**Jūjūkyō** 十住經. *See* DAŚABHŪMIKASŪTRA

**Jūjūshinron** 十住心論. *See* HIMITSU MANDARA JŪJŪSHINRON

**jūka** 住果. *See* PHALASTHITA

**jukai** 受戒. *See* UPASAṂPADĀ

**juki** 授記. *See* VYĀKARAṆA

**juko** 頌古. *See* SONGGU

**jūkō** 住劫. *See* VIVARTASTHĀYIKALPA

**Jū kokonbutsudō ronkō** 集古今佛道論衡. *See* JI GUJIN FODAO LUNHENG

**Jūmanju hannya** 十萬頌般若. *See* ŚATASAHĀSRIKĀPRAJÑĀPĀRAMITĀ

**jumyō** 壽命. *See* JĪVITA

**Junda** 準陀. *See* CUNDA

**jūnehan** 住涅槃. *See* PRATIṢṬHITANIRVĀṆA

**jungedatsubun** 順解脫分. *See* MOKṢABHĀGĪYA

**jungyaku** 順逆. *See* ANULOMAPRATILOMA

**jūnibukyō** 十二部經. *See* DVĀDAŚĀṄGA[PRAVACANA]

**Jūniinnenron** 十二因緣論. *See* PRATĪTYASAMUTPĀDAHṚDAYAKĀRIKĀ

**Jūnimonron** 十二門論. *See* SHI'ERMEN LUN

**junjishōjugō** 順次生受業. *See* UPAPADYAVEDANĪYAKARMAN

**junkan** 循觀. *See* ANUPAŚYANĀ

**junketchakubun** 順決擇分. *See* NIRVEDHABHAGĪYA

**Junse gedō** 順世外道. *See* LOKĀYATA

**junse sanmai** 順世三昧. *See* LOKIYASAMĀDHI

**Junshōriron** 順正理論. *See* *NYĀYĀNUSĀRA

**Juntei** 准提. *See* CUNDĪ

**jūnyoze** 十如是. *See* SHI RUSHI

**jūō** 十王. *See* SHIWANG

**jūriki** 十力. *See* BALA, DAŚABALA

**Jurōjin** 壽老人. *See* SHICHIFUKUJIN

**jūrokurakan** 十六羅漢. *See* ṢODAŚASTHAVIRA

**jūrokusonja** 十六尊者. *See* ṢODAŚASTHAVIRA

**Jūryōron** 集量論. *See* PRAMĀṆASAMUCCAYA

**Jūshin** 從諗. *See* ZHAOZHOU CONGSHEN

**jūsho** 住處. *See* VIHĀRA

**jūtai** 集諦. *See* SAMUDAYASATYA

**juzu** 數珠. *See* JAPAMĀLĀ

## K

**ka** 果. *See* PHALA

**ka** 過. *See* PRASAṄGA, DOṢA

**Kabirae** 迦毘羅衛. *See* KAPILAVASTU

**kachinae** 迦絺那衣. *See* KAṬHINA

**kadai** 火大. *See* TEJAS

**Kae** 菓衣. *See* SOBHITA

**kagen** 過患. *See* ĀDĪNAVA

**kahensho** 火遍處. *See* TEJOKASIṆA

**kahō** 果報. *See* VIPĀKA

**kai** 界. *See* DHĀTU

**kai** 戒. *See* ŚĪLA

**kaie** 海會. *See* HAIHUI

**Kaifukeō [nyorai]** 開敷華王[如來]. *See* SAṂKUSUMITARĀJENDRA

**kaigen** 開眼. *See* KAIYAN, NETRAPRATIṢṬHĀPANA

**Kaigen** 戒賢. *See* ŚĪLABHADRA

**kaige no kyō** 界外教. *See* JIEWAI JIAO

**Kaigen Shakkyōroku** 開元釋教録. *See* KAIYUAN SHIJIAO LU

**kaigonjuken** 戒禁取見. *See* ŚĪLAVRATAPARĀMARŚA

**kaiharamitsu** 戒波羅蜜. *See* ŚĪLAPĀRAMITĀ

**Kaihō** 戒法. *See* ŚĪLADHARMA

**Kaihon** 戒本. *See* PRĀTIMOKṢASŪTRA

**kaiinzanmai** 海印三昧. *See* SĀGARAMUDRĀSAMĀDHI

**kaike** 界繫. *See* AVACARA

**kainai no kyō** 界內教. *See* JIENEI JIAO

**kairō** 戒臘. *See* JIELA

**kaisan** 開山. *See* KAISHAN

**kaisei** 解制. *See* JIEZHI

**Kaishinron** 界身論. *See* DHĀTUKĀYA[PADA]ŚĀSTRA

**Kaishō no hōnan** 會昌法難. *See* HUICHANG FANAN

**Kaiso** 懷素. *See* HUAISU

**Kaisū** 契嵩. *See* FORI QISONG

**kaji** 加持. *See* ADHIṢṬHĀNA

**kako shichibutsu** 過去七佛. *See* SAPTATATHĀGATA

**kaku** 覺. *See* BODHI

**Kakuan Shion** 廓庵師遠. *See* KUO'AN SHIYUAN

**kakugai no zen** [alt. kakuge no zen] 格外禪. *See* GEWAI CHAN

**kakugi** 格義. *See* GEYI

**Kakuhan Ekō** 覺範慧洪. *See* JUEFAN HUIHONG

**Kakurin Genso** 鶴林玄素. *See* HELIN XUANSU

**kakushi** 覺支. *See* BODHYAṄGA

**kan** 觀. *See* VIPAŚYANĀ

**kanben** 勘辨. *See* KANBIAN

**Kan Fugen bosatsu gyōbōkyō** 觀普賢菩薩行法經. *See* GUAN PUXIAN PUSA XINGFA JING

**kangiji** 歡喜地. *See* PRAMUDITĀ

**Kanishika ō** 迦膩色迦王. *See* KANIṢKA

**Kanjizai** 觀自在. *See* GUANZIZAI; GUANYIN

**Kanjizaiō nyorai** 觀自在王如來. *See* LOKEŚVARARĀJA

**kanjō** 灌頂. *See* ABHIṢEKA

**Kanjōgyō** 灌頂經. *See* GUANDING JING

**kanjōin** 灌頂印. *See* ABHIṢEKAMUDRĀ

**Kankyū** 貫休. *See* CHANYUE GUANXIU

**Kanmuryōjukyō** 觀無量壽經. *See* GUAN WULIANGSHOU JING

**kannazen** 看話禪. *See* KANHUA CHAN

**kannin** 監院. *See* JIANYUAN

**kannō** 感應. *See* GANYING

**Kannon** 觀音. *See* AVALOKITEŚVARA, GUANYIN

**kanrin** 寒林. *See* ŚMAŚĀNA

**kanro** 甘露. *See* AMṚTA

**Kanroku** 觀勒. *See* KWALLŬK

**kanshiketsu** 乾屎橛. *See* GANSHIJUE

**Kanshoennenron** 觀所緣緣論. *See* ĀLAMBANAPARĪKṢĀ

**kansu** 監司. *See* JIANSI

**kanwazen** 看話禪. *See* KANHUA CHAN

**Kanyakabaridaja** 迦諾迦跋釐墮闍. *See* KANAKA BHARADVĀJA

**Kanyakabassa** 迦諾迦伐蹉. *See* KANAKAVATSA

**Kanzan shi** 寒山詩. *See* HANSHAN SHI

**Kanzan Tokusei** 憨山德清. *See* HANSHAN DEQING

**Kanzeon** 觀世音. *See* GUANYIN, AVALOKITEŚVARA

**Karakuda Kasen'en** 迦羅鳩馱迦旃延. *See* KAKUDA KĀTYĀYANA

**Karibatsuma** 訶梨跋摩. *See* HARIVARMAN

**Karika** 迦梨迦. *See* KĀLĪ KURURAGHARIKĀ

**Karika sonja** 迦里迦尊者. *See* KĀLIKA

**Karudai** 迦留陀夷. *See* KĀLODĀYIN

**karyōbinga chō** 迦陵頻伽鳥. *See* KALAVIṄKA

**Karyōga** 羯陵伽. *See* KALIṄGA

**Kasen'en** 迦旃延. *See* KĀTYĀYANA, MAHĀKĀTYĀYANA

**Kashin** 火神. *See* AGNI

**Kashō** 迦葉. *See* KĀŚYAPA, MAHĀKĀŚYAPA

**kashō** 和尚. *See* UPĀDHYĀYA, HESHANG

**Kashōibu** 迦葉遺部. *See* KĀŚYAPĪYA

**Kashō Matō** 迦葉摩騰. *See* KĀŚYAPA MĀTAṄGA

**Kataennishi** 迦多衍尼子. *See* KĀTYĀYANĪPUTRA

**Kataku Jinne** 荷澤神會. *See* HEZE SHENHUI

**katsuma** 羯磨. *See* KARMAN

**katsumabu** 羯磨部. *See* KARMAKULA

**kattōzen** 葛藤禪. *See* GETENG CHAN

**kazoku** 家族. *See* KULA

**ke** 悔. *See* KAUKṚTYA

**ke** 化. *See* NIRMITA

**Kechimyakuron** 血脈論. *See* XUEMO LUN

**kedai** 懈怠. *See* KAUSĪDYA

**Kegon gokyōshō** 華嚴五教章. *See* HUAYAN WUJIAO ZHANG

**Kegongyō** 華嚴經. *See* AVATAṂSAKASŪTRA

**Kegongyō den[ki]** 華嚴經傳[記]. *See* HUAYAN JING ZHUAN[JI]

**Kegongyō gōron** 華嚴經合論. *See* HUAYAN JING HELUN

**Kegongyō kannōden** 華嚴經感應傳. *See* HUAYAN JING GANYING ZHUAN

**Kegongyō shiki** 華嚴經旨歸. *See* HUAYAN JING ZHIGUI

**Kegongyōsho** 華嚴經疏. *See* HUAYAN JING SHU

**Kegongyō sōgenki** 華嚴經搜玄記. *See* HUAYAN JING SOUXUAN JI

**Kegongyō tangenki** 華嚴經探玄記. *See* HUAYAN JING TANXUAN JI

**Kegongyō zuisho engishō** 華嚴經随疏演義鈔. *See* HUAYAN JING SUISHU YANYI CHAO

**Kegon hokkai kanmon** 華嚴法界觀門. *See* HUAYAN FAJIE GUANMEN

**Kegon ichijō hokkaizu** 華嚴一乘法界圖. *See* HWAŎM ILSŬNG PŎPKYE TO

**Kegon no gokyō** 華嚴五教. *See* HUAYAN WUJIAO

**Kegon no jūgi** 華嚴十義. *See* HUAYAN SHIYI

**Kegon no jūi** 華嚴十異. *See* HUAYAN SHIYI

**Kegon no sanshō** 華嚴三聖. *See* HUAYAN SANSHENG

**Kegonsha** 華嚴社. *See* HUAYANSHE

**Kegonshū** 華厳宗. *See* HUAYAN

**Kegon wa asa** 華嚴朝. *See* HUAYAN ZHAO

**Kegon yūi** 華嚴遊意. *See* HUAYAN YOUYI

**kegyō** 加行. *See* PRAYOGA

**kegyōdō** 加行道. *See* PRAYOGAMĀRGA

**kehō** 希法. *See* ADBHUTADHARMA

**Keihō Shūmitsu** 圭峰宗密. *See* GUIFENG ZONGMI

**Keiinbu** 鷄胤部. *See* KAUKKUṬIKA

**Keika** 惠果. *See* HUIGUO

**Keikei Tannen** 荊溪湛然. *See* JINGXI ZHANRAN

**Keionji** 鶏園寺. *See* KUKKUṬĀRĀMA

**keisaku** 警策. *See* KYŌSAKU

**Keisokusen** 鶏足山. *See* KUKKUṬAPĀDA

**Keitoku dentōroku** 景德傳燈録. *See* JINGDE CHUANDENG LU

**Keiyū** 慶友. *See* NANDIMITRA

**Kejibu** 化地部. *See* MAHĪŚĀSAKA

**keka** 悔過. *See* PRATIDEŚANĀ

**kekkai** 結界. *See* SĪMĀ

**kemyō** 假名. *See* PRAJÑAPTI; PRAJÑAPTISAT

**kemyōu** 假名有. *See* PRAJÑAPTISAT

**ken** 見. *See* DARŚANA, DṚṢṬI

**ken** 慳. *See* MĀTSARYA

**kenchi** 犍稚. *See* GHAṆṬĀ

**Kendara** 健駄羅. *See* GANDHĀRA

**kendatsuba** 乾闥婆. *See* GANDHARVA

**kendatsubajō** 乾闥婆城. *See* GANDHARVANAGARA

**kendo** 犍度. *See* KHANDAKA

**kendō** 見道. *See* DARŚANAMĀRGA

**Ken'en** 賢鹽. *See* LAKUṆṬAKA BHADRIKA

**kengen** 顯現. *See* PRATIBHĀSA

**Kengo** 賢護. *See* BHADRAPĀLA

**kengō** 賢劫. *See* BHADRAKALPA

**kengoe** 堅固衣. *See* KAṬHINA

**Kengokyō** 堅固經. *See* KEVAṬṬASUTTA

**kenji** 見至. *See* DṚṢṬIPRĀPTA

**kenjō** 賢聖. *See* ĀRYAPUDGALA

**Kenjoku** 犍陟. *See* KAṆṬHAKA

**kenju** 見取. *See* DṚṢṬIPARĀMARŚA

**kenjujigoku** 劍樹地獄. *See* KṢURAMĀRGA

**kenshō** 見性. *See* JIANXING

**kenshō jōbutsu** 見性成佛. *See* JIANXING CHENGFO

**Kenshūki** 顯宗記. *See* XIANZONG JI

**kentoku** 見得. *See* DṚṢṬIPRĀPTA

**kenwaku** 見惑. *See* JIANHUO

**Ken'yōrin** 劍葉林. *See* ASIPATTRAVANA

**kerakuten** 化樂天. *See* NIRMĀṆARATI

**keron** 戲論. *See* PRAPAÑCA

**kesa** 袈裟. *See* KAṢĀYA

**Keshijō** 華氏城. *See* PĀTALIPUTRA

**keshin** 化身. *See* NIRMĀṆAKĀYA

**keshō** 化生. *See* UPAPĀDUKAYONI

**keshu** 化主. *See* HUAZHU

**kessei** 結制. *See* JIEZHI

**kessha** 結社. *See* JIESHE

**ketaku funbetsu** 計度分別. *See* ABHINIRŪPAṆĀVIKALPA

**ketchaku** 決擇. *See* NIRVEDHA

**ketsu** 結. *See* SAṂYOJANA

**ketsujō** 決定. *See* NIYĀMA

**ketsujō jaken** 決定邪見. *See* NIYATAMICCHĀDIṬṬHI

**ketsujō shushō** 決定種性. *See* NIYATAGOTRA

**ketsujū** 結集. *See* SAṂGĪTI

**ketsujūsha** 結集者. *See* SAṂGĪTĪKĀRAKA

**ki** 鬼. *See* BHŪTA

**ki** 歸. *See* LENA

**ki** 喜. *See* MUDITĀ, PRĪTI

**kichijō** 吉祥. *See* MAṄGALA

**kichijōkaiun** 吉祥海雲. *See* ŚRĪVATSA

**Kichizō** 吉藏. *See* JIZANG

**Kidō Chigu** 虛堂智愚. *See* XUTANG ZHIYU

**kie** 歸依. *See* ŚARAṆA

**kihō** 機鋒. *See* JIFENG

**Kiji** 龜茲. *See* KUCHA

**Kiki** 窺基. *See* KUIJI

**kikokuin** 祈克印. *See* TARJANĪMUDRĀ

**kikutsu** 鬼窟. *See* GUIKU

**kinhin** 經行. *See* CAṄKRAMA

**kinnara** 緊那羅. *See* KIṂNARA

**Kiroka** 呬嚕迦. *See* HERUKA

**kiseken** 器世間. *See* BHĀJANALOKA

**Kisen** 希遷. *See* SHITOU XIQIAN

**Kishimojin** 鬼子母神. *See* HĀRĪTĪ

**Kishinron** 起信論. *See* DASHENG QIXIN LUN

**kō** 好. *See* ANUVYAÑJANA

**kō** 劫. *See* KALPA

**Kō** 康. *See* KANG

**kōan** 公案. *See* GONG'AN

**Kōbō oshō zen'yō** 高峰和尚禪要. *See* GAOFENG HESHANG CHANYAO

**Kōgumyōshū** 廣弘明集. *See* GUANG HONGMING JI

**kōhahai** 劫波杯. *See* KAPĀLA

**kōhai** 光背. *See* KĀYAPRABHĀ

**Kōhō Genmyō** 高峰原妙. *See* GAOFENG YUANMIAO

**Kōhō oshō zen'yō** 高峰和尚禪要. *See* GAOFENG HESHANG CHANYAO

**Kōhyakuronpon** 廣百論本. *See* CATUḤŚATAKA

**Koin Dōsai** 湖隱道濟. *See* HUYIN DAOJI

**koji** 居士. *See* GṚHAPATI

**kojigoku** 孤地獄. *See* PRATYEKANARAKA

**Kōkaten** 廣果天. *See* BṚHATPHALA

**kokū** 虛空. *See* ĀKĀŚA

**Kokubun** 克文. *See* ZHENJING KEWEN

**kokūge** 虛空華. *See* KHAPUṢPA

**Kokugon** 克勤. *See* YUANWU KEQIN

**kokujōjigoku** 黑繩地獄. *See* KĀLASŪTRA

**Kokusei hyakuroku** 國清百録. *See* GUOQING BAILÜ

**kokushi** 國師. *See* GUOSHI

**Kokūzō bosatsu** 虛空藏菩薩. *See* ĀKĀŚAGARBHA

**komō funbetsu** 虛妄分別. *See* ABHŪTAPARIKALPA

**Kōmokuten** 廣目天. *See* VIRŪPĀKṢA

**kōmyō** 光明. *See* PRABHĀSVARA

**kōmyōshin** 光明心. *See* PRABHĀSVARACITTA

**kon** 根. *See* INDRIYA, MŪLA

**kon** 根. *See* UPANĀHA

**kongō** 金剛. *See* VAJRA

**kongōajari** 金剛阿闍梨. *See* VAJRĀCĀRYA

**Kongōbei** 金剛鉀. *See* JINGANG PI

**Kongōbuji** 金剛峰寺. *See* KŌYASAN

**Kongōchi** 金剛智. *See* VAJRABODHI

**Kongōchōkyō** 金剛頂經. *See* VAJRAŚEKHARASŪTRA

**Kongōji** 金剛持. *See* VAJRADHARA

**Kongōjō** 金剛乘. *See* VAJRAYĀNA

**kongōkafuza** 金剛跏趺坐. *See* VAJRAPARYAṄKA

**kongōke** 金剛家. *See* VAJRAKULA

**Kongōkyō** 金剛經. *See* VAJRACCHEDIKĀPRAJÑĀPĀRAMITĀSŪTRA

**Kongō ō** 金剛王. *See* HEVAJRA

**Kongō saisai darani** 金剛摧碎陀羅尼. *See* VAJRAVIDĀRAṆADHĀRAṆĪ

**Kongōsanmai** 金剛三昧. *See* VAJROPAMASAMĀDHI

**Kongōsanmaikyō** 金剛三昧經. *See* KŬMGANG SAMMAE KYŎNG

**Kongōsanmaikyōron** 金剛三昧經論. *See* KŬMGANG SAMMAEGYŎNGNON

**Kongōsatta** 金剛薩埵. *See* VAJRASATTVA

**kongōshi** 金剛師. *See* VAJRĀCĀRYA

**Kongōshu bosatsu** 金剛手菩薩. *See* VAJRAPĀṆI

**kongōyujō** 金剛喩定. *See* VAJROPAMASAMĀDHI

**kongōza** 金剛座. *See* VAJRĀSANA

**Kōnin** 弘忍. *See* HONGREN

**konjin** 惛沉. *See* STYĀNA

**Konkōmyōkyō** 金光明經. *See* SUVARṆAPRABHĀSOTTAMASŪTRA

**Konkōmyō saishōōkyō** 金光明最勝王經. *See* SURVARṆAPRABHĀSOTTAMASŪTRA

**konma** 羯磨. *See* KARMAN

**konpon bonnō** 根本煩惱. *See* MŪLAKLEŚA

**Konpon Daishubu** 根本大衆部. *See* MŪLAMAHĀSĀṂGHIKA

**Konpon Setsuissaiubu** 根本說一切有部. *See* MŪLASARVĀSTIVĀDA

**Konpon Setsuissaiubu binaya** 根本說一切有部毘奈耶. *See* MŪLASARVĀSTIVĀDA-VINAYA, VINAYAVIBHAṄGA

**konritsugi** 根律儀. *See* INDRIYASAṂVARA

**konryū** 建立. *See* PRATIṢṬHĀ

**Kon'yō** 紺容. *See* SĀMĀVATĪ

**kōonten** 光音天. *See* ĀBHĀSVARALOKA

**kore ikana** 是甚麼. *See* SHI SHEMA, IMWŎTKO

**kōro** 香爐. *See* GANDHAGHAṬIKĀ

**koromo** 衣. *See* CĪVARA

**kōsetsu** 交接. *See* MAITHUNA

**koshinkō** 擧身光. *See* JUSHENGUANG

**kōshitsu** 香室. *See* GANDHAKUṬĪ

**kōsho** 香處. *See* GANDHĀYATANA

**Kōshō baramon** 香姓婆羅門. *See* DRONA

**Kōshūshū** 洪州宗. *See* HONGZHOU ZONG

**Kōsōden** 高僧傳. *See* GAOSENG ZHUAN

**Kō Sōe** 康僧會. *See* KANG SENGHUI

**kōtōzen** 口頭禪. *See* KOUTOU CHAN

**kotsujiki** 乞食. *See* PIṆḌAPĀTA

**kōyoku** 好欲. *See* KĀMACCHANDA

**ku** 鼓. *See* DRUM

**ku** 苦. *See* DUḤKHA

**ku** 垢. *See* MALA

**kū** 空. *See* ŚŪNYATĀ

**Kubeira** 俱吠囉. *See* KUBERA

**kubukyō** 九部經. *See* NAVAṄGA[PĀVACANA]

**Kuchira** 拘絺羅. *See* KAUṢṬHILA

**Kudani** 瞿陀尼. *See* GODĀNĪYA

**kudoku** 功德. *See* ĀNISAṂSA, GUṆA

**kudokuharamitsu** 功德波羅蜜. *See* GUṆAPĀRAMITĀ

**kudokuin** 功德院. *See* GONGDE YUAN

**Kudon** 瞿曇. *See* GAUTAMA

**kūge** 空華. *See* KHAPUṢPA

**kū ge chū sangan** 空假中三觀. *See* SANGUAN

**kugedatsu** 俱解脫. *See* UBHAYATOBHĀGAVIMUKTA

**kugi** 九儀. *See* JIUYI

**kugyō** 苦行. *See* DHUTAṄGA, DUṢKARACARYĀ, TAPAS

**Kuhanda** 鳩槃荼. *See* KUMBHĀṆḌA

**kuhon** 九品. *See* JIUPIN

**kūjaku ryōchi** 空寂靈知. *See* KONGJI LINGZHI

**Kujutara** 久壽多羅. *See* KUBJOTTARĀ

**kūkō** 空劫. *See* SAṂVARTASTHĀYIKALPA

**kuku** 苦苦. *See* DUḤKHADUḤKHATĀ

**kūkū** 空空. *See* ŚŪNYATĀŚŪNYATĀ

**kukyō** 究竟. *See* NIṢṬHĀ

**kukyōdō/i** 究竟道/位. *See* NIṢṬHĀMĀRGA

**Kukyō ichijō hōshōron** 究竟一乘寶性論. *See* RATNAGOTRAVIBHĀGA

**Kumarajū** 鳩摩羅什. *See* KUMĀRAJĪVA

**Kumara Kashō** 鳩摩羅迦葉. *See* KUMĀRA-KĀŚYAPA

**Kumokushō** 孔目章. *See* KONGMU ZHANG

**kūmuhenjo** 空無邊處. *See* ĀKĀŚĀNANTYĀYATANA

**kun** 裙. *See* NIVĀSANA

**Kunaharaba** 瞿拏鉢剌婆. *See* GUṆAPRABHA

**kunjū** 薰習. *See* VĀSANĀ

**Kuntohakan** 君屠鉢漢. *See* KUṆḌADHĀNA

**Kuongyō** 苦陰經. *See* CŪḶADUKKHAKKHANDHASUTTA, MAHĀDUKKHANKKHANDHASUTTA

**Kuradantōkyō** 究羅檀頭經. *See* KŪṬADANTASUTTA

**kuse** 九世. *See* JIUSHI

**kushi mubusshō** 狗子無佛性. *See* GOUZI WU FOXING

**Kushinagara** 拘尸那揭羅. *See* KUŚINAGARĪ

**kushōki** 俱生起. *See* SAHAJA

**kushō no bonnōshō** 俱生煩惱障. *See* SAHAJAKLEŚĀVARAṆA

**kushō no gashū** 俱生我執. *See* SAHAJĀTMAGRAHA

**kushō no mumyō** 俱生無明. *See* SAHAJĀVIDYĀ

**kushō no waku** 俱生惑. *See* SAHAJAKLEŚĀVARAṆA

**kushutsukonma** 驅出羯磨. *See* PRAVRĀJANĪYAKARMAN

**kusōkan** 九想觀. *See* NAVASAṂJÑĀ

**kutai** 苦諦. *See* DUḤKHASATYA

**kutei** 俱胝. *See* KOṬI

**kutōzen** 口頭禪. *See* KOUTOU CHAN

**kuuin** 俱有因. *See* SAHABHŪHETU

**kuyō** 供養. *See* PŪJĀ

**kyakujin bonnō** 客塵煩惱. *See* ĀGANTUKAKLEŚA

**kyakuryaku** 隔歴. *See* GELI

**kyakuryaku no santai** 隔歴三諦. *See* GELI SANDI

**kyō** 教. *See* KYO

**kyō** 憍. *See* MADA

**Kyō** 脇. *See* PĀRŚVA

**kyō** 竅. *See* QIAO

**kyō** 經. *See* SŪTRA

**kyō** 境. *See* VIṢAYA

**kyōan** 輕安. *See* PRASRABDHI

**Kyōbonhadai** 憍梵波提. *See* GAVĀṂPATI

**kyōdōron** 教導論. *See* AVAVĀDA

**Kyō funbetsu** 經分別. *See* SŪTRAVIBHAṄGA

**kyōge betsuden** 教外別傳. *See* JIAOWAI BIECHUAN

**Kyōgen** 警玄. *See* DAYANG JINGXUAN

**Kyōgen Chikan** 香嚴智閑. *See* XIANGYAN ZHIXIAN

**kyōgyō** 經行. *See* CAṄKRAMA

**kyōhō** 教法. *See* ĀGAMADHARMA

**kyōhō** 敬法. *See* GURUDHARMA

**kyōkan[jigoku]** 叫喚[地獄]. *See* RAURAVA

**Kyōritsu isō** 經律異相. *See* JINGLÜ YIXIANG

**kyōroku** 經錄. *See* JINGLU

**Kyōryōbu** 經量部. *See* SAUTRĀNTIKA

**Kyōryōyasha** 畺良耶舍. *See* KĀLAYAŚAS

**Kyōsatsura koku** 憍薩羅國. *See* KOŚALA

**Kyōshika** 憍尸迦. *See* KAUŚIKA

**kyōsō hanjaku** 教相判釋. *See* JIAOXIANG PANSHI

**Kyōzan Ejaku** 仰山慧寂. *See* YANGSHAN HUIJI

**kyōzō** 經藏. *See* SŪTRAPIṬAKA

## M

**Ma** 魔. *See* MĀRA

**Machiriseita** 摩咥里制吒. *See* MĀTṚCEṬA

**Machūra** 摩偷羅. *See* MATHURĀ

**Madenchi** 末田地. *See* MADHYĀNTIKA

**Magari Kusharishi** 末伽梨拘賒梨子. *See* Maskarin Gośāla

**magoraga** 摩睺羅迦. *See* mahorāga

**Makabihara/Makabikara** 摩訶毘訶羅. *See* Mahāvihāra

**Makadaiba** 摩訶提婆. *See* Mahādeva

**Makahajahadai** 摩訶波闍波提. *See* Mahāprajāpatī

**Maka hannya haramita shingyō** 摩訶般若波羅蜜多心經. *See* Prajñāpāramitāhṛdaya

**Maka hannya haramitsukyō** 摩訶般若波羅蜜經. *See* Pañcaviṃśatisāhasrikāprajñāpāramitāsūtra

**Makakasen'en** 摩訶迦旃延. *See* Mahākātyayana

**Makakashō** 摩訶迦葉. *See* Mahākāśyapa

**Makakōhinna** 摩訶劫賓那. *See* Mahākapphiṇa

**Makamokkenren** 摩訶目犍連. *See* Mahāmaudgalyāyana

**Makanan** 摩訶男. *See* Mahānāman

**Makarata koku** 摩訶剌佗國. *See* Mahāraṭṭha

**makasatsu** 摩訶薩. *See* mahāsattva

**Makashikan** 摩訶止觀. *See* Mohe zhiguan

**Makashikan bugyōdenguketsu** 摩訶止觀輔行傳弘決. *See* Mohe zhiguan fuxing zhuanhong jue

**Makashina** 摩訶斯那. *See* Mahāsena

**Makatsuda [koku]** 摩揭陀[國]. *See* Magadha

**makatsugyo** 摩竭魚. *See* makara

**Makesamandara** [koku] 摩醯娑慢陀羅[國]. *See* Mahisa Maṇḍala

**man** 慢. *See* abhimāna, māna

**man** 鬘. *See* mālā

**Manashi** 摩那斯. *See* Manasvin

**manashiki** 末那識. *See* kliṣṭamanas

**manata** 摩那埵. *See* mānatva

**Manbutsuji** 萬佛寺. *See* Wanfosi

**mandara** 曼荼羅. *See* maṇḍala

**mani** 摩尼. *See* maṇi

**manji** 卍[alt. 萬字]. *See* svastika

**Manzen dōkishū** 萬善同歸集. *See* Wanshan tonggui ji

**Maō [Hajun]** 魔王[波旬]. *See* Namuci, Pāpīyāṃs

**mappō** 末法. *See* mofa, saddharmavipralopa

**Mara [koku]** 摩羅[國]. *See* Mallā

**Marananda** 摩羅難陀. *See* *Mālānanda

**Mari** [alt. Matsuri] 末利. *See* Mallikā

**Marishi** 摩利支. *See* Marīci

**masangin** 麻三斤. *See* ma sanjin

**masse** 末世. *See* moshi, paścimakāla

**matarika** 摩怛理迦. *See* mātṛkā

**Matsudenchi** 末田地. *See* Madhyāntika

**Maya** 摩耶. *See* Māyā

**Meitei** 明帝. *See* Mingdi

**Memyō** 馬鳴. *See* Aśvaghoṣa

**Men'ō [biku]** 面王[比丘]. *See* Mogharāja

**menpeki** 面壁. *See* mianbi

**Merōfu** 馬郎婦. *See* Malang fu

**metsu** 滅. *See* nirodha

**metsujinjō** 滅盡定. *See* nirodhasamāpatti

**metsujōhō** 滅諍法. *See* adhikaraṇaśamatha

**mettai** 滅諦. *See* nirodhasatya

**Meyūkyō** 馬邑經. *See* Cūḷāssapurasutta, Mahāssapurasutta

**mi** 味. *See* rasa

**Miroku** 彌勒. *See* Maitreya

**misho** 味處. *See* rasāyatana

**mitchi** 密意. *See* abhisaṃdhi

**Mitsugan'yukyō** 蜜丸喻經. *See* Madhupiṇḍikasutta

**Mitsuun Engo** 密雲圓悟. *See* Miyun Yuanwu

**Mizōukyō** 未曾有經. *See* Adbhutadharmaparyāyasūtra

**Mokuan Shōtō** 木菴性瑫. *See* Mu'an Xingtao

**mokugyo** 木魚. *See* muyu

**Mokukenrenshiteishu** 目犍連子帝須. *See* Moggaliputtatissa

**Mokuren** 目連. *See* Mahāmaudgalyāyana

**Mokushinrinda** 目眞隣陀. *See* Mucilinda

**mokushōzen** 默照禪. *See* mozhao chan

**mondō** 問答. *See* wenda

**mon'e** 聞慧. *See* śrutamayīprajñā

**monjizen** 文字禪. *See* wenzi chan

**Monjushiri** 文殊師利. *See* Mañjuśrī

**mōzō** 妄想. *See* WANGXIANG

**mu** 無. *See* WU

**mubonten** 無煩天. *See* AVṚHA

**muchi** 無癡. *See* AMOHA

**mufunbetsu** 無分別. *See* NIRVIKĀLPA

**mufunbetsuchi** 無分別智. *See* NIRVIKĀLPAJÑĀNA

**muga** 無我. *See* ANĀTMAN, NAIRĀTMYA

**Muga** 無我. *See* ANATTALAKKHAṆASUTTA

**mugaku** 無學. *See* AŚAIKṢA

**mugakudō** 無學道. *See* AŚAIKṢAMĀRGA

**Mugaku Sogen** 無學祖元. *See* WUXUE ZUYUAN

**mugan** 無願. *See* APRAṆIHITA

**mugegyō** 無礙行. *See* WU'AI XING

**mugyōhatsu** 無行般. *See* ANABHISAṂSKĀRAPARINIRVĀYIN

**mugyōhatsunehan** 無行般涅槃. *See* ANABHISAṂSKĀRAPARINIRVĀYIN

**muhyōjiki** 無表色. *See* AVIJÑAPTIRŪPA

**mui** 無爲. *See* ASAṂSKṚTA; WUWEI

**mui[fu]se** 無畏[布]施. *See* ABHAYADĀNA

**muihō** 無爲法. *See* ASAṂSKṚTADHARMA

**mui no shinnin** 無位眞人. *See* WUWEI ZHENREN

**Mui sanzō zen'yō** 無畏三藏禪要. *See* WUWEI SANZANG CHANYAO

**Mujaku** 無著. *See* ASAṄGA

**Muji hōkyōgyō** 無字寶篋經. *See* ANAKṢARAKARAṆḌAKA [VAIROCANAGARBHA] SŪTRA

**Mujin'i bosatsu** 無盡意菩薩. *See* AKṢAYAMATI

**Mujin'i bosatsubon** 無盡意菩薩品. *See* AKṢAYAMATINIRDEŚA

**Mujinzōin** 無盡藏院. *See* WUJINZANG YUAN

**mujishō** 無自性. *See* NIḤSVABHĀVA

**mujō** 無常. *See* ANITYA

**mujōbodai** 無上菩提. *See* MAHĀBODHI

**Mujōshōtōgaku** 無上正等覺. *See* ANUTTARASAMYAKSAṂBODHI

**mujūnehan** 無住涅槃. *See* APRATIṢṬHITANIRVĀṆA

**Mujun Shihan** 無準師範. *See* WUZHUN SHIFAN

**mukendō** 無間道. *See* ĀNANTARYAMĀRGA

**mukengō** 無間業. *See* ĀNANTARYAKARMAN

**mukenjigoku** 無間地獄. *See* AVĪCI

**mukenjō** 無間定. *See* ĀNANTARYASAMĀDHI

**muki** 無記. *See* AVYĀKṚTA

**mukihō** 無記法. *See* AVYĀKṚTADHARMA

**mukōan** 無公案. *See* WU GONG'AN

**Mukujōkō daidaranikyō** 無垢淨光大陀羅尼經. *See* MUGUJŎNGGWANG TAEDARANI KYŎNG

**mukushiki** 無垢識. *See* AMALAVIJÑĀNA

**Mumon Ekai** 無門慧開. *See* WUMEN HUIKAI

**Mumonkan** 無門關. *See* WUMEN GUAN

**mumyō** 無明. *See* AVIDYĀ

**munen** 無念. *See* WUNIAN

**munetsu** 無熱. *See* ATAPA

**munetsuten** 無熱天. *See* ATAPA

**muni** 牟尼. *See* MUNI

**Murihagunnakyō** 牟犂破群那經. *See* KAKACŪPAMASUTTA

**muro** 無漏. *See* ANĀSRAVA

**murokai** 無漏界. *See* ANĀSRAVADHĀTU

**Muryōgikyō** 無量義經. *See* WULIANG YI JING

**muryōjōten** 無量淨天. *See* APRAMĀṆAŚUBHA

**Muryōjubutsu** 無量壽佛. *See* AMITĀYUS

**Muryōjukyō** 無量壽經. *See* SUKHĀVATĪVYŪHA

**Muryōjukyō upadaisha ganshōge** 無量壽經優婆提舎願生偈. *See* WULIANGSHOU JING YOUPOTISHE YUANSHENG JI

**Muryōkōbutsu** 無量光佛. *See* AMITĀBHA

**muryōkōten** 無量光天. *See* APRAMĀṆĀBHA

**muryōshin** 無量心. *See* APRAMĀṆA

**mushae** 無遮會. *See* WUZHE HUI

**mushikikai** 無色界. *See* ĀRŪPYADHĀTU

**mushikikaijō** 無色界定. *See* ĀRŪPYĀVACARADHYĀNA

**mushikiton** 無色貪. *See* ĀRŪPYARĀGA

**mushin** 無瞋. *See* ADVEṢA

**mushin** 無心. *See* WUXIN

**Mushinron** 無心論. *See* WUXIN LUN

**mushō** 無性. *See* ASVABHĀVA, NIḤSVABHĀVA

**mushōbōnin** 無生法忍. *See* ANUTPATTIKADHARMAKṢĀNTI

**mushōchi** 無生智. *See* ANUTPĀDAJÑĀNA

**mushoi** 無所畏. *See* VAIŚĀRADYA

**mushousho** 無所有處. *See* ĀKIÑCANYĀYATANA

**musō** 無相. *See* ĀNIMITTA, NIRĀKĀRA

**musō hōrin** 無相法輪. *See* ALAKṢAṆATVADHARMACAKRA

**musōjō** 無想定. *See* ASAṂJÑĀSAMĀPATTI

**musōkai** 無相戒. *See* WUXIANG JIE

**musōten** 無想天. *See* ASAṂJÑIKA

**muton** 無貪. *See* ALOBHA

**muunten** 無雲天. *See* ANABHRAKA

**muyoku** 無欲. *See* VAIRĀGYA

**muyonehan** 無餘涅槃. *See* ANUPĀDIŚEṢANIRVĀṆA, NIRUPĀDHIŚEṢANIRVĀṆA

**myō** 明. *See* VIDYĀ

**myōgo** 明護. *See* PARITTA

**myōgokyō** 明護經. *See* PARITTA

**Myōhō rengekyō** 妙法蓮華經. *See* SADDHARMAPUṆḌARĪKA

**myōkanzatchi** 妙觀察智. *See* PRATYAVEKṢAṆĀJÑĀNA

**myōki** 妙喜. *See* ABHIRATI

**myōkon** 命根. *See* JĪVITA

**Myōkōsen** 妙高山. *See* SUMERU, MOUNT

**Myōon bosatsu** 妙音菩薩. *See* MAÑJUŚRĪ

**Myōonten** 妙音天. *See* SARASVATĪ, SHICHI FUKUJIN

**myōshiki** 名色. *See* NĀMARŪPA

**myōsho** 明處. *See* VIDYĀSTHĀNA

**Myōzen** 妙善. *See* MIAOSHAN

## N

**Nadai Kashō** 那提迦葉. *See* NADĪ KĀŚYAPA

**Nagasaina** 那伽犀那. *See* NĀGASENA

**naie** 內衣. *See* ANTARVĀSAS

**naimyō** 內明. *See* ADHYĀTMAVIDYĀ

**naishō** 內證. *See* PRATYĀTMĀDHIGAMA

**Nakura chōjamo** 諾酤羅長者母. *See* NAKULAPITṚ and NAKULAMĀTṚ

**nan** 煖. *See* ŪṢMAN

**Nanda** 難陀. *See* NANDA

**Nandaka** 難陀迦. *See* NANDAKA

**Nangaku Ejō** 南岳懷讓. *See* NANYUE HUAIRANG

**Nangaku Eshi** 南岳慧思. *See* NANYUE HUISI

**Nankai kiki naihōden** 南海寄歸內法傳. *See* NANHAI JIGUI NEIFA ZHUAN

**Nansen Fugan** 南泉普願. *See* NANQUAN PUYUAN

**nansho** 難處. *See* AKṢAṆA

**nanshōji** 難勝地. *See* SUDURJAYĀ

**Nanshū** 南宗. *See* NAN ZONG

**Nan'yō Echū** 南陽慧忠. *See* NANYANG HUIZHONG

**Nanzan Risshū** 南山律宗. *See* NANSHAN LÜ ZONG

**Naraenten** 那羅延天. *See* NĀRĀYAṆA

**Narandaji** 那爛陀寺. *See* NĀLANDĀ

**Narendairiyasha** 那連提黎耶舍. *See* NARENDRAYAŚAS

**Nasen biku** 那先比丘. *See* NĀGASENA

**Nasenbikukyō** 那先比丘經. *See* MILINDAPAÑHA

**Naurafu** 那憂羅父. *See* NAKULAPITṚ and NAKULAMĀTṚ

**nehan** 涅槃. *See* NIRVĀṆA

**Nehangyō** 涅槃經. *See* MAHĀPARINIBBĀNASUTTANTA, MAHĀPARINIRVĀNASŪTRA

**nehankai** 涅槃界. *See* NIRVĀṆADHĀTU

**Nehanshū** 涅槃宗. *See* NIEPAN ZONG

**Nehan wa yū** 涅槃夕. *See* NIEPAN XI

**nehanzō** 涅槃僧. *See* NIVĀSANA

**nen** 念. *See* ANUSMṚTI, SMṚTI

**nenbutsu** 念佛. *See* NIANFO

**nenge mishō** 拈花微笑. *See* NIANHUA WEIXIAO

**nenjo** 念處. *See* SMṚTYUPASTHĀNA

**Nenjogyō** 念處經. *See* SATIPAṬṬHĀNASUTTA

**nenju** 念誦. *See* JAPA

**nenju** 念珠. *See* JAPAMĀLĀ

**nenko** 拈古. *See* NIANGU

**nennenmujō** 念念無常. *See* ER WUCHANG

**nenshi** 念死. *See* MARAṆĀNUSMṚTI

**nenshi** 燃指. *See* YŎNJI

**Nenshō** 燃焼. *See* ĀDITTAPARIYĀYASUTTA

**Neritei** 涅哩底. *See* NIRṚTI

**nibon** 二犯. *See* ER FAN

**nidana** 尼陀那. *See* NIDĀNA

**nigashū** 二我執. *See* ER WOZHI

**nihō** 二報. *See* ER BAO

**niji** 二持. *See* ER CHI

**nijō** 二乘. *See* ER SHENG

**nijo** 二序. *See* ER XU

**nijūgoenzū** 二十五圓通. *See* ERSHIWU YUANTONG

**Nijūokuni** 二十億耳. *See* SOṆA KOLIVĪSA

**nijūsōgya** 二十僧伽. *See* VIMŚATIPRABHEDASAṂGHA

**nika** 二加. *See* ER JIA

**Nikenda'nyakudaishi** 尼揵陀若提子. *See* NIRGRANTHA-JÑĀTĪPUTRA

**Nikenshi** 尼揵子. *See* NIRGRANTHA

**nikon** 耳根. *See* ŚROTRENDRIYA

**Nikuda** 尼瞿陀. *See* NIGRODHA

**nikugen** 肉眼. *See* MĀṂSACAKṢUS

**nikukei** 肉髻. *See* UṢṆĪṢA

**Nikuritsurin** 尼拘律林. *See* NIGRODHĀRĀMA

**nikyōji** 二脇士. *See* ER XIESHI

**nimitsu** 二密. *See* ER MI

**nimujō** 二無常. *See* ER WUCHANG

**nin** 人. *See* MANUṢYA, PUDGALA, PURUṢA

**ningashū** 人我執. *See* PUDGALĀTMAGRAHA

**ninin** 二忍. *See* ER REN

**Ninken** 仁賢. *See* BHADRIKA

**ninmuga** 人無我. *See* PUDGALANAIRĀTMYA

**ninniku** 忍辱. *See* KṢĀNTI

**ninnikuharamitsu** 忍辱波羅蜜. *See* KṢĀNTIPĀRAMITĀ

**Ninniku sennin** 忍辱仙人. *See* KṢĀNTIVĀDIN

**Ninnōgyō** 仁王經. *See* RENWANG JING

**Ninnō hyakukōzae** 仁王百高座會. *See* RENWANG BAIGAOZUO HUI

**ninyū** 二入. *See* ERRU

**Ninyū shigyōron** 二入四行論. *See* ERRU SIXING LUN

**niōjin** 二應身. *See* ER YINGSHEN

**Nirenzenga** 尼連禪河. *See* NAIRAÑJANĀ

**niru** 二流. *See* ER LIU

**niseken** 二世間. see ER SHIJIAN

**nisen** 二詮. *See* ER QUAN

**nishiki** 耳識. *See* ŚROTRAVIJÑĀNA

**nisho** 耳處. *See* ŚROTRĀYATANA

**nisho san'e** 二處三會. *See* ERCHU SANHUI

**nishū** 二宗. *See* ER ZONG

**nishu no kuyō** 二種供養. *See* ERZHONG GONGYANG

**nishu no sangan** 二種三觀. *See* SANGUAN

**nishuonri** 二種遠離. *See* ERZHONG YUANLI

**nisshu** 日種. *See* ĀDITYABANDHU

**nitai** 二諦. *See* SATYADVAYA

**nitoku** 二德. *See* ER DE

**niwa** 二和. *See* ER HE

**nō** 惱. *See* PRADĀSA

**nōryū** 能立. *See* SĀDHANA

**nōsain** 能作因. *See* KĀRAṆA(HETU)

**nyogen no yu** 如幻喩. *See* AṢṬAMĀYOPĀMA

**nyogenzanmai** 如幻三昧. *See* MĀYOPAMASAMĀDHI

**nyoihōju** 如意寶珠. *See* CINTAMĀṆI

**nyojitsuchiken** 如實知見. *See* YATHĀBHŪTAJÑĀNADARŚANA

**Nyojō** 如浄. *See* TIANTONG RUJING

**nyorai** 如來. *See* TATHĀGATA

**nyoraiji** 如來地. *See* TATHĀGATABHŪMI

**nyoraike** 如來家. *See* TATHĀGATAKULA, BUDDHAKULA

**nyoraishō** 如來性. *See* TATHĀGATAGOTRA

**nyoraizō** 如來藏. *See* TATHĀGATAGARBHA

**nyorichi** 如理智. *See* YATHĀVADBHĀVIKAJÑĀNA

**nyorisai** 如理作意. *See* YONIŚOMANASKĀRA

**nyoryōchi** 如量智. *See* YĀVADBHĀVIKAJÑĀNA

**nyōyakuujō** 饒益有情. *See* SATTVĀRTHA

**nyozegamon** 如是我聞. *See* EVAṂ MAYĀ ŚRUTAṂ

**Nyūhokkaibon** 入法界品. *See* RU FAJIE PIN

**Nyū Ryōgakyō** 入楞伽經. *See* LAṄKĀVATĀRASŪTRA

## O

**ō** 誑. *See* MĀYĀ, ŚĀṬHYA

**Ōbaku Kiun** 黄檗希運. *See* HUANGBO XIYUN

**ōchō** 横超. *See* HENGCHAO

**ōgo** 擁護. *See* RĀKṢĀ

**ōgu** 應供. *See* ARHAT

**Ō I** 王維. *See* WANG WEI

**ōjō** 往生. *See* WANGSHENG

**ōka** 應訶. *See* TARJANĪYAKARMAN

**Okuni** 億耳. *See* SOṆA-KOṬIKAṆṆA

**Ōkutsumara** 央掘摩羅. *See* AṄGULIMĀLYA

**Ōkutsumarakyō** 央掘摩羅經. *See* AṄGULIMĀLĪYASŪTRA

**Ōmukyō** 鸚鵡經. *See* SUBHASUTTANTA

**ōmuzen** 鸚鵡禪. *See* YINGWU CHAN

**on** 園. *See* ĀRĀMA

**ongyōji** 遠行地. *See* DŪRAṄGAMĀ

**Onkōbu** 飲光部. *See* KĀŚYAPĪYA

**on mani padomei un** 唵嘛呢叭彌吽. *See* OṂ MAṆI PADME HŪṂ

**onri** 遠離. *See* VIVEKA

**Ōryō** [alt. Ōryū] **Enan** 黄龍慧南. *See* HUANGLONG HUINAN

**Ōryōha** [alt. Ōryūha] 黄龍派. *See* HUANGLONG PAI

**Ōshajō** 王舍城. *See* RĀJAGṚHA

**oshō** 和尚. *See* UPĀDHYĀYA, HESHANG

**oshōni** 和尚尼. *See* UPĀDHYĀYĀ

## R

**Rabanabadai** 羅婆那拔提. *See* LAKUṆṬAKA BHADRIKA

**Rada** 羅陀. *See* RĀDHA

**Ragora** 羅睺羅. *See* RĀHULA

**Ragyōbonjikyō** 倮形梵志經. *See* KASSAPASĪHANĀDASUTTA

**Raitawara** 賴吒积羅. *See* RĀṢṬRAPĀLA

**rakan** 羅漢. *See* ARHAT, LUOHAN

**raku** 樂. *See* SUKHA

**Rakuyō garanki** 洛陽伽藍記. *See* LUOYANG QIELAN JI

**Ramakyō** 羅摩經. *See* ARIYAPARIYESANĀSUTTA

**Ranbinion** 藍毘尼園. *See* LUMBINĪ

**ranjiki** 亂識. *See* BHRĀNTIJÑĀNA

**Rankei Dōryū** 蘭溪道隆. *See* LANXI DAOLONG

**rasetsu** 羅刹. *See* RĀKṢASA

**reichi** 靈知. *See* LINGZHI

**reichi** 靈地. *See* MAHĀSTHĀNA

**Rei Shō** 靈照. *See* LING ZHAO

**Reiyū** 靈祐. *See* GUISHAN LINGYOU

**Rekidai hōbōki** 歴代法寶記. *See* LIDAI FABAO JI

**Rekidai sanbōki** 歴代三寶紀. *See* LIDAI SANBAO JI

**renge** 蓮華. *See* PADMA

**rengebu** 蓮華部. *See* PADMAKULA

**Rengeshiki** 蓮華色. *See* UTPALAVARṆĀ

**Rengeshu** 蓮華手. *See* PADMAPĀṆI

**rengeza** 蓮華坐. *See* PADMĀSANA

**Retsugazō** 烈河增. *See* NADĪ VAITARAṆĪ

**ri** 理. *See* LI

**ri** 離. *See* NIḤSARAṆA, VIRATI

**Ribata** 離婆多. *See* REVATA

**rihokkai** 理法界. *See* LI FAJIE

**rijimugehokkai** 理事無礙法界. *See* LISHI WU'AI FAJIE

**Rike** 離繫. *See* NIRGRANTHA

**rikeka** 離繫果. *See* VISAṂYOGAPHALA

**rikengo** 離間語. *See* PAIŚUNYA

**rikeron** 離戲論. *See* NIṢPRAPAÑCA

**riki** 力. *See* BALA

**rikiharamitsu** 力波羅蜜. *See* BALAPĀRAMITĀ

**rikon** 利根. *See* TĪKṢṆENDRIYA

**Rikuji** 離垢地. *See* Vimalā

**rin** 輪. *See* cakra

**ringaku** 麟角. *See* khaḍgaviṣāṇa

**ringakuyu** 麟角喩. *See* khaḍgaviṣāṇakalpa

**Ringyō** 林經. *See* Vanapatthasutta

**rinne** 輪迴. *See* saṃsāra

**Rinzai Gigen** 臨濟義玄. *See* Linji Yixuan

**Rinzairoku** 臨濟錄. *See* Linji lu

**risahō** 離作法. *See* vyatireka

**risshū** 立宗. *See* pratijñā

**rita** 利他. *See* parārtha

**ritsu** 律. *See* vinaya

**Ri Tsūgen** 李通玄. *See* Li Tongxuan

**ritsugi** 律儀. *See* saṃvara

**ritsuzō** 律藏. *See* vinayapiṭaka

**riyaku** 利益. *See* ānisaṃs, arthakriyā

**riyoku** 離欲. *See* vairāgya

**rizen** 離染. *See* vairāgya

**ro** 漏. *See* āsava

**rō** 老. *See* jarā

**Rōben** 良辯. *See* Ryōben

**rojin** 漏盡. *See* kṣīṇāsrava, āsravakṣaya

**rojin[chi]** 漏盡[智]. *See* āsravakṣaya

**Rojingyō** 漏盡經. *See* Sabbāsavasutta

**Rokugunbiku** 六群比丘. *See* Ṣaḍvārgika

**rokujidaimyō** 六字大明. *See* ṣaḍakṣarī

**rokujidaimyōshu** 六字大明咒. *See* ṣaḍakṣarīvidyā

**rokujishōku** 六字章句. *See* ṣaḍakṣarī

**Rokujūju nyoriron** 六十頌如理論. *See* Yuktiṣaṣṭikā

**roku konpon bonnō** 六根本煩惱. *See* ṣaḍmūlakleśa

**Rokunamadai** 勒那摩提. *See* Ratnamati

**Rokushimo** 鹿子母. *See* Viśākhā

**Rokushimodō** 鹿子母堂. *See* Mṛgāramātuprāsāda

**rokusho** 六處. *See* ṣaḍāyatana

**rokushu** 六趣. *See* ṣaḍgati

**rokusō** 六相. *See* liuxiang

**Rokuso dangyō** 六祖壇經. *See* Liuzu tan jing

**rokusuinō** 漉水囊. *See* parisrāvaṇa

**Rokuyaon** 鹿野苑. *See* Mṛgadāva

**rokuyu** 六喩. *See* liuyu

**ron** 論. *See* śāstra, bhāṣya

**ronzō** 論藏. *See* abhidhammapiṭaka, *śāstrapiṭaka

**Roshakyō** 露遮經. *See* Lohiccasutta

**rōshi** 老死. *See* jarāmaraṇa

**Rōshi kekokyō** 老子化胡經. *See* Laozi huahu jing

**Rozan** 廬山. *See* Lushan

**Rozan Eon** 廬山慧遠. *See* Lushan Huiyuan

**ryō** 量. *See* pramāṇa

**ryōchi** 靈知. *See* lingzhi

**ryōfu** 令怖. *See* tarjanīyakarman

**Ryōga shishiki** 楞伽師資記. *See* Lengqie shizi ji

**ryōgi** 了義. *See* nītārtha

**Ryōjusen** 靈鷲山. *See* Gṛdhrakūṭaparvata

**Ryōkai** 良价. *See* Dongshan Liangjie

**Ryōshikyō** 獵師經. *See* Nivāpasutta

**ryū** 龍. *See* nāga

**Ryūchi** 龍智. *See* Nāgabodhi

**Ryūju** 龍樹. *See* Nāgārjuna

**Ryūju bosatsu kankaiōju** 龍樹菩薩勸誡王頌. *See* Suhṛllekha

**ryūzō** 龍象. *See* hastināga

## S

**sai** 作意. *See* manasikāra

**sai** 齋. *See* zhai

**saijōdaishijji** 最上大悉地. *See* uttamasiddhi

**saijōjōzen** 最上乘禪. *See* zuishangsheng chan

**Sai kō** 濟公. *See* Jigong

**saishi** 再死. *See* punarmṛtyu, rebirth

**saishinshari** 碎身舍利. *See* suishen sheli

**saishō** 最勝. *See* jina

**saishō** 再生. *See* punarjanman, rebirth

**Saishōbutchōdarani jōjogōshōjukyō** 最勝佛頂陀羅尼淨除業障呪經. *See* SARVADURGATIPARIŚODHANATANTRA

**saishōshi** 最勝子. *See* JINAPUTRA

**sanbara** 三跋羅. *See* SAṂVARA

**sanbō** 三寶. *See* RATNATRAYA

**sanbunkakyō** 三分科經. *See* SANFEN KEJING

**Sandai sennin** 羼提仙人. *See* KṢĀNTIVĀDIN

**Sandanagyō** 散陀那經. *See* UDUMBARIKASĪHANĀDASUTTA

**sandō** 三道. *See* SANDAO

**Sandōkai** 参同契. *See* CANTONG QI

**sandoku** 三毒. *See* TRIVIṢA

**san'e** [alt. sanne] 三衣. *See* TRICĪVARA

**sanfunbetsu** 三分別. *See* TRIVIKALPA

**sangai** 三界. *See* TRAILOKYA

**Sangaikyō** [alt. Sankaikyō] 三階教. *See* SANJIE JIAO

**sangaku** 三學. *See* TRIŚIKṢA

**sangan** 三觀. *See* SANGUAN

**sange** 懺悔. *See* PĀPADEŚANA

**Sange Sangai** 山家山外. *See* SHANJIA SHANWAI

**Sanhokkaiju** 讚法界頌. *See* DHARMADHĀTUSTAVA

**Sanjaya Birateishi** 刪闍耶毘羅胝子. *See* SAÑJAYA VAIRĀṬĪPUTRA

**sanjō** 三乘. *See* TRIYĀNA

**sanju** 三聚. *See* TRISKANDHAKA

**sanju jōkai** 三聚淨戒. *See* ŚĪLATRAYA

**sanjūnisō** 三十二相. *See* DVĀTRIṂŚADVARALAKṢAṆA, MAHĀPURUṢALAKṢAṆA

**Sanjūnisōgyō** 三十二相經. *See* LAKKHAṆASUTTA

**sanjūsanten** 三十三天. *See* TRĀYASTRIṂŚA

**Sanjūshichidōbon** 三十七道品. *See* BODHIPĀKṢIKADHARMA

**sankie** 三歸依. *See* TRIŚARAṆA

**sankon** 三根. *See* TRĪNDRIYA

**sanku** 三句. *See* SANJU

**sanmai** 三昧. *See* SAMĀDHI

**sanmaikyō** 三昧經. *See* SANMEI JING

**sanmaya** 三摩耶. *See* SAMAYA

**sanmayain** 三摩耶印. *See* SAMAYAMUDRĀ

**sanmayasatta** 三昧耶薩埵. *See* SAMAYASATTVA

**sanmitsu** 三密. *See* TRIGUHYA

**sanmon** 三門. *See* TRIDVĀRA

**sanmyō** 三明. *See* TRIVIDYĀ

**Sanmyōkyō** 三明經. *See* TEVIJJASUTTA

**Sannei** 贊寧. *See* ZANNING

**sanran** 散亂. *See* VIKṢEPA

**Sanron gengi** 三論玄義. *See* SANLUN XUANYI

**Sanronshū** 三論宗. *See* SANLUN ZONG; MADHYAMAKA

**sanshi** 三止. *See* SANZHI

**sanshin** 三身. *See* TRIKĀYA

**sanshi sangan** 三止三觀. *See* SANZHI, SANGUAN

**sanshō** 三性. *See* TRISVABHĀVA

**sanshuseken** 三種世間. *See* SANZHONG SHIJIAN

**sansō** 三相. *See* TRILAKṢAṆA

**santai** 三諦. *See* SANDI

**san'yō** 三要. *See* SANYAO

**sanze** 三世. *See* TRIKĀLA

**sanzendaisensekai** 三千大千世界. *See* TRISĀHASRAMAHĀSĀHASRALOKADHĀTU

**sanzō** 三藏. *See* TRIPIṬAKA

**sanzō hosshi** 三藏法師. *See* TREPIṬAKA

**saraju** [alt. sharaju] 沙羅樹. *See* ŚĀLA

**Satsubatabu** 薩婆多部. *See* SARVĀSTIVĀDA

**sedaiippō** 世第一法. *See* LAUKIKĀGRADHARMA

**segan'in** 施願印. *See* VARADAMUDRĀ

**Sego** 施護. *See* DĀNAPĀLA

**sehō** 世法. *See* LOKADHARMA

**Seigen Gyōshi** 青原行思. *See* QINGYUAN XINGSI

**seiraii** 西來意. *See* XILAI YI

**Seitasanbu** [alt. Seitasenbu] 制多山部. *See* CAITYA

**Sejizai** 世自在. *See* LOKEŚVARA

**Sejizaiō butsu** 世自在王佛. *See* LOKEŚVARARĀJA

**sekai** 世界. *See* LOKA

**sekai** 世界. *See* LOKADHĀTU

**seken** 世間. *See* LAUKIKA

**sekendō** 世間道. *See* LAUKIKAMĀRGA

**Sekishitsu koku** 石室國. *See* TAKṢAŚILĀ

**Sekitō Kisen** 石頭希遷. *See* SHITOU XIQIAN

**semui** 施無畏. *See* ABHAYADĀNA

**semuiin** 施無畏印. *See* ABHAYAMUDRĀ

**sendanjuni** 栴檀樹耳. *See* SŪKARAMADDAVA

**sendari** 旃陀利. *See* CAṆḌĀLĪ

**Sengen** 千眼. *See* SAHASRĀKṢA

**Senjū hyakuengyō** 撰集百緣經. *See* AVADĀNAŚATAKA

**Senjukyō** 千手經. *See* QIANSHOU JING

**Senju Sengen Kannon** 千手千眼觀音. *See* SĀHASRABHUJASĀHASRANETRĀVALOKITEŚVARA

**Senkan** 宣鑑. *See* DESHAN XUANJIAN

**Senni gedō** 先尼外道. *See* ŚREṆIKA HERESY

**Sennin dasho** 仙人墮處. *See* ṚṢIPATANA

**senriyokunin** 先離欲人. *See* VĪTARĀGAPŪRVIN

**Senzatsu zen'aku gōhōkyō** 占察善惡業報經. *See* ZHANCHA SHANE YEBAO JING

**Seppō Gison** 雪峰義存. *See* XUEFENG YICUN

**seppōshi** 說法師. *See* DHARMABHĀṆAKA

**Sesetsuron** 施設論. *See* PRAJÑAPTIBHĀṢYA[PĀDAŚĀSTRA]

**Seshin** 世親. *See* VASUBANDHU

**seshu** 施主. *See* DĀNAPATI

**seson** 世尊. *See* BHAGAVAN

**Seson nenge** 世尊拈花. *See* SHIZUN NIANHUA

**Sessenbu** 雪山部. *See* HAIMAVATA

**sesshin** 攝心. *See* RŌHATSU SESSHIN

**Setchō Jūken** 雪竇重顯. *See* XUEDOU CHONGXIAN

**Setsuissaiubu** 說一切有部. *See* SARVĀSTIVĀDA

**Setsukebu** [alt. Sekkebu] 說假部. *See* PRAJÑAPTIVĀDA

**setsuna** 刹那. *See* KṢAṆA

**setsunakei** 刹那頃. *See* KṢAṆIKA

**setsunagusoku** 刹那具足. *See* KṢAṆASAMPAD

**setsunaron** 刹那論. *See* KṢAṆIKAVĀDA

**setsuri** 刹利. *See* KṢATRIYA

**Setsushussebu** 說出世部. *See* LOKOTTARAVĀDA

**Seu** 世友. *See* VASUMITRA

**sezoku** 世俗. *See* SAṂVṚTI

**sezokusō** 世俗僧. *See* SAMMUTISAṄGHA

**sezokutai** 世俗諦. *See* SAṂVṚTISATYA

**sha** 遮. *See* PRATIṢEDHA

**sha** 捨. *See* UPEKṢĀ

**Shabara no tō** 遮婆羅塔. *See* CĀPĀLACAITYA

**Shabasekai** 娑婆世界. *See* SAHĀLOKA

**Shabasekaishu** 娑婆世界主. *See* SAHĀṂPATI

**shada** 捨墮. *See* NAIḤSARGIKA PĀYATTIKA

**Shae koku** 舍衛國. *See* ŚRĀVASTĪ

**shagakukaisha** 捨學戒者. *See* SIKKHĀPACCAKKHĀNA

**Shagara** 娑伽羅. *See* SĀGARA

**Shagita jō** 娑枳多城. *See* SĀKETA

**Shaka** 釋迦. *See* ŚĀKYA, cf. SHI

**shakai** 捨界. *See* SĪMĀSAMŪHANA

**Shakamuni** 釋迦牟尼. *See* ŚĀKYAMUNI

**Shakara** [alt. Shakatsura] 娑竭羅. *See* SĀGARA

**shakasō** 釋迦僧. *See* ŚĀKYABHIKṢU

**Shaku** 釋. *See* SHI

**shakujō** 錫杖. *See* KHAKKHARA

**shakunikudan** 赤肉團. *See* CHIROUTUAN

**Shakuri** 奢拘梨. *See* SAKULĀ

**shami** 沙彌. *See* ŚRĀMAṆERA

**shamini** 沙彌尼. *See* ŚRĀMAṆERIKĀ

**shamon** 沙門. *See* ŚRĀMAṆA

**Shamon fukyōōsharon** 沙門不敬王者論. *See* SHAMEN BUJING WANGZHE LUN

**Shamongakyō** 沙門果經. *See* SĀMAÑÑAPHALASUTTA

**shamonka** 沙門果. *See* ŚRĀMAṆYAPHALA

**shamuryōshin** 捨無量心. *See* UPEKṢĀPRAMĀṆA

**Shanoku** 車匿. *See* CHANDAKA

**Sharaka** 沙羅訶. *See* SARAHA

**shari** 舍利. *See* ŚARĪRA

**sharigu** 舍利具. *See* SHELIJU

**Sharihotsu** 舍利弗. *See* ŚĀRIPUTRA

**shariki** 舍利器. *See* SHELIQI

**shashin** 捨身. *See* SHESHEN, DEHADĀNA

**shi** 支. *See* AṄGA

**shi** 思. *See* CETANĀ

**shi** 師. *See* GURU

**shi** 死. *See* MARAṆA

**shi** 止. *See* ŚAMATHA

**shi** 師. *See* ŚĀSTṚ

**shi** 伺. *See* VICĀRA

**Shi** 支. *See* ZHI

**Shibara** 尸婆羅. *See* SĪVALI

**Shibi** 尸毘. *See* ŚIBI

**Shibi** 師備. *See* XUANSHA SHIBEI

**shibonzaimon** 四犯罪門. *See* *CATURĀPATTIDVĀRA

**Shibunritsu** 四分律. *See* SIFEN LÜ

**shichaku** 思擇. *See* TARKA

**shichibutsu** 七佛. *See* SAPTABUDDHA, SAPTATATHĀGATA

**shichichi** 七知. *See* QIZHI

**shichigyaku[zai]** 七逆[罪]. *See* QINI[ZUI]

**Shichihyakuju hannya** 七百頌般若. *See* SAPTAŚATIKĀPRAJÑĀPĀRAMITĀ

**shichijō rokuyoku** 七情六欲. *See* QIQING LIUYU

**shichikakushi** 七覺支. *See* BODHYAṄGA

**shichiken** 七賢. *See* QIXIAN

**shichimetsujōhō** 七滅諍法. *See* SAPTĀDHIKARAṆAŚAMATHA

**shichisaishō** 七最勝. *See* QIZUISHENG

**Shichishakyō** 七車經. *See* RATHAVINĪTASUTTA

**shichishichi** 七七. *See* QIQI

**shichishichi[nichi]sai** 七七[日]齋. *See* QIQI JI

**shichishichi no ki** 七七忌. *See* QIQI JI

**shichishisahō** 七支作法. *See* SAPTĀṄGAVIDHI

**shichishōji** 七勝事. *See* QI SHENGSHI

**shichishugo** 七種語. *See* QIZHONGYU

**shichishu no sha** 七種捨. *See* QIZHONGSHE

**shichiu** 七有. *See* QIYOU

**shichizai** 七財. *See* SAPTADHANA

**shichizen** 七善. *See* QISHAN

**shidagon** 斯陀含. *See* SAKṚDĀGĀMIN

**shidai** 支提. *See* CAITYA

**shidai** 四大. *See* MAHĀBHŪTA

**shidaien** 次第緣. *See* ANANTARAPRATYAYA

**shidai no santai** 次第三諦. *See* CIDI SANDI

**shidai sangan** 次第三觀. *See* SANGUAN

**shidai seppō** 次第說法. *See* ANUPUBBIKATHĀ

**Shiddatta** [alt. Shittatta] 悉達多. *See* SIDDHĀRTHA

**Shi Dōrin** 支道林. *See* ZHI DAOLIN, ZHI DUN

**shie** 思慧. *See* CINTĀMAYĪPRAJÑĀ

**Shifunzō** 屍糞增. *See* KUṆAPA

**shigō** 始業. *See* ĀDIKARMIKA

**shigō** 諡號. *See* SIHO

**shigu** 資具. *See* PARIṢKĀRA

**shiguzeigan** [alt. shikuseigan] 四弘誓願. *See* SI HONGSHIYUAN

**shihōkai** [alt. shihhokai] 四法界. *See* SI FAJIE

**shiin** 四印. *See* CATURMUDRĀ

**shijiki** 思食. *See* MANAḤSAṂCETANĀHĀRA

**shijinsoku** 四神足. *See* ṚDDHIPĀDA

**shijji** 悉地. *See* SIDDHI

**Shijōkō nyorai** 熾盛光如來. *See* TEJAPRABHA

**shijūku[nichi]sai** 四十九[日]齋. *See* SISHIJIU [RI] ZHAI

**Shijūnishōgyō** 四十二章經. *See* SISHI'ER ZHANG JING

**shika** 知客. *See* ZHIKE

**shikaku** 始覺. *See* SHIJUE

**shikan** 止觀. *See* ZHIGUAN, ŚAMATHA, VIPAŚYANĀ

**Shikaraka chōjamo** 室珂羅哥長者母. *See* ŚṚGĀLAKAMĀTṚ

**Shi Ken** 支謙. *See* ZHI QIAN

**shiki** 色. *See* RŪPA

**shiki** 識. *See* VIJÑĀNA, VIJÑAPTI

**shikikai** 色界. *See* RŪPADHĀTU

**shikikaijō** 色界定. *See* RŪPĀVACĀRAJHĀNA

**shikimuhenjo** 識無邊處. *See* vijñānānantyāyatana

**shikion** 識陰. *See* vijñānaskandha

**shikishamana** 式叉摩那. *See* śikṣamāṇā

**shikishamanakai** 式叉摩那戒. *See* śikṣamāṇāsaṃvara

**shikishin** 色身. *See* rūpakāya

**Shikishinsokuron** 識身足論. *See* Vijñānakāya[pādaśāstra]

**shikisho** 色處. *See* rūpāyatana

**shikisokuzekū kūsokuzeshiki** 色即是空空即是色. *See* rūpaṃ śūnyatā śunyataiva rūpaṃ

**shikiton** 色貪. *See* rūparāga

**shikiun** 色蘊. *See* rūpaskandha

**shikiun** 識蘊. *See* vijñānaskandha

**shikikukyōten** 色究竟天. *See* akaniṣṭha

**shiko** 四枯. *See* siku

**shiku funbetsu** 四句分別. *See* catuṣkoṭi

**Shikū Zenken** 指空禪賢. *See* Zhikong Chanxian

**shima** 死魔. *See* mṛtyumāra

**Shimei Chirei** 四明知禮. *See* Siming Zhili

**Shimei Jūgisho** 四明十義書. *See* Siming shiyi shu

**Shimon kyōkun/keikun** 緇門警訓. *See* Zimen jingxun

**shimugege** 四無礙解. *See* pratisaṃvid

**shin** 心. *See* citta

**shin** 瞋. *See* dveṣa, pratigha, vyāpāda

**shin** 身. *See* kāya

**shin** 信. *See* śraddhā

**Shindai** 眞諦. *See* Paramārtha

**shin'ei** 眞影. *See* chinyŏng

**shinfusōōbō** 心不相應法. *See* cittaviprayuktasaṃskāra

**shinge** 信解. *See* śraddhādhimukta

**shingedatsu** 心解脱. *See* cetovimukti

**shingi** 清規. *See* qinggui

**shingon** 眞言. *See* mantra

**shingonjō** 眞言乘. *See* mantrayāna

**Shingyō** 信行. *See* Xinxing

**shin'ikkyōshō** 心一境性. *See* cittaikāgratā

**shinji** 心地. *See* xindi

**shinjin** 信心. *See* xinxin

**Shinjinmei** 信心銘. *See* Xinxin ming

**shinjo** 心所. *See* caitta

**Shinjō** 審祥. *See* Simsang

**Shinjō Kokubun** 眞浄克文. *See* Zhenjing Kewen

**Shinka** 眞可. *See* Daguan Zhenke

**shinkan** 身觀. *See* kāyānupaśyanā

**shinkō** 身光. *See* shenguang

**shinkon** 身根. *See* kāyendriya

**Shinmōkijukyō** 身毛喜豎經. *See* Mahāsīhanādasutta

**Shinnekyō** 心穢經. *See* Cetokhilasutta

**shinnyo** 眞如. *See* zhenru, bhūtatathatā, tathatā

**shinrikaku** 親里覺. *See* qinli jue

**shinshiki** 身識. *See* kāyavijñāna

**shinsho** 身處. *See* kāyāyatana

**shinshō** 身證. *See* kāyasākṣin

**shinshōge** 信勝解. *See* śraddhāvimukta

**shinshū** 神衆. *See* sinjung

**shinsōōbō** 心相應法. *See* cittasamprayuktasaṃskāra

**shinsōzoku** 心相續. *See* cittasantāna

**shintai** 眞諦. *See* paramārthasatya

**Shion** 師遠. *See* Kuo'an Shiyuan

**Shiradatsuma** 尸羅達摩. *See* Śīladharma

**shirin** 屍林. *See* śmaśāna

**Shi Rukasen** 支婁迦讖. *See* Lokakṣema

**Shiruku rōdo** シルクロード. *See* Silk Road

**shiryō** 資糧. *See* saṃbhāra

**shiryōdō** 資糧道. *See* saṃbhāramārga

**Shi Sen** 支讖. *See* Lokakṣema

**shishiku** 師子吼. *See* siṃhanāda

**Shishikukyō** 師子吼經. *See* Cūḷasīhanādasutta

**shishiza** 師子座. *See* siṃhāsana

**shishō** 四生. *See* catvāro yonayaḥ, yoni

**shishōdai** 四聖諦. *See* four noble truths

**shishōgon** 四正勤. *See* prahāṇa

**shishōji** 四攝事. *See* saṃgrahavastu

**shisō** 四相. *See* CATURLAKṢAṆA, CATURNIMITTA

**shissui** 直歳. *See* ZHISUI

**shitai** 四諦. *See* FOUR NOBLE TRUTHS

**shitai hōrin** 四諦法輪. *See* CATUḤSATYADHARMACAKRA

**shitennō** 四天王. *See* LOKAPĀLA

**shitennōten** 四天王天. *See* CĀTURMAHĀRĀJAKĀYIKA

**Shi Ton** 支遁. *See* ZHI DUN

**shitsu** 嫉. *See* IRṢYĀ, MĀTSARYA

**shitsuji** 執事. *See* VAIYĀPṚTYAKARA

**shitsunen** 失念. *See* MUṢITASMṚTI

**Shitsuribussei** 室利佛逝. *See* ŚRĪVIJAYA

**shittan** 悉曇. *See* SIDDHAM

**Shittan jiki** 悉曇字記. *See* XITAN ZIJI

**shiwaku** 思惑. *See* SIHUO

**shiyui** 思惟. *See* BUDDHI

**shizen** 至善. *See* NIḤŚREYASA

**shizenkon** 四善根. *See* CATVĀRI KUŚALAMŪLĀNI, NIRVEDHABHĀGĪYA

**shō** 證. *See* ADHIGAMA

**shō** 聖. *See* ĀRYA

**shō** 障. *See* ĀVARAṆA

**sho** 處. *See* ĀYATANA

**shō** 生. *See* JĀTI, YONI

**shō** 聲. *See* ŚABDA

**Shōben** 清辯. *See* BHĀVAVIVEKA

**shōbō** 正報. *See* ER BAO

**shōbō** 正法. *See* SADDHARMA

**Shōbon hannyakyō** 小品般若經. *See* AṢṬASĀHASRIKĀPRAJÑĀPĀRAMITĀ

**Shōbu** 小部. *See* KHUDDAKANIKĀYA

**Shōbutsumo shōji hannya haramittakyō** 聖佛母小字般若波羅蜜多經. *See* SVALPĀKṢARAPRAJÑĀPĀRAMITĀ

**shōchi** 正知. *See* SAṂPRAJANYA

**shochishō** 所知障. *See* JÑEYĀVARAṆA

**Shōdaijōron** 攝大乘論. *See* MAHĀYĀNASAṂGRAHA

**shōdō** 聖道. *See* ĀRYAMĀRGA

**shōdōka** 聖道果. *See* ĀRYAMĀRGAPHALA

**Shōdōka** 證道歌. *See* ZHENGDAO GE

**Shōdōron** 笑道論. *See* XIAODAO LUN

**shoe** 所依. *See* ĀŚRAYA, NIŚRAYA

**shoen** 所縁. *See* ĀLAMBANA

**Shōengyō** 小緣經. *See* AGGAÑÑASUTTA

**shoennen** 所縁縁. *See* ĀLAMBANAPRATYAYA

**shōfugenka** 證不還果. *See* ANĀGĀMIPHALASTHA

**shōgaku** 正覺. *See* SAṂBODHI

**Shōgaku** 正覺. *See* HONGZHI ZHENGJUE

**shōge** 勝解. *See* ADHIMOKṢA

**shōgisō** 勝義僧. *See* PARAMĀRTHASAṂGHA

**shōgo** 正語. *See* SAMYAGVĀC

**shōgō** 正業. *See* SAMYAKKARMĀNTA

**shōgo** 證悟. *See* ZHENGWU

**shōgon** 正勤. *See* SAMYAKPRADHĀNA

**shōgusetsu** 性具說. *See* XINGJU SHUO

**shōgyō** 聖教. *See* ŚĀSANA

**shōhatsu** 生般. *See* UPAPADYAPARINIRVĀYIN

**shōhatsunehan** 生般涅槃. *See* UPAPADYAPARINIRVĀYIN

**shōhenchi** 正遍知. *See* SAMYAKSAṂBUDDHA

**shōhō** 證法. *See* ADHIGAMADHARMA

**shōichiraika** 證一來果. *See* SAKṚDĀGĀMIPHALASTHA

**shōja** 聖者. *See* MUNI

**shōja** 精舍. *See* VIHĀRA

**shōjichi** 生死智. *See* CYUTYUPAPATTIJÑĀNA

**shōjiki no shin** 正直心. *See* ADHYĀŚAYA

**shōjin** 精進. *See* VĪRYA

**shōjinharamita** 精進波羅蜜多. *See* VĪRYAPĀRAMITĀ

**shōjirinne** 生死輪迴. *See* SAṂSĀRA

**Shōjō** 小乘. *See* HĪNAYĀNA

**shōjō** 清淨. *See* PARIŚUDDHA, VAIYAVADĀNIKA, VISUDDHI

**shōjō** 正定. *See* SAMYAKSAMĀDHI

**shojō** 書狀. *See* SHUZHUANG

**shōjō bukkokudo** 清淨佛國土. *See* PARIŚUDDHABUDDHAKṢETRA, VIŚUDDHABUDDHAKṢETRA

**shōjōdōron** 清淨道論. *See* VIMOKṢAMĀRGA

**Shōjōkyō** 清淨經. *See* PĀSĀDIKASUTTA

**shojōryū** 所成立. *See* SĀDHYADHARMA

**shōjōten** 少淨天. *See* PARĪTTAŚUBHA

**shōju** 正受. *See* SAMĀPATTI

**Shōkarashu** 商羯羅主. *See* ŚAṂKARASVĀMIN

**shōken** 正見. *See* SAMYAGDṚṢṬI

**shoki** 書記. *See* SHUJI

**shōki** 生起. *See* UTPĀDA

**shōki** 性起. *See* XINGQI

**shōkishidai** 生起次第. *See* UTPATTIKRAMA

**shōkōten** 少光天. *See* PARĪTTĀBHA

**Shokyō yōshū** 諸經要集. *See* ZHUJING YAO JI

**Shōmangyō** 勝鬘經. *See* ŚRĪMĀLĀDEVĪSIṂHANĀDASŪTRA

**Shōman shishiku ichijō daihōben hōkōgyō** 勝鬘師子吼一乘大方便方廣經. *See* ŚRĪMĀLĀDEVĪSIṂHANĀDASŪTRA

**shōmon** 聲聞. *See* ŚRĀVAKA

**Shōmonji** 聲聞地. *See* ŚRĀVAKABHŪMI

**shōmonjō** 聲聞乘. *See* ŚRĀVAKAYĀNA

**shōmonshidai** 聲聞次第. *See* VIṂŚATIPRABHEDASAṂGHA

**shōmon shushō** 聲聞種姓. *See* ŚRĀVAKAGOTRA

**shōmyō** 正命. *See* SAMYAGĀJĪVA

**Shōmyōkichijō shinjitsumyōkyō** 聖妙吉祥眞實名經. *See* MAÑJUŚRĪNĀMASAṂGĪTI

**Shōnawashu** 商那和修. *See* ŚĀṆAKAVĀSIN

**shōnen** 正念. *See* SAMYAKSMṚTI

**shōnijōjaku** 照而常寂. *See* JI ER CHANGZHAO

**Shōnyakabasha** 商諾迦縛娑. *See* ŚĀṆAKAVĀSIN

**Shōrinji** 少林寺. *See* SHAOLINSI

**Shōronshū** 攝論宗. *See* SHE LUN ZONG

**Shōryōbu** 正量部. *See* SAṂMATĪYA

**shoryū** 所立. *See* SĀDHYADHARMA

**shōshi** 生支. *See* LIṄGA

**shōshin** 燒身. *See* SHAOSHEN

**shōshiyui** 正思惟. *See* SAMYAKSAṂKALPA, YONIŚOMANASKĀRA

**shōsho** 勝處. *See* ABHIBHVĀYATANA

**shōsho** 勝生. *See* ABHYUDAYA

**shōsho** 聲處. *See* ŚABDĀYATANA

**shōshōjin** 正精進. *See* SAMYAGVYĀYĀMA

**shōshōrishō** 正性離生. *See* SAMYAKTVANIYĀMĀVAKRĀNTI

**shōshu** 聖種. *See* ĀRYAVAṂŚA

**Shōshū** 性宗. *See* XING ZONG

**shoshunōshu funbetsu** 所取能取分別. *See* GRĀHYAGRĀHAKAVIKALPA

**shōsō** 聖僧. *See* ĀRYASAṂGHA

**shosoku** 所觸. *See* SPRAṢṬAVYA

**shōsoku** 床足. *See* KHAṬVĀṄGA

**shōtai** 聖諦. *See* FOUR NOBLE TRUTHS

**shotaiji** 所對治. *See* VIPAKṢABHŪTA

**Shōtennō hannya haramitsukyō** 勝天王般若波羅蜜經. *See* SUVIKRĀNTAVIKRĀMIPARIPṚCCHĀPRAJÑĀPĀRAMITĀ

**shōtenpōrin** 證轉法輪. *See* *SUVIBHAKTADHARMACAKRA

**shōtōgaku** 正等覺. *See* SAṂYAKSAṂBODHI

**shotoku** 所得. *See* UPALABDHI

**shōtokujō** 生得定. *See* DHYĀNOPAPATTI

**Shōyōroku** 從容録. *See* CONGRONG LU

**shōyoruka** 證預流果. *See* SROTAĀPANNAPHALASTHA

**shōzōmatsu** 正像末. *See* SADDHARMAPRATIRŪPAKA, SADDHARMAVIPRALOPA

**shu** 趣. *See* GATI

**shu** 珠. *See* MAṆI

**shū** 宗. *See* SIDDHĀNTA, ZONG

**shu** 取. *See* UPADĀNA

**shu** 修. *See* YOGA

**Shubatsudara** 須跋陀羅. *See* SUBHADRA

**Shubiyanyo** 須毘耶女. *See* SUPRIYĀ

**shūbō** [alt. shūhō] 宗法. *See* PAKṢADHARMA

**Shubodai** 須菩提. *See* SUBHŪTI

**shuchō** 竪超. *See* SHUCHAO

**Shudaina** 須提那. *See* SUDINNA

**Shudainu** [alt. Shudaina] 須大拏. *See* VESSANTARA

**shudaon** 須陀洹. *See* SROTAĀPANNA

**Shudatsu** 須達. *See* SUDATTA

**shudō** 修道. *See* BHAVANĀMĀRGA

**shue** 修慧. *See* BHĀVANĀMAYĪPRAJÑĀ

**shue** 衆會. *See* PARIṢAD

**shugaku** 衆學. *See* ŚAIKṢADHARMA

**Shugen** 衆賢. *See* SAṂGHABHADRA

**shugō[jigoku]** 衆合[地獄]. *See* SAṂGHĀTA

**shugyō** 修行. *See* PRATIPATTI, YOGA

**shugyōnin** 修行人. *See* YOGIN

**Shūimonsokuron** 集異門足論. *See* SAMGĪTIPARYĀYA [PĀDAŚĀSTRA]

**Shujata** 須闍多. *See* SUJĀTĀ

**shuji** 種子. *See* BĪJA

**shujinkō** 主人公. *See* ZHURENGONG

**shujō** 衆生. *See* SATTVA

**shujōjoku** 衆生濁. *See* SATTVAKAṢĀYA

**shujō seken** 衆生世間. *See* SATTVALOKA

**shujū** 修習. *See* BHĀVANĀ, YOGA

**shujukai chiriki** 種種界智力. *See* NĀNĀDHĀTUJÑĀNABALA

**Shujū shikan zazenhōyō** 修習止觀坐禪法要. *See* XIUXI ZHIGUAN ZUOCHAN FAYAO

**Shujushōge chiriki** 種種勝解智力. *See* NĀNĀDHIMUKTIJÑĀNABALA

**shukke** 出家. *See* PRAVRAJYĀ, PRAVRAJITA

**Shukō** 袾宏. *See* YUNQI ZHUHONG

**Shukōjō** 衆香城. *See* ZHONGXIANG CHENG

**shukujūzuinen** 宿住隨念. *See* PURVANIVĀSĀNUSMṚTI

**shukumyō** 宿命. *See* JĀTISMARA, PURVANIVĀSĀNUSMṚTI

**Shumisen** 須彌山. *See* SUMERU, MT

**Shūmon jikkiron** 宗門十規論. *See* ZONGMEN SHIGUI LUN

**shumonnin** 守門人. *See* DVĀRAPĀLA

**Shūmon rentōeyō** 宗門聯燈會要. *See* ZONGMEN LIANDENG HUIYAO

**Shūmon wakumon** 宗門或問. *See* ZONGMEN HUOMEN

**shūmu** 執無. *See* NĀSTIKA

**Shuna** 輸那. *See* SOṆĀ

**Shunaka** 須那迦. *See* SOṆA AND UTTARA

**Shūna monkengyō** 周那問見經. *See* SALLEKHASUTTA

**Shūnanzan** 終南山. *See* ZHONGNANSHAN

**Shūrihandoku** 周利槃特. *See* ŚUDDHIPANTHAKA

**Shurōna** 守籠那. *See* SOṆA KOLIVĪSA

**Shurona** 輸盧那. *See* ŚROṆĀPARĀNTA

**Shuryōgongyō** 首楞嚴經. *See* ŚŪRAṂGAMASŪTRA

**Shuryōgonzanmai** 首楞嚴三昧. *See* ŚŪRAṂGAMASAMĀDHI

**Shuryōgonzanmaikyō** 首楞嚴三昧經. *See* ŚŪRAṂGAMASAMĀDHISŪTRA

**Shushin yōron** 修心要論. *See* XIUXIN YAO LUN

**shushō** 種性. *See* GOTRA

**shushu** 衆主. *See* VAIYĀPṚTYAKARA

**Shushūkyō** 衆集經. *See* SAṄGĪTISUTTA

**shūshushō** 習種性. *See* SAMUDĀNĪTAGOTRA

**shussedō** 出世道. *See* LOKUTTARAMAGGA

**shusseka** 出世果. *See* LOKUTTARAPHALA

**shusseken** 出世間. *See* LOKOTTARA

**shusse sanmai** 出世三昧. *See* LOKUTTARASAMĀDHI

**Shusui** 守遂. *See* DAHONG SHOUSUI

**Shutan** 守端. *See* BAIYUN SHOUDUAN

**Shutchōgyō** 出曜經. *See* UDĀNAVARGA

**Shutokugyō** 種德經. *See* SOṆADAṆḌASUTTA

**shutokujō** 修得定. *See* DHYĀNASAMĀPATTI

**shutsuri** 出離. *See* NAIṢKRAMYA, NIRYĀṆA

**Shutsusanzōki shū** 出三藏記集. *See* CHU SANZANG JIJI

**shutsuyōshi** 出要志. *See* NAIṢKRAMYA

**shutsuzai** 出罪. *See* ABHYĀYANA

**shuun** 取蘊. *See* UPĀDĀNASKANDHA

**shuza** 首座. *See* SHOUZUO

**Shuzai** 守財. *See* DHANAPĀLA, NĀLĀGIRI

**sō** 相. *See* LAKṢAṆA, LIṄGA, NIMITTA

**sō** 想. *See* SAṂJÑĀ

**Sobakodōji shōmongyō** 蘇婆呼童子請問經. *See* SUBĀHUPARIPṚCCHĀTANTRA

**Sobinda** 蘇頻陀. *See* SUBINDA

**sōdō** 僧堂. *See* SENGTANG

**Sodōshū** 祖堂集. *See* ZUTANG JI

**Sōgen Dōshō** 曹源道生. *See* Caoyuan Daosheng

**sōgishi** 僧祇支. *See* saṃkakṣikā

**sōgya** 僧伽. *See* saṅgha

**Sōgyabatsuma** 僧伽跋摩. *See* Saṃghavarman

**Sōgyamitta** 僧伽蜜多. *See* Saṅghamittā

**sōgyari** 僧伽梨. *See* saṃghāṭī

**Sōgyase** 僧伽施. *See* Sāṃkāśya

**sōji** 總持. *See* dhāraṇī

**sōjinpen** 雙神變. *See* yamakaprātihārya

**sōjō** 相承. *See* paramparā

**Sōjō** 僧肇. *See* Sengzhao

**sōjumetsu** 想受滅. *See* saṃjñāvedayitanirodha

**sōka** 僧科. *See* sŭngkwa

**Sōka** 僧果. *See* Sengguo

**Sōkeizan** 曹溪山. *See* Caoxishan

**Sōkō** 宗杲. *See* Dahui Zonggao

**sōkonma** 僧羯磨. *See* saṃghakarman

**Sō kōsōden** 宋高僧傳. *See* Song gaoseng zhuan

**soku** 觸. *See* sparśa

**sokujiin** 觸地印. *See* bhūmisparśamudrā

**sokusai** 息災. *See* śānticāra

**sokusho** 觸處. *See* spraṣṭavyāyatana

**Sōkyō** 想經. *See* Mūlapariyāyasutta

**Sōmō** 僧猛. *See* Sengmeng

**Sondarananda** 孫陀羅難陀. *See* Sundarananda

**Sondari** 孫陀利. *See* Sundarīnandā

**songen** 損減. *See* apavāda

**sōnyū** 雙入. *See* yuganaddha

**sōō** 相應. *See* saṃprayukta

**sōōin** 相應因. *See* saṃprayuktahetu

**sōrin** 叢林. *See* conglin

**Sōri shūkyō mokuroku** 綜理衆經目錄. *See* Zongli zhongjing mulu

**Sōrō** 僧朗. *See* Sŭngnang

**Sōsan** 僧粲. *See* Sengcan

**soshi** 祖師. *See* zushi

**Soshijjikarakyō** 蘇悉地羯羅經. *See* Susiddhikarasūtra

**Sōshū** 相宗. *See* Xiang school

**Sotei jion** 祖庭事苑. *See* Zuting shiyuan

**Sotei kantsuiroku** 祖庭鉗鎚錄. *See* Zuting qianchui lu

**Sōtōshū** 曹洞宗. *See* Caodong zong

**sōun** 雙運. *See* yuganaddha

**Sōyū** 僧祐. *See* Sengyou

**sōzanhō** 僧殘法. *See* saṃghāvaśesa

**Sōzan Honjaku** 曹山本寂. *See* Caoshan Benji

**sōzanzai** 僧殘罪. *See* saṃghāvaśesa

**sōzoku** 相續. *See* saṃtāna

**sōzoku mujō** 相續無常. *See* er wuchang

**sōzokushiki** 相續識. *See* ādānavijñāna

**Sugyōroku** 宗鏡録. *See* Zongjing lu

**suidai** 水大. *See* āpas [alt. āpodhātu]

**Suigatsu Kannon** 水月觀音. *See* Shuiyue Guanyin

**suijaku** 垂迹. *See* Honji suijaku

**suiji** 垂示. *See* chuishi

**Suijōbonjikyō** 水淨梵志經. *See* Vatthūpamasutta

**Suikiyakyō** 蕤呬耶經. *See* Sarvamaṇḍalasāmānyavidhiguhyatantra

**suimen** 睡眠. *See* middha

**suirikue** 水陸會. *See* shuilu hui

**suisokuza** 垂足坐. *See* pralambapādāsana

**susokukan** 數息觀. *See* ānāpānasati

**Sūzan** 嵩山. *See* Songshan

## T

**tahiryō** 他比量. *See* parārthānumāna

**Tahō nyorai** 多寶如來. *See* Prabhūtaratna

**tai** 退. *See* parihāṇi

**tai** 諦. *See* satya

**tai** 體. *See* ti

**Taigen** 太賢. *See* T'aehyŏn

**taihō** 對法. *See* abhidharma

**taihō shashi** 對法諸師. *See* ābhidharmika

**taiji** 對治. *See* pratipakṣa

**taiki** 對機. *See* duiji

**taiki seppō** 對機說法. *See* duiji shuofa

**tairaku** 大樂. *See* mahāsukha

**Taishaku** 帝釋. *See* Śakra, Indra

**Taishakumō** 帝釋網. *See* Indrajāla

**Taishaku shomongyō** 帝釋所問經. *See* Sakkapañhasutta

**taishu** 對首. *See* pratideśanīya

**Taiyō Kyōgen** 大陽警玄. *See* Dayang Jingxuan

**tajuyūshin** 他受用身. *See* para-saṃbhogakāya

**takejizaiten** 他化自在天. *See* paranirmitavaśavartin

**Takkan Shinka** 達觀眞可. *See* Daguan Zhenke

**Tamonbu** 多聞部. *See* Bahuśrutīya

**Tamonten** 多聞天. *See* Vaiśravaṇa

**tanda** 單墮. *See* pāyattika

**Tannen Enchō** 湛然圓澄. *See* Zhanran Yuandeng

**Tara** 多羅. *See* Tārā

**tashintsū** 他心通. *See* paracittajñāna

**teikō** 提綱. *See* tichang

**teishō** 提唱. *See* tichang

**teiyō** 提要. *See* tichang

**teizen no hakujushi** 庭前柏樹子. *See* tingqian boshuzi

**ten** 天. *See* deva

**ten'ai** 天愛. *See* devānāṃ priyaḥ

**tenbōrin** 轉法輪. *See* dharmacakrapravartana

**Tenbōringyō** 轉法輪經. *See* Dhammacakkappavattanasutta

**Tenbōrin'in** 轉法輪印. *See* dharmacakramudrā

**tenchūten** 天中天. *See* devātideva

**Tendai Chigi** 天台智顗. *See* Tiantai Zhiyi

**Tendai goji** 天台五時. *See* Tiantai wushi

**Tendai hakkyō** 天台八教. *See* Tiantai bajiao

**Tendai shikyōgi** 天台四教儀. *See* Ch'ŏnt'ae sagyo ŭi

**tendō** 顚倒. *See* viparyāsa

**Tendō Nyojō** 天童如浄. *See* Tiantong Rujing

**ten'e** 轉依. *See* āśrayaparāvṛtti

**tengai** 天界. *See* devaloka

**tengen** 點眼. *See* dianyan, netrapratiṣṭhāpana

**tengerai** 天下來. *See* devāvatāra

**tengesho** 天下處. *See* devāvatāra

**Tenjiku** 天竺. *See* dianyan, netrapratiṣṭhāpana

**tenjin** 天神. *See* devatā

**tenjō** 天上. *See* devaloka, svarga

**tenni** 天耳. *See* divyaśrotra

**tennō** 天王. *See* devarājan

**tennyo** 天女. *See* apsaras

**Tenrinjōō shugyōkyō** 轉輪聖王修行經. *See* Cakkavattisīhanādasutta

**tenrin'ō** 轉輪王. *See* cakravartin

**tenryū hachibu** 天龍八部. *See* aṣṭāsena

**tensa** 展左. *See* pratyālīḍha

**tensekai** 天世界. *See* devaloka

**Tensokusai** 天息災. *See* Tianxizai

**Tensongyō** 典尊經. *See* Mahāgovindasutta

**tenzo** 典座. *See* dianzuo

**Tesshirin** 鐵刺林. *See* Ayaḥśālmalīvana

**tetchisen** 鐵圍山. *See* cakravāḍa

**tō** 塔. *See* stūpa

**Tōbamara** 沓婆摩羅. *See* Dravya Mallaputra

**Tōezō** 塘煨增. *See* Kukūla

**tōfū** 刀風. *See* daofeng

**tōin** 等引. *See* samāhita

**tōinchi** 等引智. *See* samāhitajñāna

**tōji** 等至. *See* samāpatti

**tōjinro** 刀刃路. *See* kṣuramārga

**Tojo** 都序. *See* Chanyuan zhuquanji duxu

**Tojun** 杜順. *See* Dushun

**Tōkangyō** 稲稈經. *See* Śālistambasūtra

**tōkatsu[jigoku]** 等活[地獄]. *See* saṃjīva

**tokira** 突吉羅. *See* duṣkṛta

**Tokkō** 德光. *See* Fozhao Deguang

**Tokkō** 德光. *See* Guṇaprabha

**toku** 得. *See* pattidāna

**tokuka** 得果. *See* phalapratipannaka

**Tokusan Senkan** 德山宣鑑. *See* Deshan Xuanjian

**Tokusei** 德清. *See* Hanshan Deqing

**Tokushibu** 犢子部. *See* Vātsīputrīya

**tōmuken'en** 等無間緣. *See* samanantarapratyaya

**ton** 貪. *See* abhidhyā, lobha, rāga

**tongo** 頓悟. *See* dunwu

**Tongo nyūdō yōmonron** 頓悟入道要門論. *See* Dunwu rudao yaomen lun

**tongo zenshu** 頓悟漸修. *See* dunwu jianxiu

**tongyō** 頓教. *See* dunjiao

**Tonkō** 敦煌. *See* Dunhuang

**Tōrinji** 東林寺. *See* Donglinsi

**tōriten** 忉利天. *See* trāyastriṃśa

**tōruka** 等流果. *See* niṣyandaphala

**Tōsan Shusho** 洞山守初. *See* Dongshan Shouchu

**tosotsuten** 兜率天. *See* tuṣita

**Tōsu Gisei** 投子義青. *See* Touzi Yiqing

**Tōtō Risshū** 東塔律宗. *See* Dongta lüzong

**Tōzan** 東山. *See* Pūrvaśaila

**Tōzan hōmon** 東山法門. *See* Dongshan famen

**Tōzan Ryōkai** 洞山良价. *See* Dongshan Liangjie

**tōzu** 刀塗. *See* daotu

**tsū** 通. *See* pariyatti

**tsūdatsu** 通達. *See* prativedha

**tsūsu** 都寺/司. *See* dusi

**Tsūyō** 通容. *See* Feiyin Tongrong

## U

**u** 有. *See* bhava

**U** 于. *See* Yu

**ubai** 優婆夷. *See* upāsikā

**ubaikai** 優婆夷戒. *See* upāsikāsaṃvara

**Ubakikuta** 優婆毱多. *See* Upagupta

**Ubarashiki** 優波羅色. *See* Utpalavarṇā

**Ubarikyō** 優婆離經. *See* Upālisutta

**ubasoku** 優婆塞. *See* upāsaka

**uchōten** 有頂天. *See* bhavāgra

**udai** 有大. *See* bhautika

**Udai** 優陀夷. *See* Udāyin

**udana** 優陀那. *See* udāna

**udonge** 優曇華. *See* udumbara

**ugyōhatsunehan** 有行般涅槃. *See* sābhisaṃskāraparinirvāyin

**ui** 有爲. *See* saṃskṛta

**uisō** 有爲相. *See* saṃskṛtalakṣaṇa

**ujō** 有情. *See* sattva

**ujō seken** 有情世間. *See* sattvaloka

**un** 蘊. *See* skandha

**Ungyō** 吽形. *See* Niō

**Unkō** 雲崗. *See* Yungang

**unma** 蘊魔. *See* skandhamāra

**Unmon Bun'en** 雲門文偃. *See* Yunmen Wenyan

**Unmonshū** 雲門宗. *See* Yunmen zong

**Unnan Fugan** 運庵普巖. *See* Yunan Puyan

**Unsei Shukō** 雲棲袾宏. *See* Yunqi Zhuhong

**unyō** 右遶. *See* pradakṣiṇa

**upadaisha** 優波提舍. *See* upadeśa

**Upananda** 優波難陀. *See* Upananda

**Upari** 優波離. *See* Upāli

**Upashina** 優波斯那. *See* Upasena

**urabon** 盂蘭盆. *See* ullambana, yulanpen

**Urabongyō** 盂蘭盆經. *See* Yulanpen jing

**urin** 有輪. *See* bhavacakra

**uro** 有漏. *See* sāsrava

**uroun** 有漏蘊. *See* sāsravaskandha

**Urubinra** 優樓頻螺. *See* Uruvilvā

**Urubinra Kashō** 優樓頻螺迦葉. *See* Uruvilvā-Kāśyapa

**Urukya** 優樓佉. *See* Ulūka

**ushinken** 有身見. *See* SATKĀYADṚṢṬI

**usō** 有相. *See* SĀKARA

**Uten** 于闐. *See* KHOTAN

**Uten'ō Shakazō** 優塡王 釋迦像. *See* UDĀYANA BUDDHA

**Utsukada** 欝伽陀. *See* UDGATA

**Utsuzuranhotsu** 欝頭藍弗. *See* UDRAKA RĀMAPUTRA

**Uttara** 欝多羅. *See* SOṆA AND UTTARA

**uyonehan** 有餘涅槃. *See* SOPĀDHIŚEṢANIRVĀṆA

## W

**wajō** 和尚. *See* HESHANG, UPĀDHYĀYA

**wajō** 和諍. *See* HWAJAENG

**wake** 汚家. *See* KULADŪṢAKA

**Wanshi Shōgaku** 宏智正覺. *See* HONGZHI ZHENGJUE

**watō** 話頭. *See* HUATOU

## Y

**yakukyō sanzō** 譯經三藏. *See* YIJING SANZANG

**Yakuō bosatsu** 藥王菩薩. *See* BHAIṢAJYARĀJA

**yakuseki** 藥石. *See* YAOSHI

**Yakushi hongangyō** 藥師本願經. *See* BHAIṢAJYAGURUSŪTRA

**Yakushi nyorai** 藥師如來. *See* BHAIṢAJYAGURU

**Yamaten** 夜摩天. *See* YĀMA

**yasha** 夜叉. *See* YAKṢA

**Yasha** 耶舍. *See* YAŚAS

**Yashudara** 耶輸陀羅. *See* YAŚODHARĀ

**Yō Bunkai** 楊文會. *See* YANG WENHUI

**yogaku** 與學. *See* ŚIKṢĀDATTAKA

**Yōgiha** 楊岐派. *See* YANGQI PAI

**Yōgi Hōe** 楊岐方會. *See* YANGQI FANGHUI

**Yōka Genkaku** 永嘉玄覺. *See* YONGJIA XUANJUE

**yoku** 欲. *See* KĀMA, CHANDA

**Yokukai** 欲界. *See* KĀMADHĀTU

**yokuton** 欲貪. *See* KĀMARĀGA

**Yōmei Enju** 永明延壽. *See* YONGMING YANSHOU

**Yoru[ka]** 預流[果]. *See* SROTAĀPANNA

**yorukō** 預流向. *See* SROTAĀPANNAPHALAPRATIPANNAKA

**yū** 用. *See* YONG

**yuga** 瑜伽. *See* YOGA

**Yugagyōha** 瑜伽行派. *See* YOGĀCĀRA

**Yugashiji** 瑜伽師地. *See* YOGĀCĀRABHŪMI

**Yugashijiron** 瑜伽師地論. *See* YOGĀCĀRABHŪMIŚĀSTRA

**yugyōja** 遊行者. *See* PARIVRĀJAKA

**Yūgyōkyō** 遊行經. *See* MAHĀPARINIBBĀNASUTTANTA

**yuige** 遺偈. *See* YIJI

**Yuikyōgyō** 遺教經. *See* YIJIAO JING

**Yuimagyō** 維摩經. *See* VIMALAKĪRTINIRDEŚA

**Yuimakitsu** 維摩詰. *See* VIMALAKĪRTI

**Yuimakitsu shosetsukyōchū** 維摩詰所説經註. *See* WEIMOJIE SUOSHUO JING ZHU

**Yuinichi manihōkyō** 遺日摩尼寶經. *See* KĀŚYAPAPARIVARTA

**yuishiki** 唯識. *See* VIJÑAPTIMĀTRATĀ

**Yuishiki nijūron** 唯識二十論. *See* VIṂŚATIKĀ

**Yuishiki sanjūronju** 唯識三十論頌. *See* TRIṂŚIKĀ

**Yuishikishū** 唯識宗. *See* FAXIANG ZONG, VIJÑĀNAVĀDA, WEISHI ZONG

**yuishin** 唯心. *See* CITTAMĀTRA

**yuishin** 遺身. *See* YISHEN

**yuishin no jōdo** 唯心淨土. *See* WEIXIN JINGTU

**Yuishinketsu** 唯心訣. *See* WEIXIN JUE

**yujun** 由旬. *See* YOJANA

**Yūken chōja** 勇健長者. *See* SŪRA AMBAṬṬHA

**yūmyō** 勇猛. *See* VĪRA

**yūmyōshōjin** 勇猛精進. *See* YONGMAENG CHŎNGJIN

**Yūshin anrakudō** 遊心安樂道. *See* YUSIM ALLAK TO

## Z

**za** 座. *See* ĀSANA

**zagu** 坐具. *See* NIṢĪDANA

**zahō** 坐法. *See* ĀSANA

**zai** 罪. *See* PĀPA

**zaijizai** 財自在. *See* PARIṢKĀRAVAŚITĀ

**zaike** 在家. *See* GṚHASTHA

**zaise** 財施. *See* ĀMIṢADĀNA

**zan** 慚. *See* HRĪ

**zazen** 坐禪. *See* ZUOCHAN

**zekkon** 舌根. *See* JIHVENDRIYA

**zen** 善. *See* KUŚALA

**zen** 染. *See* SAṂKLEŚA

**zenbō** 禪房/禪坊. *See* PRAHĀṆAŚĀLĀ

**zenchishiki** 善知識. *See* KALYĀṆAMITRA

**zendō** 禪堂. *See* SENGTANG

**Zendō** 善導. *See* SHANDAO

**Zen'e** 善慧. *See* SUMEDHA

**Zen'eji** 善慧地. *See* SĀDHUMATĪ

**Zengen shosenshū tojo** 禪源諸詮集都序. *See* CHANYUAN ZHUQUANJI DUXU

**zengenten** 善現天. *See* SUDṚŚA

**Zengetsu Kankyū** 禪月貫休. *See* CHANYUE GUANXIU

**Zengetsu shū** 禪月集. *See* CHANYUE JI

**zengo** 漸悟. *See* JIANWU

**zengon** 善根. *See* KUŚALAMŪLA

**zen'i seppō** 漸爲說法. *See* ANUPUBBIKATHĀ

**zenji** 禪師. *See* CHANSHI

**Zenkan sakushin** 禪關策進. *See* CHANGUAN CEJIN

**Zenke kikan** 禪家龜鑑. *See* SŎNGA KWIGAM

**Zenken** 禪賢. *See* ZHIKONG CHANXIAN

**Zenkenritsubibasha** 善見律毘婆沙. *See* SAMANTAPĀSĀDIKĀ

**zenkenten** 善見天. *See* SUDARŚANA

**zenmana** 染末那. *See* KLIṢṬAMANAS

**Zenmon kishiki** 禪門規式. *See* CHANMEN GUISHI

**Zenmon satsuyō** 禪門撮要. *See* SŎNMUN CH'WARYO

**Zenmui** 善無畏. *See* ŚUBHAKARASIṂHA

**zennanshi** 善男子. *See* KULAPUTRA

**Zennyakyō** 善夜經. *See* BHADRAKĀRĀTRĪ

**zennyonin** 善女人. *See* KULADUHITṚ

**Zen'on shingi** 禪苑清規. *See* CHANYUAN QINGGUI

**Zenpiyōhōkyō** 禪秘要法經. *See* CHAN MIYAOFA JING

**Zenrai** 善來. *See* SĀGATA

**zenrai bisshu** 善來苾芻. *See* EHIBHIKṢUKĀ

**Zenrin hōkun** 禪林寶訓. *See* CHANLIN BAOXUN

**Zenrin sōbōden** 禪林僧寶傳. *See* CHANLIN SENGBAO ZHUAN

**Zensai** 善歲. *See* SUVARṢAKA

**zenshi** 禪支. *See* DHYĀNĀṄGA

**zenshinshari** 全身舍利. *See* QUANSHEN SHELI

**Zenshō** 善星. *See* SUNAKṢATRA

**Zenshōgakusen** 前正覺山. *See* PRĀGBODHI(GIRI)

**Zenshōkyō** 善生經. *See* SIGĀLOVĀDASUTTA

**zenshu/zenshū** 漸修. *See* JIANXIU

**zenshu** 善趣. *See* SUGATI

**Zenshū Yōka shū** 禪宗永嘉集. *See* CHANZONG YONGJIA JI

**Zen'yō** 禪要. *See* CHANYAO, GAOFENG HESHANG CHANYAO

**Zenzai** 善財. *See* SUDHANA

**zenzei** 善逝. *See* SUGATA

**zesshiki** 舌識. *See* JIHVĀVIJÑĀNA

**zessho** 舌處. *See* JIHVĀYATANA

**Zetsukanron** 絶觀論. *See* JUEGUAN LUN

**zō** 藏. *See* PIṬAKA

**Zōabidon shinron** 雜阿毘曇心論. *See* SAṂYUKTĀBHIDHARMAHṚDAYA[ŚĀSTRA]

**Zōagongyō** 雜阿含經. *See* SAṂYUKTĀGAMA, SAṂYUTTANIKĀYA

**Zōbō ketsugikyō** 像法決疑經. *See* XIANGFA JUEYI JING

**zōhō** 像法. *See* XIANGFA

**Zōichiagongyō** 增壹阿含經. *See* EKOTTARĀGAMA, AṄGUTTARANIKĀYA

**zōjishōbō** 像似正法. *See* SADDHARMAPRATIRŪPAKA, XIANGFA

**zōjōegaku** 增上慧學. *See* ADHIPRAJÑĀŚIKṢA

**zōjōen** 增上緣. *See* ADHIPATIPRATYAYA

**zōjōjōgaku** 增上定學. *See* ADHISAMĀDHIŚIKṢĀ

**zōjōka** 增上果. *See* ADHIPATIPHALA

**zōjōkaigaku** 增上戒學. *See* ADHIŚĪLAŚIKṢA

**zōjōman** 增上慢. *See* ADHIMĀNA

**Zōjōshingyō** 增上心經. *See* VITAKKASAṆṬHĀNASUTTA

**Zōjōten** 增長天. *See* VIRŪḌHAKA

**zoku** 俗. *See* SAṂVṚTI

**Zoku kōsōden** 續高僧傳. *See* XU GAOSENG ZHUAN

**zokutai** 俗諦. *See* SAṂVṚTISATYA, VYAVAHĀRA

**Zōkyō** 像教. *See* XIANGJIAO

**Zōshakuyugyō** 象跡喻經. *See* CŪḶAHATTHIPADOPAMASUTTA, MAHĀHATTHIPADOPAMASUTTA

**zōshu** [alt. ZŌSU] 藏主. *See* ZANGZHU

**zōyaku** 增益. *See* SAMĀROPA

**zuda[gyō]** 頭陀[行]. *See* DHUTAṄGA

**zuibonnō** 隨煩惱. *See* UPAKLEŚA

**zuihōgyō** 隨法行. *See* DHARMĀNUSĀRIN

**zuiki** 隨喜. *See* ANUMODANA

**zuikifuku** 隨喜福. *See* PUṆYĀNUMODANA

**zuimen** 隨眠. *See* ANUŚAYA

**zuimon** 隨聞. *See* ANUŚRAVA

**zuinen funbetsu** 隨念分別. *See* ANUSMARAṆAVIKALPA

**zuirukō zenjō** 隨流向禪定. *See* SROTO'NUGATO NĀMA SAMĀDHIḤ

**zuishingyō** 隨信行. *See* ŚRADDHĀNUSĀRIN

**zuisō** 瑞相. *See* NIMITTA

**zukō** 頭光. *See* TOUGUANG

**zuzō** 圖像. *See* YANTRA

# Korean Cross-References

## A

**a** 我. *See* ĀTMAN

**abadana** 阿波陀那. *See* AVADĀNA

**Abanje [kuk]** 阿般提[國]. *See* AVANTI

**abi chiok** 阿鼻地獄. *See* AVĪCI

**abidalma** 阿毘達磨. *See* ABHIDHARMA

**Abidalma kusa non** 阿毘達磨俱舍論. *See* ABHIDHARMAKOŚABHĀṢYA

**Abidalma kyesin chok non** 阿毘達磨界身足論. *See* ABHIDHARMADHĀTUKĀYA[PĀDAŚĀSTRA], DHĀTUKĀYA[PĀDAŚĀSTRA]

**Abidalma palchi non** 阿毘達磨發智論. *See* ABHIDHARMAJÑĀNAPRASTHĀNA, JÑĀNAPRASTHĀNA

**Abidalma pŏbon chok non** 阿毘達磨法蘊足論. *See* ABHIDHARMADHARMASKANDHA[PĀDAŚĀSTRA], DHARMASKANDHA-[PĀDAŚĀSTRA]

**Abidalma taebibasa non** 阿毘達磨大毘婆沙論. *See* ABHIDHARMAMAHĀVIBHĀṢĀ

**abidalma taeronsa** 阿毘達磨大論師. *See* ĀBHIDHARMIKA

**Abidam sim non** 阿毘曇心論. *See* *ABHIDHARMAHṚDAYA

**abiraje** 阿比羅提. *See* ABHIRATI

**abujŏ** 阿嚩底. *See* AVADHŪTĪ

**Achamal posal kyŏng** 阿差末菩薩經. *See* AKṢAYAMATINIRDEŚA

**Ach'ok pul** 阿閦佛. *See* AKṢOBHYA

**Ach'ok pulguk kyŏng** 阿閦佛國經. *See* AKṢOBHYATATHĀGATASYAVYŪHA

**ae** 愛. *See* TṚṢṆĀ

**Aengmu kyŏng** 鸚鵡經. *See* SUBHASUTTANTA

**aengmu sŏn** 鸚鵡禪. *See* YINGWU CHAN

**agwi** 餓鬼. *See* PRETA

**Aham kyŏng** 阿含經. *See* ĀGAMA

**Ailta** 阿逸多. *See* AJITA

**aje aje para-aje parasŭngaje moji sabaha** 揭帝揭帝波羅揭帝波羅僧揭帝菩提薩婆訶. *See* GATE GATE PĀRAGATE PĀRASAṂGATE BODHI SVĀHĀ

**Ajiguda** 阿地瞿多. *See* ATIKŪṬA

**ajip** 我執. *See* ĀTMAGRĀHA, AHAṂKĀRA

**ak** 惡. *See* PĀPA

**akchak** 惡作. *See* DUṢKṚTA

**akch'wi** 惡趣. *See* DURGATI

**akku** 惡口. *See* PĀRUṢYA

**akkyŏn** 惡見. *See* AKUŚALADṚṢṬI, MITHYĀDṚṢṬI

**aksŏl** 惡說. *See* DURBHĀṢITA

**Allak kuk** 安楽國. *See* ANLEGUO

**am** 菴. *See* AN

**aman** 我慢. *See* AHAṂKĀRA

**Amarasik** 阿摩羅識. *See* AMALAVIJÑĀNA

**Ambaranyŏ** 菴婆羅女. *See* AMBAPĀLĪ

**amisa** 阿尾奢. *See* ĀVEŚA

**Amit'a kup'um in** 阿彌陀九品印. *See* AMITUO JIUPIN YIN

**Amit'a kyŏng** 阿彌陀經. *See* AMITĀBHASŪTRA

**Amit'a pul** 阿彌陀佛. *See* AMITĀBHA

**amsil** 庵室. *See* ANJITSU

**an** 眼. *See* CAKṢUS

**anaham** 阿那含. *See* ANĀGĀMIN

**Anan** 阿難. *See* ĀNANDA

**Anayul** 阿那律. *See* ANIRUDDHA

**Anban suŭi kyŏng** 安般守意經. *See* ANBAN SHOUYI JING

**anch'ŏ** 眼處. *See* CAKṢURĀYATANA

**Anggulmara** 央掘摩羅. *See* AṄGULIMĀLA

**Anggulmara kyŏng** 央掘摩羅經. *See* AṄGULIMĀLĪYASŪTRA

**an'gŏ** 安居. *See* ANGO

**Angsan Hyejŏk** 仰山慧寂. *See* YANGSHAN HUIJI

**an'gŭn** 眼根. *See* CAKṢURINDRIYA

**Anhye** 安慧. *See* Sthiramati

**Anju chisin** 安住地神. *See* Sthāvarā

**Annabannanyŏm** 安那般那念. *See* Ānāpānasatisūtta

**Anon** 安穩. *See* Kṣemā

**An Sego** 安世高. *See* An Shigao

**ansik** 眼識. *See* cakṣurvijñāna

**Ansik kuk** 安息國. *See* Anxi guo; Parthia

**Ansim** 安心. *See* anxin

**Ant'aek sinju kyŏng** 安宅神呪經. *See* Anzhai shenzhou jing

**Anui kyŏng** 阿㝹夷經. *See* Pāṭikasutta

**anwi in** 安慰印. *See* vitarkamudrā

**Anyang kye** 安養界. *See* Anyang jie

**anyoktara sammyak sambori** 阿耨多羅三藐三菩提. *See* anuttarasamyaksaṃbodhi

**aŏ** 我語. *See* ātmavāda

**arahan** 阿羅漢. *See* arhat

**arahan hyang** 阿羅漢向. *See* arhatpratipannaka

**[a]ranya** [阿]蘭若. *See* āraṇya

**Araragaran** 阿羅邏迦蘭. *See* Ārāḍa Kālāma

**Arit'a kyŏng** 阿梨吒經. *See* Alagaddūpamasutta

**aroeya sik** 阿賴耶識. *See* ālayavijñāna

**Asase wang** 阿闍世王. *See* Ajātaśatru

**Asat'a** 阿私陀. *See* Asita

**aso** 我所. *See* mamakāra

**Asŏlsi** 阿說示. *See* Aśvajit

**asŭnggi** 阿僧祇. *See* asaṃkhya

**asŭnggi kŏp** 阿僧祇劫. *See* asaṃkheyakalpa

**at'ana sik** 阿陀那識. *See* ādānavijñāna

**Ayakkyojinyŏ** 阿若憍陳如. *See* Ājñātakauṇḍinya

**Ayuk wang** 阿育王. *See* Aśoka

**Ayuk wang chŏn** 阿育王傳. *See* Aśokāvadāna

## C

**cha** 慈. *See* maitrī

**ch'a** 遮. *See* pratiṣedha

**Ch'abara t'ap** 遮婆羅塔. *See* Cāpālacaitya

**chabi** 慈悲. *See* maitrī

**chabiryang** 自比量. *See* svārthānumāna

**chae** 齋. *See* zhai

**chaega** 在家. *See* gṛhastha

**chaejajae** 財自在. *See* pariṣkāravaśitā

**chaengsa** 諍事. *See* adhikaraṇa

**chaengsong** 諍訟. *See* adhikaraṇa

**chaesa** 再死. *See* punarmṛtyu, rebirth

**chaesaeng** 再生. *See* punarjanman, rebirth

**chaesi** 財施. *See* āmiṣadāna

**chagak** 自覺. *See* svasaṃvedana

**chagu** 資具. *See* pariṣkāra

**chagŭi** 作意. *See* manasikāra

**Chahwanhŭi kyŏng** 自歡喜經. *See* Sampasādanīyasutta

**chaja** 自恣. *See* pravāraṇā

**chajae** 自在. *See* aiśvarya, vaṣitā

**ch'aje samgwan** 次第三觀. *See* sanguan

**ch'aje samje** 次第三諦. *See* cidi sandi

**ch'aje sŏlpŏp** 次第說法. *See* anupubbikathā

**ch'aje yŏn** 次第緣. *See* anantarapratyaya

**Chajon** 慈尊. *See* Maitreyanātha

**Cha kyŏng** 慈經. *See* Mettāsutta

**ch'alla** 刹那. *See* kṣaṇa

**ch'alla kujok** 刹那具足. *See* kṣaṇasampad

**ch'alla kyŏng** 刹那頃. *See* kṣaṇika

**ch'allaron** 刹那論. *See* kṣaṇikavāda

**ch'alli** 刹利. *See* kṣatriya

**ch'am** 慚. *See* hrī

**Ch'amdong kye** 参同契. *See* Cantong qi

**ch'amhoe** 懺悔. *See* pāpadeśana

**Chamin Hyeil** 慈愍慧日. *See* Cimin Huiri

**chang** 障. *See* āvaraṇa

**chang** 藏. *See* piṭaka

**Chang aham kyŏng** 長阿含經. *See* Dīrghāgama, Dīghanikāya

**changja** 長者. *See* gṛhapati

**changju** 藏主. *See* ZANGZHU

**Changno Chongsaek** 長蘆宗賾. *See* CHANGLU ZONGZE

**Chang Sangyŏng** 張商英. *See* ZHANG SHANGYING

**changsik** 藏識. *See* ĀLAYAVIJÑĀNA

**Changsu** 長壽. *See* KOSAMBIYASUTTA

**Ch'anik** 車匿. *See* CHANDAKA

**Ch'anjip paegyŏn kyŏng** 撰集百緣經. *See* AVADĀNAŚATAKA

**Ch'annyŏng** 贊寧. *See* ZANNING

**Ch'an pŏpkye song** 讚法界頌. *See* DHARMADHĀTUSTAVA

**Chap abidam sim non** 雜阿毘曇心論. *See* SAṂYUKTĀBHIDHARMAHṚDAYA

**Chap aham kyŏng** 雜阿含經. *See* SAṂYUKTĀGAMA, SAṂYUTTANIKĀYA

**chari** 自利. *See* SVĀRTHA

**charyang** 資糧. *See* SAṂBHĀRA

**charyang to** 資糧道. *See* SAṂBHĀRAMĀRGA

**charyŏk** 自力. *See* JIRIKI

**chasang** 自相. *See* SVALAKṢAṆA

**chasang kong** 自相空. *See* SVALAKṢAṆAŚŪNYA

**chasŏng** 自性. *See* SVABHĀVA

**chasŏng kong** 自性空. *See* SVABHĀVAŚŪNYA, SVABHĀVAŚŪNYATĀ

**chasŏng punbyŏl** 自性分別. *See* SVABHĀVAVIKALPA

**chasŏng sin** 自性身. *See* SVABHĀVAKĀYA, SVABHĀVIKAKĀYA

**chasŏng yŏlban** 自性涅槃. *See* PRAKṚTIPARINIRVṚTA

**cha suyong sin** 自受用身. *See* SVA-SAMBHOGAKĀYA

**chat'a p'yŏngdŭng** 自他平等. *See* PARĀTMASAMATA

**Chaŭn taesa** 慈恩大師. *See* KUIJI

**che** 除. *See* APOHA

**che** 諦. *See* SATYA

**ch'e** 體. *See* TI

**Cheba** 提婆. *See* ĀRYADEVA

**Chebadalta** 提婆達多. *See* DEVADATTA

**chech'ang** 提唱. *See* TICHANG

**Chedaga** 提多迦. *See* DHṚTAKA

**Chedasan pu** 制多山部. *See* CAITYA

**Chegaejang posal** 除蓋障菩薩. *See* SARVANĪVARAṆAVIṢKAMBHIN

**chegang** 提綱. *See* TICHANG

**Chegong** 濟公. *See* JIGONG

**Chegyŏng yo chip** 諸經要集. *See* ZHUJING YAO JI

**cheho** 醍醐. *See* MAṆḌA

**cheirŭi che** 第一義諦. *See* PARAMĀRTHASATYA

**chesa kwanjŏng** 第四灌頂. *See* CATURTHĀBHIṢEKHA

**Chesŏk** 帝釋. *See* ŚAKRA, INDRA

**Chesŏk mang** 帝釋網. *See* INDRAJĀLA

**Chesŏk somun kyŏng** 帝釋所問經. *See* SAKKAPAÑHASUTTA

**Chewi** 提謂. *See* TRAPUṢA

**cheyo** 提要. *See* TICHANG

**chi** 支. *See* AṄGA

**chi** 地. *See* BHŪMI

**chi** 智. *See* JÑĀNA

**ch'i** 癡. *See* MOHA

**chi** 止. *See* ŚAMATHA

**Chi** 支. *See* ZHI

**Chibimun chok non** 集異門足論. *See* SAṂGĪTIPARYĀYA-[PĀDAŚĀSTRA]

**chich'wi** 智聚. *See* JÑĀNASAṂBHĀRA

**chidae** 地大. *See* PṚTHIVĪ

**chido** 智度. *See* PRAJÑĀPĀRAMITĀ

**chigaek** 知客. *See* ZHIKE

**Chigong Sŏnhyŏn** 指空禪賢. *See* ZHIKONG CHANXIAN

**Chiguk ch'ŏn** 持國天. *See* DHṚTARĀṢṬRA

**chigwan** 止觀. *See* ŚAMATHA VIPAŚYANĀ

**Chigwang Haerin** 智光海麟. *See* WANGNYUNSA

**chigwan t'ajwa** 祇/只管打坐. *See* SHIKAN TAZA

**chigwŏn in** 智拳印. *See* BODHYAṄGĪMUDRĀ, JÑĀNAMUṢṬI

**chigyŏn** 知見. *See* JÑĀNADARŚANA

**chihye an** 智慧眼. *See* PRAJÑĀCAKṢUS

**Chijang** 地藏. *See* KṢITIGARBHA

**Chijang posal ponwŏn kyŏng** 地藏菩薩本願經. *See* KṢITIGARBHASŪTRA

**chije** 支提. *See* CAITYA

**Chiji non** 地持論. *See* BODHISATTVABHŪMI

**chijŏn** 知殿. *See* ZHIDIAN

**chikchi insim** 直指人心. *See* ZHIZHI RENXIN

**chikse** 直歲. *See* ZHISUI

**Chi Kyŏm** 支謙. *See* ZHI QIAN

**chil** 嫉. *See* ĪRṢYĀ

**chil** 嫉. *See* MĀTSARYA

**Ch'ilbaeksong panya** 七百頌般若. *See* SAPTAŚATIKĀ-PRAJÑĀPĀRAMITĀ

**ch'ilbul** 七佛. *See* SAPTABUDDHA, SAPTATATHĀGATA

**ch'il chae** 七財. *See* SAPTADHANA

**Ch'ilch'a kyŏng** 七車經. *See* RATHAVINĪTASUTTA

**ch'ilchi** 七知. *See* QIZHI

**ch'ilchi chakpŏp** 七支作法. *See* SAPTĀṄGAVIDHI

**ch'ilch'il** 七七. *See* QIQI

**ch'ilch'il [il] chae** 七七[日]齋. *See* SISHIJIU [RI] ZHAI; QIQI JI

**ch'ilch'il ki** 七七忌. *See* QIQI JI

**ch'ilch'oesŭng** 七最勝. *See* QIZUISHENG

**ch'ilchongŏ** 七種語. *See* QIZHONGYU

**ch'ilchongsa** 七種捨. *See* QIZHONGSHE

**ch'ilchŏng yugyok** 七情六欲. *See* QIQING LIUYU

**ch'ilgakchi** 七覺支. *See* BODHYAṄGA

**ch'illi kak** 親里覺. *See* QINLI JUE

**ch'il myŏlchaeng pŏp** 七滅諍法. *See* SAPTĀDHIKARAṆAŚAMATHA

**ch'ilsŏn** 七善. *See* QISHAN

**ch'ilsŏng** 七星. *See* BEIDOU QIXING

**ch'ilsŭngsa** 七勝事. *See* QI SHENGSHI

**chimmu** 執無. *See* NĀSTIKA

**Chimnyang non** 集量論. *See* PRAMĀṆASAMUCCAYA

**Ch'imun kyŏnghun** 緇門警訓. *See* ZIMEN JINGXUN

**chimyŏng** 持明. *See* VIDYĀDHARA

**chimyŏng chang** 持明藏. *See* VIDYĀDHARAPIṬAKA

**chin** 瞋. *See* DVEṢA, PRATIGHA, VYĀPĀDA

**chinbo** 珍寶. *See* RATNA

**Chin'ga** 眞可. *See* DAGUAN ZHENKE

**Chinggwan** 澄觀. *See* CHENGGUAN

**chingjŏng** 澄淨. *See* PRASĀDA

**Chinje** 眞諦. *See* PARAMĀRTHA

**chinje** 眞諦. *See* PARAMĀRTHASATYA

**chinji** 盡智. *See* KṢAYAJÑĀNA

**Chinjŏng Kŭngmun** 眞浄克文. *See* ZHENJING KEWEN

**Chinna** 陳那. *See* DIGNĀGA

**chinŏn** 眞言. *See* MANTRA

**Chi non chong** 地論宗. *See* DI LUN ZONG

**chinŏn sŭng** 眞言乘. *See* MANTRAYĀNA

**chinyŏ** 眞如. *See* ZHENRU, BHŪTATATHATĀ, TATHATĀ

**chioe** 智外. *See* PAROKṢA

**chiok pyŏn[sang]** 地獄變[相]. *See* DIYU BIAN[XIANG]

**chiok [yujŏng/chungsaeng]** 地獄[有情/衆生]. *See* NĀRAKA

**Chiŏm** 智儼. *See* ZHIYAN

**chip** 集. *See* SAMUDAYA

**chipche** 集諦. *See* SAMUDAYASATYA

**Chip kogŭm pulto nonhyŏng** 集古今佛道論衡. *See* JI GUJIN FODAO LUNHENG

**chipsa** 執事. *See* VAIYĀPṚTYA(KARA)

**ch'irhyŏn** 七賢. *See* QIXIAN

**Chi Rugach'am** 支婁迦讖. *See* LOKAKṢEMA

**ch'iryŏk[choe]** 七逆[罪]. *See* QINI[ZUI]

**ch'iryu** 七有. *See* QIYOU

**chisa** 知事. *See* ZHISHI

**chisŏn** 至善. *See* NIḤŚREYASA

**Ch'isŏnggwang yŏrae** 熾盛光如來. *See* TEJAPRABHA

**Chi Torim** 支道林. *See* ZHI DAOLIN, ZHI DUN

**Chi Tun** 支遁. *See* ZHI DUN

**Chiŭi** 智顗. *See* TIANTAI ZHIYI

**Chiuk** 智旭. *See* ZHIXU

**chiyok** 知浴. *See* ZHIYU

**ch'ŏ** 處. *See* ĀYATANA

**Chodong chong** 曹洞宗. *See* CAODONG ZONG

**choe** 罪. *See* PĀPA

**ch'oesangsŭng sŏn** 最上乘禪. *See* ZUISHANGSHENG CHAN

**ch'oesang taesilchi** 最上大悉地. *See* UTTAMASIDDHI

**ch'oesŭng** 最勝. *See* JINA

**ch'oesŭngja** 最勝子. *See* JINAPUTRA

**Ch'oesŭng pulchŏng tarani chŏngje ŏpchang chu kyŏng** 最勝佛頂陀羅尼淨除業障呪經. *See* SARVADURGATIPARIŚODHANATANTRA

**Chogyesan** 曹溪山. *See* CAOXISHAN

**chŏgyuktan** 赤肉團. *See* CHIROUTUAN

**cho i sangjŏk** 照而常寂. *See* JI ER CHANGZHAO

**Chojŏng kyŏmch'u nok** 祖庭鉗鎚錄. *See* ZUTING QIANCHUI LU

**Chojŏng sawŏn** 祖庭事苑. *See* ZUTING SHIYUAN

**Choju Chongsim** 趙州從諗. *See* ZHAOZHOU CONGSHEN

**ch'ok** 觸. *See* SPARŚA

**ch'okchi in** 觸地印. *See* BHŪMISPARŚAMUDRĀ

**ch'okch'ŏ** 觸處. *See* SPRAṢṬAVYĀYATANA

**chŏk i sangjo** 寂而常照. *See* JI ER CHANGZHAO

**Ch'ŏlcha rim** 鐵刺林. *See* AYAḤŚĀLMALĪVANA

**Chŏlgwan non** 絶觀論. *See* JUEGUAN LUN

**Chŏllyun sŏngwang suhaeng kyŏng** 轉輪聖王修行經. *See* CAKKAVATTISĪHANĀDASUTTA

**chŏllyunwang** 轉輪王. *See* CAKRAVARTIN

**chŏman** 點眼. *See* DIANYAN, NETRAPRATIṢṬHĀPANA

**Chŏmch'al sŏnak ŏppo kyŏng** 占察善惡業報經. *See* ZHANCHA SHAN'E YEBAO JING

**chŏmo** 漸悟. *See* JIANWU

**chŏmsu** 漸修. *See* JIANXIU

**chŏmwi sŏlpŏp** 漸爲說法. *See* ANUPUBBIKATHĀ

**ch'ŏn** 天. *See* DEVA

**ch'ŏnae** 天愛. *See* DEVĀNĀṂ PRIYAḤ

**Ch'ŏnan** 千眼. *See* SAHASRĀKṢA

**Ch'ŏnch'uk** 天竺. *See* TIANZHU

**ch'ŏn chung ch'ŏn** 天中天. *See* DEVĀTIDEVA

**chŏndansui** 栴檀樹耳. *See* SŪKARAMADDAVA

**chŏndari** 旃陀利. *See* CAṆḌĀLĪ

**chŏndo** 顚倒. *See* VIPARYĀSA

**Ch'ŏndong Yŏjŏng** 天童如浄. *See* TIANTONG RUJING

**chŏndŭng nok** 傳燈録. *See* CHUANDENG LU

**chong** 宗. *See* SIDDHĀNTA, ZONG

**chŏng** 頂. *See* MŪRDHAN

**chŏng** 淨. *See* VYAVADĀNA

**Chŏngban wang** 淨飯王. *See* ŚUDDHODANA

**chŏngbo** 正報. *See* ER BAO

**Ch'ŏngbyŏn** 清辯. *See* BHĀVAVIVEKA

**chŏngbyŏng** 淨瓶. *See* KUṆḌIKĀ

**Chongdŏk kyŏng** 種德經. *See* SOṆADAṆḌASUTTA

**chŏngdŭnggak** 正等覺. *See* SAMYAKSAṂBODHI

**chŏnggak** 正覺. *See* SAṂBODHI

**Chŏnggak** 淨覺. *See* JINGJUE

**Chonggo** 宗杲. *See* ZONGGAO

**chŏnggŏ ch'ŏn** 淨居天. *See* ŚUDDHĀVĀSAKĀYIKA

**chŏnggŭn** 正勤. *See* SAMYAKPRADHĀNA

**chŏnggwan chi** 定觀知. *See* YOGIPRATYAKṢA

**chŏnggye** 淨戒. *See* ŚĪLAVIŚUDDHI

**chŏnggyŏn** 正見. *See* SAMYAGDṚṢṬI

**Chonggyŏng nok** 宗鏡録. *See* ZONGJING LU

**ch'ŏnggyu** 清規. *See* QINGGUI

**chŏngin** 淨人. *See* KALPIKĀRAKA

**chongja** 種子. *See* BĪJA

**ch'ongji** 總持. *See* DHĀRAṆĪ

**chŏngji** 正知. *See* SAṂPRAJANYA

**chŏngjik sim** 正直心. *See* ADHYĀŚAYA

**chŏngjin** 精進. *See* VĪRYA

**chŏngjin paramilta** 精進波羅蜜多. *See* VĪRYAPĀRAMITĀ

**ch'ŏngjŏng** 清淨. *See* PARIŚUDDHA, VAIYAVADĀNIKA, VISUDDHI

**chŏngjŏng** 正定. *See* SAMYAKSAMĀDHI

**Ch'ŏngjŏngdo non** 清淨道論. *See* VISUDDHIMAGGA

**chongjonggye chiryŏk** 種種界智力. *See* NĀNĀDHĀTUJÑĀNABALA

**chŏngjŏngjin** 正精進. *See* SAMYAKVYĀYĀMA

**Ch'ŏngjŏng kyŏng** 清淨經. *See* PĀSĀDIKASUTTA

**ch'ŏngjŏng pulgukt'o** 清淨佛國土. *See* PARIŚUDDHABUDDHAKṢETRA, VIŚUDDHABUDDHAKṢETRA

**chongjong sŭnghae chiryŏk** 種種勝解智力. *See* NĀNĀDHIMUKTIJÑĀNABALA

**chŏngjŏn paeksuja** 庭前柏樹子. *See* TINGQIAN BOSHUZI

**Chŏngjung chong** 淨衆宗. *See* JINGZHONG ZONG

**chŏngmuk** 寂默. *See* PRATISAṂLAYANA

**chŏngmun** 迹門. *See* SHAKUMON

**Chongmun hongmun** 宗門或問. *See* ZONGMEN HUOMEN

**Chongmun sipkyu non** 宗門十規論. *See* ZONGMEN SHIGUI LUN

**Chongmun yŏndŭng hoeyo** 宗門聯燈會要. *See* ZONGMEN LIANDENG HUIYAO

**chŏngmyŏng** 正命. *See* SAMYAGĀJĪVA

**Chongnamsan** 終南山. *See* ZHONGNANSHAN

**Chongni chunggyŏng mongnok** 綜理衆經目錄. *See* ZONGLI ZHONGJING MULU

**ch'ongnu ki** 髑髏器. *See* KAPĀLA

**Chŏngnyang pu** 正量部. *See* SAṂMITĪYA

**chŏngnyŏm** 正念. *See* SAMYAKSMṚTI

**chŏngnyŏ paramilta** 靜慮波羅蜜多. *See* DHYĀNAPĀRAMITĀ

**chŏngŏ** 正語. *See* SAMYAGVĀC

**chŏngŏp** 正業. *See* SAMYAKKARMĀNTA

**Chŏngpŏbanjang** 正法眼藏. *See* ZHENGFAYANZANG

**chongpŏp** 宗法. *See* PAKṢADHARMA

**chŏngpŏp** 正法. *See* SADDHARMA

**chŏngp'yŏnji** 正遍知. *See* SAMYAKSAṂBUDDHA

**chŏngsa** 精舍. *See* VIHĀRA

**Chongsaek** 宗賾. *See* CHANGLU ZONGZE

**chŏngsang** 頂相. *See* DINGXIANG

**chŏngsayu** 正思惟. *See* SAMYAKSAṂKALPA, YONIŚOMANASKĀRA

**Chongsim** 從諗. *See* ZHAOZHOU CONGSHEN

**chongsŏng** 種性. *See* GOTRA

**chŏngsŏng isaeng** 正性離生. *See* SAMYAKTVANIYĀMĀVAKRĀNTI

**chŏngsu** 正受. *See* SAMĀPATTI

**chŏngt'o** 浄土. *See* PURE LAND

**Chŏngt'o chŏn** 淨土傳. *See* JINGTU ZHUAN

**Chŏngt'o kunŭi non** 浄土群疑論. *See* JINGTU QUNYI LUN

**Chŏngt'o non** 浄土論. *See* JINGTU LUN

**Chŏngt'o ojo** 淨土五祖. *See* JINGTU WUZU

**Chŏngt'o pyŏn** 淨土變. *See* JINGTU BIAN

**Chŏngt'o sambu kyŏng** 淨土三部經. *See* JINGTU SANBUJING

**Chŏngt'o samsŏng** 淨土三聖. *See* JINGTU SANSHENG

**Chŏngt'o sibŭi [non]** 淨土十疑[論]. *See* JINGTU SHIYI [LUN]

**Chŏngt'o sŏŭng chŏn** 浄土瑞應傳. *See* JINGTU RUIYING ZHUAN

**Ch'ŏngwŏn Haengsa** 青原行思. *See* QINGYUAN XINGSI

**ch'ŏn'gye** 天界. *See* DEVALOKA

**Chŏngyŏng Hyewŏn** 浄影慧遠. *See* JINGYING HUIYUAN

**Chongyong nok** 從容録. *See* CONGRONG LU

**ch'ŏnhach'ŏ** 天下處. *See* DEVĀVATĀRA

**ch'ŏnharae** 天下來. *See* DEVĀVATĀRA

**Chŏnjŏnggaksan** 前正覺山. *See* PRĀGBODHI(GIRI)

**Chŏnjon kyŏng** 典尊經. *See* MAHĀGOVINDASUTTA

**chŏnjwa** 典座. *See* DIANZUO

**chŏnjwa** 展左. *See* PRATYĀLĪḌHA

**ch'ŏnnyŏ** 天女. *See* APSARAS

**ch'ŏnnyong p'albu** 天龍八部. *See* AṢṬĀSENA

**Cho non** 肇論. *See* ZHAO LUN

**chŏn pŏmnyun** 轉法輪. *See* DHARMACAKRAPRAVARTANA

**chŏn pŏmnyunin** 轉法輪印. *See* DHARMACAKRAMUDRĀ

**Chŏn pŏmnyun kyŏng** 轉法輪經. *See* DHAMMACAKKAPPAVATTANASUTTA

**Chŏnpŏp chŏngjong ki** 傳法正宗記. *See* CHUANFA ZHENGZONG JI

**chŏnpŏp ke** 傳法偈. *See* CHUANFA JI, YIJI

**Chŏn pŏppo ki** 傳法寶紀. *See* CHUAN FABAO JI

**ch'ŏnsang** 天上. *See* DEVALOKA, SVARGA

**ch'ŏnse** 天世. *See* DEVALOKA

**ch'ŏnsegye** 天世界. *See* DEVALOKA

**Ch'ŏnsikchae** 天息災. *See* TIANXIZAI

**Chŏnsim pŏbyo** 傳心法要. *See* CHUANXIN FAYAO

**ch'ŏnsin** 天神. *See* DEVATĀ

**chŏnsin sari** 全身舍利. *See* QUANSHEN SHELI

**Ch'ŏnsu Ch'ŏnan Kwanŭm** 千手千眼觀音. *See* AVALOKITEŚVARASAHASRABHUJANETRA

**Ch'onsu kyŏng** 千手經. *See* QIANSHOU JING

**Ch'ŏnt'ae Chiŭi** 天台智顗. *See* TIANTAI ZHIYI

**Ch'ŏnt'ae osi** 天台五時. *See* TIANTAI WUSHI

**Ch'ŏnt'ae p'algyo** 天台八教. *See* TIANTAI BAJIAO

**chŏnŭi** 轉依. *See* ĀŚRAYAPARĀVṚTTA

**ch'ŏn wang** 天王. *See* DEVARĀJAN

**ch'ŏrwisan** 鐵圍山. *See* CAKRAVĀḌA

**chosa** 祖師. *See* ZUSHI

**Chosan Ponjŏk** 曹山本寂. *See* CAOSHAN BENJI

**chosik** 調息. *See* PRĀṆĀYĀMA

**Ch'owŏn** 超元. *See* DAOZHE CHAOYUAN

**Chowŏn Tosaeng** 曹源道生. *See* CAOYUAN DAOSHENG

**choyŏn** 助緣. *See* SAHAKĀRIPRATYAYA

**chu** 珠. *See* MAṆI

**chu** 住. *See* STHITI, VIHĀRA, LENA

**Chudobant'akka** 注荼半托迦. *See* CŪḌAPANTHAKA

**Chugoeng** 袾宏. *See* YUNQI ZHUHONG

**chugŏp** 住劫. *See* VIVARTASTHĀYIKALPA

**chugwa** 住果. *See* PHALASTHITA

**chuin'gong** 主人公. *See* ZHURENGONG

**chuji** 住持. *See* ZHUCHI

**Ch'uk** 竺. *See* ZHU

**Ch'uk Pŏpho** 竺法護. *See* DHARMARAKṢA

**ch'uksaeng** 畜生. *See* TIRYAK

**chŭksin sŏngbul** 即身成佛. *See* SOKUSHIN JŌBUTSU

**ch'ulga** 出家. *See* PRAVRAJITA, PRAVRAJYĀ

**ch'ulli** 出離. *See* NAIṢKRAMYA, NIRYĀṆA

**Ch'ul samjang kijip** 出三藏記集. *See* CHU SANZANG JIJI

**ch'ulsegan** 出世間. *See* LOKOTTARA

**ch'ulse kwa** 出世果. *See* LOKUTTARAPHALA

**ch'ulse sammae** 出世三昧. *See* LOKUTTARASAMĀDHI

**ch'ulse to** 出世道. *See* LOKUTTARAMAGGA

**Chuna mun'gyŏn kyŏng** 周那問見經. *See* SALLEKHASUTTA

**Chunda** 準陀. *See* CUNDA

**chŭng** 證. *See* ADHIGAMA

**Chung aham kyŏng** 中阿含經. *See* MADHYAMĀGAMA, MAJJHIMANIKĀYA

**Chungbong Myŏngbon** 中峰明本. *See* ZHONGFENG MINGBEN

**chŭngbŏp** 證法. *See* ADHIGAMADHARMA

**chungdo** 中道. *See* MADHYAMAPRATIPAD

**Chŭngdo ka** 證道歌. *See* ZHENGDAO GE

**chunggaŭi** 中價衣. *See* UTTARĀSAṂGA

**Chungguk** 中國. *See* MADHYAMADEŚA

**chunggŭn** 中根. *See* MADYENDRIYA

**Chunggwan non so** 中觀論疏. *See* ZHONGGUAN LUN SHU

**Chunggwan** 中觀. *See* MADHYAMAKA

**chunghak** 衆學. *See* ŚAIKṢADHARMA

**chunghap [chiok]** 衆合[地獄]. *See* SAṂGHĀTA

**chunghoe** 衆會. *See* PARIṢAD

**Chunghyŏn** 衆賢. *See* SAṂGHABHADRA

**chŭngik** 增益. *See* SAMĀROPA

**Chŭngil aham kyŏng** 增壹阿含經. *See* EKOTTARĀGAMA

**chŭng illae kwa** 證一來果. *See* SAKṚDĀGĀMIPHALASTHA

**Chŭngjang ch'ŏn** 增長天. *See* VIRŪḌHAKA

**Chungjip kyŏng** 衆集經. *See* SAṄGĪTISUTTA

**chŭngjŏn pŏmnyun** 證轉法輪. *See* *SUVIBHAKTADHARMACAKRA

**chungju** 衆主. *See* VAIYĀPṚTYA(KARA)

**Chungnimch'ong** 竹林叢. *See* VEṆUGRĀMAKA

**Chungnim chŏngsa** 竹林精舍. *See* VEṆUVANAVIHĀRA

**Chung non** 中論. *See* MŪLAMADHYAMAKAKĀRIKĀ, MADHYAMAKAŚĀSTRA

**chŭngo** 證悟. *See* ZHENGWU

**chungon yujŏng** 中蘊有情. *See* GANDHARVA

**chung pan** 中般. *See* ANTARĀPARINIRVĀYIN

**chung panyŏlban** 中般涅槃. *See* ANTARĀPARINIRVĀYIN

**chŭng purhwan kwa** 證不還果. *See* ANĀGĀMIPHALASTHA

**chungsaeng** 衆生. *See* SATTVA

**chungsaeng segan** 衆生世間. *See* SATTVALOKA

**chungsaeng t'ak** 衆生濁. *See* SATTVAKAṢĀYA

**chŭngsanggye hak** 增上戒學. *See* ADHIŚĪLAŚIKṢĀ

**chŭngsanghye hak** 增上慧學. *See* ADHIPRAJÑĀŚIKṢĀ

**chŭngsangjŏng hak** 增上定學. *See* ADHISAMĀDHIŚIKṢĀ

**chŭngsang kwa** 增上果. *See* ADHIPATIPHALA

**chŭngsang man** 增上慢. *See* ADHIMĀNA

**Chŭngsangsim kyŏng** 增上心經. *See* VITAKKASAṆṬHĀNASUTTA

**chŭngsang yŏn** 增上緣. *See* ADHIPATIPRATYAYA

**chungŭm** 中陰. *See* ANTARĀBHAVA

**chŭng yeryu kwa** 證預流果. *See* SROTAĀPANNAPHALASTHA

**chungyu** 中有. *See* ANTARĀBHAVA

**Chunje** 准提. *See* CUNDĪ

**Churibant'ŭk** 周利槃特. *See* ŚUDDHIPANTHAKA

**ch'uryoji** 出要志. *See* NAIṢKRAMYA

**Ch'uryo kyŏng** 出曜經. *See* UDĀNAVARGA

**chu yŏlban** 住涅槃. *See* PRATIṢṬHITANIRVĀṆA

**chwa** 座. *See* ĀSANA

**chwabŏp** 坐法. *See* ĀSANA

**chwagu** 坐具. *See* NIṢĪDANA

**chwasŏn** 坐禪. *See* ZUOCHAN

**ch'wi** 趣. *See* GATI

**ch'wi** 取. *See* UPĀDĀNA

**ch'wion** 取蘊. *See* UPĀDĀNASKANDHA

## H

**hae** 害. *See* VIHIṂSĀ

**haegye** 解界. *See* SĪMĀSAMŪHANA

**Haedong so** 海東疏. *See* TAESŬNG KISIN NON SO

**haehoe** 海會. *See* HAIHUI

**haein sammae** 海印三昧. *See* SĀGARAMUDRĀSAMĀDHI

**haeje** 解制. *See* JIEZHI

**haeng** 行. *See* CARITA

**haeng** 行. *See* SAṂSKĀRA

**haenggak** 行脚. *See* XINGJIAO

**haenggo** 行苦. *See* SAṂSKĀRADUḤKHATĀ

**haengja** 行者. *See* XINGZHE

**haengni** 行履. *See* XINGLI

**haeng pori sim** 行菩提心. *See* PRASTHĀNACITTOPĀDA

**Haengsa** 行思. *See* QINGYUAN XINGSI

**haengsang** 行相. *See* ĀKĀRA

**haengun yusu** 行雲流水. *See* KŌUN RYŪSUI

**haeo** 解悟. *See* JIEWU

**Haesimmil kyŏng** 解深密經. *See* SAṂDHINIRMOCANASŪTRA

**haet'ae** 懈怠. *See* KAUSĪDYA

**haet'al** 解脫. *See* MOKṢA, VIMOKṢA

**haet'al mun** 解脫門. *See* VIMOKṢAMUKHA

**haet'alto** 解脫道. *See* MOKṢAMĀRGA, VIMOKṢAMĀRGA

**Haet'alto non** 解脫道論. *See* VIMUTTIMAGGA

**hagin** 學人. *See* ŚAIKṢA

**hak** 學. *See* ŚIKṢĀ

**hakch'ŏ** 學處. *See* ŚIKṢĀPADA

**hallim** 寒林. *See* ŚMAŚĀNA

**han** 恨. *See* UPANĀHA

**Hangha** 恒河. *See* GAṄGĀNADĪ

**Hanghasa** 恒河沙. *See* GAṄGĀNADĪVĀLUKĀ

**Hangma Chang** 降魔藏. *See* XIANGMO ZANG

**Hangma kyŏng** 降魔經. *See* MĀRATAJJANĪYASUTTA

**Hangnim Hyŏnso** 鶴林玄素. *See* HELIN XUANSU

**hang samse in** 降三世印. *See* BHŪTAḌĀMARAMUDRĀ

**Hangsamse myŏngwang** 降三世明王. *See* TRAILOKYAVIJAYA

**Hansan** 寒山. *See* HANSHAN

**Hansan si** 寒山詩. *See* HANSHAN SHI

**haŏ** 下語. *See* AGYO

**hapchang** 合掌. *See* AÑJALI

**Haribalma** 訶梨跋摩. *See* HARIVARMAN

**hasa** 下士. *See* ADHAMAPURUṢA

**Hat'aek Sinhoe** 荷澤神會. *See* HEZE SHENHUI

**ho** 好. *See* ANUVYAÑJANA

**Hobŏp** 護法. *See* DHARMAPĀLA

**Hŏdang Chiu** 虛堂智愚. *See* XUTANG ZHIYU

**hoe** 悔. *See* KAUKṚTYA

**Hoech'ang pŏmnan** 會昌法難. *See* HUICHANG FANAN

**hoegwa** 悔過. *See* PRATIDEŚANĀ

**hoegwang panjo** 迴/回光返照. *See* HUIGUANG FANZHAO

**hoehyang** 迴向. *See* PARIṆĀMANĀ

**Hoejaeng non** 廻諍論. *See* VIGRAHAVYĀVARTANĪ

**hoengch'o** 横超. *See* HENGCHAO

**Hoeso** 懷素. *See* HUAISU

**Hoeyang** 懷讓. *See* NANYUE HUAIRANG

**hŏgong** 虛空. *See* ĀKĀŚA

**hŏgonghwa** 虛空華. *See* KHAPUṢPA

**Hŏgongjang posal** 虛空藏菩薩. *See* ĀKĀŚAGARBHA

**Hoguk posal hoe [kyŏng]** 護國菩薩會[經]. *See* RĀṢṬRAPĀLAPARIPṚCCHĀ

**hoguk Pulgyo** 護國佛教. *See* HUGUO FOJIAO

**hogwe** 胡跪. *See* HUGUI

**Hojae** 護財. *See* DHANAPĀLA, NĀLĀGIRI

**hŏmang punbyŏl** 虛妄分別. *See* ABHŪTAPARIKALPA

**honch'im** 惛沉. *See* STYĀNA

**Hongin** 弘忍. *See* HONGREN

**Hongju chong** 洪州宗. *See* HONGZHOU ZONG

**Hongmyŏng chip** 弘明集. *See* HONGMING JI

**hongnyŏnhwa** 紅蓮華. *See* PADMA

**Hoŭn Toje** 湖隱道濟. *See* HUYIN DAOJI

**hoyok** 好欲. *See* KĀMACCHANDA

**hudŭk chi** 後得智. *See* PṚṢṬHALABDHAJÑĀNA

**hŭi** 喜. *See* MUDITĀ, PRĪTI

**Hŭich'ŏn** 希遷. *See* SHITOU XIQIAN

**Hŭiroga** 呬嚕迦. *See* HERUKA

**hŭiron** 戲論. *See* PRAPAÑCA

**hŭksŭng chiok** 黒繩地獄. *See* KĀLASŪTRA

**hunsŭp** 薰習. *See* VĀSANĀ

**huyu** 後有. *See* PUNARBHAVA

**hwa** 化. *See* NIRMITA

**hwadae** 火大. *See* TEJAS

**hwadu** 話頭. *See* HUATOU

**Hwaji pu** 化地部. *See* MAHĪŚĀSAKA

**hwaju** 化主. *See* HUAZHU

**Hwangbyŏk Hŭiun** 黃檗希運. *See* HUANGBO XIYUN

**Hwangnyong Hyenam** 黃龍慧南. *See* HUANGLONG HUINAN

**Hwangnyong p'a** 黃龍派. *See* HUANGLONG PAI

**hwanhŭi chi** 歡喜地. *See* PRAMUDITĀ

**hwansa** 幻師. *See* MĀYĀKĀRA

**hwansin** 幻身. *See* MĀYĀDEHA

**Hwaŏm cho** 華嚴朝. *See* HUAYAN ZHAO

**Hwaŏm chong** 華嚴宗. *See* HUAYAN ZONG

**Hwaŏm kyŏng** 華嚴經. *See* AVATAṂSAKASŪTRA

**Hwaŏm kyŏng chigwi** 華嚴經旨歸. *See* HUAYAN JING ZHIGUI

**Hwaŏm kyŏng chŏn['gi]** 華嚴經傳[記]. *See* HUAYAN JING ZHUAN[JI]

**Hwaŏm kyŏng hap non** 華嚴經合論. *See* HUAYAN JING HELUN

**Hwaŏm kyŏng kamŭng chŏn** 華嚴經感應傳. *See* HUAYAN JING GANYING ZHUAN

**Hwaŏm kyŏng so** 華嚴經疏. *See* HUAYAN JING SHU

**Hwaŏm kyŏng suhyŏn ki** 華嚴經搜玄記. *See* HUAYAN JING SOUXUAN JI

**Hwaŏm kyŏng suso yŏnŭi ch'o** 華嚴經随疏演義鈔. *See* HUAYAN JING SUISHU YANYI CAO

**Hwaŏm kyŏng t'amhyŏn ki** 華嚴經探玄記. *See* HUAYAN JING TANXUAN JI

**Hwaŏm ogyo** 華嚴五教. *See* HUAYAN WUJIAO

**Hwaŏm ogyo chang** 華嚴五教章. *See* HUAYAN WUJIAO ZHANG

**Hwaŏm pŏpkye kwanmun** 華嚴法界觀門. *See* HUAYAN FAJIE GUANMEN

**Hwaŏm pu** 華嚴部. *See* HUAYAN BU

**Hwaŏmsa** 華嚴社. *See* HUAYANSHE

**Hwaŏm samsŏng** 華嚴三聖. *See* HUAYAN SANSHENG

**Hwaŏm sibi** 華嚴十異. *See* HUAYAN SHIYI

**Hwaŏm sibŭi** 華嚴十義. *See* HUAYAN SHIYI

**Hwaŏm yuŭi** 華嚴遊意. *See* HUAYAN YOUYI

**hwa p'yŏnch'ŏ** 火遍處. *See* TEJOKASIṆA

**hwarak ch'ŏn** 化樂天. *See* NIRMĀṆARATI

**hwa saeng** 化生. *See* UPAPĀDUKAYONI

**hwasang** 和尚. *See* HESHANG, OSHŌ

**hwasangni** 和尚尼. *See* UPĀDHYĀYĀ

**hwasin** 化身. *See* NIRMĀṆAKĀYA

**Hwasin** 火神. *See* AGNI

**Hwassi sŏng** 華氏城. *See* PĀTALIPUTRA

**hyang** 香. *See* GANDHA

**hyangch'ŏ** 香處. *See* GANDHĀYATANA

**hyangno** 香爐. *See* GANDHAGHAṬIKĀ

**Hyangŏm Chihan** 香嚴智閑. *See* XIANGYAN ZHIXIAN

**hyangsil** 香室. *See* GANDHAKUṬĪ

**Hyangsŏng paramun** 香姓婆羅門. *See* DROṆA

**hye** 慧. *See* MATI, PRAJÑĀ

**Hyech'ung** 慧忠. *See* NANYANG HUIZHONG

**Hyedŏk Sohyŏn** 慧德韶顯. *See* WANGNYUNSA

**Hyega** 慧可. *See* HUIKE

**Hyegae** 慧開. *See* WUMEN HUIKAI

**Hyegwa** 惠果. *See* HUIGUO

**Hyehae** 慧海. *See* DAZHU HUIHAI

**hyehaet'al** 慧解脫. *See* PRAJÑĀVIMUKTA

**hyehak** 慧學. *See* PRAJÑĀŚIKṢĀ

**Hyeil** 慧日. *See* CIMIN HUIRI

**Hyenam** 慧南. *See* HUINAN

**Hyenŭng** 慧能. *See* HUINENG

**Hyesa** 慧思. *See* NANYUE HUISI

**Hyewŏn** 慧遠. *See* LUSHAN HUIYUAN

**hyŏllyang** 現量. *See* PRATYAKṢA

**Hyŏlmaek non** 血脈論. *See* XUEMO LUN

**hyŏnch'wiin** 現取因. *See* UPĀDĀNAKĀRAṆA

**Hyŏn'gak** 玄覺. *See* YONGJIA XUANJUE

**Hyŏnggye Tamyŏn** 荊溪湛然. *See* JINGXI ZHANRAN

**hyŏn'gŏp** 賢劫. *See* BHADRAKALPA

**Hyŏn'gŏp kyŏng** 賢劫經. *See* BHADRAKALPIKASŪTRA

**hyŏn'gwan** 現觀. *See* ABHISAMAYA

**hyŏnhaeng** 現行. *See* SAMUDĀCĀRA

**Hyŏnhak** 玄學. *See* XUANXUE

**Hyŏnho** 賢護. *See* BHADRAPĀLA

**hyŏnhyŏn** 顯現. *See* PRATIBHĀSA

**Hyŏnjang** 玄奘. *See* XUANZANG

**hyŏnjŏn [chi]** 現前[地]. *See* ABHIMUKHĪ

**Hyŏnjong ki** 顯宗記. *See* XIANZONG JI

**Hyŏnjung myŏng** 玄中銘. *See* XUANZHONG MING

**Hyŏnsa Sabi** 玄沙師備. *See* XUANSHA SHIBEI

**Hyŏnsa sambyŏng** 玄沙三病. *See* XUANSHA SANBING

**hyŏnsŏng** 賢聖. *See* ĀRYAPUDGALA

**hyŏnsŏng kongan** 現成公案. *See* GENJŌ KŌAN

**Hyŏnyŏm** 賢鹽. *See* LAKUṆṬAKA BHADRIKA

**Hyŏp** 脇. *See* PĀRŚVA

## I

**i** 理. *See* LI

**i** 離. *See* NIḤSARAṆA, VIRATI

**i ajip** 二我執. *See* ER WOZHI

**Ibada** 離婆多. *See* REVATA

**Ibujongnyun non** 異部宗輪論. *See* SAMAYABHEDOPARACANACAKRA

**i che** 二諦. *See* SATYADVAYA

**i chi** 二持. *See* ER CHI

**ich'ŏ** 耳處. *See* ŚROTRĀYATANA

**i chŏn** 二詮. *See* ER QUAN

**i chong** 二宗. *See* ER ZONG

**ich'ŏ samhoe** 二處三會. *See* ERCHU SANHUI

**iganŏ** 離間語. *See* PAIŚUNYA

**igu chi** 離垢地. *See* VIMALĀ

**igŭn** 利根. *See* TĪKṢṆENDRIYA

**igŭn** 耳根. *See* ŚROTRENDRIYA

**Igye** 離繫. *See* NIRGRANTHA

**igye kwa** 離繫果. *See* VISAṂYOGAPHALA

**ihŭiron** 離戲論. *See* NIṢPRAPAÑCA

**i hwa** 二和. *See* ER HE

**i hyŏpsa** 二脇士. *See* ER XIESHI

**iik** 利益. *See* ĀNISAṂSA, ARTHAKRIYĀ

**i in** 二忍. *See* ER REN

**i ip** 二入. *See* ERRU

**Iip sahaeng non** 二入四行論. *See* Erru sixing lun

**ijakpŏp** 離作法. *See* vyatireka

**ijong kongyang** 二種供養. *See* erzhong gongyang

**ijong samgwan** 二種三觀. *See* sanguan

**ijong wŏlli** 二種遠離. *See* erzhong yuanli

**i ka** 二加. *See* er jia

**ilcha kwan** 一字關. *See* yizi guan

**ilch'e chi** 一切智. *See* sarvajñatā

**Ilch'egyŏng ŭmŭi** 一切經音義. *See* Yiqie jing yinyi

**ilch'eji chi** 一切知智. *See* sarvajñatājñāna

**ilch'ejong chi** 一切種智. *See* sarvākārajñatā

**ilch'esang chi** 一切相智. *See* vastujñāna

**Ilch'e yŏrae chinsilsŏp taesŭng hyŏnjŭng sammae taegyowang kyŏng** 一切如來眞實攝大乘現證三昧大教王經. *See* Sarvatathāgata-tattvasaṃgraha

**Ilch'e yŏrae kŭmgang samŏp ch'oesang pimil taegyowang kyŏng** 一切如來金剛三業最上秘密大教王經. *See* Guhyasamājatantra

**Ilchong** 日種. *See* Ādityabandhu

**ilch'ŏnje** 一闡提. *See* icchantika

**ilgan** 一間. *See* ekavīcika

**illae** 一來. *See* sakṛdāgāmin

**illae hyang** 一來向. *See* sakṛdāgāmiphalapratipannaka

**illyŏm samch'ŏn** 一念三千. *See* yinian sanqian

**Ilsan Illyŏng** 一山一寧. *See* Yishan Yining

**ilsim** 一心. *See* yixin

**Ilsŏl pu** 一說部. *See* Ekavyavahārika

**ilsŭng** 一乘. *See* ekayāna

**i mil** 二密. *See* er mi

**Imje nok** 臨濟錄. *See* Linji lu

**Im kyŏng** 林經. *See* Vanapatthasutta

**i musang** 二無常. *See* er wuchang

**in** 因. *See* hetu

**in** 人. *See* manuṣya, pudgala, puruṣa

**in** 印. *See* mudrā

**inajip** 人我執. *See* pudgalātmagraha

**Indara** 因陀羅. *See* Indra

**Indara mang** 因陀羅網. *See* Indrajāla

**in'ga** 印可. *See* yinke

**in'ga chŭngmyŏng** 印可證明. *See* yinke zhengming, yinke

**in'gagyu** 麟角喩. *See* khaḍgaviṣāṇakalpa

**in'gak** 麟角. *See* khaḍgaviṣāṇa

**In'get'a** 因揭陀. *See* Aṅgaja

**In'gwang** 印光. *See* Yinguang

**Inhyŏn** 仁賢. *See* Bhadrika

**Inyok sŏnin** 忍辱仙人. See Kṣāntivādin

**inmua** 人無我. *See* pudgalanairātmya

**Inmyŏng ip chŏngni non** 因明入正理論. *See* Nyāyapraveśa

**insŏng yŏmbul** 引聲念佛. *See* yinsheng nianfo

**Inwang kyŏng** 仁王經. *See* Renwang jing

**Inwang paekkojwa hoe** 仁王百高座會. *See* Renwang baigaozuo hui

**inyok** 忍辱. *See* kṣānti

**inyok paramil** 忍辱波羅蜜. *See* kṣāntipāramitā

**Inyok sŏnin** 忍辱仙人. *See* Kṣāntivādin

**in yŏn** 因緣. *See* hetupratyaya

**inyŏn** 因緣. *See* nidāna

**ipchong** 立宗. *See* pratijñā

**Ip Nŭngga kyŏng** 入楞伽經. See Laṅkāvatārasūtra

**i po** 二報. *See* er bao

**i pŏm** 二犯. *See* er fan

**i pŏpkye** 理法界. *See* li fajie

**Ip pŏpkye p'um** 入法界品. *See* Ru fajie pin

**ip'um** 異品. *See* vipakṣa

**Irhaeng** 一行. *See* Yixing

**irhaeng sammae** 一行三昧. *See* yixing sanmei

**i ryu** 二流. *See* er liu

**isa muae pŏpkye** 理事無礙法界. *See* lishi wu'ai fajie

**i segan** 二世間. *See* er shijian

**Isibŏgi** 二十億耳. *See* Soṇa Kolivīsa

**isibo wŏnt'ong** 二十五圓通. *See* ershiwu yuantong

**isik** 耳識. *See* śrotravijñāna

**isim chŏnsim** 以心傳心. *See* yixin chuanxin

**isip sŭngga** 二十僧伽. *See* VIṂŚATIPRABHEDASAṂGHA

**i sŏ** 二序. *See* ER XU

**isuk** 異熟. *See* VIPĀKA

**isuk in** 異熟因. *See* VIPĀKAHETU

**isuk kwa** 異熟果. *See* VIPĀKAPHALA

**i sŭng** 二乘. *See* ER SHENG

**it'a** 利他. *See* PARĀRTHA

**i tŏk** 二德. *See* ER DE

**i ŭngsin** 二應身. *See* ER YINGSHEN

**iyok** 離欲. *See* VAIRĀGYA

**iyŏm** 離染. *See* VAIRĀGYA

## K

**Kabimara** 迦毘摩羅. *See* KAPIMALA

**Kabirawi** 迦毘羅衛. *See* KAPILAVASTU

**kach'inaŭi** 迦絺那衣. *See* KAṬHINA

**Kadayŏnnija** 迦多衍尼子. *See* KĀTYĀYANĪPUTRA

**kae** 蓋. *See* NIVARAṆA

**kaean** 開眼. *See* KAIYAN, NETRAPRATIṢṬHĀPANA

**Kaebuhwa wang [yŏrae]** 開敷華王[如來]. *See* SAṂKUSUMITARĀJENDRA

**kaekchin pŏnnoe** 客塵煩惱. *See* ĀGANTUKAKLEŚA

**kaesan** 開山. *See* KAISHAN

**Kaewŏn Sŏkkyo nok** 開元釋教録. *See* KAIYUAN SHIJIAO LU

**kahaeng** 加行. *See* PRAYOGA

**kahaeng to** 加行道. *See* PRAYOGAMĀRGA

**kaji** 加持. *See* ADHIṢṬHĀNA

**kajok** 家族. *See* KULA

**Kajŏnyŏn** 迦旃延. *See* KĀTYĀYANA, MAHĀKĀTYĀYANA

**kak** 覺. *See* BODHI

**kakchi** 覺支. *See* BODHYAṄGA

**Kakpŏm Hyehong** 覺範慧洪. *See* JUEFAN HUIHONG

**Kallŭngga** 羯陵伽. *See* KALIṄGA

**kalma** 羯磨. *See* KARMAN

**kalma pu** 羯磨部. *See* KARMAKULA

**kaltŭng sŏn** 葛藤禪. *See* GETENG CHAN

**kambyŏn** 勘辨. *See* KANBIAN

**kamno** 甘露. *See* AMṚTA

**Kamsan Tŏkch'ŏng** 憨山德清. *See* HANSHAN DEQING

**kamŭng** 感應. *See* GANYING

**kamwŏn** 監院. *See* JIANYUAN

**kamyŏng** 假名. *See* PRAJÑAPTI, PRAJÑAPTISAT

**kamyŏng yu** 假名有. See PRAJÑAPTISAT

**Kanakkaballit'asa** 迦諾迦跋釐墮闍. *See* KANAKA BHARADVĀJA

**Kanakkabŏlch'a** 迦諾迦伐蹉. *See* KANAKAVATSA

**Kangnyangyasa** 畺良耶舍. *See* KĀLAYAŚAS

**Kang Sŭnghoe** 康僧會. *See* KANG SENGHUI

**kanhwa Sŏn** 看話禪. *See* KANHUA CHAN

**Kanisaekka wang** 迦膩色迦王. *See* KANIṢKA

**Karagut'a Kajŏnyŏn** 迦羅鳩馱迦旃延. *See* KAKUDA KĀTYĀYANA

**Karam kyŏng** 伽藍經. *See* KĀLĀMASUTTA

**Kariga** 迦梨迦. *See* KĀLĪ KURURAGHARIKĀ

**Kariga chonja** 迦里迦尊者. *See* KĀLIKA

**karura** 迦樓羅. *See* GARUḌA

**karyukpin'ga cho** 迦陸頻伽鳥. *See* KALAVIṄKA

**Karyut'ai** 迦留陀夷. *See* KĀLODĀYIN

**kasa** 袈裟. *See* KĀṢĀYA

**Kasŏbyu pu** 迦葉遺部. *See* KĀŚYAPĪYA

**Kasŏp** 迦葉. *See* KĀŚYAPA, MAHĀKĀŚYAPA

**Kasŏp Madŭng** 迦葉摩騰. *See* KĀŚYAPA MĀTAṄGA

**Kaya Kasŏp** 伽耶迦葉. *See* GAYĀ-KĀŚYAPA

**ke** 偈. *See* GĀTHĀ

**ke** 偈. *See* ŚLOKA

**Kiba** 耆婆. *See* JĪVAKA

**kibong** 機鋒. *See* JIFENG

**Kilchang** 吉藏. *See* JIZANG

**kilsang haeun** 吉祥海雲. *See* ŚRĪVATSA

**kinnara** 緊那羅. *See* KIṂNARA

**kisegan** 器世間. *See* BHĀJANALOKA

**Kisillon** 起信論. *See* DASHENG QIXIN LUN

**Kisu Kŭpkodok wŏn** 祇樹給孤獨園. *See* JETAVANA

**Kit'a t'aeja** 祇陀太子. *See* JETA

**kiya** 祇夜. *See* geya

**ko** 鼓. *See* drum

**ko** 苦. *See* duḥkha

**Kobong hwasang Sŏnyo** 高峰和尚禪要. *See* Gaofeng heshang Chanyao

**Kobong Wŏnmyo** 高峰原妙. *See* Gaofeng Yuanmiao

**ko chiok** 孤地獄. *See* pratyekanaraka

**koe** 愧. *See* apatrāpya

**koego** 壞苦. *See* vipariṇāmaduḥkhatā

**koegŏp** 壞劫. *See* saṃvartakalpa

**Koengji Chŏnggak** 宏智正覺. *See* Hongzhi Zhengjue

**kogo** 苦苦. *See* duḥkhaduḥkhatā

**kohaeng** 苦行. *See* duṣkaracaryā, dhūta, tapas

**koje** 苦諦. *See* duḥkhasatya

**kŏllip** 建立. *See* pratiṣṭhā

**kŏlsik** 乞食. *See* piṇḍapāta

**kŏmsu chiok** 劍樹地獄. *See* kṣuramārga

**kŏmyŏp im** 劍葉林. *See* asipattravana

**kŏnch'i** 犍稚. *See* ghaṇṭā

**Kŏnch'ŏk** 犍陟. *See* Kaṇṭhaka

**kŏndalba** 乾闥婆. *See* gandharva

**kŏndalba sŏng** 乾闥婆城. *See* gandharvanagara

**Kŏndara** 健馱羅. *See* Gandhāra

**kŏndo** 犍度. *See* khandaka

**kong** 空. *See* śūnyatā

**kongan** 公案. *See* gong'an

**kongdŏk** 功德. *See* ānisaṃsa, guṇa

**kongdŏk paramil** 功德波羅蜜. *See* guṇapāramitā

**kongdŏk wŏn** 功德院. *See* gongde yuan

**konggŏp** 空劫. *See* saṃvartasthāyikalpa

**konghwa** 空華. *See* khapuṣpa

**kongjŏk yŏngji** 空寂靈知. *See* kongji lingzhi, lingzhi

**kong ka chung samgwan** 空假中三觀. *See* sanguan

**Kongmok chang** 孔目章. *See* Kongmu zhang

**kong mubyŏn ch'ŏ** 空無邊處. *See* ākāśānantyāyatana

**kong pulgong ŏp** 共不共業. *See* gong bugong ye

**kongsang** 共相. *See* sāmānyalakṣaṇa

**kongyang** 供養. *See* pūjā

**kŏnsigwŏl** 乾屎橛. *See* ganshijue

**kŏp** 劫. *See* kalpa

**kŏpp'abae** 劫波杯. *See* kapāla

**kŏsa** 居士. *See* gṛhapati

**kŏsin'gwang** 擧身光. *See* jushenguang

**Kosŭng chŏn** 高僧傳. *See* Gaoseng zhuan

**Koŭm kyŏng** 苦陰經. *See* Cūḷadukkhakkhandhasutta

**Kubando** 鳩槃荼. *See* kūmbhāṇḍa

**Kubŏp kyŏng** 求法經. *See* Dhammadāyādasutta

**kubu kyŏng** 九部經. *See* navaṅga[pāvacana]

**Kuch'ira** 拘絺羅. *See* Kauṣṭhila

**kuch'ul kalma** 驅出羯磨. *See* pravrājanīyakarman

**Kudam** 瞿曇. *See* Gautama

**Kudani** 瞿陀尼. *See* Godānīya

**kudu sŏn** 口頭禪. *See* koutou chan

**kugyŏng** 究竟. *See* niṣṭhā

**kugyŏngdo/wi** 究竟道/位. *See* niṣṭhāmārga

**Kugyŏng ilsŭng posŏng non** 究竟一乘寶性論. *See* Ratnagotravibhāga

**ku haet'al** 俱解脫. *See* ubhayatobhāgavimukta

**Kuja** 龜茲. *See* Kucha

**kuja mu pulsŏng** 狗子無佛性. *See* gouzi wu foxing

**kuji** 俱胝. *See* koṭi

**kŭkch'il panyu** 極七返有. *See* saptakṛdbhavaparama

**Kukch'ŏng paengnok** 國清百録. *See* Guoqing bailu

**Kŭkkŭn** 克勤. *See* Yuanwu Keqin

**kŭkkwangjŏng ch'ŏn** 極光淨天. *See* ābhāsvaraloka

**kuksa** 國師. *See* guoshi

**Kumarajip/ Kumarasŭp** 鳩摩羅什. *See* Kumārajīva

**Kumara Kasŏp** 鳩摩羅迦葉. *See* Kumāra-Kāśyapa

**kŭmgang** 金剛. *See* vajra

**kŭmgang asari** 金剛阿闍梨. *See* vajrācārya

**Kŭmgang ch'oeswae tarani** 金剛摧碎陀羅尼. *See* Vajravidāraṇadhāraṇī

**Kŭmgangji** 金剛智. *See* Vajrabodhi, Vajramati

**Kŭmgangji** 金剛持. *See* VAJRADHARA

**kŭmgangjwa** 金剛座. *See* VAJRĀSANA

**kŭmgang ka** 金剛家. *See* VAJRAKULA

**kŭmgang kabujwa** 金剛跏趺坐. *See* VAJRAPARYAṄKA

**kŭmgang kye** 金剛界. *See* KONGŌKAI

**Kŭmgang kyŏng** 金剛經. *See* VAJRACCHEDIKĀPRAJÑĀPĀRAMITĀSŪTRA

**Kŭmgang pi** 金剛錍. *See* JINGANG PI

**kŭmgangsa** 金剛師. *See* VAJRĀCĀRYA

**Kŭmgang salt'a** 金剛薩埵. *See* VAJRASATTVA

**kŭmgang sammae** 金剛三昧. *See* VAJROPAMASAMĀDHI

**kŭmgang sŭng** 金剛乘. *See* VAJRAYĀNA

**Kŭmgang su posal** 金剛手菩薩. *See* VAJRAPĀṆI

**Kŭmgang yu chŏng** 金剛喻定. *See* VAJROPAMASAMĀDHI

**Kŭmgwangmyŏng ch'oesŭngwang kyŏng** 金光明最勝王經. *See* SURVARṆAPRABHĀSOTTAMASŪTRA

**Kŭmgwangmyŏng kyŏng** 金光明經. *See* SUVARṆAPRABHĀSOTTAMASŪTRA

**Kŭmnŭng Poji** 金陵寶誌. *See* BAOZHI

**kun** 裙. *See* NIVĀSANA

**kŭn** 根. *See* INDRIYA, MŪLA

**Kunaballaba** 瞿拏鉢剌婆. *See* GUṆAPRABHA

**Kunabalma** 求那跋摩. *See* GUṆAVARMAN

**Kunabaltara** 求那跋陀羅. *See* GUṆABHADRA

**Kŭnbon Sŏrilch'eyubu pinaya** 根本說一切有部毘奈耶. *See* MŪLASARVĀSTIVĀDA-VINAYA, VINAYAVIBHAṄGA

**kŭnbun** 近分. *See* SĀMANTAKA

**Kundobarhan** 君屠鉢漢. *See* KUṆḌADHĀNA

**kŭngmi** 極微. *See* PARAMĀNU

**Kŭngmun** 克文. *See* ZHENJING KEWEN

**kŭngnak** 極樂. *See* JILE

**kŭngnak chŏngt'o** 極樂淨土. *See* SUKHĀVATĪ

**kunji** 軍持. *See* KUṆḌIKĀ

**kŭnju** 近住. *See* UPAVĀSA

**kŭnju cheja** 近住弟子. *See* ANTEVĀSIKA

**kŭnsa yurŭi** 近事律儀. *See* UPĀSAKASAṂVARA

**kŭnyurŭi** 根律儀. *See* INDRIYASAṂVARA

**Kŭpkodok changja** 給孤獨長者. *See* ANĀTHAPIṆḌADA

**kup'um** 九品. *See* JIUPIN

**Kup'yera** 俱吠囉. *See* KUBERA

**Kuradandu kyŏng** 究羅檀頭經. *See* KŪṬADANTASUTTA

**kusaeng ajip** 俱生我執. *See* SAHAJĀTMAGRAHA

**kusaenggi** 俱生起. *See* SAHAJA

**kusaeng hok** 俱生惑. *See* SAHAJAKLEŚĀVARAṆA

**kusaeng mumyŏng** 俱生無明. *See* SAHAJĀVIDYĀ

**kusaeng pŏnnoe chang** 俱生煩惱障. *See* SAHAJAKLEŚĀVARAṆA

**kusanggwan** 九想觀. *See* NAVASAṂJÑĀ

**kuse** 九世. *See* JIUSHI

**Kusinagera** 拘尸那揭羅. *See* KUŚINAGARĪ

**kusu** 具壽. See ĀYUṢMAN

**Kusudara** 久壽多羅. *See* KUBJOTTARĀ

**kuŭi** 九儀. *See* JIUYI

**kuyuin** 俱有因. *See* SAHABHŪHETU

**kwa** 果. *See* PHALA

**kwa** 過. *See* PRASAṄGA, DOṢA

**kwabo** 果報. *See* VIPĀKA

**Kwagam Sawŏn** 廓庵師遠. *See* KUO'AN SHIYUAN

**kwagŏ ch'ilbul** 過去七佛. *See* SAPTATATHĀGATA

**kwahwan** 過患. *See* ĀDĪNAVA

**kwan** 觀. *See* VIPAŚYANĀ

**kwang** 誑. *See* MĀYĀ, ŚĀṬHYA

**kwangbae** 光背. *See* KĀYAPRABHĀ

**kwanggwa ch'ŏn** 廣果天. *See* BṚHATPHALA

**Kwang hongmyŏng chip** 廣弘明集. *See* GUANG HONGMING JI

**kwangmyŏng** 光明. *See* PRABHĀSVARA

**kwangmyŏngsim** 光明心. *See* PRABHĀSVARACITTA

**Kwang Paengnon pon** 廣百論本. *See* CATUḤŚATAKA

**Kwanhyu** 貫休. *See* CHANYUE GUANXIU

**Kwanjajae** 觀自在. *See* GUANZIZAI; GUANYIN

**Kwanjajae wang yŏrae** 觀自在王如來. *See* LOKEŚVARARĀJA

**kwanjŏng** 灌頂. *See* ABHIṢEKA

**kwanjŏng in** 灌頂印. *See* ABHIṢEKAMUDRĀ

**Kwanjŏng kyŏng** 灌頂經. *See* GUANDING JING

**Kwan Muryangsu kyŏng** 觀無量壽經. *See* GUAN WULIANGSHOU JING

**Kwan Pohyŏn posal haengpŏp kyŏng** 觀普賢菩薩行法經. *See* GUAN PUXIAN PUSA XINGFA JING

**Kwanseŭm** 觀世音. *See* GUANYIN

**Kwan soyŏn yŏn non** 觀所緣緣論. *See* ĀLAMBANAPARĪKṢĀ

**Kwanŭm** 觀音. *See* AVALOKITEŚVARA, GUANYIN

**kwi** 鬼. *See* BHŪTA

**kwigul** 鬼窟. *See* GUIKU

**Kwijamosin** 鬼子母神. *See* HĀRĪTĪ

**kwiŭi** 歸依. *See* ŚARAṆA

**kwŏn sil** 權實. *See* QUAN SHI

**kye** 界. *See* DHĀTU

**kye** 戒. *See* ŚĪLA

**Kyebŏp** 戒法. *See* ŚĪLADHARMA

**kyegŭmch'wi kyŏn** 戒禁取見. *See* ŚĪLAVRATAPARĀMARŚA

**kyegye** 界繫. *See* AVACARA

**Kyehyŏn** 戒賢. *See* ŚĪLABHADRA

**Kyejoksan** 鷄足山. *See* KUKKUṬAPĀDA

**kyenae kyo** 界內教. *See* JIENEI JIAO

**kyeoe kyo** 界外教. *See* JIEWAI JIAO

**Kye pon** 戒本. *See* PRĀTIMOKṢASŪTRA

**kyerap** 戒臘. *See* JIELA

**Kyesin non** 界身論. *See* DHĀTUKĀYA[PĀDAŚĀSTRA]

**Kyesung** 契嵩. *See* FORI QISONG

**kyet'ak punbyŏl** 計度分別. *See* ABHINIRŪPAṆĀVIKALPA

**Kyewŏnsa** 鷄園寺. *See* KUKKUṬĀRĀMA

**Kyeyun pu** 鷄胤部. *See* KAUKKUṬIKA

**kyo** 憍. *See* MADA

**Kyobŏmbaje** 憍梵波提. *See* GAVĀMPATI

**kyobŏp** 教法. *See* ĀGAMADHARMA

**kyodoron** 教導論. *See* AVAVĀDA

**kyŏgoe Sŏn** 格外禪. *See* GEWAI CHAN

**kyŏgŭi** 格義. *See* GEYI

**kyŏlche** 結制. *See* JIEZHI

**kyŏlchip** 結集. *See* SAṂGĪTI

**kyŏlchŏng** 決定. *See* NIYĀMA

**kyŏlchŏng chongsŏng** 決定種性. *See* NIYATAGOTRA

**kyŏlchŏng sagyŏn** 決定邪見. *See* NIYATAMICCHĀDIṬṬHI

**kyŏlsa** 結社. *See* JIESHE

**kyŏlt'aek** 決擇. *See* NIRVEDHA

**kyŏn** 見. *See* DARŚANA, DṚṢṬI

**kyŏnch'wi** 見取. *See* DṚṢṬIPARĀMARŚA

**kyŏndo** 見道. *See* DARŚANAMĀRGA

**kyŏndŭk** 見得. *See* DṚṢṬIPRĀPTA

**kyŏng** 經. *See* SŪTRA

**kyŏng** 境. *See* VIṢAYA

**kyŏngan** 輕安. *See* PRAŚRABDHI

**Kyŏngbunbyŏl** 經分別. *See* SŪTRAVIBHAṄGA

**kyŏngch'aek** 警策. *See* KYŌSAKU

**Kyŏngdŏk chŏndŭng nok** 景德傳燈録. *See* JINGDE CHUANDENG LU

**kyŏnghaeng** 經行. *See* CAṄKRAMA

**kyŏngjang** 經藏. *See* SŪTRAPIṬAKA

**kyŏngnok** 經錄. *See* JINGLU

**kyŏngnyŏk** 隔歷. *See* GELI

**kyŏngnyŏk samje** 隔歷三諦. *See* GELI SANDI

**Kyŏngnyul isang** 經律異相. *See* JINGLÜ YIXIANG

**Kyŏn'go kyŏng** 堅固經. *See* KEVAṬṬASUTTA

**kyŏn'goŭi** 堅固衣. *See* KAṬHINA

**kyŏngpŏp** 敬法. *See* GURUDHARMA

**Kyŏngu** 慶友. *See* NANDIMITRA

**kyŏnhok** 見惑. *See* JIANHUO

**kyŏnji** 見至. *See* DṚṢṬIPRĀPTA

**kyŏnsŏng** 見性. *See* JIANXING

**kyŏnsŏng sŏngbul** 見性成佛. *See* JIANXING CHENGFO

**kyooe pyŏlchŏn** 教外別傳. *See* JIAOWAI BIECHUAN

**Kyosalla kuk** 憍薩羅國. *See* KOŚALA

**kyosang p'ansŏk** 教相判釋. *See* JIAOXIANG PANSHI

**Kyosiga** 憍尸迦. *See* KAUŚIKA

**kyu** 竅. *See* QIAO

**Kyubong Chongmil** 圭峰宗密. *See* GUIFENG ZONGMI

**Kyugi** 窺基. *See* KUIJI

## M

**Ma** 魔. *See* Māra

**madalliga** 摩怛理迦. *See* mātṛkā

**Madu Kwanŭm** 馬頭觀音. *See* Hayagrīva

**Maekchŏksan** 麥積山. *See* Maijishan

**Magalta[guk]** 摩揭陀[國]. *See* Magadha

**magarŏ** 摩竭魚. *See* makara

**Mahabasabaje** 摩訶波闍波提. *See* Mahāprajāpatī

**Mahabihara** 摩訶毘訶羅. *See* Mahāvihāra

**Maha chigwan** 摩訶止觀. *See* Mohe zhiguan

**Maha chigwan pohaeng chŏnhong kyŏl** 摩訶止觀輔行傳弘決. *See* Mohe zhiguan fuxing zhuanhong jue

**Mahagajŏnyŏn** 摩訶迦旃延. *See* Mahākātyāyana

**Mahagasŏp** 摩訶迦葉. *See* Mahākāśyapa

**Mahagŏppinna** 摩訶劫賓那. *See* Mahākapphiṇa

**Mahajeba** 摩訶提婆. *See* Mahādeva

**Mahamokkŏllyŏn** 摩訶目犍連. *See* Mahāmaudgalyāyana

**Mahanam** 摩訶男. *See* Mahānāman

**Maha panya paramil kyŏng** 摩訶般若波羅蜜經. *See* Pañcaviṃśatisāhasrikāprajñāpāramitāsūtra

**Maharat'a kuk** 摩訶剌佗國. *See* Mahāraṭṭha

**mahasal** 摩訶薩. *See* mahāsattva

**Mahasana** 摩訶斯那. *See* Mahāsena

**mahuraga** 摩睺羅迦. *See* mahorāga

**Mahyesamandara [kuk]** 摩醯娑慢陀羅[國]. *See* Mahisa Maṇḍala

**Majillijet'a** 摩咥里制吒. *See* Mātṛceṭa

**Majo Toil** 馬祖道一. *See* Mazu Daoyi

**Malchŏnji** 末田地. *See* Madhyāntika

**Malgari-Kusarija** 末伽梨拘賒梨子. *See* Maskarin Gośāla

**malla sik** 末那識. *See* kliṣṭamanas

**Malli** 末利. *See* Mallikā

**malpŏp** 末法. *See* mofa, saddharmavipralopa

**malse** 末世. *See* moshi, paścimakāla

**Mamyŏng** 馬鳴. *See* Aśvaghoṣa

**man** 慢. *See* abhimāna, māna

**man** 鬘. *See* mālā

**man** 卍 [alt. 萬字]. *See* svastika

**Manasa** 摩那斯. *See* Manasvin

**manat'a** 摩那埵. *See* mānatva

**Manbulsa** 萬佛寺. *See* Wanfosi

**mancha** 萬字. *See* svastika

**mandara** 曼荼羅. *See* maṇḍala

**mangsang** 妄想. *See* wangxiang

**mangsin** 亡身. *See* wangshen

**mang sŏngŏn** 忘聖言. *See* upadeśasaṃpramoṣa

**mani** 摩尼. *See* maṇi

**Mansŏn tonggwi chip** 萬善同歸集. *See* Wanshan tonggui ji

**Mara [kuk]** 摩羅[國]. *See* Mallā

**Maranant'a** 摩羅難陀. *See* *Mālānanda

**Marang pu** 馬郎婦. *See* Malang fu

**Mariji** 摩利支. *See* Marīci

**ma samgŭn** 麻三斤. *See* ma sanjin

**Mat'ura** 摩偸羅. *See* Mathurā

**Maŭp kyŏng** 馬邑經. *See* Cūḷāssapurasutta, Mahāssapurasutta

**Mawang [Pasun]** 魔王[波旬]. *See* Namuci, Pāpīyāṃs

**Maya** 摩耶. *See* Māyā

**mich'ŏ** 味處. *See* rasāyatana

**Mijŭngyu kyŏng** 未曾有經. *See* Adbhutadharmaparyāyasūtra

**Milgyo** 密教. *See* Mijiao, Mikkyō

**Mirhwanyu kyŏng** 蜜丸喩經. *See* Madhupiṇḍikasutta

**mirŭi** 密意. *See* abhisaṃdhi

**Mirŭk** 彌勒. *See* Maitreya

**Mirun Wŏno** 密雲圓悟. *See* Miyun Yuanwu

**Mogam Sŏngdo** 木菴性瑫. *See* Mu'an Xingtao

**mogŏ** 木魚. *See* muyu

**Moja** 牟子. *See* Mouzi

**Moja ihok non** 牟子理惑論. *See* Mouzi lihuo lun

**Mokchillinda** 目眞隣陀. *See* Mucilinda

**Mokkŏllyŏnjajesu** 目犍連子帝須. *See* Moggaliputtatissa

**Mongnyŏn** 目連. *See* MAHĀMAUDGALYĀYANA

**moni** 牟尼. *See* MUNI

**Morip'agunna kyŏng** 牟犁破群那經. *See* KAKACŪPAMASUTTA

**mu** 無. *See* WU

**mua** 無我. *See* ANĀTMAN, NAIRĀTMYA, ANATTALAKKHAṆASUTTA

**muae haeng** 無礙行. *See* WU'AI XING

**mubŏn ch'ŏn** 無煩天. *See* AVṚHA

**mubunbyŏl** 無分別. *See* NIRVIKĀLPA

**much'a hoe** 無遮會. *See* WUZHE HUI

**Much'ak** 無著. *See* ASAṄGA

**much'i** 無癡. *See* AMOHA

**Mu Ch'ŭkch'ŏn** 武則天. *See* WU ZETIAN

**mugan chiok** 無間地獄. *See* AVĪCI

**mugan chŏng** 無間定. *See* ĀNANTARYASAMĀDHI

**mugan ŏp** 無間業. *See* ĀNANTARYAKARMAN

**mugan to** 無間道. *See* ĀNANTARYAMĀRGA

**mugibŏp** 無記法. *See* AVYĀKṚTADHARMA

**mugu sik** 無垢識. *See* AMALAVIJÑĀNA

**muhaeng pan** 無行般. *See* ANABHISAṂSKĀRAPARINIRVĀYIN

**muhaeng panyŏlban** 無行般涅槃. *See* ANABHISAṂSKĀRAPARINIRVĀYIN

**muhak** 無學. *See* AŚAIKṢA

**Muhak Chowŏn** 無學祖元. *See* WUXUE ZUYUAN

**muhakto** 無學道. *See* AŚAIKṢAMĀRGA

**mu hwadu** 無話頭. *See* WU GONG'AN, GONG'AN, HUATOU

**Muja pohyŏp kyŏng** 無字寶篋經. *See* ANAKṢARAKARAṆḌAKA [VAIROCANAGARBHA] SŪTRA

**mujasŏng** 無自性. *See* NIḤSVABHĀVA

**mujin** 無瞋. *See* ADVEṢA

**Mujinjang wŏn** 無盡藏院. *See* WUJINZANG YUAN

**Mujinŭi posal** 無盡意菩薩. *See* AKṢAYAMATI

**Mujinŭi posal p'um** 無盡意菩薩品. *See* AKṢAYAMATINIRDEŚA

**Mujun Sabŏm** 無準師範. *See* WUZHUN SHIFAN

**muju yŏlban** 無住涅槃. *See* APRATIṢṬHITANIRVĀṆA

**mukcho Sŏn** 默照禪. *See* MOZHAO CHAN

**mu kongan** 無公案. *See* WU GONG'AN

**Mumun Hyegae** 無門慧開. *See* WUMEN HUIKAI

**Mumun kwan** 無門關. *See* WUMEN GUAN

**mumyŏng** 無明. *See* AVIDYĀ

**muncha Sŏn** 文字禪. *See* WENZI CHAN

**mundap** 問答. *See* WENDA

**munhye** 聞慧. *See* ŚRUTAMAYĪPRAJÑĀ

**Munŏn** 文偃. *See* YUNMEN WENYAN

**Munsusari** 文殊師利. *See* MAÑJUŚRĪ

**munyŏm** 無念. *See* WUNIAN

**muoe[bo]si** 無畏[布]施. *See* ABHAYADĀNA

**Muoe samjang sŏnyo** 無畏三藏禪要. *See* WUWEI SANZANG CHANYAO

**mu punbyŏl chi** 無分別智. *See* NIRVIKĀLPAJÑĀNA

**mup'yosaek** 無表色. *See* AVIJÑAPTIRŪPA

**muru** 無漏. *See* ANĀSRAVA

**muru kye** 無漏界. *See* ANĀSRAVADHĀTU

**muryanggwang ch'ŏn** 無量光天. *See* APRAMĀṆĀBHA

**muryangjŏng ch'ŏn** 無量淨天. *See* APRAMĀṆAŚUBHA

**muryangsim** 無量心. *See* APRAMĀṆA

**Muryangsugyŏng ubajesa wŏnsaeng ke** 無量壽經優婆提舍願生偈. *See* WULIANGSHOU JING YOUPOTISHE YUANSHENG JI

**Muryangsu kyŏng** 無量壽經. *See* SUKHĀVATĪVYŪHA

**Muryangsu pul** 無量壽佛. *See* AMITĀYUS

**Muryang ŭi kyŏng** 無量義經. *See* WULIANG YI JING

**musaek kye** 無色界. *See* ĀRŪPYADHĀTU

**musaekkye chŏng** 無色界定. *See* ĀRŪPYĀVACARADHYĀNA

**musaek t'am** 無色貪. *See* ĀRŪPYARĀGA

**musaeng chi** 無生智. *See* ANUTPĀDAJÑĀNA

**musaeng pŏbin** 無生法忍. *See* ANUTPATTIKADHARMAKṢĀNTI

**musang** 無相. *See* ĀNIMITTA, NIRĀKĀRA

**musang** 無常. *See* ANITYA

**musang ch'ŏn** 無想天. *See* ASAṂJÑIKA

**musang chŏng** 無想定. *See* ASAṂJÑĀSAMĀPATTI

**musang chŏngdŭng kak** 無上正等覺. *See* ANUTTARASAMYAKSAṂBODHI

**musang kye** 無相戒. *See* WUXIANG JIE

**musang pŏmnyun** 無相法輪. *See* ALAKṢAṆATVADHARMACAKRA

**musang pori** 無上菩提. *See* MAHĀBODHI

**musim** 無心. *See* WUXIN

**Musim non** 無心論. *See* WUXIN LUN

**musŏng** 無性. *See* ASVABHĀVA, NIḤSVABHĀVA

**musooe** 無所畏. *See* VAIŚĀRADYA

**mu soyu ch'ŏ** 無所有處. *See* ĀKIÑCANYĀYATANA

**mut'am** 無貪. *See* ALOBHA

**muun ch'ŏn** 無雲天. *See* ANABHRAKA

**muwi** 無爲. *See* ASAṂSKṚTA; WUWEI

**muwibŏp** 無爲法. *See* ASAṂSKṚTADHARMA

**muwi chinin** 無位眞人. *See* WUWEI ZHENREN

**muwŏn** 無願. *See* APRAṆIHITA

**muyok** 無欲. *See* VAIRĀGYA

**muyŏl** 無熱. *See* ATAPA

**muyŏl ch'ŏn** 無熱天. *See* ATAPA

**muyŏ yŏlban** 無餘涅槃. *See* ANUPĀDIŚEṢANIRVĀṆA, NIRUPĀDHIŚEṢANIRVĀṆA

**Myobŏp yŏnhwa kyŏng** 妙法蓮華經. *See* SADDHARMAPUṆḌARĪKASŪTRA

**Myogosan** 妙高山. *See* SUMERU, MOUNT

**myohŭi** 妙喜. *See* ABHIRATI

**myo kwanch'al chi** 妙觀察智. *See* PRATYAVEKṢAṆĀJÑĀNA

**myŏl** 滅. *See* NIRODHA, VYAYA

**myŏlchaengpŏp** 滅諍法. *See* ADHIKARAṆAŚAMATHA

**myŏlche** 滅諦. *See* NIRODHASATYA

**myŏlchin chŏng** 滅盡定. *See* NIRODHASAMĀPATTI

**myŏnbyŏk** 面壁. *See* MIANBI

**myŏng** 明. *See* VIDYĀ

**myŏng ch'ŏ** 明處. *See* VIDYĀSTHĀNA

**myŏnggŭn** 命根. *See* JĪVITA

**myŏngho** 明護. *See* PARITTA

**myŏngho kyŏng** 明護經. *See* PARITTA

**Myŏngje** 明帝. *See* MINGDI

**myŏngsaek** 名色. *See* NĀMARŪPA

**Myŏnwang [pigu]** 面王[比丘]. *See* MOGHARĀJA

**Myosŏn** 妙善. *See* MIAOSHAN

**Myoŭm ch'ŏn** 妙音天. *See* SARASVATĪ

**Myoŭm posal** 妙音菩薩. *See* MAÑJUGHOṢA

## N

**Nabanabalche** 羅婆那拔提. *See* LAKUṆṬAKA BHADRIKA

**nach'al** 羅刹. *See* RĀKṢASA

**naejŭng** 内證. *See* PRATYĀTMĀDHIGAMA

**naemyŏng** 内明. *See* ADHYĀTMAVIDYĀ

**naeŭi** 内衣. *See* ANTARVĀSAS

**Nagasŏna** 那伽犀那. *See* NĀGASENA

**Nagyang karam ki** 洛陽伽藍記. *See* LUOYANG QIELAN JI

**nahan** 羅漢. *See* ARHAT, LUOHAN

**Nahyŏng pŏmji kyŏng** 倮形梵志經. *See* KASSAPASĪHANĀDASUTTA

**Naje Kasŏp** 那提迦葉. *See* NADĪ-KĀŚYAPA

**nak** 樂. *See* SUKHA

**Nakkora changja mo** 諾酤羅長者母. *See* NAKULAPITṚ and NAKULAMĀTṚ

**nakku** 樂求. *See* ABHILĀṢA

**Namak Hoeyang** 南嶽懷讓. *See* NANYUE HUAIRANG

**Namak Hyesa** 南嶽慧思. *See* NANYUE HUISI

**Nambini wŏn** 藍毘尼園. *See* LUMBINĪ

**Namch'ŏn Powŏn** 南泉普願. *See* NANQUAN PUYUAN

**Nam chong** 南宗. *See* NAN ZONG

**Namhae kigwi naebŏp chŏn** 南海寄歸内法傳. *See* NANHAI JIGUI NEIFA ZHUAN

**Namsan yul chong** 南山律宗. *See* NANSHAN LÜ ZONG

**namu Amit'a pul** 南無阿彌陀佛. *See* NAMU AMIDABUTSU, AMITĀBHA

**namu Myobŏp yŏnhwa kyŏng** 南無妙法蓮華經. *See* NAMU MYŌHŌRENGEKYŌ

**Namyang Hyech'ung** 南陽慧忠. *See* NANYANG HUIZHONG

**nan** 煖. *See* ūṣman

**nanch'ŏ** 難處. *See* akṣaṇa

**Nanda** 難陀. *See* Nanda

**Nandaga** 難陀迦. *See* Nandaka

**Nan'gye Toryung** 蘭溪道隆. *See* Lanxi Daolong

**nansik** 亂識. *See* bhrāntijñāna

**nansŭng chi** 難勝地. *See* sudurjayā

**Narandasa** 那爛陀寺. *See* Nālandā

**Narayŏn ch'ŏn** 那羅延天. *See* Nārāyaṇa

**Naryŏnjeriyasa** 那連提黎耶舍. *See* Narendrayaśas

**Nasŏn** 那先. *See* Nāgasena

**Nasŏn pigu** 那先比丘. *See* Nāgasena

**Nasŏn pigu kyŏng** 那先比丘經. *See* Milindapañha

**Naura pu** 那憂羅父. *See* Nakulapitṛ and Nakulamātṛ

**nidana** 尼陀那. *See* nidāna

**Nigŏnda Yajeja** 尼揵陀若提子. *See* Nirgrantha-Jñātīputra

**Nigŏnja** 尼揵子. *See* Nirgrantha

**Niguda** 尼瞿陀. *See* Nigrodha

**Niguyullim** 尼拘律林. *See* Nigrodhārāma

**Niryŏnsŏnha** 尼連禪河. *See* Nairañjanā

**no** 老. *See* jarā

**Noch'a kyŏng** 露遮經. *See* Lohiccasutta

**noe** 惱. *See* pradāsa

**Noet'ahwara** 賴吒和羅. *See* Rāṣṭrapāla

**Nogyawŏn** 鹿野苑. *See* Mṛgadāva

**Noja hwaho kyŏng** 老子化胡經. *See* Laozi huahu jing

**Nokchamo** 鹿子母. *See* Viśākhā

**Nokchamo tang** 鹿子母堂. *See* Mṛgāramātuprāsāda

**noksu nang** 漉水囊. *See* parisrāvaṇa

**non** 論. *See* śāstra, bhāṣya

**nonjang** 論藏. *See* abhidharmapiṭaka, *śāstrapiṭaka

**nosa** 老死. *See* jarāmaraṇa

**nu** 漏. *See* āsava

**nujin** 漏盡. *See* kṣīṇāsrava, āsravakṣaya

**nujin[ji]** 漏盡[智]. *See* āsravakṣaya

**Nujin kyŏng** 漏盡經. *See* Sabbāsavasutta

**Nŭngga saja ki** 楞伽師資記. *See* Lengqie shizi ji

**nŭngjak in** 能作因. *See* kāraṇa(hetu)

**Nŭngnamaje** 勒那摩提. *See* Ratnamati

**nŭngnip** 能立. *See* sādhana

## O

**o** 悟. *See* wu

**oan** 五眼. *See* pañcacakṣus

**obajesak** 鄔波題鑠. *See* upadeśa

**obŏp** 五法. *See* wufa

**obu** 五部. *See* pañcakula

**obul** 五佛. *See* pañcatathāgata

**och'aje** 五次第. *See* pañcakrama

**och'wi** 五趣. *See* pañcagati

**Odaesan** 五臺山. *See* Wutaishan

**odo** 五道. *See* pañcagati

**odo song** 悟道頌. *See* wudao song, yiji

**oe** 外. *See* bahirdhā

**oedo** 外道. *See* tīrthika

**oegyŏng** 外境. *See* bāhyārtha

**oga** 汚家. *See* kuladūṣaka

**Ŏgi** 億耳. *See* Soṇa-Koṭikaṇṇa

**ogun [pigu]** 五群[比丘]. *See* bhadravargīya, pañcavargika

**ogŭn** 五根. *See* pañcendriya

**ogye** 五戒. *See* pañcaśīla

**Ogyo chang** 五教章. *See* Huayan wujiao zhang

**ogyŏng** 五境. *See* pañcaviṣaya

**ohoe yŏmbul** 五會念佛. *See* wuhui nianfo

**oji** 五智. *See* pañcajñāna

**oji yŏrae** 五智如來. *See* pañcatathāgata, pañcajina

**ojŏnggŏ ch'ŏn** 五淨居天. *See* śuddhāvāsa

**ojong hyŏnŭi** 五種玄義. *See* wuzhong xuanyi

**Ojo Pŏbyŏn** 五祖法演. *See* WUZU FAYAN

**ojung hyŏnŭi** 五重玄義. *See* FAHUA WUCHONG XUANYI

**o ka ch'il chong** 五家七宗. *See* WU JIA QI ZONG

**o kyŏlchŏng** 五決定. *See* PAÑCANIYATA

**omi** 五味. *See* WUWEI

**om mani panme hum** 唵嘛呢叭彌吽. *See* OṂ MAṆI PADME HŪṂ

**o muganŏp** 五無間業. *See* PAÑCĀNANTARĪYA

**omyŏng** 五明. *See* PAÑCAVIDYĀ

**omyoyok** 五妙欲. *See* PAÑCAKĀMAGUṆA

**on** 蘊. *See* SKANDHA

**ongho** 擁護. *See* RĀKṢĀ

**ŏn'gyo** 言教. *See* NIRUKTI

**onma** 蘊魔. *See* SKANDHAMĀRA

**ŏnŏ** 言語. *See* VYAVAHĀRA

**oon** 五蘊. *See* PAÑCASKANDHA

**oon segan** 五蘊世間. *See* WUYUN SHIJIAN

**ŏŏp** 語業. *See* VĀKKARMAN

**ŏp** 業. *See* KARMAN

**ŏpchang** 業障. *See* KARMĀVARAṆA

**ŏpto** 業道. *See* KARMAPATHA

**ŏrok** 語録. *See* YULU

**oryŏk** 五力. *See* PAÑCABALA

**osi** 五時. *See* WUSHI

**osi p'algyo** 五時八教. *See* WUSHI BAJIAO

**ot'ak** 五濁. *See* PAÑCAKAṢĀYA

**owi** 五位. *See* PAÑCAMĀRGA

# P

**Pabu** 婆敷. *See* VĀṢPA

**Pach'a** 婆差. *See* VATSAGOTRA

**paegil kalma** 白一羯磨. *See* JÑAPTIDVITĪYĀ-KARMAVĀCANĀ

**Paegŭi Kwanŭm** 白衣觀音. *See* BAIYI GUANYIN

**Paegyŏng** 白英. *See* ŚVETAKETU

**Paek** 帛. *See* BO

**Paekchang ch'ŏnggyu** 百丈清規. *See* BAIZHANG QINGGUI

**Paekchang Hoehae** 百丈懷海. *See* BAIZHANG HUAIHAI

**Paekchŏng** 白淨. *See* ŚVETAKETU

**paekho** 白毫. *See* ŪRṆĀKEŚA

**paekkalma** 白羯磨. *See* KARMAVĀCANĀ

**Paek Kŏi** 白居易. *See* BO JUYI

**Paek non** 百論. *See* ŚATAŚĀSTRA

**paekpŏp** 百法. *See* BAIFA

**Paeksan'gae pulchŏng** 白傘蓋佛頂. *See* SITĀTAPATRĀ

**Paengmasa** 白馬寺. *See* BAIMASI

**paengnyŏnhwa** 白蓮華. *See* PUṆḌARĪKA

**Paengnyŏnsa** 白蓮社. *See* BAILIAN SHE

**Pagari** 婆迦梨. *See* VAKKALI

**Pagisa** 婆耆舍. *See* VAṄGĪSA

**P'agorap chonja** 巴沽拉尊者. *See* BAKKULA

**Paje** 婆提. *See* BHADRIKA

**Pakkura** 薄拘羅. *See* BAKKULA

**pal** 鉢. *See* PĀTRA

**p'albul** 八不. *See* AṢṬĀNTA, BABU

**p'alchaegye** 八齋戒. *See* AṢṬĀṄGASAMANVĀGATAṂ UPAVĀSAṂ

**Palch'a [kuk]** 跋蹉[國]. *See* VATSĀ

**Palche** 跋提. *See* BHADDIYA-KĀḶIGODHĀPUTTA

**p'al chŏngdo** 八正道. *See* AṢṬĀṄGAMĀRGA

**p'algak** 八覺. *See* BA JUE

**Palgija** 跋耆子. *See* VṚJIPUTRAKA

**p'algo** 八苦. *See* DUḤKHA

**p'algwan chae** 八關齋. *See* BAGUAN ZHAI

**palgwang chi** 發光地. *See* PRABHĀKARĪBHŪMI

**p'al haet'al** 八解脱. *See* AṢṬAVIMOKṢA

**Pallagŭpporisan** 鉢羅笈菩提山. *See* PRĀGBODHI(GIRI)

**p'al mi** 八味. *See* BA WEI

**pal pori sim** 發菩提心. *See* BODHICITTOTPĀDA

**P'alsŏng kyŏng** 八城經. *See* AṬṬHAKANĀGARASUTTA

**p'alssang** 八相. *See* BAXIANG

**Palt'abara** 跋陀波羅. *See* BHADRAPĀLA

**p'al taein** 八大人. *See* AṢṬĀRYAPUDGALA

**p'al tae posal** 八大菩薩. *See* AṢṬAMAHOPAPUTRA, MAHĀUPAPUTRA

**Palt'a Kundaraguiguk** 拔陀軍陀羅拘夷國. *See* BHADDĀ-KUṆḌALAKESĀ

**Palt'ara chonja** 跋陀羅尊者. *See* BHADRA

**Palt'ara Kabiriya** 跋陀羅迦卑梨耶. *See* BHADDĀ KAPILĀNĪ

**pana** 波那. *See* PRĀṆA

**Pandudalta** 槃頭達多. *See* BANDHUDATTA

**pan'ga sayu** 半跏思惟. *See* MAITREYĀSANA

**pangdŭng** 方等. *See* VAIPULYA

**Panggwang taejangŏm kyŏng** 方廣大莊嚴經. *See* LALITAVISTARA

**pangil** 放逸. *See* PRAMĀDA

**pangjang** 方丈. *See* FANGZHANG

**Pang kŏsa** 龐居士. *See* PANG YUN

**Pang kŏsa ŏrok** 龐居士語錄. *See* PANG JUSHI YULU

**Pang On** 龐蘊. *See* PANG YUN

**pangp'yŏn** 方便. *See* UPĀYA

**pangpy'ŏn sŏn'gyo** 方便善巧. *See* UPĀYAKAUŚALYA

**pangsaeng** 放生. *See* FANGSHENG

**pangsaeng hoe** 放生會. *See* FANGSHENG HUI

**Pangu p'um** 放牛品. *See* MAHĀGOPĀLAKASUTTA

**Pang Yŏmgu** 放焰口. *See* FANG YANKOU

**panjo** 返照. *See* FANZHAO

**Panju sammae kyŏng** 般舟三昧經. *See* PRATYUTPANNABUDDHASAMMUKHĀVASTHITASAMĀDHISŪTRA

**pan kabujwa** 半跏趺坐. *See* ARDHAPARYAṄKA, ARDHAPADMĀSANA

**Pant'akka** 半託迦. *See* PANTHAKA

**panya** 般若. *See* PRAJÑĀ

**Panyadŭng non sŏk** 般若燈論釋. *See* PRAJÑĀPRADĪPA

**Panya ich'wi pun** 般若理趣分. *See* ADHYARDHAŚATIKĀPRAJÑĀPĀRAMITĀSŪTRA, PRAJÑĀPĀRAMITĀNAYAŚATAPAÑCĀŚATIKĀ

**Panya muji non** 般若無知論. *See* BORE WUZHI LUN

**panya paramilta** 般若波羅蜜多. *See* PRAJÑĀPĀRAMITĀ

**Panya paramilta sim kyŏng** 般若波羅蜜多心經. *See* PRAJÑĀPĀRAMITĀHṚDAYASŪTRA

**panyŏlban** 般涅槃. *See* PARINIRVĀṆA

**pan yŏnhwajwa** 半蓮華坐. *See* ARDHAPADMĀSANA, ARDHAPARYAṄKA

**Parach'ana** 波羅遮那. *See* PAṬACĀRĀ

**parai** 波羅夷. *See* PĀRĀJIKA

**parajejesani** 波羅提提舍尼. *See* PRATIDEŚANĪYA

**parajemokch'a** 波羅提木叉. *See* PRĀTIMOKṢA

**parajemokch'aho** 波羅提木叉護. *See* PRĀTIMOKṢASAṂVARA

**paramil** 波羅蜜. *See* PĀRAMITĀ

**Parap'agaramiltara** 波羅頗迦羅蜜多羅. *See* PRABHĀKARAMITRA

**P'ari** 波利. *See* BHALLIKA

**parijiltasu** 波利質多樹. *See* PĀRIYĀTRAKA

**Pasaga** 婆呬迦. *See* BĀHIYA DĀRUCĪRIYA

**Pasanik wang** 波斯匿王. *See* PRASENAJIT

**p'asŭng** 破僧. *See* SAṂGHABHEDA

**pi** 悲. *See* KARUṆĀ

**p'ian** 彼岸. *See* PĀRA

**Pibasa sa** 毘婆沙師. *See* VAIBHĀṢIKA

**Pibasi pul** 毘婆尸佛. *See* VIPAŚYIN

**pich'ŏ** 鼻處. *See* GHRĀṆĀYATANA

**Pidan kil** 緋緞길. *See* SILK ROAD

**pidŭk** 非得. *See* APRĀPTI

**piga** 非家. *See* ANAGĀRIKĀ

**p'igap** 被甲. *See* SAṂNĀHA

**pigara** 毘伽羅. *See* VYĀKARAṆA

**pigu** 比丘. *See* BHIKṢU

**Pigu ch'ŏng kyŏng** 比丘請經. *See* ANUMĀNASUTTA

**Piguji** 毘俱胝. *See* BHṚKUTĪ

**pigŭn** 鼻根. *See* GHRĀṆENDRIYA

**piguni** 比丘尼. *See* BHIKṢUṆĪ

**Piguni chŏn** 比丘尼傳. *See* BIQIUNI ZHUAN

**pigu wiŭi** 比丘威儀. *See* ABHISAMĀCĀRIKĀ[ŚĪLA]

**Pihwa kyŏng** 悲華經. *See* KARUṆĀPUṆḌARĪKASŪTRA

**Pijeha** 毘提訶. *See* VIDEHA

**P'illŭngga Pach'a** 畢陵伽婆蹉. *See* PILINDAVATSA

**pimil kwanjŏng** 秘密灌頂. *See* GUHYĀBHIṢEKA

**Pinaya sa** 毘奈耶事. *See* Vinayavastu

**Pinbasara** 頻婆娑羅. *See* Bimbisāra

**pinch'ul** 擯出. *See* nāsana

**Pinduro Pallat'a chonja** 賓頭盧頗羅墮尊者. *See* Piṇḍola-Bhāradvāja

**Pip'an Pulgyo** 批判佛教. *See* Hihan Bukkyō

**Piraebong** 飛来峰. *See* Feilaifeng

**piri chagŭi** 非理作意. *See* ayoniśomanaskāra

**Pirojana** 毗盧遮那. *See* Vairocana

**piryang** 比量. *See* anumāṇa

**Pisagŏ** 毗舍佉. *See* Viśākha

**Pisagŏ mo** 毗舍佉母. *See* Viśākhā

**Pisamun ch'ŏn** 毘沙門天. *See* Vaiśravaṇa

**pisang pibisang ch'ŏ** 非想非非想處. *See* naivasaṃjñānāsaṃjñāyatana

**Pisari** 毘舍離. *See* Vaiśālī

**pisasa** 毘舍闍. *See* piśāca

**pisik** 鼻識. *See* ghrāṇavijñāna

**pit'aekmyŏl** 非擇滅. *See* apratisaṃkhyānirodha

**Piŭn T'ongyong** 費隱通容. *See* Feiyin Tongrong

**Poam** 普巖. *See* Yun'an Puyan

**pŏbajip** 法我執. *See* dharmātmagraha

**pŏban** 法眼. *See* dharmacakṣus

**Pŏban chong** 法眼宗. *See* Fayan zong

**Pŏban Munik** 法眼文益. *See* Fayan Wenyi

**pŏbin** 法忍. *See* dharmakṣānti

**pŏbin** 法印. *See* dharmamudrā

**pŏbŏ** 法語. *See* fayu

**Pŏbon chok non** 法蘊足論. *See* Dharmaskandha [pādaśāstra]

**pobu** 寶部. See ratnakula

**pŏbun chi** 法雲地. *See* dharmameghā

**pŏbwang** 法王. *See* dharmarāja

**Pŏbwŏn churim** 法苑珠林. *See* Fayuan zhulin

**pobyŏng kwanjŏng** 寶瓶灌頂. *See* kalaśābhiṣeka

**pŏbyu amu chong** 法有我無宗. *See* fayou wowu zong

**Pŏbyung** 法融. *See* Niutou Farong

**P'odae** 布袋. *See* Budai

**Podang chong** 保唐宗. *See* Baotang zong

**Podang Muju** 保唐無住. *See* Baotang Wuzhu

**pogŏpsa** 福業事. *See* puṇyakriyāvastu

**Pogyŏng sammae** 寶鏡三昧. *See* Baojing sanmei

**Pohaengwang chŏng non** 寶行王正論. *See* Ratnāvalī

**pohwa isin** 報化二身. *See* baohua ershen

**Pohyang** 普香. *See* Samantagandha

**Pohyŏn** 普賢. *See* Samantabhadra

**Pohyŏn posal haengwŏn ch'an** 普賢菩薩行願讚. *See* Bhadracarīpraṇidhāna

**Pojang non** 寶藏論. *See* Baozang lun

**Poji** 保誌/寶誌. *See* Baozhi

**Pojŏk** 普寂. *See* Puji

**pok** 覆. *See* mrakṣa

**pok** 福. *See* puṇya

**pokchang** 腹藏/伏藏. *See* nidhāna

**pokchangmul** 腹藏物. *See* fuzangwu

**pokchi charyang** 福智資糧. *See* puṇyajñānasaṃbhāra

**pokchŏn** 福田. *See* puṇyakṣetra

**poksaeng ch'ŏn** 福生天. *See* puṇyaprasava

**poktŏk charyang** 福德資糧. *See* puṇyasaṃbhāra

**Pŏllabasa chonja** 伐那婆斯尊者. *See* Vanavāsin

**pollae myŏnmok** 本來面目. *See* benlai mianmu

**Pŏlsarabultara** 伐闍羅弗多羅. *See* Vajraputra

**pŏmbo ch'ŏn** 梵輔天. *See* brahmapurohita

**pŏmbu** 凡夫. *See* pṛthagjana

**Pŏmch'ŏn** 梵天. *See* Brahmā

**Pŏmch'ŏn ch'ŏngbul kyŏng** 梵天請佛經. *See* Brahmanimantaṇikasutta

**Pŏmdong kyŏng** 梵動經. *See* Brahmajālasuttanta

**Pŏmgye** 梵界. *See* Brahmaloka

**pŏmhaeng** 梵行. *See* brahmacaryā

**pŏmju** 梵住. *See* brahmavihāra

**pŏmjung ch'ŏn** 梵衆天. *See* brahmakāyika

**Pŏmmang kyŏng** 梵網經. *See* Fanwang jing

**pŏmmua** 法無我. *See* dharmanairātmya

**pŏmmun** 法門. *See* dharmaparyāya

**pŏmmyŏng** 法名. *See* faming

**Pŏmnak piguni** 法樂比丘尼. *See* Dharmadinnā

**Pŏmnak piguni kyŏng** 法樂比丘尼經. *See* Cūḷavedallasutta

**pŏmnan** 法難. *See* fanan

**pŏmnap** 法臘. *See* fala

**pŏmnyul** 法律. *See* dharmavinaya

**pŏmnyun** 法輪. *See* dharmacakra

**pŏmp'ae** 梵唄. *See* fanbai

**Pŏmyŏnna** 梵衍那. *See* Bāmiyān

**ponch'o pul** 本初佛. *See* ādibuddha

**pon'gak** 本覺. *See* benjue

**ponghal** 棒喝. *See* banghe

**p'ongnyu** 暴流. *See* ogha

**Pongpŏp yo** 奉法要. *See* Fengfa yao

**ponje** 本際. *See* benji, koṭi

**Ponjŏk** 本寂. *See* Caoshan Benji

**ponmun** 本門. *See* honmon

**pŏnnoe** 煩腦. *See* kleśa

**pŏnnoe chang** 煩腦障. *See* kleśāvaraṇa

**ponsaeng kyŏng** 本生經. *See* jātaka

**ponsik** 本識. *See* mūlavijñāna, ālayavijñāna

**ponsŏng chŏng** 本性淨. *See* prakṛtiviśuddhi

**ponsŏng chu chongsŏng** 本性住種性. *See* prakṛtisthagotra

**ponwŏn** 本願. *See* purvapraṇidhāna

**Pŏnyŏk myŏngŭi taejip** 翻譯名義大集. *See* Mahāvyutpatti

**P'ooe** 怖畏. *See* Bhairava

**P'ooe Kŭmgang** 怖畏金剛. *See* Vajrabhairava

**pŏp** 法. *See* dharma

**pŏpcha** 法子. *See* fazi

**Pŏpchang** 法藏. *See* Fazang

**Pŏpchang pigu** 法藏比丘. *See* Dharmākara

**Pŏpchang pu** 法藏部. *See* Dharmaguptaka

**Pŏpch'ing** 法稱. *See* Dharmakīrti

**pŏpchip** 法執. *See* fazhi

**Pŏpchip kyŏng** 法集經. *See* Dharmasaṃgīti

**Pŏpcho** 法照. *See* Fazhao

**pŏpch'ŏ** 法處. *See* dharmāyatana

**pŏpchu** 法主. *See* fazhu

**Pŏphae** 法海. *See* Fahai

**pŏpho** 法護. *See* dharmapālā

**pŏphŭi** 法喜. *See* dharmaprīti

**Pŏphŭm** 法欽. *See* Faqin

**Pŏphwa allak haengŭi** 法華安樂行義. *See* Fahua anle xingyi

**Pŏphwa ch'ampŏp** 法華懺法. *See* Fahua chanfa

**Pŏphwa chŏn['gi]** 法華傳[記]. *See* Fahua zhuan[ji]

**Pŏphwa hyŏnch'an** 法華玄贊. *See* Fahua xuanzan

**Pŏphwa hyŏnŭi** 法華玄義. *See* Fahua xuanyi

**Pŏphwa kyŏng** 法華經. *See* Saddharmapuṇḍarīkasūtra

**Pŏphwa kyŏng ŭi ki** 法華經義記. *See* Fahua jing yi ji

**Pŏphwa kyŏng yakso** 法華經略疏. *See* Fahua jing lüeshu

**Pŏphwa mun'gu** 法華文句. *See* Fahua wenju

**Pŏphwa obaek mun non** 法華五百問論. *See* Fahua wubai wen lun

**Pŏphwa ojung hyŏnŭi** 法華五重玄義. *See* Fahua wuchong xuanyi

**Pŏphwa sambu [kyŏng]** 法華三部[經]. *See* Fahua sanbu [jing]

**Pŏphyŏn** 法顯. *See* Faxian

**Pŏphyŏn chŏn** 法顯傳. *See* Faxian zhuan

**pŏpki** 法器. *See* faqi

**Pŏpki posal** 法起菩薩. *See* Dharmodgata

**Pŏpku kyŏng** 法句經. *See* Dhammapada

**pŏpkye** 法界. *See* dharmadhātu

**pŏpkye ch'esŏngji** 法界體性智. *See* dharmadhātusvabhāvajñāna

**pŏpkye kaji** 法界加持. *See* fajie jiachi

**pŏpkye yŏn'gi** 法界緣起. *See* fajie yuanqi

**pŏpsa** 法嗣. *See* fasi

**Pŏpsang chong** 法相宗. *See* FAXIANG ZONG, KYO

**pŏpsi** 法施. *See* DHARMADĀNA

**pŏpsin** 法身. *See* DHARMAKĀYA

**pŏp[sin] sari** 法[身]舍利. *See* DHARMAŚARĪRA

**pŏpsŏng** 法性. *See* DHARMATĀ

**pŏpsu** 法數. *See* FASHU

**pŏptang** 法幢. *See* FACHUANG

**pori** 菩提. *See* BODHI

**pori charyang** 菩提資糧. *See* BODHISAṂBHĀRA

**P'orida kyŏng** 晡利多經. *See* POTALIYASUTTA

**Poridalma** 菩提達摩. *See* BODHIDHARMA

**Porihaeng kyŏng** 菩提行經. *See* BODHICARYĀVATĀRA

**pori ku** 菩提具. *See* BODHISAṂBHĀRA

**Porim chŏn** 寶林傳. *See* BAOLIN ZHUAN

**pori pun** 菩提分. *See* BODHIPAKṢA

**Poriryuji** 菩提流支. *See* BODHIRUCI

**porisim** 菩提心. *See* BODHICITTA

**Porisŏnna** 菩提僊那. *See* BODHISENA

**pori su** 菩提樹. *See* BODHI TREE

**Posaeng yŏrae** 寶生如來. *See* RATNASAṂBHAVA

**posal** 菩薩. *See* BODHISATTVA

**p'osal** 布薩. *See* UPOṢADHA

**Posalchang [kyŏng]** 菩薩藏[經]. *See* BODHISATTVAPIṬAKA

**posal chi** 菩薩地. *See* BODHISATTVABHŪMI

**Posal chiji kyŏng** 菩薩地持經. *See* BODHISATTVABHŪMISŪTRA

**Posalgye kyŏng** 菩薩戒經. *See* PUSAJIE JING

**posal kye** 菩薩戒. *See* PUSA JIE, BODHISATTVAŚĪLA, BODHISATTVASAṂVARA

**Posal kyŏnsil kyŏng** 菩薩見實經. *See* PITĀPUTRASAMĀGAMASŪTRA

**Posal ponŏp kyŏng** 菩薩本業經. *See* PUSA BENYE JING

**Posal ponsaengman non** 菩薩本生鬘論. *See* JĀTAKAMĀLĀ

**posal sŭng** 菩薩乘. *See* BODHISATTVAYĀNA

**posal wŏn** 菩薩願. *See* BODHISATTVAPRAṆIDHĀNA

**Posal yŏngnak ponŏp kyŏng** 菩薩瓔珞本業經. *See* PUSA YINGLUO BENYE JING

**posi** 布施. *See* DĀNA

**posin** 報身. *See* SAṂBHOGAKĀYA

**posi paramil** 布施波羅蜜. *See* DĀNAPĀRAMITĀ

**Posu posal** 寶手菩薩. *See* RATNAPĀṆI

**P'ot'abaru kyŏng** 布吒婆樓經. *See* POṬṬHAPĀDASUTTA

**Pot'araksan** 補陀落山. *See* POṬALAKA

**Pot'asan** 普陀山/補陀山. *See* PUTUOSHAN

**pot'ŭkkara** 補特伽羅. *See* PUDGALA

**pot'ŭkkara non** 補特伽羅論. *See* PUDGALAVĀDA

**Poŭn** 報恩. *See* DAHONG BAO'EN

**Poun kyŏng** 寶雲經. *See* RATNAMEGHASŪTRA

**Poŭn pongbun kyŏng** 報恩奉盆經. *See* BAO'EN FENGBEN JING

**Powŏn** 普願. *See* NANQUAN PUYUAN

**Poyo kyŏng** 普曜經. *See* LALITAVISTARA

**pu** 部. *See* nikāya

**pubal** 覆鉢. *See* PĀTRANIKUBJANA

**pubal kalma** 覆鉢羯磨. *See* PĀTRANIKUBJANA

**pudo** 浮屠. See FO

**pudong** 不動. *See* akopya

**pudong chi** 不動地. *See* ACALĀBHŪMI

**Pudong myŏngwang** 不動明王. *See* ACALANĀTHA-VIDYĀRĀJA

**pudongjwa** 不動坐. *See* ACALĀSANA

**pudong ŏp** 不動業. *See* ANIÑJYAKARMAN

**puhaeng** 部行. *See* VARGACĀRIN

**Puja hapchip kyŏng** 父子合集經. *See* PITĀPUTRASAMĀGAMASŪTRA

**pujŏng** 不定. *See* ANIYATA

**pujŏng** 不淨. *See* SAṂKLIṢṬA

**pujŏng chongsŏng** 不定種姓/種性. *See* ANIYATAGOTRA

**pujŏngji** 不正知. *See* ASAṂPRAJANYA

**pujŏng kwan** 不淨觀. *See* AŚUBHABHĀVANĀ

**pujŏng mul** 不淨物. *See* AKALPIKAVASTU

**pujŏng sayu** 不正思惟. *See* AYONIŚOMANASKĀRA

**Pujŭng pulgam kyŏng** 不增不減經. *See* ANŪNATVĀPŪRṆATVANIRDEŚA

**Puk chong** 北宗. *See* BEI ZONG

**pukkuro chu** 北俱盧洲. *See* UTTARAKURU

**puktu ch'ilsŏng** 北斗七星. *See* BEIDOU QIXING

**pul** 佛. *See* BUDDHA, FO

**pulbangil** 不放逸. *See* APRAMĀDA

**pulbarin** 佛鉢印. *See* BUDDHAPĀTRAMUDRĀ

**pulbijeha** 弗毘提訶. *See* VIDEHA

**pulcha** 拂子. *See* FUZI, VĀLAVYAJANA

**pulch'aje samgwan** 不次第三觀. *See* SANGUAN

**pulch'al** 佛刹. *See* BUDDHAKṢETRA

**Pulchigyŏng non** 佛地經論. *See* BUDDHABHŪMISŪTRA

**Pulchi kyŏng** 佛地經. *See* BUDDHABHŪMISŪTRA

**pulcho** 佛祖. *See* FOZU

**pulchok** 佛足. *See* BUDDHAPĀDA

**pulchŏng** 佛頂. *See* UṢṆĪṢA

**Pulcho samgyŏng** 佛祖三經. *See* FOZU SANJING

**Pulcho Tŏkkwang** 佛照德光. *See* FOZHAO DEGUANG

**Pulcho t'onggi** 佛祖統紀. *See* FOZU TONGJI

**pulgadŭk** 不可得. *See* ANUPALAMBHA

**pulgasaŭi** 不可思議. *See* ACINTYA

**pulgi** 佛紀. *See* BUDDHAVARṢA

**Pulgong** 不空. *See* AMOGHAVAJRA

**pulgong[bul] pŏp** 不共佛法. *See* ĀVEṆIKA[BUDDHA]DHARMA

**pulgongju** 不共住. *See* ASAṂVĀSA

**Pulgong Kyŏnsak** 不空羂索. *See* AMOGHAPĀŚA

**Pulgong sŏngch'wi yŏrae pul** 不空成就如來佛. *See* AMOGHASIDDHI

**pul kiŏ** 不綺語. *See* SAṂBHINNAPRALĀPĀT PRATIVIRATI

**pullae** 不來. *See* ANĀGĀMIN

**pullip muncha** 不立文字. *See* BULI WENZI

**Pulmo podŏkchang panya paramil kyŏng** 佛母寶德藏般若波羅蜜經. *See* RATNAGUṆASAṂCAYAGĀTHĀ

**pulmyŏl** 不滅. *See* ANIRUDDHA

**Pul ponhaeng chip kyŏng** 佛本行集經. *See* ABHINIṢKRAMAṆASŪTRA

**pulpŏp** 佛法. *See* BUDDHADHARMA

**pulsi haet'al** 不時解脫. *See* ASAMAYAVIMUKTA

**Pulsim chong** 佛心宗. *See* FOXIN ZONG

**pulsin** 不信. *See* ĀŚRADDHYA

**pulsin** 佛身. *See* BUDDHAKĀYA

**Pulsohaeng ch'an** 佛所行讚. *See* BUDDHACARITA

**pulsŏn** 不善. *See* AKUŚALA

**pulsŏng** 佛性. *See* FOXING

**Pulsŏng non** 佛性論. *See* FOXING LUN

**pulsŭng** 佛乘. *See* BUDDHAYĀNA

**pult'a** 佛陀. See FO

**Pult'abaltara** 佛陀跋陀羅. *See* BUDDHABHADRA

**Pult'adara** 佛陀多羅. *See* BUDDHATRĀTA

**Pult'amiltara** 佛陀蜜多羅. *See* BUDDHAMITRA

**Pult'ananje** 佛陀難提. *See* BUDDHANANDI

**Pult'ayasa** 佛陀耶舍. *See* BUDDHAYAŚAS

**pult'oejŏn** 不退轉. *See* AVAIVARTIKA

**Pultojing** 佛圖澄. *See* FOTUDENG

**P'umnyu chok non** 品類足論. *See* PRAKARAṆAPĀDA[ŚĀSTRA]

**Pumo ŭnjung kyŏng** 父母恩重經. *See* FUMU ENZHONG JING

**pun** 分. *See* BHĀGA

**pun** 忿. *See* KRODHA

**punbyŏl** 分別. *See* KALPANĀ, VIKALPA

**punbyŏl ajip** 分別我執. *See* PARIKALPITĀTMAGRAHA

**punbyŏl hok** 分別惑. *See* PARIKALPITAKLEŚĀVARAṆA

**punbyŏl mumyŏng** 分別無明. *See* PARIKALPITĀVIDYĀ

**Punbyŏlsŏl pu** 分別說部. *See* VIBHAJYAVĀDA

**pundan saengsa** 分段生死. *See* PARICCHEDAJARĀMARAṆA

**pundari hwa** 芬陀利華. *See* PUṆḌARĪKA

**p'ungdae** 風大. *See* VĀYU[DHĀTU]

**Pu pŏpchang inyŏn chŏn** 付法藏因緣傳. *See* FU FAZANG YINYUAN ZHUAN

**puran** 佛眼. *See* BUDDHACAKṢUS

**Puranna Kasŏp** 富蘭那迦葉. *See* PŪRAṆA-KĀŚYAPA

**purhae** 不害. *See* AHIṂSĀ

**purhŭiron** 不戲論. *See* NIḤPRAPAÑCA

**purhwan** 不還. *See* ANĀGĀMIN

**purhwan hyang** 不還向. *See* ANĀGĀMIPHALAPRATIPANNAKA

**puri** 不二. *See* ADVAYA

**puriji** 不二智. *See* ADVAYAJÑĀNA

**Puril Kyesung** 佛日契嵩. *See* FORI QISONG

**purŏ** 佛語. *See* BUDDHAVACANA

**Puruna** 富樓那. *See* PŪRṆA

**purwi** 不爲. *See* ABHABBAṬṬHĀNA

**puryŏm muji** 不染無知. *See* AKLIṢṬĀJÑĀNA

**puryoŭi** 不了義. *See* NEYĀRTHA

**pusa** 副司. *See* FUSI

**Pu taesa** 傅大士. *See* FU DASHI

**Puyong Tohae** 芙蓉道楷. *See* FURONG DAOKAI

**P'yesuk kyŏng** 弊宿經. *See* PĀYĀSISUTTANTA

**Pyŏgam nok** 碧巖録. *See* BIYAN LU

**pyŏkkwan** 壁觀. *See* BIGUAN

**pyŏlchu** 別住. *See* PARIVĀSA

**pyŏlgyŏng [simso]** 別境[心所]. *See* VINIYATA

**pyŏlsang samgwan** 別相三觀. *See* SANGUAN

**p'yŏn** 遍. *See* VYĀPTI

**pyŏngbul** 秉拂. *See* BINGFU

**p'yŏnch'ŏ** 遍處. *See* KASIṆA

**p'yŏngdŭngsŏng chi** 平等性智. *See* SAMATĀJÑĀNA

**Pyŏngnyŏngsa** 炳靈寺. *See* BINGLINGSI

**pyŏn'gye sojip sŏng** 遍計所執性. *See* PARIKALPITA

**pyŏn'gyŏn** 邊見. *See* ANTAGRĀHADṚṢṬI

**p'yŏnhaeng** 遍行. *See* SARVATRAGA

**p'yŏnhaeng in** 遍行因. *See* SARVATRAGAHETU

**pyŏnjae** 辯才. *See* PRATIBHĀNA

**Pyŏnjae ch'ŏn** 辯才天. *See* SARASVATĪ

**pyŏnji** 邊地. *See* BIANDI, YAVANA

**p'yŏnji** 遍至. *See* VYĀPTI

**pyŏnjŏng ch'ŏn** 遍淨天. *See* ŚUBHAKṚTSNA

**Pyŏnjŏng non** 辯正論. *See* BAIZHENG LUN

**Pyŏnjungbyŏn non** 辯中邊論. *See* MADHYĀNTAVIBHĀGA

**pyŏnyŏk saengsa** 變易生死. *See* PARIṆĀMIKAJARĀMARAṆA

**pyŏrhaet'al yurŭi** 別解脫律儀. *See* PRĀTIMOKṢASAṂVARA

## R

**Rada** 羅陀. *See* RĀDHA

**Rahura** 羅睺羅. *See* RĀHULA

**Rama kyŏng** 羅摩經. *See* ARIYAPARIYESANĀSUTTA

## S

**sa** 思. *See* CETANĀ

**sa** 師. See GURU

**sa** 死. *See* MARAṆA

**sa** 師. *See* ŚĀSTṚ

**sa** 事. *See* SHI

**sa** 捨. *See* UPEKṢĀ

**sa** 伺. *See* VICĀRA

**saba segye** 娑婆世界. *See* SAHĀLOKA

**Saba segye chu** 娑婆世界主. *See* SAHĀṂPATI

**Sabi** 師備. *See* XUANSHA SHIBEI

**sabu** 士夫. *See* PURUṢA

**Sabun yul** 四分律. *See* SIFEN LÜ

**sa chŏnggŭn** 四正勤. *See* PRAHĀṆA

**sach'ŏnwang** 四天王. *See* LOKAPĀLA

**sach'ŏnwang ch'ŏn** 四天王天. *See* CĀTURMAHĀRĀJAKĀYIKA

**sadae** 四大. *See* MAHĀBHŪTA

**sadaham** 斯陀含. *See* SAKṚDĀGĀMIN

**saek** 色. *See* RŪPA

**saekch'ŏ** 色處. *See* RŪPĀYATANA

**saek chŭksi kong kong chŭksi saek** 色即是空空即是色. *See* RŪPAṂ ŚŪNYATĀ ŚUNYATAIVA RŪPAṂ

**saek kugyŏng ch'ŏn** 色究竟天. *See* AKANIṢṬHA

**saekkye** 色界. *See* RŪPADHĀTU

**saekkye chŏng** 色界定. *See* RŪPĀVACĀRADHYĀNA

**saek on** 色蘊. *See* RŪPASKANDHA

**saeksin** 色身. *See* RŪPAKĀYA

**saek t'am** 色貪. *See* RŪPARĀGA

**saeng** 生. *See* JĀTI, YONI

**saengdŭk chŏng** 生得定. *See* DHYĀNOPAPATTI

**saenggi ch'aje** 生起次第. *See* UTPATTIKRAMA

**saengji** 生支. *See* LIṄGA

**saeng ki** 生起. *See* UTPĀDA

**saeng pan** 生般. *See* UPAPADYAPARINIRVĀYIN

**saeng panyŏlban** 生般涅槃. *See* UPAPADYAPARINIRVĀYIN

**saengsaji** 生死智. *See* CYUTYUPAPATTIJÑĀNA

**saengsa yunhoe** 生死輪迴. *See* SAṂSĀRA

**Sagalla** 娑竭羅. *See* SĀGARA

**Sagara** 娑伽羅. *See* SĀGARA

**Sagida sŏng** 娑枳多城. *See* SĀKETA

**sago** 四枯. *See* SIKU

**sagu punbyŏl** 四句分別. *See* CATUṢKOṬI

**Saguri** 奢拘梨. *See* ŚAKULĀ

**sagye** 捨界. *See* SĪMĀSAMŪHANA

**sagyŏn** 邪見. *See* AKUŚALADṚṢṬI, MITHYĀDṚṢṬI

**sahakkyeja** 捨學戒者. *See* SIKKHĀPACCAKKHĀNA

**sahok** 思惑. *See* SIHUO

**sa hongsŏwŏn** 四弘誓願. *See* SI HONGSHIYUAN

**sahye** 思慧. *See* CINTĀMAYĪPRAJÑĀ

**sain** 四印. *See* CATURMUDRĀ

**saja chwa** 師子座. *See* SIṂHĀSANA

**sajahu** 師子吼. *See* SIṂHANĀDA

**Sajahu kyŏng** 師子吼經. *See* CŪḶASĪHANĀDASUTTA

**saje** 四諦. *See* FOUR NOBLE TRUTHS, CATVĀRY ĀRYASATYĀNI, ĀRYASATYA

**saje pŏmnyun** 四諦法輪. *See* CATUḤSATYADHARMACAKRA

**saji** 邪智. *See* MITHYĀJÑĀNA

**Salbada pu** 薩婆多部. *See* SARVĀSTIVĀDA

**sallan** 散亂. *See* VIKṢEPA

**sama** 死魔. *See* MṚTYUMĀRA

**samballa** 三跋羅. *See* SAṂVARA

**sambo** 三寶. *See* RATNATRAYA

**sambun kwagyŏng** 三分科經. *See* SANFEN KEJING

**samch'ŏn taech'ŏn segye** 三千大千世界. *See* TRISĀHASRAMAHĀSĀHASRALOKADHĀTU

**samch'wi** 三聚. *See* TRISKANDHAKA

**samch'wi chŏnggye** 三聚淨戒. *See* ŚĪLATRAYA

**samdo** 三道. *See* SANDAO

**samdok** 三毒. *See* TRIVIṢA

**samgu** 三句. *See* SANJU

**samgŭn** 三根. *See* TRĪNDRIYA

**samgwan** 三觀. *See* SANGUAN

**samgwiŭi** 三歸依. *See* TRIŚARAṆA

**samgye** 三界. *See* TRAILOKYA

**Samgye kyo** 三階教. *See* SANJIE JIAO

**samhak** 三學. *See* ŚIKṢĀTRAYA

**sami** 沙彌. *See* SĀMAṆERA, ŚRĀMANERA

**samini** 沙彌尼. *See* ŚRĀMANERIKĀ

**samjang** 三藏. *See* TRIPIṬAKA

**samjang pŏpsa** 三藏法師. *See* TREPIṬAKA

**samje** 三諦. *See* SANDI

**samji** 三止. *See* SANZHI

**samji samgwan** 三止三觀. *See* SANZHI, SANGUAN

**samjong segan** 三種世間. *See* SANZHONG SHIJIAN

**sammae** 三昧. *See* SAMĀDHI

**sammae kyŏng** 三昧經. *See* SANMEI JING

**sammaeya salt'a** 三昧耶薩埵. *See* SAMAYASATTVA

**sammaya** 三摩耶. *See* SAMAYA

**sammaya in** 三摩耶印. *See* SAMAYAMUDRĀ

**sammil** 三蜜. *See* SANMITSU

**sammun** 三門. *See* TRIDVĀRA

**sammyŏng** 三明. *See* TRIVIDYĀ

**Sammyŏng kyŏng** 三明經. *See* TEVIJJASUTTA

**Samnon chong** 三論宗. *See* SANLUN ZONG; MADHYAMAKA

**Samnon hyŏnŭi** 三論玄義. *See* SANLUN XUANYI

**sam punbyŏl** 三分別. *See* TRIVIKALPA

**samsang** 三相. *See* TRILAKṢAṆA

**samse** 三世. *See* TRIKĀLA

**samsibi sang** 三十二相. *See* MAHĀPURUṢALAKṢAṆA

**Samsibi sang kyŏng** 三十二相經. *See* Lakkhaṇasutta

**samsin** 三身. *See* trikāya

**samsipch'il top'um** 三十七道品. *See* bodhipākṣikadharma

**samsipsam ch'ŏn** 三十三天. *See* trāyastriṃśa

**samsŏng** 三性. *See* trisvabhāva

**samsŭng** 三乘. *See* triyāna

**sa muae hae** 四無礙解. *See* pratisaṃvid

**samŭi** 三衣. *See* tricīvara

**samun** 沙門. *See* śrāmaṇa

**samun'gwa** 沙門果. *See* śrāmaṇyaphala

**Samun'gwa kyŏng** 沙門果經. *See* Sāmaññaphalasutta

**Samun pulgyŏng wangja non** 沙門不敬王者論. *See* Shamen bujing wangzhe lun

**sa muryangsim** 捨無量心. *See* upekṣāpramāṇa

**samyo** 三要. *See* sanyao

**Samyŏng Chirye** 四明知禮. *See* Siming Zhili

**samyŏng oedo** 邪命外道. *See* Ājīvaka

**Samyŏng sibŭi sŏ** 四明十義書. *See* Siming shiyi shu

**Sanagulta** 闍那崛多. *See* Jñānagupta

**Sandana kyŏng** 散陀那經. *See* Udumbarikasīhanādasutta

**sang** 相. *See* lakṣaṇa, liṅga, nimitta

**sang** 常. *See* nitya

**sang** 想. *See* saṃjñā

**San'ga Sanoe** 山家山外. *See* Shanjia Shanwai

**Sangbulgyŏng posal** 常不輕菩薩. *See* Sadāparibhūta

**sangbyŏn** 常邊. *See* śāśvatānta

**sangdang** 上堂. *See* shangtang

**Sanggallaju** 商羯羅主. *See* Śaṃkarasvāmin

**sanggyo** 像教. *See* xiangjiao

**sanggyŏn** 常見. *See* śāsvatadṛṣṭi

**Sanghaeng** 上行. *See* Viśiṣṭacāritra

**sanghwa sin** 上化身. *See* uttamanirmāṇakāya

**Sangje [posal]** 常啼[菩薩]. *See* Sadāprarudita

**Sangjŏgyu kyŏng** 象跡喻經. *See* Cūḷahatthipadopamasutta, Mahāhatthipadopamasutta

**sangjok** 床足. *See* khaṭvāṅga

**Sang chong** 相宗. *See* Xiang zong

**sangju** 常住. *See* changzhu

**sangjwa** 上座. *See* sthavira

**Sangjwa pu** 上座部. *See* Sthaviranikāya

**Sang kyŏng** 想經. *See* Mūlapariyāyasutta

**Sangnahwasu** 商那和修. *See* Śāṇakavāsin

**Sangnakkabaksa** 商諾迦縛娑. *See* Śāṇakavāsin

**sangnyu pan** 上流般. *See* ūrdhvasrotas

**sangnyu panyŏlban** 上流般涅槃. *See* ūrdhvasrotas

**sangpŏp** 常法. *See* nityadharma

**sangpŏp** 像法. *See* saddharmapratirūpaka, xiangfa

**Sangpŏp kyŏrŭi kyŏng** 像法決疑經. *See* Xiangfa jueyi jing

**sangsajŏngpŏp** 像似正法. *See* saddharmapratirūpaka

**sangsok** 相續. *See* saṃtāna

**sangsok sik** 相續識. *See* ādānavijñāna

**sangsu myŏl** 想受滅. *See* saṃjñāvedayitanirodha

**sangsŭng** 相承. *See* paraṃparā

**sangŭng** 相應. *See* saṃprayukta

**sangŭngin** 相應因. *See* saṃprayuktahetu

**Sanisa kyŏng** 闍尼沙經. *See* Janavasabhasuttanta

**Sanje sŏnin** 羼提仙人. *See* Kṣāntivādin

**Sansaya Pirajija** 刪闍耶毘羅胝子. *See* Sañjaya Vairāṭīputra

**sa pŏmjoe mun** 四犯罪門. *See* *caturāpattidvāra

**sa pŏpkye** 事法界. *See* shi fajie

**sa pŏpkye** 四法界. *See* si fajie

**Saraha** 沙羅訶. *See* Saraha

**sarasu** 沙羅樹. *See* śāla

**sari** 舍利. *See* śarīra

**Saribul** 舍利弗. *See* Śāriputra

**sarigi** 舍利器. *See* sheliqi

**sarigu** 舍利具. *See* sheliju

**sa saeng** 四生. *See* yoni, catvāro yonayaḥ

**sasa muae pŏpkye** 事事無礙法界. *See* shishi wu'ai fajie

**sasang** 四相. *See* caturlakṣaṇa, caturnimitta

**sase song** 辭世頌. *See* cishi song, yiji

**Sasibi chang kyŏng** 四十二章經. *See* Sishi'er zhang jing

**sasik** 思食. *See* manaḥsaṃcetanāhāra

**sasin** 捨身. *See* sheshen, dehadāna

**sasinjok** 四神足. *See* ṛddhipāda

**sasipku [il] chae** 四十九[日]齋. *See* sishijiu [ri] zhai

**sasŏngje** 四聖諦. *See* four noble truths

**sa sŏn'gŭn** 四善根. *See* catvāri kuśalamūlāni, nirvedhabhāgīya

**sa sŏpsa** 四攝事. *See* saṃgrahavastu

**sat'a** 捨墮. *See* naiḥsargikapāyattika

**sat'aek** 思擇. *See* tarka

**saŭm** 邪淫. *See* kāmamithyācāra

**Sawi kuk** 舍衛國. *See* Śrāvastī

**Sawŏn** 師遠. *See* Kuo'an Shiyuan

**sayong kwa** 士用果. *See* puruṣakāraphala

**sayu** 思惟. *See* buddhi

**sebŏp** 世法. *See* lokadharma

**Sech'in** 世親. *See* Vasubandhu

**segan** 世間. *See* laukika

**segando** 世間道. *See* laukikamārga

**segye** 世界. See loka

**segye** 世界. *See* lokadhātu

**Sejajae** 世自在. *See* Lokeśvara

**Sejajae wang pul** 世自在王佛. *See* Lokeśvararāja

**sejeilpŏp** 世第一法. *See* laukikāgradharma

**sejon** 世尊. *See* Bhagavan

**Sejon yŏmhwa** 世尊拈花. *See* Shizun nianhua

**sesok** 世俗. *See* saṃvṛti

**sesok che** 世俗諦. *See* saṃvṛtisatya

**sesok sŭng** 世俗僧. *See* sammutisaṅgha

**Seu** 世友. *See* Vasumitra

**sibang** 十方. *See* daśadiś

**sibang ch'al** 十方刹. *See* shifang cha

**Sibara** 尸婆羅. *See* Sīvali

**Sibi** 尸毘. *See* Śibi

**sibibu kyŏng** 十二部經. *See* dvādaśāṅga[pravacana]

**Sibi inyŏn non** 十二因緣論. *See* Pratītyasamutpādahṛdayakārikā

**Sibilmyŏn Kwanŭm** 十一面觀音. *See* Ekādaśamukhāvalokiteśvara

**Sibimun non** 十二門論. *See* Shi'ermen lun

**sibunjŭng** 屎糞增. *See* kuṇapa

**Sibu to** 十牛圖. *See* Oxherding Pictures, Ten

**sigak** 始覺. *See* shijue

**sigon** 識蘊. *See* vijñānaskandha

**sigŭm** 識陰. *See* vijñānaskandha

**si haet'al** 時解脫. *See* samayavimukta

**Siho** 施護. *See* Dānapāla

**sihyŏn** 示現. *See* prātihārya

**siju** 施主. *See* dānapati

**sik** 食. *See* āhāra

**sik** 識. *See* vijñāna, vijñapti

**sikchae** 息災. *See* śānticāra

**sikch'amana** 式叉摩那. *See* śikṣamāṇā

**sikch'amana kye** 式叉摩那戒. *See* śikṣamāṇāsaṃvara

**sik mubyŏn ch'ŏ** 識無邊處. *See* vijñānānantyāyatana

**Siksin chok non** 識身足論. *See* Vijñānakāya-[pādaśāstra]

**Silch'anant'a** 實叉難陀. *See* Śikṣānanda

**silche** 實際. *See* bhūtakoṭi

**silchi** 悉地. *See* siddhi

**Silgaraga changja mo** 室珂羅哥長者母. *See* Śṛgālakamātṛ

**Sillibulsŏ** 室利佛逝. *See* Śrīvijaya

**sillyŏk** 神力. *See* ṛddhi

**sillyŏm** 失念. *See* muṣitasmṛti

**silsa** 實事. *See* dravya

**silsang** 實相. *See* tattva

**Silsang panya paramil kyŏng** 實相般若波羅蜜經. *See* Adhyardhaśatikāprajñāpāramitāsūtra/ Prajñāpāramitānayapañcaśatikā

**Siltalta** 悉達多. *See* Siddhārtha

**siltam** 悉曇. *See* SIDDHAM

**Siltam chagi** 悉曇字記. *See* XITAN ZIJI

**sil yu** 實有. *See* DRAVYASAT

**sim** 心. *See* CITTA

**sim** 尋. *See* VITARKA

**simhaet'al** 心解脫. *See* CETOVIMUKTI

**Sim hŭiyu kyŏng** 甚希有經. *See* ADBHUTADHARMAPARYĀYASŪTRA

**sim ilgyŏng sŏng** 心一境性. *See* CITTAIKĀGRATĀ

**simji** 心地. *See* XINDI

**Simmansong panya** 十萬頌般若. *See* ŚATASĀHASRIKĀPRAJÑĀPĀRAMITĀ

**simnyŏk** 十力. *See* BALA, DAŚABALA

**simnyuk chonja** 十六尊者. *See* ṢODAŚASTHAVIRA

**simnyuk nahan** 十六羅漢. *See* ṢODAŚASTHAVIRA

**sim pulsangŭng pŏp** 心不相應法. *See* CITTAVIPRAYUKTASAṂSKĀRA

**sim sangsok** 心相續. *See* CITTASANTĀNA

**sim sangŭng pŏp** 心相應法. *See* CITTASAMPRAYUKTASAṂSKĀRA

**simso** 心所. *See* CAITTA

**simuoe in** 施無畏印. *See* ABHAYAMUDRA

**Simye kyŏng** 心穢經. *See* CETOKHILASUTTA

**sin** 身. *See* KĀYA

**sin** 信. *See* ŚRADDHĀ

**sina** 神我. *See* PURUṢA

**sinbyŏnsang** 神變相. *See* MAHĀPRĀTIHĀRYA

**sinch'ŏ** 身處. *See* KĀYĀYATANA

**sin'gŭn** 身根. *See* KĀYENDRIYA

**sin'gwan** 身觀. *See* KĀYĀNUPAŚYANĀ

**sin'gwang** 身光. *See* SHENGUANG

**sin'gyŏng chijŭngt'ong** 神境智證通. *See* ṚDDHIVIDHĀBHIJÑĀ

**sinhae** 信解. *See* ŚRADDHĀDHIMUKTA

**Sinhaeng** 信行. *See* XINXING

**sinjŭng** 身證. *See* KĀYASĀKṢIN

**Sinmo hŭisu kyŏng** 身毛喜豎經. *See* MAHĀSĪHANĀDASUTTA

**sinsik** 身識. *See* KĀYAVIJÑĀNA

**sinsim** 信心. *See* XINXIN

**Sinsim myŏng** 信心銘. *See* XINXIN MING

**sinsim t'allak** 身心脫落. *See* SHINJIN DATSURAKU

**Sinsu** 神秀. *See* SHENXIU

**sinsŭnghae** 信勝解. *See* ŚRADDHĀVIMUKTA

**Sinsu taejanggyŏng** 新修大藏經. *See* TAISHŌ SHINSHŪ DAIZŌKYŌ

**sint'ong** 神通. *See* ABHIJÑĀ

**siŏp** 始業. *See* ĀDIKARMIKA

**sipchi** 十地. *See* DAŚABHŪMI

**Sipchigyŏng non** 十地經論. *See* DAŚABHŪMIVYĀKHYĀNA, DI LUN ZONG

**Sipchu kyŏng** 十住經. *See* DAŚABHŪMIKASŪTRA

**sip hyŏnmun** 十玄門. *See* SHI XUANMEN

**sipkye** 十界. *See* DAŚADHĀTU

**sipkye** 十戒. *See* DAŚAŚĪLA

**sip pŏpkye** 十法界. *See* SHI FAJIE

**sip pulsŏnŏp to** 十不善業道. *See* KARMAPATHA

**Sipsang kyŏng** 十上經. *See* DASUTTARASUTTA

**sip yŏsi** 十如是. *See* SHI RUSHI

**Siradalma** 尸羅達摩. *See* ŚĪLADHARMA

**sirim** 屍林. *See* ŚMAŚĀNA

**sirŏ** 實語. *See* SATYAVACANA

**si simma** 是甚麼. *See* SHI SHENME, IMWŎTKO

**Sisŏl non** 施設論. *See* PRAJÑAPTIBHĀṢYA[PĀDAŚĀSTRA]

**siwang** 十王. *See* SHIWANG

**siwŏn in** 施願印. *See* VARADAMUDRĀ

**Sobaho tongja ch'ŏngmun kyŏng** 蘇婆呼童子請問經. *See* SUBĀHUPARIPṚCCHĀTANTRA

**Sobint'a** 蘇頻陀. *See* SUBINDA

**Sobu** 小部. *See* KHUDDAKANIKĀYA

**soch'ok** 所觸. *See* SPRAṢṬAVYA

**soch'wi nŭngch'wi punbyŏl** 所取能取分別. *See* GRĀHYAGRĀHAKAVIKALPA

**sodaech'i** 所對治. *See* VIPAKṢABHŪTA

**Sodo non** 笑道論. *See* XIAODAO LUN

**sodŭk** 所得. *See* UPALABDHI

**sŏgi** 書記. *See* SHUJI

**sogwang ch'ŏn** 少光天. *See* PARĪTTĀBHA

**sŏjang** 書狀. *See* SHUZHUANG, DAHUI PUJUE CHANSHI SHU

**sojijang** 所知障. *See* JÑEYĀVARAṆA

**sojŏng ch'ŏn** 少淨天. *See* PARĪTTAŚUBHA

**sok** 俗. *See* SAṂVṚTI

**Sŏk** 釋. *See* SHI

**sŏkchang** 錫杖. *See* KHAKKHARA

**sokche** 俗諦. *See* SAṂVṚTISATYA, VYAVAHĀRA

**Sŏkka** 釋迦. *See* ŚĀKYA, cf. SHI

**Sŏkkamoni** 釋迦牟尼. *See* ŚĀKYAMUNI

**sŏkka sŭng** 釋迦僧. *See* ŚĀKYABHIKṢU

**Sok kosŭng chŏn** 續高僧傳. *See* XU GAOSENG ZHUAN

**Sŏksilguk** 石室國. *See* TAKṢAŚILĀ

**Sŏktu Hŭich'ŏn** 石頭希遷. *See* SHITOU XIQIAN

**Sŏlbong Ŭijon** 雪峰義存. *See* XUEFENG YICUN

**sŏlch'ŏ** 舌處. *See* JIHVĀYATANA

**Sŏlch'ulse pu** 說出世部. *See* LOKOTTARAVĀDA *See* XUEDOU CHONGXIAN

**Sŏlga pu** 說假部. *See* PRAJÑAPTIVĀDA

**sŏlgŭn** 舌根. *See* JIHVENDRIYA

**Sŏllae** 善來. *See* SĀGATA

**sŏllae p'ilch'u** 善來苾芻. *See* EHIBHIKṢUKĀ

**Sŏllim pohun** 禪林寶訓. *See* CHANLIN BAOXUN

**Sŏllim sŭngbo chŏn** 禪林僧寶傳. *See* CHANLIN SENGBAO ZHUAN

**sŏlpŏpsa** 說法師. *See* DHARMABHĀṆAKA

**Sŏlsan pu** 雪山部. *See* HAIMAVATA

**sŏlsik** 舌識. *See* JIHVĀVIJÑĀNA

**Sŏltu Chunghyŏn** 雪竇重顯. *See* XUEDOU CHONGXIAN

**sŏn** 善. *See* KUŚALA

**sŏnbang** 禪房. *See* SENGTANG

**Sŏn chong Yŏngga chip** 禪宗永嘉集. *See* CHAN ZONG YONGJIA JI

**sŏnch'wi** 善趣. *See* SUGATI

**Sondaranant'a** 孫陀羅難陀. *See* SUNDARANANDA

**Sondari** 孫陀利. *See* SUNDARĪNANDĀ

**Sŏndo** 善導. *See* SHANDAO

**sŏng** 聖. *See* ĀRYA

**sŏng** 聲. *See* ŚABDA

**song** 頌. *See* ŚLOKA

**son'gam** 損減. *See* APAVĀDA

**Sŏn'gam** 宣鑑. *See* DESHAN XUANJIAN

**Sŏngbulmo soja panya p'aramilta kyŏng** 聖佛母小字般若波羅蜜多經. See SVALPĀKṢARAPRAJÑĀPĀRAMITĀ

**sŏngch'ŏ** 聲處. *See* ŚABDĀYATANA

**Sŏng chong** 性宗. *See* XING ZONG

**sŏngch'wi pŏp** 成就法. *See* SĀDHANA

**sŏngdo** 聖道. *See* ĀRYAMĀRGA

**sŏngdo kwa** 聖道果. *See* ĀRYAMĀRGAPHALA

**sŏnggi** 性起. *See* XINGQI

**songgo** 頌古. *See* SONGGU

**sŏnggŏp** 成劫. *See* VIVARTAKALPA

**sŏnggu sŏl** 性具說. *See* XINGJU SHUO

**sŏnggyo** 聖教. *See* ŚĀSANA

**sŏngja** 聖者. *See* MUNI

**sŏngje** 聖諦. *See* FOUR NOBLE TRUTHS

**sŏngjong** 聖種. *See* ĀRYAVAṂŚA

**Song kosŭng chŏn** 宋高僧傳. *See* SONG GAOSENG ZHUAN

**sŏngmun** 聲聞. *See* ŚRĀVAKA

**sŏngmun ch'aje** 聲聞次第. *See* VIṂŚATIPRABHEDASAṂGHA

**Sŏngmun chi** 聲聞地. *See* ŚRĀVAKABHŪMI

**sŏngmun chongsŏng** 聲聞種姓. *See* ŚRĀVAKAGOTRA

**sŏngmun sŭng** 聲聞乘. *See* ŚRĀVAKAYĀNA

**Sŏng myogilsang chinsil myŏng kyŏng** 聖妙吉祥眞實名經. *See* MAÑJUŚRĪNĀMASAṂGĪTI

**sŏngsil** 成實. *See* SATYASIDDHI

**Sŏngsil chong** 成實宗. *See* CHENGSHI ZONG

**Sŏngsil non** 成實論. *See* CHENGSHI LUN

**sŏngsojak chi** 成所作智. *See* KṚTYĀNUṢṬHĀNAJÑĀNA

**sŏngsŭng** 聖僧. *See* ĀRYASAṂGHA

**sŏn'gŭn** 善根. *See* KUŚALAMŪLA

**Sŏn'gwan ch'aekchin** 禪關策進. *See* CHANGUAN CEJIN

**sŏn'gyŏn ch'ŏn** 善見天. *See* SUDARŚANA

**Sŏn'gyŏnyul pibasa** 善見律毘婆沙. *See* SAMANTAPĀSĀDIKĀ

**Sŏng yusik non** 成唯識論. *See* CHENG WEISHI LUN

**Sŏng yusik non sulgi** 成唯識論述記. *See* CHENG WEISHI LUN SHU JI

**Sŏnhye** 善慧. *See* SUMEDHA

**sŏnhye chi** 善慧地. *See* SĀDHUMATĪ

**Sŏnhyŏn** 善賢. *See* BHADRIKA

**Sŏnhyŏn** 禪賢. *See* ZHIKONG CHANXIAN

**sŏnhyŏn ch'ŏn** 善現天. *See* SUDṚŚA

**Sŏnin t'ach'ŏ** 仙人墮處. *See* ṚṢIPATANA

**sŏn iyok in** 先離欲人. *See* VĪTARĀGAPŪRVIN

**Sŏnjae** 善財. *See* SUDHANA

**sŏnji** 禪支. *See* DHYĀNĀṄGA

**sŏnjisik** 善知識. *See* KALYĀṆAMITRA

**Sŏnmun kyusik** 禪門規式. *See* CHANMEN GUISHI

**Sŏnmuoe** 善無畏. *See* ŚUBHAKARASIṂHA

**sŏnnamja** 善男子. *See* KULAPUTRA

**Sŏnni oedo** 先尼外道. *See* ŚREṆIKA HERESY

**sŏnpang** 禪房/禪坊. *See* PRAHĀṆAŚĀLĀ

**Sŏn piyobŏp kyŏng** 禪秘要法經. *See* CHAN MIYAOFA JING

**sŏnsa** 禪師. *See* CHANSHI

**Sŏnsaeng kyŏng** 善生經. *See* SIGĀLOVĀDASUTTA

**Sŏnse** 善歲. *See* SUVARṢAKA

**sŏnsŏ** 善逝. *See* SUGATA

**Sŏnsŏng** 善星. *See* SUNAKṢATRA

**Sŏnwŏl chip** 禪月集. *See* CHANYUE JI

**Sŏnwŏl Kwanhyu** 禪月貫休. *See* CHANYUE GUANXIU

**Sŏnwŏn chejŏnjip tosŏ** 禪源諸詮集都序. *See* CHANYUAN ZHUQUANJI DUXU

**Sŏnwŏn ch'ŏnggyu** 禪苑清規. *See* CHANYUAN QINGGUI

**Sŏnya kyŏng** 善夜經. *See* BHADRAKĀRĀTRĪ

**Sŏnyo** 禪要. *See* CHANYAO, GAOFENG HESHANG CHANYAO

**sŏnyŏin** 善女人. *See* KULADUHITṚ

**Sŏp non chong** 攝論宗. *See* SHE LUN ZONG

**Sŏp taesŭng non** 攝大乘論. *See* MAHĀYĀNASAṂGRAHA

**Sop'um panya kyŏng** 小品般若經. *See* AṢṬASĀHASRIKAPRAJÑĀPĀRAMITĀ

**sŏrae ŭi** 西來意. *See* XILAI YI

**Sŏrilch'eyu pu** 說一切有部. *See* SARVĀSTIVĀDA

**Sorimsa** 少林寺. *See* SHAOLINSI

**sorip** 所立. *See* SĀDHYADHARMA

**sŏsang** 瑞相. *See* NIMITTA

**Sosilchi kalla kyŏng** 蘇悉地羯羅經. *See* SUSIDDHIKARASŪTRA

**sosin** 燒身. *See* SHAOSHEN

**sosŏngnip** 所成立. *See* SĀDHYADHARMA

**sosŭng** 小乘. *See* HĪNAYĀNA

**soŭi** 所依. *See* ĀŚRAYA, NIŚRAYA

**soyŏn** 所緣. *See* ĀLAMBANA

**Soyŏn kyŏng** 小緣經. *See* AGGAÑÑASUTTA

**soyŏn yŏn** 所緣緣. *See* ĀLAMBANAPRATYAYA

**ssangip** 雙入. *See* YUGANADDHA

**ssangsinbyŏn** 雙神變. *See* YAMAKAPRĀTIHĀRYA

**ssangun** 雙運. *See* YUGANADDHA

**su** 受. *See* VEDANĀ

**su** 修. *See* YOGA

**Subakka** 戌博迦. *See* JĪVAKA

**Subaltara** 須跋陀羅. *See* SUBHADRA

**Subiyanyŏ** 須毘耶女. *See* SUPRIYĀ

**subŏphaeng** 隨法行. *See* DHARMĀNUSĀRIN

**Subŏp kyŏng** 受法經. *See* CŪḶADHAMMASAMĀDĀNASUTTA

**Subŏp kyŏng** 受法經. *See* MAHĀDHAMMASAMĀDĀNASUTTA

**Subori** 須菩提. *See* SUBHŪTI

**such'o** 豎超. *See* SHUCHAO

**sudae** 水大. *See* ĀPAS

**Sudaena** 須大拏. *See* VESSANTARA

**Sudaena ponsaeng** 須大拏本生. *See* SUDĀNAJĀTAKA

**sudaham** 須陀含. *See* SAKṚDĀGĀMIN

**Sudal** 須達. *See* SUDATTA

**Sudan** 守端. *See* Baiyun Shouduan

**sudawŏn** 須陀洹. *See* srotaāpanna

**sudo** 修道. *See* bhavanāmārga

**sudŭk chŏng** 修得定. *See* dhyānasamāpatti

**sugi** 授記. *See* vyākaraṇa

**sugye** 受戒. *See* upasaṃpadā

**suhaeng** 修行. *See* pratipatti, yoga

**suhaeng in** 修行人. *See* yogin

**suhŭi** 隨喜. *See* anumodana

**suhŭibok** 隨喜福. *See* puṇyānumodana

**suhye** 修慧. *See* bhāvanāmayīprajñā

**Sujae** 守財. *See* Dhanapāla, Nālāgiri

**Sujena** 須提那. *See* Sudinna

**sujokchwa** 垂足坐. *See* pralambapādāsana

**Sujŏng pŏmji kyŏng** 水淨梵志經. *See* Vatthūpamasutta

**suju** 數珠. *See* japamālā

**sujwa** 首座. *See* shouzuo

**sukchu sunyŏm** 宿住隨念. *See* purvanivāsānusmṛti

**Sumisan** 須彌山. *See* Sumeru, Mt

**sumi tan** 須彌壇. See shumidan

**sumun** 隨聞. *See* anuśrava

**sumunin** 守門人. *See* dvārapāla

**sumyŏn** 隨眠. *See* anuśaya

**sumyŏn** 睡眠. *See* middha

**sumyŏng** 壽命. *See* jīvita

**Suna** 輸那. *See* Soṇā

**Sunaga** 須那迦. *See* Soṇa and Uttara

**sunch'a saengsuŏp** 順次生受業. *See* upapadyavedanīyakarman

**sŭng** 乘. *See* yāna

**Sŭngch'an** 僧粲. *See* Sengcan

**sŭngch'ŏ** 勝處. *See* abhibhvāyatana

**Sŭngch'ŏn wang panya paramil kyŏng** 勝天王般若波羅蜜經. *See* Suvikrāntavikrāmiparipṛcchāprajñāpāramitā

**sŭngdang** 僧堂. *See* sengtang

**sŭngga** 僧伽. *See* saṃgha

**Sŭnggabalma** 僧伽跋摩. *See* Saṃghavarman

**Sŭnggamilta** 僧伽蜜多. *See* Saṅghamittā

**sŭnggari** 僧伽梨. *See* saṃghāṭī

**Sŭnggasi** 僧伽施. *See* Sāṃkāśya

**sŭnggiji** 僧祇支. *See* saṃkakṣikā

**sŭnghae** 勝解. *See* adhimokṣa

**sŭngjanjoe** 僧殘罪. *See* saṃghāvaśesa

**sungjanpŏp** 僧殘法. *See* saṃghāvaśesa

**Sŭngjo** 僧肇. *See* Sengzhao

**sŭng kalma**僧羯磨. *See* saṃghakarman

**Sŭngkwa** 僧果. *See* Sengguo

**Sŭngmaeng** 僧猛. *See* Sengmeng

**Sŭngman kyŏng** 勝鬘經. *See* Śrīmālādevīsiṃhanādasūtra

**Sŭngman sajahu ilsŭng tae pangp'yŏn panggwang kyŏng** 勝鬘師子吼一乘大方便方廣經. *See* Śrīmālādevīsiṃhanādasūtra

**sungmyŏng** 宿命. *See* jātismara

**sŭngsaeng** 勝生. *See* abhyudaya

**Sungsan** 嵩山. *See* Songshan

**Sŭngu** 僧祐. *See* Sengyou

**sŭngŭisŭng** 勝義僧. *See* paramārthasaṃgha

**sun'gwan** 循觀. *See* anupaśyanā

**sun'gyŏlt'aekpun** 順決擇分. *See* nirvedhabhagīya

**sunhaet'albun** 順解脫分. *See* mokṣabhāgīya

**Sunjŏngni non** 順正理論. *See* *Nyāyānusāra

**Sunse oedo** 順世外道. *See* Lokāyata

**sunse sammae** 順世三昧. *See* lokiyasamādhi

**Sunŭngŏm kyŏng** 首楞嚴經. *See* Śūraṃgamasūtra

**Sunŭngŏm sammae** 首楞嚴三昧. *See* śūraṃgamasamādhi

**Sunŭngŏm sammae kyŏng** 首楞嚴三昧經. *See* Śūraṃgamasamādhisūtra

**sunyŏk** 順逆. *See* anulomapratiloma

**sunyŏm punbyŏl** 隨念分別. *See* anusmaraṇavikalpa

**sŭpchongsŏng** 習種性. *See* samudānītagotra

**sŭpki** 習氣. *See* vāsanā

**su pŏnnoe** 隨煩惱. *See* UPAKLEŚA

**Sŭptŭk** 拾得. *See* SHIDE

**Surona** 輸盧那. *See* ŚROṆĀPARĀNTA

**Surongna** 守籠那. *See* SOṆA KOLIVĪSA

**suryuhyang sŏnjŏng** 隨流向禪定. *See* SROTO'NUGATO NĀMA SAMĀDHIḤ

**suryuk hoe** 水陸會. *See* SHUILU HUI

**Susada** 須闍多. *See* SUJĀTĀ

**susi** 垂示. *See* CHUISHI

**susik kwan** 數息觀. *See* ĀNĀPĀNASATI

**Susim yo non** 修心要論. *See* XIUXIN YAO LUN

**susinhaeng** 隨信行. *See* ŚRADDHĀNUSĀRIN

**Susu** 守遂. *See* DAHONG SHOUSUI

**susŭp** 修習. *See* BHĀVANĀ, YOGA

**Susŭp chigwan chwasŏn pŏbyo** 修習止觀坐禪法要. *See* XIUXI ZHIGUAN ZUOCHAN FAYAO

**Suwŏl Kwanŭm** 水月觀音. *See* SHUIYUE GUANYIN

**swaesin sari** 碎身舍利. See SUISHEN SHELI

## T

**tabi** 荼毘. *See* KṢAPITA

**t'abiryang** 他比量. *See* PARĀRTHĀNUMĀNA

**Tabo yŏrae** 多寶如來. *See* PRABHŪTARATNA

**Taebangdŭng musang kyŏng** 大方等無想經. *See* MAHĀMEGHASŪTRA

**Taebangdŭng taejip kyŏng** 大方等大集經. *See* MAHĀSAṂNIPĀTASŪTRA

**Taebangdŭng yŏraejang kyŏng** 大方等如來藏經. *See* TATHĀGATAGARBHASŪTRA

**Taebanggwang posalchang Munsusari kŭnbon ŭigwe kyŏng** 大方廣菩薩藏文殊師利根本儀軌經. *See* MAÑJUŚRĪMŪLAKALPA

**Taebanggwang pul hwaŏm kyŏng** 大方廣佛華嚴經. *See* AVATAṂSAKASŪTRA [BUDDHĀVATAṂSAKASŪTRA], GAṆḌAVYŪHASŪTRA

**Taebanya paramilta kyŏng** 大般若波羅蜜多經. *See* MAHĀPRAJÑĀPĀRAMITĀSŪTRA

**taebi** 大悲. *See* MAHĀKARUṆĀ

**Taebi chu** 大悲咒. *See* DABEI ZHOU, QIANSHOU JING

**Taebija** 大悲者. *See* MAHĀKARUṆIKA

**Taebi kongji kŭmgang taegyo wang ŭigwe kyŏng** 大悲空智金剛大教王儀軌經. *See* HEVAJRATANTRA/HEVAJRAḌĀKINĪJĀLASAMBARATANTRA

**Taebojŏk kyŏng** 大寶積經. *See* RATNAKŪṬASŪTRA

**Taebŏm ch'ŏn** 大梵天. *See* MAHĀBRAHMĀ

**Taebon kyŏng** 大本經. *See* MAHĀPADĀNASUTTANTA, MAHĀVADĀNASŪTRA

**taebŏp** 對法. *See* ABHIDHARMA

**taebŏp chesa** 對法諸師. *See* ĀBHIDHARMIKA

**Taebŏpko kyŏng** 大法鼓經. *See* MAHĀBHERĪHĀRAKAPARIVARTA

**Taeborisa** 大菩提寺. *See* MAHĀBODHI TEMPLE

**taech'i** 對治. *See* PRATIPAKṢA

**Taech'oyŏl** 大焦熱. *See* PRATĀPANA

**taedŏk** 大德. *See* DADE

**taegaoe** 大可畏. *See* MAHĀBHAYA

**taegi** 對機. *See* DUIJI

**taegi sŏlpŏp** 對機說法. *See* DUIJI SHUOFA

**taegŏp** 大劫. *See* MAHĀKALPA

**Taeguch'ira kyŏng** 大拘絺羅經. *See* MAHĀVEDALLASUTTA

**taegyuhwan [chiok]** 大叫喚[地獄]. *See* MAHĀRAURAVA

**Taehoe kyŏng** 大會經. *See* MAHĀSAMAYASUTTANTA

**Taehong Poŭn** 大洪報恩. *See* DAHONG BAO'EN

**Taehong Susu** 大洪守遂. *See* DAHONG SHOUSUI

**Taehŭkch'ŏn** 大黑天. *See* MAHĀKĀLA

**Taehye Chonggo** 大慧宗杲. *See* DAHUI ZONGGAO

**Taehye Pogak sŏnsa chongmun mugo** 大慧普覺禪師宗門武庫. *See* DAHUI PUJUE CHANSHI ZONGMEN WUKU

**Taehye Pogak sŏnsa sŏ** 大慧普覺禪師書. *See* DAHUI PUJUE CHANSHI SHU

**Taehye sŏjang** 大慧書狀. *See* DAHUI PUJUE CHANSHI SHU

**Taehyu Chŏngnyŏm** 大休正念. *See* DAXIU ZHENGNIAN

**Taeil kyŏng** 大日經. *See* MAHĀVAIROCANĀBHISAṂBODHIASŪTRA

**Taeil kyŏng so** 大日經疏. *See* DARI JING SHU

**Taeil kyŏng ŭisŏk** 大日經義釋. *See* DARI JING YISHI

**Taeil yŏrae** 大日如來. *See* Vairocana

**taein** 大印. *See* mahāmudrā

**taein** 大人. *See* mahāpuruṣa

**taeinsang** 大人相. *See* mahāpuruṣalakṣaṇa

**taejanggyŏng** 大藏經. *See* dazangjing

**t'aejang kye** 胎藏界. *See* taizōkai

**Taejaŭnsa** 大慈恩寺. *See* Daci'ensi

**Taejido non** 大智度論. *See* Dazhidu lun

**taeji pŏp** 大地法. *See* mahābūmika

**taejong** 大種. *See* mahābhūta

**Taeju Hyehae** 大珠慧海. *See* Dazhu Huihai

**Taejung pu** 大衆部. *See* Mahāsāṃghika

**t'aengmyŏl** 擇滅. *See* pratisaṃkhyānirodha

**taeŏ** 代語. *See* daiyu

**Tae panyŏlban kyŏng** 大般涅槃經. *See* Mahāparinirvāṇasūtra, cf. Mahāparinibbānasuttanta

**Tae panyŏlban kyŏng chiphae** 大般涅槃經集解. *See* Da banniepan jing jijie

**Tae Pirojana sŏngbul sinbyŏn kachi kyŏng** 大毘盧遮那成佛神變加持經. *See* Mahāvairocanasūtra

**tae pŏnnoeji pŏp** 大煩惱地法. *See* kleśamahābhūmika

**tae pori** 大菩提. *See* mahābodhi

**tae posal** 大菩薩. *See* mahābodhisattva

**tae pulsŏnji pŏp** 大不善地法. *See* akuśalamahābhūmika

**Taep'yŏngdŭngwang** 大平等王. *See* Mahāsaṃmata

**taerak** 大樂. *See* mahāsukha

**taesa** 大事. *See* dashi

**taesa** 大士. *See* mahāsattva

**Taesalch'anigŏnja** 大薩遮尼犍子. *See* Mahāsatyanirgrantha

**taesa sang** 大師想. *See* śāstṛsamjñā

**Taeseji** 大勢至. *See* Mahāsthāmaprāpta

**taesŏl** 大說. *See* mahāpadeśa

**taesŏng** 大城. *See* mahājanapada

**Taesŏng** 大聖. *See* Mahāmuni

**taesŏng** 大聖. *See* mahāsiddha

**Tae Song sŭng sa yak** 大宋僧史略. *See* Da Song seng shi lüe

**Taesŏn'gyŏn wang kyŏng** 大善見王經. *See* Mahāsuddassanasuttanta

**taesŏnji pŏp** 大善地法. *See* kuśalamahābūmika

**taesu** 對首. *See* pratideśanīya

**Taesugu** 大隨求. *See* Mahāpratisarā

**taesuin** 大手印. *See* mahāmudrā

**Taesŭng** 大乘. *See* Mahāyāna

**Taesŭng Abidalma chip non** 大乘阿毘達磨集論. *See* Abhidharmasamuccaya

**Taesŭng changŏmgyŏng non** 大乘莊嚴經論. *See* Mahāyānasūtrālaṃkāra

**Taesŭng changŏm powang kyŏng** 大乘莊嚴寶王經. *See* Kāraṇḍavyūha

**Taesŭng chip posal hak non** 大乘集菩薩學論. *See* Śikṣāsamuccaya

**Taesŭng hyŏn non** 大乘玄論. *See* Dasheng xuan lun

**Taesŭng kisin non** 大乘起信論. *See* Dasheng qixin lun

**Taesŭng kisin non ŭi ki** 大乘起信論義記. *See* Dasheng qixin lun yi ji

**Taesŭng mirŏm kyŏng** 大乘密嚴經. *See* Ghanavyūha

**Taesŭng musaeng pangp'yŏn mun** 大乘無生方便門. *See* Dasheng wusheng fangbian men

**Taesŭng oon non** 大乘五蘊論. *See* Pañcaskandhaprakaraṇa

**Taesŭng pangp'yŏn hoe** 大乘方便會. *See* Upāyakauśalyasūtra

**Taesŭng pŏbwŏn ŭirim chang** 大乘法苑義林章. *See* Dasheng fayuan yilin zhang

**Taesŭng poyoŭi non** 大乘寶要義論. *See* Sūtrasamuccaya

**Taesŭng sŏngŏp non** 大乘成業論. *See* Karmasiddhiprakaraṇa

**Taesŭng taeŭi chang** 大乘大義章. *See* Dasheng dayi zhang

**Taesŭng ŭi chang** 大乘義章. *See* Dasheng yi zhang

**Tae Tang naejŏn nok** 大唐内典録. *See* Da Tang neidian lu

**Tae Tang Sŏyŏk ki** 大唐西域記. *See* Da Tang Xiyu ji

**Tae Tang Sŏyŏk kubŏp kosŭng chŏn** 大唐西域求法高僧傳. *See* Da Tang Xiyu qiufa gaoseng zhuan

**taeŭi** 大衣. *See* saṃghāṭī

**Taeung** 大雄. *See* Mahāvīra

**Taeun kyŏng** 大雲經. *See* *Mahāmeghasūtra

**Taewidŏk myŏngwang** 大威德明王. *See* Yamāntaka

**taewŏn'gyŏng chi** 大圓鏡智. *See* ādarśajñāna

**Taeyang Kyŏnghyŏn** 大陽警玄. *See* Dayang Jingxuan

**Taeyŏn pangp'yŏn kyŏng** 大緣方便經. *See* Mahānidānasutta

**t'ahwajajae ch'ŏn** 他化自在天. *See* paranirmitavaśavartin

**Taje kyŏng** 嗏帝經. *See* Mahātaṇhāsaṅkhayasutta

**t'ak** 濁. *See* kaṣāya

**t'akbal** 托鉢. *See* takuhatsu; cf. piṇḍapāta

**Talmadara** 達摩多羅. *See* Dharmatrāta

**Talmadara sŏn kyŏng** 達摩多羅禪經. *See* Damaduoluo chan jing

**Talmagŭpta** 達摩笈多. *See* Dharmagupta

**t'am** 貪. *See* abhidhyā, lobha, rāga

**Tammajena piguni** 曇摩提那比丘尼. *See* Dharmadinnā

**Tammuch'am** 曇無讖. *See* Dharmakṣema

**Tammudŏk pu** 曇無德部. *See* Dharmaguptaka

**Tammugal** 曇無竭. *See* Dharmodgata

**Tamnan** 曇鸞. *See* Tanluan

**Tamun ch'ŏn** 多門天. *See* Vaiśravaṇa

**Tamun pu** 多聞部. *See* Bahuśrutīya

**Tamyŏn Wŏnjing** 湛然圓澄. *See* Zhanran Yuandeng

**tan** 斷. *See* prahāṇa

**tanbyŏn** 斷邊. *See* ucchedānta

**tang** 幢. *See* ketu

**Tangoejŭng** 塘猥增. *See* Kukūla

**tan'gyŏn** 斷見. *See* ucchedadṛṣṭi

**tan'gyŏn non** 斷見論. *See* ucchedavāda

**tansŏn'gŭn** 斷善根. *See* samucchinnakuśalamūla

**tant'a** 單墮. *See* pāyattika

**tant'ŭngna** 檀特羅. *See* tantra

**tanwŏl** 檀越. *See* dānapati

**t'ap** 塔. *See* stūpa

**Tappamara** 沓婆摩羅. *See* Dravya Ma llaputra

**Tara** 多羅. *See* Tārā

**tarani** 陀羅尼. *See* dhāraṇī

**t'aryŏk** 他力. *See* tariki

**t'asimt'ong** 他心通. *See* paracittajñāna

**t'a suyong sin** 他受用身. *See* para-saṃbhogakāya

**to** 掉. *See* auddhatya

**to** 道. *See* dao, mārga, patha

**Toan** 道安. *See* Dao'an

**tobi** 荼毘. See kṣapita

**todo** 刀塗. *See* daotu

**t'oe** 退. *See* parihāṇi

**Togan kyŏng** 稻稈經. *See* Śālistambasūtra

**togu** 道具. *See* pariṣkāra

**Togyo ŭich'u** 道教義樞. *See* Daojiao yishu

**Tohae** 道楷. *See* Furong Daokai

**Toil** 道一. *See* Mazu Daoyi

**toin** 道人. *See* daoren

**toin no** 刀刃路. *See* kṣuramārga

**Toja Ch'owŏn** 道者超元. *See* Daozhe Chaoyuan

**Tojak** 道綽. *See* Daochuo

**tojang** 道場. *See* daochang

**toje** 道諦. *See* mārgasatya

**toji** 道智. *See* mārgajñatā

**tojini** 荼枳尼. *See* ḍākinī

**tokch'am** 獨參. *See* dokusan

**Tokcha pu** 犢子部. *See* Vātsīputrīya

**Tŏkch'ŏng** 德清. *See* Hanshan Deqing

**tokkak** 獨覺. *See* pratyekabuddha

**Tŏkkwang** 德光. *See* Fozhao Deguang

**Tŏkkwang** 德光. *See* Guṇaprabha

**Tokkyemo** 獨髻母. *See* Ekajaṭā, Ekajaṭī

**Tŏksan Sŏn'gam** 德山宣鑑. *See* Deshan Xuanjian

**to kwa** 道果. *See* mārgaphala

**tolgilla** 突吉羅. *See* duṣkṛta

**t'ongdal** 通達. *See* prativedha

**Tongjin** 童眞. *See* Kumārabhūta

**Tongnimsa** 東林寺. *See* Donglinsi

**tongnyuin** 同類因. *See* sabhāgahetu

**tongp'um** 同品. *See* sapakṣa

**tongsa** 同事. *See* samānārthatā

**Tongsan** 東山. *See* Pūrvaśaila

**Tongsan pŏmmun** 東山法門. *See* Dongshan famen

**Tongsan Such'o** 洞山守初. See Dongshan Shouchu

**Tongsan Yanggae** 洞山良价. *See* Dongshan Liangjie

**Tongt'ap yul chong** 東塔律宗. *See* Dongta lü zong

**ton'gyo** 頓教. *See* dunjiao

**T' ongyong** 通容. *See* Feiyin Tongrong

**Tonhwang** 敦煌. *See* Dunhuang

**tono** 頓悟. *See* dunwu

**tono chŏmsu** 頓悟漸修. *See* dunwu jianxiu

**Tono ipto yomun non** 頓悟入道要門論. *See* Dunwu rudao yaomen lun

**to pido chigyŏn ch'ŏngjŏng** 道非道智見清淨. *See* maggāmaggañāṇadassanavisuddhi

**top'ung** 刀風. *See* daofeng

**tori** 道理. *See* yukti

**tori ch'ŏn** 忉利天. *See* trāyastriṃśa

**toryang** 道場. *See* bodhimaṇḍa

**Toryung** 道隆. *See* Lanxi Daolong

**Tosaeng** 道生. *See* Daosheng, Caoyuan Daosheng

**tosang** 圖像. *See* yantra

**Tosin** 道信. *See* Daoxin

**Tosŏ** 都序. *See* Chanyuan zhuquanji duxu, Sajip

**tosol ch'ŏn** 兜率天. *See* tuṣita

**Tosŏn** 道宣. *See* Daoxuan

**tot'ong** 道通. *See* daotong

**tugwang** 頭光. *See* touguang

**T'uja Ŭich'ŏng** 投子義青. *See* Touzi Yiqing

**tŭk** 得. *See* prāpti, pattidāna

**tŭkkwa** 得果. *See* phalapratipannaka

**tŭnghwal [chiok]** 等活[地獄]. *See* saṃjīva

**tŭngin** 等引. *See* samāhita

**tŭngin chi** 等引智. *See* samāhitajñāna

**tŭngji** 等至. *See* samāpatti

**tŭngmugan yŏn** 等無間緣. *See* samanantarapratyaya

**tŭngnyu kwa** 等流果. *See* niṣyandaphala

**tun'gŭn** 鈍根. *See* mṛdvindriya

**t'uranch'a** 偸蘭遮. *See* sthūlātyaya

**tosa** 都寺/司. *See* dusi

**tusu** 頭首. *See* toushou

**Tusun** 杜順. *See* Dushun

**tut'a[haeng]** 頭陀[行]. *See* dhutaṅga

## U

**U** 于. *See* Yu

**Ubagukta** 優婆毱多. *See* Upagupta

**ubai** 優婆夷. *See* upāsikā

**ubai kye** 優婆夷戒. *See* upāsikāsaṃvara

**ubajesa** 優波提舍. *See* upadeśa

**Ubanant'a** 優波難陀. *See* Upananda

**Ubarasaek** 優波羅色. *See* Utpalavarṇā

**Ubari** 優波離. *See* Upāli

**Ubari kyŏng** 優婆離經. *See* Upālisutta

**ubasae** 優婆塞. *See* upāsaka

**Ubasana** 優波斯那. *See* Upasena

**udam hwa** 優曇華. *See* udumbara

**udana** 優陀那. *See* udāna

**udong** 愚童. *See* bāla

**Udu chong** 牛頭宗. *See* Niutou zong

**Udu Pŏbyung** 牛頭法融. *See* Niutou Farong

**Ugaksararim kyŏng** 牛角娑羅林經. *See* Cūḷagosiṅgasutta, Mahāgosiṅgasutta

**ŭi** 義. *See* abhisaṃdhi, artha

**ŭi** 衣. *See* CĪVARA

**ŭi** 意. *See* MANAS

**ŭi** 依. *See* PRATISARAṆA, UPADHI

**ŭi** 疑. *See* VICIKITSĀ

**ŭibo** 依報. *See* ER BAO

**Ŭibok** 義福. *See* YIFU

**ŭich'ŏ** 意處. *See* MANĀYATANA

**Ŭich'ŏng** 義青. *See* TOUZI YIQING

**ŭich'wi** 意趣. *See* ABHIPRĀYA

**ŭidan** 疑團. *See* YITUAN

**ŭigŭn** 意根. *See* MANENDRIYA

**ŭigwe** 儀軌. *See* VIDHI

**ŭigyŏng** 疑經. *See* APOCRYPHA

**ŭiji** 依止. *See* NIŚRAYA

**Ŭijok kyŏng** 義足經. *See* AṬṬHAKAVAGGA

**Ŭijŏng** 義淨. *See* YIJING

**ŭijŏng** 疑情. *See* YIQING

**Uik Chiuk** 蕅益智旭. See OUYI ZHIXU

**ŭiŏn** 意言. *See* MANOJALPA

**ŭiŏp** 意業. *See* MANASKARMAN

**ŭisaengsin** 意生身. *See* MANOMAYAKĀYA

**ŭisik** 意識. *See* MANOVIJÑĀNA

**ŭisuhyŏllyang** 意受現量. *See* MANONUBHAVAPRATYAKṢA

**ŭit'agi sŏng** 依他起性. *See* PARATANTRA

**Ŭiyu kyŏng** 蟻喻經. *See* VAMMIKASUTTA

**Ujŏn** 于闐. *See* KHOTAN

**Ujŏn wang Sŏkka sang** 優塡王釋迦像. *See* UDĀYANA BUDDHA

**Uju** 牛主. *See* GAVĀMPATI

**Ukka** 郁伽. *See* UGRA

**Ukka changja hoe** 郁伽長者會. *See* UGRAPARIPṚCCHĀ

**Ulgat'a** 欝伽陀. *See* UDGATA

**Ultara** 欝多羅. *See* SOṆA AND UTTARA

**Ulturambul** 欝頭藍弗. *See* UDRAKA RĀMAPUTRA

**Ŭmgwang pu** 飲光部. *See* KĀŚYAPĪYA

**Unam Poam** 運庵普巖. *See* YUN'AN PUYAN

**Un'gang** 雲崗. *See* YUNGANG

**ŭngga** 應訶. *See* TARJANĪYAKARMAN

**ŭnggong** 應供. *See* ARHAT

**Unmun chong** 雲門宗. *See* YUNMEN ZONG

**Unmun Munŏn** 雲門文偃. *See* YUNMEN WENYAN

**Unsŏ Chugoeng** 雲棲袾宏. *See* YUNQI ZHUHONG

**unsu** 雲水. *See* UNSUI

**uranbun** 盂蘭盆. *See* ULLAMBANA, YULANPEN

**Uranbun kyŏng** 盂蘭盆經. *See* YULANPEN JING

**Urubinna** 優樓頻螺. *See* URUVILVĀ

**Urubinna Kasŏp** 優樓頻螺迦葉. *See* URUVILVĀ-KĀŚYAPA

**Uruga** 優樓佉. *See* ULŪKA

**Ut'ai** 優陀夷. *See* UDĀYIN

**uyo** 右遶. *See* PRADAKṢIṆA

## W

**wagu** 臥具. *See* PRATYĀSTARAṆA

**wangsaeng** 往生. *See* WANGSHENG

**Wangsa sŏng** 王舍城. *See* RĀJAGṚHA

**Wang Yu** 王維. *See* WANG WEI

**Wiang chong** 潙仰宗. *See* GUIYANG ZONG

**wigyŏng** 僞經. *See* APOCRYPHA

**Wijehŭi** 韋提希. *See* VAIDEHĪ

**Wisan kyŏngch'aek** 潙山警策. *See* GUISHAN JINGCE

**Wisan Yŏngu** 潙山靈祐. *See* GUISHAN LINGYOU

**wisin** 威神. *See* ANUBHĀVA

**Wit'a ch'ŏn** 韋駄天. *See* WEITUO TIAN

**wiŭi** 威儀. *See* ĪRYĀPATHA

**Wŏlchang pun** 月藏分. *See* CANDRAGARBHAPARIPṚCCHĀ

**wŏlli** 遠離. *See* VIVEKA

**Wŏltŭng sammae kyŏng** 月燈三昧經. *See* SAMĀDHIRĀJASŪTRA

**wŏn** 園. *See* ĀRĀMA

**wŏn** 願. *See* PRAṆIDHĀNA

**wŏndon kyo** 圓頓教. *See* YUANDUN JIAO

**Wŏn'gak kyŏng** 圓覺經. *See* YUANJUE JING

**wŏnhaeng chi** 遠行地. *See* DŪRAṄGAMĀ

**Wŏnin non** 原人論. *See* YUANREN LUN

**Wŏnjing** 圓澄. *See* ZHANRAN YUANDENG

**Wŏn kyŏng** 願經. *See* ĀKAṄKHEYYASUTTA

**wŏnman ch'aje** 圓滿次第. *See* NIṢPANNAKRAMA

**Wŏnmyŏng non** 圓明論. *See* YUANMING LUN

**Wŏno Kŭkkŭn** 圜悟克勤. *See* YUANWU KEQIN

**wŏn paramil** 願波羅蜜. *See* PRAṆIDHĀNAPĀRAMITĀ

**wŏn pori sim** 願菩提心. *See* PRAṆIDHICITTOPĀDA

**wŏnsaengsu** 圓生樹. *See* KALPAVṚKSA

**wŏnsŏngsil sŏng** 圓成實性. *See* PARINIṢPANNA

**wŏnyung** 圓融. *See* YUANRONG

**wŏnyung samgwan** 圓融三觀. *See* SANGUAN

## Y

**yach'a** 夜叉. *See* YAKṢA

**Yagwang posal** 藥王菩薩. *See* BHAIṢAJYARĀJA

**Yaksa ponwŏn kyŏng** 藥師本願經. *See* BHAIṢAJYAGURUSŪTRA

**Yaksa yŏrae** 藥師如來. *See* BHAIṢAJYAGURU

**yaksŏk** 藥石. *See* YAOSHI

**Yama ch'ŏn** 夜摩天. *See* YĀMA

**Yanggi p'a** 楊岐派. *See* YANGQI PAI

**Yanggi Panghoe** 楊岐方會. *See* YANGQI FANGHUI

**Yang Munhoe** 楊文會. *See* YANG WENHUI

**Yangsang kŭmgang tarani kyŏng** 壤相金剛陀羅尼經. *See* VAJRAVIDĀRAṆADHĀRAṆĪ

**Yasa** 耶舍. *See* YAŚAS

**Yasudara** 耶輸陀羅. *See* YAŚODHARĀ

**Yep'um kyŏng** 穢品經. *See* ANAṄGAṆASUTTA

**yeryu [kwa]** 預流[果]. *See* SROTAĀPANNA

**yeryu hyang** 預流向. *See* SROTAĀPANNAPHALAPRATIPANNAKA

**Yi T'onghyŏn** 李通玄. *See* LI TONGXUAN

**yŏhak** 與學. *See* ŚIKṢĀDATTAKA

**yŏhwan sammae** 如幻三昧. *See* MĀYOPAMASAMĀDHI

**yŏhwan yu** 如幻喻. *See* AṢṬAMĀYOPĀMA

**yoik yujŏng** 饒益有情. *See* SATTVĀRTHA

**Yŏjŏng** 如浄. *See* TIANTONG RUJING

**yok** 欲. *See* KĀMA, CHANDA

**yŏk** 力. *See* BALA

**Yokkye** 欲界. *See* KĀMADHĀTU

**yŏkkyŏng samjang** 譯經三藏. *See* YIJING SANZANG

**yŏk paramil** 力波羅蜜. *See* BALAPĀRAMITĀ

**Yŏktae pŏppo ki** 歷代法寶記. *See* LIDAI FABAO JI

**Yŏktae sambo ki** 歷代三寶紀. *See* LIDAI SANBAO JI

**yokt'am** 欲貪. *See* KĀMARĀGA

**yŏlban** 涅槃. *See* NIRVĀṆA

**Yŏlban chong** 涅槃宗. *See* NIEPAN ZONG

**yŏlban'gye** 涅槃界. *See* NIRVĀṆADHĀTU

**Yŏlban kyŏng** 涅槃經. *See* MAHĀPARINIRVĀṆASŪTRA, cf. MAHĀPARINIBBĀNASUTTANTA

**Yŏlban sŏk** 涅槃夕. *See* NIEPAN XI

**yŏlbansŭng** 涅槃僧. *See* NIVĀSANA

**Yŏllijŏ** 涅哩底. *See* NIRṚTI

**yŏm** 念. *See* ANUSMṚTI

**yŏm** 厭. *See* NIRVEDA

**yŏm** 染. *See* SAṂKLEŚA

**yŏm** 念. *See* SMṚTI

**Yŏmbuje** 閻浮提. *See* JAMBUDVĪPA

**yŏmbul** 念佛. *See* BUDDHĀNUSMṚTI, NIANFO

**yŏmch'ŏ** 念處. *See* SMṚTYUPASTHĀNA

**Yŏmch'ŏ kyŏng** 念處經. *See* SATIPAṬṬHĀNASUTTA

**yŏmgo** 拈古. *See* NIANGU

**yŏmhwa miso** 拈花微笑. *See* NIANHUA WEIXIAO

**yŏmhye chi** 焰慧地. *See* ARCIṢMATĪ

**yŏmju** 念珠. *See* JAPAMĀLĀ

**Yŏm kyŏng** 念經. *See* DVEDHĀVITAKKASUTTA

**yŏmmalla** 染末那. *See* KLIṢṬAMANAS

**Yŏmmandŏkka** 焔曼德迦. *See* YAMĀNTAKA

**Yŏmma wang** 閻魔王. *See* YAMA

**yŏmsa** 念死. *See* MARAṆĀNUSMṚTI

**yŏmsong** 念誦. *See* JAPA

**yŏmyŏl chiok** 炎熱地獄. *See* TĀPANA

**yŏn** 緣. *See* PRATYAYA

**yong** 龍. *See* NĀGA

**yong** 用. *See* YONG

**yŏn'gak** 緣覺. *See* PRATYEKABUDDHA

**yŏn'gak sŭng** 緣覺乘. *See* PRATYEKABUDDHAYĀNA

**Yŏng Cho** 靈照. *See* LING ZHAO

**Yŏngchung** 永中. *See* YONGZHONG

**Yŏngga Hyŏn'gak** 永嘉玄覺. *See* YONGJIA XUANJUE

**Yonggŏn changja** 勇健長者. *See* ŚŪRA ĀMRAṢṬHA

**yŏn'gi** 緣起. *See* PRATĪTYASAMUTPĀDA

**yŏngji** 靈知. *See* LINGZHI

**yŏngji** 靈地. See MAHĀSTHĀNA

**Yongji** 龍智. *See* NĀGABODHI

**yongmaeng** 勇猛. *See* VĪRA

**Yŏngmyŏng Yŏnsu** 永明延壽. *See* YONGMING YANSHOU

**Yŏngnak kyŏng** 瓔珞經. *See* PUSA YINGLUO BENYE JING

**Yŏngnyŏngsa** 永寧寺. *See* YONGNINGSI

**yŏngp'o** 令怖. *See* TARJANĪYAKARMAN

**yongsang** 龍象. *See* HASTINĀGA

**Yongsu** 龍樹. *See* NĀGĀRJUNA

**Yongsu posal kwŏn'gye wang song** 龍樹菩薩勸誡王頌. *See* SUHṚLLEKHA

**Yŏngu** 靈祐. *See* GUISHAN LINGYOU

**yŏnhwa** 蓮華. *See* PADMA

**yŏnhwa chwa** 蓮華坐. *See* PADMĀSANA

**yŏnhwa pu** 蓮華部. *See* PADMAKULA

**Yŏnhwasaek** 蓮華色. *See* UTPALAVARṆĀ

**Yŏnhwasu** 蓮華手. *See* PADMAPĀṆI

**yŏnmuk** 宴默. *See* PRATISAṂLAYANA

**Yŏnsaeng non** 緣生論. *See* *PRATĪTYASAMUTPĀDAŚĀSTRA

**Yŏnso** 燃燒. *See* ĀDITTAPARIYĀYASUTTA

**Yŏnsu** 延壽. *See* YONGMING YANSHOU

**Yŏpsa kyŏng** 獵師經. *See* NIVĀPASUTTA

**yŏrae** 如來. *See* TATHĀGATA

**yŏrae chi** 如來地. *See* TATHĀGATABHŪMI

**yŏraejang** 如來藏. *See* TATHĀGATAGARBHA

**yŏrae ka** 如來家. *See* TATHĀGATAKULA, BUDDHAKULA

**yŏrae sŏng** 如來性. *See* TATHĀGATAGOTRA

**Yŏrhajŭng** 烈河增. *See* NADĪ VAITARAṆĪ

**yŏri chagŭi** 如理作意. *See* YONIŚOMANASKĀRA

**yŏri chi** 如理智. *See* YATHĀVADBHĀVIKAJÑĀNA

**yŏryang chi** 如量智. *See* YĀVADBHĀVIKAJÑĀNA

**Yŏsan** 廬山. *See* LUSHAN

**Yŏsan Hyewŏn** 廬山慧遠. *See* LUSHAN HUIYUAN

**yŏsi amun** 如是我聞. *See* EVAṂ MAYĀ ŚRUTAṂ

**yŏsil chigyŏn** 如實知見. *See* YATHĀBHŪTAJÑĀNADARŚANA

**yŏ soyu chi** 如所有智. *See* YATHĀVADBHĀVIKAJÑĀNA

**yoŭi** 了義. *See* NĪTĀRTHA

**yŏŭi poju** 如意寶珠. *See* CINTAMĀṆI

**yu** 有. *See* BHAVA

**yudae** 有大. *See* BHAUTIKA

**yuga** 瑜伽. *See* YOGA

**Yugahaeng p'a** 瑜伽行派. *See* YOGĀCĀRA

**yugan** 肉眼. *See* MĀṂSACAKṢUS

**Yugasaji** 瑜伽師地. *See* YOGĀCĀRABHŪMI

**Yugasaji non** 瑜伽師地論. *See* YOGĀCĀRABHŪMIŚĀSTRA

**yuge** 遺偈. *See* YIJI

**Yugyo kyŏng** 遺教經. *See* YIJIAO JING

**yugyu** 六喩. *See* LIUYU

**Yuhaeng kyŏng** 遊行經. *See* MAHĀPARINIBBĀNASUTTANTA

**yuhaeng panyŏlban** 有行般涅槃. *See* SĀBHISAṂSKĀRAPARINIRVĀYIN

**Yuhŭiya kyŏng** 蕤呬耶經. *See* SARVAMAṆḌALASĀMĀNYAVIDHIGUHYATANTRA

**Yuhyŏn** 有賢. *See* BHADRIKA

**Yuil manibo kyŏng** 遺日摩尼寶經. *See* KĀŚYAPAPARIVARTA

**yujŏng** 有情. *See* SATTVA

**yujŏng ch'ŏn** 有頂天. *See* BHAVĀGRA

**yujŏng segan** 有情世間. *See* SATTVALOKA

**yukcha changgu** 六字章句. *See* ṢAḌAKṢARĪ

**yukcha taemyŏng** 六字大明. *See* ṢAḌAKṢARĪ

**yukch'ŏ** 六處. *See* ṢAḌĀYATANA

**Yukcho tan kyŏng** 六祖壇經. *See* LIUZU TAN JING

**yukch'wi** 六趣. *See* ṢAḌGATI

**yuk kŭnbon pŏnnoe** 六根本煩惱. See ṢAḌMŪLAKLEŚA

**yukkun pigu** 六群比丘. *See* ṢAḌVĀRGIKA

**yukkye** 肉髻. *See* UṢṆĪṢA

**yukparamil** 六波羅蜜. *See* ṢAḌPĀRAMITĀ

**yuksang** 六相. *See* LIUXIANG

**Yuksipsong yŏri non** 六十頌如理論. *See* YUKTIṢAṢṬIKĀ

**yul** 律. *See* VINAYA

**yulchang** 律藏. *See* VINAYAPIṬAKA

**Yul chong** 律宗. *See* NANSHAN LÜ ZONG

**Yumahil** 維摩詰. *See* VIMALAKĪRTI

**Yumahil sosŏl kyŏng chu** 維摩詰所說經註. *See* WEIMOJIE SUOSHUO JING ZHU

**Yuma hoe** 維摩會. *See* YUIMAE

**Yuma kyŏng** 維摩經. *See* VIMALAKĪRTINIRDEŚA

**yun** 輪. *See* CAKRA

**yuna** 維/唯那. *See* WEINUO

**yunhoe** 輪迴. *See* SAṂSĀRA

**yuru** 有漏. *See* SĀSRAVA

**yurŭi** 律儀. *See* SAṂVARA

**yuru in** 有漏因. *See* SĀSRAVAHETU

**yuru on** 有漏蘊. *See* SĀSRAVASKANDHA

**yuryun** 有輪. *See* BHAVACAKRA

**yusang** 有相. *See* SĀKARA

**yusik** 唯識. *See* VIJÑAPTIMĀTRATĀ

**Yusik chong** 唯識宗. *See* FAXIANG ZONG, VIJÑĀNAVĀDA, WEISHI ZONG

**Yusik isip non** 唯識二十論. *See* VIṂŚATIKĀ

**Yusik samsip non song** 唯識三十論頌. *See* TRIṂŚIKĀ

**yusim** 唯心. *See* CITTAMĀTRA

**yusim chŏngt'o** 唯心淨土. *See* WEIXIN JINGTU

**Yusim kyŏl** 唯心訣. *See* WEIXIN JUE

**yusin** 遺身. *See* YISHEN

**yusin'gyŏn** 有身見. *See* SATKĀYADṚṢṬI

**yusun** 由旬. *See* YOJANA

**yuwi** 有爲. *See* SAṂSKṚTA

**yuwi sang** 有爲相. *See* SAṂSKṚTALAKṢAṆA

**yuyŏ yŏlban** 有餘涅槃. *See* SOPADHIŚEṢANIRVĀṆA

# Pāli Cross-References

## A

**abbhāna.** *See* ABHYĀYANA

**abbhutadhamma.** *See* ADBHUTADHARMA

**ābhassaraloka.** *See* ĀBHĀSVARĀLOKA

**abhibhāyatana.** *See* ABHIBHVĀYATANA

**abhidhamma.** *See* ABHIDHARMA

**abhidhammapiṭaka.** *See* ABHIDHARMAPIṬAKA

**abhijjhā.** *See* ABHIDHYĀ

**abhilāsa.** *See* ABHILĀṢA

**abhiññā.** *See* ABHIJÑĀ

**accharā.** *See* APSARAS

**acinteyya.** *See* ACINTYA

**adhikaraṇasamatha.** *See* ADHIKARAṆAŚAMATHA

**adhimokkha.** *See* ADHIMOKṢA

**adhipatipaccaya.** *See* ADHIPATIPRATYAYA

**adhiṭṭhāna.** *See* ADHIṢṬHĀNA

**ādiccabandhu.** *See* ĀDITYABANDHU

**ādikammika.** *See* ĀDIKARMIKA

**adosa.** *See* ADVEṢA

**āgantukakilesa.** *See* ĀGANTUKAKLEŚA

**Ajātasattu.** *See* AJĀTAŚATRU

**akappiyavatthu.** *See* AKALPIKAVASTU

**ākāsānañcāyatana.** *See* ĀKĀŚĀNANTYĀYATANA

**ākiñcaññāyatana.** *See* ĀKIÑCANYĀYATANA

**akkhaṇa.** *See* AKṢAṆA

**akuppa.** *See* AKOPYA

**akusala.** *See* AKUŚALA

**Āḷāra Kālāma.** *See* ĀRĀḌA KĀLĀMA

**amata.** *See* AMṚTA

**Ambapālī.** *See* ĀMRAPĀLĪ

**āmisadāna.** *See* ĀMIṢADĀNA

**anāgāmimagga.** *See* ANĀGĀMIPHALAPRATIPANNAKA

**anāgāmiphala.** *See* ANĀGĀMIPHALASTHA

**anagāriya.** *See* ANAGĀRIKĀ

**anantarapaccaya.** *See* ANANTARAPRATYAYA

**ānāpānasati.** *See* ĀNĀPĀNASMṚTI

**Anāthapiṇḍika.** *See* ANĀTHAPIṆḌADA

**anattā.** *See* ANĀTMAN

**anicca.** *See* ANITYA

**aniñjitakamma.** *See* ANIÑJYAKARMAN

**ānisaṃsa.** *See* ANUŚAṂSA

**Aññākoṇḍañña.** *See* ĀJÑĀTAKAUṆḌINYA

**Aññātakoṇḍañña.** *See* ĀJÑĀTAKAUṆḌINYA

**antaravāsaka.** *See* ANTARVĀSAS

**anulomapaṭiloma.** *See* ANULOMAPRATILOMA

**anupādisesanibbāna.** *See* ANUPADHIŚEṢANIRVĀṆA

**anusaya.** *See* ANUŚAYA

**anussati.** *See* ANUSMṚTI

**anussava.** *See* ANUŚRAVA

**apadāna.** *See* also AVADĀNA

**āpo.** *See* ĀPAS

**appamāda.** *See* APRAMĀDA

**appamāṇābha.** *See* APRAMĀṆĀBHA

**appamāṇasubha.** *See* APRAMĀṆAŚUBHA

**appamañña.** *See* APRAMĀṆA

**appaṇihita.** *See* APRAṆIHITA

**arahattamagga.** *See* ARHATPRATIPANNAKA

**ārammaṇa.** *See* ĀLAMBANA

**ārammaṇapaccaya.** *See* ĀLAMBANAPRATYAYA

**ariyamagga.** *See* ĀRYAMĀRGA

**ariyamaggaphala.** *See* ĀRYAMĀRGAPHALA

**ariyapuggala.** *See* ĀRYAPUDGALA

**ariyasacca.** *See* FOUR NOBLE TRUTHS

**ariyasaṅgha.** *See* ĀRYASAṂGHA

**ariyāṭṭhaṅgikamagga.** *See* ĀRYĀṢṬĀṄGAMĀRGA

**ariyavaṃsa.** *See* ĀRYAVAṂŚA

**arūpadhātu.** *See* ĀRŪPYADHĀTU

**arūparāga.** *See* ĀRŪPYARĀGA

**arūpāvacarajhāna.** *See* ĀRŪPYĀVACARADHYĀNA

**asaddhā.** *See* ĀŚRADDHYA

**asampajañña.** *See* ASAṂPRAJANYA

**asaṅkhata.** *See* ASAṂSKṚTA

**asaṅkhatadhamma.** *See* ASAṂSKṚTADHARMA

**asaṅkheyyakappa.** *See* ASAṂKHYEYAKALPA

**asañña.** *See* ASAṂJÑIKA

**asaññasamāpatti.** *See* ASAṂJÑĀSAMĀPATTI

**asaññasatta.** *See* ASAṂJÑIKA

**āsavakkhaya.** *See* ĀSRAVAKṢAYA

**asipattavana.** *See* ASIPATTRAVANA

**Assaji.** *See* AŚVAJIT

**atappa.** *See* ATAPA

**attagāha.** *See* ĀTMAGRAHA

**attan.** *See* ĀTMAN

**attavāda.** *See* ĀTMAVĀDA

**attha** [alt. aṭṭha]. *See* ARTHA

**aṭṭhaṅgasamannāgataṃ uposathaṃ.** *See* AṢṬĀṄGASAMANVĀGATAṂ UPAVĀSAṂ, BAGUAN ZHAI

**aṭṭhavimokkha.** *See* AṢṬAVIMOKṢA

**aviha.** *See* avṛha

**avijjā.** *See* AVIDYĀ

**āvuso.** *See* ĀYUṢMAN

**avyākata.** *See* AVYĀKṚTA

**avyākatadhamma.** *See* AVYĀKṚTADHARMA

**ayonisomanasikāra.** *See* AYONIŚOMANASKĀRA

## B

**bahiddhā.** *See* BAHIRDHĀ

**Bahulika.** *See* BAHUŚRUTĪYA

**Beluvagāmaka** [alt. Veḷugāma]. *See* VEṆUGRĀMAKA

**Bhadda.** *See* BHADRA

**Bhaddā-Kaccānā.** *See* YAŚODHARĀ

**Bhaddā-Kapilānī.** *See* BHADRA-KAPILĀNĪ

**bhaddakappa.** *See* BHADRAKALPA

**Bhaddiya.** *See* BHADRIKA

**bhavacakka.** *See* BHAVACAKRA

**bhāvanāmayapaññā.** *See* BHĀVANĀMAYĪPRAJÑĀ

**bhikkhunī.** *See* BHIKṢUṆĪ

**bodhipakkhiyadhamma.** *See* BODHIPĀKṢIKADHARMA

**bodhirukkha** [alt. bodhirukka]. *See* BODHI TREE

**bodhisatta.** *See* BODHISATTVA

**bojjhaṅga.** *See* BODHYAṄGA

**brahmacariya.** *See* BRAHMACARYA

**brahmapārisajjā.** *See* BRAHMAKĀYIKA

**buddhacakkhu.** *See* BUDDHACAKṢUS

**buddhadhamma.** *See* BUDDHADHARMA

**buddhānussati.** *See* BUDDHĀNUSMṚTI

**buddhavassa.** *See* BUDDHAVARṢA

## C

**cakka.** *See* CAKRA

**cakkavāḷa.** *See* CAKRAVĀḌA

**cakkavattin.** *See* CAKRAVARTIN

**cakkhāyatana.** *See* CAKṢURĀYATANA

**cakkhu.** *See* CAKṢUS

**cakkhundriya.** *See* CAKṢURINDRIYA

**cakkhuviññāṇa.** *See* CAKṢURVIJÑĀNA

**caṅkama.** *See* CAṄKRAMA

**cariyā.** *See* CARITA

**cātummahārājikā.** *See* CĀTURMAHĀRĀJAKĀYIKA

**catunimitta.** *See* CATURNIMITTA

**cetiya.** *See* CAITYA

**Cetiyavāda.** *See* CAITYA

**cetopariyañāṇa.** *See* PARACITTAJÑĀNA

**chabbaggiya.** *See* ṢAḌVĀRGIKA

***chagati.** *See* ṢAḌGATI

**Channa.** *See* CHANDAKA

**cintāmayapaññā.** *See* CINTĀMAYĪPRAJÑĀ

**cittasampayuttasaṅkhāra.** *See* CITTASAṂPRAYUKTASAṂSKĀRA

**cittasantāna.** *See* CITTASAṂTĀNA, SAṂTĀNA

**cittekaggatā.** *See* CITTAIKĀGRATĀ

**Cūḷapanthaka.** *See* CŪḌAPANTHAKA

**cutūpapātañāṇa.** *See* CYUTYUPAPATTIJÑĀNA

## D

**Dabba Mallaputta.** *See* DRAVYA MALLAPUTRA

**dānapāramī.** *See* DĀNAPĀRAMITĀ

**dasadisā.** *See* DAŚADIŚ

**dasasīla.** *See* DAŚAŚĪLA

**dassana.** *See* DARŚANA

**Devānampiya.** *See* DEVĀNĀṂ PRIYAḤ

**dhamma.** *See* DHARMA

**dhammabhāṇaka.** *See* DHARMABHĀṆAKA

**dhammacakka.** *See* DHARMACAKRA

**dhammacakkappavattana.** *See* DHARMACAKRAPRAVARTANA

**dhammacakkhu.** *See* DHARMACAKṢUS

**dhammadāna.** *See* DHARMADĀNA

**dhammadhātu.** *See* DHARMADHĀTU

**Dhammadinnā.** *See* DHARMADINNĀ

**dhammamuddā.** *See* DHARMAMUDRĀ

**dhammānusāri.** *See* DHARMĀNUSĀRIN

**dhammapāla.** *See* DHARMAPĀLĀ

**dhammapariyāya.** *See* DHARMAPARYĀYA

**dhammapīti.** *See* DHARMAPRĪTI

**dhammarājā.** *See* DHARMARĀJAN

**dhammavinaya.** *See* DHARMAVINAYA

**dhammāyatana.** *See* DHARMĀYATANA

**Dhammayuttika.** *See* THAMMAYUT

**Dhataraṭṭha.** *See* DHṚTARĀṢṬRA

**dibbacakkhu.** *See* DIVYACAKṢUS

**dibbasota.** *See* DIVYAŚROTRA

**diṭṭhi.** *See* DṚṢṬI

**diṭṭhiparāmāsa.** *See* DṚṢṬIPARĀMARŚA

**diṭṭhippatta.** *See* DṚṢṬIPRĀPTA

**Doṇa.** *See* DRONA

**dosa.** *See* DOṢA, DVEṢA

**dubbhāsita.** *See* DURBHĀṢITA

**duggati.** *See* DURGATI

**dukkarakārikā.** *See* DUṢKARACARYĀ

**dukkaṭa.** *See* DUṢKRTA

**dukkha.** *See* DUḤKHA

**dukkhadukkhatā.** *See* DUḤKHADUḤKHATĀ

**dundubhi.** *See* DRUM

**dvāratthaya.** *See* TRIDVĀRA

## E

**ehi bhikkhu.** *See* EHIBHIKṢUKĀ

**Ekabbohārika.** *See* EKAVYAVAHĀRIKA

**evaṃ me sutaṃ.** *See* EVAṂ MAYĀ ŚRUTAṂ

## G

**gahapati.** *See* GṚHAPATI

**gandhabba.** *See* GANDHARVA

**garuḷa.** *See* GARUḌA

**Gavampati.** *See* GAVĀṂPATI

**Gayā-Kassapa.** *See* GAYĀ-KĀŚYAPA

**geyya.** *See* GEYA

**ghānaviññāṇa.** *See* GHRĀṆAVIJÑĀNA

**ghānāyatana.** *See* GHRĀṆĀYATANA

**ghānindriya.** *See* GHRĀṆENDRIYA

**Gijjhakūṭapabbata.** *See* GṚDHRAKŪṬAPARVATA

**Gotama.** *See* GAUTAMA

**gotta.** *See* GOTRA

**goyāniya.** *See* GODĀNĪYA

**gurudhamma.** *See* GURUDHARMA

## H

**hatthināga.** *See* HASTINĀGA

**Hemavataka.** *See* HAIMAVATA

**hetupaccaya.** *See* HETUPRATYAYA

**hiri.** *See* HRĪ

## I

**iddhi.** *See* ṚDDHI

**iddhividhābhiññā.** *See* ṚDDHIVIDHĀBHIJÑĀ

**Inda.** *See* INDRA

**iriyāpatha.** *See* ĪRYĀPATHA

**Isipatana.** *See* ṚṢIPATANA

## J

**jātissara.** *See* JĀTISMARA

**jhānaṅga.** *See* DHYĀNĀṄGA

**jhānasamāpatti.** *See* DHYĀNASAMĀPATTI

**jhāpita/jhāpeti.** *See* KṢAPITA

**jivhāviññāṇa.** *See* JIHVĀVIJÑĀNA

**jivhāyatana.** *See* JIHVĀYATANA

**jivhindriya.** *See* JIHVENDRIYA

## K

**Kaccāna.** *See* KĀTYĀYANA, MAHĀKĀTYĀYANA

**Kāḷudāyin.** *See* KĀLODĀYIN

**kalyāṇamitta.** *See* KALYĀṆAMITRA

**kāmamicchācāra.** *See* KĀMAMITHYĀCĀRA

**kamma.** *See* KARMAN

**kammapatha.** *See* KARMAPATHA

**kammāvaraṇa.** *See* KARMĀVARAṆA

**Kaṅkhā-Revata.** *See* KĀNKṢĀ-REVATA, REVATA

**Kapilavatthu.** *See* KAPILAVASTU

**kappa.** *See* KALPA

**kappiyakāraka.** *See* KALPIKĀRAKA

**Kassapa.** *See* KĀŚYAPA

**Kassapīya/Kassapika.** *See* KĀŚYAPĪYA

**kāyānupassanā.** *See* KĀYĀNUPAŚYANĀ

**kāyasakkhi.** *See* KĀYASĀKṢIN

**khaṇa.** *See* KṢAṆA

**khaṇasampadā.** *See* KṢAṆASAṂPAD

**khandha.** *See* SKANDHA

**khandhaka.** *See* SKANDHAKA

**khanti.** *See* KṢĀNTI

**khantipāramī.** *See* KṢĀNTIPĀRAMITĀ

**Khantivādī.** *See* KṢĀNTIVĀDIN

**khattiya.** *See* KṢATRIYA

**Khemā.** *See* KṢEMĀ

**khīnāsava.** *See* KṢĪṆĀSRAVA

**Khujjuttarā.** *See* KUBJOTTARĀ

**kilesa.** *See* KLEŚA

**kinnara.** *See* KIṂNARA

**kodha.** *See* KRODHA

**Koṇḍañña.** *See* ĀJÑĀTAKAUṆḌINYA

**Kosala.** *See* KOŚALA

**kosiya.** *See* KAUŚIKA

**Koṭṭhita.** *See* KAUṢṬHILA

**kukkucca.** *See* KAUKṚTYA

**kuladhītā.** *See* KULADUHITṚ

**kulaputta.** *See* KULAPUTRA

**Kumāra-Kassapa.** *See* KUMĀRA-KĀŚYAPA

**kusala.** *See* KUŚALA

**kusalamūla.** *See* KUŚALAMŪLA

**Kusinārā.** *See* KUŚINAGARĪ

**kusīta.** *See* KAUSĪDYA

## L

**Lakuṇṭaka Bhaddiya.** *See* LAKUṆṬAKA BHADRIKA

**lokadhamma.** *See* LOKADHARMA

**lokiya.** *See* LAUKIKA

**Lokuttaravāda.** *See* LOKOTTARAVĀDA

## M

**macchariya.** *See* MĀTSARYA

**magga.** *See* MĀRGA

**maggaphala.** *See* MĀRGAPHALA

**maggasacca.** *See* MĀRGASATYA

**Mahākaccāna.** *See* MAHĀKĀTYĀYANA

**mahākappa.** *See* MAHĀKALPA

**Mahākappina.** *See* MAHĀKAPPHIṆA

**Mahākassapa.** *See* MAHĀKĀŚYAPA

**Mahākoṭṭhita.** *See* KAUṢṬHILA

**Mahāmoggallāna.** *See* MAHĀMAUDGALYĀYANA

**Mahānāma.** *See* MAHĀNĀMAN

**Mahānikāya.** *See* MAHANIKAI

**mahāpadesa.** *See* MAHĀPADEŚA

**Mahāpajāpatī.** *See* MAHĀPRAJĀPATĪ

**Mahāpanthaka.** *See* PANTHAKA, CŪḌAPANTHAKA

**mahāpāṭihāriya.** *See* MAHĀPRĀTIHĀRYA

**Mahāpuṇṇa.** *See* PŪRṆA

**mahāpurisa.** *See* MAHĀPURUṢA

**mahāpurisalakkhaṇa.** *See* MAHĀPURUṢALAKṢAṆA

**mahāroruva.** *See* MAHĀRAURAVA

**mahātapa.** *See* PRATĀPANA

**Mahiṃsāsaka.** *See* MAHĪŚĀSAKA

**Majjhantika.** *See* MADHYĀNTIKA

**majjhimadesa.** *See* MADHYAMADEŚA

**majjhimapaṭipadā.** *See* MADHYAMAPRATIPAD

**makkha.** *See* MRAKṢA

**Makkhali Gosāla.** *See* MASKARIN GOŚĀLIPUTRA

**mamaṃkāra.** *See* MAMAKĀRA

**maṃsacakkhu.** *See* MĀṂSACAKṢUS

**mānatta.** *See* MĀNATVA

**manindriya.** *See* MANENDRIYA

**manokamma.** *See* MANASKARMAN

**manoviññāṇa.** *See* MANOVIJÑĀNA

**manussa.** *See* MANUṢYA

**maraṇānussati.** *See* MARAṆĀNUSMṚTI

**mātikā.** *See* MĀTṚKĀ

**mettā.** *See* MAITRĪ

**Metteya.** *See* MAITREYA

**micchādiṭṭhi.** *See* MITHYĀDṚṢṬI

**Migadāya.** *See* MṚGADĀVA

**Migāramātupāsāda.** *See* MṚGĀRAMĀTṚPRĀSĀDA

**Moggallāna.** *See* MAHĀMAUDGALYĀYANA

**mokkha.** *See* MOKṢA

**Mucalinda.** *See* MUCILINDA

**mutiṅga.** *See* DRUM

**muṭṭhassati.** *See* MUṢITASMṚTI

## N

**Nadī-Kassapa.** *See* NADĪ-KĀŚYAPA

**ñāṇadassana.** *See* JÑĀNADARŚANA

**nānādhimuttikañāṇa.** *See* NĀNĀDHIMUKTIJÑĀNABALA

**nāsana.** *See* NĀŚANĪYA

**Nātaputta** [alt. Nātiputta]. *See* NIRGRANTHA-JÑĀTĪPUTRA

**natthika.** *See* NĀSTIKA

**ñatti.** *See* JÑAPTI

**navaṅga.** *See* NAVAṄGA[PĀVACANA]

**navasaññā.** *See* NAVASAṂJÑĀ

**nekkhamma.** *See* NAIṢKRAMYA

**Nerañjarā.** *See* NAIRAÑJANĀ

**nerayika.** *See* NĀRAKA

**nesajjika.** *See* CHANGJWA PURWA

**nevasaññānāsaññāyatana.** *See* NAIVASAṂJÑĀNĀSAṂJÑĀYATANA

**neyyattha.** *See* NEYĀRTHA

**nibbānadhātu.** *See* NIRVĀṆADHĀTU

**nibbidā.** *See* NIRVEDA

**nibbikappa.** *See* NIRVIKALPA

**nicca.** *See* NITYA

**nigaṇṭha.** *See* NIRGRANTHA

**Nigaṇṭha-Nātaputta.** *See* NIRGRANTHA-JÑĀTĪPUTRA

**Nigrodhārāma.** *See* NYAGRODHĀRĀMA

**nimmānarati.** *See* NIRMĀṆARATI

**nimmita.** *See* NIRMITA

**nippapañca.** *See* NIṢPRAPAÑCA

**nirodhasacca.** *See* NIRODHASATYA

**nirutti.** *See* NIRUKTI

**nisīdana.** *See* NIṢĪDANA

**nissaggiyapācittiya.** *See* NAIḤSARGIKAPĀYATTIKA, cf. PĀYATTIKA

**nissaraṇa.** *See* NIḤSARAṆA

**nissaya.** *See* NIŚRAYA

**nītattha.** *See* NĪTĀRTHA

**niṭṭhā.** *See* NIṢṬHĀ

## O

**opapātikayoni.** *See* UPAPĀDUKAYONI

**ottappa.** *See* APATRĀPYA

**ovāda.** *See* AVAVĀDA

## P

**pabbājanīyakamma.** *See* PRAVRĀJANĪYAKARMAN

**pabbajjā.** *See* PRAVRAJITA

**paccattharaṇa.** *See* PRATYĀSTARAṆA

**paccaya.** *See* PRATYAYA

**paccekabuddha.** *See* PRATYEKABUDDHA

**pācittiya.** *See* PĀYATTIKA

**padakkhiṇa.** *See* PRADAKṢIṆA

**padāleti.** *See* PRADĀSA

**padhāna.** *See* PRAHĀṆA

**padhānika.** *See* PRĀHĀṆIKA

**paduma.** *See* PADMA

**Pakudha Kaccāyana.** *See* KAKUDA KATYĀYANA

**pamāda.** *See* PRAMĀDA

**pañcakhandha.** *See* PAÑCASKANDHA, SKANDHA

**pañcasīla.** *See* PAÑCAŚĪLA

**pañcavaggiyā.** *See* PAÑCAVARGIKA

**pañcindriya.** *See* PAÑCENDRIYA

**paññācakkhu.** *See* PRAJÑĀCAKṢUS

**paññāpāramī.** *See* PRAJÑĀPĀRAMITĀ

**paññāsikkhā.** *See* PRAJÑĀŚIKṢĀ

**Paññattivādā.** *See* PRAJÑAPTIVĀDA

**paññāvimutta.** *See* PRAJÑĀVIMUKTA

**papañca.** *See* PRAPAÑCA

**Pāpimant.** *See* PĀPĪYĀṂS, NAMUCI

**paramatthasacca.** *See* PARAMĀRTHASATYA

**pāramī.** *See* PĀRAMITĀ

**paribbājaka.** *See* PARIVRĀJAKA

**parikkhāra.** *See* PARIṢKĀRA

**parinibbāna.** *See* PARINIRVĀṆA

**parisā.** *See* PARIṢAD

**parissāvana.** *See* PARISRĀVAṆA

**parittābhā.** *See* PARĪTTĀBHA

**parittasubhā.** *See* PARĪTTAŚUBHA

**Pasenadi.** *See* PRASENAJIT

**passaddhi.** *See* PRAŚRABDHI

**paṭhavī.** *See* PṚTHIVĪ

**paṭibhāna.** *See* PRATIBHĀNA

**paṭiccasamuppāda.** *See* PRATĪTYASAMUTPĀDA

**paṭidesanā.** *See* PRATIDEŚANĀ

**pāṭidesanīya.** *See* PRATIDEŚANĪYA

**pāṭihāriya.** *See* PRĀTIHĀRYA

**paṭigha.** *See* PRATIGHA

**pāṭimokkha.** *See* PRĀTIMOKṢA

**paṭipakkha.** *See* PRATIPAKṢA

**paṭisallāna.** *See* PRATISAṂLAYANA

**paṭisambhidā.** *See* PRATISAṂVID

**paṭivedha.** *See* PRATIVEDHA

**patta.** *See* PĀTRA

**pattanikkujjana.** *See* PĀTRANIKUBJANA

**pavāraṇā.** *See* PRAVĀRAṆĀ

**peta.** *See* PRETA

**phassa.** *See* SPARŚA

**phoṭṭhabba.** *See* SPARṢṬAVYA

**phoṭṭhabbāyatana.** *See* SPRAṢṬAVYĀYATANA

**Pilindavaccha.** *See* PILINDAVATSA

**pisuṇavācā.** *See* PAIŚUNYA

**pīti.** *See* PRĪTI

**pītijanana.** *See* PRĪTIJANANA

**Pubbaseliya.** *See* PŪRVAŚAILA

**pubbenivāsānussati.** *See* PŪRVANIVĀSĀNUSMṚTI

**puggala.** *See* PUDGALA

**puggalavāda.** *See* PUDGALAVĀDA

**puñña.** *See* PUṆYA

**Puṇṇa.** *See* PŪRṆA

**puññakiriyāvatthu.** *See* PUṆYAKRIYĀVASTU

**puññakkhetta.** *See* PUṆYAKṢETRA

**Puṇṇa Mantāṇīputta.** *See* PŪRṆA

**Pūraṇa-Kassapa.** *See* PŪRAṆA-KĀŚYAPA

**purisa.** *See* PURUṢA

**puthujjana.** *See* PṚTHAGJANA

## R

**Rājagaha.** *See* RĀJAGṚHA

**rakkhā.** *See* RAKṢĀ

**rakkhasa.** *See* RĀKṢASA

**ratana.** *See* RATNA

**ratanattaya.** *See* RATNATRAYA

**Raṭṭhapāla.** *See* RĀṢṬRAPĀLA

**roruva.** *See* RAURAVA

**rūpakkhandha.** *See* RŪPASKANDHA

## S

**sabbaññutāñāṇa.** *See* SARVAJÑATĀJÑĀNA

**sacca.** *See* SATYA

**saccadvaya.** *See* SATYADVAYA

**Saccaka.** *See* MAHĀSATYANIRGRANTHA

**saccakiriyā.** *See* SATYAVACANA

**saccavacana.** *See* SATYAVACANA

**sadda.** *See* ŚABDA

**saddāyatana.** *See* ŚABDĀYATANA

**saddhā.** *See* ŚRADDHĀ

**saddhamma.** *See* SADDHARMA

**saddhānusāri.** *See* ŚRADDHĀNUSĀRIN

**saddhāvimutta.** *See* ŚRADDHĀVIMUKTA

**sagga.** *See* SVARGA

**Sahampati.** *See* SAHĀṂPATI

**Sahassākkha.** *See* SAHASRĀKṢA

**sakadāgāmimagga.** *See* SAKṚDĀGĀMIPHALAPRATIPANNAKA

**sakadāgāmin.** *See* SAKṚDĀGĀMIN

**sakadāgāmiphala.** *See* SAKṚDĀGĀMIPHALASTHA

**sākiyabhikkhu.** *See* ŚĀKYABHIKṢU

**Sakka.** *See* ŚAKRA

**sakkabhikkhu.** *See* ŚĀKYABHIKṢU

**Sakkamuni.** *See* ŚĀKYAMUNI

**sakkāyadiṭṭhi.** *See* SATKĀYADṚṢṬI

**Sakulā.** *See* ŚAKULĀ

**sāla.** *See* ŚĀLA

**saḷāyatana.** *See* ṢAḌĀYATANA

**samānattatā.** *See* SAMĀNĀRTHATĀ

**sāmaṇerī.** *See* ŚRĀMANERIKĀ

**sāmaññaphala.** *See* ŚRĀMAṆYAPHALA

**samathavipassanā.** *See* ŚAMATHAVIPAŚYANĀ

**Sāmāvatī.** *See* ŚYĀMĀVATĪ

**saṃkilesa.** *See* SAṂKLEŚA

**sammādiṭṭhi.** *See* SAMYAGDṚṢṬI

**sammājīva.** *See* SAMYAGĀJĪVA

**sammākammanta.** *See* SAMYAKKARMĀNTA

**sammāpadhāna.** *See* SAMYAKPRADHĀNA

**sammāsamādhi.** *See* SAMYAKSAMĀDHI

**sammāsaṃbodhi.** *See* SAMYAKSAṂBODHI

**sammāsaṃbuddha.** *See* SAMYAKSAMBUDDHA

**sammāsaṅkappa.** *See* SAMYAKSAṂKALPA

**sammāsati.** *See* SAMYAKSMṚTI

**sammāvācā.** *See* SAMYAGVĀC

**sammāvāyāma.** *See* SAMYAGVYĀYĀMA

**sammuti.** *See* SAṂVṚTI

**sammutisacca.** *See* SAṂVṚTISATYA

**sampajañña.** *See* SAṂPRAJANYA

**samphappalāpā paṭivirata.** *See* SAṂBHINNAPRALĀPĀT PRATIVIRATI

**samudayasacca.** *See* SAMUDAYASATYA

**saṃvaṭṭakappa.** *See* SAṂVARTAKALPA

**saṃvaṭṭaṭṭhāyīkappa.** *See* SAṂVARTASTHĀYIKALPA

**saṅghabheda.** *See* SAṂGHABHEDA

**Saṅghabodhi.** *See* SIRI SANGA BŌ

**saṅghādisesa.** *See* SAṂGHĀVAŚEṢA

**saṅghakamma.** *See* SAṂGHAKARMAN

**saṅghāṭī.** *See* SAṂGHĀṬĪ

**saṅgīti.** *See* SAṂGĪTI

**Sañjaya/Sañcaya Belaṭṭiputta.** *See* SAÑJAYA VAIRĀṬĪPUTRA

**sañjīva.** *See* SAṂJĪVA

**saṅkacchika.** *See* SAṂKAKṢIKĀ

**Saṅkassa.** *See* SĀṂKĀŚYA

**saṅkhāra.** *See* SAṂSKĀRA

**saññā.** *See* SAṂJÑĀ

**saññāvedayitanirodha.** *See* SAṂJÑĀVEDAYITANIRODHA

**santāna.** *See* SAṂTĀNA

**sāsana.** *See* ŚĀSANA

**sāsava.** *See* SĀSRAVA

**sāsavakhandha.** *See* SĀSRAVASKANDHA

**sassata.** *See* ŚĀŚVATĀNTA

**sassataditthi.** *See* ŚĀŚVATADṚṢṬI

**sāṭheyya.** *See* ŚĀṬHYA

**sati.** *See* SMṚTI

**satipaṭṭhāna.** *See* SMṚTYUPASTHĀNA

**satta.** *See* SATTVA

**sattadhana.** *See* SAPTADHANA

**sattādhikaraṇasamatha.** *See* SAPTĀDHIKARAṆAŚAMATHA

**sattaloka.** *See* SATTVALOKA

**sattatathāgata.** *See* SAPTATATHĀGATA

**satthar.** *See* ŚĀSTṚ

**sāvaka.** *See* ŚRĀVAKA

**Sāvatthi.** *See* ŚRĀVASTĪ

**sekha.** *See* ŚAIKṢA

**sekhiyadhamma.** *See* ŚAIKṢADHARMA

**Setaketu.** *See* ŚVETAKETU

**Siddhattha.** *See* SIDDHĀRTHA

**Sigālakamātā.** *See* ŚṚGĀLAKAMĀTṚ

**sīhanāda.** *See* SIṂHANĀDA

**sīhāsana.** *See* SIṂHĀSANA

**sikkhamānā.** *See* ŚIKṢAMĀṆĀ

**sikkhāpada.** *See* ŚIKṢĀPADA

**sīla.** *See* ŚĪLA

**sīlabbataparāmāsa.** *See* ŚĪLAVRATAPARĀMARŚA

**sīlapāramī.** *See* ŚĪLAPĀRAMITĀ

**sīlavisuddhi.** *See* ŚĪLAVIŚUDDHI

**siloka.** *See* ŚLOKA

**simbalivana.** *See* AYAḤŚĀLMALĪVANA

**sopādisesanibbāna.** *See* SOPADHIŚEṢANIRVĀṆA

**sotāpanna.** *See* SROTAĀPANNA

**sotāpattimagga.** *See* SROTAĀPANNAPHALAPRATIPANNAKA

**sotāpattiphala.** *See* SROTAĀPANNAPHALASTHA

**sotaviññāṇa.** *See* ŚROTRAVIJÑĀNA

**sotāyatana.** *See* ŚROTRĀYATANA

**sotindriya.** *See* ŚROTRENDRIYA

**sotthika** [alt. sotthiya]. *See* SVASTIKA

**Subhadda.** *See* SUBHADRA

**subhakiṇṇā.** *See* ŚUBHAKṚTSNA

**sudassā.** *See* SUDṚŚA

**sudassī.** *See* SUDARŚANA

**suddhāvāsa.** *See* ŚUDDHĀVĀSA

**Sunakkhatta.** *See* SUNAKṢATRA

**Sunāparanta.** *See* ŚROṆĀPARĀNTA

**Suppiyā.** *See* SUPRIYĀ

**susāna.** *See* ŚMAŚĀNA

**sutamayāpaññā.** *See* ŚRUTAMAYĪPRAJÑĀ

**sutta.** *See* SŪTRA

**suttanta.** *See* SŪTRĀNTA

**suttapiṭaka.** *See* SŪTRAPIṬAKA

## T

**tajjaniyakamma.** *See* TARJANĪYAKARMAN

**Takkasilā.** *See* TAKṢAŚILĀ

**taṇhā.** *See* TṚṢṆĀ

**tapa.** *See* TAPAS

**Tapussa** [alt. Tapussu]. *See* TRAPUṢA

**tāvatiṃsa.** *See* TRĀYASTRIṂŚA

**tejo.** *See* TEJAS

**tevijjā.** *See* TRIVIDYĀ

**thina.** *See* STYĀNA

**thullaccaya.** *See* STHŪLĀTYAYA

**thūpa.** *See* STŪPA

**ticīvara.** *See* TRICĪVARA

**tikāla.** *See* TRIKĀLA

**tikkhindriya.** *See* TĪKṢṆENDRIYA

**tilakkhaṇa.** *See* TRILAKṢAṆA

**tiloka.** *See* TRILOKA

**tipeṭaka.** *See* TREPIṬAKA

**tipiṭaka.** *See* TRIPIṬAKA

**tiracchāna.** *See* TIRYAK

**tiratana.** *See* RATNATRAYA

**tisaraṇa.** *See* TRIŚARAṆA

**tisikkhā.** *See* TRIŚIKṢĀ

**titthiya.** *See* TĪRTHIKA

***tivisa.** *See* TRIVIṢA

**tusita.** *See* TUṢITA

## U

**ucchedadiṭṭhi.** *See* UCCHEDADṚṢṬI

**Uddaka Rāmaputta.** *See* UDRAKA RĀMAPUTRA

**uddhacca.** *See* AUDDHATYA

**Ugga.** *See* UGRA

**Uggata.** *See* UDGATA

**uṇhīsa.** *See* UṢṆĪṢA

**uṇṇākesa** [alt. uṇṇā]. *See* ŪRṆĀKEŚA

**upadesa.** *See* UPADEŚA

**upajjhāya/ā.** *See* UPĀDHYĀYA/Ā

**upapajjavedanīyakamma.** *See* UPAPADYAVEDANĪYAKARMAN

**upapātikayoni.** *See* UPAPĀDUKAYONI

**upāyakosalla.** *See* UPĀYAKAUŚALYA

**upekkhā.** *See* UPEKṢĀ

**upekkhāppamaññā.** *See* UPEKṢĀPRAMĀṆA

**uposatha.** *See* UPOṢADHA

**Uppalavaṇṇā.** *See* UTPALAVARṆĀ

**Uruvelā.** *See* URUVILVĀ

**Uruvela-Kassapa.** *See* URUVILVĀ-KĀŚYAPA

**uttarāsaṅga.** *See* UTTARĀSAṂGA

## V

**Vacchagotta.** *See* VATSAGOTRA

**vacīkamma.** *See* VĀKKARMAN

**Vajjiputtakā.** *See* VṚJIPUTRAKA

**Vajjiputtiyā.** *See* VĀTSĪPUTRĪYA

**Vaṃsa.** *See* VATSĀ

**Vaṃsadīpanī.** *See* WANTHADIPANI

**Vanavāsī.** *See* VANAVĀSIN

**Vappa.** *See* VĀṢPA

**vassa.** *See* VARṢĀ

**vāyo.** *See* VĀYU

**vehapphala.** *See* BṚHATPHALA

**Veḷuvanavihāra.** *See* VEṆUVANAVIHĀRA

**Vesākha.** *See* WESAK

**Vesāli.** *See* VAIŚĀLĪ

**vesārajja.** *See* VAIŚĀRADYA

**Vessavaṇa.** *See* VAIŚRAVAṆA

**veyyākaraṇa.** *See* VYĀKARAṆA

**veyyāvaccakara.** *See* VAIYĀPṚTYA(KARA)

**vicikicchā.** *See* VICIKITSĀ

**Videhī.** *See* VAIDEHĪ

**Viḍūḍabha.** *See* VIRŪḌHAKA

**vījanī.** *See* VĀLAVYAJANA

**vijjādhara.** *See* VIDYĀDHARA

**vijjāṭṭhāna.** *See* VIDYĀSTHĀNA

**vikappa.** *See* VIKALPA

**vikkhepa.** *See* VIKṢEPA

**vimokkha.** *See* VIMOKṢA

**vimokkhamukha.** *See* VIMOKṢAMUKHA

**viññāṇa.** *See* VIJÑĀNA

**viññāṇakhandha.** *See* VIJÑĀNASKANDHA

**viññāṇañcāyatana.** *See* VIJÑĀNĀNANTYĀYATANA

**vipallāsa.** *See* VIPARYĀSA

**vipariṇāmadukkha.** *See* VIPARIṆĀMADUḤKHATĀ

**Vipassī.** *See* VIPAŚYIN

**virāga.** *See* VAIRĀGYA

**viriya.** *See* VĪRYA

**viriyapāramī.** *See* VĪRYAPĀRAMITĀ

**Virūḷhaka.** *See* VIRŪḌHAKA

**Virupakkha.** *See* VIRŪPĀKṢA

**Visākhā.** *See* VIŚĀKHĀ

**visaya.** *See* VIṢAYA

**vitakka.** *See* VITARKA

**vivaṭṭakappa.** *See* VIVARTAKALPA

**vivaṭṭaṭṭhāyikappa.** *See* VIVARTASTHĀYIKALPA

**vodāna.** *See* VYAVADĀNA

## Y

**yakkha.** *See* YAKṢA

**yamakapāṭihāriya.** *See* YAMAKAPRĀTIHĀRYA

**Yasa.** *See* YAŚAS

**Yasodharā.** *See* YAŚODHARĀ

**yathābhūtañāṇadassana.** *See* YATHĀBHŪTAJÑĀNADARŚANA

**yonisomanasikāra.** *See* YONIŚOMANASKĀRA

**yutti.** *See* YUKTI

## Sanskrit Cross-References

### A

***abhavyasthāna.*** *See* abhabbaṭṭhāna

***Ādityaparyāyasūtra.*** *See* Ādittapariyāyasutta

***Amitāyurdhyānasūtra.*** *See* Guan Wuliangshou jing

**anupūrvikathā.** *See* anupubbikathā

**ārabdhavīrya.** *See* yongmaeng chŏngjin

**Arthavargīya.** *See* Aṭṭhakavagga

**āryasatya.** *See* four noble truths

**ātmabhāvaparityāga.** *See* sheshen

### B

**bali.** *See* gtor ma

**bodhidruma** [alt. bodhivṛkṣa, bodhiyaṣṭi, bodhivaṭa]. *See* bodhi tree

***Bodhisattvaśīlasūtra.*** *See* Fanwang jing, Pusajie jing

**Buddhagayā.** *See* Bodhgayā

**Buddhaghoṣa.** *See* Buddhaghosa

***Brahmajālasūtra.*** *See* Fanwang jing

**buddhakārya.** *See* twelve deeds of a buddha

### C

**cintābhūmikā.** *See* xindi

### D

**Daśottarasūtra.** *See* Dasuttarasutta

***dharmabhājana.*** *See* faqi

**Dharmacakrapravartanasūtra.** *See* also Dhammacakkappavattanasutta

***Dharmadhātupraveśanaparivarta.*** *See* Ru fajie pin

**Dharmapada.** *See* Dhammapada

**dhūta/dhuta.** *See* dhutaṅga

***Dhyānabhadra.*** *See* Zhikong Chanxian

**dṛṣṭisaṃkleśa.** *See* lta ba nyon mongs can

**dundubhi.** *See* drum

### E

**ekacitta.** *See* yixin

**ekavyūhasamādhi.** *See* yixing sanmei

### G

***garbhadhātu.*** *See* taizōkai

### J

**Janapandakalyāṇi Rūpanandā.** *See* Janapadakalyāṇī Nandā

### K

***karmadāna.*** *See* weinuo

**Kāśyapasiṃhanādasūtra.** *See* Kassapasīhanādasutta

**Kauṇḍinya.** *See* Ājñātakauṇḍinya

**kīla.** *See* phur pa

**kṛtsna/kṛtsnāyatana.** *See* kasiṇa

**kṣudrakapiṭaka.** *See* Khuddakanikāya

***Kucīna.*** *See* Kucha

**Kuṣāṇa.** *See* Kushan

### L

**laukikasamādhi.** *See* lokiyasamādhi

**layana.** *See* lena

**lokottaramārga.** *See* lokuttaramagga

***lokottaraphala.*** *See* lokuttaramagga

### M

**mahākṛtya.** *See* dashi

**mahānuśaṃsa.** *See* dashi

***Mahāprajñāpāramitāśāstra.*** *See* Dazhidu lun

***Mahāprajñāpāramitopadeśa.** *See* DAZHIDU LUN

**Mahārāṣṭra.** *See* MAHĀRAṬṬHA

***Mahāyānaśraddhotpādaśāstra.** *See* DASHENG QIXIN LUN

**mṛdaṅga.** *See* DRUM

## N

**naiṣadyika.** *See* CHANGJWA PURWA

**navāṅga[pravacana].** *See* NAVAṄGA[PĀVACANA]

**Nīlakaṇṭhakasūtra.** *See* QIANSHOU JING

## P

**pañcavārṣikapariṣad.** *See* WUZHE HUI

**Pāṇḍaravāsinī.** *See* BAIYI GUANYIN

**paryavāpti.** *See* PARIYATTI

**pluta.** *See* THOD RGAL

**poṣadha.** *See* UPOṢADHA

**Potalaka.** *See* PUTUOSHAN

**pretamukhāgnivālayaśarakāra.** *See* FANG YANKOU

## R

**Rāgavidyārāja.** *See* AIZEN MYŌŌ

**Raśmivimalaviśuddhaprabhādhāraṇī.** *See* MUGUJŎNGGWANG TAEDARANI KYŎNG

## S

***sādhāraṇāsādhāraṇakarman.** *See* GONG BUGONG YE

**samādhisūtra.** *See* SANMEI JING

**Saṃghamitrā.** *See* SAṄGHAMITTĀ

**Saṃgītisūtra.** *See* SAṄGĪTISUTTA

**saṃvṛtisaṃgha.** *See* SAMMUTISAṄGHA

**śarīre khāni.** *See* QIAO

**Śīgālovādasūtra.** *See* SIGĀLOVĀDASUTTA

***śikṣādāna.** *See* SIKKHĀPACCAKKHĀNA

**Smṛtyupasthānasūtra.** *See* SATIPAṬṬHĀNASUTTA

**Śrāmaṇyaphalasūtra.** *See* SĀMAÑÑAPHALASUTTA

**Śrīdevī.** *See* DPAL LDAN LHA MO

***Śroṇa.** *See* SOṆA AND UTTARA

**Śroṇa-Koṭikarṇa.** *See* SOṆA-KOṬIKAṆṆA

**Śrona-Koṭiviṃśa.** *See* SOṆA KOLIVĪSA

**Śrona-Viṃśatikoṭi.** *See* SOṆA KOLIVĪSA

***Śūnyadiśya-Dhyānabhadra.** *See* ZHIKONG CHANXIAN

**Supravāsā-Koliyadhītṛ.** *See* SUPPAVĀSĀ-KOḶIYADHĪTĀ

**Suvarṇabhūmi.** *See* SUVAṆṆABHŪMI

***Suvarṇadaṇḍasūtra.** *See* SOṆADAṆḌASUTTA

## U

**Uttara.** *See* SOṆA AND UTTARA

## V

**Vaiśākha.** *See* WESAK

**vajradhātu.** *See* KONGŌKAI

***Vajrasamādhisūtra.** *See* KŬMGANG SAMMAE KYŎNG

***Vijñaptimātratāsiddhi.** *See* CHENG WEISHI LUN

**Viśvantara.** *See* VESSANTARA

**vyutkrāntaka.** *See* THOD RGAL

## Y

**yānadvaya.** *See* ER SHENG

# Tibetan Cross-References

## A

**ā li kā li.** *See* ĀLIKĀLI

**A mra skyong ma.** *See* ĀMRAPĀLĪ

**a nu yo ga.** *See* ANUYOGA

**a ra pa dza na.** *See* ARAPACANA

**a ti yo ga.** *See* ATIYOGA

## B

**bag chags.** *See* VĀSANĀ

**Ba glang bdag.** *See* GAVĀṂPATI

**bag la nyal ba.** *See* ANUŚAYA

**bag med pa.** *See* PRAMĀDA

**bag yod pa.** *See* APRAMĀDA

**Ba ku la.** *See* BAKKULA

**ba lang spyod.** *See* GODĀNĪYA

**bar chad gcig pa.** *See* EKAVĪCIKA

**bar chad med lam.** *See* ĀNANTARYAMĀRGA

**bar chad med pa'i ting nge 'dzin.** *See* ĀNANTARYASAMĀDHI

**bar do.** *See* ANTARĀBHAVA

**bar do'i srid pa.** *See* ANTARĀBHAVA

**bar ma dor yongs su mya ngan las 'das pa.** *See* ANTARĀPARINIRVĀYIN

**Bcom ldan 'das.** *See* BHAGAVAT

**Bcom rlag.** *See* MATHURĀ

**Bcu gcig zhal spyan ras gzigs.** *See* EKĀDAŚAMUKHĀVALOKITEŚVARA

**bdag.** *See* ĀTMAN

**bdag 'bras.** *See* ADHIPATIPHALA

**bdag 'dzin.** *See* ĀTMAGRĀHA

**bdag 'dzin kun btags.** *See* PARIKALPITĀTMAGRAHA

**bdag 'dzin lhan skyes.** *See* SAHAJĀTMAGRAHA

**bdag gir 'dzin pa.** *See* MAMAKĀRA

**bdag gzhan brje ba.** *See* PARĀTMAPARIVARTANA

**bdag gzhan mnyam pa.** *See* PARĀTMASAMATĀ

**bdag med.** *See* ANĀTMAN, NAIRĀTMYA

**bdag po'i 'bras bu.** *See* ADHIPATIPHALA

**bdag po'i rkyen.** *See* ADHIPATIPRATYAYA

**bdag tu smra ba.** *See* ĀTMAVĀDA

**bde ba.** *See* SUKHA

**bde ba can.** *See* SUKHĀVATĪ

**Bde ba can gyi bkod pa'i mdo.** *See* SUKHĀVATĪVYŪHASŪTRA

**bde ba chen po.** *See* MAHĀSUKHA

**bde bar gshegs pa.** *See* SUGATA

**bde bar gshegs pa'i snying po.** *See* SUGATAGARBHA

**bde 'gro.** *See* SUGATI

**Bden bral.** *See* NIRṚTI

**bden bzhi'i chos khor.** *See* CATUḤSATYADHARMACAKRA

**bden bzhi rnam pa bcu drug.** *See* FOUR TRUTHS, SIXTEEN ASPECTS OF

**bden pa gnyis.** *See* SATYADVAYA

**Bden pa gnyis rnam par 'byed pa.** *See* SATYADVAYAVIBHAṄGA

**bden pa'i ngag.** *See* SATYAVACANA

**Bdud 'dul snying po.** *See* XIANGMO ZANG

**bdud rtsi.** *See* AMṚTA

**bdud rtsi lnga.** *See* PAÑCĀMṚTA

**'bebs pa.** *See* ĀVEŚA

**Bha ra dhwa dza.** *See* BHĀRADVĀJA

**Bha ra dhwa dza Bsod snyoms len.** *See* PIṆḌOLA-BHĀRADVĀJA

**Bi rū pa.** *See* VIRŪPA

**bka' bsdu.** *See* SAṂGĪTI

**bka' sdud pa po.** *See* SAṂGĪTIKĀRA

**bkra shis.** *See* MAṄGALA

**bkra shis ldan.** *See* SVASTIKA

**bkra shis rtags brgyad.** *See* AṢṬAMAṄGALA

**bla gos.** *See* UTTARĀSAṂGA

**bla ma'i rnal 'byor.** *See* GURUYOGA

**bla na med pa'i rnal 'byor rgyud.** *See* ANUTTARAYOGATANTRA

**bla na med pa yang dag par rdzogs pa'i byang chub.** *See* ANUTTARASAMYAKSAṂBODHI

**blo.** *See* BUDDHI

**Blo gros brtan pa.** *See* STHIRAMATI

**Blo gros mi zad pa.** *See* AKṢAYAMATI

**Blo gros mi zad pas bstan pa.** *See* AKṢAYAMATINIRDEŚA

**bral ba'i 'bras bu.** *See* VISAṂYOGAPHALA

**'bras bu.** *See* PHALA

**'bras bu che.** *See* BṚHATPHALA

**'bras bu la gnas pa.** *See* PHALASTHITA

**'bras bu la zhugs pa.** *See* PHALAPRATIPANNAKA

**'bras bu theg pa.** *See* PHALAYĀNA

**Bre bo.** *See* DROṆA

**Brgya byin.** *See* KAUŚIKA, ŚAKRA

**Brgyad stong 'grel chen.** *See* AṢṬASĀHASRIKĀPRAJÑĀPĀRAMITĀVYĀKHYĀBHISAMAYĀLAṂKĀRĀLOKĀ

**brjed nges.** *See* MUṢITASMṚTI

**brkyang ma.** *See* LALANĀ

**brnab sems.** *See* ABHIDHYĀ

**brten.** *See* NIŚRAYA

**brtson 'grus.** *See* VĪRYA

**brtson 'grus pha rol tu phyin pa.** *See* VĪRYAPĀRAMITĀ

**bsam gtan.** *See* DHYĀNA

**bsam gtan snyoms 'jug.** *See* DHYĀNASAMĀPATTI

**bsam gyis mi khyab pa.** *See* ACINTYA

**Bsam gyis mi khyab par bstod pa.** *See* ACINTYASTAVA

**bsam pa las byung ba'i shes rab.** *See* CINTĀMAYĪPRAJÑĀ

**bsam pa med pa.** *See* WUNIAN

**bsdigs pa'i las.** *See* TARJANĪYAKARMAN

**bsdu ba'i dngos po.** *See* SAṂGRAHAVASTU

**bse ru.** *See* KHAḌGAVIṢĀṆA

**bse ru lta bu.** *See* KHAḌGAVIṢĀṆAKALPA

**bsgoms pa las byung ba'i shes rab.** *See* BHĀVANĀMAYĪPRAJÑĀ

**bshad pa.** *See* BHĀṢYA

**Bshes pa'i spring yig.** *See* SUHṚLLEKHA

**bskal chen.** *See* MAHĀKALPA

**bskal pa.** *See* KALPA

**bskal pa bzang po.** *See* BHADRAKALPA

**Bskal pa bzang po'i mdo.** *See* BHADRAKALPIKASŪTRA

**bskal pa grangs med pa.** *See* ASAṂKHYEYAKALPA

**bskyed rim.** *See* UTPATTIKRAMA

**bslab pa.** *See* ŚIKṢĀ

**bslab pa gsum.** *See* TRIŚIKṢĀ

**bslab pa'i gzhi.** *See* ŚIKṢĀPADA

**Bslab pa kun las btus pa.** *See* ŚIKṢĀSAMUCCAYA

**bslab pa lnga.** *See* PAÑCAŚĪLA

**bslab pa sbyin pa.** *See* ŚIKṢĀDATTAKA

**bslab pa spong pa/bslab pa 'bul pa.** *See* SIKKHĀPACCAKKHĀNA

**bslabs pa'i chos.** *See* ŚAIKṢADHARMA

**Bsngags ldan.** *See* KAṆṬHAKA

**bsnyen gnas.** *See* UPAVĀSA

**bsnyen par rdzogs pa.** *See* UPASAṂPADĀ

**bsnyil ba.** *See* NĀŚANĪYA

**bsod nams.** *See* PUṆYA

**bsod nams bya ba'i dngos po.** *See* PUṆYAKRIYĀVASTU

**bsod nams dang ye shes kyi tshogs.** *See* PUṆYAJÑĀNASAṂBHĀRA

**bsod nams kyi tshogs.** *See* PUṆYASAṂBHĀRA

**bsod nams kyi zhing.** *See* PUṆYAKṢETRA

**bsod nams rjes su yi rang.** *See* PUṆYĀNUMODANA

**bsod nams skyes.** *See* PUṆYAPRASAVA

**bsod snyoms.** *See* PIṆḌAPĀTA

**bstan bcos.** *See* ŚĀSTRA

**Bstan dar lha ram pa.** *See* AGVAANDANDAR

**bstan pa.** *See* ŚĀSANA

**Bstod pa bzhi.** *See* CATUḤSTAVA

**bstod tshogs.** *See* STAVAKĀYA

**btags pa.** *See* PRAJÑAPTI

**Btags par smra ba.** *See* PRAJÑAPTIVĀDA

**Btags par smra ba'i sde.** *See* PRAJÑAPTIVĀDA

**btang snyoms.** *See* UPEKṢĀ

**btang snyoms tshad med.** *See* UPEKṢĀPRAMĀṆA

**Btsun pa zla ba.** *See* CANDRAGOMIN

**bya ba sgrub pa'i ye shes.** *See* KṚTYĀNUṢṬHĀNAJÑĀNA

**Bya gag kun ra.** *See* KUKKUṬĀRĀMA

**Bya gag 'tshong ba.** *See* KAUKKUṬIKA

**Byams ma'i bu gang po.** *See* PŪRṆA

**Byams mgon.** *See* MAITREYANĀTHA

**byams pa.** *See* MAITRĪ

**Byams pa.** *See* MAITREYA

**byams pa'i 'dug stangs.** *See* MAITREYĀSANA

**byang chub.** *See* BODHI

**byang chub chen po.** *See* MAHĀBODHI

**byang chub chen po'i sprul sku.** *See* MAHĀBODHINIRMĀṆAKĀYA

**byang chub kyi phyogs.** *See* BODHIPĀKṢIKADHARMA

**byang chub kyi sems.** *See* BODHICITTA

**byang chub kyi sems bskyed pa.** *See* BODHICITTOTPĀDA

**byang chub kyi tshogs.** *See* BODHISAṂBHĀRA

**byang chub kyi yan lag.** *See* BODHYAṄGA

**Byang chub lam gyi sgron ma.** *See* BODHIPATHAPRADĪPA

**byang chub mchog gi phyag rgya.** *See* BODHYAṄGĪMUDRĀ

**byang chub sems dpa'.** *See* BODHISATTVA

**byang chub sems dpa' chen po.** *See* MAHĀBODHISATTVA

**byang chub sems dpa'i sa.** *See* BODHISATTVABHŪMI

**Byang chub sems dpa'i sa.** *See* BODHISATTVABHŪMI

**Byang chub sems dpa'i sde snod.** *See* BODHISATTVAPIṬAKA

**byang chub sems dpa'i sdom pa.** *See* BODHISATTVASAṂVARA

**byang chub sems dpa'i smon lam.** *See* BODHISATTVAPRAṆIDHĀNA

**Byang chub sems dpa'i spyod pa la 'jug pa.** *See* BODHICARYĀVATĀRA

**byang chub sems dpa'i theg pa.** *See* BODHISATTVAYĀNA

**byang chub sems dpa'i tshul khrims.** *See* BODHISATTVAŚĪLA

**byang chub sems dpa' 'phags pa.** *See* ĀRYABODHISATTVA

**Byang chub sems dpa' zla ba'i snying pos zhus pa.** *See* CANDRAGARBHAPARIPṚCCHĀ

**Byang chub sems 'grel.** *See* BODHICITTAVIVARAṆA

**byang chub snying po.** *See* BODHIMAṆḌA

**bya rdzogs kyi skad cig ma.** *See* ER WUCHANG

**bya rgyud.** *See* KRIYĀTANTRA

**Bya rung kha shor.** *See* BODHNĀTH STŪPA

**Bye brag bshad pa chen po.** *See* MAHĀVIBHĀṢĀ

**Bye brag smra ba.** *See* VAIBHĀṢIKA

**Bye brag tu rtogs par byed pa chen mo.** *See* MAHĀVYUTPATTI

**byed pa'i rgyu.** *See* KĀRAṆAHETU

**byin gyis brlabs pa.** *See* ADHIṢṬHĀNA

**byis pa.** *See* BĀLA

**'byung ba chen po.** *See* MAHĀBHŪTA

**'byung 'gyur.** *See* BHAUTIKA

**'byung po.** *See* BHŪTA

**'byung po 'dul byed kyi phyag rgya.** *See* BHŪTAḌĀMARAMUDRĀ

**Bzang byin.** *See* SUDINNA

**Bzang po.** *See* BHADRA

**Bzang po spyod pa'i smon lam.** *See* BHADRACARĪPRAṆIDHĀNA

**Bzang skyong.** *See* BHADRAPĀLA

**Bzhi brgya pa.** *See* CATUḤŚATAKA

**bzlas brjod.** *See* JAPA

**bzlas brjod kyi 'phreng ba.** *See* JAPAMĀLĀ

**bzo bo sprul sku.** *See* ŚILPANIRMĀṆAKĀYA

**bzod pa.** *See* KṢĀNTI

**bzod pa'i pha rol tu phyin pa.** *See* KṢĀNTIPĀRAMITĀ

## C

**cha.** *See* BHĀGA

**'chab pa.** *See* MRAKṢA

**chad lta.** *See* UCCHEDADṚṢṬI

**chad mtha'.** *See* UCCHEDĀNTA

**chad par smra ba.** *See* UCCHEDAVĀDA

**chags bral sngon song.** *See* VĪTARĀGAPŪRVIN

**chags pa.** *See* LOBHA

**chags pa'i bskal pa.** *See* VIVARTAKALPA

**'Char byed nag po.** *See* KĀLODĀYIN

**'Char ka.** *See* UDĀYIN

**ched du brjod pa.** *See* UDĀNA

**Ched du brjod pa'i tshoms.** *See* UDĀNAVARGA

**chen po bstan pa.** *See* MAHĀPADEŚA

**'chi ba.** *See* MARAṆA

**'Chi ba mthar byed.** *See* MĀRATIKA

**'chi ba rjes su dran pa.** *See* MARAṆĀNUSMṚTI

**'chi bdag gi bdud.** *See* MṚTYUMĀRA

**'chi med.** *See* AMṚTA

**'Chi med ldan.** *See* AMARĀVATĪ

**'chi 'pho ba dang skye ba rjes su dran pa.** *See* CYUTYUPAPATTIJÑĀNA

**cho 'phrul.** *See* PRĀTIHĀRYA

**cho 'phrul ya ma zung.** *See* YAMAKAPRĀTIHĀRYA

**cho ga.** *See* VIDHI

**chos.** *See* DHARMA

**chos bzod.** *See* DHARMAKṢĀNTI

**chos can mthun snang.** *See* SAMĀNAPRATIBHĀSADHARMIN

**Chos dang chos nyid rnam par 'byed pa.** *See* DHARMADHARMATĀVIBHĀGA

**Chos dbyings bstod pa.** *See* DHARMADHĀTUSTAVA

**chos dbyings ye shes.** *See* DHARMADHĀTUSVABHĀVAJÑĀNA

**chos 'dul ba.** *See* DHARMAVINAYA

**chos gos.** *See* CĪVARA

**chos gos gsum.** *See* TRICĪVARA

**chos 'khor bskor ba.** *See* DHARMACAKRAPRAVARTANA

**Chos 'phags.** *See* DHARMODGATA

**chos kyi bdag 'dzin.** *See* DHARMĀTMAGRAHA

**chos kyi bdag med.** *See* DHARMANAIRĀTMYA

**Chos kyi 'byung gnas.** *See* DHARMĀKARA

**chos kyi dbyings.** *See* DHARMADHĀTU

**Chos kyi grags pa.** *See* DHARMAKĪRTI

**chos kyi 'khor lo.** *See* DHARMACAKRA

**chos kyi 'khor lo'i phyag rgya.** *See* DHARMACAKRAMUDRĀ

**chos kyi mig.** *See* DHARMACAKṢUS

**Chos kyi phung po.** *See* DHARMASKANDHA[PĀDAŚĀSTRA]

**chos kyi rgyal po.** *See* DHARMARĀJAN

**chos kyi rjes su 'brang ba.** *See* DHARMĀNUSĀRIN

**chos kyi rnam grangs.** *See* DHARMAPARYĀYA

**chos kyi sbyin pa.** *See* DHARMADĀNA

**chos kyi skye mched.** *See* DHARMĀYATANA

**chos kyi sprin.** *See* DHARMAMEGHĀ

**Chos kyis sbyin.** *See* DHARMADINNĀ

**chos la dga' ba.** *See* DHARMAPRĪTI

**chos ming.** *See* FAMING

**chos mngon pa.** *See* ABHIDHARMA

**chos mngon pa ba.** *See* ĀBHIDHARMIKA

**Chos mngon pa'i mdzod kyi bshad pa.** *See* ABHIDHARMAKOŚABHĀṢYA

**Chos mngon pa kun las btus pa.** *See* ABHIDHARMASAMUCCAYA

**chos nyid.** *See* DHARMATĀ

**chos [rtags] kyi phyag rgya.** *See* DHARMAMUDRĀ

**Chos sbas pa.** *See* DHARMAGUPTAKA

**chos sku.** *See* DHARMAKĀYA

**chos sku'i ring bsrel.** *See* DHARMAŚARĪRA

**Chos skyob.** *See* DHARMATRĀTA

**chos skyong.** *See* DHARMAPĀLA

**Chos skyong.** *See* DHARMAPĀLA

**chos smra ba.** *See* DHARMABHĀṆAKA

**Chos yang dag par sdud pa.** *See* DHARMASAṂGĪTI

**chu.** *See* ĀPAS [alt. āpodhātu]

**chu bo.** *See* OGHA

**chu bo rab med.** *See* NADĪ VAITARAṆĪ

**Chu klung 'od srungs.** *See* NADĪ-KĀŚYAPA

**chu skyes mo.** *See* APSARAS

**chu srin.** *See* MAKARA

**chu tshags.** *See* PARISRĀVAṆA

**ci yang med pa'i skye mched.** *See* ĀKIÑCANYĀYATANA

**cog bu pa.** *See* CHANGJWA PURWA

## D

**dad pa.** *See* ŚRADDHĀ, PRASĀDA

**dad pa'i rjes su 'brang ba.** *See* ŚRADDHĀNUSĀRIN

**dag pa'i zhing khams.** *See* VIŚUDDHABUDDHAKṢETRA

**dad pas lhag par mos pa.** *See* ŚRADDHĀDHIMUKTA

**dad pas rnam par grol ba.** *See* ŚRADDHĀVIMUKTA

**dag zhing.** *See* KṢETRAŚUDDHI

**dal ba brgyad.** *See* AṢṬAKṢAṆA

**dal 'byor.** *See* KṢAṆASAMPAD

**Da ltar gyi sangs rgyas mngon sum du bzhugs pa'i ting nge 'dzin gyi mdo.** *See* PRATYUTPANNABUDDHASAMMUKHĀVASTHITASAMĀDHISŪTRA

**ḍa ma ru.** *See* ḌAMARU

**dam bca'.** *See* PRATIJÑĀ

**dam pa'i chos.** *See* SADDHARMA

**dam pa'i chos kyi gzugs brnyan.** *See* SADDHARMAPRATIRŪPAKA

**dam pa'i chos nub.** *See* SADDHARMAVIPRALOPA

**Dam pa'i chos pad ma dkar po'i mdo.** *See* SADDHARMAPUṆḌARĪKASŪTRA

**Dam pa'i chos puṇḍa rī ka'i 'grel pa [rgya las bsgyur pa].** *See* FAHUA XUANZAN

**Dam pa tog dkar.** *See* ŚVETAKETU

**dam tshig.** *See* SAMAYA

**dam tshig gi phyag rgya.** *See* SAMAYAMUDRĀ

**dam tshig sems dpa'.** *See* SAMAYASATTVA

**dang ba.** *See* PRASĀDA

**dang po'i sangs rgyas.** *See* ĀDIBUDDHA

**dbang.** *See* ABHIṢEKA

**dbang bo.** *See* VAŚITĀ

**dbang bskur.** *See* ABHIṢEKA

**dbang bzhi pa.** *See* CATURTHĀBHIṢEKA

**Dbang chen.** *See* MAHINDA

**dbang du bya ba.** *See* VAŚĪKARAṆA

**Dbang gi lha mo.** *See* KURUKULLĀ

**dbang phyug.** *See* AIŚVARYA

**dbang po.** *See* INDRIYA

**Dbang po.** *See* INDRA

**dbang po 'bring.** *See* MADYENDRIYA

**dbang po gsum.** *See* TRĪNDRIYA

**dbang po'i dra ba.** *See* INDRA'S NET

**dbang po'i las.** *See* VAŚĪKARAṆA

**dbang po lnga.** *See* PAÑCENDRIYA

**dbang po rnon po.** *See* TĪKṢṆENDRIYA

**dbang po rtul ba.** *See* MṚDVINDRIYA

**dbang po sdom pa.** *See* INDRIYASAMVARA

**dben pa.** *See* VIVEKA

**Dbu ma'i bstan bcos.** *See* MADHYAMAKAŚĀSTRA

**Dbu ma'i don bsdus pa.** *See* MADHYAMAKĀRTHASAMGRAHA

**dbu ma'i lam.** *See* MADHYAMAPRATIPAD

**Dbu ma'i lung.** *See* MADHYAMĀGAMA

**Dbu ma'i snying po.** *See* MADHYAMAKAHṚDAYA

**Dbu ma la 'jug pa.** *See* MADHYAMAKĀVATĀRA

**Dbu ma pa.** *See* MADHYAMAKA

**Dbu ma rgyan.** *See* MADHYAMAKĀLAMKĀRA

**Dbu ma rin po che'i sgron ma.** *See* MADHYAMAKARATNAPRADĪPA

**Dbu ma rtsa ba'i tshig le'u byas pa.** *See* MŪLAMADHYAMAKAKĀRIKĀ

**Dbu ma snang ba.** *See* MADHYAMAKĀLOKA

**dbugs rngub pa dang 'byung ba dran pa.** *See* ĀNĀPĀNASMṚTI

**Dbugs rngub pa dang 'byung ba dran pa'i mdo.** *See* ĀNĀPĀNASATISUTTA

**Dbus mtha' rnam 'byed.** *See* MADHYĀNTAVIBHĀGA

**dbyangs bsnyad.** *See* GEYA

**Dbyangs can ma.** *See* SARASVATĪ

**dbyar gnas.** *See* VARṢĀ

**Dbyig bshes.** *See* VASUMITRA

**Dbyig gnyen.** *See* VASUBANDHU

**de bzhin gshegs pa.** *See* TATHĀGATA

**de bzhin gshegs pa bdun.** *See* SAPTATATHĀGATA

**De bzhin gshegs pa'i gtsug tor nas byung ba'i gdugs dkar po can.** *See* TATHĀGATOṢṆĪṢASITĀTAPATRĀ

**de bzhin gshegs pa'i rigs.** *See* TATHĀGATAGOTRA, TATHĀGATAKULA

**de bzhin gshegs pa'i sa.** *See* TATHĀGATABHŪMI

**de bzhin gshegs pa'i snying po.** *See* TATHĀGATAGARBHA

**De bzhin gshegs pa'i snying po'i mdo.** *See* TATHĀGATAGARBHASŪTRA

**de bzhin gshegs pa lnga.** *See* PAÑCATATHĀGATA

**De bzhin gshegs pa mi 'khrugs pa'i bkod pa.** *See* AKṢOBHYATATHĀGATASYAVYŪHA

**de bzhin nyid.** *See* TATHATĀ

**de kho na nyid.** *See* TATTVA, TATHATĀ

**De kho na nyid bsdus pa.** *See* TATTVASAṂGRAHA

**De kho na nyid rin po che'i phreng ba.** *See* TATTVARATNĀVALĪ

**de lta bu byung ba.** *See* ITIVṚTTAKA

**de ma thag pa'i rkyen.** *See* ANANTARAPRATYAYA

**de nyid.** *See* TATTVA

**dga' ba.** *See* MUDITĀ

**Dga' bo.** *See* NANDA

**Dga' byed.** *See* NANDAKA

**dgag bya.** *See* PRATIṢEDHYA

**dgag pa.** *See* PRATIṢEDHA

**dgag phye.** *See* PRAVĀRAṆĀ

**dge ba.** *See* KUŚALA

**dge ba'i bshes gnyen.** *See* KALYĀṆAMITRA

**dge ba'i rtsa ba.** *See* KUŚALAMŪLA

**dge ba'i sa mang.** *See* KUŚALAMAHĀBHŪMIKA

**dge bsnyen.** *See* UPĀSAKA

**dge bsnyen gyi sdom pa.** *See* UPĀSAKASAṂVARA

**dge bsnyen ma.** *See* UPĀSIKĀ

**dge bsnyen ma'i sdom pa.** *See* UPĀSIKĀSAṂVARA

**dge chung.** *See* PARĪTTAŚUBHA

**dge 'dun.** *See* SAṂGHA

**dge 'dun gyi dbyen byed pa.** *See* SAṂGHABHEDA

**dge 'dun gyi las.** *See* SAṂGHAKARMAN

**dge 'dun lhag ma.** *See* SAṂGHĀVAŚEṢA

**dge 'dun nyi shu.** *See* VIṂŚATIPRABHEDASAṂGHA

**Dge 'dun phal chen pa'i sde.** *See* MAHĀSĀṂGHIKA

**Dge ma.** *See* KṢEMĀ

**dge rgyas.** *See* ŚUBHAKṚTSNA

**dge rtsa bcad pa.** *See* SAMUCCHINNAKUŚALAMŪLA

**dge rtsa bzhi.** *See* CATUṢKUŚALAMŪLA

**dge sbyong.** *See* ŚRAMAṆA

**dge sbyong gi tshul gyi 'bras bu.** *See* ŚRĀMAṆYAPHALA

**dge slob ma.** *See* ŚIKṢAMĀṆĀ

**dge slob ma'i sdom pa.** *See* ŚIKṢAMĀṆĀSAṂVARA

**dge slong.** *See* BHIKṢU

**dge slong ma.** *See* BHIKṢUṆĪ

**dge slong tshur shog ces pa.** *See* EHIBHIKṢUKĀ

**dge tshul.** *See* ŚRĀMAṆERA

**dge tshul gyi sdom pa.** *See* ŚRĀMAṆERASAṂVARA

**dge tshul ma.** *See* ŚRĀMAṆERIKĀ

**dge tshul ma'i sdom pa.** *See* ŚRĀMAṆERIKĀSAṂVARA

**dgongs bshad.** *See* SANDHYĀBHĀṢĀ

**dgongs pa.** *See* ABHIPRĀYA

**dgongs skad.** *See* SANDHYĀBHĀṢĀ

**dgra bcom pa.** *See* ARHAT

**dgra bcom zhugs pa.** *See* ARHATPRATIPANNAKA

**Dgra las rnam rgyal.** *See* JITĀRI

**'di skad bdag gis thos pa.** *See* EVAṂ MAYĀ ŚRUTAM

**dka' ba spyod pa.** *See* DUṢKARACARYĀ

**dka' thub.** *See* TAPAS

**dkon mchog.** *See* RATNA

**Dkon mchog brtsegs pa'i mdo.** *See* RATNAKŪṬASŪTRA

**Dkon mchog gi rigs rnam par dbye ba.** *See* RATNAGOTRAVIBHĀGA

**Dkon mchog grags pa.** *See* RATNAKĪRTI

**dkon mchog gsum.** *See* RATNATRAYA, TRIRATNA

**Dkon mchog sprin gyi mdo.** *See* RATNAMEGHASŪTRA

**dkyil 'khor.** *See* MAṆḌALA

**dmigs med.** *See* ANUPALABDHI

**dmigs pa.** *See* ĀLAMBANA, UPALABDHI

**Dmigs pa brtag pa.** *See* ĀLAMBANAPARĪKṢĀ

**dmigs rkyen.** *See* ĀLAMBANAPRATYAYA

**dmyal ba.** *See* NĀRAKA

**dngos grub.** *See* SIDDHI

**'dod chags.** *See* RĀGA

**'dod chen.** *See* ICCHANTIKA

**'dod khams.** *See* KĀMADHĀTU

**'dod pa.** *See* ABHILĀṢA, KĀMA

**'dod pa la 'dod chags.** *See* KĀMARĀGA

**'dod pa la 'dun pa.** *See* KĀMACCHANDA

**'dod pas log par g.yem pa.** *See* KĀMAMITHYĀCĀRA

**'dod yon sna lnga.** *See* PAÑCAKĀMAGUṆA

**don.** *See* ARTHA

**don byed nus pa.** *See* ARTHAKRIYĀ

**don dam bden pa.** *See* PARAMĀRTHASATYA

**don dam byang chub kyi sems.** *See* PARAMĀRTHABODHICITTA

**don dam pa'i dge 'dun.** *See* PARAMĀRTHASAṂGHA

**don dam rnam par nges pa'i chos 'khor.** *See* PARAMĀRTHAVINIŚCAYADHARMACAKRA

**Don yod grub pa.** *See* AMOGHASIDDHI

**Don yod zhags pa.** *See* AMOGHAPĀŚA

**Dpa' bar 'gro ba'i mdo.** See *ŚŪRAṂGAMASŪTRA

**dpa' bar 'gro ba'i ting nge 'dzin.** *See* ŚŪRAṂGAMASAMĀDHI

**Dpa' bar 'gro ba'i ting nge 'dzin gyi mdo.** *See* ŚŪRAṂGAMASAMĀDHISŪTRA

**dpa' bo.** *See* ḌĀKA, VĪRA

**Dpa' bo chen po.** *See* MAHĀVĪRA

**dpag bsam shing.** *See* KALPAVṚKṢA

**dpag tshad.** *See* YOJANA

**dpal be'u.** *See* ŚRĪVATSA

**dpe byad.** *See* ANUVYAÑJANA

**Dpe med par bstod pa.** *See* NIRAUPAMYASTAVA

**Dpung bzangs kyis zhus pa'i rgyud.** *See* SUBĀHUPARIPṚCCHĀTANTRA

**dpyad sgom.** *See* VICĀRABHĀVANĀ

**dpyod pa.** *See* VICĀRA

**drag po'i las.** *See* RAUDRACĀRA

**Drag shul can.** *See* UGRA

**Drag shul can gyis zhus pa.** *See* UGRAPARIPṚCCHĀ

**drang don.** *See* NEYĀRTHA

**Drang srong lhung ba.** *See* ṚṢIPATANA

**dran pa.** *See* SMṚTI

**dran pa nye bar bzhag pa'i mdo.** *See* SATIPAṬṬHĀNASUTTA

**dran pa nyer bzhag.** *See* SMṚTYUPASTHĀNA

**dri.** *See* GANDHA

**dri gtsang khang.** *See* GANDHAKUṬĪ

**dri'i skye mched.** *See* GANDHĀYATANA

**dril bu.** *See* GHAṆṬĀ

**dri ma.** *See* MALA

**dri ma med pa.** *See* VIMALĀ

**dri ma med pa'i rnam shes.** *See* AMALAVIJÑĀNA

**Dri med bshes gnyen.** *See* VIMALAMITRA

**Dri med grags pa.** *See* VIMALAKĪRTI

**Dri med grags pas bstan pa'i mdo.** *See* VIMALAKĪRTINIRDEŚA

**Dri med 'od.** *See* VIMALAPRABHĀ

**dri za.** *See* GANDHARVA

**dri za'i grong khyer.** *See* GANDHARVANAGARA

**drod.** *See* ŪṢMAN

**drug sde.** *See* ṢAḌVĀRGIKA

**'du byed.** *See* SAṂSKĀRA

**'du byed kyi sdug bsngal.** *See* SAṂSKĀRADUḤKHATĀ

**dud 'gro.** *See* TIRYAK

**dug gsum.** *See* TRIVIṢA

**'dug stangs.** *See* ĀSANA

**'dul ba.** *See* VINAYA

**'dul ba'i gzhi.** *See* VINAYAVASTU

**'Dul ba'i mdo.** *See* VINAYASŪTRA

**'dul ba'i sde snod.** *See* VINAYAPIṬAKA

**'dul ba rnam par 'byed pa.** *See* VINAYAVIBHAṄGA

**'dun pa.** *See* CHANDA

**'Dun pa.** *See* CHANDAKA

**dur khrod.** *See* ŚMAŚĀNA

**Dur khrod bdag po.** *See* CITIPATI

**dur khrod chen po brgyad.** *See* AṢṬAMAHĀŚMAŚĀNA

**'dus byas.** *See* SAṂSKṚTA

**'dus byas kyi mtshan nyid.** *See* SAṂSKṚTALAKṢAṆA

**'Dus bzang.** *See* SAṂGHABHADRA

**dus dang mi sbyor bar rnam par grol ba.** *See* ASAMAYAVIMUKTA

**dus gsum.** *See* TRIKĀLA

**'du shes.** *See* SAṂJÑĀ

**'du shes med 'du shes med min skye mched.** *See* NAIVASAṂJÑĀNĀSAṂJÑĀYATANA

**'du shes med pa.** *See* ASAṂJÑIKA

**'du shes med pa'i snyoms par 'jug pa.** *See* ASAṂJÑĀSAMĀPATTI

**Dus kyi 'khor lo rgyud.** *See* KĀLACAKRATANTRA

**dus kyis rnam par grol ba.** *See* SAMAYAVIMUKTA

**'dus ma byas.** *See* ASAṂSKṚTA

**'dus ma byas kyi chos.** *See* ASAṂSKṚTADHARMA

**'Dzam bu gling.** *See* JAMBUDVĪPA

## G

**Ga gon.** *See* TRAPUṢA

**Ga las 'jigs med.** *See* AKUTOBHAYĀ

**Gang gā'i klung.** *See* GAṄGĀNADĪ

**Gang gā'i klung gi bye ma.** *See* GAṄGĀNADĪVĀLUKĀ

**Gang po.** *See* PŪRṆA

**Gangs ri'i sde.** *See* HAIMAVATA

**gang zag.** *See* PUDGALA

**gang zag gi bdag 'dzin.** *See* PUDGALĀTMAGRAHA

**gang zag gi bdag med.** *See* PUDGALANAIRĀTMYA

**gang zag smra ba.** *See* PUDGALAVĀDA

**gar byed pa.** *See* NṚTYĀSANA

**gar gyi tshul gyis gnas pa.** *See* NṚTYĀSANA

**gar stabs.** *See* NṚTYĀSANA

**Ga ya 'od srung.** *See* GAYĀ-KĀŚYAPA

**gcer bu pa.** *See* NIRGRANTHA

**Gcer bu pa gnyen gyi bu.** *See* NIRGRANTHA-JÑĀTĪPUTRA

**Gcig las 'phros pa'i lung.** *See* AṄGUTTARANIKĀYA

**gdags pa.** *See* PRAJÑAPTI

**Gdags pa'i gtsug lag bstan bcos.** *See* PRAJÑAPTIBHĀṢYA [PĀDAŚĀSTRA]

**gdams ngag.** *See* AVAVĀDA

**gdams ngag brjed pa.** *See* UPADEŚASAṂPRAMOṢA

**gding ba.** *See* PRATYĀSTARAṆA

**Gdugs dkar.** *See* SITĀTAPATRĀ

**gleng gzhi.** *See* NIDĀNA

**glo bur gyi nyon mongs.** *See* ĀGANTUKAKLEŚA

**gnas.** *See* ĀŚRAYA, LENA, PĪṬHA

**Gnas bcas.** *See* SĀKETA

**gnas brtan.** *See* STHAVIRA

**gnas brtan bcu drug.** *See* ṢOḌAŚASTHAVIRA

**Gnas brtan sde pa.** *See* STHAVIRANIKĀYA

**gnas chen.** *See* MAHĀSTHĀNA

**gnas gtsang.** *See* ŚUDDHĀVĀSA

**gnas gtsang ma'i ris.** *See* ŚUDDHĀVĀSAKĀYIKA

**Gnas ma.** *See* VATSĀ

**Gnas ma'i bu pa.** *See* VĀTSĪPUTRĪYA

**gnas pa.** *See* STHITI

**gnas pa'i bskal pa.** *See* VIVARTASTHĀYIKALPA

**gnas pa'i mya ngan las 'das pa.** *See* PRATIṢṬHITANIRVĀṆA

**gnas par mi bya.** *See* ASAṂVĀSA

**gnas yongs su 'gyur pa.** *See* ĀŚRAYAPARĀVṚTTI

**gnod sbyin.** *See* YAKṢA

**gnod sems.** *See* VYĀPĀDA

**gnyid.** *See* MIDDHA

**gnyis ka'i cha las rnam par grol ba.** *See* UBHAYATOBHĀGAVIMUKTA

**gnyis su med pa.** *See* ADVAYA

**gnyis su med pa'i ye shes.** *See* ADVAYAJÑĀNA

**go cha.** *See* SAṂNĀHA

**'gog pa.** *See* NIRODHA

**'gog pa'i bden pa.** *See* NIRODHASATYA

**'gog pa'i snyoms 'jug.** *See* NIRODHASAMĀPATTI

**gong du 'pho ba.** *See* ŪRDHVASROTAS

**gos.** *See* CĪVARA

**Gos dkar mo.** *See* BAIYI GUANYIN

**Go ta ma.** *See* GAUTAMA

**Grags 'dzin ma.** *See* YAŚODHARĀ

**Grags pa.** *See* YAŚAS

**Grags pa bshes gnyen.** *See* YAŚOMITRA

**grangs med pa.** *See* ASAṂKHYA

**'Grel pa don gsal.** *See* SPHUṬĀRTHĀ

**'gro ba.** *See* GATI

**'Gro ba'i rnam grangs.** *See* SAṂGĪTIPARYĀYA[PĀDAŚĀSTRA]

**'gro ba lnga.** *See* PAÑCAGATI

**'gro ba rigs drug.** *See* ṢAḌGATI

**Grol med.** *See* NAMUCI

**grong khyer chen po.** *See* MAHĀJANAPADA

**grub mtha'.** *See* SIDDHĀNTA

**grub thob.** *See* SIDDHA

**Grub thob brgyad bcu rtsa bzhi'i lo rgyus.** *See* *CATURAŚĪTISIDDHAPRAVṚTTI

**grub thob chen po.** *See* MAHĀSIDDHA

**grul bum.** *See* KUMBHĀṆḌA

**Gsal rgyal.** *See* PRASENAJIT

**gsan pa.** *See* ANUŚRAVA

**gsang dbang.** *See* GUHYĀBHIṢEKA

**gsang sngags kyi theg pa.** *See* GUHYAMANTRAYĀNA

**Gser be'u.** *See* KANAKAVATSA

**Gser gling pa.** *See* DHARMAKĪRTIŚRĪ

**Gshin rje.** *See* YAMA

**Gshin rje gshed.** *See* YAMĀNTAKA

**gsol ba.** *See* JÑAPTI

**gsol ba dang gnyis kyi las brjod pa.** *See* JÑAPTIDVITĪYĀ KARMAVĀCANĀ

**gso sbyong.** *See* UPOṢADHA

**gsung rab yan lag bcu gnyis.** *See* DVĀDAŚĀṄGA[PRAVACANA]

**gsung rab yan lag dgu.** *See* NAVAṄGA[PRAVACANA]

**Gsus po che.** *See* KAUṢṬHILA

**gtan phab.** *See* UPADEŚA

**gter.** *See* NIDHĀNA

**gti mug.** *See* MOHA

**gti mug med pa.** *See* AMOHA

**gtsang ma'i gnas.** *See* ŚUDDHĀVĀSA

**gtso sems.** *See* PRADHĀNACITTA

**gtsug lag khang.** *See* VIHĀRA

**gtsug tor.** *See* UṢṆĪṢA

**gtum mo.** *See* CAṆḌĀLĪ

**guru mtshan brgyad.** *See* PADMASAMBHAVA

**Gyad kyi yul.** *See* MALLĀ

**gya nom snang ba.** *See* SUDṚŚA

**g.yas brkyang ba.** *See* ĀLĪḌHA

**g.yo.** *See* ŚĀṬHYA

**'gyod pa.** *See* KAUKṚTYA

**g.yon brkyang pa.** *See* PRATYĀLĪḌHA

**g.yung drung.** *See* SVASTIKA

**'gyur ba'i sdug bsngal.** *See* VIPARIṆĀMADUḤKHATĀ

**gzhan dbang.** *See* PARATANTRA

**gzhan don.** *See* PARĀRTHA

**gzhan don rjes dpag.** *See* PARĀRTHĀNUMĀNA

**gzhan gyi sems shes pa.** *See* PARACITTAJÑĀNA

**gzhan 'gyur.** *See* ANIYATA

**gzhan la grags pa'i rjes dpag.** *See* PARAPRASIDDHĀNUMĀNA

**gzhan 'phrul dbang byed.** *See* PARANIRMITAVAŚAVARTIN

**gzhan sel.** *See* APOHA

**gzhi.** *See* NIDĀNA

**Gzhi dge 'dun phal chen pa.** *See* MŪLAMAHĀSĀṂGHIKA

**gzhi shes.** *See* VASTUJÑĀNA

**Gzhi thams cad yod par smra ba.** *See* MŪLASARVĀSTIVĀDA

**Gzhi thams cad yod par smra ba'i 'dul ba.** *See* MŪLASARVĀSTIVĀDA VINAYA

**Gzhung tha dad pa rim par bklag pa'i 'khor lo.** *See* SAMAYABHEDOPARACANACAKRA

**Gzi can.** *See* MANASVIN

**gzugs.** *See* RŪPA

**gzugs khams.** *See* RŪPADHĀTU

**gzugs kyi phung po.** *See* RŪPASKANDHA

**gzugs kyi skye mched.** *See* RŪPĀYATANA

**gzugs la chags pa.** *See* RŪPARĀGA

**gzugs med na spyod pa'i bsam gtan.** *See* ĀRŪPYĀVACARADHYĀNA

**gzugs med pa'i 'dod chags.** *See* ĀRŪPYARĀGA

**gzugs med pa'i khams.** *See* ĀRŪPYADHĀTU

**gzugs na spyod pa'i bsam gtan.** *See* RŪPĀVACARADHYĀNA

**gzugs sku.** *See* RŪPAKĀYA

**gzugs stong pa'o stong pa nyid gzugs so.** *See* RŪPAṂ ŚŪNYATĀ ŚUNYATAIVA RŪPAM

**gzung ba dang 'dzin pa'i rnam par rtog pa.** *See* GRĀHYAGRĀHAKAVIKALPA

**gzungs.** *See* DHĀRAṆĪ

## H

**ho thug thu.** *See* HUTUKTU

**hūm mdzad kyi phyag rgya.** *See* HŪṂKĀRAMUDRĀ

**Hwashang Mahāyāna.** *See* BSAM YAS DEBATE

## J

**'Jam dpal.** *See* MAÑJUŚRĪ

**'Jam dpal bshes gnyen.** *See* MAÑJUŚRĪMITRA

**'Jam dpal gyi mtshan yang dag par brjod pa.** *See* MAÑJUŚRĪNĀMASAṂGĪTI

**'Jam dpal gyi rtsa ba'i rgyud.** *See* MAÑJUŚRĪMŪLAKALPA

**'Jam pa'i dbyangs.** *See* MAÑJUGHOṢA

**'jig pa.** *See* VYAYA

**'jig pa'i bskal pa.** *See* SAṂVARTAKALPA

**'jig rten.** *See* LOKA

**'Jig rten 'das par smra ba.** *See* LOKOTTARAVĀDA

**'Jig rten dbang phyug.** *See* LOKEŚVARA

**'jig rten gsum.** *See* TRILOKA

**'jig rten gyi chos.** *See* LOKADHARMA

**'jig rten gyi chos brgyad.** *See* AṢṬALOKADHARMA

**'jig rten las 'das pa.** *See* LOKOTTARA

**'jig rten pa.** *See* LAUKIKA

**'jig rten pa'i chos kyi mchog.** *See* LAUKIKĀGRADHARMA

**'jig rten pa'i khams.** *See* LOKADHĀTU

**'jig rten pa'i lam.** *See* LAUKIKAMĀRGA

**'Jig rten rgyang phan pa.** *See* LOKĀYATA

**'jig rten skyong ba.** *See* LOKAPĀLA

**'jig tshogs la lta ba.** *See* SATKĀYADṚṢṬI

**'Jigs byed.** *See* BHAIRAVA

**'Jigs med 'byung gnas sbas pa.** *See* ABHAYĀKARAGUPTA

**'jigs pa chen po.** *See* MAHĀBHAYA

**ji lta ba mkhyen pa'i ye shes.** *See* YATHĀVADBHĀVIKAJÑĀNA

**ji snyed pa mkhyen pa'i ye shes.** See YĀVADBHĀVIKAJÑĀNA

**Jo bo rje.** *See* ATIŚA DĪPAṂKARAŚRĪJÑĀNA

**'jog sgom.** *See* STHĀPYABHĀVANĀ

**'jug pa'i sems bskyed.** *See* PRASTHĀNACITTOTPĀDA

## K

**ka la ping ka.** *See* KALAVIṄKA

**Ka ma la shī la.** *See* KAMALAŚĪLA

**Ka ni ska.** *See* KANIṢKA

**Kā ta'i bu mo'i bu.** *See* KĀTYĀYANĪPUTRA

**Kā ti bu mo.** *See* KĀTIYĀNĪ

**Ka tya'i bu.** *See* KĀTYĀYANA

**Ka tya'i bu chen po.** *See* MAHĀKĀTYĀYANA

**Ka tya'i bu nog can.** *See* KAKUDA KĀTYĀYANA

**Ka'u shi ka.** *See* KAUŚIKA

**khams bcu.** *See* DAŚADHĀTU

**khams gsum.** *See* TRAIDHĀTUKA

**Khams gsum rnam rgyal.** *See* TRAILOKYAVIJAYA

**Khams kyi tshogs.** *See* Dhātukāya[pādaśāstra]

**khams sna tshogs mkhyen pa'i stobs.** *See* nānādhātujñānabala

**'khar bsil.** *See* khakkhara

**'khon du 'dzin pa.** *See* upanāha

**khong du chud pa.** *See* prativedha

**khong khro.** *See* pratigha

**'khor.** *See* pariṣad

**'khor ba.** *See* saṃsāra

**'khor lo.** *See* cakra

**'Khor lo bde mchog.** *See* Cakrasaṃvara

**'Khor lo bde mchog gi rgyud.** *See* Cakrasaṃvaratantra

**'khor lo sgyur ba'i rgyal po.** *See* cakravartin

**'khor yug ri.** *See* cakravāḍa

**Khrag thung.** *See* Heruka

**khrel yod pa.** *See* apatrāpya

**khri shing.** *See* khaṭvāṅga

**'khrig pa.** *See* maithuna

**khro ba.** *See* krodha

**Khro gnyer can.** *See* Bhṛkutī

**'khrul 'khor.** *See* yantra

**'khrul shes.** *See* bhrāntijñāna

**khyab pa.** *See* vyāpti

**khyim bdag.** *See* gṛhapati

**khyim med pa.** *See* anagārikā

**khyim na gnas pa.** *See* gṛhastha

**khyim sun 'byin pa.** *See* kuladūṣaka

**khyung.** *See* garuḍa

**klu.** *See* nāga

**Klu'i byang chub.** *See* Nāgabodhi

**Klu sde.** *See* Nāgasena

**Klu sgrub.** *See* Nāgārjuna

**Ko sa la.** *See* Kośala

**Ku ṇā la'i rtogs pa brjod pa.** *See* Aśokāvadāna

**kun brtags mtshan nyid.** *See* parikalpitasvabhāva

**kun btags.** *See* parikalpita

**kun btags ma rig pa.** *See* parikalpitāvidyā

**kun 'byung.** *See* samudaya

**kun 'byung gi bden pa.** *See* samudayasatya

**Kun dga' bo.** *See* Ānanda

**kun dga' ra ba.** *See* ārāma

**kun 'gro.** *See* sarvatraga

**kun gro'i rgyu.** *See* sarvatragahetu

**kun gzhi rnam par shes pa.** *See* ālayavijñāna

**kun nas nyon mongs pa.** *See* saṃkliṣṭa; saṃkleśa

**kun rdzob.** *See* saṃvṛti

**kun rdzob bden pa.** *See* saṃvṛtisatya

**kun rdzob byang chub kyi sems.** *See* saṃvṛti bodhicitta

**kun shes.** *See* sarvajñatā

**Kun shes kauṇ ḍi nya.** *See* Ājñātakauṇḍinya

**Kun tu bzang po.** *See* Samantabhadra

**Kun tu dri bsung.** *See* Samantagandha

**kun tu rgyu.** *See* parivrājaka

**Kun tu rgyu gnag lhas kyi bu.** *See* Maskarin Gośāla

**kun tu sbyor ba.** *See* saṃyojana

**kun tu spyod pa.** *See* samudācāra

**Kye rdo rje.** *See* Hevajra

**Kye rdo rje'i rgyud.** *See* Hevajratantra

## L

**Lag na rin chen.** *See* Ratnapāṇi

**lam.** *See* mārga, patha

**lam 'bras.** *See* mārgaphala

**Lam chen bstan.** *See* Panthaka

**lam gyi bden pa.** *See* mārgasatya

**lam lnga.** *See* pañcamārga

**Lam phran bstan.** *See* Cūḍapanthaka

**lam shes.** *See* mārgajñatā

**lam yan lag brgyad pa.** *See* āryāṣṭāṅgamārga

**lan gcig phyir 'ong ba.** *See* sakṛdāgāmin

**Lang kar gshegs pa'i mdo.** *See* Laṅkāvatārasūtra

**las.** *See* karman

**las dang po pa.** *See* ĀDIKARMIKA

**Las grub pa'i rab tu byed pa.** *See* KARMASIDDHIPRAKARAṆA

**las kyi lam.** *See* KARMAPATHA

**las kyi phyag rgya.** *See* KARMAMUDRĀ

**las kyi rigs.** *See* KARMAKULA

**las kyi sgrib pa.** *See* KARMĀVARAṆA

**las su bsko ba.** *See* KARMAVĀCANĀ

**lcags kyi shing shal ma li'i nags.** *See* AYAḤŚĀLMALĪVANA

**lce'i dbang po.** *See* JIHVENDRIYA

**lce'i rnam par shes pa.** *See* JIHVĀVIJÑĀNA

**lce'i skye mched.** *See* JIHVĀYATANA

**lci ba'i chos.** *See* GURUDHARMA

**ldan min 'du byed.** *See* VIPRAYUKTASAṂSKĀRA

**ldem por dgongs pa.** *See* ABHISAṂDHI

**ldog pa.** *See* VYATIREKA

**Legs pa'i blo gros.** *See* SĀDHUMATĪ

**Legs pa'i skar ma.** *See* SUNAKṢATRA

**legs par rnam par phye ba dang ldan pa'i chos 'khor.** *See* *SUVIBHAKTADHARMACAKRA

**Legs skyes ma.** *See* SUJĀTĀ

**len pa.** *See* UPĀDĀNA

**len pa'i rnam par shes pa.** *See* ĀDĀNAVIJÑĀNA

**lha.** *See* DEVA

**Lha chen.** *See* MAHĀDEVA

**lhag bcas myang 'das.** *See* SOPADHIŚEṢANIRVĀṆA

**lhag bsam.** *See* ADHYĀŚAYA

**lhag ma med par mya ngan las 'das pa.** *See* ANUPADHIŚEṢANIRVĀṆA

**lhag med myang 'das.** *See* ANUPADHIŚEṢANIRVĀṆA

**lhag mthong.** *See* VIPAŚYANĀ

**lhag pa'i bsam pa.** *See* ADHYĀŚAYA

**lhag pa'i nga rgyal.** *See* ADHIMĀNA

**lhag pa'i shes rab kyi bslab pa.** *See* ADHIPRAJÑĀŚIKṢĀ

**lhag pa'i ting nge 'dzin gyi bslab pa.** *See* ADHISAMĀDHIŚIKṢĀ

**lhag pa'i tshul khrims kyi bslab pa.** *See* ADHIŚĪLAŚIKṢĀ

**lha'i 'jig rten.** *See* DEVALOKA

**lha'i mig.** *See* DIVYACAKṢUS

**lha'i nga rgyal.** *See* DEVAMĀNA

**lha'i rgyal po.** *See* DEVARĀJAN

**lha'i rna ba.** *See* DIVYAŚROTRA

**lha'i rnal 'byor.** *See* DEVATĀYOGA

**lha'i yang lha.** *See* DEVĀTIDEVA

**lha ma yin.** *See* ASURA

**Lha mo dpal phreng gi seng ge'i sgra'i mdo.** *See* ŚRĪMĀLĀDEVĪSIṂHANĀDASŪTRA

**lhan cig byed pa'i rkyen.** *See* SAHAKĀRIPRATYAYA

**lhan cig 'byung ba'i rgyu.** *See* SAHABHŪHETU

**lhan cig gnas pa.** *See* SĀRDHAVIHĀRIN

**lhan cig skyes pa'i ma rig pa.** *See* SAHAJĀVIDYĀ

**lhan skyes.** *See* SAHAJA

**Lha rnams kyi dga' bo.** *See* DEVĀNĀṂ PRIYAḤ

**lha srin sde brgyad.** *See* AṢṬĀSENA

**Lhas sbyin.** *See* DEVADATTA

**lha yul nas babs pa.** *See* DEVĀVATĀRA

**lhung bzed.** *See* PĀTRA

**lhung bzed khas phub pa.** *See* PĀTRANIKUBJANA

**lkog gyur.** *See* PAROKṢA

**lnga sde.** *See* PAÑCAVARGIKA

**log pa'i kun rdzob.** *See* MITHYĀSAṂVṚTI

**log par lta ba.** *See* MITHYĀDṚṢṬI

**longs spyod rdzogs pa'i sku.** *See* SAṂBHOGAKĀYA

**lta ba.** *See* DṚṢṬI

**lta ba mchog tu 'dzin pa.** *See* DṚṢṬIPARĀMARŚA

**Lteng rgyas.** *See* URUVILVĀ

**Lteng rgyas 'od srung.** *See* URUVILVĀ-KĀŚYAPA

**lto 'phye chen po.** *See* MAHORĀGA

**ltung ba'i sgo bzhi.** *See* *CATURĀPATTIDVARA

**ltung byed.** *See* PĀYATTIKA

**lugs 'byung lugs ldog.** *See* ANULOMAPRATILOMA

**Lum bi'i tshal.** *See* LUMBINĪ

**Lum bi ni.** *See* LUMBINĪ

**lung.** *See* ĀGAMA

**lung bstan pa.** *See* VYĀKARAṆA

**lung du ma bstan pa.** *See* AVYĀKṚTA

**lung gi chos.** *See* ĀGAMADHARMA

**lung ma bstan.** *See* AVYĀKṚTA

**Lung ring po.** *See* DĪRGHĀGAMA

**lus.** *See* KĀYA, ŚARĪRA

**lus dran pa nye bar bzhag pa.** *See* KĀYĀNUPAŚYANĀ

**lus kyi dbang po.** *See* KĀYENDRIYA

**lus kyi mngon sum du byed pa.** *See* KĀYASĀKṢIN

**lus kyi rnam par shes pa.** *See* KĀYAVIJÑĀNA

**lus kyi sbyin pa.** *See* DEHADĀNA

**lus kyi skye mched.** *See* KĀYĀYATANA

**lus kyi snang ba.** *See* KĀYAPRABHĀ

**Lus ngan po.** *See* KUBERA

**lus 'od.** *See* KĀYAPRABHĀ

**Lus 'phags ma.** *See* VAIDEHĪ

**lus 'phags po.** *See* VIDEHA

## M

**ma chags pa.** *See* ALOBHA

**ma 'dres pa'i chos.** *See* ĀVEṆIKA[BUDDHA]DHARMA

**ma 'gag pa.** *See* ANIRUDDHA

**Ma 'gags pa.** *See* ANIRUDDHA

**ma hā yo ga.** *See* MAHĀYOGA

**Ma li ka.** *See* MALLIKĀ

**Man da ra ba.** *See* MANDĀRAVĀ

**Mang bkur ba.** *See* SAṂMITĪYA

**Mang pos bkur pa.** *See* MAHĀSAṂMATA

**man ngag.** *See* UPADEŚA

**Ma pham pa.** *See* AJITA

**ma rgyud.** *See* MĀTṚTANTRA

**ma rig pa.** *See* AVIDYĀ

**Mar me mdzad.** *See* DĪPAṂKARA

**Ma skyes dgra.** *See* AJĀTAŚATRU

**ma skyes pa.** *See* ANUTPĀDA

**ma yin dgag.** *See* PARYUDĀSAPRATIṢEDHA

**mchod pa.** *See* PŪJĀ

**mchod rten.** *See* STŪPA; CAITYA

**Mchod rten pa.** *See* CAITYA

**mchog gi dngos grub.** *See* UTTAMASIDDHI

**mchog gi sprul sku.** *See* UTTAMANIRMĀṆAKĀYA, SPRUL SKU

**mchog sbyin gyi phyag rgya.** *See* VARADAMUDRĀ

**mdo.** *See* SŪTRA

**Mdog nag po.** *See* ASITA

**Mdo kun las btus pa.** *See* SŪTRASAMUCCAYA

**Mdo phal po che.** *See* AVATAṂSAKASŪTRA

**mdo rnam par 'byed pa.** *See* SŪTRAVIBHAṄGA

**mdo sde.** *See* SŪTRĀNTA

**Mdo sde dgongs 'grel.** *See* SAṂDHINIRMOCANASŪTRA

**mdo sde'i sde snod.** *See* SŪTRAPIṬAKA

**Mdo sde pa.** *See* SAUTRĀNTIKA

**Mdo sde spyod pa'i dbu ma rang rgyud pa.** *See* *SAUTRĀNTIKA-SVĀTANTRIKA-MADHYAMAKA

**Mdzes dga'.** *See* SUNDARANANDA

**Mdzes dga' bo.** *See* SAUNDARANANDA

**Mdzes dga' mo.** *See* SUNDARĪNANDĀ

**mdzod spu.** *See* ŪRṆĀKEŚA

**me.** *See* TEJAS

**med dgag.** *See* PRASAJYAPRATIṢEDHA

**Me lha.** *See* AGNI

**me long lta bu'i ye shes.** *See* ĀDARŚAJÑĀNA

**me ma mur.** *See* KUKŪLA

**Me tog cher rgyas.** *See* SAṂKUSUMITA

**Mgon med zas sbyin.** *See* ANĀTHAPIṆḌADA

**Mgon po skyabs.** *See* GOMBOJAB

**mgu bar bya ba.** *See* MĀNATVA

**Mi bskyod pa.** *See* AKṢOBHYA

**mi che ba.** *See* AVṚHA

**mi dge ba.** *See* AKUŚALA

**mi dge ba'i rtsa ba.** *See* AKUŚALAMŪLA

**mi dge ba'i sa mang chen po.** *See* AKUŚALAMAHĀBHŪMIKA

**mi dmigs pa.** *See* ANUPALABDHI

**mig.** *See* CAKṢUS

**mi gdung ba.** *See* ATAPA

**mig gi dbang po.** *See* CAKṢURINDRIYA

**mig gi rnam par shes pa.** *See* CAKṢURVIJÑĀNA

**mig gi skye mched.** *See* CAKṢURĀYATANA

**Mig mi bzang.** *See* VIRŪPĀKṢA

**mi gnas pa'i mya ngan las 'das pa.** *See* APRATIṢṬHITANIRVĀṆA

**Mig stong can.** *See* SAHASRĀKṢA

**Mig stong ldan pa.** *See* SAHASRĀKṢA

**mi g.yo ba.** *See* ACALĀ

**mi g.yo ba'i 'dug stangs.** *See* ACALĀSANA

**mi g.yo ba'i las.** *See* ANIÑJYAKARMAN

**mi 'jigs pa.** *See* VAIŚĀRADYA

**mi 'jigs pa'i phya rgya.** *See* ABHAYAMUDRĀ

**mi 'jigs pa sbyin pa.** *See* ABHAYADĀNA

**mi khom pa.** *See* AKṢAṆA

**mi 'khrugs pa.** *See* AKOPYA

**Mi mjed kyi bdag po.** *See* SAHĀMPATI

**mi mjed kyi 'jig rten.** *See* SAHĀLOKA

**mi mthun phyogs.** *See* VIPAKṢA

**Mi phyed pa.** *See* ABHEDA

**mi rtag pa.** *See* ANITYA

**mi sdug pa bsgom pa.** *See* AŚUBHABHĀVANĀ

**mi skye ba'i chos la bzod pa.** *See* ANUTPATTIKADHARMAKṢĀNTI

**mi skye ba shes pa.** *See* ANUTPĀDAJÑĀNA

**mi slob lam.** *See* AŚAIKṢAMĀRGA

**mi slob pa.** *See* AŚAIKṢA

**Ming chen.** *See* MAHĀNĀMAN

**ming gzugs.** *See* NĀMARŪPA

**mi 'tshe ba.** *See* AHIṂSĀ

**mkha' 'gro.** *See* ḌĀKA

**Mkha' 'gro ma.** *See* ḌĀKINĪ

**Mkha' 'gro rgya mtsho rnal 'byor ma'i rgyud.** *See* ḌĀKĀRṆAVAMAHĀYOGINĪTANTRA

**mkha' lding.** *See* GARUḌA

**mkhan mo.** *See* UPĀDHYĀYĀ

**mkhan po.** *See* UPĀDHYĀYA

**mnar med.** *See* AVĪCI

**mngon dga'.** *See* ABHIRATI

**mngon du 'gyur ba.** *See* ABHIMUKHĪ

**mngon pa'i nga rgyal.** *See* ABHIMĀNA

**Mngon par brjod pa'i rgyud bla ma.** *See* ABHIDHĀNOTTARATANTRA

**Mngon par 'byung ba'i mdo.** *See* ABHINIṢKRAMAṆASŪTRA

**mngon par 'dod pa.** *See* ABHILĀṢA

**mngon par 'du byed dang bcas pa yongs su mya ngan las 'das pa.** *See* SĀBHISAṂSKĀRAPARINIRVĀYIN

**mngon par 'du byed pa med par yongs su mya ngan las 'das pa.** *See* ANABHISAṂSKĀRAPARINIRVĀYIN

**mngon par mtho ba.** *See* ABHYUDAYA

**mngon par 'ongs.** *See* ABHYĀYANA

**mngon par rtog pa.** *See* ABHINIRŪPAṆĀVIKALPA

**Mngon par rtogs pa'i rgyan.** *See* ABHISAMAYĀLAṂKĀRA

**mngon rtogs.** *See* ABHISAMAYA

**Mngon rtogs rgyan gyi snang ba rgya cher bshad pa.** *See* ABHISAMAYĀLAṂKĀRĀLOKĀVYĀKHYĀ

**mngon shes.** *See* ABHIJÑĀ

**mngon sum.** *See* PRATYAKṢA

**mnyam bzhag.** *See* SAMĀHITA

**mnyam bzhag gi phyag rgya.** *See* DHYĀNAMUDRĀ

**mnyam bzhag ye shes.** *See* SAMĀHITAJÑĀNA

**mnyam nyid ye shes.** *See* SAMATĀJÑĀNA

**Mnyan yod.** *See* ŚRĀVASTĪ

**mos pa.** *See* ADHIMOKṢA

**mos pa sna tshogs mkhyen pa'i stobs.** *See* NĀNĀDHIMUKTIJÑĀNABALA

**Mo'u 'gal gyi bu chen po.** *See* MAHĀMAUDGALYĀYANA

**mtha' brgyad.** *See* AṢṬĀNTA

**mthar 'dzin gyi lta ba.** *See* ANTAGRĀHADṚṢṬI

**mthar gyis pa.** *See* ANUPUBBIKATHĀ

**mthar phyin pa.** *See* NIṢṬHĀ

**mthar phyin pa'i lam.** *See* NIṢṬHĀMĀRGA

**mthong ba.** *See* DARŚANA

**mthong bas thob pa.** *See* DṚṢṬIPRĀPTA

**mthong lam.** *See* DARŚANAMĀRGA

**mtho ris.** *See* SVARGA

**mthu.** *See* ANUBHĀVA

**Mthu chen thob.** *See* MAHĀSTHĀMAPRĀPTA

**Mthu ldan rin chen.** *See* PRABHŪTARATNA

**mthun phyogs.** *See* SAPAKṢA

**mtshams.** *See* SĪMĀ

**mtshams 'jig pa.** *See* SĪMĀSAMŪHANA

**mtshams med lnga.** *See* PAÑCĀNANTARYA

**mtshams med pa'i las.** *See* ĀNANTARYAKARMAN

**mtshan.** *See* LIṄGA

**mtshan bcas.** *See* SANIMITTA

**mtshan bcas kyi rnal 'byor.** *See* SANIMITTAYOGA

**mtshan gsum bcu so gnyis.** *See* DVĀTRIṂŚADVARALAKṢAṆA

**mtshan ma.** *See* NIMITTA

**mtshan ma bzhi.** *See* CATURNIMITTA

**mtshan ma med pa.** *See* ĀNIMITTA

**mtshan mar 'dzin pa.** *See* NIMITTAGRĀHA

**mtshan med kyi rnal 'byor.** *See* ANIMITTAYOGA

**Mtshan mo bzang po.** *See* BHADRAKĀRĀTRĪ

**mtshan nyid.** *See* LAKṢAṆA

**mtshan nyid med pa'i chos 'khor.** *See* ALAKṢAṆADHARMACAKRA

**mtshan nyid theg pa.** *See* LAKṢAṆAYĀNA

**mtshungs ldan.** *See* SAṂPRAYUKTA

**mtshungs ldan gyi rgyu.** *See* SAṂPRAYUKTAHETU

**mu stegs pa.** *See* TĪRTHIKA

**mya ngan las 'das pa.** *See* NIRVĀṆA

**mya ngan las 'das pa'i dbyings.** *See* NIRVĀṆADHĀTU

**Mya ngan med.** *See* AŚOKA

## N

**Nag po chen po.** *See* MAHĀKĀLA

**Nags na gnas.** *See* VANAVĀSIN

**Nam gru.** *See* REVATA

**Nam gru ma.** *See* REVATĪ

**nam mkha'.** *See* ĀKĀŚA

**nam mkha'i me tog.** *See* KHAPUṢPA

**Nam mkha'i snying po.** *See* ĀKĀŚAGARBHA

**nam mkha' mtha' yas skye mched.** *See* ĀKĀŚĀNANTYĀYATANA

**nang du yang dag 'jog pa.** *See* PRATISAṂLAYANA

**nang rig pa.** *See* ADHYĀTMAVIDYĀ

**Ne ran dza na.** *See* NAIRAÑJANĀ

**Ne'u le'i pha, Ne'u le'i ma.** *See* NAKULAPITṚ AND NAKULAMĀTṚ

**Ngag dbang.** *See* VĀṄGĪŚA

**Ngag dbang bstan dar.** *See* AGVAANDANDAR

**ngag dben.** *See* VĀGVIVEKA

**ngag gi las.** *See* VĀKKARMAN

**ngag 'khyal ba spong ba.** *See* SAṂBHINNAPRALĀPĀT PRATIVIRATI

**ngan 'gro.** *See* DURGATI

**Ngang tshul bzang po.** *See* ŚĪLABHADRA

**ngan song.** *See* APĀYA

**Ngan song thams cad yongs su sbyong ba'i rgyud.** *See* SARVADURGATIPARIŚODHANATANTRA

**ngar 'dzin.** *See* AHAṂKĀRA

**nga rgyal.** *See* MĀNA

**nges 'byung.** *See* NAIṢKRAMYA, NIḤSARAṆA, NIRYĀṆA

**nges don.** *See* NĪTĀRTHA

**nges legs.** *See* NIḤŚREYASA

**nges pa'i rigs.** *See* NIYATAGOTRA

**nges pa'i tshig.** *See* NIRUKTI

**nges pa lnga.** *See* PAÑCANIYATA

**nges par 'byed pa.** *See* NIRVEDHA

**nges par 'byed pa'i cha dang mthun pa.** *See* NIRVEDHABHĀGĪYA

**nges par 'gyur ba.** *See* NIYĀMA

**ngo bo nyid med pa gsum.** *See* TRINIḤSVABHĀVA

**ngo bo nyid sku.** *See* SVABHĀVAKĀYA

**ngo tsha shes pa.** *See* HRĪ

**ngu 'bod.** *See* RAURAVA

**ngu 'bod chen po.** *See* MAHĀRAURAVA

**ngur smrig.** *See* KĀṢĀYA

**Ni gu chos drug.** *See* NIGUMA

**nor bu.** *See* MAṆI

**Nor bzang.** *See* SUDHANA

**Nor rgyun ma.** *See* JAMBHALA

**Nor skyong.** *See* DHANAPĀLA

**Nya gro dha'i kun dga' ra ba.** *See* NYAGRODHĀRĀMA

**nyams mgur.** *See* DOHĀ

**nyan thos.** *See* ŚRĀVAKA

**nyan thos kyi rigs.** *See* ŚRĀVAKAGOTRA

**Nyan thos kyi sa.** *See* ŚRĀVAKABHŪMI

**nyan thos kyi theg pa.** *See* ŚRĀVAKAYĀNA

**nyan thos rtsa ba'i sde pa bzhi.** *See* *CATUḤŚRĀVAKANIKĀYA

**nye ba'i nyon mongs.** *See* UPAKLEŚA

**nye ba'i sras chen brgyad.** *See* MAHĀ-UPAPUTRA

**Nye bar 'khor.** *See* UPĀLI

**Nye dga' po.** *See* UPANANDA

**nye gnas.** *See* ANTEVĀSIKA

**nye 'khor ba'i dmyal ba.** *See* PRATYEKANARAKA

**nyer bsdogs.** *See* SĀMANTAKA

**nyer len gyi phung po.** *See* UPĀDĀNASKANDHA

**nyer len gyi rgyu.** *See* UPĀDĀNAKĀRAṆA

**Nyer sbas.** *See* UPAGUPTA

**nyer thob.** *See* ĀLOKASYOPALABDHIŚA

**nyes byas.** *See* DUṢKṚTA

**Nye sde.** *See* UPASENA

**nyes dmigs.** *See* ĀDĪNAVA

**nyes pa sbom po.** *See* STHŪLĀTYAYA

**nyes par bya ba.** *See* DUṢKṚTA

**nyes par smra ba.** *See* DURBHĀṢITA

**nye sras.** *See* UPAPUTRA

**Nyi ma gung pa.** *See* MADHYĀNTIKA

**Nyi ma'i gnyen.** *See* ĀDITYABANDHU

**Nyi shu pa.** *See* VIṂŚATIKĀ

**nyon mongs.** *See* KLEŚA

**nyon mongs can.** *See* SAṂKLEŚA

**nyon mongs can ma yin pa'i mi shes pa.** *See* AKLIṢṬĀJÑĀNA

**nyon mongs chen po'i sa.** *See* KLEŚAMAHĀBHŪMIKA

**nyon mongs kyi sgrib pa.** *See* KLEŚĀVARAṆA

**nyon sgrib kun btags.** *See* PARIKALPITAKLEŚĀVARAṆA

**nyon sgrib lhan skyes.** *See* SAHAJAKLEŚĀVARAṆA

**nyon yid.** *See* KLIṢṬAMANAS

## O

**'od byed pa'i sa.** *See* PRABHĀKARĪBHŪMI

**'od chung.** *See* PARĪTTĀBHA

**'Od dpag med.** *See* AMITĀBHA

**'od gsal.** *See* PRABHĀSVARA

**'od gsal ba.** *See* ĀBHĀSVARĀLOKA

**'od gsal gyi sems.** *See* PRABHĀSVARACITTA

**'Od ma can gyi grong.** *See* VEṆUGRĀMAKA

**'Od ma'i tshal.** *See* VEṆUVANAVIHĀRA

**'od 'phro ba.** *See* ARCIṢMATĪ

**'Od srung.** *See* KĀŚYAPA

**'Od srung ba'i sde.** *See* KĀŚYAPĪYA

**'Od srung chen po.** *See* MAHĀKĀŚYAPA

**'Od srung gi le'u.** *See* KĀŚYAPAPARIVARTA

**'Od srung gzhon nu.** *See* KUMĀRA- KĀŚYAPA

**'Od srung rdzogs byed.** *See* PŪRAṆA-KĀŚYAPA

**'Od zer can ma.** *See* MĀRĪCĪ

**'Od zer dri ma med pa rnam par dga pa'i 'od gzungs.** *See* MUGUJŎNGGWANG TAEDARANI KYŎNG

**'og min.** *See* AKANIṢṬHA

**O rgyan.** *See* OḌḌIYĀNA

**O rgyan pa.** *See* OḌḌIYĀNA, O RGYAN PA RIN CHEN DPAL

**O tan ta pū ri.** *See* ODANTAPURĪ

## P

**Padma 'byung gnas.** *See* PADMASAMBHAVA

**padma dkar po.** *See* PUṆḌARĪKA

**padma'i gdan.** *See* PADMĀSANA

**padma'i rigs.** *See* PADMAKULA

**Pa ṭa la yi bu.** *See* PĀṬALIPUTRA

**'phags lam.** *See* ĀRYAMĀRGA

**'phags lam gyi 'bras bu.** *See* ĀRYAMĀRGAPHALA

**'phags lam yan lag brgyad.** *See* ĀRYĀṢṬĀṄGAMĀRGA

**'phags pa.** *See* ĀRYA

**'phags pa'i bden pa.** *See* FOUR NOBLE TRUTHS

**'phags pa'i bden pa bzhi.** *See* FOUR NOBLE TRUTHS

**'phags pa'i dge 'dun.** *See* ĀRYASAṂGHA

**'phags pa'i gang zag.** *See* ĀRYAPUDGALA

**'phags pa'i gang zag brgyad.** *See* AṢṬĀRYAPUDGALA

**'phags pa'i rigs.** *See* ĀRYAVAṂŚA

**'Phags pa lha.** *See* ĀRYADEVA

**'Phags pa shing kun.** *See* SVAYAṂBHŪ/SVAYAṂBHŪNĀTH

**'Phags pa yongs su skyobs pa'i snod ces bya ba'i mdo.** *See* YULANPEN JING

**'Phags skyes po.** *See* VIRŪḌHAKA

**phan yon.** *See* ANUŚAṂSA

**pha rgyud.** *See* PITṚTANTRA

**pha rol.** *See* PĀRA

**pha rol tu phyin pa.** *See* PĀRAMITĀ

**phar phyin drug.** *See* ṢAḌPĀRAMITĀ

**phar phyin theg pa.** *See* PĀRAMITĀYĀNA

**phas pham pa.** *See* PĀRĀJIKA

**phra ma.** *See* PAIŚUNYA

**phrag dog.** *See* ĪRṢYĀ

**phran tsheg.** *See* KHUDDAKANIKĀYA

**'phreng ba.** *See* MĀLĀ

**'phrin las.** *See* KARMAN

**'Phrog ma.** *See* HĀRĪTĪ

**'phrul dga'.** *See* NIRMĀṆARATI

**phung po.** *See* SKANDHA

**phung po gsum pa.** *See* TRISKANDHAKA

**phung po'i bdud.** *See* SKANDHAMĀRA

**phung po'i lhag ma med par mya ngan las 'das ba.** *See* ANUPADHIŚEṢANIRVĀṆA

**phung po lhag ma dang bcas pa'i mya ngan las 'das pa.** *See* SOPADHIŚEṢANIRVĀṆA

**phung po lnga.** *See* PAÑCASKANDHA

**Phung po lnga'i rab tu byed pa.** *See* PAÑCASKANDHAPRAKARAṆA

**Phyag na pad mo.** *See* PADMAPĀṆI

**Phyag na rdo rje.** *See* VAJRAPĀṆI

**phyag rgya.** *See* MUDRĀ

**phyag rgya bzhi.** *See* CATURMUDRĀ

**phyag rgya chen po.** *See* MAHĀMUDRĀ

**Phyag rgya chen po'i man ngag.** *See* MAHĀMUDROPADEŚA

**phyag rgya gsum.** *See* TRILAKṢAṆA

**phyi.** *See* BAHIRDHĀ

**phyi don.** *See* BĀHYĀRTHA

**phyi ma'i dus.** *See* PAŚCIMAKĀLA

**phyi mo.** *See* MĀTṚKĀ

**phyin ci log.** *See* VIPARYĀSA

**phyir mi ldog.** *See* AVAIVARTIKA

**phyir mi 'ong ba.** *See* ANĀGĀMIN

**phyir mi 'ong 'bras gnas.** *See* ANĀGĀMIPHALASTHA

**phyir mi 'ong zhugs pa.** *See* ANĀGĀMIPHALAPRATIPANNAKA

**phyir 'ong 'bras gnas.** *See* SAKṚDĀGĀMIPHALASTHA

**phyir 'ong zhugs pa.** *See* SAKṚDĀGĀMIPHALAPRATIPANNAKA

**phyogs bcu.** *See* DAŚADIŚ

**phyogs chos.** *See* PAKṢADHARMA

**Phyogs glang.** *See* DIGNĀGA

**Pi lin da bat sa.** *See* PILINDAVATSA

## R

**Rab bzang.** *See* SUBHADRA

**Rab dga' ba.** *See* SUPRIYĀ

**Rab kyi rtsal gyis rnam par gnon pas shus pa shes rab kyi pha rol tu phyin pa.** *See* SUVIKRĀNTAVIKRĀMIPARIPṚCCHĀPRAJÑĀPĀRAMITĀ

**Rab tu byed ba'i rkang pa.** *See* PRAKARAṆAPĀDA[ŚĀSTRA]

**rab tu byung ba.** *See* PRAVRAJITA

**rab tu dga' ba.** *See* PRAMUDITĀ

**rab tu gnas pa.** *See* PRATIṢṬHĀ

**rab tu skyes ba.** *See* PRABHAVA

**rab tu tsha ba.** *See* PRATĀPANA

**Ral gcig ma.** *See* EKAJAṬĀ

**ral gri'i lo ma'i nags.** *See* ASIPATTRAVANA

**rang bzhin.** *See* SVABHĀVA

**rang bzhin gnas rigs.** *See* PRAKṚTISTHAGOTRA

**rang bzhin gsum.** *See* TRISVABHĀVA

**Rang bzhin gsum nges par bstan pa.** *See* TRISVABHĀVANIRDEŚA

**rang bzhin gyis rnam par dag pa.** *See* PRAKṚTIVIŚUDDHI

**rang bzhin gyis stong pa.** *See* SVABHĀVAŚŪNYA

**rang bzhin gyis stong pa nyid.** *See* SVABHĀVAŚŪNYATĀ

**rang bzhin gyis yongs su mya ngan las 'das pa.** *See* PRAKṚTIPARINIRVṚTA

**rang bzhin med pa.** *See* NIḤSVABHĀVA

**rang don.** *See* SVĀRTHA

**rang don rjes dpag.** *See* SVĀRTHĀNUMĀNA

**rang gi lus yongs su gtong ba.** *See* SHESHEN

**rang mtshan.** *See* SVALAKṢAṆA

**rang mtshan gyis grub pa.** *See* SVALAKṢAṆASIDDHA

**rang mtshan gyis stong pa.** *See* SVALAKṢAṆAŚŪNYA

**rang rgyal.** *See* PRATYEKABUDDHA

**rang rgyal gyi theg pa.** *See* PRATYEKABUDDHAYĀNA

**rang rgyud kyi sbyor ba.** *See* SVATANTRAPRAYOGA

**rang rgyud pa.** *See* *SVĀTANTRIKA

**rang rgyud rjes dpag.** *See* SVATANTRĀNUMĀNA

**rang rig.** *See* SVASAṂVEDANA

**rang sangs rgyas.** *See* PRATYEKABUDDHA

**Rangs byed kyi bu lhag spyod.** *See* UDRAKA RĀMAPUTRA

**Rdo 'jog.** *See* TAKṢAŚILĀ

**rdo rje.** *See* VAJRA

**Rdo rje 'chang.** *See* VAJRADHARA

**Rdo rje gcod pa shes rab kyi pha rol tu phyin pa'i mdo.** *See* VAJRACCHEDIKĀPRAJÑĀPĀRAMITĀSŪTRA

**rdo rje gdan.** *See* VAJRĀSANA

**rdo rje gzegs ma.** *See* VAJRAKAṆĀ

**rdo rje hūṃ mdzad.** *See* VAJRAHŪṂKĀRA

**Rdo rje 'jigs byed.** *See* VAJRABHAIRAVA

**rdo rje lta bu'i ting nge 'dzin.** *See* VAJROPAMASAMĀDHI

**Rdo rje mkha' 'gro rgyud.** *See* VAJRAḌĀKATANTRA

**Rdo rje mo'i bu.** *See* VAJRAPUTRA

**Rdo rje phag mo.** *See* VAJRAVĀRĀHĪ

**Rdo rje phur pa.** *See* VAJRAKĪLAYA

**rdo rje rigs.** *See* VAJRAKULA

**rdo rje rnal 'byor.** *See* VAJRAYOGA

**Rdo rje rnal 'byor ma.** *See* VAJRAYOGINĪ

**Rdo rje rnam par 'joms pa shes bya ba'i gzungs.** *See* VAJRAVIDĀRAṆADHĀRAṆĪ

**Rdo rje rtse mo.** *See* VAJRAŚEKHARASŪTRA

**Rdo rje sems dpa'.** *See* VAJRASATTVA

**rdo rje skyil krung.** *See* VAJRAPARYAṄKA

**rdo rje slob dpon.** *See* VAJRĀCĀRYA

**rdo rje theg pa.** *See* VAJRAYĀNA

**rdul phra rab.** *See* PARAMĀṆU

**rdzas.** *See* DRAVYA

**rdzas yod.** *See* DRAVYASAT

**rdzogs pa'i byang chub.** *See* SAṂBODHI

**Rdzogs pa'i rnal 'byor gyi 'phreng ba.** *See* NIṢPANNAYOGĀVALĪ

**rdzogs rim.** *See* NIṢPANNAKRAMA

**rdzu 'phrul.** *See* ṚDDHI

**rdzu 'phrul gyi rkang pa.** *See* ṚDDHIPĀDA

**rdzu 'phrul mngon shes.** *See* ṚDDHIVIDHĀBHIJÑĀ

**rdzus te skye ba.** *See* UPAPĀDUKAYONI

**reg bya.** *See* SPRAṢṬAVYA

**reg bya'i skye mched.** *See* SPRAṢṬAVYĀYATANA

**re ltar thogs na srid pa lan bdun pa.** *See* SAPTAKṚDBHAVAPARAMA

**rga ba.** *See* JARĀ

**rga shi.** *See* JARĀMARAṆA

**rgod pa.** *See* AUDDHATYA

**Rgya cher rol pa.** *See* LALITAVISTARA

**Rgya mo bza' kong jo.** *See* WENCHENG

**Rgya mtsho.** *See* SĀGARA

**rgyags pa.** *See* MADA

**rgyal ba.** *See* JINA

**rgyal ba lnga.** *See* PAÑCAJINA

**Rgyal byed.** *See* JETA

**Rgyal byed kyi tshal.** *See* JETAVANA

**rgyal chen rigs bzhi.** *See* CĀTURMAHĀRĀJAKĀYIKA

**rgyal mtshan.** *See* KETU

**Rgyal po'i khab.** *See* RĀJAGṚHA

**rgyal po rol pa'i stabs.** *See* RĀJALĪLĀSANA

**rgyal rigs.** *See* KṢATRIYA

**rgyal sras.** *See* JINAPUTRA

**Rgyan po stug po bkod pa.** *See* GHANAVYŪHA

**Rgyan snang.** *See* AṢṬASĀHARIKĀPRAJÑĀPĀRAMITĀVYĀKHYĀBHISAMAYĀLAṂKĀRĀLOKĀ

**rgyas pa'i las.** *See* PAUṢṬIKA

**rgyu.** *See* HETU

**rgyud.** *See* TANTRA

**Rgyud bla ma.** *See* UTTARATANTRA

**rgyud pa.** *See* PARAṂPARĀ

**rgyu mthun gyi 'bras bu.** *See* NIṢYANDAPHALA

**rgyun.** *See* SAṂTĀNA

**rgyun du zhugs pa.** *See* SROTAĀPANNA

**rgyun du zhugs pa'i 'bras bu la gnas pa.** *See* SROTAĀPANNAPHALASTHA

**rgyun du zhugs pa'i 'bras bu la zhugs pa.** *See* SROTAĀPANNAPHALAPRATIPANNAKA

**rgyun gyi rjes su song ba zhes bya ba'i ting nge 'dzin.** *See* SROTO'NUGATO NĀMA SAMĀDHIḤ

**rgyu rkyen.** *See* HETUPRATYAYA

**ri bo Bya rkang.** *See* KUKKUṬAPĀDA

**Ri dwags kyi gnas.** *See* MṚGADĀVA

**rig 'dzin gyi sdom pa.** *See* TANTRIC VOWS

**rig 'dzin sde snod.** *See* VIDYĀDHARAPIṬAKA

**rig gnas che ba lnga.** *See* PAÑCAVIDYĀ

**rig gsum.** *See* TRIVIDYĀ

**rig ma.** *See* VIDYĀ

**rig pa 'dzin pa.** *See* VIDYĀDHARA

**rigs.** *See* KULA, GOTRA

**rigs kyi bu.** *See* KULAPUTRA

**rigs kyi bu mo.** *See* KULADUHITṚ

**rigs lnga.** *See* PAÑCAKULA

**rigs ma nges pa.** *See* ANIYATAGOTRA

**rigs nas rigs su skye ba.** *See* KULAṂKULA

**rigs pa.** *See* YUKTI

**Rigs pa drug cu pa.** *See* YUKTIṢAṢṬIKĀ

**Rigs pa drug cu pa'i 'grel pa.** *See* YUKTIṢAṢṬIKĀVṚTTI

**rigs pa'i gnas.** *See* VIDYĀSTHĀNA

**Rigs pa'i thigs pa.** *See* NYĀYABINDU

**rigs tshogs.** *See* YUKTIKĀYA

**ril ba spyi blugs.** *See* KUṆḌIKĀ

**rim lnga.** *See* PAÑCAKRAMA

**rin chen.** *See* RATNA

**Rin chen 'byung gnas.** *See* RATNASAMBHAVA

**Rin chen 'byung gnas zhi ba.** *See* RATNĀKARAŚĀNTI

**Rin chen phreng ba.** *See* RATNĀVALĪ

**Rin chen ri bo.** *See* RATNAGIRI

**rin chen rigs.** *See* RATNAKULA

**ring bsrel.** *See* ŚARĪRA

**ring du song ba.** *See* DŪRAṄGAMĀ

**Ri rab.** *See* SUMERU, MOUNT

**rjes gnang.** *See* ANUJÑĀ

**rjes su dpag pa.** *See* ANUMĀNA

**rjes su dran pa.** *See* ANUSMṚTI

**rjes su dran pa'i rnam rtog.** *See* ANUSMARAṆAVIKALPA

**rjes su lta ba.** *See* ANUPAŚYANĀ

**rjes su yi rang.** *See* ANUMODANA

**rjes thob ye shes.** *See* PṚṢṬHALABDHAJÑĀNA

**rkang pa brkyangs pa'i 'dug stangs.** *See* PRALAMBAPĀDĀSANA

**rkyen.** *See* PRATYAYA

**rlung.** *See* VĀYU

**rlung yab.** *See* VĀLAVYAJANA

**Rma bya chen mo.** *See* MAHĀMĀYŪRĪ

**rmad du byung ba'i chos.** *See* ADBHUTADHARMA

**Rmad du byung ba'i chos kyi rnam grangs.** *See* ADBHUTADHARMAPARYĀYASŪTRA

**Rmug 'dzin.** *See* JAMBHALA

**rmug pa.** *See* STYĀNA

**rna ba'i dbang po.** *See* ŚROTENDRIYA

**rna ba'i rnam par shes pa.** *See* ŚROTAVIJÑĀNA

**rna ba'i skye mched.** *See* ŚROTĀYATANA

**rnal 'byor.** *See* YOGA

**Rnal 'byor bsgom pa'i lam.** *See* YOGABHĀVANĀMĀRGA

**rnal 'byor chen po.** *See* MAHĀYOGA

**rnal 'byor ma.** *See* YOGINĪ

**rnal 'byor ma'i rgyud.** *See* YOGINĪTANTRA

**rnal 'byor mngon sum.** *See* YOGIPRATYAKṢA

**rnal 'byor pa.** *See* YOGIN

**rnal 'byor rgyud.** *See* YOGATANTRA

**Rnal 'byor spyod pa.** *See* YOGĀCĀRA

**Rnal 'byor spyod pa'i dbu ma rang rgyud pa.** *See* YOGĀCĀRA-SVĀTANTRIKA-MADHYAMAKA

**Rnal 'byor spyod pa'i sa'i bstan bcos.** *See* YOGĀCĀRABHŪMIŚĀSTRA

**rnam bcas.** *See* SĀKĀRA

**rnam bcas pa.** *See* SĀKĀRAVĀDA

**Rnam gnon ngang tshul.** *See* VIKRAMAŚĪLA

**Rnam grol gyi bstan bcos.** *See* VIMUTTIMAGGA

**Rnam gzigs.** *See* VIPAŚYIN

**rnam pa.** *See* ĀKĀRA

**rnam pa dang bcas par smra ba.** *See* SĀKĀRAVĀDA

**rnam pa dang ldan pa.** *See* SĀKĀRA

**rnam pa med pa.** *See* NIRĀKĀRA

**rnam pa med par smra ba.** *See* NIRĀKĀRAVĀDA

**rnam par byang ba.** *See* VAIYAVADĀNIKA

**rnam par grol ba.** *See* VIMUKTI

**rnam par grol ba'i lam.** *See* VIMUKTIMĀRGA

**rnam par g.yeng ba.** *See* VIKṢEPA

**rnam par mi rtog pa'i ye shes.** *See* NIRVIKALPAJÑĀNA

**Rnam par phye ste smra ba.** *See* VIBHAJYAVĀDA

**rnam par rig byed.** *See* VIJÑAPTI

**rnam par rig byed ma yin pa'i gzugs.** *See* AVIJÑAPTIRŪPA

**rnam par rig pa tsam nyid.** *See* VIJÑAPTIMĀTRATĀ

**rnam par rtog pa.** *See* VIKALPA

**rnam par rtog pa med pa.** *See* NIRVIKALPA

**rnam par shes pa.** *See* VIJÑĀNA

**Rnam par shes pa smra ba.** *See* VIJÑĀNAVĀDA

**rnam par smin pa.** *See* VIPĀKA

**rnam par smin pa'i 'bras bu.** *See* VIPĀKAPHALA

**rnam par smin pa'i rgyu.** *See* VIPĀKAHETU

**Rnam par snang mdzad.** *See* VAIROCANA

**Rnam par snang mdzad chen po.** *See* MAHĀVAIROCANA

**Rnam par snang mdzad chen po mngon par rdzogs par byang chub pa rnam par sprul ba byin gyis rlob pa shin tu rgyas pa'i mdo.** *See* MAHĀVAIROCANĀBHISAṂBODHISŪTRA

**rnam par thar pa.** *See* VIMOKṢA

**rnam par thar pa brgyad.** *See* AṢṬAVIMOKṢA

**rnam par thar pa'i sgo.** *See* VIMOKṢAMUKHA

**rnam par 'tshe ba.** *See* VIHIṂSĀ

**rnam pa thams cad mkhyen pa.** *See* SARVĀKĀRAJÑATĀ

**rnam shes kyi phung po.** *See* VIJÑĀNASKANDHA

**Rnam shes kyi tshogs.** *See* VIJÑĀNAKĀYA[PĀDAŚĀSTRA]

**rnam shes mtha' yas skye mched.** *See* VIJÑĀNĀNANTYĀYATANA

**rnam smin gyi 'bras bu.** *See* VIPĀKAPHALA

**rnam smin gyi rgyu.** *See* VIPĀKAHETU

**rnam snang gi chos.** *See* VAIROCANADHARMA

**Rnam sras.** *See* VAIŚRAVAṆA

**Rnam thos kyi bu.** *See* VAIŚRAVAṆA

**rnga bo che.** *See* DRUM

**Rnga bo che chen po'i le'u.** *See* MAHĀBHERĪHĀRAKAPARIVARTA

**rnga yab.** *See* FUZI, VĀLAVYAJANA

**rngul gzan.** *See* SAṂKAKṢIKĀ

**rngul gzan gyi gzan.** *See* PRATISAṂKAKṢIKĀ

**ro.** *See* RASA

**ro.** *See* ŚARĪRA

**ro ma.** *See* RASANĀ

**ro'i skye mched.** *See* RASĀYATANA

**rol pa'i 'dug stangs.** *See* LALITĀSANA

**ro myags 'dam.** *See* KUṆAPA

**Rta dbyangs.** *See* AŚVAGHOṢA

**rtag pa.** *See* NITYA

**rtag pa'i chos.** *See* NITYADHARMA

**rtag pa'i mtha'.** *See* ŚĀŚVATĀNTA

**Rtag tu mi brnyas pa.** *See* SADĀPARIBHŪTA

**Rtag tu ngu.** *See* SADĀPRARUDITA

**rtags.** *See* LIṄGA

**Rta mgrin.** *See* HAYAGRĪVA

**Rta thul.** *See* AŚVAJIT

**rten cing 'brel bar 'byung ba.** *See* PRATĪTYASAMUTPĀDA

**Rten cing 'brel bar 'byung ba dang po dang rnam par dbye ba bstan pa.** *See* PRATĪTYASAMUTPĀDAVIBHAṄGANIRDEŚASŪTRA

**Rten cing 'brel bar 'byung ba'i snying po'i tshig le'ur byas pa.** *See* PRATĪTYASAMUTPĀDAHṚDAYAKĀRIKĀ

**rtog ge.** *See* TARKA

**rtog ge ba.** *See* TĀRKIKA

**Rtog ge 'bar ba.** *See* TARKAJVĀLĀ

**rtog pa.** *See* KALPANĀ

**rtog pa.** *See* VITARKA

**rtogs pa.** *See* ADHIGAMA

**Rtogs pa brjod pa brgya pa.** *See* AVADĀNAŚATAKA

**rtogs pa'i chos.** *See* ADHIGAMADHARMA

**rtogs par brjod pa.** *See* AVADĀNA

**Rtogs par brjod pa chen po'i mdo.** *See* MAHĀVADĀNASŪTRA

**rton pa.** *See* PRATISARAṆA

**rtsa.** *See* MŪLA

**rtsa.** *See* NĀḌĪ

**rtsa ba'i nyon mongs.** *See* MŪLAKLEŚA

**rtsa ba'i nyon mongs drug.** *See* ṢAḌMŪLAKLEŚA

**rtsa dbu ma.** *See* AVADHŪTĪ

**rtsa rgyud.** *See* MŪLATANTRA

**rtse mo.** *See* MŪRDHAN

**Rtsibs logs.** *See* PĀRŚVA

**rtsod pa.** *See* ADHIKARAṆA

**Rtsod pa bzlog pa.** *See* VIGRAHAVYĀVARTANĪ

**rtsod pa nye bar zhi ba.** *See* ADHIKARAṆAŚAMATHA

**rtsod pa nye bar zhi ba bdun.** *See* SAPTĀDHIKARAṆAŚAMATHA

**Rtswa mchog grong.** *See* KUŚINAGARĪ

**rung ba byed pa.** *See* KALPIKĀRAKA

**rung ba ma yin pa'i dngos po.** *See* AKALPIKAVASTU

## S

**sa.** *See* BHŪMI

**sa.** *See* PṚTHIVĪ

**sa bcu.** *See* DAŚABHŪMI

**Sa bcu'i rnam par bshad pa.** *See* DAŚABHŪMIVYĀKHYĀNA

**Sa bcu pa'i mdo.** *See* DAŚABHŪMIKASŪTRA

**sa bon.** *See* BĪJA

**sa chen po pa.** *See* MAHĀBHŪMIKA

**Sa 'dzin.** *See* GANDHĀRA

**Sa ga.** *See* VIŚĀKHA

**Sa ga ma.** *See* VIŚĀKHĀ

**sa gnon gyi phyag rgya.** *See* BHŪMISPARŚAMUDRĀ

**Sa'i dngos gzhi.** *See* YOGĀCĀRABHŪMIŚĀSTRA

**Sa'i lha mo.** *See* STHĀVARĀ

**sā la.** *See* ŚĀLA

**Sā lu ljang pa'i mdo.** *See* ŚĀLISTAMBASŪTRA

**Sang kha sa.** *See* SĀṂKĀŚYA

**sangs rgyas.** *See* BUDDHA

**Sangs rgyas bskyang.** *See* BUDDHAPĀLITA

**Sangs rgyas gsang ba.** *See* BUDDHAGUHYA

**sangs rgyas kyi bka'.** *See* BUDDHAVACANA

**sangs rgyas kyi khams.** *See* BUDDHADHĀTU

**sangs rgyas kyi mdzad pa bcu gnyis.** *See* TWELVE DEEDS OF A BUDDHA

**Sangs rgyas kyi sa'i mdo.** *See* BUDDHABHŪMISŪTRA

**sangs rgyas kyi shing yongs su dag pa.** *See* PARIŚUDDHABUDDHAKṢETRA

**sangs rgyas kyi spyan.** *See* BUDDHACAKṢUS

**Sangs rgyas kyi spyod pa.** *See* BUDDHACARITA

**sangs rgyas kyi theg pa.** *See* BUDDHAYĀNA

**sangs rgyas kyi zhabs.** *See* BUDDHAPĀDA

**sangs rgyas pa'i chos.** *See* BUDDHADHARMA

**sangs rgyas rab bdun.** *See* SAPTABUDDHA

**sangs rgyas rjes su dran pa.** *See* BUDDHĀNUSMṚTI

**sangs rgyas sku.** *See* BUDDHAKĀYA

**sangs rgyas zhing.** *See* BUDDHAKṢETRA

**Sa ston pa.** *See* MAHĪŚĀSAKA

**Sa yi snying po.** *See* KṢITIGARBHA

**Sbed byed.** *See* GOPAKA

**sbyang dka' ba.** *See* SUDURJAYĀ

**sbyang pa'i yan lag.** *See* DHUTAṄGA

**sbyin pa.** *See* DĀNA

**sbyin pa'i bdag po.** *See* DĀNAPATI

**sbyin pa'i pha rol tu phyin pa.** *See* DĀNAPĀRAMITĀ

**sbyin sreg.** *See* HOMA

**sbyor ba.** *See* PRAYOGA, YOGA

**sbyor lam.** *See* PRAYOGAMĀRGA

**sde.** *See* NIKĀYA

**sde snod.** *See* PIṬAKA

**sde snod gsum.** *See* TRIPIṬAKA

**sde snod gsum pa.** *See* TREPIṬAKA

**Sdig can.** *See* PĀPĪYĀṂS

**sdig pa.** *See* PĀPA

**sdig pa bshags pa.** *See* PĀPADEŚANĀ

**sdigs mdzub phyag rgya.** *See* TARJANĪMUDRĀ

**sdom pa.** *See* SAṂVARA

**sdom pa nyams pa'i rgyu bzhi.** See *CATURĀPATTIDVARA

**Sdong po bkod pa.** *See* GAṆḌAVYŪHA

**sdug bsngal.** *See* DUḤKHA

**sdug bsngal brgyad.** *See* AṢṬADUḤKHA

**sdug bsngal gyi bden pa.** *See* DUḤKHASATYA

**sdug bsngal gyi sdug bsngal.** *See* DUḤKHADUḤKHATĀ

**sems.** *See* CITTA

**sems byung.** *See* CAITTA

**sems can.** *See* SATTVA

**sems can gyi don.** *See* SATTVĀRTHA

**sems can snyigs ma.** *See* SATTVAKAṢĀYA

**sems dang ldan pa ma yin pa'i 'du byed.** *See* CITTAVIPRAYUKTASAṂSKĀRA

**sems dang mtshungs ldan gyi 'du byed.** *See* CITTASAṂPRAYUKTASAṂSKĀRA

**sems dpa' chen po.** *See* MAHĀSATTVA

**sems pa.** *See* CETANĀ

**sems rgyud.** *See* CITTASAṂTĀNA

**sems rtse gcig pa.** *See* CITTAIKĀGRATĀ

**sems tsam.** *See* CITTAMĀTRA

**Seng ge bzang po.** *See* HARIBHADRA

**Seng ge go cha.** *See* HARIVARMAN

**seng ge'i khri.** *See* SIṂHĀSANA

**seng ge'i nga ro.** *See* SIṂHANĀDA

**Ser skya'i gzhi.** *See* KAPILAVASTU

**ser sna.** *See* MĀTSARYA

**sgo gsum.** *See* TRIDVĀRA

**sgom lam.** *See* BHĀVANĀMĀRGA

**sgom pa.** *See* BHĀVANĀ

**sgo srungs ba.** *See* DVĀRAPĀLA

**sgra.** *See* ŚABDA

**Sgra gcan 'dzin.** *See* RĀHULA

**sgra'i skye mched.** *See* ŚABDĀYATANA

**sgra mi snyan.** *See* UTTARAKURU

**sgrib pa.** *See* ĀVARAṆA, NĪVARAṆA

**Sgrib pa thams cad rnam par sel ba.** *See* SARVANĪVARAṆAVIṢKAMBHIN

**sgro 'dogs.** *See* SAMĀROPA

**Sgrol ljang.** *See* ŚYĀMATĀRĀ

**Sgrol ma.** *See* TĀRĀ

**sgrub bya'i chos.** *See* SĀDHYADHARMA

**sgrub pa.** *See* PAṬIPATTI

**sgrub pa.** *See* SĀDHANA

**sgrub thabs.** *See* SĀDHANA

**sgyu lus.** *See* MĀYĀDEHA

**sgyu ma.** *See* MĀYĀ

**sgyu ma'i dpe brgyad.** *See* AṢṬAMĀYOPAMĀ

**sgyu ma lta bu'i ting nge 'dzin.** *See* MĀYOPAMASAMĀDHI

**sgyu ma mkhan.** *See* MĀYĀKĀRA

**Sgyu 'phrul chen mo'i rgyud.** *See* MAHĀMĀYĀTANTRA

**sgyu 'phrul dra ba.** *See* MĀYĀJĀLA

**Sgyu 'phrul ma.** *See* MĀYĀ

**Sgyu rtsal shes byed kyi bu ring du 'phur.** *See* ĀRĀḌA KĀLĀMA

**sha'i spyan.** *See* MĀṂSACAKṢUS

**Shākya.** *See* ŚĀKYA

**shākya dge slong.** *See* ŚĀKYABHIKṢU

**Shākya 'od.** *See* ŚĀKYAPRABHA

**Shākya thub pa.** *See* ŚĀKYAMUNI

**sham thabs.** *See* NIVĀSANA

**sham thabs kyi gzan.** *See* PRATINIVĀSANA

**Sha na'i gos can.** *See* ŚĀṆAKAVĀSIN

**Shan ti pa.** *See* RATNĀKARAŚĀNTI

**shar gyi ri bo.** *See* PŪRVAŚAILA

**Shā ri bu.** *See* ŚĀRIPUTRA

**sha za.** *See* PIŚĀCA

**Sher phyin brgyad stong pa.** *See* AṢṬASĀHASRIKĀPRAJÑĀPĀRAMITĀ

**shes bya'i sgrib pa.** *See* JÑEYĀVARAṆA

**shes bzhin.** *See* SAṂPRAJANYA

**shes bzhin ma yin pa.** *See* ASAṂPRAJANYA

**shes bzhin med pa.** *See* ASAṂPRAJANYA

**shes rab.** *See* PRAJÑĀ

**Shes rab 'byung gnas blo gros.** *See* PRAJÑĀKARAMATI

**Shes rab 'byung gnas sbas pa.** *See* PRAJÑĀKARAGUPTA

**shes rab kyi bslab pa.** *See* ADHIPRAJÑĀŚIKṢĀ

**shes rab kyi pha rol tu phyin pa.** *See* PRAJÑĀPĀRAMITĀ

**Shes rab kyi pha rol tu phyin pa bdun brgya pa.** *See* SAPTAŚATIKĀPRAJÑĀPĀRAMITĀ

**Shes rab kyi pha rol tu phyin pa brgyad stong pa.** *See* AṢṬASĀHASRIKĀPRAJÑĀPĀRAMITĀ

**Shes rab kyi pha rol tu phyin pa de bzhin gshegs pa thams cad kyi yum yi ge gcig ma.** *See* PRAJÑĀPĀRAMITĀSARVATATHĀGATAMĀTĀ-EKĀKṢARĀ

**Shes rab kyi pha rol tu phyin pa don bsdus pa.** *See* PRAJÑĀPĀRAMITĀPIṆḌĀRTHA

**Shes rab kyi pha rol tu phyin pa'i snying po'i mdo.** *See* PRAJÑĀPĀRAMITĀHṚDAYASŪTRA

**Shes rab kyi pha rol tu phyin pa'i tshul brgya lnga bcu pa.** *See* ADHYARDHAŚATIKĀPRAJÑĀPĀRAMITĀSŪTRA/ PRAJÑĀPĀRAMITĀNAYAŚATAPAÑCAŚATIKĀ

**Shes rab kyi pha rol tu phyin pa'i tshul brgya lnga bcu pa.** *See* PRAJÑĀPĀRAMITĀNAYAŚATAPAÑCAŚATIKĀ

**Shes rab kyi pha rol tu phyin pa man ngag gi bstan bcos mngon rtogs rgyan.** *See* ABHISAMAYĀLAṂKĀRA

**Shes rab kyi pha rol tu phyin pa stong phrag nyi shu lnga pa.** *See* PAÑCAVIṂŚATISĀHASRIKĀPRAJÑĀPĀRAMITĀSŪTRA

**Shes rab kyi pha rol tu phyin pa yi ge nyung ngu.** *See* SVALPĀKṢARAPRAJÑĀPĀRAMITĀ

**shes rab kyi spyan.** *See* PRAJÑĀCAKṢUS

**shes rab kyis rnam par grol ba.** *See* PRAJÑĀVIMUKTA

**Shes rab phar phyin man ngag gi bstan bcos mngon rtogs rgyan gyi 'grel pa.** *See* ABHISAMAYĀLAṂKĀRAVIVṚTI

**Shes rab sgron me.** *See* PRAJÑĀPRADĪPA

**shin tu mthong ba.** *See* SUDARŚANA

**shin tu rgyas pa.** *See* VAIPULYA

**shin tu sbyang ba.** *See* PRAŚRABDHI

**skad cig.** *See* KṢAṆA

**skad cig ma.** *See* KṢAṆIKA

**skal mnyam gyi rgyu.** *See* SABHĀGAHETU

**skor ba.** *See* PRADAKṢIṆA

**sku.** *See* KĀYA, ŚARĪRA

**sku gsum.** *See* TRIKĀYA

**Skul byed.** *See* CUNDA

**skur 'debs.** *See* APAVĀDA

**skyabs.** *See* ŚARAṆA

**skyabs gsum.** *See* TRIŚARAṆA

**skye ba.** *See* JĀTI, UTPĀDA

**skye ba dran pa.** *See* JĀTISMARA

**Skye dgu'i bdag mo chen mo.** *See* MAHĀPRAJĀPATĪ

**skye gnas.** *See* YONI

**skye gnas bzhi.** *See* CATVĀRO YONAYAḤ

**skye mched.** *See* ĀYATANA

**skye mched drug.** *See* ṢAḌĀYATANA

**skye med.** *See* ANUTPĀDA

**skyes bu.** *See* PURUṢA

**skyes bu chen po.** *See* MAHĀPURUṢA

**skyes bu chung ngu.** *See* ADHAMAPURUṢA

**skyes bu'i byed pa'i 'bras bu.** *See* PURUṢAKĀRAPHALA

**skyes nas myong 'gyur gyi las.** *See* UPAPADYAVEDANĪYAKARMAN

**skyes nas yongs su mya ngan las 'das pa.** *See* UPAPADYAPARINIRVĀYIN

**Skyes pa'i rabs kyi rgyud.** *See* JĀTAKAMĀLĀ

**skyes rabs.** *See* JĀTAKA

**skyil krung.** *See* SATTVAPARYAṄKA

**skyil krung phyed pa.** *See* ARDHAPARYAṄKA

**skyo ba.** *See* NIRVEDA

**skyon.** *See* DOṢA

**skyon bag.** *See* KAṢĀYA

**skyon med pa.** *See* NIYĀMA

**slob dpon.** *See* ĀCĀRYA

**slob pa.** *See* ŚAIKṢA

**smad g.yogs.** *See* ANTARVĀSAS

**Sman gyi bla baiḍūrya'i 'od kyi sngon gyi smon lam gyi khyad par rgyas pa'i mdo.** *See* BHAIṢAJYAGURUVAIḌŪRYAPRABHARĀJASŪTRA

**smon lam.** *See* PRAṆIDHĀNA

**smon lam gyi pha rol tu phyin pa.** *See* PRAṆIDHĀNAPĀRAMITĀ

**smon pa'i sems bskyed.** *See* PRAṆIDHICITTOTPĀDA

**Smra 'dod kyi bu mo'i bu yang dag rgyal ba can.** *See* SAÑJAYA VAIRĀṬĪPUTRA

**sna'i dbang po.** *See* GHRĀṆENDRIYA

**sna'i rnam par shes pa.** *See* GHRĀṆAVIJÑĀNA

**sna'i skye mched.** *See* GHRĀṆĀYATANA

**snam sbyar.** *See* SAṂGHĀṬĪ

**snang ba.** *See* PRATIBHĀSA

**Snang ba mtha' yas.** *See* AMITĀBHA

**sngags.** *See* MANTRA

**sngags kyi theg pa.** *See* MANTRAYĀNA

**Sngo bsangs can ma.** *See* ŚYĀMĀVATĪ

**sngon gyi gnas rjes su dran pa.** *See* PŪRVANIVĀSĀNUSMṚTI

**sngon gyi smon lam.** *See* PŪRVAPRAṆIDHĀNA

**snod kyi 'jig rten.** *See* BHĀJANALOKA

**Snyan pa bzang ldan.** *See* LAKUṆṬAKA BHADRIKA

**snyigs ma.** *See* KAṢĀYA

**snyigs ma lnga.** *See* PAÑCAKAṢĀYA

**snying po.** *See* MAṆḌA

**snying rje.** *See* KARUṆĀ

**snying rje chen mo.** *See* MAHĀKARUṆĀ

**Snying rje pad ma dkar po.** *See* KARUṆĀPUṆḌARĪKA

**snyom 'jug.** *See* SAMĀPATTI

**so sor brtags 'gog.** *See* PRATISAṂKHYĀNIRODHA

**so sor brtags min gyi 'gog pa.** *See* APRATISAṂKHYĀNIRODHA

**so sor bshags pa.** *See* PRATIDEŚANĀ

**so sor bshags par bya ba.** *See* PRATIDEŚANĪYA

**so sor rang gis rig pa.** *See* PRATYĀTMĀDHIGAMA

**so sor rtogs pa'i ye shes.** *See* PRATYAVEKṢAṆĀJÑĀNA

**so sor thar pa.** *See* PRĀTIMOKṢA

**So sor thar pa'i mdo.** *See* PRĀTIMOKṢASŪTRA

**so sor thar pa'i sdom pa.** *See* PRĀTIMOKṢASAṂVARA

**so sor yang dag par rig pa.** *See* PRATISAṂVID

**Sor mo'i phreng ba la phan pa'i mdo.** *See* AṄGULIMĀLĪYASŪTRA

**Sor mo phreng.** *See* AṄGULIMĀLA

**so so skye bo.** *See* PṚTHAGJANA

**spang ba.** *See* PRAHĀṆA

**spang ba'i ltung byed.** *See* NAIḤSARGIKAPĀYATTIKA

**spo ba.** *See* PARIVĀSA

**spobs pa.** *See* PRATIBHĀNA

**spong ba bsam gtan pa.** *See* PRĀHĀṆIKA

**Spos ldan ma.** *See* GANDHAVATĪ

**spos snod.** *See* GANDHAGHAṬIKĀ

**Sprin chen po'i mdo.** *See* MAHĀMEGHASŪTRA

**sprin med.** *See* ANABHRAKA

**spros pa.** *See* PRAPAÑCA

**spros pa dang bral ba.** *See* NIṢPRAPAÑCA

**sprul pa.** *See* NIRMITA

**sprul pa'i sku.** *See* NIRMĀṆAKĀYA, SPRUL SKU

**spu gri'i lam.** *See* KṢURAMĀRGA

**spyad pa.** *See* CARITA

**spyan dbye.** *See* NETRAPRATIṢṬHĀPANA

**Spyan ras gzigs.** *See* AVALOKITEŚVARA

**Spyan ras gzigs brtul zhugs.** *See* AVALOKITAVRATA

**Spyan ras gzigs phyag stong spyan stong.** *See* AVALOKITEŚVARASAHASRABHUJANETRA

**spyi mtshan.** *See* SĀMĀNYALAKṢAṆA

**spyod lam.** *See* ĪRYĀPATHA

**spyod pa.** *See* CARITA, AVACARA

**Spyod pa'i glu'i mdzod.** *See* CARYĀGĪTIKOṢA

**spyod rgyud.** *See* CARYĀTANTRA

**sra brkyang.** *See* KAṬHINA

**Sred med kyi bu.** *See* NĀRĀYAṆA

**sred pa.** *See* TṚṢṆĀ

**srid pa.** *See* BHAVA

**srid pa'i khor lo.** *See* BHAVACAKRA

**Srid pa 'pho ba.** *See* BHAVASAMKRĀNTI

**srid rtse.** *See* BHAVĀGRA

**srin po.** *See* RĀKṢASA

**srog.** *See* JĪVITA, PRĀṆA

**srog blu.** *See* FANGSHENG

**srog rtsol.** *See* PRĀṆĀYĀMA

**srung ba.** *See* RAKṢĀ

**Srung byed.** *See* AVANTI

**srung gi 'khor lo.** *See* RAKṢĀCAKRA

**srung ma.** *See* DHARMAPĀLA

**stobs.** *See* BALA

**stobs kyi pha rol tu phyin pa.** *See* BALAPĀRAMITĀ

**stobs lnga.** *See* PAÑCABALA

**stong gsum gyi stong chen po'i 'jig rten gyi khams.** *See* TRISĀHASRAMAHĀSĀHASRALOKADHĀTU

**stong pa'i bskal pa.** *See* SAṂVARTASTHĀYIKALPA

**stong pa nyid.** *See* ŚŪNYATĀ

**Stong pa nyid bdun cu pa.** *See* ŚŪNYATĀSAPTATI

**stong pa nyid kyi stong pa nyid.** *See* ŚŪNYATĀŚŪNYATĀ

**Stong pa nyid smra ba.** *See* ŚŪNYAVĀDA

**ston pa.** *See* ŚĀSTṚ

**ston par 'du shes.** *See* ŚĀSTṚSAṂJÑĀ

**Stug po bkod pa.** *See* GHANAVYŪHA

**Sum cu pa.** *See* TRIṂŚIKĀ

**sum cu rtsa gsum pa.** *See* TRĀYASTRIṂŚA

## T

**'thab bral.** *See* YĀMA

**thabs.** *See* UPĀYA

**Thabs la mkhas pa'i mdo.** *See* UPĀYAKAUŚALYASŪTRA

**thabs mkhas.** *See* UPĀYAKAUŚALYA

**thal 'gyur.** *See* PRASAṄGA

**Thal 'gyur ba.** *See* *PRĀSAṄGIKA

**thal mo sbyar ba.** *See* AÑJALI[MUDRĀ]

**Thams cad sgrol.** *See* VESSANTARA

**Thams cad yod par smra ba.** *See* SARVĀSTIVĀDA

**thar lam.** *See* MOKṢAMĀRGA, VIMOKṢAMĀRGA

**thar pa.** *See* MOKṢA

**tha snyad.** *See* VYAVAHĀRA

**Tha snyad gcig pa'i sde.** *See* EKAVYAVAHĀRIKA

**Tha snyad grub pa.** *See* VYAVAHĀRASIDDHI

**the tshom.** *See* VICIKITSĀ

**theg pa.** *See* YĀNA

**theg pa chen po.** *See* MAHĀYĀNA

**Theg pa chen po bsdus pa.** *See* MAHĀYĀNASAṂGRAHA

**Theg pa chen po'i mdo sde'i rgyan.** *See* MAHĀYĀNASŪTRĀLAṂKĀRA

**theg pa dman pa.** *See* HĪNAYĀNA

**theg pa gcig pa.** *See* EKAYĀNA

**theg pa gsum.** *See* TRIYĀNA

**thig le.** *See* BINDU

**thig nag.** *See* KĀLASŪTRA

**'thob pa.** *See* PRĀPTI

**'thob pa med pa.** *See* APRĀPTI

**Thogs med.** *See* ASAṄGA

**thos pa las byung ba'i shes rab.** *See* ŚRUTAMAYĪPRAJÑĀ

**thub pa.** *See* MUNI

**Thub pa chen po.** *See* MAHĀMUNI

**thun mong gi dngos grub.** *See* SĀDHĀRAṆASIDDHI

**ting nge 'dzin.** *See* SAMĀDHI

**Ting nge 'dzin rgyal po'i mdo.** *See* SAMĀDHIRĀJASŪTRA

**Tsa pa la.** *See* CĀPĀLACAITYA

**tsha ba.** *See* TĀPANA

**tshad ma.** *See* PRAMĀṆA

**tshad ma'i skyes bu.** *See* PRAMĀṆABHŪTA

**Tshad ma kun btus.** *See* PRAMĀṆASAMUCCAYA

**Tshad ma rigs par 'jug pa'i sgo.** *See* NYĀYAPRAVEŚA

**Tshad ma rnam 'grel.** *See* PRAMĀṆAVĀRTTIKA

**Tshad ma rnam par nges pa.** *See* PRAMĀṆAVINIŚCAYA

**tshad med bzhi.** *See* CATURAPRAMĀṆA

**tshad med dge.** *See* APRAMĀṆAŚUBHA

**tshad med 'od.** *See* APRAMĀṆĀBHA

**tshad pa med pa.** *See* APRAMĀṆA

**tshang pa chen po.** *See* MAHĀBRAHMĀ

**Tshangs pa.** *See* BRAHMĀ

**tshangs pa'i gnas.** *See* BRAHMAVIHĀRA

**tshangs pa'i 'jig rten.** *See* BRAHMALOKA

**tshangs pa'i mdun na 'don.** *See* BRAHMAPUROHITA

**tshangs ris.** *See* BRAHMAKĀYIKA

**tshangs spyod.** *See* BRAHMACARYA

**'tshe ba med pa.** *See* AHIṂSĀ

**tshe dang ldan pa.** *See* ĀYUṢMAN

**Tshe dpag med.** *See* AMITĀYUS

**tshe rabs dran pa.** *See* JĀTISMARA

**tshe thar.** *See* FANGSHENG

**tshig dbang.** *See* CATURTHĀBHIṢEKA

**'tshig pa.** *See* PRADĀSA

**Tshig rab tu gsal ba.** *See* PRASPHUṬAPADĀ, PRASANNAPADĀ

**tshig rtsub.** *See* PĀRUṢYA

**tshigs bcad/tshigs su bcad pa.** *See* GĀTHĀ, ŚLOKA

**'Tsho ba can.** *See* ĀJĪVAKA

**tshogs.** *See* KĀYA

**tshogs kyi 'khor lo.** *See* GAṆACAKRA

**tshogs lam.** *See* SAṂBHĀRAMĀRGA

**tshogs spyod.** *See* VARGACĀRIN

**tshor ba.** *See* VEDANĀ

**tshul bzhin ma yin pa'i yid la byed pa.** *See* AYONIŚOMANASKĀRA

**tshul bzhin yid la byed pa.** *See* YONIŚOMANASKĀRA

**tshul khrims.** *See* ŚĪLA

**tshul khrims bcu.** *See* DAŚAŚĪLA

**tshul khrims dang brtul zhugs mchog tu 'dzin pa.** *See* ŚĪLAVRATAPARĀMARŚA

**tshul khrims rnam par dag pa.** *See* ŚĪLAVIŚUDDHI

**tshul min yid byed.** *See* AYONIŚOMANASKĀRA

## U

**'Ug pa.** *See* ULŪKA

**Ut pa la'i mdog.** *See* UTPALAVARṆĀ

## W

**Wen tsheg.** *See* WŎNCH'ŬK

## Y

**Yab dang sras mjal ba'i mdo.** *See* PITĀPUTRASAMĀGAMASŪTRA

**yan lag.** *See* AṄGA

**yan lag bdun pa'i cho ga.** *See* SAPTĀṄGAVIDHI

**yan lag brgyad pa'i gso sbyong.** *See* AṢṬĀṄGASAMANVĀGATAṂ UPAVĀSAṂ

**yang dag pa'i dran pa.** *See* SAMYAKSMṚTI

**yang dag pa'i kun rdzob.** *See* TATHYASAMVṚTI

**yang dag pa'i las kyi mtha'.** *See* SAMYAKKARMĀNTA

**yang dag pa'i lta ba.** *See* SAMYAGDṚṢṬI

**yang dag pa'i mtha'.** *See* BHŪTAKOṬI

**yang dag pa'i ngag.** *See* SAMYAGVĀC

**yang dag pa'i rtog pa.** *See* SAMYAKSAṂKALPA

**yang dag pa'i rtsol ba.** *See* SAMYAGVYĀYĀMA

**yang dag pa'i ting nge 'dzin.** *See* SAMYAKSAMĀDHI

**yang dag pa'i 'tsho ba.** *See* SAMYAGĀJĪVA

**yang dag pa ji lta ba bzhin du yongs su shes pa.** *See* YATHĀBHŪTAJÑĀNADARŚANA

**yang dag pa ma yin pa'i kun tu rtog pa.** *See* ABHŪTAPARIKALPA

**yang dag pa nyid skyon med pa la zhugs pa.** *See* SAMYAKTVANIYĀMĀVAKRĀNTI

**yang dag par bsgrub pa'i rigs.** *See* SAMUDĀNĪTAGOTRA

**Yang dag par ldan pa'i lung.** *See* SAṂYUKTĀGAMA, SAṂYUTTANIKĀYA

**yang dag par rdzogs pa'i byang chub.** *See* SAṂYAKSAṂBODHI

**yang dar par rdzogs pa'i sangs rgyas.** *See* SAMYAKSAṂBUDDHA

**yang dag par spong ba.** *See* SAMYAKPRADHĀNA

**Yangs pa can.** *See* VAIŚĀLĪ

**yang srid pa.** *See* PUNARBHAVA

**ye nas sangs rgyas.** *See* ĀDIBUDDHA

**ye shes chos sku.** *See* JÑĀNADHARMAKĀYA

**ye shes khu tshur.** *See* JÑĀNAMUṢṬI

**ye shes kyi tshogs.** *See* JÑĀNASAṂBHĀRA

**Ye shes la 'jug pa.** *See* JÑĀNAPRASTHĀNA

**ye shes lnga.** *See* PAÑCAJÑĀNA

**ye shes mthong ba.** *See* JÑĀNADARŚANA

**ye shes phyag rgya.** *See* JÑĀNAMUDRĀ

**ye shes sems dpa'.** *See* JÑĀNASATTVA

**Ye shes snying po.** *See* JÑĀNAGARBHA

**Ye shes snying po kun las btus pa.** *See* JÑĀNASĀRASAMUCCAYA

**yid.** *See* MANAS

**yid bzhin nor bu.** *See* CINTĀMAṆI

**yid kyi dbang po.** *See* MANENDRIYA

**yid kyi las.** *See* MANASKARMAN

**yid kyi mngon sum.** *See* MĀNASAPRATYAKṢA

**yid kyi rang bzhin gyi lus.** *See* MANOMAYAKĀYA

**yid kyi rnam par shes pa.** *See* MANOVIJÑĀNA

**yid kyi skye mched.** *See* MANĀYATANA

**yid kyis myong ba'i mngon sum.** *See* MANONUBHAVAPRATYAKṢA

**yid la brjod pa.** *See* MANOJALPA

**yid la byed pa.** *See* MANASIKĀRA

**yid la sems pa'i zas.** *See* MANAḤSAṂCETANĀHĀRA

**yi dwags.** *See* PRETA

**yi ge drug pa'i rig sngags.** *See* ṢAḌAKṢARĪ

**yo byad.** *See* PARIṢKĀRA

**yo byad la dbang ba.** *See* PARIṢKĀRAVAŚITĀ

**yol ba.** *See* YAVANA

**yongs 'du sa brtol.** *See* PĀRIYĀTRAKA

**yongs su bsngo ba.** *See* PARIṆĀMANĀ

**yongs su dag pa.** *See* PARIŚUDDHA

**yongs su grub pa.** *See* PARINIṢPANNA

**yongs su mya ngan las 'das pa.** *See* PARINIRVĀṆA

**yongs su nyams pa.** *See* PARIHĀṆI

**yongs su skyob pa.** *See* PARITTA

**yongs su skyob pa'i snod.** *See* YULANPEN

**yon tan.** *See* GUṆA

**Yon tan 'od.** *See* GUṆAPRABHA

**yon tan pha rol tu phyin pa.** *See* GUṆAPĀRAMITĀ

**Yon tan rin po che sdud pa tshigs su bcad pa.** *See* RATNAGUṆASAMCAYAGĀTHĀ

**yul.** *See* VIṢAYA

**yul dbus.** *See* MADHYAMADEŚA

**Yul gyi bzang mo dga' mo.** *See* Janapadakalyāṇī Nandā

**Yul 'khor chen po.** *See* Mahāraṭṭha

**Yul 'khor skyong.** *See* Rāṣṭrapāla

**Yul 'khor skyong gis zhus pa.** *See* Rāṣṭrapālaparipṛcchā

**Yul 'khor srung.** *See* Dhṛtarāṣṭra

**yul lnga.** *See* pañcaviṣaya

**Yul ma ga dha.** *See* Magadha

**yul nges.** *See* viniyata

## Z

**zad byed.** *See* kṣapita

**zad pa shes pa.** *See* kṣayajñāna

**zag bcas kyi phung po.** *See* sāsravaskandha

**zag pa.** *See* āsrava

**zag pa dang bcas pa.** *See* sāsrava

**zag pa med pa.** *See* anāsrava

**zag pa med pa'i dbyings.** *See* anāsravadhātu

**zag pa zad pa.** *See* āsravakṣaya

**Za ma tog bkod pa'i mdo.** *See* Kāraṇḍavyūha

**zang zing gi sbyin pa.** *See* āmiṣadāna

**zas.** *See* āhāra

**Zas gtsang.** *See* Śuddhodana

**zhal ta pa.** *See* vaiyāpṛtya(kara)

**zhe sdang.** *See* dveṣa

**zhe sdang med pa.** *See* adveṣa

**zhi ba'i las.** *See* śānticāra

**Zhi ba lha.** *See* Śāntideva

**Zhi ba 'tsho.** *See* Śāntarakṣita

**Zhib mo rnam par 'thag pa.** *See* Vaidalyaprakaraṇa

**Zhib mo rnam par 'thag pa zhes bya ba'i mdo.** *See* Vaidalyasūtranāma

**zhi gnas.** *See* śamatha

**zil gyis gnon pa'i skye mched.** *See* abhibhvāyatana

**Zla ba grags pa.** *See* Candrakīrti

**zung 'jug.** *See* yuganaddha

# Tibetan Phonetic Cross-References

## A

**Amnye Machen.** *See* A MYES RMA CHEN

## B

**Bardo Tödröl Chenmo.** *See* BAR DO THOS GROL CHEN MO

**barkor.** *See* BAR BSKOR

**Barom Kagyü.** *See* 'BA' ROM BKA' BRGYUD

**barwa pündün.** *See* 'BAR BA SPUN BDUN

**Bashe.** *See* SBA BZHED

**beyul.** *See* SBAS YUL

**Bima Nyingtik.** *See* BI MA SNYING THIG

**Bodong Chokle Namgyal.** *See* BO DONG PHYOGS LAS RNAM RGYAL.

**Butön Rinchen Drup.** *See* BU STON RIN CHEN GRUB

## C

**Chakchen Chöku Dzuptsuk.** *See* PHYAG CHEN CHOS SKU MDZUB TSHUGS

**Chakchen Dawe Öser.** *See* PHYAG CHEN ZLA BA'I 'OD ZER

**Chakchen Marik Münsel.** *See* PHYAG CHEN MA RIG MUN GSAL

**Chakchen Ngedön Gyatso.** *See* PHYAG CHEN NGES DON RGYA MTSHO

**Chapa Chökyi Senge.** *See* PHYWA PA [alt. Cha pa] CHOS KYI SENG GE

**chayik.** *See* BCA' YIG

**Chekawa Yeshe Dorje.** *See* 'CHAD KA BA YE SHES RDO RJE

**chidar.** *See* PHYI DAR

**Chim Jampeyang.** *See* CHIMS [alt. Mchims] 'JAM PA'I DBYANG

**Chime Lhakang.** *See* 'CHI MED LHA KHANG

**chö.** *See* GCOD

**Chödrup.** *See* CHOS GRUB

**Chögyam Trungpa.** *See* CHOS RGYAM DRUNG PA

**Chöjung Kepe Gatön.** *See* CHOS BYUNG MKHAS PA'I DGA' STON

**Chokgyur Lingpa.** *See* MCHOG GYUR GLING PA

**choksung.** *See* MCHOG ZUNG

**chöten.** *See* MCHOD RTEN

**Chubar** [alt. Chuwar]. *See* CHU DBAR

**Chung Riwoche.** *See* GCUNG RI BO CHE

## D

**Daklha Gampo.** *See* DWAGS LHA SGAM PO

**Dakmema.** *See* BDAG MED MA

**Dakpo Kagyü.** *See* DWAGS PO BKA' BRGYUD

**Dakpo Targyan.** *See* DWAGS PO THAR RGYAN

**Dakpo Tashi Namgyal.** *See* DWAGS PO BKRA SHIS RNAM RGYAL

**Damchen Chögyal.** *See* DAM CAN CHOS RGYAL

**Damngak Dzö.** *See* GDAMS NGAG MDZOD

**Darma Dode.** *See* DAR MA MDO SDE

**Delam Lamrim.** *See* BDE LAM LAM RIM

**delok.** *See* 'DAS LOG

**Denkarma.** *See* LDAN KAR MA

**densa sum.** *See* GDAN SA GSUM

**Densa Til.** *See* GDAN SA MTHIL

**Depter Karpo.** *See* DEB THER DKAR PO

**Depter Marpo.** *See* DEB THER DMAR PO

**Depter Marpo Sarma.** *See* DEB THER DMAR PO GSAR MA

**Depter Ngonpo.** *See* DEB THER SNGON PO

**Derge.** *See* SDE DGE

**Desi Sangye Gyatso.** *See* SDE SRID SANGS RGYAS RGYA MTSHO

**Dilgo Kyentse.** *See* DIL MGO MKHYEN BRTSE

**Do Drupchen.** *See* RDO GRUB CHEN

**Doha Korsum.** *See* DO HA SKOR GSUM

**Do Kyentse Yeshe Dorje.** *See* MDO MKHYEN BRTSE YE SHES RDO RJE

**Dolpopa Sherap Gyaltsen.** *See* Dol po pa Shes rab rgyal mtshan

**domsum.** *See* sdom gsum

**Domsum Namnge.** *See* Sdom gsum rnam nges

**Domsum Rapye.** *See* Sdom gsum rab dbye

**Dorje Drak.** *See* Rdo rje brag

**Dorje Drakden.** *See* Rdo rje grags ldan

**Dorje Drolö.** *See* Rdo rje gro lod

**Dorje Lekpa.** *See* Rdo rje legs pa

**Dorje Lingpa.** *See* Rdo rje gling pa

**Dorje Shukden.** *See* Rdo rje shugs ldan

**dorje sumgyi nyendrup.** *See* rdo rje gsum gyi bsnyen sgrub

**Dorje Tsikang.** *See* Rdo rje tshig rkang

**Drakar Taso.** *See* Brag dkar rta so

**Drakpa Gyaltsen.** *See* Grags pa rgyal mtshan

**Drakyang Dzong.** *See* Sgrag yang rdzong

**Drak Yerpa.** *See* Brag yer pa

**dralha.** *See* dgra lha

**Dram.** *See* 'Gram

**Drepung.** *See* 'Bras spungs

**Drigung Kagyü.** *See* 'Bri gung bka' brgyud

**Drigung Til.** *See* 'Bri gung mthil

**Drin.** *See* Brin

**Drokmi Shākya Yeshe.** *See* 'Brog mi Shākya ye shes

**Drölma Lhakang.** *See* Sgrol ma lha khang

**Dromtön Gyalwe Jungne.** *See* 'Brom ston Rgyal ba'i 'byung gnas

**Drowolung.** *See* Gro bo lung

**Drukchen.** *See* 'Brug chen

**Drukpa Kagyü.** *See* 'Brug pa bka' brgyud

**Drukpa Künlek.** *See* 'Brug pa kun legs

**Drumpa Gyang.** *See* Grum pa rgyang

**drupa ka gye.** *See* sgrub pa bka' brgyad

**drupgyü shingta chenpo gye.** *See* sgrub brgyud shing rta chen po brgyad

**dü.** *See* bdud

**Düdjom Rinpoche.** *See* Bdud 'joms rin po che

**düdra.** *See* bsdus grwa

**Dumtsek Lhakang.** *See* Zlum brtsegs lha khang

**Dungkar.** *See* Dung dkar

**Düsum Kyenpa.** *See* Dus gsum mkhyen pa

**Dzamling Gyeshe.** *See* 'Dzam gling rgyas bshad

**dzö dün.** *See* mdzod bdun

**dzokchen.** *See* rdzogs chen

**dzokchen desum.** *See* rdzogs chen sde gsum

**dzokpa chenpo longchen nyingtik.** *See* rdzogs pa chen po klong chen snying thig

**Dzongsar.** *See* Rdzong gsar

**Dzongsar Kyentse Chökyi Lodrö.** *See* Rdzong gsar mkhyen brtse Chos kyi blo gros

## G

**Gampopa Sönam Rinchen.** *See* Sgam po pa Bsod nams rin chen

**Gampope chöshi.** *See* Sgam po pa'i chos bzhi

**Ganden.** *See* Dga' ldan

**Ganden Podrang.** *See* Dga' ldan pho brang

**Ganden Tripa.** *See* Dga' ldan khri pa

**Gangri Tökar.** *See* Gangs ris thod dkar

**Gangteng.** *See* Sgang steng

**Garap Dorje.** *See* Dga' rab rdo rje

**Gegye.** *See* Dge gyes

**Geluk.** *See* Dge lugs

**Gendün Chöpel.** *See* Dge 'dun chos 'phel

**Gendün Drup.** *See* Dge 'dun grub

**geshe.** *See* dge bshes

**Gödemchen Ngödrup Gyaltsen.** *See* Rgod ldem can Dngos grub rgyal mtshan

**gönpa.** *See* dgon pa

**Götsangpa Gönpo Dorje.** *See* Rgod tshang pa Mgon po rdo rje

**Gowo Rapjampa Sönam Senge.** *See* Go bo rab 'byams pa Bsod nams senge ge

**Guru Chökyi Wangchuk.** *See* Gu ru chos kyi dbang phyug

**Gyagar Chöjung.** *See* Rgya gar chos ’byung

**Gyalrap Salwe Melong.** *See* Rgyal rabs gsal ba’i me long

**Gyaltsap Darma Rinchen.** *See* Rgyal tshab Dar ma rin chen

**Gyalwa Karmapa.** *See* Rgyal ba karma pa

**Gyergom Tsültrim Senge.** *See* Gyer sgom Tshul khrims seng ge

**Gyijo Lotsāwa Dawe Öser.** *See* Gyi jo lo tsā ba Zla ba’i ’od zer

**Gyüme.** *See* Rgyud smad

**Gyütö.** *See* Rgyud stod

## J

**jalü.** *See* ’ja’ lus

**Jam chö de nga.** *See* Byams chos sde lnga

**Jamgön Kongtrül Lodrö Taye.** *See* ’Jam mgon kong sprul Blo gros mtha’ yas

**Jamyang Chöje Tashi Palden.** *See* ’Jam dbyangs chos rje Bkra shis dpal ldan

**Jamyang Kyentse Chökyi Lodrö.** *See* ’Jam dbyangs mkhyen brtse Chos kyi blo gros

**Jamyang Kyentse Wangpo.** *See* ’Jam dbyangs mkhyen brtse dbang po

**Jamyang Shepa Ngawang Tsöndrü.** *See* ’Jam dbyangs bzhad pa Ngag dbang brtson ’grus

**Jangchup Ö.** *See* Byang chub ’od

**je.** *See* rje

**jebang nyernga.** *See* rje ’bangs nyer lnga

**jetsün.** *See* rje btsun

**Jetsün Dampa.** *See* Rje btsun dam pa

**Jikme Lingpa.** *See* ’Jigs med gling pa

**Jikten Gönpo.** *See* ’jig rten mgon po

**Jikten Sumgön.** *See* ’Jig rten gsum mgon

**Jonang Püntsok Ling.** *See* Jo nang phun tshogs gling

**Jowo Mikyö Dorje.** *See* Jo bo mi bskyur rdo rje.

## K

**Kabap Dünden gyi Gyüpe Namtar.** *See* Bka’ ’babs bdun ldan gyi brgyud pa’i rnam thar

**kabap shi.** *See* bka’ ’babs bzhi

**Kachar Tsuklakang.** *See* Kha char gtsug lag khang

**Kachem Kakölma.** *See* Bka’ chems ka khol ma

**kachö.** *See* mkha’ spyod

**Kadam.** *See* Bka’ gdams

**Kadam Lekbam Pachö Buchö.** *See* Bka’ gdams glegs bam pha chos bu chos

**Kagyü.** *See* Bka’ brgyud

**Kagyü che shi chung gye.** *See* Bka’ brgyud che bzhi chung brgyad

**Kagyü gurtso.** *See* Bka’ brgyud mgur mtsho

**Kagyü Ngak Dzö.** *See* Bka’ brgyud sngags mdzod

**Kagyüpa.** *See* Bka’ brgyud pa

**kama.** *See* bka’ ma

**Kamtrül.** *See* Khams sprul

**Kandro Nyingtik.** *See* Mkha’ ’gro snying thig

**kangyur.** *See* bka’ ’gyur

**Karchu.** *See* Mkhar chu

**Karma Chakme.** *See* Karma chags med

**Karma Lingpa.** *See* Karma gling pa

**karpo chiktup.** *See* dkar po chig thub

**Katang Denga.** *See* Bka’ thang sde lnga

**Katang Sanglingma.** *See* Bka’ thang zangs gling ma

**Katang Sertreng.** *See* Bka’ thang gser phreng

**Katsel.** *See* Bka’ tshal

**Kawa Karpo.** *See* Kha ba dkar po

**Kedrup Gelek Palsang.** *See* Mkhas grub Dge legs dpal bzang

**Kodrakpa Sönam Gyaltsen.** *See* Ko brag pa Bsod nams rgyal mtshan

**Könchok Gyalpo.** *See* Dkon mchog rgyal po

**Kongtrül dzö gga.** *See* Kong sprul mdzod lnga

**Koting.** *See* Mkho mthing

**Kubum.** *See* Sku ’bum

**Künga Paljor.** *See* Kun dga’ dpal ’byor

**Künga Sangpo.** *See* Kun dga’ bzang po

**Künje Gyalpo.** *See* Kun byed rgyal po

**Künsang Lame Shelung.** *See* Kun bzang bla ma’i zhal lung

**kyewe tülku.** *See* skye ba’i sprul sku

**Kyirong.** *See* Skyid grong

**Kyungpo Namjor Tsültrim Gönpo.** *See* Khyung po rnam ’byor tshul khrims mgon po

## L

**Labrang Tashi Kyil.** *See* Bla brang bkra shis ’khyil

**lama.** *See* bla ma

**Lama Shang.** *See* Bla ma Zhang

**Lama Yungdrung Gönpa.** *See* Bla ma gyung drung dgon pa

**Lama Yuru Monastery.** *See* Bla ma gyung drung dgon pa

**lamdre.** *See* lam ’bras

**Lamrim Düdön.** *See* Lam rim bsdus don

**Lamrim Jampal Shelung.** *See* Lam rim ’jam dpal zhal lung

**Lamrim Nyingu.** *See* Lam rim snying gu

**Lamrim Sershünma.** *See* Lam rim gser zhun ma

**Lamrim Tarpe Lakyang.** *See* Lam rim thar pa’i lag skyang

**Langdarma.** *See* Glang dar ma

**Langkor.** *See* Glang skor

**Lapchi.** *See* La phyi

**Lekpe Sherap.** *See* Legs pa’i shes rab

**Lekshe Nyingpo.** *See* Legs bshad snying po

**Lekshe Sertreng.** *See* Legs bshad gser phreng

**Lhamo Latso.** *See* Lha mo bla mtsho

**Lhatsün Namka Jikme.** *See* Lha brtsun nam mkha’ ’jigs med

**Lhatsün Rinchen Namgyal.** *See* Lha btsun Rin chen rnam rgyal

**Lhodrak.** *See* Lho brag

**Lhoter.** *See* Lho gter

**Lingrepa Pema Dorje.** *See* Gling ras pa Padma rdo rje

**Lochen Dharmashrī.** *See* Lo chen Dharma shrī

**Lochen Tülku.** *See* Lo chen sprul sku

**lojong.** *See* blo sbyong

**Lojong Döndünma.** *See* Blo sbyong don bdun ma

**Lojong Tsikgyema.** *See* Blo sbyong tshig brgyad ma

**longchen nyingtik.** *See* klong chen snying thig

**Longchen Rapjam.** *See* Klong chen rab ’byams

**longde.** *See* klong sde

**lorik.** *See* blo rigs

**Losang Chökyi Gyaltsen.** *See* Blo bzang chos kyi rgyal mtshan

**lu.** *See* klu

**Lü Gyaltsen.** *See* Klu’i rgyal mtshan

**Lukang.** *See* Klu khang

**lüme kandro nyengyü chökor gu.** *See* lus med mkha’ ’gro snyan brgyud chos skor dgu

**lungta.** *See* rlung rta

## M

**Machen Pomra.** *See* Rma chen spom ra

**Machik Lapdrön.** *See* Ma gcig lab sgron

**Maṇi Kabum.** *See* Ma ṇi bka’ ’bum

**Marpa Chökyi Lodrö.** *See* Mar pa Chos kyi blo gros

**Marpa Kagyü.** *See* Mar pa bka’ brgyud

**Martsang Kagyü.** *See* Smar tshang bka’ brgyud

**Mebar Tso.** *See* Me ’bar mtsho

**menngak de.** *See* man ngag sde

**Menri.** *See* Sman ri

**Meru Nyingpa.** *See* Rme ru snying pa

**Mikyö Dorje.** *See* Mi bskyod rdo rje

**Milarepa.** *See* Mi la ras pa

**Milarepe Namtar.** *See* Mi la ras pa’i rnam thar

**Mile Gurbum.** *See* Mila’i mgur ’bum

**Mindröling.** *See* Smin grol gling

**Mipham Jamyang Namgyal Gyatso.** *See* Mi pham ’Jam dbyangs rnam rgyal rgya mtsho

**Mönlam Chenmo.** *See* Smon lam chen mo

## N

**Namchak Barwa.** *See* Gnam lcags bar ba

**namtar.** *See* rnam thar

**Naro chödruk.** *See* Nā ro chos drug

**Nartang.** *See* Snar thang

**Nechung.** *See* Gnas chung

**nekorwa.** *See* GNAS SKOR BA

**ngadar.** *See* SNGA DAR

**ngagyur nyingma.** *See* SNGA 'GYUR RNYING MA

**Ngakrim Chenmo.** *See* SNAGS RIM CHEN MO

**Ngalso korsum.** *See* NGAL GSO SKOR GSUM

**Ngawang Namgyal.** *See* ZHABS DRUNG NGAG DBANG RNAM RGYAL

**Ngok Lekpe Sherap.** *See* RNGOG LEGS PA'I SHES RAB

**Ngok Loden Sherap.** *See* RNGOG BLO LDAN SHES RAB

**Ngok Lotsawa.** *See* RNGOG LO TSĀ BA

**ngöndro.** *See* SNGON 'GRO

**Ngorchen Künga Sangpo.** *See* KUN DGA' BZANG PO

**Ngor Evam Chöden.** *See* NGOR E WAM CHOS LDAN

**Norbulingka.** *See* NOR BU GLING KHA

**Nupchen Sangye Yeshe.** *See* GNUBS CHEN SANGS RGYAS YE SHES

**Nyangral Nyime Öser.** *See* NYANG RAL NYI MA'I 'OD ZER

**Nyarma Tsuklakang.** *See* NYAR MA GTSUG LAG KHANG

**Nyenchen Tanglha.** *See* GNYAN CHEN THANG LHA

**nyengyü.** *See* SNYAN BRGYUD

**nyengyü kor sum.** *See* SNYAN BRGYUD SKOR GSUM

**Nyingma.** *See* RNYING MA

**Nyingmapa.** *See* RNYING MA PA

**nyingme gyü bum.** *See* RNYING MA'I RGYUD 'BUM

**Nyingtik.** *See* SNYING THIG

**nyingtik yashi.** *See* SNYING THIG YA BZHI

**Nyurlam Lamrim.** *See* MYUR LAM LAM RIM

## O

**Orgyen Lingpa.** *See* O RGYAN GLING PA

**Orgyenpa Rinchen Pal.** *See* O RGYAN PA RIN CHEN DPAL

## P

**Padampa Sangye.** *See* PHA DAM PA SANGS RGYAS

**Padma Karpo.** *See* PADMA DKAR PO

**Padma Katangyik.** *See* PADMA BKA' THANG YIG

**Padma Kö.** *See* PADMA BKOD

**Padma Ledreltsel.** *See* PADMA LAS 'BREL RTSAL

**Padma Lingpa.** *See* PADMA GLING PA

**Padma Sel.** *See* PADMA GSAL

**Pakmo Drupa Dorje Gyalpo.** *See* PHAG MO GRU PA RDO RJE RGYAL PO

**Pakpa Lodrö Gyaltsen.** *See* 'PHAGS PA BLO GROS RGYAL MTSHAN

**Pakpa Wati Lhakang.** *See* 'PHAGS PA WA TI LHA KHANG

**Palden Lhamo.** *See* DPAL LDAN LHA MO

**Palpung.** *See* DPAL SPUNGS

**Paltsek.** *See* DPAL BRTSEGS

**Palyül.** *See* DPAL YUL

**Patrül Rinpoche.** *See* DPAL SPRUL RIN PO CHE

**Patsap Lotsawa Nyima Drak.** *See* SPA TSHAB LO TSĀ BA NYI MA GRAGS

**Pawo.** *See* DPA' BO

**Pawo Tsuklak Trengwa.** *See* DPA' BO GTSUG LAG 'PHRENG BA

**Pehar Gyalpo.** *See* PE HAR RGYAL PO

**powa.** *See* 'PHO BA

## R

**Radreng Monastery.** *See* RWA SGRENG

**Ra Lotsāwa Dorje Drak.** *See* RWA LO TSĀ BA RDO RJE GRAGS

**Ralung Monastery.** *See* RWA LUNG

**rang gyü shar sum.** *See* RANG RGYUD SHAR GSUM

**Rangjung Dorje.** *See* RANG 'BYUNG RDO RJE

**Rangjung Rikpe Dorje.** *See* RANG 'BYUNG RIG PA'I RDO RJE

**rangtong shentong.** *See* RANG STONG GSHAN STONG

**Ratna Lingpa.** *See* RATNA GLING PA

**Rechung Nyengyü.** *See* RAS CHUNG BSNYAN BRGYUD

**Rechungpa Dorje Drak.** *See* RAS CHUNG PA RDO RJE GRAGS

**Rechung Puk.** *See* RAS CHUNG PHUG

**rime.** *See* RIS MED

**Rinchen Sangpo.** *See* RIN CHEN BZANG PO

**Rinchen Terdzö.** *See* RIN CHEN GTER MDZOD

**Riwoche.** *See* RI BO CHE

**Riwo Palbar.** *See* Ri bo dpal 'bar

**Rongtön Mawe Senge.** *See* Rong ston Smra ba'i seng ge

**Rongzom Chökyi Sangpo.** *See* Rong zom Chos kyi bzang po

## S

**Sachen Künga Nyingpo.** *See* Sa chen kun dga' snying po

**sadak.** *See* sa bdag

**sagadawa.** *See* sa ga zla ba

**Sakya.** *See* Sa skya

**Sakya gongma nam nga.** *See* Sa skya gong ma rnam lnga

**Sakya Kabum.** *See* Sa skya bka' 'bum

**Sakyapa.** *See* Sa skya pa

**Sakya Paṇḍita Künga Gyaltsen.** *See* Sa skya paṇḍita Kun dga' rgyal mtshan

**Sakya Tridzin.** *See* Sa skya khri 'dzin

**Samten Mikdrön.** *See* Bsam gtan mig sgron

**Samye.** *See* Bsam yas

**Sangdok Palri.** *See* Zang mdog dpal ri

**Sangpu Neutok.** *See* Gsang phu ne'u thog

**sangwe namtar.** *See* gsang ba'i rnam thar

**Sangye Lingpa.** *See* Sangs rgyas gling pa

**sarma.** *See* gsar ma

**Sekargutok.** *See* Sras mkhar dgu thog

**semde.** *See* sems sde

**se mi dün.** *See* sad mi bdun

**Serdok Panchen Shākya Chokden.** *See* Gser mdog pan chen Shākya mchog ldan

**Shalu.** *See* Zhwa lu

**Shamar.** *See* Zhwa dmar

**Shangpa Kagyü.** *See* Shangs pa bka' brgyud

**Shapkar Tsokdruk Rangdröl.** *See* Zhabs dkar tshogs drug rang grol

**Shechen.** *See* Zhe chen

**Shechen Rapjam.** *See* Zhe chen rab 'byams

**shedra.** *See* bshad grwa

**Sheja Künkyap Dzö.** *See* Shes bya kun khyab mdzod

**shentong.** *See* gzhan stong

**Sherap Gyaltsen.** *See* Shes rab rgyal mtshan

**shije.** *See* zhi byed

**shi tro.** *See* zhi khro

**Shuksep.** *See* Shug gseb

**Shuksep Kagyü.** *See* Shug gseb bka' brgyud

**shung nga.** *See* zhung lnga

**Sönam Gyatso.** *See* Bsod nams rgya mtsho

**Sönam Tsemo.** *See* Bsod nams rtse mo

**Songtsen Gampo.** *See* Srong btsan sgam po

**sumtak.** *See* sum rtags

## T

**Tadül tsuklakang.** *See* Mtha' 'dul gtsug lag khang

**Taklung.** *See* Stag lung

**Taklung Kagyü.** *See* Stag lung bka' brgyud

**Taklung Tangpa Tashipal.** *See* Stag lung thang pa Bkra shis dpal

**Taktsang.** *See* Stag tshang

**Tamshing.** *See* Gtam zhing

**Tangtong Gyalpo.** *See* Thang stong rgyal po

**Tapo Tsuklakang.** *See* Ta pho gtsug lag khang

**Tarpa Rinpoche Gyen.** *See* Thar pa rin po che'i rgyan

**Tashi Lhünpo.** *See* Bkra shis lhun po

**tashi tsering che nga.** *See* bkra shis tshe ring mched lnga

**tekpa gu.** *See* theg pa dgu

**tengyur.** *See* bstan 'gyur

**tenma chunyi.** *See* brtan ma bcu gnyis

**tenrim.** *See* bstan rim

**Terdak Lingpa.** *See* Gter bdag gling pa

**terma.** *See* gter ma

**tertön.** *See* gter ston

**tertön gyalpo nga.** *See* gter ston rgyal po lnga

**tögal.** *See* thod rgal

**Toling Tsuklakang.** *See* Tho ling gtsug lag khang

**tonglen.** *See* gtong len

**torma.** *See* gtor ma

**Tradruk.** *See* Khra 'brug

**Tradumtse.** *See* Pra dum rtse

**trekchö.** *See* khregs chod

**Trisong Detsen.** *See* Khri srong lde btsan

**Tropu Kagyü.** *See* Khro phu bka' brgyud

**Tsalpa Kagyü.** *See* Tshal pa bka' brgyud

**Tsangnyön Heruka.** *See* Gtsang smyon Heruka

**Tsangpa Gyare Yeshe Dorje.** *See* Gtsang pa rgya ras Ye shes rdo rje

**Tsangpa Karpo.** *See* Tshangs pa dkar po

**Tsangyang Gyatso.** *See* Tshangs dbyangs rgya mtsho

**Tsarchen Losel Gyatso.** *See* Tshar chen Blo gsal rgya mtsho

**tselha namsum.** *See* tshe lha rnam gsum

**Tsema dedün.** *See* tshad ma sde bdun

**Tsema rikter.** *See* Tshad ma rigs gter

**tsen.** *See* btsan

**Tsiu Marpo.** *See* Tsi'u dmar po

**tsokshing.** *See* tshogs zhing

**Tsurpu.** *See* Mtshur phu

**Tsurpu Gyaltsap.** *See* Mtshur phu rgyal tshab

**tülku.** *See* sprul sku

**Tünmong Mayinpe Dzö.** *See* Mthun mong ma yin pa'i mdzod

**Tupten Gyatso.** *See* Thub bstan rgya mtsho

## U

**uma chenpo.** *See* dbu ma chen po

## V

**Vaidūrya Karpo.** *See* Baidūrya dkar po

**Vaidūrya Ngönpo.** *See* Baidūrya mngon po

**Vaidūrya Serpo.** *See* Baidūrya gser po

## W

**Wangchuk Dorje.** *See* Dbang phyug rdo rje

## Y

**Yangdül Tsuklakang.** *See* Yang 'dul gtsug lag khang

**Yarlung.** *See* Yar klungs

**Yasang Kagyü.** *See* Gya' bzang bka' brgyud

**Yeshe De.** *See* Ye shes sde

**Yeshe Ö.** *See* Ye shes 'od

**Yeshe Tsogyal.** *See* Ye shes mtsho rgyal

**yige gyapa.** *See* yi ge brgya pa

**yönchö.** *See* yon mchod

**Yönten Gyatso.** *See* Yon tan rgya mtsho

**Yumbu Lagang.** *See* Yum bu bla sgang